D1279159

ENCYCLOPÆDIA
Britannica

2012
BOOK OF THE YEAR®

Encyclopædia Britannica, Inc. Chicago • London • New Delhi • Paris • Seoul • Sydney • Taipei • Tokyo

ENCYCLOPÆDIA
Britannica

2012 BOOK OF THE YEAR®

Library of Congress Catalog Card Number: 38-12082
International Standard Book Number: 978-1-61535-579-2
International Standard Serial Number: 0068-1156

Britannica.com may be accessed on the Internet at http://www.britannica.com.

(*Trademark Reg. U.S. Pat. Off.*) Printed in U.S.A.

Foreword

The year 2011 could best be characterized as one of constant unrest and enormous upheaval. Revolution spread through the Middle East and North Africa, giving rise to the Arab Spring, which in the course of the year led to the downfall of three powerful heads of state. In Japan a massive earthquake followed by a devastating tsunami claimed some 19,000 lives. Fracking, the process used to extract natural gas from shale, came under scrutiny as critics worried about land and water contamination. The economy failed to rebound, and countries in the euro zone faced ongoing financial crises. Sports-related brain injuries became a hot topic following the deaths, some of them suicides, of former NFL and NHL players who had suffered repeatedly from concussions. In Germany, an *E. coli* outbreak, the source of which took some time to detect, raised a panic there and in places where the disease surfaced. Meanwhile, the discovery of dinosaur skeletons in Antarctica invigorated paleontological research. The 150th anniversary of the start of the Civil War was marked, as was the first International Yarn Bombing Day, a salute and showcase for knitters and crocheters worldwide. While the U.S. released the results of its 10-year census, the world's seven billionth birth was recorded. All of these topics are featured in Special Reports.

Some relatively new gadgets and trends took flight during the year. E-readers and tablets became a huge hit, and for-profit colleges expanded their online business, but, unfortunately, the incidence of bedbug infestation skyrocketed. In a year of beginning and endings, South Sudan became the world's newest independent country, the U.S. space shuttle program ended its 30-year mission, and the *News of the World* newspaper, published in the U.K. since 1843, was silenced following confirmation that its editors had been involved in a phone-hacking scandal. India rejoiced after winning the Cricket World Cup, and the New Zealand All Blacks celebrated their victory at the Rugby Union World Cup. On a more somber note, the deaths in 2011 of the last American veteran and the final combat soldier in World War I were marked. These stories are covered in Sidebars.

Royal weddings were top news in 2011, and Catherine Middleton (the future duchess of Cambridge) captivated a worldwide audience upon her marriage to Prince William of Wales. Charlene Wittstock (the future princess of Monaco) made her vows to Prince Albert II a few months later. In the entertainment arena, pop singers Katy Perry and Rihanna took the stage by storm, *Game of Thrones* creator George R.R. Martin saw his novels turned into a television series, *Mad Men* creator-writer Matthew Weiner saw his drama series win yet another Emmy Award, and British actor Colin Firth garnered an Academy Award for best actor for his performance as a stuttering king. On the gridiron, Green Bay Packers quarterback Aaron Rodgers led his team to a Super Bowl victory, and on the baseball diamond Tony La Russa helped the St. Louis Cardinals clinch the World Series. All of these people are profiled in biographies.

Some of the most-talked-about deaths included those of militant Osama bin Laden, Libyan strongman Muammar al-Qaddafi, and North Korean leader Kim Jong Il. The accolades never seemed to stop following the passing of former first lady Betty Ford and of Apple Computer founder Steve Jobs. Hollywood lost glamour queens Elizabeth Taylor and Jane Russell as well as such beloved TV character actors as James Arness (Marshall Matt Dillon of *Gunsmoke*) and Peter Falk (Lieutenant Colombo). Readers of the funny pages mourned the deaths of Ronald Searle (St. Trinian's girls), Joe Simon (Captain America), and Jerry Robinson (the Joker and Robin, the Boy Wonder). Sports fans lost such heroes as boxer "Smokin' Joe" Frazier, golfer Seve Ballesteros, and cricketer Basil D'Oliveira. These personalities appear in obituaries.

Many more stories, personal profiles, and factoids can be found in the 2012 *Britannica Book of the Year*. In addition, there is a new country article—South Sudan—which appears in the World Affairs section. My hope is that you will continue to explore and discover the wealth of information contained between the covers of this volume.

Karen Sparks
Director and Editor

Contents 2012

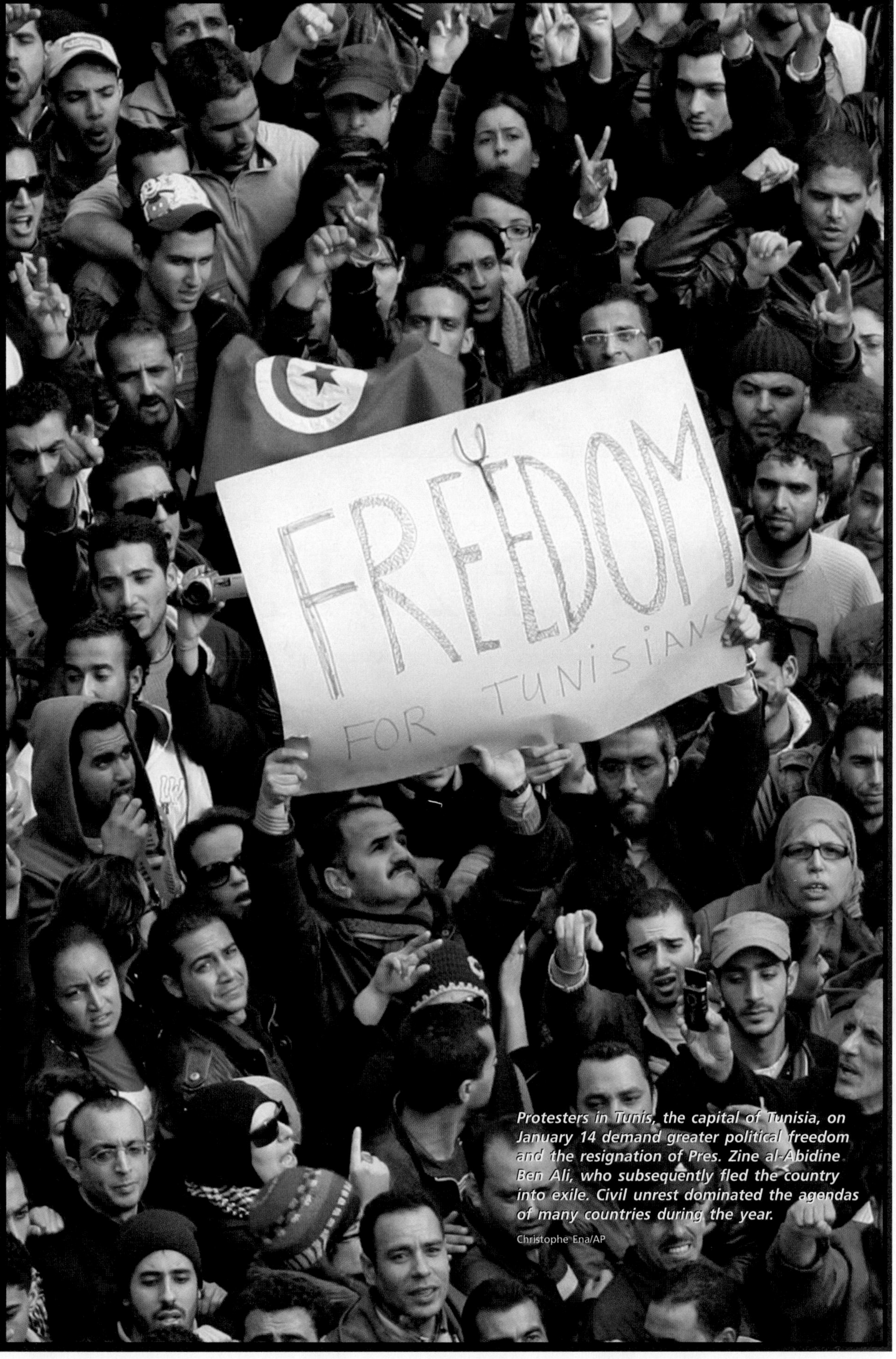

Protesters in Tunis, the capital of Tunisia, on January 14 demand greater political freedom and the resignation of Pres. Zine al-Abidine Ben Ali, who subsequently fled the country into exile. Civil unrest dominated the agendas of many countries during the year.

Christophe Ena/AP

Dates of 2011

(Top) David Freese (right) of the St. Louis Cardinals is greeted by jubilant teammates as he races to the plate after having hit his game-winning home run in the 11th inning of game six of the World Series. (Bottom left) A man in Cairo in June brandishes posters showing his own face on magazine covers as he celebrates the overthrow of Egyptian Pres. Hosni Mubarak in February.

(Top) Jeff Roberson/AP; (bottom left) Amr Nabil/AP

(Bottom right) During a nationwide strike in Chile in August, tense confrontations took place such as this face-off between a police officer and a youth.

(Bottom right) Roberto Candia/AP; (background) © a_korn/Fotolia

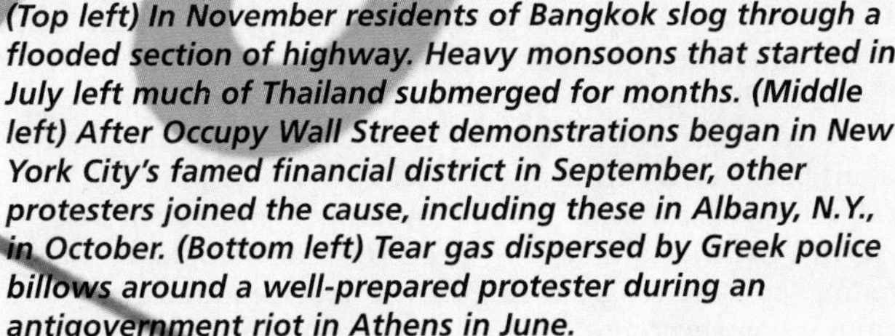

(Top left) In November residents of Bangkok slog through a flooded section of highway. Heavy monsoons that started in July left much of Thailand submerged for months. (Middle left) After Occupy Wall Street demonstrations began in New York City's famed financial district in September, other protesters joined the cause, including these in Albany, N.Y., in October. (Bottom left) Tear gas dispersed by Greek police billows around a well-prepared protester during an antigovernment riot in Athens in June.

(Top left) Sakchai Lalit/AP; (middle left) Hans Pennink/AP; (bottom left) Petros Giannakouris/AP

(Top right) A young man in the newly independent country of South Sudan displays the new national flag as he prepares for the official celebration in the capital, Juba, on July 9. (Middle right) King Jigme Khesar Namgyal Wanghuk of Bhutan presents his new queen, Jetsun Pema, after their sumptuous wedding on October 13. (Bottom right) In famine-stricken southern Somalia, children line up in August to receive hot food distributed by the World Food Programme.

(Top right) David Azia/AP; (middle right) Adrees Latif—Reuters/Landov; (bottom right) Farah Abdi Warsameh/AP

January

What happened here is going to affect the whole Arab world.

Zied Mhirsi, a demonstrator in Tunis, Tun., after the fall of Pres. Zine al-Abidine Ben Ali, January 14

1 As churchgoers leave a New Year's service a half hour after midnight at a Coptic Christian church in Alexandria, Egypt, a bomb explodes and kills at least 21 people; Christians riot in response.

•

The Estonian kroon is replaced by the euro as Estonia becomes the 17th member of the euro zone.

•

Dilma Rousseff is sworn in as the first female president of Brazil.

•

The U.S. dollar becomes the official currency in the Dutch special municipalities of Bonaire, Sint Eustatius, and Saba.

2 The Muttahida Qaumi Movement leaves the ruling coalition in Pakistan; it is the second largest component of the coalition and leaves the government without a parliamentary majority.

•

A 7.1-magnitude earthquake rattles southern Chile, causing some 50,000 people to evacuate, but there are no reports of casualties or damage.

3 Christian protests stemming from the New Year's bombing at a Coptic Christian church in Alexandria take place in Cairo, where rioting also occurs; the protests take on an antigovernment tone.

•

A second attempt by African heads of state to persuade Laurent Gbagbo, who lost the 2010 presidential election in Côte d'Ivoire, to step down fails; Gbagbo maintains that his presidency is legitimate.

4 In Islamabad, Pak., Salman Taseer, the secularist governor of Punjab, is assassinated by a member of his guard; Taseer had led a fight to repeal the country's draconian laws against blasphemy.

5 The UN Food and Agriculture Organization publishes a report saying that its world food price index went up 32% between June and December 2010, reaching a record high; the prices measured in the report are those of commodities in the export market.

•

The powerful Shi'ite cleric Muqtada al-Sadr returns to Iraq after three years of self-imposed exile in Iran; his followers greet him in Al-Najaf with jubilation.

•

In Islamabad, Pak., hundreds of people turn out in support of Malik Mumtaz Hussain Qadri, the guard member who killed Gov. Salman Taseer of Punjab for his opposition to blasphemy laws, while thousands attend Taseer's funeral.

6 Rioting over rising food prices and high unemployment spills from Algiers, the capital of Algeria, to outlying areas.

•

U.S. military officials declare that some 1,000 U.S. Marines will be deployed to Afghanistan, most of them to Helmand province, to attempt to consolidate gains.

7 After the government of Pakistani Prime Minister Yousaf Raza Gilani backs down from several planned economic reforms, the Muttahida Qaumi Movement agrees to rejoin the government.

•

Government officials in Germany shut down sales from thousands of small farms and pull millions of eggs from sale after having found feed for chickens and pigs that contained dioxin, a cancer-causing chemical.

•

The U.S. Department of Labor reports that the unemployment rate in December 2010 fell from 9.8% to 9.4% and that the economy added 103,000 jobs.

•

The First Commercial Bank of Florida, based in Orlando, becomes the first U.S. bank failure in 2011 when it is seized by regulators; 157 banks failed in 2010.

8 At a "Congress on Your Corner" event outside a supermarket in Tucson, Ariz., a deranged gunman approaches U.S. Rep. Gabrielle Giffords and shoots her in the head, gravely wounding her, and then opens fire on the crowd, shooting 18 other people attending the event before he is stopped by bystanders and taken into custody; six people, including a federal judge and a nine-year-old girl, are killed.

•

The bodies of 15 young men who were decapitated are found outside a shopping centre in Acapulco, Mex., and four bullet-riddled bodies are found in residential areas.

9 Officials in Tunisia say that protests over unemployment the previous two days left some 14 people dead; leaders of the demonstrations, which began in December 2010 after a produce vendor set himself on fire to protest the police's seizure of his cart, say the death toll is closer to 20.

•

A weeklong referendum on independence gets under way in southern Sudan; jubilant voters throng the polling places.

10 The Basque militant separatist group ETA declares a permanent cease-fire; it does not, however, offer to disarm.

•

North Korea proposes talks on economic ties to South Korea, which counters with an offer for discussions on North Korea's shelling in November 2010 of the island of Yonp'yong (Yeonpyeong) and its March 2010 sinking of the South Korean warship *Cheonan*.

•

Auburn University defeats the University of Oregon 22–19 in college football's Bowl Championship Series title game to win the NCAA Football Bowl Subdivision championship.

•

In the field of children's literature, the Newbery Medal is awarded to Clare Vanderpool for her novel *Moon over Manifest*, and Erin E. Stead wins the Caldecott Medal for her illustrations for *A Sick Day for Amos McGee* by Philip C. Stead.

11 The 123 Agreement between Russia and the U.S. on cooperation on civilian nuclear power goes into effect.

•

The telecommunications carrier Verizon announces that beginning in February the iPhone smartphone, which heretofore has been available exclusively with the AT&T network, will also be sold by Verizon.

•

The Journal of Archaeological Science publishes online a report on the finding in an Armenian cave of a complex winemaking operation that produced red wine some 6,100 years ago; it is the earliest winemaking facility to have been discovered.

•

In St. Petersburg, Fla., the new home of the Dalí Museum opens with fanfare to critical praise. *(Photo below.)*

12 Massive demonstrations take place in Tunis as well as other cities in Tunisia in spite of efforts by government forces to shut the protests down and the replacement of the minister of the interior; demonstrators call for the resignation of the president.

•

Hezbollah and its allied parties resign from Lebanon's cabinet, causing the fall of the national unity government.

•

River waters in Queensland continue to rise, and authorities in Australia urge residents of parts of Brisbane to evacuate as even a reservoir built to protect the city from flooding overflows; floodwaters inundate some 30,000 homes and businesses.

•

Torrential rainfall sets off flash flooding and landslides in Brazil's Serrana region, killing at least 842 people; the towns of Teresópolis and Nova Friburgo are particularly hard hit by the disaster.

•

The U.S. National Climatic Data Center reports that the average global temperature in 2010 was 0.62 °C (1.12 °F) above the historical average, making 2010 a tie with 2005 for the warmest year since record keeping began in 1880; 2010 was also the wettest year on record.

13 Tunisian Pres. Zine al-Abidine Ben Ali, in a televised address to the country, offers concessions to the protesters and promises not to run for reelection in 2014; protests, now against corruption, continue to grow.

•

The Organization of American States presents to Haitian Pres. René Préval a report by international experts that says that there was widespread fraud in the vote counting after the November 2010 presidential election and that the true second-place candidate who should advance to a runoff is Michel Martelly rather than Jude Célestin.

•

The Bank of Korea, South Korea's central bank, raises interest rates a quarter point, surprising economists.

•

The U.S. Environmental Protection Agency revokes the permit granted to Arch Coal for a proposed coal mine that would have removed mountain tops in a 922-ha (2,278-ac) area in West Virginia to access the coal within the mountains and would have placed the resulting debris into valleys and rivers.

14 Zine al-Abidine Ben Ali abandons the presidency of

Christian Heeb—Laif/Redux

Tunisia and flees the country in the face of relentlessly swelling protests; Prime Minister Mohamed Ghannouchi declares that he is now interim president.

•

Prosecutors in Milan announce that they are investigating Italian Prime Minister Silvio Berlusconi in connection with a prostitution case.

•

A referendum to extend the term of office of Pres. Nursultan Nazarbayev of Kazakhstan until 2020, bypassing elections scheduled for 2012 and 2017, is approved by the country's legislature; on January 31 the country's Constitutional Court rules the move unconstitutional.

•

The British-based energy company BP announces a partnership with the Russian company Rosneft to conduct oil exploration in the Russian Arctic.

15 As violent antigovernment demonstrations continue in Tunisia, Prime Minister Mohamed Ghannouchi, who the previous day declared himself interim president, relinquishes power to Fouad Mebazaa, the speaker of the Chamber of Deputies; the constitution mandates that the speaker succeed the president in case of emergency.

•

The Dakar Rally concludes in Buenos Aires; the winners are Qatari driver Nasser al-Attiyah in a Volkswagen automobile, Spanish driver Marc Coma on a KTM motorcycle, Russian driver Vladimir Chagin in a Kamaz truck, and Argentine driver Alejandro Patronelli in a Yamaha ATV.

16 Jean-Claude ("Baby Doc") Duvalier, who was dictator of Haiti from 1971 until he fled to exile in France in 1986, returns to Haiti; his motives are unclear.

•

At the Golden Globe Awards in Beverly Hills, Calif., best picture honours go to *The Social Network* and *The Kids Are All Right*; best director goes to David Fincher for *The Social Network*.

17 Pres. Michel Suleiman of Lebanon postpones planned negotiations on the formation of a new government.

•

Steven P. Jobs, CEO of the technology company Apple Inc., takes a medical leave of absence from the company but retains his title.

•

At Thoroughbred horse racing's 2010 Eclipse Awards, the nearly undefeated mare Zenyatta (19–1) is named Horse of the Year.

18 A suicide bomber detonates his explosives outside a police recruiting centre in Tikrit, Iraq, killing at least 49 people.

•

In Haiti former dictator Jean-Claude Duvalier is taken into custody and escorted to a courtroom, where prosecutors lodge charges of corruption and embezzlement against him before releasing him; he is cautioned to remain in Haiti.

•

Pres. Hu Jintao of China arrives in Washington, D.C., for a state visit.

•

The Piracy Reporting Center of the International Maritime Bureau reports that pirates attacked 445 ships in 2010 and took close to 1,200 people hostage, 8 of whom were killed; it is the fourth consecutive year of increased piracy.

19 In what appears to be part of a power struggle between Afghan Pres. Hamid Karzai and the Independent Election Commission and Electoral Complaints Commission, Karzai orders that the seating of the new legislature be delayed by a month.

•

A roadside bomb kills 13 people in a motorized rickshaw in Afghanistan's Paktika province.

20 In the face of an open revolt by members of his Fianna Fail party, Irish Prime Minister Brian Cowen calls for early elections to be held on March 11.

•

Three car bombs explode along the road to Karbala', Iraq, as thousands of Shi'ite pilgrims head to the city for a religious observance; at least 52 people are killed.

•

China's National Bureau of Statistics reports that the country's economy grew at a blistering 9.8% rate in the final quarter of 2010.

21 Some 20,000 people march in Tirana, the capital of Albania, to demand the resignation of the government; three individuals are killed in clashes with government forces.

•

Protest marches take place in several cities in Jordan, where demonstrators demand the right to elect the prime minister and object to the country's poverty.

•

Protesters return to the streets in Tunisia to demand the dissolution of the government, which is still dominated by the ousted president's ruling party.

•

Andy Coulson, communications director for British Prime Minister David Cameron, resigns because of growing questions about his involvement in the hacking of telephone messages of the royal family and various celebrities by the tabloid newspaper *News of the World* when Coulson was its editor.

•

Keith Olbermann, the most popular host on the cable television network MSNBC, suddenly announces his departure as host of *Countdown*, ending his association with MSNBC.

22 A specially created government committee formally takes command over the militia of the former Maoist insurgency in Nepal; the question of the integration of the Maoist forces into the Nepali armed forces has been a sticking point in the country's attempted transition to democracy.

•

Under pressure, Afghan Pres. Hamid Karzai backs down from his plan to postpone the seating of the country's two-chamber National Assembly.

•

Sumo *yokozuna* Hakuho defeats *ozeki* Baruto to win his 18th (and 6th consecutive) Emperor's Cup at the New Year *basho* (grand tournament) in Tokyo.

23 Some 34,000 people march in Brussels to demand the formation of a new government; Belgium has been without a government since elections in June 2010.

•

The Green Party pulls out of the governing coalition in Ireland.

24 A powerful bomb explodes outside Moscow in the public waiting area of the international arrivals hall of Domodedovo, Russia's largest airport; at least 36 people are killed.

•

Najib Miqati, the candidate put forward by Hezbollah, wins enough legislative support to become Lebanon's next prime minister; anti-Hezbollah rioting erupts in Beirut.

•

Gen. Rachid Ammar, head of the Tunisian army, for the first time addresses antigovernment protesters; he pledges the military's support for the revolution while urging the crowds to await the holding of new elections. *(Photo right.)*

Zoubeir Souissi—Reuters/Landov

25 Unexpectedly large demonstrations, apparently inspired by a Facebook page, swell in several cities in Egypt to demand the downfall of the country's government.

•

In his state of the union address, U.S. Pres. Barack Obama proposes areas for increased spending to bolster the country's international competitiveness and suggests areas for cost cutting to reduce the budget deficit.

•

Official figures released in the U.K. show that the British economy contracted by 0.5% in the final quarter of 2010.

26 Antigovernment protests continue in Egypt as government security forces unleash tear gas and truncheons in an effort to quell the uprising; hundreds are arrested.

•

The BBC World Service, citing slashing in its funding by the British government, announces that it must close five language services and reduce its workforce by a quarter over the next three years.

•

The Dow Jones Industrial Average rises above 12,000 for the first time since June 19, 2008, before falling again to close at 11,985.44.

27 A car bomb kills at least 48 people at an outdoor funeral service in a Shiʿite neighbourhood in Baghdad, and residents riot against police and security forces, angered at their failure to protect them.

•

Thousands of people march in Sanaa, Yemen, demanding reforms or the fall of the government.

•

A report published in *Science* magazine describes the finding at the Jebel Faya site in the United Arab Emirates of stone tools 127,000 years old that raise the suggestion that modern humans may have spread out from Africa earlier than the 50,000 years ago that is generally held to be the case.

28 The day after Ireland's legislature approved unpopular austerity measures, including a tax increase, the government announces that the body will be dissolved on February 1.

•

Pres. Hosni Mubarak of Egypt orders a shutdown of Internet and cell phone communications and vows to enforce security as antigovernment protests continue to grow in size and vehemence, and demonstrators fight successfully against security forces.

•

The African Union reveals its plan to set up a panel of heads of state, led by Pres. Mohamed Ould Abdel Aziz of Mauritania, to produce a resolution to the impasse that arose from the 2010 presidential election in Côte d'Ivoire.

•

The U.S. Department of Commerce reports that the country's GDP expanded at an annual rate of 3.2% in the final quarter of 2010, an improvement from the third quarter.

29 For the first time in his tenure, Egyptian Pres. Hosni Mubarak names a vice president—intelligence chief Omar Suleiman—and replaces Ahmad Nazif with Ahmed Shafiq as prime minister; meanwhile, security forces clash with tens of thousands of protesters, but the military largely remains on the sidelines.

•

Belgian Kim Clijsters defeats Li Na of China to win the Australian Open women's tennis championship; the following day Novak Djokovic of Serbia defeats Briton Andy Murray to take the men's title.

•

Japan wins the Asian Cup in association football (soccer) for a record fourth time when it defeats Australia 1–0 in extra time in the final match in Doha, Qatar.

30 It is reported that losses at Kabul Bank owing to mismanagement and fraud may be as high as $900 million, three times earlier estimates; Kabul Bank is Afghanistan's main bank.

31 A presidential election takes place in Niger as a part of a plan to restore civilian rule after a coup in February 2010; it results in the need for a runoff.

•

The legislature of Myanmar (Burma) meets in Nay Pyi Taw in its first session in 22 years.

•

The U.S. and the EU put in place new sanctions against Pres. Alyaksandr Lukashenka of Belarus and dozens of other Belarusian officials because of the government crackdown on the opposition in the wake of a flawed presidential election.

•

Illinois Gov. Pat Quinn signs a measure allowing same-sex and opposite-sex couples to enter into civil unions, which will give them most legal rights that married couples have; 10 U.S. states now permit same-sex couples to marry or enter civil unions.

February

We can breathe fresh air, we can feel our freedom. After 30 years of absence from the world, Egypt is back.

Gamal Heshamt, former Egyptian legislator, on the fall of Pres. Hosni Mubarak, February 11

1 As hundreds of thousands of antigovernment protesters fill Cairo's Tahrir Square, Egyptian Pres. Hosni Mubarak addresses the country in a televised speech in which he declares that he will not run for office again and will step down in September; the angered crowds demand his immediate resignation.

•

Irish Prime Minister Brian Cowen dissolves the legislature and schedules an election for February 25.

•

King ʿAbdullah II of Jordan responds to growing antigovernment demonstrations by dismissing the cabinet and replacing Prime Minister Samir Rifai with Marouf al-Bakhit.

2 Pres. ʿAli ʿAbd Allah Salih of Yemen offers concessions to antigovernment protesters and promises not only to abandon his effort to change the constitution to allow him to remain in office for life but also to step down at the end of his term of office in 2013.

•

NASA astronomers report that the Kepler space telescope, launched in 2009 to study part of the Milky Way, has found 1,235 possible planets, 68 of which are fairly small; other astronomers report having found a system of six planets orbiting the star Kepler 11 in a dense pack.

3 Haiti's electoral commission announces that the runoff election in March will be between Mirlande Manigat, as first announced, and Michel Martelly, who had initially been deemed to have come in third in first-round balloting.

•

On its 17th attempt to choose a new prime minister, the legislature of Nepal elects Jhalanath Kanal of the Communist Party of Nepal (Unified Marxist-Leninist) to the post.

•

In Malakal, the capital of Sudan's Upper Nile state, members of an army unit refuse deployment to the northern part of the country, and mutiny and fighting spread; at least 50 people die in the mutiny.

•

Manuel Farfán, a retired army general who a few weeks earlier was appointed police chief of Nuevo Laredo, Mex., in an attempt to deal with organized crime, is gunned down on a downtown street.

•

For the first time in nearly a decade, King ʿAbdullah II of Jordan meets with a delegation from the opposition Muslim Brotherhood.

•

Cyclone Yasi makes landfall near the village of Mission Beach and then continues inland in the Australian state of Queensland, causing major damage.

4 The legislature of Myanmar (Burma) chooses Thein Sein, who served as prime minister under Gen. Than Shwe, as the country's new president.

•

At a European Union summit meeting in Brussels, German Chancellor Angela Merkel and French Pres. Nicolas Sarkozy introduce a detailed plan to increase integration of the member countries of the euro zone.

•

The U.S. Department of Labor reports that the unemployment rate in January fell significantly from the previous month to 9% but that the economy added only 36,000 jobs.

5 Iraqi Prime Minister Nuri al-Maliki declares that he will not seek to be returned to the post in elections scheduled for 2014.

•

With signatures on instruments of ratification from U.S. Secretary of State Hillary Clinton and Russian Foreign Minister Sergey Lavrov, the New START treaty, which was agreed to in 2010 and provides for limited nuclear disarmament, goes into effect.

6 In response to the reignition of protests in Tunisia, the country's minister of the interior suspends all activities of the Democratic Constitutional Rally, the former ruling party.

•

Police evict a group of Rapa Nui indigenous people from the grounds of a resort hotel on Easter Island that they have occupied since August 2010 in protest against the development on land claimed by the Rapa Nui.

•

The Internet access company AOL reaches an agreement to acquire the news Web site the Huffington Post; Arianna Huffington of the Huffington Post is to be in charge of AOL's editorial content as president of the newly created Huffington Post Media Group.

•

In Arlington, Texas, the Green Bay Packers defeat the Pittsburgh Steelers 31–25 to win the National Football League's Super Bowl XLV.

•

The Japan Sumo Association announces that the spring *basho* (grand tournament), scheduled to begin on March 13, has been canceled because of a match-fixing scandal.

7 The results of the referendum held in southern Sudan are announced in Khartoum; 98.83% voted in favour of independence, and Pres. Omar al-Bashir declares that he accepts the results.

•

At the Laureus World Sports Awards in Abu Dhabi, U.A.E., Spanish tennis star Rafael Nadal is named sportsman of the year, while American ski champion Lindsey Vonn wins sportswoman of the year; French association football (soccer) player Zinedine Zidane takes the lifetime achievement award.

•

The Obregón Yaquis of Mexico defeat the Anzoátegui Caribes of Venezuela 3–2 to win baseball's Caribbean Series.

8 The UN Food and Agriculture Organization warns that a severe drought in China's agricultural area, particularly in Shandong province, is causing hardship and threatening the wheat crop; China is the world's largest producer of wheat.

•

For the third time in four months, the People's Bank of China raises its key lending rate by a quarter point, to 6.06%.

9 Preliminary talks between North Korea and South Korea intended to set an agenda for substantive military discussion break down when the North Korean delegation walks out.

•

A gas line explosion causes a fire that levels a half dozen row houses in Allentown, Pa.; at least five people are killed.

•

The New England Journal of Medicine publishes online the results of a much-anticipated study that found that risky prenatal surgery for the more severe form of spina bifida proved more beneficial for those with the condition than surgery that was performed on babies after they were born.

10 Hundreds of thousands of people gather in Tahrir Square in Cairo to hear a suddenly announced speech from Egyptian Pres. Hosni Mubarak in which they anticipate he will announce that he is stepping down; instead, Mubarak declares that he will not resign but will delegate authority to his new vice president, Omar Suleiman.

•

During the morning parade lineup at a military training school in Mardan, in Pakistan's Khyber Pakhtunkhwa province, a teenage suicide bomber detonates his weapon and kills at least 27 cadets.

•

Researchers from the University of Missouri and Arizona State University report in the journal *Science* the discovery of a fourth metatarsal of the hominin species *Australopithecus afarensis*, of which Lucy is the best-known example; the foot bone shows for the first time that *A. afarensis* walked upright.

11 In southern Sudan, fighting that began the previous day between members of the southern Sudanese military and members of a militia led by George Athor, which had recently integrated with the military, leaves at least 211 people dead.

•

Hundreds of thousands of Egyptians, enraged by Pres. Hosni Mubarak's failure to resign, flood the streets of Cairo *(photo below)*; as dusk falls, Vice Pres. Omar Suleiman announces that Mubarak has stepped down and handed authority to the Supreme Council of the Armed Forces.

•

Wisconsin Gov. Scott Walker proposes a budget that cuts salaries and pensions of most public employees, severely limits the right to collective bargaining for public-employee unions, and impedes the ability of such unions to collect dues.

•

The U.S. Department of Agriculture approves the commercial growing of corn that has been genetically engineered to be easy to process into ethanol; those in businesses involved in the use of corn for food products object.

12 The Palestinian Authority calls for presidential and legislative elections to be held by September; the militant organization Hamas, which won the last such elections in 2006, rejects the call.

•

A suicide bomber attacks a bus carrying Shi'ite pilgrims from Samarra', Iraq, that is stopped at a checkpoint; at least 33 people are killed.

•

A large and coordinated attack on the police headquarters in Kandahar, Afg., lasts several hours and leaves some 19 people dead.

Xu Jinquan—Xinhua/Landov

13 Egypt's Supreme Council of the Armed Forces dissolves the legislature, suspends the constitution, and calls for elections to be held in six months; the government of Prime Minister Ahmad Shafiq remains in a caretaker role.

•

Some 1,000 young people, organized via text message, march in Sanaa, Yemen, to demand the immediate resignation of the country's president; the protesters feel that the coalition of opposition parties that led earlier demonstrations is moving too slowly.

•

Voters in Switzerland reject a proposal in a referendum to restrict the keeping of army firearms in the home and to restrict the purchase of guns.

•

At the Grammy Awards in Los Angeles, the top winner is country band Lady Antebellum, which wins five awards, including both song of the year and record of the year for "Need You Now"; the album of the year is Arcade Fire's *The Suburbs*, and the best new artist is jazz bassist and vocalist Esperanza Spalding.

14 Tens of thousands of people in various cities in Iran march in protests against the government, but the demonstrations are crushed by security forces.

•

Police in Malawi prevent thousands of demonstrators from marching in Lilongwe to protest fuel shortages.

•

A judge in Ecuador orders the oil company Chevron to pay $9 billion in damages for environmental destruction caused in the 1970s by the oil company Texaco when it was operating in Ecuador in partnership with Ecuador's state oil company; Chevron bought Texaco in 2001.

15 Thousands of people gather in downtown Manama, Bahrain, in an antigovernment rally, and the opposition Islamic National Accord Association party suspends its participation in the country's legislature.

•

Egyptian Defense Minister Mohamed Hussein Tantawi, now acting chief of state, appoints a panel that is headed by Tareq al-Bishri, a retired judge who was critical of the Mubarak government, to revise the country's constitution.

•

A judge in Milan rules that Italian Prime Minister Silvio Berlusconi must stand trial on charges of having paid an underage girl for sex and of abuse of office.

•

The stock exchanges NYSE Euronext, which operates the New York Stock Exchange, and Deutsche Börse, operator of the Frankfurt (Ger.) Stock Exchange, announce a planned merger.

•

Foxcliffe Hickory Wind wins Best in Show at the Westminster Kennel Club's 135th dog show; the Scottish deerhound, known as Hickory, is the first of its breed to win the competition.

16 Large antigovernment protests take place in Benghazi, Libya; similar marches also occur in the cities of Zentan and Zawiyat al-Bayda'.

•

Thousands of protesters fill the state capital building in Madison, Wis., to oppose the bill proposed by Gov. Scott Walker that would cut public union benefits and curtail bargaining rights.

•

The bookstore chain Borders files for bankruptcy protection and plans to close about 200 of its more than 650 stores.

•

An IBM computer called Watson, programmed to understand and respond to natural language, defeats former champions Ken Jennings and Brad Rutter in a three-episode contest (filmed in January) on the popular American television game show *Jeopardy!*

17 Laurent Gbagbo, who refused to cede power in Côte d'Ivoire after having lost a presidential election in 2010, orders the government to seize major banks that suspended business in the country.

•

In Ghent, Belg., about 50 people remove their clothes in a mocking tribute to Belgium's 249th day without a formal government, a new record for time elapsed after an election.

•

Two reports are published in the journal *Nature* that use computer modeling to show that a recent worldwide increase in extreme precipitation events is likely to be connected to the rise in greenhouse gases in the atmosphere.

•

The opera *Anna Nicole*, based on the life of celebrity Anna Nicole Smith and written by composer Mark-Anthony Turnage and librettist Richard Thomas, debuts at the Royal Opera House in London.

18 Bahrain's military opens fire on protesters entering Manama's Pearl Square; an unknown number are killed.

•

Tens of thousands of demonstrators march in Tirana, Alb., demanding the resignation of the government.

•

Yoweri Museveni wins reelection as president of Uganda.

•

Japan's Ministry of Agriculture announces that the annual whale hunt, which Japan says is for scientific research, is being cut short because of harassment by the Sea Shepherd Conservation Society, which seeks to prevent the hunting of whales.

19 Several gunmen wearing explosive vests and Afghan army uniforms attack a bank in Jalalabad, Afg., as soldiers and police officers await their monthly salaries, and a three-hour gun battle ensues; at least 18 people are killed.

•

Police forces withdraw from Pearl Square in Manama, Bahrain, and joyous antigovernment protesters fill the square.

•

The Iranian film *Jodaeiye Nader az Simin* (*A Separation*), directed by Asghar Farhadi, wins the Golden Bear at the Berlin International Film Festival. *(Photo right.)*

20 Two days of battles in Somalia between African Union peacekeeping forces and Islamist insurgents using an underground system of trenches and tunnels leave at least 20 people dead.

•

In Daytona Beach, Fla., the 53rd running of the Daytona 500 NASCAR race is won by Trevor Bayne, who, at age 20, is the youngest-ever winner.

21 Antigovernment rioters take to the streets of Tripoli, the capital of Libya, and militia members loyal to Libyan leader Muammar al-Qaddafi respond with deadly force; human rights activists believe that more than 220 people have died in clashes between antigovernment

Joerg Carstensen—EPA/Landov

protesters and security forces in the country.

•

At a government census office in Afghanistan's Kunduz province, a suicide bomber detonates his weapon among people lined up to receive identification cards; at least 31 civilians are killed.

•

Crown Prince Salman ibn Hamad al-Khalifah of Bahrain announces that because of political turmoil in the country, the Bahrain Grand Prix, expected to open the Formula One automobile racing season on March 13, has been canceled.

22 A 6.3-magnitude quake, centred about 10 km (6 mi) from downtown Christchurch, N.Z., and about 5 km (3 mi) underground, causes buildings in much of the city, including skyscrapers, to collapse and kills at least 123 people, with a further 226 reported missing.

•

The legislature of Kosovo elects Behgjet Pacolli president and Hashim Thaci prime minister.

•

Former White House chief of staff Rahm Emanuel is elected mayor of Chicago.

23 U.S. Attorney General Eric Holder declares that a review has found that portions of the 1996 Defense of Marriage Act, which disallows federal recognition of same-sex marriages that are legal in other jurisdictions, are unconstitutional and that therefore the Department of Justice will no longer defend the law in suits against it.

•

The price of a barrel of light sweet crude oil briefly passes $100 for the first time since October 2008.

24 For the first time since the November 2010 election in Côte d'Ivoire, armed forces loyal to Laurent Gbagbo engage in conflict with the militia that supports the winner of the election, Alassane Ouattara; 13 combatants are reported killed.

•

Hundreds of Palestinians rally in the West Bank town of Ramallah to encourage an end to the divisions between Fatah, which dominates the West Bank, and Hamas, which controls Gaza.

•

Algeria officially ends a state of emergency that has been in place for 19 years; protest marches in Algiers, however, remain forbidden.

•

The space shuttle *Discovery* takes off on its final mission; it will deliver supplies and a storage module to the International Space Station.

•

After a public tirade against the creator of the popular television situation comedy *Two and a Half Men* by its star, Charlie Sheen, the TV network CBS and Warner Brothers halt production of the show.

25 Forces loyal to Libyan leader Muammar al-Qaddafi bloodily put down antigovernment protests in Tripoli; Libya's ambassador to the U.S. and its missions to the Arab League and the UN resign in protest against the violent response to the demonstrations.

•

In Ireland's legislative election, the opposition Fine Gael wins resoundingly, with 76 seats to the ruling Fianna Fail's 20.

•

In Baghdad what begins as protests seeking political reform devolves into rioting and clashing with Iraqi security forces; some 29 demonstrators are killed.

•

Large antigovernment protests take place in several cities in Yemen, notably in Sanaa and Ta'izz.

•

Pres. Cristina Fernández de Kirchner of Argentina and Pres. Fernando Lugo of Paraguay mark the completion of the Yacyretá hydroelectric dam project as the dam on the Paraná River between the countries reaches its full capacity; the project, begun in 1983, is expected to provide a power output of 3,100 MW.

26 Two gunmen infiltrate the Baiji Refinery, Iraq's biggest oil refinery, and set off bombs, badly damaging the facility and shutting it down.

27 Mohamed Ghannouchi resigns as prime minister of Tunisia; the interim president appoints Beji Caid Sebsi to replace him.

•

Protesters demanding political reforms, more jobs, and better pay begin fighting with Omani police when officers attempt to shut down the demonstration in Suhar, Oman; two protesters are killed.

•

Authorities in Mexico say that over the past two days at least 28 people have died in drug-related violence.

•

For the fourth time in a year, French Pres. Nicolas Sarkozy announces a cabinet reshuffle; notable is the replacement of Michèle Alliot-Marie as foreign minister, a position she had held for three months, with Alain Juppé.

•

At the 83rd Academy Awards presentation, Oscars are won by, among others, *The King's Speech* (best picture) and its director, Tom Hooper, and actors Colin Firth, Natalie Portman, Christian Bale, and Melissa Leo.

•

Frank Buckles, who was the last surviving American veteran of World War I, dies in West Virginia at the age of 110.

28 As Western countries discuss how to respond to increasing bloodshed in the country, U.S. warships begin moving closer to Libya, and the European Union announces new sanctions.

•

The Kurdistan Workers' Party in Turkey ends a six-month cease-fire.

March

I thought it would stop, but it just kept shaking and shaking and getting stronger.

Toshiaki Takahashi, a city official in Sendai, Japan, describing his experience of the 9.0-magnitude earthquake, March 11

1 Karl-Theodor zu Guttenberg resigns as Germany's minister of defense after his doctorate degree was withdrawn by the University of Bayreuth in light of revelations that parts of his doctoral dissertation were plagiarized; he is replaced the following day by Thomas de Maizière.

•

NATO helicopters gun down nine Afghan boys gathering firewood outside the village of Nanglam in Afghanistan's Pech River valley; the following day U.S. Gen. David Petraeus issues a personal apology, saying that the boys were misidentified as insurgents.

•

The French fashion house Christian Dior fires its star designer, John Galliano, after the appearance of a video in which he is seen engaging in what appears to be a drunken anti-Semitic rant.

2 Shabaz Bhatti, Pakistan's minister of minorities and the only Christian member of the cabinet, is shot dead in his car in Islamabad; he had worked to reform the country's law that makes blasphemy a capital crime.

•

The U.S. Supreme Court rules that the picketing of soldiers' funerals by members of the Westboro Baptist Church with signs saying that the deaths are God's punishment for the toleration of homosexuality in the U.S. is permitted speech under the First Amendment to the Constitution.

•

James Levine resigns as music director of the Boston Symphony Orchestra because of health difficulties; he intends to stay on, however, as music director of New York City's Metropolitan Opera.

3 Ahmad Shafiq is replaced as prime minister of Egypt by Essam Sharaf.

•

In Abidjan, Côte d'Ivoire, a militia loyal to Laurent Gbagbo fires on an all-women march protesting the refusal of Gbagbo to cede power after losing the presidential election in November 2010; at least six women are killed.

•

Fouad Mebazaa, interim president of Tunisia, announces that an election for members of a council to rewrite the country's constitution will take place on July 24.

4 Tens of thousands of pro-democracy demonstrators march in the streets of Manama, Bahrain; large pro-democracy protests also take place in Amman, Jordan, while police and military personnel prevent possible demonstrations in Djibouti.

•

The U.S. Department of Labor reports that the unemployment rate in February dropped to 8.9% and that the number of jobs added to the economy rose to 192,000; nonetheless, the percentage of adults actively involved in the workforce (either employed or seeking work) remains at a low 64.2%.

5 Forces loyal to Libyan leader Muammar al-Qaddafi lay siege to the rebel-held town of Al-Zawiyah; a day earlier, rebels had taken the port city of Ras Lanuf.

6 Japanese Foreign Minister Seiji Maehara admits having received illegal campaign donations and announces his resignation.

•

The ruling coalition is returned to power in legislative elections in Estonia.

•

Bursts of lava from new fissures that began opening the previous day between the Napau and Pu'u O'o craters on Hawaii's Kilauea volcano reach heights of 24 m (80 ft), which leads to the closure of parts of Hawaii Volcanoes National Park. *(Photo right.)*

7 Tunisia's interim government disbands the state security department.

•

Prime Minister John Key of New Zealand declares that as a result of the earthquakes on Sept. 4, 2010, and on February 22, more than 10,000 houses and other buildings in Christchurch will have to be demolished and that parts of the city will have to be abandoned because of liquefaction.

•

U.S. Pres. Barack Obama issues an executive order allowing the resumption of military trials of detainees at the U.S. detention centre at Guantánamo Bay, Cuba, and governing the treatment of the remaining 172 detainees there; the military trials had been halted two years earlier.

8 A car bomb explodes near the office of Pakistan's main intelligence agency in Faisalabad; at least 24 people are killed.

•

Ayatollah Mohammad Reza Mahdavi Kani replaces Ali Akbar Hashemi Rafsanjani as head of the Assembly of Experts in Iran; the body chooses Iran's supreme leader.

•

The Bangladesh High Court rules that the Bangladesh Bank was within its rights when it removed Muhammad Yunus as managing director of the Grameen Bank, the microfinance bank Yunus founded in 1976.

9 In Matni Adezai, Pak., a suburb of Peshawar, a suicide bomber kills at least 37 people at the funeral of the wife of an opponent of the Taliban.

•

Enda Kenny is chosen and sworn in as prime minister of Ireland.

•

The producers of the Broadway show *Spider-Man: Turn Off the Dark*, which has had 101 preview performances but is not yet ready to open, replace its star director, Julie Taymor, with Philip William McKinley.

•

The $250,000 A.M. Turing Award for excellence in computer science is granted to Leslie Valiant for his work in the mathematical foundations of computer learning and in parallel computing.

10 The Dalai Lama announces his relinquishment of political authority within the Tibetan government in exile.

11 A 9.0-magnitude earthquake rocks Japan and sets off a tsunami with waves as high as 9 m (30 ft) that engulfs towns along hundreds of kilometres of Japan's northeastern coast; some 24,000 people are feared dead.

•

Some 100,000 people engage in a sit-in in Sanaa, Yemen, to demand the resignation of the president.

U.S. Geological Survey

12 Evacuations are ordered for those living in the immediate area around Japan's Daiichi and Daini nuclear power plants after the cooling systems shut down during the earthquake and the generators to keep them running were subsequently drowned by the tsunami; later there is an explosion in the number 1 reactor at Daiichi, which is then flooded with seawater in hopes of preventing a meltdown.

•

The Arab League, which suspended Libya's membership on February 22, requests that the UN Security Council impose a no-fly zone over Libya in hopes of preventing further attacks by Muammar al-Qaddafi against those seeking democracy.

•

The runoff presidential election in Niger is held; it is won by opposition leader Mahamadou Issoufou, who handily defeats former prime minister Seïni Oumarou.

13 Antigovernment protesters in Bahrain block access to the financial district of Manama in spite of police attempts to disperse the demonstrators.

•

In London *Legally Blonde, the Musical* wins three Laurence Olivier Awards: best new musical, best actress in a musical or entertainment (Sheridan Smith), and best supporting actress in a musical or entertainment (Jill Halfpenny).

14 A large explosion occurs at the number 3 reactor at the Daiichi nuclear plant in Japan, and because the plant is off-line, the country's power company announces a planned series of rolling blackouts.

•

Some 1,200 troops from Saudi Arabia and 800 from the United Arab Emirates under the aegis of the Gulf Cooperation Council arrive in Bahrain to help the government put down antigovernment protests.

•

A Taliban suicide bomber kills 36 people outside a military recruiting centre in Kunduz, Afg.

•

In a ceremony in New York City, the Rock and Roll Hall of Fame inducts musicians Darlene Love, Neil Diamond, Alice Cooper, Dr. John, and Tom Waits; musician Leon Russell and record label owners Jac Holzman and Art Rupe are also honoured.

15 King Hamad ibn Isa al-Khalifah of Bahrain declares a three-month state of emergency as a result of continuing antigovernment protests in the country.

•

John Baker wins the Iditarod Trail Sled Dog Race, crossing under the Burled Arch in Nome, Alaska, after setting a course record time of 8 days 18 hours 46 minutes 39 seconds; Baker is the first Alaskan Inupiat to win the race.

•

The winner of the PEN/Faulkner Award for Fiction is announced as Deborah Eisenberg for her compilation *The Collected Stories of Deborah Eisenberg*.

16 Government troops in Bahrain demolish the protest tent camp in Manama's Pearl Square and clear the square of demonstrators in a crackdown that leaves at least three protesters and two security officers dead.

•

Palestinian Authority Pres. Mahmoud Abbas announces that he has accepted Hamas leader Ismail Haniya's invitation to travel to Gaza for unity talks.

•

A three-year investigation into a huge global pedophile ring culminates with the announcement of 184 arrests in more than 30 countries and the rescue of at least 230 boys.

•

The MS *Oliva* cargo ship runs aground and breaks apart on Nightingale Island in Tristan da Cunha, home of close to half the world's population of northern rockhopper penguins; more than 800 tons of oil spill from the wreck, and as many as 20,000 penguins are coated in oil.

•

The $1 million Birgit Nilsson Prize for outstanding achievement in opera and concert is awarded to Chicago Symphony Orchestra director Riccardo Muti.

17 The UN Security Council authorizes the use of force, including the establishment of a no-fly zone, to prevent forces loyal to Libyan leader Muammar al-Qaddafi from attacking civilians in the country.

•

A meeting of the Group of Seven industrialized countries results in an agreement to intervene in currency markets in order to stabilize the value of the Japanese yen, which immediately loses value against the dollar.

•

NASA's spacecraft Messenger, launched in 2004, achieves orbit around the planet Mercury.

18 Government supporters open fire on protesters in Sanaa, Yemen, killing at least 50 people, and Pres. ʿAli ʿAbd Allah Salih declares a state of emergency, but protesters are undeterred.

Hamad I Mohammed—Reuters/Landov

•

Antigovernment protests take place in four cities in Syria, the largest of them in Darʿa; they are immediately and brutally squashed.

•

The online film rental service Netflix announces that it has purchased the North American rights to 26 episodes of the political drama *House of Cards*, directed by David Fincher and starring Kevin Spacey; the show will be available only through Netflix and is expected to debut in late 2012.

•

The Pearl Monument, erected in 1982 in Manama, Bahrain, in honour of a Gulf Cooperation Council meeting there, is torn down by authorities; the monument had become a symbol of the protests in Manama's Pearl Square. *(Photos above.)*

19 Leaders of a coalition of Western and Arab countries begin a military intervention in Libya, sending missiles to fight against Libyan government forces that are attacking rebels in Banghazi and other towns in enforcement of a previously announced no-fly zone.

•

Amendments to Egypt's constitution are resoundingly approved in a referendum; amendments include a limit of two four-year terms of office for the president and judicial supervision of elections.

•

Despite a 24–8 loss to Ireland, England wins the Six Nations Rugby Union championship with a 4–1 record when France (3–2) defeats Wales (3–2).

20 Pres. ʿAli ʿAbd Allah Salih of Yemen dismisses the government of Prime Minister Ali Muhammad Mujawar.

•

Haitian voters go to the polls to choose between former first lady Mirlande Manigat and former entertainer Michel Martelly as their new president.

•

The American telecommunications giant AT&T announces that it will buy cellular telephone carrier T-Mobile; the resulting company will be the country's largest carrier.

21 A march of at least 15,000 people demanding higher spending and vastly more resources for township schools takes place in Cape Town.

•

The Dow Jones Industrial Average rises above 12,000 points, a level it sank below on March 12.

22 The U.S. Census Bureau releases figures showing that the population of Detroit fell a stunning 25% between 2000 and 2010; the city lost 237,500 people.

•

The Union for Reform Judaism in the U.S. announces that revitalizing rabbi Richard Jacobs of Scarsdale, N.Y., will succeed Eric Yoffie as its president.

23 A fourth austerity package of spending cuts and tax increases that has aroused ire in the streets is rejected by Portugal's legislature, and Prime Minister José Sócrates resigns.

•

The Egyptian stock market opens for the first time since January 27, when it was closed because of huge antigovernment protests; it immediately falls almost 9%.

•

The Norwegian Academy of Science and Letters awards its annual Abel Prize for outstanding work in mathematics to American mathematician John Milnor for his discoveries in topology, geometry, and algebra.

24 NATO agrees to take command of coalition forces maintaining the no-flight zone over Libya; later it agrees to take the lead on the entire military campaign to prevent Muammar al-Qaddafi's forces from overrunning the opposition.

•

The lower house of Germany's legislature approves the ending of military conscription beginning on July 1; service has been compulsory since the new German military was formed in 1955.

25 Thousands of pro-democracy demonstrators march in Dar'a and other cities in Syria; they are met with live fire from the military, and dozens are reported killed.

•

After fighting breaks out between pro-government and antigovernment demonstrators in Amman, Jordan, riot police clear the square of protesters, including the tent camp set up the previous day; at least one death is reported.

•

Canada's legislature votes its government in contempt, and the government falls.

•

Science magazine publishes a report on arrowheads and other tools found at the Buttermilk Creek site in central Texas that date to as long ago as 15,500 years; among the implications are that the traditional view that humans first traveled to North America 13,000 years ago over the Bering Strait cannot be correct and that the technology ascribed to the Clovis people was not imported from Asia but rather developed in North America.

26 Hundreds of thousands of people march in London to protest a package of proposed spending cuts by the government.

•

The Japanese horse Victoire Pisa wins the Dubai World Cup, the world's richest horse race.

•

Oxford defeats Cambridge in the 157th University Boat Race; Cambridge nonetheless leads the series 80–76.

27 Radiation levels high enough to cause radiation sickness are unexpectedly found in waters that have flooded turbine buildings next to reactors at Japan's stricken Daiichi nuclear complex.

•

At the American Chemical Society's annual meeting, Daniel Nocera of MIT declares that his research team has developed a practical "artificial leaf," a small, extremely efficient photovoltaic cell that can be placed in water in sunlight to produce electricity; he believes it can be put to use in less-developed countries.

28 U.S. Pres. Barack Obama makes a nationally televised speech to explain his decision to launch a military intervention in Libya.

•

India's Ministry of Environment and Forests releases the results of a survey of the population of wild tigers in the country; it found that though the area of tiger habitat is shrinking, the number of tigers rose from 1,411 in 2006 to 1,706, approximately a 20% increase.

•

The gourmet gift basket seller Harry & David files for bankruptcy protection.

•

Portuguese architect Eduardo Souto de Moura is named winner of the 2011 Pritzker Architecture Prize; among his works is a sports stadium built into a hillside in Braga, Port.

29 In Tikrit, Iraq, insurgents storm the provincial council office and seize hostages as a council meeting is breaking for lunch, and a standoff ensues for hours until Iraqi security forces attack and retake the building; at least 50 people, including all hostages and insurgents, are killed.

•

In the face of clashes between antigovernment and pro-government demonstrators, the government of Syria resigns.

•

The rating agency Standard & Poor's lowers its debt ratings for both Greece and Portugal.

•

The sixth and last installment in the best-selling Earth's Children series of novels by Jean M. Auel, *The Land of Painted Caves*, goes on sale; the first book of the series, *The Clan of the Cave Bear*, was published in 1980.

•

The winner of the Astrid Lindgren Memorial Award for children's literature is announced as Australian author and illustrator Shaun Tan.

30 Libyan Foreign Minister Moussa Koussa defects to Britain; forces loyal to Muammar al-Qaddafi, however, retake several towns recently ceded to the rebels in Libya.

•

Forces loyal to Alassane Ouattara take control of Côte d'Ivoire's administrative capital, Yamoussoukro.

•

Thein Sein is sworn in as president of Myanmar (Burma).

•

Behgjet Pacolli resigns as president of Kosovo after the country's Constitutional Court overturned his February election to the post.

31 A suicide bomber attacks the convoy of Maulana Fazlur Rehman, a member of the legislature and leader of an Islamist party in Pakistan that is viewed as insufficiently radical, killing at least 12 people; Rehman escapes, as he did an assassination attempt the previous day that killed some 10 people.

•

The Indian Ocean island of Mayotte officially becomes France's 101st *département*.

April

Today a white page opens in front of us, white like the white of our flag, symbol of hope and peace.

Alassane Ouattara, winner of the 2010 presidential election in Côte d'Ivoire, on the capture of former president Laurent Gbagbo, who refused to give up power, April 11

1 Thousands of protesters demonstrate in several cities in Syria, but security forces react with violence; at least 15 people are said to have been killed.

•

After clerics in Mazar-e Sharif, Afg., urge anti-American action in response to the virtually unreported burning of a Qu'ran by fringe pastor Terry Jones in Florida on March 20, thousands of rioters attack the UN compound in the city; 12 people, 7 of them UN workers, are killed.

•

The U.S. Department of Labor reports that the unemployment rate in March decreased to 8.8% and that the economy added 216,000 nonfarm jobs; this is seen as auspicious news.

2 UN officials and aid organizations report that they have found that hundreds of people were massacred in Duekoué, Côte d'Ivoire, the previous week during fighting between forces loyal to Alassane Ouattara and those favouring Laurent Gbagbo.

•

Officials in Japan report the discovery of a breach in a maintenance pit near the stricken Fukushima Daiichi nuclear plant that has been leaking highly radioactive water into the sea.

•

In the final of the cricket World Cup in Mumbai (Bombay), India, led by Mahendra Singh Dhoni, defeats Sri Lanka to win the title for the first time since 1983; more than one billion people worldwide watch the event on television, making it probably the most-seen sports event in history.

•

Southwest Airlines grounds 79 of its planes for inspection; the previous day one of its Boeing 737-300 aircraft had to make an emergency landing at a military base in Yuma, Ariz., when a piece of the fuselage ripped, opening a hole in the cabin ceiling.

3 A major suicide bomb attack on a popular Sufi shrine complex in Dera Ghazi Khan, Pak., kills at least 42 people.

•

Syrian Pres. Bashar al-Assad announces that the new prime minister is Minister of Agriculture Adel Safar.

•

Ai Weiwei, an internationally known artist and the designer of the Olympic stadium in Beijing, is arrested by authorities in China as part of a crackdown on critics of the government.

•

In the presidential election in Kazakhstan, incumbent Nursultan Nazarbayev wins overwhelmingly.

•

Cissé Mariam Kaïdama Sidibé is appointed prime minister of Mali.

4 Security forces fire on tens of thousands of antigovernment protesters in Ta'izz, Yemen, killing at least 10 people.

•

Preliminary results of the runoff presidential election in Haiti are released; they indicate that popular entertainer Michel Martelly won handily, with 68% of the vote.

•

Sam Abal becomes acting prime minister of Papua New Guinea when Sir Michael Somare begins a two-week suspension from office for misconduct; Somare announces an indefinite medical leave on April 19.

•

The NCAA championship in men's basketball is won by the University of Connecticut, which defeats Butler University 53–41; the following day Texas A&M University defeats the University of Notre Dame 76–70 to win the women's title.

5 China's central bank raises its key lending rate from 6.06% to 6.31% in an effort to slow inflation.

•

The government of Brazil refuses to halt construction on the giant Belo Monte hydroelectric dam in spite of a request from the Organization of American States (OAS); preliminary construction began in March.

•

With the sale of Pringles, the potato crisp brand, to Diamond Foods, Procter & Gamble Co. unloads its last food brand; Pringles were introduced by Procter & Gamble in 1971.

6 Portuguese Prime Minister José Sócrates in a televised address declares that he has requested financial aid from the European Commission.

•

Mass graves containing 59 bodies are found near San Fernando, Mex., in Tamaulipas state.

•

The IMF issues its annual report on the economies of the West Bank and Gaza; the report for the first time declares that the Palestinian Authority is capable of conducting the economic policies of an independent country.

•

Martin J. Rees, a British theoretical astrophysicist, is named the winner of the Templeton Prize for his contributions to affirming the spiritual dimension of life and to raising questions about the fundamental nature of existence. *(Photo below.)*

•

Next, a new restaurant helmed by celebrity chef Grant Achatz, opens in Chicago; the eatery sells advance tickets rather than accepting reservations or allowing walk-ins, and a thriving black market in tickets arises.

Lefteris Pitarakis/AP

7 Atifete Jahjaga is chosen as president of Kosovo and takes office the same day.

•

Mahamadou Issoufou takes office as president of Niger and appoints Brigi Rafini prime minister.

•

In a controversial move, the European Central Bank raises its benchmark interest rate for the first time since 2008; the new rate is 1.25%, a quarter point higher.

•

The publisher of *The Girl with the Dragon Tattoo*, by Stieg Larsson, announces that it has sold more than a million downloaded e-books; it is believed to be the first publication to reach that benchmark.

8 A demonstration by tens of thousands of people who feel that the military government of Egypt is failing to support democratic reform takes place in Cairo's Tahrir Square.

•

Ismail Omar Guellah is reelected president of Djibouti.

•

The Walt Disney Co. breaks ground on the Shanghai Disney Resort in China; the complex, which is planned to eventually encompass 700 ha (1,730 ac), is scheduled to open in 2015.

9 A man armed with an automatic weapon kills at least seven people, including himself, at a crowded mall in Alphen aan den Rijn, Neth.

•

The Detroit Symphony Orchestra celebrates its new contract, ending a six-month strike with a free concert in the city's Orchestra Hall.

•

Long-shot jumper Ballabriggs, ridden by jockey Jason Maguire, wins the Grand National steeplechase horse race at the Aintree course in Liverpool, Eng., by two and a quarter lengths; two horses, however, are fatally injured in the race.

10 Peru's presidential election results in the need for a runoff between Ollanta Humala and Keiko Fujimori.

•

As momentum in the battle for control of Côte d'Ivoire appears to swing in favour of Laurent Gbagbo, French and UN forces fire on Gbagbo's residence and on the presidential palace in Abidjan.

•

Charl Schwartzel of South Africa wins the Masters golf tournament in Augusta, Ga., finishing two strokes ahead of Australians Jason Day and Adam Scott.

•

Canada, led by skip Jeff Stoughton, bests Scotland to win the world men's championship in curling at the tournament in Regina, Sask.

11 In Abidjan, Côte d'Ivoire, the forces of Alassane Ouattara capture Laurent Gbagbo, who had refused to give up power after losing the 2010 presidential election to Ouattara.

•

A bomb explosion on a subway platform in downtown Minsk, Belarus, during the evening rush hour kills 12 people and injures some 150 others.

12 Japan raises its assessment of the seriousness of the crisis in mid-March at the Fukushima Daiichi nuclear power plant to a 7 on the International Nuclear Event Scale; 7 is the highest level on the scale and is the level assigned to the nuclear accident at Chernobyl in 1986.

•

A planned pro-democracy demonstration is brutally suppressed in Swaziland.

•

After a delay of nearly three weeks because of the March 11 earthquake and tsunami, the baseball season opens in Japan with a game between the Tohoku Rakuten Golden Eagles and the Chiba Lotte Marines in Chiba.

•

The winner of the 2011 Ruth Lilly Poetry Prize is named as David Ferry.

13 A suicide bomber detonates his weapon at a meeting of elders to resolve local disputes in Afghanistan's Kunar province; at least 12 people, including local leader Hajji Malik Zareen, are killed.

14 UN officials agree that Iraqi security forces killed dozens of Iranian exiles in a camp in Diyala province the previous week; Iraqi officials deny that the event occurred.

•

A summit meeting of leaders of the nascent economic organization BRICS, which comprises the emerging economic powers Brazil, Russia, India, China, and South Africa, takes place in Sanya, in China's Hainan province.

•

The journal *Science* publishes a paper by biologist Quentin Atkinson, who has applied mathematical methods to a study of phonemes in human languages and found a pattern of decreasing numbers of phonemes with distance from southern Africa, leading him to posit that language originated in that location and that the development of language made migration possible.

•

The American television network ABC announces the cancellation of two of its long-running daytime soap operas *All My Children* and *One Life to Live*.

•

The twins born January 8 to Crown Prince Frederik and Crown Princess Mary of Denmark are baptized in Copenhagen with the names Vincent Frederik Minik Alexander and Josephine Sophia Ivalo Mathilda. *(Photo right.)*

15 After a violent protest by soldiers over the failure of the government to provide promised benefits, Pres. Blaise Compaoré of Burkina Faso dismisses Prime Minister Tertius Zongo and dissolves the government.

•

Violent fighting breaks out between Salafist Muslims and supporters of King ʿAbdullah II in Al-Zarqaʾ, Jordan.

16 The first free and fair presidential election in the country's history takes place in Nigeria; Goodluck Jonathan is elected.

•

Egypt's Supreme Administrative Court formally dissolves the National Democratic Party, the party of former president Hosni Mubarak.

•

Merchants in Ouagadougou, the capital of Burkina Faso, march in protest against two nights of looting by soldiers who were protesting unpaid housing allowances; police meet the merchants' demonstration with tear gas.

•

The renowned Philadelphia Orchestra files for bankruptcy protection.

17 In legislative elections in Finland, parties opposed to participating in economic bailouts of other European Union members make gains, though the highest number of seats goes to the National Coalition Party, part of the ruling coalition and a proponent of bailouts.

•

Protests take place in cities throughout Syria; security forces respond with deadly force, with violence especially reported in Hims.

•

Emmanuel Mutai of Kenya wins the London Marathon with a time of 2 hr 4 min 40 sec, and Mary Keitany of Kenya is the fastest woman in the race, with a time of 2 hr 19 min 19 sec.

18 Supporters of losing presidential candidate Muhammad Buhari rampage in northern Nigeria; some 40 people are killed.

•

Luc Adolphe Tiao, a journalist, is appointed prime minister of Burkina Faso.

•

In New York City the winners of the 2011 Pulitzer Prizes are announced: two awards go to the *New York Times*, which wins for international reporting and commentary, and two awards go to the *Los Angeles Times*, which wins for public service and feature photography; winners in arts and letters include Bruce Norris in drama and Jennifer Egan in fiction.

•

The 115th Boston Marathon is won by Geoffrey Mutai of Kenya with an astonishing time of 2 hr 3 min 2 sec, the fastest time ever recorded for a major marathon; the fastest woman is Caroline Kilel of Kenya, who posts a time of 2 hr 22 min 36 sec.

19 British Foreign Secretary William Hague announces that the government has decided to send military advisers to assist rebels in Libya in their cause.

•

At the first Communist Party congress held in Cuba in 14 years, a program of modifications is adopted, Raúl Castro is named first secretary, and José Ramón Machado is named second secretary of the party; it is the first time a person other than a member of the Castro family has held the latter post.

Tariq Mikkel Khan—Polfoto/AP

•

Security forces in Syria violently clear a protest sit-in in Hims, and the state of emergency, in place since 1963, is officially lifted.

20 The annual summit meeting of the Arab League, delayed from March to mid-May in Baghdad, is again postponed because of turmoil in the region; a new date is to be decided on later.

•

The price of an ounce of gold for the first time exceeds $1,500.

•

India launches a rocket from Andhra Pradesh that successfully places three scientific satellites into orbit around Earth.

•

U.S. Secretary of Homeland Security Janet Napolitano announces that the colour-coded system of terrorism alerts will be replaced by a new plan in which alerts—either elevated, denoting credible general threats, or imminent, denoting credible, specific, and impending threats—will be issued as warranted and will convey information on the nature of the dangers.

•

The journal *Nature* publishes a study that suggests that all humans possess one of three microbial ecosystem types within the intestines and that the type remains constant and is unrelated to other factors, including health or ethnic background.

21 U.S. Pres. Barack Obama authorizes the use of armed drones in the fight against the forces of Libyan leader Muammar al-Qaddafi; also, rebels in Libya gain control of the town of Wazin, on the border with Tunisia.

•

Dozens of people being held in an immigration

detention centre in Sydney engage in rioting in which they burn down nine of the buildings in the centre, including laundry, kitchen, computer, and medical facilities.

22 Antigovernment protesters march in at least 20 cities throughout Syria and are met with gunfire by security forces; more than 100 demonstrators are killed, with the highest death toll in Azra.

•

Truck drivers unhappy with higher fuel prices and fees eroding their pay interfere with operations at the seaport of Shanghai for the third successive day.

23 Yemeni Pres. ʿAli ʿAbd Allah Salih agrees to a transition proposal by the Gulf Cooperation Council, saying that he will step down if a number of conditions, including the cessation of protests, are met.

•

At least 11 people are killed when Syrian security forces fire on mourners at funerals for protesters killed the previous day.

24 On the third day of shooting across a disputed border between Cambodia and Thailand, at least 10 people are killed; the area is evacuated.

•

In Vanuatu after the government loses a no-confidence vote, Serge Vohor is elected to replace Sato Kilman as prime minister.

25 Some 500 Taliban prisoners escape from the main prison in southern Afghanistan through a tunnel that had been built over a five-month period and stretched 0.8 km (0.5 mi).

•

Hungarian Pres. Pal Schmitt signs a controversial conservative constitution that was approved by the legislature in spite of boycotts by all opposition parties; it is to go into effect at the beginning of 2012.

•

Idriss Déby is overwhelmingly elected to a fourth consecutive term as president of Chad.

•

Suresh Kalmadi, the chief organizer of the 2010 Commonwealth Games in India, is arrested on charges of corruption related to the staging of the games.

26 Italian Prime Minister Silvio Berlusconi and French Pres. Nicolas Sarkozy jointly request that the European Commission make changes in the 1985 Schengen Agreement, which allows free passage between member countries of the EU, and ask for other changes to address the crisis caused by immigrants fleeing turmoil in North Africa.

•

Mexican officials report that the number of bodies found in mass graves near San Fernando has risen to 183; in addition, a mass grave in Durango state has so far yielded 75 bodies.

•

A week after an attack by hackers on Sony's PlayStation online network made the game-playing service unavailable to subscribers, Sony reveals that the attacker also gained access to personal and financial information of account holders.

27 The Palestinian political entities Fatah and Hamas announce that they have agreed to a deal brokered by the interim Egyptian government to create a unity government and hold elections within a year.

•

Tibet's government-in-exile announces that Lobsang Sangay has been elected as its prime minister.

•

Waves of tornadoes sweep through six states in the American South, leaving a large swath of devastation and killing at least 342 people; in Alabama alone some 250 people lose their lives.

•

U.S. Pres. Barack Obama releases to public view a copy of his long-form birth certificate in an attempt to put to rest rumours that seem to be gaining increasing currency among his political opposition that he was not born in the U.S. and thus is not eligible to hold the presidency.

28 The U.S. Department of Commerce reports that the country's economy grew by only 1.8% in the first quarter of 2011.

•

At lunchtime in a popular restaurant in Marrakech, Mor., a large bomb explosion kills at least 17 people, most of them French citizens.

•

Opposition leader Kizza Besigye is arrested in Uganda for the fourth time in a few weeks; the violence of the arrest leaves him partially blinded.

•

Pere López becomes acting chief executive of Andorra, replacing Jaume Bartumeu Cassany, who must resign after having been elected to the country's legislature.

29 Demonstrators attempting to break the government siege of Darʿa, Syria, where the first antigovernment protests in the country took place, are met with live fire, and at least 16 people are killed; some 25 people die in clashes in other cities in the country.

•

Large crowds of angry protesters block streets and set fires in Kampala, Ugan., and security forces use tear gas, rubber bullets, and live ammunition to disperse them; at least five people are reported killed.

•

Toshiso Kosako, who was made a nuclear adviser to the government of Japan after the March 11 earthquake and tsunami that critically damaged the Fukushima Daiichi nuclear plant, resigns in a tearful news conference in protest against the government's failure, in his view, to protect the public appropriately from radiation.

•

Prince William of Wales weds Catherine Middleton in a solemn and romantic ceremony at Westminster Abbey in London; some three billion people worldwide watch the televised nuptials.

30 Libyan leader Muammar al-Qaddafi in a televised speech offers negotiations but refuses to step down or leave the country; shortly thereafter NATO warplanes strike government targets in Tripoli, including a house in which Qaddafi's youngest son and three of his grandchildren are killed.

•

Miki Ando of Japan wins the gold medal in ladies' figure skating at the ISU world figure skating championships in Moscow, where the event was moved when the aftermath of the March 11 earthquake and tsunami prevented it from taking place in its originally scheduled location, Tokyo.

•

Frankel, ridden by Tom Queally, wins the Two Thousand Guineas Thoroughbred horse race by six lengths in Newmarket, Suffolk, Eng.

May

And on nights like this one, we can say to those families who have lost loved ones to al-Qaeda's terror: Justice has been done.

U.S. Pres. Barack Obama, announcing the killing of Osama bin Laden, May 1

1 U.S. Pres. Barack Obama makes a late-night televised appearance in the East Room of the White House to announce that U.S. military operatives entered a house in Abottabad, Pak., in which al-Qaeda leader Osama bin Laden had been living and killed bin Laden.

•

Pope Benedict XVI presides over a ceremony in St. Peter's Square at the Vatican in which Pope John Paul II (1978–2005) is beatified. *(Photo right.)*

2 In legislative elections in Canada, the ruling Conservative Party wins 39.6% of the vote, followed by the New Democrats, with 30.6%; this gives the Conservative Party a majority government, while many traditional challengers lose ground to the point of irrelevancy.

•

The U.S. Army Corps of Engineers destroys a levee on the Mississippi River, preventing flooding from washing away Cairo, Ill., and instead flooding farmland in Missouri, in a desperate attempt to save towns downriver from further catastrophic flooding.

•

The automobile manufacturer Chrysler Group announces a quarterly profit for the first time since 2006.

3 Portugal agrees to accept a plan that calls for the country to reduce its deficit in return for international funding.

•

The U.S. and Romania reach an agreement on the location of antimissile interceptors in Romania as part of the U.S.-led missile defense program.

•

Sweden's Polar Music Prize Foundation announces that the winners of the Polar Music Prize are American rock singer-songwriter Patti Smith and American string quartet the Kronos Quartet.

4 In Cairo, Palestinian Authority Pres. Mahmoud Abbas, leader of Fatah, and Khaled Meshal, head of Hamas, sign a reconciliation agreement that calls for the creation of a joint caretaker government ahead of elections.

•

China's State Council announces the formation of the State Internet Information Office, which will be charged with overseeing and regulating all Internet content in the country.

•

Francis Everitt, head of the Gravity Probe B project, in which orbiting gyroscopes measured space-time around Earth, reports that the measurements confirmed the parts of Einstein's theory of general relativity that say

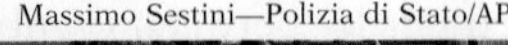

Massimo Sestini—Polizia di Stato/AP

that a spinning object should cause spinning of space-time, or "frame dragging."

5 Legislative elections in Scotland give a majority of seats to the Scottish National Party.

•

British voters defeat a proposal to change the way members of Parliament are elected from a system in which the candidate with the most votes wins to one in which a winner must achieve more than 50% of the vote.

•

Brazil's Supreme Court recognizes civil unions for same-sex couples, a legal status that entails the same rights as in marriage.

•

A suicide car bomber kills at least 25 people at a police training centre in Al-Hillah, Iraq; most of the victims are police officers.

•

Claude Choules, the last known surviving World War I combatant, dies at the age of 110 in Perth, Australia; Choules served in the British Royal Navy during World War I and in Australia's naval forces during World War II.

6 At least 41 people are killed when Syrian security forces open fire on mass protests in several cities; violence is particularly high in Hims.

•

The U.S. Department of Labor reports that in spite of a somewhat encouraging increase to 244,000 in the number of nonfarm jobs, the unemployment rate in April rose to 9%.

•

The Warner Music Group agrees to its purchase by Russian-born industrialist Len Blavatnik.

7 Syrian military forces take control of the city of Baniyas, cutting off communication, after large demonstrations took place there the previous day, and the massive crackdown continues to escalate throughout the country the following day.

•

A referendum on measures to increase the power of the president and decrease those of the judiciary is held in Ecuador; all 10 proposals are approved.

•

Unsubstantiated rumours fuel fighting between thousands of Muslims and Coptic Christians in Cairo; by the following morning two churches have been set alight and at least 15 people killed.

•

Filipino champion Manny Pacquiao wins a welterweight boxing match against American Shane Mosley by unanimous decision in Las Vegas; it is Pacquiao's 14th straight victory.

•

Animal Kingdom, ridden by John Velazquez, comes from behind to win the Kentucky Derby by 2¾ lengths.

8 The UN announces an agreement between northern Sudan and southern Sudan to withdraw forces from the disputed Abyei border region and to field a joint north-south force instead.

•

Thousands of people march in Mexico City to demand an end to the drug war in Mexico; a leader of the movement is journalist and poet Javier Sicilia, whose son was killed several weeks earlier.

9 The Standard & Poor's rating service downgrades Greece's debt from BB– to B, the same rating as that of Belarus.

•

Thai Prime Minister Abhisit Vejjajiva announces that he will, with the permission of King Bhumibol Adulyadej, dissolve the legislature and that elections will take place on July 3.

•

In a court in Guatemala, a panel of judges acquits former president Alfonso Portillo of charges of having embezzled state money.

•

India's Supreme Court overturns a ruling, made in October 2010, that the site of the Ayodhya mosque that was destroyed in 1992 should be split between Hindus and Muslims; a resolution of the problem is expected to be issued in the future.

•

A government commission in Chile approves the massive HidroAysén hydroelectric project, which will entail the building of five dams in Patagonia.

•

At the National Magazine Awards presentation in New York City, *National Geographic* wins the Magazine of the Year award; general-excellence award winners are *New York*, *Scientific American*, *Women's Health*, *Garden & Gun*, *Los Angeles*, and *Poetry*.

10 Japanese Prime Minister Naoto Kan announces that the country will cancel plans to build new nuclear reactors; 14 new reactors were planned.

•

The computer company Microsoft Corp. announces that it has reached an agreement to buy Skype, the online voice and video telecommunication corporation.

•

The Presbyterian Church (U.S.A.) agrees to a change to its constitution that will allow the ordination of people in same-sex relationships as ministers, elders, and deacons.

11 The Syrian military moves into and occupies Hims, killing at least 19 people and arresting hundreds.

•

After Belarus drops restrictions on the exchange rate of the Belarusian rubel its value plunges more quickly and deeply than anticipated.

•

Rebels in Libya seize control of the airport in Misratah.

•

Raj Rajaratnam, the billionaire founder and former manager of the Galleon Group hedge fund, is found guilty by a federal jury of 14 counts of fraud and conspiracy in an insider-trading case in New York City.

12 Opposition leader Kizza Besigye returns to Uganda after medical treatment in Kenya; the crowds welcoming him back outnumber those attending the inauguration of Pres. Yoweri Museveni to a fourth term of office.

•

The *American Journal of Public Health* publishes online a study that found that the problem of rape in the Democratic Republic of the Congo is far more widespread and pervasive than had been realized; it estimated that women in the country are raped at the rate of approximately one every minute.

•

The results of a large-scale randomized study led by the U.S. National Institute of Allergy and Infectious Diseases are made public; the study found that people who were infected with HIV and were put on the antiviral regimen used to treat AIDS were 96% less likely to infect sexual partners with HIV than people not on such medication; the current protocol is to wait for the development of AIDS before prescribing the medication.

13 A suicide attack kills at least 82 members of the

paramilitary Frontier Constabulary in Charsadda, in Pakistan's Khyber-Pakhtunkhwa province.

•

Results of state elections held in West Bengal, India, in April and May are released; for the first time in more than 30 years, the Communist Party has been ousted from power, with the majority of seats in the state legislature going to the Trinamool Congress Party.

•

George Mitchell resigns as U.S. envoy to the Middle East, despairing of the possibility of a peace agreement between Israel and Palestine.

•

Vanuatu's court of appeal rules that the selection of Serge Vohor as prime minister, following the no-confidence vote that brought down the government of Prime Minister Sato Kilman, was unconstitutional; Kilman is returned to office.

14 Syrian troops occupy the city of Tall Kalakh, on the border with Lebanon, detaining hundreds of people; residents flee over the border.

•

In Belarus, opposition leader Andrei Sannikau is sentenced to five years in prison for having led antigovernment protests after the presidential election in December 2010, which was widely viewed as fraudulent.

•

Manchester United wins the English Premier League title; it is the team's 19th English title in association football (soccer), a new record.

15 Some 200 gunmen in Petén department in Guatemala execute at least 27 people; it is feared that the massacre represents an incursion of Mexico's drug cartels into the country.

•

Palestinian protesters march on the borders of Israel from its neighbouring countries as well as the West Bank and Gaza in a coordinated confrontation.

•

Dominique Strauss-Kahn, the managing director of the IMF and a leading French politician, is arrested in New York City on suspicion of having sexually attacked a maid in his hotel room.

•

In Vicksburg, Miss., the Mississippi River reaches a height of 17.2 m (56.3 ft), 4 m (13 ft) above flood stage, breaking the record set in 1927; it has not yet crested.

•

In Düsseldorf, Ger., Azerbaijani duo Ell/Nikki wins the Eurovision Song Contest with their song "Running Scared."

16 At a meeting in Brussels, the financial leaders of the member countries of the euro zone formally approve a bailout for Portugal of €78 billion (about $110 billion).

•

China's state news agency reports that the Yangstze River area in central China has for the past five months been suffering a severe drought that has destroyed crops and left too little water for use in hundreds of reservoirs.

•

The space shuttle *Endeavour* is launched for its final flight, carrying the Alpha Magnetic Spectrometer, a detector to be deployed on the International Space Station in a particle-physics experiment that will measure cosmic radiation and search for antimatter galaxies and dark matter.

17 The joint venture between British energy giant BP and the Russian state-controlled oil-and-gas company Rosneft that was announced in January collapses.

•

John Stillwell—EPA/Landov

Queen Elizabeth II of Britain meets with Irish Pres. Mary McAleese after her arrival in Dublin for a four-day visit to Ireland; she is the first reigning British monarch to travel to the republic. *(Photo above.)*

•

The Journal of the American Medical Association publishes a study that found that the number of hospital emergency departments in the U.S. has fallen by 25% in the past 20 years; the number of visits to emergency rooms has risen even faster than the number of such departments has fallen.

18 Yemeni Pres. 'Ali 'Abd Allah Salih refuses to sign an agreement to step down that was negotiated by the Gulf Cooperation Council; he had earlier promised he would sign it.

•

Data released by Japan's Cabinet Office show that the country's economy shrank at an annual rate of 3.7% during the first fiscal quarter of 2011.

•

The U.S. imposes sanctions against Syrian Pres. Bashar al-Assad because of his regime's heavy-handed response to pro-democracy demonstrations.

•

The Portuguese association football (soccer) team FC Porto defeats Braga of Portugal 1–0 to win the UEFA Europa League title in Dublin.

•

American novelist Philip Roth is named the fourth winner of the biennial Man Booker International Prize for fiction.

19 An Afghan construction crew engaged in building a road in southeastern Afghanistan is attacked by night by insurgents; at least 35 crew members are killed.

•

A series of bomb explosions outside police and government headquarters in Kirkuk, Iraq, leave at least 29 people dead.

•

The online bookseller Amazon.com announces that since April 1 its customers have bought 105 e-books for every 100 paperback and hardcover books.

20 Israeli Prime Minister Benjamin

Netanyahu, meeting in Washington, D.C., with U.S. Pres. Barack Obama, rejects Obama's proposals for compromises in negotiating peace with Palestine, beginning with the idea of using the pre-1967 borders as a starting point.

•

Thousands of antigovernment protesters march in cities throughout Syria, defying the government crackdown, in which at least 44 protesters are killed.

21 In Yamoussoukro, Côte d'Ivoire, Alassane Ouattara is sworn in as the country's new president.

•

Bernard Hopkins wins the WBC and IBO light-heavyweight titles by unanimous decision over Jean Pascal; Hopkins, at 46, becomes the oldest fighter to win a boxing championship, as he is six months older than George Foreman was when he won the WBA and IBF heavyweight championships in 1994.

•

Shackleford wins the Preakness Stakes, the second event in U.S. Thoroughbred horse racing's Triple Crown, by a half-length over Kentucky Derby winner Animal Kingdom.

22 Supporters of Yemeni Pres. ʿAli ʿAbd Allah Salih surround the U.A.E. embassy in Sanaa, where Salih was scheduled to arrive to sign an agreement to step down, and trap diplomats within; later, after the diplomats have been flown to the presidential palace for the ceremony, Salih refuses to sign the agreement.

•

A huge tornado touches down in Joplin, Mo., devastating about a third of the city and leaving at least 160 residents dead.

•

Legislative elections in Cyprus result in a victory for the conservative opposition Democratic Rally party.

•

The American film *The Tree of Life* wins the Palme d'Or at the Cannes Festival in France.

•

In spite of his loss to *ozeki* Kaio on the final day of the May Technical Examination Tournament (held instead of the Natsu Basho [summer grand sumo tournament]), *yokozuna* Hakuho wins his seventh consecutive tournament, tying Asashoryu's record.

23 The European Union imposes sanctions against Syrian Pres. Bashar al-Assad.

•

The U.S. Supreme Court rules that California's prison system is overcrowded to the point of violating the constitutional ban on "cruel and unusual punishment" and orders the release of more than 30,000 inmates.

24 The Tokyo Electric Power Co. says that it is probably the case that three of the nuclear reactors at the Fukushima Daiichi power plant had fuel meltdowns early in the crisis caused by the March 11 earthquake and tsunami in Japan.

•

NASA reports that the rover Spirit, stuck in sand on Mars for two years, is no longer operating; the rover Opportunity continues to send data from the other side of the planet.

25 Egypt's transitional government confirms that the country will reopen its border with the Gaza Strip on May 28.

•

Riot police in Tbilisi, Georgia, break up a demonstration of citizens demanding the resignation of the country's president.

26 Former general Ratko Mladic, who is believed to have led Bosnian Serb forces that conducted the nearly four-year siege of Sarajevo in the early 1990s and the massacre at Srebenica in 1995, is arrested in Lazarevo, Serbia.

•

In Hangu, Pak., a bomb explosion kills at least 25 people.

•

Ikililou Dhoinine takes office as president of Comoros.

27 Leaders of the Group of Eight industrialized countries, meeting in Deauville, France, agree to send $20 billion in aid to Egypt and Tunisia in hopes of helping to improve economic conditions in the countries.

•

Ten of thousands of people rally in Tahrir Square in Cairo to demand more democratic reforms.

•

Ugandan Pres. Yoweri Museveni appoints Amama Mbabazi prime minister.

28 A suicide bomber wearing a police uniform infiltrates a security meeting of NATO and Afghan officials in Taliqan, Afg., and detonates his weapon, killing at least four people, among them the widely respected police commander Daoud Daoud.

•

Hundreds of Palestinians arrive by the busload to cross at the newly reopened Rafah crossing from the Gaza Strip into Egypt.

•

In association football (soccer), FC Barcelona of Spain defeats the English team Manchester United FC 3–1 to win the UEFA Champions League title in London.

29 An Islamist organization takes control of the Yemeni city of Zinjibar; the same group had earlier seized the town of Jaar.

•

As a mandated deadline for Nepal to produce a constitution passes, the country's political parties agree to extend the Constituent Assembly's term by three months, averting a crisis; the deal includes the resignation of Prime Minister Jhalanath Kanal.

•

The 95th Indianapolis 500 automobile race is won by Dan Wheldon of Britain after American front-runner J.R. Hildebrand crashed in the final lap; it is the centennial of the first Indy 500 (the race was not run during the two world wars).

30 An antigovernment demonstration takes place in Hohhot, the capital of the Chinese autonomous region of Inner Mongolia; a series of demonstrations have taken place in the region recently.

•

Germany announces a plan to phase out all of its nuclear power plants by 2022 and expand its use of renewable resources; nuclear power provides 23% of the country's electricity.

31 After Libyan leader Muammar al-Qaddafi refuses efforts by South African Pres. Jacob Zuma to persuade him to relinquish power, NATO resumes air strikes on Tripoli.

June

I think he could not have been luckier than that to have a face-saving device by leaving the country for a good medical cause.

Abdulaziz Sager, chairman of the Gulf Research Center in Saudi Arabia, on the departure from Yemen of Yemeni Pres. ʿAli ʿAbdallah Salih, June 4

1 The credit rating agency Moody's Investors Service drops the rating of Greece three levels, from B1 to Caa1.

•

Security forces in Syria stage raids on towns in the area of Hims, where large antigovernment protests have taken place in recent weeks; at least 42 people are killed.

•

A few days after the return to Honduras of former president Manuel Zelaya, the Organization of American States (OAS) reinstates Honduras as a member.

•

Brazil's environmental agency gives its final approval for the building of the giant Belo Monte hydroelectric dam on the Xingu River.

•

Although he is widely suspected of being involved in a bribery scandal, Sepp Blatter, who is credited with having increased the worldwide popularity of association football (soccer), is reelected president of the sport's governing body, FIFA.

2 Prime Minister Naoto Kan of Japan survives a no-confidence motion in the legislature with the promise to resign at an unspecified time in the future.

•

The English-language newspaper *Shanghai Daily* reports that a Chinese official says that the Three Gorges Dam on the Yangtze River is adversely affecting water levels of lakes and streams downstream, in particular in two large freshwater lakes, in ways that were not foreseen; central and southern China are enduring a major drought.

•

U.S. first lady Michelle Obama unveils a new symbol to show what a healthy diet should consist of; the symbol, a dinner plate indicating the recommended portions of each food group in a healthy meal, replaces the food pyramid most recently revised in 2005.

•

The 84th Scripps National Spelling Bee is won by Sukanya Roy of South Abington, Pa., when she correctly spells *cymotrichous*.

3 Syria shuts down Internet access in the country in an unsuccessful attempt to quell antigovernment protests, which continue to spread in spite of the government's brutal crackdown; activists report the deaths of at least 65 demonstrators in Hamah.

•

The U.S. Department of Labor reports that the unemployment rate in May rose to 9.1%; the economy added only a minuscule 54,000 nonfarm jobs.

•

Coordinated attacks at a mosque and a hospital leave at least 21 people dead in Tikrit, Iraq.

4 The day after he was wounded in an attack on the mosque in the presidential compound in Sanaa, Yemeni Pres. ʿAli ʿAbd Allah Salih agrees to travel to Riyadh, Saudi Arabia, for medical treatment; other officials, including the prime minister, also seek treatment in Riyadh.

•

The Derby at Epsom Downs in Surrey, Eng., is won by Pour Moi, ridden by Mickael Barzalona; Pour Moi beats Treasure Beach by a head.

•

Li Na of China defeats Italian Francesca Schiavone to win the women's French Open tennis title; the following day Rafael Nadal of Spain defeats Roger Federer of Switzerland to capture the men's championship for the sixth time, equaling the French Open record set in 1981 by Björn Borg.

•

In New Delhi tens of thousands of supporters of popular yoga guru Swami Ramdev gather in a large encampment for yoga and fasting in an anticorruption protest to demand the repatriation of misappropriated public money *(photo right)*; the next day the gathering is broken up by police officers using tear gas, and Swami Ramdev is forcibly returned to his ashram.

5 The opposition Social Democrats win a resounding victory in legislative elections in Portugal; Pedro Passos Coelho is sworn in as prime minister on June 21.

•

Ollanta Humala is elected president of Peru in a runoff election.

6 The government of Syria declares that police headquarters in Jisr al-Shugur were attacked by armed protesters and that 120 security officers were killed.

•

Officials in Pakistan report that U.S. drone strikes at three sites in South Waziristan killed 18 people, most of them said not to be Pakistani.

•

Steve Jobs, CEO of Apple Inc., introduces iCloud, a free service that will store content and apps on remote servers and make the content thus stored available for use on all Apple devices an individual owns.

•

The Bowl Championship Series strips the University of Southern California of its BCS national championship in 2004 because of violations regarding improper benefits given to players; the organization will recognize no champion for that season of college football.

7 NATO forces make a rare daytime bombing raid against the compound of Libyan leader Muammar al-Qaddafi in Tripoli; Qaddafi responds with an audio recording in which he declares that he will never surrender.

•

The British tabloid newspaper *News of the World*, as part of a settlement reached with actress Sienna Miller for having illegally intercepted her cell phone messages in 2005 and 2006, publicly apologizes to her; the paper published articles about her private life based on information gleaned from the messages.

8 The IMF reports internally that it has suffered a major cyberattack, the full dimensions of which have not yet been discovered.

•

Tunisia's interim government postpones an election for members of a constituent assembly, originally scheduled for July 24, to October 23, citing logistic difficulties.

•

It is reported that two new elements, with atomic numbers of 114 and 116, respectively, have been accepted by the International Union of Pure and Applied Chemistry and added to the periodic table of elements.

•

Téa Obreht wins the Orange Prize, an award for fiction written by women and published in the U.K., for her first novel, *The Tiger's Wife*.

9 Somalia's interim government reaches an agreement to extend its own mandate for a further year; the agreement includes the requirement that Prime Minister Mohamed Abdullahi Mohamed resign in 30 days, and that stipulation leads to rioting by civilians and soldiers in Mogadishu.

•

Turkey authorizes the construction of refugee camps to accommodate Syrians fleeing across the border, including much of the population of Jisr al-Shugur; Syrian security forces surround the city.

10 UN officials say that the military of Sudan is conducting house-to-house searches for opposition supporters in Kadugli, which is in northern Sudan but has many residents who support southern Sudan; tens of thousands of people have fled the area.

•

Authorities in Germany say that sprouts have been conclusively identified as the source of the *E. coli* epidemic in the country that began in May and has left at least 31 people dead.

11 The UN reports that in May 368 civilians were killed in Afghanistan, 82% by Taliban and other militant attacks, the highest monthly total since it began keeping track in 2007 and likely since the beginning of the war; also, a roadside bomb in southern Afghanistan leaves 15 civilians dead.

•

Long shot Ruler On Ice, with jockey Jose Valdivia, Jr., aboard, wins the Belmont Stakes, the last event in Thoroughbred horse racing's U.S. Triple Crown.

12 The ruling Justice and Development Party wins a resounding victory in legislative elections in Turkey.

•

The Dallas Mavericks defeat the Miami Heat 105–95 in game six of the best-of-seven tournament to secure the team's first-ever National Basketball Association championship.

•

The 65th Tony Awards are presented in New York City; winners include *War Horse*, *The Book of Mormon* (which takes nine awards), *The Normal Heart*, and *Anything Goes* and actors Mark Rylance, Frances McDormand, Norbert Leo Butz, and Sutton Foster; lifetime achievement awards go to theatre executive Philip J. Smith and South African playwright Athol Fugard.

13 In a referendum in Italy, voters overturn laws to restart the nuclear energy

Tsering Topgyal/AP

program, put the water supply in private hands, and allow the prime minister immunity from prosecution while in office.

•

Germany officially recognizes the National Transitional Council set up by rebels in Banghazi, Libya, as the government of Libya.

14 U.S. Pres. Barack Obama's visit to San Juan, P.R., marks the first visit to the commonwealth by a U.S. president since Pres. John F. Kennedy in December 1961.

•

Officials in Arizona say that the Wallow wildfire has grown to encompass more than 189,800 ha (469,000 ac), which makes it the biggest wildfire in Arizona history; it is only 18% contained.

•

After 183 preview performances, the musical *Spider-Man: Turn Off the Dark* opens on Broadway; it receives rather lukewarm reviews.

15 Hundreds of people engage in a quiet protest against economic policies that cause hardship in Minsk, Belarus.

•

The online music service Pandora Media makes its much-anticipated initial public offering of $16; though shares rise as high as $26, at market close they sell at a respectable $17.42.

•

The Boston Bruins defeat the Vancouver Canucks 4–0 to win the Stanley Cup, the National Hockey League championship trophy, for the first time since 1972; disappointed Canuck fans go on a violent rampage in Vancouver.

•

The International IMPAC Dublin Literary Award is granted to Irish-born American author Colum McCann for his novel *Let the Great World Spin*.

16 The terrorist organization al-Qaeda announces that its new leader is Ayman al-Zawahiri; he succeeds Osama bin Laden, who was killed by U.S. forces on May 2.

•

The International Labour Organization approves the Convention on Domestic Workers, requiring regular working hours and other benefits for such workers; the convention must be ratified by the ILO member countries in order to take effect.

17 King Muhammad VI of Morocco unveils a proposed new constitution that creates a prime minister but does not greatly decrease the power of the monarch.

•

Antigovernment protests in several cities in Syria are met with a military response, particularly in Hims; at least 19 people are reported killed.

18 A water-filtration system installed at the Fukushima Daiichi nuclear plant in Japan in an effort to cool the damaged reactors without adding to the amount of contaminated water breaks down after operating for only five hours; it had become clogged with radioactive cesium.

•

Three Britons, two Kenyans, and an American are given long prison sentences in Somalia for having taken into the country cash intended as ransom to be paid to pirates.

19 A Fatah spokesman declares that a meeting in Cairo between Fatah and Hamas in which it was hoped that a new Palestinian unity government could be announced has been canceled, as the factions have been unable to agree on a prime minister.

•

It is reported that two days of fighting between Islamist militants and Yemeni soldiers in Zinjibar have resulted in at least 21 deaths.

•

Rory McIlroy of Northern Ireland secures an eight-stroke victory over Jason Day of Australia to win the U.S. Open golf tournament in Bethesda, Md.

20 Zine al-Abidine Ben Ali, the former president of Tunisia, is found guilty of embezzlement and misuse of public funds and sentenced in absentia to 35 years in prison in Tunis.

•

The U.S. Supreme Court rules that a group of 1.5 million women who had worked for the retailer Wal-Mart cannot sue as a class for back pay and damages in a sex discrimination lawsuit.

•

The Office of the UN High Commissioner for Refugees reports that in 2010 there were 43.7 million refugees in the world, the highest number in 15 years.

•

A music foundation in Japan sells a Stradivarius violin known as the Lady Blunt at an online auction for $15.9 million, more than four times greater than the previous highest price for a Stradivarius; the proceeds are to go to relief for victims of the March 11 earthquake and tsunami in Japan.

21 Greek Prime Minister George Papandreou survives a legislative no-confidence vote in spite of regular street protests in Athens against austerity measures.

•

Italian Prime Minister Silvio Berlusconi wins a no-confidence vote in the country's legislature.

•

The UN General Assembly unanimously elects Ban Ki-Moon to a second term of office as secretary-general.

•

Two suicide car bombers attack the governor's compound in Al-Diwaniyah, Iraq; at least 27 people are killed, but the governor is unhurt.

22 U.S. Pres. Barack Obama announces plans to begin withdrawing troops from Afghanistan by the end of the year and to hand responsibility for security over to Afghanistan's government in 2014.

•

Chinese artist and dissident Ai Weiwei is released from prison in Beijing.

•

Legendary Boston crime boss James ("Whitey") Bulger, who has been sought by the FBI since he disappeared after being tipped off about his planned arrest in 1994, is arrested in Santa Monica, Calif.

23 Violent protests in Dakar, Senegal, against changes to the country's constitution proposed by Pres. Abdoulaye Wade that would increase his chances of being elected to a third term of office result in the quick withdrawal of the proposal.

•

A special court set up by Afghan Pres. Hamid Karzai to review the legislative election of September 2010 rules that 62 candidates either lost through fraud or were improperly disqualified and should be seated; the country's election commission denies the court's legitimacy.

Justin Lane—EPA/Landov

•

Sheikh Sharif Sheikh Ahmed, president of Somalia's transitional national government, appoints Abdiweli Mohamed Ali permanent prime minister; he has served in that capacity on a temporary basis since the resignation of Mohamed Abdullahi Mohamed on June 19.

•

Three bombs explode in a market in Baghdad, killing as many as 34 people.

24 The European Council appoints Mario Draghi of Italy to succeed Jean-Claude Trichet of France as head of the European Central Bank on November 1.

•

The state legislature of New York passes a law permitting same-sex couples to marry. *(Photo above.)*

•

The 2011 winners of the Kyoto Prize are announced: materials scientist John W. Cahn (advanced technology), astrophysicist Rashid Sunyaev (basic sciences), and Kabuki performer Tamasaburo Bando V (arts and philosophy).

25 The Basel Committee on Banking Supervision puts forth a proposal that will require that the largest and most complex of the world's banks hold a higher level of reserves to cope with unexpected losses.

•

A car bomb explodes at a hospital in Afghanistan's Logar province, near the border with Pakistan; at least 20 and perhaps as many as 50 people are killed.

•

In Pasadena, Calif., Mexico comes from behind to defeat the U.S. 4–2 and win the CONCACAF Gold Cup in association football (soccer).

26 Attackers thought to be members of the Boko Haram militant group hurl bombs at a popular drinking spot in Maiduguri, Nigeria; some 25 people are killed.

•

Yani Tseng of Taiwan wins the LPGA championship golf tournament in Pittsford, N.Y., by 10 strokes over Morgan Pressel of the U.S.

•

Treasure Beach wins the Irish Derby; it is the sixth consecutive win at the Thoroughbred horse race for animals that have been trained by Aidan O'Brien.

27 The International Criminal Court issues an arrest warrant for Libyan leader Muammar al-Qaddafi on charges of having committed crimes against humanity in February at the beginning of the uprising against him.

•

In the U.S., Abdul Qadeer Fitrat resigns as governor of the central bank of Afghanistan, citing government interference in his efforts to investigate malfeasance at the institution.

28 An official in Saudi Arabia announces that the country will withdraw most of its troops from Bahrain within a week; the Saudi military entered Bahrain in March to assist in quelling antigovernment protests.

•

French Minister of Finance Christine Lagarde is appointed managing director of the IMF.

•

Some 300 tourists travel from mainland China to Taiwan; it is the first time Chinese citizens have been permitted to travel on their own to Taiwan.

29 Greece's legislature passes the draconian austerity package required before the IMF and EU will release financial aid that will make it possible for the country to avoid defaulting on its debt, while police confront protesters in Athens; Greece has a 16% unemployment rate.

•

The African Union announces that northern and southern Sudan have agreed to the creation of a demilitarized zone between the two countries when South Sudan becomes independent on July 9.

•

The U.S. Federal Reserve announces caps on the fees that banks charge merchants for processing customers' purchases made with debit cards; the new fees, which will go into effect on October 1, are about half the current ones.

30 A UN-backed tribunal charged with investigating the 2005 assassination of Lebanese Prime Minister Rafiq al-Hariri sends indictments of four men, two of them believed to be senior members of Hezbollah, to Lebanon's state prosecutor.

•

The Jiaozhou Bay bridge, connecting Qingdao and Huangdao, opens in China; at 42.5 km (26.4 mi) in length, it is the longest bridge over water in the world, exceeding by more than 4 km (2.5 mi) the previous record holder, the Lake Pontchartrain Causeway in the U.S. state of Louisiana.

July

[He] turned a youth paradise into hell.

Norwegian Prime Minister Jens Stoltenberg, describing the previous day's massacre at a youth camp on Utoya Island, July 23

1 Proposed constitutional changes that slightly liberalize the government in Morocco are overwhelmingly approved in a popular referendum.

•

As a deadline passes with no budget agreement, all state services in Minnesota shut down.

•

An Exxon Mobil oil pipeline near Billings, Mont., ruptures, spilling as much as 1,000 bbl of oil into the flooding Yellowstone River.

•

The Las Conchas wildfire in New Mexico, the largest in the state's history, is reported to have consumed more than 41,700 ha (103,000 ac) and to be only 3% contained.

2 Finance ministers of the euro-zone countries announce that the next installment of aid for Greece, €12 billion ($17.4 billion), will be released.

•

In response to increasing demonstrations against corruption in government, King 'Abdullah II of Jordan approves changes in the cabinet, including the firing of the minister of the interior, a major focus of popular discontent.

•

Prince Albert II of Monaco weds former South African Olympic swimmer Charlene Wittstock in a religious ceremony the day after a civil ceremony in Monaco. *(Photo below.)*

•

In an upset Petra Kvitova of the Czech Republic defeats Russian Mariya Sharapova to take her first All-England (Wimbledon) women's tennis championship; the following day Novak Djokovic of Serbia wins the men's title for the first time when he defeats Rafael Nadal of Spain.

3 In legislative elections in Thailand, the For Thais party, headed by Yingluck Shinawatra, sister of deposed prime minister Thaksin Shinawatra, wins in a landslide.

•

As Pres. Alyaksandr Lukashenka of Belarus gives a speech in condemnation of popular uprisings to mark the country's independence, security officers crack down on people clapping in unison in a demonstration against the government.

•

Britons win five of the Henley Royal Regatta trophies in rowing at a tournament at which 33 records are set.

4 Thailand's victorious For Thais party announces that it has formed a coalition with four other parties, and the country's military declares that it will not intervene in the election results.

•

In response to the growing threat of famine in North Korea, the European Union announces the release of $14.5 million in emergency food aid.

•

Pres. Hugo Chávez returns to Venezuela after spending more than three weeks in Cuba, where he underwent cancer surgery.

5 The rating agency Moody's Investors Service lowers the rating of Portugal's debt from Baa1 to Ba2, which is considered junk status.

•

Two coordinated bomb attacks leave more than 30 people dead in Taji, Iraq.

•

Officials in China acknowledge that an oil spill from an offshore drilling rig in the Bohai Sea that occurred in early June and was first officially revealed on July 1

Eric Gaillard—EPA/Landov

has spread over 830 sq km (320 sq mi).

•

In a Florida case that has riveted the public, Casey Anthony is found not guilty of the murder of her daughter, Caylee, who disappeared in 2008 at the age of two and whose decomposed body was found in December of that year; the public is outraged.

6 Taliban fighters attack several border police posts in northeastern Afghanistan; 23 officers are reported to have been killed.

•

Rebels in Libya take control of the town of Qawalish from government forces, while the battle for Misurata continues.

•

The International Olympic Committee president, Jacques Rogge, announces the selection of P'yongch'ang (Pyeongchang), S.Kor., as the location of the Winter Games of 2018.

7 News Corp. announces that it is shutting down the popular British tabloid *The News of the World*, which is at the centre of the burgeoning phone-hacking scandal.

•

The U.S. Environmental Protection Agency issues new rules to go into effect in 2012 to reduce particulate emissions from power plants in 28 states that cause smog and acid rain.

•

It is reported that in June surgeons at the Karolinska University Hospital in Sweden led by Paolo Macchiarini carried out the first-ever transplant of a synthetic organ when they placed an artificial windpipe coated with stem cells from the patient's bone marrow into a cancer patient, who is recovering well; the technique eliminates the need for antirejection drugs.

8 The U.S. Department of Labor reports that the unemployment rate in June rose to 9.2% and that the economy's growth was anemic, with only 18,000 nonfarm jobs added.

•

After four days of ethnic violence in Karachi that has left at least 70 people dead, the Pakistani government orders paramilitary troops to join security forces there with instructions to shoot on sight anyone causing violence.

•

The space shuttle *Atlantis*, carrying astronauts Chris Ferguson, Doug Hurley, Sandy Magnus, and Rex Walheim, takes off on the final space shuttle mission; it will carry food and a robotic refueling facility to the International Space Station.

9 In a ceremony in the capital city of Juba, the new country of South Sudan formally becomes independent, and Salva Kiir Mayardit is sworn in as president; the first country to recognize it is Sudan.

•

A planned rally in Kuala Lumpur, Malay., to demand new rules to make elections more transparent and fair is obstructed by security forces, who arrest some 1,700 people.

•

American player Andre Agassi and tennis executive Fern Kellmeyer are inducted into the International Tennis Hall of Fame in a ceremony in Newport, R.I.

10 An official dialogue on moving toward multiparty democracy opens at a resort outside Damascus with remarks made by Syrian Vice Pres. Farouk al-Shara'; opposition groups boycott the dialogue as meaningless.

•

Russia wins the Fédération Internationale de Volleyball World League championship in men's volleyball in Gdansk, Pol., defeating Brazil to take its second World League title.

11 Organized groups of supporters of Syria's government attack the American and French embassies in Damascus; the U.S. and France have both expressed support for the antigovernment protesters.

•

Ryu So-Yeon of South Korea scores a three-stroke victory over her countrywoman Seo Hee-Kyung in a three-hole playoff to win the U.S. Women's Open golf tournament in Colorado Springs, Colo.

•

Liao Yiwu, a Chinese writer who has been persecuted for his unvarnished portrayals of the downtrodden in China, announces that he has escaped from China through Vietnam and is now in exile in Berlin.

12 Ahmed Wali Karzai, a warlord who held effective power over much of southern Afghanistan and a half brother of Afghan Pres. Hamid Karzai, is assassinated by a trusted confederate at his headquarters in Kandahar.

•

U.S. Pres. Barack Obama presents the Medal of Honor to Sgt. First Class Leroy Arthur Petry, who has served two combat tours in Iraq and six in Afghanistan, for his bravery in a battle in Afghanistan in 2008; Petry is only the second living soldier to have received the country's highest military honour since the Vietnam era.

13 Bombs explode in three crowded locations in Mumbai in a coordinated attack; at least 21 people are killed.

•

The embattled News Corp. announces the withdrawal of its vaunted bid to buy full control of the satellite television company British Sky Broadcasting, known as BSkyB.

14 The legislature in Paraguay fails to pass a plan to amend the constitution to allow the president to run for a second term of office.

•

A plan to ask the United Nations to admit Palestine as a full member is approved by the Arab League.

•

South Sudan becomes the 193rd member of the United Nations.

•

The popular European digital subscription music service Spotify becomes available in the U.S. for the first time.

15 The United States recognizes the rebel Transitional National Council as the legitimate government of Libya.

•

Police in Tunisia attempting to quell an antigovernment demonstration fire tear gas inside a mosque in Tunis, setting off three days of rioting.

•

Italy's legislature passes an austerity package that is intended to reduce the country's rising budget deficit.

•

Pres. Alan García of Peru inaugurates a bridge over the Madre de Dios River; the structure completes the 5,470-km (3,400-mi)-long Interoceanic Highway from the Atlantic coast in Brazil to the Pacific coast in Peru.

16 U.S. Pres. Barack Obama meets privately in the

White House with the Dalai Lama, the spiritual leader of Tibet, despite objections from China.

•

Joseph Huang Bingzhang, who accepted ordination as bishop of the diocese of Shantou by the Chinese state-run Catholic Patriotic Association without Vatican approval, is excommunicated by the Vatican.

17 Sir Paul Stephenson resigns as commissioner of the Metropolitan Police Service in London in the ongoing phone-hacking scandal (Scotland Yard is suspected of having had an unseemly cozy relationship with *News of the World*), and former publisher Rebekah Brooks is arrested.

•

It is reported that the movie *Harry Potter and the Deathly Hallows: Part 2* took in $168.6 million in its opening weekend, surpassing *The Dark Knight*'s ticket sales in 2008 to set a new U.S. record.

•

Japan beats the U.S. 3–1 on penalty kicks to win the FIFA Women's World Cup in association football (soccer); it is the first time an Asian country has won the title.

•

Darren Clarke of Northern Ireland defeats American golfers Phil Mickelson and Dustin Johnson by three strokes to win the British Open golf tournament at Royal St. George's in Sandwich, Eng.

18 Malaysian Prime Minister Datuk Seri Najib Tun Razak meets with Pope Benedict XVI, and an agreement is reached for the establishment of diplomatic relations between Malaysia and Vatican City.

•

Gen. David Petraeus formally hands over command of the military forces serving in the Afghanistan War to Gen. John Allen; Petraeus will become director of the CIA.

•

China's Internet search company Baidu announces an agreement with OneStop China, a joint venture between the Warner Music Group, the Universal Music Group, and Sony BMG, in which Baidu will pay licensing fees to allow its users to legally and freely download music; heretofore almost all downloaded music in China was pirated, much of it through Baidu.

•

U.S. Pres. Barack Obama nominates Richard Cordray, formerly attorney general of Ohio, to head the new Consumer Financial Protection Bureau, which begins operations three days later.

•

The Borders Group announces that the once-dominant bookstore retailer Borders will close its remaining stores and go out of business.

•

During the annual boat race from Chicago to Mackinac Island in Michigan, a storm comes up and capsizes the boat *WingNuts*, drowning the skipper and a crew member; it is the first time in the 103 runnings of the race that weather-related or accidental deaths have occurred.

19 In Hims, Syria, government forces open fire on funeral processions for the 10 protesters who were killed the previous day; at least 15 people are killed.

•

The mainstream opposition coalition in Yemen announces its formation of a national council days after such a council was announced by rebel leaders.

•

The FBI announces the arrest of 16 people in connection with Internet attacks carried out by the hacker collective Anonymous.

20 Egypt's interim government sets out a complex plan for legislative elections to take place in the fall; the vote will occur in several stages, and half the members will be elected in a winner-take-all system and half in a proportional-representation system.

•

The UN declares that the food crisis in two regions of southern Somalia, both controlled by the militia al-Shabaab, has reached the level of famine.

•

Minnesota Gov. Mark Dayton signs a new budget that allows state offices to reopen after a shutdown that began on July 1.

•

The journal *Naturwissenschaften* reports the finding in China of the fossil of a *Yabeinosaurus* lizard that contains at least 15 embryos; the fossil is 120 million years old and is the oldest example of a pregnant lizard ever found.

21 The leaders of the member countries of the euro zone agree on an extensive plan to rescue the economy of Greece; the plan will also offer debt relief to both Ireland and Portugal.

•

A NATO raid on a large insurgent encampment in Afghanistan's Paktika province, on the border with Pakistan, kills at least 80 people.

•

After two days of protests and riots over worsening economic conditions in several cities in Malawi, some 19 people have been killed by security forces and government loyalists.

•

The U.S. government sells its remaining stake in the car manufacturer Chrysler to Italian carmaker Fiat at a $1.3 billion loss.

•

The space shuttle program comes to an end with the landing at Kennedy Space Center in Florida of *Atlantis* after the completion of its final mission.

22 In Norway a powerful car bomb damages buildings in Oslo and kills 7 people, and hours later at a Labour Party youth summer camp on the island of Utoya, a man guns down at least 68 people; Norway is traumatized by the violence.

•

Mission scientists for NASA announce that the Mars Science Laboratory, a rover known as Curiosity, will have as its destination the Gale Crater, near the planet's equator; the rover is scheduled to launch later in 2011 and to reach Mars in August 2012.

23 Anders Behring Breivik, described as a right-wing fundamentalist Christian who abhors multiculturalism, is charged in Norway with both the massacre on Utoya Island and the bombing in Oslo.

•

Thousands of people march in Dakar, Senegal, to demand the resignation of Pres. Abdoulaye Wade, who they believe is subverting the intention of the country's constitution and attempting to remain in office in perpetuity.

•

A high-speed train plows into another train that is said to have lost power after being struck by lightning near Wenzhou, China; six cars derail, four of them falling off a viaduct, and at least 40 people are killed.

24 In local elections in Sri Lanka, the Tamil National Alliance wins control in 18 of the 26 councils.

•

In Argentina, Uruguay defeats Paraguay 3–0 to win its record 15th Copa América, the South American championship in association football (soccer).

•

Australian cyclist Cadel Evans wins the Tour de France.

•

The Nagoya Grand Sumo Tournament concludes in Japan; the event saw *ozeki* Harumafuji of Mongolia win his second Emperor's Cup and *ozeki* Kaio, the last Japanese *ozeki*, retire with a record 1,046 career victories.

•

The National Baseball Hall of Fame in Cooperstown, N.Y., inducts second baseman Roberto Alomar, pitcher Bert Blyleven, and manager Pat Gillick.

25 The Vatican recalls its ambassador to Ireland in response to an Irish government report conducted by an independent investigative committee; the report said, among other things, that the Vatican had encouraged Roman Catholic clergy in the country to ignore guidelines adopted in 1996 that included mandatory reporting of sexual abuse of children by clergy members to civil authorities.

26 The Millennium Challenge Corporation, a U.S. government agency, freezes a planned $350 million grant to Malawi because of that government's reaction to recent protests.

27 The British government recognizes the rebel National Transitional Council as the legitimate government of Libya and expels Libyan diplomats in London representing the current government.

Enrique Castro Mendivil—Reuters/Landov

•

The foreign ministers of India and Pakistan, meeting in New Delhi, agree on several steps to ease tensions in Kashmir, which both countries claim; the steps will make it easier for trade and travel to take place between the two sides of Kashmir.

•

A ceremony is held to mark the closing of the Walter Reed Army Medical Center in Washington, D.C.; the facility, which opened in 1909, is scheduled to move to the National Naval Medical Center in Bethesda, Md., in August, where it will be called the Walter Reed National Military Medical Center.

28 Several Taliban suicide bombers enter Tirin Kot, the capital of Oruzgan province in Afghanistan, and attempt to kill both the provincial governor and a regional warlord; neither man is hurt, but at least 21 civilians, all unintended targets, are killed.

•

Mustafa Abdul Jalil, head of Libya's rebel provisional government, announces that the top rebel military leader, Abdul Fattah Younes, who defected from Muammar al-Qaddafi's inner circle in February, has been killed by unnamed assassins.

•

Ollanta Humala (*photo above*) takes office as president of Peru.

•

At the FINA swimming world championships in Shanghai, American Ryan Lochte sets a new world record in the men's 200-m individual medley of 1 min 54 sec; it is the first world record achieved since the banning of high-tech swimming suits in January 2010.

29 In a shocking move, Turkey's top military commander, Gen. Isik Kosaner, and the heads of the country's army, navy, and air force all resign to protest the arrests of high-ranking military officers as conspiracy suspects; Prime Minister Recep Tayyip Erdogan names Gen. Necdet Ozel, head of the military police, to replace Kosaner.

•

The U.S. Department of Commerce issues revised figures showing that GDP grew at a rate of 0.4% in the first fiscal quarter of 2011 and 1.3% in the second quarter and that the 2008–09 recession had been deeper than earlier figures indicated.

•

With the chief executives of the major automobile manufacturers, U.S. Pres. Barack Obama announces new rules for gas mileage that will require mileage in new cars to improve incrementally to reach an average fuel efficiency of 54.5 mi per gal by 2025.

30 Government air strikes aimed against Islamist militants near Zinjibar, Yemen, instead hit a pro-government population, killing 14.

•

In Roses, Spain, elBulli, regarded as one of the top restaurants in the world and a lodestar in contemporary cuisine, serves its final meal; it is expected to open as a foundation for experimental cooking in 2014.

31 After weeks of brinksmanship, U.S. congressional leaders and Pres. Barack Obama reach an accord on a framework for a budget deal that Republican leaders require before agreeing to increase the government's borrowing limit.

•

Syrian government forces violently crack down in the cities of Hamah, Darʿa, and Dayr al-Zawr; at least 70 people are killed, most of them in Hamah.

•

Taiwanese golfer Yani Tseng captures the Women's British Open golf tournament for the second consecutive year with a four-stroke win over American Brittany Lang.

August

We congratulate the Libyan people for the fall of Muammar al-Qaddafi and call on the Libyan people to go into the street to protect the public property. Long live free Libya.

Mass text message from Libya's National Transitional Council on the fall of Tripoli, August 22

1 Officials in China's Xinjiang province declare that the leader of the first of two knife attacks over the previous two days, in which at least 14 people in Kashgar were stabbed to death, had trained in Pakistan.

•

Indonesian authorities say that in the past few days, political violence in the province of Papua has killed at least 22 people.

•

A report is published online by a team of astronomers who, with the use of the Herschel space telescope, became the first to see an oxygen molecule (consisting of two oxygen atoms joined by a double bond) in space; the molecule was found in a star-forming region in the constellation Orion.

2 A bill to reduce government spending and raise the debt ceiling is signed into law in Washington, D.C.

•

Peter O'Neill is chosen to replace ailing Prime Minister Sir Michael Somare of Papua New Guinea, though it is not certain that the post is legally vacant.

3 In Cairo former Egyptian president Hosni Mubarak goes on trial on charges of corruption and of complicity in the killing of antigovernment protesters; the trial is televised.

•

Syrian armed forces move into Hamah, the centre of some of the biggest antigovernment demonstrations, killing many as the government moves to crush the opposition.

•

The UN expands the area of Somalia that it deems a famine zone to include three more regions.

4 At a meeting of Turkey's Senior Military Council led by Prime Minister Recep Tayyip Erdogan, a new chief of general staff and new heads of the three branches of the armed services are named; the appointees are viewed as likely to be amenable to the primacy of the civilian government.

•

Stock markets in the U.S. experience their biggest drop in two years as the Dow Jones Industrial Average loses 4.31% of its value and the Standard & Poor's 500-stock index falls by 4.78%.

•

The U.S. government gives conditional approval to a plan of the Shell Oil Co. to drill for oil in the Beaufort Sea, north of Alaska.

5 The rating agency Standard & Poor's for the first time ever downgrades the risk rating of U.S. debt from AAA to AA+ in a controversial move; the agency cites political unpredictability in a statement.

•

The U.S. Department of Labor reports that the unemployment rate in July dropped to 9.1% and that, though the private sector added 154,000 jobs, the loss of state and local government employment brought the number of nonfarm jobs added to the economy as a whole to 117,000.

•

The NASA spacecraft Juno takes off from Cape Canaveral, Florida; it is expected to reach Jupiter in 2016 and will send back data on the planet's gravity, magnetic fields, and water content.

6 A small protest march against the killing of a local man by police in the Tottenham section of London explodes into a large riot with looting and fighting against riot police.

•

The militant organization al-Shabaab withdraws from Mogadishu, ceding control of the Somalian capital to the transitional government.

•

A transport helicopter is shot down in Afghanistan's Wardak province, and 30 Americans, among them 17 Navy Seal commandos, are killed; 7 Afghan commandos and an interpreter are also killed.

7 Manuel Pinto da Costa is elected president of Sao Tome and Principe; he previously served as president from 1975, when the country gained independence, to 1991.

•

Pender Harbour, under jockey Luis Contreras, wins the Breeders' Stakes race at Woodbine in Toronto, the final leg of the Canadian Triple Crown in Thoroughbred horse racing; Contreras also rode the winners in the first two legs of the Triple Crown.

•

The blockbuster exhibit "Alexander McQueen: Savage Beauty," which opened on May 4 at New York City's Metropolitan Museum of Art, closes; the exhibit, which attracted 661,509 visitors, was extended twice, and in the final two days it remained open until midnight to accommodate the crowds clamouring to see the retrospective of the work of fashion designer Alexander McQueen.

8 Saudi Arabia, Kuwait, and Bahrain withdraw their ambassadors from Syria to signal their displeasure with the Syrian government's violent response to protests.

•

Rioters in London set fire to a Sony Corp. warehouse that is a distribution hub for independent record labels in Britain and Ireland, destroying untold numbers of CDs and other record stock (*photo right*); an immediate effect is an announced delay of the next release by the English band Arctic Monkeys.

•

The Standard & Poor's 500-stock index loses 6.7% of its value, and the Dow Jones Industrial Average falls 634 points (5.6%), closing below 11,000 points for the first time in 2011.

•

The U.S. Department of Justice and four states file suit against the for-profit college company Education Management Corp., charging it with having illegally paid recruiters on the basis of the number of students enrolled and therefore being ineligible for state and federal financial aid; the company enrolls 150,000 students in 105 schools operating under four names.

9 Some 10,000 police officers patrol the streets of London in an effort to end the riots, looting, and arson of the past three nights, but elsewhere in England, including Birmingham, Manchester, and Liverpool, such mayhem escalates.

•

The U.S. Federal Reserve announces that it will not raise interest rates before mid-2013; stock markets respond with a surge.

•

The British Royal Navy says that it has appointed Lieut. Comdr. Sarah West commander of the frigate HMS *Portland*; when she takes up her post in April 2012, she will become the first woman in the service's history to command a warship.

10 Afghan Pres. Hamid Karzai annuls the special court he created to review the 2010 legislative election results, making the independent election commissioner the arbiter; the court in June said that 62 candidates who had lost or been disqualified should be seated.

•

North Korean and South Korean military forces exchange artillery fire near Yeonpyeong Island.

•

James H. Billington, the U.S. librarian of Congress, names Philip Levine the country's 18th poet laureate; Levine succeeds W.S. Merwin.

11 Yingluck Shinawatra takes office as Thailand's first female prime minister.

•

Israel's government approves the construction of an apartment complex in East Jerusalem, which Palestinians claim as the capital of a future state; Israel is suffering a housing shortage.

•

The Standard & Poor's 500-stock index rises 4.6% after having fallen 4.4% the previous day in a display of unprecedented volatility that is also affecting markets in Europe.

12 Italian Prime Minister Silvio Berlusconi, after an emergency cabinet meeting, announces a new austerity package that includes tax increases and cuts in local government.

•

The main Shi'ite opposition group in Bahrain announces that it will boycott elections to replace 18 legislators who resigned to protest the government's brutal response to antigovernment demonstrations in March.

•

A government report in France shows that the country's economic growth in the second quarter of the year unexpectedly fell to zero.

•

The Naismith Memorial Basketball Hall of Fame in Springfield, Mass., inducts as members NBA players Chris Mullin, Dennis Rodman, Artis Gilmore, and Tom ("Satch") Sanders, Olympic champion Teresa Edwards, Reece ("Goose") Tatum of the Harlem Globetrotters, Lithuanian player Arvydas Sabonis, and

Chris Helgren—Reuters/Landov

coaches Tex Winter, Herb Magee, and Tara VanDerveer.

13 Rebel forces in Libya seize control of much of Al-Zawiyah; the road through Al-Zawiyah is an important supply route for Tripoli.

•

At the Indiana State Fair in Indianapolis, an outflow of strong wind ahead of an approaching thunderstorm causes a concert stage to collapse; at least seven people are killed, among them six spectators and a stagehand.

14 A group of Taliban attackers make an assault on the compound of the governor of Afghanistan's Parwan province in Charikar; at least 22 people, not including the governor, are killed.

•

A brutal assault on the city of Latakia by Syrian armed and paramilitary forces leaves at least 25 people dead.

•

Jhalanath Kanal resigns as prime minister of Nepal.

•

At the Atlanta Athletic Club golf course in Johns Creek, Ga., Keegan Bradley of the U.S. defeats his countryman Jason Dufner in a three-hole play-off to win the PGA championship tournament.

•

The 52nd Edward MacDowell Medal for outstanding contributions to the arts is awarded to American playwright Edward Albee at the MacDowell Colony in Peterborough, N.H.

15 A series of 42 attacks kill at least 89 people in major cities in Iraq; in the deadliest single assault, two car bombs leave 35 people dead in Kut.

•

The Internet company Google announces its planned acquisition of Motorola Mobility Holdings, which will allow Google to add smartphones and tablet computers to its portfolio.

16 Indian authorities arrest anticorruption activist Anna Hazare in an attempt to prevent him from starting a planned hunger strike to pressure the government into creating an independent anticorruption agency.

•

Voters in Seattle approve a large highway tunnel project to run under downtown; the tunnel is expected to be completed in late 2015.

17 The Special Tribunal for Lebanon, an international court created by the UN and the government of Lebanon, issues indictments of four members of the militant organization Hezbollah for the 2005 assassination of Lebanese Prime Minister Rafiq al-Hariri.

•

More than 10,000 people march in New Delhi in support of jailed anticorruption activist Anna Hazare; similar marches take place in other cities throughout India.

18 A series of attacks near the Red Sea resort city of Elat in Israel leave at least eight Israelis dead and lead to deadly Israeli air strikes in Gaza.

•

The U.S. for the first time calls for Syrian Pres. Bashar al-Assad to step down and announces robust sanctions; Canada, France, Germany, the U.K., and the EU also call for Assad's resignation.

•

Officials in Pakistan say that gangs associated with political parties have murdered 39 people in Karachi in the past two days.

•

At the Pukkelpop Festival in Hasselt, Belg., a stage on which the Smith Westerns band is performing collapses in high winds associated with a storm; other structures also are destroyed, and at least five people are killed.

19 Militants besiege a British cultural relations agency in Kabul for several hours, and at least eight people die before the attackers are overcome and killed.

•

Belarus suspends its agreement, made in December 2010, to give up its store of highly enriched uranium in return for financial aid from the U.S.

•

A suicide bomber kills at least 47 people in a mosque in the Khyber area of Pakistan.

•

In Myanmar (Burma), opposition leader Aung San Suu Kyi meets for the first time with Pres. Thein Sein.

20 Egypt recalls its ambassador from Israel in outrage over the deaths of three Egyptians in Israel's response to the attacks in Elat two days earlier.

•

North Korean leader Kim Jong Il makes his first visit to Russia since 2002.

•

It is reported that Shane Bauer and Joshua Fattal, American hikers who were arrested in July 2009 after having apparently strayed across the Iraqi border into Iran, have been sentenced to eight years in prison for spying.

21 Afghanistan's Independent Election Commission announces that nine candidates in the 2010 legislative election who had been disqualified after winning will have their seats restored; they will be seated in place of the candidates who were elevated earlier.

•

Jorge Carlos Fonseca of the opposition Movement for Democracy party wins the run-off presidential election in Cape Verde, defeating Manuel Inocencio Sousa.

•

Prime Minister Kamla Persad-Bissessar of Trinidad and Tobago, in a nationally televised address, declares a limited state of emergency to address a spike in gang violence related to drug trafficking.

22 Rebel forces in Libya march into Tripoli and declare victory over Muammar al-Qaddafi, to general jubilation, though Qaddafi's whereabouts are unknown, and he has not surrendered.

•

Prosecutors in New York City ask to have sexual assault charges dismissed against Dominique Strauss-Kahn, the former head of the International Monetary Fund, as their case has collapsed; Strauss-Kahn was arrested with much fanfare in May.

•

Jack Layton, head of Canada's opposition New Democratic Party and a rising political star, dies in Toronto at the age of 61.

•

The UN reports that a cattle raid by ethnic Murle against Nuer villages in eastern South Sudan on August 18 resulted in the theft of some 30,000 cattle and the deaths of more than 600 people, a far greater death toll than initially believed.

23 Rebels in Libya seize Bab al-'Aziziyyah, the Tripoli compound of deposed ruler Muammar al-

Qaddafi, though in a radio address Qaddafi insists that he will continue to fight for control of the country.

•

Yemeni Prime Minister Ali Muhammad Mujawar returns to Yemen from Saudi Arabia, where he had been since an attack on the presidential compound in Sanaa in early June.

•

Voters in Liberia reject four constitutional amendments, one that would have raised the retirement age for Supreme Court justices, one lowering the number of years a presidential candidate must have resided in the country, and the others changing election laws.

24 An unmanned Russian Progress cargo spaceship carrying food and fuel for the International Space Station crashes shortly after takeoff from the Baikonur space centre in Kazakhstan.

•

Steve Jobs resigns as CEO of Apple, Inc., saying that he is no longer able to function adequately in that capacity; he will remain as chairman and be replaced as CEO by Tim Cook.

•

The ratings agency Moody's Investors Service downgrades Japan's credit rating one notch, to Aa3.

25 Members of a drug cartel set fire to a casino in Monterrey, Mex.; at least 52 people die in the blaze.

•

The journal *Nature* publishes a report of the discovery in China of a fossil of a placental mammal ancestor, *Juramaia sinensis*, that is 160 million years old; this pushes back the date of the divergence of placental and marsupial mammals about 35 million years.

26 A suicide car bomber destroys much of the UN headquarters building in Abuja, Nigeria, in a massive blast that kills at least 21 people; the Islamist militant organization Boko Haram claims responsibility.

•

A bomb explodes outside a military academy in Cherchell, Alg., and shortly thereafter a suicide bomber on a motorcycle detonates his weapon in the same place; at least 18 trainees are killed.

•

A massive public works program for Paris that includes more than 177 km (110 mi) of new subway lines and 57 new stations is approved by the French government.

•

In Monaco the Spanish club Barcelona defeats F.C. Porto of Portugal 2–0 to win the European Super Cup in association football (soccer).

27 India's legislature passes a resolution to adopt the anticorruption program championed by Anna Hazare, who vowed to fast until his program was enacted; the following day Hazare ends his 13-day hunger strike.

28 A suicide bomber kills at least 28 people in a major Sunni mosque in Baghdad; among the dead is a prominent member of the national legislature.

•

Baburam Bhattarai of the United Communist Party of Nepal (Maoist) is chosen as Nepal's new prime minister.

•

In Erin, Wis., Kelly Kraft of Denton, Texas, is the winner of the U.S. men's amateur golf championship.

•

With a bases-loaded single hit by Nick Pratto, the Ocean View team from Huntington Beach, Calif., defeats the team from Hamamatsu City, Japan, 2–1 to win baseball's 65th Little League World Series in Williamsport, Pa. *(Photo below.)*

29 Japanese Minister of Finance Yoshihiko Noda is chosen by the ruling Democratic Party to succeed Naoto Kan as prime minister; the legislature elects him prime minister the following day.

•

The large Greek lending banks Alpha Bank and Eurobank EFG announce a planned merger.

30 Two suicide bomb attacks in Grozny, the capital of the Russian republic of Chechnya, kill at least seven police officers and an emergency services worker.

•

Bolivia's Supreme Tribunal finds five former military commanders guilty of genocide in the 2003 killing of at least 64 people during a crackdown on protests and riots over poverty; two former cabinet officers are convicted of complicity in the killings, and all are given prison sentences.

•

The American oil company Exxon Mobil signs an agreement with Russian state-owned oil company Rosneft that will allow Exxon to explore for oil in the Russian Arctic; in exchange, Rosneft will be permitted to participate in Exxon projects in the U.S.

31 Solyndra, a California-based manufacturer of innovative solar cell modules that received $527 million in U.S. federal loans, goes out of business.

•

The High Court in Australia rules that a government agreement signed in July to send migrants who arrived by boat to Malaysia violates Australian law.

•

U.S. military forces in Iraq mark the first month in which no American soldier was killed; 4,465 U.S. troops have died in the Iraq War since it began in 2003, and 48,000 troops are serving in Iraq.

•

The U.S. Department of Justice sues in federal court to block the planned merger of cell phone companies AT&T and T-Mobile USA.

Tom E. Puskar/AP

September

If it is true, then we truly haven't understood anything about anything.

CERN theorist Alvaro De Rújula,
commenting on the anticipated announcement regarding neutrinos' exceeding the speed of light, September 22

1 Libya's rebel-led government extends by one week the deadline for loyalists of deposed ruler Muammar al-Qaddafi to surrender, and Qaddafi releases an audio recording declaring that Surt is now the capital of Libya.

•

The Inter American Court of Human Rights rules that Venezuela's disqualification of opposition leader Leopoldo López from seeking public office violates the Inter American Convention on Human Rights.

•

NASA scientists report that the Mars rover Opportunity, which arrived at the crater Endeavour on August 9 after a 21-km (13-mi) journey, has sent back data on a breccia rock that contains unexpectedly high levels of zinc; rocks in the crater date to an earlier geologic era of the planet than has yet been studied.

2 Turkey expels the Israeli ambassador and suspends military agreements with Israel in a display of displeasure over Israel's refusal to apologize for the killing of Turkish nationals in a raid on a Gaza-bound aid ship in 2010.

•

The U.S. Department of Labor reports that the unemployment rate in August remained at 9.1%; the economy did not see any net increase in jobs.

•

It is reported that violence between Christians and Muslims over the past week in Jos, Nigeria, has left at least 21 people dead.

3 Eight of the nine legislators ordered reinstated by Afghanistan's election commission take the oath of office in Kabul while police guard the building to prevent entry by the members who lost their seats in the ruling and their supporters.

•

The government of South Sudan announces that the capital of the country will be moved from Juba to Ramciel.

•

George Lee Andrews makes his 9,382nd and final performance in the Broadway musical *The Phantom of the Opera*, a record run; for most of the 23 years, he played the part of Monsieur André.

4 Typhoon Talas makes landfall in western and central Japan, causing massive flooding and leaving at least 20 people dead and a further 50 people missing.

•

At the world track and field championships in Taegu, S.Kor., the Jamaican team anchored by Usain Bolt breaks the world record in the 4 × 100 relay with a time of 37.04 sec; the previous record was set at the 2008 Beijing Olympic Games by a Jamaican team anchored by Asafa Powell.

5 The UN declares that the famine in Somalia has spread to the Bay region and that hundreds of people a day are dying of starvation.

•

In India the powerful mining tycoon Janardhana Reddy, who holds considerable political sway in Karnataka state, is arrested and charged with having engaged in illegal mining in the state of Andhra Pradesh.

•

Haitian Pres. Michel Martelly nominates Garry Conille as prime minister; Conille is Martelly's third nominee for the post (his first two choices were rejected).

6 A general strike takes place in Italy, where workers march to protest a proposed austerity package.

•

A wildfire in Bastrop county, Texas, has destroyed some 550 homes, making it the most destructive fire in Texas history; it is one of dozens of wildfires that have burned more than 47,900 ha (118,400 ac) in the state.

•

English recording artist P.J. Harvey, who in 2001 became the first female winner of the Mercury Prize for best album by a British or an Irish artist, wins the 2011 Mercury Prize for her album *Let England Shake*; she is the first person to win a second Mercury Prize.

7 A bomb explodes in New Delhi at a security checkpoint in the building that houses the

Chip Somodevilla—Reuters/Landov

Delhi High Court; at least 10 people are killed.

•

Two suicide bombers, one using a vehicle, attack the home of the deputy inspector general of the paramilitary Frontier Corps in Quetta, Pak., killing at least 21 people and injuring 30.

•

Germany's Constitutional Court rules that Germany has the legal right to participate in financial rescue packages for weaker members of the euro zone; it also requires that future bailouts be approved by a legislative committee.

8 Mahmoud Jibril, the head of Libya's Transitional National Council's Executive Board and de facto prime minister, makes his first public appearance in Tripoli to speak at a news conference.

•

The U.S. National Park Service signs an agreement to expand the 44,100-ha (109,000-ac) Petrified Forest National Park in Arizona by 10,700 ha (26,500 ac) with the long-sought purchase of private ranchland adjoining the park.

•

Zagat Survey, a customer-based restaurant-review company founded in 1979, sells itself to the online search company Google.

9 Protesters in Cairo pull down a protective wall outside the Israeli embassy; damage is also done to the building housing Egypt's Ministry of the Interior.

•

China's state news agency reports that some 14 million people, mostly in southwestern China, lack adequate drinking water as a result of a long-lasting drought.

•

Science magazine publishes a report by Lee Berger of the University of Witwatersrand in South Africa in which he posits the revolutionary claim that recently discovered fossils of *Australopithecus sediba* show that the species was likely a direct ancestor of *Homo* species.

10 Yoshio Hachiro resigns as Japan's minister of trade and industry after having ignited outrage with a jest that appeared to ignore his ministry's perceived failure to adequately oversee safety measures at the Fukushima Daiichi nuclear plant, which suffered meltdowns as a result of damage from the earthquake and tsunami in March.

11 Presidential, legislative, and local elections take place in Guatemala; a runoff presidential election is required.

•

In New York City the National September 11 Memorial is dedicated as part of ceremonies commemorating the 10th anniversary of the terrorist attacks of Sept. 11, 2001; the names of victims are inscribed on walls that surround subterranean fountains on the footprints of the Twin Towers. *(Photo above.)*

•

Samantha Stosur of Australia defeats American Serena Williams in an upset to win the women's U.S. Open tennis championship; the following day Novak Djokovic of Serbia defeats Rafael Nadal of Spain to take the men's title.

•

In golf's biennial Walker Cup competition in Aberdeen, Scot., Great Britain and Ireland defeat the U.S. for the first time since 2003 with a 14–12 victory.

12 A bus transporting Shi'ite pilgrims on a trip to a shrine in Damascus is attacked by gunmen in Iraq's Anbar province; the attackers force the women and children off the bus and then kill all 22 men.

•

The UN Human Rights Council announces the appointment of a three-person panel to investigate human rights abuses in Syria and estimates the number of protesters killed in Syria to date to be 2,600.

13 Insurgents attack the U.S. embassy and the NATO headquarters building in Kabul, leading to a prolonged gun battle in which at least 16 people are killed; NATO commander Gen. John R. Allen the following day accuses a Pakistan-based militia of responsibility for the attack.

•

The U.S. Census Bureau releases figures showing that in 2010 some 46.2 million Americans lived below the poverty level, 2.6 million more than the previous year, and that the poverty rate was 15.1%; also, the median household income declined 2.3% from the previous year.

14 A car bomb explodes outside a crowded restaurant in Babil province in Iraq, killing at least 13 people, and an explosive on a bus carrying Iraqi soldiers in Anbar province kills 6 soldiers.

•

Pirates seize a Cyprus-flagged fuel tanker and its 23-member crew in the Gulf of Guinea off the coast of Benin, an area that is seeing an upsurge in such attacks.

•

The Hague Civil Court orders the Dutch government to compensate the widows of seven men who were executed in Rawagedeh in western Java in 1947 during Indonesia's fight for independence from the Netherlands.

15 A centre-left coalition led by Helle Thorning-

Schmidt and the Social Democratic Party wins legislative elections in Denmark, ending 10 years of centre-right rule.

•

The European Central Bank joins with the U.S. Federal Reserve, the Bank of England, the Bank of Japan, and the Swiss National Bank to make U.S. dollars available to the European banking system in an effort to increase market confidence.

•

Turkey agrees to host a U.S.-made radar system as part of the NATO missile defense shield program.

•

Astronomers working with the Kepler planet-hunting spacecraft launched by NASA in 2009 announce the discovery of a planet circling a double-star system in the constellation Cygnus; the planet, named Kepler 16b, is informally called Tattooine for the planet with two suns in the 1977 movie *Star Wars*.

16 A South Korean government official declares that envoys from North and South Korea have scheduled a meeting to discuss restarting six-country talks on dealing with North Korea's nuclear-weapons program.

•

At the National Championship Air Races air show outside Reno, Nev., a World War II-era P-51 fighter plane crashes into a crowd of spectators; 11 people, including the pilot, are killed, and dozens are injured.

17 A two-day meeting of finance ministers of euro-zone countries at which U.S. Secretary of the Treasury Timothy Geithner urged action ends in Wroclaw, Pol., with no agreement on steps to take to solve the region's debt crisis.

•

Fighting erupts between Yemeni security forces and militias aligned with the antigovernment movement in Sanaa.

18 In Haining, Zhejiang province, China, angry protests continue for a fourth day against a solar-panel-manufacturing plant that is believed to have contaminated an adjacent river; authorities shut the factory down the following day.

•

Several armed men wearing army fatigues enter a bar in Gatumba, Burundi, near the border with the Democratic Republic of the Congo and open fire on those within, leaving at least 36 people dead.

•

Demonstrations against government corruption and excessive concentration of power in the king take place in the Moroccan cities of Casablanca and Tangier.

•

The major Swiss bank UBS explains its failure to notice rogue trading that resulted in a loss of $2.3 billion; former trader Kweku M. Adoboli has been charged in the incident.

•

The Emmy Awards are presented in Los Angeles: winners include the television shows *Modern Family* and *Mad Men* and the actors Jim Parsons, Kyle Chandler, Melissa McCarthy, Julianna Margulies, Ty Burrell, Peter Dinklage, Julie Bowen, and Margo Martindale.

19 Hundreds of civilians flee Surt, Libya; battles between rebel forces and those loyal to deposed leader Muammar al-Qaddafi have raged for five days.

•

New York Yankees pitcher Mariano Rivera notches his 602nd career save in a win over the Minnesota Twins, setting a Major League Baseball record. *(Photo below.)*

John Angelillo—UPI/Landov

20 Burhanuddin Rabbani, the head of Afghanistan's High Peace Council and a former president of the country, is assassinated by a suicide bomber who pretended to be a peace negotiator for the Taliban.

•

A string of car bombs in downtown Ankara, Tur., explode, killing at least three people and injuring more than 30; it is the first bomb attack in the city since 2007.

•

The end of "Don't Ask, Don't Tell" in the U.S. military goes into effect; henceforward openly gay and lesbian people are permitted to serve.

21 Greece's government announces further and deeper austerity measures in an effort to qualify for international aid.

•

The U.S. Federal Reserve announces a plan to shift debt holdings from short-term to long-term Treasury securities in an attempt to lower borrowing costs to businesses and consumers and thus spark economic growth.

•

Shelly Yachimovich is chosen to be the new head of Israel's Labor Party.

•

Shane Bauer and Joshua Fattal, American hikers who unintentionally crossed the border from Iraq into Iran in July 2009 and had been jailed in Iran ever since, are released from prison and leave Iran.

22 The U.S. ceremonially reopens its embassy in Tripoli, Libya; the embassy had been abandoned in February.

•

The American software and computer services company Hewlett-Packard Co.

announces that former eBay head Meg Whitman has been chosen to replace Léo Apotheker as the company's CEO.

•

Ocean's Kingdom, a ballet scored by Sir Paul McCartney (his first ballet score) and choreographed by Peter Martins, is premiered by New York City Ballet at the Koch Theater in New York City.

23 Palestinian leader Mahmoud Abbas formally requests that Palestine be admitted to the United Nations in a speech before the General Assembly that is watched by thousands in the central square of Ramallah in the West Bank.

•

Pres. ʿAli ʿAbd Allah Salih of Yemen unexpectedly returns to the country from Saudi Arabia, where he had been recuperating from injuries suffered in an attack on his compound in June.

•

Michael Sata of the opposition Patriotic Front is sworn in as president of Zambia; he won election over incumbent Rupiah Banda on September 20.

•

CERN particle physics researchers in Geneva report that they have measured neutrinos traveling faster than the speed of light; if the result is borne out by further investigation, it would violate the special theory of relativity.

•

The 2011 Lasker Awards for medical research are presented to Franz-Ulrich Hartl and Arthur Horwich for their discoveries regarding the mechanism of protein folding in cells, Tu Youyou for his discovery of artemisinin, a lifesaving treatment for malaria, and the Clinical Center of the U.S. National Institutes of Health for public service.

24 Russian Pres. Dmitry Medvedev announces at a United Russia party convention that he will not be a candidate for president in next year's election in order that Prime Minister Vladimir Putin may be the party's candidate.

•

Elections in Bahrain to fill the 18 legislative seats left open by a walkout on the part of the main Shiʿite opposition party result in extremely low turnout and a need for runoffs for half of the seats.

•

Government attacks on antigovernment protest supporters leave at least 40 people dead in Sanaa, Yemen.

•

Oswald Grübel steps down as CEO of the Swiss banking company UBS in light of the huge loss caused by a rogue trader at the bank.

•

Police appear to use pepper spray without provocation at a demonstration by a group of activists who have occupied Zuccotti Park in New York City since September 17 in the genesis of a growing protest movement called Occupy Wall Street, which is against the influence of financial interests on government at the expense of ordinary people.

25 Four successive bombs, two of them car bombs, explode outside a passport office in Karbala', Iraq; at least 15 people die.

•

King ʿAbd Allah of Saudi Arabia for the first time grants women the right to vote and to hold office beginning with the next elections, scheduled for 2015; he also says that women may be appointed to the Consultative Council.

•

Patrick Makau of Kenya wins the Berlin Marathon with a time of 2 hr 3 min 38 sec, a new record time for completing a marathon; Florence Kiplagat of Kenya is the fastest woman, with a time of 2 hr 19 min 44 sec.

•

The final bullfight takes place in La Monumental arena in Barcelona; the autonomous community of Catalonia, where Barcelona is located, has banned the traditional sport.

26 For the first time in the battle for Surt, Libya, forces of the new government succeed in taking control of part of the city.

•

The U.S. Postal Service drops its rule banning the depiction of living persons on postage stamps.

27 Greece's legislature passes a law to establish the first property tax in the country; the tax will affect about 80% of Greek households and will be a large burden to many of them.

•

Australia lifts its ban on service in combat roles by women in the armed services.

•

The U.S. Centers for Disease Control and Prevention reveals that a listeria outbreak caused by the consumption of contaminated canteloupes grown in Colorado began in late July and has caused at least 13 deaths in eight states.

28 In Afghanistan's Helmand province, an attack at a checkpoint leaves eight Afghan police officers dead; also, the UN reports a 40% increase in violent episodes in Afghanistan in June, July, and August over the same period in 2010.

•

A state of emergency is declared in Tuvalu because of an intense drought that began affecting the Pacific island country in November 2010.

•

Jeff Bezos, head of the online retailer Amazon.com, introduces the Kindle Fire, a tablet computer intended to compete with Barnes & Noble's Nook Color and Apple's iPad.

29 A security court in Bahrain issues a death sentence against a protester who is said to have run down and killed a police officer during a demonstration and also sentences eight doctors to long prison terms for having treated injured protesters; several people have recently been sentenced to prison for illegal protests.

•

Comedian and banjo player Steve Martin and his bluegrass band, the Steep Canyon Rangers, are honoured with the entertainer of the year award by the International Bluegrass Music Association.

30 A U.S. CIA drone strike in Yemen kills the American-born cleric Anwar al-Awlaki, who is believed to be a top leader of al-Qaeda in the Arabian Peninsula and to be behind several anti-American plots; an American-born editor of al-Qaeda's online magazine is also killed.

•

Japan cancels evacuation advisories for an area encompassing five towns outside the 19-km (12-mi) exclusion zone around the stricken Fukushima Daiichi nuclear power plant, which suffered meltdowns after the March 11 earthquake and tsunami.

•

The government of Myanmar (Burma) suspends a large Chinese-financed hydroelectric dam project on the Irrawaddy River as a response to strong public opposition.

October

It is the end of tyranny and dictatorship. Qaddafi has met his fate.

Abdel Hafez Ghoga,
spokesman for Libya's Transitional National Council,
on the death of former Libyan leader Muammar al-Qaddafi, October 20

1 In Pakistan, Malik Mumtaz Qadri, a member of a police guard unit, is sentenced to death for having assassinated Salman Taseer, the governor of Punjab province and an opponent of the country's harsh blasphemy law.

•

The Geelong Cats defeat the Collingwood Magpies 18.11 (119)–12.9 (81) in the Australian Football League Grand Final and thus win the AFL title.

•

"Pacific Standard Time: Art in L.A. 1945–1980," a six-month retrospective involving more than 150 exhibits at 130 museums and galleries, opens in Los Angeles.

2 The Marshall Islands passes a law creating the largest shark sanctuary in the world; it encompasses 1,900,500 sq km (750,000 sq mi) in the Pacific Ocean.

3 A Tibetan monk, Kalsang, sets himself on fire to protest Chinese policies in Tibet; he is the fourth monk from the Kirti Monastery in Tibet to self-immolate in recent months.

•

A court in Perugia, Italy, overturns the 2009 convictions of American student Amanda Knox and her former boyfriend, Raffaele Sollecito of Italy, for the 2007 murder of Knox's British roommate, Meredith Kercher; the case has aroused high emotions in all the countries concerned.

•

The Nobel Prize for Physiology or Medicine is awarded to Canadian immunologist Ralph Steinman, who died three days earlier, and to American immunologist Bruce Beutler and French immunologist Jules Hoffman for their discoveries concerning the response of the immune system to infection.

4 A large truck bomb explodes outside the gates of a government compound in Mogadishu, Som., killing more than 100 people, many of them students; the militant group al-Shabaab claims responsibility, and it is later revealed that the bomber opposed secular education.

•

China and Russia both veto a UN Security Council resolution calling on the government of Syrian Pres. Bashar al-Assad to cease using violence against antigovernment protesters.

•

In Stockholm the Nobel Prize for Physics is awarded to American astrophysicist Saul Perlmutter and to American-born Australian astronomer Brian Schmidt and American astronomer Adam Riess for their unexpected discovery that the universe is expanding at an accelerating rate, an indication of the existence of dark energy.

5 The attorney general of Bahrain revokes the convictions and sentences of medical workers who had treated antigovernment demonstrators, saying that they should be tried before an ordinary court rather than a special security court.

•

The Nobel Prize for Chemistry is awarded to Dan Schechtman of Israel for his discovery of quasicrystals, in which the arrangement of atoms exhibits regular but nonrepeating patterns.

•

Steve Jobs, the cofounder and guiding spirit of Apple Inc., dies of pancreatic cancer in California.

6 Both the European Central Bank and the Bank of England leave their benchmark interest rates unchanged, but the Bank of England expands its program of quantitative easing.

•

The Nobel Prize for Literature is awarded to Swedish poet Tomas Tranströmer.

7 A large protest takes place outside Manama, Bahrain, at the funeral of a teenage boy who was said to have been killed by police the previous day; the demonstration is broken up by security forces.

•

It is reported that the U.S. Preventive Services Task Force recommends that healthy asymptomatic men forgo PSA blood tests to check for the presence of prostate cancer, saying the tests do not save lives and result in unnecessary treatment and suffering.

•

The Nobel Peace Prize is awarded to Liberian Pres. Ellen Johnson Sirleaf, Liberian peace activist Leymah Gbowee, and Yemeni liberal Islamist antigovernment activist Tawakkol Karman.

•

The state prosecutor of Mexico's Veracruz state resigns; the previous day 32 bodies were found in a residential area of Veracruz, and three weeks earlier 35 bodies were discovered on a highway.

•

The U.S. Department of Labor reports that the unemployment rate in September remained at 9.1% and that the economy as a whole added 103,000 nonfarm jobs.

8 In Al-Qamishli, Syria, tens of thousands of protesters attend the funeral of Kurdish opposition leader Mashaal Tammo, who was assassinated the previous day.

•

In Afghanistan 70 members of the country's legislature end their monthlong boycott of the body.

9 Paul Biya is elected to a sixth term of office as president of Cameroon.

•

In legislative elections in Poland, the ruling Civic Platform party wins the largest number of seats.

•

With his third-place finish in the Japanese Grand Prix (won by Jenson Button of Britain), German driver Sebastian Vettel secures his second successive Formula One automobile racing drivers' championship.

•

In Cairo, Coptic Christians angry over the dismantling of a church in Aswan march in protest against Egypt's military government and are met by security forces and Muslim demonstrators, some opposing the Christians and some opposing the military council; at least 24 people are killed in the chaotic fighting. *(Photo right.)*

•

The Chicago Marathon is won by Moses Mosop of Kenya, with a time of 2 hr 5 min 37 sec; the women's victor for the third year in a row is Liliya Shobukhova of Russia, with a time of 2 hr 18 min 20 sec.

10 Iran's national prosecutor general announces the arrests of 14 people in connection with a $2.6 billion embezzlement at the country's biggest commercial bank, Bank Melli; 22 arrests were reported earlier, and the bank's managing director has fled to Canada.

•

China suspends boat traffic on the headwaters of the Mekong River after Thai border police find two Chinese cargo boats laden with amphetamines and one corpse and later discover the bodies of 12 murdered crew members floating on the river.

•

Pedro Pires, who was prime minister of Cape Verde in 1975–91 and president from 2001 until September 2011, wins the Mo Ibrahim Prize for Achievement in African Leadership.

•

The Nobel Memorial Prize in Economic Sciences goes to American economists Thomas Sargent and Christopher Sims for their independent work on methodology for discovering how government policies affect and are affected by the broad economy.

Ahmed Asad—APA/Landov

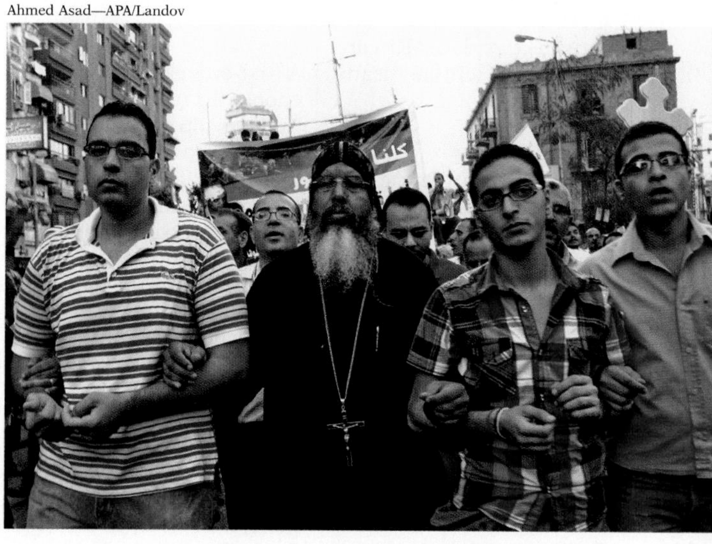

11 Israel and the Palestinian organization Hamas announce that they have agreed to an exchange of more than 1,000 Palestinian prisoners for Gilad Shalit, an Israeli soldier who was captured by Hamas in June 2006.

•

A court in Kiev, Ukr., sentences former prime minister Yuliya Tymoshenko to seven years in prison after having found her guilty of having harmed the interests of Ukraine in her negotiations in 2009 with Russia on the price Ukraine would pay for natural gas.

•

A presidential election in Liberia results in the need for a runoff between incumbent Ellen Johnson Sirleaf and challenger Winston Tubman.

12 The U.S. Congress ratifies free-trade agreements with South Korea, Colombia, and Panama that were signed in 2006; they are the first such accords approved since 2007.

•

Uganda's foreign minister resigns under suspicion of involvement in a scandal in which public money was diverted to private development; he was also accused of having received bribes from an oil-development company.

•

Insurgent attacks in Baghdad leave at least 23 people dead.

13 Slovakia's legislature approves the expansion of the euro rescue fund; it is the last of the 17 member countries whose agreement was required.

•

Former head of the Galleon Group hedge fund Raj Rajaratnam, who was convicted in May of securities fraud, is sentenced to 11 years in prison; it is the longest sentence that has ever been meted out by a U.S. court for insider trading.

•

Authorities in New Zealand close 23 km (14 mi) of beaches on its east coast after a stranded cargo ship has begun leaking an estimated 350 tons of heavy fuel oil into the sea.

•

The La Scala opera house in Milan appoints Daniel Barenboim its music director; he replaces Riccardo Muti, who left the theatre in 2005.

14 Indian Prime Minister Manmohan Singh signs an agreement with Pres. Thein Sein of Myanmar (Burma) expanding cooperation in trade and oil and gas exploration.

•

Italian Prime Minister Silvio Berlusconi narrowly survives a no-confidence vote in the legislature.

•

The rating agency Standard & Poor's lowers Spain's credit rating to AA– in the second downgrade in a month.

15 At least 19 people are killed in clashes between antigovernment demonstrators and security forces in Sanaa, Yemen; also, it is reported that air strikes thought to be from American drones killed nine people the previous day in southern Yemen.

•

In a planned day of protest against the financial system and economic inequality, demonstrations take place in cities throughout the world, including New York City, Berlin, London, Tokyo, Sydney, and Rome, where rioting breaks out.

•

Three pro-democracy activists are among the people elected to Oman's advisory council; turnout in the election is unusually high.

•

At the artistic gymnastics world championships in Tokyo, Kohei Uchimura of Japan wins a record third all-around men's title.

16 Hundreds of troops of Kenya's armed forces enter Somalia to fight against the al-Shabaab militants.

•

A first-ever election to choose the members of Bolivia's top courts takes place; more than half the ballots are deliberately spoiled to protest against Pres. Evo Morales, who championed the unconventional method of judicial selection.

•

A horrific multicar crash on lap 11 of the IndyCar season-ending Las Vegas Indy 300, kills British driver and two-time winner of the Indianapolis 500 Dan Wheldon, and the race is ruled incomplete; later Scottish driver Dario Franchitti is declared the winner of the IndyCar drivers' championship.

17 For the second time in 2011, King ʿAbdullah II of Jordan dismisses the government; he appoints Awn Khasawneh, a judge on the International Court of Justice, to replace Marouf al-Bakhit as prime minister.

•

A U.S. official says that U.S. military advisers are to be stationed in Uganda to help hunt down the guerrilla group the Lord's Resistance Army.

18 Garry Conille is sworn in as prime minister of Haiti, and five months after the presidential election, a new government is put in place.

•

The investment bank Goldman Sachs reports a quarterly loss for only the second time since it went public in 1999.

•

JP Morgan Chase passes Bank of America to become the largest American bank in terms of assets, branches, and total deposits.

•

The owner of a wild-animal menagerie in Zanesville, Ohio, releases the animals and then commits suicide; by the following day local authorities have had to kill nearly all the animals—a total of 49, including 17 lions, 18 Bengal tigers, wolves, bears, and monkeys.

19 Militant Kurds near the Turkish border with Iraq attack Turkish soldiers, killing at least 24; the Turkish military pursues the attackers over the border into Iraq.

•

In fighting between government security forces and antigovernment demonstrators in Hims, Syria, at least 24 people are killed.

•

The banking giant Citigroup agrees to a settlement with the U.S. Securities and Exchange Commission of $285 million for a complaint of negligence in having sold investors risky portfolios and then bet against the investments in those portfolios.

•

In Tokyo the Japan Art Association awards the Praemium Imperiale to Japanese conductor Seiji Ozawa, British sculptor Anish Kapoor, American painter Bill Viola, British actress Dame Judi Dench, and Mexican architect Ricardo Legorreta.

20 After a convoy attempting to flee Surt, Libya, is stopped by NATO air strikes, former Libyan leader Muammar al-Qaddafi is found hiding in a drainage ditch and is killed.

•

Violent fighting breaks out between anarchist and communist protesters in Athens as final approval of draconian austerity measures is passed in the legislature.

21 U.S. Pres. Barack Obama announces that the U.S. military will leave Iraq by the end of 2011; the date was specified in the 2008 status of forces agreement, and negotiations to extend the deadline were unsuccessful.

•

A Mexican commercial truck enters the U.S. for the first time since the 1994 passage of the North American Free Trade Agreement following the resolution of safety concerns to the satisfaction of the U.S. Department of Transportation.

22 Saudi Arabia announces the death of Crown Prince Sultan ibn ʿAbd al-ʿAziz al-Saʿud, a brother of King ʿAbd ʿAllah.

•

In Melbourne long-shot filly Pinker Pinker wins the W.S. Cox Plate under jockey Craig Williams.

23 Tunisia holds elections for an assembly that will create a new constitution and appoint an interim government; turnout is about 90% of registered voters, and Nahdah, a moderate Islamist party, wins the highest number of seats.

•

In Argentina's presidential election, Cristina Fernández de Kirchner is resoundingly elected to a second term of office.

•

Andrew Holness takes office as prime minister of Jamaica, replacing Bruce Golding, who unexpectedly stepped down in September.

•

New Zealand defeats France 8–7 to win the Rugby Union World Cup final in Auckland, N.Z.

•

The 14th annual Mark Twain Prize for American Humor is awarded to Will Ferrell in a ceremony at the John F. Kennedy Center for the Performing Arts in Washington, D.C.

24 Syria withdraws its ambassador to the U.S. in response to the departure two days earlier of Robert Ford, the U.S. ambassador to Syria; Ford, who spoke out against the Syrian government crackdown on antigovernment protests, was said to fear for his safety.

25 The Reserve Bank of India, India's central bank, raises its key interest rate for the 13th time in 19 months in an effort to lower inflation, which is running at about 10%.

•

The U.S. Congressional Budget Office releases a report saying that income inequality in the U.S. has grown significantly in the past 30 years, with government policies doing less to prevent the phenomenon; the after-tax income of the wealthiest fifth of the population in 2007 was higher than that of the remaining four-fifths together.

•

The last B53 nuclear bomb in the U.S. arsenal is dismantled in Texas; the nine-megaton bomb was put into service in 1962 and was far and away the largest remaining bomb in the U.S. nuclear arsenal.

26 Mustafa Abdel-Jalil, chairman of Libya's Transitional National Council, says in an interview that he has asked NATO to keep air patrols and military advisers in the country through the end of the year.

•

The X Prize Foundation in Playa Vista, Calif., announces a new prize of $10 million to be given to the first team that produces accurate, complete genome sequences of 100 centenarians while spending less than $1,000 per genome; the contest is to begin in January 2013 and last for one month.

27 European Union leaders meeting in Brussels reach an agreement that requires banks to accept a 50% loss on their loans to Greece; they also consent to the outline of a comprehensive plan to shore up the euro.

•

The UN Security Council unanimously agrees to end its authorization for foreign military intervention in Libya.

•

Michael Higgins of the Labour Party wins election as president of Ireland.

•

Prince Nayef ibn ʿAbd al-ʿAziz is named the new crown prince of Saudi Arabia; he serves as the country's interior minister.

•

The U.S. Department of Commerce estimates that the country's economy grew at an annual rate of 2.5% in the third quarter, a distinct improvement over the previous quarter.

28 At least 40 people participating in antigovernment demonstrations in Syria are killed by security forces.

•

British Prime Minister David Cameron announces that the Commonwealth has approved changes that will allow the oldest child, rather than only the oldest son, of the British monarch to inherit the throne and that will, for the first time since 1701, permit the monarch to be married to a member of the Roman Catholic Church.

•

In the World Series, the St. Louis Cardinals defeat the Texas Rangers 6–2 in game seven to win the Major League Baseball championship for the 11th time; St. Louis slugger David Freese is named the Series MVP.

•

In Moscow the Bolshoi Theatre reopens after a painstaking six-year effort that restored it to its pre-Soviet beauty. *(Photo below.)*

29 A suicide car bomber attacks an armoured shuttle bus in Kabul, killing at least 18 passengers, 13 of them NATO soldiers and military contractors.

30 A presidential election is held in Kyrgyzstan; former prime minister Almazbek Atambayev wins in a landslide.

•

Rosen Plevneliev is the victor in a runoff presidential election in Bulgaria.

•

Tens of thousands of people attend an antigovernment rally in Lahore, Pak., led by former cricket star Imran Khan.

31 UNESCO approves full membership for Palestine, which becomes the 195th member of the organization.

•

Libya's Transitional National Council chooses Abdel Rahim al-Keeb to serve as interim prime minister.

•

The UN estimates that the world population has reached seven billion, though it does not identify a specific infant as the seven-billionth person born; the world population reached six billion in 1999.

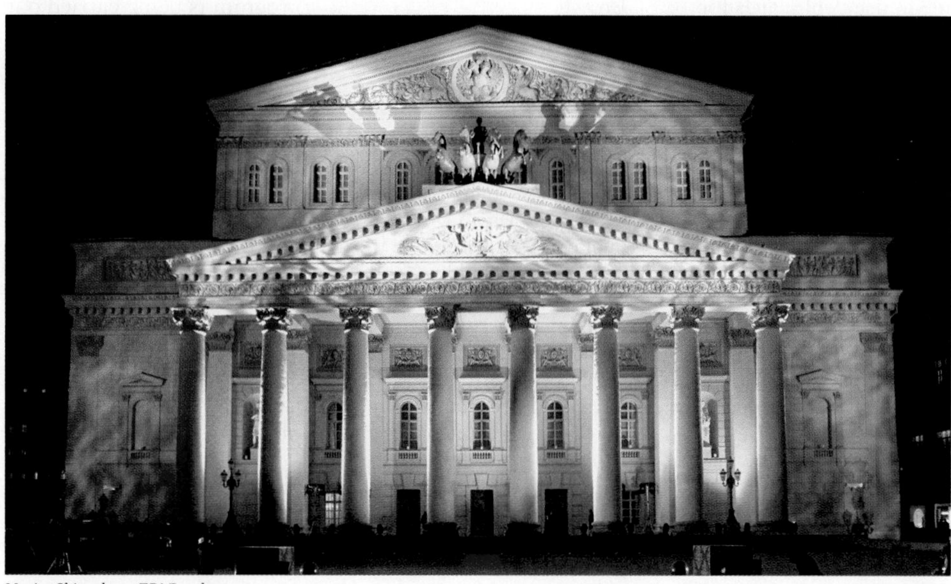

Maxim Shipenkov—EPA/Landov

November

The people didn't sacrifice hundreds of lives in the revolution so that the military would jump over their will.

Mohamed Ibrahim, one of those protesting the Egyptian military's plans to retain primacy under a new constitution, November 18

1 The leaders of Afghanistan and Pakistan agree to conduct a joint investigation into the September assassination of Burhanuddin Rabbani, head of the Afghan High Peace Council.

•

The banking giant Bank of America, in the face of a public outcry objecting to the surcharge, drops a plan announced about a month earlier to charge most of its customers a $5.00 monthly fee to use debit cards for purchases.

•

Dunaden wins Australia's Melbourne Cup Thoroughbred horse race by a nose over Red Cadeaux.

2 Greek Prime Minister George Papandreou declares that a referendum will be held in Greece to determine whether the people wish to accept the rescue package agreed to by the member countries of the euro zone; the following day he rescinds the plan.

•

Syria agrees to a peace plan brokered by the Arab League that calls for the immediate withdrawal of government forces from city streets and for talks with opposition leaders.

•

Pakistan's government chooses to normalize trade relations with India to increase trade between the countries.

•

The Dorothy and Lillian Gish Prize is awarded to American modern dance choreographer Trisha Brown.

3 In a surprise move, the European Central Bank lowers its key interest rate from 1.5% to 1.25%, and the bank's new president, Mario Draghi, declares that Europe is moving toward a mild recession.

•

A new law is announced in Cuba that will for the first time permit citizens and permanent residents to buy and sell real estate without first seeking government approval.

•

In London, Pakistani cricket players Salman Butt, Mohammad Asif, and Mohammad Amir and their agent, Mazhar Majeed, are sentenced to prison for periods ranging from 6 months (Amir) to 32 months (Majeed) for having engaged in spot-fixing during a Test match in a case that has riveted and shocked Pakistan.

4 Italy agrees to allow the IMF to oversee its books to ensure that the country's austerity program is being carried out correctly.

•

Opposition candidate Winston Tubman announces that he will boycott Liberia's runoff presidential election.

•

The U.S. Department of Labor reports that the unemployment rate in October fell to 9%, though the economy as a whole added only 80,000 nonfarm jobs.

•

Groupon, a Web site that offers daily coupon deals for a variety of goods and services, begins trading on the NASDAQ stock exchange in a much-anticipated initial public offering.

•

The General Assembly of the International Union of Pure and Applied Physics announces names for the three most recently discovered elements: darmstadtium (Ds), roentgenium (Rg), and copernicium (Cn).

5 Officials in Nigeria say that an hours-long attack in and around the town of Damaturu in Yobe state that began with a car bomb the previous day killed at least 67 people; bombings also occurred in Maiduguri.

•

The Breeders' Cup Classic Thoroughbred horse race is won by Drosselmeyer, under jockey Mike Smith; the four-year-old colt charged from 10th place for the victory at Churchill Downs in Louisville, Ky.

6 Political leaders in Greece agree to a plan that requires the formation of a unity government under a new prime minister, the passage of a new austerity package, and the acceptance of the EU rescue scheme.

•

In a presidential runoff election in Guatemala, Otto Pérez Molina emerges as the victor.

•

Daniel Ortega wins election to a third term of office as president of Nicaragua.

•

Geoffrey Mutai *(photo, below left)* of Kenya wins the New York City Marathon with a time of 2 hr 5 min 6 sec, and Ethiopia's Firehiwot Dado *(photo, below right)* is the fastest woman, with a time of 2 hr 23 min 15 sec.

•

Nicol David of Malaysia wins a record sixth squash World Open championship with her defeat of Jenny Duncalf of Britain, while Nick Matthew of the U.K. wins a second consecutive men's title when he defeats Gregory Gaultier of France.

7 Residents of Hims, Syria, report that armed forces have launched a bloody assault to take control of the city from determined antigovernment protesters; they say that more than 100 people have been killed in the past few days.

•

The U.S. and Bolivia agree to restore diplomatic relations; ties were broken in 2008 when Bolivian Pres. Evo Morales expelled the U.S. ambassador and drug-enforcement agents.

8 The International Atomic Energy Agency releases a report laying out evidence that led it to conclude that Iran has engaged in activity related to the development of nuclear weaponry.

•

Pres. Ellen Johnson Sirleaf wins more than 90% of the vote in Liberia's runoff presidential election, but turnout is only about 33%.

•

In a referendum in Ohio, voters resoundingly reject a law passed in March that greatly restricted the collective bargaining rights of public-sector unions.

•

The video game *Call of Duty: Modern Warfare 3* goes on sale and in the next 24 hours sets a new record for sales in the U.S. and the U.K. of $400 million.

9 Russia launches its first post-Soviet interplanetary space vehicle, a probe named Phobos Grunt (Phobos-Soil) that is to sample the soil of Phobos, a moon of Mars, and bring it back to Earth in August 2014; the probe, however, fails to escape Earth's gravity.

•

The Atlantic States Marine Fisheries Commission votes to reduce by as much as 37% the allowable catch of menhaden, a vital forage fish that is harvested for use in fertilizer, bait, and animal and fish feed; the population of the fish is at 10% of historic levels.

•

Legendary head football coach Joe Paterno of Pennsylvania State University is fired and Graham Spanier resigns as university president in the fallout from the pedophile scandal surrounding former assistant coach Jerry Sandusky; Paterno is faulted for having failed to act adequately when accusations against Sandusky came to his attention.

10 Bombs fall on a refugee camp in South Sudan, which blames Sudan for the attack; the following day UN officials concur.

•

The Bank of England keeps its benchmark interest rate unchanged at 0.5%.

•

Marcus Stephen resigns as president of Nauru amid accusations of misconduct; the country's legislature elects Frederick Pitcher in his place only to replace him on November 15 with Sprent Dabwido.

•

Jefferson county in Alabama files for bankruptcy protection; it is the largest U.S. municipality ever to have taken this step.

11 Lucas Papademos is sworn in as interim prime minister of Greece the day after the resignation of George Papandreou.

•

Yemeni military forces launch an assault on Ta'izz, a centre of antigovernment protests; at least 15 civilians are killed.

•

A helicopter ferrying officials from Mexico City to Cuernavaca, Mex., crashes, killing all eight aboard, including Interior Secretary Francisco Blake Mora, who is a leading figure in the government's fight against drug traffickers, four other ministry employees, and three members of the country's air force.

•

Danny Philip resigns as prime minister of Solomon Islands; Gordon Darcy Lilo is elected on November 16 to replace him.

12 The Arab League agrees to suspend Syria's membership effective in four days if Syria has not by then

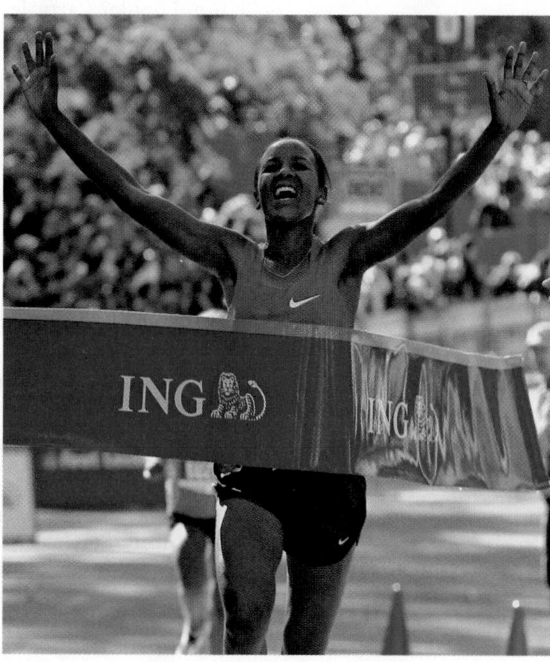

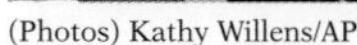
(Photos) Kathy Willens/AP

adhered to the requirements of a peace agreement.

•

Italy's legislature passes a package of austerity measures, and Silvio Berlusconi resigns as the country's prime minister.

•

According to Iranian officials, as members of the Revolutionary Guard transport munitions at a military base outside Bidganeh, Iran, an accidental explosion occurs that kills at least 17 members of the guard; one of those killed, however, is Brig. Gen. Hassan Moghaddam, a commander in the country's missile-development program.

•

In a controversial majority decision, Philippine boxer Manny Pacquiao is declared the winner of a World Boxing Organization welterweight boxing match against Mexico's Juan Manuel Márquez in Las Vegas.

13 Mario Monti, an economist and former member of the European Commission, accepts a mandate to form a new government in Italy.

•

Finnish driver Jari-Matt Latvala wins the Wales Rally GB; nonetheless, French driver Sébastien Loeb, who left the race at stage 18 after a collision, secures the drivers' championship in World Rally Championship racing for a record eighth time.

14 King ʻAbdullah II of Jordan in an interview declares that Bashar al-Assad should for the good of his country step down as president of Syria.

•

Emirates Airlines, based in Dubayy, agrees to purchase 50 777-300ER airplanes from the American manufacturer Boeing, with options for the purchase of an additional 20 aircraft; it is the biggest deal in Boeing's history.

15 Police in New York City forcibly clear the two-month-old encampment of Occupy Wall Street protesters from Zuccotti Park, though the protests continue; authorities in cities throughout the U.S. are grappling with how to handle similar encampments.

•

The troubled Swiss banking giant UBS announces that its new CEO will be Sergio Ermotti, who has been interim CEO since September, and that Axel Weber will replace Kaspar Villiger as chairman.

16 U.S. Pres. Barack Obama and Australian Prime Minister Julia Gillard announce an agreement to station 2,500 U.S. Marines in Australia.

•

Protesters force their way into the parliament building in Kuwait's capital, demanding the resignation of the country's prime minister.

17 On the anniversary of a 1973 uprising in Greece, tens of thousands of people march in Athens to protest against harsh austerity measures.

•

The UN-backed tribunal charged with trying architects of the murderous Khmer Rouge regime in Cambodia for crimes against humanity recommends that the defendant Ieng Thirith, the highest-ranked woman in the Khmer Rouge government, be released because she suffers from dementia.

18 Tahrir Square in Cairo fills with tens of thousands of Islamists who demand the end of military rule; they are enraged over the military's insistence that it retain primacy in the new constitution.

•

Former Philippine president Gloria Macapagal Arroyo is arrested on charges of corruption and election fraud.

•

At a conference in Kampala, Ugan., the Intergovernmental Panel on Climate Change reports that some recent extreme weather, including high temperatures, coastal flooding, and higher-than-normal precipitation, are likely consequences of human-enhanced climate change.

19 A Loya Jirga (grand council) called by Afghan Pres. Hamid Karzai endorses his call for American troops to remain in the country on a long-term basis, subject to restrictions as to their activities.

20 Legislative elections in Spain result in victory for the conservative opposition Popular Party, led by Mariano Rajoy.

•

It is reported that hundreds of Ethiopian troops, supported by personnel carriers and tanks, have entered Somalia in order to fight the militant al-Shabaab insurgents.

•

The Fukuoka SoftBank Hawks defeat the Chunichi Dragons 3–0 in game seven to win baseball's Japan Series.

•

After a win in the final auto race of the season, the Ford 400 in Homestead, Fla., Tony Stewart is crowned winner of the NASCAR drivers' championship; he also won the title in 2002.

21 Tunisia's governing coalition announces that the new prime minister will be Hamadi Jebali of the Nahdah Party and the president will be Moncef Marzouki of the Congress for the Republic party.

•

In the U.S. a bipartisan congressional "super committee" that was charged with finding $1.2 trillion in deficit reductions on pain of triggering unpopular automatic budget cuts declares that it has failed to agree on a plan.

•

For the first time in 10 years, King ʻAbdullah II of Jordan makes a visit to Ramallah in the West Bank, where he meets with Mahmoud Abbas, head of the Palestinian Authority.

22 Prime Minister Yousaf Raza Gilani of Pakistan accepts the resignation of Husain Haqqani as ambassador to the U.S.; Haqqani has been accused of having sought American help to prevent a possible military coup in Pakistan, and he is replaced the following day by Sherry Rehman.

•

Gov. John Kitzhaber of Oregon cancels a scheduled execution of a prisoner and declares that no further executions will take place while he is governor.

•

Astronauts Sergey Volkov of Russia, Michael Fossum of the U.S., and Satoshi Furukawa of Japan return to Earth in Kazakhstan via a Russian Soyuz capsule after five months aboard the International Space Station.

23 In Riyadh, Saudi Arabia, Pres. ʻAli ʻAbd Allah Salih of Yemen signs an agreement transferring power to his vice president; the agreement nonetheless allows Salih to retain the title of president until the next election.

•

Cyrus P. Mistry is appointed to succeed Ratan N. Tata as chairman of the enormous Indian business group Tata Sons in December 2012.

24 The Arab League tells Syria that it must agree within 24 hours to allow international monitors to enter the country or face sanctions, and the European Union issues a statement saying that there is urgent need for civilians in Syria to be protected.

•

It is announced that Kamal al-Ganzouri will replace Essam Sharaf as transitional prime minister of Egypt.

•

Yahya Jammeh is reelected president of The Gambia in elections that are marked by voter intimidation.

•

Moody's Investors Service lowers Hungary's credit rating below investment grade, to Baa3.

25 The opposition Islamist Justice and Development Party wins the largest number of seats in legislative elections in Morocco.

•

Australia's minister of immigration, Chris Bowen, announces that henceforth asylum seekers who arrive by sea in Australia may receive bridge visas that would allow them to live and work in the country while they await judgment on their applications.

26 Officials in Pakistan say that NATO air strikes the previous night struck two military posts near the country's northwestern boundary with Afghanistan, killing at least 25 Pakistani soldiers, and Pakistan shuts down NATO supply routes into Afghanistan as an expression of its outrage.

•

In Cape Canaveral, Florida, a rocket launches NASA's Mars Science Laboratory spacecraft, which includes a rover, Curiosity, that will look for organic compounds in the Martian atmosphere as well as on the surface; the spacecraft is expected to reach Mars in August 2012. *(Photo right.)*

•

NBA owners and players reach a tentative agreement in their long-running labour dispute that will allow them to begin a shortened basketball season on December 25.

Terry Renna/AP

27 The Arab League imposes economic sanctions against Syria because of the country's failure to comply with the terms of a peace treaty that it agreed to on November 2 and its refusal to accept international observers to monitor its compliance.

•

The Roman Catholic Church in English-speaking countries begins use of a new English-language translation of the Roman Missal, replacing the one that has been in use since 1973.

•

The British Columbia Lions capture the 99th Canadian Football League Grey Cup, defeating the Winnipeg Blue Bombers 34–23.

28 Emir Sheikh Sabah al-Ahmad al-Jabir al-Sabah of Kuwait accepts the resignation of Prime Minister Sheikh Nasir al-Muhammad al-Ahmad al-Jabir al-Sabah and his cabinet in the face of accusations of corruption from a broad opposition; Sheikh Jabir al-Mubarak al-Hamad al-Sabah is chosen to replace him two days later.

•

The first phase of legislative elections in Egypt gets under way with a large turnout; the final phase is scheduled for January 2012.

•

Two days of presidential and legislative elections begin in the Democratic Republic of the Congo; as expected, they are attended by violence, and Joseph Kabila is reelected president.

•

U.S. District Court Judge Jed Rakoff rejects a previously announced Securities and Exchange Commission settlement with banking giant Citigroup, saying that facts had not been established that would allow him to determine whether the settlement was adequate and reasonable.

29 The finance ministers of the member countries of the euro zone agree to release a major loan to Greece.

•

King Muhammad VI of Morocco appoints Abdelilah Benkirane of the Justice and Development Party prime minister.

•

Côte d'Ivoire unexpectedly extradites former president Laurent Gbagbo to face trial for crimes against humanity before the International Criminal Court.

•

Hundreds of Iranian students attack and ransack the British embassy in Tehran.

•

AMR, the parent company of American Airlines, files for bankruptcy protection.

30 U.S. Secretary of State Hillary Rodham Clinton arrives in Myanmar (Burma) for the first visit to that country by a U.S. secretary of state since 1955.

•

A massive one-day strike in Britain encompasses tens of thousands of public employees protesting against austerity measures.

•

Kenny Anthony of the St. Lucia Labour Party is sworn in as prime minister of St. Lucia two days after his party defeated the ruling United Workers Party in legislative elections.

December

> *Respected Comrade Kim Jong-Eun is now supreme leader of our party, military, and people.*

Kim Yong-Nam, president of North Korea's legislature, announcing Kim Jong-Eun's ascension to power, December 29

1 Yemen's political opposition declares that it has reached an agreement with the country's ruling party on the makeup of an interim government to rule until elections, which are scheduled for February 2012.

•

Almazbek Atambayev is sworn in as president of Kyrgyzstan in the country's first peaceful transfer of power.

2 The Community of Latin American and Caribbean States (CELAC), a new regional grouping with 33 member countries, holds its first summit meeting in Caracas.

•

The U.S. Department of Labor reports that the unemployment rate in November fell to 8.6%, its lowest level since March 2009, and that 120,000 nonfarm jobs were created; the rate of participation in the workforce, however, fell by 0.2%.

3 A battle takes place in Syria's Idlib province between security forces and defectors from the armed services; at least 15 individuals are killed, including people from both sides and civilians.

•

Donald Ramotar is sworn in as Guyana's new president.

4 In legislative elections in Russia, the ruling United Russia party's share of the vote falls to just under 50%; fraud is widely reported by freelance Russian observers as well as international election monitors.

•

Iranian officials say that the country's military has shot down an American stealth drone that was spying in eastern Iran.

•

Italian Prime Minister Mario Monti introduces an austerity package that includes large spending cuts and tax increases.

•

Spain defeats Argentina 3–1 to win its fifth Davis Cup in men's international team tennis.

•

The annual Kennedy Center Honors are presented in Washington, D.C., to film actress Meryl Streep, musical theatre performer Barbara Cook, pop singer and songwriter Neil Diamond, cellist Yo-Yo Ma, and saxophonist Sonny Rollins.

5 Thousands of people rally in Moscow to protest fraud in Russia's legislative elections.

•

Three bomb explosions in and around Al-Hillah, Iraq, kill at least 20 Shiʿites observing the holy day of ʿAshura'.

•

At a conference in Mountain View, Calif., it is announced that NASA's Kepler satellite has found a planet, dubbed Kepler 22b, that is some 2.4 times the size of Earth and is at a distance from its star that would make it possible for liquid water to collect on the planet's surface.

•

The U.S. Postal Service announces plans to close 252 mail-processing centres, nearly half of the total, to cut costs; the move is expected to slow mail delivery.

•

Britain's Turner Prize is presented in Gateshead, Eng., to Scottish sculptor Martin Boyce; his winning entry is a piece in which gallery pillars and a library table are reimagined as a fanciful forest. *(Photo right.)*

6 Elio Di Rupo of the Francophone Socialist Party is sworn in as prime minister of Belgium 18 months after elections; he is the country's first French-speaking leader in some 30 years.

•

Bombings targeting Shiʿites observing ʿAshura' take place in Kabul, Kandahar, and Mazar-e Sharif in Afghanistan, and at least 63 people are killed; a Pakistani militant Sunni organization claims credit for the unusual sectarian attack.

•

U.S. Pres. Barack Obama in a memorandum and Secretary of State Hillary Clinton in a speech before the UN Human Rights Council in Geneva say that the U.S. government will use the tools of diplomacy to combat violence and laws that are used against gay men, lesbians, bisexuals, or transgendered people in other countries throughout the world.

7 A member of Egypt's ruling council tells a group of American and British journalists that the military will control the writing of the constitution to protect the country from the Islamist majority that the legislature appears likely to have.

•

Police in Italy announce the arrest of Michele Zagaria, one of the heads of the powerful Camorra criminal organization.

8 The Freedom and Justice Party, the political arm of Egypt's Muslim Brotherhood, announces its withdrawal from a civilian advisory council being formed by the ruling military council in response to the news that the military plans to play a large role in the committee to write a new constitution.

•

Emir Sheikh Sabah al-Ahmad al-Jabir al-Sabah of Kuwait dissolves the country's legislature, necessitating the holding of new elections within 60 days.

•

The European Central Bank for the second time in recent weeks lowers its key interest rate by a quarter point, to 1%.

9 In a summit meeting in Brussels, the member countries of the European Union agree to a new pact to bind the union closer and allow greater EU oversight of the budgets of member countries; only the U.K. declines to sign on.

•

Egypt's ruling military council retracts its plan to oversee the writing of a new constitution, stating that the legislature will have sole responsibility for appointing a committee to create the charter.

•

UN Secretary-General Ban Ki-Moon makes an unexpected visit to Mogadishu, the capital of Somalia, and follows with a visit to a refugee camp; it is the first visit to the war-torn country by a UN secretary-general since 1993.

10 Tens of thousands of people rally in Moscow to demand electoral reforms, including the rerunning of tainted legislative elections; large demonstrations take place in other Russian cities as well.

•

The New England Journal of Medicine reports online that a team of medical researchers testing gene therapy for the form of hemophilia called hemophilia B have treated six people, all of whom saw notable improvement in a successful trial.

•

Steer roper Trevor Brazile is crowned winner of the all-around cowboy world championship for a record ninth time at the Wrangler National Finals Rodeo in Las Vegas.

11 The first legislative elections to be held in more than 10 years in Côte d'Ivoire take place peacefully.

•

Former Panamanian strongman Manuel Noriega returns to Panama for the first time since 1990; he is delivered to prison to complete a 20-year sentence that was interrupted by convictions and prison time in the U.S. and France.

12 Canada announces its intention to withdraw from the Kyoto Protocol agreement to reduce emissions of greenhouse gases.

•

Mikhail Prokhorov, a billionaire industrialist whose relations with the Kremlin have been sometimes cordial and other times chilly, announces that he will challenge Vladimir Putin for the presidency.

•

Fatou Bensouda of The Gambia is chosen to succeed Luis Moreno-Ocampo of Argentina as chief prosecutor of the International Criminal Court in June 2012; she has been the court's deputy prosecutor since 2004 and previously served as attorney general and as minister of justice in The Gambia.

•

Papua New Guinea's legislature authorizes the removal of Sir Michael Somare as prime minister, validating the August election of Peter O'Neill to the post, and hours later the Supreme Court rules that Somare remains prime minister; Somare left the country for medical treatment in April and did not return until September.

•

The United States Hockey Hall of Fame inducts ice hockey players Chris Chelios, Gary Suter, and Keith Tkachuk, announcer Mike Emrick, and Philadelphia Flyers owner Ed Snider.

13 Violence between security forces and antigovernment demonstrators leaves at least 32 people dead in Syria, 19 of them civilians in Idlib province trying to block a military convoy.

•

Moncef Marzouki takes office as president of Tunisia.

•

A man attacks people waiting at a bus stop in Liège, Belg., with grenades and an assault rifle, killing at least four and injuring dozens before killing himself.

Owen Humphreys—PA Wire/AP

14 The day after Israeli settlers in the West Bank attacked an Israeli army base, Israeli Prime Minister Benjamin Netanyahu declares that Israeli right-wing militants will henceforth be subject to the same lengthy administrative detentions that Palestinian militants endure.

•

Charges related to the 2000 murder of journalist Georgy Gongadze are dropped against former Ukrainian president Leonid Kuchma.

•

Zoran Milanovic is asked to form a new government in Croatia after legislative elections on December 4.

15 In a small ceremony at the airport in Baghdad, U.S. Secretary of Defense Leon Panetta declares an official end to the war that the U.S. began in Iraq in 2003.

•

After hearing reports that Qatar is discussing hosting peace talks for Afghanistan that include Taliban militants, Afghanistan withdraws its ambassador to Qatar.

•

Military defectors attack two military checkpoints and one military base in and around Darʿa, Syria, killing 27 soldiers.

•

A court in Paris finds former French president Jacques Chirac guilty of embezzlement and misuse of public funds; his two-year sentence is suspended.

16 After the outbreak of violence in Cairo, where soldiers attempted to break up demonstrations, and at vote-counting centres around the country, where soldiers attacked election judges and others trying to enter, the civilian advisory council recently set up by Egypt's military government suspends its operations.

•

In Zhanaozen, Kazakh., after striking oil workers who have occupied a square demanding higher wages began also seeking the right to form independent political parties, police attempt to clear the workers from the square, and violence results; at least 10 people are killed.

•

The World Trade Organization accepts Russia's application to become a member; the following day Samoa and Montenegro are also approved.

•

The online gaming company Zynga, maker of popular games played on the social network Facebook, begins trading on the NASDAQ stock exchange.

17 The Iraqi National Accord (al-Iraqiyyah) political bloc announces that it is boycotting Iraq's legislature.

•

Flash flooding caused by tropical storm Washi inundates the island of Mindanao in the southern Philippines, causing untold damage and leaving more than 927 people dead; the storm took an unusual and unexpected path.

18 The final convoy of U.S. soldiers, with 110 vehicles and about 500 troops, crosses out of Iraq into Kuwait.

•

Vaclav Havel, the playwright and dissident who became the first postcommunist president of Czechoslovakia and the first president of the Czech Republic, dies at his home in Bohemia.

•

In Yokohama, FC Barcelona of Spain, led by Argentine international Lionel Messi, defeats Santos FC of Brazil 4–0 to take the FIFA Club World Cup championship.

19 North Korea's official news media announce that the country's leader, Kim Jong Il, died on December 17 while on a train.

•

Syria signs an agreement with the Arab League to allow outside observers into the country to monitor its compliance with a peace agreement; the observer mission is to last for one month.

•

The Iraqi government orders the arrest of Vice Pres. Tariq al-Hashimi on charges of running a death squad; it is widely believed that the charges against him are politically motivated.

•

Michael Ogio, who was suspended as governor-general by Papua New Guinea's legislature on December 14 after he swore in a government headed by Sir Michael Somare, declares that he was in error and recognizes Peter O'Neill as prime minister; the legislature reinstates Ogio as governor-general.

•

The telecommunications giant AT&T withdraws its bid to purchase the smaller cellphone company T-Mobile.

20 Thousands of women march in Tahrir Square in Cairo to express outrage over the brutal treatment of women demonstrators by armed forces in recent days; videos have emerged showing military officers beating, stripping, and kicking women.

•

In an online news conference, astronomers announce that NASA's Kepler spacecraft has found the first two planets that are approximately the size of Earth in a solar system some 950 light-years away.

21 Leaders of a protest over land seizures in Wukan, China, that has kept Communist Party officials and security forces out of the city for 11 days say that provincial party officials have agreed to their demands and that the protest will end.

•

Iraqi Prime Minister Nuri al-Maliki threatens to release damaging files on his political opponents, warns Kurds not to shelter Vice Pres. Tariq al-Hashimi, and states that he will appoint replacements if the Iraqi National Accord (al-Iraqiyyah) political bloc does not end its boycott of the legislature.

•

Activists in Syria report that the government has intensified its campaign against protesters in northwestern Syria and has over three days killed at least 160 people.

•

The European Central Bank makes three-year, 1%-interest loans of €489 billion ($640 billion) to 523 European banks in hopes of easing the financial crisis in Europe.

22 A series of bombings, including car bombs and one ambulance bomb, during both the morning and the evening kill at least 63 people in Baghdad in the worst attack in the city in more than a year.

•

Legislation to set up an independent anticorruption agency is introduced in India's legislature; activist Anna Hazare objects to the proposal as being too weak.

23 Opposition leader Aung San Suu Kyi formally registers the National League for Democracy political party for participation in future elections in Myanmar (Burma).

•

Hungary's legislature passes controversial laws on financial stability, governance of the country's central bank, and the electoral system; critics maintain that the laws concentrate power in the hands of the ruling party.

•

A Russian Soyuz spacecraft delivers three astronauts to the International Space Station, increasing the number of members of the permanent crew to six; the station had been manned by only three crew members since September.

24 For the second time, tens of thousands of protesters pour into Moscow streets in a rally to demand new legislative elections.

•

A new government headed by Prime Minister Hamadi Jebali is sworn in in Tunisia.

•

Nigerian officials say that two days of fighting between government forces and those of the Islamist militant group Boko Haram in Damaturu, in northeastern Nigeria, have left at least 50 people dead and that 11 more people died in a shoot-out in Maiduguri.

25 In Madala, Nigeria, a bomb attack by the Boko Haram Islamist militant group on St. Theresa Catholic Church kills at least 38 worshippers; two other churches also suffer attacks.

•

A suicide bomber detonates his weapon at a funeral in Afghanistan's Takhar province; at least 20 people, including a member of the country's legislature and a member of the provincial council, are killed.

26 At least 30 people are killed in the Syrian government siege of Hims, and 50 members of the Arab League observer mission arrive in Damascus.

27 Afghan Pres. Hamid Karzai withdraws his objections to the opening of a Taliban office in Qatar; the purpose of the office is to make it possible for international negotiators to safely engage in peace talks with representatives of the Taliban.

•

Vladislav Surkov, regarded as the primary architect of the centralization of authority in Russia since the rise to power of Vladimir Putin, is reassigned to a position away from Russian internal politics.

•

The American retailer Sears Holdings Corp. says that after a worse-than-expected holiday season, it will need to close as many as 120 of its Sears and Kmart locations in order to cut costs.

28 Egypt's state media report that the military has given the central bank a loan of $1 billion in hopes of preventing a devaluation of the country's currency.

•

A wave of strikes at state agencies spreads through Yemen; workers demand the removal of bosses who have ties to the country's government and are accused of corruption.

29 Kim Jong-Eun is publicly declared the supreme leader in North Korea during a memorial ceremony for Kim Jong Il.

•

The upper house of India's legislature fails on the final day of its session to vote on a bill to create an anticorruption agency; the bill had been approved two days earlier by the lower house.

•

The Turkish military says that a strike that was intended to be against Kurdish militants in northern Iraq instead killed 35 Turkish cigarette smugglers; pro-Kurdish rioting takes place in Istanbul and elsewhere in response.

•

The opposition People's National Party wins legislative elections in Jamaica.

•

Samoa spends its final day in the same time zone as American Samoa, where it has been since 1892; it moves one time zone to the west, across the International Date Line, making the following day December 31.

30 Spain's government introduces an austerity package and points out that its 17 autonomous regions all face budget shortfalls.

•

At the last bell of the year at the New York Stock Exchange, the Dow Jones Industrial Average shows a rise of 5.5% since the beginning of the year, whereas the Standard & Poor's 500-stock index posts a decrease of 0.003% for the year.

31 U.S. savings bonds are sold for the last time in paper form; henceforth they will be available only online.

•

The final vessels cross the finish line in the 2011 Sydney Hobart Yacht Race in Australia; two days earlier the first-to-finish line honours were awarded to *Investec Loyal*, and the overall winner was declared to be *Loki*.

•

The Merce Cunningham Dance Company gives its final performance in New York City before disbanding at the end of its Legacy Tour following the 2009 death of its choreographer and leader, Merce Cunningham. *(Photo left.)*

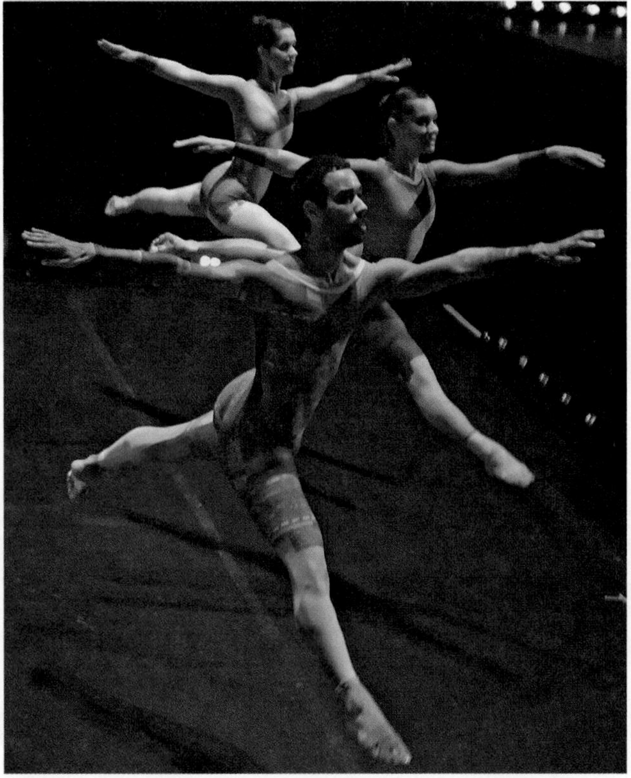

Andrea Mohin—The New York Times/Redux

Disasters

Listed here are MAJOR disasters that occurred in 2011. The list includes NATURAL and NONMILITARY mechanical disasters that claimed more than 15 lives and/or resulted in significant damage to PROPERTY.

Aviation

January 9, Iran. An IranAir Boeing 727 crashes and breaks apart as it attempts to make an emergency landing in heavy snow near the northwestern city of Orumiyeh; at least 70 of those aboard are killed. Later reports indicate that the pilot reported a technical failure prior to the crash.

April 4, Democratic Republic of the Congo. A plane carrying UN personnel from Kisangani to Kinshasa crashes upon landing; 32 of the 33 aboard perish. The plane, a Bombardier CRJ-100 jet, missed the runway. Heavy winds are thought to have been a factor.

May 7, Indonesia. A Chinese-made propeller passenger airplane crashes into the sea when attempting to land in bad weather at an airport in the province of West Papua; all 27 aboard are believed to have died.

May 18, Argentina. A Sol Líneas Aéreas commuter plane traveling from Neuquén to Comodoro Rivadavia sends out a distress signal before crashing in Río Negro province; all 22 aboard are killed. A preliminary report on the cause cites icing of the airframe.

June 20, Russia. A RusAir Tupolev Tu-134 passenger jet traveling from Moscow to Petrozavodsk crashes onto a highway just short of the runway on its approach; 44 people lose their lives. The plane's navigator is later said to have been drunk.

July 8, Democratic Republic of the Congo. A Hewa Bora Airways passenger plane crashes as it attempts to land in bad weather at Kisangani; at least 70 of those aboard are killed.

July 13, Brazil. A plane operated by regional carrier Noar Linhas Aéreas crashes shortly after takeoff from Recife as the pilot attempts an emergency landing in a populated area; all 16 aboard die. The crew of the plane, a model whose safety had been questioned, reported mechanical problems at takeoff.

July 26, Morocco. A C-130 troop transport aircraft of the Royal Moroccan Air Force crashes into a mountain near the city of Guelmim; 80 of those aboard perish in Morocco's worst air disaster since 1973.

September 2, Chile. Authorities report that an air force plane carrying 21 people has disappeared near the Juan Fernández Islands and is presumed to have crashed after wreckage is spotted in the ocean. A popular television news reporter is among those lost.

September 7, Yaroslavl, Russia. A chartered passenger plane carrying most of the Yaroslavl Lokomotiv professional ice hockey team crashes during takeoff; 44 of the 45 people aboard, including all of the team members—many of whom are former National Hockey League players—die in the disaster. Thousands of devastated hockey fans converge at the team's arena upon learning of the catastrophe.

September 25, Nepal. A sightseeing plane run by Buddha Air that has completed a tour of Himalayan mountains, including Mt. Everest, is heading back to Kathmandu when it crashes in heavy fog; all 19 passengers and crew are killed. The tourists aboard include 10 Indians, 2 Americans, and a Japanese.

September 29, Sumatra, Indonesia. A CASA/Nurtanio NC-212 passenger plane ferrying passengers between North Sumatra and Aceh provinces crashes in the mountains. When rescuers finally reach the site of the downed plane two days later, they find that all 18 aboard have perished.

October 13, Papua New Guinea. An Airlines PNG Dash 8 plane, most of whose passengers are parents planning to attend a university graduation ceremony in Madang, goes down in a storm; 28 of those aboard are killed. The pilot, the first officer, a flight attendant, and a passenger survive.

Onlookers survey the wreckage of a UN Bombardier CRJ-100 jet that missed the runway and crashed when landing in Kinshasa, Dem. Rep. of the Congo, on April 4, killing 32 of the 33 people aboard.

John Bompengo/AP

Fires and Explosions

February 16, Dar es Salaam, Tanz. A military depot explodes with a series of

Joseph Mwangi mourns after having found the charred remains of two of his children, who were among the scores of people who died in the explosion on September 12 of a gasoline pipeline that runs through a shantytown in Nairobi.
Ben Curtis/AP

detonations that continue into the next day; at least 25 people are killed. In addition, 22 armouries, 2 barracks, and 2 houses are leveled, and some 200 homes are damaged.

March 28, Yemen. Near the southern coast at a weapons factory that was abandoned by government guards and that had therefore attracted a crowd of looters, an apparently accidental explosion kills at least 150 people. The factory had been raided by al-Qaeda militants the previous day.

April 25, Beijing. A four-story clothing factory catches fire and burns; at least 17 people perish before firefighters extinguish the blaze. The structure is said to have been illegally built, and a malfunctioning electric tricycle is reported to have started the fire.

May 21, Pakistan. A tanker truck carrying fuel for NATO forces in Afghanistan is crippled by a bomb in the Khyber Agency, and as local people gather to collect the oil, it explodes; at least 15 people are incinerated.

July 10, Western Ukraine. A fire sweeps through a nursing home in the village of Beloye, killing at least 16 people. The fire begins just after midnight, and firefighters work for five hours to extinguish the blaze.

September 12, Nairobi. As people rush to collect gasoline spilling from a burst pipeline, sparks, possibly from nearby garbage fires, blow onto the gasoline, which explodes, incinerating more than 100 people. The pipeline runs through a shantytown area, and many homes are also destroyed.

November 19, Shandong province, China. An explosion at a melamine-production unit in Xintai results in the deaths of at least 14 employees. Workers were reportedly repairing a condenser at the time of the explosion.

December 9, Kolkata (Calcutta). A fire breaks out in the basement of the Advanced Medical Research Institute, an upscale private hospital, and the building fills with thick black smoke; at least 94 patients expire. The building is hermetically sealed, making both escape and rescue difficult, and doctors and staff are accused of having fled and abandoned the patients.

December 29, Myanmar (Burma). Officials say that a fire in a chemical warehouse in a suburb of Yangon (Rangoon) caused explosions that killed at least 17 people and destroyed a number of buildings nearby.

Marine

January 3, Off Yemen's south coast. Officials in Yemen report that two boats carrying migrants, largely from Ethiopia and Somalia, capsized, and some 80 people are thought to have drowned.

February 5, Off the coast of Mozambique. A boat carrying Somali and Ethiopian migrants toward South Africa sinks off Suhavo Island in Cabo Delgado province; some 50 lives are lost.

February 22, Off the coast of Yemen. Some 57 Somali refugees perish when their boat capsizes about six kilometres (four miles) from shore; a lone survivor alerts authorities to the disaster.

April 4, Myanmar (Burma). The *Weekly Eleven* news journal reports that a series of unseasonable storms in mid-March in the Andaman Sea swept thousands of fishermen into the open sea and that, while more than 15,000 were rescued, nearly 700 remain missing.

April 6, Off the coast of Lampedusa, Italy. A boat carrying refugees from sub-Saharan Africa sinks in heavy seas; though 50 migrants are rescued, some 250 are missing and feared lost.

April 10, Mediterranean Sea. A boat washes up on a beach near Zlitan, Libya; it had set sail bound for Lampedusa on March 25 carrying 72 would-be migrants but had run out of fuel and drifted for several days, ignored by European and NATO ships and coast guards, and 61 passengers had expired because of a lack of food and water.

April 25, Democratic Republic of the Congo. A boat carrying food and people across Lake Kivu tips and capsizes; at least 38 passengers drown. Bad weather may have been a factor in the disaster, but boats in the country often founder because of poor maintenance and overcrowding.

April 28, Egypt. A minibus full of passengers slides off a ferry carrying it across the Nile River in the Bani Suwayf governorate; 22 of the passengers are drowned. It appears that the driver of the vehicle, which was carrying mourners to a funeral, failed to set the emergency brake.

May 2, Democratic Republic of the Congo. A boat illegally carrying some 300 passengers after dark sinks on the Kasai River after hitting a floating tree trunk; about 100 of the passengers lose their lives.

May 5, Off the coast of southern Spain. A small boat that left Morocco carrying would-be migrants begins taking on water and sinks; the 29 passengers who are rescued say that 21 people are missing, and it is thought unlikely that they could have survived.

May 6, Off the coast of Libya. A boat carrying some 600 migrants attempting to flee violence in Libya founders shortly after its departure from Tripoli and breaks up; most of those aboard are thought to have died. Accounts from witnesses suggest that more boats carrying refugees from Libya may have sunk in recent weeks.

May 8, Togo. Boats carrying people home from a funeral across Lake Togo are caught in a storm and capsize; at least 36 of the passengers drown.

June 2, Off Tunisia. Authorities in Tunisia report that a fishing boat crowded with people attempting to migrate to Europe ran aground near the Kerkennah Islands on May 31 and that, though nearly 600 were rescued by Tunisia's coast guard, some 270 of the passengers are feared lost.

July 5, Off Tunisia. A boat carrying mostly Somali migrants to Saudi Arabia catches fire about four hours after its departure from Sudan and sinks in the Red Sea; some 200 passengers drown. Drought in the Horn of Africa is one factor driving an increase in refugees attempting to migrate by sea.

July 10, Russia. The *Bulgaria*, a riverboat dating from 1955 that is carrying families on a Volga River cruise, sinks in the Kuybyshev Reservoir; 122 of the passengers, including 28 children, lose their lives. Survivors say that the boat was caught in a storm and began to list, a situation that grew worse as the captain attempted to turn the boat around, and it began taking on water and sank in minutes.

August 1, Mediterranean Sea. Italy's Coast Guard intercepts a boat carrying migrants from Libya and finds 25 people dead in the hold. They are thought to have suffocated as a result of overcrowding.

August 9, Comoros. A passenger ferry traveling from Moroni on Grande Comore to Anjouan hits rocks and capsizes; more than 50 people are drowned.

September 10, Off Zanzibar, Tanzania. Authorities say that an overloaded ferry traveling from Zanzibar to Pemba Island overturned and capsized and that more than 200 of the passengers died. The boat sank late at night, possibly as a result of overcrowding.

December 17, Indonesia. A wooden Indonesian boat full of would-be migrants to Australia sinks in stormy weather off the coast of Java and breaks up; hundreds are missing and feared dead. The passengers included people from Afghanistan, Iran, and Turkey.

December 17, Off the Moluccas, Indonesia. An overloaded ferry carrying people trying to return to their hometowns for the Christmas holidays goes down in high seas, and at least 40 people drown, with an unknown number missing. The ferry is said to have departed port without permission.

December 18, Off Sakhalin Island, Russia. As two ships tow a Russian drilling platform toward a new assignment during a winter storm, the platform sinks; four bodies are found, and 49 of those on the platform are missing and assumed to have drowned.

Mining and Construction

January 26, Near Sardinata, Colom. A methane gas explosion during a shift change at La Preciosa coal mine leaves at least 21 workers dead.

March 20, Southwestern Pakistan. A methane gas explosion collapses part of a coal mine; all 52 miners present are killed.

May 3, Mexico. A gas explosion at a vertical-shaft mine in Coahuila state leaves 14 miners dead.

July 2, Guizhou province, China. The flooding of a privately owned coal mine traps 23 miners; rescue efforts fail. (*See* photograph on page 59.)

July 2, Guangxi autonomous region, China. Heavy rains cause a coal mine to collapse; 20 miners are trapped underground and expire.

July 6, Shandong province, China. A fire traps at least 36 miners in the Zaozhuang Fangbei coal mine; two weeks later only 8 miners have been rescued.

July 10, Shandong province, China. Flooding fatally traps 24 miners in an iron-ore mine.

July 29, Ukraine. A methane gas explosion in the Suhodolsky-Eastern coal mine in the Luhansk area leaves at least 17 miners dead and 9 others missing.

October 29, Hunan province, China. A gas explosion kills 29 miners in the state-owned Xialiuchong coal mine in the city of Hengyang.

November 10, Yunnan province, China. At least 34 workers in an unlicensed coal mine die in an explosion of coal and gas.

Natural

January 10, Queensland, Australia. Flash floods overwhelm the low-lying town of Toowoomba, leaving at least 20 people dead and some 90 missing. Witnesses describe a wall of water 8 m (26 ft) high moving with shocking swiftness.

January 12, Brazil. Flooding from rains that began on January 1 has left at least 24 people dead in São Paulo state.

January 12, Rio de Janeiro state, Braz. Landslides bury several mountain towns, leaving more than 900 dead; the cities of Teresópolis and Nova Friburgo are particularly hard hit. The area had experienced higher rainfall in a 24-hour period than is ordinarily recorded for the month as a whole.

January 13, Queensland, Australia. Days of flooding leave much of Brisbane under water; at least 35 people perish in the worst flooding the city has experienced in nearly 40 years.

January 13, Sri Lanka. The government says that flooding and mud slides from heavy rainfall in the past several days have resulted in at least 40 people's deaths and the displacement of some 300,000 as well as the devastation of farmland.

January 17, Eastern South Africa. Government officials report that storms and flooding in recent weeks have left at least 39 people dead. By the end of the month, the toll has passed 100, with thousands left homeless, as the region continues to experience unusually high rainfall.

February 22, Christchurch, N.Z. A 6.3-magnitude earthquake with its epicentre about 10 km (6 mi) from downtown and only some 5 km (3 mi) underground collapses skyscrapers and other buildings in much of the city; at least 180 people are killed. Infrastructure in the city had been weakened by a

Tanzanian police carry ashore to Zanzibar the bodies of children who died when an overcrowded ferry capsized on September 10. More than 200 of those aboard perished.

Ali Sultan/AP

EPA/Landov

Rescue workers in China's Guizhou province engage in what is ultimately a futile effort to rescue 23 coal miners who were trapped on July 2 by the sudden flooding of the mine.

stronger but less-destructive earthquake in September 2010.

March 10, Yunnan province, China. A 5.5-magnitude earthquake destroys some 1,200 homes and other buildings in Yingjiang county near the border with Myanmar (Burma); at least 25 people are killed, and more than 1,000 buildings collapse.

March 11, Japan. An underwater 9.0-magnitude earthquake causes enormous devastation and unleashes a tsunami with waves as high as 9 m (30 ft) that roars deep ashore for hundreds of kilometres along the northeastern coast; it is feared that some 24,000 people have perished, but later reports lower the number to 19,300.

March 24, Northeastern Myanmar (Burma). A shallow 6.9-magnitude earthquake is felt over a wide area, with reports of damage in Thailand, Vietnam, and Laos; government officials report that at least 74 people have been killed, though relief workers put the death toll at 120.

March 31, Southern Thailand. Rescue efforts are mounted after a week of unseasonable storms have devastated coastal provinces and islands, including many tourist areas; at least 53 people have died.

April 13, Thailand. The government says that flooding in the southern part of the country that began in late March has left at least 61 people dead; many of the fatalities resulted from flash floods and from mud slides.

April 14–16, Southern U.S. Dozens of tornadoes touch down in 12 or more states, destroying hundreds of buildings and leaving at least 45 people, 22 of them in North Carolina alone, dead; fatalities are also recorded in Virginia, Arkansas, Alabama, Oklahoma, and Mississippi.

April 27, Southern U.S. Waves of tornadoes sweep through as many as seven states, leaving a huge swath of devastation and killing some 345 people. In Alabama some 250 people die, 45 of them in Tuscaloosa, where one twister was 1.6 km (1 mi) wide; 34 in Tennessee, 34 in Mississippi, and 15 in Georgia are included in the death toll. It is the deadliest tornado outbreak to have occurred in the U.S. since 1974.

May 8, Guangxi autonomous region, China. More than 20 quarry workers in the village of Luojiang die when the area is engulfed by a landslide that followed a rainstorm. The workers are killed when their temporary dormitory is buried.

May 21, Malaysia. Two simultaneous landslides caused by heavy rainfall inundate an orphanage for ethnic Malay Muslim boys in Selangor state; 20 boys and 4 adults succumb.

May 22, Joplin, Mo. A massive tornado levels about one-third of the city and kills at least 160 residents. The multivortex twister is as much as 1.6 km (1 mi) in diameter and is categorized as an F5.

June 7, China. Officials report that heavy rains in Guizhou and Hunan provinces have caused flooding that has left at least 9 people dead and 13 missing and brought some relief from the six-month drought that has been the main focus of concern in the region.

June 7, Haiti. Flooding from storms leaves at least 20 people dead; most of the deaths are in Port-au-Prince. Officials fear that the flooding will add to the death toll from cholera, which has surpassed 5,000 since the beginning of the epidemic in October.

June 11, Central China. State media report that more than 40 people have died in flooding and landslides resulting from two days of torrential rainfall.

June 20, Southern and eastern China. Officials say that rainfall that began June 3 has caused flooding in which at least 175 people have perished, with a further 86 people missing; Zhejiang province has been particularly hard hit. Authorities report that some 70 km (43 mi) of dikes are in danger of being overtopped.

July 27, South Korea. Mud slides caused by heavy rainfall crush parts of a resort village in Chuncheon and homes on a hillside in southern Seoul, and at least 29 people succumb; subways and roadways are closed by the flooding. A total of at least 59 people die as a result of the flooding and mud slides throughout the country.

July 27, Philippines. Tropical Storm Juaning brings torrential rain and high winds to Aurora province on Luzon island; at least 27 people are killed, and thousands of families are displaced.

August 28, U.S. Hurricane Irene churns up the eastern seaboard for a second day, leaving flooding, destroyed homes and damaged property, and about 40 people dead in its wake. The storm made landfall on North Carolina's Outer Banks on August 27 and continued north, reaching New Jersey in the morning of August 28 and traveling through Vermont, which experiences historic levels of flooding.

August 29, Uganda. Landslides following heavy rain cause the deaths of at least 40 people in the eastern Bulambuli district. Deforestation on the slopes of Mt. Elgon is a contributing factor to the scale of the disaster.

August 31, New York City. The city medical examiner reports that 19 people died as a result of excessive heat in the city in late July and August.

September 4, Western and central Japan. Massive flooding results when Typhoon Talas makes landfall; at least 40 people are killed, and dozens more are said to be missing. The typhoon is the most destructive one to have struck Japan since 2004, and it unleashes a record amount of rainfall.

September 18, Himalayas. A 6.9-magnitude earthquake centred in the Indian state of Sikkim causes damage in northeastern India, Nepal, and the Chinese region of Tibet; more than 100 people are reported to have died. Monsoon rains contribute to landslides that hamper rescue and relief efforts.

September 19, Pakistan. UN and Pakistani sources say that monsoon rains have brought catastrophic flooding to Sindh province, where more than 220 people have died and 665,000 homes have been damaged or destroyed.

September 21, Japan. Typhoon Roke brings storm damage and flooding to Honshu, the main island, hitting Tokyo directly and leaving at least 16 people dead or missing.

September 26, Northeastern India. At least 80 people are said to have lost their lives in flooding resulting from monsoon rains, many of them killed by the collapse of building walls.

September 27, Philippines. Typhoon Nesat pummels the country, resulting in the deaths of at least 52 people, many of them in Manila; tens of thousands are evacuated.

September 27, Northeastern and central Thailand. A Thai newspaper reports that flooding from strong monsoon rains has caused at least 158 deaths in the area; deforestation is blamed for exacerbating the flooding.

September 30, South Asia. It is reported that weeks of flooding along the Mekong River caused by unusually heavy rains has left at least 150 people in Cambodia and southern Vietnam dead; the vast majority of the deaths occurred in Cambodia.

October 4, Thailand. Officials report that flooding since mid-July has left at least 224 people dead; also, a World Heritage site consisting of a 500-year-old temple complex in Ayutthaya has been inundated.

October 13, Thailand. Floodwaters approach Bangkok, which is ill-prepared; at least 282 people have died because of flooding in the past few months.

October 13, Cambodia. It is reported that the death toll from flooding resulting from monsoon rains has reached at least 247.

October 16, Central America. Officials say that a week of heavy rains has led to flooding and landslides in which at least 81 people perished, at least 28 of them in Guatemala, 32 in El Salvador (which experiences record amounts of rain), 13 in Honduras, and 8 in Nicaragua. The UN estimates that flooding has affected more than 100,000 people in the region.

October 20, Myanmar (Burma). Flash flooding carries away some 300 homes and leaves at least 147 people dead in Pakokku. The flooding occurs when a river overflows as a result of torrential rain, part of the unusually intense monsoon season in Southeast Asia.

October 23, Eastern Turkey. A 7.1-magnitude earthquake brings destruction to the area, causing devastation in the cities of Van and Ercis; at least 534 people perish, and hundreds of buildings are reduced to rubble.

October 25, Thailand. The death toll from catastrophic flooding in Thailand rises to 366, and floodwaters begin to encroach on Bangkok, breaching barriers that were constructed to protect the city's domestic airport.

November 5, Manizales, Colom. Heavy rains cause a landslide that sweeps away homes and kills at least 48 residents. In spite of the unusually heavy rainy season, the city previously had not been considered at risk for such a catastrophe.

November 8, Thailand. The death toll from more than three months of flooding reaches 527; floodwaters continue to inundate much of Bangkok and do not appear to be receding. The floods stem from the typhoon that struck Southeast Asia in late July.

Reuters/Landov

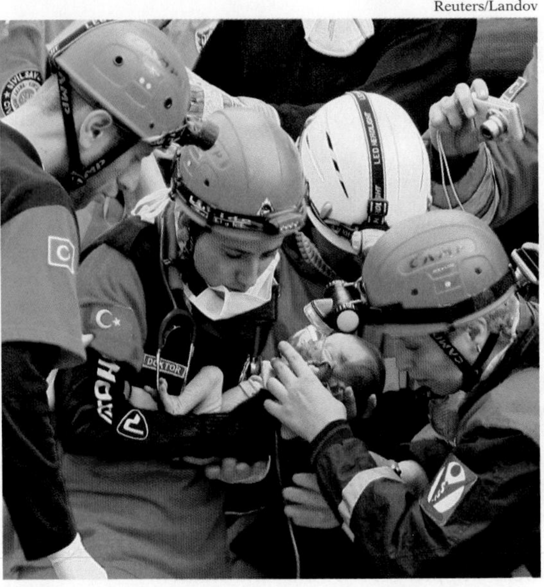

Rescue workers carry a 14-day-old baby found alive in the wreckage of a building in Ercis, Tur., two days after a 7.1-magnitude earthquake struck eastern Turkey on October 23. At least 534 people died in the cataclysm.

November 9, Southeastern Turkey. At least 40 people perish in Van province in a 5.7-magnitude earthquake, the second temblor in two weeks in the area.

December 17, Southern Philippines. Tropical storm Washi hits farther south than most storms, causing flash flooding and devastation on the island of Mindanao; more than 1,000 people die, and hundreds still remain unaccounted for at the end of the year.

Railroad

January 29, Saxony-Anhalt state, Ger. A passenger train and a freight train collide head-on near Magdeburg, and several cars of the passenger train derail; at least 10 passengers are killed, and dozens are injured. Investigators conclude that the operator of the freight train ignored signals.

July 10, Uttar Pradesh, India. A passenger train bound for New Delhi derails about 120 km (75 mi) from Lucknow, near Fatehpur; at least 69 passengers perish.

July 23, Near Wenzhou, China. A high-speed train plows into another train that has stalled on the tracks in an accident in which at least six cars derail and 40 people are killed; a subsequent investigation blames design flaws in signaling equipment that failed after a lightning strike. (*See* photograph on page 61.)

Traffic

March 4, Kampong Saom, Camb. A container truck loaded with steel crushes a passenger minibus, and at least 19 people, including the drivers of both vehicles, are killed.

March 12, New York City. The driver of a chartered bus carrying passengers home from a night of gambling in a casino in Connecticut loses control of the bus in the predawn hours; the bus hits a guardrail and tips over on its side, sliding down the highway and hitting a sign pole that shears off the roof; 15 passengers perish.

May 30, Assam state, India. As a bus carrying a wedding party crosses a wooden bridge, the bridge collapses, sending the bus into the river below; at least 25 of the passengers are killed.

July 4, Hubei province, China. A speeding truck rams into the back of a passenger bus that has stopped illegally on the highway; 23 people, including the truck driver, are killed.

Kyodo/Landov

Workers near Wenzhou, China, surround the cars of a high-speed train that derailed on July 23 when one bullet train plowed into another one that had stalled on the tracks; the crash left 40 people dead.

July 7, Uttar Pradesh, India. A bus carrying a wedding party stops on railroad tracks near Patiyali and is struck by an express train; at least 38 bus passengers perish.

July 11, Bangladesh. An open truck carrying dozens of boys returning to their school from an association football (soccer) match in Chittagong district goes off the road and flips into a roadside canal; at least 44 of the schoolboys drown in the canal.

July 22, Henan province, China. An overloaded long-distance double-decker bus on a highway in Xinyang bursts into flames, incinerating at least 41 of those aboard; the cause of the fire is unknown.

August 20, Afghanistan. A bus driver on the highway from Kandahar to Kabul loses control of his vehicle, and it goes over; at least 35 people are killed.

August 22, Uttar Pradesh. A truck carrying devotees to a temple in Ballia district overturns into a water-filled ditch; at least 41 passengers lose their lives.

September 26, Punjab province, Pak. A passenger bus plunges into a ravine after its brakes fail; at least 37 of its passengers, most of whom are schoolchildren, lose their lives, as does the driver.

October 13, Nepal. A crowded bus goes off a mountain highway and falls into the Sun Kosi River below; at least 42 of those aboard die.

November 15, Gansu province, China. A nine-seat van carrying 62 preschoolers has a head-on collision with a coal truck in Qingyang; the bus driver, a teacher, and at least 21 children are killed.

December 3, Bahia state, Braz. A tractor-trailer loaded with construction materials and heading down a hill near Milagres collides with a bus ferrying sugarcane cutters; at least 33 people perish.

December 12, Jiangsu province, China. A school bus goes off the road and overturns; at least 15 schoolchildren lose their lives.

Miscellaneous

January 14, Kerala state, India. As pilgrims return from a religious festival, a vehicle on the narrow forest path they are walking plows into them, setting off a panicked stampede in which more than 100 people lose their lives.

February 21, Bamako, Mali. As people wait to exit a stadium following a religious ceremony led by a popular imam, a stampede occurs in which at least 36 people are crushed to death. There are conflicting reports as to what set off the stampede. The stadium is reported to have been filled beyond its capacity.

February 27, Brazil. At a pre-Carnival street party in Bandeira do Sul, a power cable breaks and falls into a crowd of people dancing; at least 17 people are electrocuted.

July 17, Ecuador. The government bans the sale of alcohol for three days in response to a spate of methyl alcohol poisoning from the consumption of bootleg liquor that left at least 21 people dead.

November 8, Haridwar, India. At a religious festival, as thousands of Hindu pilgrims surge forward to make offerings, a stampede occurs when some people fall while those behind continue to push forward; some 20 people succumb.

December 15, West Bengal, India. An investigation is ordered after mass deaths result from the drinking of bootleg intoxicants that contain methyl alcohol; at least 170 people are fatally poisoned.

Thousands of Hindu pilgrims gather at a religious festival on November 8 in Haridwar, India, at which a stampede occurred that resulted in the deaths of some 20 people.

EPA/Landov

People of 2011

Catherine Middleton (left) shares a smile with her sister and maid of honour, Pippa Middleton, as she prepares to enter Westminster Abbey in London for her April 29 wedding to Britain's Prince William, duke of Cambridge.

Anwar Hussein—PA Photos/Landov

Nobel Prizes

Nobels were awarded to 10 men and 3 women in 2011; recipients included a trio of female **PEACEMAKERS** lauded for their **NONVIOLENT** efforts to include women in the peace process, an acclaimed Swedish poet noted for verse described as **"ACTIVE MEDITATIONS,"** two economists for their work on the **CAUSAL RELATIONSHIP** between economic policy and macroeconomic **VARIABLES**, and scientists who discovered the acceleration of the expansion of the **UNIVERSE**, a new form of matter called **QUASICRYSTALS**, and mechanisms underlying **IMMUNITY**.

PRIZE FOR PEACE

The 2011 Nobel Prize for Peace was shared by three women: Ellen Johnson Sirleaf and Leymah Gbowee, both of Liberia, and Tawakkul Karman, of Yemen. In its announcement the Norwegian Nobel Committee said that the three were being honoured "for their non-violent struggle for the safety of women and for women's rights to full participation in the peace-building work."

Johnson Sirleaf, president of Liberia, was born on Oct. 29, 1938, in Monrovia. She trained in economics in Africa and in the U.S. and received an M.A. degree (1971) from Harvard University. Johnson Sirleaf served as finance minister in the Liberian government, but in the 1980s she was arrested for opposing Liberia's military regime. After a brief period in prison, she spent several years in exile and worked for the World Bank and the UN before returning to Liberia. In 2005 she became the first woman to be elected head of a government in Africa. During her administration she negotiated forgiveness for billions of dollars in foreign debt, and the country enjoyed a period of calm in spite of extreme poverty and high unemployment. In the national elections held on Oct. 11, 2011, she did not win an outright majority of votes. In the November 8 runoff, she was elected to a second term.

Gbowee, born in 1972 in central Liberia, trained as a social worker. She moved to Monrovia in 1990 as the country was entering a long period of civil war. She worked to bridge the gap between Christian and Muslim women and in 2002 began to lead passive protests by women against the brutal regime of Charles Taylor. In 2003 Gbowee and her followers escalated their demands for an end to the civil war, which led to a meeting with Taylor and then to an end to the fighting. She was often credited with having created the conditions leading to the resumption, three years later, of a civilian government under Johnson Sirleaf. Gbowee was the director of Women in Peace and Security Network Africa. Her writings include an autobiography, *Mighty Be Our Powers* (2011).

Tawakkul Karman was born on Feb. 7, 1979, in Taiz in southern Yemen. A journalist, she came to be known as the

Leymah Gbowee (left), Tawakkul Karman (centre), and Ellen Johnson Sirleaf (right)

Reuters/Landov

"mother of the revolution" and as the "iron woman" for her role in the 2011 protests demanding the resignation of Yemen's president, ʿAli ʿAbdallah Salih. A cofounder of Women Journalists Without Chains, she participated in sit-ins staged in 2007 to oppose the Yemeni government's ban on the media's texting of news alerts. Although she was a member of Islah, the country's Islamist party, Karman challenged some of the restrictions commonly imposed on women, and she stopped wearing the *niqab,* or face veil, in favour of a headscarf. Living in a tent in the centre of Sanaa in 2011, she became a powerful symbol of the antigovernment protest movement. When Karman was arrested in January, the popular outcry was so great that she was released within a day. She was the first Arab woman to receive the Nobel Peace Prize.

In honouring the three women, the Nobel Committee expressed the hope that the prize would "help to bring an end to the suppression of women that still occurs in many countries, and to realise the great potential for democracy and peace that women can represent." The award to Karman was widely seen as a recognition of the so-called Arab Spring, in which autocratic governments across North Africa and in the Middle East had felt the force of demands for change. (ROBERT RAUCH)

PRIZE FOR ECONOMICS

The 2011 Nobel Memorial Prize in Economics was awarded to Americans Thomas J. Sargent and Christopher A. Sims, whose empirical research on the causal relationship between economic policy (generally as promoted by a government or a central bank) and macroeconomic variables (such as inflation and employment) led to completely new thinking and methodology to determine the nature of such relationships. The methods they developed in the 1970s and '80s enabled a better understanding of how changes in monetary and other official economic policies introduced in response to a surge in world oil prices or other unexpected events might affect economic growth or inflation in the short and long term. Previously, economic models reflected the view common in Keynesian economics that the relationships were established and the effect of policy changes was predictable. Such changes were difficult to predict, given that the new policy might be the cause of economic growth or a rise in prices, for example, but could result equally from an unexpected event that might require a different policy response. Their research showed that causal relationships can be analyzed by using historical data and resulted in methodologies capable of predicting the effects of unexpected events (or shocks) and of policy changes.

Sargent was awarded the Nobel for his research and development of methods that use historical data to understand the impact of changes in economic policy over time. Earlier economic models (including those presented by 1995 Nobel laureate Robert E. Lucas, Jr.) could not produce reliable predictions of the effect of policy changes taking into account any adjustments in expectation and behaviour by the private sector. This was why an expansionary government policy could result in rising inflation and unemployment rates. Sargent's challenge was to distinguish between cause and effect in the macroeconomy. His research focused on ways to test the new theory of rational expectations. To do this he developed a structural (macroeconomic) model of the economy that incorporated microeconomic factors that would not change unpredictably in response to policy changes. Unpredictable factors—such as consumer demand for some goods and services in the face of raised interest rates—were incorporated into the model. To perfect his model Sargent used historical data, especially on inflation, to estimate in numerical terms the fundamental values of the parameters that determine the relationships between different variables. His analysis showed that expectations of inflation were formed slowly through learning and experience, thereby blunting the effect of policy decisions.

Sims shared Sargent's skepticism for the mathematical models being used at the start of the 1970s, particularly in respect to historical relationships that were accepted as theories. Sims believed that good theories were needed to identify the economic variables that caused changes to occur in other variables. He developed a method based on vector autoregression (VAR: a statistical model used to identify mainly linear interdependencies) to analyze how the economy was affected by economic policy changes (temporary) and other factors. VAR could be used to estimate the response of one variable when another changes and determine whether one variable helped to predict another. His method identified and interpreted unexpected events, or shocks, in historical data and analyzed how they gradually affected different variables. Over the next three decades, Sims led the development and wider application of VAR in the forecasting and interpretation of macroeconomic time series.

Thomas John Sargent was born on July 19, 1943, in Pasadena, Calif., and attended the University of California, Berkeley (B.A., 1964), and Harvard University (Ph.D., 1968). In 1967 he became a research associate at the Carnegie Institute of Technology at Carnegie Mellon University, Pittsburgh. After serving in the U.S. Army as a systems analyst (1968–69), he was a professor of economics at the Universities of Pennsylvania (1970–71) and Minnesota (1971–87), where he was simultaneously an adviser to the U.S. Federal Reserve Bank of Minneapolis. Sargent then held positions as a senior fellow at the Hoover Institution, Stanford University (from 1987), the David Rockefeller Professor at the University of Chicago (1991–98), the Donald L. Lucas Professor of Economics at Stanford (1998–2002), and the William R. Berkley Professor of Economics and Business at New York University (from 2002).

Christopher Albert Sims was born on Oct. 21, 1942, in Washington, D.C., and attended Harvard (B.A., 1963; Ph.D., 1968), where he taught economics (1968–70) before serving from 1970 to 1990 as a professor at the University of Minnesota. In 1990 he joined Yale University as Henry Ford II Professor of Economics, but in 1999 he moved to Princeton University, where in 2004 he was made Harold H. Helm '20 Professor of Economics and Banking.

(JANET H. CLARK)

PRIZE FOR LITERATURE

The 2011 Nobel Prize for Literature was awarded to Swedish poet Tomas Tranströmer, cited by the Swedish Academy for his "condensed, translucent images" that "gives us fresh access to reality." During a career that spanned nearly six decades, Tranströmer produced more than 15 collections of poetry that established him as a preeminent literary figure within contemporary Scandinavian literature. He was known for his technical proficiency and detached, personal perspective and described his poems as "active meditations" intended both to engage and to challenge the reader as a means to confront the complexities of identity and to embrace the mysteries of human existence.

Tomas Gösta Tranströmer was born on April 15, 1931, in Stockholm. His

Brother Luck/Alamy

Tomas Tranströmer

parents divorced in his early childhood, and he was raised by his schoolteacher mother and nurtured by his maternal grandfather. He studied literature, psychology, and the history of religion at Stockholm University College (later Stockholm University). After completing his education in 1956, he worked at the university's Institution for Psychometrics, and in 1960 he became psychologist in residence at Roxtuna, an institution for delinquent youth near Linköping. In 1965 he moved with his wife and family to Västerås, about 100 km (60 mi) west of Stockholm, where he continued his work as a psychologist at the Labour Market Institute.

Tranströmer was influenced as a poet by diverse elements ranging from high modernism to surrealism. He published (1954) his first volume of poetry, *17 dikter* (*17 Poems*, 1987), emerging as a distinct lyrical voice in post-World War II Swedish literature. His artistic reputation was further enhanced by the subsequent publication of *Hemligheter på vägen* (1958; *Secrets on the Way*, 1987) and *Den halvfärdiga himlen* (1962; *The Half-Finished Heaven*, 1987), comprising 14 and 21 poems, respectively. Despite the limited production of just 52 poems in a 10-year period, by the mid-1960s Tranströmer was being acknowledged as a national icon and his country's foremost poet. Beginning with the publication of *Klanger och spår* (1966; *Bells and Tracks*, 1987), followed by *Mörkerseende* (1970; *Seeing in the Dark*, 1987), he gained an increasing international reputation, especially in the U.S., where his poems were first translated by American poet Robert Bly, who referred to Tranströmer's verse as "a poetry of silence and depths." Although less political and experimental than his contemporaries, Tranströmer wrote in an understated, imaginative language that communicated through bold, concrete imagery distinguished by clarity and precision. Masterful in his use of poetic metaphor, he was more accessible than other Scandinavian poets and was abundantly translated into more than 50 languages. His collected poems first appeared in English in 1987, translated by Robin Fulton, and were revised and expanded in 1997, 2006, and 2011.

Throughout his career Tranströmer celebrated the expansive and often stark beauty of the Swedish landscape, returning repeatedly to the Baltic archipelago east of Stockholm associated with his childhood and beloved by his maternal grandfather, as illustrated in the full-length poem *Östersjöar* (1974; *Baltics*, 1975). Through the inspired use of memory and perception, his poems transform everyday items into the realm of the magical and broaden the scope of poetic vision. His poetry was defined by simplicity, compression, and subtlety, exploring the seen and the unseen while offering a measure of understanding, comfort, and reconciliation.

In 1979 Tranströmer published his collected poems; he followed with *Det vilda torget* (1983; *The Wild Marketplace*, 1985; also translated as *The Wild Market Square*, 1987), a bilingual English-Swedish edition entitled *The Blue House = Det blå huset* (1987), and *För levande och döda* (1989; *For the Living and the Dead*, 1994). When he was at the height of his creative energy, however, his productivity was severely affected by a stroke in 1990 that left him physically compromised and unable to speak. Afterward, he produced a memoir of childhood and adolescence, *Minnena ser mig* (1993; *Memories Look at Me*, 1995) and additional volumes of poetry, including *Sorgegondolen* (1996; *The Sorrow Gondola*, 1997) and *Den stora gåtan* (2004; *The Great Enigma*, 2006), both of which incorporate Tranströmer's need for economic concentration based on haiku. Tranströmer, a consummate craftsman capable of juxtaposing unexpected and often ambiguous sources within poetry of spaciousness, religiosity, and transcendence, was the recipient of numerous literary awards, including the Petrarch Prize, the Neustadt International Prize for Literature, the Nordic Prize from the Swedish Academy, and the Lifetime Recognition Award from the Griffin Trust for Excellence in Poetry. (STEVEN R. SERAFIN)

PRIZE FOR CHEMISTRY

The Nobel Prize for Chemistry in 2011 went to Daniel Shechtman, of the Technion-Israel Institute of Technology, Haifa, for discovering a new form of matter called "quasicrystals." The essence of the quasicrystal is the way it differs from a crystal. Crystals have lattices in which the local structure repeats throughout the system. For example, in table salt each sodium atom is surrounded by six chlorine atoms, and likewise each chlorine is surrounded by six sodiums, in a repeating cubic arrangement. In a quasicrystal the immediate neighbourhood of each atom has a regular structure, but that structure does not repeat in a periodic way.

Shechtman was born on Jan. 24, 1941, in Tel Aviv. He received a bachelor's degree in mechanical engineering (1966) and a master's (1968) and a doctoral degree (1972) in materials engineering from Technion. From 1972 to 1975 he was a postdoctoral associate at the Aerospace Research Laboratories at Wright-Patterson Air Force Base, Dayton, Ohio. From 1975 he held various positions at Technion, finally becoming a professor in 1984. He was a visiting professor at Johns Hopkins University, Baltimore, Md. (1981–97), and at the University of Maryland (1997–2004). From 2004 he also served as a professor of materials science and engineering at Iowa State University.

The possibility of such aperiodic structures had been conjectured in the 1960s for two dimensions. Mathematicians wondered if a surface could be covered by tiles, with no vacant spaces between them, in a way that had no pe-

Daniel Shechtman

Oliver Weiken—EPA/Landov

riodic repetitions. (Examples of such tilings actually existed in medieval Islamic floors, such as in the Alhambra in Spain, but these were unknown to mathematicians and crystallographers.) The first pattern to accomplish this was completed in 1966 and used over 20,000 different tiles, but by the mid-1970s this had been reduced first to 40 and then, by Roger Penrose, to only 2. Robert Ammann extended the concept of such aperiodic structures to three dimensions. However, at that time aperiodic materials were only an idea.

While Shechtman was a guest researcher in 1982 at the National Bureau of Standards (NBS; now the National Institute of Science and Technology) in Gaithersburg, Md., he began studying alloys of aluminum with manganese or iron. He used the standard structure-probing tool of scattering electrons from the solids; the scattered electrons form regular patterns of localized spots, whose arrangement on the detector reveals the crystal's structure. The patterns from Shechtman's alloys, however, did not correspond to any known crystal lattice structure. Those lattice structures had been well understood since 1848, when they were cataloged by August Bravais—and hence became known as Bravais lattices. Bravais lattices yielded concentric circles made of four or six spots. The patterns produced in Shechtman's diffraction experiments had an unusual 10 spots on a circle, yet his materials must have had a regular pattern because a disordered material, such as a glass or a liquid, would have produced only diffuse rings, not sharp spots, in its scattering pattern. How could a solid yield such a pattern, one with regularity but not a crystal? Shechtman was able to show, by rotating his samples, that they had fivefold symmetry, which is inconsistent with any periodic lattice.

Shechtman's findings puzzled him and many others. Some disbelievers scoffed, and his supervisor asked him to leave his research group. Back at Technion he and colleague Ilan Blech prepared a paper interpreting the pattern in terms of atomic structure. The paper was rejected upon submission. Shechtman then turned to the senior scientist who had brought him to NBS, John Cahn, who in turn engaged French crystallographer Denis Gratias. The four wrote a new paper in 1984 showing that a solid could not only have long-range orientational order but also lack the translational symmetry that characterizes a crystal. The structures Shechtman had found exhibited icosahedral symmetry. The icosahedron had 20 identical pentagonal faces arranged so that an observer looking directly at one of those faces would be able to rotate the object one-fifth of the way through a circle and not be able to distinguish it from its original state. A few weeks after Shechtman's paper appeared, Dov Levine and Paul Steinhardt interpreted the result by relating it to a three-dimensional model developed by Alan Mackay; they introduced the term *quasicrystals*. Subsequent research revealed about 100 intermetallic quasicrystals.

(R. STEPHEN BERRY)

PRIZE FOR PHYSICS

The 2011 Nobel Prize for Physics was awarded to three astrophysicists who showed that the expansion of the universe is accelerating. American Saul Perlmutter received half of the prize, while the other half was shared by American Adam Riess and American-born Australian Brian Schmidt.

Saul Perlmutter was born on Sept. 22, 1959, in Urbana, Ill., and grew up in Philadelphia. He graduated with an A.B. in physics (1981) from Harvard University and received a Ph.D. in physics (1986) from the University of California, Berkeley. He remained at Berkeley in various faculty positions, finally becoming (2004) a professor of physics. Perlmutter's numerous honours include the E.O. Lawrence Award in Physics (2002); the John Scott Award (2005); the Shaw Prize in Astronomy (2006), which he also shared with Riess and Schmidt; and the Gruber Cosmology Prize (2007), which Perlmutter and his team shared with Schmidt and his team.

Adam Guy Riess was born on Dec. 16, 1969, in Washington, D.C. He graduated from MIT in 1992 and received a Ph.D. in astrophysics (1996) from Harvard. After having completed a postdoctoral fellowship (1996–99) at Berkeley, he became (1999) an astronomer with the Space Telescope Science Institute at Johns Hopkins University, Baltimore, Md., and in 2006 he joined Johns Hopkins's department of physics and astronomy as a professor. In addition to the Shaw Prize, Riess received the Astronomical Society of the Pacific's Trumpler Award (1999) and the American Astronomical Society's Helen B. Warner Prize (2003).

Brian P. Schmidt was born on Feb. 24, 1967, in Missoula, Mont. He obtained B.S. degrees in physics and astronomy (1989) from the University of Arizona and earned an M.A. (1992) and then a Ph.D. (1993) in astronomy from Harvard. In 1995 he moved to Australia and joined the Australian National University, Canberra, where in 2010 he became a professor. Schmidt's awards in Australia include the government's Malcolm McIntosh Prize (2000) and the Australian Academy of Science's Pawsey Medal (2001).

American astronomer Edwin Hubble in 1924 demonstrated that nebulae were actually galaxies far beyond the Milky Way Galaxy. Studies of these galaxies showed them to be moving away from the Milky Way; the farther away the galaxies were, the faster they seemed to be receding. These results led to the big-bang model, in which the universe expanded from an originally very small volume. It was unknown, however, if the rate of expansion of the universe had changed with time. Measurements of objects in distant galaxies made for large uncertainties. The situation was vastly improved by the discovery of Type Ia supernovas. These exploding stars produce a massive burst of light that can be used to measure distance. Because it was assumed that the mutual gravitational attraction of all the mass—including the "missing mass" that came to be known as dark matter—in the universe would work against outward expansion, scientists expected that the universe would be shown to be expanding much more slowly than at earlier times.

After having studied nearby supernovas since the early 1980s, using data from a robotic telescope, Perlmutter and his team in 1987 began a project to search for more-distant deep-space Type Ia supernovas. By 1994 this undertaking, the Supernova Cosmology Project, had identified batches of supernovas, and in January 1998 Perlmutter's team officially announced the highly unexpected discovery that the expansion of the universe was not slowing down but rather was accelerating. This discovery was independently confirmed by results announced at almost the same time by Schmidt and Riess's High-Z Supernova Search Team (established by Schmidt in 1994), which had examined the most-distant supernovas yet discovered. The accelerating expansion of the universe was attributed to the existence of dark energy, a repulsive force that permeates all of space. Dark energy was said to account for 73% of the total mass-energy of the universe, but its actual nature was a hotly debated subject in cosmological theory.

(DAVID G.C. JONES)

PRIZE FOR PHYSIOLOGY OR MEDICINE

The 2011 Nobel Prize for Physiology or Medicine was awarded to three scientists for their discoveries concerning the function of the immune system. Bruce A. Beutler, professor and chairman of the department of genetics at Scripps Research Institute, La Jolla, Calif., and Jules A. Hoffmann, former president (2007–08) of the French Academy of Sciences, Paris, shared one-half of the prize for their discoveries regarding the activation of the innate immune system, the body's first line of defense against potential pathogens. Beutler and Hoffmann had previously shared the Robert Koch Prize (2004), the Balzan Prize (2007), and the Shaw Prize (2011). The second half of the Nobel award went to Ralph M. Steinman, physician and professor at Rockefeller University, New York City, for his co-discovery of the dendritic cell and his work to uncover its role in adaptive immunity, which helped advance the development of treatments for conditions associated with immune dysfunction. Steinman died from pancreatic cancer just days before the Nobel Prize winners were announced, and although tradition dictated that the awards would not be distributed posthumously, a remarkable exception was made on his behalf.

Steinman's Nobel Prize-winning research began in the early 1970s, when, working with American cell biologist Zanvil A. Cohn, he observed unusual branching cells in the spleens of mice. The two men discovered that the cells, which Steinman named dendritic cells, were powerful immune activators, generating a response at least 100 times greater than that produced by other types of cells. Steinman later developed a method whereby large numbers of dendritic cells could be grown in a laboratory, which inspired others to generate novel immunotherapies, such as the prostate cancer agent sipuleucel-T, the first dendritic cell vaccine approved by the U.S. Food and Drug Administration.

Likewise, Beutler's research into the activation of innate immunity also led to the development of valuable new therapies. In the 1980s he isolated a protein called tumour necrosis factor (TNF), which he found contributed to immune system-generated inflammation, a normal process that fights off infection. In some persons, however, the inflammatory response is targeted against the body's own tissues, resulting in autoimmune disease. By inhibiting TNF, Beutler found that the aberrant response could be controlled. One of his inhibitors, etanercept (Enbrel), found widespread use in reducing inflammation associated with autoimmune disease.

Hoffmann's insight into the activation of the innate immune system emerged from his studies of insect immunity. In the mid-1990s, working with *Drosophila* flies, he uncovered a cell-signaling pathway that acted as a microbial sensor by detecting the presence of potential pathogens and stimulating the production of antimicrobial peptides. Hoffmann's suggestion that mechanisms of innate immunity had been evolutionarily conserved among animals led to the search for a similar microbial sensor in mammals, the eventual discovery of which spurred a surge of interest in the mechanisms of innate immunity and encouraged the development of improved antimicrobial drugs.

Ralph M. Steinman was born on Jan. 14, 1943, in Montreal and died Sept. 30, 2011, in New York City. He received a bachelor's degree (1963) from McGill University and a medical degree (1968) from Harvard Medical School. He conducted postdoctoral research at Rockefeller University, where he was later made full professor (1988). In 1998 he became director of the university's Christopher H. Browne Center for Immunology and Immune Diseases.

Bruce A. Beutler was born on Dec. 29, 1957, in Chicago. He received a medical degree (1981) from the University of Chicago and later was an assistant professor (1986) in the department of internal medicine at the University of Texas Southwestern Medical Center at Dallas. In 2000 he joined the department of immunology at Scripps, and in 2007 he became chairman of the genetics department there. He made plans in 2011 to return to the Southwestern Medical Center. He was elected to the National Academy of Sciences in 2008.

Jules A. Hoffmann was born on Aug. 2, 1941, in Echternach, Lux. He earned a Ph.D. (1969) in biology from the University of Strasbourg, France, where he also worked as a research assistant for the French National Centre for Scientific Research (CNRS). He later established and directed (1978–2005) the Immune Response and Development in Insects unit, part of the CNRS Institute of Molecular and Cellular Biology, which he also directed (1993–2005). In 2006 he became senior researcher emeritus, having retired from the CNRS. He remained a professor at the University of Strasbourg. Hoffmann was a foreign associate of the American National Academy of Sciences. (KARA ROGERS)

Bruce A. Beutler

David Gresham/UT Southwestern Medical Center

Jules A. Hoffmann

LUDOVIC—REA/Redux

Ralph M. Steinman

Lubos Stepanek/The Rockefeller University

Biographies

The SUBJECTS of these biographies are the people who in the editors' OPINIONS captured the IMAGINATION of the world in 2011—the most interesting and/or IMPORTANT personalities of the YEAR.

Abramson, Jill

(b. March 19, 1954, New York, N.Y.)

Following the resignation in September 2011 of Bill Keller, executive editor of the *New York Times*, news veteran Jill Abramson was appointed to the post and became the first woman in the history of the 160-year-old newspaper to serve in that capacity. Abramson viewed her rise to the top slot as equivalent to a religious experience, likening the promotion to "ascending to Valhalla." She was widely viewed as tough and uncompromising but revealed a softer side with the release a month later of *The Puppy Diaries: Raising a Dog Named Scout* (2011), a compilation of columns that she had written for the *Times* about her first year of caring for a golden retriever.

Jill Ellen Abramson was the daughter of a textile importer and his wife. She attended Harvard University, graduating (1976) with a bachelor's degree in history and literature. While a student, Abramson freelanced for *Time* magazine, and following her graduation she reported on the 1976 presidential election for that publication. After a stint on Virginia Democrat Henry Howell's unsuccessful gubernatorial campaign, she turned to political ad writing. Abramson then worked briefly for the election unit of NBC News—for which she covered the 1980 presidential election—before becoming (1981) an investigative reporter at the newly created magazine *The American Lawyer*. In 1986 she accepted a position as editor in chief of *Legal Times* magazine, which had just been purchased by *The American Lawyer* owner Steven Brill. Abramson remained there until 1988, when she was hired as a reporter for the Washington bureau of *The Wall Street Journal*. She covered the White House for the *Journal* and later became deputy Washington bureau chief.

In 1997 Abramson moved to the Washington bureau of the *New York Times*, where she served as enterprise editor. She was appointed Washington editor two years later, and in 2000 she became the newspaper's Washington bureau chief. She weathered frequent contretemps with *New York Times* executive editor Howell Raines over her editorial philosophy and successfully evaded his attempt to reassign her to the *Times* Book Review. After Raines's 2003 ouster in the wake of a plagiarism scandal at the *Times*, his replacement, Keller, made Abramson managing editor of the paper, and in September of that year she returned to New York City. In May 2010 Abramson took a six-month sabbatical to oversee the digital operations of the *Times*.

Abramson expanded several of her articles into books. *Where They Are Now: The Story of the Women of Harvard Law, 1974* (1986; co-written with Barbara Franklin) charts the first decade in the careers of 71 women, all Harvard Law alumni. *Strange Justice: The Selling of Clarence Thomas* (1994; co-written with Jane Mayer) covers the controversial confirmation in 1991 of Supreme Court Justice Clarence Thomas, focusing on Republican efforts to downplay allegations of sexual harassment against him. Abramson was elected to the American Academy of Arts and Sciences in 2001.

(RICHARD PALLARDY)

New York Times *executive editor Jill Abramson*

Kena Betancur—Reuters/Landov

Achatz, Grant

(b. April 25, 1974, St. Clair, Mich.)

Early 2011 set the stage for a banner year for Chicago-based chef and restaurateur Grant Achatz, whose culinary innovations made him a leader in the cuisine inspired by molecular gastronomy and earned him a place on *Time* magazine's list of the year's 100 most influential people. In April 2011 Alinea, his flagship restaurant (which in November 2010 was awarded a coveted three stars from the *Michelin Guide*), was named the best restaurant in North America and the sixth best in the world by London-based *Restaurant* magazine. That same month Achatz launched

Next, a unique themed restaurant, and Aviary, a high-concept cocktail bar. He was also publicizing *Life, on the Line: A Chef's Story of Chasing Greatness, Facing Death, and Redefining the Way We Eat* (co-written with his longtime business partner, Nick Kokonas), a memoir that chronicles not only Achatz's rise to fame but also his harrowing battle with tongue cancer.

Achatz grew up in a small town in eastern Michigan, where he worked at his parents' family restaurant. After graduating (1994) from the Culinary Institute of America, Hyde Park, N.Y., and serving a very brief—and unsuccessful—stint at chef Charlie Trotter's eponymous Chicago restaurant, he took a three-month gastronomical trip across western Europe. In 1996 Achatz persuaded California chef Thomas Keller to hire him at the French Laundry, then one of the country's most-acclaimed restaurants. After four years as "Golden Boy" under Keller's mentorship—along with a short spell at a nearby winery and an eye-opening trip to Spain to dine at Ferran Adrià's ground-breaking El Bulli—Achatz in 2001 took charge of the kitchen at Trio restaurant near Chicago. He was named Best New Chef (2002) by *Food and Wine* magazine and Rising Star Chef (2003) by the James Beard Foundation (JBF). In 2005 he and Kokonas (an enthusiastic Trio customer) launched Alinea, where Achatz had free rein for his increasingly inventive style. Within two years *Gourmet* magazine pronounced Alinea the country's best restaurant. In 2008 the JBF named Achatz the best chef in the U.S., and *Restaurant* boosted Alinea from number 36 in 2007 to number 21 in the world.

Meanwhile, Achatz, who for some time had been suffering from misdiagnosed pain in his tongue, was diagnosed in mid-2007 with stage IV nonmetastatic tongue cancer. Although most of the doctors he consulted recommended the removal of about 75% of his tongue, Achatz selected a team of University of Chicago oncologists who were running clinical trials on a protocol that relied on chemotherapy and radiation rather than radical surgery. Throughout the ordeal, Achatz prepared an Alinea cookbook (2008), began his memoir, expanded his culinary innovations, and trained Alinea's chefs to reproduce his palate.

By early 2008, tests had determined that he was cancer-free, and Achatz began to regain his lost sense of taste. In 2010 he announced the plans for Next, a revolutionary prix-fixe restaurant that would sell tickets (rather than taking reservations) for a themed menu that would be replaced four times a year. At Aviary, the cocktail lounge next door, Achatz applied the same aggressive creativity and attention to detail that made him one of the world's top chefs.

(MELINDA C. SHEPHERD)

Ai Weiwei

(b. May 18, 1957, Beijing, China)

Controversial Chinese artist and activist Ai Weiwei, who produced a multifaceted array of creative work, weathered a turbulent year in 2011. In January a studio complex in Shanghai that he had built was razed. While local authorities explained that Ai had failed to obtain a required permit, Ai himself speculated that two documentaries he had made suggesting injustices on the part of Shanghai's government may have provided the underlying motive. Then, from early April to late June, he was detained under an accusation of tax evasion in what was seen as part of a widespread crackdown on dissent. He was later levied with a tax bill of $2.4 million, which he sought to contest with the aid of private donations. On the bright side, the international media coverage of the incidents brought increased attention to Ai's art. In May, while he was still in detention, his public installation *Circle of Animals/Zodiac Heads* (2010), which featured bronze sculptures inspired by the Chinese zodiac, was unveiled in New York City and London.

Ai, whose father was Ai Qing, one of China's most renowned poets, became interested in art as a youth. In 1978 he enrolled at the Beijing Film Academy, though he found more creative and intellectual stimulation as part of a collective of avant-garde artists called Xingxing ("Stars"). Eager to escape the restrictions of Chinese society, Ai moved in 1981 to New York City, where he attended the Parsons School of Design. Although he initially focused on painting, he soon turned to sculpture, inspired by the ready-made works of the French artist Marcel Duchamp and the German sculptor Joseph Beuys. There was little market for Ai's work, however, and in 1993 he returned to Beijing.

Exploring the fraught relationship of an increasingly modernized China to its cultural heritage, Ai began creating works that irrevocably transformed centuries-old Chinese artifacts—for instance, a Han dynasty urn onto which he painted the Coca-Cola logo (1994). He also established a reputation as a promoter of avant-garde Chinese art and in 2000 cocurated an exhibition of deliberately outrageous work as an alternative to that year's Shanghai Biennale. About that time Ai turned toward architecture, and in 2003 he founded the design firm FAKE to realize his projects, which emphasized simplicity through the use of commonplace materials.

In 2005 Ai was invited to write a blog for the Chinese Web portal Sina. Through that forum, Ai publicly disavowed his role in helping to conceive the design of the National Stadium in Beijing, claiming that the 2008 Olympic Games for which the structure had been built amounted to government propaganda. Furthermore, in 2009, nearly a year after a devastating earthquake in Sichuan, Ai lambasted officials for not having released details on the fatalities and mobilized his growing readership to investigate. The blog was soon shut down, and Ai was placed under surveillance, though he refused to curtail his activities. Among the artworks that resulted from Ai's "citizen investigation" was *Remembering* (2009), an installation in Munich in which 9,000 coloured backpacks were arranged on a wall to form a quote from an earthquake victim's mother. His other notable works include a 2010 installation, at the Tate Modern in London, of 100 million hand-painted porcelain *Sunflower Seeds*.

(JOHN M. CUNNINGHAM)

Ando, Miki

(b. Dec. 18, 1987, Aichi, Japan)

At the 2011 International Skating Union (ISU) world figure skating championships, held in Moscow at the end of April, Japanese figure skater Miki Ando captured her second career world title with a dramatic come-from-behind victory over her rival Kim Yu-Na of South Korea. Ando trailed Kim, the reigning Olympic champion, by half a point following the short program, but in the ensuing showdown between the two in the final round, Ando held up better under pressure. While both skaters performed solid and graceful free skates, Ando made fewer technical mistakes. She landed five triple jumps, including two triple lutzes, and stumbled only once, while landing a double toe loop. She clinched the title with an overall score of 195.79 points to Kim's 194.50.

Ando began skating at the age of nine and quickly progressed in the sport, becoming in 2002 the first female skater to land a quadruple jump in competition. (In later years, though she still practiced the jump, she rarely included the quad as part of her competitive program.) She won the world junior championships in 2004 and back-to-back Japanese national titles in 2004–05. Ando competed for Japan at the 2006 Winter Olympics in Turin, Italy, but finished in 15th place after falling twice during her long program.

In the wake of her disappointing performance in Turin, Ando switched coaches, replacing American Carol Heiss Jenkins with Russian coach Nikolay Morozov, who challenged Ando to become a more expressive skater. She had immediate success under Morozov's guidance, taking first place at Skate America in 2006 and claiming her first world title at the 2007 ISU world figure skating championships in Tokyo. Injuries forced Ando to withdraw from the 2008 worlds, but she bounced back at the 2009 worlds to earn third-place honours.

At the 2010 Winter Olympic Games in Vancouver, Ando was in fourth place after the short program but in the end missed out on a medal once again, finishing fifth overall. Later that year, however, she won two Grand Prix events (the Cup of China and the Rostelecom Cup) and garnered her third Japanese national title by outpointing world champion Mao Asada 202.34 to 193.69. Ando added another major title to her collection in early 2011, taking gold at the Four Continents event in February in Taiwan. The world championships originally were scheduled to take place in Tokyo, but following the offshore earthquake and resultant tsunami that wreaked havoc in Japan in March, the competition was relocated to Moscow. After reclaiming her world crown, Ando dedicated her victory to those who had been affected by the disaster.

(SHERMAN HOLLAR)

Figure skating gold medalist Miki Ando

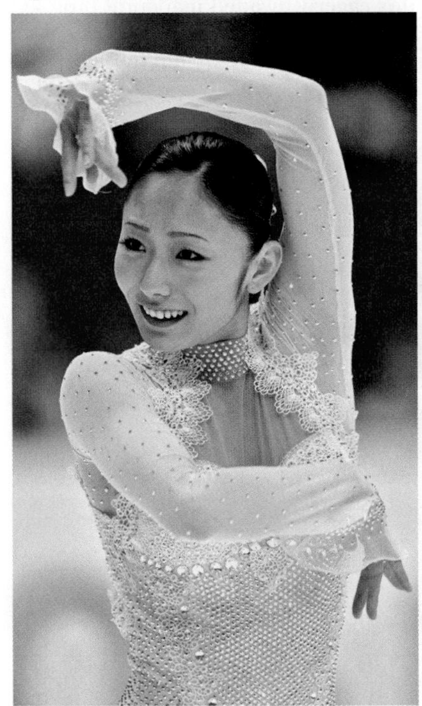

Kyodo/AP

Auel, Jean

(b. Feb. 18, 1936, Chicago, Ill.)

In March 2011 American novelist Jean Auel released *The Land of Painted Caves*, the sixth and last book in her Earth's Children series, which began with the best-selling *The Clan of the Cave Bear* (1980). Like her earlier novels, the much-anticipated finale reflected Auel's attention to detail and meticulous research on prehistoric life. Even before the release of *The Land of Painted Caves*, more than 45 million copies of Auel's novels had been sold worldwide, including translations in more than a dozen languages.

Jean Marie Untinen grew up in Chicago and married right after high-school graduation. She and her husband moved to Oregon, where she had five children and continued her education. She attended Portland State University and in 1976 received a master's degree in business administration from the University of Portland.

In 1977 Auel decided to write a short story about the social interactions of a Cro-Magnon woman with a Neanderthal clan in prehistoric Europe. After conducting extensive research into Ice Age Europe more than 30,000 years ago, however, she decided that her short story should be the first novel in a six-part series. *The Clan of the Cave Bear* introduces the main character, Ayla, a blonde blue-eyed Cro-Magnon child who is orphaned and then adopted into a foreign clan of people. The novel follows Ayla as she tries to assimilate with that Neanderthal clan, some of whom are mistrustful of her because of her fair appearance and upright stance. The book was an instant hit, and in 1986 it was adapted into a movie starring actress Daryl Hannah as a very grown-up Ayla.

In each of her subsequent books, Auel continued to explore the differences between Neanderthal and Cro-Magnon societies through Ayla's physical and emotional journey. *The Valley of Horses* (1982) follows Ayla's life after she is thrown out of her adopted clan as a teenager and attempts to live on her own. *The Mammoth Hunters* (1985) finds Ayla and her Cro-Magnon lover, Jondalar, joining a new clan. In *The Plains of Passage* (1990), Ayla and Jondalar face hardships as they travel to rejoin his tribe. It was 12 years before Auel completed the next book, *The Shelters of Stone*, which tells of Ayla, now formally mated with Jondalar, as she fights to adapt to life in his Cro-Magnon tribe, and another 9 years until the final installment, *The Land of Painted Caves*, completed Auel's story with a new family life for Ayla, Jondalar, and their young daughter.

Throughout her more-than-30-year writing career, Auel was credited with undertaking extensive research for her books and adding accurate details to her stories. She also visited archaeological sites and museums, took courses on primitive survival skills, built and experienced a snow cave, and in 1986 cosponsored a paleontology conference in Santa Fe, N.M. In 2008 she was made an Officer of the Order of Arts and Letters by the French government.

(JOAN HIBLER)

Ballmer, Steve

(b. March 24, 1956, Detroit, Mich.)

In March 2011, Steve Ballmer, CEO since 2000 of mammoth computer software company Microsoft Corp., was ranked number 46 on *Forbes* magazine's list of billionaires in the world and number 17 in the U.S., with an estimated net worth of $14.5 billion. Then in May, Microsoft announced that Ballmer, an energetic, passionate corporate leader, had helped to arrange the $8.5 billion acquisition of the Internet voice communication company Skype. It was the largest acquisition in Microsoft's history and placed the company in competition with Apple's video-chat service FaceTime and Google's Internet communication service Voice.

Steven Anthony Ballmer graduated from Harvard University in 1977 with bachelor's degrees in mathematics and economics. After working for two years at consumer products company Procter & Gamble as a product manager, he attended the Stanford University Graduate School of Business. In 1980 he left school to become a business manager for Bill Gates, a friend from Harvard who had dropped out of school and cofounded Microsoft.

In the early 1980s, after Ballmer joined Microsoft, the company started to produce the MS/DOS operating system (OS) for personal computers, and within a decade it had sold more than

David Cattanach/Alamy

Microsoft CEO Steve Ballmer

100 million copies of that OS. Microsoft then deepened its OS position with Windows, which featured a graphic user interface. By the mid-1990s Microsoft had become one of the most powerful and profitable companies in American history.

Ballmer became president of Microsoft in 1998, and two years later, when Gates stepped down, he became the company's CEO. Under Ballmer's leadership, Microsoft faced challenging hurdles as the company diversified. The company released the Xbox, an electronic game console in 2001. The next year it launched Xbox Live, a broadband gaming network for its consoles, and in 2005 it released the more-powerful Xbox 360. Microsoft, however, struggled to make consistent profits from its game consoles. Likewise, the Zune family of portable media players introduced in 2006 failed to challenge the market dominance of Apple's iPod. The Windows Mobile OS, used in smartphones made by a variety of vendors, trailed behind Research in Motion's BlackBerry and Apple's iPhone. In 2007 Microsoft released its newest OS, Vista, to mixed reviews.

Gates, in order to concentrate more fully on his philanthropic interests, left the day-to-day running of Microsoft to Ballmer and other managers in 2008. After Gates's official departure, the dynamic Ballmer became even more prominent as the public face of Microsoft. In 2009 the company expanded into the search-engine market, releasing Bing. Later that year Microsoft brokered a deal with Internet portal site Yahoo! in which Yahoo! would use Bing for its Web site and handle premium advertisements for Microsoft's Web site. Ballmer also demonstrated enthusiasm for Microsoft's future plans in the realm of cloud computing. (JOAN HIBLER)

Battle, Robert

(b. Aug. 28, 1972, Miami, Fla.)

On July 1, 2011, the up-and-coming young American choreographer Robert Battle officially took the helm of the Alvin Ailey American Dance Theater complex of troupes and schools as only the third artistic director since the company's 1958 founding by Alvin Ailey. In 2010, when Judith Jamison, the company's director since 1989, announced that Battle was to be her successor, she described him as "edgy and forward-thinking, very talented and savvy." He had already put his mark on the company with his announcement in May 2011 of the addition to the company of the first permanent workshop to focus exclusively on choreography. The New Directions Choreography Lab would grant fellowships each year to four emerging or midcareer choreographers and provide support to nurture their talent.

Battle, who was raised by his great-uncle and his cousin, studied dance under Daniel Lewis and Gerri Houlihan at the New World School of the Arts, a respected arts magnet high school in Miami. After graduation he studied at the Juilliard School in New York City, where the former Paul Taylor Dance Company star Carolyn Adams became his mentor. Upon his graduation in 1994, Battle was snapped up by the Parsons Dance Company. In 1998 Parsons began showcasing dances created by Battle, and critics took notice. Battle left Parsons in 2001 to start his own troupe. The Battleworks Dance Company debuted as the American representative at the Global Assembly of the World Dance Alliance in Düsseldorf, Ger., the following year and went on to perform at the American Dance Festival and the Jacob's Pillow Dance Festival, among other venues. Battle became known for his fast-paced, thematically challenging choreography, and among the companies that commissioned works from him or performed his dances were Hubbard Street Dance Chicago, the River North Chicago Dance Company, Koresh Dance Company of Philadelphia, and Ballet Memphis. Battle was honoured in 2005 as a Master of African American Choreography by the Kennedy Center for the Performing Arts and was a 2007 recipient of the prestigious Statue Award of the Princess Grace Foundation-USA.

Battle's association with the Alvin Ailey American Dance Theater began in 1999 when he was commissioned to create a dance for the Ailey II troupe. From that time he contributed 11 dances to the company, notably *Juba* (2003) and *In/Side* (2009). Among the highlights of the 2011–12 season—Battle's eagerly awaited inaugural program as artistic director—were the world premiere of *Home* by hip-hop choreog-

Alvin Ailey artistic director Robert Battle

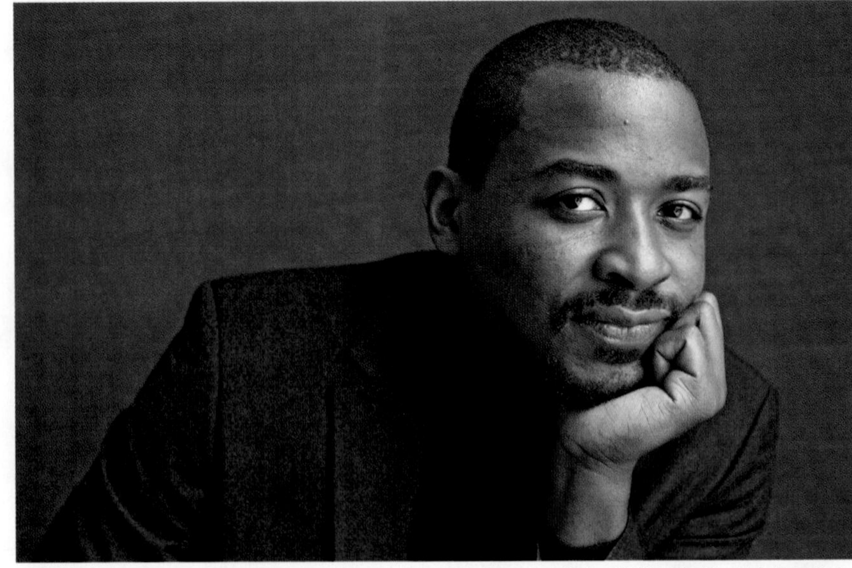

Andrea Mohin—The New York Times/Redux

rapher Rennie Harris, Paul Taylor's *Arden Court* (1981), Ailey's *Streams* (1970), and one of Battle's early works, *Takademe* (1999). (PATRICIA BAUER)

Berger, Lee

(b. Dec. 22, 1965, Shawnee Mission, Kan.) In 2011 American-born South African paleoanthropologist Lee Berger and colleagues announced the results of several follow-up studies related to *Australopithecus sediba*, a primitive hominin species whose fossils Berger had discovered in 2008. Since that species could be the most plausible link between the australopithecenes (genus *Australopithecus*) and humans (genus *Homo*), its discovery could revolutionize the timeline of human evolution.

Lee Rogers Berger received a B.A. in anthropology (1989) from Georgia Southern University and a Ph.D. in paleoanthropology (1994) from the University of the Witwatersrand in Johannesburg, where he studied under noted South African paleoanthropologist Phillip V. Tobias. He became a postdoctoral research fellow in the university's department of anatomy and human biology in 1995 and later served as the director of the university's paleoanthropology research group in the School of Anatomical Sciences. After brief appointments at Duke University (1997), Durham, N.C., and the University of Arkansas (1998), Berger returned to the University of the Witwatersrand in 1999 to serve as the director of the Palaeoanthropology Unit for Research and Exploration at the Bernard Price Institute of Palaeontology. In 2004 he became a reader in human evolution and the public understanding of science at the university's Institute for Human Evolution and the School of Geosciences.

Berger's early research involved examinations of the morphology of *A. africanus*. In 2008, however, during a fossil-hunting expedition to the Malapa Caves in the Cradle of Humankind World Heritage site near Johannesburg, he made his most significant discovery to date. His nine-year-old son, Matthew, recovered a fossilized jawbone and collarbone belonging to a juvenile male hominin, and Berger instantly noticed the mix of primitive and modern characteristics in one of the specimen's canine teeth. Shortly thereafter, Berger found the partial skeleton of an adult female with similar features. Those remains, labeled MH-2, were later recognized as the most complete early hominin skeleton known. The well-preserved bones found at the site included a pelvis, a foot, a complete right hand, and two skulls.

Courtesy of Lee Berger and the University of Witwatersrand/AP

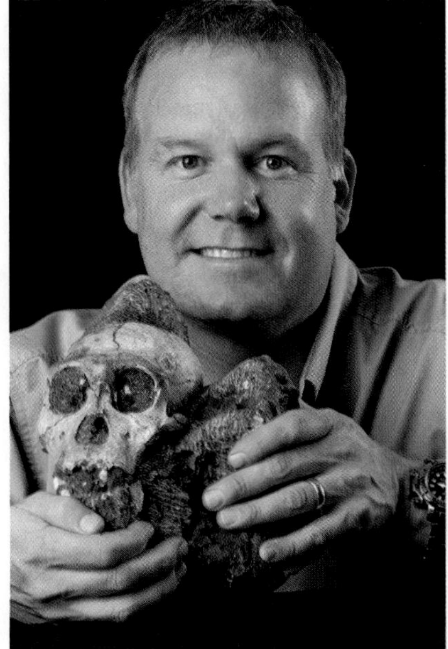

South Africa-based paleoanthropologist Lee Berger

In 2011 the results of several studies by Berger and colleagues revealed that the remains possessed a combination of apelike and humanlike features. The remains displayed more features in common with the earliest members of *Homo* than with any other australopithecine species and became the foundation of a new species called *A. sediba*. Uranium dating later determined that the remains were approximately 1,977,000 years old, which suggested that *A. sediba* could have been an ancestor to *H. erectus*. Furthermore, Berger and colleagues noted that the specimens' age and the collection of features that they shared with *Homo* could allow *A. sediba* to become the recognized transitional species that links *Australopithecus* with *Homo* or confirm it as a contemporary of the true transitional form.

Berger received the first annual National Geographic Society Prize for Research and Exploration in 1997. He became a member of the American Association for the Advancement of Science in 2001. (JOHN P. RAFFERTY)

Bhattarai, Baburam

(b. June 18, 1954, Belbas, Nepal)
In August 2011 Nepali Maoist guerrilla-turned-politician Baburam Bhattarai was elected prime minister of Nepal. A widely respected Marxist scholar, he faced significant challenges in leading a young and fragile republic that had been established only three years earlier and had already seen considerable political turmoil.

Bhattarai was raised in a remote village in the vicinity of Gurkha (Gorkha) in central Nepal. His family was poor, but he was an excellent student and was able to attend college in India on scholarship. He received a bachelor's degree in architecture (1977) from Punjab University in Chandigarh and a master's degree in planning (1979) from the School of Planning and Architecture in New Delhi. He then earned a Ph.D. (1986) in regional development planning from Jawaharlal Nehru University (also in New Delhi); his doctoral thesis was published in 2003 as *The Nature of Underdevelopment and Regional Structure of Nepal: A Marxist Analysis*.

Bhattarai became involved with Nepali antimonarchy politics while he was a student in India, and in 1981 he joined a pro-Maoist faction of the Communist Party of Nepal (CPN). He became politically active in Nepal after returning to the country in 1986 and gained respect for his intellectual achievements. Bhattarai rose to a leadership position in the CPN (Unity Centre) faction that had been established in 1990, and in 1994 he joined with Pushpa Kamal Dahal (Prachanda), who had formed a splinter party, the CPN (Maoist). Bhattarai again attained a high-ranking office in the party and had become its top ideologue by the end of the decade.

In 1996 the CPN (Maoist) launched what became a decadelong insurgency against the monarchy, and the Nepali government responded by outlawing the party. Bhattarai, Prachanda, and other insurgents went underground and operated clandestinely for several years. Peace negotiations between the Maoists and the government began in the early 21st century, with Bhattarai emerging in 2003 as the leading insurgent spokesman. In early 2005, however, Bhattarai and Prachanda disagreed on strategy, and Bhattarai spent several months under virtual house arrest before being reinstated by midyear. Bhattarai was instrumental in the negotiations between the insurgents and the government that led to peace in 2006 and, in 2008, to the end of the Nepali monarchy and the establishment of a republic in the country.

In April 2008 Bhattarai won a seat in the elections for a new national legislature, and the CPN (Maoist) gained the largest share of seats in the chamber (though not a majority). Prachanda became prime minister of a coalition government in August and named Bhattarai as finance minister. The government lasted only nine months, however; Prachanda resigned in May 2009, and Bhattarai left office then as well. Among the tasks that Bhattarai's government faced after he became prime minister in 2011 were finishing the drafting and ratification of a new constitution, determining how to reintegrate into civilian life thousands of former Maoist rebel fighters who were living in supervised camps, and reviving a stagnant economy. (KENNETH PLETCHER)

Boehner, John Andrew
(b. Nov. 17, 1949, Cincinnati, Ohio)
Tears came to the eyes of the often visibly emotional Rep. John A. Boehner on Jan. 5, 2011, when he took the gavel for the first time as the speaker of the U.S. House of Representatives, having ascended to that office after the Republican Party's stunning victory in the 2010 midterm elections. In the ensuing months he played a key role in the debate over the federal budget. As the year unfolded, however, Boehner's authority seemed to slip as he sought to manage unruly factions within his party, notably conservative freshman representatives who had been elected in 2010 as part of the populist Tea Party movement.

Boehner helped avert a government shutdown in April 2011 by negotiating a deal that cut $38 billion from the federal budget. Efforts at a compromise on raising the national debt ceiling by August 2 repeatedly collapsed, and Boehner pulled out of private talks with Democratic Pres. Barack Obama, in part because of right-wing Republican opposition to the deal. Boehner was compelled to include a provision for a balanced-budget amendment, which was popular with Tea Party supporters, but the revised bill was defeated in the Democrat-controlled Senate. Boehner finally negotiated a bipartisan agreement that passed the House on August 1 and was approved by the Senate and signed into law by Obama the following day. Another crisis was temporarily averted at year's end when the House reluctantly approved a Senate-approved two-month extension of a payroll tax break.

Boehner grew up in a large Roman Catholic family (he had 11 brothers and sisters) in southwestern Ohio. He attended an all-male high school in Cincinnati before earning a degree in business (1977) from Xavier University. He then took a job at a plastics company, Nucite Sales, where he eventually became president. In 1984 he was elected to the Ohio legislature, where he remained until his election in 1990 to the U.S. House of Representatives.

In the House, Boehner earned a reputation as a crusader against what he considered wasteful spending in the federal budget. Along with six fellow Republican representatives, he formed the so-called Gang of Seven to fight congressional corruption. He also helped draft (1994) the Republican Party's Contract with America, an ambitious 100-day conservative agenda. Boehner's anticorruption stance was questioned in 1995 after he handed out checks from tobacco-industry lobbyists to fellow Republicans on the House floor and again in 1996 when a tape was made public of a phone call in which he and other Republicans discussed how to salvage the reputation of then speaker Newt Gingrich in light of ethics charges against him.

After Obama was sworn in as president in January 2009, Boehner led the Republican opposition in the House to Obama's health care reform plan (which passed) and other legislation. Boehner's struggles throughout 2011 with a fractious Republican Party left some analysts wondering if he had lost his touch and even if he would remain speaker in the lead-up to and the aftermath of the 2012 congressional elections. (EB ED.)

Bündchen, Gisele
(b. July 20, 1980, Horizontina, Rio Grande do Sul, Braz.) Brazilian supermodel Gisele Bündchen—who graced more magazine covers than any other fashion model in history and was best known as a face of the American lingerie, clothing, and beauty retailer Victoria's Secret—achieved another major milestone in 2011. The already highest-earning model in the world (with $45 million), together with her husband of two years, NFL football quarterback Tom Brady, topped the list of American media and publishing company Forbes as the world's highest-paid celebrity couple, with an income of $76 million combined.

Gisele Caroline Bündchen was raised in the city of Horizontina—a small rural town in southern Brazil—with her five sisters, including her fraternal twin. In 1994, at age 14, Bündchen was spotted in a shopping mall by a modeling agent for Elite Model Management. In 1995 she entered the agency's Look of the Year modeling contest

Silvia Izquierdo/AP

Brazilian top model Gisele Bündchen

(later renamed Elite Model Look) and placed second nationally and fourth globally. The following year Bündchen moved to New York City to launch a professional modeling career and soon thereafter made her runway debut at New York Fashion Week—one of the industry's four major semiannual events. In 1997 Bündchen appeared on the October cover of the Brazilian edition of *Vogue*, gaining industry recognition. Despite a more curvaceous figure that stood in stark contrast to the waifish frames then in style, Bündchen continued to grace the covers of the industry's leading publications. She appeared in 1999 on the July cover of American *Vogue*, which proclaimed the "Return of the Sexy Model," thereby marking the end of the then popular and controversial look known as "heroin chic." That same year she was named Model of the Year, an honour jointly awarded by *Vogue* and the American cable-television network VH1.

In 2000 Bündchen signed a contract to become a face of Victoria's Secret (2000–07) and began dating Hollywood actor Leonardo DiCaprio. She soon became a household name, which many in the industry heralded as the return of the supermodel—a top fashion model who appears simultaneously on the covers of the world's leading fashion magazines and is globally recognized by a first name only.

Bündchen made her film debut in the comedic thriller *Taxi* (2004), and two years later she appeared in *The Devil Wears Prada* (2006). In 2007 she gained entry into the *Guinness World Records* (formerly *The Guinness Book of Records*) as the world's top-earning model. In 2009 she was appointed goodwill ambassador for the UN Environment Programme. That same year Bündchen was featured in the New York Metropolitan Museum of Art exhibition "The Model as Muse: Embodying Fashion." She launched several product lines, including footwear, clothing, jewelry, lingerie, and environmentally friendly skin care. Bündchen also founded the Luz Foundation, dedicated to empowering young women both mentally and physically through its sponsorship of various self-esteem-building programs.

(JEANNETTE L. NOLEN)

Burton, Sarah

(b. 1974, Macclesfield, Cheshire, Eng.)
English fashion designer Sarah Burton, who had been a respected behind-the-scenes worker at the Alexander McQueen fashion house for more than 10 years before becoming the company's creative director in 2010, was suddenly in the international spotlight on April 29, 2011, when she was revealed as the designer of Catherine Middleton's wedding dress for her marriage to Prince William of Wales. The long-sleeved dress was made of ivory and white satin gazar and had a v-shaped neckline, a fitted waist, an almost 2.7-m (9-ft) train, and a Victorian corset-style bodice—a trademark McQueen design. Under Burton's direction, the Royal School of Needlework crafted individual handmade lace flowers in the shapes of English roses, Scottish thistles, Welsh daffodils, and Irish shamrocks on the bodice and skirt of the dress. (The accompanying shoes, also a McQueen house creation, displayed handmade lace.) Burton also designed the sleek ivory cowl-necked maid of honour's dress worn by Middleton's sister, Pippa, as well as a second dress worn by the bride at the evening celebration. Fashion critics, some likening Middleton's formal wedding dress to an updated version of American actress Grace Kelly's when she married Prince Rainier III of Monaco in 1956, had generally positive remarks regarding Burton's designs.

Sarah Jane Heard studied art at Manchester Polytechnic before attending London's Central Saint Martin's College of Art and Design. While still in school, she became an intern (1996) at the fashion studio of McQueen, a British designer known for his groundbreaking clothes, shocking catwalk shows, and precise tailoring. When she graduated in 1997, she joined the company full-time. In 2000 Burton was promoted to head of women's wear, and the company boasted such patrons as actresses Cate Blanchett and Gwyneth Paltrow. Four years later she married David Burton, a fashion photographer responsible for the company's "lookbooks."

After McQueen's suicide in February 2010, Burton ran the company for a short time before accepting the position of creative director. As such, she became the overseer of both the men's and women's lines as well as the accessories collection. She also was tasked with completing the line's spring-summer and fall-winter collections for Paris Fashion Week, which she did to critical acclaim. Although choosing not to present the elaborate shows that McQueen did, Burton was applauded by critics for staying true to the McQueen house's dark, edgy brand while adding her own feminine style to the creations.

(JOAN HIBLER)

Alexander McQueen creative director Sarah Burton

Suzanne Plunkett—Reuters/Landov

Carlsen, Magnus

(b. Nov. 30, 1990, Tønsberg, Nor.)
When the World Chess Federation (FIDE) released its January 2011 list of the world's top-ranked chess players, 20-year-old grandmaster Magnus Carlsen of Norway sat proudly at number one. Carlsen, who had topped FIDE's bimonthly ratings for most of the previous year, had fallen to second place behind the reigning world champion, Viswanathan Anand of India, in the November 2010 list. Despite slipping a notch when he finished third at a tournament at Wijk aan Zee, Neth., in January, Carlsen regained the number one spot after winning the Kings tournament in Medias, Rom., in June.

Sven Magnus Øen Carlsen learned to play chess from his father when he was five years old; he played in his first tournament at the age of eight. In January 2004 he won his first tournament at Wijk aan Zee. Although he played in the lowest-rated group against adult players, the 13-year-old Carlsen's domination of the tournament led American player Lubomir Kavalek to dub him the "Mozart of chess." That March, at a blitz chess tournament (in which the game is played much faster than normal) in Reykjavík, Ice., he defeated former world champion Anatoly Karpov of Russia and drew a game against former world champion Garry Kasparov of Russia. Carlsen officially became a grandmaster the next month after finishing second at the Dubai Open Chess Championship.

In 2007 Carlsen became the youngest player to earn a place at the Candidate Matches, in which the top four players would receive a spot at the FIDE world championship. However, he was defeated in the first round. His victory at the Pearl Spring Chess Tournament in Nanjing, China, in October 2009 with 8 out of a possible 10 points was considered one of the all-time best tournament performances.

After rising steadily through the ranks, Carlsen topped the FIDE ratings as the world's best

Reuters/Landov

Norwegian chess prodigy Magnus Carlsen at a 2008 tournament

player in January 2010; he had recently turned 19 and thus was the youngest number one in history. Later that year the Dutch clothing company G-Star hired him to model a line of denim clothing in an advertising campaign. Carlsen surprised the chess world in November when he decided to forgo the 2011 Candidate Matches (to select a challenger to play against Anand for the FIDE world title), arguing that the reigning champion should not receive an automatic spot in the final round.

From the very beginning of his career, Carlsen used his prodigious memory to play a large variety of openings. He favoured a positional style of play in which maintaining overall control of the board, rather than attacking an opponent's pieces, is of paramount importance. Although he read chess books extensively, Carlsen, unlike most other top players, did not prepare for tournaments with intensive study but instead diverted himself with watching television or playing poker online. When asked about his training, he said, "I am chaotic and tend to be lazy."

(ERIK GREGERSEN)

Catherine, duchess of Cambridge

(b. Jan. 9, 1982, Reading, Berkshire, Eng.) On April 29, 2011, after nearly a decade of courtship, Catherine Middleton wed Prince William of Wales at Westminster Abbey in London. Upon her marriage, she assumed the title duchess of Cambridge. In addition to her new role, she became a fashion trendsetter with a remarkable flair for style.

Catherine Elizabeth Middleton was the eldest of three children of Michael and Carole Middleton; her siblings were Philippa (Pippa) and James. Her parents met while working as flight attendants at British Airways, and in 1987 they founded a mail-order business selling supplies for children's parties. The venture made them millionaires and allowed them to send Catherine to the prestigious Marlborough College in Wiltshire, Eng. At Marlborough, Catherine (then called Kate) was known as a serious, level-headed student, excelling in both athletics—she captained the school field hockey team—and academics.

In 2001 Kate went on to the University of St. Andrews in Scotland, where she met Prince William, a fellow first-year art history student who was second in line (after his father, Charles) to the British throne. The two began dating, though their relationship was not made public until they were photographed together vacationing in Switzerland in 2004. Despite the frequent intrusions of the paparazzi, Kate attempted to maintain a private life. After graduating from St. Andrews in 2005, she briefly worked as an accessories buyer for a clothing retailer, and she later assumed various roles at her parents' company while also performing a host of charity work.

Following several years of intense speculation from the British media about the couple's marriage plans—during which time Kate was dubbed "Waity Katie"—it was announced in November 2010 that the two had become engaged. In preparation for entry into the royal family, Kate reverted to the more-formal name Catherine.

Even prior to her wedding, Catherine had emerged as a fashion trendsetter. The blue dress that she wore for her public engagement announcement sold out at London's Harvey Nichols department store in a matter of hours. She reportedly also had a large role in the design of her wedding dress, which was created by Sarah Burton (*q.v.*). Catherine's image and her wardrobe choices graced hundreds of magazine covers. On her first tour of North America as duchess, Catherine dazzled Canadians with her chic white dress adorned with a maple-leaf pin and her red hat, which sported feathery maple leaves.

(JOHN M. CUNNINGHAM)

Charlene, Princess

(b. Jan. 25, 1978, Bulawayo, Rhodesia [now in Zimbabwe]) As 2011 dawned, former champion swimmer Charlene Wittstock of South Africa was preparing for her marriage in early July to one of the world's most eligible—and notorious—bachelors, Prince Albert II of Monaco. The two-day royal celebration—the first wedding of a reigning European monarch since Albert's father, Prince Rainier III, married the former American actress Grace Kelly in 1956—began on July 1, 2011, with a civil ceremony in the palace throne room. The following day a religious ceremony was held in the main courtyard on Palace Square—rather than Saint Nicholas Cathedral, where Albert's parents were married—in order to accommodate more guests. The service was followed by a procession through the streets to the St. Dévote Church, where the new Princess Charlene of Monaco placed her bouquet in accordance with tradition.

She was born Charlene Lynette Wittstock in what was then Rhodesia, but when she was 12, her parents, a sales manager and a swimming instructor, moved her and her two brothers to South Africa. There she began swimming competitively under her mother's guidance, and in 1996 she won the national championship. Wittstock represented South Africa at the 2000 Sydney Olympic Games, where she swam one leg of the women's 4 × 100-m medley relay team that finished fifth. Two years later she captured three World Cup gold medals and earned a silver medal in the women's 4 × 100-m medley relay at the Commonwealth Games. Out of the water, she worked as a teacher.

The statuesque (1.78-m [5-ft 10-in]) blonde met Prince Albert in 2000 when she went to Monaco to compete in an international swimming event, where she won gold in the 200-m backstroke. The couple were first spotted in public together at the 2006 Olympic Winter Games in Turin, Italy, and a few months later she accompanied him to a charity ball in Monaco. Although she qualified to swim for the South African team at the 2008 Beijing Games, she decided to retire from competition in 2007.

That same year she officially moved from South Africa to an apartment in Monaco. Rumours about the royal romance quickly spread as she began to learn French and Monegasque and to participate in local charitable events. Albert, a man 20 years her senior with at least two illegitimate children, had long enjoyed a reputation as an international playboy. Many believed that he would never marry, and in 2002 Monaco's parliament changed the constitution to allow the offspring of his elder sister, Princess Caroline, to succeed him if he died without a legitimate heir. The elegant South African's appearance on the scene raised hopes that Albert might marry after all, and in June 2010 Charlene and Albert put an end to the speculation and announced their engagement. (MELINDA C. SHEPHERD)

Connick, Harry, Jr.

(b. Sept. 11, 1967, New Orleans, La.)

In 2011 American singer, songwriter, musician, and actor Harry Connick, Jr., enjoyed renewed recognition for two of his greatest loves. Connick—who was known for his explorations into jazz, funk, big-band, and romantic ballads—in May helped the U.S. Library of Congress launch the National Jukebox Web site (www.loc.gov/jukebox), featuring a huge collection of pre-1925 recordings. Meanwhile, Connick was involved in the rebuilding of post-Hurricane Katrina New Orleans, where he was the cofounder (1993) of the first multiracial Mardi Gras krewe and the cosponsor, with Branford Marsalis, of the Musicians' Village for displaced New Orleans musicians and its Ellis Marsalis Center for Music.

Joseph Harry Fowler Connick, Jr., grew up in New Orleans, where his father, a longtime district attorney (1973–2003), and his mother, a judge. also owned a record store. Connick began performing when he was five years old. He subsequently studied with Ellis Marsalis and James Booker at the New Orleans Center for Creative Arts. After high school he moved to New York City to attend Hunter College and the Manhattan School of Music. He signed a contract with Columbia Records and in 1987 released his first album, *Harry Connick, Jr.*, on which he played the piano. On his second effort, *20* (1988), he also sang.

In 1989 Connick co-produced the sound track for Rob Reiner's film *When Harry Met Sally . . .*, which included performances by his jazz trio and his own rendering of such classic songs as "But Not for Me" and "I Could Write a Book." The album went multiplatinum and earned Connick his first Grammy Award for best jazz vocal performance. In 1990 he tackled his first acting role, in the movie *Memphis Belle*, and released two albums, *We Are in Love*, a big-band sound with vocals, and *Lofty's Roach Soufflé*, showcasing instrumental jazz. Connick won a second Grammy Award for best jazz vocal performance for *We Are in Love*.

Connick's later albums include *Blue Light, Red Light* (1991), *25* (1992), *She* (1994), the big-band album *Come by Me* (1999), the Grammy Award-winning pop album *Songs I Heard* (2001), *30* (2001), *Only You* (2004), *Your Songs* (2009), and *In Concert on Broadway* (2011). In 2007 he released two tributes to his hometown, *Oh, My Nola* and *Chanson du Vieux Carré*.

Simultaneously, Connick pursued an acting career, portraying a lonely little boy's grown-up friend in *Little Man Tate* (1991), a serial killer in *Copycat* (1995), a hotshot fighter pilot in *Independence Day* (1996), the doomed Lieutenant Cable in a TV version of the musical *South Pacific* (2001), and a doctor in *Dolphin Tale* (2011). He scored as a leading man in the romantic comedies *Hope Floats* (1998) and *New in Town* (2009) and in a recurring role on the TV sitcom *Will & Grace* (2002–06). Connick received Tony Award nominations for his score for the musical *Thou Shalt Not* (2001) and for his Broadway acting debut in *The Pajama Game* (2006). He was due back on Broadway in late 2011 in a reimagining of the musical *On a Clear Day You Can See Forever*.

(JOAN HIBLER)

Dhoni, Mahendra Singh

(b. July 7, 1981, Ranchi, India)

In early 2011 Mahendra Singh Dhoni was confirmed as one of the most successful captains in international cricket as he guided India to victory in the 2011 one-day World Cup. He had already led India to the inaugural Twenty20 world cup title in 2007 and to the top of the International Cricket Council (ICC) Test match rankings in 2009, and the team went into the World Cup as a solid favourite. Dhoni's dashing innings of 91 not out—in front of a home crowd in Mumbai—rescued India from potential defeat in the final of the World Cup against Sri Lanka in April and ensured Dhoni a permanent place in Indian folklore.

Although Dhoni built his reputation on his flamboyant batting in the shorter forms of the game, he also excelled at exploiting the commercial opportunities opened up by the Indian Premier League (IPL) and the fusion of Bollywood and sport. His $1.5 million contract with the Chennai Super Kings was the highest in the IPL, though he repaid the investment by leading the franchise to two successive titles (2010, 2011). He

Rajanish Kakade/AP

Indian cricketer Mahendra Singh Dhoni

also had numerous commercial endorsements, and according to a 2011 estimate by *Forbes* magazine, his total earnings of $15 million a year made him the highest-paid cricketer in history.

Dhoni, who began as a country boy from Bihar state, made his international debut in 2004. His talent with the bat came to the fore in an innings of 148 against Pakistan in only his fifth international match. Within a year he had been fast-tracked onto the India Test team, where he quickly established himself with a century against Pakistan. Despite his inexperience, Dhoni took over the captaincy of the one-day side in 2007 and led India to the Twenty20 world title, a victory that triggered the explosion of T20 cricket on the subcontinent and paved the way for the riches of the IPL. The move to make him Test captain became irresistible, and series wins over Australia and Sri Lanka, among others, moved India to the top of the Test rankings for the first time in December 2009, further enhancing Dhoni's growing popularity.

The bare facts of Dhoni's career did not seem to place him among the greats of the international game. He was no more than a competent wicketkeeper, and his batting average—48.31 for one-day internationals and 38.14 for Tests—was hardly eye-catching. His technical deficiencies were ruthlessly exposed by the England bowlers in the summer of 2011 when a hectic schedule of nonstop international cricket—and the responsibilities of captaincy, wicketkeeping, and batting—seemed to catch up with him. India lost all four Tests in England and slipped to third in the ICC rankings. Dhoni, however, was widely praised for his sportsmanship in recalling England batsman Ian Bell after a controversial run-out decision in the second Test in Nottingham. (ANDREW LONGMORE)

Djokovic, Novak
(b. May 22, 1987, Belgrade, Yugos. [now in Serbia]) The year 2011 was a banner one for Serbian tennis player Novak Djokovic, who enjoyed a meteoric rise to the number one world ranking. In January he easily defeated Britain's Andy Murray for the Australian Open title. He triumphed in six more tournaments before falling to Roger Federer of Switzerland in the semifinals of the year's second Grand Slam tournament, the French Open. Djokovic recovered from that loss, however, and followed it with victories over Rafael Nadal of Spain in both the All-England (Wimbledon) and the U.S. Open finals. At season's end Djokovic sat atop the Association of Tennis Professionals (ATP) world rankings, with 10 titles for the year, including the 3 Grand Slams.

Djokovic took up tennis at age four and quickly ascended the junior ranks. Despite the hardships that came with growing up in the war-torn Serbia of the 1990s, he became Europe's top-ranked 14-and-under player and later the number one 16-and-under player on the Continent before turning professional in 2003. Djokovic entered the top 100 of the ATP at age 18, and in July 2006 he won his first ATP event. After having advanced to the semifinals at both the French Open and Wimbledon in 2007, he reached the finals of that year's U.S. Open but lost in straight sets to Federer. Djokovic's hot play continued into 2008 as he won the Australian Open for his first Grand Slam title, thus becoming the first Serbian man to win one of tennis's four most-prestigious singles championships.

Djokovic's progress plateaued for almost three years; between February 2008 and late 2010, he won just 10 ATP men's singles tournaments and reached only one Grand Slam final, the 2010 U.S. Open, where he lost to Nadal in four sets. Djokovic's fortunes turned in December 2010 when he led the Serbian Davis Cup team to the country's first Davis Cup title. His two singles victories in the Davis Cup final against France marked the beginning of a 43-match winning steak—the third longest such streak in the Open era (since 1968). Djokovic's remarkable run ended in 2011 with his French Open semifinal loss to Federer, but his strong play helped him rise to the number one world ranking shortly after he defeated Nadal at Wimbledon. Djokovic's dream season ended on a sour note, however, as persistent injuries to his shoulder and back forced him to withdraw from several late-season tournaments—including the Davis Cup—and he lost three matches in November, which equaled his loss total for the rest of the year. (ADAM AUGUSTYN)

Draghi, Mario
(b. Sept. 3, 1947, Rome, Italy)
On Nov. 1, 2011, American-educated Italian economist Mario Draghi assumed office as president of the European Central Bank (ECB), the financial institution responsible for making monetary decisions within the euro zone. Although he had long been a leading contender to replace Jean-Claude Tichet as president, Draghi's candidacy had been complicated by Italy's role in the European sovereign debt crisis, which by mid-2011 was challenging the stability of the euro and was resurrecting old doubts about the wisdom and staying power of Italy's economic managers—particularly in Germany, where the ECB was headquartered. In the end, his long-standing reputation as a financial reformer and strict conservative on monetary policy reassured the Germans, and the presidency of the world's second most important central bank (after the U.S. Federal Reserve System) went to Draghi.

European Central Bank president Mario Draghi

Ralph Orlowski—Reuters/Landov

Draghi was raised in Rome, where he received a Jesuit secondary education and graduated from the University of Rome. He then studied economics in the U.S. at MIT under Franco Modigliani, who later won the Nobel Prize for Economics, and Stanley Fischer, future head of the central bank of Israel. Draghi received a Ph.D. from MIT in 1976. During the 1980s he taught economics at the University of Florence and worked for the World Bank in Washington, D.C.

As director general (1991–2001) of the Italian treasury, he played a central role in reducing Italy's public debt and annual budget deficits and in stabilizing interest rates and currency exchange rates. Those actions succeeded in allowing Italy to qualify for participation in the European monetary union of 1999. They also earned him the nickname "Super Mario," after the indomitable hero of the Nintendo video game. From 2002 to 2005 he was a vice-chairman and managing director at London-based Goldman Sachs International, a subsidiary of the American investment bank. In 2006 he took over the governorship of the Bank of Italy, and for the next five years, he worked at introducing responsible management and strict monetary policy in that institution as well.

As governor of Italy's central bank, Draghi was a member of the ECB's governing council, which sets interest rates in the euro zone. He also became chairman of the Financial Stability Forum, an advisory body for the Group of 20 economically advanced countries. Following the worldwide financial crisis of 2008, that forum became the Financial Stability Board, and it acquired a mandate to devise regulatory standards that would prevent another near collapse of the banking system. Draghi's appointment to the ECB therefore came at a critical time. Though he had gained a reputation for caution, Draghi in the first weeks after his appointment oversaw an interest-rate cut and called for governments to refashion the euro zone. He also hinted that he might use bank funds to combat the euro-zone debt crisis.
(ROBERT CURLEY)

Egan, Jennifer
(b. Sept. 6, 1962, Chicago, Ill.)
American novelist and short-story writer Jennifer Egan followed a meticulous work process

that had her writing and rewriting portions of her books—by hand—at least 50 times, but these time-consuming steps paid off in 2011 when she won the Pulitzer Prize for Fiction for *A Visit from the Goon Squad*. The novel, which follows the life of a record producer as well as a number of others characters, covers several decades, is told from different points of view, and does not follow a linear or chronological order. One chapter is told by using images derived from Microsoft's PowerPoint computer software in place of text. Egan's latest novel ultimately reveals time's comical and relentless changes at work on children and adults of several generations. Just days after the Pulitzer Prize was announced, it was revealed that the cable channel HBO had acquired the rights to turn *A Visit from the Goon Squad* into a television series.

Egan was born in Chicago but grew up in San Francisco. She attended the University of Pennsylvania and then went to England to study at St. John's College, Cambridge. During this period she also visited different locales in Europe. Her excursions were reflected in her first novel, *The Invisible Circus* (1995), which tells the story of a girl who travels through Europe, tracing the footsteps of her dead sister. (A movie based on the book was filmed in 1999 but was not released to general audiences until 2001.) Her short-story collection *Emerald City* (1996) was also inspired by her European travels.

In her second novel, *Look at Me* (2001)—a story about a model whose face needs to be rebuilt after she is injured in an automobile accident—Egan explored the themes of identity and reality in a world driven by consumerism. The book was a National Book Award finalist in the year of its release. She took a new direction with *The Keep* (2006), the story of an inmate in a prison writing workshop who is revealing the tale of two cousins reunited after years apart to renovate a castle in Europe. In this complex gothic mystery, Egan investigated how confinement (physical or psychological), imagination, and the past affect people in different ways.

Egan contributed short stories to such periodicals as *Harper's Magazine* and *The New Yorker*. Many of her nonfiction articles, including an exposé on homeless children, an investigation into bipolar disorder in children, and information about online dating among homosexual teenagers, appeared as cover stories in the *New York Times Magazine*.

(JOAN HIBLER)

Press Association/AP

Multifaceted British artist Tracey Emin

Emin, Tracey

(b. July 3, 1963, London, Eng.) In-your-face British artist and erstwhile bad girl Tracey Emin was much in the news in 2011 when her major midlife retrospective "Love Is What You Want" opened at the Hayward Gallery in London. She also made headlines for donating a neon installation, *More Passion*, to the government art collection by invitation of Prime Minister David Cameron. It was hung at 10 Downing Street, where—according to one report—the installation gave the hallway to the Terracotta Room the appearance of a nightclub.

Emin made her own life (with all its disappointments and messiness) the subject of her art. Her works were confessional, provocative, and transgressive, often portraying sexual acts and reproductive organs. Critics were seldom lukewarm in their response to her. Like Damien Hirst and Sarah Lucas, she was considered one of the YBAs (Young British Artists; also known as the BritArtists) who came to prominence in the 1990s.

Emin and her twin brother, Paul, were born to an unwed mother. Their father, who was married to someone other than their mother, was a Turkish Cypriot. Emin grew up in the seaside resort town of Margate. She dropped out of school at age 13 and moved to London at 15. Two years later she attended Medway College of Design (later part of the University for the Creative Arts), Rochester, where she studied fashion. She was accepted without a secondary-school certificate at nearby Maidstone College of Art (later part of the UCA) and earned a fine-arts degree in 1986. Thereafter she obtained a master's degree in painting (1989) from the Royal College of Art in London.

One of Emin's earliest exhibitions in London took place in 1993–94 at the influential White Cube gallery on Duke Street. That show, ironically titled "My Major Retrospective," gave a hint of things to come. It displayed personally significant artifacts from Emin's life. For a mostly YBA group show called "Minky Manky" (1995) at South London Gallery, she produced *Everyone I Have Ever Slept With 1963–1995* (1995; later destroyed), a tent embroidered with the names of everyone she had (literally) slept with, including her twin brother, her mother, and her two aborted fetuses, as well as assorted lovers.

In 1999 she became a finalist for the Turner Prize with the installation *My Bed* (1998), which displayed not only the artist's actual bed but also rumpled bedclothes and what one critic called "uncomfortably personal debris," including soiled underwear, empty liquor bottles, and used condoms. While critics continued to debate the merits of her self-focused and often indecorous works, Emin continued to bask in the growing recognition of her abilities, as represented by her appointment to the Royal Academy in 2007 and her representation of Britain in the Venice Biennale that same year. (KATHLEEN KUIPER)

Firth, Colin

(b. Sept. 10, 1960, Grayshott, Hampshire, Eng.) British actor Colin Firth won an Academy Award for best actor in 2011 for his poignant performance in *The King's Speech* (2010) as the future King George VI, who enlists the aid of an eccentric speech therapist to overcome a debilitating stutter. The role was a vast departure for Firth, known especially for his portrayals of aloof and articulate characters who gradually shed their reserve to become emotionally available.

Colin Andrew Firth's parents were teachers, and the family moved frequently, living in Nigeria, the U.K., and the U.S. He acted in school plays, and in 1980 he was accepted to the Drama Centre London (now part of the University of Arts London and Central Saint Martins College of Art and Design). Three years later he made his West End debut, portraying a character based on the British spy Guy Burgess in the play *Another Country*. In 1984 Firth starred in the film adaptation, though he was cast in a different role. Over the next decade Firth worked steadily, appearing in numerous stage, movie, and television productions. In 1988 he received critical praise for the TV film *Tumbledown*, in which he portrayed a Scottish soldier who is injured during the Falkland Islands War and endures a difficult recovery. The role earned Firth his first British Academy of Film and Television Arts (BAFTA) Award nomination. Notable feature films from this period include *Apartment Zero* (1988), *Valmont* (1989), and *Circle of Friends* (1995).

Firth did not receive his major breakthrough until he appeared as Fitzwilliam Darcy in the television miniseries *Pride and Prejudice* (1995), which was adapted from Jane Austen's novel. His portrayal of a repressed aristocrat whose haughtiness hides his growing affection for Elizabeth Bennet earned Firth a devoted following. A series of acclaimed films followed, including *The English Patient* (1996) and *Shakespeare in Love* (1998). In 2001 Firth garnered further attention as Mark Darcy in the romantic comedy *Bridget Jones's Diary*, an adaptation of Helen Fielding's novel. (That character, an uptight lawyer who falls in love with the title character, was based on Austen's Mr. Darcy.) Firth reprised the role in *Bridget Jones: The Edge of Reason* (2004). He continued to display his versatility in such films as *The Importance of Being Earnest* (2002); *Girl with a Pearl Earring* (2003), in which he starred as the 17th-century Dutch painter Johannes Vermeer; the family film *Nanny McPhee* (2005); and the box-office hit *Mamma Mia!* (2008), a musical based on the songs of ABBA. In the 2009 drama *A Single Man*, he portrayed a gay professor who, following the death of his lover, displays a stoic front while contemplating suicide. The role earned Firth his first Oscar nod and his first BAFTA Award; he also won a BAFTA for *The King's Speech*. In 2011 he costarred in *Tinker Tailor Soldier Spy*. (AMY TIKKANEN)

Foster, Sutton

(b. March 18, 1975, Statesboro, Ga.)
After having made her name starring in new Broadway musicals, American actress and singer Sutton Foster took on a revival in 2011. As nightclub chanteuse Reno Sweeney in Cole Porter's *Anything Goes*, she wowed audiences with her high-spirited charisma and brightly expressive voice, and she earned a bevy of honours, including her second Tony Award for best actress in a musical. Foster further displayed her easy appeal on the recording *An Evening with Sutton Foster: Live at the Café Carlyle*, released in March, which documented her one-woman cabaret act.

Sutton Lenore Foster grew up in Georgia, where she began taking dance lessons at age four. Six years later she landed the starring role in a community-theatre production of the musical *Annie*. In 1992, after having moved with her family to suburban Detroit, she was cast in the ensemble of a national touring production of *The Will Rogers Follies*. Foster then studied (1993–94) theatre at Carnegie Mellon University in Pittsburgh before resuming her stage career in a national tour of *Grease*; she later joined the show's Broadway cast as a replacement. Small roles on Broadway in *Annie*, *The Scarlet Pimpernel*, and *Les Misérables* followed. Between those productions, Foster performed a lead part in *What the World Needs Now: A Musical Fable*, a showcase for the songs of Burt Bacharach and Hal David, during its world-premiere run in San Diego in 1998.

Broadway musical star Sutton Foster

Jennifer Graylock/AP

Foster's breakthrough came in 2000 when she was cast in *Thoroughly Modern Millie*, a new musical based on the 1967 film about an independent-minded woman in the 1920s. Mere weeks before the show officially opened in La Jolla, Calif., Foster was promoted from understudy to lead, and she continued in the role when the production relocated to Broadway in early 2002. Although the show earned mixed reviews, Foster's ability to evince Millie's gawky charm was often singled out for praise, and her performance was rewarded with a Tony Award.

Having demonstrated a talent for musical comedy and a particular flair for ingenue characters, Foster remained on Broadway, originating the roles of Jo in *Little Women* (2005) and the showgirl Janet Van De Graaff in *The Drowsy Chaperone* (2006), a spoof of early Broadway musicals. Both performances earned her Tony nominations. Foster then appeared in two new musicals that were based on films, portraying the ditzy lab assistant Inga in *Young Frankenstein* (2007) and the feisty Princess Fiona in *Shrek the Musical* (2008). For the latter role, she received her fourth Tony nomination. Later, in an Off-Broadway detour, Foster played a dominatrix in the dark comedy *Trust* (2010).

Foster's admirers often commended her pliant singing voice, which conveyed subtle emotions as effortlessly as it belted out showstoppers. In 2009 she released the album *Wish*, an intimate collection of show tunes and pop songs. In addition, Foster sporadically acted on television. (JOHN M. CUNNINGHAM)

Green, Cee Lo

(b. May 30, 1974, Atlanta, Ga.)
After nearly two decades as a recording artist, American musician Cee Lo Green, known for his soulful voice and flamboyant persona, exploded into the public consciousness in 2011. Much of his sudden fame was due to "Fuck You!"—an infectious up-tempo track rooted in 1960s soul on which he assumed the role of a heartbroken lover, gleefully casting spite upon his ex-girlfriend's well-to-do new mate. The single (sanitized for radio and other contexts as "Forget You") zoomed up the charts

Charles Sykes/AP

Pop musician Cee Lo Green

early in the year and, having earned four nominations, won a Grammy Award for best urban/alternative performance. Cee Lo later ventured into television, becoming a coach on the singing competition *The Voice* and the host of the show *Talking to Strangers*, on which he interviewed other musicians.

He was born Thomas Burton and grew up in Atlanta as the son of two ordained Baptist ministers, both of whom died when he was young. As an adolescent he engaged in gang activity and committed petty theft, but after dropping out of school in the ninth grade, he earned a GED from a military academy. At the same time, he displayed an affinity for music, singing in his church and playing the piano at home.

In 1991 (by then having assumed his mother's maiden name, Callaway) he formed the hip-hop act Goodie Mob along with three friends. Four years later they released the album *Soul Food* (1995). With its optimistic attitude and its incorporation of live instrumentation infused with the sounds of classic soul and funk music, the record became a touchstone for an emerging subgenre of hip-hop based in the South. While rapping and singing under the pseudonym Cee Lo (or Cee-Lo), he earned particular praise for his spirited high-pitched delivery. Goodie Mob later recorded *Still Standing* (1998) and *World Party* (1999), though the latter was considered an artistic and commercial disappointment, and Cee Lo subsequently left the group.

Appending a surname to his moniker, Cee Lo embarked on a solo career with the stylistically varied rhythm-and-blues (R&B) record *Cee-Lo Green and His Perfect Imperfections* (2002). The album further showed off Cee Lo's rich tenor, garnering him comparisons to soul singer Al Green. *Cee-Lo Green . . . Is the Soul Machine* (2004) boasted a similarly wide-ranging sound.

For his next project, Cee Lo teamed up with the hip-hop producer Danger Mouse (byname of Brian Burton). As Gnarls Barkley, the pair released *St. Elsewhere* (2006), an offbeat R&B album on which Cee Lo mused upon such dark themes as paranoia and suicide over slick sample-based arrangements. Its first single, "Crazy," a buoyant pop-soul confection, became a surprise worldwide hit. After having won two Grammys, Gnarls Barkley returned with *The Odd Couple* (2008). In 2010 Cee Lo released the lushly orchestrated solo album *The Lady Killer*, for which "Fuck You!" served as the centrepiece. (JOHN M. CUNNINGHAM)

Hastings, Reed

(b. Oct. 8, 1960, Boston, Mass.)

In April 2011 American entrepreneur Reed Hastings, chairman and CEO of media rental service Netflix, appeared on *Time* magazine's list of the 100 most influential people in the world. It was Hastings's second appearance on *Time*'s annual list, and since the first instance, in 2005, the company that he cofounded in 1997 had grown from a mail-order DVD service with some 40,000 movie titles to the world's largest subscription-based movie and television rental enterprise, with more than 23 million members in the U.S. and, beginning in 2010, Canada.

Wilmot Reed Hastings, Jr., studied mathematics at Bowdoin College in Brunswick, Maine, earning the school's Smyth Prize in 1981 and graduating with a bachelor's degree in 1983. After an unsatisfactory stint in the U.S. Marine Corps, he spent two years with the Peace Corps, most of the time teaching math in Swaziland. He returned to the U.S. and went to Stanford University, where he received (1988) a master's degree in computer science. Subsequently, Hastings became a software developer, and in 1991 he founded Pure Software (later Pure Atria Corp.), which he sold in 1997 for a substantial profit.

That same year Hastings conceived the idea of a subscription-based movie-rental service after he incurred a large late fee when he failed to return a store-rented videocassette. DVDs were new to the market, but Hastings felt that they would travel well through the mail. He and business partner Marc Randolph (who left the company in 2004) incorporated Netflix in California in 1997 and started mail-order DVD operations in 1998. Hastings became the company's CEO in September of that year. At first customers were allowed to rent each DVD for a seven-day period, but by December 1999, subscribers could pay a set monthly fee to rent an unlimited number of DVDs. Although they made their choices and controlled their accounts via the Netflix Web site, DVDs (up to three at a time) were sent and returned by mail. Once a DVD was returned, the next movie on the customer's account list was automatically mailed.

Hastings expanded Netflix through movie studio partnerships and aggressive marketing campaigns, many of which emphasized Netflix's catalog of indie films, documentaries, and other movies not easily available through other services. In February 2007 Netflix reached a milestone when it shipped its billionth DVD. Meanwhile, the company launched special applications that permitted customers to access movies and TV shows through streaming downloads on their personal computers, video game consoles, or smartphones and other handheld devices. *Forbes* magazine named Hastings its Businessperson of the Year in 2010, and the next year *Fortune* magazine included Netflix on its list of most-admired companies.

Paul Sakuma/AP

Netflix cofounder and CEO Reed Hastings

Hastings made a rare misstep in 2011 when Netflix announced that it would increase rental prices and split the company in two, with the DVD service rebranded as Qwikster. He downplayed the resulting loss of customers and plunging stock price, but the company backtracked and canceled the Qwikster spin-off plan. (JOAN HIBLER)

Hazare, Anna
(b. June 15, 1938?, Bhingar, near Ahmadnagar, India) Indian social activist Anna Hazare spent much of 2011 pressing the government to promote rural development, increase transparency, and investigate and punish official corruption. It was the latest stage in his decadeslong career of activism. In addition to encouraging grassroots movements, Hazare frequently conducted hunger strikes to further his causes—a tactic reminiscent, to many, of the work of Mohandas K. Gandhi.

Kisan Baburao Hazare was born to a farming family. He joined the army in 1963, becoming a driver. During the India-Pakistan war, he narrowly survived an attack in 1965 by Pakistani forces. Several years prior to that incident, Hazare had discovered the writings of the Hindu leader Vivekananda, under whose spiritual philosophy he began contemplating the meaning of life. He remained in the army until 1978, when he became eligible for retirement with a pension that would enable him to pursue his activism.

After military service Hazare began a rural-development project in his hometown of Ralegan Siddhi, Maharashtra, which suffered from poverty, drought, unemployment, and crime. Working with the villagers, he started a water-conservation program that included land forestation and the building of weirs, which greatly improved the water supply. The initiative continued with agricultural reforms; eventually, full employment was restored. The transformation in Ralegan Siddhi came to the notice of state officials, who used the program as a model for similar efforts in villages across Maharashtra.

In 1991 Hazare established the People's Movement Against Corruption, which found evidence that a large number of forestry officials had been bilking the state government. To protest the government's reluctance to punish those involved, Hazare began a hunger strike that, together with other forms of activism, spurred the government eventually to remove hundreds of corrupt functionaries from their positions.

Hazare began campaigning in Maharashtra in 1997 for a "right to information" law. Such a law would provide citizens with the ability to petition public authorities for information about the workings of their government and would establish the government's legal responsibility to respond in a timely manner. Hazare and others made efforts for years to raise public awareness on the issue but without tangible results. Thus, in July 2003 he again began a public "fast unto death" to increase the pressure on authorities. Twelve days later the draft legislation was enacted. The Maharashtra law served as the model for the national Right to Information Act in 2005.

Though the government in 2010 drafted a version of a national law that would establish a Jan Lokpal—a national citizen's ombudsman to investigate corruption—Hazare and his associates believed that the legislation did not give the ombudsman power to investigate corruption at all levels. In April 2011 he began to stage a number of other hunger strikes. On August 28 he ended a 13-day fast after the parliament passed a resolution agreeing in principle to several key demands. The legislation was passed by the lower house of the parliament in late December, but Hazare initiated another brief hunger strike because he felt that the law did not go far enough.

(LORRAINE MURRAY)

Houellebecq, Michel
(b. Feb. 26, 1956/58, Réunion, France) In 2011 French writer, satirist, and provocateur Michel Houellebecq made his second foray as a *chansoniste*, releasing two new songs, "Le Film du dimanche" and "Novembre." With music by Jean-Claude Vannier and words and vocals by Houellebecq himself, the songs delighted his fans.

He was born Michel Thomas. His parents sent him to live with his maternal grandparents when he was an infant. At age five or six he was transferred to the care of his paternal grandmother, whose maiden name he later adopted. His body of work gives evidence that the abandonment by and continued absence of his parents, who divorced when he was young, deeply scarred him. Though he studied the sciences, in which he excelled, Houellebecq was drawn to the company of writers in Paris and began to write poetry. In 1980 he took a degree in agronomy, a field in which he rapidly lost interest.

After some of his poetry was accepted for publication in *Nouvelle Revue de Paris*, Houellebecq was encouraged by his editor there to write prose, and he produced *H.P. Lovecraft: contre le monde, contre la vie* (1991; *H.P. Lovecraft: Against the World, Against Life*), a biography and an appreciation of that American master of the macabre. The same year, he published a collection of short prose meditations, *Rester vivant: méthode* (*To Stay Alive: A Method*), and his first book of poetry, *La Poursuite du bonheur* (*The Pursuit of Happiness*). In order to support himself in his nascent writing career, he worked as a computer programmer, a job that inspired his first novel; *Extension du domaine de la lutte* (1994; *Whatever*; filmed 1999) featured an unnamed computer technician.

He gained his first real international attention only four years later with the publication of *Les Particules élémentaires* (1998; filmed 2006), published as *Atomised* in the U.K. and as *The Elementary Particles* in the U.S. Though the book's combination of reactionary political views and pornographic passages, as well as its misogynistic plot and scathing indictment of the 1960s "free love" generation, made it the source of much controversy, it won the 2002 IMPAC Dublin Literary Award.

Houellebecq's dark perspective brought him many fans, but the author remained a figure of controversy for expressing publicly in interviews as well as in his works what some readers considered racist, sexist, and deeply cynical views. His later works include *Plateforme* (2001; *Platform*), a consideration of sex tourism in which he drew a spiteful and savage portrait of his mother; and *La Possibilité d'une île* (2005; *The Possibility of an Island*; filmed 2008, directed by the author), a bleak futuristic tale about the implications and possibilities of reproduction by cloning. It was Houellebecq's fifth novel, *La Carte et le territoire* (2010; *The Map and the Territory*), which featured a character by the name of Houellebecq, that won the 2010 Prix Goncourt.

(KATHLEEN KUIPER)

Humala, Ollanta

(b. June 27, 1962, Lima, Peru)

On June 5, 2011, in one of the closest presidential elections in Peru's history, Ollanta Humala, a leftist former army commander and one-time military coup leader, prevailed over conservative congresswoman Keiko Fujimori in a runoff, earning a narrow 51.45–48.55% victory. The vote brought to a close a highly polarizing campaign in which Humala faced questions over his ties to Venezuelan Pres. Hugo Chávez, who had openly supported Humala's unsuccessful 2006 presidential bid, and Fujimori confronted accusations that she was a proxy for her father, former president Alberto Fujimori, who was imprisoned on human rights and corruption charges. Denying that he wished to bring Chávez's socialist revolution to Peru, Humala instead promised to pursue moderate leftist policies as he sought to reduce poverty in the country, where roughly a third of the population lived below the poverty line despite nearly a decade of robust economic growth. On July 28 Humala succeeded Pres. Alan García, who was prohibited from running for reelection.

Humala joined the army in 1982 and received training at the U.S. Army-run School of the Americas, which trained Latin American officers. In the 1990s, as an army captain, he commanded a counterinsurgency unit during the government's fight against the revolutionary organization Shining Path (Sendero Luminoso). Reports later surfaced that violent excesses had occurred under his command, though Humala denied these allegations. In October 2000 he attracted nationwide attention when he led a military rebellion against then president Fujimori that was quickly put down. Within months, however, Fujimori's government crumbled amid growing scandals; Humala subsequently received a congressional pardon for his role in the rebellion and was reinstated in the army. After serving as a military attaché at the Peruvian embassies in France and South Korea, he retired from the army in 2004 with the rank of lieutenant colonel.

In Peru's 2006 presidential election, Humala secured the most votes in the first round and advanced to a runoff with García. During the campaign Humala publicly allied himself with Chávez, and García warned that "Peru would become a colony of Venezuela" if Humala became president. García won the election by a 52.62–47.37% margin. Making an abrupt about-face in 2011, Humala attempted to downplay his association with Chávez, explicitly stating that "the Venezuelan model doesn't apply in Peru" and recasting himself as a centre-left politician in the mold of former Brazilian president Luiz Inácio Lula da Silva. Humala disavowed his earlier promises to renegotiate Peru's free-trade agreements and to rewrite the constitution in order to give the government a greater role in the economy. Although his plans included higher taxes on the country's lucrative mining sector, he insisted that he would negotiate with mining companies on taxes rather than unilaterally impose them.

Humala's critics expressed skepticism over his political transformation, but he continued to strike a moderate tone, pledging economic stability and a pragmatic approach to resolving social problems. In early December Humala drew praise from business interests when he declared a state of emergency in four provinces in response to bitter protests against a proposed gold-mine project. (SHERMAN HOLLAR)

Issoufou, Mahamadou

(b. Jan. 1, 1952, Dan Daji, Niger)

On March 12, 2011, veteran opposition leader Mahamadou Issoufou earned a decisive victory in Niger's presidential runoff election, garnering nearly 58% of the vote to defeat former prime minister Seini Oumarou, who received 42%. The election and Issoufou's subsequent inauguration on April 7 returned Niger to civilian rule a little more than a year after a military coup had ousted the government of Pres. Mamadou Tandja in February 2010. The coup took place in the wake of Tandja's 2009 constitutional revisions, which allowed him to extend his mandate by three years but provoked sharp criticism both domestically and abroad. Issoufou, as president of the Nigerien Party for Democracy and Socialism–Tarayya (PNDS), was Niger's main opposition leader during Tandja's 10-year rule.

During the late 1970s Issoufou studied in France and became a mining engineer; he returned to Niger in 1979 to work for the Société des Mines de l'Aïr (SOMAÏR), a French-controlled mining concern. In 1990 he helped found the PNDS, and two years after that he left SOMAÏR to pursue politics full-time. In 1993—when Niger held its first multiparty elections—he lost his bid for the presidency, but he served (April 1993 to September 1994) as prime minister under the newly elected president, Mahamane Ousmane, until the PNDS withdrew from the ruling coalition. Issoufou waged three additional unsuccessful presidential campaigns—placing a distant fourth to Gen. Ibrahim Baré Maïnassara in the 1996 elections, which were marred by widespread allegations of fraud, and finishing second to Tandja in 1999 and again in 2004.

In 2009 Issoufou marshaled demonstrations to protest Tandja's efforts to remain in power beyond the scheduled end of his second term in December of that year. Declaring that "the constitution has been squashed," Issoufou called on opposition parties to unite against the president, and he was briefly detained at the end of June after urging the military to disobey Tandja's orders. On Feb. 18, 2010, Tandja and other members of his government were taken into custody and were replaced by a military junta, which pledged that presidential and legislative elections would be held in January 2011. In the balloting Issoufou won the first round, although no candidates received an outright majority. Four other opposition candidates then cast their support to Issoufou, setting the stage for him to prevail in the runoff over Oumarou, who represented Tandja's party.

Among Issoufou's stated priorities as president were to fight corruption, invest in infrastructure and agricultural development, improve education, and alleviate food insecurity in Niger, which, despite having abundant mineral resources, remained one of the poorest countries in the world. He vowed to honour all peace agreements that had been signed with Tuareg rebels in northern Niger and immediately after his inauguration appointed a Tuareg, Brigi Rafini, as his prime minister. Issoufou also promised to continue efforts to counter the threat posed by al-Qaeda in the Islamic Maghrib, an Algeria-based Islamic militant group that was active in North Africa and the Sahel region.

(SHERMAN HOLLAR)

Jim O'Connell—The New York Times/Redux

Architect Toyo Ito with the model for his T'ai-chung, Taiwan, opera house

Ito, Toyo

(b. June 1, 1941, Seoul, Korea [now in South Korea]) Japanese architect Toyo Ito's innovative designs continued to spark widespread interest and discussion among critics and observers in 2011. Reflecting his belief that "all architecture is an extension of nature," Ito's buildings characteristically evoked imagery from the natural world. Among his best-known structures were the Sendai (Japan) Mediatheque (2001), a multipurpose cultural centre whose design was inspired by floating seaweed, and the Kao-hsiung (Taiwan) National Stadium (2009), whose monumental spiral-shaped roof resembled a coiled snake. During the year work progressed on one of Ito's most ambitious projects, the Metropolitan Opera House in T'ai-chung, Taiwan. The expansive venue, which some critics likened to an enormous sponge, featured a labyrinthine network of tunnels, curved walls, and cavernous spaces. The opera house was scheduled for completion in 2013.

Ito studied architecture at the University of Tokyo. After graduating (1965), he apprenticed with Kiyonori Kikutake, one of the leaders of the Metabolist school, a Japanese architectural movement of the 1960s that advocated a radically futuristic approach to design. As the Metabolist movement wound down, Ito left Kikutake's firm, and in 1971 he established his own practice, initially focusing on residential and other small-scale projects. One of his most notable early designs was the White U house (1976) in Tokyo. Intended as a place of solace and retreat for Ito's recently widowed sister, the house—built in the shape of a U around a central courtyard—featured no outward-facing windows. A few small openings in the ceiling offered the only glimpses of the outside world and created dramatic light effects within the house's pure white interior.

As Ito moved on to larger works, his designs became more experimental. In Yokohama he transformed an old concrete water tower into the visually stunning Tower of the Winds (1986) by covering the structure with a perforated aluminum plate and hundreds of lights that were configured to respond to wind speed and sound waves. By day the plate reflected the sky, but at night the tower "came alive" as the lights produced constantly changing colours and patterns.

What many critics regarded as Ito's masterpiece, the Sendai Mediatheque, took six years to complete. From the outside the approximately 22,000-sq-m (237,000-sq-ft) transparent structure resembled a gigantic aquarium; the building's seven floors were supported by slanting columns that looked like strands of seaweed swaying underwater. No walls divided the building's interior, yet the space was highly versatile, housing a great variety of art and media collections for public use.

Ito received numerous awards for his work, including a Golden Lion for lifetime achievement at the 2002 Venice Biennale, the 2006 Royal Gold Medal of the Royal Institute of British Architects, the 2008 Friedrich Kiesler Prize for Architecture and the Arts, and a 2010 Praemium Imperiale. Over the course of his career, he was also actively involved as an educator, teaching at several universities in Japan and abroad and serving as a mentor to many aspiring architects. In 2010 two of his former apprentices, Kazuyo Sejima and Ryue Nishizawa, were named winners of the Pritzker Prize; both cited Ito as a major influence on their work.

(SHERMAN HOLLAR)

Jones, Carwyn

(b. March 21, 1967, Swansea, Wales) In May 2011, having spent 18 months leading a coalition administration in Wales, Carwyn Jones finally was able to preside as first minister of a Labour-only Welsh government. Jones could boast impeccable progressive credentials. A fluent Welsh speaker, he was brought up in Bridgend in South Wales and educated at local schools and Aberystwyth University in western Wales. He joined the Labour Party as a student in 1985—during a bitter and highly politicized yearlong strike by coal miners across the U.K.

Jones qualified as a lawyer and specialized in family, criminal, and personal injury law at a legal firm in Swansea. His move into politics followed referenda in Wales and Scotland in 1997 to establish separate devolved governments. In 1999, at the age of 32, he was elected to the newly formed National Assembly for Wales. By October 2000 he had become minister for agriculture and rural development, and he became a significant public figure six months later when he led Wales's response to the foot-and-mouth outbreak that devastated livestock farms throughout Britain. Welsh farmers—never Labour's natural allies—praised his consensual approach.

For the next eight years, Jones remained a member of the Welsh cabinet in a succession of roles, including minister for education and minister for open government. After First Minister Rhodri Morgan announced in September 2009 that he would retire as Labour leader in December, Jones, still only 42, displayed youth and a relaxed television manner that appealed to the party members and trade unionists whose votes determined Labour's new leader in Wales. He defeated his two rivals outright on the first ballot, securing 52% of the vote. As Labour's new leader in Wales, Jones became first minister, leading the existing coalition with Plaid Cymru, the Welsh nationalist party, as the junior partner. When Labour lost the Britainwide May 2010 general election, Jones became the party's most-senior elected politician in the U.K.

Jones faced two major tests in 2011. The first was to secure a "yes" vote in a referendum in March to increase the powers of the Welsh government. When 63.5% of those voting approved the referendum, it was perceived as a personal triumph for Jones, especially given that the 1997 referendum on devolution had been supported by only 50.3% of the ballots. Then, in May, Jones had to lead Labour into the election for the new National Assembly. In 2007 Labour had slipped to just 26 seats (out of 60) and had been compelled to enter into coalition with Plaid Cymru. In May 2011, however, Labour gained 4 seats, to reach 30—just enough for the party to govern alone. Jones said that he would maintain his inclusive approach to politics, declaring that there would be no "triumphalism or tribalism"—which was interpreted as code for saying that Labour's left wing would be held in check. (PETER KELLNER)

Kaufman, Moisés

(b. Nov. 21, 1963, Caracas, Venez.)

In 2011 Moisés Kaufman directed not one but two plays in New York City—Tennessee Williams's *One Arm* and Rajiv Joseph's *Bengal Tiger at the Baghdad Zoo*. The former was Kaufman's adaptation of a 1940s Williams short story and three unproduced versions of a Williams screenplay. The latter, a reflection on war and its effects, featured actor and comedian Robin Williams as the title character. Although neither play was an unqualified success, both had their critical defenders, and it was clear that Kaufman was a rising star. He first came to prominence with a powerfully imagined play, *Gross Indecency: The Three Trials of Oscar Wilde* (performed 1997–98), which he both wrote and directed. The play, for which Kaufman used actual trial testimony, won an Outer Critics Circle Award for outstanding Off-Broadway play.

Kaufman was born to Orthodox Jewish parents and was of Ukrainian and Romanian descent. He attended a yeshiva (Jewish religious school) as a child and was exposed to broader culture on family trips to New York City. A Caracas theatre festival he attended as a young teenager brought him exposure to the avant-garde plays of such artists as Peter Brook, Pina Bausch, and Jerzy Grotowski, whom he cited as his early influences. While attending Metropolitan University in Caracas (B.A., 1985), Kaufman joined a touring experimental theatre group as an actor. In 1987 he moved to New York City, where he studied theatre directing at the Tisch School of the Arts, New York University, meanwhile directing a variety of plays. Four years later Kaufman, together with his partner, Jeffrey LaHoste, established Tectonic Theater Project.

Kaufman was especially interested in what he termed "watershed historical moments," events that reveal the foundations of society's beliefs. After *Gross Indecency*, Kaufman and his troupe began work on *The Laramie Project* (performed 2000, published 2001, filmed for television 2002), a work that examined the reactions of residents of the small Wyoming city in which gay college student Matthew Shepard had been brutally murdered. The play, which resulted from a multitude of citizen interviews, proved popular worldwide.

In 2003 Kaufman directed a one-man show, Doug Wright's *I Am My Own Wife: Studies for a Play About Charlotte von Mahlsdorf* (performed 2003–04), the story of a gay transvestite who survived life in Nazi Germany and Soviet East Berlin. It was critically acclaimed and resulted in two Tonys (for best play and best actor) and a nomination for Kaufman. He then directed a variety of plays, including Wilde's *Lady Windermere's Fan* and Shakespeare's *Macbeth*. He also directed his own next play, *33 Variations* (first performed 2007), which starred Jane Fonda as a musicologist obsessed with Beethoven's *Diabelli Variations* and received a Tony nomination for best play. In 2009 Kaufman and other Tectonic members arranged for 150 simultaneous readings in theatres across the globe of *The Laramie Project: Ten Years Later*, a sequel to his earlier project. (KATHLEEN KUIPER)

Kiir Mayardit, Salva

(b. 1951, Akon, Sudan [now in South Sudan]) When the southern region of Sudan seceded and became the newly independent country of South Sudan on July 9, 2011, it was under the leadership of Pres. Salva Kiir Mayardit, who for decades had played a pivotal role in the south's struggle for independence. After that hard-fought-for goal had been met, Kiir turned his attention to tackling the many challenges facing the new country.

Kiir, a Christian, was born into a family of the Dinka ethnic group in the southern region of Sudan. In the 1960s, during the first (1955–72) of Sudan's two civil wars, he joined the Anya Nya, a southern separatist movement, in the fight against the northern-based Sudanese government. After fighting ended, he was absorbed into Sudan's national army and eventually attained the rank of lieutenant colonel. When hostilities resumed in 1983, Kiir and others, including Col. John Garang de Mabior, defected from the Sudanese army. Along with Garang, Kiir helped form the Sudan People's Liberation Movement (SPLM) and the Sudan People's Liberation Army (SPLA), which would become the primary southern rebel group fighting against the government. Within the SPLA Kiir was one of Garang's top deputies. He was also an important participant in negotiations with the national government, which ultimately led to the 2005 Comprehensive Peace Agreement (CPA) that ended Sudan's second civil war.

Per the terms of the CPA, the semiautonomous region of southern Sudan was established in 2005. On July 9, 2005, Garang was named president of

South Sudan Pres. Salva Kiir

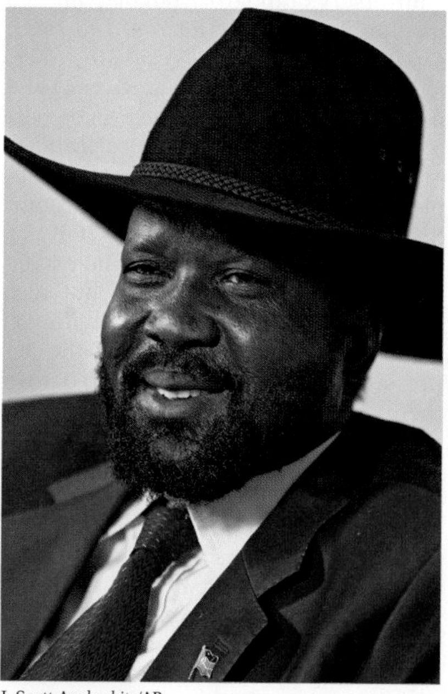

J. Scott Applewhite/AP

the region as well as first vice president in the Sudanese national government, but after his unexpected death later that month, Kiir succeeded him in both positions. In the 2010 elections Kiir received almost 93% of the vote to continue serving as southern Sudan's president; he also remained in his capacity as first vice president of the national government.

In January 2011 the southern Sudanese people voted in a referendum on whether the region should remain part of Sudan or become a separate country; the results were overwhelmingly in favour of independence. Upon the south's secession in July, Kiir became the first president of an independent South Sudan. He faced many challenges, including the daunting task of creating much-needed infrastructure to support the nascent state and handling the influx of refugees returning after the decades of war. He also had to deal with lingering skirmishes between southern rebel groups as well as navigate South Sudan's precarious relationship with the Sudanese government, particularly with regard to contested regions along the common border of the two countries. (AMY MCKENNA)

Kinkade, Thomas

(b. Jan. 19, 1958, Sacramento, Calif.)
American artist Thomas Kinkade—best known for his light-infused paintings featuring tranquil, idyllic scenes—culminated his tenure in 2011 as the official Indianapolis Motor Speedway Centennial Era Artist (2009–11) with a masterwork to commemorate the 100th anniversary of the first Indianapolis 500 race. In *A Century of Racing! The 100th Anniversary Indianapolis 500 Mile Race*, Kinkade depicted vintage race cars and modern racers dashing side by side past a waving checkered flag. In celebration of the Centennial Era kickoff, he completed the painting *Indianapolis Motor Speedway, 100th Anniversary* (2009), a work that not only captured the excitement and speed of the race but also gave a sense of the historical importance of the Brickyard raceway, the impressive pagoda landmark structure there, and the city of Indianapolis in the background. In addition to the studio paintings, Kinkade created Impressionist images of both artworks for the covers of the official 2009 and 2011 Indianapolis 500 programs.

Kinkade studied art history and took studio classes for two years at the University of California, Berkeley, before transferring to the Art Center College of Design in Pasadena, Calif. It was there that he began experimenting with techniques to create the effects of light and atmosphere in his paintings. After graduation he and a friend rode boxcars from California to New York, and Kinkade sketched the American towns and landscapes that they encountered along their journey; these works were published in the book *The Artist's Guide to Sketching* (1982). Kinkade was hired shortly thereafter to help paint some 700 backgrounds for the animated film *Fire and Ice* (1983), for which he created his trademark luminous scenes.

Kinkade's own paintings, which he began selling in local galleries, incorporated radiant effects that led him to be dubbed the "Painter of Light." His favourite subjects include cottages, bridges, gardens, and Americana scenes infused with the warm glow of sunlight. In 1984 Kinkade began to distribute his artwork with the help of investors, and in 1989 he and Ken Rausch launched Lightpost Publishing, which was dedicated exclusively to Kinkade's work. His paintings became wildly popular with the general public, which was drawn to their nostalgic quality. His skyrocketing sales made him one of the most highly collected living artists. Despite his commercial success, Kinkade was often derided by critics who considered his work to be kitschy. They also denounced the mass marketing of his work, which appeared on a wide variety of products, including calendars, notecards, and coffee mugs.

For the Disney Dream Collection, Kinkade created a series of paintings—including *Beauty and the Beast Falling in Love* (2010) and *Sleeping Beauty* (2011)—that encapsulate an entire Disney animated film in one image. In addition, beginning with *Cape Light* (2002), he created the covers for novels that he wrote (in partnership with Katherine Spencer). In 2011 the pair released a new volume in both the Cape Light series and the Angel Island series, the first installation of which appeared in 2010. (BARBARA A. SCHREIBER)

Klitschko, Vitali and Wladimir

(b. July 19, 1971, Belovodsk, Kirgiziya, U.S.S.R. [now Belovodskoye, Kyrgyz.]) and (b. March 25, 1976, Semipalatinsk, Kazakhstan, U.S.S.R. [now Semey, Kazakh.]) In 2011 boxing's heavyweight division was dominated to an unprecedented extent by Vitali and Wladimir Klitschko, a pair of Germany-based Ukrainian brothers, who, between them, held virtually every professional heavyweight title. The 2-m (6-ft 7½-in) Vitali (with a win-loss record of 43–2) was the WBC heavyweight champion, while 1.98-m (6-ft 6-in) Wladimir (56–3) held the title in the WBA and the IBF as well as the lesser-known World Boxing Organization (WBO) and International Boxing Organization (IBO). The brothers had refined what was originally a cumbersome fighting style into one that took full advantage of their prodigious size to avoid punches and gradually wear down opponents with minimum risk. Meanwhile, the Klitschkos' refusal to fight each other made it difficult to ascertain which brother was the best heavyweight of the era, creating what the media frequently referred to as a "two-headed" heavyweight champion.

Vitali and Wladimir, the sons of a Soviet air force officer, excelled at academics and athletics from a young age. Vitali, who also excelled in kickboxing as a boy, was scheduled to represent Ukraine in boxing at the 1996 Atlanta Olympic Games, but he tested positive for steroids and was dismissed from the team. Wladimir, who had followed Vitali into amateur boxing, took his place and won the super heavyweight gold medal. The brothers made their professional debuts on the same fight card in Hamburg, Ger., on Nov. 16, 1996, with each scoring a knockout victory.

Vitali lost for the first time on April 1, 2000, when he suffered a torn rotator cuff during a bout with American Chris Byrd, which resulted in a technical knockout defeat. British boxer Lennox Lewis stopped him on cuts in a thrilling defense of the WBC and *The Ring* magazine titles on June 21, 2003. Following Lewis's retirement, Vitali captured the vacant WBC and *The Ring* championships, but a series of injuries induced him to announce his retirement on Nov. 9, 2005, after having made only one defense. Vitali regained the WBC belt in his return to the ring on Oct. 11, 2008. By year-end 2011 he had made seven successful defenses. Outside the ring he played a significant role in Ukraine's 2004 Orange Revolution, which ushered Pres. Viktor Yushchenko into power. Vitali unsuccessfully ran for mayor of Kiev in 2006 and indicated his intention to return to politics following his boxing career.

Wladimir suffered knockout losses to American Ross Puritty (in 1998), South African Corrie Sanders (in 2003), and American Lamon Brewster (in 2004), which threatened to derail his career.

Herbert Knosowski/AP

Champion Ukrainian pugilists, brothers Vitali (left) and Wladmir Klitschko

He regrouped, however, under American trainer Emanuel Steward and went undefeated in his next 14 fights, winning four organization belts and recognition as champion by *The Ring*.

Although the Klitschko brothers never became major box-office attractions in the U.S., they were among Europe's leading sports stars. Many of their bouts were held in football stadiums in order to accommodate huge crowds, and they garnered record-breaking television ratings in Germany, Ukraine, and Poland. Overall, the brothers presented a far more sophisticated public image than many other boxing champions. Each held a Ph.D. in sports science—hence their nicknames, "Dr. Ironfist" (Vitali) and "Dr. Steelhammer" (Wladimir)—and both were multilingual and were involved in charitable foundations and with UNESCO. *Klitschko*, a feature-length documentary by German filmmaker Sebastian Dehnhardt, was released in October 2011. (NIGEL COLLINS)

Koch, Charles de Ganahl and David Hamilton

(b. Nov. 1, 1935, Wichita, Kan.) and (b. May 3, 1940, Wichita) In 2011 American billionaire brothers Charles and David Koch—majority co-owners of Koch Industries, Inc., and major financial backers of libertarian and conservative causes in the U.S.—found themselves unexpectedly in the media limelight. In January the public-interest group Common Cause filed a complaint with the U.S. Department of Justice, charging that Supreme Court Justices Antonin Scalia and Clarence Thomas might have violated federal law by failing to recuse themselves from *Citizens United* v. *Federal Election Commission*, the 2010 case in which the court struck down limits on independent political spending by corporations and unions. Before the court heard the case, Scalia and Thomas had allegedly attended political conferences hosted by the Koch brothers, who were direct beneficiaries of the ruling. The complaint drew further media attention to the brothers' political spending, the vast extent of which had not been widely known before the 2010 U.S. midterm elections.

Charles and David Koch both attended MIT, receiving master's degrees in engineering in 1959 and 1963, respectively. Upon the death of their father, Fred Koch, in 1967, his Rock Island Oil and Refining Co. was inherited by the pair and by David's twin brother, William, and their older brother, Frederick. Charles became chairman and CEO and renamed the company Koch Industries, Inc.; David joined the company in 1970 and eventually became executive vice president. In 1983 Charles and David purchased their brothers' stakes in Koch Industries for $1.1 billion. Under Charles's leadership, the company extended its interests into areas far beyond petroleum and increased its annual revenue 250-fold in 40 years, to an estimated $100 billion in 2009. Koch Industries became one of the largest privately held corporations in the world, and the Koch brothers made *Forbes* magazine's list of the richest persons in the world, with an estimated net worth in 2011 of more than $20 billion each.

In 1980 David was the U.S. vice presidential candidate of the Libertarian Party, which received about 1% of the popular vote. The brothers subsequently contributed millions of dollars annually to scores of think tanks, foundations, and nonprofit groups, several of which they created or controlled. One of these organizations, the Americans for Prosperity Foundation, significantly aided the growth of the antigovernment Tea Party movement from 2009 by organizing rallies, funding advertisements, and formulating policy. Koch Industries and the brothers individually also spent large sums on campaign contributions and lobbying. Starting in 2003, the brothers hosted biannual national conferences—referred to in the Common Cause complaint—at which industry executives, Republican Party leaders, and conservative activists and journalists gathered to discuss political issues, fund-raising, and electoral strategy.

Critics of the Koch brothers accused them of using their enormous wealth to manipulate public discourse and to advance policies that harmed middle- and working-class Americans and undermined public health, workers' rights, and the environment. Defenders claimed that the extent of the brothers' influence was exaggerated and that their political activities were aimed at increasing economic freedom and prosperity for all Americans.

(BRIAN DUIGNAN)

La Russa, Tony

(b. Oct. 4, 1944, Tampa, Fla.)

In 2011 St. Louis Cardinals manager Tony La Russa led his team to one of the most improbable late-season runs in baseball history. The Cardinals clinched their postseason berth after making up an 8½-game deficit in the wild-card standings with a month remaining in the regular season. Then, in the World Series against the Texas Rangers, La Russa's team was twice one strike away from elimination in game six before rallying for a victory. The Cardinals won game seven to take the Series, and La Russa retired soon after with the third championship ring of his managerial career.

Anthony La Russa, Jr., signed to play baseball with the Kansas City Athletics (or "A's") out of high school. He spent most of his 16-season playing career in the minor leagues, but he appeared sporadically in the majors with the A's (both in Kansas City and, later, in Oakland, where the franchise moved), the Atlanta Braves, and the Chicago Cubs. He was named the manager of a minor-league affiliate of the Chicago White Sox in 1978; his first big-league managerial job came when he took over the White Sox late in the 1979 season.

La Russa—who had earned a law degree from Florida State University in 1978—proved to be a natural leader. He paid great attention to the nuances and flow of each game and frequently made in-game situational substitutions (which occasionally led to criticism that he "overmanaged"). In 1983 he guided the White Sox to a 99-win season and the team's first play-off appearance in 24 years. A slow start to the 1986 campaign and La Russa's strained working relationship with the team's new general manager, however, led the Sox to fire him three months into the season. He was out of work for less than a month before he was hired by the A's.

For three straight seasons (1988–90), La Russa led the A's to the highest win total in the major leagues, as well as the American League (AL) pennant. The team was upset in two World Series, but in 1989 the A's swept the San Francisco Giants to take the Series in four games. La Russa and the A's captured another division title in 1992, but after the team posted three consecutive losing seasons (1993–95), he opted out of his contract and signed with the Cardinals. In his initial season in St. Louis, La Russa guided the Cardinals to the first of their seven division titles during his tenure. The Cardinals won National League (NL) pennants in 2004 and 2006 and in the latter year defeated the Detroit Tigers in the World Series.

LaRussa retired with the third most managerial wins (2,728) in major league history. He was named the AL's Manager of the Year three times (1983, 1988, and 1992) and was granted the NL's version of the award in 2002.

(ADAM AUGUSTYN)

Le Pen, Marine

(b. Aug. 5, 1968, Neuilly-sur-Seine, France) French politician Marine Le Pen rose to prominence in early 2011 amid a turbulent French political scene. As former IMF director and presumptive Socialist presidential candidate Dominique Strauss-Kahn battled sexual-assault charges in New York City, Le Pen's popularity in opinion polls surged. Possessed with a telegenic charm and keen political instincts forged at the side of her father, Jean-Marie Le Pen, she easily won the party election in January 2011 to succeed him as National Front leader. As the 2012 French presidential campaign began in earnest, Le Pen was expected to represent the National Front against incumbent Pres. Nicolas Sarkozy.

Chamussy—Sipa/AP

French National Front leader Marine Le Pen

Marion Anne Perrine Le Pen was the youngest of three daughters. Her childhood was coloured by the political career of her father, who espoused a range of controversial views and in 1976 was the target of a bomb attack that heavily damaged the family's apartment building. This and other, less-violent rebukes of her father's views began to inform Le Pen's own politics. She earned a law degree from the University of Panthéon-Assas (University of Paris II) in 1991 and remained there to complete an advanced degree in criminal law in 1992. That year she was certified to practice law; she worked as an attorney in Paris from 1992 to 1998.

In 1998 she joined the administrative apparatus of the National Front, which had been founded by her father in 1972 and was the main right-wing opposition to France's mainstream conservative parties. She served as the director of the National Front's legal affairs until 2003, when she became the party's vice president. The following year she made a successful run for a seat in the European Parliament, where she joined her father in that body's nonaligned bloc. Over the following years, her profile within the National Front rose, and she managed her father's presidential campaign in 2007. She served in a number of regional and municipal posts in the government of Nord-Pas-de-Calais, and she led the National Front to a strong showing there in regional elections in 2009.

As Le Pen emerged from her father's shadow to become a national figure in her own right, she distanced herself from some of his and the party's more extreme views. While Le Pen embraced the National Front's established anti-immigration stance, she rebranded the party's traditional Euroskepticism as French nationalism, and she was a vocal critic of the anti-Semitism that had marginalized the party in the past.

(MICHAEL RAY)

Lee Ufan

(b. June 24, 1936, Haman, South Kyongsang [Gyeongsang] province, Korea [now in South Korea]) Korean artist Lee Ufan in June 2011 became just the third East Asian artist to be given a solo exhibition at the Guggenheim Museum in New York City. This confirmed his position as a leading figure in the contemporary art world, a reputation that had been building since the 1960s. Lee had created a body of artistic achieve-

Wide-ranging Korean artist Lee Ufan

Gordon M. Grant—The New York Times/Redux

ment across a wide range of mediums—painting, printmaking, sculpture, installation art, and art criticism—and had had a major impact on the development of South Korean and Japanese art since the 1970s. He started receiving international recognition in the late 1980s through exhibitions in Europe and elsewhere around the world, and his reputation grew further in the 1990s.

Lee studied painting at Seoul National University's College of Fine Arts. In 1956 he went to Japan, and in 1958 he enrolled in the philosophy department at Nihon University in Tokyo. After graduating in 1961 he again turned to art and began painting and making sculptures, using natural and industrial materials such as stone, steel, rubber, and glass.

In 1968 Lee exhibited an avant-garde installation piece called *Phenomena and Perception B* (one of a series of similarly constructed works he later revisited and retitled *Relatum*, a philosophical term meaning "a thing that bears a relation of some kind to some other thing or things"). For this work Lee placed a heavy stone on a sheet of plate glass laid over a steel plate; the stone caused the glass to crack, while its placement hid the initial point of impact. The work expressed several themes that would remain significant in his art, such as the relationships between seeing and reality and between the artist's body and the material.

In the late 1960s and early '70s, Lee was the leading theorist of the Japanese art movement known as Mono-ha ("School of Things"), which promoted a minimalist aesthetic and the use of natural materials. His own work within the Mono-ha rubric consisted of sculpture, painting, and engraving. Later, his paintings in the series *From Point* and *From Line* (1972–84) were based on the brushwork and empty space of traditional Asian art and used monochromatic repeated dots and lines as a main motif. From the 1970s, Lee divided his time mainly between Japan and France, having established a studio in Paris in 1971. He also served (1973–2007) as a professor at Tama Art University in Tokyo. His published works include the books *The Search for Encounter* (1971; new edition, 2000) and *The Art of Encounter* (2004; revised edition, 2008). Lee was the recipient in 2001 of the Japan Art Association's Praemium Imperiale for painting. In 2010 the Lee Ufan Museum, designed by Ando Tadao, opened in Naoshima, Japan.

(TAE-HEE GANG)

Gary Kazanjiian/AP

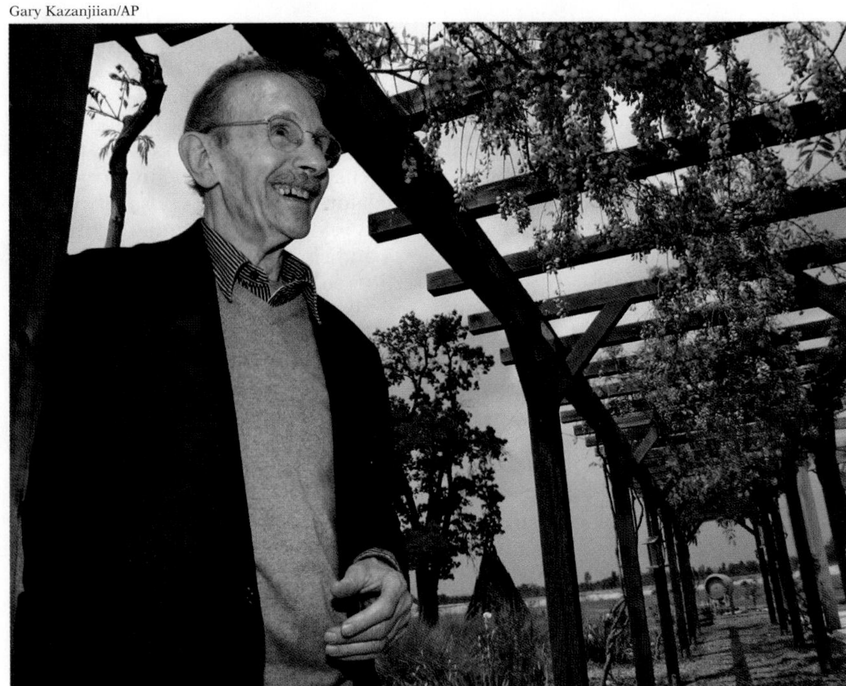

Pulitzer Prize-winning poet laureate Philip Levine

Levine, Philip

(b. Jan. 10, 1928, Detroit, Mich.)

American poet Philip Levine, whose poems reflected the struggles of urban working-class life, was in 2011 named poet laureate consultant in poetry to the Library of Congress. His verse offers graphic images of gray cities, meaningless talk and actions, subtle humiliations, dispossession, and despair.

Levine was of Russian Jewish descent. He studied at Wayne University (now Wayne State University), Detroit (B.A., 1950; M.A., 1955), and the University of Iowa (M.F.A., 1957). He worked at a series of industrial jobs before he began teaching literature and creative writing at California State University, Fresno (1958–92). Levine also served as poet-in-residence at other colleges and universities. In his poems he drew on his experiences working in factories and attempted to speak for those whose intelligence, emotions, and imagination are constrained by tedious and harsh working conditions. He wrote in free verse and in lines of variable rhythm, and his language was unambiguous.

Despite Levine's concern with modern life's brutalities, he also celebrated love and joy in his verse. His numerous poetry collections include *On the Edge* (1963), *They Feed They Lion* (1972), *Ashes* (1979; winner of a National Book Award and the National Book Critics Circle Award), *7 Years from Somewhere* (1979; winner of the National Book Critics Circle Award), and *A Walk with Tom Jefferson* (1988). Inspired by a visit to Barcelona, he wrote the poems of *The Names of the Lost* (1976) in honour of the loyalists who fought in the Spanish Civil War (1936–39).

Levine won a second National Book Award in 1991 for his collection *What Work Is*, an honour that may have partly inspired the backward look that he achieves in *The Bread of Time: Toward an Autobiography* (1994, reissued 2001), a series of essays that one critic called both elegant and tough-minded. Some of his later books of verse include the Pulitzer Prize-winning collection *The Simple Truth* (1994), filled with elegiac despair, and *Unselected Poems* (1997). Also in 1997 Levine became a member of the American Academy of Arts and Letters. *The Mercy* (1999) expresses, as another critic wrote, an acceptance of reality attended by "a sort of delight." He published more poetry in his signature vein in the volumes *Breath* (2004) and *News of the World* (2009). As poet laureate, Levine was concerned with assisting others in understanding how poetry could have an impact on their lives and with helping to showcase the works of lesser-known poets. (EB ED.)

Lieberman, Daniel E.

(b. June 3, 1964)

In 2011 American paleoanthropologist Daniel Eric Lieberman published the acclaimed *The Evolution of the Human*

Head, a comprehensive review of the human skull, its tissues, and the role played by natural selection in its development. Lieberman was already well known for his part in developing and testing the endurance-running hypothesis in hominins and for his research into the biomechanics of barefoot running.

Lieberman studied anthropology at Harvard University (A.B., 1986; A.M., 1990; Ph.D., 1993) and biological anthropology at the University of Cambridge (M.Phil, 1987). After having held faculty appointments at Rutgers University, New Brunswick, N.J. (1995–98), and George Washington University, Washington, D.C. (1998–2001), he returned to Harvard, where he served as professor of anthropology (2001–09) and then as professor and chairman of the department of human evolutionary biology. Lieberman's early research explored the structure of the skull and dentition of early hominins, but his interests quickly expanded to include the influence of biomechanical forces on the evolution of bones.

In 2004 Lieberman and American biologist Dennis M. Bramble investigated long-distance-running performance in humans and how it evolved. Building on previous work by American biologist David Carrier, Lieberman and Bramble outlined the endurance-running hypothesis, which states that the ability of humans to run long distances is an adaptation that originated approximately two million years ago with the emergence of genus *Homo*. They noted that several features that facilitated endurance running first appeared in *H. habilis* and *H. erectus*—including shortened toes and feet and lengthened legs, whose various structures both stored and released elastic energy.

In 2009 Lieberman and several colleagues became the first scientists to test the endurance-running hypothesis empirically by calculating the effects of toe length on running biomechanics. Their results suggested that reduced toe length relative to body mass in bipeds had increased locomotive efficiency and lowered the metabolic costs of running. They reported that the long toes that were observed in modern apes and early hominins had little effect on the energy expended in walking. If contemporary human toe length were increased by just 20%, however, runners would incur a greater risk of injury and would likely have to expend twice as much energy than they do at present.

Lieberman acknowledged that endurance running would not have allowed early humans to avoid faster predators over short distances, but it could have helped them travel more easily between patches of good habitat or reach animal carcasses in time to scavenge meat left behind by large predators. Lieberman also noted the utility of endurance running in tracking and chasing prey until the prey surrendered from exhaustion. Consequently, he contended, endurance running had made meat more accessible to humans; the ingestion of protein and fats found in animal flesh had in turn led to taller and narrower body forms, increased brain size, and reduced dentition. (JOHN P. RAFFERTY)

Lindquist, Susan L.

(b. June 5, 1949, Chicago, Ill.)

In 2011 American molecular biologist Susan L. Lindquist continued to make key discoveries concerning protein behaviour that advanced progress toward the development of new treatments for catastrophic neurodegenerative conditions, including Alzheimer disease, Parkinson disease, and Huntington chorea. Her latest work not only reaffirmed the importance to medicine of research focused at the most fundamental levels of cell biology but also added to her growing reputation as a leading scientist in the study of protein folding.

Lindquist (born Susan Lee McKenzie) received a bachelor's degree (1971) in microbiology from the University of Illinois at Urbana-Champaign and a doctorate (1976) in biology from Harvard University. She later joined the faculty (1978) of the department of molecular genetics and cell biology at the University of Chicago, where she remained until 2001, when she became a professor in the department of biology at MIT. From 2001 to 2004 she served as director of the MIT-affiliated Whitehead Institute for Biomedical Research.

In the 1980s and '90s, Lindquist's research centred primarily on heat-shock proteins—proteins synthesized rapidly and in large quantities following cellular exposure to sudden increases in temperature. She discovered that the proteins prevent new RNA molecules from being processed while the cell is under stress, allowing time for the cell to reset its damaged regulatory systems and restore protein homeostatis. In characterizing the process, Lindquist provided scientists with what was then one of the most complete examples of gene regulation in cells.

Lindquist's research on heat-shock proteins led her to several major discoveries about misfolded proteins known as prions. Key among these discoveries were her identification of a yeast protein that formed a cytoplasmically inherited prionlike aggregate and her finding that yeast prions are inherited without changes in genotype (genetic constitution) and expose hidden genetic variation, giving rise to new traits that enable yeast to adapt and evolve. She subsequently applied that knowledge to studies of cancer cells, which also adapt and mutate rapidly in response to environmental factors.

Lindquist later contributed to the discovery of a neuronal protein in the mammalian brain that could be converted naturally to a prionlike state and hypothesized that the prion form maintained changes at synapses (neuronal junctions) required for memory storage. She also studied a protein known as amyloid, which led to her discovery of a yeast protein capable of breaking down amyloid, opening up new avenues of research into the development of treatments for certain neurodegenerative diseases.

Lindquist was a member of the American Academy of Arts and Sciences (1996) and the National Academy of Sciences (1997). She was a recipient of the National Medal of Science (2009), the Max Delbrück Medal (2010), and the Mendel Medal (2010). (KARA ROGERS)

Lochte, Ryan

(b. Aug. 3, 1984, Rochester, N.Y.)

At the 2011 FINA world swimming championships, held in July in Shanghai, American swimmer Ryan Lochte won five gold medals and, in doing so, upstaged his longtime teammate, friend, and rival, 14-time Olympic gold medalist Michael Phelps. Lochte twice bested Phelps in head-to-head competition in Shanghai, edging him in both the 200-m freestyle event and the 200-m individual medley (IM). In the latter race Lochte set the first world record since FINA banned high-performance nontextile swimsuits in January 2010, breaking his own record (set in a high-tech suit) with a new global standard of 1 min 54.00 sec. Showcasing his exceptional versatility, he also collected wins in the 200-m backstroke and the 400-m IM and helped power the American team to gold in the 4 × 200-m freestyle relay.

Lochte attended the University of Florida, where he won seven NCAA swimming titles, including three individual titles in 2006. He first attracted international attention at the 2004 Olympic Games in Athens, where he earned a gold medal as a member of the victorious American 4 × 200-m freestyle relay team and claimed silver in the 200-m IM, behind Phelps. At the 2006 FINA short-course (25-m) world championships, Lochte set world marks in the 100-m backstroke, the 200-m backstroke, and the 200-m IM. He subsequently set his first long-course (50-m) world record in the 200-m backstroke at the FINA world championships in 2007, upsetting fellow American Aaron Peirsol to take the gold.

At the 2008 Beijing Olympic Games, Lochte and Peirsol dueled again in the 200-m backstroke. They entered the Games sharing the world record in the event, but it was Lochte who unleashed a withering kick in the final lap of the race to seize the gold and set a new global standard of 1 min 53.94 sec. With teammates Phelps, Ricky Berens, and Peter Vanderkaay, Lochte earned yet another gold and world record in the 4 × 200-m freestyle relay; he rounded out his medal haul in Beijing with bronzes in both the 200- and 400-m IM.

In 2009 and 2010 Lochte continued his string of impressive performances. At the 2009 FINA world championships, he broke Phelps's world record in the 200-m IM and also won the 400-m IM. He garnered six gold medals to Phelps's five at the 2010 Pan Pacific championships. Later that year Lochte notched an unprecedented seven medals at the FINA short-course worlds, winning all five of his individual races—two, the 200- and 400-m IM, in world-record time—and sparking the Americans to a come-from-behind victory in the 4 × 100-m medley relay; he also won silver as a member of the American 4 × 200-m freestyle relay team. At year-end 2010 *Swimming World* magazine named Lochte male World Swimmer of the Year.

(SHERMAN HOLLAR)

Ma, Jack

(b. Sept. 10, 1964, Hangzhou, Zhejiang province, China) In February 2011 Chinese Internet tycoon Jack Ma's flagship enterprise, the small-business-to-business (B2B) online marketplace Alibaba, was rocked by a scandal in which about 100 employees had certified fraudulent sources as trustworthy "Gold Suppliers." Ma responded swiftly to the scandal, firing Alibaba's CEO and chief operating officer. Later in the year he announced that he was interested in acquiring the American Internet portal Yahoo!, which owned a 40% stake in the Alibaba Group.

He was born Ma Yun, but he became interested in the English language as a young boy and later took the personal name Jack. During his teens he worked as a guide for foreign tourists to Hangzhou. Ma failed the entrance exam for the Hangzhou Teachers College twice. (His weak point was mathematics.) He was admitted on the third try, in 1984, however, and he graduated (1988) with a bachelor's degree in English. From 1988 to 1993 he taught English at the Hangzhou Institute of Electronics and Engineering (now Hangzhou Dianzi University). In 1994 he founded his first company, the Haibo Translation Agency, which provided English translation and interpretation.

Ma first encountered the Internet in 1995 on a trip to the U.S. on behalf of the Hangzhou city government. On his return home, he founded China Pages, which created Web sites for Chinese businesses and was one of China's first Internet companies. He left the company two years later, partly because of strong competition from the communications company Hangzhou Telecom, which had established a rival enterprise, Chinesepage.

From 1998 to 1999 Ma was head of a Beijing-based Internet firm that was backed by the Ministry of Foreign Trade and Economic Cooperation. In order to take advantage of the economic opportunities that the Internet offered, however, he persuaded his team at the ministry to go back to Hangzhou with him and help found the Alibaba Group. Small businesses paid a membership fee to be certified as trustworthy sellers on Alibaba.com, with a greater fee being charged to businesses that wished to sell to customers outside China. Growth was rapid, and in 2007 Alibaba.com raised $1.7 billion in its initial public offering.

In 2003 Ma created the consumer-to-consumer online marketplace Taobao (Chinese: "searching for treasure"). At the time, the American company eBay, in collaboration with the Chinese firm EachNet, had a market share of 80%. Unlike eBay-EachNet, however, Taobao did not charge a transaction fee but rather made revenue from online advertising and the sale of additional services to users. By 2007 Taobao had a 67% market share, and eBay conceded majority ownership of its Chinese operations to a local media company. In 2011 Ma announced that Taobao would split into three companies: Taobao Marketplace, where individuals could buy and sell goods; Taobao Mall, an online shopping portal; and, finally, eTao, a shopping-related search engine.

(ERIK GREGERSEN)

Mabanckou, Alain

(b. Feb. 24, 1966, Mouyondzi, Republic of the Congo) The long-awaited translation of *Mémoires de porc-épic*, the 2006 Prix Renaudot-winning work of Francophone novelist Alain Mabanckou, was finally realized in 2011 with the publication of *Memoirs of a Porcupine*. The words and the spirit of the author's poetically inclined, Congolese-influenced French were a challenge to the translator. Mabanckou confessed too that he had made a postcolonial point of flouting the rules of classical French. Yet the author's noted sense of humour could be seen in his choice of narrator—an animal double who lives on after his human associate dies—as well as his characteristic pastiche of themes and techniques. Mabanckou's wordplay, philosophical bent, and sometimes sly, often absurd sense of humour had resulted in his being known in France as "the African Samuel Beckett."

Mabanckou grew up in the Congolese port city of Pointe-Noire, the only child of a mother who could not read and a father unfamiliar with fiction. By his own account, he spoke several African languages before starting school at age six. There he learned French, and it began to dawn on him how much was lost

Congolese Francophone novelist Alain Mabanckou

Eric Gaillard—Reuters/Landov

to posterity with the use of unwritten languages and the disappearance of the rituals that served an oral tradition. He studied letters and philosophy at the Lycée Karl Marx in Pointe-Noire (B.A., 1981) and then began prelaw classes in Brazzaville. At age 22 he won a scholarship to study law in Paris, and he took an advanced degree in business law from the University of Paris-Dauphine in 1993. Prior to leaving Congo, Mabanckou had written a number of manuscripts, and he began to publish these while working for the Paris-based multinational firm Suez-Lyonnaise des Eaux. The first of his writings to see publication was a book of poems, *Au jour le jour* (1993), and more poetry followed. His first novel, *Bleu-blanc-rouge* (1998), won the Association of French-Language Writers' Literary Grand Prize of Black Africa.

Additional novels followed in rapid succession, and in 2002 Mabanckou accepted a writing fellowship from the University of Michigan. With *Verre cassé* (2005; *Broken Glass*), a comic reflection on French and Congolese cultures, he found a considerable English-language audience. His reputation was further enhanced with *Mémoires de porc-épic*. His other novels include *Black Bazar* (2009), an exposé of the differences between the several nationalities of the dark-skinned denizens of Paris.

In addition to his fiction and poetry, Mabanckou penned a tribute to American writer James Baldwin, *Lettre à Jimmy* (2007), and a memoir, *Demain j'aurai vingt ans* (2010). In 2007 he became a professor of French and Francophone studies at the University of California, Los Angeles. Mabanckou was appointed to the Legion of Honour in 2011. (KATHLEEN KUIPER)

Martelly, Michel

(b. Feb. 12, 1961, Port-au-Prince, Haiti)

In Haiti's presidential runoff election held on March 20, 2011, popular musician and political newcomer Michel Martelly trounced Mirlande Manigat, a legal scholar and the wife of a former Haitian president, by a 67.6–31.7% margin. Official results were announced on April 20, and Martelly—who prior to his entry into politics was better known to most Haitians as "Sweet Micky," a flamboyant performer of the Haitian dance music known as *compas*—was formally sworn into office on May 14. As president, Martelly faced the daunting challenge of rebuilding the country, left in ruins by the catastrophic earthquake of January 2010.

Martelly was the son of a Shell Oil plant supervisor. He graduated from Saint-Louis de Gonzague, a prestigious prep school in Port-au-Prince, and attended community colleges in the United States before returning home in the mid-1980s to embark on a musical career. He became a bandleader and adopted the moniker Sweet Micky. He quickly established himself as a star in Haiti, gaining fame for his outlandish live performances—which often included his dressing in drag or shedding his clothes onstage—and earning considerable critical acclaim as an important innovator in *compas* music. From the late 1980s into the early 21st century, he made numerous recordings and maintained a busy touring schedule. Although he was not directly involved in politics during this period, Martelly was known for offering sharp-tongued political commentary in his songs. He controversially supported the 1991 military coup that removed Pres. Jean-Bertrand Aristide from power.

Although few observers in 2010 initially took Martelly's presidential candidacy seriously, he proved to be a savvy campaigner. He hired a prominent Spanish public relations firm to manage his campaign and deftly positioned himself as a political outsider who could bring change to the poor, quake-ravaged country. First-round balloting in the presidential contest took place on Nov. 28, 2010. After Haiti's electoral commission announced that the election had resulted in the need for a runoff between Manigat and ruling-party candidate Jude Célestin, supporters of Martelly, who was said to have come in third, rioted in response. The Organization of American States later concluded that there had been widespread fraud in the vote counting, and in February 2011 the electoral commission ruled that Martelly would replace Célestin in the runoff. Strong support from young and urban voters was considered key to Martelly's eventual victory over Manigat.

As president, Martelly sought to hasten the pace of reconstruction in Haiti, where hundreds of thousands of the displaced subsisted in squalid tent settlements, and to lure more foreign investment to the country. He also pledged to improve public education and unveiled a plan to establish a fund to help guarantee access to primary schooling for all Haitian children; the fund would be financed in part through taxes on the Haitian diaspora.

(SHERMAN HOLLAR)

Martin, George R.R.

(b. Sept. 20, 1948, Bayonne, N.J.)

George R.R. Martin became the latest author to breach the confines of the fantasy ghetto with the 2011 debut of *Game of Thrones* on cable television channel HBO. The show, which took its title and the plot of its inaugural season from the first of Martin's A Song of Ice and Fire novels, steadily increased in the ratings over the course of the season, evidencing the broad appeal of his cast of schemers and heroes. Meanwhile, longtime fans were able to catch the characters' later adventures in the fifth Ice and Fire novel, *A Dance with Dragons*, released in July. Both the novels and the TV adaptation, while explicitly fantasy, pointedly avoided some of the genre's more saccharine conceits in favour of a bleak realism. Major characters—even sympathetic ones—frequently met grisly ends, and the plots were dominated by the political intriguing and battlefield savagery of those questing for the titular throne.

George Raymond Richard Martin attended Northwestern University, Evanston, Ill., graduating with bachelor's (1970) and master's (1971) degrees in journalism. He was a lifelong aficionado of science fiction and fantasy literature and sold his first short story in 1971. Having received conscientious objector status during the Vietnam War, Martin fulfilled his alternative civilian service

Game of Thrones creator George R.R. Martin

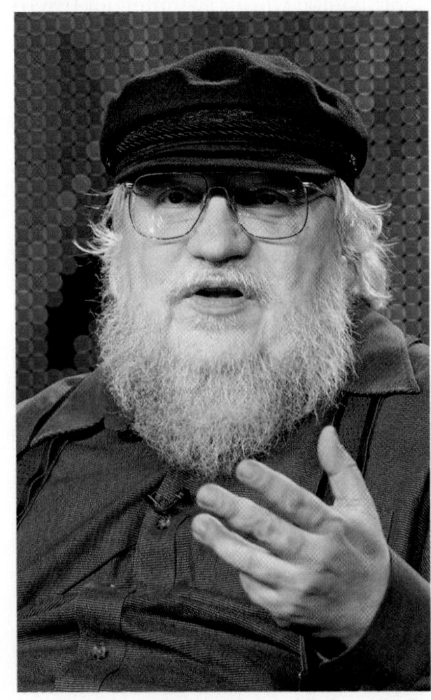

Mario Anzuoni—Reuters/Landov

by volunteering for a legal-assistance organization in Chicago while earning his living as an organizer of chess tournaments and writing short fiction. He won a Hugo Award in 1974 for his sci-fi novella *A Song for Lya*. In 1976 he accepted a position teaching journalism at Clarke College, Dubuque, Iowa.

In 1977 Martin released his first work of full-length fiction, *Dying of the Light*, about a festival on a planet nearing apocalypse, and two years later he moved to Santa Fe, N.M., to write full-time. He received both the Hugo and the Nebula Award for his novelette *Sandkings* (1981), which was adapted for TV in 1995. In 1981 he also released *Windhaven* (co-written with Lisa Tuttle), about a girl who gains the ability to fly, and he followed with two full-length efforts, the vampire novel *Fevre Dream* (1982) and the rock-and-roll horror tale *The Armageddon Rag* (1983). Though the latter sold poorly, a producer optioned the film rights. The film was never made, but in 1985 the producer suggested Martin as a writer for a remake of *The Twilight Zone* series. He wrote several screenplays for that show before accepting a position as a writer for the TV series *Beauty and the Beast* (1987–90). Martin returned to long-form fiction in 1991, having had no luck selling his TV pilots and screenplays.

One of Martin's ideas from that period evolved into *A Game of Thrones* (1996). Further installments in the Ice and Fire saga include *A Clash of Kings* (1999), *A Storm of Swords* (2000), and *A Feast for Crows* (2005). (RICHARD PALLARDY)

Matute, Ana María

(b. July 26, 1926, Barcelona, Spain)
Spanish novelist Ana María Matute, celebrated for her sympathetic treatment of the lives of children and adolescents, in 2011 was presented with the 2010 Cervantes Prize, the most prestigious literary award in the Spanish-speaking world. In her works she interjected such elements as myth, fairy tale, the supernatural, and fantasy while exploring rites of passage as well as feelings among youth of betrayal and isolation.

Matute's education suffered because of childhood illnesses, the family's frequent moves between Barcelona and Madrid, and the disruptions of the Spanish Civil War (1936–39), which left her family largely housebound in Barcelona. She broke the monotony of the war years by editing a magazine for her siblings. While in her teens, she published short stories and became a professional musician.

Matute frequently used biblical allusion in her works and often employed the story of Cain and Abel to symbolize the familial division caused by the Spanish Civil War; her first novel was titled *Los Abel* (1948). She followed up with *Fiesta al noroeste* (1953), Planeta Prize winner *Pequeño teatro* (1954), and *Los hijos muertos* (1958; *The Lost Children*, 1965), which won both the Premio Nacional de Literature (1958) and the Premio Miguel Cervantes (1959). Matute then wrote a trilogy consisting of *Primera memoria* (1959; U.K. title, *Awakening*; U.S. title, *School of the Sun*), about children thrust into an adult world by the Spanish Civil War; a war novel, *Los soldados lloran de noche* (1964; *Soldiers Cry by Night*, 1995); and *La trampa* (1969), in which the children of *Primera memoria* are presented as adults. Matute set *La torre vigía* (1971) in 10th-century Europe to examine the themes of chivalry, idealism, poverty, and prejudice. Her novel *Olvidado Rey Gudú*, a massive allegorical folk epic that spans four generations in the story of rulers, gnomes, witches, and other creatures in the mythical medieval kingdom of Olar, was published in 1996. Other works include *Aranmanoth* (2000), *En el tren* (2001), and *Paraíso inhabitado* (2008).

In addition, Matute wrote several collections of short stories, including *Los niños tontos* (1956), *Cuentos del mar* (1998), *Cuentos de infancia* (2002), and *La puerta de la luna: cuentos completos* (2010). She also penned several works for children. (EB ED.)

McKeon, Simon

(b. 1955, Dandenong, Vic., Australia)
Australian philanthropist and investment banker Simon McKeon was named Australian of the Year 2011 in recognition of his longtime support and leadership of a variety of charitable organizations in Australia and abroad. McKeon was the executive chairman of the Melbourne office of investment banking giant Macquarie Group but carried out his duties on a part-time basis so as to be able to devote much of his time to social causes, including serving on the boards of World Vision Australia and the Global Poverty Project. McKeon, who was diagnosed with multiple sclerosis (MS) in 2001, was also the founding chairman of MS Research Australia.

McKeon studied at the University of Melbourne, where he earned bachelor's degrees in commerce (1976) and law

Image provided courtesy of the National Australia Day Council

Australian of the Year Simon McKeon

(1978). After working in Sydney as an attorney for the law firm Blake Dawson Waldron, he joined the Macquarie Group in 1984, specializing in mergers and acquisitions. Aside from building a successful business career, McKeon also became an accomplished yachtsman, teaming in 1993 with co-pilot Tim Daddo to set a 500-m world speed sailing record (46.52 knots) that lasted for more than a decade. McKeon later became a patron of the Australian Olympic sailing team.

It was in 1994 that McKeon decided to limit his hours at Macquarie and make a serious commitment to philanthropy. As the director (1994–2005) of World Vision Australia, he oversaw the country's largest humanitarian organization, leading efforts to raise funds to support needy children and relief and development projects around the world. Despite being stricken with MS—which for a time left McKeon blind and paralyzed from the waist down—he continued to pursue charitable work. After guiding the establishment (2004) of MS Research Australia, he became (2007) the chairman of Business for Millennium Development, an organization that encouraged Australian companies to create economic opportunities for the poor throughout the Asia-Pacific region. The following year he took over the directorship of Red Dust Role Models, a mentoring group that aided disadvantaged youths living in remote

Australian communities. From 2009 he also served as a director of the Global Poverty Project, helping to develop education and advocacy programs related to poverty alleviation.

At the Australian of the Year awards ceremony held on Jan. 25, 2011, at Parliament House in Canberra, McKeon praised the nonprofit sector and emphasized its importance to society. "It's a sector which willingly tackles the unwanted tasks, the tasks that neither business nor government is able to do," he stated in his acceptance speech. McKeon indicated that during his time as the Australian of the Year, he would continue to promote philanthropy and challenge corporations and individuals alike to get involved in worthy causes.

(SHERMAN HOLLAR)

Mercer, Rick

(b. Oct. 17, 1969, St. John's, Nfd. [now in Newfoundland and Labrador]) The wave of activism by young voters in Canada's federal election in 2011 was credited largely to Canadian satirist, comedian, and national icon Rick Mercer. In March, on his television show, *The Rick Mercer Report*, he dedicated one of his trademark "rants" to admonishing young people to participate in the upcoming election. College students across Canada responded by celebrating the franchise with joyous demonstrations called "vote mobs."

While in high school (which he departed one credit short of graduation), Richard Vincent Mercer wrote and performed in an award-winning one-act play and cofounded a theatre troupe. In 1990 he won praise for *Show Me the Button, I'll Push It (or, Charles Lynch Must Die)*, the one-person show he first presented as an angry young man of 21. After touring with it and, later, another one-man show, *I've Killed Before, I'll Kill Again*, in 1993 Mercer began an eight-season run on the Canadian Broadcasting Corporation (CBC) in *This Hour Has 22 Minutes*, an inventive sketch-comedy-based TV show that he created with several fellow Newfoundlanders. On *This Hour*, Mercer introduced the recurring feature "Talking to Americans," a series of satiric interviews that exposed Americans' lack of knowledge regarding Canada—including an ambush of then presidential candidate George W. Bush, who accepted the endorsement of fictitious Canadian Prime Minister Jean Poutine. In 2001 an hour-long version of "Talking to Americans" gained the largest audience for a comedy special in CBC history.

Todd Korol—Reuters/Landov

Canadian funnyman Rick Mercer

In 1998 Mercer and his life partner, writer-producer Gerald Lunz, created *Made in Canada*, a sitcom about the Canadian film and television industry, with Mercer as its ruthless protagonist. After that show's five-season run, Mercer and Lunz in 2004 introduced *Rick Mercer's Monday Report*, a comedic news-focused program that drew comparisons to American TV's *The Daily Show*. Like that program's host, Jon Stewart, Mercer was commended not only as a satirist but also as a trustworthy news source. Mercer, however, was quick to define his role as more like that of an editorial cartoonist, except when performing his rant, the rapid-fire monologue he originated on *This Hour*.

In a typical rant on *The Rick Mercer Report* (renamed when it switched broadcast nights), the teleprompterless Mercer frenetically prowled a graffiti-spattered alley, delivering heartfelt harangues to a back-peddling cameraman on everything from the state of the Liberal Party to bullying. Many of Mercer's rants were collected in his books *Streeters* (1998) and *The Rick Mercer Report: The Book* (2007). On his TV show Mercer also was featured traveling the country, reveling in all manner of Canadiana, from moose tagging to the Arctic Winter Games. Politics, however, remained his forte. Among his many offbeat encounters with politicians were famous interludes with prime ministers, including eating fast food with Jean Chrétien, instructing Paul Martin about window insulation, and being read a bedtime story by Stephen Harper.

(JEFF WALLENFELDT)

Milnor, John Willard

(b. Feb. 20, 1931, Orange, N.J.)
The much-honoured American mathematician John Milnor—winner of the Fields Medal (1962), the National Medal of Science (1966), and the Wolf Prize (1989)—was awarded the 2011 Abel Prize (which carries a $1 million cash award) by the Norwegian Academy of Science and Letters. He was cited "for pioneering discoveries in topology, geometry and algebra." In addition, he was the recipient in 2011 of the Leroy P. Steele Prize for Lifetime Achievement.

Milnor attended Princeton University (A.B., 1951; Ph.D., 1954), where he held an appointment from 1953 to 1967. Following several years at other institutions, he joined (1970) the faculty of the Institute for Advanced Study, Princeton, N.J. In 1989 he became director of the Institute for Mathematical Sciences at the State University of New York, Stony Brook.

Milnor's work was part of a revival of interest in a geometric approach to topology in the 1950s. Early in the 20th century, the field had been highly geometric, but in the 1930s and '40s, algebraic approaches dominated research. In particular, Milnor's discovery in 1956 of the 28 differentiable structures for the seven-dimensional sphere, S^7, was instrumental in the development of the new field of differential topology. Milnor dubbed these differentiable structures "exotic spheres." Then, in 1963, in

Abel Prize-winning mathematician John Willard Milnor

Grott Vegard—EPA/Landov

collaboration with French mathematician Michel Kervaire, he calculated the number of exotic spheres for dimensions greater than 4.

Additionally, Milnor contributed to algebraic geometry on singular points of complex hypersurfaces, and in 1961 he showed that the *Hauptvermutung* (German: "main conjecture"), a principal conjecture in the theory of manifolds concerning triangulations of *n*-dimensional manifolds, which had been an open question since 1908, is not true for complexes in dimensions greater than 3. In the 1970s he began working on complex dynamics.

Milnor was noted as an influential teacher, particularly through his books regarding the Morse theory and the *h*-cobordism theorem, which were universally seen as models of mathematical exposition. His publications include *Differential Topology* (1958), *Morse Theory* (1963), *Topology from the Differentiable Viewpoint* (1965), and *Dynamics in One Complex Variable* (1999). His *Collected Papers* were published in five volumes from 1994 to 2010.

(ERIK GREGERSEN)

Mischel, Walter

(b. Feb. 22, 1930, Vienna, Austria)

In 2011 American psychologist Walter Mischel won the University of Louisville Grawemeyer Award for Psychology for his work on delayed gratification, self-control, and willpower. Mischel was best known for his groundbreaking study on delayed gratification known as the "marshmallow test."

Following the Nazi occupation of Vienna (1938), he and his family immigrated to the United States, settling in 1940 in Brooklyn, N.Y. Mischel's parents opened a five-and-dime shop, for which he made deliveries while maintaining various part-time jobs. He was valedictorian of his high-school class and received a scholarship to New York University.

Although he initially enrolled in premedical course work, Mischel redirected his focus toward psychology and earned a bachelor's degree in 1951. Specializing in clinical psychology, he earned a master's degree from the City College of New York (1953) and a Ph.D. from Ohio State University (1956). He thereafter held professorships at the University of Colorado (1956–58), Harvard University (1958–62), and Stanford University (1962–83).

In the late 1960s Mischel began a study on delayed gratification—the ability to abstain from instant but less-desirable outcomes in favour of deferred but more-desirable outcomes. The experimenter seated preschool-age children alone at a table with a desired treat such as a marshmallow and, before exiting the room, presented them with a choice: either (1) to ring a bell to call the researcher back and, upon his return, consume the single marshmallow or (2) to wait until the researcher's voluntary return and be rewarded with not one but two marshmallows. While some children were unable to wait a full minute ("low delayers"), others were able to wait up to 20 ("high delayers") by employing various distraction techniques (e.g., covering their eyes with their hands, singing, and turning around in their chairs) to avoid looking at the tempting object.

Upon repeating the test, Mischel advised the children to think of the treats as something inedible (e.g., cotton balls), which dramatically improved impulse control. Follow-up studies, conducted later in life via self-report, further showed that high delayers achieved greater academic success (e.g., higher standardized test scores), better health (e.g., resistance to substance abuse), and more-positive relationships (e.g., lower rates of marital separation and divorce). This breakthrough research demonstrated not only that willpower can be learned but also that it seems to be "a protective buffer against the development of all kinds of vulnerabilities later in life," as Mischel concluded, thereby implying that self-control is key to both academic and personal success.

In 1983 Mischel became a professor at Columbia University, New York City. He was elected to the American Academy of Arts and Sciences (1991) and the National Academy of Sciences (2004). Mischel served as editor of the *Psychological Review* (2000–03) and president of the Association for Psychological Science (2008–09).

(JEANNETTE L. NOLEN)

Murdoch, James

(b. Dec. 13, 1972, London, Eng.)

A sudden and public media storm battered executive James Murdoch in July 2011 when news of a phone-hacking scandal involving a newspaper owned by his family emerged. At the beginning of the month, he oversaw the publication of *News of the World*, one of the largest-circulation newspapers in the English-speaking world, was on the verge of completing a multibillion-dollar media takeover, and could look forward to taking the helm of U.S.-based News Corp., the global television and newspaper empire founded by his father, Rupert Murdoch. By the end of the month, however, the paper had closed down, the takeover had been abandoned, and the Murdoch family was in turmoil.

Facundo Arrizabalaga—EPA/Landov

News Corp. executive James Murdoch

James Rupert Jacob Murdoch was the fourth of Rupert Murdoch's six children. He attended Harvard University but dropped out in 1995 to develop a record label, Rawkus Records. He joined News Corp. when it bought Rawkus the following year. In the years that followed, he was one of three Murdoch children who were given responsibility for building parts of the group.

In 2000 the younger Murdoch was appointed CEO of Star Television, an Asian satellite service. He revived its fortunes by investing heavily in India. Three years later he became CEO of British Sky Broadcasting (BSkyB), a multinational satellite TV company in which News Corp. held a 39% stake, and he quickly overcame accusations of inexperience and nepotism to build its revenue base and profitability in Britain, Italy, and Germany. In 2007 Murdoch became nonexecutive chairman of BSkyB and chairman of News Corp. subsidiary News International (NI) when his father gave him wider responsibility for developing media business across Europe, Asia, and the Middle East.

At the start of July 2011, Murdoch was within days of consolidating his position as his father's heir-apparent; official British approval was expected for a bid by News Corp. to increase its stake in BSkyB to 100%. Then, on July 4, news emerged that a decade earlier *News of the World*, a Sunday newspaper owned by NI, had been involved in extensive phone hacking. Within days the police revealed that some thousands of phones had been targeted by, or on behalf of, *News of the World*, and the scandal mushroomed.

Murdoch insisted throughout, most notably when he gave evidence on July 19 to a committee of British MPs, that he had devoted his efforts to cleaning up NI. He had not been involved in the company when the hacking occurred and had ordered full cooperation with the police. He rejected claims that he had known in 2008 that hacking was widespread and was therefore involved in covering up the scandal for three years. On July 28 the board of BSkyB voted unanimously to confirm him as chairman of the company.

In November the MPs who had questioned Murdoch (and his father) recalled him for further questioning. The younger Murdoch still denied any past knowledge of the events in question. His long-term future, however, remained in doubt. (PETER KELLNER)

Musk, Elon

(b. June 28, 1971, Pretoria, S.Af.)

In 2011 entrepreneur Elon Musk, the CEO of Space Explorations Technologies (SpaceX), realized a few longtime dreams associated with his fascination with rocketry. In December NASA confirmed that in early 2012 SpaceX's Dragon spacecraft would become the first privately developed spacecraft to resupply the International Space Station, filling the void created when in July NASA decommissioned the space shuttles that had previously handled these flights. In addition, he shook up the commercial spaceflight industry when he announced in April that SpaceX would develop a new heavy-lift rocket, the Falcon Heavy, that would carry 53,000 kg (117,000 lb) to orbit, nearly twice the load of the Delta IV Heavy produced by the Boeing Co. (SpaceX's largest competitor) and for about one-third of the cost. Musk also declared that SpaceX had plans to develop the first fully reusable rocket.

Musk was born to a South African father and a Canadian mother. He displayed an early talent for computers and entrepreneurship. At age 12 he created a video game and sold it to a computer magazine. In 1988, after obtaining a Canadian passport, Musk left South Africa because he was unwilling to support apartheid through compulsory military service and because he sought the greater economic opportunities available in North America, particularly the U.S.

Chris Pizzello/AP

SpaceX CEO and electric car promoter Elon Musk

Musk attended Queen's University, Kingston, Ont., and in 1992 he transferred to the University of Pennsylvania, where in 1995 he received bachelor's degrees in physics and economics. Soon afterward, he left graduate school at Stanford University after only two days because he felt that the Internet had greater potential to change society than did physics, the subject he had intended to pursue. He founded (1995) Zip2, a company that provided maps and business directories to online newspapers, but four years later he sold it to computer manufacturer Compaq for $307 million. Musk founded (1999) the online financial services company X.com, which later became PayPal, a service specializing in transferring money online. The online auction site eBay purchased PayPal in 2002 for $1.5 billion.

Musk was long convinced that for life to survive, humanity had to become a multiplanet species. He was dissatisfied, however, with the staggering expense associated with building rockets. In 2002 he founded SpaceX to produce less-expensive rockets. The company's first two rockets were the Falcon 1 and the larger Falcon 9. In addition to serving as CEO of SpaceX, Musk was also the chief engineer responsible for the design of the Falcon rockets and the Dragon spacecraft.

Another Musk interest—in the possibilities of electric cars—led him in 2004 to become one of the major funders of Tesla Motors, which in 2006 introduced its first electric car. The Roadster sports car, which could travel 394 km (245 mi) on a single charge and could accelerate from 0 to 97 km/hr (60 mph) in less than four seconds, was nonetheless shelved in 2011, when Tesla halted production to concentrate on its new Model S sport sedan. (ERIK GREGERSEN)

Muti, Riccardo

(b. July 28, 1941, Naples, Italy)

Though Italian maestro Riccardo Muti had a distressing first season as conductor with the Chicago Symphony Orchestra (CSO)—he was forced to cancel several appearances because of severe stomach pain, and in early 2011 he fainted during a rehearsal, fracturing several bones in his face when he fell from the podium. After having recovered, he returned to the podium with the CSO to great acclaim. In October Muti was the recipient of both the Birgit Nilsson Prize in Sweden and the Prince of Asturias Prize in Spain.

Italian conductor Riccardo Muti

Hiroyuki Ito—The New York Times/Redux

As a child, Muti studied piano at the Conservatory of San Pietro a Majella in Naples. Later he spent five years at the Giuseppe Verdi Conservatory of Milan, studying composition and conducting. Following a successful debut with the Italian Radio Symphony Orchestra in 1968, he appeared as a conductor with leading orchestras in Europe and the United States. He served as principal conductor of the Florence Maggio Musicale from 1969 to 1980, and in 1973 he succeeded Otto Klemperer as principal conductor of the New Philharmonia (after 1977, Philharmonia Orchestra) of London. He remained principal conductor and music director until 1982. In 1977 he became the principal guest conductor of the Philadelphia Orchestra, and he served as its music director from 1980 to 1992.

Muti became music director of La Scala in Milan in 1986; he left the position in April 2005 following widely reported disputes between the administration he had led and the theatre's artistic unions. After leaving La Scala, Muti maintained a steady schedule as a guest conductor with several of the world's leading orchestras, and in 2010 he took the baton as permanent music director of the CSO.

Muti led the first modern uncut performance of Gioachino Rossini's *William Tell* in Florence in 1972, and he championed lesser-known works by Verdi as well as operas by Giacomo Meyerbeer and Gaspare Spontini. He was respected as a conductor of a wide range of orchestral and choral works, including large-scale symphonic works from the 20th century. (EB ED.)

Nocera, Daniel

(b. July 3, 1957, Winchester, Mass.)
In 2011 chemist Daniel Nocera announced the invention of the first practical "artificial leaf," a silicon-based catalyst capable of separating hydrogen and oxygen from water in the presence of sunlight. The unveiling of the working prototype at the 2011 National Meeting of the American Chemical Society was thought to mark the beginning of a new revolution in inexpensive power generation.

Nocera received a B.S. in chemistry (1979) from Rutgers University, New Brunswick, N.J., and a Ph.D. in chemistry (1984) from Caltech. While Nocera worked at Caltech in the laboratory of inorganic chemist Harry Gray, he studied the transfer of electrons in inorganic systems and in biological systems such as proteins; these studies were later regarded as the first forays into the field of biological electron transfer.

Nocera taught chemistry at Michigan State University from 1984 and at MIT from 1997. In 2007 Nocera and his colleagues at MIT announced the development of a process that liberated hydrogen and oxygen molecules in a container of water by using a cobalt-based catalyst attached to an electrode made of indium and tin. They proposed that the liberated hydrogen could be captured and either stored in fuel cells to produce electricity or mixed with carbon dioxide to make hydrocarbon fuels. In addition, Nocera and his colleagues claimed that the process would allow for the development of a large-scale generation of distributed energy that would not require the operation of large electric-power facilities, since the catalytic devices could be attached to private residences everywhere. In 2008 Nocera founded Sun Catalytix, a company designed to deliver distributed energy to parts of the world where electricity is expensive to produce by using traditional technologies.

In 2011 Nocera announced the development of an artificial leaf (actually an electrode and a playing-card-sized wafer of silicon containing a catalyst made of nickel and cobalt) that was up to 10 times more efficient at carrying out photosynthesis than a plant leaf and much less costly to produce compared with earlier devices, which used expensive platinum or ruthenium catalysts. Nocera claimed that people could power their homes, automobiles, and other devices with fuel cells and hydrocarbon fuels generated by captured hydrogen gas, which would be released by passing the equivalent of a little less than four litres (about one gallon) of water per day over two roof-mounted door-sized catalysts bathed in sunlight.

Nocera became a member of the American Academy of Arts and Sciences in 2005. Among the numerous accolades he received was the United Nations Intergovernmental Renewable Energy Organization's Science and Technology Award in 2009 for his contributions to renewable-energy development.

(JOHN P. RAFFERTY)

Noda, Yoshihiko

(b. May 20, 1957, Funabashi, Chiba prefecture, Japan) On Aug. 30, 2011, Yoshihiko Noda was named prime minister of Japan, replacing Naoto Kan, who had been in office less than 15 months. Noda was the sixth prime minister in five years and the third since the Democratic Party of Japan (DPJ) came to power in 2009. He inherited a country still reeling from two major disasters in 2011—the massive earthquake and ensuing tsunami waves that struck and devastated northeastern Honshu on March 11 and the subsequent nuclear accident at a power plant in Fukushima prefecture caused by the earthquake and tsunami.

Noda was the son of a paratrooper with the Self-Defense Force (the Japanese military) and grew up in modest means in Chiba prefecture, just east of Tokyo. He graduated in 1980 from the School of Political Science and Economics of Waseda University in Tokyo and then attended the Matsushita School (now Matsushita Institute) of Government and Management in Chigasaki, Kanagawa prefecture, graduating in 1985. It was unusual for someone like Noda, who was not from the political elite, to attend both of those institutions, long known for grooming many of Japan's top leaders.

Noda was first elected to public office in 1987 as a member of the Chiba prefectural assembly, where he served for six years. In 1992 he joined the Japan New Party (which had been established that year by Morihiro Hosokawa), and the following year he won election to the House of Representatives (lower chamber) of the Diet (national parliament) from a district in Chiba prefecture. He lost his seat in 1996, but in 2000—as a member of the DPJ—he regained it, and he retained it in subsequent elections. For the next several years, he served in relatively important but low-profile positions in the legislature and in the DPJ, including heading up the party's public relations efforts.

In 2009, when the DPJ's Yukio Hatoyama was named prime minister, Noda became senior vice finance minister. In January 2010 Naoto Kan was named finance minister, and when Kan replaced Hatoyama as prime minister in June 2010, Noda succeeded Kan as finance minister. Following Kan's resignation from office and the party leadership on Aug. 26, 2011, Noda was elected DPJ president on August 29 and was confirmed by the Diet as prime minister the next day. He faced the daunting tasks of working with a divided legislature, in which the opposition Liberal-Democratic Party controlled the upper chamber; attempting to reconcile DPJ factions in the lower house—notably the faction of party strongman Ichiro Ozawa—that had become estranged over opposition to Kan's leadership; and reviving a long-moribund economy, especially in light of overseeing the ongoing massive recovery of the country from the twin disasters in northern Japan. (KENNETH PLETCHER)

Nowitzki, Dirk

(b. June 19, 1978, Würzburg, W.Ger. [now in Germany]) In June 2011 German professional basketball player Dirk Nowitzki silenced his detractors and powered the Dallas Mavericks (established in 1980) to their first NBA title, defeating the Miami Heat by four games to two in the best-of-seven finals. Despite tearing a tendon in one finger during game one and contending with a fever throughout game four, Nowitzki averaged 26 points per game (10.3 in the fourth quarter), earning finals MVP honours and his first championship ring. The achievement confirmed for many basketball fans that he was one of the greatest foreign-born players in NBA history.

Nowitzki, whose mother was a member of the West German national basketball team, took up the sport relatively late in life, at 13, but by age 16 he was playing with DJK Würzburg, a second-division German professional team. He first gained notice outside Germany when in 1998 he scored 33 points to lead a team of international players aged 19 and under to an upset victory over American high-school stars in an exhibition game in San Antonio, Texas. As a result, Nowitzki garnered dozens of American college scholarship offers, but he instead declared his eligibility for the 1998 NBA draft. He was selected by the Milwaukee Bucks, who immediately traded him to the Mavericks.

LM Otero/AP

NBA 2011 Finals MVP Dirk Nowitzki

Nowitzki struggled during his rookie season, but he doubled his scoring average in his second season and was chosen for the All-Star Game in his fourth. Standing 2.13 m (7 ft) tall, Nowitzki was much taller than most small forwards (his natural position), but he also possessed a keen shooting ability unusual for someone his size. Over the years his fadeaway jump shot proved to be one of the most effective signature scoring maneuvers in NBA history, and he became a perennial All-Star.

Meanwhile, the Mavericks had not qualified for the play-offs for eight straight seasons when Nowitzki joined the team in 1998, but in 2000–01 he helped Dallas win 53 games and advance to the postseason. That was the first of 11 consecutive 50-win seasons for the Mavericks. In 2005–06 he led Dallas to the team's first berth in the NBA finals (a six-game loss to the Heat), and in 2006–07 he averaged 24.6 points per game while guiding the team to the best record in the league, for which he earned the 2007 NBA MVP award. During the 2007 play-offs, however, the Mavericks became the first top seed to lose a best-of-seven opening-round series, and the team's postseason disappointments—combined with its poor performance in the 2006 finals—led some to question Nowitzki's ability to win clutch games. In 2011, however, he sparked a number of fourth-quarter comebacks during a remarkable postseason run that culminated in the Mavericks' triumphant NBA finals rematch against the Heat.

(ADAM AUGUSTYN)

Ouattara, Alassane

(b. Jan. 1, 1942, Dimbokro, Côte d'Ivoire, French West Africa) Alassane Ouattara, who had endured many setbacks in his quest to become president of Côte d'Ivoire, finally had his ambition realized when he took the oath of office on May 6, 2011. Though Ouattara had initially emerged as the winner of the November 2010 election, the Constitutional Council ruled that the incumbent, Laurent Gbagbo, was the victor by a narrow margin. A political standoff ensued when both men claimed the presidency: Gbagbo refused to step down, and Ouattara, with much international support, formed a parallel government. The standoff was not resolved until April 2011, when Gbagbo was arrested and removed from power. In May the Constitutional Council reversed its previous decision and recognized Ouattara as the winner of the election.

Alassane Dramane Ouattara was born to a Muslim family of the Dioula people. There were claims that at least one of his parents hailed from neighbouring Upper Volta (now Burkina Faso); this assertion would prove to be a contentious issue during his political career. Ouattara received his primary education in Côte d'Ivoire and his secondary education in Upper Volta. He then continued his studies in the U.S., earning a B.Sc. (1965) in business administration from Drexel Institute of Technology (now Drexel University), Philadelphia, and an M.A. (1967) and a Ph.D. (1972) in economics from the University of Pennsylvania.

Ouattara was employed at the IMF as an economist (1968–73), director of the African department (1984–88), and counselor to the managing director of the IMF (1987–88). From 1973 to 1984 he worked in various positions at the Central Bank of West African States (BCEAO), and he later served as its governor (1988–90).

While maintaining his position at the BCEAO, Ouattara was appointed (1990) by Ivorian Pres. Félix Houphouët-Boigny to chair a special commission on economic recovery. That November Ouattara also assumed the newly created post of prime minister. As the president's health deteriorated, Ouattara took on greater responsibility. Shortly after Houphouët-Boigny died in December 1993, Ouattara resigned. He left the country in 1994 and returned to the IMF for five years as deputy managing director.

Meanwhile, in 1995 Ouattara joined Côte d'Ivoire's nascent Rally of Republicans (RDR) and planned on running as the RDR candidate in the country's presidential election that year. He was prevented from doing so, however, because of recent changes stipulating that both parents of a candidate had to be of Ivorian birth and that the candidate must have resided continuously in Côte d'Ivoire for at least five years prior to the election. Similar restrictions barred him from the 2000 election. Gbagbo, who had become president in 2000, found himself under international pressure to address the electoral restrictions that seemed to specifically target Ouattara, and in 2005 he declared that Ouattara was eligible to stand in the next election. That election, however, was delayed until 2010 because of lingering issues stemming from the country's 2002–03 civil war.

Ironically, the 2010 election—which was intended to be a symbol of Ivorian reconciliation and unity—threatened to leave the country even more divided than it had been, as the contested results and the increasingly violent aftermath created many problems that persisted even after Gbagbo's arrest. As president, Ouattara was faced with restoring economic stability, alleviating the humanitarian crisis, and reunifying the country. (AMY MCKENNA)

Paisley, Brad
(b. Oct. 28, 1972, Glen Dale, W.Va.)
With *This Is Country Music* earning brisk sales and generally positive reviews upon its 2011 release, American singer-songwriter and guitarist Brad Paisley proved yet again that he was one of country music's most popular performers. Compared with his previous release, *American Saturday Night* (2009), the album was a rather conventional celebration of the genre and its values, although it was still replete with the kind of skillfully crafted and often wryly humorous songs for which he had become known. In April Paisley's popularity was confirmed when the Academy of Country Music named him Male Vocalist of the Year for the fifth consecutive time.

Brad Douglas Paisley was raised in a small town in West Virginia. At age eight he received a guitar from his grandfather, who had introduced him to country music, and he soon began performing in church and at local events. When he was 12, he was invited to appear on *Jamboree USA*, a live country-music program aired by a radio station in nearby Wheeling. For the next eight years, he polished his act as a regular on the show. In 1995 he earned a bachelor's degree in music business from Belmont University in Nashville.

Paisley worked as a songwriter in Nashville before releasing his debut record, *Who Needs Pictures* (1999). The album sold more than one million copies, fueled in part by the ballad "He Didn't Have to Be," an affectionate tribute to stepfathers that was Paisley's first number one hit on the *Billboard* country singles chart. That same year he made the first of dozens of appearances at Nashville's legendary Grand Ole Opry, into which he was inducted

Wade Payne/AP

Country music's five-time Male Vocalist of the Year Brad Paisley

in 2001. After being nominated for a Grammy Award for best new artist, Paisley returned with the album *Part II* (2001). The hit single "I'm Gonna Miss Her (The Fishin' Song)" established Paisley's reputation as a playfully witty lyricist, and guest spots by Buck Owens and George Jones highlighted his appreciation for traditional country music at a time when many country artists downplayed the genre's roots in a quest for crossover success.

With the release of such albums as *Mud on the Tires* (2003), *Time Well Wasted* (2005), and *5th Gear* (2007), Paisley's popularity steadily grew. His wide-ranging appeal was partially due to the diversity of material he recorded, from lighthearted novelties like "Alcohol" and "Ticks" to the elegiac "Whiskey Lullaby," a collaboration with bluegrass singer Alison Krauss. Furthermore, while Paisley remained devoted to traditional styles—gospel standards routinely appeared on his albums—his lyrics were at times strikingly contemporary, focusing on such subjects as reality TV and the Internet.

After the mostly instrumental album *Play* (2008), Paisley recorded *American Saturday Night*, which won critical plaudits for its casual embrace of attitudes not typically associated with country music. The title track, for instance, was a sly paean to multiculturalism, and on "Welcome to the Future," which Paisley claimed was inspired by the 2008 election of U.S. Pres. Barack Obama, he marveled at cultural and technological progress. (JOHN M. CUNNINGHAM)

Panetta, Leon
(b. June 28, 1938, Monterey, Calif.)
In 2011 Leon Panetta, who was serving as director of central intelligence, was tapped to succeed retiring Robert M. Gates as secretary of defense under Pres. Barack Obama. Panetta was unanimously confirmed by the Senate and assumed the post in July. A career politician, Panetta had also served in the U.S. House of Representatives (1977–93) and held office in the administrations of two other presidents: as director of the Office of Civil Rights (1969–70) under Pres. Richard M. Nixon and as director of the Office of Management and Budget (1993–94) and chief of staff (1994–97) under Pres. Bill Clinton.

Leon Edward Panetta's parents immigrated to the U.S. from Italy and settled in central California. Panetta grew up working in the family restaurant, and he later attended Santa Clara University, where he earned a bachelor's degree in political science in 1960 and a law degree in 1963. While at Santa Clara, he was a member of the Reserve Officers' Training Corps, and after graduation he served (1964–66) in the U.S. Army as a first lieutenant. Panetta's first political job came in 1966, when he moved to Washington, D.C., to serve as a legislative assistant to Republican Sen. Thomas Kuchel. In 1969 Panetta was appointed to his Office of Civil Rights post, where he oversaw the enforcement of federal laws relating to equal opportunities in education. He recounted his experiences there in the book *Bring Us Together* (1971). Panetta returned to California in 1971, and he practiced as a private attorney until his successful run for the U.S. House of Representatives in 1976. In Congress Panetta worked on financial and budgetary issues as well as public health reform. Clinton appointed him to head the Office of Management and Budget in 1993, and he was promoted to chief of staff the following year. As chief of staff, Panetta was credited with restructuring White House operations as well as brokering deals with congressional Republicans that enabled passage of federal budgets.

Panetta left government in 1997 and later that year, with his wife, established the nonprofit Leon & Sylvia

Panetta Institute for Public Policy at California State University's Monterey Bay campus. In 2006 he was selected to serve as a member of the bipartisan Iraq Study Group, a 10-member think tank created by Congress to assess the political, economic, and security issues in Iraq following the 2003 U.S.-led invasion. Obama appointed him to head the CIA in 2009, a move that surprised some, as Panetta had no direct intelligence background. His tenure was widely regarded as a successful one, however, and it was capped with the May 2011 mission that located and killed Osama bin Laden. As defense secretary, Panetta was quick to define his agenda. He asserted that the focus in the war in Afghanistan would be a shift to using commando raids to track down insurgents rather than a continuation of a troop-heavy counterinsurgency.

(MICHAEL RAY)

Parfit, Derek

(b. Dec. 11, 1942, Chengdu, China)

No philosophical work in generations had been more eagerly anticipated than the English philosopher Derek Parfit's massive *On What Matters*, which was finally published to great acclaim in 2011. The product of 15 years of writing, the two-volume tome addressed themes in normative ethics and metaethics, personal identity, and the theory of practical rationality. Its enthusiastic reception reflected Parfit's reputation among many of his peers as the most important moral philosopher of the 20th and early 21st centuries.

Both of Parfit's parents were medical doctors who moved from England to China to teach preventive medicine; they returned to England in 1943, one year after Parfit's birth. He attended Eton College before entering the University of Oxford in 1961 to study modern history (B.A. 1964). While he was at Columbia University, New York City, and Harvard University on a Harkness fellowship in 1964–67, his interests shifted to philosophy, and in 1967 he won a prize fellowship in philosophy at Oxford's All Souls College. He was a research fellow at All Souls from 1974 to 2010, when he became an emeritus fellow. He also held visiting professorships at several American universities, including Rutgers, New Brunswick, N.J.; New York University; and Harvard.

On What Matters was only Parfit's second book. The first, *Reasons and Persons*, had created a sensation upon its publication in 1984 for its originality, ingenious argument, immense fertility, and panoramic scope. Parfit argued that conventional philosophical notions regarding the nature of persons and their presumed identity over time are mistaken. He held (following David Hume) that there is no unique entity, a "self," that underlies the mental experiences and dispositions that may be attributed to a single individual at a given time. Nor is there any necessary connection between personal identity and personal survival, because it is possible to have the latter without the former (that is, it is possible for an individual to survive into a future time without being the same person as anyone existing at that time). Personal identity, therefore, "is not what matters."

The most important thesis of *On What Matters* is that the three main theoretical traditions in normative ethics—consequentialism, Kantianism, and contractualism (the idea that morality is based on a form of social contract)—are ultimately not in conflict with one another. Given certain independently justified improvements, they can be incorporated into a single view, which Parfit called the Triple Theory, that retains what is insightful about each and discards what is problematic. Parfit described that convergence by saying that the three traditions had been "climbing the same mountain on different sides." The upshot of the convergence thesis is that there is after all a single, objectively true morality. Other sections of the book defended sophisticated views of the nature of reasons and normativity that were presupposed by the Triple Theory.

(BRIAN DUIGNAN)

Perry, Katy

(b. Oct. 25, 1984, Santa Barbara, Calif.)

American singer Katy Perry, whose anthemic and often sexually suggestive hit songs had made her a steady feature of the pop-culture landscape, remained in the spotlight in 2011. In August "Last Friday Night (T.G.I.F.)" became the fifth single from her 2010 album *Teenage Dream* to top the *Billboard* Hot 100 chart, thus matching a record set by pop legend Michael Jackson. Later that month the video for her inspirational hit "Firework" won an MTV Video Music Award for video of the year. In addition, Perry made her big-screen acting debut that summer as the voice of the animated Smurfette in the film *The Smurfs*.

Katheryn Elizabeth Hudson was raised in southern California, the middle child of two itinerant born-again Christian ministers. Nonreligious music was forbidden in the Hudson household, and she grew up singing church hymns and gospel tunes. As a teenager she learned to play the guitar and sought a musical career in Nashville with a Christian record label, but her debut album, the gospel-influenced *Katy Hudson* (2001), sold poorly. By then, however, Hudson had found new musical models in such rock artists as Freddie Mercury and Alanis Morissette, whom she had discovered through friends. She soon moved to Los Angeles to pursue success in the secular music realm, adopting her mother's maiden name, Perry, to avoid confusion with the actress Kate Hudson.

Pop music sensation Katy Perry

Victor R. Caivano/AP

Perry's initial efforts at mainstream stardom were fruitless, with two separate record labels signing and subsequently dropping her before any material was released. In 2007, however, Capitol Records put out Perry's EP *Ur So Gay*, which attracted modest attention for its cheerfully flippant title track. She made a greater splash several months later with the single "I Kissed a Girl," an assertive ode to sexual curiosity backed by a hard-edged electro-pop beat. The song quickly stirred controversy; some critics derided it for promoting same-sex relations, and others charged that the racy scenario it depicted catered to male fantasies of female sexuality. Nevertheless, it became a number one hit in multiple countries, powering sales for her album *One of the Boys* (2008). With the bouncy sharp-tongued "Hot N Cold" also proving popular, the album—much of which Perry wrote herself—eventually sold more than one million copies in the U.S.

By late 2009 Perry had become frequent tabloid fodder, largely because of her playfully cartoonish sense of style and her high-profile relationship with English comedian Russell Brand. (The couple married in 2010 and filed for divorce at the end of 2011.) Her next studio album, *Teenage Dream*, which provided a broader showcase for her full-throated voice, was even more commercially successful than its predecessor, spawning such hits as the warm-weather frivolity "California Gurls." While critics often disparaged Perry's songs as vapid, the music industry was generally kinder, with *Teenage Dream* earning a Grammy nomination for album of the year.

(JOHN M. CUNNINGHAM)

Pilati, Stefano

(b. Dec. 10, 1965, Milan, Italy)

Nearly every year since he succeeded (2004) creative director Tom Ford at the storied fashion house Yves Saint Laurent (YSL), Italian designer Stefano Pilati had been the subject of rumours foretelling his imminent forced departure, and 2011 was no exception. Rather than continue to ignore the headline-grabbing prognostications, however, Pilati rebuffed the allegations and vowed to continue at YSL, and his employers signaled their support by praising him during a financial-report meeting. His forward designs, including his tulip skirt and matador pants, had not only infused new life into the struggling brand but also increased profitability for YSL. Pilati had turned an annual loss of some $100 million in 2004 into a profit of about $15 million in 2011.

Yves Saint Laurent creative director Stefano Pilati

Christophe Ena/AP

As an unhappy youth pursuing a career as a land surveyor, Pilati found fulfillment in sketching clothing designs for his two sisters, gaining inspiration from their fashion magazines. At age 17 he became an apprentice to designer Nino Cerruti, and he later found employment at an Italian velvet manufacturer. From 1993 to 1995 he served as Giorgio Armani's menswear assistant before joining (1995) the Prada Group as the head of research and development. In 1998 Pilati was promoted to assistant designer for Miu Miu's men's and women's collections. He moved in 2000 to YSL (a subsidiary of Gucci, which was owned by conglomerate PPR) as design director under Ford. Four years later, following Ford's failed contract negotiations, Pilati replaced him—with the blessing of Yves Saint Laurent himself—as creative director of YSL's ready-to-wear line, Rive Gauche.

In Pilati's first spring-summer collection in 2005, he led fashion's new direction, with his smart ruffled YSL minidress, suede stacked-heel loafers, and thigh-grazing bell-shaped "tulip bubble" skirts. Other signature items included his cloche-shaped jackets, Muse handbag (2005), and Muse II bag (2008). Pilati managed to maintain the classic YSL sleek designs but also moved the brand forward to a more modern viewpoint. Even after Saint Laurent's death in 2008, Pilati continued to create his own aesthetic while remaining grounded in Saint Laurent's previous work. Pilati often brainstormed his own designs and then combed the YSL vaults searching for samples of Saint Laurent's work that would validate his own choices.

In 2011 Pilati, who in 2008 had unveiled his design for a YSL chic boutique, opened a retail store at Crystals at City Center in Las Vegas; it was the third establishment to embrace his design. Pilati's environmentally friendly space, which he called "the opium experience," featured reddish amber lacquer applied to the ceiling and wall panels. The rich hue was reminiscent of the shade used in the packaging of YSL's perfume Opium. Pilati had hopes that the iconic and timeless boutique design would eventually signify the brand without the necessity for a sign. (KAREN SPARKS)

Pistorius, Oscar

(b. Nov. 22, 1986, Johannesburg, S.Af.)

Track and field sprinter Oscar Pistorius, a bilateral below-the-knee amputee, won a silver medal for his contribution to South Africa's 4 × 400-m relay team at the 2011 IAAF world championships, becoming the first Paralympian to achieve podium-level distinction in open competition. He was nicknamed "Blade Runner" for the carbon-fibre prostheses on which he began breaking International Paralympic Committee world records in 2004. Pistorius ran a split of 45.58 sec for the South African foursome in the world championship heats, helping his team advance to the final, and although he did not run in the relay final, he shared the team's silver medal. He also qualified for the 400-m event with a personal best of 45.07 sec, run in July, and at the world championships he reached the semifinals.

Pistorius was born without a fibula bone in either of his lower legs. His legs were amputated below the knee when he was 11 months old, and six months after that he learned to walk on fibreglass pegs. His parents, the owners of a zinc-mining business, encouraged him to participate in sports. He played water polo and rugby in secondary school until he injured a knee in 2003 playing rugby.

Pistorius began track training to rehabilitate that knee, and under the watchful eye of his coach, Ampie Louw, he improved rapidly. After obtaining his first carbon-fibre prostheses in June 2004, Pistorius won the 200-m event at the Athens Paralympic Games and claimed a bronze medal in the 100 m. At an elite invitational competition held in Rome in July 2007, Pistorius first competed internationally against able-bodied athletes, improving his 400-m best time to 46.90 sec.

The IAAF, astounded by Pistorius's performances, asked him to participate in a series of tests by German biomechanist Peter Brüggemann in November 2007. Brüggemann concluded that Pistorius's high-tech prosthetic legs imparted an unfair advantage, enabling him to expend less energy than able-bodied athletes running at the same speed. The IAAF Council then banned him from able-bodied competition. A

Alik Keplicz/AP

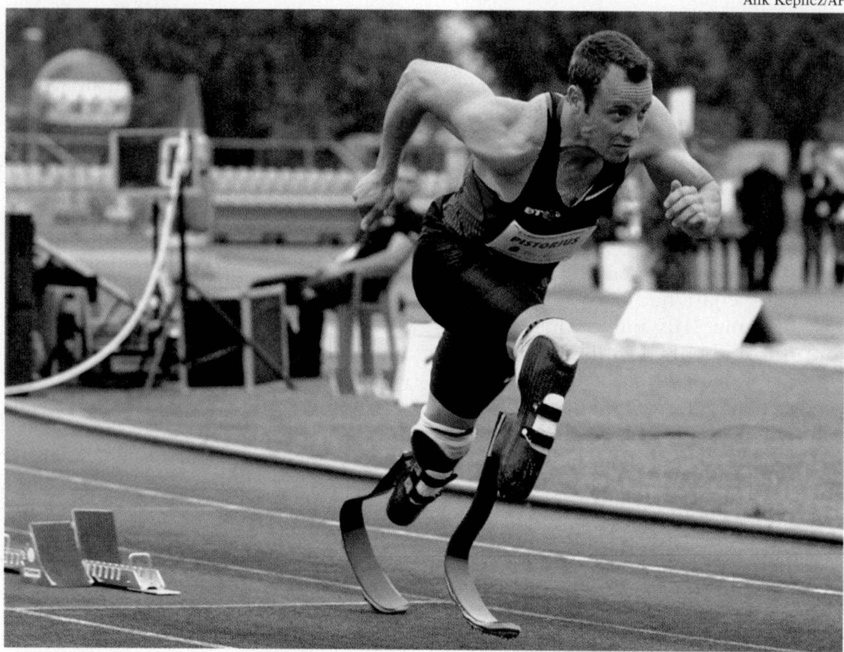

"Blade Runner" Oscar Pistorius

Court of Arbitration for Sport (CAS) appeals panel in May 2008 revoked the ban. Later that summer Pistorius won three gold medals at the Beijing Paralympics—the T43/T44 class 100 m, 200 m, and 400 m—and set a world record in his class.

Head injuries that he sustained in a boating accident in 2009 set him back throughout 2010, but he rebounded in 2011 to win gold in the 100 m and 400 m at the Paralympic World Cup before qualifying for the world championships. As the 22nd fastest 400-m runner in the world in 2011, Pistorius qualified for the 2012 London Olympics, but in order to be selected for the South African team, he would need to better 45.30 sec during the first half of the Olympic year. (SIEG LINDSTROM)

Portman, Natalie

(b. June 9, 1981, Jerusalem)

After winning the 2011 Academy Award, the Golden Globe Award, the Screen Actors Guild Award, and the BAFTA Award for best actress for her gripping portrayal of a disturbed ballerina in the thriller *Black Swan* (2010), Israeli American actress Natalie Portman took on some lighter roles in a series of 2011 box-office hits. She appeared as a scientist in the action fantasy *Thor*, a commitment-phobic doctor in *No Strings Attached*, and a warrior princess in the bawdy period comedy *Your Highness*.

Natalie Hershlag's family moved to the U.S. in 1984, and she later had a brief stint as a child model before turning to acting. She became known for the aristocratic poise and nuance with which she evinced the struggles of precocious young women. In her first film, *Léon* (1994; *The Professional*), she starred opposite French actor Jean Reno as an adolescent girl training to be an assassin after her parents have been murdered. Hershlag assumed her maternal grandmother's last name at this time in an effort to protect herself from unwanted attention as a result of the role, which had sexual overtones. She then appeared in Michael Mann's crime thriller *Heat* (1995) as a troubled teenager.

Portman worked steadily, accepting supporting roles in the relationship drama *Beautiful Girls* (1996), Woody Allen's musical *Everyone Says I Love You* (1996), and Tim Burton's alien-invasion comedy *Mars Attacks!* (1996) before appearing as the elaborately costumed Queen Amidala in the Star Wars prequel *Star Wars: Episode I—The Phantom Menace* (1999). Portman reprised the role in the film's two sequels (2002, 2005).

She starred as the resentful daughter to Susan Sarandon's flamboyant single mother in *Anywhere but Here* (1999) and as a homeless pregnant teen who gives birth in a Walmart store in *Where the Heart Is* (2000). In addition to acting, Portman attended Harvard University, graduating in 2003 with a bachelor's degree in psychology. In 2004 she won acclaim for the humanity she brought to both the romantic comedy *Garden State* and the Mike Nichols relationship drama *Closer*. The latter role earned her a Golden Globe for best supporting actress and an Academy Award nomination in the same category.

In later roles Portman continued to demonstrate the facility with which she could alternate between genres. She appeared as a shaved-headed revolutionary in the dystopian fantasy *V for Vendetta* (2006), a brassy high-stakes gambler in Wong Kar-wai's moody romance *My Blueberry Nights* (2007), and the doomed queen Anne Boleyn in *The Other Boleyn Girl* (2008). She played a grieving military spouse in *Brothers* (2009) and both directed and appeared in segments of *New York, I Love You* (2009), a compilation of short films. Portman portrayed a dowdy supermarket cashier in *Hesher* (2010).

(RICHARD PALLARDY)

Rajaratnam, Raj

(b. June 15, 1957, Colombo, Ceylon [now Sri Lanka]) In May 2011 American investor Raj Rajaratnam was convicted of securities fraud and conspiracy in one of the largest prosecutions of insider trading (trading on information not available to the public) in U.S. history. It was also the first such case to rely on evidence obtained from wiretaps, a tactic frequently employed against drug dealers and mobsters. As manager of the Galleon Group, a multibillion-dollar hedge fund (a limited-

Convicted hedge-fund founder Raj Rajaratnam

Mary Altaffer/AP

membership investment fund that uses speculative strategies to maximize returns), Rajaratnam had been at the time of his indictment (in 2009) one of the most prominent and successful investors on Wall Street.

After attending preparatory school in Sri Lanka, Rajaratnam went to England to study engineering at the University of Sussex. He entered the Wharton School at the University of Pennsylvania in 1981 and received a master's degree in business administration two years later. From 1983 to 1985 he worked for Chase Manhattan Bank as a lending officer specializing in technology companies. He became an analyst at the investment bank Needham & Co. in 1985 and rose to the presidency of the firm in 1991. The following year he established a hedge fund for Needham clients, which he later purchased with a group of investors when he left Needham in 1997. He renamed the fund the Galleon Group, after the early modern sailing ships used by the Spanish and the Portuguese to transport precious cargo.

Rajaratnam's investment strategy relied on exhaustive research and hundreds of contacts in high-tech industries and on Wall Street, many of whom belonged to informal social networks of South Asian executives, consultants, and traders. Under his leadership Galleon grew spectacularly through 2008, when it controlled approximately $7 billion in assets. Rajaratnam eventually became one of the 400 wealthiest persons in the United States, according to *Forbes* business magazine. He also became known for his philanthropic activities, which included establishing a charity to support Sri Lankan victims of the Indian Ocean tsunami of 2004 and funding AIDS programs in India.

The case against Rajaratnam involved 25 other defendants, 21 of whom pleaded guilty. During his trial prosecutors played recordings of phone conversations in which Rajaratnam received or discussed inside information or provided advice on how to disguise or cover up stock trades based on inside tips. The government charged that through his use of inside information, Rajaratnam had gained or avoided losing more than $63 million. The jury found him guilty on all counts, including nine counts of securities fraud and five counts of conspiracy, and he was fined and sentenced to 11 years in federal prison. The case was expected to result in the wider use of wiretaps in investigations involving white-collar crime.

(BRIAN DUIGNAN)

Rapace, Noomi

(b. Dec. 28, 1979, Hudiksvall, Swed.) The release in December 2011 of Swedish actress Noomi Rapace's first English-language film, *Sherlock Holmes: A Game of Shadows*, delighted American moviegoers who thus discovered for themselves what Swedish theatre and film lovers already knew: that Rapace was a compelling and meticulous actress. She had burst onto the world scene two years earlier with her masterful portrayal of the damaged but resilient hacker-turned-sleuth Lisbeth Salander in the Swedish films based on Swedish author Steig Larsson's Millennium trilogy of crime novels. The role garnered her a slew of film award nominations, including one from the 2011 British Academy of Film and Television Awards (BAFTA) for leading actress and one from the 2009 European Film Awards for best actress, both for the first film in the trilogy, *Män som hatar kvinnor* (2009; *The Girl with the Dragon Tattoo*). She went on to win both the 2011 Empire Award (U.K.) and the Swedish Film Institute's 2010 Guldbagge Award for the same motion picture.

Noomi Norén was the daughter of a Swedish actress and a Spanish flamenco singer. As a young child she lived with her mother and stepfather in Iceland, where her first acting experience was a small nonspeaking part in the film *Í skugga hrafnsins* (1988; *Shadow of the Raven*). When she was 15, she returned on her own to Sweden and studied theatre. She worked regularly on the stage, in art-house films, and on television, notably in several episodes (1996–97) of the long-running TV serial *Tre kronor*. In 2001 she married the actor Ola Rapace, who later costarred with her in *Svinalängorna* (2010; *Beyond*), in which she portrayed a woman who must come to terms with her past as the abused daughter of alcoholic parents. Notable among Rapace's other movies was the Danish picture *Daisy Diamond* (2007), in which she starred as an aspiring actress and single mother whose life spirals downward.

In 2007 Rapace was interviewed by director Niels Arden Oplev for the role of Salander. The actress was already familiar with the best-selling books on which the films were to be based, and she convinced Oplev that she could transform herself into the extraordinary character. Rapace got piercings (though not Salander's famous tattoos), trained for several months in kickboxing and other martial arts, and learned to ride a motorcycle. The three movies—*The Girl with the Dragon Tattoo*, which was directed by Oplev, *Flickan som lekte med elden* (*The Girl Who Played with Fire*), and *Luftslottet som sprängdes* (*The Girl Who Kicked the Hornet's Nest*), which were both directed by Daniel Alfredson—were filmed back to back. Rapace's success in embodying and expressing the inner life of a complex character who maintains a deliberately opaque facade delighted critics and fans alike and catapulted the actress to international fame. (PATRICIA BAUER)

Rihanna

(b. Feb. 20, 1988, St. Michael parish, Barbados) In 2011 Barbadian singer Rihanna, whose distinctive voice and fashionable appearance had made her a worldwide star, maintained her status as one of the reigning queens of pop and rhythm and blues (R&B). In February she earned a Grammy Award for a song from her 2010 album *Loud*. Two months later the album's sexually provocative single "S&M" became her 10th number one *Billboard* hit—which made her, at age 23, the youngest artist ever to reach that milestone. Not content to rest on her laurels, Rihanna in November released a new album, *Talk That Talk*, which produced yet another number one, the exuberant "We Found Love."

Robyn Rihanna Fenty grew up in Barbados with a Barbadian father and a Guyanese mother. As a child she enjoyed both Caribbean and American pop music, and in high school she won a talent show with a rendition of a Mariah Carey song. About the same time, she and two friends started a girl group, which in 2004 attracted the attention of Evan Rogers, an American record producer. For her professional career she adopted her middle name, and with Rogers's help she was signed by rapper Jay-Z to his record label Def Jam.

With the effervescent dancehall-inflected single "Pon de Replay" (2005), Rihanna immediately captured an international audience. The song's success buoyed sales for her debut full-length recording, *Music of the Sun* (2005), on which conventional R&B ballads shared space with Caribbean-flavoured dance-pop that showcased her melodious Barbadian lilt. Rihanna soon followed with the album *A Girl like Me* (2006), with the up-tempo club-oriented "S.O.S." becoming her first song to top the *Billboard* singles chart.

For *Good Girl Gone Bad* (2007), Rihanna sought to transform her youthful image. With the assistance of such high-profile collaborators as Timbaland

Fred R. Conrad—The New York Times/Redux

Pop diva Rihanna

and Justin Timberlake, she abandoned the tropical rhythms that had distinguished her first two albums and recorded a collection of sleek R&B that presented her as a fiercely independent and rebellious woman. The gambit paid off; the album sold several million copies worldwide, and its anthemic lead single, "Umbrella," featuring an introductory rap from Jay-Z, became one of the year's biggest hits.

In early 2009 Rihanna was beaten by her boyfriend, fellow R&B star Chris Brown, in an incident that was widely covered by tabloid news and gossip blogs. The album that followed later that year, *Rated R*, much of which she co-wrote, was marked by icily stark production and brooding lyrics that touched on revenge. Although her sales declined somewhat, she scored another major hit with "Rude Boy." With *Loud* she returned to less-portentous fare. Throughout her career Rihanna also collaborated with such hip-hop artists as T.I. and Eminem; many felt that her vocals on the latter's "Love the Way You Lie" (2010) lent resonance to the song's depiction of an abusive relationship.

(JOHN M. CUNNINGHAM)

Rinehart, Georgina

(b. Feb. 9, 1954, Perth, W.Aus., Australia) In February 2011 *Forbes* magazine identified mining executive Georgina (Gina) Rinehart as Australia's richest person, estimating her wealth at $9 billion; this was the first time a woman had held that position. It was a massive increase in net worth for the business executive and political activist who had first appeared on the *Forbes* list in 2007, when she became Australia's first female billionaire, and whose wealth estimate in 2010 was barely $2 billion. Rinehart built her fortune as the head of Hancock Prospecting, the privately held Western Australian mining company started by her father, as she increased its holdings and influence in the Australian iron-ore market in the two decades following his death in 1992.

Georgina Hope Hancock was the only child of Langley (Lang) George Hancock, a Western Australian pastoralist who became a mining magnate. She was educated at St. Hilda's Anglican School for Girls in Mosman Park, a suburb of Perth, and briefly studied economics at the University of Sydney. In 1973 she became her father's personal assistant at Hancock Prospecting, which had its origins in his 1952 discovery of previously unsuspected iron-rich soils in the Hamersley Range, in Western Australia's Pilbara region.

After her father's death, Rinehart (by then widowed by her second husband, American attorney Frank Rinehart) took ownership of Hancock Prospecting and became its chief executive. The business was in poor shape, however, as it carried a significant amount of debt. She kept tight control over the company's operations and built a new iron mine in the Pilbara. Under Rinehart's direction Hancock grew into one of Australia's largest exporters of iron ore, a multibillion-dollar empire that encompassed domestic and international joint ventures as well as prospecting and exploration projects for other minerals, especially coal. She diversified her holdings in the early 21st century with the purchase of shares in media companies, including Australia's Fairfax Media and Ten Network Holdings.

Although Rinehart kept a low public profile and rarely spoke to the media, she made a number of public statements on government policy issues, warning especially against excessive regulation and taxation in the resource sector, which she said would be damaging to the country's economic growth. In 2010 she came out forcefully against the federal government's proposed Resource Super Profits Tax aimed at the mining industry.

In 2011 *Forbes* also named Rinehart the 19th most powerful woman in the world, ahead of Australian Prime Minister Julia Gillard. In addition, Rinehart was inducted during the year into the WA (Western Australia) Women's Hall of Fame.

(LORRAINE MURRAY)

Rodgers, Aaron

(b. Dec. 2, 1983, Chico, Calif.)
In only his third season as the starting quarterback for the Green Bay Packers of the NFL, Aaron Rodgers led the team on Feb. 6, 2011, to a 31–25 victory over the Pittsburgh Steelers in Super Bowl XLV. Against the Steelers' top-ranked defense, Rodgers was masterful, completing 24 of 39 pass attempts for 304 yd and three touchdowns with no interceptions. He was only the fourth quarterback in Super Bowl history to eclipse the 300-yd passing mark and throw at least three touchdowns. The win gave the Packers their fourth Super Bowl title, and Rodgers was selected as the game's MVP.

Though Rodgers was a star quarterback at Pleasant Valley High School in Chico, he was not heavily recruited by college football teams. He played for a year at Butte College, a community college in nearby Oroville, before transferring in 2003 to the University of California, Berkeley. He soon took over as the starting quarterback for the school's Golden Bears, and in 2004 he guided the team to a 10–2 record and a number nine ranking in the season's final Associated Press poll. Rodgers was named first-team All-Pacific-10 Conference and was chosen by the Packers in the first round of the 2005 NFL draft. He then began a long apprenticeship as the team's backup quarterback behind starter Brett Favre. In his first three seasons (2005–07) in the league, Rodgers saw only limited action, appearing in just seven games.

That changed suddenly when in 2008 Favre—after a bitter falling-out with team management—was traded to the New York Jets before the start of the season, and the Packers' offense was handed over to Rodgers. He quickly proved himself to be an able replacement for Favre, passing that season for 4,038 yd and 28 touchdowns. Rodgers was awarded a six-year, $65 million contract extension, and in 2009 his stellar passing continued as he threw for 4,434 yd and 30 touchdowns. He thus became the only NFL player ever to post consecutive 4,000-yd passing campaigns in his first two years as a starter. He also recorded a 103.2 passer rating in 2009, second best in franchise history, behind Bart Starr's 1966 mark of 105.0, and was selected to play in the Pro Bowl.

Jeff Haynes—Reuters/Landov

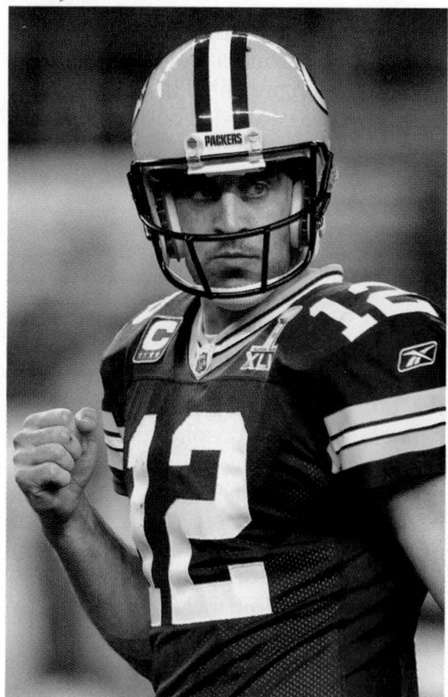

Super Bowl-winning Green Bay Packers quarterback Aaron Rodgers

In 2010 Rodgers led the Packers to a 10–6 regular-season record and a berth in the play-offs as the sixth-seeded team in the NFC. He then helped the team notch road victories over the top three seeds in the NFC—the Philadelphia Eagles, the Atlanta Falcons, and the Chicago Bears—to secure a spot in the Super Bowl. At the conclusion of the season, Rodgers's career passer rating stood at 98.4, the highest in NFL history for quarterbacks with at least 1,500 attempts. In the 2011 season Rodgers guided Green Bay to a league-best 15–1 record, but in a stunning upset the team lost its first play-off game to the 9–7 New York Giants. At season's end Rodgers had passed for 4,643 yd and set a new NFL single-season record with a quarterback rating of 122.5.

(SHERMAN HOLLAR)

Rylance, Mark

(b. Jan. 18, 1960, Ashford, Kent, Eng.)

In June 2011 British theatre actor Mark Rylance won the Tony Award for best actor for his astonishing turn as Johnny ("Rooster") Byron in *Jerusalem*, a role that had already earned him an Olivier Award in London. Instead of giving a conventional speech rattling off the standard inventory of individuals to whom he felt indebted, however, he recited a prose poem by American poet Louis Jenkins. (He had recited another Jenkins poem in 2008 when he won the Tony for *Boeing-Boeing*.) Rylance later gave away the Tony to the rural English builder who, he said, had inspired his performance.

Although he was a British citizen, David Mark Rylance Waters grew up in the U.S. His family lived in Connecticut before moving (1969) to Wisconsin, where he became involved with acting at the University School of Milwaukee. At age 16 he participated in that secondary school's Shakespeare festival, playing the title role in *Hamlet*. Later, at another local Shakespeare celebration, he was praised for his performance as Puck in *A Midsummer Night's Dream*.

After graduating in 1978, Rylance studied at the Royal Academy of Dramatic Art in London. He then joined (1980) the Citizens Theatre in Glasgow, Scot. In the early 1980s Rylance appeared with the Royal Shakespeare Company (RSC), based in Stratford-upon-Avon. Among the most memorable of his RSC performances were his interpretations of Romeo and Hamlet, both in 1989.

In the early '90s Rylance established a relationship with the Shakespeare-oriented Theatre for a New Audience in New York City. Just months after having won his first Olivier Award in 1994 for his portrayal of Benedick in Shakespeare's *Much Ado About Nothing*, Rylance was named the first artistic director of London's Globe Theatre (then under reconstruction), which opened in 1997. Under his directorship, the Globe re-created Shakespeare's era through the use of all-male casts and period-appropriate music, costumes, sets, and stage techniques. Obsessed with the historical accuracy of the productions, he played both male and female parts to great acclaim, and in 2002 he earned an Olivier nomination for his role as Olivia in *Twelfth Night*. After leaving the Globe in 2006, Rylance began to receive greater recognition for his non-Shakespearean roles, notably Robert in the French farce *Boeing-Boeing*, in which he made his Broadway debut (2007) and won his first Tony.

Rylance's films include the Shakespeare-based *Prospero's Books* (1991), *Angels and Insects* (1995), *Intimacy* (2001), and *The Other Boleyn Girl* (2008). His performance in the made-for-TV movie *The Government Inspector* (2005) won him a British Academy of Film and Television Award as best actor.

(VIRGINIA GORLINSKI)

Sangay, Lobsang

(b. 1968, Darjiling, India)

On Aug. 8, 2011, Lobsang Sangay was installed as *kalon tripa*, or prime minister, in the Tibetan Central Administration (government-in-exile). Sangay, a Harvard University legal scholar, exuded a youthful charisma and inspired confidence as he visited Tibetan exile communities in several countries, and his campaign style prompted comparisons to that of U.S. Pres. Barack Obama. Moreover, Sangay reassured exiles who had been uneasy about the prospect of having the first government-in-exile not administered by the 14th Dalai Lama, Tenzin Gyatso, who had declared in early March that he would devolve his role as head of state to the *kalon tripa*. Sangay promised that once he had been inaugurated, he would carry on the Dalai Lama's "middle way" of pursuing Tibetan autonomy within the People's Republic of China rather than seeking political independence from it. In the March 20 election (certified on April 27), Sangay won in a landslide and became both the first nonmonk and the first person born outside Tibet to be elected to the office.

Sangay was born in a refugee camp for Tibetan exiles. His father, a former Buddhist monk, kept livestock and managed to save enough funds to send his son to school. Sangay studied at the University of Delhi, earning a Bachelor of Laws degree; there he joined and soon became an executive with the Tibetan Youth Congress, a group of exiles advocating Tibetan independence. Upon graduation from Delhi in 1994, Sangay won a Fulbright scholarship to study in the United States at Harvard Law School, from which he earned (1996) a Master of Laws degree. He was awarded subsequent fellowships and contributed to reports on Tibetan issues for several nongovernmental organizations, including the International Commission of Jurists and the Pacific Basin Research Center. He then returned to Harvard, where he completed (2004) a Doctor of Juridical Science degree.

While a doctoral student, Sangay organized a conference of mainland Chinese and Tibetan scholars; the Dalai Lama, who at the time was both the spiritual and the political head of the Tibetan government-in-exile, also attended the event. Sangay remained at Harvard after graduation as a research fellow with the law school's East Asian legal studies program. In addition to performing research on human rights issues, Sangay testified on human rights abuses in Tibet before the U.S. Congress and, in 2009, organized a second conference of mainland Chinese and Tibetan scholars, again including the Dalai Lama, who also met with 100 Chinese scholars at Harvard University. Sangay also became prominent within the Tibetan Buddhist community in nearby Medford, Mass.

Sangay emerged as a surprise candidate when the election slate was chosen in 2009; however, after much personal campaigning, he garnered 55% of the more than 49,000 votes cast from among the approximately 83,000 Tibetan exiles who were eligible to vote. (MATT STEFON)

Sawa, Homare

(b. Sept. 6, 1978, Tokyo, Japan)
After 20 years at the top in women's association football (soccer) in Japan, 32-year-old Homare Sawa received her greatest accolade in 2011 as the inspirational captain leading Japan to victory in the FIFA Women's World Cup in Germany. It was Asia's first major honour in the sport, and the title lifted the spirits of her compatriots after the devastating earthquake and tsunami Japan had endured earlier in the year.

Sawa's brother taught her the basics of soccer. By the time she was 12, she was playing in Japan's first division, and at 15 she had an immediate impact on the national team, scoring four goals in a match against the Philippines. Although she was only 1.64 m (5 ft 4 in) and 55 kg (121 lb), Sawa was a tenacious tackling, fast-moving midfield player with attacking instincts and a healthy ratio of goals to her credit. (In 173 appearances for Japan, she scored 80 goals.) Well balanced and with abundant resources of stamina, despite her small stature, took physical knocks in her stride, and twice (1991, 1992) she won the fighting spirit award. In 1995 Sawa represented Japan in the first of her five consecutive World Cup appearances. She also played in three Olympic Games (1996, 2004, 2008).

Sawa's first club in Japan was Yomiuri Beleza, where she played for seven years and scored 79 goals in 136 matches. She moved to the U.S. and in 2001 joined the Women's United Soccer Association (WUSA) Atlanta Beat, scoring the franchise's first goal. When the WUSA folded in 2003, she returned to Japan and played for NTV Beleza, scoring 40 goals in 64 appearances. In 2004 she was Women's Player of the Year in Asia. The advent of the Women's Professional Soccer league in 2008 sent her back to the U.S. and the Washington Freedom until that team relocated to Florida in 2010. She went home to Japan to join INAC Kobe Leonessa.

After winning the gold medal at the 2010 Asian Games, Japan arrived at the World Cup ranked fourth. The team won its first two games, with Sawa scoring a hat trick against Mexico, but was unexpectedly beaten 2–0 by England. During the quarterfinal against Germany, Sawa was forced to help out on defense as the home team battered away at the Japanese goal. Success over Sweden in the semifinal clinched Japan's place in the final against the highly favoured U.S. Sawa was again at the fore of Japan's attacking strategy and scored the tying goal at 2–2 in overtime, cleverly flicking the ball with the outside of her boot from a corner kick. The Japanese then prevailed in the shoot-out 3–1. Sawa was awarded both the Golden Boot as the tournament's outstanding player and the Golden Ball as the top scorer, with five goals. (JACK ROLLIN)

Victorious FIFA World Cup Japanese team captain Homare Sawa celebrating a victory in 2008

Silvia Izquierdo/AP

Schiller, Daniela

(b. Oct. 26, 1972, Rishon LeZyyon, Israel) In 2011 Israeli-born cognitive neuroscientist Daniela Schiller utilized magnetic resonance imaging to scan the human brain during memory consolidation and reconsolidation in an effort to identify the neurological links between fear and memory. She was best known for her research in the area of memory reconsolidation, or the process of re-storing memories after they have been retrieved.

As a teenager Schiller spent a summer on a kibbutz (Israeli collective settlement). In 1991 she joined the Israeli army, serving in the entertainment and education division as a producer of shows for active-duty soldiers. She completed her service in 1993 and subsequently became a producer of concerts and lectures on art, history, and science for the general public while also serving as a drummer for the Israeli rock band the Rebellion Movement.

Schiller earned both a bachelor's degree in psychology and philosophy (1996) and a Ph.D. in cognitive neuroscience (2004) from Tel Aviv University. In 2004 she moved to the U.S. and began working as a postdoctoral fellow at New York University, where she led a groundbreaking study that focused on memory reconsolidation. The study participants were repeatedly exposed to a neutral visual stimulus paired with a mild electric shock—a technique known as Pavlovian conditioning, or classical conditioning—which eventually resulted in the subjects' experiencing fear after being exposed only to the visual stimulus. Schiller discovered, however, that she was able to alter that emotional response, replacing the emotion of fear through the presentation of new information during reconsolidation, when memories are relatively unstable and therefore malleable. By introducing nonfearful information (e.g., the absence of electric shock) to participants upon presentation of the stimulus and the subsequent reactivation of fearful memories—a process known as extinction training—the memory was reconsolidated in a way that was no longer associated with fear. This breakthrough discovery presented a noninvasive method of blocking fearful memories, potentially obviating the need for pharmacological interventions, which often produce a wide range of side effects. Her method potentially afforded both a safer and a less-costly means of treatment for a variety of psychological disorders, such as post-traumatic stress disorder.

Schiller's work was published in numerous scholarly journals, including *The Journal of Neuroscience* and the *Journal of Psychiatric Research*; she served as a contributing author for several books, such as *The Human Amygdala* (2009). Schiller was the recipient of multiple awards, including the New York Academy of Sciences Blavatnik Award for Young Scientists (2010) for her research on how to rewire the brain to eradicate fear as a response to memory. In 2010 she became a professor at the Mount Sinai School of Medicine in New York City, where she also directed the cognitive and affective neuroscience laboratory. In addition, Schiller performed as a drummer for the Amygdaloids, a rock band composed of New York University professors.

(JEANNETTE L. NOLEN)

Shinawatra, Yingluck

(b. June 21, 1967, San Kamphaeng, Thai.) Few in Thailand would have imagined at the beginning of 2011 that prominent businesswoman Yingluck Shinawatra, the younger sister of former prime minister Thaksin Shinawatra, would herself become prime minister during the year—especially since she had never run for nor held public office. To the surprise of many, however, she accomplished just that; in August she became the first woman prime minister of Thailand.

Sakchai Lalit/AP

Thai Prime Minister Yingluck Shinawatra

Yingluck was the youngest of nine children born into a wealthy family of Chinese descent who had settled in the Chiang Mai area of northwestern Thailand in the early 20th century. Her father was a member of the parliament from the late 1960s to the mid-1970s, and her brother also served in the parliament and in various ministerial posts before becoming prime minister in 2001. Thaksin was ousted from office in a bloodless military coup in September 2006.

Yingluck graduated from Chiang Mai University in 1988 and then attended Kentucky State University, where she earned (1991) a master's degree in public administration. After returning to Thailand, she began working in her family's various business enterprises, gradually taking on more responsibilities. She married Thai businessman Anusorn Amornchat in 1995.

Yingluck was a top executive in Advanced Info Service (AIS), the telecommunications branch of the family's large holding company in 2006 when the parent company was sold to a Singapore-based conglomerate—a controversial transaction that netted the family a huge profit but was one of the factors leading to Thaksin's downfall later that year. Yingluck then became president of the family's real-estate business while her brother went into exile. Thaksin remained popular in Thailand, however, especially among rural people in the northern part of the country. His supporters became known as the "red shirts," while his opponents, mainly urban elites, were dubbed the "yellow shirts." Tensions between the two groups mounted, culminating in prolonged mass protests by the red shirts in the spring of 2010 in central Bangkok that eventually were forcibly suppressed by the Thai military.

After Thaksin was ousted from office, his political party was outlawed, and a successor to it, the For Thais Party (Phak Puea Thai; PPT), was formed in late 2008. Parliamentary elections were announced in early May 2011 for July 3, and Yingluck declared her candidacy for office shortly thereafter. Yingluck, seen as a fresh face in Thai politics and aided considerably by being Thaksin's sister, swept to victory at the polls, along with the PPT. Although the PPT gained a majority of seats in the parliament, the party formed a ruling coalition with several smaller parties. Yingluck, emerging as party leader, was elected prime minister by the parliament on August 5 and formally took office after she was endorsed in the post by King Bhumibol Adulyadej. (KENNETH PLETCHER)

Siddique, Teepu

(b. 1947?, Pakistan)

In 2011 Pakistani American neurologist Teepu Siddique reported the groundbreaking discovery of a group of genetic mutations common to all forms of the neurological disorder amyotrophic lateral sclerosis (ALS; or Lou Gehrig disease). The finding indicated that the different forms—sporadic, familial, and dementia-associated—share a common pathological mechanism, one that could be targeted in the development of new ALS drugs. The mutations were identified in a gene known as *UBQLN2*, which encodes a protein that normally facilitates cellular recycling of damaged proteins in neurons in the spinal cord and the cortex and hippocampus of the brain. Mutation of the gene, however, causes damaged proteins to amass within the neurons, a phenomenon that Siddique concluded leads to the development of ALS.

Siddique earned a medical degree (1973) from Dow Medical College in Karachi, Pak. He then moved to the United States, where he completed an internship (1976) at Perth Amboy General Hospital in New Jersey and a residency (1979) in neurology at the University of Medicine and Dentistry of New Jersey. Fellowships in 1980 and 1981 gave Siddique the opportunity to study at the Hospital for Special Surgery in New York City (a centre specializing in orthopedics and rheumatology) and at the National Institute of Neurological Diseases and Stroke in Bethesda, Md. He later served as a physician and researcher at the University of Southern California and then at Duke University. In 1991 he joined the faculty of Northwestern University's Feinberg School of Medicine in Chicago as a professor in the departments of neurology and cell and molecular biology; he later was appointed director of the university's division of neuromuscular medicine.

Siddique began studying ALS in the early 1980s and by the end of that decade had successfully applied techniques in molecular genetics to his investigations. These efforts led to his identification of chromosome 21 as the location of a primary gene defect causing ALS, a discovery he reported in 1991. Shortly thereafter, in a study of families affected by an inherited form of the disorder, Siddique and colleagues described nearly a dozen different ALS-linked mutations in a gene known as *SOD1*. This work led to his involvement in the creation of the first transgenic mouse model for ALS (a transgenic organism is one that has been genetically modified to carry DNA from another species).

Siddique later reported the discovery of ALS-associated mutations in a gene known as *FUS/TLS*, at which point he suspected that protein accumulation in motor neurons contributes to the neuronal dysfunction underlying the disorder. This suspicion was confirmed by the report published in 2011.

Siddique was the recipient in 1995 of the International Alliance of ALS/MND Associations Forbes Norris Award. He was the corecipient in 1996 of the American Academy of Neurology Sheila Essey Award. (KARA ROGERS)

Souto de Moura, Eduardo

(b. July 25, 1952, Porto, Port.)

Portuguese architect Eduardo Souto de Moura, who was commended for integrating the clean lines of minimalism with such nonminimal elements as colour and the use of local materials, in 2011 won the Pritzker Architecture Prize. The prize jury cited the "intelligence and seriousness" of his work and noted that his architecture "appears effortless, serene, and simple."

Eduardo Elísio Machado Souto de Moura attended the Porto Higher Institute of Fine Arts (Escola Superior de Belas Artes do Porto [ESBAP]; now part of the University of Porto), where he initially studied sculpture. By his own account, he changed his focus to architecture after meeting American minimalist artist Donald Judd. Souto de Moura worked briefly with architect Noé Dinis and then for five years (1975–79) with the firm of 1992 Pritzker Prize winner Álvaro Siza. The architect counted Siza and Ludwig Mies van der Rohe as his main influences. Although Souto de Moura established his own company in 1980, he and Siza enjoyed their collaboration and continued to work together on several projects. Beginning in 1980, Souto de Moura also taught architecture at his alma mater.

His first major commission was the Municipal Market in Braga, Port. (1980–84; remodeled by the architect in 1997–2001). In the following years he steadily engaged in building single-family houses, mostly in northern Portugal. An exhibition space called Cinema House (1998–2003)—with its base that suggests a shutter gauge and its two large hooded windows that suggest camera lenses—was designed for the Portuguese film director Manoel de Oliveira. Among Souto de Moura's many other projects in Portugal were the cultural centre Casa das Artes in Porto (1981–91); the conversion of a former Cistercian monastery into a state inn, the Pousada de Santa Maria do Bouro in Amares (1989–97); Braga Municipal Stadium (2000–03); the Paula Rego Museum in Cascais (Casa das Histórias Paula Rego, 2005–09), which houses the work of that Portuguese artist; and the Burgo Tower, an office complex in Porto (2007). He also designed many other structures, including a bridge, a wine cellar, golf resorts, exposition pavilions, and several more office buildings. Before receiving the Pritzker, Souto de Moura worked chiefly in Portugal, with the occasional excursion into such countries as Italy, Spain, Switzerland, and Belgium. (KATHLEEN KUIPER)

Paulo Duarte/AP

Portuguese Pritzker Prize-winning architect Eduardo Souto de Moura

Spalding, Esperanza

(b. Oct. 18, 1984, Portland, Ore.)

American jazz bassist and singer Esperanza Spalding pulled an unexpected upset at the 53rd annual Grammy Awards presentation on Feb. 13, 2011, when she received the award for best new artist, beating four other nominees, notably fan-favourite pop singer Justin Bieber. Although Spalding, the first jazz artist to win that award, was not yet a household name, at age 26 she was already a well-respected musician who had played three times for U.S. Pres. Barack Obama, including a performance at the 2009 Nobel Prize ceremony, where he received the Prize for Peace.

Spalding grew up in a multilingual, multiethnic household (her single mother was Welsh, Hispanic, and Native American, and her father was black). As a preschooler she watched cellist Yo-Yo Ma perform on the children's television show *Mister Rogers' Neighborhood*. She subsequently taught herself to play the violin, and by the time she was five, she had earned a place in the local community orchestra, the Chamber Music Society of Oregon. Spalding performed with the group for the next 10 years, along the way learning to play the upright bass, which soon became her favoured instrument, and branching into other forms of music, including blues, hip-hop, and funk. After dropping out of high school at age 16, she received a GED and attended Portland State University before transferring to the Berklee College of Music in Boston. From there she earned a bachelor's degree in music and, in 2005 at the age of 20, became the school's youngest teacher. That same year she won a Boston Jazz Society scholarship for outstanding musicianship.

Spalding's first album, *Junjo* (2006), showcased both her instrumental and her vocal talent. *Esperanza*, released two years later, demonstrated her ability to fuse jazz with such world music as Brazilian and Argentine folk music and featured lyrics in English, Spanish, and Portuguese. The album was not only critically acclaimed but also shot up the *Billboard* contemporary jazz chart, which it stayed on for more than 70 weeks. This success brought her greater exposure, and she appeared on several television interview shows. Spalding played at the White House twice in 2009 and regularly toured with her own band while also performing with such jazz musicians as saxophonist Joe Lovano and pianists McCoy Tyner and Herbie Hancock, as well as pop stars Prince and Stevie Wonder.

In 2010 Spalding released *Chamber Music Society*, on which she combined jazz, folk, and world music components with classical chamber music traditions. She also continued to collaborate with fellow artists, including music icon Quincy Jones and Brazilian guitarist Milton Nascimento. Although her Grammy Award was likely to make her music better known to a more general audience, Spalding was staying true to her roots, and her 2011 tour included gigs at the Montreal Jazz Festival in June and the Montreux (Switz.) Jazz Festival in July. (JOAN HIBLER)

Sunyaev, Rashid

(b. March 1, 1943, Tashkent, Uzbekistan, U.S.S.R. [now in Uzbekistan]) In June 2011 Russian-German astrophysicist Rashid Sunyaev was announced as the winner of the Inamori Foundation's Kyoto Prize for Basic Sciences for his achievements in high-energy astronomy and the study of the early universe. The award was yet another accolade for a man whose previous honours included the British Royal Astronomical Society's Gold Medal (1995) and the Crafoord Prize in Astronomy (2008).

Rashid Aliyevich Sunyaev received a master's degree in physics (1966) from the Moscow Institute of Physics and Technology and a doctorate in astrophysics (1968) from Moscow State University. From 1968 to 1974 he was a scientific researcher at the Institute of Applied Mathematics of the U.S.S.R. Academy of Sciences (now the Russian Academy of Sciences) in Moscow. He remained at the academy as head of the Laboratory for Theoretical Astrophysics at the Space Research Institute (IKI; 1974–82), then as head of the high-energy astrophysics department (1982–2002), and from 1992 as the chief scientist at the IKI. From 1975 to 2001 he was a professor at the Moscow Institute of Physics and Technology. In 1995 he also joined the Max Planck Institute for Astrophysics in Garching, Ger., where he became director in 1996. At that time Sunyaev acquired dual Russian-German citizenship.

As a graduate student, Sunyaev was initially interested in particle physics, but after meeting physicist Yakov B. Zeldovich in 1965, he began working in astrophysics. Sunyaev's important early work concentrated on using the CMB (electromagnetic radiation that is a residual effect of the big bang) to uncover the early history of the universe. In 1970 Sunyaev and Zeldovich predicted the existence of baryon acoustic oscillations (regions of dense gas where galaxies would have formed in the early universe and that would appear as brightness fluctuations in the CMB). Those oscillations were first observed in 2001 by balloon-based microwave detectors. In 1972 Sunyaev and Zeldovich described the SZ effect, a phenomenon in which electrons in a galaxy cluster would collide with CMB photons, boosting the energy of the photons and raising their frequency. Thus, at certain radio frequencies, the galaxy clusters would appear as shadows against the CMB. The SZ effect was first observed in 1984 and was later used to find extremely distant galaxy clusters.

In the early 1970s, Sunyaev became interested in astronomical X-ray sources. He and astrophysicist Nikolay I. Shakura in 1973 described the physics of matter falling on the accretion disk around a black hole. The Shakura-Sunyaev model became the basis for much of the subsequent theoretical work that described cataclysmic variable stars and quasars. (ERIK GREGERSEN)

Tamasaburo Bando V

(b. April 25, 1950, Tokyo, Japan) Japanese Kabuki actor Tamasaburo Bando V, who had already been honoured with many awards during his lengthy career, in 2011 received the Kyoto Prize for his contributions to the arts. In a career that was somewhat atypical for Kabuki actors, Tamasaburo had gained international acclaim both as an *onnagata*, a man who plays female roles (in Kabuki all roles are played by men), and as a capable actor and director in film and non-Kabuki forms of drama.

Although Shin'ichi Nirehara (Tamasaburo's birth name) was not born into a performing family, he began studying performance arts at a young age as a form of rehabilitation from polio. At age six he was adopted into the family of Kabuki actor Kan'ya Morita XIV, who had no sons of his own and was looking for a successor. Tamasaburo made his stage debut under the name Kinoji Bando in 1957, playing the role of Kotaro in the drama *Terakoya* ("The Temple School"). In 1964 he inherited the prestigious stage name Tamasaburo Bando, becoming the fifth actor to perform under that moniker. The following year he appeared with his adoptive father as daughter and mother, respectively, in an adaptation of *Chushingura* ("The Treasury of Loyal Retainers"). In 1969 Tamasaburo won the role of Princess Shiranui in Yukio Mishima's new Kabuki play *Chinsetsu yumiharizuki* ("The Moon like a Drawn Bow"). His other notable roles during that period included Princess Taema in *Narukami* (1970; "The Thunder God") and Princess Nowake in *Sumidagawa gonichi no omokage* (1971; "Memories of the Sumida River").

His adoptive father forbade Tamasaburo to perform outside Kabuki, but after Kan'ya's death in 1975, Tamasaburo began to make a name for himself in other genres. He acted in *shimpa* ("new school") productions such as *Keiko ogi* (1975; "The Practice Fan") and dabbled in Shakespeare, appearing as Lady Macbeth and Desdemona. In the late 1970s he also began appearing in films, and he starred in Polish director Andrzej Wajda's *Nastasja* (1994), in which he played both a male and a female role. In the early 1990s he began directing films, and his 1992 effort *Yume no onna* ("Dream Woman") was screened at the 1993 Berlinale film festival.

In addition to his wide range of non-Kabuki projects, Tamasaburo continued to perform Kabuki throughout his career, both in Japan and abroad. In 1996 he collaborated with cellist Yo-Yo Ma, executing Kabuki dance to the music of J.S. Bach, and in 1998 he danced alongside Mikhail Baryshnikov. Tamasaburo also brought his Kabuki sensibility to traditional Chinese *kunqu* theatre, directing and starring in a production of *Mudanting* ("The Peony Pavilion") at the Shanghai International Arts Festival in 2009. The opera was widely praised, and it played in Tokyo the following year. (ALISON ELDRIDGE)

Japanese Kabuki actor Tamasaburo Bando V

Xinhua/Landov

Tseng, Yani

(b. Jan. 23, 1989, Guishan, Taiwan)
In 2011 Taiwanese golfer Yani Tseng solidified her status as the dominant player on the Ladies Professional Golf Association (LPGA) tour. In June she turned in a phenomenal performance at the LPGA Championship, winning the tournament by 10 strokes. Her 19-under-par 269 tied the record-low score at an LPGA major. In July she won the Women's British Open for the second consecutive year, edging American Brittany Lang by four strokes. The victory gave Tseng—at just 22 years of age—her fifth career major tournament title and made her the youngest golfer of either sex to reach that milestone.

Tseng played golf from the age of six and by her early teens was an accomplished amateur. In 2002 she won the girls 13–14 age division at the Callaway junior world golf championships, and two years later she captured the U.S. Women's Amateur Public Links title. She turned professional in 2007 and joined the LPGA tour the following year. At the 2008 LPGA Championship, she outdueled Maria Hjorth of Sweden in a four-hole play-off to become Taiwan's first major golf champion. Tseng also recorded five second-place finishes during her inaugural season on the tour and received the LPGA's Rookie of the Year award.

In 2010 Tseng added two major titles to her collection. At the Kraft Nabisco Championship in early April, she shot a 13-under-par 275 to secure a one-stroke victory over Suzann Pettersen of Norway. Later in the year Tseng also triumphed at the Women's British Open, again finishing on top by a single stroke, this time over Katherine Hull of Australia. At the conclusion of the season, Tseng was recognized as the LPGA's Player of the Year, becoming the second youngest player (behind American Nancy Lopez) to be accorded the honour.

In February 2011, after racking up several tournament victories at the beginning of the season, Tseng rose to the top of the women's world rankings. By April she had become the youngest women's golfer to surpass the $5 million mark in career earnings. Tseng achieved six wins on the LPGA tour during the season, notching her final victory in October at the Hana Bank Championship in Inch'on, S.Kor. That month she was named again as the LPGA Player of the Year. She was only the eighth player in history to have won the award in consecutive seasons. (SHERMAN HOLLAR)

Valiant, Leslie

(b. March 28, 1949, Budapest, Hung.)
In 2011 American computer scientist Leslie Valiant won his field's highest honour, the A.M. Turing Award. He was cited for his "fundamental contributions to the development of computational learning theory and to the broader theory of computer science."

Valiant received a bachelor's degree in mathematics (1970) from the University of Cambridge and a diploma in computer science (1973) from Imperial College, London. He earned a doctorate in computer science (1974) from the University of Warwick, Coventry, Eng. He became a lecturer at the University of Leeds and later at the University of Edinburgh. In 1982 Valiant joined the faculty at Harvard University as a professor of computer science and applied mathematics.

His most-notable paper, "A Theory of the Learnable" (1984), provided a mathematical foundation for describing how a computer could learn. In this paper Valiant introduced the "probably approximately correct" (PAC) model, in which an algorithm posits a hypothesis based on some data set and applies that hypothesis to future data. (Any hypothesis will likely have some level of error, and the PAC model gives a framework for determining that level and thus how well the algorithm can adapt.) The PAC model was greatly influential in the realm of artificial intelligence and in applications such as handwriting recognition and e-mail filtering.

Valiant made key contributions to the theory of computational complexity. In 1979 he created a new class of complexity, #P, in which a #P problem is determining the number of solutions to an NP problem. (A P [polynomial] problem can be solved in "polynomial time" when a solution algorithm exists that has a number of steps bounded by a polynomial function of n, where n is the length of input for the problem. The solution to an NP [nondeterministic polynomial] problem can be found in polynomial time, but the solution is nondeterministic because no particular rule is used to guess the solution.) Valiant discovered the unexpected result that even though it can be very easy to determine whether certain problems have a solution, it can be extremely hard to determine the number of solutions.

Valiant also wrote about the theory of parallel computing, in which a problem is broken down into several parts that are worked on simultaneously by multiple processors. In 1990 he introduced the bulk synchronous parallel (BSP) model, in which individual processors communicate with each other only after finishing their computations. Separating computation from communication avoids instances of deadlock, in which activity stops because each processor is waiting for data from another processor.

Valiant also applied methods from computer science and mathematics in an effort to understand the human brain. In his book *Circuits of the Mind* (1994), he posited a "neuroidal" model that would explain how the brain can learn and perform certain tasks faster than an electronic computer even though the individual neurons are comparatively slow and sparsely connected to each other. (ERIK GREGERSEN)

Vettel, Sebastian

(b. July 3, 1987, Heppenheim, W.Ger. [now in Germany]) One year after he took Formula One (F1) racing by storm, German Grand Prix race-car driver Sebastian Vettel dominated the circuit in 2011 as few other drivers ever had. He clinched his second straight drivers' championship nearly two months before the end of the season while help-

Formula One race-car champion Sebastian Vettel of Germany

Marius Becker—EPA/Landov

ing Red Bull Racing capture its second consecutive manufacturers' crown. When the teams arrived at the Japanese Grand Prix on October 9, Vettel had won a commanding 9 of his 15 races and had accumulated enough points to clinch the drivers' title in Japan despite a third-place finish. He wrapped up the manufacturers' title for Red Bull a week later when he won the race in South Korea. All told, he won 11 of the 19 races of the 2011 season.

Vettel grew up idolizing German racing icon Michael Schumacher, and he took up karting in 1995. He proved to have great talent and soon drew the attention of Gerhard Noack, a track owner who had shepherded Schumacher through his own youth-karting career. Noack's support (as well as that of Red Bull, which sponsored Vettel's karting career from the time he was 12 years old) helped Vettel win numerous karting titles before he switched to open-wheel racing in 2003. Vettel finished second in the overall standings in his first season of driving in the junior Formula BMW series and won the series championship handily in 2004, posting 18 victories in 20 races. He subsequently moved to the Formula Three Euro Series (placing second in 2006) and the World Series by Renault. He made his F1 race debut in 2007 after having served as an F1 test driver for two seasons.

Despite his developing reputation as a racing prodigy, Vettel was not an immediate success on the F1 circuit; he finished no higher than fourth in his first 21 races. His initial win came at the 2008 Italian Grand Prix, which made Vettel, at age 21 years and 2 months, the youngest F1 race winner ever. The impressive circumstances of that victory—on a rain-soaked track, with an inferior race car—led Red Bull to bring him on as a driver for the 2009 season.

Vettel won four races and finished second in the world drivers' championship standings in his first season with Red Bull. In 2010 he was victorious in five races, including the Brazilian Grand Prix, the penultimate race in the F1 season, which gave Red Bull its first manufacturers' championship, and the season-ending Abu Dhabi Grand Prix, which secured the drivers' crown for Vettel. In capturing the 2010 title at age 23, he became the youngest person to win an F1 Grand Prix championship and just the third driver in F1 history to win the drivers' championship after having never been atop the overall standings until the final race of the season.

(ADAM AUGUSTYN)

Fiona Hanson—PA Photos/Landov

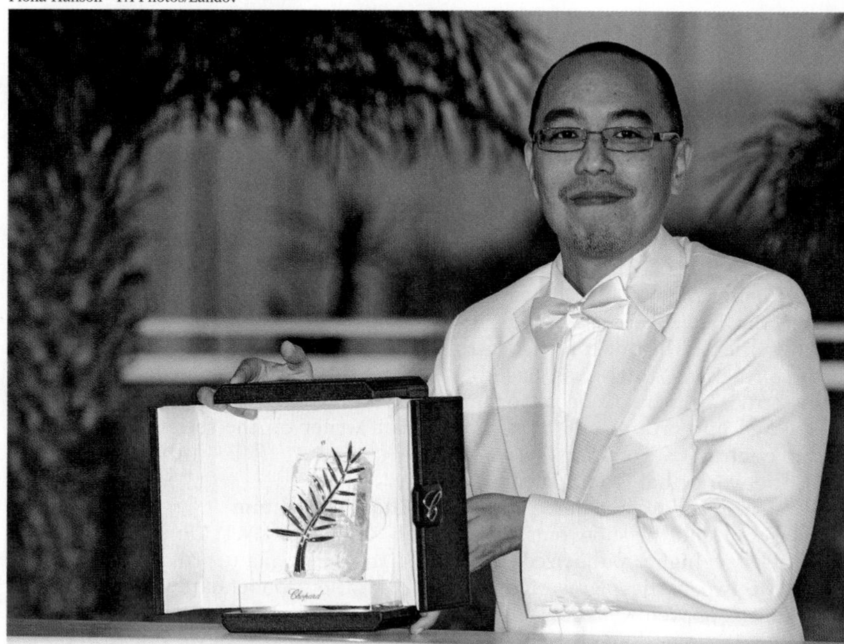

Palme d'Or-winning filmmaker Apichatpong Weerasethakul

Weerasethakul, Apichatpong
(b. July 16, 1970, Bangkok, Thai.)
In 2011 American moviegoers got their first chance to view Thai director Apichatpong Weerasethakul's lush and lyrical film *Loong Boonmee raleuk chat* (2010; *Uncle Boonmee Who Can Recall His Past Lives*), winner of the Cannes film festival's Palme d'Or. The movie, which tells the story of a dying man who is visited in turn by the ghost of his dead wife and by that of his missing son (realized as a monkey ghost), was controversial for both its nonlinear narrative structure and its dreamy pacing.

While developing *Uncle Boonmee*, the director accepted a commission to create a video installation regarding the northeastern Thai village of Nabua, where, according to a local legend, a predatory widow ghost was active. There, from the 1960s to the early '80s, the Thai army had carried on a brutal campaign to suppress the allegedly communist activities of farmers. Weerasethakul's *Primitive* (2009), which included seven videos and several short films—notably *A Letter to Uncle Boonmee* and *Phantoms of Nabua* (both 2009)—also made its American debut in 2011, at New York City's New Museum.

After studying architecture at Khon Kaen (Thai.) University (B.A., 1994), Weerasethakul took a master's degree in filmmaking from the School of the Art Institute of Chicago (M.F.A., 1997). In 1993 he produced his first film, *Bullet*, an experimental silent short. His next two films, also shorts, were *Kitchen and Bedroom* (1994), which examines the nature of memory, and *0016643225059* (1994), about the difficulty of long-distance communication. In *Like the Relentless Fury of Pounding Waves* (1996), Weerasethakul experimented with the layering of sound, light, still photography, and other elements of filmmaking.

In 1999 Weerasethakul formed a production company, Kick the Machine. His first feature-length film was *Dokfa nai meuman* (2000; *Mysterious Object at Noon*). For that movie Weerasethakul invented characters and asked his countrymen to help build a story about them. His other credits include *Sud sanaeha* (2002; *Blissfully Yours*), a diptych that concerns the problems of illegal immigrants and shifts into what seems to be a real-time picnic, and, as co-director with Thai American artist Michael Shaowanasai, *Hua jai tor ra nong* (2003; *The Adventure of Iron Pussy*), a tongue-in-cheek Asian soap opera, the third in a series featuring a transvestite secret agent. Like *Blissfully Yours* in reverse, *Sud pralad* (2004; *Tropical Malady*) is also a two-part feature. The first part examines the attraction between two young men, and the second part, set in a jungle, portrays the psychological aspects of this relationship as an unseen menace. It was a pre-*Boonmee* manifestation of Weerasethakul's interest in the rural Thai culture of his youth and the spirit world ever present there. *Sang sattawat*

(2006; *Syndromes and a Century*) also featured a two-part structure. Each part is set in a hospital—one rural, the other urban. The movie is an affectionate and poetic rumination on both memory and the options presented by cinematic storytelling. (KATHLEEN KUIPER)

Weiner, Matthew

(b. June 29, 1965, Baltimore, Md.)

In 2011, after American writer and producer Matthew Weiner completed a fourth season of his hit cable television show *Mad Men*, which was hailed by many critics as a creative peak for him, he entered into protracted and acrimonious contract negotiations with the AMC network that some media observers speculated could force him off the series or end the show outright. After weeks of highly publicized squabbling, the two parties agreed to a contract that kept Weiner in control of the show for three additional seasons, an outcome that led to countless sighs of relief from the program's many devoted fans.

Weiner moved to Los Angeles with his family at age nine. He graduated (1987) from Wesleyan University, Middletown, Conn., and received a master's degree (1990) from the University of Southern California's film school. He was an uncredited joke writer on the short-lived TV series *Party Girl* (1996) before joining the writing staff of *The Naked Truth* (1995–98). In 1999 Weiner became a writer on the sitcom *Becker* (1998–2004). He also served as a producer of the show from 2000 to 2002, and he was both a writer and a supervising producer on *Andy Richter Controls the Universe* (2002–03).

During a summer hiatus from *Becker*, Weiner wrote the pilot script for *Mad Men*, a drama set in a Madison Avenue advertising firm in the 1960s. His script circulated through show business circles for three years before it came to the attention of David Chase, creator of the critically acclaimed television drama *The Sopranos* (1999–2007). In 2002 Weiner joined the writing staff of *The Sopranos* despite the fact that his only previous professional writing experience was on comedies. He worked on the series' final three seasons, earning two Emmy Award nominations for his writing and winning two Emmys in his capacity as an executive producer of the show (he also acted in a small role in two episodes). As the production of *The Sopranos* was winding down, Weiner recirculated his *Mad Men* script, which was picked up by AMC.

Mad Men debuted in 2007 and was met with almost universal critical acclaim, becoming the flagship program of a channel that had previously been best known for showing classic films and had never before aired a scripted drama. *Mad Men* developed a sizable (by cable television standards) fan base, and the stylish program became a cultural touchstone. The show won the Emmy Award for outstanding drama series and the Golden Globe for best television drama in each of its first three seasons, and during that period Weiner won three Emmys for his work as a writer on the series as well. (ADAM AUGUSTYN)

Zhou Xiaochuan

(b. Jan. 29, 1948, Dong'an [now Mishan, Heilongjiang province], China) In 2011 Zhou Xiaochuan was well into his second term (due to expire in late 2012 or early 2013) as governor of the People's Bank of China (PBC) and had earned a reputation as one of the world's most influential financial policy makers. During his tenure the PBC amassed a great buildup of foreign reserves as a result of China's highly favourable balance of trade, which, along with Zhou's increasingly strong positions on monetary reform, gave him and China growing clout on the global economic stage.

Zhou grew up mostly in Beijing, where his father, Zhou Jiannan, was a government official. The elder Zhou was purged during the Cultural Revolution (1966–76) but later was rehabilitated and held high-ranking posts in the government and the Chinese Communist Party (CCP). Zhou Xiaochuan was sent to live (1968–72) in the countryside before attending a Beijing technical institute, graduating (1975) with a degree in engineering. He then earned a Ph.D. in economic systems engineering (1985) from Tsinghua University in Beijing.

People's Bank of China governor Zhou Xiaochuan

Imaginechina/AP

Zhou was appointed to a succession of posts in the government in the 1980s and '90s, quickly proving himself to be a capable technocrat, administrator, and policy maker. He served as vice-governor (1991–95) of the Bank of China, vice-governor (1996–98) of the PBC, president (1998–2000) of the China Construction Bank, and then chairman (2000–02) of the China Securities Regulatory Commission (CSRC). During the Asian financial crisis of the late 1990s, Zhou helped keep China's currency, the renminbi (yuan), stable without seriously affecting China's increasingly important export trade. Then, as chief of the CSRC, he instituted several reforms of the securities-trading system.

Zhou was appointed governor of the PBC in December 2002, and the following year he presided over the enactment of reform legislation that transferred the bank's regulatory functions to a new government agency. Zhou was also appointed chairman of the Monetary Policy Committee at the PBC in January 2003, and he soon addressed calls from foreign governments (notably the U.S.) for China to revalue its currency, which it did in July 2005. As the global crisis began to loom in late 2006, Zhou became a strong advocate for greater regulation of banks, including maintaining higher reserves. He also called for global financial reforms, notably reduction in dependency on the U.S. dollar at the IMF in favour of a multinational currency fund for its reserves and for a stronger presence of the renminbi in the global financial system.

In addition to his posts at the PBC, Zhou served (beginning in 2002) as a member of the CCP's Central Committee, and he maintained teaching positions at Tsinghua and other institutions. Zhou's wife, Li Ling, was also a notable public figure; she functioned as a high-level bureaucrat who handled China's trade disputes with foreign countries. (KENNETH PLETCHER)

Obituaries

In 2011 the world **LOST** many leaders, **PATHFINDERS**, newsmakers, **HEROES**, cultural icons, and **ROGUES**. The pages below **RECAPTURE** the **LIVES** and accomplishments of those we **REMEMBER** best.

Alarie, Pierrette (PIERRETTE MARGUERITE ALARIE-SIMONEAU), Canadian soprano (b. Nov. 9, 1921, Montreal, Que.—d. July 10, 2011, Victoria, B.C.), enjoyed a remarkable operatic career as a soloist and alongside her husband (from 1946 until his death in 2006), the renowned Canadian lyric tenor Léopold Simoneau. Alarie, known for her crystalline coloratura, studied (1943–46) with German American soprano Elisabeth Schumann and made her debut in 1945 at New York's Metropolitan Opera as Oscar in Verdi's *Un ballo in maschera* after having won that company's "Opera Auditions of the Air." For some three decades Alarie and her husband sang together. They also cofounded (1982) and taught at the Canada Opera Piccola in Victoria. Alarie received many honours, notably the French Order of Arts and Letters (1990) and Companion of the Order of Canada (1995).

Alekseyev, Vasily Ivanovich, Soviet weightlifter (b. Jan. 7, 1942, Pokrovo-Shishkino, Russia, U.S.S.R.—d. Nov. 25, 2011, Badenhausen, Ger.), dominated the superheavyweight class between 1970 and 1978 and was considered by many to be the greatest superheavyweight lifter of all time. Alekseyev set 80 world records and won eight European titles, eight world titles, and two Olympic gold medals (1972 and 1976). He became the first weightlifter to exceed 600 kg (1,323 lb) for a three-lift total (clean and jerk, snatch, and clean and press) and the first to clean and jerk more than 226.8 kg (500 lb). Alekseyev was the son of a lumberjack; at age 12 he was felling trees and lifting logs, and at 14 he was wrestling woodsmen. He already stood 1.8 m (6 ft) tall and weighed about 90 kg (198 lb) when he enrolled (1961) at the Archangelsk Forestry Institute and was introduced to weightlifting. (He eventually reached a body weight of about 160 kg [353 lb].) In 1972 he was awarded the Order of Lenin. He was inducted into the Weightlifting Hall of Fame in 1993.

Alia, Ramiz, Albanian politician (b. Oct. 18, 1925, Shkoder, Alb.—d. Oct. 7, 2011, Tirana, Alb.), as president of Albania (1982–92) and head of the country's communist party (1985–91), instituted mild reforms in that previously isolated country by expanding ties with its European neighbours, initiating limited economic reforms, and relaxing the communists' tight grip on Albanian society, which led to the unexpected electoral successes of democratic parties. Alia, the son of Muslim parents, attended a French secondary school in Tirana. After having served in the communist-led National Liberation Movement during World War II, Alia held leadership posts in the communist party's youth organization, and in 1948 he was elected to the party's Central Committee. He rose rapidly under party boss Enver Hoxha's patronage, serving as minister of education (1955–58). Alia played a prominent role in bitter disputes over the "revisionism" of Yugoslavia, the Soviet Union, and China and led domestic campaigns to purge the artistic and intellectual communities of "bourgeois humanism" and other "alien influences." He became the titular head of state in 1982 and the effective ruler after Hoxha's death in April 1985; he resigned on April 3, 1992. Alia (with other former communist officials) was convicted of corruption in 1994 and sentenced to nine years in prison, but he was released in 1995.

Alliluyeva, Svetlana (SVETLANA IOSIFOVNA STALINA; LANA PETERS), Russian-born daughter of Soviet ruler Joseph Stalin (b. Feb. 28, 1926, Moscow, Russia, U.S.S.R.—d. Nov. 22, 2011, Richland county, Wis.), caused an international sensation when she defected to the U.S. in 1967 and subsequently published two volumes of memoirs describing her life as Joseph Stalin's youngest child and the events surrounding her defection. Svetlana graduated (1949) from Moscow University, where she taught Soviet literature and English language (1953–65) before joining the Progres publishing house as a translator of Russian literature into English. With the help of American officials, she defected during a government-sanctioned visit to India. She burned her Soviet passport, became a U.S. citizen, and signed a lucrative publishing contract. During a brief marriage (1970–73) to architect William Wesley Peters, she took the name Lana Peters. In 1982 she went to live in England with her daughter Olga Peters before returning (1984) to the U.S.S.R., where officials restored her citizenship. After clashing with Soviet authorities, she again renounced her citizenship and in 1986 resettled in the U.S.

Anand, Dev (DHARAM DEVDUTT PISHORIMAL ANAND), Indian actor and filmmaker (b. Sept. 26, 1923, Gurdaspur, Punjab, British India—d. Dec.

Bollywood star Dev Anand

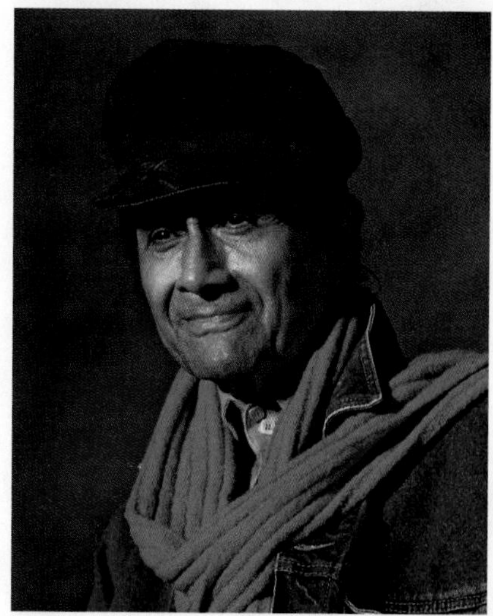

Gautam Singh/AP

3, 2011, London, Eng.), displayed his dashing good looks and on-screen charisma in more than 110 Hindi-language movies, usually as the romantic lead, over a 65-year (1946–2011) career. Anand graduated (1943) with a degree in English from Government College, Lahore (now in Pakistan), and took a government job in Bombay (now Mumbai). After his older brother, film director Chetan Anand, introduced him to the Indian People's Theatre Association, he was offered a role in the film *Hum ek hain* (1946). Within two years Anand was playing starring roles, and in 1949 he and Chetan cofounded Navketan International Films. The production company's first film, *Afsar* (1950), starred Anand in an adaptation of Nikolay Gogol's *The Government Inspector*. Anand won the Filmfare Award for best actor twice, for *Kalapani* (1958) and *Guide* (1965). Other accolades included the Indian government's Padma Bushan (2001) and Dadasaheb Phalke (2002) as well as several lifetime-achievement acting awards.

Andrianov, Nikolay Yefimovich, Soviet gymnast (b. Oct. 14, 1952, Vladimir, Russia, U.S.S.R.—d. March 21, 2011, Vladimir, Russia), won 15 Olympic medals, a record for male gymnasts, in three Olympic Games (1972, 1976, 1980). Andrianov began his gymnastics career at age 12, late for his sport. He was selected for the Soviet national team in 1970, and at the 1972 Munich Olympics he won a gold medal (floor exercise), a silver (team competition), and a bronze (vault). Andrianov was the most decorated competitor at the 1976 Montreal Games, winning seven medals, including gold in the floor exercise, rings, vault, and all-around; silver in the parallel bars and team competition; and a bronze in the pommel horse. He came away from the 1980 Moscow Olympics with gold medals in the team competition and the vault, silver in the floor exercise and the all-around, and a bronze in the horizontal bar. He also captured 12 world championship medals, including the all-around title in 1978. Andrianov's performance style was marked by innovation. He introduced the triple somersault dismount from the horizontal bar at the 1974 world championships. Andrianov was inducted into the International Gymnastics Hall of Fame in 2001.

Olympic gymnast Nikolay Andrianov

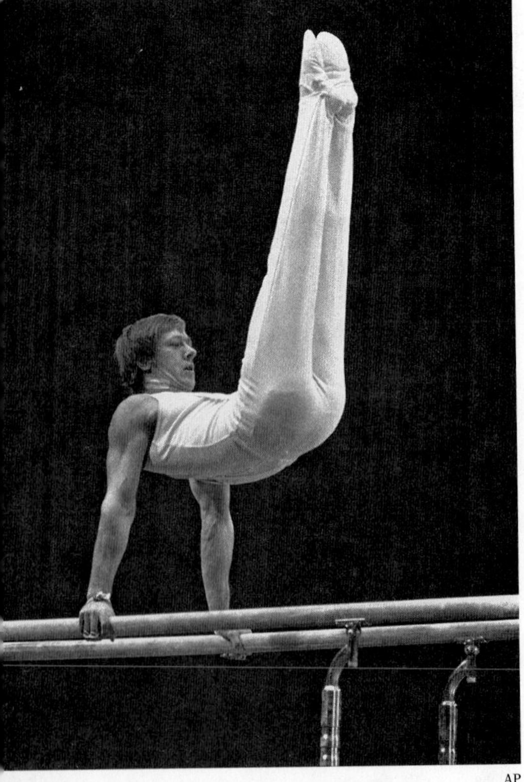

AP

Arness, James (JAMES KING AURNESS), American actor (b. May 26, 1923, Minneapolis, Minn.—d. June 3, 2011, Los Angeles, Calif.), was best known for his portrayal of Marshal Matt Dillon, the deliberate, level-headed lawman in the frontier town of Dodge City, Kan., on the long-running television series *Gunsmoke* (1955–75). Prior to his success on *Gunsmoke*, the imposing 2-m (6-ft 6-in)-tall Arness had made his big-screen debut as a strapping brother of Loretta Young in *The Farmer's Daughter*, and he was often cast in menacing film roles, notably as the space alien in *The Thing from Another World* (1951). Arness later appeared in the miniseries *How the West Was Won* (1977) as well as such TV movies as *The Alamo* (1987), *Red River* (1988), and five *Gunsmoke* sequels. His brother, Peter Graves, was also an actor.

Arroyo, Joe (ALVARO JOSÉ ARROYO GONZÁLEZ), Colombian singer (b. Nov. 1, 1955, Cartagena, Colom.—d. July 26, 2011, Barranquilla, Colom.), blended Colombian and Caribbean musical traditions to create a unique style showcased in such songs as "Rebelión" (1986), "La noche" (1988), and "En Barranquilla me quedo" (1988). Arroyo grew up poor, but by the time he was 13, he had launched his singing career. It took off in the 1970s, when he recorded 15 albums with the group Fruko y Sus Tesos and 4 more with the Latin Brothers. Arroyo produced hundreds of songs and more than 20 albums (1981–2007) with his own band, La Verdad. His contributions to music earned him a lifetime achievement award from the Latin Recording Academy. Arroyo won Colombia's highest salsa honour, the Conga de Oro, so many times that a special award, the Super Conga de Oro, was created for him.

Ashford, Nick(olas), American lyricist and singer (b. May 4, 1941, Fairfield, S.C.—d. Aug. 22, 2011, New York, N.Y.), created (1966–73) an amazing songbook together with composer Valerie Simpson (his wife from 1974) that spanned such genres as soul, rhythm and blues, and funk; their heartfelt romantic songs celebrated love, commitment, and devotion. Some of the duo's most memorable tunes include "Cry like a Baby" (1964, Aretha Franklin), "Ain't No Mountain High Enough" (1967, Marvin Gaye and Tammi Terrell; 1970, Diana Ross), "Didn't You Know (You'd Have to Cry Sometime)" (1969, Gladys Knight and the Pips), "I'm Every Woman" (1978, Chaka Khan), and "Is It Still Good to Ya?" (1980, Teddy Pendergrass). Ashford and Simpson met while singing in the choir of a church in New York City's Harlem district, and the two soon began their songwriting collaboration. They found little success until teaming with Jo ("Joshie") Armstead. Following the trio's number one hit for Ray Charles, "Let's Go Get Stoned" (1966), Ashford and Simpson joined Motown Records. Their Motown hits include "You're All I Need to Get By," "Reach Out and Touch Somebody's Hand," "Nothing like the Real Thing," and "Your Precious Love." In 1973 the couple struck out on their own, touring and performing duets that showcased their compelling harmony. They continued to write for others while also garnering hits of their own. Their single "Solid (as a Rock)" became a number one international sensation in 1984. Ashford and Simpson were inducted into the Songwriters Hall of Fame in 2002.

Babbitt, Milton Byron, American composer and theorist (b. May 10, 1916, Philadelphia, Pa.—d. Jan. 29, 2011, Princeton, N.J.), was known for

Keith Meyers—The New York Times/Redux

Composer and music theorist Milton Babbitt

the difficulty of his music and for being a leading proponent of total serialism—i.e., musical composition based on prior arrangements not only of all 12 pitches of the chromatic scale (as in 12-tone music) but also of dynamics, duration, timbre (tone colour), and register. In his youth Babbitt played violin, piano, clarinet, and saxophone and was especially attracted to jazz and other popular music. He attended New York University and also studied privately for several years with the composer Roger Sessions. Babbitt's piece *Composition for Synthesizer* (1961) displayed his interest in establishing precise control over all elements of composition. *Philomel* (1964) combines synthesizer with the voice, both live and recorded, of a soprano. More traditional in medium is *Partitions for Piano* (1957). Babbitt wrote chamber music (*Composition for Four Instruments*, 1948; *All Set*, 1957) as well as solo pieces and orchestral works. Unlike many of his contemporaries, Babbitt continued to use serialist techniques in his later works, which include *Arie da capo* (1974), *The Head of the Bed* (1982), *Swan Song No. 1* (2003), and *An Encore* (2006; commissioned by the Library of Congress) for violin and piano, among other compositions for small ensembles; solo pieces such as *Play It Again, Sam* (1989; written as a viola solo for Samuel Rhodes) and *More Melismata* (2005–06; commissioned by the Juilliard School) for cello; and *Concerti for Orchestra* (2004) and several other pieces for larger groups. In 1965 he was elected to the National Institute of Arts and Letters, and in 1982 he was honoured with a Pulitzer Prize in recognition of his lifetime compositions.

Bagapsh, Sergei Vasilyevich, Abkhazian political figure (b. March 4, 1949, Sukhumi, Georgia, U.S.S.R.—d. May 29, 2011, Moscow, Russia), as the second elected president (2005–11) of the breakaway republic of Abkhazia, struggled to sustain Abkhazia's sovereignty from Georgia, from which the autonomous republic declared its independence in 1992 and again, more formally, in 1999. As Abkhazia's prime minister (1997–99), he worked to build sustainable economic relations with foreign neighbours, notably Russia, and to implement foreign policy separate from that of Georgia. In October 2004 Bagapsh won a highly disputed presidential election against the establishment candidate, Raul Khadjimba, who ran as Bagapsh's vice president in a new ballot in January 2005 but later abrogated their power-sharing agreement. Bagapsh broke off all diplomatic talks with Georgia in 2006 after that country demanded the withdrawal of UN peacekeeping forces in Abkhazia. In 2008 the fighting between Georgia and Russia over South Ossetia, another Georgian breakaway republic, brought a measure of victory as Russia formally recognized Abkhazia and South Ossetia as independent.

Bailey, Trevor Edward, English cricketer (b. Dec. 3, 1923, Westcliff-on-Sea, Essex, Eng.—d. Feb. 10, 2011, Westcliff-on-Sea), was the best English all-rounder of the 1950s. He was one of only five players to score 25,000 runs and take 2,000 wickets in a career—having scored 1,000 runs in a season 17 times and taken the "double" (1,000 runs and 100 wickets) 8 times—and was one of *Wisden*'s Cricketers of the Year in 1950. Bailey was educated at Dulwich College, London, and (after his military service in World War II) at St. John's College, Cambridge, where he won Blues in both association football (soccer) and cricket. As a right-hand batsman, Bailey was dogged rather than dashing, earning the nickname "the Barnacle." He made his first-class debut in 1945 and his Essex debut in 1946. Bailey played in 482 matches for the county, retiring in 1967 after having served as team captain (1961–66) and as secretary (from 1955). In 682 first-class matches, Bailey scored 28,641 runs (average 33.42) with 215 not outs and 28 centuries (high score 205). His England debut was

Cricketer Trevor Bailey

AP

against New Zealand at Leeds in 1949, and in 61 Tests (1949–59), he scored 2,290 runs (average 29.74) with 14 not outs and one century (134 not out). He took 2,082 wickets for 48,170 runs (average 23.13), including 132 Test wickets for 3,856 runs (average 29.21). Bailey was made CBE in 1994.

Baker, George Morris, British actor (b. April 1, 1931, Varna, Bulg.—d. Oct. 7, 2011, West Lavington, Wiltshire, Eng.), was perhaps best known for his portrayal of the compassionate but worldly-wise Detective Chief Inspector Wexford in 49 episodes over 12 seasons (1987–2000) of the British television series *Ruth Rendell Mysteries*. Other high points in Baker's 50-year career ranged from starring roles in the World War II drama *The Dam Busters* (1955) and the swashbuckler *The Moonraker* (1958), in which his youthful matinee-idol looks were featured, to such complex character roles as the corrupt emperor Tiberius in the television miniseries *I, Claudius* (1976).

Baker, Kenny (KENNETH CLAYTON BAKER), American musician (b. June 26, 1926, Burdine, Ky.—d. July 8, 2011, Gallatin, Tenn.), drew on jazz techniques to develop a fluid style that made him one of bluegrass's premier fiddlers. Baker originally worked as a coal miner and played the guitar. He began his fiddling career in 1953 with Nashville singer-songwriter Don Gibson. Baker performed regularly with Bill Monroe's Blue Grass Boys from 1956 until he abruptly quit in 1984, and he recorded more than 230 songs with Monroe, including the classic album *Bill Monroe's Uncle Pen* (1972). Baker was inducted (1999) into the Bluegrass Hall of Fame.

Ballesteros, Severiano (SEVE), Spanish golfer (b. April 9, 1957, Pedreña, Spain—d. May 7, 2011, Pedreña), was known for his flamboyant and imaginative style of play and accumulated more than 85 wins in international tournaments, including 50 European Tour victories and 5 major championships. His fame was secured when he tied with Jack Nicklaus for second place at the 1976 British Open at Royal Birkdale, behind Johnny Miller. Also that year he received the PGA European Tour's Order of Merit (as the season's top moneymaker), which he would eventually be awarded six times. He captured his first Masters Tournament in 1980 and followed with a second win in 1983. Two years later he was on the European team that broke U.S. dominance of the Ryder Cup, marking Europe's first victory in that team event. During 1979–95 he was a Ryder Cup mainstay, with 20 wins in 37 matches; he returned in 1997 as Europe's nonplaying captain. His other achievements included three British Open victories (1979, 1984, and 1988). Ballesteros was elected to the World Golf Hall of Fame in 1999, and the next year he was named European Player of the Century.

Dave Caulkin/AP

Golfer Severiano Ballesteros

Bannister, Trevor Gordon, British actor (b. Aug. 14, 1934, Durrington, Wiltshire, Eng.—d. April 14, 2011, Thames Ditton, Surrey, Eng.), brought a sly grin and effortless charm to the cheeky junior salesman Mr. Lucas in the first seven seasons (1972–79) of the bawdy situation comedy *Are You Being Served?*, a role he repeated in the 1977 movie of the same name. Bannister studied at the London Academy of Music and Dramatic Arts and worked in repertory theatre before making his West End debut (1960) in a supporting role in *Billy Liar*. He continued to appear onstage and in pantomimes throughout his career.

Baran, Paul, American electrical engineer (b. April 29, 1926, Grodno, Pol. [now Hrodna, Belarus]—d. March 26, 2011, Palo Alto, Calif.), was the inventor of the distributed network and, contemporaneously with British computer scientist Donald Davies, of data packet switching across distributed networks. These inventions were the foundation for the Internet. In 1959 he became a researcher at the RAND Corporation, where he worked on developing a method for U.S. authorities to communicate in the event that their centralized switching facilities were destroyed by a nuclear attack. Baran conceived a "distributed" communications network in which large messages or units of computer data would be split into "message blocks"—separate packets of data that would be sent independently to the target destination, where they would be rejoined into the original message.

Barry, John (JOHN BARRY PRENDERGAST), British composer (b. Nov. 3, 1933, York, Eng.—d. Jan. 30, 2011, Oyster Bay, Long Island, N.Y.), provided the musical scores for more than 100 motion pictures and television programs, notably 11 movies featuring Ian Fleming's iconic spy James Bond and another, *Dr. No* (1962), for which Barry's score triggered a lawsuit by the credited composer, Monty Norman. He formed (1957) a rock-and-roll band, the John Barry Seven, and worked with pop singers, including Adam Faith. After agreeing to compose the scores for two films in which Faith had been cast, Barry was approached to do the musical arrangements for *Dr. No*. Barry captured five Academy Awards—for *Born Free* (1966; Oscars for both best score and best song), *The Lion in Winter* (1968), *Out of Africa* (1985), and *Dances with Wolves* (1990)—as well as nominations for *Mary, Queen of Scots* (1971) and *Chaplin* (1992). His other film scores include *Zulu* (1964), *The Ipcress File* (1965), *Midnight Cowboy* (1969), *Somewhere in Time* (1980), *Body Heat* (1981), *Peggy Sue Got Married* (1986), and *Enigma* (2001). He also composed for the stage, including the moderately successful musicals *Passion Flower Hotel* (1965) and *Billy* (1974), and won four Grammy Awards, notably best jazz instrumental performance, big band, for the film sound track of *The Cotton Club* (1984). Barry, who was made OBE in 1999, was inducted into the Songwriters Hall of Fame in 1998.

Barstow, Stan(ley), British novelist (b. June 28, 1928, Horbury, West

Yorkshire, Eng.—d. Aug. 1, 2011, Port Talbot, Wales), achieved enormous success with his first book, *A Kind of Loving* (1960; filmed 1962; stage play 1970), a frank look at a working-class man, Vic Brown, caught in an unhappy marriage. Barstow was one of several young British writers (including Alan Sillitoe, John Braine, and others collectively known as the Angry Young Men) who achieved immediate success in the 1950s and '60s with their unsentimental depiction of working-class life. He later wrote two sequels, *The Watchers on the Shore* (1966) and *The Right True End* (1976); this Vic Brown Trilogy was adapted for television in 1982. Barstow's other novels include *Joby* (1964; adapted for TV 1975), *A Raging Calm* (1968; adapted for TV 1974), *A Season with Eros* (1971), *A Brother's Tale* (1980), and *Just You Wait and See* (1986).

Bartik, Jean (BETTY JEAN JENNINGS BARTIK), American computer software pioneer (b. Dec. 27, 1924, near Stanberry, Mo.—d. March 23, 2011, Poughkeepsie, N.Y.), played an instrumental role in programming ENIAC (Electronic Numerical Integrator and Computer), the world's first all-electronic digital computer. Bartik, the only female mathematics major in her class, graduated (1945) from Northwest Missouri State Teachers College (later Northwest Missouri State University). Shortly thereafter she was recruited by the U.S. Army to calculate (by hand) artillery firing trajectories. Later that year she was one of the six women chosen by the University of Pennsylvania to program and debug ENIAC. She later went on to program BINAC (Binary Automatic Computer) as well as UNIVAC (Universal Automatic Computer), one of the earliest commercial computers. Although initially unrecognized for their work, Bartik and her ENIAC colleagues were inducted (1997) into the Women in Technology International Hall of Fame and were featured in the documentary *Top Secret Rosies: The Female Computers of World War II* (2010). Bartik received (2009) a Pioneer Award from the IEEE Computer Society.

Beier, Ulli (HORST ULRICH BEIER), German-born scholar (b. July 30, 1922, Glowitz, Ger.—d. April 3, 2011, Sydney, Australia), brought a profound new understanding and appreciation of African art and literature as the founder (1957) and coeditor (1957–68) of the Nigerian literary periodical *Black Orpheus*, which provided a previously unavailable outlet for creative writing by Africans and West Indians. After completing his studies at the University of London (B.A., 1948), Beier was appointed (1950) associate professor of extramural studies at Nigeria's University College, Ibadan (now the University of Ibadan). In 1961 he helped a group of young writers in Ibadan and Oshogbo (where he lived) organize the nonprofit Mbari Mbayo Club, which eventually encompassed an art school, a theatre, and a publisher. In the late 1960s Beier accepted a teaching position in Papua New Guinea, where he established the literary periodical *Kovave*. He returned to Nigeria in 1971 to become director of the Institute of African Studies at the University of Ife. Three years later he became the first director (1974–78) of the Institute of Papua New Guinea Studies in Port Moresby. He was also the founding director (1981–85, 1989–96) of the Iwalewa House at the University of Bayreuth (Ger.) Africa Centre. Beier's books include *Three Nigerian Plays* (1967) and *When the Moon Was Big, and Other Legends from New Guinea* (1972). He was admired for his English translations from Yoruba.

Bell, Daniel (DANIEL BOLOTSKY), American sociologist (b. May 10, 1919, New York, N.Y.—d. Jan. 25, 2011, Cambridge, Mass.), used sociological theory to reconcile what he believed were the inherent contradictions of capitalist societies. Bell received a B.S. (1939) at City College of New York, where he struck up a lifelong friendship with classmate Irving Kristol, with whom he later founded (1965) the journal *The Public Interest*. As managing editor of *The New Leader* (1941–44) magazine and labour editor for *Fortune* (1948–58), Bell wrote voluminously on various social subjects. After serving (1956–57) in Paris as director of the seminar program of the Congress for Cultural Freedom, he received a doctorate (1960) at Columbia University, New York City, where he was on the faculty from 1952 and served (1959–69) as professor of sociology. In 1969 Bell became a professor of sociology at Harvard University, where he remained until 1990. Bell's book *The Cultural Contradictions of Capitalism* (1976) was an attempt to define the relationship between science, technology, and capitalism. He was also credited with coining the terms *information economy* and *postindustrialism*.

Benacerraf, Baruj, Venezuelan-born American immunologist (b. Oct. 29, 1920, Caracas, Venez.—d. Aug. 2, 2011, Boston, Mass.), shared (with George Snell and Jean Dausset) the 1980 Nobel Prize for Physiology or Medicine for his discovery of genes that regulate immune responses and of the role that some of these genes play in autoimmune diseases. Benacerraf graduated (1942) from Columbia University, New York City, and became a naturalized U.S. citizen in 1943 while a student at the Medical College of Virginia in Richmond. Soon after receiving an M.D. (1945), he served (1946–47) in the U.S. Army Medical Corps. In 1956 he joined the faculty of the New York University (NYU) School of Medicine. He advanced to professor of pathology in 1960, a position he held until 1968. At NYU Benacerraf began conducting experiments that led to his development of the concept of immune response (Ir) genes, which control the immune system's ability to respond to antigens (infectious agents or foreign materials that enter the body). In 1968 Benacerraf became chief of the immunology laboratory at the National Institute of Allergy and Infectious Diseases in Bethesda, Md. He was appointed professor of comparative pathology and chairman of the pathology department at Harvard University Medical School in 1970 and served (1980–91) as president of the Sidney Farber Cancer Institute (now the Dana-Farber Cancer Institute) in Boston. Benacerraf was elected to the National Academy of Sciences (1973) and was awarded the National Medal of Science (1990).

Betz Addie, Pauline May, American tennis player (b. Aug. 6, 1919, Dayton, Ohio—d. May 31, 2011, Potomac, Md.), won five Grand Slam singles titles, including the U.S. national championship (now the U.S. Open) four times (1942–44, 1946) and the All-England (Wimbledon) once (1946), as well as the French Open mixed doubles title (1946). At the peak of her career, she was ranked number one in the world and was undefeated in 39 matches, but she was unable to defend her titles in 1947 when she was banned from competing in amateur tournaments after she speculated about one day turning

AP

Tennis champion Pauline Betz Addie

pro, although she had not yet done so. She was elected to the International Tennis Hall of Fame in 1965.

Bhaktipada (KEITH GORDON HAM; KIRTANANANDA SWAMI), American religious leader (b. Sept. 6, 1937, Peekskill, N.Y.—d. Oct. 24, 2011, Thane, India), led the American branch of the Hare Krishna movement before a criminal investigation resulted in his expulsion and subsequent imprisonment. He was born Keith Gordon Ham and was raised a Southern Baptist. He earned a B.A. (1959) from Maryville (Tenn.) College but failed to complete a graduate degree from Columbia University, New York City. In 1966 Ham joined the International Society for Krishna Consciousness (ISKCON; popularly known as the Hare Krishnas) soon after meeting its founder, Swami Prabhupada. In 1967 he was initiated as Swami Bhaktipada. Two years later he purchased land in the mountains of West Virginia and founded New Vrindaban, a lavish temple complex and "spiritual theme park"; he was later reprimanded by ISKCON for having allowed liturgical relaxations in order to appeal to an American audience. Allegations of sexual molestation and a federal investigation for mail fraud, racketeering, and conspiracy to murder two devotees resulted in his expulsion from ISKCON in 1987. Prabhupada ultimately served eight years in prison.

bin Laden, Osama, Saudi-born militant (b. 1957, Riyadh, Saudi Arabia—d. May 2, 2011, Abbottabad, Pak.), was the founder of the militant Islamist organization al-Qaeda and the mastermind behind numerous terrorist attacks against the U.S. and other Western powers, including the 1993 bombing of New York City's World Trade Center, the 2000 suicide bombing of the U.S. warship *Cole* in the port of Aden, Yemen, and the Sept. 11, 2001, attacks on the World Trade Center in New York City and the Pentagon near Washington, D.C. Bin Laden was one of more than 50 children of one of Saudi Arabia's wealthiest families and received a degree in civil engineering from King Abdul Aziz University, Jiddah. Shortly after the Soviet Union invaded Afghanistan in 1979, he joined the Afghan resistance, viewing it as his Muslim duty to repel the occupation. After the Soviet withdrawal (1989), bin Laden returned home a hero, but he was quickly disappointed with what he perceived as the corruption of the Saudi government and of his own family. His objection to the presence of U.S. troops in Saudi Arabia during the 1990–91 Persian Gulf War led to a growing rift with Saudi leaders, and by 1993 he had purportedly formed al-Qaeda. In 1994 the Saudi government confiscated his passport after accusing him of subversion, and he fled to Sudan, where he organized camps that trained militants in terrorist methods. He was expelled in 1996 and returned to Afghanistan, where he received protection from its ruling Taliban militia. In 1996–98 bin Laden, a self-styled scholar, issued a series of *fatwas* (religious edicts) declaring a holy war against the U.S. Following the September 11 attacks, the U.S. led a coalition that overthrew the Taliban and sent bin Laden into hiding. After having evaded a manhunt for more than nine years bin Laden was killed by U.S. forces in a military assault on a heavily fortified compound north of Islamabad, Pak. He was reportedly buried at sea with appropriate Muslim funeral rites.

Militant Osama bin Laden

AP

Binford, Lewis Roberts, American archaeologist (b. Nov. 21, 1931, Norfolk, Va.—d. April 11, 2011, Kirksville, Mo.), had a profound impact on the discipline of archaeology with his seminal paper "Archaeology as Anthropology" (1962), which was published in the journal *American Antiquity* and gave rise to what became known as "New Archaeology." The paper initially sparked controversy with its contention that archaeologists should rely less on the museum work of cataloging artifacts and instead delve into what the artifacts revealed about prehistoric cultures. Binford's enthusiasm for ethnoarchaeology, which focuses on studying contemporary societies to gain a clearer understanding of past ones, prompted him to conduct fieldwork in Australia, Africa, and Alaska to study hunter-gatherer populations. He applied the new methodology in an influential study on Mousterian artifacts and later extended it to a study of the hunting activities of the Nunamiut people of Alaska. Besides his more than 150 papers, Binford published 18 books. He became a member of the National Academy of Sciences in 2001 and was the recipient in 2008 of the Society for American Archaeology's Lifetime Achievement Award.

Blumberg, Baruch Samuel (BARRY), American research physician (b. July 28, 1925, Brooklyn, N.Y.—d. April 5, 2011, Moffett Field, near Mountain View, Calif.), discovered an antigen that provokes antibody response against hepatitis B, a finding that led in 1982 to the development by other researchers of a safe and effective vaccine against the disease. In 1976 Blumberg shared the Nobel Prize for Physiology or Medicine with D. Carleton Gajdusek for their work on the origins and spread of infectious viral diseases. After graduating (1951) from Columbia University's College of Physicians and Surgeons in New York City, Blumberg earned a Ph.D. (1957) in biochemistry from the University of Oxford. In 1960 he became chief of the Geographic Medicine and Genetics Section of the U.S. National Institutes of Health, Bethesda, Md. In 1964 he was appointed associate director for clinical research at the Institute for Cancer Research (later named the Fox Chase Cancer Center) in Philadelphia, and he also served as professor of medicine, human genetics, and anthropology at the University of Pennsylvania. In 1989 Blumberg became the first Fox Chase Distinguished Scientist, and he returned to Oxford to become master of Balliol College, a position that he held until 1994. Upon his return to the U.S., he continued to teach as professor of medicine and anthropology at the University of Pennsylvania. From 1999 to 2002 Blumberg directed the NASA Astrobiology Institute, where he embarked on investigations into the possibility of life on other planets.

Bonner, Yelena Georgiyevna, Soviet physician and human rights activist (b. Feb. 15, 1923, Merv, Turkistan, U.S.S.R. [now Mary, Turkm.]—d. June 18, 2011, Boston, Mass.), was a revered figure in the struggle against human rights abuses in the Soviet Union as a cofounder (1976) of the Moscow Helsinki Group and as the wife of Nobel Prize-winning physicist and dissident Andrey Sakharov. When Bonner was a girl, her parents were arrested during the Stalinist purges of the 1930s; her father was killed shortly thereafter. She worked as a nurse during World War II and then trained as a pediatrician and married a fellow student, but neither her marriage nor her medical career lasted. By the time she married Sakharov in 1972, Bonner had already resigned her membership in the Communist Party and joined the dissident movement. Although Sakharov spent many years confined to the Soviet Union and (from 1980) in internal exile in Gorky (now Nizhny Novgorod), Bonner remained free to travel, and in 1975 she went to Oslo to accept the Nobel Prize for Peace on her husband's behalf. In 1984, however, she was convicted of anti-Soviet activities and confined to Gorky with him. Bonner's already-fragile health suffered, and after Sakharov undertook a six-month hunger strike, she was briefly allowed to leave the country in 1985 for heart bypass surgery in the U.S. They were both permitted to return to Moscow in 1986. After Sakharov's death in 1989, Bonner continued to travel and campaign against government oppression.

Bordaberry Arocena, Juan María, Uruguayan politician (b. June 17, 1928, Montevideo, Uruguay—d. July 17, 2011, Montevideo), was president of Uruguay (1972–76), but his administration quickly devolved into a military dictatorship that lasted more than a decade. Bordaberry's November 1971 election to the presidency was followed by an army-conducted recount and accusations of fraud. Six weeks after his inauguration (March 1972), he suspended the constitution and individual liberties, allowing the military free rein in stamping out the guerrilla forces (Tupamaros) that were then terrorizing the country. By 1973 the president had become a virtual puppet of the military, passing actual control to a seven-man National Security Council. Under severe pressure from the armed forces, Bordaberry abolished the Congress, banned all political parties, and acquiesced in press censorship and political repression. Economic conditions continued to worsen, and he was removed by the military on June 12, 1976. He drew little public notice until 2006, when he was arrested and charged with having had involvement in human rights violations; convicted in 2010, Bordaberry was serving a 30-year sentence under house arrest at the time of his death.

Boyle, Willard Sterling, Canadian American physicist (b. Aug. 19, 1924, Amherst, N.S.—d. May 7, 2011, Truro, N.S.), was awarded, with American physicist George E. Smith, the Nobel Prize for Physics in 2009 for their invention in 1969 of the charge-coupled device (CCD), which responds to light and is used to store and capture image data. They shared the prize with physicist Charles Kao, who discovered how light could be transmitted through fibre-optic cables. Their discovery had widespread applications in such areas as digital photography, high-definition television, and astronomy. Boyle served in the Canadian navy during World War II. He received a bachelor's (1947), master's (1948), and doctorate (1950) in physics from McGill University, Montreal. Boyle served on the faculty (1951–53) of the Royal Military College in Kingston, Ont., before joining Bell Laboratories, the New Jersey-based research-and-development arm of AT&T. There he worked on semiconductors. In 1962, with American physicist Donald Nelson, Boyle invented the first laser capable of being operated continuously.

Bravo, Claudio (CLAUDIO NELSON BRAVO CAMUS), Chilean-born artist (b. Nov. 8, 1936, Valparaíso, Chile—d. June 4, 2011, Taroudant, Mor.), initially established himself as a society portrait painter in Chile and Spain, but he became better known for his vibrant still lifes of such everyday items as packages, crumpled paper, and draped fabric. Although he lived in Morocco for many years, it was the Spanish classical masters who inspired the provocative style of his hyperrealist paintings. Though he had some training under Chilean artist Miguel Venegas Cifuentes, Bravo was primarily self-taught. His paintings regularly sold for impressive sums, with *White Package* (1967) fetching more than $1 million in 2004.

Broder, David Salzer, American political journalist (b. Sept. 11, 1929, Chicago Heights, Ill.—d. March 9, 2011, Arlington, Va.), was greatly respected for his incisive and judicious political reporting and analysis in a career that spanned more than four decades and 11 U.S. presidential administrations. With a broad perspective

Political pundit David Broder

George Tames—The New York Times/Redux

and his ear to the ground, Broder reported on national politics for the *Washington Post* from 1966 until his death and wrote a twice-weekly column that was syndicated to more than 300 other newspapers. Broder's columns on the Watergate scandal won him a Pulitzer Prize in 1973.

Buckles, Frank Woodruff, American serviceman (b. Feb. 1, 1901, near Bethany, Mo.—d. Feb. 27, 2011, near Charles Town, W.Va.), was the last surviving American veteran of World War I. On Aug. 14, 1917, Buckles, then a 16-year-old farm boy, went to Oklahoma City and enlisted in the army after lying about his age (the navy and the Marines had already rejected him). The following December he shipped out to the European theatre, where he served as a clerk and ambulance driver in England and then France. After the end of hostilities, he was assigned to a unit that escorted former prisoners back to postwar Germany. He returned home as a corporal in January 1920 and eventually took a job with a steamship company and traveled the world. During World War II, Buckles was a prisoner of war in the Philippines, where he was working as a civilian when that country was invaded (1941) by Japan; after more than three years in a Japanese internment camp, he was freed and repatriated in early 1945. Thereafter he lived quietly as a West Virginia farmer until 2008, when it was officially determined that he was the last of the 4,734,991 Americans identified as veterans of World War I. Buckles spent his final years lobbying for the creation of a national World War I monument in Washington, D.C. In 2008 the federal government agreed to waive the usual requirements so that "the last living doughboy" could be buried in Arlington National Cemetery.

Robert D. Ward—EPA/Landov

World War I soldier Frank Buckles

Cabral, Facundo (Rodolfo Enrique Facundo Cabral; El Indio Gasparino), Argentine singer-songwriter (b. May 22, 1937, La Plata, Arg.—d. July 9, 2011, Guatemala City, Guat.), protested military dictatorships in Latin America through activism and song from the 1970s onward. Cabral's music combined mysticism and spirituality with calls for social justice, and in 1996 the UN named him a "worldwide messenger of peace." His most popular song, "No soy de aquí, ni soy de allá" (1970), inspired covers by Julio Iglesias and Neil Diamond and helped to establish him as a top Latin American singer. Cabral initially performed under the stage name El Indio Gasparino but later recorded more than two dozen albums under his birth name. He also penned numerous books and stories, despite the fact that he did not learn to read until age 14. The Argentine military coup (1976) drove Cabral into exile in Mexico, but after his return to Argentina (1984), he was even more successful than before. Cabral was killed by armed assailants in an apparent ambush.

Cano, Alfonso (Guillermo León Sáenz Vargas), Colombian Marxist guerrilla leader (b. July 22, 1948, Bogotá, Colom.—d. Nov. 4, 2011, mountains of Cauca state, Colom.), led (2008–11) the Revolutionary Armed Forces of Colombia (FARC), the country's largest rebel group. He was born into a conservative middle-class family and studied anthropology at the National University of Colombia, Bogotá. In the late 1960s, however, he became drawn to left-wing politics and joined the youth wing of the Colombian Communist Party (PCC). After imprisonment in 1981 Cano joined the FARC, rising through the ranks until he became leader. From that time Colombian armed forces made it their mission to track him down. Colombian Pres. Juan Manuel Santos called Cano's death during an army attack "the most devastating blow that this group has suffered in its history."

Scott Dalton/AP

Rebel commander Alfonso Cano

Carrington, Leonora, British-born Mexican painter and sculptor (b. April 6, 1917, Crookhey Hall, Cockerham, Lancashire, Eng.—d. May 25, 2011, Mexico City, Mex.), created often autobiographical Surrealist art peopled by fantastic Hiëronymus Bosch-influenced creatures interacting in phantasmagoric dreamscapes. She was one of a number of women associated with the Surrealist group in Paris who herself continued to produce and exhibit art in that vein to the end of her life. One of Carrington's best-known works was her self-portrait *The Inn of the Dawn Horse* (c. 1937–38), housed in New York City's Metropolitan Museum of Art.

Chamberlain, John Angus, American sculptor, painter, printmaker, and filmmaker (b. April 16, 1927, Rochester, Ind.—d. Dec. 21, 2011, New York, N.Y.), was an Abstract Expressionist who created works that were typified by *Mr. Press* (1961), a construction of fragments from automobiles, crumpled and jammed together to create an effect of isolated, frozen movement. His sculptures were often coated with bright industrial paints. Chamberlain studied at the Art Institute of Chicago (1951–52), where he began working in metals, and at Black Mountain (N.C.) College (1955–56). His early pieces were made from welded iron rods, but he later used such materials as heat-shaped Plexiglass, paper, polyurethane, industrial rubber, brown paper bags, and aluminum foil before returning in 1974 to the use of auto body parts. His first sculpture to employ car parts was *Shortstop* (1957), which featured rusty fenders that he had found in the yard of painter and friend Larry Rivers. During the 1970s oil crisis, Chamberlain often incorporated oil barrels into his work, notably in the series *Socket and Kiss* (1979).

Chedid, Andrée (ANDRÉE SAAB), Egyptian-born French writer (b. March 20, 1920, Cairo, Egypt—d. Feb. 6, 2011, Paris, France), crafted both poetry and prose in which she explored themes germane to her native Middle East and to France, where she lived from 1946. Chedid was the daughter of Lebanese Christians and was educated in Arabic, English, and French. She studied journalism (B.A., 1942) at the American University in Cairo and published her first volume of poetry, *On the Trails of My Fancy* (1943), in English. She lived in Lebanon for three years (1943–46) while her husband attended medical school, and then the family settled in Paris, where they took French citizenship. Chedid's first collection of French verse, *Textes pour une figure*, appeared in 1949; thereafter she wrote primarily in French. In addition to several more volumes of poetry, she penned short stories, plays, and novels, two of which—*Le Sixième Jour* (1960) and *L'Autre* (1969)—were adapted into films. Chedid's honours include the Académie Mallarmé's prize for poetry (1976), the Prix Goncourt for short stories (1979), the Albert Camus Prize (1996), and the Prix Goncourt for poetry (2002). She was made a grand officer of the Legion of Honour in 2009. Her son, Louis Chedid, was a successful singer, as was his son, Matthieu Chedid, the pop star known as M.

Chiluba, Frederick Jacob Titus, Zambian politician (b. April 30, 1943, Musangu, Luapula province, British Northern Rhodesia [now in Zambia]—d. June 18, 2011, Lusaka, Zambia), was hailed as a free-market reformer when he was elected president (1991) in Zambia's first multiparty election, which ended Pres. Kenneth Kaunda's 27-year single-party rule. Chiluba's administration was plagued by official corruption, however, and both criminal and civil charges were filed against him after he left office in 2002. Chiluba, who had little formal education, worked as a bookkeeper and rose through the ranks of the labour movement. After he and other labour leaders were briefly jailed in 1981 for sponsoring wildcat strikes, Chiluba cofounded the Movement for Multiparty Democracy political coalition. He defeated Kaunda with more than 75% of the vote in the 1991 ballot and was reelected in 1996 after passing legislation ensuring that Kaunda was ineligible to run. Chiluba yielded the presidency to his handpicked successor, Levy Mwanawasa. Chiluba was eventually acquitted of embezzlement and corruption.

Choules, Claude Stanley, British-born seaman (b. March 3, 1901, Pershore, Worcestershire, Eng.—d. May 5, 2011, Perth, Australia), was the last known combat veteran of World War I and the last man to serve in both world wars.

Department of Defence/AP

World War I combat veteran Claude Choules

Choules joined the British Royal Navy at age 14, and at 16 he was assigned to the battleship HMS *Revenge*, which had recently participated in the Battle of Jutland. Onboard the *Revenge* he witnessed the surrender of the German High Seas Fleet in November 1918 and the scuttling in June 1919 of that fleet at Scapa Flow in Scotland's Orkney Islands. Choules remained in the navy after the war, but in 1926 he moved to Australia, where his brothers had already settled. He eventually transferred to the Royal Australian Navy (RAN), and during World War II he served as a demolitions expert, disposing of mines that washed ashore and preparing defenses in and around the harbour at Fremantle, W.Aus., against a possible Japanese invasion. He rose to the rank of chief petty officer in the RAN and later shifted to the naval dockyard police, from which he retired in 1956. After the deaths in 2009 of fellow World War I veterans Henry Allingham of the Royal Naval Air Service and infantryman Harry Patch, Choules was identified as the last surviving British combat veteran.

Christopher, Warren Minor, American public official (b. Oct. 27, 1925, Scranton, N.D.—d. March 18, 2011, Los Angeles, Calif.), helped formulate U.S. foreign policy as deputy secretary of state (1977–81) during Pres. Jimmy Carter's administration and secretary of state (1993–97) in Pres. Bill Clinton's cabinet. During his time with the Department of State, Christopher, who was known for his low-key and methodical negotiating style, oversaw the completion (1977) of the Panama Canal Treaty, led the negotiations for the release in 1981 of 52 hostages held in the U.S. embassy in Tehran, supervised the 1995 Dayton Accords that ended the war in Bosnia, and in August 1995 became the first U.S. secretary of state to visit Hanoi. Christopher graduated (1945) from the University of Southern California while serving (1943–46) in the U.S. Naval Reserve. He obtained a law degree (1949) from Stanford University and clerked (1949–50) for Supreme Court Justice William O. Douglas before joining the Los Angeles corporate law firm O'Melveny & Myers (he was made a partner in 1958 and served as chairman from 1982 to 1992). He took his first leave of absence to serve as U.S. deputy attorney general (1967–69) under Pres. Lyndon B. Johnson. Christopher later headed the committee that in 1991 recommended substantial reforms to the Los Angeles Police Department following the beating of African American Rodney King. He also led Vice Pres. Al Gore's legal team in the disputed 2000 U.S. presidential election. Christopher was the recipient (1981) of the Presidential Medal of Freedom.

Clemons, Clarence Anicholas, American musician (b. Jan. 11, 1942, Norfolk, Va.—d. June 18, 2011, Palm Beach, Fla.), played saxophone in Bruce Springsteen's E Street Band and became one of the most celebrated

Lynne Sladky/AP

Rock saxophonist Clarence Clemons

sidemen of all time after the group's 1972 debut. Nicknamed the "Big Man" by Springsteen, with whom he had a strong fraternal bond, Clemons augmented classics such as "Born to Run" (1975) and "Tenth Avenue Freeze-Out" (1975) with his strong tenor saxophone hooks. Clemons and Springsteen met on a stormy night in 1971, a meeting that became E Street Band lore and served as the basis for one of rock and roll's most iconic album covers on *Born to Run* (1975). Springsteen put the E Street Band on hiatus in 1989. Clemons returned to the band for a recording session with Springsteen in 1995, though they did not tour again until 1999. Clemons also formed (1981) his own group, the Red Bank Rockers, and collaborated with such performers as Jackson Browne, Aretha Franklin, Twisted Sister, and Lady Gaga.

Cooper, Sir Henry ("OUR 'ENRY"), British boxer (b. May 3, 1934, London, Eng.—d. May 1, 2011, Oxted, Surrey, Eng.), held both the British and Commonwealth heavyweight titles for more than 12 years (1959–71) and the European title for 3 years (1968–71), but he was most remembered for his brutal losses to Muhammad Ali (originally Cassius Clay) in 1963 and 1966. After Cooper lost his three titles to Australia's Joe Bugner on March 16, 1971, he retired from the ring with a professional record of 40 wins (27 by knockout), 14 losses, and 1 draw. He was made OBE in 1969 and was knighted in 2000.

Cooper, Jackie (JOHN COOPER, JR.), American actor (b. Sept. 15, 1922, Los Angeles, Calif.—d. May 3, 2011, Los Angeles), was the freckled-faced star of the Our Gang comedies, starting in 1929, soon after the silent-film series moved to the talkies, and the endearing boy star of such other films as *Treasure Island* (1934), *The Champ* (1931), *The Bowery* (1933), and *O'Shaughnessy's Boy* (1935). For his title role performance in *Skippy* (1931), a tearjerker about a boy and his dog, he became the youngest Oscar nominee (at age nine) for best actor. That same year the sequel, *Sooky*, was released. As an adult, Cooper starred on such television sitcoms as *The People's Choice* (1955–58), as a local politician, and *Hennesey* (1959–62), as a navy doctor, and he became known to moviegoers for his role as editor Perry White of the *Daily Planet* in the Superman franchise.

AP

Child star Jackie Cooper

Corwin, Norman Lewis, American radio writer, producer, and director (b. May 3, 1910, Boston, Mass.—d. Oct. 18, 2011, Los Angeles, Calif.), captivated a generation of American listeners in the 1930s and '40s with moving and eloquent radio plays that earned him the nickname "the poet laureate of radio." He was best known for his coverage during World War II, particularly for the broadcasts *We Hold These Truths* (1941), a timely commemoration of the 150th anniversary of the Bill of Rights, and *On a Note of Triumph* (1945), which applauded the common soldier upon the occasion of the Allies' victory in Europe; the latter was regarded as Corwin's masterpiece. Corwin received numerous honours, including a Peabody Award (1941), and he was inducted into the Radio Hall of Fame in 1993.

Croft, David (DAVID JOHN SHARLAND), British television writer and producer (b. Sept. 7, 1922, Sandbanks, Dorset, Eng.—d. Sept. 27, 2011, Tavira, Port.), created and co-wrote scores of episodes for some of Britain's most beloved television sitcoms, including *Dad's Army* (1968–77), *It Ain't Half Hot Mum* (1974–81), *Hi-de-Hi* (1980–88), *'Allo! 'Allo!* (1982–92), *You Rang, M'Lord?* (1988–93), and both *Are You Being Served?* (1972–85) and its sequel, *Grace and Favour* (also called *Are You Being Served? Again!*; 1992–93). Croft produced several successful sitcoms before he and his sometime partner Jimmy Perry teamed up to create *Dad's Army*. (The pair won the Writers' Guild of Great Britain award for best script in 1970.) He later worked with co-writer Jeremy Lloyd. Croft was made OBE in 1978.

D'Addario, Ray(mond), American photographer (b. Aug. 18, 1920, Holyoke, Mass.—d. Feb. 13, 2011, Holyoke), produced searing images, especially his group shots, of the 21 defendants tried during the nine-month Nürnberg trials (1945–46), in which former Nazi leaders were indicted and tried as war criminals by the International Military Tribunal. His portfolio of images (all taken without the aid of flash) included close-ups of the defendants, cross-examinations by the prosecutors, and closing arguments.

Davies, John Howard, British actor, producer, and director (b. March 9, 1939, London, Eng.—d. Aug. 22, 2011, Blewbury, Oxfordshire, Eng.), was a child star in post-World War II Britain, playing the title roles in director David Lean's *Oliver Twist* (1948), *The Rocking Horse Winner* (1949), and *Tom Brown's Schooldays* (1951). After making only two more films, Davies quit acting in his teens. He later became a director and producer and went on to become a major force in British television, especially as the head (1977–82) of BBC Comedy. Davies was responsible—at least in part—for such hit comedy TV shows as *Monty Python's Flying Circus*, *Fawlty Towers*, *The Good Life* (also called *Good Neighbours*), *All Gas and Gaiters*, *The Goodies*, *Steptoe and Son*, and *No Job for a Lady*.

Davis, Al (ALLEN DAVIS), American football coach and sports executive (b. July 4, 1929, Brockton, Mass.—d. Oct. 8, 2011, Oakland, Calif.), was indelibly identified with the Oakland Raiders football franchise for more than four decades (1966–2011), first as its maverick coach and general manager and then as part owner and from 1976 full owner. After graduating (1950) from Syracuse (N.Y.) University, Davis was hired as an assistant coach at Adelphi College (now Adelphi University), Garden City, N.Y. In 1952 he became head coach of the U.S. Army football team based at Ft. Belvoir, Virginia. In the 1950s he was an assistant coach at The Citadel, Charleston, S.C., and at the University of Southern California. After three years (1960–63) as an assistant coach for the American Football League's (AFL's) Los Angeles (later San Diego) Chargers, he became the head coach and general manager of the Raiders. In his first season he led the Raiders, who had finished 1–13 the previous year, to a 10–4 record and was named the AFL's Coach of the Year. Davis became AFL commissioner in April 1966, but he was unhappy with the planned league merger with the NFL and resigned his post in July and became the Raiders' director of football operations as well as a minority owner of the franchise. As coach, Davis, who traditionally sported a black-and-silver tracksuit and dark glasses, was known for implementing an aggressive passing game, which he dubbed the "vertical game." He coined the phrase "Just win, baby," which underscored the team's notoriously rough and borderline illegal tactics. The Raiders won three Super Bowls (1977, 1981, and 1984) of the five it played and from 1963 to 1985 accrued an unmatched overall record of 229–91–11. In 1982, after having won a landmark antitrust lawsuit against the NFL, Davis relocated the Raiders to Los Angeles, but he became disenchanted (as he had in Oakland) with the quality of the stadium and returned the team to Oakland. Davis was inducted into the Pro Football Hall of Fame in 1992.

Delaney, Shelagh, British playwright (b. Nov. 25, 1939, Salford, Lancashire, Eng.—d. Nov. 20, 2011, Suffolk, Eng.), won critical acclaim and popular success at age 19 with the London production of her first play, *A Taste of Honey* (1958). Two years later she received the Drama Critics' Circle Award for the play's original Broadway production. The play, set in Delaney's birthplace in England's bleak industrial north, blends humour and pathos in its vivid account of an unwed working-class girl facing a pregnancy and a fraught relationship with her mother. In 1961 the play was adapted for film, with an award-winning screenplay by Delaney and the film's director, Tony Richardson. After a second play, *The Lion in Love* (1961), Delaney produced a volume of short stories, *Sweetly Sings the Donkey* (1963). Thereafter she focused on writing screenplays, earning wide praise for *Charlie Bubbles* (1968), *Dance with a Stranger* (1985), and *The Railway Station Man* (1992).

D'Oliveira, Basil Lewis, South African-born cricketer (b. Oct. 4, 1931, Cape Town, S.Af.—d. Nov. 19, 2011, London, Eng.), was a solid all-rounder in England for more than 15 years, but he was best remembered as the centre of an international political controversy when his selection for the 1968–69 England tour of apartheid South Africa led eventually to the banning of that country from international cricket. Young D'Oliveira excelled as a batsman and medium-pace bowler in club and nonwhite representative cricket in South Africa, but because he was classified as Cape Coloured because of his Indian-Portuguese ethnicity, he was ineligible to play for the South African national team. D'Oliveira made his first-class debut in 1961–62 for a Commonwealth XI in Rhodesia, his English county debut in 1965 for Worcestershire, scoring a century, and his debut for England in the second (Lord's) Test against the West Indies in 1966. He played well initially, but his performance declined against West Indies in 1967–68. He was dropped after the first Test against Australia in 1968 but was recalled for the fifth (Oval) Test, where his 158 in the first innings highlighted the question of his selection for the winter tour of South Africa. The South African government had made it known that D'Oliveira would not be welcome, and the English cricket authorities excluded him. A controversy ensued, and after another player withdrew owing to injury, D'Oliveira was selected as a replacement. In the face of South African opposition, the English authorities called off the tour. A proposed South Africa tour to England in 1970 elicited strong protests, and that year the governing International Cricket Conference suspended South Africa from international competition, a ban that stood until after the fall of apartheid. D'Oliveira played for England until 1972 and for Worcestershire until 1980, after which he was a coach (1980–91). D'Oliveira was made OBE in 1969 and CBE in 2005.

Duerson, Dave (DAVID RUSSELL DUERSON), American football player (b. Nov. 28, 1960, Muncie, Ind.—d. Feb. 17, 2011, Sunny Isles Beach, Fla.), was a durable safety (1983–89) for the Chicago Bears professional football team and helped the Bears capture the 1985 Super Bowl against the New England Patriots in a lopsided 46–10 victory; he won his second Super Bowl ring as a player (1990–91) for the New York Giants. Duerson was drafted by the Bears from the University of Notre Dame, where he earned (1983) a degree in economics. The four-time Pro Bowl safety ended his 11-year career with the Phoenix Cardinals (1991–93). Duerson, who was experiencing personal and financial problems, was convinced that as a result of his years on the gridiron, he suffered from a form of dementia caused by repeated brain trauma. He fatally shot himself in the chest and left instructions that his brain be assessed by the Center for the Study of Traumatic Encephalopathy at Boston University. After his death, it was revealed that Duerson did suffer from chronic traumatic encephalopathy.

Dummett, Sir Michael Anthony Eardley, English philosopher (b. June 27, 1925, London, Eng.—d. Dec. 27, 2011, Oxford, Eng.), did influential work in the philosophy of language, metaphysics, logic, the philosophy of mathematics, and the history of analytic philosophy. He was also one of the foremost expositors of the work of the late 19th-century German mathematical logician Gottlob Frege. Dummett was known chiefly for his defense of antirealism and his attempt to explicate sentence meaning in terms of "assertibility conditions" rather than truth conditions. Dummett was knighted in 1999 for his philosophical work and his decadeslong efforts to combat racism in British society. His major philosophical works include *Frege: Philosophy of Language* (1973; 2nd ed. 1981), *Frege: Philosophy of Mathematics* (1991), *The Logical Basis of Metaphysics* (1991), *The Origins of Analytical Philosophy* (1993), *Truth and the Past* (2004), and *Thought and Reality* (2006).

Eagleburger, Lawrence, American diplomat and political official (b. Aug. 1, 1930, Milwaukee, Wis.—d. June 4, 2011, Charlottesville, Va.), became acting U.S. secretary of state on Aug. 13, 1992, when Secretary of State James A. Baker resigned to become White House chief of staff for Pres. George H.W. Bush; on December 8 Eagleburger was formally sworn to serve out the secretaryship for the final weeks of President Bush's term in office. Eagleburger, who was widely respected for his long diplomatic experience, was the first career foreign service officer to hold the post. He graduated (1952) from the University of Wisconsin at Madison and, following a stint in the U.S. Army, became (1957) a foreign service officer. He worked at the U.S. embassies in Honduras and Yugoslavia and in 1969 was named an assistant to Henry Kissinger, then Pres. Richard Nixon's national security adviser. Eagleburger later served (1971–73) as deputy assistant secretary of defense before returning to the State Department. He was the U.S. ambassador to Yugoslavia (1977–81) under Pres. Jimmy Carter and, after serving in Pres. Ronald Reagan's administration as undersecretary of state for political affairs, he became (1984) the head of Kissinger's consulting firm, Kissinger Associates. In March 1989 Eagleburger returned to government service as President Bush's deputy secretary of state. Eagleburger received the State Department's Distinguished Service Award in 1992 and an honorary knighthood by Britain's Queen Elizabeth II in 1994.

Jeff Christensen—Reuters/Landov

Blues legend Honeyboy Edwards

Edwards, Honeyboy (DAVID EDWARDS), American blues singer (b. June 28, 1915, near Shaw, Miss.—d. Aug. 29, 2011, Chicago, Ill.), was the last of the Mississippi Delta bluesmen to have come of age in the 1930s. Edwards's parents were sharecroppers who moved to a plantation near Greenwood, Miss., in 1927. His father was an amateur musician, and Edwards took up the guitar under his tutelage and then under many of the other musicians who lived in or visited the Greenwood area. Edwards left the area in late 1932 to perform with Joe Lee ("Big Joe") Williams in juke joints and on the streets of Mississippi and Louisiana. Edwards traveled as an itinerant bluesman for the next 25 years and met and played with some of the most significant bluesmen of the time, including Charley Patton, Big Walter Horton, Little Walter Jacobs, Sunnyland Slim, Son House, Robert Lockwood, Jr., and Robert Johnson. In July 1942 in Clarksdale, Miss., Edwards recorded more than a dozen songs for folklorist Alan Lomax. In 1956 Edwards settled in Chicago. The interest of young whites in blues music in the 1960s provided a new impetus for his career. The recording of a 2004 concert with Pinetop Perkins (*q.v.*), Henry Townsend, and Lockwood—*Last of the Great Mississippi Bluesmen: Live in Dallas*—won a Grammy Award in 2008 for best traditional blues album. Edwards also received a Grammy in 2010 for lifetime achievement.

Erbakan, Necmettin, Turkish politician (b. 1926, Sinop, Tur.—d. Feb. 27, 2011, Ankara, Tur.), paved the way for a greater role for Islam in Turkish politics, but his tenure as the country's first Islamist prime minister (June 28, 1996–June 30, 1997) ended abruptly amid accusations that he was attempting to undermine Turkey's secular constitution. Erbakan was the son of one of the last Islamic judges of the Ottoman Empire. He received degrees in mechanical engineering from Istanbul Technical University, where he later taught, and the Rhenish-Westphalian Technical University of Aachen, then in West Germany. He was elected to the legislature as an independent in 1969 and formed his first Islamist party the following year. Over the next two decades, Erbakan's parties were repeatedly banned by the government; he was briefly imprisoned in 1980 and then prohibited from participating in politics until 1987. In the run-up to the 1995 elections, Erbakan's Islamist Welfare Party (RP) captured 158 of the 550 seats in the legislature and thereby became the first Islamic party ever to win a general election in Turkey. On July 8, 1996, the legislature confirmed a coalition government in which Erbakan and Tansu Ciller of the centre-right True Path Party would alternate as prime minister. Fears that the RP was attempting to Islamicize the country, however, led the military to force Erbakan to resign. He was convicted in 2000 of "provoking hatred"—the result of a speech he made in 1994—and again in 2002, this time of having embezzled RP funds during its dissolution, but he became politically active again in 2003.

Evora, Cesaria, Cape Verdean singer (b. Aug. 27, 1941, Mindelo, São Vicente island, Cape Verde—d. Dec. 17, 2011, Mindelo), applied her rich, haunting voice to *mornas* (traditional Cape Verdean folk songs that express sorrowful emotion-charged chronicles of the country's history of isolation, slave trade, and population loss due to emigration), as well as *coladeras*—*mornas* with a faster tempo—and other international music styles. Evora began singing as a child and as a young adult

Evocative singer Cesaria Evora

Betote Akwa—Dalle/Landov

routinely performed in the bars of Mindelo. She sang in Creole-Portuguese, usually accompanied by guitar, piano, or the *cavaquinho*, a four-stringed instrument similar to a ukulele. Frustrated by financial and personal issues and political upheaval, Evora stopped performing in public in the mid-1970s. She resumed singing in 1985 and later left home to perform in Lisbon. She won a World Music Grammy Award for *Voz d'amor* (2003). Her final album, *Cesaria Evora & . . .* (2010), was a collection of duets assembled through collaboration with musicians from more than 15 countries.

Falk, Peter Michael, American actor (b. Sept. 16, 1927, New York, N.Y. —d. June 23, 2011, Beverly Hills, Calif.), was best remembered for his portrayal of the disheveled trench-coat-wearing, cigar-smoking Los Angeles homicide detective on the television series *Columbo*. Falk played the wily Lieutenant Columbo in 69 intermittent episodes and made-for-TV movies over a period of 35 years (1968–2003) and won four Emmy Awards for the portrayal. He began acting in Off-Broadway plays in 1956 and on TV soon after. Falk later appeared on Broadway in Neil Simon's *Prisoner of Second Avenue* (1971) and in such films as *Murder Inc.* (1960) and *Pocketful of Miracles* (1961); he was nominated for an Academy Award for best supporting actor for both of those films.

Ferraro, Geraldine Anne, American politician (b. Aug. 26, 1935, Newburgh, N.Y.—d. March 26, 2011, Boston, Mass.), broke new political ground as the first woman to be nominated for vice president by a major American political party when Democratic Party presidential candidate Walter Mondale selected her in 1984 to be his running mate, but the duo lost the election to incumbent Pres. Ronald Reagan and Vice Pres. George H.W. Bush. While teaching English in public schools in Queens, she studied at night at Fordham University Law School (LL.B., 1960). She practiced law until 1974, when she became an assistant district attorney in Queens. Ferraro was elected (1978) to the U.S. House of Representatives on a platform supporting law and order, the elderly, and neighbourhood preservation and was reelected in 1980 and 1982. She was elected secretary of the Democratic caucus in 1980, and four years later she was appointed chair of the party's platform committee, the first woman to hold the post. After leaving the U.S. House in 1984, Ferraro held a fellowship at the Harvard University Institute of Politics (1988), twice ran unsuccessfully for the U.S. Senate (1992 and 1998), served as a member (1993–96) of the UN Commission on Human Rights, and was cohost (1996–98) of the political debate show *Crossfire* on the CNN cable TV network.

Bebeto Matthews/AP

Politician Geraldine Ferraro

Fischer, (Erling) Gunnar, Swedish cinematographer (b. Nov. 18, 1910, Ljungby, Swed.—d. June 11, 2011, Stockholm, Swed.), showcased his stark expressionistic style in 12 of filmmaker Ingmar Bergman's masterful black-and-white films, most notably *Det sjunde inseglet* (1957; *The Seventh Seal*) and *Smultronstället* (1957; *Wild Strawberries*). Fischer began his cinematic career in 1935 at the production company Svensk Filmindustri. There he contributed to dozens of movies, benefiting from the guidance of the renowned cinematographer Julius Jaenzon and a collaboration with Danish director Carl Theodor Dreyer on *Två människor* (1945). Fischer's career reached its peak in his partnership (1948–60) with Bergman, which began with *Hamnstad* (1948; *Port of Call*). The pair produced *Kvinnors väntan* (1952; *Secrets of Women*), *Sommaren med Monika* (1953; *Summer with Monika*), and *Sommarnattens leende* (1955; *Smiles of a Summer Night*) and closed with *Djävulens öga* (1960; *The Devil's Eye*). Fischer's later work included British director Anthony Asquith's *Two Living, One Dead* (1961) and French filmmaker Jacques Tati's television movie *Parade* (1974).

FitzGerald, Garret Michael, Irish politician (b. Feb. 9, 1926, Dublin, Irish Free State—d. May 19, 2011, Dublin, Ire.), as taoiseach (prime minister) of Ireland (June 1981–March 1982, December 1982–March 1987), pushed for liberalization of Irish laws on divorce, abortion, and contraception and strove to build bridges to Protestant leaders in Northern Ireland. In 1985 he and British Prime Minister Margaret Thatcher signed the Anglo-Irish (Hillsborough) Agreement, giving Ireland a consultative role in the governing of Northern Ireland. FitzGerald was born into a politically active family (his father was the Irish Free State's first minister of external affairs). He was educated in Dublin at University College and King's Inns and qualified as a barrister, but instead of practicing law he became (1959) an economics lecturer at University College and a journalist. He joined Fine Gael (his father's old party) and in 1969 was elected to the Dail (lower house of parliament). FitzGerald served as foreign minister (1973–77) in Prime Minister Liam Cosgrave's coalition government. When that government was resoundingly defeated in the 1977 general election, Cosgrave yielded leadership of Fine Gael to FitzGerald, who modernized and strengthened the party at the grass roots. He briefly lost power in 1982 when political instability triggered two snap elections. After Fine Gael lost in the 1987 general election, he resigned as leader; he retired in 1992.

Ford, Betty (ELIZABETH ANNE BLOOMER), American first lady (b. April 8, 1918, Chicago, Ill.—d. July 8, 2011, Rancho Mirage, Calif.), was the outspoken wife of U.S. Pres. Gerald R. Ford and the cofounder (1982) and chair (1982–2005) of the Betty Ford Center, a facility dedicated to helping people recover from drug and alcohol dependence. Ford compiled a remarkably independent record as first lady; she voiced public support for such issues as *Roe* v. *Wade*—the U.S. Supreme Court decision that legalized abortion—and the Equal Rights Amendment (ERA), then up for ratification in several state legislatures. She also candidly discussed her own struggles with breast cancer and addiction to prescription drugs and alcohol. She stud-

Wally Fong/AP

First lady Betty Ford

ied at Bennington (Vt.) College, where she came under the influence of dancer and choreographer Martha Graham, who accepted her into her New York City troupe. She performed as one of Graham's auxiliaries, but at her mother's insistence, she left the Graham troupe and returned to Grand Rapids. After an unsuccessful first marriage (1942–47), the newly divorced Betty met Gerald Ford, then a local Grand Rapids lawyer. They were married on Oct. 15, 1948. Less than a month later he was elected to Congress, and the couple moved to Washington, D.C. In the mid-1960s, when she developed a pinched nerve and spinal arthritis, doctors prescribed pain medicine, to which she became addicted. Her life as the inconspicuous wife of a congressman ended in October 1973 when Vice Pres. Spiro Agnew resigned and Pres. Richard Nixon named her husband to the job. After Nixon resigned on Aug. 9, 1974, Gerald Ford was sworn in as president. Just weeks later, on September 28, Betty Ford's doctors performed a mastectomy, removing her cancerous right breast. She continued to perform her duties as first lady, however, and openly discussed both her cancer surgery and her subsequent chemotherapy. She gained national attention in August 1975 for her appearance on the TV news program *60 Minutes* when she said that she would not be surprised to learn that her 18-year-old daughter had had premarital sex. Ford's popularity soared, and *Newsweek* magazine later named her Woman of the Year. After her husband narrowly lost the 1976 presidential election to Jimmy Carter, the Fords retired to California. Betty Ford was the recipient of a Presidential Medal of Freedom (1991) and corecipient (1999) with her husband of a Congressional Gold Medal.

Foster, Frank Benjamin, III, American jazz artist (b. Sept. 23, 1928, Cincinnati, Ohio—d. July 26, 2011, Chesapeake, Va.), played robust bop tenor saxophone solos in the Count Basie Orchestra and also composed arrangements that were essential in creating the modern Basie style in the 1950s. Foster attended Wilberforce (Ohio) University. He performed in Detroit and served in the U.S. Army before recording with Thelonious Monk and joining the Basie band in 1953. The sly, blues-hinting sophistication of his arrangements, including distinctive flute, clarinet, and muted brass voicings, graced hit albums such as *Count Basie Swings, Joe Williams Sings* (1955) and *April in Paris* (1956), which vaulted Basie to popularity. Foster provided the arrangements for the entire *Easin' It* (1960) album by Basie's orchestra. Foster's own songs, such as "Blues in Hoss' Flat," "Blues Backstage," "Down for the Count," and "Shiny Stockings" (recorded over 400 times), became familiar standards. After leaving Basie in 1964, he joined Elvin Jones's Jazz Machine and arranged for other leading big bands and singers. For much of the 1970s and until 1986, he led his New York-based Loud Minority Big Band. Two years after Basie's death, Foster led the Basie Orchestra (1986–95), which won Grammy Awards in 1987 and 1990. In 2002 Foster was named a National Endowment for the Arts Jazz Master.

Franco, Itamar Augusto Cautiero, Brazilian politician (b. June 28, 1930, at sea off the coast of Brazil—d. July 2, 2011, São Paulo, Braz.), served as vice president (1990–92) and president (1992–95) of Brazil, but he was a quiet, intensely private man who shunned most public meetings and avoided difficult decisions, and he proved to be unable to cope with government corruption scandals and inflation of up to 6,000%. He was a founding member of the opposition Brazilian Democratic Movement (now the Party of the Brazilian Democratic Movement) and was elected Juiz de Fora's mayor (1966–74); he then served (1974–90) in the federal Senate, leading committees on economy and finance and investigating corruption. He was Fernando Collor de Mello's running mate in the 1990 presidential election, which they won. Faced with charges of corruption and unable to move reforms through the legislature, however, Collor resigned in September 1992. After the National Congress voted for Collor's impeachment, Franco was sworn in as president on December 29, but his approval rating soon fell to 14.5%. He stepped down at the end of his term, on Jan. 1, 1995.

Frankenthaler, Helen, American painter (b. Dec. 12, 1928, New York, N.Y.—d. Dec. 27, 2011, Darien, Conn.), created brilliantly coloured Abstract Expressionist canvases that were much admired for their lyric qualities and introduced a new stain technique of applying colour to a canvas. In one of her major early works, the seminal *Mountains and Sea* (1952), she created diaphanous colour by means of thinned-down oils that she allowed to soak into

Abstract Expressionist Helen Frankenthaler

Suzanne Dechillo—The New York Times/Redux

the raw (unprimed) canvas. This method, known as the soak-stain technique, strongly contrasted with the use of impasto that characterized most Abstract Expressionist painting, and it seriously influenced the colour-field painters Morris Louis and Kenneth Noland. Inspired by the work of such artists as Arshile Gorky and Jackson Pollock, she eventually became known as a member of the second generation of Abstract Expressionists. Frankenthaler's first one-woman show was held in New York City in 1951. In the early 1960s she began to use acrylics, and the areas of raw canvas began to assume much greater spatial significance. Her later exhibitions included lithographs and works on paper. Although not abstractions of nature, many of her paintings, such as *This Morning's Weather* (1982) and *Yoruba* (2002), embody a strong feeling of landscape. Among her later works are *Seeing the Moon on a Hot Summer Day* (1987), *Warming Trend* (2002), and *Ebbing* (2002).

The State—MCT/Landov

Boxer Joe Frazier

Frazier, Joe (SMOKIN' JOE), American boxer (b. Jan. 12, 1944, Beaufort, S.C.—d. Nov. 7, 2011, Philadelphia, Pa.), reigned (Feb. 16, 1970–Jan. 22, 1973) as world heavyweight boxing champion until he was beaten by George Foreman at Kingston, Jam., but was probably best remembered for the bruising bouts he fought against Muhammad Ali. During Frazier's amateur career he was one of the best heavyweights in the U.S., but in 1964 he lost in the Olympic trials to Buster Mathis and made it to the Tokyo Olympic Games as a replacement boxer only when Mathis broke his thumb. Frazier won the gold medal in his weight division and then began his professional career in August 1965. Frazier (1.8 m [5 ft 11.5 in] tall and weighing 92.9 kg [205 lb]) had an aggressive style and a powerful left hook. On March 4, 1968, in a New York title bout, Frazier knocked out his rival Mathis in 11 rounds. The following month Jimmy Ellis won a championship tournament (in which Frazier declined to participate) approved by the WBA. Frazier successfully defended his New York title four times before defeating Ellis in a fifth-round technical knockout to claim the WBA heavyweight title. In "The Fight of the Century," held in New York City's Madison Square Garden on March 8, 1971, Frazier and Ali fought at a furious pace for 15 rounds, but Ali had lost some of his speed during his three-year absence from boxing, and Frazier scored a decision over him. After his loss to Foreman in 1973, Frazier faced Ali again in a nontitle bout in 1974, losing a 12-round decision. On Oct. 1, 1975, the two faced off in the Philippines for the rubber match. The fight, known as the "Thrilla in Manila," was for the heavyweight championship, and this time Ali won by technical knockout after 14 grueling rounds. Frazier retired in 1976, and after he staged an unsuccessful comeback in 1981, he retired again and began operating a gym in Philadelphia. Frazier was inducted into the International Boxing Hall of Fame in 1990.

Freud, Lucian Michael, British artist (b. Dec. 8, 1922, Berlin, Ger.—d. July 20, 2011, London, Eng.), brought a sometimes shocking realism to his figurative paintings, notably his work in portraiture and the nude. Freud painted in a highly individual style, which in his later years was characterized by impasto. His early painting *Interior at Paddington* (1951) exhibits many of his lifelong concerns—the human figure rendered in a realist manner and imbued with a stark and evocative psychological intensity. Freud often highlighted and undercut the erotics of the female nude, opting out of the idealizing tendencies of much of the history of Western art, and beginning in the 1980s, he was increasingly drawn toward what could be called extreme body types. His series of paintings and drawings of his mother, begun in 1970 and continuing until the day after her death in 1989, are particularly frank and dramatic studies of intimate life passages. Freud was the son of the architect Ernst Freud and a grandson of Sigmund Freud. He immigrated with his family to England in 1933 and became a naturalized citizen in 1939. He was trained at the Central School of Arts and Crafts in London, where he was known as much for his unconventional behaviour as for his drawing talent, and at the East Anglian School of Painting and Drawing in Dedham. Freud was a Companion of Honour (1983) and a member of the Order of Merit (1993).

Gardner, Carl Edward, American musician (b. April 29, 1928, Tyler, Texas—d. June 12, 2011, Port St. Lucie, Fla.), sang lead tenor for the Coasters for 50 years, lending his attractive vocals to such novelty rock-and-roll hits as "Yakety Yak" (1958), which reached the number one slot on *Billboard*'s Hot 100, "Charlie Brown" (1959), and "Poison Ivy" (1959). The Coasters' close harmony and often humorous songs made them one of the most popular vocal groups of the 1950s. The Coasters' roster changed over time, with Gardner as the only constant member until his retirement in 2005. During their heyday, however, the Coasters included Gardner, Billy Guy, Cornel Gunter, and Will Jones, and it was this version of the Coasters that was inducted (1987) into the Rock and Roll Hall of Fame, the first vocal group to be so honoured.

Gems, Pam (IRIS PAMELA PRICE), British playwright (b. Aug. 1, 1925, Bransgore, Hampshire, Eng.—d. May 13, 2011, London, Eng.), wrote unsentimental feminist plays and television scripts that were celebrated for their lack of pretension and frank depiction of female characters, most notably *Piaf*, a portrayal of the celebrated French chanteuse Edith Piaf. The play was produced by the Royal Shakespeare Company (1978–79) before transferring to the West End (1979–80) and to Broadway (1981). Gems had her first financial success with *Dead Fish*, or *Dusa, Fish, Stas and Vi* (1976), which follows four single women living in a shared flat. Her other biographical plays include *Queen Christina* (1982), which explores the pain of childlessness through the life of that 17th-century Swedish monarch, and *Stanley* (1996), which concerns the life of painter Stanley Spencer and was Gems's last major success with an original play.

Girardot, Annie Suzanne, French actress (b. Oct. 25, 1931, Paris, France—d. Feb. 28, 2011, Paris), achieved film stardom in France with more than 100 movies over a six-decade career (1955–2007), but she earned international acclaim—and a nomination for best foreign actress in the 1961 British Academy of Film and Television Awards—for her poignant turn as the doomed prostitute Nadia in Luchino Visconti's Italian-language film *Rocco e i suoi fratelli* (1960). She also won three César Awards: for best actress for *Docteur Françoise Gailland* (1976) and for best supporting actress for both *Les Misérables* (1995) and *La Pianiste* (2001), as well as a second best actress nomination for *La Clé sur la porte* (1978). Girardot studied at the Paris Conservatory and spent three years (1954–57) with the Comédie-Française. Her other films include *Trois Chambres à Manhattan* (1965), *Mourir d'aimer* (1971), and *La Vieille Fille* (1972).

Remy de la Mauviniere/AP

Actress Annie Girardot

Goldhaber, Maurice, American physicist (b. April 18, 1911, Lemberg, Austria-Hungary [now Lviv, Ukr.]—d. May 11, 2011, East Setauket, N.Y.), made significant contributions to nuclear physics, including the discovery that the nucleus of the deuterium atom consists of a proton and a neutron. While studying at the University of Cambridge, Goldhaber, in collaboration with James Chadwick, discovered (1934) the nuclear photoelectric effect (the disintegration of a nucleus by high-energy X-rays or gamma rays). This finding later provided evidence that the neutron is heavier than the proton. While studying slow neutrons, they discovered the neutron-induced disintegrations of the nuclei of lithium, boron, and nitrogen. Goldhaber also showed the usefulness of photographic emulsions in recording the tracks of particles formed in nuclear reactions. The slow-neutron scattering studies he made in 1937 were essential to the development of the first nuclear reactors. In 1938 Goldhaber joined the staff of the University of Illinois, where, with his wife, Gertrude Scharff Goldhaber (also a physicist), he demonstrated that electrons and beta rays are the same. In 1950 Goldhaber went to Brookhaven National Laboratory, Upton, N.Y., where, seven years later, with the American physicist Lee Grodzins, he discovered that the neutrino has a left-handed spin. Goldhaber served (1961–73) as director of Brookhaven. Goldhaber was the recipient of numerous honours, including the National Medal of Science (1983) and the Enrico Fermi Award (1999).

Gomes, Peter John, American clergyman and author (b. May 22, 1942, Boston, Mass.—d. Feb. 28, 2011, Boston), led Harvard University's Memorial Church for nearly four decades, but in 1991 the fiery Republican Baptist minister (later a registered Democrat) stunned his more conservative supporters with a public acknowledgment of his homosexuality at a rally against antigay activity on campus. Gomes, a descendant of slaves, earned a B.A. in history (1965) from Bates College, Lewiston, Maine, and a Bachelor of Divinity (1968) from Harvard. Gomes was ordained a minister in the American Baptist Church in 1968. He taught (1968–70) at the Tuskegee (Ala.) Institute before returning to Harvard to serve (1970–74) as assistant minister of its Memorial Church. In 1974 he became Pusey Minister in the Memorial Church and Plummer Professor of Christian Morals at the Divinity School, positions he held until his death. Gomes remained committed to speaking out against intolerance, and his sermons were collected in 11 volumes.

Granger, Farley Earle, American actor (b. July 1, 1925, San Jose, Calif.—d. March 27, 2011, New York, N.Y.), starred in two of director Alfred Hitchcock's most intriguing films, *Rope* (1948), in which Granger played a high-strung and somewhat reluctant murderer, and *Strangers on a Train* (1951), in which he portrayed a tennis star drawn unwittingly into a murder pact with a charming sociopath. After World War II service, he appeared in such films as *They Live by Night* (1949), *Side Street* (1950), and *Hans Christian Andersen* (1952), but he became dissatisfied with roles that relied more on his brooding good looks than his acting. After having been loaned out for Italian director Luchino Visconti's *Senso* (1954), Granger bought out his studio contract and moved to New York City to study acting and pursue a stage career. Thereafter he appeared frequently on television and on the stage, notably in several Broadway productions and at the Circle Repertory Company in Lanford Wilson's *(q.v.) Talley and Son* (1985), for which he received an Obie Award for best actor. Granger discussed his own bisexuality and the homosexual subtexts in some of his films in the documentary *The Celluloid Closet* (1995) and in his autobiography, *Include Me Out* (2007), written with his longtime partner, Robert Calhoun.

Grant, Alexander, New Zealand-born ballet dancer and artistic director (b. Feb. 22, 1925, Wellington, N.Z.—d. Sept. 30, 2011, London, Eng.), delighted audiences as a *demi-caractère* dancer who used his superb classical technique to great effect in character roles. Although he rarely played romantic leads during his 30 years (1946–76) with the Royal Ballet, Grant shone in more than 20 roles created for him by choreographer Sir Frederick Ashton, including the rejected suitor in *La Fille mal gardée* and Bottom in *The Dream* (an adaptation of Shakespeare's *A Midsummer Night's Dream*), a role that required him to perform a dazzling solo *en pointe* while wearing a donkey head. He also portrayed Peter Rabbit and danced *en pointe* as Pigling Bland in the film version of Ashton's *Tales of Beatrix Potter* (1971). Grant studied ballet in his native New Zealand and earned a scholarship to the Sadler's Wells Ballet (later the Royal Ballet) School in London, but he was quickly advanced into the main company. His other significant roles included the pirate chief in *Daphnis and Chloë* and the lead in *Petrouchka*. After he retired from the Royal Ballet, he served (1976–83) as artistic director of the National Ballet of Canada. Grant was made CBE in 1965.

Gueiler Tejada, Lidia, Bolivian politician (b. Aug. 28, 1921, Cochabamba, Bol.—d. May 9, 2011, La Paz, Bol.), was the first woman to serve (1979–80) as president of Bolivia and only the second to hold that high office in the Western Hemisphere (after Argentina's Isabel Perón). Gueiler became a member of the Nationalist Revolutionary Movement (MNR) in 1948, and three years later she cemented her reputation as a social rights activist by leading 26 women on an eight-day hunger strike to win the release of their sons and husbands, who were being held as leftist political prisoners. She was an active participant in the 1952 revolt to oust Bolivia's military leadership, but after the military overthrew the MNR-led government in 1964, she was imprisoned and then forced into exile upon her release. Following her return to Bolivia, Gueiler was elected (1979) president of the Chamber of Deputies and, later that year, president of Congress. Her eight-month term as interim president of Bolivia ended in another military coup.

Haasse, Hella S. (HÉLÈNE SERAFIA VAN LELYVELD-HAASSE), Dutch novelist (b. Feb. 2, 1918, Batavia, Dutch East Indies [now Jakarta, Indon.]—d. Sept. 29, 2011, Amsterdam, Neth.), was noted for her innovative historical fiction and for her literary examinations of colonial life in the Dutch East Indies, where she grew up. Haasse studied at the Amsterdam Toneelschool, a dramatic arts school, and published a volume of poetry, *Stroomversnelling* (1945). In her first novella, *Oeroeg* (1948), she explored race relations in the Dutch East Indies; she later returned to that setting in the novels *Heren van de thee* (1992; *The Tea Lords*, 2010) and *Sleuteloog* (2002). Her first historical novel, *Het woud der verwachting* (1949; *In a Dark Wood Wandering*, 1989), concerns Charles d'Orléans, a 15th-century French nobleman. Giovanni Borgia, a 16th-century Italian aristocrat, is the subject of *De scharlaken stad* (1952; *The Scarlet City*, 1954), while *Een nieuwer testament* (1966; *Threshold of Fire*, 1993) is set in 5th-century Rome. She revived the Marchioness of Merteuil (from Choderlos de Laclos's novel *Les Liaisons dangereuses*) in *Een gevaarlijke verhouding of Daal-en-Bergse brieven* (1976). Haasse's other novels include *Onverenigbaarheid van karakter* (1978), *De groten der aarde* (1981), and the dark thriller *Fenrir: een lang weekend in de Ardennen* (2000). Haasse won the Constantijn Huygens Prize in 1981, the P.C. Hooft Prize in 1984, and the Dutch Literature Prize in 2004. She was inducted (2000) into the French Legion of Honour.

Hamilton, Richard William, British artist (b. Feb. 24, 1922, London, Eng.—d. Sept. 13, 2011, near Oxford, Eng.), was frequently referred to as "the father of Pop art." Although much of Hamilton's work parodied contemporary culture in the 1950s and '60s, his reputation as an artistic pioneer rested largely on his landmark collage poster *Just What Is It That Makes Today's Homes So Different, So Appealing?*, a parody of bourgeois domesticity that was introduced at the exhibition "This Is Tomorrow" mounted in 1956 at London's Whitechapel Art Gallery by the circle of artists known as the Independent Group. Hamilton's later work included commercial art, photographs overcovered in paint, screenprints, found art, and, notably, the cover sleeve for the Beatles' *White Album* (1968).

Handlin, Oscar, American historian and educator (b. Sept. 29, 1915, Brooklyn, N.Y.—d. Sept. 20, 2011, Cambridge, Mass.), examined immigration and other social topics in American history in such notable works as *Boston's Immigrants, 1790–1865* (1941), a modified form of his doctoral thesis on the acculturation of Irish immigrants to that city, and the Pulitzer Prize-winning *The Uprooted* (1951), which told the story of the great waves of immigration that formed the American people. The latter work examined the psychological and cultural adjustments that people had to make after settling in the U.S. Handlin's other works include *Race and Nationality in American Life* (1956), *Fire-Bell in the Night* (1964), *Facing Life* (1971; with his first wife, Mary F. Handlin), *Truth in History* (1979), and the multivolume set *Liberty in America, 1600 to the Present* (1986–94; co-written with his second wife, Lilian Handlin).

Hardwicke, Edward Cedric, British actor (b. Aug. 7, 1932, London, Eng.—d. May 16, 2011, Chichester, West Sussex, Eng.), brought amiable dignity to his portrayal of the stalwart Dr. John Watson opposite Jeremy Brett's quintessential Sherlock Holmes on British television in the 1980s and '90s. He took on the role of Holmes's steadfast companion in the show's third series and appeared in 28 episodes and made-for-TV movies over a nine-year span (1986–94). Hardwicke, the son of actor Sir Cedric Hardwicke and actress Helena Pickard, made his film debut (uncredited) at age 10. He appeared regularly on TV from the late 1950s, notably in the World War II drama *Colditz* (1972–73), and in such films as *Shadowlands* (1993), *Richard III* (1995), and *Elizabeth* (1998).

Hauptman, Herbert Aaron, American mathematician and crystallographer (b. Feb. 14, 1917, New York, N.Y.—d. Oct. 23, 2011, Buffalo, N.Y.), shared, with Jerome Karle, the Nobel Prize for Chemistry in 1985. They developed mathematical methods for deducing the molecular structure of chemical compounds from the patterns formed when X-rays are diffracted by their crystals. Hauptman and Karle were classmates at City College of New York, from which both graduated in 1937. Hauptman went on to study mathematics further at Columbia University (M.A., 1939), New York City, and at the University of Maryland (Ph.D., 1955). After World War II, Hauptman was reunited with Karle at the Naval Research Laboratory (Washington, D.C.), where they began collaborating on the study of crystal structures. In 1970 Hauptman became a professor of biophysics at the State University of New York at Buffalo and joined the Medical Foundation of Buffalo (renamed in 1994 the Hauptman-Woodward Medical Research Institute), later serving as research director and president. Hauptman and Karle devised mathematical equations to extract phase information from the intensity of spots resulting from the diffraction of X-rays deflected off crystals. Their equations made it possible to pinpoint the location of atoms within the crystal's molecules based upon an analysis of the intensity of the spots.

Havel, Vaclav, Czech playwright, political dissident, and politician (b. Oct. 5, 1936, Prague, Czech. [now in Czech Republic]—d. Dec. 18, 2011, Hradcek, Cz.Rep.), was president of Czechoslovakia (1989–92) and of the Czech Republic (1993–2003) after having been a prominent participant in the liberal reforms of 1968 (the Prague Spring) and a leader in the human rights movement after the Soviet clampdown on Czechoslovakia that year. Havel, the son of a wealthy restaurateur whose property was confiscated by the communist government in 1948, managed to finish high school and study on the university

Petr David Josek/AP

Playwright, poet, and dissident Vaclav Havel

level. He found work in 1959 in a Prague theatrical company and began writing plays, alone and in collaboration. His first solo play, *Zahradní slavnost* (1963; *The Garden Party*), typified his work in its absurdist, satiric examination of bureaucratic routines and their dehumanizing effects. It was followed by his best-known play, *Vyrozumění* (1965; *The Memorandum*). By 1968 Havel was the resident playwright of the Theatre of the Balustrade company. After the Soviet crackdown, however, his plays were banned and his passport was confiscated. Havel was repeatedly arrested, and he served four years in prison (1979–83). When massive antigovernment demonstrations erupted in Prague in November 1989, Havel became the leading figure in the pro-democracy Civic Forum. The Communist Party soon capitulated, and in the aftermath of this bloodless Velvet Revolution, he was elected president. Havel opposed the dissolution of the Czechoslovak union and resigned from office in 1992; the following year he was elected president of the new Czech Republic. Barred constitutionally from seeking a third term, he stepped down in 2003. Havel's first new play in more than 20 years, the tragicomedy *Odcházení* (*Leaving*), premiered in 2008; he subsequently directed the 2011 film adaptation.

Haworth, (Valerie) Jill, British-born actress (b. Aug. 15, 1945, Hove, East Sussex, Eng.—d. Jan. 3, 2011, New York, N.Y.), created the role of Sally Bowles in the original Broadway production (1966–69) of the musical *Cabaret*. Many critics and audience members expressed disappointment that Haworth, who had never before sung professionally, was not a more dynamic singer in her portrayal of the decadent Kit Kat Club songstress in pre-World War II Berlin. The show's producers, however, declared that she was cast in the part precisely because she was a physically delicate ingenue with an untrained voice and therefore perfectly suited to play the self-deluded but mediocre Bowles as she was presented in Christopher Isherwood's original collection, *The Berlin Stories*, and the nonmusical play *I Am a Camera*, upon which *Cabaret* was based. Haworth made her film debut at age 15 as a Jewish refugee in *Exodus* (1960), directed by Otto Preminger. She acted in two more Preminger movies, *The Cardinal* (1963) and *In Harm's Way* (1965).

Hitchens, Christopher Eric, British American author, critic, and bon vivant (b. April 13, 1949, Portsmouth, Eng.—d. Dec. 15, 2011, Houston, Texas), proffered trenchant polemics on politics, religion, and other topics that positioned him at the forefront of public intellectual life in the late 20th and early 21st centuries. Though long an adamant leftist, Hitchens cultivated connections across the political spectrum, and after the terrorist attacks of Sept. 11, 2001, he drew criticism from the left for his support of the U.S.-led war in Iraq. With the publication of *God Is Not Great: How Religion Poisons Everything* (2007), he also moved to the forefront of the modern atheist movement. Hitchens obtained a degree in philosophy, politics, and economics (1970) from Balliol College, Oxford, where he joined the Trotskyist International Socialists. He moved to London and wrote for the *Times Higher Education Supplement*, the left-wing weekly *New Statesman*, and then the *Evening Standard* newspaper. He served as a foreign correspondent for the *Daily Express* (1977–79) before becoming foreign editor of the *New Statesman* (1979–81). In 1981 Hitchens moved to the U.S. (he became a citizen in 2007), and in 1982 he settled in Washington, D.C., where he penned columns for the liberal magazine *The Nation* (1982–2002) and *Vanity Fair* magazine (1992–2011). Hitchens frequently lambasted the mythologizing of public figures; he wrote books skewering U.S. Pres. Bill Clinton, former U.S. secretary of state Henry Kissinger, and Mother Teresa. Other books include *The Elgin Marbles: Should They Be Returned to Greece?* (1987), *Why Orwell Matters* (2002), *The Quotable Hitchens: From Alcohol to Zionism*, and *Arguably*, a collection of cultural commentary, the latter two published in 2011. In addition he appeared regularly as a TV commentator and on the lecture circuit.

Contrarian Christopher Hitchens

Stephen Shepherd—eyevine/Redux

Hoban, Russell Conwell, American novelist and children's writer (b. Feb. 4, 1925, Lansdale, Pa.—d. Dec. 13, 2011, London, Eng.), combined myth, fantasy, humour, and philosophy to explore issues of self-identity. Hoban attended the Philadelphia Museum School of Industrial Art and served in the U.S. Army (1943–45) before beginning his career as an advertising artist and copywriter. He moved to London in 1969. His first book, *What Does It Do and How Does It Work?* (1959), developed from his drawings of construction machinery. One of his most enduring fictional creations, the anthropomorphic badger Frances, was featured with her family and friends in a series of six books that began with *Bedtime for Frances* (1960). Fear and mortality intrude on the fantasy story *The Mouse and His Child* (1967; filmed 1977), one of Hoban's best-known books. Prior to 1971 most of Hoban's books for children were illustrated by his first wife, Lillian Hoban. His novels for adults include *The Lion of Boaz-Jachin and Jachin-Boaz* (1973), *Turtle Diary* (1975; filmed 1985), and *Riddley Walker*

(1980). Hoban's later writings include the novels *The Medusa Frequency* (1987) and *My Tango with Barbara Strozzi* (2007).

Holkeri, Harri Hermanni, Finnish politician (b. Jan. 6, 1937, Oripää, Fin.—d. Aug. 7, 2011, Helsinki, Fin.), devoted his life to a political career that culminated in his service as prime minister of Finland (1987–91) and his role in brokering (alongside Canadian Gen. John de Chastelain and American diplomat George J. Mitchell) the 1998 Good Friday Agreement that achieved peace in Northern Ireland. After studying political science at the University of Helsinki (M.S., 1962), Holkeri was a member of Finland's delegation (1963–65) to the UN General Assembly. He became secretary (1965–71) and then head (1971–79) of the National Coalition Party, for which he was elected a member of Parliament (1970–78). He spent many years (1978–97) as a board member of the country's central bank. Holkeri was elected president of the UN General Assembly for 2000 and in 2003–04 was a UN special representative in Kosovo.

Horton, Gladys Catherine, American singer (b. May 30, 1945, Gainesville, Fla.—d. Jan. 26, 2011, Sherman Oaks, Calif.), was a founder of the all-girl singing group called the Marvelettes (previously known as the Casinyets ["can't sing yet"] and the Marvels); she was only 15 years old when she performed the lead vocals for the quintet's debut song, "Please Mr. Postman" (1961), which reached number one on *Billboard* magazine's Hot 100 chart and scored the first number one single for fledgling Motown Records. Other hits included "Playboy" (1962), "Beechwood 4-5789" (1962), and "Too Many Fish in the Sea" (1964), but the group chose not to record the Holland-Dozier-Holland-written track "Where Did Our Love Go?" (1964), which became a smash hit for the then-struggling all-girl trio the Supremes. In 1965 Horton was replaced as lead singer by Wanda Young, and the group scored several more hits, such as "Don't Mess with Bill" (1965) and "The Hunter Gets Captured by the Game" (1967) before Horton left in 1967 to start a family. The group disbanded in the early 1970s. Horton later returned to the stage, appearing as Gladys Horton of the Marvelettes with two younger singers. She continued to perform until 2009.

Hunter, Bill (William John Bourke Hunter), Australian character actor (b. Feb. 27, 1940, Ballarat, Vic., Australia—d. May 21, 2011, Kew, Vic.), performed in more than 100 films and television programs over a five-decade career, often portraying a stereotypically strong and opinionated Australian "bloke." Hunter was a promising swimmer as a boy and qualified for the 1960 Olympics in Rome, but after a bout of meningitis ended his hopes for Olympic stardom, he worked as an extra in the film *The Shiralee* (1957) and as a swimming stuntman in *On the Beach* (1959). For some two decades he appeared mainly on TV before expanding to the big screen. He won an Australian Film Institute award for best actor in a leading role for the drama *Newsfront* (1978), one of six career AFI nominations. Hunter had pivotal roles in such iconic Australian films as *Gallipoli* (1981), for which he won the AFI award for best actor in a supporting role, *Strictly Ballroom* (1992), *Muriel's Wedding* (1994), *The Adventures of Priscilla, Queen of the Desert* (1994), and *The Cup* (2011), in which he played champion Thoroughbred horse trainer Bart Cummings.

Husky, Ferlin, American country music singer (b. Dec. 3, 1925, Flat River, Mo.—d. March 17, 2011, Westmoreland, Tenn.), was credited with helping to usher in the Nashville Sound, which featured lush string orchestrals, and the Bakersfield (Calif.) Sound, which introduced country music to the West Coast; he also was remembered for his recordings of two number one songs: the ballad "Gone" (1956), which became a pop crossover hit in 1957, and the gospel-inspired "Wings of a Dove" (1960). The engaging Husky, who also played guitar, first performed in honky-tonks under the name Terry Preston but reverted to his given name in the early 1950s after signing (1953) with Capitol Records. He also began recording under the moniker Simon Crum, his comic alter ego, and scored hits with "Cuzz You're So Sweet" (1955) and "Country Music Is Here to Stay" (1958). Husky's duet with Jean Shepard, "A Dear John Letter" (1953), vaulted to number one, and the two had another hit later that year with the follow-up "Forgive Me John." From that year to 1975—the last three with ABC Records—he charted dozens more country hit singles, including "Once" (1966). He was inducted into the Country Music Hall of Fame in 2010.

Hveger, Ragnhild (Ragnhild Tove Hveger-Andersen; "The Golden Torpedo"), Danish swimmer (b. Dec. 10, 1920, Nyborg, Den.—d. Dec. 1, 2011), was a swimming phenomenon in pre-World War II Europe, setting 44 world records in six events (200-, 400-, 800-, and 1,500-m freestyle, 4 × 100-m freestyle relay, and 200-m backstroke) over a six-year span (1936–42), including 19 records in 1941 alone. Her career was marred, however, by the wartime cancellation of the 1940 and 1944 Olympic Games (when she was in her prime) and by her Nazi associations. Hveger was only 15 years old at the 1936 Olympics in Berlin, where she earned a 400-m silver medal, missing the gold by just 1.1 seconds. She went on to win three gold medals at the 1938 European swimming championships. During the war, however, she chose to compete and coach in Nazi Germany, which resulted in her exclusion from the Danish team when the Olympics resumed in 1948 in London. Hveger was selected for the 1952 Games in Helsinki, but at age 31 she could muster only a fifth-place finish in the 400 m. When she officially retired in 1954, her records in the 200-, 400-, and 1,500-m freestyle remained unbroken. Hveger was named Danish female athlete of the 20th century in 1996, and in 1999 she was the only one of *Swimming World* magazine's top 10 swimmers of the century who had never won Olympic gold.

Iloilo, Josefa (Ratu Josefa Iloilovatu Uluivuda), Fijian politician (b. Dec. 29, 1920, Viseisei, Vuda district, British Fiji—d. Feb. 6, 2011, Suva, Fiji), served (2000–09) as president of Fiji during a period of social and political upheaval in that country. Iloilo was respected for his attempts to mediate between indigenous Fijians and the country's ethnic Indian minority. His most controversial action was in 2009 when he nullified the constitution in support of a 2006 military coup led by Commodore Voreqe Bainimarama. Iloilo taught school before being elected to Parliament (1977–82) and then appointed to the Senate (1992–99). As Tui Vuda (paramount chief of Vuda district) from 1997, he served as a vice president. He was appointed president in May 2000 after radical ethnic Fijians ousted the elected prime minister, an ethnic Indian. When Bainimarama's forces overthrew the government in 2006, Iloilo was briefly (Dec. 5, 2006–Jan. 4, 2007) removed from office, but he returned and installed Bainimarama as interim prime minister. Fiji's Court of Appeal ruled in April 2009 that Iloilo's actions were unconstitutional. He responded by abrogating the constitution, dismissing the judges, and appointing himself head of state with power to rule by decree. He stepped down from office three months later.

Jansch, Bert (HERBERT JANSCH), Scottish-born guitarist, singer, and songwriter (b. Nov. 3, 1943, Glasgow, Scot.—d. Oct. 5, 2011, London, Eng.), introduced an innovative and influential accoustic guitar technique that made him one of the leading figures in British folk music in the 1960s and early '70s, both as a solo artist and as a member of the folk-rock group Pentangle. Influenced by American folk-blues performers such as Big Bill Broonzy, Jansch honed his skills as a guitarist in the Edinburgh folk scene before moving to London. Having invested his playing style with baroque flourishes, he released several solo albums that featured both traditional material and original songs, including the highly regarded *Jack Orion* (1966). In 1967 he cofounded Pentangle, a folk-rock quintet that included another accomplished guitarist, John Renbourn (with whom Jansch also collaborated outside the group), along with vocalist Jacqui McShee, bassist Danny Thompson, and drummer Terry Cox. The group incorporated elements of jazz, blues, art rock, and traditional folk music (some dating to the Middle Ages) and gained a cult following with the albums *Basket of Light* (1969) and *Cruel Sister* (1970). After Pentangle drifted apart, Jansch returned to his solo career in 1973, eventually releasing some 20 solo albums, including *Crimson Moon* (2000) and *The Black Swan* (2006). In 2007 the original quintet reunited for the first time in more than 30 years when Pentangle was honoured with the BBC Radio 2 Folk Awards lifetime achievement award.

Jobs, Steve (STEVEN PAUL JOBS), American entrepreneur (b. Feb. 24, 1955, San Francisco, Calif.—d. Oct. 5, 2011, Palo Alto, Calif.), as the audacious cofounder of Apple Computer, Inc. (from 2007 Apple Inc.), was a charismatic pioneer of the personal computer (PC) and the visionary behind the creation and innovative marketing of the Macintosh PC (1984), which inaugurated the practical application of the user-friendly graphical interface that Jobs first saw demonstrated (1979) at Xerox Corp.'s Palo Alto Research Center. Other breakthrough consumer products developed by Apple under Jobs's leadership include the colourful egg-shaped iMac PC (1998), the stylish laptop iBook (1999), the iPod compact MP3 music player and the iTunes digital jukebox software (both 2001), the iTunes Music Store (2003), the iPhone smartphone (2007), and the iPad tablet computer (2011). Jobs was raised by adoptive parents in Cupertino, Calif., located in what later became known as Silicon Valley. Though he was interested in engineering, he dropped out of Reed College, Portland, Ore., took a job at Atari Corp. as a video game designer in 1974, and embarked on a pilgrimage to India. Later in 1974 he reconnected with Stephen Wozniak, a former high school friend who worked for Hewlett-Packard Co. (HP). After HP turned down Wozniak's design for a computer logic board in 1976, Jobs suggested that they form their own enterprise. The Apple I, as they called the new logic board, was built in Jobs's family garage with money they obtained by selling Jobs's car and Wozniak's programmable calculator. Though Jobs eschewed a traditional business appearance—a trait he retained throughout his career—he obtained financing, distribution, and publicity for Apple Computer, which they incorporated in 1977—the same year that the enormously successful Apple II was completed. In January 1984 Jobs himself introduced the Macintosh in an extraordinary publicity campaign that would later be pointed to as the archetype of "event marketing." Although Apple had a record-setting initial public stock offering (IPO) in 1980 and entered *Fortune* magazine's list of America's 500 top companies three years later, in 1985 Apple CEO John Sculley, whom Jobs had hired in 1983, persuaded the board of directors to remove him. Jobs founded (1985) another computer company, NeXT Inc., and bought (1986) the computer-graphics firm Pixar Animation Studios, which he built into a major animation studio. (Pixar's IPO in 1995 made Jobs a billionaire.) Apple, which had struggled since Jobs's departure, purchased NeXT in 1996 for more than $400 million, brought Jobs back as a consultant, and in June 1997 asked him to lead the company once again. In 2003 Jobs was diagnosed with a rare form of pancreatic cancer. He took intermittent leaves of absence from Apple as he underwent surgery (2004) and received a liver transplant (2009). Jobs resigned as CEO in August 2011.

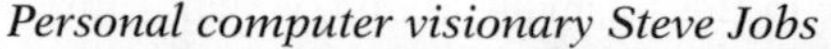

Personal computer visionary Steve Jobs

Moshe Brakha/AP

Johnson, John Henry, American football player (b. Nov. 24, 1929, Waterproof, La.—d. June 3, 2011, Tracy, Calif.), was a standout fullback who played in the National Football League (NFL) for 13 years during the 1950s and '60s. Johnson, an exceptional runner and receiver who was also a fearsome blocker, was known as one of the era's toughest and most-talented players. He played college football at St. Mary's College of California and Arizona State University, graduating in 1953. He was then placed on the roster of Canada's Calgary (Alta.) Stampeders before joining (1954) the NFL's San Francisco 49ers. With quarterback Y.A. Tittle, fullback Joe Perry (*q.v.*), and halfback Hugh

McElhenny, Johnson formed the 49ers' celebrated Million Dollar Backfield; all four players eventually entered the Pro Football Hall of Fame. In 1957 Johnson was traded to the Detroit Lions, and he led the team in rushing that season as the Lions captured the NFL championship. As a member (1960–65) of the Pittsburgh Steelers, Johnson rushed for 1,141 yd in 1962, becoming the first Steeler to eclipse the 1,000-yd rushing mark. He surpassed the mark again when in 1964 he ran for 1,048 yd. Johnson ended his career in 1966 after playing one season with the Houston Oilers. At the time of his retirement, he was the NFL's fourth leading all-time rusher, with 6,803 career yards. He ran for a total of 48 touchdowns and also made 186 career receptions for 1,478 yd, including 7 touchdowns. Johnson was elected to the Pro Football Hall of Fame in 1987.

Jones, Diana Wynne, British fantasy writer (b. Aug. 16, 1934, London, Eng.—d. March 26, 2011, Bristol, Eng.), penned more than 40 children's books, many of which centre on magic or magicians. Despite struggling with dyslexia and a difficult family life, she did well in school, developed a keen interest in reading adult works such as *The Thousand and One Nights* and Sir Thomas Malory's *Le Morte Darthur*, and began writing stories for her younger sisters. Jones studied English at St. Anne's College, Oxford (B.A., 1956), where she attended lectures by C.S. Lewis and J.R.R. Tolkien and married (1956) Chaucer scholar John Burrow. Her introduction to children's literature came when she read to her three sons, and she began to submit her own juvenile fiction to publishers and agents. *Changeover* (1970), Jones's first published novel, was originally written in 1966 and was intended for adults. Her children's books include *Wilkins' Tooth* (1973; also published as *Witch's Business*), *Eight Days of Luke* (1975), *The Ogre Downstairs* (1974), the Chrestomanci series (1977–2006), and *Howl's Moving Castle* (1986), which in 2004 was made into a Japanese animated film. She offered a humorous exploration of the clichés of her favoured genre in *The Tough Guide to Fantasyland* (1996; revised 2006). Jones was the recipient of a World Fantasy Award for lifetime achievement in 2007.

Kapoor, Shammi (SHAMSHER RAJ KAPOOR), Indian actor (b. Oct. 21, 1931, Bombay, British India [now Mumbai, India]—d. Aug. 14, 2011, Mumbai), transformed Bollywood films in the late 1950s with his spontaneous flamboyant acting and Western-style sex appeal—complete with leather jacket, swept-back hair, and smoldering eyes—that drew comparisons to American rock-and-roll icon Elvis Presley. Kapoor was born into an Indian acting dynasty, the son of stage and screen actor Prithviraj Kapoor and younger brother of Bollywood star Raj Kapoor. He made his first screen appearance in 1953, but he failed to attract much attention until *Tumsa nahin dekha* (1957) and, especially, *Junglee* (1961). He later evolved from a romantic lead into a respected character actor. Kapoor was honoured three times by the Filmfare Awards: best actor for *Brahmachari* (1968), best supporting actor for *Vidhaata* (1982), and a lifetime achievement award in 1995. His last film was *Rockstar* (2011), featuring his great nephew Ranbir Kapoor. In later years Shammi Kapoor was an active participant in the Internet, with a fan club Web site, and a founder of the Internet Users Community of India.

Cobus Bodenstein/AP

Bollywood idol Shammi Kapoor

Karzai, Ahmed Wali, Afghani government official (b. 1961, Karz, Kandahar province, Afg.—d. July 12, 2011, Kandahar, Kandahar province, Afg.), was perceived by many as a symbol of corruption in Afghanistan as the controversial younger half brother of Afghan Pres. Hamid Karzai and a predominant power broker in Afghanistan who wielded almost complete control over the country's southern provinces. Karzai was born into the powerful Pashtun Popalzai clan. He left Afghanistan after the Soviet Union began its occupation (1979) and worked in a Chicago restaurant owned by a family member. He returned to Afghanistan in 2001 and was elected to the Kandahar Provincial Council in 2005. His detractors soon accused him of involvement in the drug trade and of being on the CIA's payroll, even as others saw him as a key American ally in the heart of the Taliban's birthplace. Karzai was considered (2007) for an ambassadorial position to the U.S., but President Karzai rejected the idea. Later Ahmed Wali Karzai was accused of having manipulated the 2009 presidential elections in his half brother's favour. The Taliban claimed responsibility for Karzai's assassination after he was shot and killed by one of his own bodyguards.

Kato, David, Ugandan activist (b. 1960s, Uganda?—d. Jan. 26, 2011, Mukono, Ugan.), fought for gay rights in Uganda, where homosexuality was illegal. Kato worked as a teacher in South Africa, but after antisodomy laws there were overturned in the 1990s, he returned home to campaign against homophobia in Uganda. Despite arrests, beatings, and death threats, he publicly proclaimed his own homosexuality and cofounded Sexual Minorities Uganda, an activist group for members of the country's gay, lesbian, bisexual, and transgendered community. Kato was vocal in his opposition to the antihomosexuality bill; the bill was introduced in the Ugandan Parliament in 2009 and called for the imprisonment and, in some circumstances, the execution of gay and lesbian Ugandans. In early January 2011 he won a lawsuit against a Ugandan newspaper that had printed photographs of him and other openly homosexual individuals with a call for them to be hanged. Kato, who was believed to be in his 40s, was bludgeoned to death in his home; a suspect later confessed to the crime.

Keane, Bil (WILLIAM KEANE), American cartoonist (b. Oct. 5, 1922, Philadelphia, Pa.—d. Nov. 8, 2011, Paradise Valley, Ariz.), celebrated the humorous side of family life in the lighthearted one-panel comic *The Family Circus*, which debuted on Feb. 19, 1960, and eventually appeared in nearly 1,500 newspapers. Keane modeled the ageless characters in the strip (a suburban mother and father raising four children: Billy, Dolly, Jeffy, and P.J.) on members of his own family. The cartoon, which twice won (1967 and 1971) the National Cartoonists Society Best Syndicated Panel award, was collected in more than 40 books. In addition to *Family Circus*, Keane drew *Silly Philly*, a gag panel, and *Channel Chuckles*, amusing television tidbits.

Keating, H(enry) R(eymond) F(itzwalter), British novelist (b. Oct. 31, 1926, St. Leonards-on-Sea, Sussex, Eng.—d. March 27, 2011, London, Eng.), wrote more than 50 crime novels over a 50-year career, notably 26 books featuring the unassuming Inspector Ganesh Ghote of the Bombay (now Mumbai) police department. Keating was educated at Trinity College, Dublin, and was working as a newspaper journalist when he published his first crime novel, *Death and the Visiting Fireman* (1959). He captured the public's fancy—and a Gold Dagger Award from the Crime Writers' Association (CWA)—with *The Perfect Murder* (1964; filmed in 1988), in which he introduced his self-effacing but resolute Bombay detective. He wrote another 25 Ghote novels, ending with *A Small Case for Inspector Ghote?* (2009). Between 2000 and 2008 he took a hiatus from Ghote and published seven novels featuring British Detective Superintendent Harriet Martens. Keating also wrote crime book reviews for *The Times* newspaper (1967–83), nonfiction, several nonseries novels, and three detective novels under the pseudonym Evelyn Hervey. Keating was president of the fabled Detection Club from 1985 to 2001, and in 1996 he was awarded the CWA Diamond Dagger for lifetime achievement.

Kevorkian, Jack (JACOB KEVORKIAN; "DR. DEATH"), American physician (b. May 26, 1928, Pontiac, Mich.—d. June 3, 2011, Royal Oak, Mich.), gained international attention for his highly publicized assistance in the suicides of more than 100 patients, many of whom were terminally ill; he spent some time in jail in 1993 for his actions, but in 1999 he was convicted of second-degree murder and was incarcerated (1999–2007) after he personally administered a lethal injection to a patient who was suffering from Lou Gehrig disease (amyotrophic lateral sclerosis). Kevorkian graduated (1952) from the University of Michigan Medical School. As a pathology resident, he lobbied for carrying out medical experiments on death-row inmates at the hour set for their execution and then giving them lethal injections, a notion that earned him the sobriquet "Dr. Death." Later he advocated the establishment of suicide clinics ("obitoria"). In the 1960s and '70s, Kevorkian worked as a staff pathologist at hospitals in Michigan and southern California. After retiring (1982) from practice, he began to help patients end their lives. In response to Kevorkian's role in the February 1993 death of 70-year-old Hugh Gale, the Michigan legislature passed a bill making it a felony to knowingly provide a person with the means to commit suicide or to physically assist in the act. In 2007, after having served more than 8 years of his 10–25-year prison sentence, Kevorkian was released on parole for good behaviour.

Khorana, Har Gobind, Indian-born American biochemist (b. Jan. 9, 1922?, Raipur, British India—d. Nov. 9, 2011, Concord, Mass.), shared the Nobel Prize for Physiology or Medicine in 1968 with Marshall W. Nirenberg and Robert W. Holley for research that helped to show how the nucleotides in nucleic acids, which carry the genetic code of the cell, control the cell's synthesis of proteins. Khorana was born into a poor family and attended the University of the Punjab at Lahore (now in Pakistan) and the University of Liverpool, Eng. (Ph.D., 1948), on government scholarships. He began research on nucleic acids during a fellowship at the University of Cambridge (1951) under Sir Alexander Todd. He held fellowships and professorships in Switzerland at the Swiss Federal Institute of Technology, in Canada at the University of British Columbia (1952–59), and in the United States at the University of Wisconsin (1960–70). In 1966 Khorana became a naturalized U.S. citizen, and in 1971 he joined the faculty of MIT, where he remained until he retired in 2007. In addition to the Nobel Prize, Khorana received the Albert Lasker Basic Medical Research Award (1968) and the National Medal of Science (1987).

Killebrew, Harmon Clayton, Jr. ("KILLER"), American baseball player (b. June 29, 1936, Payette, Idaho—d. May 17, 2011, Scottsdale, Ariz.), amassed 573 home runs during his 22-year career (1954–75), which ranked him (at number 11 at the time of his death) among the greatest home-run hitters in the sport's history. Killebrew was signed by the Washington Senators at age 17, and he became an everyday player six years later. He stayed with the team through most of his career, including when it moved to Minnesota and was renamed the Twins in 1961. With 49 home runs and 140 runs batted in (RBIs), Killebrew was named the American League (AL) MVP in 1969. He finished out his career with the Kansas City Royals in 1975. The 13-time All-Star hit 40 or more home runs in 8 different seasons (1959, 1961–64, 1967, 1969–70)—the second most 40-home-run seasons in major league history, behind Babe Ruth's 11—and led the AL in homers six times. He had a lifetime batting average of .256 with 2,086 hits and 1,584 RBIs. Killebrew was elected to the National Baseball Hall of Fame in 1984.

Kim Jong Il ("DEAR LEADER"), North Korean supreme leader (b. Feb. 16, 1941, Siberia, Russia, U.S.S.R.—d. Dec. 17, 2011, North Korea?), was the son of North Korean Premier and Korean Workers' (communist) Party (KWP) Chairman Kim Il-Sung and successor to his father as the authoritarian ruler (1994–2011) of North Korea. Kim Jong Il built on the cultlike mystique surrounding his father and himself and furthered his father's national policy of self-reliance (*juche*), as well as his own "military first" (*songun chongch'i*) policy. With his country facing a struggling economy and a massive famine in the 1990s, Kim made moves toward amending North Korea's long-standing policy of isolationism and improved ties with a number of countries, including the U.S. and South Korea. Although he initially appeared to be abiding by the 1994 Agreed Framework regarding North Korea's nuclear program, it was suspected that the country was secretly enriching uranium, and in 2003 Kim announced that North Korea was pulling out of the Nuclear Nonproliferation Treaty and planning to develop nuclear weapons. Talks were suspended for several years, but another deal was struck in 2007; the matter of verifying North Korea's compliance remained unsettled, however. The official version of Kim Jong Il's life, which differed from the biography documented elsewhere, said that he was born at a guerrilla base camp on Mt. Paektu, the highest point on the Korean peninsula, and attributed many precocious abilities to him. During the Korean War (1950–53), he was reportedly placed in northeastern China (Manchuria) for his safety. After attending a pilots' training college in East Germany for two years, he graduated in 1964 from Kim Il-Sung University. He served in numerous routine posts in the KWP and in September 1973 was appointed party secretary in charge of organization, propaganda, and agitation. He was officially named his father's successor in October 1980, was given command of the armed forces in 1991, and was appointed to numerous other high-ranking posts. When Kim Il-Sung died in July 1994, Kim Jong Il became North Korea's de facto leader. He was named general secretary of the KWP in October 1997, and in September 1998 he was formally elected to the country's highest post. In 2008 speculation began that his health was deteriorating, especially after his absence from public view for several months. The following year Kim and the North Korean political establishment began a series of moves toward designating the youngest of his three officially acknowledged sons, Kim Jong-Eun, as his successor.

Kirshner, Don(ald), American music executive (b. April 17, 1934, Bronx, N.Y.—d. Jan. 17, 2011, Boca Raton, Fla.), had an uncanny ability to identify a song's hit-making potential and, as a founder (1958; with Al Nevins) of Aldon Music, cultivated prolific songwriting partnerships that included those of Neil Sedaka and Howard Greenfield ("Who's Sorry Now"), Gerry Goffin and Carole King ("Will You Love Me Tomorrow" and "Pleasant Valley Sunday"), and Barry Mann and Cynthia Weill ("You've Lost That Lovin' Feeling"). Neil Diamond also produced hits ("I'm a Believer") as a songwriter before he launched his own successful career as a performer. Kirshner's songwriters provided well-honed tunes for Connie Francis, Bobby Vee, the Drifters, and the Shirelles. In 1963 Aldon merged with the film company Screen Gems, and Kirshner became its musical director. In that role he masterminded a television project about a pop music group called *The Monkees*. The music-filled sitcom ran for two seasons (1966–68), and under Kirshner's control the quartet generated six Top Three singles and two of the best-selling albums of the decade, mostly written by in-house songwriters. When Kirshner and the Monkees had a falling out, he created a cartoon group from television's *The Archie Show*. The Archies' "Sugar, Sugar" sold six million copies in 1969. Kirshner also discovered the all-girl group the Ronettes. In 1973 he became the host of *Don Kirshner's Rock Concert*, a live TV music show that featured the Rolling Stones, the Eagles, David Bowie, and the Allman Brothers, among others.

Landau, Moshe, Israeli jurist (b. April 29, 1912, Danzig, Ger. [now Gdansk, Pol.]—d. May 1, 2011, Jerusalem), presided over the three-judge panel in the high-profile war-crimes trial (April 11–Dec. 15, 1961) of German Nazi official Adolf Eichmann, who was convicted and in 1962 executed for his role in the Holocaust. Landau obtained a law degree (1930) at the University of London and in 1933 immigrated to British Palestine, where he established a legal practice. He was called to the bar in 1937 and was made a judge three years later. In 1953 he was appointed to the Supreme Court of Israel, from which he retired in 1982 after having served his last two years as the court's president. As a Supreme Court justice, Landau issued rulings in support of freedom of information and defendants' rights while ruling against government censorship and the construction of Jewish settlements on illegally confiscated Arab land. Landau was awarded the Israel Prize in 1991.

Langham, Michael Seymour, British-born theatre director (b. Aug. 22, 1919, Bridgwater, Somerset, Eng.—d. Jan. 15, 2011, Cranbrook, Kent, Eng.), transformed the environs of the Shakespeare Festival in Stratford, Ont., from a large circus tent to a permanent 2,000-seat theatre as the festival's artistic director (1956–67). He also added Restoration drama to the festival's repertoire and gained renown as a fierce taskmaster who directed such luminaries as Sir John Gielgud (*Julius Caesar*), Peter O'Toole (*The Merchant of Venice*), Paul Scofield (*Love's Labour Lost*), Julie Harris (*Romeo and Juliet*), and Christopher Plummer (*Henry V*). After service in World War II, he had directing opportunities in London, Stratford-on-Avon, Belgium, Australia, the Netherlands, Scotland, and Canada, where, as the Shakespeare Festival's artistic head, he oversaw the construction of the thrust stage. He later led (1971–77) the Guthrie Theatre, Minneapolis, Minn., where he helped to revive the theatre's finances with measures to lengthen its season and expand its touring. From 1979 to 1992 Langham headed the drama division of the Juilliard School, New York City.

Laurents, Arthur (ARTHUR LEVINE), American playwright, director, and screenwriter (b. July 14, 1917, Brooklyn, N.Y.—d. May 5, 2011, New York, N.Y.), wrote the books for several successful Broadway productions, most notably the hit musicals *West Side Story*

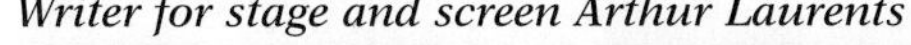
Writer for stage and screen Arthur Laurents

Sara Krulwich—The New York Times/Redux

(1957; filmed 1961) and *Gypsy* (1959; filmed 1962), during a career that spanned some 60 years. After graduating (1937) from Cornell University, Ithaca, N.Y., with an English degree, Laurents wrote scripts for such radio programs as *The Thin Man*. He was drafted (1941) into the U.S. Army and wrote for military training films and radio programs, an experience that inspired his first Broadway play, *Home of the Brave* (1945; filmed 1949). Other notable Broadway plays and musicals that he wrote and/or directed include *Time of the Cuckoo* (1952), which he later adapted into the musical *Do I Hear a Waltz?* (1965); *I Can Get It for You Wholesale* (1962), which helped launch the career of actress-singer Barbra Streisand; *Anyone Can Whistle* (1964); the Tony Award-winning musical *Hallelujah, Baby!* (1967); and *La Cage aux folles* (1983), for which Laurents won (1984) a Tony for best director. Laurents's noteworthy screenplays include *Rope* (1948), *Anastasia* (1956), *Bonjour tristesse* (1958), *The Way We Were* (1973), and *The Turning Point* (1977). In 2008 Laurents received his sixth Tony nomination, for directing a revival of *Gypsy*.

Layton, Jack (JOHN GILBERT LAYTON), Canadian politician (b. July 18, 1950, Montreal, Que.—d. Aug. 22, 2011, Toronto, Ont.), was a magnetic personality who in 2003 won the leadership of the New Democratic Party (NDP) in a landslide and helped to propel the NDP's strong showing in the 2011 Canadian federal elections as it replaced the Liberals as the official opposition party in Parliament. Layton was the son of Robert Layton (who served in the House of Commons and in the cabinet of Progressive Conservative Prime Minister Brian Mulroney) and the grandson of Gilbert Layton (a cabinet minister in Quebec's Union Nationale government). Jack Layton entered politics in 1982, running successfully for city councillor in Toronto. In that post (1982–2003), he aggressively pursued a left-leaning agenda. Layton helped engineer a strategy for combating AIDS in Toronto—the first program of its kind in Canada—and directed attention to environmental policy, championing recycling and energy-efficiency initiatives. After replacing longtime NDP leader Alexa McDonough, "Smilin' Jack" Layton spent the next year garnering public support for NDP policies. In 2004 he narrowly defeated long-serving Liberal incumbent Dennis Mills to become MP for the Toronto-Danforth riding. In the 2008 federal elections, Layton's NDP garnered more than 18% of the popular vote. Layton, who had triumphed over a bout of prostate cancer, unexpectedly resigned as NDP leader in July 2011 after announcing that he was once again battling cancer.

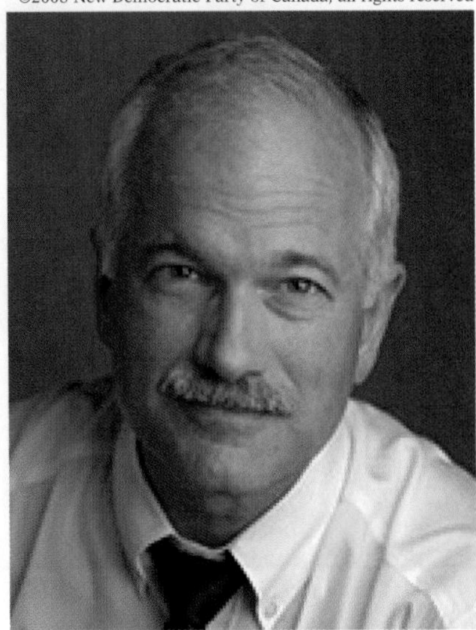

Canadian politician Jack Layton

Leacock, Richard (RICKY), British cinematographer (b. July 18, 1921, London, Eng.—d. March 23, 2011, Paris, France), crafted *cinéma vérité*-style documentary film footage that created unprecedented immediacy and naturalism through his use of innovative handheld cameras, natural ambient lighting, and synchronous sound. Leacock made his first short documentary, *Canary Bananas* (1935), to teach his schoolmates in England about his family's banana plantation in the Canary Islands. While studying physics at Harvard University, he operated a camera on David Lack's renowned expedition to the Galapagos Islands and on the classic *To Hear Your Banjo Play* (1941) in the Appalachians. After completing his military service, he was hired as cinematographer on *Louisiana Story* (1948), director Robert Flaherty's award-winning documentary. Leacock's other "direct cinema" documentaries include *Primary* (1960), a breakthrough look at the 1960 campaign for the Democratic nomination for U.S. president; *Crisis* (1963), about Pres. John F. Kennedy's confrontation with Alabama Gov. George Wallace; *Monterey Pop* (1968); and *1 P.M.* (1972). Leacock also taught cinema at MIT (1968–88). In 1987 he was awarded a lifetime achievement award by the International Documentary Association.

Leiber, Jerry (JEROME LEIBER), American songwriter and record producer (b. April 25, 1933, Baltimore, Md.—d. Aug. 22, 2011, Los Angeles, Calif.), wrote the lyrics for many enduring songs of the 1950s and '60s. He and partner Mike Stoller (who created the tunes) worked primarily for Atlantic Records and were perhaps the most successful writers and producers of the 1950s. They became partners as teenagers in Los Angeles; when their "Hound Dog" was recorded (1952) by Willie Mae ("Big Mama") Thornton, they also became producers. Major success followed with their series of novelty story-songs—e.g., "Black Denim Trousers and Motorcycle Boots" (performed by the Cheers), "Young Blood" and "Yakety Yak" (by the Coasters), and "Love Potion No. 9" (by the Clovers)—and with their songs for Elvis Presley movies, including *Love Me Tender* (1956) and *Jailhouse Rock* (1957). In 1960 Leiber teamed up with Phil Spector for "Spanish Harlem," recorded by Ben. E. King. Leiber and Stoller's early 1960s productions, particularly "Stand by Me" (by King) and "On Broadway" (by the Drifters), were especially influential. In 1964 the songwriting duo established their own label, Red Bird, on which the Shangri-Las recorded. They went on to write for films and theatre; among their last hits, in 1969, was Peggy Lee's original rendition of the world-weary "Is That All There Is?" In 1987 the pair were inducted into the Rock and Roll Hall of Fame.

Lenihan, Brian Joseph, Jr., Irish politician (b. May 21, 1959, Dublin, Ire.—d. June 10, 2011, Dublin), became finance minister for Ireland in May 2008 just months before the country succumbed to a devastating financial crisis. After the failure of the American investment bank Lehman Brothers that autumn, Lenihan produced a government guarantee of all funds in Irish banks, but it gradually became clear that the bad debts of the banks were so extensive that guaranteeing them was threatening the solvency of the Irish government. He was forced to accept a bailout in 2010 from the European Central Bank and the IMF under the condition that Ireland adopt a strict four-year austerity plan. Lenihan studied law at Trinity College, Dublin, and Sidney Sussex College, Cambridge. He was called to the Irish bar (1984) and practiced law while lecturing at Trinity College. He was introduced to politics by his father, Brian Joseph Lenihan, Sr., a cabinet minister and important figure in the centrist Fianna Fail party for more than 30 years. Lenihan Jr. was elected to Parliament for his father's party in 1996 and served as unofficial children's minister (2002–07) and minister for justice (2007–08) after a long tenure on the party's back benches. Despite Ireland's problems, Lenihan's frank demeanour and tenacity made him popular with his constituency, and he was the only Dublin-area Fianna Fail MP to retain his seat in the 2011 general elections.

Lipscomb, William Nunn, Jr., American physical chemist (b. Dec. 9, 1919, Cleveland, Ohio—d. April 14, 2011, Cambridge, Mass.), won the Nobel Prize for Chemistry in 1976 for his research on the structure and bonding of boron compounds (made up of boron and hydrogen) and the general nature of chemical bonding. By developing X-ray techniques that later proved useful in many chemical applications, he and his associates were able to map the molecular structures of numerous boranes and their derivatives. Lipscomb graduated (1941) from the University of Kentucky with a degree in chemistry, and while earning a Ph.D. (1946) from Caltech, he became a protégé of two-time Nobel Prize winner Linus Pauling. Lipscomb worked (1942–46) as a physical chemist in the Office of Scientific Research and Development before joining the University of Minnesota as an assistant professor. By 1959, when he left the university, he was professor and chief of the physical chemistry division. He then became professor of chemistry at Harvard University, where he served on the faculty from 1959 to 1990; he was chairman of the chemistry department from 1962 to 1965.

Logue, Christopher, British poet, playwright, journalist, and actor (b. Nov. 23, 1926, Portsmouth, Hampshire, Eng.—d. Dec. 2, 2011, London, Eng.), was one of the leaders of the movement to bring poetry closer to the popular experience. His own pungent verse, which owed much to the work of German playwright Bertolt Brecht and to the English ballad tradition, was read to jazz accompaniment, sung, and printed on posters. Logue's first book of verse was *Wand and Quadrant* (1953), and he adapted 20 of Pablo Neruda's poems as *The Man Who Told His Love* (1958). Other poetry volumes include *Logue's A.B.C.* (1966), *New Numbers* (1969), and *Ode to the Dodo: Poems from 1953 to 1978* (1981). From 1959 he worked on a remarkably fresh adaptation of Homer's *Iliad*, several sections of which were separately published. Logue also wrote the *True Stories* feature in the British satiric journal *Private Eye* and acted in television, movie, and stage roles. He was made CBE in 2007.

Louvin, Charlie (CHARLIE ELZER LOUDERMILK), American country singer (b. July 7, 1927, Henagar, Ala.—d. Jan. 26, 2011, Wartrace, Tenn.), together with his older brother, Ira, made up the Louvin Brothers, which was often called the greatest duet act in country music. They performed in the 1940s, '50s, and '60s and were remembered for their simple but pure gospel-tinged style and distinctive harmonies. Growing up in rural northeastern Alabama, the Loudermilk brothers were exposed to a variety of early country music influences, including the Carter Family, Charlie and Bill Monroe, and the Blue Sky Boys, as well as to shape-note hymnal singing. From the early 1940s they sang devoutly Christian songs in an artless, heartfelt manner, their high-pitched harmonies accompanied only by Charlie's guitar and Ira's mandolin. During one of their regular stints as live performers on radio stations in the Southeast, where they were billed as the "Radio Twins," they changed their name to the Louvin Brothers. Commercial success came when they adopted secular themes; among their hits were "When I Stop Dreaming," released in 1955—the year they joined Nashville's Grand Ole Opry—and "I Don't Believe You've Met My Baby" (1956). On later recordings their record companies imposed lush, elaborate accompaniments far removed from their original style. Each brother pursued a solo career after the partnership broke up in 1963, and Ira was killed in a 1965 car crash. The Louvin Brothers were also much-revered songwriters, and their compositions were covered by many performers. In 2001 the Louvin Brothers were inducted into the Country Music Hall of Fame.

Mark Humphrey/AP

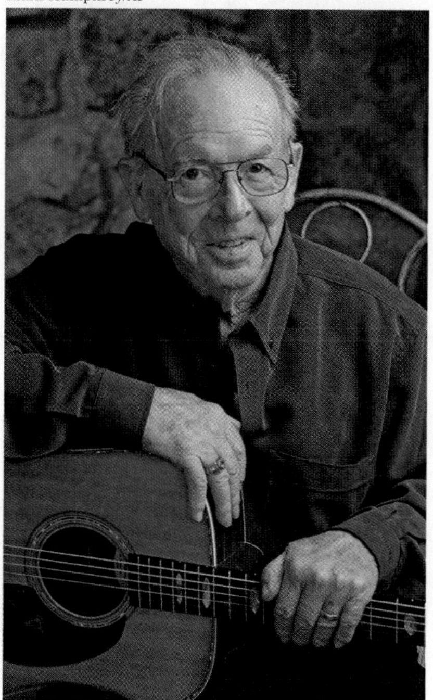

Country singer Charlie Louvin

Lumet, Sidney, American film and television director (b. June 25, 1924, Philadelphia, Pa.—d. April 9, 2011, New York, N.Y.), elicited sterling performances from his cast members in films that featured characters wrestling with moral or emotional conflicts involving betrayal, corruption, or disillusionment, notably in the taut courtroom drama *12 Angry Men* (1957), his first feature film; the gripping bank robbery thriller *Dog Day Afternoon* (1975); the satiric *Network* (1976), a study of network television; and the legal drama *The Verdict* (1982). Lumet received Academy Award nominations for best director for all of these movies but not for such classics as *Long Day's Journey into Night* (1962), *The Pawnbroker* (1965), *Serpico* (1973), or *Murder on the Orient Express* (1974). After moving with his family to New York City as a

Film director Sidney Lumet

Sam Falk—The New York Times/Redux

child, Lumet began performing on the Yiddish stage at age four and eventually moved to Broadway in the late 1930s. In 1950 he joined CBS television as a staff director of such dramatic series as *Playhouse 90* and *Studio One.* Lumet filmed many of his movies in New York City, including *The Anderson Tapes* (1971), *Prince of the City* (1981), *Deathtrap* (1982), *Night Falls on Manhattan* (1997), and *Before the Devil Knows You're Dead* (2007), his last feature film. In 1993 Lumet won a lifetime achievement award from the Directors Guild of America, and in 2005 he was the recipient of an Oscar for lifetime achievement.

Lustig, Arnošt, Czech writer (b. Dec. 21, 1926, Prague, Czech.—d. Feb. 26, 2011, Prague, Cz.Rep.), survived a series of Nazi concentration camps in World War II Europe and later used the Holocaust as the inspiration for much of his fiction. Lustig and his family were constrained in 1939 when anti-Jewish laws went into effect in Nazi-occupied Czechoslovakia, and in 1942 they were deported from Prague to the Theresienstadt camp. He was transferred to Auschwitz (1944) and then Buchenwald (1945) but escaped when the train in which he was being transported to Dachau was bombed in an American air attack. He later studied journalism at Charles University, Prague, and worked as a radio correspondent. After the Soviet suppression of the Prague Spring (1968), he immigrated to Israel and then the U.S., where he taught at American University, Washington, D.C. Lustig initially published collections of short stories, notably *Noc a naděje* (1958; *Night and Hope*, 1962) and *Démanty noci* (1958; *Diamonds in the Night*, 1962). His novels include *Dita Saxová* (1962), *Modlitba pro Kateřinu Horovitzovou* (1964; *A Prayer for Katerina Horovitzova*, 1973), and *Krásné zelené oči* (2000; *Lovely Green Eyes*, 2001). He was awarded the Franz Kafka Prize in 2008.

Maathai, Wangari Muta, Kenyan politician and environmental activist (b. April 1, 1940, Nyeri, Kenya—d. Sept. 25, 2011, Nairobi, Kenya), was awarded the 2004 Nobel Prize for Peace for her "holistic approach to sustainable development," becoming the first black African woman to win a Nobel Prize. Her work was often considered both unwelcome and subversive in her own country, where her outspokenness constituted stepping far outside traditional gender roles. Maathai was educated at Mount St. Scholastica College (now Benedictine College), Atchison, Kan. (B.S. in biology, 1964); the University of Pittsburgh (M.S., 1966); and the University of Nairobi (Ph.D. in veterinary anatomy, 1971), effectively becoming the first woman in either East or Central Africa to earn a doctorate. After graduation she remained to teach in the department of veterinary anatomy, and in 1977 she became chair of the department. While working with the National Council of Women of Kenya, Maathai developed the idea that village women could improve the environment by planting trees to provide a fuel source and to slow the processes of deforestation and desertification. The Green Belt Movement, an organization that she founded in 1977, had by the early 21st century planted some 30 million trees and had triggered similar initiatives in other African countries. Maathai was also an advocate for human rights, AIDS prevention, and women's issues, and she frequently represented those concerns to the UN General Assembly. She was elected to Kenya's National Assembly in 2002 with 98% of the vote, and in 2003 she was appointed assistant minister of environment, natural resources, and wildlife. Maathai's books include *The Green Belt Movement: Sharing the Approach and the Experience* (1988; rev. ed. 2003); an autobiography, *Unbowed* (2007); and *The Challenge for Africa* (2009).

Kimimasa Mayama—Reuters/Landov

Nobel Peace Prize laureate Wangari Maathai

Mackey, John, American football player (b. Sept. 24, 1941, New York, N.Y.—d. July 6, 2011, Baltimore, Md.), starred in the NFL in the 1960s and early '70s and was the prototype of the modern tight end—a receiver who possessed the speed to run deep patterns as well as the power to run over tacklers. Off the field Mackey served (1970–73) as president of the NFL Players Association (NFLPA), spearheading efforts to challenge free-agency restrictions. After earning All-American honours at Syracuse (N.Y.) University, Mackey joined the Baltimore Colts in 1963, becoming an integral part of the team's potent offense led by quarterback Johnny Unitas. Mackey played nine seasons with the Colts, during which time he was named to five Pro Bowls (1964, 1966–69). In helping the Colts to a 16–13 victory over the Dallas Cowboys in the 1971 Super Bowl, he made a 75-yd pass reception for a touchdown—at the time a record for the longest pass reception in a Super Bowl. Mackey was traded to the San Diego Chargers in 1972; he played one season with the team before retiring. During his NFL career, he made a total of 331 catches for 5,236 yd and 38 touchdowns. Mackey became head of the NFLPA in 1970 and led a strike that year that succeeded in winning benefits for players. Two years later he led the NFLPA in a federal antitrust lawsuit against the NFL; the suit secured improved free-agency rights for players. Mackey was elected to the Pro Football Hall of Fame in 1992. In later years he was stricken with dementia. In 2006 a new NFL labour agreement included the 88 Plan (named after Mackey's jersey number), under which former NFL players suffering from dementia were eligible to receive up to $88,000 a year for health care.

Madame Nhu (MADAME NGO DINH NHU; TRAN LE XUAN; "THE DRAGON LADY"), South Vietnamese political figure (b. April 15, 1924, Hanoi, Vietnam—d. April 24, 2011, Rome, Italy), was a significant force behind her bachelor brother-in-law Ngo Dinh Diem, who exercised dictatorial powers as president of South Vietnam from 1955 until his assassination in 1963. Tran Le Xuan was born into an aristocratic Buddhist family, but she converted to Roman Catholicism when she married (1943) Ngo Dinh Nhu, who later established the secret police in his brother's government. Madame Nhu, as she came to be called, was briefly imprisoned (1946) during the First Indochina War, but after South Vietnam gained independence (1954) and Diem rose to power, she became the country's de facto first lady and was often photographed in her trademark beehive hairdo and elegant form-fitting *ao dai* tunics. Elected to South Vietnam's National Assembly in 1956, she fought for legal rights for women and for government bans on issues opposed by the Roman Catholic Church, such as opium use, birth control, and divorce. Behind the scenes she encouraged Diem to crack down on the opposition. Madame Nhu was on a speaking tour in the U.S. when her husband and brother-in-law were killed in a military coup. She later settled in Italy, where her remaining brother-in-law, the Roman Catholic Archbishop Ngo Dinh Thuc, was ensconced.

AP

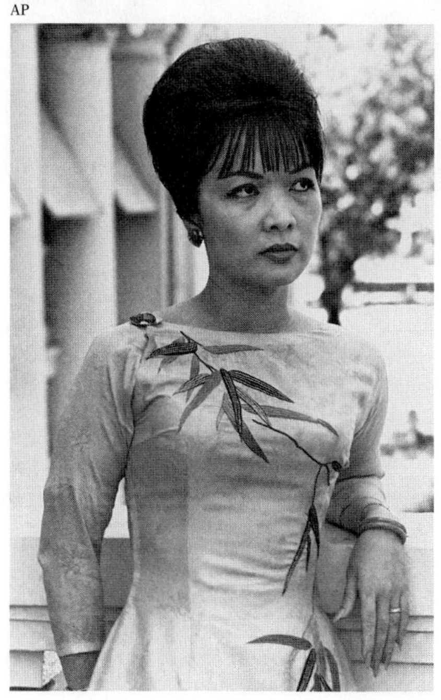

"Dragon Lady" Madame Nhu

Madl, Ferenc, Hungarian legal scholar and politician (b. Jan. 29, 1931, Band, Hung.—d. May 29, 2011, Budapest, Hung.), as president of Hungary (2000–05), oversaw his country's entry into the European Union (2004), using his legal expertise and knowledge of bipartisan politics to help ease Hungary's transition into the EU. Madl obtained a law degree (1955) from Eotvos Lorand University (ELTE) in Budapest and then studied (1961–63) at the University of Strasbourg, France, as one of the few Hungarian citizens allowed to attend a foreign university. He earned a doctorate in international law (1973) from ELTE and lectured at ELTE, the University of Munich, and various universities in the U.S. before going into politics. Madl was named to the post of minister without portfolio (1990–93) in the cabinet of Jozsef Antall, Hungary's first democratically elected prime minister; he later served as culture and education minister (1993–94) until he was first nominated to run for president in 1995. Madl's legal scholarship and work for European integration won him the Szechenyi Prize (1999), a knighthood in the French Legion of Honour (1999), and a Gold Medal from the John Monnet Foundation for Europe (2002).

Malangatana (MALANGATANA VALENTE NGWENYA), Mozambican artist (b. June 6, 1936, Matalana, Portuguese East Africa [now in Mozambique]—d. Jan. 5, 2011, Matosinhos, Port.), depicted the violence and suffering of his country during its struggle for independence (1975) from Portugal and the subsequent 16-year civil war between the Marxist-Leninist ruling party Frelimo and the rebel group Renamo through his large-scale boldly coloured paintings. After Frelimo and Renamo made peace in the early 1990s, Malangatana turned to calmer subject matter and expanded his palette to make greater use of cooler colours. He was also an accomplished ceramist and poet. As a member of the revolutionary Frelimo, Malangatana was jailed for more than a year in the mid-1960s, but his Portuguese contacts later helped him obtain a Gulbenkian Foundation grant to study art in Lisbon (1971–74). Although Malangatana had his first solo exhibition in 1961, he was not able to paint full time until the 1980s. In 1997 he was named a UNESCO artist for peace.

Margulis, Lynn, American biologist (b. March 5, 1938, Chicago, Ill.—d. Nov. 22, 2011, Amherst, Mass.), revolutionized the modern concept of how life arose on Earth with her serial endosymbiotic theory (SET) of the origin of cells, which posits that eukaryotic cells (cells with nuclei) evolved from the symbiotic merger of nonnucleated bacteria that had previously existed independently. She explained the concept in her first book, *Origin of Eukaryotic Cells* (1970). At the time, her theory was regarded as far-fetched, but it was later widely accepted. She elaborated in her classic *Symbiosis in Cell Evolution* (1981), proposing that another symbiotic merger of cells with bacteria—this time spirochetes, a type of bacterium that undulates rapidly—developed into the internal transportation system of the nucleated cell. She joined the biology department of Boston University in 1966 and taught there until 1988, when she was named Distinguished University Professor in the department of botany at the University of Massachusetts. Her 1982 book *Five Kingdoms*, written with American biologist Karlene V. Schwartz, articulates a five-kingdom system of classifying life on Earth—animals, plants, bacteria (prokaryotes), fungi, and protoctists. She also wrote numerous books interpreting scientific concepts and quandaries for a popular audience. In addition, Margulis collaborated with British scientist James Lovelock on the controversial Gaia hypothesis, which proposes that Earth can be viewed as a single self-regulating organism. Margulis was awarded the U.S. National Medal of Science in 1999 and the Darwin-Wallace Medal of the Linnean Society of London in 2008.

Markovic, Ante, Yugoslav businessman and politician (b. Nov. 25, 1924, Konjic, Kingdom of Serbs, Croats, and Slovenes [now in Bosnia and Herzegovina]—d. Nov. 28, 2011, Zagreb, Croatia), as the last premier (1989–91) of the Socialist Federal Republic of Yugoslavia, failed to prevent the outbreak of violence between the constituent republics and the breakup of the country into separate independent states. Markovic was an ethnic Croat, and after having received a degree in electrical engineering (1954) from the University of Zagreb, he remained in that Croatian city, where he was a director (1961–86) of the Rade Koncar industrial works. He joined the Communist Party at a young age and served as Croatia's reform-minded prime minister (1982–86) and president (1986–88). As the federal premier, Markovic liberalized foreign trade and instituted austerity reforms that reduced both inflation and unemployment. His attempted political reforms, however, notably his call for a directly elected federal parliament, were undermined by ethnic and interrepublic conflicts as well as his rivalry with Serbian leader Slobodan Milosevic.

UK History/Alamy

Horse trainer Ginger McCain and equine champion Red Rum

Massey, Anna Raymond, British actress (b. Aug. 11, 1937, Thakeham, West Sussex, Eng.—d. July 3, 2011, London, Eng.), captivated audiences on the stage, film, radio, and television with roles that ranged from the malevolent Mrs. Danvers (opposite her first husband, actor Jeremy Brett) in a TV adaptation of Daphne du Maurier's *Rebecca* (1979) to the dotty Miss Prism in Oscar Wilde's *The Importance of Being Earnest* (2002) to former prime minister Margaret Thatcher in the TV drama *Pinochet in Suburbia* (2006). Massey was the daughter of Canadian American actor Raymond Massey and British actress Adrianne Allen and the younger sister of actor Daniel Massey. She made her stage debut in the West End at age 17 in *The Reluctant Debutante* (1955) in a role that earned her a Tony Award nomination (1957) on Broadway. Her film debut occurred in American director John Ford's *Gideon's Day* (1958), but it was director Michael Powell's controversial *Peeping Tom* (1960) that established Massey onscreen. Other notable performances include British playwright David Hare's *Slag* (1971) and TV adaptations of Anthony Trollope's *The Pallisers* (1974) and Anita Brookner's *Hotel du Lac* (1986), for which she earned a BAFTA television award for best actress. Massey was made CBE in 2004.

Matson, Ollie Genoa, II, American football player and track star (b. May 1, 1930, Trinity, Texas—d. Feb. 19, 2011, Los Angeles, Calif.), possessed a lightning speed that resulted in his winning two Olympic track medals in 1952 (a bronze in the 400-m dash and a silver in the 4 × 400-m relay) and plaudits in the National Football League for his athleticism as a player with the Chicago Cardinals (1952 and 1954–58; 1953 was spent in the army), the Los Angeles Rams (1959–62), the Detroit Lions (1963), and the Philadelphia Eagles (1964–66). During his senior year (1951) as a defensive back for the University of San Francisco, Matson led the country with 1,556 yd rushing and 21 touchdowns. Though the team accrued a 9–0 record, the USF Dons were not invited to any of the bowl games because two of its players (Matson and Burl Toler) were African American. During his NFL career Matson was named Rookie of the Year in 1952, recorded 5,173 yd rushing, made 222 receptions, scored 438 points, and was invited to six Pro Bowl Games. He was inducted into the Pro Football Hall of Fame in 1972 and the College Football Hall of Fame in 1976.

McCain, Ginger (DONALD MCCAIN), British racehorse trainer (b. Sept. 21, 1930, Southport, Lancashire, Eng.—d. Sept. 19, 2011, Cholmondeley, Cheshire, Eng.), was the trainer of the great steeplechase horse Red Rum, which, after having been dismissed as hopelessly lame, won the Grand National an unprecedented three times (1973, 1974, 1977), the last time by some 25 lengths, and finished second twice (1975, 1976). McCain saddled his first winner, San Lorenzo, at Liverpool in 1965. He acquired the seven-year-old Red Rum in 1972 and engineered the crippled horse's miraculous recovery by running him in the sand and seawater along the shore near Southport. McCain's faith in the big bay gelding paid off, and by the time Red Rum retired in 1978, he had won 24 races, including the three Grand Nationals, and Southport had erected a statue in his honour. After Red Rum's retirement in 1978 (he died in 1995 and was buried at Aintree Racecourse, home of the Grand National), McCain continued working, and in 2004 he returned to the winner's circle for his fourth Grand National victory, with 11-year-old Amberleigh House. Two years later McCain retired and turned over his stable to his son, Donald McCain, Jr.

McCarthy, John, American mathematician and computer and cognitive scientist (b. Sept. 4, 1927, Boston, Mass.—d. Oct. 24, 2011, Stanford, Calif.), coined the term *artificial intelligence* (AI) in 1955 and was a pioneer in that field; his main research in AI involved the formalization of commonsense knowledge. McCarthy also developed (1958) the LISP programming language, which was initially used primarily by the AI community owing to its great flexibility due to its expressive power; though the use of LISP declined in the 1990s, in the 21st century there was renewed interest in it, especially in the open-source community. In addition, he developed ideas about the processing characteristics of trees (as used in computing), as distinct from nets. McCarthy earned a Ph.D. (1951) in mathematics from Princeton University, where he briefly taught. He also held professorships at Dartmouth College, Hanover, N.H. (1955–58), MIT (1958–62), and Stanford University (1953–55 and 1962–2000). His major honours were the A.M. Turing Award (1971), the Kyoto Prize (1988), the National Medal of Science (1990), and the Benjamin Franklin Medal (2003).

McCracken, John Harvey, American artist (b. Dec. 9, 1934, Berkeley, Calif.—d. April 8, 2011, New York, N.Y.), was characterized as a minimalist with works that featured simple geometric forms, especially his monochromatic columns and his signature brightly coloured planks of wood, which blurred the line between painting and sculpture because they stood on the floor (as a sculpture would) but leaned on walls (akin to a painting). The columns and planks—painted bubble gum pink, lemon yellow, deep sapphire, and ebony—were hand sanded and polished by McCracken until their enamel, lacquer, or resin surfaces shone. Working in his West Coast aesthetic, which represented the "L.A. Cool School," McCracken maintained that his works were a balance between cognitive beauty and spirituality. In what he termed a maximalist vein, he produced a series of small paintings (1971–72) based on Buddhist and Hindu mandalas. After graduating with a B.F.A. (1962) from the California College of Arts and Crafts in Oakland and earning most of his credits toward an M.F.A., McCracken began painting in an Abstract Expressionist style, but by the early 1960s he had begun to adopt simple geometric forms.

McCulloch, Ernest Armstrong, Canadian cell biologist (b. April 27, 1926, Toronto, Ont.—d. Jan. 20, 2011, Toronto), collaborated with biophysicist James E. Till in the discovery of the existence of stem cells, which thus opened new avenues for the development of regenerative therapies such as bone marrow transplantation. McCulloch received an M.D. (1948) from the University of Toronto. In the 1950s he joined the Ontario Cancer Institute in Toronto, where he met Till. Together the two investigated the biological effects of ionizing radiation and performed bone marrow transplant experiments on X-ray-irradiated mice. They determined the radiation sensitivity of marrow cells and the number of cells required to save the animals, and they found that mice surviving the procedure developed unusual spleen nodules consisting of colonies of blood cells, known as colony-forming units. In the early 1960s McCulloch and Till discovered that these units are made up of stem cells, which can reproduce and mature into different types of blood cells. Several years later, the significance of their discovery was realized when the first successful human bone marrow transplant was performed at the University of Minnesota. McCulloch and Till shared various honours for their work, including the Albert Lasker Basic Medical Research Award (2005), and in 2004 they were both inducted into the Canadian Medical Hall of Fame.

McKenna, T(homas) P(atrick), Irish actor (b. Sept. 7, 1929, Mullagh, County Cavan, Ire.—d. Feb. 13, 2011, London, Eng.), was a familiar face on British television in scores of character roles over a 40-year span. McKenna's real success as an actor, however, was onstage, notably during his many years (1955–63, 1966–68, and thereafter as an honorary life member) as a mainstay at Dublin's Abbey Theatre, where he drew acclaim for his performances in works by Irish playwrights such as J.M. Synge and for such varied roles as Jamie in Eugene O'Neill's *Long Day's Journey into Night* and George in Edward Albee's *Who's Afraid of Virginia Woolf?* In 1962 he played Cranley in *Stephen D*, an adaptation of James Joyce stories, at the Abbey, and the next year he traveled with the production to London, where he settled. McKenna's films include *Ulysses* (1967), *The Charge of the Light Brigade* (1968), *Anne of the Thousand Days* (1969), *Straw Dogs* (1971), and *The Libertine* (2004).

Moore, Gary (ROBERT WILLIAM GARY MOORE), Irish guitarist (b. April 4, 1952, Belfast, N.Ire.—d. Feb. 6, 2011, Estepona, Spain), earned acclaim for his incendiary guitar playing in stints with the hard rock band Thin Lizzy and in a solo career. Moore began his career with the quartet Skid Row in Dublin in 1969 and first played with Thin Lizzy in 1973. He was especially noted for the ballad "Parisienne Walkways" on his solo album *Back on the Streets* (1979) and for his performance on Thin Lizzy's *Black Rose: A Rock Legend* (1979), particularly on the title track. He recorded several heavy metal albums in the 1980s, with *Run for Cover* (1985) yielding the hit songs "Military Man" and "Out in the Fields," both of which featured Thin Lizzy front man Phil Lynott. Moore later focused on blues-based guitar work, notably on the albums *Still Got the Blues* (1990) and *Blues for Greeny* (1995).

Morello, Joe (JOSEPH ALBERT MORELLO), American jazz drummer (b. July 17, 1928, Springfield, Mass.—d. March 12, 2011, Irvington, N.J.), was known for his inventiveness and masterful playing as a member of the Dave Brubeck Quartet. Though he was a child violin prodigy, Morello switched to drums as a teenager. He had already amassed an impressive résumé before joining Brubeck's quartet in 1956, having worked with guitar legend Johnny Smith and big band leader Stan Kenton, among others. Morello was best remembered for his performances on such Brubeck classics as "Take Five," "The Duke," and "In Your Own Sweet Way." After Brubeck disbanded his quartet in 1967, Morello, a star in his own right, began teaching (his students included session drummer Danny Gottlieb and Bruce Springsteen's drummer Max Weinberg) and writing instructional books and videos.

Morgan, Harry (HARRY BRATSBURG), American actor (b. April 10, 1915, Detroit, Mich.—d. Dec. 7, 2011, Los Angeles, Calif.), was best known for his television work, particularly as the gruff but kindhearted Col. Sherman T. Potter (1975–83) on *M*A*S*H*, for which he won an Emmy Award for best supporting actor in 1980. Morgan made his big-screen debut in 1942 in *To the Shores of Tripoli*, a World War II recruitment film. He had a starring role in *The Ox-Bow Incident* (1943) but accepted supporting roles as a tenant farmer in *Dragonwyck* (1946) and as a lecherous soda jerk in *The Gangster* (1947). On TV he had a recurring role in the situation comedy *December Bride* (1954–59), which led to the development of *Pete and Gladys* (1960–62), a spin-off focusing on the marriage of his character, Pete Porter. Morgan later costarred as Officer Bill Gannon (1967–70) on *Dragnet 1967*, a police procedural starring Jack Webb, and he reprised the role of Colonel Potter for the short-lived spin-off *After MASH* (1983–84). Morgan also appeared as U.S. Pres. Harry Truman in *Backstairs at the White House* (1979).

Myllylä, Mika, Finnish skier (b. Sept. 12, 1969, Oulu, Fin.—found dead July 5, 2011, Kokkola, Fin.), tarnished his status as a national hero and his record of 15 Winter Olympic and world championship medals with a doping scandal in 2001 that stunned Finland and

Ski champion Mika Myllylä

Thomas Kienzle/AP

ended his career. Myllylä's awards included a gold (30-km mass start, 1998), a silver (50 km, 1994), and four bronze medals (30 km and relay, 1994; 10 km and relay, 1998) for Olympic cross country skiing. He also captured four golds, three silvers, and two bronzes in three world championships (1995, 1997, 1999). At the world championships in 2001, however, Myllylä and several teammates tested positive for an illegal performance-related drug and were banned from the sport for two years. Myllylä attempted to make a comeback but never achieved the same levels of success.

Nascimento, Abdias do, Brazilian writer, painter, activist, and scholar (b. March 14, 1914, Franca, Braz.—d. May 24, 2011, Rio de Janeiro, Braz.), was an outspoken and vibrant defender of Afro-Brazilian civil rights who supplemented his activism with his artistic endeavours. Nascimento studied economics at the University of Rio de Janeiro (B.A., 1938) and later received advanced degrees from the Higher Institute of Brazilian Studies (1957) and the Oceanography Institute (1961). He also founded numerous Afro-Brazilian rights and arts organizations. These included the Black Experimental Theater (1944), which defied the segregated tradition of using black-faced actors in Brazilian theatre; the Afro-Brazilian Democratic Committee (1945); the Museum of Black Art (1968); and the Afro-Brazilian Studies and Research Institute, known as Ipeafro (1981). He lived in exile from Brazil's military dictatorship from 1968 to 1981, and during this time he began to paint and exhibit his paintings, which drew from Afro-Brazilian religion and culture. While in exile he lectured at Yale University (1969–70), Wesleyan University, Middletown, Conn. (1970–71), the University of Ife in Ile-Ife, Nigeria (1976–77), and Temple University, Philadelphia (1990–91) and founded a chair in the department of American studies at the State University of New York at Buffalo. During this period he also cofounded the Democratic Labour Party of Brazil (1981) and led the party's Black Movement. After his return to Brazil, he served in the National Legislature as a congressman and senator, furthering his vision of Afro-Brazilian equality. In addition to his richly coloured paintings, which were exhibited and collected in the U.S. and Brazil, Nascimento crafted books, plays, and poetry that were widely read, and he edited two periodicals, *Afrodiaspora* (1983–86) and *Thoth* (1997–99).

Nelson, David Oswald, American actor (b. Oct. 24, 1936, New York, N.Y.—d. Jan. 11, 2011, Los Angeles, Calif.), starred together with his mother (Harriet), father (Ozzie), and younger brother (Ricky) on the quintessential television sitcom *The Adventures of Ozzie and Harriet* (1952–66), a portrayal of what was considered the perfect American family. Prior to the sitcom, David and Ricky joined their parents on their radio program and were dubbed "the Crown Princes of Radio." They also appeared in the comedic feature film *Here Come the Nelsons* (1952), which heralded their TV show. David's role, as the more serious older brother, was the smallest part. Though he was depicted as attending school to become a lawyer, offscreen Nelson continued to pursue a career in show business, performing in such films as *Peyton Place* (1957), *The Remarkable Mr. Pennypacker* (1959), and *The Big Circus* (1959) and taking the director's chair for some episodes of *The Adventures of Ozzie and Harriet* as well as other TV programs. He eventually formed his own production company.

Neville, John Reginald, British-born Canadian actor and director (b. May 2, 1925, London, Eng.—d. Nov. 19, 2011, Toronto, Ont.), achieved stardom with his natural and wide-ranging performances in Shakespearean plays and, as artistic director, revivified several Canadian theatres. Neville studied at the Royal Academy of Dramatic Art in London and made his stage debut in a 1947 production of Shakespeare's *Richard II*. He rapidly gained critical acclaim in leading roles as Hamlet, Othello, and Romeo. During one six-year period in the 1950s, he appeared in all 37 of Shakespeare's plays. Neville cofounded (1963) a playhouse in Nottingham, Eng., but in 1972 he moved to Canada, where he radically boosted ticket sales while serving as artistic director at the struggling Citadel (1973–78) and Neptune (1978–83) theatres before taking the helm at the Stratford Shakespeare Festival (1986–89). Neville also appeared in dozens of films and television shows, notably as the irrepressible title character in the movie *The Adventures of Baron Munchausen* (1988) and on TV in a recurring role as the "Well-Manicured Man" in *The X-Files* (1995–98). Neville was made OBE (1965) and an Officer of the Order of Canada (2006).

Nguyen Cao Ky, South Vietnamese military and political leader (b. Sept. 8, 1930, Son Tay, northern Vietnam—d. July 23, 2011, Kuala Lumpur, Malay.), was the flamboyant and vehemently anticommunist commander of South Vietnam's air force (1963–65) and the country's premier (1965–67) following the June 1965 military coup in which he (together with Maj. Gen. Nguyen Van Thieu and Gen. Duong Van Minh) unseated the government of Premier Phan Huy Quat. Ky was a member of the French forces that opposed the Vietnamese liberation movement, and he joined the South Vietnamese air force after the country was partitioned in 1954. He was highly favoured by U.S. advisers in Vietnam and with U.S. aid built up a fighting force of 10,000 men. As premier in a military triumvirate with Thieu and Minh, Ky provoked widespread opposition to his authoritarian policies. In 1967 the top military leaders agreed that Thieu would run for president and Ky for vice president of a new regime. Ky, however, became an outspoken critic of his rival, and in 1971 he attempted to oppose Thieu for the presidency. He was forced to step down and returned to the air force. Upon the fall of South Vietnam in April 1975, Ky fled to the U.S., where he lectured and promoted his books.

Nyman, Lena (ANNA LENA ELISABET NYMAN), Swedish actress (b. May 23, 1944, Stockholm, Swed.—d. Feb. 4, 2011, Stockholm), starred in the sexually explicit film *I Am Curious (Yellow)* (1967), which became a huge interna-

Film performer Lena Nyman

Evergreen Film/AP

tional box-office hit in spite of—or, according to some observers, because of—its seizure by U.S. customs officials and subsequent banning as obscene. The film was finally released in the U.S. in 1969 after a federal appeals court overturned the ban and ruled that the movie was protected under the First Amendment's clause on freedom of speech. Nyman won the Swedish Film Institute's Guldbagge Award for best actress for *I Am Curious (Yellow)* and its follow-up, *I Am Curious (Blue)* (1968). Her other movies included Ingmar Bergman's intense *Höstsonaten* (1978; *Autumn Sonata*) and the romantic comedy *Att göra en pudel* (2006; *White Trash*), for which she earned a Guldbagge nomination for best supporting actress. Nyman, who trained at the Royal Dramatic School in Stockholm, was an accomplished stage actress in works by such playwrights as Henrik Ibsen and August Strindberg.

Ohga, Norio, Japanese business executive (b. Jan. 29, 1930, Numazu, Japan—d. April 23, 2011, Tokyo, Japan), played

Richard Drew/AP

Sony leader Norio Ohga

an instrumental role in the development (1982) of the compact disc (CD), and positioned Sony Corp. to be a global leader among electronics manufacturers. In 1953 the Tokyo Telecommunications Engineering Corp. (now Sony) hired him as a part-time consultant because of his musical knowledge and technical expertise. Ohga traveled to Berlin the following year to launch a singing career, and he performed throughout Europe and Japan before joining Sony on a full-time basis in 1959. He made a rapid ascent through the corporate ranks, becoming president in 1982, CEO in 1989, and chairman in 1994. Ohga encouraged sleek product design and miniaturization, which led (1979) to the Walkman portable tape player, and insisted that Sony and its partner, Philips, devise a CD that could hold 75 minutes of music—enough for Beethoven's entire *Ninth Symphony*. He also expanded Sony's empire with the introduction (1994) of the Sony PlayStation video game system and the acquisition of CBS Records (1988) and Columbia Pictures (1989).

Ojukwu, Odumegwu (Ikemba Chukwuemeka Odumegwu Ojukwu), Nigerian military leader and politician (b. Nov. 4, 1933, Zungeru, Nigeria—d. Nov. 26, 2011, London, Eng.), was head of the secessionist state of Biafra during the Nigerian civil war (1967–70). Ojukwu was the son of a successful Igbo businessman. He graduated (1955) from the University of Oxford and returned to Nigeria as an administrative officer. After two years, however, he joined the army, and he was rapidly promoted thereafter. After a group of largely Igbo junior army officers overthrew Nigeria's civilian government in January 1966, Ojukwu was appointed military governor of the mostly Igbo Eastern Region. A countercoup in July by Hausa and Yoruba officers brought Yakubu Gowon to power as head of state, and continuing ethnic strife led in September to large-scale massacres of Igbo civilians. Ojukwu unsuccessfully proposed a weak federation-type government, which would have granted the largest ethnic groups substantial political autonomy. Mounting secessionist pressures from his fellow Igbo finally compelled Ojukwu on May 30, 1967, to declare the Eastern Region the independent Republic of Biafra. Federal troops invaded, and civil war broke out. In 1970 Ojukwu fled to Côte d'Ivoire, where he remained until 1982, when he was pardoned and returned home. He was detained for 10 months following another coup at the end of 1983. Ojukwu attempted to reenter politics and was a member of two constitutional conferences (in the 1990s), but he never again held office.

Old, Lloyd John, American cancer immunologist (b. Sept. 23, 1933, San Francisco, Calif.—d. Nov. 28, 2011, New York, N.Y.), was one of the founders of tumour immunology, a field in which he made key discoveries concerning cancer and the immune system; he pioneered a form of cancer treatment known as immunotherapy, in which specialized agents are used to strengthen the immune response against the disease. After earning a bachelor's degree in biology (1955) from the University of California, Berkeley, and a medical degree (1958) from the University of California School of Medicine, Old took a position in 1958 at Memorial Sloan-Kettering Cancer Center (MSKCC) in New York City; he stayed there for the remainder of his career. Old contributed to the discovery of an immune protein known as tumour necrosis factor (TNF) and to the discovery of substances known as cell surface markers that activate the immune system. While the notion of immunotherapy was not well received initially, Old believed that cell surface markers could be harnessed for the treatment of disease, and cancer in particular, a feat that was finally realized in 2010 with the approval of the first immunotherapeutic agent, the prostate cancer vaccine sipuleucel-T (Provenge). At MSKCC, Old was the scientific director of the Cancer Research Institute (1971–2011) as well as the director of the Ludwig Institute for Cancer Research (1988–2005).

Olsen, Kenneth Harry, American computer entrepreneur (b. Feb. 20, 1926, Bridgeport, Conn.—d. Feb. 6, 2011, Indianapolis, Ind.), cofounded (1957) and helmed Digital Equipment Corp. (DEC), which led the second wave of the computer industry in moving from large mainframe computers to smaller networked machines. Olsen graduated from the Massachusetts Institute of Technology (B.S., 1950; M.S., 1952) and from 1950 worked in MIT's Lincoln Laboratory. DEC's first offering (1960), the Programmed Data Processor, or PDP-1, incorporated technology developed at MIT, including its advanced memory design and its time-sharing capability. (The first multiuser computer game—*Spacewar!*—was created for use on the PDP-1.) The PDP-8 (1965) was the company's first commercial success, and DEC grew to become the second largest (behind IBM) computer company in the world. Olsen, however, failed to recognize the market shift toward the personal computer and was forced to resign from the company in 1992, six years before DEC was acquired by the Compaq Computer Corp. Olsen was inducted into the National Inventors Hall of Fame in 1990 and was honoured with the National Medal of Technology in 1993.

Patassé, Ange-Félix, Central African Republic politician (b. Jan. 25, 1937, Paoua, Ubangi-Shari, French Equatorial Africa [now Paoua, Central African Republic]—d. April 5, 2011, Douala, Cameroon), figured prominently in the Central African Republic (C.A.R.) as a government minister and prime minister (1976–78) under Pres. Jean-Bédel Bokassa and then later as president (1993–2003) until he was overthrown by Gen. François Bozizé. Patassé was educated in France, but in 1960 he joined the civil service in the newly independent C.A.R. After Bokassa led a coup against Pres. David Dacko, Patassé held a series of ministerial posts before being named prime minister. He unexpectedly resigned in 1978 and went into exile in France, where he formed a new anti-Bokassa political party. When Dacko was restored to the presidency (1979) through French military intervention, Patassé again returned home. He lost to Dacko in the 1981 presidential election and left the country shortly thereafter when Dacko was toppled by André Kolingba. Patassé defeated both Kolingba and Dacko in the 1993 election and was reelected in 1999. As president he instituted some political and economic reforms, but his erratic rule, along with allegations of corruption and mismanagement and his reliance on foreign peacekeeping forces, ultimately led to his ouster in March 2003.

Percy, Charles Harting (CHUCK), American politician (b. Sept. 27, 1919, Pensacola, Fla.—d. Sept. 17, 2011, Washington, D.C.), was a moderate Republican who served (1967–84) as a U.S. senator from Illinois for three terms and entered the national spotlight after proposing in May 1973 that an independent prosecutor investigate Pres. Richard Nixon's involvement in the Watergate Scandal; the Senate resolution was adopted. Percy thereafter earned a place on Nixon's notorious "enemies" list. While earning a B.A. (1941) in economics from the University of Chicago, Percy began working at photographic equipment company Bell & Howell, and following graduation he joined the firm full time. At age 29 he was named president of the company; during his tenure (1949–61) he boosted revenue from $13 million to more than $160 million. In 1964 Percy ran unsuccessfully for governor of Illinois, but two years later he defeated three-term Democrat Paul Douglas for the U.S. Senate seat; during Percy's campaign, one of his daughters was slain in the family's home in a wealthy Chicago suburb. As senator, Percy endorsed consumer protection, environmental efforts, and a strict enforcement of drug laws. Percy eventually became so identified with the more progressive wing of the party known as the Rockefeller Republicans that "decent Chuck Percy Republicans" became a synonymous phrase. Though he flirted with running for president, the resignation in 1974 of Nixon followed by the elevation of Vice Pres. Gerald Ford to that office and Ford's successful nomination in 1976 derailed Percy's plans. He served (1972–84) on the powerful Foreign Relations Committee but lost his bid in 1984 for a fourth senatorial term. After leaving politics, Percy established a consulting firm.

Perkins, Pinetop (JOE WILLIE PERKINS), American blues pianist (b. July 7, 1913, near Belzoni, Miss.—d. March 21, 2011, Austin, Texas), performed with such blues greats as Robert Nighthawk (Robert McCollum), Sonny Boy Williamson II (Aleck Miller), and Muddy Waters before launching a career as a front man in the 1980s. Perkins's piano playing was influenced by the boogie-woogie style of Clarence ("Pine Top") Smith (1904–29), whose nickname he borrowed and whose signature song, "Pine Top's Boogie Woogie," he later recorded. Perkins played in juke joints and at house parties throughout the Mississippi Delta and accompanied Nighthawk and Williamson on their rival programs on radio station KFFA in Helena, Ark. In the early 1960s Perkins moved to Chicago, where he mostly worked outside the music industry until Waters asked him in 1969 to replace Otis Spann in his band. Perkins traveled widely and recorded extensively with the Waters band, which performed as the Legendary Blues Band after Perkins and other members separated from Waters in 1980. Perkins also began to record under his own name, beginning with *After Hours* (1988). He received a Grammy lifetime achievement award in 2005 and was awarded Grammys in 2007 and 2011 for best traditional blues album. Perkins was inducted (2003) into the Blues Foundation's Hall of Fame.

Bob Fila—MCT/Landov

Blues pianist Pinetop Perkins

Perry, Joe (FLETCHER JOSEPH PERRY; "THE JET"), American football player (b. Jan. 22, 1927, Stephens, Ark.—d. April 25, 2011, Tempe, Ariz.), possessed tremendous speed and an uncanny ability to find holes in the defensive line as the powerful fullback (1948–60 and 1963) for the San Francisco 49ers of the All-America Football Conference (from 1950 the NFL). During the 1950s Perry became the first player to rush for more than 1,000 yd in two consecutive seasons (1953 and 1954) and along with his teammates—quarterback Y.A. Tittle and halfbacks Hugh McElhenny and John Henry Johnson—made up the storied Million Dollar Backfield. Perry was playing football for the navy in the San Francisco Bay area when the 49ers recruited him (their first black player) for the team. During his 16-year professional career (he also played [1961–62] for the Baltimore Colts), he had 9,723 yd rushing and 71 rushing touchdowns. For a time he held the record as the NFL's career rushing leader until Jim Brown gained that distinction in October 1963. Perry was inducted into the Pro Football Hall of Fame in 1969. He was the recipient of financial assistance from an NFL disability plan that aided former players with dementia. His brain was donated to a Boston University facility conducting research on dementia associated with football concussions.

Perry, Matthew James, Jr., American lawyer and judge (b. Aug. 3, 1921, Columbia, S.C.—d. July 29, 2011, Columbia), worked tirelessly to advance the legal status of African Americans during the civil rights movement. Perry argued several cases before the U.S. Supreme Court, which overturned more than 7,000 sit-in convictions; his most significant case, however, was *Edwards* v. *South Carolina* (1963), which upheld African Americans' right to engage in protest marches and which was cited in at least 70 other U.S. Supreme Court cases. While serving in the army (1942–46), Perry turned to activism when he saw that in the American South some Italian prisoners of war received better treatment than African American soldiers. He studied law and in 1957 became chief counsel of the South Carolina branch of the NAACP. Resigned to winning cases only on appeal, Perry often accepted food in place of payment and was restricted to the court's gallery when not arguing on the floor, but he demonstrated a perseverance and skill that led to the desegregation of such public places as parks, hospitals, restaurants, and schools, notably both Clemson (S.C.) University and the University of South Carolina in 1963. Pres. Gerald Ford appointed (1976) Perry to the U.S. Military Court of Appeals, making him its first African American judge from the Deep South. Three years later Pres. Jimmy Carter named him the first black federal district court judge in South Carolina. In 2004 Columbia's federal courthouse was named in Perry's honour.

Petit, Roland, French dancer and choreographer (b. Jan. 13, 1924, Villemomble, France—d. July 10, 2011, Geneva, Switz.), crafted dramatic ballets that combined fantasy with elements of contemporary realism. His choreography was often angular or acrobatic and was considered theatrical in its use of mime dance, occasional singing, and props such as cigarettes and telephones. Trained at the Paris Opéra Ballet school, Petit joined the company in 1940 but left in 1944 to perform his own works at the Théâtre Sarah Bernhardt in Paris. In 1945 he was instrumental in creating Les Ballets des Champs-Élysées, where he remained as principal dancer, ballet master, and choreographer until 1947. In 1948 he formed Les Ballets de Paris de Roland Petit, which made several tours of Europe and the U.S. over the next decade. Dancers who rose to prominence in his companies include Jean Babilée, Colette Marchand, Leslie Caron, and Renée ("Zizi") Jeanmaire, whom he married in 1954 and who became famous for her interpretation of the title role in one of his most erotic and popular ballets, *Carmen* (1949). Petit often worked with other major ballet companies, owned and operated (1970–75) the Casino de Paris (producing revues starring Jeanmaire), and choreographed several films, some of which featured his wife, notably *Hans Christian Andersen* (1952), *Anything Goes* (1956), and the compilation *Black Tights* (1961). In 1972 he founded and became director of the Ballet National de Marseille, a post he held until 1998.

AP

Dancer and choreographer Roland Petit

Pihos, Pete (PETER LOUIS PIHOS; "THE GOLDEN GREEK"), American football player (b. Oct. 22, 1923, Orlando, Fla.—d. Aug. 16, 2011, Winston-Salem, N.C.), was a mainstay of the NFL's Philadelphia Eagles for nine years (1947–55) and helped the team achieve unprecedented back-to-back NFL championship titles: after the Eagles lost the title to the Chicago Cardinals in Pihos's rookie season (1947), he was central to the team's 7–0 victory over the Cardinals the next year, and in the 1949 title game, he caught a 31-yd pass to score the opening touchdown in Philadelphia's 14–0 win against the Los Angeles Rams. Pihos, a versatile player who was able to switch easily between offense and defense, won All-American honours twice (1943, 1945) while at Indiana University. In his nine seasons with the Eagles, he missed only one game and made 373 catches for 6,519 yd and 61 touchdowns; he led the NFL in receptions for three seasons (1953–55) and in touchdown catches once (1953). Pihos earned All-Pro honours five times, was named to six Pro Bowls, and was inducted into both the College (1966) and the Pro (1970) Football Hall of Fame. In later years he suffered from dementia, which some doctors attributed to the head injuries that he sustained during his playing years.

Pisier, Marie-France Claire, French actress and writer (b. May 10, 1944, Dalat, French Indochina [now Da Lat, Vietnam]—found dead April 24, 2011, Saint-Cyr-sur-Mer, France), gained international recognition as the haughty Colette Tazzi in three films by director François Truffaut: the segment "Antoine et Colette" in *L'Amour à vingt ans* (1962; *Love at Twenty*), *Baisers volés* (1968; *Stolen Kisses*), and *L'Amour en fuite* (1979; *Love on the Run*), which she co-wrote with Truffaut. Pisier studied political science and obtained a law degree from the University of Paris while pursuing her acting career. She won two César Awards as best supporting actress, the first for a 1975 romantic comedy—*Cousin, cousine*, in which she played the leading man's self-centred wife—and the second a year later for her portrayal of a prostitute in the crime thriller *Barocco* (1976). Her other films include Luis Buñuel's avant-garde *Le Fantôme de la liberté* (1974; *The Phantom of Liberty*), *Céline et Julie vont en bateau* (1974; *Céline and Julie Go Boating*), which she co-wrote, *The Other Side of Midnight* (1977), *French Postcards* (1979), *Les Soeurs Brontë* (1979; *The Brontë Sisters*), and *Le Temps retrouvé* (1999; *Marcel Proust's Time Regained*). Pisier also wrote several novels, one of which she adapted and directed for the big screen.

Poly Styrene (MARIANNE JOAN ELLIOT-SAID), British musician (b. July 3, 1957, Bromley, Kent, Eng.—d. April 25, 2011, St. Leonards-on-Sea, East Sussex, Eng.), was a punk rock pioneer whose raw, intense vocals and colourful, subversive stage costumes inspired a generation of women in rock music. After seeing a concert featuring the Sex Pistols, she took the stage name Poly Styrene and in 1976 formed the band X-Ray Spex, for which she served as songwriter and vocalist. With short tight songs that used humour as well as anger to skewer sexism, racism, and consumerism, the band rapidly gained a fan base. Its best-known song was "Oh Bondage, Up Yours!" (1977). X-Ray Spex broke up a year after the 1978 release of the band's essential first-wave punk album *Germ Free Adolescents*. Poly Styrene re-formed the band in later years; she also recorded solo albums, including *Generation Indigo*, which was released about a month before her death from breast cancer.

Postlethwaite, Pete (PETER WILLIAM POSTLETHWAITE), British character actor (b. Feb. 7, 1946, Warrington, Cheshire, Eng.—d. Jan. 2, 2011, Shrewsbury, Shropshire, Eng.), was best known for *In the Name of the Father* (1993), in which he portrayed Giuseppe Conlon, the father of Gerry Conlon (played by Daniel Day-Lewis), the real-life father and son who were falsely convicted and imprisoned for Irish Republican Army terrorist bombings after Gerry Conlon and other members of the so-called Guildford Four were coerced into making false confessions. The role earned Postlethwaite an Academy Award nomination for best supporting actor. Although his prominent cheekbones and battered-looking nose gave Postlethwaite's face a distinctive working-class look, he was equally convincing as the leader of a Yorkshire miners' brass band in the sentimental comedy *Brassed Off* (1996), as the mysterious henchman Kobayashi in *The Usual Suspects* (1995), and as the antiabolition prosecutor Holabird in Steven Spielberg's *Amistad* (1997). Despite the recurrence of an earlier cancer, he appeared in three films released in 2010—the fantasy adventure *Clash of the Titans*, the crime drama *The Town*, and the science-fiction thriller *Inception*—and had completed work on *Killing Bono* (2011). Postlethwaite was made OBE in 2004.

Stefan Wermuth—Reuters/Landov

Character actor Pete Postlethwaite

Price, (Edward) Reynolds, American writer (b. Feb. 1, 1933, Macon, N.C.—d. Jan. 20, 2011, Durham, N.C.), drew on his experiences growing up and living in North Carolina for his stories and novels. Price attended Duke University, Durham (A.B. 1955), before receiving a B.Litt. degree (1958) from Merton College, Oxford, but he returned to Duke, where he began a long career teaching English. Novelist Eudora Welty, who took an interest in his writing, became a patron. Price's first novel, *A Long and Happy Life* (1961), introduced his memorable young heroine, the naive, spirited Rosacoke Mustian, who loves, becomes pregnant by, and weds an indifferent young man. A younger Rosacoke appeared in Price's short-story collection *The Names and Faces of Heroes* (1963), and in the novel *A Generous Man* (1966), her brother Milo experiences his sexual awakening while searching the backwoods for a retarded brother, a dog, and an escaped python. The third volume in the trilogy, *Good Hearts* (1988), resumes the story of Rosacoke in her middle age. Price's other novels include *Love and Work* (1968); the trilogy *A Great Circle* (2001); *Kate Vaiden* (1986), the orphaned heroine of which was based on the author's own mother; *The Tongues of Angels* (1990); and *The Good Priest's Son* (2005). While writing *Kate Vaiden*, Price became paraplegic, the aftermath of cancer of the spine. Nevertheless he continued to teach and write and also penned poetry, plays, and essays and published Bible translations.

Price, Dame Margaret Berenice, Welsh soprano (b. April 13, 1941, Blackwood, Wales—d. Jan. 28, 2011, near Ceibwr Bay, Wales), brought her rich, expressive voice to mezzo-soprano roles early in her career but later specialized in the soprano repertoire; she particularly excelled at lieder, which she recorded extensively. Price studied at Trinity College of Music in London and made her debut (1962) with the Welsh National Opera in the trouser role of Cherubino in Mozart's *Le nozze di Figaro*. Her big break came the next year when she was called on to replace Teresa Berganza in the same role at London's Royal Opera House. By the end of the 1960s, Price had developed her voice's higher register and moved into soprano roles, including the Countess in that same opera, Pamina in Mozart's *Die Zauberflöte*, and Desdemona in Verdi's *Otello*. For some years she was based in Germany, where she was associated with the Cologne Opera and the Bavarian State Opera in Munich. Price was made CBE in 1982 and advanced to DBE in 1993 and was appointed *Kammersängerin* (court singer) in both Munich and Vienna.

Prusoff, William Herman, American pharmacologist (b. June 25, 1920, Brooklyn, N.Y.—d. April 3, 2011, Branford, Conn.), developed the first antiviral drug approved by the U.S. Food and Drug Administration (FDA). The agent, idoxuridine, was used in the treatment of infant keratitis (inflammation of the cornea), which is caused by the herpes simplex virus and can lead to blindness. Prusoff also developed stavudine, an agent used to treat HIV/AIDS. In the early 1950s he synthesized idoxuridine, one of the first nucleoside analogs (so named for their similarity to subunits of DNA and RNA). The drug's success earned Prusoff the title "father of antiviral chemotherapy" and overturned the then widely held notion that safe, effective antiviral agents would be impossible to develop. In the 1980s Prusoff discovered that stavudine, another nucleoside analog, blocks replication of HIV. Approved by the FDA in 1994 under the brand name Zerit, stavudine joined three other first-generation anti-HIV/AIDS drugs—one of which was zidovudine (AZT)—that had already been approved.

Qaddafi, Muammar al-, Libyan de facto head of state (b. 1942, near Surt, Libya—d. Oct. 20, 2011, Surt), ruled Libya for more than four decades, from Sept. 1, 1969, when he seized control of the government in a military coup that deposed King Idris, until he was ousted in August 2011. The son of an itinerant Bedouin farmer, Qaddafi was born in a tent in the desert. He graduated from the University of Libya in 1963 and from the Libyan military academy in 1965. A devout Muslim and ardent Arab nationalist, he rose steadily through the military ranks, all the while plotting with fellow officers to overthrow the Libyan monarchy. After the 1969 coup Qaddafi was named commander in chief of the armed forces and chairman of Libya's new governing body, the Revolutionary Command Council. Over the next few years he consolidated his power, removed the U.S. and British military bases from Libya, expelled most members of the native Italian and Jewish communities, nationalized foreign-owned petroleum assets, and espoused a form of Islamic socialism that he expressed in *The Green Book*. His government also became known for abortive coup attempts in other countries, for financing a broad spectrum of revolutionary or terrorist groups, and for its purported involvement in the destruction of a civilian airliner in 1988 over Lockerbie, Scot. The latter event triggered UN and U.S. sanctions that were not fully lifted until 2003 following Qaddafi's announcement that Libya would cease its unconventional-weapons program. In early 2011, after antigovernment demonstrations forced out the presidents of neighbouring Tunisia and Egypt, anti-Qaddafi protests broke out in Libya. The regime attempted to violently suppress the insurgency, but opposition forces gradually took control of the country. Qaddafi survived a NATO air strike in April on his home compound in Tripoli, but he was not found in his Tripoli headquarters when rebel fighters captured the compound in August. After evading capture for several weeks, though, he was killed by rebel forces in his hometown, one of the last remaining loyalist strongholds.

Quillen, Daniel Gray, American mathematician (b. June 27, 1940, Orange, N.J.—d. April 30, 2011, Gainesville, Fla.), was awarded the Fields Medal in 1978 for contributions to algebraic *K*-theory. Quillen attended Harvard University (Ph.D., 1964), and held appointments at MIT and the Mathematical Institute of the University of Oxford. In addition to his application of geometric and topological techniques to the study of algebraic *K*-theory, he made contributions in topology to the cobordism theory of René Thom, and in 1976 Quillen solved a well-known problem that had been posed some 20 years earlier by Jean-Pierre Serre concerning the structure of certain abstract mathematical spaces. He showed that many of the highly generalized spaces that were developed extensively in 20th-century mathematics can be developed from elementary components, dimension by dimension.

Rabbani, Burhanuddin, Afghan Islamic scholar and political leader (b. 1940, Faizabad, Badakhshan, Afg.—d. Sept. 20, 2011, Kabul, Afg.), instituted strict Islamic laws as the president (1992–96) of Afghanistan but was driven into exile after the rise of the even more fundamentalist Islamist Taliban. Rabbani, who was a member of Afghanistan's Tajik minority, attended a religious school in Kabul. He then studied Islamic law and theology at Kabul University and Islamic philosophy at Cairo's al-Azhar University, from which he obtained a master's degree (1968). As a strong opponent of King Mohammad Zahir Shah's secular reforms, he became the head of an Islamic political party, which evolved into a powerful mujahideen rebel group during the Soviet occupation of Afghanistan (1979–92). Rabbani was the second president after the Soviet withdrawal, but he refused to step down from the rotating presidency. Four years later he was forced out by Taliban forces, though he retained international recognition. He returned home in the wake of the U.S.-led attacks in 2001 and briefly served as interim president until the election that November of Hamid Karzai. From 2010 Rabbani was head of the High Peace Council, which sought to pursue peace talks with the Taliban. He was assassinated by a suicide bomber claiming to be a Taliban emissary.

Afghan politician Burhanuddin Rabbani

Omar Sobhani—Reuters/Landov

Rafferty, Gerry (GERALD RAFFERTY), Scottish singer-songwriter (b. April 16, 1947, Paisley, Scot.—d. Jan. 4, 2011, Poole, Dorset, Eng.), achieved moderate success in the 1970s as a solo artist and as a member of the folk-oriented Humblebums (1968–71) and the soft-rock group Stealers Wheel (1972–75). Rafferty's smooth vocal style and often sardonic lyrics were prominently featured in Stealers Wheel's hit single "Stuck in the Middle with You" (1972) and on his second solo album, *City to City* (1978), which reached number one on the American charts and included "Right down the Line" and his biggest hit, the poignant "Baker Street." Rafferty learned Irish and Scottish folk songs from his mother, and when his hard-drinking working-class father died in 1963, he left school to work. His songwriting skills eventually attracted the attention of singer-comedian Billy Connolly, who invited him to join the Humblebums. Rafferty's other solo albums include *Night Owl* (1979), *Snakes and Ladders*

(1980), *On a Wing and a Prayer* (1993), and *Another World* (2000).

Ragovoy, Jerry (Jordan Ragovoy, Norman Margulies, Norman Meade), American songwriter and record producer (b. Sept. 4, 1930, Philadelphia, Pa.—d. July 13, 2011, New York, N.Y.), wrote some of the best-known rock-and-roll songs of the 1960s, including "Time Is on My Side," recorded by the Rolling Stones (1964), and several of Janis Joplin's hits, notably "Piece of My Heart," "Cry Baby," and "Try (Just a Little Bit Harder)." Ragovoy began as the music buyer for an appliance store in Philadelphia, but in 1953 he cofounded a small local record company. He moved to New York to become a songwriter, and by 1966 he was head of artists and repertory for Warner Brothers Records. Ragovoy's rich, soulful compositions (some of which were written under the pseudonyms Norman Margulies or Norman Meade) include the hits "Stay with Me," recorded by Lorraine Ellison (1966), and "Pata Pata," performed by Miriam Makeba (1967). Other artists who recorded his songs include Howard Tate, Erma Franklin, Elvis Costello, Dusty Springfield, Jimi Hendrix, B.B. King, the Who, Dionne Warwick, Bobby Vinton, the Drifters, Diana Ross, Louis Jordan, and Barry White. Ragovoy won a Grammy (1973) for producing the cast recording of the Broadway musical *Don't Bother Me, I Can't Cope*.

Rahal, James Joseph, Jr., American physician and educator (b. Oct. 14, 1933, Boston, Mass.—d. June 11, 2011, New York, N.Y.), was a leading expert on infectious diseases, notably the West Nile virus, and on drug-resistant bacteria, about which he publicly raised concerns in the early 1990s before the growing extent of the problem was widely understood. From 1988 Rahal was director of the infectious-diseases division of New York Hospital Medical Center of Queens, where he studied antibiotic-resistant bacteria and where in 1999 he observed an outbreak of an undiagnosed virus. After the Centers for Disease Control and Prevention in Atlanta identified the cause as West Nile virus, which had not previously been seen in the Western Hemisphere, his research led to the development of the first effective treatment (2002).

Ramsey, Norman Foster, American physicist (b. Aug. 27, 1915, Washington, D.C.—d. Nov. 4, 2011, Wayland, Mass.), was awarded one-half of the Nobel Prize for Physics in 1989 for his development of a technique to induce atoms to shift from one specific energy level to another. (The other half of the prize was split between Wolfgang Paul and Hans Georg Dehmelt.) Ramsey's innovation, called the separated oscillatory fields method, found application in the precise measurement of time and frequency. He studied physics at Columbia University, New York City, and received a Ph.D. degree there in 1940. He also earned a D.Sc. degree (1954) from the University of Cambridge. For much of his career, he taught (1947–86) at Harvard University, where he became Higgins Professor of Physics in 1966 and professor emeritus in 1986. Ramsey played an influential role in the founding of both the Brookhaven National Laboratory in Upton, N.Y., and the Fermi National Accelerator Laboratory in Batavia, Ill. In 1949 Ramsey perfected a method to study the structure of atoms by sending them through two separate oscillating electromagnetic fields. The rapid energy-level transitions thereby induced in a beam of atoms produced an interference pattern that could provide important data about the structure and behaviour of atoms. When synchronized with a microwave oscillator, the atoms' oscillations could also be used to measure the passage of time with extreme accuracy, thus providing the basis for the modern cesium atomic clock, which sets present time standards. In the 1950s Ramsey helped develop the hydrogen maser, a microwave-emitting relative of the laser.

Rapport, Maurice M., American biochemist (b. Sept. 23, 1919, Atlantic City, N.J.—d. Aug. 18, 2011, Durham, N.C.), isolated and identified the molecular structure of serotonin, which he named 5-hydroxytryptamine. His findings, published in 1949, led commercial laboratories to synthesize serotonin and to establish its properties as a neurotransmitter. It was found that serotonin has an important role in affecting a person's mood. Rapport's discovery resulted in the development of psychiatric drugs to manage depression as well as pharmaceuticals to treat cardiovascular and gastrointestinal diseases. During his career Rapport conducted significant research on cancer and diseases of the nervous system, such as multiple sclerosis, and established (1968) the division of neuroscience at the New York State Psychiatric Institute, where he functioned as division chief until 1986. In New York City he served as professor of biochemistry (1958–86) at the Columbia University College of Physicians and Surgeons, as head of the immunology section (1954–58) at the Sloan-Kettering Institute for Cancer Research, and as visiting professor of neurology (1986–2011) at the Albert Einstein College of Medicine.

Rathmann, Jim (Royal Richard Rathmann), American race-car driver (b. July 16, 1928, Alhambra, Calif.—d. Nov. 23, 2011, Palm Bay, Fla.), set a record in 1959 for the fastest-ever Indy-car race (clocking an average speed of 170 mph) at the first and only such race at Daytona (Fla.) Speedway; just months later he won the grueling 1960 Indianapolis 500 after trading the lead with Roger Ward some 20 times and edging him out at the finish line. Rathmann began racing professionally at age 16, circumventing his underage status by switching driver's licenses with the one belonging to his older brother, James, whose nickname he used for the rest of his professional career. During the 1950s Rathmann placed second in the Indianapolis 500 three times. Rathmann was inducted into the Auto Racing Hall of Fame in 1993 and the Motorsports Hall of Fame in 2007.

Rathore, Fateh Singh, Indian wildlife preservationist (b. 1938, Choradia, Jodhpur state, British India [now in Rajasthan state, India]—d. March 1, 2011, Maa Farm, near Ranthambhore National Park, Sawai Madhopur, Rajasthan), devoted more than 40 years of his life to saving the Indian tiger, notably at the tiger sanctuary at Ranthambhore National Park, where he became a game warden in 1971, and through Tiger Watch, the nongovernmental organization he founded. After joining the Rajasthan Forest Service, Rathore worked at the Mount Abu Game Reserve (1963–70) and trained (1969) at the Wildlife Institute of India, Dehradun. He was already on the staff at Ranthambhore in 1973 when the government established Project Tiger and designated that park as one of a series of tiger preserves in an attempt to prevent the extinction of the big cat. Three years after his retirement (1996), he was named Ranthambhore's honorary wildlife warden. Rathore received the World Wildlife Fund's Lifetime Conservation Award shortly before his death.

Ritchie, Dennis MacAlistair, American computer scientist (b. Sept. 9, 1941, Bronxville, N.Y.—found dead Oct. 12, 2011, Berkeley Heights, N.J.), developed, together with Kenneth L. Thompson, the UNIX operating system (OS); Ritchie also created the C programming language, which, with its family of languages (including C++ and Java), remains among the most widely used computer programming languages. The duo were awarded the 1983 A.M. Turing Award, the highest honour in computer science, and the 1998 National Medal of Technology for their development of UNIX. Ritchie earned a bachelor's degree (1963) in physics and a doctorate (1968) in applied mathematics from Harvard University. In 1967 he joined Bell Laboratories, where he first worked on the Multics OS. Multics was a time-sharing system funded by the Advanced Research Projects Agency and jointly developed by researchers at MIT, Bell Labs, and General Electric Co. AT&T Corp. (then the parent company of Bell Labs), however, withdrew from the project and removed its GE computers in 1969. Upon the removal of the GE machines, Ritchie joined Thompson in developing a more flexible OS for Bell Labs' obsolete Digital Equipment Corp. (DEC) PDP-7 minicomputer. Within a few months they had created UNIX, a new OS not completely tied to any particular computer hardware, as earlier systems had been. In 1973 Ritchie and Thompson rewrote UNIX in C. Ritchie was named a fellow by Bell Labs in 1983 and was elected to the U.S. National Academy of Engineering in 1988. In 1990 he was appointed head of the systems sciences research department at Bell Labs, where he led the development of the Plan 9 (1995) and Inferno (1996) operating systems.

Robertson, Cliff (CLIFFORD PARKER ROBERTSON III), American actor (b. Sept. 9, 1923, La Jolla, Calif.—d. Sept. 10, 2011, Stony Brook, N.Y.), enjoyed a creditable career onstage and on television but was best remembered by moviegoers for his portrayal of Lieut. John F. Kennedy in *PT 109* (1963) and for his Academy Award-winning title role in *Charly* (1968), as a mentally disabled floor sweeper who becomes a genius through the aid of surgery, only to revert after a time to his previous state. In New York City he studied at the Actors Studio. His Broadway debut, *Late Love* (1953), was followed two years later by his film bow in the romantic drama *Picnic* (1955). Most of his work during this time was on TV, however, and in 1966 he earned an Emmy Award for his lead role in the drama "The Game" (1965), which was featured on *Bob Hope Presents the Chrysler Theatre*. On the big screen Robertson was often cast as ambitious, talented, but obsessive men, notably as a sinister political candidate in *The Best Man* (1964), an amoral CIA section chief in *Three Days of the Condor* (1975), and a widower tormented by the death of his wife in *Obsession* (1976). Other film credits include *Wild Hearts Can't Be Broken* (1991), *Renaissance Man* (1994), and *Spider-Man* (2002) and its sequels (2004 and 2007).

Robinson, Jerry (SHERRILL DAVID ROBINSON), American comic book artist (b. Jan. 1, 1922, Trenton, N.J.—d. Dec. 7, 2011, New York, N.Y.), was credited with the creation (together with writer Bill Finger, 1940) of the ghoulish Joker, the ultimate comic book villain and nemesis of Batman, and Batman's ward and sidekick, Robin, the Boy Wonder, as well as such characters in the Caped Crusader franchise as Alfred (Bruce Wayne's butler) and the evildoer Two-Face. Robinson was only 17 when Bob Kane (Batman's creator), impressed with the linen jacket worn by Robinson that featured his own designs, invited him to join the team that was producing Batman for National Comics. Robinson provided detailed brushwork as Kane's primary inker and became the comics' primary penciler after Kane moved to the daily strip. Robinson later formed a studio with Mort Meskin, with Robinson penciling and Meskin inking drawings for such characters as the Black Terror, the Fighting Yank, Johnny Quick, and the Vigilante. Working for other publishing houses, Robinson originated such heroic characters as Atoman, a nuclear crime fighter, and London, a masked mercenary who battled Nazis. Robinson introduced his first newspaper strip, the science-fiction adventure *Jet Scott*, in 1953. His one-panel satiric comic strip *Life with Robinson* dispensed political commentary, and his syndicated strip *Still Life* often also offered political observations. Robinson was instrumental in securing rights and royalties for other artists' original work, successfully winning compensation and a restored byline for Superman creators Jerry Siegel and Joe Shuster, who had sold their rights for $130. Robinson's historical volume *The Comics* appeared in 1974.

Robinson, Robert Henry, British journalist and broadcaster (b. Dec. 17, 1927, Liverpool, Eng.—d. Aug. 12, 2011, London, Eng.), entertained TV and radio audiences with his intelligence and acerbic wit on a wide variety of frequently simultaneous assignments, notably as the presenter, or host, of the often-facetious TV panel show *Call My Bluff* (1967–88), the lighthearted TV game show *Ask the Family* (1967–84), and the radio quiz program *Brain of Britain* (1973–2008). After graduating from Exeter College, Oxford, Robinson began his career in the early 1950s in print media and was film critic for the weekly London *Sunday Graphic* and a columnist for the *Sunday Chronicle*. He made his first TV appearance in 1959 reviewing current cinema for *Picture Parade*. In 1962 he became the gossip columnist of *The Sunday Times* newspaper while continuing to work in TV as the host of *Points of View* (1961–65, 1969–71). Other programs included the droll *Stop the Week* (1974–92), *Word for Word*, *The Book Programme*, which included reviews and interviews with authors, and a series of popular TV travelogues.

Robustelli, Andy (ANDREW RICHARD ROBUSTELLI), American football player (b. Dec. 6, 1925, Stamford, Conn.—d. May 31, 2011, Stamford), played defensive end for the NFL's Los Angeles Rams (1951–55) and New York Giants (1956–64), earning a reputation as the whip-smart leader of a defensive lineup that raised defense players to the celebrity of their offensive counterparts. He recovered 22 fumbles and scored two touchdowns in 175 games, and he played in eight NFL championship games, winning twice, once each with the Rams (1951) and the Giants (1956). Though relatively small at 1.85 m (6 ft 1 in) and 104.3 kg (230 lb), Robustelli was drafted from Arnold College (Milford, Conn.) by the Rams. After five seasons he was traded to the Giants, and in his first season he played a central role in the team's NFL title. In his 14-year career, he was named All-Pro seven times, played in the Pro Bowl seven times, and won the Maxwell Football Club's Bert Bell Award (1962). Though he retired at the end of the 1964 season, Robustelli returned as the Giants' front office director of operations in 1974. He was elected to the Pro Football Hall of Fame in 1971.

Rojas, Gonzalo, Chilean poet (b. Dec. 20, 1917, Lebu, Chile—d. April 25, 2011, Santiago, Chile), was among Latin America's most influential and important literary figures. His lyrical poems focused on women and those people affected by the 1973 military coup that brought strongman Augusto Pinochet to power. Rojas was born into a coal-mining family and studied literature and law at the Pedagogical Institute at the University of Chile. He was a member (1938–41) of the Surrealist group La Mandrágora, whose influence was evident in his first volume of poetry, *La miseria del hombre* (1948). During the 1950s Rojas was professor of Chilean literature and literary theory and head of the Spanish department at the University of Concepción, and in 1958 he established an elite literary group, the Congress of Writers, in Concepción. Rojas traveled (1970–71) to China as the Chilean cultural counsel; he was later sent on a similar mission to Cuba. During the 1973 military coup in Chile, he was exiled from the country. Thereafter he taught at universities in East Germany, Venezuela, and the U.S., finally returning to Chillán, Chile, in 1995. Rojas's verse collections include *Contra la muerte* (1964), *Oscuro* (1976), *Del relámpago* (1981; *From the Lightning*, 2008), and *Esquizotexto y otros poemas* (1987; *Schizotext and Other Poems*, 1988). He received many awards, notably the Cervantes Prize (2003) as well as Chile's National Literature Prize and the Queen Sophia Prize for Ibero-American Poetry, both in 1992. Upon Rojas's death, the Chilean government declared two days of national mourning.

Diario La Tercera/AP

Poet Gonzalo Rojas

Rooney, Andy (ANDREW AITKEN ROONEY), American journalist and essayist (b. Jan. 14, 1919, Albany, N.Y.—d. Nov. 4, 2011, New York, N.Y.), was best known for his curmudgeonly commentaries (1978–2011) that aired at the end of the television news program *60 Minutes*. His segment, which usually featured his splenetic—and drily humorous—complaints about the vagaries of modern life, earned him three Emmy Awards (1979, 1981, and 1982) as well as a lifetime achievement Emmy in 2003. As a reporter during World War II for the U.S. Army newspaper *The Stars and Stripes*, Rooney traveled across Europe; he was among a group of journalists that flew with the U.S. Army Air Forces on a series of raids on Germany. He relayed the stories of some of the men he met while covering the aerial conflict in *Air Gunner* (1944), written with fellow reporter Oram C. ("Bud") Hutton. Following the war the two collaborated again on *The Story of the Stars and Stripes* (1946). In 1949 Rooney was hired by CBS radio and TV as a writer for on-air personality Arthur Godfrey, and he worked until 1955 on Godfrey's talk and talent shows. With presenter Harry Reasoner, Rooney collaborated on a number of TV essays that presaged the format that would catapult him to fame. Rooney's 1968 script for *Black History: Lost, Stolen, or Strayed* (narrated by Bill Cosby), an installment of CBS's *Of Black America* series, earned Rooney his first Emmy. He also produced a series of CBS specials.

Professional curmudgeon Andy Rooney

AP

Rose, Lionel Edmund, Australian boxer (b. June 21, 1948, Drouin, Vic., Australia—d. May 8, 2011, Warragul, Vic., Australia), became the first Aborigine to win a professional world boxing title on Feb. 27, 1968, when he captured both the WBC and WBA bantamweight titles with a 15-round decision over Masahiko ("Fighting") Harada of Japan. Rose's victory made him a national hero in Australia and inspired indigenous peoples around the world. He successfully defended his title three times before being knocked out by Mexican Ruben Olivares in the fifth round on Aug. 22, 1969. Rose began boxing as a boy and took the Australian amateur flyweight title in 1963. He was 16 when he made his professional boxing debut, and at age 18 he won the Australian bantamweight title. After his loss to Olivares, Rose gained a considerable amount of weight and moved up several classes to the lightweight division, but he was unable to emulate his success as a bantamweight. He retired in 1976 with a career record of 42 wins (12 by knockout) and 11 losses. He was made MBE in 1968, the same year he became the first Aborigine to be named Australian of the Year. Rose's career and his status as an Aboriginal role model are explored in the film documentary *Lionel* (2008).

Roszak, Theodore, American historian and social critic (b. Nov. 15, 1933, Chicago, Ill.—d. July 5, 2011, Berkeley, Calif.), provided incisive commentary on American cultural movements and coined the term *counterculture* in his seminal book *The Making of a Counter Culture: Reflections on the Technocratic Society and Its Youthful Opposition* (1969). Roszak, who studied history at the University of California, Los Angeles (B.A., 1955), and Princeton University (Ph.D., 1958), was a longtime professor of history (1963–98) at California State University, East Bay. A self-proclaimed "neo-Luddite," he advocated reconnection with nature in more than a dozen books. He also wrote six novels, notably *Flicker* (1991),

The Memoirs of Elizabeth Frankenstein (1995), and *The Devil and Daniel Silverman* (2003).

Roycroft, Bill (James William George Roycroft), Australian equestrian (b. March 17, 1915, Melbourne, Australia—d. May 29, 2011, Camperdown, Vic., Australia), was a five-time Olympian, a three-time medalist, and the patriarch of Australia's top eventing family. Roycroft's greatest moment came at his first Olympics, in Rome in 1960, when he secured the gold medal in the team three-day event immediately after having checked himself out of the hospital with several injuries and against doctors' wishes. He competed in the next four Olympic Games: Tokyo (1964), Mexico City (1968; team bronze medal), Munich (1972), and finally Montreal (1976), where he earned his second team bronze, becoming—at age 61 years 31 days—the oldest Australian to capture an Olympic medal. Roycroft's sons—Barry, Wayne, and Clarke—also became champion equestrians, each competing along with his father in at least one of his Olympic appearances after 1960. Roycroft was made OBE in 1969, was awarded the Australian Olympic Committee's Order of Merit in 1978, and shortly before his death was inducted into the inaugural Equestrian Australia Hall of Fame.

Rugolo, Pete (Pietro Rugulo), Italian-born American composer and arranger (b. Dec. 2, 1915, Sicily, Italy—d. Oct. 16, 2011, Sherman Oaks, Calif.), helped to invent the bombastic, brassy, dissonant "progressive jazz" of Stan Kenton's popular big band, produced important jazz albums, and composed soundtracks for many films and television shows, notably the theme songs for *The Thin Man*, *Richard Diamond: Private Detective*, and *The Fugitive*. After having studied at Mills College, Oakland, Calif., with French composer Darius Milhaud and Hungarian composer Bela Bartok and served in the U.S. Army, Rugolo composed (1945–49) more than 100 arrangements for Kenton's big band. For the Capitol and Mercury labels, he produced or arranged albums by Dinah Washington, Nat King Cole, June Christy, and others and supervised classic recordings by the Lennie Tristano Sextet, including pioneering free-improvisation works, and Miles Davis's *Birth of the Cool* nonet. Rugolo also led his own recording band. His awards include three Emmys and two Grammys, and *Down Beat* magazine named him the best arranger five times between 1947 and 1954.

Ruiz García, Samuel, Mexican Roman Catholic bishop and activist (b. Nov. 3, 1924, Irapuato, Guanajuato state, Mex.—d. Jan. 24, 2011, Mexico City, Mex.), championed the indigenous Maya in the Mexican state of Chiapas while serving (1960–99) as bishop in San Cristóbal de las Casas and was instrumental in helping to mediate the 1990s Zapatista National Liberation Army (EZLN) rebellion that pressed for land reform and redistribution for Mexico's disenfranchised Indians. In 1949 Ruiz was ordained a priest in Rome. He studied at the Pontifical Gregorian University there before being posted to Chiapas. While bishop, Ruiz, a liberation theologian, learned three of the Indians' ancient languages and organized a network of catechists who traveled to facilitate worship in remote jungle regions. Though Ruiz insisted that he had not advocated the EZLN violence that resulted in 145 deaths over 12 days in January 1994 when the EZLN occupied several towns in Chiapas, his support for EZLN principles of fighting injustice angered the government, which accused him of preaching a "theology of violence." (In 1997 he survived an attempt on his life by pro-government assassins.) In 1993 the Vatican, which feared that Ruiz had strayed from his mission of persuading the Maya to shed their ancient ways and adopt Roman Catholicism, asked for his resignation. Ruiz received the support of numerous Mexican clerics, however, and he remained bishop until mandatory retirement at age 75 forced him to step down. Ruiz was the recipient in 2000 of UNESCO's International Simón Bolivar Prize.

Ruiz Pino, Raúl Ernesto (Raoul Ruiz), Chilean-born French motion-picture director, screenwriter, and playwright (b. July 25, 1941, Puerto Montt, Chile—d. Aug. 19, 2011, Paris, France), combined his love of classic literature with his fondness for movies in more than 100 films that showcased his gifts as a superb directorial storyteller; he was also a prolific screenwriter, with more than 75 movies to his credit. His complex narratives featured twisting plots, bizarre coincidences, shocking secrets, and supernatural occurrences. His notable directorial credits include *Le Temps retrouvé* (1999; *Time Regained*), an adaptation of the last volume of Marcel Proust's seven-part classic *À la recherche du temps perdu*, and *Mistérios de Lisboa* (2010), based on Camilo Castelo Branco's 1854 novel, which explored the Portuguese aristocracy during the 19th-century civil wars. Ruiz spent his youth in Chile. He penned more than 100 plays and became a prominent moviemaker in Chile with the release of *Tres tristes tigres* (1968). Following the overthrow of Marxist Pres. Salvador Allende in 1973, Ruiz, a leftist, took sanctuary in France. Though many of his early films were confined to arthouse showings, the release of *Trois vies et une seule mort* (1996; *Three Lives and Only One Death*), starring Marcello Mastroianni, brought Ruiz international attention and attracted major stars to his films. His last effort, *La noche de enfrente* (2011), was based on stories by Chilean writer Hernán del Solar.

Rusher, William Allen, American publisher, columnist, and political strategist (b. July 19, 1923, Chicago, Ill.—d. April 16, 2011, San Francisco, Calif.), was publisher (1957–88) of the conservative political journal the *National Review* and an influential force behind the right-wing political movement in the U.S. After attending Princeton University, Rusher earned (1948) a law degree from Harvard University. He practiced law (1948–56) for a Wall Street firm before serving (1956–57) as associate counsel of the Internal Security Subcommittee of the U.S. Senate. In 1957 William F. Buckley invited him to join the *National Review* as director, publisher, and vice president. Under Rusher's leadership the *National Review's* circulation rose from 16,000 in the 1950s to some 100,000 by the 1980s. He later wrote (1973–2009) his own syndicated column, "The Conservative Advocate," in the journal. He also worked with organizations such as the Young Americans for Freedom (founded 1960) and the American Conservative Union (founded 1964).

Russ, Joanna, American writer (b. Feb. 22, 1937, Bronx, N.Y.—d. April 29, 2011, Tucson, Ariz.), introduced a feminist twist to the traditionally male-dominated science-fiction genre. She earned a B.A. in English (1957) from Cornell University, Ithaca, N.Y., and an M.A. in playwriting and dramatic literature (1960) from Yale University. Russ published her first story in 1959, and by the late 1960s she had scored notable successes with a series of stories featuring the time-hopping female adventurer Alyx, who was also the protagonist in her first novel, *Picnic on Paradise* (1968). Russ's most notable work was *The Female Man* (1975), a provocative novel that examines four women in distinctly different historical contexts. In addition, she wrote essays, short fiction, and literary criticism.

Russell, Jane (ERNESTINE JANE GERALDINE RUSSELL), American actress and singer (b. June 21, 1921, Bemidji, Minn.—d. Feb. 28, 2011, Santa Maria, Calif.), was known for her voluptuous figure and sexualized onscreen persona, notably in *The Outlaw* (1943), but she displayed her comedic skills and singing voice in two box-office hits with Bob Hope, *The Paleface* (1948) and *Son of Paleface* (1952), and, especially, as the wisecracking brunette showgirl in *Gentlemen Prefer Blondes* (1953), opposite Marilyn Monroe. Russell studied briefly at Max Reinhardt's Theatrical Workshop in Los Angeles and with acting coach Maria Ouspenskaya. She was working as a receptionist when producer and director Howard Hughes cast her in *The Outlaw*. Mainly because of Russell's provocative attire, especially in publicity shots used to promote the film, *The Outlaw* faced censorship issues and legal battles that kept it out of general release for several years. Although Hughes had signed Russell to an exclusive seven-year contract that kept her off the movie screen, except for *Young Widow* (1946), the controversy surrounding *The Outlaw* increased public curiosity, and she became a popular pinup model during World War II. After making such films as *Montana Belle* (1952), *Gentlemen Marry Brunettes* (1955), and *The Revolt of Mamie Stover* (1956), she retired from the movies. Offscreen, Russell sang on bandleader Kay Kyser's radio show in the 1940s, performed on the nightclub circuit, and in 1971 made her Broadway debut, replacing Elaine Stritch in the musical *Company*. In the 1950s Russell founded the World Adoption International Fund. Her autobiography, *Jane Russell: My Path & My Detours*, was published in 1985.

Pinup girl Jane Russell

AP

Russell, Ken (HENRY KENNETH ALFRED RUSSELL), British filmmaker (b. July 3, 1927, Southampton, Hampshire, Eng.—d. Nov. 27, 2011, Lymington, Hampshire, Eng.), gained international acclaim for *Women in Love* (1969), based on D.H. Lawrence's novel. The visual beauty of the film and its tasteful handling of erotic scenes won the approval of public and critics alike and earned Russell best director nominations from the Academy Awards, the British Academy of Film and Television Awards, and the Golden Globes. He drew both praise and reprehension for *The Music Lovers* (1970), a flamboyant look at the anguished personal life of composer Pyotr Tchaikovsky, and *The Devils* (1971), based on Aldous Huxley's novel *The Devils of Loudun*, which aroused even more vehement criticism with its story of mass sexual hysteria in a convent. Russell was the son of a shoestore owner. He became a cadet at the Nautical College at Pangbourne and subsequently joined the British Merchant Navy. After training as an electrician in the Royal Air Force, he tried acting, ballet, and photography. He took a job with the BBC directing documentaries and TV shows, notably *Monitor* and *Omnibus*. The feature films *French Dressing* (1963) and *Billion Dollar Brain* (1967), which he completed while working for the BBC, paved the way for *Women in Love*. Russell's other movies include the musical comedy *The Boy Friend* (1971); *Tommy* (1975), based on the Who's rock opera; the bawdy *Lisztomania* (1975); the science-fiction thriller *Altered States* (1980); *Crimes of Passion* (1984); and *Lair of the White Worm* (1988), based on the Bram Stoker novel.

Sábato, Ernesto Roque, Argentine novelist, journalist, and essayist (b. June 24, 1911, Rojas, Arg.—d. April 30, 2011, Buenos Aires, Arg.), wrote three important novels that delved deeply into philosophical and psychological issues, and in 1984 he won the coveted Cervantes Prize. He was perhaps most notably remembered as the principal author of *Nunca más* (1984, the "Sábato Report"), an investigation of human rights violations in Argentina; the document was vital in aiding the prosecution of military leaders responsible for the killings of some 10,000–30,000 citizens during the country's Dirty War (1976–83). Sábato attended the National University of La Plata (1929–36), where he received (1937) a doctorate in physics. He did postdoctoral work at the Curie Laboratory in Paris in 1938 and MIT in 1939 before returning in 1940 to Argentina. He taught theoretical physics (1940–45) at the National University of La Plata and at a teachers college in Buenos Aires, but because he began to contribute articles to the literary section of the newspaper *La Nación* that stated his opposition to the Juan Perón government, he was removed from his teaching posts in 1945. *Uno y el universo* (1945), a series of aphorisms, statements, and personal observations by Sábato on diverse philosophical, social, and political matters, was his first literary success. The novel *El túnel* (1948; *The Tunnel*, 1988), which portrays a man's descent into madness, won Sábato national and international notice. After the fall of Perón in 1955, Sábato published *El otro rostro del peronismo* (1956), an account of the historical and political causes of the violence and unrest of Perón's rule. His second novel, *Sobre héroes y tumbas* (1961; *On Heroes and Tombs*, 1981), is a penetrating psychological study of man, interwoven with philosophical ideas and observations. His third novel, *Abaddón el exterminador* (1974, corrected and revised, 1978; *The Angel of Darkness*, 1991), explored similar themes. In 2000 Sábato released a reflection on Western culture, *La resistencia*.

Sangster, Jimmy (JAMES HENRY KIMMEL SANGSTER), British screenwriter and director (b. Dec. 2, 1927, Kimmel Bay, Wales—d. Aug. 19, 2011, London, Eng.), gained cult status as the author of scores of stylish, often sexy, horror movies and thrillers in the 1950s and '60s for the British production company Hammer Films. Sangster's output included such titles as *The Curse of Frankenstein* (1957), *Horror of Dracula* (1958), *The Revenge of Frankenstein* (1958), *The Crawling Eye* (1958), *The Mummy* (1959), *Brides of Dracula* (1960), *Scream of Fear* (1961), *Paranoiac* (1963), *Dracula: Prince of Darkness* (1966), and *The Horror of Frankenstein* (1970). He also directed, notably *Fear in the Night* (1972). Beginning in the 1970s Sangster focused more on Hollywood, where he wrote for such TV shows as *Banacek*, *McCloud*, *Kolchak: The Night Stalker*, and *Ironside*. Sangster also wrote novels, a screenwriting guide, and an autobiography, *Do You Want It Good or Tuesday?* (1997).

Santamaría, Santi, Catalan Spanish chef and restaurateur (b. July 26, 1957, Sant Celoni, near Barcelona, Spain—d. Feb. 16, 2011, Singapore), championed locally sourced traditional Catalan food, perfectly prepared and presented at his restaurant El Racó de Can Fabes, and brought new attention and respect for Spanish cuisine as the first chef in that country to gain three stars from the vaunted *Guide Michelin*. Santamaría's passionate adherence to the simple preparation of organic seasonal ingredients put him at odds with the high-tech molecular cooking espoused by his Catalan rival, Ferran Adrià, and Santamaría publicly questioned if the chemicals used by Adrià and other avant-garde chefs might constitute a health risk for diners. Santamaría, a self-taught chef, trained as an industrial engineer before opening his first eating establishment, in his family home in 1981. The resulting restaurant, El Racó de Can Fabes, earned its first *Michelin* star in 1988 and by 1994 had amassed the maximum three stars. Santamaría opened additional restaurants and wrote several cookbooks, including the award-winning *La cocina al desnudo* (2008). He won Spain's National Gastronomy Prize in 2009.

EPA/Landov

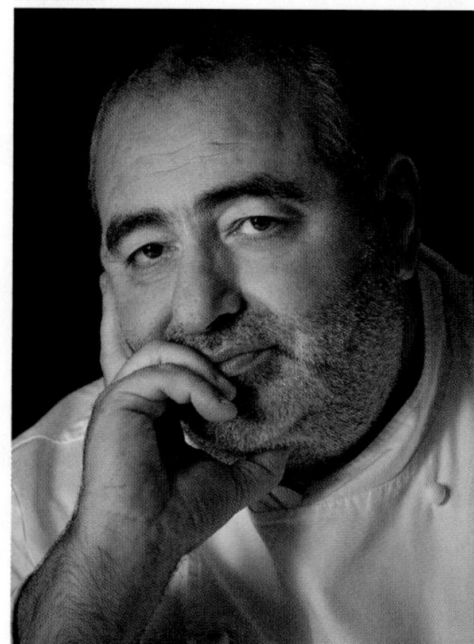

Celebrity chef Santi Santamaría

Sarrazin, Michael (JACQUES MICHEL ANDRÉ SARRAZIN), Canadian actor (b. May 22, 1940, Quebec City, Que.—d. April 17, 2011, Montreal, Que.), appeared in a slew of films during the 1960s and '70s, notably as an uneager apprentice in *The Flim-Flam Man* (1967), the forlorn dance marathoner who fatally shoots his desperate partner in what he believes to be an act of mercy in the Depression-era drama *They Shoot Horses, Don't They?* (1969), and a misunderstood son in a family of loggers in *Sometimes a Great Notion* (1971). The tall actor with the soulful eyes often portrayed drifters and flawed individuals. Other credits include *The Sweet Ride* (1968), *The Life and Times of Judge Roy Bean* (1972), *For Pete's Sake* (1974), and *Joshua Then and Now* (1985), one of his last films. In his 60s Sarrazin returned to live in Montreal, where he earned a cult following for his portrayal of the romancer Romeo Laflamme in the French-language film *La Florida* (1993).

Sathya Sai Baba (SATHYANARAYANA RAJU), Indian religious leader (b. Nov. 23, 1926, Puttaparthi, British India—d. April 24, 2011, Puttaparthi, Andhra Pradesh, India), was widely revered as a divine incarnation, but critics dismissed his claims of miracles performed, and he attracted scrutiny after allegations of sexual abuse. He claimed as a young man that he was the reincarnation of Shirdi Sai Baba (a popular religious teacher who died in 1918 and who had been revered as a saint by both Hindus and Muslims) and took the name Sathya Sai Baba. In 1950 in Puttaparthi he constructed his ashram, Prasanthi Nilayam, which served as the headquarters for his International Sathya Sai Baba Organization. His fame spread with an accessible message about divine love and the unity of religions, philanthropic endeavours such as the endowment of schools and a hospital, and the public performance of purported divine miracles and healings. In 1963 he claimed to be not only the reincarnation of Shirdi Sai Baba but also the avatar (incarnation) of both the god Shiva and his consort Shakti. As Sathya Sai Baba's fame spread, his organization grew into a multibillion-dollar empire. Yet along with popularity for his philanthropy, he also courted controversy. Six people died in his bedroom in 1993 during an apparent assassination attempt, and some young devotees alleged that they had been sexually exploited. The BBC TV documentary *The Secret Swami* (2004) brought international attention to these controversies but failed to deter his millions of followers.

Savage, Randy (RANDY POFFO; "MACHO MAN"), American professional wrestler (b. Nov. 15, 1952, Columbus, Ohio—d. May 20, 2011, Pinellas county, Fla.), was known during the 1980s and

"Macho Man" wrestler Randy Savage

Ezio Petersen—UPI/Landov

'90s for his flamboyant attire, gravelly voice, and trademark flying elbow drop. Savage came from a family of wrestlers—both his father, Angelo, and his brother Lanny (who wrestled as "Leapin' Lanny Poffo" and later as "the Genius") plied their trade in the squared circle—but Randy's "Macho Man" persona left the strongest impression. He rose to prominence at a time when professional wrestling had perhaps its greatest impact on global popular culture, facing such personalities as Hulk Hogan and Andre the Giant, and Savage's antics in the ring made him a fan favourite. He was later a successful pitchman, utilizing his catchphrase "Ohhh, yeah!" in commercials for snack products.

Savile, Sir Jimmy (SIR JAMES WILSON VINCENT SAVILE), British entertainer (b. Oct. 31, 1926, Leeds, Eng.—d. Oct. 29, 2011, Leeds), was a flamboyant radio and television personality, known as much for his platinum-dyed hair, gaudy tracksuits, and enormous cigar as he was for his zany comedic style. After working in the coal mines as a boy, Savile became a disc jockey, initially at a dance club in Leeds, then on Radio Luxembourg, the "pirate" Radio Caroline, and from 1968 on BBC Radio 1. His TV work included *Top of the Pops*, on which he appeared frequently from its premiere on Jan. 1, 1964, to its demise in July 2006, and the children's show *Jim'll Fix It*, on which he starred for some 20 years in the 1970s, '80s, and '90s. Savile was made OBE (1971) and was knighted (1990) in recognition of his charity work; he also received a knighthood (1982) from the Vatican.

Schneider, Maria (MARIE CHRISTINE GÉLIN), French actress (b. March 27, 1952, Paris, France—d. Feb. 3, 2011, Paris), gained instant international stardom at age 20 with her performance as an enigmatic young Parisian woman who enters into a passionless sexual affair with a middle-aged American (Marlon Brando) in Bernardo Bertolucci's notoriously explicit film *Last Tango in Paris* (1972). Schneider, however, was uncomfortable with her sudden status as a movie sex symbol; she later claimed that she had been mistreated by Bertolucci and coerced into doing some of *Last Tango*'s most graphic sex scenes. Her other films include Michelangelo Antonioni's *The Passenger* (1975), *La Dérobade* (1979; *Memoirs of a French Whore*), for which she earned a César Award nomination for best supporting actress, and Franco Zeffirelli's *Jane Eyre* (1996), in which she portayed the deranged Bertha Rochester.

Scliar, Moacyr Jaime, Brazilian writer (b. March 23, 1937, Porto Alegre, Braz.—d. Feb. 27, 2011, Porto Alegre), used a combination of magic realism and humour in his short stories and novels to create allegories of the experience of Jewish life in Brazil. Scliar's novella *Max e os felinos* (1981; *Max and the Cats*, 1990) was well-received, but it became famous in 2002 after it came to light that the novel that won that year's Man Booker Prize for Fiction, Yann Martel's *Life of Pi* (2001), in which an Indian boy is trapped on a lifeboat with a tiger, bore a striking resemblance to Scliar's novella, in which a Jewish boy is trapped on a lifeboat with a jaguar. Scliar first won notice with his second collection of stories, *O carnaval dos animais* (1968; *The Carnival of the Animals*, 1985). His best-known novels include *O centauro no jardim* (1980; *The Centaur in the Garden*, 1984) and *A estranha nação de Rafael Mendes* (1983; *The Strange Nation of Rafael Mendes*, 1987). He was elected to the Brazilian Academy of Letters in 2003.

Searle, Ronald William Fordham, British graphic satirist (b. March 3, 1920, Cambridge, Eng.—d. Dec. 30, 2011, Draguignan, France), lampooned politicians, clergymen, and the English class system in general but was best known for his cartoons of the anarchic girls at an imaginary school he called St. Trinian's. He created the bizarre schoolgirls in 1941 and continued to draw them until 1953; they were the subject of four motion pictures and several books. He also illustrated the Molesworth books (written by Geoffrey Willans) about a chaotic boys prep school. Searle was educated at the Cambridge School of Art and published his first humorous work in the late 1930s. During World War II he was an architectural draftsman with the Royal Engineers and was captured by the Japanese at the fall of Singapore. Grim drawings that he created during his time in Changi prison and working on the Burma railway were published in 1946 and in 1986. From 1946 Searle's satiric work appeared in British and American magazines, notably *The New Yorker*. He first contributed to *Punch* in 1949 and joined its staff in 1956. From 1961 he lived in France. Searle published more than 50 books, including *The Rake's Progress* (1955), *Searle's Cats* (1967), and *The Situation Is Hopeless* (1980), and he designed animated titles for several movies. He was made CBE in 2004 and a knight of the French Legion of Honour in 2006.

Selmon, Lee Roy, American football player (b. Oct. 20, 1954, Eufaula, Okla.—d. Sept. 4, 2011, Tampa, Fla.),

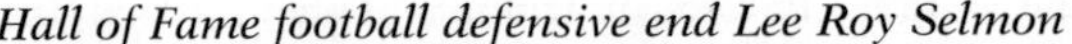
Hall of Fame football defensive end Lee Roy Selmon

Karen Fletcher/AP

was a hard-hitting, imposing defensive end who was credited with 23 sacks during his professional NFL career (1976–84) with the Tampa Bay Buccaneers. Selmon played college football with his brothers Dewey and Lucious at the University of Oklahoma, and he and Dewey helped the team capture national championships in 1974 and 1975. In 1976 he received the Lombardi trophy as the top college lineman. After moving to Tampa, Selmon played defensive tackle in his rookie year but was soon moved to defensive end. He and Dewey were also teammates (1976–80) at Tampa. A back injury forced Selmon to miss the 1985 season and ultimately retire. He was inducted into the College Football Hall of Fame in 1988 and the Pro Football Hall of Fame in 1995. Selmon later became a bank executive in Tampa, and in 1996 an expressway there was renamed in his honour. From 2001 to 2004 he served in Tampa as the athletic director at the University of South Florida.

Semprún, Jorge, Spanish writer, activist, and government official (b. Dec. 10, 1923, Madrid, Spain—d. June 7, 2011, Paris, France), embarked on a remarkable literary career after having survived 16 months (1943–45) in the Nazi concentration camp Buchenwald and laboured for the Spanish Communist Party. The grandson of five-time Spanish prime minister Antonio Maura, Semprún fled with his family to the Netherlands in 1936, during the Spanish Civil War. He enrolled at the Sorbonne in 1941, but the next year he joined the French Resistance and the Spanish Communist Party, for which he was arrested, tortured, and sent to Buchenwald. After the war he led a double life, serving as an interpreter in Paris while secretly working under the pseudonym Federico Sánchez to reorganize the banned Communist Party in Madrid. These events coloured his life and much of his writing, notably *Le Grand Voyage* (1963) and *L'Écriture ou la vie* (1994). He was later expelled (1964) from the party for his changing political views. Semprún served as Spain's minister of culture (1988–91), an experience he described in *Federico Sánchez se despide de ustedes* (1993). He continued to live and write primarily in France, however, and in 1996 he was the first non-French writer elected to the Académie Goncourt. Semprún's various honours included the Prix Femina for his French-language novel *La Deuxième Mort de Ramón Mercader* (1969), the Planeta Prize for his Spanish-language *Autobiografía de Federico Sánchez* (1977), and Academy Award nominations for two of his screenplays, director Alain Resnais's *La Guerre est finie* (1966; *The War Is Over*) and *Z* (1969), directed and co-written by Costa-Gavras.

Servan-Schreiber, David, French neuroscientist and psychiatrist (b. April 21, 1961, Neuilly-sur-Seine, France—d. July 24, 2011, Fécamp, France), wrote best-selling books about alternative approaches to cancer treatment and his own 18-year fight against that disease, notably *Guerir le stress, l'anxiété et la depression sans médicaments ni psychanalyse* (2003; *Healing Without Freud or Prozac*; U.S. title, *The Instinct to Heal*) and *Anticancer: prévenir et lutter grâce à nos défenses naturelles* (2007; *Anticancer: A New Way of Life*), which together sold more than two million copies. Servan-Schreiber, the son of journalist and politician Jean-Jacques Servan-Schreiber, studied medicine in Paris and Canada and cognitive neuroscience at Carnegie Mellon University, Pittsburgh. He then served on the faculty of Carnegie Mellon (1990–96) and the University of Pittsburgh (from 1991). He was already a celebrated researcher when his studies in brain imaging discovered (1992) his own malignant brain tumour, which eventually proved fatal. Servan-Schreiber thereafter dedicated himself to compiling and publicizing information about nutrition and other lifestyle choices that could, alongside such traditional treatments as chemotherapy and radiation therapy, assist in the fight against cancer. He also worked closely with the international humanitarian group Doctors Without Borders, the American branch of which he cofounded and served as a leader (1991–2000).

John Heller/AP

Neuroscientist David Servan-Schreiber

Shalikashvili, John Malchase David, Polish-born American army officer (b. June 27, 1936, Warsaw, Pol.—d. July 23, 2011, Tacoma, Wash.), served as supreme allied commander of NATO forces in Europe (1992–93) and as chairman of the U.S. Joint Chiefs of Staff (1993–97); he was the first immigrant—as well as the first soldier to rise from the enlisted ranks—to hold the top command in the U.S. military. Shalikashvili was descended from Georgian aristocracy. His maternal grandfather was a general in the tsarist Russian army, and his father was an officer in the Polish army until its defeat by the Germans in 1939, after which he joined a German-backed battalion of ethnic Georgians. Shalikashvili and his mother fled to Germany in 1944 to escape advancing Soviet troops. When he was 16, he and his family moved to the U.S., where he was drafted (1958) into the army. By 1968 he was a major and had been sent to Vietnam to serve as a senior district adviser to South Vietnamese forces. Shalikashvili spent most of the 1970s and '80s in Europe. He directed the 1991 campaign to airlift food and medical supplies to Kurdish refugees in Iraq in the aftermath of the Persian Gulf War, and the next year he was put in command of NATO forces. In 1993 U.S. Pres. Bill Clinton asked Shalikashvili to succeed retiring Gen. Colin Powell as chairman of the joint chiefs. Shalikashvili retired from the military in 1997. He later acted as an adviser in Sen. John Kerry's 2004 presidential campaign, and he became a vocal critic of the military's "Don't Ask, Don't Tell" policy regarding gay and lesbian members of the military.

Shearing, Sir George Albert, British pianist (b. Aug. 13, 1919, London, Eng.—d. Feb. 14, 2011, New York,

N.Y.), created a cool quintet sound that contrasted with the aggressive energy of bebop and made him a favourite modern-jazz artist. One of the many songs that he composed, "Lullaby of Birdland" (1952), written for New York City's Birdland nightclub, became a jazz standard. Shearing, who was blind from birth, played with leading swing musicians and was already one of the most popular performers in British jazz when he first visited the U.S. in 1946. After he settled in the U.S. a year later, he formed a quintet that played themes in distinctive piano-vibes-guitar unisons. The George Shearing Quintet recorded the single "September in the Rain" (1949) and a series of albums that became jazz hits, and they accompanied popular singers, including Nancy Wilson, Peggy Lee, and Nat King Cole. From 1979 he performed principally as a piano soloist, although he was often accompanied by a bassist and sometimes worked with other performers, such as singer Mel Tormé and guitarist Jim Hall; on occasion he also played classical works. Shearing's autobiography, *Lullaby of Birdland*, written with Alyn Shipton, was published in 2004. He was knighted in 2007.

Shriver, R(obert) Sargent, Jr., American public servant (b. Nov. 9, 1915, Westminster, Md.—d. Jan. 18, 2011, Bethesda, Md.), promoted public service as an administrator of such programs to aid the underprivileged as Head Start, VISTA, Community Action, Legal Services for the Poor, Neighborhood Youth Corps, and Job Corps and especially as the first director (1961–66) of the U.S. Peace Corps. A graduate (1941) of Yale Law School, Shriver served as a U.S. naval officer during World War II, and after a brief association with a Wall Street law firm, he went to work in 1946 as an assistant editor for *Newsweek* magazine. That same year he met millionaire Joseph P. Kennedy, who two years later asked him to manage the Merchandise Mart, a massive commercial building in Chicago. In 1953 Shriver married Kennedy's daughter Eunice. When his brother-in-law John F. Kennedy ran as the Democratic nominee for the presidency in 1960, Shriver proved particularly adept in his work with minority groups throughout the country, and after the election he first gained national prominence as director of the experimental overseas Peace Corps, one of the most popular ventures of the New Frontier program of the Kennedy administration. In 1964, after Kennedy's assassination, Shriver accepted appointment as head of Pres. Lyndon B. Johnson's War on Poverty in the Office of Economic Opportunity. From 1968 to 1970 he served as ambassador to France under Johnson and Republican Pres. Richard M. Nixon. In 1972 Shriver unsuccessfully ran for the vice presidency on the ticket with Sen. George McGovern, and his bid in 1976 for the Democratic presidential nomination was also unsuccessful. Shriver in 1984 was elected president of the Special Olympics, which his wife had founded in 1968. He was the recipient of numerous honours—notably the 1994 Presidential Medal of Freedom. In 2003 Shriver was diagnosed with Alzheimer disease. His daughter, Maria Shriver, a noted television journalist, produced *American Idealist* (2008), a documentary film that featured Shriver's devotion to public service.

David Kohl/AP

Civil rights hero Fred Shuttlesworth

Shuttlesworth, Fred (FREDDIE LEE ROBINSON), American civil rights leader (b. March 18, 1922, Mount Meigs, Ala.—d. Oct. 5, 2011, Birmingham, Ala.), established (1957), with Martin Luther King, Jr., and others, the Southern Christian Leadership Council (SCLC) and worked to end segregation in the South. Shuttlesworth grew up poor on his stepfather's farm in rural Alabama. He worked as a truck driver before studying at Selma (Ala.) University (B.A., 1951) and Alabama State College (now Alabama State University; B.S., 1952); while pursuing his education Shuttlesworth began preaching at the First Baptist Church in Selma. In 1953 he took over as pastor of Birmingham's Bethel Baptist Church and became increasingly involved with the civil rights movement. He worked with such organizations as the Civic League and the National Association for the Advancement of Colored People on initiatives that sought to increase voter registration among African Americans. In 1956 he founded the Alabama Christian Movement for Human Rights, which sought to overturn Birmingham's segregation laws. For his efforts—which included challenging the city's segregated schools and buses and participating in sit-ins and in the Freedom Rides of the early 1960s—Shuttlesworth survived numerous physical attacks, and his home was bombed on Christmas Day in 1956. In 1961 Shuttlesworth moved to Cincinnati, Ohio, where he founded (1966) the Greater New Light Baptist Church. He helped to organize the historic 1965 march for voting rights from Selma to Montgomery, Ala. In an effort to provide a source of low-income housing, he established the Shuttlesworth Housing Foundation in Cincinnati in the 1980s. He received the Presidential Citizens Medal in 2001. Five years later Shuttlesworth retired from the ministry.

Simon, Joe (HYMIE SIMON; JOSEPH HENRY SIMON), American cartoonist (b. Oct. 11, 1913, Rochester, N.Y.—d. Dec. 14, 2011, New York, N.Y.), created (together with Jack Kirby) a cast of superheroes that included Captain America, a star-spangled supersoldier; Manhunter, a former big-game hunter turned crime warrior; and Boy Commandos, a premier international group of young soldiers. Simon and Kirby teamed up in 1940 and collaborated on a number of titles over the following years, exploring the crime, horror, and humour genres, and in 1947 they created the first romance comic (*Young Romance*), which outsold superhero and gangster genres. The pair's professional relationship was strained by the challenges of working in an increasingly competitive and uncertain market, however, and by 1956 the duo had drifted apart. In an effort to capitalize on the popularity of *Mad* magazine, in 1960 Simon created *Sick* magazine. Simon and Kirby reunited in the 1970s to produce the Sandman comics. A longtime copyright battle with Marvel Comics over Captain America was settled out of court in 2003, and

Simon finally saw the superhero featured on the big screen in *Captain America: The First Avenger* (2011).

Simonov, Mikhail Petrovich, Soviet aircraft designer (b. Oct. 19, 1929, Rostov-on-Don, Russia, U.S.S.R.—d. March 4, 2011, Moscow, Russia), was the chief designer of the Su-27 fighter jet, a mainstay of the Soviet Union's defense industry and one of the most successful and respected military aircraft of the late 20th century. Simonov studied engineering at the Novocherkassk Polytechnic Institute and the Kazan Aviation Institute, where he remained as a designer after his graduation in 1954. After a brief spell (1969–70) with the Taganrog Aviation Co., he joined (1970) the Sukhoi Design Bureau. He left Sukhoi in 1979 to become deputy minister of aviation but returned in 1983 as chief designer and eventually served as CEO (1995–99). While at Sukhoi, Simonov was responsible for creating and marketing the twin-engine, twin-finned Su-27, which set a new standard in jet design with its extraordinary maneuverability in flight, some 3,000-km (1,865-mi) range, and maximum airspeed of Mach 2.35. The Su-27 entered service in the Soviet air force in the early 1980s after some 20 years of research and testing, and from the 1990s it was also sold abroad. Simonov was also involved in the design of the Su-24 bomber, the Su-25 ground attack plane, and the Su-30 fighter (the Su-27's successor).

Fighter jet designer Mikhail Petrovich Simonov

Vlad Lukin—Sukhoi Company Press Service/AP

Simpson, N(orman) F(rederick) ("WALLY"), British playwright (b. Jan. 29, 1919, London, Eng.—d. Aug. 27, 2011, Cornwall, Eng.), achieved spectacular verbal effects by his cunning manipulation of phrasing and his use of outrageous double entendre and, especially, of non sequitur. Simpson's absurdly comical plays influenced later farcical radio and TV shows, including *Monty Python's Flying Circus*. Simpson was educated at the University of London and served in the Intelligence Corps during World War II. In his first play, *A Resounding Tinkle* (performed 1957), which he later cut to one act, a suburban couple called the Paradocks are suddenly asked to form a new government and then discover that the elephant delivered to their garden is the wrong size. Perhaps his most successful play, *One Way Pendulum* (performed 1959), involves a plan to teach speak-your-weight machines to sing the Hallelujah Chorus from Handel's *Messiah*. Later plays include *The Hole* (performed 1958); *The Cresta Run* (performed 1965); *Was He Anyone?* (performed 1972), which he turned into the novel *Harry Bleachbaker* (1976); and *If So, then Yes* (performed 2010), which Simpson wrote after an absence from the theatre of more than 30 years.

Singh, Jagjit (JAGMOHAN SINGH), Indian singer (b. Feb. 8, 1941, Sri Ganganagar, Rajputana, British India—d. Oct. 10, 2011, Mumbai, India), excelled at the semiclassical *ghazal* song, which he performed—solo and with his wife, *ghazal* singer Chitra Singh—on more than 40 albums, for movie sound tracks, and in concert. Singh successfully broadened the appeal of traditional *ghazal* songs and reached a new, younger audience by introducing modern recording techniques (such as multitracking), incorporating Western instruments into his arrangements, and performing in several languages, including Hindi, Urdu, and Punjabi. He was awarded the Padma Bhushan in 2003.

Sisulu, Albertina (NONTSIKELELO THETHIWE), South African political activist (b. Oct. 21, 1918, Camama, Cape Province [now in Eastern Cape province], S.Af.—d. June 2, 2011, Johannesburg, S.Af.), was a revered figure in the struggle against South Africa's apartheid system as the wife of African National Congress (ANC) leader Walter Sisulu and in her own right, especially during his long imprisonment (1964–89) on charges of plotting to overthrow the government. She grew up in South Africa's Transkei region and attended Christian missionary schools, where she acquired the name Albertina. She met Sisulu in 1941 while she was training as a nurse in Johannesburg; they were married in 1944. Ma (or Mama) Sisulu, as she came to be called, was a prominent member of the ANC Women's League, the Federation of South African Women, and the antiapartheid United Democratic Front, and she participated in the historic Aug. 9, 1956, march by some 20,000 black women protesting South Africa's racist pass laws. During her husband's incarceration, she also endured periods in which she was detained, banned, or placed under house arrest. After her husband's release and the country's move to multiracial democracy, she was elected (1994) to a four-year term in the parliament.

Sladen, Elisabeth (ELISABETH CLAIRA HEATH-SLADEN), British actress (b. Feb. 1, 1946/48, Liverpool, Eng.—d. April 19, 2011, London, Eng.), played the intrepid journalist and Time Lord companion Sarah Jane Smith in the long-running BBC TV science-fiction series *Doctor Who*. Sladen did repertory theatre and a number of television roles before her first appearance as Sarah Jane in December 1973 opposite Jon Pertwee. She stayed on when Tom Baker replaced Pertwee as the Doctor a year later, and in October 1976 she appeared in her 81st—and "final"—episode. Seven years later she joined Pertwee in the show's 20th-anniversary special, *The Five Doctors*. When the series was resurrected in 2005 after a 16-year hiatus, Sladen was invited to revive Sarah Jane, and during 2006–10 she appeared in an additional five episodes. Her popularity with the show's fans was such that she starred (with the Doctor's robot dog, K-9) in the stand-alone *K-9 and Company: A Girl's Best Friend* (1981), and in 2007 she was given her own spin-off series, *The Sarah Jane Adventures*, which was still in production at the time of Sladen's death from cancer.

AP

Baseball outfielder Duke Snider

Smith, Willie ("Big Eyes"), American blues musician (b. Jan. 19, 1936, Helena, Ark.—d. Sept. 16, 2011, Chicago, Ill.), was the drummer in the Muddy Waters band primarily in the early 1960s and the '70s. Smith took up the harmonica in his youth, having been inspired by his hometown's *King Biscuit Time* radio program. A visit to his mother in Chicago in 1953 turned into a permanent move, and Smith was soon playing in a blues trio. In 1955–56 he participated in two Bo Diddley sessions for Chess Records. By the late 1950s Smith had made the drums his primary instrument and joined the Muddy Waters Jr. Band (the group that played Waters's regular club dates when Waters was touring). In 1961 he moved into the Waters band drummer's seat, which had been vacated by Francis Clay. The early 1960s were hard times for the blues, and in 1964 Smith left Waters for restaurant work and cab driving. He returned in 1968 for a dozen years, during which Waters and his group became world renowned. Smith was the drummer on four Grammy Award-winning albums during that period. In 1980 a dispute between Waters and the band over compensation and conditions caused band members, including Smith and pianist Pinetop Perkins (*q.v.*), to break with Waters and perform and record as the Legendary Blues Band. That band, comprising various personnel, recorded a number of albums and had a brief appearance in the film *The Blues Brothers* (1980). Though Smith was named the Blues Foundation's Drummer of the Year numerous times, in his last years he returned to the harmonica. He released several albums under his own name. Smith's final album, *Joined at the Hip* (2010), recorded with Perkins, won the 2010 Grammy Award for best traditional blues album.

Snider, Duke (Edwin Donald Snider; "The Silver Fox"; "The Duke of Flatbush"), American baseball player (b. Sept. 19, 1926, Los Angeles, Calif.—d. Feb. 27, 2011, Escondido, Calif.), was one of the celebrated "Boys of Summer" as the star centre fielder and left-handed power hitter for the Brooklyn Dodgers in the late 1940s and 1950s; during that "golden era" of baseball, he reigned supreme in the outfield with his crosstown rivals, Mickey Mantle of the New York Yankees and Willie Mays of the New York Giants. Snider helped the Dodgers to seven National League pennants and two World Series titles in his 16 years (1947–62) with the team, including one title (1959) a year after the franchise moved from Brooklyn to Los Angeles. He twice hit four home runs in a World Series, in 1952 and again in 1955 when the Dodgers defeated the Yankees for Brooklyn's only title. Snider signed his first contract with the Dodgers as an amateur free agent in 1943, but he did not make his major league debut until April 1947, after having played in the minors and completed his World War II military service (1944–46). He played five seasons for the Dodgers after their move to Los Angeles, but in 1963 he was sold to the Mets back in New York; he finished his career the following season in San Francisco with the Giants, who had followed the Dodgers to California in 1958. Snider played in 2,143 games in his 18-season career, retiring in 1964 with 2,116 hits, 1,333 runs batted in, a lifetime batting average of .295, and 407 home runs, including 40 or more in each of five consecutive seasons (1953–57). He was later a respected broadcaster with the Montreal Expos (1973–86). Snider was inducted into the Baseball Hall of Fame in 1980.

Sócrates (Sócrates Brasileiro Sampaio de Souza Vieira de Oliveira), Brazilian association football (soccer) player and physician (b. Feb. 19, 1954, Belém, Braz.—d. Dec. 4, 2011, São Paulo, Braz.), epitomized Brazil's quick, smooth, freewheeling style of play in the *jogo bonito* ("beautiful game") during the 1970s and '80s, scoring 22 goals in 60 international matches in a nine-year period (1979–86). Although Brazil lost in the second round of the 1982 FIFA World Cup and in the quarterfinals at the 1986 tournament, Sócrates's exuberance, clever strategy, and signature "golden heel" back-heel pass on the field made him a star. The tall (1.93 m [6 ft 4 in]), bearded Sócrates also attracted attention for his flamboyant life off the field and for his political activism on behalf of the poor and against Brazil's authoritarian government. He played (1974–78) for Botafogo football club in Ribeirão Prêto while he obtained his medical degree. He then moved up to play for the São Paulo professional club Corinthians (1978–84), for which he was a formidable midfielder, scoring 172 goals in 297 games. After a brief spell with Fiorentina in Florence, Sócrates returned home to join Flamengo in Rio de Janeiro and then Santos in São Paulo before retiring from the game in 1989. Thereafter he practiced medicine and became a noted political and sports commentator.

Spence, Augustus Andrew ("Gusty"), Northern Irish Protestant militant (b. June 28, 1933, Belfast, N.Ire.—d. Sept. 24, 2011, Belfast), was a prominent figure in the paramilitary Ulster Volunteer Force (UVF), but he later endorsed a cease-fire and the subsequent peace with the Irish Republican Army. After leaving the British military service for health reasons in 1961, Spence became active in the UVF campaign, which he continued to lead even after he was arrested in 1966 for the murder of an 18-year-old Roman Catholic and sentenced to life in the Maze prison. He was allowed out in 1972 to attend his daughter's wedding and spent four months on the run before he was recaptured. By the time Spence was released in 1984, however, he had become an advocate for peace. Spence was chosen to read the statement on a loyalist cease-fire in October 1994 and the UVF's disarmament statement in May 2007; three years later he called for the UVF to be dissolved.

Stalina, Svetlana Iosifovna, *see* Alliluyeva, Svetlana.

Steinman, Ralph Marvin, Canadian immunologist and cell biologist (b. Jan. 14, 1943, Montreal, Que.—d. Sept. 30, 2011, New York, N.Y.), shared the 2011 Nobel Prize for Physiology or Medicine with American immunologist Bruce A. Beutler and French immunologist Jules A. Hoffmann. (*See* NOBEL PRIZES.)

Sterne, Hedda (HEDWIG LINDENBERG), Romanian-born artist (b. Aug. 4, 1910, Bucharest, Rom.—d. April 8, 2011, New York, N.Y.), was indelibly identified with the New York Abstract Expressionists owing to an iconic 1951 photograph dubbed *The Irascibles*, which appeared in *Life* magazine. In the photo she loomed (as the only woman) with major practitioners of that school, including Willem de Kooning, Jackson Pollock, and Mark Rothko. She nonetheless tried to defy characterization and worked in several styles, including Surrealism and figuration; for the latter she was known for her personal portraits of friends and colleagues, notably artist Elaine de Kooning and art critic Harold Rosenberg. Sterne, who studied art in Bucharest and Vienna, was encouraged by Surrealist Victor Brauner to exhibit her works, and several of her collages were featured at a show organized by French painter Jean Arp; there she met Peggy Guggenheim, who became a patron and later invited her to exhibit at the Art of This Century gallery. After fleeing Romania in 1941, Sterne settled with her husband, Frederick Stern, in New York City, where she had her first solo show in 1943. The following year she divorced Stern, added an *e* to the end of her surname, and married cartoonist Saul Steinberg. By 1946 she was associated with the Abstract Expressionists, though she turned in the late 1940s to creating what she termed "anthropomorphic machines," which showcased her preoccupation with American tractors and other gadgets.

Stewart, Ellen, American theatre pioneer (b. Nov. 7, 1919, Chicago, Ill.—d. Jan. 13, 2011, New York, N.Y.), founded (1961) and for nearly 50 years remained the visionary artistic director of the seminal La MaMa Experimental Theatre Club (originally Café La MaMa), an Off-Off-Broadway mainstay known for presenting avant-garde international theatre in New York City's Lower East Side. La MaMa, which Stewart began in a rented basement in a tenement, produced work by aspiring playwrights and debuted hundreds of groundbreaking shows by such authors as Sam Shepard, Lanford Wilson (*q.v.*; *Balm in Gilead* among others), Stephen Schwartz (*Godspell*), and Harvey Fierstein (*Torch Song Trilogy*), as well as experimental works from around the world. In 1969 La MaMa moved to a former meatpacking plant, where two theatre spaces were created. Stewart also established La MaMa satellites in many other countries. The Annex, a larger theatre that Stewart opened in 1974 close to the La MaMa space, was renamed the Ellen Stewart Theatre in 2009. Stewart was inducted into the Broadway Theatre Hall of Fame in 1993, and in 2006 she was awarded a Tony Honor for Excellence in Theatre.

Stott, the Rev. John Robert Walmsley, British cleric and theologian (b. April 27, 1921, London, Eng.—d. July 27, 2011, Lingfield, Surrey, Eng.), transformed the Anglican Church through his dedication to evangelism and was a principal author of the Lausanne Covenant (1974), a defining document of the international evangelical Lausanne Movement. Stott attended Rugby School; Trinity College, Cambridge; and Ridley Hall Theological College, Cambridge. He was ordained in 1945 and served as curate (1945–50), rector (1950–75), and rector emeritus (from 1975) of All Souls Church in London's West End, which formed the base of the Langham Partnership, an international evangelical organization known in the U.S. as John Stott Ministries. His impact was felt around the world as he focused his considerable magnetism and exciting preaching style on increasing church involvement among the laity, college students, and the less-developed world. Stott wrote some 50 religious books (with translations into more than 60 languages), including the best-selling *Basic Christianity* (1958), *Christ the Controversialist* (1970), and *The Cross of Christ* (1986). Stott wrote many of his works while living in a small cottage without electricity, but his personal humility stood in strong contrast to the scope of his goal to bring evangelism into the Anglican mainstream, to be accomplished through the many organizations that he established, including the influential Eclectic Society (revived 1950), the Church of England Evangelical Council (1960), the Evangelical Fellowship in the Anglican Communion (1961), and the London Institute for Contemporary Christianity (1982). He also served as a chaplain (1959–91) to Queen Elizabeth II. He was made CBE in 2006.

Sullivan, John Richard Thomas, British television scriptwriter (b. Dec. 23, 1946, London, Eng.—d. April 23, 2011, Surrey, Eng.), wrote several widely acclaimed British sitcoms, most notably *Only Fools and Horses* (1981–2003), which received the BAFTA award for best comedy series in 1986, 1989, and 1997 and made actor David Jason's Derek ("Del Boy") Trotter one of Britain's favourite TV characters. After working as a member of BBC TV's props department, Sullivan approached producer Dennis Main Wilson with a script that eventually was included in the anthology series *Comedy Special* (1972–77). After it received positive reviews, a full series was commissioned, resulting in *Citizen Smith* (1977–80). After four successful seasons of *Citizen Smith*, Sullivan proposed an idea for *Only Fools and Horses* based on his own experiences as a market trader in working-class London. Sullivan went on to write the romantic comedy *Just Good Friends* (1983–86). Later in his career, he moved toward comedy-drama series such as *Over Here* (1996), *Roger Roger* (1998–2000), and *Micawber* (2001). He was made OBE in 2005.

Sultan ibn ʿAbd al-ʿAziz al-Saʿud, Prince, Saudi Arabian royal political figure (b. 1930/31?, Riyadh, Arabia [now in Saudi Arabia]—d. Oct. 22, 2011, New York, N.Y.), held a variety of cabinet posts from 1953 under a succession of Saudi kings, but it was in his role as defense minister (from 1962) that he became known as a staunch supporter of Saudi ties with the U.S. and the U.K., with which he famously negotiated a series of deals to purchase British military aircraft. Sultan was reportedly the 15th or 16th son of modern Saudi Arabia's founder, King Ibn Saʿud, and was one of seven full brothers (the Sudairi Seven) born to Ibn Saʿud's favourite wife. Sultan sought to become crown prince when his brother Fahd (another of the Sudairi Seven) ascended to the throne in 1982, but he had to yield to a half brother, ʿAbd Allah. Sultan instead was appointed second deputy prime minister. When Fahd died (2005), ʿAbd Allah succeeded him, and Sultan was named crown prince and deputy prime minister. Sultan had been undergoing medical treatment in the U.S. (reportedly for cancer) and was believed to have been suffering from Alzheimer disease.

Sumlin, Hubert, American blues musician (b. November 1931, near Greenwood, Miss.—d. Dec. 4, 2011, Wayne, N.J.), was the principal guitar player for bluesman Howlin' Wolf for more than 20 years. Sumlin's complex, inventive leads served as a counterpoint to Wolf's raw vocals in some of Wolf's biggest hits, including "Smokestack Lightnin'" (1956), "Spoonful" (1960), "Wang Dang Doodle" (1960), and "Killing Floor" (1964). Sumlin, who was raised in Arkansas, learned to play guitar as a child. While still in his teens, he worked with harmonica player James Cotton, who occasionally performed in Wolf's band. Sumlin began to play with Wolf, first on rhythm guitar and then as lead. When Wolf moved to Chicago in 1953, Sumlin soon followed, and he appeared on most of the recordings that Wolf made for Chess Records. Although Wolf often called Sumlin his son, the relationship between the two men was tempestuous and sometimes violent. One falling-out resulted in Sumlin's joining Muddy Waters's band in 1956 (which in turn led to a confrontation between Wolf and Waters), but the strain of touring with Waters drove Sumlin to return to Wolf, where he stayed until Wolf's death in 1976. Wolf's saxophonist Eddie Shaw kept the band together for a few years under the name Eddie Shaw and the Wolf Gang, but in the 1980s Sumlin launched a solo career that yielded more than a dozen albums. Sumlin was nominated for Grammys four times and was inducted into the Blues Foundation Hall of Fame in 2008. A *Rolling Stone* magazine poll of the 100 greatest guitarists of all time ranked Sumlin number 43.

Swiatek, Kazimierz Cardinal, Polish Roman Catholic cleric (b. Oct. 21, 1914, Valga, Estonia, Russian Empire [now in Estonia]—d. July 21, 2011, Pinsk, Belarus), braved a Soviet death sentence (1941) and survived harsh conditions for nearly a decade (1944–54) in the Siberian Gulag before devoting his life to providing for the Roman Catholic faithful and restoring the church after the fall of the Soviet Union. In 1922 Swiatek's family moved to Pinsk, which was then in Poland. He entered a seminary there in 1933 and was ordained a priest in 1939. He was arrested by the KGB in 1941 but escaped his death sentence in the chaos of the Nazi invasion. He was arrested again in 1944 and was sent to a forced labour lumber camp in Siberia. He faced heavy governmental opposition when he returned (1954) to preach in Pinsk (by then in Belorussia, U.S.S.R.); his church was one of the few Roman Catholic churches in the Soviet Union, drawing worshippers from thousands of kilometres away. Pope John Paul II elevated Swiatek to bishop (1989) and then archbishop (1991) of Minsk-Mogilev in Belarus. He was made a cardinal in 1994 but was too old to vote in the 2005 papal election. Pope John Paul II in 2004 awarded him the Fidei Testis award for his work.

Taseer, Salman, Pakistani political figure (b. May 31, 1944, Simla, Punjab, British India [now Shimla, Himachal Pradesh, India]—d. Jan. 4, 2011, Islamabad, Pak.), was a wealthy Muslim businessman and provincial politician known for his support of liberal reforms and his opposition to Islamic fundamentalism. Taseer, who had been appointed governor of Punjab in 2008, was assassinated by one of his own security guards, reportedly for his denunciation of Pakistan's harsh blasphemy laws and, in particular, for his public support for Aasia Bibi, a Christian woman sentenced to be hanged for blasphemy against the Prophet Muhammad. He was the son of the poet M.D. Taseer, who died when Taseer was a boy. Later his impoverished English-born mother sent him to London, where he studied chartered accountancy. He joined Zulfikar Ali Bhutto's Pakistan People's Party (PPP) in the late 1960s and was briefly imprisoned in the 1970s for his political activities. After returning to London for several years, Taseer was elected to represent the PPP in the Punjab legislature in 1988, the year that Benazir Bhutto was first elected Pakistan's prime minister.

Taylor, Elizabeth (Dame Elizabeth Rosemond Taylor), American motion picture actress (b. Feb. 27, 1932, London, Eng.—d. March 23, 2011, Los Angeles, Calif.), was noted for her sultry beauty (particularly her extraordinary violet-blue eyes) and her portrayals of emotionally volatile characters. Although she won two Academy Awards, Taylor's acting career was often overshadowed by her highly publicized personal life, which included eight marriages to seven men, notably British actor Michael Wilding, film producer Michael Todd, singer Eddie Fisher, U.S. Sen. John Warner, and British actor Richard Burton (twice). Shortly before the outbreak of World War II, her American parents, who had been living in England, moved to Los Angeles. Taylor's beauty as a child brought her to the attention of a movie studio executive, and in 1942 she made her first film, *There's One Born Every Minute*. This was closely followed by *Lassie Come Home* (1943) and *National Velvet* (1944), which made her a star. She made a smooth transition to adult roles in such films as *Life with Father* (1947), *Father of the Bride* (1950), *A Place in the Sun* (1951), *The Last Time I Saw Paris* (1954), *Giant* (1956), and *Raintree County* (1957), for which she earned

DPA/Landov

Hollywood glamour queen Elizabeth Taylor

her first Academy Award nomination. She gave Oscar-nominated performances in film adaptations of Tennessee Williams's *Cat on a Hot Tin Roof* (1958) and *Suddenly, Last Summer* (1959) and won her first Oscar for her portrayal of a New York call girl in *Butterfield 8* (1960). Taylor earned a then record $1 million for *Cleopatra* (1963) and pursued a scandalous public affair with her costar Burton during filming. The pair costarred in seven more films, notably adaptations of Edward Albee's *Who's Afraid of Virginia Woolf?* (1966), for which she won her second Oscar, and Shakespeare's *The Taming of the Shrew* (1967). After the mid-1970s,

Taylor acted only intermittently in films, onstage, and on television. An active philanthropist, she was the founder (1985) and head of the American Foundation for AIDS Research. Taylor received the American Film Institute's Life Achievement Award in 1993 and was made DBE in 2000.

Tear, Robert, Welsh tenor (b. March 8, 1939, Barry, Glamorgan, Wales—d. March 29, 2011, London, Eng.), excelled at English-language operas by Benjamin Britten and Sir Michael Tippett, as well as English choral works by Henry Purcell, Ralph Vaughan Williams, Edward Elgar, and others. He was particularly adept at character roles, many of which Britten had created for tenor Sir Peter Pears. Tear studied at King's College, Cambridge, on a choral scholarship. He made his operatic debut (1963) with the English Opera Group, starring as the Male Chorus in Britten's *The Rape of Lucretia* and Peter Quint in the composer's *The Turn of the Screw*. Tear appeared in or recorded such Britten operas as *Billy Budd*, *A Midsummer Night's Dream*, *Peter Grimes*, *The Prodigal Son*, and *Death in Venice*, as well as Britten's *War Requiem*, Tippett's *The Knot Garden*, Richard Strauss's *Salome*, Sir John Tavener's *Thérèse*, Igor Stravinsky's *The Rake's Progress*, and works by Tchaikovsky, Wagner, Puccini, and Mozart. Tear made his last appearance onstage in 2009. He was made CBE in 1984.

Thompson, Sada Carolyn, American actress (b. Sept. 27, 1929, Des Moines, Iowa—d. May 4, 2011, Danbury, Conn.), skillfully portrayed a vast array of complex characters on the stage and in films, but for many people she was best remembered as the loving matriarch Kate Lawrence on the dramatic television series *Family* (1976–80), a role for which she won (1978) an Emmy Award for outstanding lead actress in a drama series. Thompson found phenomenal success performing in such Off-Broadway productions as *Tartuffe* (1965) and *The Effect of Gamma Rays on Man-in-the-Moon Marigolds* (1970), each of which earned her an Obie Award. She captured a Tony Award, as well as a New York Drama Critics Award, for her tour de force performance as a woman and all three of her daughters in *Twigs* (1971).

Titmus, Frederick John, English cricketer (b. Nov. 24, 1932, London, Eng.—d. March 23, 2011, Hertfordshire, Eng.), was a Middlesex and England off-spinner and middle-order batsman whose first-class career spanned five decades. He was first called into the Middlesex side from the Lord's ground staff in June 1949 when the club found itself shorthanded owing to Test call-ups; although Titmus formally retired in 1976, his last first-class match was in 1982 when, having shown up to watch a match at Lord's, he was asked to play by Middlesex captain Mike Brearley. Titmus was called to the England side for two Tests against South Africa in 1955, but he took only one wicket and did not play again for England until the 1962–63 tour of Australia and New Zealand. During the 1967–68 tour of the West Indies (on which he served as vice-captain), he lost four toes on his left foot in a boating accident. Although many thought that his career was over, he returned to the Middlesex side in 1968 and was selected for the 1974–75 tour of Australia. Titmus played in 792 first-class matches, scoring 21,588 runs (average 23.11), with 208 not outs and six centuries (high score 137 not out), and taking 2,830 wickets (average 22.37). In 53 Tests he scored 1,449 runs (average 22.29), with 11 not outs and a high score of 84 not out, and took 153 wickets (average 32.22). His economy (runs per over) of 1.95 was exceeded by only four other England bowlers, and he was one of only five cricketers to have scored 20,000 runs and taken 2,500 wickets in a career. He took 100 wickets in a season 16 times and achieved the "double" of 1,000 runs and 100 wickets in a season 8 times. Titmus was appointed MBE in 1977.

Tooker, George Clair, Jr., American painter (b. Aug. 5, 1920, Brooklyn, N.Y.—d. March 27, 2011, Hartland, Vt.), created luminous canvasses of social significance that echoed themes of love, death, sex, grief, alienation, aging, isolation, and faith. Tooker's egg-tempera paintings depicted eerie and haunting situations with mythic overtones. Some of his most chilling offerings include *Children and Spastics* (1946), sadists bullying three effeminate men; *Subway* (1950), harried commuters congregating among strangers; *The Waiting Room* (1957), seemingly catatonic patrons biding their time; and *Landscape with Figures* (1965–66), the heads of office workers bobbing above a maze of cubicles.

Sam Falk—The New York Times/Redux

Surrealist artist George Tooker with one of his paintings

Though Tooker earned an A.B. (1942) from Harvard University, he became an art student of Reginald Marsh and was influenced by Paul Cadmus (who introduced him to the egg-tempera technique) and Jared French, among others. Though Tooker's narrative style fell out of favour in the late 1960s, his work enjoyed a resurgence in the early 21st century, with retrospectives held in 2008 by the National Academy Museum in New York City and in 2009 by the Pennsylvania Academy of Fine Art in Philadelphia. In 2007 Tooker was the recipient of a National Medal of Arts.

Tumba, Sven (SVEN OLOF GUNNAR JOHANSSON), Swedish ice hockey player and golfer (b. May 1, 1931, Stockholm, Swed.—d. Oct. 1, 2011, Stockholm), was a legend in Sweden in both ice hockey and golf. He was also an adept association football (soccer) player. Between 1950 and 1966, Tumba (he took the name from his hometown outside Stockholm) scored 186 goals in 245 games for the national ice hockey team and was instrumental in Sweden's winning seven world championship medals (three gold, one silver, and three bronze) and two medals (a bronze in 1952 and a silver in 1964) in four Winter Olympics. He played professionally (1950–66) with the team Djurgården, winning eight national championships, and invented a new helmet. After he retired from hockey in 1966, Tumba focused on golf. He designed golf courses, founded tournaments in the PGA European Tour, established a youth foundation, and played for Sweden in the 1971 Eisenhower Trophy (as an amateur) and the 1973 World Cup (as a professional). Tumba was inducted into the International Ice Hockey Hall of Fame (1997) and was named (2000) the country's most important player by the Swedish Hockey Federation. Meanwhile, the Swedish Golf Federation selected him (2004) the leading figure in golf and established (2011) a foundation in his honour. In 1989 King Carl Gustaf awarded Tumba the Royal Swedish Medal.

Twombly, Cy (EDWIN PARKER TWOMBLY, JR.), American painter, draftsman, and sculptor (b. April 25, 1928, Lexington, Va.—d. July 5, 2011, Rome, Italy), pursued some early experiments in an Abstract Expressionist vein before developing the calligraphic and sometimes graffiti-like repetitive and scumbled marks and gestures on canvas and paper for which he was best known. In a work such as *The Italians* (1961), Twombly made seemingly random and scrawled marks with oil paint, pencil, and crayon as if pursuing a kind of abstract and gestural handwriting in a stream of consciousness. Closer examination, though, reveals this artist's wide range of choices and emphases, with alternating and interwoven episodes of tension and release, frenetic activity and moments of calm. Many of his sculptures and paintings allude to Classical subjects and often include snippets of handwritten text. From 1947 to 1951 Twombly studied at the School of the Museum of Fine Arts in Boston, at Washington and Lee University in Lexington, Va., and at the Art Students League in New York City (where he met painter Robert Rauschenberg). With Rauschenberg, Twombly attended Black Mountain College in North Carolina in the summer of 1951, and the two traveled together (1952–53) in Italy and North Africa. After a few years of living and working in New York, Twombly moved to Italy in 1957 and made Rome his primary residence. He had retrospectives of his work at the Whitney Museum of American Art in New York in 1979 and at the Museum of Modern Art in New York in 1994, and the Cy Twombly Gallery was opened at the Menil Collection in Houston in 1995. In 1996 Twombly received a Praemium Imperiale award, presented by the Japan Art Association. In 2010 he became the first American artist and third contemporary artist following Georges Braque in 1953 to be given the honour of painting a ceiling of the Louvre Museum.

Tyzack, Margaret Maud, British actress (b. Sept. 9, 1931, London, Eng.—d. June 25, 2011, London), was a versatile character actress perhaps best known for her roles in several television miniseries in the 1960s and '70s, notably as the naive Winifred Forsyte Dartie in *The Forsyte Saga* (1967); as Princess (then Queen) Anne in *The First Churchills* (1969), for which she won a BAFTA Award; as the manipulative title character in *Cousin Bette* (1971); and as Claudius's disappointed mother, Antonia Minor, in *I, Claudius* (1976). Tyzack's greatest professional successes, however, were on the stage. She won two Olivier Awards: for her harrowing portrayal of Martha in the National Theatre's 1981 revival of *Who's Afraid of Virginia Woolf?* and in 2009 for her imperious Mrs. St. Maugham in *The Chalk Garden*. She also received a Tony Award for best featured actress in 1990 for her performance opposite Maggie Smith in *Lettice and Lovage* as the Preservation Trust bureaucrat Lotte Schoen, a role that she had originated (1987) in London opposite Smith, who refused to take the play to Broadway without Tyzack. Her last significant stage role was with Helen Mirren in *Phèdre* in 2009, the same year she undertook a recurring role in TV's *EastEnders*. Tyzack was made OBE in 1970 and advanced to CBE in 2010.

van der Meer, Simon, Dutch physical engineer (b. Nov. 24, 1925, The Hague, Neth.—d. March 4, 2011, Geneva, Switz.), was awarded, with Carlo Rubbia, the Nobel Prize for Physics in 1984 for his contribution to the discovery of the massive, short-lived subatomic particles designated W and Z that were crucial to the unified electroweak theory posited in the 1970s. After receiving a degree in physical engineering (1952) from the Delft (Neth.) Institute of Technology, van der Meer worked for Philips. In 1956 he joined the staff of CERN (the European Organization for Nuclear Research), near Geneva, where he remained until his retirement in 1990. The electroweak theory provided the first reliable estimates of the masses of the W and Z particles—nearly 100 times the mass of the proton. The most promising means of bringing about a physical interaction that would release enough energy to form the particles was to cause a beam of highly accelerated protons, moving through an evacuated tube, to collide with an oppositely directed beam of antiprotons. Van der Meer devised a mechanism that would monitor the particle scattering at a particular point in CERN's circular particle accelerator and would trigger a device on the opposite side of the ring to modify the electric fields in such a way as to keep the beams of protons and antiprotons from scattering out of the proper path.

Vang Pao, Laotian Hmong general (b. December 1929, Nonghet, Xiangkhoang province, Laos—d. Jan. 6, 2011, Clovis, near Fresno, Calif.), commanded Hmong guerrillas against communist forces in Laos as an ally of U.S. troops during the Vietnam War. He later founded the United Lao National Liberation Front, assisted in the resettlement of tens of thousands of Hmong who had been abandoned by the American forces, and became a revered leader of his people in exile. Vang Pao was already a general in the Laotian army fighting against the Pathet Lao insurgents when CIA operatives reportedly approached him in 1960 to recruit Hmong fighters from the remote mountainous areas in which they lived. Although the Hmong contribution to this "secret war" was not officially acknowledged for many years, after Laos fell (1975), Vang Pao and others were evacuated to the U.S. and other countries. In June 2007 he was arrested under the U.S. Neutrality Act and charged, along with several co-conspirators, of plotting to overthrow the Laotian government; after two years of legal wrangling, the charges were dropped in September 2009.

Vann Nath, Cambodian painter (b. 1946, Battambang province, Camb.—d. Sept. 5, 2011, Phnom Penh, Camb.), was one of only a handful of prisoners who survived the Khmer Rouge's S-21 (Tuol Sleng) prison, where more than 14,000 people were believed to have died between 1975 and 1979. Vann Nath, who was born into a farming family, studied art and worked as a bill-

Mak Remissa—EPA/Landov

Khmer Rouge survivor Vann Nath with one of his disturbing paintings

board and sign painter, but when the Khmer Rouge came to power in Cambodia (1975), he was sent to toil in the rice fields. He was arrested (he claimed that he never knew the reason) and in early 1978 was imprisoned in S-21. After Kaing Guek Eav, the prison commander known as Duch, discovered that Vann Nath could paint, he was assigned to create large portraits (reproduced from photographs) of the Khmer Rouge leader, Pol Pot. Vann Nath's artistic skills enabled him to avoid being tortured and to obtain enough food to stay alive until the prison fell in 1979 during the invasion of Cambodia by Vietnamese forces. He used recollections of his year in Tuol Sleng and the atrocities that he observed there as the basis for many of his graphic later paintings, some of which were displayed on the walls of the Tuol Sleng Genocide Museum. In 2009 Vann Nath testified at Duch's UN-sponsored war crimes trial.

Vo Chi Cong, Vietnamese communist revolutionary and government official (b. 1912, Quang Nam province, Annam, French Indochina (now in Vietnam)—d. Sept. 8, 2011, Ho Chi Minh City, Vietnam), was among the earliest fighters for Vietnam's independence from France; he later held key positions in South Vietnam's National Liberation Front (NLF) and the Provisional Revolutionary Government—both political arms of the Viet Cong guerrillas—during the Vietnam War. Cong began an activist career in 1930 under Phan Boi Chau and Phan Chau Trinh, early nationalist rebels against the French colonial regime. During World War II he participated in the underground resistance against Japan and the Vichy French, who arrested him and kept him under surveillance in 1942. It was not until 1961 that he emerged into political significance as a founding member of the NLF. Cong was the chief organizer of the People's Revolutionary Party, South Vietnam's communist party, and became a strong opponent of Saigon's U.S.-backed regime. After the reunification of Vietnam in 1976, he joined the new national government, serving as the minister of fisheries (1976–77) and of agriculture (1977–78) and as a deputy prime minister (1976–82). He also became a full member of the Politburo of the Vietnamese Communist Party in 1976.

Waitz, Grete (GRETE ANDERSEN), Norwegian athlete (b. Oct. 1, 1953, Oslo, Nor.—d. April 19, 2011, Oslo), dominated women's long-distance running for more than a decade. During 1978–88 she won the New York City Marathon nine times (she did not compete in 1981 or 1987), the London Marathon twice (1983, 1986), and the IAAF women's cross-country world championship five times (1978–81, 1983). She also captured the gold medal in the inaugural women's marathon at the 1983 IAAF track-and-field world championships and the silver medal in the first Olympic women's marathon at the 1984 Games in Los Angeles. Waitz began as a middle-distance runner and at age 17 set a 1,500-m European junior record (4 min 17 sec). She competed at that distance in the 1972 and 1976 Olympic Games and broke the 3,000-m world record in 1975 (8 min 46.6 sec) and again in 1976 (8 min 45.4 sec). Although Waitz was reluctant to attempt her first New York Marathon in 1978, she finished the race in 2 hr 32 min 30 sec, more than two minutes under the previous best time. She came back the next year to become the first woman to finish the race in under 2.5 hours (2 hr 27 min 33 sec) and broke that time by almost two minutes in 1980 (2 hr 25 min 41 sec). Her personal best race was at the 1986 London Marathon (2 hr 24 min 54 sec). Waitz retired in 1990 after finishing fourth in her final New York Marathon, but two years later she ran as race founder Fred Lebow's partner. She was the first non-American inducted (2000) into the National Distance Running Hall of Fame. In 2008 Waitz was awarded the Order of St. Olav by Norwegian King Harald V.

Norwegian marathoner Grete Waitz

Mario Suriani/AP

Wanjiru, Samuel Kamau, Kenyan athlete (b. Nov. 10, 1986, Kenya—d. May 15, 2011, Nyahururu, Kenya), set an Olympic record (2 hr 6 min 32 sec) at the 2008 Beijing Olympic Games en route to becoming the first Kenyan to capture the Olympic marathon gold medal. In 2009 Wanjiru's triumphs in the London marathon (in a personal-best 2 hr 5 min 10 sec), where he had finished second in 2008, and the Chicago marathon (in a course-record 2 hr 5 min 41 sec) earned him the men's 2008–09 World Marathon Major (WMM) title. Though he was compelled to drop out of the 2010 London race because of a recurring knee injury, his repeat victory in the Chicago marathon (in 2 hr 6 min 24 sec) later that year helped him to a second consecutive WMM series title. Wanjiru reportedly died after plummeting from a balcony following a domestic dispute with his wife.

Wheldon, Dan (DANIEL CLIVE WHELDON), British race-car driver (b. June 22, 1978, Emberton, Buckinghamshire, Eng.—d. Oct. 16, 2011, Las Vegas, Nev.), won the 2011 Indianapolis 500 after having captured both that race and the overall Indy Racing League (IRL) drivers' championship in 2005, but his career came to an abrupt end when he died from injuries he sustained in a fiery 15-car crash during the last race of the 2011 season. Wheldon moved to the U.S. in 1999 when he failed to obtain financial backing for a career in Formula Three racing. After having made his IndyCar racing debut in 2002, he was named Rookie of the Year in 2003, finished second in the IRL rankings in 2004, and in 2005 became the IRL season champion and the first British Indy 500 winner since Graham Hill in 1966. Wheldon also ranked second in the standings in 2006, the same year he was co-winner with fellow IRL driver Scott Dixon and NASCAR driver Casey Mears of the Rolex 24 Hours of Daytona race in the Grand American Sports Car Series endurance competition. Wheldon had a total of 16 IRL victories and career earnings of more than $14.6 million; in his final race he started in last place as part of a competition for a share in a special $5 million prize. In the weeks prior to the fatal accident, he had been involved in testing a new car that was designed to be safer at high speeds.

Wicker, Tom (THOMAS GREY WICKER), American journalist (b. June 18, 1926, Hamlet, N.C.—d. Nov. 25, 2011, near Rochester, Vt.), was a member of the presidential motorcade when Pres. John F. Kennedy was assassinated on Nov. 22, 1963, and his thoughtful and precise coverage of that event as a reporter for the *New York Times* newspaper established him as one of the most highly regarded political writers in the U.S. In 1964 Wicker was appointed chief of the *Times*'s Washington bureau, and two years later he began writing the "In the Nation" column, which he used until his retirement in 1991 as a forum for his opinions on such topics as the Vietnam War and the covert bombing of Cambodia during the administration of Pres. Richard M. Nixon. In September 1971, when prisoners at Attica Correctional Facility in upstate New York took 38 guards and workers hostage, the inmates named Wicker as a person they wanted as a mediator with authorities. He described the failure of communication at the prison in his most-acclaimed book, *A Time to Die* (1975). In all, Wicker wrote 20 books, including several novels (some under the pen name Paul Connolly) and nonfiction.

Widmer, Robert Henry, American aeronautical engineer (b. May 17, 1916, Hawthorne, N.J.—d. June 20, 2011, Fort Worth, Texas), designed innovative military aircraft, notably the B-58 bomber, the world's first long-range aircraft capable of sustained supersonic flight. He began working on top-secret projects for Convair, which in 1953 was acquired by General Dynamics. Widmer also led the projects that developed the F-111 medium-range fighter-bomber, the F-16 lightweight fighter, and the BGM-109 Tomahawk cruise missile. In 1962 the American Society of Mechanical Engineers awarded him the Spirit of St. Louis Medal for his work, and in 1983 the American Institute of Aeronautics and Astronautics bestowed on him the Reed Aeronautics Award for his contributions to aeronautical science and engineering. Widmer worked for several companies, and he rose to the position of vice president for science and engineering for all of General Dynamics.

Williams, Dick (RICHARD HIRSCHFIELD WILLIAMS), American baseball player and team manager (b. May 7, 1929, St. Louis, Mo.—d. June 7, 2011, Las Vegas, Nev.), during his 21 seasons (1967–88) as a Major League Baseball manager, won two consecutive World Series titles (1972–73) with the American League (AL) Oakland A's, as well as league pennants with the AL Boston Red Sox during the team's "impossible dream" season (1967) and the National League San Diego Padres (1984). He was one of seven managers to win pennants in both leagues and one of only two managers to take three different teams to the World Series. Williams played utility outfielder/infielder for 13 seasons (1951–64) with five professional baseball teams, securing 70 home runs and a .260 career batting average. His major-league managerial career began in 1967 when he was tapped to lead the Red Sox, who soared from a 72–90 season in 1966 to an AL-leading 92–70 in the first year under his guidance. Williams managed six teams, including the California Angels (1974–76), the Montreal Expos (1977–81), and the Seattle Mariners (1986–88), for a career record of 1,571 wins and 1,451 losses. He was elected to the Baseball Hall of Fame by the Veterans Committee and inducted in 2008.

Wilson, Lanford Eugene, American playwright (b. April 13, 1937, Lebanon, Mo.—d. March 24, 2011, Wayne, N.J.), was a pioneer of Off-Off-Broadway and regional theatre, notably the Circle Theater (later Circle Repertory Company) in New York City, with which he was involved from its founding in 1969 until it closed in 1996. Many of Wilson's plays, which are known for experimental staging and simultaneous dialogue, also played on Broadway. In 1980 he won a Pulitzer Prize for *Talley's Folly* (1979), the second installment in a cycle of plays about an eccentric family from Lebanon, Mo. The

Prolific playwright Lanford Wilson

Marty Reichenthal/AP

other parts of the so-called Talley Trilogy are *The Fifth of July* (1978; televised 1982) and *Talley and Son* (1985; a reworking of his 1981 play *A Tale Told*). Wilson attended schools in Missouri, San Diego, and Chicago before moving to New York City in 1962. From 1963 his plays were produced regularly at Off-Off-Broadway theatres such as Caffe Cino and La MaMa Experimental Theatre Club under its artistic director, Ellen Stewart (*q.v.*). Wilson's first one-act play, *So Long at the Fair* (1963), was followed by *Home Free!* and *The Madness of Lady Bright* (both 1964). *Balm in Gilead* (1965), his first full-length play (premiered at La MaMa), is set in a crowded world of hustlers and junkies, while *The Rimers of Eldritch* (1967) examines life in a small town. Wilson's other plays include *The Gingham Dog* (1969), *Lemon Sky* (1970; televised 1987), *The Hot l Baltimore* (1973; adapted for television 1975), *The Mound Builders* (1975), *Angels Fall* (1982), *Burn This* (1987), *Redwood Curtain* (1993; televised 1995), *Sympathetic Magic* (1997), and *Book of Days* (1998).

Wilson, Tom (THOMAS ALBERT WILSON), American cartoonist (b. Aug. 1, 1931, Grant Town, W.Va.—d. Sept. 16, 2011, Cincinnati, Ohio), was the creator of the hapless rotund cartoon character Ziggy, a short, bald everyman whose wry and self-deprecating comments framed life's tribulations; Ziggy made his debut in the cartoon collection *When You're Not Around* (1969). Though Ziggy was originally given an occupation as an elevator operator, his later encounters were mostly with his lovable pets, including Fuzz, a potato-shaped dog, and Sid, a cat that fears mice. In 1971 Universal Press Syndicate (now Universal Uclick) launched Ziggy in 15 newspapers; by 2011 the 40-year-old panel was being featured in more than 500 daily and Sunday newspaper. Wilson spent more than 35 years as an artist at American Greetings Corp., where he helped to develop humorous cards and such characters as Strawberry Shortcake and the Care Bears. He shared an Emmy Award in 1983 for the Christmas special *Ziggy's Gift*. In 1987 Wilson's son, Tom, Jr., took over the panel.

Winehouse, Amy Jade, British singer-songwriter (b. Sept. 14, 1983, London, Eng.—found dead July 23, 2011, London), skyrocketed to fame with her critically acclaimed multiple Grammy Award-winning album *Back to Black* (2006), but her tempestuous love life, erratic behaviour, and substance-abuse problems stalled her recording career even as they made her a favourite subject of tabloid journalism. While attending the prestigious BRIT School in London, Winehouse showed ability as an actor as well as a singer, and by age 16 she was performing with jazz groups. On her debut album, *Frank* (2003), she proved herself to be a shrewd, caustic lyricist, and her smoky, evocative vocals drew comparisons to jazz and rhythm-and-blues legends Sarah Vaughan, Dinah Washington, and Billie Holiday. Her follow-up, *Back to Black*, took off in Britain and entered the American music charts at number seven (the highest debut position ever for a British woman). The stick-thin and tattooed Winehouse began piling her jet-black hair in an enormous beehive that, along with heavy Cleopatra-style eye makeup, became her trademark look. After the release of a video in which she appeared to be smoking crack cocaine, she had difficulty obtaining a visa and was unable to attend the 2008 Grammy Awards ceremony in Los Angeles, where *Back to Black* won five Grammys, including two (best song and best recording) for the infectious "Rehab," with its sultry "no, no, no" refusal to enter drug and alcohol treatment. In fact, Winehouse had tried rehab, though apparently without success. In November 2008 she was named best-selling pop/rock female at the World Music Awards. Winehouse's final concert tour was cut short in June 2011 when she was unable to perform onstage.

Kevork Djansezian/AP

Troubled singer Amy Winehouse

Withers, Googie (GEORGETTE LIZETTE WITHERS), British actress (b. March 12, 1917, Karachi, British India [now in Pakistan]—d. July 15, 2011, Sydney, Australia), showed remarkable breadth of talent, portraying a variety of characters on the stage and in film, with the height of her popularity occurring in the 1940s and '50s. She often acted with her husband, Australian actor and director John McCallum, whom she married in 1948 after they performed together in *It Always Rains on Sunday* (1947). She had already appeared in several plays before her motion-picture breakthrough in *The Girl in the Crowd* (1935). Subsequent films include *The Lady Vanishes* (1938), *One of Our Aircraft Is Missing* (1942), *On Approval* (1943), *Night and the City* (1950), and *Shine* (1996). She also had a recurring role on the TV prison drama *Within These Walls* (1974–78) and continued to act on the stage in Australia and Britain, making her last appearance in 2002 in Oscar Wilde's *Lady Windermere's Fan*. Withers was the first non-Australian named to the Order of Australia (1980) and was made CBE in 2002.

Wolf, Christa (CHRISTA MARGARETE IHLENFELD), German novelist and essayist (b. March 18, 1929, Landsberg an der Warthe, Ger. [now Gorzow Wielkopolski, Pol.]—d. Dec. 1, 2011, Berlin, Ger.), was one of communist East Germany's most-admired writers. Although Wolf's reputation suffered somewhat in the West because of her opposition to German reunification (1989) and revelations in 1993 that she had cooperated (1959–62) with the Stasi secret police, in 2002 she was awarded the Deutscher Bücherpreis for lifetime achievement. Wolf was reared in a middle-class pro-Nazi family, and after World War II her family settled in East Germany. She studied at the Universities of Jena and Leipzig (1949–53) and until 1962 worked as editor of the East German Writers' Union magazine and as a reader for book publishers. Wolf's second novel, *Der geteilte Himmel* (1963; *Divided*

Heaven, 1965; filmed 1964), established her reputation and earned political favour for its story of a woman who chooses to return to East Berlin rather than remain with her lover in the West. *Nachdenken über Christa T.* (1968; *The Quest for Christa T.*, 1970), which concerns a woman who questions her beliefs and life in a socialist state, was severely attacked by the East German Writers' Congress, and its sale was forbidden in East Germany. Wolf's other novels include the semiautobiographical *Kindheitsmuster* (1976; *A Model Childhood*, 1980), *Till Eulenspiegel* (1972; filmed 1974), *Kassandra* (1983; *Cassandra*, 1984), *Störfall: Nachrichten eines Tages* (1987; *Accident: A Day's News*, 1989), *Medea* (1998), and *Leibhaftig* (2002; *In the Flesh*, 2005). *Was bleibt* (1990; *What Remains*, 1993), an account of the surveillance practices of the East German government, was her most significant nonfiction work, along with the memoir *Ein Tag im Jahr: 1960–2000* (2003; *One Day a Year*, 2007).

Wood, John, British actor (b. July 5, 1930, Derbyshire, Eng.—d. Aug. 6, 2011, Chipping Campden, Gloucestershire, Eng.), played an enormous variety of roles to great effect but was best known for his work in plays by Shakespeare and by British playwright Tom Stoppard. Wood discovered acting while studying law at Jesus College, Oxford, and began his career with the Old Vic Company (1954–56). He made his West End debut as Don Quixote in Tennessee Williams's *Camino Real* (1957) and in the early 1970s joined the Royal Shakespeare Company. His Broadway debut as Guildenstern in Stoppard's *Rosencrantz and Guildenstern Are Dead* (1967) earned him a Tony Award nomination, as did his performance as the title character in a 1974 revival of American playwright William Gillette's *Sherlock Holmes*. Wood won a Tony for his portrayal of Henry Carr in Stoppard's *Travesties* (1976), a part that was written for him. He also created the roles of Sidney Bruhl in Ira Levin's comedy thriller *Deathtrap* (1978) on Broadway and A.E. Housman in Stoppard's *The Invention of Love* (1997) for Britain's National Theatre. Wood's on-screen career included the films *WarGames* (1983), *The Purple Rose of Cairo* (1985), *Ladyhawke* (1985), and *Chocolat* (2000), as well as dozens of TV shows. He was made CBE in 2007.

Yalow, Rosalyn Sussman, American medical physicist (b. July 19, 1921, Bronx, N.Y.—d. May 30, 2011, Bronx), was the joint recipient (with Andrew V. Schally and Roger Guillemin) of the 1977 Nobel Prize for Physiology or Medicine, awarded for her development of radioimmunoassay (RIA), an extremely sensitive technique for measuring minute quantities of biologically active substances. This method could be used to measure hundreds of such substances, such as viruses and drugs. Practical applications include the screening of blood held in blood banks for the hepatitis virus and the determination of effective dosage levels of drugs and antibiotics. Yalow graduated (1941) with honours from Hunter College of the City University of New York and earned (1945) a Ph.D. in physics from the University of Illinois. From 1946 to 1950 she lectured on physics at Hunter, and in 1947 she became a consultant in nuclear physics to the Bronx Veterans Administration Hospital (now the James J. Peters Veterans Affairs Medical Center), where from 1950 to 1970 she was a physicist and the assistant chief of the radioisotope service. With a colleague, American physician Solomon A. Berson, Yalow began using radioactive isotopes to examine and diagnose various disease conditions. The duo's investigations into the mechanism underlying type II diabetes led to their development of RIA. In 1970 Yalow was appointed chief of the laboratory later renamed the Nuclear Medicine Service at the Veterans Administration Hospital. In 1976 she became the first woman to receive the Albert Lasker Basic Medical Research Award. In New York City, Yalow served (1979–85) as a distinguished professor-at-large at the Albert Einstein College of Medicine at Yeshiva University prior to accepting (1985) the position of Solomon A. Berson Distinguished Professor at Large at the Mount Sinai School of Medicine. She was awarded the National Medal of Science in 1988.

AP

Medical physicist Rosalyn Yalow

Yates, Peter James, British film director (b. July 24, 1929, Aldershot, Hampshire, Eng.—d. Jan. 9, 2011, London, Eng.), displayed enormous versatility across more than two dozen motion pictures, ranging from the cop thriller *Bullitt* (1968), with its iconic car chase through the streets of San Francisco, to the coming-of-age comedy *Breaking Away* (1979), which featured a climactic bicycle race and earned Yates his first pair of Academy Award nominations, for best picture and best director, to *The Dresser* (1983), the screen adaptation of Ronald Harwood's Tony Award-nominated play, which brought Yates his second pair of Oscar nominations. After working as assistant director on such films as *The Guns of Navarone* (1961) and *A Taste of Honey* (1961), Yates made his debut at the helm of pop singer Cliff Richard's teen musical *Summer Holiday* (1963). Yates's other films include the unconventional romance *John and Mary* (1969), the wartime drama *Murphy's War* (1971), the gangster flick *The Friends of Eddie Coyle* (1973), the undersea action adventure *The Deep* (1977), and the thriller *Eyewitness* (1981), as well as television adaptations of the novels *Don Quixote* (2000) and *A Separate Peace* (2004).

Yonamine, Wally (KANAME YONAMINE), American athlete (b. June 24, 1925, Olowalu, Maui, Hawaii—d. Feb. 28, 2011, Honolulu, Hawaii), was the first Asian American to play (1947) professional football in the U.S., but the scrappy running back for the San Francisco 49ers left the team after a wrist injury and became (1951) the first American to play professional baseball in Japan, leading off for the Yomiuri Giants. His career in Japan was distinguished by his aggressive play, which was initially derided by fans and players. When it became evident that his drag bunts and hook slides helped the team to win games, Yonamine became a beloved figure in the sport. A three-time batting champion, he led the Giants to eight pennants and was named MVP in 1957. During his 12 seasons, he had a career batting average of .311 with 1,337 hits and 482 runs batted in. After retiring in 1962 he became a successful coach and manager. He was inducted into the Japanese Baseball Hall of Fame in 1994.

York, Susannah (SUSANNAH YOLANDE FLETCHER), British actress (b. Jan. 9, 1939, London, Eng.—d. Jan. 15, 2011, London), was initially cast as a blue-eyed blonde ingenue, but her gamine beauty belied acting skills that came to the fore in such roles as the feisty Sophie Western, the object of the eponymous hero's affections in *Tom Jones* (1963), and as Sir Thomas More's daughter, Margaret, in *A Man for All Seasons* (1966). York finally overcame this "English rose" typecasting with powerful performances as the duplicitous lesbian "Childie" in the X-rated *The Killing of Sister George* (1968) and as the deluded dance marathon participant Alice in *They Shoot Horses, Don't They?* (1969), which earned her an Academy Award nomination and a British Academy of Film and Television Arts (BAFTA) award for best supporting actress. York grew up in Scotland, and after graduating (1958) from the Royal Academy of Dramatic Art in London, she earned her first major role as Alec Guinness's daughter in *Tunes of Glory* (1960). Other motion pictures include *Freud* (1962), *Kaleidoscope* (1966), *Happy Birthday, Wanda June* (1971), *The Maids* (1975), and three Superman movies in which she played the Man of Steel's biological mother. York secured an Emmy Award nomination for a TV adaptation of *Jane Eyre* (1970) and won best actress honours at the 1972 Cannes film festival for her portrayal of a woman suffering from schizophrenia in Robert Altman's film *Images*. She later focused on the stage and TV, including the miniseries *We'll Meet Again* (1982) and roles on *Trainer* (1991–92) and *Holby City* (2003).

AP

British actress Susannah York

Yuan Xuefen, Chinese performer and administrator (b. May 26, 1922, Zhejiang province, China—d. Feb. 19, 2011, Shanghai, China), initiated a series of reforms in the lyrical genre of Chinese Yue opera (Shaoxing opera). Yue opera, founded in the early 1900s, was originally performed by men and was based on a loose outline that allowed the performers freedom of improvisation. Yuan incorporated elements from traditional Kunqu drama with techniques from Western theatre and film. As an actress she was best known for her starring role in the Yue opera *Xianglin Sao* (1946), which was adapted from Lu Xun's story *Zhufu* (1924; *The New Year's Sacrifice*, 1956). Yuan broadcast on radio in the 1930s and beginning in the 1940s performed in films, notably a 1978 adaptation of *Xianglin Sao*. She also established (1944) the Xuefen Yueju troupe, and in the 1950s she became head of the Shanghai Yueju Academy. When traditional performing arts were banned during the Cultural Revolution, Yuan was forced to leave her position at the academy and endure imprisonment, torture, and separation from her young son. She was restored to her position in 1976 and later won numerous domestic and foreign awards.

Chinese opera innovator Yuan Xuefen

Xinhua/Landov

Zanzotto, Andrea, Italian poet (b. Oct. 10, 1921, Pieve di Soligo, Italy—d. Oct. 18, 2011, Conegliano, Italy), was known for his innovative engagement with language and his rootedness in the landscape of the Veneto. He was considered one of the foremost Italian poets of the 20th century. Zanzotto, who graduated (1942) from the University of Padua with a degree in Italian literature, made his living as a teacher. His first book of poetry, *Dietro il paesaggio* (1951), won a literary award juried by noteworthy poets. His verse, consistently erudite and creative, took a noticeable stylistic turn with his sixth volume, *La beltà* (1968), in which he questioned the ability of words to reflect truth. He contributed poetry in dialect to filmmaker Federico Fellini's *Casanova* (1976). Together with other verse reflecting the dialect of his native region, the work was published in *Filò: per il Casanova di Fellini* (1976; *Peasants Wake for Fellini's Casanova, and Other Poems*, 1997). Zanzotto's masterworks are the trilogy *Il galateo in bosco* (1978), *Fosfeni* (1983; Eng. trans., 2010), and *Idioma* (1986). English translations of his writings include *Poems by Andrea Zanzotto* (1993) and *The Selected Poetry and Prose of Andrea Zanzotto* (2009).

2011 Special Reports

On October 23, Libyans in Tripoli celebrate their country's liberation from former head of state Muammar al-Qaddafi, who had been captured and killed by rebels just days earlier. Libya's civil war began in February as part of the pro-democracy movement known as the Arab Spring, which swept across the Middle East and North Africa during the year.

Abdel Magid al-Fergany/AP

The Elusive Economic Recovery

by Joel Havemann

As 2011 drew to a merciful close in Europe, the continent's economy seemed to fall deeper into crisis by the hour. It threatened to drag the rest of the Western world behind it. The global recession that began in late 2008 officially lasted for 18 months and ended in June 2009. The optimists in 2011 hoped that the world economy could avoid a "double dip," while pessimists thought that a second recession had already begun.

Many observers believed that Europe had been brought low by an instinct to do good and that the gold-plated social-welfare systems that many European countries inaugurated in the 19th century were simply unaffordable. New debt piled onto old debt, driving interest rates on government bonds to levels that governments could not afford. Five EU countries avoided bankruptcy only because their creditor banks forgave up to half their debt or the 27-member EU provided them with financial aid—or both. Typically, assistance was conditioned on deep cuts in social-welfare programs, but when governments acceded to those conditions, their citizens poured into the streets in sometimes violent protest.

Greece, where the situation was the most dire, nearly defaulted on its massive debt, the largest in the EU relative to the size of the country's economy. It came close to being dumped from the roster of 17 euro-zone members, an outcome that could have produced exchange-rate chaos. Greece escaped that ignominy—at least temporarily—when its creditor banks, under pressure from German Chancellor Angela Merkel and French Pres. Nicolas Sarkozy, accepted 50% losses on their Greek bonds. The EU and the IMF provided Greece with $140 billion in new bailout loans.

As in Greece, governments fell in Denmark, Finland, Ireland, Portugal, Slovakia, and Spain. Italy, the third largest economy in the EU and second only to Greece in the relative size of its debt, joined the parade in November when longtime Prime Minister Silvio Berlusconi was replaced in office just days after Greek Prime Minister George Papandreou.

The EU giants were not much better off. France, the second largest member, was thought to have an unsustainable mountain of debt. Even though traditional economic powerhouse Germany's growth rate had outpaced that of its major EU partners and the U.S. during the previous two years, by the end of 2011, it could find no buyers at any price for some of its bonds. Overall EU growth in the third quarter of 2011 was only 0.2% greater than in the second, and many analysts judged that several EU countries had sunk back into the recessions that they had escaped just a year or two earlier.

The euro was perhaps the most visible expression of Europe's effort at harmony after two terrible world wars in the first half of the 20th century. Failure to preserve the currency would have raised questions about the Continent's commitment to move ahead as one instead of many. In the end, leaders of 26 of the 27 European Union member countries—all but the U.K.—supported a measure to enforce rules for fiscal discipline and to pledge additional funds to member countries whose debt threatened to swamp them. The agreement came 20 years to the day after the European Council gathered on Dec. 9, 1991, in Maastricht, Neth., to negotiate the economic and monetary union that ultimately led to the common currency.

Unlike the 2008 financial crisis, which began in the U.S. housing market, the 2011 version was distinctly European in origin and style. Its effects, however, were similar—there was precious little loan money to be had—and the consequences washed over the entire free-market world. Would-be lenders feared that even their most-reliable European borrowers would be unable to pay them back. They demanded high interest rates—if they were willing to lend

Michael Probst/AP

Demonstrators concerned about job losses and other economic issues rally on October 13 outside a federal courthouse in Las Vegas. In November Nevada's unemployment rate of 13% was the highest in the U.S., well above the national average of 8.6%.

Rioting broke out in several European countries faced with crushing debt and new economic austerity measures; protesters in Rome torched cars, smashed windows, and fought with police on October 15.

at all. Without loans, companies could not secure the money they needed to cover their costs and meet their financial obligations. More pointedly in the high-unemployment economy of 2011, they could not get funds to hire new workers. At the same time, Europe could not afford to invest in the U.S., thus decreasing the funds available for growth there. Trade between Europe and North America receded.

The U.S. economy, reflecting Europe's troubles, grew at an annual rate of only 1.8% in the third quarter of 2011 and 1.5% for the year ended in the third quarter. For the four years ended in that quarter, the U.S. economy was essentially stagnant, growing at an anemic 0.4% average annual rate. Late in November the Organisation for Economic Co-operation and Development slashed its estimate of U.S. growth in 2012 from 3.1% to 2%. Other forecasters made similar adjustments.

The U.S. worried that it was losing the global dominance that it had enjoyed for the more than 60 years following World War II. In 2010 China had overtaken Japan as the world's second largest economy, and it seemed only a matter of time before its economy, growing at a reliable 8–12% a year, passed that of the U.S.

China benefited from its economic as well as its geographic distance from the Western financial powers. It was barely grazed, at least for the time being, by the debt crisis. Although Chinese manufacturing had declined slightly by year's end as its overseas markets took a pounding, foreign direct investment continued to flourish as investors looked for more-dependable markets than those they found in the West. For the future, however, some analysts argued that China's housing prices were too high to last, and they forecast a bursting housing bubble akin to the one that triggered the U.S. financial crisis in 2008. Poor working conditions continued to cast a shadow over China's labour force, which in any case was not expected to keep pace with the population as a whole because the country's long-standing one-child limit ensured that fewer young adults were entering the workforce.

India could not achieve China's consistent pace, but its GDP growth had rebounded from a quarterly low of 5.8% during the global recession (2009) to a quarterly high of 9.4% in 2010. The World Bank, in line with other forecasters, estimated that India's economy grew by 8% in 2011 and that it would continue to grow 8–9% for the next two years. Largely sheltered from the effects of the European debt crisis, India deregulated some industries and privatized others. Although more than half of India's workforce was in agriculture, the large English-speaking workforce accounted for half of the country's GDP.

For Japan the earthquake and resulting tsunami of March 11 could hardly have come at a worse time. In addition to killing more than 19,000 people, the natural disaster was an economic calamity, forcing several nuclear power plants, most notably Fukushima Daiichi, to shut down and causing rolling blackouts. Companies such as Toyota, Honda, Nissan, Toshiba, Sony, and Texas Instruments were compelled to shutter plants. Exports, the lifeblood of the Japanese economy, fell more than 10% from May 2010 to May 2011. According to the World Bank, Japan's overall GDP growth of 0.1% brought it closer than any other major industrial country to negative growth in 2011. (*See* Special Report on page 176.)

After the 2008 financial crisis, the U.S. and the EU adopted very different strategies for keeping ahead of the soaring Asians. The Europeans, obsessed by inflation, insisted on tight budgetary discipline related to requirements for EU membership (though even the fastidious Germans did not meet the national debt limit of 60% of GDP and only occasionally held their annual deficit below the maximum 3%). Meanwhile, for the American Democratic Party, which controlled the White House and both houses of Congress in 2009 and 2010, averting a deep recession or even a depression following the 2008 financial crisis was paramount. U.S. Pres. Barack Obama pushed legislation through Congress that authorized more than $700 billion in programs designed to propel economic growth.

Whether the stimulus package had achieved that goal was still a matter of dispute in 2011, but it certainly had contributed to a U.S. deficit that reached $14 trillion during the crisis. Republicans demanded spending cuts, whereas their Democratic opponents said that the ailing economy needed more medicine. The stalemate persisted through much of 2011 and seemed likely to affect the 2012 presidential election campaign.

Joel Havemann is a Former Editor and National and European Economics Correspondent for the Washington, D.C., and Brussels bureaus of the Los Angeles Times.

(Top left) Isaac Brekken/AP; (top right) Gregorio Borgia/AP

The Arab Spring: The End of the Beginning

Protesters against the Syrian regime raise their hands in the victory sign in Hims province on December 21. Two days earlier the regime had agreed to allow an Arab League observer mission into the country.

by Mark Almond

No one could say for certain what Tunisian street vendor Mohamed Bouazizi was thinking when he set fire to himself on Dec. 17, 2010, in the town of Sidi Bouzid, but he probably could not have imagined that his action would spark in his own country a Jasmine Revolution, which in 2011 evolved into a wider revolt that became known throughout the world as the Arab Spring. His self-immolation galvanized citizens in North Africa and the Middle East to protest against government repression and corruption and in the process bring about the downfall of three heads of state (Tunisia, Egypt, and Libya). As reports of his desperate act soon spread far beyond Tunisia, various media—satellite television news, mobile phones, and social networking Web sites—turned a local suicide viral. What made Bouazizi's self-destructive response to an alleged shakedown by a local policewoman so electrifying was the sense among residents across the Arab world that it could have happened to them.

The Unrest. Even prior to Bouazizi's death, public protests had erupted in Tunisia. Local corruption as well as rumours of corruption at the top echelons of the government combined to destabilize the 23-year-old regime of Pres. Zine al-Abidine Ben Ali. Like other de facto presidents for life, Ben Ali favoured family members' involvement in government affairs. The Trabelsi extended family of his wife, Leila, reportedly had fingers in every pie, and this association had corroded the authority of the regime. Within a month of Bouazizi's lighting himself on fire, Ben Ali and his family had fled into exile. This development broke the decadeslong logjam in the Arab world, as some of the world's longest-serving rulers suddenly faced real challenges to their leadership. Only a few months earlier in Surt, Libya, Muammar al-Qaddafi, in power there since 1969, had hosted Ben Ali, along with Egyptian Pres. Hosni Mubarak (head of state since 1981) and Yemeni Pres. 'Ali 'Abd Allah Salih (in power since 1978).

The contrast between the aging rulers and their very young populace was striking. Most people could not remember a time before "Him." Listening to the dreary litany of praise and the rambling speeches of a "leader for life" was becoming intolerable for teenagers and twentysomethings whose parents had heard the same voice addressing them at that age. Demographic pressure was a constant from Morocco to Yemen, but inside the

AP

regimes discontent with family rule was growing. The very longevity of Arab leaders made the succession issue increasingly urgent. Older loyalists were irritated by the emergence of presidential sons, who not only were much younger than they were but also seemed to want to combine the pleasures of a playboy lifestyle with an accelerated promotion to the top.

Rumours of corruption as well as the disclosure by Wikileaks of U.S. diplomatic cables that provided Washington's inside knowledge all helped to corrode public respect for rulers, but what proved disastrous for them was the unwillingness of previously loyal generals to deploy tanks against protesters in a crisis. Mubarak had faced serious protests prior to late January 2011, but he had never lacked tools of repression. That month, however, his longtime defense minister, Mohamed Hussein Tantawi, turned against Mubarak and sent tanks to Cairo's Tahrir Square to protect demonstrators from Mubarak's police. The military's refusal to back Mubarak was rooted in tensions over Mubarak's grooming of his son Gamal as his successor as well as a push by Gamal's friends to advance their business interests at the expense of the Egyptian army's vast economic empire.

Both Ben Ali and Mubarak had alienated the generals by fostering their own clans, especially by promoting the prospect of turning the authoritarian republic into a dynastic regime by passing the presidency to a son. Qaddafi's fostering of his son Sayf al-Islam as heir apparent turned his old comrades in arms, notably Minister of the Interior Abdel Fattah Younis, into enemies when the crisis broke out in Libya only a week after the fall on February 11 of Mubarak.

Whereas the generals' refusal to support their regimes with tanks on the streets was decisive in the swift removal of both Ben Ali and Mubarak, Qaddafi's regime survived not only the defections of several senior figures but also seven months of assaults by NATO airstrikes. In the cases of Tunisia and Egypt, the West had many more subtle means of influence than it did over Libya. U.S. and European governments had spent years forging security cooperation ties with Tunis and Cairo to combat al-Qaeda–affiliated terrorist groups. The West had much less influence over Libya and Syria, which were considered two "rogue" states.

The prolonged violence in Libya, Syria, and Yemen reflected the role of

Riot police in Tunisia's capital, Tunis, drag away a protester on January 14. Later that day Zine al-Abidine Ben Ali abandoned the presidency and fled the country, less than a month after antigovernment protests in the country had begun.

clan loyalties and religious affiliation in helping to entrench regimes that faced considerable opposition. Though Qaddafi's was the weakest—owing to his eccentric rule that had left him without an effective military—defectors from his ramshackle forces had little to rely on to organize resistance to him.

Without NATO intervention, Qaddafi would probably have retained control over Libya, but his flamboyant televised threats to pursue the rebels in Benghazi *"zanga zanga"* ("from alley to alley") backfired because they raised the spectre in the Western media of a massacre. Already unpopular with the other members of the Arab League—and also with Iran for sectarian reasons—Qaddafi had no friends in the international community. When Libyan diplomats at the UN peeled away and called on the international community to step in, France and Britain in particular were ready to heed calls for "humanitarian intervention."

NATO, aware of the primitive level of Qaddafi's armaments and seeing evidence of desertion by senior figures such as Younis, used air power to protect Libyan civilians from Qaddafi's loyalists. Though NATO had confidence that Qaddafi's regime was already imploding, its combined forces, local rebels, and special forces from Arab states took from March 18 until late August to capture the capital, Tripoli. It was another two months before NATO airstrikes drove Qaddafi out of his final stronghold—his birthplace, Surt—and to a grisly fate at the hands of rebel forces. (*See* OBITUARIES.) The prolonged nature of the struggle for power in Libya indicated that Qaddafi had a significant minority of support and that many Libyans stood aside unsure of whom to support. Infighting among Qaddafi's enemies raised the spectre of civil war between them once the "Brother Leader" was gone. Libya lacked the religious mosaic of a country such as Syria. Libya's regional and tribal divisions meant that rivalries among Qaddafi's opponents were pronounced even as they struggled against his regime.

Protests in Syria began soon after the Libyan crisis turned into an armed conflict. Although Syrian Pres. Bashar al-Assad's uncle Rifʿat played the role of regime insider-turned-dissident from his exile in London, few Syrians respected the man whom many held responsible for having directed the brutal suppression of the uprising in Hamah some 30 years earlier. The absence of senior regime defectors meant that the Syrian regime maintained effective coordination over the state machine, whereas Qaddafi had relied on ad-hoc leadership by his sons, clan members, and a few mercenaries.

Though the West had deep security and economic ties in the Gulf states, it chose not to exert hard pressure on monarchies there to move toward

Christophe Ena/AP

democracy. When Bahrain's Sunni monarchy came under pressure from largely Shi'ite pro-democracy activists imitating the tactics employed by Egyptian demonstrators in Tahrir Square, it received active military support from Saudi forces. Saudi Arabia, which had a restive Shi'ite population in its eastern province, saw a risk of spillover from Bahrain's Shi'ite majority if protests there succeeded. The fact that Bahrain hosted the U.S. 5th Fleet and was an ally against Iran led U.S. politicians to downplay the repression there and to emphasize King Hamad ibn 'Isa al-Khalifah's public declarations in favour of reform rather than the heavy hand of his security forces.

The Gulf states supported opposition to the would-be republican dynasts but carefully protected their own monarchies. Oil and gas revenues gave them the resources to buy social peace—at least in the short term. Though Qatar's emir, Sheikh Hamad ibn Khalifah Al Thani, both funded the al-Jazeera satellite TV network (its reports stimulated more protests) and sent troops to support the rebellion against Qaddafi, at home he offered only to "consult" his own subjects on government policy.

The fall of the secular dictators Ben Ali and Mubarak left the Sunni Gulf monarchs in a much stronger position in the Arab League, which they used to legitimize calls for intervention against Libya and sanctions on Syria. Public opinion might have been more aroused against the regimes openly fighting their rebellious peoples, but in the Gulf countries there was a growing gap between the promotion of democracy abroad and the firm suppression of domestic dissent.

Religious Overtones. The motive for the oil-rich monarchs to promote political change seemed to have been less political than religious. Saudi and Qatari financial backing and satellite media openly promoted political parties associated with the Muslim Brotherhood in North Africa and Syria. Their hope, presumably, that the triumph of such parties in any new democracy would cement a Saudi-style Islamic social order was one of the reasons secular people, non-Muslim religious minorities, and Shi'ites reluctantly backed regimes that were similar to that of Assad's.

The reluctance of the Shi'ite-led Iraqi government to follow its U.S. ally in denouncing the Assad regime baffled Washington. It was not just that prominent Iraqis from the prime minister down were given asylum in Syria prior to 2003 as refugees escaping Iraqi leader Saddam Hussein. The main enemies of the post-Saddam democracy in Iraq were precisely the armed Sunni Muslim radicals whom Baghdad saw as the vanguard of the anti-Assad movement. Given that Syria's Alawites were seen in the same negative light by Sunnis as other Shi'ites—and were also allies of Iran—the regional struggle for power between the Wahhabi Sunni regime in Saudi Arabia and the Shi'ite Islamic Republic of Iran was threatening to erupt into a regional religious civil war.

The proponents of a secular democracy in Syria as the alternative to the secular Ba'thist dictatorship led by the Alawite Assad clan appeared to be hopelessly squeezed between the extremes. Other religious minorities, such as Syria's Christians and Druze, seemed to fear a Muslim Brotherhood regime and remained loyal to Assad. Over the border in Lebanon, an alliance made up of Shi'ite Hezbollah, Christians, and Druze had a parliamentary majority and rejected Arab League sanctions on Syria.

The other major regional player was Turkey. After initially denouncing foreign intervention, Turkish Prime Minister Recep Tayyip Erdogan became a vocal critic of Qaddafi's regime and a proponent of NATO intervention. As 2011 progressed, Erdogan also became fiercely critical of Assad's regime. Erdogan's Justice and Development Party (AKP) was widely seen as the model for an Islamic democratic movement in the Arab world. The AKP's electoral successes since 2002 were based on its successful handling of the economy (even during a worldwide crisis), and its characterization as an Islamic party gave it particular appeal to the religious-based opposition to secular dictatorships in the Arab world. The AKP model seemed to offer a reassuring mix of constitutional government, economic competence, and respect for the religious sentiments of the majority.

By metamorphosing into an active opponent of the Arab dictators, Erdogan reinforced the appeal of the "Turkish model." "Freedom and Justice" parties sprang up across the Arab-speaking world from Morocco to Syria, but they also emerged from the local branches of Muslim Brotherhood, raising fears among secularists and non-Muslim minorities that their electoral victories might provide democratic legitimation in any new constitutions for religious discrimination.

Tensions between Christian Copts and Muslims, which had been rising in 2010, became acute in 2011 after Mubarak's fall. Although the crowds in Tahrir Square and Alexandria included prominent Coptic supporters of democratization, so-called Salafists—or Wahhabi extremist groups—denounced

A Libyan rebel implores people to retreat as shelling from forces loyal to leader Muammar al-Qaddafi begins landing at the rebel position some 150 km (90 mi) east of Surt on March 29. Though NATO forces had begun airstrikes in support of the rebels, it took another five months for the opposition to dislodge the regime.

Anja Niedringhaus/AP

Protesters against the regime in Yemen roar their defiance in Sanaa on September 29 during a prolonged spasm of clashes between government and antigovernment forces. Throughout the year, Pres. ʿAli ʿAbd Allah Salih repeatedly agreed to step down and then reneged.

them as an alien and un-Islamic element. Disputes over new church-building projects spiraled out of control into street clashes, with more than 30 people killed in October. Intracommunal tensions as well as secular-Islamic rivalries could destabilize the tortuous process of democracy building in Egypt.

Outlook. Although the Arab Spring revolution was often compared to the "Velvet Revolutions" of 1989 that led to the collapse of communism, there were significant differences between the two. Whereas eastern Europeans had a clear alternative to communism—the market democracy in western Europe that seemed to offer the recipe for freedom and prosperity—Arabs had another apparent alternative other than widely discredited Marxism: Islam.

In the Arab world, aspirations for democracy and prosperity were also widespread, but Islam in its various forms offered either a strong modifying force or even outright opposition to the Western model of human rights and liberation of sexual minorities. Though Shariʿah (Islamic) law had been reinterpreted to take into account the needs of modern finance, it did not yet tolerate deviations from the personal code of morality that had been laid down 14 centuries earlier.

Though the would-be Mubarak, Qaddafi, and Salih republican dynasties were scotched by popular uprisings, some of the opposition movements continued to have a strong family element. Previous Arab revolutions, especially in the 1950s, had promised both democracy and republicanism but produced dictatorship and clan rule. Whether old family loyalties would trump new civic values was not certain but could not be ruled out.

Though it was probably too early to give a final verdict on the meaning of the Arab Spring, it was clear that it reenergized political engagement in the region, both by many of the people who actually lived there and by powerful actors such as the U.S. and its NATO allies. Given the region's oil reserves and the tensions surrounding Arab-Israeli and Arab-Iranian relations, the importance of the permutations of the eventual outcome could not be exaggerated.

Democratic Arab states might converge in their policies with the West's priorities.Whereas aging autocrats cooperated easily with the West, genuine Arab democracies could be assertive and uncomfortable neighbours. Israel, for instance, had enjoyed a regional monopoly on functioning democracy for decades, a factor that had given it a huge advantage in appealing for Western support. If a democratic Syria posed demands for the return of the Golan Heights, however, then Western acceptance of the status quo might crumble. Though Syrian exiles had reassured the West that they would be cooperative and drop Assad's alliance with Iran, Iraqi exiles had been similarly soothing about a post-Saddam Iraq.

In 2011, decades of authoritarian stability in the Arab world came to an end. Three alternatives beckoned: the advance of democracy, a return to another kind of authoritarian regime, or chaos. The teeming population of frustrated young people had had their ambitions and hopes raised, but the economic sources of their frustration had worsened in the previous 12 months. Clan and religious structures might prove stronger than the appeal of new nationwide democratic arrangements. The very drama of political revolution has worsened the economies, especially in Egypt and Tunisia, which are highly dependent on tourism and foreign investment. Past new democratic dawns had floundered when economic downturns destroyed the consensus for change. Successful Muslim democracies, such as Turkey and Malaysia, had enjoyed decades of peace to build up their economic foundations. Impatience for rapid change on all fronts after decades of authoritarian immobility could undermine the hopes of the Arab Spring, ironically, because it expressed the popular mood for complete change—now.

Mark Almond is a Visiting Professor in International Relations at Bilkent University, Ankara, Tur., and a member of the University of Oxford's History Faculty.

Hani Mohammed/AP

Japan's Deadly Earthquake and Tsunami

by Kenneth Pletcher and John P. Rafferty

On March 11, 2011, a massive earthquake—that was variously called the Great Sendai Earthquake or the Great Tohoku Earthquake—struck at 2:46 PM local time off the northeastern coast of Honshu, Japan's main island. The earthquake caused widespread havoc across northeastern Japan (the Tohoku region) and lesser amounts of damage farther to the south and west, but this destruction was dwarfed by the subsequent arrival of a series of relentless tsunami waves that devastated many coastal areas and instigated a major nuclear accident at a power station along the coast.

The Earthquake and Tsunami. The magnitude-9.0 temblor was caused by the rupture of a stretch of the subduction zone associated with the Japan Trench, the boundary that separates the Eurasian Plate from the subducting Pacific Plate. (Some geologists have argued that this portion of the Eurasian Plate is actually a fragment of the North American Plate called the Okhotsk microplate.) The epicentre of the earthquake was located in the western Pacific Ocean, some 130 km (80 mi) east of the city of Sendai, Miyagi prefecture, and the focus occurred at a depth of about 30 km (19 mi) below the ocean floor. A part of the subduction zone measuring approximately 300 km (190 mi) long by 150 km (95 mi) wide lurched about 50 m (about 165 ft) to the southeast and thrusted upward by some 10 m (33 ft). The force of the quake was so intense that it moved Honshu 2.4 m (7.9 ft) to the east. One geophysicist noted that the quake redistributed Earth's mass and reduced the length of the 24-hour day by 1.8 microseconds.

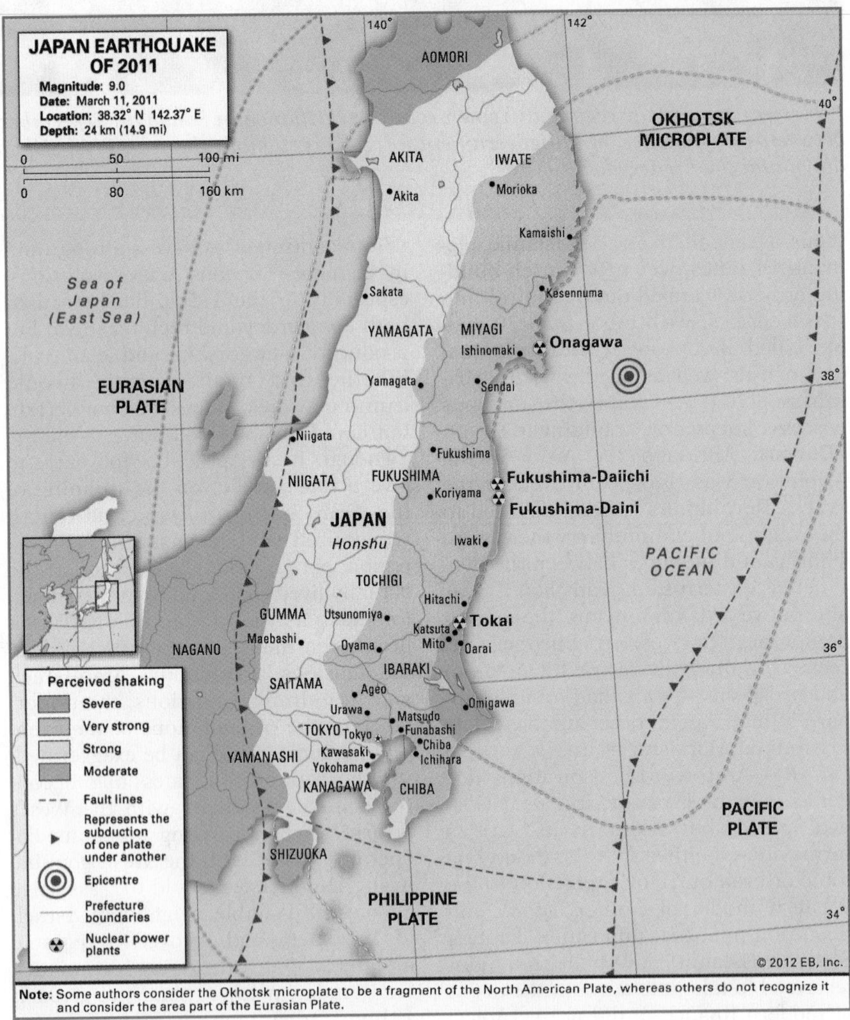

Map of the northern part of Japan's main island of Honshu depicting the intensity of shaking caused by the earthquake of March 11.

Shaking was felt as far away as Petropavlovsk-Kamchatsky, Russia; Kao-hsiung, Taiwan; and Beijing, China. It was preceded by several foreshocks, including a magnitude-7.2 event centred approximately 40 km (25 mi) away from

Houses are engulfed in flames while tsunami waves flood the Natori River and devastate parts of Natori, Miyagi prefecture, after a strong earthquake hit the area.

the epicentre of the main quake. Hundreds of aftershocks, dozens of magnitude 6.0 or greater and two of magnitude 7.0 or greater, followed in the days and weeks after the main quake. The magnitude-9.0 earthquake was the strongest to strike the region since the beginning of record keeping in the late 19th century. Only three earthquakes in recorded history were larger: the Chile earthquake of 1960 (magnitude 9.5), the Alaska earthquake of 1964 (magnitude 9.2), and the Sumatra earthquake of 2004 (magnitude 9.1).

The sudden horizontal and vertical thrusting of the Pacific Plate, which had been slowly advancing under the Eurasian Plate near Japan, displaced the water above and spawned a series of highly destructive tsunami waves. A wave measuring approximately 10 m (33 ft) high inundated the coast and flooded parts of the city of Sendai, including its airport and the surrounding countryside. According to some reports, one wave penetrated some 10 km (6 mi) inland after causing the Natori River, which separates Sendai from the city of Natori to the south, to overflow. Damaging tsunami waves also struck the coasts of Iwate prefecture, just north of Miyagi prefecture, and Fukushima, Ibaraki, and Chiba, the prefectures extending along the Pacific coast south of Miyagi. In addition to Sendai, other communities hard hit by the tsunami included Kamaishi and Miyako in Iwate; Ishinomaki, Kesennuma, and Shiogama in Miyagi; and Kitaibaraki and Hitachinaka in Ibaraki. As the floodwaters retreated back to the sea, they carried with them hundreds of vehicles and enormous quantities of debris, as well as thousands of victims caught in the deluge. Large stretches of land were left submerged under seawater, particularly in lower-lying areas, for weeks and even months.

The earthquake triggered tsunami warnings throughout the Pacific basin. The tsunami raced outward from the epicentre at speeds that approached 800 km (500 mi) per hour. It generated waves 3.3–3.6 m (11–12 ft) high along the coasts of Kauai and Hawaii in the Hawaiian Islands chain and 1.5-m (5-ft) waves along the island of Shemya in the Aleutian Islands chain. Several hours later 2.7-m (9-ft) tsunami waves struck the coasts of California and Oregon in North America. Finally, some 18 hours after the quake, waves roughly 0.3 m (1 ft) high reached the coast of Antarctica and caused a portion of the Sulzberger Ice Shelf to break off its outer edge.

Casualties and Property Damage. Initial reports of casualties following the tsunami put the death toll in the hundreds, with hundreds more missing. That number in both categories increased dramatically in the following days as the extent of the devastation—especially in coastal areas—became known and rescue operations got under way. Within two weeks of the disaster, the official count of deaths had exceeded 10,000; more than one and a half times that number were still listed as missing and presumed dead. By then it was evident that the earthquake and tsunami had produced one of the deadliest natural disasters in Japanese history, rivaling the major earthquake and tsunami that had occurred off the coast of Iwate prefecture in June 1896. As the search for victims continued, the official count of those confirmed dead or still missing rose to about 28,500. As more people thought to be missing were found to be alive, however, that figure began to drop; by the end of the year, it had been reduced to fewer than 19,300.

Most of those killed were victims of the tsunami waves. Coastal cities and towns as well as vast areas of farmland in the tsunami's path were inundated by swirling waters that swept enormous quantities of houses, boats, cars,

Yasushi Kanno—The Yomiuri Shimbun/AP

Aerial view of the destruction in Sendai, Miyagi prefecture, Japan, three days after being struck by the March 11 earthquake and tsunami.

trucks, and other debris along with them. As the extent of the destruction became known, it became clear how many thousands of people were missing—including, in some cases, half or more of a locality's population. Among those who initially were unaccounted for were people on a ship that was washed away by the tsunami and passengers on several trains reported as missing in Iwate and Miyagi prefectures. The ship was later found (and the people on board rescued), and all trains were located as well.

Although much of the destruction was caused by the tsunami waves along Japan's Pacific coastline, the earthquake was responsible for considerable damage over a wide area. Notable were fires in several cities, including a petrochemical plant in Sendai, a portion of the city of Kesennuma in Miyagi prefecture, northeast of Sendai, and an oil refinery at Ichihara in Chiba prefecture, near Tokyo. In Fukushima, Ibaraki, and Chiba prefectures, thousands of homes were completely or partially destroyed by the temblor and aftershocks. Infrastructure was also heavily affected throughout eastern Tohoku as roads and rail lines were damaged, electric power was knocked out, and water and sewerage systems were disrupted. In Fukushima a dam burst close to the prefectural capital of Fukushima city.

The Fukushima Nuclear Emergency. Of significant concern following the main shock and the tsunami was the status of several nuclear power stations in the Tohoku region. The reactors at the three nuclear power plants closest to the quake's epicentre were shut down automatically following the earthquake. This process also cut the main power to those plants and their cooling systems. The subsequent inundation by the tsunami waves damaged the backup generators at some of those plants, most notably at the Fukushima Daiichi ("Number One") plant operated by the Tokyo Electric Power Co. (TEPCO). Fukushima Daiichi, made up of six boiling-water reactors constructed between 1971 and 1979, was situated along the Pacific coast in northeastern Fukushima prefecture about 100 km (60 mi) south of Sendai. At the time of the accident, only reactors 1–3 were operational, and reactor 4 served as temporary storage for spent fuel rods.

With power gone, the cooling systems failed in three reactors within the first few days of the disaster, and their cores subsequently overheated, which led to partial meltdowns of the fuel rods. (Some plant workers, however, attributed at least one partial meltdown to coolant pipe bursts caused by the earthquake's ground vibrations.) Melted material fell away from the rods and landed on the bottom of the containment vessels in reactors 1 and 2 and burned sizable holes in the floor of each vessel. These holes partially exposed the nuclear material in the cores. Explosions resulting from the buildup of pressurized hydrogen gas in the outer containment buildings enclosing reactors 1, 2, and 3, along with a fire touched off by rising temperatures in the spent fuel rods placed in reactor 4, led to the release of significant levels of radiation from the facility in the days and weeks following the earthquake. Workers sought to cool and stabilize the damaged reactors by pumping seawater and boric acid into them.

Because of concerns over possible radiation exposure, Japanese officials established a 30-km (18-mi) no-fly zone around the facility, and an area of 20 km (12.5 mi) around the plant was evacuated. The evacuation zone was later expanded to coincide with the borders of the 30-km no-fly radius. Within this 10-km (6.2-mi) outer ring, residents were asked to either leave or remain indoors. The appearance of increased levels of

Airman 1st Class Katrina R. Menchaca/U.S. Air Force photo

radiation in some local food and water supplies prompted officials in Japan and overseas to issue warnings about their consumption. At the end of March, seawater near the Daiichi facility was discovered to have been contaminated with high levels of radioactive iodine-131. The contamination stemmed from the exposure of pumped-in seawater to radiation inside the facility; this water later leaked into the ocean through cracks in water-filled trenches and tunnels located between the facility and the ocean. On April 6, plant officials announced that the cracks had been sealed, and later that month workers began to pump the irradiated water to an on-site storage building until it could be properly treated.

In mid-April Japanese nuclear regulators elevated the severity level of the nuclear emergency at the Fukushima Daiichi facility from 5 to 7—the highest level on the scale created by the International Atomic Energy Agency—placing the Fukushima accident in the same category as the Chernobyl accident, which occurred in the Soviet Union in 1986. At year's end, radiation levels remained high in the evacuation zone, and government officials remarked that the area might be uninhabitable for decades. However, they also announced that radiation levels had declined in five towns located just beyond the original 20-km evacuation zone to levels low enough that residents would be allowed to return to their homes. Japanese Prime Minister Yoshihiko Noda declared the facility stable after the cold shutdown of the reactors was completed on December 16.

Relief Efforts. In the first hours after the earthquake, then Japanese Prime Minister Naoto Kan moved to set up an emergency command centre in Tokyo, and a large number of rescue workers and some 100,000 members of the Japanese Self-Defense Force were rapidly mobilized to deal with the crisis. In addition, the Japanese government requested that U.S. military personnel stationed in the country be available to help in relief efforts, and a U.S. Navy aircraft carrier was dispatched to the area. Several countries, including Australia, China, India, New Zealand, South Korea, and the United States, sent search-and-rescue teams, and dozens of other countries and major international relief organizations, such as the Red Cross and Red Crescent, pledged financial and material support to Japan. In addition, a large number of private and nongovernmental organizations within Japan and worldwide soon established relief funds to aid victims and assist with rescue and recovery efforts.

The rescue work itself was hampered initially by the difficulty in getting personnel and supplies to the devastation zone; compounding the difficulty were periods of inclement weather that curtailed air operations. Workers in the disaster zones then faced widespread seas of destruction: vast areas, even whole towns and cities, had been washed away or covered by great piles of mud and debris. Although some people were rescued from the rubble in the first several days following the main shock and tsunami, most of the relief work involved the recovery of bodies, including hundreds that began washing ashore in several areas after having been swept out to sea.

In the immediate aftermath of the disaster, several hundred thousand people were in shelters, often with limited or negligible supplies of food or water, and tens of thousands more remained stranded and isolated in the worst-hit areas as rescuers worked to reach them. Within days the number of displaced people in the Fukushima area grew as the situation with the nuclear reactors on the coast deteriorated and people left the quarantined area. Gradually many people were able to find other places to stay in the Tohoku area, or they relocated to other parts of the country; some quarter million people were still in hundreds of shelters in the region two weeks after the quake, but by the end of the year, that number had been reduced by more than two-thirds. Tens of thousands of these displaced residents were living in some 50,000 prefabricated temporary housing units that had been set up in Sendai and other tsunami-damaged locations.

In the weeks following the disaster, much of northern Honshu's transportation and services infrastructure was at least partially restored, and repairs continued until train lines and major highways were again fully operational. The region's power supply continued to be affected, however, by the ongoing situation at the Fukushima plant, resulting in temporary power outages and rolling blackouts. The loss of businesses and factories from earthquake and tsunami damage, as well as the uncertainties surrounding the power supply, severely reduced the region's postdisaster manufacturing output. Industries most affected included those producing semiconductors and other high-technology items and automobiles.

Kenneth Pletcher is the Senior Editor for East and South Asian Geography and History for Encyclopædia Britannica.

John P. Rafferty is the Associate Editor of Earth and Life Sciences for Encyclopædia Britannica.

Nuclear safety workers scan an evacuee for radiation exposure after civilians were evacuated from the quarantine area around a nuclear power station in Fukushima prefecture, Japan, that was damaged in the earthquake and tsunami.

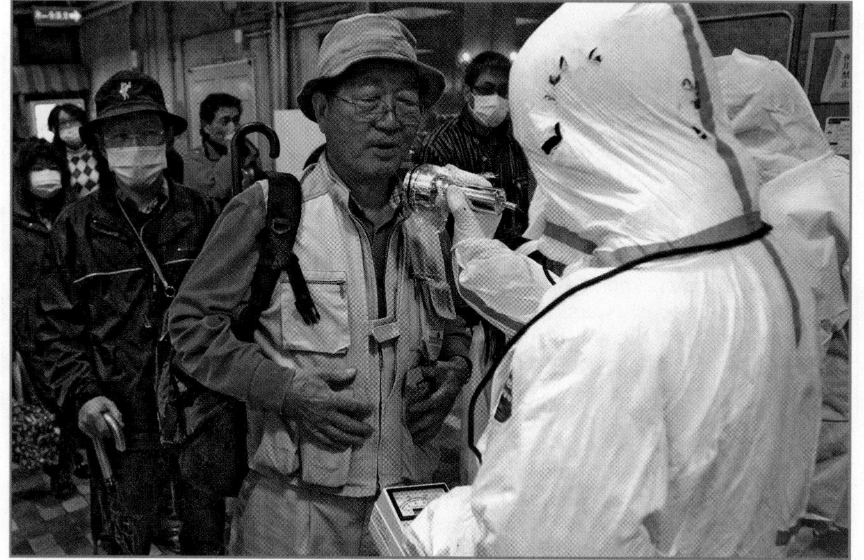

Wally Santana/AP

SPECIAL REPORT

The U.S. Census of 2010: Foreshadowing a Century of Change

by William H. Frey

In 2011 the U.S. government released detailed data from the national census taken on April 1, 2010. As the country's demographic yardstick, the 2010 census came at a time when the U.S. was undergoing notable transitions. The first decade of the 21st century showed a country whose growth not only had slowed but also had become more dependent on "new" minorities than in the past—fostered by continuing waves of immigrants and their children. Yet a vestige of that past—the large baby-boom generation—was leading the trajectory toward a further aging of the country's population. Those dynamics, along with changing social mores, affected the kinds of households that were formed—different not only from those of the 1950s but also from those of the 1990s. While there was a continued shift toward the Sun Belt states and the suburbs, there were some new turns—affected in part by the decade's volatile economy. Also affecting those shifts were reversals in long-standing African American population movements.

The 2010 census questionnaire was one of the shortest in U.S. history; only 10 questions were asked. The answers, however, revealed some startling changes in the country's growth, along with race, aging, and household makeup, as fundamental demographic transitions took place that were likely to shape the U.S. population in the decades to come.

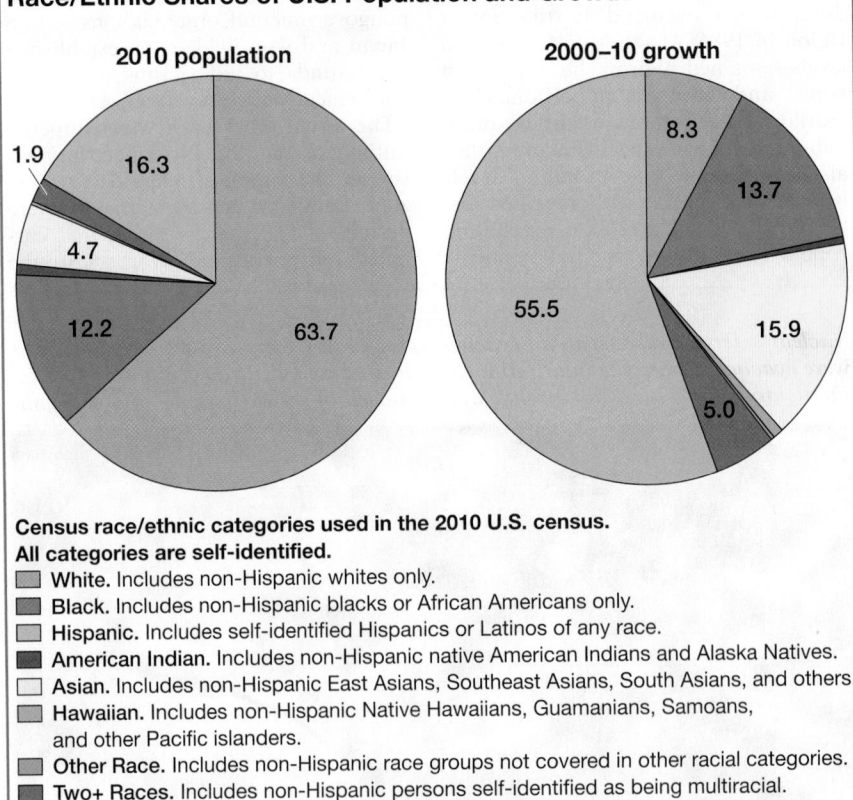

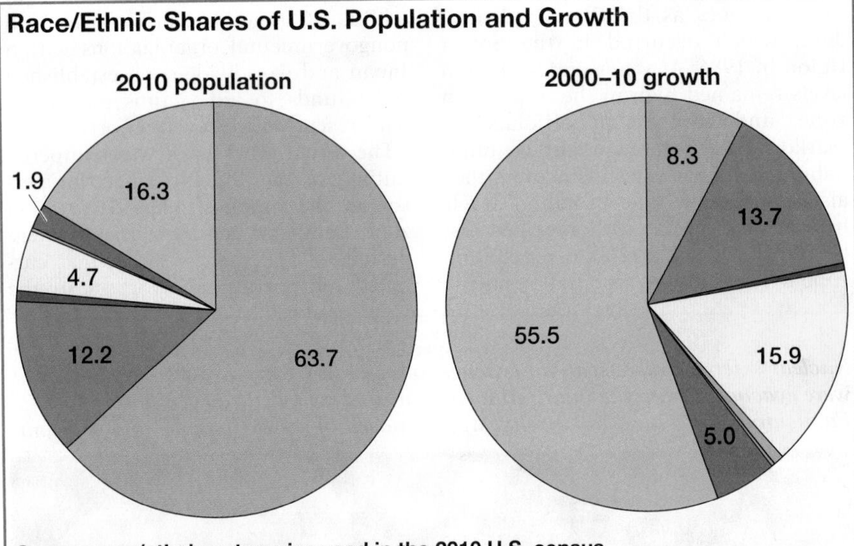

Race/Ethnic Shares of U.S. Population and Growth
2010 population
2000–10 growth

16.3
4.7
12.2
63.7
8.3
13.7
55.5
15.9

Census race/ethnic categories used in the 2010 U.S. census.
All categories are self-identified.
White. Includes non-Hispanic whites only.
Black. Includes non-Hispanic blacks or African Americans only.
Hispanic. Includes self-identified Hispanics or Latinos of any race.
American Indian. Includes non-Hispanic native American Indians and Alaska Natives.
Asian. Includes non-Hispanic East Asians, Southeast Asians, South Asians, and others.
Hawaiian. Includes non-Hispanic Native Hawaiians, Guamanians, Samoans, and other Pacific islanders.
Other Race. Includes non-Hispanic race groups not covered in other racial categories.
Two+ Races. Includes non-Hispanic persons self-identified as being multiracial.
Source: William H. Frey analysis

The Slowest Population Growth Rate in 70 Years. The 2010 census demonstrated that the image of the U.S. as both a fast-growing and a youthful country can now be laid to rest. The 2000–10 population growth rate of 9.7% was the lowest since the Great Depression (when the 1940 census showed that the

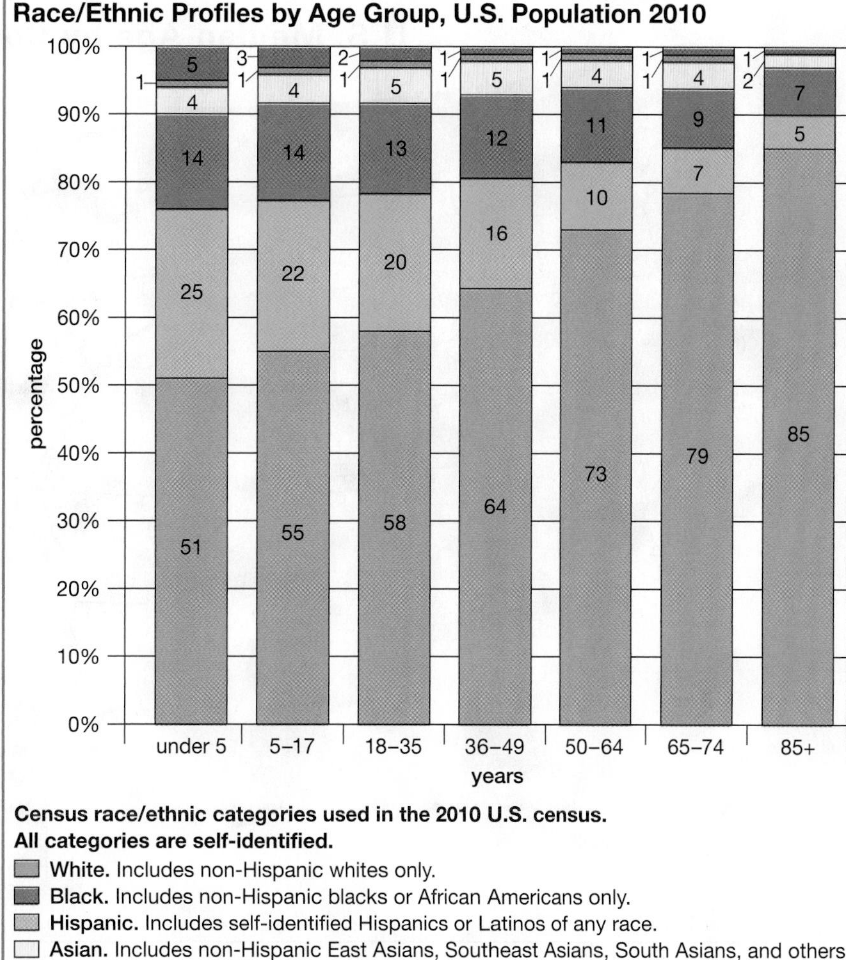

Source: William H. Frey analysis

growth rate during the 1930s was just 7.3%). That may seem surprising, given the 13.2% growth in the 1990s or even the 9.8% growth in the recession-ridden 1980s. There are two reasons why growth slowed. The short-term reason is the downturn in immigration associated with the widespread economic woes late in the decade. Longer-term, however, there is a continuing issue: the aging of the population, leading to a continued natural-increase slowdown. The country's median age in 2010 was 37.2, up from 32.6 in 1990, and it will continue to rise. The country's official 2010 population of 308,745,538 was the world's third largest (after China and India), with growth outpacing "older" countries such as Japan and Germany. Even continued immigration will not likely bring a return in the U.S. to 1990s-level growth, however.

The Growth in "New" Minorities. The more-tepid growth of the U.S. population would have slowed even further had it not been for the "new" fast-growing minorities: Hispanics, Asians, and a smaller multiracial population. Although whites still make up 64% of the population, they contributed only 8% to the country's 2000–10 gain of some 27 million people, compared with contributions of 55% by Hispanics and 16% by Asians. (*See* Figure on page 180.) The Hispanic population is now 50 million strong, composing 16% of the population, compared with 12% for blacks and 4.7% for Asians.

Minority growth was especially important for the population under the age of 18. The sharp aging of the country's white population and consequent lower fertility led to a decline of 4.3 million white children over the decade. Were it not for the 5.5 million gain in Hispanic and Asian children, there would have been an absolute loss in the number of people under age 18. That shift was also reflected in the disparate median ages of 41 for whites and 27 for Hispanics.

Aging Baby Boomers. Over the course of the past decade, the large 75+ million baby-boom generation moved squarely into advanced middle age—thus inflating the over-45 age group. The 10-year growth rate for the population aged 45 and older was 25.6%—18 times larger than for the population under age 45. Among other milestones, that marks the first time that more than half the U.S. voting-age population is older than 45—a statistic that is not likely to reverse. Perhaps just as important for the future is the 50% growth in the group aged 55–64—reflecting the ascension of leading-edge baby boomers into their "presenior" years. In January 2011 the baby-boom train began inflating the senior age group, 65 and over, which is projected to increase as a share of the population from 13% in 2010 to 20% in 2030.

Racial/Ethnic Generational Disparities. The new minority-driven growth of the younger part of the population—coupled with the aging of the mostly white baby-boom and senior generations—is creating something of a cultural generation gap between the young and the old. Among those aged 50 and over, who were born before 1960, whites make up more than 70% of the population, and blacks are the largest minority group. Among those under age 35, born since 1975, whites make up less than 60% of the population, and Hispanics are the largest minority. (*See* Figure above.) The generation gap is more pronounced in the 2010 census and is likely to continue for the next decade or two. In some cases it will create political divisions on issues that appeal to older segments of the population, such as social security and health care, versus those of more concern to younger citizens, such as education and affordable housing.

Decline in Traditional Households. The aging of the population and the changing mores of young people with regard to marriage have combined to further reduce two historical staples of American life: "traditional" households—those with a husband, a wife, and at least one child—and married couples.

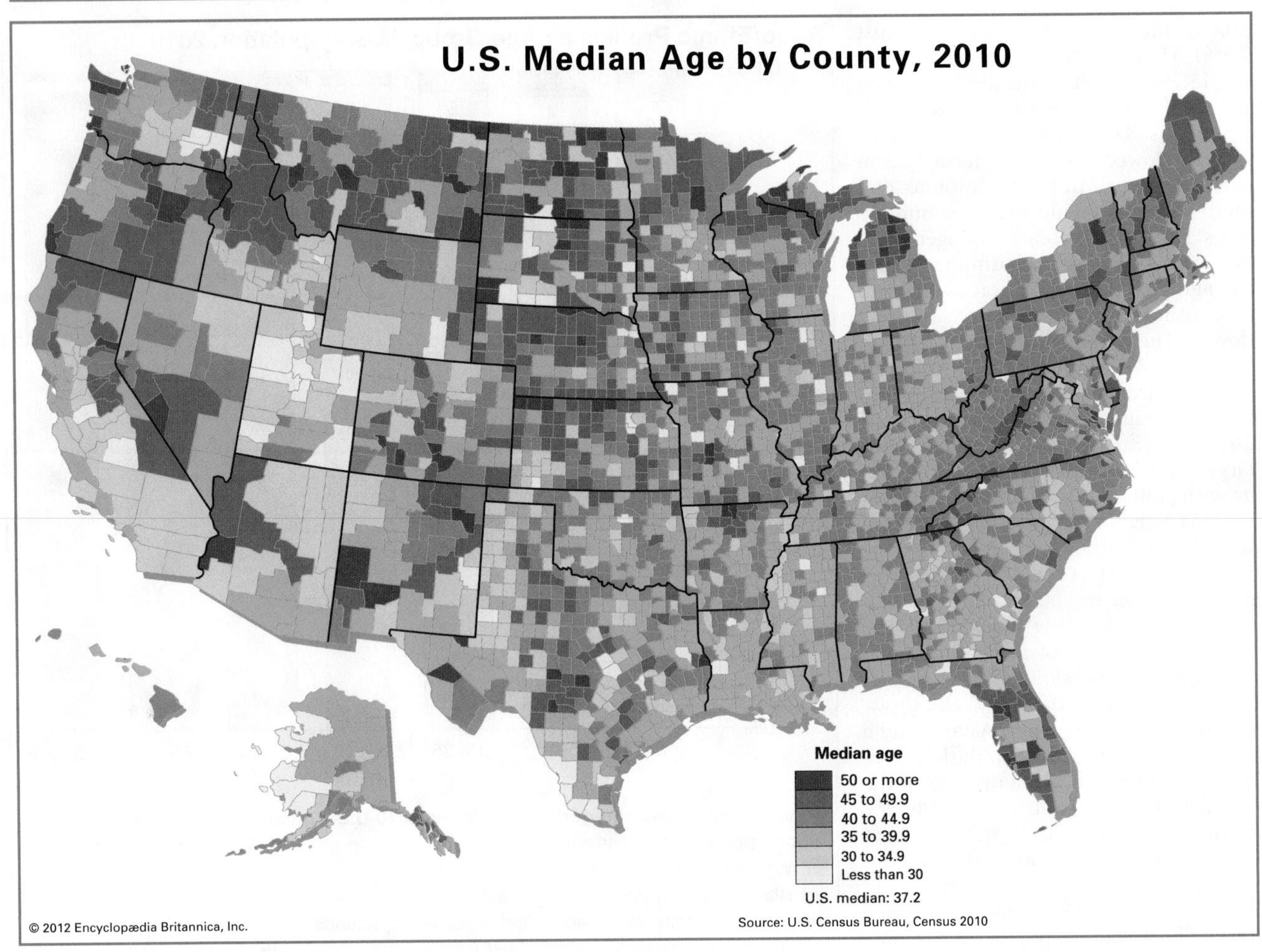

There was an absolute decline in the former, which now make up barely one-fifth of all households—down from 23% in 2000 and 40% in 1970. The number of married couples, once the mainstay of American life, dipped to less than half of all households. Among household types on the rise are persons living alone (both young and old), which account for 27% of the whole. Unmarried-partner households are also more prevalent, though they still make up only 2.5% of all households in the U.S. The census also reported that there are more than 600,000 same-sex couples, a tiny but rising portion of the population.

Gains in the Sun Belt and Suburbs. Although all regions grew more slowly in the past decade, the South and West Sun Belt states continued to outpace the states in the Northeast and Midwest, with about 14% population growth for the former, compared with less than 4% for the latter. The gains in the West have finally led to a larger population in that region than in the Midwest; at the same time, one Midwestern state, Michigan, showed a net population decline. The middecade housing bubble propelled population growth in states such as Arizona and Nevada before the subsequent "mortgage meltdown" and recession deflated some of that growth. Still, the latter two states led all others, with growth rates of 25% and 35%, respectively. "New minorities," including Hispanics, Asians, and persons classed as multiracial, were important sources of growth in both fast- and slow-growing states. Of the 49 states that gained population, those minorities accounted for more than half the growth in 33.

The congressional reapportionment implications of those shifts led to a net gain of 10 seats for the Sun Belt, with only Louisiana, of the Sun Belt states, showing a loss. Texas, which was immune to much of the decade's economic woes, was the big winner—gaining four congressional seats—while Florida added two. The coast-to-interior movement within the West left California without a seat gain for the first time since it achieved statehood, whereas nearby Arizona, Nevada, Utah, and Washington each picked up one seat. Georgia and South Carolina were the other winners. The biggest losers of seats in the Frost Belt were New York and Ohio, each dropping two, with Illinois, Iowa, Massachusetts, Michigan, Missouri, New Jersey, and Pennsylvania losing one each.

The decade continued to favour growth in metropolitan areas and especially the suburbs, the latter now home to more than half the country's population. Once again, the late-decade housing crisis reduced suburban gains, especially in large metropolitan areas. Minorities were particularly important for gains in metropolitan areas, as 42 of the 100 largest areas showed absolute declines in their white populations due to both out-migration and aging.

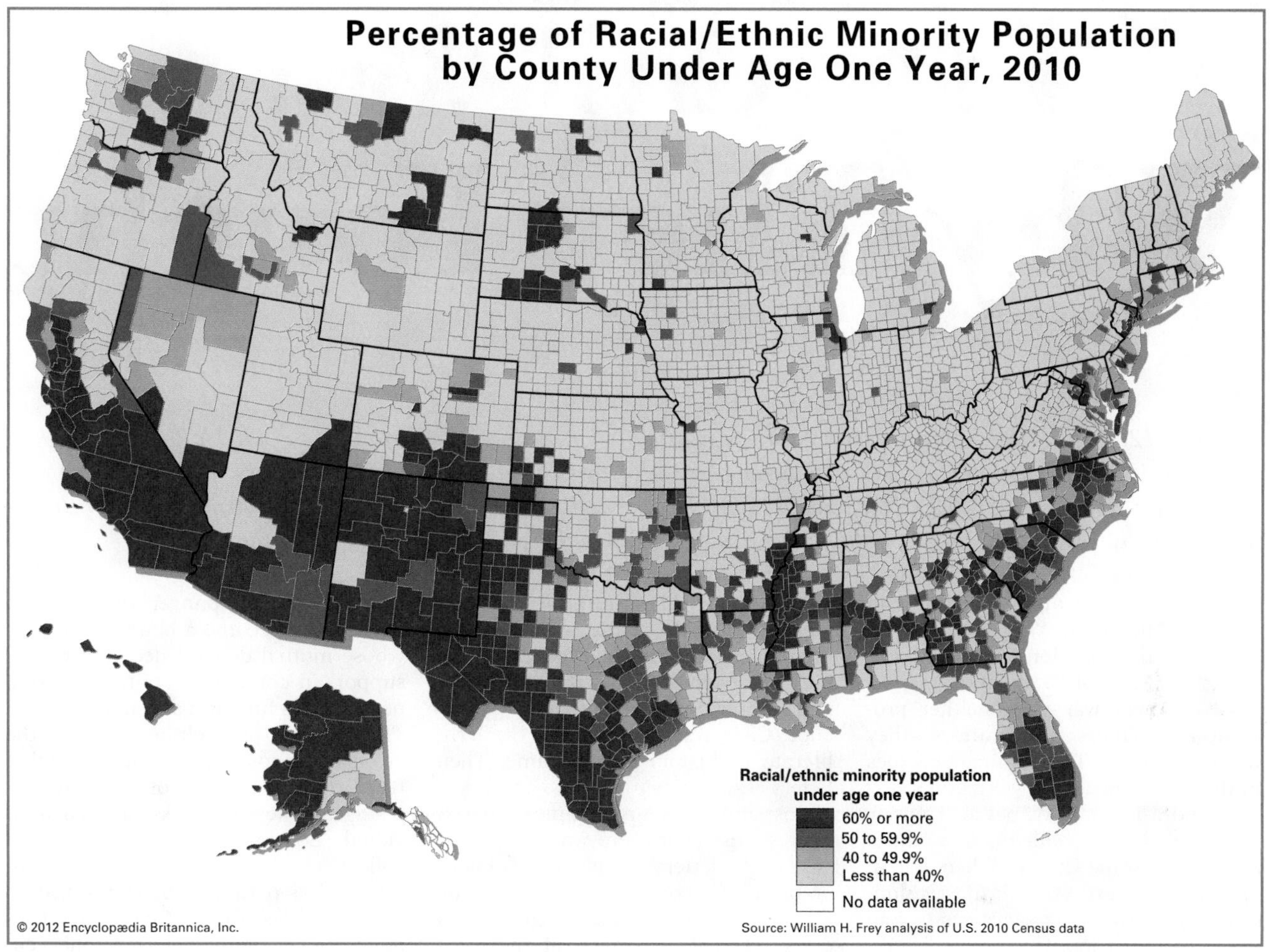

Black Population Reversals. The census revealed two reversals of well-known shifts in the black population. The first was the sharp shift of blacks away from the Northeast, the Midwest, and the West to the Southern regions. For the first time, the metropolitan areas of Detroit, Chicago, and New York City—three historical destinations of South-to-North black migrants—showed absolute losses of blacks. The major metropolitan gainers, led by Atlanta, Dallas, and Houston, were primarily in the South. Over the course of the decade, more than three-quarters of the country's black population growth occurred in the South.

The second reversal was a decline in urban black populations within most metropolitan areas with large black populations, as part of a wholesale black relocation to the suburbs. For the first time, more blacks lived in the suburbs than in the cities, leading to lower levels of neighbourhood segregation between whites and blacks overall.

Geographic Transformations. The 2010 census points up several demographic transformations. New minority populations propel growth, especially in younger parts of the population and in faster-growing states. At the same time, the less-diverse baby boomers are aging everywhere. Although new minorities are gradually dispersing, they have not heavily affected a swath of states in the interior and northern parts of the country that are rapidly aging and experiencing declines in families with children. Those states tend to have the highest median ages and lowest shares of traditional families, with 23 of them showing absolute declines in their child populations in the past decade. (*See* Map on page 182.)

On the other hand, the faster-growing states, located primarily in the South, the West, and the coastal areas, are aging less rapidly and exhibiting gains in their increasingly diverse child populations. Texas, for example, over the decade gained nearly one million children, 95% of whom were Hispanic. Similar minority gains among Hispanics, blacks, and others propelled large gains in child populations in Florida, Georgia, North Carolina, and other Sun Belt states, most of which showed healthy gains in married-with-children households. Those increases are in parts of the country where large shares of infants are minorities. (*See* Map above.)

Eventually, the rest of the country will look like those more-diverse, faster-growing states. As that transformation takes place, however, politics, policies, and civic activities will need to accommodate parts of the country that bear a greater resemblance to the past and others that point toward the future.

William H. Frey is a demographer and Senior Fellow with the Brookings Institution in Washington, D.C., and Research Professor in Population Studies at the University of Michigan.

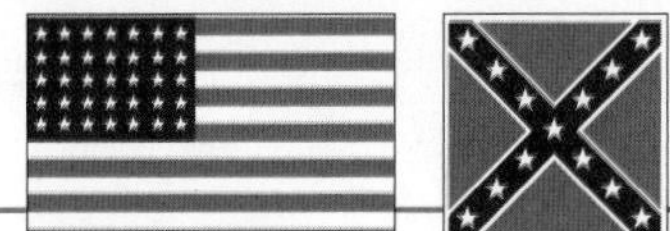

The Civil War: Why They Fought

by James M. McPherson

On April 12, 2011, the 150th anniversary of the Battle of Fort Sumter, historian James M. McPherson presented in Charleston, S.C., a slightly longer version of this lecture on Civil War soldiers. It was the last lecture in a series (April 8–12, 2011) called "Why They Fought: Reflections on the 150th Anniversary of the American Civil War," produced by the Fort Sumter–Fort Moultrie Historical Trust, Charleston.

The motivation of soldiers in the Civil War is a subject that has long intrigued me. Most of the fighting men in that war were neither professional soldiers nor draftees—they were volunteers. The dominant themes in their wartime letters were homesickness and a longing for peace. The pay was poor; the large enlistment bounties received by some Union soldiers late in the war were exceptional; most volunteers made economic sacrifices to join the army. What motivated them to give up several of the best years of their lives—indeed, to give up life itself in a war that killed almost as many American soldiers as all the rest of the wars this country has fought combined? What enabled them to overcome that most basic of instincts, self-preservation, and risk their lives in combat?

This is a vital question in all wars, for without such sacrificial behaviour by soldiers, armies could not fight. For the American Civil War, the question is perhaps more baffling than for most wars, because some traditional answers have little if any relevance. Religious fanaticism and ethnic hatreds do not apply; discipline was notoriously lax in Civil War armies; training was minimal; the coercive power of the state was relatively weak; subordination and unquestioning obedience to orders were alien to this most democratic and individualistic of 19th-century societies. Yet the Union and Confederate armies mobilized three million men. What made these men tick? What motivated them to fight and if necessary to die—a fate suffered by more than 600,000 of them?

To answer this question, the best place to go is the writings of these soldiers themselves, in their letters to families and friends during the war or the diaries they kept during their experience. Civil War armies were the most literate in history to that time. Their letters and diaries constitute a rich and almost unique source—almost unique in the sense that there was no censorship of the letters of Civil War soldiers, no prohibition or discouragement of diary keeping, as there has been in many other wars. Thus, many of these letters—and diaries—were remarkably candid and detailed about important matters that would not get into censored letters: morale, relations between officers and men, details of marches and battles, politics and ideology and war aims, and so on.

There is a large literature on combat motivation in modern armies—especially in World War II armies and more recent wars. When I began my research in Civil War soldiers' letters and diaries, I was guided in what to look for by this literature. It investigated the traditional assumptions about what motivates soldiers to fight: patriotism, ideology, religion, ideals of duty and honour and manhood; glory and adventure; training and discipline; and coercion. These studies found that while some or all of these factors in combination may have been important for some soldiers, for most of them the key factor was what the social psychologists called "primary group cohesion."

What is that? The soldier's primary group consists of his comrades in the squad or platoon or gun crew. Bonded by the common danger they face in battle, they become a band of brothers whose mutual dependence and mutual support in combat create the cohesion necessary to function as a fighting unit. The survival of each member of the group depends on the others' doing their jobs; the survival of the group depends on the steadiness of each individual. So does their individual and collective self-respect. If any of them falters or is paralyzed by fear—skedaddles or skulks, to use Civil War terminology—that individual not only endangers his own and the others' survival but also courts their contempt and ostracism, loses face, and loses self-respect as a man. The compulsion of the peer group is a greater force than coercion by officers or by the state. As one of the leading writers on combat motivation in World War II, S.L.A. Marshall, put it in his book *Men Against Fire*: "No man wants to die; what induces him to risk his life bravely?" It is not "belief in a cause"; "when the chips are down, a man fights to help the man next to him. . . . Men do not fight for a cause but because they do not want to let their comrades down."

Given the prominence of this theme in studies of 20th-century soldiers, it was one of the most important things I was sensitive to in my research. And I found a great deal of evidence for it in the writings of Civil War soldiers. An Ohio colonel felt forever bonded to the men with whom he endured the horrible carnage of Shiloh: "Those who had stood shoulder to shoulder during the two terrible days of that bloody battle,

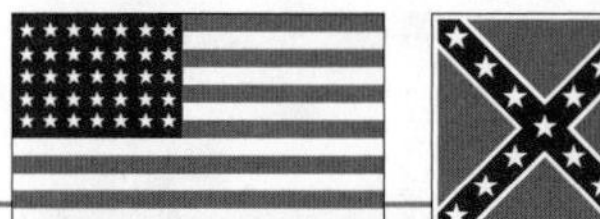

were hooped with steel, with bands stronger than steel."

The fear of giving way to fear, the shame of cowardice in the eyes of one's peers, was also a powerful motivator in Civil War armies. The greatness of Stephen Crane's novel about a young Civil War soldier, *Red Badge of Courage*, is that it brilliantly portrays this sentiment. And so do many of the soldiers' letters I have read. A Connecticut private wrote just before his first battle: "I am so afraid I shall prove a coward. I can hardly think of anything else." Afterward he uttered a sigh of relief that he had passed the test: "A little shaky at first but soon got used to the music. I know no one will say that I behaved cowardly in the least." An Ohio soldier confessed in his diary that he was shaking like a leaf before he went into his first action, but he was determined nevertheless to "stand up to my duties like a man, let the consequences be as they might. I had rather die like a brave man, than have a coward's ignominy cling around my name and live. . . . Of all names most terrible and to be dreaded is *coward*."

One important factor that made this motivation so important was that most Civil War companies were recruited from the same community or region. Many of the men in a regimental company had been friends and neighbours back home. Their families knew each other. Thus, any reports of cowardice or other nonperformance in battle not only ruined a man's reputation among his comrades but also brought disgrace to his family and community. He could never hold up his head again in the army or at home. An Ohio officer wrote to his wife about another officer from their town who had "proved himself a coward on the battlefield . . . what a stigma for men to transmit to their posterity—your father a coward!" A North Carolina sergeant said that if any man in his regiment showed "the white feather, he should never return to live in N. Carolina."

Soldiers' letters and diaries contain much evidence of other kinds of motivation for fighting: for example, leadership, especially leadership by example of officers who would not ask their men to do anything they were not willing to do themselves; the motives of defending hearth and home against an invading enemy, and of revenge against a foe that has ravaged one's country, which of course operated mainly for Confederate rather than Union soldiers; the physiological effects of extreme stress and fear, and of rage, which causes the adrenal glands to pump an extraordinary amount of adrenalin into the body, producing an altered state of consciousness wherein men sometimes lost all sensation of fear and danger, gained almost superhuman strength, and behaved with a sort of fighting madness that defied the normal instinct of self-preservation. Civil War soldiers did not understand the body chemistry that produced this phenomenon, but their descriptions of feelings and actions during combat make it clear that many of them experienced it.

Religion is another complex factor in combat behaviour that was important for Civil War soldiers. Prayer to God for protection from danger is a common theme in letters and diaries. It probably helped many of them to face that danger more readily. A powerful theme in the letters is a kind of fatalism, a belief that if one's time had come, God would take him no matter what; if not, God would protect him even in the midst of bullets—and this too helped soldiers face those bullets. As a captain in the 4th Alabama Infantry expressed it in a letter to his wife: "I might as well die at home as in battle, [for] we are feeble instruments in the hands of the Supreme Power [and] no man can die before the day appointed by God, or live after that hour."

Civil War soldiers belonged to a generation powerfully affected by the Second Great Awakening in the history of American Protestantism. Many soldiers believed literally in salvation, in a life after death. The travail of life on Earth was merely preparation for a better existence hereafter. Thus, they could confront the possibility of death with greater equanimity than could a nonbeliever, for whom death was the end of existence. A South Carolina artillery officer confessed that the prospect of death terrified him because "I am not a christian—a christian can afford to be a philosopher because he believes in a certain reunion hereafter but a poor devil who cant believe it hasn't that support." For those who did have that support, it played a part in nerving them to face the prospect of death in battle, to act with courage in the belief that even a terrible death was not the end of life. A Massachusetts soldier told his wife that "if I shall fall in this contest it is but going home to my *savior* whom I love . . . if we meet not again on earth prepare to meet me in Heaven." This religious conviction was not a motive for fighting, but a way of overcoming the greatest inhibition to combat, the fear of death.

One of the more controversial findings in my research on Civil War soldiers' motivation is the role of ideology. In much of the literature on this subject, one might get the impression that such a role did not exist. In some quarters there has been a belief that most Civil War soldiers had little or no idea what they were fighting for. Some years ago the commander of the New York branch of the Sons of Union Veterans said that "it wasn't because our fathers knew what they were fighting for that they were heroes. They didn't know what they were fighting for, exactly, and they fought on anyway. That's what made them heroes."

But, to the contrary, the prevalence of ideological themes in the letters and diaries of many soldiers jumps out at the reader. Many, many soldiers were intensely aware of the issues at stake in the war and passionately concerned about them. Their expressions on these issues ranged from simple but heartfelt avowals of patriotism to well-informed and often quite sophisticated discussions of the Constitution, state's rights, nationalism, majority rule, self-government, democracy, liberty, and slavery.

To provide some background and context for understanding this, remember that these were the most literate armies in history to that time. They also came from the world's most democratic and highly politicized society. They had grown up in the highly charged political culture of the 1850s with its polarization between slavery and antislavery, South and North, the Southern Rights Democratic Party and the new antislavery Republican Party. Their median age at the time of enlistment was 23½, which meant that most of them had voted in the election of 1860, the most heated and momentous election in American history, which brought out almost 85% of eligible voters. These citizen soldiers continued to vote during the war, not only electing some of their officers in these volunteer regiments but also voting in state and national elections by absentee ballot. Americans were the world's preeminent newspaper-reading people in the 19th century. Soldiers continued this habit during the war, when they eagerly snapped up newspapers available in camp a few days after publication.

A Mississippi private wrote in his diary during the winter of 1862: "Spend much time in reading the daily papers & discussing the war question in general." Two years later an Alabama officer in the trenches at Petersburg wrote to his wife: "We have daily access to the Richmond papers. . . . We spend much of our time in reading these journals and discussing the situation." A New York captain wrote home in 1864: "It is a very great mistake to suppose that the soldier does not think. Our soldiers are closer thinkers and reasoners than the people at home. It is the soldiers who have educated the people at home . . . to a just perception of our great duties in this contest. . . . Every soldier [knows] he [is] fighting not only for his own liberty but [even] more for the liberty of the human race for all time to come."

On May 20, 1864, James Gardner, one of Mathew Brady's field photographers, recorded this image of Union soldiers who had been wounded earlier that month in the Battle of the Wilderness near Fredericksburg, Va. Citizen soldiers on both sides of the Civil War retained their ideological convictions despite the long years of bloody fighting and the high casualty rates.

Several units established debating societies during less-active times in winter quarters, especially in the Union Army. An Illinois sergeant's diary described some of these debates in camp near Vicksburg during the winter of 1863–64: "Took part on the affirmative of Resolved that the Constitutional relations of the rebel states should be fixed by Congress only." Another debate, he wrote, "discussed the question of reducing rebel states to territories." Still another: "Sergeants Rollins & Need discussed ably the rights of the South. Sergt. Miller expanded on the revolution of ideas." The following winter a New York private recovering from a wound described a debating society among convalescent soldiers, which discussed among other subjects the following: "Resolved that the present struggle will do more to establish and maintain a republican form of government than the Revolutionary war."

This last debate topic suggests one of the dominant themes of Civil War ideology: the self-conscious awareness of parallels with the generation that fought the Revolution and gave birth to the nation. Americans in both the Union and the Confederacy believed themselves custodians of the legacy of the founding fathers. The crisis of 1861 to 1865 was the great test of their worthiness of that heritage. Soldiers on both sides felt intensely this honourable burden: on their shoulders rode the fate of that great experiment of republican self-government launched in 1776.

The tragic irony of the Civil War was that Confederate and Union soldiers interpreted this heritage in opposite ways. In the image of the founders, Confederates professed to fight for liberty and independence from what they considered a tyrannical government; Unionists fought to preserve the nation created by the founders from dismemberment and destruction. A Virginia officer filled letters to his mother with comparisons of the North's "war of subjugation against the South" to "England's war upon the [American] colonies." He was certain the Confederacy would win this "second War for American Independence" because "Tyranny cannot prosper in the nineteenth century" against "a people fighting for their liberties." An Alabama corporal referred in his diary to the Confederacy's struggle for "the same principles which fired the hearts of our ancestors in the revolutionary struggle."

Northern consciousness of the duty to defend the legacy of 1776 was equally powerful. A Wisconsin private considered "this second war . . . equally as holy as the first . . . by which . . . our fathers . . . gained those liberties and privileges which have made us such a great and prosperous nation." A 29-year-old lieutenant from Ohio wrote to his wife, who complained to him about the burdens of raising three young children while worrying about the fate of their father: "Remember that thousands went forth and poured out their lifs blood in the Revolution to establish this government; and twould be a disgrace to the whole American people if she had not noble sons enough who had the spirit of seventy six in their hearts to stand up nobly in defence of the flag of our country." Many Union soldiers also echoed Lincoln's words that the Union cause represented the last best hope for the survival of republican self-government in the world. A 21-year-old Ohio corporal thought "we may better die . . . than allow the glorious fabric of American Liberty to crumble into the dust and the grand experiment of man's capability to devise laws for his own government be frustrated by the vile hands of infernal rebels. Then would . . . tyranny rejoice in victory."

Union convictions often tended to focus on somewhat abstract principles: national unity, constitutional liberty, survival of the republican experiment, the principle of majority rule. Principles of liberty and self-government were, of course, important in Confederate ideology as well. But many Southern soldiers tied these principles to the more visceral, concrete motives of defending their land and homes against the hated invader they believed had come south to despoil and enslave them. Hatred and revenge were a dominant motif. A Texas officer told his wife to teach their children "a bitter and unrelenting hatred to the Yankee race" that had "invaded our country . . . [and] murdered our best citizens." Many Confederate soldiers tied this motive to the theme of slavery—but not in the way one might expect. A Mississippian said he was fighting to help "drive from our soil the ruthless invader who is seeking to reduce us to abject slavery. . . . Let our last entrenchments be our graves before we will be conquered." He got his wish—at Chickamauga. A Georgia soldier met the same fate at Spotsylvania less than

Library of Congress, Washington, D.C. (neg. no. LC-USZC4-4582)

three months after he had written to a friend that "the Deep still quiet peace of the grave is more desirable than Vassalage or Slavery."

These soldiers were using the word *slavery* in the same sense that American revolutionists of 1776 had used it to refer to their subordination to Britain. Some Confederates could go on in the next breath to affirm the protection of property rights in black slaves as a reason for fighting. If the Confederacy lost the war, said a Texas officer in 1864, the South would "lose slaves, liberty, and all that makes life dear." A Georgia captain who owned 40 slaves wrote to his wife in 1863 from the front in Virginia of "the arch of liberty we are trying to build"—and several sentences later advised her to sell a troublesome slave. Three weeks later he reassured his wife, who had expressed doubts about the survival of slavery as an institution, that if the Confederacy won the war, slavery "is established for centuries." A Georgia officer fighting in the Atlanta campaign during 1864 wrote his wife that "in two months more we will perhaps be an independent nation or a nation of slaves." If we lose, "not only will the negroes be free but . . . we will all be on a common level." But a Texas private remained confident even in 1864 that Confederate victory would prevent this from happening, because "we are fighting for matters real and tangible . . . our property and our homes . . . they for matters abstract and intangible . . . for the flimsy and abstract idea that a negro is equal to an Anglo American."

Few Yankees professed to fight for racial equality, however. Nor did many white Union soldiers claim to fight solely or even primarily for emancipation. But from the beginning of the war, there were some soldiers whose nationalism fused with antislavery conviction to produce an ideological mix of Liberty and Union, one and inseparable. A Massachusetts private told his parents that he considered "the object of our government as one worth dying to attain—the maintenance of our free institutions which must of necessity result in the freedom of every human being over whom the stars and stripes wave. Who desires peace while such an institution as slavery exists among us?"

But this question badly divided Union soldiers, especially during the six or eight months surrounding Lincoln's issuance of the Emancipation Proclamation. It contributed to a severe morale crisis in Union armies during the winter of 1862–63. A New York artillery officer wrote in 1862 that the war must be "for the preservation of the Union, the putting down of armed rebellion, and for that purpose only." If Lincoln gave in to radical pressure to make it "an abolition war . . . I for one shall be sorry that I ever lent a hand to it." An Indiana private told his parents that "if emancipation is to be the policy of this war . . . I do not care how quick the country goes to pot." In the officers' mess of a New York regiment, a lieutenant in January 1863 reported "several pretty spirited, I may call them *hot*, controversies about slavery, the Emancipation Edict and kindred subjects. It is not a very acceptable idea to me that we are Negro Crusaders. Anything, however, as I have often said, to crush the rebellion and give us back the Union with all its stars."

This lieutenant's last sentence provides the key to understanding a significant change that occurred in the Union Army after mid-1863. Many soldiers previously opposed to or skeptical about emancipation came to accept it, not as an ideological war aim but as a means to weaken the Confederacy and win the war. Some of these soldiers eventually became full-fledged abolitionists. My favourite example of this transformation of attitude toward slavery is a young private in the 103rd Ohio, who wrote several letters home in the early months of 1863 after the issuance of the Emancipation Proclamation. "I enlisted to fight for and vindicate the supremacy of the constitution," he wrote, but "we did not enlist to fight for the negro and I can tell you that *we never shall* . . . sacrafise [our] lives for the liberty of a miserable black race of beings." By the fall of 1863, however, he was changing his tune. He now wrote to his horrified father that he believed the abolition of slavery would be "a means of haistening the speedy Restoration of the Union and the termination of the war." Having denounced the Emancipation Proclamation in January 1863, he was praising it a year later. "It was intended to weaken the rebellion and I can asshure you it was a great blow to them." By January 1865, another year later, he had made the pilgrimage all the way to genuine abolitionism when he wrote in joyous anticipation of a restored nation *"free free free* yes free from that blighting curs *Slavery* the cause of four years of Bloody Warfare."

I want to sum up by classifying the motivation of these volunteer citizen soldiers of the Civil War into three separate but related categories: initial motivation, sustaining motivation, and combat motivation. My discussion in the latter part of this lecture on ideological convictions deals with initial motivation—the reason many of these men enlisted in the first place—and sustaining motivation—their convictions about what they were fighting for, convictions that kept them going and motivated many of them to reenlist. Combat motivation relates more to the themes of primary group cohesion, fear of being considered a coward, and religion—the factors that enabled men to go forward into a hail of bullets, that enabled them to face the music at the moment of truth. Of these three categories of motivation, the most controversial, the one on which I have been challenged by some critics, is sustaining motivation. They argue that even if many soldiers were patriotic, ideological, and gung-ho when they first enlisted, their enthusiasm and convictions waned and turned more cynical or weary as the war went on and on. There is some truth to this. But what impressed me in my research was the degree to which these ideological convictions persisted in the minds of many soldiers. A couple of examples. A Texas Confederate officer wrote to his wife in 1864: "I am sick of war" and of "the separation from the dearest objects of life," his wife and children, but "were the contest again just commenced I would willingly undergo it again for the sake of . . . our country's independence and [our children's] liberty." About the same time, a Pennsylvania Union officer wrote to his wife that he had to fight it out to the end because, "sick as I am of this war and bloodshed as much oh how much I want to be home with my dear wife and children . . . every day I have a more religious feeling, that this war is a crusade for the good of mankind. . . . I [cannot] bear to think of what my children would be if we were to permit this hell-begotten conspiracy to destroy this country." These persisting convictions were the glue that held both the Confederate and Union armies together through four bloody years and enabled them to endure far higher casualties than any other armies in American history and keep fighting.

James M. McPherson is a Pulitzer Prize-winning Civil War historian and a senior adviser to Encyclopædia Britannica.

Yarn Bombing

by Kristan M. Hanson

By 2011 the cultural phenomenon known as *yarn bombing*, a knitted or crocheted graffiti that had sprung up worldwide in 2005, had become a global cultural phenomenon in which artists and craft enthusiasts publicly displayed their stitching skills. Unlike graffiti artists who typically spray-paint marks or tags, yarn bombers knit or crochet impermanent tactile works for the urban environment. Yarn bombing is associated with the do-it-yourself subculture and various activist movements; practitioners typically infuse traditionally feminine needlework techniques with the subversive edginess of street art. Yarn interventions have ranged in scale from an enormous pink blanket with which the Danish artist Marianne Jorgensen swaddled a military tank to the corseting by Polish-born artist Agata Olek of the iconic *Charging Bull* bronze sculpture located near Wall Street in New York City and to a tiny sidewalk mushroom attributed to the Swedish artist Stickkontakt. Because of the ephemeral and often illegal nature of yarn graffiti (official approval for works displayed on public property is not generally secured), many bombers take pseudonyms and use blogs and other forms of social media to document their projects.

Artist Agata Olek, crocheting in the early hours of Christmas day 2010, used neon-coloured yarn to adorn the Charging Bull *sculpture near Wall Street; in less than two hours, her work was dismantled by New York City officials.*

Whether they covered urban objects or added humorous elements to public sculpture, yarn bombers sought to beautify the urban landscape and communicate ideas in 2011. On March 13 the Philadelphia artist Ishknits surreptitiously covered seats in the cars of three Southeastern Pennsylvania Transportation Authority (SEPTA) trains with whimsical cozies for the rush-hour commute. The following month the artist fashioned a bright pink sweater vest—emblazoned with the phrase "Go see the art"—for a bronze statue depicting fictional boxer Rocky Balboa. The tag urged viewers to visit the nearby Philadelphia Museum of Art. In a quieter and more intimate gesture, Chicagoan Jessie Magyar in December covertly installed some book cozies in the stacks of the School of the Art Institute of Chicago's John M. Flaxman Library.

Yarn bombers also use their craft to enhance the natural world and to bring people together through collaborative, site-specific installations. In January, Mandy Moore and Leanne Prain hosted community knit- and crochet-ins, where participants made pink blossoms to adorn a cherry tree during the winter. The event raised awareness for the activities of the Historic Joy Kogawa House in Vancouver. That same month Ohio-based artist Carol Hummel enlisted volunteers to help crochet *Lichen It!*, a plantlike bloom wrapped around a large tree at the Morton Arboretum in Lisle, Ill. Elsewhere Magda Sayeg, the Texan widely recognized as yarn bombing's originator, collaborated with more than 170 volunteers who embellished tree trunks on the University of Texas at Austin campus with candy-coloured sleeves.

In 2011 yarn bombing further infiltrated mainstream culture through ad campaigns and museum happenings; a clothing company commissioned Sayeg to craft tree, tire-swing, see-saw, and park-bench cozies for a series of ads featuring people bundled in winter wear. In addition, members of the British group Knit the City "yarnstormed" London by placing crocheted paint tubes and brushes at the Tate Britain and stitched squid at the Natural History Museum. Perhaps the year's biggest event occurred on June 11, when Joann Matvichuk of Lethbridge, Alta., inaugurated the first International Yarn Bombing Day to celebrate this distinctly soft, cozy form of guerrilla art.

Kristan M. Hanson is the Visual Resources Librarian at the School of the Art Institute of Chicago.

Olek/Jonathan LeVine Gallery

(Counterclockwise from top left) On June 10, in preparation for the first International Yarn Bombing Day the following day, an Australian participant shows her support by festooning a pole in Martin Place, Sydney; Rocky, the fictional boxer of movie lore, wears a hot pink sweater vest that is emblazoned with a directive to passersby to "go see the art" at the nearby Philadelphia Museum of Art; A rock outside the Barbara Barker Center for Dance at the University of Minnesota sports a striped cover; Jessie Magyar fashioned knitted covers for some of the books that are housed in the stacks at the library at the Art Institute of Chicago; The limbs and trunk of a tree in a park in Southsea, Hampshire, Eng., are decorated with colourful cozies; (centre) A passerby speeds by two of the four poles outside the Berkeley (Calif.) Repertory Theatre that were covered in rainbow-coloured cozies; one pole's design includes a business card.

(Counterclockwise from top left) Tracey Nearmy—EPA/Landov; Photo courtesy of Conrad Benner/Streetsdept.com; Tom Sweeney—MCT/Landov; Courtesy of Jenn Smith; Martyn Evans/Alamy; (centre) Laura A. Oda—MCT/Landov

Fracking

by Robert Curley

On Jan. 25, 2011, the Academy of Motion Picture Arts and Sciences announced that *Gasland*, a documentary about fracking by New York theatre and film director Josh Fox, had been nominated for an Oscar for best documentary feature of 2010. This ignited a war of words between Fox's supporters on the one hand and partisans of the natural-gas industry on the other. Fracking, or hydraulic fracturing, is a technique in which water, sand, and chemicals are injected underground in order to crack open rock formations and allow liberated gas to flow to the surface for capture. Fox, a self-styled "natural-gas detective," had created a film record of the polluted tap water, health problems, and releases of explosive methane that he was convinced were caused by fracking. The gas industry retorted that *Gasland* was so biased that it ought to win a prize for propaganda. As it turned out, the Oscar was awarded in February to another documentary, but by then it was too late: Fox's scene of a kitchen faucet bursting into flames in Fort Lupton, Colo., had defined fracking for many people around the world.

Old Gas, New Technology. The technique of hydraulic fracturing has been known since the 1940s, but it entered its modern phase only in the 1990s, when steerable drill-bit motors and electronic telemetering systems allowed developers to exploit previously inaccessible deposits of shale gas. Shales are fine-grained sedimentary rocks that were laid down hundreds of millions of years ago as organic-rich mud at the bottom of ancient seas. Over time, heat and pressure transformed the mud into shale and the organic matter into gas. Enormous quantities of gas are locked in the hard,

(Left to right) Three steps in hydraulic fracturing for shale gas: drilling the well, fracking the shale formation, and production of the liberated gas.

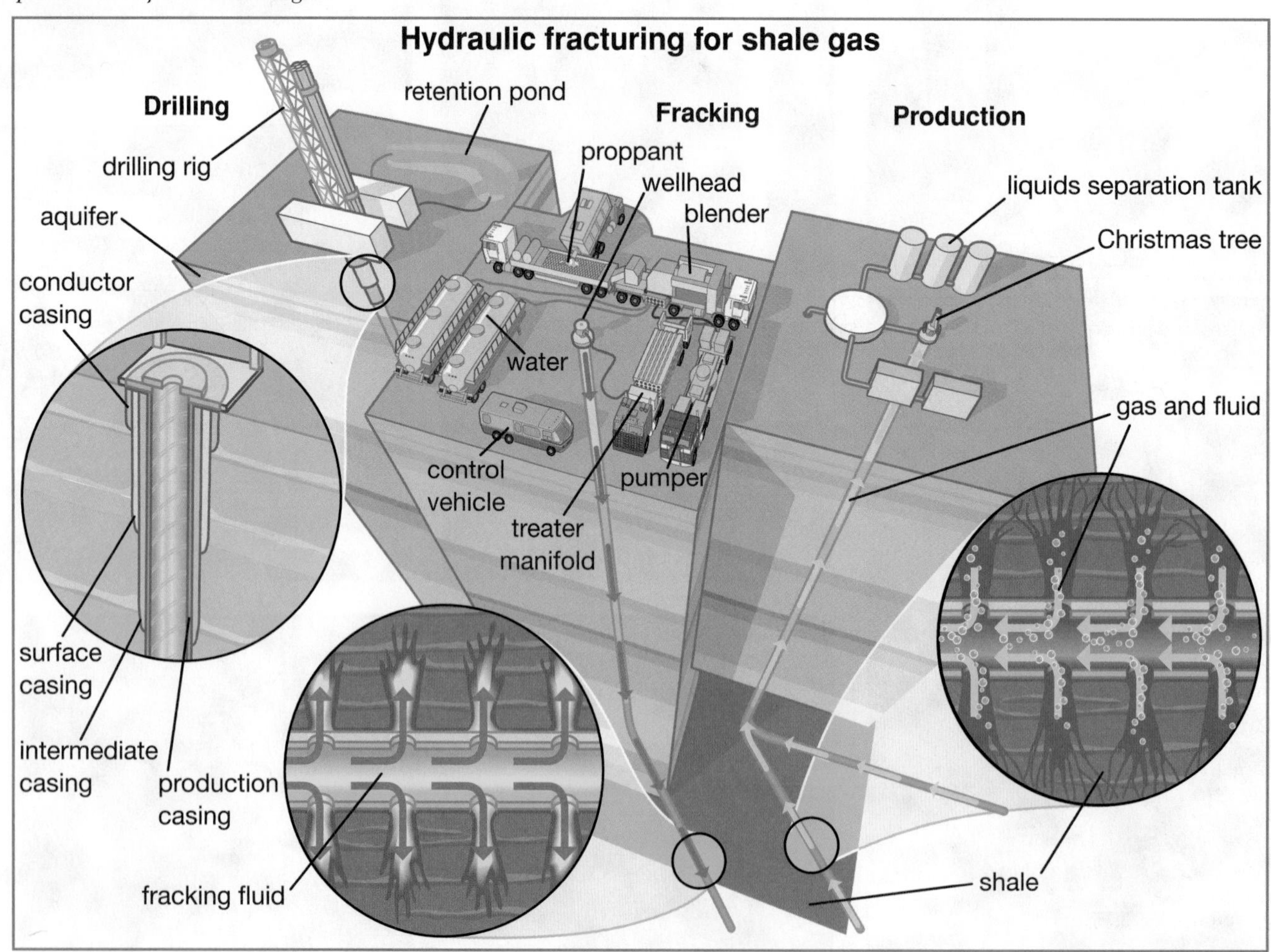

dense rock; the problem is how to extract it easily.

The most productive method is horizontal drilling followed by fracking. In this combined technique, a borehole is drilled straight down through thousands of metres of rock to the shale. This portion of the well is lined with one and sometimes two cemented steel pipes called casing. At a predetermined "kickoff point," the borehole is turned to the horizontal; from there drilling can continue for thousands of metres more. When this lateral section is done, the entire borehole is lined with yet another casing, which is perforated by a series of small explosive charges.

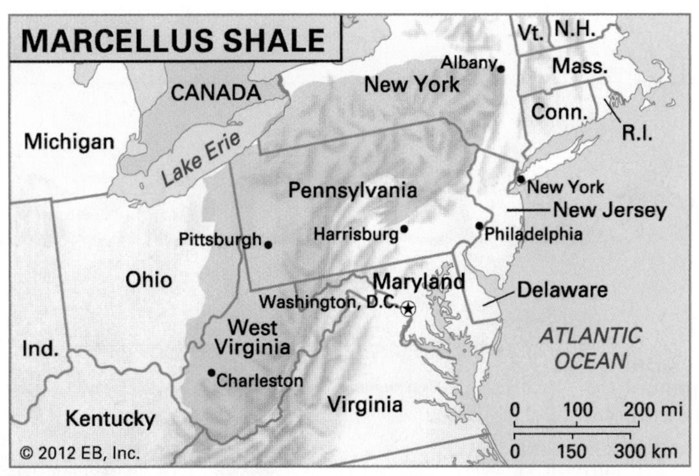

At this point fracking commences, typically with the arrival of a fleet of tanker trucks at the drilling pad. The amount of fresh water used in fracking a single shale-gas well varies greatly: industry and regulatory sources give figures ranging from approximately 7.5 million to 20 million litres (2 million to 5 million gal)—roughly equivalent to the water contained in three to eight Olympic-size swimming pools.

A fluid is blended that consists of some 90% water, less than 10% sand "proppant" to hold open the fissures in the rock, and 0.5–2% chemical additives, including such items as borehole-cleaning acids, corrosion-preventing stabilizers, and petroleum-based friction reducers. The fluid is pumped at high pressure down the borehole and through the perforations in the casing. Once fracturing has completed, production tubing is inserted into the well, and gas flows to the surface. Fracking fluid returns along with the gas, in some cases mixed with brines from the shale formation. These liquids are diverted for further treatment to steel tanks or to settling ponds that have been excavated out of the ground and lined with plastic. A finished production site may eventually be denuded of all but a network of valves called the "Christmas tree," connections to a gas pipeline, tanks for storing condensed liquids, and support and maintenance equipment.

Environmental Concerns. Since the 1990s fracking has opened up vast natural-gas deposits in the U.S., mainly in traditional oil- and gas-producing regions of Texas, Arkansas, Oklahoma, and Louisiana but also as far afield as Colorado and North Dakota. In the early 2000s, gas developers began to drill in the Marcellus shale, a huge basin they called the "Saudi Arabia of natural gas" that lay under most of Pennsylvania but also extended into New York, Ohio, and West Virginia. This sudden influx of development brought much-needed jobs and tax revenue to depressed areas of Pennsylvania during the recession of 2008–09. At the same time, it triggered concerns about the environment.

One frequently expressed fear was that hydraulic fracturing would allow shale gas and contaminated liquids to migrate upward into water tables. Industry officials insisted, and environmental officials agreed, that this was extremely unlikely, as fracking was typically done at 1,500–2,500 m (5,000–8,000 ft) below the surface. A more likely scenario might be the diffusion of shale gas through old, unused wells that had not been adequately cased or plugged. Also, well operators had frequently been cited for defective casing that had allowed production gas and liquids to pass into an aquifer.

Drilling of all kinds was known occasionally to disturb gas pockets close to an aquifer, enabling methane gas to permeate well water. The flaming faucet in *Gasland* inspired a number of imitation videos on the Internet. The gas industry conceded that some of these events could be traced to drilling but insisted that they almost certainly had nothing to do with fracking.

Recovered fracturing fluid contained not only the original additives (some of which could be carcinogenic) but also subsurface brines as well as minerals that might include toxic barium and radium. In some areas such as the Marcellus, flowback water was commonly taken to wastewater-treatment plants—some of which, environmentalists warned, were not equipped to treat fracking water and might be releasing dangerous chemicals into aquatic ecosystems. Partly in response to environmental regulations, producers were developing various methods for recycling fracking water.

In other oil and gas basins, used fracking water was routinely pumped into disposal wells deep underground. According to some geologists, this threatened to alter pressure balances or even lubricate existing faults in rock formations that were already liable to slip. During 2011, in locations as far apart as Arkansas and England, fracking or disposal operations had been halted after unusual seismic activity was noted in their vicinity.

Regulation and Further Study. These environmental concerns called into question the value and practice of shale-gas exploitation—especially in the Marcellus, a region blanketed by the scenic Allegheny Mountains that was home to powerful environmentalist groups long before anyone had ever heard of fracking. Using records kept by the Pennsylvania Department of Environmental Protection, conservationists found that gas drillers in that state had been cited for violations of environmental regulations more than 1,600 times from January 2008 to August 2010. In July 2011 the New York Department of Environmental Conservation recommended that horizontal drilling and high-volume hydraulic fracturing be banned within the watersheds that were supplying drinking water to New York City and Syracuse.

Such moves were well received in western Europe. In June France became the first country in the world to ban the exploration and extraction of gas and oil by hydraulic fracturing.

Meanwhile, the safe exploitation of shale gas remained a pillar of U.S. Pres. Barack Obama's energy policy. The Environmental Protection Agency announced in June that it would conduct detailed case histories of seven well sites around the U.S. A preliminary report was to be issued in 2012 and a final report in 2014.

Robert Curley is a Senior Editor of Science and Technology for Encyclopædia Britannica.

Antarctic Dinosaurs

by Peter J. Makovicky

Two stories involving Antarctic dinosaurs captured the imagination of paleontologists and the public in 2011. Early in the year, William Hammer and colleagues revealed the discovery of two nearly 200-million-year-old dinosaur skeletons and the partial remains of a massive sauropod (a large herbivorous dinosaur) on the slopes of Mt. Kirkpatrick in the Central Transantarctic Mountains. They speculated that one of the new dinosaurs may have been an ornithischian (bird-hipped dinosaur); however, closer analysis suggested that both skeletons belonged to small basal sauropodomorphs possibly related to *Plateosaurus* or *Massospondylus*. Since most of Antarctica was unexplored and the collected remains of dinosaurs were few, paleontologists believed that these finds provided critical pieces to the puzzle of dinosaur evolution.

Cryolophosaurus, a dinosaur discovered in Antarctica, is the largest-known predator of the Early Jurassic Epoch.

In August a second study, led by Holly Woodward, examined the bone histologies (the microstructural framework of fossilized bone) of several Australian dinosaurs, which would have lived inside the Antarctic circle in the Cretaceous, for evidence of hibernation. The team reported that there were no significant differences in bone growth between these polar dinosaurs and dinosaurs from other regions. They also noted that the examination of seasonal growth lines in bones did not provide enough information to determine whether a dinosaur hibernated.

Although the 2011 discoveries added much to the study of paleontology, dinosaur research in Antarctica continued to be limited by the continent's extensive ice coverage and brutal climate. Dinosaur finds were restricted to the rocky regions of some nearshore islands and the Central Transantarctic Mountains. Even in these ice-free areas, fieldwork on the continent remained extremely difficult and required unusual resources. All Antarctic vertebrate fossils had been recovered by expeditions mounted by governmental agencies, such as the U.S. National Science Foundation and the British Antarctic Survey. Many excavations had been extended over a number of years because of short field seasons, infrequent visits to the field sites, and difficult conditions. Some standard paleontological practices, such as wrapping bones in plaster jackets, could not be applied in Antarctica owing to freezing conditions. Along the coast, many skeletons were damaged by freeze thawing, and sea ice often complicated access. All operations in the interior required helicopter support, and the hardness of the strata required that excavations be performed with power tools.

Despite the logistic challenges, the first Antarctic dinosaur was discovered on James Ross Island in 1986. Since then, additional remains had been found there and on nearby Seymour and Vega islands. All but one of these fossils were recovered in nearshore marine sediments that were deposited during the last three stages of the Cretaceous Period, which lasted from 85 million to 65 million years ago. It was thought that carcasses floated out to sea from terrestrial areas before sinking to the sea bottom where they were buried in the rock. Antarctica was thought to have had a warm, temperate climate during the Cretaceous, since the region harboured coals (which could not form under cold conditions) dating back to that period.

Between 1986 and 2003, parts of five nonavian dinosaurs were collected from these islands, along with numerous bird remains. The oldest (89 million–83 million years old) was a tibia of a large theropod (a carnivorous dinosaur) that was 3–5 m (1 m = 3.3 ft) long. Another notable specimen, made up of skull fragments, vertebrae, and the girdle and foot bones of a small nodosaur (armoured dinosaur), was discovered in 1986. Argentine paleontologists named the specimen *Antarctopelta oliveroi*; it measured less than four metres long. Two partial skeletons of other ornithopod dinosaurs measuring up to five metres long were collected from James Ross Island in 1989 and about 2000. American and Argentine paleontologists described a hadrosaur tooth in 1998, and the jawbones, tooth fragments, and partial leg, of a two-metre-

Walter Myers—Stocktrek Images, Inc./Alamy

long dromaeosaurid carnivore were discovered in 2003. These last four specimens appeared in rocks that were 83 million–65 million years old.

Although their fragmentary nature renders their evolutionary affinities uncertain, these dinosaurs became important biogeographic data for Antarctica. Four were members of lineages that had inhabited the continent since at least Early Cretaceous times, whereas the hadrosaur tooth demonstrated that various Northern Hemisphere species could have dispersed to Antarctica via South America near the end of the Cretaceous. *Antarctopelta* appeared to be the only reliable example of a nodosaurid from the Southern Hemisphere.

Bird remains dated to the Cretaceous, however, were more abundant. *Vegavis*, an extinct Cretaceous bird collected from Vega Island, was thought to be related to ducks and geese. *Polarornis*, a loonlike diving bird, was also likely related to an extant bird order. These fossils were considered to be the best evidence that the diversification of modern bird lineages started prior to the end-Cretaceous extinction event, which wiped out all nonavian dinosaurs.

In 1990 geologist David Elliot discovered several large bones in Early Jurassic floodplain sediments about 4,000 m above sea level on Mt. Kirkpatrick. That same year Hammer and colleagues began to excavate the site, collecting parts of two dinosaurs from one quarry. The remains included the skull and thighbone of a large theropod, which was described in 1994 as *Cryolophosaurus elliot*i. The other, more fragmentary remains were part of the knee and ankle of a large quadrupedal sauropodomorph, which was described in 2007 as *Glacialisaurus hammeri*.

Cryolophosaurus—named for the unusual furrowed and fan-shaped crest on its skull—was approximately 6.6 m long. It was the largest predator known from the Early Jurassic, and it marked the ascent of dinosaurs to the ranks of the world's top predators after the rauisuchians (a group of crocodile-like archosaurs) and other large predators died out at the end of the Triassic Period. *Cryolophosaurus* was related to other Early Jurassic theropods with crests, such as *Dilophosaurus* from the American Southwest.

Glacialisaurus was estimated at more than 0.9 metric ton (1 short ton). It belonged to a cosmopolitan group of sauropodomorphs that also included *Massospondylus* from South Africa, *Riojasaurus* from South America, and *Lufengosaurus* from China. Other limb and girdle bones, which were presumed to have belonged to *Glacialisaurus*, were also collected. Additional research was initiated to determine whether the sauropodomorph skeletons found in 2011 were juvenile *Glacialisaurus* or whether they represented new species.

The Mt. Kirkpatrick quarry and its immediate surroundings also yielded several teeth of a small primitive theropod species, the molarlike tooth of a large tritylodont cynodont (a mammal-like reptile), and the wing bone of a pterosaur (flying archosaur) during its first excavation season. This Early Jurassic fauna lived when all of Earth's continents were part of the supercontinent called Pangea. Many scientists maintain that this continental arrangement aided faunal dispersal. Paleogeographic reconstructions posited that Antarctica was warm and temperate during the Jurassic, an inference that was supported both by the fossil fauna and by the discoveries of fossilized wood on Mt. Kirkpatrick.

Cryolophosaurus, *Glacialisaurus*, and the tritylodont belong to groups that possessed widespread distributions. More important, these dinosaurs differed with respect to the continent on which their nearest relative was discovered. Fossils of the closest relative of *Cryolophosaurus* were recovered from North America, while the closest relative of *Glacialisaurus*'s group was found in Asia. This lack of congruence between biogeographic patterns was consistent with facile and rapid dispersal between continents. Remarkably, many of the species found on Mt. Kirkpatrick, such as *Cryolophosaurus* and the tritylodont were larger than their relatives from more-temperate latitudes. *Glacialisaurus*, however, was comparable in size to large early-Jurassic sauropodomorphs from other continents. Whether this pattern was a sampling artifact or the result of a biological reason—such as Bergmann's Rule, which states that animals from higher latitudes are generally larger than their relatives from more temperate regions—had not yet been determined.

Peter J. Makovicky is the Associate Curator and Chair of the Department of Geology at the Field Museum of Natural History in Chicago.

(Left) On display at the Australian Museum in Sydney is this cast of a Cryolophosaurus ellioti *dinosaur skull that was unearthed in Antarctica in 1990–91. The red areas denote markers used in excavation. (Right) During the austral (Southern Hemisphere) summer of 2010–11, scientists work at the quarry on Mt. Kirkpatrick, Antarctica, where fossil remains of the dinosaur* Cryolophosaurus *were excavated 20 years earlier.*

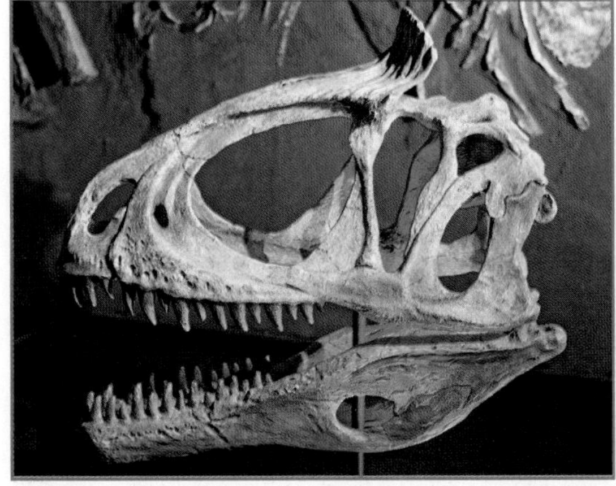

(Left) Bosiljka Zutich/Alamy; (right) Courtesy of Peter Makovicky

Sports-Related Brain Injuries

by Christopher Nowinski

Research and Advocacy. By 2011 it had been estimated that up to 3.8 million traumatic brain injuries per year were attributable to sports and recreation. A growing body of research revealed that concussions—defined as a type of traumatic brain injury caused by a bump, blow, or jolt to the head that changes the way a person's brain works—were a far more serious injury than previously believed. For decades, athletes had been taught to ignore concussions, and medical professionals would allow players to return to a game after they had suffered one. A convergence of research—combined with strong advocacy from health care professionals, the media, and others—helped to change those long-held practices. Much of the scientific evidence came from the Boston University Center for the Study of Traumatic Encephalopathy (BU CSTE), founded in 2008 by BU's School of Medicine in partnership with the Sports Legacy Institute and the U.S. Department of Veterans Affairs, which by 2011 had studied the brains of nearly 100 athletes, mostly boxers and gridiron-football and ice-hockey players. BU neuropathologist Ann McKee and colleagues found that nearly three out of four of the athletes examined tested positive for a degenerative brain disease cause by trauma, including the first three NHL players studied and an 18-year-old football player.

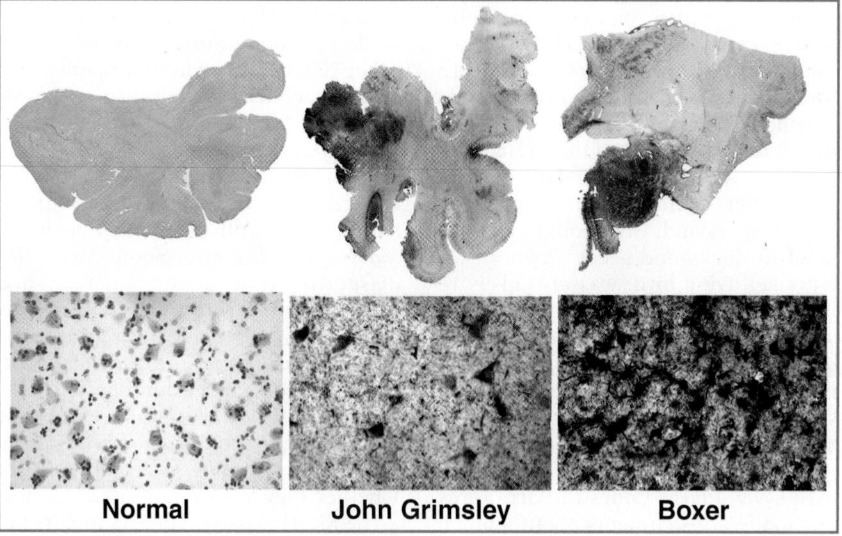

Sections of brain tissue from a 65-year-old with a normal brain (left), from John Grimsley, a 45-year-old former NFL player (centre), and from a 73-year-old former professional boxer (right). Microscopic images of the tissue samples reveal abnormal protein accumulation (brown colour) indicative of chronic traumatic encephalopathy (CTE) in the subjects at centre and right.

A study conducted by biomedical engineer Thomas Talavage, a professor at Purdue University, West Lafayette, Ind., revealed that subconcussive hits (those that did not cause concussion symptoms) might be just as damaging as hits that caused concussions, and data from sensors implanted in football helmets showed that athletes were exposed to shocking amounts of brain trauma. Sports exercise scientist Steve Broglio, a specialist in sports concussions, discovered that the average high-school football player received 652 hits to the head per season that exceeded 15 g of force (15 times the force the brain experiences from Earth's gravity), and he found that one student had sustained a whopping 2,235 hits.

It also became clear that up to 90% of concussions were not being diagnosed, because the symptoms were subtle and athletes had not been encouraged to report them. One study of youth ice hockey conducted by London, Ont., sports medicine specialist Paul Echlin found that concussion diagnosis increased from 5% of players per season to 35% simply by allowing a physician sitting in the stands to watch for suspected concussions and permitting him to remove and evaluate the players exhibiting signs of trauma.

The spotlight on the afflicted players themselves was intensified when on Feb. 17, 2011, former NFL safety Dave Duerson (*see* OBITUARIES) committed suicide. He left behind a note pleading, "Please, see that my brain is given to the NFL's brain bank." It was presumed that he had shot himself in the chest to preserve his brain for study.

Duerson suspected that he was suffering from chronic traumatic encephalopathy, or CTE, a degenerative brain disease linked to repeated concussions and subconcussive hits to the head that causes cognitive impairment as well as behavioral and mood disorders prior to leading to dementia. CTE was first diagnosed in boxers and was called *dementia pugilistica* or punch-drunk syndrome. It could be diagnosed only after death, by physical examination of the brain, and there was no known treatment. The BU CSTE confirmed that Duerson had been suffering from advanced CTE; he was the 14th out of only 15 NFL players examined to have been diagnosed with CTE.

The NFL and the NHL React. Two of the major sports organizations eventually

Dr. Ann McKee—Center for the Study of Traumatic Encephalopathy/BU Photography

began changing their approaches to brain trauma. In 2007 an NFL spokesperson maintained that "there is absolutely no evidence to suggest a connection between the NFL and dementia," but that same year the NFL introduced the 88 Plan, named for Pro Football Hall of Famer John Mackey. (*See* OBITUARIES.) The plan supplied compensation of $88,000 annually to retired players for custodial care necessitated by dementia, including Alzheimer disease. Rule changes designed to lessen opportunities for brain trauma were also enacted. In 2011 the NFL moved the kickoff from the 30- to the 35-yd line, and in the players' new collective-bargaining agreement, the two-a-day preseason practices were eliminated and only 14 full-padded practices were required during the regular season. The league also agreed to pay a certified athletic trainer to monitor play and provide injury feedback to teams from an upstairs booth, where visibility was clearer and instant replay available. Team medical staffs were permitted to use cell phones during games to assess injured players' conditions.

Jeremy Maclin of the NFL Philadelphia Eagles sustains an illegal hit to the head by Dunta Robinson of the Atlanta Falcons on September 18. The NFL, which had been criticized for not doing enough to reduce the incidence of brain trauma among players, slapped Robinson with a large fine.

Concussions were a major issue in the 2010–11 NHL season. Pittsburgh Penguins superstar Sidney Crosby suffered two concussions within one week, missed the last five months of that season, and sat out when the 2011–12 season began. Three other NHL players, all of whom played the "enforcer" role and were involved in frequent fights, died between May and September: New York Ranger Derek Boogaard (age 28) died of a drug overdose; Winnipeg Jet Rick Rypien (27) and recently retired Wade Belak (35) both committed suicide. Many suspected that all three had suffered from CTE, which could have contributed to addiction and suicidal thoughts. Boogaard's family donated his brain to the BU CSTE.

The NHL continued to make incremental changes to its concussion program, which in 2011 included alterations to Rule 48 (which had severely penalized intentional blindside hits to the head) to cover all intentional hits to the head from any direction. In addition, the NHL said that it would investigate possibilities for making equipment safer, reexamine the size and safety of skating rinks, and require that players showing signs or reporting symptoms of concussion be evaluated by a team physician in a quiet room away from the playing surface.

Youth Sports. While concussions in professional sports dominated the headlines, the situation was most dire in youth sports: tens of millions of children regularly suffered brain trauma and concussions. Children are far more vulnerable to brain trauma than are adults for a host of reasons, including having poorer-quality equipment, a lack of medical resources, and a brain that was still growing. In October 2011 the U.S. Centers for Disease Control and Prevention reported a 62% increase (from 2001 to 2009) in traumatic brain injuries in people aged 19 or younger.

In reaction to such findings, 32 states passed sports concussion laws, most modeled on that of Washington state's Zachery Lystedt Law (enacted after Lystedt, a 13-year-old football player, became permanently disabled after resuming play too soon following a concussion), which required that (1) stakeholders (coaches, athletes, and parents) receive concussion education, (2) athletes under age 18 be removed from play when a concussion is suspected, and (3) athletes removed from play be forbidden to return to play without clearance from a medical professional trained in diagnosing and treating concussions.

USA Hockey raised the age at which players were allowed to bodycheck from 11 to 13. The American Academy of Pediatrics (AAP) in August issued a policy statement recommending that physicians "vigorously oppose" boxing by children and adolescents.

There was little leadership at the collegiate level until the Ivy League announced in July that it had assembled a concussion committee to review protocols in football. As a result of the committee's recommendations, the number of days per week in which full-contact practice was allowed was reduced from five to two.

The Future. It was clear that further changes needed to be made to ensure that athletes' brains were protected. Though educational efforts appeared to be working—NFL players reported 21% more concussions in 2010 than in 2009 and 34% more than in 2008—most concussions remain undiagnosed.

Sporting leagues needed to revisit the question of what activities were "age appropriate." In football and soccer, for example, the youth and adult games were indistinguishable. Practice methods needed to change, as studies had revealed that most of the brain trauma an athlete received occurred in practice. Better equipment was also required. In a helmet-rating system (of zero to five stars, from least to most protective) devised by researchers at Virginia Tech, it was found that the Riddell VSR-4 helmet, used by most professional football players in the 2010–11 season, earned a one-star rating.

To accelerate science-based reform, efforts were under way to measure total brain trauma by using new technologies, and age-appropriate activity limits were expected to help reduce the amount of brain trauma athletes received. Though some safeguards had been implemented quickly, much more work needed to be done before modern athletes could be assured that they would not suffer a fate similar to that of Duerson.

Christopher Nowinski is the Cofounder and CEO of the Sports Legacy Institute and Codirector of the Center for the Study of Traumatic Encephalopathy, Boston University School of Medicine. The former Harvard University football player and professional wrestler is the author of Head Games: Football's Concussion Crisis *(2006).*

John Amis/AP

The German *E. coli* Outbreak

by Kara Rogers

The year 2011 witnessed the deadliest and second largest *E. coli* outbreak in history. Though limited primarily to Germany, the episode raised fears in other countries and caused some 4,321 cases of illness and 50 deaths, nearly all of which were associated with hemolytic uremic syndrome (HUS), in which infection of the gastrointestinal tract by toxin-producing bacteria results in the destruction of red blood cells and sometimes leads to kidney failure.

Stages of the Outbreak. In late April a small number of people in Germany were hospitalized with HUS, the cause of which was determined to be a strain of *E. coli* that produced a substance called Shiga toxin, named for its similarity to toxins produced by the bacterium *Shigella dysenteriae*. The unusual spike in *E. coli*-related HUS prompted German health officials to begin providing case data to the World Health Organization (WHO) on May 1.

Over the course of the next several weeks, the outbreak developed slowly; just 138 cases had been reported by the third week of May. By the end of that month, however, the number of confirmed cases in Germany had jumped to 373, and more than two dozen additional cases had been reported in other European Union member states. As many as 12 to 16 deaths had also been disclosed by local authorities. About the same time, scientists reported that the causative agent appeared to be a strain of *E. coli* known as O104:H4, a rare form of the bacterium. While most *E. coli* infections are self-limiting, infection with O104:H4 was associated with an unusually high rate of progression to HUS. Those affected—nearly 900 individuals—experienced symptoms typical of gastrointestinal infection (e.g., diarrhea, abdominal cramps, and vomiting) followed by onset of fatigue, decreased consciousness, and indications of anemia. For most, treatment with corticosteroids, dialysis, and blood transfusion facilitated recovery.

A digger unloads discarded vegetables suspected of having E. coli *contamination at the Albahida vegetable-recycling plant in Nijar, Almería province, Spain.*

In early June the European Centre for Disease Prevention and Control (ECDC), which had been providing daily updates on the number of HUS cases and deaths, also began supplying data on non-HUS *E. coli* infections, revealing that hundreds of other people were affected, many of whom, for reasons that were unclear, were women. Most cases were reported in and around Hamburg in northern Germany. The minority of cases and deaths reported outside Germany, in places such as Denmark, Sweden, the Netherlands, and the United Kingdom, occurred in persons who had visited the country just prior to their illness.

The number of afflicted rose into the thousands through mid-June, which marked the peak of the outbreak. The

Francisco Bonilla—Reuters/Landov

last reported onset of illness was documented on July 4. On July 26, after the three-week incubation, diagnosis, and reporting period for infection had passed with no new cases, German officials declared the outbreak over.

***E. coli* O104:H4.** In the 2011 outbreak one-third of O104:H4 victims were hospitalized with HUS, compared with about one-tenth to one-fourth of victims of other pathogenic (disease-causing) *E. coli*. *E. coli* pathogenicity is determined by the type and abundance of virulence factors the bacterium produces. At the close of the outbreak, American scientists based at the University of Maryland School of Medicine published a study revealing that O104:H4 possessed a rare combination of virulence factors as well as an additional set of these factors. The researchers speculated that the unusual traits enabled the bacterium to aggressively colonize the mucosa and thereby facilitate absorption of Shiga toxin, which promoted progression to HUS in susceptible individuals.

The investigation also revealed that the German O104:H4 strain differed from other O104:H4 strains in that during the course of its evolution it came to possess not only a prophage (a viral genome integrated into bacterial DNA) that produced Shiga toxin but also a plasmid (an extrachromosomal genetic element) expressing a gene for antibiotic resistance. Furthermore, when treated with the antibiotic ciprofloxacin, often used to treat infectious diarrhea, the bacterium increased its production of Shiga toxin.

Tracking the Source. In late May, following analyses carried out at the Hamburg Institute for Hygiene and Environment, German authorities announced that traces of the bacterium had been found in cucumbers imported from Spain. Officials at the Robert Koch Institute in Hamburg advised consumers not to eat cucumbers, and the suspect vegetables were pulled from store shelves and those in Spain were destroyed or fed to livestock. On June 1, however, officials with the European Commission (EC) announced that follow-up studies had failed to confirm the initial findings. The EC immediately lifted a food-safety alert that had been issued for Spanish cucumbers. The economic impact in Spain, however, was not so easily reversed. Estimates of the losses suffered by the Spanish agriculture industry amounted to some €200 million (about $290 million), and the country's leaders sought

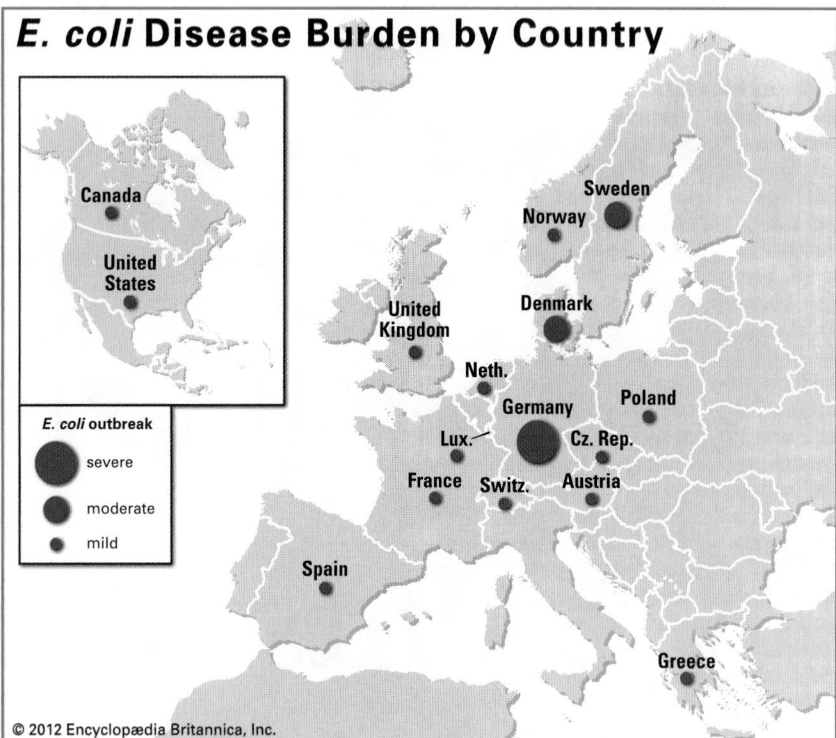

The severity of the E. coli *disease outbreak shown by country.*

financial compensation from the EU and Germany.

Investigators were next led to sprouts produced at a farm in northern Germany, just south of Hamburg. Growing sprouts require warm, humid conditions, and such conditions also support the growth of various types of bacteria. Hence, sprouts often are associated with outbreaks of foodborne illness. However, similar to the cucumbers, sprouts grown at the farm tested negative for the O104:H4 strain.

On June 24, as German authorities were ready to dismiss sprouts, French health officials reported a small number of HUS cases linked to Shiga toxin-producing *E. coli* near Bordeaux, where eight people had been hospitalized after consuming arugula, fenugreek, and mustard sprouts. The same strain of O104:H4 was at fault for the outbreak. A task force set up by the European Food and Safety Authority (EFSA) tracked the source to a single lot of fenugreek seeds imported from Egypt by a German distributor in November 2009. The distributor sold the seeds to about 70 companies, more than 50 of which were in Germany. The task force believed that it was likely that this single lot of sprouts was the common link between the French and German outbreaks. Consumers were discouraged from growing sprouts for consumption and were advised to avoid eating raw sprouts. Suspected Egyptian seeds were pulled from the European market, and the import of fenugreek seeds into Europe from Egypt was temporarily banned. Egyptian officials responded by arguing that *E. coli* could not have survived for two years on dried seeds and that handling by the distributor or the use of unclean water by growers could have resulted in contamination of the sprouts.

The Issue of Food Safety. While improvements in food regulation and surveillance were expected to emerge following the O104:H4 outbreak, progress was slow, particularly in Europe. Among the first to take action were two U.S. companies, Costco Wholesale and the lean beef manufacturer Beef Products, Inc., both of which in July introduced new *E. coli*-testing requirements for their products. Costco's new measures included mandatory testing for a range of *E. coli* strains by its produce suppliers, and Beef Products introduced testing for the six most potent *E. coli* strains—the so-called "Big Six" associated with foodborne illness—in its lean beef. In September the U.S. Department of Agriculture announced a long-awaited extension of its *E. coli* ban in ground beef that would require ground beef suppliers to test for the Big Six in addition to the previously banned strain, *E. coli* O157:H7.

Kara Rogers is the Senior Editor of Biomedical Sciences for Encyclopædia Britannica.

Events of 2011

A massive tsunami, generated by a powerful undersea earthquake, engulfs a residential area in Natori, Miyagi prefecture, northeastern Honshu, Japan, on March 11.

Kyodo/AP

Anthropology and Archaeology

Several studies provided compelling evidence of **HYBRIDIZATION** between *Homo sapiens* and other archaic **HOMININ** populations. After 90 years scholars completed the 21-volume ***CHICAGO ASSYRIAN DICTIONARY***. Researchers determined that **CHILDREN HELPED** make cave art. They also suggested earlier dates for **HORSE DOMESTICATION** and discovered the intact 13th-century hull of one of **KUBLAI KHAN'S SHIPS**. Researchers found evidence of **CHOCOLATE** at an Olmec site.

ANTHROPOLOGY

Key developments in the field of physical anthropology in 2011 were highlighted by rapidly growing evidence for hybridization between *Homo sapiens* and multiple archaic hominin populations in different geographic locations. In 2010 an international team of geneticists and anthropologists led by American geneticist David Reich and Swedish geneticist Svante Pääbo published the nuclear genome of a 30,000–50,000-year-old female from Denisova Cave in the Altai Mountains of Siberia. This individual belonged to a group of archaic hominins provisionally designated as "the Denisovans," and comparisons with the Vindija Cave Neanderthal and 12 present-day human genome sequences determined that the Denisovans were a sister group of the Neanderthals. Denisovan DNA sequences diverged from those of Neanderthals 640,000 years ago. Surprisingly, 4–6% of the genome of present-day Melanesians from Papua New Guinea and Bougainville Island came from the Denisovans, while Neanderthal DNA made up an additional 2.5%. Two Denisovan molar teeth were recovered in addition to the original juvenile finger bone that provided the nuclear DNA sequence. The primitive morphology and very large size of these molars supported the DNA-based conclusion that the Denisovans were a distinct population of archaic hominins.

In 2011 a subsequent Reich-Pääbo study with a different international team of collaborators quantified the Denisovan admixture in 33 additional populations from Asia and Oceania. Data on over 350,000 single nucleotide polymorphisms (SNPs), or genetic variations, were assembled for 243 individuals. Several modern groups—including Aboriginal Australians, Polynesians, Fijians, individuals from eastern Indonesia, and a Negrito group from the Philippines called the Mamanwa—inherited genetic material from the Denisovans. On the other hand, mainland East Asians, western Indonesians, and Negrito groups from Malaysia and the Andaman Islands contained no Denisova genetic material. To explain this geographic distribution, Reich and Pääbo hypothesized that gene flow from Denisovans to modern humans occurred in Southeast Asia after the migration of a single group of modern humans from Africa became the source of several subsequent dispersals to southern and eastern Asia. The proposed Southeast Asian location for the Denisovan homeland and human admixture suggested an extremely wide ecological and geographic distribution for the Denisovans, extending from the tropics to the deciduous forests of Siberia. Given that modern inhabitants of the island of Flores in Indonesia had detectable Denisovan genetic material, a phylogenetic relationship between the Denisovans and *H. floresiensis*—a hominin whose existence as a distinct species continued to be questioned by many paleontologists—was a distinct possibility that awaited the discovery of ancient DNA from the Flores fossil record.

Eske Willerslev, a Danish geneticist, headed an international team that published the first Australian Aboriginal genome from a hair sample collected almost a century earlier. Approximately 450,000 high-confidence SNPs were compared with data representing 1,220 individuals from 79 modern human populations. The Australian genome clustered with the Highland Papua New Guinea samples and was positioned between South and East Asians. The Bougainville Islanders and Aeta people of the Philippines were the next-closest matches to the Australian genome. The Denisovan and Australian Aboriginal genomes displayed almost as much allele sharing as the Denisovan-Papuan comparison. (An allele is an alternate form of a gene.) The authors proposed a two-wave model for the peopling of Asia; a single out-of-Africa migration, which occurred 75,000–62,000 years ago along a southern Asian route to Australia, was followed by a second migration to Europe and mainland Asia 38,000–25,000 years ago. Admixture with Denisovans may have occurred in Melanesia or in southern Eurasia during the early migratory wave. However, substantial admixture and population replacement involving the two waves of *H. sapiens* also probably occurred with the Aboriginal Australians, Papua New Guinea Highlanders, and the Aeta as remnants of the first dispersal. Thus, the contemporary Australian Aboriginal people were deemed to be the direct descendants of the first human inhabitants of Australia, who arrived there approximately 50,000 years ago.

British biologist Peter Parham from Stanford University and an international team of geneticists discovered that adaptive introgression (gene infiltration from one gene pool to another) of archaic alleles from Neanderthals and Denisovans to *H. sapiens* had significantly shaped modern human immune systems. Specifically, human leukocyte antigen (HLA) haplotypes carrying functionally distinct alleles spread from these two archaic hominin groups to modern human populations in Eurasia and Oceania. (Haplotypes are sets of alleles that tend to be inherited together.) Later these alleles moved from modern Eurasians to Africans by back-migration. Six Denisovan and six Neanderthal HLA alleles were analyzed. Five of the six Denisovan alleles were identical to their modern human counterparts, whereas all six Neanderthal alleles were identical to modern human HLA Class I alleles. The authors estimated the putative archaic HLA-A system ancestry to be more than 50% in Europe, more than 70% in Asia, and more than 95% in parts of Papua New Guinea. These estimates for HLA Class I genetic material suggested that limited interbreeding with archaic humans and the subsequent incorporation of foreign DNA conferred selective advantages that, over time, significantly shaped the modern human immune system outside Africa.

Polish-born Canadian biologist Damian Labuda and his colleagues determined that a region of the modern human X-chromosomal DNA known as dys44 (which is part of the dystrophin gene) contained a haplotype, B006, that came from admixture with Neanderthals. They analyzed 6,092 X chromosomes from modern humans from all of Earth's inhabited continents and found that the average frequency of this Neanderthal-derived segment was 9% for all populations outside Africa. Interbreeding was thought to have taken place prior to, or during the very early stages of, the worldwide expansion of *H. sapiens* between 80,000 and 50,000 years ago. The authors also discovered the B006 haplotype in Africa; however, each of these instances was ascribed to gene flow from non-African modern human sources.

Such extensive archaic introgression, occurring on an almost global scale, was documented in a variety of different genetic systems. This evidence suggested that genetic exchange between morphologically divergent populations may have been a common feature of human evolution, and the multiregional model of human origins—which posited that discrete archaic populations of *Homo* evolved locally in Africa, Asia, and Europe and contributed genes to modern *Homo sapiens*—thus gained significant genetic support in 2011.

(STEPHEN L. ZEGURA)

ARCHAEOLOGY

Eastern Hemisphere. In early 2011 a team of researchers led by Ulf Büntgen of the Swiss Federal Research Institute for Forest, Snow, and Landscape Research in Birmensdorf, Switz., issued a study linking many of the events in European history over the past 2,500 years to climate change and its impact on agrarian wealth and overall economic growth in the region. The team's extensive analysis of tree rings—prime indicators of temperature and precipitation—showed that wet and warm summers facilitated Roman and medieval prosperity, while increased climate variability between 250 and 600 CE coincided with the demise of the Western Roman Empire and the turmoil that pervaded the migration period. Many scientists believed that periods of large-scale climate change associated with cooler, wetter conditions in the 6th and 14th centuries were inextricably linked to the onset of the Black Death.

The year 2011 also witnessed a major milestone in Near Eastern studies with the completion of the *Chicago Assyrian Dictionary* after some 90 years of work undertaken by scholars who were associated with the University of Chicago's Oriental Institute.

A tablet written in the Old Babylonian language was one of the documents used to compile the **Chicago Assyrian Dictionary.** *The hand holding the tablet is that of Robert Biggs, professor emeritus at the University of Chicago, who worked on the 90-year project for more than half of that period.*

M. Spencer Green/AP

In Scotland evidence of a settlement dating to the late prehistoric period (*c.* 500 BCE–500 CE) was found on the craggy islet of Boreray—which lies more than 65 km (40 mi) west of the Outer Hebrides and which was previously thought to have been home only to seabirds and feral sheep. Inhabitants of Hirta, the largest island of the St. Kilda group, were known to have frequented Boreray to hunt birds and gather wool during the summer months, but until the 2011 excavations Boreray islet, which has an area of less than one square kilometre (247 ac), had been considered too inhospitable for permanent settlement.

Also in Scotland, a well-preserved 10th-century-CE Viking boat burial—the first to be found on the west coast of the British mainland—was discovered at Ardnamurchan in the West Highlands. Further evidence of Norse maritime activity in Scotland was found at Loch na h-Airde on the Isle of Skye's Rubh an Dunain peninsula, where Colin Martin of the Morvern Maritime Centre and his survey team identified a stone-built quay, a canal, and boat timbers associated with a 12th-century-CE Viking shipbuilding site.

At the Cave of a Hundred Mammoths in Rouffignac, France, Leslie Van Gelder of Walden University, Minneapolis, Minn., and Jessica Cooney of the University of Cambridge determined through forensic analysis that many of the 13,000-year-old engravings were made by children aged three to seven, a number of them the work of one five-year-old girl. (Three-fingered flutings that are 34 mm [1.3 in] wide or smaller are by children aged seven or younger, and males typically have a longer ring finger, while females have index fingers that are the same as or slightly longer than those of males.)

Analysis of the wreck of a mid-2nd-century-CE trading vessel that sank 10 km (6 mi) off the coast of Grado in northeastern Italy suggested that ancient Roman merchants plied the seas in vessels equipped with onboard fish tanks, enabling them to supply local fishmongers

Andrew Milligan—PA Photos/Landov

A sword, an ax head, and a bronze ring pin were among the contents of a Viking burial site at Ardnamurchan in the West Highlands of Scotland.

with live varieties caught throughout the Adriatic and Mediterranean seas. According to Carlo Beltrame of the Ca' Foscari University in Venice, the 16.5-m (54-ft)-long trader had a lead pipe in its stern section, which penetrated the hull near the keel. The pipe, he said, was likely part of a hand-driven piston pump that kept oxygenated seawater circulating in the onboard tank.

Also in Italy, the remains of a 2,400-year-old furnished Etruscan house were found at the site of Poggiarello Renzetti in Vetulonia, Tuscany. The two-story dwelling—the first of its kind to be unearthed—measured 10 × 15 m (33 × 50 ft) and had stone walls and a terracotta tile roof supported by wooden beams. Domestic items uncovered to date included grain-storage vessels, a number of large jars for storing wine and oil, amphorae, what may be an olive press, and a household altar topped with an offering of five bronze Roman coins. According to project director Simona Rafanelli of the Isidoro Falchi Archaeological Museum, the house—known to researchers as the Domus dei Dolia ("House of the Jars")—appeared to have collapsed in a fire—possibly ignited by the Roman dictator Lucius Cornelius Sulla, who set Vetulonia ablaze in 79 BCE.

The oldest-known winepress in the world was found within a Chalcolithic cave complex at Areni, Armenia. Dated to between 4100 and 4000 BCE, the installation included a shallow grape-trampling basin, a fermentation vat, and drinking cups. The remains of domesticated grapes—desiccated skins, stems, and seeds—were found within the basin, and traces of malvidin, the plant pigment that makes red wine red, were detected within the cups.

Ongoing excavations carried out by Christopher S. Henshilwood of the University of Bergen, Nor., and his team at Blombos Cave on the southern tip of Africa yielded two tool kits used to produce and store a liquefied red ochre-rich mixture some 100,000 years ago. The tool kits consisted of storage containers made of abalone (*Haliotis midae*) shells, quartzite cobble pestles used to crush ochre powder, traces of ground trabecular bones (rich in marrow and fat) that may have been used as a binder, and coarse quartzite slabs to grate or extract ochre oxides from host matrices such as rocks and compacted earth. The processed pigment, remains of which had adhered to the nacre on the shell interiors, was likely used for body decoration or to colour leather clothing.

High-resolution satellite images revealed the presence of more than 100 previously unknown sites—mudbrick fortresses known as *qsur*, settlements, cemeteries, wells, agricultural fields, and underground irrigation works for extracting groundwater known as *foggaras*—belonging to the Garamantes, a little-known people whose culture flourished in the Murzuk region of the Libyan Sahara *c.* 500 BCE–500 CE. David Mattingly of the University of Leicester, Eng., and his team carried out a preliminary investigation of the tightly clustered sites, which attested the existence of a vast, complex, and highly organized African kingdom well beyond the frontiers of the Roman Empire.

A 9,000-year-old settlement at Al-Magar in southwestern Saudi Arabia yielded abundant artifacts bearing equine imagery, including a metre (3.3-ft)-high bust of a horse, as well as a "horse cemetery," which prompted site excavators to contend that the locale offered the world's earliest-known evidence for horse domestication. Thus far, the earliest morphological evidence for horse domestication was from a suite of 5,500-year-old Botai sites in northern Kazakhstan.

In Japan the remains of a late 13th-century wreck thought to have been part of the second Mongolian invasion fleet led by Kublai Khan were found buried in the seabed off the coast of Nagasaki and were excavated by Yoshifumi Ikeda of the University of the Ryukyus, Okinawa, Japan. The 12-m (39-ft)-long keel section contained some 4,000 artifacts, among them cannonballs, stone anchors, ceramics, and ballast bricks. According to Japanese legend, both of Kublai's fleets (which were sent to invade Japan in 1274 and 1281) were decimated by "divine winds" known as the Kamikaze. Collectively, the typhoons were purported to have laid waste to an estimated 5,300 Yuan dynasty vessels.

(ANGELA M.H. SCHUSTER)

Western Hemisphere. In 2011 a number of important discoveries and research developments took place along the west coast of North America. Prominent among these findings was the dating of a mastodon kill site in Washington state to 13,800 years BP (before the present). Fossilized mastodon remains, including a rib with an embedded bone projectile and other bones bearing cut marks, were originally excavated from the Manis site near Sequim, Wash., in the late 1970s. Debate over the antiquity of these remains was put to rest in 2011 by a series of new and more refined radiocarbon dates. These new dates demonstrated that the rib and other associated mastodon remains from the Manis site predate the Clovis era (*c.* 9050 to 8800 BCE) by 800 years. Documenting the presence of mastodon hunters with projectile weaponry in the Pre-Clovis era lends support to the argument that humans played an important role in the extinction of this species.

A team of archaeologists from the University of Oregon and the Smithsonian Institute uncovered evidence of some of North America's earliest inhabitants on the Channel Islands off the coast of southern California. A variety of undisturbed thin and well-made stone projectile points found there were dated to as early as 12,000 years ago. The makers of these stone tools would have been contemporaries of the Clovis people who occupied other parts of North America. However, the distinctive tool forms and flaking techniques that characterized these coastal southern California artifacts distinguished the islanders from Clovis mainlanders. This finding added to growing evidence that there were multiple paths of migration into ancient North America, some of which preceded Clovis.

Archaeologists confirmed the location of the shipwreck of the *Queen Anne's Revenge*, once sailed by the English pirate Blackbeard. Originally a French slave vessel, the *Queen Anne's Revenge* was commandeered by Blackbeard and was later run aground on a sandbar off the coast of North Carolina in 1718. A team of underwater archaeologists recently recovered a 3.4-m (11-ft 4-in)-long anchor and a 2.4-m (8-ft)-long one-ton cannon from the shipwreck. These and other artifacts from the sunken ship were being curated and displayed at the North Carolina Maritime Museum in Beaufort.

An archaeologist from the University of Colorado at Boulder recently unearthed an ancient Asian bronze artifact from a 1,000-year-old house in western Alaska. The artifact—a portion of a small mold-made bucklelike object—was recovered from a house built by Inupiat Eskimos (Inuit) at Cape Espenberg on the Seward Peninsula, inside what is now the Bering Land Bridge National Preserve. How this ancient metal object arrived in Alaska was unclear. However, the Bering Land Bridge was thought to have been the principal route by which the ancestors of the Inupiat migrated into North America from Asia; the bronze buckle may have been transported to Alaska by these early immigrants.

Dozens of previously unknown archaeological sites along the Gulf Coast of North America were discovered and documented in 2011. These finds were the result of attempts to protect known sites threatened by the Deepwater Horizon oil spill of 2010. Among the more important discoveries were a number of small coastal residential and cemetery sites associated with larger villages farther inland that were occupied by mound-building cultures.

(GREG WILSON)

Two of the important archaeological discoveries made in Mesoamerica in 2011 were related to the Preclassic Olmec culture of southern Mexico. A residue analysis published by Terry Powis of Kennesaw (Ga.) State University and colleagues confirmed the use of cacao (possibly as a beverage) at the Early Preclassic Olmec capital of San Lorenzo, located in the southern Veracruz lowlands. Ceramic vessel fragments from both domestic and ritual contexts were tested, and theobromine (a chemical compound unique to cacao) was identified on several types of vessels. The earliest documented use of cacao at San Lorenzo (1800–1600 BCE) was contemporaneous with similar findings from the site of Paso de la Amada along the Pacific coast of Chiapas; collectively these data represent the earliest evidence of cacao processing and consumption in Mesoamerica. The evidence from San Lorenzo suggested that cacao products were used in at least one elite mortuary ceremony involving ritual sacrifice. The second Olmec-related discovery was a stone monolith depicting three cats (interpreted as either jaguars or mountain lions) at the well-known site of Chalcatzingo, located about 100 km (60 mi) south of Mexico City. Chalcatzingo was known for its connections to the Olmec heartland, and the monolith was carved in a classic Olmec style. The carving dated to 700 BCE and appeared to have been part of a collection of similar monoliths situated along a hillside wall. Archaeologists interpreted this "Triad of Felines" as part of a broader set of ritual imagery that would have been visible on the landscape as ancient Olmecs traveled this route as part of a spiritual "pilgrimage."

In the jungles of Guatemala, archaeologists were able in 2010 to identify nearly a hundred structures at the lost Mayan city of Holtun (meaning "head of stone"). Although the site's existence had been known for some time, it was buried under significant jungle cover, which made it impossible to assess the site's size or importance within the Mayan world. Research using GPS and electronic distance-measurement technology allowed archaeologists to map the locations and elevations of several structures, including a pyramid, a ball court, and an astronomical observatory. Documenting Holtun's site layout had the potential to illuminate the role of lesser Mayan cities vis-à-vis the more densely populated urban centres, such as Tikal, located only 35 km (22 mi) to the north.

A new dendrochronological study conducted in 2011 by David Stahle of the University of Arkansas at Fayetteville produced the longest and most precise climate reconstruction for Mesoamerica to date. Stahle examined 74 tree-ring cores from 30 Montezuma bald cypress trees (*Taxodium mucronatum*), a species that can grow and survive for more than a millennium. Stahle's sampling stretched back 1,238 years, which enabled him to document the timing of several significant periods of drought, including the event during the Terminal Classic period that was credited with the collapse of the Mayan civilization. Not only did Stahle's study bracket the timing of the drought to 897–922 CE, but it also revealed that this drought event was more widespread than previously surmised, affecting regions as far north as central Mexico. The study also expanded the geographic range of impact of a subsequent drought (1149–1167 CE) documented in the dendrochronological record of the American Southwest. It appeared that the later drought also extended into central Mexico and may have contributed to the collapse of the Toltec civilization.

(AMBER VANDERWARKER)

Holger Bennewitz—Reuters/Landov

A cannon from the shipwrecked Queen Anne's Revenge, *a slave ship commandeered by the pirate Blackbeard, was scavenged from waters off the coast of North Carolina.*

Architecture and Civil Engineering

The **GREENING** of architecture trumped starchitecture as a concern in 2011, though Steven Holl, Zaha Hadid, and Frank Gehry continued to **MAKE WAVES**. Notable Canadian-Israeli architect Moshe Safdie and **WALMART** heiress Alice Walton brought high culture to Arkansas with the opening of **CRYSTAL BRIDGES** Museum of American Art.

ARCHITECTURE

In 2011 many observers pointed to a change in architecture. Architects and their clients seemed less interested in fame and publicity, and after several years of economic recession in many countries, they appeared to be exercising some restraint. Social concerns seemed on the rise. There was a lot of interest in the greening of the environment, especially in cities. New York City, for example, was in the process of creating nearly 300 ha (about 750 ac) of new parks and announced a goal of planting one million trees. In Germany, which was a leader in the environmental movement, 10 million sq m (12 million sq yd) of "green roofs" were being constructed each year. Green roofs, covered with a layer of soil and plant materials, saved energy by serving as insulation. They also cooled and freshened the outside air through evaporation and the release of oxygen.

As a result of the growing interest in architecture as environment, the three design professions—architecture, landscape architecture, and urban design—collaborated with one another more than they had in the recent past. Often they worked as equals on large projects. Some designers called themselves "landscape urbanists," thus merging two of the disciplines. Other architects, believing that architecture should embody a strong social purpose, designed affordable housing for areas devastated by climate disasters. As one American writer put it, "Humanitarian design, in its various guises, has . . . become the single-most-visible architectural concern of the moment, at least among designers younger than 40."

Another widely noticed trend of 2011, especially among younger architects, was a keen interest in digital design. A variety of computer programs offered innovative ways for designers to imagine and investigate pictorial representations of future architecture. On the technical side, there was rapidly growing use of a technology called BIM (Building Information Modeling). With BIM, all the details of a building could be recorded, coordinated, and transmitted in a database format rather than by means of traditional plans and specifications.

Awards. The Pritzker Prize, considered the world's top honour for lifetime achievement in architecture, was presented to Portuguese architect Eduardo Souto de Moura. (*See* BIOGRAPHIES.) Not widely known outside his own country, Souto de Moura was a creator of architecture that was admired for its restraint, craftsmanship, and modesty. The selection of Souto de Moura, like other trends of the year, was seen as a move away from what one magazine called "the extroverted formal experimentation that has marked the most conspicuous world architecture leading up to the financial crisis of 2008." The Stirling Prize for the best British building of the year went, for the second year in a row, to Iraqi-born British architect Zaha Hadid. Hadid won this time for the Evelyn Grace Academy in London, described as "a highly stylized zigzag of steel and glass." It was the first time that a school building had been chosen for the Stirling. The prestigious Royal Gold Medal of the Royal Institute of British Architects (RIBA), for lifetime achievement, was awarded to Dutch architect Herman Hertzberger. New York-based architect Steven Holl was the winner of the highest American honour, the Gold Medal of the American Institute of Architects (AIA), also awarded for lifetime achievement. The Twenty-Five Year Award, given by the AIA to a building that has proved its merit for at least a quarter century, went to the John Hancock Tower in Boston. The Hancock, a 240-m (790-ft) office tower with an all-glass surface that often mirrored the passing clouds, was considered one of the great Modernist skyscrapers. It

The Crystal Bridges Museum of American Art, designed by Moshe Safdie, opened in Bentonville, Ark., in November.

Danny Johnston/AP

was designed by Henry Cobb of the firm I.M. Pei & Partners and was completed in 1976.

Other Notable Buildings of the Year. Despite slowed economies around the world, major buildings continued to be completed. In Spain the City of Culture of Galicia opened in Santiago de Compostela. The project, a vast cultural complex covering 70 ha (173 ac), was the work of American architect Peter Eisenman, whose proposed design won an international competition in 1999. An archive and library were completed in 2011, with an opera house, a technology centre, and other structures yet to be finished. The buildings were shaped like a series of natural mounds faced with a rock-hard gray quartzite. They seemed to grow naturally out of the landscape. In China, Hadid designed the Guangzhou Opera House. Like many Hadid buildings, the Opera House featured free-flowing curved shapes instead of rectangular forms, and its grottolike performance space was an acoustical marvel.

In the small city of Bentonville, Ark., the Crystal Bridges Museum of American Art opened. It was funded by Walmart heiress Alice Walton and was praised for the quality of its collection of American paintings. The museum's architect was Moshe Safdie, who designed it as a circle of pavilions surrounding a landscaped courtyard. Safdie was also the architect of the Khalsa Heritage Centre, a new museum of Sikh culture located in Punjab, India. In Miami Beach, Fla., California-based architect Frank Gehry designed the New World Center, a music hall for the New World Symphony orchestra and a building with a spectacular multistory indoor performance space. The Center's exterior was finished in white stucco to harmonize with the celebrated Art Deco historic district located nearby. Another Gehry design was an apartment tower in Manhattan known as New York by Gehry. At 265 m (870 ft), it was the tallest residential building in the Western Hemisphere. Three of its exterior walls were covered in strips of stainless steel that looked rumpled and wavy.

In rural Vardø, Nor., above the Arctic Circle, Swiss architect Peter Zumthor and American sculptor Louise Bourgeois collaborated on a shrine to the memory of persons burned for witchcraft in Vardø in the 17th century. Zumthor contributed a long delicate bridgelike wooden pavilion filled with a stretched-canvas object, and Bourgeois's burning chair was situated in a smoked-glass cube nearby. (*See* photograph on page 208.) Also in far northern Norway was the Knut Hamsun Centre in Hamarøy, by Holl, a museum honouring the life of the Nobel Prize-winning author, who died in 1952. Both projects were seen as part of a trend to assert national and local identity in an increasingly global world culture. In Israel the Tel Aviv Museum of Art opened an orthogonal addition by American architect Preston Scott Cohen. It was notable for an interior skylighted atrium, which the architect called Lightfall, five stories tall with many angles and curves. In Boston the British architecture firm Foster + Partners designed an addition to the city's Museum of Fine Arts. It formed a major new wing and added 53 galleries. In New York the hugely popular public park known as the High Line, built on an abandoned elevated freight-rail line, was extended another 10 blocks to the north, with a third and final section to open in the future. The success of the High Line led to much redevelopment in its formerly industrial neighbourhood, most of it in the form of fashionable and expensive apartment buildings by well-known "name" architects.

Architect Frank Gehry's Manhattan residential building, known as New York by Gehry, featured numerous curvy corners, as evidenced in the top floors of the structure.
Mary Altaffer/AP

Exhibitions, Conferences, and Other News. Several exhibitions in 2011 presented some aspect of the style known as Postmodernism, which flourished in the 1970s and '80s and in which there seemed to be renewed interest. The Victoria and Albert Museum in London mounted an exhibition entitled "Postmodernism: Style and Subversion," and the National Academy in New York City offered "Parabolas to Post-Modern: Architecture from the Collection." A two-day conference called "Reconsidering Postmodernism" took place in New York in November. Postmodernist architecture was a style that was critical of Modernism and often produced buildings that made reference to architecture of the past.

The Flagler Museum in Palm Beach, Fla., showed "The Extraordinary Joseph Urban," on the work of an architect often associated with the Art Deco style of the 1920s. In Montreal the Canadian Centre for Architecture presented "Palladio at Work," an exhibit of drawings by the Italian Renaissance master Andrea Palladio. The Milwaukee Art Museum (MAM) showed "Frank Lloyd Wright: Organic Architecture for the 21st Century," a collection of objects, photos, never-before-shown drawings, and rare film footage of one of the greatest American architects.

Preservation Issues. The National Trust for Historic Preservation held its annual convention in Buffalo, N.Y., a so-called rust-belt city that still possessed a remarkable range of works from its heyday as a wealthy industrial centre. There were massive grain elevators, parks, and parkways by Frederick Law Olmsted and buildings by Wright, Louis Sullivan, H.H. Richardson, Stanford White, Eliel and Eero Saarinen, and other well-known architects. In New York City the American Folk Art Museum, an admired work completed in 2001 by architects Tod Williams and Billie Tsien, was sold to its next-door neighbour, the Museum of Modern Art (MoMA). Another New York museum, the Whitney Museum of American Art by Modernist master Marcel Breuer, was sold to the Metropolitan Museum of Art, which planned to recycle it as gallery space. The Whitney planned to move its collection to a new building designed by Italian architect Renzo Piano and under construction on the High Line.

In New Orleans, neighbourhoods devastated by Hurricane Katrina (2005) were beginning to sport new houses, many of them sponsored by film actor

(continued on page 208)

Notable Civil Engineering Projects (in work or completed, 2011)

Name	Location		Year of completion	Notes
Airports		**Terminal area (sq m)**		
New Doha International (phases 1 and 2)	near Doha, Qatar	465,000	2013	Being built on 22 sq km of Persian Gulf landfill; new departures terminal opened in June 2011
Muscat International	west of Muscat, Oman, near Al-Sib	332,000	2014	Terminal expanded
Miami International (North Terminal)	northwest of central Miami	316,000	2012	Largest U.S. airport expansion under way in 2011; original terminal is being remodeled and expanded to become the North Terminal
Berlin Brandenburg International	Schönefeld airport, southeast of Berlin	220,000	2012	Schönefeld to be expanded; other Berlin airports closed in 2008 (Tempelhof) or will close in 2012 (Tegel); new terminal to be U-shaped
McCarran International (new Terminal 3)	Las Vegas	173,750	2012	To become new international terminal, with almost double the number of gates
Frankfurt Airport (new Terminal 3)	Frankfurt am Main, Ger.	106,700	2015	To increase passenger capacity at Europe's 2nd busiest airport by half
Spaceport America	Sierra county, N.M.	62,250	2012	To be the world's first purpose-built commercial facility for private space travel
San Francisco International (Terminal 2)	San Francisco	59,500	2011	Opened April 14
Winnipeg International	west of Winnipeg, Man.	51,000	2011	LEED-certified, Canada's "greenest" airport terminal opened Oct. 30
Al Maktoum International (phase 1)	at Jebel Ali, southwest of Dubai, U.A.E.	41,000*	2012	Cargo operations began in 2010; to become largest commercial airport in the world; *size of cargo terminals
Bridges		**Length (main span; m)**		
Hong Kong–Zhuhai Crossing	Hong Kong to China link (via Macau) (in Pearl River estuary)	c. 50 km	2016	To include world's largest sea bridge (c. 30 km) and world's longest immersed tube tunnel (5.6 km)
Jiaozhou Bay Bridge	between Qingdao and Huangdao, China, over Jiaozhou Bay	41,380	2011	Opened to traffic June 30; world's longest transoceanic bridge
Hangzhou Bay #2 (Jia-Shao)	between Jiaxing and Shaoxing, China	2,680	2012	Will be world's longest all-span cable-stayed bridge
Bridge Crossing to the Russky Island	Vladivostok–Russky Island, Russia (across the Eastern Bosporus Strait)	1,104	2012	To be world's longest cable-stayed bridge
San Francisco–Oakland Bay (East Span)	Yerba Buena Island–Oakland, Calif.	611	2013	To be world's longest self-anchored suspension span; last deck segment lifted into place Oct. 28, 2011
John James Audubon Bridge	New Roads–St. Francisville, La. (across the Mississippi)	483	2011	Opened May 5—the longest cable-stayed bridge in the Western Hemisphere
Chenab River Rail Bridge	Katra, Jammu-Kashmir, India	460	2015	To be world's highest vehicular bridge at 359 m
New Mississippi River Bridge	St. Louis, Mo.–Fairmount City, Ill.	457	2014	To be first new Mississippi bridge at St. Louis in more than 40 years
Tokyo Gate Bridge	Tokyo (on reclaimed land [in part] outside central breakwater)	440	2012?	Part of Tokyo Port Seaside Road; to enhance movement of international trade cargo; will be world's longest fully welded steel truss bridge
Manaus–Iranduba Bridge	Manaus–Iranduba, Braz.	400	2011	Inaugurated Oct. 24—1st bridge across a major Amazon river; 3.6 km in length and supported by 74 pylons
Deh Cho Bridge	at Fort Providence, N.W.Terr., across Mackenzie River	190	2012	Unique redesigned (1,045 m in length) composite steel truss bridge with 190-m cable-assisted main span; creates first permanent road link between Yellowknife, N.W.Terr., and the Alberta border
Danube Bridge #2 (2nd bridge between Bulgaria and Romania)	Vidin, Bulg.–Calafat, Rom.	180	2012	To stimulate economic development in an economically depressed part of Europe (NW Bulgaria/SW Romania); total length of bridge is 1,971 m
Buildings, Towers		**Height (rooftop; m)**		
Ping An Finance Centre	Shenzhen, China	660	2015	To be among the world's 10 tallest buildings
Tokyo Sky Tree	Tokyo	634	2012	To be world's tallest stand-alone communications tower; topped 500 m on Dec. 1, 2010
Shanghai Tower	Shanghai	632	2014	To be the tallest building in China
Abraj Al Bait ("Royal Clock") Towers	Mecca, Saudi Arabia	601	2012	Ceremonially inaugurated Aug. 19, 2011; 6 residential/hotel towers to house 65,000 people
Goldin Finance 117	Tianjin, China	597	2015	To be among the world's 10 tallest buildings
Lotte Jamsil Super Tower	Seoul	556	2015	To be South Korea's tallest building
1 World Trade Center (Freedom Tower)	New York City	"1,776 ft" (541.3 m)	2013	Complex to include 6 new buildings, a memorial, and a museum; construction reached structural halfway point in Feb. 2011
Pentominium	Dubai, U.A.E.	516	2013?	Will be world's tallest residential tower
Kingkey 100	Shenzhen, China	442	2011?	Topped out April 23
World One	Mumbai	442	2015	To be the tallest building on the Indian subcontinent
Ryugyong Hotel	Pyongyang, N.Kor.	330	2012	Work on North Korea's tallest building began in 1987, halted in 1993, and resumed in 2008; work on exterior thought to be completed in early 2011
Trump Ocean Club International Hotel and Tower	Panama City, Pan.	284	2011	Opened July 6; tallest building in Latin America
Dams		**Crest length (m)**		
Santo Antonio (SA)/Jirau (J) (2 dams on the Madeira River)	(SA): near Porto Velho, Rondônia, Braz. (J): between Porto Velho and Bolivian border	(SA) 1,173 (J) 550	2012 2012	Together will provide 8% of the electricity for Brazil by 2016
Diamer-Bhasha	on Indus River near Diamer, Pak.	1,169	2019	To be world's highest concrete dam; would satisfy all of Pakistan's current electricity needs and regulate water level of the flood-prone Indus River
Bakun Hydroelectric Project	Balui River, Sarawak, Malay.	750	2011	Began producing electricity Aug. 16; 2nd largest concrete-faced rockfill dam in the world
Xiluodu (part of upper Yangtze hydropower development scheme)	184 km upriver of Yibin, China, on Jinsha River	700	2015	First of 4-dam scheme that will generate more electricity than Three Gorges Dam
Gilgel Gibe III	Omo River, southwestern Ethiopia	610	2013	Electricity will be exported to Sudan and Kenya; largest hydropower project in sub-Saharan Africa
Sangtuda 2	on Vakhsh River, south of Dushanbe, Tajik.	385	2011	Electricity production began Sept. 5; Tajikistan will be energy self-sufficient when this Iranian-built dam reaches full power
Manuel Piar (Tocoma) (4th of 4-dam lower Caroní development scheme)	Caroní River, northern Bolívar, Venez.	360	2012	To be final unit of world's 3rd largest hydroelectric complex
Xiaowan	on Mekong (Lancang) River, southwestern Yunnan, China	?	2012	World's tallest (292 m) arch dam; 2nd only to Three Gorges Dam in hydroelectric potential
Zangmu	on Tsangpo (Brahmaputra) River southeast of Lhasa, Tibet, China	?	2015	First of 5 planned dams to be built on Tsangpo (Brahmaputra) River and its tributaries; possible water diversion is controversial with India
Highways		**Length (km)**		
South Interoceanic Highway	Iñapari (at Brazilian border)–Ilo/Matarani/San Juan de Marcona, Peru	2,603	2012	To be paved road for Brazilian imports/exports from/to Asia via 3 Peruvian ports; to link the Atlantic and Pacific oceans
Mombasa–Nairobi–Addis Ababa Road Corridor	Addis Ababa, Eth.–Mombasa, Kenya	1,284	2014	To facilitate trade between landlocked Ethiopia and the world through the Kenyan port of Mombasa

1 m=3.28 ft; 1 km=0.62 mi

Notable Civil Engineering Projects (in work or completed, 2011) continued

Name	Location		Year of completion	Notes
Highways (continued)		**Length (km)**		
East-West Highway (across northern Algeria)	Tunisian border (near Annaba)–Algerian border (near Tlemcen)	1,216	2012?	To facilitate economic development and trade across North Africa
Moscow–St. Petersburg M11 Motorway	Moscow–St. Petersburg	650	2017?	To reduce congestion in traffic between Russia's two largest cities
A2 Motorway ("east to west expressway across Poland")	Polish border near Frankfurt an der Oder, Ger.–Brest, Belarus (via Warsaw)	610	2012	Will link to German autobahn; 106-km section from German border to Nowy Tomysl, Pol., opened Nov. 30, 2010
Bamenda–Enugu Multinational Highway Corridor	Bamenda, Cameroon–Enugu, Nigeria	433	2013	To be a component of a planned Pan-African highway
Upper Egypt–Red Sea Road	Safaga–Assiut/Sohag/Qena, Egypt	414	2014	To link three vital communities on the Nile with the Red Sea via a modern multilane highway
Kaladan Multimodal Transport Project	Mizoram, India–Patetwa, Myanmar (Burma)	129	2013	To be part of a land and sea route connecting landlocked northeastern India to Myanmar ports
Canals and Floodgates		**Length (m)**		
Southern Delivery System (phase I)	Pueblo Reservoir to Colorado Springs and Denver suburbs	100,000	2016	To provide needed water from the Arkansas River to Colorado Springs and Denver
Inner Harbor Navigation Canal Surge Barrier	near confluence of Gulf Intracoastal Waterway and Mississippi River Gulf Outlet, east of New Orleans	2,897	2012	To be the largest design-build civil works project in U.S. Army Corps of Engineers history; central component of flood-protection system after Hurricane Katrina
MOSE Project (flood-protection plan)	lagoon openings near Venice	—	2015	Rows of 78 20-m-wide submerged gates in 3 lagoon openings will rise in flood conditions
Panama Canal Expansion	between Panama City and Colón, Pan.	—	2014	Will include new wider and longer 3-chamber locks, doubling the canal's capacity and allowing the passage of world's biggest container ships
Eastmain-1-A Powerhouse and Rupert Diversion	Rupert River watershed to Eastmain River watershed, northern Quebec	—	2012	Water diversion scheme to create an additional capacity of 918 MW; commissioning of first power-generating unit took place in June 2011
South-to-North Water Transfer Project (Middle Route)	Danjiangkou Reservoir (on Haijiang River) to Beijing	—	2014	Water will be canalized north to drought-prone Beijing area; total length of canal-pipeline system will be more than 1,273 km
Railways (Heavy)		**Length (km)**		
North South Rail Project (freight)	Al-Zubairah–Ras Al-Zour, Saudi Arabia	1,486	2011	Completed in May; will facilitate the export of phosphate and bauxite from mines in the interior via the Persian Gulf
Benguela Railway (rehabilitation; closed by civil war 1975–2002)	Lobito–Luau, Angola (at Dem. Rep. of the Congo border)	1,344	2012	Will enable resumption of copper exports from Dem. Rep. of the Congo and Zambia; 423-km section from Lobito to Huambo completed in Aug. 2011
Xinqiu–Bayan Ul Railway	Xinqiu, Liaoning–Bayan Ul, Inner Mongolia, China	487	2012?	To be used for coal transport; future 230-km link to Mongolian border expected
KATB rail project	Baku, Azer.–Kars, Tur. (via Tbilisi, Georgia)	258	2012	Caspian Sea to Turkey link, bypassing Armenia; 98 km of new rail, remainder modernized; new transport outlet for Georgia
Lhasa–Xigaze railway	Lhasa–Xigaze, Tibet, China	253	2015	Extension of the world's highest railroad will include 29 tunnels
North Luzon Railway System project (phase 1)	Caloocan (north Metro Manila)–Clark international airport, Philippines	82	2013?	To accelerate development of central Luzon
Northern line	Hairatan (on the Uzbekistan border)–Mazar-i-Sharif, Afg.	75	2011	First trial run took place Dec. 21; provides Afghanistan with it first rail service and link to neighbours' lines
Railways (High Speed)		**Length (km)**		
Jinghu High-Speed	Beijing–Shanghai	1,318	2011	Put into commercial service June 30; halves travel time between capital and financial centre
Turkish High-Speed	Ankara–Istanbul	533	2013	To connect capital with largest city; 212-km Ankara–Konya section inaugurated Aug. 23, 2011
Illinois High-Speed	Chicago–St. Louis	460	2015?	To cut travel time between Chicago and St. Louis by one-third
Haramain High Speed Rail Project (phase II)	Mecca–Medina, Saudi Arabia	444	2013?	To connect the holy cities of Mecca and Medina with Jeddah and King Abdullah Economic City in Rabigh
Morocco High-Speed	Tangier–Casablanca	348	2015	To link Morocco's two largest cities
Gautrain (second phase)	Johannesburg–Pretoria	77	2011	Opened Aug. 2; links South Africa's administrative capital with its commercial centre
Subways/Metros/Monorails/ Commuter Rails		**Length (km)**		
Delhi Metro	Delhi	111.7	2012?	111.7 km represents lengths of lines or extensions opened Jan. 2010–Feb. 2011; total length of planned lines equals 189.6 km
Namma Metro (phase I)	Bangalore (Bengaluru), India	42.3	2013	2 lines to be built; 7-km section inaugurated Oct. 20, 2011
Circle MRT	Singapore	35.7	2012	To be longest fully automated metro in the world; 33.3 km had opened by Oct. 8, 2011
Rome Metro (Line C)	Rome	25.5	2012	Crosses the city from NW to SE; 20 km completed by year-end 2011
Dubai Metro (Green Line)	Dubai, U.A.E.	22.5	2011	Opened Sept. 9; part of world's longest fully automated driverless transport system
Tel Aviv Mass Transit (Red Line)	Petah Tikva–Bat Yam (suburban Tel Aviv)	22.5	2017	To be Tel Aviv's first subway system; will link north and south suburbs through downtown
Lima Metro (Line 1)	Lima	21.5	2011	Opened July 11; includes 9.8-km refurbishment of existing line and 11.7-km new extension
Métro d'Alger (Line 1)	Algiers	21.0	2014	8.5-km phase I opened Oct. 31, 2011; delayed by archaeological finds
Houston Metro (north and southeast lines)	Houston	19.2	2015	First light-rail construction in Houston in a decade
Tunnels		**Length (m)**		
Brenner Base Tunnel	Innsbruck, Austria–Fortezza, Italy	55,392	2015	To be the longest underground railway tunnel in the world; more than 19 km of tunnel had been completed by year-end 2011
Alimineti Madhava Reddy Project	Krishna River to Nalgonda district, Andhra Pradesh state, India	43,500	2012	To provide irrigation and drinking water to drought-prone Nalgonda; will be world's longest tunnel without intermediate access
Marmaray railroad project tunnels	connecting European and Asian portions of Istanbul	13,600	2013/14	Includes 1.4-km-long bored tunnel, world's deepest sunken-tube tunnel (56 m under the Bosporus strait); opening delayed by discovery of historic artifacts at the construction site
East and West tunnels of A86 ring road	western outskirts of Paris	10,000/7,500	2011	Opened Jan. 8–9; two tunnels under Versailles and nearby protected woodlands
Portland East Side Big Pipe	underneath the Willamette River, Portland, Ore.	9,650	2011	Completed in December; capped a 20-year effort to upgrade Portland's sewerage system
Bay Tunnel Project	Menlo Park–Newark, Calif.	8,047	2015	To replace San Francisco-area water system and make it quake resistant

1 m=3.28 ft; 1 km=0.62 mi

(continued from page 205)
Brad Pitt. The houses were often painted in bright Caribbean-inspired colours. All were raised at least one metre (3.3 ft) aboveground to guard against flooding. In Japan, regions of which were devastated in March by an earthquake and tsunami, architect Shigeru Ban responded by creating a system of inexpensive indoor partitions to give privacy to homeless families living in public shelters.

Issues in Architecture. In the U.S. and elsewhere, business remained slow for architectural firms. Increasingly they responded to their economic problems by merging with one another. They hoped that the result would be larger firms with a greater variety of marketable skills.

The death of Apple founder Steve Jobs (*see* OBITUARIES) stirred the architectural community. He was not an architect, but he had inspired architects and hired them. Notable were the nearly 350 Apple stores, many of them all glass, including the roof; most of the buildings were designed for Jobs by architect Peter Bohlin. At his death Jobs was planning a vast new headquarters in California by the British firm Foster + Partners.

In London work on the Olympic Park, for the Games of 2012, involved many notable architects. The most-talked-about building was Hadid's London Aquatics Centre, a structure noted for its fluid lines. Most of the major Olympic buildings were planned so that they could be converted to public use after the Games were over. In Dresden, Ger., the Museum of Military History reopened after a 10-year reconstruction. Architect Daniel Libeskind created a five-story element that seemed to slice through the traditional building like a shard of shrapnel.

In New York City work on the seemingly endless redevelopment of the World Trade Center site plodded on. Of all the new elements planned for the site, only the National September 11 Memorial, designed by architect Michael Arad and landscape architect Peter Walker, opened during 2011, 10 years after the attack. The memorial preserved the footprints of the former Twin Towers in the form of two deep square holes, down the sides of which water cascaded. The two voids were surrounded by a public park that was planted with a dense grove of white oaks.

Controversy surrounded a proposed addition to the Glasgow (Scot.) School of Art. The original building, considered the most important work of Scots architect Charles Rennie Mackintosh, was finished in 1909. The school had proposed to expand into a new and entirely different building across the street by Holl, whose design for the building's exterior consisted almost entirely of translucent or transparent glass, in contrast to the darker stonework of the older building. Influential critic and historian William Curtis considered Holl's proposed building "far from being a worthy neighbour to a universally admired masterpiece." Gehry aroused controversy with his proposed memorial to U.S. Pres. Dwight D. Eisenhower. Intended to fill the length of a block near the Mall in Washington, D.C., the memorial design featured a row of 25-m (80-ft)-tall columns, with metal mesh tapestry stretched between them. At year's end it was in the process of being revised to address criticisms that it was too big and grand. (ROBERT CAMPBELL)

Scanpix Norway—Reuters/Landov

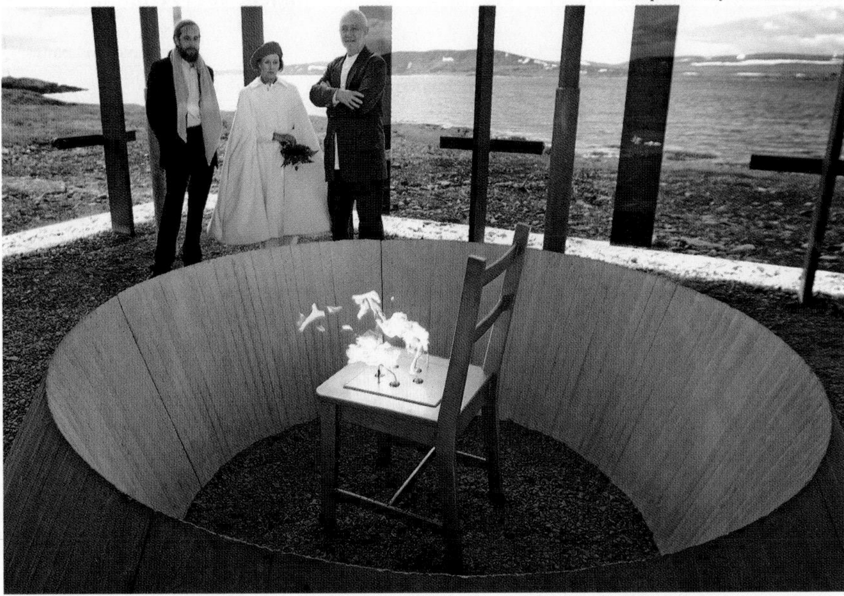

At a ceremony in Vardø, Nor., to dedicate a shrine to the victims of 17th-century witch trials there, Queen Sonja stands between Jerry Gorovoy (left), the former assistant to sculptor Louise Bourgeois, and architect Peter Zumthor (right), June 23. Prior to Bourgeois's death in 2010, she and Zumthor had collaborated on the design of the shrine and the glass house that enclosed an installation by Bourgeois.

Following a dramatic redesign by American architect Daniel Libeskind that featured the inclusion of a five-story wedge of glass, concrete, and steel, the Museum of Military History in Dresden, Ger., reopened in October.

Jens Meyer/AP

Art and Art Exhibitions

A sense of renewed **VITALITY** marked many of the global art fairs during the year, and **REASONABLE** prices for artworks helped to **BOOST** interest among collectors. **ASIAN** works were highly sought after among collectors, and China's **BOOMING** art market overtook the auction and gallery sales of the U.K. to **COMMAND** second place behind that of the U.S. Portraits of the stars of **HOLLYWOOD'S GOLDEN AGE** and the heretofore lost works of Chicago-based nanny **VIVIAN MAIER** were among the year's photo exhibits.

ART

In January 2011 New York City's Museum of Modern Art (MoMA) jumped into the ongoing debate over art and freedom of speech when it acquired two versions of David Wojnarowicz's video *A Fire in My Belly* (1986–87) for its permanent collection. The latest censorship controversy was ignited in November 2010 when the Smithsonian Institution acquiesced to demands from the Catholic League and some conservative members of the U.S. Congress that the video be removed from the National Portrait Gallery exhibition "Hide/Seek: Difference and Desire in American Portraiture." Other institutions, including the New Museum in New York City and Tate Modern in London, also chose to screen the controversial video. Also in January the Shanghai studio of Chinese artist Ai Weiwei was destroyed in advance of an agreed-upon official demolition date; two months earlier the artist-activist had been placed under house arrest in Beijing. On April 3 the police apprehended Ai as he tried to board a flight to Hong Kong. The art world demonstrated support for him in the form of petitions and withdrawals from planned exhibitions in China; Tate Modern, which was exhibiting Ai's *Sunflower Seeds* in the Turbine Hall, mounted letters spelling "Release Ai Weiwei" on the side of a light box facing the Thames from the top of the museum. In early June, as part of the Incidental Art Fest in Beijing, an otherwise blank wall at the CCD 300 gallery bore Ai's name; the police promptly closed the exhibition and took Lin Bing and the other organizers into custody. On June 22, after 81 days in prison, Ai was released; he faced heavy fines for charges related to "economic crimes" and remained under surveillance in Beijing with restricted access to the press and prohibitions against the use of social media. (*See* BIOGRAPHIES.)

In the art market a strong showing in early sales sparked expectations, but buyers were conservative in their choices. The Old Master sale in January at Sotheby's New York realized $90.6 million for 26 works, including Titian's *Sacra Conversazione: The Madonna and Child with Saints Luke and Catherine of Alexandria* (c. 1560), which sold for $16.1 million, breaking a 20-year record. Similarly, at London's postwar and contemporary sales in February, buyers chose reputation over risk. At Sotheby's, Francis Bacon's 1964 triptych of his friend Lucian Freud brought $37 million, more than doubling the auctioneer's high estimate. At Christie's, Gerhard Richter's subtle *Abstraktes Bild* (1990), which the seller had acquired in 2005 for less than $500,000, realized $5.1 million, nearly tripling the high estimate. Andy Warhol's monumental red-and-white *Self-Portrait* (1967), unseen by the public for more than 30 years, sold for $17.4 million. At Christie's New York Post-War and Contemporary sale in May, records were shattered for Warhol, Cindy Sherman, Cy Twombly, Urs Fischer, Richard Diebenkorn, and Anselm Kiefer. Warhol's photo-booth *Self-Portrait* (1963–64) set off a rowdy bidding war; the audience roared encouragement until the hammer came down at $38.4 million.

Among the year's surprises was the fierce bidding at Sotheby's in January that drove the price of Claude-Joseph Vernet's *A Grand View of the Seashore* (1776), estimated at $2 million, to $6.2 million. In July at Christie's Old Master

The interior view of Anish Kapoor's massive balloon sculpture Leviathan, *which was installed in May in the nave of the Grand Palais in Paris for the site's annual Monumenta exhibition.*

Benoit Tessier—Reuters/Landov

sale in London, George Stubbs's horse portrait *Gimcrack on Newmarket Heath* (c. 1765), realized a staggering $36 million. Hans Holbein the Younger's *The Madonna with the Family of Mayor Meyer* (1525–26), since 2003 on loan from a collector to the Städel Museum in Frankfurt am Main, Ger., changed hands in a record-breaking private sale for Germany at more than $70 million, far exceeding a previous offer from the museum for $57 million.

Sales in Asia were closely watched as they held steady, but the previous years' intense interest in Chinese contemporary artists abated among Western buyers. Chinese buyers acquired works in all areas, and, with combined auction and gallery sales of more than $8.3 billion, China displaced the U.K. for second place in the world market, surpassed only by the U.S. In response, Western dealers began expanding their Asian venues. In June Art Basel bought a majority stake in Art HK, Hong Kong's contemporary fair, and London's White Cube gallery was scheduled to open a branch in Hong Kong in early 2012. By the fall, global financial insecurity had drained the energy out of all markets. Christie's Post-War and Contemporary sale in October in London sold only 47 of 53 important lots; despite this, the sale, at $59.9 million, fell just short of the total high estimate. The year's trend toward blue-chip works continued, with the strongest returns for works by Richter, Antony Gormley, and Martin Kippenberger.

Site-specific installations in public buildings transformed existing space. Anish Kapoor's *Leviathan*—a monumentally scaled four-chambered balloon whose interior was bathed in red light—filled the main hall of the Grand Palais in Paris, forcing visitors to either pass through its chambers or walk around them. Gormley linked his sculpture *Transport* to its site, Canterbury (Eng.) Cathedral, by crafting a human figure out of lead nails removed from the cathedral's transept roof during a recent renovation. The otherworldly quality of the openwork figure, suspended from the ceiling over the tomb of Thomas Becket, evoked the transitory nature of existence; Gormley commented, "We are all the temporary inhabitants of a body." Equally ethereal was Jaume Plensa's *Echo*, a 13-m (44-ft)-high head—cast in resin that was painted glowing white and covered in lustrous marble dust—installed on the lawn of New York City's Madison Square Park. Plensa modeled the serenely beautiful face after that of a nine-year-old girl from his Barcelona neighbourhood and deliberately evoked the aesthetic of Constantin Brancusi through smooth surfaces and elongation. Rob Pruitt's 2-m (7-ft)-tall polished chrome *The Andy Monument*—featuring Warhol toting a Bloomingdale's shopping bag and wearing a Polaroid camera on a strap—was on temporary display in New York City's Union Square at 17th Street and Broadway (near the former locations of Warhol's studio, the Factory) and prompted critics and local residents alike to call for its permanent installation.

Antony Gormley's hanging sculpture Transport, *composed of nails that had been removed from the roof of Canterbury (Eng.) Cathedral, was displayed inside that cathedral beginning in January.*

Gareth Fuller—PA Photos/Landov

Although Christian Marclay's 24-hour film montage *The Clock* had debuted in autumn 2010, it took the 2011 art year by storm. After winning the Golden Lion at the Venice Biennale, the film—which combines documentary footage from across the globe with movie clips that blur the distinction between real and composed time—was copied and purchased by several museums, including MoMA and the Los Angeles County Museum of Art. The moving image was also the subject of *FILM*, Tacita Dean's Unilever Series installation in Tate Modern's Turbine Hall. Her celebratory elegy, created on 35-mm film and projected on a towering white block at the east end of the vast hall, offers a breathtaking array of images created on celluloid through analogue methods, a tribute to what Dean called "this beautiful medium" that had been eclipsed by digital technology.

The winner of the 2011 Turner Prize was environmental artist Martin Boyce, whose atmospheric sculptural installations drew inspiration from design history and attained the sensibility of the natural landscape through the human-made elements of utilitarian objects and sleek materials. Other nominees included environmental artist Karla Black, who used everything from swags of painted polyethylene and sugar paper to topsoil and bath products in an exploration of the physical realities of colour and form, George Shaw, a painter who portrayed the rundown Coventry (Eng.) neighbourhood of his youth in glossy Humbrol enamel (commonly used for model making), and Hilary Lloyd, a video artist whose blurred imagery expresses tactile ideas in a nontactile medium. Only one MacArthur fellowship went to an artist: Ubaldo Vitali, a fourth-generation traditional silversmith. Jasper Johns was awarded the Presidential Medal of Freedom. The Japan Art Association selected video artist Bill Viola and Kapoor to receive the Praemium Imperiale, an honour that recognized lifetime achievement.

Among the losses in the art world were figurative painters George Tooker and Lucian Freud, painter, draftsman, and sculptor Cy Twombly, "L.A. Cool School" sculptor John McCracken, Abstract Expressionist sculptor John Chamberlain, Pop art pioneer Richard Hamilton, Mozambican painter Malangatana, painter M.F. Husain, known as "India's Picasso," Abstract Expressionist Helen Frankenthaler, and British-born Mexican surrealist Leonora Carrington. (*See* OBITUARIES.) Conceptual and land artist Dennis Oppenheim and printmaker June Wayne also died.

(DEBRA N. MANCOFF)

ART EXHIBITIONS

The debates that challenged the viability of global art fairs in recent years were muted as the 2011 season opened in January with the inaugural edition of Art Stage Singapore. The new fair, led by Lorenzo Rudolf (former director of Art Basel), attracted 121 galleries from 26 countries and more than 32,000 visitors. Sales were strong for Asian and European galleries; Takashi Murakami's triptych *Snow Moon Flower* (2002) brought $2.2 million. The success was seen to rival the popular ART HK show, and Rudolf compared the excitement and energy of the Singapore show to his early days with Art Basel.

The vitality continued at the 13th edition of the Armory Show in New York City, where more than 270 galleries and dealers countered rumours of declining participation. Critic Roberta Smith credited an "egalitarian, free-for-all spirit" for making the fair feel "fresher" than in previous years. That scenario was certainly evident in the prominence of such affordable—and often playfully subversive—works as Andrew Hahn's $2,000 silk screen *Why Not Purchase Art?* and a $26,000 set of Gilbert and George's found and altered postcards. Reasonable prices for works by reputable artists provided a strategy for success and might help build a new audience base for future fairs. For other fairs expansion brought new vigour. In May the seventh edition of SP-Arte in São Paolo hosted 89 galleries and occupied double the space of previous editions; it saw sales rise 35%. In June the 42nd edition of Art Basel opened to great enthusiasm, but there was an estimable drop in American buyers. Noted works by Andy Warhol and Francis Bacon did not sell.

With 89 countries participating, the 54th Venice Biennale was the largest to date. The headline exhibition *ILLUMInations*, conceived by Bice Curiger of the Kunsthaus Zürich for the Central Pavilion in the Giardini and for the Arsenale, featured 83 artists ranging from Tintoretto and established contemporary artists Sigmar Polke and Cindy Sherman to the new generation, including light-and-sound artist Haroon Mirza. Curiger's themes of history, heritage, and contrast extended to other installations; Chinese artist Song Dong constructed a labyrinthine parapavilion of 100 doors salvaged in Beijing as a showcase for Moroccan artist Yto Barrada and British artist Ryan Gander. Swiss sculptor Urs Fischer replicated Giambologna's *Rape of the Sabines* (c. 1580) in candle wax, which was to melt through the duration of the fair. Iraq hosted a pavilion for the first time since 1976, and Israeli film and video artist Yael Bartana represented Poland with *... and Europe Will Be Stunned*, an ironic trilogy employing the style of Nazi and Zionist propaganda films to urge a Jewish return to revitalize Polish culture. The United States hosted an imposing installation by Jennifer Allora and Guillermo Calzadilla; *Track and Field* featured an upended military tank with a treadmill fixed to its right track. Once an hour an athlete ran on the treadmill to make the tank's wheels turn for 15 minutes; nearby, a gymnast performed on wooden replicas of airline first-class and business-class seats. Germany was awarded the Golden Lion for national participation with the late Christoph Schlingensief's total environment *A Church of Fear vs. the Alien Within*, and Christian Marclay took the Golden Lion for an individual artist with his 24-hour film, *The Clock* (2010). Mirza won the Silver Lion for most-promising young artist, and Golden Lions for lifetime achievement were given to the American artist Sturtevant and the Austrian artist Franz West.

In museum exhibitions the controversial *Art in the Streets*, organized by the Museum of Contemporary Art, Los Angeles, made headlines prior to its opening in April. Early in December 2010, a mural on an outside wall of LA MOCA's Geffen Contemporary building that featured dollar-draped coffins by the Italian street artist Blu was whitewashed just hours after it was unveiled; the subject was deemed potentially offensive to the patrons of a nearby Veterans' Affairs hospital. Through the duration of the exhibition, this survey of street art, ranging from urban tagging of the 1960s to Shepard Fairey's campaign image of U.S. Pres. Barack Obama, *Hope* (2008), inspired heated debate: Did it validate street art as a "museum-worthy" enterprise? Did it extinguish the authenticity of maverick expression by absorbing it into the mainstream? A simultaneous spike in graffiti in local neighbourhoods was attributed by the police to the exhibition, and the Brooklyn Museum canceled its planned showing for 2012. The headlines, no doubt, also contributed to the success of the exhibition; an influx of more than 200,000 visitors—including patrons who gained free admission each Monday owing to sponsorship by British street artist Banksy—broke the museum's attendance record.

Two outstanding midcareer retrospective exhibitions presented artists wrestling with self-identity in strikingly different ways. Glen Ligon's *AMERICA*, at the Whitney Museum of American Art in New York City, traced the conceptual artist's engagement with racial issues over more than two decades, featuring words and images of such iconic African American figures as Zora Neale Hurston, Malcolm X, and Richard Pryor. Ligon also interrogated perceptions of colour through such diverse objects as colouring books of the 1970s and Robert

Visitors to the Geffen Contemporary branch of the Museum of Contemporary Art, Los Angeles, stand in front of an artwork displayed in the Art in the Streets *exhibition, which was on view from April to August; the show was the first major graffiti and street-art exhibit mounted by an American museum.*

Lucy Nicholson—Reuters/Landov

Mapplethorpe's photographs of black men in more than 100 works in various media. At London's Hayward Gallery, *Love Is What You Want* presented the work of Tracey Emin (*see* BIOGRAPHIES) from her initial recognition as one of the Saatchi Gallery's Young British Artists to her recent reflections on turning 50. Her media ranged from assemblages to quilts to videos in a full theatrical installation. Emin's fearless self-exposure remained undiminished in an exhibition that evoked a trove of relics, profane objects made sacrosanct by the artist's self-inscribed hagiography.

Two retrospectives offered new insights into artists whose careers spanned the 20th century. The Whitney's *Lyonel Feininger: At the Edge of the World* overturned perceptions about an artist who had been conventionally linked with the Bauhaus. In an uneven but absolutely fascinating and fluid career, Feininger adapted his work to the turmoil of his times. The discoveries displayed—from early cartoons to a daring modernist palette for his urban scenes to the whimsical yet disturbing wooden figures that he carved throughout his career—demanded that his work be reevaluated. That eye-opening exhibition won Feininger new respect. For *De Kooning: A Retrospective*, at the Museum of Modern Art (MoMA), curator John Elderfield organized nearly 200 of Willem de Kooning's paintings, drawings, and sculptures into seven galleries. The definitive survey spanned seven decades—from his early explorations through his breakthrough expression at midcentury to the late lyricism of his final works in the late 1980s—and confirmed de Kooning's undisputed position as a modern master. Also of note were a trio of exhibitions exploring the figure in motion by Edgar Degas: *Degas and the Ballet: Picturing Movement* at London's Royal Academy of Arts, *Degas and the Nude* at Boston's Museum of Fine Arts, and *Degas's Dancers at the Barre: Point and Counterpoint* at the Phillips Collection in Washington, D.C.

In museum news New York City's American Folk Art Museum vacated its West 53rd Street premises; its neighbour MoMA had purchased the building for $31.2 million. The Metropolitan Museum of Art (the Met) planned to take over the Whitney's Madison Street building, designed by Marcel Breuer, in 2015; ground was broken on Gansevoort Street near the High Line for the Whitney's new home; it was designed by Renzo Piano. After 10 years of planning, the suite of galleries for the former Islamic Wing at the Met reopened; the suite was renamed Art of the Arab Lands, Turkey, Iran, Central Asia, and Later South Asia to rightly acknowledge, in curator Navina Najat Haidar's words, "Not one world, but many." In staff changes, James Cuno left his post as Eloise W. Martin Director of the Art Institute of Chicago to become president and CEO of the J. Paul Getty Trust; he was replaced by Douglas Druick, the Art Institute's most-accomplished curator. Deaths included those of Françoise Cachin, cofounder and first director of the Musée d'Orsay in Paris, Islamic art historian Oleg Grabar, and controversial scholar Leo Steinberg. (DEBRA N. MANCOFF)

Love Is What You Want, *a major retrospective of the work of British artist Tracey Emin, showed at the Hayward Gallery in London from May to August.*

David Levene—eyevine/Redux

PHOTOGRAPHY

When the year 2011 dawned, the media were anticipating the 10th anniversary of the September 11 terrorist attacks on the United States and the subsequent invasion of Afghanistan by U.S. and British forces. The most prominent photography exhibition related to the anniversary was "Burke + Norfolk: Photographs from the War in Afghanistan" (May 6–July 10), Tate Modern, London. The exhibition featured British landscape photographer Simon Norfolk, who took as his subject daily life in Kabul and at U.S. and British military bases in Afghanistan. Norfolk's photographs, made over the course of several visits in 2010 and early 2011, were arranged alongside images made by 19th-century Irish photographer John Burke during the Second Anglo-Afghan War (1878–80). Coinciding with the exhibition opening was publication of a book of the same name.

In Afghanistan a complementary exhibition, "Views of Kabul" (March 6–28), opened at the Queen's Palace, Bagh-e Babur, Kabul. The exhibition was organized by the Tate Modern in collaboration with the Aga Khan Trust for Culture and the World Collections Programme (a U.K. initiative to broaden cultural links between institutions in the U.K., Asia, the Middle East, and Africa) and featured colour photographs by Fardin Waezi and other Afghan photographers who had participated in workshops led by Norfolk.

One of Britain's most respected contemporary photographers, John Blakemore, held his first major retrospective exhibition, "John Blakemore: Photographs 1955–2010" (September 16–October 14), at Hoopers Gallery, London. In 2010 his photographic archive was purchased for the nation by Birmingham Central Library. On the other side of the Atlantic, the Klompching Gallery, New York City, eschewed the retrospective exhibition in favour of photographs by new and unknown artists. That influential gallery, co-owned by *Photo District News* creative director Darren Ching and Debra Klomp Ching, exhibited "Fresh 2011" (July 20–August 13), its first annual open photography exhibition to showcase images that were "fresh in ap-

Charles Rex Arbogast/AP

A light box frames 12 of the more than 100,000 recently discovered negatives made by unknown amateur photographer Vivian Maier, who worked as a nanny for a living. The negatives, auctioned off after her death, were purchased by John Maloof, and a portion of them were printed and formed into a remarkable traveling show.

proach and vision." Four photographers—Harold Ross, Skott Chandler, Donna J. Wan, and Ahron D. Weiner—were chosen by Darren Ching and New York-based collector and curator W.M. Hunt to exhibit at the gallery and online.

The death of film star Elizabeth Taylor (*see* OBITUARIES) added poignancy to the exhibition "Glamour of the Gods: Hollywood Portraits" (July 7–October 23) at the National Portrait Gallery, London. Comprising photographic portraits from the John Kobal Foundation, the exhibition featured vintage prints from 1920 to 1960 of some of Hollywood's greatest stars, including Greta Garbo, Marlene Dietrich, Clark Gable, Jean Harlow, Jane Russell (*see* OBITUARIES), Humphrey Bogart, and Marlon Brando, as well as Taylor, whom many regarded as the last major star to emerge from the old Hollywood studio system.

Taylor was one of the featured stars in another London exhibition, "Herb Ritts" (June 27–September 11), at Hamiltons Gallery, which showed limited-edition prints of celebrities, including Madonna, Cindy Crawford, and Naomi Campbell. Ritts, who died in 2002, had made those prints at the time of the shoots and kept them aside for himself. Consequently, most had never been reproduced or shown until released for the exhibition by the Ritts Foundation.

The difficulties faced by the global economy in 2011 did not appear to affect the market for fine-art photography. A major auction of 170 lots by Bonhams New York on May 10 brought in total sale proceeds in excess of $1.2 million. The auction featured works by renowned 20th-century photographers such as Edward Weston, Irving Penn, Ansel Adams, Hiroshi Sugimoto, and Helmut Newton. Four of the prints—Lucien Clergue's *Picasso à la cigarette à la Californie, Cannes* (1956), Flor Garduño's *Basket of Light, Sumpango, Guatemala* (1989), Richard Avedon's *Humphrey Bogart, Actor, New York* (1953), and Irving Penn's *Alfred Hitchcock, New York, May 23* (1947)—sold for at least double their presale high estimates. The last print sold for $54,900, the highest bid of the day. Two prints from Sugimoto's *Colors of Shadow* (both 2006) collection brought $30,500 and $24,400, respectively.

In China 30-year-old photographer Chi Peng presented his latest work in the exhibition "Mood and Memory" (July 2–August 28) at the m97 Gallery, Shanghai. His photographs explored themes of identity, freedom, and elusive love in images that featured recurring symbols of water, sky, and seabirds. The exhibition coincided with the publication of Chi Peng's latest book, *Me, Myself, and I*, which was printed in English and featured an interview with the photographer by fellow artist and political activist Ai Weiwei. (*See* BIOGRAPHIES.)

American photographer Bruce Davidson on April 27 received the Outstanding Contribution to Photography Award at the Sony World Photography Awards ceremony in London. The same ceremony honoured the memory of photographers Tim Hetherington and Chris Hondros, who were killed in Misratah, Libya, on April 20 while covering the Libya Revolt of 2011. Hetherington was co-director (with writer Sebastian Junger) of the film *Restrepo* (2010), which was nominated for an Academy Award for best documentary feature. In remembrance, Aperture Foundation, New York City, from May 25 to June 23 screened two of Hetherington's works: the five-minute three-screen video installation *Sleeping Soldiers* (2009) and the 19-minute personal video *Diary* (2010).

A photographic discovery of 2011 that generated significant media attention and public interest was a cache of the photographs and home movies of Vivian Maier, a Chicago nanny and street photographer who died in 2009, leaving more than 100,000 negatives only she had seen. "Vivian Maier: A Life Uncovered," at the German Gymnasium, London, was the headline exhibition of the first London Street Photography Festival (July 1–24). Forty-eight framed prints in black-and-white as well as colour documented daily life on the streets of several cities, notably Chicago. It prompted *The Telegraph* newspaper to compare her to the great American photographer Harry Callahan, especially in the way "she looked for drama in the streets" and used high-contrast black-and-white to "lend the ordinary a sense of the extraordinary."

Photography returned to the Royal Academy of Arts, London, for the first time in the century with an exhibition *This Is London* magazine described as "unmissable." "Eyewitness: Hungarian Photography in the 20th Century" (June 30–October 2) brought together works of the well-known Hungarian photographers Brassai, Robert Capa, Martin Munkacsi, Andre Kertesz, and Laszlo Moholy-Nagy, as well as lesser-known Hungarian photographers from the early 20th century to the present day. In the exhibition catalog, curator Colin Ford quoted the Hungarian-born British author Arthur Koestler's explanation of why Hungary had produced so many artists: "Hungarians are the only people in Europe without racial or linguistic relatives, … therefore they are the loneliest on this continent. This … perhaps explains the peculiar intensity of their existence. … Hopeless solitude feeds their creativity." Capa had a simpler explanation: "It's not enough to have talent, you also have to be Hungarian."

(KEITH WILSON)

Business Overview

The year 2011 was marked by **VOLATILITY** as spikes in energy and raw materials prices, widespread political **INSTABILITY**, and destructive weather in Japan and elsewhere hit the **BOTTOM LINE** for industries ranging from airlines to chemical manufacturers. There were **POSITIVE** signs, however, including the sharp recovery of the American **AUTO SECTOR** and an unprecedented **SURGE** in new energy sources, including shale gas released through **FRACKING**.

Petroleum and Natural Gas. With new oil and natural gas finds seemingly everywhere that producers looked in 2011—from the Arctic Circle to the coast of Mozambique—many observers believed that the collective potential of these new supplies could alter the nature and distribution of energy production over the next two decades, with the power of Middle Eastern oil producers possibly on the wane. In the U.S., domestic oil and gas production was increasing for the first time in decades. Global deepwater-well oil production stood at 7 million bbl per day, up from 1.5 million in 2000, and that amount could double by 2020. Production from Canadian oil sands was generating 1.5 million bbl of synthetic oil daily, up from 600,000 bbl a decade earlier. In September a shale find in the U.K. was announced that could meet British gas demand for 64 years. Meanwhile, despite ongoing environmental concerns, a growing supply of natural gas from the hydraulic fracturing, or fracking, of shale deposits made the U.S. the world's largest producer of shale gas. (*See* Special Report on page 190.) The promise of an ample global supply flattened natural gas prices, which stood at $4 per million British thermal units (BTU) in October 2011, compared with $13 per million in July 2008.

Kinder Morgan reported in October that it would buy its rival El Paso Corp. to form the largest natural gas pipeline operator—and the fourth largest energy company—in the U.S. The Kinder Morgan–El Paso deal, which would control more than 107,000 km (about 67,000 mi) of natural gas pipelines from New York to California, would likely herald other mergers in a fragmented industry that had more than 50 pipeline operators and no nationwide pipeline network.

Exxon Mobil Corp. in August announced an oil find of potentially a billion barrels in the Gulf of Mexico. "Hadrian," possibly the largest oil discovery yet made in the Gulf, faced delays in development, however, as Exxon and Norway's Statoil sued the U.S. government after Department of the Interior regulators provisionally denied the companies lease extensions for the find. Regulators claimed that the companies had not followed correct procedures to obtain the extensions. Finding new production sources was vital for Exxon, which, although it posted record capital and exploration expenses of $26.7 billion for the first nine months of 2011, saw its oil and gas output fall by 4%, its first decline since 2009.

Oil producers' profits generally spiked owing to higher crude oil prices; Brent crude rose 46% in the third quarter year-over-year, with average prices at $112.09 a barrel. Exxon profits rose 41% in the third quarter. ConocoPhillips, which was to split its production and refining businesses into two publicly traded companies in 2012, had its profits rise by roughly 30%, and Chevron, which was more concentrated in oil than natural gas, had an 80% boost. Oil prices cooled to $107.38 as the year ended, however, reflecting tentative political stability in the Middle East and signs of a persistently weak economic recovery.

BP PLC was still recovering from the Gulf of Mexico oil spill in 2010, with its share price in October some 44% lower than before the Deepwater Horizon disaster. Seeking to rebound from the spill, BP announced a deal in January with Russia's OAO Rosneft to develop fields in the Russian Arctic shelf. BP subsidiary TNK-BP, which was partially owned by Russian billionaire consortium AAR, fought the deal, claiming that it violated a shareholder agreement specifying TNK-BP as BP's primary vehicle for investing in Russian oil. After court injunctions and rejected compromises (BP and Rosneft offered to buy out AAR's stake in TNK-BP, to no avail), the deal collapsed. Exxon Mobil took BP's place in the Rosneft deal, agreeing to invest $2.2 billion. BP, which posted a third-quarter profit of $5.3 billion, was seeking new exploration projects as the year ended.

Producers in Asian countries, which were increasingly dependent on oil and gas imports, spent the year securing new energy sources. China's Sinopec was financing a pipeline across Canada to move oil from Alberta to British Columbia ports, from which oil could be transported via tanker to China. CNOOC, China's largest offshore oil producer, purchased the bankrupt Canadian oil-sands developer OPTI Canada Inc. for $2.1 billion and was trying to buy BP's stake in Argentina's Pan American Energy LLC for $7 billion as the year closed.

Automobiles. The Big Three U.S. automakers—Ford, General Motors (GM), and Chrysler—which had come close to collapse in 2008 and had required $80 billion from the federal government to stay alive, were all profitable in 2011. They negotiated new agreements with their labour unions to reduce costs (each signed agreements with the United Auto Workers [UAW] union to keep in place a two-tier system in which new hires earned roughly half that of veterans) and pushed into growing markets, such as China and India. By contrast, formerly strong Japanese automakers suffered a terrible year. Global automakers sold more than 12.7 million cars and light trucks in the U.S. in 2011, up from 11.5 million in 2010.

General Motors Corp. began 2011 with its first annual profit since 2004 and its best yearly performance since 1999. In the previous three years, GM had reduced its employee count to 208,000 from 263,000 and slashed its production to 49 models from 86. GM posted an 89% increase in net income—$2.5 billion on revenue of $39.4 billion—for the second quarter of 2011, though its performance cooled later in the year, with profits falling 15% in the third quarter to $1.7 billion. GM also pushed to extend its reach into China (where it hoped to double its sales to five million units by 2015) via its joint venture with SAIC Motor Corp.

Chrysler Group LLC repaid $7.5 billion in loans that it had received from the U.S. and Canadian governments and posted its first quarterly profits since 2006, including $212 million in the third quarter. Chrysler was on pace for its first profitable year since 2005, with a projected annual net income of $600 million. Fiat SpA took a majority stake in Chrysler in July and soon afterward combined senior management of both companies into one executive committee, headed by CEO Sergio Marchionne. The merger, which was to be completed by 2014, hinged on the UAW's health care trust fund, which owned 41.5% of Chrysler, selling its shares.

For the first nine months of 2011, Ford Motor Co.'s pretax operating profit was $7.7 billion, and its net income was $6.6 billion. Ford consolidated and renovated brands throughout the year, discontinuing Mercury after a 71-year-run and redesigning most of its Lincoln models. Ford faced declining profit margins, however, owing partially to higher raw materials costs, while losses in its European operations rose 56% in the third quarter alone. Ford was also playing catch-up to its domestic rivals in China and India: it planned to expand its low-cost Chinese models to 15 models from 5 and its Indian models from 3 to 8. Ford hoped to expand its global auto sales by 50% to roughly eight million vehicles per year by 2015.

By contrast, Toyota Motor Co. and Honda Motor Co. endured sales declines for much of the year. Production slowdowns after the massive earthquake and subsequent tsunami in northern Japan in March at times left car dealers with scant inventories and an inability to find replacement parts. Just as Japanese automakers had returned to full production in late September, flooding temporarily closed their factories in Thailand. Japanese automakers were also hurt by the yen's strong performance against the dollar, which made Japanese cars more costly to export (for example, every one-yen drop in the dollar's value cut Toyota's annual profit by roughly $450 million). Toyota's net profit fell 99% in its fiscal first quarter, though the company projected a net profit for the year. One of Toyota's few pieces of good news came when in February the National Highway Traffic Safety Administration and NASA engineers absolved Toyota of responsibility for unintended accelerations in its vehicles. The commission found that the accelerations, a public relations debacle for Toyota, were due primarily to driver error.

Narong Sangnak—EPA/Landov

Floodwaters surround a bridge holding dozens of cars at the site of a Honda Motor Co. factory in Phra Nakhon Si Ayutthaya province, Thai., on October 18. Japanese car production throughout the world was disrupted by massive flooding in Thailand, where various parts were manufactured.

Honda, which was slower than Toyota or Mitsubishi to recover from earthquake-related production slowdowns, experienced a 61% drop in profit for the second quarter. Honda's redesigned Civic, which had been expected to anchor sales in 2011, experienced substantial production slowdowns, and Honda's planned launch of the redesigned CR-V was put on hold owing to parts shortages. By contrast, Nissan Motor Co. was the swiftest of the Japanese automakers to recover from the earthquake, aided by having had a larger inventory on hand than its rivals.

Prospering at the expense of the Japanese automakers were South Korea's Hyundai Motor Co. and its affiliate, Kia Motors Corp. Hyundai posted a 21% increase in quarterly net profit for the July–September period, and the two automakers were on pace to meet their combined target of moving 6.5 million units for the year. At year's end, Hyundai and Kia's market share in the U.S. was 8.9%.

Volvo, which China's Zhejiang Geely Holding Group acquired from Ford in 2010, was pushed by its new owners to concentrate on the luxury market. Volvo sought to double its annual sales to 800,000 vehicles by 2020 and to challenge top luxury-car models such as Volkswagen AG's Audi and Daimler AG's Mercedes. Geely was expected to invest as much as $11 billion in Volvo over the next five years. Volvo reported an operating profit in the first nine months of 2011 of about $72.5 million.

European automakers suffered from declining sales, owing in part to the ongoing economic crisis in the euro zone, which sapped demand. Daimler, whose premium car sales had slumped, in October dismissed Ernst Lieb, the CEO of its U.S.-based Mercedes-Benz operations, after allegations of financial impropriety. Lieb had been credited with Mercedes' strong performance in 2011, when it was the largest luxury-car maker in the U.S. Volkswagen also blamed the debt crisis for weak demand in western European markets, although VW posted a quarterly operating profit of €9 billion (about $12 billion). Renault SA fired three executives for allegedly having stolen secrets associated with its electric car program but then recanted, admitting that the claims were false. Saab Automobile filed for liquidation in mid-December after a possible deal collapsed between Saab's parent company, Swedish Automobile and two Chinese carmakers, Zhejiang Youngman Lotus Automobile and Pang Da Automobile Trade.

Airlines. The global airline industry, after a mild recovery in 2010, was facing another double punch of high fuel costs and declining profits. The International Air Transport Association said that the average profit margin in the industry could fall to a mere 0.8% in 2012, a decline from 2011's already small 1.2%.

AMR Corp. (American Airlines' parent) was in the roughest shape of the legacy carriers in the U.S. AMR posted a third-quarter loss of $162 million, compared with $143 million in revenue in third-quarter 2010, owing in part to a 41% increase in fuel costs in the year-over-year period. AMR had higher labour expenses than its rivals, lacked the variety of routes of merged rivals such as Delta–Northwest, and was the only legacy carrier to remain unprofitable; it was on course to post its fourth-straight annual loss. AMR, the sole legacy airline to escape bankruptcy in the previous decade, filed for Chapter 11 bankruptcy protection in late November.

The newly merged United Continental, the world's largest airline, projected a $1.4 billion profit for 2011, though it faced challenges, including a federal lawsuit by the Air Line Pilots Association (representing United pilots) that claimed that United's revised post-merger operating procedures would not maintain safety standards. Delta Air Lines, the second largest global airline, posted a 51% spike in earnings in third-quarter 2011. While it was on course to be profitable for the year, Delta's fuel spending rose sharply, up 42% to $2.88 billion in the third quarter.

Discount airlines were also plagued by high fuel costs. JetBlue Airways Corp. reported third-quarter income of $35 million, down from $59 million the previous year. JetBlue blamed a 56% rise in fuel costs, a 35% increase in mechanical costs in the same period, and Hurricane Irene, which caused JetBlue to cancel 1,400 flights in late August. Southwest Airlines posted a $140 million loss in the third quarter, partially because of $227 million of noncash markdowns resulting from the company's inadequate fuel hedges (the airline had anticipated roughly $90-per-barrel oil prices but paid about $120). Southwest raised fares eight times between December 2010 and October 2011, which thus pushed its average ticket price up 39% in five years.

European and Asian airlines saw demand sapped by everything from the Japanese earthquake to ongoing political turmoil in Europe. All Nippon Airways Co. (ANA) reported that it would likely post a loss in the second half of its fiscal year through March 2012 as a result of the strong yen, high fuel costs, and slowing demand. ANA, which ordered 55 of Boeing's new 787s, planned to use the new Dreamliner to extend its global presence. International Consolidated Airlines Group SA (IAG; the former British Airways and Iberia Lineas Aereas) said that its Spanish unit might not be profitable until 2013 owing to poor domestic demand and a 10% increase in fuel costs in the previous year. IAG in October unveiled Iberia Express, a new low-cost carrier designed for the Spanish market. Lufthansa, whose nine-month operating profit fell 5.6% owing to fuel costs and declining customers, made a deal to sell its ailing U.K. subsidiary, British Midland International, which posted an operating loss of €154 million (about $208 million) in the first nine months of 2011.

Aircraft. In mid-October ANA conducted the first charter passenger flight of Boeing Co.'s 787 Dreamliner, signaling an end to more than three years of production delays. The Dreamliner was intended to be Boeing's primary aircraft for the next 25 years, with Boeing hoping that the new jet would turn a profit by 2020. The Dreamliner's debut was part of a strong year for Boeing, which reported a 31% increase in its third-quarter profit and a batch of future orders, including a $35 billion contract for fueling tankers from the U.S. Air Force and Delta's $8 billion 100-plane order of 737-900s. Deliveries of Boeing's 787 and 747-8 jetliners were still behind schedule, however, with Boeing expecting to deliver only up to 20 of the new planes by the end of 2011, compared with earlier projections of 25–30. While Boeing intended to increase 787 production to 10 jets a month by late 2013 from its 2011 pace of 2.5 per month, it delayed plans to introduce a larger version of the 787, the 787-9, until 2014.

Airbus SAS managed a win against Boeing when American Airlines split a $40 billion order of 460 new aircraft between the two and gave Airbus the greater share (260 A320s to 200 Boeing 737s). It was the first order that American had placed with Airbus since the 1980s. Airbus also received orders for more than 100 A320s from the Indian budget carrier Go Airlines and the Philippines' Cebu Air Inc. During the year, Airbus began production of its rival to the Dreamliner, the A350, which was due to reach the market in 2014.

Metals. The metals price boom that began with the recession in 2008 continued for much of 2011. On September 6 gold hit a new all-time high (in nominal, not inflation-adjusted terms) of $1,923.70 per ounce before slipping to $1,566.80 at year's end. In what some read as a sign that the global economy would not recover in the near future, governments nearly tripled their net gold purchases in a year. Silver in April rallied to 31-year highs of nearly $50 per ounce after having already broken a 30-year high in October 2010, but it tumbled to a year-end $27.92. Copper prices, which topped $4.63 per pound in February, also fell to close at $3.44.

Prices for commodities such as iron ore and coal rose between 22% and 52% in the first half of 2011 compared with the same period in 2010. This was attributed to strong demand (in part from emerging market economies) and constrained supply brought about by a host of factors, from labour strikes in African mines to weather-related production delays. Some 25 countries announced plans to increase tax and royalty rates. Australia's BHP Billiton Ltd., the world's largest mining company, broke a streak of failed merger attempts with a $12.1 billion purchase in August of U.S.-based Petrohawk Energy. At year's end BHP, whose net profits rose 85% to hit $23.6 billion in its fiscal year ended June 30, was considering buying Brazil's Ferrous Resources.

Aluminum prices generally softened during the year, falling to $2,185 per metric ton as of mid-October, down from a peak of $2,786 per metric ton in May, and dropping below $2,000 in December. Alcoa Inc. reported third-quarter net income of $172 million due to strong demand from automobile and airplane makers, along with Chinese manufacturers. The company was likely to reduce smelting capacity in 2012, however, in order to reduce costs. Two Alcoa officials were arrested in October by global law-enforcement agencies as part of an investigation into alleged overcharges and kickbacks in its dealings with Aluminum Bahrain BSC (Alba).

Steelmakers faced both falling demand and lower prices. According to the World Steel Association, world steel demand was expected to grow by 6.5% for the year, compared with the 15.1% growth of 2010, and 2012 was expected to slow further, with growth predictions in the 5% range. Prices of hot-rolled steel fell to roughly $670 per ton in October, compared with almost $900 a ton in April. These declines left steelmakers scrambling to scale down production; ThyssenKrupp AG indicated that it would reduce output by 500,000 tons by early 2012, and ArcelorMittal planned to permanently close two blast furnaces in Liège, Belg., and temporarily shutter plants in France and Germany. ArcelorMittal in October pulled out of a $5 billion joint bid for Macarthur Coal.

Steelmakers pushed to renegotiate raw material contracts at lower prices (spot iron-ore prices dropped to below $150 a ton by year's end, and coal prices also fell) as steel buyers sought to reduce inventories and shorten lead times. Less-developed markets were expected to account for nearly three-quarters of global steel demand in 2012.

Pharmaceuticals. With many of the pharmaceutical industry's top-selling drugs facing the expiration of their patents, the struggle between generic manufacturers and name-brand producers intensified, with regulators occasionally called in to referee. In September the Federal Trade Commission claimed that some drug manufacturers were trying to delay competition by offering to defer their own generic version of their patented drug if generics manufacturers delayed their versions. U.S. regulators were also examining Warner Chilcott's novel attempt to delay generic competition. The Irish drugmaker added a second line to the surface of its Doryx pills (to make it easier to divide the pill in thirds) and then claimed that generics issued with only one line would "raise public health concerns."

Pfizer Inc., whose Lipitor lost U.S. patent protection in November, looked to introduce a new version of the cholesterol drug to be sold over the counter, hoping to retain some of Lipitor's $11 billion in annual sales. A federal judge upheld Pfizer's patent on Viagra until 2019, delaying a bid by Teva Pharmaceutical Industries Ltd. to develop a generic version. Viagra generated $1 billion in sales in the U.S. annually; keeping exclusivity could increase Pfizer's earnings by as much as 3% for each remaining year of patent protection. Pfizer and other pharmaceutical companies were laying the groundwork for a post-"blockbuster" era by reducing research-and-development spending by 30% and concentrating more on lucrative "niche" drugs such as Xalkori, which treated a rare form of lung cancer at an annual price of $115,200.

Teva, the world's largest generic drug manufacturer, got a taste of its own medicine when its brand-name drug Copaxone faced the threat of generic competition. Mylan Inc. and Momenta Pharmaceuticals Inc. asked the FDA for approval to sell generics before the patent expired in 2014. The threat of expiring patents also spurred some industry consolidation, such as Canada's Valeant Pharmaceuticals International Inc.'s hostile offer for Cephalon Inc., which Teva eventually purchased for $6.8 billion. The patent on Cephalon's leading drug, the narcolepsy treatment Provigil, would expire in April 2012.

Drugmakers were also challenged by regulators on a variety of fronts. In November the FDA revoked its previous approval of Roche Holding AG's breast cancer drug Avastin after the agency concluded that clinical trials showed that the drug did not improve the conditions of breast cancer sufferers. In March co-developers GlaxoSmithKline PLC and Human Genome Sciences won approval from the FDA for Benlysta, the first new drug to treat lupus in a half century. The U.K.'s National Institute for Health and Clinical Excellence, however, subsequently recommended that the National Health Service not pay for the new drug, which it considered overpriced.

Finance. Although the global economy managed to avoid a "double dip" recession in 2011, growth in most Western countries faltered. (*See* Special Report on page 170.) As the euro-zone debt crisis expanded, governments fell in several EU member countries during the year, notably Greece and Italy. Unemployment in the U.S. finally showed signs of improvement, declining to 8.5% in December. Investors and consumers in the U.S. remained nervous, however, in the face of the unresolved crisis in the euro zone, political upheaval in the Middle East and North Africa, a still-moribund U.S. housing market, and uncertainty over the upcoming 2012 elections. After two years of gains, most world stock markets showed losses for the year, with the notable exception of the Dow Jones Industrial Average, which closed up 5.5% at 12,217.60.

(CHRISTOPHER O'LEARY)

Selected Major World Stock Market Indexes[1]

Country and Index	2011 range[2] High	Low	Year-end close	Percent change from 12/31/2010
Argentina, Merval	3665	2287	2463	–30
Australia, Sydney All Ordinaries	5065	3928	4111	–15
Brazil, Bovespa	71,633	48,668	56,754	–18
Canada, Toronto Composite	14,271	11,178	11,955	–11
China, Shanghai A	3202	2269	2304	–22
France, Paris CAC 40	4157	2782	3160	–17
Germany, Frankfurt Xextra DAX	7528	5072	5898	–15
Hong Kong, Hang Seng	24,396	16,250	18,434	–20
India, Sensex (BSE-30)	20,561	15,175	15,455	–25
Italy, S&P/MIB	23,178	13,474	15,090	–25
Japan, Nikkei 225	10,858	8160	8455	–17
Mexico, IPC/BOLSA	38,696	31,716	37,078	–4
Russia, RTS	2124	1217	1380	–22
Singapore, Straits Times	3280	2529	2646	–17
South Africa, Johannesburg All Share	33,094	28,391	31,986	0
South Korea, KOSPI	2229	1653	1826	–11
Spain, Madrid Stock Exchange	1138	770	858	–15
Taiwan, Weighted Price	9145	6633	7072	–21
United Kingdom, FTSE 100	6083	4944	5572	–6
United States, Dow Jones Industrials	12,811	10,655	12,218	6
United States, Nasdaq Composite	2874	2336	2605	–2
United States, NYSE Composite	8671	6574	7477	–6
United States, Russell 2000	865	609	741	–5
United States, S&P 500	1364	1099	1258	0
United States, Wilshire 5000	14,495	11,459	13,190	–1
World, MS Capital International	1392	1075	1183	–8

[1]Index numbers are rounded. [2]Based on daily closing price.
Sources: Bloomberg.com, wilshire.com, *Financial Times, The Wall Street Journal.*

Computers and Information Systems

SOCIAL networking, tablet computers, and E-BOOK readers were hot areas of technology in 2011. Public SCRUTINY was focused on GOOGLE'S business practices, AT&T's attempt to acquire T-MOBILE, and such online services as GROUPON and Netflix.

The technology news that affected the most consumers in 2011 was the death in October of Apple Inc.'s legendary CEO and cofounder Steve Jobs, who had been diagnosed with pancreatic cancer in 2003. (*See* OBITUARIES.) There was a worldwide outpouring of grief and tribute for Jobs, who was widely seen as a visionary who had changed the world and in the process had become the symbol of Silicon Valley innovation.

Just weeks earlier, Jobs, aged 56, had issued his resignation announcement. He gave few details, but his three previous sick leaves from the company and his gaunt physical appearance had led many to believe that he was again seriously ill. In an August letter to the board and the "Apple Community," Jobs said, "I have always said if there ever came a day when I could no longer meet my duties and expectations as Apple's CEO, I would be the first to let you know. Unfortunately, that day has come."

Jobs's chosen successor, Apple chief operating officer Tim Cook, 50, was named CEO. The loss of Jobs set off a firestorm of speculation about Apple's future; many wondered if the company could prosper without Jobs, who had rock-star status in the public eye for his seemingly unerring knack for intuitively knowing consumers' wants. Cook was given credit for one of Apple's major strengths, however: its ability to keep the prices of its consumer electronics devices relatively low as a result of supplier contracts that allowed Apple to buy electronic parts at favourable prices. That pricing strategy was a major barrier for Apple's competitors because it limited their ability to sell similar products for less than those from Apple.

Apple's success in 2011 went beyond products. For one day in August, it surpassed Exxon Mobil Corp. in value (as measured by the price of its stock times the number of shares). That made it briefly the world's most highly valued company, at $337.2 billion. Some observers said that the rise of Apple—the world's best-known manufacturer of mobile electronic devices and the acknowledged trendsetter in the field—was symbolic of the rising influence of consumer technology in modern life.

Social Networking. Social-networking Web sites continued to thrive. According to the Pew Research Center, half of all American adults questioned in a survey said that they used social-networking sites such as Facebook and LinkedIn. Facebook reported that it had more than 800 million active monthly users worldwide; LinkedIn revealed that it had 100 million users, although it did not say how many were active. Microblogging service Twitter stated that it had attracted 100 million monthly active users worldwide and that half of them "tweeted" (i.e., sent a Twitter message) daily. Pew said that its survey showed that among Internet users social networking was most popular with women and "young adults under age 30." There was also significant growth in social-networking usage among people over age 50.

Facebook in 2011 sought to expand from just connecting people with friends to linking consumers to information—a move that put it on a collision course with Google, the world's leading Internet search company. Rather than have Facebook users search on their own for content, Facebook's approach was to enable a person's friends to recommend content from Facebook partner companies, including video firms Netflix and Hulu, music firm Spotify, Yahoo!, the *Washington Post* newspaper, and Ticketmaster. Facebook's expansion came at a time when studies showed that Americans spent more time on its service than on any other top Web site.

In an effort to compete with Facebook for users and advertisers, Google in June debuted its own social-networking service, called Google+. The new service sought to make social networking more private by allowing users to communicate with just a portion of their online friends at any one time. At year's end, however, Google+ lagged far behind Facebook in the number of people accessing the service.

Twitter sought to take advantage of its popularity by expanding its advertising. Using what it called "promoted tweets," the firm displayed advertising messages in a user's list of incoming messages.

There were also social-networking failures during the year. Myspace, once synonymous with social networking, was sold by News Corp. for about $35 million. Myspace had been the fastest-growing social network in 2005, when it was acquired by News Corp. for $580 million, but it could not keep up with the growth of Facebook.

The widespread use of social media tested the boundaries of the law when it came to freedom of speech. A man accused of the online stalking of a female Buddhist leader in the U.S. was jailed on the basis of his Twitter posts about her, including one that suggested that she commit suicide. His arrest raised questions of whether Twitter was a public forum protected under free-speech laws or a personal communication, akin to an old-fashioned letter, in which unwanted intrusive remarks could be considered threats. Unlike other Twitter cases involving civil lawsuits, this was a criminal case filed in a Maryland federal court and was based on a seldom-used cyberstalking law. On December 15 a federal judge ruled that Twitter posts were protected as free speech.

Two other forms of social networking, texting and cell phone calling, appeared to be no longer growing. A survey of American cell phone users by the Pew Research Center found that text messaging and cell phone calling levels were about the same as in 2010, with the average texting user sending or receiving an average of just over 41 texts

E-Readers and Tablets: The New Frontier in Technology

Two high-tech items once regarded as the playthings of early gadget adopters and the technorati had clearly broken into the mainstream in 2011. Electronic reading devices, or e-readers, and tablet computers were ubiquitous throughout the year, with the market's two leading products—the Amazon Kindle and the Apple iPad—posting especially impressive numbers. In March, Apple Inc. CEO Steve Jobs (*see* OBITUARIES) returned from a medical leave of absence to unveil the iPad 2, a slimmer, faster model of the popular tablet. Debuting less than a year after its predecessor had essentially created the tablet computer market, the iPad 2 incorporated front and rear cameras for the capturing of video and still images, an enhancement that allowed it to perform as an all-in-one videoconferencing device. Both the iPad and the iPad 2 sold well in spite of a soft global economy—consumers purchased more than 25 million of the devices within the first nine months of the year, and they were available in more than 90 countries.

Tablets on the whole were estimated to represent about 15% of the personal computing market in 2011, an increase of more than 300% over the previous year and a bright spot in an otherwise sluggish sales period for computer hardware. This was outstanding news for Apple, and the company posted a string of record-setting quarterly earning statements that put it on track to easily surpass $100 billion in revenue for the year. Such attractive numbers drew a host of imitators to the burgeoning tablet market, but they did little more than compete for second place behind the iPad juggernaut. Hewlett-Packard debuted its Touchpad tablet with much fanfare in July only to discontinue it a month later. BlackBerry manufacturer Research in Motion and mobile phone giant Motorola fared little better with their tablet offerings, which approached the iPad in price but not in popularity. In terms of quality, only Sony Corp.'s Tablet S and Samsung's Galaxy Tab series could credibly compete with the iPad, but their sales remained a dim shadow of Apple's throughout the year.

Compared with the iPad, the Kindle, which debuted in 2007, was an established presence in the consumer electronics market. Improvements to Amazon's e-reader had made it progressively lighter and sturdier, and later models possessed a longer battery life and antiglare screens that made reading easier in less-than-ideal lighting conditions. Seeking to capture market share at the expense of per-unit sales returns, Amazon slashed prices on its entry-level Kindles, with the cheapest models dipping below the psychologically significant $100-price point. Amazon sought to make up for the low (or even negative) profit margins on these units through the sale of content at Amazon.com's online store. This tactic appeared to bear fruit; Amazon in May announced that it currently sold more Kindle titles than traditional hardcover and softcover books combined. Analysts estimated that more than 300 million Kindle e-books were sold in 2011 alone, and that figure was projected to more than double in 2012. The Amazon Web site offered nearly one million titles in the proprietary Kindle format, and American Kindle owners could borrow virtual books from more than 10,000 public libraries through the OverDrive distribution service.

Amazon-created applications had previously allowed iPhone and iPad owners to read Kindle titles on their Apple devices, but Amazon staked its own claim on the Apple-dominated tablet market in November with the debut of the Kindle Fire. Bowing with a price point below $200, the Fire featured a roughly 18-cm (7-in) colour LCD touchscreen and an extensive library of Amazon-supplied media content. Interest in the device was so intense that Amazon registered more than 2,000 presales per hour in the weeks prior to its release. Although it was dubbed an "iPad killer" by some in the media, it lacked many of the features that defined a true tablet computer, leading critics to dub it a "tablet lite." Brick-and-mortar bookseller Barnes & Noble challenged Amazon in the colour e-reader market with its Nook Tablet. Although more expensive than the Fire, it featured more storage and a crisper display than Amazon's offering. Released within days of each other, both devices operated on Google's Android operating system platform, and each made use of Wi-Fi technology to allow Web surfing and the streaming of audio and video content (indeed, the Fire's limited storage space was mitigated by its extensive reliance on Internet-based "cloud" technology to provide users with virtual storage). As the Fire and the Nook were a fraction of the cost of even a first-generation iPad, the two devices came to define the entry-level tablet market. They also fueled a marketing war between Amazon and Barnes & Noble as the two retailers attempted to secure exclusive licensing agreements with publishers and application developers. One notable deal, which granted Amazon the exclusive right to distribute the digital versions of 100 of DC Comics' most popular graphic novels, led Barnes & Noble to pull the physical copies of the books from its shelves. Weeks later Barnes & Noble announced a partnership with DC rival Marvel Comics. The tug-of-war demonstrated not only the commitment of Amazon and Barnes & Noble to their respective devices but also the desire of traditional publishers to see their products prominently displayed in the emerging e-book and tablet paradigm. (MICHAEL RAY)

per day and cell phone callers making or receiving an average of 12 calls a day.

Tablets and E-Book Readers. About 62.5 million tablet computers were expected to be shipped worldwide in 2011, a stronger performance than some analysts had predicted, reported market researcher IDC. Apple's iPad 2, which was introduced in March—nearly a year after the first iPad—made up more than two-thirds of tablet sales. Tablets from manufacturers that used Google's Android operating system (OS) were in second place, with about a quarter of the market. RIM's PlayBook tablet was a distant third. Hewlett-Packard Co. (HP), which reassessed its expenditures and withdrew its TouchPad tablet from the market just seven weeks after it was launched, was also a factor in the market as HP sold off its supply of discontinued TouchPads for $99 each. Other tablets ranged in price into the hundreds of dollars. (*See* Sidebar.)

Many thought the iPad's biggest rival would be Amazon.com's Kindle Fire tablet computer, which was introduced in November. It sold for $199, less than half the price of the least-expensive $499 iPad. One trade-off for the lower price was that the Kindle Fire had a smaller colour screen than the iPad. The Fire's access to content rivaled that of the iPad, however, and included millions of preexisting Amazon e-books, music tracks, TV shows, and movies. The Amazon tablet also ran some, but not all, Android apps and took advantage of Amazon's huge data centres by offering free online data storage. By the time the Kindle Fire was introduced, however, Apple had already sold more than 40 million iPads.

Microsoft Corp. announced a plan to develop a new version of its OS, Windows 8, for touch-screen tablet computers, to be available in 2012. (The company confirmed that the OS would also work with notebook laptops and desktop PCs.) Some observers viewed a tablet-friendly version of Windows as particularly important for the company because tablets were cutting into sales of traditional Windows PCs. In addition, Microsoft's existing Windows 7 OS had not been particularly successful on tablet computers.

E-book readers, which were themselves specialized computers, remained popular. Sales of e-reader devices continued to accelerate, and slightly more than 20 million units were expected to be in use in the U.S. by the end of 2011, up from 12.7 million in 2010, according to research firm eMarketer. Sales of e-books reflected the popularity of both e-readers (which were aimed primarily at book and magazine reading) and tablet computers (which were aimed at people interested in consuming all types of digital content). Amazon, a major bookseller of both print books and digital editions, said that its unit sales of e-books had, for the first time, slightly exceeded its unit sales of printed books. *Publishers Weekly* reported that e-book sales in the U.S. rose nearly 160% in the first quarter of 2011, to about $233.1 million. Sales of all types of print books declined in the same quarter.

Smartphones. Smartphones continued to increase as a percentage of wireless phones in use. As cellular-network data speeds increased, wireless-service companies were able to compete more directly with landline telephone companies and cable TV networks for high-speed Internet customers.

One big name in smartphones, BlackBerry, found itself in difficulty despite the booming market. Research In Motion (RIM), which created the BlackBerry, reported that it would lay off 2,000 workers, or about 10.5% of its employees. As the year ended, dissident shareholders were demanding changes in the management and direction of the company, potentially including a sale or split-up of RIM, or a merger with another firm. According to industry analysts, the BlackBerry suffered from competition from Apple's iPhone and from the multitude of phones using Google's Android OS. RIM was not helped by lower-than-anticipated shipments of its PlayBook tablet computer. As a result, RIM was betting heavily on a new BlackBerry OS that was to be introduced in 2012.

The first Nokia smartphones powered by Microsoft's Windows OS appeared late in the year. The devices represented an important strategic push by both firms, since Finnish cell-phone maker Nokia had seen its smartphone market share dwindling, and Microsoft ranked behind Apple and Google in smartphone software.

The role of smartphones in society was poised to change again as new phones that incorporated "near field communication" began to enter the American market. (European deployment was already under way.) Using magnetic technology, cell phones could be used as electronic payment systems in place of magnetic-strip credit or debit cards. The phones could be waved near a terminal to complete transactions. Google introduced a near field communication app called Google Wallet for its Android smartphone OS.

The popularity of mobile devices from Apple and other firms gave a big boost to the market for downloadable mobile-device programs, called apps. According to the telecommunications research firm Ovum, worldwide app downloads for smartphones were expected to exceed 18 billion in 2011, up from 7.4 billion in 2010. Some smartphone apps were free and typically made money for their creators by including advertising with their content. Other smartphone apps were bought by users, and Ovum reported that those were expected to generate $3.7 billion in revenue in 2011, up from $1.95 billion in 2010.

Traditional PCs. Two former winners of the A.M. Turing Award died in October. Dennis M. Ritchie was cocreator in the 1970s of both the UNIX operating system and the C computer programming language. John McCarthy was a pioneer in the field of artificial intelligence. (*See* OBITUARIES.)

Because of their small size and easy-to-use touch screens, tablets soon became viewed as a real threat to sales of laptop computers, particularly the smallest laptops, called netbooks. According to California market researcher IHS iSuppli, netbook shipments in 2011 were projected to drop by a third from 2010, to 21.5 million units, and to dip further, to 13.5 million units, in 2015. Shipments of larger notebook laptop computers were still projected to continue growing.

In an effort to improve its position in the laptop market, Intel Corp. indicated that it would invest $300 million over three to four years in what the chip manufacturer called "ultrabook" PCs. These devices would be thin but full-featured and would incorporate some of the touch-screen features made popular by the iPad. Intel planned to develop more power-efficient chips for the new PCs.

HP, the market-leading PC manufacturer, revealed that it was considering spinning off its low-profit-margin PC business into a separate company and instead focusing on business products and services. The new strategy announcement was followed shortly by the news that HP's board of directors had replaced CEO Léo Apotheker with Meg Whitman, the former CEO of online auction company eBay and an unsuccessful candidate for governor of California. She was the company's third CEO in a little more than a year. (Apotheker had replaced the previous CEO, Mark Hurd, who was fired in 2010 after the board learned that he had filed a false expense account in connection with his relationship with a female executive, who was an HP contract employee.) In October HP reversed Apotheker's decision to abandon the PC market.

IBM announced in October that the sales and marketing chief, Virginia Rometty, would succeed Sam Palmisano as CEO in January 2012. Rometty had been closely involved in IBM's earlier move away from the PC market into business services.

One of the most unusual PCs to debut in 2011 was the Google Chromebook, which came not with an operating system but rather with a browser that provided access to most computer functions and data storage online. This meant that the Chromebook operated mostly through online "cloud computing" and was largely nonfunctional when an Internet connection was not available. There was no rush to embrace Google's unusual computer design.

Apple introduced a new OS code named Lion in an attempt to bring to traditional computers some of the features of tablet computers and smartphones, such as touch to control items on the screen. Lion, however, relied on the computer's touch pad rather than a tabletlike touch screen and continued to use conventional computer programs. As a result, Lion was not compatible with apps for Apple's iPhone or iPad.

Online Marketing. Groupon and a new generation of other Internet-based firms were changing online advertising in ways that accommodated consumers' daily lives. One that applied to smartphones was "location-based marketing," in which online advertising was directed at smartphone users on the basis of where they were at that moment.

Groupon, Living Social, and others began selling coupons via smartphones for ongoing discount deals at stores, restaurants, and other outlets in the immediate vicinity of a user, as determined by the phone's GPS chips or its proximity to specific cell phone network antennas. Consumers could pay for discounted goods or services by displaying the coupon on their smartphone screens. Consumers using stationary computers could also find nearby "deals" by typing in a zip code on a Web site to access a coupon that could be printed. The marketing companies also offered discounts for future events, but those offers were based on citywide locations, not where consumers were at that moment.

Struggling newspaper companies, which saw traditional advertising campaigns plummet, tried to compete with location-based marketing services. The Associated Press claimed that its new iCircular service would deliver to smartphones some of the same advertisements that were routinely printed and inserted into the Sunday newspaper. Consumers could receive the advertising via the smartphone apps of participating newspapers.

Antitrust Concerns. Google became the target of critics who claimed that it had abused its influence in ways that violated antitrust laws. At midyear the U.S. Federal Trade Commission (FTC) launched a civil antitrust investigation of Google's search-engine business. The investigation was an effort to determine whether there was anything anticompetitive about the order in which Google search results and their associated advertising appeared on the computer screens of users.

The U.S. Senate held hearings to air such grievances. Google maintained at the hearings that by being a leader in online search and advertising, it had helped other businesses, not hurt them. Critics charged that Google in subtle ways favoured online searches for its own e-commerce offerings, such as travel, over those of other companies.

Justin Lane—EPA/Landov

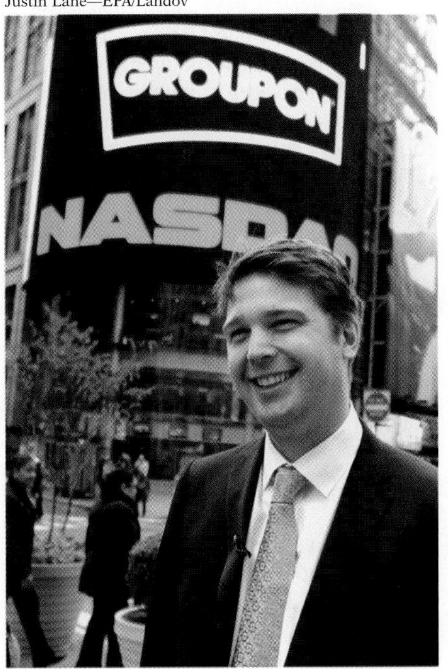

Groupon Inc. CEO Andrew Mason enjoys the moment in New York City's Times Square on November 4, the day his three-year-old Internet company joined the NASDAQ stock exchange with an initial public offering worth $700 million.

One Google critic was Yelp, an online restaurant- and business-review service that Google had unsuccessfully sought to acquire. Yelp claimed that Google had subsequently started a competing service called Places and had often given Places a higher ranking in Google search listings than Yelp received. Google maintained that it did not favour its own businesses in Google search listings.

Hanging over the dispute was the argument by some that there was a parallel between Google in 2011 and Microsoft during the 1990s, when the U.S. government sued it for antitrust law violations. In the Microsoft suit, which was later settled, the government painted Microsoft as a firm with an operating system monopoly that had overstepped the bounds of fair competition.

Separately, Google agreed to pay a $500 million fine to the U.S. government to settle allegations that it had illegally showed ads in the U.S. for Canadian pharmacies. The complaint centred on Canadian pharmacies alleged to have illegally sold prescription drugs without a prescription or to have sold counterfeit drugs.

There was new management at Google. Eric Schmidt was replaced as CEO by company cofounder Larry Page, and Schmidt became chairman. It was unclear how much that would change the company, which previously was jointly managed by Schmidt, Page, and the other cofounder, Sergey Brin.

Google's 2011 acquisitions included its largest-ever deal, the $12.5 billion purchase of Motorola Mobility Holdings, the former Motorola, Inc., cell phone manufacturing business that was spun off early in the year as a separate company. By acquiring the Motorola unit, one of 39 companies that made mobile devices using Google's Android OS, Google positioned itself to compete more directly with Apple.

Google also acquired, for undisclosed terms, a social-media analytics company called SocialGrapple, which led to speculation that it wanted to interpret more data about the users of its Google+ service. Google received approval from the U.S. Department of Justice (DOJ) for its $700 million acquisition in 2010 of ITA Software, which made search software for making air-travel arrangements. Google was required by the government to continue licensing the ITA software to other firms.

A U.S. federal judge rejected a $125 million proposed settlement in the long-running Google Books case but gave both sides until mid-2012 to reach a new settlement agreement. The lawsuit, which involved Google's project to digitize millions of library books around the world, began in 2005 when the Authors Guild and the Association of American Publishers sued Google for copyright infringement. A settlement reached in 2008 was later revised to meet DOJ concerns, and it was this revision that the federal court rejected in early 2011. The judge ruled that the settlement would effectively have given Google monopoly power over the books and the right to earn money with them without the express permission of the books' copyright owners, many of whom were unknown.

When AT&T Corp. announced in March its intention to acquire smaller wireless rival T-Mobile from Deutsche Telekom for $39 billion, a major political battle began over whether the U.S. Federal Communications Commission (FCC) should approve the deal. The acquisition would create the largest American wireless company by combining the second largest firm (AT&T) with the fourth largest (T-Mobile). That would leave Verizon Wireless as the second largest wireless provider and make Sprint Nextel a distant third.

AT&T insisted that the combined companies could more rapidly introduce broadband data service in rural areas where it was lacking, long a major goal of U.S. Pres. Barack Obama's administration. Opponents expressed misgivings, saying that the acquisition would reduce wireless competition, which for consumers would mean fewer choices, higher prices, and less technical innovation in the smartphone market.

The debate seemed to shift in favour of the opponents when in August the DOJ filed a civil suit opposing the acquisition under the U.S. antitrust laws. Following the DOJ's action, Sprint Nextel also filed a civil suit opposing the acquisition on antitrust grounds. At year's end, AT&T and Deutsche Telekom agreed to cancel the deal.

Other Developments. Microsoft made its largest acquisition ever, the $8.5 billion cash purchase of Skype Global, the leading provider of Internet phone service and personal video conferencing. The purchase was designed to help Microsoft compete with Google, whose Internet voice service lagged behind Skype's. As an independent company, Skype had difficulty sustaining profitability because most of its calls, made from one computer to another, were provided free of charge. Skype charged users who made long-distance calls to telephones. Skype had previously been owned by eBay.

Microsoft also made a strategic gamble by taking one of its most successful packaged software products, Microsoft Office, into the cloud to compete with Google Docs, which was Office-like software that was already available online. Office 365 was an online version of the familiar Office collection of word processing, spreadsheet, presentation, whiteboard, and other programs that could be accessed through a computer's Web browser. It was unclear how the online version of Office would affect sales of the traditional disk-based software.

A struggling Yahoo! fired its CEO, Carol Bartz, after a two-year tenure in which a turnaround failed to materialize. Yahoo! had undergone a corporate makeover that involved layoffs, management changes, and a deal with Microsoft that essentially outsourced Yahoo!'s search service to the PC software giant. Despite its huge online audience, Yahoo! had not been able to expand its advertising revenue significantly, and investors had pressured the firm to sell all or parts of its operations. Previously, the company had resisted being acquired. In 2008, before Bartz took over as CEO, Yahoo! had refused a takeover offer from Microsoft. As 2011 ended, Yahoo! was the subject of takeover rumours, including talk of a possible deal with Alibaba Group, a Chinese e-commerce giant in which Yahoo! held a 40% stake. Chinese entrepreneur Jack Ma, Alibaba's founder and CEO, had expressed an interest in acquiring the Internet portal. (*See* BIOGRAPHIES.)

Despite uncertain economic conditions, technology companies such as LinkedIn, Facebook, and Groupon were either having or preparing to launch big initial public stock offerings (IPOs). For some investors the situation was reminiscent of the overvalued stocks of the late 1990s dotcom boom era, which later resulted in huge financial losses when stock values began to implode.

Groupon, which raised $700 million in its IPO, smoothed the way for its stock offering by changing its accounting methods, which had come under the scrutiny of U.S. regulators. The change resulted in a restatement of the company's financial results for the prior three years and altered the way that revenue was reported, by excluding money that Groupon took in but later paid out to merchants that used its services.

Netflix struggled with the differing economics of two separate digital content businesses. The company, a movie-rental service that had begun with DVDs delivered by mail and then moved aggressively into online video streaming of movies and TV shows, saw its rapid growth falter when it raised prices for a combination of its two services. The company claimed that it needed to raise prices in order to afford more licensing of streaming video content while continuing its mail service. Following that decision, Netflix suffered a one-million-customer decline in its 25 million U.S.-based subscribers. Netflix then decided to split the firm into two companies, one that handled DVDs by mail, called Qwikster, and the other in charge of its video-streaming business, to retain the Netflix name. When customers rebelled again, Netflix relented and called off the split. Netflix founder and CEO Reed Hastings (*see* BIOGRAPHIES) downplayed the loss of subscribers and the drop in the company's share price, which plunged from more than $298 in July to about $75 in October.

Sony, Toshiba, and Hitachi agreed to merge their liquid crystal display (LCD) businesses with a Japanese government fund at a time when analysts were predicting a strong market for LCDs used in cell phones and digital cameras. Pending approval under Japanese antitrust laws, a government fund called the Innovation Network Corp. was to invest $2.6 billion for a 70% ownership share in the combined company, which would have 22% of the world market for small and midsize LCD screens. The three manufacturers would each own 10% of the new company.

Cisco Systems, a maker of computer-networking equipment, eliminated 9% of its workforce, or 6,500 employees, in an effort to reduce its corporate expenses by $1 billion a year, about 6% of its total expenses. Cisco reportedly made the cuts to cope with increasing competition in the networking market.

LightSquared, a company proposing to build a wireless data network using a combination of ground-based antennas and satellites, continued to face government scrutiny over interference with GPS signals. Under current plans the data network would cover 260 million people in the U.S. by the end of 2015. While LightSquared said that it would use a slightly different frequency to minimize interference problems, it also asserted that the GPS industry should bear some financial responsibility for refitting existing GPS units with filters to prevent their sensing capabilities from straying into LightSquared's assigned frequencies. LightSquared said that it would provide $50 million to help federal agencies fix interference problems, but the U.S. Air Force Space Command remained opposed to the network, on the basis of concerns that it would cost the military billions of dollars in technical adjustments to avoid having LightSquared's network interfere with GPS.

Cloud computing—the outsourcing of corporate computer operations to remote data centres run by companies that included Amazon, Microsoft, and Google—continued to be more talked about than adopted. Cloud computing did not gain much traction because of concerns about cloud data security and because of a shortage of corporate technical expertise in the field. A survey of corporations in 38 countries by security firm Symantec found that fewer than 20% of the firms in the study had moved their company computer applications software to the cloud. Symantec also reported that some corporations were using cloud computing to expand their existing information technology operations or to outsource parts of their computing operations, such as data storage or backup.

Casual games for cell phones, tablet computers, and other portable devices continued to expand their appeal, and their market was projected to rival that for traditional video games played on computers, game consoles such as the Xbox 360 and Sony PlayStation 3, and handheld gaming devices from Nintendo and others. One of the most high-profile companies in the casual-games market was Zynga, the leading creator of games for Facebook. In December Zynga Inc. raised $1 billion in its highly anticipated IPO.

Despite the rise in casual computer games that could be played on smartphones and other portable devices, IDC predicted that the traditional market for gaming on consoles would experience growth again in 2012. A weak economy was expected to result in a modest year-to-year decline in worldwide sales of consoles and their game software in 2011 versus 2010. In the longer run, however, IDC predicted that revenue for consoles and their software would grow at a compound annual rate of 3.6% from 2010 to 2015, when it would reach $39.7 billion worldwide.

Changing Technology. IBM's Watson computer system beat two human champions to win the *Jeopardy* TV game show and in the process displayed its unusual ability to quickly correlate an encyclopedic amount of information while exercising judgment about the reliability of its answers. IBM identified Watson as "a natural language processor" that accepted questions spoken in plain English, broke them into several parts, and rapidly compared them with information in a data bank. Watson gave answers that were rated on the basis of its "confidence level" in a particular response. IBM stated that it was seeking practical applications for Watson, potentially including the role of automated physician's assistant.

Spotify, an online music service already available in the U.K., made its debut in the U.S. in July. The service allowed consumers to listen for several hours to its 15-million-song library for free and to specify which songs they wanted to hear rather than rely on the service to stream music on the basis of a broad set of preferences, as was commonly done in the U.S. After listening to Spotify for free for 10 hours a month, users would be charged for additional music. In addition, the free service included advertising. Alternatively, the company offered a subscription music-streaming service. Less than one month after its debut in the U.S., Spotify was sued for patent infringement by PacketVideo, a firm that licensed its software to companies such as Verizon Wireless. PacketVideo claimed that its software was used in more than 260 million devices worldwide.

Hacking and Privacy. Data breaches continued at an alarming pace. In one of the largest security disasters of its kind, data stolen from online marketing firm Epsilon revealed the names and e-mail addresses of millions of consumers who did business with big firms such as Citibank and Walgreens. Epsilon handled e-mail marketing for hundreds of corporations, and the fear was that hackers would use the stolen data to devise plausible but phony e-mails—so-called "phishing attacks"—to steal money from consumers or take over their computers.

Britain was stunned and its government stung by a cell phone hacking scandal that involved a prominent British newspaper, the *News of the World*. (*See* WORLD AFFAIRS: *United Kingdom*: Sidebar.) While the fallout from the story shook the government, the level of hacking involved was minor: intruders used a default voicemail password that British cell phone companies had given their users and which the users had never changed to more secure passwords.

The hacking group Anonymous was in the news during the year for brazen social-issue-oriented attacks on companies and Web sites, sometimes called "hacktivism." Among the Anonymous victims were computer security firms ManTech, Booz Allen Hamilton, and HBGary Federal, all of which Anonymous sought to ridicule by breaching their security defenses, releasing stolen internal documents, and then bragging about it.

The arrest of an 18-year-old man in Scotland, who went by the code name "Topiary," suggested that even the members of Anonymous—who, as its name implied, took great care to hide their identities—could not avoid identification forever. Believed to be one of the leaders of the organization, he was charged with having violated the U.K.'s Computer Misuse Act and other laws in connection with attacks by Anonymous and LulzSec, another online activist group, on Sony Corp., Britain's National Health Service, and Rupert Murdoch's newspaper properties. The man's defense attorney said that there might be evidence that his client belonged to the hacktivist groups, but there was none to show that he participated in the attacks.

In addition, 14 lower-level Anonymous members were arrested in the U.S. in connection with a late 2010 attack on PayPal, an Internet firm that facilitated financial transactions. PayPal was hit with a distributed denial of service attack, in which Web servers were paralyzed as a result of being flooded with Internet traffic. Anonymous let it be known that the attack was a way to get even with PayPal for having cut its ties to WikiLeaks, a Web

Mark Pincus, the CEO of Zynga Inc., addresses the audience at Zynga Unleashed, an event held on October 11, at which the social-media casual-games company announced "a gaggle of new social games."

Jeff Chiu/AP

Dominic Lipinski—PA Photos/Landov

On November 10 a protester representing media executive James Murdoch appears at a demonstration by the activist organization Avaaz outside the British Houses of Parliament, where Murdoch was testifying about the cell-phone-hacking scandal that brought down the News of the World *newspaper earlier in the year.*

site devoted to the unauthorized release of secret government documents.

Separately, hackers who attacked the Dutch company DigiNotar managed to imitate Google's Web site for Internet users in Iran, enabling the hackers to spy on Google online communications there. The attack called into question the safety of electronic "certificates" that were supposed to guarantee the authenticity of Web sites—an important safety feature at a time when it was difficult for Internet users to discern when a legitimate-looking Web site was a phony. Earlier there had been complaints that the authentication system in use lacked a standards-enforcement group, as well as calls to overhaul the whole system. DigiNotar was just one of several companies that were authorized to issue the digital certificates. Google acknowledged the attack but provided no details.

Several months after WikiLeaks disclosed a huge cache of classified U.S. government documents that had allegedly been stolen by an American soldier with computer access to the data, the government adopted new security measures designed to prevent similar incidents. The new rules approved emergency measures already taken, such as sharply reducing the number of military computers that could copy sensitive data onto portable memory devices, and also sought to make computer security policies more consistent. In addition, the rules established ways to search for unusual patterns of data usage on government computer networks handling classified information.

China released an imprisoned blogger who had been arrested after having addressed human rights issues and gained a huge following in that country. Ran Yunfei had faced up to 15 years in prison after his arrest early in the year, an event that some observers said coincided with uprisings against authoritarian governments in the Middle East and North Africa and signaled China's willingness to crack down on dissent. Several other dissidents were arrested after Ran, and some received prison sentences.

After a series of riots in London and other British metropolitan areas, British Prime Minister David Cameron suggested curtailing the use of social media by those suspected of planning violence. He was met by a barrage of protests by groups claiming that such a move would restrict basic freedoms and, in any event, would be difficult to carry out. The protest groups also drew an unflattering comparison between Cameron's proposal and efforts by the government of Egypt to block protesters from using the Internet and cell phones.

In response to European pressure, Google backed down on its plan to help locate cell phone users by mapping the locations of privately owned Wi-Fi routers in the U.S. and Europe. Google agreed to let citizens opt out of having their Wi-Fi hot spots included in Google's Wi-Fi listings, which the search giant said were designed to more precisely locate cell phone users who wanted to use location-based services, such as navigation and advertising. Without the use of Wi-Fi hot spots, phones could be located with somewhat less precision via cell phone towers and satellites. While mapping Wi-Fi hot spots did not personally identify any individuals, European officials had frowned on unauthorized use of the private Wi-Fi data.

The FTC sought to update rules governing online privacy for American children; the measures in place at the time had been written prior to the existence of social-media Web sites. The original Children's Online Privacy Protection Act said that companies need to secure parental permission before collecting personal information about children under age 13. The FTC wanted to expand the scope of coverage of "personal information" to include the kind of data collected online in 2011, including a person's location, online habits (as revealed by browser cookies), and facial features (as monitored by facial-recognition software). Web sites would have to make provisions to protect that information and to keep it only for a limited time. The FTC indicated that it would create final rules in 2012.

Responding to privacy concerns, Facebook introduced a new set of controls that allowed people to opt out of some information sharing on its social-networking service. In the past, the world's largest social network had been criticized by the U.S. government and the American Civil Liberties Union for not having adequate privacy protection in its sharing options. In the latest changes, Facebook users were allowed to restrict access to messages posted on their pages rather than having to rely on more general settings. In addition, users were allowed to decide after posting information or photos how widely those items and images should be viewed. Users could also require that they give personal approval before any photos of them in which they were "tagged," or identified, could appear on their profile pages. Some privacy experts warned that Facebook had yet to safeguard another type of personal information: location. Facebook users remained free to post another person's whereabouts without having obtained that person's permission. (STEVE ALEXANDER)

Earth Sciences

Scientists in 2011 found signs that **MANTLE CONVECTION CYCLING** under **HAWAII** had been extremely rapid and uncovered evidence that the **PERMIAN EXTINCTION** was caused in large part by **OCEAN ACIDIFICATION**. Large **EARTHQUAKES** caused tremendous damage in **NEW ZEALAND** and **JAPAN**, and several devastating **TORNADOES** struck the southern and midwestern U.S.

GEOLOGY AND GEOCHEMISTRY

The new wave of studies of the Moon continued in 2011 as geochemists applied new analytic tools to samples from the Apollo missions. Some of the results challenged the consensus paradigm, which maintained that the Moon originated from a collision between Earth and a giant asteroid or a small planet approximately 4.5 billion years ago. A high-temperature lunar magma ocean was commonly assumed to have followed, implying that volatile materials such as water were lost to space; indeed, original analyses of lunar samples brought back by Apollo detected essentially no water. In 2006, however, scientists identified trace water in lunar volcanic glass spheres, which implied that the Moon's lava possessed a much higher water content prior to eruption events. This line of thought was greatly strengthened in May when the same group of scientists, led by Erik Hauri of the Carnegie Institution of Washington, unveiled evidence of rare inclusions of glass trapped within olivine crystals in the same lunar samples. These glass inclusions, which would have been protected from eruptive and posteruptive modification, preserved water concentrations similar to those found in basalts in Earth's midocean ridges—indicating that at least some of the lunar mantle was as wet as Earth's upper mantle.

Another major line of evidence supporting the lunar magma ocean model was the age of lunar anorthosites, crystalline igneous rocks found on the Moon's highlands that were thought to have formed more than 4.45 billion years ago from plagioclase minerals floating atop a sea of magma. The hypothesis was disputed by Lars Borg of Lawrence Livermore (Calif.) National Laboratory, and others, who calculated the precise age of 4.36 billion years for one such rock, and led some scientists to believe that some aspects of the prevailing lunar origins paradigm would need to be revised.

A team of geochemists who examined terrestrial rocks from modern and ancient hotspots identified candidates for the oldest pristine mantle reservoir. Flood basalts are voluminous outpourings of lava that often evolve into persistent hot spots of ongoing volcanic activity far from tectonic plate boundaries. Most scientists think of flood basalts and hot spots as the surface expression of deep mantle plumes. Matthew Jackson of Boston University and Richard Carlson of the Carnegie Institution studied rock samples from the six largest flood basalts erupted over the last 250 million years and found isotopic ratios of helium, lead, neodymium, and hafnium consistent with those rocks' having derived from a magma reservoir that would have separated from the rest of the mantle in the first 100 million years of Earth's history. Even though convective mixing occurred in the mantle, this reservoir apparently remained isolated for the next 4.5 billion years and was possibly associated with the large, low shear velocity provinces that have been imaged seismically in the lower mantle.

Alexander V. Sobolev and paper: Sobolev, A.V., Hofmann, A.W., Jochum, K.-P. Kuzmin, D.V. and B. Stoll (2011). A young source for the Hawaiian plume. Nature 476 (7361), 434-437/Max Planck Institute for Chemistry

In these olivine crystals taken from the Mauna Loa volcano, Hawaii, the brown ovals represent solid glassy inclusions that were trapped as droplets of melt whose presence indicated that the recycling of subducted material occurred over a relatively short time span.

In August, Alexander Sobolev of the Max Planck Institute for Chemistry, Mainz, Ger., and others documented the surprisingly rapid recycling of subducted material to the bottom of the mantle and back to the surface in hotspot-associated magmas by examining melt inclusions from the Mauna Loa volcano in Hawaii. They uncovered a rare class of material that combined extremely high ratios of strontium isotopes (specifically, $^{87}Sr/^{86}Sr$) with an extremely low abundance of unstable rubidium isotopes (^{87}Rb, the radioactive parent of ^{87}Sr). There were many possible explanations for this anomaly, but Sobolev and co-workers discarded all of them except the idea that a component of the Hawaiian plume had been contaminated by seawater. This component was then subducted into the deep mantle between 200 million and 600 million years ago, the only time in Earth's history when the strontium in seawater was high enough in $^{87}Sr/^{86}Sr$. The scientists noted that it was unusual that such recently subducted material would rise in a mantle plume. They remarked that this phenomenon would have required extremely rapid cycling of material by mantle convection.

Paleontologists revealed several surprising findings about dinosaurs and other Mesozoic reptiles during the year. Traditionally, absolute ages of fossils older than a few million years (that is, too old for radiocarbon or uranium-thorium dating) were only indirectly dated by the analysis of stratigraphically associated igneous rocks. Retired United States Geological Survey geologist James Fassett and co-workers succeeded, however, in directly dating two dinosaur bones by using an advanced uranium-lead technique. Meanwhile, the question of whether dinosaurs were cold-blooded like their reptile cousins or warm-blooded like their avian descendants was addressed by Robert Eagle and co-workers at the California Institute of Technology. (*See* LIFE SCIENCES: *Paleontology*.) Paradoxically, the challenge for such large animals was not cold blood but the export of body heat. In order to maintain body temperatures as low as modern mammals, they must have had efficient cooling mechanisms. In addition, F.R. O'Keefe of Marshall University, Huntington, W.Va., and Luis Chiappe of the Natural History Museum of Los Angeles County described, and placed on public display, a fossil of a pregnant plesiosaur, which stood as evidence that this ancient reptile gave birth to live young—just like modern marine mammals.

Throughout Earth's geologic history, the diversity of life had been dramatically altered by mass extinctions. Much attention had been focused on the causes of these events and evidence of mass extinction in the fossil record. The development of the Cretaceous-Paleogene, or K–Pg, boundary some 65 million years ago was generally attributed to climatic effects caused by the impact of an asteroid or a comet at the Chicxulub crater near Mexico's Yucatán Peninsula, perhaps in combination with massive volcanic eruptions of the Deccan Traps in India. However, most dramatic climatic shifts and mass extinctions in Earth's history were less well understood. In June the results of a high-resolution geochronology study of the Paleocene-Eocene Thermal Maximum (PETM) were published by Adam Charles and co-workers at the National Oceanography Centre, Southampton, Eng. They showed that a dramatic warming took place about 55.8 million years ago during a time when global climate should have been cooling as a result of variations in Earth's orbit around the Sun. Thus, evidence of warming pointed not to astronomical forcing but instead to an internal mechanism that would have released large amounts of carbon dioxide into the atmosphere.

The most dramatic mass extinction in the fossil record, which occurred near the Permian-Triassic boundary some 251 million years ago, was traditionally attributed to the effects of volcanism from the large Siberian Traps igneous province—though exactly how this massive pulse of volcanic material affected the climate and caused the extinction of most marine organisms was frequently debated. Many scientists were attracted to the idea of widespread deep-ocean anoxia (oxygen depletion); however, climate model simulations published in August by Alvaro Montenegro of St. Francis Xavier University, Antagonish, N.S., and others showed no decrease in the supply of oxygenated water to the deep ocean. Instead, the simulations pointed to ocean acidification as the cause. Under the modeling scenarios, the carbon dioxide emitted by volcanic eruptions would have been absorbed by seawater, lowering the pH of the oceans so much that the building of carbonate structures by mollusks, corals, and other marine life would have been severely impeded.

Scientists continued to present surprising evidence concerning the past distribution of Earth's continents and oceans. Traditionally, Earth's paleogeography over the most recent 200 million years of Earth's history was well known because seafloor spreading left a precise record of plate movement. Reconstructions of the deeper past were always more difficult, however, with various proposed arrangements of continents remaining controversial for years as evidence was compiled and examined. In August, Zhu Dicheng of China University of Geosciences, Beijing, and others reported on the distribution of ages and isotopic compositions of 1.1-billion-year-old zircon fragments from the Lhasa Terrane, a landmass now surrounded by India and southern Tibet. On the basis of their data, the team proposed that the Lhasa Terrane originally formed as part of the northern margin of Australia, which was India's eastern neighbour when both were part of the continent of Gondwana during the Paleozoic Era. That same month Staci Loewy of California State University, Bakersfield, and others presented results of their analysis of rocks from two tiny outcrops beneath Antarctic ice; their data supported the hypothesis that the southwestern United States and eastern Antarctica were connected approximately 1.1 billion years ago.

(PAUL D. ASIMOW)

GEOPHYSICS

A giant earthquake with a moment magnitude of 9.0 occurred off the coast of Honshu, Japan, on March 11, 2011. (*See* Special Report on page 176.) It was the fourth largest earthquake ever recorded, and it ruptured a fault plane approximately 300 km (1 km = 0.6 mi) long and 150 km wide. Just over 100 km east of the Japanese coastline, near the Japan Trench, the crust slipped about 50 m (165 ft). Here the Pacific plate subducted westward beneath the North American plate at a speed of 8 cm (about 3 in) per year. The sudden uplift of the seafloor over such a broad area spawned a massive tsunami that caused substantially more damage than the ground shaking produced by the earthquake itself. Along some parts of the Japanese coast, tsunami run-ups reached over 30 m (98 ft) in height, and smaller waves were recorded across the entire Pacific basin. In Japan more than 19,000 people were killed, another 4,000 were missing, and over 5,000 were injured. Hundreds of thousands of buildings were destroyed, and four nuclear reactors, which were thought to be earthquake-proof, were critically damaged; some leaked radioactive material into the environment. The economic cost of the disaster was estimated at over $300 billion. Although Japan's disaster preparedness was recognized as being the best in the world, the size and location of the earthquake were a surprise. It had previously been thought that the geology of the region could produce earthquakes up to magnitude 8, and thus seawalls were built to accommodate only moderate-sized tsunamis. Government officials had placed more emphasis on defending against the possibility of a large earthquake coming from the Nankai Trough, a feature located along the southeastern coast of Japan that formed the boundary between the Philippine Sea plate and the Eurasian plate.

In early September 2010 a magnitude-7.0–7.1 earthquake struck New Zealand's Canterbury Plains region. It shook the city of Christchurch but caused relatively little damage. In February 2011, however, a destructive aftershock (magnitude 6.3) located only five kilometres beneath Heathcote Valley, a Christchurch suburb on the Banks Peninsula, caused tremendous damage and loss of life. The aftershock's depth and close proximity to Christchurch contributed in the metropolitan area to substantial shaking, surface cracking, and soil liquefaction (ground failure that causes solid soil to behave temporarily as a viscous liquid). Many buildings and roads across the region, which had been weakened by the September main shock and its initial aftershocks, were severely damaged or destroyed by the February aftershock. In the following months it was established that more than 180 died in the earthquake; many of them had been killed outright as structures collapsed and falling debris crushed cars and buses. By June more than 50,000 of the residents of Christchurch had moved out of the city permanently.

In April scientists from Pennsylvania State University and the United States Geological Survey announced the results of laboratory measurements on rocks that had been extracted from a borehole drilled into the San Andreas Fault zone. Core samples and cuttings were taken near a depth of 2.7 km from two actively deforming shear zones (areas with rocks altered by shearing stress) located between the North American and Pacific plates. Using sophisticated laboratory equipment, the scientists measured the frictional strength of the rocks and found that they were significantly weaker than the rocks sampled outside the shear zone. These rocks were also generally weaker than most rocks found at Earth's surface, a quality that the scientists attributed to the presence of smectite, a weak clay mineral that acted as a lubricant for the other rocks in the shear zone. The discovery provided a compelling explanation for why relatively little heat was generated by the movement of the tectonic plates bordering the San Andreas Fault. In addition, the rock samples tended to become stronger as stress was applied more quickly. This rheological (deformational) property, known as velocity strengthening, helped to explain the absence of large, destructive earthquakes along this segment of the San Andreas Fault. The scientists also noted that the rocks in the samples lacked the ability to regain their strength after laboratory-induced sliding ceased and that this inability to recover was also consistent with the absence of large earthquakes.

SAFOD—National Science Foundation/USGS

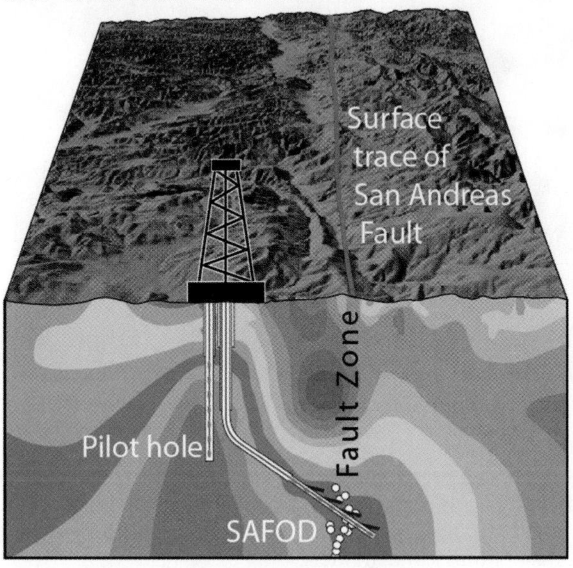

A cross section of the San Andreas Fault zone at Parkfield, Calif., displays the drill hole for the San Andreas Fault Observatory at Depth (SAFOD) and the project's pilot hole. The locations of monitoring instruments are indicated by red dots, and sites of continuing minor seismicity are indicated by white dots. Rocks with the lowest electrical resistivity, indicated by red coloration, were thought to make up a fluid-rich geologic zone.

A milestone in solar system exploration was reached in March when the Messenger spacecraft began to orbit Mercury, which is the closest planet to the Sun. NASA's past mission to Mercury (Mariner 10 in 1974 and 1975) consisted of brief flybys that imaged only about half of the planet's surface. Messenger was launched in 2004, and its mission was designed to answer several fundamental questions about Mercury—such as why the planet is so dense, how its magnetic field was generated, and what the unusually reflective material at its poles is composed of. As of September 8, Messenger had delivered 1.1 terabytes of data to the publicly accessible Planetary Data System, including more than 18,000 images taken while in orbit around Mercury. Some of the notable features in the images included the broad plains located near Mercury's north pole. These smooth expanses likely represented Mercury's largest volcanic province and confirmed that its surface had been shaped by volcanism throughout its history. Scientists were also intrigued by bits of reflective material discovered at the bottoms of many craters; some of these areas were permanently shadowed, and the images raised the possibility that ice exists on the planet's surface.

(KEITH D. KOPER)

METEOROLOGY AND CLIMATE

The year 2011 featured several especially notable weather events across the United States. According to the National Climatic Data Center of the National Oceanic and Atmospheric Administration (NOAA), there were a record number of weather-related disasters (12 for the January–September period)—including tornado outbreaks across the South and Midwest, a record drought in Texas, and major flooding events caused by heavy rains and melting snow as well as from Hurricane Irene—whose damage estimates exceeded $1 billion each. Since 1980 the U.S. had experienced 112 weather-related disasters that totaled $1 billion or more in damages each, and total losses from those disasters exceeded $750 billion.

Deadly tornadoes devastated parts of the southern and midwestern U.S. during the spring of 2011. Two enormous outbreaks in April spawned a combined 455 tornadoes. The second episode, which was the largest tornado outbreak of its kind on record, killed at least 321 people across the central and southern U.S. Some 240 deaths occurred in the state of Alabama alone. In addition, a 1.6-km (1-mi)-wide tornado cut across the city of Joplin, Mo., in late May, killing approximately 160 and damaging or destroying roughly one-third of the buildings in the city.

In August NOAA announced that it would be launching a "weather-ready"

Mike Gullett/AP

A view of the damage along 26th Street in Joplin, Mo., after an EF5 tornado struck the city on May 22.

initiative to save lives and protect livelihoods as the exposure of many communities to severe weather events increased. The components of the plan included partnering with governmental agencies, researchers, and the private sector to improve weather and water forecasts and weather-decision-support services and implement enhanced radar and satellite systems.

The National Hurricane Center's forecast track for Hurricane Irene, which skimmed the eastern seaboard of the U.S. in August, was especially accurate, implying that investments in hurricane research and forecast models had paid off. In contrast, the storm's intensity was less than had been forecast, which indicated that the greatest challenge for meteorologists continued to be predicting storm intensity. Data compiled since 1980 demonstrated little or no improvement in forecasts of intensity within 24–120 hours of an event. In response, NOAA's Hurricane Forecast Improvement Project, which began in 2008, continued its work to improve track and intensity forecasts by 20% in five years. Research performed in 2011 revealed that the best path toward improved intensity forecasts would lie in leveraging observations within the storm environment to initialize and evaluate high-resolution hurricane models.

While the North Atlantic experienced a second consecutive year with above-average tropical cyclone activity, with 18 named storms, data compiled by Ryan Maue at Florida State University showed that global tropical cyclone activity had decreased in recent years. The years 2006–10 saw the lowest levels of accumulated cyclone energy (ACE) since the late 1970s. The variability of ACE, which was calculated from storm wind speeds, was related to large-scale mechanisms such as the El Niño Southern Oscillation (ENSO) and the Pacific Decadal Oscillation (PDO).

At the 17th Conference of the Parties, which concluded in December in Durban, S.Af., delegates agreed to extend the Kyoto Protocol, the international agreement governing greenhouse gas emissions, until at least 2017. The delegates also pledged to create a new, comprehensive, legally binding climate treaty by 2015 that would require greenhouse gas-producing countries—including major carbon emitters that had not abided by the Kyoto Protocol (such as China, India, and the United States)—to limit and reduce their emissions of carbon dioxide and other greenhouse gases and thus keep global temperature increases to less than 2 °C (3.6 °F) from pre-industrial levels.

Data from the U.S. National Snow and Ice Data Center (NSIDC) indicated that the average Arctic sea-ice extent calculated for August 2011 reached its second lowest level for the month since the satellite record began in 1979. The linear trend for the month showed a decline of 9.3% per decade. Furthermore, the annual minimum ice extent, which was calculated in September, was the second smallest in the satellite record.

The steady downward trend in sea-ice extent led to concerns that once Arctic summer ice had melted away, the ice cap would not recover. Scientists at the Max Planck Institute for Meteorology, Hamburg, however, used a general circulation model to show that no critical threshold in ice extent existed that would lead to an irreversible loss of ice. Simulations of 21st-century climate in the model, when prescribed with ice-free summer scenarios, showed Arctic ice extent recovering within two years to the state dictated by climate conditions occurring during that time.

Two studies released in 2011 attempted to explain the pause in the trend of rising average global temperatures between 1998 and 2008. A NOAA study showed that stratospheric aerosols (fine solid or liquid airborne particles) had been reflecting sunlight back into space, offsetting part of the warming effect produced by increased carbon dioxide concentrations. In addition, small volcanic eruptions or sulfur dioxide emissions could have contributed to the increase in the amount of aerosols in the atmosphere. A second study, published by researchers from Boston University, Harvard University, and the University of Turku, Fin., pointed to sulfur emissions from Chinese coal consumption, which more than doubled from 2003 to 2007, as being a major source of the cooling aerosols. They found that declining solar insolation and the change from El Niño to La Niña conditions in the tropical Pacific Ocean also contributed to the observed slowdown of global warming in their statistical model.

(DOUGLAS LE COMTE)

Education

The **PISA** report in 2011 revealed that countries with **ACADEMICALLY** or financially **SEGREGATED** school systems, such as **GERMANY** and **CHILE**, had lower test scores. Primary-school enrollment gained worldwide, but high **DROPOUT** rates and youth **UNEMPLOYMENT** pushed some countries to emphasize **VOCATIONAL** education. In the U.S. more students attended privately run **FOR-PROFIT** colleges.

PRIMARY AND SECONDARY EDUCATION

During 2011 conflicting definitions of the purpose of education shaped national and international debates. The broad attention garnered by international test-score results focused countries' attention on rankings races based on the premise that high test scores lead to national economic competitiveness. The resulting policy initiatives, however, varied greatly from country to country. China shifted toward universal education and away from an emphasis on elite institutions. Poland looked to decentralization as the key. The U.S. proposed a stronger national test-based accountability system and punitive consequences for schools and educators turning in low scores. Reactions against a too-rigid approach to education were played out in many countries, but perhaps nowhere more prominently than in Japan, where the student suicide rate was the highest among those member countries in the Organisation for Economic Co-operation and Development (OECD). Japan was a top scorer on international tests, and suicides peaked on national examination day.

Policy debates followed the release in late 2010 of the Programme for International Student Assessment (PISA) test scores for 2009 (the latest year available), which provided scores for 65 countries or economies in reading, math, and science for 15-year-old students. While there was near-universal agreement that rank-order ratings were an incomplete and narrow way to measure an educational system, the rankings nevertheless precipitated national attention and commentary around the globe.

Perhaps more interesting and thought-provoking, however, was the publication of the characteristics of the educational systems of high- and low-scoring countries. The high-scoring countries provided greater and more universal learning opportunities and more socioeconomic equality. In general, Asian and other more culturally homogenous countries recorded higher scores. Looking closer, countries that tracked students into different educational or career paths, retained (held back) students in grade levels, or segregated students into different schools or classes (by race, mental or physical disability, behaviour, etc.) showed lower results. Germany found that its test-based curriculum, which assigned students to different tracks at age 10, was causing economic and social segregation, maintaining an achievement gap, and depressing its international scores.

The PISA report also concluded that schools that had greater autonomy to set their own curriculum and conduct their own assessments performed higher on international tests. While such locations as Poland, the German state of Saxony, Victoria state in Australia, and the province of Ontario in Canada decentralized, the U.S. pressed forward with its Common Core State Standards and the formation of two national testing consortia with the aim of universal testing in grades three through eight (plus a high school examination). Centralization and standardization into core subjects became a reform motif for the U.K., as well. Centralized but economically depressed Cuba scored higher than other countries in the region on the World Bank's school ratings. Commentators pointed to the island country's very high adult literacy, equality of educational opportunities, and support programs for children as key positive factors.

Competition-based market-model reforms also received extensive attention during 2011, even though the PISA results found that schools that competed for students scored no higher once socioeconomic and other background factors were taken into account. Nevertheless, competition and privatization of schools grew rapidly in some countries. In the U.S. the number of publicly financed but privately operated charter schools increased, and in late 2011 some 40 states had laws that authorized those schools, which were designed to be competitive with traditional public schools. Paralleling the PISA findings, charter schools in the U.S. were shown to have segregative effects—although they remained highly popular with the parents of charter-school children. In the U.K. "independent academies" and "free schools" were the equivalent of charter schools. Australia had a public/private combination where private schools were publicly subsidized, but the private schools often charged additional fees. This disparate funding excited extensive growth in the private-school sector and kindled a national debate as to whether the resulting fragmentation would result in an irreversible dissolution of the public education system. Chile had the broadest and longest-lasting privatized voucher system, in which each child received a voucher, but more-affluent parents were allowed to supplement this sum and use it for more-expensive private schools. The result was a highly segregated system with affluent students in private schools and poorer students in the less-well-funded public schools. Chile ranked 64th out of 65 countries in OECD rankings regarding equality of education and scored well below international averages. Chilean students had repeatedly taken to the streets in protest, but the outcome of this political ferment was yet to be determined.

Enrollment. The UNESCO goal of universal primary education by 2015 showed overall worldwide gains over the past 10 years, and in 2011 it averaged 90% across the world. The great-

Aliosha Marquez/AP

Young protesters demanding that Chile's government institute educational reforms to the country's highly segregated school system are pummeled by Santiago police with spray from water cannons in October.

est growth was seen in the lowest-access countries, found predominately in sub-Saharan Africa, the Arab states, and South and West Asia. Less-developed countries (LDCs) in general showed the greatest growth (and likewise had the most room to grow), though Mozambique and Ethiopia both registered below 40% completion of primary education for eligible students. Another troubling factor was that 30% of the students in two-thirds of sub-Saharan countries were expected to drop out before completing primary education. While the worldwide trend was positive, small but worrisome losses were registered for developed countries and for countries in transition. In North America and western Europe enrollment dropped from 97% to 96%.

Upper-secondary dropouts became a political issue in the U.S. with the adoption of a new metric that defined a dropout as anyone who did not complete upper-secondary education "on time." By excluding those who took longer or followed alternate paths, the effect was to generate a political crisis by posting a new and much higher dropout rate of 30%. Nevertheless, because dropouts are generally less likely to be in the labour force, and traditionally earn considerably less when employed, the issue was an international concern. The Netherlands, with a noncompletion rate of 11%, employed a literal recapture program, while Norway (12%) shortened vocational programs and integrated work and learning programs. South Korea, second only to Canada in higher education completion rates, took a different tack and started a program to discourage higher education and encourage vocational programs. According to the OECD's 16-country study, the most successful countries in retaining students had larger proportions of students in vocational school and sought to match training to labour-force needs.

Funding. Spending on education increased faster than inflation from 1975 on and represented 6.1% of GDP in OECD countries, though the effects of the 2008 global recession were yet to be seen in the international statistics. The correlation between level of education and earnings led many observers to urge ever-increasing higher educational levels as a means of advancing economies as well as benefiting the welfare of individuals. The increasing technical sophistication of the world was likewise put forward as a rationale for higher investment in education. Education was also encouraged as a means of closing the socioeconomic gap and was an explicit part of the reform rationale in the U.K. and the U.S.

On the other hand, some proponents of lower education spending pointed to the PISA results and noted the high achievement scores of some low-spending countries and the low achievement of some high-spending countries. Of course, countries varied dramatically in culture, breadth of educational program offerings, and the defined number of extra services that schools were obliged to provide, such as social programs and drug, sex, and health education. PISA's analysis concluded that after a sufficient level of programs had been provided to all students, further expenditures did not increase test scores in any significant fashion. This broad sweep did not consider the vast spending inequalities within countries, which PISA highlighted as a major concern.

Funding distribution was an ongoing problem in the U.S., Australia, Chile, the U.K., and many other countries. Rural students received disproportionately less, and advocates for poor populations challenged fund distributions in U.S. courts. The judicial decisions tended to favour the plaintiffs, but the pace of such cases waned with the economic downturn.

Socioeconomic advancement remained the great personal motivator for pursuing education. This truism was shifting as the effects of the recession, the changing nature of the job force, and the advent of technology began to weaken that path to personal prosperity. Finland, among the highest-scoring countries, was beset by more than 20% youth unemployment, and Japan experienced a similar problem. The U.S. faced 16% underemployment and about 9% unemployment overall. For OECD countries, youth unemployment stood at about 17%, and for those aged 15 to 19 who were not in school, the unemployment rate was over 50%.

Technology also displaced manufacturing jobs and, paradoxically, simplified many jobs—thereby reducing the necessary skill levels and the amount of pay offered. The result was an increase in educated but unemployed or underemployed youth. The unemployment rate for university graduates in OECD countries stood at 4.4%, while the rate for secondary school noncompleters was 11.5%.

Teachers. There was broad international agreement that a high-quality teaching force is essential for all students, and reflecting the highly labour-intensive nature of education, teacher salaries represented 63% of school spending. Thus, having well-qualified faculties was an economic as well as a labour-force issue.

Of 208 countries, 54% faced shortages in the number of primary teachers needed to attain the goal of universal literacy, according to UNESCO. The greatest shortage was in sub-Saharan Africa, followed by South Asia and

West Asia. Moderate shortages were projected in Western countries, including Ireland, Italy, Spain, Sweden, and the U.S. Much of the need was based on the number of students, but teacher attrition was a major problem in such diverse locations as the U.S., China, Indonesia, Nigeria, and Ethiopia. At the primary level, the proportion of teachers who were female had risen from 56% to 62% since 1990.

The PISA results indicated that teacher pay was a more important factor in high test scores than was class size. Teacher salaries increased in real terms in most countries; since 2000 the Czech Republic, Estonia, and Turkey had registered more than 50% cumulative pay increases. As part of their education-quality reforms, Finland and South Korea focused on recruiting top-quality teachers and paying them accordingly. Only Australia, Japan, New Zealand, and Switzerland showed a decrease in teacher pay.

Policy actions affecting the teaching force were not all in the same direction. Kenya declared universal free primary and secondary education, but the allocation of government funds to the military rather than to teacher pay resulted in 200,000 teachers' going on strike.

In the U.S., 46% of teachers left the profession within the first five years, and political attacks against teachers' unions and teacher pay were common. Rolling back teacher benefits had political repercussions in several states, gaining the most notoriety in Wisconsin, where the governor faced a recall petition, in part because of that issue. In England and Wales, nearly half of schools were closed on June 30 because of nationwide teacher strikes that were staged to protest political efforts to cut teacher pensions.

Evaluating teachers and teacher-preparation programs by standardized-test scores was on the agenda in the U.S. and Canada. Proponents argued for merit pay, but the primary objections were that such a practice would narrow the curriculum and that attaching test score gains to a particular teacher was not scientifically reliable. In Florida and some other states, hiring teachers who had not undergone a formal training program as a teacher was becoming commonplace, and efforts were under way to advance these plans in more states.

Computers, Technology, and Distance Education. While computer technology had been forecast to fundamentally change education, UNESCO reported that this had yet to happen. Use of computerized technology showed no gains in achievement scores above those produced in traditional classrooms. The common model was a teacher in front of a classroom, albeit with computer-assisted projectors and devices. Teacher professional development, however, was changing to include the use of technology. Transformed and adaptive-computerized student assessment also continued to be promoted, and the two major assessment consortia in the U.S. promised to deliver such programs by 2015, but the necessary software had not yet been designed, much less tested.

The most pronounced shifts were in student computer literacy and the immediate access to knowledge by all. For remote and rural schools, satellite linkages took the world of knowledge to any location, as evidenced by Australia's "School of the Air" and India's "Digital Study Hall." Personal communications devices had become ubiquitous in the Western world, while cell phones compensated for the lack of infrastructure in LDCs.

A number of "cyberschools" provided complete educational programs online. These were particularly prominent for higher education and technical training, though distance-learning providers in primary and secondary education were on the rise.

Quality control over the diverse online educational offerings remained an unresolved issue. As distance-learning providers increasingly sought governmental subsidies and supports, concerns increased regarding the monitoring of the quality of the offerings and standards for such courses. In the U.S. some critics continued to express apprehension over low completion rates, uneven quality, and the lack of employer acceptance of electronically earned credentials.

Students in New Delhi test a low-cost tablet computer in October. The device, which used Google's Android operating system, was designed to improve computer literacy and access to the Internet for those in remote and rural areas in India and elsewhere.

EPA/Landov

HIGHER EDUCATION

Student participation in higher education dramatically increased in recent years, with the European Union showing annual market increases averaging 7%. OECD countries saw a cumulative increase of nearly 20% from 1995 to 2008. More students were receiving their postsecondary education from privately owned, for-profit schools, especially in the U.S., where by 2009 some 10% of all postsecondary students were enrolled in a for-profit institution. (*See* Sidebar.)

One of the most dramatic problems facing higher education in 2011 was the continuing increase in costs, which had the effect of excluding those less able to pay high tuitions. In the U.S. many students left school with a staggering debt load, including those attending for-profit institutions, where up to 92% of those enrolled had student loans. In real terms, since 2000 international higher education costs had risen 14%, with some countries showing even greater increases. In the U.S. costs were dramatically higher for private institutions. Private funding for higher education increased in 20 of 26 countries, with the private share of costs increasing by 6% on average. Portugal, Slovakia, and the U.K. saw private-share increases of 15 percentage points or more.

According to an OECD report released in 2011, international students (those attending higher education outside their country of citizenship) increased from 800,000 in 1975 to 3.7 million in 2009. Greater international mobility led this number to be projected to increase, but it was a shifting and nuanced phenomenon. The U.S. attracted 37% of international students in 1970, but this share steadily dropped to 22% in 2009. The decline was exacerbated by the terrorist attacks of Sept. 11, 2001, with the

The Proliferation of For-Profit Colleges

In 2011 providers of postsecondary education fell into three broad categories: private nonprofit institutions, public institutions (operated by national, provincial/state, or local government entities), and privately owned for-profit institutions, many of which initially focused on trades and other career training. DeVry University, for example, was founded as DeForest Training School in 1931 to train people in emerging technical fields such as electronics, but by 2011 the for-profit school was offering undergraduate and graduate degrees, both online and at over 90 locations in the U.S. and Canada.

For-profit institutions grew dramatically in the U.S. after World War II, in large measure because the G.I. Bill, passed in 1944, provided federal government financial support for returning U.S. service members to attend postsecondary schools. Subsequently, the 1972 reauthorization of the Higher Education Act of 1965 allowed students to use tuition subsidies such Pell Grants to attend for-profit institutions. In 1986 for-profit schools enrolled about 2% of U.S. postsecondary students; by 2009, however, there were some 2,800 for-profit institutions, enrolling approximately 10% of all postsecondary students and about 7% of all postsecondary students attending degree-granting institutions. *The Chronicle of Higher Education* reported that the industry grew an average of 9% per year from 1980 to 2010. The overall growth rate among postsecondary institutions was about 1.5% over the same period.

By 2010 five firms—Apollo Group, Education Management Corp., Career Education Corp., Corinthian Colleges, and DeVry University—enrolled more than 40% of all students attending for-profit institutions. The Apollo Group, which operated the University of Phoenix, accounted for more than 20% of students enrolled in for-profit postsecondary schools and was, according to Bloomberg News, the second largest postsecondary institution in the U.S. (after the State University of New York system).

The U.S. government General Accountability Office (GAO) reported that in 2009 students attending for-profit colleges received more than $4 billion in Pell Grants and $20 billion in federal loans provided by the Department of Education. Data from various sources indicated that individually and as a group for-profit postsecondary schools received more than three-fourths of their revenue from government loan and grant programs. *Bloomberg Businessweek* magazine reported that the amount of federal aid going to students at for-profit colleges grew nearly sixfold from $4.6 billion in 2000 to $26.5 billion in 2009. Individual companies reported even higher reliance on federal sources for their revenues, with some nearing a federally imposed cap of 90% (set in 1998). In 2010, for example, 80% of the revenue generated by Career Education Corp. came from federal sources, according to the *New York Times* newspaper, as did 86% of revenue generated by the University of Phoenix in 2009, according to Bloomberg News. For-profit institutions benefited when Congress in 2006 repealed a rule that students had to receive at least 50% of their instruction in a physical location rather than online for their school to be eligible to collect federal student financial aid.

Students attending for-profit institutions were found to carry much more student debt than their counterparts at public and nonprofit schools. The Institute on College Access and Success reported that as of 2007–08, some 92% of students enrolled in for-profit schools had student loans, compared with 60% at nonprofit schools, 27% at public colleges, and 13% at community colleges. In 2009 students who had attended for-profit institutions and were entering repayment defaulted on their loans at twice the rate of students from public colleges and at three times the rate of students at nonprofit schools.

Critics argued that the rapid growth of the industry in general and the largest firms in particular might, in part, be the result of unethical or illegal practices and that students at for-profit schools not only took on more debt but also dropped out at higher rates and often failed to find jobs in the careers for which they were trained. In 2010 the GAO conducted an investigation of the recruiting practices of for-profit firms and reported, among other things, that recruiters exaggerated the salaries graduates would potentially receive and the school's graduation rate while understating the cost of programs and the length of time it took to complete them. The GAO report also documented the use of high-pressure recruitment tactics, among other questionable practices, and noted that for-profit schools charged substantially more for degrees and certificates than nearby public schools.

Allegations of high costs, failure to provide the education promised, high dropout rates, and poor job placement for graduates led to calls for stricter oversight of the for-profit postsecondary education industry. As of 2011, however, the extent of new regulations fell short of what U.S. Pres. Barack Obama's administration originally sought.

Although its full scope was difficult to accurately quantify, international agreements that favoured privatization and deregulation, along with the expansion of Web-based virtual education, suggested that internationally the for-profit education industry was on a high-growth trajectory. In 2011, for example, the Apollo Group had holdings in the U.K., Chile, and Mexico; Kaplan Education was doing business in the U.K., Ireland, and parts of Asia; and Career Education Corp. claimed 90 campuses in five countries. (ALEX MOLNAR)

resulting restrictions on international travel. The leading host countries, as measured by percentage of students, were Australia, the U.K., Austria, Switzerland, and New Zealand. China was the leading source country, contributing 18.2% of all visiting students in OECD countries. In a shift in gender roles, young women were more likely to finish higher education than men. Women dominated in education, health, welfare, humanities, and the arts, while men dominated in engineering, manufacturing, and construction.

In an attempt to keep their students at home—and as a reflection of the expanding international face of higher education—previously high-sending countries were building their own universities and forming new international partnerships. Malaysia, with 300,000 university-educated citizens working abroad, established branches of three British universities at home. With online communication, courses originating in one country were easily accessible in others. In another example of internationalization, the European Union was moving to standardize degrees.

(WILLIAM J. MATHIS)

The Environment

Scientists reported that Earth contains about **8.7 MILLION SPECIES**, mapped the migratory routes of **LEATHERBACK TURTLES**, observed the hatching of a **SHORT-TAILED ALBATROSS** outside Japan, and documented the **SIGNIFICANT DECLINE** in springtime **OZONE COVERAGE** in the Northern Hemisphere. The planned construction of **BRAZIL'S BELO MONTE DAM** was shut down, whereas **CHILE'S HIDROAYSEN DAM PROJECT** was approved.

INTERNATIONAL ACTIVITIES

Wangari Maathai. On Sept. 25, 2011, Kenyan social activist and environmental campaigner Wangari Maathai, who was the winner of the 2004 Nobel Peace Prize, died from ovarian cancer at the age of 71. She had received the Nobel Prize for her work supporting democracy, human rights, and the environment. (*See* OBITUARIES.)

Arctic. On May 12, indigenous leaders and foreign ministers of Arctic countries met in Nuuk, Greenland, to develop a plan for oil-spill preparedness and response. The participants also consented to form a working group charged with developing an ecosystem-based management plan to administer the region's resources, including fish stocks. After the representatives considered the results of a study showing that black carbon, ozone, and methane may account for up to 40% of the warming observed in the Arctic, they decided to establish another working group charged with undertaking projects to reduce black carbon and other climate-forcing emissions.

European Union. On April 13 the Nuffield Council on Bioethics in London issued a report calling for the lifting of production targets for biofuel raw materials grown in the EU or imported from other countries until new safeguards were in place. It urged that biofuel production be environmentally sustainable, contribute to the reduction in greenhouse-gas emissions, and adhere to fair-trade principles. The report also called for the equitable distribution of the resource's costs and benefits and for its production not to occur at the expense of human rights.

In July the European Commission approved 7 voluntary schemes and was considering 18 more that were aimed at ensuring that biofuels used in the EU were produced in accordance with the Renewable Energy Directive (RED), which forbade biofuel-crop cultivation in areas of high biodiversity or in recently cleared regions, such as filled-in wetlands or harvested forests. The European Commission also mandated that the biofuel production chain must emit amounts of greenhouse gases at least 35% less than the fossil-fuel production chain did, in accordance with RED, which came into force in December 2010. This figure would rise to 50% by 2017 for existing production facilities and to 60% by 2018 for new installations.

NATIONAL DEVELOPMENTS

Australia. In March rallies protesting the planned introduction of a carbon tax by the Labor government of Prime Minister Julia Gillard included hundreds of people in Canberra, Melbourne, Brisbane, Adelaide, and Perth. The demonstrators insisted that the tax would damage the economy by increasing the cost of living and eroding competitiveness, thereby eliminating jobs. On July 9 the government unveiled its \$A 24.5 billion (\$A 1 = about \$1.02) clean-energy legislative package. The carbon tax, which from July 1, 2012, would be imposed on the country's top 500 emitters, was set at \$A 23 per metric ton (1 metric ton = about 2,205 lb). The rate would increase annually until 2015, when the tax would be replaced by an emissions trading scheme. The measure's aim was to reduce carbon emissions to 5% below 2000 levels by 2020; such reductions would increase to 80% by 2050. Gillard presented her bill to Parliament in

On March 23, protesters demonstrate outside Parliament House in the Australian capital of Canberra to voice their disapproval of the Australian Labor government's proposed carbon tax, which was designed to reign in the country's greenhouse gas emissions.

Mark Graham/AP

Dolores Ochoa/AP

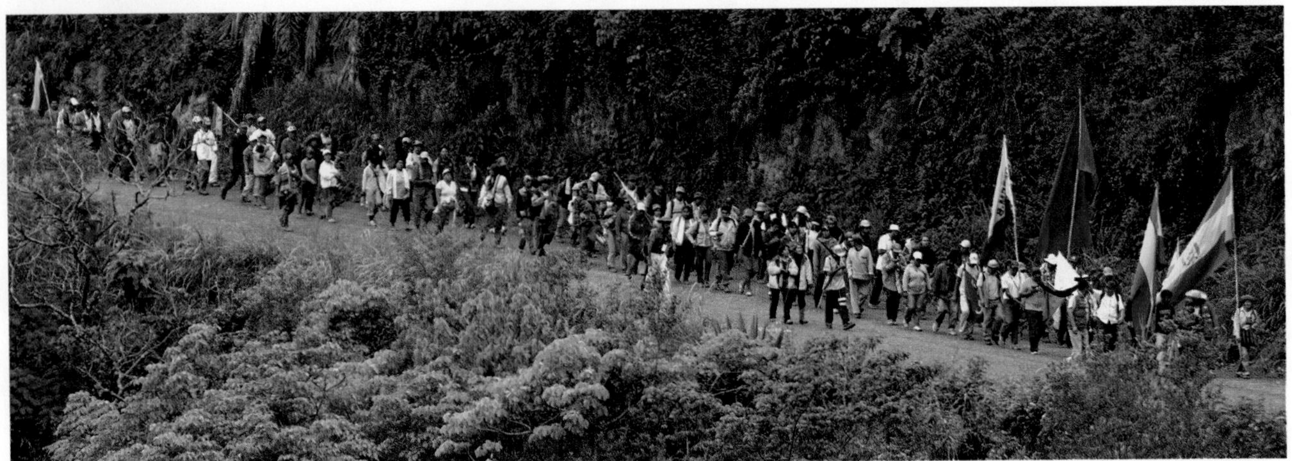

Marchers protesting against the construction of a road that would connect the Bolivian cities of Cochabamba and San Ignacio de Moxos advance toward the county's capital, La Paz, on October 14.

September; the lower house of Parliament approved the measure on October 12, and the upper house followed on November 8.

Bolivia. In August more than 500 protesters belonging to several indigenous groups began a 500-km (1 km = 0.6 mi) march from the city of Trinidad to the capital, La Paz. The goal was to demonstrate their opposition to plans for a road linking Cochabamba in the highlands with San Ignacio de Moxos in the Amazon lowlands. The road, funded by Brazil and contracted to a Brazilian company, would help connect Brazil's southern Amazon region with Pacific ports in Peru and Chile. It would, however, pass through the Isiboro Sécure Indigenous Territory and National Park, which was home to the Chiman, Yurucare, and Moxos peoples. Despite the government's assurances that environmental safeguards were in place for what some considered to be a much-needed road, the protesters believed that its construction would encourage deforestation and illegal settlement, particularly by growers of coca leaf, the raw material for making cocaine.

On September 26, after a heated confrontation in which police arrested hundreds of protesters in the Yucumo region, Pres. Evo Morales announced the road project's suspension, stating that the two provinces concerned, Cochabamba and Beni, should decide whether the project should resume. In response to criticism of the police crackdown, Interior Minister Sacha Llorenti and his deputy both resigned. On September 28 tens of thousands of demonstrators critical of the president's handling of the crisis brought traffic to a standstill in the centre of La Paz.

Brazil. In September, Judge Carlos Castro Martins ruled in favour of a fisheries group that had argued that the Belo Monte dam on the Xingu River would affect local fish stocks and subsequently harm families who made their living from fishing. The judge barred the Norte Energia company from doing any infrastructure work that would interfere with the natural flow of the Xingu River. The dam would generate 11 gigawatts of power, which, according to the government, was necessary to meet the country's energy needs.

China. On August 14 in the city of Dalian, scuffles broke out between police and about 12,000 protesters, who took part in a "group stroll." The use of the term, which was code for "rally," was a favoured tactic for critics of official policies. The protesters aimed to close a chemical factory that made paraxylene—a chemical used to make fibres, films, and bottle resins—which they feared might leak into the environment. Immediately following the clashes, authorities ordered the plant's closure and said that it would be relocated.

In September, following a vigorous three-day demonstration at a solar-panel factory near Shanghai, the owner, Shanghai-based Jinko Solar, suspended operations at the plant. Large numbers of fish had died in a nearby river, and tests showed high levels of fluoride in the water. Villagers accused the company of having discharged hazardous chemicals into the water supply. The company said that it had stored chemicals in the open and that unexpectedly severe weather had torn off covers.

Ecuador. On February 14 a court fined Chevron $8.6 billion for polluting rivers in the Amazon region. In addition, Chevron would have to pay a 10% reparations fee, including $5 billion for soil restoration and $2 billion for health care for local residents. The pollution had occurred between 1972 and 1992 when Texaco, which Chevron bought in 2001, dumped billions of litres of toxic substances into unlined pits and rivers. Campaigners maintained that the pollution had damaged crops, killed farm animals, and raised the local incidence of cancer. The case, brought on behalf of 30,000 persons, had continued for 17 years. Following the decision, local people said that they would file an appeal demanding higher compensation, as their lawyers had assessed the reparations at up to $113 billion. Chevron called the judgment "illegitimate and unenforceable," and on March 9 it also launched an appeal. In addition, the company claimed that Texaco had spent $40 million cleaning up the area during the 1990s and had signed an agreement with the government absolving it of further responsibility.

Nigeria. A report published early in August by the UN Environment Programme assessed the extent of pollution in the coastal region of Ogoniland that resulted from more than 50 years of oil production there. The report, requested by the Nigerian government and paid for in part by the multinational oil-producing company Shell, estimated that it would take 25–30 years for the region to recover from oil spills and that the cleanup would cost up to $1 billion. In at least 10 Ogoniland communities, drinking water was contaminated with hydrocarbons. In one community residents consumed drinking water containing benzene at 900 times the maximum levels recommended by WHO, oil

Akintunde Akinleye—Reuters/Landov

A boy stands on oil-contaminated land in the Ikarama community in Bayelsa state in Nigeria's delta region on August 20.

slicks up to 8 cm (3 in) thick floated on the water, and oil had soaked at least 5 m (16 ft) into the ground in some locations. Shell accepted the responsibility for two spills, which occurred in 2008 and 2009. It also agreed to settle claims under Nigerian law from members of the Bodo fishing community, who alleged that the spills had ruined their livelihoods.

United States. The year 2011 began with the termination of carbon credit trade by the Chicago Carbon Exchange and the introduction by the Environmental Protection Agency (EPA) of new controls on greenhouse-gas emissions—regulations that came into force on January 2. Those new rules covered carbon dioxide emissions from new industrial plants. But the EPA's authority to regulate greenhouse-gas emissions was called into question by Congress and challenged by lawsuits.

On February 19 the House of Representatives passed a budget amendment offered by Blaine Luetkemeyer, a Republican representative from Missouri, that prohibited the government from contributing $13 million to the UN Intergovernmental Panel on Climate Change (IPCC). Luetkemeyer argued that American taxpayers should not be forced to support the IPCC, because it was "an entity that is fraught with waste and fraud and engaged in dubious science." The Senate subsequently rejected the amendment.

On September 2 Pres. Barack Obama directed EPA administrator Lisa Jackson to withdraw a proposed regulation intended to cut permitted concentrations of ground-level ozone, the principal ingredient of photochemical smog. Under the regulation, the legal average concentration of the chemical over 8 hours would have declined from 75 parts per billion (ppb) (set in 2008) and 80 ppb (set in 1997) to 70 ppb.

ENVIRONMENTAL ISSUES

Intergovernmental Panel on Climate Change. In May, at the end of an eight-day meeting held in Abu Dhabi, U.A.E., representatives of 194 countries agreed to policies aimed at restoring the IPCC's integrity and credibility. The new policies covered conflicts of interest, protocols for handling errors in reports, guidance on communication, and recommendations on the use of non-peer-reviewed material. The meeting also approved an IPCC summary of a special report on renewable energy.

That summary, issued halfway through the meeting, claimed that renewable resources could supply 77% of the world's energy by 2050. When the full report was released on June 15, however, it revealed that Sven Teske, a lead author of the chapter from which the 77% figure had come, was a renewable-energy campaigner employed by Greenpeace International. The renewable-resource calculation erroneously assumed a decline in energy consumption over the following 40 years, ignored any contribution from nuclear power, and was based on the most optimistic of 164 scenarios the IPCC had investigated.

Clean Development Mechanism (CDM). In August the WikiLeaks Web site published a diplomatic cable sent on July 16, 2008, from the U.S. consulate in Mumbai to the secretary of state that summarized a CDM discussion between consulate representatives, the U.S. Government Accountability Office, Indian government officials, and executives of large Indian companies. It reported that most of the carbon-offset projects in India approved under the CDM failed to meet the requirements set by the UN Framework Convention on Climate Change (UNFCCC) because they did not reduce carbon emissions beyond those that would have occurred anyway, without foreign investment. A former chairman of the Indian CDM authority said that in approving projects, its officials had accepted the developer's word and had known about the problem for at least two years. Eva Filzmoser, program director at Brussels-based CDM Watch, commented that the leaked information confirmed "our view that in its present form the CDM is basically a farce."

In July a report by an international fact-finding mission was presented to the European Parliament's Subcommittee on Human Rights concerning the murder between January 2010 and March 2011 of 23 peasants, one journalist, and the journalist's partner by security forces in the Bajo Aguán region of northern Honduras. The report noted that the killings occurred because the deceased had attempted to repossess land that they said had been sold illegally to large CDM-funded oil-palm plantations.

On September 21 Oxfam, an international group seeking solutions to poverty and injustice, issued a report stating that in recent years more than 20,000 people had been evicted from their homes around Kicucula, Ugan., to make way for pine and eucalyptus trees grown by the British-owned New Forests Company. The company, to which the Ugandan government had granted a 50-year license in 2005, grew forests in African countries in order to sell carbon credits under the CDM.

Climate Change. The climate summit held in Cancún, Mex., in late 2010 opened with wide divisions between countries and few expectations of any substantial agreement. Many industrialized countries stated that they intended to reduce their greenhouse-gas emissions to 25–40% below 1990 levels by 2020 to ensure that the average global temperature did not rise by more than 2 °C (3.6 °F). Even though delegates were not presented with concrete proposals for legally binding limits, the conference concluded with an understanding that deeper cuts in emissions were needed. The details of the cuts considered were to be approved at the 2011 Conference of the Parties (COP17) in Durban, S.Af., from November 28 to December 9. On the final day of COP17, there was still no agreement on a text that would produce a legally binding agreement on greenhouse gas emissions. As a result, talks were allowed to continue, and the conference ended on December 11 with a compromise agreement under which discussions on a replacement to the Kyoto Protocol would begin in 2012. This new pact, which would have legal force and apply to all countries, would be finalized in 2015 and would come into force in 2020. In addition, delegates agreed to develop a fund for climate aid to poor countries; however, they could not concur on how the finances would be raised.

Ozone Layer. On April 5, at the annual meeting of the European Geosciences Union in Vienna, scientists from the World Meteorological Organization and the Alfred Wegener Institute for Polar and Marine Research released figures showing that the combination of sunshine and low temperatures in the upper atmosphere had reduced stratospheric ozone levels over the Arctic by 40%. That was the largest reduction in ozone levels ever recorded.

It was reported in May that a team led by meteorologist Murry Salby of Macquarie University, Sydney, might have detected the first sign of Antarctic ozone recovery. A paper in *Geophysical Research Letters* revealed that since the late 1990s a 15% increase in stratospheric ozone levels had occurred.

Deepwater Horizon. In December 2010 the U.S. government launched legal action under the Clean Water Act and the Oil Pollution Act against BP Exploration and Production, Inc., Transocean Holdings LLC, and their partners. The companies were accused of having violated a number of federal regulations covering operations and safety measures, and those violations were thought to have contributed to the 2010 Deepwater Horizon disaster. Specific charges included failure to take necessary precautions to keep the Macondo oil well under control in the period leading up to the April 20 oil-rig explosion and failure to use the best and safest drilling technology to monitor the well's conditions. The presidential commission's report on the disaster, published in January 2011, placed the blame for the accident on BP, which owned the well; on Transocean, which owned the rig; and on Halliburton, which managed the well-sealing operation. The report said that corner cutting by all three companies contributed to the accident, and federal government oversight failed to provide an acceptable level of protection for workers on the rig as well as for the environment. In September the Bureau of Ocean Energy Management, Regulation, and Enforcement and the U.S. Coast Guard Joint Investigation Team issued their own joint report, which blamed the accident on operational errors, poor leadership, and a poor job of using cement to seal the well.

Marine Pollution. At a meeting held in London in July, the Marine Environment Protection Committee of the International Maritime Organization (IMO) consented to new rules that from 2016 onward would ban new passenger ships from discharging untreated sewage into the Baltic Sea. The IMO also agreed to introduce a mandatory energy-efficiency standard for new ships. Ships constructed in 2015–19 would have to be 10% more efficient than those constructed in 2013–14. Also, overall efficiency would have to improve by 20% for ships built between 2020 and 2024 and 30% for those built after 2024. Ships built in LDCs would be exempt from these rules until 2019.

A five-day meeting of the Greenhouse Gas Working Group of the IMO, held in London at the beginning of April, failed to produce a consensus on a path to reduce carbon dioxide emissions from shipping. Participants discussed an emission-trading scheme, emission charges for all shipping, and levies on ships that failed to reach efficiency standards. A group of LDCs led by India, China, Brazil, and South Africa, however, contested the IMO's equality principle, demanding instead that LDCs be allowed to meet conditions different from those that developed countries had to meet, in line with the concept of common but differentiated responsibility contained in the UNFCCC.

In August representatives of Russia, Iran, Kazakhstan, Azerbaijan, and Turkmenistan met in Aktau, Kazakh., to discuss the legally binding Framework Convention for the Protection of the Marine Environment of the Caspian Sea (Tehran Convention). The representatives sanctioned the text of a protocol that would introduce common rules for environmental-impact statements prepared by companies operating in the area. The new protocol dealt largely with the topics of oil-spill preparedness and response.

Pesticides. At the final meeting of parties to the Stockholm Convention on Persistent Organic Pollutants, which was held in Geneva on April 25–29, India acceded to international pressure and agreed to a global ban on endosulfan, an organochlorine insecticide and acaricide (tick and mite killer), in return for financial assistance in replacing it. Participants endorsed a six-year phaseout of endosulfan for most countries; however, LDCs such as India would have 11 years. They also agreed to create a program to find safer alternatives. Endosulfan was banned because of its acute toxicity, its potential for bioaccumulation, and its role as an endocrine disrupter. (MICHAEL ALLABY)

WILDLIFE CONSERVATION

In January 2011 Brazil's environment agency, IBAMA, allowed work to begin on the Belo Monte hydroelectric dam on the Xingu River, a tributary of the Amazon. After years of protests, the contracts for the dam were signed in August 2010. Opponents said that the 6-km (3.7-mi) dam would threaten the survival of indigenous groups and leave 50,000 people homeless, since roughly 500 sq km (about 190 sq mi) of land would be flooded. A judge blocked the plans in February because IBAMA had approved the project without ensuring that environmental conditions had been met. This decision was countered by a higher court ruling in March, which stated that there was no need for all conditions to be met for work to begin. In late September, however, a judge sided with a fisheries group that argued that the dam would affect fish stocks and harm indigenous families and ordered a halt to construction, thereby barring any work that would interfere with the natural flow of the Xingu.

In October a Chilean appeals court ruled in favour of the multibillion-dollar HidroAysen Dam project in Patagonia, which lifted a previous suspension order that supported objections made by environmentalists who claimed that the project would damage Patagonia's fragile ecosystem. Five dams would be built on two rivers that run into the Pacific, draining lakes in a region famous for its glaciers, ice fields, mountains, and fjords. Opponents of the dam filed seven objections, which included citing the project's detrimental effects on the Laguna San Rafael National Park and threats to the Patagonian huemul (*Hippocamelus bisulcus*), an endangered Andean deer.

A five-year satellite-tracking study published in January revealed, for the first time, the migratory routes of leatherback turtles (*Dermochelys coriacea*). The study tracked 25 female

David Dow/U.S. Fish and Wildlife Service

*The first short-tailed albatross chick (*Phoebastria albatrus*) that hatched in the Midway Atoll National Wildlife Refuge was banded by wildlife biologists on June 8.*

leatherbacks across the South Atlantic. Three migratory routes were identified between the largest leatherback breeding colony in Gabon and its feeding grounds in the equatorial Atlantic, off South America and off southern Africa. The longest recorded journey for an individual leatherback was 7,563 km (4,700 mi) across the South Atlantic from Africa to South America. Such increased knowledge of the migratory patterns and routes would likely improve conservation strategies for the protection of leatherback turtles.

It was reported in January that for the first time in recorded history, a short-tailed albatross (*Phoebastria albatrus*) hatched outside Japan, emerging on Eastern Island in the Midway Atoll National Wildlife Refuge, Hawaii. The species' main breeding grounds, located on Japan's Torishima Island, were regularly threatened by volcanic activity, and the establishment of a new breeding ground thus would be significant. (The species is listed as vulnerable on the International Union for Conservation of Nature's [IUCN's] Red List of Threatened Species.) It was thought that the population of the short-tailed albatross once had numbered more than five million; however, in 1939 only 10 pairs remained. Through conservation efforts, however, the population had risen to roughly 2,400 individuals by 2011.

In July the first global assessment of the conservation status of scombrids and billfish—which include commercially valuable species, such as albacore, tuna, marlin, and mackerel—was published. Of 61 species assessed by means of the IUCN Red List categories and criteria, 5 were considered vulnerable. In addition, the Atlantic bluefin tuna (*Thunnus thynnus*) was considered endangered, and the southern bluefin tuna (*T. maccoyii*) was considered critically endangered, which helped to confirm that several species were already overexploited.

In August, using a new approach based on the higher taxonomic classification of species (assignment to phylum, class, order, family, and genus), it was estimated that the natural world contained approximately 8.7 million species (not including bacteria and some types of other microorganisms). The majority had not yet been identified, and many would become extinct before they could be studied. The research quantified the relationship between the discovery of new species and the discovery of new higher groups, such as phyla and orders. This information was then used to predict how many species likely exist.

In early June the International Tropical Timber Organization reported that the area of tropical forest under sustainable management had grown by 50% in five years; this area, however, still accounted for less than 10% of global tropical forest. Some countries, including Brazil, Malaysia, and Peru, made progress toward sustainable forest management. In other countries, such as Cambodia, Liberia, and Guatemala, major military conflicts hindered the development of the institutions required for sustainable forest management. The growth of sustainability was further complicated by the fact that in still other countries, such as Nigeria and Papua New Guinea, forest administrations did not have sufficient resources to supervise forest management. The report also warned that forces that favour forest destruction may overwhelm those favouring forest conservation.

In June 25 new sites were added to the UNESCO World Heritage List, which brought the total number of locations up to 936. The new sites included the Kenya Lake System in the Great Rift Valley, a region with numerous bird species; the Ningaloo Coast in Australia, a site with one of the longest near-shore reefs; and the Ogasawara Islands in Japan, home to the critically endangered Bonin flying fox (*Pteropus pselaphon*). Human activity occurring in two existing World Heritage sites, the Tropical Rainforest Heritage of Sumatra and the Río Plátano Biosphere Reserve in Honduras, led to their inclusion on the list of World Heritage Sites in Danger.

On October 5 the MV *Rena* container ship struck Astrolabe Reef, located some 12 nautical miles off New Zealand's northern coast in the Bay of Plenty. Oil leaking from the ship created a 5-km (3.1-mi) slick. In an attempt to prevent an environmental disaster in this ecologically sensitive area, work began immediately to remove the remaining fuel and oil containers. On October 10 the first oil was found ashore, on Mount Maunganui beach on North Island.

(MARTIN FISHER)

Part of the oil slick from the Rena, *a Liberian-flagged container ship that struck Astrolabe Reef in early October, washed up on a beach on New Zealand's North Island.*

Reuters/Landov

Fashions

WEDDING attire flaunted by notable women and **STYLISH** high-profile personalities dominated the fashion scene, and a number of **TRENDS** emerged, including elaborate **FLORAL MOTIFS**, tropical patterns, and **ACCESSORIES** made of **SNAKESKIN**.

The dramatic buildup to the April 29, 2011, royal wedding of Prince William of Wales and Catherine Middleton (*see* BIOGRAPHIES) prompted intense sartorial scrutiny of the historic occasion as well as the ceremonies that followed it. Middleton also emerged as the uncontested fashion icon of the year as she topped a number of best-dressed lists, notably that produced by *Vanity Fair* magazine.

During her eight-year courtship by the prince, Middleton had rarely earned plaudits for her style because of its conservative nature, but as the new duchess of Cambridge gradually fulfilled royal duties alongside her husband, her look appeared more sophisticated, forging a regal yet relaxed dress mode that genuinely reflected her low-key character, levelheaded demeanour, and inherent refinement. Her polished appearance in ladylike and mostly affordably priced clothing—including pieces with graceful flourishes (such as the frill finishing a Burberry London ruffled wool trench coat that she wore in March to visit City Hall in Belfast, N.Ire.)—unleashed a huge demand for the items she favoured. She repeatedly flaunted Sledge 2, a nude-hued medium-heel patent pump by L.K. Bennett (the luxury women's fashion brand that opened its first American boutique in the spring), and that footwear was among the myriad items associated with her wardrobe that sold out around the world.

In the lead-up to the royal wedding, blogs chronicling Middleton's style proliferated as excitement developed about the make of her bridal gown. *Daily Mail* columnist and biographer Katie Nicholl, who chronicled the royal wedding for *Vanity Fair,* later revealed the many measures employed to keep secret that the gown's designer was Sarah Burton (*see* BIOGRAPHIES), the creative director at the Alexander McQueen fashion house. The members of the team working on the dress there were asked to sign confidentiality agreements. In addition, "Kate switched cars several times on her visit to the atelier. Seamstresses worked night shifts in order to keep the project clandestine, and some parts of the dress were assembled outside the atelier."

John Stillwell/AP

Newly married Catherine, duchess of Cambridge, wears the second dress created for her wedding day by British designer Sarah Burton at her reception.

Burton's ivory and white satin gazar gown featured a flattering "sweetheart bodice." In concert with a suggestion by the bride (who reportedly had a 50% input into the design), the gown's pleated and draped skirt was conceived to evoke the "opening of a flower." The Royal School of Needlework produced the lace appliqué on the bodice as well as the skirt of the gown and crafted individual handmade lace flowers in the shapes of English roses, Scottish thistles, Welsh daffodils, and Irish shamrocks. Those who created the lace manually washed their hands at 30-minute intervals to ensure that it was kept pristine. The gown's hourglass silhouette and padded hips drew on McQueen's hallmark "Victorian tradition of corsetry." (*See* photograph on page 62.) The duchess donned a strapless white Burton gown that was adorned with a sparkling diamanté sash for her Buckingham Palace wedding reception.

Burton's design flair transformed the image of Philippa (Pippa) Middleton, the maid of honour and sister of the bride. Pippa appeared in a cream cowl-neck dress that featured an intricate network of silk-covered buttons that descended down its back. A bridal dress based on the look sold out swiftly after it was launched in November on the Net-A-Porter fashion retail Web site.

Earlier in the year, controversy swirled over the gown that Burton had designed for U.S. first lady Michelle Obama. The red organza floor-length frock that she wore to the state dinner for visiting Chinese Pres. Hu Jintao featured a black petal print from the 2011 McQueen resort collection and proved a critical hit with Chinese guests, as its hue symbolized happiness and prosperity in China. Nevertheless, a debate was sparked after fashion designer Oscar de la Renta spoke out against the propriety of the first lady wearing "European clothes" at a fête that promoted "American-Chinese" trade relations.

Casting a shadow over the July royal nuptials in Monaco—and the sumptuous Armani Privé bridal gown that was known to be worn by the bride, Charlene Wittstock (*see* BIOGRAPHIES)—were persistent rumours that the former South African Olympic swimmer had repeatedly attempted to escape from the principality upon discovering that her fiancé, Prince Albert II, had fathered another illegitimate child. Nevertheless, Wittstock walked down the aisle on July 1 in one of two identical gowns upon which three seamstresses had spent 2,500 hours of manual labour. The second gown was made in the event of an unforeseen mishap with the first. Each was adorned with 40,000 Swarovski crystals, 20,000 mother-of-pearl teardrops, and a 4.9-m (16-ft) train.

Roger L. Wollenberg—UPI/Landov

First lady Michelle Obama sported a striking red gown by British fashion designer Sarah Burton at a White House state dinner welcoming Chinese Pres. Hu Jintao in January.

Though the allegedly $10 million nuptials of reality-television star Kim Kardashian and NBA basketball star Kris Humphries was hyped as the "wedding of the year," only 72 days later the bride filed for divorce. Her unexpected move prompted retail analysts to predict dire future sales for the trio of replica dresses that Vera Wang had created for David's Bridal, the largest American bridal retailer. The "wedding wardrobe" consisted of three custom-made ivory designs, including a strapless full-skirted ceremonial ballgown, a mermaid-style dress (in which Kardashian posed for photographs), and a bias-cut satin party dress.

Ralph Lauren designed the gown worn by his daughter, Dylan (the founder of confectionery chain Dylan's Candy Bar), at her wedding on June 11 to Paul Arrouet, a hedge-fund founder. The handmade duchesse-satin, silk-tulle, and georgette-embroidered dress featured a tiered train. Lauren conceived an ivory Victorian-inspired gown for future daughter-in-law Lauren Bush (the granddaughter of former U.S. president George H.W. Bush), who on September 4 married David Lauren (Ralph's son and executive vice president of Ralph Lauren). The bride sported cowboy boots with her gown at a Western-themed ceremony that was staged at the Lauren family's 6,880-ha (17,000-ac) Double RL Ranch in Ridgway, Colo.

A comprehensive fashion retrospective, "Alexander McQueen: Savage Beauty," was staged over the summer at the Metropolitan Museum of Art's Costume Institute in New York City and featured 100 pieces that McQueen produced before and during his 19-year career. The popular show attracted 650,000 visitors and was extended one week past its original July 31 closure.

Another popular museum show, "Hussein Chalayan, Récits de Mode," was held at Les Arts Décoratifs in Paris and showcased the "distinctive" creative process of Chalayan, the London-based Cypriot designer whose conceptual work explored an array of multimedia, including furniture design, sculpture, and video. "The Fashion World of Jean Paul Gaultier: From the Sidewalk to the Catwalk" charted the erotically charged and humble origins of designs produced by the gifted Paris haute couturier. The exhibit had originated at the Montreal Museum of Fine Arts and later traveled to Dallas and San Francisco. Marking its 90th anniversary, Gucci opened a lavish museum in a 14th-century Florentine palazzo as a permanent space to display its historic designs alongside the contemporary art collection of François Pinault, proprietor of PPR, the luxury brand's parent company. On December 5 Valentino Garavani launched an eponymous "virtual museum." Once downloaded onto a computer, the free interactive program presented 300 iconic designs produced by the Italian master over his 48-year career.

John Galliano was fired in March as designer in chief of Christian Dior following the posting on *The Sun* tabloid's Web site of an embarrassing 45-second cell-phone video that captured a severely inebriated Galliano at a Paris bar taunting two patrons with anti-Semitic slurs. After his dismissal Galliano retreated to a rehabilitation treatment centre. In June he appeared "remorseful" in a one-day trial in a Paris court but was found guilty of a hate crime and given a suspended fine of €6,000 (about $8,100). Nonetheless, despite much speculation by the media and the fashion industry, model Kate Moss wore a Galliano cream wedding gown to her July 1 marriage to British guitarist Jamie Hince, the frontman for the Kills rock band. Her dress was threaded with sequins and gold filigree and featured a 1930s-inspired bias-cut style, a Galliano signature.

Among the rumoured replacements for Galliano at Dior were Haider Ackermann, Burton, Marc Jacobs, Raf Simons, Riccardo Tisci, Alexander Wang, and Jason Wu. Bill Gaytten—Galliano's longtime associate, with whom he had worked since 1994—fulfilled his former roles in the interim.

Bebeto Matthews/AP

"Alexander McQueen: Savage Beauty," a record-breaking retrospective show at the Metropolitan Museum of Art in New York City featured the endlessly creative clothing designs of an original mind.

Another notable departure was that of designer Christophe Decarnin, who had recently revitalized Balmain but suffered a stress-induced nervous breakdown around the same time as Galliano's leave-taking and was replaced in April by Olivier Rousteing. A month later, following the dismissal of Hannah MacGibbon, Claire Waight Keller, the former creative director of Pringle of Scotland, assumed the designer post at Chloé.

Stella McCartney proved to be one of the year's most high-profile design forces. Aside from producing a white trouser suit as Moss's postceremony "going-away" look and also the "demure" knee-length ivory gown that bride Nancy Shevell wore at the October 9 civil-service ceremony to Sir Paul McCartney (Stella's father), her work proved trendsetting. A perky citrus print incorporating lemons and grapefruit motifs in McCartney's spring-summer 2011 collection spearheaded a tropical pattern summer trend. Prada also evoked the exotic theme with a Josephine Baker-inspired banana print, while a lemon pattern was featured upon white chiffon Moschino Cheap & Chic separates.

Figure-enhancing dresses from McCartney's "womanly" fall-winter collection altered a pattern of red-carpet dressing as a number of actresses flaunted the same silhouettes. After Kate Winslet resplendently appeared at a trio of film premieres in McCartney ensembles, notably Lucia—a black knee-length cocktail dress featuring polka-dots embroidered upon "stretchy, transparent *point d'espirit*"—numerous actresses followed her lead. The September issue of *Harper's Bazaar* featured Jane Fonda modeling Lucia, and Susan Sarandon was spotted wearing the dress in October to a New York fund-raising gala.

McCartney's two-toned sleeveless Octavia sheath became known as the "miracle dress" because its cotton stretch fabric and wide black side panels delivered a slimming hourglass silhouette, suggesting that its wearer was "two sizes smaller." Retail chains Topshop and ASOS swiftly produced affordable variations of the frock.

Ethical accessories entrepreneur Blake Mycoskie's profile was also heightened owing to the prevalence on city streets of TOMS Shoes—an affordable unisex cloth shoe that he based on the "alpargata" Argentine espadrille. For each pair of his casual footwear sold, Mycoskie donated another to an individual in need. Mary Kate and Ashley Olsen—who topped *Vogue*'s Best Dressed list and graced the cover of its special edition annual magazine revealing their selection—introduced a collaboration with Mycoskie and the Row, their luxury brand, entitled "TOMS + The Row." It featured three models of Mycoskie's alpargata in plaid, wool-cashmere, and herringbone. According to *Women's Wear Daily*, the venture (launched in February) had the aim of trying to "heighten the exposure of [Mycoskie's] charitable mission," although as the year progressed, TOM'S Shoes became known as one of the world's fastest-growing shoe companies.

A craze for snakeskin developed in the autumn. Prada deftly crafted luxuriant accessories made from it, including knee-high high-heel boots, which graphically juxtaposed jewel-tone suede or leather with natural python. The Spanish retail chain Zara produced similar inexpensive models. Shoe designer Christian Louboutin lost his court battle with Yves Saint Laurent over a trade infringement; Louboutin had sued the venerable label upon noticing that it had produced shoes featuring his trademark "red outsole."

Loulou de la Falaise, the former muse of Saint Laurent and designer of costume jewelry for the brand, died on November 5. François Lesage—who ran his family's eponymous couture embroidery atelier, which since the 1920s had produced textiles for the finest Paris haute couture houses—left the fashion scene on December 1.

(BRONWYN COSGRAVE)

Designer Stella McCartney's bold fabric pattern of citrus fruits in her ready-to-wear spring-summer line started a trend for the tropical.

Valerio Mezzanotti—The New York Times/Redux

Health and Disease

A rise in HIV/AIDS treatment was attributed to increased availability of **ANTIRETROVIRAL DRUGS** in the world's poorest countries, while China reported **POLIO** for the first time since 1999, and **MEASLES** claimed the lives of child refugees in Somalia. Researchers found that a large percentage of young people are affected by **ATHEROSCLEROSIS**.

HIV and AIDS. In a summary published in 2011, the World Health Organization reported that by the end of 2010, an estimated 6.6 million people with HIV/AIDS were receiving antiretroviral therapy in low- and middle-income countries, an increase of 1.4 million over the previous year. WHO Director-General Margaret Chan called the new estimates "an important milestone in the public health response to HIV that began 30 years ago." The rise in the number of people receiving treatment was attributed to increased availability of antiretroviral drugs in some of the world's poorest countries. The number was predicted to increase even further following an agreement among pharmaceutical companies to sell the drugs at lower prices. Eight pharmaceutical companies in India agreed to reduce prices for first-line drugs as well as second-line regimens. The treatments were made available for $200 in poor countries, which represented a dramatic decrease relative to wealthy countries, where combinations of the drugs had sold for more than $12,000 per year. The Clinton Health Access Initiative, established in 2002 as the Clinton HIV/AIDS Initiative by former U.S president Bill Clinton, negotiated the lower prices and was supported in this effort by the Bill and Melinda Gates Foundation and by British foreign aid.

While more infected people were receiving treatment, there was progress on the prevention front. Two U.S.-based studies showed evidence that taking daily drugs containing AIDS medications could prevent people from becoming infected with the virus. Researchers from the University of Washington conducted a study in Uganda and Kenya in which they gave uninfected participants who had an infected sexual partner the drug Truvada, a mix of the agents tenofovir and emtricitabine. Those who took the pill daily had a 73% lower chance of becoming infected compared with those who did not take the pill. Other participants took a Viread pill containing just tenofovir and had a 62% lower chance of becoming infected with the virus. In Botswana researchers with the U.S. Centers for Disease Control and Prevention conducted an additional study of Truvada in 1,200 sexually active young adults. The risk of infection was reduced by 63% in participants who had taken the drug.

Though treatment for AIDS continued to expand internationally, several reports released in August 2011 revealed increasing rates of HIV infection among specific groups. In the United States, for example, researchers found that from 2006 to 2009 HIV infections increased by 48% among black gay and bisexual men, even though the rate of infection across all groups of Americans had remained stable overall. In addition, while the overall infection rate in the United States held steady at 0.47%, some 2% of low-income heterosexuals in that country were found to have been infected with HIV. In the journal *PLoS Medicine*, an international team of researchers reported increased rates of HIV infection among men who have sex with men (MSM) in the Middle East and North Africa. The report suggested that the increase might have been attributable to fear and shame among MSM—particularly those who are Muslim—about their homosexuality and their unwillingness to be tested. Lack of education on risk and treatment of the disease, low rates of condom use, the possibility of intravenous drug use, and the tendency toward contact with male sex workers were other factors cited in the rise of HIV infections in the study population.

Polio. In August China experienced its first outbreak of polio since 1999, prompting a massive immunization effort. At least one person died, and 17 people were paralyzed by the disease, which surfaced in the Hotan prefecture in Xinjiang province. Chinese health officials led a campaign to vaccinate more than nine million people in the region, which had poor access to health care services. The strain of polio, known as PV1, was believed to have originated in Pakistan. By the end of November, Pakistan had reported 161 polio cases, an increase over the total number of cases recorded in 2010. Pakistan's prime minister, Yousaf Raza Gilani, who in 2011 chaired the country's first meeting of the National Task Force

In preparation for a nationwide polio-immunization campaign in Nigeria, a health worker in Lagos transports vaccination kits, February 21.

Akintunde Akinleye—Reuters/Landov

on Polio Eradication, launched a national emergency action plan to address immunization efforts, which had been hampered in high-risk areas, and to address the disease's spread within and from the country.

Although polio outbreaks were documented in some areas of Africa, WHO officials reported progress in their efforts to eradicate the disease. From 2010 to May 2011, more than 214 million African children under age five were immunized against polio as a result of campaigns in Angola, Chad, the Democratic Republic of the Congo, and Nigeria. At the same time, WHO reported that 11 West African countries had become reinfected since mid-2009, leaving many children dead and hundreds paralyzed. Nigeria remained the only endemic country in Africa. The number of cases in Nigeria had been reduced by 95% as a result of greater immunization efforts; in late 2011, however, the country experienced a more than fourfold increase in polio cases relative to the year before.

More than 550 new cases of polio were reported worldwide in 2011; more than 25% of those occurred in Pakistan. By comparison, there were 1,352 new cases reported in 2010. Polio remained endemic in Afghanistan, India, Nigeria, and Pakistan.

Bird Flu. In December in Hong Kong, 17,000 chickens were slaughtered after the bird flu virus H5N1 was detected at a poultry market. The incident resulted in the temporary closure of the market, in increased bird flu surveillance, and in the shutdown of poultry import and export for 21 days. At the end of the month, bird flu claimed the life of a man from Shenzhen, China. The two reports coincided with an unprecedented step taken by the U.S. government, which asked scientific journals not to publish papers by researchers who had engineered a bird flu virus in ferrets that could conceivably jump from ferrets to humans.

Measles. Widespread drought and famine were responsible for an outbreak of measles among Somali refugees who fled their homes and sought relief in the country's capital, Mogadishu, as well as in Ethiopia and Kenya. In Ethiopia's Kobe refugee camp alone, an estimated 10 children under age five died daily from a combination of measles and malnutrition. Although measles, which is caused by a highly contagious virus, is not often fatal, severe malnutrition had left the refugees especially vulnerable to its effects. As a result, the United Nations High Commissioner for Refugees and Ethiopia's government initiated a massive measles vaccination campaign in August. In the town of Marere and surrounding areas where refugees had sought shelter, physicians associated with Doctors Without Borders (Médecins Sans Frontières) worked to control cholera and measles. Although the famine had eased in some areas by mid-November, measles remained a significant threat to the health of children suffering from the lingering effects of malnutrition.

Eduardo Verdugo/AP

On June 30 a man carries a child suffering from symptoms of cholera to a treatment centre in Mirebalais, Haiti. A report published midyear suggested that the strain of cholera responsible for an outbreak in Haiti in late 2010 may have been transmitted by UN peacekeepers from Nepal.

Cholera. Haiti continued to experience a widespread cholera epidemic nearly two years after being hit by a deadly earthquake. Scientists in the United States predicted in April in the journal *Lancet* that some 779,000 cases and more than 11,000 deaths from cholera would occur by the end of November. However, in a health bulletin published in early November by the Pan American Health Organization, which had been closely monitoring the cholera situation in Haiti, the cumulative number of cases and deaths recorded in the outbreak totaled 473,649 and 6,631, respectively. WHO officials estimated that roughly 25,000 more cases would arise by the end of the year. Although the estimates from the *Lancet* study turned out to be too high, the researchers did point out that the epidemic was in fact larger than had been predicted. In the first year following the earthquake, which occurred on Jan. 12, 2010, more than 3,651 people died from cholera, out of more than 171,300 cases of the disease, which had spread through contaminated food and water.

Tuberculosis. In 2011 the number of new cases of tuberculosis diagnosed worldwide was found to have been in steady decline over a multiyear period. According to the WHO Global Tuberculosis Control Report released in October, the number of people who had become ill with the disease dropped to 8.8 million in 2010, having fallen from 9 million in 2005. The report also indicated that the number of people dying from the disease fell to its lowest level in a decade and had dropped 40% between 1990 and 2010. With the exception of Africa, all regions were expected to see a 50% decline in tuberculosis death rates by 2015. While treatment and cure rates had improved, UN Secretary-General Ban Ki-Moon warned that many more millions of people would still develop the disease and that the world's poorest and most vulnerable populations still required vigorous support for prevention and treatment. In addition, there remained a growing threat of multidrug-resistant tuberculosis.

Malaria. What could emerge as the world's first effective vaccine against malaria showed promising results in a major clinical trial conducted in African children. The study, published online in October in *The New England Journal of Medicine*, reported that the risk of infection fell by half among children aged 5–17 months who received the shot. The experimental vaccine, RTS,S (Mosquirix), was developed by GlaxoSmithKline, which, along with the nonprofit PATH (Program for Appropriate Technology in Health) Malaria Vaccine Initiative, also funded the study. In the trial 6,000 children received three doses of the vaccine. Follow-up 12 months after vaccination revealed that RTS,S reduced the children's risk of clinical and severe malaria by 56% and 47%, respectively. Health experts believed that the vaccine represented a significant achievement but warned that it would not likely eradicate malaria any time soon.

Cancer. The American Cancer Society's *Global Cancer Facts and Figures 2nd Edition* (2011) indicated that death rates from many types of cancers had dropped significantly in the United States, the United Kingdom, and other economically developed countries. At the same time, less-developed countries, such as India and many countries in Africa, experienced an increase in the number of cancer cases and deaths. The rise in cancer rates in those countries was likely due to a shift in behaviours, with people leading more sedentary lifestyles, smoking more often, and acquiring poor dietary habits. The report suggested that such behavioral and lifestyle changes may accompany better economic prosperity and noted that people making unhealthy lifestyle choices were particularly vulnerable to lung, breast, and colorectal cancers. Citing statistics from 2008, the latest global figures available, the publication reported that there were 7.1 million new cancer cases and 4.8 million deaths in less-developed countries. Worldwide, there were 12.7 million new cancer cases and 7.6 million deaths. Those numbers were expected to nearly double by 2030 owing to an increasing and aging world population. More encouraging news came from the United States, where death rates from all types of cancer fell by 22% for men and 14% for women. A report released in June by the American Association for Cancer Research indicated that 900,000 deaths from cancer had been avoided in the United States between 1990 and 2007, resulting in a decline in cancer death rate. Some of the biggest successes came in the treatment of breast, cervical, and colorectal cancers, which all had significant decreases in death rates.

Cardiovascular Disease. People in the Mediterranean, thought to be healthier than people in other regions of the world because of their diet and lifestyle, were found to have a high risk for cardiovascular disease, similar to that of people living in the United States and the United Kingdom. The study, published in the January issue of the *International Journal of Clinical Practice*, challenged the long-held belief that people living in the Mediterranean region were less susceptible to heart disease. The scientists analyzed patients at a health centre in Andalusia, a region with one of the highest rates of cardiovascular disease in Spain. The researchers found that more than 60% of patients were overweight or obese and that 77% did not get enough exercise. Other risk factors were also at play. For example, it was found that 28% smoked, 33% had high blood pressure, 7% had diabetes, and 65% had high cholesterol. In addition, the cost of foods such as olive oil, vegetables, and fruits, which are traditionally associated with the Mediterranean diet, may be too high for some segments of the population, leaving those people prone to a poor diet and susceptible to cardiovascular disease.

Canadian researchers found that atherosclerosis, believed to affect mostly those of advanced age, strikes a significant number of younger people as well. According to one researcher, the number of young adults who appear healthy but have atherosclerosis was "staggering." The study, by Canada's Heart and Stroke Foundation, found evidence of fat buildup in the arteries of a large percentage of 168 men and women between the ages of 18 and 35. The study subjects did not have traditional risk factors for atherosclerosis.

Victims of heart attacks recover in the emergency department of a hospital in Beijing, September 7. Heart disease was reportedly on the rise in China, with experts citing the rapid urbanization of the country as a factor.

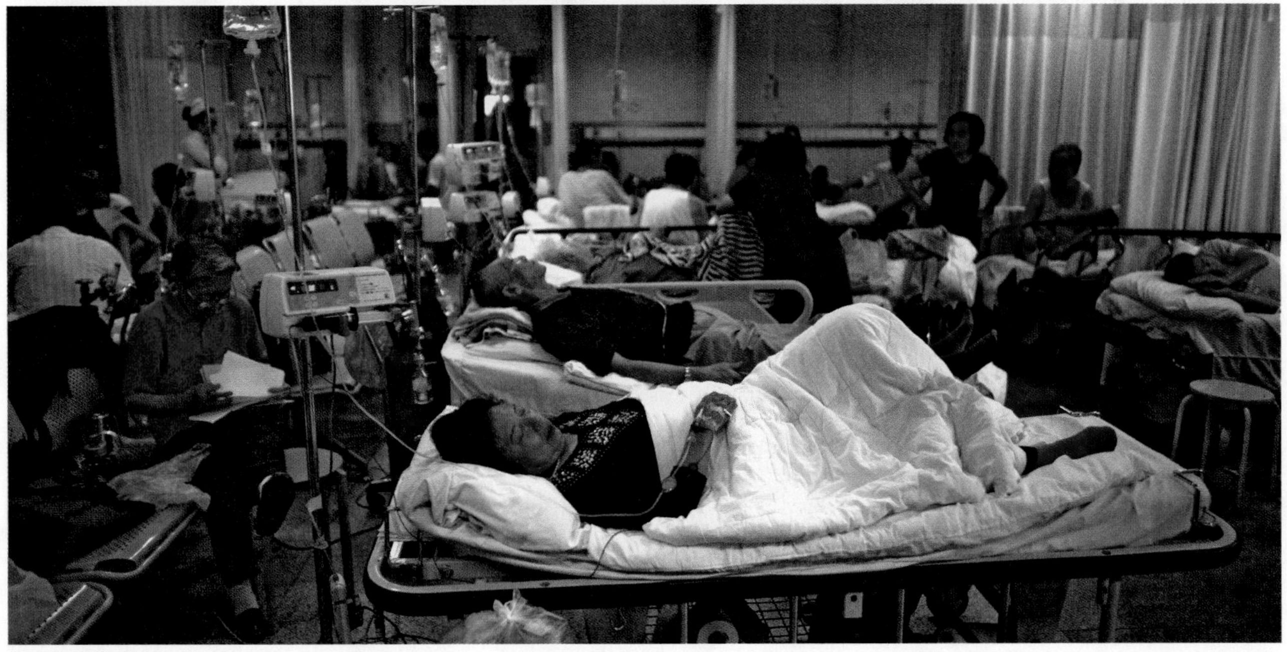

Alexander F. Yuan/AP

The Bedbug Resurgence

The United States experienced a resurgence in bedbug (*Cimex lectularius*) infestations in 2011 as the tiny pests took up residence in hotels, apartments, office buildings, and homes. The National Pest Management Association (NPMA), an industry trade group, reported that one in five Americans had had a bedbug infestation at home or knew someone who had encountered the pests. The problem became so rampant that the U.S. government held national summits, enlisting the aid of top entomologists and health officials. Bedbug fever also inspired entrepreneurs to seize on the demand for products and services to detect and control bedbugs. Pest-sniffing dogs and wasps were among the novel ideas employed in the fight to root out the tiny bugs.

The latest infestation was likely caused by increased pesticide resistance among bedbugs and by a rise in domestic and international travel that allowed the bugs to hitch rides in luggage and on clothing. Other possible causes included inbreeding by bedbugs, believed to facilitate their spread, and inadequate public pest-control programs. The bedbugs, reddish brown and about one to seven millimetres (1 mm = 0.04 in) in length, were difficult to see, and their flat bodies allowed them to slip into cracks and crevasses. They often lived in or near places where people slept and found their way into bedding and furniture. They fed on human and animal blood, and, although generally not harmful or known to transmit disease, their bites were capable of causing skin irritation and mild allergic reactions.

While bedbug sightings were reported across the country, New York City was hit particularly hard. From 2008 to 2010, complaints there increased by nearly 70%, and, according to researchers at the University of Massachusetts, because residents there had been battling the pests for years, bedbugs in the city were 250 times more resistant to the standard pesticide than bedbugs in Florida were. The bugs may have been generating higher levels of enzymes that cleansed them of poisons, according to entomologists at the Ohio State University.

The NPMA indicated that the best way to prevent an infestation was to closely inspect the places the bugs tend to inhabit. The association recommended vacuuming suitcases after vacations, avoiding taking used furniture or bedding items into a home without having thoroughly inspected them, and regularly inspecting areas where pets slept. Government officials urged people with infestations to contact certified pest-control companies, and the U.S. Centers for Disease Control and Prevention (CDC) encouraged the use of nonchemical pesticides. Because of the bugs' increasing resistance to pesticides, however, many people overused or misused chemical insecticides, which failed to eliminate the bugs but did cause illness. A CDC report released in September documented 111 cases in which people had fallen ill with symptoms of pesticide poisoning. In nearly 40% of the cases, the people had applied the pesticides themselves.

(KEVIN DAVIS)

(Below) Matt Rourke/AP; (top right) Blaine Mathison/CDC

*(Above) As part of a scent-detection certification test held during the National Canine Conference, a dog, led by a pest-control professional, sniffs for bedbugs at a Philadelphia hotel, June 2. (Top right) Dorsal view of an adult bedbug (*Cimex lectularius*).*

They did, however, have signs of enlarged waist circumference and visceral fat covering internal organs in the chest and the abdomen. The study found that waist circumference, which could be measured easily during a routine physical examination, was predictive of unhealthy levels of visceral fat and early-onset atherosclerosis.

An American Heart Association report released in January in the journal *Circulation* warned that an increasing aging population was driving up the cost of treating heart disease and stroke in the United States. The cost was expected to triple—reaching $818 billion—by 2030. The increase threatened to limit the country's ability to care for those affected unless additional steps were taken to prevent cardiovascular disease. About 36.9% of the U.S. population had some form of cardiovascular disease in 2011; this number was expected to rise to 40.5%, or 116 million people, by 2030. Nancy Brown, CEO of the association, said that "unhealthy behaviors and unhealthy environments have contributed to a tidal wave of risk factors among many Americans."

Pharmaceuticals. U.S. health officials and drug manufacturers took steps to curb the use of acetaminophen in medications for adults and children, citing concerns that the popular pain reliever could cause liver damage if taken in excess. Acetaminophen overdose, the leading cause of acute liver failure in the United States, sent more than 50,000 Americans to the emergency room each year. According to the U.S. Center for Drug Evaluation and Research, nearly half of all cases in the U.S. occurred when people used products that combined acetaminophen with other drugs. Often, patients were unaware that the products contained acetaminophen. To address the problem, the Food and Drug Administration (FDA) announced that it would lower the amount of acetaminophen allowed in Vicodin and Percocet as well as other prescription pain relievers that combined acetaminophen with other substances. The drugs previously could contain up to 750 mg of acetaminophen, but the new regulations limited the dose to 325 mg. The new regulations, however, did not apply to over-the-counter products, which could contain up to 500 mg of acetaminophen. Those products included labels warning of possible liver damage. In the children's medication market, manufacturers said that they would discontinue infant-drops versions of cold and fever medications that contained acetaminophen. Such medications, which had been sold in concentrated forms, were to be packaged in one formula that could be used for all children under age 12. Children's products were sold in 160 mg/5 mL (millilitre) concentrations, but infant formulas were sold in 80 mg/0.8 mL and 80 mg/1 mL. This discrepancy often made it confusing for parents to determine how much their infant needed and increased the risk for accidental overdose, which was exacerbated by poorly marked dropper and measuring devices.

The widely used diabetes drug Avandia fell under heavy restriction in the U.S. in 2011. The FDA limited the sale of Avandia owing to mounting evidence that it increased the risk of heart attack or stroke. The drug remained available only to a restricted number of patients who already had been taking it safely or new patients who were unable to control their diabetes with other medications and were informed about the risks. Such patients were required to enroll in a program to qualify and were allowed to receive the drug only by mail order from certified pharmacies. In 2010 the European Medicines Agency suspended all marketing of the drug.

Vaccines. In February the U.S. Supreme Court ruled that drug manufacturers were protected from lawsuits by families claiming injuries from childhood vaccinations. Instead, families were required to seek compensation through the country's vaccine court, which had been established in 1988 to handle such claims. The Supreme Court voted six to two against a couple from Pennsylvania who had sought damages on behalf of their daughter, who suffered from developmental disabilities. The couple filed suit against the drug company Wyeth, later acquired by Pfizer, claiming that the diphtheria, tetanus, and pertussis vaccine that their daughter had received at six months caused her developmental problems. In the majority opinion, Justice Antonin Scalia noted that the Vaccine Injury Compensation Program was created to help families receive compensation while preventing drug companies from leaving the vaccine market. The court awards compensation only if plaintiffs can prove the victim suffers from complications and injuries that have been officially recognized as caused by vaccination. The court had awarded more than $1.9 billion to an estimated 2,500 people since its creation.

Deaths from chickenpox had been nearly eliminated in the U.S. as a result of the use of the varicella vaccine, which was introduced in 1995 and was first given in one dose and later (2006) in two doses. A study by the National Center for Immunization and Respiratory Diseases found that the vaccine was responsible for having reduced chickenpox deaths by 88% overall and by 97% in people aged 20 and under. The decrease in deaths, however, mostly occurred when one dose was recommended. While chickenpox-related deaths were rare, researchers had believed that the two-dose vaccine could eliminate them altogether.

Alzheimer Disease. New guidelines in diagnosing Alzheimer disease issued in April by the Alzheimer's Association and the U.S. National Institute on Aging were likely to more than double the number of Americans considered to be in the early stages of the disease. The measure represented the first time that the guidelines had been changed in 27 years. Under the new approach, Alzheimer disease was recognized as a continuum of stages, from preclinical stages to mild cognitive impairment (MCI) to Alzheimer dementia. The guidelines recognized MCI with mild symptoms, which progresses to Alzheimer disease in some cases but previously had been disregarded as a diagnostic measure owing to controversy surrounding its value as such. Its inclusion, however, suggested that the number of people diagnosed with Alzheimer disease would increase. The guidelines also incorporated biomarkers, such as levels of certain proteins in the blood or spinal fluid, to diagnose the disease and monitor its progress. The new guidelines were not expected to cause changes in treatment; rather, they would be used to help investigate the disease, for which there was no cure. For those diagnosed with inherited Alzheimer disease, researchers found that some forms might be detectable as early as age 20. Early detection could lead to treatment that prevents brain damage.

In an international study of inherited forms of the disease, researchers for the Dominantly Inherited Alzheimer Network (DIAN) found that children whose parents developed dementia were likely to develop the condition at the same age if the child inherited the genetic mutation. The researchers were able to detect changes in brain chemistry in such people up to 20 years before the symptoms began to appear, allowing for preventive treatment.

In a study published in the *Journal of the American Medical Association*, scientists described the use of a brain-scanning technology known as PET (positron emission tomography) for the detection of beta-amyloid, a plaque that appears in the brains of those with Alzheimer disease. Only autopsies have allowed researchers to confirm the disease, and although the study's results were promising, they were preliminary; autopsy thus remained the only reliable method.

Other Developments. A new and virulent strain of *E. coli* that originated in Germany caused more than 4,300 people to become sick and killed 50 others. The bacterium was believed to have been harboured in contaminated vegetables, namely sprouts. The new strain, which scientists had never before seen, produced a harmful substance known as Shiga toxin, which caused hemolytic uremic syndrome, a condition in which the bacterial toxin destroyed red blood cells. The dead cells interfered with the normal function of the kidneys and led to kidney failure in some instances. (*See* Special Report on page 196.) (KEVIN DAVIS)

Life Sciences

Scientists sequenced the **POTATO GENOME**, discovered a new group of **FUNGI**, found what could be the most-primitive **BASAL DINOSAUR**, took away the title of **"WORLD'S OLDEST BIRD"** from *Archaeopteryx*, and uncovered evidence that **CLIMATE CHANGE** was already altering the geographic ranges of many groups of animals.

ZOOLOGY

In January 2011 a study examining 8 species of bumblebees (*Bombus*) provided convincing evidence that in recent years at least 4 of the approximately 50 species that occur in North America had undergone marked population declines. The study, which was conducted by Sydney A. Cameron of the University of Illinois at Champaign-Urbana and colleagues, noted that the four species declined by as much as 96% in relative abundance (total population in a given area) compared with four bumblebee species with stable populations that occupied overlapping areas. More than 16,000 specimens of the eight study species were sampled in the field between 2007 and 2009, and their current geographic ranges were compared with those of more than 73,000 specimens of earlier collections stored in museums. The geographic ranges of the four declining species shrank by 23–87% from those based on historical records.

The investigators examined individual bumblebees to determine infection levels of *Nosema bombi*, a fungal pathogen that had been shown to reduce the survival of worker bees in infected colonies and increase the susceptibility of individual bees to other pathogens and diseases. They also examined the genetic diversity of bee populations by analyzing microsatellites (short, repetitive DNA sequences that are useful markers of genetic variation in populations). The four declining populations had significantly higher infection levels and lower genetic diversity than the four species with stable populations. The ecological importance of bumblebees as pollinators of a wide variety of native plants as well as agricultural crops such as tomatoes, alfalfa, and legumes could not be overstated. The investigators called for further studies to establish the cause of bumblebee declines in North America.

In February an international team of researchers led by Marina S. Ascunce and Chin-Cheng Yang of the USDA–Agricultural Research Service in Gainesville, Fla., provided empirical documentation of a phenomenon known as the "invasive bridgehead effect," in which a recent invasive species served as a source of colonists to remote locations. The red imported fire ant (*Solenopsis invicta*), a species native to South America, was introduced between the late 1930s and early 1940s into the southeastern United States, where it quickly became a naturalized pest that delivered painful stings to people and animals that disturbed their mounds. Ascunce and colleagues used genetic markers to assess more than 2,000 colonies of red imported fire ants from 75 sites—including ones in China, Hong Kong, New Zealand, Australia, and the Caribbean—to determine the origin of the introductions into those regions. The findings supported the conclusion that red imported fire ants that were initially introduced into the United States were indeed from Argentina, but most of the current worldwide distribution of the species originated with southeastern U.S. populations. After examining the ant's genetic variation, the researchers also determined that the source of the ants introduced into one area in Taiwan was California, for which the southeastern U.S. was the origin. The spread of the species worldwide highlighted one of the negative ecological effects of unchecked global trade and underscored the need for better invasive-species-detection techniques in the world's transportation systems.

Rapid climate warming in portions of the Antarctic have led to significant increases in average winter temperatures and noticeable declines in the amount of sea-ice coverage in some regions. In April American scientist Wayne Z. Trivelpiece of the National Oceanic and Atmospheric Administration and colleagues published an analysis of 30 years of population data on Adélie penguins (*Pygoscelis adeliae*) and chinstrap penguins (*P. antarctica*) of the West Antarctic Peninsula and the Scotia Sea. The study was designed to test a widely held hypothesis that population sizes of "ice-loving" top predators declined with decreasing ice coverage, whereas "ice-avoiding" species increased in population size as ice coverage diminished. (Adélie penguins are an ice-loving species, whereas chinstrap penguins are an ice-avoiding species.) The findings, however, did not offer support for the diminishing-ice hypothesis. Instead, the investigators concluded that the fluctuations in the population sizes of both species were driven by changes in the abundance of Antarctic krill (*Euphausia superba*), a small crustacean that served as the primary prey of both species and of many other vertebrates in the region.

Increases in the number of Adélie and chinstrap penguins in the Antarctic were reported after predators (such as fur seals) and competitors (such as baleen whales and certain krill-eating fish) had gone nearly extinct in the region by the 1950s from harvesting pressure caused by the sealing and commercial-fishing industries. With few fish and marine mammals to prey on them, krill populations rose during the 1960s and 1970s. Adélie and chinstrap penguins took advantage of this nearly exclusive food source, and their populations subsequently increased. Since the 1970s, however, krill density, which correlates with the amount of sea-ice coverage, had declined by up to 80%. Previous studies had shown that the underside of Antarctic pack ice served as a substrate for phytoplankton, which was an important source of food for krill during the coldest months of the year. In recent years sea-ice loss had reduced the size of this substrate, and fewer phytoplankton had thus been available for the krill. Although the populations of all krill-eating predators in the Antarctic had also declined, the researchers maintained that the loss of sea ice became a special concern for chinstrap penguin populations, which had once been wrongly believed to increase with decreasing ice coverage.

Climate change was also implicated in the seasonal timing (phenology) of reproductive cycles in some groups of organisms. In July, Brian D. Todd of the University of California, Davis, and colleagues released the results of an analysis of three decades of field data that documented the migration patterns of 10 species of amphibians at a natural wetland in South Carolina. In six of the species, shifts in reproductive timing were not observed. The findings, however, provided the first evidence that in recent years two fall-breeding species of amphibians (the dwarf salamander, *Eurycea quadridigitata*, and the marbled salamander, *Ambystoma opacum*) had been arriving at their breeding grounds significantly later (76.4 days and 15.3 days, respectively) than in previous years. In contrast, during the same period, two of the winter-breeding amphibian species (the tiger salamander, *A. tigrinum*, and the ornate chorus frog, *Pseudacris ornata*) had been arriving for breeding at the wetland significantly earlier (56.4 days and 59.5 days, respectively). The shifts in breeding schedules coincided with an increase in nighttime air temperatures of more than 1.2 °C (about 2 °F) from 1979 to 2008 for the September-to-March prereproductive and reproductive periods. The rates of phenological change for the four species during the 30-year interval were some of the greatest yet confirmed for amphibians and other groups of animals. The investigators also pointed out that their findings demonstrated that breeding-site arrival times for a variety of amphibian species were likely to be correlated with climatic factors because of how sensitive amphibians were to environmental conditions.

In August a team of researchers led by Chris Thomas of the University of York, Eng., published the results of a meta-analysis, a statistical examination of previous scientific studies, to examine the shifts in the geographic distribution of several groups of animal species caused by changes in climate. The meta-analysis considered various animal groups, including arthropods, mollusks, fish, amphibians, reptiles, birds, and mammals. In addition to reporting that many animals had indeed shifted their ranges, the research revealed evidence that the rates of change with respect to latitude and elevation were at least double those reported in earlier studies. The shift to higher elevations occurred at a rate of 11 m (about 36 ft) per decade, whereas geographic range shifts to higher latitudes occurred at a rate of almost 17 km (about 11 mi) per decade. The distances of both latitudinal and elevational range shifts of species observed in different studies reflected the average increase in temperature of an area. The investigators indicated that several processes were probably responsible for the high diversity of geographic range shifts among species and that this diversity made the identification of global patterns difficult. For example, different species in the analysis varied greatly in how long they took to respond to climate change, in part because each species differed physiologically in how sensitive it was to environmental variability. Also, the direct responses of some species to climate change may have been masked by latitudinal or elevational range adjustments that occurred in response to other ecological phenomena, such as changes in habitat, food and water resources, and interactions with other species. The scientists also noted that the variation between and within taxonomic groups was great when each species or group of species was examined independently. Therefore, the researchers maintained that determining and predicting the climate-change responses for individual species would require detailed studies of their unique physiology and ecology, as well as comprehensive surveys of the environments in which they lived.

(J. WHITFIELD GIBBONS)

*On average, the barred tiger salamander (*Ambystoma tigrinum*) arrived in its breeding grounds about two months earlier in 2011 than it did in 1981.*

BOTANY

In February 2011 one of the fastest plant movements in the world was described in detail by a team of scientists led by physicist Philippe Marmottant of the Laboratoire Interdisciplinaire de Physique in France. It was known that the carnivorous bladderwort (*Utricularia*) uses a submerged suction trap to capture tiny aquatic creatures, such as water fleas. The expulsion of water from the plant's bladder-shaped traps creates a partial vacuum that is sealed with a watertight trap door. When the plant's prey touches trigger hairs at the trap's entrance, the trap door opens and closes within a fraction of a second, sucking the animal inside. The study used ultra-high-speed video technology that was capable of recording 15,000 frames per second and revealed that the movement of the trap door lasts less than a millisecond, much faster than previously

Carmen Weisskopf

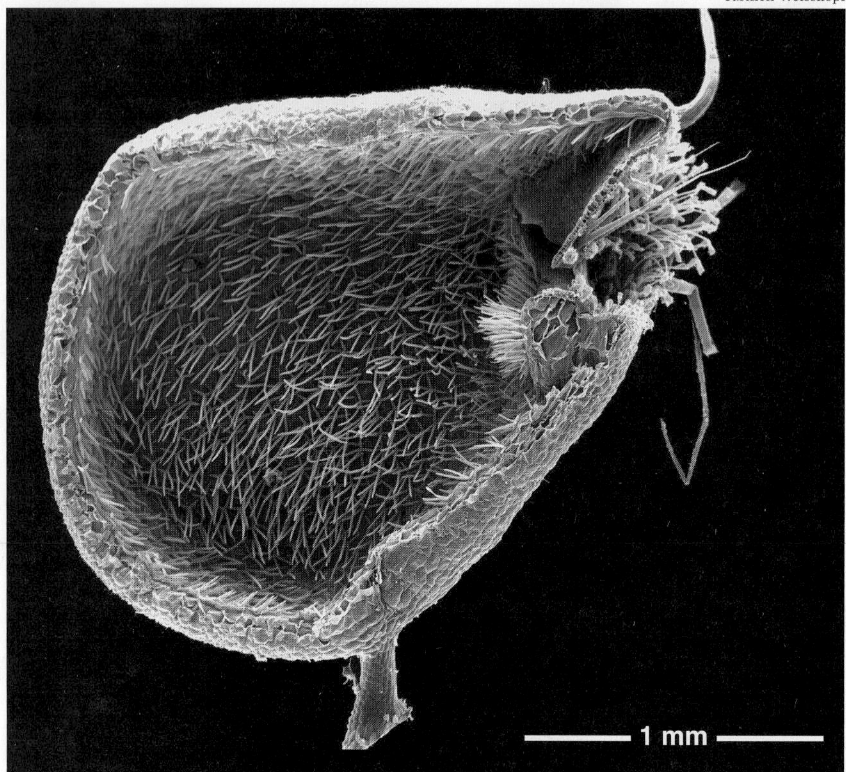

*The common bladderwort (*Utricularia vulgaris*) evolved a suction trap, which has been imaged by a scanning electron microscope, to capture prey. It was discovered that the trap door, displayed on the right side of the image, opens for less than one millisecond before the plant's prey is sucked in.*

thought. In contrast, the Venus's-flytrap (*Dionaea muscipula*) reacts to its prey in 100 milliseconds. The trap door of *Utricularia* plays a key part in the movement, because it functions as an elastic valve that buckles inward when it opens and unbuckles when it closes. The suction is so strong that it causes water to accelerate with a force of up to 600 *g* (600 times the force of gravity), which leaves little chance of escape for any prey.

In July the genetic code of the potato (*Solanum tuberosum*) was sequenced for the first time, revealing traits that could be exploited by plant breeders to improve the genetic stock of the crop. The potato is the world's fourth most important food crop, and it was estimated that by 2020 more than two billion people worldwide would depend on it for food, animal feed, or income from cash crops. The potato, however, had been susceptible to pests, diseases, and inbreeding depression (a loss of fitness in later generations that results from crossing between closely related individuals). The Potato Genome Sequencing Consortium, an international team of 29 research groups from 14 countries, sequenced more than 39,000 genes of the genome. The project was particularly difficult because of the complex genetics of the potato, with up to four copies of each chromosome and variations occurring between the corresponding four copies of each gene. Hence, the researchers used a potato variety with two copies of every gene. They selected one copy of each chromosome and duplicated it to produce a clone in which the genes in each pair were identical. The completed genetic sequence of the clone contained 408 genes that were involved in disease resistance and had the potential for use in fighting devastating diseases, such as the potato cyst nematode and potato blight, the fungal infection that ruined the Irish potato crop in 1845. Other sequenced genes were linked to the quality and yield of the potato tuber. Because of its complex genetics, the potato had been notoriously difficult to improve through artificial selection, with new varieties taking about 10–12 years to breed. The sequencing of the potato genome was expected to speed efforts to develop new varieties.

In August a paper by Stuart West of the University of Oxford and an international research team uncovered evidence that plants and fungi trade with each other in a biological "marketplace" that ensures that both partners receive a fair "deal." For many millions of years, plant roots and mycorrhizal fungi in the soil have been intertwined in a symbiotic partnership that benefits both parties: the fungi provide roots with phosphorus, and the plants supply the fungi with carbohydrates. This symbiosis, perhaps the most widespread mutualism in the world, is tremendously important for the nutrition of plants. With an elaborate network of different fungi entangled among several different plant roots, the system would seem to make it easy for one party to gain the maximum benefit without giving much in return. West and colleagues tracked changes in the amount of phosphorus produced by three different mycorrhizal fungi that colonized the roots of the barrel clover (*Medicago truncatula*).

Using radioactive carbon isotopes, the researchers traced the flow of carbohydrates from the roots to the fungi. They found that the more phosphorus a plant received, the more carbohydrates it would reward to the fungus. The fair-trading system also worked the other way, so that when plants supplied fewer carbohydrates, the fungi provided reduced amounts of phosphorus. The researchers pointed out that "cheating" partners were penalized and generous partners were rewarded. They also noted that both plants and fungi could be selective in their partnerships to ensure that both partners received the best rate of exchange, thereby preventing the "enslavement" of one partner by another.

Also in August researchers at Australia's Commonwealth Scientific and Industrial Research Organisation (CSIRO) in Canberra revealed that they had made significant progress toward understanding how viruses cause disease in plants. In most organisms, DNA serves as their genetic material and RNA as a carrier of genetic information. Some viruses, however, such as cucumber mosaic virus (CMV), had been shown to use RNA as their genetic material.

CMV attacks tobacco (*Nicotiana tabacum*) and many other plant species, causing a disease characterized by yellow blotches on leaves and poor growth and development in the host plant. CSIRO researchers Ming-Bo Wang, Andrew Eamens, and Neil Smith discovered that part of an extra piece of the virus's RNA (known as the "satellite") is an exact match for the host plant's gene *CHL1*, which controls the production of chlorophyll, the green pigment vital for photosynthesis. The virus satellite RNA locks onto the plant's *CHL1* gene and slices it apart. This action stops the production of chlorophyll and thus causes leaf yellowing. The researchers blocked the disease by creating an altered *CHL1* gene that no longer matched the viral satellite RNA. This altered gene protected the plant from the disease, and the leaves continued to produce chlorophyll, which allowed the plant to grow normally. That finding enabled the researchers to search for genes in other viruses that match known genetic sequences in plants.

(PAUL SIMONS)

MOLECULAR BIOLOGY AND GENETICS

Meet the Cryptomycota. In 2011 an international team of researchers led by British scientists Thomas Richards and Meredith Jones applied molecular tools to the exploration of biodiversity in soil, fresh water and marine water, and aquatic sediments from different locations worldwide. DNA sequences derived from samples of the different habitats revealed a fungal diversity so extreme as to require the establishment of an entirely new branch on the fungal "tree of life," a branch known as the cryptomycota (or "hidden fungi"; also known as Rozellida). The diversity represented by the cryptomycota was comparable to that of all other known fungi combined.

The discovery of cryptomycota raised important questions about how organisms that were so abundant in the environment managed to go unnoticed for so long. One explanation was that these single-celled life-forms were more fragile than already-identified microorganisms and therefore were unable to survive in laboratory culture. Indeed, unlike all other fungi, it appeared that cryptomycota did not produce a tough chitin-rich cell wall at any stage of their development.

To further confirm the existence of cryptomycota, the researchers used a technique known as fluorescence in situ hybridization (FISH), which allowed them to attach fluorescent tags specifically to cells harbouring the DNA sequences attributed to cryptomycota and then observe the cells under a fluorescence microscope. Consistent with the sequencing results, the FISH procedure revealed populations of tiny single-celled eukaryotes, each cell measuring about 3 to 5 micrometres (1 micrometre = 3.9×10^{-5} inch) in diameter and therefore similar in size to many types of bacteria. The team also confirmed that cryptomycota possess flagella. That finding was accomplished by using a technique that was known as immunofluorescence, in which the researchers labeled an antibody directed against the flagellar protein alpha-tubulin. During the evolution of higher fungi, the chytrid flagellum was lost (chytrids represent the ancestors of an ancient group of fungi), and hence the discovery of flagella on cryptomycota suggested that these organisms may be an evolutionary link between the fungi and other single-celled eukaryotes. While the idea that the cryptomycota had existed in abundance on Earth and yet escaped notice for so long was humbling, perhaps even more sobering was the realization that human knowledge of the diversity of life on the planet was far from complete.

Meredith Jones

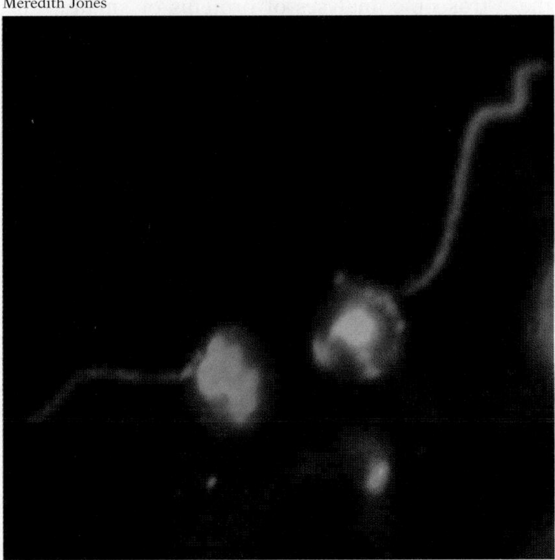

A fluorescence micrograph of two cryptomycota cells found in water samples collected from a pond by British scientists at the University of Exeter.

The discovery of the cryptomycota highlighted the significant role that the development of new scientific tools and careful observation fulfill in advancing scientists' understanding of life on Earth. Indeed, what scientists were able to observe depended on the tools they had at hand. For example, the realization that an organism new to science was present in soil, water, and sediment samples came only after the cryptomycota researchers combined the precision of DNA sequencing technology with the power of fluorescence microscopy. While such an approach was not new to molecular biology, it was aided significantly by refinements in the tools and how the tools were used. Furthermore, as new tools were developed and existing ones improved, scientists' knowledge about living organisms changed, a principle illustrated elegantly by the discovery of the cryptomycota.

The new group of "hidden fungi" also drew attention to the significance of contemporary molecular genetics technologies, which had enabled scientists to distinguish life-forms on the basis of subtle variations in their DNA sequence. For example, all living creatures contain in their genomes genes that encode ribosomal RNA, which is required for protein synthesis and therefore is essential for life. The precise nucleotide sequence of ribosomal RNA genes, however, varies from species to species. This variation is a reflection of the accumulation of subtle changes through the span of evolutionary time that has elapsed since species diverged from their common ancestors. The degree of similarity between any two ribosomal RNA gene sequences may therefore be used to define the degree of relationship between life-forms.

Biology in silico. In 2011 numerous papers reporting discoveries in the fields of genetics and molecular biology highlighted the rapid advance of bioinformatics, the science that brings together biological data and information storage, distribution, and analysis. Indeed, bioinformatics has come of age—it has become a fully integrated branch of science, supported by peer-reviewed journals, interdisciplinary academic departments, in addition to its own annual international conference.

The field of bioinformatics emerged in the 1980s from the growing realization that increasingly powerful computers and software could be applied to interpret increasingly diverse and complex sets of biological data. In the early 2000s its value became self-evident with its successful application in the Human

Genome Project. The key to speeding completion of the project, which began in 1990 and was completed in 2003, was the realization that large pieces of DNA could be sequenced more rapidly by breaking them into small fragments, sequencing those simultaneously, and then reassembling the predicted full sequence by aligning the short sequences, using their inevitable regions of overlap. This strategy previously had been applied to the sequencing of proteins. Applying this method to the sequencing of genomic quantities of DNA, however, would have been impossible without powerful computers and software to manipulate the sequence files, find the regions of overlap, and then assemble the fragment sequences into a final reconstituted whole.

Leveraging this same strategy with yet further improved wet-lab methods, computers, and software, DNA sequencing was later achieved on an even larger scale and at lower cost. Refinements in sequencing techniques and the development of new algorithms for bioinformatics were central to the success of a wide range of projects, including those designed to uncover the extent of human genetic diversity, to explore the evolutionary relationships between known species, and to compare known and previously unknown DNA sequences, the approach taken in the discovery of the cryptomycota. The development of large databases of biological information, the improvement of information retrieval technology, and the ability to integrate data from different biological sources—all of which fall under the umbrella of bioinformatics—gave scientists the power to explore the immense volumes of data generated by their research. The types of data sets to be analyzed became as varied as the biological questions posed.

In the field of molecular genetics, bioinformatics was used for the analysis of data sets generated from microarrays, which consisted of small glass plates or chips imprinted with tens of thousands of DNA samples, each of which represented a single gene or a single segment of DNA of interest. Microarrays produced enormous amounts of data. For example, the relative expression levels of all the genes on a microarray chip translated into thousands of pieces of information. Some microarrays were used to interrogate a given DNA sample for the presence or absence of hundreds to thousands of known sequence variants. The resulting data were then analyzed by using sophisticated software and statistical methods to identify biologically relevant patterns.

Bioinformatic approaches, however, were not restricted to genetic endeavours. So-called in silico—meaning "virtual"—screens were utilized to search extensive small-molecule chemical libraries for candidates predicted to bind to a region of a three-dimensional structure of a given macromolecule, such as the active site of an enzyme. In other projects computers were used to analyze the massive data sets generated by mass spectroscopic or even tandem (multiple and simultaneous) mass spectroscopic analyses of proteins or small metabolites in biological samples. Indeed, this was the basis for what became the recommended approach to newborn screening in many countries. With ever-increasing speed and decreasing price, improved computer hardware and software became integral components of contemporary biomedical science at essentially all levels, paving the way for untold future discoveries.

(JUDITH FRIDOVICH-KEIL)

PALEONTOLOGY

In January 2011 Argentine paleontologist Ricardo Martínez and colleagues noted that a small Late Triassic theropod known as *Eodromaeus murphi*, which was found at the Ischigualasto Formation of Argentina, might represent the most primitive basal dinosaur yet discovered. The animal was excavated from the same rock formation as the famous *Eoraptor*, which had for 20 years been considered to be the most basal dinosaur known. Reevaluation of the phylogenetic position of *Eoraptor* resulted in its movement from the clade Theropoda, which contains all flesh-eating dinosaurs, to clade Sauropodomorpha, which contains all plant-eating forms.

During the evolution of theropod dinosaurs, the number of fingers on their hands declined from five to three in most theropods and down to two in the tyrannosaurs. In January 2011, however, scientists discovered the first single-fingered form, *Linhenykus monodactylus*, from the Late Cretaceous of Inner Mongolia. The 1-m (3.3-ft)-tall animal belonged to the alvarezsauroid group of theropods. The study, led by Xing Xu of the Institute of Vertebrate Paleontology and Paleoanthropology in Beijing, suggested that the single-clawed digit might have been used for digging up insects.

Also in January an article by Isabelle Kruta of the National Museum of Natural History, Paris, and her colleagues described the use of synchrotron X-ray microtomography, which employs high-energy X-rays to generate cross-sectional images with micrometre resolution of three-dimensional objects, in the discovery of new information about ammonite paleobiology. Ammonites, a type of cephalopod with an external shell, were among the most abundant marine invertebrates of the Mesozoic Era. Since the ammonites lacked living descendants, their feeding habits were poorly understood. With the aid of synchrotron X-ray microtomography, however, the researchers documented the presence of jaws, a radula, and possible food remains within the buccal mass (the mouth and pharynx) of the Late Cretaceous ammonite *Baculites*. In addition, the team identified the remains of isopods, a type of crustacean plankton, within the buccal mass, which suggested that cephalopods fed on zooplankton.

In March a 260-million-year-old therapsid fossil from Brazil that possessed a unique dentition was described. Therapsids, called "mammal-like reptiles," spanned the Middle Permian through the Late Triassic periods and were the ancestors of the first mammals, which probably first appeared during the Middle Triassic. The therapsid *Tiarajudens* was classified with the herbivorous anomodonts. Between the Late Permian and the Middle Triassic periods, the anomodonts' postcanine teeth (those located directly behind the canines) were replaced by large rounded tusks. *Tiarajudens*, however, was unique. It possessed postcanine teeth that occluded (came into contact when the mouth closed), as well as large flattened saber-shaped canine teeth. Juan Carlos Cisneros of the Federal University of Piauí in Brazil and colleagues suggested that the palatal teeth (those near the roof of the mouth) were adapted for chewing high-fibre food, whereas the canines might have been used for defense and sexual displays.

In May a study of the morphology of the orbit and scleral ring in the eyes of Mesozoic archosaurs (a reptile group containing the dinosaurs and pterosaurs ["flying reptiles"], as well as the living and ancestral forms of birds and crocodiles) published by University of California, Davis, researchers Lars Schmitz and Ryosuke Motani indicated that archosaurs had ecological characteristics similar to those of modern amniotes

Matt Colbert—University of Texas at Austin/DigiMorph.org

*Computed tomography (CT) scans of the braincases of the modern short-tailed opossum (*Monodelphis*, upper left) and the extinct* Hadrocodium *(bottom right) increased the scientific understanding of the evolution of the mammalian brain.*

(reptiles, birds, and mammals). They also determined that flying archosaurs, such as the pterosaurs, were largely diurnal (active during the day), that terrestrial predators were partially nocturnal (active during the night), and that herbivores were cathemeral (active during the day and night).

On May 20 Timothy Rowe of the University of Texas at Austin and colleagues published the results of a study that used high-resolution X-ray tomography to create brain endocasts (casts of the cranial cavity), providing new insight into the early evolution of mammalian brains. Brain endocasts of two basal mammals, *Morganucodon* and *Hadrocodium*, revealed that mammalian brain evolution occurred in three major steps. Brain endocasts of Triassic cynodont reptiles, a group of therapsids that gave rise to the first mammals, revealed that cynodonts lacked fine motor coordination and had relatively poor olfaction, vision, and hearing. The *Morganucodon* endocast indicated that its brain was almost 50% larger than that of cynodonts, with the olfactory lobes and cerebral hemispheres showing the greatest increase in size. This suggested an improvement in the sense of smell and neuromuscular coordination. The endocast belonging to the more advanced *Hadrocodium*, which had a brain-to-body size ratio comparable to that of living mammals, showed another 50% increase during a second stage of brain development. The third phase, involving improvements to the sense of smell, occurred later.

On May 26 Yale University researchers Peter Van Roy and Derek Briggs announced the discovery of a new group of anomalocaridids (primitive predatory marine arthropods) in rocks found in southeastern Morocco that dated to the Early Ordovician Period. Anomalocaridids were the largest animals to appear in Cambrian marine faunas. The oldest specimens that had been found previously occurred in the Middle Cambrian rocks of Utah, and arthropods with anomalocaridid characteristics had been found in deposits dating to the Devonian Period, nearly 100 million years later. The new group contained specimens larger than any previously described. The specimens confirmed the presence of flexible dorsal blades, which probably functioned as gills, attached to a rachis (central column) on the trunk segments of the animal.

The finding of what appeared to be the youngest dinosaur fossil to date was reported in July in a paper published by Tyler Lyson of Yale University and his research team. The fossil is a 45-cm (17.7-in)-long horn of either a *Triceratops* or a *Torosaurus* from the Late Cretaceous Hell Creek Formation in southeastern Montana. It was found just 13 cm (about 5 in) below the Cretaceous-Tertiary (K-T) boundary, which falls within a 3-m (10-ft) "gap" in the stratigraphic record from the end of the Cretaceous that is generally devoid of dinosaurs. Some paleontologists claimed that this finding proved that dinosaurs were killed off by a large meteorite impact at the end of the Cretaceous, since the fossil was found so close to the boundary layer. Others concluded that the discovery of a single bone is inconclusive and that multiple causes were responsible for the extinction event.

Also in July, Robert Eagle of Caltech and colleagues published a paper describing the use of clumped isotope thermometry on fossilized teeth to determine the body temperature of Jurassic sauropods. (Clumped isotope thermometry is a method for determining past temperatures that is based on the extent to which isotopes bond with or cluster near each other.) The authors estimated that the body temperatures of sauropods averaged 36–38 °C (about 97–100 °F), similar to those of modern mammals.

That same month the authenticity of a paleontological icon was challenged following the discovery of *Xiaotingia zhengi*, a small theropod from the Late Jurassic Tiaojishan Formation of western Liaoning, China. The results of the phylogenetic analysis performed by Xing Xu, who had reported the discovery of *L. monodactylus* earlier in the year, and colleagues suggested that *Archaeopteryx*, which for 150 years had been considered the most primitive bird in the fossil record, was not actually a bird. The new study placed *Archaeopteryx* in a clade with the nonavian deinonychosaur theropods.

(WILLIAM R. HAMMER)

Literature

In the U.S. **E-BOOKS** outsold **TRADITIONAL** print books in 2011, and in the U.K. controversy **SWIRLED** over the nominees for the **MAN BOOKER PRIZE.** Chinese literati reveled in the awarding of the **MAO DUN LITERATURE PRIZE,** while Japanese intellectuals bestowed the **AKUTAGAWA PRIZE** (given twice yearly) to the country's most **PROMISING** writers. In Russian literature **FIGL-MIGL** struck again. Meanwhile, Arab writers and poets took their cue from the events of the **ARAB SPRING.** German and Italian writers for the most part **SHUNNED CONTEMPORARY EVENTS** to examine phenomena of the 20th century. Two Latin American literary giants left the scene during the year: Chilean poet **GONZALO ROJAS** and Argentine novelist **ERNESTO SÁBATO.** Also vanished from the scene were French Canadian writer **GIL COURTEMANCHE,** Italian poet **ANDREA ZANZOTTO,** and many others.

ENGLISH

U**nited Kingdom.** Few literary controversies filled newspaper columns in 2011 as much as the commentary about the short list for the Man Booker Prize, which critics claimed had prioritized readability over literary excellence and damaged the award's prestige. While journalists and former judges penned their own short lists in defiance of Man Booker judges, literary agent Andrew Kidd announced the creation of the Literature Prize, a new award for novels "unsurpassed in their quality and ambition." The chair of the Man Booker judges, thriller writer and former MI5 director Dame Stella Rimington, countered by accusing the London literati of elitism.

Critics were particularly incensed by the absence from the short list of Alan Hollinghurst's *The Stranger's Child*, his first novel since having won the Man Booker in 2004 with *The Line of Beauty*. His latest work, lauded widely as one of the year's best offerings, certainly fulfilled notions of highbrow literature. Described by one commentator as an "ironic meditation on the evolution of literary memory," it was peppered with allusions to Alfred Lord Tennyson, Evelyn Waugh, Ford Madox Ford, Henry James, and the Bloomsbury group. The novel, written in five sections, told the story of a Georgian poet slain in World War I and then chronicled his posthumous literary reputation over the next century. Hollinghurst's exquisite phrasing extended equally to descriptions of architecture and social behaviour, while his masterly ability to weave character and social history drew comparisons to George Eliot's *Middlemarch*.

The winner of the Man Booker Prize was fourth-time short-listed Julian Barnes (the only short-listed author to receive the blessing of critics) for his novel *The Sense of an Ending*. Inviting comparisons to Ford and James with his device of an unreliable narrator, Barnes explored the way people edit and reedit their memories in order to create selves that they can live with. Tony, the protagonist, is a lacklustre 60-year-old whose conventional life has featured a job in arts administration, fatherhood, and an amicable divorce. When he is mysteriously bequeathed the diary of a truth-seeking, Camus-reading school friend who committed suicide 40 years earlier, Tony is confronted with the limitations of his own personal fiction. *The Daily Telegraph* newspaper called *The Sense of an Ending* "brief but masterful."

The British-dominated Man Booker short list also contained Carol Birch's 11th novel, *Jamrach's Menagerie*, likened by one reviewer to the best work of two-time Booker winner Peter Carey. Birch tells the story of an eight-year-old boy who is plucked from the jaws of a marauding tiger by its owner, Mr. Jamrach, and plunged into an outlandish new life. The story was based on such historical figures as Charles Jamrach, the 19th-century importer of wild animals and birds, and such events as the sinking in 1820 of the whaling ship *Essex*. Birch's novel was rich with historically accurate detail: streets awash with blood and brine, three-masted clippers from India resting in the Thames, and colourful seafaring misfits.

While Birch made convincing use of the 19th-century vernacular in her novel, Stephen Kelman, also short-listed, provided insight into the language and culture of a contemporary Peckham housing estate in his first novel, *Pigeon English*. Kelman's rite-of-passage saga, based on the highly publicized murder in 2000 of black schoolboy Damilola Taylor and narrated from the perspective of an 11-year-old boy from Ghana living in a public housing tenement, was the subject of fierce bidding wars between publishers. Also short-listed was *Snowdrops*, the debut of A.D. Miller (former Moscow correspondent for *The Economist* magazine), about a British lawyer who is seduced by Moscow's gangster-driven culture. *Snowdrops* derived its name from the Moscow slang for a corpse hidden under the snow.

With two debut and two second-time novelists on the Man Booker short list, it was a year for notable newcomers. Not least among them was Indian-born British writer Kishwar Desai, who had won the 2010 Costa First Novel Award with *Witness the Night* (2010), about a teenage girl who is found surrounded by 13 dead bodies and the social worker who tries to help her. Desai's twin theme was the culling of female fetuses in India and the oppression in Indian society of girls who survive birth. Her novel was commended for combining fiction with facts about a social issue while keeping readers captivated.

Matt Crossick—PA Photos/Landov

Maggie O'Farrell won the Costa Novel Award for The Hand That First Held Mine *(2010), a complex look at the unreliability of memory and the ties that connect people across time.*

The winner of the Costa 2010 Novel Award was Maggie O'Farrell's fifth novel, *The Hand That First Held Mine* (2010). Like *The Stranger's Child* and *The Sense of an Ending*, O'Farrell's novel posed questions about the unreliability of memory. Set in two time frames, it opened with the story of a bored graduate who runs away from a Devon backwater to become a groundbreaking journalist, single mother, and free spirit in the heart of Soho's post-World War II art scene. It then treated the postpartum blues of Elina, a Finnish artist living in 21st-century London, after the traumatic birth of her son. As Elina's partner, Ted, begins to unravel—experiencing hazy flashbacks, blank spots in his memories, and panic attacks—the connection between the stories is revealed. Emma Hagestadt in *The Independent* newspaper described O'Farrell's focus on "a father's postnatal ravings" as an "inspired upending of literary convention."

One of 2011's best-selling novels was David Nicholls's sleeper hit *One Day* (2009), voted Galaxy Book of the Year for 2010. The novel opens on July 15, 1988, with a postfinals fling between two students in Edinburgh and revisits their subsequent friendship on the same date for the next 20 years. *The Guardian* newspaper ascribed its phenomenal success (over a million copies sold) to the fact that it was both "roaringly funny" and "in its own unassuming, unpretentious way, rather profound," while Iain Hollingshead in *The Telegraph* called it "the best British novel of the past 20 years." Its detractors were equally hyperbolic, accusing Nicholls of having served up clichés and one-dimensional stereotypical characters.

A more serious novel to top the best-seller list (albeit briefly) was Jewish Ukrainian Vasily Grossman's *Life and Fate*, a book completed in 1960 but published only after having been smuggled out of the Soviet Union in 1980. BBC Radio 4's massive adaptation of the book, featuring actors Kenneth Branagh and David Tennant (and made available for free download), was part of a deliberate campaign by Mark Damazer, former controller of Radio 4, to rehabilitate the neglected masterpiece as the *War and Peace* of the 20th century. Historian Antony Beevor shored up Damazer's project, declaring Grossman's 900-page account of the struggle between Stalinism and Nazism to be "more important than *Doctor Zhivago* and *The Gulag Archipelago*."

While commentators in 2010 had predicted that a glut of fiscal calamity novels would emerge in 2011, little notable fiction was published on this theme. One exception was Robert Harris's financial thriller *The Fear Index*. Unfolding over 24 hours in Geneva, Harris's novel featured a mathematical genius who made billions for himself and his hedge-fund investors with a computer program that traded by predicting fear in the market. The novel was fast-paced and gripping, but as Charles Cumming wrote in *The Spectator* magazine, its real purpose was to "skewer the hubris and greed of the financial classes."

The political and social angst precipitated by the financial crisis was treated more directly in nonfiction, though the onslaught of books on this theme abated compared with recent years. *Masters of Nothing: How the Crash Will Happen Again Unless We Understand Human Nature* captured headlines with its description of the ire of Sir Fred Goodwin (former chief executive of the Royal Bank of Scotland) over the serving of a plate of pink wafers during afternoon tea. Highlighting the role of irrational and self-interested behaviour in economic decision making, Conservative backbencher Matthew Hancock and his co-writer, Nadhim Zahawi (also a Conservative MP), presented a blueprint for legislation to protect the public against corporate negligence. Meanwhile, Owen Jones's *Chavs: The Demonization of the Working Class* expressed indignation over the segregation along lines of class and income that deepened in British society after the financial crash. Besides analyzing the causes of the imbalance of power in Britain's economic and social structure, Jones attacked middle-class stereotypes of the working class that reinforced their "invisible prison." *Back from the Brink: 1,000 Days at Number 11*, a memoir by Alistair Darling (a Labour MP) of his tenure as chancellor of the Exchequer during the collapse of Northern Rock bank, painted Gordon Brown's leadership during the recession as opportunistic, dishonest, and self-defeating. Notwithstanding Darling's damning portrayal of the former prime minister, reviewers described Darling as "a decent man who does not exaggerate."

Soul-searching about less-recent British history appeared in an impressive spate of new writing about the legacies of the Empire. Richard Gott's *Britain's Empire: Resistance, Repression and Revolt* examined Britain's record of cruelty and genocidal repression from the 1750s to the Indian revolt of 1857–58, further debunking the myth of Britain's "civilizing mission." BBC presenter Jeremy Paxman took a similarly antiheroic approach to the subject of imperial agents in *Empire: What Ruling the World Did to the British*. While Paxman's book was well received as a witty and colourful introduction to imperial history, commentators pointed out that its subtitle was misleading, as its analysis of the corrosive effect of empire on its so-called builders was fleeting and superficial. The anti-Empire chorus was joined by Tory MP and historian Kwasi Kwarteng, who countered the celebration of empire among neoconservative elements in his party with *Ghosts of Empire: Britain's Legacies in the Modern World*. Kwarteng argued that the overly self-confident public-school-bred individualism of Empire builders paired with the autonomy granted them led to messy and tragic decision making.

Simon Sebag Montefiore's *Jerusalem: The Biography* was widely hailed as an encyclopaedic, impartial, and magnificent account of the city's 3,000-year history of spirituality, conquest, and conflict. As Beevor dryly observed in his review for *The Guardian*, Montefiore's sweeping chronicle of war, rape, sadistic torture, and religion-inspired slaughter was "likely to confirm atheist prejudices."

(continued on page 256)

WORLD LITERARY PRIZES 2011

All prizes are annual and were awarded in 2011 unless otherwise stated. Currency equivalents as of July 1, 2011, were as follows: €1 = $1.449; £1 = $1.606; Can$1 = $1.035; ¥1 = $0.155; SEK 1 = $0.158; DKK 1 = $0.194; and 1 Russian ruble = $0.036.

Nobel Prize for Literature

Awarded since 1901; included at the behest of Alfred Nobel, who specified a prize for those who "shall have produced in the field of literature the most outstanding work in an ideal direction." The prizewinners are selected in October by the Swedish Academy and receive the award on December 10 in Stockholm. Prize: a gold medal and a monetary award that varies from year to year; in 2011 the award was SEK 10 million.

Tomas Tranströmer (Sweden)

International IMPAC Dublin Literary Award

First awarded in 1996; this is the largest international literary prize and is open to books written in any language. The award is a joint initiative of Dublin City Council, the Municipal Government of Dublin City, and the productivity-improvement company IMPAC. It is administered by Dublin City Public Libraries. Prize: €100,000, of which 25% goes to the translator if the book was not written in English, and a Waterford crystal trophy. The awards are given at Dublin Castle in May or June.

Let the Great World Spin by Colum McCann (U.S.)

Neustadt International Prize for Literature

Established in 1969 and awarded biennially by the University of Oklahoma and *World Literature Today*. Novelists, poets, and dramatists are equally eligible. Prize: $50,000, a replica of an eagle feather cast in silver, and a certificate.

Duo Duo (China), awarded in 2010

Man Booker International Prize

This prize is awarded every other year (beginning in 2005) to a living author of fiction of any nationality who writes in English or whose work is widely translated into English for the body of his work. The prize is supported by the Man Group PLC. Winners are announced in midyear. Prize: £60,000.

Philip Roth (U.S.)

Astrid Lindgren Memorial Award for Literature

This award, first bestowed in 2003 by the government of Sweden, is given annually to one or more living authors who, in the words of the organizers, "in their writing have produced literature for children and young people of absolutely the highest artistic quality and in the humanistic spirit associated with Astrid Lindgren." Organizations that contribute to the literary welfare of children and young people are also eligible. Prize: SEK 5 million.

Shaun Tan (Australia)

Commonwealth Writers' Prize

Established in 1987 by the Commonwealth Foundation. In 2011 there was one award of £10,000 for the best book submitted, as well as an award of £5,000 for the best first book. In each of the four regions of the Commonwealth, two prizes of £1,000 are awarded: one for the best book and one for the best first book.

Best Book	*The Memory of Love* by Aminatta Forna (Sierra Leone)
Best First Book	*A Man Melting* by Craig Cliff (New Zealand)
Regional winners—Best Book	
Africa	*The Memory of Love* by Aminatta Forna (Sierra Leone)
Caribbean & Canada	*Room* by Emma Donoghue (Canada)
Europe & South Asia	*The Thousand Autumns of Jacob de Zoet* by David Mitchell (U.K.)
Southeast Asia & Pacific	*That Deadman Dance* by Kim Scott (Australia)

Man Booker Prize

Established in 1969, sponsored by Booker McConnell Ltd. and, beginning in 2002, the Man Group; administered by Booktrust in the U.K. Awarded to the best full-length novel written by a citizen of the Commonwealth or the Republic of Ireland and published in the U.K. during the 12 months ended September 30. Prize: £50,000.

The Sense of an Ending by Julian Barnes

Costa Book of the Year

Established in 1971 as the Whitbread Literary Awards (from 1985 Whitbread Book of the Year); Costa Coffee assumed sponsorship in 2006. The winners of the Costa Book Awards for Poetry, Biography, Novel, and First Novel as well as the Costa Children's Book of the Year each receive £5,000, and the winner of the Costa Book of the Year prize receives an additional £30,000. Winners are announced early in the year following the award.

Of Mutability by Jo Shapcott (2010 award)

Orange Prize for Fiction

Established in 1996. Awarded to a work of published fiction written by a woman in English and published in the U.K. during the 12 months ended March 31. Prize: £30,000 and a bronze figurine called the "Bessie."

The Tiger's Wife by Téa Obreht (U.S.)

Frank O'Connor International Short Story Award

The prize was first awarded in 2005 and recognizes a collection of short stories in English by a living author and published in the previous 12 months. The award is organized by the Munster Literature Centre in Cork, Ire., and is underwritten by the Cork City Council in association with the *Irish Times*. Prize: €35,000, shared by the writer and the translators (if any).

Saints and Sinners by Edna O'Brien (Ireland)

Bollingen Prize in Poetry

Established in 1948 by Paul Mellon. It is awarded to an American poet every two years by the Yale University Library. Prize: $100,000.

Susan Howe (2011 prize)

PEN/Faulkner Award

The PEN/Faulkner Foundation each year recognizes the best published works of fiction by contemporary American writers. The award, named for William Faulkner, was founded by writers in 1980 to honour their peers. Prize: $15,000.

The Collected Stories of Deborah Eisenberg by Deborah Eisenberg

Pulitzer Prizes in Letters and Drama

Begun in 1917. Awarded by Columbia University, New York City, on the recommendation of the Pulitzer Prize Board for books published in the previous year. Five categories in Letters are honoured: Fiction, Biography, and General Nonfiction (authors of works in these categories must be American citizens); History (the subject must be American history); and Poetry (for original verse by an American author). The Drama prize is for "a distinguished play by an American author, preferably original in its source and dealing with American life." Prize: $10,000 for each award.

Fiction	*A Visit from the Goon Squad* by Jennifer Egan
Drama	*Clybourne Park* by Bruce Norris
History	*The Fiery Trial: Abraham Lincoln and American Slavery* by Eric Foner
Poetry	*The Best of It: New and Selected Poems* by Kay Ryan
Biography	*Washington: A Life* by Ron Chernow
General Nonfiction	*The Emperor of All Maladies: A Biography of Cancer* by Siddhartha Mukherjee

National Book Awards

Awarded since 1950 by the National Book Foundation, a consortium of American publishing groups. Categories have varied, beginning with 3—Fiction, Nonfiction, and Poetry—swelling to 22 in 1983, and returning to the following 4 in 1996. Prize: $10,000 and a bronze sculpture in each category.

Fiction	*Salvage the Bones* by Jesmyn Ward
Nonfiction	*The Swerve: How the World Became Modern* by Stephen Greenblatt
Poetry	*Head Off & Split* by Nikky Finney
Young People's Literature	*Inside Out & Back Again* by Thanhha Lai

Frost Medal

Awarded annually since 1930 by the Poetry Society of America for distinguished lifetime achievement in American poetry.

Charles Simic

Association for Library Service to Children (ALSC) Awards

The ALSC, a branch of the American Library Association (ALA), presents a series of awards each year for excellence in children's literature. The two best-established and best-known are the following:

WORLD LITERARY PRIZES 2011 (continued)

The **Newbery Medal,** first bestowed in 1922 (the oldest award in the world for children's literature), honours the author of the most distinguished contribution in English to American literature for children. The award consists of a bronze medal.

Clare Vanderpool, for *Moon over Manifest*

The **Caldecott Medal,** first bestowed in 1938, is awarded to the artist of the most distinguished picture book for children. The award consists of a bronze medal.

Erin E. Stead, for *A Sick Day for Amos McGee* (written by Philip C. Stead)

Governor General's Literary Awards

Canada's premier literary awards. Prizes are given in 14 categories altogether: Fiction, Poetry, Drama, Translation, Nonfiction, and Children's Literature (Text and Illustration), each in English and French. Established in 1937. Prize: Can$25,000.

Fiction (English)	*The Sisters Brothers* by Patrick deWitt
Fiction (French)	*L'Homme blanc* by Perrine Leblanc
Poetry (English)	*Killdeer* by Phil Hall
Poetry (French)	*Plus haut que les flammes* by Louise Dupré

Griffin Poetry Prize

Established in 2000 and administered by the Griffin Trust for Excellence in Poetry. The award honours first-edition books of poetry published during the preceding year. Prize: Can$65,000.

Canadian Award	*Ossuaries* by Dionne Brand
International Award	*Heavenly Questions* by Gjertrud Schnackenberg (U.S.)

Büchner Prize

Georg-Büchner-Preis. Awarded for a body of literary work in the German language. First awarded in 1923; now administered by the German Academy for Language and Literature. Prize: €50,000.

Friedrich Christian Delius (Germany)

P.C. Hooft Prize

P.C. Hooft-prijs. The Dutch national prize for literature, established in 1947. Prize: €60,000.

H.J.A. Hofland

Nordic Council Literature Prize

Established in 1961. Selections are made by a 10-member jury from among original works first published in Danish, Norwegian, or Swedish during the previous two years or in other Nordic languages (Finnish, Faroese, Sami, etc.) during the previous four years. Prize: DKK 350,000.

Milli trjánna by Gyrðir Elíasson (Iceland)

Prix Goncourt

Prix de l'Académie Goncourt. First awarded in 1903 from the estate of French literary figure Edmond Goncourt, to memorialize him and his brother, Jules. Prize: €10.

L'Art français de la guerre by Alexis Jenni

Prix Femina

Established in 1904. The awards for works "of imagination" are announced by an all-female jury in the categories of French fiction, fiction in translation, and nonfiction. Announced in November together with the Prix Médicis. Prize: not stated.

French Fiction	*Jayne Mansfield 1967* by Simon Liberati

Strega Prize

Premio Strega. Awarded annually since 1947 for the best work of prose (fiction or nonfiction) by an Italian author in the previous year. The prize is supported by the beverage company Liquore Strega and Telecom Italia. Prize: not stated.

Storia della mia gente by Edoardo Nesi

Cervantes Prize for Hispanic Literature

Premio Cervantes. Established in 1975 and awarded by the Spanish Ministry of Culture for a body of work in the Spanish language. Announced in November or December and awarded the following April. Prize: €125,000.

Nicanor Parra (Chile)

Planeta Prize

Premio Planeta de Novela. Established in 1952 by the Planeta Publishing House for the best original novel in Spanish. Awarded in Barcelona in October. Prize: €601,000.

El imperio eres tú by Javier Moro

Camões Prize

Prémio Camões. Established in 1988 by the governments of Portugal and Brazil to honour a "representative" author writing in the Portuguese language. Prize: €100,000.

Manuel António Pina (Portugal)

Russian Booker Prize

Awarded since 1992; the Russian Booker Prize has sometimes carried the names of various sponsors—e.g., Smirnoff in 1997–2001. In 2004 it was underwritten by the Open Russia Charitable Organization and called the Booker/Open Russia Literary Prize. Awards: $20,000 for the winner, $2,000 for each finalist. In 2011 the award was for the Book of the Decade.

Lozhitsya mgla na staryye stupeni (2000; *A Gloom Is Cast upon the Ancient Steps*) by Aleksandr Chudakov

Big Book Prize

Premiya Bolshaya Kniga. First given out in 2006; it is sponsored by the government of Russia and underwritten by a number of prominent businessmen, who also serve as the jury. Awards: 3 million rubles for first prize, 1.5 million for second, and 1 million for third.

Mikhail Shishkin for his novel *Pismovnik* ("A Compilation of Letters")

Naguib Mahfouz Medal for Literature

Established in 1996 and awarded for the best contemporary novel published in Arabic. Prize: $1,000 and a silver medal. The winning work is translated into English and published in Cairo, London, and New York. The award in 2011 was symbolic.

The revolutionary creativity of the Egyptian people during the popular uprising that began on 25 January 2011

Caine Prize for African Writing

The Caine Prize for African Writing is awarded annually for a short story written by an African writer and published in English. The prize is named for Sir Michael Caine, longtime chairman of Booker PLC, the publishing company, and chairman of the Booker Prize management committee for 25 years. The Caine Prize was first given out in 2000. Award: £10,000 plus a travel allowance.

NoViolet Bulawayo (Zimbabwe) for "Hitting Budapest"

Man Asian Literary Prize

This prize, inaugurated in 2007, is awarded annually for an Asian novel written in English or translated into English. In 2010 it was announced that, as part of a new format, the previous year's winner would be announced in spring. The prize is underwritten by the Man Group PLC. Prize: $30,000 for the author and $5,000 for the translator.

Three Sisters by Bi Feiyu (China) (2010 award)

Jun'ichirō Tanizaki Prize

Tanizaki Jun'ichirō Shō. Established in 1965 to honour the memory of novelist Jun'ichirō Tanizaki. Awarded annually (except in 2009) to a Japanese author for an exemplary literary work. Prize: ¥1,000,000 and a trophy.

Mayumi Inaba for *Hantō e* ("To the Peninsula")

Ryūnosuke Akutagawa Prize

Akutagawa Ryūnosuke Shō. Established in 1935 and now sponsored by the Association for the Promotion of Japanese Literature; the prize is awarded in January and June for the best serious work of fiction by a promising new Japanese writer published in a magazine or journal. Prize: ¥1,000,000 and a commemorative gift.

Kueki ressha ("Labour Train") by Kenta Nishimura and *Kikotowa* by Mariko Asabuki (144th prize, second half of 2010)

No award for first half of 2011

Mao Dun Literature Prize

Established in 1982 to honour contemporary Chinese novels and named after novelist Shen Yanbing (1896–1981), whose nom de plume was Mao Dun; awarded roughly every three years. The latest awards were given on Aug. 20, 2011.

Ni zai gaoyuan (2010; "You on the Plateau") by Zhang Wei

Tian xingzhe (2009; "Skywalker") by Liu Xinglong

Tuina (2008; "Massage") by Bi Feiyu

Wa (2009; "Frog") by Mo Yan

Yi ju ding yiwan ju (2009; "One Sentence Worth Ten Thousand") by Liu Zhenyun

(PATRICIA BAUER)

(continued from page 253)

Like *Jerusalem: The Biography*, the winner of the 2010 Costa Biography Award and one of 2011's best-selling books was not, strictly speaking, a biography. Edmund de Waal's *The Hare with Amber Eyes* (2010) told the story of a collection of netsuke, traditional carved wood or ivory toggles from Japan. De Waal traced their movement from his distant cousin Charles, through the hands of Charles's cousin's baroness wife Emmy, their rescue from the Nazis by Emmy's personal maid (who hid them in her mattress), and their eventual miraculous reunion with Emmy's daughter, de Waal's grandmother. The book captivated readers with its evocations of Paris, Tokyo, and Vienna and its historical anecdotes. Part family memoir, part travelogue, it was also a meditation on the way objects accumulate meaning.

The short list of the recently renamed Royal Society Winton Prize for Science Books featured works that combined anecdote with fact, making engaging reading for the nonspecialist. Alex Bellos's *Alex's Adventures in Numberland* (2010), for example, opened with a description of a linguist's onerous month-long journey to reach the Amazonian Munduruku, a people who cannot count higher than the number five. Bellos went on to describe the history and personalities of mathematics from Euclid to the supercomputer, from the Greek cult of Pythagoras to the importance of geometry in origami. As one reviewer noted, "Even those suffering from a phobia about maths would find his book revealing and insightful." Ian Sample similarly made quantum physics accessible in *Massive: The Hunt for the God Particle* (2010), a book about the human drama behind the search for the world's most elusive subatomic particle.

The science writer who grabbed the most headlines was once again atheist Richard Dawkins, this time for his children's book *The Magic of Reality: How We Know What's Really True*. Designed, in part, to counter what he regarded as the pernicious effects of fairy tales and religion, *The Magic of Reality* opened with a definition of reality as "everything that exists" and then sought to answer questions such as "Who was the first person?" and "What is an earthquake?" Many critics berated Dawkins for his crude ultramaterialist view and unsophisticated understanding of religion.

Judges of the Forward Prize for Poetry were more concerned with consciousness than materialism when they awarded Scottish poet John Burnside the £10,000 (about $15,900) prize for his collection *Black Cat Bone*. The judges, including former poet laureate Sir Andrew Motion, said that it had "a vitality of language, an undertow of complexity, and an evocative dream logic." Eyebrows were raised, however, by the absence of women from the Forward Prize's six-poet short list. The winner of the 2010 Costa Poetry Award was female poet Jo Shapcott for *Of Mutability* (2010), a collection written after she was diagnosed with breast cancer. Kate Kellaway in *The Observer* newspaper remarked that the poem "Procedure" was simple but moving, "a hymn to tea and a thank you—to whom it may concern—for being alive to drink it." At year's end nonagenarian crime writer P.D. James's *Death Comes to Pemberley*, a sequel to Jane Austen's *Pride and Prejudice*, was issued. (CAROL PEAKER)

United States. Social historians would probably mark 2011 as the year in American literature when electronic books, or e-books, surpassed hardcover books in sales. According to *Publisher's Weekly* magazine, in the first six months of 2011, sales of adult hardcover books declined 23.7%, and adult paperbacks dropped 26.6%. Meanwhile e-books recorded a staggering 161.3% increase in sales. In the mass market, sales of paperbacks ($232.5 million) were less than half of those of e-books ($473.8 million). (*See* COMPUTERS: Sidebar.)

Fiction lovers would also recall 2011 as a period rich in new work by some of the masters of modern fiction and some startlingly talented younger writers. The Library of America issued *Novels & Stories, 1963–1973*, an offering of some of Kurt Vonnegut's best novels, including *Slaughterhouse-Five*, *Breakfast of Champions*, *God Bless You, Mr. Rosewater*, *Cat's Cradle*, and some of Vonnegut's better-known short stories. *Slaughterhouse-Five*, first published in 1969, introduces World War II veteran Billy Pilgrim, a survivor of the Allied firebombing raid on Dresden, where he was interned in early 1945 as a German prisoner of war. A batch of previously uncollected Vonnegut stories also appeared under the title *While Mortals Sleep*.

A few octogenarians published novels during the year. Pulitzer Prize winner William Kennedy (83) brought out *Changó's Beads and Two-Tone Shoes*, set in Cuba in 1957 (with a cameo appearance by novelist Ernest Hemingway) and his native Albany, N.Y., which he had celebrated so vividly in many of his other books. Distinguished and much-lauded John Barth (81) released *Every Third Thought: A Novel in Five Seasons*, which begins with the opening of *The Adventures of Huckleberry Finn* and progresses from there to allude to various other novels and poems as it tells a story that Barth began with protagonist George I. Newett in his 2008 short-story sequence *The Development*. The novel explores a number of coincidences related to the visions that Newett sees on the first day of the seasons. Multi-prizewinning novelist and storyteller E.L. Doctorow (80) issued *All the Time in the World: New and Selected Stories*, which revealed news not just about the world but also about the mysteries that lie at the heart of human behaviour, thus bringing the reader near to the resonance at the heart of ordinary life. Septuagenarian Don DeLillo (75), one of the most respected and admired novelists of the 21st century, released his first collection of short stories, *The Angel Esmeralda*, which gathered pieces published between 1979 and 2011.

The year also offered a pair of spectacular literary debuts. Balkan-born Téa Obreht signed in with *The Tiger's Wife*, set in the Balkans in the aftermath of war; the work was nominated for the National Book Award. Chad Harbach (the cofounder and coeditor of *n+1*, a journal published thrice yearly) made his bow with *The Art of Fielding*, set in a college town in Wisconsin (where Harbach was reared). This graceful book, a novel about how to read and how to write, could also be categorized as a baseball novel, a college novel, and thus a coming-of-age novel about families (by birth and by life choices), and a novel about how to live, how to love, and how to die. *Cleaning Nabokov's House* by Leslie Daniels was also an extremely pleasurable debut, or as charming as a book on the subject of the perils of love and single parenthood could be. The narrator, while cleaning her upstate New York rental house (purportedly once the residence of the great novelist Vladimir Nabokov when he taught at Cornell University), unearths the manuscript of a novel that may or may not have been written by the former resident. This find leads her to discover her own latent powers as a writer and as a person in her own right.

What seems merely descriptive in Denis Johnson's spare and straightforwardly narrated short novel *Train Dreams* becomes emotionally evocative, a beautifully made word engraving on the page. The memorable narrative, which finally came out in hardcover, was slightly different when it was initially published in 2002 in the *Paris Review*. In *When the Killing's Done*, T.C. Boyle sailed out to the Channel Islands of Anacapa and Santa Cruz for a raucous battle between animal rights activists and a government biologist. *Caleb's Crossing*, by Pulitzer Prize winner Geraldine Brooks, visits Martha's Vineyard in the 17th century and dramatizes quite effectively the life of the first Native American to graduate from Harvard University. Bruce Duffy's novel *Disaster Was My God* is a fictional biography of French poet and adventurer Arthur Rimbaud, and longtime writer and reviewer Alan Cheuse chimed in with *Song of Slaves in the Desert*, a historical fiction set mainly in slaver Africa and a mid-19th-century Charleston, S.C., plantation, where a family of Sephardic Jews hold slaves and cultivate rice.

New Mexico and New York served as the settings for Laura Furman's latest story collection, *The Mother Who Stayed*, which includes a beautifully made story cluster that examines the relationships between mothers and daughters. *Widow: Stories*, by California writer Michelle Latiolais, a story miscellany with a focus on widowhood and bereavement, includes an investigation of the very word: "In Sanskrit the word means empty. And in the Old Testament, God instructs Moses that a widow is in the same category as profane and whore." The widowed author goes on to produce an incisive exploration of her state of being: the constancy of grief. Another talented California writer, San Francisco-based Carol Edgarian, after 17 years of silence delivered a novel titled *Three Stages of Amazement*. An ambitious doctor, a troubled wife, and a mysterious San Francisco family inheritance all make for a beautifully written and deeply engaging novel set in the depths of the economic crisis.

Impressive novels came from Russell Banks, whose *Lost Memory of Skin* (a searing look at the dark lives of sex offenders) would not be easily forgotten; Kate Christensen, whose *The Astral* told the story of a middle-aged Brooklyn poet as his marriage unravels at the seams; Bonnie Jo Campbell, who released *Once upon a River*, a delightful coming-of-age novel set in Michigan; and Ann Patchett, whose *State of Wonder*, an Amazonian journey, stayed on the best-seller list for many weeks. Peter Orner, a writer with a slow-growing but deserved reputation for deeply felt and intelligent novels, showed off his latest, *Love and Shame and Love*, which explores the individual secret shame and search for love by three generations of a Chicago family. Mexican-born Chicago-based writer Luis Alberto Urrea continued the saga he began in *The Hummingbird's Daughter* (2005) with *Queen of America*.

Though few American writers attempted to experiment in the vein in which James Joyce had in *Ulyssses*, Chicago writer Jesse Ball led the way with *The Curfew*, his third novel. In his second work, *The Way Through Doors* (2009), he had tipped his hat to Joyce by opening with a giant letter Y. In *The Curfew*, the story of one family's struggle against an unnamed totalitarian regime, Ball suppresses the urge to deploy giant type until fully 50 pages into the story, but used thusly it feels, alas, more like mannerism than experiment. Cuban American writer Ana Menéndez (based variously in Amsterdam and Miami) produced *Adios, Happy Homeland!*, a brilliant meld of tradition and Modernism based on the work of an imaginary cadre of Cuban writers and poets. Ann Beattie, one of the country's most applauded short-story writers, relied on her imagination and information gleaned from magazines and relatives and friends of Pat Nixon to shape *Mrs. Nixon*, the story of the writer's struggle to portray the world as seen through the eyes of the former first lady.

New Mexico's Rudolfo Anaya, a foremost Chicano writer, played successfully with allegory in his novel *Randy Lopez Goes Home*. California novelist Percival Everett employed the police procedural in *Assumption*, a novel in three parts about a black New Mexico sheriff's deputy with an overriding problem of perception. The title of West Coast writer Maxine Hong Kingston's *I Love a Broad Margin to My Life* was borrowed from a line by Henry David Thoreau. The work showed her in full-blown experimental mode, making personal and social explorations in a long narrative poem.

Story collections came in from Midwestern writer Valerie Laken (*Separate Kingdoms*), Idaho writer Alan Heathcock (*Volt*), and Los Angeles-based Danzy Senna (*You Are Free*). Two of the country's most popular and successful novelists, John Grisham and Stephen King, signed in with new books, *The Litigators* and *11/22/63*, respectively.

The year was replete with new poetry volumes from prizewinning and highly treasured poets. Former poet laureate Robert Pinsky offered *New and Selected Poems*, and another former laureate, Billy Collins, released *Horoscopes for the Dead*. *The Chameleon Couch* by Pulitzer Prize winner Yusef Komunyakaa appeared, along with *Money Shot*, a new collection by Rae Armantrout.

Come, Thief, by Marin county, Calif., resident Jane Hirshfield included the popular poem "A Blessing for Wedding":

> Today when persimmons ripen
> Today when fox-kits come out of
> their den into snow
> Today when the spotted egg
> releases its wren song
> Today when the maple sets down
> its red leaves

Other pleasing poetry volumes included *Traveling Light* by Linda Pastan, *Lucifer at the Starlite* by Kim Addonizio, *In the Shadow of Al-Andalus* by Victor Hernandez Cruz, and *New and Selected Poems, 1957–2011* by Robert Sward.

Among translations, John Ashbery's translation of Rimbaud's *Illuminations* stood out, as did Stephen Mitchell's milestone version of the *Iliad*, based on recently established texts.

Two fine fiction writers overtook the memoir market in both substance and style. Joyce Carol Oates released *A Widow's Story*, and Francisco Goldman offered his account of his young wife's death in *Say Her Name*. Story writer Tracy Daugherty's biography of Joseph Heller—*Just One Catch*—was followed

***The Pulitzer Prize for Fiction was awarded to American novelist and short-story writer Jennifer Egan for her inventive novel* A Visit from the Goon Squad.**

Henny Ray Abrams/AP

by the appearance of *Yossarian Slept Here: When Joseph Heller Was Dad, the Apthorp Was Home, and Life Was a Catch-22* by Heller's daughter, Erica. There were mixed reviews for Kenneth Slawenski's *J.D. Salinger: A Life* (2010).

Some volumes were published that were of great interest to historians. They included *Elizabeth Bishop and The New Yorker: The Complete Correspondence*, edited by Joelle Biele, and *What There Is to Say We Have Said: The Correspondence of Eudora Welty and William Maxwell*, edited by Suzanne Marrs.

The Pulitzer Prize for Fiction went to 2010's *A Visit from the Goon Squad* by Jennifer Egan (*see* BIOGRAPHIES); the prize for history was awarded to *The Fiery Trial: Abraham Lincoln and American Slavery* (2010) by Eric Foner; the biography prize was claimed by *Washington: A Life* (2010) by Ron Chernow; the poetry prize was bestowed on *The Best of It: New and Selected Poems* (2010) by former poet laureate Kay Ryan; and the general nonfiction prize was captured by *The Emperor of All Maladies: A Biography of Cancer* (2010) by Siddhartha Mukherjee.

The Collected Stories of Deborah Eisenberg took the PEN/Faulkner Award for Fiction, and the PEN/Malamud Award for Excellence in the Short Story went to Edith Pearlman. The five nominees for the National Book Award for Fiction were Andrew Krivak (*The Sojourn*), Obreht (*The Tiger's Wife*), Julie Otsuka (*The Buddha in the Attic*), Pearlman (*Binocular Vision*), and Jesmyn Ward (*Salvage the Bones*). Ward took the fiction award for her novel about a poor black Louisiana family riding out Hurricane Katrina. The award for nonfiction went to Stephen Greenblatt for his intellectually stimulating book—*The Swerve*—on the work of Roman writer Lucretius and its links to modern life. Nikky Finney won the prize in poetry for *Head Off & Split*, her fourth book of poems.

Among the deaths during the year were those of writers Reynolds Price (*see* OBITUARIES), Wilfrid Sheed, and Lillian Jackson Braun. Also leaving the literary scene was feminist writer E.M. Broner, who wrote of the difficulties she encountered as a woman and a Jew.

(ALAN CHEUSE)

Canada. Tales of the frontier were abundant in Canadian literature in 2011. Patrick deWitt's *The Sisters Brothers* was an account of a fraternal pair of outlaws' belligerent excursion through the underworld of the Old West; Pauline Holdstock's *Into the Heart of the Country* explored how the tragic clash of European and indigenous cultures in western Canada continued to affect events many years later, and Guy Vanderhaeghe's *A Good Man* crossed many borders—political, emotional, physical, and factual—in this tale of love and revenge. On the opposite coast, Wayne Johnston's *A World Elsewhere* crisscrossed eastern borderlands in a sweeping story of ambition, remorse, and hope that reached from St. John's, Nfd., to Princeton, N.J., and to a grand mansion, Vanderland, in the hills of North Carolina.

Moving forward in time, Marina Endicott's *The Little Shadows*, set in the early 20th century, followed three intrepid young women as they danced and sang in vaudeville shows throughout the west, and Alexi Zentner's *Touch*, in a story that spanned three generations in a boom-and-bust town in northern British Columbia, introduced golden caribou and dogs that sang. Esi Edugyan's *Half Blood Blues*, a jazz-soaked saga of love, fear, opportunism, and defiance, took place in Paris in 1940. An ocean liner in the '50s was the setting for *The Cat's Table* by Michael Ondaatje, the surreal sea-bound sojourn of a Ceylonese boy at the beginning of a lifelong odyssey.

Canadian author Esi Edugyan's novel **Half Blood Blues** *won the Scotiabank Giller Prize and was short-listed for both the Man Booker Prize in the U.K. and the Governor General's Literary Award in Canada.*

Lefteris Pitarakis/AP

The Free World by David Bezmozgis, set in Italy in the 1970s, related how three generations of Russian Jews coped with the long wait for visas to a new life. In Frances Itani's *Requiem*, a road trip west became an extended metaphor for an inner journey, with many side trips, through the driver's long-neglected memories, while in Lynn Coady's *The Antagonist*, a man psychologically dismembers himself in order to become whole. Suzette Mayr's *Monoceros* revealed how a young man's suicide affected many, even those beyond his immediate circle of family and friends.

Short-story collections included Zsuzsi Gartner's *Better Living Through Plastic Explosives*, in which lively juxtapositions of lifestyles, values, and expectations (arranged for best satiric effect) were set in the urban wilderness of Vancouver. *The Meagre Tarmac* by Clark Blaise, which centred on the Indo-American experience (about people from various parts of India immigrating to the U.S.) and featured a collection of memorable individuals who encountered one another with often disruptive force; Michael Christie's *The Beggar's Garden*, the place where a ragged coterie of characters searched for the missing bits of their lives; and Jessica Westhead's *And Also Sharks*, which was a study (both humorous and disconcerting) of characters who seem to act without a normal moral compass and yet elicit excited laughter more than condemnation.

The themes of death and mourning as well as life and acceptance informed several poetry collections, including Lorna Crozier's *Small Mechanics*, which was involved with the powerful interlocking gears of aging, bereavement, and hope as one's life rolls forward; *Oyama Pink Shale* by Sharon Thesen, which celebrated the life and mourned the passing of a colleague, poet Robin Blaser; and *Origami Dove* by Susan Musgrave, a sometimes in-your-face, sometimes delicate rendition of the intermingled shades of grief and comic despair.

Some books of poetry were extended variations on other literary forms. Garry Thomas Morse's *Discovery Passages*, based on stories both oral and written, resurrected and reconstructed the acts and consequences of European interventions in traditional indigenous cultures, and Phil Hall's *Killdeer* contained a collection of thoughtful passages on becoming a poet, combined with elegiac musings on the lives and deaths of fellow Canadian poets.

Science inspired some poets, as evidenced by Anne Simpson's *Is*, wherein the cell was envisioned as a microcosm within a macrocosm that was itself a microcosm, elements of each intricately intertwined. From a more skeptical angle, Leigh Kotsilidis's *Hypotheticals* challenged the underpinnings of the scientific method itself with a collection of questions based on a double reading of the title, while in Jacob McArthur Mooney's *Folk*, a tragic airplane crash launched an investigation into the internal psychological geometry of modern civilized humans and their varied societies as well as their limits and structural values.

Graphic novels came into their own during the year. *The Listener* by David Lester combined a well-structured story, illustrated in a mix of styles, that reflected back upon itself how art can be both used and abused as a vehicle for ends beyond art.

(ELIZABETH RHETT WOODS)

Other Literature in English. Much of sub-Saharan Africa and Australasia's literary resources remained vibrant during 2011, as evidenced by the production of notable works written in English that were published and honoured throughout the year. This occurred even as widespread famine and drought persisted throughout the Horn of Africa and wildfires, floods, and earthquakes halfway across the globe in Australia and New Zealand took their toll.

In Africa internationally acclaimed Somali-born author Nuruddin Farah brought out his 11th novel—the last in a trilogy (following *Links* [2003] and *Knots* [2006])—entitled *Crossbones*, which offered a timely and engaging look at the extreme conditions in his native country. Two Ethiopian authors, Maaza Mengiste (*Beneath the Lion's Gaze*, 2010) and Dinaw Mengestu (*How to Read the Air*, 2010) were short-listed in the fiction category of the 2011 Dayton Literary Peace Prize, "the first and only U.S. literary award recognizing the power of the written word to promote peace." The Commonwealth Writers' Prize for Best Book went to Aminatta Forna (a Scottish-born author raised in Sierra Leone) for her novel *The Memory of Love* (2010), praised by the judges for its "risk-taking, elegance, and breadth."

Elsewhere, Zimbabwe's NoViolet Bulawayo garnered the 12th edition of Africa's Caine Prize for African Writing for her short story "Hitting Budapest," and Kenya's Binyavanga Wainaina, winner of the 2002 Caine Prize, continued to impress with his memoir *One Day I Will Write About This Place*.

Matthias Schumann—dpa/Landov

Somali-born Nuruddin Farah published Crossbones, *the long-awaited finale to his most recent trilogy of novels, Past Imperfect.*

Acclaimed Australian poet, novelist, and short-story writer David Malouf brought out *The Happy Life: The Search for Contentment in the Modern World*, a monograph in which he called for a return to the "highest wisdom" of the classics to find meaning and fulfillment. Tim Winton, one of Australia's finest novelists and short-story writers, saw the production of his first play, *Rising Water*. The annual Miles Franklin Literary Award for best novel, the Regional Commonwealth Writers' Prize, the Association for the Study of Australian Literature Gold Medal, and other major prizes went to Kim Scott's third novel, *That Deadman Dance* (2010), which was set in early 19th-century Western Australia and examined the initial contact between the Aboriginal Noongar people and the first European settlers.

In nearby New Zealand, many of the country's outstanding and most promising writers were recognized by the second annual *New Zealand Post* Book Awards. Among the 2011 recipients (for books published in 2010) were Laurence Fearnley, for *The Hut Builder* (Fiction); Kate Camp, for *The Mirror of Simple Annihilated Souls* (Poetry); and triple winner Chris Bourke, for *Blue Smoke: The Lost Dawn of New Zealand Popular Music, 1918–1964* (Book of the Year, General Nonfiction Book of the Year, and People's Choice Award).

The year 2011 also marked the passing of a number of important literary figures, including British-born Australian writer Hazel Rowley; New Zealand diplomat, civil servant, author, and academic Denis McLean; South African poet Stephen Watson; South African poet and biographer Patrick Cullinan; Australian fiction writer Tom Hungerford; New Zealand journalist, publisher, and author Dame Christine Cole Catley; Kenyan author Margaret A. Ogola; Australian fantasy writer Sara Douglass; Australian author and Aboriginal historian Ruby Langford Ginibi; and Australian publisher Diana Gribble.

(DAVID DRAPER CLARK)

GERMAN

The winner of the German Book Prize for 2011 was Eugen Ruge for *In Zeiten des abnehmenden Lichts*, his historical novel about East Germany (the former German Democratic Republic; GDR). The book told the moving story of three generations of socialists, their relationship to the East German state, and their gradual loss of faith in their political ideals. The grandson ultimately leaves East Germany in the final years of its existence—just as the novel's author did. Antje Rávic Strubel's novel *Sturz der Tage in die Nacht* also dealt with the former East German state, especially with the legacy of Stasi, its secret-police agency. The novel's protagonist, as an adolescent girl, enters into a sexual relationship with a Stasi officer, is abandoned by him, bears his child, and gives it up for adoption. After the collapse of the GDR, these long-ago events return to haunt the now middle-aged protagonist as she once again encounters both the son she gave up and her former lover; this meeting has a tragic, Oedipal outcome because a love affair develops between mother and son, suggesting that it may be impossible for the present generation to escape the burden of East German history.

Another family novel that examined 20th-century German history—this time events in Adolf Hitler's Third Reich—was Astrid Rosenfeld's *Adams Erbe*, which told the story in a lighthearted vein of several generations of a German-Jewish family and in particular of the relationship in the late 1930s between a woman named Anna and the Adam of the title. Their relationship throughout the terrible events of 1938 is detailed in Adam's diary, discovered by the book's narrator, his grandnephew Eddy.

Ilija Trojanow's *EisTau* addressed the ecological endangerment of Earth. The protagonist of this novel is a scientist who studies the gradual melting of the

Alex Domanski—Reuters/Landov

German writer Eugen Ruge won the German Book Prize for his first novel, In Zeiten des abnehmenden Lichts, *which treated an extended family's relationship to East Germany.*

world's great ice sheets and who gives lectures on a cruise ship bound for Antarctica. His pessimism about the human race and the future of Earth culminates in a radical act of desperation. He leaves behind the message: "The individual human being is a riddle, but several billions of human beings, organized into a parasitical system, are a catastrophe."

Almost as critical of the contemporary world was Thomas Melle's novel *Sickster*, which detailed the relationship between two former high-school acquaintances who have taken different paths in the corporate world. One is an apparently successful businessman who fills the emptiness of his life with sex and alcohol; the other is a frustrated and sidelined writer. When one becomes interested in the other's girlfriend, events begin to spin out of control. Jan Peter Bremer's *Der amerikanische Investor* also concerned the globalized world of contemporary capitalism, exploring the life of a Berlin writer whose apartment building was purchased by the eponymous American investor. The question posed in the novel was whether it is possible to address or even locate a capitalism that knows neither borders nor resting points.

Austrian authors Marlene Streeruwitz and Ludwig Laher both explored the potential for violence and pain in contemporary Europe. Streeruwitz's novel *Die Schmerzmacherin* concerned a woman who decides to leave the private security company she works for because of moral qualms about the violence that characterizes the company's working methods; however, she finds that leaving such a company is far more difficult than she had imagined. Laher's novel *Verfahren* examined the plight of political and economic refugees and the difficulty they have gaining admittance into prosperous first-world countries such as Austria. Its protagonist, Jelena, a survivor of unspeakable brutality in the former Yugoslavia, is forced to deal with an uncaring bureaucracy in the very country where she has sought refuge.

One of the most talked-about novels of the year was Charlotte Roche's erotic and semiautobiographical novel *Schossgebete*, which dealt with a woman's effort to overcome a horrible family tragedy by means of sex.

The 84-year-old Martin Walser published the novel *Muttersohn*, a grand summary of some of the themes that had long been present in his oeuvre: love, literature, language, and neurosis. The novel's protagonist has a particularly close relationship to his mother and therefore a strong sense of belonging in and to the world, but when he starts to work at a psychiatric institution, he must learn to deal with people who do not share his sense of belonging.

Finally, Niklas Maak's novel *Fahrtenbuch*—really a series of interconnected stories—presented the recent history of Germany by looking at a Mercedes 350 SL automobile and its diverse owners, from 1971 through the postunification period. (STEPHEN M. BROCKMANN)

FRENCH

France. The surprise best seller in 2011 was an essay barely longer than a pamphlet, *Indignez-vous!* (2010) by Stéphane Hessel, a 93-year-old former French Resistance fighter and prisoner at Buchenwald who later helped write the UN's *Universal Declaration of Human Rights*. In *Indignez-vous!* (which was published in English in 2011 as *Time for Outrage!*), Hessel called upon youths in France to renew their indignation for all political injustice, including the growing gap between rich and poor, the treatment of illegal immigrants, the slow death of the free press, and the Palestinians' plight. Hessel's message quickly crossed French borders once his book had been translated into more than a dozen languages, selling 3.5 million copies worldwide.

The success of the nonfictional *Indignez-vous!* set the tone for the year's French literature, which showed a clear preponderance of works based in fact rather than fiction, especially with the heavy representation of *autofiction*, the genre of fictionalized autobiography widely practiced in France for two decades. In *Comment gagner sa vie honnêtement* (2010), Jean Rouaud continued his famous series of *autofictions*, concentrating this time on the 1970s, when refusing to compromise and embark on a steady career path, he instead wandered from job to job, discovering in his adventures the writer he would later become. In *Le Livre des brèves amours éternelles*, Andreï Makine recounted 50 years of his life—from the Soviet orphanage of his childhood to the Russia of his youth and the France of his later life—through the prism of his encounters with women, each of whom contributed a lesson to his sentimental education. In *Un Homme de passage*, Serge Doubrovsky cast a backward glance at his life's path and reflected on the women who accompanied him. It was a voyage he saw as increasingly overshadowed by ever-approaching decrepitude and death.

Three of the year's best-selling autofictional works discussed the loss of a loved one. For Annie Ernaux, in *L'Autre*

Ninety-three-year-old former French Resistance fighter and diplomat Stéphane Hessel caused a worldwide literary sensation with his essay Indignez-vous!*—a rallying cry that went viral.*

Antonio Calanni/AP

Fille, the inspiration was her sudden discovery at age 10 of a sister who had fallen victim to diphtheria two years before the author's birth and who had been idealized in death, to whom the author would always come second in her parents' eyes. This circumstance produced in the celebrated author a deep heartache to which she suspected she might owe her career as a writer. In *Rien ne s'oppose à la nuit*, Delphine de Vigan wrote of her mother, dead by suicide, in an attempt to determine what in her mother's seemingly joyful life could have led her to such unsupportable despair. Finally, in the autofictional *Ce qu'aimer veut dire*, winner of the year's Médicis literary prize, Mathieu Lindon wrote of the death of the two men who most helped him grow to maturity—his father, publisher Jérôme Lindon, and his friend, the world-renowned philosopher Michel Foucault.

Three volumes of *biofiction*, a genre that blurred the boundary between biography and fiction, also proved to be best sellers. Laurent Mauvignier, in *Ce que j'appelle oubli*, spun his story from an actual crime committed in 2009. The book featured a down-and-out immigrant from Martinique who was beaten to death in a Lyon, France, supermarket by four security guards for drinking a can of beer without having paid. In *Limonov*, Emmanuel Carrère sketched the stranger-than-fiction life of the Russian adventurer Eduard Limonov. From life as a Ukrainian hoodlum to a literary life in Paris, Limonov went to soldiering in the Balkans, to street life in the United States as well as life among the American jet set, and later to the leadership of an extremist party in Russia. The book won the Prix Renaudot. The Prix Femina was awarded to Simon Liberati for his biofictional *Jayne Mansfield, 1967*, which retraced the life of American starlet Jayne Mansfield backward from her death in a car accident in 1967 to the start of her career in 1950s Hollywood through those decades' transformative upheaval. The double win of literary prizes for biofictional works gave the genre a new cachet likely to ensure its further expansion.

Best-selling works of historical fiction also straddled the boundary between fact and fiction, placing themselves by the precision of their research closer to documentary treatises than to novels in their frank examination of France's often disastrous colonial relations. In *Kampuchéa*, Patrick Deville documented the role of the French in the history of Cambodia, beginning with Henri Mouhot's discovery of the temples of Angkor in 1860. He described the concurrent spread of the ideas the French occupation brought of Jean-Jacques Rousseau, Karl Marx, and the Reign of Terror, all of which combined in the 1970s to help produce the genocidal reign of the Khmer Rouge. In *Plantation Massa-Lanmaux*, Yann Garvoz set his tale of racism largely on an 18th-century Antillean sugarcane plantation. The landlord's son attempts to apply the ideas of the Enlightenment to his father's slave-run farm and thereby foments a slave revolt and brings about the plantation's destruction by fire and his own paranoiac insanity. In Alexis Jenni's *L'Art français de la guerre*, a former captain of the French army recounted 18 years of French wars—starting with the disgrace of World War II and continuing into the dirty wars of French imperialist colonization in Indochina and Algeria, with all the savagery and torture that were their hallmark—a story with little fictional about it besides its narrator. Together with Carrère's Renaudot prize, Liberati's Femina, and Lindon's Médicis, Jenni's Prix Goncourt meant that works in which nonfiction outweighed fiction had swept all four main literary prizes in an official recognition of the nonfiction trend that had long been growing in France's literature. (VINCENT AURORA)

Canada. During the 2011 Salon du Livre, Montreal's French-language book fair considered the publishing event of the year, the entertainment paper *Voir* featured a stark front-page announcement: "49% of Québécois can't read this paper." Despite another successful year in book publishing, the truth remained that half the population did not have the skills to read a book. It was a big year for novelist, essayist, screenwriter, and all-around provocateur Victor-Lévy Beaulieu. He won French Quebec's Prix Gilles-Corbeil—at $100,000, Canada's richest French-language prize—as well as finishing his monumental Beauchemin saga with the novel *Antiterre*. Among other winners was Élise Turcotte, who picked up the Grand Prix du Livre de Montréal for her novel *Guyana*, which used the events at Jonestown as a starting point. Writers from far-flung areas of the province of Quebec had their say too. Jocelyne Saucier from the Abitibi region of northwestern Quebec was the surprise winner of Le Prix des Cinq Continents de la Francophonie with her novel *Il pleuvait des oiseaux*; the prize was open to French-language writers throughout the world. Samuel Archibald made a name for himself with *Arvida* (the name of a town in the Abitibi), a grab bag of stories and legends and cock-eyed characters. A rapper-turned-author who went by the name Biz attracted media attention with *La Chute de Sparte*, a story of suicide set in a high school. His novel explored the difficulty of growing up male in today's society. In the realm of nonfiction, two works based on Quebec social phenomena were noteworthy. They included Pierre Nepveu's biography of poet Gaston Miron (*Gaston Miron: la vie d'un homme*), whose career was intimately involved with the Quebec independence movement, and longtime left-wing feminist and activist Françoise David chipped in with *De colère et d'espoir*, an expression of anger and hope.

Quebec society mourned the passing in August of novelist and journalist Gil Courtemanche, who was best known for his novel *Un Dimanche à la piscine à Kigali* (2000). The work, which chronicled the 1994 Rwandan genocide, was translated into more than 20 languages and was adapted for the large screen in 2006.

(DAVID HOMEL)

ITALIAN

The winner of the Campiello Prize for 2011 was Andrea Molesini's historical novel *Non tutti i bastardi sono di Vienna* (2010). A magisterially written war bildungsroman, it narrated the coming-of-age of an aristocratic boy in occupied Veneto after the 1917 Battle of Caporetto. After the family villa is requisitioned by the enemy, Paolo, a prisoner in his own home, finds a path to dignity by becoming a spy against the enemy army. Eight stories set in the provincial Sicilian town of Vigata made up Andrea Camilleri's *Gran circo Taddei e altre storie di Vigàta*. The stories, set during the years between the rise of Benito Mussolini and the '60s, combined elements in the Boccaccian tradition of eroticism, wit, and practical jokes with characteristics of commedia dell'arte.

The protagonist of Marco Malvaldi's mystery novel *Odore di chiuso* was the historical figure Pellegrino Artusi, author of the celebrated cookbook *La scienza in cucina e l'arte di mangiar bene* (1891). The novel portrayed the decline of an aristocratic family, taken aback by the transformations in power relations imposed by the newly unified state of Italy. The beginning of the post-unitarian era was also the background for Giuseppina Torregrossa's novel *Manna e miele, ferro e fuoco*. Romilda—

the daughter of a master of the art of harvesting manna and a bee breeder—is herself gifted with a power to enchant humans and insects. She comes of age in a Sicily that is undergoing deep changes following social and political upheavals. In order to gain control of her spiritual gifts, fully develop her femininity, and achieve emancipation, she must endure the hardships of a repressive marriage.

Several other works of 2011 revolved around female protagonists. Simonetta Agnello Hornby's *Un filo d'olio* was an autobiographical account structured around the leitmotif of family cooking and Sicilian peasant culture. The author recounted her golden childhood, growing up, summer after summer, in her family's country villa and farm. In describing the rituals of a family of the Sicilian landed aristocracy, its close interaction with the peasants, and the many shared traditions, Agnello Hornby composed a complex portrait of post-World War II rural Sicily. Another woman from southern Italy, Mimì Orlando, was the protagonist of Mario Desiati's novel *Ternitti* (the word is a Pugliese dialectal variation of the term Eternit). In Mimì, Desiati presented the free-spirited and strong-willed daughter of immigrants who worked for several years in an Eternit fibre cement factory in Switzerland. Mimì returns to her native Puglia, and through her vicissitudes—her commitment to fighting for the rights of returning workers affected by asbestos-related illnesses and of her co-workers threatened by their employer's plan to relocate production in eastern Europe—Desiati gave a snapshot of contemporary Puglia: a tourist mecca, a land of ancient traditions, an industrialized territory affected by globalization, and a society deeply marked by the tragic consequences of emigration.

After losing her mother at age six, Mandorla—the protagonist of Chiara Gamberale's novel *Le luci nelle case degli altri*—is raised by the tenants of an apartment building in a Roman suburb. As she matures, moving from one household to the other, from ground to top floor, the secret lives of others are revealed through Mandorla's naive and curious gaze. Michela Murgia dedicated to contemporary women her theological essay on the myth of the Virgin Mary, *Ave Mary e la Chiesa inventò la donna*. Murgia, herself a theologian, drew attention to the passive role of women in the Christian tradition. Elena Loewenthal spent more than a year volunteering at Italian health facilities to understand how illness affects human existence. She wrote of this experience in *La vita è una prova d'orchestra*, which described illness from the point of view of patients and their loved ones, an unconventional perspective on the subject. Fulvio Ervas's *L'amore è idrosolubile* was a mystery novel with a comedic twist. Through the multicultural gaze of a half-Persian police inspector and through the diary of the crime victim (an unconventional travel agent with a special gift for portraying her lovers' idiosyncrasies), the productive and yet provincial Italian northeast was revealed as a complex social fabric made up of unscrupulous entrepreneurs, exploited immigrants, depraved professionals, single mothers, disillusioned spinsters, and troubled teenagers. Giulia and Camilla, the protagonists of Enzo Fileno Carabba's noir, grotesque, and surreal novel *Con un poco di zucchero*, are representatives of the "threatened species" of old Florentine aristocracy. They lack an ethical sense, and the only consciousness they have is the one of their class, while the values they cherish are elegance and each other's friendship. By following them in their adventurous, exhilarating endeavours, the reader was transported to a fantastic and yet realistic Florence. Edoardo Nesi won the Strega Prize with his book *Storia della mia gente* (2010), which stood midway between autobiography and economics essay. It analyzed how globalization affected small- and medium-sized enterprises in the textile city of Prato. Finally, on a sad note, the year also saw the passing of Andrea Zanzotto, one of Italy's greatest and most acclaimed contemporary poets. (*See* OBITUARIES.) (CRISTINA GRAGNANI)

The Strega Prize was awarded to Italian novelist, translator, and filmmaker Edoardo Nesi for his book Storia della mia gente *(2010).*

Alberto Cristofari—A3/Contrasto/Redux

SPANISH

Spain. Universal human emotions and, as in several past years, Spain's recent history were common themes in Spanish literature of 2011. Unsatisfied, hidden, or forbidden wishes were the connecting thread of Marina Mayoral's *Deseos*, which narrated the lives of several characters tormented by wishes that they dared not act on or secrets they kept locked in their memories. *Los enamoramientos* by Javier Marías reflected on the condition known as infatuation, which is generally considered to be positive and sometimes redeeming but could produce bad and even evil behaviour as well as noble and selfless actions. Luis Mateo Díez's *Pájaro sin vuelo* traced an unforgettable day when Ismael Cieza's fragile will was forced to confront the complex contradictions of his life and the shirked responsibilities of his past; the reader was presented with a life conditioned by irresolution in which feelings and ideas were constantly at war.

Several books relating to the Spanish Civil War and its aftermath were also published. Raúl del Pozo's *El reclamo*, which was awarded the Primavera Prize, told the story of a former guerrilla fighter, or maquis, living in exile in South America on the banks of the Paraná River who is asked by an American historian for help investigating the maquis that remained in Spain after the Civil War. Another novel on that period was crime novelist Alicia Giménez Bartlett's *Donde nadie te encuentre*, which took the Nadal Prize. It was based on the true life of a mysterious figure, Teresa Pla Meseguer, who joined the maquis after being humiliated by the Guardia Civil. In the spy novel *Operación Gladio*, Benjamín Prado guided the reader through Spain's devious path filled with conquests and renunciations, historical agreements and shameful pacts, during the Transition, as the period from dictatorship to democracy is known. Rafael Reig's *Todo está perdonado* depicted the postwar period in both a realistic and an ironic light.

Adventure, mystery, and emotion are the predominant elements of *El prisionero del cielo* by Carlos Ruiz Zafón, third in the author's Cemetery of Forgotten Books series set in Barcelona of the 1940s and '50s.

The Planeta Prize went to Javier Moro for his novel *El imperio eres tú*, about the first emperor of Brazil, Dom Pedro I, who supported the nationalist cause against Portugal's imperial power. The Colombian writer Juan Gabriel Vásquez received Spain's Alfaguara Prize for his work *El ruido de las cosas al caer*, written under the pseudonym Raúl K. Fen. The novel begins with the escape and hunting of a hippopotamus from the exotic zoo kept by Colombian drug kingpin Pablo Escobar.

The 2011 National Prize for Narrative was awarded to Marcos Giralt Torrente for his *Tiempo de vida* (2010), and the National Prize for Poetry went to Francisca Aguirre for her *Historia de una anatomía* (2010).

The most renowned Spanish-language literary prize, the Cervantes Prize, was awarded to Chilean poet and mathematician Nicanor Parra.

(VERÓNICA ESTEBAN)

Latin America. In 2011 Colombian author Juan Gabriel Vásquez received the Alfaguara award for his novel *El ruido de las cosas al caer*. When the protagonist of that work witnesses the murder of a circumstantial friend by hired assassins, his life is shattered by the experience. The narrative reflects Colombian life during the late 1970s, when drug trafficking was pervasive and any sense of the ordinary was obliterated by violence and fear.

Colombian writer Juan Gabriel Vásquez won the Alfaguara award for El ruido de las cosas al caer, *his novel about life in the violent drug-trafficking world of 1970s Colombia.*

Alberto Estevez—EPA/Landov

Los días del arcoíris, by Chilean author Antonio Skármeta, was awarded the Premio Planeta-Casamérica. In the novel the opposition to Gen. Augusto Pinochet devises a means of winning the 1988 referendum on the dictatorship. The rainbow (*arcoíris*) of the title was a symbol of hope and also reflected the colours of the political coalition that eventually won the referendum. The narration depicts a hard reality with good humour and cheerfulness.

In his novel *Hotel DF* (2010), Mexican writer Guillermo Fadanelli presented a microcosm of the Federal District (D.F.) of Mexico. The novel cast a caustic and despairing look at a group of Mexican hotel residents who openly pursue lives of criminality that include illegal dealings, notably in drugs, for individual gain. The narrator is part of the reality depicted, and at times he uses black humour to express his pain for the city he both loves and hates.

Formas de volver a casa, by Chilean Alejandro Zambra, had a postmodern structure: history and fiction were deliberately confused; the narrative perspectives were mixed; and narrator, author, and character seemed to merge. The novel was clear, however, in its criticism of the Pinochet dictatorship as well as of Chile's transitional governments. The impotence and failure depicted in the novel's social and political reality also had an impact on the narration's form and content.

Another novel that mixed fiction and historical fact, this time in an autobiographical key, was *Entre dos aguas* (2010), by Colombian Plinio Apuleyo Mendoza. The story was set in Paris, Rome, and Bogotá, all cities in which the author had lived. The protagonist returns to Colombia when he learns that his brother, a colonel in the Colombian army, has committed suicide. Trying to understand his brother's death, he encounters violence and corruption wherever he goes.

In *La muerte de Montaigne*, Chilean author Jorge Edwards selected scenes from the life of Michel de Montaigne and showed a fascination with his character that he effortlessly transmitted to the reader. Montaigne wrote that he himself was the topic of his *Essays*, and the narrator of Edwards's novel, who identifies with Montaigne, mixes his character's and his own autobiographical experiences. Montaigne lived in dangerous times, but he managed to avoid involvement in wars and intrigues.

In his novel *La fugitiva*, Nicaraguan Sergio Ramírez presented another fusion of fiction and biography. Three female narrative voices tell the story of a fictional Costa Rican novelist, Amanda Solano, who represents (the author informs the reader) the real-life writer Yolanda Oreamuno. Unconventional and defiant, Oreamuno rejected the bourgeois traditions of her times and her country and led a stormy, tormented, and peripatetic life. The novel offers an ample view of life in each of the Central American countries in which this singular woman lived.

La vida privada, by the Argentine Rodolfo Rabanal, was a literary experiment: the author avoided traditional narrative conventions in his depiction of space, time, and character. His impersonal narrator, called "the one who perceives," remained without a name and, but for a few personal experiences he relates, almost unknown to the reader. Using these techniques, the author associated this novel with the so-called *novela de la mirada* or *nouveau roman*. During a hot summer the "perceiver" contemplates daily life from his balcony in Buenos Aires. From time to time, images of the past and images of the narrator's childhood neighbourhood are superposed on the perceived reality.

Betibú, by Argentine author Claudia Piñeiro, was an ambitious work that went beyond the usual limits of the detective novel. It centred on two journalists and a writer nicknamed Betibú, who are forced to confront, at their own risk, the power of political pressure and corruption, and they agonize over the best way to convey to their readers the truth about a series of murders in a high-class neighbourhood. The novel succeeds in cleverly showing some of the conflicts between private and public language and between journalism and political power.

Leonora, by Mexican author Elena Poniatowska, was yet another example of the blending of history and fiction. The book, a novelized biography of English-born Mexican painter and writer Leonora Carrington (*see* OBITUARIES), was awarded the Premio Biblioteca Breve. The narrative depicts Carrington's life among her lovers and friends in Italy and Spain and later in Mexico and the United States, where the Surrealists took refuge during World War II.

Colombian Darío Jaramillo won the José María de Pereda Award with his short novel *Historia de Simona*. The work was exceptional for the beauty of its language—a quality not surprising to readers of Jaramillo's poetry. It relates the story of a passionate love affair between a young man of 21 and a sophisticated woman 21 years his senior. The city of Bogotá provided the setting for the story, but it was not part of the story, because the lovers were too obsessed with themselves to look at their surroundings. *Historia de Simona* was a rare example of a commonplace topic transformed into a masterpiece.

Two monumental figures in Latin American letters died during the year. Chilean poet Gonzalo Rojas and Ernesto Sábato both left the scene. (*See* OBITUARIES.) (LEDA SCHIAVO)

PORTUGUESE

Portugal. In 2011, as in several previous years, much of Portuguese fiction addressed the political and social transformations of the 1970s and 1980s, examining the end of empire and the transition to democracy. Dulce Maria Cardoso's novel *O retorno* received much more media and critical attention than had her earlier works *Os meus sentimentos* (2005) and *O chão dos pardais* (2009), despite their having been awarded literary prizes of, respectively, the European Union and the Portuguese PEN Club in 2009. The narrator of *O retorno* was a troubled teenage boy torn between the cultures of Luanda and Lisbon at the time of the mass exodus of Portuguese colonists from Angola—a social and cultural phenomenon known as the *retornados*—shortly before that country's independence in 1975. Cardoso tried to distinguish her book from Isabela Figueiredo's acclaimed *Caderno de memórias coloniais* (2009), also about the decolonization of Lusophone Africa in the 1970s, stating in a TV interview that her own work was neither autobiography nor therapeutically oriented.

Portugal's most internationally acclaimed living author, António Lobo Antunes, who worked as a military doctor in Angola in the 1970s, also tackled the end-of-empire subject in his latest novel, *Comissão das lágrimas*; the title evoked a postindependence Angolan tribunal that was responsible for the summary sentencing of thousands of citizens in 1977. Another major novelist, Lídia Jorge, published her 10th novel, *A noite das mulheres cantoras*. Setting her narrative between the 1980s and the present, Jorge dealt with postimperial remembrance by way of a monologue about the perils of success and stardom in Portugal's musical milieu. Another novel dealing with recent history was Pedro Rosa Mendes's *Peregrinação de Enmanuel Jhesus* (2010), a fictionalized work of journalism that took place in East Timor. About José Saramago's *Claraboia*, written in the 1950s and rejected by publishers at that time, critic Inês Pedrosa wrote in the *O Estado de São Paulo* that "the repeated references to the 'international crisis' link this novel to our days in a strangely prophetic way." Other novels of interest were Mário de Carvalho's *Quando o diabo reza*, Rui Zink's *O amante é sempre o último a saber*, and Maria Teresa Horta's *As luzes de Leonor*.

Several biographies were also published in 2011, notably two volumes on Portuguese writers—the magisterial António Mega Ferreira's portrait of José Agostinho de Macedo, *Macedo: uma biografia da infâmia*, and João Pedro George's *Puta que os pariu!: a biografia de Luiz Pacheco*. In the realm of poetry, acclaimed author Ana Luísa Amaral published a new collection entitled *Vozes*, and Margarida Vale de Gato's *Mulher ao mar* (2010) was praised as the best first collection by a female poet in a few decades. (VICTOR K. MENDES)

Brazil. Brazilian publishers brought out several noteworthy books in 2011. One of these, *Toupeira: a história do assalto ao Banco Central*, by lawyer and former police investigator Roger Franchini, fictionalized the 2005 real-life bank heist of 170 million reais (about $100 million) from the Banco Central de Fortaleza, Ceará. On a different note, writer and editor Nelson de Oliveira published *Geração Zero Zero: fricções em rede*, an anthology of short stories by 21 young writers who had garnered fame in the first decade of the 21st century and had published at least two books. Oliveira himself was awarded a Cuban Casa de las Américas prize for his 2010 novel *Poeira: demônios e maldições*, a work of science fiction set in a futuristic city. *Antes das primeiras estórias* collected for the first time some of the early short stories (1929–30) of João Guimarães Rosa.

In a version of *cordel* literature ("literature on a string"), Moreira de Acopiara's *Colcha de retalhos* told the story of the Alvorada family, a tale that paralleled that of the author's own life. The International Year of African Descent was launched in honour of Brazil's most widely known and respected novelist, Joaquim Maria Machado de Assis.

Two notable Brazilian cultural figures, artist and activist Abdias do Nascimento and writer Moacyr Scliar, died in 2011. (*See* OBITUARIES.) Among his many other activities, Nascimento in 1944 founded the Black Experimental Theatre in Rio de Janeiro to celebrate Afro-Brazilian culture and to train black actors. During the following 60 years, he became a preeminent defender and promoter of black culture in Brazil through his writings, paintings, and lectures both in Brazil and abroad. He also established Ipeafro, the Rio-based Afro-Brazilian Studies and Research Institute, which remained a vital centre. Also an outsider of sorts, Scliar wrote novels and short fiction that examined through allegories and from a Jewish perspective the questions of Brazilian identity. His book *O centauro no jardim* (1980; *The Centaur in the Garden*, 1984), for example, was the tale of Guedali Tratskovsky, born a centaur to his immigrant Russian Jewish parents in Rio Grande do Sul, the southernmost state of Brazil. In this first work of fiction to confront Jewish immigration to Brazil, Scliar sought to reconcile intimate Jewish life (e.g., eating gefilte fish and observing Shabbat) with the realities of Brazilian street life (e.g., playing football [soccer] and dancing the samba).

(IRWIN STERN)

RUSSIAN

In 2011 the competition continued between the highly consolidated large publishing houses, with an orientation toward mass-market fiction, and the smaller publishers, known as defenders of a more "elitist" conception of Russian literature. *Uroki russkogo* ("Russian Lessons"), an important series launched by KoLibri in 2010 with works by Anatoly Gavrilov, Vladislav Otroshchenko, and Oleg Zobern, ceased publication in 2011 owing to losses. Before doing so, however, it managed to release books by Nikolay Baytov and others. Perhaps the most significant publication in the series was Denis Osokin's *Ovsyanki* ("Yellowhammers" [a type of bird]), a story collection and his second published book. Osokin was generally regarded as one of the most talented discoveries of the 21st century and was already well known because of the film adaptations that had been made of several of his stories, including *Ovsyanki* (2010). Osokin's work was marked by an intense sensuality, a masterly style, and a subject matter that to many Russian readers was exotic: the contemporary survivors of the ancient Finno-Ugric and Turkic cultures of the Volga River (Os-

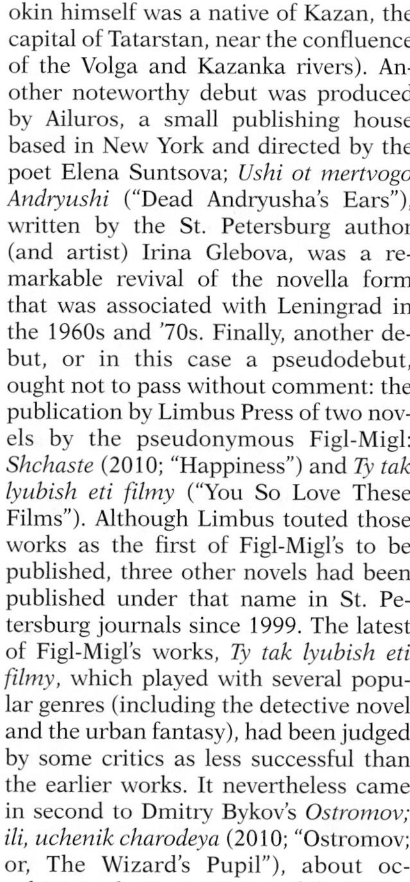

okin himself was a native of Kazan, the capital of Tatarstan, near the confluence of the Volga and Kazanka rivers). Another noteworthy debut was produced by Ailuros, a small publishing house based in New York and directed by the poet Elena Suntsova; *Ushi ot mertvogo Andryushi* ("Dead Andryusha's Ears"), written by the St. Petersburg author (and artist) Irina Glebova, was a remarkable revival of the novella form that was associated with Leningrad in the 1960s and '70s. Finally, another debut, or in this case a pseudodebut, ought not to pass without comment: the publication by Limbus Press of two novels by the pseudonymous Figl-Migl: *Shchaste* (2010; "Happiness") and *Ty tak lyubish eti filmy* ("You So Love These Films"). Although Limbus touted those works as the first of Figl-Migl's to be published, three other novels had been published under that name in St. Petersburg journals since 1999. The latest of Figl-Migl's works, *Ty tak lyubish eti filmy*, which played with several popular genres (including the detective novel and the urban fantasy), had been judged by some critics as less successful than the earlier works. It nevertheless came in second to Dmitry Bykov's *Ostromov; ili, uchenik charodeya* (2010; "Ostromov; or, The Wizard's Pupil"), about occultists in the Soviet Union of the 1920s, for the 2011 National Bestseller Prize.

Both the National Bestseller and the Russian Booker committees decided in 2011 to award a prize for the best work of the previous 10 years. The National Bestseller awarded its prize to Zakhar Prilepin for his 2007 *Grekh* ("Sin"). Prilepin's work, intensely emotional and politically radical (he was a member of the outlawed National Bolshevik Party, although this did not prevent him from participating in Kremlin receptions for leading cultural figures), had long been the object of critical controversy; some saw his work as an eloquent expression of the times, whereas others saw it as aesthetically primitive. The 2011 Russian Booker was awarded only for the achievement of the decade. Initially there was strong support for Ruben David Gonsales Gallego, whose *Beloe na chernom* (2002; *White on Black*, 2006) had won the Russian Booker in 2003. In his book Gallego, a Russian of Spanish and Venezuelan extraction, described his experiences of having been disabled from birth and orphaned early in childhood. In 2011 he was critically injured in an accident in Washington, D.C. (where he lived). That circumstance provoked a flurry of letters calling for him

Igor Kubedinov—Itar-Tass/Landov

Russian author Zakhar Prilepin took the National Bestseller Prize for his novel Grekh *(2007; "Sin").*

to be awarded the Russian Booker of the Decade. When he regained consciousness, however, Gallego requested instead that he be put on the panel that determined the winner. The short list included Oleg Pavlov's 2002 Booker winner *Karagandinskiye devyatiny; ili, povest poslednikh dney* ("Karaganda Commemorations; or, A Tale of the Last Days"), Zakhar Prilepin's 2006 finalist *Sankya*, Roman Senchin's 2009 finalist *Yeltyshevy* ("The Yeltyshevs"), Lyudmila Ulitskaya's 2007 finalist *Daniel Shtayn, perevodchik* (*Daniel Stein, Interpreter*, 2011), and Aleksandr Chudakov's 2001 finalist *Lozhitsya mgla na staryye stupeni* (*A Gloom Is Cast upon the Ancient Steps*, 2004–). Chudakov was the winner.

The 2010 Andrey Bely Prize in poetry was awarded to Sergey Stratanovsky, a leading poet of the Leningrad underground of the 1970s and '80s; to Anatoly Gavrilov for his minimalist prose; to the literary scholar Lyudmila Zubova for her studies of the language of contemporary Russian poetry; to Aleksey Prokopiev, a gifted translator of German Expressionist works; and to the directors of two publishing houses: Yevgeny Kolchuzhin of Vodoley and Sergey Kudryavtsev of Giley, whose houses published the collected works of two very talented deceased contemporary poets, Sergey Petrov (Vodoley) and Gennady Aygi (Giley).

The Russian Prize, given to Russian-language writers living abroad, was awarded in 2011 to, among others, the 75-year-old poet and human rights activist Natalya Gorbanevskaya. That award and her recent books bore witness to a burst of creative energy not usually associated with poets of advanced age. The Debut Prize for young writers underwent a change of rules in 2011 that extended the age limit from 25 to 35. As a result, the nominees included many mature and well-established writers.

Among new books of poetry for 2011 was a posthumous title from Elena Shvarts, *Pereletnaya ptitsa* ("The Migratory Bird"). Significant new works of poetry came from Oleg Yuryev, who lived in Frankfurt am Main, Ger.; Aleksandr Belyakov from Yaroslavl; Aleksey Porvin from St. Petersburg; Yekaterina Simonova from the Ural city of Nizhny Tagil; Polina Barskova, who taught at Hampshire College, Amherst, Mass.; Marianna Geyde, who lived in Moscow; Andrey Polyakov from the Crimea; and Ilya Rissenberg of Kharkiv, Ukr. The geographic diversity of the Russian muse was a fundamental sign of the times. Another such sign was the gradual loss of standing of the old-guard "thick journals" and their replacement by Web-based publications.

(VALERY SHUBINSKY)

PERSIAN

In Iran old tensions between the state censorship apparatus, private publishing enterprises, and the reading public escalated in 2011, with the result that while fewer new titles appeared on the market, more copies of previously published literary works were issued, read, and reviewed. Meanwhile, state production of literature and sponsorship of academic literary studies, particularly in relatively safe areas such as children's literature, took new strides. Shiraz University, which in recent years had emerged as a prominent centre for the study of children's literature, in May hosted a conference on the subject and in April and September published two more issues of the *Journal of Iranian Children's Literature Studies*, launched in 2010.

The perennial tug of war between the Ministry of Culture and Islamic Guidance and Iran's publishers reached new heights in August when a brawl over a few lines in a classic epic poem resulted in baseless reports, fanned by the intellectual opposition both in Iran and abroad, that Persian classics were now fair game for the censors of the Islamic Republic.

Muṣṭafā Mastur's *Tehrān dar ba'd az ẓuhr* ("Tehran in the Afternoon"), a collection of six short stories revolving around women, love, and prostitution first published in late 2010, became the latest sensation in prose fiction, going through a dozen editions in less than a year. Maziar Ouliaeinia's *Hindisah-yi jahān-i darun* ("The Geometry of the World Within"), also published in 2010 in Esfahan, became one of the most popular poetry collections of the year. Meanwhile, among the works published in 2011, the urge to revisit the Iran-Iraq War of the 1980s found contemporary expression in Kāmrān Muḥammadī's novel, *Ān jā kih barfhā āb namīshavand* ("Where Snows Will Not Melt"), conceived as the first volume of a trilogy. Muḥammadī's book attracted much attention on the part of a public eager to develop new perspectives on that war.

Veteran novelist Mahmoud Dowlatabadi's latest major work, "Zaval-i sarhang," which in Iran was placed on the list of "unpublishable books," first appeared in German as *Der Colonel* (2009; *The Colonel*, 2011). It was one of 12 novels long-listed for the Man Asian Literary Prize. On a more sombre note, the death in March of internationally recognized textual scholar Iraj Afshar in Tehran was the first of several literary losses in 2011.

(AHMAD KARIMI-HAKKAK)

ARABIC

The events of the Arab Spring—which had its roots in Tunisia, where protests began in December 2010, and subsequently spread throughout the Arab countries of the Middle East and North Africa—were central to the literature of the Arab world in 2011. Oral poetry was the literary form that most speedily addressed those events; much of it was spontaneously composed in Cairo's Tahrir Square, which was the centre of the uprising in Egypt. The most prominent poem in colloquial Arabic (*al-ʿammiyyah*) was ʿAbd al-Raḥmān Abnūdī's "Lissa al-nizām mā saqatch/sa'atch" ("The System Has Not Fallen Yet"), in which he denounced the abuses of the regime of Hosni Mubarak—who stepped down from the presidency of Egypt in February 2011—and welcomed the young revolution. The Egyptian Fārūq Juwaydah attacked all oppressive leaders in his poem "Ilā kull jallad taghā" ("To Every Tyrannical Executioner") and praised the revolutionaries of the Arab Spring. The events in Tunisia that came to be known as the Jasmine Revolution prompted Tunisian poet Tahar Bakri to change the title of his most-recent collection of verse from *Chants pour la Tunisie* to *Je te nomme Tunisie*. His poems are filled with a nostalgic love for his country of origin and with references to the bloody events of the revolution.

Other works that engaged with the uprising in Egypt included *Li-kull arḍ mīlād: ayyām al-Taḥrīr* ("Every Land Has a Birth: The Days of Tahrir"), in which the novelist Ibrāhīm ʿAbd al-Majīd recorded his personal experiences among the demonstrators. In his novel *Ajniḥat al-farāshah* ("The Wings of the Butterfly"), Egyptian writer Muḥammad Salmāwī denounced the political corruption in Egypt that contributed to the anger underlying the uprising.

Multifaceted Moroccan French writer Tahar Ben Jelloun managed to respond quickly to the events of the Arab Spring, constructing his short novel *Par le feu* around his imagining of the Tunisian street vendor Mohamed Bouazizi's family life and the circumstances that led to Bouazizi's self-immolation, which resulted in the Jasmine Revolution. Ben Jelloun also analyzed the Arab Spring in his long essay *L'Étincelle*.

Elsewhere, writers used their books to defend the causes that had become their raison d'être. In *Ḥubbī al-awwal* ("My First Love"), a novel released at the end of 2010 that centres on the armed struggle of the Palestinians and the role of Palestinian Liberation Organization official Fayṣal ibn ʿAbd al-Qādir al-Ḥusaynī within it, Saḥar Khalīfah continued to tell the life story of the narrator of her previous novel *Aṣl wa faṣl* (2009; "Of Noble Origin"). Writing from Haifa, Israel, Salmān Nāṭūr offered in his novel *Hiya, anā wa-al-kharīf* ("She, Me, and the Autumn") a symbolic account of what he depicted as the slow usurpation of Palestinian heritage in Israel. Francophone Algerian writer Yasmina Khadra set the action of his novel *L'Équation africaine* in Africa, specifically in Somalia and Darfur, in an effort to understand the psychology of Somali pirates and their brutal acts. In *Al-Jalīd* ("Ice"), Egyptian author Ṣunʿ Allāh Ibrāhīm traveled back in time to 1973 and recorded the life of a graduate student in the Soviet Union. His novel had a bold narrative style that resembles a personal journal while using techniques associated with documentary filmmaking.

Dec. 11, 2011, was the 100th anniversary of the birth of Egyptian novelist Naguib Mahfouz, who was the first Arabic writer to win the Nobel Prize for Literature. Plans to commemorate the event were reduced to a modest size because of political conditions, but the Egyptian press and numerous cultural organizations still celebrated the life and works of Mahfouz, who died in 2006.

Moroccan novelist Muḥammad Ashʿarī was one of two recipients of the 2011 International Prize for Arabic Fiction—the so-called Arabic Booker—with *Al-Qaws wa al-farāshah* (2010; "The Arch and the Butterfly"). The other recipient, Rajāʾ ʿĀlim of Saudi Arabia, became the first woman to win the prize, for her novel *Ṭawq al-ḥamām* (2010; "The Dove's Necklace"), which revolves around a crime committed in Mecca.

In Kuwait the shaky literary scene was somewhat stirred by the Arab Spring, though the regime maintained its control over the country. Kuwaiti critic and writer Fahd Tawfīq al-Hindāl blamed the weakness of cultural activities in his country on the lack of support from the country's cultural institutions, the subjugation of culture to politics, and a pervasive consumerism. There were similar concerns among Jordanian intellectuals, who called for governmental transparency, freedom, and the end of the status quo. Although neither Kuwait nor Jordan saw the violent protests that other countries did, the engagement of their writers with the concerns of the Arab Spring demonstrated the strong sense of community generated among Arabs. They increased their pan-Arab meetings and set plans for sustained cooperation in the future.

Prominent among the writers who died in 2011 were Khayrī Shalabī of Egypt and ʿAbd Allāh Rakībī of Algeria.

(AIDA A. BAMIA)

CHINESE

The most eye-catching event in Chinese literature in 2011 was the awarding of the Mao Dun Literature Prize, which was founded in 1982 and was the most important national prize for fiction written in Chinese. The prize had been bestowed only seven times previously. In 2011 it was shared by five writers: Zhang Wei, Liu Xinglong, Bi Feiyu, Mo Yan, and Liu Zhenyun.

Zhang's novel *Ni zai gaoyuan* ("You on the Plateau"), as published in 2010, ran to 10 volumes and consisted of 4.5 million Chinese characters, which placed it among the longest contemporary novels in the world. Zhang first began publishing the material that became *Ni zai gaoyuan* in the 1990s. Zhang's novel sharply criticizes the modernization that deeply changed rural China over the past century. It presents a sadly lyrical description of the village life that the Chinese people have lost.

Liu Xinglong received a share of the Mao Dun Prize for *Tian xingzhe* (2009; "Skywalker"), a novel that describes the hard life of the young teacher Zhang Yingcai and his colleagues, who struggle to educate the children of their village while they suffer from poor material conditions—such as a lack of classrooms, nonexistent books, and low wages—as well as the corruption of local officials. Among the novelists born in the 1960s, Bi was probably the most popular in mainland China. The novel for which he received the prize, *Tuina* (2008; "Massage"), details the darkness as well as the brightness in the inner world of several blind massage therapists who tenaciously seek dignity and love in the midst of their often-painful lives.

Mo and Liu Zhenyun were recognized for their novels *Wa* (2009; "Frog") and *Yi ju ding yiwan ju* (2009; "One Sentence Worth Ten Thousand"), respectively. Both books were unique in style. *Wa* tells bitter stories about the one-child policy and other family-planning programs undertaken by the Chinese government since the 1960s, and *Yi ju ding yiwan ju* considers the subject of a uniquely Chinese form of loneliness and friendship. (WANG XIAOMING)

Winners of the Mao Dun Prize received exposure to an audience beyond China by way of a new English-language version of *Renmin wenxue* ("People's Literature"), the first periodical founded in the People's Republic, in which selections from fiction and nonfiction were published. The release in late 2011 of the first volume of the new magazine, called *Pathlight: New Chinese Writing* and overseen by the editor in chief of *Renmin wenxue*, marked a significant effort by one of China's most prestigious publications to raise worldwide awareness of contemporary Chinese writing.

Artist and writer Mu Xin, who had lived for more than two decades in the U.S., died in his place of birth, Wuzhen, in 2011. He was born Sun Pu in 1927 and grew up in a wealthy family that provided him a classical Chinese education; he also had early exposure to Western literature. He was a prolific writer and painter, but his works were destroyed in 1966, at the start of the Cultural Revolution. He was subsequently jailed and held under house arrest multiple times, and he left China in 1982. During his time in the U.S., Mu Xin published a wide range of poetry and prose in Chinese that found a small but devoted audience. He returned to China in 2006. His stories were collected in English translation for the first time in *An Empty Room* (2011).

(EB ED.)

JAPANESE

Though the Great Tohoku Earthquake of March 11, 2011, and its aftermath were not depicted in any of the year's major literary works in Japanese, the disaster made clear the power of the printed word in the aftermath of calamity. In spite of another year in which the Japanese publishing industry as a whole contracted, sales of printed publications increased at many bookstores in the region most affected by the earthquake, where people were seeking books that provided both spiritual and practical remedies. (*See* Special Report on page 176.)

The committee responsible for awarding the Akutagawa Prize, presented twice a year for the best work of fiction by a promising Japanese writer, declined in July to select the year's first winner. Amy Yamada, one of the judges, commented that the committee had tried hard to select a winner but found none deserving of the prize. Some thought that the judges might have set a particularly—and unachievably—high standard in the hopes of supplying a piece of good news via the announcement of a new writer amid the gloom of the disaster.

Setsuko Tsumura, who won the year's Yasunari Kawabata Prize with her short story "Ikyō" ("A Foreign Land," which appeared in the January issue of the literary magazine *Bungakukai*), responded directly to the earthquake; she donated the royalties from sales of a work by her deceased husband, Akira Yoshimura, to relief efforts. Yoshimura's book on historical tsunamis, originally published in 1970 and subsequently reissued as *Sanriku kaigan ōtsunami* ("The Sanriku Coast Giant Tsunamis"), was widely reread in 2011 after the events of March 11.

In January the second Akutagawa Prize of 2010 was announced. It went to two contrasting works: *Kikotowa*, a story by Mariko Asabuki about the reunion of two women, Kiko and Towako, which was first published in the September 2010 issue of *Shinchō*, and Kenta Nishimura's story about a miserable day labourer, *Kueki ressha* ("Labour Train"), which first appeared in the December 2010 issue of *Shinchō*.

Kyodo/Landov

Japanese writer Mariko Asabuki received an Akutagawa Prize for her novel Kikotowa, *which explored the memories and dreams of two women reunited after 25 years.*

Among the remarkable literary works of 2011 were another book by Tsumura, *Kōbai* ("Red Blossomed Plum Tree"), about her last days with Yoshimura; Teru Miyamoto's family chronicle *Jiu no oto* ("The Sound of a Blessed Rain"); and two collections of essays by Haruki Murakami, *Zatsubunshū* ("Miscellaneous Writings") and *Ōkina kabu muzukashii abokado* ("A Big Turnip, a Difficult Avocado").

Tokuya Higashigawa won the Booksellers Award, an annual prize designating the best book as selected by sales clerks of Japanese bookstores, for his *Nazotoki wa dinā no ato de* (2010; "Let's Solve a Riddle After the Dinner"). Natsuo Kirino's *Nanika aru* (2010; "There Is Something") received the Yomiuri Prize for Literature. The Kenzaburō Ōe Prize was awarded to Tomoyuki Hoshino's *Ore ore* (2010; "It's Me, It's Me"), and Mayumi Inaba received the Tanizaki Prize for *Hantō e* ("To the Peninsula").

Deaths in 2011 included science-fiction author Sakyo Komatsu, in July, and essayist, novelist, and psychiatrist Morio Kita (pen name of Sokichi Saitō), in October. Some of Komatsu's final writings appeared in *San ichiichi no mirai* ("For the Future After March 11"). Kita, a winner of the Akutagawa Prize, was famous for his humorous Dokutoru Manbō ("Doctor Sunfish") series.

(YOSHIHIKO KAZAMARU)

Military Affairs

NATO conducted a six-month **AIR CAMPAIGN** in Libya, and the **LAST U.S. TROOPS** left Iraq. Following the **ARAB SPRING** uprisings across North Africa and the Persian Gulf, Yemen and Syria came to the brink of all-out **CIVIL WAR**. Preparations for **CYBERWAR** occupied militaries around the world. Germany abolished the **PEACETIME DRAFT**, and Australia cleared the way for **WOMEN IN COMBAT**.

In Libya a coalition of rebel groups, with crucial support from the North Atlantic Treaty Organization (NATO), overthrew the 42-year-old regime of strongman Col. Muammar al-Qaddafi (*see* OBITUARIES) in what became the bloodiest episode of the dramatic "Arab Spring" uprising against authoritarian rulers. Beginning on March 19, over 300 aircraft from NATO and allied countries bombed nearly 6,000 targets, and NATO ships intercepted over 3,000 vessels to help enforce a UN arms embargo against Qaddafi. Dubbed Operation Unified Protector, the NATO effort ended in October after 204 days. Shortly after the war Qatar admitted that it had sent hundreds of troops to support the Libyan rebels.

WMD, ARMS CONTROL, AND DISARMAMENT

The New Strategic Arms Reduction Treaty (New START) between Russia and the U.S. was ratified by Russia's Duma (parliament) in January. New START, which aimed to reduce the number of nuclear warheads owned by both sides by about 30%, had been ratified by the U.S. Senate in December 2010. Also, the Duma ratified an agreement supporting the Treaty of Pelindaba, which declared a nuclear-weapons-free zone in Africa. The only declared nuclear weapons state that had not ratified its support of the treaty was the U.S.

The last B53 thermonuclear bomb was dismantled. The B53 weighed 4,500 kg (10,000 lb) and was the most lethal weapon in the U.S. arsenal, being 600 times more destructive than the atomic bomb dropped on Hiroshima, Japan, in 1945. The B53 was first deployed at the height of the Cold War in 1962 and remained in service until 1997.

CONFLICTS

Africa. Conflict in Africa drew increasing attention from NATO countries. The U.S. constructed a secret base in Ethiopia from which it was operating Predator unmanned aerial vehicles (UAVs) as part of the campaign against radical Islamist groups in Somalia and Yemen. The U.S. also announced that it was sending about 100 soldiers to Uganda to help regional forces combat the Lord's Resistance Army, blamed for the deaths of 30,000 people during the previous 20 years.

French troops and combat aircraft helped UN peacekeepers quell civil war in Côte d'Ivoire, which erupted when forces loyal to former president Laurent Gbagbo refused to accept that he had lost the November 2010 election. Post-election violence left an estimated 3,000 people dead and 500,000 displaced.

With assistance from French military aircraft, Kenya sent hundreds of troops into neighbouring Somalia to battle al-Shabaab, a militant group with ties to the al-Qaeda terrorist organization. A 9,000-strong African Union force led by Uganda and Burundi was in Somalia supporting the weak transitional government. British Royal Marines participated in an operation in Somalia to seize a tribal leader with suspected terrorist links.

The Americas. Alfonso Cano, leader of the left-wing Revolutionary Armed Forces of Colombia (FARC), was killed in a raid in November. (*See* OBITUARIES.) Colombia's civil war had lasted more than four decades. Although weakened in recent years by a sustained government offensive, FARC rebels were still able to launch over 1,100 attacks in the first six months of 2011.

Middle East. The last contingent of U.S. troops withdrew from Iraq in December, nearly nine years after the invasion to topple Saddam Hussein. U.S. and Iraqi authorities had failed to agree

A Rafale fighter lands on the deck of the French aircraft carrier Charles de Gaulle *in March, during NATO's enforcement of a no-fly zone over Libya.*

Benoit Tessier—Reuters/Landov

on plans to keep an American military mission in Iraq past the end of the year. At the Iraq War's peak in 2007, there were 165,000 U.S. troops in Iraq.

Conflict continued between Israel and the Palestinians over the future of the Gaza Strip and the West Bank. Israel responded to frequent rocket attacks from Gaza by launching air strikes against suspected guerrilla positions.

Syrian troops backed by tanks and aircraft battled pro-democracy demonstrators across the country, resulting in thousands of casualties on both sides. In November the Free Syrian Army, composed of army defectors, attacked a military base near the capital, Damascus.

Turkey responded to an increasing number of attacks by the Kurdistan Workers' Party (PKK) by launching artillery and air strikes against separatist bases in northern Iraq. More than 40,000 people had been killed in the 27-year insurgency against the Turkish state.

Yemen teetered on the brink of civil war for much of 2011. Following violent demonstrations across the country, several senior government leaders, including Gen. Ali Mohsen al-Ahmar, commander of an armoured division based in the capital, defected to the opposition. Al-Qaeda in the Arabian Peninsula captured a city in the south and held it for four months before control was regained by government forces.

South and Central Asia. Despite the presence of more than 130,000 troops in the NATO-led International Security Assistance Force (ISAF), the number of attacks by the Taliban and other insurgent groups across Afghanistan increased. These included a 20-hour siege of the U.S. embassy and an attack on ISAF headquarters in the capital, Kabul. Canada, Denmark, and Poland all withdrew or substantially reduced the number of troops they had in ISAF.

Southeast Asia. Fighting between the Philippine armed forces and Moro Islamic Liberation Front (MILF) rebels in the country's southern islands intensified in 2011. After more than four decades of conflict, 120,000 people had been killed and two million displaced.

MILITARY TECHNOLOGY

The U.K. company BAE Systems developed a technology called ADAPTIV, which used hexagonal tiles that could change temperature to disguise a tank's infrared signature. By means of an onboard computer, ADAPTIV heated or cooled individual tiles either to hide the tank from enemy infrared sensors or to mimic the image of other objects such as a car or a pile of rocks.

China publicly revealed its first stealth fighter, the J-20, a single-seat twin-engine aircraft, bigger and heavier than Russia's new Sukhoi T-50 or the U.S. F-22 Raptor. The Russian company Concern Morinformsystem-Agat exhibited a working model of its controversial Club-K Container Missile System. The system featured ballistic missiles housed in a series of standard commercial shipping containers; the missiles could be launched discretely from nonmilitary ships, railways, and trucks. Existence of the Club-K had alarmed arms-control experts because of its ability to launch surprise attacks.

The U.S. conducted the first test flight of the Advanced Hypersonic Weapon (AHW), a new generation of nonnuclear missile with the eventual goal of being able to hit a target 6,000 km (3,700 mi) away in 35 minutes, with an accuracy of 10 m (33 ft).

ARMED FORCES AND POLITICS

Australia agreed to the basing of up to 2,500 U.S. Marines on its territory. This move was seen as an effort to help counter China's growing influence in the Asia-Pacific region.

Global economic woes squeezed military budgets. The U.K. announced cuts in the size of its army beyond those planned in a 2010 strategic review. By 2020 the regular British army would shrink from 102,000 troops to 82,000—its lowest level since the Boer War at the end of the 19th century. To help reduce its massive deficit, the U.S. government committed itself to cutting at least $450 billion from the defense budget over the next decade. NATO defense ministers approved a series of reforms to reduce the overall size of the alliance's command structure. An estimated 4,500 personnel would be eliminated from the existing pool of 13,000.

Russia purchased for €1.7 billion ($2.4 billion) two *Mistral*-class amphibious assault ships from the French company DCNS. The contract marked the first-ever sale of a major military system by a NATO member to Russia. Russia's Defense Ministry announced that it would no longer be buying the legendary Kalashnikov assault rifle, which had been in continuous production since 1947. The armed forces had huge overstocks of the weapon and wanted to acquire a new generation of small arms. Kalashnikovs, with an estimated production of over 100 million, had been the weapon of choice for armed forces and insurgent groups around the world.

The head of the Turkish armed forces, Gen. Isik Kosaner, resigned along with the heads of the army, navy, and air force to protest the arrest of several other officers accused of having plotted to undermine the government. The replacement of the four marked the first time that a civilian government in Turkey had been able to decide who would command the armed forces.

The U.S. delayed a $53 million deal to sell missiles and armoured vehicles to Bahrain until results from an investigation into alleged human rights abuses that took place during the Arab Spring uprising in February had been published. Germany's government, however, approved the controversial sale of 200 Leopard 2 tanks to Saudi Arabia, which had sent its armed forces to help Bahrain suppress pro-democracy demonstrations.

MILITARY AND SOCIETY

Acts of piracy rose to record levels in the first nine months of 2011, according to the International Maritime Bureau. It blamed Somali pirates for 56% of the 352 attacks on ships around the world. The total number of ships hijacked was reduced, however, in part because of NATO's ongoing Operation Ocean Shield, which stationed warships off the Horn of Africa.

The growing number of cyber attacks worldwide prompted the U.S. Department of Defense to reveal its strategy for defending against threats to the country's information infrastructure. Under some circumstances a computer attack would be considered an act of war, which for the first time would open the way for the U.S. to respond by using conventional military weapons. In May, Lockheed Martin, the largest U.S. defense contractor, announced that it had suffered a "significant and tenacious" cyber attack. Mitsubishi Heavy Industries, Japan's largest defense manufacturer, announced that viruses were found on more than 80 of its computers. U.S. Air Force officials admitted in October that computers used by pilots controlling the UAVs operating over war zones were infected by malware usually associated with online games. In

The Revered Last Veterans of World War I

The end of an era in U.S. history was marked on Feb. 27, 2011, when Frank Buckles, the last surviving American veteran of World War I, died at the age of 110. On May 5, just over two months later, 110-year-old British-born Claude Choules, the last known combat veteran of the Great War (1914–18) and the last man to see action in both world wars, died in Perth, Australia. (*See* OBITUARIES.)

"The war to end all wars" was triggered by the assassination on June 28, 1914, of Austrian Archduke Francis Ferdinand by a Serbian nationalist in Sarajevo, Bosnia, then part of Austria-Hungary. After more than a month of threats, ultimatums, and troop mobilizations across Europe, formal hostilities began on the night of August 3–4 when German forces crossed into Belgium. More than 65 million troops were eventually mobilized, an estimated 42.2 million from the Allied Powers—mainly the British Empire (including Great Britain, Australia, Canada, British India, New Zealand, and South Africa), Belgium, France, Greece, Italy, Japan, Montenegro, Portugal, Romania, Russia, Serbia, and the U.S.—and some 22.8 million from the Central Powers—Austria-Hungary, Germany, Bulgaria, and the Ottoman Empire. Newly developed weaponry, including machine guns and rapid-fire field artillery, took the carnage and destruction on the battlefield to unprecedented levels. Casualty figures for the war were estimated at more than 37 million, including 8.5 million dead, 21 million wounded, and 7.7 million missing or imprisoned. By the time the armistice was signed on Nov. 11, 1918, the empires of Germany, Austria-Hungary, Russia, and Ottoman Turkey had fallen; national boundaries across Europe and the Middle East had been altered; and the groundwork for World War II had been laid.

In the early 21st century, historians noted that the last members of the generation that fought World War I were more than 100 years old. In 2008 several countries marked the deaths of their own last official veterans, notably Hungary (Franz Künstler of Austria-Hungary, who died at age 107), Germany (Erich Kästner, age 107), Turkey (Yakup Satar, age 110), Ukraine/Russia (Mikhail Krichevsky, age 111), Italy (Delfino Borroni, age 110), and France, which recorded the death of 110-year-old Lazare Ponticelli, who served in both the French (1914–15) and Italian (1915–18) armies during the war. These were soon followed by the demise of Australia's last known veteran, John Campbell Ross, in 2009 at age 110 and Canada's John Babcock in 2010 at age 109. This series of deaths left only one official veteran from the Great War: 110-year-old Florence Patterson Green, who worked at a British air base after joining the Women's Royal Air Force in 1918. (MELINDA C. SHEPHERD)

March, one day after Norwegian F-16s first took part in the NATO bombing in Libya, about 100 military employees received an e-mail with an attachment containing a computer virus.

Japan deployed at least 100,000 soldiers to provide humanitarian assistance following the earthquake and tsunami that devastated the country in March. (*See* Special Report on page 176.) In addition, approximately 20,000 American troops as well as 140 aircraft and 20 ships participated in Operation Tomodachi ("Friends" in Japanese). Other countries, such as Australia, India, and South Korea, provided military aircraft and personnel to assist with rescue efforts.

Alfredo Astiz and 11 other former Argentine military and police officers were given life sentences for crimes against humanity committed during military rule in 1976–83. Brazil and Uruguay also addressed issues of human rights abuse during their military dictatorships. Brazil established a "truth and reconciliation" commission to investigate crimes committed by its former military government, and Uruguay's parliament passed legislation to revoke a military amnesty granted for crimes committed between 1973 and 1985.

Kyodo—Reuters/Landov

Soldiers in Japan's Self-Defense Force rescue a resident of Kesennuma in Miyagi prefecture after an earthquake and tsunami devastated the area in March. Within 24 hours of the disaster, the first of some 100,000 Japanese troops had been mobilized to provide supplies and search for survivors.

An appeals court in the Netherlands ruled that the Dutch state was responsible for the 1995 murder of three Muslim refugees by Serb forces during the civil war in former Yugoslavia. The refugees were under the protection of Dutch UN peacekeeping troops. The ruling reversed an earlier court decision, opening the way for compensation claims against other international peacekeeping operations.

A panel of UN experts reported an "alarming resurgence" in the global use of mercenaries in 2011. For example, the number of armed employees working for licensed private military and security companies in Iraq was about 35,000, compared with 45,000 employees in the Iraqi federal police. The panel highlighted conflicts in countries such as Iraq, Côte d'Ivoire, and Libya, where mercenaries were involved in serious human rights violations.

Germany became the latest country to abolish conscription in peacetime. The last draftees began their six months of compulsory service in January. Australia dropped its ban on women's serving in combat. It joined Canada, Israel, and New Zealand as the only countries with no restrictions on women's serving in front-line capacities. The 18-year-old "Don't Ask, Don't Tell" law, which prevented serving U.S. military personnel from disclosing that they were gay, was formally repealed. (PETER SARACINO)

Performing Arts

British and American theatre companies **MARKED** several seminal **ANNIVERSARIES** in 2011: the birth (100 years ago) of **TENNESSEE WILLIAMS**, the founding (50 years earlier) of the **ROYAL SHAKESPEARE COMPANY**, and the 10th observance of the **SEPTEMBER 11 ATTACKS**. The international music scene was dominated by **FUSION** styles that blended the modern and the traditional, while British vocalist **ADELE** vied with American pop tart **KATY PERRY** for dominance of the charts. Europe's premiere dance companies battled major budget cuts, while a number of North American troupes staged *Giselle*, savvily tapping the popular appeal of the **SUPERNATURAL**. Live **JAZZ** was heard—perhaps for the **FIRST** time—in **GAZA**, Palestine. Film director **TERRENCE MALICK** returned after a six-year absence with the award-winning *The Tree of Life*, and there were movie offerings from **MARTIN SCORSESE** and **STEVEN SPIELBERG**, among other **DELIGHTS**.

MUSIC

Classical. East met West in a moment of symbolic harmony on October 12 when the Royal Opera House of Oman opened its doors in Oman's capital city, Muscat. The building, which blended the striking architecture of the country's ancient castles with cutting-edge Western stage technology, was the first opera house to be built in the Persian Gulf.

Conductor Plácido Domingo, who led the opening-night performance of Giacomo Puccini's *Turandot*, evoked the vision of the country's leader, Sultan Qaboos bin Said, when he said that the goal of the opera house was to "show the new culture we are heading toward, from the great collections of Islam and the world cultures."

This meeting of cultures was mirrored in the various collaborations involved in the building's design, planning, and execution. Jeffrey Wheel, formerly of London's Royal Opera House at Covent Garden, served as its technical director; Italian director Franco Zeffirelli and Domingo were among its artistic advisers; and members of Washington, D.C.'s Kennedy Center for the Performing Arts supervised the opening-night festivities.

The continuing ability of classical music to transcend cultural, political, and artistic borders was highlighted throughout 2011. In August Israeli pianist-conductor Daniel Barenboim was nominated for the Nobel Prize for Peace by his native country, Argentina. Barenboim, who cofounded the West-Eastern Divan Orchestra in 1999, had during the past decade tirelessly promoted a reconciliation between Israel and its Arab neighbours via a series of concerts by the orchestra, which comprised young Arab and Israeli musicians.

Chinese American composer Zhou Long's opera *Madame White Snake* won the Pulitzer Prize for music in 2011. The work, which made its debut in February 2010 in a production by Opera Boston, was based on an ancient Chinese folk tale, and its score was an amalgam of Eastern and Western musical forms. French-born Chinese American cellist Yo-Yo Ma, whose performing career had encompassed everything from Bach cello suites to Appalachian folk songs and East-West fusions with his Silk Road Ensemble, was awarded the Presidential Medal of Freedom by U.S. Pres. Barack Obama in February and in December was named a Kennedy Center honoree.

The Philadelphia Orchestra announced in September that it would embark on a cultural exchange program with China starting in May 2012 to discover and nurture young Chinese classical musicians and composers. The Philadelphia, which nearly four decades earlier had been the first U.S. orchestra to tour communist China, also announced that it would commission a new work by a young Chinese composer to be performed as part of the program during its first year. The orchestra would also give concerts at the National Centre for the Performing Arts in Beijing and later hold a series of master classes in Shanghai, Guangzhou, and Tianjin.

Meanwhile, in June, conductor Riccardo Muti (see BIOGRAPHIES) announced that he would lead the Chicago Symphony Orchestra in the first performance by a U.S. orchestra in Russia since its previous performances in that country in 1990. The concerts, scheduled to be held in Moscow and St. Petersburg in April 2012, were a part of the yearlong "American Seasons in Russia" cultural festival sponsored by the Bilateral Presidential Commission, established by President Obama and Pres. Dmitry Medvedev of Russia.

Finally, the calamitous earthquake and tsunami that struck Japan on March 11 also had an impact on the classical-music world. The Manchester, Eng.-based BBC Philharmonic was forced to cut short its ongoing tour of the country. Subsequently, Germany's Bavarian State Orchestra canceled a scheduled tour, and Austria's Salzburg Mozarteum Orchestra called off a series of performances at the Tongyeong International Music Festival in South Korea owing to fears of radiation leaks from Japan's Fukushima nuclear power plant, which had been critically damaged in the natural disaster. While the rest of New York City's Metropolitan Opera (the Met) went on with the show in performances in Nagoya and Tokyo in May, Russian soprano Anna Netrebko and Maltese tenor Joseph Calleja refused to appear because of similar

Pete Souza—Official White House Photo

Following a ceremony on February 15 at which he received the Presidential Medal of Freedom, Chinese American cellist Yo-Yo Ma (seated, left) performs with the Marine Band String Quartet at the White House before an audience that includes Pres. Barack Obama.

concerns. But New York's Carnegie Hall pitched in to help with relief efforts. Officials of the hall announced, three days after the tsunami, that their ongoing festival of Japanese culture would be dedicated to the victims of the disaster and provided a list of relief organizations on their festival's Web site.

New music got a boost when the Santa Fe (N.M.) Opera announced its intention to produce one new opera per year for three years, beginning in 2013. The first to be announced was *Oscar*, composed by Theodore Morrison with a libretto by John Cox and based on the life of Oscar Wilde. The others were the U.S. premiere of British composer Judith Weir's *Miss Fortune* in 2014 and the 2015 debut of Pulitzer Prize-winning composer Jennifer Higdon's operatic version of the Civil War novel *Cold Mountain*, whose film adaptation, starring Jude Law, was released in 2003.

While it did not inspire a second coming of Beatlemania among critics, the debut of Sir Paul McCartney's first ballet, *Ocean's Kingdom*, in September did attract the media's attention. The work, staged by the New York City Ballet, was the result of a meeting in 2010 between the former Beatle and the company's longtime artistic leader Peter Martins. The ballet, which McCartney described as a tale of lovers caught between their opposing worlds, featured dancers representing members of a "pure" ocean kingdom and their counterparts on land, who are "sort of baddies." In addition, an album of the ballet was released in October.

The New York Philharmonic attempted to undo a cinematic wrong when in September it performed a reconstructed score of the film version of Leonard Bernstein's *West Side Story*. The film, whose score (adapted by others from the musical) Bernstein famously detested, was shown with its dialogue and singing intact, while the orchestra performed the new music.

Music and film also made news in July, when the London 2012 Festival announced a plan to commission new scores for early silent films by Sir Alfred Hitchcock. British composer Daniel Cohen was picked to score the famed director's first film, *The Pleasure Garden* (1925), and Nitin Sawhney was commissioned to provide a sound track for the 1926 thriller *The Lodger: A Story of the London Fog*. The films were being restored by the British Film Institute.

The worlds of film and music crossed in July again when orchestral scores by Oscar-winning actor Sir Anthony Hopkins were performed by the City of Birmingham (Eng.) Symphony Orchestra. The concerts, which featured Hopkins's scores for his films *August* (1996) and *Slipstream* (2007), also included excerpts from the sound tracks of two of his most celebrated films, *Remains of the Day* (1993) and *The Silence of the Lambs* (1991).

In October the Los Angeles Philharmonic and conductor Gustavo Dudamel became the stars of their own "movie" when they offered the first of their new season of live broadcasts to movie theatres from the city's Walt Disney Concert Hall. The performance, featuring works by Felix Mendelssohn, also came with backstage interviews and rehearsal videos. Dudamel and the orchestra planned another such event in Caracas in February 2012, featuring a performance of Gustav Mahler's Eighth Symphony, with 1,000 musicians taking part.

A "folk opera" based on the teenage years of former U.S. president Bill Clinton debuted in June in a production by New York's Metropolis Opera Project at the Medicine Show Theatre. *Billy Blythe*, which drew its title from the name of Clinton's biological father, followed the president-to-be during a day in the late 1950s in Hot Springs, Ark. The opera was composed by Bonnie Montgomery with libretto by Britt Barber. Montgomery noted that "[Clinton's] personality is mythical and where he came from provides the perfect mythical backdrop."

The year was not without its controversies. The same month that the Philadelphia Orchestra's cultural exchange program was unveiled, officials from the National Centre for the Performing Arts in Beijing announced the last-minute cancellation, apparently for political reasons, of *Dr. Sun Yat-sen*, an opera based on the life of China's first president. The work, by Chinese-born American composer Huang Ruo, was to have been produced by Opera Hong Kong and performed with Western instruments. Instead, the opera had its premiere in Hong Kong in October and used Chinese instruments.

In July Mikhail Arkadyev, conductor of the Pacific Symphony Orchestra in Vladivostok, Russia, was informed that his contract with the orchestra would not be renewed. Arkadyev claimed that the decision was made because of his opposition to the All-Russia People's Front, a movement affiliated with Russian Prime Minister Vladimir Putin, who was seeking a return to the country's presidency.

In Washington, D.C., National Public Radio officials announced that NPR would no longer distribute the program *World of Opera* because host Lisa Simeone had participated in a demonstration by the protest movement Occupy D.C. The show's producers at classical music station WDAV in North Carolina replied that they would take over distribution and retain Simeone as host.

Four musicians of the London Philharmonic Orchestra (LPO) were suspended in September when they protested a performance by the Israel Philharmonic Orchestra at London's Royal Albert Hall. In a media statement LPO officials said, "The LPO has no political or religious affiliations and strongly believes in the power of music to bring peace and harmony to the world, not war, terror and discord. The orchestra would never restrict the right of its players to express themselves freely; however, such expression has to be independent of the LPO itself."

In Germany, Bayreuth Festival codirectors (and half sisters) Eva Wagner-Pasquier and Katharina Wagner announced that noted film director Wim Wenders would not be leading a production of their great-grandfather Richard Wagner's *Ring* cycle in 2013. The two cited the expense of Wenders's plan to film the performances in 3-D.

The Salzburg (Austria) Easter Festival, which was rocked by allegations in 2010 that two officials of the festival had misappropriated $5 million in funds, threatened legal action against the Berlin Philharmonic Orchestra when the latter announced that it would end its more than four-decade-long association with the annual event after the 2012 festival. In May orchestra officials responded with an announcement that they were founding an Easter event of their own, to debut in 2013, at the Festspielhaus in Baden-Baden.

Another longtime musical partnership came to an end in May when French pianist Hélène Grimaud and conductor Claudio Abbado became embroiled in a dispute over an 80-second cadenza in a recording they were making of a Mozart piano concerto. Grimaud favoured a cadenza by Italian composer Ferruccio Busoni (1866–1924), while Abbado preferred Mozart's original. The dispute escalated to the point that the two canceled upcoming joint appearances, and eventually another recording of the work, which Grimaud had made with the Bavarian Radio Symphony Orchestra, was included on an album she released in November.

American minimalist composer Steve Reich was accused of being "insensitive" for his album cover—a photo of a hijacked airplane as it was about to strike the World Trade Center on Sept. 11, 2001. The album, titled *WTC 9/11*, featured a 15-minute title track based on the terrorist attacks. Responding to the furor, Reich said: "As a composer I want people to listen to my music without something distracting them. The present cover of *WTC 9/11* will, for many, act as a distraction from listening and so, with the gracious agreement of [the record label] Nonesuch, the cover is being changed."

Finally, the classical world was saddened by the death of Italian tenor Salvatore Licitra in September. Licitra, 43, died of injuries suffered in August in a motor-scooter accident in Sicily. He began to make a name for himself in the opera world in the late 1990s and became a full-fledged star when he was a last-minute substitute for Luciano Pavarotti at the Met in 2002. In fact, over the next few years, Licitra came to be referred to as "the next Pavarotti."

(HARRY SUMRALL)

Jazz. When in 2011 veteran producer and concert impresario George Wein chose not to organize a festival to succeed his many CareFusion, JVC, Kool, Newport, and other festivals of previous years, New York City was left without a large-scale jazz event for the first time in nearly four decades. There were smaller festivals, however, to help maintain the city's reputation as the jazz centre of the U.S. By far the largest of those was the Blue Note Jazz Festival, which offered concerts and club dates by jazz and pop musicians throughout June, both at the Blue Note nightclub and at other venues. Other events included the greatly expanded two-year-old Undead Jazzfest in Brooklyn and Manhattan and the 16-year-old Vision Festival, which gave German saxophonist Peter Brötzmann its lifetime-achievement award. A full schedule of Jazz at Lincoln Center (JALC) events included artistic director Wynton Marsalis playing trumpet and leading the JALC Orchestra in a concert with guitarist Eric Clapton; a CD of the concert was issued in September.

The year was a disappointing one for fans of pianist Cecil Taylor, whose widely heralded series of weekly performances at the nightclub Le Poisson Rouge was canceled. Also canceled were the plans for a museum in his Brooklyn home and a fund-raising concert at the Brooklyn Borough Hall. Perhaps Taylor's fans should have taken a clue from other jazz artists who sought new ways to finance their creative work. Clarinetist James Falzone used the social-media fund-raising Web site Kickstarter to finance his Benny Goodman tribute album *Other Doors*, released in April on his own label. Also in early 2011, the Tri-Centric Foundation Web site was relaunched in a significantly expanded form to produce and distribute composer-saxophonist Anthony Braxton's music. From the site the foundation offered subscribers two album-length downloads per month of recordings on the online New Braxton House Records label. It also offered, free of charge, assorted bootleg recordings.

Saxophonist, composer, and bandleader Angelika Niescier and the 12-woman German Women Jazz Orchestra played what may have been the first jazz concert in Gaza, Palestine. The show, organized by Germany's Goethe-Institute, was a challenging one, with the Israeli military firing on Gaza targets during both the rehearsal and the concert. Two Gazan rappers were included on the program, but because Hamas forbade solo rapping, their role was limited to performing with the orchestra for part of the concert.

The "war on terrorism" threatened to disrupt the July lineup at the St. Moritz, Switz., jazz festival. When festival organizers tried to advance $10,000 to the American pianist Ahmad Jamal, U.S. authorities froze the bank transfer because Jamal's name was similar to that of a wanted terrorist. After the incident was reported in Swiss newspapers and the authorities were invited to the festival as guests of honour, Jamal received his front money and was allowed to perform at the event.

In other news, bassist-singer Esperanza Spalding (*see* BIOGRAPHIES) won a Grammy for best new artist, becoming one of the rare jazz musicians to receive that honour. In March, U.S. Pres. Barack Obama presented tenor saxophonist Sonny Rollins and musician, composer, arranger, and producer Quincy Jones each with a National Medal of Arts. The versatile Afro-Cuban percussionist-composer Dafnis Prieto became the most recent jazz musician to receive a MacArthur Foundation "genius" grant. Meanwhile, tenor saxophonist Von Freeman, drummer Jack DeJohnette, trumpeter Jimmy Owens, singer Sheila Jordan, and bassist Charlie Haden were announced as 2012 Jazz Masters by the National Endowment for the Arts.

Imaginative revivals of traditional jazz works of the 1920s were the material of a new album, *Fireworks*, by Les Rois du Fox-Trot. On a less-traditional note, the earliest recording by free-jazz saxophonist Roscoe Mitchell and his quartet—*Before There Was Sound* (1965)—was discovered and released in October. Pianist Chick Corea's *Forever*, featuring bassist Stanley Clark and drummer Lenny White, was essentially a reunion album of his popular 1970s group Return to Forever. *Standing on the Rooftop* by singer Madeleine Peyroux, *Road Shows, Vol. 2* by Sonny Rollins with fellow saxophone legend Ornette Coleman, and *Celebrating Mary Lou Williams* by Trio 3 and pianist Geri Allen were among the year's other notable new recordings.

The year's large reissue projects included *The Complete Atlantic Studio Recordings of the Modern Jazz Quartet*, a seven-CD set, and *Jazz: The Smithsonian Anthology*, which comprised six discs containing 111 historically significant recordings. For more than 40 years, Berlin-based FMP Records produced albums of free improvisation and European jazz. In 2011 it released several historic downloads and *FMP: im Rückblick—In Retrospect*, a box set of 12 CDs and a 218-page book; the CDs included works by major European figures such as Brötzmann, by the Globe Unity Orchestra, and by American saxophonist Steve Lacy.

The year's deaths included pianist George Shearing, tenor saxophonist, composer, and bandleader Frank Foster, and arranger-composer Pete Rugolo. (*See* OBITUARIES.) The jazz world also lost American violinist-composer Billy Bang, American drummer and composer Paul Motian, and South African saxophonist Zim Ngqawana.

(JOHN LITWEILER)

Popular. *International.* Fusion styles dominated in 2011, and Asian artists were among those mixing folk or classical themes with contemporary influences. Raghu Dixit, from the Indian city of Bangalore, the capital of Karnataka state, succeeded because of his powerful, soulful voice and songs that he described as "Indian folk rock." Many of his songs were in the Kannada language, and his aim was to promote Kannada because he considered the language to be "under threat" because of the number of Hindi or Tamil speakers moving into Karnataka. The approach won him acclaim in the region, but he also amassed a growing global following, thanks to his engaging stage presence, his sturdy Western-influenced melodies, and English language ballads such as "No Man Will Ever Love You like I Do." He toured extensively during the year, including concerts in the U.S. and the U.K., where his debut album was a World Music best seller and where he was invited to become an artist in residence at London's Southbank Centre.

Asha Bhosle, India's legendary queen of the Bollywood "playback singers," recorded the easygoing *Naina Lagaike*, on which she was joined by the classical singer and sitar player Shujaat Khan. There was further Indian fusion work from the U.K.-based singer Susheela Raman, whose stirring album *Vel* reflected her travels in India with a clash of Indian and contemporary Western styles, in which she was joined by the passionate Rajasthani singer Kutle Khan.

In the U.K. itself, there were further experiments in mixing different global styles by the new band JuJu. Formed by British guitarist Justin Adams and featuring astonishing improvised solos on the one-stringed *ritti* by Gambian musician Juldeh Camara, the duo was later joined by bass and drums.

There were also adventurous new projects in the British folk music scene, most notably by the veteran singer June Tabor, who released two exceptional albums during the year—the often bleak and chilling *Ashore*, a concept album about the sea, and *Ragged Kingdom*, recorded with the folk-rock group Oysterband, their first recording together since the acclaimed *Freedom and Rain* in 1990. The album mixed traditional material with cover versions of songs by Bob Dylan, PJ Harvey, and Joy Division. Tabor also appeared on *Purpose + Grace*, an eclectic album by the British guitarist Martin Simpson, which also featured appearances by British folk stars Richard Thompson, Jon Boden, and Dick Gaughan.

The year was a good one for female singers around the world. Turkish star Sezen Aksu had been the undisputed queen of her country's contemporary music scene for three decades, but remarkably, her 2011 album *Optum* was her first international release. It demonstrated her powerful, passionate style on songs that dealt with love, fate, and politics. The Malian singer Fatoumata Diawara released a cool, confident debut album, *Fatou*, which drew comparisons to her country's two greatest female stars, Rokia Traore and Oumou Sangare, with whom Diawara once worked.

From the Americas one of the most intriguing newcomers of the year was Aurelio Martínez, who had enjoyed a successful career as a politician in Honduras. He was a spokesman of the Garifuna community—the descendants of slaves and Caribs who were exiled from British colonies in the eastern Caribbean and later became scattered across Central America. His album *Laru Beya* mixed lilting, languid songs with a lament for the victims of slavery and included contributions from the Senegalese star Youssou N'Dour.

British guitarist Justin Adams (left) performs with Gambian musician Juldeh Camara, playing the ritti *(a one-stringed violin-like instrument), at a music festival in Basel, Switz., Oct. 23, 2010.*

Georgios Kefalas—EPA/Landov

In the U.S. there were impressive releases from two great veterans. Gregg Allman, best known for his work with the Allman Brothers Band, released his first solo album in 14 years, *Low Country Blues*, an album that proved that his distinctive voice and Hammond keyboard work were both in excellent shape. Ry Cooder recorded an often angry but bleakly witty album, *Pull Up Some Dust and Sit Down*, that dealt with bankers, war, and politics and was hailed as one of his finest solo recordings since the 1970s.

The year saw the death of British folk guitarist Bert Jansch, acclaimed for his solo playing and work with Pentangle. (*See* OBITUARIES.) Other deaths included Mauritanian singer Dimi Mint Abba and the Tanzanian singer and guitarist Remmy Ongala.

(ROBIN DENSELOW)

United States. It was not exactly a British Invasion reprise, but a pair of very different U.K. acts accounted for two of 2011's biggest U.S. success stories. Adele was the undisputed queen of the American charts. By midyear her *21* had sold more than four million units, including over one million digital versions. And nouveau-folk ensemble Mumford & Sons relished a breakout year with 2010's *Sigh No More*. Unlike Adele, whose ailing vocal cords forced her to twice cancel a slate of concert dates, Mumford et al. managed to mount a successful American tour.

American-born Katy Perry (*see* BIOGRAPHIES), Lady Gaga, and Taylor Swift extended their winning streaks, presiding over slick theatrical arena tours. Kings of Leon, by contrast, canceled the final 26 dates of a summer tour after singer Caleb Followill quit the stage at a July 29 show in Dallas. Country legend Glen Campbell embarked on a farewell tour after announcing that he had Alzheimer disease.

On August 13 a sudden violent windstorm toppled stage scaffolding at the Indiana State Fair moments before contemporary country duo Sugarland was to perform. Seven deaths, dozens of injuries, and multiple lawsuits resulted from the stage collapse.

Lil Wayne demonstrated staying power as his *Tha Carter IV* received lukewarm reviews yet still sold 964,000 copies in its first week of release. Such upstarts as Wiz Khalifa and Tyler, the Creator represented hip-hop's crop of new talent, while Miami-based rapper Pitbull and DJ duo LMFAO found chart success with club anthems that filled dance floors throughout the summer.

Robert E. Klein/AP

British pop singer Adele, whose album 21 topped charts worldwide in 2011, demonstrates her vocal prowess at a concert in Boston on May 15.

Kanye West and Chris Brown made great strides toward rehabilitating their public personas. Brown's *F.A.M.E.* sold well, as did his arena tour. West joined forces with Jay-Z as a duo dubbed the Throne. They promoted their joint CD, *Watch the Throne*, with a highly anticipated fall arena tour.

Joining the indefatigable television show *American Idol* were two new TV shortcuts to pop stardom, *The Voice* and *The X Factor*. Hirsute Canadian blues-rock quartet the Sheepdogs became the first unsigned act to grace the cover of *Rolling Stone* magazine after winning a readers' contest.

The National Academy of Recording Arts and Sciences reduced the number of Grammy categories from 109 to 78, much to the chagrin of musicians in such deleted categories as Cajun/zydeco music. Meanwhile, Arcade Fire's *The Suburbs* was the surprise winner for best album at the 2011 Grammy Awards, and jazz bassist-singer Esperanza Spalding (*see* BIOGRAPHIES) bested the more commercial Justin Bieber, Mumford & Sons, and Florence + the Machine as best new artist. Less surprisingly, country-pop trio Lady Antebellum's omnipresent "Need You Now" won both record and song of the year.

A deluxe box-set reissue marked the 20th anniversary of Nirvana's landmark *Nevermind*. Grunge survivors Pearl Jam celebrated the band's 20th anniversary with 54,000 fans at a two-day festival in Wisconsin. After 31 years R.E.M., among the most respected and successful American bands of the 1980s and '90s, disbanded.

The popularity of the costumed deejay Deadmau5 was indicative of electronic music's deeper inroads into the American mainstream. Critical darlings Wilco released *The Whole Love*, the band's first album on its own record label. Ageless crooner Tony Bennett scored a hit with *Duets II*, on which he shared the microphone with such artists as Lady Gaga, Willie Nelson, Aretha Franklin, John Mayer, Norah Jones, and, in what turned out to be her final recording, Amy Winehouse. (*See* OBITUARIES.)

During the MTV Video Music Awards, comedian and actor Russell Brand delivered a heartfelt, sobering eulogy for Winehouse, whose July death saddened fans on both sides of the Atlantic. The music community also mourned the passing of "Stand by Me" and "Hound Dog" cocomposer Jerry Leiber, longtime E Street Band saxophonist Clarence Clemons, R&B singer-songwriter Nick Ashford of Ashford & Simpson, avant-jazz spoken-word artist Gil Scott-Heron, country music pioneer Charlie Louvin, early bluesmen Pinetop Perkins and Honeyboy Edwards, and manager and music publisher Don Kirshner, host of the TV show *Don Kirshner's Rock Concert*. (*See* OBITUARIES.) Other notable deaths included Warrant singer Jani Lane, TV on the Radio bassist Gerard Smith, original Alice in Chains bassist Mike Starr, West Coast rapper Nate Dogg, classic R&B singer Benny Spellman, and veteran New Orleans music arranger and bandleader Wardell Quezergue. (KEITH SPERA)

DANCE

North America. In 2011 several ballet companies across North America staged the standard ballet *Giselle* with the idea that the menacing vampirelike Wilis in its second act might resonate with those interested in the vampires of the blockbuster book and film series *Twilight*. American Ballet Theatre (ABT), San Francisco Ballet (SFB), and various other companies throughout the U.S. offered performances of the work, while Britain's Royal Ballet and Russia's Bolshoi Ballet brought their own versions of the romantic tale to movie screens in the U.S. via live telecasts from their home stages. Additionally, Russia's Mariinsky Ballet presented its production at the Kennedy Center for the Performing Arts (KC), Washington, D.C. Perhaps the freshest entry into the *Giselle* mix, however, was the production by Pacific Northwest

Ballet (PNB) in June. Overseen by artistic director Peter Boal and guided by music and dance historian Marian Smith and others, the production aimed to reclaim more of the atmosphere of the ballet's 19th-century origins.

ABT's year was highlighted by a number of works from Alexei Ratmansky, its artist in residence, whose contract was extended for 10 more years. His comic ballet *The Bright Stream*, a two-act rendering of a Soviet "tractor ballet" from 2003, entered ABT's repertory, and his new dance, *Dumbarton*, set to Igor Stravinsky's *Dumbarton Oaks*, was part of a mixed bill at the troupe's annual season at New York City's (NYC's) Metropolitan Opera House. Ratmansky's much-admired version of *The Nutcracker*, new the previous year, returned to the Brooklyn Academy of Music (BAM), and his new version of *Romeo and Juliet* opened National Ballet of Canada's (NBC's) 60th anniversary season in November.

Much of ABT's NYC season was distinguished by the presence of guest dancers—some of them announced, others brought in when ABT principal Herman Cornejo canceled his full season of performances owing to injury. Joining the company's ranks for some eagerly attended performances were several dancers from abroad, including Polina Semionova (Berlin), Alina Cojocaru (London), Natalya Osipova (Moscow), Roberto Bolle (Milan), and Ivan Vasiliev (Moscow). Stellar dancer Ethan Stiefel, who also canceled his performances because of injury, in September assumed the directorship of Royal New Zealand Ballet, and principal dancer David Hallberg made history as the first American to join the Bolshoi Ballet. Cuban-born José Manuel Carreño in June gave his farewell ABT performance.

Ballet Nacional de Cuba, which initially nurtured both Carreño and the Feijóo sisters, toured the U.S. and Canada and received much acclaim for its staging of *Giselle*. Copenhagen's Royal Danish Ballet (RDB) made a four-city U.S. tour, highlights of which included revised versions of *A Folk Tale* and *Napoli*, classic 19th-century creations of the troupe's legendary artistic force, August Bournonville, as envisioned by RDB director Nikolaj Hübbe. In keeping with a focus on performing arts from China, KC presented the National Ballet of China and Beijing Dance Theater.

In the spring New York City Ballet (NYCB) presented a lacklustre new version of Kurt Weill and Bertolt Brecht's *The Seven Deadly Sins* (sung by Patti LuPone and choreographed by Lynn Taylor-Corbett). NYCB's fall season featured Paul McCartney's new (and first) ballet score, *Ocean's Kingdom*, choreographed by NYCB ballet master in chief Peter Martins, with costume designs by Stella McCartney, the composer's daughter. Longtime NYCB principal dancer Charles Askegard gave a farewell performance in October.

© Andrea Mohin—The New York Times/Redux

New York City Ballet principal dancers Robert Fairchild and Sara Mearns perform in Ocean's Kingdom *in September. The new piece, with choreography by Peter Martins, was the first ballet score composed by Sir Paul McCartney.*

Another choreographer in the news was Christopher Wheeldon. His *Alice's Adventures in Wonderland* joined NBC's repertory to much acclaim, and his new *Number Nine* had its world premiere at SFB. Meanwhile, Morphoses, the company that Wheeldon had founded and later left, made its first NYC appearances without him at its helm. With Luca Veggetti as the first to hold the rotating post of resident artistic director, the company presented *Bacchae*, based on the play by Euripides.

SFB choreographer in residence Yury Possokhov gave Chicago's Joffrey Ballet a new production of *Don Quixote* in October. Russia's Boris Eifman took his *Don Quixote, or Fantasies of a Madman* to four U.S. cities midyear. Jorma Elo, resident choreographer of Boston Ballet (BB), gave his home base a program called *Elo Experience* and choreographed a new work, *ONE/end/ONE*, for Houston Ballet (HB). For *A Midsummer Night's Dream*, which he created for the Vienna State Opera Ballet in 2010, Elo won the Benois de la Danse prize, awarded out of Moscow by the International Dance Union.

Both HB and Kansas City Ballet (KCB) opened new state-of-the-art headquarters during the year. To help mark its transfer to the Kauffman Center for the Performing Arts, KCB presented *Tom Sawyer*, a new three-act ballet by artistic director William Whitener. Ballet Arizona celebrated its 25th anniversary in part by presenting *Mosaik*, a ballet for which artistic director Ib Andersen created not only the choreography but also the painted costumes and backdrops. Miami City Ballet returned from a successful tour of Paris and later saw itself nationally telecast on the PBS Arts Fall Festival, which featured the troupe's performances of George Balanchine's *Square Dance* and *Western Symphony* and Twyla Tharp's *The Golden Section*. Despite that success, it was announced that the company's founding artistic director, Edward Villella, would be stepping down in 2013. Also in the fall, Tharp's 2009 tribute to Frank Sinatra, *Come Fly Away*, got trimmed from two acts to one 80-minute production in advance of a national tour.

On a tour sponsored by the U.S. Department of State, the Merce Cunningham Dance Company (MCDC) made its first-ever appearances in Moscow. Back in the U.S., the troupe performed at BAM and then hosted a special event at NYC's Park Avenue Armory in honour of the company's founder before disbanding permanently at the end of the year. Also in celebration of Cunningham's achievements, the Walker Arts Center of Minneapolis, Minn., acquired and, in November, displayed portions of a collection of props, sets, costumes, and other items made for MCDC.

The Paul Taylor Dance Company helped the American Dance Festival (ADF) recognize the legacy of longtime and retiring ADF director Charles Reinhart through performances of Taylor's new work, *The Uncommitted*. Under the guidance of Robert Battle, who succeeded Judith Jamison as artistic director, the Alvin Ailey American Dance Theater presented *Arden Court* (1981), its first-ever dance by Taylor, as part of its annual NYC season.

In other dance news, the Mark Morris Dance Group continued its 30th-anniversary celebration with special performances of Morris's most recent work, *Renard*, set to music by Stravinsky, at Lincoln Center's (LC's) Mostly Mozart Festival. As part of the 40th-anniversary retrospective project of husband-and-wife performing artists Eiko and Koma, the couple's installation-like production *Naked* was presented at NYC's Baryshnikov Arts Center. They also mounted a multimedia exhibition, *Residue*, at the New York Public Library for the Performing Arts and staged a presentation called *Water* in LC's Out of Doors summer series. The popular performing collective Pilobolus marked its 40th anniversary at NYC's Joyce Theater with a monthlong run that included the premiere of *Seraph*, a creation made in collaboration with the MIT Distributed Robotics Laboratory. The Martha Graham Dance Company commemorated its 85th anniversary with a weeklong season in NYC.

In Canada NBC celebrated Greta Hodgkinson's 20 years with the company by featuring her in Jerome Robbins's *Other Dances*, and the Royal Winnipeg Ballet (RWB) presented Shawn Hounsell's *Wonderland*, a new interpretation of Alice's fabled adventures. Later in the year RWB offered Mark Godden's *Svengali*. Alberta Ballet artistic director Jean Grand-Maître presented his latest pop-icon work, *Fumbling Towards Ecstasy*, which paid homage to singer Sarah McLachlan. Beijing Modern Dance Company took part in Vancouver's DanceHouse series. Canadian choreographer Crystal Pite, director of her own contemporary dance company, received the fifth annual Jacob's Pillow Dance award. Louise Lecavalier, long associated with Canada's Edouard Lock and his La La La Human Steps company, was named Choreographic Personality of the Year by the Syndicat de la Critique Théâtre, Musique et Danse, the French organization that sponsors the award.

There were several deaths. They included Canadian dancer Lois Smith and American dancers Jerry Ames, Garry Reigneborn, Edward Bigelow, Marnee Morris, Ruth Currier, and Mark Goldweber. (ROBERT GRESKOVIC)

Europe. Economic uncertainty continued to affect the European dance world in 2011. The international reputation of the Royal Ballet of Flanders, cultivated under the leadership of Kathryn Bennetts, had proved to be of little consequence in late 2010 when the regional government proposed a consolidation of the ballet and the Flemish Opera. As of 2013, the two companies would operate under a single intendant. Assuming that the company would lose its autonomy, Bennetts responded by announcing that she would resign from the artistic directorship when her contract ended in 2012. The resulting outcry from the worldwide dance community included a petition, a deluge of letters to the Flemish government, and two parliamentary hearings. By year's end, the future of the proposed merger was still unclear.

The government of the Netherlands also announced cuts. The Netherlands Dance Theatre suffered the most devastating blow, with a 40–50% loss in funding and a proposed downgrade from an international to a regional company. The Dutch National Ballet escaped more lightly, with a proposed 26% reduction, and was able to proceed with an interesting array of shows. Highlights of its season included the first European performance of Alexei Ratmansky's *On the Dnieper* (2009), originally created for American Ballet Theatre, and world premieres of works by noted young choreographers Sidi Larbi Cherkaoui and David Dawson. In addition, the troupe took to London a program of works by the leading Dutch choreographer Hans van Manen. In September the company commenced its 50th-anniversary celebration, with a gala evening event that was simulcast to cinemas around the country. In the weeks that followed, the company presented a program of ballets from its "golden age," featuring choreography by Rudi van Dantzig, Toer van Schayk, and van Manen.

The Stuttgart Ballet also celebrated an important anniversary: 50 years since South African-born John Cranko arrived in Stuttgart and began the transformation of a minor German regional company into an acclaimed international troupe. A three-week festival included performances, conferences, discussions and talks, and some special events.

Both the Stuttgart and Hamburg ballets reported that their funding was intact. The cultural budget for Hamburg actually increased as the city prepared to become the home of Germany's new National Youth Ballet. The Hamburg Ballet Days—traditionally marking the close of the season—were held in late June and early July with 10 programs in 13 days, culminating, as usual, in a marathon Vaslav Nijinsky gala. December brought an item of particular interest: *Lilliom*, a new full-evening work by Hamburg Ballet director John Neumeier, based on the play of the same name by Ferenc Molnar. The ballet was created for the Romanian-born star of Britain's Royal Ballet, Alina Cojocaru.

In Britain the major dance companies prepared for a 15% reduction in funding, and at least two contemporary dance troupes were forced to close when they lost all government support. A significant event at the Royal Ballet was the world premiere in February of Christopher Wheeldon's *Alice's Adventures in Wonderland*, a joint production with the National Ballet of Canada and the first full-evening commission by the Royal Ballet in 16 years. Although there had been a number of attempts by various choreographers to turn Lewis Carroll's famous tales of Alice into dance, none of them had been entirely successful, largely because the book itself has no overarching narrative structure. Wheeldon had the advantage of a specially commissioned score by Joby Talbot and brilliant set designs from Bob Crowley. Indeed, many observers felt that the designs and special effects outdid the choreography. There was, however, high praise for the dancers, especially Lauren Cuthbertson as Alice.

Offstage at the Royal Ballet, the big news was the appointment of a new artistic director to succeed Monica Mason in 2012. The surprise choice was Kevin O'Hare, the current administrative director of the troupe and a former dancer with the Birmingham Royal Ballet. He was responsible for another highlight of the company's year: a run of performances of Sir Kenneth MacMillan's *Romeo and Juliet* at the O_2 Arena, a space usually reserved for large-scale pop concerts. The Birmingham-based Royal Ballet followed the London troupe into the arena at the end of the year with a run of *The Nutcracker*.

Scottish Ballet artistic director Ashley Page also created a full-evening *Alice*. This was a darker version, featuring Carroll himself as a character; once again, the structure of the story proved to be a stumbling block. The troupe appeared at the Edinburgh International Festival with a double bill consisting of a new work, *Kings 2 Ends*, by the Finnish choreographer Jorma Elo and the company's first performance of MacMillan's *Song of the Earth*, danced to Gustav Mahler's song cycle. In late 2010, following a disagreement with the ballet's board, Page had said that he would resign as artistic director in 2012 when his contract expired.

The English National Ballet revived Rudolf Nureyev's production of *Romeo and Juliet* and added two mixed bills to its repertory. The first of these included an excellent production of Serge Lifar's *Suite en blanc*; the second, an evening of ballets by Roland Petit (*see* OBITUARIES), was dampened by the choreographer's death a few days prior to its premiere. The company's young Russian star Vadim Muntagirov was promoted to principal dancer.

Promotions came too at the Royal Danish Ballet, where both Marcin Kupinski and the young Alban Lendorf were named principal dancers by artistic director Nicolaj Hübbe. Highlights of the company's season included a new production of the August Bournonville classic *A Folk Tale*, updated by 300 years and given some additional choreography by Hübbe himself. The company toured the U.S. in May and June to mixed reviews.

The Mariinsky Ballet also included the U.S. on its extensive touring schedule, but the high point of its year was the home production of Angelin Preljocaj's *Le Parc* (1994), originally created for the Paris Opéra Ballet. Whereas previous examples of Preljocaj's work had been very much disliked in St. Petersburg, the 2011 production was received with great enthusiasm. The talented Vladimir Shklyarov was promoted to principal, while Olga Smirnova, outstanding graduate of the Vaganova Academy, stirred up consternation when she decided to join the Bolshoi Ballet as a soloist rather than remain in St. Petersburg.

The Bolshoi itself began the year in some disarray when a controversy erupted over the choice of a new artistic director to succeed Yury Burlaka. After several weeks of rumour, and a couple of rounds of recruitment and resignation, the former Bolshoi principal Sergey Filin was lured away from his job at the Stanislavsky Theatre to head the company. The major premiere of the season was a full-evening ballet by Ratmansky based on Honoré de Balzac's novel *Lost Illusions*. Other new additions were Wayne McGregor's *Chroma* (2006) and Jiri Kylian's *Symphony of Psalms* (1978). The company moved back to the refurbished Bolshoi Theatre for the new season, opening with a new production of *The Sleeping Beauty* (1965) by former balletmaster Yuri Grigorovich.

The Mikhailovsky Ballet showed a well-received first evening of ballets by artistic director Nacho Duato, including a new work inspired by the company's Yekaterina Borchenko. The dancers evidently adapted well to Duato's style. Elsewhere in Europe, Duato's former company, the Compañía Nacional de Danza of Spain, in late 2010 had appointed a new artistic director, José Martínez, former *étoile* (principal dancer) of the Paris Opéra Ballet. Another former Paris *étoile*, Manuel Legris, head of the Vienna State Opera Ballet, reported soaring attendance figures at the end of his first season, which culminated in June 2011 in a gala honouring the late Rudolf Nureyev, holder of an Austrian passport and Legris's own mentor.

Lauren Cuthbertson (centre) dances as Alice in the British Royal Ballet's much-anticipated Alice's Adventures in Wonderland *in February. The world premiere ballet, a joint production with the National Ballet of Canada, featured Christopher Wheeldon's choreography and a score by Joby Talbot.*

In addition to Roland Petit, the ballet world lost New Zealand-born Royal Ballet star Alexander Grant. (*See* OBITUARIES.) Sergey Berezhnoy, former dancer with the Kirov Ballet and longtime coach of the Boston and Mariinsky ballets, also left the scene.

(JUDITH CRUICKSHANK)

THEATRE

Great Britain and Ireland. The year 2011 brought yet another fizzing, ambitious, and highly entertaining piece of ensemble theatre from director Rupert Goold. Following his *Enron* (2009) and *Earthquakes in London* (2010), Goold and his Headlong Theatre touring company occupied a disused trading centre in East London to present *Decade*, a surprisingly successful and moving 10th-anniversary memorial to the September 11 attacks in the U.S. Eighteen British and American writers—including historian Simon Schama and playwrights Christopher Shinn, Lynn Nottage, Mike Bartlett, and Beth Steel—provided texts for a virtuoso company of 12 actors, with the audience seated at tables and banquettes in a nostalgic replication of the Windows on the World restaurant, which occupied the 107th floor of one of the World Trade Center towers. The horrors of the attacks were subtly recreated, with flight crews desperately issuing safety instructions to an accelerating overture by Gioachino Rossini. The audience lingered in the aftermath among widows, innocent Muslims, eyewitnesses, and even the assassination of Osama bin Laden, all of it molded into poetic stage imagery and dance movement.

Happier anniversaries were celebrated in 2011: the centenary year of the birth of playwright Terence Rattigan; the 50th birthday of the Royal Shakespeare Company (RSC); the 40th birthday of the redoubtable little Orange Tree Theatre in Richmond, Surrey, which offered the U.K. premiere of *The Conspirators*, a bilious farce by Czech playwright and politician Vaclav Havel (*see* OBITUARIES) about the fragility of a postrevolutionary government in an unspecified country; and the 30th birthday of two other significant fringe venues, BAC (Battersea Arts

Centre) in South London and the Tricycle at Kilburn in North London. The Rattigan anniversary drew an outpouring of critical affirmation of his status. The highlight was Trevor Nunn's sumptuous revival of Rattigan's wartime *Flare Path* at the Theatre Royal Haymarket, with fine performances by Sheridan Smith, Sienna Miller, James Purefoy, and Harry Hadden-Paton.

The mood in London was also ripe for revisiting a newer, modern repertoire. Dominic West, the British star of the American television series *The Wire* (2002–08), gave a coruscating performance as the dissolute English lecturer in Simon Gray's *Butley*, while Kristin Scott Thomas led an acclaimed revival of *Betrayal*, Harold Pinter's shimmering play on adultery. Max Stafford-Clark, the original director of Caryl Churchill's brilliant feminist drama *Top Girls*, served up a gleaming new production for a post-Margaret Thatcher-era audience of working women.

West End drama otherwise was fairly ordinary, though Keira Knightley and Elisabeth Moss, a star of the American television series *Mad Men*, proved a potent box-office combination in Lillian Hellman's *The Children's Hour*, directed by Ian Rickson. Nunn supervised a string of hits as resident artistic director at the Haymarket; *Flare Path* was followed by Tom Stoppard's *Rosencrantz and Guildenstern Are Dead*, and then came Ralph Fiennes as a beautifully spoken middle-aged and conciliatory Prospero in Shakespeare's *The Tempest* as well as Robert Lindsay and Joanna Lumley in James Goldman's *The Lion in Winter*. That nostalgic turn continued with Vanessa Redgrave's and James Earl Jones's reprise of their acclaimed 2010 Broadway roles in Alfred Uhry's *Driving Miss Daisy*.

In his last season in charge of the Donmar Warehouse, Michael Grandage presented a beautiful, burnished production of Friedrich Schiller's *Luise Miller*. Also at the Donmar were Jude Law and Ruth Wilson in a glistening revival, directed by Rob Ashford, of Eugene O'Neill's *Anna Christie*, Douglas Hodge in a rare revival of John Osborne's *Inadmissible Evidence*, and Eddie Redmayne, winner of a Tony Award in 2010 (for his Broadway appearance in the Donmar's *Red* by John Logan), as Shakespeare's Richard II.

The musical theatre had a mixed year. The RSC's delightful version of Roald Dahl's *Matilda*, with music and lyrics by Tim Minchin and book by Dennis Kelly, arrived from Stratford-upon-Avon at the Cambridge Theatre in London buoyed by the most unanimously positive reviews for a British musical since the West End premiere of *Billy Elliot* in 2005. But other musicals struggled to be hits, even in the big musical houses, the London Palladium and the Theatre Royal, Drury Lane. At the first, *The Wizard of Oz* was a curiously flat affair, despite a handful of new songs by Andrew Lloyd Webber and his writing partner Tim Rice. At the second, the Broadway import of *Shrek the Musical* seemed a tepid compromise between an American children's show and English pantomime. Neither musical compared well with its movie original.

Three of the most interesting new musicals all performed poorly at the box office and were soon withdrawn. The best of them was producer Cameron Mackintosh's *Betty Blue Eyes*, based on a 1984 movie by Malcolm Mowbray; the score was by Anthony Drewe and George Stiles, and the book was by little-known Americans Ron Cowen and Daniel Lipman, who adapted it from Alan Bennett's screenplay. Richard Eyre's nimble direction translated the movie into a genuine musical comedy of rationing and provincial snobbery in a Yorkshire village, complete with an animatronic pig voiced by Kylie Minogue. The show, which centred on a street party to celebrate the 1947 wedding of Queen Elizabeth II and Prince Philip, was fortuitously timed to coincide with the immensely popular 2011 marriage of Prince William of Wales and Catherine Middleton. But even that hook failed to land an audience, and the show closed within six months. *The Umbrellas of Cherbourg* was charmingly adapted and staged by Kneehigh Theatre director Emma Rice, but audiences seemed not to be in the mood for the soft-focus romantic heart of Jacques Demy's 1964 movie in a new format, even though Michel Legrand's music was a civilized pleasure. And then a musical version of Ken Ludwig's snappy backstage farce *Lend Me a Tenor* slumped at the Gielgud.

Hopes were high for the Barbican Theatre opening of *South Pacific*, directed by Bartlett Sher. Paulo Szot, winner of a 2008 Tony Award for his performance in the musical's run at the Lincoln Center Theater in New York City, joined the British cast as the French plantation owner Emile de Becque, alongside Loretta Ables Sayre as Bloody Mary. The revival proved less exciting, however, and more staid, than Trevor Nunn's 10 years previous.

The Royal National Theatre under Nicholas Hytner remained buoyant, with three standout productions during 2011. The first was Danny Boyle's new look at Mary Shelley's *Frankenstein*, scripted by Nick Dear and sensationally designed by Mark Tildesley in the Olivier Theatre, with a great tolling bell, a canopy of countless electric light bulbs, and for the first 15 minutes a naked, writhing Creature ripping through a membrane, learning how to walk and move, and eventually entering a hostile world. Jonny Lee Miller and Benedict Cumberbatch played both the Creature and his creator, Victor Frankenstein, alternating in the roles throughout the run.

The second landmark production at the National was Rufus Norris's staging in the small Cottesloe Theatre of *London Road* by Alecky Blythe (book and lyrics) and sound-score specialist Adam Cork (music and lyrics), based on the improbable subject of the murder in 2006 of five prostitutes in the Suffolk town of Ipswich. That example of ver-

Geraint Lewis/Alamy

Jonny Lee Miller (left) as Victor Frankenstein stands over Benedict Cumberbatch as the tormented Creature in playwright Nick Dear's adaptation of Mary Shelley's Frankenstein *at the Royal National Theatre. Danny Boyle directed the powerful production in which the two actors alternated performances in the roles.*

batim theatre, using taped interviews of local residents who lived near the rented room of the convicted killer (now serving a life sentence), related the crimes' reverberations through the community as well as the healing process achieved, perhaps unexpectedly, through flower competitions. *London Road* was an extraordinary and unforgettable show, one of the finest and most innovative achievements, in the National Theatre's history.

And third, in the Lyttelton Theatre, Hytner directed an update of Carlo Goldoni's classic 18th-century farce *Il servitore di due padrone*. Richard Bean's new script, *One Man, Two Guvnors*, relocated the action from Venice to Brighton on England's southern coast and featured James Corden (an original cast member of Alan Bennett's *The History Boys* who had since become a popular television actor) as the overrun gofer of divided loyalties. Plump and amiable, like a faster-moving version of Oliver Hardy, Corden was brilliantly funny, embroiling the audience in some of his stunts, slapping himself about the face, and even turning up in the musical interludes to play xylophone with the onstage skiffle band.

The National slipped up badly only with a surprisingly dull *Twelfth Night*—directed by Peter Hall with his own daughter, Rebecca Hall, as Viola and Simon Callow as an all-too-obvious Sir Toby Belch—and with a committee-authored climate-change play, *Greenland*. Jonathan Kent's British premiere of Henrik Ibsen's unruly epic of the later Roman Empire, *Emperor and Galilean*, was a vivid collector's item; Bijan Sheibani's thrilling balletic staging of Arnold Wesker's *The Kitchen* was a well-controlled riot; and Mike Leigh's new play, *Grief*, was a total joy.

The first RSC production in the revamped and rebuilt Royal Shakespeare Theatre at Stratford-upon-Avon was Michael Boyd's *Macbeth*, with Jonathan Slinger and Aislin McGuckin acting out their murderous marriage on what looked like a desecrated re-creation of Shakespeare's nearby baptismal and burial site. In recognition of its half-centenary season, the company revisited mid-1960s glories—Pinter's *The Homecoming* and Peter Weiss's *Marat/Sade* (one of Peter Brook's greatest productions)—with decidedly mixed results.

Kevin Spacey led his Old Vic company in a so-so production of Shakespeare's *Richard III* directed by Sam Mendes. At the Royal Court, Juliet Stevenson starred in Richard Bean's *The Heretic*, and a striking new actor, Kyle Soller—who had previously made a big impression in Richard Jones's brilliant Young Vic revival of Nikolay Gogol's *The Government Inspector*—scored again as a floppy New Yorker in Alexi Kaye Campbell's ambitious "religion and capitalism" drama, *The Faith Machine*.

Beyond London, Dominic West was a charmingly malevolent Iago to Clarke Peters's baffled Othello at the Crucible in Sheffield. Ian McKellen was a Neapolitan godfather in a touring production of Eduardo De Filippo's *The Syndicate*, which started at the resurgent Chichester Festival Theatre. Edward Hall's touring all-male Propeller company excelled in a riotously Mexican *The Comedy of Errors* and a satanic knockabout *Richard III*. (Hall was making a big difference too as the artistic director of the Hampstead Theatre in London.)

At the Edinburgh International Festival, director Tim Supple unveiled *One Thousand and One Nights*, a beautiful six-hour drama (split neatly into two parts) that was drawn by Lebanese novelist Hanan al-Shaykh from the classic collection of tales *The Thousand and One Nights*. Performed in English, French, and Arabic by a mostly Middle Eastern and African cast, it seemed to provide an essential cultural counterweight to the contemporaneous upheavals of the Arab Spring.

A notable co-production—by Great Britain's National Theatre and the Abbey Theatre in Dublin—of Sean O'-Casey's *Juno and the Paycock*, starring Sinead Cusack and Ciaran Hinds, was the centrepiece of the Dublin Theatre Festival; the play later joined the National's repertoire in London. Dublin's other festival offerings included Lynne Parker's Rough Magic Theatre Company in a rumbustious new version of Ibsen's *Peer Gynt* and a new play by the novelist Colm Toibin, *Testament*, in which Marie Mullen played a woman described as "forced to bear an unimaginable burden in tumultuous times."

Actors who died in 2011 included the potato-faced Pete Postlethwaite; the pyrotechnical John Wood, one of Stoppard's greatest interpreters; much-loved stalwarts Anna Massey and Margaret Tyzack; and the Irish favourite T.P. McKenna. Pam Gems, author of sprightly plays about famous women—*Piaf*, *Marlene*, *Camille*, and *Queen Christina*—also passed away. (*See* OBITUARIES.) (MICHAEL COVENEY)

U.S. and Canada. The centennial of the birth of that quintessentially American playwright Tennessee Williams did not go uncelebrated in 2011. In fact, the year was marked by a flurry of productions, publishing, exhibits, and special events honouring the author of *A Streetcar Named Desire*, *Cat on a Hot Tin Roof*, and more than 40 other plays, some of them so obscure as to be virtually unknown, even to Williams aficionados. Champions of the Mississippi-born writer, seizing the occasion to try to redeem Williams's wildly inconsistent reputation, delved more deeply into his body of work than ever before. There were new productions of Williams's major works, ranging from straightforward interpretations to radical experimental versions; mountings of his rarely seen late-career one-acts and stage adaptations of his short stories; and even original plays about Williams himself, assaying aspects of his life and his creative impact on American drama.

Among the notable revivals of Williams classics were Williamstown Theatre Festival's *Streetcar*, with Jessica Hecht playing the fragile heroine Blanche DuBois; well-received stagings of *Cat* at Ontario's Shaw Festival and the Irish Classical Theatre Company of Buffalo, N.Y.; and a wave of *The Glass Menageries* in Utah, Wisconsin, California, and North Carolina. More adventurously, the New York City-based Wooster Group applied its deconstructionist techniques to Williams's autobiographical meditation *Vieux Carré*, baffling some critics and audiences, and iconoclastic director Lee Breuer teamed up with puppeteer and designer Basil Twist to reconceive *Streetcar* as a high-concept Kabuki-flavoured performance piece. The latter work became the first non-European play ever presented (in French, under the title *Un Tramway nommé Désir*) at the venerable Comédie-Française in Paris, and it was expected to arrive in the United States in 2012 unless objections from the estate of Williams prevented its remounting.

Another playwright with an all-American pedigree, Texan Horton Foote, who died in 2009—and, like Williams, frequently adapted his stage work into Hollywood screenplays—was honoured with multiple productions and academic attention. A two-month-long festival of Foote's earthy, emotionally fraught works was presented in Dallas–Fort Worth, and no fewer than 10 resident theatres across the U.S. mounted revivals of such Foote staples as *The Trip to Bountiful* and *Dividing the Estate*.

There were significant new works from established writers, among them Tony Kushner and Adam Rapp. Kushner's voluminously titled Off-Broadway drama *The Intelligent Homosexual's Guide to Capitalism and Socialism with a Key to the Scriptures* brought together the noisy, combative family of a retired Brooklyn longshoreman intent on killing himself, while Rapp's the Hallway Trilogy, also mounted Off-Broadway, depicted the unsavoury denizens of a single apartment building in three plays set 50 years apart.

Tony Taccone, artistic director of California's Berkeley Repertory Theatre, tried his hand at playwriting, revisiting in *Ghost Light* the 1978 assassination of San Francisco Mayor George Moscone through the eyes of Moscone's son Jonathan, who was 14 at the time (and who became, in 2000, the artistic leader of neighbouring California Shakespeare Theatre; he directed the play's premiere co-production at Oregon Shakespeare Festival and Berkeley Rep). One of the biggest musical successes of the year occurred at San Francisco's flagship American Conservatory Theater, where librettist Jeff Whitty and musicians Jake Shears and John Garden (of the alt-dance band Scissor Sisters) transformed Armistead Maupin's Tales of the City series, about Bay Area gay life in the 1970s, into a conventional but wildly popular piece of musical theatre.

Sara Krulwich—The New York Times/Redux

From left, Rema Webb, Andrew Rannells, and Josh Gad perform on March 17 in the hit Broadway musical The Book of Mormon.

The uninhibited creators of the animated television series *South Park*, Trey Parker and Matt Stone, became Broadway celebrities in 2011 with their raucous, frequently blasphemous musical *The Book of Mormon*, which swept the year's Tony Awards and continued through year's end to be the commercial theatre's hottest ticket. Best play, best direction, and a cluster of design honours went to *War Horse*, an adaptation by British dramatist Nick Stafford of a 1981 novel about a cavalry horse in World War I, in which the titular character was a life-size puppet manipulated with astonishing verisimilitude by a team of puppeteers. The show continued to draw enthusiastic audiences at Lincoln Center Theater at year's end, even as a Steven Spielberg film version of the same story opened.

War was also on the mind of the organizers of the Theater of War project, which targeted veterans across the United States with performances of Sophocles' *Ajax* and of contemporary playwright K.J. Sanchez's *ReEntry*, a powerful documentary-theatre piece based on interviews with Marines returning from service. Another interaction between theatre and the military came with Tricycle Theatre of the U.K.'s *The Great Game: Afghanistan*, an amalgam of history plays performed for Pentagon personnel and at American theatres.

Leadership changes in 2011 included the appointment of two noted playwright-directors to top positions at important companies. Chay Yew, a major figure in contemporary Asian American drama, took over the reins of Chicago's Victory Gardens Theater from Dennis Zacek, who had held the position for more than three decades. Yew was born and raised in Singapore and served for 10 years as director of the Asian Theatre Workshop at the Mark Taper Forum in Los Angeles. At Centerstage in Baltimore, Md., artistic director Irene Lewis was succeeded (after 19 years in the post) by Kwame Kwei-Armah, an award-winning playwright, director, and actor of African-Caribbean descent. Kwei-Armah relocated from London, where he had lived most of his life, to take the job.

In Canadian theatre a new awards organization—the Toronto Theatre Critics Awards (established by J. Kelly Nestruck of the *Globe and Mail*, Richard Ouzounian of the *Toronto Star*, Robert Cushman of the *National Post*, and John Coulbourn of the *Toronto Sun*)—was formed out of discontent with the long-standing Dora Awards, Toronto's equivalent of the Tonys. Alberta playwright Stephen Massicotte's *The Clockmaker* was named best Canadian play of 2010–11 by the new organization.

Among other notable new works of the year were Hannah Moscovitch's *The Children's Republic*, a drama about a Polish Jewish pediatrician in Warsaw circa 1939, premiered by Toronto's Tarragon Theatre; and the antic musical *Ride the Cyclone*, devised by the British Columbia-based troupe Atomic Vaudeville, about six members of a youth choir who died in a tragic amusement park accident. The latter show gained buzz during a national tour and ended the year in a critically acclaimed run at Toronto's Theatre Passe Muraille.

In terms of classical work, the Stratford Festival's artistic director, Des McAnuff, scored again with a top-flight production of *Twelfth Night*, and auteur Robert Lepage packed an unlikely venue—the First Nations Huron-Wendat Reserve just outside Quebec city—with enthusiastic young Francophone audiences for his site-specific *The Tempest*. More than a decade of a legal investigation and a trial also came to an end in 2011 when Garth Drabinsky, former CEO of the now-defunct theatre company Livent, Inc., began serving a five-year sentence in an Ontario federal prison after having been convicted on fraud and forgery charges related to his big-musical-import empire.

Deaths affecting the North American theatre community included those of distinguished playwright Lanford Wilson, musical-theatre legend Arthur

Laurents, and director Michael Langham, who headed the Stratford Festival and later taught at Juilliard. (*See* OBITUARIES.) Other notable deaths were those of playwright Romulus Linney; Philip Rose, the Broadway producer of *A Raisin in the Sun*; Tennessee-based poet and playwright Jo Carson; Los Angeles producer Gil Cates; Romanian-born master director Liviu Ciulei; costumer Theoni V. Aldredge; and pioneering gay playwright Doric Wilson. (JIM O'QUINN)

MOTION PICTURES

United States. Two films stood out in 2011 for their sophisticated cinema magic. Terrence Malick's *The Tree of Life*, winner of the Palme d'Or at the Cannes Festival, paid elaborate homage to the human family. It was most convincing in the jaw-dropping visualization of the world's creation and the meticulous description of a boy's life in Texas. Martin Scorsese spread more consistent delight in *Hugo*, an adult homage to cinema's dreamland and its early pioneers, disguised as a fantasy for children. As its young hero, Asa Butterfield veered toward the wooden; not so Ben Kingsley's enchanting performance as a toy-shop owner (gradually revealed to be the French filmmaker Georges Méliès) or the design and photography imaginatively exploiting 3-D. Other interesting films appeared during the year. Early cinema received a pleasurable if superficial valentine in the heartfelt and wordless *The Artist* (Michel Hazanavicius), financed in France and filmed in black-and-white in the United States. Jean Dujardin won the Cannes Festival's best actor award for his role as the silent star who fails to adapt in the new world of the talkies. A box of tissues was needed for Steven Spielberg's *War Horse*, an emotionally draining version of Michael Morpurgo's story about a British horse and its fortunes in World War I. Spielberg also directed *The Adventures of Tintin*, a busy 3-D animation adventure based on the classic Belgian comic books by Hergé.

Nourished neither by blockbuster publicity nor critical approval, Tate Taylor's adaptation of Kathryn Stockett's novel *The Help*, a warmhearted tale set in the 1960s in which a young white woman learns about the lives of African American women who have spent their lives working as maids for white families in the South, became a substantial hit. Star power failed to attract spectators to the romantic comedy *Larry Crowne* (Tom Hanks), a lukewarm vehicle for Hanks and Julia Roberts. George Clooney, another actor-director, had no problem finding viewers for *The Ides of March*, a smartly acted film about corruption in American politics. Clooney also appeared in *The Descendants*, Alexander Payne's thoughtful drama about a Hawaiian land baron's family crisis. Clint Eastwood's *J. Edgar*, featuring Leonardo DiCaprio as J. Edgar Hoover, provided dainty and old-fashioned treatment of the feared FBI chief. A sharper sensibility surfaced in *Moneyball* (Bennett Miller), an unflinching look at the business of baseball featuring Brad Pitt as Oakland Athletics general manager Billy Beane. Woody Allen offered sophisticated entertainment in his time-traveling diversion *Midnight in Paris*; wider audiences enjoyed *Crazy, Stupid, Love* (Glenn Ficarra, John Requa), an unusually mature romantic comedy. Comedy entered trickier terrain in *Young Adult* (Jason Reitman), the prickly tale of a young-adult author returning to the scene of her high-school social triumphs.

Martin Scorsese's 3-D fantasy Hugo *starred Asa Butterfield as an orphan inhabiting a Paris train station in the 1930s.*

Fantasy franchise products and sequels proliferated. The enormously successful Harry Potter series concluded with *Harry Potter and the Deathly Hallows: Part 2* (David Yates), whose urgent excitements dwarfed those of *The Twilight Saga: Breaking Dawn—Part 1* (Bill Condon), the penultimate installment of the vampire series. Director Guy Ritchie's mission to transform Sherlock Holmes into a modern action hero continued in the frenetic *Sherlock Holmes: A Game of Shadows*, notable for the Hollywood debut of Noomi Rapace (*see* BIOGRAPHIES), original Swedish star of *The Girl with the Dragon Tattoo* and its sequels. Stieg Larsson's crime story received its own slick and sophisticated American remake, directed by David Fincher, with Rooney Mara in Rapace's role as the ravaged Goth heroine.

In the animation field, *Cars 2* (John Lasseter) improved on its original; *Happy Feet Two* (George Miller) did not. The Muppets returned after a 12-year absence in the ebullient *The Muppets* (James Bobin), while the animated *Puss in Boots* (Chris Miller) revamped the fairy tale with 3-D, cheeky twists, and Antonio Banderas's purring voice. Other animation features included the adult-friendly *Rango* (Gore Verbinski), about an ordinary chameleon's adventures in the Wild West, and *Rio* (Carlos Saldanha), almost as colourful as its leading character, a macaw parrot.

British Isles. Three films displayed the continuing vibrancy of British social realism. Lynne Ramsay's *We Need to Talk About Kevin*, featuring a high-density performance by Tilda Swinton, took a harrowing look at the domestic damage wrought by a psychopathic son. Steve McQueen's *Shame* continued in the uncompromising vein of his first feature *Hunger* (2008); Michael Fassbender won the Volpi Cup for best actor at the Venice International Film Festival for his part as a Manhattan sex addict. Only slightly easier to watch, Paddy Considine's gritty *Tyrannosaur* followed the fortunes of an angry widower and the charity shop manager who gives him shelter. On the lighter side, *Arthur Christmas* (Sarah Smith, Barry Cook), Aardman Animations Ltd.'s holiday offering, found ample jokes in Santa's dysfunctional family.

Meryl Streep's adroit impersonation of the former British prime minister Margaret Thatcher dominated *The Iron Lady* (Phyllida Lloyd), an otherwise fuzzy and ungallant drama about a still-controversial figure; while Michelle Williams's lustre aided *My Week with Marilyn* (Simon Curtis), an uneven divertissement about Marilyn Monroe in mid-1950s England. Among high-profile literary adaptations, Cold War ethics came under chilly examination in *Tinker Tailor Soldier Spy*, an incisive if emotionally distancing version of John le Carré's novel, directed with a foreigner's eye by Swedish director Tomas Alfredson. Andrea Arnold, known for her realistic urban dramas, adapted Emily Brontë's *Wuthering Heights* with raw images, an emphasis on primal forces, and a Heathcliff remodeled as an Afro-Caribbean outsider. Charlotte Brontë's *Jane Eyre* received subtler treatment from director Cary Fukunaga in a sharply focused film with persuasive performances by Mia Wasikowska and Fassbender.

In *The Deep Blue Sea* Terence Davies handled Sir Terence Rattigan's stage drama of marital infidelity with visual poise and a strong sense of period but failed to make the material seem compelling. Lone Scherfig's *One Day*, starring Anne Hathaway (seriously miscast), was an overly neat adaptation of David Nicholls's novel about a couple's slow journey from flirtation to commitment. Michael Winterbottom, ever eclectic, repositioned Thomas Hardy's *Tess of the d'Urbervilles* in modern India in *Trishna*, while actor-director Ralph Fiennes aimed his fire at Shakespeare's *Coriolanus* in a bellicose modern adaptation. Ireland's principal films were chiefly notable for their leading actors: Glenn Close in *Albert Nobbs* (Rodrigo García), the dour tale of a 19th-century woman working in male disguise, and Brendan Gleeson in the crime comedy *The Guard* (John Michael McDonagh).

Canada, Australia, and New Zealand. Canadian director David Cronenberg abandoned shock tactics for cerebral musings in *A Dangerous Method*, concerning the relationship between pioneer psychiatrists Sigmund Freud and Carl Jung. Greater emotional involvement was supplied by Sarah Polley's *Take This Waltz*, a bittersweet comedy about a young woman's crisis of conscience. Philippe Falardeau's *Monsieur Lazhar* intelligently handled the problems of an Algerian immigrant teacher in Montreal, while maverick Guy Maddin polished his eccentricities in the crazed ghost story *Keyhole*. From Australia, Justin Kurzel's fiercely bleak serial killer drama *Snowtown* was easy to admire but hard to enjoy, while Fred Schepisi's *The Eye of the Storm* wrestled gamely with Patrick White's source novel and lost. New Zealand's brightest offering was *My Wedding and Other Secrets* (Roseanne Liang), a funny, touching autobiographical tale of cross-cultural conflicts.

Western Europe. Two leading European directors dominated the landscape. Danish controversialist Lars von Trier showed a gentler side in *Melancholia*, a visionary fable promoting calm acceptance of the Earth's impending destruction. Dazzling special effects were balanced with intimate drama and piercing acting; Kirsten Dunst won the Cannes Festival's best actress prize. The film also won the top prize at the European Film Awards. Another individual stylist, Spain's Pedro Almodóvar pursued various obsessions in *La piel que habito* (*The Skin I Live In*), the tortuous saga of a plastic surgeon who invents a damage-resistant synthetic skin.

Valérie Donzelli's modestly scaled *La Guerre est déclarée* (*Declaration of War*), following the fortunes of a family with a child diagnosed with cancer, achieved unexpected success at the French box office. *Omar m'a tuer* (*Omar Killed Me*; Roschdy Zem), about a Moroccan gardener accused of murdering his wealthy employer, also pleased many with its straightforward treatment of a true story. Acid laughter dominated *Carnage*, Roman Polanski's highly dramatic version of *God of Carnage*, Yazmina Reza's hit play about middle-class couples abandoning the social niceties. *L'Exercice de l'état* (Pierre Schöller) presented a talkative investigation into the working life of an imaginary French politician, while Vincent Garenq's searing *Présumé coupable* (*Guilty*) explored the true case of a bailiff wrongly jailed for child molestation. In a different vein, Mia Hansen-Løve's *Un Amour de jeunesse* (*Goodbye First Love*) offered an emotionally satisfying story about the lingering power of first love.

In Belgium, Jean-Pierre and Luc Dardenne, specialists in closely observed dramas about broken souls and underdogs, continued their investigations in *Le Gamin au vélo* (*The Kid with a Bike*), a moving story about a young boy's struggles after having been abandoned by his father. The film shared the Cannes Grand Prix. Michael R. Roskam made an ambitious directing debut with the dark, complex *Rundskop* (*Bullhead*), inspired by the murder of a Belgian veterinarian. In the Netherlands *Rabat*, Victor Ponten and Jim Taihuttu's pleasant road movie following three boys from the Netherlands to Morocco, proved an unexpected hit.

Norway provided Scandinavia's biggest success of the year in *Trolljegeren* (*Trollhunter*), André Øvredal's entertaining thriller about the country's secret troll menace. *Sykt lykkelig* (*Happy, Happy*), Anne Sewitsky's winning comedy about two households behaving badly, was also popular. City life went under the microscope in Joachim Trier's melancholy *Oslo, 31. august* (*Oslo, August 31st*), tracing one day in a recovering drug addict's life. Aki Kaurismäki's agreeable *Le Havre* applied the Finnish director's usual mix of morose drama and deadpan comedy to a French setting. Sweden's boldest offering was *Apflickorna* (*She Monkeys*; Lisa Aschan), an unsettling account of equestrian gymnastics, competition, and girls' developing sexualities. Featuring domestic abuse and alcoholism, Pernilla August's *Svinalängorna* (*Beyond*), starring Noomi Rapace, boasted its own inflammable elements but treated them too mechanically. In Iceland, Rúnar Rúnarsson made a small but impressive debut with the realist drama *Eldfjall* (*Volcano*).

Germany's past continued to haunt its filmmakers. Achim von Borries's *4 tage im Mai* (*4 Days in May*) coasted along the surface of its story about Russian soldiers occupying a German children's home at the end of World War II. Dubious comedy ruled in *Hotel Lux* (Leander Haussmann), the tale of a refugee comedian in Moscow, mistaken for Hitler's astrologer. Popular actor-director Til Schweiger scored a hit with *Kokowääh*, about a womanizing writer suddenly faced with the arrival on his doorstep of a small child who proves to be his daughter.

The pedigree and subject matter of Nanni Moretti's *Habemus Papam* (*We Have a Pope*) earned the film attention. The Italian director's satire of the Roman Catholic Church proved too gentle, but Michel Piccoli's humane performance as the newly elected pope paralyzed by fear was worth watching. Other films paddling in shallow waters included Emanuele Crialese's *Terraferma*, a sweetly packaged social drama, and the popular comedy *Che bella giornata* (*What a Beautiful Day*; Gennaro Nunziante). Stronger entertainment came with Gianni Di Gregorio's *Gianni e le donne* (*The Salt of Life*), a wistfully comic investigation into the aging Italian male, and Paolo Sorrentino's English-language *This Must Be the Place*, a bizarre but meaningful road movie about a retired rock star trying to find his late father's Auschwitz persecutor.

In Spain, Max Lemcke's *Cinco metros cuadrados* (*Five Square Metres*) drew

© Magnet Releasing/Everett Collection

*An enormous troll looms over the snowy Norwegian landscape in André Øvredal's comic thriller Trolljegeren (*Trollhunter*).*

dark comedy from corruption in the country's construction business, while Enrique Urbizu's *No habrá paz para los malvados* delivered a damning report on police incompetence. Benito Zambrano's *La voz dormida* (*The Sleeping Voice*) shaped a harrowing drama from the plight of female prisoners after the Spanish Civil War. Portugal's most striking film was *América* (João Nuno Pinto), a grimly humorous portrait of immigrants, criminals, and multiculturalism gone wrong.

Eastern Europe. Leading Turkish director Nuri Bilge Ceylan shared the Grand Prix at Cannes with *Bir zamanlar Anadolu'da* (*Once upon a Time in Anatolia*), a poignant, beautifully crafted analysis of the human condition through the medium of a hunt for a murder victim's body. Other significant Turkish films included *Hayde bre* (Orhan Oguz), a cross-generational drama, and *Press* (Sedat Yilmaz), the powerful story of journalists in the 1990s risking their lives to expose injustice. Greece came forward with *Alpeis* (*Alps*), a typically eccentric offering from the director of *Dogtooth* (2009), Giorgos Lanthimos; and *Kanenas* (*Nobody*; Christos Nikoleris)—essentially *Romeo and Juliet* transported to the immigrant communities of modern Athens.

The 3-D revival reached Poland with veteran director Jerzy Hoffman's rousingly old-fashioned *1920 Bitwa Warszawska* (*Battle of Warsaw 1920*). Other films resurrecting the country's turbulent past included *Czarny czwartek* (Antoni Krauze), Wojciech Smarzowski's *Róża* (*Rose*), and Agnieszka Holland's provocatively harsh *W ciemnósci* (*In Darkness*), a tale of Jewish survival, chiefly set in the sewers underneath Nazi-occupied Lviv (now in Ukraine). Contemporary Poland was featured in *Cudowne lato* (*Wonderful Summer*), Ryszard Brylski's winningly eccentric romantic comedy with a tinge of the macabre. Artistically more ambitious, Lech Majewski's *Mlyn i krzyz* (*The Mill and the Cross*) took the spectator inside the narrative of Pieter Bruegel, the Elder's painting *The Way to Calvary*.

In Russia, Aleksandr Sokurov concluded a series of films about powerful figures in history with the challenging and very talkative *Faust*; it won the Golden Lion award for best film at the Venice Film Festival. Wider audiences welcomed Victor Ginzburg's *Generation P*, a whirlwind satiric fantasy of life in post-Soviet Russia. Andrey Zvyagintsev's well-mounted *Elena* incisively explored the domestic travails of a fragile family, and Angelina Nikonova made a striking debut as director in *Portret v sumerkakh* (*Twilight Portrait*), a challenging drama that explored a privileged woman's extreme reaction to sexual violence.

Actress Nihan Okutucu clutches her onscreen son in the haunting Turkish drama Bir zamanlar Anadolu'da (Once upon a Time in Anatolia), *directed by Nuri Bilge Ceylan.*

© Cinema Guild/Everett Collection

Romania, a recent hotbed of film activity, offered little of note. Hungarian director Béla Tarr entered deeper into his artistic cul-de-sac in *A Torinói ló* (*The Turin Horse*), another of his bleak epics of futile rural life. It was announced as his last film. In Georgia new blood pulsed through *Marilivit tetri* (*Salt White*), Ketevan Machavariani's debut feature following three characters interacting at a Black Sea resort. Another new talent, Viktor Chouchkov, engineered thoughtful youth-oriented entertainment in the Bulgarian film *Tilt*. The Czech Republic and Slovakia joined forces for *Cigan* (*Gypsy*), Martin Sulík's poignant drama about a Roma teenager.

Latin America. Argentina easily dominated the region's activity. Opinion was divided about Milagros Mumenthaler's *Abrir puertas y ventanas* (*Back to Stay*), a coolly stylized drama about the lives of three sisters in the wake of their grandmother's death; the film won the Golden Leopard prize at the Locarno International Film Festival. Sprightlier filmmaking emerged with *Aballay, el hombre sin miedo* (*Aballay, the Man Without Fear*), Fernando Spiner's brazenly surreal tale of a young man aiming to avenge his father's death. Sergio Teubal's engagingly whimsical *El dedo* (*The Finger*) followed the election process in a locality where a murdered candidate's finger casts the crucial vote. Santiago Mitre's *El estudiante* (*The Student*) aimed its own arrows at Argentine politics with a sharp treatment of university machinations. Chile's new generation of filmmakers produced an artistic triumph in *Bonsái*, Cristián Jiménez's subtly pitched version of a popular novella by Alejandro Zambra about an ultimately doomed love affair between college students. The intense life of the Chilean singer-songwriter Violeta Parra came under the spotlight in Andrés Wood's *Violeta se fue a los cielos* (*Violeta*).

Middle East. In a gesture both artistic and political, the Berlin International

Film Festival competition jury awarded three major awards to the Iranian *Jodaeiye Nader az Simin* (*A Separation*). Asghar Farhadi's thoughtful drama about the plight of a middle-class family besieged by moral and practical dilemmas, won the prize for best film, and its cast collectively won the trophies for best actor and actress. Other new Iranian films courageously tackled contemporary issues. In *Be omid e didar*, director Mohammad Rasoulof found a parallel for his own problems with the country's government in the quietly devastating story of a female lawyer struggling to obtain a visa. Israeli films continued a trend away from politics toward domestic and personal matters. Yossi Madmoni's impressive *Boker tov adon Fidelman* (*Restoration*) followed the rancorous fortunes of a family struggling with an antique-restoration business. Less disciplined, Joseph Cedar's *Hearat shulayim* (*Footnote*) plunged into the hothouse of academia, while new director Nadav Lapid showed promise in *Ha-Shoter* (*Policeman*), a strong drama about an anti-terrorism unit clashing with young radicals. Two films from Egypt dealt bravely with previously taboo subjects: women's sexual harassment in *678* (Mohamed Diab) and *Asmaa* (Amr Salama), the true story of an HIV-positive woman who made her condition public.

India. Although no Indian film hit the heights internationally, Mangesh Hadawale's *Dekh Indian Circus* (*Watch Indian Circus*) earned respect for its attractive visuals and resonant story about an impoverished mother determined to take her children to the circus. Raj Kumar Gupta's *No One Killed Jessica* vigorously dramatized the real-life case of a murdered model in Delhi and the resulting miscarriage of justice. Pleasanter tales were told in *Adaminte makan Abu* (*Abu, Son of Adam*; Salim Ahmed), a dramatically quiet story about an elderly Muslim couple's plans to join the annual hajj pilgrimage; and *Deool* (*The Temple*), from Maharashtra, Umesh Vinayak Kulkarni's sweet-tempered satire of consumerism and village life.

East and Southeast Asia. Propaganda weighed heavily in China's physically impressive *1911* (Zhang Li, Jackie Chan), commissioned to mark the centenary of the revolution that overthrew China's last imperial dynasty. Less stiff as cinema, *Jian dang wei ye* (*Beginning of the Great Revival*; Han Sanping, Huang Jianxin) celebrated the birth of the Chinese Communist Party. But the films that scored at the box office avoided doctrinal politics. Chen Kaige's medieval drama *Zhao shi gu er* (*Sacrifice*) told a domestic tale of parental love and revenge. China's Oscar submission, Zhang Yimou's *Jin ling shi san chai* (*The Flowers of War*), boasted sumptuous visuals and Christian Bale as a Westerner caught in the chaos as the Japanese overran Nanjing in 1937. Lou Ye's more confrontational French co-production *Love and Bruises* offered a sharply pessimistic view of human relationships. In Taiwan and Hong Kong, audiences flocked to Ko Giddens's bawdy *Na xie nian, wo men yi qi zhui de nu hai* (*You Are the Apple of My Eye*), based on his autobiographical novel. Quieter pleasures ruled in Ann Hui's *Tao jie* (*A Simple Life*), a tender comedy-drama about elderly people and their caregivers.

Japanese director Takashi Miike, known for films of unbuttoned violence, displayed admirable restraint in the samurai drama *Ichimei* (*Hara-Kiri: Death of a Samurai*), an elegant remake of Masaki Kobayashi's 1962 classic *Harakiri*. Contemporary problems occupied Takahisa Zeze's *Antoki no inochi* (*Life Back Then*), a full-blooded melodrama concerning the aftereffects of high-school bullying. Subtler notes were struck by Hirokazu Koreeda in this stylish director's most audience-friendly film, *Kiseki* (*I Wish*), the naturalistic tale of two youngsters trying to cope with their parents' divorce.

At international festivals South Korean films displayed a lower profile than usual. Most attention fell on *Musanilgi* (*The Journals of Musan*), Park Jung-Bum's brilliantly observed if overlong drama about a North Korean refugee struggling to survive in the South. Local box-office hits included *Go-ji-jeon* (*The Front Line*; Jang Hun), a sober action drama revisiting the Korean War; Na Hong-Jin's *Hwanghae* (*The Yellow Sea*), a ferociously brutal thriller; and the richly humane *Sseo-ni* (*Sunny*), Kang Hyeong-Cheol's emotional rollercoaster about seven teenage girlfriends reunited in adulthood.

Elsewhere in East Asia, Marlon Rivera took satiric aim at trends in Filipino independent cinema in the lively comedy *Ang babae sa septic tank* (*The Woman in the Septic Tank*), a local hit. Indonesia came forth with *Madame X* (Lucky Kuswandi), the irreverent tale of a transsexual superhero who battles intolerance.

Africa. Significant product from the African continent continued to shrink. From South Africa, Darrell Roodt's *Winnie* offered superficial treatment of the early life of Nelson Mandela's second wife. Better entertainment arrived with the classic man-and-his-dog tale *Jock* (Duncan MacNeillie), the continent's first locally produced 3-D animation. Audiences were also attracted to *Spud* (2010; Donovan Marsh), a breezy boarding-school drama based on a popular series of novels by John van de Ruit. (GEOFF BROWN)

Documentary Films. In 2011 veteran German director Werner Herzog's chilling *Into the Abyss: A Tale of Death, a Tale of Life*, about inmates on death row in a Texas prison, won the Grierson Award for Best Documentary at the 2011 London Film Festival.

Blurring the lines between reality and fiction, Vikram Gandhi's *Kumaré* documented the filmmaker's experiment in creating a gurulike character and the surprising results that occurred for both his "students" and himself. The Grand Jury Prize winner at the 2011 Sundance Film Festival, *How to Die in Oregon* by Peter Richardson, examined the results of the state's legalization of physician-assisted death by choice and with dignity.

Cindy Meehl's *Buck* proved to be quite popular with festival viewers, winning audience awards at several film festivals. It explored the work of Buck Brannaman, a horse trainer with unusual abilities to communicate with horses and to enlighten humans as well. The winner of the World Cinema Audience Award at Sundance, *Senna*, chronicled the life of legendary Brazilian Formula One driver Ayrton Senna, whose tragic death in a 1994 race resulted in major reforms in the Formula One race-car design.

Marshall Curry's *If a Tree Falls: A Story of the Earth Liberation Front* scrutinized the efforts of a militant environmental group labeled by the FBI as the "number one domestic terrorism threat," while *The Whale*, directed by Suzanne Chisholm and Michael Parfit, looked at an extraordinary connection between a killer whale and the people of Nootka Sound, British Columbia.

Director Frederick Wiseman added to his prolific documentary legacy with *Crazy Horse*, a backstage look at the legendary Parisian entertainment venue. It premiered at the 2011 Venice Film Festival and was also an official selection for the New York, London, Tokyo, Toronto, and Telluride film festivals.

(BEN LEVIN)

INTERNATIONAL FILM AWARDS 2011

Golden Globes, awarded in Beverly Hills, California, in January 2011	
Best drama	*The Social Network* (U.S.; director, David Fincher)
Best musical or comedy	*The Kids Are All Right* (U.S.; director, Lisa Cholodenko)
Best director	David Fincher (*The Social Network,* U.S.)
Best actress, drama	Natalie Portman (*Black Swan,* U.S.)
Best actor, drama	Colin Firth (*The King's Speech,* U.K./Australia/U.S.)
Best actress, musical or comedy	Annette Bening (*The Kids Are All Right,* U.S.)
Best actor, musical or comedy	Paul Giamatti (*Barney's Version,* Canada/Italy)
Best foreign-language film	*Hæven* (*In a Better World*) (Denmark/Sweden; director, Susanne Bier)

Sundance Film Festival, awarded in Park City, Utah, in January 2011	
Grand Jury Prize, dramatic film	*Like Crazy* (U.S.; director, Drake Doremus)
Grand Jury Prize, documentary	*How to Die in Oregon* (U.S.; director, Peter Richardson)
Audience Award, dramatic film	*Circumstance* (France/U.S./Iran; director, Maryam Keshavarz)
Audience Award, documentary	*Buck* (U.S.; director, Cindy Meehl)
World Cinema Jury Prize, dramatic film	*Sykt lykkelig* (*Happy, Happy*) (Norway; director, Anne Sewitsky)
World Cinema Jury Prize, documentary	*Hell and Back Again* (U.S./U.K./Afghanistan; director, Danfung Dennis)
U.S. directing award, dramatic film	Sean Durkin (*Martha Marcy May Marlene,* U.S.)
U.S. directing award, documentary	Jon Foy (*Resurrect Dead: The Mystery of the Toynbee Tiles,* U.S.)

British Academy of Film and Television Arts, awarded in London in February 2011	
Best film	*The King's Speech* (U.K./Australia/U.S.; director, Tom Hooper)
Best director	David Fincher (*The Social Network,* U.S.)
Best actress	Natalie Portman (*Black Swan,* U.S.)
Best actor	Colin Firth (*The King's Speech,* U.K./Australia/U.S.)
Best supporting actress	Helena Bonham Carter (*The King's Speech,* U.K./Australia/U.S.)
Best supporting actor	Geoffrey Rush (*The King's Speech,* U.K./Australia/U.S.)
Best foreign-language film	*Män som hatar kvinnor* (*The Girl with the Dragon Tattoo*) (Sweden/Denmark/Germany/Norway; director, Neils Arden Oplev)

Berlin International Film Festival, awarded in February 2011	
Golden Bear	*Jodaeiye Nader az Simin* (*A Separation*) (Iran; director, Asghar Farhadi)
Silver Bear, Jury Grand Prix	*A Torinói ló* (*The Turin Horse*) (Hungary/France/Germany/Switzerland/U.S.; director, Béla Tarr)
Silver Bear, best director	Ulrich Köhler (*Schlafkrankheit* [*Sleeping Sickness*]; Germany/France/Netherlands)
Silver Bear, best actress	the ensemble of the actresses of *Jodaeiye Nader az Simin* (*Jodaeiye Nader az Simin* [*A Separation*], Iran)
Silver Bear, best actor	the ensemble of the actors of *Jodaeiye Nader az Simin* (*Jodaeiye Nader az Simin* [*A Separation*], Iran)

Césars (France), awarded in Paris in February 2011	
Best film	*Des hommes et des dieux* (*Of Gods and Men*) (France; director, Xavier Beauvois)
Best director	Roman Polanski (*The Ghost Writer,* France/Germany/U.K.)
Best actress	Sara Forestier (*Le Nom des gens* [*The Names of Love*], France)
Best actor	Eric Elmosnino (*Gainsbourg* (*Vie héroïque*) [*Gainsbourg: A Heroic Life*], France)
Most promising actress	Leïla Bekhti (*Tout ce qui brille* [*All That Glitters*], France)
Best first film	*Gainsbourg* (*Vie héroïque*) (*Gainsbourg: A Heroic Life*) (France; director, Joann Sfar)

Academy of Motion Picture Arts and Sciences (Oscars; U.S.), awarded in Los Angeles in February 2011	
Best film	*The King's Speech* (U.K./Australia/U.S.; director, Tom Hooper)
Best director	Tom Hooper (*The King's Speech,* U.K./Australia/U.S.)
Best actress	Natalie Portman (*Black Swan,* U.S.)
Best actor	Colin Firth (*The King's Speech,* U.K./Australia/U.S.)
Best supporting actress	Melissa Leo (*The Fighter,* U.S.)
Best supporting actor	Christian Bale (*The Fighter,* U.S.)
Best foreign-language film	*Hæven* (*In a Better World*) (Denmark/Sweden; director, Susanne Bier)
Best animated film	*Toy Story 3* (U.S.; director, Lee Unkrich)

Cannes Festival, France, awarded in May 2011	
Palme d'Or	*The Tree of Life* (U.S.; director, Terrence Malick)
Grand Prix	*Bir zamanlar Anadolu'da* (*Once upon a Time in Anatolia*) (Turkey/Bosnia and Herzegovina; director, Nuri Bilge Ceylan); *Le Gamin au vélo* (*The Kid with a Bike*) (Belgium/France/Italy; directors, Jean-Pierre Dardenne and Luc Dardenne)
Jury Prize	*Polisse* (France; director, Maïwen)
Best director	Nicolas Winding Refn (*Drive,* U.S.)
Best actress	Kirsten Dunst (*Melancholia,* Denmark/Sweden/France/Germany)
Best actor	Jean Dujardin (*The Artist,* France)
Caméra d'Or	*Las acacias* (Argentina/Spain; director, Pablo Giorgelli)

INTERNATIONAL FILM AWARDS 2011 (continued)

Locarno International Film Festival, Switzerland, awarded in August 2011	
Golden Leopard	*Abrir puertas y ventanas* (*Back to Stay*) (Argentina/Switzerland/Netherlands; director, Milagros Mumenthaler)
Special Jury Prize	*Tokyo Kouen* (Japan; director, Shinji Aoyama)
Best actress	María Canale (*Abrir puertas y ventanas* [*Back to Stay*], Argentina/Switzerland/Netherlands)
Best actor	Bogdan Dumitrache (*Din dragoste cu cele mai bune intentii* [*Best Intentions*], Hungary/Romania)
Montreal World Film Festival, awarded in August 2011	
Grand Prix of the Americas (best film)	*Hasta la vista!* (*Come as You Are*) (Belgium; director, Geoffrey Enthoven)
Best actress	Fatemeh Motamed-Arya (*Inja bedoone man* [*Here Without Me*], Iran)
Best actor	Borys Szyc (*Kret* [*The Mole*], Poland/France); Danny Huston (*Playoff*, Germany/France/Israel)
Best director	Brigitte Bertele (*Der Brand* [*The Fire*], Germany)
Special Grand Prix of the Jury	*Waga haha no ki* (*Chronicle of My Mother*) (Japan; director, Masato Harada)
Best screenplay	*L'Art d'aimer* (*The Art of Love*) (France; screenplay by Emmanuel Mouret)
International film critics award	*Czarny czwartek* (*Black Thursday*) (Poland; director, Antoni Krauze)
Venice Film Festival, awarded in September 2011	
Golden Lion	*Faust* (Russia; director, Aleksandr Sokurov)
Special Jury Prize	*Terraferma* (Italy/France; director, Emanuele Crialese)
Volpi Cup, best actress	Deanni Yip (*Tao jie* [*A Simple Life*], Hong Kong)
Volpi Cup, best actor	Michael Fassbender (*Shame*, U.K.)
Silver Lion, best director	Shanjung Cai (*Ren shan ren hai* [*People Mountain People Sea*], China/Hong Kong)
Marcello Mastroianni Award (best new young actor or actress)	Shota Sometani and Fumi Nikaido (*Himizu*, Japan)
Luigi De Laurentiis Award (best first film)	*Là-bas* (Italy; director, Guido Lombardi)
Toronto International Film Festival, awarded in September 2011	
Best Canadian feature film	*Monsieur Lazhar* (director, Philippe Falardeau)
Best Canadian first feature	*Edwin Boyd* (director, Nathan Morlando)
Best Canadian short film	*Doubles with Slight Pepper* (director, Ian Harnarine)
International film critics award	*Avalon* (Sweden; director, Axel Petersen)
People's Choice Award	*Et maintenant, on va où* (*Where Do We Go Now?*) (France/Lebanon/Egypt/Italy; director, Nadine Labaki)
San Sebastián International Film Festival, Spain, awarded in September 2011	
Best film	*Los pasos dobles* (*The Double Steps*) (Spain/Switzerland; director, Isaki Lacuesta)
Special Jury Prize	*Le Skylab* (France; director, Julie Delpy)
Best director	Filippos Tsitos (*Adikos kosmos* [*Unfair World*], Greece/Germany)
Best actress	María León (*La voz dormida* [*The Sleeping Voice*], Spain)
Best actor	Antonis Kadetzopoulos (*Adikos kosmos* [*Unfair World*], Greece/Germany)
Best cinematography	Ulf Brantås (*Happy End*, Sweden)
New directors prize	Jan Zabeil (*Der Fluss war einst ein Mensch* [*The River Used to Be a Man*], Germany)
International film critics award	*The Tree of Life* (U.S.; director, Terrence Malick)
Vancouver International Film Festival, awarded in October 2011	
Most Popular Canadian Film Award	*Starbuck* (director, Ken Scott)
People's Choice Award	*Jodaeiye Nader az Simin* (*A Separation*) (Iran; director, Asghar Farhadi)
National Film Board Most Popular Canadian Documentary Award	*Peace Out* (director, Charles Wilkinson)
Shaw Media Award for Best Canadian Feature Film	*Nuit #1* (director, Anne Émond)
Environmental Film Audience Award	*People of a Feather* (Canada; director, Joel Heath)
Dragons and Tigers Award for Young Cinema	*Tai yang zong zai zuo bian* (*The Sun-Beaten Path*) (China; director, Sonthar Gyal)
Chicago International Film Festival, awarded in October 2011	
Gold Hugo, best film	*Le Havre* (Finland/France/Germany; director, Aki Kaurismäki)
Gold Hugo, best documentary	*Cinema komunisto* (Serbia and Montenegro; director, Mila Turajlic)
Silver Hugo, Special Jury Award	*678* (*Cairo 678*) (Egypt; director, Mohamed Diab)
European Film Awards, awarded in December 2011	
Best European film	*Melancholia* (Denmark/Sweden/France/Germany; director, Lars von Trier)
Best actress	Tilda Swinton (*We Need to Talk About Kevin*, U.K./U.S.)
Best actor	Colin Firth (*The King's Speech*, U.K./Australia/U.S.)

(PATRICIA BAUER)

Physical Sciences

Scientists made **ADVANCES** in the study of **HYDROGEN BONDS**, the use of sunlight and water for **GENERATING** hydrogen gas, and the detection of water **POLLUTANTS** such as petroleum. Physicists created long-lasting **ANTIHYDROGEN**, induced a cell to shine laser light, and may have observed **FASTER-THAN-LIGHT** neutrinos. Astronomers discovered a new **MOON** of **PLUTO** and many interesting extrasolar planets. The American **SPACE SHUTTLE** program **ENDED** after 30 years, and China **LAUNCHED** its first space station module.

CHEMISTRY

Physical Chemistry. Two studies reported in 2011 concerned advances in the understanding of hydrogen bonding. Hydrogen bonds involve highly changeable interactions that are individually very weak but that in bulk are of fundamental importance to a wide range of phenomena, from the workings of climate to the formation of DNA molecules. Since hydrogen atoms have a very small mass, they tend to behave according to quantum-mechanical rules rather than by Newtonian rules governing larger masses. Using computational techniques, Angelos Michaelides of University College, London, and co-workers found that these quantum-mechanical effects weaken already weak hydrogen bonds but add strength to stronger ones. The scientists expected that this discovery would lead to more precise calculations of the strength and other characteristics of hydrogen bonds in any given hydrogen compound and therefore would allow chemists to predict more precisely the behaviour of hydrogen-containing bulk materials such as water.

The second study dealt with the discovery that the hydrogen bonds of water molecules at the boundary between a body of water and air are not strictly liquid or gaseous. The nature of this interface between water and air, which exists over more than 70% of Earth's surface, affects the atmosphere and the environment. Alexander Benderskii from the University of Southern California and colleagues found that the interface is only one molecule thick and that water molecules at this boundary have one of their two hydrogen atoms in the water and the other in the air. The hydrogen atom in the air acts as if it is in the gas phase, whereas the hydrogen atom below, in the water, acts as if it is in the liquid phase. This is important because many of the properties of water are determined by how the hydrogen atoms in its molecules bond chemically. The bonding of a molecule that straddles the water's surface is slightly weaker in comparison with the hydrogen bonds of molecules deeper in the bulk section of water and is similar to that of free water molecules in the air. The molecules at the surface change in and out constantly and are sometimes in the liquid phase, sometimes at the surface, and sometimes in the gas phase. As a result, there is a very fast transition of water molecules from gas-phase to liquid-phase behaviour and vice versa.

Applied Chemistry. Cheap, efficient solar-energy conversion has long been a goal of scientists. In 2011 Daniel Nocera (*see* BIOGRAPHIES) from MIT and colleagues reported on the development of a device that uses sunlight and water to produce hydrogen gas. The apparatus, about the size of a playing card, incorporated a silicon solar cell coated with catalytic materials. In one version of the device, one side of the solar cell was coated with a cobalt-based catalyst on a thin protective layer of indium tin oxide and the other side was coated with an alloy of nickel, molybdenum, and zinc. When the device is placed in water and illuminated by sunlight, the solar cell absorbs light and produces electrical energy that promotes chemical reactions between its coated surfaces and the water, effectively splitting water into its component elements, hydrogen and oxygen. In the version described, oxygen bubbles from the side of the solar cell coated with the cobalt-based catalyst

When placed in water and exposed to sunlight, this "artificial leaf," a silicon solar cell lined with catalytic materials, is able to split water into hydrogen and oxygen.

Dominick Reuter/Massachusetts Institute of Technology

and hydrogen from the other side. The hydrogen gas generated can then be collected and used as a fuel (in a fuel cell, for example). The device represented an advance over related technology by not requiring relatively rare chemical elements and for its ability to operate in ordinary fresh water and seawater. The resulting "artificial leaf" was inexpensive to produce, and the researchers envisioned the device's being used in poor countries that do not have easy access to large amounts of energy.

Organic Chemistry. In the 1950s Stanley Miller from the University of Chicago conducted a set of now-famous experiments to probe the origins of life on Earth. These experiments involved sending an electric charge, meant to simulate lightning, through a chamber filled with gasses thought to have formed the early atmosphere and then determining whether chemical precursors of life had been produced in the chamber. Miller followed up his published results with additional experiments in which he varied the composition of the gasses in the chamber. Miller, who died in 2007, left unanalyzed samples from these experiments with a former student, Jeffrey Bada. Bada, of the Scripps Institution of Oceanography, La Jolla, Calif., and colleagues used modern techniques such as high-performance liquid chromatography and time-of-flight mass spectrometry to study the preserved samples. These modern techniques, which were many times more sensitive than those used in the 1950s, detected a total of 23 amino acids, including 7 organosulfur compounds in a sample that Miller had produced by using a gaseous mixture of hydrogen sulfide, methane, ammonia, and carbon dioxide. Hydrogen sulfide was not included in Miller's earlier experiments, but he later used the compound because, according to some scenarios, it may have entered the early terrestrial environment in the plumes of volcanic eruptions. The samples, which had been stored in vials for more than 50 years, had roughly equal proportions of left-handed and right-handed varieties of many of the amino acids. This finding was an indication that the amino acids analyzed were generated by the experiment and not introduced later accidentally, since all living organisms produce only left-handed amino acids. The experiment was the first to show that sulfur-containing amino acids, vital to life, can be produced from a spark-discharge experiment. In addition, the overall quantities of the amino acids that were analyzed were comparable to those found in a type of meteorite rich in carbon, perhaps signifying that hydrogen sulfide may have had a key role in the environments of the early solar system.

Environmental Chemistry. Environmental chemists made advances during the year in the detection of water pollutants. Sang-Eun Oh and researchers from Arizona State University and Kangwon (S.Kor.) National University developed a system that uses *Acidithiobacillus*, a genus of sulfur-oxidizing bacteria found in wastewater, to monitor the overall toxicity of the water. Scientists usually monitored water pollution by looking at changes in the activity of specific microorganisms. This approach, however, was generally expensive and slow and could detect only certain pollutants. In the presence of oxygen and water, the *Acidithiobacillus* bacteria digest elemental sulfur and convert it to sulfate salts and protons. When nitrates, perchlorates, dichromates, or other pollutants are present, the bacteria's conversion of sulfur is slowed, reducing the yield of sulfate and protons. As a result, the pH of the water rises and the water's electrical conductivity decreases. These properties can be easily monitored, and the system can be used to measure water pollution as low as 5 to 50 parts per billion. The bacteria-based biosensor can detect toxicity within minutes to hours, which may be fast enough for use as an early-warning system to circumvent environmental pollution and threats to public health.

As known from such major oil spills as the Deepwater Horizon oil spill in 2010, petroleum can be a very serious water pollutant. To detect the amount of petroleum in water, oil workers use both ultraviolet fluorescence and infrared spectroscopy. Researchers from the University of Liverpool, Eng., used a technique that can measure oil levels in seawater more precisely and at lower concentrations than these methods. Stephen Taylor and colleagues tested the technique, called membrane inlet mass spectrometry, in the harsh conditions of the North Sea off Scotland. This type of mass spectrometry uses a membrane to keep water and salt from entering the instrument while letting through molecules of petroleum and other organic substances. It enabled the scientists not only to detect low levels of pollutants but also to identify what types of toxic hydrocarbons, such as benzene, toluene, and xylene, were in the oil. Use of this technique would allow oil workers to identify problems in the oil-extraction process and correct them more easily. The research conducted by Taylor and co-workers represented the first time that the technology had been used out in the field in harsh sea conditions. They were able to detect oil concentrations as low as 15 mg per litre, one-half the legal oil-discharge limit in the United Kingdom and, on the basis of the hydrocarbons found in the samples, were able even to distinguish contamination from two types of petroleum.

Industrial Chemistry. Renewable-energy production presents a number of challenges that need to be addressed for successful large-scale commercialization. It requires economical energy storage that can hold high levels of energy over extended electrical cycling (charging and discharging). By depositing manganese dioxide on porous textiles coated with an atom-thick layer of graphene, Zhenan Bao and colleagues at Stanford University created a flexible electrode material for high-performance capacitors. They placed the electrode in a solution of sodium sulfate together with a second electrode made from a textile coated with carbon nanotubes to create a supercapacitor with a maximum power density of 110 kW/kg that could hold 95% of its energy through 5,000 recharging cycles. The key to its high-energy load was the large surface area of the electrodes, and the scale of the reaction could be easily increased to industrial levels, making the technique easily transferable to large-scale energy production.

(LEIGH KRIETSCH BOERNER)

PHYSICS

Particle Physics. In 2011 technological developments enabled physicists to close in on the answers to outstanding problems in the physics of fundamental particles. One such problem concerns antimatter, the mirror image of normal matter; when matter and antimatter interact, they annihilate each other. Antihydrogen, consisting of a positively charged electron (or positron) and a negatively charged nucleus, was detected for the first time in 1995. The ALPHA international consortium at CERN, near Geneva, succeeded in producing and storing antihydrogen for up to 17 minutes, making it possible to compare its properties with those of normal hydrogen. Any observed differences might suggest a solution to the problem of the vast preponderance of normal matter over antimatter in the universe. On the other hand, they would also contradict the standard model of fundamental particle physics, which assumes identical properties for matter and antimatter. In a different approach, Masaki Hori and co-workers at the Max Planck Institute, Garching, Ger., examined a molecule made up of a helium atom and an antiproton, giving a relative mass of the electron and antiproton agreeing with that of the electron and proton. The STAR collaboration at the Relativistic Heavy Ion Collider, Brookhaven National Laboratory, Upton, N.Y., produced the first antihelium nuclei, which may also provide a test of matter-antimatter asymmetry.

Fundamental particle theory was tested in another way. One popular extension of the standard model is the theory of supersymmetry, which postulates that each particle has a heavier "supersymmetrical" partner that rarely interacts with normal matter. However, first results from the Large Hadron Collider at CERN produced no evidence of such particles.

Condensed State. The study of graphene—a two-dimensional lattice of carbon atoms on an insulating substrate—produced results that may lead to a new generation of electronic devices, since electrons can travel in graphene 100 times faster than in silicon. Yanqing Wu and co-workers at the IBM Thomas J. Watson Research Center, Yorktown Heights, N.Y., studied graphene transistors that had cut-off frequencies as high as 155 GHz and that, unlike conventional devices, worked well at temperatures as low as 4.3 K (–268.9 °C, or –451.9 °F). Ming Liu and colleagues at the NSF Nanoscale Science and Engineering Center, Berkeley, Calif., demonstrated a high-speed broadband electro-optical modulator with high efficiency and an active device area of only 25 μm^2. Such a device could lead to new designs of optical communications on chips. Vinay Gupta and colleagues from the National Physical Laboratory, New Delhi, made luminescent graphene quantum dots blended with organic polymers for use in solar cells and light-emitting diodes, which could offer better performance at lower cost than other polymer-based organic materials. By combining graphene with extremely small metal wires called plasmonic nanostructures, T.J. Echtermeyer, of the University of Cambridge, and co-workers created graphene-based photodetectors that were 20 times more efficient than those made in previous experiments.

Other two-dimensional systems were studied. A.F. Santander-Syro's group at Université de Paris-Sud, Orsay, France, showed that there was a two-dimensional electron gas at the surface of the material $SrTiO_3$.

One possible way for future computers to store information would be to encode data in the spin of electrons; such a computer has been called "spintronic." Kuntal Roy and colleagues at Virginia Commonwealth University made a great step to producing a spintronic device by making a small spintronic switch in which very small amounts of energy would cause a piezoelectric material to move and thus change the spins of electrons in a thin magnetic layer. Devices using such switches could be powered by only very slight movements.

Optics and Lasers. Two new types of laser appeared in 2011. Yao Xiao and colleagues at the department of optical instrumentation, Zhejiang University, Hangzhou, China, reported lasing action at 738 nm (nanometres), using a folded wire 200 nm in diameter. The configuration made possible a tunable single-mode nanowire laser. Malte Gather and Seok-Hyun Yun at Harvard Medical School created a "living laser" by using biological material. Green fluorescent protein that had been inserted into human embryo kidney cells was used in a tiny optical cavity to produce laser light. This technique could be used to study processes in a living cell.

In a different region of the electromagnetic spectrum, J.R. Hird, C.G. Camara, and S.J. Putterman at the department of physics and astronomy, University of California, Los Angeles, investigated the triboelectric effect, in which electric currents are generated by friction. When the team pulled apart silicon and a metal-coated epoxy, a current generated by the friction was found to produce a beam of X-rays. This method could lead to a new generation of simple and cheap sources for X-ray imaging.

Lasers and optical devices for high-speed communications and information processing were being studied in many laboratories, with an emphasis on efficiency and reproducibility. Bryan Ellis and co-workers at Stanford University developed an electrically pumped quantum dot laser that produced continuous wave operation with the lowest current threshold yet observed. Matthew T. Rakher and colleagues at National Institute of Standards and Technology, Gaithersburg, Md., devised a system for simultaneous wavelength translation and amplitude modulation for single photons, using the "blending" in a crystal of photons from two separate laser sources. Georgios Ctistis and colleagues at the University of Twente, Enschede, Neth., built a switch that changed state in just one-trillionth of a second (10^{-12} s).

Quantum Information. Quantum information systems involve photons that are "entangled"—perfectly correlated over long distances. For storage and transmission of such photons, practical

(Left) A cell that is genetically designed to produce the light-emitting molecule, green flourescent protein, produces green laser light. (Right) The cell emits green laser light when placed inside an optical resonator consisting of two mirrors 20 micrometres apart and after a beam of blue light shines on the cell.

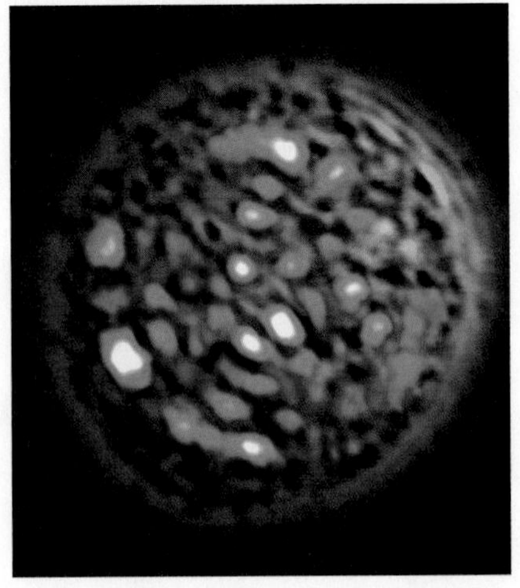

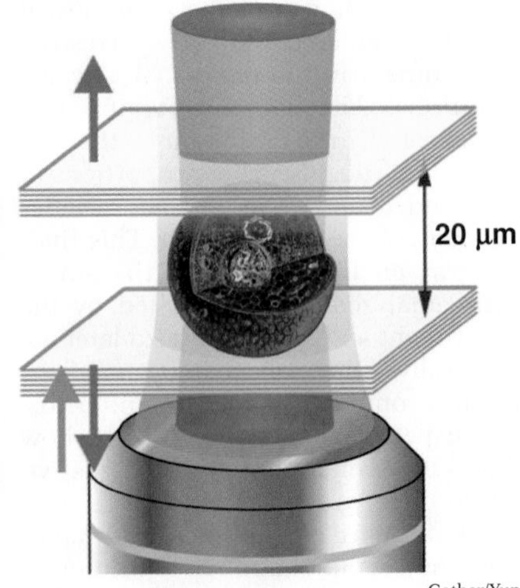

Gather/Yun

quantum memories are required for storing and recalling quantum states on demand with high efficiency and low noise. For transmission occurring over long distances, memory repeaters are required for receiving input data and retransmitting.

In 2011 a number of groups demonstrated designs for such devices. M. Hosseini and colleagues at the Australian National University in Canberra reconstructed quantum states that had been stored in the ground states of rubidium vapour with up to 98% fidelity. Christoph Clausen and co-workers at the University of Geneva demonstrated entanglement between a photon and a physical system. One photon from an entangled pair was stored in a Nd:Y_2SiO_5 crystal and then later released, but it still retained its entanglement with the unstored photon.

Holger P. Specht and co-workers at the Max Planck Institute for Quantum Optics, Garching, demonstrated a system in which a quantum bit, or qubit (a photon whose polarization states contain information), was absorbed by a single rubidium atom trapped inside an optical cavity. The rubidium atom later emitted a photon containing the original polarized information. Thus, the rubidium atom served as a quantum computer memory.

In a very different approach, Christian Ospelkaus of Leibniz University, Hannover, Ger., and colleagues used a waveguide integrated on a microchip to produce the first microwave quantum gate—that is, a logic gate for a quantum computer. Two ions were trapped just above the chip's surface. Multiple pulses of microwave radiation entangled the two ions, which acted as a quantum gate. N. Timoney and colleagues at the University of Siegen, Ger., trapped individual ions and applied microwave pulses to them to decouple them from outside noise and thus make an undisturbed quantum processor. Such developments could aid the production of large ion-trap quantum computers in the foreseeable future.

Relativity. Results from Gravity Probe B, one of NASA's longest-running missions, confirmed two predictions of Einstein's general theory of relativity. It observed geodetic precession, in which the curvature of space-time around Earth induces a slight wobble in an orbiting gyroscope, and also gravitomagnetism, in which the spin of a massive object such as Earth tugs space-time in the direction of its rotation.

However, the OPERA group at the Gran Sasso National Laboratory, near Aquila, Italy, studying a beam of neutrinos generated 730 km (454 mi) away at CERN, caused a stir when they announced results that appeared to show that the particles had traveled faster than the speed of light, the fundamental limiting speed that underlies the special theory of relativity. If confirmed, this would call into question the whole basis of modern physics. The group made their results public in the hope that the experiment would be repeated independently and reasons would be identified for their unexpected finding. (DAVID G.C. JONES)

ASTRONOMY

Solar System. New discoveries about planets in the solar system provided some of the major astronomical headlines in 2011. In August scientists announced that cameras on board Mars Reconnaissance Orbiter (MRO) captured images of what appeared to be water flowing on the surface of Mars. MRO took pictures of dark streaks emerging from a slope in Newton crater and then flowing downhill. These streaks began during Martian spring and increased in length through Martian summer. The best candidate for a material that would begin melting at the right temperature was salty water. The likely presence of surviving underground water on Mars buoyed hopes that perhaps microbial life still survived there.

Minor planets and asteroids are among the smallest members of the solar system, along with comets and some of the moons of the major planets. On July 16 NASA's Dawn spacecraft arrived at Vesta, the second largest main-belt asteroid. Vesta revolved around the Sun in an orbit lying between the orbits of Mars and Jupiter. During the following months the spacecraft mapped Vesta's surface with unprecedented spatial resolution. Images showed that the asteroid has a diameter of 530 km (330 mi) and is highly pockmarked with many meteor-impact craters, particularly in its northern hemisphere. The southern hemisphere's surface appeared to be somewhat smoother. Scientists speculated that a collision with another solar system body might have obliterated some of the southern hemisphere's earlier craters. The most notable feature on the surface of Vesta is a large circular depression at its south pole, which is surrounded by cliffs several kilometres in height. Vesta also has a long set of ridges and grooves running along its equator. A mountain about 22 km (13 mi) high, roughly three times the height of Mt. Everest, was discovered on the southernmost part of the body. The Dawn spacecraft would continue to make a variety of scientific measurements of the properties of Vesta until July 2012, at which time it would depart for the even larger main-belt asteroid and dwarf planet Ceres.

In 2006 the International Astronomical Union demoted Pluto from being one of the nine major planets to one of the tens of thousands of minor planets. Nevertheless, the object continued to surprise and fascinate scientists and the public alike. In July astronomers using the Hubble Space Telescope announced the discovery of a new moon of Pluto; they also checked earlier Hubble images and found faint traces of what appeared to be the moon in images from 2006 and 2010. This brought to four the total number of moons discovered for this minor planet. The new moon, P4, is only about 13–34 km

Earth Perihelion and Aphelion, 2012	
Jan. 5	Perihelion, approx. 00:00[1]
July 5	Aphelion, approx. 03:00[1]
Equinoxes and Solstices, 2012	
March 20	Vernal equinox, 05:14[1]
June 20	Summer solstice, 23:09[1]
Sept. 22	Autumnal equinox, 14:49[1]
Dec. 21	Winter solstice, 11:12[1]
Eclipses, 2012	
May 20	Sun, annular (begins 20:56[1]), the beginning visible in eastern Asia; with the ending visible in most of North America and Greenland.
June 4	Moon, partial (beginning 08:46[1]), the beginning visible in most of North and South America; the middle visible in Australia; the end visible in eastern Asia.
Nov. 13	Sun, total (beginning 19:38[1]), visible along a path beginning in northern Australia and ending in the South Pacific Ocean near South America; with a partial phase visible beginning in some of Indonesia, Papua New Guinea, Australia, and New Zealand; the middle visible in some of Antarctica; the end visible in southern Argentina and Chile.
Nov. 28	Moon, partial (begins 12:12[1]), the beginning visible in most of North America; the middle visible in Asia and Australia; the end visible in the Middle East and most of Europe and Africa.

[1] Universal time.
Source: *The Astronomical Almanac for the Year 2012* (2011).

(8–21 mi) across. The three previously discovered moons—Nix, Hydra, and Charon—have diameters ranging from about 81 km (50 mi) for Hydra to about 1,200 km (750 mi) for Charon.

Stars and Extrasolar Planets. By the end of 2011, more than 700 extrasolar planets had been discovered. Of these, more than 210 planets were in multiplanet systems, a few of these somewhat similar to the solar system. On the basis of the European Southern Observatory's High Accuracy Radial velocity Planet Searcher (HARPS) survey, it was estimated that at least half of the stars in the Milky Way Galaxy that are similar to the Sun have planets in orbit around them. NASA's Kepler spacecraft science team announced that it had identified over 2,000 additional planet candidates. The Kepler satellite in 2011 came closer to its goal of finding an Earth-size planet in another star's habitable zone (the region where liquid water could survive on a planet's surface) when it found the first Earth-size planets, Kepler-20e and Kepler-20f, which are 0.87 and 1.03 times the radius of Earth, respectively. However, with orbital periods of 6.1 and 19.6 days, respectively, they orbit too close to their star for liquid water to survive. Kepler also detected a planet orbiting in the habitable zone. The planet Kepler-22b orbits a star similar to the Sun every 290 days and has a radius 2.4 times that of Earth. Another Kepler discovery was in orbit around two stars. The planet Kepler-16b is part of an eclipsing binary star system where the stars and planet pass in front of one another periodically blocking some of the light from the telescope on board Kepler. This planet is a cold inhospitable place roughly the size of Saturn, and it orbits the two stars in about 229 days. Another planet studied by the Kepler mission, TrES-2b, is in a very close orbit around its central star and has a temperature of about 1,000 °C (1,800 °F). What was most unusual about the planet was that it reflects less than 1% of the light striking it, making its surface blacker than coal or any other natural substance found on Earth. Another remarkable discovery was KeplerH-10b. It orbits so close to its star that it appears to be tidally locked to it, with one side of the planet always facing the star. The planet is about 40% larger in diameter than Earth but has a mass of about 4.6 Earth masses. This meant that the average density of the planet is about 8.8 g/cc. (Earth has a mean density of 5.5 g/cc.) This suggested that the planet consists almost entirely of rock and metal.

The first reported candidates for black holes within the Milky Way Galaxy were objects that were detected as members of binary star systems. These objects were not seen directly in visible light. Instead, they were detected as X-ray sources, where the X-rays were thought to be radiated by disks of hot gas surrounding the purported black holes. Since the 1960s Cygnus X-1, the brightest X-ray source in the constellation Cygnus, had been the most prominent of the black hole candidates. The case for the X-ray emitter's being a black hole, however, was somewhat circumstantial. Using rough estimates of the distance to the source and best estimates for the mass of the fairly normal companion star in the binary system, scientists concluded that the mass of the unseen star was 5–10 times the mass of the Sun. This mass was too high for the optically invisible star to be either a white dwarf or a neutron star, which led to the conclusion that it must be a black hole. In 2011, some 40 years after the system's discovery, detailed properties of it were finally determined, leaving very little room for ambiguity. The new findings were published in a series of three papers. The first study, by M.J. Reid and collaborators from the Harvard-Smithsonian Center for Astrophysics, Cambridge, Mass., used the Very Long Baseline Array of radio telescopes that were distributed around the world to determine an accurate distance to the source of approximately 6,070 light-years. This facilitated the second study, which used a variety of optical and X-ray observations to determine the mass of the black hole. The result, reported by J.A. Orosz and colleagues from San Diego State University, was that the black hole has a mass of 15 solar masses with an uncertainty of less than one solar mass. The third study, by L. Gou and collaborators from the Harvard-Smithsonian Center for Astrophysics, showed that the black hole is spinning at a rate of more than 800 rotations per second. This was very nearly the maximum rotation rate that the general theory of relativity allows for a black hole of this mass.

The first planet found to orbit two stars, Kepler-16b, appears in this artist's conception.

T. Pyle—JPL-Caltech/NASA

Galaxies and Cosmology. The beginning of 2011 saw the record broken for the most-distant astronomical object ever detected. Using the Hubble Ultra Deep Field image 09, a team led by Rychard Bouwens of the University of California, Santa Cruz, found a galaxy with a redshift of 10.3. The light from the galaxy took 13.2 billion years to arrive at Earth. This meant that it formed a mere 500 million years after the big bang.

According to the best observational evidence, the universe began with a hot dense phase that resulted in the synthesis of hydrogen and helium with only trace amounts of heavier elements. Most of the heavier elements were made much later through nuclear fusion in the interiors of stars. However, no truly primordial gas had been observed until now; all the previous detections of gas at high redshifts contained some heavier elements. In November, Michele Fumagalli and colleagues from the University of California, Santa Cruz, announced that they had observed two clouds of intergalactic gas at redshifts of 3.5 and 3.3 (originating when the universe was only about two billion years old). These clouds were truly "pristine," containing mainly hydrogen and helium. In one cloud the team observed deuterium, an isotope of hydrogen, in the amount predicted by the best theoretical model.

(KENNETH BRECHER)

SPACE EXPLORATION

Manned Spaceflight. The U.S. space shuttle program ended with three final missions to the International Space Station (ISS) and left Americans uncertain about their next steps in manned spaceflight. Although the ISS's mission was to last through 2020, future access to it and plans for flights beyond Earth orbit were still being worked out. In the near future, astronauts would be carried to the ISS by Russia's Soyuz, and supplies would be delivered by unmanned craft from Russia, Japan, and Europe. (*See* Sidebar.)

Each of the three space shuttle orbiters made a final flight in 2011. *Discovery* (STS-133, February 24–March 9) carried the Leonardo Multi-Purpose Logistics Module (MPLM), which was added to the ISS as a permanent storage module. The most interesting payload was the "seventh crewmember" for the ISS, Robonaut 2 (R2), a humanoid robot developed by NASA and General Motors. The 150-kg (330-lb) R2 was designed to take over mundane operational tasks aboard the ISS, allowing the six-person human crew to focus on scientific research. Eventually R2 would be rated for operations outside the ISS. In the long term, NASA hoped to deploy R2 successors on planetary-exploration missions.

Endeavour (STS-134, May 16–June 1) attached the Alpha Magnetic Spectrometer (AMS), the most sophisticated particle detector in space, to the ISS. At one point the project had been canceled because of ISS costs and because of problems with the AMS's superconducting magnet. International protests and replacement of the magnet led to its eventual flight.

Atlantis (STS-135, July 8–21) carried the Raffaello MPLM filled with supplies, spares, and other equipment. A small crew of only four astronauts was launched to maximize the payload carried up and to minimize the time the four would have to stay on the ISS if *Atlantis* could not return to Earth.

The ramp-down from the shuttle program began even before *Atlantis* landed. On April 12, the 30th anniversary of the first shuttle launch, NASA announced the final disposition of the orbiters. Each orbiter would be displayed as a museum piece: *Atlantis* at the Kennedy Space Center at Cape Canaveral, Florida; *Discovery* at the National Air and Space Museum's Udvar-Hazy Center, Chantilly, Va.; and *Endeavour* at the California Science Center in Los Angeles.

Four Soyuz crew-exchange missions to the ISS were launched, with the last two being delayed by a launch failure on August 24 of the same rocket used for Soyuz flights, caused by the blockage of a fuel duct in the third stage. Although the ISS had adequate supplies, temporarily abandoning it was considered because of the limited orbital life of the Soyuz spacecraft that served as the station's lifeboats.

China took a major step toward assembly of its own space station with the launch on September 29 of Tiangong 1 ("Heavenly Palace 1"). It had a single docking port and two solar arrays. The unmanned Shenzhou 8 spacecraft docked with it on November 3. Shenzhou 9 and 10 with two- or three-man crews were scheduled for docking in 2012. Assembly of a much larger Chinese space station was expected to be completed in 2020–22.

NASA announced that it would redesign the canceled Constellation spacecraft Orion as the Orion Multi-Purpose Crew Vehicle for carrying up to four astronauts. The first unmanned orbital flight was set for 2014 and the first manned flight in 2016. The new vehicle would initially be launched by existing rockets and later by NASA's proposed Space Launch System.

Bigelow Aerospace, which was developing its own BA 330 six-person space

Human Spaceflight Launches and Returns, 2011

Country	Flight	Crew[1]	Dates[2]	Mission/payload
U.S.	STS-133, *Discovery*	Steven Lindsey Eric Boe Benjamin Alvin Drew, Jr. Michael Barratt Stephen Bowen Nicole Stott	February 24–March 9	delivery of robot Robonaut 2 and ESA-built Permanent Multipurpose Module to ISS
Russia	Soyuz TMA-01M (down)	Scott J. Kelly, NASA Aleksandr Kaleri Oleg Skripochka	March 16	crew exchange
Russia	Soyuz TMA-21 (up)	Andrey Borisenko Aleksandr Samokutyayev Ronald Garan, NASA	April 5	crew exchange
U.S.	STS-134, *Endeavour*	Mark Kelly Gregory Johnson Edward Michael Fincke Gregory Chamitoff Andrew Feustel Roberto Vittori, ESA	May 16–June 1	delivery of Alpha Magnetic Spectrometer to ISS
Russia	Soyuz TMA-20 (down)	Dmitry Kondratyev Catherine Coleman, NASA Paolo Nespoli, ESA	May 24	crew exchange
Russia	Soyuz TMA-02M (up)	Michael Fossum, NASA Sergey Volkov Satoshi Furukawa, JAXA	June 7	crew exchange
U.S.	STS-135, *Atlantis*	Christopher Ferguson Douglas Hurley Sandra Magnus Rex Walheim	July 8–21	delivery of ESA-built Raffaello Multipurpose Logistics Module with supplies
Russia	Soyuz TMA-21 (down)	Andrey Borisenko Aleksandr Samokutyayev Ronald Garan, NASA	September 16	crew exchange
Russia	Soyuz TMA-22 (up)	Daniel Burbank, NASA Anatoly Ivanishin Anton Shkaplerov	November 14	crew exchange
Russia	Soyuz TMA-02M (down)	Michael Fossum, NASA Sergey Volkov Satoshi Furukawa, JAXA	November 22	crew exchange
Russia	Soyuz TMA-03M (up)	Oleg Kononenko Donald Pettit, NASA André Kuipers, ESA	December 21	crew exchange

[1] For shuttle flights, mission commander and pilot are listed first. For Soyuz flights, ISS commander is listed first.
[2] Flight dates for shuttle; Soyuz launch or return dates for ISS missions.

The Culmination of the U.S. Space Shuttle Program

On July 21, 2011, the 30-year-old U.S. space shuttle program reached its end when the final shuttle, *Atlantis,* landed at NASA's Kennedy Space Center after having concluded a 12-day mission. It was the 135th mission in a flight program that began with the launch of the first space shuttle on April 12, 1981, and comprised four test flights, 129 operational missions, and two flights that were cut short by catastrophic accidents, each resulting in the death of the seven-person crew. Though the space shuttle program achieved significant accomplishments, a number of promises remained unfulfilled.

Each space shuttle consisted of three elements: the shuttle orbiter, the winged vehicle that accelerated into orbit, carried out its mission, and then glided to a runway landing; the external tank, the large cigar-shaped body that carried the system's extremely cold liquid hydrogen and liquid oxygen fuel and burned up as it reentered the atmosphere after it was jettisoned a few minutes after liftoff; and two solid rocket boosters that attached to the sides of the external tank and provided most of the lifting power during the first two minutes after launch, after which they separated and fell into the ocean, from which they were recovered to be refurbished and reused. After the solid rockets were jettisoned, three main engines on the rear of the orbiter accelerated the orbiter to its orbital speed of 28,000 km/hr (17,500 mph).

Six shuttle orbiters were built. The first, *Enterprise,* was a test vehicle not intended for space travel. On the basis of a letter-writing campaign, it was named after the spacecraft in the television series *Star Trek.* The other orbiters were named after research ships. The first to fly, *Columbia,* engaged in 27 successful missions before breaking up on reentry on Feb. 1, 2003. A piece of the external tank's insulation foam had punched a hole in the orbiter's wing two minutes after launch; this allowed the heat of reentry 16 days later to melt the wing's internal structure. The next, *Challenger,* flew nine missions before it broke up 73 seconds after launch on Jan. 28, 1986, after its fuel ignited as a solid rocket booster failed because of a faulty rubber O-ring. *Discovery* flew the most, completing 39 missions between 1984 and 2011; *Atlantis* performed 33 missions, beginning in 1985, including the final shuttle mission in July 2011. *Endeavour* replaced *Challenger* and had 25 flights between 1992 and 2011. The five orbiters carried 355 different people (306 men and 49 women) from the U.S. and 15 other countries into orbit; many of those people made multiple trips to space.

The space shuttle was one of the most complex machines ever built, with more than 2.5 million parts. The shuttle orbiter was 37 m (122 ft) long and had a wingspan of 24 m (78 ft); its payload bay measured 5 × 18 m (15 × 60 ft). Its heaviest payload, the Chandra X-ray Observatory and its upper stage and support equipment (launched in 1999), weighed some 25 tons at launch. When attached to its external tank, the shuttle stood 56 m (184 ft) high; it weighed up to 2 million kg (4.5 million lb) on liftoff. The shuttle could fly only to low Earth orbit, ranging from 185 to 640 km (115 to 400 mi) above the planet. On most missions it carried a crew of seven. Prior to the *Challenger* accident, the shuttle was thought safe enough to carry passengers such as politicians and a teacher.

The space shuttle, with its large payload bay, orbital maneuvering capability, and robotic arm, was capable of many different operations in space. It carried various spacecraft, including communications satellites and probes to Jupiter and Venus, to Earth orbit for launch to their final orbits. The shuttle served as an orbiting laboratory, carrying out many onboard experiments. It retrieved satellites that were launched into incorrect orbits and returned them to Earth for relaunch. It also carried out classified missions for the national security community.

Among the space shuttle's most notable achievements were:

- Five missions to the Hubble Space Telescope—the first one to install the corrective optics that allowed Hubble to operate at full capability despite a misshapen primary mirror and the others to give it additional capabilities and to extend its life
- Nine dockings (1995–98) with the Russian space station Mir as a first step in U.S.-Russian cooperation in human spaceflight
- Thirty-seven flights between 1998 and 2011 to assemble and provision the International Space Station

The space shuttle set a precedent for international cooperation in human spaceflight. Canada contributed the robotic arm, and Europe provided a small laboratory—Spacelab—that could be carried in the shuttle's payload bay.

Despite these significant accomplishments, the space shuttle program did not fulfill many of the promises made by its proponents to gain program approval. When Pres. Richard Nixon announced in 1972 that the U.S. would develop the shuttle, he envisioned that the reusable vehicle would "revolutionize transportation into near space, by routinizing it." The shuttle was very difficult to operate safely, however. It remained experimental, and its complexity carried inherent safety risks. In 1972 NASA estimated that a shuttle mission would cost $10.5 million ($54.7 million in 2010 dollars); the average cost was $775 million in 2010 dollars. The total shuttle program cost through development and 135 flights was $113.7 billion ($209.1 billion in 2010 dollars, or $1.55 billion per flight). The shuttle was projected to fly as many as 55 missions annually, but the most shuttle launches in one year (1985) turned out to be nine. When the space shuttle was retired, there was not an immediate replacement for its crew-carrying capability. (JOHN M. LOGSDON)

station with inflatable modules for use by both governments and private companies, announced in September that it was laying off roughly half of its workforce. The company cited the lack of immediate means of carrying astronauts to the BA 330.

In October Iran announced that it had failed in an attempt to send a monkey on a suborbital flight on the Kavoshgar-5 vehicle, despite the success in March of the Kavoshgar-4 test vehicle. Iran hoped to send a human into space in 2020.

Space Probes. The NASA spacecraft Messenger entered orbit around Mercury on March 17. It was the first spacecraft to orbit Mercury and only the second to visit it. Its nominal mission at Mercury was planned to last one Earth year, or four Mercury years.

Kim Shiflett/NASA

The orbiter Atlantis *lands on July 21, marking the end of the U.S. space shuttle program.*

Its instruments investigated the planet's magnetic field, surface chemistry, and geology. Messenger was placed in a highly elliptical orbit, 200 × 15,000 km (120 × 9,300 mi), designed to reduce exposure to infrared radiation from the planet's surface.

On the final stage of its exploration of Mars, the rover *Opportunity* prepared to enter Endeavour crater. *Opportunity* had started its drive to the crater in January and reached its edge on August 9. Since landing on Mars in 2004, it had traveled more than 33.6 km (20.9 mi). Its sister rover *Spirit* was declared lost on May 24 after repeated attempts to contact it failed.

A new rover, the Mars Science Laboratory, called *Curiosity*, launched to Mars on November 26 and would arrive in August 2012. *Curiosity* weighed 900 kg (2,000 lb), more than twice as much as *Spirit* and *Opportunity* combined. *Curiosity* was targeted for Gale crater, which was believed to contain materials washed down by liquid water. The exploration plan included an area believed to be an ancient lake bed possibly holding organic compounds.

Russia launched the Phobos-Grunt (Phobos-Soil) probe on November 9. Phobos-Grunt, which also carried the Chinese Mars orbiter Yinghuo-1, was scheduled to arrive at the Martian moon Phobos in 2012, but it failed to leave Earth orbit.

The Cassini spacecraft orbiting Saturn continued its second mission extension, the Cassini Solstice mission, which should run through 2017. The name referred to the position of Saturn relative to the Sun. During the year Cassini executed 11 close flybys of Saturnian moons—six of Titan, three of Enceladus, and one each of Rhea and Dione.

The Juno spacecraft was launched to Jupiter on August 5. It was the first outer solar system mission to use solar rather than nuclear power and would go into polar orbit around Jupiter in July 2016. The use of the polar orbit would allow the study of the planet's gravitational field and magnetosphere.

The Gravity Recovery and Interior Laboratory (GRAIL) mission comprised twin spacecraft launched on September 10 on a nine-month mission to orbit the Moon. The first spacecraft arrived in lunar orbit on December 31, and the other arrived the next day. Precision radio tracking of the separation between the two would allow for the mapping of the Moon's gravitational field.

Unmanned Satellites. A second X-37B spacecraft was launched by the U.S. Air Force into Earth orbit on a classified mission on March 5. The craft resembled a miniature space shuttle and was designed to carry a small payload for several months and then reenter the atmosphere, glide to Earth, and land like a shuttle. The air force did not reveal its mission.

Several smaller countries entered space or expanded their presence. Iran launched its second satellite, the Earth-observing Rasad 1, on June 15, using a Safir B1 rocket derived from the Scud ballistic missile. The United States launched Satélite de Aplicaciones Científicas (SAC-D)/Aquarius, built by Argentina, on June 10. Aquarius was an American instrument designed to measure ocean salinity. SAC-D contained other instruments, such as a microwave radiometer that complemented Aquarius by measuring rainfall and wind speed over the oceans.

Two unmanned satellites made headlines with uncontrolled returns to Earth. The Upper Atmosphere Research Satellite, launched Sept. 12, 1991, had been decommissioned in 2005. Its orbit decayed, and it entered the atmosphere on September 24 over the Pacific Ocean. No large parts were known to have struck land. The German Röntgensatellit (ROSAT), which was launched June 1, 1990, and defunct since 1999, reentered Earth's atmosphere on October 23. Few of its large glass and ceramic parts were thought to have survived reentry.

Launch Vehicles. NASA announced that it would develop the Space Launch System (SLS), which would be less ambitious than the Ares V launcher of the canceled Constellation program. The new SLS would have a core vehicle based on the shuttle external tank and five RS-25 engines derived from the space shuttle main engine and use five-segment solid rocket boosters. A second stage would use the J-2X engine based on the Saturn rocket's J-2. The first flight with an unmanned Orion Multi-Purpose Crew Vehicle flight around the Moon was expected in 2017, followed by a manned trip in 2019. Through 2032 only 13 NASA launches were expected—the same number of launches that took place during the Apollo and Skylab programs in 1967–73.

(DAVE DOOLING)

Religion

VIOLENCE between adherents of different faith groups, government **RESTRICTIONS** on religious practices, new developments in the **SEXUAL ABUSE** scandals in the Roman Catholic Church, and continuing debates concerning the **ORDINATION** of women and **HOMOSEXUALS** were among the major developments in the world of religion in 2011.

Religious Violence. Two major political figures were killed in Pakistan for having opposed the country's anti-blasphemy laws. Salman Taseer, governor of Punjab province, was assassinated in January by one of his bodyguards at a shopping centre in Islamabad. Five hundred Islamic scholars from the Jamaat-e-Ahl-e-Sunnat, a group within the Barelvi movement, warned that anyone who expressed grief over the assassination could suffer the same fate. Barelvis spearheaded rallies to call for the release of the assassin. The group had been known for its opposition to suicide bombings and other violence, but Mohammed Ziaul Haq, a spokesman for the Barelvis' Sunni Ittehad Council, distinguished between terrorism and killing in response to blasphemy. Shahbaz Bhatti, Pakistan's federal minorities minister and the only Christian in the Pakistani cabinet, was gunned down in March in Islamabad as he left for work from his mother's house. Like Taseer, he had publicly stated that the blasphemy laws had been used to persecute members of religious minorities. In April two Taliban suicide bombers detonated explosives at the Sakhi Sarwar Sufi shrine in Dera Ghazi Khan, Pak., killing 42 people.

Boko Haram, a militant Nigerian Islamist group, killed more than 400 people in attacks throughout the year. Attempts to negotiate with the group were complicated by its apparent split into three factions following the 2009 death of its leader, Mohammed Yusuf.

Deadly clashes between Muslims and Christians erupted in Egypt throughout the year. In Alexandria an apparent suicide bombing after a New Year's mass at the Saints Church, a Coptic Orthodox house of worship, killed 21 people. The Coptic Church of the Two Martyrs St. George and St. Mina in the village of Sool was destroyed by a Muslim mob in March after an imam had called for the killing of Christians in response to a rumour of an adulterous affair between a Muslim woman and a Christian man. The church was later rebuilt by the Egyptian military. After two days of clashes in May between Christians and Muslims, in which 12 people were reportedly killed, Justice Minister Mohamed el-Guindy said that gatherings around places of worship would be banned to protect their sanctity and prevent sectarian strife. Mohammed Badie, leader of the Islamist organization the Muslim Brotherhood, condemned the burning of churches by Muslims and said, "There is nothing like this criminality present in Islam."

In Ethiopia a court in Addis Ababa sentenced 558 people in July to jail terms ranging from six months to 25 years for attacks in March in which 69 churches were burned down. The attacks on Protestants were prompted by rumours that desecrated pages from the Qur'an, the holy book of Islam, had been found at a church construction site near the town of Asendabo. At least 20 people were killed in Afghanistan in April during protests against the burning of a Qur'an at the Dove World Outreach Center, a small church in Gainesville, Fla., that had made international headlines the previous year for having announced a public Qur'an burning. In November U.S. federal authorities raided the compound of a breakaway Amish group in eastern Ohio and arrested seven men, including group leader Sam Mullet and three of his sons, on charges of hate crimes

Onlookers assess the scene outside the Sakhi Sarwar Sufi shrine in Dera Ghazi Khan, Pak., following a pair of suicide bomb attacks that claimed dozens of lives, April 3.

Naeem Sindhu—EPA/Landov

Amy Sancetta/AP

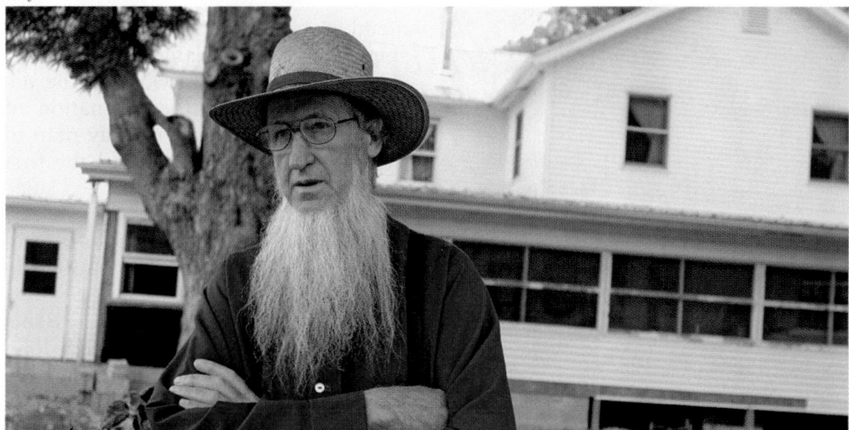

Sam Mullet, the leader of a breakaway Amish group that was responsible for having forcibly cut the hair of other Amish men and women during a series of attacks in late 2011, stands in front of his house in Bergholz, Ohio, on October 10. In December Mullet and 11 others were federally indicted on various charges.

in hair-cutting attacks against six other Amish. Hair-cutting violates the Amish belief that men are biblically enjoined to grow beards. The attacks occurred during a dispute between Mullet and bishops who objected to his desire to excommunicate several Amish.

Church-State Relations. The European Court of Human Rights ruled in March that displaying crucifixes in schools in Italy does not breach the rights of non-Catholic families. In so doing, the court overturned its own decision of November 2009 that such displays could be disturbing for non-Christian pupils. In an appeal that was the first of its kind, 17 house churches (which lack official sanction) in the People's Republic of China petitioned the National People's Congress in May to provide legal protection of religious freedom after police detained dozens of members of a congregation in Beijing that had been trying to hold outdoor services. In July the Vatican excommunicated Joseph Huang Bingzhang, who had been installed without the approval of the Holy See as bishop of Shantou by the state-sanctioned Chinese Patriotic Catholic Association. In a statement, the Vatican said that Pope Benedict XVI deplored the way that Chinese authorities had coerced some bishops loyal to the Vatican to attend the ordination service against their will. Both the Vatican and Chinese authorities agreed in November upon the consecration as a bishop coadjutor of Peter Luo Xuegang.

The centuries-old ban on the marriage of the British monarch to a Roman Catholic was overturned in October by the 16 countries that recognize the monarch as their head of state. However, the rule reserving the throne to Protestants remained; the position is linked to the monarch's title as head of the Church of England. In a visit to Zimbabwe in October, Rowan Williams, archbishop of Canterbury and head of the Anglican Communion (the worldwide administrative body of mainstream Anglicanism), criticized violence against churches in the country that was initiated by supporters of Pres. Robert Mugabe. In August the Zimbabwean Supreme Court had issued a ruling giving control of Anglican properties to Bishop Nolbert Kunonga, the leader of a breakaway faction. The establishment of South Sudan as an independent country in July was marked by services of thanksgiving in churches throughout the country. The new country, three-fifths of whose citizens were Christian, won independence from the predominantly Islamic Sudan after decades of civil war in which 1.5 million people died. In a mass James Wani Igga, the president of South Sudan's parliament, said, "Let our Muslim brothers and sisters know that independence means freedom of religion for all" without fear of reprisal or persecution.

Kazakhstan's Parliament passed a law in September requiring existing religious organizations in the mainly Muslim country to dissolve and register again. To register nationwide, a group had to have 5,000 members across all the country's regions. Critics objected because of the likelihood that two-thirds of existing religious groups could be abolished as a result of the law. Turkish Prime Minister Recep Tayyip Erdogan announced in August that the country's government would return hundreds of properties that had been confiscated from religious minorities since 1936 and would pay compensation for those that had been sold. Lobsang Sangay (*see* BIOGRAPHIES), a Fulbright scholar at Harvard Law School, was sworn in as *kalon tripa* (prime minister) of the Tibetan Central Administration (government-in-exile) in August in Dharmshala, India. He was elected in March with about 55% of the more than 49,000 votes cast to become the first nonmonk to hold the position of *kalon tripa*; he was also the first secular head of the Tibetan government-in-exile, as Tenzin Gyatso, the 14th Dalai Lama, had earlier relinquished his political authority. The self-immolation of a young Buddhist monk in March to protest China's campaign of forced reeducation at the Kirti monastery led to a series of such protests by monks and nuns during the year that claimed the lives of at least six.

In the U.S. two federal appeals courts issued rulings with implications for religious liberty. A Denver court ruled in March that a law restricting the use of eagle feathers to American Indian tribes for religious purposes does not violate the religious freedoms of non-Indians, including Native Americans who are not a member of a federally recognized Indian tribe. A New York court ruled in June that the city may ban Sunday worship services conducted by churches in public school buildings. In September the U.S. Conference of Catholic Bishops established an Ad Hoc Committee for Religious Liberty in response to concerns about both government policies and a more permissive American culture. In a letter to bishops announcing its formation, Archbishop Timothy M. Dolan of New York declared that religious freedom "is now increasingly and in unprecedented ways under assault in America," and cited the impact on church-run health and adoption services of government policies concerning access to contraception and same-sex unions. In Houston, Texas Gov. Rick Perry addressed a crowd estimated at 30,000 people at a seven-hour prayer service. Titled "The Response" and occurring on August 6,

Tsering Topgyal/AP

On August 8, at his inauguration in Dharmshala, India, as kalon tripa *(prime minister) of the Tibetan Central Administration (government-in-exile), Lobsang Sangay (left) greets the crowd alongside the 14th Dalai Lama (right), whose political authority he assumed.*

which he had proclaimed "a day of prayer and fasting for our nation," the event took place one week before Perry announced his candidacy for the Republican nomination for U.S. president. Nine days earlier a federal judge had dismissed a lawsuit filed by the Freedom from Religion Foundation, which had claimed that Perry's official sanction of the event would violate the separation of church and state.

Sexual Abuse. In January Irish broadcaster RTE and the Associated Press reported that a 1997 letter signed by the late Archbishop Luciano Storero, the Vatican envoy to Ireland, had cautioned the country's bishops against enforcing their new policy of mandatory reporting of suspected child abuse cases to police, instructing them instead to handle abuse allegations within the church according to canon law. In July a report sponsored by the Irish government revealed that church leaders in the diocese of Cloyne had failed to report all sexual abuse complaints to the police as recently as 2009. Prime Minister Enda Kenny denounced what he called "the dysfunction, disconnection, elitism and the narcissism that dominate the culture of the Vatican to this day." In response, the Vatican recalled its ambassador to Ireland, Archbishop Giuseppe Leanza. In November Ireland closed its embassy to the Vatican; it cited budget cuts rather than deteriorating ties as the reason for the closure. In February a Pennsylvania grand jury reported that the archdiocese of Philadelphia had allowed as many as 37 priests accused of the sexual abuse of minors to remain in active ministry. In response, the archdiocese placed a number of these priests on administrative leave. In December an independent investigation commissioned by two Dutch Catholic bodies found that tens of thousands of children had been victims of sexual abuse by the church in the Netherlands during 1945–2010. The groups that commissioned the report, the Conference of Bishops and the Dutch Religious Conference, said that the decadeslong abuse "fills us with shame and sorrow."

Gender Issues. In May, Benedict XVI removed Australian Bishop William Morris of Toowoomba from office five years after he said that he would be open to ordaining women and married men if the church changed its rules on such matters. In an open letter following his removal, he declared that his 2006 letter had been misinterpreted by a small group within the diocese. The United Methodist Church's Judicial Council ruled in April that a resolution adopted by the church's New York regional conference that would have allowed clergy to marry someone of the same sex was "neither valid nor constitutional." A majority of presbyteries of the Presbyterian Church (U.S.A.) voted in May to overturn a provision of the denomination's constitution that effectively prohibited members in open same-sex relationships from being ordained as ministers, elders, or deacons. In October the denomination upheld the ordination of Scott Anderson, an openly gay man in a committed relationship and the first openly gay person to be ordained since the constitution was changed.

Roman Catholic Issues. Pope John Paul II, who died in 2005, was beatified in May in a mass at the Vatican that drew an estimated 1.5 million pilgrims. Benedict XVI had previously placed John Paul on a fast track to beatification, thus opening the way to a rapid canonization. Some critics of the beatification had faulted John Paul II for having failed to speak out more forcefully against the clergy sex scandals that occurred during his papacy. In November Catholic parishes in the United States began using a new English translation of the Latin Missal, replacing the one that had been in use since the 1970s. The new version was a more formal, more word-for-word translation and included 17 additions to the Proper of Saints, the section that includes a calendar of saints' days, such as new memorials for St. Teresa Benedicta of the Cross, better known as Edith Stein, and St. Pio of Pietrelcina, better known as Padre Pio.

Islamic Issues. A study of Muslim population trends found that more Muslims lived in Asia than in the rest of the globe combined and composed 23.4% of the world's population of seven billion. It also indicated that the world's Muslim population would grow at double the rate of non-Muslims over the next 20 years. The study was issued by the Pew Research Center and the John Templeton Foundation. Among other projections that it made were that by 2030 Pakistan would overtake Indonesia as having the largest Muslim community and that the Muslim population in the U.S. would grow to 6.2 million, or 1.7% of the total, in the following two decades. The Fiqh Council of North America, a group of Islamic legal scholars, issued a religious ruling in September that stated, "It is false and misleading to suggest that there is a contradiction between being faithful Muslims committed to God [Allah] and being loyal American citizens." The ruling, which its authors had said was prompted by "erroneous perceptions and Islamophobic propaganda" in the decade following the Sept. 11, 2001, attacks, added that "Islamic teachings require respect of the laws of the land where Muslims live as minorities, including the Constitution and the Bill of

Rights, so long as there is no conflict with Muslims' obligation for obedience to God."

Ecumenical and Interfaith Relations. On a visit to his native Germany in September, Benedict XVI became the first pope to visit the monastery in Erfurt where Martin Luther lived before he started what became the Protestant Reformation. Lutheran Bishop Nikolaus Schneider, head of the Evangelical Church in Germany, told the pope that Luther was "a hinge between our two churches, because he belongs to both." In June three ecumenical bodies—the Pontifical Council for Interreligious Dialogue, the World Council of Churches, and the World Evangelical Alliance—issued a document that provided recommendations for Christian evangelism in multifaith societies. "If Christians engage in inappropriate methods of exercising mission by resorting to deception and coercive means," the document said, "they betray the Gospel and may cause suffering to others." Muslim and Jewish communities in the Netherlands joined in protest against a vote in June by the lower house of the Dutch parliament to ban ritual slaughter of animals. The bill stipulated that livestock had to be stunned before being slaughtered, an action contrary to Islamic halal and Jewish kosher practices. The Conference of European Rabbis, gathering in Warsaw in November for the largest meeting of Jewish religious leaders in Poland since World War II, stated in response to the bill that the proposed regulation "has become an issue of the utmost concern to European Jewry." The Dutch Senate had been scheduled to vote on the bill in December but postponed a vote until 2012 in order to consider whether it may pass without infringing upon religious traditions. Muslim and Jewish groups also worked together in San Francisco to protest against a proposed anticircumcision city ordinance. Religious, medical, and civil liberties groups sued to stop the vote, and a judge blocked the initiative in July. Three months later California Gov. Jerry Brown signed a bill prohibiting all local bans on circumcision in the state. In October 300 representatives of various religious traditions met with Benedict XVI in Assisi, Italy, to promote peace. The event, which commemorated one held 25 years earlier by Pope John Paul II, was noteworthy for including Buddhist monks and a small group of agnostics and atheists. The lack of communal prayer at the close of the meeting drew criticism from conservative Catholics.

Bibles. The 400th anniversary of the King James Version of the Bible (KJV; also Authorized Version), widely considered an exemplar of English letters, was marked by conferences, exhibits, and commemorative worship services in several countries. The Saint John's Bible, the first complete illuminated manuscript of the Bible commissioned by a Benedictine monastery since the invention of printing by movable type, was finished in May for St. John's Abbey and University in Collegeville, Minn. The bible was notable for integrating both traditional and modern techniques. In November the National Museum of American History at the Smithsonian Institution in Washington, D.C., displayed the "Jefferson Bible." In 1820 Thomas Jefferson cut selections from the New Testament and pasted them together into an 84-page work, *The Life and Morals of Jesus of Nazareth*. Jefferson's narrative portrayed Jesus as a moral teacher but made no mention of miracles, the resurrection, or eschatology (the doctrine of last things).

People in the News. The British theoretical astrophysicist Martin J. Rees won the $1.6 million Templeton Prize, which goes to "a living person who has made an exceptional contribution to affirming life's spiritual dimension, whether through insight, discovery, or practical works." Rees had been recognized for his encouragement of the notion that tensions between science and religion may be overcome. In his acceptance remarks, he said that "the effective efforts of natural scientists, environmentalists, social scientists, and humanists" were needed for humanity to grapple with the challenges that face it. "All must be guided," he said, "by the knowledge that 21st-century science can offer, but inspired by an idealism, vision, and commitment that science alone can't provide."

A Dutch court in June acquitted Geert Wilders, leader of the Freedom Party in the Netherlands, of charges of inciting hatred of Muslims. The presiding judge said that although Wilders's remarks were sometimes hurtful, shocking, or offensive, they were not criminal. In India Swami Ramdev, a popular teacher of Yoga, led an eight-day hunger strike in June to denounce government corruption. During the fast, police used batons and tear gas to disperse a demonstration that he and his followers conducted in New Delhi.

Harold Camping, the 90-year-old founder of the Family Radio network, apologized when the Rapture did not occur on either of the two days that he had predicted for it. Camping's predictions had prompted some of his followers to sell their belongings and donate money to his ministry to enable it to spread the end-times predictions through billboards in several cities. Camping had originally predicted that the world would end on May 21; when that did not happen, he proclaimed that he had miscalculated the date, which would be October 21. Rob Bell, founding pastor of the 10,000-member Mars Hill Bible Church in Grand Rapids, Mich., stirred debate among Christians with the publication of *Love Wins: A Book About Heaven, Hell and the Fate of Every Person Who Ever Lived*. The book raised questions about the nature of hell and whether belief in the divinity of Jesus Christ was necessary in order for a person to be saved. In response, the annual meeting of the Southern Baptist Convention, held in Phoenix, adopted a resolution in June affirming "our belief in the biblical teaching on eternal, conscious punishment of the unregenerate in Hell."

Prominent figures who died in 2011 included Edwin S. Gaustad, the author of several books on the history of religion in the United States; Sathya Sai Baba, a Hindu guru who had ashrams in more than 126 countries; the Rev. Fred Shuttlesworth, a Baptist minister and a pioneer in the American civil rights movement; the Rev. John Stott, a former rector of All Souls Church in London and author of several influential books on Christian theology; and Swami Bhaktipada, who led the U.S. branch of the Hare Krishna movement until his expulsion following federal criminal charges and allegations of sexual abuse. (*See* OBITUARIES.) Other losses included those of John Cardinal Foley, head of the Pontifical Council for Social Communications and host of the annual NBC broadcast of the pope's Christmas mass; retired Catholic Archbishop Philip Hannan of New Orleans; the Rev. Eugene A. Nida, who headed the American Bible Society's translation program for four decades and pioneered the dynamic equivalence method of translation; the Rev. David Wilkerson, founding pastor of Times Square Church in New York City and the author of *The Cross and the Switchblade*; José Comblin, a renowned liberation theologian; and Paula Hyman, a prominent historian of modern Judaism and advocate for a greater role for women within Conservative Judaism. (DARRELL J. TURNER)

ANALYZING THE MEGACENSUS OF RELIGIONS, 1900–2011

Each year since 1750, churches and religions around the world have generated increasing volumes of new statistical data. Much of this is uncovered in decennial governmental censuses: half the countries of the world have long asked their populations to state their religions, if any, and they still do today. The other major source of data each year consists of the decentralized censuses undertaken by many religious headquarters. Each year almost all Christian denominations ask and answer statistical questions on major religious subjects. A third annual source is the total of 27,000 new books on the religious situation in each country, as well as some 9,000 printed annual year-

Worldwide Adherents of All Religions by Six Continental Areas, Mid-2011

	Africa	Asia	Europe	Latin America	Northern America	Oceania	World	%	Change Rate (%)	Number of Countries
Christians	498,856,000	354,835,000	588,538,000	552,147,000	275,032,100	28,684,900	2,298,093,000	33.0	1.27	232
Affiliated	474,168,000	350,765,000	562,928,000	545,969,000	224,144,100	24,036,900	2,182,011,000	31.3	1.30	232
Roman Catholics	182,564,000	140,001,000	277,858,000	488,414,000	86,540,000	8,981,000	1,184,358,000	17.0	1.34	232
Protestants	143,411,000	88,298,000	67,683,000	59,437,000	59,426,000	7,810,000	426,065,000	6.1	1.55	229
Independents	104,528,000	133,656,000	10,619,000	40,101,000	58,334,000	1,273,000	348,511,000	5.0	2.13	221
Orthodox	44,990,000	18,173,000	203,104,000	1,060,000	7,493,000	988,000	275,808,000	4.0	0.39	137
Anglicans	52,140,000	865,000	26,434,000	870,000	2,780,000	4,836,000	87,925,000	1.3	1.47	162
Marginal Christians	4,086,000	3,183,000	4,110,000	11,491,000	11,965,000	676,000	35,511,000	0.5	1.74	217
Doubly affiliated	*–57,551,000*	*–33,411,000*	*–26,880,000*	*–55,404,000*	*–2,393,900*	*–527,100*	*–176,167,000*	*–2.5*	*2.53*	*181*
Unaffiliated	24,688,000	4,070,000	25,610,000	6,178,000	50,888,000	4,648,000	116,082,000	1.7	0.73	227
Muslims	426,923,400	1,084,836,900	40,910,000	1,611,000	5,561,000	549,000	1,560,391,300	22.4	1.76	211
Hindus	2,973,000	952,725,000	1,044,000	790,000	1,866,000	543,000	959,941,000	13.8	1.37	127
Nonreligious (agnostics)	5,590,000	503,509,000	86,551,500	17,111,010	46,952,200	5,355,700	665,069,410	9.5	0.16	231
Chinese folk-religionists	134,000	466,791,000	442,000	191,000	789,000	104,000	468,451,000	6.7	0.66	120
Buddhists	258,000	459,625,000	1,796,000	767,000	4,503,000	597,000	467,546,000	6.7	0.86	151
Ethnoreligionists	107,886,000	154,712,000	1,168,000	3,884,000	1,226,000	376,000	269,252,000	3.9	1.27	146
Atheists	575,000	115,503,000	15,450,000	2,939,000	2,028,000	496,000	136,991,000	2.0	–0.09	221
New religionists	117,000	59,132,000	366,000	1,756,000	1,724,000	106,000	63,201,000	0.9	0.17	119
Sikhs	75,000	23,032,000	507,000	7,200	613,000	50,800	24,285,000	0.3	1.49	55
Jews	133,000	6,167,000	1,923,000	970,000	5,563,000	119,000	14,875,000	0.2	0.71	140
Spiritists	2,800	2,100	144,000	13,413,000	245,000	8,000	13,814,900	0.2	0.84	57
Daoists (Taoists)	0	8,469,000	0	0	12,500	4,600	8,486,100	0.1	0.67	6
Baha'is	2,197,000	3,477,000	144,000	913,000	573,000	113,000	7,417,000	0.1	1.55	222
Confucianists	20,200	6,384,000	15,700	490	0	50,100	6,470,490	0.1	0.34	16
Jains	96,600	5,162,000	19,100	1,400	101,000	3,300	5,383,400	0.1	1.27	19
Shintoists	0	2,693,000	0	7,900	63,000	0	2,763,900	0.0	0.09	8
Zoroastrians	1,000	168,000	5,700	0	21,200	2,600	198,500	0.0	0.62	27
Other religionists	85,000	225,000	275,000	120,000	690,000	12,000	1,407,000	0.0	1.31	79
Total population	**1,045,923,000**	**4,207,448,000**	**739,299,000**	**596,629,000**	**347,563,000**	**37,175,000**	**6,974,037,000**	**100.0**	**1.17**	**232**

Continents. These follow current UN demographic terminology, which now divides the world into the six major areas shown above. *See* United Nations, *World Population Prospects: The 2010 Revision* (New York: UN, 2011), with populations of all continents, regions, and countries covering the period 1950–2100, with 100 variables for every country each year. Note that "Asia" includes the former Soviet Central Asian states, and "Europe" includes all of Russia eastward to the Pacific.

Change rate. This column documents the annual change in 2011 (calculated as an average annual change from 2005 to 2010) in worldwide religious and nonreligious adherents. Note that from 2005 to 2010 the annual growth of world population was 1.17%, or a net increase of 77,851,600 persons per year.

Countries. The last column enumerates sovereign and nonsovereign countries in which each religion or religious grouping has a numerically significant and organized following.

Adherents. As defined in the 1948 Universal Declaration of Human Rights, a person's religion is what he or she professes, confesses, or states that it is. Totals are enumerated for each of the world's 232 countries following the methodology of the *World Christian Encyclopedia*, 2nd ed. (2001), and *World Christian Trends* (2001), using recent censuses, polls, surveys, yearbooks, reports, Web sites, literature, and other data. *See* the *World Christian Database* (www.worldchristiandatabase.org) and *World Religion Database* (www.worldreligiondatabase.org) for more detail. Religions (including nonreligious and atheists) are ranked in order of worldwide size in mid-2011.

Atheists. Persons professing atheism, skepticism, disbelief, or irreligion, including the militantly antireligious (opposed to all religion). A flurry of recent books have outlined the Western philosophical and scientific basis for atheism. Ironically, the vast majority of atheists today are found in Asia (primarily Chinese communists).

Buddhists. 56% Mahayana, 38% Theravada (Hinayana), 6% Tantrayana (Lamaism).

Chinese folk-religionists. Followers of a unique complex of beliefs and practices that may include universism (yin/yang cosmology with dualities earth/heaven, evil/good, darkness/light), ancestor cult, Confucian ethics, divination, festivals, folk religion, goddess worship, household gods, local deities, mediums, metaphysics, monasteries, neo-Confucianism, popular religion, sacrifices, shamans, spirit-writing, and Taoist and Buddhist elements.

Christians. Followers of Jesus Christ, enumerated here under **Affiliated**, those affiliated with churches (church members, with names written on church rolls, usually total number of baptized persons, including children baptized, dedicated, or undedicated): total in 2011 being 2,181,982,000, shown above divided among the six standardized ecclesiastical megablocs and with (negative and italicized) figures for those **Doubly affiliated** persons (all who are baptized members of two denominations) and **Unaffiliated**, who are persons professing or confessing in censuses or polls to be Christians though not so affiliated. **Independents**. This term here denotes members of Christian churches and networks that regard themselves as postdenominationalist and neoapostolic and thus independent of historical, mainstream, organized, institutionalized, confessional, denominationalist Christianity. **Marginal Christians**. Members of denominations who define themselves as Christians but on the margins of organized mainstream Christianity (e.g., Unitarians, Mormons, Jehovah's Witnesses, Christian Science, and Religious Science).

Confucianists. Non-Chinese followers of Confucius and Confucianism, mostly Koreans in Korea.

Ethnoreligionists. Followers of local, tribal, animistic, or shamanistic religions, with members restricted to one ethnic group.

Hindus. 68% Vaishnavites, 27% Shaivites, 2% neo-Hindus and reform Hindus.

Jews. Adherents of Judaism. For detailed data on "core" Jewish population, *see* the annual "World Jewish Populations" article in the American Jewish Committee's *American Jewish Year Book*.

Muslims. 84% Sunnis, 14% Shi'ites, 2% other schools.

New religionists. Followers of Asian 20th-century neoreligions, neoreligious movements, radical new crisis religions, and non-Christian syncretistic mass religions.

Nonreligious (agnostics). Persons professing no religion, nonbelievers, agnostics, freethinkers, uninterested, or dereligionized secularists indifferent to all religion but not militantly so.

Other religionists. Including a handful of religions, quasi-religions, pseudoreligions, parareligions, religious or mystic systems, and religious and semireligious brotherhoods of numerous varieties.

Total population. UN medium variant figures for mid-2011, as given in *World Population Prospects: The 2010 Revision*.

books or official handbooks. Together, these three major sources of data constitute a massive annual megacensus, although decentralized and uncoordinated. The two tables below combine all these data on religious affiliation. The first table summarizes worldwide adherents by religion. The second goes into more detail for the United States of America. There are two recent publications both supporting and mapping the data below. First, the *Atlas of Global Christianity* (Edinburgh University Press, 2009) puts Christian data in the context of 1910–2010. Second, the *World Religion Database* (www.worldreligiondatabase.org) offers sources and a detailed analysis of global religious dynamics.

(DAVID B. BARRETT, TODD M. JOHNSON, PETER F. CROSSING)

Religious Adherents in the United States of America, 1900–2010

	1900	%	mid-1970	%	mid-1990	%	mid-2000	%	mid-2010	%	Annual Change, 2000–2010 Natural	Conversion	Total	Rate (%)
Christians	73,260,000	96.4	189,873,000	90.6	215,961,600	85.2	231,732,200	82.0	247,319,900	79.7	2,287,700	–728,900	1,558,800	0.65
Affiliated	54,425,000	71.6	152,752,300	72.9	174,682,600	69.0	189,125,000	66.9	202,293,000	65.2	1,867,000	–550,200	1,316,800	0.68
Roman Catholics	10,775,000	14.2	48,305,000	23.1	56,500,000	22.3	62,970,000	22.3	70,656,000	22.8	621,600	147,000	768,600	1.16
Independents	5,850,000	7.7	33,656,000	16.1	42,900,000	16.9	52,749,000	18.7	56,858,000	18.3	520,700	–109,800	410,900	0.75
Protestants	35,000,000	46.1	57,185,000	27.3	60,216,000	23.8	56,921,000	20.1	56,008,000	18.0	561,900	–653,200	–91,300	–0.16
Marginal Christians	800,000	1.1	6,114,000	2.9	8,440,000	3.3	10,080,000	3.6	11,305,000	3.6	99,500	23,000	122,500	1.15
Orthodox	400,000	0.5	4,395,000	2.1	5,150,000	2.0	5,595,000	2.0	6,386,000	2.1	55,200	23,900	79,100	1.33
Anglicans	1,600,000	2.1	3,196,000	1.5	2,450,000	1.0	2,300,000	0.8	2,191,000	0.7	22,700	–33,600	–10,900	–0.48
Doubly affiliated	*0*	*0.0*	*–98,700*	*0.0*	*–973,400*	*–0.4*	*–1,490,000*	*–0.5*	*–1,111,000*	*–0.4*	*–14,700*	*52,600*	*37,900*	*–2.89*
Evangelicals	*32,068,000*	*42.2*	*33,625,000*	*16.1*	*38,400,000*	*15.2*	*41,520,000*	*14.7*	*44,752,000*	*14.4*	*409,900*	*–86,700*	*323,200*	*0.75*
evangelicals	*11,000,000*	*14.5*	*45,500,000*	*21.7*	*85,656,000*	*33.8*	*95,900,000*	*33.9*	*103,121,000*	*33.2*	*946,700*	*–224,600*	*722,100*	*0.73*
Unaffiliated	18,835,000	24.8	37,120,700	17.7	41,279,000	16.3	42,607,200	15.1	45,026,900	14.5	420,600	–178,600	242,000	0.55
Nonreligious (agnostics)	1,000,000	1.3	10,270,000	4.9	21,442,000	8.5	31,487,000	11.1	41,922,000	13.5	310,800	732,700	1,043,500	2.90
Jews	1,500,000	2.0	6,700,000	3.2	5,535,000	2.2	5,341,000	1.9	5,122,000	1.7	52,700	–74,600	–21,900	–0.42
Muslims	10,000	0.0	800,000	0.4	3,500,000	1.4	3,959,000	1.4	4,696,000	1.5	39,100	34,600	73,700	1.72
Black Muslims	0	0.0	200,000	0.1	1,250,000	0.5	1,650,000	0.6	1,850,000	0.6	16,300	3,700	20,000	1.15
Buddhists	30,000	0.0	200,000	0.1	1,880,000	0.7	3,456,000	1.2	3,955,000	1.3	34,100	15,800	49,900	1.36
New religionists	10,000	0.0	560,000	0.3	1,155,000	0.5	1,475,000	0.5	1,625,000	0.5	14,600	400	15,000	0.97
Hindus	1,000	0.0	100,000	0.0	750,000	0.3	1,222,000	0.4	1,445,000	0.5	12,100	10,200	22,300	1.69
Atheists	1,000	0.0	200,000	0.1	770,000	0.3	1,156,000	0.4	1,310,000	0.4	11,400	4,000	15,400	1.26
Ethnoreligionists	100,000	0.1	70,000	0.0	780,000	0.3	970,000	0.3	1,085,000	0.3	9,600	1,900	11,500	1.13
Baha'is	2,800	0.0	138,000	0.1	600,000	0.2	431,000	0.2	513,000	0.2	4,300	3,900	8,200	1.76
Sikhs	0	0.0	10,000	0.0	160,000	0.1	237,000	0.1	279,000	0.1	2,300	1,900	4,200	1.64
Spiritists	0	0.0	0	0.0	120,000	0.0	193,000	0.1	225,000	0.1	1,900	1,300	3,200	1.55
Chinese folk-religionists	70,000	0.1	90,000	0.0	76,000	0.0	98,900	0.0	109,000	0.0	1,000	0	1,000	0.98
Shintoists	0	0.0	3,000	0.0	5,000	0.0	73,400	0.0	85,400	0.0	700	500	1,200	1.53
Zoroastrians	0	0.0	0	0.0	50,000	0.0	57,100	0.0	62,700	0.0	600	0	600	0.94
Daoists (Taoists)	0	0.0	0	0.0	14,400	0.0	16,100	0.0	17,600	0.0	200	0	200	0.89
Jains	0	0.0	0	0.0	10,000	0.0	11,300	0.0	12,400	0.0	100	0	100	0.93
Other religionists	10,200	0.0	450,000	0.2	530,000	0.2	580,000	0.2	600,000	0.2	5,700	–3,700	2,000	0.34
U.S. population	**75,995,000**	**100.0**	**209,464,000**	**100.0**	**253,339,000**	**100.0**	**282,496,000**	**100.0**	**310,384,000**	**100.0**	**2,789,000**	**0**	**2,789,000**	**0.95**

Methodology. This table extracts and analyzes a microcosm of the world religion table. It depicts the United States, the country with the largest number of adherents to Christianity, the world's largest religion. Statistics at five points in time from 1900 to 2010 are presented. Each religion's **Annual Change** for 2000–2010 is also analyzed by **Natural** increase (births minus deaths, plus immigrants minus emigrants) per year and **Conversion** increase (new converts minus new defectors) per year, which together constitute the **Total** increase per year. **Rate** increase is then computed as percentage per year.

Structure. Vertically the table lists 30 major religious categories. The major categories (including nonreligious) in the U.S. are listed with largest (Christians) first. Indented names of groups in the "Adherents" column are subcategories of the groups above them and are also counted in these unindented totals, so they should not be added twice into the column total. Figures in italics draw adherents from all categories of Christians above and so cannot be added together with them. Figures for Affiliated Christians are built upon detailed head counts by churches, often to the last digit. Totals are then rounded to the nearest 1,000. Because of rounding, the corresponding percentage figures may sometimes not total exactly to 100%. Religions are ranked in order of size in 2010.

Christians. All persons who profess publicly to follow Jesus Christ as God and Savior. This category is subdivided into **Affiliated** (church members) and **Unaffiliated** (nominal) Christians (professing Christians not affiliated with any church). *See also* the note on Christians below the world religion table. The first six lines under "Affiliated Christians" are ranked by size in 2010 for each of the six megablocs (Anglican, Independent, Marginal Christian, Orthodox, Protestant, Roman Catholic).

Evangelicals/evangelicals. These two designations—italicized and enumerated separately here—cut across all six Christian traditions or ecclesiastical blocs listed above and should be considered separately from them. The **Evangelicals** (capitalized "E") are mainly Protestant churches, agencies, and individuals who call themselves by this term (for example, members of the National Association of Evangelicals); they usually emphasize 5 or more of 7, 9, or 21 fundamental doctrines (salvation by faith, personal acceptance, verbal inspiration of Scripture, depravity of man, Virgin Birth, miracles of Christ, atonement, evangelism, Second Advent, et al.). The **evangelicals** (lowercase "e") are Christians of evangelical conviction from all traditions who are committed to the evangel (gospel) and involved in personal witness and mission in the world.

Jews. Core Jewish population relating to Judaism, excluding Jewish persons professing a different religion.

Other categories. Definitions are as given under the world religion table.

Sports and Games

Three sports held **WORLD CUP** tournaments in 2011: **JAPAN** upset the U.S. to capture its first **WOMEN'S** FIFA association football (soccer) trophy, **INDIA** topped Sri Lanka for the **CRICKET** title, and the New Zealand **ALL BLACKS** defeated France in the **RUGBY UNION** final.

AUTOMOBILE RACING

Grand Prix Racing. In 2011 the Fédération Internationale de l'Automobile (FIA) Formula One (F1) world drivers' championship was won for the second straight year by Sebastian Vettel of Germany. (*See* BIOGRAPHIES.) Vettel—who finished second to Jenson Button of the U.K. in the 2009 drivers' standings and grabbed the 2010 title with a victory in the season-ending Abu Dhabi (U.A.E.) Grand Prix—sewed up the 2011 title with four races to go when he finished in third place at the Japanese Grand Prix on October 9. Vettel dominated the 2011 season with 11 victories—including five of the first six races. He also broke British driver Nigel Mansell's 19-year-old record for the most pole positions in a season with 15 by taking the pole at the season-ending Brazilian Grand Prix on November 27. Vettel never started lower than third and was in the front row in all but one race. He failed to reach the podium in only two races, taking fourth place in the German Grand Prix on July 24 and retiring after a tire puncture during the first lap in Abu Dhabi on November 13.

Vettel finished 2011 with a total of 392 points, an astounding 122 more than McLaren's Button, who won three races. Australian Mark Webber, Vettel's teammate, earned his only win in Brazil to finish third in the drivers' standings by just one point over Spaniard Fernando Alonso of Ferrari. The 2008 champion, McLaren's Lewis Hamilton of the U.K., had three victories but finished in fifth place. Vettel and Webber also helped Red Bull win its second straight constructors' championship, earning 650 points to top McLaren (497) and Ferrari (375). Ferrari had gone three full seasons without any title; the team's record 16th constructors' title was in 2008, and Kimi Räikkönen of Finland last won the drivers' championship for Ferrari in 2007.

The race in Bahrain that was intended to be the season opener in March was called off amid violent antigovernment protests, but F1 chief Bernie Ecclestone said that the 2012 Bahrain Grand Prix would take place. The Turkish Grand Prix, which had been on the F1 calendar since 2005, was run on May 8, but it was dropped from the 2012 calendar amid complaints from local organizers about the cost of staging the race.

There were rule changes in the sport in 2011 that succeeded in encouraging drivers to pass more and that led to exciting racing. Most of the passing occurred because of the new drag-reduction system (DRS), which enabled drivers to adjust their rear wings from inside the car on certain occasions to increase their speed. The return of the hybrid KERS power-boost system, which had been banned in 2010 only one year after its introduction, also added to the excitement, and the use of Pirelli tires led to more pit stops and in-race strategy.

Team Lotus's number one driver, Robert Kubica, suffered massive injuries to the right side of his body in a crash on February 6 at the Ronde di Andora rally in Italy. The Polish driver almost had his forearm severed and endured fractures to his leg and shoulder; he was expected to miss the start of the 2012 season. Nick Heidfeld of Germany initially took over for Kubica in 2011, but Team Lotus replaced Heidfeld with Brazilian Bruno Senna, the nephew of F1 great Ayrton Senna (who died from injuries he sustained in a crash during the 1994 San Marino Grand Prix). Team Lotus failed to earn a point in the 2011 constructors' standings. There was going to be just one team bearing the Lotus name in 2012 after F1's ruling body approved Renault's switch to call itself Lotus, with Team Lotus becoming Caterham. Virgin Racing also rebranded as Marussia.

Webber extended his contract with Red Bull and was scheduled to race for the team until at least the end of the 2012 season, while Ferrari prolonged Alonso's deal through the end of 2016. German Nico Rosberg, who finished seventh in the 2011 drivers' standings with 89 points, agreed to a contract extension that was going to keep him with Mercedes GP through 2013. Sauber decided to stick with its driver lineup of Japan's Kamui Kobayashi and Mexican Sergio Perez for 2012 after they helped the team to a seventh-place finish in the 2011 constructors' standings with 44 points. France's Charles Pic was slated to drive for Marussia in 2012 and replace Belgian driver Jerome d'Ambrosio, who failed to earn a point in the 2011 drivers' standings while never finishing higher than 14th in a race. Pic was to drive alongside Germany's Timo Glock, who also did not pick up a point in 2011 for Virgin Racing. Williams cofounder Patrick Head announced in 2011 that he was ending his involvement in F1. Head established the team with Frank Williams in 1977, and it went on to win nine constructors' championships and seven drivers' titles but scored only five points in the constructors' standings in 2011. Williams confirmed that Venezuela's Pastor Maldonado would return in 2012 despite having claimed only one point in the 2011 drivers' standings with a 10th-place finish in the Belgian Grand Prix on August 28. Räikkönen, who quit Ferrari in 2009 to try his hand at rallying and stock-car racing, was slated to return to F1 in 2012 with the Lotus team. (PAUL DIGIACOMO)

U.S. Auto Racing. Both NASCAR, with its stock-appearing vehicles, and the Indy Racing League (IRL), with its open-wheeled single seaters, altered rules and changed personnel in 2011 in an effort to keep relevance with their fans and sponsors despite a volatile economy. NASCAR cut one man from the crew allowed to service the car during a pit stop and altered its point-scoring method for the first time since 1975. It also permitted tandem racing wherein one contestant can push an-

Stephen A. Arce—CSM/Landov

Rookie NASCAR driver Trevor Bayne, age 20, celebrates his upset victory in the Daytona 500 stock-car auto race on February 20.

other and relaxed its penalty for hitting another car. These led to changes in car construction, as did a new fuel with 15% corn-based ethanol.

The championship of NASCAR's signature 36-event Sprint Cup series, the Chase for the Sprint Cup, comprised the final 10 events with a separate point total. For the first time, however, the champion was determined by the number of races won. The new titlist, driver-owner Tony Stewart in a Chevrolet, tied Aflac Ford's Carl Edwards in points by winning the final race, the rain-delayed Ford 400 at Homestead-Miami Speedway, with Edwards second. Stewart won five of the Chase events, however, to Edwards's one and thus ended the five-year reign of Chevrolet's Jimmie Johnson.

At the $18.7 million Daytona 500, which began the NASCAR Sprint Cup season, 20-year-old rookie Trevor Bayne upset Edwards by 0.118 sec. Edwards had been pushed by Ford's David Gilliland, who finished third. Bayne was driving a Ford for the Wood Brothers, part-time competitors. He was ineligible for Sprint Cup points, however, because he had chosen to compete in the subsidiary Nationwide Series. That series crown was won by Ricky Stenhouse, Jr., driving a Roush Fenway Ford. Austin Dillon, age 21, in a Chevrolet, was the youngest winner of the Camping World truck title.

The 95th running of the Indianapolis 500 generated excitement as Englishman Dan Wheldon won unexpectedly, collecting $2.57 million of the $13.5 million purse. Rookie J.R. Hildebrand hit the wall 300 m (1,000 ft) from the finish after swerving to avoid another car and then slid down the embankment to place second. Hildebrand earned $1.06 million. Graham Rahal was third. All 33 qualifiers drove Dallara-chassied Hondas for the last time before the advent of a new turbocharged formula in 2012. Wheldon's average speed was 170.265 mph, and Scott Dixon of New Zealand led the most laps (73).

The IRL, still recovering from a 12-year internal battle among single-seat organizations, hired promoter Randy Bernard away from the Professional Bull Riders to preside over its revival. Under his aegis the new Baltimore Grand Prix weekend, held in September on a 2.04-mi street circuit, drew 75,000 spectators. It was won by Will Power of the Penske team. The event included a 71-lap American Le Mans Series (ALMS) sports-car race, which was won by a Mazda-Lola driven by Northern Ireland's Steven Kane and Humaid Al Masaood from the U.A.E. The event's future immediately became a political issue, although the promoters had a five-year contract with the city.

The scheduled 18-event IRL season was cut short at the 1.5-mi Las Vegas Motor Speedway on October 16. On the 11th lap of the race, Wheldon suffered fatal injuries in a fiery crash than involved 15 of the 34 cars. (*See* OBITUARIES.) That left the season title to the defending champion, Scotsman Dario Franchitti of the Chip Ganassi team.

(ROBERT J. FENDELL)

Rallies and Other Races. Sébastien Loeb (Citroën) of France was less dominant in the 2011 World Rally Championship (WRC), but 5 victories and 222 points in 13 races was enough to earn him (and co-driver Daniel Elena of Monaco) a record eighth consecutive WRC drivers' title. Loeb's Citroën teammate, Sébastien Ogier of France, also won five races but earned only 196 points and finished in third place behind Mikko Hirvonen (Ford) of Finland. Hirvonen (214 points) captured two races, including the season-opening Sweden Rally for the second straight year. In fourth place was Jari-Matti Latvala (Ford) of Finland, whose victory in the Wales Rally of Great Britain season finale was his first since the Rally of Finland in July 2010.

Audi secured the 24-Hour Le Mans (France) Grand Prix d'Endurance by 13.854 sec with Marcel Fässler of Switzerland, Germany's André Lotterer, and Benoît Tréluyer of France behind the wheel. The other two Audi R18 cars, driven by 2010 winner Mike Rockenfeller of Germany and two-time champion Allan McNish of Scotland, respectively, crashed out of the race in separate accidents.

The 12 Hours of Sebring (Fla.), part of the ALMS, was run in 2011 on a 3.7-mi course. For the second year in a row a Peugeot 908 diesel won, covering 1,227.5 mi. The winning drivers were the all-French team of Loïc Duval, Nicolas Lapierre, and Olivier Panis. ALMS class winners and runners-up for the season received an automatic bid to the 24-Hour Le Mans Grand Prix. The victory also counted toward the new Intercontinental Le Mans Cup.

Across the state the Rolex 24 at Daytona was held on a 3.56-mi course that included most of the 2.5-mi high-banked NASCAR Speedway. The locale and the race's close relationship with NASCAR ensured the entry of many Indy Racing League and NASCAR drivers. Telmex Ganassi Racing had captured three of the previous five races, using a Riley MKXI chassis with various drivers and manufacturers' engines. Ganassi won again in 2011, with a BMW engine and Americans Graham Rahal, Scott Pruett, and Joey Hand and Memo Rojas of Mexico covering 2,566.76 mi for the victory.

(ROBERT J. FENDELL; MELINDA C. SHEPHERD)

BASEBALL

North America. Culminating a sequence of remarkable comebacks, the St. Louis Cardinals defeated the visiting Texas Rangers 6–2 on Oct. 28, 2011, before a record Busch Stadium crowd of 47,399 to win the Major League Baseball (MLB) World Series four games to three. David Freese, a St. Louis native, stroked a game-tying two-run double in the first inning; Allen Craig hit a go-ahead home run in the third inning off Rangers pitcher Matt Harrison; and ace Chris Carpenter pitched six innings on three days' rest to earn the victory as the Cardinals claimed their 11th World Series title, the most of any franchise in the National League (NL). Freese, a third baseman, batted .348 for the series with seven runs batted in (RBIs) and was named MVP, repeating an honour that he had received for the NL Championship Series (NLCS).

The triumph occurred one night after the Cardinals had outlasted the Rangers to prevail 10–9 in 11 innings in game six, a matchup that was hailed as one of the most memorable in World Series history. The Rangers squandered five different leads (a Series record) and twice were within one strike of securing the first championship in the franchise's history. Trailing 7–5 with two out in the ninth, the Cardinals rallied on Freese's two-run triple. After Texas's Josh Hamilton hit a two-run home run in the 10th inning, the Cardinals again achieved a tie before Freese launched a dramatic home run in the 11th inning off Mark Lowe, the eighth pitcher for the Rangers.

"Amazing," said Cardinals manager Tony LaRussa, who announced his retirement a few days later. (*See* BIOGRAPHIES.) It was LaRussa's third World Series title and his second with the resilient Cardinals, who had appeared destined to miss the postseason in 2011 before winning 23 of their last 32 games and surging past the Atlanta Braves to qualify as the NL wild-card team on the final day.

In game one of the Series in St. Louis on October 19, the Cardinals defeated the Rangers 3–2 on a tie-breaking single by pinch hitter Craig in the sixth inning. Craig was batting for Carpenter, who received the victory after members of the bullpen held the Rangers to one hit over the last three innings. One night later the visiting Rangers played excellent defense and beat the Cardinals 2–1 when Hamilton and Michael Young each batted in a ninth-inning run with a sacrifice fly. For the second consecutive game, Craig had a pinch-hit single to put the Cardinals ahead, this time in the seventh inning.

When the Series moved to Texas for game three on October 22, the Cardinals routed the Rangers 16–7. Cardinals first baseman Albert Pujols hit three home runs, a feat only Babe Ruth (1926 and 1928) and Reggie Jackson (1977) had achieved in a single World Series game. Pujols collected five hits overall and six RBIs, both tying single-game Series marks held by Paul Molitor (1982) and by Bobby Richardson (1960) and Hideki Matsui (2009), respectively. Craig also hit a home run, and Yadier Molina drove in four runs for St. Louis. The Rangers responded the next night by defeating the visiting Cardinals 4–0 behind Derek Holland, who yielded just two hits over 8⅓ innings. Mike Napoli blasted a three-run home run in the sixth inning for the Rangers.

On October 24 the Rangers gained a lead in the Series by beating the visiting Cardinals 4–2 when Napoli hit a tie-breaking two-run double in the eighth inning. Napoli's hit came against St. Louis's Marc Rzepczynski, the second relief pitcher after Carpenter had pitched seven innings. Darren Oliver was the winning pitcher, and Neftali Feliz earned his second save of the Series. Back in St. Louis for games six and seven, the Rangers, who were trying to avenge their 2010 World Series loss to the San Francisco Giants, fell short for the second straight year.

Play-offs and Regular Season. The Rangers earned their second consecutive American League (AL) pennant by defeating the Detroit Tigers four games to two in the AL Championship Series (ALCS). The Rangers clinched by trouncing the Tigers 15–5 at home on October 15 behind Nelson Cruz, who hit his record sixth home run of the series. He had 13 RBIs during the ALCS, also a postseason record, and was voted MVP of the series. The Rangers, who had finished first in the AL West, defeated the wild-card Tampa Bay Rays in the AL Division Series (ALDS) three games to one. The Tigers advanced in the ALDS by besting the East champion New York Yankees three games to two.

The Cardinals secured their 18th NL pennant by overpowering the NL Central champion Milwaukee Brewers 12–6 in Milwaukee on October 16 to win the NLCS four games to two. Freese hit his third home run of the series in the first inning of game six. The Philadelphia Phillies compiled 102 victories during the regular season to ease to the NL East title but fell to the Cardinals in the NL Division Series (NLDS), losing the decisive fifth game at home 1–0. The Brewers won their NLDS against the Arizona Diamondbacks, who had finished first in the NL West, by prevailing in the fifth game at home 3–2.

Individual Accomplishments. Detroit's Miguel Cabrera led the AL with a .344 batting average, and Jose Reyes of the New York Mets topped the NL with a .337. Jose Bautista of the AL Toronto Blue Jays hit the most home runs (43). Curtis Granderson of the Yankees won AL honours with 119 RBIs. Matt Kemp of the Los Angeles Dodgers topped the NL in home runs (39) and RBIs (126), but he lost out to Brewers slugger Ryan Braun (.332 and 33 home runs) in the NL MVP voting. Detroit starter Justin Verlander won 24 games, the most for AL pitchers, and led the league with a 2.40 earned run average (ERA), enough to earn him both the AL Cy Young and MVP awards. Dodgers pitcher Clayton Kershaw, the NL Cy Young winner, and Arizona's Ian Kennedy each won 21 games in the NL, which Kershaw led with a 2.28 ERA. Verlander's 250 strikeouts were the most in MLB, as were the 49 saves by his Detroit teammate Jose Valverde. John Axford of Milwaukee and Atlanta's Craig Kimbrel, the NL Rookie of the Year, tied for the NL lead with 46 saves.

Verlander pitched his second career no-hitter on May 7, beating the Blue Jays 9–0. Ervin Santana of the Los Angeles Angels recorded a no-hitter while yielding an unearned run against the Cleveland Indians on July 27. The final score was 3–1. Francisco Liriano of the Minnesota Twins threw a no-hitter against the Chicago White Sox in a 1–0 triumph on May 3. Yankees shortstop Derek Jeter registered the 3,000th hit of his career, and his teammate Mariano Rivera recorded 44 saves, bringing his 17-year career total to 603 and thereby breaking the record of 601 set by the recently retired Trevor Hoffman.

All-Star Game. The NL defeated the AL 5–1 on July 12 before 47,994 spectators at Chase Field in Phoenix to win the annual All-Star Game and secure home-field advantage for the league representative (St. Louis) in the World Series. Prince Fielder of the Brewers hit a three-run home run in the fourth inning off Texas's Wilson (the losing pitcher) to earn the MVP honours. Andre Ethier of the Dodgers and the Giants' Pablo Sandoval batted in the other runs for the NL, which had lost 12 All-Star Games before its 2010 triumph in Anaheim, Calif. Boston's Adrian Gonzalez hit a home run off Philadelphia's Cliff Lee for the only AL run. Tyler Clippard of the Washington Nationals, the third of 10 NL pitchers, received the victory despite yielding a single while pitching only one-third of an inning.

Little League World Series. A team from Huntington Beach, Calif., bested Hamamatsu City, Japan, 2–1 on August 28 in South Williamsport, Pa., to capture the 2011 Little League World Series (LLWS). Braydon Salzman pitched a complete game, yielding just three hits, and Nick Pratto singled with the bases loaded and two out in the bottom of the sixth inning to provide the winning run. California's other run resulted from a homer by Hagen Danner off Shoto Totsuka, Japan's starting pitcher. Teams from the U.S. had won six of the last seven LLWS.

(ROBERT VERDI)

Fred Thornhill—Reuters/Landov

Pitcher Justin Verlander of the Detroit Tigers focuses on his follow-through in the ninth inning of his no-hitter against the Toronto Blue Jays on May 7. He finished the season as the American League's MVP and Cy Young Award winner.

Latin America. The 2011 Caribbean Series was held in Mayagüez, P.R., February 2–7. The Yaquis de Obregón, representing Mexico, won the championship with a 4–2 record. Puerto Rico's Criollos de Caguas and the Dominican Republic's Toros del Este from La Romana, tied for second with 3–3 records. The Caribes de Anzoátegui, representing Venezuela, finished last with a 2–4 record.

In Cuba, Pinar del Río defeated Ciego de Ávila four games to two to win the 50th Serie Nacional (National Series). It was the third Serie Nacional title for Pinar del Río, which had beaten Sancti Spiritus four games to two in the quarterfinals and Cienfuegos four games to two in the semifinals to reach the final. Cienfuegos infielder José Abreu won the batting title with a .453 average. Abreu and Granma outfielder Yoenis Cespedes each had 33 home runs to set a Serie Nacional record. Freddy Álvarez from Villa Clara posted a 1.89 earned run average (ERA) to lead the league.

The Quintana Roo Tigers (Tigres) defeated the Mexico City Red Devils (Diablos Rojos) in a four-game sweep to win their 10th Mexican League title. It was the eighth time that the two teams had met in the championship series. Oaxaca first baseman Bárbaro Cañizares, with a .396 average, led the league in hitting. Marco Tovar, from Reynosa, with a 3.11 ERA, led all pitchers and tied for first in victories while compiling a 12–4 record.

(MILTON JAMAIL)

Japan. The Fukuoka SoftBank Hawks defeated the Chunichi Dragons four games to three in 2011 to win their first Japan Series title since 2003, when they were the Daiei Hawks. The Hawks dropped games one and two at their own Yahoo! Dome but won all three games in Nagoya before the Dragons evened the series at 3–3. In game seven back in Fukuoka, starting pitcher Toshiya Sugiuchi combined with three relievers on a four-hit shutout as the Hawks won 3–0. Hawks first baseman Hiroki Kokubo, aged 40, was named MVP.

The March 11 earthquake and subsequent tsunami in northeastern Japan pushed back the start of the season by more than two weeks to April 12. The Hawks finished the regular season 17½ games ahead of the second-place Hokkaido Nippon-Ham Fighters. The Hawks were able to advance to the Japan Series by sweeping the third-place Saitama Seibu Lions in three games in the final round of the Pacific League (PL) Climax Series play-offs. Hawks outfielder Seiichi Uchikawa was named the PL MVP after having a league-high .338 average to become only the second player in Japanese baseball history to have won the batting title in both leagues. Rakuten Golden Eagles right-hander Masahiro Tanaka won the Sawamura Award for best pitcher after a close vote. Tanaka led the PL with 19 wins and a 1.27 earned run average (ERA), and Fighters ace Yu Darvish struck out 276 batters over 232 innings. The Dragons rallied from a 10-game deficit against the Yakult Swallows to win the Central League (CL) title. Chunichi reliever Takuya Asao, with a 0.41 ERA in 79 appearances, was named the CL MVP.

(HIROKI NODA)

BASKETBALL

Professional. The Dallas Mavericks won the NBA championship for the first time in the franchise's history with a 105–95 victory over the Miami Heat on June 12, 2011, to complete the best-of-seven series in six games. Dirk Nowitzki, who captured his first title at age 32 in his 13th season in the league, scored 21 points in the clinching game and was named the MVP of the Finals. (*See* BIOGRAPHIES.) The German-born Nowitzki played with a torn tendon in his left middle finger, and he still scored 10 key points in the fourth quarter to help lift the Mavericks to that previously elusive championship.

The same two teams had competed in the Finals in 2006, when the Heat overcame a 2–0 series deficit to win in six games. In 2011, however, the Mavericks won four of the series' last five games, thanks in part to the only two remaining players from the team that had lost in '06—Nowitzki and Jason Terry, who led the Mavericks with 27 points in the decisive sixth game. Terry picked up his first championship after 12 seasons at the age of 33. The Dallas bench also excelled in game six, scoring 43 of the team's 105 points. Point guard Jason Kidd earned his first title at 38 years old after 17 seasons in the league and two previous failed trips to the Finals with the New Jersey Nets.

Michael Laughlin—MCT/Landov

Jason Terry (centre) of the Dallas Mavericks reaches for the basket in game six of the NBA finals against the Miami Heat on June 12. The 33-year-old 12-season veteran scored 27 points in the game, which clinched the NBA title for the Mavericks.

The victory made Mavericks coach Rick Carlisle the 11th man to achieve an NBA title both as a player and as a coach. Carlisle, who gained the 2002 Coach of the Year award with the Detroit Pistons, won 50 or more regular-season games in each of his three seasons with the Mavericks. Before owner Mark Cuban bought the franchise in January 2000, the Mavericks had been to the play-offs only six times in 19 seasons, had never advanced to the Finals, and had won only four play-off series. Since 2000, however, Dallas had advanced to the postseason in 11 straight seasons, including the last three under Carlisle.

In 2010 the Heat signed marquee free agents LeBron James and Chris Bosh to team with Dwyane Wade. The additions helped the Heat finish 58–24, an 11-game improvement over the previous season. Miami then defeated the Philadelphia 76ers in five games in the first round of the play-offs, followed by series wins over the Boston Celtics and the Chicago Bulls. Dallas (57–25) reached the Finals after having bested the Portland Trail Blazers, the Los Angeles Lakers, and the Oklahoma City Thunder (formerly the Seattle Supersonics), which qualified for the play-offs in only the team's second year in Oklahoma.

The Minnesota Lynx won their first WNBA championship with a 73–67 victory over the Atlanta Dream on October 7 to finish a three-game sweep. Seimone Augustus, the Finals MVP, scored 16 points, and Maya Moore contributed 15 points for the Lynx, who ended the play-offs with six consecutive victories. (Minnesota also swept the Phoenix Mercury in the Western Conference Finals.) The Lynx did their best to contain Atlanta star Angel McCoughtry, who scored 22 points in game three after having poured in a WNBA Finals-record 38 points in game two. (Atlanta was also swept by the Seattle Storm in the 2010 WNBA Finals.) The regular-season MVP was Tamika Catchings of the Indiana Fever, which lost to Atlanta two games to one in the Eastern Conference championship. (ANDY JASNER)

College. The 2011 NCAA men's college basketball tournament had just about everything—except a truly satisfying final game. The final, held on April 4 in Reliant Stadium in Houston before 70,376 fans, was not nearly as well played as most of the 66 tournament games that preceded it, as Connecticut (32–9) defeated Butler (28–10) by 53–41 in the lowest-scoring championship game since 1949. Butler shot just 12-for-64 (18.8%), the lowest shooting percentage in any title game. It was UConn's third NCAA championship in school history, all since 1999, and made Jim Calhoun, 68, the oldest coach to have won the title. Connecticut star Kemba Walker was named Most Outstanding Player of the Final Four. Walker was spectacular all season, scoring 965 points for a team that won all three of the major tournaments in which it played (Maui Invitational, Big East, NCAA).

Butler and Connecticut survived to play in a championship game that few would have predicted when the tournament began. The two teams had combined to lose 18 games during the regular season. Connecticut, which lost four of its last five regular-season games, had to win five games in five days to prevail in the Big East tournament. Butler took the Horizon League tournament.

In the expanded 68-team NCAA tournament, Virginia Commonwealth (VCU), a team that had to win a game just to advance into the main 64-team draw, won five consecutive games to get all the way to the Final Four. There, it played Butler, which had lost the 2010 championship in a classic game against Duke. VCU was unable to contain a resurgent Butler, however, which won 70–62. In the other semifinal Connecticut squeaked past Kentucky 56–55.

In the women's NCAA tournament, Texas A&M (32–5) beat Notre Dame (31–7) by 76–70 on April 5 at Conseco Fieldhouse in Indianapolis, for the school's first championship. The Aggies shot a solid 29-for-53 (54.7%) in the championship game behind the brilliant play of Danielle Adams, who scored 22 of her 30 points in the second half and was named Most Outstanding Player of the Final Four.

Nearly everyone had expected that the final would be between two-time defending champion Connecticut and Stanford, the team that ended UConn's epic 90-game winning streak during the regular season. The script was dramatically altered in the semifinals as Texas

Texas A&M star Danielle Adams (right) drives past Becca Bruszewski of Notre Dame in the final game of the women's NCAA basketball tournament on April 5. Adams's aggressive play and 30 points led the Aggies to the school's first title.

John Sommers II—Reuters/Landov

A&M upset Stanford and Notre Dame beat Connecticut. Texas A&M reached the Final Four by defeating Baylor in a regional final after having lost three times to the Bears during the regular season. Notre Dame's upset of Tennessee in their regional final set up its semifinal game against Connecticut. After the season, Tennessee's legendary head coach Pat Summitt, aged 59, revealed that she had been diagnosed with early-onset Alzheimer disease.

(DICK JERARDI)

International. The 2012 London Olympic Games were the target for the men and women's teams that contested the five continental basketball championships in 2011. As the year began, only the U.S., which won both the men's and women's Fédération Internationale de Basketball (FIBA) world championships in 2010, was assured of a place in both of the 12-team Olympic contests. Meanwhile, the U.K. faced being the first Olympic host to be refused a place in the tournament. In December 2005 FIBA had insisted that the individual associations of England, Scotland, and Wales form a joint team as they chased their first FIBA EuroBasket finals slot since 1981. It was only in March 2011—after both the British men, with a team built around Luol Deng of the NBA Chicago Bulls, and women qualified for their second successive EuroBasket tournaments—that FIBA confirmed their places in the 2012 Games.

Spain defended its EuroBasket title at the 2011 finals in Lithuania, beating France 98–85, inspired by 27 points from Juan Carlos Navarro. Both teams earned a place in London. Tunisia qualified for its first Olympic appearance after beating Angola 67–56, denying the Angolan men the FIBA African championship for only the second time in 22 years. Argentina and Brazil were guaranteed qualification with semifinal victories in the FIBA Americas championship. Australia clinched Oceania's Olympic slot at the expense of New Zealand. China's American coach Bob Donewald scheduled a return to London, where he formerly had coached a club team, after the Chinese team secured a nervy 70–69 FIBA Asian championship win over Jordan.

In women's competition, Mariya Stepanova's "double double" (18 points and 12 rebounds) led Russia to qualification with a 59–42 victory over Turkey in EuroBasket. China and Australia qualified in their respective women's FIBA continental tournaments. In the Americas, Brazil routed Argentina 74–33 to qualify. Angola, beaten heavily by defending champion Senegal in its first-round group, bounced back to win the FIBA Africa final 62–54.

Extra qualifying tournaments were scheduled for early summer 2012. In the men's event Angola, the Dominican Republic, Greece, Jordan, Lithuania, Macedonia, New Zealand, Nigeria, Puerto Rico, Russia, South Korea, and Venezuela would compete for the three remaining Olympic slots. Five places were available in the women's tournament to be contested by Argentina, Canada, Croatia, Cuba, the Czech Republic, France, Japan, Mali, New Zealand, Senegal, South Korea, and Turkey.

(RICHARD TAYLOR)

BOBSLEIGH, SKELETON, AND LUGE

Bobsleigh. During the 2010–11 bobsleigh season, his first year on the World Cup circuit, German pilot Manuel Machata earned 10 medals, securing the season title in the four-man competition and finishing second overall in the two-man rankings. He also drove to four-man gold and tied for two-man silver with fellow German Thomas Florschütz at the world championships in Königssee, Ger., in February 2011. Fellow German Karl Angerer placed second in the world championships four-man event, with American Steven Holcomb third. Aleksandr Zubkov of Russia, who won the two-man race at the world championships, was named the two-man World Cup champion and runner-up in the four-man standings.

In women's bobsleigh Sandra Kiriasis led the German charge throughout the season, topping the podium five times and earning her ninth consecutive World Cup title, but she failed to win a medal at the world championships in Königssee. Germany's Cathleen Martini won gold in Königssee and collected four World Cup medals to end the season in second place. American Shauna Rohbock, also a four-World Cup medalist and a silver medalist at the world championships, was third in the season rankings . Kaillie Humphries of Canada took the world championship bronze.

Skeleton. Latvian slider Martins Dukurs dominated the 2010–11 men's skeleton season, landing on the podium in seven of eight World Cup events (including five wins) and earning the overall title. He also gained the gold at the world championships in Königssee. Aleksandr Tretiakov of Russia placed second both at the world championships and in the season rankings. Germany's Frank Rommel earned the world championship bronze medal.

Anja Huber of Germany claimed the top spot in the women's rankings, with four gold medals on the World Cup circuit, but she faltered slightly at the world championships and had to settle for the silver medal behind fellow German Marion Thees. Canadian Mellisa Hollingsworth took the bronze at the world championships. British slider Shelley Rudman finished second in the overall season standings, with Thees third.

(JULIE PARRY)

Luge. Italian luger Armin Zöggeler raced to his 10th World Cup title in 2010–11 after winning five of the nine

On January 15, German lugers Tobias Wendl (left) and Tobias Arlt (right) slide to victory in the doubles competition at the World Cup event in Oberhof, Ger. The duo won four of the season's nine World Cup races and earned their first overall crown.

Jens Meyer/AP

season races. The perennial favourite, Zöggeler also took gold at the world championships in Cesana, Italy, in January 2011. Germany's Felix Loch was second at the world championships and in the overall World Cup standings. Russian Albert Demchenko finished with the overall bronze.

In the women's competition, Germany's Tatjana Hüfner swept the first four races of the season, and seven out of nine events, to race her way to the 2011 luge world championship and her fourth consecutive overall World Cup title. Hüfner's German teammates Natalie Geisenberger and Anke Wischnewski finished in second and third place, respectively. Canadian Alex Gough captured the bronze at the world championships behind silver medalist Geisenberger.

The German domination continued in the double's event, with Tobias Wendl and Tobias Arlt securing their first overall World Cup title. The 2010 Olympic gold medalists, Andreas and Wolfgang Linger, captured gold at the world championships, but the Austrian brothers were inconsistent in World Cup competition and finished second overall, despite winning five races, including the last three of the season. Italy's Christian Oberstolz and Patrick Gruber picked up the silver at the world championships and the World Cup bronze. (JANELE M. MAREK)

Jae Hong/AP

WBC light heavyweight champion Bernard Hopkins struggles to rise from the canvas after having been sent sprawling by his opponent, fellow American Chad Dawson, in their title bout on October 15. The title, which Hopkins had captured in May at age 46, was awarded to Dawson but in December was restored to Hopkins on appeal.

BOXING

Former middleweight and light heavyweight boxing champion Bernard Hopkins (U.S.) made history on May 21, 2011, by becoming the oldest boxer ever to win a major world title when he regained *The Ring* magazine and WBC light heavyweight championships in a unanimous 12-round decision over 28-year-old Jean Pascal (Canada) in front of a capacity crowd of 17,560 fans at the Bell Centre in Montreal. The 46-year-old Hopkins broke the record previously held by George Foreman (U.S.), who had won the heavyweight title in 1994 at age 45 by knocking out Michael Moorer (U.S.). Hopkins's first defense of his second reign as light heavyweight champion was nowhere near as glorious. In the second round of a bout held on October 15 at the Staples Center in Los Angeles, Hopkins missed with a right hand and ended up draped over challenger Chad Dawson's shoulder. Dawson (U.S.) extricated himself by lifting Hopkins off his feet and depositing him on the canvas. Hopkins claimed that he had injured his left shoulder in the fall and could not continue, at which point referee Pat Russell (U.S.) ruled Hopkins a technical knockout (TKO) loser and awarded the titles to Dawson. Hopkins appealed the referee's decision to the California Athletic Commission, and at a December 13 hearing, the commission voted 5–1 (with one commissioner recusing himself) to overturn the original result and change it to a no decision, which meant that the titles reverted back to Hopkins.

Although welterweights Manny Pacquiao (Philippines) and Floyd Mayweather, Jr. (U.S.), continued to be the sport's leading box-office attractions, both had a disappointing year that could possibly detract from a long-anticipated match between them. Pacquiao's 12-round unanimous decision over Shane Mosley (U.S.) on May 7 in Las Vegas was a financial success; 15,422 fans paid at total of $8,882,600 to watch the bout live at the MGM Grand, and approximately 1.25 million pay-per-view packages were sold, generating an estimated $75 million in TV revenue. The fight, however, degenerated into a friendly, albeit one-sided, sparring session after Pacquiao knocked down Mosley in the third round. Pacquiao's second fight of the year, a 12-round majority decision over Juan Manuel Márquez (Mexico) on November 12, was an even bigger moneymaker: a live crowd of 15,498 at the MGM Grand paid $11,648,300, and approximately 1.4 million pay-per-view packages were sold, creating more than $80 million in TV revenue. An additional $575,000 in revenue was generated by the sale of 11,504 closed-circuit tickets at various Las Vegas casinos, making the Pacquiao-Márquez bout the biggest moneymaking match of the year. The fight itself, however, was marred by the controversial nature of the decision, which was booed by the crowd and widely criticized by the media, most of whom thought that Márquez deserved the verdict because of his clever boxing and accurate counterpunching. Pacquiao's status was further eroded by the fact that Mayweather had easily beaten Márquez via a 12-round unanimous decision in 2009.

Mayweather's only bout of 2011, a fourth-round knockout of defending (WBC) titleholder Victor Ortiz (U.S.) on September 17 at the MGM Grand in Las Vegas, also ended in controversy. After losing the first three rounds, Ortiz bulled Mayweather into a corner and landed what appeared to be an intentional head butt. Referee Joe Cortez (U.S.) stopped the action and penalized Ortiz a point. Ortiz apologized and hugged Mayweather, after which Cortez told the boxers to resume fighting. Ortiz, however, attempted to again embrace Mayweather, at which point Mayweather landed a left-right combination to the head that put Ortiz down for the full count. Although Mayweather's actions were technically legal, he was criticized for having exhibited poor sportsmanship and was booed by the crowd of 13,364. Approximately 1.25 million pay-per-view packages were sold, generating $78.44 million, but consumers were generally unhappy with the quality of the match and the contentious ending.

The popular super middleweight tournament sponsored by subscription cable TV network Showtime came to a conclusion on December 17, when Andre Ward (U.S.) won a 12-round unanimous decision over Carl Froch (U.K.) in Atlantic City, N.J. The convincing victory boosted the undefeated Ward's reputation as one of the sport's finest technicians and also added the WBC and *Ring* magazine title to the WBA belt that he already held.

Ukrainian brothers Vitali and Wladimir Klitschko (*see* BIOGRAPHIES) both defended their heavyweight titles in 2011. There were high hopes for a competitive fight when International Boxing Federation (IBF) and *Ring* magazine champion Wladimir faced WBA titleholder David Haye (U.K.) on July 2 in Hamburg. Many pundits believed that Haye's speed and athleticism would present problems for the much larger Klitschko, but Klitschko prevailed in his usual manner, carefully boxing his way to a unanimous 12-round decision in a boring one-sided bout. Vitali tallied two successful defenses of the WBC heavyweight title. He scored a first-round knockout of Odlanier Solis (Cuba) on March 19 in Cologne, Ger., and then he stopped former light heavyweight and cruiserweight titleholder Tomasz Adamek (Poland) in the 10th round of a bout held on September 10 in front of a standing-room-only crowd of 42,000 at Stadion Miejski in Wroclaw, Pol.

WBA junior middleweight super champion Miguel Cotto underlined his status as Puerto Rico's most popular boxer when he attracted a sellout crowd of 21,239 to New York City's Madison Square Garden for a December 3 rematch with Antonio Margarito (Mexico), who had handed Cotto a gory TKO loss in July 2008. Cotto controlled the rematch with lateral movement and stinging combinations, forcing referee Steve Smoger (U.S.) to halt the contest three seconds into the 10th round owing to Margarito's badly swollen right eye. Earlier in the year Cotto had pounded shopworn Ricardo Mayorga (Nicaragua) into an 11th-round TKO victim on March 12 in Las Vegas. (NIGEL COLLINS)

CRICKET

On April 2, 2011, India, led by captain Mahendra Singh Dhoni (*see* BIOGRAPHIES), defeated Sri Lanka by six wickets (with 10 balls remaining) to win its second International Cricket Council (ICC) World Cup and its first since 1983. The final, held in front of an enthusiastic home crowd in Mumbai's Wankhede Stadium, brought to an end the 14-team tournament that began with India's win over Bangladesh in the first match, which was held on February 19. (*See* Sidebar.)

In Test cricket India, number one in the ICC ranking since December 2009, was comprehensively outplayed in a four-Test summer series against England, which rose to the top of the international Test rankings for the first time. England won 8 of its 12 Tests in 2010–11 (6 of them by an innings) and lost just one. Two of the other three tests were affected by rain. The long-dominant Australia slumped to fifth in the rankings.

England, ably led by Andrew Strauss and meticulously prepared by coach Andy Flower, demonstrated its dominance during the November 2010–January 2011 tour down under, beating Australia in Australia for the first time in 24 years to retain the Ashes (represented by the historic urn that symbolizes the oldest and fiercest cricketing rivalry). England won 3–1, with Alastair Cook and Jonathan Trott the outstanding batsmen in the five-match series. In an unprecedented show of supremacy, all three England Test victories were achieved by the margin of an innings.

England's long-awaited success was based more on excellent teamwork than individual brilliance. The players bowled and batted to a well-rehearsed plan and, like all great teams, always found someone to take responsibility in a crisis. Cook's 766 runs (at an average of 127) was the fifth highest total for an Ashes series. His unbeaten 235 rescued England from a difficult position in the first Test in Brisbane and instilled confidence in the whole team. England's nine centuries in the series were scored by six different batsmen; Australia mustered just three hundreds. James Anderson led the England bowling attack with 24 wickets (average 26.04), but Chris Tremlett, with 17 (23.35), and Tim Bresnan, with 11 (19.54), provided highly effective support as the Australian batsmen, with the exception of Mike Hussey (570 runs at 63.33), failed to match England's skill and discipline.

Ricky Ponting, long the mainstay of Australia's batting, had a miserable series and gave up the captaincy soon after the final comprehensive defeat in Sydney. After having leveled the series 1–1 with a victory in Perth, Australia collapsed to 98 all out on the opening day of the Fourth Test in Melbourne and could not recover. Unfortunately, Ponting, considered one of Australia's greatest batsmen, was likely to be remembered as the captain who lost three Ashes series.

India began the 2010–11 season at home, sweeping Australia 2–0 and then defeating New Zealand 1–0, with two draws. A mark of India's mental strength was a 1–1 draw in a three-Test series in South Africa against the hostile fast bowling of Dale Steyn and Morne Morkel. India lost the opening Test by an innings after a double century by Jacques Kallis but leveled the series in Durban. Another hard-fought win in the West Indies, with a depleted team, confirmed India's resilience under Dhoni's charismatic captaincy.

A confident Indian squad arrived in England in July 2011 but then lost all four Tests by wide margins, despite the consistent batting of Rahul Dravid. With its major batsmen, Sachin Tendulkar and V.V.S. Laxman, out of form and its main strike bowler, Zaheer Khan, suffering an injury early in the tour, India could not match a rampant England side in testing conditions. Kevin Pietersen (533 runs at 106.6) and Ian Bell (504 at 84.00) led the way for England, while the impeccable Dravid (461 at 76.83) upheld India's cause virtually on his own. Tendulkar, seeking to become the first batsman to score 100 international centuries, failed to make any impact. Stuart Broad (25 wickets at 13.84) was England's leading wicket taker. India's players looked weary after a heavy schedule of competition in one-day cricket, and fears were again expressed by commentators and analysts about the future of Test cricket in a market dominated by one-day and Twenty20 cricket.

The 2011 Cricket World Cup

In early 2011 the 10th World Cup of cricket was held in India, Sri Lanka, and Bangladesh. Pakistan had been forced to withdraw as one of the host countries after terrorist attacks were launched there against the Sri Lankan team in 2009. India, a strong favourite under captain Mahendra Singh Dhoni (*see* BIOGRAPHIES), won its second World Cup title, beating Sri Lanka by six wickets in the final in Mumbai on April 2. The tournament lasted nearly seven weeks, and several players and administrators objected to the length of the event. The players had to cover countless kilometres across the three countries to fulfill their fixtures and by the end were close to exhaustion. The organizers, however, had few alternatives. There were 14 teams participating—the 10 Test-playing teams plus Kenya, the Netherlands, Canada, and Ireland—and the major broadcasters, ESPN Star Sports and Star Cricket, demanded maximum coverage for their $2 billion investment.

India had two of the most effective bowlers in the tournament, Yuvraj Singh and Zaheer Khan, while the ageless Sachin Tendulkar, nearing his 100th international century, held the occasionally brittle Indian batting lineup together with a series of superb innings. The low, slow pitches favoured the teams from the subcontinent, and three of them—India, Sri Lanka, and Pakistan—reached the semifinals, joined by New Zealand. Reigning champion Australia, England, and South Africa never came to terms with the creativity and variety required to flourish in the conditions. In the quarterfinals, Pakistan easily defeated the West Indies, Australia was handily beaten by India, and South Africa, a favourite of many, surprisingly lost to New Zealand.

England, though humbled by Sri Lanka in the quarterfinals, featured in two of the most memorable matches of an otherwise lacklustre tournament. The group match with India in Bangalore, India, ended in a tie after England just failed to get the two runs needed off the final ball to top India's total of 338. Many described it as the greatest one-day match of all time, but another was to follow a few days later. Kevin O'Brien hit 13 fours and 6 sixes in an innings of 113 to lift Ireland to victory over England in one of the biggest one-day upsets of all time. Chasing England's total of 327 for 8, Ireland was 106 for 4 when the red-haired Irishman went to the wicket. His century, off 50 balls, was the fastest in World Cup history.

India's politically charged semifinal against Pakistan failed to live up to expectations, and Sri Lanka easily overcame a lightweight New Zealand side to set up the final. A century by Mahela Jayawardene ensured a competitive Sri Lankan total of 274 for 6 in Mumbai, but Dhoni's innings of 91 off 79 balls lifted the home team to a victory that was celebrated the length and breadth of the cricket-mad country. Tillakaratne Dilshan of Sri Lanka was the leading run scorer, with a total of 500. Shaheed Afridi of Pakistan and India's Zaheer Khan each took 21 wickets, the most in the tournament.

(ANDREW LONGMORE)

Michael Clarke replaced Ponting as Australia's captain and recorded his first win in Sri Lanka, though the aftershocks of the Ashes defeat continued to rock Australian cricket. New Zealand captain Daniel Vettori resigned after an indifferent year. Sri Lanka, under its new captain, Tillakaratne Dilshan, was in a process of transformation after the retirement from the international game of Muttiah Muralitharan, the world's best spin bowler. After renewed infighting between the Cricket Board and the players, Chris Gayle, the West Indian batsman and captain, was dropped from the Test series against both Pakistan and India. Meanwhile, Pakistan, which was struggling with an ongoing investigation into spot fixing by players in 2010 and still forced to play its "home" Tests in the U.A.E. because of political unrest, chose Misbah-ul-Haq to lead a young and talented side. One of the unnoticed highlights of the year was the return to Test cricket of Zimbabwe, which in August defeated Bangladesh in its first Test in six years. Hamilton Masakadza, one of a new generation of Zimbabwean cricketers, scored a century.

In domestic cricket in England, Lancashire won the county championship outright for the first time in 77 years with an unfashionably home-grown team, and Leicestershire, one of the smallest counties, defied the odds to win the T20 tournament. The Chennai Super Kings, led by Dhoni, won the Indian Premier League for the second time, beating Royal Challengers Bangalore in the final. (ANDREW LONGMORE)

CURLING

Canada's Jeff Stoughton made the most of home-ice advantage by winning the 2011 men's world curling championship, held in Regina, Sask., in early April. The Canadians edged Scotland's skip, Tom Brewster, 6–5 in the final. It was Stoughton's second men's crown, his first having been won in 1996. Sweden, under skip Niklas Edin, took the bronze medal.

Anette Norberg of Sweden captured the women's world title in March in Esbjerg, Den., by stealing two points in the last end to defeat Canada's Amber Holland 7–5. Norberg, the reigning Olympic champion, won her third women's championship with a new, young team. China, skipped by Bingyu Wang, earned the bronze.

At the world junior curling championship in Perth, Scot., Oskar Eriksson's Swedish team won the men's title with a 6–5 victory over Switzerland's Peter de Cruz. Norway's Steffen Mellemseter came in third. Eve Muirhead captured the fourth junior women's title of her career, skipping Scotland to a commanding 10–3 victory over Canada's Trish Paulsen in the final. Meanwhile, Anna Sidorova of Russia secured the bronze.

Canada swept the world senior curling championships, held in April in St. Paul, Minn. Mark Johnson's team stole a point in an extra end to win 5–4 in the men's final against Geoff Goodland of the U.S. Christine Jurgenson defeated Sweden's Ingrid Meldahl 9–2 in the women's final. Australia's Hugh Millikin and Switzerland's Chantal Forrer were the men's and women's bronze medalists, respectively. In the world mixed doubles tournament, which was also held in St. Paul, Switzerland's Sven Michel and Alina Pätz dominated the final with an 11–2 victory over Russia's Aleksey Tselousov and Alina Kovaleva. Amaury Pernette and Pauline Jeanneret of France finished in third place. (DONNA SPENCER)

CYCLING

Cycling's premier road event, the Tour de France, was won in 2011 by Cadel Evans, the first Australian to triumph in the race since its inception in 1903. Evans, the runner-up in 2007 and 2008, claimed the yellow jersey of the race leader on the penultimate stage, a 42.5-km (26.5-mi) time trial based in Grenoble. He had an overall advantage of 1 min 34 sec over Andy Schleck of Luxembourg when the 21-stage three-week race finished in Paris on July 24 after having covered 3,430.5 km (about 2,130 mi). Schleck, whose brother Frank finished in third place, took the yellow jersey on stage 19 with a lead of 57 seconds over Evans, but the Australian's time-trial ability proved decisive the next day when he beat his rival by 2 min 31 sec. Mark Cavendish of Great Britain won five stages, including the traditional finale on Paris's Avenue des Champs-Élysées for an unprecedented third successive year. (Cavendish went on to win the men's elite title at the Union Cycliste Internationale [UCI] road-racing world championships held in Copenhagen in September.)

Laurent Cipriani/AP

Australian cyclist Cadel Evans races down a cobbled street in Paris past the Arc de Triomphe on July 24 at the end of the 21st and final stage of the Tour de France. Evans, a two-time runner-up, won the race by 1 min 34 sec.

Three-time Tour de France winner Alberto Contador of Spain, who finished fifth overall, was cleared to ride in the 2011 Tour when a Court of Arbitration for Sport postponed a hearing into his positive test for the banned substance clenbuterol, from a sample taken during the 2010 race. The hearing originally had been due to be held after the Tour of Italy (Giro d'Italia), which Contador won in May by a margin of 6 min 10 sec over Michele Scarponi of Italy. The Spaniard held the overall Giro lead from the ninth stage, which finished on Mt. Etna. The 21-stage race was marred by the death of Belgian rider Wouter Weylandt after a crash on the descent of the Passo del Bocco on the third stage.

The third of the sport's three Grand Tours, the Tour of Spain (Vuelta a España) was won by home rider Juan José Cobo. The early-season round of elite road-race classics was dominated by Philippe Gilbert of Belgium, who became only the second rider to achieve the Ardennes treble by winning the Amstel Gold, the Flèche Wallonne, and the Liège-Bastogne-Liège races in the space of eight days.

Australia dominated the UCI world track championships, held in Apeldoorn, Neth., in March, winning eight titles. Australia's Anna Meares, the most successful individual rider, captured gold medals in the women's sprint and keirin and defended the team sprint title with partner Kaarle McCulloch. Jack Bobridge took the men's 4,000-m pursuit and was a member of Australia's gold-medal-winning team pursuit quartet. Just weeks earlier Bobridge had set a new world record for the individual event (4 min 10.534 sec), breaking the record set in 1996 by Britain's Chris Boardman. (JOHN R. WILKINSON)

EQUESTRIAN SPORTS

Thoroughbred Racing. *United States.* For many Thoroughbred horse-racing enthusiasts, the high point of the 2011 racing year was the Breeders' Cup, held at Churchill Downs, Louisville, Ky., on November 4–5. In the final race Drosselmeyer, winner of the 2010 Belmont Stakes, surged past nine opponents in the final quarter of a mile to capture the 1¼-mi Breeders' Cup Classic. As significant a victory as it was for the four-year-old colt, which was sent off at odds of 14.80–1, it was equally special for his Hall of Fame trainer, Bill Mott, and jockey Mike Smith. That victory, coupled with the winning of the Breeders' Cup Ladies' Classic with Royal Delta the previous day, made Mott only the second trainer to have won both showcase main track races in the same year. (John Shirreffs accomplished the feat in 2009.) In addition, the victory put Smith into a tie with retired jockey Jerry D. Bailey for the most wins in Breeders' Cup history: 15. Drosselmeyer was then retired from racing to begin in 2012 his first season of stud duty at WinStar Farm in Versailles, Ky.

Total attendance for the two-day Breeders' Cup spectacular was 105,820, the second highest in Breeders' Cup history but down 7.5% from the 2010 record of 114,353. Total wagering from all sources worldwide was $155,525,947, a 4.9% drop from the $163,619,784 bet in 2010.

On May 7 lightly raced Animal Kingdom, a 20.90–1 outsider ridden by John Velazquez, captured the Kentucky Derby at Churchill Downs before a record crowd of 164,858. In defeating 18 opponents, the colt became the first Derby champion since Exterminator in 1918 to win with only four previous career starts.

Any hope of Animal Kingdom's becoming American Thoroughbred racing's first Triple Crown champion since Affirmed in 1978 was dashed two weeks later in Baltimore, Md., when Shackleford, a 12.60–1 long shot ridden by Jesus Castanon, defeated the Derby winner by half a length in the Preakness Stakes at Pimlico Race Course. Animal Kingdom was diagnosed in June with a slab fracture in his left hind leg and was sidelined for the remainder of the season. Following successful surgery, the colt was considered likely to return to competition in 2012.

The Triple Crown season ended with yet another upset winner, Ruler On Ice at 24.75–1, taking the demanding 1½-mi Belmont Stakes over a muddy track. Shackleford and Animal Kingdom, which got off to a bumpy start, were fifth and sixth, respectively. The win-

Darren Calabrese—The Canadian Press/AP

On June 26 Thoroughbred filly Inglorious, ridden by Mexican-born jockey Luis Contreras, charges to a 2½-length victory in the Queen's Plate Stakes, the first leg in Canadian horse racing's Triple Crown. Contreras won the other two legs on the gelding Pender Harbour.

ner's time of 2 min 30.88 sec was more than six seconds slower than Secretariat's stakes and track record established in 1973.

Rapid Redux, a five-year-old gelding that competed in ordinary (mainly starter allowance) races, proved to be far from ordinary. In winning his 20th straight race, on November 21 at Mountaineer Race Track, Chester, W.Va., he broke the modern North American record of 19 consecutive victories held jointly by 2010 Horse of the Year Zenyatta and Peppers Pride. On December 13 at Laurel Park in Maryland, he captured his 27th victory in 41 starts and extended the streak to 21, equaling the calendar-year record of 19 wins set by Citation during his 1948 Triple Crown-winning season. Rapid Redux began his winning streak on Dec. 2, 2010, in an $8,000 claiming race at Penn National Race Course, Grantville, Pa. His trainer, David Wells, had claimed (purchased) the horse for $6,250 for owner Robert Cole, Jr., earlier in the year. Rapid Redux's 21 victories came at seven racetracks around the country, with seven different jockeys.

Following a trouble-filled 33-year career, jockey Patrick Valenzuela retired on December 9 with 4,333 victories, including 213 in graded stakes competition, and earnings of nearly $164 million. The 49-year-old Valenzuela, who rode Sunday Silence to victory in the 1989 Kentucky Derby and Preakness Stakes, had served numerous drug-related suspensions during his career.

Trainer Jerry Hollendorfer, a member of the Racing Hall of Fame, notched his 6,000th career victory on September 3 at Golden Gate Fields, Berkeley, Calif., when he saddled Just Tappin It to win the sixth race. On November 18, Eclipse Award-winning trainer Steve Asmussen recorded the 6,000th win of his career with Basalt at Remington Park in Oklahoma City. Hollendorfer and Asmussen were the fourth and fifth trainers, respectively, to reach 6,000 wins.

Hall of Fame trainer Elliott Burch died on January 29 in Rhode Island at age 86. During his 31-year career (1955–85), the third-generation horseman trained three Belmont Stakes winners. Carl Hanford, who trained five-time Horse of the Year Kelso (1960–64), died August 15 at age 95. (JOHN G. BROKOPP)

International. Sadler's Wells, the most influential Thoroughbred stallion in Europe in the past quarter century, died on April 26, 2011, at the age of 30. He was a champion on the track in 1984 and had been retired at Coolmore, Ire., in May 2008 after 22 years of stud service, but his legacy was assured. In 2011 offspring of three of his sons based at Coolmore—Galileo, Montjeu, and High Chaparral—dominated the flat season. Frankel, sired by Galileo, ended his second season undefeated in nine races—five of them in 2011, including the 2,000 Guineas, the Sussex Stakes, and the Queen Elizabeth II Stakes, all with jockey Tom Queally on board. (Khalid Abdullah, the leading owner in Britain in 2011, had named his champion after the late trainer Bobby Frankel.) Frankel's trainer, Henry Cecil, was credited with making the most of his "wonder horse." Cecil was knighted in June for his services to racing.

In late 2010 John Magnier, Michael Tabor, and Derrick Smith, the Coolmore partners, bought shares in So You Think, which was sired by High Chaparral. The New Zealand-bred five-year-old So You Think added four Group 1 prizes in 2011, including the Coral-Eclipse in England and the Irish Champion Stakes, to the eight races that he had already won in Australia, notably the 2009 and 2010 Cox Plates.

The 2011 Epsom Derby winner, Pour Moi, was the third offspring sired by Montjeu to take that race in the space of seven years. Pour Moi did not race again, however. He suffered an injury on August 26 while being prepared for the Prix de l'Arc de Triomphe in Paris and was retired. Pour Moi, which was also owned by Coolmore, was trained by André Fabre, the champion trainer in France for the 23rd time.

When Christophe Soumillon rode the French-trained Cirrus des Aigles to victory in the Champion Stakes at Ascot on October 15, the Belgian-born jockey was suspended for five days for having used his whip six times in the final furlong, one more than the permitted number under a new set of rules in the U.K. He was also deprived of his share of the prize—£52,000 (about $80,000), but that part of the rules was abandoned six days later. There was general anger each time a rider was banned under the rule, but threats of a jockeys' strike came to nothing.

The Champion Stakes, the richest race in Britain, was traditionally run at Newmarket Racecourse. In 2011, however, it was part of a reorganization that created a new Champions Day at Ascot, sponsored by QIPCO, the investment arm of the government of Qatar. The Prix de l'Arc de Triomphe had been sponsored by Qatar since 2008. In the 2011 Arc, fillies took the first three places, with the victorious Danedream the first German-trained winner since Star Appeal in 1975.

Sheikh Fahad al Thani, who engineered the QIPCO sponsorship, had bought his first horses in 2010. Racing as Pearl Bloodstock, he won his first Group 1 race on Sept. 24, 2011, with the Irish-trained Lightening Pearl in the Cheveley Park Stakes at Newmarket. He was also the owner of the French-trained Dunaden, which triumphed in Australia's Melbourne Cup on November 1.

Mexican-born jockey Luis Contreras was a Triple Crown winner in Canada—on two different horses. He captured the Queen's Plate Stakes on June 26 aboard Inglorious, but the filly's owner chose not to run her in the Prince of Wales Stakes on July 17. For that race Contreras switched to Pender Harbour, a gelding that had finished third in the Queen's Plate. Contreras and Pender Harbour charged to a come-from-behind photo finish in the Prince of Wales, and on August 7 they claimed the third leg, the Breeders' Stakes, by a nose. Contreras was the winning jockey in an astonishing 6 of the 10 races on the Breeders' Stakes card. He was the first jockey to secure a North American Triple Crown on different horses, though American D. Wayne Lukas had accomplished the feat in 1995 as a trainer.

(ROBERT W. CARTER)

Harness Racing. People made bigger headlines than horses did in harness racing in 2011, most notably New York real-estate mogul Jeff Gural, who saved the Meadowlands Racetrack in New Jersey from closure. New Jersey Gov. Chris Christie had said that the state-owned facility, which had been the premier harness track in recent decades, would cease operation because it was running at a loss that was a burden on taxpayers. Gural, a longtime harness racing fan, owner, and breeder, made saving the Meadowlands a personal crusade. He overcame numerous obstacles to reach an agreement with state officials to lease the facility.

The standout trotter of the season was San Pail, a seven-year-old Canadian gelding given plenty of time to mature by trainer Rod Hughes (who was also co-owner with breeder Glenn Van Camp). San Pail previously had competed in Ontario, but in 2011 he was shipped to the U.S. and emerged victorious in several races, notably the Nat Ray Invitational in August.

There was no dominant three-year-old among either the trotters or the pacers in North America. Broad Bahn took the Hambletonian at the Meadowlands in August, and his rival Manofmanymissions got revenge when he won the Kentucky Futurity in October. Daylon Magician prevailed in the Canadian Trotting Classic, and Leader Of The Gang won the Yonkers Trot.

Among sophomore pacers, Up The Credit gained prominence by winning the North America Cup in June, but Roll With Joe took the Meadowlands Pace in July. Big Bad John then scored in the Little Brown Jug in September.

For the first part of the season, the three-year-old pacing filly See You At Peelers was in the spotlight as she triumphed in her first nine races. Combined with her perfect 13-for-13 freshman season, she had a 22-race winning streak over two seasons. In late summer, however, she lost two races and underwent extensive veterinary testing before she returned to the track in October.

In January the best European trotters gathered at the Vincennes racecourse in Paris for the Prix d'Amerique, which was voted by a poll of experts as the greatest trotting race in the world. In the 2011 race French star Ready Cash got the best of a duel with Sweden's Maharajah to win the 1⁵/₈-mi marathon.

The world's fastest trotters over the mile distance gathered at the Solvalla track in Stockholm in May for the Elitlopp. The American star Arch Madness was impressive in winning his elimination heat, but the French speedster Rapide Lebel was just as good in his. Those two were the heavy favourites in the eight-horse final, but Arch Madness faded abruptly in the homestretch. Brioni, a longshot from Germany, came from last place in the stretch to nose out Rapide Lebel.

In April, Blacks A Fake was going for his fifth straight victory in the Inter-Dominion Pacing Final held in Auckland, N.Z. Driver Natalie Rasmussen put her pacer in front of the pack at the start and then yielded to Smoken Up. In the stretch drive favoured Themightyquinn challenged Smoken Up but failed to catch him and finished second. Blacks A Fake settled for third place.

(DEAN A. HOFFMAN)

Steeplechasing. Long Run won both the King George VI Chase and the Cheltenham Gold Cup in 2011, setting a new course record in the Gold Cup. Sam Waley-Cohen rode him in both races and was the first amateur to win the Gold Cup since 1981. He also rode Oscar Time to second place behind Ballabriggs in the Grand National. It was the first Grand National success for Ballabriggs' trainer, Donald McCain, whose father, known as Ginger McCain (*see* OBITUARIES), had won the race on four occasions, three of them with Red Rum. Jason Maguire, who rode Ballabriggs, was banned for five days for excessive use of the whip. He had hit the horse 17 times after the last fence—one of the principal reasons for new whip rules that were introduced in September. Two horses died in the race, and extensive modifications to the Grand National fences were announced as well as tighter age and ability qualifications for runners. Paul Nicholls was champion trainer in Britain for the sixth time, and A.P. ("Tony") McCoy claimed his 16th jockeys' championship. Willie Mullins was Irish champion trainer for the sixth time. Mid Dancer won his second Grand Steeple-Chase de Paris.

(ROBERT W. CARTER)

FOOTBALL

Association Football (Soccer). *Europe.* In 2011 national association football (soccer) teams in Europe were occupied with qualifying for the final stages of Euro 2012, the European championship to be held jointly in Poland and Ukraine, but overshadowing the overall game were the accusations of bribery and corruption leveled at certain members of the FIFA executive committee. This scandal emerged in the aftermath of the controversial campaign to decide the host countries for the FIFA World Cup finals of 2018 and 2022, eventually awarded to Russia and Qatar, respectively.

Two FIFA committee members had already received bans for breaches of the organization's code of ethics. Chuck Blazer, FIFA executive committee member and its U.S. representative, raised the levels of alarm by reporting Mohamed Bin Hammam, a Qatari candidate for the FIFA presidency, and the

FIFA vice president, Jack Warner, to the ethics committee on suspicion of wrongdoing. Bin Hammam insisted that the incumbent president, Josep S. Blatter, should also be investigated. Blatter was cleared, but both Bin Hammam and Warner were suspended pending an inquiry, and Warner subsequently resigned. Bin Hammam withdrew his candidacy and later received a lifetime ban by FIFA for offering cash for votes. The English Football Association led a call for the postponement of the election, but Blatter was reelected unopposed, with the world governing body's standing severely damaged.

Fortunately, the Champions League final between FC Barcelona, the ultimate victor, and Manchester United on May 28 at Wembley Stadium in London, before a crowd of 87,695, bristled with the finest qualities of the beautiful game. Josep ("Pep") Guardiola, the 40-year-old coach of the favourite, Barcelona, was looking for a repeat of the team's 2009 final triumph in Rome. Meanwhile, Sir Alex Ferguson—at age 69 the longest-serving manager in England, having led United from 1986 to 24 various league and cup honours—was chasing his third such trophy.

Manchester United's game plan was to contain and frustrate Barcelona to prevent the Spanish team from developing its passing game at the midfield source. The scheme worked for 10 or 15 minutes before Barcelona adjusted tactics. With the momentum that allowed the player in possession to have the luxury of three of four options for passing to a colleague, Barcelona gradually gained supremacy, with the nearly faultless midfielder Xavi (Xavier Hernández) the focal point of this strategy.

Significantly, it was Xavi who fed the ball through for Pedro Rodríguez to drill in a shot from inside the penalty area in the 27th minute. The match seemed within the Spanish team's control, so it was a complete surprise when United equalized seven minutes later. Wayne Rooney exchanged passes with Ryan Giggs and curled a shot high into the net. It was to be United's only shot on target. Nine minutes into the second half, Barcelona restored its lead. Argentine international Lionel Messi characteristically darted through to hit a left-foot snap shot from just outside the penalty area. It was his 12th goal in the competition and his 53rd of the season in only 55 matches. David Villa made it 3–1 with a chip from long range in the 69th minute. Incredibly, it was Barcelona's 152nd goal of the season. Messi, voted UEFA's inaugural Best Player in Europe, became the first player to be outright Champions League leading scorer in three consecutive seasons, taking his tally to 12.

It was an all-Portuguese Europa League final between FC Porto and SC Braga on May 18 at the Aviva Stadium in Dublin, before a crowd of 45,391. Braga went on the offensive from the start but then retreated in defense as the game developed into a stalemate. The deadlock was broken a minute before halftime when Porto's leading scorer, Colombian international Radamel Falcao, headed in a cross-field pass from Fredy Guarin, who had picked up the ball from a Braga defensive error. It was Falcao's 17th goal in the competition and proved to be the only one of the game. He was subsequently transferred to Atlético Madrid for €40 million (€1 = about $1.45).

Spanish international Raúl (Raúl Gonzalez), the former Real Madrid striker, added to his impressive total of appearances and goals in the Champions League, topping both charts with 144 matches and 71 goals in his first season with Schalke 04 in the German Bundesliga. Real Madrid provided the leading marksman in Europe when the Portugal international Cristiano Ronaldo hit 40 goals, a season record for Spain's La Liga. The Madrid club also scored 102 league goals. In Estonia, Tallinn clubs Flora and Levadia hit 104 and 100 goals, respectively. Conversely, Estonia's Lootus club posted the most porous defense, with 103 goals conceded.

Manchester United became the most successful championship team in England, with its 19th overall title and 12th in the Premier League. The club was almost invincible in the league when playing at its home field of Old Trafford, dropping only two points in a drawn match with West Bromwich Albion. Goals in the Premier League reached a new high, with 1,063 being scored. United's Giggs overtook legendary Sir Bobby Charlton's record of appearances for the club and finished the season with a record 12 championship medals, 613 League appearances, and the honour of having been the only player to have scored in every one of his 18 Premier League seasons.

United's neighbour Manchester City had its best season since winning the League Cup in 1976, annexing the FA Cup and finishing third in the Premier League. The club also announced a record £400 million (£1 = about $1.60) naming rights deal with Etihad Airways. Chelsea set a new British transfer record by trading Spain's international striker Fernando Torres from Liverpool

MVP Homare Sawa (centre) raises the trophy aloft as she and her Japanese teammates celebrate their upset of the U.S. in a penalty shoot-out in the final of the FIFA women's World Cup on July 17.

Michael Probst/AP

for £50 million. The record for an English player was broken when Liverpool replaced Torres with Andy Carroll from Newcastle United in a £35 million deal. Samuel Eto'o of Cameroon was believed to have become the world's highest-paid soccer player when he was traded by Milan's Internazionale to Anzhi Makhachkala, from oil-rich Dagestan on the Caspian Sea in Russia. Eto'o was rumoured to have signed a three-year contract for an annual salary of about €20 million, or €385,000 per week.

Sectarian rivalry between Protestants and Catholics reached unacceptable proportions in Scotland with Rangers and Celtic matches attracting violence on and off the pitch. Death threats were made to Celtic manager Neil Lennon; parcel bombs and bullets were sent in the post; and he was even attacked by a spectator. Some 229 arrests were made at one Glasgow match, and Lennon was placed under 24-hour protection. Rangers won the title for the third season in a row.

While Real Madrid and Barcelona were the soccer world's top two richest clubs, the Spanish La Liga suffered in the economic downturn. The season due to start in August 2011 was delayed a week because of a players' strike. Their union claimed that €50 million was owed to them by clubs. The Italian opening was postponed for two weeks by players seeking improved conditions.

Spain's stock continued to rise at the national level. Already reigning World Cup champion, it added UEFA trophies at Under-19 and Under-21 levels in 2011. At the FIFA women's World Cup, France, which lost to the U.S. in the semifinals, and Sweden, which fell to the eventual champion, Japan, faced off in the bronze medal match, where the Swedish women defeated the French 2–1.

(JACK ROLLIN)

The Americas. Uruguay, the South American country that placed the best (fourth) in the 2010 FIFA association football (soccer) World Cup, in 2011 confirmed its regional supremacy by beating Paraguay 3–0 in the final of the 43rd Copa América. Venezuela, until recently the continent's poor relation in soccer, reached the semifinal, while favourites Argentina (the host) and Brazil were knocked out in the quarterfinals. The invited CONCACAF teams, Mexico and Costa Rica, sent B teams while their best players were engaged in the CONCACAF Gold Cup at almost the same time. The latter was won by Mexico for its second straight and record sixth victory, beating the U.S. 4–2 in the final. Mexico also captured the Pan American Games tournament with a 1–0 final triumph over Argentina.

Brazil did better at the club level; Santos won the Libertadores Cup against Uruguay's Peñarol (0–0, 2–1), and Internacional of Porto Alegre defeated Argentina's Independiente (1–2, 3–1) in the Recopa (held between the 2010 Libertadores and South American Cup winners, respectively). The CONCACAF Champions League trophy went to a Mexican club for the sixth straight year as Monterrey edged (2–2, 1–0) Real Salt Lake (Utah), which reached the final with a 37-match unbeaten run.

Argentina's Boca Juniors finally secured a title again (an unbeaten 2011–12 opening tournament) after three years and returned to international competition (the Libertadores) after a two-year absence. Nacional won the Uruguay title and the opening tournament of the 2011–12 season. Meanwhile, Universidad de Chile won that country's opening tournament as well as the South American Cup final against Ecuador's Liga Deportiva Universitaria (1–0, 3–0) and, after a 36-match unbeaten run, won in the final in Chile's closing tournament.

In the U.S. the Los Angeles Galaxy captured the Major League Soccer (MLS) title for the first time with a 1–0 win over the Houston Dynamo in the MLS Cup. The Seattle Sounders took the U.S. Open Cup for the third straight year, beating the Chicago Fire 2–0 in the final.

(ERIC WEIL)

Africa and Asia. Japan's status rose higher on the association football (soccer) scene in 2011. In January an overtime goal by substitute Lee Tadanari gave the Japanese men's national team victory over Australia in the final of the Asian Cup, its fourth title in the quadrennial tournament. The timing of the finals in Doha, Qatar, was of special interest as the temperatures dropped considerably in evening matches amid the ongoing controversy over the 2022 FIFA World Cup, due to be held in Qatar during the hot summer.

Japan raised its international soccer profile even more in July when it won the FIFA women's World Cup in Germany. The Japanese team, led by MVP Homare Sawa (*see* BIOGRAPHIES), defeated the highly favoured U.S. in a penalty shoot-out in the final match.

The Democratic Republic of the Congo team TP Mazembe, playing in its home field in Lubumbashi, retained its African Super Cup title but needed a penalty shoot-out to dispose of FUS Rabat from Morocco in the final. Peter Odemwingie, the Nigerian striker with West Bromwich Albion, was voted the English Premier League's African Player of the Year, beating Ghana's Asamoah Gyan of Sunderland and the Ivorian Yaya Toure from Manchester City, who finished second and third, respectively.

(JACK ROLLIN)

U.S. Football. *College.* The story that garnered the most attention during the 2011–12 college football season was the sex-abuse scandal at Pennsylvania State University, which on Nov. 9, 2011, cost longtime coach Joe Paterno his job. Paterno was fired four days after former Penn State assistant coach Jerry Sandusky was charged with having sexually assaulted eight boys over a 15-year period. The school deemed that Paterno did not do enough when then graduate assistant Mike McQueary reported to Paterno in 2002 that he saw Sandusky sexually assaulting a boy in the shower at the school's practice facility. Paterno started his career at Penn State as an assistant coach in 1950 before taking over the program in 1966. He finished his career with 409 wins, a Football Bowl Subdivision (FBS) record.

On the field Alabama (12–1) secured its second Bowl Championship Series (BCS) title in three seasons by upsetting top-ranked Southeastern Conference (SEC) champion Louisiana State University (LSU; 13–1) by a score of 21–0 in New Orleans on Jan. 9, 2012. The game was a rematch between teams that had met on November 5, when LSU secured a 9–6 overtime win over the Crimson Tide. Big 12 Conference champion Oklahoma State (12–1) won its first BCS bowl game with a thrilling 41–38 overtime victory over Stanford University (11–2) in the Fiesta Bowl. The Rose Bowl also was wildly entertaining, with Pacific-12 Conference champion Oregon (12–2) defeating Big Ten Conference winner Wisconsin (11–3) by a margin of 45–38 in the highest-scoring Rose Bowl ever. It was the Ducks' first Rose Bowl victory since the 1916–17 season. Michigan (11–3) won its first BCS bowl since the 1999–2000 season with a 23–20 overtime victory over Virginia Tech (11–3) in the Sugar Bowl. Big East Conference champion West Virginia (10–3) set a bowl scoring record in the Orange Bowl when it beat Atlantic Coast Conference winner Clemson (10–4) by a margin of 70–33.

Quarterback Robert Griffin III became Baylor's first Heisman Trophy winner, beating out the preseason favourite, Stanford quarterback Andrew

Luck. Griffin, a junior, received 1,687 points, 280 more than Luck, who was the fourth player to be Heisman runner-up in consecutive seasons. Griffin led Baylor (10–3) to its first bowl win since 1992 in an incredible 67–56 victory over Washington in the Alamo Bowl. He completed 24 of 33 passes for 295 yd, throwing one touchdown pass and running for another score in a contest that featured the most points ever in regulation for a bowl game. Griffin finished the season with 4,293 passing yards, 37 touchdown passes, a completion percentage of 72.4, and a quarterback rating of 189.5, as well as 699 rushing yards and 10 touchdowns on the ground. In addition to the Heisman, Griffin received the Davey O'Brien National Quarterback Award. Luck won the Maxwell Award for most outstanding player, the Walter Camp Player of the Year Award, and the Johnny Unitas Golden Arm Award as the quarterback who best exemplified character and scholastic and athletic achievement. Alabama's Trent Richardson, the third-place finisher in the Heisman voting, took the Doak Walker Award for top running back. For the second straight season, Oklahoma State's Justin Blackmon, who caught eight passes for 186 yd and three touchdowns in the Fiesta Bowl, won the Fred Biletnikoff Award for most outstanding wide receiver. LSU cornerback Tyrann Mathieu won the Chuck Bednarik Award for defensive player of the year. Running back Montee Ball of Wisconsin led the FBS with 1,923 yd rushing and 33 touchdowns and caught 6 touchdown passes to tie Barry Sanders's 23-year-old FBS single-season record of 39 total scores.

Professional. The NFC Green Bay Packers defeated the AFC Pittsburgh Steelers 31–25 in Super Bowl XLV in Arlington, Texas, on Feb. 6, 2011, winning their first NFL championship in 14 years and their league-record 13th title—9 of which came before the Super Bowl era. Quarterback Aaron Rodgers (*see* BIOGRAPHIES) captured the Super Bowl MVP award after completing 24 of 39 passes for 304 yd and three touchdowns without an interception as the Packers became just the second number six seed to win the Super Bowl.

The 2011–12 season was threatened by a labour dispute between players and owners, but the sides agreed to a deal after a lockout of nearly four and a half months, and the season started on time. Green Bay finished the 2010–11 season on a six-game winning streak—including the play-offs—and opened the 2011–12 campaign with 13 consecutive victories before falling 19–14 on the road to the Kansas City Chiefs on Dec. 18, 2011. The Packers came up two wins short of tying the NFL record of 21 consecutive victories set by the 2003–04 and 2004–05 New England Patriots but still finished 15–1 to win the NFC North. Rodgers threw for Packers records of 4,643 yd and 45 touchdown passes while setting an NFL mark with a 122.5 passer rating. In their first year under coach Jim Harbaugh, the San Francisco 49ers (13–3) locked up their first NFC West title since the 2002–03 season. The New Orleans Saints (13–3) won the NFC South for the second time in three seasons behind a slew of record-setting performances. Saints quarterback Drew Brees threw for 5,476 yd to break former Miami Dolphin Dan Marino's 27-year-old single-season passing record of 5,084 yd. Brees also threw 46 touchdown passes, the fourth most in NFL history, and set other records with 468 completions, a 71.2 completion percentage, and 13 games—7 of them consecutive—with at least 300 yd passing. As a team, New Orleans set league records with 7,474 offensive yards, 5,347 passing yards, and 416 first downs. Saints running back Darren Sproles set an NFL record with 2,969 combined yards. The New York Giants (9–7) clinched the NFC East title in the final game of the regular season with a 31–14 win over the Dallas Cowboys. Quarterback Eli Manning set a Giants passing record with 4,933 yd. The Atlanta Falcons (10–6) and the Detroit Lions (10–6) reached the play-offs as wild cards.

In the AFC the New England Patriots (13–3) won the East Division for the eighth time in nine seasons behind quarterback Tom Brady, who threw for 5,235 yd and 39 touchdowns. The Patriots' Rob Gronkowski set an NFL record for receiving yards by a tight end with 1,327. The Baltimore Ravens and the Pittsburgh Steelers each posted a 12–4 record, but the Ravens won the AFC North over the Steelers with a tiebreaker, pushing Pittsburgh to wild-card status and a first-round play-off matchup with the AFC West champion Denver Broncos (8–8). Denver reached the postseason for the first time since the 2005–06 season as quarterback Tim Tebow became the starter in October and led the Broncos to 7 wins in 12 games. The Houston Texans (10–6) earned their first play-off berth, winning the AFC South despite losing their top two quarterbacks, Matt Schaub and Matt Leinart, to injuries. Houston's first play-off game was against the Cincinnati Bengals (9–7), who earned a wild-card berth on the last day of the season.

Quarterback Tim Tebow (centre) of the NFL Denver Broncos shakes off a defensive tackle as he scrambles to gain yardage during the Broncos' December 11 game against the Chicago Bears. The Broncos edged the Bears 13–10 in overtime for the team's sixth straight victory.

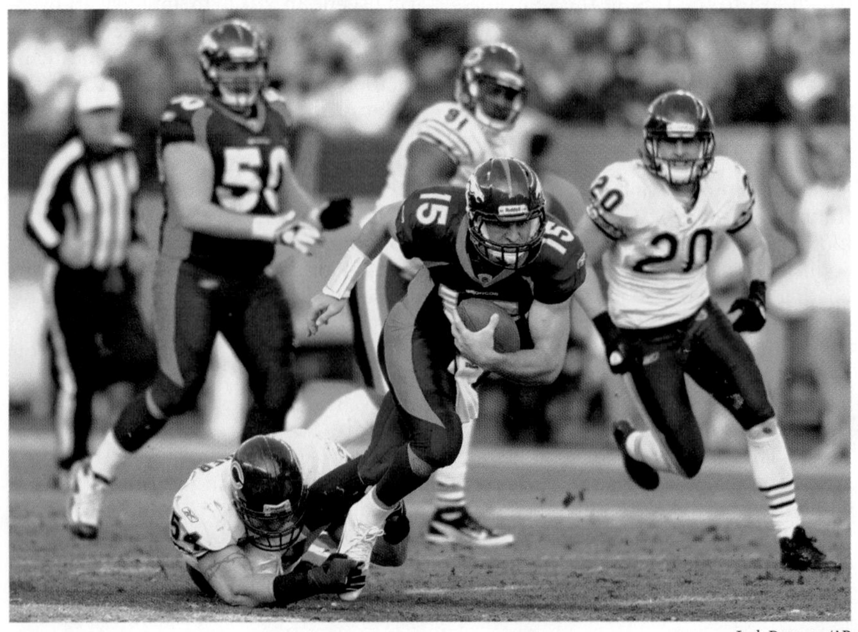

Jack Dempsey/AP

Other clubs had disappointing seasons—none more than the Indianapolis Colts (2–14). Indianapolis entered 2011–12 on a run of nine straight double-digit win seasons with Peyton Manning at quarterback, but he missed the 2011–12 season after multiple neck surgeries. The poor campaign cost vice-chairman Bill Polian and his son Chris Polian, the team's general manager, their jobs, and it seemed unlikely that head coach Jim Caldwell would keep his for very much longer.

(PAUL DIGIACOMO)

Canadian Football. The British Columbia Lions won the Canadian Football League (CFL) championship for the sixth time with a 34–23 Grey Cup victory over the Winnipeg Blue Bombers on Nov. 27, 2011, at BC Place Stadium in Vancouver. The Lions were the fourth team to win the Grey Cup at home but the first in CFL history to capture a championship after having started the season with five straight losses. Lions quarterback Travis Lulay, the Grey Cup MVP, completed 21 of 37 passes for 320 yd and threw a pair of touchdowns in the second half. During the regular season Lulay had earned the CFL Most Outstanding Player honours as he passed for 4,815 yd and 32 touchdowns in helping B.C. win 11 of its final 13 games to finish first in the West Division at 11–7. B.C. reached the Grey Cup with a 40–23 victory over the Edmonton Eskimos (11–7) in the Playoffs Finals. Winnipeg (10–8) topped the East Division and beat the Hamilton Tiger-Cats (8–10) by a score of 19–3 in the other Playoffs Final.

The Montreal Alouettes (10–8), winner of the last two Grey Cups, lost 52–44 in overtime to Hamilton in the Playoffs Semi-Finals. Meanwhile, Montreal quarterback Anthony Calvillo broke three of Damon Allen's career CFL records with 73,412 passing yards, 418 touchdowns, and 5,444 completions. Winnipeg defensive back Jovon Johnson was the CFL's Most Outstanding Defensive Player, and Edmonton running back Jerome Messam was named the Canadian Player of the Year.

(PAUL DIGIACOMO)

Australian Football. On Oct. 1, 2011, the Australian Football League (AFL) season's two most powerful clubs, the Geelong Cats and the Collingwood Magpies, met in the AFL Grand Final for the first time since 1953. Geelong triumphed 18.11 (119)–12.9 (81), notching the club's ninth premiership before a crowd of 99,537 at the Melbourne Cricket Ground. Geelong started as the favourite for the big match and won the game with a powerful second half, when players such as Tom Hawkins, Joel Selwood, and Norm Smith Award winner James Bartel stood out. The Cats—with three victories (2007, 2009, 2011), a second-place finish (2008), and a third-place finish (2010) in five seasons—were being compared to the greatest past premiership teams. Collingwood was attempting to win its 16th premiership and join Essendon and Carlton at the head of the AFL premierships table, but after opening up a lead in the second quarter of the Grand Final, the Magpies could not maintain the pressure and were held goalless in the last quarter.

Collingwood midfielder Dane Swann captured the Brownlow Medal as the home-and-away season's best and fairest player. Hawthorn's Lance Franklin, with 71 goals, earned the Coleman Medal as the season's top goal-kicker, and 19-year-old Dyson Heppell of Essendon was named the Rising Star.

(GREG HOBBS)

Rugby Football. The biggest event in Rugby Union in 2011 was the quadrennial World Cup, which took place in New Zealand from September 9 to October 23. New Zealand's 8–7 victory over France in the final confirmed that the All Blacks were the number one rugby team in the world. (*See* Sidebar.) In the Southern Hemisphere, new winning-team names were inscribed on two major rugby trophies: the Tri-Nations and the former Super 14 club tournament.

After eight winless years in Europe, England finally climbed to the top of the Six Nations table as manager Martin Johnson showed genuine development of his young team. Johnson came

The 2011 Rugby Union World Cup

It took 24 years, but in 2011 the New Zealand All Blacks, Rugby Union's most famous national team, finally confirmed themselves as the number one side in the sport by winning the World Cup. Although New Zealand was undefeated, the team fought every inch of the way, winning the final on October 23—in front of an enthusiastic home crowd at Eden Park in Auckland—only by the slimmest of margins, 8–7, against a resurgent France.

In the first World Cup in 1987, New Zealand, the cohost with Australia, was the inaugural winner, but despite having been considered the world's best team in many of the subsequent years, the All Blacks had failed to secure the Webb Ellis Cup a second time. When the World Cup returned to New Zealand in 2011, 24 cities on both islands offered a warm welcome to rugby teams and fans from around the world. Thus, the final victory touched almost every area of a rugby-mad country of some 4.5 million people.

The All Blacks found an unlikely hero in the 2011 final in fourth-choice outside-half Stephen Donald, who was playing only because of injuries suffered by Dan Carter, Colin Slade, and Aaron Cruden. Donald was called up at the last minute, but in the final he kicked the winning penalty to send New Zealanders into raptures. France had limped through the tournament until the final, even having suffered a loss to Tonga in the pool stage. In the final, however, the French players were inspired into a world-class performance by team captain Thierry Dusautoir, who scored the try to bring his side back into the match until Donald's final point.

Among the 20 teams that qualified for the six-week tournament, France led the Northern Hemisphere challenge. The French were backed up by a resurgent Wales, which also produced its best performance since 1987 and finished fourth. The Australian Wallabies, who knocked out defending champion South Africa in the quarterfinals before losing badly to New Zealand in the semifinals, beat Wales in the bronze-medal match to finish third. England suffered a disappointing tournament: matching its worst-ever finish, losing to France in the quarterfinals, and ensuring that the English dream of reaching three successive finals ended prematurely.

A major theme of the tournament was the development of the emerging nations. There were none of the 100-point defeats that had blighted previous World Cups. Tonga even beat France, and Argentina reached the quarterfinals. Russia made its debut in the tournament, although it lost to the U.S., Italy, Ireland, and Australia in the pool round.

(PAUL MORGAN)

close to turning that championship into a Grand Slam (victories in all five matches) until the final day, when England fell 24–8 to Ireland in Dublin. Even that defeat could not dampen England's joy at triumphing in a campaign that included a stunning tournament debut for Northampton wing Chris Ashton, who scored twice in his first game—against Wales—and then followed it up with an incredible four tries against Italy, becoming the first England player to hit that mark since 1914. Johnson, aged 41, resigned as manager in November, however, after England's poor showing in the World Cup.

Italy finished at the bottom of the table, but the tournament was likely to be remembered for that country's incredible 22–21 victory over the reigning Grand Slam holder, France. Since the Italians joined the tournament in 2000, their improved performances had hinted at a breakthrough win, and it came in 2011 before coach Nick Mallett confirmed his departure from the job.

Ireland's Leinster picked up the Heineken Cup for the second time in three years as that team overcame a 22–6 deficit against Northampton at Millennium Stadium in Cardiff, Wales, inspired by second-half displays from Jonathan Sexton and Brian O'Driscoll. The second tier of European competition, the Amlin Challenge Cup, went to the English side Harlequins. Saracens won England's Aviva Premiership for the first time, trouncing Leicester 50–25 in the final, while Munster won the final Magners League title, beating Leinster 19–9 before the tournament was renamed the RaboDirect PRO 12.

Down under, Australia had not won the Tri-Nations tournament for 10 years. In 2011, however, the Wallabies bucked their losing trend, overcoming New Zealand 25–20 before a home crowd in the final match in Brisbane. The tournament was the last Tri-Nations, with Argentina joining the newly renamed Rugby Championship competition in 2012. Most observers saw this as a welcome expansion to the annual tournament that decided the best side in the Southern Hemisphere.

Super Rugby (formerly the Super 14 competition) had a new winner as the Reds (from Queensland, Australia) completed a remarkable reverse in their fortunes. The Reds had finished in the bottom three of the table every year from 2004 to 2009, but they went to the top in 2011, beating the Canterbury (N.Z.) Crusaders 18–13 in the final.

(PAUL MORGAN)

GOLF

For the first time in eight years, in 2011 all four of golf's major championships were shared among players winning for the first time; three of the new champions were in the early days of their professional careers, while the fourth achieved victory two decades after he made his initial attempt. This meant that the last 13 majors had 13 different winners, with the last 7 victors never before having tasted such success, a record sequence.

In the Masters Tournament at the Augusta (Ga.) National Golf Club in April, the early spotlight fell on 21-year-old Rory McIlroy, from Northern Ireland. Having finished third in the final two majors of 2010, the highly fancied McIlroy opened with a 65 and with a round to play was four strokes clear of the field, but his inexperience was exposed as the pressure mounted on the final day, and in a collapse that raised questions about his future, he shot 80 (the highest score of the day) and lost by 10 strokes. The eventual victor, 26-year-old South African Charl Schwartzel, chipped in for a birdie on the first hole, pitched in for an eagle on the third, and closed with four birdies for a round of 66 (the lowest of the day). Schwartzel beat Australians Adam Scott and Jason Day by two with a 14-under-par total of 274.

Eldrick ("Tiger") Woods—unable to add to his 14 majors since the 2008 U.S. Open and since a sex scandal in which he was involved hit the headlines late in 2009—finally achieved his first tournament victory in more than two years in December when he birdied the last two holes of the limited-field Chevron World Challenge at Sherwood Country Club in Thousand Oaks, Calif. He had briefly led at Augusta after a front-nine charge, but he had to settle for a share of fourth place in what proved to be his last major appearance until August. Although it was not apparent at the time, the former world number one had suffered knee and Achilles tendon injuries playing one particular shot. After an attempt to return to action at the Players Championship at Sawgrass in Ponte Vedra Beach, Fla., a month later—he played nine holes in six over par before withdrawing—he missed both the U.S. Open at the Congressional Country Club in Bethesda, Md., and the British Open at Royal St. George's, Sandwich, Eng.

At the U.S. Open, McIlroy began with a 65 (as he had at Augusta), but there was to be no repeat of what had happened there two months earlier. His three-stroke first-day lead was doubled when he added a 66 on day two. With records tumbling, he increased his lead to eight strokes with a third-round 68 and maintained that advantage with a closing 69. At age 22 McIlroy was the youngest winner of the title since American amateur Bobby Jones in 1923, and his 16-under-par aggregate of 268 was the lowest by four in the championship's history. Day, only one year older than McIlroy, was runner-up for the second major in a row.

McIlroy's victory came a year after Graeme McDowell had become the first player from Northern Ireland to take the title, yet only four weeks later the British Open trophy was heading in the same direction. Ranked only 111th in the world but a former runner-up in the event, Northern Ireland's Darren Clarke triumphed at Royal St. George's by three strokes over Americans Phil Mickelson and Dustin Johnson with a five-under-par total of 275. The 42-year-old Clarke, who made his professional debut in 1991, was the oldest winner since Roberto de Vicenzo in 1967 and a hugely popular one, not least following the death of his wife from breast cancer in 2006.

Woods was back for the Professional Golfers' Association (PGA) Championship at the Atlanta Athletic Club but not for long. He missed the halfway cut by six strokes in the worst major performance of his career and thereby failed to qualify for the PGA Tour's end-of-season FedEx Cup play-offs during a decline that took him outside the world's top 50 golfers—an unimaginable outcome a few years earlier. There was an American winner for the first time in seven majors, though. It looked as if it would be Jason Dufner when he led by five with four holes to play, but he bogeyed the next three holes, while Keegan Bradley, having triple-bogeyed the 15th, birdied the next two and tied Dufner with the eight-under-par mark of 272. Bradley—a 108th-ranked PGA Tour rookie whose aunt, former Ladies Professional Golf Association (LPGA) star Pat Bradley, won six majors in her career—prevailed by one shot in a three-hole play-off to become only the second player since 1913 to win on his first appearance in a major. (American Ben Curtis was the other at the 2003 British Open.)

Lee Westwood began the year as world number one but lost that position first to Germany's Martin Kaymer and then to fellow Englishman Luke Donald when they clashed in a play-off for the

BMW PGA Championship at Wentworth, Surrey, Eng. Prior to that tournament, Donald had captured the first of the World Golf Championships, the Accenture Match Play; he later added both the Barclays Scottish Open and the Children's Miracle Network Hospitals Classic at the Walt Disney Resort in Florida, a win that enabled him to overtake American Webb Simpson and become the PGA Tour's leading money winner, with $6,683,214. He was the first European to do so, and in December he topped the European tour "Race to Dubai" money list as well, with £4,577,103 (about $7,300,000).

The other World Golf Championship victors were American Nick Watney (Cadillac Championship), Scott (Bridgestone Invitational), and Kaymer (HSBC Champions), while South Korean K.J. Choi captured the Players Championship. The $10 million bonus for winning the FedEx Cup play-off series went to American Bill Haas. Despite his lack of success at the time, Woods was still handed a wild card onto the United States team for the Presidents Cup at Royal Melbourne, Australia, where the United States retained the title by winning 19–15 over the International team in November. Matt Kuchar followed that up by combining with Gary Woodland to give the Americans victory in the World Cup at Mission Hills, China.

Yomiuri Shimbun/AP

Yani Tseng of Taiwan poses with the trophy that she won at the LPGA Championship tournament in June. A month later the 22-year-old Tseng captured her second straight Women's British Open, thus breaking Tiger Woods's record as the youngest golfer to take five major titles.

While there was no dominant player among the men, Taiwan's Yani Tseng (*see* BIOGRAPHIES) again led the way in the women's game. For the second successive year she claimed two of the four majors and at age 22 took over from Woods as the youngest player to win five majors in his or her career. After finishing runner-up to American Stacy Lewis at the Kraft Nabisco Championship in Rancho Mirage, Calif., Tseng took the Wegmans LPGA Championship at Locust Hill in Rochester, N.Y., by 10 strokes from American Morgan Pressel with a 19-under-par aggregate of 269 that matched the record in majors. South Korean Ryu So-Yeon beat compatriot Seo Hee-Kyung in a three-hole play-off for the U.S. Women's Open at the Broadmoor in Colorado Springs, Colo., but world number one Tseng added to her haul with a successful defense of the Ricoh Women's British Open at Carnoustie, Scot., where she defeated American Brittany Lang by four strokes.

Europe's women regained the Solheim Cup with a 15–13 victory at Killeen Castle in Ireland, while there was also defeat for the U.S. in the men's amateur Walker Cup. Britain and Ireland unexpectedly triumphed 14–12 at Royal Aberdeen in Scotland over an American side that included Nationwide Tour winners Russell Henley and Harris English, as well as world number one Patrick Cantlay, who some three months earlier had achieved a round of 60 during the PGA Tour's Travelers Championship. Another top amateur, England's Tom Lewis, had the lowest round ever by an amateur in the British Open (a 65 that gave him a share of the first-round lead), and the 20-year-old's rich promise was confirmed when he won the European Tour's Portugal Masters in only his third start as a professional.

Golf's saddest day of 2011 came in May with the news that former world number one Severiano Ballesteros of Spain had lost a two-year battle with brain cancer at age 54. Seve was the winner of more than 85 international tournaments, including five majors, and was one of the sport's most charismatic characters. (*See* OBITUARIES.)

(MARK GARROD)

GYMNASTICS

At the 2011 artistic gymnastics world championships, held in Tokyo in October, China earned the most medals—12, including 4 gold. The U.S. and Japan each secured seven medals, while Russia took six.

The U.S. scored its third world team title in women's gymnastics, despite losing a top contender, Alicia Sacramone, to injury prior to the competition. Defending champion Russia placed second, and China, the 2008 Olympic gold medalist, was third. There was a close race in the women's all-around competition between American Jordyn Wieber and Russia's Victoriya Komova, but in the end Wieber triumphed. China's Yao Jinnan took the bronze.

In the women's apparatus finals, American McKayla Maroney prevailed in the vault ahead of 36-year-old Oksana Chusovitina, who had competed for the Soviet Union and Uzbekistan before immigrating to Germany. Phan Thi Ha Thanh of Vietnam took the bronze—her country's first world gymnastics medal. Komova easily won the uneven bars title, followed by her teammate Tatiyana Nabiyeva and China's Huang Qiushuang. Two other Chinese gymnasts, Sui Lu and Yao Jinnan, finished 1–2 on the balance beam, while Wieber was third. Kseniya Afanaseva of Russia won the floor exercise gold medal, with Sui and American Alexandra Raisman in second and third place, respectively.

China continued its supremacy in men's gymnastics, capturing its 10th team title. Japan and the U.S. battled for second in a close finish, but in the end Japan ruled. Kohei Uchimura of Japan won his third consecutive world all-around title. Germany's Philipp Boy took the all-around silver medal for the second straight time, and Japan's Koji Yamamuro earned the bronze.

Chen Xiaowei—Xinhua/Landov

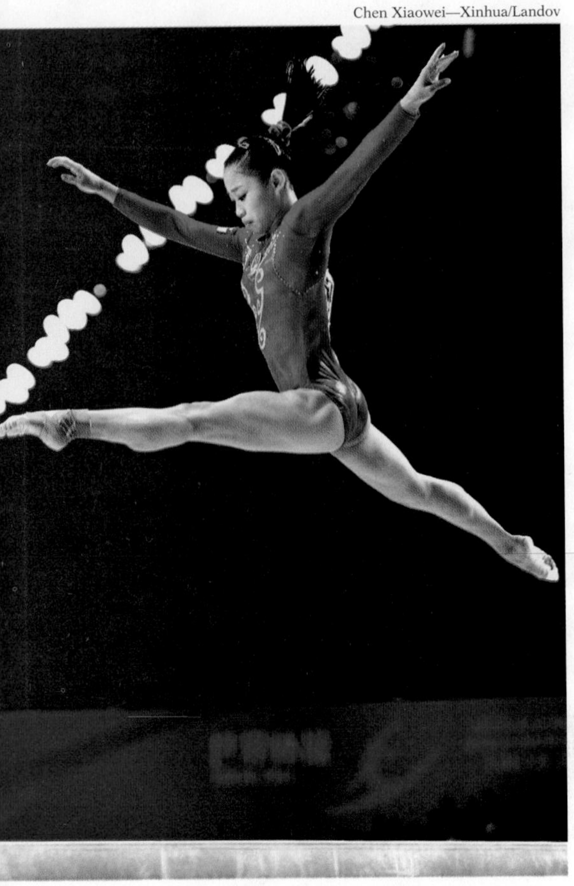

Sui Lu of China, the ultimate gold medalist, soars above the balance beam in the apparatus finals of the artistic gymnastics world championships on October 16.

Uchimura was the only gymnast to qualify and compete in five of the six men's event finals. He won the floor exercise title, ahead of China's Zou Kai. There was a tie for the bronze medal between Brazilian Diego Hypolito and Alexander Shatilov of Israel. On pommel horse Hungary's Krisztian Berki won the title for the second straight year, with Cyril Tommasone of France in second and Britain's Louis Smith in third. Chen Yibing of China won his fifth rings title in six years, ahead of Brazil's Arthur Nabarrete Zanetti and Yamamuro. South Korean Yang Hak-Seon secured the vault title, followed by Russian Anton Golotsutskov and Japan's Makoto Okiguchi. American Danell Leyva won the parallel bars; Vasileios Tsolakidis of Greece and China's Zhang Chenglong tied for second. On the horizontal bar Zou and Zhang finished 1–2, respectively, and Uchimura took third.

Russia reigned at the rhythmic gymnastics world championships, held in Montpellier, France, in September, and defended its team title ahead of Belarus and Ukraine. Yevgeniya Kanayeva of Russia earned her third consecutive all-around title and won all four event titles. Russian teammate Darya Kondakova took second in the all-around final, and Aliya Garayeva of Azerbaijan was third. (LUAN PESZEK)

ICE HOCKEY

North America. When 2.06-m (6-ft 9-in) Boston Bruins captain Zdeno Chara hoisted the iconic Stanley Cup trophy on June 15, 2011, it meant that Boston's historic ice hockey franchise had captured its first NHL championship since 1972. In a rollicking best-of-seven final series against the Vancouver Canucks, Boston won game seven on Vancouver ice by a 4–0 score to take the title four games to three. The Bruins victory earned the team its sixth Stanley Cup. The Canucks, who entered the league in 1970 but had never won a championship, fell short this time despite being the NHL's best and highest-scoring team during the regular season, with a league-leading 54–19–9 record.

Boston's win also capped a remarkable story of redemption and determination for Tim Thomas, the Bruins' acrobatic goaltender who was at the heart of the club's championship run. The 37-year-old netminder went into the 2010–11 season uncertain of his role on the team. He had lost his number one status the previous season because of a hip injury that required off-season surgery, and there was no guarantee that he would regain his prominence. A late pick in the 1994 NHL entry draft, Thomas played in Europe and bounced around ice hockey's minor leagues before he finally found steady work with the Bruins at age 32. In 2011 he not only regained his starting position but also set an NHL record for the highest save percentage (.938) and won his second Vezina Trophy as the NHL's top regular-season goaltender. Then, at the end of the play-offs, Thomas was presented with the Conn Smythe Trophy as the postseason MVP. He was the second American to win that award. In the play-offs, Thomas set a record for the most saves with 798, and during the seven-game final series, he allowed only eight goals and recorded two shutouts. Thomas became the first player to win the Vezina and Conn Smythe trophies, along with the Stanley Cup, in the same season since Philadelphia's Bernie Parent did it consecutively in 1974 and 1975.

The Hart Trophy, for the league's regular-season MVP, was given to Corey Perry, who led the league in goals with 50. Perry, of the Anaheim Ducks, scored 19 goals in the final 16 games of the season, a finishing kick that likely allowed him to surge ahead of Vancouver's Daniel Sedin in the media voting. Sedin won the Art Ross Trophy as the league's top point producer, with 104, and was the only player to reach the 100-point plateau. His twin brother, Henrik, who also played for Vancouver, had captured the Art Ross the previous season.

Other major trophy winners included Detroit's Nicklas Lidstrom, who gained his seventh Norris Trophy as the league's best defenseman. (Legendary Bruin Bobby Orr, who earned eight, was the only player with more Norris trophies than the 41-year-old Lidstrom.) Carolina's Jeff Skinner, aged 18, won the Calder Trophy as the NHL's top rookie, while with the Selke Trophy, Vancouver's Ryan Kesler was acknowledged as the league's top defensive forward.

The Atlanta Thrashers left Georgia after poor performances on the ice and at the gate for 11 seasons. During the team's time in Atlanta, it qualified for the postseason only once and never won a single play-off game. During the summer the Thrashers relocated to Winnipeg, Man., a city that had lost its former NHL franchise in 1996 when the Jets moved to Phoenix and became the Coyotes. The new Winnipeg franchise, which again adopted the name Jets, was set to begin play in the 2011–12 season. Meanwhile, the Phoenix franchise continued to struggle financially and was owned by the NHL, which had been unable to find a buyer for the club.

The off-season brought its usual share of retirements and free-agent shuffling. Among the biggest names to walk away from the NHL were Brian Rafalski (Detroit), Paul Kariya (St. Louis), Mark Recchi (Boston), Adam Foote (Colorado), and Doug Weight (New York Islanders). Kariya did not play a game during the 2010–11 season, because he was sidelined with a concussion that eventually forced him out of the league. Concussions continued to be a major talking point in the NHL, and in hopes of limiting similar injuries, the league approved a stiffer penalty for hits to the head. (*See* Special Report on page 194.)

Jonathan Hayward—The Canadian Press/AP

After having helped his team win the NHL Stanley Cup, Boston Bruins goalie Tim Thomas shows off the Conn Smythe Trophy that he was awarded as the postseason MVP. Thomas also won the Vezina Trophy as the best goaltender in the regular season.

Among the prominent end-of-season free agents to change teams were Brad Richards, who went from Dallas to the New York Rangers; Simon Gagne, who moved to Los Angeles from Tampa; and Tim Connolly, who left Buffalo for Toronto. Former NHL star winger and league MVP Jaromir Jagr returned to North America after three seasons of playing professionally in Russia. He signed a one-year contract with the Philadelphia Flyers.

In June the Hockey Hall of Fame's selection committee announced that four new members would be inducted in November. Going into the Hall were Ed Belfour, Doug Gilmour, Mark Howe, and Joe Nieuwendyk. Belfour, who won the Vezina Trophy twice during his stellar career, was admitted in his first year of eligibility. Howe had been eligible since 1998.

Three NHL players, all known for on-ice fighting, died during the 2011 off-season. The deaths of New York Rangers enforcer Derek Boogaard (age 28) and Rick Rypien (27), who had signed with Winnipeg after having played with Vancouver, prompted commissioner Gary Bettman to say that the league would review its substance abuse and behavioral health program. Both players had spent time in the program. Recently retired Nashville forward Wade Belak (35) died in an apparent suicide.

International. At the International Ice Hockey Federation (IIHF) men's world championship gold-medal final, held at the Orange Arena in Bratislava, Slvk., on May 15, 2011, Finland rolled to a 6–1 victory over Sweden to capture its first world championship in 16 years. There was little to indicate that the floodgates would open when Finland's Jarkko Immonen scored his tournament-leading ninth goal with seven seconds left in the second period, but open they did. Immonen's goal tied the score at 1–1, and when Petteri Nokelainen made it 2–1 for the Finns less than three minutes into the third period, the rout was officially on, as four more Finns scored in the next 17 minutes. The score was particularly stunning because, not only did Sweden have tournament MVP Viktor Fasth in the net but Finland also had a history of heartbreak in similar big games. Although they did capture a bronze at the 2010 Winter Olympics, in four previous trips to the IIHF world final since their only previous title in 1995, the Finns had lost all four times. Television ratings indicated that viewership in Finland peaked at 2.6 million, about half the country's population, during the gold-medal game. An estimated 100,000 revelers then gathered in downtown Helsinki to fete the team after it returned home.

In addition to his MVP honours, Fasth was named the tournament's top goaltender, while Canada's Alex Pietrangelo was the top defenseman, and Jaromir Jagr of the Czech Republic was named best forward. Earlier, in what many called the most entertaining bronze medal ice hockey game ever, the Czech Republic had upended Russia 7–4, the countries combining for a record 11 goals in a world or Olympic third-place showdown. Roman Cervenka led the Czechs with three goals and an assist in a game in which defense was virtually forgotten.

On the women's side, it took overtime, but the U.S. won its third consecutive IIHF world championship when Hilary Knight scored at 7 min 48 sec of extra time to give the Americans a 3–2 victory over Canada in the gold medal game in Zürich on April 25, 2011. The Americans played solid defense against a talented Canadian team and earned a measure of revenge for Canada's win over the U.S. at the 2010 Winter Olympics. The bronze medal game also required overtime to settle; Finland's Karoliina Rantamaki scored to give the Finns a 3–2 victory over Russia. Slovakia goaltender Zuzana Tomcikova was named the tournament MVP.

In early September the entire sport was in mourning after a Yak-42 plane carrying most of Russia's professional ice hockey team Lokomotiv Yaroslavl crashed soon after takeoff in Yaroslavl. The fiery accident killed 44 people, including all 37 of Lokomotiv's players and staff members on board. Swedish legend Sven Tumba died less than a month later at age 80. (*See* OBITUARIES.)

(PAUL HUNTER)

ICE SKATING

Figure Skating. The 2011 International Skating Union (ISU) world figure skating championships were scheduled to start in Tokyo on March 21, but the extensive damage caused by the earthquake and tsunami that hit Japan's northeastern coast 10 days earlier prompted the ISU to move the event to April 25–May 1 in Moscow. Fittingly, a Japanese woman stole the show in Russia as Miki Ando (*see* BIOGRAPHIES) defeated 2010 Winter Olympics champion Kim Yu-Na of South Korea by 1.29 points to win her first world title since 2006–07. Italy's Carolina Kostner took the bronze medal. Ando also captured gold medals at the 2010–11 Four Continents event, Japanese championships, Rostelecom Cup, and Cup of China. On the men's side at worlds, Canada's Patrick Chan finally broke through to win the gold medal, setting three world records along the way, after having taken home silver the previous two seasons. Takahiko Kozuka of Japan secured the silver, his first medal at worlds, and Russia's Artur Gachinski placed third. Meryl Davis and Charlie White won the first world gold medal for the U.S. in ice dance, beating 2010 world and Olympic champions Tessa Virtue and Scott Moir of Canada. The American sister-brother team of Maia and Alex Shibutani earned the bronze. In pairs, Germany's Aliona Savchenko and Robin Szolkowy took the gold medal for the third time in four years over Russia's Tatiyana Volosozhar and Maksim Trankov, with defending champions Pang Qing and Tong Jian of China settling for the bronze.

Like Ando, Chan and Kozuka had dominating seasons. Chan also captured gold medals at the Grand Prix Final, Skate Canada, and the Canadian championships. Kozuka won gold medals at the Cup of China, Trophée Eric Bompard, and the Japanese championships. France finished one-two at the European championships in Bern, Switz., as 20-year-old Florent Amodio, skating in his first European finals, narrowly upset three-time winner Brian Joubert.

In the women's field, U.S. champion Alissa Czisny won gold medals at the Grand Prix Final and Skate Canada. Kostner was the gold medalist at the NHK Trophy and Italian championships, but at the European championships she struggled in the short program and lost to Switzerland's Sarah Meier, who at age 26 was skating in her last competition.

Pairs were dominated by the Savchenko/Szolkowy and Pang/Tong teams, who combined to win 8 of the 11 gold medals on offer, including the European championship, which the Germans secured for the fourth time. In ice dance, Davis and White also captured gold medals at the Four Continents, the Grand Prix Final, and Skate America. The French duo of Nathalie Pechalat and Fabian Bourzat took home the gold medal at the European championships, as well as Trophée Eric Bompard and the Cup of China.

Yuri Kochetkov—EPA/Landov

Charlie White glides across the ice as his ice dance partner, Meryl Davis, balances on one skate on his leg during their free-skate program at the world figure skating championships in April. The American duo's elegant performance was enough to secure their first world title.

The 2010–11 season was without 2010 Olympic men's champion Evan Lysacek of the U.S., who decided to sit out because of a heavy schedule of promotions and appearances. In Lysacek's absence, Ryan Bradley took gold at the U.S. championship. Meanwhile, Yevgeny Plushchenko, who finished second to Lysacek at the 2010 Olympics, was stripped of his eligibility by the ISU after he appeared in exhibitions without having gained permission. Plushchenko had his amateur status restored in June.

Speed Skating. American Shani Davis continued his dominance in the 1,500 m during the 2010–11 speed-skating season, but his reign in the 1,000 m came to an end. Davis won the 1,500-m World Cup title for the fourth straight season and was attempting to do the same in the 1,000 m, but Stefan Groothuis of the Netherlands came away with the World Cup crown in that distance, and Davis ended up third behind Lee Kyou-Hyuk of South Korea. Bob de Jong of the Netherlands won the 5,000-m and 10,000-m season titles. In the absence of four-time champion Sven Kramer of the Netherlands, Russia's Ivan Skobrev won the world all-around championship in February.

On the women's side, Canada's Christine Nesbitt had her two-year run as 1,000-m World Cup season champion ended by American Heather Richardson, who edged the defending champion by just 15 points. Nesbitt did capture the 1,500-m title as fellow Canadian Kristina Groves failed to secure that crown for a fourth straight year. Germany's Jenny Wolf won her sixth consecutive season title in the 500 m, and Martina Sablikova of the Czech Republic captured the 3,000-m/5,000-m season crown for the fifth straight time. Sablikova failed to take her third straight all-around title, however, as Ireen Wüst of the Netherlands finished on the podium in all four events and claimed the crown.

The 2011 world single-distance championships were held in Germany in March, and the Netherlands was the big winner, with 14 total medals. Coming in second was Germany, with six medals, and Canada and the U.S. followed with four apiece. Davis earned three of those medals for the U.S., picking up gold in the 1,000 m and team pursuit while taking a silver in the 1,500 m.

South Korea dominated short-track speed skating in 2011, with Noh Jin-Kyu and Cho Ha-Ri capturing the overall men's and women's titles, respectively, at the individual world short-track championships, held in Sheffield, Eng., in March. Just days later South Korea won the gold medal in both the men's and women's events at the world team championships in Warsaw.

(PAUL DIGIACOMO)

SAILING (YACHTING)

Interest in the 34th America's Cup was heating up in 2011 as rivals faced off in the new AC World Series. This five-regatta "feeder series" would give AC crews a chance to work together to hone the skills that they would need in the Louis Vuitton Cup—the match-racing event used to select the challenger for the 2013 America's Cup.

Race organizers designated a 14-m (45-ft) wing-mast rigged carbon-fibre catamaran (AC45) as the one-design sailboat for the AC World Series. The boat was quick to reach speeds of more than 20 knots but proved to be a handful in a heavy breeze. After Emirates Team New Zealand won the first AC World Series event off Cascais, Port., in August, more than 100,000 spectators lined the seawalls of Plymouth, Eng., during the second event in September. On the final day of racing, gusty winds confronted the fleet, setting the stage for spectacular mark-rounding action and even more dramatic maneuvering as sailors worked hard to avoid catapult-like capsizes. Emirates Team New Zealand emerged with a slight lead over Oracle Racing.

Brad Van Liew, an American adventure sailor from Charleston, S.C., won the Velux 5 Oceans Race. On his way to a decisive victory, Van Liew chalked up a string of five first-place finishes. During eight months and some 48,000 km (about 30,000 mi) of solo sailing, punctuated by five stopovers, Van Liew never relinquished his lead. This was his third solo around-the-world race and his second win, but it was the first time that an American had claimed overall honours in a race that previously had been dominated by Europeans.

Racing sailors from around the world flocked to Key West, Fla., in January to trade tacks with other top-tier competitors. The 2011 event saw fewer boats than past Key West Race Weeks but no reduction in the caliber of the Grand Prix competition. From the start the RC 44 one-design class epitomized exciting sailing. The battle for first place went to the wire, with the last leg of the last race deciding the victor. Team Aqua (U.S.) lost out to Mascalzone Latino (Italy) in a tiebreaker. The Italians had tallied up more first-place finishes in the 10 races, and in accordance with the rules, the win went their way. Oracle Racing, under former America's Cup-winning skipper Russell Coutts of New Zealand (co-designer of the RC 44), came in third.

The first few days of 2011 saw competitors returning to Sydney after a grueling Sydney Hobart Race at year-end 2010. A protest over the provisional victor's problems with radio communication was resolved in favour of the boat and the crew of *Wild Oats XI*, which laid claim to a sailing hat trick (first-to-finish, first on corrected time, and a new course record). In the 2011 Sydney Hobart Yacht Race, which culminated in late December, the overall winner was declared to be *Loki*, and the first-finish line honours went to Ivestec Loyal.

In July the nearly 350 sailboats entered in the Chicago–Mackinac Race had an easy sail until the last leg, when a volatile band of severe weather moved in. Gusts in excess of 60 knots knocked vessels down, tore sails, and tragically capsized the Kiwi 35 *WingNuts*. Six of the eight crew were rescued, but the skipper and another crew member were trapped beneath the vessel and drowned. A review of the incident, conducted by US Sailing, the national governing body, concluded that *WingNuts* had not been suited to compete because its sail area was unusually large in proportion to the boat's light weight.

(RALPH NARANJO)

SKIING

Alpine Skiing. American Lindsey Vonn's quest for a fourth straight International Ski Federation (FIS) World Cup overall women's title came down to the final day of the 2010–11 Alpine skiing season, but she lost the crown to Maria Riesch of Germany despite the fact that the longtime rivals and friends never had to ski that day. Although Vonn won eight overall World Cup races to Riesch's six, the German held a three-point lead heading into the season-ending giant slalom (GS) race in Lenzerheide, Switz. The race was canceled because of poor weather, thus giving the overall title to Riesch in the smallest margin of victory since 2005. Vonn continued her dominance in other World Cup disciplines: she was the downhill champion for the fourth straight season, took the supergiant slalom (super G) crown for the third consecutive season, and was the super combined champion for the second year in a row. This matched the record Vonn set in 2009–10, when she became the first American to win three World Cup discipline titles in a single season. Austria's Marlies Schild won her third career slalom title and first since 2008 by ending Riesch's two-year run in the discipline. Viktoria Rebensburg of Germany took the GS crown for her first career World Cup title.

Croatia's Ivica Kostelic was the runaway victor of the men's overall 2010–11 World Cup title, beating Didier Cuche of Switzerland by 400 points. He also took the slalom and super combined crowns after winning seven World Cup races (all in January 2011). Kostelic, whose younger sister, Janica Kostelic, achieved three women's overall World Cup titles before retiring in 2006, had not won a season crown since being the slalom champion in 2002. Cuche earned the downhill title for the second straight season, as well as the super G crown, and American Ted Ligety was the GS champion for the second year in a row and the third time in four seasons.

At the 2011 FIS Alpine world ski championships, held in Garmisch-Partenkirchen, Ger., in February, the men's gold medal winners were Ligety in GS, Canadian Erik Guay in downhill, Italy's Christof Innerhofer in super G, Jean-Baptiste Grange of France in slalom, and Norway's Aksel Lund Svindal in super combined. In the women's events, Austria's Elisabeth Görgl won gold in both downhill and super G, with the other golds going to Schild in slalom, Slovenia's Tina Maze in GS, and Anna Fenninger of Austria in super combined. Vonn had to settle for the silver in downhill, and Riesch took bronze medals in downhill and super G.

Nordic Skiing. Switzerland's Dario Cologna beat 2009–10 overall Nordic World Cup title winner Petter Northug of Norway by 330 points to capture the 2010–11 cross-country season title. Cologna, who also had beaten Northug in 2008–09, added the distance crown, and Sweden's Emil Jönsson won the sprint title for the second straight season. In the women's field, Poland's Justyna Kowalczyk captured the overall and distance titles for the third consecutive season. In 2009–10 Kowalczyk also had been the sprint champion, ending the two-year run of Slovenia's Petra Majdic, but Majdic reclaimed that title in 2011. Northug shone brightly in his home country by winning three gold and two silver medals at the 2011 FIS Nordic world ski championships in Oslo, and countrywoman Marit Bjørgen earned four gold medals and a silver. Kowalczyk won two silver medals and a bronze.

France's Jason Lamy Chappuis again dominated in Nordic combined, securing the overall World Cup title for the second straight season and winning a gold medal at the world championships. Thomas Morgenstern of Austria took the season crown in ski jumping, as well as three gold medals and a

David W. Cerny—Reuters/Landov

Thomas Morgenstern of Austria dominated ski jumping competition, winning three gold medals and a silver at the world championships as well as the overall World Cup.

silver at the worlds. Fellow Austrian Daniela Iraschko reigned in women's ski jumping, winning 17 of 24 events, including the world championship.

Freestyle Skiing. Guilbaut Colas of France and American Hannah Kearney won, respectively, the men's and women's overall World Cup freestyle skiing titles, while France's Ophélie David had her string of seven straight women's season titles in ski cross ended by Anna Holmlund of Sweden. Colas also took the moguls season crown and earned a gold medal in the discipline at the 2011 FIS freestyle world ski championships in Park City, Utah, in February. Qi Guangpu of China was the men's aerials season champion and Austrian Andreas Matt took the season crown in ski cross. On the women's side, Kearney also took the moguls title, and Cheng Shuang of China was the aerials champion.

Snowboarding. Austria's Benjamin Karl won the overall World Cup snowboarding title and the parallel crown for the second straight season, as well as two gold medals at the FIS snowboarding world championships, held in La Molina, Spain, in January 2011. Australian Alex Pullin took the season championship in snowboardcross (SBX) after having finished second in 2009–10. Austrian Clemens Schattschneider earned the season title in big air, and Nathan Johnstone of Australia was the halfpipe winner. The women's overall World Cup title and parallel crown went to Russia's Yekaterina Tudegesheva. Dominique Maltais of Canada was the SBX champion; China's Cai Xuetong captured the season crown in halfpipe; and Poland's Katarzyna Rusin took home the big air championship. (PAUL DIGIACOMO)

SQUASH

Egyptian players dominated most of the squash world titles in 2011. At the inaugural World Squash Federation (WSF) World Cup, held in March in Chennai, India, Egypt's top-seeded mixed team defeated second-ranked England 2–0 in the final without recourse to a deciding match. Australia topped Malaysia for the bronze medal.

Both the men's and the women's world junior individual events—held in Herentals, Belg., and Boston, respectively—featured all-Egyptian finals. In July, Marwen El Shorbagy followed his older brother, two-time champion Mohamed El Shorbagy, to complete the first family double for the men's title, beating Mohamed Abouelghar. Nour El Tayeb, who had come up short in 2009 and 2010, made it third time lucky in the women's junior final in May when she overcame former champion Nour El Sherbini. Egypt also took the women's junior team title as the individual finalists paired up to spearhead a 2–1 victory over the U.S. host.

The men's world team championship, staged in Paderborn, Ger., in August, seemed like a near replay of the World Cup. Egypt, headed by Ramy Ashour and Karim Darwish, topped England 2–1 to retain the title, with Australia beating France 2–1 to take the bronze.

The Egyptians faltered at the men's and women's World Open championships, staged together on October 28–November 6 in Rotterdam, Neth. Malaysia's Nicol David captured her sixth World Open crown to become the all-time women's record holder, overtaking Australia's Sarah Fitz-Gerald, who had five. David overwhelmed England's Jenny Duncalf 11–2, 11–5, 11–0 in the final. Meanwhile, Nick Matthew of England won his second consecutive title when he beat France's Gregory Gaultier 6–11, 11–9, 11–6, 11–5 in the men's final. During the tournament David became the 12th "legend" of the sport when she was inducted into the WSF Hall of Fame. (ANDREW SHELLEY)

SWIMMING

With the 2012 London Olympic Games only one year away, in 2011 there were a host of very fast international swimming meets, including those at the World University Games and regional contests such as the Pan-American Games. The highlight of the year, however, was the XIV FINA world championships, held July 16–31 at the Oriental Sports Center in Shanghai. Though the American men and women both dominated with nearly identical medal counts, including eight golds each, the wealth was spread around as swimmers from 15 countries took home gold, while aquatic athletes from 20 countries earned at least one medal of silver or bronze.

Only two long-course world records were set during the year—the first since December 2009—a legacy of the performance-enhancing "high-tech suits" outlawed by FINA as of January 2010. A better measure of the quality of swimming in 2011 was the fact that the fastest swims ever recorded in textile suits were bettered in 13 of the 26 individual Olympic events.

The first world record to fall was that in the men's 200-m individual medley (IM), which American Ryan Lochte (*see* BIOGRAPHIES) cut to a phenomenal 1 min 54.00 sec in Shanghai on July 28. Two years earlier, at the Rome world championships, Lochte had lowered the suit-aided mark to 1 min 54.10 sec. In Shanghai, wearing a low-tech textile suit, Lochte overtook teammate Michael Phelps, the previous world record holder, just before the halfway mark. He then withstood Phelps's challenge, setting the record and winning the race by 0.16 sec.

Three days later China's Sun Yang, buoyed by a boisterous home crowd, unleashed an incredible finishing sprint to nip the oldest record in the book: the men's 1,500-m freestyle. Sun's time of 14 min 34.14 sec carved 0.42 sec off the former mark, set in 2001 by Australian distance legend Grant Hackett. Sun's final 50 m—timed at 25.94 sec—was faster than the final 50 m of the 200-m freestyle swimmers. The 19-year-old Sun also stroked to victory in the 800-m freestyle and placed second in the 400-m final. That lapse was corrected two months later when he swam the fastest 400 m of the year (3 min 40.29 sec), just missing the high-tech world record of 3 min 40.07 sec.

Despite Sun's many accomplishments, Lochte was the biggest story at the worlds. Aside from his world record, he also registered 2011 world-leading times in the 200-m freestyle (1 min 44.44 sec), the 200-m backstroke (1 min 52.96 sec), and the 400-m IM (4 min 07.13 sec). In addition, he anchored the American team's golden 4 × 200-m freestyle relay and swam in the preliminaries of the 4 × 100-m freestyle relay, in which the U.S. eventually took the bronze. Lochte's total of five gold medals and one bronze was unmatched. Phelps came the closest, with four golds (100- and 200-m butterfly, 4 × 100-m medley relay, and 4 × 200-m freestyle relay), two silvers (200-m freestyle and 200-m IM), and one bronze (4 × 100-m freestyle relay).

At the swimming world championships in Shanghai, local favourite Sun Yang of China glides through the water in the 1,500-m final on July 31 en route to a gold medal and a new world record.

Gero Breloer/AP

There were other remarkable men's performances in Shanghai. Norway's Alexander Dale Oen won his country's first world championship gold with a brilliant 58.71-sec swim in the 100-m breaststroke, the fastest time ever in a textile suit. Although no Frenchman had ever won a backstroke medal at a world championship, in Shanghai France collected two gold medals—in the same event. That unlikely outcome was the result of a first-place tie (52.76 sec) in the 100-m backstroke between teammates Camille Lacourt and Jeremy Stravius.

Italy's Federica Pellegrini and American Rebecca Soni were the only women to earn two gold medals in individual events in Shanghai. Pellegrini reprised her triumphs of 2009 in the 200- and 400-m freestyle events with excellent times of 1 min 55.58 sec and 4 min 01.97 sec, respectively. In addition to repeating her winning breaststroke effort in Rome two years earlier by notching a victory in the 100 m (1 min 05.05 sec), Soni also won the 200 m (2 min 21.47 sec). She scored a third gold as the U.S. lowered its national record to 3 min 52.36 sec in the women's 4 × 100-m medley relay.

The outstanding swim by a woman, however, came in the 200-m backstroke when 16-year-old American Melissa ("Missy") Franklin recorded 2 min 05.10 sec, the second fastest time in history in the event. (The world record, set by Zimbabwe's Kirsty Coventry in a high-tech suit in 2009, stood at 2 min 04.81 sec.) Almost unnoticed was Franklin's leadoff swim in the 4 × 200-m freestyle relay, where her time of 1 min 55.06 sec was half a second faster than Pellegrini's winning swim in the 200 m and ranked the third-year high-school student first in the world at the distance. Franklin achieved her first world record in October, a blistering 2 min 0.03 sec in the 200-m backstroke at the short-course (25-m) World Cup meet in Berlin.

Among the other outstanding women swimmers, Sweden's Therese Alshammar, just 26 days shy of her 34th birthday, became history's oldest female swimming world champion when she won the 50-m freestyle. She was also second in the 50-m butterfly. Two long shots tied for the gold in the 100-m freestyle at 53.45 sec: Denmark's Jeanette Ottesen and Aleksandra Herasimenia of Belarus.

Diving. China proved yet again that its team was the dominant power in the diving world. Chinese divers had not been seriously challenged at the very highest level of international meets in well over a decade, and their intrasquad meets were often deemed more competitive than the world championships. It seemed unlikely that they could get even better, but that was precisely what the Chinese divers showed at the 2011 FINA world aquatics championships, held July 16–24 in Shanghai. Led by Olympic veterans Wu Minxia and Chen Ruolin and by teenage phenomenon Qiu Bo, the Chinese scored a perfect 10, winning every gold medal (and four silver) at the global diving fest.

Wu and synchronized-diving partner He Zi breezed to victory in the women's 3-m synchro springboard final with 356.40 points. The two women later battled each other in the individual 3 m, with Wu nipping her teammate by a razor-thin 1.70 points. Shi Tingmao and Wang Han took the top two spots in the women's 1-m springboard, and Chen and Hu Yadan duplicated that one–two finish on the 10-m platform.

The Chinese men proved every bit as formidable as the women, with Qiu setting the pace as he teamed with two-time champion Huo Liang to take the men's 10-m platform synchro crown. Li Shixin and He Min took the two top spots in the 1-m springboard, and in the 3-m springboard the defending champion, He Chong, was again victorious. Qin Kai and Luo Yutong took gold in the men's 3-m synchro event. The competition ended much as it had begun, with Qiu bagging the individual 10 m.

Synchronized Swimming. Since the turn of the 21st century, Russia had dominated the elegant world of synchronized swimming, having won all of the gold medals at the last three Olympic Games and all but one of the gold medals on offer at each of the last three world championships. Led by the incomparable Nataliya Ischenko, who earned six golds, the Russians outdid themselves in 2011, sweeping all seven events at the FINA world championships in Shanghai.

China overtook perennial runner-up Spain for the number two position with six silver medals and one bronze. The Spaniards placed third with one silver and five bronze. Canada earned the remaining bronze medal, in free combination, and finished fourth in every other event. (PHILLIP WHITTEN)

TENNIS

Having concluded the previous four tennis seasons (2007–10) with a ranking of number three in the world, Serbia's charismatic Novak Djokovic (*see* BIOGRAPHIES) lifted his game to a newfound level in 2011, moving past Spaniard Rafael Nadal and Roger Federer of Switzerland to number one. Djokovic's banner year included a season-opening 41-match winning streak, 10 tournament triumphs, 3 Grand Slam championship titles, and a remarkable 10–1 combined record against Federer and Nadal. Denmark's Caroline Wozniacki garnered the number one women's ranking for the second year in a row but once again failed to secure a major title.

For the first time since 2002, Federer did not win a major championship, failing in his bid to become the first man to win at least one Grand Slam event for nine consecutive years. Nadal, however, captured his sixth French Open singles championship to tie Sweden's Björn Borg for the men's record at Roland Garros. In a compelling year for the women, four different competitors claimed the most prestigious prizes. Belgium's Kim Clijsters was victorious at the Australian Open; China's Li Na prevailed at the French Open; Petra Kvitova of the Czech Republic won the All-England (Wimbledon) title; and Australian Samantha Stosur was the victor at the U.S. Open. Djokovic was the year's top prize-money earner among the men with $11,019,803. Kvitova was the top earner for the women, making $5,145,943.

Mike Groll/AP

Samantha Stosur of Australia demonstrates her powerful serve during her astonishing upset victory over American Serena Williams in the final of the U.S. Open tennis tournament on September 11.

Australian Open. Having led Serbia to its first Davis Cup title at the end of 2010, Djokovic, the 2008 Australian Open champion, arrived in Melbourne in January 2011 brimming with confidence. During the fortnight of competition, Djokovic, the number three seed, dropped only one set in seven matches, toppling Federer 7–6 (3), 7–5, 6–4 in a high-quality semifinal. In the final Djokovic upended Britain's Andy Murray, the number five seed, with surprising ease, coming through 6–4, 6–2, 6–3.

Number three seed Clijsters did not concede a set on her way to a final-round confrontation with Li Na, casting aside number two seed Vera Zvonareva of Russia 6–3, 6–3 in the semifinals. Li upset top-seeded Wozniacki 3–6, 7–5, 6–3 in their semifinal, saving a match point in the second set. At the outset of the final, Li seemed ready to replicate her triumph over Clijsters a few weeks earlier in Sydney, but the Belgian rallied gamely to take her fourth career major, registering a 3–6, 6–3, 6–3 victory.

French Open. Heading into the world's most significant clay court tournament, Djokovic was viewed as the favourite among most of the cognoscenti. After winning his fourth-round contest easily over Frenchman Richard Gasquet, however, Djokovic did not play again for five days because his quarterfinal opponent defaulted. Facing an inspired Federer in the semifinals, Djokovic was knocked out in a sparkling four-set encounter for his first defeat of the year. Federer performed prodigiously in the final against Nadal, but the Spaniard rallied from 2–5 and set point down in the critical opening set and eventually achieved a 7–5, 7–6 (3), 5–7, 6–1 triumph. Nadal had cut down number four seed Murray in a straight-set semifinal.

Li followed up on her sterling run in Australia, becoming the first Chinese player—male or female—to secure a major singles tennis title. The gritty and perspicacious 29-year-old—seeded sixth—overcame Kvitova in a come-from-behind three-set fourth-round victory and then ousted number four seed Victoria Azarenka of Belarus in the quarterfinals and number seven Mariya Sharapova of Russia in the semifinals. Confronting defending champion Francesca Schiavone of Italy in the championship match, Li was the better big-point player, and her superior power from the backcourt carried her to a 6–4, 7–6 (0) victory.

Wimbledon. When six-time Wimbledon champion Federer built a commanding two-set lead over Frenchman Jo-Wilfried Tsonga in the quarterfinals, he seemed certain to prevail. (In 178 previous clashes at the majors when he had been up by that margin, he had never been beaten.) Tsonga, seeded 12th, gallantly recovered, however, for a startling 3–6, 6–7 (3), 6–4, 6–4, 6–4 triumph; he never faced a break point after having lost his serve once early in the first set. Tsonga was subsequently picked apart 7–6 (4), 6–2, 6–7 (9), 6–3 in the semifinals by number two seed Djokovic. Nadal, the defending champion, hurt his foot during a fourth-round victory over Argentina's Juan Martín del Potro and received numbing injections for the remainder of the tournament. He rallied for a four-set victory over Murray in the semifinals but fell to a masterful Djokovic in a four-set final.

Kvitova was dazzling and uncompromising during her journey through the women's draw. The free-flowing left-hander—one of the sport's finest shot makers—halted number four seed Azarenka in a three-set semifinal. Sharapova, who was in pursuit of her first major title since the 2008 Australian Open, did not lose a set in six matches on her way to the final with Kvitova, dismissing Germany's big-serving Sabine Lisicki (a surprise second-round winner over Li, the number three seed) in the semifinals. Many authorities believed that Sharapova's record and reputation would give her an edge over Kvitova, who was appearing in her first major final at age 21. Kvitova was remarkably poised, however, going boldly for her shots, playing an uninhibited brand of aggressive baseline tennis, while Sharapova seemed ill at ease and off balance. Kvitova took the title convincingly in two sets, 6–3, 6–4.

U.S. Open. A year earlier on the same Arthur Ashe Stadium court, Nadal had beaten Djokovic in a spirited four-set final to claim his first U.S. Open crown. They reversed roles in 2011 when Djokovic had too much firepower for Nadal, who could no longer intimidate his Serbian rival with his trademark topspin forehand crosscourt. Djokovic had the answer to Nadal's signature shot, retaliating with his powerful two-handed backhand. Djokovic bested Nadal 6–2, 6–4, 6–7 (3), 6–1 in a final that was far better and more competitive than the score suggested, securing his first U.S. Open title. The match of the tournament was surely Djokovic's semifinal comeback over Federer. Not only did he rally from two sets down, but he also saved two match points in the fifth set. Federer was serving at 5–3, 40–15 in the fifth set when Djokovic uncorked an astonishing forehand service return winner that left Federer dazed and the crowd in a frenzy. Djokovic saved one more match point, captured four games in a row, and defeated Federer 6–7 (7), 4–6, 6–3, 6–2, 7–5.

American Serena Williams returned to tennis in June after an absence of nearly a year. She won two tournaments on the Olympus U.S. Open Series and arrived at the U.S. Open as the number 28 seed. The three-time champion struck down number four seed Azarenka in the third round and the top-seeded Wozniacki in the semifinals, but she was caught thoroughly off guard by Stosur in the final. Stosur, the number nine seed, made only 12 unforced errors, 13 fewer than Williams, in her 6–2, 6–3 triumph, one of the most stunning upsets in the history of women's tennis.

Other Events. For the fifth time since 2000, Spain won the Davis Cup, defeating Argentina in the final on clay in Seville, Spain. Nadal clinched the victory for his country, overcoming a tenacious del Potro 1–6, 6–4, 6–1, 7–6 (0). The Czech Republic, spearheaded by the surging Kvitova, defeated Russia 3–2 in Moscow to capture the Fed Cup. At the Barclays ATP World Tour Finals in London, Federer became the first man to have taken the season-ending event six times, overcoming Tsonga in the final. The Swiss ended an otherwise disappointing year with a 17-match, three-tournament winning streak. At the season-concluding TEB BNP Paribas WTA Championships in Istanbul, Kvitova underlined her status as a champion of growing stature, defeating Azarenka to secure the number two world ranking. (STEVE FLINK)

TRACK AND FIELD SPORTS (ATHLETICS)

In 2011 Usain Bolt, the Jamaican sprinter whose world record-setting gold medal victories in 2008 and 2009 made him the most renowned active athlete in track and field, hoped, after an injury-shortened 2010 campaign, to get back to his self-proclaimed goal of establishing himself as a legend. While he met with some success, he false-started the most important 100-m race of the year, at the world championships. His training partner Yohan Blake stepped up to win that dash and with subsequent victories wrote a rivalry into the story line ahead of the 2012 London Olympics.

World Outdoor Championships. The 100-m dash at the 13th IAAF world championships, held August 27–September 4 in Daegu, S.Kor., drew heightened attention as Bolt's first international title race in two years. He mugged for the crowd before settling into the blocks and then shot out from the set position 0.104 sec before the gun to earn an instant disqualification under a controversial rule established in 2010, which allowed for no second chances. Bolt ripped off his singlet, immediately cognizant of his gaffe, leaving the in-stadium crowd of some 32,000 spectators—plus millions of television viewers—shocked as he exited the track. On the restart the 21-year-old Blake charged to a nearly two-metre lead and finished in 9.92 sec against a 2.25-km/hr (1.4-mph) headwind. Walter Dix of the U.S., the 2008 Beijing Olympic bronze medalist, placed second in 10.08-sec, just 0.01 sec ahead of Kim Collins of Saint Kitts and Nevis, the 2003 gold medalist. Collins, age 35, became the oldest man to earn a world championships 100-m medal. Bolt patched his reputation by winning the 200-m six nights later in 19.40 sec. In the final event of the championships, Jamaica's 4 × 100-m relay team, with Blake and Bolt running the last two legs, won in 37.04 sec, a world record that cut 0.06 sec from the mark another Bolt-led Jamaican team had set to win the 2008 Olympics. South African Oscar Pistorius, a double below-the-knee am-

Jamaican sprinter Usain Bolt (left) accepts the baton handoff from his teammate Yohan Blake (right) on September 4 in the final of the men's 4 × 100-m relay at the track and field world championships. The Jamaican foursome (Nesta Carter, Michael Frater, Blake, and Bolt) won the gold medal in world-record time.

Chen Xiaowei—Xinhua/Landov

putee who raced on carbon-fibre prosthetics, became the first Paralympic athlete to win an open world championships medal, a silver in the men's 4 × 400-m relay. (*See* BIOGRAPHIES.)

Distance runner Vivian Cheruiyot of Kenya was the championships' only double gold medalist in individual events. On the meet's first night, she won the women's 10,000-m in 30 min 48.98 sec, leading teammates Sally Kipyego, Linet Masai, and Priscah Cherono to the first 1–2–3–4 team finish in meet history in any event. In the 5,000 m Cheruiyot preceded fellow Kenyan Sylvia Kibet and Meseret Defar of Ethiopia across the line to defend her title from 2009 with a time of 14 min 55.36 sec. Britain's Mo Farah very nearly won the same double in men's competition. He led the closing stages of the 10,000 m and sprinted the last of the 25 laps in 53.4 sec, but he was overtaken in the final 20 m by Ibrahim Jeilan, a Japan-trained Ethiopian. Jeilan won in 27 min 13.81 sec to Farah's second-place 27 min 14.07 sec mark. In a tactical 5,000 m that Farah won in 13 min 23.36 sec, he ran his last lap in 52.6 sec to just hold off American Bernard Lagat, the 2007 champion.

David Rudisha, the Kenyan 800-m runner who swept all before him in 2010 with two world records and no losses in the two-lap event, captured gold by half a second over Abubaker Kaki of Sudan. For 22-year-old Rudisha the win snapped a frustrating major championships streak that had seen him miss the Beijing Olympics because of injury and fail to advance from the semifinals at the 2009 world championships. Kirani James of Grenada won gold in the men's 400 m with a time of 44.60 sec just two days before his 19th birthday. James defeated American LaShawn Merritt, the defending world and Olympic champion, who had recently returned from a 21-month doping suspension for inadvertent consumption of a banned substance contained in a male enhancement product. At the opposite end of the age spectrum from James, 36-year-old hammer champion Koji Murofushi of Japan became the oldest men's throws winner in meet history. He led throughout the competition and made his best mark, 81.24 m (266 ft 6 in), in round five. He then had to wait out the measurement of the final throw by favoured Krisztian Pars of Hungary, which taped out 6 cm (2 in) shy of the win. Murofushi's was the smallest winning margin ever in the hammer at a world championships.

Sally Pearson of Australia and Lashinda Demus of the U.S. turned in fast women's hurdles wins. Pearson took the 100-m hurdles in 12.28 sec, advancing to fourth all-time best performer. Demus's winning mark in the 400-m hurdles, 52.47 sec, was the third fastest performance ever recorded. The women's javelin competition, won by Mariya Abakumova of Russia, was the deepest in event history. After Olympic champion and world record holder Barbora Spotakova of the Czech Republic threw 71.58 m (234 ft 10 in), the third farthest throw ever, Abakumova bettered it with a 71.99-m (236-ft 2-in) meet-record heave, just 29 cm (12 in) shorter than the world record. Spotakova's mark and the 63.38-m (224-ft 4-in) throw by bronze medalist Sunette Viljoen of South Africa were the longest-ever marks by second- and third-place finishers.

As 11 individuals (7 men and 4 women) successfully defended their titles from 2009, American Dwight Phillips in the men's long jump and New Zealander Valerie Adams (formerly Valerie Vili) in the women's shot put stretched their world championships win streaks to four in a row. The women's 20-km walk victory by Olga Kaniskina of Russia, also the Beijing Olympic champion, marked her third world title in succession.

International Competition. In the second year of the IAAF's Diamond League series, Blake produced the most stunning single performance. On September 16, at the final meet of the series in Brussels, he raced 200 m in 19.26 sec. Suddenly Blake, who had previously broken 20 seconds just twice in his career, was history's second fastest half lapper, with only Bolt's 19.19-sec world record ahead of him on the all-time list. Rudisha, as in 2010, showed fabulous consistency. He won 10 elite-level 800-m races before losing his last race of the season to Ethiopian teenager Mohamed Aman. The loss snapped Rudisha's finals win streak since 2009 at 26 meets. Discus world champion Robert Harting of Germany led men's field-event athletes for consistency. Rival Zoltan Kovago of Hungary had the year's longest throw, and Lithuania's Virgilijus Alekna won the Diamond League discus title, but Harting never lost during his 16-meet season.

In women's competition Adams had a season without blemishes. She won all 13 of her meets and the Diamond League shot-put title and led the seasonal list. The season's top women performers on the track, most experts agreed, were Cheruiyot and Pearson, respective winners of the Diamond League in the 5,000 m and the 100-m hurdles. Cheruiyot ran undefeated in nine races at 3,000 m, 5,000 m, and 10,000 m. Pearson won 10 of her 11 races against top-flight competition, losing only when she fell in Brussels, her last competition of the year.

Bolt and Pearson were named the men's and women's IAAF Athletes of the Year, respectively. Both decisions drew some criticism from commentators, with charges leveled that online voting, which carried weight in the process, favoured popularity over performance and left African athletes, particularly Cheruiyot, at a disadvantage because access to the Web was limited on that continent compared with other parts of the world.

Cross Country and Marathon Running. Never before had one country dominated the men's marathon as Kenya did in 2011; Kenyans ran 27 of the top 32 times. The extraordinary performances began at the Boston Marathon in April. As a tailwind blew, Geoffrey Mutai (2 hr 3 min 2 sec) and Moses Mosop (2 hr 3 min 6 sec) both ran far under the world record (2 hr 3 min 59 sec) set by Ethiopia's Haile Gebrselassie in 2008. Mutai's winning time could not count as a record, however, because of Boston's point-to-point, net downhill configuration. Emmanuel Mutai set a course record (2 hr 4 min 40 sec) at the London Marathon the same month. At the Berlin Marathon in September, 26-year-old Patrick Makau raced to a new world record, 2 hr 3 min 38 sec. Mosop prevailed at the Chicago Marathon in October, but Mutai secured the 2010–11 men's World Marathon Majors (WMM) title when he demolished the course record for the notoriously challenging New York City Marathon with a time of 2 hr 5 min 6 sec.

Russian Liliya Shobukhova sewed up the women's WMM crown and became history's second fastest woman marathoner when she won the Chicago Marathon in 2 hr 18 min 20 sec, her third straight victory there. Firehiwot Dado of Ethiopia won in New York, while Kenyan women took the other major marathons: Caroline Kilel (Boston), Mary Keitany (London), and Florence Kiplagat (Berlin).

At the world cross country championships, held in Punta Umbria, Spain, on March 20, Ethiopian Imane Merga and Cheruiyot were the men's and women's senior champions, respectively. Only Ethiopia's team win in the women's junior race stopped Kenya from sweeping the team titles.

(SIEG LINDSTROM)

VOLLEYBALL

In indoor volleyball Russia captured the 2011 Fédération Internationale de Volleyball (FIVB) men's World Cup title, beating Poland in five sets on December 4, the final day of the two-week competition held in Tokyo. It was Russia's sixth title in the competition. Maksim Mikhaylov of Russia was tabbed the World Cup MVP. Russia and Poland both qualified for the 2012 London Olympic Games. Brazil, the two-time defending World Cup winner, clinched the third and final berth for the Olympics with a victory over Japan in straights sets.

Despite losing to the Americans, Italy in November retained the women's World Cup title. The U.S. could have clinched its first women's World Cup title with a victory on the final day but instead fell to Japan in three sets. Italy's Carolina del Pilar Costagrande was named MVP. Italy, the U.S., and third-place China each clinched a spot at the London Olympics.

Russia gained revenge over defending champion Brazil to win its second men's World League crown. Mikhaylov was named the tournament MVP. Poland claimed the bronze medal after beating Argentina. The U.S. women in August retained the World Grand Prix title as they swept Brazil in three straight sets. Serbia finished in third.

On the sand Brazil's Alison Cerutti and Emanuel Rego defeated countrymen Marcio Araujo and Ricardo Santos to win the FIVB men's beach volleyball world championship. Defending champions Julius Brink and Jonas Reckermann of Germany captured the bronze. Juliana Felisberta Silva and Larissa Franca of Brazil earned a hard-fought decision over three-time champions Misty May-Treanor and Kerri Walsh of the U.S. at the women's beach volleyball world championships. In the bronze-medal match, China's Chen Xue and Xi Zhang downed Czech Republic's Lenka Hajeckova and Hana Klapalova.

(RICHARD S. WANNINGER)

Tolga Bozoglu—EPA/Landov

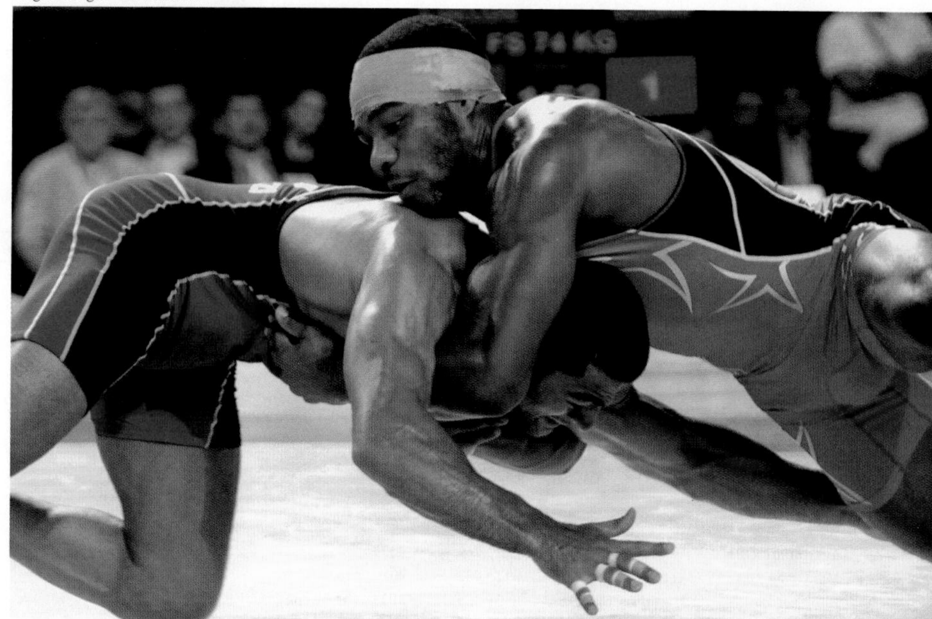

American Jordan Burroughs (right) grapples with Sadegh Goudarzi of Iran in the 74-kg freestyle final at the world wrestling championships in Istanbul in September. Burroughs added the world gold medal to his two NCAA wrestling titles.

WRESTLING

Freestyle and Greco-Roman. Russia swept the men's freestyle and Greco-Roman team titles and earned three men's individual gold medals at the Fédération Internationale des Luttes Associées (FILA) world wrestling championships, held in Istanbul on Sept. 12–18, 2011. Russia (43 points) edged Iran (41) and the resurgent U.S. (38) in the freestyle competition. Russians Victor Lebedev at 55 kg and Besik Kudukhov at 60 kg were the only repeat winners from 2010. Two Iranians, Reza Yazdani at 96 kg and Mehdi Taghavi Kermani at 66 kg, also won gold. Coming off a worst-ever 23rd-place finish in 2010, the U.S. finished solidly in 3rd place behind Jordan Burroughs's gold-medal performance at 74 kg. Burroughs, a two-time NCAA champion at Nebraska, became the first American since 2006 to win a world freestyle title and the first since 1999 to win collegiate and world championships in the same year.

In the Greco-Roman tournament, Russia won the team race with 41 points, followed by Turkey (35) and Iran (30). Roman Vlasov won gold for Russia at 74 kg. Riza Kayaalp of host Turkey led his team to second place by capturing the 120-kg division. Iran picked up gold from Omid Haji Noroozi at 60 kg and Saeid Morad Abdvali at 66 kg and had one bronze medalist.

In women's freestyle, Japan rolled to a 52–33 margin over Canada; Mongolia and the U.S. tied for third at 32 points. Three Japanese women won gold medals: Hitomi Obara Sakamoto at 48 kg, Saori Yoshida at 55 kg, and Kaori Icho at 63 kg.

(J. CARL GUYMON)

Sumo. *Yokozuna* (grand champion) Hakuho won his sixth consecutive sumo *yusho* (championship) in January 2011. Trouble began early the next month when an ongoing investigation by the Tokyo police into the 2010 gambling scandal uncovered irrefutable evidence of bout-fixing on cell phones used by top-division wrestlers. In the face of a lack of confidence from the public and the government ministry overseeing the sport, officials canceled the March *basho* (grand tournament) in Osaka. The May Technical Examination Tournament was not televised and tickets were not sold, but contributions were collected for earthquake and tsunami relief. More than 20 athletes, coaches, and employees of the Sumo Association either resigned or were expelled, and oversight of the daily administration was put in the hands of outsiders.

Hakuho prevailed in the May tournament, and fellow Mongolian *ozeki* (champion) Harumafuji took the Emperor's Cup in the July *basho*. Hakuho won again in September, with runner-up Kotoshogiku earning promotion to *ozeki* rank. Hakuho's victory in November was his 21st *yusho*.

Midway through the July *basho*, *ozeki* Kaio announced his retirement, leaving no Japanese champion-class men in the sport. Tosanoumi and Hokutoriki also retired and became coaches.

(KEN COLLER)

Sporting Record

ARCHERY

FITA Outdoor World Target Archery Championships*

Year	Men's individual		Men's team		Women's individual		Women's team	
	Winner	Points	Winner	Points	Winner	Points	Winner	Points
2007	Im Dong Hyun (S.Kor.)	110	South Korea	224	N. Valeeva (Italy)	108	South Korea	226
2009	Lee Chang-Hwan (S.Kor.)	113	South Korea	222	Joo Hyun-Jung (S.Kor.)	113	South Korea	224
2011	**Kim Woo-Jin (S.Kor.)**	**113**	**South Korea**	**226**	**D. Van Lamoen (Chile)**	**108**	**Italy**	**210**

*Olympic (recurve) division.

AUTOMOBILE RACING

Formula One Grand Prix Race Results, 2011

Race	Driver	Winner's time (hr:min:sec)
Australian GP	S. Vettel (Ger.)	1:29:30.259
Malaysian GP	S. Vettel (Ger.)	1:37:39.832
Chinese GP	L. Hamilton (U.K.)	1:36:58.226
Turkish GP	S. Vettel (Ger.)	1:30:17.558
Spanish GP	S. Vettel (Ger.)	1:39:03.301
Monaco GP	S. Vettel (Ger.)	2:09:38.373
Canadian GP	J. Button (U.K.)	4:04:39.537*
European GP	S. Vettel (Ger.)	1:39:36.169
British GP	F. Alonso (Spain)	1:28:41.196
German GP	L. Hamilton (U.K.)	1:37:30.334
Hungarian GP	J. Button (U.K.)	1:46:42.337
Belgian GP	S. Vettel (Ger.)	1:26:44.893
Italian GP	S. Vettel (Ger.)	1:20:46.172
Singapore GP	S. Vettel (Ger.)	1:59:06.757
Japanese GP	J. Button (U.K.)	1:30:53.427
Korean GP	S. Vettel (Ger.)	1:38:01.994
Indian GP	S. Vettel (Ger.)	1:30:35.002
Abu Dhabi GP	L. Hamilton (U.K.)	1:37:11.886
Brazilian GP	M. Webber (Austl.)	1:32:17.464

*Includes rain delay of more than two hours.

WORLD DRIVERS' CHAMPIONSHIP: Vettel 392 points; Button 270 points; Webber 258 points.

CONSTRUCTORS' CHAMPIONSHIP: RBR-Renault 650 points; Mclaren-Mercedes 497 points; Ferrari 375 points.

National Association for Stock Car Auto Racing (NASCAR) Sprint Cup Champions

Year	Winner
2009	J. Johnson
2010	J. Johnson
2011	**T. Stewart**

Daytona 500

Year	Winner	Avg. speed in mph
2009	M. Kenseth	132.816
2010	J. McMurray	137.284
2011	**T. Bayne**	**130.326**

IndyCar Champions

Year	Indy Racing League
2009	D. Franchitti (Scot.)
2010	D. Franchitti (Scot.)
2011	**D. Franchitti (Scot.)**

Indianapolis 500

Year	Winner	Avg. speed in mph
2009	H. Castroneves (Braz.)	150.318
2010	D. Franchitti (Scot.)	161.623
2011	**D. Wheldon (Eng.)**	**170.265**

Le Mans 24-Hour Grand Prix d'Endurance

Year	Car	Drivers
2009	Peugeot 908	D. Brabham, M. Gené, A. Wurz
2010	Audi R15	T. Bernhard, R. Dumas, M. Rockenfeller
2011	**Audi R18 TDI**	**M. Fässler, A. Lotterer, B. Tréluyer**

Monte-Carlo Rally*

Year	Car	Driver
2009	Peugeot 207 S2000	S. Ogier (Fr.)
2010	Ford Fiesta S2000	M. Hirvonen (Fin.)
2011	**Peugeot 207 S2000**	**B. Bouffier (Fr.)**

*Race not considered part of the World Rally Championship series.

Paul Sancya/AP

English race-car driver Dan Wheldon celebrates his second victory in the Indianapolis 500. He also won the iconic Indy 500 in 2005. Wheldon died as the result of a fiery crash in the final race of the IndyCar season.

BADMINTON

All England Open Championships—Singles

Year	Men	Women
2009	Lin Dan (China)	Wang Yihan (China)
2010	Lee Chong Wei (Malay.)	T. Rasmussen (Den.)
2011	**Lee Chong Wei (Malay.)**	**Wang Shixian (China)**

Thomas Cup (men)

Year	Winner	Runner-up
2005–06	China	Denmark
2007–08	China	South Korea
2009–10	China	Indonesia

Uber Cup (women)

Year	Winner	Runner-up
2005–06	China	Netherlands
2007–08	China	Indonesia
2009–10	South Korea	China

World Badminton Championships

Year	Men's singles	Women's singles	Men's doubles	Women's doubles	Mixed doubles
2009	Lin Dan (China)	Lu Lan (China)	Cai Yun, Fu Haifeng (China)	Zhang Yawen, Zhao Tingting (China)	T. Laybourn, K. Rytter Juhl (Den.)
2010	Chen Jin (China)	Wang Lin (China)	Cai Yun, Fu Haifeng (China)	Du Jing, Yu Yang (China)	Zheng Bo, Ma Jin (China)
2011	**Lin Dan (China)**	**Wang Yihan (China)**	**Cai Yun, Fu Haifeng (China)**	**Wang Xiaoli, Yu Yang (China)**	**Zhang Nan, Zhao Yunlei (China)**

BASEBALL

Final Major League Standings, 2011

AMERICAN LEAGUE

East Division

	Won	Lost	G.B.†
*N.Y. Yankees	97	65	—
*Tampa Bay	91	71	6
Boston	90	72	7
Toronto	81	81	16
Baltimore	69	93	28

Central Division

	Won	Lost	G.B.†
*Detroit	95	67	—
Cleveland	80	82	15
Chicago W.Sox	79	83	16
Kansas City	71	91	24
Minnesota	63	99	32

West Division

	Won	Lost	G.B.†
*Texas	96	66	—
L.A. Angels	86	76	10
Oakland	74	88	22
Seattle	67	95	29

NATIONAL LEAGUE

East Division

	Won	Lost	G.B.†
*Philadelphia	102	60	—
Atlanta	89	73	13
Washington	80	81	21½
N.Y. Mets	77	85	25
Florida	72	90	30

Central Division

	Won	Lost	G.B.†
*Milwaukee	96	66	—
*St. Louis	90	72	6
Cincinnati	79	83	17
Pittsburgh	72	90	24
Chicago Cubs	71	91	25
Houston	56	106	40

West Division

	Won	Lost	G.B.†
*Arizona	94	68	—
San Francisco	86	76	8
L.A. Dodgers	82	79	11½
Colorado	73	89	21
San Diego	71	91	23

*Qualified for play-offs. †Games behind.

Caribbean Series

Year	Winning team	Country
2009	Aragua Tigers (Tigres)	Venezuela Republic
2010	Escogido Lions (Leones)	Dominican Republic
2011	**Obregón Yaquis**	**Mexico**

World Series*

Year	Winning team	Losing team	Results
2009	New York Yankees (AL)	Philadelphia Phillies (NL)	4–2
2010	San Francisco Giants (NL)	Texas Rangers (AL)	4–1
2011	**St. Louis Cardinals (NL)**	**Texas Rangers (AL)**	**4–3**

*AL—American League; NL—National League.

Japan Series*

Year	Winning team	Losing team	Results
2009	Yomiuri Giants (CL)	Nippon-Ham Fighters (PL)	4–2
2010	Chiba Lotte Marines (PL)	Chunichi Dragons (CL)	4–2†
2011	**Fukuoka SoftBank Hawks (PL)**	**Chunichi Dragons (CL)**	**4–3**

*CL—Central League; PL—Pacific League. †Seven-game series included one tie game.

BASKETBALL

NBA Final Standings, 2010–11

EASTERN CONFERENCE

Atlantic Division

	Won	Lost	G.B.†
*Boston	56	26	—
*New York	42	40	14
*Philadelphia	41	41	15
New Jersey	24	58	32
Toronto	22	60	34

Central Division

	Won	Lost	G.B.†
*Chicago	62	20	—
*Indiana	37	45	25
Milwaukee	35	47	27
Detroit	30	52	32
Cleveland	19	63	43

Southeast Division

	Won	Lost	G.B.†
*Miami	58	24	—
*Orlando	52	30	6
*Atlanta	44	38	14
Charlotte	34	48	24
Washington	23	59	35

WESTERN CONFERENCE

Northwest Division

	Won	Lost	G.B.†
*Oklahoma City	55	27	—
*Denver	50	32	5
*Portland	48	34	7
Utah	39	43	16
Minnesota	17	65	38

Pacific Division

	Won	Lost	G.B.†
*L.A. Lakers	57	25	—
Phoenix	40	42	17
Golden State	36	46	21
L.A. Clippers	32	50	25
Sacramento	24	58	33

Southwest Division

	Won	Lost	G.B.†
*San Antonio	61	21	—
*Dallas	57	25	4
*New Orleans	46	36	15
*Memphis	46	36	15
Houston	43	39	18

*Qualified for play-offs. †Games behind.

National Basketball Association (NBA) Championship

Season	Winner	Runner-up	Results
2008–09	Los Angeles Lakers	Orlando Magic	4–1
2009–10	Los Angeles Lakers	Boston Celtics	4–3
2010–11	**Dallas Mavericks**	**Miami Heat**	**4–2**

Women's National Basketball Association (WNBA) Championship

Season	Winner	Runner-up	Results
2009	Phoenix Mercury	Indiana Fever	3–2
2010	Seattle Storm	Atlanta Dream	3–0
2011	**Minnesota Lynx**	**Atlanta Dream**	**3–0**

David Goldman/AP

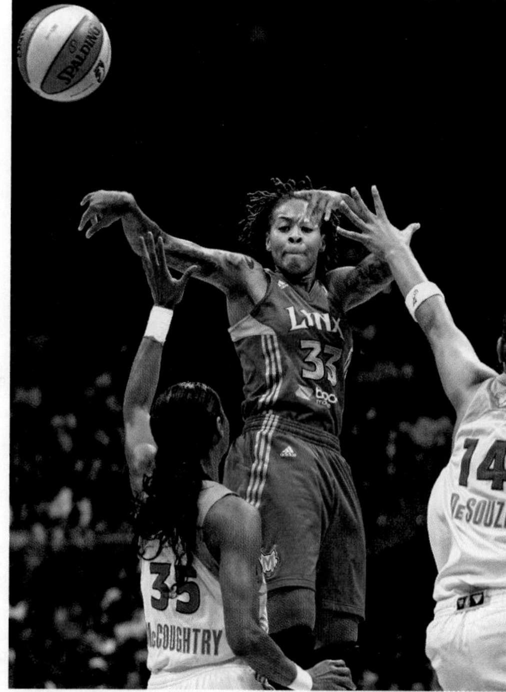

In game three of the WNBA finals, Seimone Augustus of the Minnesota Lynx passes the ball over Atlanta Dream players en route to a three-game sweep over Atlanta and the franchise's first title.

BASKETBALL (continued)

Division I National Collegiate Athletic Association (NCAA) Championship—Men

Year	Winner	Runner-up	Score
2009	North Carolina	Michigan State	89–72
2010	Duke	Butler	61–59
2011	**Connecticut**	**Butler**	**53–41**

Division I National Collegiate Athletic Association (NCAA) Championship—Women

Year	Winner	Runner-up	Score
2009	Connecticut	Louisville	76–54
2010	Connecticut	Stanford	53–47
2011	**Texas A&M**	**Notre Dame**	**76–70**

World Basketball Championship—Men

Year	Winner	Runner-up
2006	Spain	Greece
2008*	United States	Spain
2010	United States	Turkey

*Olympic champion.

World Basketball Championship—Women

Year	Winner	Runner-up
2006	Australia	Russia
2008*	United States	Australia
2010	United States	Czech Republic

*Olympic champion.

BILLIARD GAMES

World Three-Cushion Championship*

Year	Winner
2009	F. Kasidokostas (Greece)
2010	D. Sánchez (Spain)
2011	**D. Jaspers (Neth.)**

*Union Mondiale de Billard champion.

WPA World Nine-Ball Championships

Year	Men's champion
2009	*not held*
2010	F. Bustamante (Phil.)
2011	**Y. Akagariyama (Japan)**

Year	Women's champion
2009	Liu Shasha (China)
2010	Fu Xiaofang (China)
2011	**Bi Zhuqing (China)**

World Professional Snooker Championship

Year	Winner
2009	J. Higgins (Scot.)
2010	N. Robertson (Austl.)
2011	**J. Higgins (Scot.)**

BOBSLEIGH AND LUGE

Bobsleigh and Skeleton World Championships

Year	Two-man bobsleigh	Four-man/driver	Women's bobsleigh	Men's skeleton	Women's skeleton	Team
2009	I. Rüegg, C. Grand (Switz.)	United States/ S. Holcomb	N. Minichiello, G. Cooke (Gr.Brit.)	G. Stähli (Switz.)	M. Trott (Ger.)	Germany
2010*	A. Lange, K. Kuske (Ger.)	United States/ S. Holcomb	K. Humphries, H. Moyse (Can.)	J. Montgomery (Can.)	A. Williams (Gr.Brit.)	
2011	**A. Zubkov, A. Voevoda (Russia)**	**Germany/ M. Machata**	**C. Martini, R. Logsch (Ger.)**	**M. Dukurs (Latvia)**	**M. Trott Thees (Ger.)**	**Germany**

*Olympic champions.

Luge World Championships*

Year	Men	Women	Doubles	Team
2009	F. Loch (Ger.)	E. Hamlin (U.S.)	G. Plankensteiner, O. Haselrieder (Italy)	Germany
2010†	F. Loch (Ger.)	T. Hüfner (Ger.)	A. Linger, W. Linger (Austria)	
2011	**A. Zöggeler (Italy)**	**T. Hüfner (Ger.)**	**A. Linger, W. Linger (Austria)**	***canceled***

*Artificial track. †Olympic champions.

BOWLING

USBC Open Bowling Championships—Regular Division

Year	Singles	Score	All-events	Score
2009	B. Goergen	862	R. Vokes	2,321
2010	T. Syring	833	M. McNiel	2,326
2011	**M. Weggen**	**826**	**M. Weggen**	**2,268**

USBC Women's Bowling Championships—Classic Division*

Year	Singles	Score	All-events	Score
2009	M. Feldman	816	R. Romeo	2,172
2010	K. Howard	792	J. Woessner	2,330
2011	**S. Pluhowsky**	**763**	**D. Davidson**	**2,199**

*From 2010 overall scratch champions.

World Tenpin Bowling Championships—Men

Year	Singles	Doubles	Trios	Team (fives)
2006	R. Ong (Sing.)	Sweden	South Korea	United States
2008	W.R. Williams, Jr. (U.S.)	United States	South Korea	United States
2010	B. O'Neill (U.S.)	Sweden	United States	United States

World Tenpin Bowling Championships—Women

Year	Singles	Doubles	Trios	Team (fives)
2007	S. O'Keefe (U.S.)	South Korea	Sweden	Malaysia
2009	S. Nation (U.S.)	South Korea	Taiwan	South Korea
2011	**J. Sijore (Malay.)**	**United States**	**United States**	**United States**

PBA Tournament of Champions

Year	Champion
2008–09	P. Allen
2009–10	K. Kulick
2010–11	**M. Koivuniemi (Fin.)**

PBA World Championship

Year	Winner
2008–09	N. Duke
2009–10	T. Smallwood
2010–11	**C. Barnes**

BOXING

World Heavyweight Champions
No Weight Limit

WBA

David Haye (U.K.; 11/7/09)
Wladimir Klitschko (Ukr.; 7/2/11)
declared super champion in 2011
Aleksandr Povetkin (Russia; 8/27/11)

WBC

Vitali Klitschko (Ukr.; 10/11/08)

IBF

Wladimir Klitschko (Ukr.; 4/22/06)

World Cruiserweight Champions
Top Weight 200 Pounds

WBA

Guillermo Jones (Pan.; 9/27/08)

WBC

Krzysztof Wlodarczyk (Pol.; 5/15/10)

IBF

Steve Cunningham (U.S.; 6/5/10)
Yoan Pablo Hernández (Cuba; 10/1/11)

World Light Heavyweight Champions
Top Weight 175 Pounds

WBA

Beibut Shumenov (Kazakh.; 1/29/10)

WBC

Jean Pascal (Can.; 6/19/09)
Bernard Hopkins (U.S.; 5/21/11)

IBF

Tavoris Cloud (U.S.; 8/28/09)

World Super Middleweight Champions
Top Weight 168 Pounds

WBA

Andre Ward (U.S.; 11/21/09)
declared super champion in 2009
Karoly Balzsay (Hung.; 8/26/11)

WBC

Carl Froch (U.K.; 11/27/10)
Andre Ward (U.S.; 12/17/11)

IBF

Lucian Bute (Can.; 10/19/07)

World Middleweight Champions
Top Weight 160 Pounds

WBA

Felix Sturm (Ger.; 4/28/07)
declared super champion in 2010
Gennady Golovkin (Kazakh.; 12/16/10)

WBC

Sergio Martínez (Arg.; 4/17/10)
declared super champion emeritus in 2011
Sebastian Zbik (Ger.; 1/18/11; interim from 7/11/09)
Julio César Chávez, Jr. (Mex.; 6/4/11)

IBF

Sebastian Sylvester (Ger.; 9/19/09)
Daniel Geale (Austl.; 5/7/11)

World Junior Middleweight Champions
Top Weight 154 Pounds
(also called super welterweight)

WBA

Miguel Cotto (P.R.; 6/5/10)
declared super champion in 2010
Austin Trout (U.S.; 2/5/11)

WBC

Manny Pacquiao (Phil.; 11/13/10)
title declared vacant in 2011
Saúl Álvarez (Mex.; 3/5/11)

IBF

Cornelius Bundrage (U.S.; 8/7/10)

Puerto Rican boxer Miguel Cotto (right), the WBA junior middleweight super champion, pounds Antonio Margarito of Mexico in their title bout on December 3. Cotto retained the title he captured in 2010.

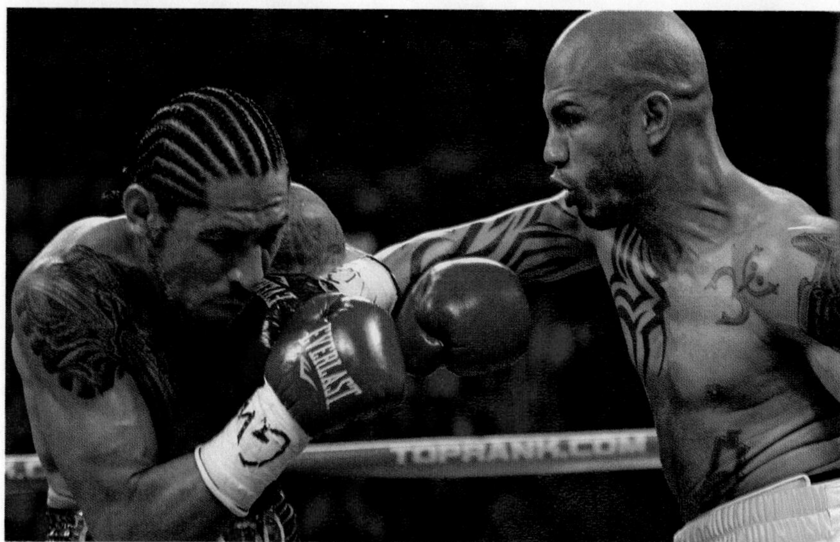

Frank Franklin II/AP

World Welterweight Champions
Top Weight 147 Pounds

WBA

Vyacheslav Senchenko (Ukr.; 4/10/09)

WBC

Andre Berto (U.S.; 6/21/08)
Victor Ortiz (U.S.; 4/16/11)
Floyd Mayweather, Jr. (U.S.; 9/17/11)

IBF

Jan Zaveck (Slvn.; 12/11/09)
Andre Berto (U.S.; 9/3/11)
gave up title in 2011

World Junior Welterweight Champions
Top Weight 140 Pounds
(also called super lightweight)

WBA

Amir Khan (U.K.; 7/18/09)
Lamont Peterson (U.S.; 12/10/11)

WBC

Devon Alexander (U.S.; 8/1/09)
Timothy Bradley (U.S.; 1/29/11)
stripped of title in 2011
Erik Morales (Mex.; 9/17/11)

IBF

Devon Alexander (U.S.; 3/6/10)
stripped of title in 2010
Zab Judah (U.S.; 3/5/11)
Amir Khan (U.K.; 7/23/11)
Lamont Peterson (U.S.; 12/10/11)

World Lightweight Champions
Top Weight 135 Pounds

WBA

Juan Manuel Márquez (Mex.; 2/28/09)
declared super champion in 2009
Miguel Acosta (Venez.; 5/29/10)
Brandon Rios (U.S.; 2/26/11)
stripped of title in 2011

WBC

Humberto Soto (Mex.; 3/13/10)
gave up title in 2011
Antonio DeMarco (Mex.; 10/15/11)

IBF

Miguel Vázquez (Mex.; 8/14/10)

World Junior Lightweight Champions
Top Weight 130 Pounds
(also called super featherweight)

WBA

Takashi Uchiyama (Japan; 1/11/10)

WBC

Takahiro Aoh (Japan; 11/26/10)

IBF

Mzonke Fana (S.Af.; 9/1/10)
stripped of title in 2011
Juan Carlos Salgado (Mex.; 9/10/11)

BOXING (continued)

World Featherweight Champions
Top Weight 126 Pounds

WBA

Yuriorkis Gamboa (Cuba; 10/10/09)
declared unified champion in 2010
stripped of unified title in 2011
Jonathan Barros (Arg.; 12/4/10)
Celestino Caballero (Pan.; 10/14/11)

WBC

Elio Rojas (Dom.Rep.; 7/14/09)
declared champion in recess in 2010
Hozumi Hasegawa (Japan; 11/26/10)
Jhonny González (Mex.; 4/8/11)

IBF

Yuriorkis Gamboa (Cuba; 9/11/10)
stripped of title in 2011
Billy Dib (Austl.; 7/29/11)

World Junior Featherweight Champions
Top Weight 122 Pounds
(also called super bantamweight)

WBA

Ryol Li Lee (Japan; 10/2/10)
Akifumi Shimoda (Japan; 1/31/11)
Rico Ramos (U.S.; 7/9/11)

WBC

Toshiaki Nishioka (Japan; 1/3/09)

IBF

Steve Molitor (Can.; 3/27/10)
Takalani Ndlovu (S.Af.; 3/6/11)

World Bantamweight Champions
Top Weight 118 Pounds

WBA

Anselmo Moréno (Pan.; 5/31/08)
declared super champion in 2010
Koki Kameda (Japan; 12/26/10)

WBC

Fernando Montiel (Mex.; 4/30/10)
Nonito Donaire (Phil.; 2/19/11)
gave up title in 2011
Shinsuke Yamanaka (Japan; 11/6/11)

IBF

Joseph Agbeko (Ghana; 12/11/10)
Abner Mares (U.S.; 8/13/11)

World Junior Bantamweight Champions
Top Weight 115 Pounds
(also called super flyweight)

WBA

Vic Darchinyan (Austl.; 11/1/08)
declared unified champion in 2008
Hugo Cazares (Mex.; 5/8/10)
Tomonobu Shimizu (Japan; 8/31/11)

WBC

Tomas Rojas (Mex.; 9/20/10)
Suriyan Sor Rungvisai (Thai.; 8/19/11)

IBF

Cristian Mijares (Mex.; 12/11/10)
gave up title in 2011
Rodrigo Guerrero (Mex.; 10/8/11)

World Flyweight Champions
Top Weight 112 Pounds

WBA

Daiki Kameda (Japan; 2/7/10)
vacated title in 2011
Luis Concepción (Pan.; 1/11; interim from 9/5/09)
Hernan Márquez (Mex.; 4/2/11)

WBC

Pongsaklek Wonjongkam (Thai.; 3/27/10)

IBF

Moruti Mthalane (S.Af.; 11/20/09)

World Junior Flyweight Champions
Top Weight 108 Pounds

WBA

Juan Carlos Reveco (Arg.; 8/28/10)
gave up title in 2011
Román González (Nic.; 2/4/11; interim from 10/24/10)

WBC

Gilberto Keb Baas (Mex.; 11/6/10)
Adrian Hernández (Mex.; 4/30/11)
Kompayak Porpramook (Thai.; 12/23/11)

IBF

Luis Alberto Lazarte (Arg.; 5/29/10)
Ulises Solis (Mex.; 4/30/11)

World Mini-flyweight Champions
Top Weight 105 Pounds
(also called strawweight)

WBA

Kwanthai Sithmorseng (Thai.; 11/5/10)
Muhammad Rachman (Indon.; 4/19/11)
Pornsawan Porpramook (Thai.; 7/30/11)
Akira Yaegashi (Japan; 10/24/11)

WBC

Oleydong Sithsamerchai (Thai.; 11/29/07)
Kazuto Ioka (Japan; 2/11/11)

IBF

Nkosinathi Joyi (S.Af.; 3/26/10)

CHESS

FIDE Olympiad—Open

Year	Winner	Runner-up
2006	Armenia	China
2008	Armenia	Israel
2010	Ukraine	Russia

FIDE Olympiad—Women

Year	Winner	Runner-up
2006	Ukraine	Russia
2008	Georgia	Ukraine
2010	Russia	China

Gurinder Osan/AP

Indian cricket star Sachin Tendulkar displays his elegant batting style during India's win over Sri Lanka in the ICC World Cup final on April 2.

CRICKET

Test Match Results, October 2010–September 2011

Host/Ground	Date	Scores	Result
India/Mohali	Oct. 1–5	Austl. 428 and 192; India 405 and 216 for 9	India won by 1 wicket
India/Bangalore	Oct. 9–13	Austl. 478 and 223; India 495 and 207 for 3	India won by 7 wickets; India won series 2–0
India/Ahmedabad	Nov. 4–8	India 487 and 266; N.Z. 459 and 22 for 1	Match drawn
India/Hyderabad	Nov. 12–16	N.Z. 350 and 448 for 8 dec; India 472 and 68 for 0	Match drawn
India/Nagpur	Nov. 20–23	N.Z. 193 and 175; India 566 for 8 dec	India won by an innings and 198 runs; India won series 1–0
U.A.E./Dubai*	Nov. 12–16	S.Af. 380 and 318 for 2 dec; Pak. 248 and 343 for 3	Match drawn
U.A.E./Abu Dhabi*	Nov. 20–24	S.Af. 584 for 9 dec and 203 for 5 dec; Pak. 434 and 153 for 3	Match drawn; series drawn 0–0
Sri Lanka/Galle	Nov. 15–19	W.Ind. 580 for 9 dec; SriL. 378 and 241 for 4	Match drawn
Sri Lanka/Colombo	Nov. 23–27	SriL. 387 for 9 dec and 57 for 1 dec; W.Ind. 243 and 12 for 2	Match drawn
Sri Lanka/Pallekele	Dec. 1–5	W.Ind. 303 for 8	Match drawn; series drawn 0–0
Australia/Brisbane	Nov. 25–29	Eng. 260 and 517 for 1 dec; Austl. 481 and 107 for 1	Match drawn
Australia/Adelaide	Dec. 3–7	Austl. 245 and 304; Eng. 620 for 5 dec	Eng. won by an innings and 71 runs
Australia/ Perth	Dec. 16–19	Austl. 268 and 309; Eng. 187 and 123	Austl. won by 267 runs
Australia/Melbourne	Dec. 26–29	Austl. 98 and 258; Eng. 513	Eng. won by an innings and 157 runs
Australia/Sydney	Jan. 3–7	Austl. 280 and 281; Eng. 644	Eng. won by an innings and 83 runs; Eng. won series 3–1
South Africa/Centurion	Dec. 16–20	India 136 and 459; S.Af. 620 for 4 dec	S.Af. won by an innings and 25 runs
South Africa/Durban	Dec. 26–29	India 205 and 228; S.Af. 131 and 215	India won by 87 runs
South Africa/Cape Town	Jan. 2–6	S.Af. 362 and 341; India 364 and 166 for 3	Match drawn; series drawn 1–1
New Zealand/Hamilton	Jan. 7–9	N.Z. 275 and 110; Pak. 367 and 21 for 0	Pak. won by 10 wickets
New Zealand/Wellington	Jan. 15–19	N.Z. 356 and 293; Pak. 376 and 226 for 5	Match drawn; Pak. won series 1–0
West Indies/Guyana	May 12–15	W.Ind. 226 and 152; Pak. 160 and 178	W.Ind. won by 40 runs
West Indies/St. Kitts	May 20–24	Pak. 272 and 377 for 6 dec; W.Ind. 223 and 230	Pak. won by 196 runs; series drawn 1–1
England/Cardiff	May 26–30	SriL. 400 and 82; Eng. 496 for 5 dec	Eng. won by an innings and 14 runs
England/London (Lord's)	June 3–7	Eng. 486 and 335 for 7 dec; SriL. 479 and 127 for 3	Match drawn
England/Southampton	June 16–20	SriL. 184 and 334 for 5; Eng. 377 for 8 dec	Match drawn; Eng. won series 1–0
West Indies/Jamaica	June 20–23	India 246 and 252; W.Ind. 173 and 262	India won by 63 runs
West Indies/Barbados	June 28–July 2	India 201 and 269 for 6 dec; W.Ind. 190 and 202 for 7	Match drawn
West Indies/Dominica	July 6–10	W.Ind. 204 and 322; India 347 and 94 for 3	Match drawn; India won series 1–0
England/London (Lord's)	July 21–25	Eng. 474 for 8 dec and 269 for 6 dec; India 286 and 261	Eng. won by 196 runs
England/Nottingham	July 29–Aug. 1	Eng. 221 and 544; India 288 and 158	Eng. won by 319 runs
England/Birmingham	Aug. 10–13	India 224 and 244; Eng. 710 for 7 dec	Eng. won by an innings and 242 runs
England/London (The Oval)	Aug. 18–22	Eng. 591 for 6 dec; India 300 and 283	Eng. won by an innings and 8 runs; Eng. won series 4–0
Zimbabwe/Harare	Aug. 4–8	Zimb. 370 and 291 for 5 dec; Bangl. 287 and 244	Zimb. won by 130 runs
Sri Lanka/Galle	Aug. 31–Sept. 3	Austl. 273 and 210; SriL. 105 and 253	Austl. won by 125 runs
Sri Lanka/Pallekele	Sept. 8–12	SriL. 174 and 317 for 6; Austl. 411 for 7 dec	Match drawn
Sri Lanka/Colombo	Sept. 16–20	Austl. 316 and 488; SriL. 473 and 7 for 0	Match drawn; Austl. won series 1–0
Zimbabwe/Bulawayo	Sept. 1–5	Zimb. 412 and 141; Pak. 466 and 88 for 3	Pak. won by 7 wickets

*Pakistan "home" match played at neutral venue.

Cricket World Cup

Year	Result			
2003	Australia	359 for 2	India	234
2007	Australia	281 for 4	Sri Lanka	215 for 8
2011	**India**	**277 for 4**	**Sri Lanka**	**274 for 6**

CURLING

World Curling Championship—Men

Year	Winner	Runner-up
2009	Scotland	Canada
2010	Canada	Norway
2011	**Canada**	**Scotland**

World Curling Championship—Women

Year	Winner	Runner-up
2009	China	Sweden
2010	Germany	Scotland
2011	**Sweden**	**Canada**

CYCLING

Cycling Champions, 2011

Event	Winner	Country
WORLD CHAMPIONS—TRACK		
Men		
Sprint	G. Baugé*	France
Individual pursuit	J. Bobridge	Australia
Kilometre time trial	S. Nimke	Germany
Points	E. Alcibiades	Colombia
Team pursuit	J. Bobridge, R. Dennis, L. Durbridge, M. Hepburn	Australia
Keirin	S. Perkins	Australia
Team sprint	G. Baugé, M. D'Almeida, K. Sireau*	France
Madison	L. Howard, C. Meyer	Australia
Scratch	Kwok Ho Ting	Hong Kong
Omnium	M. Freiberg	Australia
Women		
Sprint	A. Meares	Australia
Individual pursuit	S. Hammer	United States
500-m time trial	O. Panarina	Belarus
Points	T. Sharapova	Belarus
Team pursuit	W. Houvenaghel, D. King, L. Trott	Great Britain
Keirin	A. Meares	Australia
Team sprint	K. McCulloch, A. Meares	Australia
Scratch	M. Vos	Netherlands
Omnium	T. Whitten	Canada
WORLD CHAMPIONS—ROAD		
Men		
Individual road race	M. Cavendish	Great Britain
Individual time trial	T. Martin	Germany
Women		
Individual road race	G. Bronzini	Italy
Individual time trial	J. Arndt	Germany
WORLD CHAMPIONS—CYCLO-CROSS		
Men	Z. Stybar	Czech Republic
Women	M. Vos	Netherlands
WORLD CHAMPIONS—MOUNTAIN BIKES		
Men		
Cross-country	J. Kulhavy	Czech Republic
Downhill	D. Hart	Great Britain
4-cross	M. Prokop	Czech Republic
Cross-country team relay	F. Canal, V. Koretzky, J. Bresset, M. Marotte	France
Women		
Cross-country	C. Pendrel	Canada
Downhill	E. Ragot	France
4-cross	A. Beerten	Netherlands
MAJOR ELITE ROAD-RACE WINNERS		
Tour de France	C. Evans	Australia
Tour of Italy	A. Contador	Spain
Tour of Spain	J. Cobo	Spain
Tour of Switzerland	L. Leipheimer	United States
Milan–San Remo	M. Goss	Australia
Tour of Flanders	N. Nuyens	Belgium
Paris–Roubaix	J. van Summeren	Belgium
Amstel Gold	P. Gilbert	Belgium
Liège–Bastogne–Liège	P. Gilbert	Belgium
Flèche Wallonne	P. Gilbert	Belgium
Vattenfall Cyclassics	E. Boasson Hagen	Norway
GP Ouest-France	G. Bole	Slovenia
San Sebastian Classic	P. Gilbert	Belgium
Tour of Lombardy	O. Zaugg	Switzerland
Paris–Nice	T. Martin	Germany
Ghent–Wevelgem	T. Boonen	Belgium
Tour of Romandie	C. Evans	Australia
Critérium du Dauphiné	B. Wiggins	Great Britain
Tirreno–Adriatico	C. Evans	Australia

*Later stripped.

EQUESTRIAN SPORTS

The Kentucky Derby

Year	Horse	Jockey
2009	Mine That Bird	C. Borel
2010	Super Saver	C. Borel
2011	**Animal Kingdom**	**J. Velazquez**

The Preakness Stakes

Year	Horse	Jockey
2009	Rachel Alexandra	C. Borel
2010	Lookin At Lucky	M. Garcia
2011	**Shackleford**	**J. Castanon**

The Belmont Stakes

Year	Horse	Jockey
2009	Summer Bird	K. Desormeaux
2010	Drosselmeyer	M. Smith
2011	**Ruler On Ice**	**J. Valdivia, Jr.**

2,000 Guineas

Year	Horse	Jockey
2009	Sea The Stars	M. Kinane
2010	Makfi	C.-P. Lemaire
2011	**Frankel**	**T. Queally**

The Derby

Year	Horse	Jockey
2009	Sea The Stars	M. Kinane
2010	Workforce	R. Moore
2011	**Pour Moi**	**M. Barzalona**

The St. Leger

Year	Horse	Jockey
2009	Mastery	T. Durcan
2010	Arctic Cosmos	W. Buick
2011	**Masked Marvel**	**W. Buick**

Triple Crown Champions—U.S.

Year	Horse
1973	Secretariat
1977	Seattle Slew
1978	Affirmed

Triple Crown Champions—British

Year	Winner
1918	Gainsborough
1935	Bahram
1970	Nijinsky

Melbourne Cup

Year	Horse	Jockey
2009	Shocking	C. Brown
2010	Americain	G. Mosse
2011	**Dunaden**	**C.-P. Lemaire**

The Hambletonian Trot

Year	Horse	Driver
2009	Muscle Hill	B. Sears
2010	Muscle Massive	R. Pierce
2011	**Broad Bahn**	**G. Brennan**

EQUESTRIAN SPORTS (continued)

Major Thoroughbred Race Winners, 2011

Race	Won by	Jockey
United States		
Acorn Stakes	It's Tricky	E. Castro
Alabama Stakes	Royal Delta	J. Lezcano
Alcibiades Stakes	Stephanie's Kitten	J. Velazquez
American Oaks Invitational	Cambina*	M. Garcia
	Nereid*	J. Talamo
Apple Blossom Handicap	Havre de Grace	R. Dominguez
Arkansas Derby	Archarcharch	J. Court
Arlington Million	Cape Blanco	J. Spencer
Ashland Stakes	Lilacs and Lace	J. Castellano
Beldame Stakes	Havre de Grace	R. Dominguez
Belmont Stakes	Ruler On Ice	J. Valdivia
Beverly D. Stakes	Stacelita	R. Dominguez
Blue Grass Stakes	Brilliant Speed	J. Rosario
Breeders' Cup Classic	Drosselmeyer	M. Smith
Breeders' Cup Dirt Mile	Caleb's Posse	R. Maragh
Breeders' Cup Filly and Mare Sprint	Musical Romance	J. Leyva
Breeders' Cup Filly and Mare Turf	Perfect Shirl	J. Velazquez
Breeders' Cup Juvenile	Hansen	R. Dominguez
Breeders' Cup Juvenile Fillies	My Miss Aurelia	C. Nakatani
Breeders' Cup Ladies' Classic	Royal Delta	J. Lezcano
Breeders' Cup Mile	Court Vision	R. Albarado
Breeders' Cup Sprint	Amazombie	M. Smith
Breeders' Cup Turf	St Nicholas Abbey	J. O'Brien
Breeders' Futurity	Dullahan	K. Desormeaux
Carter Handicap	Morning Line	J. Velazquez
CashCall Futurity	Liaison	R. Bejarano
Champagne Stakes	Union Rags	J. Castellano
Cigar Mile Handicap	To Honor and Serve	J. Lezcano
Clark Handicap	Wise Dan	J. Velazquez
Coaching Club American Oaks	It's Tricky	E. Castro
Diana Stakes	Zagora	J. Castellano
Donn Handicap	Giant Oak	S. Bridgmohan
Eddie Read Stakes	Acclamation	J. Rosario
Florida Derby	Dialed In	J. Leparoux
Flower Bowl Invitational	Stacelita	R. Dominguez
Haskell Invitational	Coil	M. Garcia
Hollywood Derby	Ultimate Eagle	M. Pedroza
Hollywood Gold Cup	First Dude	M. Garcia
Hopeful Stakes	Currency Swap	R. Maragh
Jockey Club Gold Cup	Flat Out	A. Solis
Joe Hirsch Turf Classic Invitational	Cape Blanco	J. Spencer
Just A Game Stakes	C.S. Silk	J. Castellano
Kentucky Derby	Animal Kingdom	J. Velazquez
Kentucky Oaks	Plum Pretty	M. Garcia
Man o' War Stakes	Cape Blanco	J. Spencer
Manhattan Handicap	Mission Approved	J. Espinoza
Matriarch Stakes	Star Billing	V. Espinoza
Metropolitan Handicap	Tizway	R. Maragh
Mother Goose Stakes	Buster's Ready	J. Velazquez
Pacific Classic	Acclamation	P. Valenzuela
Personal Ensign Stakes	Ask the Moon	J. Castellano
Preakness Stakes	Shackleford	J. Castanon
Queen Elizabeth II Challenge Cup	Together	C. O'Donoghue
Ruffian Handicap	Ask the Moon	J. Castellano
Santa Anita Derby	Midnight Interlude	V. Espinoza
Santa Anita Handicap	Game On Dude	C. Sutherland
Secretariat Stakes	Treasure Beach	C. O'Donoghue
Spinster Stakes	Aruna	R. Dominguez
Stephen Foster Handicap	Pool Play	M. Mena
Sword Dancer Invitational Stakes	Winchester	C. Velasquez
Travers Stakes	Stay Thirsty	J. Castellano
Turf Classic Stakes	Get Stormy	R. Dominguez
Turf Mile Stakes	Gio Ponti	R. Dominguez
United Nations Stakes	Teaks North	E. Castro
Vosburgh Stakes	Giant Ryan	C. Velasquez
Whitney Handicap	Tizway	R. Maragh
Wood Memorial	Toby's Corner	E. Castro
Woodward Stakes	Havre de Grace	R. Dominguez
Yellow Ribbon Stakes	Dubawi Heights	J. Rosario

Race	Won by	Jockey
England		
Two Thousand Guineas	Frankel	T. Queally
One Thousand Guineas	Blue Bunting	F. Dettori
Epsom Derby	Pour Moi	M. Barzalona
Epsom Oaks	Dancing Rain	J. Murtagh
St. Leger	Masked Marvel	W. Buick
Coronation Cup	St Nicholas Abbey	R. Moore
Ascot Gold Cup	Fame and Glory	J. Spencer
Coral-Eclipse Stakes	So You Think	S. Heffernan
King George VI and Queen Elizabeth Diamond Stakes	Nathaniel	W. Buick
Sussex Stakes	Frankel	T. Queally
Juddmonte International Stakes	Twice Over	I. Mongan
Champion Stakes	Cirrus Des Aigles	C. Soumillon
France		
Poule d'Essai des Poulains	Tin Horse	T. Jarnet
Poule d'Essai des Pouliches	Golden Lilac	O. Peslier
Prix du Jockey-Club (French Derby)	Reliable Man	G. Mosse
Prix de Diane (French Oaks)	Golden Lilac	M. Guyon
Grand Prix de Paris	Meandre	M. Guyon
Grand Prix de Saint-Cloud	Sarafina	C.-P. Lemaire
Prix Jacques Le Marois	Immortal Verse	G. Mosse
Prix Vermeille	Galikova	O. Peslier
Prix de l'Arc de Triomphe	Danedream	A. Starke
Prix Jean-Luc Lagardère–Grand Critérium	Dabirsim	F. Dettori
Prix Royal-Oak	Be Fabulous	M. Guyon
Ireland		
Irish Two Thousand Guineas	Roderic O'Connor	J. O'Brien
Irish One Thousand Guineas	Misty for Me	S. Heffernan
Irish Derby	Treasure Beach	C. O'Donoghue
Irish Oaks	Blue Bunting	F. Dettori
Irish Champion Stakes	So You Think	S. Heffernan
Irish St. Leger	Duncan*	E. Ahern
	Jukebox Jury*	J. Murtaugh
Italy		
Derby Italiano	Crackerjack King	F. Branca
Gran Premio del Jockey Club	Campanologist	F. Dettori
Germany		
Deutsches Derby	Waldpark	J. Bojko
Grosser Preis von Baden	Danedream	A. Starke
Preis von Europa	Campanologist	F. Dettori
Australia		
Caulfield Cup	Southern Speed	C. Williams
Cox Plate	Pinker Pinker	C. Williams
Melbourne Cup	Dunaden	C.-P. Lemaire
United Arab Emirates		
Dubai World Cup	Victoire Pisa	M. Demuro
Dubai Sheema Classic	Rewilding	F. Dettori
Dubai Duty Free	Presvis	R. Moore
Asia		
Japan Cup	Buena Vista	Y. Iwata
Hong Kong Gold Cup	California Memory	M. Chadwick
Singapore Airlines International Cup	Gitano Hernando	G. Schofield
Canada		
Queen's Plate Stakes	Inglorious	L. Contreras
Prince of Wales Stakes	Pender Harbour	L. Contreras
Breeders' Stakes	Pender Harbour	L. Contreras
Woodbine Mile	Turallure	J. Leparoux
Canadian International Stakes	Sarah Lynx	C. Soumillon

*Dead heat.

FENCING

World Fencing Championships—Men

Year	Individual			Team		
	Foil	Épée	Sabre	Foil	Épée	Sabre
2009	A. Baldini (Italy)	A. Avdeyev (Russia)	N. Limbach (Ger.)	Italy	France	Romania
2010	P. Joppich (Ger.)	N. Novosjolov (Est.)	Won Woo-Young (S.Kor.)	China	France	Russia
2011	**A. Cassarà (Italy)**	**P. Pizzo (Italy)**	**A. Montano (Italy)**	**China**	**France**	**Russia**

World Fencing Championships—Women

Year	Individual			Team		
	Foil	Épée	Sabre	Foil	Épée	Sabre
2009	A. Shanayeva (Russia)	L. Shutova (Russia)	M. Zagunis (U.S.)	Italy	Italy	Ukraine
2010	E. Di Francisca (Italy)	M. Nisima (France)	M. Zagunis (U.S.)	Italy	Romania	Russia
2011	**V. Vezzali (Italy)**	**Li Na (China)**	**S. Velikaya (Russia)**	**Russia**	**Romania**	**Russia**

FIELD HOCKEY

World Cup Field Hockey Championship—Men

Year	Winner	Runner-up
2002	Germany	Australia
2006	Germany	Australia
2010	Australia	Germany

World Cup Field Hockey Championship—Women

Year	Winner	Runner-up
2002	Argentina	Netherlands
2006	Netherlands	Australia
2010	Argentina	Netherlands

FOOTBALL

FIFA World Cup—Men

Year	Result			
2002	Brazil	2	Germany	0
2006	Italy*	1	France	1
2010	Spain	1	Netherlands	0

*Won on penalty kicks.

FIFA World Cup—Women

Year	Result			
2003	Germany	2	Sweden	1
2007	Germany	2	Brazil	0
2011	**Japan***	**2**	**United States**	**2**

*Won on penalty kicks.

Lucy Nicholson—Reuters/Landov

Mike Magee of the victorious Los Angeles Galaxy outmaneuvers Danny Cruz of the Houston Dynamo in the Major Soccer League (MLS) Cup on November 20.

Association Football National Champions, 2010–11

Nation	League Champions	Cup Winners
Algeria	Chlef	Kabylie
Argentina	Estudiantes (Opening)	Velez Sarsfield (Closing)
Australia	Brisbane Roar	
Austria	Sturm Graz	Ried
Belgium	Racing Genk	Standard Liège
Bolivia	Bolivar	
Brazil	Fluminense	Vasco da Gama
Bulgaria	Litex	CSKA Sofia
Cameroon	Cotonsport	
Chile	Univ. de Chile (Opening)	Univ. de Chile (Closing)
China	Guangzhou	Tianjin Teda
Colombia	Atlético Nacional (Opening)	Junior (Closing)
Costa Rica	Alajuelense	
Côte d'Ivoire	Africa Sports	ASEC
Croatia	Dinamo Zagreb	Dinamo Zagreb
Czech Republic	Viktoria Plzen	Mlada
Denmark	FC Copenhagen	Nordsjælland
Ecuador	Deportivo Quito	
England	Manchester United	Manchester City
Finland	HJK Helsinki	HJK Helsinki
France	Lille	Lille
Georgia	Zestafoni	Gagra
Germany	Borussia Dortmund	Schalke
Ghana	Berekum Chelsea	
Greece	Olympiakos	AEK Athens
Honduras	Real España (Opening)	Motagua (Closing)
Hungary	Videoton	Kecskemeti
Ireland Republic	Shamrock Rovers	Sligo Rovers
Israel	Maccabi Haifa	Hapoel Tel Aviv
Italy	AC Milan	Internazionale
Japan	Kashiwa Reysol	
Mexico	Monterrey	UNAM
Morocco	Raja Casablanca	Maghreb Fes
Netherlands	Ajax	Twente
New Zealand	Waitakere United	
Nigeria	Dolphin Port Harcourt	
Northern Ireland	Linfield	Linfield
Norway	Molde	Aalesund
Paraguay	Nacional (Opening)	Olimpia (Closing)
Peru	Juan Aurich	Real Atlético Garcilaso
Poland	Wisla Krakow	Legia Warsaw
Portugal	Porto	Porto
Qatar	Lekhwiya	Al Sadd
Romania	Otelul Galati	Steaua Bucuresti
Russia	*postponed until 2012*	CSKA Moscow
Saudi Arabia	Al Hilal	Al Hilal
Scotland	Rangers	Celtic
Senegal	Ouakam	
Serbia	Partizan Belgrade	Partizan Belgrade
Slovakia	Slovan Bratislava	Slovan Bratislava
Slovenia	Maribor	Domzale
South Africa	Orlando Pirates	Orlando Pirates
South Korea	Jeonbuk Motors	
Spain	Barcelona	Real Madrid
Sweden	Helsingborg	Helsingborg
Switzerland	Basel	Sion
Tunisia	ES Tunis	ES Tunis
Turkey	Fenerbahce	Besiktas
Ukraine	Shakhtar Donetsk	Shakhtar Donetsk
United States (MLS)	Los Angeles Galaxy	
Uruguay	Nacional	
Venezuela	Deportivo Táchira (Opening)	Zamora (Closing)

FOOTBALL (continued)

UEFA Champions League

Season	Result			
2008–09	FC Barcelona (Spain)	2	Manchester United (Eng.)	0
2009–10	Internazionale Milan (Italy)	2	Bayern Munich (Ger.)	0
2010–11	**FC Barcelona (Spain)**	**3**	**Manchester United (Eng.)**	**10**

UEFA Europa League*

Season	Result			
2008–09	Shakhtar Donetsk (Ukr.)†	2	Werder Bremen (Ger.)	1
2009–10	Atlético de Madrid (Spain)†	2	Fulham FC (Eng.)	1
2010–11	**Porto (Port.)**	**1**	**Braga (Port.)**	**0**

*UEFA Cup until 2009–10. †Won in overtime.

Libertadores de América Cup

Year	Winner (country)	Runner-up (country)	Scores
2009	Estudiantes La Plata (Arg.)	Cruzeiro (Braz.)	0–0, 2–1
2010	Internacional (Braz.)	Chivas Guadalajara (Mex.)	2–1, 3–2
2011	**Santos FC (Braz.)**	**Peñarol (Uruguay)**	**0–0, 2–1**

Copa América

Year	Winner	Runner-up	Score
2004	Brazil	Argentina	2–2, 4–2*
2007	Brazil	Argentina	3–0
2011	**Uruguay**	**Paraguay**	**3–0**

*Winner determined in penalty shoot-out.

MLS Cup

Year	Result			
2009	Real Salt Lake*	1	Los Angeles Galaxy	1
2010	Colorado Rapids†	2	FC Dallas	1
2011	**Los Angeles Galaxy**	**1**	**Houston Dynamo**	**0**

*Won on penalty kicks. †Won in overtime.

U.S. College Football National Championship*

Season	Result			
2009–10	Alabama	37	Texas	21
2010–11	Auburn	22	Oregon	19
2011–12	**Alabama**	**21**	**Louisiana State**	**0**

*BCS championship game.

Rose Bowl

Season	Result			
2009–10	Ohio State	26	Oregon	17
2010–11	Texas Christian	21	Wisconsin	19
2011–12	**Oregon**	**45**	**Wisconsin**	**38**

Orange Bowl

Season	Result			
2009–10	Iowa	24	Georgia Tech	14
2010–11	Stanford	40	Virginia Tech	12
2011–12	**West Virginia**	**70**	**Clemson**	**33**

Fiesta Bowl

Season	Result			
2009–10	Boise State	17	Texas Christian	10
2010–11	Oklahoma	48	Connecticut	20
2011–12	**Oklahoma State**	**41**	**Stanford**	**38**

Sugar Bowl

Season	Result			
2009–10	Florida	51	Cincinnati	24
2010–11	Ohio State	31	Arkansas	26
2011–12	**Michigan**	**23**	**Virginia Tech**	**20**

NFL Final Standings, 2011–12

AMERICAN CONFERENCE

East Division	Won	Lost	Tied	North Division	Won	Lost	Tied	South Division	Won	Lost	Tied	West Division	Won	Lost	Tied
*New England	13	3	0	*Baltimore	12	4	0	*Houston	10	6	0	*Denver	8	8	0
New York Jets	8	8	0	*Pittsburgh	12	4	0	Tennessee	9	7	0	San Diego	8	8	0
Miami	6	10	0	*Cincinnati	9	7	0	Jacksonville	5	11	0	Oakland	8	8	0
Buffalo	6	10	0	Cleveland	4	12	0	Indianapolis	2	14	0	Kansas City	7	9	0

NATIONAL CONFERENCE

East Division	Won	Lost	Tied	North Division	Won	Lost	Tied	South Division	Won	Lost	Tied	West Division	Won	Lost	Tied
*New York Giants	9	7	0	*Green Bay	15	1	0	*New Orleans	13	3	0	*San Francisco	13	3	0
Philadelphia	8	8	0	*Detroit	10	6	0	*Atlanta	10	6	0	Arizona	8	8	0
Dallas	8	8	0	Chicago	8	8	0	Carolina	6	10	0	Seattle	7	9	0
Washington	5	11	0	Minnesota	3	13	0	Tampa Bay	4	12	0	St. Louis	2	14	0

*Qualified for play-offs.

NFL Super Bowl

	Season	Result			
XLIII	2008–09	Pittsburgh Steelers (AFC)	27	Arizona Cardinals (NFC)	23
XLIV	2009–10	New Orleans Saints (NFC)	31	Indianapolis Colts (AFC)	17
XLV	**2010–11**	**Green Bay Packers (NFC)**	**31**	**Pittsburgh Steelers (AFC)**	**25**

CFL Grey Cup*

Year	Result			
2009	Montreal Alouettes (ED)	28	Saskatchewan Roughriders (WD)	27
2010	Montreal Alouettes (ED)	21	Saskatchewan Roughriders (WD)	18
2011	**British Columbia Lions (WD)**	**34**	**Winnipeg Blue Bombers (ED)**	**23**

*ED—Eastern Division; WD—Western Division.

FOOTBALL (continued)

AFL Grand Final

Year	Result			
2009	Geelong Cats	12.8 (80)	St. Kilda Saints	9.14 (68)
2010*	Collingwood Magpies	16.12 (108)	St. Kilda Saints	7.10 (52)
2011	**Geelong Cats**	**18.11 (119)**	**Collingwood Magpies**	**12.9 (81)**

*Grand Final Replay after Grand Final ended in a draw: Collingwood 9.14 (68)–St. Kilda 10.8 (68).

Rugby Union World Cup

Year	Result			
2003	England	20	Australia	17
2007	South Africa	15	England	6
2011	**New Zealand**	**8**	**France**	**7**

Rugby League World Cup

Year	Result			
1995	Australia	16	England	8
2000	Australia	40	New Zealand	12
2008	New Zealand	34	Australia	20

Six Nations Championship

Year	Result
2009	Ireland*
2010	France*
2011	**England**

*Grand Slam winner.

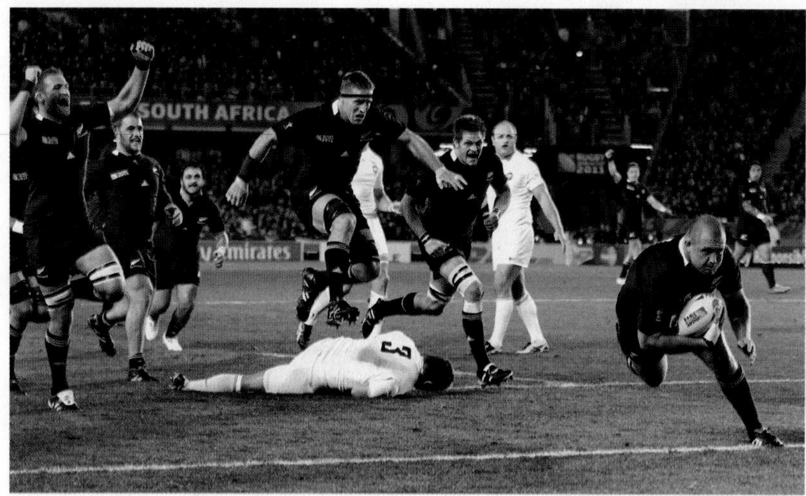

Rob Griffith/AP

Tony Woodcock (right) races ahead of his delighted New Zealand All Blacks teammates to score a try in New Zealand's 8–7 victory over France in the final of the Rugby Union World Cup on October 23.

GOLF

Masters Tournament

Year	Winner
2009	A. Cabrera (Arg.)
2010	P. Mickelson (U.S.)
2011	**C. Schwartzel (S.Af.)**

United States Open Championship (men)

Year	Winner
2009	L. Glover (U.S.)
2010	G. McDowell (N.Ire.)
2011	**R. McIlroy (N.Ire.)**

British Open Tournament (men)

Year	Winner
2009	S. Cink (U.S.)
2010	L. Oosthuizen (S.Af.)
2011	**D. Clarke (N.Ire.)**

U.S. Professional Golfers' Association (PGA) Championship

Year	Winner
2009	Yang Yong-Eun (S.Kor.)
2010	M. Kaymer (Ger.)
2011	**K. Bradley (U.S.)**

United States Amateur Championship (men)

Year	Winner
2009	An Byeong-Hun (S.Kor.)
2010	P. Uihlein (U.S.)
2011	**K. Kraft (U.S.)**

British Amateur Championship (men)

Year	Winner
2009	M. Manassero (Italy)
2010	Jeong Jin (S.Kor.)
2011	**B. Macpherson (Austl.)**

United States Women's Open Championship

Year	Winner
2009	Ji Eun-Hee (S.Kor.)
2010	P. Creamer (U.S.)
2011	**Ryu So-Yeon (S.Kor.)**

Women's British Open Championship

Year	Winner
2009	C. Matthew (Scot.)
2010	Y. Tseng (Taiwan)
2011	**Y. Tseng (Taiwan)**

Ladies Professional Golf Association (LPGA) Championship

Year	Winner
2009	A. Nordqvist (Swed.)
2010	C. Kerr (U.S.)
2011	**Y. Tseng (Taiwan)**

United States Women's Amateur Championship

Year	Winner
2009	J. Song (U.S.)
2010	D. Kang (U.S.)
2011	**D. Kang (U.S.)**

Ladies' British Amateur Championship

Year	Winner
2009	A. Muñoz (Spain)
2010	K. Tidy (Eng.)
2011	**L. Taylor (Eng.)**

World Cup (men; professional)

Year	Winner
2008	Sweden (R. Karlsson and H. Stenson)
2009	Italy (E. Molinari and F. Molinari)
2011*	**United States (M. Kuchar and G. Woodland)**

*Changed to biennial event.

Solheim Cup (women; professional)

Year	Result
2007	United States 16, Europe 12
2009	United States 16, Europe 12
2011	**Europe 15, United States 13**

Ryder Cup (men; professional)

Year	Result
2006	Europe 18½, United States 9½
2008	United States 16½, Europe 11½
2010	Europe 14½, United States 13½

GYMNASTICS

World Gymnastics Championships—Men

Year	All-around team	All-around individual	Horizontal bar	Parallel bars
2009	*not held*	K. Uchimura (Japan)	Zou Kai (China)	Wang Guanyin (China)
2010	China	K. Uchimura (Japan)	Zhang Chenglong (China)	Feng Zhe (China)
2011	**China**	**K. Uchimura (Japan)**	**Zou Kai (China)**	**D. Leyva (U.S.)**
Year	**Pommel horse**	**Rings**	**Vault**	**Floor exercise**
2009	Zhang Hongtao (China)	Yan Mingyong (China)	M. Dragulescu (Rom.)	M. Dragulescu (Rom.)
2010	K. Berki (Hung.)	Chen Yibing (China)	T. Bouhail (Fr.)	E. Kosmidis (Greece)
2011	**K. Berki (Hung.)**	**Chen Yibing (China)**	**Yang Hak-Seon (S.Kor.)**	**K. Uchimura (Japan)**

World Gymnastics Championships—Women

Year	All-around team	All-around individual	Balance beam
2009	*not held*	B. Sloan (U.S.)	Deng Linlin (China)
2010	Russia	A. Mustafina (Russia)	A. Porgras (Rom.)
2011	**United States**	**J. Wieber (U.S.)**	**Sui Lu (China)**
Year	**Uneven parallel bars**	**Vault**	**Floor exercise**
2009	He Kexin (China)	K. Williams (U.S.)	E. Tweddle (U.K.)
2010	E. Tweddle (U.K.)	A. Sacramone (U.S.)	L. Mitchell (Austl.)
2011	**V. Komova (Russia)**	**M. Maroney (U.S.)**	**K. Afanaseva (Russia)**

Xinhua News Agency—Eyevine/Redux

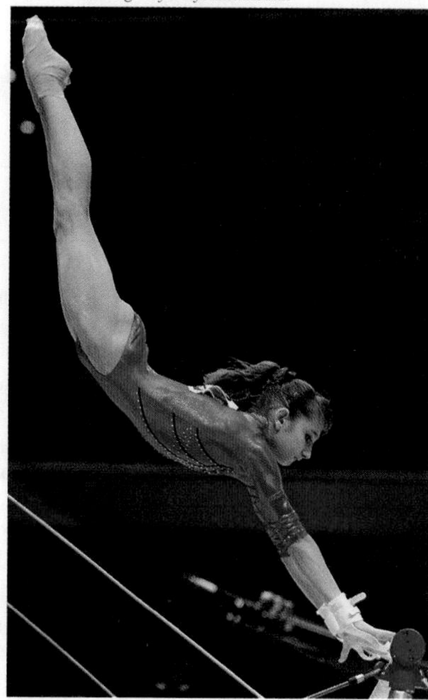

Russian gold medalist Victoriya Komova soars on the uneven bars at the world gymnastics championships in October.

ICE HOCKEY

NHL Final Standings, 2010–11

EASTERN CONFERENCE

Northeast Division	Won	Lost	OTL*
†Boston	46	25	11
†Montreal	44	30	8
†Buffalo	43	29	10
Toronto	37	34	11
Ottawa	32	40	10

Atlantic Division	Won	Lost	OTL*
†Philadelphia	47	23	12
†Pittsburgh	49	25	8
†N.Y. Rangers	44	33	5
New Jersey	38	39	5
N.Y. Islanders	30	39	13

Southeast Division	Won	Lost	OTL*
†Washington	48	23	11
†Tampa Bay	46	25	11
Carolina	40	31	11
Atlanta	34	36	12
Florida	30	40	12

WESTERN CONFERENCE

Central Division	Won	Lost	OTL*
†Detroit	47	25	10
†Nashville	44	27	11
†Chicago	44	29	9
St. Louis	38	33	11
Columbus	34	35	13

Northwest Division	Won	Lost	OTL*
†Vancouver	54	19	9
Calgary	41	29	12
Minnesota	39	35	8
Colorado	30	44	8
Edmonton	25	45	12

Pacific Division	Won	Lost	OTL*
†San Jose	48	25	9
†Anaheim	47	30	5
†Phoenix	43	26	13
†Los Angeles	46	30	6
Dallas	42	29	11

*Overtime losses, worth one point. †Qualified for play-offs.

The Stanley Cup

Season	Winner	Runner-up	Results
2008–09	Pittsburgh Penguins	Detroit Red Wings	4–3
2009–10	Chicago Blackhawks	Philadelphia Flyers	4–2
2010–11	**Boston Bruins**	**Vancouver Canucks**	**4–3**

World Ice Hockey Championship—Men

Year	Winner
2009	Russia
2010	Czech Republic
2011	**Finland**

World Ice Hockey Championship—Women

Year	Winner
2009	United States
2010*	Canada
2011	**United States**

*Olympic champion.

ICE SKATING

World Figure Skating Champions—Men

Year	Winner
2009	E. Lysacek (U.S.)
2010	D. Takahashi (Japan)
2011	**P. Chan (Can.)**

World Figure Skating Champions—Women

Year	Winner
2009	Kim Yu-Na (S.Kor.)
2010	M. Asada (Japan)
2011	**M. Ando (Japan)**

World Figure Skating Champions—Pairs

Year	Winners
2009	A. Savchenko, R. Szolkowy (Ger.)
2010	Pang Qing, Tong Jian (China)
2011	**A. Savchenko, R. Szolkowy (Ger.)**

World Ice Dancing Champions

Year	Winners
2009	O. Domnina, M. Shabalin (Russia)
2010	T. Virtue, S. Moir (Can.)
2011	**M. Davis, C. White (U.S.)**

ICE SKATING (continued)

World Ice Speed-Skating Records Set in 2011 on Major Tracks*

Event	Name	Country	Result
MEN			
none			
WOMEN			
5,000 m	Martina Sablikova	Czech Republic	6 min 42.66 sec

*May include records awaiting ISU ratification at year's end.

World All-Around Speed-Skating Champions

Year	Men	Women
2009	S. Kramer (Neth.)	M. Sablikova (Cz.Rep.)
2010	S. Kramer (Neth.)	M. Sablikova (Cz.Rep.)
2011	**I. Skobrev (Russia)**	**I. Wüst (Neth.)**

World Short-Track Speed-Skating Championships—Overall Winners

Year	Men	Women
2009	Lee Ho-Suk (S.Kor.)	Wang Meng (China)
2010	Lee Ho-Suk (S.Kor.)	Park Seung-Hi (S.Kor.)
2011	**Noh Jin-Kyu (S.Kor.)**	**Cho Ha-Ri (S.Kor.)**

World Speed-Skating Sprint Champions

Year	Men	Women
2009	S. Davis (U.S.)	Wang Beixing (China)
2010	Lee Kyou-Hyuk (S.Kor.)	Lee Sang-Hwa (S.Kor.)
2011	**Lee Kyou-Hyuk (S.Kor.)**	**C. Nesbitt (Can.)**

World Ice Speed-Skating Records Set in 2011 on Short Tracks*

Event	Name	Country	Time
MEN			
1,500 m	Noh Jin-Kyu	South Korea	2 min 09.042 sec
3,000 m	Noh Jin-Kyu	South Korea	4 min 31.891 sec
5,000-m relay	Great Britain National Team (Jack Whelbourne, Richard Shoebridge, Paul Stanley, Jon Eley)	Great Britain	6 min 37.877 sec
	South Korea National Team (Noh Jin-Kyu, Kwak Yoon-Gy, Sin Da-Woon, Lee Ho-Suk)	South Korea	6 min 35.884 sec
WOMEN			
none			

*May include records awaiting ISU ratification at year's end.

Misha Japaridze/AP

South Korea's Noh Jin-Kyu speeds across the ice in a 1,500-m short-track race in February. During the year Noh secured the men's overall title at the short-track world championships and set three world records.

JUDO

World Judo Championships—Men

Year	Open weights	60 kg	66 kg	73 kg
2009	T. Riner (Fr.)*	G. Zantaraia (Ukr.)	T. Hashbaatar (Mong.)	Wang Ki-Chun (S.Kor.)
2010	D. Kamikawa (Japan)	R. Sobirov (Uzbek.)	J. Morishita (Japan)	H. Akimoto (Japan)
2011	***not held***	**R. Sobirov (Uzbek.)**	**M. Ebinuma (Japan)**	**R. Nakaya (Japan)**
Year	**81 kg**	**90 kg**	**100 kg**	**+100 kg**
2009	I. Nifontov (Russia)	Lee Kyu-Won (S.Kor.)	M. Rakov (Kazakh.)	T. Riner (France)
2010	Kim Jae-Bum (S.Kor.)	I. Iliadis (Greece)	T. Anai (Japan)	T. Riner (France)
2011	**Kim Jae-Bum (S.Kor.)**	**I. Iliadis (Greece)**	**T. Khaybulayev (Russia)**	**T. Riner (France)**

*Competition held separately in December 2008.

World Judo Championships—Women

Year	Open weights	48 kg	52 kg	57 kg
2009	Tong Wen (China)*	T. Fukumi (Japan)	M. Nakamura (Japan)	M. Ribout (Fr.)
2010	M. Sugimoto (Japan)	H. Asami (Japan)	Y. Nishida (Japan)	K. Matsumoto (Japan)
2011	***not held***	**H. Asami (Japan)**	**M. Nakamura (Japan)**	**A. Sato (Japan)**
Year	**63 kg**	**70 kg**	**78 kg**	**+78 kg**
2009	Y. Ueno (Japan)	Y. Alvear (Colom.)	M. Verkerk (Neth.)	Tong Wen (China)
2010	Y. Ueno (Japan)	L. Decosse (Fr.)	K. Harrison (U.S.)	M. Sugimoto (Japan)
2011	**G. Emane (Fr.)**	**L. Decosse (Fr.)**	**A. Tcheuméo (Fr.)**	**Tong Wen (China)**

*Competition held separately in December 2008.

RODEO

Men's World All-Around Rodeo Championship

Year	Winner
2009	T. Brazile
2010	T. Brazile
2011	**T. Brazile**

ROWING

World Rowing Championships—Men

Year	Single sculls	Min:sec	Double sculls	Min:sec	Quadruple sculls	Min:sec	Coxed pairs	Min:sec
2009	M. Drysdale (N.Z.)	6:33.35	E. Knittel, S. Krüger (Ger.)	6:07.02	Poland	5:38.33	T. Kepper, H. Rummel (U.S.)	6:53.58
2010	O. Synek (Cz.Rep.)	6:47.49	N. Cohen, J. Sullivan (N.Z.)	6:22.63	Croatia	6:15.78	C. Morgan, D. Grimm (Austl.)	7:03.32
2011	**M. Drysdale (N.Z.)**	**6:39.56**	**N. Cohen, J. Sullivan (N.Z.)**	**6:10.76**	**Australia**	**5:39.31**	**V. Capelli, P. Frattini (Italy)**	**6:56.45**

Year	Coxless pairs	Min:sec	Coxless fours	Min:sec	Eights	Min:sec
2009	E. Murray, H. Bond (N.Z.)	6:15.93	Great Britain	5:47.28	Germany	5:24.13
2010	E. Murray, H. Bond (N.Z.)	6:30.16	France	6:45.38	Germany	5:33.84
2011	**E. Murray, H. Bond (N.Z.)**	**6:14.77**	**Great Britain**	**5:55.18**	**Germany**	**5:28.81**

World Rowing Championships—Women

Year	Single sculls	Min:sec	Coxless pairs	Min:sec
2009	Ye. Karsten-Khodotovich (Bela.)	7:11.78	Z. Francia, E. Cafaro (U.S.)	7:06.28
2010	F. Svensson (Swed.)	7:47.61	J. Haigh, R. Scown (N.Z.)	7:17.12
2011	**M. Knapkova (Cz.Rep.)**	**7:26.64**	**J. Haigh, R. Scown (N.Z.)**	**6:58.16**

Year	Double sculls	Min:sec	Coxless fours	Min:sec
2009	M. Fularczyk, J. Michalska (Pol.)	6:47.18	Netherlands	6:31.34
2010	A. Watkins, K. Grainger (Gr.Brit.)	7:04.70	Netherlands	7:21.09
2011	**A. Watkins, K. Grainger (Gr.Brit.)**	**6:44.73**	**United States**	**6:30.30**

Year	Quadruple sculls	Min:sec	Eights	Min:sec
2009	Ukraine	6:18.41	United States	6:05.34
2010	Great Britain	7:12.78	United States	6:12.42
2011	**Germany**	**6:18.37**	**United States**	**6:03.65**

The Boat Race*

Year	Winner	Winner's time (min:sec)	Margin of victory
2009	Oxford	17:00	3½ lengths
2010	Cambridge	17:35	1⅓ lengths
2011†	**Oxford**	**17:32**	**4 lengths**

*Annual race between the Universities of Cambridge and Oxford. †Historical record: Cambridge 80, Oxford 76, 1 draw.

SAILING (YACHTING)

America's Cup

Year	Winning yacht	Owner	Skipper	Losing yacht	Owner
2003	*Alinghi* (Switz.)	Alinghi Swiss Challenge	R. Coutts	*New Zealand* (N.Z.)	Team New Zealand
2007	*Alinghi* (Switz.)	Alinghi	B. Butterworth	*New Zealand* (N.Z.)	Team New Zealand
2010	*USA-17* (U.S.)	BMW Oracle Racing	J. Spithill	*Alinghi 5* (Switz.)	Alinghi

World Class Boat Champions, 2011

Class	Winner	Country
Etchells 22	B. Hardesty	United States
Finn	G. Scott	Great Britain
J/24	A. Rigoni	Argentina
Laser	T. Slingsby	Australia
Laser Women	M. Bouwmeester	Netherlands
RS:X (men's boards)	D. van Rijsselberghe	Netherlands
RS:X (women's boards)	L. Korzits	Israel
470 (men's)	M. Belcher/M. Page	Australia
470 (women's)	T. Pacheco/ B. Betanzos	Spain
49er	N. Outteridge/ I. Jensen	Australia
2.4 metre	T. Schmitter	Netherlands
Moth	N. Outteridge	Australia
Star	R. Scheidt/B. Prada	Brazil
Tornado	I. Paschalidis/ K. Trigonis	Greece
Farr 40	G. Belgiorno-Nettis	Australia
Transpac 52 (TP52)	Quantum Racing (E. Baird)	United States
Eliot 6m	A. Tunnicliffe	United States

Bermuda Race*

Year	Winning yacht	Owner
2006	*Sinn Fein*†	P. Rebovich
	Lively Lady II‡	W. Hubbard III
2008	*Sinn Fein*	P. Rebovich
2010	*Carina*	R. Potts

*St. David's Lighthouse Trophy winner.
†Winner under Offshore Rating Rule (ORR) scoring.
‡Winner under IRC scoring.

Transpacific Race*

Year	Winning yacht	Owner/Skipper
2007	*Reinrag2*	T. Garnier
2009	*Samba Pa Ti*	J. Kilroy, Jr.
2011	***Grand Illusion***	**J. McDowell**

*Overall winner based on corrected time.

Richard Langdon—Ocean Images/Reuters/Landov

At the sailing world championships, Nathan Outteridge (right) and Iain Jensen of Australia cheer after having triumphed in the 49er class.

SKIING

World Alpine Skiing Championships—Slalom

Year	Men's slalom	Men's giant slalom	Men's supergiant slalom	Women's slalom	Women's giant slalom	Women's supergiant slalom	Team
2009	M. Pranger (Austria)	C. Janka (Switz.)	D. Cuche (Switz.)	M. Riesch (Ger.)	K. Hölzl (Ger.)	L. Vonn (U.S.)	*canceled*
2010*	G. Razzoli (Italy)	C. Janka (Switz.)	A. Svindal (Nor.)	M. Riesch (Ger.)	V. Rebensburg (Ger.)	A. Fischbacher (Austria)	
2011	**J.-B. Grange (Fr.)**	**T. Ligety (U.S.)**	**C. Innerhofer (Italy)**	**M. Schild (Austria)**	**T. Maze (Slvn.)**	**E. Görgl (Austria)**	**France**

*Olympic champions.

World Alpine Skiing Championships—Downhill

Year	Men	Women
2009	J. Kucera (Can.)	L. Vonn (U.S.)
2010*	D. Defago (Switz.)	L. Vonn (U.S.)
2011	**E. Guay (Can.)**	**E. Görgl (Austria)**

*Olympic champions.

World Alpine Skiing Championships—Combined

Year	Men	Women
2009	A. Svindal (Nor.)	K. Zettel (Austria)
2010*	B. Miller (U.S.)	M. Riesch (Ger.)
2011	**A. Svindal (Nor.)**	**A. Fenninger (Austria)**

*Olympic champions.

World Nordic Skiing Championships—Men

Year	Sprint	Team sprint	15 km	30 km	50 km	Relay
2009	O.V. Hattestad (Nor.)	Norway	A. Veerpalu (Est.)	P. Northug (Nor.)	P. Northug (Nor.)	Norway
2010*	N. Kriyukov (Russia)	Norway	D. Cologna (Switz.)	M. Hellner (Swed.)	P. Northug (Nor.)	Sweden
2011	**M. Hellner (Swed.)**	**Canada**	**M. Heikkinen (Fin.)**	**P. Northug (Nor.)**	**P. Northug (Nor.)**	**Norway**

*Olympic champions.

World Nordic Skiing Championships—Women

Year	Sprint	Team sprint	10 km	15 km	30 km	Relay
2009	A. Follis (Italy)	Finland	A.-K. Saarinen (Fin.)	J. Kowalczyk (Pol.)	J. Kowalczyk (Pol.)	Finland
2010*	M. Bjørgen (Nor.)	Germany	C. Kalla (Swed.)	M. Bjørgen (Nor.)	J. Kowalczyk (Pol.)	Norway
2011	**M. Bjørgen (Nor.)**	**Sweden**	**M. Bjørgen (Nor.)**	**M. Bjørgen (Nor.)**	**T. Johaug (Nor.)**	**Norway**

*Olympic champions.

World Nordic Skiing Championships—Ski Jump

Year	Normal hill*	Large hill†	Women (normal hill)*	Team jump (normal hill)*	Team jump (large hill)†
2009	W. Loitzl (Austria)	A. Küttel (Switz.)	L. Van (U.S.)		Austria
2010‡	S. Ammann (Switz.)	S. Ammann (Switz.)			Austria
2011	**T. Morgenstern (Austria)**	**G. Schlierenzauer (Austria)**	**D. Iraschko (Austria)**	**Austria**	**Austria**

Year	Nordic combined (mass start; 10 km)*	Nordic combined (10 km)*	Nordic combined (large hill; 10 km)†	Nordic combined team (normal hill; 4×5 relay)*	Nordic combined team (large hill; 4×5 relay)†
2009	T. Lodwick (U.S.)	T. Lodwick (U.S.)	B. Demong (U.S.)		Japan
2010‡		J. Lamy Chappuis (France)	B. Demong (U.S.)		Austria
2011		**E. Frenzel (Ger.)**	**J. Lamy Chappuis (France)**	**Austria**	**Austria**

*100-m hill in 2009; 106-m hill in 2010 and 2011. †134-m hill in 2009 and 2011; 140-m hill in 2010. ‡Olympic champions.

Alpine World Cup

Year	Men	Women
2009	A. Svindal (Nor.)	L. Vonn (U.S.)
2010	C. Janka (Switz.)	L. Vonn (U.S.)
2011	**I. Kostelic (Cro.)**	**M. Riesch (Ger.)**

Freestyle Skiing World Cup

Year	Men	Women
2009	A. Bilodeau (Can.)	O. David (Fr.)
2010	A. Kushnir (Bela.)	Li Nina (China)
2011	**G. Colas (Fr.)**	**H. Kearney (U.S.)**

Nordic World Cup

Year	Men	Women
2009	D. Cologna (Switz.)	J. Kowalczyk (Pol.)
2010	P. Northug (Nor.)	J. Kowalczyk (Pol.)
2011	**D. Cologna (Switz.)**	**J. Kowalczyk (Pol.)**

Snowboard World Cup

Year	Men	Women
2009	S. Grabner (Austria)	D. Günther (Austria)
2010	B. Karl (Austria)	M. Ricker (Can.)
2011	**B. Karl (Austria)**	**Ye. Tudegesheva (Russia)**

SQUASH

British Open Championship—Men

Year	Winner
2009	N. Matthew (Eng.)
2010	*not held*
2011	***not held***

British Open Championship—Women

Year	Winner
2009	R. Grinham (Austl.)
2010	*not held*
2011	***not held***

World Open Championship—Men

Year	Winner
2009	A. Shabana (Egypt)
2010	N. Matthew (Eng.)
2011	**N. Matthew (Eng.)**

World Open Championship—Women

Year	Winner
2009	N. David (Malay.)
2010	N. David (Malay.)
2011	**N. David (Malay.)**

SWIMMING

World Swimming Records Set in 2011 in 25-m Pools*

Event	Name	Country	Time
MEN			
none			
WOMEN			
200-m backstroke	Melissa Franklin	United States	2 min 00.03 sec
4 × 100-m medley relay	United States (Natalie Coughlin, Rebecca Soni, Dana Vollmer, Melissa Franklin)	United States	3 min 45.56 sec

*May include records awaiting FINA ratification at year's end.

World Swimming Records Set in 2011 in 50-m Pools*

Event	Name	Country	Time
MEN			
1,500-m freestyle	Sun Yang	China	14 min 34.14 sec
200-m individual medley	Ryan Lochte	United States	1 min 54.00 sec
WOMEN			
none			

*May include records awaiting FINA ratification at year's end.

World Swimming and Diving Championships—Men

	Freestyle					
Year	50 m	100 m	200 m	400 m	800 m	1,500 m
2007	B. Wildman-Tobriner (U.S.)	F. Magnini (Italy)	M. Phelps (U.S.)	Park Tae-Hwan (S.Kor.)	P. Stanczyk (Pol.)*	M. Sawrymowicz (Pol.)
2009	C. Cielo (Braz.)	C. Cielo (Braz.)	P. Biedermann (Ger.)	P. Biedermann (Ger.)	Zhang Lin (China)	O. Mellouli (Tun.)
2011	**C. Cielo (Braz.)**	**J. Magnussen (Austl.)**	**R. Lochte (U.S.)**	**Park Tae-Hwan (S.Kor.)**	**Sun Yang (China)**	**Sun Yang (China)**

	Backstroke			Breaststroke		
	50 m	100 m	200 m	50 m	100 m	200 m
2007	G. Zandberg (S.Af.)	A. Peirsol (U.S.)	R. Lochte (U.S.)	O. Lisogor (Ukr.)	B. Hansen (U.S.)	K. Kitajima (Japan)
2009	L. Tancock (U.K.)	J. Koga (Japan)	A. Peirsol (U.S.)	C. Van der Burgh (S.Af.)	B. Rickard (Austl.)	D. Gyurta (Hung.)
2011	**L. Tancock (U.K.)**	**C. Lacourt (Fr.)† J. Stravius (Fr.)†**	**R. Lochte (U.S.)**	**F. Franca da Silva (Braz.)**	**A. Dale Oen (Nor.)**	**D. Gyurta (Hung.)**

	Butterfly			Individual medley		Team relays
	50 m	100 m	200 m	200 m	400 m	4 × 100-m freestyle
2007	R. Schoeman (S.Af.)	M. Phelps (U.S.)	M. Phelps (U.S.)	M. Phelps (U.S.)	M. Phelps (U.S.)	United States
2009	M. Cavic (Serbia)	M. Phelps (U.S.)	M. Phelps (U.S.)	R. Lochte (U.S.)	R. Lochte (U.S.)	United States
2011	**C. Cielo (Braz.)**	**M. Phelps (U.S.)**	**M. Phelps (U.S.)**	**R. Lochte (U.S.)**	**R. Lochte (U.S.)**	**Australia**

			Diving				
	4 × 200-m freestyle	4 × 100-m medley	1-m springboard	3-m springboard	Platform	3-m synchronized	10-m synchronized
2007	United States	Australia	Luo Yutong (China)	Qin Kai (China)	G. Galperin (Russia)	China	China
2009	United States	United States	Qin Kai (China)	He Chong (China)	T. Daley (U.K.)	China	China
2011	**United States**	**United States**	**Li Shixin (China)**	**He Chong (China)**	**Qiu Bo (China)**	**China**	**China**

*Original winner stripped after failing drug test. †Tied.

World Swimming and Diving Championships—Women

	Freestyle					
Year	50 m	100 m	200 m	400 m	800 m	1,500 m
2007	L. Lenton (Austl.)	L. Lenton (Austl.)	L. Manaudou (Fr.)	L. Manaudou (Fr.)	K. Ziegler (U.S.)	K. Ziegler (U.S.)
2009	B. Steffen (Ger.)	B. Steffen (Ger.)	F. Pellegrini (Italy)	F. Pellegrini (Italy)	L. Friis (Den.)	A. Filippi (Italy)
2011	**T. Alshammar (Swed.)**	**J. Ottesen (Den.)* A. Herasimenia (Bela.)***	**F. Pellegrini (Italy)**	**F. Pellegrini (Italy)**	**R. Adlington (U.K.)**	**L. Friis (Den.)**

	Backstroke			Breaststroke		
	50 m	100 m	200 m	50 m	100 m	200 m
2007	L. Vaziri (U.S.)	N. Coughlin (U.S.)	M. Hoelzer (U.S.)	J. Hardy (U.S.)	L. Jones (Austl.)	L. Jones (Austl.)
2009	Zhao Jing (China)	G. Spofforth (U.K.)	K. Coventry (Zimb.)	Yu. Efimova (Russia)	R. Soni (U.S.)	N. Higl (Serbia)
2011	**A. Zueva (Russia)**	**Zhao Jing (China)**	**M. Franklin (U.S.)**	**J. Hardy (U.S.)**	**R. Soni (U.S.)**	**R. Soni (U.S.)**

	Butterfly			Individual medley		Team relays
	50 m	100 m	200 m	200 m	400 m	4 × 100-m freestyle
2007	T. Alshammar (Swed.)	L. Lenton (Austl.)	J. Schipper (Austl.)	K. Hoff (U.S.)	K. Hoff (U.S.)	Australia
2009	M. Guehrer (Austl.)	S. Sjöström (Swed.)	J. Schipper (Austl.)	A. Kukors (U.S.)	K. Hosszu (Hung.)	Netherlands
2011	**I. Dekker (Neth.)**	**D. Vollmer (U.S.)**	**Jiao Liuyang (China)**	**Ye Shiwen (China)**	**E. Beisel (U.S.)**	**Netherlands**

			Diving				
	4 × 200-m freestyle	4 × 100-m medley	1-m springboard	3-m springboard	Platform	3-m synchronized	10-m synchronized
2007	United States	Australia	He Zi (China)	Guo Jingjing (China)	Wang Xin (China)	China	China
2009	China	China	Yu. Pakhalina (Russia)	Guo Jingjing (China)	P. Espinosa (Mex.)	China	China
2011	**United States**	**United States**	**Shi Tingmao (China)**	**Wu Minxia (China)**	**Chen Ruolin (China)**	**China**	**China**

*Tied.

TABLE TENNIS

World Table Tennis Championships—Men

Year	St. Bride's Vase (singles)	Iran Cup (doubles)
2007	Wang Liqin (China)	Chen Qi, Ma Lin (China)
2009	Wang Hao (China)	Chen Qi, Wang Hao (China)
2011	**Zhang Jike (China)**	**Ma Long, Xu Xin (China)**

World Table Tennis Championships—Women

Year	G. Geist Prize (singles)	W.J. Pope Trophy (doubles)
2007	Guo Yue (China)	Wang Nan, Zhang Yining (China)
2009	Zhang Yining (China)	Guo Yue, Li Xiaoxia (China)
2011	**Ding Ning (China)**	**Guo Yue, Li Xiaoxia (China)**

World Table Tennis Championships—Mixed

Year	Heydusek Prize
2007	Guo Yue, Wang Liqin (China)
2009	Cao Zhen, Li Ping (China)
2011	**Cao Zhen, Zhang Chao (China)**

World Table Tennis Championships—Team

Year	Swaythling Cup (men)	Corbillon Cup (women)
2006	China	China
2008	China	China
2010	China	Singapore

Table Tennis World Cup

Year	Men
2009	V. Samsonov (Bela.)
2010	Wang Hao (China)
2011	**Zhang Jike (China)**

Year	Women
2009	Liu Shiwen (China)
2010	Guo Yan (China)
2011	**Ding Ning (China)**

TENNIS

Australian Open Tennis Championships—Singles

Year	Men	Women
2009	R. Nadal (Spain)	S. Williams (U.S.)
2010	R. Federer (Switz.)	S. Williams (U.S.)
2011	**N. Djokovic (Serbia)**	**K. Clijsters (Belg.)**

Australian Open Tennis Championships—Doubles

Year	Men	Women
2009	B. Bryan, M. Bryan	S. Williams, V. Williams
2010	B. Bryan, M. Bryan	S. Williams, V. Williams
2011	**B. Bryan, M. Bryan**	**G. Dulko, F. Pennetta**

French Open Tennis Championships—Singles

Year	Men	Women
2009	R. Federer (Switz.)	S. Kuznetsova (Russia)
2010	R. Nadal (Spain)	F. Schiavone (Italy)
2011	**R. Nadal (Spain)**	**Li Na (China)**

French Open Tennis Championships—Doubles

Year	Men	Women
2009	L. Dlouhy, L. Paes	A. Medina Garrigues, V. Ruano Pascual
2010	D. Nestor, N. Zimonjic	S. Williams, V. Williams
2011	**M. Mirnyi, D. Nestor**	**A. Hlavackova, L. Hradecka**

All-England (Wimbledon) Tennis Championships—Singles

Year	Men	Women
2009	R. Federer (Switz.)	S. Williams (U.S.)
2010	R. Nadal (Spain)	S. Williams (U.S.)
2011	**N. Djokovic (Serbia)**	**P. Kvitova (Cz.Rep.)**

All-England (Wimbledon) Tennis Championships—Doubles

Year	Men	Women
2009	D. Nestor, N. Zimonjic	S. Williams, V. Williams
2010	J. Melzer, P. Petzschner	V. King, Y. Shvedova
2011	**B. Bryan, M. Bryan**	**K. Peschke, K. Srebotnik**

United States Open Tennis Championships—Singles

Year	Men	Women
2009	J. del Potro (Arg.)	K. Clijsters (Belg.)
2010	R. Nadal (Spain)	K. Clijsters (Belg.)
2011	**N. Djokovic (Serbia)**	**S. Stosur (Austl.)**

United States Open Tennis Championships—Doubles

Year	Men	Women
2009	L. Dlouhy, L. Paes	S. Williams, V. Williams
2010	B. Bryan, M. Bryan	V. King, Y. Shvedova
2011	**J. Melzer, P. Petzschner**	**L. Huber, L. Raymond**

Davis Cup (men)

Year	Winner	Runner-up	Results
2009	Spain	Czech Republic	5–0
2010	Serbia	France	3–2
2011	**Spain**	**Argentina**	**3–1**

Fed Cup (women)

Year	Winner	Runner-up	Results
2009	Italy	United States	4–0
2010	Italy	United States	3–1
2011	**Czech Republic**	**Russia**	**3–2**

Charlie Riedel/AP

Serbian Novak Djokovic follows through on his serve in the final of the U.S. Open tennis tournament on September 12. Djokovic beat defending champion Rafael Nadal of Spain for his third major title of the year.

TRACK AND FIELD SPORTS (ATHLETICS)

World Outdoor Track and Field Championships—Men

Event	2009	2011
100 m	U. Bolt (Jam.)	Y. Blake (Jam.)
200 m	U. Bolt (Jam.)	U. Bolt (Jam.)
400 m	L. Merritt (U.S.)	K. James (Grenada)
800 m	M. Mulaudzi (S.Af.)	D.L. Rudisha (Kenya)
1,500 m	Y.S. Kamel (Bahrain)	A. Kiprop (Kenya)
5,000 m	K. Bekele (Eth.)	M. Farah (Gr.Brit.)
10,000 m	K. Bekele (Eth.)	I. Jeilan (Eth.)
steeplechase	E. Kemboi (Kenya)	E. Kemboi (Kenya)
110-m hurdles	R. Brathwaite (Barb.)	J. Richardson (U.S.)
400-m hurdles	K. Clement (U.S.)	D. Greene (Gr.Brit.)
marathon	A. Kirui (Kenya)	A. Kirui (Kenya)
20-km walk	V. Borchin (Russia)	V. Borchin (Russia)
50-km walk	S. Kirdyapkin (Russia)	S. Bakulin (Russia)
4 × 100-m relay	Jamaica (S. Mullings, M. Frater, U. Bolt, A. Powell)	Jamaica (N. Carter, M. Frater, Y. Blake, U. Bolt)
4 × 400-m relay	United States (A. Taylor, J. Wariner, K. Clement, L. Merritt)	United States (G. Nixon, B. Jackson, A. Taylor, L. Merritt)
high jump	Y. Rybakov (Russia)	J. Williams (U.S.)
pole vault	S. Hooker (Austl.)	P. Wojciechowski (Pol.)
long jump	D. Phillips (U.S.)	D. Phillips (U.S.)
triple jump	P. Idowu (Gr.Brit.)	C. Taylor (U.S.)
shot put	C. Cantwell (U.S.)	D. Storl (Ger.)
discus throw	R. Harting (Ger.)	R. Harting (Ger.)
hammer throw	P. Kozmus (Slov.)	K. Murofushi (Japan)
javelin throw	A. Thorkildsen (Nor.)	M. de Zordo (Ger.)
decathlon	T. Hardee (U.S.)	T. Hardee (U.S.)

World Indoor Track and Field Championships—Men

Event	2008	2010
60 m	O.A. Fasuba (Nigeria)	D. Chambers (Gr.Brit.)
400 m	T. Christopher (Can.)	C. Brown (Bah.)
800 m	A. Kaki Khamis (Sudan)	A. Kaki Khamis (Sudan)
1,500 m	D. Mekonnen (Eth.)	D. Mekonnen (Eth.)
3,000 m	T. Bekele (Eth.)	B. Lagat (U.S.)
60-m hurdles	Liu Xiang (China)	D. Robles (Cuba)
4 × 400-m relay	United States (J. Davis, J. Torrance, G. Nixon, K. Willie)	United States (J. Torrance, G. Nixon, T. Tate, B. Jackson)
high jump	S. Holm (Swed.)	I. Ukhov (Russia)
pole vault	Ye. Lukyanenko (Russia)	S. Hooker (Austl.)
long jump	G.K. Mokoena (S.Af.)	F. Lapierre (Austl.)
triple jump	P. Idowu (Gr.Brit.)	T. Tamgho (France)
shot put	C. Cantwell (U.S.)	C. Cantwell (U.S.)
heptathlon	B. Clay (U.S.)	B. Clay (U.S.)

2011 World Indoor Records—Men*

Event	Competitor and country	Performance
triple jump	Teddy Tamgho (France)	17.91 m (58 ft 9¼ in)
	Teddy Tamgho (France)	17.92 m (58 ft 9½ in)
	Teddy Tamgho (France)	17.92 m (58 ft 9½ in)†
heptathlon	Ashton Eaton (U.S.)	6,568 points

*May include records awaiting IAAF ratification at year's end. †Equals world record.

2011 World Outdoor Records—Men*

Event	Competitor and country	Performance
25,000 m	Moses Mosop (Kenya)	1 hr 12 min 25.4 sec
30,000 m	Moses Mosop (Kenya)	1 hr 26 min 47.4 sec
30-km road race	Peter Kirui (Kenya)	1 hr 27 min 37 sec
marathon†	Geoffrey Mutai (Kenya)	2 hr 03 min 02 sec‡
	Patrick Makau (Kenya)	2 hr 03 min 38 sec
50,000-m walking	Yohan Diniz (France)	3 hr 35 min 27.2 sec
4 × 100-m relay	Jamaica (Nesta Carter, Michael Frater, Yohan Blake, Usain Bolt)	37.04 sec

*May include records awaiting IAAF ratification at year's end. †Not an officially ratified event; best performance on record. ‡Wind aided.

World Outdoor Track and Field Championships—Women

Event	2009	2011
100 m	S.-A. Fraser (Jam.)	C. Jeter (U.S.)
200 m	A. Felix (U.S.)	V. Campbell-Brown (Jam.)
400 m	S. Richards (U.S.)	A. Montsho (Bots.)
800 m	C. Semenya (S.Af.)	M. Savinova (Russia)
1,500 m	M.Y. Jamal (Bahrain)	J. Simpson (U.S.)
5,000 m	V. Cheruiyot (Kenya)	V. Cheruiyot (Kenya)
10,000 m	L.C. Masai (Kenya)	V. Cheruiyot (Kenya)
steeplechase	M. Domínguez (Spain)	Y. Zaripova (Russia)
100-m hurdles	B. Foster-Hylton (Jam.)	S. Pearson (Austl.)
400-m hurdles	M. Walker (Jam.)	L. Demus (U.S.)
marathon	Bai Xue (China)	E. Kiplagat (Kenya)
20-km walk	O. Kaniskina (Russia)	O. Kaniskina (Russia)
4 × 100-m relay	Jamaica (S. Facey, S.-A. Fraser, A. Bailey, K. Stewart)	United States (B. Knight, A. Felix, M. Myers, C. Jeter)
4 × 400-m relay	United States (D. Dunn, A. Felix, L. Demus, S. Richards)	United States (S. Richards-Ross, A. Felix, J. Beard, F. McCorory)
high jump	B. Vlasic (Cro.)	A. Chicherova (Russia)
pole vault	A. Rogowska (Pol.)	F. Murer (Braz.)
long jump	B. Reese (U.S.)	B. Reese (U.S.)
triple jump	Y. Savigne (Cuba)	O. Saladuha (Ukr.)
shot put	V. Vili (N.Z.)	V. Adams (N.Z.)
discus throw	D. Samuels (Austl.)	Li Yanfeng (China)
hammer throw	A. Wlodarczyk (Pol.)	T. Lysenko (Russia)
javelin throw	S. Nerius (Ger.)	M. Abakumova (Russia)
heptathlon	J. Ennis (Gr.Brit.)	T. Chernova (Russia)

World Indoor Track and Field Championships—Women

Event	2008	2010
60 m	A. Williams (U.S.)	V. Campbell-Brown (Jam.)
400 m	O. Zykina (Russia)	D. Dunn (U.S.)
800 m	T. Lewis (Austl.)	M. Savinova (Russia)
1,500 m	Ye. Soboleva (Russia)	K. Gezahegne (Eth.)
3,000 m	M. Defar (Eth.)	M. Defar (Eth.)
60-m hurdles	L. Jones (U.S.)	L. Jones (U.S.)
4 × 400-m relay	Russia (Yu. Gushchina, T. Levina, N. Nazarova, O. Zykina)	United States (D. Dunn, D. Trotter, N. Hastings, A. Felix)
high jump	B. Vlasic (Cro.)	B. Vlasic (Cro.)
pole vault	Ye. Isinbaeva (Russia)	F. Murer (Braz.)
long jump	N. Gomes (Port.)	B. Reese (U.S.)
triple jump	Y. Savigne (Cuba)	O. Rypakova (Kazakh.)
shot put	V. Vili (N.Z.)	N. Ostapchuk (Bela.)
pentathlon	T. Hellebaut (Belg.)	J. Ennis (Gr.Brit.)

2011 World Indoor Records—Women*

Event	Competitor and country	Performance
4 × 800-m relay	Moscow (Aleksandra Bulanova, Yekaterina Martynova, Yelena Kofanova, Anna Balakshina)	8 min 6.24 sec

*May include records awaiting IAAF ratification at year's end.

2011 World Outdoor Records—Women*

Event	Competitor and country	Performance
20-km road race	Mary Keitany (Kenya)	1 hr 2 min 36 sec
half marathon†	Mary Keitany (Kenya)	1 hr 5 min 50 sec
hammer throw	Betty Heidler (Ger.)	79.42 m (260 ft 7 in)
20-km road walking	Vera Sokolova (Russia)	1 hr 25 min 08 sec

*May include records awaiting IAAF ratification at year's end. †Not an officially ratified event; best performance on record.

TRACK AND FIELD SPORTS (ATHLETICS) (continued)

World Cross Country Championships—Men

Year	Individual	Team
2009	G. Gebremariam (Eth.)	Kenya
2010	J. Ebuya (Kenya)	Kenya
2011	**I. Marga (Eth.)**	**Kenya**

World Cross Country Championships—Women

Year	Individual	Team
2009	F. Kiplagat (Kenya)	Kenya
2010	E. Chebet (Kenya)	Kenya
2011	**V. Cheruiyot (Kenya)**	**Kenya**

Juan Jose Ubeda/AP

Vivian Cheruiyot of Kenya breaks the tape at the world cross country championships in March. She also won the 5,000- and 10,000-m finals at the track world championships.

Boston Marathon

Year	Men	hr:min:sec
2009	D. Merga (Eth.)	2:08:42
2010	R. (Kiprono) Cheruiyot (Kenya)	2:05:52
2011	**G. Mutai (Kenya)**	**2:03:02***
Year	**Women**	**hr:min:sec**
2009	S. Kosgei (Kenya)	2:32:16
2010	T. Erkesso (Eth.)	2:26:11
2011	**C. Kilel (Kenya)**	**2:22:36**

*Fastest official time.

London Marathon

Year	Men	hr:min:sec
2009	S. Wanjiru (Kenya)	2:05:10
2010	T. Kebede (Eth.)	2:05:19
2011	**E. Mutai (Kenya)**	**2:04:40***
Year	**Women**	**hr:min:sec**
2009	I. Mikitenko (Ger.)	2:22:11
2010	L. Shobukhova (Russia)	2:22:00
2011	**M. Keitany (Kenya)**	**2:19:19**

*Fastest official time.

Berlin Marathon

Year	Men	hr:min:sec
2009	H. Gebrselassie (Eth.)	2:06:08
2010	P. Makau (Kenya)	2:05:08
2011	**P. Makau (Kenya)**	**2:03:38**
Year	**Women**	**hr:min:sec**
2009	A. Habtamu Besuye (Eth.)	2:24:47
2010	A. Kebede (Eth.)	2:23:58
2011	**F. Kiplagat (Kenya)**	**2:19:44**

Chicago Marathon

Year	Men	hr:min:sec
2009	S. Wanjiru (Kenya)	2:05:41
2010	S. Wanjiru (Kenya)	2:06:24
2011	**M. Mosop (Kenya)**	**2:05:37**
Year	**Women**	**hr:min:sec**
2009	L. Shobukhova (Russia)	2:25:56
2010	L. Shobukhova (Russia)	2:20:25
2011	**L. Shobukhova (Russia)**	**2:18:20**

New York City Marathon

Year	Men	hr:min:sec
2009	M. Keflezighi (U.S.)	2:09:15
2010	G. Gebremariam (Eth.)	2:08:14
2011	**G. Mutai (Kenya)**	**2:05:06**
Year	**Women**	**hr:min:sec**
2009	D. Tulu (Eth.)	2:28:52
2010	E. Kiplagat (Kenya)	2:28:20
2011	**F. Dado (Eth.)**	**2:23:15**

VOLLEYBALL

Beach Volleyball World Championships

Year	Men	Women
2007	P. Dalhausser, T. Rogers (U.S.)	M. May-Treanor, K. Walsh (U.S.)
2009	J. Brink, J. Reckermann (Ger.)	J. Kessy, A. Ross (U.S.)
2011	**A. Cerutti, E. Rego (Braz.)**	**L. Franca, J. Felisberta Silva (Braz.)**

World Volleyball Championships

Year	Men	Women
2006	Brazil	Russia
2008*	United States	Brazil
2010	Brazil	Russia

*Olympic champions.

WEIGHTLIFTING

World Weightlifting Champions, 2011

MEN

Weight class	Winner and country	Performance
56 kg (123.5 lb)	Wu Jingbiao (China)	292 kg (643.7 lb)
62 kg (136.5 lb)	Zhang Jie (China)	321 kg (707.7 lb)
69 kg (152 lb)	Tang Deshang (China)	341 kg (751.8 lb)
77 kg (169.5 lb)	Liu Xiaojun (China)	375 kg (826.7 lb)
85 kg (187 lb)	Kianoush Rostami (Iran)	382 kg (842.2 lb)
94 kg (207 lb)	Ilya Ilyin (Kazak.)	407 kg (897.3 lb)
105 kg (231.5 lb)	Khadzhimurat Akkayev (Russia)	430 kg (948.0 lb)
+105 kg (+231.5 lb)	Behdad Salimikordasiabi (Iran)	464 kg (1,023.0 lb)

WOMEN

Weight class	Winner and country	Performance
48 kg (106 lb)	Tian Yuan (China)	207 kg (456.4 lb)
53 kg (117 lb)	Zulfiya Chinshanlo (Kazak.)	227 kg (500.4 lb)
58 kg (128 lb)	Nastassiya Novikava (Bela.)	237 kg (522.5 lb)
63 kg (139 lb)	Svetlana Tsarukayeva (Russia)	255 kg (562.2 lb)
69 kg (152 lb)	Oksana Slivenko (Russia)	266 kg (586.4 lb)
75 kg (165 lb)	Nadezda Yevstyukhina (Russia)	293 kg (646.0 lb)
+75 kg (+165 lb)	Zhou Lulu (China)	328 kg (723.1 lb)

WRESTLING

World Wrestling Championships—Freestyle

Year	55 kg	60 kg	66 kg	74 kg
2009	Yang Kyong-Il (N.Kor.)	B. Kudukhov (Russia)	M. Taghavi (Iran)	D. Tsargush (Russia)
2010	V. Lebedev (Russia)	B. Kudukhov (Russia)	S. Kumar (India)	D. Tsargush (Russia)
2011	**V. Lebedev (Russia)**	**B. Kudukhov (Russia)**	**M. Taghavi (Iran)**	**J. Burroughs (U.S.)**
Year	**84 kg**	**96 kg**	**120 kg**	
2009	Z. Sokhiev (Uzbek.)	K. Gatsalov (Russia)	B. Makhov (Russia)	
2010	M. Ganev (Bulg.)	K. Gazyumov (Azer.)	B. Makhov (Russia)	
2011	**S. Sharifov (Azer.)**	**R. Yazdani (Iran)**	**A. Shemarov (Bela.)**	

World Wrestling Championships—Greco-Roman Style

Year	55 kg	60 kg	66 kg	74 kg
2009	H. Soryan-Reihanpour (Iran)	I.-B. Albiyev (Russia)	F. Mansurov (Azer.)	S. Cebi (Tur.)
2010	H. Soryan-Reihanpour (Iran)	H. Aliyev (Azer.)	A. Vachadze (Russia)	S. Cebi (Tur.)
2011	**R. Bayramov (Azer.)**	**O. Noroozi (Iran)**	**S. Abdvali (Iran)**	**R. Vlasov (Russia)**
Year	**84 kg**	**96 kg**	**120 kg**	
2009	N. Avluca (Tur.)	B. Kiss (Hung.)	M. López (Cuba)	
2010	H. Marinov (Bulg.)	A. Aliakbari (Iran)	M. López (Cuba)	
2011	**A. Selimau (Bela.)**	**E. Guri (Bulg.)**	**R. Kayaalp (Tur.)**	

Sumo Tournament Champions, 2011

Tournament	Location	Winner	Winner's record
Hatsu Basho (New Year's tournament)	Tokyo	Hakuho	14–1
Haru Basho (spring tournament)	Osaka	*canceled*	
Technical Examination Tournament*	Tokyo	Hakuho	14–1
Nagoya Basho (Nagoya tournament)	Nagoya	Harumafuji	14–1
Aki Basho (autumn tournament)	Tokyo	Hakuho	13–2
Kyushu Basho (Kyushu tournament)	Fukuoka	Hakuho	14–1

*Held instead of Natsu Basho (summer tournament).

Kyodo/Landov

Yokozuna (grand champion) Hakuho performs his ceremonial entry to the ring at the Nagoya basho *(grand tournament) in July. The tournament marked Hakuho's first loss in more than a year and his only loss in 2011.*

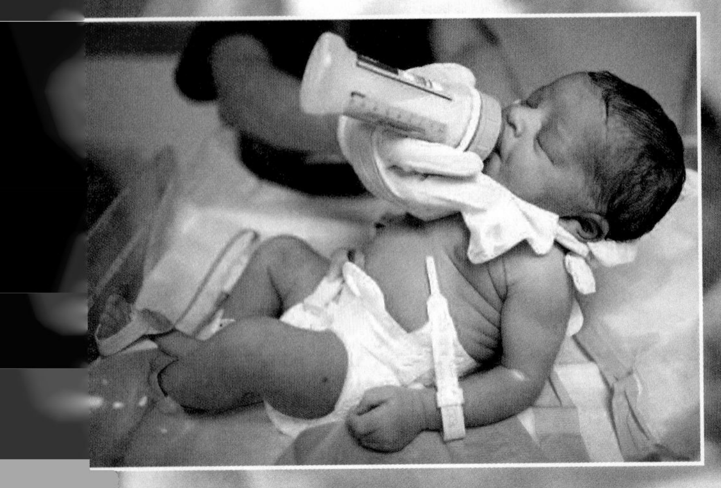

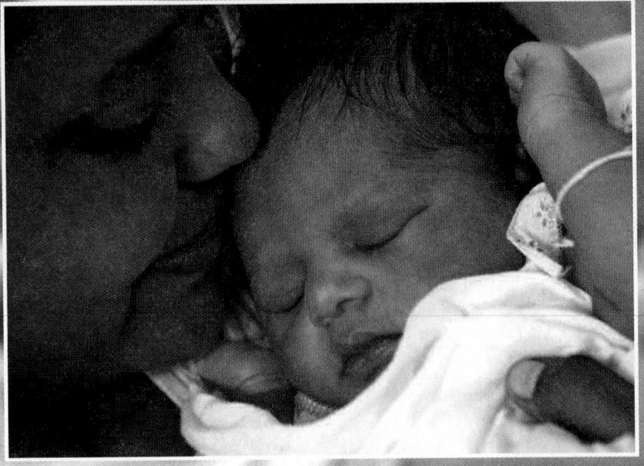

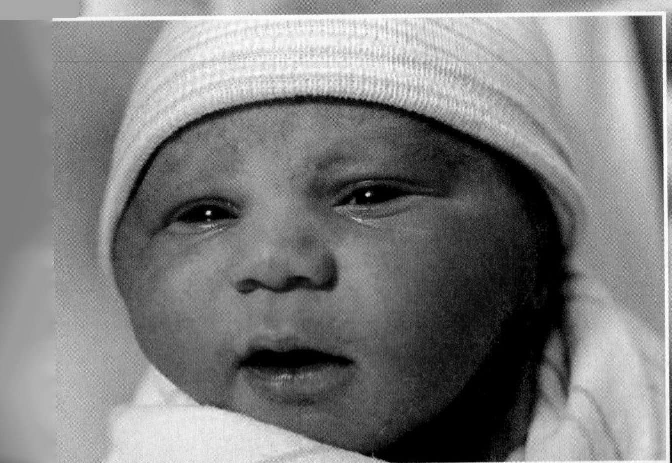

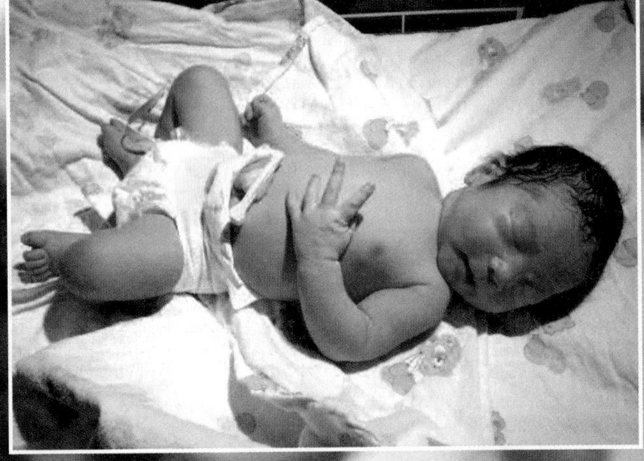

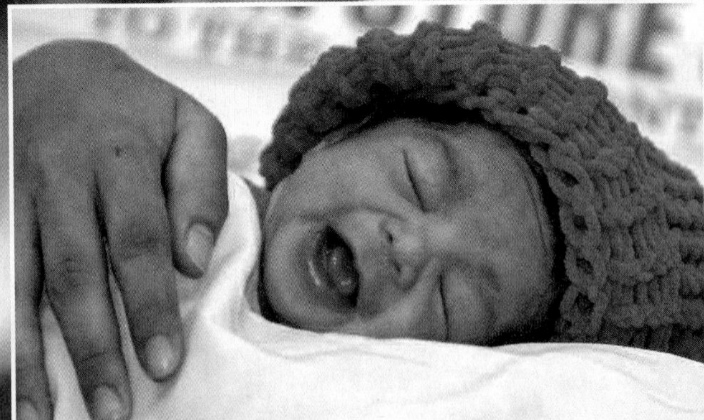

The World in 2011

The United Nations estimated that the population of the world reached seven billion on October 31, the day on which all of these babies were born.

(Facing page clockwise starting top left) Lucas Jackson—Reuters/Landov; M.A. Pushpa Kumara—EPA/Landov; Rick Wilking—Reuters/Landov; Bullit Marquez/AP; Reuters/Landov; Brian Snyder—Reuters/Landov; (background) Mohammed Zaatari/AP

World Affairs

In 2011 SOUTH SUDAN became an INDEPENDENT country, Paraguay and VENEZUELA celebrated their 200TH anniversaries of independence from Spain, and Sierra Leone marked 50 years of independence. Discontent was rampant across the globe: the so-called ARAB SPRING pro-democracy revolts spread across the Middle East and North Africa, and demonstrators took part in cities around the world in "OCCUPY" protests that railed against GREED and disproportionate WEALTH. The EU struggled for survival as a few of its member states coped with CRUSHING debt. Severe FAMINE affected Djibouti, Eritrea, Ethiopia, Kenya, and Somalia. Meanwhile, CRIPPLING natural DISASTERS—especially temblors in New Zealand and Turkey and an earthquake and TSUNAMI in Japan—battered ALREADY-FRAGILE economies affected by the worldwide economic DOWNTURN.

UNITED NATIONS

As the economic, food, and energy crises continued to have a heavy impact on most countries around the world in 2011, the hardest-hit and the least able to cope were the poor, many of whom turned to the UN for help. With only four years remaining before the 2015 deadline for achieving the Millennium Development Goals, most of the seven substantive problem-focused goals remained unlikely to be achieved. Against this rather dire backdrop emerged glimmers of hope for peoples in North Africa and the Middle East as waves of democratic movements spread in the so-called Arab Spring. (*See* Special Report on page 172.) The hope of Palestinian peoples for peace and a state of their own took a giant step forward as the Palestine state was voted full membership in UNESCO. After an internationally monitored referendum in January, on July 9 South Sudan joined the UN as the 193rd member state. In parts of Africa and Asia, several emerging economies were moving forward. The UN designated the year 2011 as the International Year of Forests to increase awareness of sustainable development and management of forests. In addition, 2011 was deemed the International Year of Youth, with a focus on integrating youths into planning and decision making about future governance arrangements.

At United Nations headquarters in New York City on September 23, Mahmoud Abbas (left), president of the Palestinian Authority, presents UN Secretary-General Ban Ki-Moon with a letter requesting the organization's recognition of Palestinian statehood.

Seth Wenig/AP

Peace and Security. The year was a busy one for UN peace and security operations. As of September 30 the UN Department of Peacekeeping (DPKO) was fielding 15 peacekeeping operations and one political mission in Afghanistan; these consisted of 121,744 personnel, of which 97,675 were in uniform. The figures were down somewhat from the historic high of the previous year. Protection of civilian populations was the core task of 7 of the 15 peacekeeping missions. This function faced critical challenges in Darfur (a region in western Sudan), the Democratic Republic of the Congo (DRC), Côte d'Ivoire, and South Sudan. The UN Integrated Mission in East Timor successfully completed the handover of policing and security responsibilities to national authorities. The total approved peacekeeping budget was set at $7.06 billion for the period from July 1, 2011, to June 30, 2012. As of Oct. 13, 2011, however, the peacekeeping budget was about $3.3 billion in arrears for 2010. Some 114 member states provided uniformed personnel, with the largest contributors being Bangladesh, Pakistan, and India, followed by Nigeria, Ethiopia, and Nepal. In Central Africa conflict persisted as the Ugandan-based Lord's Resistance Army (LRA) continued its attacks on civilian and other targets. The UN Security Council on November 14 called on UN peacekeepers in Central African countries to increase measures to stop such attacks. Although the civil war in Uganda had ended five years earlier, the LRA continued its violent attacks in the Central African Republic (CAR), the DRC, South Sudan, and Uganda. LRA leaders, who were under indictment by the International Criminal Court for crimes against humanity, had eluded capture.

During the year the UN enhanced its peacemaking activities and deployed missions in Central Africa, Central Asia, Gabon, Guinea, Lebanon, Libya, and Somalia. In all, the UN fielded 18 special political missions that employed about 4,000 staff and required nearly $645 million in funding. Most political missions were in Africa, which hosted four regionally focused missions: UN Office to the African Union (UNOAU), UN Office in Central Africa (UNOCA), UN Office in West Africa (UNOWA), and the UN Regional Center for Preventive Diplomacy for Central Asia (UNRCCA). Though U.S. Pres. Barack Obama announced on October 31 that all U.S. troops would be out of Iraq by the end of 2011, the mandate for the UN Assistance Mission for Iraq extended to July 2012.

UN Secretary-General Ban Ki-Moon placed particular focus on preventing election-related violence and fraud. Through the mechanism of his "good offices," technical assistance, and strategic advice, the UN provided assistance in 50 countries, including the CAR, Comoros, Côte d'Ivoire, Guinea, Haiti, Kyrgyzstan, Niger, South Sudan, and Tanzania.

The Middle East peace process continued to limp along, and direct peace talks were deadlocked as 2011 came to a close. Robert Serry, the UN secretary-general's special envoy to the region, publicly criticized Israel for its settlement-building policy. He reported to the Security Council that the weekly average of attacks by Israeli settlers on Palestinians in occupied territories had increased by 40% in 2011 over 2010 and by 165% over 2009. After the Palestinian state was admitted in October as a member of UNESCO, the Israeli government froze value-added tax (VAT) and customs payments to the Palestinian Authority, amounting to about two-thirds of its annual income.

Nonproliferation. In regard to nuclear nonproliferation, the Security Council continued its pressure on Iran, which was already under Security Council sanctions, to make its nuclear activities under the NPT convention more transparent. In mid-November the International Atomic Energy Agency (IAEA) passed a resolution expressing "deep and increasing concern" over Iran's nuclear program, stating that Iran had carried out tests relevant to the development of a nuclear device. The U.S., Canada, and European countries responded by tightening sanctions against Iran, which involved cutting off Iran's access to foreign banks and credit. Meanwhile, the IAEA and South Korea agreed to increase their collaboration in an effort to deal with North Korea's nuclear-weapons-development program.

Counterterrorism. The UN Counter-Terrorism Implementation Task Force continued to move forward with the implementation of the UN Counter-Terrorism Strategy. The main foci of this work included strengthening coordination in the event of nuclear or radiological terrorist attacks, countering the use of the Internet for terrorist purposes, introducing border-control measures for countering terrorism, and protecting human rights in instances in which people were stopped and searched. Special attention was also focused on building awareness in the international community of the Counter-Terrorism Strategy and on how to assist in making its implementation more effective.

Piracy. In 2011 piracy off the coast of Somalia in the Indian Ocean continued to be an important issue. The threat of piracy to ships operating in the Indian Ocean had increased, resulting in higher shipping costs and greater risk to human security. The pirates operated at distances of up to 1,750 nautical miles off the coast, and the number of attacks continued to increase. In the first nine months of the year, there were 185 attacks and 28 hijackings against ships in the waters off Somalia. As of October 2011, 316 individuals were being held hostage. This represented a very small reduction from the previous period, perhaps reflecting the impact of the monsoon season. Frustrated by the lack of success in dealing with pirates, the UN-backed Contact Group on Piracy off the Coast of Somalia in late 2011 called for member states to provide adequate financial, human, and material resources needed to tackle the problem.

Humanitarian Affairs and Human Rights. In 2011 the impacts of the 2010 Haitian catastrophic earthquake and Pakistani flooding persisted to threaten human security in those regions. On top of these crises, in 2011 flooding in Australia, major earthquakes in New Zealand and China, and the disastrous earthquake and tsunami in Honshu, Japan (*see* Special Report on page 176), that resulted in a major nuclear power-plant disaster presented the UN with extraordinary challenges. The UN sent its Disaster Assessment Coordination Team (UNDAC) to Japan to assist in support of relief operations.

In the wake of the so-called Arab Spring that led to the downfalls of the governing regimes in Tunisia, Egypt, and Libya, unrest still smoldered as 2011 came to a close as the populace in those societies struggled with issues of succession. The situation in Egypt had grown so bad, with the military killing more than 30 protesters, that both Secretary-General Ban and the UN High Commissioner for Human Rights in late November publicly deplored the excessive use of force by Egypt's transitional authority. In Yemen the political crisis continued as government forces allied with warlords battled militants seeking to oust authoritarian Pres. ʿAli ʿAbd Allah Salih. The UN secretary-general's special envoy met with President Salih on November 13 to persuade him to peacefully transfer power under a proposal initiated by Yemen's Gulf-state neighbours but to no avail.

In March the UN Security Council passed a mandate to establish a no-fly zone over Libya and authorized NATO and other military forces to use "all necessary means" to protect Libyan citizens. The resulting NATO intervention led to the toppling of the Libyan regime and the killing on October 20 of Libyan leader Muammar al-Qaddafi. (*See* OBITUARIES.)

UN sources estimated that between March and November 2011, more than 3,500 people were killed in Syria in antigovernment protests. A resolution by the UN Security Council calling for sanctions against Syria was blocked in October by China and Russia. On November 22, however, the UN General Assembly's Human Rights Committee overwhelmingly passed a resolution calling on Syria to implement a peace plan initiated by the Arab League and demanding an immediate end to government violence against its citizens. The 66th session of the UN General Assembly passed resolutions condemning human rights violations in Iran, North Korea, and Myanmar (Burma).

According to UN High Commissioner for Refugees (UNHCR) statistics, 43.7 million persons were forcibly displaced in 2010. This was the highest number since the mid-1990s. The year ended with 10.55 million refugees under the care of UNHCR and 4.82 million receiving assistance from the UN Relief and Works Agency for Palestinian Refugees (UNRWA). An overwhelming number—about 80%—were located in less-developed countries that were ill equipped to deal with them. Pakistan, Iran, and Syria hosted the largest number of refugees worldwide with 1.9 million, 1.1 million, and 1 million refugees, respectively. At the end of 2010, there were nearly 850,000 asylum seekers, with close to 20% in South Africa alone. During 2010 only 197,600 refugees were able to return home—the lowest number in more than two decades. In 2010 an estimated 27.5 million people were internally displaced (IDPs) within their own countries because of conflict or violations of human rights, with another 42.3 million displaced because of natural disasters. In 2011 UNHCR assisted more than 17 million IDPs in 25 countries and served as the lead agency in 21 humanitarian-assistance operations. UNHCR launched the Protection Capacity Initiative, which established 42 new protection posts and bolstered capacity, especially in UNHCR's largest operations.

Administration, Finance, and Reform. Secretary-General Ban announced four complementary reform initiatives aimed at increasing the world body's efficiency and effectiveness. First, he proposed an overall budget reduction of 3% aimed at making the organization more lean. Second, he called on the UN System Chief Executive Board for Coordination to collaborate on a systemwide reform effort. Third, he challenged all senior UN managers to propose specific ways to improve the way the UN operated and did business. Finally, he shook up his senior management team, bringing in new personnel with fresh perspectives. The UN's facelift continued, and the $1.9 billion Capital Master Plan project to refurbish the 60-year-old UN headquarters in New York City remained on budget.

Legally binding dues assessments for the regular UN budget in 2011 were $2.4 billion, which represented a slight increase from 2010. The peacekeeping budget had fallen from $9.67 billion in 2010 to $7.43 billion in 2011. The budgetary situation at the UN in mid-October 2011 was sobering but did not create a panic. As of October 2011, member states were in arrears to the UN regular budget for their legally binding dues for a total of $867 million. The United States accounted for 87.4% of this total. Other arrears included Mexico ($40 million), Spain ($19 million), and Venezuela ($11 million), and 57 others accounted for the remaining $39 million. In terms of peacekeeping, $3.3 billion was outstanding as of Oct. 5, 2011. Although the peacekeeping budget was more than $2 billion less than in 2010, the outstanding payment total was up by $113 million. Japan in 2011 led the list of unpaid peacekeeping dues, with an outstanding balance of $648 million. Spain and the U.S. came in second and third, with $490 million and $405 million in unpaid legally binding dues, respectively.

In terms of building UN systemwide coherence, the United Nations Entity for Gender Equality and the Empowerment of Women (UN-Women) became operational, creating a single administrative entity dedicated to gender issues. Also of note, the UN System Chief Executive Board for Coordination made progress toward implementing the Plan of Action for Harmonization of Business Practices in the United Nations System. (ROGER A. COATE)

EUROPEAN UNION

It was a measure of the troubles that beset Europe throughout 2011 that toward year's end its weary and desperate leaders were talking of the possible collapse of the entire EU. Following 10 months of battling to save the euro—the common currency established in 1999 as glue to bind the economies of many member states—the EU was faced in the closing months of the year with an existential crisis. Chancellor Angela Merkel of Germany attempted to shake fellow leaders to their senses in late October, warning that unless EU countries could muster sufficient resolve and financial firepower to support the euro and its indebted member states, the currency, and with it the whole EU project, could disintegrate. The result, she said, could mean a return to nationalism in Europe with all the dangers that that would entail. "No one should believe that another half a century of peace and prosperity in Europe is a given. It is not," Merkel said. "Therefore I say: If the euro fails, then Europe fails." It was a sobering message from the leader of a country that, since soon after the end of World War II, had championed closer integration as the only way to secure true and lasting peace and prosperity on a continent scarred by the memory of conflict.

Merkel was not alone. French Pres. Nicolas Sarkozy conceded in October what EU leaders had never before said—that some countries might have to decouple from the euro if the existence of the EU was being threatened. Sarkozy declared that if Greece could not agree to austerity measures to turn around its debt-ridden economy, it would have to quit the euro and go its own way: "We have said clearly that we want Greece to stay in the euro, but we cannot wish for this if she does not want it herself."

As the year opened, Estonia joined the single-currency area, becoming the 17th country in the 27-member EU to abandon its own notes and coins and enter the community's inner economic core. In addition, pro-democracy movements stirred on the EU's southern doorstep across the Mediterranean Sea in Tunisia. In the early part of the year, the same impulse toward democracy spread across North Africa, first to Egypt and then to Libya. Soon after, the rebellion penetrated the Middle East, where mass protests in Syria demanded political reform. The so-called Arab Spring demanded swift and clear foreign-policy responses from the European Union. (*See* Special Report on page 172.)

The year 2011 was scarcely under way before it became clear that the EU's 2010 economic-rescue loans to bail out Greece (€110 billion [about $146 billion]) and Ireland (€85 billion [about $113 billion]) represented the tip of the iceberg and that the euro's problems could not be fixed quickly. Fears spread that other high-spending euro countries might also need help from their neighbours. Spain, Portugal, and even Italy, one of the world's biggest economies, were seen as vulnerable, because the financial markets saw the huge national debts of those countries as reason to force up interest rates on lending. As with Greece and Ireland, the problem was that the costs of servicing the debts were increasing by the week, but because the countries were locked inside the currency zone, they had limited means to do anything about the problem. As euro-zone members they were unable to use their own central banks to pump more money into their economies, because they had surrendered control of the money supply to the European Central Bank (ECB), based in Frankfurt am Main, Ger. Nor could they devalue their currencies to gain a competitive edge, because interest rates were set centrally by the ECB, which had to set rates suitable for all 17 countries—not just those in trouble.

By early May, as the markets continued to push up the cost of borrowing, Portugal was obliged to reluctantly accept a €78 billion (about $114 billion) rescue package, thereby becoming the latest euro-zone state to enter intensive care. All the while, Greece's problems mounted. The government in Athens faced unremitting protests from its citizens as it tried to enforce tax increases, public-sector job cuts, and pension reforms—the price that the EU was demanding in return for further tranches of rescue money. Before Greek Prime Minister George Papandreou narrowly won support in the Hellenic Parliament during the summer for an austerity bill, he said that the choice was simple and stark: "We can choose deficit or prosperity. . . .This is the time to build our house on concrete foundations. . . . We have to stop our country from collapsing." Even after the vote was won, there were continuing doubts in Brussels and in the financial markets about whether Greece was doing enough to put its house in order, and the sense of deep instability remained.

The Arab Spring was both an opportunity and a problem for the EU. In recent years it had sought to develop a coherent, stronger voice in foreign policy in an effort to speak as one on the global stage on behalf of its 27 members. Encouraging democracy in neighbouring countries that had grown used to dictatorships was the easy part, but agreeing on military intervention—in this case in Libya, after the regime of Col. Muammar al-Qaddafi had unleashed bloody revenge on pro-democracy protesters—was quite another.

On March 17 the UN Security Council voted to establish a no-fly zone over Libya. The EU, however, was divided. Germany, the largest EU member state, refused to back the move called for by its key European allies—France and the U.K.—as well as the United States. Because Germany was haunted by its history—and nervous about backing military intervention—its unique position again undermined the idea that modern Europe could act as one in foreign policy. Later in the year, however, after exhaustive negotiations, the EU did rally behind the imposition of sanctions on Syrian oil exports as the bloc intensified pressure on Pres. Bashar al-Assad to end a crackdown on antigovernment protests that had begun in March.

The democracy movements raised other problems for the EU; citizens who had been caught up in the violent conflicts outside the borders of the EU sought refuge in the EU. An influx of North African migrants into the internally borderless EU during the Arab Spring triggered tensions between France and Italy. The latter—although concerned by the number of people fleeing political violence in Tunisia and Libya—nonetheless admitted large numbers. Sarkozy became alarmed that many of the French-speaking migrants who had entered the EU via Italy would be pouring into France. As a result, France asked for a revision to the Schengen Agreement, which allowed goods and people to move freely between most of the member states. The European Commission—the EU's executive, in Brussels—said that it would be possible for member states to reimpose border controls to prevent exceptional inflows but insisted that such measures be temporary and not mean the imposition of "fortress Europe" or the reintroduction of permanent borders within the EU.

By autumn, with Qaddafi deposed and killed, Sarkozy and British Prime Minister David Cameron were able to claim victory for their strategy in Libya. The Arab Spring promised to deliver democracy to countries on the EU's doorstep and thus deliver political and economic benefits to Europe. There was no letup, however, in the EU's own economic difficulties. Fears grew that Greece was about to default on its debts, which would leave the European and global banking sector with huge losses that would then trigger economic crises farther afield.

At a summit in Brussels at the end of October, EU leaders finally announced an agreement under which banks and insurers would have to accept, as part of the effort to reduce national liabilities to sustainable levels, 50% losses on the Greek debt they held. It was also agreed that the bloc would increase its rescue fund, the European Financial Stability Facility (EFSF), from €440 billion (about $592 billion) to €1 trillion (about $1.4 trillion). Initially, the agreement appeared to calm the markets (though details about the source of the funding remained sketchy), but pandemonium broke out after Papandreou made the deal conditional on a referendum that would not take place in his country until early 2012. Other EU members were furious and summoned Papandreou to meetings to explain why he had created yet more instability over a package designed to help his country avoid economic collapse. Within days, under huge pressure, Papandreou withdrew the referendum plan and resigned.

No sooner had that crisis been dealt with than the focus of Europe's economic and political turmoil became Italy. Like Greece, Italy was struggling to finance a huge debt as the markets pushed up the interest rate on Italian bonds to record levels. The prospect of the EU's having to rescue mighty Italy—one of the leading industrial countries of the Group of Eight—was raising its head. Many member states said that the only way to calm the markets was for the ECB to step in as the "lender of last resort"—a move strongly opposed by Germany, which said that such a move would take the pressure off countries to undertake necessary structural reforms. Other EU countries backed the idea of a new tax on bank transactions, but the U.K.—although not a member of the euro zone—resisted, fearing a negative effect on the City of London.

Amid growing turmoil in Italy, long-serving Prime Minister Silvio Berlusconi resigned on November 12. Nevertheless, the markets were unconvinced that a change of government would resolve Italy's fiscal crisis, and they pushed up the cost of lending to the country to a point at which it looked to be on the brink of bankruptcy. A sense of uncertainty haunted the financial markets in the first week of December, and it was then that France and Germany announced detailed plans to establish tough new rules for euro-zone member countries. Their plan involved setting up a fiscal union in which all euro countries obeyed the same rules to limit their deficits and debts and advancing ideas for a transaction tax on banks. They were keen that all 27 member states—the 17 inside the euro zone and the 10 outsiders—should sign so that the accord could be entered as a formal change into the EU rule book. A summit convened in Brussels in December ended amid acrimony, however; the U.K. refused to sign because France and others would not agree to safeguards it demanded for the City of London. As a result, the other 26 countries opted to form their own agreement outside the EU institutions. Though there was a determination to save the euro despite the traumatic year, the means of doing so were causing division and had left one of the EU's biggest and most important countries on the sidelines.

(TOBY HELM)

MULTINATIONAL AND REGIONAL ORGANIZATIONS

In 2011 the Group of 20 (G20) struggled to retain the global prominence that it had enjoyed since 2008, thanks to its vigorous response to the global financial crisis. As the locus of the financial crisis shifted to Europe, however, the spotlight was turned on the EU, particularly at the G20 summit in Cannes, France, in November.

During deliberations in France and the U.S., the G20 promised continued vigilance against the lingering repercussions of the global financial crisis. The September 22 meeting of the finance ministers and central bank governors in Washington, D.C., pledged to

Amid massive antigovernment protests in Idlib, Syria, on December 30, an Arab League monitor takes photographs of the assembled crowd.

Reuters/Landov

provide liquidity to the banks as needed and to support the world economy while maintaining price stability. Earlier, at the Group of Eight (G8) summit in Deauville, France, in May, the members pledged $20 billion to support the Tunisian and Egyptian revolutions.

The IMF had a more dramatic year but for an entirely different reason. Dominique Strauss-Kahn, the IMF executive director, was arrested over allegations that he had sexually assaulted a hotel maid in New York City. Charges against him were eventually dropped, owing to doubts about the credibility of his accuser. French Finance Minister Christine Lagarde succeeded Strauss-Kahn on June 28.

The OPEC conference held in June in Iran was marred by differences between Saudi Arabia and Iran over the issue of lifting oil production in an effort to lower prices. Iraq asked to rejoin OPEC's quota system in 2014, a move that would lead to a boost in production from 2.9 million bbl a day in 2011 to 3.4 million bbl a day in 2012 and to 4.5 million bbl a day in 2014.

The African Union (AU) continued to steadily expand its role in peace operations and conflict resolution. It mediated a border-security agreement between Sudan and South Sudan as the latter gained independence. The AU's peacekeeping contingent in Somalia, numbering nearly 10,000, earned praise from the international community for its surprising resilience and effectiveness in enforcing security against warlords, criminals, and Islamic militants and factional armies in and around Mogadishu, the Somali capital.

In answer to the Arab Spring revolts, the Arab League took a strong stand against the killing of pro-democracy protesters in Libya and Syria. In February the league barred Libya from its meetings. At its gathering in Cairo on March 12, the league affirmed the "necessity to respect international humanitarian law and the call for an end to the crimes against the Libyan people" while urging the UN Security Council to impose a no-fly zone over Libya. Without the support of the Arab League, the NATO intervention that eventually led to the overthrow of the regime of Muammar al-Qaddafi would have been far more controversial, even unlikely. The Arab League in August condemned the Syrian government for its repression of the pro-democracy uprisings and in November imposed sanctions on Syria. This surprising show of resolve was backed by Saudi Arabia and the other Gulf Cooperation Council member states, which feared that a continuation of atrocities might aggravate resentment within their own populations and spark uprisings of the kind that occurred in Bahrain. On December 22 the Arab League sent a monitoring group to Syria to establish ground rules for an observer mission intended to ensure that the government maintained its promise to end the violence against the protesters; observers entered the country on December 27.

In November, U.S. Pres. Barack Obama attended the East Asia Summit (EAS), the region's newest (set up in 2005) multilateral forum; it was the first time that a U.S. president had been in attendance. While the U.S. also deepened its engagement with the 10-member Association of Southeast Asian Nations (ASEAN) and the ASEAN Regional Forum (ARF), China's relations with ASEAN deteriorated because of the territorial dispute over the South China Sea, which involved five ASEAN members. At the July 2011 ARF meeting in Bali, Indon., U.S. Secretary of State Hillary Clinton criticized China's recent actions in the South China Sea as a threat to regional stability and freedom of navigation. China asked the U.S. to keep out of the dispute. As China became assertive in pressing its claims in the South China Sea, however, ASEAN welcomed a greater U.S. role in the security of the region.

The Shanghai Cooperation Organization (SCO) summit in Kazakhstan in June reaffirmed cooperation against the three evil forces: terrorism, separatism, and extremism. With observer states Pakistan and India seeking full membership, the SCO risked a possible dilution of its coherence and unity. Meanwhile, Iran sought to use SCO as an anti-Western platform.With the return in May to Honduras from exile of Manuel Zelaya, the country's former president who in 2009 had been ousted in a coup, the Organization of American States lifted the ban on the country. In December, Latin American and Caribbean leaders formed the 33-member Community of Latin American and Caribbean States (CELAC), which excluded the U.S. and Canada. That month Russia became the newest member of the World Trade Organization.

(AMITAV ACHARYA)

DEPENDENT STATES

Europe and the Atlantic. On Dec. 8, 2011, Gibraltarians went to the polls in a hard-fought general election. Chief Minister Peter Caruana of the Gibraltar Social Democrats (GSD), who was seeking his fifth four-year term, had faced accusations of misuse of power when he delayed the ballot past the October 11 anniversary of the 2007 election. The final result, with a turnout of 82.5%, was a reversal of the 2007 vote. The GSD (46.76%) dropped from 10 seats to 7 in the 17-seat parliament, while the opposition Gibraltar Socialist Labour Party–Liberal Party Alliance (48.88%) increased from 7 to 10 seats. The Progressive Democratic Party (PDP) took the remaining 4.36%.

Fabian Raymond Picardo, who had defeated then opposition leader and former chief minister (1988–96) Joe Bossano in an Alliance leadership battle in April, was sworn in as Gibraltar's new chief minister on December 9. Picardo declared his intention to improve relations with Morocco and with Spain, but he reiterated that his government would not accept a return to bilateral talks between the U.K. and Spain regarding Gibraltar's future status. Picardo also led the territory in mourning the death of former chief minister (1969–72) Sir Robert Peliza, who was responsible, at least in part, for the founding of the Integration with Britain Party, the drafting of Gibraltar's original 1969 constitution, and the securing in 1981 of full British citizenship for Gibraltarians. Peliza died on December 12 at age 91.

After two years of exploration, Scotland-based Cairn Energy announced in late 2011 that it had failed to discover commercially viable sources of oil or natural gas off Greenland. Just weeks earlier the company had reported that it had spent some £500 million (about $785 million) on the six completed wells and that it might reconsider its plans for an additional six wells.

Rockhopper Exploration, Falkland Oil & Gas, and other energy companies had better luck drilling in the South Atlantic off the Falkland Islands/Islas Malvinas. The South American economic group Mercosur backed Argentina's claim of sovereignty over the Falklands, and in December member countries agreed to ban from their ports all ships bearing the Falklands flag.

(MELINDA C. SHEPHERD)

Gibraltarian politician Fabian Picardo embraces a supporter on December 9, the day after his Gibraltar Socialist Labour Party won parliamentary elections. Picardo replaced Peter Caruana, who had governed since 1996, as chief minister of the British overseas territory.

Carrasco Ragel—EPA/Landov

Caribbean and Bermuda. Anguilla Chief Minister Hubert Hughes in January 2011 called on the people of the British overseas territory to start considering whether the island should begin "seriously to move towards independence." Gov. Alistair Harrison refused to sanction Anguilla's 2011 budget passed by the local executive council, but Anguilla capitulated in February and agreed to a revised budget assisted by U.K. government officials. Harrison indicated in May that Anguilla could eventually become independent once the decision had been approved by the majority of the population.

According to a January report by the U.S. ratings agency Fitch, Puerto Rico was expected to return to real economic growth of about 0.4% in 2011. Puerto Rico was said to have lost more than 100,000 jobs during 2007–11. In the U.S. Virgin Islands, the major employer in St. Croix—the Hovensa oil refinery—decided in January to reduce its capacity from 500,000 bbl per day to 350,000 bbl per day, in a bid to reduce losses.

In May the two sets of Virgin Islands—U.S. and British— jointly convened the fourth meeting of the Inter-Virgin Islands Council. Subjects such as immigration, crime, natural disasters, and cultural exchanges were discussed, and both governments signed a Memorandum of Understanding, which provided for collaboration between law-enforcement agencies from the two sides, particularly in the area of fingerprinting and ballistics. French overseas departments in the region also moved to strengthen relations with their English-speaking compatriots as Guadeloupe reached an agreement with Antigua and Barbuda on joint action in such areas as tourism, agriculture, and disaster preparedness.

The British Virgin Islands government changed hands in November when the National Democratic Party, led by Orlando Smith, won 9 of the 13 seats at stake in the general election to the Virgin Islands Party's 4. Smith was subsequently sworn in as premier.

The British Virgin Islands and the Cayman Islands were criticized by the U.S. State Department's 2011 International Narcotics Control Strategy Report in March for not taking sufficient steps to combat money laundering. In July the U.K.-appointed governor of the Caymans, Duncan Taylor, confirmed that Premier McKeeva Bush was the subject of a police investigation into alleged "financial irregularities."

Curaçao advanced its renewable energy credentials in July when it was announced that two new 15-MW wind farms would be built. The developer, NuCapital Inc., said that the $76 million investment would provide electricity at half the cost of oil-fired generation.

Bermuda played host to the Organisation for Economic Co-operation and Development Global Forum on Transparency and Exchange of Information for Tax Purposes on May 31–June 1. Premier and Finance Minister Paula Cox also attended international finance meetings in Europe and Canada. According to industry sources in March, Bermuda housed the largest number of captive insurance companies in the world—845 at the end of 2010. The Caymans harboured 738, and Anguilla had 252.

(DAVID RENWICK)

Pacific Ocean. The Cook Islands in 2011 sought to reduce its financial dependence on New Zealand. The government sent a delegation to China for bilateral aid talks and explored the possibility of bringing the Spanish fishing fleet back into its southern exclusive economic zone. In another attempt to increase revenue, the Cooks extended the length of New Zealanders' visitors permits and offered retirees from New Zealand opportunities for extended residence of up to 12 months. The plan appeared to be working, with the number of visitors increasing solidly for the second straight year. In September the Cooks won the right to host the annual South Pacific Islands Forum in 2012.

On April 1 the French Polynesian assembly ousted Pres. Gaston Tong Sang and designated former president Oscar Temaru as his replacement. In a close vote the assembly in August approved a resolution asking French Pres. Nicolas Sarkozy to reinscribe French Polynesia on the UN's decolonization list. President Temaru lobbied the Pacific Islands Forum at its annual meeting, held in September in New Zealand, but he failed to secure the organization's support. The Pacific Conference of Churches agreed to help lobby the UN for reinscription (and eventual independence). Former president Gaston Flosse criticized the attempts, arguing that Temaru should not confront France. Flosse, who was convicted in 2010 of corruption during his time as president, was sentenced in October to four years' imprisonment.

In mid-August the New Caledonian Congress elected pro-independence advocate Roch Wamytan its president by a solid majority after a court in Paris had ruled his previous election, in

April, invalid. A dispute over ownership of the airport on the island of Maré, triggered by increases in domestic airfares, resulted in August in the deaths of four young men and injuries to another 23 who were occupying the airport, which was built on disputed land. The government moved quickly to negotiate a compromise with customary land owners and imposed a moratorium on fare raises.

Niue opened a new visitors centre in August, but the Chamber of Commerce admitted that there were challenges in building a sustainable tourism industry. The resident population of Niue was only 1,400, and few Niueans living in Australia and New Zealand were willing to return permanently with the necessary skills and funds. Chinese interest in noni juice led to a joint venture to double existing noni production on Niue to 120 ha (about 297 ac) over the following four years, which could generate income and jobs.

American Samoa's economic situation deteriorated further following the closure of canneries in the territory and the attendant loss of revenue. By midyear the government owed its power company more than $5 million and lacked the funds to pay $2 million in mandated subsidies to the LBJ Tropical Medical Center, without which it could not draw down matching U.S. Medicaid funds.

The three atolls of the Tokelau Islands experienced prolonged drought in 2011 and by October had only one week's water supply for their 1,300 inhabitants. A joint New Zealand–U.S. operation oversaw the distribution of containers flown from New Zealand to American Samoa, where water was loaded for delivery to the atolls by the U.S. Coast Guard. (CLUNY MACPHERSON)

Indian Ocean. Mayotte, the only island in the Comoros group that voted in 1974 to remain a French dependency instead of joining independent Comoros, was admitted on March 31, 2011, as the 101st *département* of France. Residents of Mayotte had voted overwhelmingly for department status in a referendum held in 2009. Daniel Zaidani of the Mayotte Departmentalist Movement was elected council president.

Rioting broke out in March and again in July among asylum seekers held in the Australian detention centre on Christmas Island. At least 170 detainees escaped from the centre, where more than 2,500 people were housed. Meanwhile, an investigation began into the tragic December 2010 shipwreck off Christmas Island, in which some 50 people were believed to have died; charges of people smuggling and reckless conduct were brought against an Iranian-born Australian. Some 70 vessels carrying more than 4,500 asylum seekers who arrived from such places as Afghanistan, Pakistan, and Iran were intercepted off Christmas Island during 2011, with at least one additional ship foundering off the Indonesian island of Java in December.

(MELINDA C. SHEPHERD)

Dependent States[1]

Australia
- Christmas Island
- Cocos (Keeling) Islands
- Norfolk Island

Denmark
- Faroe Islands
- Greenland

France
- French Guiana[2]
- French Polynesia
- Guadeloupe[2]
- Martinique[2]
- Mayotte
- New Caledonia
- Réunion[2]
- Saint-Barthélemy
- Saint-Martin
- Saint-Pierre and Miquelon
- Wallis and Futuna

Netherlands
- Aruba
- Curaçao
- Sint Maarten

New Zealand
- Cook Islands
- Niue
- Tokelau

United Kingdom
- Anguilla
- Bermuda
- British Virgin Islands
- Cayman Islands
- Falkland Islands
- Gibraltar
- Guernsey
- Isle of Man
- Jersey
- Montserrat
- Pitcairn Islands
- Saint Helena Tristan da Cunha
- Turks and Caicos Islands

United States
- American Samoa
- Guam
- Northern Mariana Islands
- Puerto Rico
- Virgin Islands (of the U.S.)

[1]Excludes territories (1) to which Antarctic Treaty is applicable in whole or in part, (2) without permanent civilian population, (3) without internationally recognized civilian government (Western Sahara), or (4) representing unadjudicated unilateral or multilateral territorial claims. [2]Legally classified as overseas *département* of France.

ANTARCTICA

Ice averaging roughly 2,160 m (7,085 ft) in thickness covers more than 98% of the continent of Antarctica, which has an area of 14.2 million sq km (5.5 million sq mi). There is no indigenous human population, and there is no land-based industry. Human activity consists mainly of scientific research. The 49-country Antarctic Treaty is the managerial mechanism for the region south of latitude 60° S, which includes all of Antarctica. The treaty reserves the area for peaceful purposes, encourages cooperation in science, prescribes environmental protection, allows inspections to verify adherence, and defers the issue of territorial sovereignty.

On Oct. 31, 2011, Malaysia acceded to the Antarctic Treaty, as a nonconsultative party; it planned to become a consultative party in the future. Since 1997, when New Zealand opened its facilities at Scott Base to Malaysia, the Malaysians had supported about 62 research projects in Antarctica involving some 60 scientists.

At the 34th Antarctic Treaty Consultative Meeting (ATCM), held in Buenos Aires on June 20–July 1, 2011, approximately 350 diplomats, Antarctic program managers, logistics experts, and polar scientists from 48 countries—including the 28 consultative parties with a scientific presence in the Antarctic—gathered to discuss environmental and management issues. Representatives of 16 international and intergovernmental organizations also participated as observers, and the Committee for Environmental Protection (CEP) met as well.

The ATCM representatives reviewed reports from station inspections conducted by representatives from Japan and Australia. While those reports demonstrated that most consultative parties were adhering to the requirements of the treaty's Protocol on Environmental Protection, they also pointed out that sharing information and technology could improve management of the facilities. Other matters the representatives deliberated included proposals on how to prevent unauthorized access to Antarctica and preliminary discussions regarding the risks that tsunamis could pose to the large number of coastal research stations.

The CEP's discussions included contemplating the potential environmental effects of drilling into subglacial Lake Ellsworth, revising the management plan governing 10 Antarctic Specially Protected Areas, and airing concerns about ways to maintain a pristine environment on the continent under sustained human presence; special attention was focused on preventing the introduction of nonnative species. The committee also reviewed the plans for South Korea's Jang Bogo research station at Terra Nova Bay, commenting on how an appropriately designed structure, sustainable energy production, and other factors would reduce the station's environmental impact.

During the 2010–11 austral summer, 33,824 tourists visited the continent, with some 33,438 arriving by ship. Compared with 2009–10, the number of tourists decreased by 8.3%, primarily because several cruise-only programs were canceled after the International

NASA—Reuters/Landov

In October 2011 scientists discovered a crack 29 km (18 mi) long across the ice shelf of Pine Island Glacier in Antarctica that was believed would result in the formation of an iceberg.

Maritime Organization ban on using heavy fuel oil in the Antarctic Treaty area took affect in August. Of the 2010–11 visits, 19,065 landed in the Antarctic Treaty area, and 14,373 participated in large cruise-only trips. About 386 participated in multiday land-based expeditions to the continental interior, and another 531 traveled by air and ship to Antarctica and landed on the continent.

In January the U.S. completed construction of a $271 million neutrino detector array at the South Pole when the final basketball-sized optical sensor was installed in a hole 1.5 km (0.9 mi) deep in the ice sheet. The array was designed to use the clear bubble-free ice as a medium to detect faint flashes of light generated when fast-moving neutrinos collided with the ice to produce muons.

The massive magnitude-9.0 earthquake that shook Japan on March 11, 2011, was felt as far south as Antarctica. A team of researchers from the University of California, Santa Cruz, who were remotely monitoring the Whillans Ice Stream that feeds into the Ross Ice Shelf, observed that the surface seismic waves generated by the temblor caused the ice stream to slide by 0.5 m (1.6 ft), but they did not believe that the shock destabilized the ice stream. A tsunami produced by the quake arrived in Antarctica about 18 hours later after having traveled some 12,880 km (8,000 mi), and it battered the Suzerberger Ice Shelf in West Antarctica. A piece of ice the size of Manhattan Island broke off the ice shelf, which until then had been stable for 46 years. The largest of the resulting icebergs was about 6.5 × 9.5 km (4 × 5.9 mi) and some 80 m (260 ft) thick.

The hole in the atmosphere's ozone layer that forms above Antarctica during the austral spring on September 12 reached its peak size of 25.9 million sq km (10 million sq mi), the ninth largest hole on record. Australian scientists, reporting in the journal *Geophysical Research Letters*, however, believed that they had evidence that the hole was becoming smaller, something that most scientists had not expected to see until after 2020. By identifying the natural influences on the year-to-year variations in the quantity of atmospheric ozone and then subtracting their estimates of those from the actual changes, they found that a clear upward trend in ozone recovery had been occurring since the 1990s.

In 1958 scientists discovered Earth's most extraordinary mountain range—the Gamburstsev Subglacial Mountains—buried beneath the East Antarctic Ice Sheet. The mountains were located where it was believed that the vast ice sheet first formed, but how the mountains themselves had formed had been a mystery for more than 50 years. A seven-country team of researchers analyzed new geophysical data and published its findings in November. They concluded that multiple tectonic events, rather than a single one, had formed the mountains. A billion years ago tectonic collisions crushed what had been a mountain range there, but they also created and preserved a crustal root beneath the former mountains and formed the East Antarctic rift system—a fracture in Earth's surface 3,000 km (1,860 mi) long extending from East Antarctica to India. Later, about 250 million–100 million years ago, the breakup of the supercontinent Gondwana caused the rock of the old root to warm, and that action, together with tectonic movements along the rift, forced the land upward into a new range of mountains.

Scientists flying over Pine Island Glacier in October made an unexpected discovery: a massive crack running about 29 km (18 mi) across the glacier's floating tongue. The rift, 80 m (260 ft) wide, marked the creation of a new iceberg with an area of some 880 sq km (340 sq mi). The glacier, one of Antarctica's fastest moving, drained about 10% of the West Antarctic Ice Sheet.

(WINIFRED REUNING)

ARCTIC REGIONS

The Arctic regions may be defined in physical terms (astronomical [north of the Arctic Circle, latitude 66° 30′ N], climatic [above the 10 °C (50 °F) July isotherm], or vegetational [above the northern limit of the tree line]) or in human terms (the territory inhabited by the circumpolar cultures—Inuit [Eskimo] and Aleut in North America and Russia, Sami [Lapp] in northern Scandinavia and Russia, and 29 other peoples of the Russian North, Siberia, and East Asia). No single national sovereignty or treaty regime governs the region, which includes portions of eight countries: Canada, the United States, Russia, Finland, Sweden, Norway, Iceland, and Greenland (part of Denmark). The Arctic Ocean, 14.09 million sq km (5.44 million sq mi) in area, constitutes about two-thirds of the region. The land area consists of permanent ice cap, tundra, or boreal forest (taiga). The population (2011 est.) of peoples belonging to the circumpolar cultures is about 530,000 (Aleuts [in Russia and Alaska], more than 4,000; Athabascans [North America], 40,000; Inuits [or Eskimos, in Russian Chukhotka, North America, and Greenland], 150,000; Sami [Northern Europe], 85,000; and 41 indigenous peoples of the Russian North, totaling about 250,000). International organizations concerned with the Arctic include the Arctic Council, the Barents Euro-Arctic Council, the Inuit Circumpolar Council, and the Indigenous Peoples' Secretariat. International scientific cooperation in the Arctic is the focus of the International Arctic Research Center of the University of Alaska at Fairbanks and the University of the Arctic, a circumpolar network of member institutions.

The warming of the north continued to have a profound impact on all dimensions of the Arctic in 2011. This included the increased melt of land and sea ice, loss of habitat for ice-dependent species such as polar bears and ringed seals, access to open shipping lanes, oil and natural-gas development, search and rescue in response to increased activity in the region, and Arctic sovereignty. The Greenland ice sheet, the world's second largest ice sheet, after the Antarctic ice mass, accelerated its overall melt. NASA estimated that Greenland was losing approximately 220 cu km (53 cu mi) of ice each year and that the melt appeared to be increasing by 9 cu km (2 cu mi) per year. As the Greenland glacier melted, both fresh water and icebergs were released to the North Atlantic Ocean. In the spring of 2011, a massive 250-sq-km (100-sq-mi) iceberg approached the northeastern coast of Canada.

Summer Arctic sea ice reached its annual minimum coverage on September 9. This represented 35% less ice compared with the 20-year average minimum coverage between 1980 and 2000. The Polar Science Center at the University of Washington estimated that the overall minimum volume of Arctic sea ice had dropped even further, to a record low of some 4,200 cu km (1,000 cu mi), or 66% less ice compared with the 20-year average. According to projections by researchers, in coming decades the Arctic would be ice-free during the summer.

Warm surface temperatures were accompanied by cooling in the upper atmosphere of the high north. The prolonged low temperatures in the stratosphere activated ozone-depleting chemicals and produced the first significant ozone hole ever recorded over the Arctic. NASA warned that ozone depletion in the Arctic was similar in magnitude to that in the Antarctic and was likely to occur again in coming years.

Lower levels of summer sea ice resulted in more open water along the Northeast Passage (called the Northern Sea Route in Russia) and the Northwest Passage. The Northeast Passage, along the Russian Arctic coast, opened in June, earlier than in previous years. For the first time, a Suezmax-class tanker (i.e., the largest vessel that can transit the Suez Canal), the *Vladimir Tikhonov*, sailed from Europe to Asia along the route. In addition, a new speed record was set when two tankers crossed the Russian Arctic in only eight days. Also set in 2011 was a record for the volume of goods shipped through the Arctic: more than 800,000 metric tons, which was a fivefold increase over 2010. Gas condensates represented more than half of the bulk of the goods transported. Oil and iron ore were also shipped in quantity.

Russia pledged to support the growing shipping activity along the route. In July, Deputy Prime Minister Sergey Ivanov announced plans for six new Russian icebreakers. Russia also committed to providing more port and rail facilities along its northern coast. Other countries also increased their activity in the Arctic. A Chinese icebreaker navigated to latitude 88° N on its fourth scientific expedition into the Arctic Ocean. The two U.S. heavy icebreakers were out of commission in 2011. Canada's flagship icebreaker, the *Louis S. St. Laurent*, was forced to dry dock with a broken propeller. The *St. Laurent* had been working on a joint mission with the U.S. cutter *Healy* to map the subsea continental shelf.

Interest in offshore oil and natural gas increased in 2011. The U.S. continued to approve offshore drilling projects in the Arctic, although it moved cautiously owing to concerns regarding oil spills and the challenges of cleanup in icy waters. Russia launched its first offshore oil rig capable of operating in Arctic waters. The rig was scheduled to begin operations in 2012. The Scotland-based company Cairn Energy began exploratory drilling off the west coast of Greenland, although operations were delayed when protesters occupied the drilling rig. In November the company announced promising results from one of the exploratory wells. Demand for metallic-mineral commodities also rose in 2011, and mining in the north boomed. Two abandoned iron-ore mines were reopened in Norway, and a new mine was planned in Sweden. As northern shipping opened up, the possibility of locating a mine in the high Arctic became viable. Planning was under way for an open-pit iron-ore mine at latitude 71° N in Canada's Nunavut territory. The mine was expected to ship 18 million metric tons annually and triple the economy of the region.

As human activity increased across the Arctic, pressure grew to find ways to coordinate disaster response with limited facilities and overlapping jurisdictions. In May the eight Arctic countries signed an international treaty to cooperate on air and marine search and rescue, the first legally binding agreement created through the Arctic Council. In conjunction with the treaty, council ministers established a task force to address Arctic prevention and preparedness in the event of an oil spill. As a result of the Arctic Council's growing mandate and demand on regional issues, the council decided to make its secretariat, located in Tromsø, Nor., a permanent facility.

In May 2008 the U.S. had set the status of polar bears as threatened under the Endangered Species Act because of the loss of sea ice. Gov. Sean Parnell and the state of Alaska opposed the classification with a legal challenge, expressing concern over offshore development. In June 2011 the status of polar bears as a species threatened by climate change was upheld by U.S. federal courts. Several months later Canada added polar bears to its Species at Risk registry in the "special concern" category.

Although the reduction of summer sea ice negatively affected polar bear habitat, the opening of the Northwest Passage allowed the transoceanic migration of species. In 2010 a gray whale apparently passed from the Pacific to the Atlantic, where those whales had been extinct for centuries, and in 2011 microscopic plankton from the Pacific were reported in North Atlantic waters.

(JOHN STREICKER)

Protesting plans by the company Cairn Energy to conduct deepwater oil drilling in Arctic waters, Kumi Naidoo (left), the executive director of Greenpeace International, and activist Ulvar Arnkværn approach by speedboat a Cairn oil rig off the coast of western Greenland, June 17. The two were subsequently arrested for having scaled the rig in defiance of an injunction.

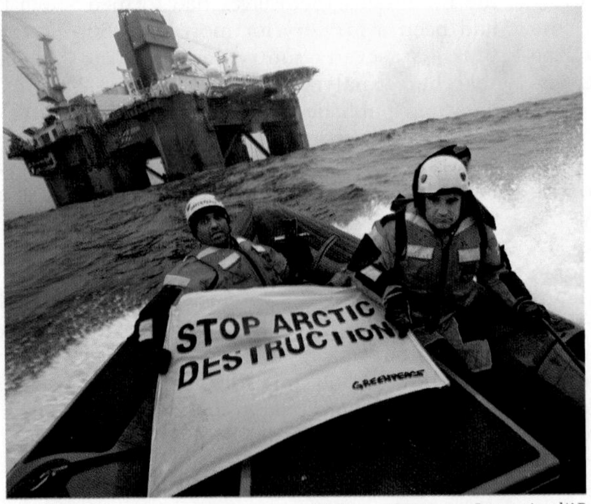

Jiri Rezac—Greenpeace International/AP

AFGHANISTAN

Area: 652,864 sq km (252,072 sq mi)
Population (2011 est.): 26,442,000 (excluding Afghan refugees in Pakistan and Iran)
Capital: Kabul
Head of state and government: President Hamid Karzai

Despite the presence of 130,000 NATO and U.S. troops in Afghanistan in 2011, the level of violence throughout the country did not decline. Taliban activity was contained in some areas, but deadly strikes at military and civilian targets continued. As the 2014 deadline for the departure of international forces neared, the country's democracy was tested by a prolonged deadlock between the branches of government.

Groups fighting the government of Hamid Karzai made extensive use of improvised explosive devices in roadside bombings, suicide attacks, and assassinations. Mindful of its announced pullout, NATO focused on training Afghan army and police forces and gradually transferring security responsibilities to them. Insurgent activity became more frequent in the north and in Kabul. The Haqqani network, an arm of the Taliban with bases in Pakistan and links to al-Qaeda, was particularly adept at carefully planned and executed assaults. They were credited with high-profile suicide attacks on civilian, diplomatic, and government centres in Kabul and elsewhere.

Encouraged by his Western allies, President Karzai pressed ahead with a reconciliation program. The High Peace Council, founded in 2010 to engage the Taliban, attempted to draw opposition figures into dialogue. Some Afghan leaders worried that Karzai might compromise too many basic values, and many women feared that their expanding freedoms would be threatened. Analysts saw the influence of Pakistan behind the Taliban as a threat to Afghanistan's sovereignty.

After a U.S. raid inside Pakistan in May killed Osama bin Laden, suicide attacks in Afghanistan aimed at local and national leaders increased. Suspicions that Pakistan's military was supporting Taliban activity in Afghanistan, especially that of the Haqqani network, increased. In September a suicide bomber killed the head of the High Peace Council, former Afghan president Burhanuddin Rabbani (*see* OBITUARIES), and Afghan officials claimed to have evidence of Pakistani involvement. In October Karzai admitted that peace talks with the Taliban were futile and said that he would instead deal directly with Pakistan.

After the September 2010 parliamentary election, contention had emerged between the Wolesi Jirga (the lower house of the parliament) and the Karzai-appointed Supreme Court and attorney general. The Independent Election Commission (IEC) had reacted to widespread corruption by disqualifying 24 winning candidates, an action that the attorney general called illegal. By the end of that year, Karzai had appointed a special court to reconsider the IEC's findings, while the new MPs demanded that the president inaugurate the new session. In late January 2011 Karzai consented but insisted that the special court's decisions to replace any MPs would be binding. Observers accused Karzai of having pressured the parliament in order to weaken it and worried that prolonged uncertainty would erode the people's trust in government.

The tense situation lasted for months while Karzai's government carried on, seemingly unaffected. In June the court ruled that 62 MPs whom the IEC had declared winners should be replaced, but when MPs decried the decision, Karzai established yet another commission to evaluate the matter. In August, under orders from Karzai, the IEC reluctantly conceded that 9 of the MPs should be replaced. The new MPs were sworn in, but the episode provoked a walkout, which thus left the parliament without a quorum. Only in October was the parliament able to fully function. The constitutional standoff between the parliament on one side and the government and the judiciary on the other served to magnify the authority of the president.

Throughout the year talks continued between the Afghan and U.S. governments over a formal agreement regulating the status of U.S. forces in the country following Afghanistan's assumption of responsibility for its own security. The Afghan public largely saw the matter as a question of allowing permanent U.S. bases in Afghanistan. Some felt that such bases would limit Afghanistan's sovereignty while disturbing its neighbours, whereas others saw U.S. bases as a guarantee against interference from neighbouring countries. U.S. officials repeatedly denied having any interest in establishing permanent bases. A Loya Jirga, or assembly of national leaders, agreed in November that U.S. bases ought to be allowed for 10 years so long as Afghanistan's sovereignty and traditions were guaranteed. In December an international peace conference met in Bonn, Ger., to review Afghanistan's peace process, but hopes for greater cooperation were weakened when, in response to a NATO air strike inside Pakistan, Pakistan refused to participate. (STEPHEN SEGO)

Following the killing of Afghan political leader Burhanuddin Rabbani, supporters hold posters bearing his image during a protest in Herat, September 23.

Jalil Rezayee—EPA/Landov

ALBANIA

Area: 28,703 sq km (11,082 sq mi)
Population (2011 est.): 3,196,000
Capital: Tirana
Head of state: President Bamir Topi
Head of government: Prime Minister Sali Berisha

The beginning of 2011 in Albania saw the culmination of 18 months of organized protest by the opposition Socialist Party of Albania (PS). On January 21 guards fired shots from within the prime minister's office complex in Tirana, killing three protesters, when demonstrators tried to break through a fence surrounding the grounds. The protests followed the resignation on January 14 of Deputy Prime Minister Ilir Meta, the leader of the Socialist Movement for Integration (LSI), the junior partner in the governing coalition led by the Democratic Party (PD). Meta was at the centre of a corruption scandal sparked by a video that allegedly showed him trying to influence then economy minister Dritan Prifti to intervene on behalf of a private company in the government concession for a hydroelectric power plant.

On May 8 former foreign minister Lulzim Basha of the PD challenged PS leader Edi Rama for the Tirana mayor's office. Rama, the incumbent, was declared the narrow winner, but he lost the recount that was ordered because of ballot-box irregularities. On June 27 Albania's central election commission announced that Basha had won the race, and on July 8 a court confirmed the decision.

In the wake of the events surrounding the Tirana mayoral race, the PS resumed the partial parliamentary boycott it had maintained since disputed general elections on June 28, 2009. PS members returned to their seats on September 5, however, to vote on constitutional amendments essential to Albania's progress toward EU association and integration. Albanian law required the consent of three-fifths of the members of Parliament for changes to the constitution, and PS support was necessary for passage. The late move was not sufficient to satisfy repeated demands by the EU's enlargement commissioner for an end to the political stalemate. Presenting the EU's progress reports on October 11, Stefan Fule made clear that Albania was not ready to attain candidate status in 2011.

The opposition criticized the decision by PD legislators to raze a pyramid-shaped building that once had served as a museum for Stalinist leader Enver Hoxha to construct a new parliament building at that location to honour the 100th anniversary of Albania's independence in 1912. Pres. Bamir Topi also announced on June 15 that Albania would begin paying Russia for a €25 million ($36 million) Hoxha-era debt to the Soviet Union.

Albania's economy stabilized as GDP growth in the first quarter of 2011 was 3.4% greater than in the same period in 2010. Midyear unemployment and inflation rates dropped slightly but continued to hover at about 13% and 3%, respectively.

Aided by Europol and several European police forces, Albanian police foiled two major shipments of cocaine to the country, seizing 200 kg (about 440 lb) of the illegal drug on March 22 and almost a ton on May 31.

On April 2 Haxhi Ded Reshat Bardhi, who had led the Albanian Islamic Sufi order for 18 years, died. On November 30 Leka Zogu, the son of Zog I (the king of precommunist Albania) and claimant to the throne, died at age 72 in Tirana. The government declared periods of national mourning for both men. (FABIAN SCHMIDT)

ALGERIA

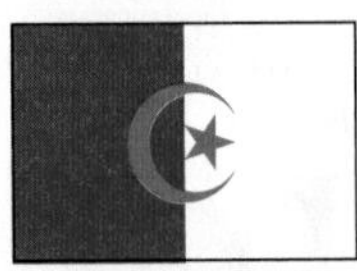

Area: 2,381,741 sq km (919,595 sq mi)
Population (2011 est.): 35,930,000
Capital: Algiers
Head of state and government: President Abdelaziz Bouteflika, assisted by Prime Minister Ahmed Ouyahia

Confronted by increasingly violent demonstrations and riots over escalating food prices at the end of 2010 and in January 2011, the government of Algeria moved swiftly to address popular demands. On January 8 it announced subsidies, which were expected to reduce prices by 41% for staples such as sugar and cooking oil. By January 10 the riots had subsided, leaving three dead, and more than 800 injured. More than 1,000 were arrested by the police and gendarmerie. The unrest highlighted the severe poverty and deprivation that Algerians faced despite the country's bulging foreign reserves, which reached $165 billion by midyear. The riots were followed by a spate of protest self-immolations—30 occurring up to the beginning of June.

Surprisingly, however, neither riots nor acts of individual protest sparked political protests of the kinds that occurred at the start of the year in other North African countries. Instead, sporadic local rioting betrayed Algerians' frustration with endless examples of maladministration and official incompetence. The antiriot police reported that there had been 2,777 violent incidents involving the police in the first six months of 2011, and Said Sadi, a leading opposition politician, claimed that there were 9,700 riots in 2010 alone.

In the wake of the January riots, opposition political parties, particularly those close to the Berber movement, sought to organize regular mass demonstrations against the government in Algiers. Because demonstrations had been banned in Algiers since 2001, the government warned that it would not tolerate the initiative and flooded the capital with up to 30,000 police on the days when protests were planned. Pres. Abdelaziz Bouteflika, in his first public response at the start of February, also promised to rescind the state-of-emergency legislation, which had been in force since 1992, and to liberalize access to audio-visual media, which up to then had been a state monopoly. He also vowed to promote job creation—a major popular demand.

In mid-April, President Bouteflika also pledged to amend the constitution, inviting political parties to submit their proposals for amendments to a parliamentary committee. On August 8 proposed reforms to the laws governing political parties, the electoral process, and nongovernmental organizations were announced. The proposed reforms were greeted with general disappointment and rejected even by parties within the president's coalition. Similar disappointment greeted the announcement in late September (after the annual meeting between the government and the trade union confederation) of a $40 increase in the monthly minimum wage, to $240.

Meanwhile, terrorist violence continued throughout northern rural Algeria, albeit concentrated in Kabylia. Govern-

AP

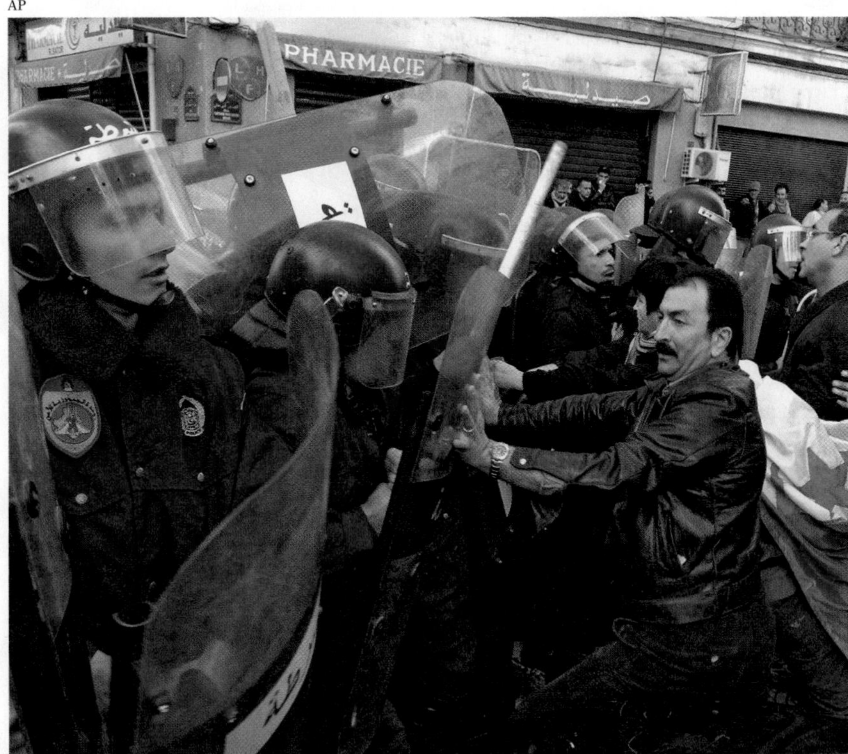

In Algiers protesters attempting to hold a political demonstration in defiance of a government ban clash with police, January 22.

ment sources reported that 171 members of the security forces had been killed in counterterrorism operations in 2010, together with 235 civilians—131 civilians were also injured—and 463 terrorists, while 1,473 persons suspected of terrorism were arrested. The level of violence rose slightly in 2011, culminating in an attack on the military academy at Cherchell on August 27 in which 18 persons died. Al-Qaeda in the Islamic Maghrib also continued its operations in the deep Sahara.

(GEORGE JOFFÉ)

ANDORRA

Area: 464 sq km (179 sq mi)
Population (2011 est.): 85,600
Capital: Andorra la Vella
Heads of state: Co-princes of Andorra, the president of France and the bishop of Urgell, Spain
Head of government: Chief Executives Jaume Bartumeu Cassany, Pere López Agràs (acting) from April 28, and, from May 12, Antoni Martí Petit

On April 28, 2011, Chief Executive Jaume Bartumeu Cassany was ousted as the head of government in Andorra because he was unable, for the second consecutive year, to get a budget passed. As a result, the ruling Social Democratic Party was forced to call parliamentary elections two years earlier than scheduled. In the balloting held on April 3, the Social Democrats were soundly defeated by the Democrats for Andorra, which won 20 of the 28 seats in the legislature. Antoni Martí Petit took office as the head of government on May 12. He had previously served as mayor of Escaldes-Engordany.

The worldwide economic crisis was felt in Andorra as well. The economic downturn led to unprecedented calls for changes in the tax structure, which were set to begin in 2012 with the introduction of a business tax of up to 10%, to be followed by a sales tax in 2013. Even a theretofore widely resisted income tax appeared to be in the offing. During the year Andorra, along with San Marino and Monaco, requested increased involvement and integration in European Union tax and trade matters. The European Commission took the issue under advisement.

(ANNE ROBY)

ANGOLA

Area: 1,246,700 sq km (481,354 sq mi)
Population (2011 est.): 19,618,000
Capital: Luanda
Head of state and government: President José Eduardo dos Santos

The rise of oil revenue and foreign investment throughout 2011 ensured Angola's robust economic growth. Real GDP was forecast to peak at 8.5% in 2012, although inflation remained high at over 14%, driven by continuing currency depreciation, rising fuel prices resulting from steep reductions in subsidies, and frequent obstruction in processing imported food supplies and consumer goods. Meanwhile, the capital, Luanda, gained the dubious reputation of being the world's most expensive city for political, diplomatic, and commercial elites. In stark contrast, the gap between the wealthy minority and the poor majority grew wider, with few signs of government success in ameliorating socioeconomic problems. Key challenges were the declining infrastructure, youth unemployment, low education levels, and an urban housing shortage, particularly in the capital, where almost three million people resided. Unfortunately, much of the recent residential construction represented gentrification at the expense of the poor, who were forced to move to the city's peripheries after their housing was demolished. The country ranked near the bottom of the United Nations Development Programme's Human Development Index: 148 of 187.

The Popular Movement for the Liberation of Angola (MPLA), the ruling party, maintained a tight grip on the country's political system and government resources. It held 191 of the 220 seats in the national legislature. The main opposition party, the National Union for the Total Independence of Angola (UNITA), with only 16 seats, offered little significant opposition. By the end of the year, it was bedeviled by leadership rivalry and could not even build a consensus to hold a congress to consider its platform and candidates for the upcoming general election.

Preparations for a lengthy preelection period ahead of Angola's general election in September 2012 dominated politics. An MPLA victory seemed certain. Speculation increased that Pres. José Eduardo dos Santos, in power for 32 years, intended to name Manuel Vicente, former head of the state oil company, Sonangol, as his successor. This was dampened when President dos Santos indicated that he would be ready to serve as president again and later reappointed Vicente to another three-year term as head of Sonangol.

In March a shadowy group of diasporic origin, styling itself as the Angolan People's Revolution, became active. Inspired by events in North Africa and the Middle East known as the Arab Spring, the group mobilized several significant, although low-key, antigovernment demonstrations. Two possible reasons why this movement failed to gain support were persistent memories of civil war and limited access to cell phones and the Internet among the disenfranchised youth.

International relations highlighted Angola's desire for an assertive role in continental affairs. Unfortunately, early in the year President dos Santos's attempt to mediate in Côte d'Ivoire's electoral crisis in support of former president Laurent Gbagbo failed and was heavily criticized. Meanwhile, economic ties with China and Brazil were further strengthened. In August Angola assumed the presidency of the Southern African Development Community.

In the scientific world, archaeologists leading the PaleoAngola Project, the first such expedition since the 1960s, announced the discovery in Angola of the fossil remains of *Angolatitan adamastor*, a sauropod. It was reputed to be a new type of gigantic plant-eating dinosaur. (LARAY DENZER)

ANTIGUA AND BARBUDA

Area: 442 sq km (171 sq mi)
Population (2011 est.): 91,400
Capital: Saint John's
Chief of state: Queen Elizabeth II, represented by Governor-General Dame Louise Lake-Tack
Head of government: Prime Minister Baldwin Spencer

In the early months of 2011, Antigua and Barbuda began to experience the crime upsurge that had troubled so many Caribbean territories, facilitated by what the national security minister, Errol Cort, described as "the proliferation of illegal firearms and ammunition." In May a series of bomb threats resulted in the closure of 13 police stations.

Antigua and Barbuda in March found itself on the list of countries in the region criticized by the U.S. State Department in its 2011 International Narcotics Control Strategy Report for not taking sufficient steps to control money laundering and financial crime. The country's Office of National Drug and Money Laundering Control Policy, however, countered that its efforts were, in fact, being held up by others as a good example of a Caribbean anti-money-laundering unit.

In March the IMF announced that it was pleased with Antigua and Barbuda's economic progress and would disburse an additional $10.7 million under the current standby agreement. The amount provided so far totaled about $42.7 million.

Antigua Labour Party opposition leader Lester Bird in July forcefully criticized the government's plan to offer "economic citizenship" to foreigners. He stressed that such a policy would do "irreparable harm" to the country's international standing.

(DAVID RENWICK)

ARGENTINA

Area: 2,780,403 sq km (1,073,520 sq mi)
Population (2011 est.): 40,365,000
Capital: Buenos Aires
Head of state and government: President Cristina Fernández de Kirchner

On Oct. 23, 2011, Cristina Fernández de Kirchner was reelected president of Argentina in a landslide over a demoralized and divided opposition. Fernández de Kirchner, of the Peronist Front for Victory (FPV), garnered 54% of the vote and outdistanced her nearest competitor by 37 points. She also won a plurality in every province but one (San Luis). Fernández de Kirchner's impressive victory was principally the product of the country's robust economic growth (GDP expanded by about 7% in 2011), the increasingly uneven political and economic playing field on which the opposition was forced to compete, a lack of voter confidence in the opposition candidates' ability to govern, and a host of errors made by the principal opposition leaders.

Martin Acosta—Reuters/Landov

Argentine Pres. Cristina Fernández de Kirchner hoists a photo of herself and her late husband, former president Néstor Kirchner, while celebrating her reelection on October 23 in Buenos Aires.

The non-Peronist opposition, which in 2009 had performed well in the country's midterm congressional elections under the banner of the Civic and Social Agreement (AyC), was unable to unite for the 2011 elections because of ideological, personal, and strategic disagreements between the AyC's principal players: the Radical Civic Union (UCR), the Socialist Party (PS), the Civic Coalition (CC), and the Generation for a National Encounter (GEN). As a result, the AyC splintered into three separate groups, each of which supported a different presidential candidate. The PS and the GEN joined to create the Progressive Broad Front, which backed the candidacy of Hermes Binner (PS), the governor of Santa Fe province, who finished second in the race, with 17%. The UCR allied with Francisco de Narváez (who in 2009 had defeated former president Néstor Kirchner in the congressional election for Buenos Aires province) to form the Union for Social Development (UDESO). De Narváez ran for governor in Buenos Aires, where 38% of Argentine voters resided. UDESO's presidential candidate, Ricardo Alfonsín (UCR), finished a disappointing third, with 11% of the vote. The remaining candidate from that sector, Elisa Carrió (CC), captured a dismal 2% to finish last among the seven presidential candidates.

Disputes between leading anti-Fernández de Kirchner Peronists resulted in the sector's implosion during 2011. Many of those dissidents returned to the fold of President Fernández de Kirchner; others allied with non-Peronist opposition groups; and still others opted to not participate at all in the 2011 electoral process. The remaining dissidents split into two camps, one of which supported the presidential candidacy of Alberto Rodríguez Saá (Federal Commitment), governor of San Luis province, while the other backed former president Eduardo Duhalde (Popular Front). Rodríguez Saá placed fourth in the presidential race, with 8% of the vote; Duhalde finished fifth, with 6%.

One-half of the Chamber of Deputies (130 of 257 seats) and one-third of the Senate (24 of 72 seats) also were elected on October 23. Fernández de Kirchner's FPV and its allies won 87 seats in the Chamber and 17 seats in the Senate. That result meant that Fernández de Kirchner would enjoy the support of an absolute majority in both new houses when they convened on December 10. The remaining seats were distributed across nearly a dozen opposition parties, which ensured the continued fragmentation of the anti-Fernández de Kirchner forces.

Despite Argentina's booming economy, concerns grew throughout the year over increasing inflation. The government reported the inflation rate at 9.5% in December, but other sources, including skeptical international financial organizations, believed the figure to be more than twice that.

(MARK P. JONES)

ARMENIA

Area: 29,743 sq km (11,484 sq mi). About 13% of neighbouring Azerbaijan (including the 4,400-sq-km [1,700-sq-mi] disputed region of Nagorno-Karabakh [Armenian: Artsakh]) has been under Armenian control since 1993.
Population (2011 est.): 3,100,000 (plus 142,500 in Nagorno-Karabakh)
Capital: Yerevan
Head of state: President Serzh Sarkisyan
Head of government: Prime Minister Tigran Sarkisyan

Armenia experienced a wave of protest demonstrations in 2011 launched by the extraparliamentary opposition Armenian National Congress (HAK). Inspired by the revolutions in Egypt and Tunisia, protests began in February and continued throughout the year. The authorities acceded to HAK demands for the release of persons jailed in connection with the post-presidential-election violence in Yerevan in March 2008 and for the reopening of the official investigation into 10 deaths, but they refused to hold preterm elections. In July the HAK and the ruling coalition began talks, but the HAK walked out in September to protest the arrest of one of its youth activists and late that month began a one-week sit-in in Yerevan's Liberty Square.

The opposition Heritage party boycotted parliamentary proceedings from February to August to protest an agreement under which the ruling coalition's junior partners, Prosperous Armenia and Rule of Law, pledged to support incumbent Pres. Serzh Sarkisyan's bid for reelection in February 2013. The opposition Armenian Revolutionary Federation failed in May to force a vote of no confidence in the government of Prime Minister Tigran Sarkisyan. On September 9 the Central Election Commission chairman, Garegin Azarian, died suddenly of heart failure at the age of 50, days after publication of a WikiLeaks cable suggesting that the 2008 presidential election results had been rigged.

Economic growth slowed during the first half of 2011 and amounted to 4.6% for the year. The authorities failed to reduce annual inflation to 5–6%.

Armenian-Turkish relations remained strained. President Sarkisyan threatened twice, in January and in August, to annul the protocols signed in October 2009 on the normalization of bilateral relations if Ankara continued to tie the ratification of the protocols by the Turkish parliament to progress toward resolving the Nagorno-Karabakh conflict. In July, Turkish Prime Minister Recep Tayyip Erdogan demanded an apology from President Sarkisyan for remarks that Erdogan asserted were an Armenian claim on Turkish territory.

Iranian Pres. Mahmoud Ahmadinejad canceled a visit to Yerevan in June, but in September he affirmed his desire to expand bilateral ties. Armenia continued to make progress in negotiations with the European Union on expanding political and economic ties within the framework of the Eastern Partnership and Cooperation Agreement.

(ELIZABETH FULLER)

AUSTRALIA

Area: 7,702,501 sq km (2,973,952 sq mi)
Population (2011 est.): 22,651,000
Capital: Canberra
Head of state: Queen Elizabeth II, represented by Governor-General Quentin Bryce
Head of government: Prime Minister Julia Gillard

In Australia the year 2011 began with all eyes in the country focused on an unfolding natural disaster in the northern state of Queensland, where the wettest December on record had triggered flood conditions across vast swaths of the state. On January 10 a flash flood swept through the main street of the city of Toowoomba, killing four people. In the nearby Lockyer Valley, a wall of water, described by Queensland Premier Anna Bligh as an "inland tsunami," swept through a series of small towns, including the settlement of Grantham, causing the deaths of at least 16 people in the region. The state capital, Brisbane, was also heavily flooded; some 20,000 homes were inundated. By the end of January, 35 people across the state were confirmed dead, and 9 were missing.

Queenslanders had only a brief rest between natural disasters when on

Janie Barrett/AP

During a disastrous spate of flooding across the Australian state of Queensland, waters submerge major thoroughfares south of Rockhampton, January 4.

February 3 a category 5 tropical cyclone, Yasi, struck the state's east coast with wind speeds of up to 285 km/hr (177 mph). The storm caused damages estimated at $A 3.5 billion (about U.S.$3.5 billion), though it claimed only one life.

In January, Prime Minister Julia Gillard began her first full calendar year in power. The year proved difficult for her, however, as her initial popularity after her party's electoral wins in August 2010 began to fade during 2011.

The prime minister's political authority was undermined by her government's inability to find a way to reduce the number of unauthorized asylum seekers arriving by boat from Southeast and Central Asia. Gillard pursued plans to create an offshore processing system, in which the claims of refugees seeking asylum would be assessed in a third country, after which only genuine asylum seekers would be allowed into Australia. After the High Court ruled on August 31 that Gillard's plan to exchange refugees with Malaysia was invalid, the government announced on November 25 that refugees arriving by sea would be processed onshore and could live in the country while their claims were considered.

In July the complexion of Australian politics changed when the winning candidates of the 2010 federal elections took their seats in the Senate (the upper house of Parliament) as the new session began. The Greens, who had won 13% of the vote in 2010, assumed the balance of power; their six seats represented a voting bloc that could decide the fate of new legislation awaiting parliamentary approval.

The government's popularity was also harmed by its pursuit of a carbon emissions tax as Australia's main weapon for reducing greenhouse gas emissions. It did so despite Gillard's preelection pledge that she would not introduce such a scheme. The measure was fiercely opposed by the Liberal-National coalition and was largely unpopular with voters. Nevertheless, the bill eventually passed by a narrow majority in Parliament in November. Later that month the lower house passed a second major reform, the Minerals Resource Rent Tax, which was to be levied on 30% of the so-called superprofits made by large iron-ore and coal-mining companies. The proposal for the tax sparked a fierce debate between mining companies—which argued that it would damage the country's most profitable economic sector—and those who believed that the massive profits of the largest miners should be used to help the country's overall fiscal position.

Gillard's popularity suffered to such an extent that rumours abounded in October and November about a possible return to leadership by Kevin Rudd, whom Gillard had deposed as prime minister in an internal party coup in 2010. By December, however, she had stemmed her slide and not only had quelled the speculation as to possible leadership changes but was slowly gaining ground against her main political opponent, Tony Abbott.

The Economy. During the year the economy was dominated by a mining investment boom, powered by Chinese demand for raw minerals. That boom greatly benefited the mining states of Western Australia and Queensland, but it had little impact on nonmining states. The result was what was described as a "two-speed economy" across Australia. The boom also ensured that Australia outperformed most other Western economies in 2011, but it also helped to create a strong dollar, which exceeded parity with the U.S. dollar for most of the year and hurt the manufacturing and tourism sectors. Late in the year the European financial crisis helped to erode consumer confidence and spending, which forced the Reserve Bank of Australia to reduce interest rates twice.

Foreign Affairs. Australia's foreign policy during the year was driven by the activities of Rudd, Gillard's foreign minister. Rudd sought to raise the country's profile on the international stage via its activities in multilateral bodies such as the UN, the G20 leaders' meeting, and regional economic and security forums. Australia hosted both the Commonwealth Heads of Government Meeting in Perth in October and the visit of U.S. Pres. Barack Obama to Canberra and Darwin the following month. Obama used the visit to pledge an enhanced U.S. presence in the Asia-Pacific region and a permanent presence of up to 2,500 U.S. Marines for training purposes in northern Australia. China reacted angrily to what it identified as an expansion of U.S. military alliances in the region. The situation reinforced the diplomatic challenge facing Gillard's government as it attempted to balance its priorities between its closest military ally, the U.S., and its largest trading partner, China.

Public support for the continued deployment of 1,550 Australian troops in Afghanistan declined sharply as the death toll of Australian soldiers reached 32. In December the government signaled the possibility that troops could be withdrawn before the previously stated target of 2014.

(CAMERON STEWART)

AUSTRIA

Area: 83,879 sq km (32,386 sq mi)
Population (2011 est.): 8,419,000
Capital: Vienna
Head of state: President Heinz Fischer
Head of government: Chancellor Werner Faymann

Though Austria continued to be governed in 2011 by a grand coalition made up of the Austrian People's Party (ÖVP) and the Social Democrats (SPÖ), a fundamental shift in Austrian politics took place during the year. That largely occurred as a number of negative developments for the ÖVP left a political power vacuum that the right-wing Freedom Party (FPÖ) filled. In April, ÖVP leader Josef Pröll stepped down as party chairman and vice-chancellor because of severe illness. His resignation came at a time of crisis for the party owing to high-profile corruption scandals involving two ÖVP members of the European Parliament. The FPÖ, which had benefited most from the weak ÖVP, had surpassed it in recent opinion polls and ranked about even with the SPÖ.

The FPÖ continued to base its program in part on anti-immigrant sentiment, with the party's leader, Heinz-Christian Strache, making highly provocative comments with respect to foreigners and especially Muslims. In particular, the FPÖ came out vehemently against a proposed program to teach Turkish as an elective that would be covered on the final school-leaving exams (*Matura*), claiming that such a plan would allow Turkish immigrants to pass their exams by doing less work than other students.

Relations between Austria and Turkey deteriorated during the year, with Turkey vetoing the candidacy of Austrian diplomat Ursula Plassnik for the secretary-generalship of the Organization for Security and Co-operation in Europe. That veto was motivated by Turkey's perception that Plassnik was opposed to Turkish EU membership. The Austrian government remained officially open to Turkey's joining the EU, but Austrian public opinion was staunchly against it.

The Austrian government submitted a stability program to the European Commission in early 2011 designed to reduce the country's deficit to less than 3% of GDP by 2013. To comply with the European System of Accounts, however, Austria revised its deficit for 2010 upward by one percentage point, to 4.6%, with knock-on effects for the 2011 government balance. While Austria's deficit and debt levels were relatively low by EU standards, the government would have to implement further measures to hit its targets over the next few years. One such measure adopted in 2011 was a series of funding cuts for entities and individuals in the academic arena.

While Austria's two largest banks passed the EU-wide stress tests in July 2011, the smaller Österreichische Volksbanken was one of only nine banks to fail the stress tests. Austrian banks' exposure to the weaker euro-zone countries was modest, though Bank Austria was part of Italian UniCredit and therefore was affected by decreased confidence in Italy's ability to service its debt.

On May 1 Austria opened its labour market to citizens of the eight central and eastern European states that had joined the EU in 2004. Workers from those countries helped to fill a void in skilled labour in certain sectors.

Austria's GDP grew robustly in the first half of 2011 owing to strong domestic and foreign demand. Consumer and business confidence improved significantly in the first few months of the year, and unemployment fell. By year's end, Austria boasted the lowest unemployment rate in the EU. Inflation increased forcefully in the first half of 2011, and, consequently, overall real wages fell. That dampened private-consumption growth, but improved competitiveness boosted Austrian exports. Exports recovered strongly in early 2011 as the country's largest export market—Germany—staged a strong economic revival. Export growth slowed in the second half of the year, however, as Germany's economy stalled and fiscal tightening hampered growth throughout the euro zone. (MEGAN GREENE)

AZERBAIJAN

Area: 86,600 sq km (33,436 sq mi), including the 5,500-sq-km (2,100-sq-mi) exclave of Nakhichevan and the 11,400-sq-km (4,400-sq-mi) disputed area (with Armenia) comprising the Nagorno-Karabakh region and surrounding territory
Population (2011 est.): 9,150,000
Capital: Baku
Head of state and government: President Ilham Aliyev, assisted by Prime Minister Artur Rasizade

In January 2011 several Azerbaijani opposition groups that were excluded from the new parliament elected in November 2010 formed an opposition alliance called the Public Chamber. That body organized demonstrations

Aida Sultanova/AP

Police officers detain a protester at a rally for democratic reform held in Baku, Azer., April 2. Azerbaijani authorities cracked down on several opposition-led demonstrations in the capital during the year.

in Baku in March, April, and May to demand democratic reforms and measures to eradicate corruption. On each occasion the police apprehended dozens of protesters. Thirteen participants in a protest on April 2 were sentenced in September and October to prison terms ranging from one to three years for having violated public order. In May the Public Chamber unveiled a three-stage plan for a transition to genuine democracy, including the holding of free parliamentary elections.

Seven members of the unregistered Islamic Party of Azerbaijan were arrested in early January after its leader, Movsum Samedov, protested the ban on female students' wearing the *hijab* and called for the overthrow of the country's "despotic" leadership. On October 7 they were sentenced to 10–12 years in jail on charges of having planned a terrorist act and having plotted to seize power.

On May 26 Pres. Ilham Aliyev pardoned journalist Eynulla Fatullayev, who had been sentenced to prison for extremism and alleged possession of drugs. Fatullayev's sentencing had been condemned by the European Court of Human Rights in April 2010. Government interference in the media continued, however. The property of the *Khural*, a newspaper, was confiscated on October 19, and its editor, Avaz Zeynalli, was arrested on October 28 on a bribery charge. On August 11 the Baku municipal authorities demolished without warning the privately owned office belonging to the Institute of Peace and Democracy, a human rights organization.

Azerbaijan's economy stagnated in 2011 despite a modest increase in agricultural output. Annual inflation was estimated at 8%. President Aliyev and visiting European Commission president José Manuel Barroso signed an agreement in January on expanding the so-called Southern Energy Corridor.

Six visits to the region by the Organization for Security and Co-operation in Europe's Minsk Group and two meetings between the Armenian and Azerbaijani presidents mediated by Russian Pres. Dmitry Medvedev yielded little progress toward resolving the Nagorno-Karabakh conflict. In July talks began on the terms for extending Russia's use of the Gabala radar station in central Azerbaijan beyond 2012. On October 24 Azerbaijan was elected a nonpermanent member of the UN Security Council. (ELIZABETH FULLER)

BAHAMAS, THE

Area: 13,939 sq km (5,382 sq mi)
Population (2011 est.): 360,000
Capital: Nassau
Chief of state: Queen Elizabeth II, represented by Governor-General Sir Arthur Foulkes
Head of government: Prime Minister Hubert Ingraham

The Bahamas privatized a major public utility when in February 2011 the U.K.'s Cable and Wireless took over 51% of The Bahamas Telecommunications Co. (BTC) at a cost of $210 million. The Free National Movement government said that it planned to sell another 9% of BTC in the near term and up to 25% in the future. In August BTC pledged some $2 million in aid to assist islanders affected by Hurricane Irene.

In January U.S. petroleum distributor Buckeye Partners bought an 80% stake in The Bahamas Oil Refining Co. storage terminal in Grand Bahama from private equity firm First Reserve for $1.36 billion; Buckeye, which later took over the remaining 20% held by Royal Vopak (for $340 million), said that it planned to increase capacity from 21.6 million bbl to 45 million.

In May The Bahamas and Cuba agreed "in principle" on the delimitation of their respective exclusive economic zones to help facilitate offshore oil exploration. (DAVID RENWICK)

BAHRAIN

Area: 757 sq km (292 sq mi)
Population (2011 est.): 1,325,000
Capital: Manama
Head of state: King Hamad ibn Isa al-Khalifah
Head of government: Prime Minister Khalifah ibn Sulman al-Khalifah

Following the example of popular uprisings in other Arab countries in 2011, the Bahraini Shiʿite opposition, comprising some 60% of the population, rose up against the Sunni-led regime on February 14. Demonstrators' demands ranged from fundamental constitutional reforms to the downfall of the monarchy. This unrest was met by a violent reaction from the government that tried, unsuccessfully, to suppress the demonstrations, and Shiʿite protesters continued to occupy the main square of the capital, Manama. In the face of intransigence, the Bahraini government declared martial law on March 15 and asked for military help

At a demonstration march in Al-Rifaʿ, Bahrain, on March 11, antigovernment protesters attempt to evade tear gas sprayed by riot police.

Isa Ebrahim—UPI/Landov

from Saudi Arabia and other Arab Gulf countries. The Saudis responded swiftly, sending 1,000 soldiers to Bahrain; the United Arab Emirates sent 500 policemen, and other Gulf Cooperation Council countries added token military forces. Using live ammunition, these combined forces cleared the square and the main streets in Manama of protesters, but sporadic clashes with demonstrators continued in Shi'ite villages. The unrest left at least 33 people dead and hundreds wounded or in prison.

Confident that it had quelled the rebellion and under pressure from the U.S., the Bahraini government lifted martial law on June 1 and called for a dialogue with Shi'ite leaders. In July, Shi'ite politicians walked out of government-led reconciliation talks, claiming that key issues had not been addressed. The main Shi'ite political group, al-Wifaq (Accord), announced that it would boycott the upcoming parliamentary elections called to replace the 18 al-Wifaq deputies who had resigned during the crisis. Following a runoff election on October 1, the number of Shi'ite deputies in the parliament was reduced to 8 out of a total of 40. All were pro-government. (LOUAY BAHRY)

BANGLADESH

Area: 147,570 sq km (56,977 sq mi)
Population (2011 est.): 142,875,000
Capital: Dhaka
Head of state: President Zillur Rahman
Head of government: Prime Minister Sheikh Hasina Wazed (Wajed)

The major news in Bangladesh in 2011 concerned the continued efforts to bring to trial those Islamist elements that were involved in atrocities (including genocide, murder, and torture) that were committed some 40 years earlier during the country's fight for independence in 1971 from Pakistan. In November 2011 the first defendant, Delwar Hossain Sayeede (the senior leader of the opposition party Jama'at-i Islami), went on trial, charged with crimes against humanity. Those accused of having committed war crimes during the bloody nine-month struggle for independence (in which as many as three million people were killed), included six others: four suspects belonging to the Jama'at-i and two members of the main opposition Bangladesh Nationalist Party. Observers, however, voiced concerns about whether international standards for fairness were being met. Human Rights Watch disclosed that the tribunal had been established in 2010 without UN participation. Though the leading prosecutor maintained that the trial would be impartial and that it would not entail "political ax-grinding," questions were raised about the vetting process for the prosecutors, judges, and chairman of the tribunal. Analysts warned that political tensions could escalate unless the trials were seen as unquestionably fair.

Bangladesh was affected monetarily in the wake of the Arab Spring revolts that swept across the Middle East. The country depended heavily on remittances from labourers working in that region, especially Saudi Arabia. Some two-thirds of Bangladesh's recorded remittances were derived from countries in the Middle East, and they accounted for 12% of Bangladesh's GDP. Fortunately, the country's textile industry was booming, with an annual increase of 40% recorded in the previous eight months to March, and this $14 billion rise helped to offset the revenue lost by the decline in remittances.

In March Bangladesh Bank removed bank executive Muhammad Yunus (who in 2006 had won the Nobel Prize for Peace) as managing director of the microfinance Grameen Bank, which he had founded in 1976 and headed for more than three decades. Yunus, who challenged the decision, appealed to the Bangladesh High Court, which ruled that the central Bangladesh Bank was within its rights to remove him. Though his dismissal was reportedly due to his age (he had turned 60 in 2000, the mandatory retirement age in Bangladesh for bankers), observers believed that he had probably run afoul of the government. Yunus appealed to the Supreme Court, which rejected his petition on May 5.

Following the implementation of a new government policy that allowed women to inherit equally with men, hard-line Islamist protesters on April 4 staged a general strike that shuttered businesses and schools. The demonstrators demanded that the policy be rescinded and that Islamic law be adopted. The previous day a student had been killed and some 25 protesters injured in a violent encounter with the police.

In July a three-day joint census was conducted for the first time of Indian enclaves within Bangladesh and Bangladeshi enclaves within India. The purpose of the census was to seek a solution for the difficulties faced by these orphaned populations.

(KAREN SPARKS)

BARBADOS

Area: 430 sq km (166 sq mi)
Population (2011 est.): 277,000
Capital: Bridgetown
Head of state: Queen Elizabeth II, represented by Governors-General Sir Clifford Husbands and, from November 1, Elliot Belgrave (acting)
Head of government: Prime Minister Freundel Stuart

Barbados was criticized in a January 2011 report from the Organisation for Economic Co-operation and Development's Global Forum on Transparency and Exchange of Information for Tax Purposes for allegedly having failed to share full details on tax matters with international partners. It was urged to "remove any impediments or uncertainties" in this regard, and in February the government indicated that it would comply with the request. In March, however, the minister of finance and economic affairs, Chris Sinckler, declared that Barbados would not "roll over and play dead" in the face of the OECD's efforts to portray the country as an "uncooperative" offshore tax jurisdiction.

Barbados obtained a $10 million loan from the Inter-American Development Bank in February to establish an Energy Smart Fund. The country—already a leader in renewable energy in the Caribbean through its widespread use of solar energy in water heating—planned to use the funds for initiatives in photovoltaics and energy efficiency.

In June, Moody's Investors Service downgraded Barbados's domestic currency debt rating to the lowest investment-grade level, citing the erosion of what had been its primary credit strength, a large captive market for domestic currency government paper. Also in June, Prime Minister Freundel

Stuart visited China. The two countries agreed to increase cooperation on issues such as climate change, trade, and infrastructure development.

(DAVID RENWICK)

BELARUS

Area: 207,595 sq km (80,153 sq mi)
Population (2011 est.): 9,472,000
Capital: Minsk
Head of state and government: President Alyaksandr Lukashenka, assisted by Prime Minister Mikhail Myasnikovich

Belarus experienced a difficult year in 2011 as it dealt with spiraling inflation, a currency crisis, shortages of basic products, and heightened international criticism of the country's record on human rights. The Belarusian economy reportedly grew by 8% from January to September, and industrial production rose by 10.6%. Inflation, however, skyrocketed by 75% over that same period. In March a shortage of reserves forced the government to seek from Russia and the Eurasian Economic Community's Anti-Crisis Fund $3 billion in loans. A request to the IMF in June for $8 billion was met with the demand that the Belarusian government cut spending and raise interest rates as a precursor to any bailout negotiations. On September 19 China agreed to loan Belarus $1 billion, and additional funds were sought through year's end. An independent survey conducted in December reported that 54% of Belarusians blamed Pres. Alyaksandr Lukashenka for the country's economic crisis, and his personal approval rating dropped from over 50% in December 2010 to 24.9%.

In May, Russian Finance Minister Aleksey Kudrin stated that Belarus needed to sell $7.5 billion in state assets to receive further Russian loans. Prime Minister Mikhail Myasnikovich announced in July that 250 enterprises would be privatized by the end of the year, mainly in the light-industry and housing sectors.

Excessive state expenditure during the 2010 presidential elections also weakened the national currency, the Belarusian ruble. On May 24 the national bank devalued it from 3,155 rubles to 4,930 rubles against the dollar, and then in September the ruble was devalued to 8,600 rubles per dollar.

Reverberations of the widely disputed December 2010 elections continued into 2011. The EU expanded its travel ban on Belarusian officials in January, and in May the government imposed prison sentences on former presidential candidates Andrei Sannikau, Dzmitry Vus, and Mikalay Statkevich. Vus was unexpectedly released on October 1, one day after EU officials had appealed for the release of Belarus's political prisoners. Former candidate Ales Mikhalevich had fled to the Czech Republic after his conditional release in March, and he reported the widespread use of torture in the Minsk detention centre.

In August the United States imposed sanctions on four Belarusian state-owned enterprises in an effort to pressure Lukashenka into releasing imprisoned political activists. Later that month, after a clandestine meeting with Bulgarian Foreign Minister Nikolai Mladenov, Lukashenka bowed to Western influence and freed a handful of prisoners. Fourteen people were killed and more than 200 injured on April 11 when a bomb exploded at Minsk's busiest metro station during the evening rush hour. Two men were charged with the crime, and authorities linked one of them to prior bomb attacks in Minsk and Vitsyebsk.

The summer was marked by youth protests organized through social media and dubbed a "revolution by social network." The government responded by blocking the organizer's Web sites, and a protest rally on October 8 was undermined by mass arrests of potential participants the day prior to the event.

(DAVID R. MARPLES)

BELGIUM

Area: 30,528 sq km (11,787 sq mi)
Population (2011 est.): 10,971,000
Capital: Brussels
Head of state: King Albert II
Head of government: Prime Ministers Yves Leterme (acting) and, from December 6, Elio Di Rupo

Belgium was locked in political stalemate throughout almost the whole of 2011 as repeated efforts to form a coalition government came to naught. The deadlock was finally broken on December 6, when the Francophone Socialist Party leader, Elio Di Rupo, was sworn in as prime minister at the head of a six-party coalition of Dutch- and French-speaking Socialists, Christian Democrats, and Liberals. Di Rupo was the first premier from Belgium's French-speaking community since 1979.

The breakthrough was only achieved after a succession of senior politicians, appointed by King Albert II, had earlier failed in numerous attempts since the June 13, 2010, general election to forge an agreement between different political parties. The departure in the summer from the government negotiations of the strongly nationalist New Flemish Alliance, the largest party in Flanders, helped to end the stalemate. In all, it took 541 days to form the coalition, which earned Belgium an unwelcome designation in the Guinness World Records as the country without a government for the longest period in peacetime, easily eclipsing the 207-day record set by the Netherlands in 1977.

The 177-page agreement between the government parties involved one of the largest transfers of financial and political power from the federal level to the country's three regions. It also provided

Geert Vanden Wijngaert/AP

In October, Elio Di Rupo (left), the leader of Belgium's French-speaking Socialist Party, chats with Wouter Beke (centre) of the Flemish Christian Democrats and Laurette Onkelinx (right) of the Francophone Socialists during negotiations to form a coalition government. An agreement was reached in December after nearly 18 months of talks, and Di Rupo was sworn in as prime minister.

a solution to the long-running dispute in the large Brussel-Halle-Vilvoorde constituency on the edge of the capital to the satisfaction of both linguistic groups and introduced savings of €11.3 billion (€1 = about $1.35) in the 2012 national budget.

While the political maneuvers continued, the country was led by a caretaker government under Prime Minister Yves Leterme, whose previous coalition had collapsed in April 2010. Leterme's administration could manage only day-to-day business and did not have the powers to introduce the structural reforms and budget cuts widely considered necessary. Leterme confirmed that he would leave domestic politics when he announced in September that he would become deputy secretary-general of the Organisation for Economic Co-operation and Development in Paris.

While Belgium was in better economic health than many other euro-zone members, the political stagnation was having an effect. The European Commission, using new budget rules, warned in November that the country would face heavy fines if public spending was not brought under control. On November 25 the ratings agency Standard & Poor's had downgraded Belgium's credit from AA+ to AA, raising the cost of government borrowing.

In October the Franco-Belgian bank Dexia, once a leading lender to local authorities, became the first European bank to fall victim to the euro crisis after having been heavily exposed to Greek sovereign debt. The Belgian government agreed to guarantee 60.5% of the €90 billion rescue plan, which included splitting the bank's operations, while France shouldered 36.5% and Luxembourg backed 3%.

In sports, runner Kevin Borlée, the winner of the 400-m gold medal at the 2010 European championships, earned a bronze at the same distance at the 2011 IAAF world championships. His twin brother, Jonathan, finished in fifth place. Tennis star Kim Clijsters won the Australian Open in January and briefly regained the world number one ranking, but she was forced to cut her season short in August after having sustained several injuries.

One of Belgium's most prominent Flemish Liberal politicians, Willy De Clercq—a former deputy prime minister, European commissioner (1985–89), and member (1989–2007) of the European Parliament—died on October 28 at the age of 84. A little more than a month earlier, Gerard Brackx (age 80), a pioneer of Belgium tourism who founded Jetair in 1971, had died in Ostend. (RORY WATSON)

BELIZE

Area: 22,965 sq km (8,867 sq mi)
Population (2011 est.): 322,000
Capital: Belmopan
Head of state: Queen Elizabeth II, represented by Governor-General Sir Colville Young
Head of government: Prime Minister Dean Barrow

Belize's economic growth between January and June 2011 edged up to 2.8%, compared with 2.2% in the same period in 2010. Despite a strong showing in the wholesale and retail trade (8.4%) and manufacturing (6.5%) sectors, a decline in construction (16.3%) and agriculture (4.5%) dampened the overall activity. The critical agricultural sector (especially the banana and sugarcane crops) was impacted by extreme weather and fiscal problems.

After Belize Electricity Ltd. announced that it was insolvent, the government expropriated the company on June 20. The Court of Appeals then ruled that the government's 2009 takeover of Belize Telemedia Ltd. was unconstitutional, but the government renationalized Telemedia. It then introduced in the legislature a controversial ninth amendment to the constitution to give it majority ownership of public utilities. Meanwhile, the cabinet proposed and then abandoned an eighth amendment, which included, inter alia, preventive detention to combat a surge in violent crimes. The ninth (renamed eighth) amendment passed and was enacted in late October.

Belizeans began a week of mourning following the death on September 19 of the 92-year-old Right Honourable George Cadle Price, who is considered Father of the Nation and had been awarded (2000) the National Hero of Belize gold medal. He served as first minister (1961–64), premier (1964–81), prime minister (1981–84 and 1989–93), and leader (1956–96) of the People's United Party. (HERMAN J. BYRD)

BENIN

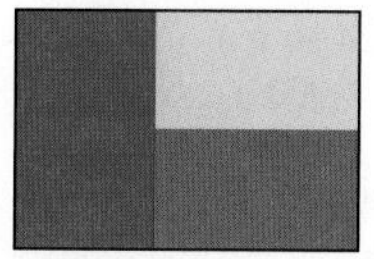

Area: 114,763 sq km (44,310 sq mi)
Population (2011 est.): 9,100,000
Capital: Porto-Novo (executive and ministerial offices remain in Cotonou)
Head of state and government: President Thomas Yayi Boni, assisted from May 28 by Prime Minister Pascal Koupaki

Following widespread protests over the voter-registration process, and international calls for delay, Benin's Constitutional Court twice postponed the 2011 presidential election. Opposition parties accused the National Electoral Commission of not having issued more than one million voter cards for an electorate estimated at 4.5 million. When the election was held, on March 13, Pres. Thomas Yayi Boni easily won his second term, taking 53% of the vote. Adrien Houngbédji came in second, with 36% of the vote. Houngbédji challenged the result, claiming that fraud had robbed him of his victory. On March 24, police in Cotonou used tear gas to drive off hundreds of Houngbédji's youthful supporters. The Constitutional Court rejected all opposition appeals and declared Yayi the undisputed winner. He was sworn in on April 6. Parliamentary elections held in April gave parties supporting the president an absolute majority, taking 52 of the 83 seats.

The severe floods of October 2010, which had a devastating effect on the country's always fragile economy, threatened to cause further damage in 2011 as the Ouémé River began rising to record levels again in August. Although the U.S. forgave $460 million in Benin's debt and the IMF approved a $16.9 million aid package, the economy remained weak and overdependent on its main cash crop, cotton.

The National Assembly voted on August 18 to ratify an international covenant calling for the abolition of the death penalty. If approved by Yayi, Benin would be the 74th signatory to the treaty. (NANCY ELLEN LAWLER)

BHUTAN

Area: 38,394 sq km (14,824 sq mi)
Population (2011 est.): 701,000
Capital: Thimphu
Head of state: Druk Gyalpo (King) Jigme Khesar Namgyal Wangchuk
Head of government: Prime Minister Lyonchen Jigmi Thinley

In 2011 Bhutan completed the transformation of its political process, continuing with reforms initiated by the abdication of King Jigme Singye Wangchuck in 2006 and the promulgation of a new constitution in 2008. The country's first local government elections were conducted on July 27. Another important national event was the marriage on October 13 of King Jigme Khesar Namgyal Wangchuk to Jetsun Pema, who was the daughter of an airline pilot with distant royal connections. (*See* photograph on page 7.)

Bhutan continued to enjoy robust economic growth in 2011. In his annual report to the parliament in July, Prime Minister Lyonchen Jigmi Thinley predicted that Bhutan would continue to grow by 9–10% annually until 2015. Sustaining that high rate, however, was dependent on Bhutan's increasing hydroelectric generating capacity to 10,000 MW by 2020, with most of that power to be exported.

Little progress was made on the issue of Bhutanese refugees of Nepalese origin in Nepal. By 2011 nearly half of the roughly 108,000 who fled to Nepal in the early 1990s had been resettled in third countries, and the original seven refugee camps had been largely consolidated into two. Bilateral talks, however, remained stalled after eight years, despite Prime Minister Thinley's offer in 2011 to resume them. In March the king paid an official visit to Bangladesh. On September 18 an earthquake of magnitude 6.9 in the Bhutan-India border region killed one person in Bhutan and damaged thousands of structures.

(KESHAB POUDEL)

BOLIVIA

Area: 1,098,581 sq km (424,164 sq mi)
Population (2011 est.): 10,088,000
Capitals: La Paz (administrative); Sucre (constitutional)
Head of state and government: President Evo Morales Ayma

Pres. Evo Morales faced growing hostility in 2011 from Bolivia's poor indigenous majority (the very people who had brought him to power) over proposed changes to fiscal and development programs. Late in 2010 the government had announced plans to cut gasoline subsidies, saying this action was necessary to stimulate investment and stem the smuggling of cheap fuel to neighbouring countries. Street protests and a strike by bus drivers erupted in response to a more than 70% increase in gas prices, and as 2011 dawned, Morales said that the cuts instead would be phased in over time. In the Amazon basin Morales faced criticism for plans to dam pristine rivers for hydroelectric projects and to allow petroleum exploration in the rainforest. A two-month-long protest forced him to cancel a proposed Brazil-financed road through indigenous territory. Nevertheless, millions of Bolivians continued to benefit from wealth redistribution carried out by Morales's administration, and Morales accused his critics of exaggerating economic problems and opposing development of any kind.

Having earlier nationalized many foreign oil operations, Morales softened his approach to international firms, offering production and investment incentives in an attempt to boost oil and gas output. Petrobras (the Brazilian state petroleum company) and the Argentine unit of Spain's Repsol-YPF said that they would begin exploration in six new fields. Morales said that his government would provide significant new investment in the industry. Morales also announced that a major discovery by the French company Total would increase proven gas reserves by 30%.

Tension with the U.S. over the illegal cocaine trade resurfaced in 2011. René Sanabria Oropeza, an official in the Interior Ministry and the former head of Bolivian antinarcotics efforts, was arrested in Panama in February and sent to Miami, where he pleaded guilty to drug-smuggling charges. The U.S. Drug Enforcement Administration (DEA) said that he had accepted $250,000 in return for having allowed more than 100 kg (220 lb) of cocaine to be shipped to the U.S. In November, however, the two countries restored diplomatic relations, which had been suspended in 2008. Meanwhile, UN drug-control officials maintained that illegal coca

In the face of an international ban supported by the United States, an indigenous Bolivian woman chews coca leaves at a January 26 gathering outside the U.S. embassy in La Paz aimed at promoting the cultural practice.

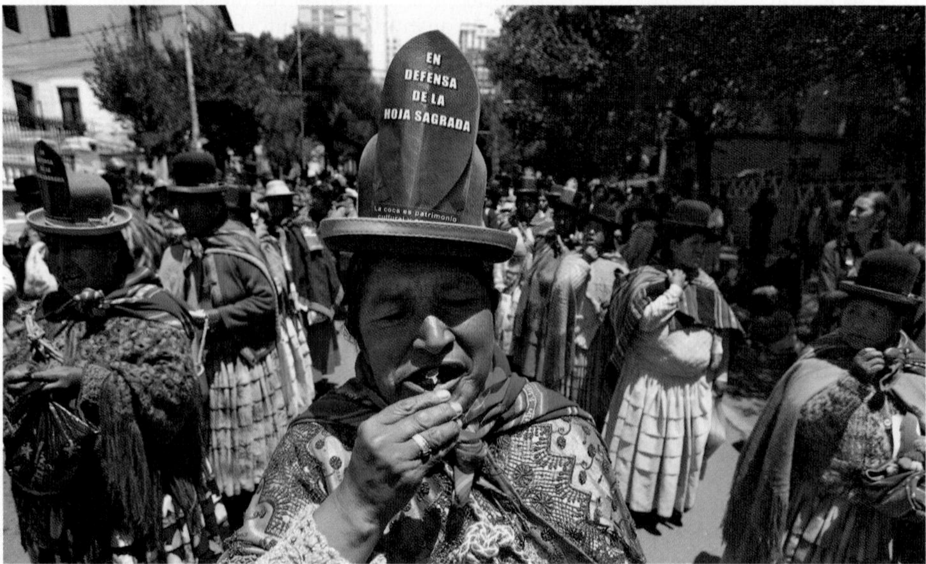

Juan Karita/AP

growing in Bolivia had increased by 22% since 2008, when Bolivia expelled the DEA. In August five former military commanders and two former cabinet ministers were convicted of having committed genocide in 2003 when troops fired on antigovernment protesters, killing more than 60 people.

Prices for quinoa, an Andean plant rich in nutrients, rose in response to increased demand among health-conscious North Americans and Europeans, pushing it beyond the means of many indigenous Bolivians. Some worried about the effect on the diet of those Bolivians who substituted rice and noodles for the traditional food. On the environmental front, atmospheric warming caused continued melting of glaciers near La Paz, exposing the well-preserved remains of air-crash victims and mountain climbers. The government planned to grant legal rights to Pachamama (Mother Earth), including the rights to clean water, clean air, undisturbed life cycles, and freedom from disturbance by large development projects. (PAUL KNOX)

BOSNIA AND HERZEGOVINA

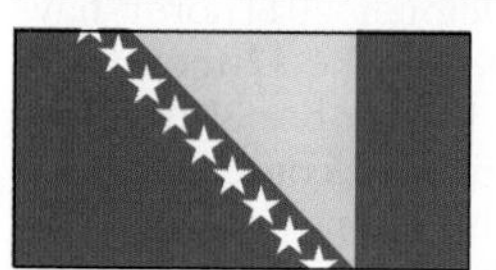

Area: 51,209 sq km (19,772 sq mi)
Population (2011 est.): 3,843,000
Capital: Sarajevo
Heads of state: Nominally a tripartite (Serb, Croat, Bosniak [Bosnian Muslim]) presidency with a chair that rotates every eight months; members in 2011 were Nebojsa Radmanovic (Serb; chairman until July 10), Zeljko Komsic (Croat; chairman from July 10), and Bakir Izetbegovic (Bosniak). Final authority resides in the Office of the High Representative and EU Special Representative, Valentin Inzko (Austria)
Head of government: Prime Minister Nikola Spiric

The government of Bosnia and Herzegovina was deadlocked throughout 2011 as the country's six principal political parties failed until year-end to reach an agreement on the formation of the national government in the wake of the October 2010 general election. The resultant paralysis represented the country's longest political crisis since the end of the four-year war in 1995. In the meantime, the acting government was both unwilling and unable to institute the reforms necessary to position Bosnia for entry into the EU. On December 28 the parties ended the 15-month stalemate by agreeing to form a coalition government, with Croat Vjekoslav Bevanda at its head, that would take power in January 2012.

The lack of compromise between political parties within the country's two entities—the Bosniak-Croat Federation and Republika Srpska (RS)—for several years had retarded progress toward European integration. International observers expressed concern that a renewal of conflict was impending, and in May the high representative in Bosnia, Valentin Inzko, reported to the UN Security Council that Bosnia was on the "brink of collapse." In its annual progress report on Bosnia and Herzegovina, the European Commission noted "little progress" in reforms necessary for entry to the EU. On the other hand, Bosniaks gained a measure of closure in May when Bosnian Serb military commander Ratko Mladic, the suspected mastermind of the Srebrenica massacre, was apprehended after a decade at large.

In an effort to avert losing €96 million ($132 million) in aid, the acting government in October agreed to implement a list of EU-stipulated steps toward reform of public administration, the judiciary, and infrastructure. More than €8 million ($11 million) was earmarked for demining and assistance to refugees of the 1992–95 war. Also in October the Bosnian parliament began procedures to amend the constitution regarding discrimination against minorities, such as Jews and Roma (Gypsies), seeking elected office.

The economy showed subdued and uneven growth. Unemployment continued to hover at about 43%, and the International Labour Organization reported an unemployment rate of 57.9% among Bosnia's youths 15–24 years of age. Observers iterated concerns regarding the lack of administrative and legal procedures aimed at confronting widespread corruption and inflammatory nationalist rhetoric. During the first nine months of 2011, industrial production grew significantly in the RS but only slightly in the Federation, by 6.8% and 1.8%, respectively. Overall, the economy was projected to grow nearly 2.8%, and Bosnia's central bank expected the economy to show further improvement in 2012.

The Royal Dutch/Shell Group and the federation agreed upon a two-year research project on fossil-fuel exploration. The RS signed similar agreements with Russia's state-owned Zarubezhneft and Serbia's NIS (majority-owned by Russia's Gazprom). Geologists estimated potential oil reserves in Bosnia, Serbia, and Croatia at about 70 million bbl apiece.

(MILAN ANDREJEVICH)

BOTSWANA

Area: 581,730 sq km (224,607 sq mi)
Population (2011 est.): 2,033,000
Capital: Gaborone
Head of state and government: President Ian Khama

In 2011 Botswana's economy was boosted by the recovery of the world diamond market in 2010. After dwindling by 4.9% in 2009, GDP grew by 7.2% in 2010, although growth was predicted to be lower for 2011. A two-month nationwide strike by public servants, including teachers, after a three-year pay freeze, was ended in May when the government conceded a 3% salary raise.

On September 16 the government signed a 10-year contract by which De Beers would transfer its worldwide rough diamond collection and sales operations from London to Gaborone by the end of 2013. De Beers also agreed that the government could sell 10% of local diamond production on the world free market.

In January an appeals court affirmed the right of Bushmen in the Central Kalahari Game Reserve to reopen wells around Mothomelo, with financial assistance from a company that planned to open a diamond mine there. In August four security servicemen were convicted of the "murder with extenuating circumstances" of alleged criminal mastermind John Kalafatis in May 2009. Corruption charges against Ndelu Seretse, who resigned from the cabinet as minister of defense, justice, and security in 2010, were dropped in October 2011.

Relations with South Africa were highlighted by the accusation by Julius Malema, leader of South Africa's ANC Youth League, that Botswana's president was the "puppet" of U.S. imperialism. Botswana was the first African state to cut ties with the Qaddafi

Libyan government during that country's revolution. Relations with Zimbabwe continued to improve, with the export of cattle from Botswana in August reviving meat production at Bulawayo's state slaughterhouse.

(NEIL PARSONS)

BRAZIL

Area: 8,514,877 sq km (3,287,612 sq mi)
Population (2011 est.): 192,813,000
Capital: Brasília
Head of state and government: President Dilma Rousseff

On Jan. 1, 2011, Dilma Rousseff, a former political prisoner who had been persecuted by the military regime (1964–88), was sworn in as the first woman president of Brazil. She outlined a domestic agenda that focused on the maintenance of economic stability, poverty eradication, political and tax reform, improvement in the quality of government spending, job creation, and an increase in prosperity and wages. She articulated a foreign policy that stressed human rights, multilateralism, peace, and nonintervention. On August 2 President Rousseff launched a new industrial policy, "Larger Brazil," that included "buy Brazilian" provisions and tax cuts for industry. On its way through Congress but not yet passed by the year's end was the new forestry code that sought to address deforestation. A landmark law that established a truth commission to investigate the disappearances and human rights abuses during military rule was signed by Rousseff on November 18.

Throughout 2011 the Rousseff administration faced accusations of corruption. The first and most important of these surfaced in mid-May when the media reported that Chief of Staff Antonio Palocci's consulting company had profited substantially from government decisions that favoured its clients. Palocci resigned on June 7, and Rousseff immediately replaced him with female Sen. Gleisi Hoffmann of Paraná state and the Workers' Party (PT). Evidence of overinvoicing for railroad and highway contracts resulted in wholesale changes at the Transport Ministry in late June and July, most notably the resignation of Transport Minister Alfredo Nascimento on June 24.

By the end of 2011, investigations into multiple allegations of corruption and the potential of congressional inquiries had led to the resignation of five cabinet ministers, all holdovers from the administration of Luiz Inácio Lula da Silva ("Lula"), of which Rousseff had been the chief of staff. In addition, the minister of defense stepped down because of misgivings with the government's direction. The constant stream of allegations and evidence sparked protests on September 7 (Brazilian Independence Day) and October 12 (the feast day of Brazil's patron saint, Our Lady of Aparecida) in dozens of cities—including Brasília, Rio de Janeiro, and São Paulo—by tens of thousands of Brazilians, led by the Movement Against Corruption.

The exit of members of Rousseff's cabinet under clouds of corruption was accompanied by a series of judicial decisions that highlighted the dysfunction of the judiciary and the impunity of those accused of certain crimes. On March 23 the Supreme Court voted 6 to 5 to nullify the application of the 2010 Clean Slate Law to the results of the October 2010 elections, having ruled that the law needed to have been in effect for at least a year prior to the election. By a vote of 3–2, on June 7 the 5th Chamber of the Superior Federal Appeals Court overturned the 10-year jail sentence for bribery imposed on investment banker Daniel Dantas by Judge Fausto de Sanctis. Moreover, in September the use of illegal wiretaps and search and seizures were cited by the 6th Chamber of the Superior Federal Appeals Court as it annulled federal police investigations of the son of the Senate president and former president of the republic, José Sarney.

In advance of the mayoral elections in 2012, a major political realignment began with the announcement of the founding of the Party of Social Democracy (PSD) in Salvador (Bahia) and São Paulo on March 20 and 21, respectively. Led by São Paulo Mayor Gilberto Kassab, the PSD attracted a migration of more than 600 mayors, 50 federal deputies, and several prominent politicians. On October 29 Lula was diagnosed with cancer of the larynx and immediately began treatment.

Concerns about security and violence were addressed in Rio de Janeiro, the future site of the 2014 association football (soccer) World Cup final and the 2016 Summer Olympic Games. In June and November, respectively, state police, supported by the armed forces, pacified Mangueira and Roçinha, two major favelas (slums) that had been controlled by drug traffickers. Prior to the Roçinha operation, police arrested prominent drug kingpin Antonio Bonfim Lopes. Despite these actions, Rio de Janeiro continued to be plagued by high-profile violence. On April 6 in the Rio de Janeiro suburb of Realengo, a 23-year-old gunman entered a school and killed 12 people, injured dozens of others, and was wounded by police before he turned a gun on himself. On August 12 Patricia Acioli, a federal judge who was instrumental in handing down stiff sentences to drug traffickers and corrupt police, was found murdered. On September 27 State Police Lieut. Col. Claudio Luiz de Oliveira, implicated in organizing the Acioli execution, turned himself in to authorities. Torrential rains in early January flooded towns in Rio de Janeiro state and created mud slides that killed more than 750 people, left more than 10,000 people homeless, and caused billions of dollars in damage.

The Brazilian economy cooled down in 2011. It grew 3.7% in the 12 months that ended in October 2011 after having soared 7.6% over the 12-month period that ended in October 2010. Measured by the expanded consumer price index (IPCA), inflation over the 12-month period that ended in November 2011 reached 6.64% to exceed the federal government's inflation target of 6.5%. Because the high price of commodities such as sugar and ethanol contributed to inflationary pressures, on April 28 ethanol was subjected to price controls by the National Petroleum Agency. President Rousseff subsequently ordered the required levels of ethanol in Brazilian gasoline to be reduced from 25% to 20%. Later the government reduced federal taxes on imported and domestic petroleum products by more than 15% to stabilize prices, and state-owned Petrobrás reduced the price of gas by 18.6%, effective in November. On August 20, after five successive rate increases from January through July, the central bank's Open Market Committee decreased the overnight discount rate (SELIC rate) at which banks could borrow from the central bank from 12.5% to 12%. By the end of the year, the SELIC rate was down to 11%, with the likelihood of further reductions to come. Brazil's GDP in 2010 was $2.2 trillion.

(JOHN CHARLES CUTTINO)

BRUNEI

Area: 5,765 sq km (2,226 sq mi)
Population (2011 est.): 422,000
Capital: Bandar Seri Begawan
Head of state and government: Sultan and Prime Minister Sir Haji Hassanal Bolkiah Mu'izzaddin Waddaulah

In 2011 Brunei and Malaysia continued to work on details of a joint resource-exploitation project in the South China Sea that resulted from the 2010 settlement of a long-standing border dispute between the two countries. Brunei retained sovereign rights over two oil-rich areas of the seabed located along the maritime boundary between the two countries. In return, Brunei entered into a 40-year production-sharing agreement with Malaysia. The project was expected to generate billions of dollars for each country.

The 2011 Arab Spring popular agitations against authoritarian regimes in the Middle East raised concerns in Brunei. A major state-sponsored conference was held in May on the national ideology—Malay Islamic Monarchy (MIB)—to reinforce its value as a bulwark against political ideas from abroad deemed potentially subversive.

In late May and early June, Brunei staged a 50th-anniversary celebration of the founding of Royal Brunei Armed Forces that included an international tattoo (performances by military bands), and it hosted the third Bridex (Brunei military exposition) in July; both events attracted large local and international audiences. An unprecedented five senior military officers received promotions to the rank of brigadier general, one of whom, Pehin Tawih bin Abdullah, was appointed to the newly created post of deputy commander of the armed forces.

Brunei Shell Petroleum (BSP—50% owned by Royal Dutch Shell PLC) announced a significant new oil discovery in the coastal waters about 100 km (60 mi) offshore. The water depth there was approximately 1,000 m (3,300 ft), which made those hydrocarbon reserves the deepest identified to date by BSP in the Brunei region.

(B.A. HUSSAINMIYA)

BULGARIA

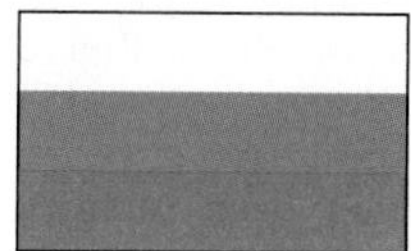

Area: 111,002 sq km (42,858 sq mi)
Population (2011 est.): 7,333,000
Capital: Sofia
Head of state: President Georgi Parvanov
Head of government: Prime Minister Boiko Borisov

Bulgaria experienced a year of financial stability in 2011. In December its annual economic growth was projected at 1.9%, a healthier rate than those of many other members of the European Union. Despite no-confidence votes and documents released by the Web site WikiLeaks that linked Prime Minister Boiko Borisov to special interests in Russia, his cabinet successfully navigated the backlash of the global financial crisis with its fiscally conservative policy. Voters voiced their support for the ruling party by electing as president Rosen Plevneliev, a former minister in Borisov's cabinet, in an October runoff. He would assume the office in January 2012. The budget deficit shrank by 1.3%, and Moody's upgraded Bulgaria's credit rating to Baa2 (a low-end investment-grade rating). The stock exchange in Sofia, which went public in December 2010, posted impressive gains throughout the first half of 2011. By August, however, declining markets in the U.S. and Europe had sent the SOFIX, the bourse's main index, plunging. On a more positive note, tourism grew at 4.5% and was on track to generate record revenues of €2.7 billion.

While these developments were viewed as positive, Bulgaria's economic competitiveness did not improve. The country's weak labour market persisted, with 60% of unemployed workers having looked for a job for more than a year. At the same time, labour productivity remained among the lowest in Europe, and employers reported that talent was hard to find.

In the international arena, Bulgaria's demands upon its European peers remained largely unmet. Bulgaria and Romania were denied entry into Europe's "borderless" Schengen area, despite the two countries' having met the technical requirements for accession. Bulgarian-Russian relations were exposed to additional tension over the year as the Burgas-Alexandroupolis pipeline project was put on hold by the Russian oil-pipeline monopoly Transneft after Bulgaria refused to deliver its promised investment in response to the plan's environmental instability. The Bulgarian government also temporarily froze the building of a nuclear plant at Belene because of allegations that the Russian state-owned Rosatom had not provided sufficient documentation on plant equipment environmental-security checks.

In the world of sports, Tzvetana Pironkova reached the women's singles quarterfinals of the Wimbledon Championships, while Grigor Dimitrov became the country's highest-ranked male tennis player in history.

(IVA TEIXEIRA; BORIS YOVCHEV)

In Sofia, Bulg., Rosen Plevneliev (left) and Margarita Popova—both of whom had served as ministers in the ruling centre-right government—exalt upon their election on October 30 as Bulgaria's president and vice president, respectively.

Stoyan Nenov—Reuters/Landov

BURKINA FASO

Area: 270,764 sq km (104,543 sq mi)
Population (2011 est.): 16,968,000
Capital: Ouagadougou
Head of state: President Blaise Compaoré
Head of government: Prime Ministers Tertius Zongo and, from April 18, Luc Adolphe Tiao

Though Pres. Blaise Compaoré claimed victory in the Burkina Faso 2010 presidential elections, a tide of demonstrations and strikes swept the country throughout much of 2011. In late February demonstrators demanded the president's ouster. Anger over the unexplained death on February 20 of student leader Justin Zongo while under arrest led to violent clashes between security forces and students, resulting in five deaths in Koudougou. The unrest spread quickly to the entire country. Soldiers mutinied on April 14 in Ouagadougou, where they looted shops and markets for three nights. President Compaoré responded by putting the city under curfew; firing his government, including the commander of the army; and naming himself defense minister. There were similar incidents by troops in Pô and Bobo-Dioulasso. On April 18 a new government was formed, headed by Prime Minister Luc Adolphe Tiao.

Unrest in the capital by the police and others at the end of April was attributed to low wages and huge increases in the price of basic foodstuffs. In May the government lowered the price of rice, cooking oil, and sugar, and cotton producers saw a reduction in the price of seeds. On August 23, three policemen were convicted of having fatally beaten Zongo; two were given 10-year prison sentences, and the other received 8 years. (NANCY ELLEN LAWLER)

BURUNDI

Area: 27,816 sq km (10,740 sq mi)
Population (2011 est.): 8,575,000
Capital: Bujumbura
Head of state and government: President Pierre Nkurunziza

After the election boycotts and intermittent violence surrounding the uncontested reelection of Pres. Pierre Nkurunziza in 2010, Burundi struggled to secure its fragile stability and peace during 2011. Concerns over security were heightened amid ongoing grenade attacks as well as threats from the al-Qaeda-linked Somalian militant group al-Shabaab, owing to Burundi's deployment of thousands of troops as part of the African Union's peacekeeping force in Mogadishu, Som. Sporadic grenade attacks that had started after the 2010 elections continued into 2011 with a New Year's Day assault in the capital, Bujumbura, that left three dead. As the year progressed, a spate of grenade and gun attacks perpetrated by men in police uniforms flared up throughout Burundi. International concern was raised in June over the alleged extrajudicial killings and cases of torture carried out against opposition parties by the ruling National Council for the Defense of Democracy–Forces for the Defense of Democracy (CNDD-FDD). Agathon Rwasa, the self-exiled leader of the opposition National Liberation Forces (FNL), maintained in September that since January 169 members of the FNL had gone missing, 20 of whom were arrested and later found dead.

In February Burundi signed the River Nile Cooperative Framework Agreement, a multilateral initiative involving the securing of water resources by countries in the Nile basin to enable hydropower projects and the construction of dams and to safeguard agriculture in the region. More than 90% of Burundians depended on agricultural food production for their livelihoods.

Aid workers raised concerns over the alarming rise in hunger, malnutrition, and food insecurity in several provinces. Outbreaks of cholera, which infected more than 400 and killed 4 in Bujumbura and several surrounding provinces, compounded worries over a growing crisis. Nearly 60% of Burundians continued to face food insecurity due to drought, high food prices, land scarcity, and weather phenomena, such as La Niña.

The British government announced that by 2016 it would cut all development aid to Burundi, which was ranked by the World Bank as the world's second poorest country. Since the genocide in the 1990s and the ensuing 13-year civil war, Burundi had been struggling to rebuild and develop its society and infrastructure.

(MARY EBELING)

CAMBODIA

Area: 181,035 sq km (69,898 sq mi)
Population (2011 est.): 14,702,000
Capital: Phnom Penh
Head of state: King Norodom Sihamoni
Head of government: Prime Minister Hun Sen

Cambodia and Thailand made progress near the end of 2010 in border-dispute negotiations, but tensions between the two countries resurged in 2011 after a group of nationalist Thai politicians crossed the border into Cambodia and were arrested on Dec. 29, 2010; two remained in prison after the others were released. A subsequent troop buildup led in February to four days of fighting in the disputed area near the ancient temple of Preah Vihear, with at least 11 soldiers killed. The case was discussed in the UN Security Council and within the Association of Southeast Asian Nations. Attempts to broker a cease-fire and bring in Indonesian observers failed, and more fighting broke out in late April at a border site about 150 km (95 mi) southwest of Preah Vihear, near two other ancient temples; at least 15 were killed. On April 28, during the fighting, Cambodia appealed to the International Court of Justice to interpret its 1962 ruling on Preah Vihear in light of the latest conflict. The court's initial judgment, in July, called for the creation of a provisional demilitarized zone. Both sides complied, but agreement on troop withdrawal was not reached until December. In addition, optimism rose after Yingluck Shinawatra (*see* BIOGRAPHIES) became the new Thai prime minister in July and visited Phnom Penh in September. During talks, she and Cambodian Prime Minister Hun Sen agreed to revive bilateral relations.

The Khmer Rouge Tribunal (known officially as the Extraordinary Chambers in the Courts of Cambodia [ECCC]) reached another milestone on June 27 with the start of the joint trial of Khieu Samphan, Nuon Chea, Ieng Sary, and Ieng Thirith, the surviving leaders most identified in the public mind with the brutal 1975–79 regime. Nevertheless, there were acrimonious internal disputes about the future of

Heng Sinith/AP

A Cambodian soldier stands at the ancient Preah Vihear temple on February 8, following four days of nearby skirmishes between Cambodia and Thailand over their disputed border.

two additional cases—one believed to involve Khmer Rouge military leaders and another focused on those thought to be responsible for inhuman conditions at a dam-construction site—after ECCC judges discontinued their investigation. Public disagreement between judges and the international prosecutor, leaked documents, and the resignation of UN legal officers and a key consultant brought the dispute to public attention. Hun Sen opposed the tribunal's proceeding to those cases, and critics claimed that failing to pursue them demonstrated that the court was not independent from government pressure. In the meantime, proceedings of the ongoing trial were delayed while the judges considered whether Ieng Thirith, whom doctors reported as suffering from dementia, was fit to stand trial.

As opposition parties prepared for local elections in 2012, their increasing marginalization was evident. The best-known opposition leader, Sam Rainsy, remained in exile. His appeals against a prison sentence were denied, and in March he was stripped of his National Assembly seat. There were negotiations in early 2011 for a merger between the Sam Rainsy Party (SRP) and another opposition party, the Human Rights Party (HRP), but a recording of a conversation between HRP president Kem Sokha and Hun Sen that was leaked to the press gave the impression—perhaps falsely—of collaboration between the two, which effectively ended talks with the SRP. (JOHN A. MARSTON)

CAMEROON

Area: 476,350 sq km (183,920 sq mi), including the 700-sq-km (270-sq-mi) Bakassi Peninsula
Population (2011 est.): 20,073,000
Capital: Yaoundé
Chief of state: President Paul Biya
Head of government: Prime Minister Philémon Yang

Election-related news dominated in Cameroon in 2011. In apparent response to opposition parties' criticisms of the country's electoral commission, Pres. Paul Biya increased its size by one-half, appointing six new members from outside the political structure. The appointments on July 7 followed an earlier reform of the commission that removed its power to determine the final result of any election. In anticipation of the country's October 9 presidential election, many candidacies were declared, including those of John Fru Ndi of the Social Democratic Front and Pierre Mila Assouté of the Democratic Assembly for the Modernization of Cameroon. As expected, the 78-year-old Biya, in power since 1982, was the candidate for the ruling party, the Cameroon People's Democratic Movement. He easily won reelection, garnering more than 77% of the vote. The election, however, was marred by numerous complaints of fraud and irregularities.

The government was accused of having used the police to prevent journalists from reporting on activities of the regime's opponents. Raphaël Kamtchuen, editor of the monthly journal *La Boussole*, was held for six days in February and charged with possession of a leaked letter containing evidence of public corruption.

Gangs of robbers struck two banks in Douala on March 18, killing seven bystanders. While the gangs attempted to escape in speedboats, security forces caught up with them as they neared the coast of Nigeria. In the ensuing gun battle, at least 18 of the criminals were shot to death.

An agreement in principle was announced in Yaoundé on August 19 that would indemnify 350 people who lost their jobs during the 1980s when 48 publicly owned enterprises were privatized. This followed an August 9 sit-in at the Ministry of Finance by at least 400 people who were demanding redundancy payments.

(NANCY ELLEN LAWLER)

CANADA

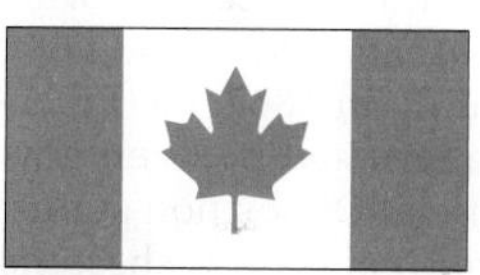

Area: 9,984,670 sq km (3,855,103 sq mi)
Population (2011 est.): 34,447,000
Capital: Ottawa
Head of state: Queen Elizabeth II, represented by Governor-General David Johnston
Head of government: Prime Minister Stephen Harper

Domestic Politics. Canadians went to the polls in 2011 for the fourth time in seven years after the minority Conservative government was brought down by an opposition no-confidence motion on March 25. The three parties that collectively held a majority of the seats in the House of Commons—the centrist Liberal Party, the left-wing New Democratic Party (NDP), and the separatist Bloc Québécois—voted in favour of a motion that found the government in contempt of Parliament for having failed to share information needed to assess proposed legislation. The historic motion, which passed by a 156–145 vote, marked the first time

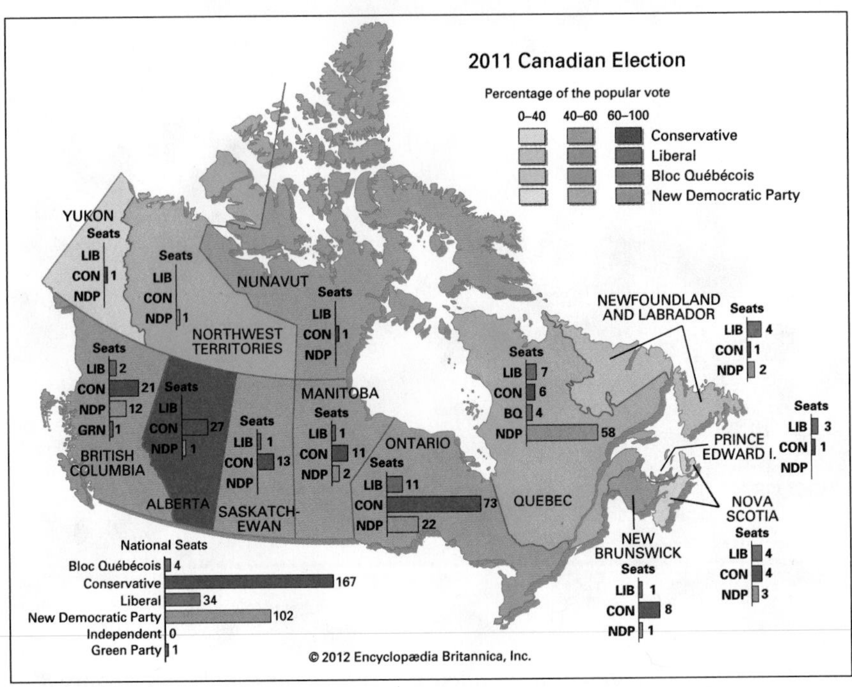

that the national government of a Commonwealth country had ever been found in contempt of Parliament.

Prime Minister Stephen Harper asked voters to return his party to government with a stable majority and suggested that if the election resulted in another hung Parliament (in which no political party had a majority), the Liberals and New Democrats would attempt to govern with help from the Bloc. Liberal leader Michael Ignatieff denied that he would form a coalition government, but he stated that the Liberal minority government would work cooperatively with all other parties. Midway through the campaign, polls showed startling growth in support for the NDP, largely at the expense of the Bloc Québécois in Quebec. Some speculated that NDP leader Jack Layton's performance in the televised debates and the general softening of support for sovereignty in Quebec prompted voters to consider the party.

The May 2 election resulted in a historic change in the country's political standing. Despite having increased their popular support by less than 2% over their 2008 election vote, the Conservatives won 166 of 308 constituencies and formed a majority government. The Liberals posted the worst result in party history and fell to third place, with only 34 MPs and less than 20% of the vote. Since Confederation in 1867, the Liberals had always alternated between government and Official Opposition status. Driven by dramatic gains in Quebec, the NDP achieved its best result ever and formed the Official Opposition with 31% of the popular vote and 103 seats—including 59 from Quebec. Prior to the vote, in its 50-year history the party had elected only two MPs from the predominantly francophone province. The success of the NDP was disastrous for the Bloc Québécois, which fell from 47 seats to 4 and lost official party status in the House of Commons. Although support for the Green Party declined overall, its leader, Elizabeth May, became the first Green to be elected an MP when she won in British Columbia. In all, an unprecedented 76 women were elected to the House of Commons. Voter turnout increased from a historic low of 58.8% in 2008 to 61.1%.

Following the election three of the country's opposition parties were in disarray. Defeated in their own ridings, Liberal leader Ignatieff and Bloc Québécois leader Gilles Duceppe both resigned their leadership positions. Daniel Paillé was chosen to lead Bloc Québécois on December 11; the Liberals decided to wait until 2013. NDP leader Layton, only months into his new role as leader of the Official Opposition, announced that he would be taking a leave of absence to seek cancer treatment. He had previously been diagnosed with prostate cancer in 2010, and he had used a cane during the campaign while recovering from a hip fracture and operation. Although Layton expected his leave to be temporary, his condition deteriorated, and he died on August 22. (*See* OBITUARIES.) Newly elected Quebec MP Nycole Turmel became interim NDP leader and then leader of the Official Opposition upon Layton's death. The party scheduled a leadership election for March 24, 2012.

The newly emboldened Conservative government reintroduced bills that had been held up by the minority Parliament and tabled new legislation to fulfill long-standing promises. Major initiatives included eliminating public subsidies for political parties, ending the Canadian Wheat Board's monopoly on prairie wheat and barley sales, continuing the process of Senate reform, requiring more fiscal accountability among First Nations (Native American) chiefs and band councillors, abolishing the national long-gun registry, and passing an omnibus crime bill. The omnibus legislation contained nine bills that had failed to pass in the former Parliament, including acts to impose mandatory minimum sentences for a range of sexual offenses involving those under age 16 as well as for certain drug-related crimes, an act to eliminate pardons for serious crimes and replace them with "record suspensions," and an act that would prevent judges from imposing conditional sentences for certain crimes.

Canadians also voted in general elections in five provinces and two territories in 2011. Incumbent governments were returned to office in six out of seven cases. Canada's smallest province, Prince Edward Island, saw its centrist Liberal government elected to a second, albeit smaller, majority government with 22 seats. The centre-right Progressive Conservatives took the remaining five seats. Manitoba's voters elected the centre-left NDP to a fourth consecutive majority government. The NDP won 37 seats; the Progressive Conservatives were elected to 19; and the Liberals gained 1. In Ontario the Liberals were reduced on October 6 to a minority government with 53 seats to the Progressive Conservatives' 37 and the NDP's 17. Contesting her first election as Progressive Conservative leader and premier, Kathy Dunderdale led her party to a third consecutive majority government in Newfoundland and Labrador on October 11 with 37 seats. The Liberals remained the Official Opposition with six seats, and the NDP achieved a best-ever showing with five seats. On November 7 the right-of-centre Saskatchewan Party led by Premier Brad Wall won a second consecutive majority government in a landslide. Wall's party captured 64% of the vote and 49 of 58 seats. The NDP won the remaining nine seats and polled 32% of the vote, a historic low. The Yukon Party secured a third consecutive majority government in Yukon with 11 of

19 seats under new leader Darrell Pasloski. The NDP became Official Opposition with six seats, and the Liberals fell to third place with two seats. Under the Northwest Territories' nonpartisan system of government, incumbents were reelected in 13 of 19 ridings. Bob McLeod was elected premier by the legislature to replace a retiring Floyd Roland.

Governing parties in two other provinces selected new leaders in 2011. Christy Clark was not sitting in the legislature when she became leader of the centre-right British Columbia Liberal Party on February 26. On May 11 she narrowly emerged as the winner in a by-election. Alison Redford became Alberta's first female premier on October 7 after winning the leadership of the Progressive Conservatives.

Economy. The snap federal spring election prevented the national government from passing its March 22 budget. Finance Minister Jim Flaherty tabled a new but substantively similar budget on June 6. Key measures included an austerity plan as well as a pledge to reduce the country's deficit and return to a balanced budget by 2014–15, one fiscal year earlier than originally forecast. In a November 8 budget update, the government once again pushed back the date to the 2015–16 fiscal year in response to a worsening economy.

Canada's GDP declined for the first time since 2009 during the second quarter of 2011. Flaherty suggested that the 0.1% drop should not raise fears that the country was heading into another recession, however. He noted that although exports declined by 2.1%, oil and gas production fell by 3.6%, and manufacturing declined by 0.9%, steady business investment and consumer spending indicated Canadians' confidence in the economy.

British Columbians successfully repealed their province's unpopular harmonized sales tax (HST) in a mail-in referendum during the summer. Of the 1.6 million ballots cast, 55% favoured eliminating the tax, which combined the federal goods and services tax with the old provincial sales tax. The HST, which was promoted as a tax that simplified accounting for businesses, had previously been adopted by Quebec, Nova Scotia, New Brunswick, Newfoundland and Labrador, and Ontario. In a bid to keep the tax, provincial Finance Minister Kevin Falcon had announced a reduction in the HST from 12% to 10% by 2014 and a one-time transition payment of Can$175 (Can$1 = about U.S.$0.98) to all families with children under age 18. Falcon said that reverting to the two-tax system would require the province to repay the Can$1.6 billion it received from the federal government to assist in the transition and would cost a total of Can$2.3 billion.

On September 30 Prime Minister Harper delivered a Can$2.2 billion check to the Quebec government to cover the cost of the HST. Although Quebec had been the first province to adopt the HST in 1991, unlike other provinces it had not previously received transition funding from the federal government.

Supervised Injection Site Preserved. On September 30, in a 9–0 decision, the Supreme Court ruled in favour of the continued operation of Vancouver's Insite clinic. The medically supervised injection site located in the city's Downtown Eastside—one of the poorest urban areas in the country and home to many intravenous drug users—had been opened in 2003 as a pilot project supported by all three levels of government. The federal government had declined to continue granting the clinic any further extensions to its renewable exemption under the Controlled Drugs and Substances Act. The court's majority opinion held that the federal government had the constitutional power to restrict the use of illicit drugs; however, the government's reasons for interfering with the clinic were deemed "grossly disproportionate" to Insite's benefit to its clients and the community. During the hearings lawyers noted that since 2006 Insite staff had offered assistance and treatment for 336 overdoses. The clinic had no fatalities, and the crime rate in the surrounding area had remained unchanged. The landmark decision would allow other supervised drug-injection clinics to open across the country. Federal Health Minister Leona Aglukkaq said that the government would comply with the court's ruling while reviewing its options.

Government Cyberattack. The federal Finance Department, Treasury Board, and one of the Department of National Defense's civilian agencies were the target in January of unprecedented cyber espionage. Hackers using Chinese networks were able to access highly classified material from computers in the offices of senior government executives. Although the federal government had not revealed the extent of the system's compromise, reports suggested that the cyberattack targeted passwords for data systems that held Canadians' sensitive personal information. On October 30 the press reported that an intelligence assessment released by the Canadian Security Intelligence Service two months prior to the breach had raised concerns over the same techniques used in the attacks. A regularly scheduled evaluation of the Finance Department and the Treasury Board prior to the attacks also revealed that neither department had been meeting all the government's information-technology security requirements.

(WILL STOS)

CAPE VERDE

Area: 4,033 sq km (1,557 sq mi)
Population (2011 est.): 498,000
Capital: Praia
Head of state: Presidents Pedro Pires and, from September 9, Jorge Carlos Fonseca
Head of government: Prime Minister José Maria Neves

Cape Verde's democratic credentials were enhanced by two elections and a leadership award in 2011. In the February parliamentary election, the African Party for the Independence of Cape Verde (PAICV) gained a majority in the National Assembly. Having been president for two terms, Pedro Pires of the PAICV was not able to stand in the presidential election, and the PAICV chose Manuel Inocencio Sousa as its candidate. Sousa and Jorge Carlos Fonseca of the Movement for Democracy (MpD) were the top two finishers in the first round of voting, held on August 7. In the runoff election, which took place on August 21, Fonseca polled 54.2% of the votes, and Sousa, who won 45.8%, immediately conceded defeat. Fonseca, who then had to govern with a PAICV prime minister, promised measures to attract foreign investment and boost tourism, both of which were sorely needed, given the island state's lack of resources and fragile ecology.

In October Pires was the recipient of the Mo Ibrahim Prize for Achievement in African Leadership. The prize included a $5 million award over 10 years.

Cape Verde ended the year on a sad note with the death of Cesaria Evora on December 17. The Grammy-winning singer was 70. (*See* OBITUARIES.)

(CHRISTOPHER SAUNDERS)

CENTRAL AFRICAN REPUBLIC

Area: 622,436 sq km (240,324 sq mi)
Population (2011 est.): 4,950,000
Capital: Bangui
Head of state: President François Bozizé
Head of government: Prime Minister Faustin-Archange Touadéra

The Central African Republic held presidential and legislative elections on Jan. 23, 2011. Pres. François Bozizé won an overwhelming victory, with 66% of the vote. Former president Ange-Félix Patassé, in exile since his ouster in 2003, was a distant second, taking 21%. Bozizé's party, National Convergence (Kwa Na Kwa; "Work, Only Work"), won more than two dozen seats outright in the 105-member National Assembly. Opposition calls of fraud were dismissed by the Constitutional Court, which certified the results on February 12. The second round of legislative elections, held on March 27, was boycotted by opposition parties, and the KNK won enough additional seats to guarantee that the party would hold a majority in the legislature. The results of a third round, held on September 4 in 14 districts where results of the previous round had been invalidated, maintained the KNK's majority.

On January 12 former president Jean-Bédel Bokassa's chateau in a Paris suburb was auctioned off to an anonymous bidder for €915,000 ($1.2 million), a month after Bozizé had granted a posthumous rehabilitation of Bokassa by presidential decree. On April 5, Patassé died in Cameroon at the age of 74. (*See* OBITUARIES.)

The UN continued to express its concern at the kidnapping and recruitment of children to serve in various rebel armies, including the Lord's Resistance Army (LRA). It was reported that the LRA alone had abducted more than 3,000 people in Central Africa since September 2008.

The economy showed some signs of improvement as the agricultural, forestry, and diamond sectors grew. Overall growth was small, however, owing in large part to global increases in the price of oil. Health care outside the capital was virtually unobtainable, and the level of poverty remained extremely high. (NANCY ELLEN LAWLER)

CHAD

Area: 1,284,000 sq km (495,755 sq mi)
Population (2011 est.): 12,018,000
Capital: N'Djamena
Head of state: President Lieut. Gen. Idriss Déby
Head of government: Prime Minister Emmanuel Nadingar

In February 2011 Chad held parliamentary elections, the first since 2002. Pres. Idriss Déby's Patriotic Salvation Movement won 113 of the 188 seats, but the opposition claimed that there had been widespread fraud. The presidential election was held in April. Déby stood for a fifth term, but the country's main opposition leaders boycotted the election; only two candidates from small parties challenged Déby. After he won nearly 89% of the vote, he was sworn in for another five-year term. Sudanese Pres. Omar al-Bashir attended Déby's inauguration, despite a warrant for his arrest having been issued by the International Criminal Court. Déby continued his rapprochement with Sudan, signing an agreement with that country and the Central African Republic in May.

Earlier in the year there had been unconfirmed reports that Chadian troops were in Libya fighting for Libyan leader Muammar al-Qaddafi in that country's civil conflict. One outcome of the Libyan conflict was that the many Chadians who had been working in Libya had to return to Chad, and their families lost the remittances they had been sending home, sending many into dire poverty.

The United Nations Mission in the Central African Republic and Chad (MINURCAT) completed its withdrawal and the handover of its programs to the government of Chad at the end of 2010. The mission had been established in 2007 to promote regional security, including the protection of Chadians.

Once again, nothing came of efforts either to try Hissène Habré or to extradite him from Senegal. The former Chadian president was accused of having committed crimes against humanity, war crimes, and torture.

(CHRISTOPHER SAUNDERS)

CHILE

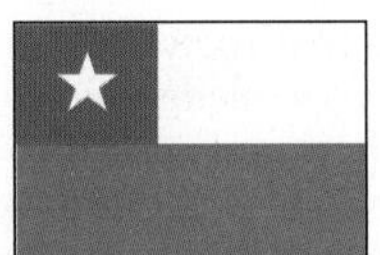

Area: 756,096 sq km (291,930 sq mi)
Population (2011 est.): 17,270,000
Capitals: Santiago (national) and Valparaíso (legislative)
Head of state and government: President Sebastián Piñera

Sebastián Piñera, Chile's first right-wing president since redemocratization

Men suspected of being Chadian mercenaries fighting on behalf of Libyan ruler Muammar al-Qaddafi are detained by antigovernment forces at a roadblock in eastern Libya, February 27.

Kevin Frayer/AP

Eliseo Fernandez—Reuters/Landov

On May 21, opposition members of the Chilean parliament in Valparaíso display a banner to protest the HidroAysén dam planned for southern Chile; environmental concerns had been raised about the hydroelectric project.

in 1990, watched his popularity sink below 30% in 2011 as he finished his second year in office. Piñera's popularity had soared during his first year as president, especially in the aftermath of the October 2010 rescue of 33 Chilean miners trapped deep below ground. As the national euphoria wore off, however, the Piñera government faced a major challenge, beginning in May, when large student protests broke out demanding reform of the outdated, underfunded, and class-based public education system. Protesters also opposed the government's decision to move ahead with the controversial HidroAysén dam project in southern Chile. Student protests against the education system had first broken out in 2006 during Michelle Bachelet's presidency. She had promised that a high-level committee would study the problem and offer remedies, but the lack of major reform led to renewed student action. Neither Piñera's first education minister, Joaquín Lavín, a former presidential candidate, nor his replacement, Felipe Bulnes (who resigned in late December), was able to quell the crisis.

One of the protesters' principal demands was for the public education system to again come under the oversight of the national government, a reversal of the existing policy, which had begun under the dictatorship of Augusto Pinochet; that policy mandated that municipalities oversee and finance public schools. Pinochet had pushed the "municipalization" of education as part of a strategy to shrink national government that had been formulated by the "Chicago Boys," a group of Chilean economists who embraced the free-market theories they had encountered as students at the University of Chicago. Because the financial resources of local governments in Chile varied enormously, however, public schools in poorer areas lacked adequate funding.

As the student protesters' numbers swelled in 2011, the students undertook other actions, including an October sit-in at the former Congress building in Santiago. Over the months of the burgeoning protests, the students also broadened their demands to include a referendum on the 1980 constitution, which had been written by the Pinochet military regime. Opinion polls showed a high level of support for the students, who seemed to reflect a long-simmering discontent with a political system that still contained vestiges of the military regime's rule and with an economic system that perpetuated sharp class differences despite years of rapid economic growth.

The Chilean economy, which continued to thrive despite the global downturn, grew by 8.4% in the first half of the year. The country's export-oriented economy maintained a positive balance of trade, facilitated by the government's successful pursuit of free-trade agreements with countries around the globe. Moreover, the overall level of exports also rose in 2011. Trade continued to increase with China, which remained the largest consumer of Chilean exports; prior to 2007 the U.S. had been the prime destination for Chilean exports. Although Chile had signed free-trade agreements with both countries, China's appetite for Chilean copper was a major factor in that historic shift.

There were, however, some clouds on the economic horizon. Despite Chile's efforts to diversify its exports, copper still accounted for about half the country's exports, and its declining price on the international market in 2011 prompted Chile's minister of the economy to predict that the country's economic growth would slow significantly. Finally, Chile's salmon industry faced challenges. In 2007 infectious salmon anemia (ISA) had hit the domestic salmon-farming industry, the second largest in the world. Although the industry appeared to have recuperated, there was a growing consensus that salmon farming might not be sustainable. Producers faced the prospect of having to make significant investments in the fish-farming system so that it would not destroy lakes and marine waters or leave the industry vulnerable to future infestations.

(LOIS HECHT OPPENHEIM)

CHINA

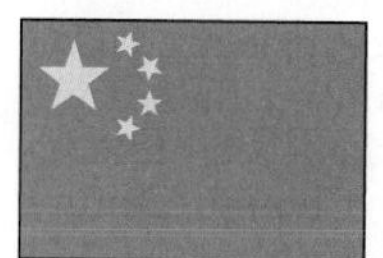

Area: 9,572,900 sq km (3,696,100 sq mi), including Tibet and excluding Taiwan and the special autonomous regions of Hong Kong and Macau
Population (2011 est., excluding Taiwan, Hong Kong, and Macau): 1,342,274,000
Capital: Beijing
Head of state: President Hu Jintao
Head of government: Premier Wen Jiabao

Domestic Affairs. In 2011 China consolidated its status as the world's second largest economy, managing significant continued economic growth despite a weak world economy. Domestically, China prepared for an expected leadership transition in 2012, but the government appeared anxious about the effects of the Arab Spring uprisings, both at home and abroad.

In March the National People's Congress ratified the country's 12th Five-Year Plan for 2011–15. Reporting on the plan, Premier Wen Jiabao projected that China's economic growth would slow to 7% annually, that the country would achieve 51.5% urbanization by 2015, and that research and development would make up 2.2% of the national budget. Wen and Pres. Hu Jintao were to begin relinquishing power in late 2012.

Yan Runbo—Xinhua/Landov

One of the longest overwater bridges in the world, the 42-km (26-mi) Jiaozhou Bay Bridge—which connected the urban centre of Qingdao, China, with an outlying district—opened in June.

A powerful symbol of the uncertainty that gripped China was a 17-ton statue of Confucius that appeared in Tiananmen Square early in the year near the tomb of Mao Zedong. Although Mao had once criticized Confucius as a feudal thinker, the ancient Chinese philosopher had been rehabilitated to emphasize Chinese cultural values. The statue was removed four months later, however, with no official explanation offered.

In October China marked the 100th anniversary of the start of the Chinese Revolution by hanging paintings of Sun Yat-sen and Mao next to each other. While hailing the 1911 revolution as the beginning of the rejuvenation of China and promoting an officially sponsored film on the revolution, the government nervously canceled an opera based on Sun's life and an academic conference on the Republican period.

The Chinese Communist Party (CCP) also marked the 90th anniversary of its founding in Shanghai, with ceremonies at the Great Hall of the People in Beijing. A film version of the party's history, entitled *Beginning of the Great Revival,* was released, along with a wave of television shows designed to highlight the central role of the CCP in creating the country's current prosperity and maintaining social order. A nostalgic "Red Culture" movement celebrating the music and culture of the Mao era also spread nationwide from Chongqing. At the National People's Congress earlier in the year, Wu Bangguo, a high-ranking CCP official, assured delegates that China would not allow multiparty democracy or Western-style separation of powers.

Problems with China's high-speed rail network, a symbol of its modernization, troubled the country at large. First, Minister of Railways Liu Zhijun was arrested for having embezzled millions of dollars while in office. Second, China's high-speed rail system, already the world's largest, with some 8,000 km (5,000 mi) of track, had had a projected cost of $300 billion, but $306 billion had been borrowed to finance the system. In late June, though, a 1,318-km (819-mi) high-speed link between Shanghai and Beijing was opened. Also in June, one of the world's longest overwater bridges was opened, connecting Qingdao and Huangdao with a span of 42 km (26 mi).

Against that backdrop, the crash of two high-speed trains near Wenzhou on July 23 that killed some 40 people shocked the public, as did a less-serious accident on the Shanghai Metro commuter system in September. Authorities were especially concerned about the use of such microblogging services as Twitter to criticize the government's handling of those incidents. In April dissident artist Ai Weiwei (*see* BIOGRAPHIES) was arrested on tax-evasion charges at the Beijing airport and was held for 81 days.

Unrest continued to sporadically rock China's vast border regions, which, for the first time in many years, included demonstrations in Inner Mongolia. Students there were confined to campus, and Internet communications were limited after they had protested the killing of an ethnic Mongolian herdsman by a Han Chinese truck driver. In July, 18 were killed in riots in Hotan in far western Xinjiang as ethnic unrest continued between native Uighurs and immigrant Han Chinese. At least 4 Uighurs were shot dead by police after rioting in Kashgar; authorities claimed that the dead Uighurs were religious extremists who had been trained in Pakistan. More than 10 Tibetan monks set themselves on fire to protest Chinese rule in the ethnic Tibetan Kham region of Sichuan.

In China proper more than 10,000 people demonstrated in the northeastern industrial city of Dalian to protest the pollution from a $1.5 billion petrochemical plant; the plant was then closed. The central government's State Council also admitted that the Three Gorges Dam, the world's largest hydroelectric project, had ecological and environmental problems that could cause catastrophe, but it also stated that the project—a symbol of the success of China's modernization and reform since the 1980s—had comprehensive benefits that outweighed its drawbacks.

A large section of central China's grain-producing provinces was hit by the country's worst drought in 60 years. By February some 7.73 million ha (19.1 million ac) of wheat were affected. Drought also gripped southwestern China between July and October, leaving some 14.5 million people without access to drinking water. In June more than five million people were affected by floods in Zhejiang province on China's eastern seaboard.

China's military demonstrated its ongoing modernization by pointedly testing its new J-20 stealth fighter just before U.S. Secretary of Defense Robert M. Gates visited China in January on a mission to restore direct relations between the U.S. and Chinese military. China had suspended those relations after the U.S. sold $6.4 billion in weapons to Taiwan in 2010. A subsequent $5.85 billion arms sale to Taiwan in 2011, however, did not lead to a resumption of the suspension. China tested its first aircraft carrier in August.

Economy. China, which surpassed Japan in 2010 to become the world's second largest economy, solidified this position with robust GDP growth of 9% in 2011, despite the financial crisis in Europe and North America. Inflation was about 6%, and the urban unemployment rate was 4.1% at the end of September. The country began the year with some 534,500 millionaires and 115 billionaires. Average urban household income was about $8,000, and consumer spending accounted for just 35% of GDP.

To control rising real-estate prices, Beijing cut back on credit, which had been widely available over the previous two years to stoke China's economy during the global recession. The credit crunch, however, triggered a wave of factory closings in Wenzhou as exports declined by 0.6% in the third quarter after two straight quarters of strong growth. Wenzhou's many entrepreneurs had leveraged credit lines available to their core manufacturing operations to speculate in booming property markets across China. As 2011 came to a close, China's property bubble appeared to be bursting; housing prices declined for the first time in two years, and the government raised interest rates. Low incomes, high property prices, and rising consumer prices also led to strikes by taxi drivers in Hangzhou and by railway workers in Changsha.

The minimum wage increased in many urban areas, including Guangzhou (up by 18%) and Beijing (20%). Shenzhen, a major manufacturing centre near Guangzhou, reported wage increases of nearly 20%. As a result, factories in southern China with considerable Taiwanese investment continued their exodus to countries with lower manufacturing costs, such as Vietnam.

By December initial public offerings (IPOs) overseas had raised an estimated $15.4 billion, which accounted for more than 10% of the world's annual total of IPOs. Reports of fraudulent financial accounting at Chinese companies listed overseas, however, drove down the share prices of firms such as Longtop Financial Technologies Ltd. Longtop was eventually delisted by the New York Stock Exchange and became the subject of a U.S. federal investigation.

By November there were some 300 million registered users of microblogging services in China. Censors nonetheless worked hard to remove angry comments on the Wenzhou high-speed rail crash as well as references to the Arab Spring and the demonstrations in Dalian. China also had some 500 million total Internet users, but censors deleted an estimated 790,000 posts and articles. Facebook, YouTube, and Twitter remained banned through technical measures put in place by the government that became known as the "Great Firewall." In addition, the Great Firewall began to more effectively block virtual private networks used by Chinese Internet users to make encrypted connections to servers outside China.

In July in a case brought by the EU, Mexico, and the United States, the WTO found that the controls China put on its export of rare-earth minerals in 2010 violated WTO rules. China subsequently appealed the ruling.

Foreign Relations. In 2011 China and North Korea celebrated the 50th anniversary of their friendship treaty, which committed both sides to assisting one another militarily. China was North Korea's closest ally, and its leader, Kim Jong-Il, made a rare visit to China in May, ostensibly to learn from China's economic success but also to shore up support from China's leadership for the planned succession of Kim's youngest son, Kim Jong-Eun. In June, China and North Korea announced the joint development of two special economic zones: one at the North Korean border city of Rajin-Sonbong and the other on offshore islands near the China–North Korea border.

The South China Sea remained a point of contention between China and neighbours such as Vietnam and the Philippines, all of which had territorial claims there. In May and in June, Vietnam complained that Chinese fishing vessels had interfered with oil-exploration activities. China countered that Vietnamese naval vessels had expelled Chinese fishing boats from contested waters. Meanwhile, the Philippines complained that China was building structures on reefs claimed by the Philippines and harassing its oil-exploration activities. In August, Philippine Pres. Benigno S. Aquino III met with President Hu in Beijing and discussed the need to defuse regional tensions.

Construction of a China-Thailand-Laos high-speed rail link, scheduled to begin in 2011, was put on hold after corruption problems in the Chinese Railway Ministry. Myanmar (Burma), one of China's closest allies, ordered a state-owned Chinese company to halt construction of a $3.6 billion dam on the Irrawaddy River in northeastern Myanmar.

China responded nervously to the Egypt Uprising of 2011, deploying scores of police officers to a busy Beijing shopping area after the spread of online rumours about homegrown demonstrations. Notably, China briefly broke with its long-standing policy of noninterference in the internal affairs of other countries by voting for UN sanctions against the government of Libyan dictator Muammar al-Qaddafi. (*See* OBITUARIES.) China joined Russia, however, in voting against a Security Council resolution condemning violence in Syria.

Hu made a state visit in January to the U.S., where he was given a formal White House state dinner with U.S. Pres. Barack Obama, the first such event for a Chinese leader in 13 years. Despite this cordial beginning to 2011, relations with the U.S. were strained by the U.S. sale of weapons to Taiwan that included upgrades to Taiwan's F-16 A/B fighter jets. Relations were further tested in October when the U.S. Senate passed the Currency Exchange Rate Oversight Reform Act of 2011. Although the U.S. House of Representatives declined to take up the bill because of concerns that it might unleash a trade war, the provisions of the act would allow the U.S. government to impose tariffs on countries such as China that kept their currency value artificially low.

In August Gary Locke, a former governor of Washington state, became the first Chinese American to serve as U.S. ambassador to China. After he was photographed buying his own coffee at the Seattle airport and flew economy class without a retinue, many Chinese people compared his low-key style favourably against Chinese officials' love of formality. Similar public interest was sparked when Locke dined with U.S. Vice Pres. Joe Biden at a Beijing noodle shop. The state media, however, claimed that Locke was putting on a show to further U.S. interests.

At the beginning of 2011, the exchange rate was about 6.83 renminbi (yuan) per U.S. dollar. In line with China's policy of allowing the yuan to appreciate slowly, by the end of December, the yuan had risen slightly, to about 6.35 per dollar. While U.S. lawmakers wanted China to allow the yuan to appreciate more, China feared that appreciation would make its exports less competitive and could affect domestic stability. Throughout 2011 China urged the U.S. to manage its economy wisely, citing concerns that continued U.S. economic weakness might threaten China's dollar-denominated investments of its foreign-currency reserves. Those reserves had reached about $3.5 trillion by the end of the year. Although nearly two-thirds of those reserves were held in U.S. bonds, China had rapidly increased its euro-denominated holdings to nearly one-quarter of the total. China also began further diversifying its holdings after the U.S.'s credit rating was downgraded in August and the sovereign debt crisis in Europe roiled markets. Also in August, China bought some $2.3 billion in Japanese debt as part of this diversification.

In October China took a first step toward making the yuan an international currency when it began allowing some foreign direct investment (FDI) to be made in yuan. Total FDI investment in China for 2011 exceeded $110 billion. Through November some $68.35 billion entered China from Hong Kong. Taiwan and Japan, the second and third largest sources of FDI, invested $6.25 billion and $5.94 billion, respectively.

Premier Wen visited the U.K., Hungary, and Germany in June, promising that Chinese investment in the region would increase. In the U.K. Wen visited the Chinese-owned MG Motor UK Ltd. and spoke about China's determination to implement democracy and the rule of law in the future. His visit to Germany yielded an order by China of 88 Airbus Industrie jet aircraft and $15 billion in bilateral investment agreements. China failed to increase its purchases of sovereign debt from European countries, however, despite express invitations to do so from Italy and other countries.

China's territory became slightly larger in January when it implemented an agreement with neighbouring Tajikistan that gave China an additional 1,158 sq km (447 sq mi) of disputed territory. With the important exception of India, China no longer had any land border disputes with the 14 countries that border it. Tensions remained over the disputed border in India's Arunachal Pradesh state, but bilateral trade between China and India was expected to reach $70 billion in 2011.

(MICHAEL R. FAHEY)

COLOMBIA

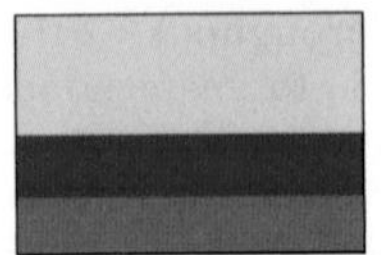

Area: 1,141,748 sq km (440,831 sq mi)
Population (2011 est.): 44,726,000
Capital: Bogotá
Head of state and government: President Juan Manuel Santos

Colombia started 2011 with a historically heavy rainy season, leaving behind about $5 billion in damages and more than three million people without homes. Aid transfers during the emergency became the focus of yet another corruption scandal, which paved the road for Congress to grant Pres. Juan Manuel Santos extraordinary powers to restructure many state agencies that were suspected of engaging in corrupt practices.

Perhaps the administration's greatest accomplishment in 2011 was pushing land reform through Congress as a major part of the Victims and Land Restitution Law, a response to the armed conflict between the government, left-wing guerrilla groups, and right-wing paramilitaries that had displaced an estimated 3.4 million people by the end of 2010. The initiative, though spearheaded in Congress by left-of-centre Liberal members, was supported by members of all ideological stripes. The law, commended by UN Secretary-General Ban Ki-Moon and referred to as "historic" by President Santos, recognized violence in Colombia as the result of an "armed conflict"—a designation that former president Álvaro Uribe had adamantly refused to accept, insisting instead on referring to the ongoing clash as "acts of terrorism."

Tensions between Uribe and his similarly popular successor Santos, once Uribe's minister of defense, escalated after Uribe's comments on the performance of Santos's administration regarding issues such as corruption and national security. This, combined with an increasing public perception that security had deteriorated during his mandate, prompted Santos to display a renewed interest in security matters, signaled by an unexpected change of both the minister of defense and the joint chiefs of staff. Santos got a major boost when, on November 4, a military operation killed top guerrilla leader Alfonso Cano (*see* OBITUARIES) in the southwestern mountains. Meanwhile, Uribe and Minister of the Interior Germán Vargas Lleras engaged in repeated inflammatory exchanges.

Vargas Lleras's accusations revolved around Uribe's former aides. Warrants for the arrest of high-ranking officials in the previous administration—including then minister of agriculture Andrés Felipe Arias, former chief of staff Bernardo Moreno, and former National Intelligence Agency director María del Pilar Hurtado—were issued in response to two investigations: the *Agro Ingreso Seguro* (a farm-subsidies program) embezzlement and the "DAS-gate" (DAS is the acronym for the internal security services) illegal-tapping scandals (in which U.S. aid money was allegedly implicated). Meanwhile, Uribe was called before Congress to give a statement regarding the latter incident as part of an investigation that probed the extent of his knowledge and involvement. Despite this, Uribe's popularity remained high among the general electorate, which made him relevant during the latest round of local elections.

In addition to the selection of departmental governors and municipal mayors around the country, the mayoralty of Bogotá—often referred to as the second most important position in Colombian politics—was also decided during the 2011 local elections. The campaign for the capital's main elected post was held under the shadow of the infrastructure-related corruption scandal known as the "hiring carousel," which led to the suspension of former mayor Samuel Moreno, who, along with his brother Iván, was the subject of judicial prosecution. The race in Bogotá also prompted a schism in the Green Party as Antanas Mockus (runner-up in the 2010 presidential election) decided to run (alone at first and then in alliance with independent Gina Parody) against the party's official candidate and the former mayor of Bogotá, Enrique Peñalosa, who accepted Uribe's support during his campaign. The race was won by former presidential candidate (and former guerrilla) Gustavo Petro. In other parts of the country—especially Antioquia, Arauca, Caquetá, and Putumayo—the competitiveness and legitimacy of elections were put at risk by the actions of newly rising organized-crime groups, or *BACRIM* (for *bandas criminales*), and by political fraud more generally. Accusations brought by independent watchdogs (such as Misión de Observación Electoral) of rising political violence against left-wing candidates were particularly prominent during this round of local elections.

In economic matters Colombia saw a marginal increase in the cost of living with respect to 2010, putting inflation at about 3.6%. As expected, unemployment decreased in 2011 by a small amount, with an estimated rate of 11.6%—still one of the highest in the region. Nevertheless, and despite the global uncertainty, the economy continued to grow, at an estimated rate of 6%. With a proposed free-trade agreement with the United States approved in the U.S. Congress after seven years of stalled negotiations, Colombia also began negotiating free-trade agreements with several Asian countries, including Japan and South Korea.

(BRIAN F. CRISP; SANTIAGO OLIVELLA)

COMOROS

Area: 1,862 sq km (719 sq mi), excluding the 374-sq-km (144-sq-mi) island of Mayotte, a de facto dependency of France since 1976
Population (2011 est.): 754,000 (excluding 210,000 on Mayotte)
Capital: Moroni
Head of state and government: Presidents Ahmed Abdallah Mohamed Sambi and, from May 26, Ikililou Dhoinine

The tiny Indian Ocean country of Comoros opened 2011 with news of a new government. On January 13 the Electoral Commission announced that former vice president Ikililou Dhoinine had won the Dec. 26, 2010, election for president, with 61% of the vote. President Dhoinine and the elected governors of the three islands were inaugurated into office in May. The December elections were the result of a 2009 constitutional reform intended to streamline Comoros's bloated government by reducing the status of the federal presidents of the semiautonomous Grande Comore, Anjouan, and Mohéli islands to governors.

Demobilization efforts stalled in January when it was revealed that hundreds of weapons used in the 2008 revolt on Anjouan island were still unaccounted for. The National Disarmament, Demobilization and Reintegration Program, organized by the Comorian government with support from the United Nations Development Programme, had begun in June 2010 to disarm former combatants and place them into reskilling and reintegration programs. Officials estimated that about 400 small arms remained on the island, but by January only a handful of weapons had been turned in.

(MARY EBELING)

At his inauguration ceremony in Moroni on May 26, Comorian Pres. Ikililou Dhoinine (left) speaks with Chinese special envoy Hao Ping.

Xinhua/Landov

CONGO, DEMOCRATIC REPUBLIC OF THE

Area: 2,345,410 sq km (905,568 sq mi)
Population (2011 est.): 67,758,000
Capital: Kinshasa
Head of state and government: President Joseph Kabila, assisted by Prime Minister Adolphe Muzito

Predictions that the November 2011 elections in the Democratic Republic of the Congo would be marred by tension, sporadic violence, and wide-ranging logistic problems were amply borne out. On November 28 more than 18 million voters (58.8% of registered voters) turned out to vote for 11 presidential candidates and about 19,000 legislative candidates. Because of logistic obstacles, voting was extended for two days in some areas and the overall vote-tallying process was slow. On December 9 the electoral commission declared Pres. Joseph Kabila the victor with 48.95% of the vote, followed by former prime minister Étienne Tshisekedi with 32.33% and former National Assembly president Vital Kamerhe with 7.74%. Both Tshisekedi and Kamerhe disputed the outcome, claiming fraudulent results. Their case was supported by statements from several quarters, including the Carter Center, MONUSCO (the UN stabilization mission in Congo), the European Union, and the archbishop of Kinshasa. The country's Supreme Court, however, upheld the results, which were also supported by the African Union. Kabila was inaugurated on December 20; meanwhile, Tshisekedi unilaterally declared himself president but had not garnered widespread support by year's end. Analysts speculated that international governments and agencies preferred to deal with the younger, perhaps more progressive, Kabila (40) rather than the older Tshisekedi (78), considered to be a rabble-rouser.

Accusations of voting irregularities and fraud notwithstanding, Kabila's victory stemmed more from his well-funded, well-organized political machine than personal popularity among the electorate. Many were dissatisfied with his failure to implement his 2006 election campaign promises to build socioeconomic infrastructure, reduce unemployment, and hold local elections. In his favour, however, was the fact that he faced a disparate opposition split among 277 parties. Another important factor that supported Kabila's victory was a constitutional amendment, instituted in January, that reduced the election from two rounds to one, allowing him to win without having obtained more than 50% of the vote.

During the year, fighting continued in the eastern provinces, stemming from the expansion of the National Congress for the Defense of the People (CNDP), which was controlled by Tutsi militants. Their quest for more land and greater access to mineral resources was a source of conflict with other ethnic groups and militias in the area. Although most CNDP fighters belonged to the national military, there was a concern that they could opt to sever that tie and return to war as a means of obtaining more land and resources. The actions of the Rwandan government also were a factor in this situation. Previously the government had supported the CNDP, but it reevaluated this policy after some CNDP militants allied themselves with Hutu Rwandan rebels, who could eventually become a credible threat to the Rwandan government.

On June 28 the UN Security Council ignored the Congolese government's demands to withdraw MONUSCO troops and personnel by the end of the year. In renewing the mission mandate, the UN Security Council declared that its objective was to remain until stability had been restored in the east; however, it limited its role in the election to providing technical and logistic support, promoting dialogue between the stakeholders, and investigating human rights violations. Total strength of the mission stood at 23,305, including 16,819 military personnel.

(LARAY DENZER)

CONGO, REPUBLIC OF THE

Area: 342,000 sq km (132,047 sq mi)
Population (2011 est.): 3,920,000
Capital: Brazzaville
Head of state and government: President Denis Sassou-Nguesso

In 2011 health issues remained a concern in the Republic of the Congo. Congolese citizens welcomed a February 21 announcement that the Global Fund to Fight AIDS, Tuberculosis, and Malaria would provide Congo with $35 million for the provision of services. Other health issues, however, continued to take their toll. By June chikungunya, a viral disease related to dengue fever and carried by mosquitoes, had afflicted more than 7,000 people, mainly in and around Brazzaville and the Pool region. An outbreak of measles also claimed 32 victims, with over 800 infected. On June 22 a campaign to vaccinate all children between six and eight months of age began in Pointe Noire and the Koulilou region. The same month also saw a cholera epidemic that killed 20 people of the 341 reported infected. On June 20 a train derailment 60 km (37 mi) from Pointe-Noire resulted in the deaths of at least 75 passengers and crew. Three days of national mourning were declared.

On March 10, in an effort to improve food security, the government granted 30-year leases on 80,000 ha (about 197,700 ac) of uncultivated land to a company owned by 14 South Africans that planned to grow cereal crops and breed livestock. Approximately 40 South African farmers were involved in the project, which included the construction of a food-processing factory in Malolo II, southeastern Congo. The government announced on May 21 that over the next 10 years it would plant trees on one million ha (about 2.5 million ac) in order to fight deforestation and to improve the lives of the 1.5 million people who depended upon the forests for their livelihoods.

Elections for 36 of the Senate's 72 seats were held on October 9. In the balloting the ruling Congolese Labour Party and its allies won a majority of the seats contested.

(NANCY ELLEN LAWLER)

COSTA RICA

Area: 51,100 sq km (19,730 sq mi)
Population (2011 est.): 4,577,000
Capital: San José
Head of state and government: President Laura Chinchilla Miranda

The year 2011 in Costa Rica was marked by a major easing of international tensions but an increase in domestic political conflict. The longstanding northern border dispute with Nicaragua boiled over in late 2010 in the area of Calero Island along the San Juan River, which divided the two countries and was considered to be of strategic importance. When Nicaragua began dredging the river, Costa Rica protested that the action was a violation of its sovereignty and was causing environmental damage to the wetlands in the area. Nicaragua sent troops, and Costa Rica mobilized members of its police force. After the Organization of American States requested that both countries remove their forces from the area, Nicaragua refused. Costa Rica filed a brief with the International Court of Justice, which in March handed down a provisional ruling that instructed both sides to remove their forces. Nicaragua was allowed to continue dredging the river, but Costa Rica was permitted to send civilians to monitor potential environmental damage. Both sides claimed victory, and the matter was largely defused.

Political conflict over taxes and spending emerged over proposed tax increases to deal with the growing fiscal deficit, which had risen to more than 5% of GDP, and over a security plan unveiled in February by the government of Pres. Laura Chinchilla. The plan involved increasing the number of trained security forces and implementing measures to deal with violence against women as well as gang and drug-related violence. In May Chinchilla suffered a major political defeat when her party (the National Liberation Party [PLN]) lost control of the legislature. A strikingly ideologically diverse coalition of five parties took control on May 2; however, late in the year Chinchilla and the leading opposition party, the Citizen's Action Party (PAC), agreed on a fiscal-reform package. A major trade agreement that was struck with China in 2010 came into force in August.

(MITCHELL A. SELIGSON)

CÔTE D'IVOIRE

Area: 320,803 sq km (123,863 sq mi)
Population (2011 est.): 21,504,000
Capital: Yamoussoukro
De facto capital: Abidjan
Head of state: Presidents Laurent Gbagbo and also Alassane Ouattara (parallel administration), and, from April 11, Ouattara
Head of government: Prime Ministers Gilbert N'gbo Aké (under Gbagbo) and also Guillaume Soro (under Ouattara), and, from April 11, Soro

Juan Carlos Ulate—Reuters/Landov

On April 5 Costa Rican environmental officials survey protected northern wetlands that were feared to have been damaged as a result of Nicaragua's dredging of the nearby San Juan River. The river was at the centre of a border dispute between the two countries.

On March 8, several days after a violent attack by government forces in Côte d'Ivoire claimed the lives of at least six women demonstrating their support of presidential contender Alassane Ouattara, women in Abidjan march to mourn the victims.

Rebecca Blackwell/AP

Côte d'Ivoire began the year 2011 in the grips of the tense and increasingly violent political standoff stemming from the disputed results of the previous year's presidential election. On Dec. 2, 2010, the Independent Electoral Commission had declared that Alassane Ouattara (*see* BIOGRAPHIES) had won with 54% of the vote. Despite this, and worldwide recognition of the results, the Constitutional Council announced that the incumbent, Laurent Gbagbo, was the victor. Thus began a desperate struggle by Gbagbo to retain power by seizing banks, taking personal charge of the cocoa industry, and severely disrupting supplies of electricity and water to the north, Ouattara's stronghold. In January the UN bolstered its peacekeeping force in the country, ignoring Gbagbo's demand to withdraw. Repeated efforts by African leaders to mediate the dispute failed, and by February extensive violence had erupted in virtually all the cities and towns in western, central, and southern regions.

On February 28 a UN team in Yamoussoukro was attacked. Three days later in Abidjan, security forces opened fire on some 5,000 women demonstrating support for Ouattara, killing at least 6. Within days, however, the tide began to turn as western cities fell to former rebels who now fought in support of Ouattara. On March 30 Ouattara's troops took Yamoussoukro. After intense fighting in Abidjan, Gbagbo was captured on April 11. The International Criminal Court, which was investigating postelection violence, issued a warrant for Gbagbo's arrest in late November. He was taken into custody and moved to The Hague, where he was charged with crimes against humanity. Meanwhile, the country began to recover from the standoff. Banks were reopened in late April, and on May 6 Ouattara was officially sworn in by the Constitutional Council. In December legislative elections (boycotted by Gbagbo's party) Ouattara's coalition easily won a large majority of the seats.

The human and economic cost of the crisis was considerable. Hundreds of thousands of Ivoirians had fled their homes, and it was believed that at least 3,000 had died. Both sides were under investigation for human rights abuses, and as one of the means to that end, the Truth, Reconciliation, and Dialogue Commission was inaugurated in September. The economy was weakened, as exports of cocoa had collapsed, and the government predicted a 6.3% drop in GDP for 2011. (NANCY ELLEN LAWLER)

CROATIA

Area: 56,542 sq km (21,851 sq mi)
Population (2011 est.): 4,287,000
Capital: Zagreb
Head of state: President Ivo Josipovic
Head of government: Prime Ministers Jadranka Kosor and, from December 23, Zoran Milanovic

In June 2011 Croatia provisionally closed negotiations to join the European Union, an achievement that was the culmination of more than a decade's efforts to undertake necessary political and economic reforms. On December 9 the country signed the accession treaty that would allow it to join the EU as the 28th member in July 2013.

Moreover, Prime Minister Jadranka Kosor had worked hard to defuse potential sources of criticism from existing member states, particularly on corruption, which proved a thorny issue for Bulgaria and Romania. The United States and the EU both commended Kosor for having led a strong fight against corruption by establishing effective interagency bodies for such investigations and declaring that there were no "untouchables." Indeed, Kosor oversaw the launch of investigations into such high-ranking individuals as Ivo Sanader, her predecessor, who had served (2003–09) as prime minister.

Sanader's arrest was precipitated by a December 2010 WikiLeaks release of a secret U.S. embassy cable in which U.S. diplomats revealed that Croatian Chief State Prosecutor Mladen Bajic had disclosed to them that he was investigating links between Sanader and several major corruption probes. As a result, the Office for Suppressing Corruption and Organized Crime (USKOK) announced that an international warrant for Sanader's arrest was being issued on suspicions that he had abused his office and conspired to commit criminal acts. Sanader was arrested on an Austrian highway and was held in Salzburg until he could be extradited in July 2011; he denied any wrongdoing and maintained that he was the target of a witch hunt.

Other corruption investigations resulted in the arrest of a senior army commander in July and the arrest of 23 customs officers and policemen from Krapina-Zagorje county on charges of having accepted bribes to permit the import of commodities. At the end of 2010, former defense minister Berislav Roncevic was convicted of having mismanaged state funds and abused his office, and a former treasurer of Kosor's party, the Croatian Democratic Union (HDZ), pleaded guilty to charges relating to another corruption case.

The positive conclusion of EU accession negotiations helped to rebuild domestic support for Kosor and for Croatia's integration into the West after a difficult spring. In February demonstrators in Zagreb called for the government's resignation, accusing it of having engaged in corruption and criticizing it for having allowed war veteran Tihomir Purda to be held in Bosnia and Herzegovina for extradition to Serbia on war crimes charges. In April further demonstrations followed when the International Criminal Tribunal for the Former Yugoslavia sentenced two former senior military officers, Ante Gotovina and Mladen Markac, to 24 years' and 18 years' imprisonment, respectively, for war crimes committed in the 1991–95 war.

Moreover, political protests were fueled by general dissatisfaction over the state of the economy and the government's perceived failure to ease the pain of the global crisis. The economy entered recession in 2009 and made only a meagre recovery in 2011, with GDP growth expected to be about 1% and the unemployment rate at 17%.

As Croatia struggled with the economic doldrums that afflicted the rest of Europe, Kosor and her HDZ government could not rebuild enough domestic support to remain in power. In the general election held on December 4, the opposition Kukuriku coalition, comprising the Social Democratic Party (SDP) and other left-liberal parties that were in power during 2000–03, claimed an overall majority in Parliament, winning 80 of 151 seats. SDP leader Zoran Milanovic was sworn in as prime minister on December 23.

(LIZ DAVID-BARRETT)

CUBA

Area: 109,886 sq km (42,427 sq mi)
Population (2011 est.): 11,240,000
Capital: Havana
Head of state and government: President of the Council of State and President of the Council of Ministers Raúl Castro Ruz

Cuba entered the 53rd year of its revolution in 2011 confronted by the urgent necessity for economic reform. Efforts focused on the development of strategies designed to decentralize economic planning. Specifically, the government sought to expand nonstate retail and private agricultural sectors, increase the efficiency of state-run enterprises, and lower government expenditures, principally through a reduction of social expenditures and the furlough of some 500,000 state employees.

The authorization of licenses in the nonstate retail (*cuenta propia*) sector proceeded steadily. The government authorized local state-run banks to provide start-up loans to small-business entrepreneurs and microcredit grants to farmers. By midyear the number of licenses the government had issued to self-employed entrepreneurs had reached a record high of 325,000. Nearly two million hectares (about five million acres) of vacant state-owned land was leased to about 140,000 small farmers. Moreover, farmers were authorized to bypass inefficient state-controlled distribution systems and sell directly to the public.

The sixth Communist Party Congress convened in April, and members ratified a number of wide-ranging economic reforms designed to improve production and shift the economy toward private enterprise. In all, about 300 legal changes were ratified, including the removal of some of the more onerous restrictions of the old order. Once again it was legal to buy and sell private homes as well as to purchase automobiles, computers, and cell phones. There were also changes in the rationing system and a relaxation of controls on foreign travel.

The economy expanded erratically through much of the year. According to 2011 reports, tourism and remuneration for medical services rendered abroad combined to contribute $4.4 billion of foreign-exchange earnings to the Cuban economy in 2010. Tourism receipts were estimated to have risen by more than 10% in the first half of 2011, while the number of visitors to the country was expected to grow from 2.5 million in 2010 to 2.7 million in 2011. Earnings from the export of nickel, tobacco, and rum also increased. The agricultural sector remained in crisis, however, with the production of traditional cash crops—including sugar, coffee, tobacco, citrus, and cacao—well below the norms of 2005. Economic hardship continued to contribute to emigration from the island. Nearly 40,000 Cubans emigrated in 2011, the largest annual departure since the emigration crisis in the summer of 1994.

Relations with the United States remained largely unchanged. The administration of Pres. Barack Obama relaxed restrictions on travel to Cuba in January 2011 and expanded contact between individuals through increased academic, educational, religious, and cultural exchanges. The number of Cuban American visitors to the island had risen markedly in 2010 to about 300,000 and was expected to reach nearly 400,000 in 2011. On average, they stayed for seven days and spent $100 per day in 2010. The $210 million they spent was equivalent to the total value of sugar exports that year. Not only were more Americans authorized to travel to Cuba, but also more Cubans received visas to visit the United States.

The Obama administration also authorized U.S. citizens to send up to $2,000 annually to individual Cubans and unlimited funds to religious organizations. Remittances from friends and family abroad promised to play a vital role in the expansion of private enterprise. Wire transfers and funds delivered by visiting friends and family infused an estimated $1.4 billion directly into the Cuban economy in 2011.

The prospects for improved relations between the Cuban and U.S. governments hardly improved, however. As late as September, Obama stipulated that the improvement of bilateral relations depended on Cuban respect for human rights, including the right to work, to change jobs, to get an education, and to start a business—conditions that immediately foreclosed the possibility of engagement. Certainly the continued imprisonment of four of the so-called Cuban Five, who in 2001 were convicted in the U.S. of espionage, did not serve to promote better ties. Nor did the conviction and imprisonment in Cuba of American technology consultant Alan Gross for having distributed communication equipment in Cuba. Gross was not among the more than 2,900 prisoners pardoned by the Cuban government as a "humanitarian gesture" in December. It seemed that relations between the two countries remained stalled in a Cold War time warp.

(LOUIS A. PÉREZ, JR.)

CYPRUS

Area: 9,251 sq km (3,572 sq mi) for the entire island; the area of the Turkish Republic of Northern Cyprus (TRNC), proclaimed unilaterally (1983) in the occupied northern third of the island, 3,355 sq km (1,295 sq mi)
Population (2011 est.): island, 1,118,000; TRNC only, 302,000 (including Turkish settlers)
Capital: Nicosia (also known as Lefkosia/Lefkosa)
Head(s) of state and government: President Dimitris Christofias; of the TRNC, President Dervis Eroglu

Cyprus remained divided in 2011, but engagement and negotiation increasingly took the place of confrontation.

Philippos Christou/AP

In Mari, Cyprus, smoke billows from the Vasilikos power station, the country's largest, which was damaged by an explosion at a nearby naval base on July 11.

Reunification talks between the two presidents, now in their third year, made progress on issues such as citizenship and power sharing, although disagreements remained. The Greek Cypriots sought one government, whereas their Turkish counterparts insisted on two sovereignties.

Both sides felt the effects of the worldwide economic downturn. Greek Cyprus's Standard & Poor's credit rating was lowered in February, partly because of ties to Greek banks, and Turkish Cyprus underwent strikes and demonstrations against austerity measures.

Cypriot life was interrupted on July 11 when confiscated contraband ammunition stored at a Greek Cypriot naval base exploded, killing 13 and injuring many more. The blast disabled a major power plant, depriving Greek Cyprus of about half of its electricity. In the aftermath the cabinet and military leaders resigned and the ruling coalition collapsed. Greek Cyprus's credit rating, having already been lowered once, fell further. Emergency measures included procurement of generators overseas, rolling blackouts, a strict austerity program to maintain the economy, and, significantly, purchase of power from Turkish Cyprus.

Despite continuing problems, interzone contact increased. The two economies were increasingly intertwined, and zone crossing was routine. A new crossing point was opened, and the UN completed removal of some 27,000 land mines from the buffer zone.

Projects to solve the island's chronic water shortage did not come to fruition in 2011, but plans for the near future included an underwater pipeline from Turkey and dams and desalination plants on the Greek side.

Cyprus remained one of the world's archaeological treasures. Archaeologists excavated sites ranging from Neolithic remains to Templar structures, often exposed by landslides or construction projects. (GEORGE H. KELLING)

CZECH REPUBLIC

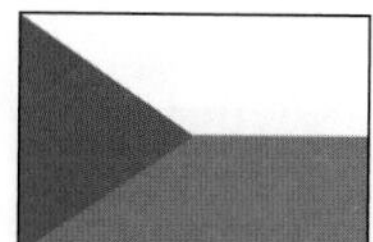

Area: 78,865 sq km (30,450 sq mi)
Population (2011 est.): 10,551,000
Capital: Prague
Head of state: President Vaclav Klaus
Head of government: Prime Minister Petr Necas

The Czech Republic cabinet remained intact in 2011, but the three-party ruling coalition underwent several crises that damaged its credibility among voters. The popularity of Prime Minister Petr Necas's centre-right government was further hit by the approval of long-awaited pension, taxation, and health care reforms, which attracted large-scale protests from trade unions, as well as harsh criticism from the political opposition.

The first political crisis of 2011 began in March when a series of corruption-related scandals and ministers' resignations threatened to bring down the government. Following some initial personnel changes, the leaders of the three coalition parties—the Civic Democrats (ODS), Tradition Responsibility Prosperity 09 (TOP 09), and Public Affairs (VV)—reached a tentative agreement in mid-May. The government was thrown into another wave of uncertainty in early June after newly reelected VV leader Radek John threatened to remove his party from the ruling coalition unless it gained additional ministerial positions. On July 1 the VV was given the posts of deputy prime minister and transport minister, and the dispute was resolved.

Conflicts continued to emerge as Necas struggled to retain control of both the government and his own party, the ODS. In August, TOP 09 began boycotting government sessions with the aim of removing an Education Ministry clerk who was accused of having neo-Nazi affiliations. The clerk was transferred to another position. Another dispute soon emerged over the government's appointment of a coordinator for EU affairs, a move that Foreign Minister Karel Schwarzenberg, the TOP 09 leader, saw as impinging on his own position. In October an internal conflict was exposed within the ODS after Necas dismissed his party's own agriculture minister, citing dissatisfaction with his performance. In November the ODS-appointed industry and commerce minister resigned on suspicion of fraud.

On the policy front, fiscal reforms ranked among the Czech Republic's key challenges in 2011, given the cabinet's aim of reducing the budget deficit to 3% of GDP by 2013. Despite the ruling coalition's strong parliamentary majority, moving ahead with those changes was more difficult than imagined because of squabbling among the governing parties.

In September the Chamber of Deputies backed the government's pension-reform legislation as well as preliminary changes to the health care system, but the approval process was slowed by the opposition's majority in the Senate. Although the Chamber of Deputies managed to override a Senate veto of reform legislation in November, the opposition threatened to take the legislation before the Constitutional Court. The new pension plan, which was widely viewed as insufficient and poorly prepared, maintained the pay-as-you-go system while allowing workers to voluntarily divert 3% from their social tax payment to private pension funds, on the condition that they add 2% from their salaries. The cabinet planned to finance those changes through an increase in the value-added tax.

The Czech economy performed fairly well in 2011, boosted by continued strong growth in industrial production and exports. In contrast, domestic demand was dampened by fiscal austerity measures that took effect at the start of the year. By mid-2011 industry had begun to weaken as the situation elsewhere in Europe deteriorated. Consumer price inflation—which remained under the Czech National Bank's 2% target band most of the year—allowed for continued low interest rates, which stood below those of the European Central Bank throughout 2011.

In December the world mourned the loss of Czech statesman and intellectual Vaclav Havel. Arguably the most successful dissident-turned-leader to emerge from the ashes of the Soviet sphere, Havel played a key role in the Velvet Revolution that led to a democratic Czechoslovakia; he served two terms as president of the Czech Republic (1993–2003). (*See* OBITUARIES.)

(SHARON FISHER)

DENMARK

Area: 43,098 sq km (16,640 sq mi)
Population (2011 est.): 5,574,000
Capital: Copenhagen
Head of state: Queen Margrethe II
Head of government: Prime Ministers Lars Løkke Rasmussen and, from October 3, Helle Thorning-Schmidt

Ten years of centre-right rule in Denmark ended on Sept. 15, 2011, when the centre-left opposition "Red Bloc" won a narrow victory in the general elections to the Folketing (parliament), and Helle Thorning-Schmidt, aged 44, the leader of the Social Democrats and daughter-in-law of former British Labour leader Neil Kinnock, became the country's first female prime minister. After 16 days of thorny negotiations, the centrist Social Liberals and the left-wing Socialist People's Party joined the Social Democrats in a three-party minority ruling coalition. The economy had been the main theme of the election as Denmark, like a number of other European states, continued to experience its worst economic downturn since World War II, with recession compounded by a banking crisis and budgetary problems. A state budget deficit equal to at least 5.5% of GDP was forecast for 2012, with growth estimated at only 1–1.5%. The new government announced a 10 billion krone (about $50 billion) growth package to kick-start the economy, including tax and welfare reforms, wage restraint, and improved education and training schemes. The government's climate policy called for a record 40% reduction in CO_2 levels by 2020.

The tight immigration policies of the previous government, which had brought Denmark much criticism, were largely set to be relaxed by the new ruling coalition. "We must integrate, not exclude," Thorning-Schmidt told the Folketing on October 4. "We must build people up, not break them down." Asylum seekers, she said, should be treated "with care and respect."

On the foreign-policy front, the new government pledged to withdraw Denmark's 750 troops from NATO's International Security Assistance Force in Afghanistan by the end of 2014. It also vowed to set up a commission to investigate Danish involvement in the Allied intervention in Iraq that began in 2003. In the summer Denmark unilaterally introduced tighter border controls with Sweden and Germany, in defiance of the European Union's 25-country Schengen Agreement on the free movement of people throughout Europe. The border controls—which upset the Germans in particular—were the price the former government of Liberal Prime Minister Lars Løkke Rasmussen had to pay to gain the support of the anti-immigration Danish People's Party for a pension and welfare reform deal. In July 50 new customs officers were deployed to Denmark's borders, a controversial move that the new government later rescinded. Denmark's isolationist mood was also reflected in the sharp rebuke delivered to Copenhagen by the UN High Commissioner for Refugees (UNHCR) following the country's rejection, in breach of two United Nations conventions, of applications for citizenship by 36 stateless young people. That criticism led in March to the dismissal of Birthe Rønn Hornbech, then integration and ecclesiastical affairs minister. Also that month Denmark contributed six F-16 fighter aircraft and a military transport plane to the international effort to protect civilians through the enforcement of the UN Security Council's no-fly zone during the civil war in Libya.

(CHRISTOPHER FOLLETT)

Danish Prime Minister Helle Thorning-Schmidt attends a summit of the European Union in Brussels, October 23. Thorning-Schmidt, the leader of the Social Democratic Party, was appointed prime minister following parliamentary elections held in September.

Eric Vidal—Reuters/Landov

DJIBOUTI

Area: 23,200 sq km (8,960 sq mi)
Population (2011 est.): 840,000
Capital: Djibouti
Head of state and government: President Ismail Omar Guelleh, assisted by Prime Minister Dileita Muhammad Dileita

The tiny yet strategically important Red Sea country of Djibouti faced civil unrest early in 2011 in the lead-up to the April presidential election. The previous year the country's parliament had passed a constitutional amendment that allowed Pres. Ismail Omar Guelleh to run for a third term. Thousands of Djiboutians gathered in the capital on

Katherine Bundra Roux—IFRC/Reuters/Landov

Women in southern Djibouti gather with representatives of the International Federation of Red Cross and Red Crescent Societies to discuss the severe drought affecting the area, August 2.

Feb. 18, 2011, to demand the immediate resignation of President Guelleh. Security forces detained four opposition party members at the illegal demonstration. The government banned another opposition protest in March, and by the end of the month, opposition parties had announced their boycott of the upcoming poll. Adding to the tense political climate, weeks prior to the balloting, Djibouti's government deported an American election-monitoring group. President Guelleh was the winner of the April 8 election, capturing more than 80% of the vote.

A severe drought, compounded with regional instability, plunged Djibouti—along with its Horn of Africa neighbours Somalia, Kenya, and Ethiopia—into one of the worst famines in decades. More than 12 million people in the region needed urgent humanitarian aid, with close to 120,000 Djiboutians—approximately 15% of the country's population—facing starvation.

(MARY EBELING)

DOMINICA

Area: 751 sq km (290 sq mi)
Population (2011 est.): 72,500
Capital: Roseau
Head of state: President Nicholas Liverpool
Head of government: Prime Minister Roosevelt Skerrit

In 2011 Dominica, like most other Caribbean states, was reeling under budgetary restraints. In February the government began a drive to control public-sector costs, instructing state-owned agencies and companies to reduce their spending by 20%. That same month, however, the country also accessed an unusual source of funds—Morocco—to finance a new 50-room, $40 million government hotel project to add to its modest existing stock of 700 hotel rooms.

In April Dominica signed a $6.29 million deal with an Icelandic agency to look into developing its geothermal energy resources. The government's long-term goal was to build a 120-MW power station that could export power to the neighbouring French overseas *départements* of Guadeloupe and Martinique.

The country's membership (since 2008) in Venezuelan Pres. Hugo Chavez's Bolivarian Alliance for the Peoples of Our America (ALBA) group seemed to be paying off. In April the government announced that over 10 projects, particularly in the area of arts and culture, would be pursued with financial support from ALBA. Improvements were slated for the Old Mill Cultural Center and the Arawak House of Culture.

The IMF said in June that it expected the Dominica economy to grow by only 0.8% in fiscal 2011 and, if this performance was to be improved in the future, the government would have to make "concerted efforts to create an environment propitious for private-sector investment." (DAVID RENWICK)

DOMINICAN REPUBLIC

Area: 48,671 sq km (18,792 sq mi)
Population (2011 est.): 9,440,000
Capital: Santo Domingo
Head of state and government: President Leonel Fernández Reyna

Leonel Fernández, the president of the Dominican Republic, was intensely pressured in 2011 by his partisans and political appointees to pursue the removal of the constitutional statute that prevented him from running for a consecutive presidential term in 2012. Enactment of the necessary constitutional change and Fernández's reelection seemed like a foregone conclusion, given that his party, the Dominican Liberation Party (PLD), held nearly two-thirds of the seats in the Chamber of Deputies. Nevertheless, Fernández opposed the change and instead shrewdly positioned himself for a run in 2016. The PLD nominated Fernández's less-charismatic colleague Danilo Medina as its candidate for the 2012 election. Some observers believed that Medina would be defeated by the Dominican Revolutionary Party candidate, former president Hipólito Mejía. The reputations of both candidates, however, were damaged by documents released by WikiLeaks.

Following tradition, the 2012 presidential campaign started early, and because there were no official limits on campaign spending, the country was quickly awash in propaganda. Little attention was paid, though, to the Dominican Republic's litany of problems: high unemployment, the growing gulf between rich and poor, declining GNP (a reflection of the volatility of the U.S. economy and of diminished remittances and tourism), 8% inflation, the growth of drug-oriented organized crime (along with its apparent linkage to government security institutions), excessive patronage, rampant corruption, and chronic and economically debilitating electricity blackouts. Increasingly tested, Dominican tolerance for mismanagement and adversity remained high.

The Dominican landscape was by no means all bleak. Investment in the minerals sector was strong, with Canada having overtaken the United States as the principal foreign investor in the Dominican Republic. Moreover, Fernández maintained his profile as an activist whose concerns spanned the hemisphere. He engaged constructively with Haiti despite ancient and ongoing grievances concerning illegal Haitian immigration, and he steadily advocated for former Honduran president Manuel Zelaya's return from exile in Santo Domingo. (JOHN W. GRAHAM)

EAST TIMOR (TIMOR-LESTE)

Area: 14,919 sq km (5,760 sq mi)
Population (2011 est.) 1,092,000
Capital: Dili
Head of state: President José Ramos-Horta
Head of government: Prime Minister Xanana Gusmão

In March 2011 East Timor applied to join the Association of Southeast Asian Nations (ASEAN), a move that was surprisingly welcomed by Indonesia; the latter's occupation of East Timor from 1975 to 1999 had devastated the country. Other ASEAN members expressed concern about East Timor's application, however, citing the burden of the group's existing responsibilities toward its poorer members. East Timor also applied to join the Melanesian Spearhead Group, which shared a preferential trade agreement between its five members.

A United Nations police force that had taken charge of security in East Timor when violence erupted in 2006 between the country's military and police returned full control of security operations to East Timorese police in late March. Some UN police were scheduled to remain until the elections scheduled for 2012.

East Timor's economy grew rapidly in 2011, with GDP growth forecast at about 8.5%. In the decade following independence, development had slowly led to improved living conditions. The infant mortality rate declined from 79 to 46 per 1,000 live births between 2000 and 2010, and life expectancy rose from 56 to 61. More than 40% of the people remained below the country's poverty line, however, and only half were literate.

(JANET MOREDOCK)

ECUADOR

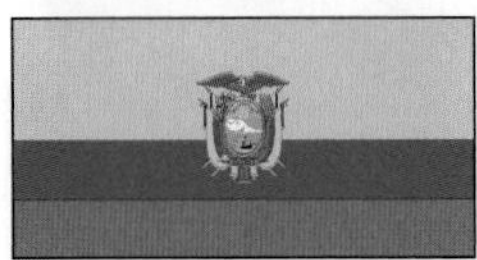

Area: 256,370 sq km (98,985 sq mi), including the 8,010-sq-km (3,093-sq-mi) Galapagos Islands
Population (2011 est.): 14,650,000 (Galapagos Islands, about 25,000)
Capital: Quito
Head of state and government: President Rafael Correa Delgado

Pres. Rafael Correa of Ecuador scored a major political victory in May 2011 when voters approved all 10 questions put forth in a national referendum. Voters supported measures to outlaw bullfighting and casino gambling and to institute reform that would grant courts wider powers in dealing with criminal suspects. Presidential powers were given a significant boost when approval was secured for Correa to appoint a commission to overhaul the judicial system and to direct the National Assembly to form a commission (reporting to him) that would regulate media content. In addition, banks and media firms were prohibited from owning other types of businesses. Correa's older brother, Fabricio, an affluent businessman, characterized the measures as a power grab and an attempt to gag opponents. The criticism grew louder after a court ruled in a one-day trial that a columnist and three directors of the daily newspaper *El Universo* had libeled Correa. In print, columnist Emilio Palacio had called the president a dictator and questioned his actions in the abortive police uprising of September 2010. The four received three-year jail terms and were fined a total of $40 million. Palacio fled to Miami. A higher court upheld the sentence, but the newspaper planned further appeals.

Ecuador expelled the U.S. ambassador, Heather M. Hodges, in March after she divulged in a confidential diplomatic cable that became public that senior police officials, and possibly Correa himself, were aware that senior police official Jaime Hurtado was involved in bribery and extortion when he was appointed national police chief by Correa in 2008. Hurtado denied the allegations. In retaliation the U.S. expelled the Ecuadoran ambassador, Luis Gallegos.

In February a judge ordered U.S.-based Chevron Corp. to pay damages of $8.6 billion and a 10% surcharge to residents of the Ecuadoran Amazon. Plaintiffs in the long-running lawsuit maintained that the region remained heavily polluted after extensive oil production in the 1970s and '80s by Texaco, later taken over by Chevron. Several levels of appeal were expected. Though several foreign oil companies withdrew from Ecuador over a law that replaced production-sharing deals with service contracts, major Spanish, Italian, and Chinese firms remained. Ecuadoran and Chinese officials signed a $2 billion loan agreement in June, pushing Ecuador's indebtedness to China to more than $6 billion. By year-end, "crowdfunding" from national and regional governments as well as prominent individuals throughout the world had raised some $116 million to surpass the $100 million in donations required by the Ecuadoran government to forgo oil development in 2012 in the ecologically sensitive Yasuní rainforest. (PAUL KNOX)

On May 7 voters in Quito, Ecuador, celebrate the results of a national referendum in which 10 ballot measures proposed by Pres. Rafael Correa, some of which aimed to strengthen presidential powers, were approved.

Patricio Realpe/AP

EGYPT

Area: 1,002,000 sq km (386,874 sq mi)
Population (2011 est.): 82,537,000
Capital: Cairo
Head of state: President Hosni Mubarak and, from February 11, Chairman of the Supreme Council of the Armed Forces Mohamed Hussein Tantawi (de facto)
Head of government: Prime Ministers Ahmad Nazif, Ahmad Shafiq from January 31, Essam Sharaf from March 7, and, from December 7, Kamal al-Ganzouri

Amr Nabil/AP

An Egyptian man injured in clashes with security forces protests against the country's ruling military council during a sit-in outside the cabinet office in Cairo, December 4.

Egypt experienced major upheaval in 2011 when mass protests toppled the regime of Pres. Hosni Mubarak. Between two million and three million protesters clashed with security forces in Cairo, Alexandria, and Suez, turning January 25—a minor holiday dedicated to the Egyptian police—into the start of a full-fledged revolution that ousted Mubarak, his family, and the National Democratic Party (NDP). Mubarak's ouster left Egypt under the control of the Supreme Council of the Armed Forces, a group of senior military officers who suspended the constitution and dismissed the two houses of the parliament. Violence by security forces left 850 Egyptians dead and 6,000 wounded.

Demonstrations organized by the "We Are All Khaled Said" group, the 6th April Movement, and the National Association for Change began peacefully on January 25 but soon became violent as security forces beat protesters and fired tear gas, water cannons, and rubber bullets into crowds. The protesters' demands for "bread, freedom, and social justice" escalated into slogans of "Down with Mubarak." Mubarak announced a dusk-to-dawn curfew in major cities and deployed the army to maintain public order. In a surprise move the Supreme Council of the Armed Forces convened without Mubarak. When troops and tanks were deployed to Tahrir Square, the hub of the protests, they did not fire on demonstrators, and military officers announced that they would support the people's "legitimate demands." As the military deployed, the 1.5 million-strong Central Security Forces belonging to the Ministry of the Interior were withdrawn from most demonstration areas. To appease protesters, Mubarak replaced the government of Prime Minister Ahmad Nazif with a cabinet of loyalists headed by Gen. Ahmad Shafiq. Mubarak announced that he would not run for a sixth term in the 2011 presidential elections. He also appointed Omar Suleiman, the head of the Egyptian General Intelligence Service, as vice president, after having refused for nearly 30 years to name a deputy.

For several days protesters were divided by Mubarak's assurances. Some believed that his promises were genuine, but others staged a sit-in Tahrir Square to continue demonstrating until their demands were met. On February 2 a few hundred pro-Mubarak loyalists, organized and paid by senior NDP officials and businessmen, rode into the square on horses and camels, attacking the protesters with knives, cudgels, stones, and petrol bombs as snipers fired on demonstrators from rooftops. The bloody episode strengthened the protesters' resolve and ignited a nationwide outcry that continued until Mubarak stepped down on February 11.

A reportedly ailing Mubarak, his two sons, Alaa and Gamal, and Habib al-Adly, the minister of the interior, were arrested, interrogated, and brought to trial on charges of having allegedly ordered the shooting of protesters, illegally enriched themselves, laundered money, and abused power. The heads of the dissolved Consultative Assembly and the People's Assembly were similarly indicted and tried. A high court ruling disbanded the NDP, confiscating its assets and returning them to the state while suspending senior NDP members' rights to form political parties, run for office, and vote for a period of five years. The final report of a special commission of the Ministry of Justice confirmed that the minister of the interior and his top lieutenants gave shoot-to-kill orders but did not offer evidence that the orders had come from Mubarak himself.

With the fall of the Mubarak regime, including the much-dreaded state security apparatus, a new sense of the people's power reigned. Freedom of political action led to the creation of many new political parties, including liberal and extreme right-wing parties. The six-decade ban on the Muslim Brotherhood was lifted. In preparation for parliamentary elections scheduled for November 28, the Brotherhood's new Freedom and Justice Party joined with over 45 other parties to form the Democratic Alliance, and liberal parties formed a coalition called the Egyptian Bloc.

Coalitions and alliances soon unraveled, however, as leaders bickered over the priority listing of candidates, the distribution of parliamentary quotas, and their discordant agendas. The lack of security in Egypt led to increases in crime and sectarian violence, including the burning of four Coptic churches.

In the first two rounds of the three-round parliamentary election, some 70% of seats were won by Salafist parties and by the Muslim Brotherhood's Freedom and Justice Party. The results stirred fears among liberals that Egypt's next parliament would be dominated by Islamists. (AYMAN M. EL-AMIR)

EL SALVADOR

Area: 21,040 sq km (8,124 sq mi)
Population (2011 est.): 6,072,000
Capital: San Salvador
Head of state and government: President Carlos Mauricio Funes Cartagena

The left-of-centre government of El Salvadoran Pres. Mauricio Funes battled the consequences in 2011 of the global recession and criminal gangs. Funes proposed a new tax to fund increased law enforcement as well as a controversial plan for military conscription of 5,000 potential gang members, youths between the ages of 16 and 18. U.S. Pres. Barack Obama visited El Salvador in March and promised $200 million to combat organized crime and drug trafficking in Central America. During a trip to Mexico, however, Funes said that any comprehensive solution to the problem had to include an American reduction in demand for narcotics. Economic recovery was slow, and rising food and fuel prices increased the cost of living. Moreover, the economic recession in the U.S. slowed remittances from Salvadorans living there to relatives and associates in El Salvador. Nonetheless, the country enjoyed a sizable increase in apparel and textile exports as a result of the Central America–Dominican Republic Free Trade Agreement (CAFTA-DR).

The Supreme Court ordered the dissolution of the two longtime dominant (1960s–80s) political parties—the Christian Democratic Party (PDC) and the National Conciliation Party (PCN), which had failed to win the required minimum 3% of the votes in the last presidential election. Two newer parties, the leftist Farabundo Martí National Liberation Front (FMLN) and the conservative Nationalist Republican Alliance (ARENA), emerged as the new principal parties.

President Funes accelerated the process of reconciliation in the country following its bloody civil war (1980–92). Measures included investigations and arrests of military personnel suspected of having violated human rights during that period. The Spanish government charged some 20 officers with the assassination in 1989 of six Jesuits (five of whom were Spaniards) along with their housekeeper and her daughter in San Salvador and requested their extradition. El Salvador also enacted a new Public Information Access Law and made media reforms that gave state-owned radio and television stations legal autonomy to broadcast independent content apart from the special interests of the government. Budgetary constraints delayed the implementation of a child-protection law.

A dispute over environmental damage from gold and silver mining by American and Canadian companies in El Salvador resulted in the government shutdown of some mining operations owing to compelling protests by local inhabitants and environmentalists over water-supply contamination. The mining companies claimed that the shutdowns violated the CAFTA-DR agreement. Violence, including a death, ensued, and journalists reporting on the issue received death threats warning them to stop publicizing the dispute.

(RALPH LEE WOODWARD, JR.)

EQUATORIAL GUINEA

Area: 28,051 sq km (10,831 sq mi)
Population (2011 est.): 720,000
Capital: Malabo
Head of state and government: President Brig. Gen. (ret.) Teodoro Obiang Nguema Mbasogo, assisted by Prime Minister Ignacio Milam Tang

Having been appointed head of the African Union (AU) for 2011, Equatorial Guinea's leader, Teodoro Obiang Nguema Mbasogo, was able to host the meeting of AU heads of state in Malabo at the end of June. Prior to the meeting, a state-funded public-relations campaign tried to challenge the general perception of the country as having one of Africa's most corrupt and repressive regimes. Vast sums were spent on creating a new venue for the meeting so that visitors did not see the squalor in which most of the population continued to live.

Several constitutional changes were approved in a November referendum, reportedly by more than 97% of voters. Although the government claimed that the revisions would provide for democratic improvements, critics charged that the changes amounted to a power grab by Obiang.

Rebecca Blackwell/AP

On June 28, during a summit of the African Union held at a multimillion-dollar luxury complex (built specifically for the meeting) in Sipopo, Equatorial Guinea, security agents sit guard outside the site's conference centre.

Obiang's son Teodorin, the agriculture minister and the favourite to succeed his 69-year-old father, was reported to be building a yacht costing three times what the country spent on health and education annually. The sole opposition member of the 100-seat parliament, Placido Mico, meanwhile, charged that the country's oil revenues trumped any leverage anyone had on Obiang's administration with regard to encouraging improvement in the area of human rights.

(CHRISTOPHER SAUNDERS)

ERITREA

Area: 121,144 sq km (46,774 sq mi)
Population (2011 est.): 5,415,000
Capital: Asmara
Head of state and government: President Isaias Afwerki

Eritrea in 2011 maintained its long-standing stance of isolationism amid growing signs that a devastating famine afflicting the Horn of Africa and a host of internal problems were hurting its people. Eritrean Pres. Isaias Afwerki's government deflected attention from the problems by denying that there was an existence of hunger in the small country. He also cut economic ties with Europe and muzzled the media.

Following years of drought in the Horn of Africa, a food shortage rose to its apex in 2011. More than 12 million people were affected in Djibouti, Eritrea, Ethiopia, Kenya, and Somalia. International news agencies estimated that the famine, which drew global attention, was affecting a large proportion of Eritreans. Despite the severe hunger, evidenced by the flight of thousands of Eritreans to neighbouring countries in search of food, the Afwerki government insisted that Eritrea could feed itself. The regime also stuck to its policy of rejecting international monetary and humanitarian aid and barring international journalists from entering the country.

On the economic front, Eritrea remained one of the world's poorest countries, but a new mining deal brought some hope for progress. Early in the year Canada-based Nevsun Resources Ltd. announced that it had begun commercial production of gold at Bisha mine, which it owned in partnership with an Eritrean government entity. The commencement of mining at Bisha mine coincided with a historic rise in the price of gold, driven by investor concerns about the economic health of developed countries. While Eritrea stood to gain from the newfound gold, its poor and often tense relations with its neighbours and many other countries became a hindering block.

In December the United Nations Security Council passed a resolution that strengthened existing sanctions against Eritrea. The resolution, which accused the Eritrean government of having fomented trouble in the Horn of Africa region and having aided al-Shabaab (an Islamist insurgent group in Somalia), required that countries with companies involved in mining operations in Eritrea exercise diligence in making sure that funds from the sector were not used to destabilize the region. It also required that Eritrea disengage from any destabilizing activities. Eritrea angrily denied the accusations presented in the resolution.

Toward year's end Eritrea severed its nearly $163 million economic-development agreement with the European Union following a disagreement between the two parties. Under the pact the EU would have initially provided Eritrea with more than $60 million in ongoing agricultural and other government projects and more than $91 million for future projects.

(PATRICK L. THIMANGU)

ESTONIA

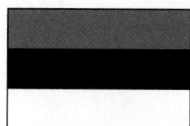

Area: 45,227 sq km (17,462 sq mi)
Population (2011 est.): 1,340,000
Capital: Tallinn
Head of state: President Toomas Hendrik Ilves
Head of government: Prime Minister Andrus Ansip

Two major elections took place in Estonia during 2011, and both reflected the growing stability in the country's political life. On March 6, in the sixth regularly scheduled parliamentary election since the restoration of independence, only four parties obtained representation in the 101-member Riigikogu (parliament), led by Prime Minister Andrus Ansip's Reform Party with 33 seats. Edgar Savisaar's Centre Party fell to 26 seats in the wake of reports that he had actively sought financial assistance from Russia. On April 5 Ansip began his seventh consecutive year as prime minister, at the head of a coalition that included the Pro Patria and Res Publica Union parties. On August 29 Pres. Toomas Hendrik Ilves easily won reelection on the first ballot in the Riigikogu by a vote of 73–25, which marked the first time since independence that the process had been completed in the parliament rather than in the larger and more cumbersome electoral college.

Voters clearly gave Ansip credit for having skillfully navigated Estonia through the recent recession and having brought the country into the euro zone on January 1. The economy rebounded very well during the year. Not only did Estonia lead all European Union countries in GDP growth rates, but unemployment fell considerably. While inflation rose, the state budget deficit remained minimal. On balance Estonia's first year of experience with the euro was clearly positive despite concerns about participation in the compulsory bailout for Greece and possibly other member states with weak economies.

For the entire year Tallinn, along with the city of Turku in neighbouring Finland, served as a European Capital of Culture. The Estonian capital emphasized its seaside location and medieval roots and offered a wide range of events to celebrate both Estonian and international culture.

(TOIVO U. RAUN)

ETHIOPIA

Area: 1,063,652 sq km (410,678 sq mi)
Population (2011 est.): 82,102,000
Capital: Addis Ababa
Head of state: President Girma Wolde-Giyorgis
Head of government: Prime Minister Meles Zenawi

The ruling Ethiopian Peoples' Revolutionary Democratic Front and allied parties continued to dominate the political landscape of Ethiopia in 2011. Arrests of several groups of activists in March, August, and September, including those charged with having affiliation with disparate opposition groups, such as the Oromo Liberation Front and the Ginbot 7, signaled that the ruling regime continued to take threats to its rule seriously. Arrests in September included those of a number of prominent journalists, such as Eskinder Nega. Two Swedish journalists were arrested in the Somali region in July and were later charged with having entered the country illegally and having aided terrorists; in December they were each convicted and sentenced to 11 years in prison.

The heavily agriculture-based Ethiopian economy was expected to grow at an average rate of about 7.5–10% in 2011. The government's continued emphasis on infrastructure and public-service expenditure resulted in substantial improvements in sectors such as health care and primary education. The poverty rate fell from 39% in 2005 to 32% in 2010, and the country was on track to achieve the UN Millennium Development Goals. In January the government responded to rising food prices by introducing price controls but had to abandon them by June because of severe shortages of basic items such as sugar and cooking oil. After the removal of the controls, prices rose dramatically and continued to register higher than in previous years.

The government's five-year economic strategy, the Growth and Transformation Plan, was released in late 2010. It

Carola Frentzen—DPA/Landov

Somali children at a refugee camp in southeastern Ethiopia, July 19. Thousands of Somalis were displaced during the year by a devastating drought in the region.

continued to keep focus on agricultural development, though more attention was given to industrial growth than in previous periods. Among the plans were large-scale commercial farms in parts of western Ethiopia, and several high-profile purchases were made by foreign companies during the year. These commercial ventures would also require the controversial resettlement of communities in those areas. While the government viewed hydropower as one of the country's most valuable resources, large-scale hydropower projects such as the Gibe (I, II and III) dam projects on the Omo River remained controversial. Though plans for the Grand Millennium Dam along the Nile River were highly publicized during the year, they were still in early stages and involved substantial diplomatic negotiations with Egypt in particular.

The Horn of Africa drought, the worst in 60 years, left more than 13 million people in the subregion in need of emergency food assistance. Though most of the victims were in southern Somalia, Ethiopia experienced drought in some of its arid regions and saw a considerable increase in refugee flows.

The border dispute with Eritrea continued with little change. Neither country had taken steps to demarcate the border in line with the 2002 ruling of the Eritrea-Ethiopia Boundary Commission, which Ethiopia had rejected. The Ethiopian military continued to engage in periodic battles with small but persistent domestic armed insurgencies, particularly those in the Somali region of the country. Later in the year Ethiopia's military also crossed over the border into neighbouring Somalia to aid that country in its battle against the Islamic insurgent group al-Shabaab.

(LAHRA SMITH)

FIJI

Area: 18,272 sq km (7,055 sq mi)
Population (2011 est.): 852,000
Capital: Suva
Head of state: President Ratu Epeli Nailatikau
Head of government: Prime Minister Voreqe Bainimarama (interim)

Some of the popular support that Fiji's interim administration had earlier enjoyed seemed to be eroding in 2011. In May a senior soldier facing charges of sedition and mutiny against the military regime, Col. Tevita Mara—the son of Fiji's first prime minister, Ratu Sir Kamisese Mara—fled to Tonga and obtained a Tongan passport. He then toured Australia and New Zealand criticizing the administration of Prime Minister Voreqe Bainimarama for its suppression of civil liberties. In August the government canceled the Fiji Methodist Church's annual conference after church leaders—active critics of the regime—refused to submit to restrictions on speakers.

Organized labour objected to the government's Essential National Industries (Employment) Decree announced in July, which banned strikes and similar actions in key industries. The following month union leaders were detained after a meeting and charged with unlawful assembly. Further, the government ceased deducting union dues from public servants' pay, a move seen by the unions as harmful and discriminatory. In December entry was denied to trade-union leaders from Australia and New Zealand who sought to meet Fiji union members on workers' rights.

Despite these pressures, the economy held steady, with tourism as its main support, although the once-central sugar industry continued its decline. In August, Standard & Poor's upgraded the country's long-term sovereign credit rating from B– to B.

(CLUNY MACPHERSON)

FINLAND

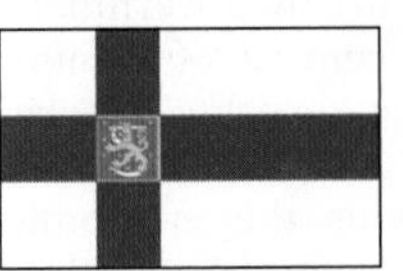

Area: 338,424 sq km (130,666 sq mi)
Population (2011 est.): 5,387,000
Capital: Helsinki
Head of state: President Tarja Halonen
Head of government: Prime Ministers Mari Kiviniemi and, from June 22, Jyrki Katainen

In early 2011 Finland's parliament decided to let former prime minister Matti Vanhanen off the hook in the long-running campaign contributions scandal, in which he was implicated, and not try him in the High Court of Impeachment. Vanhanen had been accused of receiving political donations from Nuorisosäätiö, a foundation close to his Centre Party, while granting the foundation public subsidies in his role as prime minister.

The April general elections became a peaceful demonstration of democracy at work. Prime Minister Mari Kiviniemi's Centre Party lost its status as the biggest party, with only 15.8% of the vote (down from 23.1% in 2007) and 35 seats (down from 51) in the 200-seat Parliament. The True Finns, a populist party with an anti-European Union agenda, quadrupled its votes (19.1%) and emerged with 39 seats, up from 5 in 2007. This put the True Finns close behind the Social Democrats (42 seats) and the conservative National Coalition Party (NCP; 44 seats).

The True Finns' election victory rested mainly on disappointment among voters over the EU, most notably its bailout packages for debt-ridden euro-zone countries such as Greece. Popular opinion saw the share asked of Finland as excessive and regarded the bailouts as a handout to reckless German, British, and French banks, while cautious Finnish banks had refrained from lending to unstable economies.

As head of the NCP, Jyrki Katainen led the negotiations on the formation of a new cabinet. He insisted on an unusually detailed government program, which resulted in lengthy talks. Ultimately, the True Finns chose to remain in opposition. The Social Democrats joined the coalition, on the condition that collateral be mentioned in the government program as a prerequisite for the Greek bailout.

Jutta Urpilainen, the finance minister and head of the Social Democratic Party, negotiated collateral unilaterally with Greece, but other EU countries refused to accept her plan. In September Finland agreed to join the bailout package, and it was later granted a collateral plan, though only for 20% of the sum. In return, Finland would have to pay in one installment its share (€1.44 billion [about $2 billion]) of the European Financial Stability Facility and give up any possible profits. Also, should Greece default, collateral would be paid only some 15–30 years later.

Cell-phone maker Nokia Corp. announced in February that the company would adopt Microsoft Corp.'s operating system for its smartphones. Nokia CEO Stephen Elop, the Canadian-born executive who was recruited from Microsoft in 2010, assured investors, however, that he was not a "Trojan horse" plotting to sell Nokia to his former employer and that Nokia research and development would remain in Finland.

(SUSANNA BELL)

FRANCE

Area: 543,965 sq km (210,026 sq mi)
Population (2011 est.): 63,278,000
Capital: Paris
Head of state: President Nicolas Sarkozy
Head of government: Prime Minister François Fillon

For France, 2011 was a year in which the country's politics and economy were rocked by external events. The political landscape appeared totally altered by the apparently career-ending arrest on May 15 of Dominique Strauss-Kahn in New York City for the alleged attempted rape of a hotel chambermaid. To the world Strauss-Kahn was important as the managing director of the International Monetary Fund at a time of unprecedented global financial instability. To the French, who knew him as DSK, he was important as the yet undeclared Socialist candidate with the best chance of denying Gaullist Pres. Nicolas Sarkozy reelection in 2012. That contest was expected to be closer after François Hollande was chosen in October to carry the Socialist standard. The external shocks to the French economy came from the pounding that the whole euro zone had taken from financial markets worried about the more-indebted and weakest members of the single currency union. From August on, the worries extended to the creditworthiness of France itself. French banks held large amounts of Greek, Spanish, and Italian government debt, and ratings agencies debated lowering France's AAA grade. It was therefore not a year in which it was easy for Sarkozy, as president of both the Group of Eight and Group of 20 countries for most of 2011, to focus on the wider agenda of these international bodies.

Politics. Sarkozy started the year at a low point in the polls, having felt pressure from both ends of the political spectrum. In January the far-right National Front elected Marine Le Pen (*see* BIOGRAPHIES) to succeed her father, Jean-Marie, as its leader. She brought a softer leadership style but no change in the party's hard-line anti-European and anti-immigration stances. To some French these positions seemed an appropriate response to growing friction inside the European Union caused by the financial ructions in the euro zone and to the waves of North African refugees from the unrest caused by the Arab Spring. At the other end of the spectrum, the mainstream Socialist opposition gained from popular discontent with some of Sarkozy's earlier reforms to public pensions and widespread dislike of his hyperactive presidential style.

The result was a very poor showing by Sarkozy's ruling Union for a Popular Movement (UMP) at local cantonal elections in March, the only large-scale election of the year. In the second and decisive round of these elections, the Socialists garnered nearly twice the votes (36%) won by the UMP (20%). All of the left-wing parties together captured just over 50% of the votes, while what might be called the "presidential majority" for Sarkozy totaled just under 36%. Moreover, Sarkozy was expected to face competition from a centre-right candidate in 2012. On the far right the National Front polled 11.5%, which made it the third largest single party.

Within two months, however, Sarkozy was to benefit from the bombshell of

Prime Minister Jyrki Katainen of Finland arrives at a European Union summit in Brussels on June 23, a day after assuming the premiership.

Thierry Charlier/AP

Strauss-Kahn's arrest. Indeed, the very convenience of having his most-feared Socialist rival removed from the scene fueled conspiracy theories that somehow the Élysée Palace was behind the chambermaid's accusations. According to all the polls, at the time of his arrest, DSK appeared to have been the leading candidate to beat Sarkozy. DSK was hauled off a Paris-bound Air France jet, briefly jailed, and then let out on bail in New York. The photographs of him in handcuffs were part of the U.S. judicial ritual but scandalized many in France, where public images of crime suspects are believed to damage the presumption of innocence. In August U.S. prosecutors dropped the charges because of inconsistencies in the testimony of DSK's accuser, and he was allowed to return to France, albeit with his presidential hopes over. DSK's arrest had one immediate consequence—it opened the way for Christine Lagarde, France's highly regarded and Anglophone finance minister (she had headed an American law firm), to succeed him at the IMF in Washington, D.C. François Baroin, once a close protégé of former president Jacques Chirac, replaced her as finance minister. Chirac's long-pending trial on charges of political corruption as mayor of Paris (1977–95) finally ended in December, when the 79-year-old Chirac received a two-year suspended prison sentence.

Economy. The French economy, like those of other northern members of the euro zone, started 2011 well. The expectation that it would exceed its 1.4% growth performance of 2010 seemed entirely possible when growth came in at 0.9% in the first quarter. The economy flatlined in the second quarter and grew only marginally in the third quarter, however, as the failure of repeated attempts to solve the euro-zone debt crisis began to sap the confidence of domestic businesses and consumers as well as foreign bondholders. Both France and Germany began to realize the need for closer integration if the 17 members of the euro zone were to hold together. While Germany expressed anxiety about the financial implications of this integration, the creation of an "economic government" for the euro zone had long been a French policy aim. In a series of Franco-German agreements and declarations—often presented as a fait accompli to their euro-zone partners—France accepted Germany's insistence on the euro zone's adoption of pacts on fiscal discipline and competitiveness. In return Germany accepted the French desire for closer budget coordination and tax harmonization among the 17 euro-zone members.

By August France had to look to its own financial salvation as the euro zone's crisis of confidence reached it. The government of Prime Minister François Fillon had already set the goal of reducing the public deficit from 7.1% of GDP in 2010 to 5.7% in 2011, to 4.6% in 2012, and finally to 3% in 2013. Sarkozy ordered a further tightening of the 2012 budget plans, including a temporary extra income tax on the very rich. But in September, for the first time since the Fifth Republic's creation in 1958, the Socialists won a majority in the Senate. Members of this upper chamber, less powerful than the National Assembly, are elected indirectly by establishment figures, largely local government officials. This put paid to Sarkozy's plans for a deficit-limiting constitutional amendment, as he would have had to muster a 60% majority in both houses for its passage.

Foreign Policy. France began 2011 with two military interventions under way. One was in Côte d'Ivoire in support of the UN-backed presidential candidate, Alassane Ouattara (*see* BIOGRAPHIES), against incumbent Pres. Laurent Gbagbo. Gbagbo claimed that he had won the disputed 2010 election, but the conflict was resolved in April, when pro-Ouattara forces captured and arrested Gbagbo. They were supported by French troops, who acted discreetly in an effort to minimize accusations of neocolonialism in the former French colony. France's bigger commitment had been in Afghanistan, but on a visit there in July, Sarkozy announced that 1,000 French troops would leave by the end of 2012 and the remaining 3,000 by 2014.

Despite these commitments, French forces found themselves virtually leading the UN-authorized international intervention in Libya. These actions were spurred by Sarkozy's embarrassment at having been not only slow to back the Arab Spring revolts in Tunisia and Egypt but also initially unsupportive on the advice of his foreign minister, Michèle Alliot-Marie. In January, just days before Tunisian Pres. Zine al-Abidine Ben Ali was deposed, Alliot-Marie had offered him French security assistance. It was later revealed that Alliot-Marie had received holiday hospitality from those close to the regime. She was forced to resign in February and was replaced as foreign minister by Alain Juppé, who had served as prime minister under Chirac. French planes were among the first to strike military targets associated with Muammar al-Qaddafi's forces in Libya, and France was the first country to recognize the rebel Libyan government. France also dropped arms to the rebels, arguing that this was for the rebels' "self-defense" and therefore not in contravention of the United Nations Security Council resolution.

Sarkozy had hoped that the G20 summit in Cannes in early November would produce significant reforms to the international economy, but the unresolved euro crisis dominated the agenda. Sarkozy and German

On September 15 French Pres. Nicolas Sarkozy (right) and British Prime Minister David Cameron greet a crowd in Benghazi, Libya, during a joint visit to the country in which they pledged support to its new leadership.

Philippe Wojazer/AP

Chancellor Angela Merkel failed to win any commitments from non-European G20 members to contribute to the European Financial Stability Facility, the euro zone's main bailout fund. There was, however, G20 agreement on exempting emergency supplies from food-export bans and on the need to completely recast the Doha round of World Trade Organization talks.

By year's end the future of the euro was very unclear. After the U.K. vetoed an amendment to the existing EU treaty, the remaining 26 EU countries agreed in December to negotiate by March 2012 a separate treaty on tighter economic discipline rules. This embryo of economic government appeared to satisfy Sarkozy, but many in France, and particularly Socialist presidential candidate Hollande, argued that only massive intervention by the European Central Bank could solve the immediate euro crisis. (DAVID BUCHAN)

Joel Bouopda Tatou/AP

Declaring himself the winner of the disputed 2009 presidential election in Gabon, which he claimed had been marred by fraud, opposition leader André Mba Obame takes a self-administered oath of office at the Libreville headquarters of his National Union party, January 25.

GABON

Area: 267,667 sq km (103,347 sq mi)
Population (2011 est.): 1,534,000
Capital: Libreville
Head of state: President Ali Ben Bongo Ondimba
Head of government: Prime Minister Paul Biyoghé Mba

In 2011 opposition parties in Gabon continued to dispute the results of the 2009 presidential elections, maintaining their charges of widespread electoral fraud. There was general consternation when, on January 25, National Union (NU) party leader and presidential candidate André Mba Obame declared himself the victor and took the oath of office at his party headquarters. Hours later the Council of State, a Gabonese judicial organ, dissolved the NU for treason. Obame and some 30 party members took refuge at UN headquarters in Libreville. Negotiations under the auspices of UN Secretary-General Ban Ki-Moon ended the immediate crisis, but the Council of State refused to lift the dissolution order on the NU.

Preparations were made for legislative elections scheduled for December. In March, after consultations with opposition parties, Pres. Ali Ben Bongo Ondimba announced plans to introduce biometric voting cards, featuring photographs and digitized fingerprints, and in May proposed that the elections be delayed until 2012 to allow adequate time for implementing the biometric system. The government also wished to delay elections in order to avoid conflict with its hosting of the African Cup of Nations tournament in January 2012. On June 3 the Constitutional Court denied the request to postpone the elections. The government later stated that biometrics would not be able to be used in the 2011 elections. The elections, held in December, were boycotted by some opposition groups over the lack of biometrics. Not surprisingly, Bongo's coalition won the vast majority of the legislative seats.

On February 25 Bongo and Pres. Teodoro Obiang Nguema Mbasogo of Equatorial Guinea met with Ban regarding a border dispute. They agreed to take their dispute to the International Court of Justice.

(NANCY ELLEN LAWLER)

GAMBIA, THE

Area: 11,632 sq km (4,491 sq mi)
Population (2011 est.): 1,776,000
Capital: Banjul
Head of state and government: President Col. Yahya Jammeh

As The Gambia moved toward its November 2011 presidential election, there were widespread reports of human rights abuses against those opposed to Pres. Yahya Jammeh, who was serving his third term as elected president. The official period for opposition parties to campaign was reduced to only 11 days in November. Journalists and civil society activists were harassed, and the president controlled the judiciary. With independent radio stations banned, only the state-run radio broadcast news. The state's Intelligence Agency was said to be involved in extrajudicial detentions and the torture of journalists and opposition protesters. In June treason charges were brought against a former government minister and others for having distributed T-shirts carrying slogans that called for an end to dictatorship in the country. In July, as Jammeh celebrated the 17th anniversary of the coup by which he had come to power, international human rights organizations reported that a climate of fear had gripped the country.

Government-appointed local leaders rallied behind Jammeh, though they had not been successful in the previous year's campaign to have him crowned the king of Gambia. As the Nov. 24, 2011, election drew near, Jammeh said that no election or coup would remove him from office because God had placed him there. He was reelected with 72% of the vote, although the poll was clouded by accusations of intimidation, fraud, and media bias in favour of Jammeh during the run-up to the election. (CHRISTOPHER SAUNDERS)

GEORGIA

Area: 57,160 sq km (22,070 sq mi), excluding the disputed areas (from the early 1990s)/autonomous regions of Abkhazia (8,640 sq km [3,336 sq mi]) and South Ossetia (3,900 sq km [1,506 sq mi])
Population (2011 est.): 4,474,000, excluding the populations of Abkhazia and South Ossetia
Capital: Tbilisi
Head of state and government: President Mikheil Saakashvili, assisted by Prime Minister Nikoloz (Nika) Gilauri

On August 27, a day after his election as president of the Republic of Abkhazia (a separatist region of Georgia), Aleksandr Ankvab poses with a portrait of himself at a news conference in Sokhumi.
Mikhail Metzel/AP

The Georgian authorities moved resolutely in 2011 to neutralize any new opposition alliance. On May 21 the People's Representative Assembly, a new alliance of radical parties, launched a series of demonstrations in Tbilisi to demand early parliamentary and presidential elections. Police and security forces intervened on May 26, using force to disperse the protesters. A police officer and a demonstrator were killed by a car leaving the venue, allegedly driven by Badri Bitsadze, the husband of former parliament speaker Nino Burjanadze. Bitsadze was tried in absentia and sentenced to five and a half years in prison for "attacking police."

Difficult talks between the government and six moderate opposition parties ended in June with the formulation of amendments to the election law. The amendments, however, failed to incorporate measures proposed by the opposition to preclude malpractice.

On October 7 billionaire Bidzina Ivanishvili announced his intention to seek the position of prime minister or parliament speaker in 2012 in order to fight corruption, attract foreign investment, and ease tensions with Russia. Georgian Pres. Mikheil Saakashvili revoked Ivanishvili's Georgian citizenship. In December Ivanishvili formed an opposition movement known as Georgian Dream.

Sergei Bagapsh, president of the breakaway Republic of Abkhazia, died unexpectedly on May 29. (*See* OBITUARIES.) Vice Pres. Aleksandr Ankvab was elected his successor on August 26. In South Ossetia the Supreme Court annulled the results of the presidential runoff ballot in November and scheduled a repeat election for March 2012.

Visiting Tbilisi in November, NATO Secretary-General Anders Fogh Rasmussen held out the prospect that Georgia might be offered a Membership Action Plan, a step toward NATO membership, at the alliance's May 2012 summit in Chicago. The European Union formally announced on December 5 that it would begin the talks on a free-trade agreement with Georgia.

Under pressure from the U.S., in November Georgia shelved its longstanding veto of Russia's application for membership in the World Trade Organization in return for the deployment of international inspectors to monitor trade between the Russian Federation and Georgia's breakaway republics of Abkhazia and South Ossetia.

GDP grew by 6.5% during the first 10 months. Annual inflation for January–August was 7.2%. By October Georgia's foreign debt had soared to more than $4.25 billion. (ELIZABETH FULLER)

GERMANY

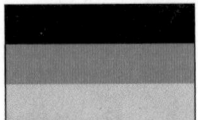

Area: 357,104 sq km (137,879 sq mi)
Population (2011 est.): 81,604,000
Capital: Berlin; some ministries remain in Bonn
Head of state: President Christian Wulff
Head of government: Chancellor Angela Merkel

All in all, 2011 was an unpredictable year for Germany. As the German economy enjoyed a remarkable recovery from the global slowdown, optimism would have been expected to reign throughout the country. Chancellor Angela Merkel's government struggled, however, with apparent indecisiveness, political challenges from opposition parties, a euro crisis involving a bailout for Greece, and an academic-corruption scandal, all of which left a general feeling of uncertainty and precariousness. The financial crises drew into doubt many financial ideals that Germans had long held, while fundamental constitutional precepts were threatened by new security measures and by the political battle over Stuttgart 21, a controversial building project. On the international stage Germany showed what appeared to be a lack of resolve, drawing into question all that it had stood for over the previous few decades. As a result, Germany faced a period of deep reflection in which traditional values and ideals were questioned.

Domestic Affairs. The year started with high hopes in the face of the first signs of economic recovery in 2010. Positive perceptions quickly became obscured, however, by the continuation of the euro-zone crises. The financial emergency in Greece and the ever-increasing need to boost the level of aid to that country caused high levels of strife in the German Bundestag (parliament) and within Merkel's governing coalition. Challenges in Germany's Federal Constitutional Court came to a head in

September when the court finally rendered the decision that the aid packet to Greece was constitutional. The court added a warning, however, as a reminder to the government that the Bundestag needed to be more involved in the decision-making process. This was symptomatic of one of the large social debates throughout the year: was Germany, like many other Western democracies, moving toward a political climate in which the executive would increasingly usurp and undermine the powers of the legislature?

The Constitutional Court's decision in regard to financial aid to Greece was not a surprise to observers. When the court issued its decision in 2009 concerning the passage of the European Union's Lisbon Treaty, it had cautioned Germany's executive branch of government to observe the legitimate separation of powers and called for a strengthening of the parliament at the national level. The fact that two consecutive warnings had been handed to Merkel's government—both admonishing it to involve the Bundestag more prominently in decisions relating to the EU—added further fuel to the public debate on the executive usurpation of power. The continued reluctance of the government to commit to an early phaseout of nuclear power was another indication of the power struggle between the parliament and the government. Following the nuclear catastrophe that took place in the wake of the earthquake and massive tsunami in Japan early in the year, subsequent high levels of fear and nuclear hysteria in Germany led Merkel's administration to retrench and fix on a nuclear power phaseout by 2022.

The local parliamentary elections held in many parts of the country in 2011 proved to be a major contributor to the apparent difficulties of the government. *Länder* (state) elections in Hamburg, Saxony-Anhalt, Rhineland-Palatinate, Hesse, Bremen, Mecklenburg–West Pomerania, Lower Saxony, Berlin, and, especially, Baden Württemberg recorded significant losses for the ruling party. The latter election overshadowed many national and international decisions—from German abstention in the UN Security Council decision in favour of intervention in Libya to decisive financial action in Greece and to the nuclear energy phaseout. Baden Württemberg had been a Christian Democratic Union (CDU) stronghold since the foundation of West Germany after World War II. Therefore, a loss for Merkel's CDU party in Baden Württemberg would be interpreted as a major loss of face for the chancellor.

For many weeks prior to the elections, doubt was cast over a CDU win in Baden Württemberg because of a controversial building project in Stuttgart, the state's capital city. Stuttgart 21 was an ambitious building and city-development project that was intended to serve as an international role model for environmental and energy-neutral building and to support the flagging local economy, thus allowing Stuttgart to compete with the other two large economic centres in the country's south, Frankfurt and Munich. During the election campaign the opposition parties denounced the enterprise and encouraged xenophobic hysteria among voters relating to fears that the building project would be opening Stuttgart's inner-city area to large-scale apartment-building projects. This and worries over the initial high cost of the development, which included an enlarged main railway station complex, were enough to win the regional elections within the capital for the opposition and to seriously damage the Christian Democrats. In the end the CDU, which had controlled the state for over 50 years, took 39% of the vote in Baden Württemberg, and the party was forced to give way to a coalition government between the Green Party (24.2%) and the Social Democratic Party (SPD; 23.1%).

Even after the elections, Stuttgart 21 continued to wreak havoc with German politics. The opposition's promise to halt the project was neither legally nor economically feasible. Moreover, the opposition promised moves toward direct democracy with an increased use of referenda. This would necessitate a constitutional change because the German constitution, as a result of lessons learned from the Third Reich, did not accommodate referenda. Although this would be a difficult promise to keep, especially in a coalition government, it did open a nationwide public and political debate on the desirability of constitutional change to permit referenda and to create pathways for increased public involvement in day-to-day political decision making.

International Affairs. In the international arena, Germany unexpectedly found itself on the same side as Russia and China, in opposition to all of the other Western powers, in its refusal to support military intervention in Libya. In Germany, where the country's history under the Third Reich still had repercussions, there was a deep-seated public abhorrence of making a commitment to military intervention. Any decision to send troops into any form of conflict was widely unpopular in Germany—and with the CDU's precarious situation in the state elections scheduled to take place just days later—Merkel ordered the German representative to abstain in the UN Secu-

On July 9 in Stuttgart, Ger., a woman protests against the planned Stuttgart 21 project, which included the demolition of Stuttgart's historic train station.

Kai Pfaffenbach—Reuters/Landov

rity Council vote that would have committed Germany to aiding in the action in Libya.

The decision for a quick nuclear phaseout, which was very popular with the German public, made the governments of some other Western countries uncomfortable, especially since it would increase Germany's reliance on Russian natural gas resources to a level of almost absolute dependency. The fact that the international heads of state learned of this resolution from the news agencies rather than through a courtesy phone call from Merkel did not endear the chancellor to those other leaders and changed Merkel's image in the international community from the "new iron lady" to that of a political leader desperately grappling to preserve her power base.

Economic Affairs. This image of a struggling government was reinforced by the slow and constantly changing postures Germany took throughout the Greek crisis and the wider critical implications for the survival of the euro. During the previous two decades, Germany had increasingly resented its position as the paymaster of Europe, and even prior to 2011, it had been slow to commit funds that were greater than those that other large member countries designated to EU ventures. Germany had always been decisive in its actions and ready to align the EU interests with its own. Therefore, the evident indecisiveness regarding aid to Greece not only undermined Germany's position in the international community but also contributed to the lack of trust in the euro. In late September the Bundestag finally gave its approval for Germany to join the eurozone bailout of Greece.

Internally, Germany completed its stringent social security reforms and austerity measures, and the continued increase in GDP growth, even with the looming euro crisis, led to initial economic optimism. After GDP growth of more than 3.5% in 2010, economists anticipated a slowdown to 2.9% in 2011, and in October analysts predicted a drop to only 0.8% in 2012. The debate continued on whether the top 20% of income earners in Germany should pay more than 50% of the federal income tax collected, a dispute that aggravated the traditional political alienation between the left-wing parties and the centrist parties. Nonetheless, unemployment, which had hovered around 9.7% from 1991 to 2010, dropped to 6.8% in December 2011.

Cultural Affairs. The German trust in the country's educational system as well as its government was further undermined by various corruption scandals surrounding the academic titles granted to a number of individuals. In early March, Defense Minister Karl-Theodor zu Guttenberg resigned from office after he admitted that he had plagiarized parts of his doctoral dissertation. Guttenberg had been a distinguished figure in the Christian Social Union (CSU), the CDU's Bavarian partner. Other prominent politicians were also found guilty of having plagiarized in their Ph.D. theses, notably Silvana Koch-Mehrin, a Free Democratic Party member of the European Parliament. German universities were notoriously insular and disconnected from the international arena in most subjects, but nationally high levels of trust and pride had existed in the educational system. Over the previous decade there had been recurrent political attempts to force German universities into greater transparency and competitiveness, and it was yet to be seen if the plagiarism scandal could achieve what politicians had failed to accomplish.

As elsewhere in the Western world, German authorities expressed worries that citizens were increasingly willing to resort to violent protests. On the occasion of an anti-neo-Nazi demonstration in February, protesters from both sides clashed, and violence ensued. Tempers flared regarding Stuttgart 21 throughout the year, with individuals on both sides resorting to violence and inflicting property damage. The dispute over Stuttgart 21 culminated in the summer with the serious injury of nine policemen, who had been attempting to regulate a demonstration against the project.

In sports, Germany hosted the FIFA women's association football (soccer) World Cup in 2011. The title was taken by newcomer Japan in a final against the highly favoured U.S. Although Germany, the two-time defending champion, lost to Japan in the quarterfinals, the enthusiastic German fans showed the same high hospitality standards they had shown throughout the men's FIFA World Cup in 2006. In Formula 1 Grand Prix auto racing, 24-year-old Sebastian Vettel (*see* BIOGRAPHIES), competing for Red Bull, managed to secure the world drivers' title for a second consecutive year, becoming the youngest double world champion in the history of Formula 1 racing.

(NICOLA CORKIN)

GHANA

Area: 238,533 sq km (92,098 sq mi)
Population (2011 est.): 24,661,000
Capital: Accra
Head of state and government: President John Evans Atta Mills

In 2011 Ghanian Pres. John Evans Atta Mills and his ruling National Democratic Congress (NDC) confronted the twin tasks of implementing their electoral platform and stabilizing economic recovery. Mills dealt with significant party factionalism arising from a growing lack of faith in his ability to formulate a strategy to lead the NDC to victory in the forthcoming 2012 presidential and legislative elections. Further exacerbating tension within the NDC was a struggle for party leadership between Mills and Konadu Agyeman Rawlings, the wife of former president Jerry Rawlings, at its congress in Sunyani early in July. She lost decisively, mustering a paltry 90 votes out of 2,861 (or 3.1%).

Traditional rulers posed a potential source of unrest, stemming from resentment over Parliament's rejection (in November 2010) of the Western Regional House of Chiefs' demand that 10% of the country's new oil revenue be earmarked for their region. They argued that the commencement of oil production in the offshore Jubilee oilfield directly impinged on local livelihoods and environment. While the chiefs' position was supported by Vice Pres. John Dramani Mahama and some members of the opposition New Patriotic Party, it was ignored in the final version of the Petroleum Revenue Management Act enacted in March.

Oil production and related activity boosted the country's economic growth to 8.9%. Agriculture also maintained a robust growth rate of more than 5%. Cocoa farmers had high yields; despite falling world prices, they benefited from the political turmoil in neighbouring Côte d'Ivoire, the world's largest cocoa producer. The mining and quarrying sector grew by 7.6%, with increases in gold (6.8%), bauxite (27.1%), and manganese (55.4%) production.

(LARAY DENZER)

GREECE

Area: 131,957 sq km (50,949 sq mi)
Population (2011 est.): 11,372,000
Capital: Athens
Head of state: President Karolos Papoulias
Head of government: Prime Ministers George Papandreou and, from November 11, Lucas Papademos.

On November 14, three days after he was installed as Greece's prime minister, Lucas Papademos delivers a speech before the Greek Parliament.
Thanassia Stavrakis/AP

Throughout 2011 Greece struggled to cope with its deep financial and economic crisis and to implement reforms aimed at averting default. In the face of increasing public dissatisfaction with the course and cost of reforms, a deepening political crisis culminated in November in the resignation of the government headed by Panhellenic Socialist Movement (PASOK) leader George Papandreou and the appointment of a broader-based transitional government led by technocrat Lucas Papademos.

As part of the aid agreements negotiated with the EU and the IMF the previous year, the government's fiscal and economic policies were under constant scrutiny by the so-called troika that consisted of the European Commission, the European Central Bank (ECB), and the IMF. While the troika's progress reports generally acknowledged the government's efforts to tackle the crisis, they nevertheless called for additional reforms and measures, including further spending cuts and the privatization of state assets. The relatively slow pace of reforms repeatedly threatened the disbursement of aid to Greece. In June euro-zone ministers stipulated that Greece had to implement new austerity measures in order to receive the next tranche of its loan.

In mid-June Papandreou hinted at his willingness to step down if the centre-right New Democracy (ND) party would agree to enter a government of national unity. After ND leader Antonis Samaras turned down the offer, Papandreou reshuffled his government on June 17. Most notably, Evangelos Venizelos moved from defense to the crucial Finance Ministry and became deputy prime minister.

On June 29 Parliament passed the so-called midterm fiscal plan, a new austerity package that called for €28 billion (about $41 billion) to be raised over the following five years through tax hikes, public-sector layoffs, and cuts to health care, social benefits, defense, and public investments, along with another €50 billion (about $72 billion) through privatization of public assets. In September the government announced a reformed tax system, as well as a new property tax, to be collected via electricity bills to fight tax evasion. These and other reforms met with significant resistance from opposition parties, trade unions, and citizens. Throughout the year Greece experienced a series of strikes as well as civil disobedience, which at times erupted in violence.

On July 21 euro-zone leaders agreed on a new aid deal for Greece that totaled €109 billion (about $158 billion) and, for the first time, involved private lenders. On October 27 those leaders raised the amount of the bailout to some €130 billion (about $183 billion). Under this arrangement, private banks agreed to write off 50% of the money Greece owed them, which amounted to about €100 billion (about $141 billion).

Papandreou's announcement on October 31 that he would call a referendum on the latest agreement triggered negative reactions both domestically and from Greece's partners, who brought into question the country's continued membership in the EU and the euro zone. As resistance increased, even within his own party, Papandreou reneged on the referendum and proposed the formation of a coalition government, though he insisted that a vote of confidence be held first. On November 5 Parliament voted in favour of the government. Papandreou then called for talks on a new government under the auspices of Pres. Karolos Papoulias. After days of negotiations and Papandreou's formal resignation on November 9, the two main parties and the rightist Popular Orthodox Rally (LAOS) agreed on a new government. Its main tasks would be to see the October 27 bailout agreement, as well as the measures required for its implementation, through Parliament and to lead the country toward elections in early 2012. The new government, headed by Papademos—formerly the governor of the Bank of Greece and an ECB vice president—took office on November 11. Venizelos and many other key PASOK ministers retained their posts. ND took over the Ministries of Foreign Affairs and of National Defense but declined to name any sitting MPs as government ministers. LAOS took over the Ministry of Infrastructure, Transport and Networks. The interim government won a vote of confidence on November 16.

The Greek economy was estimated to have shrunk by about 5.5% in 2011, while the budget deficit was estimated at about 9%. Unemployment stood at 18.4% in August, a 50% increase over the previous year. A significant drop in domestic consumption caused by the crisis forced many small businesses to close. During the first half of 2011, the major rating agencies repeatedly downgraded Greece's credit rating, and it became the world's least-creditworthy country.

Greece's foreign relations remained stable despite some friction with Turkey over the latter's opposition to Cyprus's plans to drill for oil and gas off its southern coast. On December 5 the International Court of Justice ruled that Greece had violated the 1995 accord on Macedonia by blocking a 2008 invitation for Macedonia to join NATO.

(STEFAN KRAUSE)

GRENADA

Area: 344 sq km (133 sq mi)
Population (2011 est.): 108,000
Capital: Saint George's
Head of state: Queen Elizabeth II, represented by Governor-General Sir Carlyle Glean
Head of government: Prime Minister Tillman Thomas

As it tried to recover in 2011 from the economic slump affecting most Caribbean states, Grenada was heartened by good financial news. In late 2010 the IMF stated that Grenada would be allowed to continue to draw down portions of the more than $13 million three-year Extended Credit Facility it had provided in April 2010. The government predicted in January that it expected an actual return to economic growth in 2011, about 2–2.5%, following the downturn of 1.4% in 2010. The expansion was expected to come from increased tourist receipts, construction activity, and the growing light manufacturing and agriculture sectors.

Grenada moved to better secure its borders in March by signing a Memorandum of Understanding with the U.S. The agreement committed Washington to providing maritime equipment—including two interceptor vessels, communications equipment, and information systems—in support of Grenada's ongoing battle against seaborne drug trafficking and other threats.

Grenada enhanced its relations with China in May, when a visiting delegation of Chinese business leaders pledged to invest about $250 million in various areas of the economy, including hotels and cocoa processing. In June the country secured a $26.2 million loan from the World Bank to improve risk assessment in the public sector and to make public buildings as safe as possible from the expected impact of climate change.

(DAVID RENWICK)

GUATEMALA

Area: 109,117 sq km (42,130 sq mi)
Population (2011 est.): 14,729,000
Capital: Guatemala City
Head of state and government: President Álvaro Colom Caballeros

Guatemala suffered deadly violence by organized-crime gangs during 2011. Harsh crackdowns on gangs in El Salvador, Colombia, and Mexico had pushed criminals from those countries into Guatemala to traffick arms and drugs as well as to launder their profits. Despite efforts by the government of Pres. Álvaro Colom to combat these criminals, the violence worsened. In addition to perpetrating street violence, gangs demanded protection money from bus companies and individual households in the capital and elsewhere. They murdered those who refused to pay. Moreover, some 35 political candidates or activists were killed in 2011, and on July 9 Argentine singer-songwriter Facundo Cabral (*see* OBITUARIES) died in Guatemala City when he was attacked in the car in which he was riding with a concert promoter, who was believed to have been the actual target of the assault. In June, U.S. Secretary of State Hillary Clinton visited Guatemala and promised to increase U.S. aid for antidrug efforts in Central America. Cocaine farmers were accused of having destroyed large portions of Guatemala's rainforest to build airstrips, an action that threatened the UNESCO Maya biosphere reserve that included ancient Mayan ruins. In July Colom proposed a "NATO-style" Central American military force to rid the region of gangs.

The Colom government was only partly successful in its prosecution of members of earlier administrations for alleged criminal activity. Notably, former president Alfonso Portillo was found innocent of embezzlement of government funds. He remained incarcerated, however, to await extradition to the United States on money-laundering charges.

Crime and corruption were thus major issues in the presidential election held on September 11. Retired army general Otto Pérez Molina of the Patriotic Party, who had promised to employ "iron fist" policies against the gangs, finished atop the field of 10 candidates with 36% of the first-round votes. His principal opposition was the wife of President Colom, Sandra Torres, of the National Unity of Hope–Grand National Alliance (UNE-GANA) coalition, who divorced her husband in an attempt to skirt a constitutional provision prohibiting close relatives from succeeding to the presidency. Eventually, the constitution court ruled that she was still ineligible to run. Out of time, UNE-GANA did not run a presidential candidate. Pérez Molina and second-place finisher (24%) Manuel Baldizón, of the conservative Renewed Democratic Liberty Party (Líder), collided in the

Otto Pérez Molina, a retired army general who founded and led the Patriotic Party of Guatemala, addresses supporters in Guatemala City on November 7, a day after winning election as president of the country.

Rodrigo Abd/AP

November 6 runoff election, which was won by Pérez Molina, who captured some 54% of the vote.

(RALPH LEE WOODWARD, JR.)

GUINEA

Area: 245,857 sq km (94,926 sq mi)
Population (2011 est.): 10,222,000
Capital: Conakry
Head of state and government: President Alpha Condé; assisted by Prime Minister Mohamed Said Fofana

In Guinea many political developments in 2011 stemmed from events in late 2010. On Dec. 30, 2010—nine days after his inauguration as Guinea's first democratically elected president since independence—Alpha Condé announced that all civil servants in both his and the prime minister's office would be replaced. He then undertook a reform of the security services, which won commendation from the UN as a model for other West African countries. President Condé admitted that Guinea was virtually bankrupt and accused the previous military junta of having spent more in its two-year rule than had all the governments since independence. Nearly $130 million in unpaid taxes and royalties was owed to the state by individuals, mining companies, and politicians. On September 12, Mines Minister Mohamed Lamine Fofana stated that the government had annulled an agreement reached between the junta and the China International Fund that gave the latter the right to exploit all undeveloped mineral resources. Two days later Prime Minister Mohamed Said Fofana implemented a new mining code intended to prevent multinational corporations from bribing government officials to obtain cheap concessions.

On March 8 hundreds of army recruits rioted at their training camp in Kissidougou, 600 km (375 mi) southeast of Conakry. Having already spent two years in training, they were demanding immediate induction into the army. At least one recruit died in the violence.

Simmering trouble between Kpelle and Malinke peoples in the southeastern town of Galakpaye erupted on May 2. At least 25 died, including 10 who were reportedly burned alive.

On July 19 soldiers still loyal to the former junta launched a rocket attack on President Condé's residence. The president was uninjured, but at least one guard was killed as government forces repelled the attack. Afterward, 37 soldiers, including some top officers, were arrested, and by early August, 16 people had been charged with the attempted assassination of the president.

(NANCY ELLEN LAWLER)

GUINEA-BISSAU

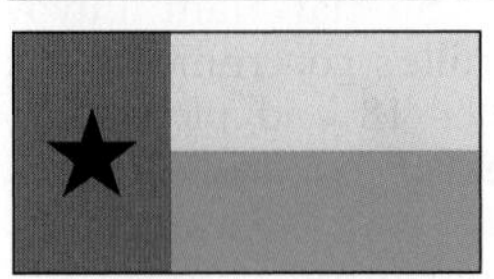

Area: 36,125 sq km (13,948 sq mi)
Population (2011 est.): 1,606,000
Capital: Bissau
Head of state and government: President Malam Bacai Sanhá, assisted by Prime Minister Carlos Gomes Júnior

Though Guinea-Bissau remained one of the poorest countries in the world, it saw relative political stability in 2011 after the chaos of previous years. In late 2010 tensions had flared between Pres. Malam Bacai Sanhá and Prime Minister Carlos Gomes Júnior after Gomes suspended the interior minister for contravening cabinet instructions to freeze promotions in the defense and security forces. Still, Sanhá retained Gomes in his post when he reshuffled the cabinet in August 2011.

In preparation for a national conference on reconciliation, regional conferences for defense and security personnel were held. The Community of Portuguese-Speaking Countries and the Economic Community of West African States helped to prepare a road map for security-sector reform, while Angola provided support for the restructuring of the armed forces.

Improvements were seen in the economic sector; Guinea-Bissau's international debt was cut by 87%, and production of the country's main crop, cashew nuts, increased significantly. This positive news was tempered by the fact that drug trafficking continued, as did food shortages, and that those responsible for the assassination of the president and others in 2009 still had not been brought to justice. In late December, while Sanhá was abroad for medical treatment, a coup attempt was quickly put down. Naval chief and reputed drug kingpin Rear Adm. José Americo Bubo Na Tchuto, allegedly the mastermind of the plot, was arrested.

(CHRISTOPHER SAUNDERS)

GUYANA

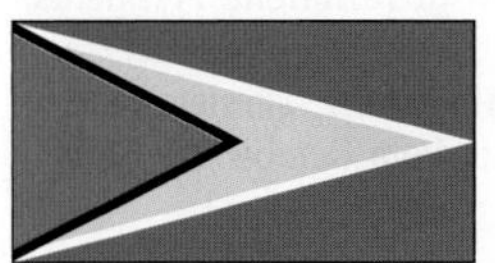

Area: 214,999 sq km (83,012 sq mi)
Population (2011 est.): 756,000
Capital: Georgetown
Head of state: Presidents Bharrat Jagdeo and, from December 3, Donald Ramotar
Head of government: Prime Minister Sam Hinds

An ongoing battle between the People's Progressive Party (PPP) administration and the Guyana media heated up in March 2011. Pres. Bharrat Jagdeo called on PPP supporters to boycott newspapers and television stations "hostile" to the government by not "putting money" in their "pockets." The PPP's Donald Ramotar won the presidency in elections held on November 28 and was sworn in on December 3.

The cost projections for Guyana's first major move into renewable energy increased in April when the promoters of the proposed 165-MW Amaila Falls hydropower project on the Kuribrong River 250 km (about 155 mi) southwest of the capital, Georgetown, revised the sum to around $700 million; that figure was $50 million more than the 2010 estimate. Nevertheless, the proposed operator and shareholder in the project, the U.S.-based company Sithe Global Power, predicted that the project could still become a reality by 2015.

Determined to keep its sugar industry alive, even though other Caribbean countries had opted out of the sector, Guyana obtained a $27 million loan in March from the European Union for developing and increasing sugar production. In September Guyana asked the UN Commission on the Limits of the Continental Shelf to approve the extension of its exclusive economic zone by an additional 150 nautical miles.

(DAVID RENWICK)

HAITI

Area: 27,700 sq km (10,695 sq mi)
Population (2011 est.): 9,720,000, including 1,300,000 people displaced by the January 2010 earthquake
Capital: Port-au-Prince
Head of state and government: Presidents René Préval and, from May 14, Michel Martelly, assisted by Prime Ministers Jean-Max Bellerive and, from October 18, Garry Conille

In 2011 elections and politics took centre stage as Haiti struggled to recover from the 2010 earthquake. On March 20 Michel Martelly (*see* BIOGRAPHIES), a singer-turned-politician, won two-thirds of the vote in an unprecedented presidential runoff election that attracted fewer than 30% of eligible voters. Outgoing president René Préval's Unity party won a majority in the Senate and the largest bloc in the lower house.

At the National Palace in Port-au-Prince, Haiti, a man costumed as national hero Toussaint Louverture leads a crowd in cheering as Michel Martelly delivers his first public address as the country's president, May 14.

Carl Juste—MCT/Landov

Martelly's desire to move quickly on campaign promises in education, employment, environment, and rule of law was delayed by parliamentary rejections of his first two nominations for prime minister. The parliament confirmed his third nominee, Garry Conille, a physician and UN program manager who had also served as chief of staff for UN Special Haiti Envoy Bill Clinton. Conille's government took office on October 18 and pledged to end the months of political gridlock that had stalled postquake recovery, slowed public and private investment, and further disillusioned Haiti's impoverished people—including some 500,000 displaced persons still living in tents in the Port-au-Prince quake zone.

Other challenges in the import-dependent country included rising global food and fuel prices, which pushed up costs by 9% and 8%, respectively. In addition, the number of cholera cases resurged toward year's end; the health ministry reported that the death toll from the epidemic, which began in 2010, had reached more than 6,900, and at least 515,000 people had been infected. Despite widespread dissatisfaction among Haitians with the UN Stabilization Mission in Haiti (MINUSTAH)—the introduction of cholera was traced to Nepalese peacekeepers, and an incident of sexual abuse involved Uruguayan soldiers—Martelly requested a one-year extension of MINUSTAH through mid-October 2012. He concurrently pledged to restore Haiti's long-disbanded army.

Slow disbursement of aid pledged by international donors for the country's recovery added to the frustration. Only 43% of a promised $4.6 billion had been disbursed by October. Those funds—applied largely to international contractors, road projects, and an industrial park under construction in northern Haiti—rendered little tangible change among Haiti's poor, who remained dependent on services of uneven quality provided by nongovernmental organizations and on remittances sent from Haitians living overseas.

The unexpected January return of former dictator Jean-Claude Duvalier, followed by the arrival two months later of exiled former president Jean-Bertrand Aristide, heightened Haiti's unease. Duvalier was under house arrest on charges of corruption and embezzlement, while Aristide worked to reopen his shuttered private university.

(ROBERT MAGUIRE)

HONDURAS

Area: 112,492 sq km (43,433 sq mi)
Population (2011 est.): 7,755,000
Capital: Tegucigalpa
Head of state and government: President Porfirio Lobo

Multiple events in 2011 enabled a resolution to the ouster on June 28, 2009, of former Honduran president Manuel Zelaya. Among them was the Honduras Truth and Reconciliation Commission's ruling that his removal had been an illegal coup but one that had been instigated by actions by Zelaya, including his refusal to call off a referendum that the courts had declared illegal. In early May an appeals court dropped all corruption charges against Zelaya. On May 22 he and Honduran Pres. Porfirio Lobo signed an accord (brokered by Colombia's and Venezuela's presidents) in Cartagena, Colom., that permitted Zelaya and his associates to return to Honduras without prosecution and to participate again in politics. When Zelaya returned on May 28 from exile in the Dominican Republic to the Honduran capital, Tegucigalpa, he called for "peaceful resistance" from the thousands of supporters who greeted him at Toncontin airport.

Zelaya's return eliminated the final obstacle to Honduras's readmission to the Organization of American States (OAS), from which it had been suspended after Zelaya's removal from power. In a special session on June 1, the OAS voted 32–1 to readmit Honduras. Only Ecuador dissented.

It seemed likely that Honduras's return to the OAS would promote foreign investment; however, several developments mitigated against that investment, not least the spread of violent crime in the country, much of which was related to drug trafficking. Moreover, some 40 people had been killed during 2011 in conflicts in the Bajo Aguán region. Farmworkers had occupied land there that wealthy landowners had purchased in the 1990s from farm cooperatives under circumstances the farmworkers claimed were illegal. In January Congress amended the constitution to cede Honduran sovereignty temporarily in special development zones where foreign investors would be given autonomy to develop "model cities."

(MICHELLE M. TAYLOR-ROBINSON)

HUNGARY

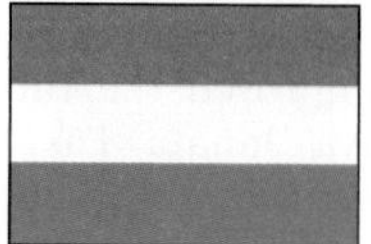

Area: 93,030 sq km (35,919 sq mi)
Population (2011 est.): 9,972,000
Capital: Budapest
Head of state: President Pal Schmitt
Head of government: Prime Minister Viktor Orban

As a result of its stewardship of the rotating presidency of the European Union (EU) during the first six months of 2011, Hungary could claim several significant EU-wide achievements, but its time in the limelight also brought international criticism of the media regulations that the Hungarian government had promulgated early in the year. Although Hungary assumed the presidency one year after the EU had weakened the power of the rotating post by creating the position of the permanent president of the European Council, the country's accomplishments at the helm included an agreement on an integrated European energy market to be established by 2014, a new EU framework for national strategies to integrate the Roma (Gypsies), and the closing of EU-accession negotiations with Croatia. Meanwhile, the media legislation that had been passed in late 2010 by Prime Minister Viktor Orban's centre-right government was criticized by European human rights institutions and the European Parliament for having stifled freedom of the press in Hungary and for having established a new media council that was too powerful and too closely related to Orban's ruling Fidesz (Fidesz–Hungarian Civic Alliance)-led coalition. In response, the National Assembly modified the legislation in 2011.

In March the government presented plans to reduce public debt from about 80% of GDP to 65–70% by the end of 2014. The government called for cuts in health care, education subsidies, and unemployment benefits to accompany a radical overhaul of the pension system. The first debt-reduction step was immediate and involved the transfer of $15 billion of so-called mandatory private pension savings back into the state pension system.

In April the National Assembly (dominated by the more than two-thirds majority enjoyed by the Fidesz coalition) adopted a new constitution. Highly critical of the new document, some intellectuals and the opposition parties accused Fidesz of having attempted to systematically remove checks and balances that restrained the government. The Hungarian Socialist Party (MSzP) and the green Politics Can Be Different (LMP) party boycotted the assembly's debates and vote on the new constitution, which the far-right Jobbik party voted against.

The new constitution, signed in April by Pres. Pal Schmitt, went into force on Jan. 1, 2012, amid widespread protests. It strengthened the powers of the president while restricting those of the Constitutional Court and the National Bank. Rather conservative in tone, the new text included references to the "Holy Crown," Christianity, and traditional family values, defining marriage as a union between a man and a woman. It also codified that the life of a fetus would be protected from the moment of conception, opening the possibility for future restrictions on abortion. Finally, the country's name was changed from Republic of Hungary to Hungary.

Economic growth stagnated throughout the year, owing to the impact of the global financial downturn and in particular to the sharp strengthening of the Swiss franc. With over $25 billion in Swiss franc-denominated loans, Hungary had the highest rate of foreign-currency borrowing in central Europe—equal to about two-thirds of total household debt. In September the government adjusted its early-year economic growth forecast from 3.1% of GDP to under 2% and announced a new package of austerity measures for 2012. The package included an in-

Bela Szandelszky/AP

In Budapest on June 16, trade union members dressed as clowns protest against the Hungarian government's austerity measures and its increasing restrictions on workers' rights.

crease in value-added tax—with the top bracket rising from 25% to 27%, the highest rate in the EU—and included a rise in compulsory health insurance contributions and excise taxes, affecting the price of gasoline, alcohol, and tobacco products. Given the ongoing debt crisis within the euro zone and because of Hungary's own macroeconomic imbalances, the country's planned entry into the euro zone was reset to 2018–20.

(ZSOFIA SZILAGYI)

ICELAND

Area: 103,000 sq km (39,769 sq mi)
Population (2011 est.): 319,000
Capital: Reykjavík
Head of state: President Ólafur Ragnar Grímsson
Head of government: Prime Minister Jóhanna Sigurðardóttir

The Icelandic economy began to show signs of an upturn in 2011, on the heels of the sharp contractions it had experienced in 2009 and 2010. Real GDP increased by an estimated 2.5% in 2011, having declined by 4% the previous year. Unemployment averaged 6% for the year, down from 9% in 2010.

The Icelandic government continued to be plagued by the losses incurred by foreign depositors when the country's

Landsbanki collapsed in 2008. Having compensated their citizens who lost money in the bank's collapse, the British and Dutch governments continued to seek restitution from Iceland. Although the Althingi (Parliament) had voted to settle this debt, Pres. Ólafur Ragnar Grímsson refused to sign the resulting legislation and instead put the repayment matter to the public in plebiscite, which was soundly rejected by the electorate. This was the second time in two years that the president had exercised his power of plebiscite referral. Following the vote, the government announced that no further attempts would be made to settle the issue, which would be left to the international courts to resolve.

On May 21 an eruption at Grímsvötn, a volcano in the Vatnajökull glacier, emitted ash that reached high altitudes and disrupted air traffic for several days. It was the second major ash-emitting eruption in two years, but the interruption to air travel was not nearly as great as that caused by the 2010 eruption at Eyjafjallajökull, which had an impact on European and transatlantic flights for two weeks.

Following a parliamentary resolution, a special court of government governance was convened to prosecute former prime minister Geir H. Haarde. He was charged with dereliction of duty relating to his role in the bank collapse in 2008.

(BJÖRN MATTHÍASSON)

INDIA

Area: 3,166,414 sq km (1,222,559 sq mi)
Population (2011 est.): 1,216,728,000
Capital: New Delhi
Head of state: President Pratibha Patil
Head of government: Prime Minister Manmohan Singh

Despite remaining relatively insulated from the impact of the debt and financial crisis in Europe and the persistent slowdown of the transatlantic economies, India witnessed a terrible year in 2011. Though there was good political news—at least for some—notably the historic defeat of the 34-year-old Left Front government in the eastern state of West Bengal (which produced a satisfactory outcome for the national government and the economy), overall, India performed below par. The country experienced a deceleration in the rate of economic growth, a persistent high rate of inflation, and a slide in the dollar value of the Indian rupee.

Domestic Politics. The key political challenge for the ruling United Progressive Alliance (UPA) government in New Delhi, headed by Prime Minister Manmohan Singh, was a widespread populist movement against corruption and cronyism in public life. The India Against Corruption campaign—led by Anna Hazare, a social activist little known outside his home state, Maharashtra, until 2011—captured the imagination of middle-class India with the help of 24-hour television news channels and the use of social media. Hazare's "indefinite" hunger strike, which began on August 16 (a day after India's national Independence Day) and ended 12 days later, mobilized public opinion countrywide against corruption and immobilized the national government and the parliament. Hazare broke his fast only after the Indian parliament unanimously resolved to consider legislation that would create an office of an independent anticorruption ombudsman. (*See* BIOGRAPHIES.)

With corruption becoming the number one political issue, several figures, including Andimuthu Raja (the minister for telecommunications), Suresh Kalmadi (the chief organizer of the 2010 Commonwealth Games in Delhi), and B.S. Yeddyurappa (the chief minister of the southern state of Karnataka), were all incarcerated while awaiting trials. Several businessmen who had allegedly been involved in the manipulation of "second-generation" (2G) telecom licenses were also jailed while awaiting trial.

Those corruption scandals, the arrests, and the decline in the influence of the Indian National Congress (Congress Party), the major partner in the UPA coalition, contributed to what the Indian media dubbed a "policy paralysis." While many believed that those events should have improved the ratings of the Bharatiya Janata Party (BJP), the main opposition, a number of issues held it back. One notable obstacle was an illegal mining scam in Karnataka, which was ruled by the BJP; another was a power struggle of sorts between the party's octogenarian leader, Lal Krishna Advani, and a clutch of contenders for the post, including Arun Jaitley, Sushma Swaraj, Narendra Modi, and Nitin Gadkari. Though willing, the BJP was unable to unseat Prime Minister Singh. Even the

After the Indian parliament took action in response to his crusade against corruption, Indian activist Anna Hazare (centre) ends a 12-day hunger strike by drinking coconut water and honey in New Delhi, August 28.

Manish Swarup/AP

Congress Party, led by Sonia Gandhi (the widow of former prime minister Rajiv Gandhi and the mother of the party's main prime ministerial aspirant, Rahul Gandhi), was unable to engineer a change of leadership at the national level or make a strong political impact.

The Economy. Inflation, slowing growth, and a depreciating rupee emerged as the three main concerns of economic policy makers in India. Inflation was triggered partly by the overextension of the fiscal stimulus provided after the economic crisis of 2008. The Reserve Bank of India, the country's central bank, stepped in to increase interest rates by more than 200 basis points during the year. Despite monetary tightening, loose fiscal policy remained a problem. In addition, the depreciation of the rupee and rising world energy prices intensified India's inflation woes. Economic and political uncertainty, both at home and abroad, took their toll on the spirit of enterprise, with private investment (both direct and portfolio) remaining subdued. A decline in the gross investment rate, especially in manufacturing, contributed to the slowing of the overall growth rate. A robust monsoon helped to push agricultural growth up and kept food-grain prices in check, but rising demand for proteins exerted pressure on the prices of fruits, vegetables, poultry, and meat (lamb).

The lack of consensus on fiscal reform and the introduction of a nationwide goods and services tax (GST) imposed additional burdens on the economy. The government, faced with the prospect of a further decline in national income growth in fiscal 2011–12 and with the likelihood of the economy's growing at closer to 7% against the forecast of 8.6%, tried to rush through policy initiatives in the winter session (November–December) of the parliament. In early December the parliament failed to approve a plan put forward by the cabinet to allow multibrand retailers, such as Wal-Mart, to open businesses in India. Given the fractured nature of Prime Minister Singh's coalition government, the defeat of the measure illustrated India's limits to attaining economic liberalization.

Foreign Affairs. India entered 2011 on a high note in foreign affairs as a unanimously elected member of the UN Security Council. The heads of government of all five permanent members (the U.S., China, Russia, the U.K., and France) had visited New Delhi in 2010, setting the tone for high-profile diplomacy. However, the persistent global economic slowdown and a focus on domestic affairs by most major powers, including India, left limited room for diplomatic maneuver. Consequently, no major diplomatic initiatives were spearheaded or concluded in 2011. Prime Minister Singh's visit to Dhaka helped strengthen relations with Bangladesh, and a "creeping normalization" of relations with Pakistan enabled Pakistan's beleaguered civilian leadership to approve extending to India the World Trade Organization's most-favoured-nation status.

India was slow and cautious in expressing solidarity with the people of the Arab world as many of them revolted against tyranny. After some initial hesitation, India came out in support of democracy in the Middle East and North Africa. India's main concern was the safety and security of the nearly four million Indians working in the region. Indian diplomacy scored some victories in East Asia, with India increasingly engaged in the East Asian community-building process. Prime Minister Singh participated in the East Asia Summit in Bali, Indon., and India was to be the host of the ASEAN-India Summit in New Delhi in 2012. Singh also traveled to Cannes, France, to participate in the Group of 20 (G20) summit; those gathered, however, failed to find a way forward for the euro-zone economies, and questions were raised about the G20's effectiveness.

Neighbourhood diplomacy was in focus in 2011, with the political environment improving in countries such as Nepal, Myanmar (Burma), and Sri Lanka. In October Singh and Myanmar Pres. Thein Sein agreed to bolster ties in several areas, including trade and oil and gas exploration. The possibility of a new strategic partnership between India and Australia was raised in November when the latter signaled its willingness to allow the sale of uranium to New Delhi. That month India won election (106–77) over China to a key UN post, capturing the Asia-Pacific region's lone seat in the UN Joint Inspection Unit. The continuing uncertainty in the Afghanistan-Pakistan region, however, remained the main problem for Indian security and foreign-policy planners.

(SANJAYA BARU)

INDONESIA

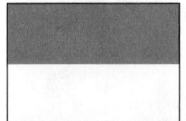

Area: 1,910,931 sq km (737,815 sq mi)
Population (2011 est.): 241,343,000
Capital: Jakarta
Head of state and government: President Susilo Bambang Yudhoyono

In 2011 Indonesia won plaudits for its impressive economic growth and stable democratic political system. Pres. Susilo Bambang Yudhoyono, in particular, continued to be widely praised by Western leaders for his moderate and statesmanlike leadership. There were, however, signs of democratic regression and increasing religious intolerance, which tarnished Indonesia's and Yudhoyono's positive international image.

Economically, Indonesia was one of the best-performing countries in Southeast Asia; in the year June 2010–June 2011, overall growth stood at 6.5%, inflation fell below 5%, international investment was strong, unemployment declined, and foreign reserves swelled to $120 billion, the highest in more than decade. The size of Indonesia's middle class (estimated by the World Bank to be greater than 80 million) had doubled in seven years, and that group's high-spending behaviour fueled robust domestic retail sales and demand. Industries that were previously shrinking, such as footwear and textiles, bounced back strongly, reflecting Indonesia's relatively cheap labour costs compared with those of competitor Asian countries. Indonesia's high GDP growth, abundant food and energy, favourable demographic trends, and high consumption patterns led the World Bank to predict that by 2040 the country would rank as one of the fastest-growing economies, along with those of such countries as China, India, and Turkey. Despite the glowing forecasts, Indonesia suffered mounting infrastructure problems (such as inadequate roads and ports), shortfalls in electricity generation, and chronic transportation bottlenecks.

Indonesian politics remained stable throughout 2011, though there was the usual mix of high-level corruption scandals and political tensions within the ruling coalition. The scandal that seized the most public attention centred on Muhammad Nazaruddin, a par-

Irwin Fedriansyah/AP

A participant in an antigovernment protest in Jakarta clashes with police officers, October 28. Demonstrators criticized the Indonesian government as negligent in its handling of corruption, human rights, and the economy.

liamentarian and treasurer to President Yudhoyono's Democrat Party (PD). Nazaruddin was accused of having taken bribes relating to the construction of facilities for the Southeast Asian Games, which Indonesia hosted in late 2011. Other senior party officials were soon implicated in the scandal, including PD chairman Anas Urbaningrum and Youth and Sports Minister Andi Mallarangeng, both of whom were seen as prospective presidential candidates. The scandal exposed the manner in which parties systematically extracted money from budgetary processes within the parliament and also laid bare the deep divisions within the PD between Yudhoyono and Anas. Anas was increasingly seen by Yudhoyono's circle as intent on pursuing his own political objectives and lacking sufficient loyalty to the president. Having served two five-year presidential terms, Yudhoyono could not run for office in 2014, and the succession issue preoccupied Jakarta's political elite.

There were also signs in 2011 of slippage in Indonesia's democratization process. The parliament, with support from the government, sought to undermine the independence and authority of the Corruption Eradication Commission (KPK), a far more successful and publicly trusted antigraft institution than either the police or the attorney general's department. One reason for the parliament's hostility toward the KPK was that more than 20 MPs had been prosecuted for graft and numerous others were under investigation. Thanks to pressure from civil society groups and the media, most of these moves against the KPK failed, but the threat to it remained. The parliament also passed legislation that allowed that the newly installed Election Commission contain party representatives, rather than nonparty professionals, as occurred for the previous two elections. The inclusion of politicians, however, was likely to diminish the commission's perceived neutrality and competence in managing the 2014 elections. Furthermore, the government was seeking to wind back direct elections for regional heads and proposed that provincial governors be selected by local legislatures rather than be popularly elected. The government was also pushing for the elimination of paired district head and deputy candidates. The existing system, though not without its drawbacks, inclined parties to form broader alliances to maximize their chances of victory, in the process reducing the risk of interethnic and interreligious tensions. These initiatives by the government and the parliament were criticized by commentators as attempts to limit the scrutiny of political leaders and entrench the power of the existing elite.

During the year religious intolerance also rose. Although Indonesia remained, on the whole, a religiously harmonious society, research by nongovernmental organizations showed that since 2010 abuses of religious freedom had increased 30–50%. The most prominent target of religious intolerance was the Ahmadiyah sect, which regarded itself as part of the Islamic community but which many Muslims viewed as heretical. In February 2011 three Ahmadis were brutally slain in an attack on an Ahmadiyah house in western Java. Twelve people were eventually sentenced to three to six months' jail terms. Following the attack Islamic groups renewed calls for the government to ban the sect on the grounds that it caused disorder. Government ministers remained unsympathetic to the Ahmadis' plight. In September religious conflict erupted between Muslims and Christians in Ambon, the site of savage sectarian violence a decade earlier. Seven died in clashes, indicating that reconciliation efforts had failed to overcome simmering religious tensions on the island.

Papua also reemerged as a site of separatist agitation and conflict for the government. In mid-2011 the Papuan People's Council (MRP) voted to reject the province's special autonomy status and called for a referendum on independence. Late in the year, tensions escalated further when security services brutally disbanded a Papuan People's Congress, which had called for independence; at least 6 died, and another 96 were injured in police attacks. The government announced measures to accelerate development in Papua, but Papuan sentiment toward Jakarta was hardening. (GREG FEALY)

IRAN

Area: 1,648,200 sq km (636,374 sq mi)
Population (2011 est.): 75,276,000
Capital: Tehran
Supreme political and religious authority: *Rahbar* (Spiritual Leader) Ayatollah Sayyed Ali Khamenei
Head of state and government: President Mahmoud Ahmadinejad

Iran experienced economic difficulties in 2011 as reforms to the subsidy system took effect and pushed the annual inflation rate to more than 20%. Rising costs of living hit lower-income families hard and engendered considerable criticism. Some 55% of all Iranians fell below the poverty line. The Central Bank of the Islamic Republic of Iran claimed that conditions for a slump prevailed. Other economic indicators, with the sole exception of hydrocarbons, showed deterioration during the year. According to the Central Bank, unemployment stood at 17.5%; that figure included a significant proportion of recent graduates. In addition, there were reportedly one million illegal migrants workers in the country.

The economy's dismal performance was the product of long-term deficiencies in the management of oil revenues, which were often used to fund social welfare objectives. It was estimated that $80 billion was spent annually on subsidies to the poor for food, medicine, and other items. During the year the government gave cash payments to 58 million Iranians to compensate for the removal of subsidies.

The draft national budget for 2011–12 was set at $513 billion, of which $168 billion was slated for ordinary expenditures and $345 billion for state-aligned companies. OPEC estimated oil output at 3,706,000 bbl per day, and the industry earned $40 billion in the first half of 2011. Public-sector activities dominated the economy, with privatization providing opportunities for state-aligned companies to acquire substantial new holdings.

Chased by police, a protester storms the British embassy in Tehran on November 29, several days after the U.K. announced new sanctions against Iran.

Reuters/Landov

Pres. Mahmoud Ahmadinejad was blamed for the economic downturn and the removal of subsidies. Ahmadinejad's attempts to concentrate power by reconfiguring key government ministries and replacing powerful ministers with his own allies led to a public power struggle with the supreme leader, Ali Khamenei, and his allies in the Majlis (parliament). In April Ahmadinejad refused to make appearances for 11 days to protest Khamenei's reinstatement of Heydar Moslehi as minister of intelligence after Ahmadinejad had fired him. In May Ahmadinejad dismissed the minister of oil and declared himself acting oil minister. The Guardian Council and the Majlis decried the move as illegal, forcing Ahmadinejad to back down and appoint another caretaker. In an effort to block Ahmadinejad's grab for additional power, in July Khamenei established a board to arbitrate claims by government departments.

Ahmadinejad's position seemed further weakened when an investigation into the embezzlement of $2.6 billion from Iranian banks widened to include several of his associates, nearly forcing him to appear before the Majlis for questioning. His feud with Khamenei came into the open again when in October Khamenei commented pointedly that Iran was evolving toward a parliamentary system and eventually would no longer need a president elected by popular vote.

Opposition parties supporting Mir Hossein Mousavi and Mehdi Karroubi were involved in street demonstrations against the regime in March, and unrest persisted into June. Iran experienced attacks by regional autonomist groups in the Kurdish and Balochi regions of Iran. In April Iranian officials announced the construction of a fence on the border with Pakistan to prevent infiltration by Balochi militants.

Iran took a hard line against the Bahraini government during its crackdown against protesters there, and on April 15 Iranian Foreign Minister Ali Akbar Salehi requested UN intervention to stop further bloodshed. Unrest in Bahrain led to the deterioration of Iranian relations with Saudi Arabia and the U.A.E., a sign of deepening rifts between Sunni and Shi'ite communities in the Persian Gulf region. Iran's links with Syria were strained by the uprising there and the authorities' heavy-handed crackdown. The official Iranian stance—that its leadership role in the Persian Gulf was strengthened by the effects of the Bahrain uprising—became increasingly untenable. Tehran's power to intervene in regional initiatives was shown to be limited by administrative paralysis and intergroup political strife.

Iran remained embroiled in international disputes over the proliferation of nuclear weapons and the development of nuclear-production facilities but agreed to talks in Istanbul in late January with China, Russia, Germany, France, the U.K., and the U.S. A Russian proposal for a uranium swap was not accepted by the European powers, and Iran rejected any capitulation on its right to produce weapons-grade uranium for peaceful research purposes. In response to the talks' failure, Iran announced in July that it would move its uranium-enrichment program to a site deep underground. In November international attention was again focused on Iran's nuclear activities when the International Atomic Energy Agency issued a report presenting evidence that Iran was secretly developing nuclear weapons. Iran denied the accusation and denounced the report as biased and sloppy. Later that month Iranian officials announced that they were fighting a recently discovered computer worm similar to the Stuxnet worm that was believed to have been employed in a cyber attack on Iran's nuclear facilities in 2010. In late November the U.S., the U.K., and Canada announced new sanctions against Iran. Days later a mob broke into the British embassy in Tehran, ransacking offices and burning documents. The U.K. responded to the attack, which it claimed had the support of the Iranian government, by withdrawing its diplomatic staff from the country and expelling Iranian diplomats in the U.K.

The U.S. was irritated by Iranian intransigence on the issue of atomic development, Tehran's interventions in Lebanon, and its support for Hezbollah. Tension between the two countries increased in October when the U.S. announced that it had foiled a plot by Iranian operatives to hire members of a Mexican drug cartel to assassinate the Saudi ambassador to the U.S. The allegations, forcefully denied by Iran, were greeted with skepticism by many experts, who noted that the details of the far-fetched plot did not match the pattern of the past Iranian covert operations. (KEITH S. MCLACHLAN)

IRAQ

Area: 434,128 sq km (167,618 sq mi)
Population (2011 est.): 32,665,000 (including about 1,700,000 Iraqi refugees, of which about 1,000,000 are in Syria and about 450,000 are in Jordan)
Capital: Baghdad
Head of state: President Jalal Talabani
Head of government: Prime Minister Nuri al-Maliki

Iraq in 2011 saw the continuation of a political struggle between Nuri al-Maliki, the prime minister, and his rival, Ayad ʿAllawi, head of the Iraqi National Accord (al-Iraqiyyah) political coalition. In a conference held in November 2010, the major factions in the Council of Representatives had tried to solve the impasse, concluding an agreement that left Maliki as prime minister and awarded ʿAllawi leadership of a new institution, the National Council for Strategic Policies, whose functions had yet to be determined. Despite ʿAllawi's efforts, the new council was never formed.

Feuds between political factions continued to prevent Maliki from filling the most-sensitive posts in his cabinet, those of the ministers of defense and the interior. Ultimately, both the cabinet and the Council of Representatives were paralyzed by the struggle between factions for a share of political power. Meanwhile, in January 2011 Maliki made an attempt to broaden his authority by pressuring the Supreme Court to issue a ruling placing several independent institutions under his control. Those included the Independent High Electoral Commission, charged with overseeing elections and certifying their results, the Integrity Commission, charged with investigating corruption, and the central bank. The move was quickly rejected by both the public and the major political factions. In the end the court issued a "clarification" stating that cabinet supervision of the institutions would not undermine their independence. Corruption at all levels of government continued to obstruct economic, political, and human development.

Despite political difficulties, security in Iraq improved in comparison with past years, although some assassinations, political violence, and kidnappings persisted. A notable exception to the improved security situation occurred on September 12 when gunmen, presumably Sunni extremists, stopped a bus carrying Shiʿite pilgrims near the town of Al-Nukhayb and killed 22 men aboard. The incident provoked outrage and calls for revenge among Iraq's Shiʿites. Maliki and Sunni leaders had to intervene to contain the incident and calm both Shiʿite and Sunni communities.

Iraqi army officers, along with a U.S. serviceman, salute during a flag ceremony in Baghdad on December 15 that marked the formal end of U.S. military presence in Iraq after nearly nine years.

Shannon Stapleton—Reuters/Landov

Chronic water shortages persisted in parts of Iraq as increased irrigation and the construction of hydroelectric dams in Turkey, Iran, and Syria lowered the water levels of Iraq's main rivers. The water shortages, exacerbated by the poor condition of Iraq's irrigation infrastructure, threatened the livelihoods of thousands of Iraqi farmers and caused the abandonment of thousands of hectares of farmland each year.

In the summer Usama al-Nujayfi, the Sunni speaker of the Council of Representatives, openly stated that unless conditions for Sunnis improved, they might call for the creation of a Sunni semiautonomous region, similar to that of the Kurds in northern Iraq, which would incorporate at a minimum the three Sunni-dominated governorates of Salah al-Din, Anbar, and Ninawa. In the months that followed, Iraqi public opinion regarding the proposal remained split. The notion of a Sunni semiautonomous region gained strength in October when the government arrested hundreds of Sunnis across Iraq after vague accusations of plans for a Baʿthist coup following the withdrawal of U.S. forces. In addition, the government fired 145 faculty and staff members from the University of Tikrit, all of them Sunnis. The government justified the firings by claiming that it was implementing a 2008 de-Baʿthification law that had replaced a decree issued after the U.S. occupation began in 2003. The dismissals resulted in widespread protests and demonstrations in Salah al-Din governorate and strengthened calls for an autonomous Sunni region. Protesters accused Maliki, a Shiʿite, of adopting anti-Sunni policies.

According to an agreement between Iraq and the United States signed in 2008, all American troops were scheduled to leave the country by the end of 2011. Throughout the year negotiations between the two countries took place over whether to allow some troops to stay in Iraq to train the Iraqi army and security forces. Iraqis firmly rejected the Americans' insistence on legal immunity for any troops left in Iraq. Although some Iraqi factions remained open to the possibility of a continued U.S. military presence, the staunchly anti-American cleric Muqtada al-Sadr, whose political support Maliki required in order to remain in power, used pressure and threats to force a complete U.S. withdrawal from Iraq. After months of internal debate and hesitation, the Iraqi government finally decided to ask the U.S. to withdraw all its troops by the end of the year.

The American withdrawal raised questions such as whether Iran would try to fill the vacuum left in Iraq and how Iraqi forces would be trained to use the U.S. equipment purchased by the Iraqi military. In addition, there were fears that sectarian violence might resume. In an effort to address uncertainties related to the American withdrawal, Nuri al-Maliki visited Washington on December 12 for talks with Pres. Barack Obama and his administration. The last remaining U.S. troops left Iraq on December 18.

The renewal of sectarian conflict seemed increasingly likely after Iraqi authorities issued an arrest warrant on December 19 for the country's Sunni vice president, Tariq al-Hashimi, whom they accused of orchestrating attacks on officials and police officers. Hashimi was able to evade arrest by fleeing to the Kurdish autonomous region of Iraq.

Relations with Kuwait remained strained over disputed oil fields, border issues, and Kuwait's plans to build a giant port on the island of Bubiyan near an inlet that provided Iraq with access to the Persian Gulf. In March Iraqis hailed a popular uprising against Syrian Pres. Bashar al-Assad as a step toward democracy, but the Iraqi government soon signaled its support for the Assad regime. The Iraqi government's refusal to withdraw its support for Assad stemmed from its fear of a possible takeover by Sunni extremists in Syria as well as its rejection of what it characterized as international interference in the domestic affairs of an Arab country. At the same time, Iraq did give its support to popular protests in Bahrain that were led by the country's marginalized Shi'ite majority, who demanded increased political rights from Bahrain's Sunni royal family. (LOUAY BAHRY)

IRELAND

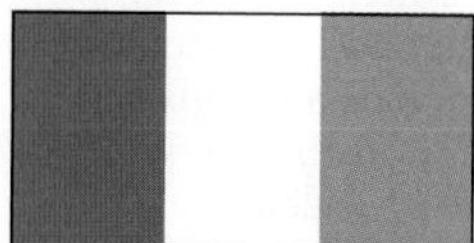

Area: 70,273 sq km (27,133 sq mi)
Population (2011 est.): 4,606,000
Capital: Dublin
Head of state: Presidents Mary McAleese and, from November 11, Michael D. Higgins
Head of government: Prime Ministers Brian Cowen and, from March 9, Enda Kenny

Although 2011 would be remembered for the crushing defeat of the outgoing Irish government in February, the state visit of Queen Elizabeth II to Ireland might prove to have more lasting resonance. The first British monarch to visit in a century began her speech at a formal dinner in Dublin Castle on May 18 by speaking in Gaelic; she then said, "To all those who have suffered as a consequence of our troubled past I extend my sincere thoughts and deep sympathy." The queen and her husband, Prince Philip—whose uncle, Lord Mountbatten, had been killed by the Irish Republican Army in 1979—were warmly greeted during their historic four-day visit, particularly in the southern city of Cork, which long had been a centre of antimonarchist sentiment. A few days later U.S. Pres. Barack Obama and first lady Michelle Obama stopped in Ireland on their way to a summit conference in London. President Obama briefly visited a village in the Irish midlands from which some of his ancestors had emigrated. He also addressed an open-air meeting in Dublin. The cumulative effect of both visits was a shot in the arm to the Irish tourist industry. May also saw the death of former prime minister Garret FitzGerald (*see* OBITUARIES).

The parliamentary election in February—triggered by the Green Party's withdrawal of support for its senior partner in the ruling coalition, Fianna Fail—was a total disaster for the outgoing government. Fianna Fail, previously the largest party in the 166-seat Dail (lower house), was reduced to a rump of 20 seats. The Green Party lost all six of its seats. On March 9 Enda Kenny of Fine Gael replaced Brian Cowen as taoiseach (prime minister), with Eamon Gilmore of Labour as deputy prime minister. They took office with a mandate to continue the austerity program agreed to by the outgoing government as the price of an €85 billion (about $113 billion) IMF–European Central Bank rescue package. Another winner in the election was Gerry Adams, who in 2010 had relinquished his West Belfast seat in the Northern Ireland Assembly to lead the 2011 Dail campaign of Sinn Fein, which won 14 seats. In June Fianna Fail's woes were further compounded by the death of its popular deputy leader Brian Lenihan. (*See* OBITUARIES.)

Having benefited from its large parliamentary majority and a modest reduction in the interest rate on the IMF loan, the new government enjoyed a political honeymoon during its first six months in office. Although some progress was

Reuters/Landov

Irish politician Michael D. Higgins, leader of the Labour Party, beams during a ceremony at Dublin Castle at which he was inaugurated as his country's ninth president, November 11.

made on bank recapitalization, economic indicators remained bleak. Year on year, September rates for inflation and unemployment rose by 2.6% and 14.3%, respectively, though the underlying rate of increase for unemployment had moderated. The housing market continued to decline, with residential property prices in July down 12.5% from the July 2010 figure. Moreover, nationwide the average asking price for residential properties was 43% lower than its highest level in 2007.

On December 5 and 6, respectively, Minister for Public Expenditure and Reform Brendan Howlin and Finance Minister Michael Noonan outlined the budget for 2012. The government's new austerity plan called for €1.4 billion (about $1.8 billion) in spending cuts—mainly in health, education, and social welfare services—and €1.6 billion (about $2.1 billion) in new revenue to be generated in part by inceases to value-added (2%), tobacco, and carbon taxes.

In November Pres. Mary McAleese stepped down after two widely praised terms as head of state. A low-key campaign, in which Fianna Fail did not run a candidate, was enlivened by the entry of Sinn Fein's Martin McGuinness, deputy first minister of Northern Ireland and a former IRA leader. Balloting took place on October 27. Michael D. Higgins, age 70, a popular veteran

Labour Party parliamentarian, emerged the clear winner to become the ninth president of Ireland.

The most unexpected development in 2011 involved a diplomatic row with the tiny Vatican City state. On July 20 Kenny made a forceful speech criticizing the Vatican for its lack of cooperation with the tribunal set up by the Irish government to investigate child sexual abuse by clergy. He accused the Vatican of having frustrated a lawful inquiry established by a sovereign republic and later parsed the report's finding of humiliation and betrayal inflicted on children with "the gimlet eye of the canon lawyer." Kenny, an avowed Catholic, surprised listeners with the vehemence of his arguments.

The Vatican's 25-page reply, issued in September, rejected the accusation of hindering the inquiry's work and said that Kenny had misrepresented church documents quoted in his speech. There was no reconciling the two positions, and Ireland found itself at odds with its longest-standing diplomatic ally, as well as with the leadership of the church to which the majority of its citizens gave allegiance. (KIERAN FAGAN)

Ariel Hermoni—Defense Ministry/AP

On October 18 Israeli soldier Gilad Shalit (second from right) arrives at the Tel Nof air base with Defense Minister Ehud Barak (far left), Prime Minister Benjamin Netanyahu (second from left), and Israeli Defense Forces Chief of Staff Benny Gantz (right). Shalit, who had become a cause célèbre in 2006 after he was taken captive by Palestinian militants, was released in a prisoner exchange.

ISRAEL

Area: 21,643 sq km (8,357 sq mi), including the Golan Heights and disputed East Jerusalem, excluding the Emerging Palestinian Autonomous Areas
Population (2011 est.): 7,431,000, excluding 312,000 Jews in the West Bank
Capital: Jerusalem is the proclaimed capital of Israel (since Jan. 23, 1950) and the actual seat of government, but recognition has generally been withheld by the international community
Head of state: President Shimon Peres
Head of government: Prime Minister Benjamin Netanyahu

The Emerging Palestinian Autonomous Areas (the West Bank and the Gaza Strip)
Total area under disputed administration: West Bank 5,655 sq km (2,183 sq mi); Gaza Strip 365 sq km (141 sq mi)
Population (2011 est.): West Bank 2,551,000, including 2,239,000 Arabs and 312,000 Jews; Gaza Strip 1,574,000
Principal administrative centres: Ramallah and Gaza
Head of government: President Mahmoud Abbas, assisted by Prime Minister Salam Fayyad

For Israel, 2011 carried the seeds of potentially significant change. A Palestinian drive for UN membership challenged Israel's continued occupation of the West Bank, while popular uprisings across the Middle East raised questions about its future ties with the Arab world and mass protests at home generated pressure for reform of what had become a quintessentially neoliberal socioeconomic system.

The year began with the Palestinians pressing ahead with a new unilateralist strategy. They warned that in the event of the failure to relaunch a credible peace process by September, they would seek UN membership for a Palestinian state. With peace talks stalled, mainly over Israel's refusal to halt construction of Jewish settlements in the West Bank, their declared aim was to intensify international pressure for a two-state solution.

On September 23 Palestinian Pres. Mahmoud Abbas submitted a formal request for membership to UN Secretary-General Ban Ki-Moon. Explaining the move in the UN General Assembly, Abbas excoriated Israel for building Jewish settlements in the West Bank and accused it of forcing Palestinians off their land. Israel's Prime Minister Benjamin Netanyahu retorted that in adopting a unilateralist policy and refusing to engage in peace talks, the Palestinians were trying to get a state without having to negotiate key issues, such as borders and security. Abbas was able to muster overwhelming support for a Palestinian state among the 193 members of the General Assembly, but according to UN procedure, his membership bid required prior recommendation by the 15-member Security Council, where the U.S. made clear that it would cast a veto blocking Palestinian membership. After Abbas submitted his request to Ban, the Security Council formed a committee to study it, delaying a vote.

The international "Quartet" (the U.S., the EU, the UN, and Russia), concerned that unilateral moves could raise false hopes that when dashed could lead to violence, made strenuous efforts to get the parties to reengage. The Palestinians, however, continued to demand that Israel first stop building Jewish settlements and commit to border negotiations based on the 1967 lines. Israel insisted on negotiations without preconditions. That meant ignoring the results of earlier exchanges between Abbas and the previous Israeli prime minister, Ehud Olmert, who, according to both men, had come within a whisker of agreement. The Palestinians viewed Netanyahu's insistence on starting from scratch as a means to buy time and an indication that he was not serious about cutting a deal.

In May, U.S. Pres. Barack Obama seemed to favour the Palestinian position, calling for a resumption of peace talks based on the 1967 lines with agreed land swaps. In the UN General Assembly in September, however, he took a strong stand against Palestinian unilateralism, insisting that Israel's security concerns were legitimate and needed to be addressed in negotiations.

An unprecedented sequence of popular uprisings, dubbed the "Arab Spring," created more regional uncertainty for Israel. The uprisings, which began in Tunisia in December 2010 and quickly spread across the Arab world, toppled long-standing dictatorships in Tunisia, Egypt, and Libya and precipitated protracted sectarian violence in Syria. While Western leaders welcomed the process in the hope that it would lead to democracy, Israeli analysts feared that the collapse of the secular dictatorships could bring radical anti-Israeli and anti-Western Islamists to power. Their biggest fear was that the Islamist Muslim Brotherhood could gain control in Egypt and abrogate the 32-year-old peace treaty with Israel.

Israel's regional troubles were compounded by further deterioration in relations with Turkey. The Turks continued to insist on two conditions for any improvement in ties: that Israel apologize for having killed eight Turkish activists and a Turkish-born American attempting to breach the Israeli naval blockade of the Gaza Strip in May 2010 and that Israel pay compensation to the families of those killed. A report on the affair by a UN commission headed by former New Zealand prime minister Geoffrey Palmer, leaked in early September, added fuel to the flames. Although it found Israel's use of force "excessive and unreasonable," it declared the blockade of the Gaza Strip to be "a legitimate security measure" and accused Turkish activists of acting "recklessly" in their attempts to breach it. Angry at the findings and at Israel's concomitant refusal to apologize, the Turkish government expelled Israel's ambassador to Ankara and suspended the once-extensive military ties between the two countries.

Relations with Egypt also grew tense after a cross-border incident on August 18 in which Palestinian militants killed eight Israelis and fled to the Sinai Peninsula. Egyptians were outraged when units of the Israel Defense Forces (IDF) in hot pursuit accidently killed five Egyptian border guards on Egyptian territory. Three weeks later a seething Egyptian mob stormed the Israeli embassy in Cairo, tearing down the Israeli flag, hurling Hebrew documents into the street, and threatening the lives of six security guards hiding in a barricaded safe room. Only after intervention by President Obama and his defense secretary, Leon Panetta, did the Egyptians send in commandos to extricate the besieged Israelis.

Ties between Israel and the transitional military government in Egypt, still part of a moderate pro-American axis, were too important for either side to allow an open rift. In October, Israel's Defense Minister Ehud Barak formally apologized for the killing of the Egyptian border guards, and the Egyptians played a key behind-the-scenes role in securing the release of IDF Corp. Gilad Shalit, who had been held by Hamas militants in a secret location in Gaza for more than five years. Shalit was handed over to Israeli authorities on October 18 in exchange for 477 jailed Palestinian militants named by Hamas and another 550 to be named by Israel and freed at a later date. Shalit's release was greeted with euphoria in Israel and significantly enhanced Netanyahu's domestic standing.

Like the rest of the region, Israel was rocked by widespread protests led by a young "social network" generation, but in its case the demand was for "social justice." Grievances were initially directed against the high cost of living, especially the lack of affordable housing, but quickly broadened to target the wide gap between rich and poor and the concentration of wealth in the hands of relatively few tycoons. Students and young middle-class professionals demanded a reallocation of national resources, with higher taxation of the rich and more government spending on health care, education, and welfare services, along with government moves to lower housing and other living costs. In mid-July, Daphni Leef, a 25-year-old video editor, pitched a tent in central Tel Aviv to protest high apartment rents and opened a Facebook page inviting others to join her. The response was overwhelming. Protest tent camps sprang up across the country, and protest rallies throughout the summer drew hundreds of thousands of people. Netanyahu made proposals to bring down housing costs and set up a committee to consider the demonstrators' wider demands. But its recommendations—which involved reallocating government spending without increasing the budget—were rejected by the protest leaders as merely cosmetic, and in late October the protests started anew.

Israel's economy continued to outperform most others in the West, with growth of about 4.7%. Unemployment fell from about 6.3% in 2010 to about 5.4%; inflation (at about 2%) was well within the 1–3% target range; and exports were expected to reach a record \$89 billion. By the end of the year, though, the economy was clearly slowing down, and the growth forecast for 2012 was a significantly lower 3.2%.

(LESLIE D. SUSSER)

ITALY

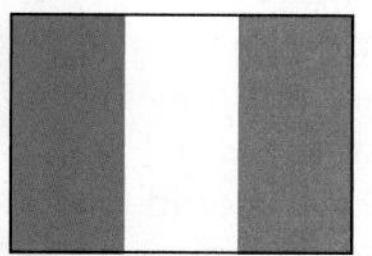

Area: 301,336 sq km (116,346 sq mi)
Population (2011 est.): 60,769,000
Capital: Rome
Head of state: President Giorgio Napolitano
Head of government: Prime Ministers Silvio Berlusconi and, from November 16, Mario Monti

The dramatic downturn in 2011 in the fortunes of Europe's decade-old common currency, the euro, produced a 90-day tidal wave of events in Italy. The country witnessed the collapse of longtime Prime Minister Silvio Berlusconi's government, his replacement by nonpartisan leader Mario Monti, and the introduction of sweeping austerity measures intended to restore debt-ridden Italy's tarnished status within the financially battered European Union.

Italy's sudden unraveling began when in mid-September it was downgraded by international credit agencies Standard & Poor's and Moody's, both citing the country's debt, its anemic economic growth prospects, and ongoing government instability. Though Italy represented the euro zone's third largest economy (after Germany and France), its debt was estimated at €1.9 trillion (about \$2.57 trillion), some 120% of its GDP.

Until the two scathing report cards were issued, Berlusconi, a 75-year-old billionaire media mogul who had risen to power in 1994 and had led the country for 8 of the previous 10 years, appeared to maintain a solid grip on power, notwithstanding continuing allegations of sexual misconduct and abuse of office. Though his conservative People of Freedom party (PdL), which reclaimed power in 2008, spent much of 2010 and 2011 resisting the corrosive effects of the scandals, few of its members openly rebelled.

The double downgrading, coupled with the precarious status of euro neighbour Greece, dramatically changed the focus, revealing a landscape of fearful investors worried about Italy's chances of refinancing more than $530 billion in public debt owed in 2012. Yields on the country's benchmark 10-year bonds began inching toward the 7% levels seen when Greece and Ireland were forced to seek EU bailout funds. Throughout a bleak October and early November, economists debated not only what Italy's future in the euro was but also whether it could stave off national bankruptcy. Berlusconi was further battered by criticism from esteemed 86-year-old Pres. Giorgio Napolitano, who suggested that the prime minister's scandal-ridden incumbency was diminishing Italy's global credibility.

Pier Paolo Cito/AP

After being sworn in as prime minister of Italy on November 16 in Rome, Mario Monti (left) receives from his predecessor, Silvio Berlusconi (right), a small bell used for calling attention in cabinet meetings.

On November 9, as markets continued their plunge and Italian bond issues faltered, Napolitano helped to facilitate Berlusconi's ouster by elevating Monti, a respected economist and former EU commissioner, to the largely ceremonial post of senator for life. The move gave Italy's parties a feasible apolitical alternative to Berlusconi in lieu of holding early national elections, seen by economists as a potentially fatal delay, given the widening breadth of the euro crisis. Monti's ascension immediately triggered a series of defections within Berlusconi's party and was met with applause from the opposition Democratic Party, which called for Berlusconi to step aside in favour of a technocratic Monti-led cabinet charged with confronting the economic emergency. No longer able to muster a parliamentary majority, Berlusconi reluctantly resigned on November 12, pledging to support Monti's efforts to keep Italy's economy afloat.

The unelected Monti and his new cabinet, sworn in four days later, won applause from EU leaders after immediately promising a debt-reduction package intended to balance the Italian budget by 2013. Monti also faced the daunting task of imposing austerity measures in a country with powerful labour unions. His emergency decrees, announced in early December and dubbed the "Save Italy" package, called for a rise in the retirement age, the introduction of pension reform, the imposition of higher property taxes, and an effort to rein in endemic tax evasion. The ambitious plan, fraught with unpopular moves, was intended to save some $40 billion over two years. "We're faced with an alternative between the current situation, with the required sacrifices, or an insolvent state, and a euro destroyed perhaps by Italy's infamy," Monti said bluntly.

Some labour leaders criticized Monti for having targeted the country's middle class and its blue-collar workforce while failing to rein in political and bureaucratic costs, rated as among the highest in Europe. (To set an example, Monti agreed to forgo his salary as prime minister.) The Roman Catholic Church also questioned the austerity measures, noting that Monti's corporate and banking-oriented leadership seemed aloof from the well-being of Italy's families. Industrialists wondered how a package based on cutbacks could stimulate growth and reduce unemployment in an already recession-stricken country. Near year's end the World Bank ranked the country 87th of 183 in its global "ease of doing business" survey.

Political observers noted that Monti's nonpartisan government could last only as long as it received majority support from both the left and the right, a prospect seemingly guaranteed only for the duration of the euro crisis. Though Monti had asked for a mandate through spring 2013, which would have marked the end of Berlusconi's abbreviated term, he was unable to receive a clear promise from the country's politicians. Nevertheless, he remained undeterred, particularly in his commitment to the euro. "You can do without me, but not without Europe," Monti said.

Media commentators also continued to rue what they called Italy's widening social malaise, an unofficial condition that key statistics seemed to bear out. In a country known for large families, the number of single Italians of all ages rose by 39% in the decade (2000–10), according to Censis, a respected statistical agency. Censis also noted that more than 7 million Italians lived alone, or 13.6% of the population over age 15; an additional 3.3 million people aged 65 or older were also on their own.

Reinforcing the gloom, autumn statistics showed that some 27.6% of youths aged 15–24 were unemployed; that age group amounted to 23 million people in a country of 60 million. Gender was also a sticking point. Though more Italian women than men had university degrees, only 46% had jobs, compared with the EU average of 59%. The details of the Berlusconi sex scandals made this gulf even more evident by featuring unemployed young women ready to use any means necessary to get ahead in a society deemed to be hostile to their presence in the mainstream workplace.

Though Emma Marcegaglia, the first woman to lead Confindustria, Italy's largest association of industrialists, repeatedly blamed this biased mentality in the political arena for helping to make Italy into an "international laughingstock," her outrage appeared to fall on deaf ears. Monti's Equal Opportunity Minister Elsa Fornero, appointed in November, expressed "surprise and disappointment" when a delegation of youth leaders named to meet with her did not include a single female representative.

Though Berlusconi was undone by the euro crisis, disenchantment was already evident during May regional elections. In Naples, where underworld corruption had been blamed for an ongoing waste-disposal crisis, Berlusconi's mayoral candidate was soundly defeated. His party earlier had lost control of Milan, and his Northern League allies were beaten in the party's critical northern strongholds of Pavia and Novara.

On the foreign policy front, the ouster of Tunisian Pres. Zine al-Abidine Ben Ali and Libyan leader Muammar al-Qaddafi undermined Italy's efforts to reduce the steady flow of illegal immigrants. With sea-patrol pacts between Libya and Italy in limbo, waves of North African refugees tried to reach Italian shores. Some boats were turned away, while other vessels foundered, producing hundreds of casualties. An estimated 50,000 immigrants passed through the island of Lampedusa, off Sicily; Italy repatriated many of them after a series of violent outbreaks occurred at a holding centre.

In other news, media attention turned to Perugia, where American student Amanda Knox, convicted of having murdered her British roommate in 2007, saw her controversial verdict overturned in October after a lengthy appeal. In a story that mesmerized domestic and international media, the court ruled that forensic evidence had been mishandled and ordered Knox's immediate release.

In association football (soccer) news, defending titleholder Inter Milan surrendered its domestic Serie A title to Berlusconi-owned city rival AC Milan. Inter Milan was also unable to defend its Champions League trophy, losing in the quarterfinals to Germany's Schalke 04.

(CHRISTOPHER P. WINNER)

JAMAICA

Area: 10,991 sq km (4,244 sq mi)
Population (2011 est.): 2,709,000
Capital: Kingston
Head of state: Queen Elizabeth II, represented by Governor-General Sir Patrick Allen
Heads of government: Prime Ministers Bruce Golding and, from October 23, Andrew Holness

In January 2011 the prime minister of Jamaica, Bruce Golding, conceded that the government lacked sufficient resources for dealing effectively with drug traffickers. Spending funds on the effort, he said, would mean sacrificing the construction of hospitals and schools. The government continued with plans to restore Jamaica's passenger rail service, defunct for almost 20 years. The project, expected to be completed in 2012, had a ceremonial opening in April with a test run between two towns, May Pen and Linstead (about 50 km [30 mi]).

The World Bank said in April that Jamaica could increase its annual GDP by as much as 5.4% if it reduced its crime levels to those of Costa Rica, whose homicide rate was 11 per 100,000 people, compared with Jamaica's 55 per 100,000. The World Bank cited the indirect costs of violence, such as victims' stress and lower productivity at work, as the major expense of crime.

The report from the commission of enquiry into the extradition of gang leader Christopher ("Dudus") Coke to the U.S., and the involvement of law firm Manatt, Phelps and Phillips, was released in June. Prime Minister Golding was also reprimanded for having been too closely involved with the case. His popularity declined, and in September he decided to step down. His replacement as Jamaica Labour Party leader, Andrew Holness, took office as prime minister on October 23. Holness miscalculated in calling an early election for December 29. It was won in a landslide by the opposition People's National Party and its leader, former prime minister Portia Simpson-Miller. (DAVID RENWICK)

JAPAN

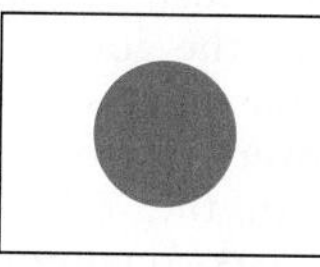

Area: 377,950 sq km (145,927 sq mi)
Population (2011 est.): 127,937,000
Capital: Tokyo
Symbol of state: Emperor Akihito
Head of government: Prime Ministers Naoto Kan and, from August 30, Yoshihiko Noda

Domestic Affairs. The massive earthquake and tsunami of March 11 sent shock waves through all aspects of domestic affairs in Japan in 2011. (*See* Special Report on page 176.) The most devastating effects of the disaster were in northeastern Honshu (Tohoku), where a magnitude-9.0 tremor—one of the strongest ever recorded—struck offshore east of Sendai, Miyagi prefecture. The initial quake and its dozens of powerful aftershocks were felt throughout Japan. Damage from the temblor was serious, but it paled in comparison with the overwhelming devastation caused by a series of powerful quake-generated tsunami waves, which rushed inland over low-lying areas of the eastern Tohoku coast, sweeping away cities and towns and inundating vast areas of farmland. According to official government statistics, at the end of the year, some 19,300 people had died or were listed as missing, the bulk of them victims of the tsunami. Tens of thousands more were displaced or living in temporary housing.

The most enduring effects of the March 11 disaster, however, unfolded at the Fukushima Daiichi nuclear power complex along the coast of Fukushima prefecture south of Sendai, where, following the earthquake and tsunami, the plant's cooling systems failed. That led to partial meltdowns in three reactors and to the release of radioactive materials into the environment. The situation developed into the worst nuclear emergency since the Chernobyl accident in 1986. The Japanese government ordered the evacuation of residents living within a 20-km (12.5-mi) radius of the plant. At the end of 2011, the area remained off-limits to those residents. Many others fled areas outside the evacuation zone.

The March 11 catastrophe and its aftermath had a deep impact on Japanese politics in the months that followed. It allowed Prime Minister Naoto Kan—who had been in imminent danger of losing his position—to extend his time in office to lead the country's response to the disaster. Nevertheless, Kan's perceived failures in that effort ultimately forced him to announce his resignation on August 26. A quick leadership election within the Democratic Party of Japan (DPJ) four days later led to the selection of Yoshihiko Noda (*see* BIOGRAPHIES) as Japan's new prime minister. Noda was the sixth prime minister in five years and the third leader from the DPJ since that party won a landslide legislative election in 2009.

Kan lost support for several reasons, the most important of which was the general perception that he had mishandled the Fukushima nuclear emergency. In the days after the disaster, the government provided only limited information about the status of the reactor cores and the radiation levels outside the evacuation zone. For weeks the government denied that there had been a meltdown, and Kan's cabinet thus faced criticism when it admitted a month after the disaster began that Japan had experienced a Chernobyl-level nuclear event. Similarly, when residents of villages that had not been evacuated learned that the government had recorded radiation levels there that exceeded the threshold for ordering evacuation, they blasted the government for having failed to alert them sooner.

Kan's other significant problems were that his party lacked a majority in the upper house of the Diet (parliament) and that the DPJ itself continued to suffer from internal divisions. Short of the necessary upper-house votes, Kan's government scaled back and delayed some emergency spending on disaster recovery. Meanwhile, Kan had to fend off a no-confidence motion in the lower house of the Diet on June 2 brought by the opposition Liberal-Democratic Party (LDP), which his DPJ rival Ichiro Ozawa and Ozawa's supporters threatened to back. Although the prime minister survived the confidence vote (Ozawa did not vote on the motion), his subsequent effort to revive support for his leadership by promising to phase out Japan's reliance on nuclear energy fell flat. Kan then offered to resign in exchange for legislation that provided emergency funding for the Tohoku crisis.

Noda was not expected to emerge as the winner of the DPJ's internal leadership contest that followed Kan's departure, but he ultimately prevailed as a compromise candidate after two better-known candidates backed by pro- and anti-Ozawa wings of the party failed to win a majority on the first ballot. Noda's subsequent cabinet and party leadership selections demonstrated that he intended to bridge the party divide, as he named top figures from each side to leadership positions. Noda chose Seiji Maehara, who had run against him with support from anti-Ozawa elements, to head the party's Policy Research Committee, and he tapped Ozawa supporter Azuma Koshiichi to serve as DPJ secretary-general.

After assuming leadership Noda made a series of politically difficult decisions. On November 1 his minister responsible for the nuclear industry announced that the government would allow a nuclear reactor to restart in Saga prefecture on Kyushu; the reactor had been off-line for a month after human error caused it to shut down. The decision, which led opponents of nuclear power to question Noda's commitment to reducing reliance on that energy source, sparked protests in the nearby city of Fukuoka. Two weeks later, at the Asia-Pacific Economic Cooperation (APEC) summit in Honolulu, he announced that Japan would participate in ongoing talks regarding the proposed Trans-Pacific Partnership (TPP) trade agreement (*see* below). That decision was opposed by some 200 members of the DPJ caucus in the Diet.

The Economy. The earthquake and tsunami also contributed to dramatic swings in the Japanese economy during 2011. Already operating at close to stall speed at the start of the year, the economy shrank sharply in the first two quarters largely because of the damage to ports, supply networks, and the power grid in northeastern Japan. With many businesses closed in the weeks immediately following March 11, the economy shrank by 0.7% in the first quarter. In the second quarter the economy shrank by another 0.3% as automobile and electronics firms struggled to find replacements for off-line suppliers in the disaster zone.

Also slowing the economy was the loss of electric power produced by nuclear plants as reactors across the country were shut down for inspections and then left off-line. Prime Minister Kan accelerated the trend when he ordered a shutdown of the reactors at the Hamaoka power station on the coast of Shizuoka prefecture until greater safety measures could be implemented. That area, about 190 km (120 mi) southwest of Tokyo, was one that seismologists judged to be the most prone in the country to earthquakes and tsunamis. As summer started, with just 17 of Japan's 54 reactors online, the government issued advice to consumers and worked with large employers to reduce electricity consumption in the Tokyo area by 15% during peak daylight hours. The country avoided major blackouts and brownouts, but only by limiting factory operations to weekends and nights and setting thermostats to a higher level.

Those disruptions caused a decline in Japanese exports to the point that Japan was on track in 2011 to record its first annual trade deficit in decades. Exports of automobiles in the first half of fiscal 2011 stood at 1.98 million units, down almost 17% from the previous year. With other export sectors also hit hard by the quake, Japan ran a trade deficit of about $12.4 billion (¥1 trillion) over the first eight months of 2011. By late summer, however, the economy had reversed direction. It grew briskly in the third quarter, by 1.4% (an annualized rate of 5.6%), as disruptions in supply chains and energy markets eased and recovery work in Tohoku began in earnest. Reflecting that recovery, the unemployment rate fell to 4.3% in August, 0.4% lower than in the previous month.

Although the rebound in growth and the decline in unemployment were good news, economic analysts remained worried that the economy faced serious challenges going forward, including slowdowns in Japan's major export markets: Europe, North America, and China. The turmoil surrounding public-debt levels in the euro zone in 2011 and the resulting loss of confidence in the euro, following closely on the agonizing debate in the U.S. over the federal debt ceiling, threatened to stymie growth by boosting the value of the yen. The yen reached near-record

While touring a school in Yokohama on October 14, Prime Minister Yoshihiko Noda puts his hands together before eating lunch with children.

Kyodo News/AP

highs over the summer, prompting Japanese authorities to intervene unilaterally in currency markets out of concern that a yen-dollar rate at that level would lead to the loss of export markets and an exodus of manufacturing to lower-cost countries. After the yen reached a record high level of ¥75.35 to the dollar on October 31, Japanese monetary authorities intervened for the third time during the calendar year. Although those interventions helped to put a ceiling on the yen's rise, the yen still stood at ¥77–¥78 to the dollar at year's end.

Throughout the autumn the Noda government pressed for passage of a $155 billion third supplementary budget that was aimed primarily at providing more funds for rebuilding the devastated areas of Tohoku. The budget was passed in late November with the support of the opposition parties in the upper house. Finally, in early December the government proposed a nearly unprecedented fourth supplementary budget for 2011. The additional $25 billion—which was to be voted on in January 2012—was slated to assist companies affected by the high yen rate or by heavy flooding in Thailand earlier in the year.

Monetary policy remained unchanged throughout the year. The Bank of Japan (BOJ) maintained a target overnight call rate as close to zero as possible (between 0.0% and 0.1%). The BOJ also continued a policy, begun in November 2010, of purchasing long-term securities—including government bonds and real-estate investment trusts—in an effort to lower long-term rates.

Foreign Affairs. Japan began 2011 with troubled relations with its primary partners. Its long-standing security alliance with the U.S. was under stress as the two countries struggled to implement a U.S. military base-realignment plan on Okinawa that the DPJ's first prime minister, Yukio Hatoyama, had tried but failed to renegotiate. Protests continued in Okinawa, and local governments there made it extremely difficult to implement the plan. Japan's relations with China, meanwhile, were suffering from the aftermath of a September 2010 incident involving a Chinese fishing trawler that had collided with Japanese coast guard vessels patrolling disputed waters near the Senkaku (Chinese: Daiyu) Islands. Japanese authorities had detained the captain of the fishing boat in Okinawa, prompting Chinese officials to take into custody four Japanese construction workers in China and to look the other way when Japanese firms found that they could not buy vital rare-earth minerals from China (which had near-monopoly control of those commodities). Within the following two months, however, the workers had been returned to Japan, and the mineral shipments had resumed.

The March 11 disaster helped Japan improve its relationships with both the U.S. and China. Among the first to respond to the scenes of devastation in the Japanese cities and towns along the Tohoku coast hit by the tsunami were vessels of the U.S. Navy sent from bases in Japan. At the peak of the relief efforts, some 20,000 U.S. personnel, 20 ships, and 140 aircraft were in the disaster area as part of Operation Tomodachi ("Friend"). The media coverage of the disaster recovery, showing U.S. troops assisting Tohoku residents, helped Japanese see the benefits offered by the military alliance.

In the aftermath of the successful cooperation between U.S. forces and the Japanese Self-Defense Force in the area, the two governments reemphasized their commitment to the alliance. The Okinawa base-realignment plan remained in limbo, but questions about it were raised by both sides. Okinawa's governor, Hirokazu Nakaima, visited Washington, D.C., in September to promote changes to the plan; several influential U.S. senators called for the U.S. to reexamine the details after they visited the island in April and concluded that the existing approach was "unrealistic, unworkable, and unaffordable." The two sides announced in May that they would miss a 2014 deadline for carrying out the plan.

Japan's relations with China also improved after March 11, as the disaster provided the Chinese with a chance to reciprocate the help Japan had given China following earthquakes in that country—notably the 2008 Sichuan quake. The Japanese government greatly appreciated the visit Chinese Premier Wen Jiabao and South Korean Pres. Lee Myung-Bak made in May to a refugee centre near the stricken Fukushima plant prior to a planned trilateral summit in Tokyo. The photo opportunity of the two leaders sampling local strawberries and vegetables was set up by the Japanese side in an effort to reassure residents of China and South Korea that Japan was safe to visit and that its products were safe to eat. That scene, however, also pointed to lingering distrust among Japan's neighbours. After it became known that the plant had released radioactive materials into the environment, the most vociferously expressed concerns came from residents and officials of China and South Korea. Both countries promptly imposed restrictions on imports of food from the Fukushima area.

Despite that distrust, Japan moved forward with a variety of initiatives aimed at lowering trade barriers and deepening economic ties with its neighbours. At the trilateral summit in May, Wen, Lee, and Kan reiterated their support for a proposed three-way free-trade area, and the draft of an initial study was released in mid-December. In late December, Prime Minister Noda and Chinese officials meeting together in Beijing agreed to begin direct currency trading between the two countries.

In early November, Noda took his most dramatic step to date when he announced prior to the Honolulu APEC summit that Japan would begin discussions with TPP countries about Japan's participation in negotiations on the TPP agreement. The government had been giving mixed signals about whether Japan was ready to join the nine countries attempting to draft the agreement—a comprehensive economic pact aimed at eliminating tariffs within 10 years of its launch. Over the summer Prime Minister Kan had postponed making a decision on Japan's participation after he faced strong objections from DPJ members worried about the effects of such an agreement on Japan's farmers and rural areas.

After the U.S. Congress approved a free-trade agreement between South Korea and the U.S. in October, however, Noda signaled that he did not want to see Japan left out of the move toward deeper economic integration. Noda encountered significant opposition within his own party—with some members threatening to leave the DPJ—but he was able to avoid a rift by carefully qualifying his statement to indicate that Japan was agreeing only to negotiate, not to accept any specific terms. After U.S. Pres. Barack Obama announced plans to move forward quickly, with the aim of completing the TPP agreement by November 2012, however, it was not clear that Japan would be able to keep up. If it did agree to such a pact, the move would represent a dramatic shift from its long-standing protection of its agricultural markets and a gamble that the agreement would help Japan pull out of its prolonged period of slow economic growth. (LEONARD SCHOPPA)

JORDAN

Area: 88,778 sq km (34,277 sq mi)
Population (2011 est.): 6,180,000 (including about 2,000,000 Palestinian refugees, most of whom hold Jordanian citizenship; excluding roughly 500,000 Iraqi refugees)
Capital: Amman
Head of state and government: King ʿAbdullah II, assisted by Prime Ministers Samir Rifai, Marouf al-Bakhit from February 9, and, from October 24, Awn Khasawneh

The political scene in Jordan in 2011 was dominated by struggles over political reform. Following extensive protests, Jordanian ruler King ʿAbdullah II announced a series of constitutional reforms with the stated intention of evolving toward parliamentary government—albeit gradually over an undefined time frame.

In January Jordanian protesters called for reforms to the political system rather than advocating for the overthrow of the monarchy. Corruption and unemployment were also key grievances. The king responded in February by replacing the unpopular prime minister, Samir Rifai, with Marouf al-Bakhit; increasing subsidies and public-sector pay; and establishing two national committees to develop reform proposals. In March several well-connected businesspeople were arrested in a corruption investigation.

Protests continued, however, and in July the king reshuffled the cabinet, replacing the ministers of interior and information, among others. Still, criticisms of the government did not subside. In August the king announced proposed constitutional reforms, including the establishment of a constitutional court and an independent electoral commission, the prohibition of torture and phone tapping, limitations on the government's ability to dissolve the parliament and pass its own temporary laws, and a reduction in the jurisdiction for the state security court. A key demand of the protesters—making the office of the prime minister elective—was not addressed. The parliament approved the key elements of the proposals, but the opposition Islamic Action Front called for deeper changes and threatened to boycott the December municipal elections, which were subsequently postponed until no later than mid-March 2012. In October the king replaced the prime minister for the second time in eight months, selecting Awn Khasawneh. He also appointed a new cabinet and replaced the head of intelligence. The king said that following parliamentary elections, members of the parliament would be consulted on his choice of prime minister.

Israel temporarily withdrew embassy staff from Jordan in September after protesters attacked its embassy in Egypt. In November, the prime minister said that Jordan's 1999 decision to expel the Palestinian political and military organization Hamas had been "a legal and constitutional mistake."

Tourism suffered from regional unrest, and there were indications that trade with Syria was suffering from instability there. The economy, however, was bolstered by greater foreign aid and rising trade with Iraq. Social spending was increased by $1 billion, and the sales tax was cut on 150 items.

Jordan expected to receive $2.8 billion in foreign aid in 2011, compared with $1.1 billion in 2010. In September it bid for new aid from the Deauville Partnership, a G8-led program for Arab countries undergoing political transitions. Saudi Arabia, keen to bolster the Jordanian monarchy, promised Jordan $1.4 billion in direct budgetary support. In May the Gulf Cooperation Council, comprising six oil-exporting Arab monarchies, said that it would welcome membership bids from Jordan and Morocco. (JANE KINNINMONT)

KAZAKHSTAN

Area: 2,724,900 sq km (1,052,090 sq mi)
Population (2011 est.): 16,560,000
Capital: Astana
Head of state and government: President Nursultan Nazarbayev, assisted by Prime Minister Karim Masimov

Kazakhstan continued its march toward becoming an industrial power in 2011. In August the minister for industry and new technology, Asset Issekeshev, announced that in the previous 18 months, 227 industrial projects had been launched in the country, resulting in 29,000 jobs. The introduction in September of a Kazakhstan edition of *Forbes* magazine indicated that the country's status as the economic powerhouse of Central Asia had gained international recognition. In July Kazakh officials reported that negotiations over conditions for U.S. and EU firms to enter the Kazakhstan market had been completed, and the country had entered the final stage of preparation for its long-desired goal of accession to the World Trade Organization.

International attention was focused on a strike by oil workers in western Kazakhstan that began in May. Thousands of disgruntled oil workers demanded increased pay, equal to the compensation given to foreigners working in the same oil fields, and the removal of restrictions on independent trade unions. In late August the affected oil company, KazMunaiGaz, asserted that despite the strike, production was almost back to normal. Independent media covering the strike experienced harassment, and a lawyer representing the strikers was sentenced to six years in prison for "inciting social hatred." Human rights activists denounced the sentence as stifling dissent and labour union activity. In December 16 people were reportedly killed when police fired on striking oil workers in the oil town of Zhanaozen.

In April an early presidential election confirmed Nursultan Nazarbayev in his long-held position as head of state; his two opponents received only minuscule percentages of the vote. In August an Astana court blocked several popular Internet blog sites, asserting that the sites were promoting extremism.

Human rights activists inside Kazakhstan and abroad were highly critical of a hastily drafted law on religion that was adopted by the lower house of Parliament in late September and approved by the upper house a few days later. Critics objected to the lack of public discussion of the draft, which banned prayer in state institutions, including schools and military units, set minimum membership sizes for religious organizations to register, and restricted the activity of missionaries. Defenders of the law asserted that it was necessary to prevent the spread of religious extremism, pointing to the arrest in August of 18 persons for allegedly having plotted terrorist activity. In a speech to Parliament in support of the draft law, President Nazarbayev called for increased monitoring of the activities of foreign Muslims but denied that the draft law was intended to limit freedom of conscience. (BESS BROWN)

KENYA

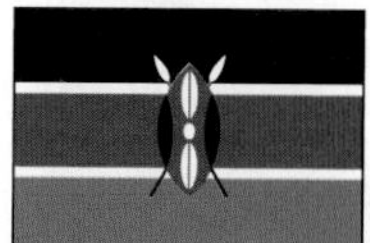

Area: 582,646 sq km (224,961 sq mi)
Population (2011 est.): 40,770,000
Capital: Nairobi
Head of state and government: President Mwai Kibaki, assisted by Prime Minister Raila Odinga

Bitter infighting in 2011 threatened to split Kenya's governing coalition, which faced the challenge of implementing a new constitution and preparing for the 2012 elections. The requirement that Pres. Mwai Kibaki stand down in 2012 inevitably resulted in a leadership struggle within the Party of National Unity (PNU), the ruling party. Political tension was further exacerbated when six influential politicians were summoned to the International Criminal Court (ICC) in The Hague for confirmation hearings relating to electoral violence in 2007. Three were supporters of Kibaki: Uhuru Kenyatta (deputy prime minister, finance minister, and son of Kenya's founding president), Francis Muthaura (head of civil service and cabinet secretary), and Hussein Ali (the police chief during the violence). The other three were members of the opposition Orange Democratic Movement (ODM): William Ruto (former minister of higher education), Henry Kosgey (former minister of industrialization and ODM chairman), and Joshua arap Sang (reporter and radio station executive). On October 5 the ICC accused Kenyatta, Muthaura, and Ali of conspiracy with the Mungiki criminal gang to attack civilians in reprisals for violence perpetrated by ODM followers after the election. A verdict on whether the six defendants would stand trial was expected in January 2012.

The ramification of the ICC's actions substantively reoriented the national political landscape. Two of the ICC suspects—Kenyatta and Ruto—had declared their intention to run as presidential candidates in the forthcoming election. Meanwhile, both the prime minister and the president were damaged by the ICC move. Prime Minister Raila Odinga, considered the front-runner for the presidency, was rumoured to have engineered the names for inclusion on the ICC's list, thus driving the supporters of the ODM suspects to the ruling party. President Kibaki, however, stood to lose the most because of his overt role in forestalling the ICC investigation as well as his known alliances with some ICC suspects. Meanwhile, Vice Pres. Kalonzo Musyoka, leader of the government's anti-ICC campaign, emerged with strengthened credentials for a presidential bid.

Ongoing interparty conflict impaired legislative progress, bringing the key justice committee in the parliament to a standstill. Nonetheless, the two main parties, the PNU and the ODM, managed to support—despite strong dissenting voices on both sides—the new constitution that had been passed the previous year and was gradually being implemented. One of the provisions of the 2010 constitution was for the creation of a Supreme Court, which was established in June 2011. Only two justices were sworn in at that time, as the other five appointments were being challenged by several women's groups on the basis that the new court would lack an equitable gender balance. In August the challenge was dismissed, and the remaining justices took their oaths. Another provision, for the establishment of a new anticorruption agency, was implemented in August.

A thorny historical issue was reopened in July when the London High Court declared in favour of four Kenyan elders, former warriors in the 1950s anticolonial Land and Freedom Movement (Mau Mau), who won an appeal to try the United Kingdom for atrocities experienced during the decolonization era. The case raised fundamental issues: should former colonial powers pay compensation for undermining indigenous property rights and human rights violations?

On October 15 Kenya declared war on al-Shabaab (an Islamist militant group) at home and abroad to bring to justice the Somali-based group believed to have orchestrated the kidnappings of tourists in northeastern Kenya. Kenyan troops entered Somalia the next day. It became apparent, however, that the action represented a longer-term strategy, coordinated with Somalia's Transitional Federal Government, to reinforce security in the Somali capital, Mogadishu, and destroy the networks of the rebel militias, pirates, and drugs and arms traffickers, some with possible links to corrupt officials in Nairobi. African Union forces from Uganda and Burundi that were already in Somalia supported this crackdown.

The world mourned the death of Nobel laureate Wangari Maathai, aged 71. Maathai died in Nairobi from ovarian cancer on September 25. (*See* OBITUARIES.) (LARAY DENZER)

On April 7 four Kenyan elders outside the Royal Courts of Justice in London demand reparations from the United Kingdom for abuses suffered at detention camps in Kenya during the anticolonial resistance movement of the 1950s.

Lefteris Pitarakis/AP

KIRIBATI

Area: 811 sq km (313 sq mi)
Population (2011 est.): 101,400
Capital: Government offices on three islets of South Tarawa
Head of state and government: President Anote Tong

Kiribati in 2011 remained a strong voice in global forums for small island states facing the catastrophic consequences of climate change. The country scored a coup in September when UN Secretary General Ban Ki-Moon visited and saw firsthand the consequences of climate change and sea-level rise on the low-lying atolls of Kiribati. He agreed to seek a commitment of funds from wealthy countries to mitigate the changes.

Kiribati held the first round of elections for its 46-seat legislature on October 21 and followed with a second round the next week and a runoff vote in early November to decide the final seat. Pres. Anote Tong held on to his seat, along with 29 other incumbents, but four cabinet ministers were among those voted out. The new parliament nominated three candidates for president: Tong, opposition leader Rimeta Beniamina, and Tetaua Taitai, a physician who had served in former president Teburoro Tito's government. The scheduled December presidential election was postponed until Jan. 13, 2012.

(CLUNY MACPHERSON)

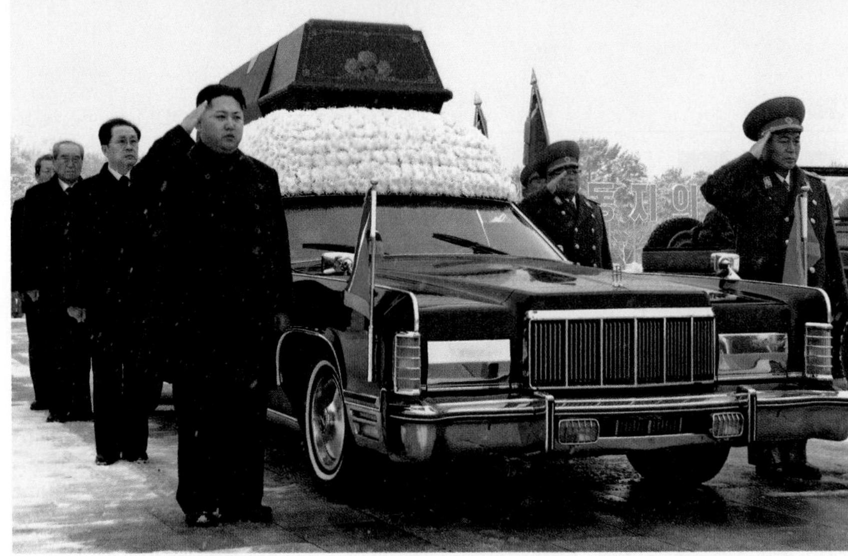

During a funeral procession for deceased North Korean ruler Kim Jong Il on December 28 in Pyongyang, his youngest son, Kim Jong-Eun (front left), who was named to succeed him, salutes next to the hearse transporting his father's body.
AP

KOREA, DEMOCRATIC PEOPLE'S REPUBLIC OF

Area: 122,762 sq km (47,399 sq mi)
Population (2011 est.): 24,336,000
Capital: Pyongyang
Head of state and government: Supreme Leader/Chairman of the National Defense Commission Kim Jong Il and, from December 17, Kim Jong-Eun (unofficial leader); Supreme Leader from December 29 Kim Jong-Eun

The event that overshadowed all others in North Korea during 2011 was the death of the country's leader, Kim Jong Il. The death of Kim, who had been in power officially since 1998, was unexpected; he had appeared to have recovered substantially from a suspected stroke in 2009. International observers were left waiting to see which of the previously theorized post-Kim scenarios would take shape. Contributing to the uncertainty were instability in the country's economy and in its relationship with South Korea. Further, although Kim's successor, his son Kim Jong-Eun, had been named to a high position on the powerful National Defense Commission in February, he apparently had had little formal experience to prepare him for the country's leadership.

Kim Jong-Eun was front and centre during the national 10-day mourning period and memorial services. On December 29 Kim Yong-Nam, leader of the Supreme People's Assembly (the national legislature), announced the status of Kim Jong-Eun as "supreme leader," a designation that was believed to indicate his leadership of the military and the Korean Workers' Party. Two days later he was officially named commander of the Korean People's Army.

Although no South Korean government delegation attended the services, a small number of prominent South Koreans did, including the chairwoman of Hyundai Asan, which had business relations with North Korea, and the widow of former South Korean president Kim Dae-Jung, who had pursued a cooperative "sunshine policy" with North Korea in the early 2000s that resulted in joint business initiatives. Afterward North Korea announced its desire to restore cooperative programs that had halted in recent years with a chill in North-South relations.

Earlier in the year Kim Jong Il had made moves toward increasing foreign ties. In August he traveled to Russia, his first trip there since 2002, presumably to discuss energy deals that included the building of a Russian natural-gas pipeline through his country to South Korea. Although North and South Korea exchanged artillery fire in August near Yonpyong Island, the site of a North Korean attack in 2010, Kim's government also signaled openness to resuming six-party talks on North Korea's denuclearization. Negotiators from the U.S. and North Korea met in Geneva in October.

The country's economic hardships continued. Food and fuel shortages were reported throughout the year, and in July the EU pledged $14.5 million in emergency aid. Food imports remained inadequate to rectify shortages, and in November UN agencies called for greater international help.

(LORRAINE MURRAY)

KOREA, REPUBLIC OF

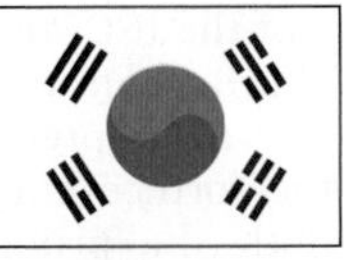

Area: 99,678 sq km (38,486 sq mi)
Population (2011 est.): 48,755,000
Capital: Seoul
Head of state and government: President Lee Myung-Bak, assisted by Prime Minister Kim Hwang-Sik

South Korea got off to a dramatic start in 2011 when a South Korean freighter was hijacked off the coast of Somalia on January 15. It was retaken by South Korean special forces a week later in a battle that killed eight of the Somali pirates. All 21 members of the ship's international crew were rescued.

As ever, relations with North Korea made news throughout the year. In February military representatives from both countries met for talks in the border town of Panmunjom. Little more than a day later, however, the North Korean delegation walked out after the South Koreans pressed for an apology for the sinking of the South Korean ship *Chonan* and the shelling of Yonpyong Island, near a disputed maritime border, the previous year. Nevertheless, North Korean leader Kim Jong Il seemed willing to reconvene talks on the North's denuclearization. Nuclear negotiators from both sides met in Bali, Indon., in July and in Beijing in September. Tensions continued along the maritime border, however, and on August 10 the two countries briefly exchanged artillery fire near Yonpyong without causing injury. Kim's death on December 17 brought uncertainty as to his country's future direction, but his son and successor, Kim Jong-Eun, indicated some openness to pursuing improvement in inter-Korean relations. (*See* OBITUARIES.)

Events in Seoul signaled a possible shift in the domestic political climate ahead of the presidential election planned for December 2012. Seoul Mayor Oh Se-Hoon—who was, like his ally Pres. Lee Myung-Bak, a member of the conservative Grand National Party—resigned on August 26 after his loss in a citywide referendum on the city's universal free-lunch program for elementary- and middle-school students. Oh had sought to restrict the program to cover only lower-income children. Liberals urged a boycott of the vote, which was invalidated by a low turnout, and the existing program remained in place. In an October 26 special election, independent Park Won-Soon was elected the new mayor. He was a prominent civic activist and critic of President Lee, who had once held that office himself (2002–06). Opposition to the referendum and Park's election were considered evidence of a growing liberalism in South Korea.

In late November the National Assembly ratified the long-planned free-trade pact with the U.S. The governing Grand National Party pushed for the vote in the absence of many opposition members, and with only 170 members of the 299-seat legislature in attendance, the deal passed 151–7, though not before a minority-party member detonated a can of tear gas in the chamber in protest.

The economy showed signs of weakness in 2011. The Bank of Korea raised interest rates three times during the year in an effort to control inflation, which reached a three-year high of 5.3% in August, dropped to 3.6% in October, and ticked back up to just over 4% in December. At year's end the central bank forecast a recovery but warned that troubles in the euro zone and political uncertainty in North Korea could have adverse effects on South Korea's economy.

There was good news on July 6 with the announcement by the International Olympic Committee that it had chosen Pyongchang—180 km (110 mi) east of Seoul and 80 km (50 mi) south of the North Korean border in Kangwon province—as the site of the 2018 Winter Games. South Korea had proposed the ski resort twice before without success.

The country was saddened by the death on December 30 of pro-democracy activist Kim Geun-Tae. Kim had been tortured as a dissident in the 1980s, during the country's military dictatorship. He later became a member of the National Assembly and a government minister. (LORRAINE MURRAY)

KOSOVO

Area: 10,908 sq km (4,212 sq mi)
Population (2011 est.): 1,826,000
Capital: Pristina
International Authority: Final authority resides with the UN interim administrators, Lamberto Zannier (Italy), Robert Sorenson (U.S.; acting) from July 1, and, from August 3, Farid Zarif (Afghanistan) in conjunction with the EU special representatives in Kosovo, Pieter Feith (Netherlands) until April 30 and Fernando Gentilini (Italy) from May 6 to July 31, and international civilian representative Pieter Feith (Netherlands)
Head of state: Presidents Jakup Krasniqi (acting), Behgjet Pacolli from February 22, Krasniqi (acting) from March 30, and, from April 7, Atifete Jahjaga
Head of government: Prime Minister Hashim Thaci

In January 2011 some 100,000 voters were eligible to recast their ballots in five regions of Kosovo to redress widespread fraud in the December 2010 general election. The vote confirmed that incumbent Prime Minister Hashim Thaci's Democratic Party of Kosovo had won the election. On February 22 the Assembly elected Thaci to a second term, and businessman Behgjet Pacolli,

Near Zubin Potok in northern Kosovo, a NATO soldier atop an armoured vehicle fires tear gas in an attempt to disperse a group of ethnic Serbs blocking a contested border crossing with Serbia, October 20.

Reuters/Landov

of the New Kosovo Alliance, was elected president. Having denounced Pacolli's ties with Russia, which had opposed Kosovo's independence, the opposition parties boycotted the vote. On April 7 Pacolli was replaced by Atifete Jahjaga, the former deputy general director of Kosovo's police forces. For his part Thaci had been reelected despite a Council of Europe report and an ongoing EU investigation that linked the former military leader to organ trafficking and other war crimes committed during the 1999 war against Serbia. Thaci rebutted the allegations.

In October the Assembly opened debate on a constitutional change that would provide for the direct election of the president. No real progress was reported in any aspect of the country's fragile economy. The World Bank and the IMF estimated that 45% of Kosovars lived below the poverty line and that unemployment approached 50%.

Unrest continued in northern Kosovo, where ethnic Serbs, backed by the Serbian government, established parallel institutions in defiance of Kosovo's sovereign authority. In contrast, southern enclaves of Serbs had achieved some degree of integration into Kosovo's legal, political, and economic life. Living conditions and access to educational and employment opportunities for Kosovo's minority Roma (Gypsy), Ashkali, and Egyptians remained a concern.

Negotiations between Serbia and Kosovo were conducted in an effort to settle the status of Kosovo's Serb community and to normalize relations between Belgrade and Pristina. At stake was Serbia's candidacy to the EU and Kosovo's place in the international community. Since Kosovo's declaration of independence in 2008, 85 countries had recognized the country.

(MILAN ANDREJEVICH)

KUWAIT

Area: 17,818 sq km (6,880 sq mi)
Population (2011 est.): 3,650,000
Capital: Kuwait
Head of state and government: Emir Sheikh Sabah al-Ahmad al-Jabir al-Sabah, assisted by Prime Ministers Sheikh Nasir al-Muhammad al-Ahmad al-Jabir al-Sabah and, from December 4, Sheikh Jabir al-Mubarak al-Hamad al-Sabah

Although Kuwait avoided the massive popular demonstrations seen in a number of Arab countries in 2011, some youth-led rallies were held. These groups demanded political reforms and the eradication of corruption. Early in the year the government tried to mollify the population by distributing 1,000 Kuwaiti dinars (about $3,650) to each Kuwaiti. Nonetheless, social agitation continued in the form of strikes and sit-ins by different professional unions and by government employees demanding better employment conditions.

Tensions between the parliament and the cabinet continued as opposition deputies pressed for greater accountability. Prime Minister Sheikh Nasir al-Muhammad al-Ahmad al-Jabir al-Sabah refused demands that he be "questioned" by the parliament, and on March 31 he submitted his resignation to Emir Sheikh Sabah al-Ahmad al-Jabir al-Sabah. The emir then reappointed Sheikh Nasir and charged him with forming a new government, his sixth since 2006.

In August Kuwaitis were astonished when some Kuwaiti banks announced that they would take legal action against members of parliament whom they accused of having engaged in money laundering. The amounts in question totaled at least $92 million, which the banks claimed came from cash deposits with unverifiable origins. A public outcry ensued, sparked by suspicions that this cash was derived from bribes and kickbacks. The Kuwaiti public prosecutor opened an investigation of the matter, and on September 25 the government sent an anticorruption draft law to the parliament that included articles on financial disclosure and made money laundering punishable by seven years' imprisonment. The prime minister, blamed for the spread of corruption and facing demands from members of parliament for government accountability, resigned on November 28. This was followed by the dissolution of the parliament. On December 4 Sheikh Jabir al-Mubarak al-Hamad al-Sabah was appointed prime minister, and his cabinet was sworn in on December 14.

Relations between Kuwait and Iraq soured in April when Kuwait began to build a megaport on the island of Bubiyan near an inlet that provided Iraq access to the Persian Gulf. In Iraq, which has only a few kilometres of shoreline on the Gulf, public opinion turned against Kuwait over fears that the port would stifle Iraqi trade.

(LOUAY BAHRY)

KYRGYZSTAN

Area: 199,945 sq km (77,199 sq mi)
Population (2011 est.): 5,168,000
Capital: Bishkek
Head of state: Presidents Rosa Otunbayeva (interim) and, from December 1, Almazbek Atambayev
Head of government: Prime Ministers Almazbek Atambayev and, from September 23, Omurbek Babanov (acting)

Much of Kyrgyzstan's political life in 2011 revolved around the aftermath of events in 2010: the ousting of former president Kurmanbek Bakiyev in April and ethnic violence in southern Kyrgyzstan in June. A trial that sought to determine blame for violence during the uprising that ousted Bakiyev dragged on for months, often becoming unruly as relatives of victims of what was seen as the state-sponsored violence tried to attack the defendants and defense witnesses. In July the defense claimed that

On November 1, a day after his election as president of Kyrgyzstan, Almazbek Atambayev holds a press conference in Bishkek.

Vladimir Voronin/AP

the prosecution was inciting the courtroom disturbances.

Unemployment, poverty, and corruption continued to plague Kyrgyzstan, with little sign of improvement. In September the International Monetary Fund announced a new three-year strategy for Kyrgyzstan's economy that focused on developing agribusiness, stabilizing business operations, and continuing the Local Currency Lending Program to build up domestic funding. In the same month, a World Food Programme official reported that the number of families with low levels of food security was increasing and added that the WFP was trying to expand the Food for Work program started in 2010. As part of the effort to improve Kyrgyzstan's poor ratings for corruption, interim president Roza Otunbayeva set up a body to ensure transparency in the use of U.S. rental payments for the facilities at Manas Airport, a major supply base for U.S. forces in Afghanistan.

The national parliament set October 30 as the date for a presidential election, with the official start of the presidential campaign set for September 25. As of September 26, 20 candidates remained in the race after dozens had been disqualified by election officials for failing to meet candidacy requirements. The election was held on time and was subsequently hailed as the most democratic in the country's history. Former prime minister Almazbek Atambayev garnered over 60% of the vote, and interim president Otunbayeva resigned in Kyrgyzstan's first peaceful transfer of power. The new president indicated that he would pursue closer cooperation with Russia than had his predecessor.

Election law required that retransmission of foreign television channels be suspended during the presidential campaign to prevent foreign interference in the election process. The suspension mainly affected popular Russian television channels. Kyrgyz authorities quickly pointed out that satellite reception was not affected.

Tensions between ethnic Kyrgyz and ethnic Uzbeks remained strong in the south, and fearing another outbreak of the violence that cost several hundred lives in 2010, UN Secretary-General Ban Ki-Moon appealed for preelection reconciliation among the peoples of Kyrgyzstan. On July 20 the Batken region of southern Kyrgyzstan was struck by an earthquake that caused considerable damage. (BESS BROWN)

LAOS

Area: 236,800 sq km (91,429 sq mi)
Population (2011 est.): 6,392,000
Capital: Vientiane
Head of state: President Choummaly Sayasone
Head of government: Prime Minister Thongsing Thammavong

The year 2011 was mixed for the leadership of Laos. It started well with a perfectly orchestrated ninth Congress of the Lao People's Revolutionary Party (LPRP), the party's most important political event, convened on March 17–21 in Vientiane. The 576 delegates to the congress, representing some 191,700 party members, elected 61 members to the party's Central Committee, and the Central Committee then selected the 11 members of the Politburo, the regime's highest political body. As expected, the leadership remained in place, with Choummaly Sayasone and Thongsing Thammavong being reelected as LPRP secretary-general (he also was president of the Lao People's Democratic Republic) and prime minister, respectively. The Politburo did welcome three new members: Bounthong Chitmany, Bounpone Bouttanavong, and Phankham Viphavanh. The congress also endorsed the seventh National Socio-Economic Development Plan (2011–15).

Elections for the National Assembly were held in April. The 190 candidates had been carefully vetted beforehand by the LPRP's executive organs, and all of the 132 newly elected deputies, with the exception of one, were party members. The National Assembly had acquired more powers and had gained more visibility in the past few years, especially after the adoption of the country's amended constitution in 2003 and the passage in 2006 of revisions to the laws governing the National Assembly. It was highly unlikely, however, that the deputies would attempt to censure, block, or overturn the government's policies or decisions, as the assembly had, at most, an advisory role, not a lawmaking one.

On the economic front, the year did not go as smoothly for the country, as new government projects encountered some serious setbacks. In April the start of construction of a much-publicized high-speed rail line in Laos, cofinanced by Chinese investors (70%) and the Lao government (30%), was suddenly postponed to a later, unspecified date. The project, which was to link Boten (on the border with China) to Vientiane, was delayed allegedly because of concerns at the highest levels of the LPRP over the terms of the contract—one provision of which was for a massive number of Chinese labourers to be hired to work on it. About a month later the controversial Xayaboury dam project on the Mekong River in northwestern Laos was also shelved for the time being by the Lao government following protests from international nongovernmental organizations and some Southeast Asian governments (including Vietnam) that the dam could have harmful transboundary environmental impacts. (VATTHANA PHOLSENA)

LATVIA

Area: 64,589 sq km (24,938 sq mi)
Population (2011 est.): 2,217,000
Capital: Riga
Head of state: Presidents Valdis Zatlers and, from July 8, Andris Berzins
Head of government: Prime Minister Valdis Dombrovskis

Internal political turbulence and economic issues figured prominently in Latvia in 2011. Stability was preserved by Valdis Dombrovskis, who began his third successive term as prime minister on October 25. On the international front, Latvian soldiers continued serving in the International Security Assistance Force (ISAF) in Afghanistan, and Latvia also provided transit facilities for supplies routed to the ISAF.

GDP grew by about 4.5% in 2011, and unemployment rates were down from their peak of more than 20% in 2010. They remained stubbornly high throughout the year, however, at an average of roughly 16%, and preliminary results from a census taken in the spring suggested that many Latvians were seeking employment abroad. Lawmakers continued to take steps to balance Latvia's budget with the intention of joining the euro zone in 2014.

The erratic behaviour of the parliament that was elected in October 2010 frustrated the populace and raised suspicions that many deputies had ties to the oligarchs backing their parties. On May 28 Pres. Valdis Zatlers proposed dissolving the current parliament and holding new elections. The parliament voted on June 2 to replace Zatlers and chose as his successor Andris Berzins, a former banker affiliated with the Greens' and Farmers' Union. After Berzins's inauguration on July 8, the former president formed Zatlers' Reform Party (ZRP).

With nearly 60% voter participation in the election on September 17, five parties and alliances won representation in the 100-seat parliament: the leftist, pro-Russian Harmony Center—31 seats; the centrist ZRP—22; the right-leaning Unity—20; the nationalist National Association (NA)—14; and the Greens' and Farmers' Union—13. The ZRP led negotiations with other parties on the composition of the new government, but President Berzins entrusted Valdis Dombrovskis (Unity) with the formation of the new Cabinet of Ministers.

(DZINTRA BUNGS)

Bilal Hussein/AP

At the seat of the Maronite church in Bkirki, Leb., Bishara al-Ra'i prays shortly after his election as Maronite patriarch, March 15.

LEBANON

Area: 10,452 sq km (4,036 sq mi)
Population (2011 est.): 4,143,000 (including registered Palestinian refugees estimated to number about 455,000)
Capital: Beirut
Head of state: President Michel Suleiman
Head of government: Prime Ministers Sa'ad al-Hariri and, from June 13, Najib Mikati

Lebanon began 2011 with the forced collapse of Prime Minister Sa'ad al-Hariri's cabinet on January 13, following the resignations of ministers belonging to the March 8 bloc led by Hezbollah and Gen. Michel Aoun. After five months of deliberations, a Hezbollah-backed cabinet led by Najib Mikati was formed on June 13. In July the new cabinet won a parliamentary vote of confidence, receiving 68 of the 128 votes.

On June 30 the UN-backed Special Tribunal for Lebanon accused four members of Hezbollah of having assassinated former prime minister Rafiq al-Hariri in Beirut in 2005. Hassan Nasrallah, Hezbollah's leader, refused to cooperate with the tribunal, denouncing it as part of an Israeli and U.S. agenda for Lebanon. The new government's stance regarding Lebanon's commitment to the tribunal remained ambivalent. In August the government announced that it had been unable to apprehend the suspects, setting the stage for trials in absentia.

The new government renewed Riad Salameh's term as central bank governor for another six years. It also appointed Maj. Gen. 'Abbas Ibrahim head of the General Security Directorate. Since Ibrahim was well known for having close relations with Hezbollah, the March 14 bloc accused the new cabinet of having a bias.

In February the U.S. Treasury Department accused the Lebanese Canadian Bank of having laundered hundreds of millions of dollars a month for an international drug-trafficking ring associated with Hezbollah. Although the bank denied the allegations, a liquidity problem ensued, forcing the bank to merge with the Lebanese subsidiary of Société Général.

Seven Estonians kidnapped and held for about four months were released on July 14 in the Biqa' Valley. The identity of their captors was not revealed, but in September two of the alleged kidnappers were killed in a battle with security forces.

Amid a dispute with Israel over offshore oil and gas fields, the Lebanese cabinet delineated the boundaries of Lebanon's exclusive economic zone. Soon after the cabinet's decision, Nabih Berri, the speaker of the parliament, called for Lebanon to begin drilling in the area.

Lebanon took over the rotating presidency of the UN Security Council in September, and Pres. Michel Suleiman and Prime Minister Mikati each chaired some of its sessions in New York City. Both men affirmed that Lebanon would uphold its commitments to international resolutions, especially those regarding Lebanon and the Middle East.

Bishara al-Ra'i was chosen to replace Nasrallah Sfeir as the patriarch of the Maronite Church. While on a visit to Paris, Ra'i drew attention for statements that seemed to offer indirect support for Hezbollah's military activities. He also signaled his support for the Palestinian right of return to Palestine and for Syrian Pres. Bashar al-Assad, saying that the embattled leader deserved more time to implement reforms as he confronted a six-month popular uprising. In addition, the patriarch warned that if the Muslim Brotherhood took power in Syria, it would threaten Christians there and in Lebanon.

(MAHMOUD HADDAD)

LESOTHO

Area: 30,355 sq km (11,720 sq mi)
Population (2011 est.): 1,925,000
Capital: Maseru
Head of state: King Letsie III
Head of government: Prime Minister Bethuel Pakalitha Mosisili

Already beset by wide-scale unemployment and a high incidence of HIV/AIDS, in 2011 much of Lesotho's population battled to survive in the face of rising food costs and poor harvests. The country's budget was hard hit by the large reduction in the amount of funds that the country received from the Southern Africa Customs Union. Mediation by the Southern African Development Community on Lesotho's electoral system came to an end, but it remained to be seen if the political instability of the past was over. In September the trial began in the country's high court of eight men who were charged with having plotted to assassinate the prime minister in April 2009. The men were arrested in South Africa and extradited to Lesotho in April 2011. A leaked United States diplomatic cable revealed that the secretary-general of the ruling party, the Lesotho Congress for Democracy, had expressed concerns over the dictatorial leadership of Prime Minister Bethuel Pakalitha Mosisili, who had not agreed to retire at the end of his term in 2012.

In August government officials from South Africa and Lesotho signed an agreement for the implementation of Phase II of the Lesotho Highlands Water Project. In October a South African company signed a deal with the Lesotho government for a $15 billion renewable energy venture known as the Lesotho Highlands Power Project, which was expected to generate wind power and hydro-power. (CHRISTOPHER SAUNDERS)

Luc Gnago—Reuters/Landov

After unrest broke out on November 7, the day before Liberia's presidential runoff election, riot police in Monrovia confront supporters of opposition presidential candidate Winston Tubman.

LIBERIA

Area: 96,917 sq km (37,420 sq mi)
Population (2011 est.): 3,953,000
Capital: Monrovia
Head of state and government: President Ellen Johnson Sirleaf

A few days prior to Liberia's general election on Oct. 11, 2011, Pres. Ellen Johnson Sirleaf won the Nobel Prize for Peace, along with her compatriot peace activist Leymah Gbowee and Tawakkul Karman of Yemen. (*See* NOBEL PRIZES.) While women's associations welcomed this reflection of women's empowerment, Winston Tubman, the flag bearer of the Congress for Democratic Change (CDC) and Johnson Sirleaf's major rival for the presidency, viewed it as a "provocative intervention" in Liberian politics. "She does not deserve it. She is a warmonger," he declared. His remarks demonstrated that Johnson Sirleaf was far less popular at home than she was abroad. Her political opponents harshly criticized her for having reneged on a promise to step down after one term, for her complicity with former military governments, and for not having done more to rein in corruption or promote socioeconomic development. The country ranked among the poorest on the UN human development index.

On November 8 President Johnson Sirleaf won her second term by default when Tubman—former international civil servant and nephew of a former president—carried out his threat to boycott the runoff election, on charges of irregularities. Although she won 90.8% of the votes, the result was marred by an extremely low turnout of only 37.4%, only about half of the first voter turnout in October. This signified widespread apprehension concerning possible outbreaks of violence, reinforced by rioting the day before the election that resulted in at least one death and some abusive police behaviour. In contrast, the first electoral round had proceeded peacefully, but Johnson Sirleaf had failed to secure the majority vote she desired, with only a 43.9% return to Tubman's 32.7%.

The election over, Johnson Sirleaf faced the difficult task of repairing relations with her opponents; however, U.S. Pres. Barack Obama and other international leaders issued strong statements dismissing the opposition's claims of fraud. Meanwhile, the 8,000-strong UN peacekeeping force remained in place to ensure peace. (LARAY DENZER)

LIBYA

Area: 1,676,198 sq km (647,184 sq mi)
Population (2011 est.): 6,423,000
Capital: Tripoli
Head of state: (de facto) Col. Muammar al-Qaddafi and, from August 23, Chairman of the Transitional National Council Mustafa Abdul Jalil
Head of government: Secretary of the General People's Committee (Prime Minister) Al-Baghdadi ʿAli al-Mahmudi and interim Prime Ministers Mahmoud Jibril from August 23, Ali Tarhouni from October 23, and, from November 24, Abdel Rahim al-Keeb

In 2011 Libya experienced a protracted period of protest and conflict that culminated in a shift to an interim government under the control of the Transitional National Council (TNC) and in the capture and death of the country's longtime ruler Muammar al-Qaddafi. (*See* OBITUARIES.) Protests began in late February, after the overthrow of

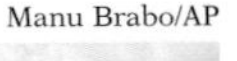
Manu Brabo/AP

Libyan rebels launch a missile during an attack on the city of Surt, the hometown of ousted ruler Muammar al-Qaddafi, October 5.

Tunisian leader Zine al-Abidine Ben Ali, but quickly descended into armed conflict. Libya's leader of more than 40 years used the Libyan military as well as mercenaries, mostly from sub-Saharan Africa, in an ultimately unsuccessful attempt to crush the opposition.

Key regime officials, including ministers and ambassadors, defected to the opposition forces, which soon began to call for international support. As civilian casualties mounted, the UN Security Council approved a no-fly zone and other measures to protect civilians from Qaddafi's forces. Under the UN resolution, NATO forces and forces from some Arab countries implemented the no-fly zone. In addition, the foreign assets of the Libyan government (which totaled more than $150 billion) were frozen. Despite those efforts, a stalemate persisted for many months, with many thousands of lives lost and extensive internal displacement. By late summer, however, the TNC forces had gained the upper hand, capturing Tripoli from Qaddafi's forces at the end of August.

In October, after opposition forces had effectively taken over governing Libya, Qaddafi was found and killed by TNC forces. The leader's death brought an end to the stalemate, formalizing the shift in power that had already begun. On October 31, TNC members elected Abdel Rahim al-Keeb as Libya's head of government. His interim administration promised to hold elections in 2012.

The civil war hit Libya's economy hard, with the collapse in oil output and destruction of infrastructure leading to a sharp recession. The conflict caused food, fuel, and water shortages, and oil output decreased from 1.6 million bbl a day in 2010 to a trickle, eliminating an important source of government revenue. The freezing of Libyan government assets abroad, including stakes in European companies such as the Italian bank UniCredit and the energy company Eni, helped choke off the Qaddafi regime's resources. At the end of 2011, most of those assets were still being unfrozen and were likely to be used for the reconstruction then under way. (RACHEL ZIEMBA)

LIECHTENSTEIN

Area: 160 sq km (62 sq mi)
Population (2011 est.): 36,300
Capital: Vaduz
Head of state: Prince Hans Adam II
Head of government: Klaus Tschütscher

The observance of Liechtenstein's August 15 national holiday, an occasion when the royal family traditionally invited everyone in the country (some 36,000 people) to the castle grounds, was marked in 2011 by one glaring absence. To protest the country's legalization of same-sex civil unions, the bishop of Vaduz refused to perform the mass that had traditionally been part of the celebration. The civil union act was supported by Prince Alois (who since 2004 had assumed the day-to-day duties of his father, Prince Hans Adam II), passed by the parliament in March, and approved by 68% of the voters in a June referendum. The law went into effect on September 1. A referendum on September 18 to legalize abortion in the first 12 weeks of a pregnancy or if a fetus is severely disabled resulted in a rejection of the plan. Prince Alois, who had earlier promised to veto the measure, stated that it could prompt late-term abortions to prevent the birth of children with disabilities.

In international affairs Liechtenstein was cited by the Organisation for Economic Co-operation and Development's Global Forum on Transparency and Information Exchange for Tax Purposes as having made "rapid progress in developing exchange of information mechanisms." The forum noted, however, that Liechtenstein still needed to meet international standards in combating tax evasion and bank secrecy.

The economy continued to prosper. About half (51%) of the 33,000 jobs available were filled by workers who commuted from nearby Switzerland, Austria, and Germany. (ANNE ROBY)

LITHUANIA

Area: 65,300 sq km (25,212 sq mi)
Population (2011 est.): 3,218,000
Capital: Vilnius
Head of state: President Dalia Grybauskaite
Head of government: Prime Minister Andrius Kubilius

In 2011 Lithuania marked 20 years of independence from the Soviet Union, but the formal anniversary celebration was dampened by the remembrance of events that had occurred on Jan. 13, 1991, when Soviet troops stormed a television station in Vilnius, the capital, where hundreds of unarmed civilians had gathered to guard the tower in a sign of defense of the country's independent broadcasting. Soviet tanks drove over and killed 14 people, and

Mindaugas Kulbis/AP

Lithuanians carrying a banner in the pattern of their country's flag march through Vilnius on January 13, the 20th anniversary of a brutal Soviet siege there that aimed to quell Lithuanian independence activities.

more than 500 were injured in the attempted coup.

During 2011 Lithuania continued to preside over the Community of Democracies. From June 30 to July 1, U.S. Secretary of State Hillary Clinton visited Lithuania to participate in the sixth Ministerial Conference of the Community of Democracies in Vilnius. The U.S. and Lithuania also commemorated the 20th anniversary of the resumption of diplomatic relations. In late September a high-level American trade delegation led by Rep. John Shimkus visited Lithuania on this occasion. During the year Lithuania chaired the Organization for Security and Co-operation (OSCE) in Europe, promoting human rights, democracy, and rule of law. On December 6–7 the meeting of the Council of Ministers of the OSCE took place in Vilnius.

In economic news, Lithuania continued its recovery. In comparing the third quarter of 2010 with that of 2011, unemployment decreased from 18.3% to 15.3%, but real earnings dropped by 2.9%, owing to inflation, which increased 3.8%. GDP increased 6.6%, exports rose 26%, and industrial production went up by 6.9%, while foreign direct investment dipped 43.9%.

In the realm of sports, the FIBA EuroBasket championship took place August 31–September 18 in Lithuania. The Lithuanian team took fifth place among the 24 competing teams.

(DARIUS FURMONAVICIUS)

LUXEMBOURG

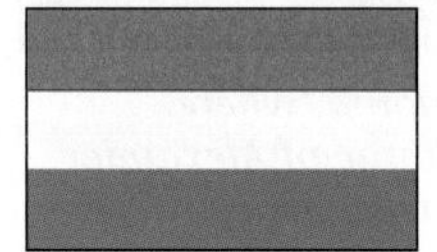

Area: 2,586 sq km (999 sq mi)
Population (2011 est.): 517,000
Capital: Luxembourg
Head of state: Grand Duke Henri
Head of government: Prime Minister Jean-Claude Juncker

Luxembourg's Prime Minister Jean-Claude Juncker worked tirelessly in 2011 to find some consensus among the euro zone countries to help with the continuing fiscal crisis. Finland demanded collateral for any loan it made to Greece, and Greece claimed an assault on its sovereignty. Nevertheless, Juncker, as chairman of the Eurogroup, led finance ministers to approve an additional €12 billion (about $17.43 billion) installment for the bailout of Greece. He stated that "the current package of measures, which Athens has agreed to, will bring a solution to the Greek question."

Luxembourg's internal economy continued to be quite strong. In September Russian steelmaker Magnitogorsk formed a new mining unit in Luxembourg. Alcatel-Lucent and P&TLuxembourg launched one of Europe's fastest high-capacity data networks, at 100 gigabits per second—beginning with a link between Luxembourg and Frankfurt, Ger.—and had plans to expand the enhanced network to additional major business capitals. Cargolux, headquartered in Luxembourg and ranked ninth worldwide in cargo traffic, refused the delivery on September 19 of the first of 13 Boeing 747-8Fs. Boeing's delivery of the new aircraft was already two years behind schedule. It was not clear whether Cargolux's decision was a financial move because of the long delay or, as some aviation experts suspected, a dispute centred on performance issues.

(ANNE ROBY)

MACEDONIA

Area: 25,713 sq km (9,928 sq mi)
Population (2011 est.): 2,060,000
Capital: Skopje
Head of state: President Gjorge Ivanov
Head of government: Prime Minister Nikola Gruevski

Macedonia entered 2011 in a state of political crisis after raids on the privately owned television station A1 and three newspapers, along with the subsequent arrest of their owner, Velija Ramkovski, on criminal charges, including tax evasion. Opposition parties, media representatives, and nongovernmental organizations claimed that the move had been motivated by the antigovernment stance these media outlets had taken. In late January, after the outlets' accounts were frozen, the opposition boycotted the parliament and demanded new parliamentary elections. The government forced the newspapers to suspend publication in early July and revoked the broadcasting license of A1. On July 31 the Broadcasting Council, dominated by the ruling parties, sacked the entire managing board of public Macedonian Radio-Television.

The government initially rejected the opposition's demand for elections, but on February 20 Prime Minister Nikola Gruevski of the ruling Internal Macedonian Revolutionary Organization—Democratic Party for Macedonian National Unity (VMRO–DPMNE) reversed that decision, and on April 14 the parliament was dissolved after having

Ognen Teofilovski—Reuters/Landov

On September 8 fireworks illuminate the sky in Skopje, Macedonia, where thousands of citizens have gathered around a newly erected statue of Alexander the Great to celebrate the 20th anniversary of Macedonian independence.

paved the way for new elections, which were scheduled for June 5. The VMRO–DPMNE-led coalition won the elections with 39% of the vote but, having captured 56 seats, fell short of an outright majority. The opposition coalition led by the Social Democratic Union of Macedonia (SDSM) increased its representation considerably to 42 seats, having garnered 32.8% of the vote. Three ethnic-Albanian parties also made their mark: the Democratic Union for Integration (BDI), with 10.2% of the vote and 15 seats; the Democratic Party of Albanians (PDSh), with 5.9% and 8 seats; and the newly formed National Democratic Revival (RDK), with 2.7% and 2 seats. For the first time, three MPs were elected by the diaspora. The OSCE and the Council of Europe concluded that the elections were "competitive, transparent, and well-administered throughout the country, although certain aspects require attention."

Gruevski renewed the coalition with the BDI, and the new government was approved by the parliament on July 28. The biggest change was the replacement of Foreign Minister Antonio Milososki (who left the government citing private and family reasons) by Nikola Popovski. Interethnic relations remained largely calm, despite a violent incident on February 13 in Skopje's Kale fortress, where ethnic Macedonians and Albanians clashed over plans to build a museum in the shape of a church. In mid-October, however, the national census, which was already under way, was canceled after ethnicity-related disagreements over procedures resulted in the resignation of the census commission.

Macedonia's economy was expected to continue its slight upward trend, with GDP growth estimated at 3%. Inflation, however, was projected to increase to 5%. Unemployment was expected to remain extremely high at 32.2%.

In foreign policy, the dispute over the country's name with Greece was no closer to resolution, despite continued UN-brokered talks and a meeting between Gruevski and then Greek prime minister George Papandreou, at which both affirmed their political will to solve the problem. This issue continued to hold up negotiations over Macedonia's membership in NATO and the EU. (STEFAN KRAUSE)

MADAGASCAR

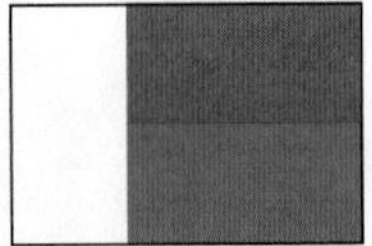

Area: 587,041 sq km (226,658 sq mi)
Population (2011 est.): 21,307,000
Capital: Antananarivo
Head of state and government: President Andry Rajoelina, assisted by Prime Ministers Albert Camille Vital and, from November 2, Omer Beriziky

While Madagascar remained suspended from the Southern African Development Community (SADC) and the African Union in 2011, the SADC continued to mediate the crisis that had existed since the 2009 de facto coup that brought Andry Rajoelina to power. After a series of SADC talks mediated by former president Joaquim Chissano of Mozambique failed to resolve the dispute, it was announced in September 2011 that the SADC road map to a free and fair election, to be held within a year, had finally been accepted by the main parties in Madagascar. Part of the agreement's terms dictated that former Malagasy president Marc Ravalomanana, who had been living in exile since the coup, would be allowed to return to the Indian Ocean island, despite having been found guilty in absentia of causing civilian deaths and given a life sentence by a Malagasy court during the previous year. In November a unity government was formed by Omer Beriziky, the new prime minister. Days later another former president, Didier Ratsiraka, returned after several years of exile.

It was anticipated that the political developments might make possible the return of donor support, which had been cut off after the coup, at a cost to Madagascar of an estimated $500 million. One consequence of the lost aid was the higher poverty levels that were reported, especially in rural areas, where 80% of the country's 20 million people lived.

In February 2011 a cyclone struck northeastern Madagascar, causing extensive damage to crops and deepening food insecurity. Meanwhile, the southern part of the island suffered from recurrent droughts.

(CHRISTOPHER SAUNDERS)

MALAWI

Area: 118,484 sq km (45,747 sq mi)
Population (2011 est.): 15,381,000
Capital: Lilongwe; judiciary meets in Blantyre
Head of state and government: President Bingu wa Mutharika

Malawi's progress in economic recovery and democratic governance completely reversed in 2011. Pres. Bingu wa Mutharika and an ethnic clique consolidated their grip on state institutions, moving toward one-party rule reminiscent of the Hastings Kamuzu Banda era (1963–94). In December 2010, Vice Pres. Joyce Banda was expelled from the ruling Democratic Progressive Party, although she retained her official position. Other influential officials were also dismissed in late 2010 and in 2011.

In response to tightening autocracy, widespread discontent erupted in nationwide demonstrations on July 20. Protesters were mobilized by civil society activists, opposition politicians, trade unions, and faith-based groups. The army brutally quelled the disturbances, killing 19 protesters, wounding hundreds, and forcing activists into hiding. Homes of some leading human rights activists were fire-bombed. On August 19 the president dissolved his 42-member cabinet, interpreted as a move to assuage his critics. At year's end the government and civil society remained at loggerheads, despite mediation efforts by the UN.

A bonfire that was set to protest a court ruling that curbed public demonstrations in Malawi burns on a street in Lilongwe, July 20.

Diane Boles/AP

Meanwhile, the market price of tobacco, the main cash crop, plunged. Civil servants did not receive salaries for months; consumer prices surged; and there were severe shortages of foreign exchange, fuel, electricity, and water. Economic troubles were further exacerbated when international donors, concerned with how the government was handling Malawi's economic and political problems, withheld considerable amounts of aid. (LARAY DENZER)

MALAYSIA

Area: 330,803 sq km (127,724 sq mi)
Population (2011 est.): 28,161,000
Capital: Kuala Lumpur; administrative centre, Putrajaya
Head of state: *Yang di-Pertuan Agong* (Paramount Rulers) Tuanku Mizan Zainal Abidin ibni al-Marhum Sultan Mahmud and, from December 13, Tuanku Abdul Halim Muadzam Shah ibni al-Marhum Sultan Badlishah
Head of government: Prime Minister Datuk Seri Najib Tun Razak

Malaysia made some progress toward reestablishing its image as a diverse and tolerant country in 2011, but questions remained about the government's commitment to safeguarding constitutional freedoms. In mid-September, Prime Minister Najib Razak announced the repeal of the repressive Internal Security Act, under which individuals could be detained indefinitely without trial if the government deemed them a threat to national security. In an effort to improve relations with Malaysia's significant Christian minority, the prime minister established diplomatic ties with the Vatican in July. Earlier in the year, the government released 35,000 Malay-language Bibles that had been impounded because they referred to God as Allah. While Razak emphasized that the move was simply in recognition of the constitution's guarantee of religious freedom, critics noted that it came just ahead of an important election in Sarawak state, which had a large Christian population. In March a Christian lawyer was barred from arguing cases before the country's Shari'ah (Islamic law) courts. In July police in Kuala Lumpur fired tear gas and water cannons on thousands of protesters who were demanding the reform of election procedures. The government's harsh response to the rally was criticized by officials in other countries, who saw the protest as an exercise of free speech.

In October the Australian government abandoned plans to send seekers of political asylum in Australia to Malaysia while their applications were being processed. The reversal came after Australia's High Court ruled that offshore processing of refugees was unlawful.

Malaysia's GDP was forecast to grow at a rate of about 4.5% in 2011. Domestic demand was projected to rise slightly from one-time payouts to the poor and bonuses for civil servants that were announced in early October, but the increase was not expected to offset a drop in demand for exports. Almost 35% of Malaysian workers had incomes below the official poverty line, and the government announced in April that it was considering instituting a minimum wage. The government also raised the mandatory retirement age to 60.

The first meeting of the Global Science and Innovation Advisory Council took place in May. The council advised the government on how best to encourage green development in Malaysia, with a focus on such issues as the handling of industrial waste, water management, and reforestation. A new rare-earth metals refinery being built in Kuantan prompted environmental concerns when engineers associated with the project said in June that design and construction flaws could result in radiation leaks. Analysts predicted that the refinery could supply almost one-third of world demand for rare-earth metals (used in many high-technology applications) and could generate more than $1.7 billion in exports annually.

Malaysia-based low-cost airline AirAsia signed a deal in August to take over budget routes belonging to Malaysia Airlines, leaving the latter to concen-

Lai Seng Sin/AP

In Kuala Lumpur, Malay., a young activist attempts to kick a tear-gas canister deployed by police during a rally calling for electoral reform, July 9.

trate on its premium service. In June AirAsia ordered 200 jet airliners worth $18 billion from Airbus Industrie.

(JANET MOREDOCK)

MALDIVES

Area: 298 sq km (115 sq mi)
Population (2011 est.): 325,000, excluding about 100,000 foreign workers employed on the resort islands
Capital: Male
Head of state and government: President Mohamed Nasheed

Economic issues dominated the political agenda of the Maldives government of Pres. Mohamed Nasheed and the opposition parties in 2011, threatening to cause instability in the country. In May a series of protests erupted in Male against soaring prices after the Maldivian currency, the rufiyaa, was devalued by 20%. The demonstrations allegedly were orchestrated by former president Maumoon Abdul Gayoom's faction in the Dhivehi Rayyithunge Party (DRP). In response, the ruling Maldivian Democratic Party (MDP) organized counter-protests defending the government's economic policies.

Gayoom, who had returned to politics after having retired, split in September from the DRP to form the Progressive Party of Maldives. In addition, the People Alliance (PA) headed by Gayoom's half brother, Abdulla Yameen, withdrew from the DRP-led opposition coalition in the parliament, and the PA emerged as the leader of a new coalition. The government was jolted when the religiously conservative Adhaalath Party ended its alliance with the MDP after it accused the government of making "secret deals" with Israel and criticized a new law intended to control and prevent extremist and unlicensed preaching of Islam in Maldives. In February, in the country's first-ever local-council elections, the DRP won majorities in island and atoll constituencies, while the MDP prevailed in the city.

The government's major economic concern was to reduce the fiscal deficit, which represented 16.4% of GDP in the 2011 budget. As an effective cost-cutting measure, it decided not to raise the wages of civil servants—which accounted for 49% of the budget—until 2012.

(PONMONI SAHADEVAN)

MALI

Area: 1,248,574 sq km (482,077 sq mi)
Population (2011 est.): 15,525,000
Capital: Bamako
Head of state: President Amadou Toumani Touré
Head of government: Prime Ministers Modibo Sidibé and, from April 3, Cissé Mariam Kaïdama Sidibé

In 2011 political change was in the air in Mali. Prime Minister Modibo Sidibé, along with his cabinet, resigned on March 30. It was presumed that he was preparing his candidacy for the April 2012 presidential elections. Under the terms of the constitution, Pres. Amadou Toumani Touré was not able to run for a third term. Cissé Mariam Kaïdama Sidibé was named prime minister on April 3; she was the first woman to serve in that office. The National Assembly on August 2 adopted a bill to revise the constitution to allow for the creation of a Senate and to strengthen the powers of the president. The changes were to be put to a referendum to seek public approval.

On January 5, 24-year old Tunisian citizen Bechir Sinoun, claiming to be a member of al-Qaeda in the Islamic Maghrib (AQIM), was captured after having launched a rocket attack on the French embassy in Bamako. Two people were injured. He escaped from prison on February 28 but was recaptured in Gao on March 3.

On May 20, following a conference of ministers from Algeria, Mali, Mauritania, and Niger, Algeria announced that it would hold an international meeting to discuss means of dealing with AQIM. It was estimated that over the previous two years, Islamic militancy had cost Mali's tourism sector at least 50 billion CFA francs (about $110 million), with a loss of 8,000 jobs. On June 25 a combined Malian-Mauritanian ground force, supported by fighter planes, attacked an AQIM camp in the western Wagadou forest. Casualties were reported to have been heavy.

(NANCY ELLEN LAWLER)

Malian Prime Minister Cissé Mariam Kaïdama Sidibé on September 23 addresses the United Nations General Assembly, calling on the international body to support continued democratic efforts in Mali.

Jason DeCrow/AP

MALTA

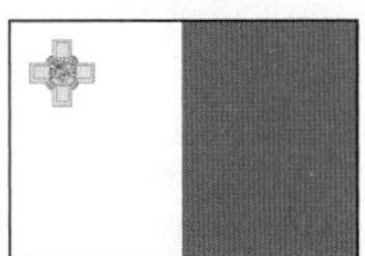

Area: 316 sq km (122 sq mi)
Population (2011 est.): 419,000
Capital: Valletta
Head of state: President George Abela
Head of government: Prime Minister Lawrence Gonzi

When the Libyan conflict escalated in 2011, Malta became a harbour of refuge and the base for a huge humanitarian mission. In a single week in February, nearly 12,000 people fled from Libya to Malta. Some Libyans wounded in fighting were treated in Malta, and water, food, and medical supplies were sent to Libya from Malta. The government did not provide a military base, but it allowed military planes to fly through Maltese airspace.

The influx of immigrants, which had declined considerably in 2010, once more became an insurmountable crisis. In April 820 sub-Saharan Africans landed in Malta in one 24-hour period. A conference was organized by the European Commission of the EU to tackle Malta's immigration crisis, but only 10 EU member states volunteered to take a total of 323 refugees from Malta.

A movement for the legalization of divorce won a referendum that was held in May. With a turnout of 72% of eligible voters, 53.2% were in favour and 46.8% against. While more than 230,000 persons voted, more than 92,000 persons abstained from voting or did not collect their vote. The Nationalist Party's official position was against divorce, but the Labour Party was in favour. On July 25 the parliament approved the divorce legislation, effective from October 2011. While 52 members voted in favour, 11 were against and 5 abstained.

A World Health Organization report on cancer rates in 50 countries ranked Malta with the eighth lowest rate. A United Nations study reported that Malta and Qatar were the two safest countries in the world.

(ALBERT GANADO)

Hundreds of sub-Saharan African migrants who fled Libya as military activity there intensified arrive at a harbour in Malta, March 28.

Lino Arrigo Azzopardi—EPA/Landov

MARSHALL ISLANDS

Area: 181 sq km (70 sq mi)
Population (2011 est.): 55,000
Capital: Majuro
Head of state and government: President Jurelang Zedkaia

The economic woes of the Marshall Islands continued throughout 2011. For the fourth consecutive year, the Social Security Administration had to sell investments to meet retirees' benefit payments. It was believed that if the trend continued, the fund could be exhausted by 2020. The country's national trust fund, a key component of the economy, lost 10% of its value in a single month (August) as international equity markets, in which the money was invested, fell steeply amid global concerns about sovereign debt. In an attempt to increase revenue, the government, which had been repeatedly criticized by auditing agencies for lack of accountability, considered partial privatization of the heavily indebted national airline, Air Marshall Islands.

The government realized financial benefits from its membership in the consortium of Pacific Islands countries known as the Parties to the Nauru Agreement. The group regulated access to members' tuna fisheries and allowed its members to sell or trade designated "fishing days" within their waters. In August the Marshall Islands received some $1 million from the sale of such rights to Papua New Guinea. The government managed to pass a 2012 budget in September, but only because 70% of the budget was funded by contributions from the U.S. and Taiwan. The U.S. demanded the inclusion of tuberculosis- and leprosy-control programs, which had not been part of the original budget. (CLUNY MACPHERSON)

MAURITANIA

Area: 1,030,700 sq km (398,000 sq mi)
Population (2011 est.): 3,282,000
Capital: Nouakchott
Head of state: President Mohamed Ould Abdel Aziz
Head of government: Prime Minister Moulaye Ould Mohamed Laghdaf

In Mauritania, militant attacks and popular protests dominated the news in 2011. On February 2 Mauritanian troops prevented an attack on the capital by firing on a car loaded with explosives 12 km (7 mi) south of Nouakchott. Three men believed to be members of al-Qaeda in the Islamic Maghrib (AQIM) were killed. Col. Mohamed Ould Ahmed confirmed that the vehicle was one of three that had come from Mali and was being tracked by intelligence services. One man was arrested in a second car; however, those in the third vehicle escaped. On March 15 Mohamed Abdallahi Ould Ahmednah, believed to belong to AQIM, was sentenced to death for the 2009 murder of Christopher Legget, an American. Two others received prison terms. Mauritania's army stated that on June 24 it had destroyed a new AQIM base camp in the Wagadou forest along the border with Mali. On July 5 AQIM responded by attacking a military outpost in Bassiknou, near Mali's western border. Troops fought off the attackers.

Protests against Pres. Mohamed Ould Abdel Aziz's government, which began in Nouakchott in February, escalated to a "day of rage" held on April 25. Using tear gas, police prevented demonstrators, who stretched for an estimated half a kilometre through the streets, from entering the main square. Opposition deputies were forcibly kept from joining the march.

Four antislavery activists were arrested on August 4 for "rebellion." Although the government had taken some steps to eliminate the practice of slavery, sentencing a woman on January 17 to six months in prison for keeping two young girls as virtual slaves, the problem continued in some parts of the country. (NANCY ELLEN LAWLER)

MAURITIUS

Area: 2,040 sq km (788 sq mi)
Population (2011 est.): 1,288,000
Capital: Port Louis
Head of state: President Sir Anerood Jugnauth
Head of government: Prime Minister Navin Ramgoolam

In 2011 widespread accusations of government corruption threatened to destabilize Mauritius's sound political and economic base. Health Minister Santi Bai Hanoomanjee was arrested for graft in July for her part in the inflation of the value of a government tender. The high-profile arrest was the first to be made after the seven-month investigation by the Independent Commission Against Corruption. Tensions over corruption and declining living standards, such as an 8% unemployment rate, led several thousand Mauritians to protest in Port Louis in September. After the implementation of two fiscal-stimulus packages in response to the global economic downturn, the Mauritian economy grew almost 4% in 2011 in spite of a slow rate of growth worldwide.

One of the Indian Ocean country's core industries, tourism, was tainted after the brutal murder of an Irish tourist in January. Michaela McAreavey was killed by two staff members of the hotel where she was vacationing. Mauritius's $10 billion economy depended heavily upon tourism, along with other key sectors such as sugar production, textiles, and financial services.

Mauritius also took part in the expanding antipiracy efforts launched by Indian Ocean countries. The country entered into an accord with the European Union to prosecute in Mauritian courts suspected pirates caught at sea by European military vessels.

(MARY EBELING)

MEXICO

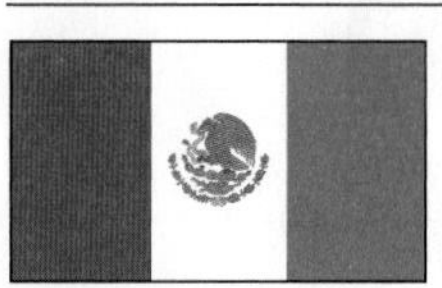

Area: 1,964,375 sq km (758,450 sq mi)
Population (2011 est.): 114,492,000
Capital: Mexico City
Head of state and government: President Felipe Calderón Hinojosa

The extreme violence produced by the country's long-running drug war remained the most prominent public issue in Mexico in 2011. The government reported 12,903 deaths from drug-related violence from January to September 2011, bringing to 47,515 the total number of deaths since the administration of Pres. Felipe Calderón began its assault on drug-trafficking cartels in December 2006. The government's antidrug effort received a blow in November when Secretary of the Interior Francisco Blake Mora, one of the fiercest opponents of the cartels, died in a helicopter crash. Although the government continued to score notable successes in the capture or killing of cartel leaders, the press reported drug-violence atrocities on a regular basis.

In public-opinion polls, a substantial majority of respondents expressed growing doubts about the efficacy of the government's use of military forces in the fight against the cartels and concerns about worsening public security. Indeed, a national survey conducted by the National Institute of Statistics, Geography, and Informatics found that 24% of the population aged 18 years and older (and 36% of all households) had been victims of robbery, extortion, fraud, or other crimes during 2010. Human Rights Watch, a New York City-based nongovernmental organization, and Mexico's National Human Rights Commission both criticized the Calderón administration for the mounting human rights violations that had resulted from military operations. Furthermore, Ministry of Finance and Public Credit officials acknowledged that violence had discouraged business investment in some parts of the country and reduced the country's annual growth rate by about 1%.

Deepening public concerns about drug-related violence and the government's response to the crisis led to the formation of an important civic protest movement named Caravan for Peace (Caravana por la Paz). It was founded by Javier Sicilia, a poet whose son had been murdered in March when he was caught up in a cartel vendetta in the city of Cuernavaca. The movement garnered widespread public support and backing from leading human rights groups as it organized marches throughout the country to protest the militarization of the drug war. Although he declined to alter the government's overall strategy, President Calderón did hold a televised meeting with Sicilia and publicly acknowledged the importance of his movement. Widespread endorsement of Sicilia's efforts won the activist a role in negotiations with government officials and political party representatives over how to safeguard citizen rights in a controversial draft national security law.

In a development that held important implications for the government's strategy in its struggle against the drug-trafficking cartels, in July the Supreme Court ruled that human rights violations committed against civilians by military forces must henceforth come under the jurisdiction of civilian (rather than military) tribunals. In addition, the court concluded that Mexico was legally bound by its obligations under international human rights treaties and therefore subject to the decisions of the Inter-American Court of Human Rights. Rights campaigners regarded the decision as a major victory in the struggle to prevent arbitrary actions by security forces and strengthen the rule of law.

The drug war also featured prominently in Mexican-U.S. relations. The United States continued to provide Mexico with substantial financial sup-

Bernandino Hernandez/AP

On August 16 two shooting victims lie dead near a beach in Acapulco, Mex. The once-peaceful resort city was ravaged by drug-related violence throughout the year.

port, intelligence assistance, equipment, and police training under the terms of the $1.5 billion multiyear Mérida Initiative. Despite domestic political sensitivities, the Mexican government permitted U.S. Drug Enforcement Agency officers, CIA operatives, and retired U.S. military personnel to operate (albeit without firearms) from a military base in northern Mexico. At the same time, President Calderón lobbied strenuously for the U.S. government to take tougher measures to block the smuggling of guns and ammunition into Mexico, disrupt drug cartels' money-laundering operations, and reduce U.S. consumption of illegal drugs. Among the measures taken by the U.S. government was a presidential decree requiring the thousands of gun stores located along the U.S.-Mexican border to report multiple sales of military-style assault rifles made within five days to the same person. Moreover, the U.S. government permitted Mexican police to launch cross-border drug raids from staging posts within the United States.

After years of political controversy and Mexico's decision in 2009 to impose retaliatory tariffs on imports of U.S. goods and agricultural products valued at up to $2.5 billion, the U.S. government finally agreed in July to permit Mexican long-distance truckers to operate freely in the United States. The agreement settled the longest-running dispute resulting from the 1994 North American Free Trade Agreement and removed a significant irritant from bilateral relations.

Partisan politics focused heavily on the 2012 presidential election. Opinion polls consistently showed Enrique Peña Nieto, a former governor of the state of México (2005–11) and the nominee of the Institutional Revolutionary Party (PRI), as the front-runner. In the incumbent National Action Party (PAN), the leading contenders were (in alphabetical order) Ernesto J. Cordero, secretary of social development (2008–09) and secretary of finance and public credit (2009–11) in the Calderón cabinet; Santiago Creel Miranda, a PAN senator, secretary of the interior (2000–05) during the PAN administration of Pres. Vicente Fox (2000–06), and a leading candidate for the PAN presidential nomination in 2006; and Josefina Vázquez Mota, secretary of social development under President Fox, secretary of public education under President Calderón (2006–09), and leader of the PAN's delegation in the federal Chamber of Deputies between 2009 and 2011. In November, Andrés Manuel López Obrador, the 2006 presidential nominee of the centre-left Party of the Democratic Revolution (PRD), triumphed over Marcelo Ebrard Casaubon, governor of the Federal District (2006–12), in an opinion poll that the two agreed would determine the PRD's 2012 candidate.

The economy, which in early 2010 had begun to recover from the sharp recession caused by the 2008–09 international financial crisis, slowed in late 2010 and early 2011. GDP expanded by 4% during the year, but forecasters predicted a lower growth rate in 2012. Inflation averaged 3.4% in 2011. International reserves reached a record $136 billion in September 2011.

(KEVIN J. MIDDLEBROOK)

MICRONESIA, FEDERATED STATES OF

Area: 701 sq km (271 sq mi)
Population (2011 est.): 102,000
Capital: Palikir, on Pohnpei
Head of state and government: President Emanuel (Manny) Mori

In a move to increase government revenue in 2011, the government of the Federated States of Micronesia (FSM) sold short-term fishing rights in its waters to Papua New Guinea for $1 million. The agreement was enabled by the FSM's membership in the Parties to the Nauru Agreement (PNA), a consortium of countries whose goals included the extraction of more revenue from member states' tuna fisheries by strictly limiting the access given to deepwater fishing countries. The FSM hoped to gain additional benefits from its membership in the PNA through the group's pursuit of a prized "ecolabel" from the Marine Stewardship Council that would certify that its tuna had come from a sustainably managed fishery. The label would bring a premium price and allow the FSM into markets that favoured sustainably managed food.

In September a crisis loomed as the U.S. sought to restrict the privilege of visa-free access to the U.S. that had been given to citizens of the FSM as a provision of the Compact of Free Association, which governed the relationship between the U.S. and the FSM. The U.S. Senate Appropriations Committee directed the Department of Homeland Security to review the policy. The move was seen by the FSM as a violation of the spirit of the compact.

(CLUNY MACPHERSON)

MOLDOVA

Area: 33,843 sq km (13,067 sq mi), including the 4,163-sq-km (1,607-sq-mi) area of the disputed territory of Transdniestria (Transnistria; Pridnestrovie)
Population (2011 est.): 3,927,000 (excluding Moldovans working abroad but including the more than 515,000 persons in Transdniestria)
Capital: Chisinau
Head of state: President Marian Lupu (acting).
Head of government: Prime Minister Vlad Filat

Having survived a recount of the disputed November 2010 parliamentary elections in which it had retained power, Moldova's ruling three-party coalition, the Alliance for European Integration (AEI), formed a new government on Jan. 14, 2011. Vlad Filat, whose Liberal Democrat Party had made the biggest gains in the election, remained as prime minister. Nevertheless, the AEI lacked the necessary votes in Parliament to fill the position of president (vacant since 2009). Moreover, despite AEI gains in many local elections in June, the fragility of its grip on power was evidenced when it barely held on to the mayoralty of Chisinau in the face of a strong Communist challenge.

European Union efforts in 2011 to reinforce Moldova's Western orientation and to limit the gravitational pull of Russia included €78.6 million (about $104 million) from the EU's bilateral assistance program and a relaxation of visa requirements. There were also a number of visits to Moldova in 2011 by top-level Western diplomats, including U.S. Vice Pres. Joseph Biden and the president of the European Council, Herman Van Rompuy. Meanwhile, relations between the Moldovan Communists and the Russian government remained strained, reducing the likelihood of Moscow's actively contesting EU influence in Moldova. Although the surprising meeting between Igor Smirnov, the leader of the breakaway region of Transdniestria, and Filat at an Organization for Security and Co-operation in Europe conference in Germany in September signaled another success for the EU's Eastern Partnership program, there was little other evidence that relations between Moldova and Russian-backed Transdniestria were likely to fundamentally improve. In economic news, GDP increased by 7.5% in the first half of 2011 over the comparable period of 2010.

(TOM GALLAGHER)

MONACO

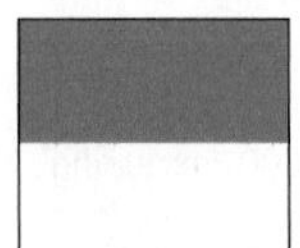

Area: 2.02 sq km (0.78 sq mi)
Population (2011 est.): 36,000
Head of state: Prince Albert II
Head of government: Minister of State Michel Roger

In July 2011 Prince Albert II of Monaco married South African swimmer Charlene Wittstock in a lavish wedding. A civil service took place in the throne room of the palace on Friday, July 1, followed on Saturday by an extravagant religious ceremony, attended by international celebrities and royalty. Both days were declared public holidays.

Afterward, the couple flew to Durban, S.Af., where Albert attended a weeklong business meeting, and Princess Charlene stayed 16 km (10 mi) away, at the seaside town of Umhlanga Rocks, where she organized a luxurious reception for South African friends. Another "secret" honeymoon was promised. In August the newlyweds were in Monaco to preside over the 63rd Red Cross Ball. Speculation about the marriage was raised, however, when in September Albert attended two functions without his wife; he escorted his sister Princess Caroline to a sailing launch and attended a charity auction with American singer Beth Hart. Previously, rumours had spread that the bride was considering returning to South Africa after having discovered that Albert might have fathered a third out-of-wedlock child.

The Prince Albert of Monaco Foundation continued to work on environmental issues. A major concern was that of increasing seawater temperatures, thought to alter the resilience of corals and mollusks, affected by ocean acidification in the Mediterranean Sea.

(ANNE ROBY)

MONGOLIA

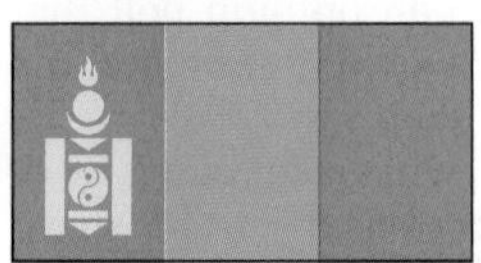

Area: 1,564,116 sq km (603,909 sq mi)
Population (2011 est.): 2,765,000
Capital: Ulaanbaatar (Ulan Bator)
Head of state: President Tsakhiagiin Elbegdorj
Head of government: Prime Minister Sükhbaataryn Batbold

In 2011 those in Mongolia who opposed the decision in 2010 of the majority Mongolian People's Revolutionary Party (MPRP) to revert to its earlier name, the Mongolian People's Party (MPP), moved to reestablish the MPRP. Under the leadership of former MPRP chairman Nambaryn Enkhbayar, the new MPRP was registered in June, but he split from that in September to form the All Mongol Labour Party. Having agreed to amalgamate in January, the Green and Civil Courage parties, led by Dangaasürengiin Enkhbat and Sanjaasürengiin Oyuun, respectively, faced difficulties with registration and challenges from the Greens Alliance.

The Democratic Party (DP) leader, Chief Deputy Prime Minister Norovyn Altankhuyag, said in September that he would continue the government coalition with the MPP. With Great Khural elections due in May 2012, however, the partners disagreed about the voting system that was to be specified in a new election law: simple majority (MPP) or proportional representation (DP). A law intended to make government functioning more transparent and give citizens access to information was passed in August.

Andy Wong/AP

Mongolian Prime Minister Sükhbaataryn Batbold (left) and U.S. Vice Pres. Joe Biden pose with camels while attending a cultural festival in Ulaanbaatar, Mong., August 22.

After his state visit to Japan in November 2010, Pres. Tsakhiagiin Elbegdorj attended a NATO summit in Lisbon. In 2011 President Elbegdorj led visits to Moscow (May), the United States (June), and the United Kingdom (October). On August 22, U.S. Vice Pres. Joe Biden made a six-hour stopover in Ulaanbaatar. Prime Minister Sükhbaataryn Batbold paid official visits to Moscow (December 2010) and to China, including Hong Kong (June 2011).

The mining industry was booming, thanks to high market prices for copper and gold and to China's great demand for coal. Foreign exchange reserves exceeded $2 billion in 2010, when China accounted for 56% of the value of Mongolia's total trade and Russia for another 21%. Mongolian GDP growth was expected to reach 9% in 2011 and 12% in 2012.

In 2011 Mongolia celebrated the centenary of its declaration of independence and the 2,220th anniversary of the Xiongnu empire, described by President Elbegdorj as the "first state" of the Mongols.

(ALAN J.K. SANDERS)

MONTENEGRO

Area: 13,812 sq km (5,333 sq mi)
Population (2011 est.): 620,000
Capital: Podgorica (Cetinje is the old royal capital)
Head of state: President Filip Vujanovic
Head of government: Prime Minister Igor Luksic

Montenegro moved a step closer to membership in the European Union in 2011. In October the European Commission recommended that the EU set a date for formal accession talks. The Commission's positive assessment recognized Montenegro for having improved its legislative and institutional framework, its electoral system, and its public administration and judiciary.

The country experienced a modest economic recovery and made further progress toward achieving a functioning market economy. Manufacturing output, overall industrial production, and the value of construction projects increased. The number of tourists for the first nine months of the year rose 8.4% over the same period in 2010. In October the government announced that it would privatize the country's postal and telephone system in 2012.

Inflation averaged about 3%, and unemployment remained high at 19%. Almost 7% of the population lived below the poverty line (set at €170 [about $230] per month), with most of the poor concentrated in the rural northern municipalities. Average gross earnings per capita in November were €721, which amounted to an annual income of some €8,500 (about $11,400). The average cost of food and rent per capita that month was about €430.

In November Montenegro signed free-trade agreements with members of the European Free Trade Association (EFTA) and Ukraine that allowed Montenegro to resume its accession negotiations with the World Trade Organization. Montenegrin officials signed separate agreements with Russia and Serbia that called for increased cooperation in tourism, commerce, and energy.

The World Bank's *Doing Business* report, which measured business regulations, ranked Montenegro 56th on the list of 183 economies. The United Nations Development Programme's *Sustainability and Equity: A Better Future for All* annual report, which assessed countries' efforts to create and enable the well-being of their citizens, ranked Montenegro 54th of 187 countries.

(MILAN ANDREJEVICH)

MOROCCO

Area: 694,420 sq km (268,117 sq mi), including the 252,120-sq-km (97,344-sq-mi) area of the disputed Western Sahara annexation
Population (2011 est.): 32,476,000, of which Western Sahara 507,000
Capital: Rabat
Head of state: King Muhammad VI
Head of government: Prime Ministers ʿAbbas al-Fassi and, from November 29, Abdelilah Benkirane

Protests in Morocco were less intense than those elsewhere in North Africa and the Middle East in 2011 and reflected different grievances. On February 20, thousands of Moroccans participated in demonstrations organized by a coalition of youth activist groups and formal political parties to demand constitutional reform. Although the protests were generally peaceful, violence occurred in some areas; five bank employees were burned to death in Al-Hoceima when their place of work was set alight.. Demonstrations continued throughout the year, keeping up pressure for reform. At the end of May, the police, who had not previously interfered, began intervening to disperse protesters.

In a televised speech on March 9, King Muhammad VI promised comprehensive constitutional reform and appointed a commission to draft the legislation. Despite the government's invitation to political parties to submit proposals for reform, most opposition leaders boycotted the commission. Nonetheless, the king announced a series of proposals in mid-June, to be approved by referendum on July 1. The proposed reforms included greater executive authority for the parliament and the cabinet, particularly for the prime minister. The king, however, would remain the highest authority in matters of national security, foreign policy, and religious affairs. Objecting to the affirmation of supreme royal authority, the protest movement called for a boycott of the referendum. The constitutional reforms, however, were approved by a suspiciously large 98.5% of voters, with a 73.5% turnout. The king subsequently called for rapid implementation of the reforms. Parliamentary elections, due in September 2012, were brought forward to Nov. 25, 2011. The Justice and Development Party, a moderate Islamist party, won the most votes, and the party's leader, Abdelilah Benkirane, was appointed prime minister.

Protests also erupted in the Moroccan-controlled Western Sahara in February after a riot by Moroccan residents of Dakhla led to attacks on the indigenous Sahrawi population. Peaceful demonstrations and sit-ins continued until mid-May.

An eighth round of UN-sponsored talks between Morocco and the Polisario Front ended in an impasse in July. Morocco continued to insist on its plan to grant the territory greater autonomy, while the Polisario Front, with Algerian support, continued to seek a referendum on self-determination. Moroccan relations with Algeria remained tense over the issue, and Morocco's attempts to persuade Algeria to open the border between the two countries were rejected.

(GEORGE JOFFÉ)

MOZAMBIQUE

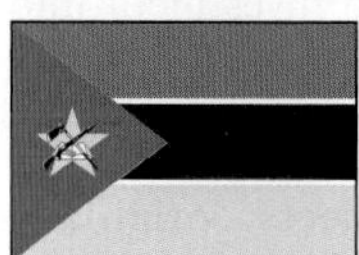

Area: 799,380 sq km (308,642 sq mi)
Population (2011 est.): 22,949,000
Capital: Maputo
Head of state and government: President Armando Guebuza, assisted by Prime Minister Aires Ali

The Mozambican government declared 2011 as "Samora Machel Year," marking the 25th anniversary of the death on Oct. 19, 1986, of Machel and a 33-member delegation in a plane crash near Mbuzini, just inside South Africa. At the time, the South African apartheid government had conducted a unilateral inquiry that attributed the crash to pilot error, although the Mozambican government always suspected that an assassination had taken place. At a ceremony to unveil a statue of Machel in Independence Square in

Maputo, Graca Machel, his widow and the wife of Nelson Mandela, demanded that the investigation into the crash be reopened.

The ruling Mozambique Liberation Front (Frelimo) remained generally popular and inclusive, while the opposition Mozambique National Resistance (Renamo) and Mozambique Democratic Movement (MDM) failed to mount any serious political challenges. The ruling party, however, was embarrassed by the WikiLeaks publication of U.S. diplomatic communications implicating high-level Mozambican officials in money laundering and drug trafficking. Meanwhile, the parliament established a committee to "modernize" the constitution, which prompted speculation by the opposition that the ruling party intended to allow the incumbent to stand for another presidential term, although no such proposal had been put forward.

Late in January unusually heavy rains in the south caused widespread flooding along the banks of the Zambezi, Limpopo, Púnguè, and Save rivers. About 100,000 people were evacuated. The damage to cropland and pasture did not significantly affect agricultural production, as the main producing areas of the country were in the north.

The government made considerable progress in its economic and social plan for the year. Real GDP growth stood at 7.4%, backed by increasing foreign aid and foreign investment into minerals and infrastructure megaprojects. The government announced the possibility of introducing legislation to renegotiate megaprojects, originally signed in the late 1990s, to increase revenue. These included the Mozal aluminum smelter operated by Australian-based BHP Billiton, the gas export pipeline run by Sasol (a South African company), and the Moma titanium mine in Nampula province, operated by Kenmare Resources of Ireland. In May Brazilian mining conglomerate Vale began coal production in Moatize in the Tete province, which transformed life in a previously neglected area. Trade with Brazil rose from $25 million in 2010 to $60 million early in the year and was expected to expand once coal exports began. In the last quarter of the year, massive gas fields were discovered off the northern coast of Mozambique. Although the fields would not be productive for several years, the news nonetheless buoyed hopes of a future economic windfall for the country. (LARAY DENZER)

MYANMAR (BURMA)

Area: 676,577 sq km (261,228 sq mi)
Population (2011 est.): 54,000,000
Capital: Nay Pyi Taw (Naypyidaw)
Head of state and government: Chairman of the State Peace and Development Council Gen. Than Shwe, assisted by Prime Minister Thein Sein (from March 30, President)

In 2011 Myanmar experienced significant change and promises of reform. The new government was formed on March 30, with Pres. Thein Sein announcing a broad agenda that included economic and social reform, a push against corruption, and promises to respect basic freedoms. The national parliament and 14 regional and state assemblies convened, with members fairly free to raise issues formerly deemed too sensitive for public debate. Press restrictions were relaxed, and relatively open debate within Myanmar was permitted. Opposition leader Aung San Suu Kyi had talks with government interlocutors and was permitted to travel around the country. Her party was allowed to open offices, conduct public events without official harassment, and, in December, register for the upcoming elections.

High-level visitors to Myanmar in 2011 included Vijay Nambiar, the special representative of the UN secretary-general; Australian Foreign Minister Kevin Rudd; and, late in the year, U.S. Secretary of State Hillary Clinton. In August, Tomás Ojea Quintana, the UN special envoy for human rights in Myanmar, visited the country, met with senior government officials, and saw political detainees at Insein Prison near Yangon (Rangoon). Myanmar applied to become chair of ASEAN for 2014.

Ethnic conflict resumed in several parts of Myanmar during 2011 as long-standing cease-fires with ethnic Kachin and Shan insurgents broke down. More than 50,000 civilians were displaced in those areas, while ethnic conflict between Karen rebels and the Myanmar military in eastern regions displaced an estimated 500,000 civilians. The government proposed peace talks with various ethnic militias.

In September the president announced the suspension of the controversial Myitsone hydroelectric-dam project in Kachin state, responding to mounting local discord and to rare open disagreements between government ministers over the dam's potentially damaging environmental and human rights effects. Construction of

Released inmates exit Insein Prison in Yangon, Myanmar, May 17. During the year the newly installed government of Myanmar freed thousands of prisoners and commuted the sentences of many others.

Soe Zeya Tun—Reuters/Landov

crude oil and natural gas pipelines from Myanmar into southern China continued, as did major hydro-dam projects on the Salween River.

The UN estimated real GDP growth in Myanmar at 5.8% in 2011. Foreign investment, mostly in the energy sector, exceeded $16 billion. The kyat appreciated dramatically in 2011—from some 1,000 kyat to the U.S. dollar to around 800—causing difficulties for exporters. Economists in Myanmar advised the government to align the exchange rates as a first step in promised economic reforms intended to rejuvenate the crucial agricultural sector. Commodity prices and inflation rose in 2011, causing increased hardships for rural and poor populations even as urban elites experienced a boom.

(DAVID SCOTT MATHIESON)

NAMIBIA

Area: 824,116 sq km (318,193 sq mi)
Population (2011 est.): 2,324,000
Capital: Windhoek
Head of state and government: President Hifikepunye Pohamba, assisted by Prime Minister Nahas Angula

Severe floods in northern Namibia in early 2011 caused many deaths and great disruption. In late March, Pres. Hifikepunye Pohamba announced that $4.4 million had been allocated for relief. With the use of nuclear power on the wane worldwide, the price of uranium dropped, but Namibia continued to benefit from the relatively high price of minerals. In the spring the minister of mines and energy announced new taxes on mines, but a few months later the cabinet backpedaled in the face of criticism from potential investors. The most important news of the year was the announcement in early July that Namibia might have more than 10 billion tons of oil offshore, which would make it one of the largest oil producers on the continent. Drilling had yet to confirm that the oil was present, but the announcement caused a flurry of excitement.

There was much speculation about who would succeed Pohamba as the SWAPO candidate for the national presidency. If former prime minister Hage Geingob retained his position as vice president of SWAPO at the 2012 party congress, party rules dictated that he would become the party's candidate to succeed Pohamba. He was likely to be challenged, however, by others, including Pendukeni Iivula-Ithana, the secretary-general of SWAPO. If Iivula-Ithana emerged as the SWAPO presidential candidate and then was elected to the national presidency, she would become Namibia's first female president. Though there continued to be much criticism of the secrecy with which the SWAPO-led government conducted its affairs, the government did withdraw its 10-year boycott of the country's leading newspaper, *The Namibian*.

(CHRISTOPHER SAUNDERS)

NAURU

Area: 21.2 sq km (8.2 sq mi)
Population (2011 est.): 9,300
Capital: Government offices in Yaren district
Head of state and government: Presidents Marcus Stephen, Frederick Pitcher from November 10, and, from November 15, Sprent Dabwido

As supplies of phosphate, its primary resource, neared exhaustion, Nauru continued in 2011 to seek new sources of income and ways to conserve its other resources. In August, Israeli Pres. Shimon Peres announced that his country would provide technological assistance to help Nauru improve its freshwater supply, which had been contaminated by decades of phosphate mining. Nauru was also one of the beneficiaries of a Secretariat of the Pacific Community project to restore the native forests of the Pacific Islands, which included teak, eucalyptus, and mahogany trees.

By far the most prominent of Nauru's conservation efforts, however, was its participation in the expansion of the Nauru Agreement, which sought to protect tuna stocks in a region of the Pacific Ocean some 4.5 million sq km (1.7 million sq mi) in area. In January the eight partners to the agreement began enforcing quotas on the number of days a particular country's vessels could fish the protected waters and requiring payment for additional days.

Plans to reopen a processing centre on the island for people seeking asylum in Australia suffered a blow in August when that country's High Court ruled illegal the Australian government's proposed deal with Malaysia to exchange refugees processed offshore. The ruling, construed broadly, implied that any offshore processing of refugees could also be considered unlawful.

(JANET MOREDOCK)

NEPAL

Area: 147,181 sq km (56,827 sq mi)
Population (2011 est.): 26,629,000
Capital: Kathmandu
Head of state: President Ram Baran Yadav
Head of government: Prime Ministers Madhav Kumar Nepal, Jhalanath Khanal from February 6, and, from August 29, Baburam Bhattarai

In 2011 the peace process in Nepal came closer to completion following an agreement on November 1 between the four major political parties: the Nepali Congress; Communist Party of Nepal (Unified Marxist-Leninist), or CPN (UML); Unified Communist Party of Nepal (Maoist), or UCPN-M; and Madheshi People's Rights Forum (Democratic). According to the agreement, some 6,500 former rebel combatants were to be integrated into the Nepali military, and other fighters who chose not to remain with the armed forces were to be provided with financial incentives. Despite that major breakthrough, the country experienced political turbulence during the year. Madhav Kumar Nepal, leader of CPN (UML), resigned as prime minister in June 2010 but stayed in office until fellow party member Jhalanath Khanal succeeded him in February. Khanal's government collapsed in August, and UCPN-M leader Baburam Bhattarai (*see* BIOGRAPHIES) became prime minister.

In October the government released the third Nepal Living Standards Survey, conducted with support from the World Bank. It revealed that Nepal had recorded a 5.7% decline in absolute poverty between 2003–04 and 2009–10.

As concern grew in neighbouring India and China over Nepal's protracted political crisis, Prime Minister Bhattarai visited India in October and signed the Bilateral Investment Promotion and

Binod Joshi/AP

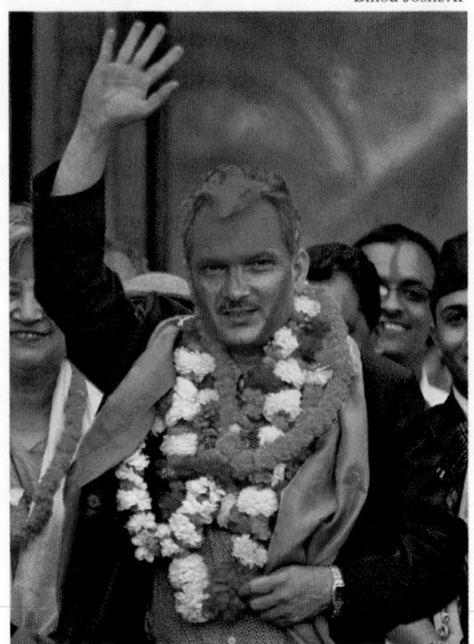

With vermilion powder smeared on his face in a traditional symbol of victory, Nepalese politician Baburam Bhattarai waves as he emerges from the parliament building in Kathmandu upon his election as prime minister, August 28.

Protection Agreement. In March China's top army general, Chen Bingde, had visited Nepal, where he pledged $20 million in aid to the Nepali army.

Krishna Prasad Bhattarai (*see* OBITUARIES), Nepal's first prime minister after the restoration of multiparty democracy in 1990, died in March. The former prime minister had spent 14 years in prison in the 1960s and '70s for demanding political reforms.

(KESHAB POUDEL)

NETHERLANDS

Area: 41,543 sq km (16,040 sq mi)
Population (2011 est.): 16,683,000
Capital: Amsterdam; seat of government, The Hague
Head of state: Queen Beatrix
Head of government: Prime Minister Mark Rutte

In 2011 the Netherlands avoided massive unemployment and drastic increases in bankruptcies, despite the worldwide economic crisis. The government kept a watchful eye on the European debt crisis and on international developments, recognizing that the Dutch dependence on international trade made the country vulnerable to fluctuations in the world economy. The Netherlands, which ranked 60th in the world by population, had the 16th largest economy and the 8th biggest financial sector and was ranked 5th among investor countries worldwide. Prime Minister Mark Rutte's right-centre government announced substantial budget cuts. Proposals for reductions in educational subsidies were met with public protest by students and university professors. Before year's end there were plans for additional cuts, including steep progressive cost increases to individuals for health care benefits. The government also announced rollbacks for some government regulations, such as environmental protections, stating that these changes would permit innovation and economic growth. In addition, it acknowledged that the retirement age would need to be raised in the future.

The government, which was formed after the 2010 general election, consisted of a minority coalition of Rutte's right-of-centre People's Party for Freedom and Democracy (VVD) and the centre-right Christian Democrats that was made possible only by the consent—and a promise of supporting votes in the parliament—of the anti-immigrant Party for Freedom (PVV). In 2011, however, the government showed signs of strain. Geert Wilders, the leader of the PVV and a member of the parliament, continued to exercise more political independence than would thus far be expected of a politician in his position and thus required Prime Minister Rutte to show an unprecedented level of restraint and tact.

Wilders's trial before the District Court of Amsterdam, which had been interrupted in late 2010, resumed in April. Wilders faced charges, brought in 2009, that he had engaged in "group defamation" by insulting a group of people (Muslims) on the basis of their religion and that he had incited hatred and discrimination of people (Muslims) because of their religion and their race. The court had investigated first whether Wilders should be held responsible for those statements that had been attributed to him, and if so, whether they were indeed illegal. In the end, the court acquitted him in June on all charges. In part, it found that his negative utterances concerned Islam generally and not specific people and that under the law his statements were considered within the bounds of political debate and did not incite hatred or discrimination.

In the Netherlands the sale of so-called soft drugs (cannabis products) remained legal, with limited quantities available for purchase in carefully monitored retail venues known as "coffee shops." In an effort to mitigate traffic problems and challenges to public order, however, and in a move that might prove to be a test case for a national policy, the border city of Maastricht banned the sale of soft drugs to residents of countries other than the Netherlands, Belgium, or Germany and thus significantly curtailed drug tourism.

(JOLANDA VANDERWAL TAYLOR)

NEW ZEALAND

Area: 270,692 sq km (104,515 sq mi)
Population (2011 est.): 4,407,000
Capital: Wellington
Head of state: Queen Elizabeth II, represented by Governors-General Sir Anand Satyanand, Dame Sian Elias (acting) from August 23, and, from August 31, Sir Jerry Mateparae
Head of government: Prime Minister John Key

Earthquakes, the economy, elections, and the environment dominated the events of New Zealand in 2011. Following Christchurch's 7.1-magnitude earthquake on Sept. 4, 2010, the city sustained months of aftershocks; the strongest of them (magnitude 6.3) struck on February 22, causing more than 180 fatalities, ravaging the central business district, and rendering thousands of residences uninhabitable. Prime Minister John Key declared a state of national emergency in the quake area. Thousands of additional aftershocks, some exceeding magnitude 5.5, were recorded through the end of the year. The Reserve Bank of New Zealand estimated the cost to rebuild the city at NZ$20 billion (NZ$1 = U.S.$0.85), equal to 10% of GDP.

Finance Minister Bill English designated NZ$8.8 billion for earthquake recovery in his May budget, projecting a government operating deficit of NZ$16.7 billion for the 2011–12 fiscal year. He also announced several policies to stimulate exports, savings, and investment.

During the year Key and Australia's Julia Gillard became their countries' first prime ministers to address each other's parliament. In June, Key discussed trade and foreign affairs with Indian Prime Minister Manmohan Singh in New Delhi and did the same with U.S. Pres. Barack Obama at the White House in July.

Two New Zealand soldiers were killed in Afghanistan, where about 200 troops were deployed in a mentoring role. Another 80 troops were serving in the International Stabilisation Force in East Timor. That force was scheduled to be withdrawn in 2012.

The ruling National Party retained office in the November 26 elections, winning 59 seats in the 121-member parliament and maintaining its partnership with the smaller parties in the governing coalition. In a companion referendum, voters retained the mixed-member proportional voting system.

The Greek-owned container vessel *Rena* grounded on a reef near Tauranga on October 5 with 1,700 tons of heavy fuel oil on board. It was expected that the cleanup of some 350 tons of spilled oil and the salvage of 2,100 containers and the remainder of the oil would continue into 2012.

In other news, New Zealand's longest-serving female MP (1967–96), Whetu Tirikatene-Sullivan, died in July at age 79. The country's first Maori governor-general (1985–90), Sir Paul Reeves, died in August at age 78. In October, New Zealand defeated France 8–7 in the final of the quadrennial Rugby Union World Cup. (NEALE MCMILLAN)

NICARAGUA

Area: 130,373 sq km (50,337 sq mi)
Population (2011 est.): 5,870,000
Capital: Managua
Head of state and government: President Daniel Ortega Saavedra

Daniel Ortega handily defeated his rivals to win reelection as the president of Nicaragua in 2011. Ortega tallied about 62% of the vote, while Fabio Gadea of the Independent Liberal Party (PLI) received 31%. Despite preelection polls that had shown Ortega with a commanding lead that seemed to guarantee his reelection, his opponents claimed that there was widespread election fraud. Still, Ortega seemed to have benefited from the popularity of strong antipoverty measures enacted under his leadership and the pro-business climate he helped foster. His party, the Sandinista National Liberation Front (FSLN), also thrived in the election, achieving a supermajority of 63 seats in the National Assembly, three votes more than the 60 required to ratify constitutional changes. Ever since Ortega's election to the presidency in 2006, relations with the United States had remained tense, but in 2011 the two countries continued to work together against organized crime and narcotics trafficking.

Despite political uncertainties, Nicaragua's economic stability, its deficit reduction, and its implementation of other structural reforms continued to win support from the IMF. Moreover, the Inter-American Development Bank authorized approximately $220 million in loans to Nicaragua for infrastructure development and poverty reduction. Aid of approximately $500 million from Venezuela, under the auspices of Pres. Hugo Chávez's Bolivarian Alliance for the Peoples of Our America, helped the Ortega government make significant investments in food security, housing, education, and health care. In addition, Nicaragua reached the first of eight UN Millennium Development Goals when, well ahead of the 2015 target date, it cut in half the percentage of its population suffering from hunger. Despite strong public support for the government's social programs, debate continued over whether any real structural reform had been achieved.

Nicaragua remained the largest beneficiary of the Central America–Dominican Republic Free Trade Agreement (CAFTA-DR) with the United States. Notwithstanding the ongoing global economic downturn, GDP in Nicaragua was projected to grow by 4%, with inflation expected to average at least 8%. Overall, Nicaragua experienced strong investment in the energy, manufacturing, mining, and tourism sectors. High unemployment (over 7%) and persistent poverty, however, continued to promote emigration and dampen consumer demand.

The UN, the U.S., and European countries provided aid for more than 130,000 Nicaraguan victims of torrential hurricane-season rains. Work continued on a Venezuelan-built oil refinery in Miramar, while plans for a deepwater port at Monkey Point stirred resistance from indigenous people and Creoles in the South Atlantic Autonomous Region. Tensions also remained high in the North Atlantic Autonomous Region over the control of indigenous lands. (JUSTIN WOLFE)

On February 24, two days after a deadly earthquake struck New Zealand, a rescue worker examines a pile of rubble near the damaged Cathedral of the Blessed Sacrament in Christchurch.

Simon Baker—Reuters/Landov

NIGER

Area: 1,267,000 sq km (489,191 sq mi)
Population (2011 est.): 16,469,000
Capital: Niamey
Head of state and government: Presidents Maj. Salou Djibo, assisted by Prime Minister Mahamadou Danda, and, from April 7, Mahamadou Issoufou, assisted by Prime Minister Brigi Rafini

On Jan. 31, 2011, Niger held the first round of presidential elections since the overthrow in 2010 of Mamadou Tandja. Longtime opposition leader Mahamadou Issoufou (*see* BIOGRAPHIES) and former prime minister Seïni Oumarou took 36% and 23% of the vote, respectively. In the March 12 runoff, Issoufou was victorious, garnering 58% of the vote. International observers praised the transparency and conduct of the poll. The peaceful transition to democracy was completed on April 7, when Issoufou took the oath of office. In June most international donors who had frozen development funds following the coup announced the resumption of aid programs for Niger.

Tens of thousands of Nigeriens who had been working in Libya fled after a revolt against Libyan leader Muammar al-Qaddafi began in February. Nearly 65,000 were residing in refugee camps in Niger around the city of Agadez. By August thousands of Qaddafi's African mercenaries were flooding out of Libya into Niger. Libyan army convoys began entering Niger in early September. They included Gen. Ali Kana, commander of Qaddafi's southern forces, and Saadi Qaddafi, Qaddafi's third son. President Issoufou stated that neither would be extradited to Libya.

Two French citizens, kidnapped by al-Qaeda in the Islamic Maghrib (AQIM) on January 7 in Niamey, were found dead after a failed rescue attempt. Three other hostages taken in Niger were released on February 24, but four remaining French captives appeared in a video on April 26, calling for the withdrawal of French troops from Afghanistan. On September 15, Defense Minister Mahamadou Karidio announced that an army unit in the Agadez region had attacked and destroyed a convoy of AQIM militants, killing 3 and releasing 50 men who claimed to have been forcibly recruited.

(NANCY ELLEN LAWLER)

NIGERIA

Area: 923,768 sq km (356,669 sq mi)
Population (2011 est.): 162,471,000
Capital: Abuja
Head of state and government: President Goodluck Jonathan

Nigerian Pres. Goodluck Jonathan and his party, the People's Democratic Party (PDP), were returned to power in the April 16, 2011, elections with a solid majority. Jonathan won 58.9% of the vote, almost twice the amount of his nearest opponent, former military ruler Muhammad Buhari, a northern Muslim and the flag bearer of the Congress for Progressive Change (CPC), who polled 32% of the vote. Although local and international observers praised the conduct of the election as the most credible since the end of military rule in 1999, Buhari challenged the results in court, but his petition was thrown out on November 1. The PDP retained control of the bicameral legislature and held 23 of the 36 state governorships. While the PDP lost some federal legislators and state governors, it remained the only one of the 63 registered parties with a national power base. Despite Buhari's large presidential vote, his party won only one state governorship and just a few legislative seats. The Action Congress of Nigeria (ACN) emerged as the strongest opposition group, particularly in the southwest, where it took back five governorships from the PDP.

The election campaign was generally peaceful, but Buhari's rejection of the results sparked three days of violence in CPC strongholds in 12 northern states. About 800 people were killed, most of whom were Muslim. More than 65,000 people were forced to flee; 350 churches were destroyed; and many vehicles were burned. In some predominantly Christian communities in Kaduna state, Christians retaliated in kind. Buhari distanced himself from the rioting. While religious conflict appeared to be the overt cause of violence, analysts cautioned that the more-important reasons for the vio-

In Zonkwa, Nigeria, a man inspects the debris of a market destroyed by rioting, April 21. Violence broke out across the predominantly Muslim northern states of Nigeria following the election of Goodluck Jonathan, a Christian from the south, as president.

Sunday Alamba/AP

lence were stemming from poverty and economic marginalization.

Meanwhile, on April 29 the president announced his intention to form a government of national unity along the lines of his predecessors, Olusegun Obasanjo and Umaru Yar'Adua, who both had included rival political leaders in their cabinets to placate opposition parties after controversial elections. At the close of President Jonathan's first 100 days, many reserved judgment concerning his approach to socioeconomic development, reform, and conflict management. Throughout the year many serious outbreaks of violence occurred in the oil-producing Niger Delta, the Plateau state, where the predominantly Muslim north met the predominantly Christian south, and Borno state. Much of it was exacerbated by electoral politics and existing intercommunal tensions; however, the terrorist activities of the fundamentalist Islamist sect Boko Haram (meaning "Western education is a sin") escalated.

Boko Haram, originally centred in northeastern Borno state, was believed to have links to al-Qaeda in the Islamic Maghrib in Algeria and Niger and al-Shabaab in Somalia. By the end of the year, it had staged increasingly sophisticated attacks, including the use of suicide bombers, on government, police, and military targets in northern Nigeria. Boko Haram militants bombed the UN headquarters in Abuja on August 26 and unleashed coordinated attacks in Borno and Yobe states on November 4 that left an estimated 100 dead. High-profile arrests were made, including that of Sen. Ali Ndume of Borno state, and a former Boko Haram spokesperson, Ali Sanda Umar Konduga, received a three-year prison sentence. In mid-December the police captured a number of militants and seized a significant amount of arms and bomb-making materials in the cities of Maiduguri and Kano. Militants retaliated with a series of bombings and armed attacks across the northeast and in Abuja on Christmas Day, leaving more than 40 dead and 90,000 displaced in Damaturu (Yobe state). On December 31 President Jonathan declared a state of emergency in Yobe, Borno, Plateau, and Niger states and temporarily closed segments of the country's international borders with Chad, Niger, and Cameroon.

In November, Odumegwu Ojukwu, leader of the defunct Republic of Biafra, died in London of a stroke. (*See* OBITUARIES.) (LARAY DENZER)

NORWAY

Area: 385,179 sq km (148,718 sq mi), including the overseas Arctic territories of Svalbard (61,020 sq km [23,560 sq mi]) and Jan Mayen (377 sq km [146 sq mi])
Population (2011 est.): 4,953,000
Capital: Oslo
Head of state: King Harald V
Head of government: Prime Minister Jens Stoltenberg

Norway entered the world spotlight in shocking fashion on July 22, 2011, when a heavily armed Norwegian killed 69 people and injured about 100 others in an attack upon the Labour Party's youth camp on the island of Utøya, roughly 40 km (25 mi) from Oslo. Prior to his assault on the island, the gunman had detonated a bomb in Oslo, where eight died. Prime Minster Jens Stoltenberg responded to the event with a call for more openness and greater democracy. Some 200,000 people carrying flowers filled the streets of Oslo, and elsewhere Norwegians gathered to protest terror and hate. A pall fell over the country as Norwegians collectively watched the burials of the victims on television. (*See* Sidebar on page 444.) The government's reaction to the tragedy included the creation of a commission to assess Norway's antiterrorist measures and an increase in police funding in the national budget for 2012.

Despite expectations that there would be increased participation in local elections in September in response to the attack on Utøya, the turnout was typically low, at 63.8% of eligible voters. The Labour Party registered the strongest support, with 31.7% of the votes. Although the Conservative Party's total was 28%, most large cities continued to be governed by Conservatives. The anti-immigrant Progress Party suffered significant losses and ended up with only 11.4% of the vote. One of the parties in Stoltenberg's red-green government coalition, the Socialist Left Party, fared even worse, with only 4%.

The Norwegian economy remained strong. At 3.3% in November, unemployment was low, while at midyear GDP for mainland Norway was projected to grow by 2.8%. Two massive oil discoveries, in the Barents and North seas, mitigated Norwegian concerns over the country's declining hydrocarbon reserves. The ecologically vulnerable Lofoten-Vesterålen archipelago was protected from oil and gas exploration for two more years under a compromise reached by the partners in the coalition government. Drilling was, however, allowed in nearby offshore sectors and along the coast of the far northern counties of Troms and Finnmark. Housing prices continued to climb, and many first-time buyers were forced to go deeply into debt even as economists warned against the risks of incurring such debt in the climate of high interest rates brought about by financial unrest in the EU. The relative strength of the national currency, the krone, created problems for Norwegian industries that depended on exports, and manufactures in general declined by about 5%.

Abroad, Norwegian F-16 jets participated in the UN mission to protect the opposition in Libya against the forces of the country's strongman ruler, Muammar al-Qaddafi. In Afghanistan a Norwegian UN employee was killed in an uprising in Mazar-e Sharif.

In February the world Nordic skiing championship was held in the forests around Oslo. Athletes from some 50 countries took part in 21 competitions. Finally, the University of Oslo celebrated its 200th anniversary.

(HILDE SANDVIK)

OMAN

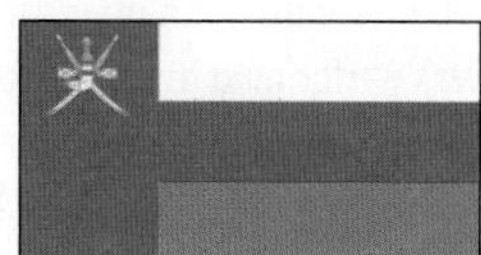

Area: 309,500 sq km (119,500 sq mi)
Population (2011 est.): 2,810,000
Capital: Muscat
Head of state and government: Sultan and Prime Minister Qaboos bin Said (Qabus ibn Sa'id)

Oman in 2011 was not spared the kind of unrest experienced by many Arab countries in what was termed the Arab Spring. In every major city, citizens from all walks of life, especially youths, used social media to organize protests decrying unemployment and the high cost of housing and calling for greater transparency and accountability to curb abuse of privilege by government officials. Sultan Qaboos bin Said reacted more effectively than most of his counterparts elsewhere. He did so by declar-

Terror in Norway

At 3:26 PM on July 22, 2011, an explosion shattered the peace in the Norwegian capital of Oslo. The blast, which was centred just outside the government offices of Norwegian Prime Minister Jens Stoltenberg, killed eight people and injured dozens more. Had the bombing occurred at another time of the year, the casualty list likely would have been much longer; because many Norwegians take their vacations at the end of July, this unofficial "common holiday" meant that many public offices in the area of the blast were largely empty on the afternoon of the attack. As events continued to unfold throughout the day, Norwegians would take little comfort from the fact that the deadliest attacks on Norway since World War II could have been far worse.

Police officials determined that the explosion had been caused by a car bomb, and they drew parallels to the Oklahoma City bombing of 1995 in the U.S. The Norwegian military established a cordon around downtown Oslo. Fearing the detonation of additional devices, officials warned residents to remain in their homes. As the rescue and recovery effort continued in Oslo, police received reports of gunshots on the resort island of Utøya, some 40 km (25 mi) to the northwest.

Joerg Carstensen—EPA/Landov

On July 25 thousands of Norwegians gathered in Oslo hold up roses in tribute to the 77 people killed in related bombing and shooting attacks in the area three days earlier.

About 5:00 PM, roughly an hour and a half after the bomb detonated in Oslo, a man dressed as a police officer took a ferry from the mainland to the island of Utøya. Stating that he was performing a security check in connection with the bombing, he gained access to a youth camp hosted by the Norwegian Labour Party. At 5:26 PM police began to receive reports of gunfire on the island. Armed with a semiautomatic rifle and pistol, the gunman spent the next hour methodically targeting the roughly 600 young people at the camp. Many of the campers were teenagers—and one survivor was just 10 years old—and the gunman used his police disguise to lure some of his victims closer with the promise of rescue. A shortage of transport helicopters delayed the law-enforcement response, and by the time police arrived on the island at 6:25 PM, 69 people were dead or dying. Police apprehended the suspected gunman, Anders Behring Breivik, minutes later without incident. The combined death toll of the bombing and shooting ultimately reached 77, and the overwhelming majority of the dead were between 14 and 19 years old.

Breivik, the 32-year-old Norwegian accused of having executed the two attacks, had no previous criminal record. He was active on neo-Nazi and anti-Islamic Web sites; however, he had not demonstrated a propensity for violent rhetoric. After his arrest a 1,500-page manifesto attributed to "Andrew Berwick," an Anglicization of Breivik's name, was found online. Titled *2083: A European Declaration of Independence*, the tract borrowed heavily from the antitechnology manifesto issued by Ted Kaczynski (the so-called Unabomber, who conducted a 17-year bombing campaign in the United States), and it was filled with anti-Islamic language and imagery that evoked the Crusades and the Templar religious military order. It also detailed the day-to-day preparations that Breivik had made prior to the attacks. He spent several years amassing the funds to finance what he called his "martyrdom operation," and he leased a secluded farmhouse in eastern Norway, which made his purchase of several tons of fertilizer in the weeks prior to the blast look less suspicious. Ammonium nitrate fertilizer can be combined with fuel oil to create a powerful improvised explosive device.

Breivik stated that the Labour Party had failed to prevent the encroachment of "cultural Marxism" (a pejorative term for multiculturalism) and a "Muslim takeover," so he sought to precipitate an armed revolt. His attack on the Labour Party youth camp was designed to limit the party's ability to recruit in the future, and he intended to target former Labour prime minister Gro Harlem Brundtland, who delivered a speech at Utøya just hours before the massacre. Although Breivik admitted to both the bombing in Oslo and the shootings at Utøya, he pleaded not guilty to the criminal charges that were filed against him. In November 2011 court-appointed psychiatrists concluded that Breivik suffered from paranoid schizophrenia. Had he been deemed mentally fit for trial, Breivik could have been sentenced to a maximum of 30 years in prison. With an insanity diagnosis, however, he faced the possibility of spending the rest of his life in psychiatric care. (MICHAEL RAY)

ing the complete independence of the state accounting authority, sacking half a dozen prominent executive branch officials, increasing the power of elected officials within the country's national consultative body, and pledging 50,000 new employment opportunities—35,000 in the country's armed forces and the balance in other sectors of the economy. Oman's overall economic situation also benefited from unprecedented pledges of $10 billion in economic support from Oman's five fellow Gulf Cooperation Council member countries, to be distributed in annual payments spread over the following decade.

Tourism, a major generator of employment and a key feature of efforts to diversify the economy and lessen reliance on oil and gas income, suffered as a result of the global economic downturn. The setback was cushioned by progress in extending the country's road and rail infrastructure.

In mid-October, elections for the country's seventh Consultative Council (Majlis al-Shura) took place without incident. The number of female candidates increased to 77 among a record high of 1,333 candidates vying for the council's 84 seats representing 61 provincial districts. (JOHN DUKE ANTHONY)

PAKISTAN

Area: 881,889 sq km (340,499 sq mi), including the 85,793-sq-km (33,125-sq-mi) Pakistani-administered portion of Jammu and Kashmir
Population (2011 est.): 187,343,000 (including the nearly 5,000,000 residents of Pakistani-administered Jammu and Kashmir as well as Afghan refugees)
Capital: Islamabad
Head of state and government: President Asif Ali Zardari, assisted by Prime Minister Yousaf Raza Gilani

Pakistan's religious and political tensions continued to erupt sporadically into violence in 2011, and a series of confrontations with the U.S. pushed relations between the two countries to new lows. In January, Salman Taseer, the governor of Punjab province, was shot to death by one of his security guards. After being arrested, the guard stated that he had killed Taseer for his vocal criticism of the country's blasphemy laws, under which those convicted of defaming Islam could be sentenced to life in prison or death. Several prominent Pakistani religious groups made statements praising the assassination and condemning Taseer as an apostate. Following the attack Prime Minister Yousaf Raza Gilani met with Pakistani religious leaders to reassure them that the blasphemy laws would not be altered. In March a second critic of the laws, Shabaz Bhatti, the federal minister for minority religious affairs, was assassinated. The only Christian member of the cabinet, Bhatti had argued that the blasphemy laws were used to repress Pakistan's religious minorities.

Sectarian tensions repeatedly erupted into violence. A series of bombings at shrines, mosques, and religious gatherings resulted in dozens of deaths in 2011. In Karachi violence by ethnic gangs aligned with political parties surged, claiming more than 800 lives over the course of the year.

In May militants launched a sophisticated attack against a major naval base in Karachi. Attackers infiltrated the base and destroyed or damaged maritime surveillance airplanes recently acquired from the United States. Syed Saleem Shahzad, a journalist who reported that the assault may have involved links between navy officials and al-Qaeda operatives, disappeared. Days later he was found dead, his body bearing signs of torture.

Events in 2011 strained the military and political alliance between the U.S. and Pakistan. In January, Raymond Davis, a U.S. citizen later revealed to be a private contractor working undercover for the CIA, shot and killed two men in Lahore. Davis claimed that the men had tried to rob him after approaching his car on a motorcycle. In addition, a pedestrian was struck and killed by a support vehicle from the U.S. consulate as it made an abortive attempt to aid Davis, who was arrested by Pakistani police and charged with murder. U.S. officials frantically tried to secure Davis's release while enraged Pakistanis held demonstrations calling for his execution. Despite pleas by the U.S. government, the Pakistani authorities insisted on bringing Davis to trial. In March, after considerable diplomatic maneuvering, Davis was released in exchange for payment of reparations to relatives of the two men. In April Pakistani officials ordered the departure of 400 U.S. special forces soldiers working in Pakistan as counterterrorism trainers, fearing that the soldiers might also be involved in spying.

On May 1 U.S. Pres. Barack Obama announced that a U.S. special operations task force had killed Osama bin Laden in a raid on a residence in Abbottabad, Pak., after U.S. intelligence located him there. The revelation that bin Laden had lived for years in an affluent town near Islamabad in a home less than a kilometre from a major Pakistani military academy fueled speculation that the Pakistani government may have concealed knowledge of bin Laden's whereabouts. The administration of Pres. Asif Ali Zardari decried the raid as a violation of Pakistan's sovereignty and denied that the country had sheltered bin Laden.

Tensions between Pakistan and the United States intensified later in May when two NATO helicopters that had been flying in Afghanistan strayed over the border into North Waziristan and were fired upon by Pakistani forces. The helicopters returned fire, wounding two Pakistani soldiers and prompting a new round of heated exchanges between Islamabad and Washington. In spite of the tension, the U.S. continued its campaign of armed drone strikes in Pakistan, killing several high-ranking members of militant groups over the course of the year. The strikes remained deeply unpopular with the Pakistani public, who deplored the strikes' civilian toll and the violations of Pakistan's sovereignty. In June Pakistani officials announced that they had ordered the U.S. to vacate Shamsi airfield, a base in southwestern Pakistan that the U.S. had used to launch drones.

U.S. officials continued to pressure Pakistan to take greater action to combat militant groups fighting Afghan and NATO forces in Afghanistan. In September an assault by insurgents on the

Khalid Tanveer/AP

On February 4 protesters in Multan, Pak., demand punishment for Raymond Davis, an undercover CIA contractor who killed two Pakistani men in Lahore a week earlier in what he claimed was self-defense.

U.S. embassy and NATO's International Security Assistance Force (ISAF) headquarters in Kabul was allegedly traced to the Pakistan-based Haqqani network, a militant group allied to the Taliban. Testifying before a congressional committee, Adm. Michael Mullen, the chairman of the U.S. Joint Chiefs of Staff, charged that the assault had been organized with assistance from Pakistan's Inter-Services Intelligence (ISI) agency and called the Haqqani network "a veritable arm of Pakistan's ISI."

In late September, Burhanuddin Rabbani (*see* OBITUARIES), a former Afghan president and the leader of an initiative to negotiate a reconciliation with the Taliban, was assassinated. The attack was also linked to the Haqqani network, and Washington again expressed its dismay over Islamabad's reluctance to combat the organization. That reluctance prompted the United States to step up its drone strikes and launch a ground offensive at the Afghanistan-Pakistan border specifically targeting Haqqani fighters. A U.S. delegation that included Secretary of State Hillary Clinton, CIA director Gen. David Petraeus, and Gen. Martin Dempsey, the new head of the Joint Chiefs of Staff, visited Islamabad during the intensified campaign. Focused on the projected U.S. withdrawal from Afghanistan in 2014, the delegation emphasized that the elimination of the Haqqani network was a primary objective, and Clinton bluntly informed Islamabad that time was running out.

In November NATO helicopter gunships and fighter aircraft killed 24 Pakistani soldiers posted at the border with Afghanistan, angering Islamabad. Pakistan closed its border to NATO shipments and once again declared the Shamsi airfield off-limits to U.S. drone activity. The U.S. removed all equipment and personnel from the base on December 11. U.S.-Pakistan relations, long strained, were close to the breaking point. (LAWRENCE ZIRING)

PALAU

Area: 488 sq km (188 sq mi)
Population (2011 est.): 20,600
Capital: Melekeok (on Babelthuap)
Head of state and government: President Johnson Toribiong

Although effects of the global financial crisis appeared to be easing in Palau, the country faced challenges in 2011. Tourism, the leading domestic source of income, rebounded strongly, with the number of visitors in 2010 up almost 20% from 2009. The government had an operating deficit of about $13 million through 2009, according to an independent audit. With some budget cuts in place, the government projected a slight surplus for 2011. Meanwhile, the $250 million aid package included in the Compact of Free Association with the United States was awaiting approval by the U.S. Congress. Palau's legislators sought to boost revenues by raising the excise tax on hotel rooms and charging registration fees for foreign visitors, but the Supreme Court declared the fees were unconstitutional.

A November fire at a main power plant led to electricity rationing. As a result, a Pacific regional fisheries meeting scheduled for December in Palau was postponed and moved to Guam.

Palau's potential as an ecotourism destination grew as the country took steps to protect its wildlife and marine ecosystems. Pres. Johnson Toribiong in January signed a law strictly limiting the hunting of sea turtles. Micronesian leaders enacted a regional ban in July on the possession or sale of shark fins and announced plans to develop a five-million-square-kilometre (about two-million-square-mile) shark sanctuary in regional waters by December 2012.

(JANET MOREDOCK)

PANAMA

Area: 74,177 sq km (28,640 sq mi)
Population (2011 est.): 3,643,000
Capital: Panama City
Head of state and government: President Ricardo Martinelli

The removal of Vice Pres. Juan Carlos Varela of the Panameñista Party from the post of foreign minister on Aug. 30, 2011, marked the end of the coalition that had brought Pres. Ricardo Martinelli to power in Panama in 2009. Conflict between the two politicians erupted over proposed constitutional reforms that would replace the country's first-past-the-post presidential electoral system with one that would require a runoff if no candidate won an outright majority. Martinelli also seemed intent on eliminating the constitutional prohibition against a president's serving more than one five-year term and tried to coax legislators to switch to his Democratic Change party. Martinelli's dismissal of Varela as foreign minister (he remained vice president) triggered the resignations of other cabinet members. Varela declared that even as a member of the executive, he would now play the role of "leader of the opposition." In the process, Martinelli's approval rating plummeted 20 points in September, the biggest decline in the popularity of a Panamanian president in 20 years.

On October 21, U.S. Pres. Barack Obama promulgated the long-pending Free Trade Agreement (FTA) with Panama. This action came nine days after the deal was ratified by the U.S. Congress but four years after approval by Panama's National Assembly. Panama Canal administrator Alberto Alemán Zubieta forecast that in 2011 the Panama Canal would set a new record for tonnage shipped through it and tolls paid. Panama's economy, the fastest growing in Latin America, expanded by 11.4% (year on year) in the second quarter of 2011. According to one analysis, Panama also had become the region's top recipient of foreign direct investment as a share of GDP. In December former dictator Manuel Noriega returned to Panama to complete three 20-year prison sentences for murder. He had been imprisoned abroad for some 20 years for drug trafficking and money laundering.

(ORLANDO J. PEREZ)

PAPUA NEW GUINEA

Area: 462,840 sq km (178,704 sq mi)
Population (2011 est.): 6,188,000
Capital: Port Moresby
Head of state: Queen Elizabeth II, represented by Governor-General Michael (from May 6, Sir Michael) Ogio (acting to February 25)
Head of government: Prime Ministers Sir Michael Somare (Sam Abal [acting] until January 17 and from April 4 to August 2), Peter O'Neill from August 2, and, from December 14, Somare and O'Neill (disputed)

Papua New Guinea experienced governmental instability in 2011. In early April, days before he was to begin a two-week suspension for official misconduct, Prime Minister Sir Michael Somare (in whose place Sam Abal acted for much of the year) traveled to Singapore, where he underwent three heart operations. He was ousted on August 2, and Parliament elected Peter O'Neill, a former businessman and treasury minister, to replace him. After Somare's return to Papua New Guinea in September, he made a bid for reinstatement that was ultimately supported in mid-December by the Supreme Court. O'Neill, however, maintained the legitimacy of his own claim. On December 19 the governor-general, who had previously supported Somare, reversed his position and endorsed O'Neill. The standoff continued through the end of the year as the rival administrations vied for power. The high court decision meant that Somare's claim had the weight of law behind it, but O'Neill continued to have much support in Parliament.

In September the media organization WikiLeaks released confidential U.S. diplomatic cables suggesting that Papua New Guinea politicians had enriched themselves with public funds. Although the country received substantial foreign aid—more than $400 million annually from Australia alone—many hospitals lacked basic medications and equipment.

Critics demanded greater transparency regarding plans to exploit the country's abundant mineral resources. In Southern Highlands province, popular opposition to the construction of Exxon Mobil's multibillion-dollar liquefied natural gas facility continued. In July a national court rejected environmentalists' request for a permanent injunction against the Ramu nickel mine in Madang province.

(JANET MOREDOCK)

A hot-air balloon is launched in Asunción, Para., on May 15 at a celebration marking the 200th anniversary of Paraguayan independence from Spain.

Ubaldo Gonzalez—Xinhua/Landov

PARAGUAY

Area: 406,752 sq km (157,048 sq mi)
Population (2011 est.): 6,459,000
Capital: Asunción
Head of state and government: President Fernando Lugo

Even as Paraguay celebrated the bicentennial of its independence from Spain in 2011, the country's internal political and economic struggles reflected the challenges of overcoming its troubled past. Many of those struggles pitted Pres. Fernando Lugo—swept into office three years earlier by a populist alliance that ended 61 years of Colorado Party (CP) rule but quickly fractured—against a legislature and government bureaucracy still controlled by the CP. That party, dominated by powerful oligarchs and agribusiness interests, blocked most of Lugo's reform efforts. Large landholders, who produced most of the country's soybeans and beef, blocked his plans for land redistribution (less than 2% of the population controlled 80% of the country's arable land) and environmental protection. About 19% of Paraguay's population, and 42% of the rural population, lived below the poverty line, but Lugo's campaign to improve economic opportunities for the poor largely foundered after soybean producers blocked his efforts to increase taxes.

Lugo's administration had limited successes in tackling cocaine trafficking, with a series of large seizures during the year (including one of nearly a ton), mostly in the three-borders region with Brazil and Argentina, long a haven for smugglers. Paraguay served as a way station en route from the Andean countries to Africa and Europe.

Paraguay's economy, highly dependent on exports of soybeans and other agricultural products, followed record-setting growth of 15.3% in 2010 with a solid increase estimated at 6.4% in 2011. The country settled a dispute with Brazil over revenue sharing from the massive Itaipú hydroelectric dam, bringing in a badly needed $240 million annually in additional revenue. The environmentally contentious Yacyretá hydroelectric dam was inaugurated and brought to full capacity, 37 years after Paraguay and Argentina signed the treaty to build it. In late September an outbreak of foot-and-mouth disease forced Paraguay to ban beef exports, which usually earned some $800 million annually.

Former interior minister Sabino Montanaro, dubbed the "cruel right hand" of the late dictator Alfredo Stroessner, died in September in Asunción while under house arrest on charges of having killed opponents of the regime in the 1970s and '80s. Earlier in the year, the government began making an additional $40 million in reparation payments to victims of the Stroessner regime. (ROBERT ORTEGA)

PERU

Area: 1,285,216 sq km (496,225 sq mi)
Population (2011 est.): 29,249,000
Capital: Lima
Head of state and government: Presidents Alan García and, from July 28, Ollanta Humala

Peru was enveloped in presidential and congressional elections in 2011, and little else seemed to matter. Pres. Alan García could not succeed himself, and, absent his candidacy, the Peruvian Aprista Party (PAP, also called the American Popular Revolutionary Alliance) nominated no one. The race was considered wide open, with five major candidates: Ollanta Humala (*see* BIOGRAPHIES), a former military officer and the 2006 candidate of the Peru Wins (Gana Perú); former president Alejandro Toledo of Peru Possible; the former mayor of Lima, Luís Castañeda of the National Solidarity Party; Pedro Pablo Kuczynski of the Alliance for Great Change; and Keiko Fujimori of Fuerza 2011, the daughter of former president Alberto Fujimori.

Under the Peruvian constitution a candidate had to win a simple majority of the popular vote to be elected. Given that the polls showed substantial support for all five major candidates, it was all but certain that no one would win the first round in April 2011 outright. However, because Peru's political parties were less parties than admiration societies for their leaders—with little institutional durability of their own—the electorate was highly fluid and volatile. Most Peruvian voters were centrists, but in the April election the centrist candidates—Toledo, Kuczynski, and Castañeda—split about 42% of the total vote, which meant that none of them could advance to the runoff round. Instead, the two extreme candidates, Humala (with 31% of the vote) and Fujimori (23%), moved on. Both carried considerable baggage. Fujimori, a conservative, was accused of having been guided by her father's legacy and advisers. Humala had led a failed coup attempt against the elder Fujimori and had presented himself in 2006 as a fervent nationalist with open backing from Venezuela's Hugo Chávez (a strategy that backfired badly in that election). Humala tried to convince voters that he had moved away from Chávez and was modeling himself after Brazil's popular former president Luiz Inácio Lula da Silva ("Lula"). Meanwhile, Fujimori claimed that she would build on her father's popularity in provincial areas and would continue Peru's neoconservative economic model, but she tried to convince voters that her father and his advisers would not be in charge from behind the scenes. Many Peruvians expressed their frustration with both candidates. In the second round, held on June 5, Humala won by the slim margin of 51.4% to Fujimori's 48.6%.

The response among Lima's elite was instantaneous, and the stock market fell precipitously on the assumption that Humala would move rapidly to the left and that investment would disappear. Humala quieted such fears early on, however, by reappointing Julio Velarde, the highly regarded head of the Central Reserve Bank under García, and making Luis Castilla, a centrist, his minister of economics. Moreover, Humala named confidant Salomón Lerner, a high-profile businessman, as the head of his somewhat eclectic cabinet.

Nevertheless, Humala's basic campaign platform—a commitment to maintaining Peru's rapid economic growth and to sharing that growth with the country's indigenous population—was reflected in his creation of a new Ministry of Development and Inclusion. The new president also raised mining royalties substantially (with the consent of the international corporation involved) and signed a prior-consultation law that required dialogue with indigenous groups before mining operations could proceed.

Peru still faced many difficulties. Its economy depended largely on mineral exports that in turn rested on shifting world prices and the economic well-being of China, the United States, and other more-developed countries. Remnants of the brutal Shining Path insurgency that had paralyzed the country were still active in some remote areas of Peru, and drug production and corruption persisted. Nevertheless, the country had weathered the global economic downturn much better than most of its neighbours and had seen a contentious election come and go with no major hitches. (HENRY A. DIETZ)

PHILIPPINES

Area: 300,000 sq km (115,831 sq mi)
Population (2011 est.): 95,849,000
Capital: Manila (some government offices and ministries are located in Quezon City and other Manila suburbs)
Head of state and government: President Benigno S. Aquino III

A long dispute between the Philippines and China escalated in 2011 over tiny islands in a portion of the South China Sea that the Philippines announced on June 13 it had renamed the West Philippine Sea. China, however, claimed the entire South China Sea, including areas off the coasts of five other countries that may contain petroleum and natural gas beneath major shipping lanes. This led to several naval incidents between China and the Philippines during 2011. In March two Chinese patrol boats harassed an oil-exploration vessel sent by the Philippines to Reed Bank, an area claimed by the Philippines. The Philippines also accused Chinese forces of having shot at Filipino fishermen and having marked some islands as Chinese property.

Pres. Benigno S. Aquino III ordered an improvement in the Philippines' limited ability to defend the islands. Armed forces—mostly using half-century-old equipment—were to be modernized with U.S. help, he said. As a start, a decommissioned U.S. Coast Guard patrol vessel was acquired.

Aquino visited China in late summer to discuss the dispute and trade with Chinese Pres. Hu Jintao. Aquino told reporters that the two agreed on the need for a maritime code of conduct to defuse tensions. Both countries also pledged to double bilateral trade—which had reached $27.7 billion in 2010, an increase of 35% from 2009—to $60 billion by 2016.

In his July 25 address, Aquino claimed that production of rice, a staple of the Filipino diet, had increased 15.6% as irrigation and other agricultural improvements had spread. He added that this pointed toward an end to rice imports and maintained that the proportion of people not getting enough to eat had dropped from 20.5% to 15.1%. Some 1.4 million jobs had been created in 2011 up to April, Aquino said, reducing the unemployment rate from 8% to 7.2%.

Government revenues increased 18% in the first four months of 2011, almost twice as fast as the economy grew, as Aquino emphasized attacks on corruption and introduced easier methods for paying income taxes. The country depended heavily on remittances from its large overseas workforce, but turmoil and policy changes in the Middle East had reduced the amount of money being sent home.

Despite Aquino's claimed accomplishments, he was heavily criticized. Oscar V. Cruz, a retired archbishop of the Roman Catholic Church, said that Aquino

Rolex Dela Pena/AP

On July 20 on Philippine-occupied Thitu Island—one of the Spratly Islands in the South China Sea—a group of legislators, military officials, and local residents display a banner in a symbolic assertion of their country's claim to the region, which was disputed by China.

was incompetent and should resign. A leading media commentator, Amando Doronila, faulted Aquino for lacking a vision for the country and for such judgment lapses as buying an expensive sports car.

Former president Gloria Macapagal Arroyo was arrested on November 18 and was charged with having fixed votes in the 2007 legislative elections. President Aquino also accused her of other corrupt practices while she was in office. On December 12 the House of Representatives voted to impeach Supreme Court Chief Justice Renato Corona for alleged breach of public trust by favouring Arroyo in court rulings. Both Arroyo and Corona denied all charges.

Insurgencies continued to plague the Philippines. On August 4 Aquino met in Tokyo with the chief of the Moro National Liberation Front (MNLF), which had fought sporadically for decades for a separate state in the southern islands. That meeting in Japan and additional discussions that took place in Malaysia, however, failed to reconcile the two sides.

Typhoon-generated rains in late September and early October flooded parts of the northern Philippines and killed at least 100 people. In December some 1,250 people died and hundreds were missing after storms produced flash floods that devastated parts of Mindanao in the south.

(HENRY S. BRADSHER)

POLAND

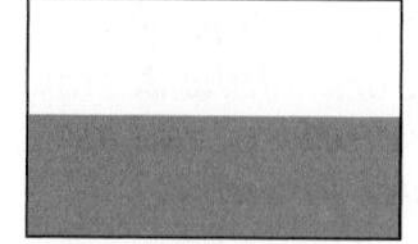

Area: 312,679 sq km (120,726 sq mi)
Population (2011 est.): 38,216,000
Capital: Warsaw
Head of state: President Bronislaw Komorowski
Head of government: Prime Minister Donald Tusk

Much of the political debate in Poland in 2011 continued to centre on the plane crash in April 2010 in Smolensk, Russia, that killed then president Lech Kaczynski and 95 other high-ranking Polish officials. The Russian Interstate Aviation Committee's final report on the crash, published in January, sparked a heated political dispute in Poland that lasted through the year's parliamentary election campaign when it laid the blame for the crash squarely on the Polish side. The report identified the main cause of the crash as the decision by the pilots to land in unfavourable conditions. In addition, it alleged that officials from the presidential entourage had pressured the pilots to land. While the Polish government did not reject the report's findings, it argued that the report was incomplete because it failed to address the Russian air traffic controllers' responsibility for the safety of the flight. Prime Minister Donald Tusk promised to publish in a timely fashion the findings of the Polish commission investigating the crash. The Civic Platform (PO), the principal party of the governing coalition, showed awareness of the sensitivity of the crash issue in the report it published in the summer. It blamed poor training of the pilots for the tragic event. As a consequence, Tusk accepted the resignation of Defense Minister Bogdan Klich.

On July 1 Poland began its first tenure in the six-month rotating presidency of the European Union. Although the post had become increasingly administrative and ceremonial, Poland used its chairing and hosting of official EU gatherings to promote the country and its achievements. Among the goals set by the Polish government for its presidency were the assurance of the continued flow of structural funds to the new member states of the EU; the strengthening of the EU's food, military, and energy security; and a commitment to making progress on further enlargement of the organization. Finally, Poland sought to enhance cooperation with the EU's neighbours to the east through the Eastern Partnership Program, an initiative that had suffered setbacks during the previous year and that Warsaw hoped to strengthen.

Prime Minister Tusk used the EU presidency to boost the PO's chances of winning the elections for the Sejm (parliament) on October 9. The campaign was unusually long, but it was more subdued and less confrontational than previous contests had been. The party platforms were very general, and candidates refrained from running on concrete policy proposals. The PO was the winner, with 39.2% of the vote, followed by the Law and Justice party (PiS), with 29.9%. The big surprise was the success of the Palikot Movement (Ruch Palikota), a liberal and anticlerical party, which came in third, with 10% of the vote, and entered the Sejm for the first time. The Polish Peasant Party (PSL) received 8.4%, about the same as its showing in the previous general election, in 2007. The big loser was the Democratic Left Alliance (SLD), which received only 8.2%. In the new Sejm the PO had 207 seats, the PiS 157, Ruch Palikota 40, the PSL 28, and the SLD 27. The PO and its junior partner in the ruling coalition, the PSL, won enough seats (235) to form another government. That marked the first time since the collapse of communism that the prime minister and the governing party had been reelected to a second term. The markets reacted favourably to the outcome of the elections, under the assumption that it would provide political stability for Poland and foster economic growth.

Poland continued to grow its GDP in 2011, with an estimated increase of 3.8%. In December the country's inflation rate stood at 4.6%, while the unemployment rate was 12.5%, slightly higher than the December 2010 figure. The government continued to express a commitment to adopting the euro, even though Greece's economic crisis dampened Polish enthusiasm for the common currency. The government did, however, refuse to set a new target date for adoption until the economic situation had stabilized. Despite the economic slowdown in much of Europe, Poland was still perceived as a relatively safe haven in terms of economic development, a view that was supported by the country's decision not to use the $20.5 billion flexible credit line established for it in 2009 by the International Monetary Fund.

(MICHAEL WYGANOWSKI)

PORTUGAL

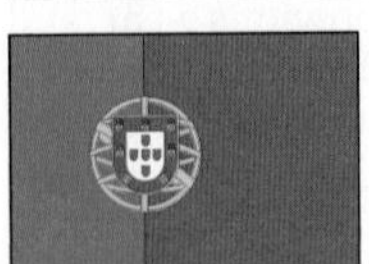

Area: 92,094 sq km (35,558 sq mi)
Population (2011 census est.): 10,556,000
Capital: Lisbon
Head of state: President Aníbal Cavaco Silva
Head of government: Prime Ministers José Sócrates and, from June 21, Pedro Passos Coelho

Portugal's political and economic crisis came to a head in 2011 as the ruling Socialist government struggled to put together a credible package to fix the country's huge fiscal imbalances and reduce the budget deficit. Bond yields soared, and speculation grew that Portugal would be forced to follow Greece and Ireland in seeking outside economic help. Finally, in March, the minority government of Prime Minister José Sócrates was defeated in the parliament in a crucial vote on economic reform. Sócrates tendered his resignation, setting the stage for a snap election against a backdrop of an increasingly grim economy, with sovereign debt yields rising steadily to levels deemed unsustainable. The election was set for early June, but before the vote was held, Sócrates's caretaker government caved in and called for a bailout, agreeing to negotiate financial assistance from the EU, the European Central Bank, and the IMF. The deal would provide Portugal with €78 billion (€1 = about $1.30), including €12 billion earmarked for the banking sector. In exchange, Portugal agreed to apply tough economic measures designed to slash the deficit by cutting public spending and raising taxes—steps that were supported by the main opposition Social Democratic Party (PSD).

Paulo Duarte/AP

In advance of Portuguese legislative elections, Pedro Passos Coelho, leader of the centre-right Social Democratic Party, waves to supporters during a campaign march in Porto, June 2. He ultimately emerged victorious and as the new prime minister formed a coalition government.

Pedro Passos Coelho, leader of the right-leaning PSD, won the general election, though his party fell short of an absolute majority in the parliament. He formed a government in coalition with the conservative Social Democratic Centre–Popular Party and quickly began implementing the measures required by the bailout deal.

The austerity measures were dramatic—the bailout required Portugal to reduce its deficit to 5.9% of GDP in 2011, from more than 9% in 2010. Taxes, including the value-added-tax scale as well as income taxes and real-estate taxes, were pushed higher. One-off measures were introduced, notably the decision to cancel the Christmas bonus for state employees. Public transport prices rose, while all government services were required to cut budgets drastically. A new slate of privatizations also was announced.

The early criticism of the Passos Coelho government centred on what appeared to be its singular focus on raising revenue, with more tentative steps taken to cut spending. Even so, the economic fix was seen by most Portuguese as both essential and inevitable, and while unions and other workers' groups contested the many measures, there was none of the violent public protest seen in other countries implementing austerity plans.

The outlook for Portugal over the following two years was for continued recession as the austerity effects worked their way through the economy. Banks were actively deleveraging—reducing loans and boosting deposits—while public and private investment was shrinking. Unemployment was predicted to rise to at least 13% by 2013, though by the third quarter of 2011, it had stabilized at about 12%. Exports remained the only bright spot, with the government encouraging investment and expansion in regions that had so far proved resistant to the global economic downturn, including Africa.

A further blow to Portugal's economic credibility came when in September the Finance Ministry revealed a €6 billion gap in the accounts for the autonomous Madeira Islands. The Bank of Portugal said that the unexpected overrun, the equivalent of about 0.5% of Portugal's GDP, meant that the country was unlikely to meet its budget deficit targets without additional measures. Opposition politicians called on the prime minister to publicly chastise Pres. Alberto Jardim of Madeira, a highly popular PSD member who had won successive elections over more than 30 years.

Meanwhile, Portugal carried out a census in 2011, and the initial data showed a 1.9% increase in population from the 2001 census, to about 10.56 million people. The country's population was boosted by immigration, with 182,100 new residents arriving from abroad, but natural population growth also showed a net increase of 17,600 people.

(ERIK T. BURNS)

QATAR

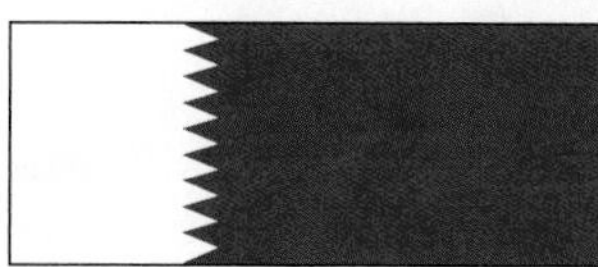

Area: 11,571 sq km (4,468 sq mi)
Population (2011 est.): 1,624,000
Capital: Doha
Head of state and government: Emir Sheikh Hamad ibn Khalifah Al Thani, assisted by Prime Minister Sheikh Hamad ibn Jasim ibn Jabr Al Thani

When in late 2010 Qatar won the competition to host the Fédération Internationale de Football Association (FIFA) World Cup in 2022, the privilege gave Qatar a place on the 2011 world map like no previous development had in the country's history. Qatar pledged to build seven new "minicities" and nine new stadiums and have 84,000 hotel rooms available. The country's selection also ensured that Qatar would undergo a continuous construction boom in its accommodation, catering, and tourism sectors alongside completion of a new $10 billion airport capable of handling 24 million passengers annually.

Internationally, the energy-resource-rich country, together with Brunei, remained one of the world's wealthiest countries; its GDP per capita soared to more than $100,000. Qatar also held fast to its activist role as a regional diplomatic arbiter and would-be peacemaker. The country was in the forefront in persuading the Arab League to request and support an international no-fly zone over Libya. Qatar sent a third of its air force to Souda, Crete, to help police the UN-backed and NATO-led aerial security zone in support of the Libyan rebels who ousted leader Muammar al-Qaddafi from power. In so doing, Qatar took the lead in financing, hosting, and being the first Arab country to recognize the rebels' provisional and later transitional government while also agreeing to help market Libya's oil exports.

With its fellow Gulf Cooperation Council members, Qatar also sought to end the violence that erupted in neighbouring Bahrain and Yemen, pledged $10 billion in investments for Egypt in the wake of the ousting of Pres. Hosni Mubarak by antiregime protesters, and recalled its ambassador from Damascus to protest the Syrian government's violence against its dissenting citizens. In addition, throughout the so-called Arab Spring of regional political tumult, Qatar's government-owned al-Jazeera satellite television excelled at providing worldwide exposure to the region's revolutionary changes.

(JOHN DUKE ANTHONY)

ROMANIA

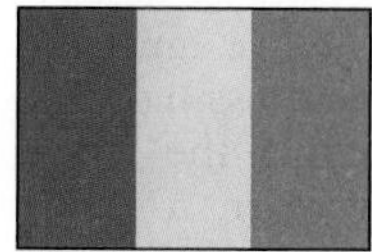

Area: 238,391 sq km (92,043 sq mi)
Population (2011 est.): 21,393,000
Capital: Bucharest
Head of state: President Traian Basescu
Head of government: Prime Minister Emil Boc

In Romania, Prime Minister Emil Boc's government, made up of his party of Democratic Liberals (PDL) and smaller allies, clung to office in 2011 despite lacking the parliamentary votes to pass important bills. For this reason, in July, legislation designed to regionalize government in the hope of making an unwieldy bureaucracy more efficient had to be shelved. In September, however, there was consensus behind the establishment of a coordinator for the absorption of funds from the European Union. Romania continued to be a net contributor to the EU budget, despite being the second poorest member of the body.

The PDL had very low poll ratings, owing to tough cuts imposed on the public sector in 2010 in an effort to stabilize finances. In the run-up to the 2012 parliamentary elections, the Social Liberal Union, a hybrid alliance of left- and right-wing parties, remained well ahead in the polls, but those polled believed that regardless of the outcome there would be little change in the standards of government.

In 2011 Romania enjoyed good economic news compared with much of the rest of Europe. One major credit agency, Fitch, upgraded its assessment of Romania's investment potential. In July the EU offered Romania as a model for Greece to emulate because of the country's success since 2010 in lowering a very high budget deficit.

Romania's relations with the Netherlands were badly strained owing to the latter's refusal to allow Romania to join the visa-free Schengen zone. Romania insisted that the Netherlands' fears that organized crime and corruption could be exported westward were groundless and pointed to a crackdown on bribe taking in the customs service and other antigraft efforts. When the issue flared up, Poland held the EU's rotating presidency, and Polish Interior Minister Jerzy Miller pointed out on September 22 that Romania was being treated unfairly because it had fulfilled the technical criteria meant to ensure that it could join the Schengen zone. Only Finland supported the Netherlands in blocking Romania's accession. Romanian Pres. Traian Basescu branded their actions "non-European behaviour." In a move that was viewed as possibly retaliatory, on September 19 Romania halted at the border 15 truckloads of flowers and seed imports from the Netherlands on suspicion of contamination with harmful bacteria. What quickly became known as "the Tulip War" had been pre-

Vadim Ghirda/AP

After the Romanian government approved plans for a Canadian company to open an open-pit gold mine in Transylvania, protesters wearing gas masks demonstrate against the project in Bucharest, July 19.

ceded in July by Spain's decision, owing to an unemployment crisis, to impose labour restrictions on Romania, which had nearly one million of its citizens living in Spain. Resentment was growing in Romania over the readiness of established EU members to restrict membership benefits after Romania had agreed to rapidly liberalize its economy, enabling top western European firms to acquire control of many of its strategic industries.

Relations were smoother with the U.S. On September 13 in Washington, D.C., Basescu and Pres. Barack Obama signed an agreement on the deployment in Romania of new antimissile shields. At home Basescu supported a planned gold-mining operation in Rosia Montana, Transylvania, but he encountered strong opposition from environmental groups, intellectuals, and the country's influential Orthodox Church over the risk of serious pollution's arising from the open-cyanide pit and the disruption of the heritage-rich area. (TOM GALLAGHER)

RUSSIA

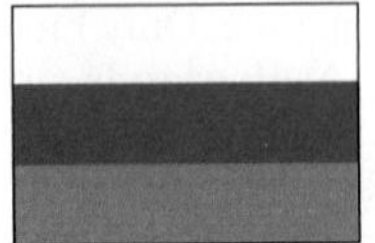

Area: 17,098,200 sq km (6,601,700 sq mi)
Population (2011 est.): 142,707,000
Capital: Moscow
Head of state: President Dmitry Medvedev
Head of government: Prime Minister Vladimir Putin

Domestic Affairs. Addressing a congress of Russia's ruling United Russia party on Sept. 24, 2011, Pres. Dmitry Medvedev announced that he was nominating Prime Minister Vladimir Putin to be the party's presidential candidate in the elections set for March 2012. In that way Medvedev ended months of increasingly tense speculation over whether he himself would stand for a second presidential term. Earlier that day Putin had proposed that Medvedev head United Russia's list of candidates for the elections to be held on December 4 for the State Duma, the lower house of the Russian parliament. After having agreed to run for the presidency, Putin said that should he win the election, Medvedev would likely be his nominee for prime minister. Effectively, Putin and Medvedev were announcing that they would be swapping jobs. Putin's popularity with the public declined slowly but steadily throughout the year—but even so, he was virtually certain to be elected for what would be his third presidential term. The news took even the elite by surprise. Two days later Finance Minister Aleksey Kudrin—one of Putin's closest colleagues—handed in his resignation, having received a public dressing-down from Medvedev for telling the media that he would not serve in a future Medvedev-led government.

September's announcement resolved one mystery but did not end speculation over the policies that Putin would follow after returning to the Kremlin. Putin's statement on October 4 that he aspired to form a "Eurasian Union" of former Soviet states suggested to some that he might devote his presidency to foreign policy, which would free Medvedev to pursue some of the modernization reforms about which Medvedev had spoken while president but had failed to implement. In late December Medvedev surprisingly advocated changes that would reverse Putin initiatives, including direct election of governors and creation of a TV station free from Kremlin interference.

In a surprise move on May 6, Putin announced the creation of the All-Russia Popular Front. His aim appeared to be to bolster the United Russia party by recruiting fresh blood from trade unions, youth organizations, World War II and Afghanistan war veterans, and women's associations. The Popular Front cast its support behind Putin but in the event did little to boost popular enthusiasm for United Russia. Also in May, Russia's third richest man, billionnaire entrepreneur Mikhail Prokhorov—who had made his fortune in the precious-metals sector and was owner of the NBA's New Jersey Nets basketball team—announced his intention to assume leadership of Right Cause, Russia's small pro-business political party. At the time, Prokhorov denied that he had received any encouragement from the Kremlin to revitalize the party. Once Prokhorov had assumed the party leadership, however, he began to behave in ways that did not suit the Kremlin's agenda, such as his declaration that he might himself run for president. In September law-enforcement officers raided the Moscow offices of the International Finance Club, a bank partially owned by Prokhorov, although they made no arrests. Within a week of the raid, Prokhorov had been ousted from the party leadership by an internal coup. At that point he denounced Right Cause as "a puppet Kremlin party" micromanaged by a "puppet master" in the presidential administration—Kremlin ideologist Vladislav Surkov. Stripped of Kremlin support, Right Cause sank back into obscurity.

Misha Japaridze/AP

Having a few days earlier announced his intention to run for president of Russia, billionaire businessman Mikhail Prokhorov addresses supporters at a meeting in Moscow, December 15.

Opinion polls indicated that popular discontent was increasing. Much of the blame was laid on rising utility prices and, even more so, on corruption among state officials. According to Medvedev himself, for example, a trillion rubles (about $31 billion) was being embezzled annually from the state procurement system. The expression of public disgust with corruption was spearheaded by Aleksey Navalny, a 34-year-old lawyer who in December 2010 had launched the whistle-blowing Web site RosPil (short for "Russian Saw"—*saw* being Russian slang for "to embezzle," as in "to saw" off a piece of a contract). The site publicized cases in which state contracts appeared to have been awarded corruptly. Navalny invited visitors to anonymously post details of suspicious government requests for tender and discuss the allegations online. Within six months the site was reportedly getting a million hits a month. When Navalny went on to coin the term "party of crooks and thieves" to describe the United Russia party, it quickly became the catchphrase of Russian protest.

According to the Levada Centre polling agency, 60% of Russians said that they were not interested in December's Duma elections, because they believed that the balloting would not be conducted honestly. The opposition People's Freedom Party (PARNAS) was not permitted to register for the Duma elections; its leaders—Boris Nemtsov, Mikhail Kasyanov, and Vladimir Ryzhkov—called on voters to spoil their votes as a sign of protest. The party's fourth leader, Vladimir Milov, followed Navalny's lead in exhorting Russians to vote for any party other than United Russia, a controversial tactic, given that it risked boosting the Communist vote. In the December 4 elections, all four parties represented in the outgoing Duma—United Russia, the Communist Party, A Just Russia, and the Liberal Democratic Party—won seats in the new parliament. However, in what was seen as a setback for the prestige of the Putin-Medvedev leadership, United Russia won only 49.3% of the vote. While the party was assured of a majority of seats in the new Duma, it would lose the constitutional majority it had enjoyed until then. The Communist Party came second with 19.19% of the vote, followed by A Just Russia with 13.24% and the Liberal Democrats with 11.67%. Voter turnout was 60%. On December 10 allegations of vote rigging provoked demonstrations across Russia; these represented the largest popular protests since the fall of the U.S.S.R. 20 years earlier. Two weeks later Moscow was the site of another huge demonstration.

On March 1 the name of Russia's police force was officially changed from the Soviet-era *militsia* to *politsia* as part of an effort by Medvedev to increase the efficiency and improve the public image of the law-enforcement bodies. The number of police officers was to be reduced by 20% by 2012, from 1.28 million to 1.1 million. That reduction was to be accomplished by assessing each officer's disciplinary record, physical and mental fitness, and knowledge of Russian law; those who were found wanting would lose their jobs, whereas the salaries of those who passed the evaluation would increase by 30%. The new policy also delineated new rights for detainees, including the right to consult a lawyer immediately upon arrest.

Violent unrest continued in Russia's largely Muslim North Caucasus region and periodically spilled over into other portions of the country. In January, 36 people were killed in a suicide bombing at Domodedovo, Moscow's busiest airport.

In October Moscow's historic Bolshoi Theatre reopened following a six-year restoration that returned the theatre, founded in 1776, to its former glory. As winter set in, Russia remained on summer time after Medvedev had ordered that clocks should no longer be put back in Russia. The change promised darker mornings but lighter evenings and potential energy savings of up to 3%.

In June human rights activist Yelena Bonner, widow of Soviet dissident and Nobel Peace Prize laureate Andrey Sakharov, died in Boston. In November, Joseph Stalin's daughter, Svetlana, known in later life as Lana Peters, died in Wisconsin. (*See* OBITUARIES.)

Economy. The economy continued to recover from the global financial crisis, and in October it was announced that unemployment had returned to below precrisis levels. GDP was expected to grow by about 4% in 2011 (the same rate as in 2010). With the aid of increased world oil prices, Russia's recovery was projected to be sufficient to reduce the federal budget deficit in 2011 to 1.3% of GDP. Even so, there was considerable disarray in economic policy making. In particular, there was disagreement between the Ministry of Economic Development (headed by Elvira Nabiullina) and the Ministry of Finance (headed by Kudrin) over implementation of modernization policies. Kudrin had fought hard for prudent budgetary policies, having built up Russia's reserve fund and steered its public finances through the downturn in 2008–09. There was also disagreement between Medvedev and Kudrin, ostensibly over Medvedev's insistence on increased defense spending. The clash exacerbated what was reported to be an already difficult relationship between the two men, and it culminated in September in Kudrin's forced resignation.

In March expert groups were set up under the leadership of economists Vladimir Mau and Yaroslav Kuzminov and commissioned to work on a revised economic strategy to extend from the present to 2020. That would replace the "Putin Plan" of 2007–08, which predated the global financial crisis and had as a result been rendered ineffective. In August the experts published a lengthy interim report that spelled out many liberal reform proposals without explaining how, politically, they would be put into effect. The measures included, for example, strengthening the rule of law and establishing a level playing field for all businesses operating in Russia. The experts also indicated that Russia badly needed a continuing flow of immigration to increase the labour force, which would otherwise decline in absolute terms. Such a move would likely be highly unpopular with the general public, as would anticipated recommendations for an increase in the age at which retirees could begin to receive their pensions (in 2011 age 55 for women and age 60 for men). The experts were expected to submit a final agreed-upon document toward the end of the year.

There was much discussion in the Russian media about the need for changes in the business environment. An underlying problem was a lack of confidence on the part of the business community, both domestic and foreign. That was reflected in a net outflow of private capital from Russia, with a significant part of Russian savings having moved offshore. According to credible reports, small and medium-sized businesses, unsettled by uncertainty and corruption within the Russian political system, accounted for much of that traffic. September's dramatic public clash between Medvedev and Kudrin threatened to further damage both domestic and international business confidence in the Russian economy.

Concern was also expressed about a "brain drain," linked in the Russian media to the high number of young, well-educated Russian citizens reportedly emigrating from Russia or to those who told pollsters that they would like to do so. Officially, only 33,000 people emigrated in 2010, but that figure omitted those who left Russia to work or study abroad and might not plan to return. The actual number of emigrants was believed to be substantially higher.

In 2010 the rate of fixed investment in the economy as a share of GDP was 20.5%, well below the investment rate of other emerging markets, such as India and China, and it was not expected to increase significantly in 2011. That outlook reflected Russia's relatively poor business environment, including weak protection of property rights. The World Bank's ease-of-doing-business index ranked Russia 120th out of 183

Mikhail Klimentyev—Presidential Press Service/RIA Novosti/AP

At a military base in Kaliningrad, Russian Pres. Dmitry Medvedev stands in front of a graphic display inside an early-warning radar station that he inaugurated, November 29.

countries in 2011 (up four places since 2010), while Transparency International ranked Russia 143rd out of 183 countries in its 2011 Corruption Perceptions Index. Confidence in the health of the economy was shaken in the autumn by reports of worsening economic conditions in the U.S. and the EU. Russian government officials began to plan for worst-case scenarios involving a double-dip recession in the Western economies. Such a recession would threaten the Russian economy because it would likely lead to a drop in the price of oil and because about half of Russian exports (dominated by oil and gas) went to the EU. In November Russia and Georgia reached a compromise agreement that would allow Russia to complete its 18-year-long effort to join the World Trade Organization. On December 16 Russia was invited to join the WTO and was given until mid-June 2012 to ratify its membership.

Foreign Affairs. Thanks to the "reset" begun after U.S. Pres. Barack Obama took office, relations between Moscow and Washington remained cooperative. The year began well, with the entry into force on February 5 of the New START (Strategic Arms Reduction Talks) between Russia and the U.S.; that replaced an earlier treaty, signed in 1991, which had expired in December 2009. Disagreements between the two countries remained, however, over U.S. plans for ballistic missile defense. Moscow called on Washington to provide it with a legally binding guarantee that any U.S. installation of a ballistic missile defense system would not weaken Russia's own system of strategic deterrence. In November Medvedev warned that failure by the U.S. and its allies to take Moscow's concerns into consideration could spark a new arms race and announced the inauguration of an early-warning radar system in the Baltic exclave of Kaliningrad.

Moscow was slow to react to the Arab Spring uprisings, and Russian leaders seemed divided over the appropriate response. While Moscow recognized that the unrest had been provoked by the corrupt and inefficient nature of the existing regimes, it expressed concern that democratization might undermine rather than enhance regional stability. Moscow's main concern appeared to be the danger that instability might spread from the Middle East and North Africa to Central Asia and Russia's own North Caucasus region. In March, under Medvedev's auspices, Russia abstained from the vote on UN Security Council Resolution 1973, thereby removing an obstacle to authorization of NATO-led military intervention in Libya.

Following Iran's refusal to disclose details about its nuclear program, Moscow continued to support UN Security Council sanctions against Iran and to block delivery of the S-300 air-defense systems that Russia had earlier contracted to deliver. Nevertheless, Moscow continued to assist Iran in developing its nuclear-energy infrastructure, and toward year's end Russia warned that it would not agree to the imposition of further international sanctions against Iran.

In an article in the newspaper *Izvestiya* on October 4, Putin called for a new "Eurasian Union." He explicitly ruled out comparisons with the Soviet Union, saying that "it would be naive to try to revive or emulate something that has been consigned to history"; rather, he seemed to have in mind a Eurasian version of the EU. He proposed that the existing Russia-Belarus-Kazakhstan Customs Union gradually expand to include other former Soviet states (with the first of these to be Kyrgyzstan and Tajikistan) and develop into a "bridge between Europe and the dynamic Asia-Pacific region." Reactions from other former Soviet republics were not initially enthusiastic, but the project seemed set to form a major plank of Putin's third presidential term. On October 18 Putin unexpectedly announced that Russia and seven other former Soviet republics had signed a free-trade agreement, which scrapped export and import tariffs on a range of goods. There was speculation during the year that the Collective Security Treaty Organization (of which Russia was a leading member) might widen its activities to include cooperating in military action to quell social unrest within a member state. (ELIZABETH TEAGUE)

RWANDA

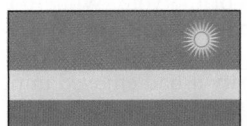

Area: 26,379 sq km (10,185 sq mi)
Population (2011 est.): 10,943,000
Capital: Kigali
Head of state and government: President Maj. Gen. Paul Kagame, assisted by Prime Ministers Bernard Makuza and, from October 7, Pierre Damien Habumuremyi

In 2011 Rwanda continued rapid realization of Millennium Development Goals in facilitating state building, alleviating poverty, diminishing corruption, and improving health and education. Real GDP growth stood at 7.2%. Rural agricultural production of food and export crops increased, with a 14% rise in coffee export revenues. On August 24 the first-ever comprehensive business census reported that since 2010, 60,202 new businesses had been created; all but 1.2% of them were owned by Rwandan nationals, and of these, women operated 26.3%.

Shant Fabricatorian/AP

Vital Uwumuremyi (left), Noel Habiyambere (centre), and Tharcisse Nditurende (right), former commanders of the Democratic Forces for the Liberation of Rwanda rebel group who were accused of terrorist activities, arrive at court in Kigali, September 7. All three men pleaded guilty to the charges against them.

Regrettably, while socioeconomic achievements attracted foreign donors and investors, the woeful political transparency record of the Tutsi-dominated ruling Rwandan Patriotic Front (RPF) raised increasing criticism at home and abroad. Journalists and political opponents experienced frequent intimidation and oppression, and many opted for exile, where they urged international groups to apply pressure for reform in governance. Meanwhile, former government supporters, including some senior army officers (notably South African-based Faustin Kayumba Nyamwasa, a former armed forces chief of staff), became disillusioned with RPF corruption and nepotism. In January Nyamwasa was sentenced in absentia by a military court to 24 years' imprisonment on charges of desertion and threatening state security. In May six alleged terrorists were arrested and charged with having plotted to overthrow the Rwandan regime.

Several notable changes occurred in government. In local elections that took place in June, 54.5% of the registered voters were women, and women also made up 41% of candidates for district advisory committees. On May 6 the first cabinet reshuffle since 2009 changed the technocratic lineup. Five months later long-serving Bernard Makuza was replaced as prime minister by Pierre Damien Habumuremyi.

The International Criminal Tribunal for Rwanda (ICTR) in Arusha, Tanz., responsible for trying the alleged leaders of the 1994 genocide, returned verdicts against several notorious suspects. Pauline Nyiramasuhuko (former minister for family and women's affairs) and her son, Arsene Ntahobali (a former militia leader), received life sentences for their roles in the abduction, murder, or rape of hundreds of ethnic Tutsis. Several others received sentences ranging from 25 to 35 years, including former ministers Justin Mugenzi and Prosper Mugiraneza. The ICTR Appeals Chamber reduced the life sentences of former military leaders Théoneste Bagosora and Anatole Nsengiyumva to 35 and 15 years, respectively. In France an appeals court rejected Rwanda's international warrant for the extradition of Agathe Habyarimana, the widow of former president Juvénal Habyarimana (assassinated in 1994). She was suspected by some of having been a master planner of the 1994 genocide. (LARAY DENZER)

SAINT KITTS AND NEVIS

Area: 269 sq km (104 sq mi)
Population (2011 est.): 50,300
Capital: Basseterre
Head of state: Queen Elizabeth II, represented by Governor-General Sir Cuthbert Sebastian
Head of government: Prime Minister Denzil Douglas

Although in 2011 Saint Kitts and Nevis continued to face significant economic challenges because of its high public debt, in November 2010 the IMF had still expressed confidence in the country's ability to foster growth. In July 2011 the IMF approved a three-year agreement to provide some $84 million in financial assistance to Saint Kitts and Nevis. Prime Minister Denzil Douglas hailed the economic union between six members of the Organisation of Eastern Caribbean States that came into force on January 21. The union with Antigua and Barbuda, Dominica, Grenada, St. Lucia, and St. Vincent and the Grenadines was expected to allow the free movement of people, goods, services, and capital.

The government denied in January that it planned to reintroduce personal income tax as alleged by the official opposition People's Action Movement. In May the Nevis Island Administration approved a guarantee for a $57 million loan sought by West Indies Power for the construction of an 8.5-MW geothermal power plant at Spring Hill.

The incumbent Nevis Reformation Party (NRP) won three of the five seats in the Nevis Island Assembly in July elections. The Concerned Citizens Movement retained the other two but, alleging voter tampering by the NRP, filed a legal challenge to the results.

(DAVID RENWICK)

SAINT LUCIA

Area: 617 sq km (238 sq mi)
Population (2011 est.): 167,000
Capital: Castries
Head of state: Queen Elizabeth II, represented by Governor-General Dame Pearlette Louisy
Head of government: Prime Ministers Stephenson King and, from November 30, Kenny Anthony

In early 2011 Saint Lucia's electric utility, Lucelec, explored a number of renewable-energy initiatives. As planning continued for a geothermal power plant at Sulphur Springs, Lucelec held discussions with Canadian companies Island Green Energy and Elementa on a project to convert 40,000 tons of waste into electricity.

Saint Lucia's police commissioner, Vernon Francois, in March strongly denied the existence of an alleged "hit list" of known criminals being pursued by a "death squad" within the Royal Saint Lucia Police Force. The allegations came after the killing of five suspects by police in the preceding months during a crime crackdown known as Operation Restore Confidence.

The governing United Workers Party (UWP), led by Prime Minister Stephenson King, found itself with only a one-seat majority in the 17-seat House of Assembly in September after the deputy minister resigned from the party. He was the second of two sitting MPs to do so during the year. The Saint Lucia Labour Party (SLP) was swept back into office in the November 27 general elections, winning 11 seats in the House of Assembly; the UWP won just six. The leader of the SLP, Kenny Anthony, assumed the post of prime minister on November 30.

(DAVID RENWICK)

SAINT VINCENT AND THE GRENADINES

Area: 389 sq km (150 sq mi)
Population (2011 est.): 101,000
Capital: Kingstown
Head of state: Queen Elizabeth II, represented by Governor-General Sir Frederick Ballantyne
Head of government: Prime Minister Ralph Gonsalves

The Saint Vincent and the Grenadines government began work in January 2011 after Prime Minister Ralph Gonsalves's Unity Labour Party (ULP) won a third consecutive term in the December 2010 general election. The ULP held only a one-seat majority in the 15-member parliament, however—eight seats to the opposition New Democratic Party's seven—which seemed likely to make governing more difficult during the new term of office.

In January Gonsalves announced that the police had arrested a man who had allegedly been hired after the election to kill him. According to Gonsalves, two major drug-trafficking and money-laundering organizations were behind the plot, targeting him primarily because they were "feeling the heat" from his administration.

The country continued its recovery from the destruction caused by Hurricane Tomas in October 2010. Help came in early January from a short-term interest-free loan of about $3.26 million from the IMF's Rapid Credit Facility and from the World Bank, which extended $5 million in interest-free credit to the country. The government estimated that the damage caused by Tomas to infrastructure and private property amounted to at least 5% of GDP. In April flooding and landslides caused further damage, and in July the IMF granted Saint Vincent another loan for $2 million. (DAVID RENWICK)

SAMOA

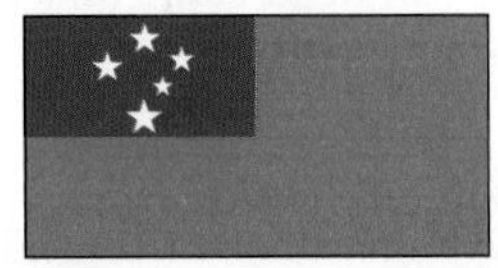

Area: 2,785 sq km (1,075 sq mi)
Population (2011 est.): 184,000
Capital: Apia
Head of state: *O le Ao o le Malo* (Head of State) Tuiatua Tupua Tamasese Efi
Head of government: Prime Minister Tuila'epa Lupesoliai Sailele Malielegaoi

The March 2011 national election in Samoa saw the Human Rights Protection Party (HRPP) returned to power with a reduced, but still significant, majority in the parliament. A more organized opposition with strong candidates made a better showing than in previous elections, although a series of election petitions resulted in four by-elections that were all won by HRPP candidates.

Prime Minister Tuila'epa Lupesoliai Sailele Malielegaoi persuaded the parliament to relocate Samoa to the west of the international dateline after 119 years on the east side of that demarcation. The shift, which received parliamentary approval in June, was intended to reflect evolving patterns of Samoan trade, which was increasingly with New Zealand, Australia, and Asian countries, notably China. The change, which occurred at the end of 2011, resulted in the elimination of December 30 on the Samoan calendar in 2011.

Increasing Chinese demand for nonu juice and kava, New Zealand interest in Samoa's chili sauce and organic products, and a plan to use biomass to produce energy looked likely to stimulate opportunities for growers of those commodities, reducing dependence on taro exports. Tourism continued to grow, and new hotels and other tourism-related businesses were producing much-needed employment for Samoan youth. The prime minister came under considerable pressure from churches and the general population, however, over his plan to license two casinos in Samoa, from which he planned to ban Samoan gamblers.

(CLUNY MACPHERSON)

SAN MARINO

Area: 61.2 sq km (23.6 sq mi)
Population (2011 est.): 32,000
Capital: San Marino
Heads of state and government: The republic is governed by two *capitani reggenti,* or coregents, appointed every six months by a popularly elected Great and General Council.

In 2011 San Marino continued to renew its image in the financial world. During her speech to the UN General Assembly, Antonella Mularoni, secretary of state for foreign affairs, underscored the importance of San Marino's international ties. Both the World Bank and the International Monetary Fund acknowledged the significance of the country's banking-reform efforts.

It was especially alarming during the year to discover, following investigations by the Italian police, that powerful criminal organizations from Naples were well integrated into San Marino's financial fabric. Allegedly, these organizations had the capacity to manipulate the country's political system. Italian Finance Minister Giulio Tremonti noted that the per capita personal savings in San Marino was 20 times greater than that of the Italian savings rate. Such high liquidity could not, he asserted, be attributed to legitimate family savings alone. Evidently such distorted financial conditions were detrimental to the overall economy; during the year 7% of all San Marino companies closed.

One way for San Marino to circumvent this anomalous status would be to attain full membership in the European

Union. The country already had many ties with the EU, but a popular initiative was launched in 2011 to mandate a process that could lead to full membership. To some, this step could guarantee future stability, while others held that such a commitment could undermine the tiny state's unique character.

(GREGORY O. SMITH)

SAO TOME AND PRINCIPE (SÃO TOMÉ E PRÍNCIPE)

Area: 1,001 sq km (386 sq mi)
Population (2011 est.): 169,000
Capital: São Tomé
Head of state: Presidents Fradique de Menezes and, from September 3, Manuel Pinto da Costa
Head of government: Prime Minister Patrice Trovoada

In Sao Tome and Principe, the key event of 2011 was the presidential election. Pres. Fradique de Menezes had served two five-year terms and was not eligible for a third. In the first round of the election, there was no clear winner, but in the runoff held in August, the archipelago's first president, Manuel Pinto da Costa, emerged victorious. He had ruled as a virtual dictator from independence in 1975 until the first multiparty elections in 1991 but now promised to tackle the country's endemic poverty, political instability, and corruption. His main challenger, former prime minister Evaristo Carvalho, was a leading figure in the National Assembly and enjoyed the backing of Prime Minister Patrice Trovoada, but he won only 47% of the vote to Pinto da Costa's 53%. Election observers from the African Union, the Community of Portuguese Speaking Countries, and elsewhere proclaimed the election free and fair.

The island state remained highly dependent on foreign aid and agriculture despite the vast oil fields that had been discovered offshore. Most of the population remained very poor, and with the global economic downturn, the challenge for the new president would be to bring the oil onstream, without destabilizing the country, and to diversify the economy.

(CHRISTOPHER SAUNDERS)

SAUDI ARABIA

Area: 2,149,690 sq km (830,000 sq mi)
Population (2011 est.): 28,572,000
Capital: Riyadh
Head of state and government: King ʿAbd Allah

Events in Saudi Arabia in 2011 were dominated by the Arab Spring, a wave of mass protests in Arab countries. In February and March, wary of possible unrest in Saudi Arabia, King ʿAbd Allah announced two programs, with a combined cost of $130 billion, that would provide for massive social spending and handouts. Although it was feared that this spending would trigger inflation, Finance Minister Ibrahim al-Assaf said that the country's economy was in "excellent shape."

After witnessing the sudden collapse of rulers in both Egypt and Tunisia, Saudi Arabia—along with the U.A.E. and Kuwait—sent troops to Bahrain in March to help crush pro-democracy protests there. In March and April, Saudi Arabia attempted to broker a peace deal in Yemen. In June, Yemeni Pres. ʿAli ʿAbd Allah Salih was injured during an attack on his palace and was taken to Riyadh for hospitalization, but he returned to Yemen in September.

Analysts claimed that there were disagreements among senior princes and officials over whether to intervene in—either in support of or against—the pro-democracy protest movements in the Middle East. Some commentators suggested that the advanced age and ill health of many senior Saudi princes were to blame for apparent inconsistencies in Saudi Arabia's policies regarding the Arab Spring. The crown prince, Sultan ibn ʿAbd al-ʿAziz, died in October after a long illness. (*See* OBITUARIES.) He was succeeded by Prince Nayef ibn ʿAbd al-ʿAziz, the interior minister.

In July, Saudi authorities announced that they had uncovered a plot by al-Qaeda and a group of citizens to overthrow the government. Sixteen people were arrested. Interior Minister Prince Nayef ibn ʿAbd al-ʿAziz stated at the end of August that terrorism remained a threat to the kingdom. Referring to conflicts in Yemen and Iraq he said, "Evil surrounds us from all sides." He also accused Iran of having plotted against Saudi Arabia. In October, American authorities accused Iranian operatives of having plotted to assassinate the Saudi ambassador to the U.S. Tehran denied the allegation.

In September, King ʿAbd Allah announced that women would have the right to run and vote in municipal elections, starting in 2015. He also canceled an order from a religious court calling for a woman to receive 10 lashes for having disobeyed a law pro-

At the royal palace in Riyadh, Saudi Arabia, King ʿAbd Allah (right) applauds after witnessing ʿAli ʿAbd Allah Salih (left) sign an agreement to step down as president of Yemen, November 23.

Saudi Press Agency/AP

hibiting females from driving cars. Nationwide, municipal council elections in 2011 were characterized by low voter participation, with turnout rates less than 50% of those in the 2006 election cycle.

Saudi Arabian crude oil output hit 9.7 million bbl per day in July owing to increased prices and soaring demand. Statistics showed that Saudi Arabia imported 90% of its food.

A $60 billion–$90 billion arms agreement with the U.S. was under way for the purchase of at least 84 new F-15 fighter jets and 178 combat helicopters. In addition, Riyadh reached an agreement to buy 200 Leopard 2A7 tanks from Germany. The sale ended Germany's decadeslong refusal to sell heavy artillery to Saudi Arabia.

Saudi Arabia announced that it was planning to build its first nuclear plant by 2020. A surge in the demand for electricity made it imperative for the country to at least double its electricity-generating capacity by that date.

(MAHMOUD HADDAD)

Protesting against proposed changes to Senegal's constitution that some claimed would strengthen Pres. Abdoulaye Wade's hold on power, demonstrators cast rocks at police outside the National Assembly building in Dakar, June 23.

Rebecca Blackwell/AP

SENEGAL

Area: 196,722 sq km (75,955 sq mi)
Population (2011 est.): 12,644,000
Capital: Dakar
Head of state and government: President Abdoulaye Wade, assisted by Prime Minister Souleymane Ndéné Ndiaye

Political controversy was a source of tension in Senegal during 2011. On June 23, after often violent demonstrations, Pres. Abdoulaye Wade withdrew a proposed constitutional amendment that would have declared as outright winner a presidential candidate who had taken only 25% of the vote in the first round. Another controversial change, to create an elected vice presidency, was also dropped. Opposition supporters accused Wade of planning a "monarchic" succession by handing power over to his son, Karim, should the president be reelected in 2012.

Protests against unemployment and constant power outages were widespread in June. In Mbour rioters torched government buildings on June 28, including those of the state electricity company. On July 21 the government banned political protests in central Dakar, but this did not prevent hundreds of thousands of pro-Wade demonstrators from rallying on July 23 in support of a third term. An announcement in late August that presidential candidates would be required to deposit nearly $145,000 that would be forfeit should they not garner 5% of the vote was met with protest from the opposition. After a period of relative calm, the Casamance region saw a resurgence of violence by some rebel factions late in the year.

On July 8 the government announced that it would accede to Chad's request to extradite former president Hissène Habré, detained in Senegal since 2005, in order to face trial for crimes he committed while in power. Two days later, following an appeal by the head of the UN Human Rights Commission, the decision was reversed on grounds that Habré, sentenced to death in absentia in 2008, would be tortured and likely executed if he was returned to Chad.

(NANCY ELLEN LAWLER)

SERBIA

Area: 77,498 sq km (29,922 sq mi) (excluding Kosovo)
Population (2011 est.): 7,262,000
Capital: Belgrade
Head of state: President Boris Tadic
Head of government: Prime Minister Mirko Cvetkovic

The European Commission's report for 2011 recommended that Serbia become an official EU candidate country. The Commission noted Serbia's significant progress toward establishing the required criteria for bringing about the "stability of institutions guaranteeing democracy, rule of law, human rights and respect for and protection of minorities." The report also cited continued progress in establishing a functioning market economy. In addition, it recommended that Serbia pursue structural reforms to upgrade productivity and to create a more conducive climate for foreign investment.

On December 9, however, EU member states decided to postpone a decision on Serbia's candidate status until February or March 2012. EU ministers stipulated that Serbia had to prove itself capable of normalizing relations with Kosovo. The decision came after months of tension and violence in the Serb-dominated areas of northern Kosovo. Clashes between local Serbs, NATO peacekeepers, and ethnic Albanians were commonplace, and Serbs had erected numerous roadblocks to resist attempts by the government of Kosovo to assume customs control over the border with Serbia. Kosovo's Serb minority in the north and Serbia did not recognize Kosovo's independence, declared in 2008.

In May, Ratko Mladic, commander of the Bosnian Serb forces during the 1992–95 war in Bosnia and Herzegovina, was arrested in Serbia. Mladic—indicted by the UN's International Criminal Tribunal for the Former Yugoslavia in 1995 on charges of genocide, war crimes, and crimes against humanity—

was held pending trial at The Hague. Serbia's action did receive considerable recognition by the EU as a move in the right direction regarding negotiations over the country's EU membership drive.

According to preliminary census data, Serbia's population had deceased by 5% over the previous nine years. Government officials attributed the decline to such factors as a negative birth rate, migration, and a general boycott of the census by many of the estimated 57,000 ethnic Albanians living in southern Serbia, who protested Belgrade's lack of interest in the general welfare of the region's minorities.

Unemployment fluctuated between 20% and 27%. Those under age 35 constituted half of the republic's jobless rate. More than 9% of the population lived below the poverty line. After having peaked at 14.7% in April, inflation trended downward throughout 2011 and settled at about 8% by year's end. Amid rising unemployment, poverty, and government corruption, opposition parties demanded early elections and in February staged the largest demonstrations in Belgrade since the fall of Slobodan Milosevic in 2000. Nevertheless, parliamentary elections remained scheduled for May 2012.

In September external debt stood at €23.86 billion (about $32 billion). The European Bank for Reconstruction and Development in July projected Serbia's GDP growth to come to about 3.3%. Serbia's national bank and the IMF revised this figure in November, however, and projected modest growth of 2%. In September the IMF agreed to a standby loan of about €1 billion ($1.38 billion) aimed at underwriting Serbia's economic stability and attracting much-needed foreign investment. Since 2000 Serbia had canceled some 30% of privatization deals; more than 650 companies had yet to attract foreign offers, including the Nikola Tesla Airport in Belgrade, valued at €140 million (about $182 million), and the Commercial Bank, valued at €70 million (about $91 million).

In keeping with its long-term goal of transforming Serbia into a major energy hub in southeastern Europe, the government signed an agreement in October with a consortium of Chinese companies. The agreement called for the construction of an additional power-generating plant at the Nikola Tesla complex in Obrenovac and for investment in the research of renewable energy sources. Serbian Foreign Minister Vuk Jeremic stated that relations between China and Serbia were "excellent." He expected China to become the largest foreign investor in Serbia in 2012. (MILAN ANDREJEVICH)

SEYCHELLES

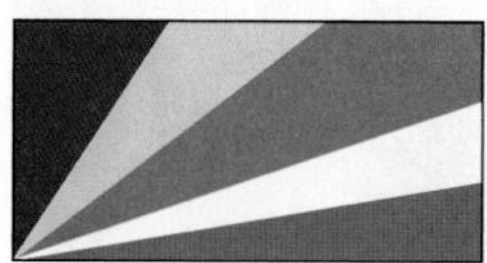

Area: 452 sq km (about 174 sq mi)
Population (2011 est.): 92,000
Capital: Victoria
Head of state and government: President James Michel

In May 2011 voters in Seychelles reelected James Michel to the presidency, which marked his second five-year presidential term. President Michel won 55% of the vote. When voters returned to the polls in late September for the National Assembly elections, Michel's People's Party swept all 25 seats, owing in large part to the election boycott by the Seychelles National Party (SNP). In response to allegations of electoral misconduct lobbed by SNP opposition leader Wavel Ramkalawan, Michel tasked the Electoral Commission to commence a national consultation to discuss reforming the electoral process.

The Indian Ocean country continued to play a central role in global antipiracy efforts. In March the Seychellois Supreme Court sentenced 10 Somali pirates to 20 years in prison, and another 5 pirates were sentenced in late June. Early in the year Seychelles and Somalia signed an agreement to transfer convicted Somali pirates to Somalia. Seychelles received supplies, aircraft, and financial support for antipiracy operations from the European Union and Interpol, as well as from China and the United Arab Emirates, among other countries.

Diplomatic cables leaked in 2011 (part of WikiLeaks) indicated that a secret U.S. military base, dubbed "Ocean Look," had been built in Seychelles in 2009. The leaked correspondence revealed that the operation had been billed as part of ongoing antipiracy activities but also was intended as a drone-launching site for counterterrorism operations in the region.

(MARY EBELING)

SIERRA LEONE

Area: 71,740 sq km (27,699 sq mi)
Population (2011 est.): 5,997,000
Capital: Freetown
Head of state and government: President Ernest Bai Koroma

On April 27, 2011, Sierra Leone staged a lavish celebration to mark its 50th anniversary of independence. A number of western African leaders were in attendance, including the presidents of Liberia, Equatorial Guinea, Mali, Guinea, and Senegal. Various analysts and organizations seized the opportunity to assess the country's achievements, while Pres. Ernest Bai Koroma proclaimed a "Year of Unity" in preparation for the forthcoming general election in 2012.

Notable progress was made in restoring democracy and socioeconomic programs since the end of the 10-year civil war in 2002. According to the 2011 Mo Ibrahim Index of African Governance, Sierra Leone rose three places to number 30 of 53 countries for governance quality. The goals of the national Agenda for Change and the second Poverty Reduction Strategy (2008–12) achieved partial realization. Expanded road and bridge construction throughout the country, both north and south, facilitated internal trade and movement. The free health care program increased the number of children receiving health care by 214%, reduced the maternal mortalities in difficult pregnancies by 61%, and diminished malaria deaths in children treated in hospitals by 85%. The completion of the Bumbuna hydroelectric dam in 2009 promised to extend the electricity supply beyond the capital, Freetown, and in the meantime, the government had distributed generators to some cities, allowing them to benefit from a reliable supply of electricity. Unfortunately, corruption remained intractable. The Anti-Corruption Commission (ACC) declared that 86% of the police force had engaged in corruption at some level, followed closely by customs officers and the judiciary. In the interim the ACC had successfully prosecuted several eminent politicians.

Meanwhile, economic development proceeded slowly. The country stood

Simon Akam—Reuters/Landov

On April 27, Sierra Leonean Pres. Ernest Bai Koroma (third from left) arrives at a ceremony at the National Stadium in Freetown that marked the 50th anniversary of Sierra Leone's independence.

near the bottom of the UN Human Development Index, ranking 180th of 187 countries. Real GDP was forecast to increase from 5% to 6% in 2011, but the government depended on donors for more than half of its revenue. Agriculture, the mainstay of much of the population, accounted for 5% of GDP, but mining generated 80% of national exports. The largest earner of foreign exchange was the diamond sector, but improved production of bauxite and rutile reduced dependence on diamonds. Prospects for the resumption of large-scale iron mining, once a major industry, and offshore oil exploration bolstered concerns that the government should take legislative action to ensure that the people of Sierra Leone, rather than foreign companies, reap the benefits of the country's natural resources. (LARAY DENZER)

SINGAPORE

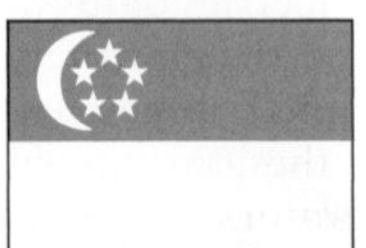

Area: 710 sq km (274 sq mi)
Population (2011 est.): 5,182,000
Head of state: Presidents S.R. Nathan and, from September 1, Tony Tan
Head of government: Prime Minister Lee Hsien Loong

For Singapore, where since 1997 only two opposition members had been in Parliament at any given time, the political landscape underwent a major transformation in 2011. On May 7, in its worst showing in a general election since independence in 1965, the ruling People's Action Party (PAP) lost a record 6 seats out of 87 contested and garnered a vote share of only 60.1%. The results pushed the PAP toward deep soul-searching and pledges to transform itself both as a party and in the way that it governed the country. Three months later it received another sharp jolt when Tony Tan, the PAP-backed candidate in the presidential election, won by only a razor-thin margin following a recount.

Taken together, the results of the two elections marked what became known as the "new normal" in Singapore politics, although that term came to be used in different ways. To some it meant the emergence of a strong—or, at least, stronger—opposition and the end of one-party dominance. To others it heralded the ascendancy of a new set of political values and aspirations among voters, marked by a desire for greater pluralism, political participation, and government transparency. The old social compact, in which voters supported the PAP in return for material well-being, was no longer sufficient, it was argued. Pundits raised questions about the continued viability of the prevailing model of elite, technocratic rule. The PAP responded with a promise to not just "get its policies right" but also to "get its politics right."

A week after the general election, in what Prime Minister Lee Hsien Loong billed as an "epochal change," Lee Kuan Yew, Singapore's founding prime minister (1959–90), and Goh Chok Tong, prime minister from 1990 to 2004, both stepped down from the cabinet. It was a tacit admission that their continued presence there—Lee as minister mentor and Goh as senior minister—hampered new approaches and styles of governance. Both, however, remained in Parliament and acted as occasional envoys of the country overseas. Several other ministers also stepped down, which resulted in a cabinet with fewer members who were of a much lower median age. Of the 14 ministries, 11 had new people at their helm. Policy shifts followed rapidly in areas that had been contentious during the two elections. The supply of public-housing units was increased, for example, in response to complaints of long waiting times for housing. A review of ministerial pay—long criticized as too high—recommended reducing salaries significantly for top government officials. (CHUA LEE HOONG)

SLOVAKIA

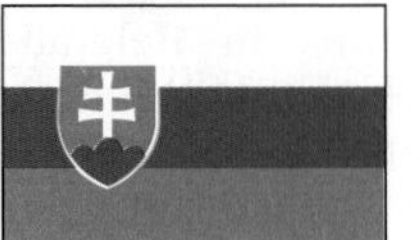

Area: 49,034 sq km (18,932 sq mi)
Population (2011 est.): 5,440,000
Capital: Bratislava
Head of state: President Ivan Gasparovic
Head of government: Prime Minister Iveta Radicova

The centre-right coalition government in Slovakia made considerable strides during the first nine months of 2011 before collapsing in a parliamentary vote of no confidence on October 11 amid a controversy over the country's contribution to the EU's enlarged European Financial Stability Facility (EFSF). Several squabbles had rocked the four-party ruling coalition prior to that vote, raising concerns about the loyalty of one of the junior coalition partners, Freedom and Solidarity (SaS). While the SaS was new and untested, politicians from the other three parties—Prime Minister Iveta Radicova's Slovak Democratic and Christian Union (SDKU), the Christian Democratic Movement (KDH), and Bridge (Most-Hid)—had worked together effectively in the past. Still, internal conflicts also emerged within the SDKU, pitting Radicova against party leader Mikulas

Dzurinda, who previously had served (1998–2006) as prime minister.

Despite such tensions, the parliament finally elected Jozef Centes as attorney general in June, ending a dispute that had threatened to unravel the government in late 2010. In mid-September Radicova survived a confidence vote advanced by the opposition, gaining support from all four coalition parties. In terms of policy, the Radicova cabinet pushed through measures to help reduce unemployment, including labour code amendments and incentives for attracting investment to poorer regions. With the aim of fighting corruption, the coalition also took steps to improve the transparency of the judicial system and the public tender process.

Prior to the October vote, SaS leader Richard Sulik voiced opposition to the EFSF, claiming that Slovakia—as the second poorest euro-zone member—should not be liable for the "irresponsible" fiscal policies of Greece. To try to bring SaS in line, Radicova tied the EFSF to a confidence vote, but to no avail. Slovaks were divided over whether the country should contribute to the bailout: while the payment was unduly large (at nearly 12% of 2010 GDP) and the impact of the EFSF's expansion was uncertain, failure to support the measure would have damaged Slovakia's international credibility.

The opposition Direction-Social Democracy party (Smer-SD) helped push the EFSF forward; however, in return for its support, Smer-SD demanded new parliamentary elections, which were set for March 2012, more than two years ahead of schedule. Meanwhile, a minority government of the SDKU, the KDH, and Bridge was appointed, and planned changes to the pension and taxation systems and upgrades to anticorruption legislation were put on hold. Still, the 2012 state budget bill was approved in December when Smer-SD legislators walked out on the vote, which lowered the quorum and permitted the bill's passage.

On the economic front, Slovakia continued to recover from the 2009 downturn, and in the first quarter of 2011, GDP returned to its precrisis level. Industrial output and exports were the biggest drivers of growth. Though there were signs of weakening by midyear, as the European debt crisis heightened, Slovakia's reliance on Germany as a key export market helped to guarantee stability. Household demand in Slovakia remained weak in 2011 owing to fiscal consolidation measures and high inflation. Despite public-sector job cuts, total employment rose substantially in 2011; jobless rates, however, remained well above 2008 lows. (SHARON FISHER)

SLOVENIA

Area: 20,273 sq km (7,827 sq mi)
Population (2011 est.): 2,052,000
Capital: Ljubljana
Head of state: President Danilo Turk
Head of government: Prime Minister Borut Pahor

Political uncertainty complicated efforts in 2011 to put Slovenia's economy back on track. The inflation rate began the year at 1.8% and finished it at 2%; unemployment went from 12.3% (the highest rate since 2000) at the beginning of the year to 11.9% in November. In September the government's economic growth forecast was revised downward from 2.2% to 1.5%, with spending to be reduced by $500 million to deal with a loss of revenue and to meet the year's planned public deficit of 5.5% of GDP.

Internal disputes, resignations, and the rejection of two referenda (held on June 5) on pension reform and regulating part-time employment led to a no-confidence vote for the centre-left government on September 20 and resulted in its dissolution on October 21. Rating services soon lowered Slovenia's credit rating one level owing to concerns over a worsening fiscal position among euro-zone countries.

Pres. Danilo Turk called for an early parliamentary election on December 4. In October Ljubljana's popular mayor, millionaire businessman Zoran Jankovic, created a new centre-left party, Positive Slovenia, and announced his candidacy for prime minister. Polls predicted a centre-right victory for Janez Jansa, an opposition leader and former prime minister (2004–08). Against expectations, Jankovic upset Jansa, and Positive Slovenia captured the most seats (28 out of 88). Jansa and four others went on trial on September 5 for alleged bribery in Slovenia's 2006 deal with state-run Finnish defense contractor Patria.

In the realm of foreign affairs, in October Slovenia withdrew its bid for a nonpermanent seat on the UN Security Council, ceding to Azerbaijan. That same month the government announced a timeline for the withdrawal of Slovenia's 89-member military contingency from Afghanistan. A new constitutional law in Austria regulated the rights of the native Slovenian minority, including the posting of some bilingual city-limit signs.

In domestic affairs, on June 16 a family law bill granted same-sex civil partnerships the identical rights of married couples but limited adoptions. The third referendum held on June 5 on restricting access to communist-era intelligence archives was also defeated. Adria Airways, Slovenia's primary airline, received a $70 million bailout from the government and its largest shareholder, state-run PDP Corp. The "Occupy" movement reached Slovenia on October 15, with protests in Ljubljana, Maribor, and Koper.

In other news, NASA awarded a $1.35 million prize (the largest in history) to an electric ultralight plane built by Slovenian light-aircraft manufacturer Pipistrel and Penn State University. *Gremo mi po svoje* (2010; *Going Our Way*), a summer-camp comedy directed by Miha Hocevar, became the all-time hit Slovenian film both in terms of attendance and as the highest-grossing Slovenian-made movie. The country's first film museum opened in Divaca on July 8, and the first museum of contemporary art opened in Ljubljana on November 26. As part of the celebrations for Slovenia's 20th anniversary of independence, 1,100 musicians gathered in Ljubljana to perform Gustav Mahler's *Symphony No. 8*.

(JOSEPH VALENCIC)

SOLOMON ISLANDS

Area: 28,370 sq km (10,954 sq mi)
Population (2011 est.): 535,000
Capital: Honiara
Head of state: Queen Elizabeth II, represented by Governor-General Sir Frank Kabui
Heads of government: Prime Ministers Danny Philip and, from November 16, Gordon Darcy Lilo

The Regional Assistance Mission to Solomon Islands (RAMSI) continued its activities in the Solomon Islands in

2011, maintaining order and providing technical aid to the government. In eight years in the country, RAMSI had trained 2,000 civil servants, overseen the introduction of competition in the telecommunications market, and provided stability that spurred the growth of foreign investment. In response to a growing desire in the Solomons to reduce the size of the mission, however, a midyear meeting of the Pacific Islands Forum standing committee on RAMSI focused on the issue of scaling it back. Also in July, as a move toward national unity, Gov.-Gen. Sir Frank Kabui pardoned convicted murderer Andrew Te'e, the former commander of the Guadalcanal Revolutionary Army, on condition that he become involved in the national reconciliation process and refrain from criminal activity for three years. The fragile state of national unity was highlighted by a short-lived riot following the election of Gordon Darcy Lilo as prime minister in November.

The Solomons' government extended its diplomatic representation abroad, establishing posts in Switzerland, New Zealand, and Cuba. The value of external linkages for economic development was evident in July, when the government received a grant of some $4.3 million from Australia through the Asian Development Bank to improve transport infrastructure.

(CLUNY MACPHERSON)

SOMALIA

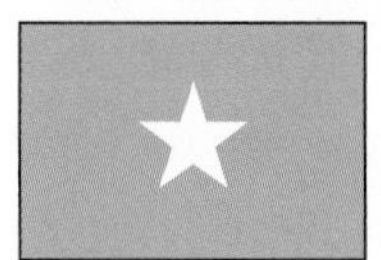

Area: 637,657 sq km (246,201 sq mi), including the 176,000-sq-km (68,000-sq-mi) area of the unilaterally declared (in 1991) and unrecognized Republic of Somaliland
Population (2011 est.): 9,926,000 (including roughly 3,500,000 in Somaliland); at the beginning of the year, nearly 700,000 refugees were in neighbouring countries and 1,465,000 were internally displaced
Capital: Mogadishu; Hargeysa is the capital of Somaliland
Head of state and government: Somalia's transitional government comprised President Sheikh Sharif Sheikh Ahmed, assisted by Prime Ministers Mohamed Abdullahi Mohamed and, from June 19, Abdiweli Mohamed Ali

In 2011 Somalia's Transitional Federal Government (TFG) continued to falter in its efforts to establish political stability and security. Al-Shabaab, an Islamist youth movement with ties to al-Qaeda, remained more powerful than the TFG and, for the first half of the year, controlled much of southern Somalia and part of Mogadishu. The TFG did little to prevent the spread of al-Shabaab's control, instead falling prey to a power struggle between the executive branch and the parliament, which ended with the resignation of popular Prime Minister Mohamed Abdullahi Mohamed. The TFG's mandate was set to expire in August, but the president and the parliament agreed to extend it until August 2012.

Meanwhile, a drought led to skyrocketing food prices and widespread hunger. By late July five regions of the country were suffering from famine, and just weeks later al-Shabaab unexpectedly withdrew from Mogadishu. Analysts said that the withdrawal indicated that the group was weakening, but they warned that it may continue to launch guerrilla attacks from southern Somalia. Because al-Shabaab had banned most humanitarian aid agencies from entering Somalia in 2009, many Somalis blamed the group for the severity of the famine.

In August a limited number of humanitarian aid agencies began sending food aid to Somalia; however, there were widespread reports of theft. Thousands of Somalis fled across the border to Kenya's Dadaab refugee-camp complex, swelling its population to over 440,000. Al-Shabaab opened its own camps in southern Somalia, and there were reports of starving Somalis' being imprisoned in the camps for attempting to flee the country.

By early September the famine had spread to a sixth area. Seasonal rains and an increase in delivered aid led to three of the six areas being downgraded to prefamine status by November. Officials warned that the situation was still critical, though. More than four million people were estimated to be in crisis, with 250,000 in imminent danger of starvation. By mid-November international donors had provided $802 million in assistance, which fell short of the $1 billion the UN had said it needed.

Throughout the fall the security situation in southern Somalia grew more tenuous. Clans fought to take control of areas of southern Somalia from al-Shabaab, and in early October, fighting between al-Shabaab and militias affiliated with the TFG spilled over the Kenyan border. The Kenyan government was increasingly worried that al-Shabaab might attack inside Kenya and in October sent troops into Somalia to fight the group, citing al-Shabaab's abduction of individuals in Kenya and the need to secure the border. It was Kenya's first military invasion of another country.

Piracy off the coast of Somalia in the Gulf of Aden showed no signs of abating. In February four Americans held on a hijacked yacht were killed by their captors. By mid-December, 26 ships had been hijacked (of 42 global hijackings), and 450 people had been taken hostage in 2011, according to the International Maritime Bureau's Piracy Reporting Centre. There was evidence that some pirates were giving a percentage of their ransoms to factions of al-Shabaab.

(STEPHANIE HANSON)

SOUTH AFRICA

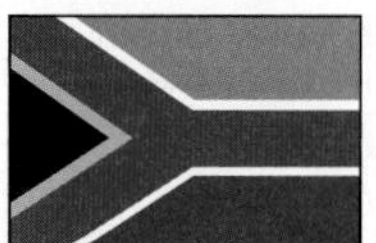

Area: 1,220,813 sq km (471,359 sq mi)
Population (2011 est.): 50,587,000
Capitals (de facto): Pretoria (executive); Bloemfontein (judicial); Cape Town (legislative)
Head of state and government: President Jacob Zuma

South African Pres. Jacob Zuma, in his state of the nation address in early February, declared 2011 a year of job creation through meaningful economic transformation and incisive growth. A total of 9 billion rand (1 rand = about $0.15) would be spent over the following three years in subsidies to industry for job creation; 20 billion rand in tax breaks would be given for the same purpose.

In February, Public Protector Thuli Madonsela declared that a controversial 500 million rand police headquarters property deal was illegal and found that police commissioner Bheki Cele's involvement was "improper, unlawful and amounted to maladministration." Madonsela also criticized the equally controversial 1.1 billion rand police lease deal in Durban and stated that the minister of public works, Gwen Mahlangu Nkabinde, was guilty of improper conduct in allowing the two deals to go ahead. In October, President

Zuma dismissed Nkabinde from his cabinet, suspended Cele, and appointed a commission of inquiry to investigate Cele's dealings. At the same time, Zuma announced the names of three judges who would conduct an inquiry into the controversial 1990s arms deal.

Also in February, the Solidarity trade union called attention to a statement that government spokesperson Jimmy Manyi had made a year earlier when he was serving as director-general of the national Department of Labour. He stated that Coloureds (persons of mixed European and African or Asian ancestry, as classified under apartheid) were "overconcentrated" in the Western Cape province and should spread out around the country. Trevor Manuel, minister of planning in the president's office, called Manyi a racist, and various other senior African National Congress (ANC) members weighed in on one side or the other. The organization as a whole issued a condemnation of Manyi's comments, and he later apologized for his remarks. The renewed attention on Manyi's statement occurred in the context of a pending amendment to the Employment Equity Act, which some thought would require that national, rather than provincial, demographic standards be used in determining employment equity targets. It was feared that the proposed change would threaten job opportunities in the Western Cape province for Coloured workers and in KwaZulu-Natal province for Indian workers, as both groups made up a much higher percentage of the population in those provinces than they did nationally. The government disputed this interpretation of the amendment.

Local elections were held on May 18. The ANC maintained its dominance, winning 63.65% of the votes. The Democratic Alliance (DA), however, was able to increase its percentage of the vote from 14.8% in 2006 to 21.97% in 2011 and won the most votes in Western Cape province. Support for the ANC fell in every province, except for KwaZulu-Natal, where its percentage of votes rose at the expense of the Inkatha Freedom Party (IFP). Nationally, the IFP came in third, with a percentage vote of 3.94%, down from 8.1% in 2006.

President Zuma was criticized for elevating an inexperienced and controversial judge when in September he appointed Mogoeng Mogoeng to the position of chief justice of the Constitutional Court. Zuma had previously attempted to extend the appointment of the sitting chief justice, an action that was ruled unconstitutional.

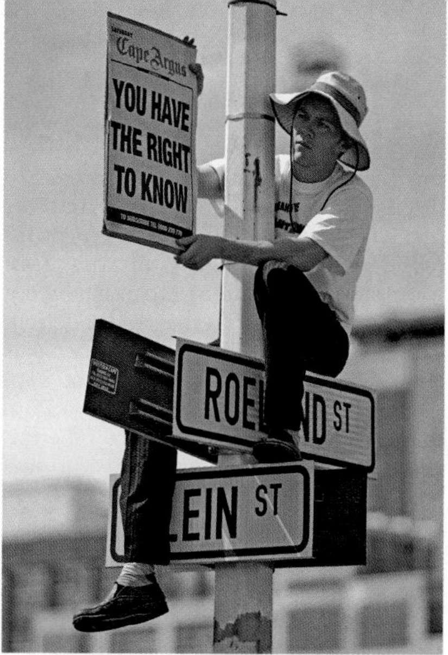

On September 17 a man perched atop a street sign in Cape Town demonstrates his opposition to the South African Parliament's protection of information bill. The bill's detractors contended it would erode freedom of speech and transparency in government.
Schalk van Zuydam/AP

In August the ANC Youth League's president, Julius Malema, was charged for the second time by the ANC for bringing the organization into disrepute. He was also charged with sowing intolerance and provoking divisions within the ANC. A disciplinary hearing was held, and in November Malema, along with other youth leaders, was suspended from the ANCYL. He appealed the decision.

The ANC Youth League was also in the news when it called for nationalization of the mines, banks, and other big companies at its national congress in June. The call was supported by the Congress of South African Trade Unions (COSATU), which was part of the Tripartite Alliance with the ANC and the South African Communist Party. Spokespersons for the ANC, however, insisted that nationalization was not the policy of government.

The debate continued on a controversial protection of information bill that had been introduced to Parliament in 2010. Opposition parties, civil society organs, and even some senior ANC members said that the bill threatened freedom of speech. It was, however, passed by the National Assembly in November and was due to be considered by the other chamber of Parliament, the National Council of Provinces, in 2012.

A record number of working days (more than 27 million) were lost as a result of strikes that broke out in midyear. Striking employees included those in the metal, mine, food, petroleum, engineering, packaging, catering, and municipal industries.

Economy. The economy grew by 2.8% in 2010 and by 4.5% in the fourth quarter. In the first quarter of 2011, growth stood at 4.5%, but it slowed to 1.3% in the second quarter and was 1.4% in the third quarter. At the end of June, the governor of the Reserve Bank commented on the "fragility" of economic recovery, noting the contraction in the manufacturing sector in April 2011 and the continued slow pace of growth in the construction sector and in private-sector fixed capital formation.

Job creation was the central focus of the 2011 budget, with 100 billion rand direct spending on plans for employment and skills training. A youth job subsidy would be launched in April 2012, to be reviewed in three years. This was opposed by COSATU. There was tax relief of 8.1 billion rand. The 2011–12 budget deficit was projected at 5.3%.

Despite economic growth, the unemployment rate increased to 25.7% in the second quarter of 2011. It did decline slightly to 25% in the third quarter, but was still higher than the 24% unemployment rate of the fourth quarter of the previous year.

In January inflation was up slightly (3.7%) from December 2010 (3.5%), but by November it had increased to 6.1%. There was no change in the bank repurchase rate during the year.

Foreign Affairs. The South African government was accused of bending to the will of China when it failed to issue a visa for the Dalai Lama to visit South Africa in October. It was also alleged to have lent support to Muammar al-Qaddafi in Libya and the government of Syria, despite uprisings against their rule. While the United Nations and the African Union declared Alassane Ouattara the victor in the 2010 Côte d'Ivoire election, the South African government for a while appeared to be pushing for compromise between Ouattara and the former president, Laurent Gbagbo. On the occasion of the independence of South Sudan, President Zuma praised former president Thabo Mbeki for his role in ending the Sudanese conflict. In August the government committed 8 million rand for famine relief in Somalia.

(MARTIN LEGASSICK)

SPAIN

Area: 505,991 sq km (195,364 sq mi)
Population (2011 est.): 47,215,000
Capital: Madrid
Head of state: King Juan Carlos I
Head of government: Prime Ministers José Luis Rodríguez Zapatero and, from December 21, Mariano Rajoy

The economic crisis in the euro zone overshadowed all else in Spain throughout 2011. During the first half of the year, the optimists, led by the Socialist (PSOE) government, took a hopeful view as a result of a slight upturn in exports, a booming tourist season, and a reduction in the deficit that had been spurred by austerity measures introduced in 2010. Additional measures were spearheaded to bolster the public finances and prospects for medium-term growth. Those included congressional approval in June for a raise in the standard retirement age from 65 to 67 and a plan for adding flexibility to Spain's rigid collective-bargaining arrangements. Meanwhile, the forced merger of many of Spain's regionally based savings banks, which had been highly exposed to bad mortgage debts, helped somewhat to reinforce the banking system.

Any illusions of a swift recovery were shattered in the summer by the onset of the European sovereign-debt crisis. In August the stock and bond markets turned on Spain. The real threat of intervention by the EU or the IMF prompted the Socialists to introduce a constitutional cap on the public deficit. The measure, which in September was rushed through Congress with the support of the conservative opposition Popular Party (PP), was rejected by the minority parties and by unions but was welcomed by the EU and the markets, particularly as the latter's attention briefly turned away from Spain. Nevertheless, in November Spain moved back into the spotlight, and interest rates on new government bond issues hit 7%, the level that had forced the Irish, Greek, and Portuguese bailouts. With 0% growth in the third quarter, unemployment topping 21%, and youth unemployment running at a staggering 46%, there was still no light at the end of what promised to be a very long tunnel.

In those circumstances the Socialists' fumbling response to the crisis only hastened their demise. The regional (in 13 of Spain's 17 autonomous communities) and local elections held on May 22 signaled the beginning of the end. The PSOE took just 27.8% of the vote nationally and was left in power in just two regions where elections had not taken place (the Basque Country and Andalusia). With 37.6% of the vote, the PP obtained its best results ever and was positioned to govern, alone or in coalition, in 11 autonomous communities.

The PSOE was not helped by the sudden appearance of the so-called *indignados* ("angry ones"), also known as the 15-M movement, which was inspired by the popular uprisings of the Arab Spring. On May 15, less than a week prior to the local and regional elections, the 15-M occupied squares throughout Spain in an ill-defined protest against the economic and political system and all its failings. Though the demonstrator camps had been dismantled by the summer, on October 15 the 15-M brought hundreds of thousands of protesters onto the streets of some 80 towns and cities across the country. Given the left-wing leanings of most of the activists, the antiestablishment rhetoric and calls to boycott from within the 15-M further undermined the Socialists' electoral support.

In July, Prime Minister José Luis Zapatero, who in April had confirmed that he would not stand for a third term, announced that early general elections would take place on November 20. The race pitted veteran Socialist strongman Alfredo Pérez Rubalcaba against the PP's lacklustre leader, Mariano Rajoy, who was running for the third time.

The downbeat election campaign ended in an expected PP victory. By capturing nearly 45% of the vote and a comfortable overall majority of 186 of the 350 seats in Congress, Rajoy secured the parliamentary support and popular mandate necessary to push through his plans, even though he was vague about their nature. It was a victory by default, due above all to the PSOE's collapse; the Socialists' 110 seats and less than 29% share of the vote represented their worst result since the return in 1977 to democracy. The PSOE vote went to the PP but above all to nationalists and other minority parties, including the centrist Progress and Democracy Union (UPD), up from 1 seat in 2008 to 5, and the left-wing United Left (IU), up from 2 seats to 11.

Overshadowed by the economic meltdown, the declarations on January 10 of a permanent, general, and verifiable cease-fire and on October 20 of "the complete cessation of armed activity" by Euskadi Ta Askatasuna (ETA) offered the prospect of a definitive end to the organization's 40-year armed struggle for Basque independence. After nearly 850 deaths and a dozen broken cease-fires, many Spaniards remained skeptical, but others considered that ETA—facing a decimation of its ranks due to arrests and flagging support by members tired of the violence—was, however reluctantly, committed to peace. (JUSTIN BYRNE)

Young people in Madrid protest against the poor condition of the Spanish economy, April 7. The youth unemployment rate in Spain topped 40% during the year.

Andres Kudacki/AP

SRI LANKA

Area: 65,610 sq km (25,332 sq mi)
Population (2011 est.): 21,045,000
Capitals: Colombo (executive and judicial); Sri Jayewardenepura Kotte (legislative)
Head of state and government: President Mahinda Rajapakse, assisted by Prime Minister D.M. Jayaratne

In 2011 Sri Lanka continued to recover from its 26-year civil war, which had ended in 2009. Pres. Mahinda Rajapakse enjoyed great popularity among the majority Sinhalese community for having defeated the Tamil Tigers (Liberation Tigers of Tamil Eelam; LTTE). As expected, the United People's Freedom Alliance, led by Rajapakse, dominated local government elections held in March and July. Predominantly Tamil areas formerly held by the LTTE in the north and east of the country voted for the Tamil National Alliance.

During 2011 the president moved to consolidate political power (much of it held by members of his family) in the executive branch of government while placing limits on media freedom, the role of civil society in Sri Lankan politics, and the expression of antigovernment dissent. In August it was announced that emergency regulations in place for nearly three decades were being lifted, but this still left many powers in government hands and failed to allay fears of repression among some Sri Lankans.

International attention was directed throughout the year toward alleged violations of human rights in Sri Lanka. A highly critical report submitted to the UN Human Rights Council in September charged that both the LTTE and government forces deliberately targeted civilians during the civil war. The government refused to permit an international investigation into human rights violations in Sri Lanka, and in October it announced the creation of a National Action Plan designed to protect and promote human rights and support reconciliation between the communities.

Economic growth in Sri Lanka, which had continued throughout the war period, slowed in 2009 because of the global recession but then accelerated rapidly. GDP was expected to rise by at least 8% in 2011, despite floods in January that displaced more than a million people and damaged rice and other crops. Major economic issues included continued poverty, employment creation and skill provision, the reconstruction of war-damaged areas, a large deficit in the government budget, and persistent inflation. Nevertheless, an IMF mission to Sri Lanka in August–September pronounced macroeconomic conditions there satisfactory and stated that monetary and fiscal policies were appropriate. Yet many believed that to sustain high growth rates in the future, significant policy reforms would be required. Foreign aid and remittances from Sri Lankan workers employed abroad were important sources of foreign exchange. Foreign direct investment was rising, but a conference held in September suggested that fears regarding political risk were holding back that investment.

(DONALD SNODGRASS)

SUDAN

Area: 1,844,797 sq km (712,280 sq mi)
Population (2011 est.): 36,787,000, including about 300,000 refugees in Chad
Capital: Khartoum
Head of state and government: President Omar Hassan Ahmad al-Bashir

In Sudan, 2011 was dominated by the secession of its southern region in July. Despite considerable apprehension, Sudan abided by the terms of the 2005 Comprehensive Peace Agreement (CPA) and accepted the overwhelming majority vote of the South Sudanese for secession in the January referendum. The Sudanese president, Omar al-Bashir, attended the July 9 independence day celebrations in Juba, the new country's capital, and the swearing in of Salva Kiir Mayardit (*see* BIOGRAPHIES), its new president. Once the formalities were over, however, both countries faced the difficult task of settling unresolved issues, principally those of oil revenue, water resources, borders, and debt. (*See* Sidebar on page 466.)

Southern Sudanese independence had profound implications for Sudan's politics, economy, and security. Its success in gaining autonomy weakened the power of Sudan's ruling National Congress Party. Key opposition parties—the Ummah Party, the Popular Congress Party, and the Sudanese Communist Party—pushed for increased political and economic reform, inspired by the Arab Spring revolts in North Africa and the Middle East and underscored by frequent demonstrations against inflation and high prices. In May the government established a consultative committee on constitutional reforms.

Rebel militias in Southern Kordofan and Blue Nile states, often led by the Sudan People's Liberation Movement–North (SPLM–N), stepped up activities against the Khartoum government. Alluding to the obvious connection to the SPLM-led government of South Sudan, the opposition referred to them as the "New South." As in the earlier case of Darfur, the Khartoum government launched a brutal campaign to quell resistance in those states, deploying air bombardment, tanks, and sophisticated weaponry. By December more than 400,000 people had been displaced, with many fleeing into the Nuba Mountains, South Sudan, and Ethiopia.

In July the Khartoum government and one of Darfur's rebel groups, the Liberation and Justice Movement, signed the Darfur Peace Agreement. Other Darfur rebel groups refused to sign, however. In November the SPLM–N and three of the refusing groups, including the powerful Justice and Equality Movement (JEM), said that they had formed an alliance to overthrow the government. In late December JEM leader Khalil Ibrahim was killed by the Sudanese army.

Meanwhile, Sudan faced the task of restructuring its political and economic landscape. A major problem concerned recovery from the loss of its oil wealth. Three-quarters of the oil that had hitherto fueled its prosperity derived from the south. Under the 2005 CPA the two Sudans had shared equally the revenue generated from southern oil, but under the new order northern policy makers calculated a 36% shortfall in their budget. They expected to replace much of this through negotiations concerning South Sudan payments for access to the north's pipelines, refineries, and export terminal. Further, policy makers renewed emphasis on agriculture, which accounted for one-third of the GNP and supported more than two-thirds of the population. They also focused on increasing mining. Gold was the second most valuable export. The surge in world prices had spurred a gold rush in some remote desert areas.

(LARAY DENZER)

The Challenges Confronting South Sudan

On July 9, 2011, South Sudan seceded from Sudan after having fought two civil wars (1955–72 and 1983–2005) and having engaged in years of negotiations. Although South Sudan's declaration of independence was met with much celebration and international recognition, attention was also focused on the many challenges facing the nascent country.

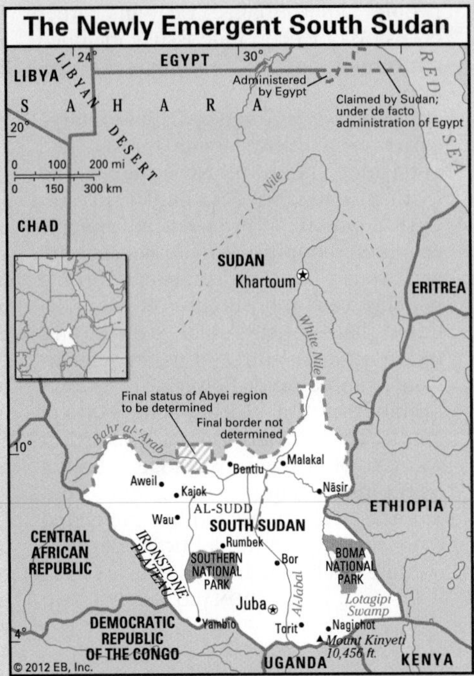

The region of South Sudan declared its independence from the rest of Sudan on July 9.

Internal Security. The leaders of rebel militias (between 7 and 12) operating within South Sudan had fought in or beside the Sudan People's Liberation Army (SPLA) during the second civil war against Sudan. Some of them had lost electoral contests, while others viewed rebellion as a strategic career move. At independence their followers flaunted brand-new weapons, uniforms, and boots, believed to have arrived from Sudan. Typically, a militia was based in a specific state and was composed of a specific ethnic group. One of the most important militias was the South Sudan Liberation Army (SSLA), based in Unity state and made up mostly of Nuer (the second largest ethnic group) rebels who resented the dominance of the Dinka, the largest ethnic group. Such militias had great potential for destabilizing the new government.

Border Disputes and Displaced Persons. Several issues remained unresolved at the time of independence. By year's end Sudan had undertaken military action in several places, including the disputed Abyei region and two South Sudanese border states, Unity and Upper Nile. All were oil-producing regions and gateways for refugees or returning displaced persons. Nearly 200,000 people of southern origin had returned from the north, with the potential that many more would follow, which put pressure on already limited resources.

Resource Dependence. Although presecession Sudan had exported billions of dollars' worth of oil annually, the region that became South Sudan had produced more than 80% of it but had received only 50% of the revenue. The pipelines, however, ran north, where the refineries and port facilities were located. Renegotiation of the modalities for sharing future oil wealth was bitter and remained unsettled. Moreover, more than 95% of South Sudan's revenue was derived from oil, which made it necessary for the country to begin to develop policies for the diversification of the economy.

Corruption. Although a stand-alone ranking for doing business in South Sudan did not exist for 2011, Transparency International had ranked presecession Sudan as one of the world's most corrupt states: 172nd out of 178. Observers noted that corruption was endemic throughout the government and society. That was exacerbated by ethnicity, for a high proportion of the official positions were filled by Dinka, which prompted deep resentment among the many other ethnic groups.

Poverty, Poor Health Infrastructure, and Low Education Levels. South Sudan placed near the bottom of the UN Human Development Index, as 51% of the people lived below the poverty line and 78% earned their livelihoods through agriculture or animal husbandry without much aid from modern technology. Health indicators were very low. Infant mortality was high: one in 10 children died in its first year, and one in 7 children died before the age of five. Maternal mortality was among the highest in the world, with one out of seven pregnant women likely to die from pregnancy-related causes. In addition, about 80% of medical care was provided by international aid groups. Another problem stemmed from a lack of education. Only 27% of the population over the age of 15 was literate, with a 40% literacy rate for males and a 16% rate for females.

(LARAY DENZER)

SUDAN, SOUTH

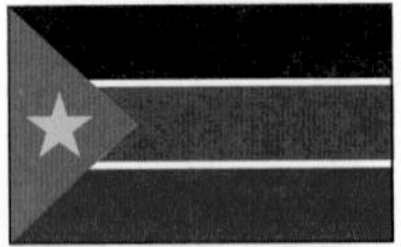

Area: 644,330 sq km (248,777 sq mi)
Population: (2011 est.): 9,150,000
Capital: Juba
Head of state and government: President Salva Kiir Mayardit

South Sudan raised its flag as Africa's newest independent country on July 9, 2011. That ended more than a century of struggle against alien rule, first by the British from the 1890s and then by the government of independent Sudan from 1956. The fight for independence involved two hard-fought civil wars (1955–72 and 1983–2005), resulting in an estimated 2.5 million casualties. The Comprehensive Peace Agreement, which concluded military hostilities in 2005, laid the groundwork for power sharing, with a separate government in the south, and specified a popular referendum at the beginning of 2011 to determine if the south desired complete political autonomy. In January a 99% vote for secession left no doubt about the wishes of the people.

South Sudan continued under the rule of the Sudan People's Liberation Movement (SPLM), the majority political party that had emerged from the

Thomas Mukoya—Reuters/Landov

A crowd in Juba, South Sudan, cheers as a statue of John Garang, the South Sudanese rebel leader and politician, is unveiled during independence celebrations, July 9.

rebel army that fought the second civil war. Unfortunately, the young country faced a fragile future and numerous challenges. (*See* Sidebar.) South Sudan ranked among the poorest countries on the UN Human Development Index, lacking basic infrastructure, education and social-welfare systems, and a skilled modern labour force. Endemic corruption and interethnic rivalry raised questions about transparency in governance and internal stability. In addition, the government inherited a series of disputes with Sudan that had been left unresolved in the rush for political autonomy.

At the heart of those disputes were oil and national boundaries. Oil accounted for more than 95% of South Sudan's revenue and, prior to secession, some 75% of Sudan's. Signs of future trouble occurred even before secession when in May Sudanese troops forcibly occupied the Abyei region, an oil-producing borderland area and a gateway for southward-bound refugees from conflict areas in Sudan that was claimed by both Sudan and South Sudan. In November the Sudan Armed Forces (SAF) bombed a number of sites in South Sudan's Unity and Upper Nile states, both oil-producing areas. Some analysts believed that this was a strategic move by SAF generals to push Sudan's borders south and regain control of oil-producing areas. In the meantime, international nongovernmental organizations reported the attacks, the UN called for an investigation, the South Sudanese government asked for the establishment of a no-fly zone, and Sudan adamantly denied any military incursion or other interference.

(LARAY DENZER)

SURINAME

Area: 163,820 sq km (63,251 sq mi)
Population (2011 est.): 529,000
Capital: Paramaribo
Head of state and government: President Dési Bouterse, assisted by Prime Minister Robert Ameerali

Former dictator and convicted narcotics trafficker Dési Bouterse completed a full year as the president of Suriname in 2011, which proved to be less disastrous than many observers had expected. The president's unwieldy 14-party multiethnic governing coalition held together, albeit precariously, with control of 36 of the 51 seats in the legislature. GDP grew by 4%. The independent central bank imposed fiscal austerity measures, which helped to cushion the negative impact of inexperienced cabinet ministers and rising inflation. The modest macroeconomic success owed much to the robust price of gold.

Bouterse benefited from the continued suspension of his trial for the murder of 15 political opponents in 1982. His unsavory past and questions about his willingness to curb organized crime, however, softened the confidence of international donors and investors. China was a principal exception, increasing its engagement in Surinamese infrastructure, gold mining, and petroleum exploration. Chinese interests included bauxite, despite the depletion of that resource. Suriname was less afflicted by violence than neighbouring Guyana but retained its reputation as a major route for narcotics moving to Europe via West Africa.

After several tense years, relations improved with Guyana. Planning was initiated to build a bridge over the Courantyne River, which would be the first road linkage between the two countries.

(JOHN W. GRAHAM)

SWAZILAND

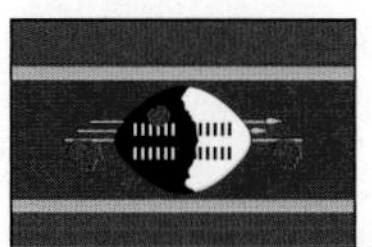

Area: 17,364 sq km (6,704 sq mi)
Population (2011 est.): 1,203,000
Capitals: Mbabane (administrative and judicial); Lobamba (legislative)
Head of state: King Mswati III, assisted by Prime Minister Barnabas Sibusiso Dlamini

Swaziland faced serious financial challenges in 2011 that resulted in cash-flow problems for all government ministries as well as the state-supported University of Swaziland. In response to these pecuniary woes, the newly operational Swaziland Revenue Authority began its efforts to become "a highly efficient and modern revenue collection agency." The financial situation grew worse, however, and in November the IMF declared that it was critical.

In January Sam Mkhombe, King Mswati III's private secretary, and Mathendele Dlamini, a member of the king's Advisory Council, were dismissed for allegedly having attempted to revive the Imbokodvo National Movement. On April 12 a rally held to demand democratic and economic reforms was contained by Swazi security forces.

Lawyers boycotted the courts from August to November because of what they saw as judicial irregularities in the suspension and dismissal of High

Court Judge Thomas Masuku for his alleged criticism of the king. Moreover, in October Minister for Justice and Constitutional Affairs David Matse was also sacked for his alleged refusal to endorse Masuku's dismissal. Despite the ongoing suppression of political activity and nonrecognition of political parties, former trade union leader Jan Sithole launched a new party, the Swaziland Democratic Party (SWADEPA), in September.

Food and energy prices steadily increased. Unemployment and poverty, like corruption, remained a major challenge. The HIV/AIDS prevalence rate still stood at 26%.

(NHLANHLA DLAMINI)

SWEDEN

Area: 450,295 sq km (173,860 sq mi)
Population (2011 est.): 9,451,000
Capital: Stockholm
Head of state: King Carl XVI Gustaf
Head of government: Prime Minister Fredrik Reinfeldt

Sweden entered 2011 with a strong economic rebound as its GDP grew by about 5% in the first half of the year. Most economic forecasters had speculated that the country would recover swiftly from the financial crisis of 2008–09; however, the European sovereign debt crisis that had so adversely afflicted Greece, Portugal, and Ireland, as well as Spain and Italy, also had consequences for Sweden. By the autumn Sweden's bright economic prospects seemed to have dimmed considerably, yet GDP still grew by 4.6% year-on-year in the third quarter. In its budget for 2012, the centre-right government led by Prime Minister Fredrik Reinfeldt predicted that economic growth would slow considerably, from 4.1% in 2011 to only 1.3% in the coming year—less than half the growth that was previously expected.

Sweden enjoyed strong public finances, and at 40% of GDP its national debt was among the lowest in Europe (the EU average was 80% of GDP). Thus, while the country needed neither budget cuts nor other drastic measures to bolster its own economy, it could not escape the economic turmoil elsewhere, especially in Europe, which remained the main export market for Swedish manufactures. Finance Minister Anders Borg repeatedly warned that Sweden's situation might worsen, contingent upon European developments. In an effort to prepare for the worst, the government decided to postpone promised tax relief for wage earners and retirees in order to save ammunition should the economy need more stimulus later.

In the absence of an absolute majority, Reinfeldt's coalition government kept a relatively low profile in 2011. It favoured political compromises where necessary, as in the matter of the nature of Swedish participation in the NATO military efforts to protect the rebels engaged in the overthrow of Muammar al-Qaddafi in Libya. After strong demands from the leading opposition party, the Swedish Social Democratic Party (SAP), Sweden did not allow its Gripen jet fighters to participate in bombing missions and instead restricted their participation to reconnaissance flights.

Having lost consecutive general elections in 2006 and 2010, after decades as Sweden's ruling party, the SAP chose Hakan Juholt as its new leader in spring of 2011. Juholt set his sights on challenging Reinfeldt in the next general election, scheduled for 2014, but the new leader's credibility received a strong blow in the autumn when it was disclosed that during his tenure as an MP, he had received housing allowances from the Riksdag (parliament) for which he was not qualified. Issues related to his personal conduct also emerged to spark public fury against him, create strong tensions within his party, and raise the prospect that Juholt might be forced from his post early in his short tenure. Swedes were also shocked and deeply moved by the tragedy in July in neighbouring Norway surrounding the attack on the Labour Party's youth camp on the island of Utöya, where dozens were killed. Hitherto Scandinavians had felt that they lived in a peaceful part of the world where such horrific actions had been almost impossible to imagine.

In happier news, the future of the popular Swedish monarchy seemed to be assured by the announcement that Crown Princess Victoria and Prince Daniel, who were married in 2010, were expecting their first child in March 2012. Sports-minded Swedes were relieved when the national association football (soccer) team finally qualified for the 2012 European Championship by beating the Netherlands in the last and decisive qualification match.

(MARTIN HAAG)

SWITZERLAND

Area: 41,285 sq km (15,940 sq mi)
Population (2011 est.): 7,913,000
Capital: Bern
Head of state and government: President Micheline Calmy-Rey

Parliamentary elections in October 2011 halted the advance of the nationalist Swiss People's Party (SVP), which for two decades had wooed increasing numbers of voters in Switzerland with its anti-European and antiforeigner rhetoric in a country in which about one-quarter of the people were immigrants. The SVP won 26.6% of the vote in the House of Representatives. This was down 2.4% from its 2007 record result and dashed its ambition of breaking the 30% barrier, but it was still well ahead of the left-of-centre Social Democrats and two other centrist parties. All of the established parties lost ground to two newcomers, the Conservative Democrats (a moderate breakaway faction of the SVP) and the Liberal Greens, both of which picked up 5.4% of the vote. The SVP failed in its target of regaining a second seat on the seven-member Federal Council, which it had lost when a former representative switched to the Conservative Democrats.

Switzerland, which was not a member of the EU, was spared the acute financial crises elsewhere on the continent. Swiss exports and key economic sectors such as tourism were battered by the strengthening of the Swiss franc, which became a safe haven from the euro zone's debt crisis and stock-market turmoil. The Swiss franc had gained about 25% in value against the euro and the dollar over the previous four years—a trend that accelerated during 2011.

The parliament in September approved a package of financial measures to inject 870 million Swiss francs (about $1 billion) into the economy to cushion vulnerable sectors of the economy and jobs. The measure came in August after the Swiss National Bank moved to halt the "massive overvaluation" of the franc by setting a minimum exchange rate target of 1.20 Swiss francs to the euro. (The franc nearly touched parity with the euro in early August.) The State Secretariat for Economic Affairs reduced its GDP growth forecast for 2011 from 2.1% to 1.9% and predicted that growth would be below 1% in 2012.

Financial markets were jolted in September by revelations that UBS, Switzerland's biggest bank, had lost about $2.3 billion owing to rogue dealing by Kweku Adoboli, a trader in the bank's London-based investment unit. CEO Oswald Gruebel, who had done much to turn UBS around in the previous two years, stood down as a result of the scandal.

Switzerland continued to make progress in shaking off its reputation as a tax haven by exchanging tax data with other countries. It managed to stay off the Organisation for Economic Co-operation and Development's "grey list" of uncooperative countries, although an international review of its performance found that there was still room for improvement to greater transparency. Following a 2009 settlement in which UBS paid $780 million to settle a U.S. Department of Justice complaint, U.S. authorities increased their pressure on other Swiss banks to hand over the names of American clients who were accused of evading taxes at home by hiding their assets offshore.

In an effort to prove that it was no longer a refuge for dictators' ill-gotten gains, Switzerland moved rapidly during the "Arab Spring" to freeze assets belonging to the erstwhile leaders of Tunisia, Egypt, and Libya. The historically neutral country also aligned itself with the EU to impose sanctions against Syria.

The disaster at the Fukushima power plant resulting from the massive earthquake and tsunami in Japan was the decisive factor in Switzerland's long-running debate about nuclear energy. Both houses of the parliament voted to shut down Swiss nuclear power plants by 2034 and to boost renewable-energy resources—while leaving a loophole for the parliament to revisit the issue later. Approximately 40% of the country's energy needs were supplied by five domestic nuclear power plants.

(CLARE KAPP)

SYRIA

Area: 185,180 sq km (71,498 sq mi)
Population (2011 est.): 22,262,000 (including some 1,000,000 Iraqi refugees and nearly 500,000 long-term Palestinian refugees)
Capital: Damascus
Head of state and government: President Bashar al-Assad, assisted by Prime Ministers Muhammad Naji al-Otari and, from April 14, Adel Safar

Large-scale popular unrest shook Syria throughout 2011. In late January troops moved into Kurdish districts of Aleppo to preclude antiregime demonstrations. Small protests by activists were broken up in Damascus in February. Security forces dispersed a crowd gathered in front of the Interior Ministry on March 16, sparking a protest in central Damascus. These events were eclipsed by the uprising that broke out in Dar'a a week later. Fighting quickly spread to Latakia and Hamah. Government officials blamed the unrest on criminal gangs in the south and Palestinian militants in the northwest and deployed armoured units to restore order. Nevertheless, violence erupted in the countryside outside Damascus at the end of March.

As clashes escalated, former minister of agriculture Adel Safar was appointed prime minister. Violence erupted in the oil port of Baniyas in early April. By mid-April the industrial city of Hims had emerged as the centre of antiregime activity. Even as the security forces deployed snipers to pick off leaders of the Hims protests, the government made a few conciliatory gestures, including the announcement of the abolition of the emergency law and the state security court, two key sources of popular anger. State officials also charged that Islamist radicals were responsible for the continuing disorders.

Early June saw renewed unrest in Hamah, Idlib, Rastan, and Jisr al-Shughur. A massive military assault on Jisr al-Shughur sent refugees streaming across the border into Turkey. Troops then enveloped Hamah, where on July 3 Ibrahim Qashush, a local poet whose anthems had inspired protesters across the country, was kidnapped and killed. A month later tanks occupied the city, prompting a condemnation from the United Nations Security Council. Assad responded by issuing a decree authorizing the formation of opposition political parties.

In August masked men seized the cartoonist 'Ali Farzat and severely beat him after he published a drawing in which Assad appeared to be asking Muammar al-Qaddafi for a ride out of town. Russian Foreign Minister Sergey Lavrov told reporters on September 3 that the Syrian government needed more time to carry out reforms, and on October 4 Russia joined with China in vetoing a Security Council resolution that condemned the Syrian government for egregious human rights violations. Also in late September, reports of clashes between Syrian government

Wearing T-shirts emblazoned with a demand that Pres. Bashar al-Assad be executed, demonstrators march through the streets of Idlib, Syria, September 23.

Reuters/Landov

forces and armed opposition groups began to emerge, raising the prospect of a civil war.

On November 2 the Syrian government accepted an Arab League plan calling for the withdrawal of security forces from cities, the release of prisoners, and the deployment of a delegation of Arab League monitors in Syria. Bloodshed in Syria continued in spite of the agreement, causing the Arab League to vote to suspend Syria's membership.

Following a threat by Arab countries to take the matter to the UN Security Council, the Syrian government agreed in December to allow Arab League monitors into the country. Although the monitors arrived in Syria in late December, violence continued. (FRED H. LAWSON)

Pichi Chuang—Reuters/Landov

On June 28, days after the Taiwanese government lifted a prohibition on visits to the country by individuals from mainland China, Chinese tourists hold aloft gift packages presented to them by the government of Taipei upon their arrival at the city's airport.

TAIWAN (REPUBLIC OF CHINA)

Area: 36,191 sq km (13,973 sq mi)
Population (2011 est.): 23,190,000
Capital: Taipei
Head of state: President Ma Ying-jeou
Head of government: President of the Executive Yuan (Premier) Wu Den-yih

In April 2011 the Democratic Progressive Party (DPP) nominated Tsai Ying-wen as its candidate for Taiwan's presidential election scheduled for Jan. 14, 2012. Tsai, the first woman to run for president in Taiwan and in East Asia, was to face incumbent Ma Ying-jeou of the Nationalist Party, or Kuomintang (KMT). Her platform attempted to appeal to middle-of-the-road voters by stressing domestic social issues with a strong emphasis on growing economic inequality in one of the world's most equitable societies. Concerning relations with China, Tsai argued that Taiwan was becoming overly dependent on China, and she sought to replace the KMT's 1992 Consensus on One China policy with a broadly defined "Taiwan consensus."

The KMT nominated Ma Ying-jeou and selected Premier Wu Den-yih, a native Taiwanese, as his running mate. Ethnic issues once again came to the fore in the campaign, with Tsai emphasizing her Hakka and aboriginal Taiwanese ethnic heritage in contrast to Ma, whose parents were KMT refugees from China. Ma's platform focused on his achievements in building relations with China and his successes in cleaning up corruption. After Ma suggested that he might sign a peace treaty with China if elected to a second term, polls showed Tsai in a statistical dead heat with him. Yet another variable in the election was James Soong, a renegade KMT politician who had nearly won the 2000 election and who entered the 2012 race in November.

In August jailed former president Chen Shui-bian was given an additional two years on one of his corruption convictions. He was sentenced to 18 more years in October in another case.

Although security was a major topic during the election campaign, the economy was the central issue for voters. Taiwan's GDP grew by an estimated 4.4% in 2011, but the economy showed clear signs of cooling in the second half of the year in response to the European debt crisis and political uncertainty. Unemployment stayed above 4%. Those figures were at the heart of Ma's political difficulties in the campaign, since in the 2008 campaign he had promised to achieve an annual GDP growth rate of 6% and to reduce unemployment to less than 3% by improving relations with China.

The crowning achievement of Ma's China policy had been the Economic Cooperation Framework Agreement (ECFA), signed with China in 2010. Although Taiwan's exports under the ECFA increased by $11.8 billion (14.4% annually) in the first half of 2011, that rate was lower than the 17.5% annual increase reached in 2006–08 before the global financial downturn.

The New Taiwan dollar traded at or slightly below NT$30 per U.S. dollar throughout 2011 as the central bank mobilized Taiwan's vast foreign currency reserves to stabilize a market buffeted by turbulence in the European economy. Taiwan held approximately $400 billion in foreign currency reserves by the end of the year.

Chinese tourism to Taiwan held steady at more than 1.2 million arrivals in 2011. Independent travel for Chinese nationals from Beijing, Shanghai, and Xiamen was also liberalized in June. In September Chinese students were allowed to enroll as full-time degree students in Taiwan.

Taiwan needed to attract the additional Chinese students because it was reported in August that Taiwan's fertility rate for 2010 had dropped to 0.9 birth per woman, the lowest in the world. The government blamed the drop on the inauspiciousness of that year on the Chinese calendar, but the rate had been declining for years.

As Taiwan prepared for the 2012 election, President Ma's government gingerly tried to step away from China by signaling Taiwan's willingness to join the U.S.-proposed Trans-Pacific Partnership pact. At the same time, economic ties between Taiwan and China hit a sticking point when the two sides were unable to reach an agreement on investor protection after several rounds of negotiations. The U.S., meanwhile, announced arms sales to Taiwan worth $5.85 billion, including upgrades for Taiwan's aging fighter jets. In addition, Ma paid a symbolic visit to an exhibition by dissident Chinese artist Ai Weiwei in Taipei. Ma's visit was intended to show his support for greater freedoms in China.

In September one of Taiwan's leading filmmakers, Wei Te-sheng, released his two-part epic *Seediq Bale*. It depicted a bloody uprising of aboriginal Taiwanese against Japanese colonial rule in 1930. (MICHAEL R. FAHEY)

TAJIKISTAN

Area: 143,100 sq km (55,300 sq mi)
Population (2011 est.): 7,681,000
Capital: Dushanbe
Head of state: President Imomali Rakhmon
Head of government: Prime Minister Akil Akilov

The government of Tajikistan's heavy-handed dealings with the country's Muslim community, which included most of the population, continued in 2011, ostensibly intended to prevent the growth of extremism. The Islamic Renaissance Party of Tajikistan (IRPT)—the only legal religious party in Central Asia—continued to warn that government measures were frequently counterproductive. In the summer two pieces of legislation restricting freedom of religion were approved by the parliament and signed by Pres. Imomali Rakhmon, despite warnings in the independent media and from opposition parliamentarians that one of the laws, which restricted young people's participation in religious communities, would be unenforceable. At the end of August, police reportedly were overzealous in enforcing the new law, preventing persons under age 18 from attending end of Ramadan services in mosques, although the law permitted participation in religious festivals.

In 2010 young people studying at religious schools abroad had been ordered home by Rakhmon himself, with the promise that they could continue their religious education in Tajikistan. In July 2011, however, worried officials in the southern Khatlon region noted that returnees were encountering difficulties finding jobs or continuing their religious education.

Tajikistan's relations with Russia intensified during the year, reaching a high point during a Commonwealth of Independent States (CIS) summit at the beginning of September with an agreement on a Russian military presence in Tajikistan for the next 49 years. In lieu of rent for the facilities used by Russian forces, Tajikistan was to receive military technology and training. Russian authorities were eager for Russian border troops to return to the Tajik border, but despite pressure from Moscow, Tajikistan resisted the Russian proposals.

Iran also was eager to intensify relations with Persian-speaking Tajikistan. In September, Iranian Pres. Mahmoud Ahmadinejad formally opened the Iranian-financed Sangtuda-2 power plant, which would make a huge contribution to solving Tajikistan's energy problems.

Independent journalists continued to be harassed by the authorities. The arrest of BBC correspondent Urinboy Usmonov in June on charges that he was a member of an extremist organization because he interviewed persons associated with the banned Hizb ut-Tahrir caused an international outcry. He was sentenced to three years in jail but was given amnesty. In early October journalist Mahmadyusuf Ismoilov was convicted on charges of defamation arising from his having written articles in the independent weekly *Nuri Zindagi* that revealed high-level corruption in the Sughd Region. He was ordered to pay a fine and banned from practicing journalism for three years. (BESS BROWN)

TANZANIA

Area: 945,090 sq km (364,901 sq mi)
Population (2011 est.): 45,030,000
De facto capital: Dar es Salaam; only the legislature meets in Dodoma, the longtime planned capital
Head of state and government: President Jakaya Kikwete, assisted by Prime Minister Mizengo Pinda

Tanzania retained its reputation in 2011 as one of Africa's most stable governments. Though Pres. Jakaya Kikwete and the ruling party, the Revolutionary Party of Tanzania (CCM), controlled politics, internal dissension developed in the party leadership. Kikwete's 2010 electoral victory, however, allowed him to initiate a more-vigorous campaign for reform and liberalization in his final term in office. His new cabinet agreed with his general policy concerning infrastructure development, economic diversification, and anticorruption. In addition, a government of national unity was created that crafted an acceptable compromise with the new Zanzibari president, Ali Mohammed Shein, who shared Kikwete's political outlook.

Meanwhile, political opposition became more vocal. The main opposition party, the Party for Democracy and Progress (Chadema), gained new strength in the 2010 elections. Its demand for a new constitution, however, was preempted by the CCM, which established a Constitutional Review Commission mandated to outline a reform agenda. Throughout 2011 occasional violent clashes between protesters and police disrupted the political scene. In January Chadema claimed that five people had been killed in a protest in the northern city of Arusha, although the government maintained that there were only three deaths. In November the police banned all demonstrations by opposition and government supporters alike when Chadema renewed demands for the release of its members arrested in Arusha as well as for the president's resignation.

Corruption remained a major issue. Transparency International's East African Bribery Index 2011 ranked Tanzania as the third most corrupt country in the region, behind Burundi and Uganda. Financial malfeasance was rampant in the police force, the judiciary and the courts, immigration services, government ministries, and other official bodies.

For five years the country's annual economic growth rate averaged 6.7%. The government sought to increase growth in an effort to reduce poverty, diversify the economy, and create new opportunities. Fundamental to implementing these objectives were initiatives to improve the electricity supply, further develop the Kilimo Kwanza (agriculture first) policy, expand the business sector, and widen the tax base. A new agreement was reached with gold-mining companies that established a 4% royalty tax; payments were expected by year's end. Tanzania ranked as the fourth largest gold producer in Africa.

Late in June environmentalists and the East African tourist industry breathed a sigh of relief when the government changed its plan to build a highway across the Serengeti National Park to a southern route from Serengeti to Mukoma. The initial northern route would have interfered with the Serengeti–Maasai Mara ecosystem, especially the wildebeest migration route, a major attraction to the region. Another boost to tourism was the announcement by a team of Dutch speleologists (cave experts) of a discovery of lava tunnels on Kibo, the largest volcano of Mt. Kilimanjaro.

(LARAY DENZER)

THAILAND

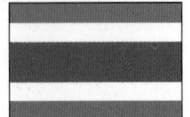

Area: 513,120 sq km (198,117 sq mi)
Population (2011 est.): 65,856,000
Capital: Bangkok
Head of state: King Bhumibol Adulyadej
Head of government: Prime Ministers Abhisit Vejjajiva and, from August 8, Yingluck Shinawatra

In Thailand the year 2011 centred on the general election held on July 3, following the dissolution in May of the National Assembly by unelected Prime Minister Abhisit Vejjajiva. The dissolution came a year after Abhisit's bloody crackdown on the antigovernment demonstration organized by the United Front for Democracy Against Dictatorship (UDD), popularly known as red shirts. The election involved a fierce contest between the ruling Democrat Party, led by Abhisit, and the largest opposition party, the For Thais Party (Phak Phuea Thai; PPT), led by Yingluck Shinawatra (*see* BIOGRAPHIES), the younger sister of former prime minister Thaksin Shinawatra. The PPT won a majority, sweeping seats in Thailand's rural north and northeast, where Thaksin had remained popular for policies he had implemented to benefit the poor while in office (2001–06). Subsequently, Yingluck, aged 44, formed a six-party coalition government and assumed office in August as Thailand's first female prime minister.

Although Yingluck won admiration for her striking beauty, she faced daunting challenges from the start. The Democrat Party, which moved into opposition, dismissed her for being a proxy for Thaksin and a political neophyte who had managerial experience only in her family's telecommunications companies. She vowed to achieve national reconciliation in Thailand, which had remained sharply divided along ideological and regional lines between the urban rich and the rural poor following the 2006 coup that ousted Thaksin. For anti-Thaksin Thais, however, her familial link to Thaksin (an alleged financier for the UDD) only complicated the reconciliation process. She came under heavy attack in August when Thaksin—in exile to escape imprisonment at home on corruption charges—traveled to Japan on a special visa arranged by Foreign Minister Surapong Towichukchaikul, a distant relative of the Shinawatras. The business community, meanwhile, openly opposed Yingluck's move to deliver on her populist campaign promises—to raise Thailand's minimum daily wage to 300 baht (about $10), set the starting monthly salary for university graduates at 15,000 baht (about $480), and distribute tablet computers to primary schoolchildren throughout Thailand.

The most urgent problem Yingluck faced was the catastrophic flood caused by heavy monsoon rains from July onward. The flood, reportedly the worst in half a century, inundated more than 60 of Thailand's 76 provinces and killed more than 650 people. Particularly hard hit was Ayutthaya province, a site of massive foreign investment located 80 km (50 mi) north of Bangkok. Many multinational corporations—vital earners of Thailand's foreign currency—were forced to suspend their operations. Transportation by road and rail was paralyzed. Yingluck ordered reinforcement of embankments in Bangkok to prevent the capital from being submerged. By December the floodwaters had largely subsided, and cleanup operations were under way.

On the diplomatic front, in September Yingluck paid her first official visit to Thailand's neighbour Cambodia. Ties between the two countries had been seriously strained since 2008, when Cambodia won UNESCO World Heritage site status for Preah Vihear, an ancient temple located along its border with Thailand. Troops from both sides clashed in February and again in April, and more than two dozen people were killed. Yingluck's visit, warmly welcomed by Cambodia, helped ease the tension.

(YOSHINORI NISHIZAKI)

On October 29 a Buddhist monk stands on sandbags at the Amarakire temple in Bangkok, which was engulfed in floodwaters following torrential rains throughout Thailand.

Sakchai Lalit/AP

TOGO

Area: 56,600 sq km (21,853 sq mi)
Population (2011 est.): 5,830,000
Capital: Lomé
Head of state: President Faure Gnassingbé, assisted by Prime Minister Gilbert Houngbo

In 2011 several people on trial for allegedly having plotted a coup in Togo

Ange Obafemi—Maxppp/Landov

Demonstrating against perceived government threats to press freedom, Togolese journalists march through the capital city of Lomé, August 6.

had their fates decided. On September 15 the Supreme Court sentenced Gen. Assani Tidjani, Maj. Abi Atti, and former defense minister Kpatcha Gnassingbé, the half brother of Pres. Faure Gnassingbé, to 20 years in prison for having planned a military coup in 2009. Twenty other suspects, including another half brother, Essolizam, were acquitted.

Relations with the news media remained tense as three independent radio stations were shut down for the first quarter of the year. On August 6 a group of journalists demonstrated in Lomé, calling for the preservation of press freedom. The magazine *Tribune d'Afrique*, banned from distribution in Togo following a libel suit brought by a third half brother of the president, Mey Gnassingbé, resumed sales on August 29 following a sharp reduction of its fine by an appeals court.

In late February ceremonies marked the agreement to construct two joint border posts between Togo and the neighbouring countries of Ghana to the west and Benin to the east. The project was sponsored jointly by the EU and the Economic and Monetary Union of West Africa and was designed to facilitate inter-African trade, leading eventually to a free-trade zone.

The Truth, Justice, and Reconciliation Commission, investigating the political violence that gripped Togo between 1958 and 2005, began hearings on September 7. More than 20,000 depositions had been taken by the commission.

(NANCY ELLEN LAWLER)

TONGA

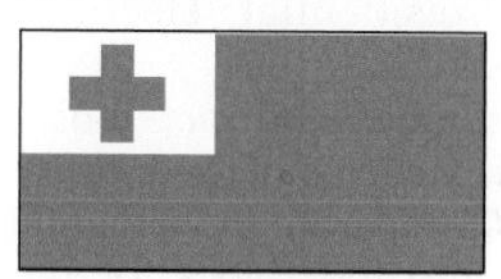

Area: 748 sq km (289 sq mi)
Population (2011 est.): 104,000
Capital: Nuku'alofa
Head of state: King Siaosi (George) Tupou V
Head of government: Prime Minister of Privy Council Tu'ivakano

The voters of Tonga showed continuing interest in and commitment to their new electoral system in 2011 following the first postreform general election in November 2010. In September 2011 the country's first by-election, held to fill a vacant seat from a Tongatapu constituency, had a 75% voter turnout and returned pro-democracy candidate Falisi Tupou, a journalist and member of the Democratic Party of the Friendly Islands. Much of the impetus for the transition to more-democratic government had come from the large Tongan diasporic population, whose remittances accounted for some two-fifths of Tonga's GDP.

In April a Tongan court found four people guilty of manslaughter for the deaths of 74 passengers in the 2009 sinking of the ferry *Princess Ashika*. Relations with Fiji became strained in May when the Tongan navy assisted Lieut. Col. Ratu Tevita Uluilakeba Mara, a senior Fijian soldier and a critic of the Fijian military government, as he fled Fiji by sea. Tonga denied Fiji's extradition petitions and provided Mara with a passport, which allowed him to travel through the region, criticizing the actions of the Fijian administration.

In October the government began the first phase of a plan to provide the country's high schools with solar power. The project, funded in part by aid from New Zealand, would reduce electricity bills and address the schools' annual power shortages.

(CLUNY MACPHERSON)

TRINIDAD AND TOBAGO

Area: 5,155 sq km (1,990 sq mi)
Population (2011 est.): 1,325,000
Capital: Port of Spain
Head of state: President George Maxwell Richards
Head of government: Prime Minister Kamla Persad-Bissessar

Against a backdrop of credit downgrades in the rest of the Caribbean in 2011, Standard & Poor's in January reaffirmed Trinidad and Tobago's A foreign-currency and its A+ local-currency long-term sovereign-credit ratings. In July Moody's Investor Service maintained its Baa1 rating on Trinidad and Tobago government bonds.

Trinidad and Tobago's economy continued to benefit significantly in 2011 from the country's successful exploitation of offshore natural gas deposits. In August, however, an annual audit revealed that in 2010 proven reserves were at 13.4 trillion cu ft, some 7% lower than the 2009 level, which prompted a desire for new exploration. In order to expedite the search for additional offshore gas reserves, the government in April had approved production-sharing contracts for four shallow-water blocks, three of which were located off Trinidad's north coast. In an effort to extend the search for oil and gas into a previously unexplored region, three deepwater blocks in the Atlantic Ocean off the east coast of Trinidad were also awarded in July.

In late August the government imposed a nationwide state of emergency (SOE), with nighttime curfews in so-called "crime hot spots." Earlier that month 11 people were murdered. The government said that this involved the temporary suspension of some human rights but asserted that the SOE was necessary to enable the police and military to crack down on criminal gangs. The SOE was further extended in September. (DAVID RENWICK)

TUNISIA

Area: 163,610 sq km (63,170 sq mi)
Population (2011 est.): 10,594,000
Capital: Tunis
Head of state: Presidents Gen. Zine al-Abidine Ben Ali, Fouad Mebazaa from January 15, and, from December 13, Moncef Marzouki
Head of government: Prime Ministers Mohamed Ghannouchi, Beji Caid Sebsi from February 27, and, from December 24, Hamadi Jebali

On December 13, one day after Tunisia's constituent assembly elected him president of the country, Moncef Marzouki—a human rights activist who had led the secular centre-left Congress for the Republic party—takes the oath of office in Tunis.

EPA/Landov

The self-immolation of Mohamed Bouazizi in Sidi Bouzid on Dec. 17, 2010, ushered in a series of demonstrations throughout Tunisia that on Jan. 14, 2011, led to the hurried departure of Pres. Zine al-Abidine Ben Ali from power. Accompanied by his immediate family, he fled into exile in Saudi Arabia. Meanwhile, Tunisia's dominant political party and former presidential vehicle, the Democratic Constitutional Rally (RCD), attempted to reestablish control of the government, and Tunisia's small army sought to restore public order.

Continued public protest stymied the RCD takeover, and the party itself was formally banned within a month of the president's departure from office. A series of short-lived caretaker cabinets persisted until the end of February, when veteran politician Beji Caid Sebsi formed a transitional government, which was able to plan for elections in October to form a constituent assembly that would elect an interim president and draw up a new constitution. Once this had been done, new parliamentary and presidential elections were to be held.

In 2011 many new and previously banned political parties emerged, eventually totaling 103 separate movements. Most coalesced into four blocs for the upcoming elections. The two most important blocs gave support to the Islamist Nahdah Party, persecuted by the previous regime, and the Progressive Democratic Party (PDP), which had enjoyed a limited legal existence.

Constituent Assembly elections were held October 23 to determine the composition of the 217-member body. The well-organized Nahdah Party won 90 seats with more than 40% of the vote. The Constituent Assembly began holding meetings in November. It elected Moncef Marzouki interim president, and Marzouki appointed Hamadi Jebali interim prime minister; both took office in December.

The Tunisian economy was seriously affected by the disruption caused by the mass demonstrations. Tourism throughout the year declined 30–40%, and unemployment soared. As a result, illegal immigration to Europe also rose. In the Tunisian hinterland, poverty and unemployment led to violent clashes, often along tribal lines. Much of the Tunisian private sector feared that its interests might be threatened by the collapse of the previous regime. The new authorities also had to deal with a massive influx of refugees from Libya, fleeing from the conflict there. (GEORGE JOFFÉ)

TURKEY

Area: 785,347 sq km (303,224 sq mi)
Population (2011 est.): 74,306,000
Capital: Ankara
Head of state: President Abdullah Gul
Head of government: Prime Minister Recep Tayyip Erdogan

In 2011 Turkey's ruling conservative Justice and Development Party (AKP), led by Prime Minister Recep Tayyip Erdogan, won a third consecutive victory in general elections in June, raising its share of the poll to 50% and winning 326 seats in the 550-member single-chamber legislature. It was followed by the centre-left Republican People's Party (CHP), under its new leader, Kemal Kilicdaroglu, with 135 seats, and Devlet Bahceli's far-right Nationalist Action Party (MHP) with 53 seats. Kurdish nationalists, who stood as independents to circumvent a rule dictating that parties had to win 10% of the national poll to qualify for representation in the parliament, improved their position as candidates sponsored by their Peace and Democracy Party (BDP) won 36 seats. Subsequently, 29 independents rejoined BDP. After the elections the CHP and Kurdish nationalists boycotted the parliament to protest the court's decision to disqualify several newly elected candidates on the basis of their having been charged with political offenses. Both parties had ended their boycott by October 1, when the parliament embarked on the new legislative program that it had endorsed on July 13. The government gave priority to the drafting of a new and more liberal constitution, and all parties represented in the parliament assigned members to a committee formed for the purpose.

Strengthened by the election results, the AKP proceeded to break the political power of the armed forces, which had traditionally seen themselves as guardians of the secularist regime. On July 29 Chief of the General Staff Gen. Isik Kosaner and the commanders of the three services resigned to protest the detention of serving and retired senior officers on charges of having plotted to overthrow the government. The resignations did not prevent further arrests in a slow-moving series of

AP

On December 29, near the southeastern Turkish village of Ortasu, people gaze at some of the 35 Kurdish civilians killed in a botched military air raid along the Iraq border the night before. The Turkish government admitted that the victims, who were identified as cigarette smugglers, had been mistaken for guerrillas.

trials, which also led to the detention of two prominent investigative journalists, a former police chief, and other civilians. The prolonged detention of government opponents, sometimes on unspecified charges, was criticized in the report released by the European Commission in October on Turkey's progress toward meeting European Union membership criteria. The report commended, however, the steps taken by Erdogan's government to curb the political power of the military.

The armed militants of the Kurdistan Workers' Party (PKK), listed as a terrorist organization in the EU and the U.S., reduced the scope of their attacks in the preelectoral period. They ended their poorly observed unilateral truce, however, when the government failed to deal with their demands for Kurdish as a language of instruction in schools and for autonomy for Kurdish-majority provinces in southeastern Turkey. In retaliation for the killing of 13 soldiers on July 14 and of another 24 on October 19, the Turkish air force launched air strikes against the PKK's base in the mountains of northern Iraq. In October the parliament extended by a year the authority of the government to employ armed forces outside the country's borders. Also in October Turkey assumed command of the NATO assistance and stabilization force in Afghanistan for another year. In September Turkey agreed to host NATO radar installations as part of an antimissile shield.

Turkey continued to disagree with U.S. policy toward Israel. Following the publication of the Palmer report on the killing of nine Turkish activists by Israeli commandos enforcing the blockade of Gaza, Turkey downgraded its diplomatic relations and ended military procurement and defense cooperation with Israel, while preserving nondefense trade links. Speaking at the UN, Prime Minister Erdogan advocated the immediate recognition of Palestinian statehood. In September Erdogan visited Egypt, Tunisia, and Libya to declare his support for their new regimes. Previously close relations with Syrian Pres. Bashar al-Assad approached a breaking point as Turkey offered support to opponents of his regime.

Erdogan's popularity was underpinned by strong growth in the economy. In the first half of the year, GDP grew by 10%. By the end of September, exports had increased by 21% and imports by 36%, while consumer price inflation dropped from 8.6% in December 2010 to 7.9% by the end of October 2011. The reliance of the economy on the continued inflow of foreign funds affected market confidence, however, and between January 1 and November 9, the index of the Istanbul stock exchange dropped by 15%. (ANDREW MANGO)

TURKMENISTAN

Area: 491,210 sq km (189,657 sq mi)
Population (2011 est.): 4,998,000
Capital: Ashgabat
Head of state and government: President Gurbanguly Berdymukhammedov

Turkmenistan continued to be a difficult partner for the international community in 2011. Although officially supportive of NATO coalition activities in Afghanistan, as of late 2011 the country was still refusing involvement in land transport via the Northern Distribution Network. In late May, during a visit of Afghan Pres. Hamid Karzai to Ashgabat, cooperation agreements were signed on a wide range of issues, including transport and communications and the acceleration of construction of a Turkmen-Afghan-Pakistani-Indian gas pipeline. Despite the efforts of European diplomats, Turkmen participation in the proposed Nabucco gas pipeline remained uncertain, partly because of the unpredictable behaviour of Turkmenistan's absolute ruler, Pres. Gurbanguly Berdymukhammedov.

In May, Berdymukhammedov signed a decree permitting recognition of foreign diplomas on the grounds that Turkmenistan needed all the educated personnel it could get, thereby overruling a decision of his predecessor, Saparmurad Niyazov. In September, however, the Turkmen Migration Service prevented nearly 900 Turkmen students from returning to their studies at Tajik universities. Also in September, it was reported that for the first time, Turkmen first-grade pupils were required to fill out forms at the beginning of the school year listing such information as the ethnicity, occupations, and criminal records of their immediate families dating back three generations.

Turkmenistan continued to have one of the lowest rates of Internet use in the world. During a visit to the country in September by the Organization for Security and Co-operation in Europe (OSCE), Dunja Mijatovic, the representative on freedom of the media, appealed for the Turkmen authorities to ease restrictions on the media and permit greater Internet access. In August the president ordered the removal of private satellite dishes on the grounds that they were unsightly and suggested the restoration of cable systems that his predecessor had shut down. Berdymukhammedov had made a similar demand in 2007, but it was largely ignored.

The Turkmen authorities' restriction of access to information was sorely tried in July when an ammunition depot exploded in the town of Abadan, near Ashgabat. Official sources claimed that the explosions were only fireworks and that there had been only 15 fatalities. Persons on the spot used their mobile phones and whatever other means they could obtain to contradict the official version. An independent exile Web site reported from unofficial sources that the death toll could have been as high as 1,382, with one-third of the fatalities said to have been children. Turkey and Uzbekistan offered assistance to Turkmenistan in dealing with the aftermath of the explosions, but the Turkmen authorities made clear that they wanted no outsiders near the site.

(BESS BROWN)

Alastair Grant/AP

In an attempt to alleviate significant freshwater shortages in Tuvalu, members of the New Zealand Defence Force on October 13 pump seawater into holding tanks on Funafuti Atoll for later desalinization.

TUVALU

Area: 25.6 sq km (9.9 sq mi)
Population (2011 est.): 11,200
Capital: Government offices in Vaiaku, Fongafale islet, of Funafuti Atoll
Head of state: Queen Elizabeth II, represented by Governor-General Sir (from June 21) Iakoba Taeia Italeli
Head of government: Prime Minister Willy Telavi

Climate change had a marked impact on Tuvalu in 2011. Rising tides and aquifers contaminated by sea-water infiltration left the Pacific island country's atolls dependent on roof-water collection and limited desalinization, while a prolonged drought caused by La Niña's extended presence in the area caused not only freshwater deficiencies but also crop failures and consequent food shortages. In July a small group of Tuvaluan families with ancestral links to Futuna in the French territory of Wallis and Futuna moved to Futuna to settle. By September, after the second driest year in 78 years, Tuvalu faced disastrous freshwater shortages and began rationing; in some places residents had only a few days' supply left. With drought predicted to continue, Prime Minister Willy Telavi's government declared a state of emergency. Water, desalinization equipment, and other supplies were flown from New Zealand and provided limited reserves for the capital while the islands' desalinators were being repaired.

In December the World Bank announced its first Country Assistance Strategy for Tuvalu. It also approved $14.4 million in grants for a three-year period beginning in 2012.

(CLUNY MACPHERSON)

UGANDA

Area: 241,551 sq km (93,263 sq mi)
Population (2011 est.): 34,509,000
Capital: Kampala
Head of state and government: President Yoweri Museveni, assisted by Prime Ministers Apolo Nsibambi and, from May 24, Amama Mbabazi

On Feb. 18, 2011, Ugandan voters returned Yoweri Museveni for his fourth presidential term with a resounding 68.4% of the votes. His closest rival was Kizza Besigye, flag bearer of the coalition Inter-Party Cooperation and three-time contender, who followed with 26%. International monitors from the European Union, the East African Community, and other regional blocs agreed that the election met "minimum international benchmarks for free elections," despite glaring irregularities. Besigye immediately charged that outright fraud and voter intimidation had occurred and vowed to step up opposition.

Museveni's victory rested in part on the steady economic growth and stability achieved by the development policies of his ruling party, the National Resistance Movement (NRM). The IMF estimated that economic growth rose to 6.1% from 5.8% in 2010. Policy makers looked forward to an oil boom in 2012 to accelerate growth, raise the country to middle-income status by 2016, possibly create half a million jobs, and nearly double the annual per capita income to $800. Unfortunately, such optimism soured in October when parliamentarians—NRM and opposition alike—forced a recall of Parliament to debate matters relating to the nascent oil industry. After a dramatic debate, Parliament demanded an end to secrecy relating to oil agreements. It also passed nonbinding resolutions that demanded inter alia the resignation of three ministers—Prime Minister Amama Mbabazi, Foreign Minister Sam Kutesa, and former energy minister Hilary Onek, who held the internal affairs portfolio—on charges of corruption. Although Mbabazi and Onek did not heed the call, Kutesa "stepped aside" from his post and two other officials resigned. Parliament voted to freeze activities in the oil industry until a petroleum law had been passed and existing agreements had been reviewed.

Meanwhile, Besigye, influenced by the antigovernment movements in North Africa known as the Arab Spring, gained more traction in stimulating protest against increasing NRM autocracy and corruption. Although his efforts to mobilize displays of resistance initially were slow to bear fruit—many of his party's newly elected parliamentarians flatly refused a directive to boycott Parliament—Besigye had more success from the end of April as rising prices of food and fuel, coupled with worsening electricity failures and anger over corruption, sparked new public demonstrations. In late April Besigye mounted a "walk-to-work" protest, during which he was pepper sprayed by the police, brutally beaten, and arrested. Such disproportionate police force ignited three weeks of demonstrations in the capital, Kampala, and resulted in two deaths, injuries to 120 people, and 360 arrests. In October the walk-to-work protest revived. During the year Besigye was arrested several times and endured periods of confinement to his home by police. Many other protesters were also arrested, and the government claimed to have foiled a coup plot. By year's end it was clear that although the government had succeeded in quelling public demonstration, Museveni's credibility had suffered a serious blow while Parliament had expanded its power to insist on public accountability. The events created the climate for a significant challenge to Museveni's grip on power.

(LARAY DENZER)

UKRAINE

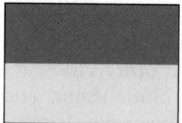

Area: 603,628 sq km (233,062 sq mi)
Population (2011 est.): 45,672,000
Capital: Kiev (Kyiv)
Head of state: President Viktor Yanukovych
Head of government: Prime Minister Mykola Azarov

The year 2011 in Ukraine was dominated by the public trial of former prime minister Yuliya Tymoshenko. Her arrest was considered by many to have been politically motivated.

On May 24 Tymoshenko was charged with having abused the powers of her office during her tenure as Ukrainian prime minister by signing a gas deal in 2009 with Russian Prime Minister Vladimir Putin. The trial began the following month in Kiev. On August 7 former Ukrainian president Viktor Yushchenko testified on behalf of the government. The court found Tymoshenko guilty on October 11 and sentenced her to seven years' imprisonment and a fine of $188 million. The EU promptly suspended a scheduled visit of Pres. Viktor Yanukovych to Brussels, having expressed its belief that the government of Ukraine should follow the rule of law. On October 13 new charges were brought against Tymoshenko, alleging that she had transferred some $400 million of debt from her company, United Energy Systems, to the government in 1996, when her then ally Pavlo Lazarenko was prime minister. The case also raised questions regarding the participation of Tymoshenko, who remained popular, in the parliamentary elections scheduled for October 2012.

Other trials also made news in 2011. In March former president Leonid Kuchma (1994–2005) was formally charged with abuse of power in connection with the murder of Georgy Gongadze, the editor of *Ukrainska Pravda*. In July the main suspect in that case, Oleksiy Pukach, formerly the head investigator for the Interior Ministry's foreign surveillance units, was also put on trial. Meanwhile, the trial of former minister of the interior Yuri Lutsenko continued, following his arrest on Dec. 26, 2010, for allegedly having overpaid his chauffeur.

On October 27 the European Parliament proposed an EU-Ukraine meeting with the goal of achieving an association agreement between the two parties. A summit in December was inconclusive, with the EU president, Herman Van Rompuy, stating that the approval of such an agreement would be tied to "political cirumstances" within Ukraine.

GDP growth of 4.7% was predicted for the year, with inflation projected at 8.9%, but the economy in general was in difficulty. In March the IMF froze its quarterly payment to Ukraine of $1.5 billion because of the country's failure to meet its agreed economic targets. In September Ukraine's foreign-currency reserves dropped by 8.3% to $35 billion, which led the country to seek new loans. In late October an IMF mission arrived in Ukraine to discuss revisions to the standby program and a potential allocation of $3 billion in credit.

According to the International Organization for Migration, an estimated 6.5 million Ukrainians were working abroad. The average domestic wage in September was 2,700 hryvnya (about $337), but it averaged much lower in western regions. On October 1 the min-

On April 26 the 25th anniversary of the calamitous nuclear accident at the Chernobyl power station in Ukraine, a flame at a monument in Kiev burns in memory of the accident's victims.

Efrem Lukatsky/AP

imum wage was increased to 800 hryvnya (about $100) after taxes. Ukraine's outlook for long-term foreign and currency default ratings was revised from "positive" to "stable" by Fitch on October 19.

April 26 marked the 25th anniversary of the Chernobyl disaster. A commemorative ceremony attended by President Yanukovych and Russian Pres. Dmitry Medvedev was held at the site of the abandoned nuclear plant, and a conference in Kiev attracted many world leaders. Yanukovych requested a further $1 billion in international aid to help construct a permanent roof over the destroyed fourth reactor. The European Bank for Reconstruction and Development (EBRD) had gathered $1.43 billion to date.

On September 29 the EBRD provided a loan of €200 million ($276 million) to the state company Ukrhydroenergo to help upgrade hydroelectric stations. Also that month, U.S. Secretary of State Hillary Clinton and Ukrainian Foreign Minister Kostiantyn Hryshchenko signed a memorandum of understanding on nuclear security whereby the U.S. would provide technical and financial assistance for the elimination of Ukraine's enriched uranium and for the improvement of civil nuclear research enterprises.

On July 29 a methane-gas explosion at the Sukhodilska-Vostochnaya coal mine in eastern Luhansk killed 17 miners. On October 8 Yanukovych and Colombian pop star Shakira opened Kiev's new association football (soccer) stadium, which was set to host the 2012 finals of the European Championship.

(DAVID R. MARPLES)

UNITED ARAB EMIRATES

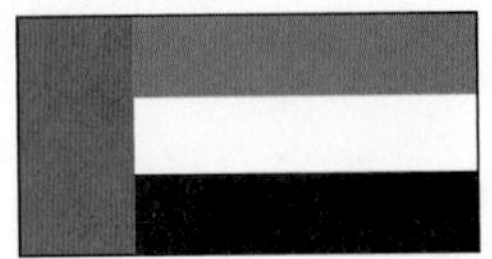

Area: 83,600 sq km (32,280 sq mi)
Population (2011 est.): 7,891,000, of whom about 900,000 are citizens
Capital: Abu Dhabi
Head of state: President Sheikh Khalifah ibn Zayid Al Nahyan
Head of government: Prime Minister Sheikh Muhammad ibn Rashid al-Maktum

The United Arab Emirates (U.A.E.) did not experience the popular uprisings that shook the Arab world in 2011. Demands for political reform, however, were voiced by intellectuals and professionals in letters and petitions. In April five well-known activists were jailed, charged with having insulted the country's leaders. The bloggers were convicted on November 27 and given jail sentences, only to be pardoned the following day.

The government deported hundreds of Shi'ite and Islamist expatriate Arabs working in the country. The move was interpreted as a precautionary measure to ensure political stability. Despite the Shi'ite uprising in neighbouring Bahrain, U.A.E. Shi'ites, constituting 15% of the native population, generally remained calm.

In February the U.A.E. was one of the first countries to support a rebellion in Libya against the regime of Muammar al-Qaddafi, offering the rebels military and financial aid. In March, when the Bahraini government asked the U.A.E. for military support against the Shi'ite opposition, the U.A.E. sent some 500 police officers. They were joined by some 1,000 Saudi soldiers.

General elections for the country's Federal National Council (FNC) were held on September 24. The FNC, which functioned only as an advisory body to the government, was composed of 40 members; half were elected, and half were appointed by the rulers of the seven emirates of the U.A.E. Voter turnout was weak, with about 28% of the 129,000 eligible voters casting ballots. (LOUAY BAHRY)

UNITED KINGDOM

Area: 243,073 sq km (93,851 sq mi)
Population (2011 est.): 62,675,000
Capital: London
Head of state: Queen Elizabeth II
Head of government: Prime Minister David Cameron

Domestic Affairs. In 2011 the Conservative–Liberal Democrat coalition, which had been formed after the 2010 general election and was the United Kingdom's first peacetime coalition since the 1930s, survived a number of stressful events. The greatest of these was a referendum held on May 5 on a possible change to the system for electing MPs. The Liberal Democrats had long wanted to replace the existing system, which gave them fewer than one in 10 MPs despite having won almost a quarter of the popular vote. The Conservatives had reluctantly agreed to hold a referendum on the Alternative Vote, a preferential voting system that would have given the Liberal Democrats more MPs, though not as many as they would gain in a fully proportional system. In the event, the public voted by 68–32%, on a 41% turnout, to keep the existing system. Nick Clegg, the leader of the Liberal Democrats, admitted that electoral reform would stay off the agenda for the foreseeable future.

One constitutional innovation that did take place occurred on September 5, when the Fixed Term Parliament Act became law. This removed from the prime minister the power to choose the date of a general election. The legislation laid down that general elections would be held every five years unless the government lost a vote of confidence or two-thirds of MPs voted to hold an early election. The next election was scheduled for May 7, 2015. Another innovation required MPs to debate any proposition that attracted 100,000 supporters in an online petition. On October 24 the House of Commons debated a call for a referendum on the U.K.'s relationship with the European Union. The leaders of all three main parties opposed the idea. It was defeated 483–111, but 81 Conservative MPs—more than one in three of the party's backbench MPs—defied the government and supported a referendum.

Riots that erupted in London and elsewhere in August forced the government to recall Parliament during its summer break. Police in Tottenham, north London, shot dead Mark Duggan, a gangster and drug dealer, while trying to arrest him on August 4. Two days later, following a peaceful protest march regarding Duggan's death, rioting broke out in Tottenham. In the days that followed, the disorder spread to other parts of London and to other cities, including Birmingham, Manchester, and Liverpool. The riots appeared to involve looting and arson, however, rather than any organized political protests. The turmoil was able to flare up quickly because participants spread the news via mobile phone messaging that shops had been broken into and that the police were failing to protect property.

Following criticism of the initial police response, including rebukes by government ministers, all police leave was can-

Tom Hevezi/AP

British royal Prince William and his bride, Catherine, leave Westminster Abbey in London after their highly publicized wedding, April 29.

celed as of August 11, and widespread looting ceased. Eventually more than 3,000 people were arrested, many on the basis of actions recorded by surveillance cameras. The riots sparked a fierce debate about whether the turbulence was caused by fundamental social problems or the opportunist actions of a minority of criminals. In a speech on August 15, Prime Minister David Cameron blamed "a broken society" for a "slow-motion moral collapse." In a separate statement he promised tougher measures, especially against people living in rented social housing in the event that any member of the family broke the law.

A more specific challenge confronted the prime minister in October when the media reported that Defense Secretary Liam Fox had broken the rules that governed ministerial behaviour by allowing Adam Werritty (a close friend and the best man at his wedding) into his inner circle without having obtained security clearance from, or having received sufficient supervision by, Fox's civil servants. When it became known that Werritty had personal links to right-wing groups in the U.K. and abroad, Fox was accused of having privately backed his own, alternative foreign policy. Fox resigned on October 14, having accepted that he had allowed the line between his personal and governmental activities to be blurred. Sir Gus O'Donnell, the U.K.'s most senior civil servant, on October 18 published a report in which he stated that Fox had breached ministerial rules on a number of occasions and ignored warnings in the past by senior officials in the Ministry of Defence about Werritty's access to him.

During the second half of the year, the government was swept up in a phone-hacking scandal that led to upheaval in Rupert Murdoch's News Corp. media empire and the arrest of numerous people, including Cameron's former director of communications. Murdoch and his son James Murdoch (*see* BIOGRAPHIES) were among those called to testify before Parliament. (*See* Sidebar on page 480.)

The government's first major social innovation started to bear fruit in September with the opening of the first 24 "Free Schools." These schools were free to students and funded by the government but able to operate independently of local councils. Education Secretary Michael Gove argued that councils often stifled initiative and prevented government-funded schools from being as consistently good as they should be. He allowed free schools to be set up by groups of parents, voluntary organizations, religious bodies, private companies, or private schools that wished to cooperate with the state sector. Gove expressed his hope that, over time, Free Schools would be available to every parent and that local councils would play a far smaller role in organizing local education.

Millions of people were granted a brief respite from Britain's problems by the marriage on April 29 of Prince William—the eldest son of Prince Charles, the heir to the throne—to Catherine Middleton. (*See* BIOGRAPHIES.) The day was made a public holiday, and thousands of people crowded the streets to join in the celebration. The wedding, held in Westminster Abbey, confirmed the U.K.'s continuing ability to stage spectacular pageants. Queen Elizabeth II, William's grandmother, granted the young couple the titles of duke and duchess of Cambridge on their wedding day.

Their marriage reopened a simmering controversy over whether the law of primogeniture should be changed. For centuries the British crown passed to the eldest male child of the monarch, and many people regarded this gender bias as anachronistic. Cameron consulted the other 15 countries that also had the British monarch as their head of state, and they agreed on October 28, at a meeting of Commonwealth leaders in Australia, to change the rules so that the crown would in future pass to the first-born child, regardless of sex, and also lift the more than 300-year-old ban on a British monarch's marrying a Roman Catholic.

Economic Affairs. The recovery in the U.K.'s economy faltered in 2011. Growth of about 1% over the year was too slow to prevent a rise in unemployment to 2.6 million, or 8% of the labour force—the highest figure since 1994. An increase in private-sector jobs was not enough to offset a reduction in the number of jobs in the public sector, which was triggered by the government's program of spending cuts designed to reduce government borrowing, which amounted to £137 billion (£1 = about $1.60) in the year to March 2011, or 9% of GDP.

Some previously announced tax increases took effect during the year, most notably a rise in the value-added tax from 17.5% to 20% in January. George Osborne, the chancellor of the Exchequer, resisted calls from some economists, industrial leaders, and Conservative MPs to reduce the top rate of income tax, which the previous Labour Party government had increased in 2010 to 50% on incomes above £150,000 a year. The chancellor did, however, commission an inquiry to investigate whether the 50% rate raised the expected revenue.

A wider controversy concerned the impact of the government's debt-reduction program on economic growth. Osborne insisted that this was necessary to retain the confidence of the financial markets and thus keep interest rates

The U.K. Phone-Hacking Scandal

In July 2011 a simmering scandal erupted in the U.K., which led to the closure of the *News of the World* (*NOTW*), the country's best-selling newspaper; the resignation of Britain's most senior police officer; turmoil in one of the world's largest media empires; and the arrest of numerous people, including Prime Minister David Cameron's former communications director. The scandal centred on phone hacking by the *NOTW*, a tabloid Sunday newspaper that sold almost three million copies a week by uncovering the corrupt actions, sexual exploits, and personal trivia of politicians, celebrities, and sports stars.

The seeds of the scandal were sown in November 2005 when Prince William—Queen Elizabeth II's grandson and second in line to the British throne—suspected that intercepted voice mails had been the source of two *NOTW* stories about him. A police investigation led to Clive Goodman, the paper's royal editor, and Glenn Mulcaire, a private investigator, who were charged with having hacked the phone of one of William's aides. Both defendants pleaded guilty and were sent to prison. During the trial it emerged that Mulcaire had hacked into the voice mails of a handful of other people. Andy Coulson, then editor of the *NOTW*, accepted responsibility and resigned his position in January 2007, when the trial ended. Cameron, the Conservative opposition leader at the time, subsequently appointed Coulson as his director of communications. When Cameron became prime minister in May 2010, Coulson retained his post inside the government.

For almost four years the police and *NOTW* maintained that no journalists other than Goodman had been involved. Investigations by other newspapers, however—notably *The Guardian* and the *New York Times*—suggested that hacking was widespread while Coulson was editor of the *NOTW*. On Jan. 21, 2011, he announced his resignation as Cameron's director of communications. Five days later London police started a new investigation, known as Operation Weeting, to examine "significant new information." This led to the arrest of three more *NOTW* journalists in April. In the same month, News International—the British newspaper division of the parent company, News Corporation Ltd. (News Corp.)—offered to compensate eight public figures for having hacked their phones.

Up to this point, the News International was embarrassed rather than gravely threatened by the unfolding scandal. This changed when on July 4 *The Guardian* disclosed that Mulcaire had hacked into the voice mail of Milly Dowler, a 13-year-old girl who had gone missing in 2002 and was subsequently discovered to have been murdered. When hacking into Dowler's voice mail, Mulcaire deleted some messages when her mailbox was full. Dowler's parents, trying to call the missing girl, suddenly found that space had been freed up; they assumed that she had deleted messages and was therefore still alive. This hacking took place while Rebekah Brooks was the *NOTW*'s editor; by 2009, however, she was News International's chief executive and a protégé of News Corp.'s founder, Rupert Murdoch.

Public revulsion at the Dowler disclosure provoked an acute crisis inside News International—a crisis that was exacerbated by subsequent disclosures that Mulcaire had hacked thousands of telephones on behalf of the *NOTW*, including the relatives of British soldiers killed in action. Rupert Murdoch's son James Murdoch (*see* BIOGRAPHIES), the chairman of News International, announced on July 7 that the *NOTW*, which launched in 1843, would cease publication the following Sunday. On July 13 News Corp. withdrew its controversial bid to take full control of BSkyB, Britain's dominant satellite broadcaster, in which News Corp. held a 39% stake. On July 15 Brooks resigned as CEO of News International, and one of Rupert Murdoch's closest and longest-serving colleagues, Les Hinton, quit as CEO of News Corp.'s Dow Jones & Co., publisher of *The Wall Street Journal*. (Hinton had been CEO of News International between 1995 and 2007 and, in testimony before Parliament, had defended the company's internal investigation into the hacking.)

The ripples quickly spread beyond the News Corp. empire. Sir Paul Stephenson stepped down as commissioner of the Metropolitan Police (Britain's most senior police officer) on July 17, when he admitted that he had accepted free hospitality at a luxury health spa with connections to Neil Wallis, a former *NOTW* executive editor. Stephenson's assistant commissioner, John Yates, resigned the next day in response to criticism that his original investigation in 2006 into phone hacking had failed to probe deeply enough.

More generally, the crisis broke the spell that News International papers, especially the mass-circulation daily *The Sun*, had cast over politicians of all parties. Both Cameron and Labour Party leader Ed Miliband accepted that they and their predecessors had been too close to News International executives, possibly because of the fear of incurring the wrath of News Corp.'s journalists. Cameron announced on July 13 that a senior judge, Lord Justice (Brian) Leveson, would head a public inquiry into both the hacking scandal and the system of media regulation.

Rupert and James Murdoch endured a torrid two-hour interrogation on July 19 by a committee of MPs. They expressed their horror and deep regret at what had happened but insisted that they had no personal knowledge of phone hacking at the time. The final *NOTW* editor, Colin Myler, declared that James Murdoch had been told in 2008 that hacking had been widespread at the *NOTW*, but Murdoch denied the allegation.

By the end of 2011, Operation Weeting had led to a number of further arrests of former *NOTW* reporters and executives, including Brooks and Coulson. Rupert Murdoch survived an attempt by some shareholders at News Corp.'s annual meeting on October 21 to remove him as chairman. He announced that the company would pay the Dowler family £2 million (about $3.2 million) compensation and that he would personally pay another £1 million to charities chosen by the family. Two-thirds of external shareholder votes were cast for James's removal as a director; he needed the votes of the Murdoch family, which controlled 40% of the stock, to retain his position.

(PETER KELLNER)

low. His critics, including Ed Balls, Labour's shadow chancellor, averred that the deficit should be reduced more slowly, as should public spending on services such as health, education, and the police.

The Bank of England (BOE) used monetary policy to offset fiscal tightening. Even though the inflation rate peaked at 5.2% in September—well above the 2% target rate set by the government—the BOE held the base interest rate at just 0.5% all year. The BOE announced on October 6 that it would inject a further £75 billion into the economy by means of "quantitative easing."

The impact of this policy depended on the banks' increasing their lending to businesses and home buyers. Osborne on February 9 announced an agreement with four leading banks to increase lending to business, especially smaller companies. Under the deal, called Project Merlin, the banks also agreed to reduce the bonuses paid to their staff and to disclose the incomes of more of their senior executives.

Pay rates remained frozen for public-sector workers who earned more than £21,000 annually, while those earning less received a flat-rate £250 increase. In March the government announced that the freeze would be extended to 2013 and that from 2012 most public-sector workers would have to pay more toward their pensions. Treasury Minister Danny Alexander (a Liberal Democrat) in June announced that the retirement age, traditionally 60 for most public-sector workers, would rise in stages to 66 by 2020. Public-sector unions reacted to the combined impact of these measures by holding a series of one-day strikes, starting on June 30, which closed a number of schools, law courts, and government offices. Additional strikes were held on November 30. Another measure, designed to encourage more people to delay retirement, came into effect on October 1, when it became illegal for companies to force employees to retire. Previously, employers could require workers to retire when they reached their 65th birthday.

Foreign Affairs. The U.K. played a significant role in Libya during the year. Cameron joined with French Pres. Nicolas Sarkozy to secure NATO and UN support for a no-fly zone to prevent Libyan forces from attacking civilians. When military operations started on March 19, British forces took part in "Operation Ellamy," deploying eight naval vessels (including submarines) and more than 30 aircraft. Cameron and Sarkozy visited Libya's newly liberated capital, Tripoli, on September 15.

The U.K.'s military presence in Iraq came to an end on May 22, eight years after the U.S.-led 2003 war, with the conclusion of a Royal Navy mission to train Iraqi sailors. Cameron announced on July 6 that the U.K. would withdraw an additional 500 troops from Afghanistan in 2012. By the end of 2011, 394 British troops had been killed in Afghanistan since the start of military operations in 2001.

In May the European Union Act came into force. This legislation mandated that in the future the British government had to obtain the people's consent in a national referendum in order to approve any European Union treaty that would transfer any powers or areas of policy from the U.K. to the EU. No such referendum had been held for previous treaties. With opinion polls showing consistently that most Britons wanted the EU to have fewer, not more, powers, this act made it unlikely that any new major EU treaty would be adopted for the foreseeable future because new treaties needed the unanimous support of all member states, and the U.K. would be forced by a "no" majority in a referendum to veto it. In Brussels on December 9, Cameron blocked a proposal supported by the other 26 EU heads of government to amend the EU's rules to reduce the risks of future financial crisis in the euro zone.

Queen Elizabeth made a state visit to Ireland on May 17–20, the first such trip by a British monarch since Ireland seceded from the U.K. in 1922. She laid a wreath at Dublin's Garden of Remembrance, which commemorates the deaths of Irish people who fought for independence from British rule. Her visit was both symbolically important and immensely popular in Ireland.

Scotland, Wales, and Northern Ireland. Elections were held on May 5 in each of the three U.K. countries with devolved powers. Scotland provided the most dramatic outcome. The pro-independence Scottish National Party (SNP) won 69 seats (22 more than in 2007), an absolute majority in the 129-seat Parliament. For the previous four years Alex Salmond, the SNP's leader, had been Scotland's first minister. As the head of a minority administration, however, he had been unable to secure the approval of Scotland's Parliament for a referendum on independence. With an overall SNP majority, Salmond could proceed, but with most opinion polls suggesting that an early referendum on full independence would be lost, he indicated that the vote would not be held until 2014 or 2015. Salmond on October 23 told his party's annual conference that the Scottish people would be offered three choices: the status quo, full independence, or greater autonomy within the U.K. Under the "autonomy" option, Scotland would have full control over its finances while accepting that defense and foreign policy would continue to be decided in London.

The SNP's triumph meant losses for the other main parties, with Labour winning 37 seats (9 fewer than in 2007), the Conservatives taking 15 (down 2), and the Liberal Democrats dropping to only 5 (a loss of 11). The Greens won 2 seats, the same as in 2007. Following the election Iain Gray and Annabelle Goldie stepped down as leaders of, respectively, Labour and the Conservatives in Scotland. On November 4 Ruth Davidson won the contest to lead Scotland's Conservatives; on December 17 Johann Lamont was elected the new leader of Scotland's Labour Party.

In Wales a referendum was held on March 3, with the approval of the U.K. Parliament, on whether the Welsh Assembly should be granted the kind of lawmaking powers that Scotland's Parliament had enjoyed since 1999. (When devolution was instituted after the U.K.'s 1997 general election, more power was transferred to Scotland than to Wales.) On a 35% turnout, Welsh voters backed these extra powers by 63–37%. This contrasted with the original referendum in 1997, when just over 50% voted to establish a Welsh assembly.

In the elections on May 5, Labour won 30 seats in the 60-seat Welsh Assembly, 4 more than in 2007. The Conservatives secured 14 seats (a gain of 2); the Welsh nationalist Plaid Cymru fell to third place with 11 seats (a loss of 4); the Liberal Democrats finished with 5 seats (down 1); and the independents lost their 1 seat. Carwyn Jones (*see* BIOGRAPHIES) remained first minister in a Labour-only administration; prior to the election he had headed a coalition with Plaid Cymru.

In Northern Ireland's assembly elections, the two main parties consolidated their positions, with the mainly Protestant Democratic Unionist Party (DUP) winning 38 seats (up 2 from 2007) and the predominantly Roman Catholic Sinn Fein taking 29 (an increase of 1). The Ulster Unionist Party and Social Democratic and Labour Party each lost 2 seats, to finish with 16 and 14, respectively. The cross-community Alliance Party won 8 seats (up 1), and three other parties each captured 1. The DUP's Peter Robinson remained first minister, and Sinn Fein's Martin McGuinness stayed on as deputy first minister, though the latter briefly stepped down while he contested (and lost) the election in October for president of Ireland. (PETER KELLNER)

UNITED STATES

Area: 9,526,468 sq km (3,678,190 sq mi), including 233,798 sq km of inland water and 155,293 sq km of the Great Lakes that lie within U.S. boundaries but excluding 111,849 sq km of coastal water and 193,148 sq km of territorial water
Population (2011 est.): 313,387,000
Capital: Washington, D.C.
Head of state and government: President Barack Obama

For decades friends and adversaries alike had prematurely forecast the end of the American era, and 2011 was at best a plateau year for the United States, which showed signs of actual decline for the first time. With its economy and political system weakened, the U.S. struggled to maintain the world-leadership role it had long shouldered. It continued to live well beyond its means and recorded a $1.3 trillion deficit even as the country's economy again failed to generate its traditional robust growth. Moreover, the federal government became even more deeply immobilized by partisan gridlock.

Although the U.S. was accustomed to directing affairs abroad, it became more collegial in 2011 and encouraged other prominent countries to assume their share of ensuring world security. Many U.S. allies, particularly in Europe, faced their own economic problems, however. Meanwhile, Russia, China, Iran, and some of the West's other traditional rivals continued their resurgence without serious interference. The U.S. took major steps to wind down its 10-year war on terrorism, but while it reduced its overt military presence in Afghanistan and Iraq, it generated new controversy with expanded use of unmanned drones for spy missions and military attacks in several areas of the world.

Domestic Policy. Handcuffed by the struggling economy, ongoing deficits, and paralyzing political partisanship and led by a politically weakened Pres. Barack Obama maneuvering for reelection in 2012, Washington claimed few domestic accomplishments during 2011. In its least-productive year in recent history, Congress approved only 80 new public measures (most of them inconsequential), the lowest number since World War II—a stark contrast to 2010, when the federal government produced a host of new legislation, including a historic revamping of the country's health care system. A year of deadlock resulted after a Republican majority took control of the U.S. House of Representatives in January 2011, having vowed to stop and even undo President Obama's agenda.

Republicans and Democrats split sharply over the proper corrective course for a national economy that showed little sign of improvement for most of the year. Democrats generally favoured more government stimulus spending and higher taxes on the wealthy; Republicans pushed for reducing government and holding the line on taxes. As a result, virtually nothing was done to assist the economy other than stimulating it with a third consecutive year of more than $1 trillion in deficit spending. Brinksmanship ruled the day, with four near shutdowns of government during the year, which generated even more uncertainty and prompted an unprecedented lowering of the U.S. credit rating.

Obama pushed for a $447 billion job-creation bill that included an extension of the 2% payroll tax cut he had negotiated in late 2010, to be paid for by additional taxes on high-income earners. With the federal government already having borrowed some 36 cents of every dollar spent, however, Republicans balked. They cited scant evidence of progress from an even larger 2010 stimulus program that had failed to keep unemployment from rising well above 9%. The Obama measure was rejected, and his administration spent the remainder of the year attempting to get pieces of it approved, with mixed success.

The most-dramatic confrontation occurred in midsummer when congressional leaders faced a deadline on increasing the country's debt ceiling. Failure to act could have meant another potential government shutdown and an unprecedented default on federal debt obligations. Republicans demanded spending reductions at least equal to the debt-level increase and opposed measures to increase revenue. On August 2, just hours before a possible default, Congress passed the Budget Control Act of 2011, which increased the debt ceiling and aimed at trimming some $2.4 trillion in spending over 10 years. It required a vote on a balanced-budget amendment to the U.S. Constitution, specified $917 billion in cuts, and mandated the creation of a congressional "supercommittee" to propose by late November another $1.5 trillion in cuts. The failure to identify the required spending reductions would trigger $1.2 trillion in cuts, to be split evenly between defense and nondefense programs.

Ultimately, only $21 million of the first $917 billion in reductions would be effective during the 2012 financial year, and balanced-budget-amendment drafts were voted down in both congressional chambers. Standard & Poor's, citing a lack of real progress in Washington's debt-reduction initiatives, lowered the U.S. credit rating. In late November the 12-member supercommittee, equally divided between Democrats and Republicans, announced that it had failed to reach agreement on the remaining spending reductions.

At year-end, after another unproductive showdown over continuing the payroll-tax reduction and extending long-term unemployment benefits, Congress agreed to a mere two-month extension of both measures, to which it added a provision that attempted to force Obama to approve the politically charged Keystone XL oil pipeline from Alberta to Texas.

As these events unfolded, a populist movement on the left of the political spectrum gained steam in the autumn of 2011. Inspired by the mass protests of the Arab Spring, a disparate group of protesters calling themselves Occupy Wall Street took up residence in a park near New York City's financial district to call attention to a list of what they saw as injustices. Among the protesters' concerns were that the wealthy were not paying what the protesters considered a fair share of income taxes and that major corporations—particularly banks and other financial institutions—needed to be held more accountable for risky practices. The protesters identified themselves as "the 99 percent," the have-nots who would no longer put up with the corruption and greed that they perceived among "the 1 percent," the wealthiest Americans. In the succeeding weeks the movement spread to other cities across the country.

Among the handful of relatively uncontroversial new laws approved during the year was the first major overhaul of the country's patent system in 50 years. The new law provided increased funding to reduce the Patent Office backlog and sought to lessen disputes and widespread frivolous lawsuits by changing the patent-granting standard from "first invented" to "first filed." The USA PATRIOT Act was extended until June 2015, with only minor modifications, even after several

As part of the Occupy Wall Street protests, which called attention to corporate greed and income inequality in the United States, demonstrators swarm Zuccotti Park in New York City's financial district, October 10.
Andrew Burton/AP

legislators warned that federal officials had secretly abused the act to invade personal privacy. Results of the 2010 census began to be released early in the year. (*See* Special Report on page 180.)

After a four-year delay, the White House successfully pushed Congress to approve free-trade agreements with Panama, Colombia, and South Korea that were originally negotiated by the administration of George W. Bush. The agreement with South Korea was the largest new trade pact since the North American Free Trade Agreement. Congress also approved a defense-appropriations bill that contained a controversial measure allowing indefinite detention of U.S. citizens suspected of terrorist activities. Obama signed the bill but declared that he would not authorize such detention without trial.

The Economy. Historically the U.S. had not only snapped sharply back from most economic recessions but often led the world out of downturns. In 2011, however, the U.S. economy continued to languish, with minimal growth, high unemployment, and expansion insufficient to absorb new job seekers. External events—including an economic slowdown in Asia, the Japanese earthquake and tsunami that disrupted auto-parts supply, and the European sovereign debt crisis—seemed to stall every U.S. economic rally. The Federal Reserve System, which kept its short-term interest rates just above zero for the third straight year, had seemingly exhausted its ability to encourage economic activity, and as a consequence of legislative gridlock, the federal government offered but minimal assistance to the struggling economy. For the first three quarters, GDP grew at a woeful 1.8% or less, and although economic activity appeared to accelerate in the fourth quarter (with predicted growth of about 3%), the underperforming economy remained the country's most-serious concern.

U.S. equity markets recorded an uneventful year. The broad S&P 500 started 2011 at 1257 points, drifted up in the spring, and plunged in late summer, amid the congressional budget crises and economic worries in Europe, only to finish the year back at 1257. The narrower Dow Jones average gained 5.5%. Intermediate and long-term investment rates took a dive when investors rushed to the safety of U.S. bonds and treasury notes after a midyear sell-off in equity markets. Long-term interest rates on mortgages fell to historic lows.

The U.S. housing situation remained stuck in a backlog of foreclosures, with more looming; it was estimated that more than 30% of borrowers held mortgages that were greater than the value of their homes. Banks, backed by lower borrowing costs, made extraordinary efforts to clear the backlog, but progress was glacial, in part because of high unemployment and general economic malaise. Average housing prices in major metropolitan areas continued to hover near their crisis lows of spring 2009, remaining about one-third below their peaks of summer 2006.

Even so, at year-end, economic reports indicated a more robust recovery might be getting under way. In November unemployment dropped from 9% to 8.6%, its lowest level in 30 months, although much of the improvement was attributed to a reduction in the number of those still actively seeking work. Inflation, as measured by the consumer price index, was slated to rise by only 2.2% for the year; housing starts actually began climbing; and corporate earnings were reported to have reached record levels. Although major economic problems abroad created obstacles to renewed U.S. growth, they also provided an opportunity for American economic leadership. (*See* Special Report on page 170.)

Foreign Policy. For the two decades following the end of the Cold War, the United States enjoyed unquestioned primacy in world affairs. As the world's sole superpower, it pursued foreign-policy goals backed by a mighty military empowered by deficit spending. In 2011, however, there were unmistakable signs that U.S. influence was ebbing, particularly in the Middle East.

In his 2008 presidential campaign, Obama had criticized U.S. "unilateralism" and promised a more collegial foreign policy. The first major achievement of that approach occurred when France and Britain led a NATO intervention assisting rebels against longtime Libyan strongman Muammar al-Qaddafi. U.S. planes and drones helped establish a no-fly zone over Libya early in the intervention but later left manned flight operations to non-U.S. NATO pilots, which prompted jibes that Obama had "led from behind." Even though the operation took longer than expected (seven months) and culminated in the untoward execution of Qaddafi, the Obama administration hailed it as a model of international cooperation.

The U.S. struggled to keep abreast of the events of the Arab Spring (*see* Special Report on page 172), alternately viewed in Washington as a refreshing expansion of democracy or as an ominous resurgence of Islamic fundamentalism against secular regimes that were friendly to the U.S. The American response to Egypt's demonstrations was particularly mixed. Secretary of State Hillary Rodham Clinton initially appeared to back longtime U.S. ally Hosni Mubarak. However, after having declared his regime stable and well-intentioned, she turned against the Egyptian president when he was deposed by the military. The U.S. openly provided aid to a pro-Western regime in Bahrain that was under assault but helped lead international opposition to the brutal suppression of an uprising against the regime of Bashar al-Assad in Syria.

Declining U.S. influence was also evident as the Israeli-Palestinian peace process crumbled during the year amid failed U.S. efforts to spark serious talks. In May U.S.-Israeli relations hit a low point when Obama pressured Israel to negotiate after Palestinian rivals Hamas and Fatah reconciled. Obama's suggestion that Israel use its pre-1967 borders as a starting point for talks was rebuffed by Israel, which said those borders were "indefensible." In September Palestinians attempted an unprecedented end run around the dormant U.S.-sponsored peace process when they appealed directly to the United Nations for statehood status, but the effort was stymied by opposition in the Security Council from the U.S and several other countries.

The hostile U.S. relationship with Iran deteriorated even further as international diplomatic efforts to prevent the development of nuclear weapons in that country again met with Iranian instransigence. After the International Atomic Energy Agency stated in November that Iran had "carried out" critical steps toward nuclear-weapons production, the U.S., Britain, and Canada imposed strict sanctions on the Iranian government, commercial banking, and energy production. Although the UN chose not to join in the sanctions regime, intelligence reports at year-end suggested that the U.S.-led effort had played havoc with Iran's currency and economy. Iran released two young Americans whom it had convicted of spying after they wandered into Iranian territory from Iraq while hiking, but it let them go only after receiving payment of nearly $1 million in "bail money." At year-end, Iran threatened to blockade the vital Strait of Hormuz, but the U.S. pledged to keep the area open to international shipping.

China and Russia provided little overt help in reigning in Iran and actively opposed more-serious sanctions. The U.S. continued its long-term diplomatic chess game with China and sought to prepare for future rivalry with the fast-growing Asian military and economic power. After China arranged to set up a military outpost in far-off Seychelles, ostensibly to help counter Indian Ocean piracy, Obama announced a new U.S.-Australian military arrangement, which began with permanent detachment of a U.S. Marine brigade to Darwin, on Australia's northern shore. Secretary of State Clinton paid a high-profile visit to Myanmar (Burma) in what some observers saw as an effort to wean that country from its longtime ally China. Obama's efforts to "reset" the sometimes-tense relationship with Russia, which had thus far proved only modestly successful, seemed to evaporate in December when Clinton declared that recent Russian parliamentary elections had been neither free nor fair. Russian Prime Minister Vladimir Putin icily accused the U.S. of fomenting disruptive street protests in Russia.

Mohammad Zubair/AP

On May 2, during the U.S. military raid on Osama bin Laden's compound in Abbottabad, Pak., that resulted in his death, a stealth Black Hawk helicopter crashed into one of the compound's walls.

War on Terrorism. During 2011 the U.S. passed several milestones in reducing its involvement in the 10-year-old war on terrorism. On May 2 a U.S. Navy Seal team invaded a walled compound in Pakistan and killed Osama bin Laden (*see* OBITUARIES), the mastermind of the September 11 attacks. The Seals used two helicopters to storm the residence—located only some 730 m (about 800 yd) from the Pakistani army's chief officer-training academy—and shot bin Laden when he allegedly went for a weapon. The team buried bin Laden's body at sea. President Obama, who had authorized the hazardous raid, later declared bin Laden's death "the most significant achievement to date in our nation's effort to defeat al-Qaeda."

The incident further strained an already-tenuous U.S. relationship with Islamic Pakistan, which had long been suspected of playing both sides in the war on Muslim extremism. Rankled by the U.S. failure to alert it to the bin Laden raid, the Pakistani government allowed Chinese technicians to inspect a technologically advanced U.S. helicopter abandoned by the raiders. In September the Pakistani-based Haqqani network mounted a raid on U.S. embassy and NATO facilities in Kabul. U.S. Adm. Mike Mullen, who later retired from the chairmanship of the Joint Chiefs of Staff, declared that the Haqqani network had acted "as a veritable arm" of Pakistan's Inter-Service Intelligence Directorate. Also in September, 22 Navy Seals, most from the same unit that had provided the forces for the bin Laden raid, were killed when their helicopter was shot down over Afghanistan. Later in the year, in an apparent case of mistaken targeting, NATO aircraft killed 24 Pakistani soldiers manning a border station near Afghanistan. In response the Pakistani government shut down, at least temporarily, one of the key routes used to supply NATO forces in Afghanistan and demanded that the U.S. end its use of unmanned drones over Pakistani territory.

At midyear, in a symbolic but important step, the U.S. began a drawdown of its forces in Afghanistan, as Obama had promised in 2009 when he authorized a controversial surge of U.S. troops. The phased withdrawal, which removed 10,000 of 100,000 U.S. personnel in Afghanistan over six months, was largely well received by Americans who had grown weary of the 10-year conflict and the absence of clear progress toward the mission's pacification goals. Nevertheless, the withdrawal clearly discomfited U.S. military leaders, whose forces were fully engaged with a resurgent Taliban and other local opposition. Bin Laden's death paradoxically bolstered critics of the war who argued that the U.S. mission was now complete and should be ended. At year-end, Pakistan boycotted an international conference on Afghanistan held in Bonn, Ger.

Afghan leaders promised to continue efforts toward self-sufficient defense and against rampant corruption. They called on their Western allies to continue military and economic assistance for a decade beyond the scheduled 2014 withdrawal of NATO troops.

In late December the departure of the final U.S. troops from Iraq brought an end to a nearly nine-year regime-change effort that had cost the U.S. some $800 billion and 4,400 lives. A sizable U.S. diplomatic mission, complete with hundreds of security contractors, remained in Iraq at year-end to help the country with an expected bumpy transition to self-sufficiency in internal security.

During the year the U.S. continued a dramatic escalation in the use of unmanned aerial vehicles (UAVs), or drones, to conduct surveillance and missile strikes around the world. The CIA and the military ran separate drone programs, which critics complained were not properly coordinated and lacked both adequate congressional oversight and clear rules of engagement. Major drone programs aimed at suspected al-Qaeda targets in Yemen and Somalia continued throughout the year. U.S.-provided UAVs also played a large part in NATO operations in the Libyan campaign. The expanding use of drones generated several controversies. In September a U.S. drone killed an American-born al-Qaeda propagandist, Anwar al-Awlaki, in Yemen. That assassination without trial of a U.S. citizen abroad raised only nominal opposition from U.S. civil rights groups, in large part because Awlaki had clearly led, or at least inspired, anti-U.S. terrorists. In November a drone conducting nuclear-program surveillance over eastern Iran either malfunctioned or was shot down and fell into Iranian hands largely intact. That event provided Iran with a major propaganda victory and led to speculation that Iran would share its newly acquired knowledge of advanced U.S. drone technology with China or other U.S. rivals.

(DAVID C. BECKWITH)

DEVELOPMENTS IN THE STATES 2011

For a fourth consecutive year in 2011, U.S. state governments were preoccupied with the effects of a national recession and the associated controversy with the federal government over power and funding. Financial difficulties stifled state innovation. Most states, under a mandate to balance their budgets, opted for still more spending cuts and service reductions instead of raising taxes and fees. As the economy appeared to stabilize late in the year, most states reported a brighter fiscal outlook, but the improvement did not bring overall state revenue up to prerecession levels.

Minor gains in limited off-year elections added slightly to the Republicans' overall advantage nationwide in state governments. Four states held gubernatorial balloting. Democrats were reelected in West Virginia and Kentucky, and Republicans in Mississippi and Louisiana. Therefore, the lineup in 2012, as in 2011, would be 29 Republican governors, 20 Democrats, and 1 independent. In legislative balloting Republicans won the Mississippi house for the first time since Reconstruction and gained enough seats to deadlock the Virginia state Senate. For 2012 both houses of legislature would be controlled by Republicans in 26 states and by Democrats in 15 states, with split control in 8 states. Nebraska had a nonpartisan unicameral legislature.

The year was notable for contentious recall elections. Prominent Republican legislators were removed from office in Arizona (in an intraparty challenge) and Michigan. A year of political turmoil in Wisconsin began when newly elected Republican officials removed collective-bargaining rights from state workers, a decision narrowly affirmed by the state's highest court. In subsequent recall elections, two Republican senators were removed, which narrowed the upper-house Republican majority to one vote, but a conservative state Supreme Court justice survived a high-profile recall challenge that was mounted by labour unions and Democrats.

Structures, Powers. Concerns over possible voter fraud led to partisan divisions and tough new voter-identification laws in Alabama, Kansas, Mississippi, Rhode Island, South Carolina, Tennessee, Texas, and Wisconsin. Most measures required a photo ID for registration or voting. Democratic governors in Minnesota, Missouri, Montana, New Hampshire, and North Carolina vetoed similar new laws. Maine restored same-day registration and voting.

New Jersey became the first state to order all new state workers to live within the state's boundaries. Arizona joined more than 20 other states that had established a state militia to augment the National Guard. A plan to privatize 29 south Florida state prisons was ruled unconstitutional by a state judge.

Finances. Affected by the end of federal assistance from the 2009 stimulus bill, the 50 states started the year with an estimated $82 billion budget shortfall, and most balanced their books with spending reductions rather than increased taxes during an economic slowdown. By spring, signs of national economic recovery had reduced spending pressure on social programs and increased revenue, particularly through sales taxes,

At a military base near Al-Nasiriyyah, Iraq, U.S. soldiers departing from the country board a transport plane, December 17. The withdrawal of U.S. troops from Iraq was completed the next day, marking the end of nearly nine years of war.

Mario Tama—Reuters/Landov

Tom Lynn—Milwaukee Journal Sentinel/AP

At the Wisconsin State Capitol in Madison on June 14, people demonstrate against the state Supreme Court's upholding of a law passed earlier in the year that abrogated public workers' collective-bargaining rights.

but failed to bring the states back to prerecession fiscal levels by year's end.

With recovery finally in sight, many states were forced into contentious negotiations with state workers over pay and benefits, including pensions. In Rhode Island, where an unsustainable 10% of state revenue went to retirement pay, the state initiated an innovative reform plan that suspended cost-of-living increases for retirees, raised the retirement age for current workers, and melded a defined-pension benefit with 401(k)-style plans to reduce future state obligations.

In an effort to avoid tax increases, some states delayed state payments and accelerated revenue collection. Connecticut and Illinois bucked the no-tax trend, however. Connecticut increased a variety of income, sales, and service levies by $1.5 billion, the largest tax increase in state history. Illinois raised its personal income tax rate from 3% to 5% and increased business taxes by nearly 50%. Hawaii and New York boosted personal taxes on high-income earners. Michigan began taxing pension and retirement income.

Most states, however, held the line on revenue increases. Kansas, Missouri, and Oklahoma, persuaded by the example of fast-growing Texas, made preliminary moves to repeal their personal income tax. After having turned down three major tax- cut proposals in 2010, Colorado voters in 2011 overwhelmingly rejected increased sales and income taxes to fund education. Business taxes were trimmed in Arizona, Florida, Indiana, Kansas, and Missouri. Michigan reduced corporate taxes by $1.8 billion and increased personal income taxes by $1.5 billion. Nevada extended $620 million in business and sales taxes due to expire at midyear.

State spending was cut in every budget area. Many states reduced aid to municipalities. New York eliminated 3,700 prison beds and cut funding for state courts. Florida reduced payments to social workers. Washington cut monthly welfare benefits. Illinois planned to transfer half of its Medicaid caseload to managed care by 2015, and Florida began making arrangements for expanding managed care to all patients. In an attempt to close a $26.6 billion deficit, California made across-the-board cuts.

Florida, Ohio, and Wisconsin canceled ambitious high-speed rail projects backed by the administration of Pres. Barack Obama, while, as cost estimates ballooned to $98.5 billion, California legislators reconsidered a high-speed rail project linking San Francisco, Sacramento, Los Angeles, and San Diego that was scheduled to begin in 2012. In a major development with long-term financial ramifications, California and Tennessee obtained a promise for eventual collection of state sales taxes from Amazon, the country's largest online retailer. The breakthrough created a likely road map for future congressional action to make sales-tax collection universal in U.S. online merchandising.

Social Issues. New York became the sixth state to legalize same-sex marriage. Illinois, Rhode Island, Hawaii, and Delaware approved laws establishing civil unions, which meant nine states had granted gay couples substantial legal rights short of full marriage. Several states enacted novel laws designed to restrict abortion, but almost all were enjoined by federal courts. Notably, Texas specified that a woman seeking an abortion had to be offered a sonogram view of the fetus, while Kansas and Idaho banned late-term abortions because of "fetal pain." Indiana banned the use of Medicaid funds for abortion, and several states reduced or eliminated state funding for Planned Parenthood facilities. Utah allowed hospital employees to refuse to participate in any abortion-related procedure. In Mississippi, however, voters rejected a referendum that would have conferred legal rights on the fetus by defining "personhood" as beginning at conception.

Law, Ethics. Absent new federal legislation on immigration, states struggled to cope with issues related to undocumented residents. Alabama, South Carolina, and Utah—like Arizona before them—gave local law enforcement enhanced powers to determine the immigration status of individuals stopped in the course of normal police activity. As it did with Arizona's 2010 law, the Justice Department promptly sued on the grounds of state interference with a federal responsibility. Federal courts enjoined enforcement of the state statutes, and the U.S. Supreme Court put the Arizona case on its 2012 docket.

Connecticut, Illinois, and Maryland enacted local versions of the proposed federal DREAM Act that allowed children of illegal immigrants to receive tuition aid. California passed a limited version that allowed private-school tuition assistance. Efforts to rescind similar DREAM laws that had been passed by Kansas, Texas, and Wisconsin failed. Only three states (New Mexico, Utah, and Washington) continued to allow illegal aliens to obtain driver's licenses. Illinois and New York exited the federal Secure Communities program, an effort established to screen jail inmates and deport serious criminals that critics said was ineffective and undermined law enforcement.

Legislators in Indiana, Ohio, Tennessee, and Wisconsin reduced collective-bargaining rights for state workers. The particularly controversial Wisconsin and Ohio measures dramatically affected how local governments and school districts could deal with public unions, and Ohio voters overwhelmingly rejected their new law in a November referendum. The vote capped a year of confrontation between state employees and state governments that had resulted in worker layoffs, frozen wages, reduced benefits, increased health-insurance premiums, narrower parameters for striking employees, and other cost-cutting measures.

Wisconsin became the 49th state to authorize citizens to carry a concealed weapon, which left only Illinois and the District of Columbia without a concealed-carry law. In an attempt to encourage economic activity, 11 states enacted tort-reform measures that limited lawsuits against businesses, with particularly strong measures passed by Alabama, Oklahoma, Tennessee, and Wisconsin. Delaware became the 16th state to legalize medicinal marijuana use. In an apparent reversal of a 2009 position, however, the Obama administration threatened to prosecute if the medical-marijuana laws were seen to violate federal antidrug laws.

M. Spencer Green/AP

After signing into law the Illinois DREAM Act, which made privately funded college scholarships available to undocumented immigrants in the state, Gov. Pat Quinn (centre) celebrates with students and supporters at a predominantly Latino high school in Chicago, August 1.

Statistics released during 2011 indicated that the incidence of both violent and property crime declined, despite the national economic recession. In addition, the imposition of capital punishment continued to wane. Illinois joined New Jersey and New Mexico in legislatively abolishing executions. Only 43 men were executed in 14 jurisdictions during the year, all by lethal injection, down from 46 the previous year. Former Illinois governor Rod Blagojevich was sentenced to 14 years' imprisonment after being found guilty on 18 corruption counts, including attempting to sell the U.S. Senate seat vacated by Obama.

Health, Welfare. As the 2010 Patient Protection and Affordable Care Act headed to the U.S. Supreme Court, states were split on how to prepare for the law, which would reach full effect in 2014. Several states accepted Obama administration grants to begin implementation, but others refused to establish the private insurance exchanges anticipated by the new law. Some 28 states sued the federal government to invalidate the law. They alleged that the individual mandate to acquire health insurance was unconstitutional and complained about increased state costs. Some states accepted federal grants even as they filed suit.

In a symbolic test of public sentiment, Ohio voters approved a state constitutional amendment that prohibited the government from mandating the purchase of health insurance. Vermont, however, set up a new public-option health plan. Washington had earlier appropriated supplemental money to assist states in the costly transition to an expanded Medicaid program, but those extra federal funds were largely exhausted during 2011.

States experimented with methods to cut public benefits. Florida became the first state to require public-assistance applicants to submit to drug testing. Missouri and Pennsylvania added a drug-test requirement for some welfare applicants. Michigan and California put a four-year time limit on welfare payments, and eight states reduced unemployment benefits or toughened qualification standards. Florida forged a link between the length of unemployment benefits and the unemployment rate.

Environment, Education. Numerous governors initiated wide-ranging education reform that typically provided for more school choice, linked student performance to teacher evaluations, and encouraged business to fund private-school scholarships. Indiana approved a school-voucher plan.

Environmental advocates sustained several reverses during 2011. New Jersey withdrew from the Northeast's Regional Greenhouse Gas Initiative, the only operating cap-and-trade system to reduce greenhouse gas emissions. A similar pullout was also approved by the New Hampshire legislature, but it was vetoed by the governor. A judge in California ruled that the state could not implement its own cap-and-trade system until alternative methods, such as carbon taxes, were explored. In June the U.S. Supreme Court unanimously rejected a 2004 lawsuit by six states against various power companies over their greenhouse gas emissions.

(DAVID C. BECKWITH)

Upon signing into law a bill that provided for an expansive school-voucher program, Indiana Gov. Mitch Daniels chats with children in attendance at the Statehouse in Indianapolis, May 5.

Michael Conroy/AP

URUGUAY

Area: 177,879 sq km (68,679 sq mi)
Population (2011 est.): 3,380,000
Capital: Montevideo
Head of state and government: President José Mujica

In 2011, Pres. José Mujica's second year in office, Uruguay continued to enjoy solid economic growth and international respect for its political stability. Although inflation exceeded 8% in November, GDP was projected to grow by 5.7% for the year, and unemployment stood at a historic low at 6.4%. Moreover, exports were at record levels, and tourism became the single-greatest source of foreign exchange.

Politically, two issues dominated the year. The first occurred in late October, when both houses of the parliament passed contentious legislation to nullify the Amnesty Law that had been in effect since 1987. This law absolved the military for its crimes—especially human rights violations—committed during its dictatorial rule from 1973 to 1985. The original legislation had been upheld in two national referenda (1989 and 2009). New court cases were expected to begin almost immediately, but most observers anticipated that Uruguay's Supreme Court would ultimately determine whether the new legislation was constitutional.

The other major conflict erupted in November, when the teachers union and local school boards rejected a national pilot project for educational reform that had been painstakingly negotiated. President Mujica promised to take a firm stand to see that the reform project was implemented. Educational reform was long overdue in a country that, despite experiencing significant economic improvement and holding fiercely middle-class values, had a very high dropout rate in secondary school, especially among poorer students.

In the realm of sports, Uruguay's national association football (soccer) team experienced a dream year. After having finished fourth in the 2010 FIFA World Cup in South Africa, the team in 2011 captured the Copa América, the most prestigious soccer event in Latin America football, and in November beat Italy in a match in Rome. The team's fourth-place world ranking was the highest position Uruguay had enjoyed in at least a generation. (MARTIN WEINSTEIN)

Watching from Montevideo, fans of Uruguay's national association football (soccer) team celebrate a goal scored during the final match of the Copa América tournament, July 24. Uruguay defeated Paraguay 3–0 in Buenos Aires to win the continental competition for the first time since 1995.

Jorge Silva—Reuters/Landov

UZBEKISTAN

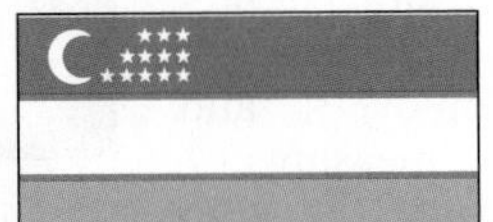

Area: 444,103 sq km (171,469 sq mi)
Population (2011 est.): 28,129,000
Capital: Tashkent
Head of state and government: President Islam Karimov, assisted by Prime Minister Shavkat Mirziyayev

In September 2011 the U.S. Congress voted to remove restrictions that had been imposed in 2004 on military aid to Uzbekistan because of the country's poor human rights record. Human Rights Watch, however, had appealed for the restrictions to remain intact, claiming that the Uzbek human rights record had hardly improved, despite the U.S. administration's assertions to the contrary. U.S. officials' eagerness to remove the restrictions indicated the importance of Uzbek support for the Northern Distribution Network (NDN), which supplied the NATO military in Afghanistan. An unidentified U.S. official was quoted as saying that the objective of providing military aid was to ensure that Uzbekistan could defend itself if it was attacked for its support of the NDN.

In September more than 60 prominent international clothing firms signed a pledge to boycott Uzbek cotton because of the use of child labour in its production. While Uzbek officials denied that children were being forced into the cotton fields, human rights activists were being detained for photographing child cotton pickers. UNICEF attempted to document child labour in the Uzbek cotton harvest, but the organization insisted that its efforts could not substitute for monitoring by the International Labour Organization, which Uzbekistan categorically rejected. President Islam Karimov's daughter Gulnara Karimova felt the weight of international disapproval of Uzbek child labour when her fashion show was canceled during New York Fashion Week. The boycott threatened to have serious consequences for Uzbekistan's foreign currency earnings, though the country was increasingly shipping cotton to the Middle East and Asia.

In April Karimov visited China in an effort to secure investment. The visit resulted in approval of a cooperative plan for joint uranium production.

President Karimov indicated a desire to interest European Union organizations in modernizing his country's energy sector, though at the beginning of October the European Parliament's foreign affairs committee excluded textiles from the Partnership and Cooperation Agreement that since 1999 had been the basis for EU-Uzbek trade. The committee cited disapproval of child labour in the cotton fields as the reason for the exclusion.

The year 2011 was officially designated the Year of Small Business and Entrepreneurship, and in August Karimov issued a decree that was allegedly designed to enhance the freedom of entrepreneurs by removing bureaucratic barriers to the development of small business. Small businesspeople, however, complained that new taxes and license costs were forcing many into bankruptcy. (BESS BROWN)

VANUATU

Area: 12,190 sq km (4,707 sq mi)
Population (2011 est.): 251,000
Capital: Port Vila
Head of state: President Iolu Abil
Head of government: Prime Ministers Sato Kilman, Serge Vohor from April 24, Kilman from May 13, Edward Natapei from June 16, and, from June 26, Kilman

Vanuatu experienced political instability in mid-2011 because of disputes over the constitutionality of procedures used to replace prime ministers; the position changed hands four times in a relatively short period. By July, however, the reform-minded Sato Kilman—who had been prime minister as the year began—and his parliamentary allies seemed to be firmly back in power. Tensions arose again in August as Maxime Carlot Korman, the speaker of Parliament and an opposition MP, repeatedly adjourned legislative sessions in order to stall the passage of a supplementary budget. In September Korman was suspended from Parliament until the end of the term. After Vanuatu's foreign minister made moves toward establishing relations with Taiwan, China issued a clear warning in July to remind Vanuatu of the dangers of trying to play the two entities against each other.

The economy remained strong. Remittances from horticultural and viticultural seasonal workers employed in Australia and New Zealand through government programs helped support the Vanuatu economy. In addition, Vanuatu established a trade office in Hong Kong to encourage foreign (primarily Chinese) companies to register in Vanuatu. In October the WTO approved Vanuatu's accession, but ratification was delayed by domestic opposition to membership. (CLUNY MACPHERSON)

VATICAN CITY STATE

Area: 44 ha (109 ac)
Population (2011 est.): about 800, of whom about 450 have Vatican citizenship (including about 225 living abroad mostly as diplomatic personnel)
Head of state: (sovereign pontiff) Pope Benedict XVI
Head of administration: Secretary of State Tarcisio Cardinal Bertone

Through countless actions and statements, Vatican City in 2011 expressed its advocacy of ethics in every sphere, including the conduct of government and business. Pope Benedict XVI addressed a letter to Italian Pres. Giorgio Napolitano calling for ever more intense ethical renewal, apparently prompted by charges that Italian Prime Minister Silvio Berlusconi had paid for sex with minors. Equally, the appointment of Angelo Cardinal Scola to head the diocese of Milan, the Roman Catholic Church's second most important diocese, was hailed as a "pro-Vatican" choice because of Scola's strong commitment to religious renewal as a bulwark against ethical decline in modern society. Meanwhile, the Vatican warned that the confession application (app) available for download on some smartphones could in no way substitute for the authentic sacramental encounter.

The Vatican's most cogent action in international diplomacy was in regard to China, where the government-sanctioned Chinese Catholic Patriotic Association continued to ordain Roman Catholic bishops without the approval of the Holy See. Under Vatican canon law such action entailed automatic excommunication for all those involved, but the intricacies of the issue were not always clear to the Chinese laity. For this reason a blog was launched to clarify the Vatican's position in a popular question-and-answer format.

The Vatican in 2011 reported that in 2010 it had shown a budget surplus for the first time in four years, notwithstanding a dip in direct donations and transfers from the international dioceses to the Holy See. A significant surplus source was the successful Vatican Museums. The budget was still small, however, and the Vatican called on governments in other countries to provide financial support for such activities as Roman Catholic education, a system that served almost 60 million students worldwide. (GREGORY O. SMITH)

VENEZUELA

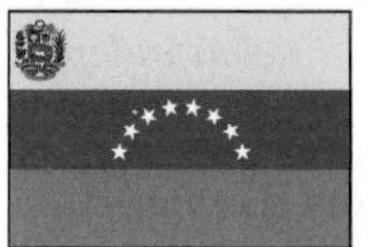

Area: 916,445 sq km (353,841 sq mi)
Population (2011 est.): 29,437,000
Capital: Caracas
Head of state and government: President Hugo Chávez Frías

Even though a newly elected National Assembly had taken office on Jan. 5, 2011, Pres. Hugo Chávez of Venezuela used the special powers given to him for 18 months by the outgoing Assembly in December 2010 to legislate unilaterally in 2011. With these powers Chávez was able to end the autonomy of the central bank, increase the influence of communes, and establish military districts to enforce government policies in regions of strong resistance. Implementation of these policies slowed after June 30, when Chávez revealed that he had undergone surgery to remove a cancerous tumor from his abdomen. While the president claimed that he was headed for a rapid recovery, there were reports that he had only a 50% chance of living more than 18 months. Vice Pres. Elías Jaua and leaders of the United Socialist Party of Venezuela (PSUV) were quick to voice their support, but uncertainty over the seriousness of Chávez's illness initiated the most contentious infighting within the Chavismo movement since Chávez was elected president in 1998. The military was at the centre of one of two important factions that emerged; the other included Marx-

Veronica Canino—Xinhua/Landov

Thousands of people parade through Caracas on July 3 in commemoration of the bicentennial of Venezuelan independence.

ist civilians such as Jaua, Foreign Minister Nicolas Maduro, and the president's older brother, Adán Chávez.

Some opposition leaders saw the prospect of life-threatening or incapacitating illness for the president as an opportunity to triumph over the Chavistas in free elections. Others feared that Chávez's passing would intensify instability, with unpredictable political consequences. Opposition leaders attended services at which various clergy prayed for Chávez's recovery. Prospective candidates in the Feb. 12, 2012, opposition primary elections took their cues from the popular governor of Miranda state, Henrique Capriles Radonski, who said that he relished the opportunity to campaign against a healthy Chávez.

The internecine conflict between the two factions of the Chavismo movement brought the president back from Cuba earlier than planned. On July 7, soon after his return, Chávez declared that he remained in control. On July 17, as he left to undertake a new round of chemotherapy in Havana, Chávez appeared satisfied that he had restored the political status quo and promised that he would rise "like a phoenix." Another trip to Cuba, for a fourth round of chemotherapy, followed in September. Soon after he returned home this time, Chávez announced his intention to seek reelection. In October he claimed that he was cancer-free.

Economic conditions in Venezuela were mixed. Accumulated inflation for 2011 was 25.4%, up slightly from 2010. The government increased its expropriation of farms and urban land. This continuation of the assault on private property rattled investors, and the central bank reported that foreign investment had declined by 15.4% over the previous three years. Meanwhile, GDP grew by 4%, and unemployment hovered around 8.5%. Industrial production was up 7.8%, and with the exception of the construction sector, the economy had recovered from the recession of 2009. Government spending was scheduled to increase by one-third, to the benefit of the "Boliburgésia," the pro-government middle class. Crime and personal safety, along with the deterioration of the country's infrastructure, remained problematic. For most Venezuelans, however, their concern with the state's increasing social control paled in comparison with their satisfaction with economic gains.

Chávez's ongoing crusade to build multinational Latin American organizations that excluded the United States bore fruit in December when 33 countries formed the Community of Latin American and Caribbean States (CELAC) without the U.S. or Canada. Although the organization was structured as an annual summit without a permanent headquarters or secretariat, it sought to increase regional trade and integration. The Bolivarian Alliance of the Americas (ALBA), a group of seven countries governed by anticapitalist populist leaders, was another element of Chávez's strategy. (DAVID J. MYERS)

VIETNAM

Area: 331,212 sq km (127,882 sq mi)
Population (2011 est.): 88,145,000
Capital: Hanoi
Head of state: Presidents Nguyen Minh Triet and, from July 25, Truong Tan Sang
Head of government: Prime Minister Nguyen Tan Dung

Two major developments dominated Vietnam in 2011: the selection of new party and state leaders and the approach to take with China on competing sovereignty claims in the South China Sea without harming bilateral relations. The 11th National Congress of the Vietnam Communist Party (VCP) met on January 12–19 and was attended by some 1,400 delegates representing 3.6 million party members. The congress adopted two major policy documents: the new five-year (2011–15) socioeconomic development plan and the political report by the party's secretary-general. The congress also approved revisions to the party's statutes and platform.

In addition, delegates elected a new leadership. They used their prerogative to make nominations from the floor to add to the list provided by the outgoing Central Committee. In the end, 218 candidates vied for 175 full-member seats, and 64 candidates stood for 25 alternate, or nonvoting, slots. The results indicated that 10 incumbent cabinet ministers had lost their posts. The new Central Committee then elected the executive leadership. The outgoing Politburo had consisted of 15 members, 6 of whom were retiring. The Central Committee rejected a proposal to expand membership to 17 and elected only 14 members. Nguyen Phu Trong, the chair of the National Assembly Standing Committee, was given an exemption from the mandatory retirement age of 65 and was elected the new party secretary-general. The VCP Central Committee met twice more during the year. The second plenum, in July, approved its five-year work program. The third plenum was held in October and deliberated socioeconomic-development issues.

On May 22 Vietnam held elections for the 500-member National Assembly. Those elections, usually conducted the year after a national congress, had been moved forward to speed up the leadership transition. At the first session of the 13th National Assembly, held in July, former deputy prime minister Nguyen Sinh Hung was chosen as its chairman; Truong Tan Sang was selected as state president; and Nguyen Tan Dung was reelected to a second term as prime minister. Assembly deputies then approved Prime Minister Dung's nominations for the cabinet, including 22 ministers and 4 deputy prime ministers.

The territorial dispute with China in the South China Sea heated up as a result of two altercations involving Chinese navy patrol boats and Vietnamese commercial oil-exploration vessels on May 26 and June 9. The incidents sparked weeks of unprecedented anti-China demonstrations in Vietnam during June, July, and August before authorities banned them. After the June 9 incident, Prime Minister Dung and Pres. Nguyen Minh Triet made speeches vowing to defend national sovereignty. In addition, Dung issued a decree outlining eligibility for military conscription in the event of a national emergency. On June 13 the Vietnamese navy conducted well-publicized live-fire exercises. Two weeks later Vietnam dispatched a special envoy to China to discuss a diplomatic resolution to the dispute.

Tensions subsequently subsided after China and ASEAN adopted guidelines to implement an accord on the South China Sea that had been reached in 2002. China hosted a visit by Secretary-General Trong in October, during which an agreement on basic principles guiding the settlement of sea issues was reached, including a proposal for joint economic development. In September Vietnam had sought to bolster its position vis-à-vis China by signing a memorandum on defense cooperation with the United States.

While Trong was in Beijing, Vietnam sent Pres. Truong Tan Sang to India to solicit diplomatic support and military assistance. It was announced in New Delhi that Vietnam had awarded an oil-exploration contract to an Indian company and that India was considering selling cruise missiles to Vietnam. Prime Minister Dung traveled to the Netherlands and indicated interest in purchasing up to four Dutch-built naval vessels. In late autumn Dung also visited Japan to reaffirm bilateral socioeconomic and security ties.

(CARLYLE A. THAYER)

YEMEN

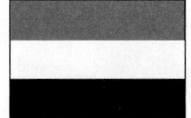

Area: 528,076 sq km (203,891 sq mi)
Population (2011 est.): 24,800,000
Capital: Sanaa
Head of state: President Maj. Gen. ʿAli ʿAbd Allah Salih
Head of government: Prime Ministers Ali Muhammad Mujawar and, from December 10, Muhammad Basindwah

Inspired by the uprisings in Tunisia and Egypt, Yemeni protesters rallied on Feb. 3, 2011, to demand democratic reforms and an end to the nearly 33-year rule of Pres. ʿAli ʿAbd Allah Salih. The first protesters were mainly students, young people, and intellectuals, but in March they were joined by tribal forces and army units that had defected.

As demonstrations continued, the government used force to suppress the revolt, killing and injuring thousands. A U.S.-supported Gulf Cooperation Council (GCC) initiative to ease Salih out of power failed. The chaos enabled Islamic militants to seize territory in southern Yemen, but they were weakened by battles with government forces. On June 3 an attack on Salih's compound left him badly injured. He was flown to Saudi Arabia for treatment, returning to Yemen on September 23. On November 23 Salih signed the GCC plan, transferring his powers to his vice president, Abd Rabbuh Mansur Hadi, who then ordered presidential elections for Feb. 21, 2012. In December, Muhammad Basindwah became prime minister.

On October 7 Tawakkul Karman, a Yemeni human rights activist, was awarded the Nobel Prize for Peace for her nonviolent role in the uprising. She shared the prize with two Liberian women who were recognized for similar efforts in their country. (*See* NOBEL PRIZES.)

(LOUAY BAHRY)

A defector from the Yemeni army stands watch over a demonstration in Sanaa on September 30 in which protesters are demanding the resignation of Pres. ʿAli ʿAbd Allah Salih.

Hani Mohammed/AP

ZAMBIA

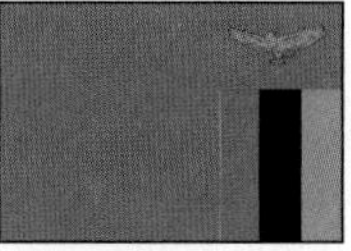

Area: 752,612 sq km (290,585 sq mi)
Population (2011 est.): 13,306,000
Capital: Lusaka
Head of state and government: Presidents Rupiah Banda and, from September 23, Michael Sata

Political change was in the air in Zambia during 2011. Michael Sata, popularly known as "King Cobra" and the flag bearer of the Patriotic Front (PF), came from behind with 42% of the votes to win the September 20 presidential election. His surprise victory ended two decades of rule by the Movement for Multiparty Democracy (MMD), headed since 2008 by Rupiah Banda, who received 36% of the vote. Although Banda briefly toyed with the idea of ignoring the results and declaring himself the victor, he quickly yielded to persuasion to accept the results and ensure a peaceful transition of power. Banda's concession of defeat ended two days of violent demonstrations by voters who were frustrated by the slow release of electoral results and feared that the MMD had interfered with balloting in the main towns of the Copperbelt and the capital, Lusaka.

As president, Sata faced the difficult task of implementing his campaign promises: creating new employment opportunities; raising workers' wages, especially those of miners; and curtailing rampant corruption. His constituency included 1.3 million mostly young people who had voted for the first time, composing 24.5% of the electorate. Although the new president promised to start actualizing his policies within 90 days of taking office, the PF did not have a clear majority in the National Assembly and had to build alliances with other parties to obtain approval of fiscal budgets and other legislation. Of crucial importance was economic policy related to Chinese investment and trade, especially in the mining sector.

Guy Scott, a Zambian of European descent, was appointed vice president, becoming the highest-ranking white politician in sub-Saharan Africa. The new cabinet included a number of politicians from previous regimes, raising questions concerning Sata's prospects for genuine reform; however, he did initiate a tough anticorruption campaign. In October he dismissed many senior officials, including the heads of the armed forces, the police, the Anti-Corruption Commission, and other key agencies. In addition, investigations into existing government contracts were announced.

Late in October an outbreak of strikes took place in both foreign and locally owned businesses. Worker demands included higher wages and better conditions. Employers first capitulated to government pressure to meet these demands but reneged. Then, on November 1, they agreed to enter a two-month negotiation period.

Disgraced former president Frederick Chiluba died on June 18. Although he was convicted by a British court of stealing $46 million from Zambian government coffers, he was acquitted of this charge at home. (*See* OBITUARIES.)

(LARAY DENZER)

Jerome Delay/AP

On September 23, three days after his unexpected election as president of Zambia, populist politician Michael Sata takes the oath of office at the Supreme Court building in Lusaka.

ZIMBABWE

Area: 390,757 sq km (150,872 sq mi)
Population (2011 est.): 12,084,000, of which about 3,000,000 people might be living outside the country
Capital: Harare
Head of state: President Robert Mugabe
Head of government: Prime Minister Morgan Tsvangirai

Speculation was rampant in 2011 about Zimbabwean Pres. Robert Mugabe, who had held office for 31 years and adamantly refused advice to step down. By the time the annual conference of the Zimbabwe African National Union–Patriotic Front (ZANU-PF) was held in December, he had secured its endorsement as presidential candidate in the next general election, expected in either 2012 or 2013. This apparent unity, however, belied the well-known view within the party inner circle that his advancing age—he was 87—and deteriorating health meant that he did not have the stamina to withstand the rigor of campaigning. In September the WikiLeaks publication of a series of U.S. diplomatic cables from 2004 to 2010 revealed that some of Mugabe's closest allies and army officers considered him to be a liability and privately discussed his exit from power or death. Although information concerning his health was guarded, it was believed that he suffered from prostate cancer and diabetes and experienced strokelike episodes. During the year he made more than eight visits to Asia, most of them suspected to include medical treatment. Unflattering photographs in the local press underscored his frail appearance, depicting Mugabe asleep during meetings or being helped to walk by aides.

Although Mugabe was stunned to learn about the disloyalty of certain officials implicated in disclosing confidential matters to U.S. officials, their control of powerful party constituencies meant that he could not afford to alienate them. These included two politicians frequently mentioned as his possible successors: First Vice Pres. Joice Mujuru, the widow of a powerful kingmaker, and Defense Minister Emmerson Mnangagwa, believed to be floating the idea of forming a new party. Aside from the ZANU-PF inner circle, younger politicians, known as Generation 40, openly called on the "geriatrics" to retire and make way for younger leaders. Two new independent and outspoken newspapers supported their reform agenda.

Incessant disagreements between the three constituent members of the power-sharing unity government (ZANU-PF, the Movement for Democratic Change–Tsvangirai, and the Movement for Democratic Change–Ncube) delayed the drafting of a new constitution. The Constitution Select Committee had still not hammered out an agreement on the issues of citizenship, systems of governance, and other matters. The new constitution was a prerequisite to ending the unity government and preparing the groundwork for presidential and legislative elections.

Economic life remained difficult for ordinary Zimbabweans; four out of five people had no form of modern employment. The production of food and export crops had still not recovered the levels realized before the government accelerated its land-redistribution strategy in the early 21st century. HIV/AIDS had reduced life expectancy for women to 34 years. Meanwhile, new diamond-mining activities produced substantial new wealth for a favoured sector of the population, but analysts and civic leaders worried that this windfall might be funneled into ZANU-PF patronage and repression.

(LARAY DENZER)

Acharya, Amitav. UNESCO Chair in Transnational Challenges and Governance, American University, Washington, D.C. Author of *Whose Ideas Matter? Agency and Power in Asian Regionalism.* •WORLD AFFAIRS: *Multinational and Regional Organizations*

Alexander, Emma. Freelance Writer. •OBITUARIES *(in part)*

Alexander, Steve. Freelance Technology Writer. •COMPUTERS AND INFORMATION SYSTEMS

Allaby, Michael. Freelance Writer. Author of *Encyclopedia of Weather and Climate* and *Basics of Environmental Science.* •THE ENVIRONMENT: *Environmental Issues; International Activities*

Almond, Mark. Visiting Professor in International Relations, Bilkent University, Ankara, Tur., and the University of Oxford. Author of *Uprising! Political Upheavals That Have Shaped the World.* •SPECIAL REPORT: *The Arab Spring: The End of the Beginning*

Andrejevich, Milan. Professor of History, Ivy Tech Community College, South Bend (Ind.) campus; Adjunct Professor of Communication, Valparaiso (Ind.) University. •WORLD AFFAIRS: *Bosnia and Herzegovina; Kosovo; Montenegro; Serbia*

Anthony, John Duke. President and CEO, National Council on U.S.-Arab Relations; International Economic Policy Advisor, U.S. Department of State. Author of *The United Arab Emirates: Dynamics of State Formation.* •WORLD AFFAIRS: *Oman; Qatar*

Asimow, Paul D. Professor of Geology and Geochemistry, California Institute of Technology. •EARTH SCIENCES: *Geology and Geochemistry*

Augustyn, Adam. Assistant Editor, Encyclopædia Britannica. •BIOGRAPHIES *(in part)*

Aurora, Vincent. Lecturer in French and Romance Philology, Columbia University, New York City. Author of *Michel Leiris' Failles: Immobile in Mobili.* •LITERATURE: *French:* France

Bahry, Louay. Adjunct Professor of Political Science, University of Tennessee. Author of *The Baghdad Bahn.* •WORLD AFFAIRS: *Bahrain; Iraq; Kuwait; United Arab Emirates; Yemen*

Bamia, Aida A. Professor Emeritus of Arabic Language and Literature, University of Florida; Visiting Professor, University of Michigan. Author of *The Graying of the Raven: Cultural and Sociopolitical Significance of Algerian Folk Poetry.* Translator of Sahar Khalifeh's *The Inheritance* and *The Image, the Icon, and the Covenant,* Ali Bader's *Papa Sartre: A Modern Arabic Novel,* and Naguib Mahfouz's *Heart of the Night.* •LITERATURE: *Arabic*

Barrett, David B. Research Professor of Missiometrics, World Evangelization Research Center. Author of *World Christian Encyclopedia* and *Schism and Renewal in Africa.* Coauthor of *World Christian Trends, AD 30–AD 2200: Interpreting the Annual Christian Megacensus.* •RELIGION: *Tables (in part)*

Baru, Sanjaya. Director for Geo-Economics and Strategy, International Institute for Strategic Studies, London; Honorary Senior Fellow, Centre for Policy Research, New Delhi. Author of *Strategic Consequences of India's Economic Performance.* •WORLD AFFAIRS: *India*

Bauer, Patricia. Assistant Editor, Encyclopædia Britannica. •BIOGRAPHIES *(in part);* CALENDAR; DISASTERS; LITERATURE: *Table;* OBITUARIES *(in part);* PERFORMING ARTS: *Motion Pictures (table)*

Beckwith, David C. Freelance Writer. •WORLD AFFAIRS: *United States; United States:* Developments in the States

Bell, Susanna. Journalist. •WORLD AFFAIRS: *Finland*

Berry, R. Stephen. Professor Emeritus, University of Chicago. Coauthor of *Phase Transitions of Simple Systems.* •NOBEL PRIZES *(in part)*

Boerner, Leigh Krietsch. Science Writer. •PHYSICAL SCIENCES: *Chemistry*

Bradsher, Henry S. Foreign Affairs Analyst and Lecturer. Author of *Afghan Communism and Soviet Intervention.* •WORLD AFFAIRS: *Philippines*

Brecher, Kenneth. Professor of Astronomy and Physics; Director, Science and Mathematics Education Center, Boston University. •PHYSICAL SCIENCES: *Astronomy*

Brockmann, Stephen. Professor of German, Carnegie Mellon University, Pittsburgh. Author of *A Critical History of German Film, Literature and German Reunification, German Literary Culture at the Zero Hour,* and *Nuremberg: The Imaginary Capital.* •LITERATURE: *German*

Brokopp, John G. Media Relations Consultant, Freelance Journalist, and Syndicated Columnist on casino gambling. Author of *Thrifty Gambling* and *Insider's Guide to Internet Gambling: Your Sourcebook for Safe and Profitable Gambling.* •SPORTS AND GAMES: *Equestrian Sports:* Thoroughbred Racing: *United States*

Brown, Bess. Regional Economic and Environmental Advisor, Organization for Security and Co-operation in Europe. Author of *Authoritarianism in the New States of Central Asia.* •WORLD AFFAIRS: *Kazakhstan; Kyrgyzstan; Tajikistan; Turkmenistan; Uzbekistan*

Brown, Geoff. Critic and Historian. Editor of *Alistair Cooke at the Movies.* •PERFORMING ARTS: *Motion Pictures*

Buchan, David. Political and Energy Consultant. Author of *Energy and Climate Change: Europe at the Crossroads.* •WORLD AFFAIRS: *France*

Bungs, Dzintra. Senior Research Fellow, Latvian Institute of International Affairs, Riga. Author of *The Baltic States: Problems and Prospects of Membership in the European Union.* •WORLD AFFAIRS: *Latvia*

Burns, Erik T. Writer. •WORLD AFFAIRS: *Portugal*

Byrd, Herman J. Director, Belize Archives and Records Service. •WORLD AFFAIRS: *Belize*

Byrne, Justin. Independent Scholar. •WORLD AFFAIRS: *Spain*

Campbell, Robert. Architect and Architecture Critic. Author of *Cityscapes of Boston: An American City Through Time.* •ARCHITECTURE AND CIVIL ENGINEERING: *Architecture*

Carter, Robert W. Journalist. •SPORTS AND GAMES: *Equestrian Sports:* Steeplechasing; Thoroughbred Racing: *International*

Cheuse, Alan. Writing Faculty, English Department, George Mason University, Fairfax, Va.; Book Commentator, National Public Radio. Author of *Song of Slaves in the Desert, To Catch the Lightning: A Novel of American Dreaming, The Fires, The Light Possessed, A Trance After Breakfast: And Other Passages,* and *Listening to the Page: Adventures in Reading and Writing.* •LITERATURE: *English:* United States

Chua Lee Hoong. Political Editor, *The Straits Times,* Singapore. •WORLD AFFAIRS: *Singapore*

Clark, David Draper. Editor and Translator. •LITERATURE: *English:* Other Literature in English

Clark, Janet H. Editor, Independent Analyst, and Writer on international economic and financial topics. •NOBEL PRIZES *(in part)*

Coate, Roger A. Paul Coverdell Chair of Public Policy, Georgia College and State University; Distinguished Professor Emeritus of Political Science, University of South Carolina. Coauthor of *United Nations Politics: International Organization in a Divided World* and *The United Nations and Changing World Politics.* •WORLD AFFAIRS: *United Nations*

Coller, Ken. President, West Seattle Productions. •SPORTS AND GAMES: *Wrestling:* Sumo

Collins, Nigel. Former Editor of *The Ring.* •BIOGRAPHIES *(in part);* SPORTS AND GAMES: *Boxing*

Corkin, Nicola. Ph.D., European Research Institute, University of Birmingham, Eng. •WORLD AFFAIRS: *Germany*

Cosgrave, Bronwyn. Author, Journalist, and Broadcaster. Founding Chairperson, The Dorchester Collection Fashion Prize. Author of *Made for Each Other: Fashion and the Academy Awards* and *Costume and Fashion: A Complete History.* Editor of *Sample: 100 Fashion Designers, 010 Curators: Cuttings from Contemporary Fashion.* •FASHIONS

Coveney, Michael. Theatre Critic. Author of *Ken Campbell: The Great Caper, The World According to Mike Leigh, The Andrew Lloyd Webber Story,* and others. •PERFORMING ARTS: *Theatre:* Great Britain and Ireland

Crisp, Brian F. Associate Professor of Political Science, Washington University, St. Louis, Mo. Author of *Democratic Institutional Design.* •WORLD AFFAIRS: *Colombia (in part)*

Crossing, Peter F. Data Analyst, World Christian Database; Center for the Study of Global Christianity. Associate Editor of *World Christian Encyclopedia.* •RELIGION: *Tables (in part)*

Cruickshank, Judith. Journalist. •PERFORMING ARTS: *Dance:* Europe

Cunningham, John M. Research Editor, Encyclopædia Britannica. Former Staff Writer, *Stylus Magazine.* •BIOGRAPHIES *(in part)*

Curley, Robert. Senior Editor, Science and Technology, Encyclopædia Britannica. •BIOGRAPHIES *(in part);* SPECIAL REPORT: *Fracking*

Cuttino, John Charles. President, Portal Commerce & Logistics, LLC. •WORLD AFFAIRS: *Brazil*

David-Barrett, Liz. Research Fellow, University of Oxford. Author of *Business in the Balkans: The Case for Cross-Border Co-Operation.* •WORLD AFFAIRS: *Croatia*

Davis, Kevin. Journalist; Author; Part-Time Journalism Instructor, Loyola University, Chicago; Adjunct Faculty, Graham School of General Studies, University of Chicago. Author of *Defending the Damned: Inside Chicago's Cook County Public Defender's Office* and *The Wrong Man.* •HEALTH AND DISEASE; HEALTH AND DISEASE: Sidebar

Denselow, Robin. World Music Correspondent, *The Guardian* (London); Producer/Correspondent, BBC TV and Radio. Author of *When the Music's Over: The Story of Political Pop.* •PERFORMING ARTS: *Music:* Popular (International)

Denzer, LaRay. Lecturer, specializing in West African history and biography, Northwestern University, Evanston, Ill. Author of *Folayegbe M. Akintunde-Ighodalo: A Public Life.* Coeditor of *Gendering the African Diaspora: Women, Culture, and Historical Change in the Caribbean and Nigerian Hinterland.* •WORLD AFFAIRS: *Angola; Congo, Democratic Republic of the; Ghana; Kenya; Liberia; Malawi; Mozambique; Nigeria; Rwanda; Sierra Leone; Sudan; Sudan, South; Sudan, South: Sidebar; Tanzania; Uganda; Zambia; Zimbabwe*

Dietz, Henry A. Professor, Department of Government, University of Texas at Austin. •WORLD AFFAIRS: *Peru*

DiGiacomo, Paul. Deputy Manager, STATS LLC. •SPORTS AND GAMES: *Automobile Racing:* Grand Prix Racing; *Football:* Canadian; U.S.; *Ice Skating; Skiing*

Dlamini, Nhlanhla. Lecturer and Head of History Department, University of Swaziland. •WORLD AFFAIRS: *Swaziland*

Dooling, Dave. Education and Public Outreach Officer, National Solar Observatory, Sacramento Peak, New Mexico. Author of *The Christmas Planet;* Coauthor of *Engineering Tomorrow.* •PHYSICAL SCIENCES: *Space Exploration*

Duignan, Brian. Senior Editor, Philosophy, Encyclopædia Britannica. Editor of *The Executive Branch of the Federal Government: Purpose, Process, and People.* •BIOGRAPHIES *(in part)*

Ebeling, Mary. Assistant Professor of Sociology, Department of Culture and Communication, Drexel University, Philadelphia. •WORLD AFFAIRS: *Burundi; Comoros; Djibouti; Mauritius; Seychelles*

El-Amir, Ayman M. Columnist, *Al-Ahram Weekly;* Media Consultant. •WORLD AFFAIRS: *Egypt*

Eldridge, Alison. Research Editor, Encyclopædia Britannica. •BIOGRAPHIES *(in part)*

Esteban, Verónica. Journalist and Bilingual Editor. •LITERATURE: *Spanish:* Spain

Fagan, Kieran. Journalist; Media Consultant; Former Assistant Editor, *The Irish Times.* •WORLD AFFAIRS: *Ireland*

Fahey, Michael R. Journalist. •WORLD AFFAIRS: *China; Taiwan (Republic of China)*

Fealy, Greg. Associate Professor of Indonesian Politics, Australian National University, Canberra. Coauthor of *Joining the Caravan?: The Middle East, Islamism and Indonesia.* •WORLD AFFAIRS: *Indonesia*

Fendell, Robert J. Freelance Writer on automobiles and racing. Author of *The New Era Car Book and Auto Survival Guide* and *The Encyclopedia of Auto Racing Greats.* •SPORTS AND GAMES: *Automobile Racing:* U.S. Auto Racing; Rallies and Other Races *(in part)*

Fisher, Martin. Editor, *Oryx.* Coeditor of *The Natural History of Oman: A Festschrift for Michael Gallagher.* •THE ENVIRONMENT: *Wildlife Conservation*

Fisher, Sharon. Ph.D., Central European and Balkan Specialist, IHS Global Insight, Inc., Washington, D.C. Author of *Political Change in Post-Communist Slovakia and Croatia: From Nationalist to Europeanist.* •WORLD AFFAIRS: *Czech Republic; Slovakia*

Flink, Steve. Columnist for www.tennischannel.com. Inducted into the Eastern Tennis Hall of Fame, 2010. Author of *The Greatest Tennis Matches of the Twentieth Century.* •SPORTS AND GAMES: *Tennis*

Follett, Christopher. Freelance Journalist. Author of "The Danish Composer Asger Hamerik and Berlioz." •WORLD AFFAIRS: *Denmark*

Frey, William H. Senior Fellow, The Brookings Institution; Research Professor of Population Studies, University of Michigan. Coauthor of *America by the Numbers: A Field Guide to the U.S. Population.* •SPECIAL REPORT: *The U.S. Census of 2010: Foreshadowing a Century of Change*

Fridovich-Keil, Judith L. Professor, Department of Human Genetics, Emory University School of Medicine, Atlanta. •LIFE SCIENCES: *Molecular Biology and Genetics*

Fuller, Elizabeth. Editor, Radio Free Europe/Radio Liberty. •WORLD AFFAIRS: *Armenia; Azerbaijan; Georgia*

Furmonavičius, Darius. Director, Lithuanian Research Centre, Nottingham, Eng. Author of *Lithuania Rejoins Europe.* •WORLD AFFAIRS: *Lithuania*

Gallagher, Tom. Professor of Ethnic Peace and Conflict, University of Bradford, Eng. Author of *Theft of a Nation: Romania Since Communism* and others. •WORLD AFFAIRS: *Moldova; Romania*

Ganado, Albert. Lawyer; Former Chairman, Malta National Archives Advisory Committee; Past President, Malta Historical Society. Author of *Miniature Maps of Malta; Valletta, Città Nuova: A Map History (1566–1600);* and *Malta in World War II: Contemporary Watercolours by Alfred Gerada (1940–1942).* •WORLD AFFAIRS: *Malta*

Garrod, Mark. Golf Correspondent, PA Sport, U.K. •SPORTS AND GAMES: *Golf*

Gibbons, J. Whitfield. Professor Emeritus of Ecology, Savannah River Ecology Laboratory, University of Georgia. Coauthor of *Ecoviews: Snakes, Snails, and Environmental Tales.* •LIFE SCIENCES: *Zoology*

Gorlinski, Virginia. Editor, Arts and Culture, Encyclopædia Britannica. •BIOGRAPHIES *(in part)*

Gragnani, Cristina. Assistant Professor of Italian, Temple University, Philadelphia. Coauthor, *Sottoboschi letterari: sei case studies tra otto e novecento;* Coeditor of *Taccuino di Harvard.* •LITERATURE: *Italian*

Graham, John W. Chair Emeritus, Canadian Foundation for the Americas; Former Canadian Ambassador. •WORLD AFFAIRS: *Dominican Republic; Suriname*

Greene, Megan. Independent Eurozone Economist. •WORLD AFFAIRS: *Austria*

Gregersen, Erik. Associate Editor, Encyclopædia Britannica. •BIOGRAPHIES *(in part);* OBITUARIES *(in part)*

Greskovic, Robert. Dance Writer, *The Wall Street Journal.* Author of *Ballet 101.* •PERFORMING ARTS: *Dance:* North America

Guymon, J. Carl. Columnist, *Amateur Wrestling News.* Television Broadcaster for Wrestling, Fox Sports Net; Radio Play-by-Play, Takedown Radio. •SPORTS AND GAMES: *Wrestling:* Freestyle and Greco-Roman

Haag, Martin. Business and Economics Writer. Author of *Percy Barnevik.* •WORLD AFFAIRS: *Sweden*

Haddad, Mahmoud. Associate Professor of History, University of Balamand, Leb. Author of *The Rise of Arab Nationalism Reconsidered.* •WORLD AFFAIRS: *Lebanon; Saudi Arabia*

Hammer, William R. Fritiof Fryxell Professor of Geology, Augustana College, Rock Island, Ill., and Director, Augustana Center for Polar Studies. Author of *Gondwana Dinosaurs from the Jurassic of Antarctica.* •LIFE SCIENCES: *Paleontology*

Hanson, Kristan M. Visual Resources Librarian, MacLean Visual Resource Center, Flaxman Library, The School of the Art Institute of Chicago. •SPECIAL REPORT: *Yarn Bombing*

Hanson, Stephanie. Director of Policy and Outreach, One Acre Fund. •WORLD AFFAIRS: *Somalia*

Havemann, Joel. Retired Editor and National and European Economics Correspondent, Washington and Brussels Bureaus, *Los Angeles Times.* Author of *A Life Shaken: My Encounter with Parkinson's Disease.* •SPECIAL REPORT: *The Elusive Economic Recovery*

Helm, Toby. Political Editor, *The Observer.* •WORLD AFFAIRS: *European Union*

Hibler, Joan. Associate Editor, Encyclopædia Britannica. •BIOGRAPHIES *(in part)*

Hobbs, Greg. Senior Contributing Writer; Football Historian; longtime writer with newspapers and the Australian Football League. Author of *Allen Aylet: My Game* and several books on Australian football. •SPORTS AND GAMES: *Football:* Australian

Hoffman, Dean A. Member, Communicators Hall of Fame, Harness Racing Museum. Author of *Yankeeland: The Farm the Kellers Built, Castleton Farm: A Tradition of Standardbred Excellence, Quest for Excellence: Hanover Shoe Farms: The First 75 Years,* and *The Hambletonian: America's Trotting Classic.* •SPORTS AND GAMES: *Equestrian Sports:* Harness Racing

Hollar, Sherman. Associate Editor, Encyclopædia Britannica. •BIOGRAPHIES *(in part)*

Homel, David. Freelance Writer; Lecturer, Concordia University, Montreal. Author of *Midway* and others. •LITERATURE: *French:* Canada

Hunter, Paul. Hockey Reporter, *Toronto Star.* •SPORTS AND GAMES: *Ice Hockey*

Hussainmiya, B.A. Associate Professor, Department of History, University of Brunei Darussalam. Author of *The Brunei Constitution of 1959: An Inside History.* •WORLD AFFAIRS: *Brunei*

Jamail, Milton. Author of *Full Count: Inside Cuban Baseball* and *Venezuelan Bust, Baseball Boom: Andrés Reiner and Scouting on the New Frontier.* •SPORTS AND GAMES: *Baseball:* Latin America

Jasner, Andy. Freelance Writer. Author of *Baltimore Ravens (Inside the NFL).* •SPORTS AND GAMES: *Basketball:* Professional

Jerardi, Dick. Writer, *Philadelphia Daily News.* •SPORTS AND GAMES: *Basketball:* College

Joffé, George. Lecturer, Department of Politics and International Studies, University of Cambridge; Department of Geography, King's College, University of London; Director, RUSI Qatar. Editor of *Journal of North African Studies.* •WORLD AFFAIRS: *Algeria; Morocco; Tunisia*

Johnson, Todd M. Director, Center for the Study of Global Christianity. Coauthor of *World Christian Encyclopedia.* •RELIGION: *Tables (in part)*

Jones, David G.C. Author of *Atomic Physics.* •NOBEL PRIZES *(in part);* PHYSICAL SCIENCES: *Physics*

Jones, Mark P. Joseph D. Jamail Chair in Latin American Studies, Rice University, Houston. Author of *Electoral Laws and the Survival of Presidential Democracies.* •WORLD AFFAIRS: *Argentina*

Kapp, Clare. Freelance Consultant •WORLD AFFAIRS: *Switzerland*

Karimi-Hakkak, Ahmad. Professor and Founding Director, Center for Persian Studies, University of Maryland. Poetry Editor of *Strange Times, My Dear: The PEN Anthology of Contemporary Iranian Literature.* Coeditor of *Essays on Nima Yushij: Animating Modernism in Persian Poetry.* •LITERATURE: *Persian*

Kazamaru, Yoshihiko. Literary Critic; Professor, Morioka University, Takizawa, Japan. •LITERATURE: *Japanese*

Kelling, George H. Ph.D.; Lieutenant Colonel, U.S. Army (ret.). Author of *Countdown to Rebellion: British Policy in Cyprus, 1939–1955.* •WORLD AFFAIRS: *Cyprus*

Kellner, Peter. President, YouGov PLC. Author of *Democracy: 1,000 Years in Pursuit of British Liberty* and others. •BIOGRAPHIES *(in part);* WORLD AFFAIRS: *United Kingdom; United Kingdom:* Sidebar

King, Thad. Manager, Encyclopædia Britannica Almanac. •ARCHITECTURE AND CIVIL ENGINEERING: *Table*

Kinninmont, Jane. Senior Research Fellow, Middle East and North Africa, Chatham House. Contributor to *Power and Politics in the Persian Gulf Monarchies.* •WORLD AFFAIRS: *Jordan*

Knox, Paul. Associate Professor, School of Journalism, Ryerson University, Toronto. •WORLD AFFAIRS: *Bolivia; Ecuador*

Koper, Keith D. Associate Professor of Geophysics, University of Utah, Salt Lake City. •EARTH SCIENCES: *Geophysics*

Krause, Stefan. Freelance Analyst. •WORLD AFFAIRS: *Greece; Macedonia*

Kuiper, Kathleen. Senior Editor, Arts and Culture, Encyclopædia Britannica. Editor of *Merriam-Webster's Encyclopedia of Literature, The Britannica Guide to Ancient Civilizations* series, *The Britannica Guide to Literary Elements* series, and others. •BIOGRAPHIES *(in part)*

Lawler, Nancy Ellen. Professor Emerita, Oakton Community College, Des Plaines, Ill. Author of *Soldiers, Airmen, Spies, and Whisperers: The Gold Coast in World War II* and others. •WORLD AFFAIRS: *Benin; Burkina Faso; Cameroon; Central African Republic; Congo, Republic of the; Côte d'Ivoire; Gabon; Guinea; Mali; Mauritania; Niger; Senegal; Togo*

Lawson, Fred H. Professor of Government, Mills College, Oakland, Calif. Author of *Why Syria Goes to War.* •WORLD AFFAIRS: *Syria*

Le Comte, Douglas. Retired Meteorologist, Climate Prediction Center, U.S. National Oceanic and Atmospheric Administration. •EARTH SCIENCES: *Meteorology and Climate*

Legassick, Martin. Professor Emeritus of History, University of the Western Cape, Bellville, S.Af. Author of *Subjugation and the Roots of Democracy in South Africa: The Struggle for the Eastern Cape, 1800–1854.* •WORLD AFFAIRS: *South Africa*

Levin, Ben. Documentary Filmmaker; Professor, Department of Radio, Television, and Film, University of North Texas. Co-producer and Co-director, *Verso Negro: Black Verse Poetry of the Spanish Caribbean.* •PERFORMING ARTS: *Motion Pictures:* Documentary Films

Lindstrom, Sieg. Managing Editor, *Track & Field News.* •BIOGRAPHIES *(in part);* SPORTS AND GAMES: *Track and Field Sports (Athletics)*

Litweiler, John. Contributing Jazz Critic, *Chicago Sun-Times, www.pointofdeparture.org,* and *www.goodbaitbooks.com.* Author of *Mojo Snake Minuet: A Novel.* •OBITUARIES *(in part);* PERFORMING ARTS: *Music:* Jazz

Logsdon, John M. Professor Emeritus, Space Policy Institute, Elliott School of International Affairs, The George Washington University, Washington, D.C. Author of *John F. Kennedy and the Race to the Moon.* •PHYSICAL SCIENCES: *Space Exploration:* Sidebar

Longmore, Andrew. Senior Sports Writer, *The Sunday Times* (London); Former Assistant Editor, *The Cricketer.* Author of *Kieren Fallon: The Biography of the Controversial Jockey.* •BIOGRAPHIES *(in part);* SPORTS AND GAMES: *Cricket; Cricket:* Sidebar

Macpherson, Cluny. Professor, College of Humanities and Social Sciences, Massey University, Albany campus, Auckland, N.Z. Coauthor of *Samoan Medical Belief and Practice* and *Warm Winds of Change: Globalisation in Contemporary Samoa.* •WORLD AFFAIRS: *Dependent States:* Pacific Ocean; *Fiji; Kiribati; Marshall Islands; Micronesia, Federated States of; Samoa; Solomon Islands; Tonga; Tuvalu; Vanuatu*

Maguire, Robert E. Professor, Elliott School of International Affairs, The George Washington University, Washington, D.C. Author of *Haiti Held Hostage: International Responses to the Quest for Nationhood 1986–1996.* •WORLD AFFAIRS: *Haiti*

Makovicky, Peter V. Associate Curator and Chair, Department of Geology, The Field Museum of Natural History, Chicago. •SPECIAL REPORT: *Antarctic Dinosaurs*

Mancoff, Debra N. Adjunct Professor of Art History, School of the Art Institute of Chicago. Author of

Icons of Beauty: Art, Culture, and the Image of Women; 50 American Artists You Should Know; and *The Garden in Art.* •ART AND ART EXHIBITIONS: *Art; Art Exhibitions*

Mango, Andrew. Foreign Affairs Analyst. Author of *Atatürk: The Biography of the Founder of Modern Turkey, The Turks Today,* and *From the Sultan to Atatürk—Turkey (Makers of the Modern World).* •WORLD AFFAIRS: *Turkey*

Marek, Janele M. Account Supervisor, BarkleyREI. •SPORTS AND GAMES: *Bobsleigh, Skeleton, and Luge:* Luge

Marples, David R. Distinguished University Professor, Department of History and Classics, University of Alberta. Author of *Heroes and Villains: Creating National History in Contemporary Ukraine, Belarus: A Denationalized Nation,* and *Motherland: Russia in the Twentieth Century.* •WORLD AFFAIRS: *Belarus; Ukraine*

Marston, John A. Professor, Centro de Estudios de Asia y África, El Colegio de México. Editor of *Anthropology and Community in Cambodia: Reflections on the Work of May Ebihara.* •WORLD AFFAIRS: *Cambodia*

Mathieson, David Scott. Senior Researcher, Asia Division of Human Rights Watch. Coauthor of *Militia Redux; or, Sor and the Revival of Paramilitarism in Thailand.* •WORLD AFFAIRS: *Myanmar (Burma)*

Mathis, William J. Managing Director, National Education Policy Center, University of Colorado Boulder. Coeditor of *The Obama Education Blueprint: Researchers Examine the Evidence.* •EDUCATION

Matthíasson, Björn. Economist, Iceland. •WORLD AFFAIRS: *Iceland*

McKenna, Amy. Senior Editor, Encyclopædia Britannica. •BIOGRAPHIES *(in part)*

McLachlan, Keith S. Professor Emeritus, School of Oriental and African Studies, University of London. Author of *The Boundaries of Modern Iran.* Coeditor of *Technology, Tradition and Survival.* Contributor to *Boundary Politics and International Boundaries of Iran.* •WORLD AFFAIRS: *Iran*

McMillan, Neale. Managing Editor, South Pacific News Service. Author of *Top of the Greasy Pole: New Zealand Prime Ministers of Recent Times.* •WORLD AFFAIRS: *New Zealand*

McPherson, James M. George Henry Davis '86 Professor Emeritus of American History, Princeton University. Author of *Battle Cry of Freedom: The Civil War Era, This Mighty Scourge: Perspectives on the Civil War,* and others. •SPECIAL REPORT: *The Civil War: Why They Fought*

Mendes, Victor K. Associate Professor and Graduate Program Director, University of Massachusetts Dartmouth. •LITERATURE: *Portuguese:* Portugal

Middlebrook, Kevin J. Professor of Politics, Institute for the Study of the Americas, University of London. Coauthor of *Mexico Since 1980 (The World Since 1980).* •WORLD AFFAIRS: *Mexico*

Molnar, Alex. Director of Publications, National Education Policy Center; Research Professor, University of Colorado Boulder. •EDUCATION: Sidebar

Moredock, Janet. Freelance Writer and Editor. •WORLD AFFAIRS: *East Timor; Malaysia; Nauru; Palau; Papua New Guinea*

Morgan, Paul. Communications Director of *Premiership Rugby.* •SPORTS AND GAMES: *Football:* Rugby; Rugby: Sidebar

Murray, Lorraine. Associate Editor, Encyclopædia Britannica. •BIOGRAPHIES *(in part);* WORLD AFFAIRS: *Korea, Democratic People's Republic of; Korea, Republic of*

Myers, David J. Professor of Political Science, Pennsylvania State University. Coeditor of and contributor to *The Unraveling of Representative Democracy in Venezuela.* •WORLD AFFAIRS: *Venezuela*

Naranjo, Ralph. Technical Editor, *Practical Sailor Magazine.* Author of *Boatyards and Marinas: A Boat Owner's Guide to Smart Shopping.* •SPORTS AND GAMES: *Sailing (Yachting)*

Nishizaki, Yoshinori. Assistant Professor, Department of Political Science, National University of Singapore. Author of *Political Authority and Provincial Identity in Thailand: The Making of Banharn-buri.* •WORLD AFFAIRS: *Thailand*

Noda, Hiroki. Sporting News Reporter, *Kyodo News,* Tokyo. •SPORTS AND GAMES: *Baseball:* Japan

Nolen, Jeannette L. Social Science Editor, Encyclopædia Britannica. •BIOGRAPHIES *(in part)*

Nowinski, Christopher. Cofounder and CEO, Sports Legacy Institute; Co-director, Center for the Study of Traumatic Encephalopathy, Boston University School of Medicine. Author of *Head Games: Football's Concussion Crisis from the NFL to Youth Leagues.* •SPECIAL REPORT: *Sports-Related Brain Injuries*

O'Leary, Christopher. Managing Editor, *The M&A Lawyer.* Contributing Writer, *Absolute Return; Investment Dealers Digest; eFinancialCareers.com.* •BUSINESS OVERVIEW

Olivella, Santiago. Ph.D. Student, Department of Political Science, Washington University, St. Louis, Mo. •WORLD AFFAIRS: *Colombia (in part)*

Oppenheim, Lois Hecht. Professor of Political Science, American Jewish University, Los Angeles. Author of *Politics in Chile: Socialism, Authoritarianism, and Market Democracy,* 3rd ed. Coeditor of *After Pinochet: The Chilean Road to Democracy and the Market.* •WORLD AFFAIRS: *Chile*

O'Quinn, Jim. Editor in Chief, *American Theatre.* Editor, *The American Theatre Reader: Essays and Conversations from American Theatre Magazine.* •PERFORMING ARTS: *Theatre:* U.S. and Canada

Ortega, Robert. Senior Reporter, *Arizona Republic.* Author of *In Sam We Trust: The Untold Story of Sam Walton and How Wal-Mart Is Devouring America.* •WORLD AFFAIRS: *Paraguay*

Pallardy, Richard T. Research Editor and Assistant Manager, Encyclopædia Britannica. •BIOGRAPHIES *(in part);* OBITUARIES *(in part)*

Parry, Julie. Merchandising Communications Manager, Sprint Nextel. •SPORTS AND GAMES: *Bobsleigh, Skeleton, and Luge:* Bobsleigh; Skeleton

Parsons, Neil. Former Professor of History, University of Botswana. Author of *Clicko: The Wild Dancing Bushman.* •WORLD AFFAIRS: *Botswana*

Peaker, Carol. English Lecturer, University of Oxford. Author of *The Penguin Modern Painters: A History.* •LITERATURE: *English:* United Kingdom

Pérez, Louis A., Jr. J. Carlyle Sitterson Professor of History, University of North Carolina at Chapel Hill. Author of *Cuba: Between Reform and Revolution.* •WORLD AFFAIRS: *Cuba*

Pérez, Orlando J. Professor of Political Science, Central Michigan University. Author of *Political Culture in Panama: Democracy After Invasion.* Editor of *Post-invasion Panama: The Challenges of Democratization in the New World Order.* Coeditor of *Latin American Democracy: Emerging Reality or Endangered Species?* and others. •WORLD AFFAIRS: *Panama*

Peszek, Luan. Publications Director and Editor, *U.S.A. Gymnastics.* Author of *The Gymnastics Almanac.* •SPORTS AND GAMES: *Gymnastics*

Pholsena, Vatthana. Research Fellow, IRASEC-CNRS (National Centre for Scientific Research), Singapore. Author of *Post-war Laos: The Politics of Culture, History and Identity.* •WORLD AFFAIRS: *Laos*

Pletcher, Kenneth. Senior Editor, Geography, Encyclopædia Britannica. •BIOGRAPHIES *(in part);* SPECIAL REPORT: *Japan's Deadly Earthquake and Tsunami (in part)*

Ponmoni Sahadevan. Professor, Jawaharlal Nehru University, New Delhi. Author of *Conflict and Peacemaking in South Asia.* •WORLD AFFAIRS: *Maldives*

Poudel, Keshab. Managing Editor, *New Spotlight.* •WORLD AFFAIRS: *Bhutan; Nepal*

Rafferty, John P. Associate Editor, Earth and Life Sciences, Encyclopædia Britannica. •BIOGRAPHIES *(in part);* OBITUARIES *(in part);* SPECIAL REPORT: *Japan's Deadly Earthquake and Tsunami (in part)*

Rauch, Robert. Freelance Editor and Writer. •NOBEL PRIZES *(in part)*

Raun, Toivo U. Professor of Central Eurasian Studies, Indiana University. Author of *Estonia and the Estonians.* •WORLD AFFAIRS: *Estonia*

Ray, Michael. Assistant Editor, Encyclopædia Britannica. •BIOGRAPHIES *(in part);* COMPUTERS AND INFORMATION SYSTEMS: Sidebar; OBITUARIES *(in part);* WORLD AFFAIRS: *Norway:* Sidebar

Renwick, David. Freelance Journalist. •WORLD AFFAIRS: *Antigua and Barbuda; Bahamas, The; Barbados; Dependent States:* Caribbean and Bermuda; *Dominica; Grenada; Guyana; Jamaica; Saint Kitts and Nevis; Saint Lucia; Saint Vincent and the Grenadines; Trinidad and Tobago*

Reuning, Winifred. Editor and Web Manager, Office of Polar Programs, National Science Foundation. •WORLD AFFAIRS: *Antarctica*

Roby, Anne. Freelance Journalist; Program Associate, Institute for Mathematics and Science Education, University of Illinois at Chicago. •WORLD AFFAIRS: *Andorra; Liechtenstein; Luxembourg; Monaco*

Rogers, Kara. Senior Editor, Biomedical Sciences, Encyclopædia Britannica. •BIOGRAPHIES *(in part);* NOBEL PRIZES *(in part);* OBITUARIES *(in part);* SPECIAL REPORT: *The German E. coli Outbreak of 2011*

Rollin, Jack. Editor, *Sky Sports Football Yearbook* and *Playfair Football Annual.* Author of *Soccer at War 1939–45.* Coauthor of *The Forgotten FA Cup: The Competition of 1945–46* and others. •BIOGRAPHIES *(in part);* SPORTS AND GAMES: *Football:* Association Football (Soccer): *Africa and Asia; Europe*

Sale, Jennifer. Senior Copy Editor, Encyclopædia Britannica. •OBITUARIES *(in part)*

Sanders, Alan J.K. Freelance Mongolist; Former Lecturer in Mongolian Studies, School of Oriental and African Studies, University of London. Author of *Historical Dictionary of Mongolia.* Coauthor of *Colloquial Mongolian.* •WORLD AFFAIRS: *Mongolia*

Sandvik, Hilde. Doctor of Philosophy; Associate Professor, Department of History, University of Oslo. Author of *Norsk historie 1300–1625.* •WORLD AFFAIRS: *Norway*

Saracino, Peter. Freelance Defense Journalist. •MILITARY AFFAIRS; OBITUARIES *(in part)*

Saunders, Christopher. Professor Emeritus of Historical Studies, University of Cape Town. Coauthor of *Historical Dictionary of South Africa* and *South Africa: A Modern History.* •WORLD AFFAIRS: *Cape Verde; Chad; Equatorial Guinea; Gambia, The; Guinea-Bissau; Lesotho; Madagascar; Namibia; Sao Tome and Principe (São Tomé e Príncipe)*

Schiavo, Leda. Professor Emerita, University of Illinois at Chicago. Author of *El éxtasis de los límites: temas y figuras del decadentismo* and *Naufragios y comentarios.* Contributor to *Historia crítica de la literatura Argentina.* •LITERATURE: *Spanish:* Latin America

Schmidt, Fabian. Balkan Expert, Research and Education desk of Deutsche Welle Radio. •WORLD AFFAIRS: *Albania*

Schoppa, Leonard. Professor, Department of Politics, University of Virginia. Author of *Race for the Exits: The Unraveling of Japan's System of Social Protection.* •WORLD AFFAIRS: *Japan*

Schreiber, Barbara A. Editorial Assistant, Encyclopædia Britannica. •BIOGRAPHIES *(in part);* OBITUARIES *(in part)*

Schuster, Angela M.H. Contributing Editor, *Archaeology* magazine; Contributor, *New York Times;* Editor in Chief, *The Explorers Journal.* •ANTHROPOLOGY AND ARCHAEOLOGY: *Archaeology:* Eastern Hemisphere

Sego, Stephen. Freelance Journalist; Former Director, Radio Free Afghanistan. •WORLD AFFAIRS: *Afghanistan*

Seligson, Mitchell A. Centennial Professor of Political Science, Vanderbilt University, Nashville. Editor of *Elections and Democracy in Central America, Revisited.* Coauthor of *The Legitimacy Puzzle in Latin America: Political Support and Democracy in Eight Nations.* •WORLD AFFAIRS: *Costa Rica*

Serafin, Steven R. Director, Writing Center, Hunter College, City University of New York. Coeditor of *The Continuum Encyclopedia of American Literature* and *The Continuum Encyclopedia of British Literature.* •NOBEL PRIZES *(in part)*

Shelley, Andrew. Chief Executive, World Squash Federation. Author of *Squash Rules: A Player's Guide.* •SPORTS AND GAMES: *Squash*

Shepherd, Melinda C. Senior Editor, Encyclopædia Britannica. •BIOGRAPHIES *(in part);* MILITARY AFFAIRS: Sidebar; OBITUARIES *(in part);* SPORTS AND GAMES: *Automobile Racing:* Rallies and Other Races *(in part);* WORLD AFFAIRS: *Dependent States:* Europe and the Atlantic; Indian Ocean

Shubinsky, Valery. Poet, Writer, and Critic. Author of *Daniil Kharms: zhizn cheloveka na vetru, Mikhail Lomonosov: vserossiiskii chelovek,* and *Nikolay Gumilyov: zhizn poeta.* •LITERATURE: *Russian*

Simons, Paul. Freelance Journalist. Author of *The Action Plant.* •LIFE SCIENCES: *Botany*

Smith, Gregory O. Director, European Management Institute, Rome. •WORLD AFFAIRS: *San Marino; Vatican City State*

Smith, Lahra. Assistant Professor, Georgetown University, Washington, D.C. •WORLD AFFAIRS: *Ethiopia*

Snodgrass, Donald. Institute Fellow Emeritus, Harvard University. Coauthor of *Economics of Development,* 5th ed. •WORLD AFFAIRS: *Sri Lanka*

Sparks, Karen J. Director and Editor, Encyclopædia Britannica. •BIOGRAPHIES *(in part);* OBITUARIES *(in part);* WORLD AFFAIRS: *Bangladesh*

Spencer, Donna. Journalist, The Canadian Press. •SPORTS AND GAMES: *Curling*

Spera, Keith. Music Writer, *The Times-Picayune* (New Orleans). Author of *Groove Interrupted: Loss, Renewal and the Music of New Orleans.* •PERFORMING ARTS: *Music:* Popular (United States)

Stefon, Matt. Assistant Editor, Religion, Encyclopædia Britannica. •BIOGRAPHIES *(in part);* OBITUARIES *(in part)*

Stern, Irwin. Teaching Associate Professor of Foreign Languages, North Carolina State University. Editor of *Dictionary of Brazilian Literature.* Coauthor of *Spanish for Mental Health Professionals: A Step by Step Handbook.* •LITERATURE: *Portuguese:* Brazil

Stewart, Cameron. Associate Editor, *The Australian.* •WORLD AFFAIRS: *Australia*

Stos, William. Ph.D. Candidate, York University, Toronto. •WORLD AFFAIRS: *Canada*

Streicker, John. Lecturer, Yukon College; Researcher, Northern Climate Exchange, Northern Research Institute. Coauthor of *Quilt Sensations.* •WORLD AFFAIRS: *Arctic Regions*

Sumrall, Harry. Classical Operations Manager, Gracenote, Inc. •PERFORMING ARTS: *Music:* Classical

Susser, Leslie D. Diplomatic Correspondent, *The Jerusalem Report.* Coauthor of *Shalom Friend: The Life and Legacy of Yitzhak Rabin.* •WORLD AFFAIRS: *Israel*

Szilagyi, Zsofia. Political Analyst and Freelance Writer. •WORLD AFFAIRS: *Hungary*

Tae-Hee Gang. Professor, Korea National University of the Arts. Art Critic. President, Korea Association for History of Modern Art. Author of *Modern Art and Visual Culture.* •BIOGRAPHIES *(in part)*

Taylor, Jolanda Vanderwal. Associate Professor of Dutch and German, University of Wisconsin at Madison. Author of *A Family Occupation: Children of the War and the Memory of World War II in Dutch Literature of the 1960s.* •WORLD AFFAIRS: *Netherlands*

Taylor, Richard. Deputy Editor, *BCA Chronicle,* Cairo, Egypt. •SPORTS AND GAMES: *Basketball:* International

Taylor-Robinson, Michelle M. Professor of Political Science, Texas A&M University. Author of *Do the Poor Count? Democratic Institutions and Accountability in a Context of Poverty.* •WORLD AFFAIRS: *Honduras*

Teague, Elizabeth. Research Analyst, U.K. Foreign and Commonwealth Office. (The opinions expressed are personal and do not necessarily represent those of the British government.) •WORLD AFFAIRS: *Russia*

Teixeira, Iva. Consultant, Bain & Company. •WORLD AFFAIRS: *Bulgaria (in part)*

Thayer, Carlyle A. Professor Emeritus, University of New South Wales. Author of *The Vietnam People's Army Under Doi Moi.* •WORLD AFFAIRS: *Vietnam*

Thimangu, Patrick L. Journalist. •WORLD AFFAIRS: *Eritrea*

Tikkanen, Amy. Corrections Manager, Encyclopædia Britannica. •BIOGRAPHIES *(in part)*

Turner, Darrell J. Freelance Writer; Former Religion Writer, *Fort Wayne* (Ind.) *Journal Gazette;* Former Associate Editor, Religion News Service. •RELIGION

Valencic, Joseph. Author, Film Writer, and Slovenian Scholar. •WORLD AFFAIRS: *Slovenia*

VanDerwarker, Amber. Associate Professor of Anthropology, University of California, Santa Barbara. Author of *Farming, Hunting and Fishing in the Olmec World.* Coeditor of *Integrating Zooarchaeology and Paleoethnobotany: A Consideration of Issues, Methods, and Cases.* •ANTHROPOLOGY AND ARCHAEOLOGY: *Archaeology:* Western Hemisphere *(in part)*

Verdi, Robert. Team Historian, Chicago Blackhawks. Author of *Chicago Blackhawks: Seventy-five Years.* Coauthor of *The Golden Jet; McMahon!: The Bare Truth About Chicago's Brashest Bear; Once a Bum, Always a Dodger: My Life in Baseball from Brooklyn to Los Angeles;* and *Holy Cow!* Contributor to *One Goal Achieved: The Inside Story of the 2010 Stanley Cup Champions.* •SPORTS AND GAMES: *Baseball:* U.S. and Canada

Wallenfeldt, Jeff. Senior Editor and Manager, Geography and History Group, Encyclopædia Britannica. •BIOGRAPHIES *(in part)*

Wang Xiaoming. Zijiang Lecture Professor of Chinese Literature and Chair of the Board of the Center for Modern Chinese Literature, East China Normal University; Professor of Cultural Studies and Director of the Center for Contemporary Culture Studies, Shanghai University. Author of *Life Cannot Be Faced Straight-On: A Biography of Lu Xun.* •LITERATURE: *Chinese*

Wanninger, Richard S. Freelance Journalist. •SPORTS AND GAMES: *Volleyball*

Watson, Rory. Freelance Journalist, specializing in European Union affairs; Brussels Correspondent, *The Times* (London). Coauthor of *The Belgian House of Representatives.* Contributor to *The European Union: How Does It Work?* •WORLD AFFAIRS: *Belgium*

Weil, Eric. Columnist and Contributor, *Buenos Aires Herald;* Reporter, Associated Press; South America Correspondent, *World Soccer;* Contributor, *FIFA Magazine.* •SPORTS AND GAMES: *Football:* Association Football (Soccer): *The Americas*

Weinstein, Martin. Professor Emeritus, Department of Political Science, William Paterson University of New Jersey. Author of *Uruguay: Democracy at the Crossroads* and numerous articles and book chapters on Uruguay. •WORLD AFFAIRS: *Uruguay*

Wereley, Sophie. Freelance Writer. •OBITUARIES *(in part)*

White, Martin L. Freelance Writer. •OBITUARIES *(in part)*

Whitten, Phillip. Executive Director, College Swimming Coaches Association of America; Former Editor in Chief, *Swimming World.* Author and/or editor of 18 books, including *The Complete Book of Swimming.* •SPORTS AND GAMES: *Swimming*

Wilkinson, John R. Freelance Sportswriter, United Kingdom. •SPORTS AND GAMES: *Cycling*

Wilson, Gregory D. Associate Professor, Department of Anthropology, University of California, Santa Barbara. Author of *The Archaeology of Everyday Life at Early Moundville.* •ANTHROPOLOGY AND ARCHAEOLOGY: *Archaeology:* Western Hemisphere *(in part)*

Wilson, Keith. Former Editorial Director, *Outdoor Photography* and *Black & White Photography.* Author of *The AVA Guide to Travel Photography.* •ART AND ART EXHIBITIONS: *Photography*

Winner, Christopher P. Editor and Publisher, *The American* (Rome). •WORLD AFFAIRS: *Italy*

Wolfe, Justin. Associate Professor, Department of History, Tulane University, New Orleans. Author of *The Everyday Nation-State: Community and Ethnicity in Nineteenth-Century Nicaragua.* •WORLD AFFAIRS: *Nicaragua*

Woods, Elizabeth Rhett. Writer. Author of *Coyote: A Tale of Unexpected Consequences; Woman Walking: Selected Poems; 1970: A Novel Poem; Beyond the Pale,* and other works. Web site: www.elizabethrhettwoods.ca. •LITERATURE: *English:* Canada

Woodward, Ralph Lee, Jr. Professor Emeritus of Latin American History, Tulane University, New Orleans. Author of *A Short History of Guatemala.* •WORLD AFFAIRS: *El Salvador; Guatemala*

Wyganowski, Michael. International Consultant. •WORLD AFFAIRS: *Poland*

Yovchev, Boris. Graduate Student, Ross School of Business, University of Michigan. •WORLD AFFAIRS: *Bulgaria (in part)*

Zegura, Stephen L. Professor Emeritus of Anthropology, University of Arizona. •ANTHROPOLOGY AND ARCHAEOLOGY: *Anthropology*

Ziemba, Rachel. Director of Global Macroeconomics at Roubini Global Economics. •WORLD AFFAIRS: *Libya*

Ziring, Lawrence. Arnold E. Schneider Professor Emeritus of Political Science, Western Michigan University. Author of *Pakistan in the Twentieth Century: A Political History* and *Pakistan: At the Crosscurrent of History.* Coauthor of *The United Nations: International Organization and World Politics.* Contributor to *South Asia's Weak States: Understanding the Regional Insecurity Predicament.* •WORLD AFFAIRS: *Pakistan*

Selected New and Revised Encyclopædia Britannica Articles

This section of the *Britannica Book of the Year* consists of articles that have been revised or added to the Britannica database and published at *Britannica Online* in 2011. The articles appearing here have been chosen by the yearbook editorial staff for their general interest or their timeliness.

The year 2011 marked the 10th anniversary of the September 11 attacks, a series of airline hijackings and suicide attacks against targets in the United States. Britannica observed the anniversary by publishing the substantially expanded article "September 11 Attacks" by Peter L. Bergen, CNN national security analyst and director of the national security studies program at the New America Foundation. A comprehensive revision of the article "Communitarianism" was undertaken in 2011 by Amitai Etzioni, a professor of sociology at George Washington University and a significant figure in the philosophy's emergence during the 1980s. The article "Blessed John Paul II," by ABC News correspondent William B. Blakemore, was revised to acknowledge John Paul's beatification in May 2011. A month later Britannica added the new article "Museum of Modern Art," in which Glenn D. Lowry, director of the Museum of Modern Art in New York City, describes the history of museums that collect modern and contemporary art and identifies the challenges they face in the 21st century. The article "Gothic Art" was also revised.

A new bibliography was added to the article "Stand-Up Comedy," which traces the evolution of this comedic form from Mark Twain through the Monty Python troupe to Jon Stewart. It was written by Richard Zoglin, author of *Comedy at the Edge: How Stand-Up in the 1970s Changed America*. In September 2011 the U.S. policy known as "Don't Ask, Don't Tell," governing the service of homosexuals in the military, came to an end; the article "Don't Ask, Don't Tell" was updated accordingly. The International Monetary Fund named its first female managing director in 2011, a landmark noted in the articles "International Monetary Fund," by Lawrence McQuillan of the Pacific Research Institute, and "Christine Lagarde," by analyst and writer Janet H. Clark. The year 2011 also witnessed the continued dwindling of the disease sometimes called dracunculiasis, described in the new article "Guinea Worm Disease" by Kara Rogers, Britannica's biomedical sciences editor.

September 11 Attacks

The deadliest terrorist attacks on American soil in U.S. history, the September 11 attacks were a series of airline hijackings and suicide attacks committed in 2001 by 19 militants associated with the Islamic extremist group al-Qaeda against targets in the United States. The attacks against New York City and Washington, D.C., caused extensive death and destruction and triggered an enormous U.S. effort to combat terrorism. Some 2,750 people were killed in New York, 184 at the Pentagon, and 40 in Pennsylvania (where one of the hijacked planes crashed after the passengers attempted to retake the plane); all 19 terrorists died. Police and fire departments in New York were especially hard-hit: hundreds had rushed to the scene of the attacks, and more than 400 police officers and firefighters were killed.

THE PLOT

The September 11 attacks, also called the 9/11 attacks, were precipitated in large part because Osama bin Laden, the leader of the militant Islamic organization al-Qaeda, held naive beliefs about the United States in the run-up to the attacks. Abu Walid al-Masri, an Egyptian who was a bin Laden associate in Afghanistan in the 1980s and '90s, explained that, in the years prior to the attacks, bin Laden became increasingly convinced that America was weak. "He believed that the United States was much weaker than some of those around him thought," Masri remembered, and "as evidence he referred to what happened to the United States in Beirut when the bombing of the Marines base led them to flee from Lebanon," referring to the destruction of the marine barracks there in 1983, which killed 241 American servicemen. Bin Laden believed that the United States was a "paper tiger," a belief shaped not just by America's departure from Lebanon following the marine barracks bombing but also by the withdrawal of American forces from Somalia in 1993, following the deaths of 18 U.S. servicemen in Mogadishu, and the American pullout from Vietnam in the 1970s.

The key operational planner of the September 11 attacks was Khalid Sheikh Mohammed (often referred to simply as "KSM" in the later *9/11 Commission Report* and in the media), who had spent his youth in Kuwait. Khalid Sheikh Mohammed became active in the Muslim Brotherhood, which he joined at age 16, and then he went to the United States to attend college, receiving a degree from North Carolina Agricultural and Technical State University in 1986. Afterward he traveled to Pakistan and then Afghanistan to wage jihad against the Soviet Union, which had launched an invasion against Afghanistan in 1979.

According to Yosri Fouda, a journalist at the Arabic-language cable television channel al-Jazeera who interviewed him in 2002, Khalid Sheikh Mohammed planned to blow up some dozen American planes in Asia during the mid-1990s, a plot (known as "Bojinka") that failed, "but the dream of Khalid Sheikh Mohammed never faded. And I think by putting his hand in the hands of bin Laden, he realized that now he stood a chance of bringing about his long awaited dream."

In 1996 Khalid Sheikh Mohammed met bin Laden in Tora Bora, Afghanistan. The 9-11 Commission (formally the National Commission on Terrorist Attacks Upon the United States), set up in 2002 by Pres. George W. Bush and the U.S. Congress to investigate the attacks of 2001, explained that it was then that Khalid Sheikh Mohammed "presented a proposal for an operation that would involve training pilots who would crash planes into buildings in the United States." Khalid Sheikh Mohammed dreamed up the tactical innovation of using hijacked planes to attack the United States, al-Qaeda provided the personnel, money, and logistical support to execute the operation, and bin Laden wove the attacks on New York and Washington into a larger strategic framework of attacking the "far enemy"—the United States—in order to bring about regime change across the Middle East.

The September 11 plot demonstrated that al-Qaeda was an organization of global reach. The plot played out across the globe with planning meetings in Malaysia, operatives taking flight lessons in the United States, coordination by plot leaders based in Hamburg, Germany, money transfers from Dubai, and recruitment of suicide operatives from countries around the Middle East—all activities that were ultimately overseen by al-Qaeda's leaders in Afghanistan.

Key parts of the September 11 plot took shape in Hamburg. Four of the key pilots and planners in the "Hamburg cell" who would take operational control of the September 11 attacks, including the lead hijacker Mohammed Atta, had a chance meeting on a train in Germany in 1999 with an Islamist militant who struck up a conversation with them about fighting jihad in Chechnya. The militant put the Hamburg cell in touch with an al-Qaeda operative living in Germany who explained that it was difficult to get to Chechnya at that time because many travelers were being detained in Georgia. He recommended they go to Afghanistan instead.

Although Afghanistan was critical to the rise of al-Qaeda, it was the experience that some of the plotters acquired in the West that made them simultaneously more zealous and better equipped to carry out the attacks. Three of the four plotters who would pilot the hijacked planes on September 11 and one of the key planners, Ramzi Binalshibh, became more radical while living in Hamburg. Some combination of perceived or real discrimination, alienation, and homesickness seems to have turned them all in a more militant direction. Increasingly cutting themselves off from the outside world, they gradually radicalized each other, and eventually the friends decided to wage battle in bin Laden's global jihad, setting off for Afghanistan in 1999 in search of al-Qaeda.

Atta and the other members of the Hamburg group arrived in Afghanistan in 1999 right at the moment that the September 11 plot was beginning to take shape. Bin Laden and his military commander Muhammad Atef realized that Atta and his fellow Western-educated jihadists were far better suited to lead the attacks on Washington and New York than the men they had already recruited, leading bin Laden to appoint Atta to head the operation.

The hijackers, most of whom were from Saudi Arabia, established themselves in the United States, many well in advance of the attacks. They traveled in small groups, and some of them received commercial flight training.

Throughout his stay in the United States, Atta kept Binalshibh updated on the plot's progress via e-mail. To cloak his activities, Atta wrote the messages as if he were writing to his girlfriend "Jenny," using innocuous code to inform Binalshibh that they were almost complete in their training and readiness for the attacks. Atta wrote in one message, "The first semester commences in three weeks . . . Nineteen certificates for private education and four exams." The referenced 19 "certificates" were code that identified the 19 al-Qaeda hijackers, while the four "exams" identified the targets of the attacks.

In the early morning of August 29, 2001, Atta called Binalshibh and said he had a riddle that he was trying to solve: "Two sticks, a dash and a cake with a stick down—what is it?" After considering the question, Binalshibh realized that Atta was telling him that the attacks would occur in two weeks—the two sticks being the number 11 and the cake with a stick down a 9. Putting it together, it meant that the attacks would occur on 11-9, or 11 September (in most countries the day precedes the month in numeric dates, but in the United States the month precedes the day; hence, it was 9-11 in the United States). On September 5 Binalshibh left Germany for Pakistan. Once there he sent a messenger to Afghanistan to inform bin Laden about both the day of the attack and its scope.

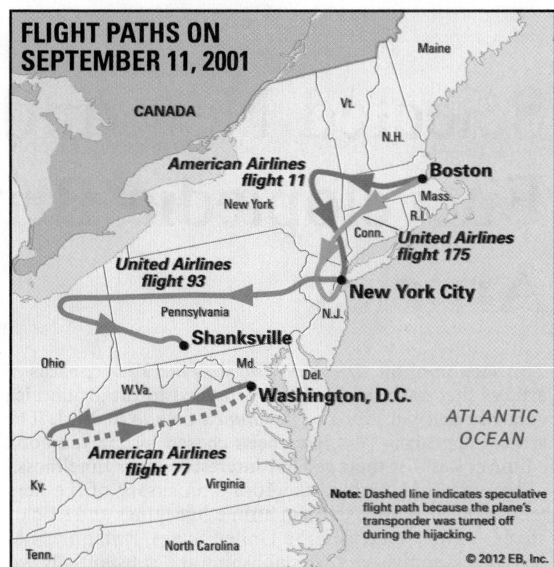

The routes of the four U.S. planes hijacked during the terrorist attacks of September 11, 2001.

THE ATTACKS

On September 11, 2001, groups of attackers boarded four domestic aircraft at three East Coast airports, and soon after takeoff they disabled the crews, some of whom may have been stabbed with box cutters the hijackers were secreting. The hijackers then took control of the aircraft, all large and bound for the West Coast with full loads of fuel. At 8:46 AM the first plane, American Airlines flight 11, which had originated from Boston, was piloted into the north tower of the World Trade Center in New York City. Most observers construed this initially to be an accident involving a small commuter plane. The second plane, United Airlines flight 175, also from Boston, struck the south tower 17 minutes later. At this point there was no doubt that the United States was under attack. Each structure was badly damaged by the impact and erupted into flames. Office workers who were trapped above the points of impact in some cases leapt to their deaths rather than face the infernos now raging inside the towers. The third plane, American Airlines flight 77, taking off from Dulles Airport near Washington, D.C., struck the southwest side of the Pentagon (just outside the city) at 9:37 AM, touching off a fire in that section of the structure. Minutes later the Federal Aviation Authority ordered a nationwide ground stop, and within the next hour (at 10:03 AM) the fourth aircraft, United Airlines flight 93 from Newark, New Jersey, crashed near Shanksville in the Pennsylvania countryside after its passengers—informed of events via cellular phone—attempted to overpower their assailants.

At 9:59 AM the World Trade Center's heavily damaged south tower collapsed, and the north tower fell 29 minutes later. Clouds of smoke and debris quickly filled the streets of Lower Manhattan. Office workers and residents ran in panic as they tried to outpace the billowing debris clouds. A number of other buildings adjacent to the twin towers suffered serious damage, and several subsequently fell. Fires at the World Trade Center site smoldered for more than three months.

Rescue operations began almost immediately as the country and the world sought to come to grips with the enormity of the losses. Nearly 3,000 people had perished: some 2,750 people in New York, 184 at the Pentagon, and 40 in Pennsylvania; all 19 terrorists also died. Included in the total in New York City were more than 400 police officers and firefighters, who had lost their lives after rushing to the scene and into the towers.

On the morning of September 11, President Bush had been visiting a second-grade classroom in Sarasota, Florida, when he was informed that a plane had flown into the

World Trade Center. A little later Andrew Card, his chief of staff, whispered in the president's right ear: "A second plane hit the second tower. America is under attack." To keep the president out of harm's way, Bush subsequently hopscotched across the country on Air Force One, landing in Washington, D.C., the evening of the attacks. At 8:30 PM Bush addressed the nation from the Oval Office in a speech that laid out a key doctrine of his administration's future foreign policy: "We will make no distinction between the terrorists who committed these acts and those who harbor them."

On September 14 Bush visited "Ground Zero," the smoking pile of debris of what remained of the World Trade Center and the thousands who had perished there. Standing on top of a wrecked fire truck, Bush grabbed a bullhorn to address the rescue workers working feverishly to find any survivors. When one of the workers said that he could not hear what the president was saying, Bush made one of the most memorable remarks of his presidency:

> I can hear you. The rest of the world hears you. And the people who knocked these buildings down will hear from all of us soon.

Bush's robust response to the attacks drove his poll ratings from 55 percent favourable before September 11 to 90 percent in the days after, the highest ever recorded for a president.

THE AFTERMATH

The emotional distress caused by the attacks—particularly the collapse of the twin towers, New York City's most visible landmark—was overwhelming. Unlike the relatively isolated site of the Pearl Harbor attack of 1941, to which the September 11 events were soon compared, the World Trade Center lay at the heart of one of the world's largest cities. Hundreds of thousands of people witnessed the attacks firsthand (many onlookers photographed events or recorded them with video cameras), and millions watched the tragedy unfold live on television. In the days that followed September 11, the footage of the attacks was replayed in the media countless times, as were the scenes of throngs of people, stricken with grief, gathering at "Ground Zero"—as the site where the towers once stood came to be commonly known—some with photos of missing loved ones, seeking some hint of their fate.

Moreover, world markets were badly shaken. The towers were at the heart of New York's financial district, and damage to Lower Manhattan's infrastructure, combined with fears of stock market panic, kept New York markets closed for four trading days. Markets afterward suffered record losses. The attacks also stranded tens of thousands of people throughout the United States, as U.S. airspace remained closed for commercial aviation until September 13, and normal service, with more rigid security measures, did not resume for several days.

The September 11 attacks were an enormous tactical success for al-Qaeda. The strikes were well coordinated and hit multiple targets in the heart of the enemy, and the attacks were magnified by being broadcast around the world to an audience of untold millions. The September 11 "propaganda of the deed" took place in the media capital of the world, which ensured the widest possible coverage of the event. Not since television viewers had watched the abduction and murder of Israeli athletes during the Munich Olympics in 1972 had a massive global audience witnessed a terrorist attack unfold in real time. If al-Qaeda had been a largely unknown organization before September 11, in the days after it became a household name.

After the attacks of September 11, countries allied with the United States rallied to its support, perhaps best symbolized by the French newspaper *Le Monde*'s headline, "We are all Americans now." Even in Iran thousands gathered in the capital, Tehrān, for a candlelight vigil.

Evidence gathered by the United States soon convinced most governments that the Islamic militant group al-Qaeda was responsible for the attacks. The group had been implicated in previous terrorist strikes against Americans, and bin Laden had made numerous anti-American statements. Al-Qaeda was headquartered in Afghanistan and had forged a close relationship with that country's ruling Taliban militia, which subsequently refused U.S. demands to extradite bin Laden and to terminate al-Qaeda activity there.

For the first time in its history, the North Atlantic Treaty Organization (NATO) invoked Article 5, allowing its members to respond collectively in self-defense, and on October 7 the U.S. and allied military forces launched an attack against Afghanistan. Within months thousands of militants were killed or captured, and Taliban and al-Qaeda leaders were driven into hiding. In addition, the U.S. government exerted great effort to track down other al-Qaeda agents and sympathizers throughout the world and made combating terrorism the focus of U.S. foreign policy. Meanwhile, security measures within the United

J01 Preston Keres/U.S. Navy

Firefighter calling for 10 additional rescue workers to make their way into the rubble of the World Trade Center in New York City following the September 11, 2001, terrorist attacks.

States were tightened considerably at such places as airports, government buildings, and sports venues. To help facilitate the domestic response, Congress quickly passed the USA PATRIOT Act (the Uniting and Strengthening America by Providing Appropriate Tools Required to Intercept and Obstruct Terrorism Act of 2001), which significantly but temporarily expanded the search and surveillance powers of the Federal Bureau of Investigation (FBI) and other law-enforcement agencies. Additionally, a cabinet-level Department of Homeland Security was established.

Despite their success in causing widespread destruction and death, the September 11 attacks were a strategic failure for al-Qaeda. Following September 11, al-Qaeda—whose name in Arabic means "the base"—lost the best base it ever had in Afghanistan. Later some in al-Qaeda's leadership—including those who, like Egyptian Saif al-Adel, had initially opposed the attacks—tried to spin the Western intervention in Afghanistan as a victory for al-Qaeda. Al-Adel, one of the group's military commanders, explained in an interview four years later that the strikes on New York and Washington were part of a far-reaching and visionary plan to provoke the United States into some ill-advised actions:

> Such strikes will force the person to carry out random acts and provoke him to make serious and sometimes fatal mistakes.... The first reaction was the invasion of Afghanistan.

But there is not a shred of evidence that in the weeks before September 11 al-Qaeda's leaders made any plans for an American invasion of Afghanistan. Instead, they prepared only for possible U.S. cruise missile attacks or air strikes by evacuating their training camps. Also, the overthrow of the Taliban hardly constituted an American "mistake"—the first and only regime in the modern Muslim world that ruled according to al-Qaeda's rigid precepts was toppled, and with it was lost an entire country that al-Qaeda had once enjoyed as a safe haven. And in the wake of the fall of the Taliban, al-Qaeda was unable to recover anything like the status it once had as a terrorist organization with considerable sway over Afghanistan.

Bin Laden disastrously misjudged the possible U.S. responses to the September 11 attacks, which he believed would take one of two forms: an eventual retreat from the Middle East along the lines of the U.S. pullout from Somalia in 1993 or another ineffectual round of cruise missile attacks similar to those that followed al-Qaeda's bombings of American embassies in Kenya and Tanzania in 1998. Neither of these two scenarios happened. The U.S. campaign against the Taliban was conducted with pinpoint strikes from American airpower, tens of thousands of Northern Alliance forces (a loose coalition of mujahideen militias that maintained control of a small section of northern Afghanistan), and more than 300 U.S. Special Forces soldiers on the ground working with 110 officers from the Central Intelligence Agency (CIA). In November, just two months after the September 11 attacks, the Taliban fell to the Northern Alliance and the United States. Still, it was just the beginning of what would become the longest war in U.S. history, as the United States tried to prevent the return of the Taliban and their al-Qaeda allies.

In December 2001, faced with the problem of where to house prisoners as the Taliban fell, the administration decided to hold them at Guantánamo Bay, which the U.S. had been leasing from Cuba since 1903. As Secretary of Defense Donald Rumsfeld put it on December 27, 2001, "I would characterize Guantánamo Bay, Cuba, as the least worst place we could have selected." Guantánamo was attractive to administration officials because they believed it placed the detainees outside the reach of American laws, such as the right to appeal their imprisonment, yet it was only 90 miles (145 km) off the coast of Florida, making it accessible to the various agencies that would need to travel there to extract information from what was believed to be a population of hundreds of dangerous terrorists. Eventually, some 800 prisoners would be held there, although the prison population was reduced to less than 175 by the time of the 10th anniversary of the September 11 attacks.

In his State of the Union speech on January 29, 2002, President Bush laid out a new doctrine of preemptive war, which went well beyond the long-established principle that the United States would go to war to prevent an adversary launching an attack that imminently threatened the country. Bush declared:

> I will not wait on events while dangers gather. I will not stand by as peril draws closer and closer. The United States of America will not permit the world's most dangerous regimes to threaten us with the world's most destructive weapons.

Bush identified those dangerous regimes as an "axis of evil" that included Iran, Iraq, and North Korea. At the graduation ceremony for West Point cadets on June 1, 2002, Bush elaborated on his preemptive war doctrine, saying to the assembled soon-to-be graduates and their families, "If we wait for threats to fully materialize, we will have waited too long." Bush believed that there would be a "demonstration effect" in destroying Saddam Hussein's regime in Iraq that would deter groups like al-Qaeda or indeed anyone else who might be inclined to attack the United States. Undersecretary of Defense Douglas J. Feith later explained,

> What we did after 9/11 was look broadly at the international terrorist network from which the next attack on the United States might come. And we did not focus narrowly only on the people who were specifically responsible for 9/11. Our main goal was preventing the next attack.

Thus, though there was no evidence that Saddam Hussein's government in Iraq had collaborated with al-Qaeda in the September 11 attacks, the United States prepared for conflict against Iraq in its global war against terror, broadly defined.

On March 19, 2003, on the eve of the invasion of Iraq, President Bush issued the order for war:

> For the peace of the world and the benefit and freedom of the Iraqi people, I hereby give the order to execute Operation Iraqi Freedom. May God bless the troops.

On March 20 the American-led invasion of Iraq began. Within three weeks U.S. forces controlled Baghdad, and the famous pictures of the massive statue of Saddam Hussein being toppled from its plinth were broadcast around the world.

THE SEPTEMBER 11 COMMISSION AND ITS FINDINGS

In 2002 President Bush had appointed a commission to look into the September 11 attacks, and two years later it issued its final report. The commission found that the key pre-September 11 failure at the CIA was its not adding to the State Department's "watch list" two of the "muscle" hijackers (who were trained to restrain the passengers on the plane), the suspected al-Qaeda militants Nawaf al-Hazmi and Khalid al-Mihdhar. The CIA had been tracking Hazmi and Mihdhar since they attended a terrorist summit meeting in Kuala Lumpur, Malaysia, on January 5, 2000. The failure to watch-list the two al-Qaeda suspects with the Department of State meant that they entered the United States under their real names with ease. On January 15, 2000, 10 days after the Malaysian meeting, Hazmi and Mihdhar flew into Los Angeles. The CIA also did not alert the FBI about the identities of the suspected terrorists, which could have helped the bureau locate them once they were inside the United States. According to the commission, this was the failure of not just a few employees at the CIA but a large number of CIA officers and analysts. Some 50 to 60 CIA employees read cables about the two al-Qaeda suspects without taking any action. Some of those officers knew that one of the al-Qaeda suspects had a visa for the United States, and by May 2001 some knew that the other suspect had flown to Los Angeles.

The soon-to-be hijackers would not have been difficult to find in California if their names had been known to law enforcement. Under their real names they rented an apartment, obtained driver's licenses, opened bank accounts, purchased a car, and took flight lessons at a local school; Mihdhar even listed his name in the local phone directory.

It was only on August 24, 2001, as a result of questions raised by a CIA officer on assignment at the FBI, that the two al-Qaeda suspects were watch-listed and their names communicated to the FBI. Even then the FBI sent out only a "Routine" notice requesting an investigation of Mihdhar. A few weeks later Hazmi and Mihdhar were two of the hi-

One of the two reflecting pools that are part of the National September 11 Memorial. Located on the site of the World Trade Center, the memorial opened to the public September 12, 2011.
9/11 Memorial/Joe Woolhead

jackers on the American Airlines flight that plunged into the Pentagon.

The CIA inspector general concluded that "informing the FBI and good operational follow-through by CIA and FBI might have resulted in surveillance of both al-Mihdhar and al-Hazmi. Surveillance, in turn, would have had the potential to yield information on flight training, financing, and links to others who were complicit in the 9/11 attacks."

The key failure at the FBI was the handling of the Zacarias Moussaoui case. Moussaoui, a French citizen of Moroccan descent, was attending flight school in the summer of 2001 in Minnesota, where he attracted attention from instructors because he had little knowledge of flying and did not behave like a typical aviation student. The flight school contacted the FBI, and on August 16 Moussaoui was arrested on a visa overstay charge. Although Moussaoui was not the "20th hijacker," as was widely reported later, he had received money from one of the September 11 coordinators, Ramzi Binalshibh, and by his own account was going to take part in a second wave of al-Qaeda attacks following the assaults on New York and Washington.

The FBI agent in Minneapolis who handled Moussaoui's case believed that he might have been planning to hijack a plane, and the agent was also concerned that Moussaoui had traveled to Pakistan, which was a red flag as militants often used the country as a transit point to travel to terrorist training camps in Afghanistan. On August 23 (or 24, according to some reports) CIA director George Tenet was told about the case in a briefing titled "Islamic Extremist Learns to Fly." But FBI headquarters determined that there was not sufficient "probable cause" of a crime for the Minneapolis office to conduct a search of Moussaoui's computer hard drive and belongings. Such a search would have turned up his connection to Binalshibh, according to Republican Sen. Charles Grassley, a leading member of the Senate Judiciary Committee, which has oversight of the FBI. The 9-11 Commission also concluded that "a maximum U.S. effort to investigate Moussaoui conceivably could have unearthed his connection to Binalshibh."

THE HUNT FOR BIN LADEN

In September 2001 President Bush announced that he wanted Osama bin Laden captured—dead or alive—and a $25 million bounty was eventually issued for information leading to the killing or capture of bin Laden. Bin Laden evaded capture, however, including in December 2001, when he was tracked by U.S. forces to the mountains of Tora Bora in eastern Afghanistan. Bin Laden's trail subsequently went cold, and he was thought to be living somewhere in the Afghanistan-Pakistan tribal regions.

U.S. intelligence eventually located bin Laden in Pakistan, living in the garrison city of Abbottabad, and in the early morning hours of May 2, 2011, on orders from U.S. Pres. Barack Obama, a small team of U.S. Navy SEALs assaulted his compound and shot and killed the al-Qaeda leader.

BIBLIOGRAPHY. The authoritative account of the planning, execution, and aftermath of the September 11 attacks is *The 9/11 Commission Report: Final Report of the National Commission on Terrorist Attacks Upon the United States* (2004). Any history of the attacks must examine how the 19 hijackers became motivated. A comprehensive study of this process of radicalization is the focus of MARC SAGEMAN, *Understanding Terror Networks* (2004). TERRY MCDERMOTT, *Perfect Soldiers: The Hijackers: Who They Were, Why They Did It* (2005), provides a narrative picture of the hijackers. A discussion of the religious motivations of the hijackers forms the basis for KANAN MAKIYA and HASSAN MNEIMNEH, "Manual for a 'Raid'," *The New York Review of Books* (January 17, 2002).

Background information on al-Qaeda's history, ideology, and internal discussions can be found in PETER L. BERGEN, *The Osama bin Laden I Know: An Oral History of al-Qaeda's Leader* (2006), and *Holy War, Inc.: Inside the Secret World of Osama bin Laden* (2001); and MICHAEL SCHEUER, *Through Our Enemies' Eyes: Osama bin Laden, Radical Islam and the Future of America*, rev. ed., 2nd ed. (2006).

A broad explanation of how al-Qaeda evolved from other jihadist strands is LAWRENCE WRIGHT, *The Looming Tower: Al-Qaeda and the Road to 9/11* (2006). The definitive history of the CIA's role during the Soviet war in Afghanistan and al-Qaeda's presence in Afghanistan up until the September 11 attacks is STEVE COLL, *Ghost Wars: The Secret History of the CIA, Afghanistan, and Bin Laden, from the Soviet Invasion Until September 10, 2001* (2004). A discussion of the ideologies that fueled and continue to fuel al-Qaeda's recruitment and appeal appears in FAWAZ A. GERGES, *The Far Enemy: Why Jihad Went Global*, 2nd ed. (2009). Another discussion of the factors leading to the September 11 attacks forms the basis of PETER BERGEN, "What were the causes of 9/11?" *Prospect*, issue 126 (September 2006).

Perspectives on al-Qaeda from personal interviews with bin Laden and his key lieutenants can be found in ABDEL BARI ATWAN, *The Secret History of al-Qaeda* (2006); and YOSRI FOUDA and NICK FIELDING, *Masterminds of Terror: The Truth Behind the Most Devastating Attack the World Has Ever Seen* (2003). An analysis based on on-the-ground reporting from the places in which al-Qaeda operated prior to and after 9/11 is JASON BURKE, *Al-Qaeda: Casting a Shadow of Terror* (2003). (Peter L. Bergen)

Communitarianism

Communitarianism is a social and political philosophy that emphasizes the importance of community in the functioning of political life, in the analysis and evaluation of political institutions, and in understanding human identity and well-being. It arose in the 1980s as a critique of two prominent philosophical schools: contemporary liberalism, which seeks to protect and enhance personal autonomy and individual rights in part through the activity of government, and libertarianism, a form of liberalism (sometimes called "classical liberalism") that aims to protect individual rights—especially the rights to liberty and property—through strict limits on governmental power.

There are strong communitarian elements in many modern and historical political and religious belief systems—e.g., in the Hebrew Bible (Old Testament) and the Christian New Testament (Acts 4:32: "Now the whole group of those who believed were of one heart and soul, and no one claimed private ownership of any possessions, but everything they owned was held in common"); in the early Islamic concept of *shūrā* ("consultation"); in Confucianism; in Roman Catholic social thought (the papal encyclical *Rerum Novarum* [1891]); in moderate conservatism ("To be attached to the subdivision, to love the little platoon we belong to in society, is the first principle . . . of public affections"—Edmund Burke); and in social democracy, especially Fabianism. Communitarian ideas have also played a significant role in public life through their incorporation into the electoral platforms and policies of Western political leaders of the late 20th and early 21st centuries, including British Prime Minister Tony Blair, Dutch Prime Minister Jan Peter Balkenende, and U.S. Presidents Bill Clinton and Barack Obama.

VARIETIES OF COMMUNITARIANISM

The term *communitarian* was coined in 1841 by John Goodwyn Barmby, a leader of the British Chartist movement, who used it to refer to utopian socialists and others who experimented with unusual communal lifestyles. It was rarely used in the generations that followed.

It was not until the 1980s that the term gained currency through its association with the work of a small group of mostly American political philosophers who argued for the importance of the common good in opposition to contemporary liberals and libertarians, who emphasized the good for individuals, particularly including personal autonomy and individual rights. The Canadian philosopher Charles Taylor and the American political theorist Michael Sandel were among the most prominent scholars of this brand of communitarianism. Other political theorists and philosophers who were often cited as communitarians in this sense, or whose work exhibited elements of such communitarian thinking, included Shlomo Avineri, Seyla Benhabib, Avner de-Shalit, Jean Bethke Elshtain, Amitai Etzioni, William A. Galston, Alasdair MacIntyre, Philip Selznick, and Michael Walzer.

During the same period, students of East Asian politics and society used *communitarianism* to describe the social thinking within authoritarian societies such as China, Singapore, and Malaysia, which extolled social obligations and the importance of the common good and accorded much less weight to autonomy and rights. Indeed, these societies viewed individuals as more or less interchangeable cells who find meaning in their contribution to the social whole rather than as free agents. Scholars of this kind of communitarianism included the American political theorist Russell A. Fox and the Singaporean diplomat Bilahari Kausikan.

In 1990 Etzioni and Galston founded a third school, known as "responsive" communitarianism. Its members formulated a platform based on their shared political principles, and the ideas in it were eventually elaborated in academic and popular books and periodicals, gaining thereby a measure of political currency, mainly in the West. The main thesis of responsive communitarianism is that people face two major sources of normativity, that of the common good and that of autonomy and rights, neither of which in principle should take precedence over the other.

THE COMMON GOOD VERSUS INDIVIDUAL RIGHTS

Whereas the classical liberalism of the Enlightenment can be viewed as a reaction to centuries of authoritarianism, oppressive government, overbearing communities, and rigid dogma, modern communitarianism can be considered a reaction to excessive individualism, understood by communitarians as an undue emphasis on individual rights, leading people to become selfish or egocentric. Excessive individualism was discussed in an oft-cited communitarian work, *Habits of the Heart: Individualism and Commitment in American Life* (1985), by the American sociologist Robert Neelly Bellah, who observed that by the early 1980s most Americans had become self-centred. Increasing prosperity from the 1950s, among other factors, had contributed to a decline in respect for traditional authority and institutions, such as marriage, and fostered a kind of materialistic hedonism, according to many communitarians. Earlier sociologists such as Ferdinand Tönnies and Émile Durkheim had discussed such antisocial tendencies in the context of modernization, which they viewed as a historical transition from oppressive but nurturing communities (*Gemeinschaft*) to liberating but impersonal societies (*Gesellschaft*). They warned of the dangers of anomie (normlessness) and alienation in modern societies composed of atomized individuals who had gained their liberty but lost their social moorings. Essentially the theses of Tönnies and Durkheim were supported with contemporary social-scientific data in *Bowling Alone: The Collapse and Revival of American Community* (2000), by the American political scientist Robert Putnam.

The close relation between the individual and the community was discussed on a theoretical level by Sandel and Taylor, among other academic communitarians, in their criticisms of philosophical liberalism, including especially the work of the American liberal theorist John Rawls and that of the German Enlightenment philosopher Immanuel Kant. They argued that contemporary liberalism and libertarianism presuppose an incoherent notion of the individual as existing outside and apart from society rather than embedded within it. To the contrary, they argued, there are no generic individuals but rather only Germans or Russians, Berliners or Muscovites, or members of some other particularistic community. Because individual identity is partly constituted (or "constructed") by culture and social relations, there is no coherent way of formulating individual rights or interests in abstraction from social contexts. In particular, according to these communitarians, there is no point in attempting to found a theory of justice on principles that individuals would choose in a hypothetical state of ignorance of their social, economic, and historical circumstances (from behind a Rawlsian "veil of ignorance"), because such individuals cannot exist, even in principle.

Liberal scholars argued that this line of criticism is overstated or misconceived. Despite its emphasis on autonomy and rights, they contended, contemporary liberalism is not incompatible with the notion of a socially embedded self. Indeed, Rawls himself, in his foundational work *A Theory of Justice* (1971), recognized the importance of what he called "social unions" and asserted that "only in a social union is the individual complete." Thus, according to liberals, the communitarian critique does not rebut the core of liberal theory but merely serves as a corrective to "stronger" liberal doctrines such as libertarianism, which does embrace an atomized notion of individual identity (*see below* A synthesis: Rights and responsibilities).

Academic communitarians also drew upon Aristotle and the German idealist philosopher Georg Friedrich Wilhelm Hegel to argue that some conception of the good must be formulated on the social level and that the community cannot be a normative-neutral realm. Unless there is a social formulation of the good, there can be no normative foundation upon which to draw to settle conflicts of value between different individuals and groups. Such an overriding good (e.g., the national well-being) enables persons with different moral outlooks or ideological backgrounds to find principled (rather than merely prudential) common ground.

Liberals and libertarians responded by characterizing the communitarian position as akin to East Asian authoritarian communitarianism. They also argued that social formulations of the good—and the obligations they generate, which individuals must then discharge—can sometimes be oppressive. Some libertarians cited taxes and mandatory vaccinations as examples of such obligations.

A SYNTHESIS: RIGHTS AND RESPONSIBILITIES

Responsive communitarianism may be considered a synthesis of both liberal and academic-communitarian concerns. Sandel and Taylor in effect held that many forms of philosophical liberalism, especially libertarianism, overemphasize autonomy and rights at the expense of the common good. However, in doing so, they were less than clear about the standing of individual rights, including human rights. Indeed, Alasdair MacIntyre asserted that rights were merely figments of the imagination, like unicorns. Responsive communitarians attempted to bridge this divide. In their platform and in their academic works, they posited that all societies must heed the moral claims of two core values, the common good and autonomy and rights. They also held that, because actual societies tend to tilt toward one core value or the other, they need to be pulled back toward the centre. Thus Japan, in their view, was strongly dedicated to the common good but insufficiently committed to the rights of women, ethnic minorities, and the disabled, while the United States during the presidential administration of Ronald Reagan (1981–89) and the United Kingdom during the prime ministership of Margaret Thatcher (1979–90) attached undue importance to individual rights. The early prime ministership of Tony Blair demonstrated a concern for the common good through its policies of devolution and the "stakeholder society" (the idea that businesses should be responsive to workers, consumers, and other groups whose interests they affect), as did the early administration of George W. Bush through its dedication to "compassionate conservatism." After the 2001 September 11 attacks, however, the common good in the United States was increasingly identified with national security, and some individual rights (e.g., the right to habeas corpus) were curtailed.

In the same vein, responsive communitarians also warned against excessively expansive definitions of rights and championed modern communities in which people find both a rich web of social relations and considerable degrees of freedom. In the early 21st century, responsive communitarians believed that the Scandinavian countries had achieved the best balance, though even there some individual rights were being curtailed for security reasons and in response to anti-immigrant sentiment.

POLICY IMPLICATIONS

Responsive communitarianism developed criteria for the formulation of policies that would enable societies to cope with the potential conflicts between the common good and individual rights, including in areas such as public health versus individual privacy and national security versus individual liberty. These criteria, which must be applied jointly, included the following:

1. No change is justified in governing public policies and norms unless society encounters serious challenges, because these kinds of changes exact considerable societal costs. (The September 11 attacks constituted such a challenge.)

2. Limitations on rights can be considered only if there are significant gains to the common good—what the U.S. courts refer to as a "compelling interest"—and if the intrusion is as limited as possible.

3. Adverse side effects that result from policy changes must be treated, above all, by introducing stronger mechanisms of accountability and oversight.

An example of the application of these criteria can be seen in the debate in the United States concerning whether to improve public health by testing newborn babies for HIV. According to communitarians, such tests would be justified if: (1) they saved lives (an infant infected with HIV has a strong chance of not developing AIDS if it is not breastfed and is treated with the drug AZT), (2) the intrusion were limited to testing blood that would be collected anyway, and (3) the adverse side effects could be limited by regulations that ban the disclosure of test results to nonmedical personnel.

SOCIALLY CONSTRUCTED PREFERENCES

The communitarian approach challenges the liberal view—reflected in many social sciences, especially neoclassical economics and the study of law—that the political and economic preferences of individuals should be respected and that their aggregation should guide the governance of the polity (through voting) and the economy (through the influence of consumer spending on the production and distribution of consumer goods). It is fully legitimate, for example, for public authorities to urge people to resist the appeals of political extremists or to encourage them to save more of their money. Communitarianism also challenges the libertarian position that it is paternalistic to interfere with individual choices based on personal preferences. In keeping with their view concerning the social constitution of individual identity, communitarians argue that personal preferences are to a significant extent not autonomous but rather a reflection of the larger culture, aspects of which can be heavily influenced by nonrational forces such as commercial advertising. Hence, public efforts to influence such preferences in beneficial ways, say in campaigns against smoking and obesity, do not undermine personal autonomy and are not a violation of human dignity.

THE THIRD SECTOR

Communitarianism adds a major element to a centuries-old debate in the West over the proper roles of government on the one hand and the market on the other. Communitarians argue that attention also must be paid to the role of civil society, including families, local and nonresidential communities, voluntary associations, schools, places of worship, foundations, and nonprofit corporations. It stresses that much of the behaviour that must be regulated in any society, as well as the factors that encourage people to discharge their social responsibilities (e.g., caring for children), are influenced by this third sector. Communitarians point to the importance of social norms and informal social controls in fostering pro-social conduct and in providing the moral foundations (e.g., trust) required for the successful operation of both governments and markets. The American political journalist Jonathan Rauch introduced the term "soft communitarianism" to refer to communitarianism that focuses on the role of civil society, in contrast to "hard," East Asian communitarianism, which views the state as the primary social agent.

CULTURAL RELATIVISM AND THE GLOBAL COMMUNITY

Because communitarians favour communal formulations of the good, which are necessarily particular to each community, they are vulnerable to the charge of ethical relativism, or to the claim that there is no absolute good but only different goods for different communities, cultures, or societies. Walzer adopted a clearly relativistic position in his book *Spheres of Justice* (1983), in which he asserted that the caste system is "good" by the standards of traditional Indian society. Critics argued, however, that his position was untenable. One simply needs to consider a community that champions honour killings, lynchings, or book burnings to realize that communities should not be the ultimate arbiters of that which is good. While acknowledging that different communities may have different ultimate values, Taylor argued—as did Rawls—that an "overlapping consensus" on specific norms and policies is still possible, though different communities may have different reasons for believing that a given norm or policy is right. In the United States, for example, abortion-rights and antiabortion activists have worked together to make adoption easier and to improve the quality of day-care centres. According to a much more-contested argument, advanced by the American scholar of religion Don Browning, there are some substantive universal values, such as human rights and the integrity of the global climate, that can provide a foundation for particularistic, communal ones.

Closely related to the question of the scope of morality is the question of the scope of community itself. Historically, communities have been local. However, as the reach of economic and technological forces extended, more-expansive communities became necessary in order to provide effective normative and political guidance to and control of these forces—hence the rise of national communities in Europe in the 17th century. Since the late 20th century there has been a growing recognition that the scope of even these communities is too limited, as many challenges that people now face, such as the threat of nuclear war and the reality of global environmental degradation, cannot be handled on a national basis. This has led to the quest for more-encompassing communities. The most advanced experiment in building a supranational community is the European Union (EU). However, so far the EU has not developed the kind of social integration and shared values that a strong community requires.

A similar issue arises with regard to the global community, currently more an ideal than a reality. Could such a community be constructed top-down, say, through some kind of enhanced United Nations (UN)? Or will it arise from the bottom up, through societal processes and institutions such as international nongovernmental organizations (NGOs), the transnational sharing of norms (e.g., for protecting the environment), a global second language (about one quarter of the world's population has at least a functional command of English), and other informal social networks? The question remains whether, ultimately, world governance can thrive without a worldwide community.

BIBLIOGRAPHY

Communitarianism and liberalism. Discussion of communitarianism as a response to liberalism can be found in DANIEL BELL, *Communitarianism and Its Critics* (1993). Liberal responses to communitarian critiques are discussed in STEPHEN MULHALL and ADAM SWIFT, *Liberals and Communitarians,* 2nd ed. (1996).

Academic communitarianism. Various philosophical perspectives within academic communitarianism are represented in ALASDAIR MacINTYRE, *After Virtue: A Study in Moral Theory*, 2nd ed. (1984); WILLIAM A. GALSTON, *Liberal Purposes: Goods Virtues, and Diversity in the Liberal State* (1991); CHARLES TAYLOR, *Sources of the Self* (1989); AMITAI ETZIONI, *The New Golden Rule* (1996); and MICHAEL J. SANDEL, *Liberalism and the Limits of Justice*, 2nd ed. (1998), and *Justice* (2009).

Responsive communitarianism. Discussions of communitarian theory, as well as responsive-communitarian answers to particular policy questions, can be found in PHILIP SELZNICK, *The Communitarian Persuasion* (2002); and AMITAI ETZIONI, *My Brother's Keeper: A Memoir and a Message* (2003), also containing an exposition of the formation of the responsive-communitarian movement, and *From Empire to Community: A New Approach to International Relations* (2004). A useful anthology is AMITAI ETZIONI, ANDREW VOLMERT, and ELANIT ROTHSCHILD (eds.), *The Communitarian Reader* (2004).

East Asian communitarianism. East Asian communitarianism is discussed in RUSSELL A. FOX, "Confucian and Communitarian Responses to Liberal Democracy," in *The Review of Politics,* 59(3):561–592 (Summer 1997); and JOSEPH CHAN, "A Confucian Perspective on Human Rights for Contemporary China," in J. BAUER and D. BELL (eds.), *The East Asian Challenge for Human Rights* (1999), pp. 212–237.

Modern Western societies. The role of rights and individualism in modern American society is outlined in MARY ANN GLENDON, *Rights Talk* (1991). A British perspective is presented in HENRY TAM, *Communitarianism* (1998).

(Amitai Etzioni)

Blessed John Paul II

The bishop of Rome and head of the Roman Catholic Church from 1978 to 2005, John Paul II was the first non-Italian pope in 455 years and the first from a Slavic country. His pontificate of more than 26 years was the third longest in history. As part of his effort to promote greater understanding between nations and between religions, he undertook numerous trips abroad, traveling far greater distances than had all other popes combined, and he extended his influence beyond the church by campaigning against political oppression and criticizing the materialism of the West. He also issued several unprecedented apologies to groups that historically had been wronged by Catholics, most notably Jews and Muslims. His unabashed Polish nationalism and his emphasis on nonviolent political activism aided the Solidarity movement in communist Poland in the 1980s and ultimately contributed to the peaceful dissolution of the Soviet Union in 1991. More generally, John Paul used his influence among Catholics and throughout the world to advance the recognition of human dignity and to deter the use of violence. His centralized style of church governance, however, dismayed some members of the clergy, who found it autocratic and stifling. He failed to reverse an overall decline in the numbers of priests and nuns, and his traditional interpretations of church teachings on personal and sexual morality alienated some segments of the laity.

EARLY LIFE AND INFLUENCES

Karol Józef Wojtyła was born in Wadowice, Poland, on May 18, 1920. His childhood coincided with the only period of freedom that Poland would know between 1772 and 1989: the two decades between Marshal Józef Piłsudski's defeat of the Soviet Red Army in 1920 and the German invasion in 1939. Wojtyła thus grew up experiencing national freedom but also understanding its vulnerability. Although Wadowice, a town of about 8,000 Catholics and 2,000 Jews, lay only 15 miles (24 km) from the future site of Auschwitz, a Nazi death camp, there was apparently little anti-Semitism in the town before the war. One of Wojtyła's close boyhood friends was a son of the leader of Wadowice's Jewish community.

Wojtyła's father, Karol senior, was a lieutenant in the Polish army. His mother, Emilia Kaczorowska, died when he was eight years old; his brother, Edmund, who had become a physician, died less than four years later. Wojtyła was an outgoing youth, though always with a serious side. He excelled in academics and dramatics, played football (soccer), and, under his father's guidance, lived a disciplined life of routine religious observance. He regularly assisted Father Kazimierz Figlewicz, his confessor and first teacher in Catholicism, in Wadowice's main church, which was next door to the Wojtyła family's tiny apartment.

After graduating from secondary school as valedictorian, Wojtyła moved with his father to Kraków, where he attended the Jagiellonian University. His studies ended abruptly when Nazi Germany invaded Poland on September 1, 1939. In the months that followed, Jews as well as non-Jewish cultural and political leaders, including professors and priests, were killed or deported to concentration camps by the Nazis, who considered the Slavs an inferior race.

Wojtyła and his father fled with thousands to the east but soon returned after learning that the Russians had also invaded Poland. Back in Kraków, Wojtyła continued his studies in clandestine classes. For the next four years, in order to avoid arrest and deportation, he worked in a factory owned by Solvay, a chemical firm that the Nazis considered essential to their war effort. Wojtyła was thus the only pope, at least in modern times, to have been a labourer.

During these years Wojtyła began to write nationalistic plays, and he joined the Rhapsodic Theatre, an underground resistance group that aimed to sustain Polish culture and morale through covert readings of poetry and drama. Through Jan Tyranowski, a tailor who conducted a youth ministry for the local church, Wojtyła was introduced to the teachings of St. John of the Cross, a Carmelite mystic who held that redemption could be gained through suffering and a "spirituality of abandonment." Tyranowski's example helped to convince Wojtyła that the church, even more than a renewed Polish theatre, might improve the world. Wojtyła's confessor continued to be his childhood mentor, Figlewicz, who had transferred to Wawel Cathedral in Kraków.

DECISION TO JOIN THE PRIESTHOOD

In February 1941 Wojtyła returned from work one day to discover that his father had died alone; he prayed by the body all night. By the autumn of 1942 he had decided to enter the priesthood. For two years, while still working at the chemical factory, he attended illegal seminary classes run by Kraków's cardinal archbishop, Prince Adam Sapieha. After narrowly escaping a Nazi roundup of able-bodied men and boys in 1944, Wojtyła spent the rest of the war in the archbishop's palace, disguised as a cleric. As pope, Wojtyła recalled that witnessing Nazi horrors, including the murder of many priests, showed him the real meaning of the priesthood.

In 1945 the Soviets replaced the Germans as occupiers of Poland. In November 1946 Wojtyła was ordained by Sapieha into the Catholic priesthood. He chose to say his first mass, assisted by Figlewicz, in Wawel Cathedral's crypt chapel amid the sarcophagi of Polish monarchs and heroes, including those who had defended national freedom and European Christendom. He then began two years of study in Rome, where he completed his first doctorate, an examination of the theology of St. John of the Cross. Assigned to Kraków's St. Florian's parish in 1949, he studied, wrote, and lectured on philosophy and social and sexual ethics. During the next decade he completed a second doctorate, taught theology and ethics at the Jagiellonian University, and eventually was appointed to a full professorship at the Catholic University of Lublin.

The young priest wrote poetry, published anonymously, on a variety of religious, social, and personal themes. He also became the spiritual leader and mentor of a circle of young adult friends whom he joined on kayaking and camping trips. Together, they celebrated mass in the open at a time when unapproved worship outside of churches was forbidden by the communist regime. Experiences with these friends contributed to the ideas in his first book of nonfiction, *Love and Responsibility* (1960), an exploration of the several graces available in conjugal sexual relationships. The work was considered radical by those who held the traditional church view that sex was solely for the purpose of procreation.

Church leaders were impressed by Wojtyła's ability to operate a dynamic pastorate despite communist restrictions. In 1958 Pope Pius XII appointed him an auxiliary bishop of Kraków. At the Second Vatican Council (1962–65) Wojtyła so distinguished himself that halfway through the council, in December 1963, Pope Paul VI named him archbishop of Kraków.

The Second Vatican Council introduced Wojtyła to issues including the role of the laity, the church's relations with other religions, and its relations with the secular world. After the council's conclusion in 1965, Wojtyła was appointed to Pope Paul VI's Commission for the Study of Problems of the Family, Population, and Birth Rate. His work appears to have influenced *Humanae vitae* (1968;

"Of Human Life"), Paul VI's encyclical rejecting artificial contraception, which became one of the church's most ignored teachings. Some bishops also disagreed with it, saying privately that, on this issue, Wojtyła may have made basic theological mistakes.

ACTIONS AS CARDINAL

Wojtyła was made a cardinal in June 1967. As cardinal archbishop of Kraków, he worked closely with Poland's powerful primate cardinal, Stefan Wyszyński, archbishop of Warsaw, who declared that Christianity, not communism, was the true protector of the poor and oppressed. In an effort that spanned two decades, Wojtyła lobbied for permission to build a church in Kraków's new industrial suburb, Nowa Huta. He planted a cross in the field where the church was to stand and defied communist authorities by holding masses there. He also applied for permission to hold traditional religious processions in the streets, though he was often turned down. Eventually Wojtyła prevailed, and he consecrated Nowa Huta's new Ark Church in 1977. Meanwhile, he had written his major philosophical work, *The Acting Person* (1969), which argues that moral actions—not simply thoughts or statements—create authentic personality and define what a person truly stands for.

Ironically, the authorities forced Wojtyła to develop a public speaking style that would eventually work against them: denied access to the media, he and fellow church leaders traveled ceaselessly among the people and grew skilled at communicating with large crowds. This ability would enhance the impact of the messages he delivered as pope to the faithful around the world, especially during his trips, when his ability to appeal to the millions who gathered to see him was captured in global television broadcasts.

ELECTION AS POPE

When Pope Paul VI died in August 1978, the College of Cardinals, split between two powerful Italians, elected the Venetian Albino Luciani as Pope John Paul I. He died only 33 days later. When the cardinals entered the second conclave of 1978, the world did not know that Wojtyła had received votes in the first conclave. Wojtyła seemed in some ways a good compromise candidate who could hold together a divided church. Liberal interpretations of religious life that followed the Second Vatican Council had created rifts and defections; religious conservatives were digging in, claiming that the council had betrayed the church. Wojtyła appeared to be traditional in church discipline but forward-looking in his acceptance of Vatican Council reforms. The cardinals also hoped that his relative youthfulness would attract young people to the church. Wojtyła's election on October 16, 1978, made him the first non-Italian pope since the Dutch Adrian VI (reigned 1522–23).

In taking the name John Paul II—which his predecessor, John Paul I, had said honoured the two popes of the Second Vatican Council—he signaled his intention to continue with the council's reforms. His homily at an installation mass on October 22, 1978, repeated the refrain "Be not afraid!"—a Biblical phrase announcing the presence of God and Jesus Christ and calling for Christian courage. It also presaged the bold but nonviolent human rights campaigns that John Paul would conduct around the world.

FIRST YEAR OF TRAVELS

John Paul's characteristic mixture of religion and politics—and its deep roots in Poland—became evident during the first year of his pontificate in his first four trips abroad. He went first to Mexico (January 1979), where he reaffirmed for the bishops of Latin America, leaders of half the world's Catholics, that politics—especially as it concerns human rights, personal dignity, and religious freedom—is an area of human life in which priests as well as laity must be involved. While there, he attracted what was called the largest crowd ever assembled—estimated at some five million people.

His second trip (June 1979) was to Poland, where he declared to his audiences that their Catholic faith dictated that they had a right to be free. Many Poles said later that the sight of themselves assembled in enormous but orderly gatherings made them realize their own political strength and encouraged their subsequent defiance of the communist regime. John Paul's speeches and activities served as models for the Polish priests who would carry out his independence campaigns in the country after he returned to Rome.

John Paul's third trip (October 1979) took him to Ireland, where he condemned violence done in the name of religion, and to the United States, where he was given a Wall Street ticker-tape parade. To the chagrin of some Americans, John Paul used his U.S. visit to express serious disagreements with the West, including aspects of American capitalism. In particular, he decried the neglect of the poor and denounced the exploitation of poor nations by wealthy ones.

On his fourth trip (November 1979) he visited Turkey to meet with the titular head of the Eastern Orthodox Church, which included most of the state-allied churches of what was then the Soviet Union. He thereby indicated a possible intention to pressure Soviet leaders by means of church congregations across eastern Europe. Although such an eastern arm of his anti-Soviet campaign never materialized, the Soviet government viewed it as a serious threat.

POLITICAL AND CULTURAL MESSAGES

In travels during the next 10 years, John Paul preached to the world his messages of religious freedom, national independence, and human rights. He declared that all of Europe—"from the Atlantic to the Ural Mountains" (east of Moscow)—should be reunited through its common Christian heritage. Some Vatican clergy said privately that the new pope was traveling too much, giving a triumphalist face to Catholicism when he should have been concentrating more on rebuilding the church from behind his desk in the Vatican. John Paul kept traveling.

From the start of his papacy, John Paul strictly reasserted the canon law banning priests from any active participation in party politics. His intention was not to weaken Catholicism's political impact but to unify the church and to strengthen its moral authority. He wanted Catholic social doctrine—developed in part from Pope Leo XIII's seminal encyclical on workers' rights, *Rerum novarum* (1891; "Of New Things")—to be delivered with the singular political authority of the Vatican, unaltered by local politics.

On May 13, 1981, John Paul was shot and nearly killed by a 23-year-old Turkish man, Mehmet Ali Agca. Meanwhile, the Poles' other spiritual leader, Primate Cardinal Wyszyński, lay dying of cancer. The sudden prospect of losing both men unsettled the Solidarity movement. Although no conspiracy in the assassination attempt was ever proved in court, the widespread suspicion that the Soviets were involved (in the hope of demoralizing Solidarity) did much to diminish world opinion of the Soviet Union at the time. John Paul later publicly forgave his would-be assassin, who had shot him on the feast day of the Virgin of Fátima. John Paul said the Virgin had saved his life by guiding the bullet away from vital organs. He made a pilgrimage to the shrine of the Virgin in Fátima, Portugal, on the first anniversary of the assassination attempt, but, during a ceremony in which John Paul consecrated the modern world to the Immaculate Heart of Mary, a priest ordained by (and subsequently disowned by) the dissident French archbishop Marcel Lefebvre lunged at the pope with a bayonet, narrowly missing him.

As the Polish Solidarity movement gained momentum, John Paul repeatedly emphasized to his fellow Poles the importance of pressing for change peacefully, so as not to give the communist regime a justification for using force and dismantling the trade union. In December 1981 Poland's premier, General Wojciech Jaruzelski, declared martial law. Despite the arrest of thousands of Solidarity members and years of uncertainty, the movement persevered. In April 1989 the communists legalized the trade union, and in June of that year Solidarity made a strong

Pope John Paul II at Shea Stadium, Queens, N.Y., October 1979.
USN&WR—Thomas J. O'Halloran/Library of Congress, Washington, D.C. (LC-U9-38282-12)

showing in free elections. In December 1989 Mikhail Gorbachev became the first Soviet leader to visit the Vatican. The collapse of the Soviet Union occurred two years later. Throughout the 1980s John Paul's continuing private discussions with Polish and Soviet leaders, and his persistent success in keeping Solidarity a nonviolent movement, helped inspire similar movements in other Soviet-bloc countries and eventually led Gorbachev to write that John Paul's approach had made a new kind of thinking possible.

John Paul's visits to other countries ruled by nondemocratic regimes, especially in Latin America, raised the political expectations of the people and thus contributed, in the opinion of some analysts, to the eventual emergence of democratic governments in those regions. In a 1995 address to the General Assembly of the United Nations (UN), he said that universal moral law could help the world move from "a century of violent coercion" to "a century of persuasion." His intervention in a territorial dispute between Chile and Argentina during the first year of his pontificate was credited with preventing a war between the two countries. Not all his political initiatives were successful, however. His fierce criticism of some U.S. actions, such as the First and Second Persian Gulf wars against Iraq and the economic embargo against Cuba, had little visible effect. His popular visit to communist Cuba in 1998, however—where he was openly welcomed by President Fidel Castro, who admired John Paul's criticisms of unbridled American capitalism—did lead to greater acceptance and freedom for the Roman Catholic Church there.

After the dissolution of the Soviet Union, John Paul continued to criticize what he considered the pernicious effects of materialism in the West, including consumerism and pornography. Western societies, he believed, were falling prey to a "culture of death" characterized by acceptance of abortion and euthanasia; he also chided their indifference to the suffering of the poor and the widely held belief that modern technologies can assure fundamental happiness. In the later years of his papacy, he strongly emphasized the message of nonviolence, reflecting a concern borne of his experience of the German and Soviet occupations of his homeland. He frequently made personal appeals for clemency in cases of prisoners sentenced to death, and he repeatedly insisted that religion should never be used as an excuse for violence of any kind.

DIALOGUE WITH OTHER FAITHS

World religions. In 1986 John Paul invited the leaders of all major religions to Assisi, Italy, for a universal prayer service for world peace. The meeting was scorned by the ultraconservatives of several religions, including his own. The traditionalist archbishop Lefebvre called the pope's action a "scandal" and a betrayal of "the one true faith." Lefebvre also cited it as one of the reasons he consecrated his own bishops (without papal approval) in 1988—the first significant schism in reaction to the reforms of the Second Vatican Council and an act Lefebvre knew would result in his excommunication. Nevertheless, by the mid-1990s John Paul had orchestrated some dramatic acts of interfaith reconciliation, especially with the two other religions that stem from Abraham—Judaism and Islam. He worked to improve relations with these two faiths through frequent meetings that often garnered little public attention. Crucial to John Paul's approach to other religions was his unprecedented campaign to involve Catholics in general apologies for the sins of Catholics against others throughout history, including those committed during the Crusades and against indigenous peoples, women, suspected heretics, non-Catholic Christians, Muslims, and Jews.

From the start of his pontificate, John Paul cultivated personal contacts with Jewish leaders and continued to assert, as he had in Poland, that the Jews are, for Christians, "our elder brothers in faith." In 1986 he became the first pontiff known to have entered a synagogue, when he embraced the chief rabbi at the Great Synagogue of Rome. In 1990 he declared anti-Semitism a sin against God and humanity, and throughout his papacy he used his influence in efforts to help end nearly 2,000 years of oppression and violence inflicted on Jews by Christians. By the end of 1993 he had pushed the Vatican to recognize the State of Israel, overriding the objections of Vatican officials who worried about the consequences for Christian minorities in Arab countries, and on Holocaust Remembrance Day in 1994 he hosted Jews and Christians at an unprecedented memorial concert inside the Vatican. On the controversial question of Pope Pius XII's policy of neutrality during World War II, John Paul did not criticize his silence but asserted that Pius had acted with deep conscience in a terrible situation. The Vatican document *We Remember: A Reflection on the Shoah* (1998) reviewed various aspects of Catholic anti-Jewish prejudice that contributed to the Holocaust.

A few reconciliation efforts failed. John Paul's canonization of Jewish convert Edith Stein, a nun killed at Auschwitz because she was Jewish, offended many Jews who felt it usurped a Jewish tragedy for Catholic purposes. For them, John Paul only added to this offense by saying her new saint's day should be a Catholic remembrance of the Holocaust's Jewish victims. In March 2000 in Jerusalem, Israeli Prime Minister Ehud Barak welcomed John Paul to Yad Vashem, a memorial to Holocaust victims, with the words "Blessed are you in Israel." Three days later the pope prayed alone at the Western Wall, into which he placed a printed prayer requesting forgiveness and citing a desire for "genuine brotherhood with the People of the Covenant." These gestures were favourably received by most Israelis.

One month earlier, in Cairo, John Paul had become the first head of his church to meet with the Sheikh al-Azhar, one of Sunni Islam's highest religious authorities. The next year, in May 2001, John Paul became the first pope ever to enter a mosque, the Great Mosque of Damascus (also known as the Umayyad Mosque), where, in the company of Muslim clerics, he prayed at the shrine of St. John the Baptist. From the beginning of his pontificate, he held nearly 50 substantive meetings with Muslim leaders—far more than those of all previous popes combined.

Christian ecumenism. John Paul's highly personalized encyclical *Ut unum sint* (1995; "That They May Be One") reviewed 30 years of ecumenical relations, including his visits—the first by any pope—to Canterbury Cathedral and to Lutheran churches in Germany and Sweden. Its invitation to non-Catholic churches to join John Paul in rethinking the role of the papacy in world Christianity sparked new ecumenical discussions.

Although his hopes of mending the 1,000-year rift with the Eastern Orthodox Church were advanced with his visits to a few nations of the former Soviet Union, the Russian Orthodox Church remained suspicious and did not invite him to visit the country.

ECCLESIASTICAL AND THEOLOGICAL CONTRIBUTIONS

During his long pontificate, John Paul directed the rewriting of several major church texts. The revisions included the new *Codex Juris Canonici* (1983), the first update of the Code of Canon Law since 1917; *Pastor Bonus* (1988; "Good Shepherd"), the first reform of the Roman Curia since 1967; and the new *Codex Canonum Ecclesiarum Orientalium* (1990; "Code of Canons for the Eastern Churches"). In 1992 he promulgated the new *Catechism of the Catholic Church*, its first revision in more than four centuries.

John Paul admired and encouraged the scientific search for truth but warned against the misuse of science in ways that undermine human dignity. He saw no basic contradiction between the findings of modern science and biblical accounts of the Creation, stating in a series of brief homilies (published as *Original Unity of Man and Woman*, 1981) that some stories in Genesis, including the story of Adam and Eve, should be understood as inspired metaphor. In 1984 the Vatican declared that the church's condemnation of Galileo in 1633 had been in error; John Paul subsequently stated that Galileo had been "imprudently opposed" by the church. In his encyclical *Fides et ratio* (1998; "Faith and Reason"), he argued for the importance of reason in the development of any meaningful faith. He was also the first pope to link the protection of the natural environment firmly to Catholic theology, declaring in 1999 that destruction of the environment "can be a grave sin" and "a sign of real contempt for man."

(William B. Blakemore)

FINAL YEARS

Beginning in the early 1990s, the once-robust John Paul was increasingly slowed by Parkinson disease and by a series of operations. Nonetheless, he maintained a rigorous schedule, insisting that his visible suffering was part of his ministry. To aides urging him to slow down, he reportedly said simply, "Si crollo, crollo" ("If I collapse, I collapse"). Although he may have considered the possibility of resignation, he remained silent on the subject (few popes had resigned, the last being Gregory XII in 1415). Even in old age he continued to attract enormous crowds; four million were estimated to have joined him at a mass in Manila in 1995, and two million assembled at a Kraków mass in 2002. After 2003, he appeared in public only when seated. By Easter 2005, following a tracheotomy, he was unable to speak to the people he blessed from his apartment window, and he died on April 2, 2005, in Vatican City. His funeral drew to Rome millions of pilgrims, as well as a number of the world's former and current political leaders. In May

Jerome Delay—AP/Wide World Photos

John Paul II leaving a message at the Western Wall during his pilgrimage to Jerusalem, March 26, 2000.

2005 his successor, Pope Benedict XVI, waiving the usual five-year waiting period, allowed review to begin in the cause of John Paul II for beatification and canonization. In January 2011 the Vatican recognized the recovery of a French nun from Parkinson disease as a miracle performed by John Paul II; he was beatified on May 1. His feast day is celebrated on October 22. (William B. Blakemore/Ed.)

ASSESSMENT

John Paul II was, in a real sense, the first globally oriented pope. His election coincided with the arrival of routine, worldwide, instantaneous audiovisual communications, and many of his major efforts were intended to adjust—though not to challenge—the essential tenets of Catholicism for an open, interconnected world in which nations and religions must live in daily contact with one another. By publishing unprecedented papal meditations about other faiths, he showed how a Catholic may approach them with reverence. He also hoped to strengthen Catholicism in many cultures around the world by canonizing far more saints—drawn from a broader geographical and occupational spectrum—than had any of his predecessors.

In 2000 John Paul centralized ecclesiastical and theological control over Catholic educational institutions around the world, prompting renewed criticism from members of the church hierarchy who believed that the Second Vatican Council had called upon the pope to be less of an autocrat and more of a collegial moderator. John Paul also proscribed the teachings of some dissident Catholic theologians. For example, early in his pontificate he censured Hans Küng for arguing that the Catholic church was wrong to invoke papal infallibility. In the 1980s John Paul's uneasiness with liberation theology (which he regarded as too closely allied with Marxism and Soviet communism) prompted him to withdraw bureaucratic and moral support from ecclesial base communities in parts of Latin America, a move that may have contributed to the defection of large numbers of Catholics in the region to Evangelical Protestantism.

Throughout his pontificate John Paul maintained traditional church positions on gender and sexual issues, denouncing abortion, artificial contraception, premarital sex, and—through Vatican teachings—homosexual practices (though not homosexual orientation). He continually rebuffed pleas for priests to be allowed to marry and denied requests from Catholic nuns who wanted a greater role in the church. And, though he often spoke out for full equality for women outside religious vocations, he rejected even any discussion of the ordination of women as priests—a stance that evoked sharp and continuing criticism from some quarters.

Some critics charged that John Paul's autocratic style of governing greatly discouraged American and European bishops from seeking the Vatican's help in responding to accusations, which began in the late 20th century, of sexual abuse of minors by clergy. Even as revelations of the abuse grew into a worldwide scandal, the church did little to confront the problem, allowing it to fester without intervention or punishment. In April 2002 the U.S. cardinals received an unprecedented papal summons to Rome, during which time John Paul declared that there was "no place in the priesthood" for anyone who would abuse children. In June 2002 all American bishops met in Dallas, Texas, to adopt strict new policies for investigating any charges of clergy abuse of minors and removing proven offenders. Ultimately, however, the church's reputation in the United States and Europe was gravely damaged. By 2005 the church in the United States had spent more than $1 billion in litigation and legal settlements.

John Paul's emphasis on human rights and national and religious freedom suggested to some a theology that was excessively "human-centred" and insufficiently "Christ-centred." A related criticism was that his political campaigns involved the church too directly in worldly affairs and thereby threatened to obscure its spiritual mission. His defenders argued that his humanistic Catholicism was based upon the person and inspiration of Christ and that his campaigns could be justified by the Catholic belief that it was his duty as the Vicar of Christ to help alleviate the world's suffering. Moreover, they urged, his activism only helped the church by showing that its essential values, advanced with commitment and courage, could improve the world. Other critics claimed that his pontifical writings were often unfocused, but supporters insisted that his encyclicals and other assertions were simply so numerous, varied, and farsighted that it would take years for their impact on Catholicism to be understood.

From the start of his pontificate, John Paul tried to reassert a sense of religious challenge and discipline by making firm declarations about personal morality and the religious life. This effort generally did not reverse a dramatic decline in vocations to the priesthood and sisterhood, nor did it improve church attendance in many Catholic countries. The cardinals who elected him had asked that he end the sense of confusion among many Catholics that seemed to stem from the reforms of the Second Vatican Council, but there was no consensus that he did. Nevertheless, John Paul is generally seen as having increased the global prestige of the papacy and thus to have laid a foundation for possible future revival within the church. (William B. Blakemore)

BIBLIOGRAPHY. Biographies of John Paul II include TAD SZULC, *Pope John Paul II, The Biography* (1995), which is especially valuable for perspectives on Karol Wojtyła's early development and accomplishments in Poland; GEORGE WEIGEL, *Witness to Hope: The Biography of Pope John Paul II* (1999), which offers rich detail but little criticism of the pope; and JONATHAN KWITNEY, *Man of the Century: The Life and Times of Pope John Paul II* (1997), valuable for analysis of John Paul's geopolitical impact. An assessment of John Paul relative to two of his predecessors is WILTON WYNN, *Keepers of the Keys: John XXIII, Paul VI, and John Paul II—Three Who Changed the Church* (1988). Critical examinations include GARRY WILLS, *Papal Sins* (2000). LUIGI ACCATTOLI, *When a Pope Asks Forgiveness: The Mea Culpas of John Paul II* (1999), documents his unprecedented church apologies. (Ed.)

Museum of Modern Art

A museum of modern art is an institution devoted to the collection, display, interpretation, and preservation of "avant-garde" or "progressive" art of the late 19th, 20th, and 21st centuries. This article describes the history of these institutions, which can be found around the world, as well as the challenges they face today.

HISTORY

Museums of modern art, as they are understood today, owe their origins to the Musée du Luxembourg in Paris. Designated by Louis XVIII in 1818 as a venue for the collection and display of the work of living artists, the Musée du Luxembourg acted as a kind of testing ground for recent art to judge its worthiness for admission to the permanent collection of the state. Works acquired by the museum were kept there for a number of years after the death of the artist, at which point those works whose "glory had been confirmed by universal opinion" and that were deemed of national significance were transferred to the Louvre, while others were dispersed to regional museums.

Similar institutions and arrangements developed in Germany and Britain, among other places. In Munich, for instance, the Pinakothek (later renamed the Alte Pinakothek)—established by Louis I of Bavaria (ruled 1825–48) in 1826—was designed to display the Old Masters collection owned by the house of Wittelsbach, while the Neue Pinakothek (opened 1853) contained the collection of "modern" (that is to say, 19th-century) paintings that Louis had begun forming in 1809, while crown prince. In Britain the Tate Gallery (now the Tate Britain, one of four Tate galleries)—founded in 1897 as the National Gallery of British Art (later officially renamed the Tate Gallery in honour of Henry Tate, its initial donor) and part of the National Gallery of Art until 1954, when it formally became an independent institution—was in 1917 charged with collecting British historical art and forming a national collection of international modern art, while the National Gallery focused on art prior to 1900.

The idea of a museum devoted to modern art was given fresh impetus early in the 20th century by several pioneering directors, including Alexander Dorner in Germany and Alfred H. Barr, Jr., in the United States. Dorner, director (1925–37) of the Landesmuseum in Hanover, was deeply interested in the work of contemporary artists such as Piet Mondrian, László Moholy-Nagy, and Kazimir Malevich and sought to integrate their ideas into the Landesmuseum by inviting several of them to design displays for modern art that would fit the museum's sequence of historical galleries. Dorner saw the museum not simply as an instrument of the Enlightenment that was designed to order and classify works of art of the past but as an "educational facility whose purpose is first to develop a taste for the subject—and secondly, and more importantly, to illustrate the developments of the human spirit in its most independent and liveliest object—in art." It was this idea of the museum as an educational institution and a place for the discovery and interpretation of the work of contemporary artists that so influenced Barr, the founding director of the Museum of Modern Art (MoMA) in New York City.

Barr traveled to Europe in 1927 to study contemporary European culture and to gather material for his intended thesis on the machine in modern art. Much of his thinking about modern art, and ultimately about MoMA, was formulated during this trip. He visited London, Rotterdam, The Hague, Amsterdam, Berlin, Moscow, Leningrad (now St. Petersburg), Warsaw, and Vienna, but he was particularly impressed by Dessau, Ger., which at that time was the home of the Bauhaus. Founded in 1919 by architect Walter Gropius, the Bauhaus was a radical school that endeavoured to teach the interdisciplinarity of the arts and crafts, including painting, textile design, architecture, and photography. Gropius brought together some of the most daring and progressive architects and artists of the day, such as Hannes Meyer, Ludwig Mies van der Rohe, Johannes Itten, Marianne Brandt, Oskar Schlemmer, Wassily Kandinsky, and Paul Klee, the work of all but one of whom (Meyer) would ultimately be collected by MoMA.

Barr was predisposed to the Bauhaus approach, having previously taught a course on modern art at Wellesley College that focused on painting and sculpture—as well as graphic design, decorative arts, music, literature, film, theatre, and architecture—and saw in it a model for approaching art by discipline or medium rather than by epoch or geography. The most important idea he absorbed from Dorner was that of the museum as a place of learning and discovery committed to living artists. These concepts coalesced in the Museum of Modern Art, the first museum in North America to declare itself "modern"; it identified itself with the most progressive tendencies in art, which meant work that was original and daring and challenged traditional or established canons. The museum, as Barr understood it, was to be a laboratory in which the

Nicolas Asfouri—AFP/Getty Images

A visitor looking at enigmatic American artist Andy Warhol's *Campbell's Soup Cans* at the Tate Modern in London, 2002.

A series of eight massive sculptures by Richard Serra, collectively titled *A Matter of Time* (completed 2005), on display at the Guggenheim Museum Bilbao, a museum devoted to modern and contemporary art.

Rafa Rivas—AFP/Getty Images

public was invited to participate, and it was organized in its early years around departments of painting and sculpture, architecture and design, film, and photography; departments of prints and illustrated books, drawings, and media and performance art were added later.

By emphasizing innovation, MoMA was able to rapidly develop outstanding collections and inventive programs that appealed to an audience that had not been served by preexisting institutions, which paid little, if any, attention to modern art. The catalyst for this was the financial and moral support the museum received in 1929 from its founding trustees, especially Lillie P. Bliss, Mary Quinn Sullivan, and Abby Aldrich Rockefeller, who were determined to create a museum devoted exclusively to the most progressive tendencies in modern art. The museum's success was based on its willingness to take a great deal of risk in the selection of art as well as how that art was displayed and interpreted.

The recognition that the Museum of Modern Art achieved for the artists it championed, combined with the impact of its publications and exhibitions, made it a model for other institutions in North America, Europe, Asia, and Latin America. In some cases, such as those of the San Francisco Museum of Modern Art (1935), the Musée National d'Art Moderne (1947; which succeeded the Musée du Luxembourg) in Paris, the São Paulo and Rio de Janeiro museums of modern art (which opened within nine months of each other in 1948) in Brazil, and the Museum of Modern Art, Kamakura (1951) in Japan, entirely new museums were founded; at other institutions, such as the Art Institute of Chicago and the Metropolitan Museum of Art in New York, new departments of modern art were created in the 1960s.

Many smaller museums of modern art were also established around this time, often based on private collections. These include the Museum Folkwang in Hagen, Ger., founded in 1902 by Karl Ernst Osthaus and moved to Essen in 1922; the Kröller-Müller State Museum in Otterlo, Neth., (1938), the result of a large donation from Helene Kröller-Müller; the Barnes Foundation Galleries in Merion, Pa., which housed Albert C. Barnes's extensive collection of Impressionist, Post-Impressionist, and early Modernist masterworks and which opened to the public by appointment in 1925; the Ōhara Museum of Art in Kurashiki, outside Ōsaka, Japan, which opened to the public in 1930 and was based on Ōhara Magosaburō's collection of 19th- and 20th-century French paintings and sculptures; and the Solomon R. Guggenheim Museum designed by Frank Lloyd Wright (1959) to house Guggenheim's collection of nonobjective art.

CONTEMPORARY CHALLENGES

Growing in tandem with the increased interest in and increasing number of museums of modern and contemporary art is the number of challenges facing such institutions. For example, to what extent is it practical or even desirable to present a coherent overview of a tradition or an era whose history is not yet fully developed or understood? Is it really possible to relate the most recently made art to works now more than a hundred years old? Does it still make sense to divide an institution's collections by medium? How should Western museums deal with art from Latin America, Asia, or the Middle East, where terms such as *progressive* or *avant-garde* might have very different meanings? Is there something distinct and unique about the impact of globalization and the explosion of interest in contemporary art that changes what a museum of modern art should be?

There are no easy answers to these questions, and museums of modern art must constantly grapple with how to remain "disruptive" and new while becoming increasingly part of an established order or accepted canon. How can they balance, for instance, their commitment to new and progressive art while simultaneously collecting and displaying works by such artists as Georges Seurat, Vincent van Gogh, and Paul Cézanne, whose still wildly popular works were radical and progressive when they were made but are now well over a century old? Some institutions, like MoMA, have endeavoured to engage with this challenge by imagining the collection as "metabolic" (to use Barr's word) and constantly evolving, but it has proved problematic, and at times contentious, to shed works of art that have become recognized masterpieces in favour of the new and not yet fully appreciated. More productively, many museums are experimenting with different ways of presenting their collections, whether through refreshed historical narratives, through new thematic investigations, or by periodic rehangings designed to explore modern and contemporary art from particular perspectives, such as those of gender and identity. To the degree that a museum of modern art implies a dedication to art whose history is not yet fixed, or fully fixed, any attempt to articulate a cohesive and concise narrative about such work is more likely to be provisional than definitive.

One of the most pressing issues for museums of modern art is how to contend with the growth in, and changing nature of, their audiences. Of special concern is the impact of the Internet, given its ability to engage large numbers of art lovers who may never physically visit a museum. This circumstance requires a reconceptualization of both the intellectual and the physical space of a museum. While museums of modern art are committed first and foremost to the artists and works of art they collect and display, the need to engage the public has become an increasingly important aspect of their efforts. Museum space in this context is not simply artistic or intellectual but also social. It encompasses a complex nexus of relationships between viewers and art objects and between viewers and other viewers. What once was an intimate experience shared by a relatively small number of people from similar social and intellectual backgrounds has become a hugely popular experience shared by many people from far more diverse backgrounds. Some critics have seen this explosion of attendance as a detriment to the visitor's ability to engage directly with discrete objects, thereby undermining the importance of the institution; others have seen this as a fulfillment of modern art's democratic and populist impulses. Whatever one's perspective, the idea of the museum as a laboratory must include the notion of the museum as a crucible of experience in both the real world of the physical museum and the virtual world of the Internet that can engage audiences with the most daring and significant works of the day.

(Glenn D. Lowry)

Gothic Art

The painting, sculpture, and architecture characteristic of the second of two great international eras that flourished in western and central Europe during the Middle Ages is categorized as Gothic art. It evolved from Romanesque art and lasted from the mid-12th century to as late as the end of the 16th century in some areas. The term Gothic was coined by classicizing Italian writers of the Renaissance, who attributed the invention (and what to them was the nonclassical ugliness) of medieval architecture to the barbarian Gothic tribes that had destroyed the Roman Empire and its classical culture in the 5th century CE. The term retained its derogatory overtones until the 19th century, at which time a positive critical revaluation of Gothic architecture took place. Although modern scholars have long realized that Gothic art has nothing in truth to do with the Goths, the term Gothic remains a standard one in the study of art history.

ARCHITECTURE

Architecture was the most important and original art form during the Gothic period. The principal structural characteristics of Gothic architecture arose out of medieval masons' efforts to solve the problems associated with supporting heavy masonry ceiling vaults over wide spans. The problem was that the heavy stonework of the traditional arched barrel vault and the groin vault exerted a tremendous downward and outward pressure that tended to push the walls upon which the vault rested outward, thus collapsing them. A building's vertical supporting walls thus had to be made extremely thick and heavy in order to contain the barrel vault's outward thrust.

Medieval masons solved this difficult problem about 1120 with a number of brilliant innovations. First and foremost they developed a ribbed vault, in which arching and intersecting stone ribs support a vaulted ceiling surface that is composed of mere thin stone panels. This greatly reduced the weight (and thus the outward thrust) of the ceiling vault, and since the vault's weight was now carried at discrete points (the ribs) rather than along a continuous wall edge, separate widely spaced vertical piers to support the ribs could replace the continuous thick walls. The round arches of the barrel vault were replaced by pointed (Gothic) arches which distributed thrust in more directions downward from the topmost point of the arch.

Since the combination of ribs and piers relieved the intervening vertical wall spaces of their supportive function, these walls could be built thinner and could even be opened up with large windows or other glazing. A crucial point was that the outward thrust of the ribbed ceiling vaults was carried across the outside walls of the nave, first to an attached outer buttress and then to a freestanding pier by means of a half arch known as a flying buttress. The flying buttress leaned against the upper exterior of the nave (thus counteracting the vault's outward thrust), crossed over the low side aisles of the nave, and terminated in the freestanding buttress pier, which ultimately absorbed the ceiling vault's thrust.

These elements enabled Gothic masons to build much larger and taller buildings than their Romanesque predecessors and to give their structures more complicated ground plans. The skillful use of flying buttresses made it possible to build extremely tall, thin-walled buildings whose interior structural system of columnar piers and ribs reinforced an impression of soaring verticality.

Three successive phases of Gothic architecture can be distinguished, respectively called early, High, and late Gothic.

Early Gothic. This first phase lasted from the Gothic style's inception in 1120–50 to about 1200. The combination of all the aforementioned structural elements into a coherent style first occurred in the Île-de-France (the region around Paris), where prosperous urban populations had sufficient wealth to build the great cathedrals that epitomize the Gothic style. The earliest surviving Gothic building was the abbey of Saint-Denis in Paris, begun in about 1140. Structures with similarly precise vaulting and chains of windows along the perimeter were soon begun with Notre-Dame de Paris (begun 1163) and Laon Cathedral (begun 1165). By this time it had become fashionable to treat the interior columns and ribs as if each was composed of a bunch of more slender parallel members. A series of four discrete horizontal levels or stories in the cathedral's interior were evolved, beginning with a ground-level arcade, over which ran one or two galleries (tribune, triforium), over which in turn ran an upper, windowed story called a clerestory. The columns and arches used to support these different elevations contributed to the severe and powerfully repetitive geometry of the interior. Window tracery (decorative ribwork subdividing a window opening) was also gradually evolved, along with the use of stained (coloured) glass in the windows. The typical French early Gothic cathedral terminated at its eastern end in a semicircular projection called an apse. The western end was much more impressive, being a wide facade articulated by numerous windows and pointed arches, having monumental doorways, and being topped by two huge towers. The long sides of the cathedral's exterior presented a baffling and tangled array of piers and flying buttresses. The basic form of Gothic architecture eventually spread throughout Europe to Germany, Italy, England, the Low Countries, Spain, and Portugal.

In England the early Gothic phase had its own particular character (epitomized by Salisbury Cathedral) that is known as the early English Gothic style (c. 1200–1300). The first mature example of the style was the nave and choir of Lincoln Cathedral (begun in 1192).

Early English Gothic churches differed in several respects from their French counterparts. They had thicker, heavier walls that were not much changed from Romanesque proportions; accentuated, repeated moldings on the edges of interior arches; a sparing use of tall, slender, pointed lancet windows; and nave piers consisting of a central column of light-coloured stone surrounded by a number of slimmer attached columns made of black purbeck marble.

Early English churches also established other stylistic features that were to distinguish all of English Gothic: great length and little attention to height; a nearly equal emphasis on horizontal and vertical lines in the stringcourses and elevations of the interior; a square termination of the building's eastern end rather than a semicircular eastern projection; scant use of flying buttresses; and a piecemeal, asymmetrical conception of the ground plan of the church. Other outstanding examples of the early English style are the nave and west front of Wells Cathedral (c. 1180–c. 1245) and the choirs and transept of Rochester Cathedral.

High Gothic. The second phase of Gothic architecture began with a subdivision of the style known as Rayonnant (1200–80) on the Continent and as the Decorated Gothic (1300–75) style in England. This style was characterized by the application of increasingly elaborate geometrical decoration to the structural forms that had been established during the preceding century.

During the period of the Rayonnant style a significant change took place in Gothic architecture. Until about 1250, Gothic architects concentrated on the harmonious distribution of masses of masonry and, particularly in France, on the technical problems of achieving great height; after that date, they became more concerned with the creation of rich visual effects through decoration. This decoration took such forms as pinnacles (upright members, often spired, that capped piers, buttresses, or other exterior elements), moldings, and, especially, window tracery. The most characteristic and finest achievement of the Rayonnant style is the great circular rose window adorning the west facades of large French cathedrals; the typically radial patterns of the tracery inspired the designation Rayonnant for the new style. Another typical feature of Rayonnant architecture is the thinning of vertical supporting members, the enlargement of windows, and the combination of the triforium gallery and the clerestory until walls are largely undifferentiated screens of tracery, mullions (vertical bars of tracery dividing windows into sections), and glass. Stained glass—formerly deeply coloured—became lighter in colour to increase the visibility of tracery silhouettes and to let more light into the interior. The most notable examples of the Rayonnant style are the cathedrals of Reims, Amiens, Bourges, Chartres, and Beauvais.

The parallel Decorated Gothic style came into being in England with the general use of elaborate stone window tracery. Supplanting the small, slender, pointed lancet windows of the early English Gothic style were windows of great width and height, divided by mullions into two to eight brightly coloured main subdivisions, each of which was further divided by tracery. At first, this tracery was based on the trefoil and quatrefoil, the arch, and the circle, all of which were combined to form netlike patterns. Later, tracery was based on the ogee, or S-shaped curve, which creates flowing, flamelike forms. Some of the most outstanding monuments of the Decorated Gothic style are sections of the cloister (c. 1245–69) of Westminster Abbey; the east end, or Angel Choir, of Lincoln Cathedral (begun 1256); and the nave and west front of York Minster (c. 1260–1320).

Late Gothic. In France the Rayonnant style evolved about 1280 into an even more decorative phase called the Flamboyant style, which lasted until about 1500. In England a development known as the Perpendicular style lasted from about 1375 to 1500. The most conspicuous feature of the Flamboyant Gothic style is the dominance in stone window tracery of a flamelike S-shaped curve.

In the Flamboyant style wall space was reduced to the minimum of supporting vertical shafts to allow an almost continuous expanse of glass and tracery. Structural logic was obscured by the virtual covering of the exteriors of buildings with tracery, which often decorated masonry as well as windows. A profusion of pinnacles, gables, and other details such as subsidiary ribs in the vaults to form star patterns further complicated the total effect.

By the late Gothic period greater attention was being given to secular buildings. Thus, Flamboyant Gothic features can be seen in many town halls, guild halls, and even residences. There were few churches built completely in the Flamboyant style, attractive exceptions being Notre-Dame d'Épine near Châlons-sur-Marne and Saint-Maclou in Rouen. Other important examples of the style are the Tour de Beurre of Rouen Cathedral and the north spire of Chartres. Flamboyant Gothic, which eventually became overly ornate, refined, and complicated, gave way in France to Renaissance forms in the 16th century.

In England the parallel Perpendicular Gothic style was characterized by a predominance of vertical lines in the stone tracery of windows, an enlargement of windows to great proportions, and the conversion of the interior stories into a single unified vertical expanse. The typical Gothic pointed vaults were replaced by fan vaults (fan-shaped clusters of tracery-like ribs springing from slender columns or from pendant knobs at the centre of the ceiling). Among the finest examples of the Perpendicular Gothic style are Gloucester Cathedral (14th–15th centuries) and King's College Chapel, Cambridge (1446–1515).

SCULPTURE

Gothic sculpture was closely tied to architecture, since it was used primarily to decorate the exteriors of cathedrals and other religious buildings. The earliest Gothic sculptures were stone figures of saints and the Holy Family used to decorate the doorways, or portals, of cathedrals in France and elsewhere. The sculptures on the Royal Portal of Chartres Cathedral (c. 1145–55) were little changed from their Romanesque predecessors in their stiff, straight, simple, elongated, and hieratic forms. But during the later 12th and the early 13th centuries sculptures became more relaxed and naturalistic in treatment, a trend that culminated in the sculptural decorations of the Reims Cathedral (c. 1240). These figures, while retaining the dignity and monumentality of their predecessors, have individualized faces and figures, as well as full, flowing draperies and natural poses and gestures, and they display a classical poise that suggests an awareness of antique Roman models on the part of their creators. Early Gothic masons also began to observe such natural forms as plants more closely, as is evident in the realistically carven clusters of leaves that adorn the capitals of columns.

Monumental sculptures assumed an increasingly prominent role during the High and late Gothic periods and were placed in large numbers on the facades of cathedrals, often in their own niches. In the 14th century, Gothic sculpture became more refined and elegant and acquired a mannered daintiness in its elaborate and finicky drapery. The elegant and somewhat artificial prettiness of this style was widely disseminated throughout Europe in sculpture, painting, and manuscript illumination during the 14th century and became known as the International Gothic style. An opposite trend at this time was that of an intensified realism, as displayed in French tomb sculptures and in the vigorous and dramatic works of the foremost late Gothic sculptor, Claus Sluter.

Gothic sculpture evolved into the more technically advanced and classicistic Renaissance style in Italy during the 14th and early 15th centuries but persisted until somewhat later in northern Europe.

PAINTING

Gothic painting followed the same stylistic evolution as did sculpture; from stiff, simple, hieratic forms toward more relaxed and natural ones. Its scale grew large only in the early 14th century, when it began to be used in decorating the retable (ornamental panel behind an altar). Such paintings usually featured scenes and figures from the New Testament, particularly of the Passion of Christ and the Virgin Mary. These paintings display an emphasis on flowing, curving lines, minute detail, and refined decoration, and gold was often applied to the panel as background colour. Compositions became more complex as time went on, and painters began to seek means of depicting spatial depth in their pictures, a search that eventually led to the mastery of perspective in the early years of the Italian Renaissance. In late Gothic painting of the 14th and 15th centuries secular subjects such as hunting scenes, chivalric themes, and depictions of historical events also appeared. Both religious and secular subjects were depicted in manuscript illuminations—i.e., the pictorial embellishment of handwritten books. This was a major form of artistic production during the Gothic period and reached its peak in France during the 14th century. The calendar illustrations in the *Très Riches Heures du duc de Berry* (c. 1409–16) by the Limbourg brothers, who worked at the court of Jean de France, duc de Berry, are perhaps the most eloquent statements of the International Gothic style as well as the best known of all manuscript illuminations.

Manuscript illumination was superseded by printed illustrations in the second half of the 15th century. Panel and wall painting evolved gradually into the Renaissance style in Italy during the 14th and early 15th centuries but retained many more of its Gothic characteristics until the late 15th and early 16th centuries in Germany, Flanders, and elsewhere in Northern Europe.

Stand-Up Comedy

Comedy that generally is delivered by a solo performer speaking directly to the audience in some semblance of a spontaneous manner is called stand-up comedy.

ORIGINS

Stand-up, at least in the form it is known today, is a fairly recent entertainment phenomenon. In the United States, where it developed first and reached its greatest popularity, it had its origins in the comic lecturers, such as Mark Twain, who toured the country in the 19th century. It began to emerge as populist entertainment in vaudeville in the early decades of the 20th century. While comedy was a staple of every vaudeville bill, it most often took the form of packaged routines delivered by comedy teams (who spoke to each other, not to the audience). But a few performers, such as Frank Fay, became known for their facility at off-the-cuff patter while serving as emcees in vaudeville houses such as the famed Palace Theatre in New York City. This solo style was honed further in the resorts of the Catskill Mountains region of New York in the 1930s and '40s. The predominantly Jewish comedians of the so-called Borscht Belt developed a brash gag-filled monologue style that played on familiar comic tropes—the bossy mother-in-law, the henpecked husband—exemplified by Henny Youngman's famous line "Take my wife—please."

Yet the comedian who probably did the most to make stand-up comedy a staple of American popular entertainment was Bob Hope, a British-born former vaudeville song-and-dance man. Hope, an admirer of Fay, developed an engaging rapid-fire style as an vaudeville emcee and, beginning in 1938, as host of his own top-rated radio program. Forced to come up with fresh material for his weekly radio monologues—and for the military audiences that he frequently traveled to entertain—Hope hired a team of writers who came up with jokes that played off the day's news, local gossip in the towns and military bases he visited, and the offstage doings of Hope and his show business friends. This was a significant departure from the vaudeville and Borscht Belt comics, whose gags were generic, were largely interchangeable, and could be repeated almost endlessly.

THE NEW WAVE

Hope and the Borscht Belt comics established the classic stand-up style that dominated popular entertainment well into the television era, when it became a staple of television variety programs such as *The Ed Sullivan Show*. But in the 1950s a new wave of stand-up comics emerged who rejected the detached mechanical style of the old joke tellers. The groundbreaker was Mort Sahl, who appeared onstage sitting on a stool with a rolled-up newspaper in his hand and talked in normal conversational tones—delivering not gag lines but caustic commentary on the political leaders, popular culture, and pillars of respectability of American society during the conservative 1950s. ("Are there any groups here I haven't offended?" he would typically crack.) Sahl's brainy politically dissenting comedy became a hit in the hip night spots of the Beat era and inspired a spate of new comedians who showed that stand-up could be smart, personal, and socially engaged.

Bob Newhart, Shelley Berman, and the comedy team of Mike Nichols and Elaine May created extended improv-style bits—one-sided phone conversations, people talking to their psychiatrists—that satirized various aspects of an uptight conformist era. Jonathan Winters blew apart the set-up/punch-line structure of traditional stand-up, pummeling the audience with a wild stream-of-consciousness barrage of characters, jokes, fragmented scenes, and physical bits. African American comedians such as Dick Gregory used stand-up as a vehicle for acerbic commentary on the racial tensions of the period of the civil rights movement, while Woody Allen turned himself into the butt of his own comic confessionals: the neurotic, sexually insecure New York Jewish nebbish.

The most influential comedian of this group, however, was Lenny Bruce, who spent much of his early career entertaining in strip clubs and other small-time venues and developed a cult following as the most audacious provocateur of stand-up's new wave. Bruce attacked America's most sacred cows—from organized religion to moralistic attitudes toward sex and drugs—and exposed himself more nakedly than any comedian had before. His renegade, free-form, often X-rated comedy made him a pariah for most of mainstream show business (Bruce was almost totally shunned by television); after numerous arrests for his performing allegedly obscene material in nightclubs, it also thrust him into a series of legal battles that virtually destroyed his career. Bruce's death from a drug overdose in 1966 solidified his legend and made him an inspiration for a new generation just coming of age in the turbulent late 1960s.

COUNTERCULTURAL COMEDY

The first of these Bruce acolytes to break through was George Carlin. Though already a successful relatively straitlaced comedian known for his parodies of television commercials and game shows, Carlin at the end of the 1960s let his hair and beard grow long, turned away from mainstream nightclubs, and reinvented himself as the comedic voice of the counterculture—skewering the war culture, middle-class hypocrisy, and his own Catholic upbringing. In his most famous routine, Carlin parsed, with devilish flair, the "seven words you can never say on television"; the taboo words that had gotten Bruce thrown in jail a few years earlier helped make Carlin a star.

Carlin's close contemporary Richard Pryor went through a similar reinvention. Outgrowing his youthful clean-cut television persona, in the early 1970s he transitioned to hard-edged, racially charged, brilliantly improvisational comedy that drew on the characters—winos, pimps, junkies, street preachers—he had grown up with in the Peoria, Ill., ghetto, as well as the increasingly baroque details of his troubled private life. Robert Klein, the third major comic of the early '70s to colonize the territory that Bruce had opened up, was a veteran of Chicago's Second

AP

Richard Pryor, 1977

City comedy troupe who developed a smart, supple, socially aware style of stand-up that was widely influential among a younger generation of comics.

By the 1970s stand-up comedy had become as potent a voice of the Vietnam War generation as rock music and Hollywood's new independent films such as *Easy Rider*. Comedy clubs sprouted in New York and Los Angeles, giving a bumper crop of young comics a place to hone their craft and develop an audience. Working night after night for little or no money, these young, mostly New York City-based comedians—among them Richard Lewis, Freddie Prinze, Elayne Boosler (one of the few women in a largely male-dominated crowd), and later Jerry Seinfeld—developed an intimate "observational" style, less interested in sociopolitical commentary than in chronicling the trials of everyday urban life, dealing with relationships, and surviving in the ethnic melting pot.

As the best young stand-ups began moving from New York to Los Angeles—where their most important television showcase, *The Tonight Show*, hosted by Johnny Carson, was located—experimentation flourished. For a popular culture now awash in stand-up comedy, many of these innovators turned to self-parody and ironic put-on. Albert Brooks, the son of a radio comedian known as Parkyakarkus, became a regular on TV talk and variety shows in the early 1970s with a string of put-on bits in which he parodied bad show-business acts—a terrible mime, a bumbling ventriloquist, and a succession of amateur songwriters trying to rewrite the U.S. national anthem. Andy Kaufman started out in New York clubs by posing as an inept wannabe comedian with a vaguely middle-European accent and unleashed series of deadpan Dadaist stunts, from singing children's songs to testing the audience's patience by reading F. Scott Fitzgerald's novel *The Great Gatsby* (1925) out loud or doing his laundry onstage.

The vogue for stand-up self-parody reached its pinnacle with the phenomenal success of Steve Martin, a former television writer who poked fun at old-time show business by impersonating the worst practitioner imaginable: a smug, ludicrously un-self-aware clown who puts arrows through his head and dubs himself a "wild and crazy guy." By the end of the 1970s, Martin was selling out 20,000-seat arenas and releasing best-selling comedy albums, becoming arguably the most popular stand-up comedian in history. This set the stage for a boom in the 1980s, when at least 300 comedy clubs blanketed the United States and cable TV shows such as *An Evening at the Improv* gave even mediocre stand-ups their moment in the national spotlight.

THE BRITISH TRADITION AND THE SPREAD OF STAND-UP COMEDY

Stand-up comedy—which depends so much on shared experiences, assumptions, even nuances of language—has rarely traveled well beyond its national borders. As the form was flourishing in the United States, parallel but largely separate stand-up traditions were developing in other countries, most notably the United Kingdom. British stand-up comedy had its origins in the music-hall performers of the 19th and early 20th centuries, especially Max Miller, who dressed in flashy suits and delivered cheeky fast-paced comedy patter in between song-and-dance bits. The more progressive British comedy of the 1950s and '60s was largely an outgrowth of the Universities of Oxford and Cambridge tradition of satirical college revues, including the Beyond the Fringe quartet (Peter Cook, Dudley Moore, Alan Bennett, and Jonathan Miller) and the wilder, mixed-media antics of the Monty Python troupe. A more working-class breed of solo stand-up, meanwhile, was emerging in Britain's equivalent of America's Borscht Belt: the workingmen's club circuit in the north of England, where comics assaulted the audience with brash joke-driven monologues that often traded on racial and sexual stereotypes. Stars of these clubs, such as Frank Carson and Bernard Manning, gained national fame in the 1970s via the popular British TV show *The Comedians*. Television, at the same time, provided an ideal platform for a far different kind of stand-up comic, Dave Allen. Allen, an urbane Irishman, hosted several popular talk-variety shows on British TV and would typically sit on a stool, cigarette in one hand and drink in the other, as he delivered wry stories and commentary on everything from the minor annoyances of life to the hypocrisies of the Roman Catholic Church, one of his favorite targets.

With the opening of the first American-style comedy club in London, the Comedy Store, in 1979, a new generation of alternative comedians began to emerge who rejected the retro joke-driven monologues of the old school and experimented with new styles and subject matter. One of the biggest stars of this new generation had actually made a splash a few years earlier: Billy Connolly, a former folksinger from Glasgow who achieved huge popularity in the mid-1970s with his irreverent, high-energy observational stand-up. He was followed in the 1980s by a rush of younger comics, including Alexei Sayle, emcee of the influential Comic Strip club that was a hothouse for new comedy stars in the '80s; the comedy team of Dawn French and Jennifer Saunders, the latter of whom starred in the situation comedy *Absolutely Fabulous*; and, a bit later, Eddie Izzard, whose flamboyant free-form stand-up made him one of the few British comedians whose work translated successfully in the United States. By the turn of the 21st century, stand-up comedy had taken root around the world, from Australia—where Barry Humphries, in the guise of Dame Edna Everage, became that country's most popular comedy export—to nascent stand-up scenes in countries ranging from Argentina to the Philippines.

JERRY SEINFELD AND BEYOND

Back in the United States, meanwhile, the stand-up explosion had faded considerably as the glut of comedy clubs and TV outlets led to overexposure and a dilution of the talent pool. TV sitcoms were cannibalizing many of the best and brightest—from Bill Cosby, whose gentle family-friendly monologues became the basis for a hugely popular NBC sitcom, *The Cosby Show* (1984–92), to Jerry Seinfeld, whose self-described "comedy about nothing" gave rise to *Seinfeld* (1989–98), the most critically acclaimed sitcom of the 1990s.

Seinfeld, who resumed a thriving stand-up career after walking away from his still-popular TV series, became a model for American stand-up comedy success well into the new century. But his small-bore, PG-rated comedy was increasingly an aberration as the proliferation of cable TV outlets (with their more permissive standards) and an increasingly freewheeling club scene encouraged comics to work even harder to demolish the last taboos of language and subject matter. At the same time, the institutionalization of the late-night-TV monologue—led by David Letterman, Jay Leno, and (with the help of his *Daily Show* repertory company) Jon Stewart—reinforced stand-up's role as American culture's primary means of processing and commenting on political leaders, Hollywood gossip, and the headline news of the day.

BIBLIOGRAPHY. WILLIAM ROBERT FAITH, *Bob Hope: A Life in Comedy* (2003), provides the most authoritative account thus far of the life and work of the father of American stand-up. GERALD NACHMAN, *Seriously Funny: The Rebel Comedians of the 1950s and 1960s* (2003), profiles the comedians who reinvented stand-up in the 1950s and '60s, from Mort Sahl to Woody Allen. ALBERT GOLDMAN and LAWRENCE SCHILLER, *Ladies and Gentlemen—Lenny Bruce!!* (1974), offers a quirky and flamboyant but nonetheless definitive account of the life of stand-up's most influential rebel. LARRY GELBART et al., *Stand-Up Comedians on Television* (1996), is a collection of essays for the Museum of Radio and Television that includes an excellent survey of the origins of American stand-up by David Bushman. RICHARD ZOGLIN, *Comedy at the Edge: How Stand-Up in the 1970s Changed America* (2008), is a critical and historical survey of the stand-up explosion that followed the death of Lenny Bruce, from Bruce acolytes such as George Carlin to comedy superstars such as Steve Martin. PHIL BERGER, *The Last Laugh: The World of Stand-Up Comics*, updated ed. (2000), presents a flavourful and entertaining look at the world of stand-up comedy, more impressionistic than historical but probably the best inside glimpse of stand-up comedians at work. WILLIAM COOK, *Ha Bloody Ha: Comedians Talking* (1994), among the relatively few books about British stand-up, nicely surveys Britain's new wave that began with the opening of London's Comedy Store in 1979.

(Richard Zoglin)

Don't Ask, Don't Tell

"Don't Ask, Don't Tell" is the byname for the former official U.S. policy (1993–2011) regarding the service of homosexuals in the military. The term, often abbreviated as DADT, was coined after Pres. Bill Clinton in 1993 signed a law (consisting of statute, regulations, and policy memoranda) directing that military personnel "don't ask, don't tell, don't pursue, and don't harass." When it went into effect on October 1, 1993, the policy theoretically lifted a ban on homosexual service that had been instituted during World War II, though in effect it continued a statutory ban. In December 2010 both the House of Representatives and the Senate voted to repeal the policy, and Pres. Barack Obama signed the legislation on December 22. The policy officially ended on September 20, 2011.

In the period between winning election as president in November 1992 and his inauguration in January 1993, Clinton announced his intention to quickly seek an end to the U.S. military's long-standing ban on homosexuals in the ranks. Although the move was popular among many Americans, notably gay activists who had supported Clinton's campaign, and Clinton had promised action during the election campaign, few political analysts thought he would move on such a potentially explosive issue so quickly. The move met with strong opposition, including from Sen. Sam Nunn, a Democrat from Georgia who headed the Senate Armed Services Committee. Indeed, Clinton's declaration put the president at odds with top military leaders and with a number of key civilians who had oversight responsibilities for the armed forces. After heated debate, Clinton managed to gain support for a compromise measure under which homosexual servicemen and servicewomen could remain in the military if they did not openly declare their sexual orientation, a policy that quickly became known as "Don't Ask, Don't Tell." Yet military officers were overwhelmingly opposed to that approach, fearing that the mere presence of homosexuals in the armed forces would undermine morale. The policy was further subverted by discrimination suits that upheld the right of gays to serve in the military without fear of discrimination.

Under the terms of the law, homosexuals serving in the military were not allowed to talk about their sexual orientation or engage in sexual activity, and commanding officers were not allowed to question service members about their sexual orientation. Although Clinton introduced "Don't Ask, Don't Tell" as a liberalization of existing policy, saying it was a way for gays to serve in the military when they had previously been excluded from doing so, many gay rights activists criticized the policy for forcing military personnel into secrecy and because it had fallen far short of a policy of complete acceptance. For a variety of reasons, the policy did little to change the behaviour of commanders; gay and lesbian soldiers continued to be discharged from service. During the Iraq War, which began in 2003, the policy came under further scrutiny, as many Arab linguists who were gay were discharged by the military.

By the 15-year anniversary of the law in 2008, more than 12,000 officers had been discharged from the military for refusing to hide their homosexuality. When Barack Obama campaigned for the presidency in 2008, he pledged to overturn "Don't Ask, Don't Tell" and to allow gay men and lesbians to serve openly in the military (a stance that was, according to public opinion polls, backed by a large majority of the public). During Obama's transition, Robert Gibbs, his press secretary, unequivocally reiterated that position. Although gay activists hoped that Obama would overturn "Don't Ask, Don't Tell" quickly, discharges continued during Obama's first year in office. In February 2010 the Pentagon announced its plan to reevaluate the policy and soon began a study, due in late 2010, that would determine how a repeal would affect the military. The following month, new measures were introduced to immediately relax the enforcement of "Don't Ask, Don't Tell" to make it more difficult for openly gay military service members to be expelled. The measures included permitting only high-ranking officers to oversee discharge proceedings and requiring higher standards for evidence presented in such cases. For example, under the new guidelines all third-party testimony had to be made under oath.

In May 2010 the U.S. House of Representatives and a U.S. Senate panel voted to allow the repeal of "Don't Ask, Don't Tell," pending completion of the Pentagon study and certification by the president, the secretary of defense, and the chairman of the Joint Chiefs of Staff that lifting the ban would not adversely affect military readiness. While the Pentagon review was being carried out, the policy was subject to a lawsuit claiming that it violated the First and Fifth Amendment rights of service members. In September a federal judge agreed with the plaintiffs, holding that it was unconstitutional, though the ruling did not invalidate the law immediately. Later that month efforts to end "Don't Ask, Don't Tell" stalled in the Senate, when the annual National Defense Authorization Act—which included several contentious bills, including the one that would allow for the law's repeal—was filibustered by Republicans.

In October "Don't Ask, Don't Tell" was halted after a federal judge in California issued an injunction banning the military from enforcing the policy. Later that month, however, "Don't Ask, Don't Tell" was reinstated after a stay was granted as the U.S. Justice Department appealed the injunction. Amid uncertainty concerning the policy's future, Defense Secretary Robert M. Gates issued stricter guidelines for its enforcement, requiring that the secretary of the air force, army, or navy consult with both the undersecretary of defense and the Pentagon's top legal official before expelling a gay service member.

On November 30, 2010, the Pentagon released its report of its study on "Don't Ask, Don't Tell," which found that repealing the policy would pose little risk to military effectiveness. Some 70 percent of service members surveyed believed that ending the policy would have mixed, positive, or no impact. However, some 40–60 percent of those in the Marine Corps expressed negative views or concerns about overturning "Don't Ask, Don't Tell." After a continued filibuster of the National Defense Authorization Act, independent U.S. Sen. Joe Lieberman and Maine Republican Sen. Susan Collins introduced in the U.S. Senate a stand-alone bill that would repeal "Don't Ask, Don't Tell." A similar bill was introduced in the House of Representatives, where it passed 250–174 on December 15. Three days later the measure overcame a Republican filibuster attempt by a vote of 63–33, and the repeal bill was passed later that day 65–31. President Obama praised the vote, releasing a statement that said, "It is time to recognize that sacrifice, valor and integrity are no more defined by sexual orientation than they are by race or gender, religion or creed." Obama signed the bill on December 22. Before the law could be officially enacted, however, the Pentagon had to devise a plan for implementing the repeal, which included updating various policies and regulations as well as developing education and training programs for troops. On July 22, 2011, Obama certified that the military was ready to end "Don't Ask, Don't Tell" after Defense Secretary Leon Panetta and Joint Chiefs of Staff Chairman Adm. Mike Mullen also signed off on the certification. After a mandatory 60-day time period passed, the repeal took effect on September 20, 2011.

International Monetary Fund

The International Monetary Fund (IMF) is a United Nations (UN) specialized agency, founded at the Bretton Woods Conference in 1944 to secure international monetary cooperation, to stabilize currency exchange rates, and to expand international liquidity (access to hard currencies).

ORIGINS

The first half of the 20th century was marked by two world wars that caused enormous physical and economic destruction in Europe and a Great Depression that wrought economic devastation in both Europe and the United States. These events kindled a desire to create a new international monetary system that would stabilize currency exchange rates without backing currencies entirely with gold; to reduce the frequency and severity of balance-of-payments deficits (which occur when more foreign currency leaves a country than enters it); and to eliminate destructive mercantilist trade policies, such as competitive devaluations and foreign exchange restrictions—all while substantially preserving each country's ability to pursue independent economic policies. Multilateral discussions led to the UN Monetary and Financial Conference in Bretton Woods, New Hampshire, U.S., in July 1944. Delegates representing 44 countries drafted the Articles of Agreement for a proposed International Monetary Fund that would supervise the new international monetary system. The framers of the new Bretton Woods monetary regime hoped to promote world trade, investment, and economic growth by maintaining convertible currencies at stable exchange rates. Countries with temporary, moderate balance-of-payments deficits were expected to finance their deficits by borrowing foreign currencies from the IMF rather than by imposing exchange controls, devaluations, or deflationary economic policies that could spread their economic problems to other countries.

After ratification by 29 countries, the Articles of Agreement entered into force on December 27, 1945. The fund's board of governors convened the following year in Savannah, Georgia, U.S., to adopt bylaws and to elect the IMF's first executive directors. The governors decided to locate the organization's permanent headquarters in Washington, D.C., where its 12 original executive directors first met in May 1946. The IMF's financial operations began the following year.

ORGANIZATION

The IMF is headed by a board of governors, each of whom represents one of the organization's approximately 180 member states. The governors, who are usually their countries' finance ministers or central bank directors, attend annual meetings on IMF issues. The fund's day-to-day operations are administered by an executive board, which consists of 24 executive directors who meet at least three times a week. Eight directors represent individual countries (China, France, Germany, Japan, Russia, Saudi Arabia, the United Kingdom, and the United States), and the other 16 represent the fund's remaining members, grouped by world regions. Because it makes most decisions by consensus, the executive board rarely conducts formal voting. The board is chaired by a managing director, who is appointed by the board for a renewable five-year term and supervises the fund's staff of nearly 3,000 employees from more than 120 countries. The managing director is usually a European and—by tradition—not an American. The first female managing director, Christine Lagarde of France, was appointed in June 2011.

Each member contributes a sum of money called a quota subscription. Quotas are reviewed every five years and are based on each country's wealth and economic performance—the richer the country, the larger its quota. The quotas form a pool of loanable funds and determine how much money each member can borrow and how much voting power it will have. For example, the United States' approximately $50 billion contribution to date is the most of any IMF member, accounting for approximately 18 percent of total quotas. Accordingly, the United States receives about 18 percent of the total votes on both the board of governors and the executive board. The Group of Seven industrialized nations (Canada, France, Germany, Italy, Japan, the United Kingdom, and the United States) controls nearly 50 percent of the fund's total votes.

OPERATION

Since its creation, the IMF's principal activities have included stabilizing currency exchange rates, financing the short-term balance-of-payments deficits of member countries, and providing advice and technical assistance to borrowing countries.

Stabilizing currency exchange rates. Under the original Articles of Agreement, the IMF supervised a modified gold standard system of pegged, or stable, currency exchange rates. Each member declared a value for its currency relative to the U.S. dollar, and in turn the U.S. Treasury tied the dollar to gold by agreeing to buy and sell gold to other governments at $35 per ounce. A country's exchange rate could vary only 1 percent above or below its declared value. Seeking to eliminate competitive devaluations, the IMF permitted exchange rate movements greater than 1 percent only for countries in "fundamental balance-of-payments disequilibrium" and only after consultation with, and approval by, the fund. In August 1971 U.S. President Richard Nixon ended this system of pegged exchange rates by refusing to sell gold to other governments at the stipulated price. Since then each member has been permitted to choose the method it uses to determine its exchange rate: a free float, in which the exchange rate for a country's currency is determined by the supply and demand of that currency on the international currency markets; a managed float, in which a country's monetary officials will occasionally intervene in international currency markets to buy or sell its currency to influence short-term exchange rates; a pegged exchange arrangement, in which a country's monetary officials pledge to tie their currency's exchange rate to another currency or group of currencies; or a fixed exchange arrangement, in which a country's currency exchange rate is tied to another currency and is unchanging. After losing its authority to regulate currency exchange rates, the IMF shifted its focus to loaning money to developing countries.

Financing balance-of-payments deficits. Members with balance-of-payments deficits may borrow money in foreign currencies, which they must repay with interest, by purchasing with their own currencies the foreign currencies held by the IMF. Each member may immediately borrow up to 25 percent of its quota in this way. The amounts available for purchase are denominated in Special Drawing Rights (SDRs), whose value is calculated daily as a weighted average of four currencies: the U.S. dollar, the euro, the Japanese yen, and the British pound sterling. SDRs are an international reserve asset created by the IMF in 1969 to supplement members' existing reserve assets of foreign currencies and gold. Countries use the SDRs that have been allocated to them by the IMF to settle international debts. More than 20 billion SDRs were allocated to members in successive allocations from 1969 through 1981. SDRs are not part of the quota subscriptions supplied by members, and thus they are not part of the general asset pool available for loans to members. The IMF uses the SDR as its unit of account for all transactions. Drawing on the IMF by a country raises the fund's holdings of that country's currency but lowers its holdings of another country's currency by an equal amount. Thus the composition of the fund's resources changes, but the total resources as measured in SDRs remains the same. The country repays the loan over a specified period (usually three to five years) by using member currencies acceptable to the IMF to repurchase its own national currency. Only about 20 currencies are borrowed during a typical year, with most borrowers exchanging their currency for the major convertible currencies: the U.S. dollar, the Japanese yen, the euro, and the British pound sterling. Countries whose currencies are borrowed by other member governments receive remuneration—about 4 percent of the amount borrowed.

Additional loans are available for members with financial difficulties that require them to borrow more than 25 percent of their quotas. The IMF uses an analytic framework known as financial programming, which was first fully formulated by IMF staff economist Jacques Polak in 1957, to determine the amount of the loan and the macroeconomic adjustments and structural reforms needed to reestablish the country's balance-of-payments equilibrium. The IMF has several financing programs, or facilities, for providing these loans, including a standby arrangement, which makes short-term assistance available to countries experiencing temporary or cyclical balance-of-payments deficits; an extended-fund facility, which supports medium-term relief; a supplemental-reserve facility, which provides loans in cases of extraordinary short-term deficits; and, since 1987, a poverty-reduction and growth facility. Each facility has its own access limit, disbursement plan, maturity structure, and repayment schedule. The typical IMF loan, known as an upper-credit tranche arrangement, features an annual access limit of 100 percent of a member's quota, quarterly disbursements, a one- to three-year maturity structure, and a three- to five-year repayment schedule. The IMF charges the same interest rate to every country that borrows from a particular financing facility. Loans typically carry annual interest charges of approximately 4.5 percent.

Each of these loans is accompanied by a "letter of intent" that specifies the macroeconomic adjustments and structural reforms required by the IMF as conditions for assistance. Loan conditions, or "conditionality," have been explicitly authorized by the Articles of Agreement since 1968. Typical conditionalities require borrowing governments to reduce budget deficits and rates of money growth; to eliminate monopolies, price controls, interest rate ceilings, and subsidies; to deregulate selected industries, particularly the banking sector; to lower tariffs and eliminate quotas; to remove export barriers; to maintain adequate international currency reserves; and to devalue their currencies if faced with fundamental balance-of-payments deficits. These adjustments are intended to reduce imports and increase exports to enable the country to earn sufficient foreign exchange in the future to pay its foreign debts, including the newly incurred IMF debt. Most lending programs specify quarterly targets for key economic variables that, in theory, must be met to receive the next loan installment.

Advising borrowing governments. The IMF consults annually with each member government. Through these contacts, known as "Article IV Consultations," the IMF attempts to assess each country's economic health and to forestall future financial problems. The fund also operates the IMF Institute, a department that provides training in macroeconomic analysis and policy formulation for officials of member countries.

CRITICISM AND DEBATE

The impact of IMF loans has been widely debated. Opponents of the IMF argue that the loans enable member countries to pursue reckless domestic economic policies knowing that, if needed, the IMF will bail them out. This safety net, critics charge, delays needed reforms and creates long-term dependency. Opponents also argue that the IMF rescues international bankers who have made bad loans, thereby encouraging them to approve ever riskier international investments.

IMF conditionalities have also been widely debated. Critics contend that IMF policy prescriptions provide uniform remedies that are not adequately tailored to each country's unique circumstances. These standard, austere loan conditions reduce economic growth and deepen and prolong financial crises, creating severe hardships for the poorest people in borrowing countries and strengthening local opposition to the IMF. (Lawrence McQuillan)

Christine Lagarde

A French lawyer and politician, Christine Lagarde is the first woman to serve as France's finance minister (2007–11) and as the managing director of the International Monetary Fund (IMF; 2011–).

Born in Paris on January 1, 1956, Lagarde was educated in the United States and France. After graduating (1974) from the prestigious Holton-Arms girls' college-preparatory school in Bethesda, Md., she studied at the Law School of the University of Paris X-Nanterre, where she lectured after graduation before going on to specialize in labour law, in which she obtained a postgraduate diploma (DESS). She also acquired a master's degree in English. In 1981 Lagarde joined the international law firm Baker & McKenzie in Paris. She was made a partner in 1987 and became the first female member (1995–99) of the executive committee. She was made chairman of the executive committee in 1999 (reelected 2002) and moved to Chicago. At Baker & McKenzie, she promulgated a "client first" approach whereby lawyers anticipated client needs rather than solely reacting to exigent situations. As a result, profits at the firm rose strongly.

While a member of the Center for Strategic & International Studies (CSIS), Lagarde led the U.S.-Poland Defense Industry Working Group, advancing the interests of aircraft companies Boeing and Lockheed Martin against those of Airbus and Dassault Aviation. In 2003 she was a member of the CSIS commission that culminated in a $3.5-billion contract for the sale of 48 Lockheed Martin jet fighters to Poland. Despite what struck some French observers as a conflict of interest, Lagarde in March 2004 received an appointment to France's highest order, the Legion of Honour, from Pres. Jacques Chirac, who described her as a role model and a charismatic leader.

Lagarde returned to France in June 2005 to join Prime Minister Dominique de Villepin's government as trade minister before becoming (briefly) minister for agriculture and fisheries in 2007. As trade minister she encouraged foreign investment in France and the opening of new markets for French products, particularly in the technology sector, helping exporters through the Cap Export mechanism, which she launched in September 2005.

In June 2007 Lagarde was designated finance minister by newly elected Pres. Nicolas Sarkozy. She was the first woman in the Group of Eight countries to hold this influential position. Her appointment reflected the end of a political leadership dominated by antiglobalization and the burgeoning (if tacit) acceptance of the unpleasant measures needed to revitalize France's increasingly uncompetitive and flagging economy. In contrast to her predecessors, Lagarde held the controversial view that the country's 35-hour workweek was a symbol of indolence. She advocated a stronger work ethic, a sentiment mirrored by the French business community. In June 2011 Lagarde was appointed managing director and chairman of the board of the IMF. The following month she officially replaced Dominique Strauss-Kahn, who had resigned in May. (Janet H. Clark)

Guinea Worm Disease

Guinea worm disease is an infection in humans caused by a parasite known as the guinea worm (*Dracunculus medinensis*). The disease's alternate name, dracunculiasis, is Latin for "affliction with little dragons," which adequately describes the burning pain associated with the infection. Historically a fairly common disease, affecting millions of people each year in the Middle East, India, and Africa, it is now relatively rare, being isolated to just a handful of countries in Africa. Death from guinea worm disease is infrequent; however, because it is debilitating, affected persons often have limited mobility and are unable to perform work.

COURSE OF THE DISEASE

Humans become infected with guinea worm by drinking water contaminated with water fleas (*Cyclops*), which are crustaceans that harbour the worm larvae. Gastric juices in the human host's intestinal tract kill the water fleas, thereby freeing the larvae to migrate and bore from the intestinal tract into the tissues of the abdomen, where they grow and where male and female worms mate. Whereas males die after mating, the fertilized females travel to other tissues (possibly by migrating along bones or by tunneling through tissues), usually moving to the legs.

About one year after initial infection, the adult worm, which can reach 1 metre (3.3 feet) in length, bores through subcutaneous tissues, headed toward the skin surface, and emerges from a blister. Guinea worm victims often enter ponds, streams, or other water sources to relieve the burning pain caused by the emerging worm. Once in the water, the worm sheds thousands of immature (or first-stage) larvae, which are then eaten by water fleas. Within two weeks of their ingestion, the larvae undergo two molts to become mature (or third-stage) larvae. Although still inside the fleas at this stage, they are infectious to humans upon ingestion of the fleas via contaminated water.

Symptoms of infection begin to appear just prior to the worm's emergence and include fever and pain and swelling in the area of the body housing the worm. The formation of a blister is a signal that the worm will soon emerge, and when it does so, it produces extreme pain.

TREATMENT AND PREVENTION

There is no specific drug treatment for guinea worm disease. Rather, the infection typically is managed through the careful removal of the worm in its entirety. Soaking the site of the blister in a container of water encourages the worm to emerge. Once it has broken through the skin, gentle traction is applied to the worm, speeding its emergence, which may take several days or weeks. The worm usually is wrapped around a piece of gauze or a stick to maintain tension and prevent the worm from retracting into the body. Topical antibiotics often are applied to the site of the wound to prevent infection with another organism during the extraction period. Aspirin or ibuprofen may be administered to relieve pain and reduce inflammation.

Prevention is the first line of defense against guinea worm disease. Prevention is effected through a combination of surveillance, including control of water fleas and early detection of cases, and health education. In addition, the availability of clean drinking water is key to long-term prevention in affected communities. Other approaches to prevention include the filtration of water to remove infected water fleas from suspect water sources and the treatment of contaminated water supplies with pesticides to kill the fleas.

GUINEA WORM DISEASE THROUGH HISTORY

Some of the earliest known evidence of guinea worm disease comes from the *Ebers Papyrus*, an ancient Egyptian compilation of medical texts dated to about 1550 BCE. The texts described the process of extracting the worm from the body by winding it around a stick. It is thought that in the Old Testament (Numbers 21:6) the fiery serpents that descended upon the Israelites in the 12th or 13th century BCE at the shores of the Red Sea were in fact guinea worms. (The parasite was later found to occur throughout the region of the Red Sea, and the disease was once endemic there.) Texts found in the ancient Assyrian city of Nin-

Encyclopædia Britannica, Inc.

Life cycle of the guinea worm

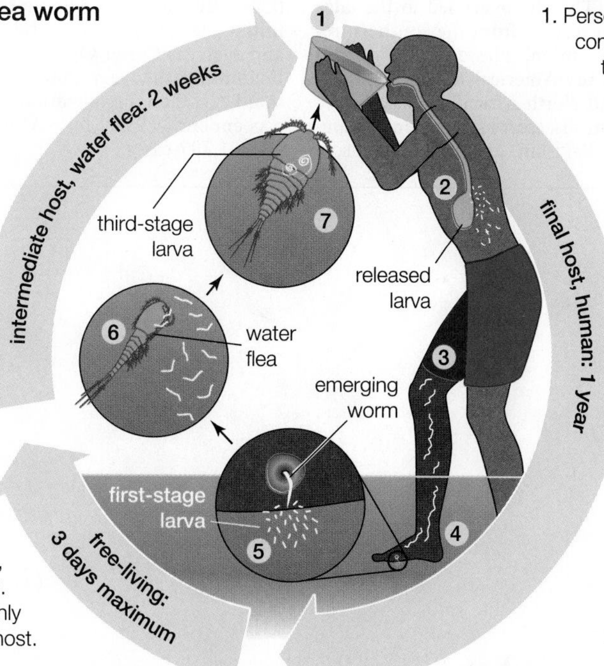

1. Person drinks well or pond water containing water fleas (*Cyclops*) that are infected with mature (third-stage) worm larvae.

2. Gastric juices in the human stomach digest the water fleas. Worm larvae are released and move to the abdominal tissues, where they grow and mate.

3. Fertilized female worms migrate to various body regions, usually the lower limbs. (Males die soon after mating.)

4. A year after infection the worm begins to emerge through the skin at the site of a painful blister.

5. On contact with water the emerging worm releases immature (first-stage) larvae into the water source, often a pond or shallow well. A free-living larva survives only three days unless it finds a host.

6. Water flea consumes worm larvae, which resist digestion.

7. In two weeks the larvae undergo two molts within the water flea to become third-stage larvae, which can infect humans.

eveh, in the library of King Ashurbanipal, who flourished in the 7th century BCE, included descriptions of infections of the feet and legs, and guinea worm disease is believed to be among the infections described. The existence of guinea worm disease in the ancient world was confirmed in the 1970s with the discovery of a calcified male guinea worm in a mummy dated to approximately 1000 BCE.

Guinea worm disease was also documented in ancient Greece, most notably by the writer Plutarch and by the physician Galen of Pergamum. In fact, Galen, who admitted to never having encountered a patient with the disease, is credited with giving it the name dracontiasis. There is some speculation that he may have mistaken the worm for a protruding nerve (a similar mistake was rumoured to have been made in the 16th century by French physician Ambroise Paré). The ancient Greeks are also believed to have uncovered the association between the infection and water and to have discovered the importance of keeping the worm intact during the extraction process. Some scholars contend that the serpent coiled around the healing staff of Asclepius, the Greco-Roman god of medicine, is a guinea worm, rather than a snake. The portrayal of the worm as being wound around the staff would have been associated with healing.

Physicians of the medieval world provided additional details about guinea worm disease. Al-Rāzī, a physician of the Islamic world, believed that the swellings on afflicted individuals were the result of a parasite, and in the 11th century Avicenna, another of the Islamic world's great physicians, provided the first clinical account of the disease and its treatment. In the centuries that followed, European physicians and explorers provided further documentation of the disease, confirming its presence in Egypt, India, Africa, and the Persian Gulf proper. The infection was given its common name, guinea worm disease, because European travelers who visited the coast of Guinea in Western Africa often either encountered people with the disease or were themselves afflicted.

In 1674 Italian physician Georgius Hieronymus Velschius published *Exercitatio de Vena Medinensis*, an illustrated work that included a depiction of the process of worm extraction from a patient's leg. The following century, Swedish naturalist Carolus Linnaeus assigned the Latin name *Dracunculus medinensis* to the guinea worm, and a short while later, suspicions that the parasite was transmitted to humans through contaminated drinking water intensified. About 1870 Russian scientist Aleksey P. Fedchenko confirmed these suspicions with his description of the guinea worm life cycle and the involvement of water fleas as intermediate hosts. This discovery led to the later eradication of guinea worm disease from the southern regions of the former Soviet Union. The disease was also eventually eradicated from the Americas and from many parts of the Middle East and North Africa.

By the 1980s, guinea worm disease was prevalent primarily in sub-Saharan Africa, Pakistan, and India, with several million new cases occurring each year collectively in those places in the middle part of that decade. In 1986 former U.S. president Jimmy Carter initiated a campaign for the complete eradication of the disease from the world. Following a visit in 1988 to Ghana, where tens of thousands of people were affected, Carter expanded his eradication campaign. Multiple organizations were involved in eradication efforts, including the World Health Organization (WHO), the United Nations Children's Fund (UNICEF), and the Atlanta-based Carter Center. WHO's initial goal of eradication by 1995 proved too ambitious, and even the Carter Center's aim to rid the world of the affliction by the year 2000 was not achieved. However, thanks to these organizations' efforts, by 2010 the disease was endemic in just four African countries and was limited to 1,797 cases. (Kara Rogers)

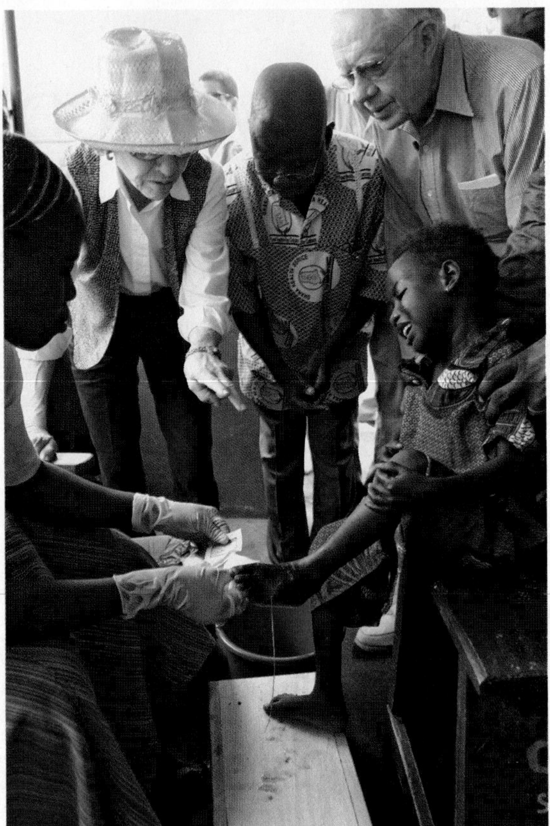

At Savelugu Hospital in the Northern Region of Ghana, former U.S. president Jimmy Carter and his wife, Rosalynn, watch as a health worker dresses a child's extremely painful guinea worm wound.

Louise Gubb/The Carter Center

Thomas Mukoya—Reuters/Landov

INTRODUCING CURAÇAO, SINT MAARTEN, AND SOUTH SUDAN IN 2012

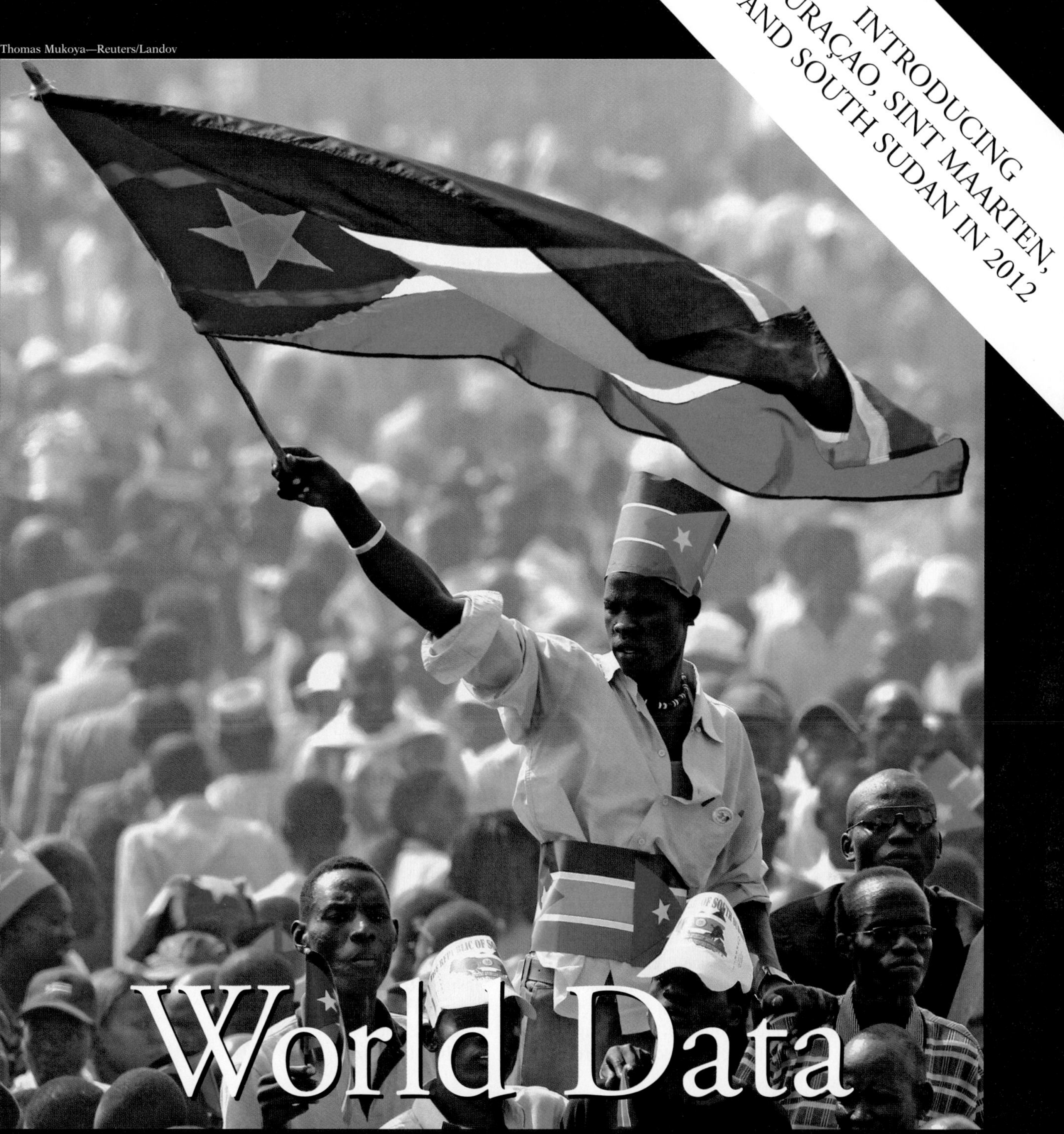

World Data

South Sudanese celebrate their independence on July 9, 2011. Independence was voted on by referendum, which overwhelmingly passed, in January 2011. Formal declaration came in July after decades of struggle.

CONTENTS

INTRODUCTION

Britannica World Data provides a statistical portrait of some 220 countries, dependencies, and territories of the world, at a level appropriate to the significance of each. It contains 219 country statements, ranging in length from one to five pages, and permits, in the 11 major thematic tables (the "Comparative National Statistics" [CNS] section), comparisons among these larger countries and 3 other states.

Updated annually, *Britannica World Data* is particularly intended as direct, structured support for many of Britannica's other reference works—encyclopaedias, yearbooks, atlases—at a level of detail that their editorial style or design do not permit.

Like the textual, graphic, or cartographic modes of expression of these other products, statistics possess their own inherent editorial virtues and weaknesses. Two principal goals in the creation of *Britannica World Data* were up-to-dateness and comparability, each possible to maximize separately, but not always possible to combine. If, for example, research on some subject is completed during a particular year (x), figures may be available for 100 countries for the preceding year ($x - 1$), for 140 countries for the year before that ($x - 2$), and for 180 countries for the year before that ($x - 3$).

Which year should be the basis of a thematic compilation for 219 countries so as to give the best combination of up-to-dateness and comparability? And, should $x - 1$ be adopted for the thematic table, ought up-to-dateness in the country table (for which year x is already available) be sacrificed for agreement with the thematic table? In general, the editors have opted for maximum up-to-dateness in the country statistical boxes and maximum comparability in the thematic tables.

Comparability, however, also resides in the meaning of the numbers compiled, which may differ greatly from country to country. The headnotes to the thematic tables explain many of these methodological problems; the Glossary serves the same purpose for the country statistical pages. Published data do not always provide the researcher or editor with a neat, unambiguous choice between a datum compiled on two different bases (say, railroad track length, or route length), one of which is wanted and the other not. More often a choice must be made among a variety of official, private, and external intergovernmental (UN, FAO, IMF) sources, each reporting its best data but each representing a set of problems: (1) of methodological variance from (or among) international conventions; (2) of analytical completeness (data for a single year may, successively, be projected [based on 10 months' data], preliminary [for 12 months], final, revised or adjusted, etc.); (3) of time frame, or accounting interval (data may represent a full Gregorian calendar year [preferred], a fiscal year, an Islamic or other national or religious year, a multiyear period or average [when a one-year statement would contain unrepresentative results]); (4) of continuity with previous data; and the like. Finally, published data on a particular subject may be complete and final but impossible to summarize in a simple manner. The education system of a single country may include, for example, public and private sectors; local, state, or national systems; varying grades, tracks, or forms within a single system; or opportunities for double-counting or fractional counting of a student, teacher, or institution. When no recent official data exist, or they exist, but may be suspect, the tables may show unofficial estimates, a range (of published opinion), analogous data, or no data at all.

The published basis of the information compiled is the statistical collections of Encyclopædia Britannica, Inc., some of the principal elements of which are enumerated in the Bibliography. Holdings for a given country may include any of the following: the national statistical abstract; the constitution; the most recent censuses of population; periodic or occasional reports on vital statistics, social indicators, agriculture, mining, labour, manufacturing, domestic and foreign trade, finance and banking, transportation, and communications. Further information is received in a variety of formats—telephone, letter, fax, microfilm and microfiche, and most recently, in electronic formats such as computer disks, CD-ROMs, and the Internet. So substantial has the resources of the Internet become that it was decided to add uniform resource locators (URLs) to the great majority of country pages and a number of the CNS tables (summary world sites with data on all countries still being somewhat of a rarity) so as to apprise the reader of the possibility and means to access current information on these subjects year-round.

The recommendations offered are usually to official sites (national statistical offices, general national governments, central banks, embassies, intergovernmental organizations [especially the UN Development Programme], and the like). Though often dissimilar in content, they will usually be updated year-round, expanded as opportunity permits, and lead on to related sites, such as parliamentary offices, information offices, diplomatic and consular sites, news agencies and newspapers, and, beyond, to the myriad academic, commercial, and private sites now accessible from the personal computer. While these URLs were correct and current at the time of writing, they may be subject to change.

The great majority of the social, economic, and financial data contained in this work should not be interpreted in isolation. Interpretive text of long perspective, such as that of the *Encyclopædia Britannica* itself; political, geographic, and topical maps, such as those in the *Britannica Atlas;* and recent analysis of political events and economic trends, such as that contained in the articles of the *Book of the Year,* will all help to supply analytic focus that numbers alone cannot. By the same token, study of those sources will be made more concrete by use of *Britannica World Data* to supply up-to-date geographic, demographic, and economic detail.

GLOSSARY

A number of terms that are used to classify and report data in the "Countries, Dependencies, and Territories" section require some explanation.

Those italicized terms that are used regularly in the country compilations to introduce specific categories of information (*e.g., birth rate, budget*) appear in this glossary in italic boldface type, followed by a description of the precise kind of information being offered and how it has been edited and presented.

All other terms are printed here in roman boldface type. Many terms have quite specific meanings in statistical reporting, and they are so defined here. Other terms have less specific application as they are used by different countries or organizations. Data in the country compilations based on definitions markedly different from those below will usually be footnoted.

Terms that appear in small capitals in certain definitions are themselves defined at their respective alphabetical locations.

Terms whose definitions are marked by an asterisk (*) refer to data supplied only in the larger two- to four-page country compilations.

activity rate, *see* participation/activity rates.

age breakdown, the distribution of a given population by age, usually reported here as percentages of total population in 15-year age brackets except for, when available, the 75–84 group. When substantial numbers of persons do not know, or state, their exact age, distributions may not total 100.0%.

aquatic plants production, the weight of aquatic plants (primarily seaweeds) harvested in freshwater or marine areas; the share harvested by farming is *aquaculture* production.

area, the total surface area of a country or its administrative subdivisions, including both land and inland (nontidal) water area. Land area is usually calculated from "mean low water" on a "plane table," or flat, basis.

area and population, a tabulation usually including the first-order administrative subdivisions of the country (such as the states of the United States), with capital (headquarters, or administrative seat), area, and population. When these subdivisions are especially numerous or, occasionally, nonexistent, a planning, electoral, census, or other nonadministrative scheme of regional subdivisions has been substituted.

associated state, *see* state.

atheist, in statements of religious affiliation, one who professes active opposition to religion; "nonreligious" refers to those professing only no religion, nonbelief, or doubt.

balance of payments, a financial statement for a country for a given period showing the balance among: (1) transactions in goods, services, and income between that country and the rest of the world, (2) changes in ownership or valuation of that country's monetary gold, SPECIAL DRAWING RIGHTS, and claims on and liabilities to the rest of the world, and (3) unrequited transfers and counterpart entries needed (in an accounting sense) to balance transactions and changes among any of the foregoing types of exchange that are not mutually offsetting. Detail of national law as to what constitutes a transaction, the basis of its valuation, and the size of a transaction visible to fiscal authorities all result in differences in the meaning of a particular national statement.*

balance of trade, the net value of all international goods trade of a country, usually excluding reexports (goods received only for transshipment), and the percentage that this net represents of total trade.

Balance of trade refers only to the "visible" international trade of goods as recorded by customs authorities and is thus a segment of a country's BALANCE OF PAYMENTS, which takes all visible and invisible trade with other countries into account. (Invisible trade refers to imports and exports of money, financial instruments, and services such as transport, tourism, and insurance.) A country has a favourable, or positive (+), balance of trade when the value of exports exceeds that of imports and negative (–) when imports exceed exports.

barrel (bbl), a unit of liquid measure. The barrel conventionally used for reporting crude petroleum and petroleum products is equal to 42 U.S. gallons, or 159 litres. The number of barrels of crude petroleum per metric ton, ranging typically from 6.20 to 8.13, depends upon the specific gravity of the petroleum. The world average is roughly 7.33 barrels per ton.

birth rate, the number of live births annually per 1,000 of midyear population. Birth rates for individual countries may be compared with the estimated world annual average of 20.3 births per 1,000 population in 2005.

Abbreviations

Measurements

cu m	cubic metre(s)
kg	kilograms(s)
km	kilometre(s)
kW	kilowatt(s)
kW-hr	kilowatt-hour(s)
metric ton-km	metric ton-kilometre(s)
mi	mile(s)
passenger-km	passenger-kilometre(s)
passenger-mi	passenger-mile(s)
short ton-mi	short ton-mile(s)
sq km	square kilometre(s)
sq m	square metre(s)
sq mi	square mile(s)
troy oz	troy ounce(s)
yr	year(s)

Political Units and International Organizations

ASEAN	Association of Southeast Asian Nations
Bos.-Her.	Bosnia and Herzegovina
CACM	Central American Common Market
Caricom	Caribbean Community and Common Market
CFA	Communauté Financière Africaine
CFP	Change franc Pacifique
CIS	Commonwealth of Independent States
CUSA	Customs Union of Southern Africa
EC	European Communities
ESCWA	Economic and Social Commission for Western Asia
EU	European Union
FAO	United Nations Food and Agriculture Organization
ILO	International Labour Organisation
IMF	International Monetary Fund
Neth.	Netherlands
OECD	Organization for Economic Cooperation and Development
OECS	Organization of Eastern Caribbean States
Serb.-Mont.	Serbia and Montenegro
Trin./Tob.	Trinidad and Tobago
U.A.E.	United Arab Emirates
UNDP	United Nations Development Programme

Months

Jan.	January	Oct.	October
Feb.	February	Nov.	November
Aug.	August	Dec.	December
Sept.	September		

Miscellaneous

AIDS	Acquired Immune Deficiency Syndrome
avg.	average
c.i.f.	cost, insurance, and freight
commun.	communications
CPI	consumer price index
est.	estimate(d)
excl.	excluding
f.o.b.	free on board
GDP	gross domestic product
GNP	gross national product
govt.	government
incl.	including
LNG	liquefied natural gas
n.a.	not available (in text)
n.e.s.	not elsewhere specified
no.	number
pl.	plural
pub. admin.	public administration
SDR	Special Drawing Right
SITC	Standard International Trade Classification
svcs.	services
teacher tr.	teacher training
transp.	transportation
VAT	value-added taxes
Voc.	Vocational
$	dollar (of any currency area)
£	pound (of any currency area)
. . .	not available (in tables)
—	none, less than half the smallest unit shown, or not applicable (in tables)

budget, the annual receipts and expenditures—of a central government for its activities only; does not include state, provincial, or local governments or semipublic (parastatal, quasi-nongovernmental) corporations unless otherwise specified. Figures for budgets are limited to ordinary (recurrent) receipts and expenditures, wherever possible, and exclude capital expenditures—*i.e.,* funds for development and other special projects originating as foreign-aid grants or loans.

When both a recurrent and a capital budget exist for a single country, the former is the budget funded entirely from national resources (taxes, duties, excises, etc.) that would recur (be generated by economic activity) every year. It funds the most basic governmental services, those least able to suffer interruption. The capital budget is usually funded by external aid and may change its size considerably from year to year.

capital, usually, the actual seat of government and administration of a state. When more than one capital exists, each is identified by kind; when interim arrangements exist during the creation or movement of a national capital, the de facto situation is described.

Anomalous cases are annotated, such as those in which (1) the de jure designation under the country's laws differs from actual local practice (*e.g.,* Benin's designation of one capital in constitutional law, but another in actual practice), (2) international recognition does not validate a country's claim (as with the proclamation by Israel of a capital on territory not internationally recognized as part of Israel), or (3) both a state and a capital have been proclaimed on territory recognized as part of another state (as with the Turkish Republic of Northern Cyprus).

capital budget, *see* budget.

causes of death, as defined by the World Health Organization (WHO), "the disease or injury which initiated the train of morbid events leading directly to death, or the circumstances of accident or violence which produced the fatal injury." This principle, the "underlying cause of death," is the basis of the medical judgment as to cause; the statistical classification system according to which these causes are grouped and named is the *International List of Causes of Death*, the latest revision of which is the Tenth. Reporting is usually in terms of events per 100,000 population. When data on actual causes of death are unavailable, information on morbidity, or illness rate, usually given as reported cases per 100,000 of infectious diseases (notifiable to WHO as a matter of international agreement), may be substituted.

chief of state/head of government, paramount national governmental officer(s) exercising the highest executive and/or ceremonial roles of a country's government. In general usage, the chief of state is the formal head of a national state. The primary responsibilities of the chief of state may range from the purely ceremonial—convening legislatures and greeting foreign officials—to the exercise of complete national executive authority. The head of government, when this function exists separately, is the officer nominally charged (by the constitution) with the majority of actual executive powers, though they may not in practice be exercised, especially in military or single-party regimes in which effective power may reside entirely outside the executive governmental machinery provided by the constitution. A prime minister, for example, usually the actual head of government, may in practice exercise only Cabinet-level authority.

In communist countries an official identified as the chief of state may be the chairman of the policy-making organ, and the official given as the head of government the chairman of the nominal administrative/executive organ.

c.i.f. (trade valuation): *see* imports.

commonwealth (U.K. and U.S.), a self-governing political entity that has regard to the common weal, or good; usually associated with the United Kingdom or United States. Examples include the Commonwealth (composed of independent states [from 1931 onward]), Puerto Rico since 1952, and the Northern Marianas since 1979.

communications, collectively, the means available for the public transmission of information within a country. Data are tabulated for: paid-for daily newspapers and their total circulation; television as total numbers of receivers; telephone data as landlines, or the number of subscriber lines (not receivers) having access to the public switched network; cellular telephones and Internet broadband users as number of subscribers; and personal computers and Internet users as number of units. For each, a rate per 1,000 persons is given.

constant prices, an adjustment to the members of a financial time series to eliminate the effect of inflation year by year. It consists of referring all data in the series to a single year so that "real" change may be seen.

constitutional monarchy, *see* monarchy.

consumer price index (CPI), also known as the retail price index, or the cost-of-living index, a series of index numbers assigned to the price of a selected "basket," or assortment, of basic consumer goods and services in a country, region, city, or type of household in order to measure changes over time in prices paid by a typical household for those goods and services. Items included in the CPI are ordinarily determined by governmental surveys of typical household expenditures and are assigned weights relative to their proportion of those expenditures. Index values are period averages unless otherwise noted.

coprincipality, *see* monarchy.

current prices, the valuation of a financial aggregate as of the year reported.

de facto population, for a given area, the population composed of those actually present at a particular time, including temporary residents and visitors (such as immigrants not yet granted permanent status, "guest" or expatriate workers, refugees, or tourists), but excluding legal residents temporarily absent.

de jure population, for a given area, the population composed only of those legally resident at a particular time, excluding temporary residents and visitors (such as "guest" or expatriate workers, refugees, or tourists), but including legal residents temporarily absent.

death rate, the number of deaths annually per 1,000 of midyear population. Death rates for individual countries may be compared with the estimated world annual average of 8.6 deaths per 1,000 population in 2005.

density (of population), usually, the DE FACTO POPULATION of a country divided by its total area. Special adjustment is made for large areas of inland water, desert, or other uninhabitable areas—*e.g.,* excluding the ice cap of Greenland.

dependency, an area annexed to, or controlled by, an independent state but not an integral part of it; a non-self-governing territory. A dependency has a charter and may have a degree of self-government. A crown dependency is a dependency originally chartered by the British government (*see* Table).

direct taxes, taxes levied directly on firms and individuals, such as taxes on income, profits, and capital gains. The *immediate* incidence, or burden, of direct taxes is on the firms and individuals thus taxed; direct taxes on firms may, however, be passed on to consumers and other economic units in the form of higher prices for goods and services, blurring the distinction between direct and indirect taxation.

divorce rate, the number of legal, civilly recognized divorces annually per 1,000 population.

doubling time, the number of complete years required for a country to double its population at its current rate of natural increase.

earnings index, a series of index numbers comparing average wages in a collective industrial sample for a country or region with the same industries at a previous period to measure changes over time in those wages. It is most commonly reported for wages paid on a daily, weekly, or monthly basis; annual figures may represent total income or averages of these shorter periods. The scope of the earnings index varies from country to country. The index is often limited to earnings in manufacturing industries. The index for each country applies to all wage earners in a desig-

Dependencies[1]

Australia
Christmas Island
Cocos (Keeling) Islands
Norfolk Island

Denmark
Faroe Islands
Greenland

France
French Guiana[2]
French Polynesia
Guadeloupe[2]
Martinique[2]
Mayotte
New Caledonia
Réunion[2]
Saint-Barthélemy
Saint-Martin
Saint-Pierre and Miquelon
Wallis and Futuna

Netherlands
Aruba
Curaçao
Sint Maarten

New Zealand
Cook Islands
Niue
Tokelau

United Kingdom
Anguilla
Bermuda
British Virgin Islands
Cayman Islands
Falkland Islands
Gibraltar
Guernsey
Isle of Man
Jersey
Montserrat
Pitcairn Island
Saint Helena
Tristan da Cunha
Turks and Caicos Islands

United States
American Samoa
Guam
Northern Mariana Islands
Puerto Rico
Virgin Islands (of the U.S.)

[1]Excludes territories (1) to which Antarctic Treaty is applicable in whole or in part, (2) without permanent civilian population, (3) without internationally recognized civilian government (Western Sahara, Gaza Strip), or (4) representing unadjudicated unilateral or multilateral territorial claims. [2]Legally classified as overseas department of France.

nated group and ordinarily takes into account basic wages (overtime is normally distinguished), bonuses, cost-of-living allowances, and contributions toward social security. Some countries include payments in kind. Contributions toward social security by employers are usually excluded, as are social security benefits received by wage earners.

economically active population, *see* population economically active.

education, tabulation of the principal elements of a country's educational establishment, classified as far as possible according to the country's own system of primary, secondary, and tertiary levels (the usual age limits for these levels being identified in parentheses), with total number of teachers and students (whether full- or part-time). The student-teacher ratio and enrollment rates (net for primary and secondary, gross for tertiary) are calculated whenever available data permit.

educational attainment, the distribution of the population age 25 and over with completed educations by the highest level of formal education attained or completed; it must sometimes be reported, however, for age groups still in school or for the economically active only.

emirate, *see* monarchy.

enrollment rates, if net (for primary and secondary levels of education): number of students in a theoretical age group for a given level of education expressed as a percentage of the total population of that age group; if gross: number of (domestically enrolled) students, regardless of age, expressed as a percentage of a theoretical age group (for the tertiary level of education UNESCO Institute for Statistics defines the theoretical age group as being the 5-year age group following the secondary school-leave).

enterprise, a legal entity formed to conduct a business, which it may do from more than one establishment.

ethnic/linguistic composition, ethnic, racial, or linguistic composition of a national population, reported here according to the most reliable breakdown available, whether published in official sources (such as a census) or in external analysis (when the subject is not addressed in national sources).

exchange rate, the value of one currency compared with another, or with a standardized unit of account such as the SPECIAL DRAWING RIGHT, or as mandated by local statute when one currency is "tied" by a par value to another. Rates given usually refer to free market values when the currency has no, or very limited, restrictions on its convertibility into other currencies.

exports, material goods legally leaving a country (or customs area) and subject to customs regulations. The total value and distribution by percentage of the major items (in preference to groups of goods) exported are given, together with the distribution of trade among major trading partners (usually single countries or trading blocs). Valuation of goods exported is free on board (f.o.b.) unless otherwise specified. The value of goods exported and imported f.o.b. is calculated from the cost of production and excludes the cost of transport.

external debt, public and publicly guaranteed debt with a maturity of more than one year owed to nonnationals of a country and repayable in foreign currency, goods, or services. The debt may be an obligation of a national or subnational governmental body (or an agency of either), of an autonomous public body, or of a private debtor that is guaranteed by a public entity. The debt is usually either outstanding (contracted) or disbursed (drawn).

external territory (Australia), *see* territory.

federal, consisting of first-order political subdivisions that are prior to and independent of the central government in certain functions.

federal constitutional monarchy, *see* monarchy.

federal republic, *see* republic.

federation, union of coequal, preexisting political entities that retain some degree of autonomy and (usually) right of secession within the union.

fertility rate, *see* total fertility rate.

financial aggregates, tabulation of seven-year time series, providing principal measures of the financial condition of a country, including: (1) the exchange rate of the national crurency against the U.S. dollar, the pound sterling, and the International Monetary Fund's SPECIAL DRAWING RIGHT (SDR), (2) the amount and kind of international reserves (holdings of SDRs, gold, and foreign currencies) and reserve position of the country in the IMF, and (3) principal economic rates and prices (central bank discount rate, government bond yields, and industrial stock [share] prices). For BALANCE OF PAYMENTS, the origin in terms of component balance of trade items and balance of invisibles (net) is given.*

fisheries production, the live-weight equivalent of the aquatic animals (including fish, crustaceans, mollusks, and other aquatic mammals) caught in freshwater or marine areas by national fleets and landed in domestic or foreign harbours for commercial, industrial, or subsistence purposes. The share of fisheries production that is harvested by farming is *aquaculture* production.

f.o.b. (trade valuation), *see* exports.

food, *see* daily per capita caloric intake.

foreign direct investment (FDI), a long-term investment with a significant degree of control by a business entity or individual of one country into another country's economy. FDI comprises three components—equity capital, reinvested earnings, and intra-company loans. The net balance of the three FDI components is often volatile from one year to the next. If negative for a particular time period, the balance of the three components is called a reverse investment, or disinvestment.

form of government/political status, the type of administration provided for by a country's constitution—whether or not suspended by extralegal military or civil action, although such de facto administrations are identified—together with the number of members (elected, appointed, and ex officio) for each legislative house, named according to its English rendering. Dependent states (*see* Table) are classified according to the status of their political association with the administering country.

gross domestic product (GDP), the total value of the final goods and services produced by residents and nonresidents within a given country during a given accounting period, usually a year. Unless otherwise noted, the value is given in current prices of the year indicated. The *System of National Accounts* (SNA, published under the joint auspices of the UN, IMF, OECD, EC, and World Bank) provides a framework for international comparability in classifying domestic accounting aggregates and international transactions comprising "net factor income from abroad," the measure that distinguishes GDP and GNP.

gross national income (GNI), also called gross national product (GNP), the total value of final goods and services produced both from within a given country *and* from external (foreign) transactions in a given accounting period, usually a year. Unless otherwise noted, the value is given in current prices of the year indicated. GNI is equal to GROSS DOMESTIC PRODUCT adjusted by net factor income from abroad, which is the income residents receive from abroad for factor services (labour, investment, and interest) less similar payments made to nonresidents who contribute to the domestic economy.

head of government, *see* chief of state/head of government.

health, a group of measures including number of accredited physicians currently practicing or employed and their ratio to the total population; total hospital beds and their ratio; and INFANT MORTALITY RATE.

household, economically autonomous individual or group of individuals living in a single dwelling unit. A family household is one composed principally of individuals related by blood or marriage.

household income and expenditure, data for average size of a HOUSEHOLD (by number of individuals) and median household income. Sources of income and expenditures for major items of consumption are given as percentages.

In general, household income is the amount of funds, usually measured in monetary units, received by the members (generally those 14 years old and over) of a household in a given time period. The income can be derived from (1) wages or salaries, (2) nonfarm or farm SELF-EMPLOYMENT, (3) transfer payments, such as pensions, public assistance, unemployment benefits, etc., and (4) other income, including interest and dividends, rent, royalties, etc. The income of a household is expressed as a gross amount before deductions for taxes. Data on expenditure refer to consumption of personal or household goods and services; they normally exclude savings, taxes, and insurance; practice with regard to inclusion of credit purchases differs markedly.

imports, material goods legally entering a country (or customs area) and subject to customs regulations; excludes financial movements. The total value and distribution by percentage of the major items (in preference to groups of goods) imported are given, together with the direction of trade among major trading partners (usually single countries), trading blocs (such as the European Union), or customs areas (such as Belgium-Luxembourg). The value of goods imported is given free on board (f.o.b.) unless otherwise specified; f.o.b. is defined above under EXPORTS.

The principal alternate basis for valuation of goods in international trade is that of cost, insurance, and freight (c.i.f.); its use is restricted to imports, as it comprises the principal charges needed to bring the goods to the customs house in the country of destination. Because it inflates the value of imports relative to exports, more countries have, latterly, been estimating imports on an f.o.b. basis as well.

incorporated territory (U.S.), *see* territory.

independent, of a state, autonomous and controlling both its internal and external affairs. Its date usually refers to the date from which the country was in effective control of these affairs within its present boundaries, rather than the date independence was proclaimed or the date recognized as a de jure act by the former administering power.

indirect taxes, taxes levied on sales or transfers of selected intermediate goods and services, including excises, value-added taxes, and tariffs, that are ordinarily passed on to the ultimate consumers of the goods and services. Figures given for individual countries are limited to indirect taxes levied by their respective central governments unless otherwise specified.

infant mortality rate, the number of children per 1,000 live births who die before their first birthday. Total infant mortality includes neonatal mortality, which is deaths of children within one month of birth.

invisibles (invisible trade), *see* balance of trade.

kingdom, *see* monarchy.

labour force, portion of the POPULATION ECONOMICALLY ACTIVE (PEA) comprising those most fully employed or attached to the labour market (the unemployed are considered to be "attached" in that they usually represent persons previously employed seeking to be reemployed), particularly as viewed from a short-term perspective. It normally includes those who are self-employed, employed by others (whether full-time, part-time, seasonally, or on some other less than full-time, basis), and, as noted above, the unemployed (both those previously employed and those seeking work for the first time). In the "gross domestic product and labour force" table, the majority of the labour data provided refer to population economically active, since PEA represents the longer-term view of working population and, thus, subsumes more of the marginal workers who are often missed by shorter-term surveys.

land use, distribution by classes of vegetational cover or economic use of the land area only (excluding inland water, built-up areas, and wasteland), reported as percentages. The principal categories utilized include: (1) arable land under temporary cultivation, (2) arable land left fallow for less than five years, (3) land under permanent cultivation (significantly tree crops but also grapes, pineapples, and bananas), (4) pastures and rangeland, which includes land in temporary or permanent use whose principal purpose is the growing of animal fodder, and (5) forest areas (without permanent tree crops); forest areas may include scrub forests, forest plantations, and recently afforested or reforested land.

life expectancy, the number of years a person born within a particular population group (age cohort) would be expected to live, based on actuarial calculations.

literacy, the ability to read and write a language with some degree of competence; the precise degree constituting the basis of a particular national statement is usually defined by the national census and is often tested by the census enumerator. Elsewhere, particularly where much adult literacy may be the result of literacy campaigns rather than passage through a formal educational system, definition and testing of literacy may be better standardized.

major cities, usually the five largest cities/towns proper (national capitals are almost always given, regardless of size); fewer cities/towns may be listed if there are fewer urban localities in the country. For multipage tables, 10 or more may be listed.* Populations for cities/towns will usually refer to the city/town proper—*i.e.,* the legally bounded corporate entity, or the most compact, contiguous, demographically urban portion of the entity defined by the local authorities. Occasionally figures for METROPOLITAN AREAS, urban areas, or urban agglomerations are cited when the relevant civil entity at the core of a major agglomeration had an unrepresentatively small population.

marriage rate, the number of legal, civilly recognized marriages annually per 1,000 population.

material well-being, a group of measures indicating the percentage of households or dwellings possessing certain goods or appliances, including automobiles, telephones, television receivers, refrigerators, air conditioners, and washing machines.*

metropolitan area, a city and the region of dense, predominantly urban, settlement around the city; the population of the whole usually has strong economic and cultural affinities with the central city.

military expenditure, the apparent value of all identifiable military expenditure by the central government on hardware, personnel, pensions, research and development, etc., reported here both as a percentage of the GNP, with a comparison to the world average, and as a per capita value in U.S. dollars.

military personnel, *see* total active duty personnel.

mobility, the rate at which individuals or households change dwellings, usually measured between censuses and including international as well as domestic migration.*

monarchy, a government in which the CHIEF OF STATE holds office, usually hereditarily and for life, but sometimes electively for a term. The state may be a coprincipality, emirate, kingdom, principality, sheikhdom, or sultanate. The powers of the monarch may range from absolute (*i.e.,* the monarch both reigns and rules) through various degrees of limitation of authority to nominal, as in a constitutional monarchy, in which the titular monarch reigns but others, as elected officials, effectively rule.

monetary unit, currency of issue, or that in official use in a given country; name and abbreviation or symbol according to local practice or name and 3-digit code according to the ISO (International Organization for Standardization); and valuation in U.S. dollars and U.K. pounds sterling, usually according to free-market rates.

See also exchange rate.

natural increase, also called natural growth, or the balance of births and deaths, the excess of births over deaths in a population; the rate of natural increase is the difference between the BIRTH RATE and the DEATH RATE of a given population. The estimated world average during 2005 was 11.7 per 1,000 population, or 1.35% annually. Natural increase is added to the balance of migration to calculate the total growth of that population.

nonreligious, *see* atheist.

official development assistance, officially administered grants and concessional loans that donors (usually developed countries) give to developing countries to promote economic development and welfare.

official language(s), that (or those) prescribed by the national constitution for day-to-day conduct and publication of a country's official business or, when no explicit constitutional provision exists, that of the constitution itself, the national gazette (record of legislative activity), or like official documents. Other languages may have local protection, may be permitted in parliamentary debate or legal action (such as a trial), or may be "national languages," for the protection of which special provisions have been made, but these are not deemed official. The United States, for example, does not yet formally identify English as "official," though it uses it for virtually all official purposes.

official name, the local official form(s), short or long, of a country's legal name(s) taken from the country's constitution or from other official documents. The English-language form is usually the protocol form in use by the country, the U.S. Department of State, and the United Nations.

official religion, generally, any religion prescribed or given special status or protection by the constitution or legal system of a country. Identification as such is not confined to constitutional documents utilizing the term explicitly.

organized territory (U.S.), *see* territory.

overseas department (France), *see* department.

overseas territory (France), *see* territory.

parliamentary state, *see* state.

part of a realm, a dependent Dutch political entity with some degree of self-government and having a special status above that of a colony (*e.g.,* the prerogative of rejecting for local application any law enacted by The Netherlands).

participation/activity rates, measures defining differential rates of economic activity within a population. Participation rate refers to the percentage of those employed or economically active who possess a particular characteristic (sex, age, etc.); activity rate refers to the fraction of the total population who *are* economically active.

passenger-miles, or **passenger-kilometres,** aggregate measure of passenger carriage by a specified means of transportation, equal to the number of passengers carried multiplied by the number of miles (or kilometres) each passenger is transported. Figures given for countries are often calculated from ticket sales and ordinarily exclude passengers carried free of charge.

people's republic, *see* republic.

place of birth/national origin, if the former, numbers of native- and foreign-born population of a country by actual place of birth; if the latter, any of several classifications, including those based on origin of passport at original admission to country, on cultural heritage of family name, on self-designated (often multiple) origin of (some) ancestors, and on other systems for assigning national origin.*

political status, *see* form of government/political status.

population, the number of persons present within a country, city, or other civil entity at the date of a census of population, survey, cumulation of a civil register, or other enumeration. Unless otherwise specified, populations given are DE FACTO, referring to those actually present, rather than DE JURE, those legally resident but not necessarily present on the referent date. If a time series, noncensus year, or per capita ratio referring to a country's total population is cited, it will usually refer to midyear of the calendar year indicated.

population economically active, the total number of persons (above a set age for economic labour, usually 10–15 years) in all employment statuses—self-employed, wage- or salary-earning, part-time, seasonal, unemployed, etc. The International Labour Organisation defines the economically active as "all persons of either sex who furnish the supply of labour for the production of economic goods and services." National practices vary as regards the treatment of such groups as armed forces, inmates of institutions, persons seeking their first job, unpaid family workers, seasonal workers and persons engaged in part-time economic activities. In some countries, all or part of these groups may be included among the economically active, while in other countries the same groups may be treated as inactive. In general, however, the data on economically active population do not include students, persons occupied solely in family or household work, retired persons, persons living entirely on their own means, and persons wholly dependent upon others.

See also labour force.

population projection, the expected population in the years 2020 and 2030, embodying the country's own projections wherever possible. Estimates of the future size of a population are usually based on assumed levels of fertility, mortality, and migration. Projections in the tables, unless otherwise specified, are medium (*i.e.,* most likely) variants, whether based on external estimates by the United Nations, U.S. Bureau of the Census, or on those of the country itself.

price and earnings indexes, tabulation comparing the change in the CONSUMER PRICE INDEX over a period of seven years with the change in the general labour force's EARNINGS INDEX for the same period.

principality, *see* monarchy.

production, the physical quantity or monetary value of the output of an industry, usually tabulated here as the most important items or groups of items (depending on the available detail) of primary (extractive) and secondary (manufactured) production, including construction. When a single consistent measure of value, such as VALUE ADDED, can be obtained, this is given, ranked by value; otherwise, and more usually, quantity of production is given.

public debt, the current outstanding debt of all periods of maturity for which the central government and its organs are obligated. Publicly guaranteed private debt is excluded. For countries that report debt under the World Bank Debtor Reporting System (DRS), figures for outstanding, long-term EXTERNAL DEBT are given.

purchasing power parity, an economic theory used to determine the number of units in a country's currency that are required to buy the same amount of goods and services in another country. As such it is often used to compare the standards of living between countries expressed in a common currency which is usually U.S.$. *Britannica World Data* publishes only purchasing power parity rates as calculated by the World Bank method.

quality of working life, a group of measures including weekly hours of work (including overtime); rates per 100,000 for job-connected injury, illness, and mortality; coverage of labour force by insurance for injury, permanent disability, and death; workdays lost to labour strikes and stoppages; and commuting patterns (length of journey to work in minutes and usual method of transportation).*

railroads, mode of transportation by self-driven or locomotive-drawn cars over fixed rails. Length-of-track figures include all mainline and spurline running track but exclude switching sidings and yard track. Route length, when given, does not compound multiple running tracks laid on the same trackbed.

recurrent budget, *see* budget.

religious affiliation, distribution of nominal religionists, whether practicing or not, as a percentage of total population. This usually assigns to children the religion of their parents.

remittances, amount of a migrant's earnings sent from the migration destination to the place of origin. Remittance data are compiled somewhat differently from one country source to another but usually include cash transfers of long-term legal migrants. Cash transfers of short-term ("for less than one year of residence") legal migrants or the cash transfers of illegal migrants and refugees are also often included with remittances. The standard (but not universal) sources used in BWD for national remittances are the latest editions of World Bank publications and UNCTAD *Handbook of Statistics*. These two sources may also (1) include net wages and salaries of all nonresident migrants and (2) approximate the value of migrants' transfers of household and personal effects to their place of origin as part of a broader remittances definition.

republic, a state with elected leaders and a centralized presidential form of government, local subdivisions being subordinate to the national government. A *federal republic* (as distinguished from a unitary republic) is a republic in which power is divided between the central government and the constituent subnational administrative divisions (*e.g.,* states, provinces, or cantons) in whom the central government itself is held to originate, the division of power being defined in a written constitution and jurisdictional disputes usually being settled in a court; sovereignty usually rests with the authority that has the power to amend the constitution. A *unitary republic* (as distinguished from a federal republic) is a republic in which power originates in a central authority and is not derived from constituent subdivisions. A *people's republic,* in the dialectics of Communism, is the first stage of development toward a communist state, the second stage being a *socialist republic.* An *Islamic republic* is structured around social, ethical, legal, and religious precepts central to the Islamic faith.

retail price index, *see* consumer price index.

retail sales and service enterprises, *see* manufacturing, mining, and construction enterprises/retail sales and service enterprises.

roundwood, wood obtained from removals from forests, felled or harvested (with or without bark), in all forms. Roundwood used for fuel is fuelwood; other roundwood used in construction, paper products, flooring, furniture manufacture, etc., is called industrial roundwood.

rural, *see* urban-rural.

self-employment, work in which income derives from direct employment in one's own business, trade, or profession, as opposed to work in which salary or wages are earned from an employer.

self-governing, of a state, in control of its internal affairs in degrees ranging from control of most internal affairs (though perhaps not of public order or of internal security) to complete control of all internal affairs (*i.e.,* the state is autonomous) but having no control of external affairs or defense. In this work the term self-governing refers to the final stage in the successive stages of increasing self-government that generally precede independence.

service/trade enterprises, *see* manufacturing, mining, and construction enterprises/retail sales and service enterprises.

sex distribution, ratios, calculated as percentages, of male and female population to total population.

sheikhdom, *see* monarchy.

social deviance, a group of measures, usually reported as rates per 100,000 for principal categories of socially deviant behaviour, including specified crimes, alcoholism, drug abuse, and suicide.*

social participation, a group of measures indicative of the degree of social engagement displayed by a particular population, including rates of participation in such activities as elections, voluntary work or memberships, trade unions, and religion.*

social security, public programs designed to protect individuals and families from loss of income owing to unemployment, old age, sickness or disability, or death and to provide other services such as medical care, health and welfare programs, or income maintenance.

socialist republic, *see* republic.

sources of income, *see* household income and expenditure.

Special Drawing Right (SDR), a unit of account utilized by the International Monetary Fund (IMF) to denominate monetary reserves available under a quota system to IMF members to maintain the value of their national currency unit in international transactions.*

state, in international law, a political entity possessing the attributes of: territory, permanent civilian population, government, and the capacity to conduct relations with other states. Though the term is sometimes limited in meaning to fully independent and internationally recognized states, the more general sense of an entity possessing a *preponderance* of these characteristics is intended here. It is, thus, also a first-order civil administrative subdivision, especially of a federated union. An associated state is an autonomous state in free association with another that conducts its external affairs and defense; the association may be terminated in full independence at the instance of the autonomous state in consultation with the administering power. A *parliamentary state* is an independent state of the Commonwealth that is governed by a parliament and that may recognize the British monarch as its titular head.

structure of gross domestic product and labour force, tabulation of the principal elements of the national economy, according to standard industrial categories, together with the corresponding distribution of the labour force (when possible POPULATION ECONOMICALLY ACTIVE) that generates the GROSS DOMESTIC PRODUCT.

sultanate, *see* monarchy.

territory, a noncategorized political dependency; a first-order administrative subdivision; a dependent political entity with some degree of self-government, but with fewer rights and less autonomy than a colony because there is no charter. An *external territory* (Australia) is a territory situated outside the area of the country. An *organized territory* (U.S.) is a territory for which a system of laws and a settled government have been provided by an act of the United States Congress. An *overseas territory* (France) is an overseas subdivision of the French Republic with elected representation in the French Parliament, having individual statutes, laws, and internal organization adapted to local conditions.

ton-miles, or **ton-kilometres,** aggregate measure of freight hauled by a specified means of transportation, equal to tons of freight multiplied by the miles (or kilometres) each ton is transported. Figures are compiled from waybills (nationally) and ordinarily exclude mail, specie, passengers' baggage, the fuel and stores of the conveyance, and goods carried free.

total active duty personnel, full-time active duty military personnel (excluding militias and part-time, informal, or other paramilitary elements), with their distribution by percentages among the major services.

total fertility rate, the sum of the current age-specific birth rates for each of the child-bearing years (usually 15–49). It is the probable number of births, given present fertility data, that would occur during the lifetime of each woman should she live to the end of her child-bearing years.

tourism, service industry comprising activities connected with domestic and international travel for pleasure or recreation; confined here to international travel and reported as expenditures in U.S. dollars by tourists of all nationalities visiting a particular country and, conversely, the estimated expenditures of that country's nationals in all countries of destination.

transfer payments, *see* household income and expenditure.

transport, all mechanical methods of moving persons or goods. Data reported for national establishments include: for railroads, route length and volume of traffic for passengers and cargo (excluding mail); for roads, length of network and numbers of passenger cars and of commercial vehicles (*i.e.,* trucks and buses) and volume of traffic for passenger cars/buses and cargo; and for air transport, traffic data for passengers and cargo.

undernourished population, the number of persons according to an FAO study whose daily caloric consumption (based on a weighted average of all age and sex groups) is below a minimum level needed for maintaining a healthy life and performing light physical activity.

unincorporated territory (U.S.), *see* territory.

unitary republic, *see* republic.

urban-rural, social characteristic of local or national populations, defined by predominant economic activities, "urban" referring to a group of largely nonagricultural pursuits, "rural" to agriculturally oriented employment patterns. The distinction is usually based on the country's own definition of urban, which may depend only upon the size (population) of a place or upon factors like employment, administrative status, density of housing, etc.

value added, also called value added by manufacture, the gross output value of a firm or industry minus the cost of inputs—raw materials, supplies, and payments to other firms—required to produce it. Value added is the portion of the sales value or gross output value that is actually created by the firm or industry. Value added generally includes labour costs, administrative costs, and operating profits.

Countries, Dependencies, and Territories

Afghanistan

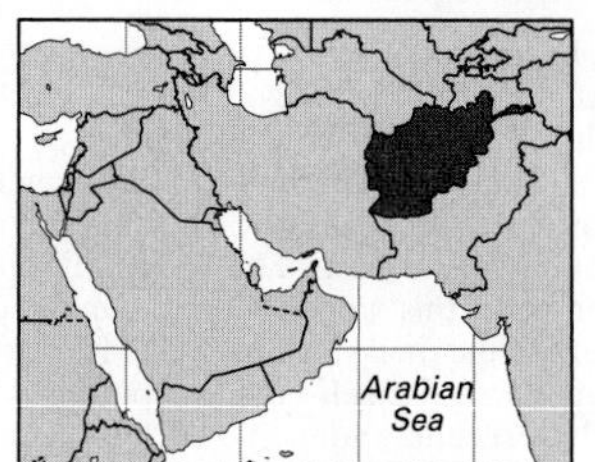

Official name: Islamic Republic of Afghanistan (Jomhūrī-ye Eslāmī-ye Afghānestān [Dari]); Da Afghanestan Eslami Jamhuriyat (Pashto)[1].
Form of government: Islamic republic[1] with two legislative bodies (House of Elders [102]; House of the People [249]).
Head of state and government: President.
Capital: Kabul.
Official languages: Dari; Pashto[2].
Official religion: Islam.
Monetary unit: (new) afghani (Af); valuation (Sept. 1, 2011) 1 U.S.$ = Af 43.34; 1 £ = Af 70.04[3].

Population (2009 estimate)[4]

Province	population ('000)	Province	population ('000)	Province	population ('000)
Badakhshān	860.3	Jowzjān	485.3	Orūzgān	317.2
Bādghīs	448.8	Kābol (Kabul)	3,568.5	Paktīā	499.2
Baghlān	818.6	Kandahār	1,080.3	Paktīkā	393.8
Balkh	1,169.0	Kāpīsā	399.5	Panjshīr[5]	139.1
Bāmīān	404.7	Khowst	520.2	Parvān	600.0
Dāykundi[6]	417.3	Konar	407.8	Samangān	350.4
Farāh	458.5	Konduz	900.3	Sar-e Pol	505.4
Fāryāb	900.0	Laghmān	403.5	Takhār	886.4
Ghaznī	1,111.3	Lowgar	354.9	Vardak	540.1
Ghowr	625.2	Nangarhār	1,358.4	Zābol	275.1
Helmand	835.8	Nīmrūz	148.5	TOTAL	23,993.5
Herāt	1,676.0	Nūrestān	134.1		

Demography

Area: 252,072 sq mi, 652,864 sq km.
Population (2011): 26,442,000[7].
Density (2011): persons per sq mi 104.9, persons per sq km 40.5.
Urban-rural (2006): urban 21.5%; rural 78.5%.
Sex distribution (2010): male 50.78%; female 49.22%.
Age breakdown (2010): under 15, 44.2%; 15–29, 27.9%; 30–44, 15.4%; 45–59, 8.4%; 60–74, 3.5%; 75–84, 0.5%; 85 and over, 0.1%.
Population projection: (2020) 30,222,511; (2030) 36,580,048.
Ethnolinguistic composition (2004): Pashtun *c.* 42%; Tajik *c.* 27%; Ḥazāra *c.* 9%; Uzbek *c.* 9%; Chahar Aimak *c.* 4%; Turkmen *c.* 3%; other *c.* 6%.
Religious affiliation (2009): Sunnī Muslim *c.* 80%; Shīʿī Muslim *c.* 19%.
Major cities (2009): Kabul 2,938,300; Herāt 395,400; Kandahār (Qandahār) 363,100; Mazār-e Sharīf 333,800; Jalālābād 188,300; Konduz 129,500.

Vital statistics

Birth rate per 1,000 population (2010): 39.8 (world avg. 19.2).
Death rate per 1,000 population (2010): 19.6 (world avg. 8.2).
Total fertility rate (avg. births per childbearing woman; 2010): 5.85.
Life expectancy at birth (2010): male 47.7 years; female 50.2 years.

National economy

Budget (2009–10). Revenue: Af 132,698,000,000 (grants 60.4%, domestic tax revenue 30.3%, domestic nontax revenue 9.3%). Expenditures: Af 215,880,000,000 (capital expenditure 55.1%, current expenditure 44.9%).
Public debt (external, outstanding; 2009): U.S.$2,203,000,000.
Gross national income (2009): U.S.$12,853,000,000 (U.S.$457 per capita).

Structure of gross domestic product and labour force

	2009–10 in value Af '000,000	2009–10 % of total value	2002–03 labour force[4]	2002–03 % of labour force[4]
Agriculture	196,990	31.4	5,181,400	69.6
Mining	2,921	0.5	362,200	4.9
Manufacturing	80,435	12.8		
Public utilities	629	0.1		
Transp. and commun.	111,784	17.8	169,500	2.3
Construction	49,955	8.0	98,600	1.3
Trade, hotels, restaurants	49,812	7.9	509,600	6.8
Finance, real estate	11,745	1.9	1,126,000	15.1
Pub. administration	67,170	10.7		
Services	34,171	5.4		
Other	21,782[8]	3.5[8]		
TOTAL	627,394	100.0	7,447,300	100.0

Production (metric tons except as noted). Agriculture, forestry, fishing (2009–10): wheat 5,064,000, barley 480,000, rice 469,000, grapes 350,000, potatoes 302,400, corn (maize) 300,000, almonds 77,200, apricots (2009) 46,895, berries 32,300, opium poppy (2009) 6,900[9]; livestock (number of live animals; 2009–10) 12,287,000 sheep, 5,810,000 goats, 190,000 camels; roundwood (2009) 3,357,549 cu m, of which fuelwood 48%; fisheries production (2008) 1,000 (from aquaculture, none). Mining and quarrying (2009): salt *c.* 12,000; chromite *c.* 7,000; lapis lazuli *c.* 9,000 kg; marble, n.a. Manufacturing (value added in Af '000,000; 2005–06): food 48,575; chemicals 1,206; cement, bricks, and ceramics 809; textiles, wearing apparel, and fur 569; base metals 139. Energy production (consumption): electricity (kW-hr; 2008–09) 826,990,000 (589,640,000); coal (metric tons; 2009) *c.* 150,000 ([2007] 33,000); crude petroleum (barrels; 2009) *c.* 20,000 (none); petroleum products (metric tons; 2007) none (191,000); natural gas (cu m; 2009) *c.* 50,000,000 ([2007] 3,000,000).
Household income and expenditure (2003). Average household size 8.0; sources of income: wages and salaries 49%, self-employment 47%; expenditure (2004)[10]: food 60.6%, housing and energy 16.5%, clothing 9.1%.
Population economically active (2008): total 8,728,000[11]; activity rate of total population 32.1%[11] (participation rates: ages 15–64, 60.4%[11]; female 26.5%[11]; unemployed [January 2009] *c.* 33%).

Price index (2005 = 100)

	2004	2005	2006	2007	2008	2009	2010
Consumer price index	89.2	100.0	103.5	121.0	148.5	128.9	145.5

Land use as % of total land area (2009): in temporary crops 5.3%, left fallow 6.6%, in permanent crops 0.2%, in pasture 46.0%, forest area 2.1%.
Selected balance of payments data. Receipts from (U.S.$'000,000): tourism (1998) 1.0; remittances, n.a.; foreign direct investment (2007–09 avg.) 243; official development assistance (2009) 6,070. Disbursements for (U.S.$'000,000): n.a.

Foreign trade[12]

Balance of trade (current prices)

	2004–05	2005–06	2006–07	2007–08	2008–09	2009–10
U.S.$'000,000	–1,872	–2,087	–2,328	–2,567	–2,475	–2,933
% of total	75.4%	73.1%	73.7%	73.8%	69.4%	78.4%

Imports (2009–10): U.S.$3,336,000,000 (petroleum products 22.2%; food 17.6%, of which wheat 10.8%; passenger cars 9.8%; fabricated metals 9.5%). *Major import sources:* Uzbekistan 26.3%; China 10.8%; Japan 10.1%; Pakistan 9.2%; Kazakhstan 8.7%.
Exports (2009–10): U.S.$403,000,000 (dried fruits/nuts 44.9%, of which almonds 14.7%, raisins 14.5%, pistachios 4.9%; high-quality carpets 16.6%; fresh fruits 5.6%; licorice roots 4.4%)[13]. *Major export destinations:* Pakistan 47.4%; India 18.9%; Iran 10.2%; Russia 6.5%; U.S. 4.2%.

Transport and communications

Transport. Railroads (2006): route length 6.2 mi, 10 km. Roads (2006): total length 26,190 mi, 42,150 km (paved 29%). Vehicles (2009–10): passenger cars 621,937; trucks and buses 241,318. Air transport (2009–10): passenger-km 3,540,000,000; metric ton-km cargo 22,913,000.

Communications

Medium	date	number in '000s	units per 1,000 persons	Medium	date	number in '000s	units per 1,000 persons
Televisions	2003	312	14	PCs	2006	1.4	4.0
Telephones				Dailies	2009	32[14]	1.7[14]
Cellular	2010	13,000[15]	414[15]	Internet users	2010	1,256	40
Landline	2010	140	4.5	Broadband	2010	1.5[15]	—[15]

Education and health

Educational attainment: n.a. *Literacy* (2006): total population age 15 and over literate 28.1%; males 43.1%; females 12.6%.

Education (2008)

	teachers	students	student/ teacher ratio	enrollment rate (%)
Primary (age 7–12) / Secondary/Voc. (age 13–18)	164,783	6,350,734	38.5	… / …
Tertiary	3,378	68,026	20.1	1[16] (age 19–23)

Health: physicians (2008) 4,834 (1 per 5,847 persons); hospital beds (2008) 12,095 (1 per 2,337 persons); infant mortality rate (2010) 126.2.

Military

Total active duty personnel (November 2010): 136,106 (army 96.9%, air force 3.1%)[17]. *Military expenditure as percentage of GDP* (2008): 1.5%[18]; per capita expenditure *c.* U.S.$7[18].

[1]From promulgation of new constitution on Jan. 26, 2004. [2]Six additional locally official languages per the 2004 constitution are Uzbek, Turkmen, Balochi, Kafiri (Nuristani), Pashai, and Pamiri. [3]The afghani was redenominated on Oct. 7, 2002; from that date 100 (old) afghanis equaled 1 (new) afghani. [4]Refers to settled population only and excludes refugees in Pakistan and Iran. [5]Created in 2004 from part of Parvān. [6]Created in 2004 from part of Orūzgān. [7]Excludes Afghan refugees in Pakistan and Iran but includes nomadic population; the first complete national census since 1979 was to be conducted in Sept.–Oct. 2010. [8]Taxes on imports. [9]Represents 95% of world production; in 2009, Afghanistan was also the world's leading producer of cannabis. [10]Weights of consumer price index components. [11]ILO estimate. [12]Exports f.o.b.; imports c.i.f. [13]Exports of illegal opiates equaled *c.* U.S.$2,800,000,000 in 2009. [14]Circulation. [15]Subscribers. [16]2003–04. [17]Foreign troops (August 2010): 47-country NATO-sponsored security and development force 119,800, of which U.S. 78,400, U.K. 9,500, Germany 4,600, France 3,800, Italy 3,400, Canada 2,800, Poland 2,600. [18]Domestic budget only.

Internet resource for further information:
- **Central Statistics Office http://www.cso.gov.af**

Albania

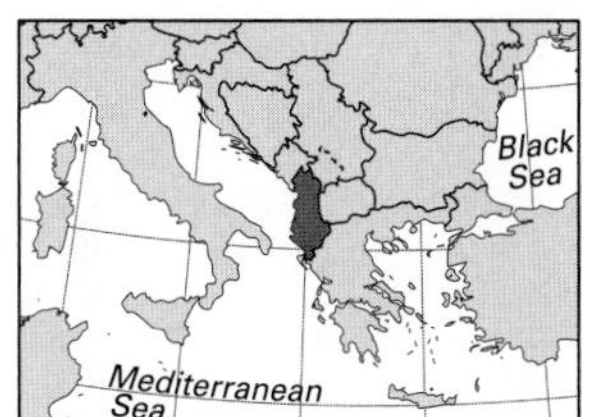

Official name: Republika e Shqipërisë (Republic of Albania).
Form of government: unitary multiparty republic with one legislative house (Kuvendi, or Parliament [140]).
Head of state: President.
Head of government: Prime Minister.
Capital: Tirana (Tiranë).
Official language: Albanian.
Official religion: none.
Monetary unit: lek (L); valuation (Sept. 1, 2011) 1 U.S.$ = 98.54 leks; 1 £ = 159.24 leks.

Area and population

		area		population
Counties	**Capitals**	sq mi	sq km	2010[1] estimate
Berat	Berat	696	1,802	170,845
Dibër	Peshkopi	968	2,507	140,002
Durrës	Durrës	319	827	310,499
Elbasan	Elbasan	1,266	3,278	343,115
Fier	Fier	729	1,887	374,074
Gjirokastër	Gjirokastër	1,113	2,883	102,549
Korçë	Korçë	1,433	3,711	257,576
Kukës	Kukës	916	2,373	79,303
Lezhë	Lezhë	610	1,581	158,829
Shkodër	Shkodër	1,375	3,562	246,060
Tiranë	Tirana (Tiranë)	612	1,586	800,347
Vlorë	Vlorë	1,045	2,706	211,773
TOTAL		11,082	28,703	3,194,972

Demography

Population (2011): 3,196,000.
Density (2011): persons per sq mi 288.4, persons per sq km 111.3.
Urban-rural (2005[1]): urban 44.5%; rural 55.5%.
Sex distribution (2010): male 50.26%; female 49.74%.
Age breakdown (2006[1]): under 15, 25.3%; 15–29, 26.4%; 30–44, 19.9%; 45–59, 16.2%; 60–74, 9.2%; 75–84, 2.5%; 85 and over, 0.5%.
Population projection: (2020) 3,376,000; (2030) 3,455,000.
Ethnic composition (2000): Albanian 91.7%; Greek 2.3%; Aromanian 1.8%; Rom 1.8%; other 2.4%.
Traditional religious groups (2005)[2]: Muslim *c.* 68%, of which Sunnī *c.* 51%, Bektashi *c.* 17%; Orthodox *c.* 22%; Roman Catholic *c.* 10%.
Major cities (2010[1]): Tirana (Tiranë) 540,000; Durrës 145,000; Vlorë 110,000; Elbasan 90,400; Shkodër 83,400.

Vital statistics

Birth rate per 1,000 population (2009): 9.1 (world avg. 19.2).
Death rate per 1,000 population (2009): 4.9 (world avg. 8.2).
Natural increase rate per 1,000 population (2009): 4.2 (world avg. 11.0).
Marriage/divorce rates per 1,000 population (2009): 5.6/1.6.
Total fertility rate (avg. births per childbearing woman; 2008): 1.40.
Life expectancy at birth (2008): male 72.9 years; female 77.8 years.
Major causes of death per 100,000 population (2009): diseases of the circulatory system 286.2; malignant neoplasms (cancers) 82.2; accidents, injury, and violence 28.0; diseases of the respiratory system 15.2; diseases of the digestive system 8.9.

National economy

Budget (2010[3]). Revenue: 293,448,000,000 leks (tax revenue 89.1%, nontax revenue 10.0%, grants 0.9%). Expenditures: 316,505,000,000 leks (current expenditure 84.3%, capital expenditure 17.2%, other –1.5%).
Public debt (external, outstanding; September 2010): U.S.$2,436,000,000.
Gross national income (GNI; 2010): U.S.$12,677,000,000 (U.S.$4,000 per capita); purchasing power parity GNI (U.S.$8,840 per capita).

Structure of gross domestic product and labour force

	2009		2006	
	in value '000,000 leks	% of total value	labour force	% of labour force
Agriculture	193,730	16.8	542,000	50.0
Mining	9,729	0.8	5,000	0.5
Manufacturing	92,860	8.1	58,000	5.4
Public utilities	...	...	10,900	1.0
Construction	146,015	12.7	53,200	4.9
Transp. and commun.	97,453	8.5	19,000	1.8
Trade, restaurants	215,505	18.7	83,900	7.7
Finance, real estate Pub. admin., defense Services	276,165	24.0	162,700	15.0
Other	119,563[4]	10.4[4]	150,000	13.8
TOTAL	1,151,020[5]	100.0	1,084,000[6]	100.0[6]

Production (metric tons except as noted). Agriculture, forestry, fishing (2009): wheat 333,100, corn (maize) 265,100, potatoes 200,000, watermelons 195,430, grapes 162,800, tomatoes 162,376, olives 48,000; livestock (number of live animals) 1,768,000 sheep, 772,000 goats, 494,000 cattle, 5,138,000 chickens; roundwood (2010) 430,000 cu m, of which fuelwood 81%; fisheries production 8,128 (from aquaculture 27%). Mining and quarrying (2009): chromite (gross weight) 256,000. Manufacturing (value added in U.S.$'000,000; 2008): glass and glass products 98; iron and steel 98; textiles 70; basic chemicals 59; leather (all forms) 45; grain mill products 32. Energy production (consumption): electricity (kW-hr; 2008) 3,771,000,000 (6,246,000,000); lignite (metric tons; 2007) 92,000 (105,000); crude petroleum (barrels; 2008) 2,190,000 ([2007] 3,759,000); petroleum products (metric tons; 2007) 231,000 (1,000,000); natural gas (cu m; 2007) 17,170,000 (17,170,000).
Population economically active (2007): total 1,383,000; activity rate of total population 43.6% (participation rates: ages 15–64, 65.8%; female 43.4%; unemployed [December 2010] 13.5%).

Price and earnings indexes (2005 = 100)

	2004	2005	2006	2007	2008	2009	2010
Consumer price index	95.2	100.0	102.4	105.4	108.9	111.4	115.3
Monthly earnings index	91.0	100.0	107.8	129.6	136.4	152.5	162.7

Household income and expenditure. Average household size (2002) 4.3; average annual income per household (2002) 416,556 leks (U.S.$2,972); sources of urban income (2000): wages and salaries/self-employment 64.2%, transfers/pensions 14.8%; expenditure (2001)[7]: food and nonalcoholic beverages 42.6%, housing/energy 24.4%, hotels and restaurants 7.3%.
Selected balance of payments data. Receipts from (U.S.$'000,000): tourism (2009) 1,827; remittances (2010) 1,285; foreign direct investment (FDI; 2007–09 avg.) 876; official development assistance (2009) 359. Disbursements for (U.S.$'000,000): tourism (2009) 1,585; remittances (2009) 10; FDI (2007–09 avg.) 44.
Land use as % of total land area (2009): in temporary crops or left fallow 15.0%, in permanent crops 3.2%, in pasture 25.7%, forest area 28.4%.

Foreign trade[8]

Balance of trade (current prices)

	2004	2005	2006	2007	2008	2009
'000,000,000 leks	–174	–196	–221	–279	–327	–329
% of total	58.3%	59.9%	58.6%	58.9%	59.0%	61.4%

Imports (2009): 431,997,000,000 leks (manufactured goods 25.3%, of which iron and steel 5.5%; machinery and apparatus 16.4%; food 12.1%; chemicals and chemical products 9.9%; road vehicles 6.2%; refined petroleum 6.0%). *Major import sources:* Italy 26.1%; Greece 15.5%; China 7.2%; Germany 6.5%; Turkey 6.4%.
Exports (2009): 103,329,000,000 leks (clothing and accessories 26.8%, of which men's or boys' outerwear 12.5%; footwear/parts 19.4%; crude petroleum 7.6%; locksmiths' wares 4.0%; iron and steel 4.0%; chromium 3.9%). *Major export destinations:* Italy 62.8%; Greece 7.4%; Slovakia 5.5%; China 4.8%; Germany 3.4%.

Transport and communications

Transport. Railroads (2008): route length 399 km; passenger-km 41,000,000; metric ton-km cargo 52,000,000. Roads (2002): total length 11,184 mi, 18,000 km (paved 39%); passenger-km (2001) 197,000,000[9]; metric ton-km cargo (2001) 2,200,000,000. Vehicles (2007): passenger cars 237,932; trucks and buses 89,151. Air transport: passenger-km (2005) 149,000,000; metric ton-km (2007) less than 500,000.

Communications

Medium	date	number in '000s	units per 1,000 persons	Medium	date	number in '000s	units per 1,000 persons
Televisions	2003	989	318	PCs	2007	120	38
Telephones				Dailies	2009	70[10]	25[10]
Cellular	2010	4,548[11]	1,419[11]	Internet users	2010	1,442	450
Landline	2010	332	104	Broadband	2010	110[11]	25[11]

Education and health

Educational attainment (2001). Population age 20 and over having: no formal schooling/incomplete primary education 7.8%; primary 55.6%; lower secondary 2.7%; upper secondary 17.9%; vocational 8.8%; university 7.2%.
Literacy (2008): total population age 15 and over literate 99.0%.

Education (2008–09)

	teachers	students	student/ teacher ratio	enrollment rate (%)
Primary (age 6–9)	11,701	236,102	20.2	85
Secondary/Voc. (age 10–17)	24,193	354,587	14.7	74[12]
Tertiary	1,699[13]	53,014[12]	25.7[13]	19[12] (age 18–22)

Health: physicians (2004) 3,699 (1 per 845 persons); hospital beds (2007) 9,191 (1 per 346 persons); infant mortality rate per 1,000 live births (2008) 6.0; undernourished population (2005–07) less than 5.0% of total population based on the consumption of a minimum daily requirement of 1,910 calories.

Military

Total active duty personnel (November 2010): 14,295[14]. *Military expenditure as percentage of GDP* (2008): 1.9%; per capita expenditure U.S.$80.

[1]January 1. [2]In actuality, a majority of citizens are secular after decades of rigidly enforced atheism. [3]Excludes December. [4]Net taxes less subsidies and less imputed bank service charges. [5]Excludes legal but unauthorized gray economy that may be as large as 50% of official GDP. [6]Detail does not add to total given because of rounding. [7]Weights of consumer price index components. [8]Imports c.i.f.; exports f.o.b. [9]Buses only. [10]Circulation. [11]Subscribers. [12]2003–04. [13]2002–03. [14]Primarily a land-oriented force supported by naval and air units.

Internet resources for further information:
- **Bank of Albania http://www.bankofalbania.org**
- **Institute of Statistics http://www.instat.gov.al**

Algeria

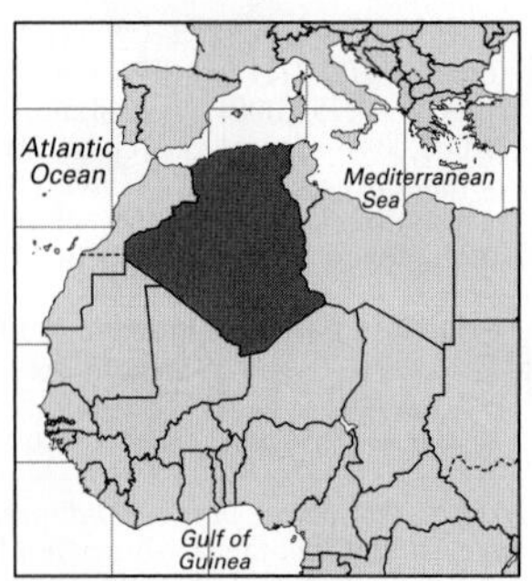

Official name: Al-Jumhūriyyah al-Jazā'iriyyah al-Dīmuqrāṭiyyah al-Sha'biyyah (Arabic) (People's Democratic Republic of Algeria).
Form of government: multiparty republic with two legislative bodies (Council of the Nation [144[1]]; National People's Assembly [389]).
Head of state and government: President assisted by Prime Minister.
Capital: Algiers.
Official language: Arabic[2].
Official religion: Islam.
Monetary unit: Algerian dinar (DA); valuation (Sept. 1, 2011) 1 U.S.$ = DA 72.87; 1 £ = DA 117.75.

Population (2008 preliminary census)

Provinces	population	Provinces	population	Provinces	population
Adrar	402,197	El-Bayadh	262,187	Ouargla	552,539
Aïn Defla	771,890	El-Oued	673,934	Oum el-Bouaghi	644,364
Aïn Temouchent	368,713	El-Tarf	411,783	Relizane	733,060
Alger	2,947,461	Ghardaïa	375,988	Saïda	328,685
Annaba	640,050	Guelma	482,261	Sétif	1,496,150
Batna	1,128,030	Illizi	54,490	Sidi bel-Abbès	603,369
Béchar	274,866	Jijel	634,412	Skikda	904,195
Bejaïa	915,835	Khenchela	384,268	Souk Ahras	440,299
Biskra	730,262	Laghouat	477,328	Tamanrasset	198,691
Blida	1,009,892	Mascara	780,959	Tébessa	657,227
Bordj Bou Arreridj	634,396	Médéa	830,943	Tiaret	842,060
Bouira	694,750	Mila	768,419	Tindouf	58,193
Boumerdes	795,019	Mostaganem	746,947	Tipaza	617,661
Constantine	943,112	M'Sila	991,846	Tissemsilt	296,366
Djelfa	1,223,223	Naâma	209,470	Tizi Ouzou	1,119,646
Ech-Cheliff	1,013,718	Oran	1,443,052	Tlemcen	945,525
				TOTAL	34,459,729[3]

Demography

Area: 919,595 sq mi, 2,381,741 sq km.
Population (2011): 36,649,000.
Density (2011): persons per sq mi 39.9, persons per sq km 15.4.
Urban-rural (2010): urban 66.5%; rural 33.5%.
Sex distribution (2010): male 50.60%; female 49.40%.
Age breakdown (2007): under 15, 27.2%; 15–29, 32.1%; 30–44, 21.8%; 45–59, 11.9%; 60–74, 5.2%; 75–84, 1.5%; 85 and over, 0.3%.
Population projection: (2020) 41,569,000; (2030) 48,877,000.
Doubling time: 35 years.
Ethnic composition (2000): Algerian Arab 59.1%; Berber 26.2%, of which Arabized Berber 3.0%; Bedouin Arab 14.5%; other 0.2%.
Religious affiliation (2000): Muslim 99.7%, of which Sunnī 99.1%, Ibāḍīyah 0.6%; Christian 0.3%.
Major cities (2009): Algiers 2,740,000; Oran 770,000; Constantine (2005) 475,000; Annaba (2004) 410,700; Batna (2004) 285,800.

Vital statistics

Birth rate per 1,000 population (2010): 24.7 (world avg. 19.2).
Death rate per 1,000 population (2010): 4.4 (world avg. 8.2).
Natural increase rate per 1,000 population (2010): 20.3 (world avg. 11.0).
Total fertility rate (avg. births per childbearing woman; 2008): 1.82.
Marriage rate per 1,000 population (2010): 9.6.
Life expectancy at birth (2010): male 75.6 years; female 77.0 years.
Major causes of death per 100,000 population (2002): cardiovascular diseases 150.0; infectious and parasitic diseases 96.5; malignant neoplasms (cancers) 54.2; respiratory infections 45.2; accidents 41.2.

National economy

Budget (2009). Revenue: DA 3,672,900,000,000 (hydrocarbon revenue 65.7%, nonhydrocarbon revenue 34.3%). Expenditures: DA 4,224,800,000,000 (current expenditure 54.4%, capital expenditure 45.6%).
Public debt (external, outstanding; 2009): U.S.$2,871,000,000.
Production (metric tons except as noted). Agriculture, forestry, fishing (2009): wheat 2,953,117, potatoes 2,636,057, barley 2,203,359, onions 980,160, tomatoes 641,034, oranges 626,091, dates 600,696, grapes 492,525, olives 475,182; livestock (number of live animals) 20,000,000 sheep, 3,800,000 goats; roundwood 8,174,209 cu m, of which fuelwood 99%; fisheries production (2008) 141,615 (from aquaculture 2%). Mining and quarrying (2008): iron ore 2,077,000; phosphate rock 1,805,000; liquid helium 20,000,000 cu m; gold 647 kg. Manufacturing (value added in U.S.$'000,000; 2005): food and beverages 1,230; fabricated metals 880; refined petroleum/manufactured gas 720; motor vehicles and parts 400. Energy production (consumption): electricity (kW-hr; 2007) 37,196,000,000 (37,202,000,000); hard coal (metric tons; 2007) none (938,000); crude petroleum (barrels; 2009) 435,000,000 ([2007] 170,307,000); petroleum products (metric tons; 2007) 38,732,000 (11,527,000); natural gas (cu m; 2009) 79,500,000,000 (20,400,000,000).
Land use as % of total land area (2009): in temporary crops 1.7%, left fallow 1.5%, in permanent crops 0.4%, in pasture 13.8%, forest area 0.6%.
Household income and expenditure. Average household size (2004) 6.2; disposable income per household (2002) *c.* U.S.$5,700; sources of income (2008): self-employment 43.1%, wages and salaries 36.8%, transfers 20.1%; expenditure: n.a.
Gross national income (GNI; 2010): U.S.$157,939,000,000 (U.S.$4,460 per capita); purchasing power parity GNI (U.S.$8,130 per capita).

Structure of gross domestic product and labour force

	2009		2004	
	in value DA '000,000	% of total value	labour force[4]	% of labour force[4]
Agriculture	926,400	9.2	1,616,200	17.1
Petroleum and natural gas	3,109,100[5]	31.0[5]	135,100[5] (with Other mining)	1.4[5]
Other mining / Manufacturing	573,100[5]	5.7[5]		
Manufacturing			846,700[5]	8.9[5]
Public utilities / Construction	1,094,800	10.9		
Public utilities			79,100	0.8
Construction			967,600	10.2
Transp. and commun. / Trade, restaurants / Finance, real estate / Services	2,515,300	25.1		
Transp. and commun.			435,900	4.6
Trade, restaurants			1,339,200	14.1
Finance, real estate			141,200	1.5
Services			1,113,300	11.8
Pub. admin., defense	1,087,700	10.9	1,104,100	11.7
Other	711,100[6]	7.1[6]	1,691,600[7]	17.9[7]
TOTAL	10,017,500	100.0[8]	9,470,000	100.0

Population economically active (2010): total 10,812,000; activity rate of population 30.1% (participation rates: ages 15–64 [2004] *c.* 74%; female 16.9%; unemployed [October–December 2010] 10.6%).

Price index (2005 = 100)

	2004	2005	2006	2007	2008	2009	2010
Consumer price index	98.6	100.0	102.3	106.1	111.2	117.6	122.2

Selected balance of payments data. Receipts from (U.S.$'000,000): tourism (2009) 267; remittances (2010) 2,031; foreign direct investment (FDI; 2007–09 avg.) 2,385; official development assistance (2009) 319. Disbursements for (U.S.$'000,000): tourism (2009) 456; FDI (2007–09 avg.) 307.

Foreign trade[9]

Balance of trade (current prices)

	2004	2005	2006	2007	2008	2009
U.S.$'000,000	+13,774	+25,645	+33,157	+32,532	+39,823	+5,936
% of total	27.3%	38.6%	43.6%	37.1%	33.5%	7.0%

Imports (2009): U.S.$39,258,000,000 (nonelectrical machinery 17.9%; iron and steel 15.4%, of which tubes and pipes 8.8%; food and live animals 14.3%; road vehicles/parts 12.2%). *Major import sources:* France 15.7%; China 12.1%; Italy 9.3%; Spain 7.6%; Germany 7.0%.
Exports (2009): U.S.$45,194,000,000 (crude petroleum 47.1%; natural gas [gaseous] 17.7%; LNG 14.4%; refined petroleum 11.0%). *Major export destinations:* U.S. 22.9%; Italy 12.6%; Spain 12.0%; France 9.8%; Neth. 7.2%.

Transport and communications

Transport. Railroads (2006): route length 2,468 mi, 3,973 km; (2003) passenger-km 946,000,000; (2003) metric ton-km cargo 2,041,000,000. Roads (2004): total length 67,295 mi, 108,302 km (paved 70%). Vehicles (2006): passenger cars 2,042,824; trucks and buses 1,221,000. Air transport (2009)[10]: passenger-km 3,526,000,000; metric ton-km cargo 4,010,000.

Communications

Medium	date	number in '000s	units per 1,000 persons	Medium	date	number in '000s	units per 1,000 persons
Televisions	2003	3,633	114	PCs	2007	377	11
Telephones				Dailies	2009	2,600[11]	102[11]
Cellular	2010	32,780[12]	924[12]	Internet users	2010	4,435	125
Landline	2010	2,923	82	Broadband	2010	900[12]	25[12]

Education and health

Educational attainment (2006). Percentage of population age 25 and over having: no formal schooling 35.5%; incomplete primary education 17.8%; complete primary 22.4%; lower secondary 16.5%; upper secondary/higher 7.6%; other 0.2%. *Literacy* (2005): total population age 15 and over literate 76.3%; males literate 84.5%; females literate 68.0%.

Education (2008–09)

	teachers	students	student/ teacher ratio	enrollment rate (%)
Primary (age 6–11)	169,701[13]	3,931,874[13]	23.2[13]	94
Secondary/Voc. (age 12–17)	176,375[14]	3,755,821[15]	21.3[14]	66[14]
Tertiary	37,168	1,149,666	30.9	31 (age 18–22)

Health: physicians (2003) 36,347 (1 per 877 persons); hospital beds (2004) 55,089 (1 per 588 persons); infant mortality rate per 1,000 live births (2009) 24.8; undernourished population (2005–07) less than 5.0% of total population based on the consumption of a minimum daily requirement of 1,830 calories.

Military

Total active duty personnel (November 2010): 147,000 (army 86.4%, navy 4.1%, air force 9.5%). *Military expenditure as percentage of GDP* (2009): 3.3%; per capita expenditure U.S.$150.

[1]Includes 48 nonelected seats. [2]The Berber language, Tamazight, became a national language in April 2002. [3]Reported total; summed total equals 34,459,731; includes nomads, excludes other non-household residents. [4]Based on labour force survey. [5]Petroleum and natural gas excludes (and Manufacturing includes) refined petroleum. [6]Import taxes and duties. [7]Nearly all unemployed including 1,149,400 seeking first employment. [8]Detail does not add to total given because of rounding. [9]Imports c.i.f. in balance of trade and c.i.f. in commodities and trading partners. [10]Air Algérie. [11]Circulation. [12]Subscribers. [13]2007–08. [14]2003–04. [15]2004–05.

Internet resources for further information:
- **Statistiques Algérie http://www.ons.dz**
- **Banque d'Algerie http://www.bank-of-algeria.dz**

American Samoa

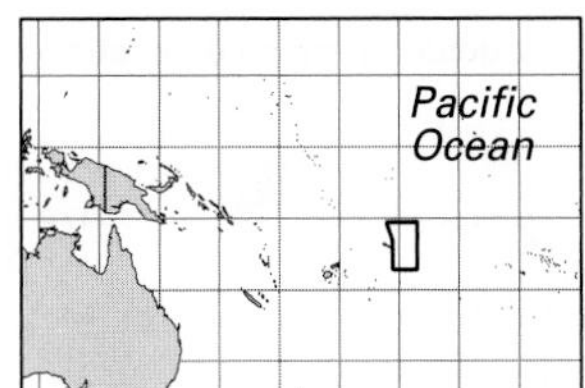

Official name: American Samoa (English); Amerika Samoa (Samoan).
Political status: unincorporated and unorganized territory of the United States with two legislative houses (Senate [18]; House of Representatives [21[1]]).
Head of state: President of the United States.
Head of government: Governor.
Capital: Fagatogo[2] (legislative and judicial) and Utulei (executive).
Official languages: English; Samoan.
Official religion: none.
Monetary unit: dollar (U.S.$); valuation (Sept. 1, 2011) 1 U.S.$ = £0.62.

Area and population

Districts and islands	area sq mi	area sq km	population 2000 census
Eastern District	25.9	67.1	23,441
Tutuila Island (part)	25.3	65.5	21,673
Aunu'u Island	0.6	1.6	1,768
Western District	28.8	74.6	32,435
Tutuila Island (part)	28.8	74.6	32,435
Manu'a District (Manu'a Islands)	21.9	56.7	1,378
Ofu Island	2.8	7.2	289
Olosega Island	2.0	5.2	216
Ta'u Island	17.1	44.3	873
Rose Island[3]	0.1	0.3	0
Swains Island[3]	0.6	1.5	37
TOTAL	77.3[4]	200.2[4]	57,291

Demography

Population (2011): 66,700.
Density (2011): persons per sq mi 862.9, persons per sq km 333.2.
Urban-rural (2007): urban 92.0%; rural 8.0%.
Sex distribution (2007): male 50.68%; female 49.32%.
Age breakdown (2007): under 15, 35.4%; 15–29, 25.7%; 30–44, 19.7%; 45–59, 13.1%; 60–74, 5.1%; 75–84, 0.8%; 85 and over, 0.2%.
Population projection: (2020) 75,000; (2030) 84,000.
Doubling time: 41 years.
Ethnic composition (2005): Samoan 91.6%, of whom born in the nearby independent nation of Samoa 29.3%; Tongan 3.2%; other 5.2%.
Religious affiliation (2005): Protestant *c.* 38%, of which Congregational *c.* 21%; Mormon *c.* 19%; Roman Catholic *c.* 15%; other (including nonreligious) *c.* 28%.
Major villages (2000): Tafuna 8,406; Nu'uuli 5,154; Pago Pago 4,278 (urban agglomeration [2001] 15,000); Leone 3,568; Fagatogo 2,096[2].

Vital statistics

Birth rate per 1,000 population (2010): 23.5 (world avg. 19.2); within marriage (2006) 65.3%; outside of marriage (2006) 34.7%.
Death rate per 1,000 population (2010): 4.5 (world avg. 8.2).
Natural increase rate per 1,000 population (2010): 17.0 (world avg. 11.0).
Total fertility rate (avg. births per childbearing woman; 2008): 3.35.
Marriage/divorce rates per 1,000 population: (2006) 2.6/(1993) 0.5.
Life expectancy at birth (2008): male 70.6 years; female 76.6 years.
Major causes of death per 100,000 population (2004): diseases of the circulatory system 121.7; malignant neoplasms (cancers) 59.3; diseases of the respiratory system 54.6; diabetes mellitus 39.0; accidents, injuries, and violence 34.3.

National economy

Budget (2005). Revenue: U.S.$182,014,612 (U.S. government grants 48.5%, taxes 27.7%, charges for services 4.6%, other 19.2%). Expenditures: U.S.$192,498,724 (education and culture 34.2%, general government 23.7%, health and welfare 16.6%, economic development 10.4%, public safety 6.1%, capital projects 3.9%, public works and parks 3.0%, debt 2.1%).
Public debt: n.a.
Gross domestic product (2007): U.S.$532,000,000 (U.S.$7,801 per capita).

Structure of labour force

	2005 labour force	2005 % of labour force
Agriculture, forestry, and fishing	360	1.5
Mining	30	0.1
Manufacturing	5,030	21.3
Construction	1,210	5.1
Public utilities	500	2.1
Transp. and commun.	800	3.4
Trade and hotels	2,690	11.4
Finance, real estate	1,200	5.1
Public administration	1,410	6.0
Services	4,530	19.1
Other	5,890[5]	24.9[5]
TOTAL	23,650	100.0

Production (metric tons except as noted). Agriculture, forestry, fishing (2009): taros 9,315, coconuts 5,595, bananas 997, yams 693, pineapples 319, coconut oil 71, citrus fruits 32; livestock (number of live animals) 10,500 pigs, 40,000 chickens; roundwood, n.a.; fisheries production (2008) 4,451[6] (from aquaculture, none). Mining and quarrying: pumice, n.a. Manufacturing (value of exports in U.S.$; 2009): canned tuna 471,100,000; pet food 8,600,000; other manufactures include garments, handicrafts, soap, and alcoholic beverages. Energy production (consumption): electricity (kW-hr; 2007) 196,000,000 (196,000,000); coal, none (n.a.); crude petroleum, none (n.a.); petroleum products (metric tons; 2007) none (none); natural gas, none (none).
Population economically active (2005): total 23,650; activity rate of total population 37.1% (participation rates: ages 16 and over 59.9%; female 43.7%; unemployed 10.0%).

Price index (2000 = 100)

	2002	2003	2004	2005	2006	2007
Consumer price index	103.4	108.4	116.1	122.1	125.8	134.2

Household income and expenditure. Average household size (2005) 5.7; average annual income per household (2004) U.S.$32,028; sources of income: n.a.; expenditure (1995): food and beverages 30.9%, housing and furnishings 25.8%, church donations 20.7%, transportation and communications 9.4%, clothing 2.9%, other 10.3%.
Selected balance of payments data. Receipts from (U.S.$'000,000): tourism (1998) 10; remittances, n.a.; foreign direct investment, n.a. Disbursements for (U.S.$'000,000): tourism (1996) 2.0; remittances, n.a.
Land use as % of total land area (2009): in temporary crops or left fallow 10%, in permanent crops 15%, in pasture, n.a.; overall forest area (overlapping with other categories) 88.8%.

Foreign trade

Balance of trade (current prices)

	2001	2002	2003	2004	2005	2006
U.S.$'000,000	–203.0	–111.1	–164.3	–158.1	–132.4	–140.7
% of total	24.2%	12.5%	15.2%	15.1%	15.0%	13.8%

Imports (2006): U.S.$579,200,000 (fish for cannery 41.0%, other food 24.4%, tin plates 8.3%, mineral fuels 6.1%). *Major import sources* (2006): United States 39.1%; New Zealand 9.1%; Singapore 8.0%; Thailand 6.6%; Fiji 6.6%.
Exports (2009): U.S.$487,648,000[7] (canned albacore tuna 48.3%, canned skipjack tuna 46.0%, pet food 1.8%). *Major export destination:* nearly all United States.

Transport and communications

Transport. Railroads: none. Roads (1991): total length 217 mi, 350 km (paved, 43%). Vehicles (2006): passenger cars 7,758; trucks and buses 602. Air transport (2006): passenger arrivals 75,116, passenger departures 81,907; incoming cargo 1,376 metric tons, outgoing cargo 1,411 metric tons.

Communications

Medium	date	number in '000s	units per 1,000 persons	Medium	date	number in '000s	units per 1,000 persons
Televisions	2000	13	211	PCs	2007	...	...
Telephones				Dailies	2009	6.0[8]	140[8]
Cellular	2006	8.5[9]	127[9]	Internet users	2010	...	...
Landline	2010	10	152	Broadband	2010	...	...

Education and health

Educational attainment (2005). Percentage of population age 25 and over having: no formal schooling to some secondary education 31.2%; completed secondary 42.6%; some college 19.0%; bachelor's degree 5.0%; graduate degree 2.2%. *Literacy* (2000): total population age 10 and over literate 99.4%; males literate 99.4%; females literate 99.5%.

Education (2006)

	teachers	students	student/ teacher ratio	enrollment rate (%)
Primary	450	11,100	24.7	...
Secondary/Voc.	213	5,074	23.8	...
Tertiary[10]	...	1,607	...	...

Health (2003): physicians 49 (1 per 1,253 persons); hospital beds 128 (1 per 480 persons); infant mortality rate per 1,000 live births (2008) 10.5; undernourished population, n.a.

Military

Military defense is the responsibility of the United States.

[1]Including the appointed nonvoting delegate from Swains Island. [2]The seat of the legislature, as defined by the Constitution of American Samoa, is at Fagatogo, one of a number of villages within an urban agglomeration collectively known as Pago Pago. [3]Not within district administrative structure. Swains Island is administered by a village government and a representative of the governor. [4]Area of American Samoa including deeply indented harbour is 84.4 sq mi (218.6 sq km). [5]Includes 3,530 inadequately defined and 2,360 unemployed. [6]Mostly tuna. [7]To U.S. only. [8]Circulation. [9]Subscribers. [10]American Samoa Community College at Mapusaga.

Internet resource for further information:

- **American Samoa Department of Commerce http://www.spc.int/prism/Country/AS/stats**

Andorra

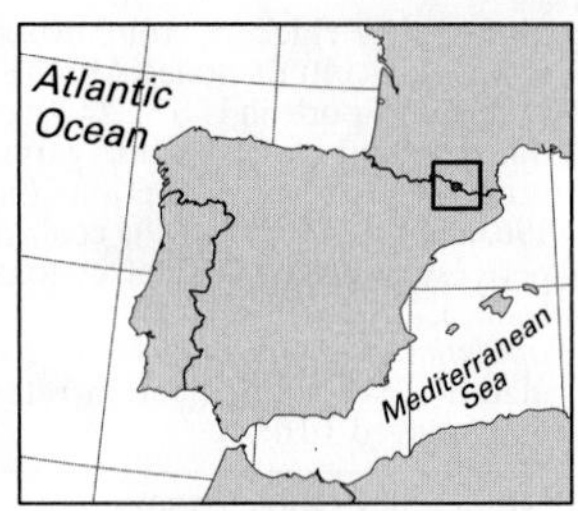

Official name: Principat d'Andorra (Principality of Andorra).
Form of government: parliamentary coprincipality with one legislative house (General Council [28]).
Heads of state: President of France; Bishop of Urgell, Spain.
Head of government: Head of Government.
Capital: Andorra la Vella.
Official language: Catalan.
Official religion: none[1].
Monetary unit: euro (€)[2]; valuation (Sept. 1, 2011) 1 U.S.$ = €0.70; 1 £ = €1.13.

Area and population		area		population
				2011[3]
Parishes	**Capitals**	sq mi	sq km	estimate
Andorra la Vella	Andorra la Vella	11	27	23,505
Canillo	Canillo	47	121	6,194
Encamp	Encamp	29	74	14,357
Escaldes-Engordany	Escaldes-Engordany	12	32	16,920
La Massana	La Massana	23	61	9,937
Ordino	Ordino	34	89	4,396
Sant Julià de Lòria	Sant Julià de Lòria	23	60	9,706
TOTAL		180[4]	468[4]	85,015

Demography

Population (2011): 85,600.
Density (2011): persons per sq mi 478.2, persons per sq km 184.5.
Urban-rural (2005): urban 91%; rural 9%.
Sex distribution (2010[3]): male 52.08%; female 47.92%.
Age breakdown (2010[3]): under 15, 14.5%; 15–29, 17.3%; 30–44, 28.6%; 45–59, 22.0%; 60–74, 11.1%; 75–84, 4.3%; 85 and over, 2.2%.
Population projection: (2020) 98,000; (2030) 112,000.
Doubling time: 98 years.
Ethnic composition (by nationality; 2008[3]): Andorran 36.7%; Spanish 33.0%; Portuguese 16.3%; French 6.3%; British 1.3%; Argentinian 0.8%; Moroccan 0.6%; other 5.0%.
Religious affiliation (2009): Roman Catholic *c.* 90%, of which *c.* 45% active church attendees; Muslim *c.* 2%; remainder (mostly other Christian) *c.* 8%.
Major towns (2011[3]): Andorra la Vella 20,526; Escaldes-Engordany 16,920; Encamp 8,830; Sant Julià de Lòria 8,101; La Massana 5,067.

Vital statistics

Birth rate per 1,000 population (2010): 9.7 (world avg. 19.2).
Death rate per 1,000 population (2010): 2.8 (world avg. 8.2).
Natural increase rate per 1,000 population (2010): 6.9 (world avg. 11.0).
Total fertility rate (avg. births per childbearing woman; 2007): 1.17.
Marriage rate per 1,000 population (2010): 3.4.
Life expectancy at birth (2007): male 80.4 years; female 85.4 years.
Major causes of death per 100,000 population (2002–06 avg.): malignant neoplasms (cancers) 108.2; diseases of the circulatory system 100.6; diseases of the respiratory system 28.5; injuries and poisoning 27.7; diseases of the digestive system 18.2.

National economy

Budget (2009). Revenue: €357,800,000 (indirect taxes 87.3%, other taxes 8.7%, investment income 4.0%). Expenditures: €357,600,000 (current expenditures 67.9%, development expenditures 32.1%).
Production. Agriculture, forestry, fishing (2008): tobacco 244 metric tons; other traditional crops include hay, potatoes, and grapes; livestock (number of live animals; 2009) 2,126 sheep, 1,560 cattle, 904 horses; roundwood, n.a.; fisheries production, n.a. Quarrying: small amounts of marble are quarried. Manufacturing (2006): local manufactured goods include cigarettes, furniture, food and beverages, newspapers and magazines, and worked metals; many manufactures are imported for resale to tourists. Energy production (consumption): electricity (kW-hr; 2009) 101,000,000 (599,000,000); coal, none (n.a.); crude petroleum, none (n.a.); petroleum products (metric tons; 2007) none (175,000); natural gas, none (n.a.).
Household income and expenditure (2009): average household size 2.4; expenditure per household €42,541 (U.S.$30,621); sources of income: n.a.; expenditure: housing and energy 25.8%, transportation 17.9%, food, beverages, and tobacco products 12.2%, recreation and culture 8.3%, health care 7.9%, hotels and restaurants 6.0%.
Population economically active (2007): total 43,234; activity rate of total population *c.* 55% (participation rates: ages 15–64 [2003] 75.1%; female 46.6%; unemployed, n.a.[5]).

Price and earnings indexes (2005 = 100)[6]	2003	2004	2005	2006	2007	2008	2009
Consumer price index	93.8	97.0	100.0	103.2	107.2	109.3	109.3
Monthly earnings index	89.8	95.0	100.0	106.5	...	...	...

Selected balance of payments data. Receipts from (U.S.$'000,000): tourism[7]; remittances, n.a.; foreign direct investment, n.a. Disbursements for (U.S.$'000,000): tourism, n.a.; remittances (2001–02) 12.
Gross national income (at current market prices; 2009): U.S.$3,743,000,000 (U.S.$43,770 per capita)[8].

Structure of gross domestic product and labour force	2007		2009	
	value in U.S.$'000,000	% of total value	labour force	% of labour force
Agriculture	17.2	0.5	148	0.4
Mining }	21.2	0.7	4	—
Public utilities }			154	0.4
Manufacturing	84.9	2.6	1,765	4.3
Construction	332.6	10.2	5,410	13.2
Transportation and communications	104.5	3.2	1,220	3.0
Trade }	829.9	25.6	10,362	25.3
Restaurants, hotels }			5,136	12.5
Finance, real estate }	1,475.0	45.4	5,811	14.2
Pub. admin., defense }			4,698	11.5
Services }			6,088	14.8
Other	380.1[9]	11.7[9]	223	0.5
TOTAL	3,245.4	100.0[4]	41,019	100.0[4]

Public debt (2009): *c.* U.S.$898,000,000.
Land use as % of total land area (2009): in temporary crops, left fallow, or in permanent crops 2.1%, in pasture 36.2%, forest area 34.0%.

Foreign trade

Balance of trade (current prices)	2004	2005	2006	2007	2008	2009
€'000,000	−1,313	−1,328	−1,297	−1,303	−1,248	−1,093
% of total	87.0%	85.4%	84.4%	87.5%	95.3%	92.3%

Imports (2009): €1,138,000,000 (machinery and apparatus 14.2%; food 12.8%; clothing and knitwear 9.5%; perfumes, cosmetics, and soaps 8.9%; mineral fuels 8.5%; motor vehicles 6.9%; alcoholic beverages 4.8%). *Major import sources:* Spain 59.5%; France 19.1%; Germany 4.3%; China 3.5%; Italy 3.1%.
Exports (2009): €45,000,000 (motor vehicles 19.9%; alcoholic beverages 14.7%; electrical machinery and apparatus 9.7%; clothing 7.2%; perfumes, cosmetics, and soaps 6.8%). *Major export destinations:* Spain 70.2%; France 20.0%; Italy 2.1%; Switzerland 1.4%.

Transport and communications

Transport. Railroads: none; however, both French and Spanish railways stop near the border. Roads (1999): total length 167 mi, 269 km (paved 74%). Vehicles (2008): passenger cars 51,648; trucks and buses 5,560.

Communications Medium	date	number in '000s	units per 1,000 persons	Medium	date	number in '000s	units per 1,000 persons
Televisions	2000	36	461	PCs	...	...	...
Telephones				Dailies	2009	27[10]	380[10]
Cellular	2010	66[11]	772[11]	Internet users	2010	69	810
Landline	2010	38	450	Broadband	2010	25[11]	289[11]

Education and health

Educational attainment (2006). Percentage of population age 25 and over having: no formal schooling 6.9%; primary 42.6%; secondary 19.3%; postsecondary/vocational 12.3%; university 17.8%; unknown 1.1%. *Literacy:* resident population is virtually 100% literate.

Education (2008–09)	teachers	students	student/ teacher ratio	enrollment rate (%)
Primary (age 6–11)	433	4,474	10.3	82
Secondary/Voc. (age 12–17)	482[12]	3,914	7.8[12]	70
Tertiary	113	459[13, 14]	5.3[13]	10[13] (age 18–22)

Health (2006): physicians 244 (1 per 327 persons); hospital beds 208 (1 per 385 persons); infant mortality rate per 1,000 live births (2006–07) 2.4; undernourished population, n.a.

Military

Total active duty personnel: none. France and Spain are responsible for Andorra's external security; the police force is assisted in alternate years by either French gendarmerie or Barcelona police. Andorra has no defense budget.

[1]Roman Catholicism enjoys special recognition in accordance with Andorran tradition. [2]Andorra uses the euro as its official currency even though it is not a member of the EU. [3]January 1. [4]Detail does not add to total given because of rounding. [5]The restricted size of the indigenous labour force necessitates immigration to serve the tourist trade, especially seasonal cross-border workers from Portugal and Spain. [6]All indexes are end of year. [7]In 2008, Andorra had 10,193,749 visitors, of which daily excursionists from Spain 4,406,985, daily excursionists from France 3,561,090. [8]Tourism and the banking system (*c.* 60% in 2007) are the primary sources of gross national income. [9]Includes taxes and customs duties. [10]Circulation. [11]Subscribers. [12]2004–05. [13]2007–08. [14]Other students are enrolled in Spain (460 in 2008–09), in France (74 in 2008–09), and elsewhere (9 in 2008–09).

Internet resources for further information:
- **Andorra Statistical Yearbook** **http://www.estadistica.ad**
- **Cambra de Comerç Indústria i Serveis d'Andorra** **http://www.ccis.ad/ing/index.html**

Angola

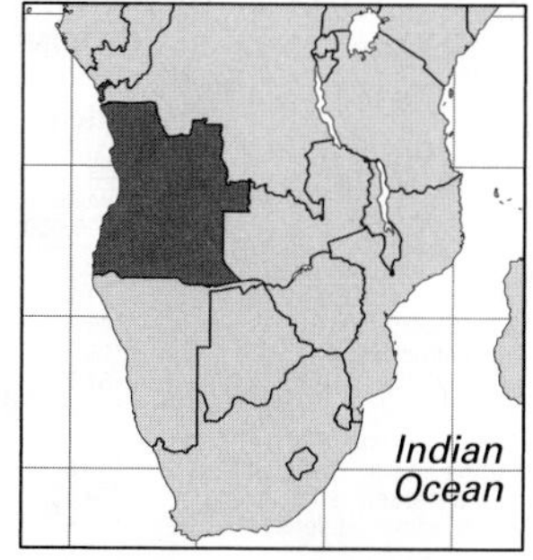

Official name: República de Angola (Republic of Angola).
Form of government: unitary multiparty republic with one legislative house (National Assembly [220[1]]).[2]
Head of state and government: President.
Capital: Luanda.
Official language: Portuguese.
Official religion: none.
Monetary unit: kwanza (AOA); valuation (Sept. 1, 2011) 1 U.S.$ = AOA 93.44; 1 £ = AOA 151.00.

Area and population

Provinces	Capitals	area sq mi	area sq km	population 2004 estimate
Bengo	Caxito	12,112	31,371	242,000
Benguela	Benguela	12,273	31,788	912,000
Bié	Kuito	27,148	70,314	1,625,000
Cabinda	Cabinda	2,807	7,270	320,000
Cuando Cubango	Menongue	76,853	199,049	177,000
Cuanza Norte	N'dalatando	9,340	24,190	556,000
Cuanza Sul	Sumbe	21,491	55,660	901,000
Cunene	Ondjiva	34,495	89,342	323,000
Huambo	Huambo	13,233	34,274	2,197,000
Huíla	Lubango	28,959	75,002	1,214,000
Luanda	Luanda	934	2,418	2,571,000
Lunda Norte	Lucapa	39,685	102,783	406,000
Lunda Sul	Saurimo	17,625	45,649	210,000
Malanje	Malanje	37,684	97,602	1,293,000
Moxico	Luena	86,110	223,023	457,000
Namibe	Namibe	22,447	58,137	193,000
Uíge	Uíge	22,664	58,698	1,249,000
Zaire	M'banza Congo	15,494	40,130	332,000
TOTAL		481,354	1,246,700	15,178,000

Demography

Population (2011): 19,618,000.
Density (2011): persons per sq mi 40.8, persons per sq km 15.7.
Urban-rural (2009): urban 57.6%; rural 42.4%.
Sex distribution (2010): male 50.97%; female 49.03%.
Age breakdown (2010): under 15, 44.6%; 15–29, 27.2%; 30–44, 15.4%; 45–59, 8.3%; 60–74, 3.8%; 75–84, 0.7%; 85 and over, negligible.
Population projection: (2020) 24,780,000; (2030) 30,801,000.
Ethnic composition (2000): Ovimbundu 25.2%; Kimbundu 23.1%; Kongo 12.6%; Lwena (Luvale) 8.2%; Chokwe 5.0%; Kwanyama 4.1%; Nyaneka 3.9%; Luchazi 2.3%; Ambo (Ovambo) 2.0%; Mbwela 1.7%; Nyemba 1.7%; mixed race (Eurafrican) 1.0%; white 0.9%; other 8.3%.
Religious affiliation (2006): Roman Catholic *c.* 55%; independent Christian *c.* 30%, of which African indigenous *c.* 25%, Brazilian evangelical *c.* 5%; Protestant *c.* 10%; Muslim *c.* 0.7%; traditional beliefs/other *c.* 4.3%.
Major cities (2004): Luanda (urban agglomeration; 2009) 4,772,000; Huambo 173,600; Lobito 137,400; Benguela 134,500; Namibe 132,900.

Vital statistics

Birth rate per 1,000 population (2010): 39.7 (world avg. 19.2).
Death rate per 1,000 population (2010): 12.6 (world avg. 8.2).
Natural increase rate per 1,000 population (2010): 27.1 (world avg. 11.0).
Total fertility rate (avg. births per childbearing woman; 2010): 5.66.
Life expectancy at birth (2010): male 52.6 years; female 54.7 years.
Major causes of death (percentage of total deaths; 2002): diarrheal diseases 16%; respiratory infections 15%; HIV/AIDS 7%; perinatal conditions 6%; malaria 6%.
Adult population (ages 15–49) *living with HIV* (2009): 2.0% (world avg. 0.8%).

National economy

Budget (2009). Revenue: AOA 1,848,000,000,000 (petroleum tax revenue 63.1%, nonpetroleum tax revenue 29.2%, nontax revenue 7.7%). Expenditure: AOA 2,363,000,000,000 (current expenditure 68.6%, development expenditure 31.4%).
Household income and expenditure (2002). Average household size 5.0; annual income per household: n.a.; sources of income: n.a.; expenditure[3]: food and nonalcoholic beverages 46.1%, housing and energy 12.3%, household furnishings 6.5%, transportation 6.5%.
Production (metric tons except as noted). Agriculture, forestry, fishing (2009): cassava 12,827,580, sweet potatoes 982,588, corn (maize) 970,231, potatoes 823,266, sugarcane (2008) 360,000, bananas (2008) 300,000, oil palm fruit (2008) 280,000, dry beans 247,314, peanuts (groundnuts) 110,828, millet 40,348, pineapples (2008) 40,000, natural honey (2008) 23,000; livestock (number of live animals) 3,604,608 cattle, 2,500,000 goats, (2008) 785,000 pigs; roundwood 5,013,158 cu m, of which fuelwood 78%; fisheries production (2008) 317,452 (from aquaculture, negligible). Mining and quarrying (2009): diamonds 7,000,000 carats (90% gem grade); granite 50,000 cu m. Manufacturing (2007): liquefied petroleum gas 711,000; residual fuel oil 601,000; gas-diesel oil 513,000; cement (2009) 500,000; jet fuel 351,000; wheat flour 38,168[4]; frozen fish 36,173[4]; beer 1,920,000 hectolitres[4]. Energy production (consumption): electricity (kW-hr; 2007) 3,171,000,000 (3,171,000,000); coal, none (none); crude petroleum (barrels; 2009) 664,300,000 ([2007] 13,990,000); petroleum products (metric tons; 2007) 2,308,000 (2,673,000); natural gas (cu m; 2007) 830,000,000 (830,000,000).
Selected balance of payments data. Receipts from (U.S.$'000,000): tourism (2009) 534; remittances (2008) 82; foreign direct investment (FDI; 2007–09 avg.) 13,159; official development assistance (2009) 239. Disbursements for (U.S.$'000,000): tourism (2009) 133; remittances (2009) 716; FDI (2007–09 avg.) 1,163.
Gross national income (GNI; 2010): U.S.$75,150,000,000 (U.S.$3,960 per capita); purchasing power parity GNI (U.S.$5,430 per capita).

Structure of gross domestic product and labour force

	2007 in value AOA '000,000	2007 % of total value	2010 labour force	2010 % of labour force
Agriculture	424,070	9.0	5,853,000	69.3
Mining and quarrying[5, 6]	3,175,661	67.4		
Manufacturing	41,313	0.9	2,594,000	30.7
Construction	26,707	0.6		
Public utilities	9,385	0.2		
Trade, hotels, restaurants	620,689	13.2		
Finance; Transp. and commun.; Pub. admin., defense; Services	313,304	6.6		
Other[7]	100,500	2.1	...	...
TOTAL	4,711,629	100.0	8,447,000	100.0

Public debt (external, outstanding; 2009): U.S.$13,721,768,000.
Population economically active (2008)[8]: total 8,011,000; activity rate of total population 44.5% (participation rates: ages 15–64, 82.6%; female 46.7%; unemployed, n.a.).

Price index (2005 = 100)

	2004	2005	2006	2007	2008	2009	2010
Consumer price index	81.3	100.0	113.3	127.2	143.0	162.7	186.2

Land use as % of total land area (2009): in temporary crops or left fallow 3.0%, in permanent crops 0.2%, in pasture 43.3%, forest area 47.0%.

Foreign trade

Balance of trade (current prices)

	2004	2005	2006	2007	2008	2009
U.S.$'000,000	+7,142	+15,316	+19,483	+33,835	+57,634	+18,168
% of total	38.0%	47.8%	45.6%	63.8%	66.5%	28.6%

Imports (2009): U.S.$22,660,000,000 (nonpetroleum sector 80.9%, petroleum sector 19.1%). *Major import sources:* Portugal *c.* 19%; China *c.* 17%; U.S. *c.* 9%; Brazil *c.* 8%; South Korea *c.* 7%.
Exports (2009): U.S.$40,828,000,000 (crude petroleum 96.2%, diamonds 2.0%, refined petroleum/manufactured gases 1.3%). *Major export destinations:* China *c.* 36%; U.S. *c.* 26%; France *c.* 9%; South Africa *c.* 4%.

Transport and communications

Transport. Railroads (2008): route length of lines in operation *c.* 750 km; passenger-km (2006) 69,900,000[9]; metric ton-km cargo (2006) 510,000[9]. Roads (2006): total length *c.* 44,700 mi, 72,000 km (paved *c.* 25%)[10]. Vehicles (2001): passenger cars 117,200; trucks and buses 118,300. Air transport: passenger-km (2005) 479,000,000; metric ton-km cargo (2007) 73,000,000.

Communications

Medium	date	number in '000s	units per 1,000 persons	Medium	date	number in '000s	units per 1,000 persons
Televisions	2003	582	52	PCs	2006	84	7.0
Telephones				Dailies	2009	42[11]	5.8[11]
Cellular	2010	8,909[12]	467[12]	Internet users	2010	1,545	81
Landline	2010	303	16	Broadband	2010	20[12]	1.0[12]

Education and health

Educational attainment: n.a. *Literacy* (2006): percentage of population age 15 and over literate 67.4%; males literate 82.9%; females literate 54.2%.

Education (2005–06)

	teachers	students	student/ teacher ratio	enrollment rate (%)
Primary (age 6–9)	...	3,931,583[13]	...	...
Secondary/Voc. (age 10–16)	21,818[14]	458,111	19.0[14]	...
Tertiary	1,286	48,694	37.9	3 (age 17–21)

Health: physicians (2004) 1,165 (1 per 9,890 persons); hospital beds (2005) 1,170 (1 per 10,000 persons); infant mortality rate (2010) 87.2; undernourished population (2005–07) 7,100,000 (41% of total population based on the consumption of a minimum daily requirement of 1,740 calories).

Military

Total active duty personnel (November 2010): 107,000 (army 93.5%, navy 0.9%, air force 5.6%). *Military expenditure as percentage of GDP* (2009): 3.6%; per capita expenditure U.S.$150.

[1]Excludes 3 unfilled seats reserved for Angolans living abroad. [2]New constitution promulgated on Feb. 5, 2010; the post of prime minister was abolished at this time. [3]Weights of consumer price index components; Luanda only. [4]2003. [5]Primarily crude petroleum and diamonds. [6]In 2008 about half of crude petroleum production came from offshore Cabinda, an exclave separated from Angola proper by a sliver of the Dem. Rep. of the Congo. Onshore production in Cabinda has been stymied by the possibility of secessionist unrest. [7]Indirect taxes and taxes on products less subsidies. [8]ILO estimates. [9]Benguela Railway only. [10]General condition of even paved roads is poor. [11]Circulation of daily newspapers. [12]Subscribers. [13]2007–08. [14]2000–01.

Internet resources for further information:

- **Bank of Angola http://www.bna.ao**
- **Ministério das Finanças http://www.minfin.gv.ao**

Antigua and Barbuda

Official name: Antigua and Barbuda.
Form of government: constitutional monarchy with two legislative houses (Senate [17]; House of Representatives [17[1]]).
Head of state: British Monarch represented by Governor-General.
Head of government: Prime Minister.
Capital: Saint John's.
Official language: English.
Official religion: none.
Monetary unit: Eastern Caribbean dollar (EC$); valuation (Sept. 1, 2011) 1 U.S.$ = EC$2.70; 1 £ = EC$4.36.

Area and population	area		population
			2001
Parishes (of Antigua)[2]	sq mi	sq km	census
Saint George	9.3	24.1	6,673
Saint John's (city)	2.9	7.5	24,451
Saint John's (rural)	25.6	66.3	20,895
Saint Mary	22.0	57.0	6,793
Saint Paul	18.5	47.9	7,848
Saint Peter	12.7	32.9	5,439
Saint Phillip	17.0	44.0	3,462
Other islands[2]			
Barbuda	62.0	160.6	1,325
Redonda	0.5	1.3	0
TOTAL	170.5	441.6	76,886[3]

Demography

Population (2011): 91,400.
Density (2011): persons per sq mi 536.0, persons per sq km 206.9.
Urban-rural (2003): urban 37.7%; rural 62.3%.
Sex distribution (2007): male 47.61%; female 52.39%.
Age breakdown (2005–06): under 15, 26.6%; 15–29, 21.8%; 30–44, 23.7%; 45–59, 14.2%; 60 and over, 13.7%.
Population projection: (2020) 98,700; (2030) 106,900.
Ethnic composition (2005–06): black 92.0%; mixed race 2.8%; Indian 1.1%; Caucasian 1.0%; Amerindian/Carib 0.4%; other 2.7%.
Religious affiliation (2005–06): Christian 83.9%, of which Anglican 22.6%, Seventh-day Adventist 13.8%, Moravian 10.1%, Methodist 7.3%; Rastafarian 1.3%; atheist/nonreligious 4.7%; other/unknown 10.1%.
Major town (2009): Saint John's 22,000.[4]

Vital statistics

Birth rate per 1,000 population (2007): 17.0 (world avg. 20.3); within marriage (2001) 25.7%; outside of marriage (2001) 74.3%.
Death rate per 1,000 population (2007): 6.4 (world avg. 8.5).
Natural increase rate per 1,000 population (2007): 10.6 (world avg. 11.8).
Total fertility rate (avg. births per childbearing woman; 2007): 2.09.
Marriage/divorce rates per 1,000 population (2007): 21.7[5]/1.2.
Life expectancy at birth (2007): male 71.9 years; female 75.7 years.
Major causes of death per 100,000 population (2004): diseases of the circulatory system 215, of which cerebrovascular disease 63, ischemic heart disease 59, hypertensive diseases 42; malignant neoplasms (cancers) 118; diabetes mellitus 81; perinatal conditions 37.

National economy

Budget (2009). Revenue: EC$599,830,000 (tax revenue 95.7%, of which taxes on international transactions 36.4%, sales tax 34.0%, taxes on income and profits 16.3%; nontax revenue 4.3%). Expenditures: EC$1,037,800,000 (current expenditures 76.3%, of which transfers and subsidies 21.2%; development expenditures 23.7%).
Production (metric tons except as noted). Agriculture, forestry, fishing (2008): cow's milk 5,400, mangoes, mangosteens, and guavas 1,500, melons 900, tomatoes 395, eggplants 345, lemons and limes 305, "Antiguan Black" pineapples 210; livestock (number of live animals) 20,000 sheep, 14,600 cattle; roundwood, n.a.; fisheries production 3,521 (from aquaculture, none). Mining and quarrying: crushed stone for local use. Manufacturing: manufactures include cement, bricks, and tiles, handicrafts, alcoholic and nonalcoholic beverages, and jams and jellies. Energy production (consumption): electricity (kW-hr; 2007) 118,000,000 (118,000,000); coal, none (none); crude petroleum, none (none); petroleum products (metric tons; 2007) none (142,000); natural gas, none (none).
Land use as % of total land area (2007): in temporary crops or left fallow 18.2%, in permanent crops 2.3%, in pasture 9.1%, forest area 21.4%.
Population economically active (2005–06): total 39,943; activity rate of total population 47.8% (participation rates: ages 15–64, 72.8%; female 53.4%; unemployed 2.7%).

Price index (2005 = 100)	2003	2004	2005	2006	2007	2008	2009
Consumer price index	94.9	97.5	100.0	100.0	105.2	106.0	108.5

Household income and expenditure (2001). Average household size (2005–06) 3.8; income per household: n.a.; sources of income: n.a.; expenditure[7]: housing 21.8%, food 21.4%, transportation and communications 15.4%, household furnishings 12.6%, clothing and footwear 11.1%.

Gross national income (GNI; 2010): U.S.$939,000,000 (U.S.$10,610 per capita); purchasing power parity GNI (U.S.$15,380 per capita).

Structure of gross domestic product and labour force	2009		2005–06	
	in value EC$'000,000	% of total value	labour force	% of labour force
Agriculture, fishing	92.5	3.0	981	2.5
Quarrying	61.6	2.0	...	...
Manufacturing	45.5	1.5	496	1.2
Construction	535.3	17.5	4,031	10.1
Public utilities	87.7	2.9	...	...
Transp. and commun.	531.0	17.4	987	2.5
Trade, restaurants, and hotels	454.8	14.9	4,513	11.3
Finance, real estate	454.5	14.9	...	...
Pub. admin., defense	403.5	13.2	4,395	11.0
Services	175.6	5.7	16,057	40.2
Other	213.9[8]	7.0[8]	8,483[9]	21.2[9]
TOTAL	3,055.8[10]	100.0	39,943	100.0

Public debt (external, outstanding; December 2009): U.S.$443,700,000[6].
Selected balance of payments data. Receipts from (U.S.$'000,000): tourism (2009) 304; remittances (2010) 27; foreign direct investment (2007–09 avg.) 217; official development assistance (2009) 6. Disbursements for (U.S.$'000,000): tourism (2009) 54; remittances (2009) 2.

Foreign trade[11]

Balance of trade (current prices)	2006	2007	2008	2009	2010
U.S.$'000,000	–562	–474	–704	–565	–537
% of total	79.2%	70.5%	85.9%	88.9%	89.2%

Imports (2007): U.S.$573,000,000 (machinery and apparatus 20.3%, manufactured goods 16.3%, food and live animals 15.0%, road vehicles 8.1%, refined petroleum 6.2%[12]). *Major import sources:* U.S. 58.2%; U.K. 6.4%; Japan 4.3%; Netherlands Antilles 4.2%; Trinidad and Tobago 3.9%.
Exports (2007): U.S.$99,000,000 (refined petroleum 57.6%[12], telecommunications equipment 6.6%, generators 3.0%, sails 2.9%). *Major export destinations:* Netherlands Antilles 30.9%; U.S. 23.5%; Barbados 8.2%; Dominica 6.1%; U.K. 4.2%.

Transport and communications

Transport. Railroad[13]. Roads (2002): total length 725 mi, 1,165 km (paved 33%). Vehicles: n.a. Air transport (2006): passenger-km 118,200,000; metric ton-km cargo 200,000.

Communications Medium	date	number in '000s	units per 1,000 persons	Medium	date	number in '000s	units per 1,000 persons
Televisions	2001	34	449	PCs	...	...	...
Telephones				Dailies	2009	9[14]	143[14]
Cellular	2009	135[15]	1,540[15]	Internet users	2009	65	742
Landline	2009	37	426	Broadband	2009	15[15]	170[15]

Education and health

Educational attainment (2001). Percentage of population age 25 and over having: no formal schooling 0.6%; incomplete primary education 2.6%; complete primary 27.9%; secondary 43.6%; higher (not university) 14.4%; university 10.9%. *Literacy* (2009): percentage of total population age 15 and over literate 99.0%.

Education (2008–09)	teachers	students	student/ teacher ratio	enrollment rate (%)
Primary (age 5–11)	695	11,276	16.2	88
Secondary/Voc. (age 12–16)	678	8,557	12.6	88
Tertiary	147	1,037	7.1	15 (age 17–21)

Health: physicians, n.a.; hospital beds (2009) 211 (1 per 420 persons); infant mortality rate per 1,000 live births (2007) 18.8; undernourished population (2005–07) 18,500 (22% of total population based on the consumption of a minimum daily requirement of 1,870 calories).

Military

Total active duty personnel (November 2009): a 170-member defense force (army 73.5%, navy 26.5%).[16] *Military expenditure as percentage of GDP* (2008): 0.6%; per capita expenditure U.S.$79.

[1]Directly elected seats only; attorney general and speaker may serve ex officio if they are not elected to House of Representatives. [2]Community councils on Antigua and the local government council on Barbuda are the organs of local government. [3]Based on table of detailed de facto census results released in July 2004. [4]Large settlements include (2009): All Saints 4,600; Liberta 3,000; Potters Village 2,900; Codrington (on Barbuda; 2006) 680. [5]Includes nonresident marriages. [6]Includes short-term public external debt. [7]Weights of consumer price index components. [8]Net indirect taxes less subsidies and imputed bank service charges. [9]Includes 1,462 unemployed and 7,021 not adequately defined activities. [10]Detail does not add to total given because of rounding. [11]Imports c.i.f.; exports f.o.b. [12]Fuel storage facilities on Antigua supply petroleum to eastern Caribbean countries. [13]Mostly nonoperative privately owned tracks. [14]Circulation. [15]Subscribers. [16]Foreign forces: 2 (1 U.S. detection and tracking radar is located on Antigua).

Internet resources for further information:
- **Eastern Caribbean Central Bank http://www.eccb-centralbank.org**
- **Government of Antigua and Barbuda http://www.antigua.gov.ag**

Argentina

Official name: República Argentina (Argentine Republic).
Form of government: federal republic with two legislative houses (Senate [72]; Chamber of Deputies [257]).
Head of state and government: President.
Capital: Buenos Aires.
Official language: Spanish.
Official religion: none[1].
Monetary unit: peso (ARS); valuation (Sept. 1, 2011) 1 U.S.$ = ARS 4.19; 1 £ = ARS 6.78.

Area and population

Provinces	area sq km	population 2010 census[2]	Provinces	area sq km	population 2010 census[2]
Buenos Aires	307,571	15,594,428	Neuquén	94,078	550,344
Catamarca	102,602	367,820	Río Negro	203,013	633,374
Chaco	99,633	1,053,466	Salta	155,488	1,215,207
Chubut	224,686	506,668	San Juan	89,651	680,427
Córdoba	165,321	3,304,825	San Luis	76,748	431,588
Corrientes	88,199	993,338	Santa Cruz	243,943	272,524
Entre Ríos	78,781	1,236,300	Santa Fe	133,007	3,200,736
Formosa	72,066	527,895	Santiago del Estero	136,351	896,461
Jujuy	53,219	672,260	Tierra del Fuego[3]	21,571	126,190
La Pampa	143,440	316,940	Tucumán	22,524	1,448,200
La Rioja	89,680	331,847	**Autonomous city**		
Mendoza	148,827	1,741,610	Buenos Aires	203	2,891,082
Misiones	29,801	1,097,829	TOTAL	2,780,403	40,091,359

Demography

Population (2011): 40,365,000.
Density (2011): persons per sq mi 37.6, persons per sq km 14.5.
Urban-rural (2009): urban 92.2%; rural 7.8%.
Sex distribution (2010): male 48.83%; female 51.17%.
Age breakdown (2007): under 15, 25.9%; 15–29, 24.9%; 30–44, 19.2%; 45–59, 15.4%; 60–74, 9.8%; 75–84, 3.6%; 85 and over, 1.2%.
Population projection: (2020) 43,448,000; (2030) 46,326,000.
Ethnic composition (2000): European extraction 86.4%; mestizo 6.5%; Amerindian 3.4%; Arab 3.3%; other 0.4%.
Religious affiliation (2008): Roman Catholic *c.* 76%[4]; Pentecostal *c.* 8%; Muslim (mostly Sunnī) *c.* 1.5%; Jewish *c.* 0.7%; nonreligious/atheist *c.* 11%; other (significantly Middle East–based Christian) *c.* 2.8%.
Major urban agglomerations (2010): Buenos Aires 13,361,000; Córdoba 1,427,500; Rosario 1,286,500; Mendoza 947,000; San Miguel de Tucumán 836,200; La Plata 798,400.

Vital statistics

Birth rate per 1,000 population (2008): 18.8 (world avg. 20.3).
Death rate per 1,000 population (2008): 7.6 (world avg. 8.5).
Natural increase rate per 1,000 population (2008): 11.2 (world avg. 11.8).
Total fertility rate (avg. births per childbearing woman; 2007): 2.39.
Marriage/divorce rates per 1,000 population (2007): 3.5/n.a.
Life expectancy at birth (2007): male 72.9 years; female 79.6 years.
Major causes of death per 100,000 population (2008): diseases of the circulatory system 224.5; malignant neoplasms (cancers) 141.8; communicable diseases 76.2; accidents and violence 48.3; diabetes mellitus 19.2.
Adult population (ages 15–49) *living with HIV* (2007): 0.5% (world avg. 0.8%).

National economy

Budget (2009). Revenue: ARS 242,949,000,000[2] (tax revenue 71.5%, social security contributions 24.0%, remainder 4.5%). Expenditure: ARS 249,914,000,000[5] (social security 39.4%, public debt servicing 10.4%, transportation 8.4%, energy/mineral fuels/mining 7.0%, education/culture 6.9%, health 3.8%, public order 3.4%, defense 2.5%).
Public debt (external, outstanding; 2009): U.S.$72,923,000,000.
Gross national income (GNI; 2010): U.S.$343,636,000,000 (U.S.$8,450 per capita); purchasing power parity GNI (U.S.$15,150 per capita).

Structure of gross domestic product and labour force

	2008		2001	
	in value ARS '000,000	% of total value	labour force	% of labour force
Agriculture	93,179	9.0	910,996	6.0
Mining	35,688	3.5	37,979	0.2
Manufacturing	201,175	19.5	1,245,544	8.2
Construction	56,554	5.5	638,566	4.2
Public utilities	12,321	1.2	90,165	0.6
Transp. and commun.	80,279	7.8	717,573	4.7
Trade, restaurants	137,564	13.3	2,213,065	14.5
Finance, real estate	152,892	14.8	898,264	5.9
Pub. admin., defense	58,186	5.6	969,280	6.3
Services	119,370	11.6	2,762,447	18.1
Other	85,551[6]	8.3[6]	4,780,904[7]	31.3[7]
TOTAL	1,032,759	100.0[8]	15,264,783	100.0

Production (metric tons except as noted). Agriculture, forestry, fishing (2009): soybeans 30,993,379, sugarcane 29,950,000, corn (maize) 13,121,380, cow's milk 10,500,000, wheat 7,573,254, grapes 2,900,000, beef 2,830,000, sunflower seeds 2,483,437, apples 1,300,000, lemons and limes 1,260,000, maté 300,000, natural honey 81,000; livestock (number of live animals) 50,750,000 cattle, 12,450,000 sheep, 3,680,000 horses; roundwood 13,551,000 cu m, of which fuelwood 32%; fisheries production 862,543 (from aquaculture, negligible). Mining and quarrying (2009): boron 500,433; copper (metal content) 143,084; silver 415,235 kg; gold 46,588 kg. Manufacturing (value added in U.S.$'000,000; 2002): food products 10,152, of which vegetable oils and fats 3,864; base metals 4,031; industrial and agricultural chemicals 2,770; refined petroleum products 2,514; beverages 1,977; transport equipment 1,958. Energy production (consumption): electricity (kW-hr; 2007) 115,296,000,000 (122,949,000,000); coal (metric tons; 2007) 110,000 (1,573,000); crude petroleum (barrels; 2008) 241,400,000 ([2007] 215,280,000); petroleum products (metric tons; 2007) 28,053,000 (23,244,000); natural gas (cu m; 2007) 51,040,000,000 (49,933,000,000).
Selected balance of payments data. Receipts from (U.S.$'000,000): tourism (2009) 4,478; remittances (2010) 682; foreign direct investment (FDI; 2007–09 avg.) 7,031. Disbursements for (U.S.$'000,000): tourism (2009) 5,759; remittances (2009) 701; FDI (2007–09 avg.) 1,191.
Population economically active (2006)[9]: total 11,089,700; activity rate of total population 46.2% (participation rates: ages 15–64, 68.5%; female 43.4%; unemployed [April 2007–March 2008] 8.1%).

Price index (2005 = 100)

	2004	2005	2006	2007	2008	2009	2010
Consumer price index	91.2	100.0	110.9	120.7	131.1	139.3	154.3

Household size and expenditure. Average household size (2001) 3.6; average annual income per household (1996–97) ARS 12,972 (U.S.$12,978); sources of income: n.a.; expenditure (1996–97): food products 26.8%, transportation and communications 15.0%, housing and energy 13.4%, health 10.2%.
Land use as % of total land area (2007): in temporary crops or left fallow 11.9%, in permanent crops 0.4%, in pasture 36.5%, forest area 12.0%.

Foreign trade[10]

Balance of trade (current prices)

	2004	2005	2006	2007	2008	2009
U.S.$'000,000	+13,265	+13,087	+13,958	+13,456	+15,423	+18,528
% of total	23.7%	19.3%	17.6%	13.7%	12.3%	20.0%

Imports (2009): U.S.$40,293,000,000 (machinery and apparatus 29.0%, of which industrial machinery 5.8%; chemicals and chemical products 18.7%; road vehicles/parts 14.5%; mineral fuels 6.0%). *Major import sources:* Brazil 29.3%; China 13.4%; U.S. 13.4%; Germany 5.3%; Mexico 3.0%.
Exports (2009): U.S.$55,669,000,000 (food 36.3%, of which soybean animal foodstuffs 14.5%, cereals 7.0%, fruits/vegetables 4.3%, meats 4.1%; road vehicles/parts 9.6%; petroleum 7.5%; soybean oil 5.9%). *Major export destinations:* Brazil 20.4%; Chile 7.9%; China 6.6%; U.S. 6.6%; Neth. 4.3%.

Transport and communications

Transport. Railroads: (2008) route length 31,409 km; (2007) passenger-km 8,248,000,000; (2007) metric ton-km cargo 12,871,000,000. Roads (2003): total length 143,768 mi, 231,374 km (paved 30%). Vehicles (2005): passenger cars 5,230,000; trucks and buses 1,775,000. Air transport (2008): passenger-km 12,108,000,000[11]; metric ton-km cargo 129,700,000[11].

Communications

Medium	date	number in '000s	units per 1,000 persons	Medium	date	number in '000s	units per 1,000 persons
Televisions	2004	12,500	323	PCs	2006	3,500	90
Telephones				Dailies	2009	1,129[12]	37[12]
Cellular	2010	57,300[13]	1,418[13]	Internet users	2009	12,244	304
Landline	2010	10,000	247	Broadband	2010	3,862[13]	96[13]

Education and health

Educational attainment (2001). Percentage of population age 15 and over having: no formal schooling 3.7%; incomplete primary education 14.2%; complete primary 28.0%; secondary 37.1%; higher 17.0%. *Literacy* (2009): percentage of total population age 15 and over literate 97.7%.

Education (2006–07)

	teachers	students	student/ teacher ratio	enrollment rate (%)
Primary (age 6–11)	302,654	4,700,176	15.5	99[14]
Secondary/Voc. (age 12–17)	285,764	3,483,089	12.2	79
Tertiary	176,810	2,208,291	12.5	68 (age 18–22)

Health: physicians (2005) 120,978 (1 per 319 persons); hospital beds (2004) 76,446 (1 per 500 persons); infant mortality rate (2008) 12.5; undernourished population (2005–07) less than 5.0% of total population based on the consumption of a minimum daily requirement of 1,890 calories.

Military

Total active duty personnel (November 2010): 73,100 (army 52.7%, navy 27.3%, air force 20.0%); paramilitary 31,240, of which coast guard 13,240. *Military expenditure as percentage of GDP* (2009): 0.8%; per capita expenditure U.S.$55.

[1]Roman Catholicism has special status and receives financial support from the state, but it is not an official religion. [2]Preliminary. [3]Area of Tierra del Fuego excludes claims to British-held islands in the South Atlantic Ocean. [4]Less than 20% practicing. [5]Final. [6]Import duties and VAT less imputed bank service charges. [7]Includes 427,307 (2.8%) not defined and 4,351,596 (28.5%) unemployed. [8]Detail does not add to total given because of rounding. [9]Based on a survey of 31 urban agglomerations. [10]Import figures are f.o.b. in balance of trade and c.i.f. in commodities and trading partners. [11]Aerolineas Argentinas and Austral airlines only. [12]Circulation. [13]Subscribers. [14]2004–05.

Internet resource for further information:
- **National Institute of Statistics and Censuses http://www.indec.mecon.ar**

Armenia

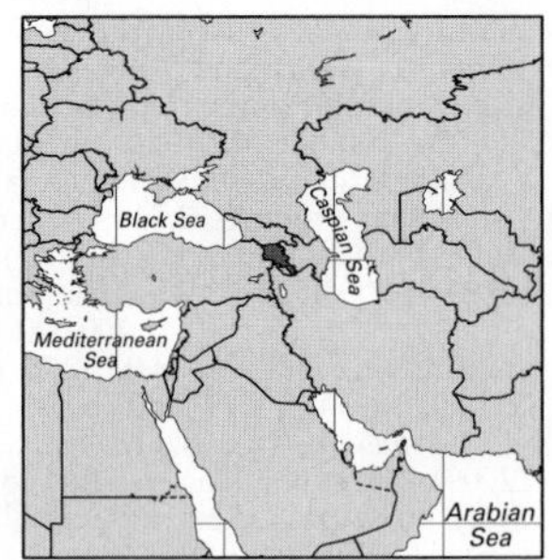

Official name: Hayastani Hanrapetut'yun (Republic of Armenia).
Form of government: unitary multiparty republic with a single legislative body (National Assembly [131]).
Head of state: President.
Head of government: Prime Minister.
Capital: Yerevan.
Official language: Armenian.
Official religion: none[1].
Monetary unit: dram (AMD); valuation (Sept. 1, 2011) 1 U.S.$ = AMD 365.50; 1 £ = AMD 590.63.

Area and population

		area		population
Provinces	**Centres**	sq mi	sq km	2010[2] estimate
Aragatsotn	Ashtarak	1,063	2,753	141,700
Ararat	Artashat	809	2,096	278,800
Armavir	Armavir	479	1,242	284,100
Gegharkunik	Gavar	2,065[3]	5,348[3]	241,500
Kotayk	Hrazdan	807	2,089	280,600
Lori	Vanadzor	1,463	3,789	281,600
Shirak	Gyumri	1,035	2,681	281,500
Syunik	Kapan	1,740	4,506	152,900
Tavush	Ijevan	1,044	2,704	134,400
Vayots-Dzor	Yeghegnadzor	891	2,308	55,800
City[4]				
Yerevan	—	88	227	1,116,600
TOTAL		11,484[5]	29,743[5]	3,249,500

Demography

Population (2011)[6]: 3,100,000.
Density (2011): persons per sq mi 270.0, persons per sq km 104.2.
Urban-rural (2009[2]): urban 64.0%; rural 36.0%.
Sex distribution (2009[2]): male 48.43%; female 51.57%.
Age breakdown (2005): under 15, 20.9%; 15–29, 27.2%; 30–44, 19.5%; 45–59, 17.9%; 60–74, 10.2%; 75–84, 3.8%; 85 and over, 0.5%.
Population projection[6]: (2020) 3,146,000; (2030) 3,105,000.
Ethnic composition (2001): Armenian 97.9%; Kurdish 1.3%; Russian 0.5%; other 0.3%.
Religious affiliation (2005): Armenian Apostolic (Orthodox) 72.9%; Roman Catholic 4.0%; Sunnī Muslim 2.4%; other Christian 1.3%; Yazidi 1.3%; other/nonreligious 18.1%.
Major cities (2010[2]): Yerevan 1,116,600; Gyumri 146,272; Vanadzor 104,849; Vagharshapat 57,465; Hrazdan 53,196.

Vital statistics

Birth rate per 1,000 population (2010): 13.8 (world avg. 19.2); within marriage (2007) 64.5%; outside of marriage (2007) 35.5%.
Death rate per 1,000 population (2010): 8.6 (world avg. 8.2).
Natural increase rate per 1,000 population (2010): 5.2 (world avg. 11.0).
Total fertility rate (avg. births per childbearing woman; 2009): 1.6.
Marriage/divorce rates per 1,000 population (2010): 5.5/0.9.
Life expectancy at birth (2009): male 70.6 years; female 77.0 years.
Major causes of death per 100,000 population (2008): diseases of the circulatory system 423.0; malignant neoplasms (cancers) 170.2; diseases of the respiratory system 55.4; diseases of the digestive system 47.0; endocrine and metabolic disorders 42.3.

National economy

Budget (2009). Revenue: AMD 689,995,000,000 (VAT 36.8%, social insurance contributions 14.9%, tax on profits 11.9%, income tax 8.7%, excise tax 6.2%). Expenditures: AMD 929,109,000,000 (social security 26.2%, economic services 14.4%, defense 14.0%, education 11.6%, public order 7.5%, health 6.0%).
Public debt (external, outstanding; 2009): U.S.$2,376,000,000.
Household income and expenditure (2005). Average household size 3.8; money income per household AMD 1,720,195 (U.S.$3,758); sources of money income: rent, self-employment, and remittances 38.9%, wages and salaries 34.5%, transfers 7.1%, other 19.5%; expenditure: food and beverages 56.6%, services 24.0%, non-food goods 14.3%, tobacco 5.1%.
Land use as % of total land area (2007): in temporary crops or left fallow 14.4%, in permanent crops 1.9%, in pasture 41.0%, forest area 9.7%.
Gross national income (GNI; 2010): U.S.$9,556,000,000 (U.S.$3,090 per capita); purchasing power parity GNI (U.S.$5,450 per capita).

Structure of gross domestic product and labour force

	2010		2007	
	in value AMD '000,000	% of total value	labour force	% of labour force
Agriculture, forestry	609,378	17.4	434,200	26.2
Mining	87,940	2.5	17,100	1.0
Manufacturing	331,914	9.5	81,500	4.9
Public utilities	99,186	2.8	35,400	2.1
Construction	600,305	17.1	91,400	5.5
Transp. and commun.	237,390	6.8	72,200	4.4
Trade, hotels	480,463	13.7	127,300	7.7
Finance, real estate	292,186	8.3	31,300	1.9
Pub. admin., defense	131,703	3.8	70,500	4.2
Services	295,204	8.4	227,600	13.7
Other	335,970[7]	9.6[7]	470,900[8]	28.4[8]
TOTAL	3,501,638[9]	100.0[9]	1,659,400	100.0

Production (metric tons except as noted). Agriculture, forestry, fishing (2009): cow's milk 609,000, potatoes 593,551, tomatoes 278,582, watermelons 216,101, grapes 208,649, wheat 206,505, barley 145,141, cabbages 115,888[10], apples 110,000; livestock (number of live animals) 584,779 cattle, 526,638 sheep; roundwood 42,000 cu m, of which fuelwood 95%; fisheries production 5,859 (from aquaculture 89%). Mining and quarrying (2008): copper concentrate (metal content) 18,800; molybdenum (metal content) 4,250; gold (metal content) 1,400 kg. Manufacturing (value of production in AMD '000,000; 2007): food products and beverages 208,733; base metals 122,269; construction materials 40,207; 320,000 carats of cut diamonds were processed in 2004. Energy production (consumption): electricity (kW-hr; 2008) 6,114,000,000 ([2007] 5,866,000,000); coal (metric tons; 2007) none (3,000); crude petroleum, none (none); petroleum products (metric tons; 2007) none (301,000); natural gas (cu m; 2008) none (1,930,000,000).
Population economically active: total (2008) 1,194,600; activity rate of total population (2001) 49.5% (participation rates: ages 15–64 [2001] 72.1%; female [2008] 49.8%; officially unemployed [2009] 6.9%).

Price and earnings indexes (2005 = 100)

	2004	2005	2006	2007	2008	2009	2010
Consumer price index	99.4	100.0	102.9	107.4	117.0	121.0	130.9
Monthly earnings index	80.4	100.0	122.9	148.5	177.3	193.3	...

Selected balance of payments data. Receipts from (U.S.$'000,000): tourism (2009) 334; remittances (2010) 824; foreign direct investment (2007–09 avg.) 877; official development assistance (2009) 528. Disbursements for (U.S.$'000,000): tourism (2009) 326; remittances (2009) 145.

Foreign trade[11]

Balance of trade (current prices)

	2005	2006	2007	2008	2009	2010[12]
U.S.$'000,000	–755	–1,190	–1,932	–3,046	–2,491	–2,471
% of total	28.7%	37.2%	46.3%	59.1%	64.5%	58.0%

Imports (2009): U.S.$3,175,000,000 (machinery and apparatus 19.9%; food products 14.1%; chemicals and chemical products 10.3%; refined petroleum 7.5%; natural gas 7.3%; iron and steel 4.1%). *Major import sources:* Russia 24.8%; China 9.0%; Ukraine 6.4%; Turkey 5.6%; Iran 4.2%.
Exports (2009): U.S.$684,000,000 (nonferrous metals 18.8%, of which unrefined copper 8.9%, aluminum foil 8.5%; copper ore and concentrates 14.4%; ferroalloys 12.6%; wine/grape brandy 10.4%; cut diamonds 8.2%; food 5.6%). *Major export destinations:* Germany 16.8%; Russia 15.6%; U.S. 9.7%; Bulgaria 8.8%; Neth. 7.6%.

Transport and communications

Transport. Railroads (2007): length 732 km; passenger-km (2008) 26,600,000; metric ton-km cargo (2008) 705,000,000. Roads (2007): length 4,669 mi, 7,515 km (paved 68%); passenger-km (2008) 2,742,000,000[13]; metric ton-km cargo (2008) 179,000,000. Vehicles: n.a. Air transport (2008): passenger-km 1,127,000,000; metric ton-km cargo 13,100,000.

Communications

Medium	date	number in '000s	units per 1,000 persons	Medium	date	number in '000s	units per 1,000 persons
Televisions	2003	687	229	PCs	2007	980	319
Telephones				Dailies	2009	42[14]	16[14]
Cellular	2010	3,865[15]	1,250[15]	Internet users	2009	208	68
Landline	2010	590	191	Broadband	2010	83[15]	27[15]

Education and health

Educational attainment (2001). Percentage of population age 25 and over having: no formal schooling 0.7%; primary education 13.0%; completed secondary and some postsecondary 66.0%; higher 20.3%. *Literacy* (2009): total population age 15 and over literate 99.5%; male 99.7%; female 99.4%.

Education (2008–09)

	teachers	students	student/ teacher ratio	enrollment rate (%)
Primary (age 7–9)	6,606[16]	114,528	19.3[16]	84[16]
Secondary/Voc. (age 10–16)	41,708[17]	304,116	7.4[17]	87
Tertiary	11,258	154,639	13.7	50 (age 17–21)

Health (2008): physicians 12,929 (1 per 232 persons); hospital beds 12,358 (1 per 242 persons); infant mortality rate per 1,000 live births (2010) 11.3; undernourished population (2005–07) 700,000 (22% of total population based on the consumption of a minimum daily requirement of 1,920 calories).

Military

Total active duty personnel (November 2010): 48,570 (army 93.5%, air force/air defense 6.5%); Russian troops 3,214. *Military expenditure as percentage of GDP* (2009): 4.7%; per capita expenditure U.S.$130.

[1]The Armenian Apostolic Church (Armenian Orthodox Church) has special status per 1991 religious law. [2]January 1 de jure estimate. [3]Includes the 485 sq mi (1,256 sq km) area of Lake Sevan. [4]City has province status. [5]In addition, about 13% of neighbouring Azerbaijan (including the 1,700 sq mi [4,400 sq km] geographic region of Nagorno-Karabakh [Armenian: Artsakh]) has been occupied by Armenian forces since 1993. [6]De facto population. [7]Taxes less subsidies and less imputed bank service charges. [8]Unemployed. [9]Detail does not add to total given because of rounding. [10]Includes other brassicas. [11]Imports c.i.f.; exports f.o.b. [12]Excludes December. [13]Buses only. [14]Circulation. [15]Subscribers. [16]2006–07. [17]2007–08.

Internet resources for further information:
- **National Statistical Service http://www.armstat.am**
- **Central Bank of Armenia http://www.cba.am**

Aruba

Official name: Aruba[1].
Political status: autonomous state of the Netherlands with one legislative house (Staten/Parlamento di Aruba, or Parliament of Aruba [21]).
Head of state: Dutch Monarch represented by Governor.
Head of government: Prime Minister.
Capital: Oranjestad.
Official languages: Dutch; Papiamentu.
Official religion: none.
Monetary unit: Aruban florin (Af.); valuation (Sept. 1, 2011) 1 U.S.$ = Af. 1.79; 1 £ = Af. 2.89.

Area and population	area[2]		population
			2010
Census region	sq mi	sq km	census
Noord/Tanki Leendert	14	37	21,495
Oranjestad East	5	13	14,318
Oranjestad West	4	10	13,976
Paradera	10	25	12,024
San Nicolas North	9	23	10,433
San Nicolas South	4	10	4,850
Santa Cruz	18	47	12,870
Savaneta	11	28	11,518
TOTAL	75	193	101,484

Demography

Population (2011): 102,000.
Density (2011): persons per sq mi 1,360.0, persons per sq km 528.5.
Urban-rural (2003): urban 45.4%; rural 54.6%.
Sex distribution (2008): male 47.85%; female 52.15%.
Age breakdown (2008): under 15, 19.9%; 15–29, 18.8%; 30–44, 23.9%; 45–59, 23.4%; 60–74, 10.7%; 75–84, 2.6%; 85 and over, 0.7%.
Population projection: (2020) 106,000; (2030) 107,000.
Linguistic composition (2000): Papiamento 69.4%; Spanish 13.2%; English 8.1%; Dutch 6.1%; Portuguese 0.3%; other 2.0%; unknown 0.9%.[3]
Religious affiliation (2010): Roman Catholic 75.3%; Protestant 2.7%; Jehovah's Witness 1.7%; other/nonreligious 20.3%.
Major urban areas (2010): Oranjestad 28,294; San Nicolas 15,284.

Vital statistics

Birth rate per 1,000 population (2010): 10.6 (world avg. 19.2); within marriage (2009) 41.6%; outside of marriage (2009) 58.4%.
Death rate per 1,000 population (2010): 5.7 (world avg. 8.2).
Natural increase rate per 1,000 population (2010): 4.9 (world avg. 11.0).
Total fertility rate (avg. births per childbearing woman; 2008): 1.70.
Marriage/divorce rates per 1,000 population (2008): 3.8[4]/2.8.
Life expectancy at birth (2006): male 76.0 years; female 82.8 years.
Major causes of death per 100,000 population (2001–04): diseases of the circulatory system 177.7; malignant neoplasms (cancers) 129.2; communicable diseases 36.2; diabetes mellitus 32.5; suicide or accidents 31.5; violence 13.2.

National economy

Budget (2009–10). Revenue: Af. 1,275,300,000 (tax revenue 88.4%, of which taxes on income and profits 29.7%, turnover taxes 26.3%, taxes on commodities 19.2%; nontax revenue 9.5%; grants 2.1%). Expenditures: Af. 1,338,600,000 (wages/wage subsidies 37.7%; transfer to general health insurance 11.4%; interest 9.7%).
Production (metric tons except as noted). Agriculture, forestry, fishing: aloes are cultivated for export; small amounts of tomatoes, beans, cucumbers, gherkins, watermelons, and lettuce are grown on hydroponic farms; divi-divi pods, sour orange fruit, sorghum, and peanuts (groundnuts) are nonhydroponic crops of limited value; livestock (number of live animals) Aruba has very few livestock; roundwood (2009) 1,705 cu m, of which fuelwood 100%; fisheries production (2009) 163 (from aquaculture, none). Mining and quarrying: excavation of sand for local use. Manufacturing[5]: refined petroleum, rum, cigarettes, aloe products, and soaps. Energy production (consumption): electricity (kW-hr; 2007) 936,000,000 (936,000,000); coal, none (none); crude petroleum (barrels; 2007) 916,000 (77,900,000); petroleum products (metric tons; 2007) 10,100,000 (256,000); natural gas, none (none).
Land use as % of total land area (2007): in temporary crops, left fallow, or in permanent crops 11.1%; in pasture, n.a.; forest area 2.2%.
Gross national income (2009): U.S.$2,466,000,000 (U.S.$23,148 per capita).

Structure of gross domestic product and labour force	2006		2008	
	in value Af. '000,000	% of total value	labour force[6]	% of labour force[6]
Agriculture, fishing	16.8	0.4	246	0.6
Mining	...	...	26	0.1
Manufacturing	160.9[7]	3.7[7]	2,728	6.2
Construction	313.4	7.2	4,442	10.2
Public utilities	397.1[8]	9.2[8]	507	1.2
Transp. and commun.	347.6	8.0	2,079	4.8
Trade, restaurants	826.2	19.1	18,281	41.8
Finance, real estate	1,156.7	26.7	7,868	18.0
Pub. admin., defense	534.2	12.3	166	0.4
Services	417.4	9.6	7,366	16.9
Other	163.7[9]	3.8[9]	4	—
TOTAL	4,334.1[10]	100.0	43,713	100.0[10]

Public debt (June 2010): U.S.$1,300,800,000.
Population economically active (2007): total 54,729; activity rate of total population 52.5% (participation rates: ages 15–64, 73.8%; female 47.7%; unemployed 5.7%).

Price index (2005 = 100)	2004	2005	2006	2007	2008	2009	2010
Consumer price index	96.6	100.0	103.6	109.2	119.0	116.4	118.9

Household income and expenditure (2006): average household size 2.8; average annual expenditure per household Af. 50,421 (U.S.$28,168); sources of income: n.a.; expenditure: housing 26.8%, transportation 14.9%, energy and water 9.5%, household furnishings and operation 9.5%, food and nonalcoholic beverages 8.4%, recreation and culture 7.6%, communications 5.3%.
Selected balance of payments data. Receipts from (U.S.$'000,000): tourism (2009) 1,295; remittances (2010) 20; foreign direct investment (2008–10 avg.) 145. Disbursements for (U.S.$'000,000): tourism (2009) 305; remittances (2009) 77.

Foreign trade[11, 12, 13]

Balance of trade (current prices)	2004	2005	2006	2007	2008	2009
U.S.$'000,000	–796.5	–923.8	–932.3	–1,016.0	–1,011.7	–955.8
% of total	83.3%	81.3%	81.0%	83.8%	83.4%	77.6%

Imports (2009): U.S.$1,093,500,000 (machinery and apparatus 21.5%, of which power-generating machinery 7.4%; food products 17.3%; chemicals and chemical products 10.3%; whiskey 5.4%; road vehicles 5.0%). *Major import sources:* United States 49.2%; Netherlands 15.8%; United Kingdom 4.9%; Colombia 3.8%; Panama 3.2%.
Exports (2009): U.S.$137,700,000 (whiskey 48.1%; cigarettes 19.0%; machinery and apparatus 5.4%; food 4.6%). *Major export destinations:* Panama 23.9%; Netherlands Antilles 20.5%; Colombia 17.4%; Venezuela 12.6%; United States 9.4%.

Transport and communications

Transport. Railroads: none. Roads (1995): total length 497 mi, 800 km (paved 64%). Vehicles (2008): passenger cars 49,372; trucks and buses 1,292. Air transport: n.a.[14]

Communications Medium	date	number in '000s	units per 1,000 persons	Medium	date	number in '000s	units per 1,000 persons
Televisions	2001	20	218	PCs	...	...	...
Telephones				Dailies	2009	54[15]	651[15]
Cellular	2010	132[16]	1,226[16]	Internet users	2009	24	225
Landline	2010	35	326	Broadband	2010	19[16]	179[16]

Education and health

Educational attainment (2000). Percentage of population age 25 and over having: no formal schooling or incomplete primary education 9.7%; primary education 33.9%; secondary/vocational 39.2%; advanced vocational/higher 16.2%; unknown status 1.0%. *Literacy* (2009): percentage of total population age 15 and over literate 98.2%.

Education (2008–09)	teachers	students	student/ teacher ratio	enrollment rate (%)
Primary (age 6–11)	582	9,944	17.1	97
Secondary/Voc. (age 12–16)	553	7,439	13.5	77
Tertiary	231	2,196	9.5	31 (age 17–21)

Health (2008): physicians (2009) 172 (1 per 620 persons); hospital beds 292[17] (1 per 360 persons); infant mortality rate per 1,000 live births 1.6; undernourished population, n.a.

Military

Total active duty naval/coast guard personnel (in Dutch Caribbean; 2010): 50 Dutch and 190 locals from Aruba, Curaçao, or Sint Maarten.

[1]Same official name in Dutch and Papiamentu. [2]Areas for census regions are approximate. [3]Most Arubans are racially and ethnically mixed; the 4 major ethnic groups are Amerindian, Dutch, Spanish, and black. [4]Excludes tourists. [5]Service facilities include a free zone, offshore corporate banking facilities, casino/resort complexes, a petroleum transshipment terminal, a cruise ship terminal, and ship repair and bunkering facilities. [6]Employees on payrolls only. [7]Excludes refined petroleum. [8]Includes refined petroleum. [9]Taxes less subsidies and less imputed bank service charges. [10]Detail does not add to total given because of rounding. [11]Includes imports and exports of Aruba free zone. [12]Imports c.i.f.; exports f.o.b. [13]Excludes trade in petroleum. [14]Air Aruba ceased operations in 2000. [15]Circulation. [16]Subscribers. [17]Excludes hospital beds in geriatric homes.

Internet resources for further information:
- **Centrale Bank van Aruba http://www.cbaruba.org**
- **Central Bureau of Statistics http://www.cbs.aw/cbs/home.do**

Australia

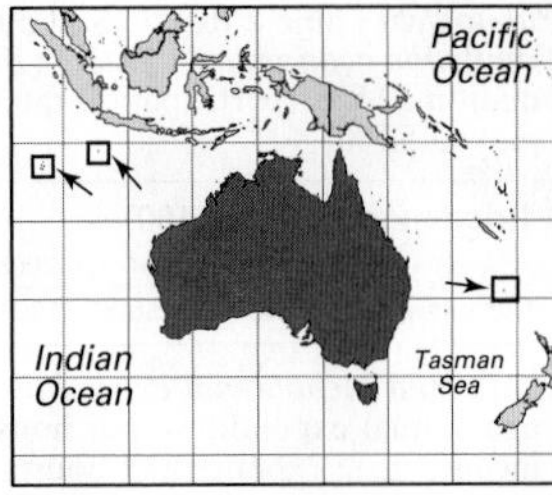

Official name: Commonwealth of Australia.
Form of government: federal parliamentary state (formally a constitutional monarchy) with two legislative houses (Senate [76]; House of Representatives [150]).
Head of state: British Monarch represented by Governor-General.
Head of government: Prime Minister.
Capital: Canberra.
Official language: English.
Official religion: none.
Monetary unit: Australian dollar ($A); valuation (Sept. 1, 2011) 1 U.S.$ = $A 0.93; 1 £ = $A 1.50.

Area and population

		area		population
States	**Capitals**	sq mi	sq km	2010[1] estimate
New South Wales (NSW)	Sydney	309,389	801,315	7,232,589
Queensland (QLD)	Brisbane	669,568	1,734,174	4,513,850
South Australia (SA)	Adelaide	380,441	985,338	1,644,582
Tasmania (TAS)	Hobart	26,222	67,914	507,643
Victoria (VIC)	Melbourne	87,805	227,415	5,545,932
Western Australia (WA)	Perth	977,442	2,531,562	2,293,510
Territories[2]				
Australian Capital Territory (ACT)	Canberra	908	2,352	358,571
Christmas Island	The Settlement	53	137	1,462
Cocos (Keeling) Islands	West Island	5	14	605
Jervis Bay	—	26	68	392
Norfolk Island	Kingston	14	35	1,863[3]
Northern Territory (NT)	Darwin	522,079	1,352,178	229,711
TOTAL		2,973,952	7,702,501[4]	22,330,710[5]

Demography

Population (2011): 22,651,000.
Density (2011): persons per sq mi 7.6, persons per sq km 2.9.
Urban-rural (2005): urban 88.2%; rural 11.8%.
Sex distribution (2008): male 50.09%; female 49.91%.
Age breakdown (2008): under 15, 18.7%; 15–29, 20.8%; 30–44, 22.0%; 45–59, 20.0%; 60–74, 12.2%; 75–84, 4.5%; 85 and over, 1.8%.
Population projection: (2020) 25,355,000; (2030) 27,896,000.
Ethnic composition (2007): white and others not elsewhere classified 90.2%; Asian (excl. Middle East) 7.3%; aboriginal 2.5%.
Religious affiliation (2006): Christian 63.9%, of which Roman Catholic 25.6%, Anglican Church of Australia 18.7%, other Christian 19.6% (Uniting Church 5.7%, Presbyterian 2.9%, Orthodox 2.6%, Baptist 1.6%, Lutheran 1.3%); Buddhist 2.1%; Muslim 1.7%; Hindu 0.7%; Jewish 0.4%; no religion 18.7%; other 12.5%.
Major urban centres/metropolitan areas (2006): Sydney 3,641,422/4,119,191; Melbourne 3,371,888/3,592,590; Brisbane 1,676,389/1,763,132; Perth 1,256,035/1,445,077; Adelaide 1,040,719/1,105,840; Gold Coast (QLD)–Tweed Heads (NSW) 454,436/541,675; Newcastle 288,732/493,467; Canberra (ACT)–Queanbeyan (NSW) 356,120/368,128; Gosford (Central Coast) 282,726/n.a.; Wollongong 234,482/263,535; Sunshine Coast (Caloundra) 184,662/209,578; Hobart 128,577/200,524; Geelong 137,220/160,992; Townsville 128,808/143,330; Cairns 98,349/122,731; Toowoomba 95,265/114,480; Darwin 66,291/105,990; Launceston 71,395/99,674; Albury (NSW)–Wodonga (VIC) 73,497/96,292.
Place of birth (2006): 70.9% native-born; 29.1% foreign-born, of which Europe 10.5% (United Kingdom 5.2%, Italy 1.0%, Greece 0.6%, Germany 0.5%, Netherlands 0.4%, Poland 0.3%), Asia and Middle East 7.3% (China [including Hong Kong] 1.4%, Vietnam 0.8%, India 0.7%), New Zealand 2.0%, Africa, the Americas, and other 9.3%.
Mobility (1999). Population age 15 and over living in the same residence as in 1998: 84.4%; different residence between states, regions, and neighbourhoods 15.6%.
Households (2006). Total number of households 8,058,248. Average household size 2.6; 1 person (2003–04) 25.4%, 2 persons (2003–04) 33.9%, 3 or more persons (2003–04) 40.7%. Family households 5,665,000 (70.3%), nonfamily 2,393,000 (29.7%), of which 1-person 26.5%.
Immigration (2006–07): permanent immigrants admitted 140,148, from New Zealand 17.1%, United Kingdom 16.6%, India 9.6%, China 8.6%, Philippines 4.0%, South Africa 2.9%, Vietnam 2.2%, Malaysia 2.1%, Sri Lanka 1.9%, Sudan 1.8%. *Emigration* (2006–07): 72,100, to New Zealand 19.3%, United Kingdom 18.2%, United States 10.0%, Hong Kong 7.5%. Refugee arrivals (2006–07) 13,017.

Vital statistics

Birth rate per 1,000 population (2009–10): 13.5 (world avg. 19.2); within marriage (2009) 65.4%; outside of marriage (2009) 34.6%.
Death rate per 1,000 population (2009–10): 6.3 (world avg. 8.2).
Natural increase rate per 1,000 population (2009–10): 7.2 (world avg. 11.0).
Total fertility rate (avg. births per childbearing woman; 2009–10): 1.92.
Marriage/divorce rates per 1,000 population (2009): 5.5/2.3.
Life expectancy at birth (2009): male 79.3 years; female 83.9 years.
Major causes of death per 100,000 population (2009): diseases of the circulatory system 208.1, of which ischemic heart disease 101.7; malignant neoplasms (cancers) 189.4; diseases of the respiratory system 49.9; accidents and violence 38.6; mental and behavioral disorders 29.4; diseases of the nervous system 26.7; endocrine, nutritional, and metabolic diseases 26.5.

Social indicators

Quality of working life. Average workweek (2008): 34.5 hours. Working 50 hours a week or more (2006) 22.5%. Annual rate per 100,000 workers for: accidental injury and industrial disease (2008) 1,020; death (2006) 2.0. Proportion of employed persons insured for damages or income loss resulting from: injury 100%; permanent disability 100%; death 100%. Working days lost to industrial disputes per 1,000 employees (2008): 21. Means of transportation to work (2003): private automobile 74.5%; public transportation 12.0%; motorcycle, bicycle, and foot 5.7%. Discouraged job seekers (2006): 52,900 (0.5% of labour force).

Distribution of household income (2007–08)

percentage of household income by quintile

lowest	second	third	fourth	highest
7.6%	12.7%	17.4%	22.9%	39.4%

Educational attainment (2005). Percentage of population age 15–64 having: no formal schooling and incomplete secondary education 48.5%; completed secondary and postsecondary, technical, or other certificate/diploma 28.9%; bachelor's degree 14.2%; incomplete graduate and graduate degree or diploma 5.4%; unknown 3.0%.
Social participation. Eligible voters participating in last national election (2010): 90%; voting is compulsory. Trade union membership in total workforce (2008): *c.* 20%. Volunteerism rate of population age 18 and over (2006) 34.1%.
Social deviance (2009). Offense rate per 100,000 population for: murder 1.2; sexual assault 86.0; assault (2007) 839; auto theft 272.7; burglary and housebreaking 1,018.0; robbery 69.7, of which armed robbery 29.8. Incidence per 100,000 in general population of: prisoners (2008) 169; suicide (2006) 8.7.
Material well-being (2005). Households possessing: refrigerator 99.9%; washing machine 96.4%; dishwasher 41.5%; automobiles per 1,000 population (2006) 544.

National economy

Gross national income (GNI; 2009): U.S.$957,529,000,000 (U.S.$43,770 per capita); purchasing power parity GNI (U.S.$38,210 per capita).

Structure of gross domestic product and labour force

	2008–09		2008	
	in value $A '000,000[6]	% of total value	labour force	% of labour force
Agriculture, forestry, fishing	31,460	2.6	354,800	3.2
Mining and quarrying	81,575	6.8	133,100	1.2
Manufacturing	103,431	8.6	1,102,100	9.8
Construction	84,596	7.1	987,000	8.8
Public utilities	28,605	2.4	98,500	0.9
Transp. and commun.	93,624	7.8	695,600	6.2
Trade, restaurants	134,751	11.3	2,555,400	22.8
Finance, real estate	239,689	20.0	1,727,800	15.4
Pub. admin., defense	60,790	5.1	644,500	5.7
Services	249,168	20.8	2,441,700	21.8
Other	89,307[7]	7.5[7]	470,900	4.2
TOTAL	1,196,996	100.0	11,211,400	100.0

Budget (2009–10). Revenue: $A 290,612,000,000 (tax revenue 92.1%, of which individual income tax 42.2%, company income tax 18.9%, sales tax 15.4%; nontax revenue 7.9%). Expenditures: $A 338,213,000,000 (social security and welfare 32.8%; health 15.1%; education 10.4%; defense 6.2%; general administration 5.2%; interest on public debt 1.9%).
Public debt (December 2010): U.S.$184,700,000,000.
Production (metric tons except as noted). Agriculture, forestry, fishing (2009): sugarcane 31,456,900, wheat 21,656,000, cow's milk 9,388,000, barley 8,098,000, sorghum 2,691,790, beef 2,147,910, rapeseed 1,910,000, grapes 1,797,010, oats 1,244,000, potatoes 1,178,530, chicken meat 832,456, sheep meat 658,390, lupins 614,000, cottonseed 465,000, tomatoes 440,093, wool 370,601, oranges 347,724, pork 323,959, apples 295,134, bananas 270,393, mushrooms 43,416; livestock (number of live animals) 72,739,700 sheep, 27,906,800 cattle, 2,301,710 pigs, 95,409,000 chickens; roundwood 30,132,000 cu m, of which fuelwood 16%; fisheries production 237,537 (from aquaculture 27%); aquatic plants production 1,923 (from aquaculture, none). Mining and quarrying (2008): iron ore (metal content) 209,000,000 (world rank: 3), bauxite (2010) 63,000,000 (world rank: 1), manganese (metal content) 2,320,000 (world rank: 2), ilmenite 2,199,000 (world rank: 1), zinc (metal content) 1,477,000 (world rank: 3), copper (metal content) 886,000 (world rank: 5), lead (metal content) 645,000 (world rank: 2), rutile 325,000 (world rank: 1), lithium minerals 200,000 (world rank: 1), nickel (metal content) 199,200 (world rank: 3), uranium 9,989 (world rank: 2), opal (value of production) $A 41,000,000 (world rank: 1), industrial diamonds 15,400,000 carats (world rank: 2), gold (2009) 220,000 kg (world rank: 2). Manufacturing (gross value added in $A '000,000; 2006–07): base metals 15,158; food 14,455; machinery and apparatus 10,538; fabricated metal products 9,076; transport equipment 9,003; chemicals and chemical products 6,831; beverages and tobacco products 5,787; bricks, cement, and ceramics 5,019.
Population economically active (2008): total 11,211,400; activity rate of total population 52.5% (participation rates: ages 15–64, 76.2%; female 45.4%; unemployed [October 2009–September 2010] 5.3%).

Price and earnings indexes (2005 = 100)

	2004	2005	2006	2007	2008	2009	2010
Consumer price index	97.4	100.0	103.5	106.0	110.6	112.6	115.3
Weekly earnings index	94.8	100.0	103.8	108.6	113.0	119.6	125.5

Household income and expenditure (2007–08). Average household size (2007–08) 2.6; average annual equivalised disposable income per household[8] $A 42,172 (U.S.$35,330); sources of income (2006): wages and salaries 59.3%, transfer payments 26.1%, self-employment 6.1%, other 8.5%; expenditure (2007–08): housing 17.2%, recreation and culture 12.1%, transportation 11.7%, food and nonalcoholic beverages 11.0%, hotels and cafés 7.5%, household furnishings and operation 5.6%, health 5.4%, alcohol and cigarettes 3.7%, clothing and footwear 3.7%, education 3.4%.

Financial aggregates

	2004	2005	2006	2007	2008	2009	2010
Exchange rate, $A per[9]:							
U.S. dollar	1.28	1.36	1.26	1.13	1.44	1.12	0.98
£	2.47	2.34	2.47	2.26	2.10	1.81	1.53
SDR	1.99	1.95	1.90	1.79	2.22	1.75	1.51
International reserves (U.S.$)[9]							
Total (excl. gold; '000,000)	35,803	41,941	53,448	24,768	30,691	38,950	38,659
SDRs ('000,000)	195	193	200	193	174	4,856	4,764
Reserve pos. in IMF ('000,000)	1,706	776	428	339	649	1,092	1,102
Foreign exchange ('000,000)	33,901	40,972	52,821	24,237	29,867	33,002	32,793
Gold ('000,000 fine troy oz)	2.56	2.57	2.57	2.57	2.57	2.57	2.57
% world reserves	0.3	0.3	0.3	0.3	0.3	0.3	0.3
Interest and prices							
Govt. bond yield (short-term; %)	5.27	5.28	5.68	6.30	5.73	4.22	4.89
Industrial share prices (2005 = 100)	82.5	100.0	119.2	143.9	113.7	95.4	105.8
Balance of payments[9] (U.S.$'000,000)							
Balance of visible trade	–18,064	–13,372	–9,596	–17,784	–4,915	–4,215	+18,180
Imports, f.o.b.	–105,230	–120,383	–134,509	–160,205	–193,972	–159,003	–194,670
Exports, f.o.b.	87,166	107,011	124,913	142,421	189,057	154,788	212,850
Balance of invisibles	–20,790	–27,660	–31,908	–40,248	–42,871	–39,676	–50,170
Balance of payments, current account	–38,854	–41,032	–41,504	–58,032	–47,786	–43,891	–31,990

Energy production (consumption): electricity (kW-hr; 2009) 229,848,000,000 ([2007] 254,965,000,000); hard coal (metric tons; 2007) 287,545,000 (35,899,000); lignite (metric tons; 2007) 101,838,000 (102,464,000); crude petroleum (barrels; 2009) 173,900,000 ([2007] 229,300,000); petroleum products (metric tons; 2007) 30,618,000 (35,814,000); natural gas (cu m; 2009) 42,334,000,000 ([2007] 31,660,000,000).

Selected balance of payments data. Receipts from (U.S.$'000,000): tourism (2009) 25,594; remittances (2010) 5,057; foreign direct investment (FDI; 2008–10 avg.) 35,010. Disbursements for (U.S.$'000,000): tourism (2009) 17,575; remittances (2009) 3,000; FDI (2008–10 avg.) 25,398.

Land use as % of total land area (2009): in temporary crops 3.6%, left fallow 2.5%[10], in permanent crops 0.05%, in pasture 47.1%, forest area 19.6%.

Foreign trade

Balance of trade (current prices)

	2004	2005	2006	2007	2008	2009
U.S.$'000,000	–17,322	–13,170	–9,328	–16,535	–4,731	–5,174
% of total	9.1%	5.9%	3.6%	5.6%	1.3%	1.7%

Trade by commodity group (2009)

	imports		exports	
SITC Group	U.S.$'000,000	%	U.S.$'000,000	%
00 Food and live animals	6,844	4.3	16,965	11.0
01 Beverages and tobacco	1,385	0.9	2,033	1.3
02 Crude materials, excluding fuels	1,588	1.0	39,333	25.6
03 Mineral fuels, lubricants, and related materials	20,135	12.7	45,372	29.5
04 Animal and vegetable oils, fat, and waxes	448	0.3	385	0.3
05 Chemicals and related products, n.e.s.	17,088	10.7	6,312	4.1
06 Basic manufactures	17,189	10.8	10,763	7.0
07 Machinery and transport equipment	60,658	38.2	9,340	6.1
08 Miscellaneous manufactured articles	21,661	13.6	3,974	2.6
09 Goods not classified by kind	11,945	7.5	19,290	12.5
TOTAL	158,941	100.0	153,767	100.0

Direction of trade (2009)

	imports		exports	
	U.S.$'000,000	%	U.S.$'000,000	%
Africa	1,271	0.8	2,579	1.7
Asia	88,140	55.4[4]	116,118	75.5
East Asia	50,432	31.7	83,021	54.0
China	28,351	17.8	33,360	21.7
Japan	13,223	8.3	29,988	19.5
Southeast Asia	31,125	19.6	15,374	10.0
South Asia	1,984	1.3	12,781	8.3
West Asia	3,812	2.4	4,942	3.2
undefined Asia	787	0.5	—	—
South America and Caribbean	2,542	1.6	2,078	1.4
North America	19,484	12.3	8,586	5.6
United States	18,005	11.3	7,461	4.9
Europe	33,922	21.3	14,362	9.3
United Kingdom	4,908	3.1	7,071	4.6
Oceania	7,735	4.9	8,505	5.5
New Zealand	5,201	3.3	6,216	4.0
other	5,847	3.7	1,539	1.0
TOTAL	158,941	100.0	153,767	100.0

Imports (2009): U.S.$158,941,000,000 (machinery and apparatus 27.1%, of which general industrial machinery 6.0%, telecommunications/sound recording equipment 5.6%, electrical machinery 4.8%; motor vehicles/parts 10.0%; crude petroleum 6.1%; refined petroleum 5.1%; medicines and pharmaceuticals 4.7%; gold 4.6%; food 4.3%). *Major import sources:* China 17.8%; U.S. 11.3%; Japan 8.3%; Thailand 5.8%; Singapore 5.6%; Germany 5.3%; Malaysia 3.8%; New Zealand 3.3%; South Korea 3.3%; U.K. 3.1%.

Exports (2009): U.S.$153,767,000,000 (mineral fuels 29.5%, of which bituminous coal 20.1%, petroleum 4.9%, LNG 3.9%; metal ore and scrap 22.8%, of which iron ore and concentrates 15.3%; food 11.0%, of which meat and meat preparations 3.4%, cereals [mostly wheat] and cereal preparations 3.3%; gold 7.6%; nonferrous metals [particularly aluminum and refined copper] 4.8%; machinery and apparatus 4.1%; wine 1.2%; wool 0.9%). *Major export destinations:* China 21.7%; Japan 19.5%; South Korea 8.0%; India 7.4%; U.S. 4.9%; U.K. 4.6%; New Zealand 4.0%; Taiwan 3.3%; Singapore 2.7%; Thailand 2.2%.

Transport and communications

Transport. Railroads (2008): route length 37,855 km; passenger-km (2007) 13,240,000,000; metric ton-km cargo (2007) 198,700,000,000. Roads (2004): total length 503,709 mi, 810,641 km (paved 42%); passenger-km (2007) 301,500,000,000[11]; metric ton-km cargo (2007) 182,500,000,000. Vehicles (2008): passenger cars 11,848,326; trucks and buses 2,880,647. Air transport (2008): passenger-km 79,224,000,000; metric ton-km cargo 2,206,000,000.

Communications

Medium	date	number in '000s	units per 1,000 persons	Medium	date	number in '000s	units per 1,000 persons
Televisions	2003	14,371	722	PCs	2006	15,671	757
Telephones				Dailies	2009	2,482[12]	143[12]
Cellular	2010	22,500[13]	1,010[13]	Internet users	2009	15,757	740
Landline	2010	8,660	389	Broadband	2010	5,165[13]	232[13]

Education and health

Literacy (2006): total population literate, virtually 100%[14].

Education (2007–08)

	teachers	students	student/teacher ratio	enrollment rate (%)
Primary (age 5–11)	...	1,977,837	...	97
Secondary/Voc. (age 12–17)	...	2,538,385	...	88
Tertiary	...	1,117,804	...	77 (age 18–22)

Health: physicians (2006) 55,063 (1 per 375 persons); hospital beds (2006–07) 82,587 (1 per 255 persons); infant mortality rate per 1,000 live births (2009) 4.3; undernourished population (2005–07) less than 5% of total population.

Military

Total active duty personnel (November 2010): 56,552[15] (army 49.9%, navy 25.2%, air force 24.9%). *Military expenditure as percentage of GDP* (2009): 2.5%; per capita expenditure U.S.$1,264[16].

[1]July 1. [2]With permanent civilian population only. [3]Revised 2006 census results. [4]Detail does not add to total given because of rounding. [5]Total includes 2006 revised census results for Norfolk Island. [6]At constant prices of 2007–08. [7]Taxes on products less subsidies and less statistical discrepancy. [8]Income that a single-person household would require to maintain the same standard of living as the average person living in all households in Australia; average annual gross income per household (2007–08) was $A 85,748 (U.S.$71,837). [9]At end of year. [10]Includes temporary meadows and pastures. [11]Passenger cars and buses. [12]Circulation. [13]Subscribers. [14]A national survey conducted in 1996 put the number of persons who had very poor literacy and numeracy skills at about 17% of the total population (age 15 to 64). [15]Troops deployed abroad (November 2010) 2,582, of which to Afghanistan 1,550, to East Timor 404. [16]Includes military pensions.

Internet resources for further information:

- **Australian Bureau of Statistics http://www.abs.gov.au**
- **Reserve Bank of Australia http://www.rba.gov.au**

Austria

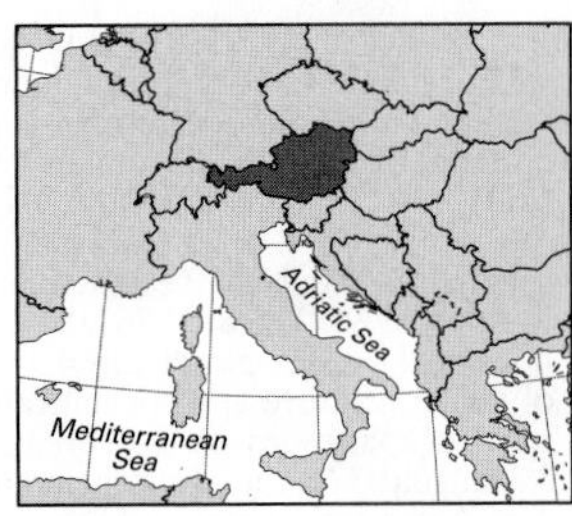

Official name: Republik Österreich (Republic of Austria).
Form of government: federal state with two legislative houses (Federal Council [62]; National Council [183]).
Head of state: President.
Head of government: Chancellor.
Capital: Vienna.
Official language: German.
Official religion: none.
Monetary unit: euro (€); valuation (Sept. 1, 2011) 1 U.S.$ = €0.70; 1 £ = €1.13.

Area and population

		area		population
States	**Capitals**	sq mi	sq km	2011[1] estimate
Burgenland	Eisenstadt	1,530	3,962	284,897
Kärnten	Klagenfurt	3,683	9,538	558,271
Niederösterreich	Sankt Pölten	7,408	19,186	1,611,981
Oberösterreich	Linz	4,626	11,980	1,412,640
Salzburg	Salzburg	2,763	7,156	531,721
Steiermark	Graz	6,332	16,401	1,210,614
Tirol	Innsbruck	4,880	12,640	710,048
Vorarlberg	Bregenz	1,004	2,601	369,938
Wien (Vienna)	—	160	415	1,714,142
TOTAL		32,386	83,879	8,404,252

Demography

Population (2011): 8,419,000.
Density (2011): persons per sq mi 260.0, persons per sq km 100.4.
Urban-rural (2005): urban 66.5%; rural 33.5%.
Sex distribution (2007): male 48.66%; female 51.34%.
Age breakdown (2007): under 15, 15.5%; 15–29, 18.7%; 30–44, 23.3%; 45–59, 20.3%; 60–74, 14.3%; 75–84, 6.0%; 85 and over, 1.9%.
Population projection: (2020) 8,722,000; (2030) 9,018,000.
Population composition by country of birth (2008[1]): Austria 84.8%; former Serbia and Montenegro 2.3%; Germany 2.2%; Turkey 1.9%; Bosnia and Herzegovina 1.6%; Poland 0.7%; Romania 0.7%; other 5.8%.
Religious affiliation (2009): Christian 73.3%, of which Roman Catholic 66.0%, Protestant (mostly Lutheran/Reformed) 3.9%, Orthodox 2.2%; Muslim 4.2%; atheist 12.0%; other/unknown 10.5%.
Major cities (2011[1]): Vienna 1,714,142 (urban agglomeration 2,013,941); Graz 261,540; Linz 189,367; Salzburg 148,078; Innsbruck 120,147.

Vital statistics

Birth rate per 1,000 population (2010): 9.4 (world avg. 19.2); within marriage 59.9%; outside of marriage 40.1%.
Death rate per 1,000 population (2010): 9.2 (world avg. 8.2).
Natural increase rate per 1,000 population (2010): 0.2 (world avg. 11.0).
Total fertility rate (avg. births per childbearing woman; 2010): 1.44.
Marriage/divorce rates per 1,000 population (2010): 4.5/2.1.
Life expectancy at birth (2010): male 77.7 years; female 83.2 years.
Major causes of death per 100,000 population (2008): diseases of the circulatory system 387.4; malignant neoplasms (cancers) 245.0; accidents and violence 52.8; diseases of the respiratory system 49.5.

National economy

Budget (2009)[2]. Revenue: €133,858,000,000 (social security contributions 34.1%; taxes on products and imports 30.2%; income/wealth taxes 26.2%). Expenditures: €143,527,000,000 (social protection 41.7%, of which for the elderly 24.8%; health 15.7%; education 11.1%; economic services 9.5%; public debt 5.4%; defense 1.6%).
Production (metric tons except as noted). Agriculture, forestry, fishing (2009): sugar beets 3,083,140, corn (maize) 1,890,500, wheat 1,523,370, barley 835,107, potatoes 722,098, apples 485,609, grapes 313,583, triticale 254,451, rye 183,642, currants 19,375; livestock (number of live animals) 3,064,230 pigs, 1,997,210 cattle; roundwood (2010) 17,830,956 cu m, of which fuelwood 26%; fisheries production 2,491 (from aquaculture 86%). Mining and quarrying (2009): iron ore (metal content) 480,000; manganese (metal content) 10,000; tungsten (metal content) 1,000. Manufacturing (value added in €'000,000; 2008): nonelectrical machinery and apparatus 6,171; fabricated metal products 4,785; electrical machinery and apparatus 4,067; base metals 3,860; food products 3,362; motor vehicles/parts 3,153; cement, bricks, and ceramics 2,402; wood products (excl. furniture) 2,030. Energy production (consumption): electricity (kW-hr; 2009) 68,856,000,000 ([2007] 69,976,000,000); coal (metric tons; 2008) none ([2007] 4,387,000); crude petroleum (barrels; 2009) 5,960,000 ([2007] 62,700,000); petroleum products (metric tons; 2007) 7,208,000 (11,524,000); natural gas (cu m; 2009) 1,670,000,000 ([2007] 8,969,000,000).
Land use as % of total land area (2009): in temporary crops 15.4%, left fallow 0.5%, in permanent crops 0.8%, in pasture 21.7%, forest area 47.1%.
Population economically active (2008)[3]: total 4,252,300; activity rate of total population 51.7% (participation rates: ages 15–64 75.0%; female 45.8%; unemployed [December 2009–November 2010] 6.8%).

Price and earnings indexes (2005 = 100)

	2004	2005	2006	2007	2008	2009	2010
Consumer price index	97.7	100.0	101.4	103.6	107.0	107.5	109.5
Annual hourly index	97.7	100.0	102.7	105.2	108.5	112.1	113.9

Gross national income (GNI; 2010): U.S.$391,511,000,000 (U.S.$46,710 per capita); purchasing power parity GNI (U.S.$39,410 per capita).

Structure of gross domestic product and labour force

	2009		2008	
	in value €'000,000	% of total value	labour force[3]	% of labour force
Agriculture, forestry	3,790	1.4	228,200	5.4
Mining	990	0.4	10,600	0.3
Manufacturing	46,160	16.8	694,800	16.3
Construction	18,200	6.6	332,000	7.8
Public utilities	6,940	2.5	25,600	0.6
Transp. and commun.	14,550	5.3	244,900	5.8
Trade, restaurants	43,750	15.9	914,900	21.5
Finance, real estate	58,710	21.4	540,900	12.7
Pub. admin., defense	15,070	5.5	278,300	6.5
Services	39,820	14.5	812,700	19.1
Other	26,320[4]	9.6[4]	169,500[5]	4.0[5]
TOTAL	274,320[6]	100.0[6]	4,252,300[6]	100.0

Public debt (December 2009): U.S.$243,035,000,000.
Household income and expenditure. Average household size (2006) 2.3; median annual disposable income per household (2009) €28,849 (U.S.$40,079); sources of income: n.a.; expenditure (2004–05): housing and energy 22.3%, transportation 16.1%, recreation and culture 12.6%, food 11.7%.
Selected balance of payments data. Receipts from (U.S.$'000,000): tourism (2009) 19,176; remittances (2010) 3,340; foreign direct investment (FDI; 2008–10 avg.) 6,827. Disbursements for (U.S.$'000,000): tourism (2009) 10,817; remittances (2009) 3,339; FDI (2008–10 avg.) 15,896.

Foreign trade[7]

Balance of trade (current prices)

	2004	2005	2006	2007	2008	2009
U.S.$'000,000	–431	–2,228	–187	+533	–2,798	–5,031
% of total	0.2%	0.9%	0.1%	0.2%	0.8%	1.9%

Imports (2009): U.S.$136,418,000,000 (machinery and apparatus 22.1%; chemicals and related products 12.5%; mineral fuels 10.4%; road vehicles/parts 9.2%; food products 6.4%). *Major import sources:* Germany 40.7%; Italy 6.7%; Switzerland 6.0%; China 4.6%; Czech Republic 3.5%.
Exports (2009): U.S.$131,387,000,000 (machinery and apparatus 27.7%, of which electrical machinery 6.7%, general industrial machinery 6.5%; base and fabricated metals 12.2%; road vehicles/parts 7.7%; medicine and pharmaceuticals 5.8%; food 5.5%). *Major export destinations:* Germany 31.1%; Italy 8.2%; Switzerland 5.0%; U.S. 4.3%; France 4.0%.

Transport and communications

Transport. Railroads: (2008) route length 6,399 km; (2007) passenger-km 9,167,000,000; (2007) metric ton-km cargo 21,371,000,000. Roads (2007): total length 66,649 mi, 107,262 km (paved 100%); (2006) passenger-km 81,300,000,000[8]; (2008) metric ton-km cargo 34,327,000,000. Vehicles (2010): passenger cars 4,441,000; trucks and buses 380,000. Air transport (2008): passenger-km 16,464,000,000; metric ton-km cargo 421,000,000.

Communications

Medium	date	number in '000s	units per 1,000 persons	Medium	date	number in '000s	units per 1,000 persons
Televisions	2008	3,218	386	PCs	2006	5,027	607
Telephones				Dailies	2009	2,305[9]	325[9]
Cellular	2010	12,241[10]	1,458[10]	Internet users	2009	6,144	735
Landline	2010	3,245	387	Broadband	2010	2,002[10]	239[10]

Education and health

Educational attainment (2008). Percentage of population age 25 and over having: up to lower secondary education 27.5%; upper secondary 48.9%; higher vocational 8.4%; university 15.2%. *Literacy:* virtually 100%.

Education (2007–08)

	teachers	students	student/ teacher ratio	enrollment rate (%)
Primary (age 6–9)	29,017	337,448	11.6	...
Secondary/Voc. (age 10–17)	72,856	770,792	10.6	...
Tertiary	32,686	284,791	8.7	55 (age 18–22)

Health: physicians (2008[1]) 20,318 (1 per 410 persons); hospital beds (2008[1,11]) 57,646 (1 per 144 persons); infant mortality rate per 1,000 live births (2010) 3.9; undernourished population (2005–07) less than 5.0% of total population.

Military

Total active duty personnel (November 2010): 25,900 (army 49.4%, air force 11.2%, support 39.4%); reserve 195,000. *Military expenditure as percentage of GDP* (2009): 0.7%; per capita expenditure U.S.$375.

[1]January 1. [2]For general (central and local) government. [3]Excludes conscripts on compulsory military service. [4]Taxes less subsidies. [5]Includes 7,200 inadequately defined and 162,300 unemployed. [6]Detail does not add to total given because of rounding. [7]Imports c.i.f.; exports f.o.b. [8]Passenger cars 72,000,000,000; buses 9,300,000,000. [9]Circulation. [10]Subscribers. [11]Excludes hospital beds in nursing homes and sanatoriums.

Internet resource for further information:

- **Austrian Central Office of Statistics http://www.statistik.at**

Azerbaijan

Official name: Azərbaycan Respublikası (Republic of Azerbaijan).
Form of government: unitary multiparty republic with a single legislative body (National Assembly [125[1]]).
Head of state and government: President assisted by Prime Minister.
Capital: Baku (Bakı).
Official language: Azerbaijanian.
Official religion: none.
Monetary unit: (new) manat (AZN)[2]; (Sept. 1, 2011) 1 U.S.$ = AZN 0.79; 1 £ = AZN 1.27.

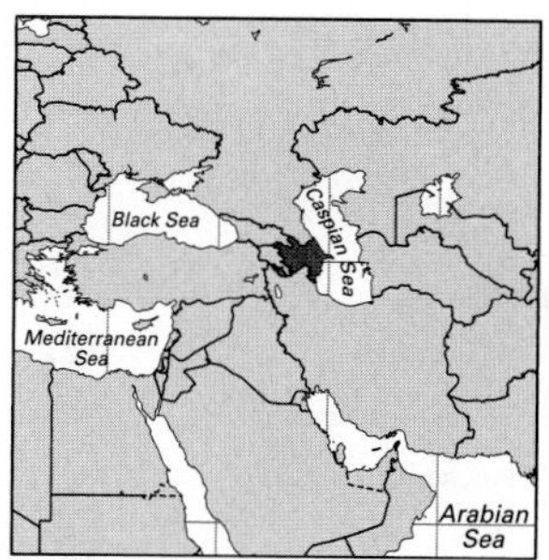

Area and population

Economic regions[3]	area sq km	population 2009 census[4]	Economic regions[3]	area sq km	population 2009 census[4]
Abşeron	3,290	514,200	Yuxarı Qarabağ (part)	2,200[5]	110,000[5]
Aran	21,430	1,797,300			
Bakı (Baku)	2,130	2,046,100	**Autonomous republic**		
Dağlıq Şirvan	6,060	281,200	Naxçıvan	5,500	398,400
Gəncə-Qazax	12,480	1,172,200			
Kəlbəcər-Laçın[6]	0	0			
Lənkəran	6,070	823,900	**Conflicted area**[6]	11,450[7]	...[7]
Quba-Xaçmaz	6,960	488,300	REMAINDER	—	724,800[8]
Şəki-Zagatala	8,960	565,900	TOTAL	86,530[9]	8,922,300

Demography

Population (2011): 9,150,000[10].
Density (2011): persons per sq mi 273.9, persons per sq km 105.7.
Urban-rural (2010[11]): urban 54.1%; rural 45.9%.
Sex distribution (2010[11]): male 49.53%; female 50.47%.
Age breakdown (2011[11]): under 15, 22.6%; 15–29, 29.6%; 30–44, 21.9%; 45–59, 17.7%; 60 and over, 8.2%.
Population projection: (2020) 10,080,000; (2030) 10,647,000.
Ethnic composition (1999): Azerbaijani 90.6%; Lezgian (Dagestani) 2.2%; Russian 1.8%; Armenian 1.5%; other 3.9%.
Religious affiliation (2009): Muslim *c.* 96%[12], of which Shīʿī *c.* 63%[12], Sunnī *c.* 33%[12]; Jewish *c.* 0.2%; Christian (significantly Orthodox)/other *c.* 3.8%.
Major cities (2009[4]): Baku 1,145,000 (urban agglomeration 1,950,000); Gəncə 313,300; Sumqayıt (Sumgait) 309,700; Mingəçevir (Mingechaur) 96,400; Qaraçuxur (2007) 74,700.

Vital statistics

Birth rate per 1,000 population (2010): 18.5 (world avg. 19.2); within marriage 84.7%; outside of marriage 15.3%.
Death rate per 1,000 population (2010): 6.0 (world avg. 8.2).
Natural increase rate per 1,000 population (2010): 12.5 (world avg. 11.0).
Total fertility rate (avg. births per childbearing woman; 2010): 1.94.
Marriage/divorce rates per 1,000 population (2010): 8.9/1.0.
Life expectancy at birth (2010): male 70.9 years; female 76.2 years.
Major causes of death per 100,000 population (2010): diseases of the circulatory system 364.4; malignant neoplasms (cancers) 74.2; accidents, poisoning, and violence 28.3; diseases of the respiratory system 26.6.

National economy

Budget (2009). Revenue: AZN 10,326,000,000 (nontax revenue 50.3%; tax revenue 48.8%, of which VAT 19.5%, taxes on enterprise profits 12.9%, individual income taxes 5.6%; other 0.9%). Expenditures: AZN 10,568,000,000 (national economy 41.5%; education 10.9%; social security 9.8%; defense/police 6.1%; health 3.8%).
Production (metric tons except as noted). Agriculture, forestry, fishing (2009): wheat 2,096,200, cow's milk 1,460,090, potatoes 982,979, tomatoes 392,927, apples 204,237, persimmons 135,549, grapes 129,159, hazelnuts 30,430, tobacco leaves 2,609, cranberries 2,200; livestock (number of live animals) 7,685,240 sheep, 2,280,720 cattle; roundwood (2010) 6,500 cu m, of which fuelwood 49%; fisheries production 1,303 (from aquaculture 8%). Mining and quarrying (2008): limestone 1,364,000; bromine 3,500. Manufacturing (value of production in AZN '000,000; 2009): food, beverages, and tobacco products 1,645; refined petroleum products 1,346; transport equipment 203; base and fabricated metals 171. Energy production (consumption): electricity (kW-hr; 2009) 18,552,000,000 ([2008] 17,700,000,000); coal, none (none); crude petroleum (barrels; 2009) 367,000,000 ([2008] 53,529,000); petroleum products (metric tons; 2007) 6,819,000 (3,139,000); natural gas (cu m; 2009) 16,407,000,000 ([2008] 10,133,000,000).
Household income and expenditure (2009). Average household size 4.5; annual income per household AZN 4,736 (U.S.$5,519); sources of income: wages and salaries 31.9%, self-employment 24.5%, agriculture 16.1%, transfers 14.8%; expenditure: food 48.8%, housing and energy 6.5%, hotels and cafés 5.9%.
Population economically active (2009): total 4,331,800[13]; activity rate of total population 48.7% (participation rates: ages 15–64, 73.2%; female 49.2%; unemployed 6.0%).

Price index (2005 = 100)

	2004	2005	2006	2007	2008	2009	2010
Consumer price index	89.6	100.0	108.3	126.4	152.7	154.9	161.1

Gross national income (GNI; 2010): U.S.$45,983,000,000 (U.S.$5,180 per capita); purchasing power parity GNI (U.S.$9,220 per capita).

Structure of gross domestic product and labour force

	2009 in value AZN '000,000	% of total value	labour force	% of labour force
Agriculture	2,321	6.7	1,573,020	36.3
Petroleum and natural gas, other mining	15,495	44.8	41,220	1.0
Manufacturing	1,396	4.1	196,545	4.5
Public utilities	391	1.1	65,926	1.5
Construction	2,562	7.4	220,750	5.1
Transp. and commun.	2,948	8.5	209,811	4.8
Trade, hotels	2,777	8.0	679,886	15.7
Finance, real estate	1,494	4.3	104,204	2.4
Services	2,519	7.3	720,101	16.6
Pub. admin., defense	634	1.9	260,132	6.0
Other	2,042[14]	5.9[14]	260,192	6.0
TOTAL	34,579	100.0	4,331,787	100.0[15]

Public debt (external, outstanding; 2009): U.S.$3,402,930,000.
Selected balance of payments data. Receipts from (U.S.$'000,000): tourism (2009) 350; remittances (2010) 1,472; foreign direct investment (FDI; 2008–10 avg.) 350; official development assistance (2009) 232. Disbursements for (U.S.$'000,000): tourism (2008) 341; remittances (2009) 652; FDI (2008–10 avg.) 371.
Land use as % of total land area (2009): in temporary crops 22.2%, left fallow 0.5%, in permanent crops 2.7%, in pasture 32.1%, forest area 11.3%.

Foreign trade[16]

Balance of trade (current prices)

	2004	2005	2006	2007	2008	2009
U.S.$'000,000	+99	+136	+1,105	+346	+40,594	+8,570
% of total	1.4%	1.6%	9.5%	2.9%	73.9%	41.2%

Imports (2009): U.S.$6,119,000,000 (machinery and apparatus 35.4%, of which specialized machinery 7.5%, electrical machinery 7.1%; food 10.5%; road vehicles 9.0%; chemicals and chemical products 8.1%; iron and steel products 6.9%). *Major import sources:* Russia 17.5%; Turkey 14.8%; Germany 9.0%; Ukraine 8.3%; China 7.9%.
Exports (2009): U.S.$14,689,000,000 (crude petroleum 81.6%; refined petroleum 10.1%; natural gas 0.9%; floating cranes/fire-floats 0.8%; hazelnuts/fruits 0.7%). *Major export destinations:* Italy 25.8%; U.S. 11.9%; France 9.0%; Israel 8.4%; Russia 5.1%.

Transport and communications

Transport. Railroads (2009): route length 2,079 km; passenger-km 1,024,000,000; metric ton-km cargo 7,952,000,000. Roads (2009): total length 36,748 mi, 59,141 km (paved 49%); passenger-km (2007) 12,893,000,000[17]; metric ton-km cargo (2009) 10,634,000,000. Vehicles (2009): passenger cars 759,203; trucks and buses 147,363. Air transport (2009): passenger-km 1,275,000,000; metric ton-km cargo 7,388,000.

Communications

Medium	date	number in '000s	units per 1,000 persons	Medium	date	number in '000s	units per 1,000 persons
Televisions	2003	2,750	334	PCs	2007	207	24
Telephones				Dailies	2009	120[18]	13[18]
Cellular	2010	9,100[19]	990[19]	Internet users	2009	3,689	418
Landline	2010	1,500	163	Broadband	2010	500[19]	54[19]

Education and health

Educational attainment (2008). Percentage of population age 25 and over having: no formal schooling/incomplete primary education 2.8%; complete primary 4.4%; some secondary 9.8%; complete secondary 49.7%; higher vocational 19.4%; university 13.9%. *Literacy* (2007): 99.4%.

Education (2008–09)

	teachers	students	student/ teacher ratio	enrollment rate (%)
Primary (age 6–9)	44,232	490,242	11.1	85
Secondary/Voc. (age 10–16)	139,109	1,114,356	8.0	93
Tertiary	25,836	180,276	7.0	19 (age 17–21)

Health (2010): physicians 33,200[11] (1 per 271 persons); hospital beds 68,300[11] (1 per 132 persons); infant mortality rate per 1,000 live births 11.2; undernourished population (2005–07) less than 5% of total population.

Military

Total active duty personnel (November 2010): 66,940 (army 84.9%, navy 3.3%, air force 11.8%). *Military expenditure as percentage of GDP* (2009): 2.9%; per capita expenditure U.S.$170.

[1]Statutory number. [2]The (new) manat was introduced on Jan. 1, 2006, at a rate of 4,500 (old) manats (AZM) to 1 (new) manat (AZN). [3]Administratively, Azerbaijan is divided into 66 districts, 13 cities, and 1 autonomous republic (Naxçıvan). [4]Preliminary. [5]Part not occupied by Armenian forces; estimated population. [6]Occupied by Armenian forces since 1992/93. [7]Area controlled by Armenian forces including all of Nagorno-Karabakh (4,400 sq km; pop. [2010] *c.* 142,000), all of Kəlbəcər-Laçın (5,420 sq km; pop. [1999] n.a.), and part of Yuxarı Qarabağ (1,630 sq km; pop. [1999] n.a.). [8]Refugee population from Nagorno-Karabakh and other conflicted areas. [9]Summed total; reported total is 86,600 sq km. [10]Excludes Armenian population of Nagorno-Karabakh. [11]January 1. [12]Includes large number of nominal Muslims. [13]Excludes military. [14]Includes taxes less subsidies. [15]Detail does not add to total given because of rounding. [16]Imports c.i.f.; exports f.o.b. [17]Buses/taxis only. [18]Circulation. [19]Subscribers.

Internet resource for further information:

- **The State Statistical Committee of Azerbaijan Republic http://www.azstat.org**

Bahamas, The

Official name: The Commonwealth of The Bahamas.
Form of government: constitutional monarchy with two legislative houses (Senate [16]; House of Assembly [41]).
Head of state: British Monarch represented by Governor-General.
Head of government: Prime Minister.
Capital: Nassau.
Official language: English.
Official religion: none.
Monetary unit: Bahamian dollar (B$); valuation (Sept. 1, 2011) 1 U.S.$ = B$1.00; 1 £ = B$1.62.

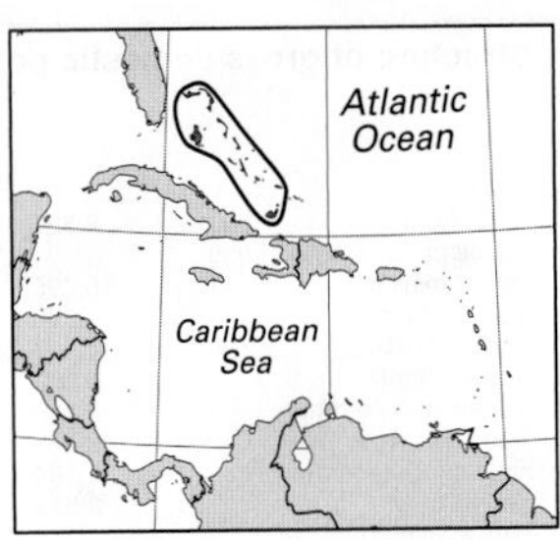

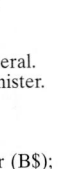

Area and population

Islands and Island Groups[2]	area[1] sq km	population 2010 census	Islands and Island Groups[2]	area[1] sq km	population 2010 census
Abaco, Great and Little	1,681	16,692	Inagua, Great and Little	1,551	911
Acklins	497	560	Long Island	596	3,024
Andros	5,957	7,386	Mayaguana	285	271
Berry Islands	31	798	New Providence Island (Nassau)	207	248,948
Bimini Islands	23	2,008	Ragged Island	36	70
Cat Island	388	1,503	Rum Cay	78	99
Crooked and Long Cay	241	323	San Salvador	163	930
Eleuthera	484	7,826	Spanish Wells	26	1,537
Exuma, Great, and Exuma Cays	290	7,314	Other uninhabited cays and rocks	23	—
Grand Bahama	1,373	51,756	TOTAL	13,939[3]	353,658
Harbour Island	8	1,702			

Demography

Population (2011): 360,000.
Density (2011)[4]: persons per sq mi 92.5, persons per sq km 35.7.
Urban-rural (2009): urban 83.9%; rural 16.1%.
Sex distribution (2010): male 48.63%; female 51.37%.
Age breakdown (2010): under 15, 26.4%; 15–29, 24.3%; 30–44, 24.2%; 45–59, 16.1%; 60–74, 7.0%; 75–84, 1.5%; 85 and over, 0.5%.
Population projection: (2020) 398,000; (2030) 431,000.
Doubling time: 89 years.
Ethnic composition (2007): local black/mixed race *c.* 74%; Haitian *c.* 15%; white/European *c.* 11%.
Religious affiliation (2000): Baptist 35.4%; Anglican 15.1%; Roman Catholic 13.5%; other Christian 32.3%; other/nonreligious 3.7%.
Major cities and towns (2006): Nassau (2010) 248,948; Freeport (on Grand Bahama) 47,100; West End (on Grand Bahama) 12,900; Cooper's Town (on Great Abaco) 8,600; Marsh Harbour (on Great Abaco) 5,400.

Vital statistics

Birth rate per 1,000 population (2010): 13.8 (world avg. 19.2); within marriage (2008) 40.7%; outside of marriage (2008) 59.3%.
Death rate per 1,000 population (2010): 6.0 (world avg. 8.2).
Natural increase rate per 1,000 population (2010): 7.8 (world avg. 11.0).
Total fertility rate (avg. births per childbearing woman; 2010): 1.94.
Marriage/divorce rates per 1,000 population (2010): 11.8[5]/1.2.
Life expectancy at birth (2007): male 71.0 years; female 77.0 years.
Major causes of death per 100,000 population (2008): diseases of the circulatory system 185.2; malignant neoplasms (cancers) 104.9; HIV/AIDS 34.6; accidents 27.8; diabetes 24.2; diseases of the respiratory system 23.9.
Adult population (ages 15–49) *living with HIV* (2009): 3.1%[6] (world avg. 0.8%).

National economy

Budget (2009–10). Revenue: B$1,400,046,000 (tax revenue 88.4%, of which taxes on international trade and transactions 47.2% [including import duties 32.9%, excise taxes 13.5%], property tax 7.6%, business and professional licenses 7.2%; nontax revenue 10.1%; grants 0.8%; capital revenue 0.7%). Expenditures: B$1,639,300,000 (education 17.4%; health 16.9%; general administration 14.5%; interest on public debt 10.8%; public works and water supply 10.7%; public order 10.5%; defense 2.8%).
Public debt (external, outstanding; September 2010): U.S.$1,324,000,000[7].
Production (metric tons except as noted). Agriculture, forestry, fishing (2009): vegetables 24,027, grapefruit (incl. pomelos) 20,244, lemons and limes 9,535; livestock (number of live animals) 3,000,000 chickens; roundwood (2010) 49,896 cu m, of which fuelwood 66%; fisheries production 9,106 (mainly lobsters, crayfish, and conch; from aquaculture, negligible). Mining and quarrying (2009): salt 1,000,000; aragonite 1,100. Manufacturing (value of export production in B$'000; 2009): polystyrene 122,500; heterocyclic compounds 106,900; yachts/boats 8,300; blow torches 7,200.[8] Energy production (consumption): electricity (kW-hr; 2008) 2,206,500,000 ([2007] 2,110,000,000); crude petroleum, none (none); petroleum products (metric tons; 2006) none (693,000).
Household income and expenditure. Average household size (2009) 3.3; income per household (2009) B$38,314 (U.S.$38,314); sources of income: n.a.; expenditure (1995)[9]: housing 32.8%, transportation and communications 14.8%, food and beverages 13.8%, household furnishings 8.9%.
Land use as % of total land area (2009): in temporary crops or left fallow 0.4%, in permanent crops 0.4%, in pasture 0.2%, forest area 51.4%.
Gross national income (2009): U.S.$6,941,000,000 (U.S.$20,312 per capita).

Structure of gross domestic product and labour force

	2008		2009	
	in value B$'000[10]	% of total value	labour force	% of labour force
Agriculture, fishing	88,500	1.2	4,530	2.5
Mining	23,500	0.3	2,595	1.4
Public utilities	179,800	2.5		
Manufacturing	234,600	3.3	5,315	2.9
Construction	821,800	11.4	17,345	9.4
Transp. and commun.	602,200	8.4	10,985	6.0
Trade	807,900	11.2	46,500	25.3
Hotels, restaurants	732,300	10.2		
Finance, real estate	2,086,700	28.9	19,405	10.5
Pub. admin., defense	440,200	6.1	50,550	27.5
Services	966,100	13.4		
Other	224,400[11]	3.1[11]	26,795[12]	14.5[12]
TOTAL	7,208,200[3]	100.0	184,020	100.0

Population economically active (2009): total 184,020; activity rate of total population 73.4% (participation rates: ages 15–64 [2007] 76.2%; female 51.0%; unemployed 14.2%).

Price index (2005 = 100)

	2004	2005	2006	2007	2008	2009	2010
Consumer price index	98.4	100.0	102.4	104.9	109.7	111.9	113.4

Selected balance of payments data. Receipts from (U.S.$'000,000): tourism (2009) 1,938; remittances, n.a.; foreign direct investment (2008–10 avg.) 912. Disbursements for (U.S.$'000,000): tourism (2009) 240; remittances (2009) 96.

Foreign trade[13]

Balance of trade (current prices)

	2004	2005	2006	2007	2008	2009
B$'000,000	–1,575	–2,296	–2,475	–2,433	–2,528	–2,114
% of total	66.2%	80.9%	70.8%	64.5%	64.3%	64.4%

Imports (2009): B$2,699,000,000 (refined petroleum 19.9%[14], food products 15.5%, machinery and equipment 14.5%, chemicals and chemical products 10.1%, metal manufactures 5.4%). *Major import sources:* U.S. 90.9%; Venezuela 1.8%; Trinidad and Tobago 1.6%.
Exports (2009): B$585,000,000 (polystyrene 20.9%, refined petroleum 19.2%[14], organic chemicals 18.3%, crustaceans [significantly crayfish] 10.4%). *Major export destinations:* U.S. 71.7%; Neth. 6.9%; Canada 4.3%; France 4.0%.

Transport and communications

Transport. Railroads: none. Roads (2002): total length 1,688 mi, 2,717 km (paved 57%). Vehicles (2002): passenger cars 112,900; trucks and buses 19,200. Air transport (2006): passenger-km 275,700,000; metric ton-km cargo 600,000.

Communications

Medium	date	number in '000s	units per 1,000 persons	Medium	date	number in '000s	units per 1,000 persons
Televisions	2001	77	247	PCs	…	…	…
Telephones				Dailies	2009	39[15]	114[15]
Cellular	2010	428[16]	1,249[16]	Internet users	2009	116	420
Landline	2010	129	377	Broadband	2010	25[16]	71[16]

Education and health

Educational attainment (2000). Percentage of population age 15 and over having: no formal schooling 1.5%; primary education 8.7%; incomplete secondary 19.9%; complete secondary 53.7%; higher 15.2%; not stated 1.0%.
Literacy (2005): total percentage age 15 and over literate 95.8%.

Education (2007–08)

	teachers	students	student/ teacher ratio	enrollment rate (%)
Primary (age 5–10)	2,333	36,833	15.8	91
Secondary/Voc. (age 11–16)	2,716	34,399	12.7	85
Tertiary	…	…	…	… (age 17–21)

Health: physicians (2006) 849 (1 per 389 persons); hospital beds (2007) 1,057 (1 per 316 persons); infant mortality rate per 1,000 live births (2010) 16.1; undernourished population (2005–07) 20,000 (6% of total population based on the consumption of a minimum daily requirement of 1,890 calories).

Military

Total active duty personnel (November 2010): 860 (marines with coast guard duties 100%). *Military expenditure as percentage of GDP* (2008): 0.7%; per capita expenditure U.S.$145.

[1]Includes areas of lakes and ponds, as well as lagoons and sounds almost entirely surrounded by land; area of land only is about 10,070 sq km (3,890 sq mi). [2]For local administrative purposes, The Out (Family) Islands of the Bahamas are divided into 32 districts; New Providence Island is administered directly by the national government. [3]Detail does not add to total given because of rounding. [4]Land area only. [5]Includes nonresident marriages. [6]Statistically derived midpoint within range. [7]Includes public corporations. [8]No rum exported in 2009. [9]Weights of retail price index components. [10]At constant prices of 2006. [11]Indirect taxes less imputed bank service charges. [12]Includes 26,215 unemployed. [13]Imports c.i.f.; exports f.o.b. [14]Much of which is transshipped from the petroleum storage terminal near Freeport. [15]Circulation. [16]Subscribers.

Internet resources for further information:
- **The Central Bank of The Bahamas http://www.bahamascentralbank.com**
- **Department of Statistics http://statistics.bahamas.gov.bs**

Bahrain

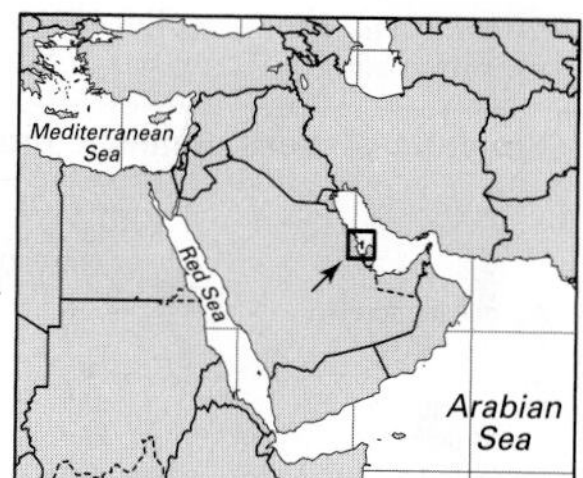

Official name: Mamlakat al-Baḥrayn (Kingdom of Bahrain).
Form of government: constitutional monarchy with a parliament comprising two bodies (Shura Council [40[1]]; Council of Representatives [40]).
Head of state: King.
Head of government: Prime Minister.
Capital: Manama.
Official language: Arabic.
Official religion: Islam.
Monetary unit: Bahraini dinar (BD); valuation (Sept. 1, 2011) 1 BD = U.S.$2.65 = £1.64.

Area and population

		area		population
				2010
Governorates	Principal cities	sq mi	sq km	census
Capital	Manama	14.5	37.5	329,510
Central	Al-Rifāʿ al-Gharbī	32.7	84.8	326,305
Al-Muḥarraq	Al-Muḥarraq	21.7	56.1	189,114
Northern	Madīnat Ḥamad	54.4	140.8	276,949
Southern[2]	ʿAwālī	169.2	438.3	101,456
TOTAL		292.5[3]	757.5[3]	1,234,571[4]

Demography

Population (2011): 1,325,000.
Density (2011): persons per sq mi 4,529.9, persons per sq km 1,749.2.
Urban-rural (2009): urban 88.5%; rural 11.5%.
Sex distribution (2010): male 62.24%; female 37.76%.
Age breakdown (2010): under 15, 20.1%; 15–29, 29.8%; 30–44, 32.3%; 45–59, 14.3%; 60–74, 2.8%; 75–84, 0.6%; 85 and over, 0.1%.
Population projection: (2020) 1,491,000; (2030) 1,635,000.
Doubling time: 56 years.
Ethnic composition (2010): Arab 51.4%, of which Bahraini 46.0%; other Asian (mostly Indian, Pakistani, Persian, or Filipino) 45.5%; African 1.6%; European 1.0%; other 0.5%.
Religious affiliation (2010): Muslim 70.2%, of which Shīʿī c. 46%, Sunnī c. 24%; other (significantly Christian or Hindu) 29.8%.
Major urban areas (2001): Manama (2009) 163,000; Al-Muḥarraq 91,307; Al-Rifāʿ al-Gharbī 79,550; Madīnat Ḥamad 52,718; Al-ʿAlī 47,529; Madīnat ʿIsā 36,833.

Vital statistics

Birth rate per 1,000 population (2009): 15.1 (world avg. 20.3).
Death rate per 1,000 population (2009): 2.6 (world avg. 8.5).
Natural increase rate per 1,000 population (2009): 12.5 (world avg. 11.8).
Total fertility rate (avg. births per childbearing woman; 2009): 1.94.
Marriage/divorce rates per 1,000 population (2008): 4.5/1.1.
Life expectancy at birth (2009): male 75.8 years; female 80.0 years.
Major causes of death per 100,000 population (2008): diseases of the circulatory system 40.0; malignant neoplasms (cancers) 23.1; accidents, poisoning, and violence 20.4; endocrine, metabolic, and immunity diseases 20.3; diseases of the respiratory system 16.5; ill-defined conditions 51.1.

National economy

Budget (2009). Revenue: BD 1,708,200,000 (petroleum and natural gas revenue 83.0%, other 17.0%). Expenditures: BD 2,082,200,000 (current expenditure 81.3%, development expenditure 18.7%).
Production (metric tons except as noted). Agriculture, forestry, fishing (2009): dates 14,068, cow's milk 11,000, tomatoes 4,300, hen's eggs 2,700, eggplant 1,200, lemons and limes 1,125, onions 850, okra 700; livestock (number of live animals) 40,000 sheep, 19,000 goats, 525,000 chickens; roundwood (2010) 6,506 cu m, of which fuelwood 100%; fisheries production 16,360 (from aquaculture, negligible). Mining (2009): sand, n.a., rocks, n.a. Manufacturing (value added in BD '000,000; 2009): petroleum products 364.4; aluminum 220.7; other metal industries (including iron ore pellets) 164.9; food products 100.6; bricks, cement, tiles 100.0. Energy production (consumption): electricity (kW-hr; 2008) 11,657,000,000 ([2007] 10,908,000,000); coal, none (none); crude petroleum (barrels; 2009) 66,500,000[5] ([2007] 95,160,000); petroleum products (metric tons; 2007) 11,176,000 (1,359,000); natural gas (cu m; 2009) 15,388,000,000 ([2007] 8,685,000,000).
Gross national income (2009): U.S.$16,919,000,000 (U.S.$14,362 per capita[6]).

Structure of gross domestic product and labour force

	2009		2001	
	value in BD '000,000	% of total value	labour force[7]	% of labour force[7]
Agriculture, fishing	31.7	0.4	4,483	1.5
Crude petroleum, nat. gas	1,677.0	23.1 }	2,780	0.9
Quarrying	50.8	0.7 }		
Manufacturing	1,070.8	14.7	49,979	16.2
Construction	324.7	4.5	26,416	8.6
Public utilities	105.9	1.5	2,515	0.8
Transp. and commun.	515.7	7.1	13,769	4.5
Trade, restaurants	733.1	10.1	47,570	15.5
Finance, real estate	2,069.0	28.5	24,797	8.1
Pub. admin., defense	942.9	13.0	52,389	17.0
Services	374.3	5.1	61,256	19.9
Other	–632.1[8]	–8.7[8]	21,560[9]	7.0[9]
TOTAL	7,263.8	100.0	307,514	100.0[10]

Public debt (September 2010): U.S.$5,402,000,000.
Population economically active (2005): total 350,000; activity rate of total population 48.3% (participation rates: ages 15 and over c. 67%; female 23.2%; unemployed [Bahrainis only; July–September 2010] 3.7%).

Price and earnings indexes (2005 = 100)

	2004	2005	2006	2007	2008	2009	2010
Consumer price index	97.5	100.0	102.0	105.3	109.0	112.1	114.3
Monthly earnings index[11]	104.7	100.0	96.7	100.0	...	...	...

Household income and expenditure (2005–06): Average household size (2001) 5.9; average annual income per household BD 14,227 (U.S.$37,838); sources of income: wages and salaries 70.2%, real estate 14.5%, transfers 8.4%, self-employment 6.7%; expenditure: food, beverages, and tobacco 20.4%, other 79.6%.
Land use as % of total land area (2009): in temporary crops or left fallow 6.9%, in permanent crops 3.3%, in pasture 5.3%, forest area 0.7%.
Selected balance of payments data. Receipts from (U.S.$'000,000): tourism (2009) 1,118; remittances, n.a.; foreign direct investment (FDI; 2008–10 avg.) 736. Disbursements for (U.S.$'000,000): tourism (2009) 408; remittances (2009) 1,391; FDI (2008–10 avg.) 54.

Foreign trade[12]

Balance of trade (current prices)

	2002	2003	2004	2005	2006	2007
U.S.$'000,000	+798	+974	+932	+899	+2,705	+2,150
% of total	7.4%	7.9%	6.6%	4.6%	13.1%	8.5%

Imports (2007): U.S.$11,515,000,000 (crude petroleum 50.9%, machinery and apparatus 10.0%, road vehicles 7.9%, aluminum oxide 5.8%, food and live animals 4.0%). *Major import sources* (2008): Saudi Arabia c. 74%; Australia c. 2%; Japan c. 2%; China c. 2%; U.S. c. 2%.
Exports (2007): U.S.$13,665,000,000 (refined petroleum 79.1%, aluminum [all forms] 9.0%, urea 2.4%, iron ore agglomerates 1.4%, methanol 1.3%). *Major export destinations* (2008)[13]: U.A.E. 32.8%; Saudi Arabia 26.9%; Qatar 14.5%; U.S. 8.1%; Australia 4.4%.

Transport and communications

Transport. Railroads: none. Roads (2008): total length 2,449 mi, 3,942 km (paved 81%). Vehicles (2008): passenger cars 310,221; trucks and buses 59,362. Air transport (2008)[14]: passenger-km 13,656,000,000; metric ton-km cargo 614,000,000.

Communications

Medium	date	number in '000s	units per 1,000 persons	Medium	date	number in '000s	units per 1,000 persons
Televisions	2002	273	386	PCs	2004	121	147
Telephones				Dailies	2009	189[15]	160[15]
Cellular	2010	1,567[16]	1,242[16]	Internet users	2009	649	551
Landline	2010	228	181	Broadband	2010	154[16]	122[16]

Education and health

Educational attainment (2001). Percentage of population age 15 and over having: no formal education 24.0%; primary education 37.1%; secondary 26.4%; higher 12.5%. *Literacy* (2008): percentage of population age 15 and over literate 90.8%; males literate 91.7%; females literate 89.4%.

Education (2009–10)

	teachers	students	student/teacher ratio	enrollment rate (%)
Primary (age 6–11)	4,953[17]	88,281[18]	16.4[17]	97[18]
Secondary/Voc. (age 12–17)	5,198[17]	79,162[18]	12.4[17]	89[18]
Tertiary	1,727	35,848	20.8	51 (age 18–22)

Health (2008): physicians 2,322 (1 per 474 persons); hospital beds 2,104 (1 per 526 persons); infant mortality rate per 1,000 live births (2009) 9.8; undernourished population, n.a.

Military

Total active duty personnel (November 2010): 8,200 (army 73.2%, navy 8.5%, air force 18.3%)[19]. *Military expenditure as percentage of GDP* (2009): 2.0%; per capita expenditure U.S.$597.

[1]All seats are appointed by the king. [2]Includes the area of Ḥawār island and other nearby islets awarded to Bahrain by the International Court of Justice in 2001. [3]An extensive land reclamation scheme was under way in 2009. [4]Includes 11,237 non-Bahrainis not assigned to a governorate. [5]Includes offshore production totaling 54,800,000 barrels. [6]Includes non-Bahrainis temporarily working in Bahrain. [7]Excludes small number of unemployed non-Bahrainis. [8]Import duties less imputed bank service charges. [9]Includes 5,424 inadequately defined and 16,136 unemployed Bahrainis. [10]Of which c. 59% non-Bahrainis; non-Bahrainis constituted 76.1% of labour force in March 2010. [11]Private sector. [12]Imports c.i.f.; exports f.o.b. [13]Excluding petroleum; petroleum accounted for 79.6% of all exports in 2008. [14]Gulf Air and DHL International only. [15]Circulation. [16]Subscribers. [17]2001–02. [18]2008–09. [19]U.S. troops in Bahrain (November 2010): 1,339.

Internet resources for further information:
- **Central Bank of Bahrain http://www.cbb.gov.bh**
- **Central Informatics Organisation http://www.cio.gov.bh/cio_eng/**

Bangladesh

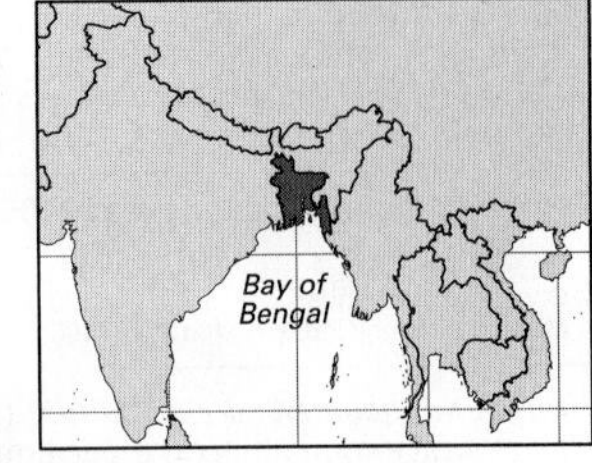

Official name: Gana Prajatantri Bangladesh (People's Republic of Bangladesh).
Form of government: unitary multiparty republic with one legislative house (Parliament [345[1]]).
Head of state: President.
Head of government: Prime Minister.
Capital: Dhaka.
Official language: Bengali (Bangla).
Official religion: Islam.
Monetary unit: Bangladesh taka (Tk); valuation (Sept. 1, 2011) 1 U.S.$ = Tk 73.85; 1 £ = Tk 119.34.

Area and population

		area		population
Divisions	**Administrative centres**	sq mi	sq km	2011 census[2]
Barisal	Barisal	5,134	13,297	8,147,000
Chittagong	Chittagong	13,039	33,771	28,079,000
Dhaka	Dhaka	12,015	31,119	46,729,000
Khulna	Khulna	8,600	22,274	15,563,000
Rajshahi	Rajshahi	7,025	18,195	18,329,000
Rangpur[3]	Rangpur	6,301	16,318	15,665,000
Sylhet	Sylhet	4,863	12,596	9,807,000
TOTAL		56,977[4]	147,570[4]	142,319,000

Demography

Population (2011): 142,875,000.
Density (2011)[5]: persons per sq mi 2,655.8, persons per sq km 1,025.4.
Urban-rural (2009): urban 27.6%; rural 72.4%.
Sex distribution (2010): male 48.70%; female 51.30%.
Age breakdown (2010): under 15, 34.8%; 15–29, 26.6%; 30–44, 19.5%; 45–59, 12.0%; 60–74, 5.5%; 75–84, 1.2%; 85 and over, 0.4%.
Population projection: (2020) 158,789,000; (2030) 172,657,000.
Ethnic composition (1997): Bengali 97.7%; tribal 1.9%, of which Chakma 0.4%, Saontal 0.2%, Marma 0.1%; other 0.4%.
Religious affiliation (2005): Muslim (nearly all Sunnī) 88.3%; Hindu 10.5%; Buddhist 0.6%; Christian (mostly Roman Catholic) 0.3%; other 0.3%.
Major cities/metropolitan areas (2008): Dhaka 7,000,940/12,797,394[6]; Chittagong 2,579,107/3,858,093; Khulna 855,650/1,388,425; Rajshahi 472,775/775,495; Tungi (2009) 417,500; Sylhet (2009) 399,400.

Vital statistics

Birth rate per 1,000 population (2010): 23.4 (world avg. 19.2).
Death rate per 1,000 population (2010): 5.8 (world avg. 8.2).
Total fertility rate (avg. births per childbearing woman; 2010): 2.65.
Marriage/divorce rates per 1,000 population (2008): 11.6/n.a.
Life expectancy at birth (2010): male 67.6 years; female 71.3 years.
Major causes of death per 100,000 population (2004)[7]: old age 100.2; infectious and parasitic diseases 98.3; diseases of the respiratory system 90.5; high blood pressure, heart disease, and stroke 61.0; suicide, accidents, and poisoning 35.7; malignant neoplasms (cancers) 26.6; unspecified 80.8.

National economy

Budget (2009–10). Revenue: Tk 794,800,000,000 (tax revenue 80.5%, of which VAT 28.7%, taxes on income and profits 20.8%, import duties 13.1%; nontax revenue 19.5%). Expenditures: Tk 1,105,200,000,000 (current expenditure 62.2%; development expenditure 25.8%; other 12.0%).
Production (metric tons except as noted). Agriculture, forestry, fishing (2009): paddy rice 47,724,000, potatoes 5,268,000, sugarcane 5,232,650, goat's milk 2,226,900, jute 923,500, wheat 849,000, bananas 836,183, mangoes, mangosteens, and guavas 828,161, pulses 204,877, spices 140,113, dry chilies and peppers 109,337, areca and betel nuts 105,448, ginger 72,608, lentils 60,537; livestock (number of live animals) 60,600,000 goats, 22,970,000 cattle; roundwood (2010) 27,641,263 cu m, of which fuelwood 99%; fisheries production (2009) 2,885,864 (from aquaculture 37%). Mining and quarrying (2009): granite 600,000; marine salt 360,000. Manufacturing (value added in Tk '000,000,000; 2007–08)[8]: small-scale 273.6, of which handloom-based 36.0; wearing apparel 222.7; food 120.9; textiles 63.8; cigarettes 40.0; medicine and pharmaceuticals 36.1.[9] Energy production (consumption): electricity (kW-hr; 2009) 26,904,000,000 ([2007] 21,383,000,000); hard coal (metric tons; 2007) 1,000,000 (700,000); crude petroleum (barrels; 2007) 2,100,000 (9,033,000); petroleum products (metric tons; 2007) 797,000 (3,594,000); natural gas (cu m; 2008–09[10]) 19,303,000,000 ([2008] 17,896,000,000).
Household income. Average household size (2006) 4.7; average annual income per household (2005) Tk 86,438 (U.S.$1,344); sources of income (2000): self-employment 56.9%, wages and salaries 28.1%, transfer payments 9.1%, other 5.9%; expenditure (2005): food and beverages 53.8%, housing 12.3%, energy 6.0%, clothing and footwear 5.5%.
Land use as % of total land area (2009): in temporary crops or left fallow 50.6%, in permanent crops 7.5%, in pasture 4.6%, forest area 11.1%.
Population economically active (2004–05): total 49,461,000; activity rate of total population 36.0% (participation rates: ages 15–64, 59.7%; female 24.5%; unemployed or underemployed [2008] 38%).

Price and earnings indexes (2004–05 = 100)

	2004–05	2005–06	2006–07	2007–08	2008–09	2009–10
Consumer price index	100.0	106.8	116.5	126.9	133.7	144.6
Average wage index	100.0	109.8	114.7	128.3	152.5	168.8

Gross national income (GNI; 2010): U.S.$104,478,000,000 (U.S.$640 per capita); purchasing power parity GNI (U.S.$1,620 per capita).

Structure of gross domestic product and labour force

	2008–09		2004–05	
	in value Tk '000,000,000[11]	% of total value	labour force	% of labour force
Agriculture, forestry	526	15.4	21,672,000	43.8
Fishing	150	4.4	1,095,000	2.2
Mining	41	1.2	51,000	0.1
Manufacturing	583	17.1	5,224,000	10.6
Construction	299	8.8	1,524,000	3.1
Public utilities	52	1.5	76,000	0.2
Transp. and commun.	348	10.2	3,976,000	8.0
Trade, hotels	497	14.6	7,820,000	15.8
Finance, real estate	302	8.9	746,000	1.5
Public admin., defense	91	2.7	882,000	1.8
Services	391	11.5	4,290,000	8.7
Other	126	3.7	2,104,000	4.3
TOTAL	3,406	100.0	49,461,000[12]	100.0[12]

Public debt (external, outstanding; 2009): U.S.$21,206,000,000.
Selected balance of payments data. Receipts from (U.S.$'000,000): tourism (2009) 69; remittances (2010) 10,804; foreign direct investment (FDI; 2008–10 avg.) 900; official development assistance (2009) 1,227. Disbursements for (U.S.$'000,000): tourism (2009) 249; remittances (2009) 8; FDI (2008–10 avg.) 18.

Foreign trade[13]

Balance of trade (current prices)

	2004	2005	2006	2007	2008	2009
U.S.$000,000	–3,006	–3,199	–2,890	–4,195	–6,004	–4,693
% of total	15.6%	14.7%	11.1%	14.4%	16.2%	13.5%

Imports (2007): U.S.$17,623,000,000 (machinery and apparatus 18.0%, food 12.5%, refined petroleum 8.8%, vegetable fats and oils 8.8%, textile yarn and fabrics 6.8%, cotton 6.0%). *Major import sources:* China 15.6%; India 13.2%; Kuwait 7.2%; Japan 5.1%; Indonesia 5.1%.
Exports (2007): U.S.$13,143,000,000 (knitted or woven clothing or accessories 71.5%, shrimp 4.6%, leather 2.2%, textile yarn 2.2%, bed linen 1.8%, refined petroleum 1.6%, jute 1.4%). *Major export destinations:* U.S. 25.7%; Germany 15.2%; U.K. 9.5%; France 6.5%; Italy 4.0%.

Transport and communications

Transport. Railroads (2008): route length 2,822 km; passenger-km (2007–08) 5,690,000,000; metric ton-km cargo (2007–08) 869,000,000. Roads (2007): total length 168,121 mi, 270,565 km (paved 30%). Vehicles (2007): passenger cars 158,109; trucks and buses 200,271. Air transport (2007–08)[14]: passenger-km 4,717,000,000; metric ton-km cargo 244,000,000.

Communications

Medium	date	number in '000s	units per 1,000 persons	Medium	date	number in '000s	units per 1,000 persons
Televisions	2004	11,531	85	PCs	2006	3,050	22
Telephones				Dailies	2009	1,500[15]	0.9[15]
Cellular	2010	68,650[16]	462[16]	Internet users	2009	617	3.8
Landline	2010	900	6.1	Broadband	2010	60[16]	0.4[16]

Education and health

Educational attainment (2004)[17]. Percentage of population age 25 and over having: no formal schooling 48.8%; incomplete primary education 17.9%; complete primary 7.7%; incomplete secondary 15.1%; complete secondary[18] or higher 10.5%. *Literacy* (2009): total population age 15 and over literate 55.3%; males literate 61.7%; females literate 48.9%.

Education (2008–09)

	teachers	students	student/ teacher ratio	enrollment rate (%)
Primary (age 6–10)	361,450	16,539,389	45.8	86
Secondary/Voc. (age 11–17)	370,800[19]	10,036,889[19]	27.1[19]	41[20]
Tertiary	61,569	1,294,535	21.0	8 (age 18–22)

Health (2008): physicians 49,994 (1 per 3,081 persons); hospital beds 74,415 (1 per 2,070 persons); infant mortality rate (2010) 52.5; undernourished population (2005–07) 41,700,000 (27% of total population based on the consumption of a minimum daily requirement of 1,750 calories).

Military

Total active duty personnel (November 2010): 157,053[21] (army 80.3%, navy 10.8%, air force 8.9%). *Military expenditure as percentage of GDP* (2009): 1.4%; per capita expenditure U.S.$8.

[1]Includes 45 indirectly elected seats reserved for women. [2]Preliminary. [3]New division approved January 2010. [4]The total area excluding the river area equals 53,797 sq mi (139,334 sq km). [5]Based on the total area excluding the river area. [6]Includes Narayanganj metro area (2009 est. 1,450,000). [7]Based on national sample registration system. [8]Including small-scale manufacturers. [9]Export processing zone manufactures (particularly ready-made garments) are of the greatest value. [10]December 2008–November 2009. [11]At constant prices of 1995–96. [12]Detail does not add to total given because of rounding. [13]Import figures are f.o.b. in balance of trade and c.i.f. in commodities and trading partners. [14]Biman Bangladesh Airlines only. [15]Circulation. [16]Subscribers. [17]Sample survey based on 21,405 people. [18]Through 5th year of secondary education (out of 7 years). [19]2007–08. [20]2006–07. [21]Of which deployed as UN peacekeepers 8,729.

Internet resources for further information:
- **Bangladesh Bank http://www.bangladesh-bank.org**
- **Bangladesh Bureau of Statistics http://www.bbs.gov.bd**

Barbados

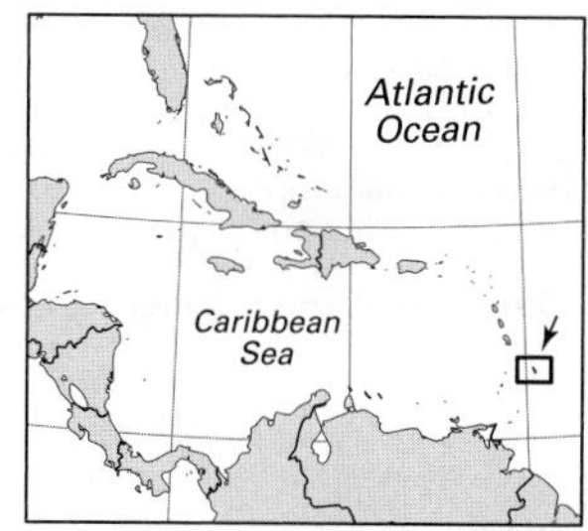

Official name: Barbados.
Form of government: constitutional monarchy with two legislative houses (Senate [21]; House of Assembly [30]).
Head of state: British Monarch represented by Governor-General.
Head of government: Prime Minister.
Capital: Bridgetown.
Official language: English.
Official religion: none.
Monetary unit: Barbados dollar (Bds$); valuation (Sept. 1, 2011) 1 U.S.$ = Bds$2.00; 1 £ = Bds$3.23.

Area and population

	area		population
Parishes[1]	sq mi	sq km	2005 projection
Christ Church	22	57	55,900
St. Andrew	14	36	5,600
St. George	17	44	18,100
St. James	12	31	28,100
St. John	13	34	9,400
St. Joseph	10	26	7,100
St. Lucy	14	36	9,600
St. Michael[2]	15	39	92,300
St. Peter	13	34	11,200
St. Philip	23	60	22,800
St. Thomas	13	34	11,900
TOTAL	166	430[3]	272,000[4]

Demography

Population (2011): 277,000.
Density (2011): persons per sq mi 1,668.7, persons per sq km 644.2.
Urban-rural (2009): urban 43.7%; rural 56.3%.
Sex distribution (2008): male 48.37%; female 51.63%.
Age breakdown (2008): under 15, 19.4%; 15–29, 22.3%; 30–44, 24.4%; 45–59, 20.8%; 60–74, 8.9%; 75–84, 3.1%; 85 and over, 1.1%.
Population projection: (2020) 282,000; (2030) 284,000.
Ethnic composition (2000): local black 87.1%; mixed race 6.0%; British expatriates 4.3%; U.S. white 1.2%; Indo-Pakistani 1.1%; other 0.3%.
Religious affiliation (2000): Christian 72.5%, of which Anglican 28.3%, Pentecostal 18.7%, Adventist 5.5%, Methodist 5.1%; Rastafarian 1.1%; Muslim 0.7%; Hindu 0.3%; nonreligious 17.3%; other/unknown 8.1%.
Major urban areas (2009): Bridgetown 93,300; Speightstown 2,400; Bathsheba 1,600; Holetown 1,500; Oistins 1,400.

Vital statistics

Birth rate per 1,000 population (2008): 12.9 (world avg. 20.3).
Death rate per 1,000 population (2008): 9.0 (world avg. 8.5).
Natural increase rate per 1,000 population (2008): 3.9 (world avg. 11.8).
Total fertility rate (avg. births per childbearing woman; 2008): 1.68.
Marriage/divorce rates per 1,000 population: (2000) 13.1/n.a.
Life expectancy at birth (2008): male 71.4 years; female 76.0 years.
Major causes of death per 100,000 population (2002): diseases of the circulatory system 270.5; malignant neoplasms (cancers) 165.0; communicable diseases 84.1; diabetes mellitus 70.0; accidents, poisonings, and violence 29.3.
Adult population (ages 15–49) *living with HIV* (2009) 1.4%[5] (world avg. 0.8%).

National economy

Budget (2008–09). Revenue[6]: Bds$2,622,000,000 (tax revenue 90.3%, of which taxes on goods and services 41.1%, taxes on income and profits 34.1%, taxes on international trade 8.4%; nontax revenue 9.7%). Expenditures: Bds$3,580,000,000 (debt service 22.1%; general public service 19.2%; education 14.6%; health 12.5%; economic services 12.2%; defense/public order 1.6%).
Public debt (December 2008): U.S.$3,002,000,000.
Production (metric tons except as noted). Agriculture, forestry, fishing (2009): sugarcane 320,000, sweet potatoes 2,400, coconuts (2008) 2,100, string beans 1,200, cucumbers and gherkins 1,200, yams 1,100, chilies and green peppers 800, okra (2008) 650; livestock (number of live animals) 20,000 pigs, 11,500 sheep, 3,600,000 chickens; roundwood (2010) 11,000 cu m, of which fuelwood 46%; fisheries production 3,496 (from aquaculture, none). Mining and quarrying (2009): limestone 1,900,000, clay and shale 145,000. Manufacturing (2007): cement 294,184, raw sugar 34,700, rum (2005) 132,000 hectolitres, beer (2005) 87,000 hectolitres; other manufactures include industrial chemicals, electronic components, garments, and wooden furniture. Energy production (consumption): electricity (kW-hr; 2008) 1,011,000,000 (945,000,000); coal, none (none); crude petroleum (barrels; 2010) 270,000 ([2007] negligible); petroleum products (metric tons; 2007) 1,000 (367,000); natural gas (cu m; 2008) 28,300,000 (28,300,000).
Land use as % of total land area (2009): in temporary crops or left fallow 37.2%, in permanent crops 2.3%, in pasture 4.7%, forest area 4.0%.
Population economically active (2008): total 143,800; activity rate of total population 52.2% (participation rates: ages 15 and over, 67.6%; female 48.7%; unemployed [2010] 10.8%).

Price index (2005 = 100)

	2004	2005	2006	2007	2008	2009	2010
Consumer price index	94.3	100.0	107.3	111.6	120.7	125.1	132.4

Gross national income (2009): U.S.$3,438,000,000 (U.S.$13,438 per capita).

Structure of gross domestic product and labour force

	2008			
	in value Bds$'000,000	% of total value	labour force	% of labour force
Agriculture, fishing	161.4	2.3	3,700	2.6
Mining and quarrying	56.0	0.8	[7]	[7]
Manufacturing	384.7	5.4	6,700	4.7
Construction	365.8	5.2	13,600[7]	9.5[7]
Public utilities	214.4	3.0	1,600	1.1
Transp. and commun.	356.3	5.0	5,800	4.0
Trade, tourism	1,720.3	24.3	33,000	22.9
Finance, real estate[8]	1,079.8	15.2	10,600	7.4
Pub. admin., defense	971.2	13.7	26,600	18.5
Services	366.0	5.2	30,100	20.9
Other	1,406.2[9]	19.9[9]	12,100	8.4
TOTAL	7,082.1	100.0	143,800	100.0

Household income and expenditure. Average household size (2004) 2.8; income per household: n.a.; expenditure (2001): food 33.8%, medical and personal care 17.0%, housing 12.3%, household furnishings and operations 10.1%, education and recreation 7.4%, energy 6.3%.
Selected balance of payments data. Receipts from (U.S.$'000,000): tourism (2009) 1,068; remittances (2010) 161; foreign direct investment (FDI; 2007–09 avg.) 305; official development assistance (2009) 12. Disbursements for (U.S.$'000,000): tourism (2009) 71; remittances (2008) 40; FDI (2007–09 avg.) 69.

Foreign trade[10]

Balance of trade (current prices)

	2005	2006	2007	2008	2009	2010
U.S.$'000,000	–1,311	–1,187	–985	–1,290	–1,018	–883
% of total	64.5%	57.4%	61.0%	58.7%	61.2%	58.4%

Imports (2009): U.S.$1,341,000,000 (machinery and apparatus 16.7%; food 15.8%; chemicals and chemical products 13.2%; refined petroleum 11.9%; road vehicles 4.7%). *Major import sources:* U.S. 39.7%; Trin./Tob. 15.8%; U.K. 5.0%; China 4.0%; Canada 3.8%.
Exports (2009): U.S.$323,000,000 (food 14.8%, of which raw sugar 5.6%; medicines 12.0%; rum 9.0%; machinery and apparatus 7.2%; gold/silver jewelry 4.5%; wristwatches 4.2%; perfumery/cosmetics 4.0%). *Major export destinations:* U.S. 27.9%; U.K. 10.2%; Trin./Tob. 10.0%; St. Lucia 7.8%; Jamaica 5.4%.

Transport and communications

Transport. Railroads: none. Roads (2006): total length 1,025 mi, 1,650 km (paved virtually 100%). Vehicles (2007): passenger cars 103,535; trucks and buses 15,782. Air transport: passenger-km, n.a.; (2003) metric ton-km cargo 200,000.

Communications

Medium	date	number in '000s	units per 1,000 persons	Medium	date	number in '000s	units per 1,000 persons
Televisions	2004	78	291	PCs	2005	40	148
Telephones				Dailies	2009	48[11]	209[11]
Cellular	2010	350[12]	1,281[12]	Internet users	2007	280	997
Landline	2010	138	503	Broadband	2010	56[12]	206[12]

Education and health

Educational attainment (2003). Percentage of employed labour force[13] having: no formal schooling 0.5%; primary education 14.9%; secondary 58.7%; technical/vocational 5.4%; university 19.6%; other/unknown 0.9%. *Literacy* (2008): total population age 15 and over literate 99.7%.

Education (2008–09)

	teachers	students	student/ teacher ratio	enrollment rate (%)
Primary (age 5–10)	1,607	22,727	14.1	...
Secondary/Voc. (age 11–15)	1,430[14]	19,928	14.6[14]	...
Tertiary	786[15]	14,324	14.5[15]	... (age 16–20)

Health: physicians (2003) 369 (1 per 751 persons); hospital beds (2007) 630 (1 per 446 persons); infant mortality rate per 1,000 live births (2008) 18.3; undernourished population (2005–07) less than 5.0% of total population.

Military

Total active duty personnel (November 2010): 610 (army 82.0%, navy 18.0%). *Military expenditure as percentage of GDP* (2009): 0.9%; per capita expenditure U.S.$118.

[1]Parishes and city (urban area) of Bridgetown have no local administrative function. [2]Includes most of the city (urban area) of Bridgetown. [3]Detail does not add to total given because of rounding. [4]Official projection based on adjusted total (268,792) of 2000 census. [5]Statistically derived midpoint within range. [6]Current revenue only. [7]Construction includes Mining and quarrying. [8]Offshore banking and information services are important sources of revenue. [9]Net indirect taxes. [10]Imports c.i.f.; exports f.o.b. [11]Circulation. [12]Subscribers. [13]Represents about 129,300 people. [14]2005–06. [15]2006–07.

Internet resources for further information:

- **Central Bank of Barbados http://www.centralbank.org.bb**
- **Barbados Statistical Service http://www.barstats.gov.bb**

Belarus

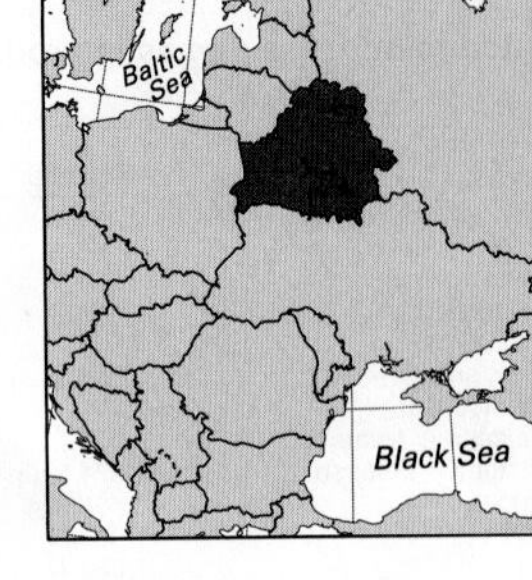

Official name: Respublika Belarus (Republic of Belarus).
Form of government: republic with two legislative bodies (Council of the Republic [64[1]]; House of Representatives [110]).
Head of state and government: President assisted by Prime Minister.
Capital: Minsk.
Official languages: Belarusian; Russian.
Official religion: none[2].
Monetary unit: Belarusian rubel (or ruble; Br); valuation (Sept. 1, 2011) 1 U.S.$ = Br 5,131; 1 £ = Br 8,291.

Area and population

		area		population
Provinces	**Capitals**	sq mi	sq km	2011[3] estimate
Brest	Brest	12,500	32,300	1,394,668
Homyel (Gomel)	Homyel	15,600	40,400	1,434,974
Hrodna (Grodno)	Hrodna	9,650	25,000	1,066,010
Mahilyow (Mogilev)	Mahilyow	11,200	29,000	1,088,093
Minsk (Myensk)	Minsk	14,800	38,300	1,411,528
Vitsyebsk (Vitebsk)	Vitsyebsk	15,500	40,100	1,221,830
City				
Minsk (Myensk)	—	950	2,500	1,864,090
TOTAL		80,200[4]	207,600[4]	9,481,193

Demography

Population (2011): 9,472,000.
Density (2011): persons per sq mi 118.1, persons per sq km 45.6.
Urban-rural (2011): urban 75.1%; rural 24.9%.
Sex distribution (2009): male 46.51%; female 53.49%.
Age breakdown (2009): under 15, 14.3%; 15–29, 23.2%; 30–44, 21.3%; 45–59, 22.3%; 60–74, 12.4%; 75–84, 5.4%; 85 and over, 1.1%.
Population projection: (2020) 9,193,000; (2030) 8,798,241.
Ethnic composition (2009): Belarusian 83.7%; Russian 8.3%; Polish 3.1%; Ukrainian 1.7%; Jewish 0.1%; other 3.1%.
Religious affiliation (2007): nonreligious/atheist *c.* 50%; Belarusian Orthodox *c.* 40%; Roman Catholic *c.* 7%; other Christian *c.* 1%; Jewish *c.* 0.6%; other *c.* 1.4%.
Major cities (2011[3]): Minsk 1,864,090; Homyel 491,790; Mahilyow 360,918; Vitsyebsk 354,566; Hrodna 338,287; Brest 315,824.

Vital statistics

Birth rate per 1,000 population (2010): 11.4 (world avg. 19.2); within marriage (2008) 79.9%; outside marriage (2008) 20.1%.
Death rate per 1,000 population (2010): 14.5 (world avg. 8.2).
Natural increase rate per 1,000 population (2010): –3.1 (world avg. 11.0).
Total fertility rate (avg. births per childbearing woman; 2008): 1.42.
Marriage/divorce rates per 1,000 population (2010): 8.2/3.9.
Life expectancy at birth (2008): male 64.7 years; female 76.5 years.
Major causes of death per 100,000 population (2007): diseases of the circulatory system 731.9; malignant neoplasms (cancers) 186.7; accidents, poisoning, and noxious substances 84.4; diseases of the respiratory system 48.7.

National economy

Budget (2009). Revenue: Br 67,495,000,000 (taxes on goods and services 30.8%, taxes on income and profits 16.6%, other taxes 25.0%, social security contributions 21.5%, nontax revenue 6.1%). Expenditures: Br 63,222,000,000 (economic affairs 26.4%, social protection 25.6%, education 11.6%, health 8.5%, public order 3.9%, defense 2.2%).
Public debt (external, outstanding; 2009): U.S.$4,758,000,000.
Household income and expenditure (2004)[5]. Average household size 2.6; average annual income per household Br 6,520,956 (U.S.$3,019); sources of income (2009): wages and salaries 56.4%, transfers 18.7%, property income 2.6%, other 22.3%; expenditure: food and nonalcoholic beverages 46.1%, housing and energy 11.0%, clothing and footwear 10.0%, recreation and culture 7.3%, health 5.2%.
Population economically active (2010): 4,693,000; activity rate of total population 49.5% (participation rates: ages 15–64, 77.3%; female [1999] 52.8%; officially/unofficially unemployed [2010] 0.7%/*c.* 15–20%).

Price and earnings indexes (2005 = 100)

	2004	2005	2006	2007	2008	2009	2010
Consumer price index	90.7	100.0	107.0	115.9	133.1	150.3	161.8
Monthly earnings index[6]	77.3	100.0	118.5	141.2	…	140.7	162.6

Production (metric tons except as noted). Agriculture, forestry, fishing (2009): potatoes 7,124,980, cow's milk 6,549,100, sugar beets 3,972,990, barley 2,123,420, wheat 1,979,000, rye 1,226,750, rapeseed 610,968, apples 431,573, plums and sloes 80,914, sour cherries 54,686; livestock (number of live animals) 4,130,500 cattle, 3,704,000 pigs; roundwood (2010) 10,364,200 cu m, of which fuelwood 22%; fisheries production 5,050 (from aquaculture 82%). Mining and quarrying (2009): potash 2,485,000; peat 2,485,000. Manufacturing (2009): cement 4,350,000; fertilizers 3,390,000; crude steel 2,449,000; sausages 294,900; butter 116,800; beer 3,370,000 hectolitres; footwear 10,900,000 pairs; refrigerators/freezers 1,007,000 units; tractors 45,300 units. Energy production (consumption): electricity (kW-hr; 2010) 34,700,000,000 ([2007] 36,173,000,000); coal (metric tons; 2007) none (83,000); crude petroleum (barrels; 2009) 12,500,000 ([2007] 156,605,000); petroleum products (metric tons; 2009) 21,634,000 ([2007] 5,689,000); natural gas (cu m; 2009) 205,000,000 ([2007] 20,687,000,000).
Gross national income (GNI; 2010): U.S.$58,169,000,000 (U.S.$6,030 per capita); purchasing power parity GNI (U.S.$14,020 per capita).

Structure of gross domestic product and labour force

	2009			
	in value Br '000,000,000	% of total value	labour force	% of labour force
Agriculture, forestry	11,265	8.2	430,000	9.2
Mining, Manufacturing	34,600	25.3	1,211,000	26.0
Construction	14,654	10.7	416,000	8.9
Transp. and commun.	12,263	9.0	351,000	7.5
Trade, hotels	14,673	10.7	2,213,000 (Trade, hotels; Finance; Public admin., defense; Services)	47.5
Finance, Public admin., defense, Services	30,036	22.0		
Other	19,299[7]	14.1[7]	42,000[8]	0.9[8]
TOTAL	136,790	100.0	4,663,000	100.0

Land use as % of total land area (2009): in temporary crops or left fallow 26.7%, in permanent crops 0.6%, in pasture 16.1%, forest area 42.4%.
Selected balance of payments data. Receipts from (U.S.$'000,000): tourism (2009) 369; remittances (2010) 375; foreign direct investment (2008–10 avg.) 1,805; official development assistance (2009) 98. Disbursements for (U.S.$'000,000): tourism (2009) 588; remittances (2009) 112.

Foreign trade[9]

Balance of trade (current prices)

	2004	2005	2006	2007	2008	2009
U.S.$'000,000	–2,593	–721	–2,585	–4,418	–6,581	–7,282
% of total	8.6%	2.2%	6.1%	8.3%	9.1%	14.6%

Imports (2009): U.S.$28,564,000,000 (crude petroleum 24.7%; nonelectrical machinery 10.8%; chemicals and chemical products 9.8%; natural gas 9.1%; food 6.2%; iron and steel 4.5%). *Major import sources:* Russia 58.5%; Germany 7.8%; Ukraine 4.5%; China 3.8%; Poland 2.8%.
Exports (2009): U.S.$21,282,000,000 (refined petroleum 32.9%; food 10.0%, of which dairy products 4.7%; potassium chloride 6.4%; road vehicles/parts 4.0%; iron and steel 3.9%; agricultural machinery/tractors 3.9%). *Major export destinations:* Russia 31.5%; Neth. 17.3%; Ukraine 8.0%; Latvia 7.8%; Germany 4.6%.

Transport and communications

Transport. Railroads (2008): route length 5,538 km; passenger-km 8,188,000,000; metric ton-km cargo 48,994,000,000. Roads (2005): total length 58,904 mi, 94,797 km (paved 89%); passenger-km (2008) 8,104,000,000[10]; metric ton-km cargo (2008) 24,231,000,000. Vehicles (2007): passenger cars 2,329,243; trucks and buses 409,191. Air transport (2008): passenger-km 1,280,000,000; metric ton-km cargo 55,000,000.

Communications

Medium	date	number in '000s	units per 1,000 persons	Medium	date	number in '000s	units per 1,000 persons
Televisions	2003	3,809	386	PCs	2007	78	80
Telephones				Dailies	2009	1,796[11]	119[11]
Cellular	2010	10,333[12]	1,077[12]	Internet users	2009	4,437	460
Landline	2010	4,139	431	Broadband	2010	1,666[12]	174[12]

Education and health

Education (2009–10)

	teachers	students	student/ teacher ratio	enrollment rate (%)
Primary (age 6–9)	23,907	358,055	15.0	94[13]
Secondary/Voc. (age 10–16)	101,663[14]	654,216	8.1[14]	87[14]
Tertiary[15]	42,728	586,434	13.7	77 (age 17–21)

Educational attainment (2009). Percentage of population age 15 and over having: incomplete/complete primary education 15.8%; secondary/vocational 61.7%; higher 18.9%; unknown 3.6%. *Literacy* (2007): total population age 15 and over literate 99.7%.
Health (2010): physicians 50,400 (1 per 189 persons); hospital beds 106,500 (1 per 89 persons); infant mortality rate per 1,000 live births 4.0; undernourished population (2005–07) less than 5.0% of total population based on the consumption of a minimum daily requirement of 1,940 calories.

Military

Total active duty personnel (November 2010): 72,940 (army 40.6%, air force and air defense 24.9%, centrally controlled units 34.5%); paramilitary 110,000. *Military expenditure as percentage of GDP* (2008): 1.1%; per capita expenditure U.S.$70.

[1]Statutory number. [2]However, a 2003 concordat grants the Belarusian Orthodox Church privileged status. [3]January 1. [4]Rounded area figures; exact area figures are 80,153 sq mi (207,595 sq km). [5]Based on a sample survey of 4,831 households. [6]All calculations based on December only. [7]Taxes less subsidies. [8]Registered unemployed only. [9]Imports c.i.f.; exports f.o.b. [10]Buses only. [11]Circulation. [12]Subscribers. [13]2007–08. [14]2006–07. [15]2008–09.

Internet resource for further information:
- **Ministry of Statistics and Analysis**
http://www.belstat.gov.by/homep/en/main.html

Belgium

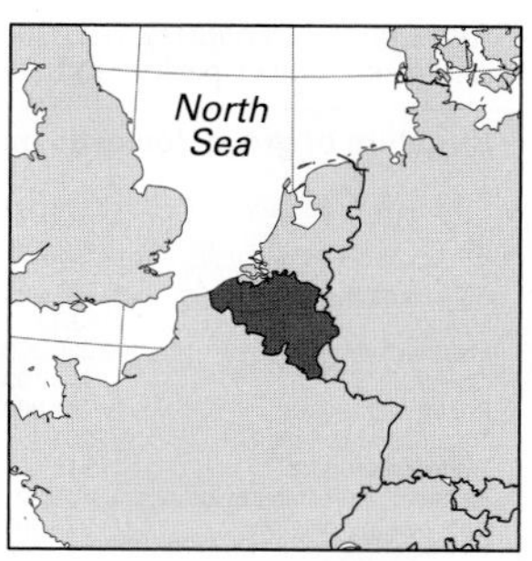

Official name: Koninkrijk België (Dutch); Royaume de Belgique (French); Königreich Belgien (German) (Kingdom of Belgium).
Form of government: federal constitutional monarchy with two legislative bodies (Senate [71[1]]; House of Representatives [150]).
Head of state: Monarch.
Head of government: Prime Minister.
Capital: Brussels.
Official languages: Dutch; French; German.
Official religion: none.
Monetary unit: euro (€); valuation (Sept. 1, 2011) 1 U.S.$ = €0.70; 1 £ = €1.13.

Area and population

Regions[2] Provinces	Capitals	area sq mi	area sq km	population 2010[3] estimate
Brussels[4]	Brussels	62	161	1,089,538
Flanders	Brussels[5]	5,221[6]	13,522[6]	6,251,983
Antwerp	Antwerp	1,107	2,867	1,744,862
East Flanders	Gent (Ghent)	1,151	2,982	1,432,326
Flemish Brabant	Leuven	813	2,106	1,076,924
Limburg	Hasselt	935	2,422	838,505
West Flanders	Brugge	1,214	3,144	1,159,366
Wallonia[7]	Namur[8]/Brussels[9]	6,504[6]	16,844[6]	3,498,384
Hainaut	Mons	1,462	3,786	1,309,880
Liège	Liège	1,491	3,862	1,067,685
Luxembourg	Arlon	1,714	4,440	269,023
Namur	Namur	1,415	3,666	472,281
Walloon Brabant	Wavre	421	1,091	379,515
TOTAL		11,787	30,528[6]	10,839,905

Demography

Population (2011): 10,971,000.
Density (2011): persons per sq mi 930.8, persons per sq km 359.4.
Urban-rural (2009): urban 97.4%; rural 2.6%.
Sex distribution (2008[3]): male 48.98%; female 51.02%.
Age breakdown (2008): under 15, 16.9%; 15–29, 18.5%; 30–44, 21.2%; 45–59, 20.8%; 60–74, 14.1%; 75–84, 6.5%; 85 and over, 2.0%.
Population projection: (2020) 11,639,000; (2030) 12,253,000.
National composition (2008[3]): Belgian 90.9%, of which Flemish-speaking 53.6%, French-speaking 36.4%, German-speaking 0.9%; Italian 1.6%; French 1.2%; Dutch 1.2%; Moroccan 0.7%; other 4.4%.
Religious affiliation (2010): Roman Catholic *c.* 60%; Muslim *c.* 4%; Protestant *c.* 2%; Jewish *c.* 1%; nonreligious *c.* 31%; other *c.* 2%.
Major cities/urban agglomerations (2010[3]): Brussels 157,673/1,883,447; Antwerp 483,505/970,801; Liège 192,504/648,895; Gent 243,366/432,408; Charleroi 202,598/407,292; Mons 91,759/234,298.

Vital statistics

Birth rate per 1,000 population (2010): 11.7 (world avg. 19.2); within marriage 53.0%; outside of marriage 47.0%.
Death rate per 1,000 population (2010): 9.6 (world avg. 8.2).
Total fertility rate (avg. births per childbearing woman; 2009): 1.84.
Marriage/divorce rates per 1,000 population (2010): 4.2/3.0.
Life expectancy at birth (2009): male 77.3 years; female 82.8 years.
Major causes of death per 100,000 population (2004): circulatory system diseases 338.8; malignant neoplasms 256.2; respiratory system diseases 107.6.

National economy

Budget (2009). Revenue: €161,024,000,000 (social security contributions 30.7%; personal income tax 23.2%; taxes on goods and services 22.7%). Expenditures: €181,448,000,000 (social insurance benefits 47.1%, of which health 13.1%; wages 24.0%; interest on debt 7.0%; capital expenditure 6.1%).
Public debt (December 2010): U.S.$431,360,000,000.
Production (metric tons except as noted). Agriculture, forestry, fishing (2009): sugar beets 5,186,180, potatoes 3,296,080, cow's milk 2,954,390, wheat 1,909,770, pork 1,028,100, chicory roots 474,423, apples 310,600, pears 280,600, leeks 164,500, mushrooms/truffles 42,208; livestock (number of live animals) 6,321,060 pigs, 2,600,450 cattle; roundwood (2010) 4,827,425 cu m, of which fuelwood 15%; fisheries production 22,298 (from aquaculture 3%). Mining and quarrying (2009): stone 340,000. Manufacturing (value added in €'000,000; 2009): chemicals and chemical products 8,435; base and fabricated metals 6,369; food/beverages/tobacco 6,178; nonelectrical machinery and equipment 2,882; transport equipment 2,721. Energy production (consumption): electricity (kW-hr; 2009) 90,780,000,000 ([2007] 84,884,000,000); coal (metric tons; 2008) none (6,530,000); crude petroleum (barrels; 2009) none (222,000,000); petroleum products (metric tons; 2007) 28,178,000 (15,841,000); natural gas (cu m; 2008) none ([2009] 16,877,000,000).
Household income and expenditure. Avg. household size (2005) 2.4; average net income per household (2003) €24,455 (U.S.$27,602); sources of disposable income (2008): wages and salaries 40.6%, transfers 27.7%, property 10.7%; expenditure (2006): housing and energy 22.8%, transportation 14.9%, food and nonalcoholic beverages 13.1%, recreation and culture 9.4%.
Land use as % of total land area (2009): in temporary crops 24.8%, left fallow 0.3%, in permanent crops 0.7%, in pasture 19.2%, forest area 22.4%.
Population economically active (2008): total 4,779,600; activity rate 44.6% (participation rates: ages 15–64, 67.1%; female 45.0%; unemployed [2010] 8.5%).

Price and earnings indexes (2005 = 100)

	2004	2005	2006	2007	2008	2009	2010
Consumer price index	97.5	100.0	101.8	103.6	108.3	108.2	110.6
Annual earnings index	97.6	100.0	102.3	104.0	106.9	109.7	110.9

Gross national income (GNI; 2010): U.S.$493,526,000,000 (U.S.$45,420 per capita); purchasing power parity GNI (U.S.$37,840 per capita).

Structure of gross domestic product and labour force

	2009		2008	
	in value €'000,000	% of total value	labour force	% of labour force
Agriculture	2,047	0.6	80,400	1.7
Mining	333	0.1	6,200	0.1
Manufacturing	42,494	12.5	727,500	15.2
Construction	16,358	4.8	321,800	6.7
Public utilities	6,684	2.0	40,400	0.8
Transp. and commun.	24,002	7.1	331,800	7.0
Trade, restaurants	41,782	12.3	712,900	14.9
Finance, real estate	92,666	27.3	593,600	12.4
Pub. admin., defense	23,192	6.8	436,900	9.2
Services	53,819	15.9	1,121,500	23.5
Other	35,796[10]	10.6[10]	406,500[11]	8.5[11]
TOTAL	339,162[6]	100.0	4,779,600[6]	100.0

Selected balance of payments data. Receipts from (U.S.$'000,000): tourism (2009) 9,967; remittances (2010) 10,068; foreign direct investment (FDI; 2008–10 avg.) 75,783. Disbursements for (U.S.$'000,000): tourism (2009) 19,673; remittances (2009) 4,278; FDI (2008–10 avg.) 60,127.

Foreign trade[12]

Balance of trade (current prices)

	2004	2005	2006	2007	2008	2009
U.S.$'000,000	+20,983	+13,976	+15,466	+17,451	+6,473	+18,169
% of total	3.5%	2.1%	2.1%	2.1%	0.7%	2.5%

Imports (2009): U.S.$351,781,000,000 (machinery and apparatus 13.2%, road vehicles/parts 10.2%, medicines 9.6%, petroleum 8.6%, food 7.3%, organic chemicals 6.8%, base and fabricated metals 6.1%). *Major import sources:* Neth. 17.9%; Germany 17.1%; France 11.7%; Ireland 6.3%; U.S. 5.8%.
Exports (2009): U.S.$369,950,000,000 (machinery and apparatus 11.6%, medicines 10.6%, road vehicles/parts 9.5%, food 8.3%, base and fabricated metals 7.5%, organic chemicals 6.5%, refined petroleum 4.7%, plastics [in primary form] 4.5%, diamonds 3.0%[13]). *Major export destinations:* Germany 19.6%; France 17.7%; Neth. 11.8%; U.K. 7.2%; U.S. 5.3%.

Transport and communications

Transport. Railroads (2007): route length 2,217 mi, 3,568 km; passenger-km 9,403,000,000; metric ton-km cargo 9,258,000,000. Roads (2006): total length 95,113 mi, 153,070 km (paved 78%); passenger-km 128,100,000,000[14]; metric ton-km cargo 38,356,000,000. Vehicles (2007): passenger cars 5,006,294; trucks and buses 725,697. Air transport (2008)[15]: passenger-km 7,567,000,000; metric ton-km cargo 1,167,000,000.

Communications

Medium	date	number in '000s	units per 1,000 persons	Medium	date	number in '000s	units per 1,000 persons
Televisions	2004	5,800	557	PCs	2006	3,977	377
Telephones				Dailies	2009	1,382[16]	128[16]
Cellular	2010	12,154[17]	1,135[17]	Internet users	2009	8,113	762
Landline	2010	4,640	433	Broadband	2010	3,373[17]	315[17]

Education and health

Educational attainment (2008). Percentage of population age 25 and over having: incomplete primary education 7.0%; complete primary 14.7%; secondary/vocational 50.9%; higher 27.4%.

Education (2007–08)

	teachers	students	student/ teacher ratio	enrollment rate (%)
Primary (age 6–11)	65,574	733,052	11.2	98
Secondary/Voc. (age 12–17)	81,873[18]	817,258	10.0[18]	87[18]
Tertiary	26,619	401,652	15.1	63 (age 18–22)

Health: physicians (2008[3]) 38,402 (1 per 278 persons); hospital beds (2008) 70,084 (1 per 153 persons); infant mortality rate (2010) 3.5.

Military

Total active duty personnel (November 2010): 37,882 (army 35.9%, navy 4.2%, air force 18.0%, medical service 5.0%, joint service 36.9%)[19]. *Military expenditure as percentage of GDP* (2008): 1.1%[20]; per capita expenditure U.S.$519[20].

[1]Excludes children of the monarch serving ex officio from age 18. [2]Belgium has a complex division of responsibilities between 3 administrative regions and 3 linguistic communities. [3]January 1. [4]Officially, Brussels Capital Region. [5]Dual capital of Flemish region and community. [6]Detail does not add to total given because of rounding. [7]The German community (within Wallonia [Jan. 1, 2008, pop. est. 74,169]) lacks expression as an administrative region. [8]Capital of Walloon Region. [9]Capital of French Community. [10]Taxes less subsidies. [11]Includes 333,700 unemployed. [12]Imports c.i.f.; exports f.o.b. [13]World's leading diamond-trading centre. [14]Passenger cars 110,000,000,000; buses 18,100,000,000. [15]Brussels Airlines, EAT, and TNT Airways only. [16]Circulation. [17]Subscribers. [18]2005–06. [19]Foreign forces at NATO headquarters (November 2010) U.S. 1,261. [20]Includes military pensions.

Internet resource for further information:
- **Statistics Belgium http://www.statbel.fgov.be**

Belize

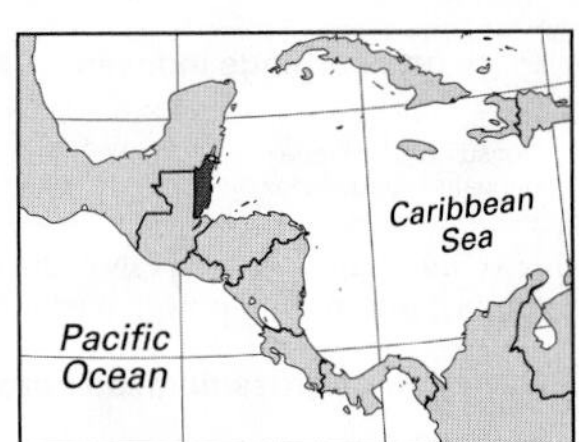

Official name: Belize.
Form of government: constitutional monarchy with two legislative houses (Senate [12[1, 2]]; House of Representatives [31[2]]).
Head of state: British Monarch represented by Governor-General.
Head of government: Prime Minister.
Capital: Belmopan.
Official language: English.
Official religion: none.
Monetary unit: Belize dollar (BZ$); valuation (Sept. 1, 2011) 1 U.S.$ = BZ$1.99; 1 £ = BZ$3.21.

Area and population

		area		population
				2010
Districts	Capitals	sq mi	sq km	census
Belize	Belize City	1,663	4,307	89,247
Cayo	San Ignacio/Santa Elena	2,006	5,196	72,899
Corozal	Corozal	718	1,860	40,354
Orange Walk	Orange Walk	1,790	4,636	45,419
Stann Creek	Dangriga	986	2,554	32,166
Toledo	Punta Gorda	1,704	4,413	30,538
TOTAL		8,867[3]	22,965[3, 4]	312,698[5]

Demography

Population (2011): 322,000.
Density (2011): persons per sq mi 36.3, persons per sq km 14.0.
Urban-rural (2008): urban 51.4%; rural 48.6%.
Sex distribution (2009): male 49.97%; female 50.03%.
Age breakdown (2009): under 15, 36.8%; 15–29, 26.6%; 30–44, 18.3%; 45–59, 11.1%; 60–74, 5.0%; 75–84, 1.6%; 85 and over, 0.6%.
Population projection: (2020) 380,000; (2030) 442,000.
Doubling time: 31 years.
Ethnic composition (2004): mestizo (Spanish-Indian) 48.4%; Creole (predominantly black) 27.0%; Mayan Indian 10.0%; Garifuna (black-Carib Indian) 5.7%; white 3.9%, of which Mennonite 3.2%; East Indian 3.0%; Chinese 0.9%; other 1.1%.
Religious affiliation (2000): Roman Catholic 49.6%; Protestant 31.8%, of which Pentecostal 7.4%, Anglican 5.3%, Seventh-day Adventist 5.2%, Mennonite 4.1%; other Christian 1.9%; nonreligious 9.4%; other 7.3%.
Major cities (2010): Belize City 53,532; San Ignacio/Santa Elena 16,977; Orange Walk 13,400; Belmopan 13,351; San Pedro (on Ambergris Caye) 11,500.

Vital statistics

Birth rate per 1,000 population (2007): 28.3 (world avg. 20.3).
Death rate per 1,000 population (2007): 5.7 (world avg. 8.5).
Natural increase rate per 1,000 population (2007): 22.6 (world avg. 11.8).
Total fertility rate (avg. births per childbearing woman; 2007): 3.52.
Marriage/divorce rates per 1,000 population (2003): 6.3/0.6.
Life expectancy at birth (2007): male 66.4 years; female 70.1 years.
Major causes of death per 100,000 population (2005): diseases of the circulatory system 108.3; malignant neoplasms (cancers) 56.9; accidents 49.7; infectious and parasitic diseases 44.2; diseases of the respiratory system 42.8; violence/poisoning 41.4.
Adult population (ages 15–49) *living with HIV* (2009): 2.3%[6] (world avg. 0.8%).

National economy

Budget (2010/11). Revenue: BZ$811,589,000 (tax revenue 86.7%, of which taxes on goods and services 33.7%, taxes on income and profits 30.5%, taxes on international trade 21.7%; nontax revenue 9.9%; grants 2.8%; other 0.6%). Expenditures: BZ$877,102,000 (current expenditure 82.3%; capital expenditure 17.7%).
Production (metric tons except as noted). Agriculture, forestry, fishing (2009): sugarcane 917,728, oranges 225,331, bananas 68,070, corn (maize) 45,041, grapefruit 40,796, concentrated orange juice (2008) 33,405, papayas 24,653, cashew nuts 1,080; livestock (number of live animals) 91,129 cattle, 1,500,000 chickens; roundwood 715,196 cu m, of which fuelwood 94%; fisheries production 14,642 (from aquaculture 66%). Mining and quarrying (2009): limestone 300,000; sand and gravel 200,000 cu m. Manufacturing (value added in U.S.$'000,000; 2008): food products and beverages (significantly citrus concentrate, flour, sugar, and beer) 62.4; textiles, clothing, and footwear 0.1; other (incl. crude petroleum extraction) 65.4. Energy production (consumption): electricity (kW-hr; 2007) 197,000,000 (445,000,000); coal, none (none); crude petroleum (barrels; 2009) 1,610,000 (n.a.); petroleum products (metric tons; 2007) none (139,000); natural gas, none (none).
Household income and expenditure. Average household size (2010) 3.9; average annual household income: n.a.; sources of income: n.a.; expenditure[7]: food, beverages, and tobacco 34.7%, transportation 17.0%, housing and energy 16.8%, clothing and footwear 9.2%.
Population economically active (2005): total 110,786; activity rate of total population 38.2% (participation rates: ages 15–64, 64.2%; female 36.7%; unemployed [2009] 13.1%).

Price index (2005 = 100)

	2004	2005	2006	2007	2008	2009	2010
Consumer price index	96.6	100.0	104.2	106.6	113.5	112.2	113.2

Gross national income (GNI; 2010): U.S.$1,288,000,000 (U.S.$3,740 per capita); purchasing power parity GNI (U.S.$5,970 per capita).

Structure of gross domestic product and labour force

	2008		2007	
	in value BZ$'000	% of total value	labour force	% of labour force
Agriculture, fishing, forestry	287,900	10.6	24,837	20.3
Mining	13,500[8]	0.5[8]	507	0.4
Manufacturing	339,200[9]	12.5[9]	8,367	6.8
Construction	124,100	4.6	6,769	5.5
Public utilities	61,000	2.2	1,047	0.9
Transp. and commun.	283,400	10.4	3,996	3.3
Trade, restaurants	518,100	19.1	36,143	29.6
Finance, real estate, insurance	402,200	14.8	3,672	3.0
Pub. admin., defense	277,600	10.2	10,562	8.6
Services	177,000	6.5	15,246	12.5
Other	233,400[10]	8.6[10]	11,112[11]	9.1[11]
TOTAL	2,717,400	100.0	122,258	100.0

Public debt (external, outstanding; November 2010): U.S.$1,009,000,000[12].
Selected balance of payments data. Receipts from (U.S.$'000,000): tourism (2009) 256; remittances (2010) 88; foreign direct investment (2008–10 avg.) 125; official development assistance (2009) 28. Disbursements for (U.S.$'000,-000): tourism (2009) 43; remittances (2009) 23.
Land use as % of total land area (2007): in temporary crops or left fallow 3.1%, in permanent crops 1.4%, in pasture 2.2%, forest area 72.5%.

Foreign trade[13]

Balance of trade (current prices)

	2004	2005	2006	2007	2008	2009
U.S.$'000,000	–303.0	–231.1	–385.9	–417.7	–541.4	–417.6
% of total	41.8%	32.4%	41.3%	43.9%	52.0%	45.5%

Imports (2009): U.S.$668,200,000 (machinery and transport equipment 20.0%, mineral fuels [mostly refined petroleum] 15.7%, manufactured goods 13.3%, food products 11.7%, chemicals and chemical products 9.4%). *Major import sources:* U.S. 34.7%; Netherlands Antilles 10.7%; Mexico 10.2%; China 9.2%; Panama 5.8%.
Exports (2009): U.S.$250,600,000 (crude petroleum 24.1%, raw cane sugar 17.8%, orange concentrate 16.9%, bananas 13.3%, shrimp 5.4%, papayas 4.4%, lobster 2.6%). *Major export destinations:* U.S. 32.4%; U.K. 31.7%; other Central American countries 18.4%; Caricom 5.4%.

Transport and communications

Transport. Railroads: none. Roads (2006): total length 1,868 mi, 3,007 km (paved 19%). Vehicles (2003): passenger cars 36,952; trucks and buses 7,380. Air transport (2001)[14]: passenger arrivals 256,564, passenger departures 240,900; cargo loaded 186 metric tons, cargo unloaded 1,272 metric tons.

Communications

Medium	date	number in '000s	units per 1,000 persons	Medium	date	number in '000s	units per 1,000 persons
Televisions	2003	52	190	PCs	2002	35	132
Telephones				Dailies	2007	0[15]	0[15]
Cellular	2010	194[16]	623[16]	Internet users	2009	36	117
Landline	2010	30	97	Broadband	2010	8.9[16]	29[16]

Education and health

Educational attainment (2005). Percentage of population age 25 and over having: no formal schooling 6.2%; incomplete primary education 25.1%; complete primary 42.9%; secondary 13.6%; higher 10.9%; other/unknown 1.3%.
Literacy (2003): total population age 15 and over literate 76.9%; males 77.1%; females 76.7%.

Education (2008–09)

	teachers	students	student/ teacher ratio	enrollment rate (%)
Primary (age 5–10)	2,325	52,629	22.6	97
Secondary/Voc. (age 11–16)	1,895	31,721	16.7	65
Tertiary	97[17]	3,581	7.4[17]	11 (age 17–21)

Health: physicians (2006) 263 (1 per 1,140 persons); hospital beds (2005) 436 (1 per 665 persons); infant mortality rate per 1,000 live births (2007) 21.2; undernourished population (2004–06) less than 5.0% of total population based on the consumption of a minimum daily requirement of 1,750 calories.

Military

Total active duty personnel (November 2010): 1,050 (army 100%)[18]. *Military expenditure as percentage of GDP* (2007): 1.4%; per capita expenditure U.S.$58.

[1]All seats nonelected. [2]Excludes speaker, who may be designated from outside either legislative house. [3]Includes offshore cays totaling 266 sq mi (689 sq km). [4]Detail does not add to total given because of rounding. [5]Includes 2,075 homeless and institutionalized population. [6]Statistically derived midpoint within range. [7]Weights of consumer price index published by central bank in 2008. [8]Excludes crude petroleum extraction. [9]Includes crude petroleum extraction. [10]Taxes less subsidies on products and less financial services indirectly measured. [11]Includes 689 not adequately defined and 10,423 unemployed. [12]Includes short-term debt. [13]Imports c.i.f.; exports f.o.b. [14]Belize international airport only. [15]Circulation; the only daily newspaper is online only. [16]Subscribers. [17]2003–04. [18]Foreign forces (2010): British army 30.

Internet resources for further information:
- **Central Bank of Belize http://www.centralbank.org.bz**
- **Statistical Institute of Belize http://statisticsbelize.org.bz**

Benin

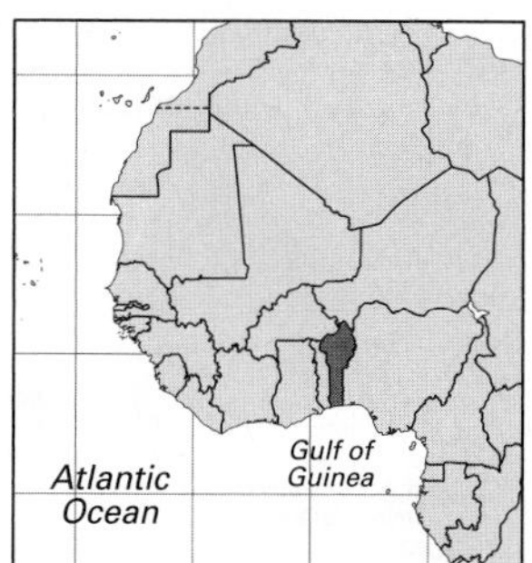

Official name: République du Bénin (Republic of Benin).
Form of government: multiparty republic with one legislative house (National Assembly [83]).
Head of state and government: President, assisted by Prime Minister[1].
Capital: Porto-Novo.[2]
Official language: French.
Official religion: none.
Monetary unit: CFA franc (CFAF); valuation (Sept. 1, 2011) 1 U.S.$ = CFAF 460.31; 1 £ = CFAF 743.83.

Area and population

		area		population
Departments	Capitals	sq mi	sq km	2007 estimate
Alibori	Kandi	10,132	26,242	612,605
Atakora	Natitingou	7,915	20,499	645,903
Atlantique	Ouidah	1,248	3,233	942,471
Borgou	Parakou	9,983	25,856	851,346
Collines	Savalou	5,379	13,931	630,039
Couffo	Dogbo	928	2,404	616,711
Donga	Djougou	4,296	11,126	411,538
Littoral	Cotonou	31	79	781,902
Mono	Lokossa	620	1,605	423,265
Ouémé	Porto-Novo	495	1,281	859,107
Plateau	Sakété	1,260	3,264	478,612
Zou	Abomey	2,024	5,243	705,315
TOTAL		44,310[3]	114,763	7,958,813[3]

Demography

Population (2011): 9,100,000.
Density (2011): persons per sq mi 205.4, persons per sq km 79.3.
Urban-rural (2009): urban 41.6%; rural 58.4%.
Sex distribution (2010): male 49.31%; female 50.69%.
Age breakdown (2008): under 15, 45.5%; 15–29, 27.3%; 30–44, 15.7%; 45–59, 7.4%; 60–74, 3.4%; 75–84, 0.6%; 85 and over, 0.1%.
Population projection: (2020) 11,523,000; (2030) 14,630,000.
Doubling time: 23 years.
Ethnic composition (2002)[4]: Fon 39.2%; Adjara 15.2%; Yoruba (Nago) 12.3%; Bariba 9.2%; Fulani 7.0%; Somba (Otomary) 6.1%; Yoa-Lokpa 4.0%; other 7.0%.
Religious affiliation (2002): Christian 42.8%, of which Roman Catholic 27.1%, Protestant 5.4%, indigenous Christian 5.3%; Muslim 24.4%; traditional beliefs 23.3%, of which voodoo 17.3%; nonreligious 6.5%; other 3.0%.
Major urban localities (2006): Cotonou (2009) 815,041; Porto-Novo (2009) 276,993; Godomey 187,836; Parakou 178,304; Abomey-Calavi 75,226; Bohicon 74,070.

Vital statistics

Birth rate per 1,000 population (2009): 39.0 (world avg. 20.3).
Death rate per 1,000 population (2009): 8.9 (world avg. 8.5).
Natural increase rate per 1,000 population (2009): 30.1 (world avg. 11.8).
Total fertility rate (avg. births per childbearing woman; 2009): 5.40.
Marriage rate per 1,000 population (2002): n.a.[5]
Life expectancy at birth (2008): male 57.4 years; female 59.8 years.
Adult population (ages 15–49) *living with HIV* (2009): 1.2% (world avg. 0.8%).

National economy

Budget (2009). Revenue: CFAF 672,800,000,000 (tax revenue 74.4%, of which taxes on international trade 38.5%; grants 14.4%; nontax revenue 11.2%). Expenditures: CFAF 805,400,000,000 (current expenditure 60.9%; development expenditure 37.5%; net lending 1.6%).
Public debt (external, outstanding; 2009): U.S.$990,000,000.
Gross national income (GNI; 2010): U.S.$6,945,000,000 (U.S.$750 per capita); purchasing power parity GNI (U.S.$1,510 per capita).

Structure of gross domestic product and labour force

	2009		2002	
	in value CFAF '000,000	% of total value	labour force[6]	% of labour force[6]
Agriculture, fishing	1,038,000	32.7	1,324,000	46.8
Mining	7,600	0.2	39,400	1.4
Public utilities	30,700	1.0	2,800	0.1
Manufacturing	225,500	7.1	253,100	8.9
Construction	139,000	4.4	70,300	2.5
Transp. and commun.	264,400	8.3	95,600	3.4
Trade, restaurants	544,200	17.1	815,400	28.8
Finance	338,100	10.7	2,800	0.1
Pub. admin., defense	322,000	10.1	205,300	7.2
Services	—	—		
Other	264,700[7]	8.3[7]	22,200	0.8
TOTAL	3,174,200	100.0[3]	2,830,900	100.0

Production (metric tons except as noted). Agriculture, forestry, fishing (2009): cassava 3,996,420, yams 2,370,860, corn (maize) 1,205,200, oil palm fruit 260,000, pineapples 222,223, tomatoes 159,034, cotton lint (2008) 125,300, sorghum 123,960, peanuts (groundnuts) 121,000, dry beans 115,944, cashews 49,487, okra 49,143, fonio (local grain) 947; livestock (number of live animals) 1,954,250 cattle, 1,580,000 goats, 16,000,000 chickens; roundwood (2010) 6,655,500 cu m, of which fuelwood 94%; fisheries production 39,328 (from aquaculture, negligible). Mining (2009): clay 77,000, gold 20 kg. Manufacturing (2009): cement 1,500,000; beer of barley 120,000; palm oil 44,000; cottonseed oil 16,500; soft drinks are also produced. Energy production (consumption): electricity (kW-hr; 2008) 130,000,000 (650,000,000)[8]; coal, none (none); crude petroleum, none (none); petroleum products (metric tons; 2007) none (1,011,000); natural gas, none (none).
Population economically active (2009)[9]: total 3,652,000; activity rate of total population 42.5% (participation rates: ages 15–64 [2008] 73.7%; female 40.7%; unemployed, n.a.).

Price index (2005 = 100)

	2004	2005	2006	2007	2008	2009	2010
Consumer price index	94.9	100.0	103.8	105.1	113.5	115.9	118.6

Household income and expenditure. Average household size (2002) 5.6; income per household: n.a.; sources of income: n.a.; expenditure (1996)[10]: food and nonalcoholic beverages 38.2%, transportation 10.1%, expenditures in cafés and hotels 9.8%, housing and energy 9.5%, clothing and footwear 6.9%.
Land use as % of total land area (2009): in temporary crops or left fallow (2007) 24.4%, in permanent crops 2.7%, in pasture 5.0%, forest area 41.7%.
Selected balance of payments data. Receipts from (U.S.$'000,000): tourism (2008) 236; remittances (2010) 236; foreign direct investment (2008–10 avg.) 139; official development assistance (2009) 683. Disbursements for (U.S.$'000,000): tourism (2008) 64; remittances (2008) 67.

Foreign trade[11, 12]

Balance of trade (current prices)

	2003	2004	2005	2006	2007	2008
U.S.$'000,000	–620.5	–595.5	–610.5	–778.7	–1,097.9	–1,276.1
% of total	53.3%	49.9%	51.4%	63.4%	52.1%	55.1%

Imports (2006): U.S.$1,003,300,000 (food products 24.9%, of which rice 11.1%, poultry cuts 4.4%; refined petroleum 15.3%; machinery and apparatus 7.0%; electricity 5.6%; fabrics 4.9%; used clothing 4.4%; road vehicles 4.3%; cement clinker 4.2%). *Major import sources:* France 17.2%; China 8.5%; Côte d'Ivoire 6.9%; Ghana 6.8%; U.K. 6.3%; Togo 5.3%.
Exports (2006): U.S.$224,600,000 (raw cotton 40.4%; cigarettes 15.6%; food products 13.6%, of which cashews 7.4%). *Major export destinations:* China 24.0%; Nigeria 8.7%; India 8.6%; Niger 7.2%; Côte d'Ivoire 5.7%.

Transport and communications

Transport. Railroads (2008): route length 578 km[13]; passenger-km (2005) 17,000,000; metric ton-km cargo (2006) 28,900,000. Roads (2004): total length 11,800 mi, 19,000 km (paved 9.5%). Vehicles (2007): passenger cars 149,310; trucks and buses 36,770. Air transport (2003): passenger-km, n.a.; metric ton-km cargo 7,000,000.

Communications

Medium	date	number in '000s	units per 1,000 persons	Medium	date	number in '000s	units per 1,000 persons
Televisions	2004	431	59	PCs	2007	58	7.0
Telephones				Dailies	2009	50[14]	10[14]
Cellular	2010	7,075[15]	799[15]	Internet users	2009	200	22
Landline	2010	133	15	Broadband	2010	26.1[15]	2.9[15]

Education and health

Educational attainment (2002). Percentage of population age 25 and over having: no formal schooling 69.6%; primary education 16.0%; secondary 12.2%; higher 2.2%. *Literacy* (2006): total percentage of population age 15 and over literate 34.7%; males literate 47.9%; females literate 23.3%.

Education (2008–09)

	teachers	students	student/teacher ratio	enrollment rate (%)
Primary (age 6–11)	38,321	1,719,390	44.9	95
Secondary/Voc. (age 12–18)	14,410[16]	435,449[17]	23.9[16]	...
Tertiary	...	42,603[18]	...	6[18] (age 19–23)

Health: physicians (2005) 334 (1 per 23,256 persons); hospital beds (2001) 590 (1 per 11,238 persons); infant mortality rate per 1,000 live births (2008) 66.2; undernourished population (2004–06) 1,600,000 (19% of total population based on the consumption of a minimum daily requirement of 1,730 calories).

Military

Total active duty personnel (November 2010): 4,750[19] (army 90.5%, navy 4.2%, air force 5.3%). *Military expenditure as percentage of GDP* (2009): 1.1%; per capita expenditure U.S.$9.

[1]Office of Prime Minister vacant from May 1998 was filled in May 2011; the post of prime minister is not required per the constitution. [2]Porto-Novo, the official capital established under the constitution, is the seat of the legislature, but the president and most government ministers reside in Cotonou. [3]Detail does not add to total given because of rounding. [4]Data combine principal and related ethnic groups. [5]In 2002, 27% of all marriages were polygamous. [6]Age 10 years and over. [7]Indirect taxes less subsidies and less imputed service charges. [8]Mostly imported from Ghana. [9]Estimates of ILO Employment Trends Unit. [10]Weights of consumer price index components. [11]Imports c.i.f.; exports f.o.b. [12]Excludes reexports (notably petroleum and food products particularly from Nigeria and Niger) valued at U.S.$473,000,000 in 2006. [13]Includes 140 km of railroad not in use. [14]Circulation. [15]Subscribers. [16]2003–04. [17]2004–05. [18]2005–06. [19]Of which UN peacekeepers 878.

Internet resources for further information:

- **Institut National de la Statistique et de l'Analyse Economique http://www.insae-bj.org**
- **La Banque de France: La Zone Franc http://www.banque-france.fr/fr/eurosys/zonefr/zonefr.htm**

Bermuda

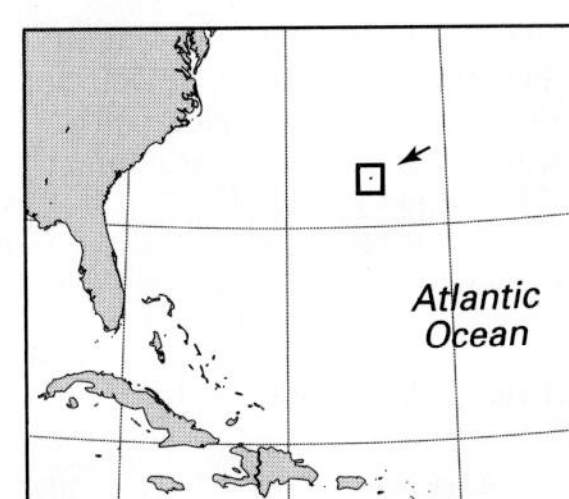

Official name: Bermuda.
Political status: overseas territory (United Kingdom) with two legislative houses (Senate [11[1]]; House of Assembly [36]).
Head of state: British Monarch, represented by Governor.
Head of government: Premier.
Capital: Hamilton.
Official language: English.
Official religion: none.
Monetary unit: Bermuda dollar (Bd$); valuation (Sept. 1, 2011) 1 U.S.$ = Bd$1.00[2]; 1 £ = Bd$1.62.

Area and population	area		population
			2000
Municipalities	sq mi	sq km	census
Hamilton	0.3	0.8	969
St. George	0.5	1.3	1,752
Parishes			
Devonshire	2.0	5.1	7,307
Hamilton	2.0	5.1	5,270
Paget	2.1	5.3	5,088
Pembroke[3]	1.8	4.6	10,337
St. George's[4]	3.5	8.0	3,699
Sandys	2.1	5.4	7,275
Smith's	1.8	4.7	5,658
Southampton	2.2	5.6	6,117
Warwick	2.0	5.1	8,587
TOTAL	20.5[5, 6]	53.1[5, 6]	62,059[7]

Demography

Population (2011): 65,300.
Density (2011): persons per sq mi 3,185, persons per sq km 1,230.
Urban-rural (2009): urban 100.0%; rural, none.
Sex distribution (2008): male 48.22%; female 51.78%.
Age breakdown (2008): under 15, 18.5%; 15–29, 18.0%; 30–44, 20.1%; 45–59, 24.1%; 60–74, 13.3%; 75–84, 4.5%; 85 and over, 1.5%.
Population projection: (2020) 66,300; (2030) 66,100.
Ethnic composition (2000): black 50.4%; British expatriates 29.0%; mixed black/white 10.0%; U.S. white 6.0%; Portuguese 4.5%; other 0.1%.
Religious affiliation (2000): Protestant 64.3%, of which Anglican 22.6%, Methodist 14.9%; Roman Catholic 14.9%; nonreligious 13.8%; other 6.0%; unknown 1.0%.
Major municipalities and settlements (2000): St. George 1,752; Hamilton 969; Tucker's Town, n.a.; Flatts Village, n.a.

Vital statistics

Birth rate per 1,000 population (2009): 12.7 (world avg. 20.3); within marriage (2002) 64.2%; outside of marriage (2002) 35.8%.
Death rate per 1,000 population (2009): 7.3 (world avg. 8.5).
Natural increase rate per 1,000 population (2009): 5.4 (world avg. 11.8).
Total fertility rate (avg. births per childbearing woman; 2010): 2.00.
Marriage/divorce rates per 1,000 population (2008): 11.2[8]/3.3.
Life expectancy at birth (2010): male 77.4 years; female 83.9 years.
Major causes of death per 100,000 population (2006): diseases of the circulatory system 240; malignant neoplasms (cancers) 145; diseases of the respiratory system 45; accidents, injuries, and poisonings 30.

National economy

Budget (2010–11). Revenue: Bd$977,200,000 (payroll taxes 40.9%, customs duties 23.8%, taxes on international companies 6.9%, taxes on land 5.1%, stamp duties 4.7%, other 18.6%). Expenditures: Bd$1,073,400,000 (general administration 28.6%, health 18.3%, education 13.1%, public order 8.8%, transport 7.6%, youth/families 6.6%, defense 0.8%).
Production (value in Bd$'000 except as noted). Agriculture, forestry, fishing (2009): vegetables (including cabbages, carrots, and potatoes) 4,232, milk 1,802, eggs 344, fruits 241, honey 183, flowers (particularly lilies) 180; livestock (number of live animals) 1,000 horses, 650 cattle, 50,000 chickens; roundwood, n.a.; fisheries production 387 (from aquaculture, none). Mining and quarrying: crushed stone for local use. Manufacturing (2008): industries include pharmaceuticals, paints, fish processing, handicrafts, and small boat building.[9] Energy production (consumption): electricity (kW-hr; 2007) 643,000,000 (643,000,000); coal, none (none); crude petroleum, none (none); petroleum products (metric tons; 2007) none (167,000); natural gas, none (none).
Household income and expenditure (2004). Average household size 2.3; average annual income per household Bd$106,233 (U.S.$106,233); sources of income: wages and salaries 65.1%, imputed income from owner occupancy 14.4%, self-employment 9.2%, net rental income 4.1%, other 7.2%; expenditure (2009): housing 33%, household furnishings 13%, food and nonalcoholic beverages 15%, transportation 9%, foreign travel 5%, health care 5%.
Population economically active (2000): total 37,879; activity rate of total population 61.0% (participation rates: ages 16–64, 84.8%; female 48.3%; unemployed [May 2009] 4.5%).

Price index (2005 = 100)	2004	2005	2006	2007	2008	2009	2010
Consumer price index	97.0	100.0	103.1	107.0	112.1	114.1	116.8

Gross national income (2009): U.S.$8,127,000,000 (U.S.$125,287 per capita).

Structure of gross domestic product and labour force	2009			
	in value Bd$'000,000	% of total value	labour force[10]	% of labour force[10]
Agriculture, fishing	45	0.8	710	1.8
Quarrying / Construction	317	5.5	3,488	8.8
Manufacturing	77	1.3	907	2.3
Public utilities	97	1.7	409	1.0
Transp. and commun.	282	4.9	2,471	6.3
Trade, restaurants	665	11.6	9,426	23.9
Finance, real estate[11]	2,066	36.2	7,584	19.2
International business[11]	1,490	26.1	4,431	11.2
Pub. admin., defense	337	5.9	4,318	10.9
Services	518	9.1	5,776	14.6
Other	−179[12]	−3.1[12]	—	—
TOTAL	5,715	100.0	39,520[13]	100.0

Public debt (March 2010): U.S.$1,047,000,000.
Selected balance of payments data. Receipts from (U.S.$'000,000): tourism (2009) 350; remittances, n.a.; foreign direct disinvestment (2008–10 avg.) –8. Disbursements for (U.S.$'000,000): tourism (2009) 407; remittances, n.a.; foreign direct investment (2008–10 avg.) 488.
Land use as % of total land area (2007): in temporary crops, left fallow, or in permanent crops (including land occupied by golf courses) *c.* 20%, forest area *c.* 20%.

Foreign trade

Balance of trade (current prices)	2004	2005	2006	2007	2008	2009
Bd$'000,000	−930	−936	−1,069	−1,066	−1,121	−1,022
% of total	93.0%	90.5%	95.5%	95.5%	95.6%	94.7%

Imports (2009): Bd$1,028,000,000 (machinery and apparatus 13.5%; food products 11.9%; refined petroleum 10.7%; chemicals and chemical products 7.0%; manufactures of metal 5.6%; printed matter 5.1%). *Major import sources:* U.S. 68.6%; Venezuela 8.7%; Canada 6.8%; U.K. 4.5%.
Exports (2008): Bd$29,000,000 (including sales of fuel to aircraft and ships and reexports of pharmaceuticals; also rum and flowers). *Major export destinations:* more than 80% to the EU.

Transport and communications

Transport. Railroads: none. Roads (2006): total length 140 mi, 225 km (paved 100%)[14]. Vehicles (2009): passenger cars 22,626; trucks and buses 4,802. Air transport: visitor arrivals (2010) 232,262.[15] Cruise-ship transport: visitor arrivals (2010) 347,931.

Communications Medium	date	number in '000s	units per 1,000 persons	Medium	date	number in '000s	units per 1,000 persons
Televisions	2001	68	1,077	PCs	2004	34	535
Telephones				Dailies	2009	16[16]	236[16]
Cellular	2010	88[17]	1,352[17]	Internet users	2009	54	833
Landline	2010	58	890	Broadband	2010	40[17]	618[17]

Education and health

Educational attainment (2000). Percentage of total population age 15 and over having: no formal schooling 0.4%; primary education 7.0%; secondary 39.3%; postsecondary technical 25.7%; higher 26.8%; not stated 0.8%. *Literacy* (2005): total population age 15 and over literate 98.5%.

Education (2009–10)	teachers	students	student/ teacher ratio	enrollment rate (%)
Primary (age 5–10)	608	4,473	7.4	74
Secondary/Voc. (age 11–17)	825	4,418	5.4	59
Tertiary[18]	83	1,366	16.5	32 (age 18–22)

Health: physicians (2009) 157 (1 per 432 persons); hospital beds (2008–09) 228 (1 per 297 persons); infant mortality rate per 1,000 live births (2007–09 avg.) 3.6; undernourished population (2004–06) 5,000 (8% of total population based on the consumption of a minimum daily requirement of 1,920 calories).

Military

Total active duty personnel (2009): 530; part-time defense force assists police and is drawn from Bermudian conscripts.

[1]All seats are appointed. [2]The Bermuda dollar is at par with the U.S. dollar. [3]Excludes the area and population of the city of Hamilton. [4]Excludes the area and population of the town of St. George. [5]Includes 0.4 sq mi (1.1 sq km) of uninhabited islands. [6]Detail does not add to total given because of rounding. [7]Excludes 8,335 short-term visitors, 901 institutionalized persons, and 39 transients. [8]Marriages between nonresidents constitute 60% of all marriages. [9]The economy of Bermuda is overwhelmingly based on service industries such as tourism, insurance companies, offshore financial centres, e-commerce companies, and ship repair facilities. [10]Employed only. [11]Bermuda is a major international financial centre, mainly due to its importance as an operating base for the international insurance and reinsurance industry. [12]Taxes less imputed bank service charges. [13]68% Bermudian, 32% non-Bermudian with work permits. [14]Excludes 138 mi (222 km) of paved private roads. [15]No airlines are headquartered in Bermuda. [16]Circulation. [17]Subscribers. [18]2008–09; many students attend universities abroad because Bermuda does not have a degree-conferring university, business school, or law school.

Internet resources for further information:

- **Bermuda Government, Department of Statistics http://www.statistics.gov.bm**
- **Bermuda Online: Economy http://bermuda-online.org/economy.htm**

Bhutan

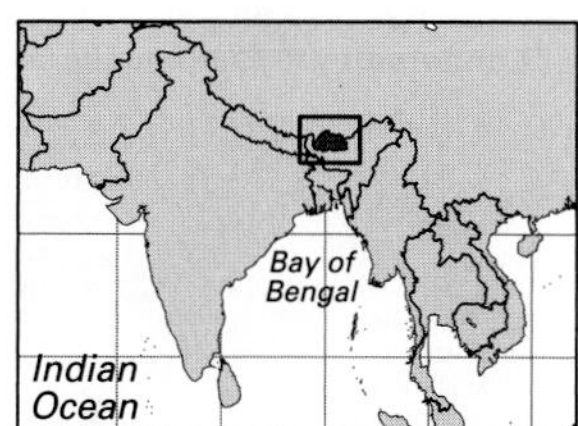

Official name: Druk-Yul (Kingdom of Bhutan).
Form of government: constitutional monarchy[1] with two legislative houses (National Council [25[2]]; National Assembly [47]).
Head of state: Monarch.
Head of government: Prime Minister.
Capital: Thimphu.
Official language: Dzongkha (a Tibetan dialect).
Official religion: [3].
Monetary unit: ngultrum[4] (Nu); valuation (Sept. 1, 2011) 1 U.S.$ = Nu 46.05; 1 £ = Nu 74.41.

Area and population

Districts	area sq km[5]	population 2005 census	Districts	area sq km[5]	population 2005 census
Bumthang	2,611	16,116	Sarpang (Geylegphug)	2,188	41,549
Chukha (Chhukha)	1,728	74,387	Thimphu	1,843	98,676
Dagana	1,344	18,222	Trashigang	2,188	51,134
Gasa	4,185	3,116	Trashiyangtse	1,382	17,740
Haa	1,651	11,648	Trongsa	1,728	13,419
Lhuentse (Lhuntse)	2,764	15,395	Tsirang (Chirang)	614	18,667
Mongar (Monggar)	1,881	37,069	Wangdue Phodrang	3,878	31,135
Paro	1,229	36,433	Zhemgang	2,035	18,636
Pemagatshel	499	13,864	unallocated population		37,443
Punakha	922	17,715	TOTAL	38,394	672,425[6]
Samdrup Jongkhar	2,227	39,961			
Samtse (Samchi)	1,497	60,100			

Demography

Population (2011): 701,000.
Density (2011): persons per sq mi 47.3, persons per sq km 18.3.
Urban-rural (2010): urban 34.7%; rural 65.3%.
Sex distribution (2008): male 52.50%; female 47.50%.
Age breakdown (2008): under 15, 30.9%; 15–29, 31.9%; 30–44, 18.6%; 45–59, 10.6%; 60–74, 6.3%; 75–84, 1.5%; 85 and over, 0.2%.
Population projection: (2020) 809,000; (2030) 887,000.
Doubling time: 54 years.
Ethnic composition (2005): Bhutia (Ngalops) *c.* 50%; Nepalese (Gurung) *c.* 35%; Sharchops *c.* 15%.
Religious affiliation (2005): Buddhist *c.* 74%; Hindu *c.* 25%; Christian *c.* 1%.
Major towns (2005): Thimphu 79,185; Phuntsholing 20,537; Gelaphu 9,199; Wangdue 6,714; Samdrup Jongkhar 5,952; Samtse 4,981.

Vital statistics

Birth rate per 1,000 population (2008): 20.6 (world avg. 20.3).
Death rate per 1,000 population (2008): 7.5 (world avg. 8.5).
Natural increase rate per 1,000 population (2008): 13.1 (world avg. 11.8).
Total fertility rate (avg. births per childbearing woman; 2008): 2.48.
Life expectancy at birth (2010): male 68.4 years; female 69.4 years.
Major causes of death per 100,000 population (2009)[7]: diseases of the digestive system 25.2, of which alcohol-related liver diseases 18.5; diseases of the respiratory system 15.0; neonatal deaths 10.7; diseases of the circulatory system 9.8.

National economy

Budget (2008–09). Revenue: Nu 20,624,000,000 (nontax revenue 36.7%, of which transfers of profits 16.5%, dividends 9.3%; grants 31.9%; tax revenue 31.4%, of which corporate income taxes 11.4%). Expenditures: Nu 20,891,000,000 (current expenditure 52.9%; capital expenditure 47.1%).
Public debt (external, outstanding; July 2009): U.S.$695,000,000[8].
Production (metric tons except as noted). Agriculture, forestry, fishing (2009): rice 66,393, corn (maize) 61,158, potatoes 48,513, oranges 30,000, dry chilies and peppers 10,448, nutmeg, mace, and cardamom 9,082, ginger 3,766, mustard seed 1,741; livestock (number of live animals) 326,017 cattle, (2008) 39,609 yaks, 26,000 horses; roundwood (2010) 5,040,068 cu m, of which fuelwood 95%; fisheries production 226 (from aquaculture 20%). Mining and quarrying (2009): dolomite 1,029,000; limestone 649,952; gypsum 299,700; ferrosilicon 36,600. Manufacturing (value of sales in Nu '000,000; 2009): cement 1,785; ferroalloys 1,712; chemical products 1,158; wood board products 414. Energy production (consumption): electricity (kW-hr; 2008/09) 6,960,000,000 (1,203,000,000); coal (metric tons; 2009) 48,500 ([2007] 101,000); crude petroleum, none (none); petroleum products (metric tons; 2007) none (73,000); natural gas, none (none).
Household income and expenditure. Average household size (2007) 5.0; income per household: n.a.[9]; sources of income: n.a.; expenditure (2007): food and beverages 31.6%, education 15.6%, housing/energy 14.6%, clothing and footwear 6.5%, transportation and communication 6.3%, food away from home 6.1%.
Population economically active (2010): total 331,900; activity rate of total population 45.9% (participation rates: ages 15–64, 71.6%; female 48.6%; officially unemployed 3.3%).

Price index (2005 = 100)

	2004	2005	2006	2007	2008	2009	2010
Consumer price index	95.0	100.0	105.0	110.4	119.6	124.8	133.6

Gross national income (GNI; 2010): U.S.$1,361,000,000 (U.S.$1,920 per capita); purchasing power parity GNI (U.S.$5,070 per capita).

Structure of gross domestic product and labour force

	2009 in value Nu '000,000	2009 % of total value	2010 labour force	2010 % of labour force
Agriculture, forestry	11,159	18.2	190,600	57.4
Mining	1,392	2.3	900	0.3
Manufacturing	5,017	8.2	12,400	3.7
Construction	7,470	12.2	2,700	0.8
Public utilities	11,816	19.3	5,200	1.6
Trade, restaurants	3,473	5.7	34,700	10.4
Transportation and communications	5,990	9.8	9,500	2.9
Finance and real estate	4,962	8.1	15,700	4.7
Pub. admin., defense	4,728	7.7	25,600	7.7
Services	3,511	5.7	22,500	6.8
Other	1,705[10]	2.8[10]	12,200[11]	3.7[11]
TOTAL	61,224[12]	100.0	331,900[12]	100.0

Land use as % of total land area (2009): in temporary crops or left fallow (2007) 3.3%, in permanent crops 0.8%, in pasture 3.9%, forest area 72.5%.
Selected balance of payments data. Receipts from (U.S.$'000,000): tourism (2009) 42; remittances (2009–10) 4.0; foreign direct investment (2008–10 avg.) 18; official development assistance (2009) 125. Disbursements for (U.S.$'000,000): tourism (2009) 39; remittances (2009–10) 28.

Foreign trade[13]

Balance of trade (current prices)

	2005	2006	2007	2008	2009
U.S.$'000,000	–128.6	…	…	–21.9	–33.6
% of total	19.9%	…	…	2.1%	3.3%

Imports (2009): U.S.$529,400,000 (machinery and apparatus 20.8%, refined petroleum 11.8%, food 11.6%, road vehicles 8.9%, iron and steel 8.1%). *Major import sources:* India 77.8%; Singapore 2.9%; Japan 2.2%; China 1.9%; Sweden 1.8%.
Exports (2009): U.S.$495,800,000 (electricity 42.1%, ferrosilicon 17.7%, portland cement 5.8%, vegetables/fruits 4.7%, copper wire 4.1%). *Major export destinations:* India 93.5%; Bangladesh 3.2%; Hong Kong 2.8%.

Transport and communications

Transport. Railroads: none. Roads (2009): total length 3,717 mi, 5,982 km (paved 45%). Vehicles (2009): passenger cars 29,189; trucks and buses 6,608. Air transport (2005): passenger-km 74,000,000; metric ton-km cargo 7,000,000[14].

Communications

Medium	date	number in '000s	units per 1,000 persons	Medium	date	number in '000s	units per 1,000 persons
Televisions	2004	25	33	PCs	2005	13	16
Telephones				Dailies	2009	18[15]	37[15]
Cellular	2010	394[16]	543[16]	Internet users	2009	50	72
Landline	2010	26	36	Broadband	2010	8.7[16]	12[16]

Education and health

Educational attainment (2005). Percentage of population age 25 and over having: no formal schooling 12.9%; incomplete/complete primary education 52.7%; incomplete/complete secondary 21.4%; higher vocational 4.1%; university 8.9%. *Literacy* (2007): total population age 6 and over literate 55.5%; males literate 65.7%; females literate 45.9%.

Education (2008–09)

	teachers	students	student/ teacher ratio	enrollment rate (%)
Primary (age 6–12)	3,929	108,842	27.7	87
Secondary/Voc. (age 13–18)	2,739	56,543	20.6	47
Tertiary	375[17]	5,051[18]	11.0[17]	7[18] (age 19–23)

Health (2009): physicians 176 (1 per 3,883 persons); hospital beds 1,186 (1 per 576 persons); infant mortality rate per 1,000 live births (2008) 51.9; undernourished population, n.a.

Military

Total active duty personnel (2009): about 8,000[19, 20]. *Military expenditure as percentage of GDP* (2005): *c.* 1.0%; per capita expenditure U.S.$11.

[1]Bhutan's first constitution was promulgated on July 18, 2008. [2]Includes 5 nonelected members. [3]Buddhism is the spiritual heritage of Bhutan per article 3.1 of the 2008 constitution. [4]Indian currency is also accepted legal tender; the ngultrum is at par with the Indian rupee. [5]Estimated district areas are derived from district area percentages of total national area as published in the *Statistical Yearbook of Bhutan* (2003). [6]Includes 634,972 residents and 37,453 temporary residents. [7]Hospital-diagnosed deaths only. [8]Includes private external debt. [9]Bhutan reports household consumption expenditure in lieu of income data; in 2007 average annual household consumption expenditure was Nu 165,876 (U.S.$4,012). [10]Taxes less subsidies. [11]Includes 11,000 unemployed and 1,200 in armed forces. [12]Detail does not add to total given because of rounding. [13]Imports c.i.f.; exports f.o.b. [14]Includes weight of passengers and mail. [15]Circulation of daily newspapers. [16]Subscribers. [17]2005–06. [18]2007–08. [19]Includes army, royal bodyguard, police, forest guards, and militia. [20]India maintains a permanent military training presence.

Internet resources for further information:
- **Royal Monetary Authority of Bhutan http://www.rma.org.bt**
- **National Statistics Bureau http://www.nsb.gov.bt**

Bolivia

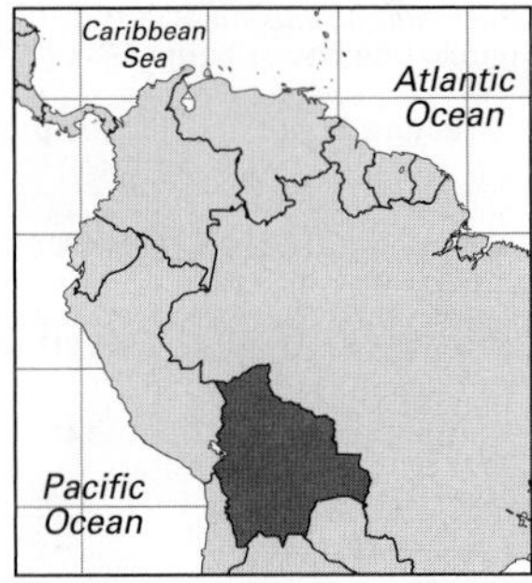

Official name: Estado Plurinacional de Bolivia (Plurinational State of Bolivia).
Form of government: unitary multiparty republic[1] with two legislative houses (Chamber of Senators [36]; Chamber of Deputies [130]).
Head of state and government: President.
Capitals: La Paz (administrative)[2]; Sucre (constitutional)[2, 3].
Official languages: Spanish and 36 indigenous languages[3].
Official religion: none[3].
Monetary unit: boliviano (Bs); valuation (Sept. 1, 2011) 1 U.S.$ = Bs 6.92; 1 £ = Bs 11.18.

Area and population

Departments	area sq km	population 2001 census	Departments	area sq km	population 2001 census
Beni	213,564	362,521	Pando	63,827	52,525
Chuquisaca	51,524	531,522	Potosí	118,218	709,013
Cochabamba	55,631	1,455,711	Santa Cruz	370,621	2,029,471
La Paz	133,985[4]	2,350,466	Tarija	37,623	391,226
Oruro	53,588	391,870	TOTAL	1,098,581	8,274,325

Demography

Population (2011): 10,088,000.
Density (2011): persons per sq mi 23.8, persons per sq km 9.2.
Urban-rural (2010): urban 66.4%; rural 33.6%.
Sex distribution (2010): male 49.89%; female 50.11%.
Age breakdown (2009): under 15, 36.3%; 15–29, 28.0%; 30–44, 18.3%; 45–59, 10.6%; 60–74, 5.3%; 75 and over, 1.5%.
Population projection: (2020) 11,591,000; (2030) 13,391,000.
Doubling time: 37 years.
Ethnic composition (2006): Amerindian *c.* 55%, of which Quechua *c.* 29%, Aymara *c.* 24%; mestizo *c.* 30%; white *c.* 15%.
Religious affiliation (2001): Roman Catholic *c.* 78%; Protestant/independent Christian *c.* 16%; other Christian *c.* 3%, of which Mormon 1.8%; nonreligious 2.5%; other 0.5%.
Major cities (2001): Santa Cruz 1,116,059 (urban agglomeration [2009] 1,584,000); La Paz 789,585 (urban agglomeration [2009] 1,642,000); El Alto 647,350[5]; Cochabamba 516,683; Oruro 201,230; Sucre 193,873.

Vital statistics

Birth rate per 1,000 population (2010): 26.1 (world avg. 19.2).
Death rate per 1,000 population (2010): 7.3 (world avg. 8.2).
Natural increase rate per 1,000 population (2010): 18.8 (world avg. 11.0).
Total fertility rate (avg. births per childbearing woman; 2010): 3.29.
Marriage/divorce rates per 1,000 population (2006): 2.2/n.a.
Life expectancy at birth (2010): male 64.2 years; female 68.5 years.
Major causes of death per 100,000 population (2002): malignant neoplasms (cancers) 145.6; infectious and parasitic diseases 140.6; cardiovascular diseases 129.8; respiratory infections 78.2; accidents 63.9.

National economy

Budget (2010). Revenue: Bs 41,803,000,000 (income taxes 50.3%, taxes on hydrocarbons 29.2%). Expenditures: Bs 42,160,000,000 (current expenditure 69.4%, capital expenditure 30.6%).
Production (metric tons except as noted). Agriculture, forestry, fishing (2009): sugarcane 7,437,700, soybeans 1,499,380, corn (maize) 813,586, potatoes 762,719, plantains 466,401, rice 395,651, beef 254,552, sunflower seeds 206,466, Brazil nuts 39,080, quinoa 28,276; livestock (number of live animals) 9,529,650 sheep, 8,079,580 cattle, 2,843,030 llamas, alpacas, vicuñas, and guanacos, 2,760,000 pigs; roundwood (2010) 3,238,950 cu m, of which fuelwood 72%; fisheries production 8,343 (from aquaculture 9%). Mining and quarrying (2009): zinc 430,879[6]; lead 84,537[6]; tin 19,581[6]; tungsten 1,023[6]; silver 1,325,700 kg[6]; gold 7,217 kg. Manufacturing (value added in Bs '000,000; 2009): beverages 1,914; bricks, cement, and ceramics 1,893; meat products 1,795; petroleum products 1,703; textiles, clothing, and leather products 1,084; flour and bakery products 1,038.[7] Energy production (consumption): electricity (kW-hr; 2007) 5,550,000,000 ([2009] 4,596,000,000); coal, none (none); crude petroleum (barrels; 2009) 13,102,000 (22,995,000); petroleum products (metric tons; 2007) 1,866,000 (2,310,000); natural gas (cu m; 2009) 12,788,000,000 ([2008] 2,407,000,000).
Household income and expenditure. Average household size (2004) 4.3; annual income per household (1999) Bs 16,980 (U.S.$2,920); expenditure (2000): food 28.6%, transportation and communications 23.1%, rent and energy 10.3%, expenditures in cafés and hotels 9.5%, recreation and culture 7.1%.
Population economically active (2007): total 4,927,400; activity rate of total population 49.8% (participation rates: ages 15–64 [2000] 71.8%; female 45.2%; registered unemployed [2009] 7.9%).

Price and earnings indexes (2005 = 100)

	2004	2005	2006	2007	2008	2009	2010
Consumer price index	94.9	100.0	104.3	113.4	129.2	133.6	136.9
Annual earnings index[8]	96.6	100.0	100.4	101.8	109.6	113.2	...

Gross national income (GNI; 2010): U.S.$17,982,000,000 (U.S.$1,790 per capita); purchasing power parity GNI (U.S.$4,560 per capita).

Structure of gross domestic product and labour force

	2009		2007	
	in value Bs '000,000	% of total value	labour force[9]	% of labour force[9]
Agriculture	13,575	11.2	1,686,700	34.2
Mining	9,664	7.9	72,400	1.5
Crude petroleum, nat. gas	6,115	5.0		
Manufacturing	14,141	11.6	514,900	10.5
Construction	3,028	2.5	316,300	6.4
Public utilities	2,631	2.2	15,400	0.3
Transp. and commun.	10,724	8.8	272,400	5.5
Trade, hotels	11,848	9.7	833,100	16.9
Finance, real estate	10,643	8.8	164,900	3.4
Pub. admin., defense	14,508	11.9	152,300	3.1
Services	5,239	4.3	641,900	13.0
Other	19,611[10]	16.1[10]	257,100	5.2
TOTAL	121,727	100.0	4,927,400	100.0

Public debt (external, outstanding; September 2010): U.S.$2,735,000,000.
Selected balance of payments data. Receipts from (U.S.$'000,000): tourism (2009) 279; remittances (2010) 1,088; foreign direct investment (2008–10 avg.) 519; official development assistance (2009) 726. Disbursements for (U.S.$'000,000): tourism (2009) 290; remittances (2009) 106.
Land use as % of total land area (2009): in temporary crops 2.4%, left fallow 0.8%, in permanent crops 0.2%, in pasture 30.5%, forest area 53.1%.

Foreign trade[11]

Balance of trade (current prices)

	2004	2005	2006	2007	2008	2009
U.S.$'000,000	+301.8	+457.1	+1,060.3	+1,003.6	+1,445.2	+483.1
% of total	7.6%	8.9%	15.9%	12.7%	12.5%	5.2%

Imports (2007): U.S.$3,522,000,000 (chemical products 17.2%; road vehicles 13.4%; specialized machinery 8.1%; food products 7.9%; refined petroleum 7.6%; iron and steel 7.3%). *Major import sources* (2009): Argentina 18.4%; Brazil 17.6%; U.S. 13.5%; China 8.4%; Peru 7.2%; Japan 7.0%.
Exports (2009): U.S.$4,917,500,000 (natural gas 36.1%; minerals 33.9%, of which zinc 12.6%, silver 11.2%, tin 4.3%, gold 2.1%; soybeans [all forms] 8.8%; petroleum 2.2%). *Major export destinations* (2009): Brazil 30.6%; U.S. 8.7%; Argentina 8.3%; Japan 5.6%; Colombia 5.4%.

Transport and communications

Transport. Railroads (2008): route length 3,504 km; (2004) passenger-km 286,000,000; (2004) metric ton-km cargo 1,058,000,000. Roads (2004): total length 38,823 mi, 62,479 km (paved 7%). Vehicles (2007): passenger cars 175,000; trucks and buses 475,759. Air transport (2007)[12]: passenger-km 287,000,000; metric ton-km cargo 9,000,000.

Communications

Medium	date	number in '000s	units per 1,000 persons	Medium	date	number in '000s	units per 1,000 persons
Televisions	2004	1,210	134	PCs	2006	224	24
Telephones				Dailies	2009	155[13]	16[13]
Cellular	2010	7,179[14]	723[14]	Internet users	2009	1,103	112
Landline	2010	848	85	Broadband	2010	96[14]	9.7[14]

Education and health

Educational attainment (2007). Percentage of population age 19 and over having: no formal schooling 10.7%; some to complete primary education 37.5%; some to complete secondary 27.2%; some to complete higher 24.4%; not specified 0.2%. *Literacy* (2007): total population age 15 and over literate 90.7%; males literate 96.0%; females literate 86.0%.

Education (2006–07)

	teachers	students	student/ teacher ratio	enrollment rate (%)
Primary (age 6–11)	62,430	1,508,389[15]	24.2	91[15]
Secondary/Voc. (age 12–17)	57,912	1,059,641[15]	18.1	69[15]
Tertiary	15,685	352,554	22.5	38 (age 18–22)

Health: physicians (2007) 4,058 (1 per 2,323 persons); hospital beds (2008) 15,017 (1 per 639 persons); infant mortality rate per 1,000 live births (2010) 41.7; undernourished population (2005–07) 2,500,000 (27% of total population based on the consumption of a minimum daily requirement of 1,730 calories).

Military

Total active duty personnel (November 2010): 46,100 (army 75.5%, navy 10.4%, air force 14.1%). *Military expenditure as percentage of GDP* (2009): 1.3%; per capita expenditure U.S.$25.

[1]New constitution promulgated Feb. 8, 2009; actual implementation of changes per new constitution will take time. [2]Executive and legislative branches meet in La Paz, judiciary in Sucre. [3]Per 2009 constitution. [4]Includes the 3,690 sq km area of the Bolivian part of Lake Titicaca. [5]Within La Paz urban agglomeration. [6]Metal content. [7]In 2008 Bolivia ranked third in the world in coca production; 113 metric tons of cocaine were produced. [8]Private sector; second quarter only. [9]Population 10 years of age and over. [10]Import duties and indirect taxes less imputed bank service charges. [11]Imports c.i.f.; exports f.o.b. [12]AeroSur, LAB (closed down in 2007), and Amaszonas airlines only. [13]Circulation. [14]Subscribers. [15]2007–08.

Internet resources for further information:
- **Instituto Nacional de Estadística http://www.ine.gob.bo**
- **Banco Central de Bolivia http://www.bcb.gob.bo**

Bosnia and Herzegovina

Official name: Bosna i Hercegovina (Bosnia and Herzegovina).
Form of government: emerging republic with bicameral legislature (House of Peoples [15[1]]; House of Representatives [42]).
Heads of state: nominally a tripartite presidency.
International authority: [2].
Head of government: Prime Minister (Chairman of the Council of Ministers).
Capital: Sarajevo.
Official languages: Bosnian; Croatian; Serbian.
Official religion: none.
Monetary unit: convertible marka (KM[3, 4]); valuation (Sept. 1, 2011) 1 U.S.$ = KM 1.37; 1 £ = KM 2.22.

Area and population

Autonomous regions / Cantons	area sq km	population 2008 estimate	Autonomous regions / Cantons	area sq km	population 2008 estimate
Federation of Bosnia and Herzegovina (FBH)	26,110	2,327,195	Una-Sana	4,125	287,998
Bosnia-Podrinje	505	33,225	West Herzegovina	1,362	81,833
Canton 10	4,934	81,396	Zenica-Doboj	3,343	400,848
Central Bosnia	3,189	255,648	Republika Srpska (RS)	24,857	1,437,500
Herzegovina-Neretva	4,401	226,632	**District**		
Posavina	325	40,513	Brčko	208	75,635
Sarajevo	1,277	421,289	REMAINDER	34	—
Tuzla	2,649	497,813	TOTAL	51,209	3,840,330

Demography

Population (2011): 3,843,000.
Density (2011): persons per sq mi 194.4, persons per sq km 75.0.
Urban-rural (2005): urban 45.7%; rural 54.3%.
Sex distribution (2005): male 48.11%; female 51.89%.
Age breakdown (2005): under 15, 16.6%; 15–29, 22.7%; 30–44, 22.6%; 45–59, 20.4%; 60–74, 13.3%; 75–84, 3.9%; 85 and over, 0.5%.
Population projection: (2020) 3,739,000; (2030) 3,560,000.
Ethnic composition (1999): Bosniak 44.0%; Serb 31.0%; Croat 17.0%; other 8.0%.
Religious affiliation (2009): Muslim *c.* 45%; Serbian Orthodox *c.* 36%; Roman Catholic *c.* 15%; Protestant *c.* 1%; nonreligious/other *c.* 3%.
Major cities (2008): Sarajevo 393,000; Banja Luka 164,200; Tuzla 83,800; Zenica 83,300; Mostar 66,900.

Vital statistics

Birth rate per 1,000 population (2009): 9.1 (world avg. 20.3); within marriage 89.5%; outside of marriage 10.5%.
Death rate per 1,000 population (2009): 9.1 (world avg. 8.5).
Total fertility rate (avg. births per childbearing woman; 2009): 1.30.
Marriage/divorce rates per 1,000 population (2009): 5.4/0.2.
Life expectancy at birth (2007): male 66.9 years; female 72.5 years.
Major causes of death per 100,000 population (2009): diseases of the circulatory system 476.5; neoplasms 181.5; endocrine, metabolic, and nutritional disorders 52.1; accidents, violence 32.8.

National economy

Budget (2009). Revenue: KM 10,697,000,000 (tax revenue 83.1%, of which social security contributions 33.7%, VAT/sales tax 26.4%, excise tax 11.7%; nontax revenue 11.3%; grants 4.5%; dividends 1.1%). Expenditures: KM 12,054,000,000 (current expenditures 87.1%; development expenditures 12.9%).
Public debt (external, outstanding; 2009): U.S.$3,569,000,000.
Gross national income (GNI; 2010): U.S.$18,015,000,000 (U.S.$4,790 per capita); purchasing power parity GNI (U.S.$8,970 per capita).

Structure of gross domestic product and labour force

	2009 in value KM '000,000	2009 % of total value	2008 labour force	2008 % of labour force
Agriculture, forestry	1,803	7.5	19,160	1.6
Mining	501	2.1	20,153	1.7
Manufacturing	2,556	10.7	147,115	12.7
Construction	1,269	5.3	42,658	3.7
Public utilities	1,060	4.4	22,792	2.0
Transp. and commun.	1,643	6.8	44,653	3.8
Trade, restaurants	3,611	15.1	166,147	14.3
Finance, real estate	3,025	12.6	40,576	3.5
Pub. admin., defense	2,361	9.8	67,597	5.8
Services	2,735	11.4	127,556	11.0
Other	3,430[5]	14.3[5]	463,593[6]	39.9[6]
TOTAL	23,994	100.0	1,162,000	100.0

Production (metric tons except as noted). Agriculture, forestry, fishing (2009): corn (maize) 962,921, potatoes 413,658, wheat 255,848, plums and sloes 155,767, cabbages 81,684, apples 71,507, dry chilies and peppers 20,429, raspberries 8,487; livestock (number of live animals) 1,054,690 sheep, 529,095 pigs, 457,743 cattle; roundwood (2010) 3,614,000 cu m, of which fuelwood 35%; fisheries production 9,625 (from aquaculture 79%). Mining (2009): iron ore (metal content) 678,000; bauxite 555,800; lime 280,900. Manufacturing (value of sales in KM '000,000; 2009): food, beverages, and tobacco products 1,650; base and fabricated metals 1,352; cement, bricks, and ceramics 391; wood and wood products 340; paper and paper products 335. Energy production (consumption): electricity (kW-hr; 2008) 14,823,000,000 (9,984,000,000); hard coal (metric tons; 2007) 3,876,000 (4,552,000); lignite (metric tons; 2009) 11,515,000 ([2007] 10,308,000); crude petroleum (barrels; 2009) none ([2007] 777,000,000); petroleum products (metric tons; 2007) 98,000 (1,169,000); natural gas (cu m; 2009) none (225,000,000).
Population economically active (2008): total 1,162,000; activity rate of total population 36.2% (participation rates: ages 15–64, 53.4%; female 37.3%; unemployed [2010] 27.2%).

Price index (2005 = 100)

	2004	2005	2006	2007	2008	2009	2010
Consumer price index	...	100.0	106.1	107.7	115.7	115.3	117.8

Household expenditure (2007). Average household size 3.3; average annual household expenditure KM 18,497 (U.S.$12,944)[7]; sources of income: n.a.; expenditure: food and nonalcoholic beverages 31.9%, housing 14.7%, transport 11.2%, energy/water 7.4%, household furnishings 5.4%.
Selected balance of payments data. Receipts from (U.S.$'000,000): tourism (2009) 681; remittances (2010) 2,228; foreign direct investment (FDI; 2008–10 avg.) 414; official development assistance (2009) 415. Disbursements for (U.S.$'000,000): tourism (2009) 236; remittances (2009) 61; FDI (2008–10 avg.) 17.
Land use as % of total land area (2007): in temporary crops 10.9%, left fallow 9.1%, in permanent crops 1.9%, in pasture 20.2%, forest area 42.7%.

Foreign trade

Balance of trade (current prices)

	2004	2005	2006	2007	2008	2009
U.S.$'000,000	–4,068	–4,665	–4,131	–5,568	–7,167	–4,410
% of total	50.9%	49.4%	37.6%	40.1%	41.6%	35.8%

Imports (2009): U.S.$8,364,000,000 (machinery and apparatus 15.0%, food 14.1%, chemicals and chemical products 12.5%, petroleum 11.2%, base and fabricated metals 8.5%, road vehicles 6.0%). *Major import sources:* Croatia 15.0%; Germany 11.3%; Serbia 10.4%; Italy 10.1%; Russia 7.0%.
Exports (2009): U.S.$3,954,000,000 (machinery and apparatus 10.9%, furniture/parts 9.0%, electricity 8.3%, manufactures of metal 6.5%, footwear 6.2%, aluminum 6.0%, food 6.0%). *Major export destinations:* Croatia 17.1%; Germany 14.7%; Serbia 13.3%; Italy 12.7%; Slovenia 8.4%.

Transport and communications

Transport. Railroads (2008): route length 632 mi, 1,017 km; passenger-km 78,000,000; metric ton-km cargo 1,284,000,000. Roads (2008): total length 10,875 mi, 17,502 km (paved, n.a.); passenger-km 2,108,000,000; metric ton-km cargo 1,872,000,000. Vehicles: n.a. Air transport (2009): passenger-km 108,000,000; metric ton-km (2003) 6,000,000.

Communications

Medium	date	number in '000s	units per 1,000 persons	Medium	date	number in '000s	units per 1,000 persons
Televisions	2002	950	248	PCs	2007	246	64
Telephones				Dailies	2009	190[8]	48[8]
Cellular	2010	3,014[9]	802[9]	Internet users	2009	1,422	377
Landline	2010	999	266	Broadband	2010	391[9]	104[9]

Education and health

Educational attainment (2004). Percentage of population age 18 and over having: no formal schooling 8.7%; incomplete primary education 11.4%; complete primary 21.4%; incomplete/complete secondary 49.8%; technical/university 8.7%. *Literacy* (2008): total population age 15 and over literate 97.6%; males literate 99.4%; females literate 95.9%.

Education (2008–09)

	teachers	students	student/ teacher ratio	enrollment rate (%)
Primary (age 6–9)	...	173,647	...	87
Secondary/Voc. (age 10–17)	...	334,355	...	...
Tertiary	5,193	105,488	20.3	37 (age 18–22)

Health: physicians (2005) 5,540 (1 per 694 persons); hospital beds (2004) 11,414 (1 per 337 persons); infant mortality rate per 1,000 live births (2009) 5.3; undernourished population (2004–06) less than 5.0% of total population.

Military

Total active duty personnel (November 2010): 10,577[10, 11]. *Military expenditure as percentage of GDP* (2010): 1.4%; per capita expenditure U.S.$59.

[1]All seats are nonelective. [2]High Representative of the international community per the 1995 Dayton Peace Agreement/EU Special Representative. [3]The KM is pegged to the euro. [4]The euro also circulates as semiofficial legal tender. [5]Taxes on products and imports less subsidies and imputed bank service charges. [6]Includes 272,000 unemployed. [7]Less consumption of self-produced food and imputed rent equals KM 15,352 (U.S.$10,743). [8]Circulation. [9]Subscribers. [10]A formally combined military was established in 2006. [11]EU-sponsored (EUFOR) peacekeeping troops (November 2010) 1,795.

Internet resources for further information:
- **Statistics of Bosnia and Herzegovina http://www.bhas.ba**
- **Central Bank http://www.cbbh.ba**

Botswana

Official name: Republic of Botswana.
Form of government: multiparty republic with one legislative body[1] (National Assembly [63[2]]).
Head of state and government: President.
Capital: Gaborone[3].
Official language: English[4].
Official religion: none.
Monetary unit: pula (P); valuation (Sept. 1, 2011) 1 U.S.$ = P 6.69; 1 £ = P 10.81.

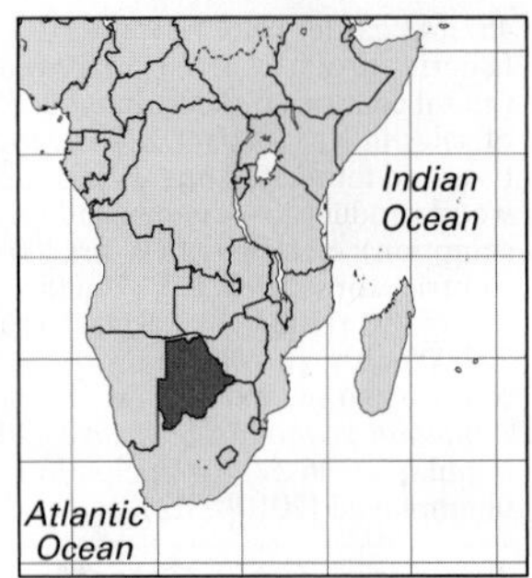

Area and population

Districts	area sq km	population 2011 census[5]	Districts	area sq km	population 2011 census[5]
Central	147,730	640,443	North East	5,120	159,908
Ghanzi	117,910	43,370	North West	129,930	181,553
Kgalagadi	106,940	50,500	South East	1,780	349,208
Kgatleng	7,960	92,247	Southern	28,470	216,325
Kweneng	35,890	304,674	TOTAL	581,730	2,038,228

Demography

Population (2011): 2,033,000.
Density (2011): persons per sq mi 9.1, persons per sq km 3.5.
Urban-rural (2009): urban 60.4%; rural 39.6%.
Sex distribution (2008): male 49.99%; female 50.01%.
Age breakdown (2008): under 15, 35.3%; 15–29, 32.9%; 30–44, 17.4%; 45–59, 9.0%; 60–74, 3.9%; 75–84, 1.2%; 85 and over, 0.3%.
Population projection: (2020) 2,290,000; (2030) 2,602,000.
Ethnic composition (2000): Tswana 66.8%; Kalanga 14.8%; Ndebele 1.7%; Herero 1.4%; San (Bushman) 1.3%; Afrikaner 1.3%; other 12.7%.
Religious affiliation (2005): independent Christian 41.7%; traditional beliefs 35.0%; Protestant 12.8%; Muslim 0.3%; Hindu 0.2%; other 10.0%.
Major cities (2009): Gaborone 230,900; Francistown 96,300; Molepolole 72,100; Selebi-Pikwe 57,200; Mogoditshane 56,300; Maun 56,000.

Vital statistics

Birth rate per 1,000 population (2010): 25.0 (world avg. 19.2).
Death rate per 1,000 population (2010): 12.0 (world avg. 8.2).
Natural increase rate per 1,000 population (2010): 13.0 (world avg. 11.0).
Total fertility rate (avg. births per childbearing woman; 2008): 2.66.
Life expectancy at birth (2008): male 61.5 years; female 62.1 years.
Adult population (ages 15–49) *living with HIV* (2009): 24.8%[6] (world avg. 0.8%).

National economy

Budget (2008–09). Revenue: P 30,455,000,000 (tax revenue 89.3%, of which mineral royalties 33.4%, non-mineral income tax 15.2%, general sales tax/VAT 14.4%; nontax revenue 8.7%; grants 2.0%). Expenditures: P 35,151,000,000 (government services including defense 26.0%; education 22.0%; housing/urban development 8.8%; health 8.6%; electricity/water supply 8.1%).
Public debt (external, outstanding; 2009): U.S.$1,388,000,000.
Population economically active (2008): total 653,200[7]; activity rate of total population 35.6%[7] (participation rates: ages 15–59 [2001] 58.1%[7]; female [2001] 49.1%[7]; unemployed [2008] 17.5%).

Price and earnings indexes (2005 = 100)

	2004	2005	2006	2007	2008	2009	2010
Consumer price index	92.1	100.0	111.6	119.5	134.6	145.4	155.5
Monthly earnings index[8]	82.7	100.0	120.8	137.4	...	...	...

Production (metric tons except as noted). Agriculture, forestry, fishing (2009): cow's milk 112,350, roots and tubers 87,628, pulses 40,142, sorghum 37,581, game meat 21,469, corn (maize) 13,193, sunflower seeds 6,000, goat's milk 3,900; livestock (number of live animals) 2,467,260 cattle, 2,000,000 goats, 169,603 sheep; roundwood (2010) 783,556 cu m, of which fuelwood 87%; fisheries production 86 (from aquaculture, none). Mining and quarrying (2009): soda ash 265,000; salt 170,000; nickel ore (metal content) 28,595; copper ore (metal content) 27,700; cobalt (metal content) 330; semiprecious gemstones (mostly agate) 30,000 kg; gold 1,530 kg; diamonds 17,700,000 carats[9, 10]. Manufacturing (value added in U.S.$'000,000; 2007): beverages 61; textiles 18; tanned and processed leather 2; unspecified 290. Energy production (consumption): electricity (kW-hr; 2008) 590,000,000 (2,850,000,000); hard coal (metric tons; 2009) 1,036,000 (1,039,000); crude petroleum, none (none); petroleum products (metric tons; 2007) none (678,000); natural gas, none (none).
Land use as % of total land area (2009): in temporary crops/left fallow 0.4%; in permanent crops, less than 0.01%; in pasture 45.2%; forest area 20.4%.
Household income and expenditure (2002–03). Average household size (2004) 4.3; average annual disposable income per household P 29,095 (U.S.$5,320), of which cash income P 25,519 (U.S.$4,670); expenditure (2006)[11]: food and nonalcoholic beverages 21.8%, transportation 19.0%, housing and energy 11.5%, alcoholic beverages and tobacco 9.3%, clothing and footwear 7.5%, household furnishings 6.8%.
Gross national income (GNI; 2010): U.S.$13,633,000,000 (U.S.$6,890 per capita); purchasing power parity GNI (U.S.$13,910 per capita).

Structure of gross domestic product and labour force

	2009 in value P '000,000	2009 % of total value	2008 labour force[7]	2008 % of labour force[7]
Agriculture	2,478	3.0	161,400	24.7
Mining	21,621	26.0	14,200	2.2
Manufacturing	3,343	4.0	36,000	5.5
Construction	4,313	5.2	27,600	4.2
Public utilities	2,409	2.9	4,200	0.6
Transp. and commun.	4,050	4.9	16,100	2.5
Trade, hotels	11,328	13.6	92,100	14.1
Finance, real estate	10,301	12.4	33,700	5.2
Pub. admin., defense	15,364	18.5	60,200	9.2
Services	3,809	4.6	93,700	14.3
Other	4,257[12]	5.1[12]	114,000[13]	17.5[13]
TOTAL	83,272[14]	100.0[14]	653,200	100.0

Selected balance of payments data. Receipts from (U.S.$'000,000): tourism (2009) 452; remittances (2010) 100; foreign direct investment (2008–10 avg.) 545; official development assistance (2009) 280. Disbursements for (U.S.$'000,000): tourism (2009) 230; remittances (2009) 145.

Foreign trade[15]

Balance of trade (current prices)

	2004	2005	2006	2007	2008	2009
U.S.$'000,000	+276	+1,268	+1,453	+1,086	–261	–1,272
% of total	4.1%	16.7%	19.2%	13.5%	2.6%	15.5%

Imports (2009): U.S.$4,728,000,000 (machinery and apparatus 17.3%, refined petroleum 10.9%, food products 10.3%, road vehicles 9.4%, unworked diamonds 7.6%, manufactures of metal 6.5%). *Major import sources:* South Africa 76.1%; U.K. 6.1%; China 3.3%; U.S. 2.2%; France 1.4%.
Exports (2009): U.S.$3,456,000,000 (unworked diamonds 56.3%, nickel matte 12.3%, worked diamonds 6.3%, apparel and clothing accessories 5.2%, bovine meat 3.3%, copper ore/copper matte 2.2%). *Major export destinations:* U.K. 53.1%; South Africa 14.7%; Norway 9.8%; Zimbabwe 4.5%; Israel 3.2%.

Transport and communications

Transport. Railroads (2008): route length 552 mi, 888 km; (2003) passenger-km 572,000,000; (2004) metric ton-km cargo 636,700,000. Roads (2007)[16]: total length 5,540 mi, 8,916 km (paved 72%). Vehicles (2007): passenger cars 104,926; trucks and buses 105,754. Air transport (2008)[17]: passenger-km 120,000,000; metric ton-km cargo, 1,100,000.

Communications

Medium	date	number in '000s	units per 1,000 persons	Medium	date	number in '000s	units per 1,000 persons
Televisions	2003	78	44	PCs	2006	84	45
Telephones				Dailies	2009	11[18]	8.5[18]
Cellular	2010	2,363[19]	1,178[19]	Internet users	2009	120	62
Landline	2010	137	69	Broadband	2010	12[19]	6.0[19]

Education and health

Educational attainment (2001). Percentage of population age 25 and over having: no formal schooling 27.9%; primary education, n.a.; secondary, n.a.; post-secondary, n.a. *Literacy* (2008): total population over age 15 literate 83.3%; males literate 83.1%; females literate 83.5%.

Education (2006–07)

	teachers	students	student/ teacher ratio	enrollment rate (%)
Primary (age 6–12)	12,989	327,617	25.2	87
Secondary/Voc. (age 13–17)	12,798	177,615	13.9	60
Tertiary	529[20]	16,239[21]	29.7[20]	8[21] (age 18–22)

Health: physicians (2007) 478 (1 per 3,798 persons); hospital beds (2008) 3,543[22] (1 per 551 persons); infant mortality rate per 1,000 live births (2008) 13.4; undernourished population (2005–07) 500,000 (25% of total population based on the consumption of a minimum daily requirement of 1,830 calories).

Military

Total active duty personnel (November 2010): 9,000 (army 94.4%, navy, none [landlocked], air force 5.6%). *Military expenditure as percentage of GDP* (2008): 2.2%; per capita expenditure U.S.$150.

[1]In addition, the Ntlo ya Dikgosi (known as the House of Chiefs in English), a 35-member body consisting of chiefs, subchiefs, and associated members, serves in an advisory capacity to the government. [2]Includes 4 specially elected members and 2 ex officio members (the president and attorney general); the statutory number (63) includes the speaker who may be appointed from outside the National Assembly. [3]The high court meets in Lobatse. [4]Tswana is the national language. [5]Preliminary results of de facto population. [6]Statistically derived midpoint within range. [7]Excludes military. [8]Citizens only. [9]About 70% gem and near-gem quality (Botswana is the world's leading producer of diamonds by value). [10]The world's most advanced diamond-sorting and diamond-valuing centre was opened at Gaborone in 2008. [11]Weights of cost of living index. [12]Import duties and indirect taxes less subsidies and less imputed bank service charges. [13]Unemployed. [14]Detail does not add to total given because of rounding. [15]Imports c.i.f.; exports f.o.b. [16]Roads maintained by central government only. [17]Air Botswana only. [18]Circulation. [19]Subscribers. [20]2004–05. [21]2005–06. [22]Excludes 696 beds in clinics.

Internet resources for further information:

- **Central Statistical Office http://www.cso.gov.bw**
- **Bank of Botswana http://www.bankofbotswana.bw**

Brazil

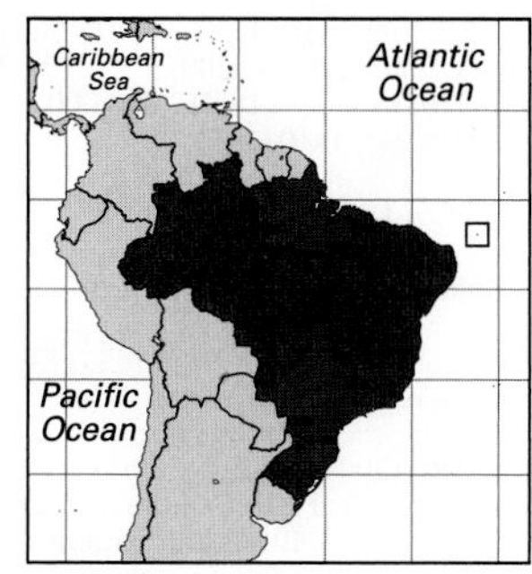

Official name: República Federativa do Brasil (Federative Republic of Brazil).
Form of government: multiparty federal republic with 2 legislative houses (Federal Senate [81]; Chamber of Deputies [513]).
Head of state and government: President.
Capital: Brasília.
Official language: Portuguese.
Official religion: none.
Monetary unit: real (R$; plural reais); valuation (Sept. 1, 2011) 1 U.S.$ = R$1.61; 1 £ = R$2.59.

Area and population

States	Capitals	area sq mi	area sq km	population 2010 census[1]
Acre	Rio Branco	58,912	152,581	732,793
Alagoas	Maceió	10,721	27,768	3,120,922
Amapá	Macapá	55,141	142,815	668,689
Amazonas	Manaus	606,468	1,570,746	3,480,937
Bahia	Salvador	218,029	564,693	14,021,432
Ceará	Fortaleza	57,462	148,826	8,448,055
Espírito Santo	Vitória	17,791	46,078	3,512,672
Goiás	Goiânia	131,308	340,087	6,004,045
Maranhão	São Luís	128,179	331,983	6,569,683
Mato Grosso	Cuiabá	348,788	903,358	3,033,991
Mato Grosso do Sul	Campo Grande	137,887	357,125	2,449,341
Minas Gerais	Belo Horizonte	226,460	586,528	19,595,309
Pará	Belém	481,736	1,247,690	7,588,078
Paraíba	João Pessoa	21,792	56,440	3,766,834
Paraná	Curitiba	76,956	199,315	10,439,601
Pernambuco	Recife	37,958	98,312	8,796,032
Piauí	Teresina	97,116	251,529	3,119,015
Rio de Janeiro	Rio de Janeiro	16,871	43,696	15,993,583
Rio Grande do Norte	Natal	20,385	52,797	3,168,133
Rio Grande do Sul	Porto Alegre	108,784	281,749	10,695,532
Rondônia	Porto Velho	91,729	237,576	1,560,501
Roraima	Boa Vista	86,602	224,299	451,227
Santa Catarina	Florianópolis	36,813	95,346	6,249,682
São Paulo	São Paulo	95,834	248,209	41,252,160
Sergipe	Aracaju	8,459	21,910	2,068,031
Tocantins	Palmas	107,190	277,621	1,383,453
Federal District				
Distrito Federal	Brasília	2,240	5,802	2,562,963
TOTAL		3,287,612[2, 3]	8,514,877[2, 3]	190,732,694

Demography

Population (2011): 192,813,000.
Density (2011): persons per sq mi 58.6, persons per sq km 22.6.
Urban-rural (2010): urban 84.3%; rural 15.7%.
Sex distribution (2010): male 48.96%; female 51.04%.
Age breakdown (2005): under 15, 27.6%; 15–29, 27.7%; 30–44, 21.7%; 45–59, 14.1%; 60–74, 6.6%; 75–84, 1.8%; 85 and over, 0.5%.
Population projection: (2020) 207,143,000; (2030) 216,410,000.
Doubling time: 70 years.
Racial composition (2008): white 48.4%; mulatto and mestizo 43.8%; black and black/Amerindian 6.8%; Asian 0.6%; Amerindian 0.3%; other/unknown 0.1%.
Religious affiliation (2005)[4]: Roman Catholic 65.1%; Protestant 12.7%, of which Assemblies of God 9.2%; independent Christian 10.7%, of which Universal Church of the Kingdom of God 2.2%; Spiritist (Kardecist) 1.3%; Jehovah's Witness 0.7%; African and syncretic religions 0.4%; Muslim 0.4%; nonreligious/other 8.7%.
Major cities[5] and metropolitan areas (2010)[1]: São Paulo 11,125,243 (19,672,582); Rio de Janeiro 6,323,037 (11,875,063); Belo Horizonte 2,375,444 (5,413,627); Porto Alegre 1,409,939 (3,895,168); Brasília 2,476,249 (3,710,543); Recife 1,536,934 (3,688,428); Fortaleza 2,447,409 (3,525,564); Salvador 2,675,875 (3,459,377); Curitiba 1,746,896 (3,124,044); Campinas 1,062,453 (2,798,477); Goiânia 1,296,969 (2,052,794); Belém 1,380,836 (2,040,843); Manaus 1,793,416 (1,802,525); Vitória 325,453 (1,668,356).

Other principal cities[5]/metropolitan areas (2010)

	population		population
Santos	419,443/1,663,082	Londrina	493,457/733,541
São Luís	955,600/1,306,029	Santo André	673,914[6]
Natal	803,811/1,255,856	Blumenau	294,968/668,715
Guarulhos	1,222,357[6]	Osasco	666,469[6]
Maceió	931,984/1,156,278	Jaboatão	630,683[7]
Joinville	497,788/1,115,764	São José dos Campos	615,610/627,544
João Pessoa	720,789/1,068,937	Ipatinga	236,678/615,004
Florianópolis	405,243/1,012,831	Ribeirão Preto	603,401/605,114
São Gonçalo	999,161[8]	Contagem	601,009[9]
Duque de Caxias	852,131[8]	Uberlândia	583,879/600,285
Teresina	767,777/814,439	Sorocaba	580,340/586,311
Campo Grande	776,654/787,204	Aracaju	570,937/570,937
Nova Iguaçu	786,536[8]	Maringá	349,120/567,178
São Bernardo do Campo	752,414[6]		

Families. Average family size (2005) 3.2; (1996) 1–2 persons 25.2%, 3 persons 20.3%, 4 persons 22.2%, 5–6 persons 23.3%, 7 or more persons 9.0%.
Emigration (2000): Brazilian emigrants living abroad 1,887,895; in the U.S. 42.3%, in Paraguay 23.4%, in Japan 12.0%.
Immigration (2000): foreign-born immigrants living in Brazil 683,830; from Europe 56.3%, of which Portugal 31.2%; South/Central America 21.0%; Asia 17.8%, of which Japan 10.4%.

Vital statistics

Birth rate per 1,000 population (2008): 16.4 (world avg. 20.3).
Death rate per 1,000 population (2008): 6.4 (world avg. 8.5).
Natural increase rate per 1,000 population (2008): 10.0 (world avg. 11.8).
Total fertility rate (avg. births per childbearing woman; 2008): 1.90.
Life expectancy at birth (2008): male 68.7 years; female 76.0 years.
Marriage/divorce rates per 1,000 population (2008): 5.1[10]/1.0[10].
Major causes of death per 100,000 population (2005)[11]: diseases of the circulatory system 180.5, of which cerebrovascular disease 57.2, ischemic heart disease 54.0; malignant neoplasms (cancers) 92.5; external causes 81.1, of which accidents 37.0, violence 30.2 (excl. suicide 5.4); diseases of the respiratory system 61.9; diseases of the digestive system 31.8; infectious and parasitic diseases 25.8; diabetes mellitus 25.3; causes unknown 66.4.
Adult population (ages 15–49) *living with HIV* (2009): 0.4% (world avg. 0.8%).

Social indicators

Educational attainment (2007). Percentage of population age 25 and over having: no formal schooling 13.6%; incomplete primary education 12.9%; complete primary 25.9%; lower secondary 13.9%; upper secondary 24.4%; higher 9.3%.

Distribution of income (2008)

percentage of national income by quintile

1	2	3	4	5 (highest)
3.3	7.2	11.6	18.5	59.4

Quality of working life. Proportion of employed population receiving minimum wage (2002): 53.5%. Number and percentage of children (age 5–17) working: 5,400,000 (12.6% of age group).
Access to services. Proportion of urban households having access to (2008): safe public (piped) water supply 92.1%; public (piped) sewage system 68.5%; garbage collection 89.4%. Rural households have far less access to services.
Social participation. Voter turnout at last (October 2010) national legislative election: 81.9%. Trade union membership in total workforce (2001): 19,500,000. Practicing Roman Catholic population in total affiliated Roman Catholic population (2000): large cities 10–15%; towns and rural areas 60–70%.
Social deviance. Annual murder rate per 100,000 population (2005): Brazil 29.6; Rio de Janeiro only (2002) 56; São Paulo only (2002) 54.
Leisure. Favourite leisure activities include: playing and watching football (soccer), dancing, practicing *capoeira,* rehearsing all year in neighbourhood samba groups for celebrations of Carnival, and competing in water sports, volleyball, and basketball.
Material well-being. Urban households possessing (2006): electricity 99.7%; colour television receiver 94.8%; refrigerator 93.3%; washing machine 42.2%; computer 25.5%; Internet access 19.6%; freezer 16.1%.

National economy

Gross national income (GNI; 2010): U.S.$1,830,392,000,000 (U.S.$9,390 per capita); purchasing power parity GNI (U.S.$10,920 per capita).

Structure of gross domestic product and labour force

	2009		2007[12]	
	in value U.S.$'000,000	% of total value	labour force	% of labour force
Agriculture, forestry	82,000	5.2	16,578,900	16.8
Mining }	65,200	4.2	378,500	0.4
Public utilities }			362,700	0.4
Manufacturing	209,500	13.3	13,105,100	13.3
Construction	68,700	4.4	6,107,000	6.2
Transportation and communications	118,300	7.5	4,374,000	4.4
Trade, hotels	277,900	17.7	19,659,800	19.9
Finance, real estate }			6,680,700	6.8
Pub. admin., defense }	529,900	33.7	4,504,200	4.6
Services }			18,825,800	19.0
Other	220,500	14.0	8,269,000[13]	8.4[13]
TOTAL	1,572,000	100.0	98,845,600[3]	100.0[3]

Budget (2008). Revenue: R$716,647,000,000 (taxes and welfare contributions 67.6%, social security contributions 22.8%, other 9.6%). Expenditures: R$645,246,000,000 (social security and welfare 33.4%, transfers to state and local governments 20.6%, personnel 20.3%, other 25.7%).
Public debt (external, outstanding; December 2009): U.S.$86,800,000,000.
Production ('000 metric tons except as noted). Agriculture, forestry, fishing (2009): sugarcane 671,395, soybeans 57,345, corn (maize) 51,232, cow's milk 29,112, cassava 24,404, oranges 17,619, rice 12,652, chicken meat 9,967, cattle meat 9,508, bananas 6,783, wheat 5,056, tomatoes 4,310, dry beans 3,487, potatoes 3,444, seed cotton 2,928, pig meat 2,924, coffee 2,440, watermelons 2,056, coconuts 1,973, hen's eggs 1,922, sorghum 1,854, papayas 1,793, cashew apples[14] 1,593, dry onions 1,512, pineapples 1,471, grapes 1,365, apples 1,223, mangoes and guavas 1,198, tangerines, mandarins, and clementines 1,094, lemons and limes 972, oil palm fruit 914, tobacco 863, maté 443, peanuts (groundnuts) 293, cashews 221, cacao beans 218, natural rubber 127, garlic 87, pepper 65, Brazil nuts 28; livestock (number of live animals) 205,292,000 cattle, 38,045,200 pigs, 16,812,100 sheep, 5,496,460 horses; roundwood (2010) 264,149,139 cu m, of which fuelwood 54%; fisheries production 1,241,048 (from aquaculture 33%). Mining and quarrying (metric tons; 2008): columbium (niobium) 82,000 of pyrochlore in concentrates[15] (world rank: 1); iron ore (metal content) 233,514,000 (world rank: 2); tantalum 180 (world rank: 2); bauxite 28,097,500 (world rank: 3); asbestos fibre 287,673 (world rank: 3); graphite 76,200 (world rank: 3); kaolin (marketable product) 2,618,000; manganese (metal content) 2,091,200; copper (metal content) 245,633; nickel (metal content in ore) 54,060; tin (mine output, metal content) 10,558; gold 48,373 kg; diamonds 182,000 carats.

Land use as % of total land area (2009): in temporary crops or left fallow 7.2%, in permanent crops 0.9%, in pasture 23.2%, forest area 61.7%.

Manufacturing enterprises (2007)

	number of employees	value added[16] (in U.S.$'000,000)
Food products	1,299,436	37,956
Petroleum products	34,782	33,055
Motor vehicles and parts	413,148	26,508
Nonelectrical machinery and apparatus	501,543	19,216
Paints, soaps, pharmaceuticals, and related products	260,190	18,792
Iron and steel	127,051	17,407
Electrical machinery and apparatus[17]	338,549	14,774
Industrial chemicals	99,887	12,833
Beverages	228,604	12,082
Paper and paper products	168,437	10,387
Fabricated metal products	319,997	8,865
Bricks, tiles, cement, and related products	314,804	7,758
Plastics	272,915	6,842
Textiles	330,028	5,855
Publishing	111,075	5,777
Clothing	552,508	5,620
Nonferrous base metals	50,810	5,538
Footwear, leather processing	404,112	4,832
Wood and wood products (excl. furniture)	225,022	3,872
Rubber products	92,814	3,423

Population economically active (2007[12]): total 98,845,600; activity rate of total population 52.2% (participation rates: ages 15–64, 73.5%; female 43.5%; unemployed [December 2009–November 2010] 6.9%).

Price index (2005 = 100)

	2004	2005	2006	2007	2008	2009	2010
Consumer price index	93.6	100.0	104.2	108.0	114.1	119.7	125.7

Selected balance of payments data. Receipts from (U.S.$'000,000): tourism (2009) 5,305; remittances (2010) 4,234; foreign direct investment (FDI; 2008–10 avg.) 33,148; official development assistance (2009) 338. Disbursements for (U.S.$'000,000): tourism (2009) 10,898; remittances (2009) 1,003; FDI (2008–10 avg.) 7,297.

Direction of trade (2009)

	imports		exports	
	U.S.$'000,000	%	U.S.$'000,000	%
Africa	8,465	6.6	8,688	5.7
Asia-Pacific	40,596	31.8	48,330	31.6
China	15,911	12.5	20,191	13.2
Japan	5,368	4.2	4,270	2.8
South Korea	4,818	3.8	2,622	1.7
India	2,191	1.7	3,415	2.2
Europe	33,904	26.6	40,200	26.3
Germany	9,866	7.7	6,175	4.0
Italy	3,664	2.9	3,016	2.0
France	3,625	2.8	2,949	1.9
United Kingdom	2,408	1.9	3,727	2.4
Western Hemisphere	44,682	35.0	53,137	34.7
United States	20,214	15.8	15,745	10.3
Argentina	11,281	8.8	12,785	8.4
Mexico	2,783	2.2	2,676	1.7
Chile	2,616	2.0	2,657	1.7
Canada	1,601	1.3	1,712	1.1
NOT SPECIFIED	—	—	2,640	1.7
TOTAL	127,647	100.0	152,995	100.0

Family income and expenditure. Average household size (2002–03) 3.6; average annual income per family (2008–09) R$31,516 (U.S.$15,093); sources of income (2008–09): work-related 63.9%, transfers 19.4%, nonmonetary income 13.4%, rent 1.8%; expenditure (2002–03): housing, energy, and household furnishings 35.9%, food and beverages 20.8%, transportation and communications 18.4%, health care 6.4%, education 4.1%.

Financial aggregates[18]

	2005	2006	2007	2008	2009	2010
Exchange rate, R$ per:						
U.S. dollar	2.34	2.14	1.77	2.34	1.74	1.67
£	4.03	4.19	3.55	3.41	2.71	2.61
SDR	3.34	3.21	2.80	3.60	2.73	2.56
International reserves (U.S.$)						
Total (excl. gold; '000,000)	53,245	85,156	179,433	192,844	237,364	287,056
SDRs ('000,000)	29	8	2	1	4,527	4,450
Reserve pos. in IMF ('000,000)	—	—	—	—	950	2,037
Foreign exchange ('000,000)	53,216	85,148	179,431	192,843	231,888	280,570
Gold ('000,000 fine troy oz)	1.08	1.08	1.08	1.08	1.08	1.08
% world reserves	0.1	0.1	0.1	0.1	0.1	0.1
Interest and prices						
Central bank discount (%)	25.34	19.98	17.85	20.48	15.17	17.30
Govt. bond yield (%)	...	...	...	...	...	...
Industrial share prices	...	...	...	...	...	...
Balance of payments (U.S.$'000,000)						
Balance of visible trade	+44,703	+46,458	+40,031	+24,746	+25,290	+20,221
Imports, f.o.b.	–73,606	–91,350	–120,618	–173,197	–127,705	–181,694
Exports, f.o.b.	118,308	137,807	160,649	197,942	152,995	201,915
Balance of invisibles	–30,719	–32,838	–38,481	–53,046	–49,592	–67,586
Balance of payments, current account	+13,984	+13,620	+1,550	–28,300	–24,302	–47,365

Energy production (consumption): electricity (kW-hr; 2008) 454,830,000,000 (419,960,000,000); hard coal (metric tons; 2009) 6,218,000 (23,010,000); crude petroleum (barrels; 2009) 711,900,000 ([2007] 634,000,000); petroleum products (metric tons; 2007) 82,210,000 (76,687,000); natural gas (cu m; 2009) 10,279,000,000 (18,717,000,000); ethanol (litres; 2008/09) 27,200,000,000 (22,050,000,000).

Foreign trade

Balance of trade (current prices)

	2004	2005	2006	2007	2008	2009
U.S.$'000,000	+33,842	+44,928	+46,463	+40,028	+24,746	+25,347
% of total	21.2%	23.4%	20.3%	14.2%	6.7%	9.0%

Imports (2009): U.S.$127,647,000,000 (machinery and apparatus 28.9%, of which general industrial machinery 6.0%, power-generating machinery 4.2%, telecommunications equipment 3.6%, specialized machinery for particular industries 3.4%; chemicals and chemical products 19.8%, of which organic chemicals 5.0%, medicines and pharmaceuticals 4.0%, fertilizers 3.0%; mineral fuels 14.8%, of which crude petroleum 7.2%, refined petroleum 3.6%; road vehicles/parts 8.9%; base and fabricated metals 6.2%; food 4.4%). *Major import sources:* United States 15.8%; China 12.5%; Argentina 8.8%; Germany 7.7%; Japan 4.2%; South Korea 3.8%; Nigeria 3.7%; Italy 2.9%; France 2.8%; Mexico 2.2%.

Exports (2009): U.S.$152,994,000,000 (food 23.4%, of which meat 7.5%, raw cane sugar 3.9%, soybean animal foodstuffs 3.0%, coffee 2.5%; machinery and apparatus 9.0%, of which power-generating machinery 2.2%, general industrial machinery 2.2%; iron ore and concentrates 8.7%; soybeans 7.5%; chemicals and chemical products 6.9%, of which organic chemicals 2.5%; crude petroleum 6.2%; road vehicles/parts 5.3%; iron and steel 4.9%; aircraft/spacecraft 2.7%; wood pulp and waste paper 2.2%; refined petroleum 2.0%; tobacco 2.0%). *Major export destinations:* China 13.2%; United States 10.3%; Argentina 8.4%; Netherlands 5.3%; Germany 4.0%; Japan 2.8%; U.K. 2.4%; Venezuela 2.4%; India 2.2%; Belgium 2.1%.

Transport and communications

Transport. Railroads (2006): route length 29,605 km; (2005) passenger-km 5,852,000,000[19]; (2005) metric ton-km cargo 154,870,000,000[19]. Roads (2004): total length 1,088,558 mi, 1,751,868 km (paved [2000] 6%). Vehicles (2007): passenger cars 30,282,855; trucks and buses 7,694,824. Air transport (2008): passenger-km 66,144,000,000; metric ton-km cargo 1,807,000,000.

Communications

Medium	date	number in '000s	units per 1,000 persons	Medium	date	number in '000s	units per 1,000 persons
Televisions	2003	65,949	369	PCs	2006	29,340	161
Telephones				Dailies	2009	8,193[20]	57[20]
Cellular	2010	202,944[21]	1,041[21]	Internet users	2009	75,944	392
Landline	2010	42,141	216	Broadband	2010	14,087[21]	72[21]

Education and health

Literacy (2007/2008): total population age 15 and over literate/functionally literate 90.5%/79.0%; males literate/functionally literate 90.1%/78.4%; females literate/functionally literate 90.9%/79.5%.

Education (2007–08)

	teachers	students	student/ teacher ratio	enrollment rate (%)
Primary (age 7–10)	773,624	17,812,436	23.0	94
Secondary/Voc. (age 11–17)	1,375,114	23,645,669	17.2	82
Tertiary	375,202	5,958,135	15.9	34 (age 18–22)

Health: physicians (2005) 505,841 (1 per 356 persons); hospital beds (2008) 443,210 (1 per 428 persons); infant mortality rate per 1,000 live births (2008) 23.5; undernourished population (2005–07) 12,100,000 (6% of total population based on the consumption of a minimum daily requirement of 1,850 calories).

Military

Total active duty personnel (November 2010): 318,480 (army 59.7%, navy 18.5%, air force 21.8%); paramilitary (public security forces) 395,000; reserve 1,340,000. *Military expenditure as percentage of GDP* (2009): 1.7%; per capita expenditure U.S.$155.

[1]Preliminary census. [2]Total area including inland water per survey of 2002. [3]Detail does not add to total given because of rounding. [4]Christian data include nominal Christians. [5]Urban populations of *municípios*. [6]Within São Paulo metropolitan area. [7]Within Recife metropolitan area. [8]Within Rio de Janeiro metropolitan area. [9]Within Belo Horizonte metropolitan area. [10]Excludes Amerindian population of interior Brazil. [11]Projected rates based on c. 86% of total deaths. [12]September. [13]Includes 209,400 not adequately defined and 8,059,600 unemployed. [14]Edible stalks to which cashew nuts are attached. [15]Niobium oxide content. [16]At factor values. [17]Includes televisions, radios, and telecommunications equipment. [18]End-of-period figures. [19]Includes suburban services. [20]Circulation. [21]Subscribers.

Internet resources for further information:

- **IBGE: Instituto Brasileiro de Geografia e Estatística**
  http://www.ibge.gov.br/english
- **Central Bank of Brazil: Economic Data**
  http://www.bcb.gov.br/?english

Brunei

Official name: Negara Brunei Darussalam (State of Brunei Darussalam).
Form of government: monarchy (sultanate) with one advisory body (Legislative Council [29][1]).
Head of state and government: Sultan.
Capital: Bandar Seri Begawan.
Official language: Malay[2].
Official religion: Islam.
Monetary unit: Brunei dollar (B$)[3]; valuation (Sept. 1, 2011) 1 U.S.$ = B$1.20; 1 £ = B$1.95.

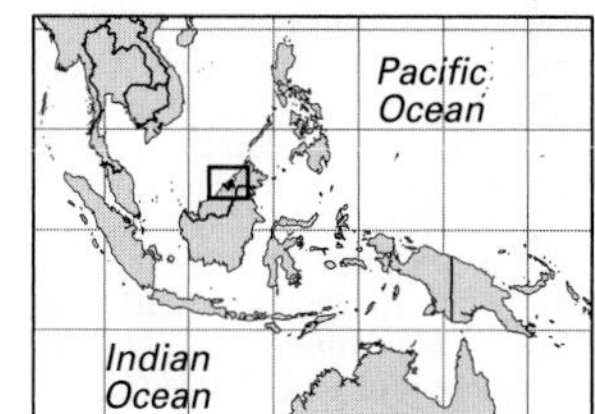

Area and population		area		population
				2009
Districts	Capitals	sq mi	sq km	estimate
Belait	Kuala Belait	1,052	2,724	67,100
Brunei and Muara	Bandar Seri Begawan	220	571	283,300
Temburong	Bangar	504	1,304	10,100
Tutong	Tutong	450	1,166	45,700
TOTAL		2,226	5,765	406,200

Demography

Population (2011): 422,000.
Density (2011): persons per sq mi 189.6, persons per sq km 73.2.
Urban-rural (2009): urban 75.2%; rural 24.8%.
Sex distribution (2009): male 52.93%; female 47.07%.
Age breakdown (2008): under 15, 27.2%; 15–29, 27.7%; 30–44, 25.1%; 45–59, 14.8%; 60–74, 4.1%; 75–84, 0.9%; 85 and over, 0.2%.
Population projection: (2020) 483,000; (2030) 542,000.
Doubling time: 53 years.
Ethnic composition (2009): Malay 66.3%; Chinese 11.0%; other 22.7%.
Religious affiliation (2006)[4]: Muslim 80.4%; Buddhist 7.9%; Christian 3.2%; traditional beliefs/other 8.5%.
Major cities (2009): Bandar Seri Begawan 74,500; Kuala Belait 27,700; Seria 27,600; Tutong 21,000.

Vital statistics

Birth rate per 1,000 population (2008): 16.1 (world avg. 20.3).
Death rate per 1,000 population (2008): 2.7 (world avg. 8.5).
Natural increase rate per 1,000 population (2008): 13.4 (world avg. 11.8).
Total fertility rate (avg. births per childbearing woman; 2008): 1.70.
Marriage/divorce rates per 1,000 population (2008): 6.0/1.3[5].
Life expectancy at birth (2008): male 76.6 years; female 79.8 years.
Major causes of death per 100,000 population (2006): diseases of the circulatory system 91.9; malignant neoplasms (cancers) 57.4; diabetes mellitus 30.3; diseases of the respiratory system 29.5; accidents and violence 21.4.

National economy

Budget (2008–09). Revenue: B$11,378,000,000 (tax revenue 65.3%, of which taxes on petroleum and natural gas companies 62.4%, other company taxes 1.5%; nontax revenue 34.7%, of which dividends paid by petroleum companies 20.7%, petroleum and natural gas royalties 9.6%). Expenditures: B$5,975,000,000 (current expenditure 83.0%; capital expenditure 17.0%).
Production (metric tons except as noted). Agriculture, forestry, fishing (2009): chicken meat 18,900, hen's eggs 6,847, vegetables 4,072, cassava 2,993, rice 1,371, pineapples 988, buffalo meat 153; livestock (number of live animals) 4,600 buffalo, 16,600,000 chickens; roundwood 118,968 cu m, of which fuelwood 10%; fisheries production 2,791 (from aquaculture 16%). Mining and quarrying: other than petroleum and natural gas, none except sand and gravel for construction. Manufacturing (value added in B$'000,000; 2008): liquefied natural gas 2,628; textiles and apparel 103; other manufactures 65. Energy production (consumption): electricity (kW-hr; 2009) 3,220,000,000 (3,050,000,000); coal, none (none); crude petroleum (barrels; 2009) 47,700,000 ([2007] 2,452,000); petroleum products (metric tons; 2007) 1,250,000 (1,068,000); natural gas (cu m; 2009) 11,497,000,000 (2,690,000,000).
Land use as % of total land area (2009): in temporary crops or left fallow (2007) 0.6%, in permanent crops 0.9%, in pasture 0.6%, forest area 72.4%.
Gross national income (at current market prices; 2009): U.S.$10,546,000,000 (U.S.$26,385 per capita).

Structure of gross domestic product and labour force	2008		2001	
	in value B$'000,000	% of total value	labour force	% of labour force
Agriculture, fishing, forestry	130	0.6	1,994	1.3
Petroleum, natural gas	11,672	57.2	3,954	2.5
Mining	...	...		
Manufacturing[6]	2,796	13.7	12,455	7.9
Construction	534	2.6	12,301	7.8
Public utilities	115	0.6	2,639	1.7
Transportation and communications	534	2.6	4,803	3.0
Trade, hotels	616	3.0	20,038	12.7
Finance, real estate	1,646	8.1	8,190	5.2
Pub. admin., defense	2,152	10.6	79,880	50.7
Services	203	1.0		
Other	—	—	11,340[7]	7.2[7]
TOTAL	20,398	100.0	157,594	100.0

Population economically active (2008): total 188,800[8]; activity rate of total population 47.4% (participation rates: ages 15–64 [2001] 65.9%; female 39.4%; unemployed [2010] 2.7%).

Price index (2005 = 100)	2005	2006	2007	2008	2009	2010
Consumer price index	100.0	100.2	101.1	103.2	104.3	104.5[9]

Public debt (external, outstanding; 2010): none.
Household income and expenditure. Average household size (2002) 5.6; income per household: n.a.; sources of income: n.a.; expenditure (2002)[10]: food and nonalcoholic beverages 28.8%, transportation 22.5%, housing and energy 8.8%, household furnishings 8.6%, recreation and entertainment 8.1%, clothing and footwear 5.6%, communications 5.5%.
Selected balance of payments data. Receipts from (U.S.$'000,000): tourism (2009) 254; remittances, n.a.; foreign direct investment (FDI; 2008–10 avg.) 368. Disbursements for (U.S.$'000,000): tourism (2009) 477; remittances (2009) 420; FDI (2008–10 avg.) 10.

Foreign trade[11]

Balance of trade (current prices)	2003	2004	2005	2006	2007	2008
U.S.$'000,000	+3,094	+3,635	+4,758	+5,939	+5,567	+8,178
% of total	53.8%	56.1%	61.5%	64.0%	57.0%	61.7%

Imports (2008): U.S.$2,574,000,000 (machinery and transport equipment 43.8%, manufactured goods 22.0%, food products 12.3%). *Major import sources:* Singapore 20.4%; Malaysia 18.7%; United States 13.7%; Japan 8.5%; China 6.9%.
Exports (2008): U.S.$10,543,000,000 (crude petroleum 53.2%, liquefied natural gas 44.6%, garments 0.8%, other domestic exports 0.1%, reexports 1.3%). *Major export destinations*[12]: Japan 43.8%; Indonesia 20.3%; South Korea 15.0%; Australia 10.5%; India 3.2%.

Transport and communications

Transport. Railroads (2004)[13]: length 19 km. Roads (2008): total length 1,847 mi, 2,972 km (paved 81%). Vehicles (2007): passenger cars 252,679; trucks and buses 18,266. Air transport (2008)[14]: passenger-km 3,818,000,000; metric ton-km cargo 106,000,000.

Communications Medium	date	number in '000s	units per 1,000 persons	Medium	date	number in '000s	units per 1,000 persons
Televisions	2001	215	648	PCs	2004	31	87
Telephones				Dailies	2009	41[15]	103[15]
Cellular	2010	435[16]	1,091[16]	Internet users	2009	319	798
Landline	2010	80	200	Broadband	2010	22[16]	54[16]

Education and health

Educational attainment (1991). Percentage of population age 25 and over having: no formal schooling 17.0%; primary education 43.3%; secondary 26.3%; postsecondary and higher 12.9%; not stated 0.5%. *Literacy* (2008): percentage of total population age 15 and over literate 95.0%; males literate 96.6%; females literate 93.3%.

Education (2008–09)	teachers	students	student/ teacher ratio	enrollment rate (%)
Primary (age 6–11)	3,739	44,681	11.9	93
Secondary/Voc. (age 12–18)	4,601	48,119	10.5	89
Tertiary	638	6,107	9.6	17 (age 19–23)

Health (2008): physicians 564 (1 per 706 persons); hospital beds 1,122 (1 per 355 persons); infant mortality rate per 1,000 live births 7.0; undernourished population (2004–06) less than 5.0% of total population based on the consumption of a minimum daily requirement of 1,880 calories.

Military

Total active duty personnel (November 2010): 7,000 (army 70.0%, navy 14.3%, air force 15.7%). British troops (November 2010) 550; Singaporean troops (2008) 500. *Military expenditure as percentage of GDP* (2009): 3.2%; per capita expenditure U.S.$817.

[1]Legislative Council (suspended from 1984) reinstated September 2004 and enlarged September 2005; all seats are nonelected. [2]All official documents that must be published by law in Malay are also required to be issued in an official English version. [3]Pegged to the Singapore dollar at a ratio of 1:1. [4]Based on governmental statistics for 185,430 citizens and 32,765 permanent residents. Religion data for *c.* 162,000 temporary residents (nearly all foreign workers) are unavailable. [5]Muslim divorces only. [6]Includes manufacture of liquefied natural gas (B$2,628,000,000; 12.9% of total value). [7]Unemployed. [8]Foreign workers accounted for 70% of the 160,500 economically active in 2004. [9]End of 3rd quarter. [10]Weights of consumer price index components. [11]Imports c.i.f.; exports f.o.b. [12]For crude petroleum, liquefied natural gas, and garments only. [13]Privately owned light railway. [14]Royal Brunei Airlines. [15]Circulation. [16]Subscribers.

Internet resource for further information:
- **Asian Development Bank http://www.adb.org**

Bulgaria

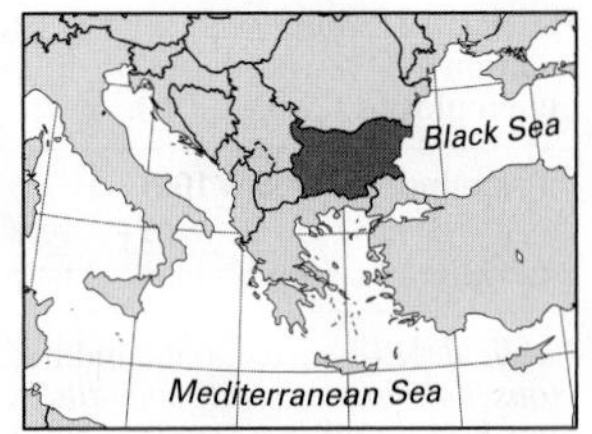

Official name: Republika Bŭlgaria (Republic of Bulgaria).
Form of government: unitary multiparty republic with one legislative body (National Assembly [240]).
Head of state: President.
Head of government: Prime Minister.
Capital: Sofia.
Official language: Bulgarian.
Official religion: none[1].
Monetary unit: lev (Lv; plural leva); valuation (Sept. 1, 2011) 1 U.S.$ = 1.37 leva; 1 £ = 2.22 leva.

Area and population

Districts	area sq km	population 2011 census	Districts	area sq km	population 2011 census
Blagoevgrad	6,449	323,552	Ruse	2,803	235,252
Burgas	7,748	415,817	Shumen	3,390	180,528
Dobrich	4,720	189,677	Silistra	2,846	119,474
Gabrovo	2,023	122,702	Sliven	3,544	197,473
Khaskovo	5,533	246,238	Smolyan	3,193	121,752
Kŭrdzhali	3,209	152,808	Sofiya[2]	7,062	247,489
Kyustendil	3,052	136,686	Sofiya-Grad[3]	1,349	1,291,591
Lovech	4,129	141,422	Stara Zagora	5,151	333,265
Montana	3,636	148,098	Tŭrgovishte	2,559	120,818
Pazardzhik	4,457	275,548	Varna	3,819	475,074
Pernik	2,394	133,530	Veliko Tŭrnovo	4,662	258,494
Pleven	4,335	269,752	Vidin	3,033	101,018
Plovdiv	5,973	683,027	Vratsa	3,938	186,848
Razgrad	2,640	125,190	Yambol	3,355	131,447
			TOTAL	111,002	7,364,570

Demography

Population (2011): 7,333,000.
Density (2011): persons per sq mi 171.1, persons per sq km 66.1.
Urban-rural (2010): urban 71.4%; rural 28.6%.
Sex distribution (2010): male 48.38%; female 51.62%.
Age breakdown (2010): under 15, 13.6%; 15–29, 19.4%; 30–44, 21.8%; 45–59, 20.9%; 60–74, 16.5%; 75–84, 6.5%; 85 and over, 1.3%.
Population projection: (2020) 6,897,000; (2030) 6,359,000.
Ethnic composition (2001): Bulgarian 83.9%; Turkish 9.4%; Rom (Gypsy) 4.7%; other 2.0%.
Religious affiliation (2005)[4]: Bulgarian Orthodox *c.* 81%; Sunnī Muslim *c.* 12%; Evangelical Protestant *c.* 2%; Catholic *c.* 1%; other *c.* 4%.
Major cities (2011): Sofia 1,204,685; Plovdiv 338,153; Varna 334,870; Burgas 200,271; Ruse 149,642; Stara Zagora 138,272.

Vital statistics

Birth rate per 1,000 population (2009): 10.7 (world avg. 20.3); within marriage 46.6%; outside of marriage 53.4%.
Death rate per 1,000 population (2009): 14.2 (world avg. 8.5).
Total fertility rate (avg. births per childbearing woman; 2009): 1.57.
Life expectancy at birth (2008): male 69.5 years; female 76.6 years.
Marriage/divorce rates per 1,000 population (2009): 3.4/1.5.
Major causes of death per 100,000 population (2009): diseases of the circulatory system 939.3; malignant neoplasms (cancers) 226.0; diseases of the respiratory system 54.7; accidents, injuries, and poisonings 45.0; diseases of the digestive system 43.0.

National economy

Budget (2009)[5]. Revenue: 27,313,000,000 leva (tax revenue 81.2%, of which VAT 27.4%, social insurance 15.7%, excise taxes 14.8%; nontax revenue 14.3%; grants 4.1%). Expenditures: 25,323,000,000 leva (current expenditure 80.3%; capital expenditure 17.0%; other 2.7%).
Public debt (January 2011): U.S.$7,155,000,000.
Gross national income (GNI; 2010): U.S.$47,159,000,000 (U.S.$6,240 per capita); purchasing power parity GNI (U.S.$13,210).

Structure of gross domestic product and labour force

	2009		2008	
	in value U.S.$'000,000	% of total value	labour force	% of labour force
Agriculture, forestry	2,355	4.9	251,200	7.1
Mining }	2,629	5.4	35,000	1.0
Public utilities }			79,100	2.2
Manufacturing	6,338	13.0	769,700	21.6
Construction	3,717	7.6	340,300	9.6
Transp. and commun.	5,652	11.6	260,700	7.3
Trade, restaurants	4,970	10.2	698,800	19.6
Finance }			71,100	2.0
Pub. admin., defense }	16,184	33.2	235,300	6.6
Services }			619,400	17.4
Other	6,877[6]	14.1[6]	199,800[7]	5.6[7]
TOTAL	48,722	100.0	3,560,400	100.0

Production (metric tons except as noted). Agriculture, forestry, fishing (2009): wheat 3,976,850, sunflower seeds 1,317,980, corn (maize) 1,290,830, cow's milk 1,073,400, barley 858,679, grapes 281,302, potatoes 231,745, anise, fennel, and coriander 33,957; livestock (number of live animals) 1,474,850 sheep, 783,649 pigs, 564,904 cattle; roundwood (2010) 5,668,000 cu m, of which fuelwood 47%; fisheries production 15,701 (from aquaculture 43%). Mining and quarrying (2009): copper 105,000[8]; zinc 10,700[8]; gold 4,300 kg. Manufacturing (value added in U.S.$'000,000; 2007): refined petroleum products, n.a.; food products 637; nonelectrical machinery and apparatus 596; wearing apparel 533; cement, bricks, ceramics 528; fabricated metals 369. Energy production (consumption): electricity (kW-hr; 2009) 42,789,000,000 ([2008] 34,684,-000,000); hard coal (metric tons; 2009) 39,000 ([2007] 4,916,000); lignite (metric tons; 2009) 27,174,000 ([2007] 28,687,000); crude petroleum (barrels; 2009) 176,000 ([2007] 52,057,000); petroleum products (metric tons; 2007) 5,938,000 (3,625,000); natural gas (cu m; 2009) 12,000,000 (2,661,000,000).
Household income and expenditure (2009). Average household size 2.5; income per household 9,122 leva (U.S.$6,485); sources of income: wages and salaries 52.2%, transfers 30.8% (of which pensions 27.6%), self-employment 4.8%; expenditure: food and nonalcoholic beverages 36.5%, housing and energy 14.5%, transportation 6.0%, health 5.3%, communications 4.5%.
Population economically active (2009): total 3,491,600; activity rate of total population 46.0% (participation rates: ages 15–64 *c.* 67%; female 47.5%; unemployed [September 2009–August 2010] 9.2%).

Price index (2005 = 100)

	2004	2005	2006	2007	2008	2009	2010
Consumer price index	95.2	100.0	107.3	116.3	130.6	134.2	137.5

Selected balance of payments data. Receipts from (U.S.$'000,000): tourism (2009) 3,776; remittances (2010) 1,403; foreign direct investment (FDI; 2008–10 avg.) 5,125. Disbursements for (U.S.$'000,000): tourism (2009) 1,755; remittances (2009) 101; FDI (2008–10 avg.) 291.
Land use as % of total land area (2007): in temporary crops 22.6%, left fallow 5.2%, in permanent crops 1.8%, in pasture 17.5%, forest area 34.3%.

Foreign trade[9]

Balance of trade (current prices)

	2004	2005	2006	2007	2008	2009
U.S.$'000,000	–3,688	–5,450	–7,028	–10,572	–12,624	–5,775
% of total	15.7%	18.8%	18.9%	21.4%	21.9%	15.0%

Imports (2009): U.S.$23,341,000,000 (mineral fuels 20.1%; machinery and apparatus 19.8%; chemicals and chemical products 11.1%; food 7.9%; base and fabricated metals 7.4%). *Major import sources:* Russia 15.6%; Germany 11.0%; Italy 8.0%; Greece 5.6%; Turkey 5.6%; China 5.4%.
Exports (2009): U.S.$16,502,000,000 (base and fabricated metals 16.7%, of which refined/unrefined copper 7.4%; machinery and apparatus 14.9%; refined petroleum 10.2%; food 10.2%; clothing and accessories 9.6%). *Major export destinations:* Germany 11.2%; Greece 9.4%; Italy 9.3%; Romania 8.6%; Turkey 7.3%; Belgium 5.6%.

Transport and communications

Transport. Railroads (2008): route length 4,294 km; (2008–09[10]) passenger-km 2,161,000,000; (2008–09[10]) metric ton-km cargo 3,200,000,000. Roads (2005): length 24,998 mi, 40,231 km (paved 98%); (2006) passenger-km 43,900,000,000[11]; (2008) metric ton-km cargo 11,027,000,000. Vehicles (2008): cars 2,366,196; trucks and buses 324,760. Air transport (2008): passenger-km 4,467,000,000; metric ton-km cargo 3,000,000.

Communications

Medium	date	number in '000s	units per 1,000 persons	Medium	date	number in '000s	units per 1,000 persons
Televisions	2002	3,620	453	PCs	2007	682	89
Telephones				Dailies	2009	870[12]	115[12]
Cellular	2010	10,585[13]	1,412[13]	Internet users	2009	3,395	450
Landline	2010	2,200	294	Broadband	2010	1,102[13]	147[13]

Education and health

Educational attainment (2008). Percentage of population age 25 and over having: no formal schooling to complete primary education 7.8%; lower secondary 24.5%; upper secondary 47.5%; higher vocational/university 20.2%.
Literacy (2008): total population age 15 and over literate 98.3%; males 98.6%; females 97.9%.

Education (2009–10)

	teachers	students	student/ teacher ratio	enrollment rate (%)
Primary (age 7–10)	15,054	260,340	17.3	93
Secondary/Voc. (age 11–18)	48,291	531,980	11.0	81
Tertiary	22,662	287,086	12.7	41 (age 19–23)

Health (2010): physicians 27,988 (1 per 271 persons); hospital beds (2009) 49,507 (1 per 153 persons); infant mortality rate per 1,000 live births (2009) 9.0; undernourished population (2005–07) less than 5.0% of total population.

Military

Total active duty personnel (November 2010): 31,315 (army 52.1%, navy 11.1%, air force 21.4%, central staff 15.4%). *Military expenditure as percentage of GDP* (2009): 2.2%; per capita expenditure U.S.$146.

[1]Bulgaria has no official religion; the constitution, however, refers to Eastern Orthodoxy as the "traditional" religion. [2]District nearly encircles Sofiya-Grad district on north, east, and south. [3]Sofiya-Grad includes Sofia city and immediately adjacent urban and rural areas. [4]Unofficially up to 40% of the population is estimated to be atheist or agnostic. [5]General government. [6]Taxes less subsidies and imputed bank charges. [7]Unemployed. [8]Metal content of mine output. [9]Imports f.o.b. in balance of trade and c.i.f. for commodities and trading partners. [10]November–October. [11]Passenger cars 31,000,000,000; buses 12,900,000,000. [12]Circulation. [13]Subscribers.

Internet resources for further information:
- **National Statistical Institute http://www.nsi.bg**
- **Bulgarian National Bank http://www.bnb.bg**

Burkina Faso

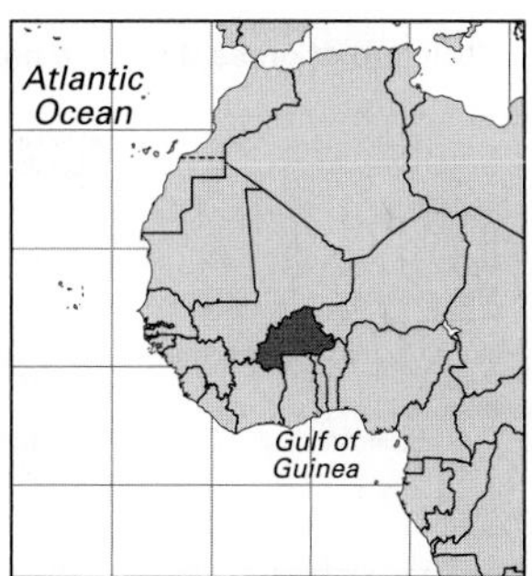

Official name: Burkina Faso (Burkina Faso).
Form of government: multiparty republic with one legislative body (National Assembly [111]).
Head of state: President.
Head of government: Prime Minister.
Capital: Ouagadougou.
Official language: French.
Official religion: none.
Monetary unit: CFA franc (CFAF); valuation (Sept. 1, 2011) 1 U.S.$ = CFAF 460.31; 1 £ = CFAF 743.83.

Area and population

Regions	Capitals	area sq mi	area sq km	population 2006 census[1]
Boucle du Mouhoun	Dédougou	13,190	34,162	1,442,749
Cascades	Banfora	7,117	18,434	531,808
Centre	Ouagadougou	1,083	2,805	1,727,390
Centre-Est	Tenkodogo	5,659	14,656	1,132,016
Centre-Nord	Kava	7,660	19,840	1,202,025
Centre-Ouest	Koudougou	8,388	21,726	1,186,566
Centre-Sud	Manga	4,368	11,313	641,443
Est	Fada N'gourma	17,849	46,228	1,212,284
Hauts-Bassins	Bobo-Dioulasso	9,785	25,343	1,469,604
Nord	Ouahigouya	6,255	16,199	1,185,796
Plateau Central	Ziniaré	3,299	8,545	696,372
Sahel	Dori	13,653	35,360	968,442
Sud-Ouest	Gaoua	6,237	16,153	620,767
TOTAL		104,543	270,764	14,017,262

Demography

Population (2011): 16,968,000.
Density (2011): persons per sq mi 159.6, persons per sq km 61.6.
Urban-rural (2009): urban 24.8%; rural 75.2%.
Sex distribution (2009): male 48.26%; female 51.74%.
Age breakdown (2006): under 15, 46.4%; 15–29, 26.2%; 30–44, 14.3%; 45–59, 7.6%; 60–74, 3.8%; 75–84, 0.9%; 85 and over, 0.3%; unknown 0.5%.
Population projection: (2020) 22,150,000; (2030) 29,112,000.
Doubling time: 23 years.
Ethnic composition (2000): Mossi 46.4%; Fulani 5.9%; Bobo 5.8%; Busansi (Bissa) 3.8%; Gurma 3.4%; Dogara 2.7%; Lobi 2.6%; other 29.4%.
Religious affiliation (2006): Muslim 60.5%[2]; Roman Catholic 19.0%[2]; traditional beliefs 15.3%; Protestant/independent Christian 4.2%[2]; nonreligious 0.4%; other 0.6%.
Major urban localities (2006): Ouagadougou 1,475,223; Bobo-Dioulasso 489,967; Koudougou 88,184; Banfora 75,917; Ouahigouya 73,153.

Vital statistics

Birth rate per 1,000 population (2009): 44.3 (world avg. 20.3).
Death rate per 1,000 population (2009): 13.3 (world avg. 8.5).
Natural increase rate per 1,000 population (2009): 31.0 (world avg. 11.8).
Total fertility rate (avg. births per childbearing woman; 2009): 6.28.
Marriage/divorce rates per 1,000 population: n.a.
Life expectancy at birth (2009): male 51.0 years; female 54.9 years.
Major causes of death per 100,000 population (2002): lower respiratory infections *c.* 414; HIV/AIDS *c.* 256; malaria *c.* 207; diarrheal diseases *c.* 174; perinatal conditions *c.* 108.
Adult population (ages 15–49) *living with HIV* (2009): 1.2%[3] (world avg. 0.8%).

National economy

Budget (2009). Revenue: CFAF 771,524,000,000 (tax revenue 64.1%, of which taxes on goods and services 36.7%, taxes on international transactions 11.6%; grants 30.1%; nontax revenue 5.8%). Expenditures: CFAF 959,595,000,000 (current expenditure 52.0%; development expenditure 47.7%; other 0.3%).
Public debt (external, outstanding; 2009): U.S.$1,725,000,000.
Household income and expenditure. Average household size (2006) 5.9; average annual income per household: n.a.; sources of income: n.a.; expenditure (2003): food, beverages, and tobacco 48.8%, housing and energy 17.8%, transportation 7.0%, clothing 6.8%, health 4.4%, recreation and culture 4.1%.
Production (metric tons except as noted). Agriculture, forestry, fishing (2009): sorghum 1,521,470, millet 970,927, corn (maize) 894,558, seed cotton 483,865, sugarcane 455,000, peanuts (groundnuts) 330,624, dry cowpeas 325,000, rice 213,584, shea nuts 68,841, sesame seed 56,252, bambara beans 44,712; livestock (number of live animals) 11,983,000 goats, 8,234,000 cattle, 8,003,160 sheep; roundwood (2010) 13,770,731 cu m, of which fuelwood 91%; fisheries production 12,075 (from aquaculture 2%). Mining and quarrying (2009): gold 13,181 kg; granite 300,000 cu m. Manufacturing (2009): beer of barley (2008) 60,900; cottonseed oil 47,520; cement 30,000; cattle hides 18,930; goatskins 7,844. Energy production (consumption): electricity (kW-hr; 2008) 590,000,000 (680,000,000); coal, none (none); crude petroleum, none (none); petroleum products (metric tons; 2008) none ([2007] 678,000); natural gas, none (none).
Population economically active (2006): total 6,703,681[4]; activity rate 47.8%[4] (participation rates: ages 15–64, 72.3%; female 45.3%; officially unemployed 2.3%).

Price index (2005 = 100)

	2004	2005	2006	2007	2008	2009	2010
Consumer price index	94.0	100.0	102.3	102.1	113.0	115.9	115.0

Gross national income (GNI; 2010): U.S.$9,031,000,000 (U.S.$550 per capita); purchasing power parity GNI (U.S.$1,260 per capita).

Structure of gross domestic product and labour force

	2009 in value CFAF '000,000	2009 % of total value	2010 labour force	2010 % of labour force
Agriculture	1,224,500	31.8	6,835,000	92.1
Mining	99,900	2.6	590,000 (Mining through Other)	7.9 (Mining through Other)
Manufacturing	424,800	11.1		
Public utilities	48,500	1.3		
Construction	259,400	6.7		
Transp. and commun.	276,700	7.2		
Trade, hotels	424,900	11.1		
Finance, real estate	181,200	4.7		
Pub. admin., defense; Services	601,200	15.6		
Other	305,000[5]	7.9[5]		
TOTAL	3,846,100	100.0	7,425,000	100.0

Land use as % of total land area (2007): in temporary crops or left fallow 19.0%, in permanent crops 0.2%, in pasture 21.9%, forest area 24.7%.
Selected balance of payments data. Receipts from (U.S.$'000,000): tourism (2008) 62; remittances (2010) 43; foreign direct investment (2008–10 avg.) 115; official development assistance (2009) 1,084. Disbursements for (U.S.$'000,000): tourism (2008) 63; remittances (2009) n.a.

Foreign trade[6]

Balance of trade (current prices)

	2004	2005	2006	2007	2008	2009
U.S.$'000,000	–870.7	–828.4	...	...	...	–1,074.8
% of total	59.5%	55.5%	...	...	...	40.3%

Imports (2009): U.S.$1,870,300,000 (petroleum products 22.4%, machinery and apparatus 14.8%, food 12.7%, base and fabricated metals 7.6%, road vehicles 7.5%). *Major import sources:* Côte d'Ivoire 14.5%; France 12.8%; China 9.8%; Neth. 5.3%; U.S. 4.9%.
Exports (2009): U.S.$795,500,000 (gold 47.7%, raw cotton 31.4%, sesame seed 6.0%, food 5.3%). *Major export destinations:* Switzerland 55.4%; Singapore 11.8%; France 5.2%; Ghana 4.2%; Belgium 4.1%.

Transport and communications

Transport. Railroads: (2006) route length 509 km[7]; (2003) passenger-km 9,980,000; (2005) metric ton-km cargo 674,900,000. Roads (2007): total length 9,490 mi, 15,272 km (paved 18%). Vehicles (2007): passenger cars 97,052; trucks and buses 43,553. Air transport (2005): passenger-km 37,000,000; metric ton-km cargo, n.a.

Communications

Medium	date	number in '000s	units per 1,000 persons	Medium	date	number in '000s	units per 1,000 persons
Televisions	2004	156	12	PCs	2007	88	6.0
Telephones				Dailies	2009	36[8]	2.3[8]
Cellular	2010	5,708[9]	347[9]	Internet users	2009	178	11.3
Landline	2010	144	8.7	Broadband	2010	13.7[9]	0.8[9]

Education and health

Educational attainment (2003)[10]. Percentage of population age 25 and over having: no formal schooling or unknown 85.4%; incomplete to complete primary education 7.9%; incomplete to complete secondary 5.5%; higher 1.2%.
Literacy (2007): percentage of total population age 15 and over literate 28.3%; males literate 36.7%; females literate 21.0%.

Education (2008–09)

	teachers	students	student/ teacher ratio	enrollment rate (%)
Primary (age 7–12)	38,983	1,906,279	48.9	63
Secondary/Voc. (age 13–19)	18,251	467,658	25.6	15
Tertiary	2,515	47,587	18.9	3 (age 20–24)

Health: physicians (2008) 473 (1 per 32,207 persons); hospital beds (2006) 12,200 (1 per 1,111 persons); infant mortality rate per 1,000 live births (2009) 84.5; undernourished population (2004–06) 1,300,000 (9% of total population based on the consumption of a minimum daily requirement of 1,730 calories).

Military

Total active duty personnel (November 2010): 11,200 (army 57.1%, air force 5.4%, gendarmerie 37.5%). *Military expenditure as percentage of GDP* (2009): 1.3%; per capita expenditure U.S.$7.

[1]Final. [2]Adherence to beliefs often nominal. [3]Statistically derived midpoint within range. [4]Includes 1,417,821 persons deemed economically active between the ages of 5 and 14. [5]Indirect taxes less imputed bank service charges. [6]Imports c.i.f.; exports f.o.b. [7]Burkina Faso part of Abidjan, Côte d'Ivoire–Ouagadougou railway; 103 km of railway beyond Ouagadougou is operational but not in use. [8]Circulation. [9]Subscribers. [10]Based on the 2003 Burkina Faso Demographic and Health Survey, comprising 57,737 people in 9,097 households, about 80% of which are located in rural areas.

Internet resources for further information:
- **Institut National de la Statistique et de la Démographie http://www.insd.bf**
- **La Banque de France: La Zone Franc http://www.banque-france.fr/fr/eurosys/zonefr/zonefr.htm**

Burundi

Official name: Republika y'u Burundi (Rundi); République du Burundi (French) (Republic of Burundi).
Form of government: republic with two legislative bodies (Senate [41[1]]; National Assembly [106[2]]).
Head of state and government: President assisted by Vice Presidents.
Capital: Bujumbura[3].
Official languages: Rundi; French.
Official religion: none.
Monetary unit: Burundi franc (FBu); valuation (Sept. 1, 2011) 1 U.S.$ = FBu 1,260; 1 £ = FBu 2,036.

Area and population

Provinces	area sq km	population 2008 preliminary census	Provinces	area sq km	population 2008 preliminary census
Bubanza	1,089	348,188	Muyinga	1,836	632,346
Bujumbura	1,232	565,070	Mwaro	840	269,048
Bururi	2,465	570,929	Ngozi	1,474	661,310
Cankuzo	1,965	221,391	Rutana	1,959	336,394
Cibitoke	1,636	460,626	Ruyigi	2,339	400,818
Gitega	1,979	715,080			
Karuzi	1,457	433,061	**Urban Province**		
Kayanza	1,233	586,096	Bujumbura	87	478,155
Kirundo	1,703	636,298	TOTAL LAND AREA	25,950	
Makamba	1,960	428,917	INLAND WATER	1,867	
Muramvya	696	294,891	TOTAL	27,834[4]	8,038,618

Demography

Population (2011): 8,575,000.
Density (2011)[5]: persons per sq mi 855.8, persons per sq km 330.4.
Urban-rural (2009): urban 10.7%; rural 89.3%.
Sex distribution (2009): male 49.02%; female 50.98%.
Age breakdown (2005): under 15, 41.4%; 15–29, 30.8%; 30–44, 14.7%; 45–59, 8.7%; 60–74, 3.5%; 75–84, 0.8%; 85 and over, 0.1%.
Population projection: (2020) 10,057,000; (2030) 11,441,000.
Doubling time: 34 years.
Ethnic composition (2000): Hutu 80.9%; Tutsi 15.6%; Lingala 1.6%; Twa Pygmy 1.0%; other 0.9%.
Religious affiliation (2009): Roman Catholic *c.* 60%; indigenous religious groups/traditional beliefs *c.* 20%; Protestant *c.* 15%; Muslim (mostly Sunnī) *c.* 3.5%; other *c.* 1.5%.
Major city and towns (2004): Bujumbura (2009) 454,866; Gitega 25,500; Ngozi 21,500; Bururi 20,500.

Vital statistics

Birth rate per 1,000 population (2009): 41.8 (world avg. 20.3).
Death rate per 1,000 population (2009): 10.1 (world avg. 8.5).
Natural increase rate per 1,000 population (2009): 31.7 (world avg. 11.8).
Total fertility rate (avg. births per childbearing woman; 2009): 6.33.
Life expectancy at birth (2009): male 56.2 years; female 59.4 years.
Adult population (ages 15–49) *living with HIV* (2009): 3.3%[6] (world avg. 0.8%).
Major causes of death per 100,000 population (2002): HIV/AIDS-related *c.* 370; lower respiratory infections *c.* 185; diarrheal diseases *c.* 128; war-related *c.* 114; perinatal conditions *c.* 100; malaria *c.* 57.

National economy

Budget (2009). Revenue: FBu 1,627,100,000,000 (grants 81.3%, of which HIPC relief[7] 65.7%; tax revenue 17.1%, of which taxes on goods and services 9.1%, income taxes 5.2%; nontax revenue 1.6%). Expenditures: FBu 643,300,000,000 (current expenditure 65.6%; capital expenditure 33.8%; net lending 0.6%).
Public debt (external, outstanding; September 2010): U.S.$414,400,000[8].
Production (metric tons except as noted). Agriculture, forestry, fishing (2009): bananas 620,028, sweet potatoes 484,207, cassava 235,369, dry beans 202,934, sugarcane 132,769, corn (maize) 120,379, sorghum 81,176, rice 78,432, taros 44,502, dry peas 37,316, cow's milk 26,000, coffee 25,130, cattle meat 15,210, tea 6,729; livestock (number of live animals) 1,687,370 goats, 553,528 cattle, 291,522 sheep; roundwood (2010) 9,994,143 cu m, of which fuelwood 91%; fisheries production 17,900 (from aquaculture 1%). Mining and quarrying (2008): columbite-tantalite ore 83,854 kg; gold 750 kg. Manufacturing (2009): soap (2008) 5,671,000; sugar 14,300; beer 1,366,500 hectolitres; carbonated beverages 287,100 hectolitres; cottonseed oil 31,500 litres; cigarettes 514,240,000 units; fabrics (2006) 2,866,000,000 sq m. Energy production (consumption): electricity (kW-hr; 2009) 121,150,000 (206,700,000); coal, none (none); crude petroleum, none (none); petroleum products (metric tons; 2007) none (52,000); natural gas, none (none); peat (metric tons; 2009) 9,800 ([2007] 5,000).
Household income and expenditure (2004)[9]. Average household size 5.6; average annual income per household *c.* FBu 168,000 (*c.* U.S.$153); sources of income: agriculture/livestock *c.* 91%, other *c.* 9%; expenditure: food *c.* 46%, housing, n.a., debt service *c.* 14%, alcoholic beverages and tobacco *c.* 8%, transportation *c.* 6%, health *c.* 5%, clothing *c.* 4%.
Land use as % of total land area (2009): in temporary crops or left fallow (2007) 38.7%, in permanent crops 13.6%, in pasture 35.0%, forest area 6.8%.
Gross national income (GNI; 2010): U.S.$1,402,000,000 (U.S.$160 per capita); purchasing power parity GNI (U.S.$390 per capita).

Structure of gross domestic product and labour force

	2009 in value U.S.$'000	2009 % of total value	2010 labour force[10]	2010 % of labour force[10]
Agriculture	525,300	42.0	3,801,000	89.2
Mining; Public utilities	13,200	1.1	459,000	10.8
Manufacturing	112,600	9.0		
Construction	41,800	3.3		
Transp. and communications	182,600	14.6		
Trade	130,100	10.4		
Finance; Pub. admin., defense; Services	150,100	12.0		
Other	94,900[11]	7.6[11]		
TOTAL	1,250,600	100.0	4,260,000	100.0

Population economically active (2008)[12]: total 4,406,000; activity rate of total population 54.6% (participation rates: ages 15–64, 89.9%; female 52.6%; unemployed, n.a.).

Price index (2005 = 100)

	2004	2005	2006	2007	2008	2009	2010
Consumer price index	88.1	100.0	102.8	111.4	138.2	153.4	163.2

Selected balance of payments data. Receipts from (U.S.$'000,000): tourism (2009) 1.5; remittances (2010) 3.0; foreign direct investment (2008–10 avg.) 13; official development assistance (2009) 549. Disbursements for (U.S.$'000,000): tourism (2009) 71; remittances (2009) negligible.

Foreign trade[13]

Balance of trade (current prices)

	2004	2005	2006	2007	2008	2009
U.S.$'000,000	−90.0	−144.4	−205.1	−266.8	−173.4	−231.9
% of total	35.2%	38.8%	31.0%	46.1%	37.9%	50.7%

Imports (2009): U.S.$344,800,000 (machinery and apparatus 21.8%, road vehicles 10.6%, base and fabricated metals 8.2%, cereals 7.7%, telecommunications equipment/parts 7.5%, kraft paper 7.5%, medicines 7.4%). *Major import sources:* Belgium 13.5%; China 9.4%; Kenya 9.3%; Uganda 8.6%; India 5.6%.
Exports (2009): U.S.$112,900,000 (coffee 35.1%, gold 25.7%[14], tea 6.7%, goods vehicles 4.6%, metal ore/scrap metal 3.5%). *Major export destinations:* U.A.E. 25.6%; Switzerland 18.3%; Tanzania 8.4%; Germany 7.4%; Kenya 6.5%.

Transport and communications

Transport. Railroads: none. Roads (2004): total length 7,657 mi, 12,322 km (paved 10%). Vehicles (2007): passenger cars 15,466; trucks and buses 32,717. Air transport (2007–08)[15]: passenger arrivals 96,175, passenger departures 62,845; cargo unloaded 2,116 metric tons, cargo loaded 317 metric tons.

Communications

Medium	date	number in '000s	units per 1,000 persons	Medium	date	number in '000s	units per 1,000 persons
Televisions	2004	280	37	PCs	2006	57	7.0
Telephones				Dailies	2009	20[16]	2.4[16]
Cellular	2010	1,151[17]	137[17]	Internet users	2009	65	7.8
Landline	2010	33	3.9	Broadband	2010	0.2[17]	—

Education and health

Educational attainment: n.a. *Literacy* (2008): percentage of total population age 15 and over literate 65.9%; males literate 72.3%; females literate 59.9%.

Education (2008–09)

	teachers	students	student/teacher ratio	enrollment rate (%)
Primary (age 7–12)	33,867	1,739,450	51.4	99
Secondary/Voc. (age 13–19)	10,895	288,956	26.5	9[18]
Tertiary	1,487	24,290	16.3	3 (age 20–24)

Health (2004): physicians 200 (1 per 37,581 persons); hospital beds (2006) 5,663 (1 per 1,429 persons); infant mortality rate per 1,000 live births (2009) 64.9; undernourished population (2004–06) 4,900,000 (63% of total population based on the consumption of a minimum daily requirement of 1,720 calories).

Military

Total active duty personnel (November 2010): 20,000 (army 100%)[19]. *Military expenditure as percentage of GDP* (2009): 3.2%; per capita expenditure U.S.$5.

[1]34 seats are indirectly elected; additional seats are designated for the Twa ethnic group (3) and former presidents (4). [2]Includes 6 additional appointed or co-opted seats. [3]Future move of capital to Gitega announced by president in March 2007. [4]Detail does not add to total given because of statistical discrepancy. [5]Based on land area. [6]Statistically derived midpoint within range. [7]Debt relief for Heavily Indebted Poor Countries funded by the World Bank and IMF. [8]Includes short-term debt. [9]Based on a survey of 4,300 households in rural Burundi. [10]FAO estimate. [11]Nearly all indirect taxes less subsidies. [12]ILO estimates. [13]Imports c.i.f.; exports f.o.b. [14]Nearly all gold smuggled from neighbouring countries. [15]Figures for Bujumbura airport only. [16]Circulation. [17]Subscribers. [18]2006–07. [19]Burundian troops in Somalia as part of African Union (AU) peacekeeping mission (November 2010) 3,000.

Internet resource for further information:
- **Banque Centrale du Burundi http://www.brb-bi.net**

Cambodia

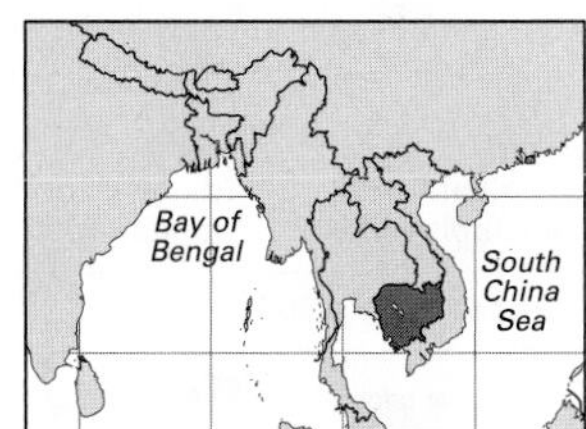

Official name: Preahreacheanachakr Kampuchea (Kingdom of Cambodia).
Form of government: constitutional monarchy with two legislative houses (Senate [61[1]]; National Assembly [123]).
Head of state: King.
Head of government: Prime Minister.
Capital: Phnom Penh.
Official language: Khmer.
Official religion: Buddhism.
Monetary unit: riel (KHR); valuation (Sept. 1, 2011) 1 U.S.$ = KHR 4,075; 1 £ = KHR 6,585.

Area and population

Provinces	area sq km	population 2008 census	Provinces	area sq km	population 2008 census
Banteay Meanchey	6,679	677,872	Prey Veng	4,883	947,372
Battambang	11,702	1,025,174	Pursat	12,692	397,161
Kampong Cham	9,799	1,679,992	Ratanak Kiri	10,782	150,466
Kampong Chanang	5,521	472,341	Siemreap	10,299	896,443
Kampong Speu	7,017	716,944	Sihanoukville	868	221,396
Kampong Thom	13,814	631,409	Stung Treng	11,092	111,671
Kampot	4,873	585,850	Svay Rieng	2,966	482,788
Kandal	3,568	1,265,280	Takeo	3,563	844,906
Kep	336	35,753			
Koh Kong	11,160	117,481	**Municipality**		
Kratie	11,094	319,217	Phnom Penh	290	1,327,615
Mondul Kiri	14,288	61,107	TOTAL LAND AREA	178,035	
Oddar Meanchey	6,158	185,819	INLAND WATER	3,000	
Pailin	803	70,486	TOTAL	181,035	13,395,682
Preah Vihear	13,788	171,139			

Demography

Population (2011): 14,702,000.
Density (2011)[2]: persons per sq mi 213.9, persons per sq km 82.6.
Urban-rural (2008): urban 19.5%; rural 80.5%.
Sex distribution (2008): male 48.64%; female 51.36%.
Age breakdown (2008): under 15, 33.7%; 15–29, 31.5%; 30–44, 17.0%; 45–59, 11.4%; 60–74, 4.9%; 75 and over, 1.5%.
Doubling time: 41 years.
Population projection: (2020) 16,927,000; (2030) 19,031,000.
Ethnic composition (2000): Khmer 85.2%; Chinese 6.4%; Vietnamese 3.0%; Cham 2.5%; Lao 0.6%; other 2.3%.
Religious affiliation (2009): Buddhist *c.* 93%; Muslim *c.* 4%; Christian (mostly Protestant) *c.* 2%; other *c.* 1%.
Major urban areas (2008): Phnom Penh 1,242,992; Siemreap 168,662; Battambang 140,533; Paoy Paet 89,549; Preah Seihanu 89,447; Ta Khmau 80,141; Sisophon 61,631.

Vital statistics

Birth rate per 1,000 population (2009): 26.2 (world avg. 20.3).
Death rate per 1,000 population (2009): 8.3 (world avg. 8.5).
Natural increase rate per 1,000 population (2009): 17.8 (world avg. 11.8).
Total fertility rate (avg. births per childbearing woman; 2009): 3.00.
Life expectancy at birth (2009): male 59.6 years; female 64.3 years.
Major causes of death per 100,000 population (2002): cardiovascular diseases *c.* 158; HIV/AIDS-related *c.* 114; tuberculosis *c.* 90; diarrheal diseases *c.* 86; perinatal conditions *c.* 84.

National economy

Budget (2009). Revenue: KHR 6,091,800,000,000 (tax revenue 71.1%, grants 16.6%, nontax revenue 11.8%, other 0.5%). Expenditures: KHR 7,548,600,000,000 (current expenditure 60.9%, development expenditure 39.1%).
Production (metric tons except as noted). Agriculture, forestry, fishing (2009): rice 7,586,000, cassava 3,497,000, corn (maize) 924,000, sugarcane 350,000, bananas 160,768, soybeans 137,000, coconuts 71,000, oranges 50,458, rubber (2008) 31,676, tobacco leaves 18,599; livestock (number of live animals) 3,550,000 cattle, 2,200,000 pigs, 750,000 buffalo, (2005) 120,000 crocodiles; roundwood (2010) 8,668,835 cu m, of which fuelwood 99%; fisheries production 515,000 (from aquaculture 10%); aquatic plants production, none. Mining and quarrying (2008): gold, n.a.; gemstones, n.a.; crude stones 2,039,336; salt 454,750. Manufacturing (value added in KHR '000,000,000; 2005): wearing apparel/footwear 3,158; food, beverages, tobacco products 657; wood and paper products and publishing 144; rubber products 125. Energy production (consumption): electricity (kW-hr; 2008) 1,380,000,000 (1,560,000,000); coal (metric tons; 2009) none (none); petroleum products (metric tons; 2007) none (1,432,000); crude petroleum (barrels; 2009) none (none); natural gas (cu m; 2009) none (none).
Household income and expenditure. Average household size (2008) 4.7; average annual extrapolated monetary and nonmonetary income (1993–94) KHR 2,031,000 (U.S.$787); sources of income (1993–94): monetary 67.4% (of which nonagricultural [mostly self-employment] 36.8%, agricultural 18.1%, wages and salaries 9.1%), non-monetary 32.6% (of which agricultural 11.4%); household expenditure (2002): food, beverages, and tobacco 62.6%, housing and energy 19.7%, health 6.0%, transportation and communications 3.4%.
Selected balance of payments data. Receipts from (U.S.$'000,000): tourism (2009) 1,312; remittances (2010) 369; foreign direct investment (FDI; 2008–10 avg.) 712; official development assistance (2009) 722. Disbursements for (U.S.$'000,000): tourism (2009) 162; remittances (2009) 215; FDI (2008–10 avg.) 20.

Gross national income (GNI; 2010): U.S.$10,686,000,000 (U.S.$760 per capita); purchasing power parity GNI (U.S.$2,040 per capita).

Structure of gross domestic product and labour force

	2008 in value KHR '000,000,000	2008 % of total value	2007 labour force	2007 % of labour force
Agriculture	13,593	30.5	4,670,000	55.9
Mining	165	0.4	22,000	0.3
Manufacturing	6,441	14.5	944,000	11.3
Construction	2,571	5.8	299,000	3.6
Public utilities	212	0.5	21,000	0.3
Transp. and commun.	3,102	7.0	228,000	2.7
Trade, hotels	5,619	12.6	1,282,000	15.3
Finance, real estate	5,805	13.0	52,000	0.6
Public admin., defense	768	1.7	185,000	2.2
Services	3,560	8.0	308,000	3.7
Other	2,694[3]	6.0[3]	343,000	4.1
TOTAL	44,530	100.0	8,354,000	100.0

Public debt (external, outstanding; 2009): U.S.$2,128,000,000.
Population economically active (2008): total 7,053,398; activity rate of total population 52.7% (participation rates: ages 15–64, 80.0%; female 51.2%; unemployed[4] 1.7%).

Price index (2005 = 100)

	2004	2005	2006	2007	2008	2009	2010
Consumer price index	94.0	100.0	106.1	114.3	142.9	141.9	147.6

Land use as % of total land area (2007): in temporary crops or left fallow 21.5%, in permanent crops 0.9%, in pasture 8.5%, forest area 56.7%.

Foreign trade[5]

Balance of trade (current prices)

	2004	2005	2006	2007	2008
U.S.$'000,000	–735	...	...	...	–59
% of total	15.1%	...	...	...	0.7%

Imports (2008): U.S.$4,417,000,000 (textile yarns/fabrics 31.9%; machinery and apparatus 11.9%; road vehicles 10.5%, of which motorcycles/parts 3.5%; refined petroleum 7.0%). *Major import sources:* China 21.1%; Thailand 15.8%; Hong Kong 13.3%; Vietnam 10.7%; Taiwan 8.3%.
Exports (2008): U.S.$4,358,000,000 (wearing apparel and accessories 69.2%, of which women's/girls' outerwear 26.2%, men's/boys' outerwear 16.1%; printed matter 20.7%; crude fertilizers 2.7%). *Major export destinations:* U.S. 45.2%; China 19.3%; Canada 6.7%; Vietnam 3.9%; U.K. 3.6%.

Transport and communications

Transport. Railroads (2008): route length 613 km; passenger-km (2005) 45,000,000; metric ton-km (2000) 92,000,000. Roads (2009[6]): total length 24,617 mi, 39,618 km (paved 7%); passenger-km (1999) 201,000,000; metric ton-km cargo (1999) 3,200,000. Vehicles (2005): passenger cars 195,268; trucks and buses 35,272. Air transport (2007): passenger-km 432,000,000; metric ton-km cargo 2,000,000.

Communications

Medium	date	number in '000s	units per 1,000 persons	Medium	date	number in '000s	units per 1,000 persons
Televisions	2008	1,646	113	PCs	2008	103	7.1
Telephones				Dailies	2009	58[7]	5.9[7]
Cellular	2009	5,593[8]	378[8]	Internet users	2009	78	5.3
Landline	2009	54	3.7	Broadband	2009	30[8]	2.0[8]

Education and health

Educational attainment (2008). Percentage of literate population age 25 and over having: no formal schooling 3.2%; incomplete primary education 47.2%; complete primary 26.8%; incomplete secondary 18.8%; secondary/vocational 2.2%; higher 1.8%. *Literacy* (2008): percentage of total population age 15 and over literate 77.6%; males literate 85.1%; females literate 70.9%.

Education (2006–07)

	teachers	students	student/ teacher ratio	enrollment rate (%)
Primary (age 6–11)	46,658[9]	2,289,759[9]	49.1[9]	89[10]
Secondary/Voc. (age 12–17)	30,258	875,120	28.9	34
Tertiary	3,261[11]	122,633[10]	23.3[11]	7[10] (age 18–22)

Health: physicians (2008) 3,542 (1 per 3,953 persons); hospital beds (2002) 9,800 (1 per 1,405 persons); infant mortality rate per 1,000 live births (2009) 58.4; undernourished population (2004–06) 3,500,000 (25% of total population based on the consumption of a minimum daily requirement of 1,750 calories).

Military

Total active duty personnel (November 2010): 124,300 (army 60.3%, navy 2.3%, air force 1.2%, provincial forces 36.2%). *Military expenditure as percentage of GDP* (2009): 2.2%; per capita expenditure U.S.$15.

[1]Includes 59 indirectly elected seats and 2 nonelected seats. [2]Based on land area. [3]Indirect taxes less subsidies and less imputed bank service charges. [4]Registered; for population age 7 and over. [5]Imports c.i.f.; exports f.o.b. [6]January 1. [7]Circulation. [8]Subscribers. [9]2008–09. [10]2007–08. [11]2005–06.

Internet resource for further information:

- **National Institute of Statistics http://www.nis.gov.kh**

Cameroon

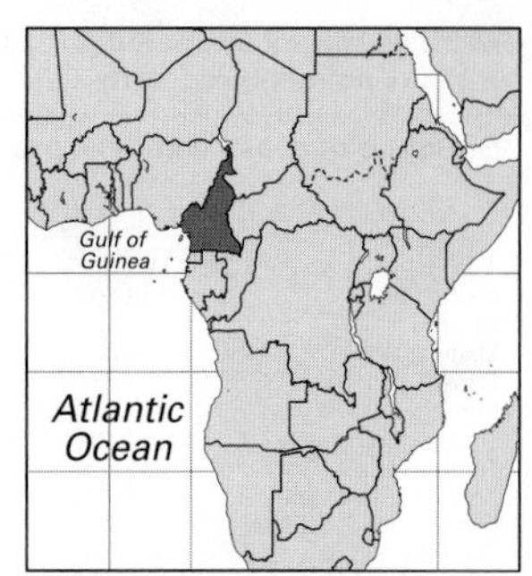

Official name: République du Cameroun (French); Republic of Cameroon (English).
Form of government: unitary multiparty republic with one legislative house (National Assembly [180])[1].
Head of state: President.
Head of government: Prime Minister.
Capital: Yaoundé.
Official languages: French; English.
Official religion: none.
Monetary unit: CFA franc (CFAF); valuation (Sept. 1, 2011) 1 U.S.$ = CFAF 460.31; 1 £ = CFAF 743.83.

Area and population		area		population
				2010[2]
Regions	**Capitals**	sq mi	sq km	projection[3]
Adamoua	Ngaoundéré	24,595	63,701	1,015,622
Centre	Yaoundé	26,623	68,953	3,525,664
Est	Bertoua	42,086	109,002	801,968
Extrême-Nord	Maroua	13,229	34,263	3,480,414
Littoral	Douala	7,818	20,248	2,865,795
Nord	Garoua	25,517	66,090	2,050,229
Nord-Ouest	Bamenda	6,680	17,300	1,804,695
Ouest	Bafoussam	5,364	13,892	1,785,285
Sud	Ebolowa	18,221	47,191	692,142
Sud-Ouest	Buea	10,081[4]	26,110[4]	1,384,286
LAND AREA		180,213[5]	466,750	
INLAND WATER		3,707	9,600	
TOTAL		183,920[4, 5]	476,350[4]	19,406,100

Demography

Population (2011): 20,073,000.
Density (2011)[6]: persons per sq mi 111.4, persons per sq km 43.0.
Urban-rural (2010[2]): urban 52.0%; rural 48.0%.
Sex distribution (2010[2]): male 49.46%; female 50.54%.
Age breakdown (2010[2]): under 15, 43.6%; 15–29, 28.5%; 30–44, 15.2%; 45–59, 7.7%; 60–74, 3.8%; 75–84, 0.9%; 85 and over, 0.3%.
Population projection: (2020) 24,193,000; (2030) 28,902,000.
Ethnic composition (2006): "western highlanders" *c.* 38.0%, including Bamileke *c.* 11.5%; "coastal tropical forest peoples" *c.* 12.0%, including Bassa *c.* 2.5%; "southern tropical forest peoples" *c.* 18.0%, including Ewondo (Yaunde) *c.* 8.0%; "mostly Islamic central highlanders" *c.* 14.0%, including Fulani *c.* 8.5%; "mostly traditional believers of central highlands and far north" or "Kirdi" *c.* 18.0%, including Mofa *c.* 2.5%.
Religious affiliation (2005): Roman Catholic 38.4%; Protestant 26.3%; Sunnī Muslim 20.9%; animist 5.6%; nonreligious/other 8.8%.
Major urban areas (2006): Douala 2,125,000[7]; Yaoundé 1,801,000[7]; Kousséri 476,600; Garoua 461,300; Bamenda 419,400; Maroua 335,800.

Vital statistics

Birth rate per 1,000 population (2009): 36.4 (world avg. 20.3).
Death rate per 1,000 population (2009): 14.0 (world avg. 8.5).
Natural increase rate per 1,000 population (2006): 22.6 (world avg. 11.8).
Total fertility rate (avg. births per childbearing woman; 2006): 4.58.
Life expectancy at birth (2006): male 51.7 years; female 53.0 years.
Adult population (ages 15–49) *living with HIV* (2009): 5.3%[8] (world avg. 0.8%).
Major causes of death per 100,000 population (2002): HIV/AIDS-related *c.* 308; lower respiratory infections *c.* 201; malaria *c.* 119; diarrheal diseases *c.* 88.

National economy

Budget (2009). Revenue: CFAF 1,978,000,000,000 (non-oil revenue 69.0%, oil revenue 25.5%, grants 5.5%). Expenditures: CFAF 1,925,000,000,000 (current expenditure 69.5%, capital expenditure 30.5%).
Public debt (external, outstanding; 2009): U.S.$2,128,000,000.
Gross national income (GNI; 2010): U.S.$23,169,000,000 (U.S.$1,160 per capita); purchasing power parity GNI (U.S.$2,190 per capita).

Structure of gross domestic product and labour force	2008		2006	
	in value CFAF '000,000,000	% of total value	labour force[9]	% of labour force
Agriculture, fishing, forestry	2,257	21.2	4,013,000	53.9
Mining	1,086	10.2	3,660,000	46.1
Manufacturing	1,533	14.4		
Construction	275	2.6		
Public utilities	102	1.0		
Transp. and commun.	621	5.8		
Trade, hotels	2,053	19.3		
Finance, real estate	1,047	9.9		
Public admin., defense	791	7.4		
Services	114	1.1		
Other	750[10]	7.1[10]		
TOTAL	10,629	100.0	7,673,000	100.0

Selected balance of payments data. Receipts from (U.S.$'000,000): tourism (2008) 154; remittances (2010) 148; foreign direct investment (2008–10 avg.) 344; official development assistance (2009) 649. Disbursements for (U.S.$'000,000): tourism (2008) 340; remittances (2009) 94.
Land use as % of total land area (2009): in temporary crops or left fallow (2007) 12.6%, in permanent crops 3.0%, in pasture 4.2%, forest area 43.0%.

Household income and expenditure (2004). Average household size 4.8; expenditure: food and nonalcoholic beverages 44.1%, clothing and footwear 13.1%, cafés and hotels 8.6%, transportation 7.4%, housing and energy 7.0%.
Population economically active (2008): total 7,518,000[11]; activity rate of total population 39.4%[11] (participation rates: ages 15–64, 68.1%[11]; female 39.9%[11]; unemployed 9.3%[12], underemployed 68.8%[12]).

Price index (2005 = 100)	2004	2005	2006	2007	2008	2009	2010
Consumer price index	98.0	100.0	105.1	106.1	111.7	115.2	116.6

Production (metric tons except as noted). Agriculture, forestry, fishing (2009): cassava 2,800,000, taro 1,668,130[13], plantains 1,627,610[13], oil palm fruit 1,600,000, sugarcane 1,450,000, corn (maize) 1,300,000, bananas 1,000,000, sorghum 600,000, tomatoes 570,000, yams 400,000, dry beans 270,000, cacao 226,000, seed cotton 175,000, peanuts (groundnuts) 160,000, dry cowpeas 130,000, game meat 66,208[13], melonseed 59,612, coffee 48,123; livestock (number of live animals) 6,000,000 cattle, 4,400,000 goats, 3,800,000 sheep; roundwood (2010) 12,434,344 cu m, of which fuelwood 79%; fisheries production 138,400 (from aquaculture, negligible). Mining and quarrying (2009): pozzolana 600,000; limestone 100,000; gold 1,800 kg. Manufacturing (value added in U.S.$'000,000; 2002): food products 97; refined petroleum 88; beverages 78; paints, soaps, and varnishes 51; wood products (excl. furniture) 48; rubber products 38. Energy production (consumption): electricity (kW-hr; 2008) 5,420,000,000 (4,883,000,000); coal, none (none); crude petroleum (barrels; 2010) 23,725,000 ([2009] 9,855,000); petroleum products (metric tons; 2007) 2,030,000 (1,636,000); natural gas (cu m; 2007) 412,000,000 (412,000,000).

Foreign trade[14]

Balance of trade (current prices)	2005	2006	2007	2008	2009	2010
CFAF '000,000,000	+66.6	+221.1	–285.5	–492.6	–439.3	–470.5
% of total	2.3%	6.3%	7.6%	11.3%	12.1%	10.9%

Imports (2006): CFAF 1,647,600,000,000 (crude petroleum 29.4%, chemicals and chemical products 11.1%, machinery and apparatus 10.9%, cereals 9.0%, road vehicles 5.8%). *Major import sources* (2006): Nigeria 23.3%; France 17.2%; China 6.3%; Belgium 4.1%; Equatorial Guinea 3.5%.
Exports (2008): CFAF 2,230,800,000,000 (crude petroleum 52.2%, refined petroleum [2007] 15.0%, sawn and rough wood 13.0%, cocoa 6.4%, aluminum 4.7%, raw cotton 2.0%, coffee 1.6%). *Major export destinations* (2006): Spain 25.9%; Italy 23.1%; France 10.7%; U.S. 6.4%; Neth. 6.3%.

Transport and communications

Transport. Railroads (2009): route length 990 km; passenger-km 481,000,000; metric ton-km cargo 1,015,000,000. Roads (2006): total length 17,834 mi[15], 28,702 km[15] (paved 17%). Vehicles (2007): passenger cars 190,341; trucks and buses 63,113. Air transport: passenger-km (2005) 797,000,000; metric ton-km cargo (2007) 26,000,000.

Communications			units				units
Medium	date	number in '000s	per 1,000 persons	**Medium**	date	number in '000s	per 1,000 persons
Televisions	2004	720	43	PCs	2006	194	11
Telephones				Dailies	2009	75[16]	3.9[16]
Cellular	2010	8,156[17]	416[17]	Internet users	2009	750	38
Landline	2010	497	25.3	Broadband	2010	1.0[17]	0.1[17]

Education and health

Educational attainment (2004)[18]: Percentage of population age 25 and over having: no formal schooling 32.9%; primary education 35.3%; secondary 26.2%; higher 4.2%; other/unknown 1.4%. *Literacy* (2007): percentage of total population age 15 and over literate 70.7%; males 78.9%; females 63.0%.

Education (2008–09)	teachers	students	student/ teacher ratio	enrollment rate (%)
Primary (age 6–11)	72,344	3,350,662	46.3	92
Secondary/Voc. (age 12–18)	43,193[19]	1,268,655	16.2[19]	...
Tertiary	3,834[20]	174,144	38.5[20]	9 (age 19–23)

Health: physicians (2009) 1,555[21] (1 per 12,315 persons); hospital beds (2006) 26,589 (1 per 667 persons); infant mortality rate (2006) 67.2; undernourished population (2004–06) 4,000,000 (23% of total population based on the consumption of a minimum daily requirement of 1,800 calories).

Military

Total active duty personnel (November 2010): 14,100 (army 88.7%, navy 9.2%, air force 2.1%). *Military expenditure as percentage of GDP* (2009): 1.6%; per capita expenditure U.S.$18.

[1]The 1996 Constitution calls for the parliament to comprise also a Senate, which has yet to be formed. [2]January 1. [3]Official projection based on analysis of demographic trends from the 1976, 1987, and 2005 censuses. [4]Includes the 270 sq mi (700 sq km) area of Bakassi peninsula, which was formally ceded by Nigeria to Cameroon on Aug. 14, 2008; the 2008 pop. est. for Bakassi is roughly 250,000. [5]Detail does not add to total given because of rounding. [6]Based on land area. [7]2010. [8]Statistically derived midpoint within range. [9]FAO estimate. [10]Indirect taxes less imputed bank service charges. [11]ILO estimate. [12]Per government survey. [13]Based on FAO imputation methodology. [14]Imports c.i.f. [15]National roads only. [16]Circulation. [17]Subscribers. [18]Based on 2004 survey of 17,506 persons. [19]2005–06. [20]2007–08. [21]Public health only.

Internet resource for further information:

- **National Institute of Statistics http://www.statistics-cameroon.org**

Canada

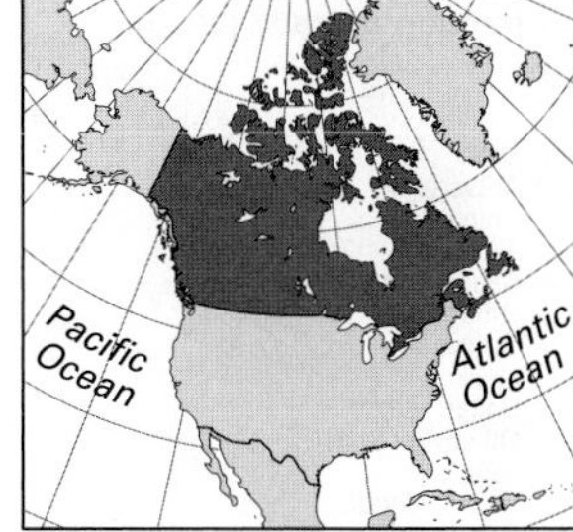

Official name: Canada.
Form of government: federal multiparty parliamentary state with two legislative houses (Senate [105[1, 2]]; House of Commons [308]).
Head of state: Queen of Canada (British Monarch).
Representative of chief of state: Governor-General.
Head of government: Prime Minister.
Capital: Ottawa.
Official languages: English; French.
Official religion: none.
Monetary unit: Canadian dollar (Can$); valuation (Sept. 1, 2011) 1 U.S.$ = Can$0.98; 1 £ = Can$1.58.

Area and population

		area		population
				2011[3]
Provinces	Capitals	sq mi	sq km	estimate
Alberta	Edmonton	255,541	661,848	3,742,753
British Columbia	Victoria	364,764	944,735	4,554,085
Manitoba	Winnipeg	250,116	647,797	1,243,653
New Brunswick	Fredericton	28,150	72,908	753,232
Newfoundland and Labrador	St. John's	156,453	405,212	509,148
Nova Scotia	Halifax	21,345	55,284	943,414
Ontario	Toronto	415,599	1,076,395	13,282,444
Prince Edward Island	Charlottetown	2,185	5,660	143,481
Quebec	Quebec	595,391	1,542,056	7,942,983
Saskatchewan	Regina	251,367	651,036	1,052,050
Territories				
Northwest Territories	Yellowknife	519,735	1,346,106	43,554
Nunavut	Iqaluit	808,185	2,093,190	33,303
Yukon	Whitehorse	186,272	482,443	34,306
TOTAL		3,855,103[4]	9,984,670[4]	34,278,406

Demography

Population (2011): 34,447,000.
Density (2011)[5]: persons per sq mi 9.8, persons per sq km 3.8.
Urban-rural (2006): urban 80.2%; rural 19.8%.
Sex distribution (2007): male 49.53%; female 50.47%.
Age breakdown (2007): under 15, 17.0%; 15–29, 20.5%; 30–44, 21.9%; 45–59, 22.0%; 60–74, 12.2%; 75–84, 4.7%; 85 and over, 1.7%.
Population projection: (2020) 37,211,000; (2030) 39,901,000.
Population by mother tongue (2006): English 57.8%; French 22.1%; other 20.1%, of which Chinese languages 3.3%, Italian 1.5%, German 1.5%, Punjabi 1.2%, Spanish 1.2%, Arabic 0.9%, Tagalog 0.9%, Portuguese 0.7%, Polish 0.7%, Urdu 0.5%, Ukrainian 0.5%.
Aboriginal population (2006): North American Indian 1,172,790 (2.2% of total population); Métis 698,025 (1.3%); Inuit (Eskimo) 50,485 (0.2%); other/multiple 34,500 (0.1%).
Religious affiliation (2001): Christian 77.1%, of which Roman Catholic 43.2%, Protestant 28.3%, unspecified Christian 2.6%, Orthodox 1.7%, other Christian 1.3%; Muslim 2.0%; Jewish 1.1%; Hindu 1.0%; Buddhist 1.0%; Sikh 0.9%; nonreligious 16.5%; other 0.4%.
Major metropolitan areas (2006): Toronto 5,113,149; Montreal 3,635,571; Vancouver 2,116,581; Ottawa-Gatineau 1,130,761; Calgary 1,079,310; Edmonton 1,034,945; Quebec 715,515; Winnipeg 694,668; Hamilton 692,911; London 457,720; Kitchener 451,235; St. Catharines–Niagara 390,317.

Other metropolitan areas (2006)

	population		population		population
Abbotsford	159,020	Oshawa	330,594	Sherbrooke	186,952
Barrie	177,061	Regina	194,971	Sudbury	158,258
Halifax	372,858	Saguenay	151,643	Trois-Rivières	141,529
Kelowna	162,276	St. John's	181,113	Victoria	330,088
Kingston	152,358	Saskatoon	233,923	Windsor	323,342

Place of birth (2006): 80.2% native-born; 19.8% foreign-born, of which Asian 8.1%, European 7.3%, Latin American 1.2%, African 1.2%.
Mobility (2006). Population living in the same residence as in 2001: 59.1%; different residence, same municipality 22.0%; same province, different municipality 12.1%; different province 2.9%; different country 3.9%.
Households. Total number of households (2006) 12,437,470. Average household size 2.5; 1 person 26.8%, 2 persons 33.6%, 3 persons 15.9%, 4 persons 15.0%, 5 or more persons 8.7%.
Immigration (2007): permanent immigrants admitted 236,758; from Asia/Pacific 47.6%, of which China 11.4%, India 11.0%, Philippines 8.1%; Africa/Middle East 20.5%; Europe 16.5%; Latin America 10.9%; U.S. 4.4%; refugee population (end of 2007) 175,741.

Vital statistics

Birth rate per 1,000 population (2008–09): 11.3 (world avg. 20.3); within marriage (2007) 61.7%; outside of marriage (2007) 38.3%.
Death rate per 1,000 population (2008–09): 7.3 (world avg. 8.5).
Natural increase rate per 1,000 population (2008–09): 4.0 (world avg. 11.8).
Total fertility rate (avg. births per childbearing woman; 2007): 1.66.
Marriage/divorce rates per 1,000 population: (2007) 4.6/(2004) 2.2.
Life expectancy at birth (2005–07): male 78.3 years; female 83.0 years.
Major causes of death per 100,000 population (2004): diseases of the circulatory system 226.4; malignant neoplasms (cancers) 208.3; diseases of the respiratory system 61.0; diseases of the nervous system 31.9; accidents 27.6; diseases of the digestive system 26.9; diabetes mellitus 24.3.

Social indicators

Educational attainment (2006). Percentage of population age 25–64 having: less than complete secondary education 15.5%; complete secondary 23.9%; higher vocational 12.4%; some college/university 25.3%; bachelor's degree 14.6%; beyond bachelor's/master's 7.5%; doctorate 0.8%.

Distribution of income (2006)

percentage of family after-tax income by quintile

1	2	3	4	5 (highest)
2.3%	7.6%	14.8%	24.3%	51.0%

Quality of working life. Average workweek (2007): 35.6 hours. Annual rate per 100,000 workers for (2006): injury, accident, or industrial illness 1,998; death 5.9. Days lost to labour stoppages per 1,000 employees (2008): 60.4. Average round-trip commuting time (2005): 63 minutes; mode of transportation (2006): auto driver 72.3%, auto passenger 7.7%, public transportation 11.0%, walking 6.4%, bicycling 1.3%, other/unknown 1.3%. Labour force covered by a pension plan (2006): 38.1%.
Social participation. Eligible voters participating in last national election (May 2011): 61.4%. Trade union membership as percentage of civilian labour force (2007) 29.4%. Attendance at religious services on a weekly basis (2006): 17%.
Social deviance (2007). Offense rate per 100,000 population for: violent crime 929.6, of which battery/aggravated battery/dangerous operation of vehicle 718.5, robbery 89.8, sexual assault 65.0, homicide 1.8; property crime 3,319.7, of which breaking and entering 700.3, auto theft 443.2, fraud 267.7.
Leisure. Favourite leisure activities (hours weekly): television (2004) 21.4; radio (2006) 18.6; annual visits per capita to movie theatres (2006) 3.3; percentage of population participating in organized sports (2005) 28% (notably ice hockey and football [soccer]).
Material well-being (2006). Households possessing: automobile 59.7%; truck/van 36.9%; landline telephone only (December 2007) 24.0%; cellular phone (December 2007) 72.4%; air conditioner 48.1%; cable television 65.2%; computer 75.4%; Internet access 68.1%; dishwasher 57.7%.

National economy

Gross national income (GNI; 2009): U.S.$1,422,977,000,000 (U.S.$42,170 per capita); purchasing power parity GNI (U.S.$37,590 per capita).

Structure of gross domestic product and labour force

	2008		2009	
	in value Can$'000,000[6]	% of total value	labour force	% of labour force
Agriculture, fishing, forestry	25,965	2.1	320,500[7]	1.8[7]
Mining	55,311[8]	4.5[8]	316,200[9]	1.7[9]
Manufacturing	175,617	14.3	1,790,600	9.7
Construction	74,570	6.1	1,161,400	6.3
Public utilities	31,143	2.5	147,800	0.8
Transportation	56,755	4.6	820,300	4.5
Trade, hotels, and restaurants	172,669	14.1	3,695,700	20.1
Finance, real estate	305,532[10]	24.9[10]	1,099,000	6.0
Pub. admin., defense	69,438	5.7	926,600	5.0
Services	260,259	21.2	6,570,800	35.8
Other	—	—	1,520,100	8.3
TOTAL	1,227,259[11]	100.0	18,369,000	100.0

Budget (2007–08)[12]. Revenue: Can$256,575,000,000 (personal income tax 46.2%, corporate income tax 16.3%, general sales tax 13.8%, contributions to social security 8.5%, other 15.2%). Expenditures: Can$242,814,000,000 (social services 37.0%, defense/police 11.8%, transfers to government subsectors 11.3%, health 10.6%, debt charges 8.4%, resource conservation and industrial development 4.5%, foreign affairs/international assistance 2.4%, education 2.3%).
Public debt (May 2011): U.S.$839,460,000,000.
Production (metric tons except as noted). Agriculture, forestry, fishing (2009): wheat 26,847,600, rapeseed 11,825,400, corn (maize) 9,561,200, barley 9,517,200, cow's milk 8,213,300, potatoes 4,581,100, soybeans 3,503,700, dry peas 3,379,400, oats 2,798,200, pork 2,785,010, lentils 1,510,200, cattle meat 1,247,100, linseed 930,100, tomatoes 457,695, apples 413,096, mustard seed 208,300, canary seed 141,900, blueberries 103,070, cranberries 86,776, mushrooms 77,017, maple syrup 2,403,965 litres; livestock (number of live animals) 13,180,000 cattle, 12,180,000 pigs, 165,000,000 chickens, 5,600,000 turkeys; roundwood (2010) 132,461,009 cu m, of which fuelwood 2%; fisheries production (2009) 1,093,247 (from aquaculture 14%); aquatic plants production (2009) 13,876 (from aquaculture, none). Mining and quarrying (value of production in Can$'000,000; 2008)[13]: potash 8,243 (1); nickel 5,856 (2); copper 4,438; gold 2,824; iron ore 2,427; diamonds 2,404; sand and gravel 1,496; uranium 1,488 (1); stone 1,373; zinc 1,268 (5); platinum group 592 (3); salt 538 (5); cobalt 434 (2); gypsum 76 (4); ilmenite 816,000[14] (3); molybdenum (metal content) 7,724[14] (5). Manufacturing (value added in Can$'000,000,000; 2008)[6]: transportation equipment 30.8; food 19.3; base chemicals, medicines, and soaps 15.6; machinery 13.7; fabricated metal products 13.4; base metals 11.8; wood products (excl. furniture) 9.6; paper products 9.5; rubber and plastic products 9.0; information and communication technologies 8.5.
Population economically active (2007[3]): total 17,825,800; activity rate of total population 55.6% (participation rates: ages 15 and over, 67.5%; female 46.7%; unemployed [2009] 8.3%).

Price and earnings indexes (2005 = 100)

	2004	2005	2006	2007	2008	2009	2010
Consumer price index	97.8	100.0	102.0	104.2	106.7	107.0	108.9
Hourly earnings index[15]	97.3	100.0	99.7	105.1	106.9	101.5	106.4

Household income and expenditure. Average household size (2006) 2.5; average annual income per family (2006) Can$65,500 (U.S.$57,740); sources of income (2001): wages, salaries, and self-employment 71.8%, transfer payments 14.0%, other 14.2%; expenditure (2005): housing and energy 23.0%, transportation 14.4%, recreation and culture 10.3%, food and nonalcoholic beverages 9.6%, restaurants and hotels 7.0%, household furnishings and operations 6.6%, clothing 4.8%, health 4.2%, alcoholic beverages and tobacco 4.0%, communications 2.3%, education 1.4%.

Financial aggregates[16]

	2005	2006	2007	2008	2009	2010
Exchange rate, Can$ per:						
U.S. dollar	1.16	1.17	0.99	1.22	1.05	1.00
£	2.20	2.30	1.98	1.79	1.64	1.57
SDR	1.66	1.75	1.56	1.89	1.64	1.54
International reserves (U.S.$)						
Total (excl. gold; '000,000)	32,962	34,994	40,991	43,778	54,238	56,998
SDRs ('000,000)	897	963	1,016	991	9,212	9,054
Reserve pos. in IMF ('000,000)	1,401	833	661	1,249	2,424	3,056
Foreign exchange ('000,000)	30,664	33,198	39,314	41,537	42,602	44,888
Gold ('000,000 fine troy oz)	0.11	0.11	0.11	0.11	0.11	0.11
% world reserves	0.01	0.01	0.01	0.01	0.01	0.01
Interest and prices						
Central bank discount (%)	3.50	4.50	4.50	1.75	0.50	1.25
Govt. bond yield (long-term; %)[17]	4.39	4.30	4.34	4.04	3.89	3.66
Industrial share prices (2005 = 100)[17]	100.0	118.5	134.8	123.5	100.6	119.5
Balance of payments (U.S.$'000,000)						
Balance of visible trade,	+51,736	+43,655	+43,770	+43,803	–4,394	–8,682
of which:						
Imports, f.o.b.	–320,209	–356,594	–388,313	–417,849	–328,915	–401,865
Exports, f.o.b.	371,945	400,249	432,083	461,651	324,521	393,183
Balance of invisibles	–30,022	–25,571	–31,767	–37,427	–35,630	–40,625
Balance of payments, current account	+21,714	+18,084	+12,003	+6,376	–40,024	–49,307

Energy production (consumption): electricity (kW-hr; 2007) 639,841,000,000 (614,530,000,000); hard coal (metric tons; 2007) 32,811,000 (23,258,000); lignite (metric tons; 2007) 35,635,000 (37,777,000); crude petroleum (barrels; 2008) 946,000,000[18] ([2007] 652,188,000); petroleum products (metric tons; 2007) 89,483,000 (80,829,000); natural gas (cu m; 2007) 187,000,000,000 (92,900,000,000).

Land use as % of total land area (2009): in temporary crops or left fallow 4.2%, in permanent crops 0.8%, in pasture 1.7%, forest area 34.1%.

Selected balance of payments data. Receipts from (U.S.$'000,000): tourism (2009) 13,707; remittances, n.a.; foreign direct investment (FDI; 2008–10 avg.) 33,999. Disbursements for (U.S.$'000,000): tourism (2009) 24,169; remittances, n.a.; FDI (2008–10 avg.) 53,348.

Foreign trade

Balance of trade (current prices)

	2004	2005	2006	2007	2008	2009
Can$'000,000,000	+41.0	+43.2	+46.2	+40.0	+51.5	–6.9
% of total	5.5%	5.2%	5.5%	4.7%	5.4%	1.0%

Imports (2008): Can$447,904,000,000 (machinery and apparatus 24.0%, of which nonelectrical machinery 12.2%; road vehicles 13.8%, of which cars 6.0%, parts for road vehicles 4.3%; mineral fuels 12.0%, of which crude petroleum 7.6%; chemicals and chemical products 10.3%; food products 5.1%). *Major import sources:* U.S. 52.6%; China 10.1%; Mexico 4.1%; Japan 3.5%; Germany 2.9%; U.K. 2.9%; Algeria 1.7%; South Korea 1.4%; Norway 1.4%; France 1.4%.

Exports (2008): Can$499,384,000,000 (mineral fuels 26.9%, of which crude petroleum 13.6%, natural gas in gaseous state 6.6%; machinery and apparatus 11.6%; road vehicles 10.7%, of which cars 7.0%; chemicals and chemical products 8.3%; food products 6.6%; sawn wood, wood pulp, and paper products 6.2%; base nonferrous metals 4.3%). *Major export destinations:* U.S. 76.9%; U.K. 2.9%; China 2.4%; Japan 2.3%; Mexico 1.2%; Germany 0.9%; South Korea 0.9%; Belgium 0.8%.

Trade by commodities (2006)

	imports		exports	
SITC Group	U.S.$'000,000	%	U.S.$'000,000	%
00 Food and live animals	16,403	4.7	22,627	5.8
01 Beverages and tobacco	2,826	0.8	2,227[19]	0.6[19]
02 Crude materials, excluding fuels	9,852	2.8	29,354	7.6
03 Mineral fuels, lubricants, and related materials	31,903	9.1	77,534	20.0
04 Animal and vegetable oils, fats, and waxes	567	0.1	...	...
05 Chemicals and related products, n.e.s.	35,912	10.3	29,441	7.6
06 Basic manufactures	46,215	13.2	59,438	15.3
07 Machinery and transport equipment	156,759	44.8	123,224	31.8
08 Miscellaneous manufactured articles	40,779	11.7	22,510	5.8
09 Goods not classified by kind	8,673	2.4	21,665	5.6
TOTAL	349,889	100.0[20]	388,020	100.0[20]

Direction of trade (2006)

	imports		exports	
	U.S.$'000,000	%	U.S.$'000,000	%
Africa	7,429	2.1	2,251	0.6
Asia-Oceania	70,188	20.1	30,737	7.9[20]
China	30,424	8.7	6,755	1.7
Japan	13,521	3.9	8,302	2.1
South Korea	5,084	1.5	2,880	0.7
Other	21,159	6.0	12,800	3.3
Americas	220,619	63.1[20]	325,643	83.9
Mexico	14,123	4.0	3,867	1.0
United States	191,996	54.9	316,665	81.6
Other Americas	14,500	4.1	5,111	1.3
Europe	51,642	14.8[20]	29,376	7.6
United Kingdom	9,569	2.7	8,935	2.3
Germany	9,817	2.8	3,418	0.9
Other Europe	32,256	9.2	17,023	4.4
TOTAL	349,889[20]	100.0[20]	388,020[20]	100.0

Transport and communications

Transport. Railroads (2008): route length 46,688 km; passenger-km (2007) 1,444,656,000; metric ton-km cargo (2007) 357,444,000,000. Roads (2007): total length 1,409,000 km (paved [2004] *c.* 35%); passenger-km, n.a.; metric ton-km cargo (2006) 234,294,000,000. Vehicles: passenger cars (2007) 12,266,332; trucks and buses (2005) 785,649. Air transport[21]: passenger-km (2008) 74,400,000,000; metric ton-km cargo (2007) 1,184,921,000.

Communications

Medium	date	number in '000s	units per 1,000 persons	Medium	date	number in '000s	units per 1,000 persons
Televisions	2003	22,384	707	PCs	2007	31,051	943
Telephones				Dailies	2009	4,117[22]	147[22]
Cellular	2010	24,037[23]	707[23]	Internet users	2009	26,225	781
Landline	2010	17,021	500	Broadband	2010	10,139[23]	298[23]

Education and health

Literacy (2006): total population age 15 and over literate virtually 100%.

Education (2005–06)

	teachers	students	student/ teacher ratio	enrollment rate (%)
Primary (age 6–11)	...	2,305,211	17.4[24]	99
Secondary/Voc. (age 12–17)	...	2,632,432	17.7[24]	...
Tertiary	132,230[25]	1,326,711[26]	9.5[25]	53[26] (age 18–22)

Health: physicians (2006) 62,307 (1 per 524 persons); hospital beds (2005) 110,113 (1 per 294 persons); infant mortality rate per 1,000 live births (2007) 5.1; undernourished population (2005–07) less than 5.0% of total population.

Military

Total active duty personnel (November 2010): 65,722[27] (army 52.9%, navy 16.8%, air force 30.3%); reserve 33,967; civilian coast guard 4,554. *Military expenditure as percentage of GDP* (2009): 1.5%; per capita expenditure U.S.$581.

[1]Statutory number. [2]All seats are nonelected. [3]January 1. [4]Total area equals 3,855,103 sq mi (9,984,670 sq km), of which land area equals 3,511,023 sq mi (9,093,507 sq km), inland freshwater area equals 310,296 sq mi (803,663 sq km), and Great Lakes freshwater area equals 33,784 sq mi (87,500 sq km). [5]Based on land area. [6]At prices of 2002. [7]Excludes fishing, forestry. [8]Includes extraction of petroleum and natural gas (Can$39,989,000,000; 3.3%). [9]Includes fishing, forestry. [10]Includes professional, scientific, and technical services (Can$58,515,000,000; 4.8%). [11]Summed total; reported total equals Can$1,225,687,000,000. [12]Federal government revenue and expenditure only. [13]World ranking by production volume is in parentheses. [14]In metric tons; value of production data are confidential. [15]Manufacturing only. [16]End of period unless otherwise footnoted. [17]Period average. [18]From (in 2007): the Alberta oil sands *c.* 50%, conventional on land sources *c.* 38%, offshore Newfoundland in the Atlantic Ocean *c.* 12%. [19]Includes 04 SITC group. [20]Detail does not add to total given because of rounding. [21]Air Canada and Air Transat only. [22]Circulation. [23]Subscribers. [24]1999–2000. [25]2001–02. [26]2003–04. [27]Canadian troops in Afghanistan as part of the NATO International Security Assistance Force (November 2010): 2,922.

Internet resource for further information:

- **Statistics Canada http://www.statcan.gc.ca**

Cape Verde

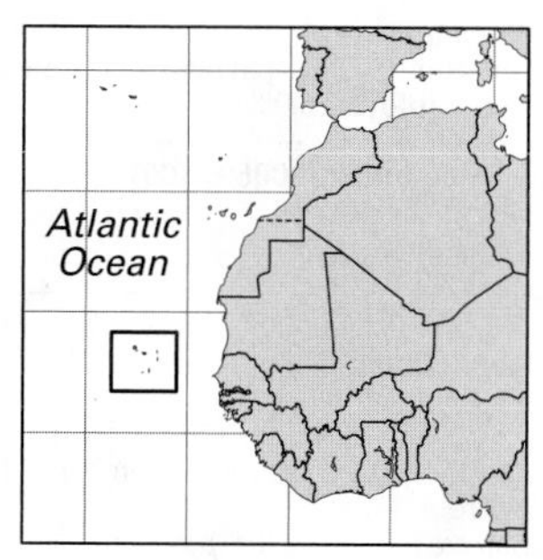

Official name: República de Cabo Verde (Republic of Cape Verde).
Form of government: multiparty republic with one legislative house (National Assembly [72[1]]).
Head of state: President.
Head of government: Prime Minister.
Capital: Praia.
Official language: Portuguese[2].
Official religion: none.
Monetary unit: escudo (C.V.Esc.); valuation (Sept. 1, 2011) 1 U.S.$ = C.V.Esc. 74.96; 1 £ = C.V.Esc. 121.13.

Area and population

Island Groups Islands/Counties	Principal towns	area sq mi	area sq km	population 2010 census
Leeward Islands		693[3]	1,796	323,917
Brava[4]	Nova Sintra	25	64	5,995
Fogo[5]	São Filipe	182	472	37,051
Maio[6]	Vila do Maio	104	269	6,952
Santiago[7]	Praia	383	991	273,919
Windward Islands		864[3]	2,237	167,766
Boa Vista[6]	Sal Rei	239	620	9,162
Sal[6]	Santa Maria	83	216	25,765
Santa Luzia, Branco, and Raso[8]	—	19	49	0
Santo Antão[5]	Porto Novo	300	779	43,915
São Nicolau[9]	Ribeira Brava	134	346	12,817
São Vicente[6]	Mindelo	88	227	76,107
TOTAL		1,557	4,033	491,683[10]

Demography

Population (2011): 498,000.
Density (2011): persons per sq mi 319.8, persons per sq km 123.5.
Urban-rural (2010): urban 61.8%; rural 38.2%.
Sex distribution (2010): male 49.52%; female 50.48%.
Age breakdown (2010): under 15, 31.6%; 15–29, 31.8%; 30–44, 17.9%; 45–59, 11.0%; 60–74, 4.3%; 75–84, 2.6%; 85 and over, 0.8%.
Population projection: (2020) 541,000; (2030) 585,000.
Doubling time: 45 years.
Ethnic composition (2000): Cape Verdean *mestico* (black-white admixture) 69.6%; Fulani 12.2%; Balanta 10.0%; Mandyako 4.6%; Portuguese white 2.0%; other 1.6%.
Religious affiliation (2000): Christian 95.1%, of which Roman Catholic 88.1%, Protestant 3.3%, independent Christian 2.7%; Muslim 2.8%; other 2.1%.
Major urban localities (2010): Praia (on Santiago) 127,832; Mindelo (on São Vicente) 70,468; Santa Maria (on Sal) 23,839; Assomada (on Santiago) 12,026; Pedra Badejo (on Santiago) 9,345.

Vital statistics

Birth rate per 1,000 population (2009): 22.2 (world avg. 20.3).
Death rate per 1,000 population (2009): 6.5 (world avg. 8.5).
Natural increase rate per 1,000 population (2009): 15.7 (world avg. 11.8).
Total fertility rate (avg. births per childbearing woman; 2009): 2.62.
Life expectancy at birth (2009): male 68.0 years; female 72.3 years.
Major causes of death per 100,000 population (2007): diseases of the circulatory system 136.3; malignant neoplasms (cancers) 54.5; diseases of the respiratory system 46.8; accidents and violence 42.5; infectious and parasitic diseases 35.0.

National economy

Budget (2008). Revenue: C.V.Esc. 40,129,000,000 (tax revenue 73.7%, of which VAT 29.2%, taxes on income and profits 21.2%, taxes on international transactions 14.7%; grants 16.0%; nontax revenue 6.5%; other 3.8%). Expenditures: C.V.Esc. 41,304,000,000 (current expenditure 60.6%; capital expenditure 39.4%).
Public debt (external, outstanding; 2008): U.S.$689,200,000.
Gross national income (GNI; 2010): U.S.$1,620,000,000 (U.S.$3,160 per capita); purchasing power parity GNI (U.S.$3,670 per capita).

Structure of gross domestic product and labour force

	2008		1990	
	in value C.V.Esc. '000,000	% of total value	labour force	% of labour force
Agriculture, fishing	9,673	7.4	29,876	24.7
Manufacturing	9,164	7.0	5,520	4.6
Public utilities			883	0.7
Mining			410	0.3
Construction	15,162	11.6	22,722	18.9
Transp. and commun.	25,999	19.8	6,138	5.1
Trade, hotels	30,293	23.1	12,747	10.6
Finance, real estate	12,717	9.7	821	0.7
Pub. admin., defense	15,789	12.1	17,358	14.4
Services	2,397	1.8		
Other	9,826[11]	7.5[11]	24,090	20.0
TOTAL	131,020	100.0	120,565	100.0

Production (metric tons except as noted). Agriculture, forestry, fishing (2009): sugarcane 28,500, cow's milk 11,300, goat's milk 11,000, bananas 9,424, pig meat 8,110, corn (maize) 7,380, mangoes 7,002, coconut 6,109, sweet potatoes 5,754, tomatoes 5,203, pulses 2,584; livestock (number of live animals) 231,640 pigs, 215,850 goats, 45,000 cattle; roundwood (2010) 1,542 cu m, of which fuelwood 100%; fisheries production 16,828 (from aquaculture, none). Mining and quarrying (2009): salt 1,600. Manufacturing (2003): cement (2009) 160,000; frozen fish 900; canned fish 200; other manufactured goods include clothing, footwear, and rum. Energy production (consumption): electricity (kW-hr; 2008) 257,000,000 (239,000,000); coal, none (none); crude petroleum, none (none); petroleum products (metric tons; 2007) none (100,000); natural gas, none (none).
Population economically active (2008): total 207,000[12]; activity rate of total population *c.* 41.5%[12] (participation rates: ages 15–64 *c.* 68.6%[12]; female *c.* 43%[12]; unemployed [2006] 18.3%, underemployed [2006] *c.* 26%).

Price index (2005 = 100)

	2004	2005	2006	2007	2008	2009	2010
Consumer price index	99.6	100.0	105.4	110.0	117.5	118.6	121.1

Household income and expenditure. Average household size (2006) 4.9; expenditure (2004): food 36.9%, transportation 14.1%, alcoholic beverages 10.1%, housing 7.9%, household furnishings and operation 6.4%, energy 5.2%.
Land use as % of total land area (2007): in temporary crops or left fallow 12.4%, in permanent crops 0.7%, in pasture 6.2%, forest area 21.0%.
Selected balance of payments data. Receipts from (U.S.$'000,000): tourism (2009) 292; remittances (2010) 144; foreign direct investment (2008–10 avg.) 146; official development assistance (2009) 196. Disbursements for (U.S.$'000,000): tourism (2009) 136; remittances (2009) 10.0.

Foreign trade[13]

Balance of trade (current prices)

	2003	2004	2005	2006	2007	2008
U.S.$'000,000	–308.6	–377.9	–348.8	–463.8	–663.9	–715.0
% of total	74.5%	76.7%	66.3%	70.8%	80.2%	75.5%

Imports (2008): U.S.$824,200,000 (food products 21.7%, machinery and apparatus 14.3%, refined petroleum 9.9%, fabricated/structural metals 9.8%, road vehicles 8.8%, chemicals and chemical products 6.0%). *Major import sources* (2008): Portugal 45.6%; Netherlands 14.6%; Spain 6.9%; Brazil 5.9%; Japan 3.4%.
Exports (2007): U.S.$114,800,000 (refined petroleum [significantly for refueling services for ships and aircraft] 49.8%, transport containers 15.8%, fresh fish 8.3%, clothing 5.7%, footwear 4.0%). *Major export destinations* (2007): Côte d'Ivoire 30.7%; Portugal 21.6%; Netherlands 15.2%; Spain 9.1%; France 4.1%.

Transport and communications

Transport. Railroads: none. Roads (2007): total length 1,398 mi, 2,250 km (paved [mostly with cobblestones] 78%). Vehicles (2004[14]): passenger cars 23,811; trucks and buses 5,032. Air transport (2005): passenger-km 1,078,000,000; metric ton-km cargo, n.a.

Communications

Medium	date	number in '000s	units per 1,000 persons	Medium	date	number in '000s	units per 1,000 persons
Televisions	2003	48	105	PCs	2004	48	102
Telephones				Dailies	2009	[15]	[15]
Cellular	2010	372[16]	750[16]	Internet users	2009	150	297
Landline	2010	72	145	Broadband	2010	15.1[16]	30[16]

Education and health

Educational attainment (1990). Percentage of population age 25 and over having: no formal schooling 47.9%; primary 40.9%; incomplete secondary 3.9%; complete secondary 1.4%; higher 1.5%; unknown 4.4%. *Literacy* (2007): total population age 15 and over literate 79.4%; males 87.5%; females 72.6%.

Education (2007–08)

	teachers	students	student/ teacher ratio	enrollment rate (%)
Primary (age 6–11)	3,132	76,299	24.4	84
Secondary/Voc. (age 12–17)[17]	3,195	60,783	19.0	61
Tertiary	792	6,658	8.4	12 (age 18–22)

Health (2007): physicians 230 (1 per 2,137 persons); hospital beds 1,016[18] (1 per 484 persons); infant mortality rate per 1,000 live births (2009) 28.9; undernourished population (2004–06) 70,000 (14% of total population based on the consumption of a minimum daily requirement of 1,800 calories).

Military

Total active duty personnel (November 2010): 1,200 (army 83.3%, air force 8.3%, coast guard 8.4%). *Military expenditure as percentage of GDP* (2009): 0.6%; per capita expenditure U.S.$19.

[1]Six members, two each, elected to represent Cape Verdeans living in the Americas, Africa, and Europe. [2]Cape Verdean Creole (Crioulo) is the national language. [3]Detail does not add to total given because of rounding. [4]Island/county areas are coterminous (including the nearby islets of Rei and Rombo). [5]Administratively split into 3 counties. [6]Island/county areas are coterminous. [7]Administratively split into 9 counties. [8]Islands administered from São Nicolau. [9]Administratively split into 2 counties. [10]Excludes some 700,000 Cape Verdeans living abroad. [11]Taxes and duties on imports less imputed bank service charges. [12]ILO estimate. [13]Imports f.o.b. in balance of trade and c.i.f. in commodities and trading partners. [14]January 1. [15]No daily newspapers in 2009; Cape Verde has 4 weeklies, however. [16]Subscribers. [17]2006–07. [18]Includes 259 beds in health centres.

Internet resources for further information:
- **Instituto Nacional de Estatística de Cabo Verde http://www.ine.cv**
- **Banco de Cabo Verde http://www.bcv.cv**

Cayman Islands

Official name: Cayman Islands.
Political status: overseas territory (United Kingdom) with one legislative house (Legislative Assembly [18[1]]).
Head of state: British Monarch, represented by Governor.
Head of government: Premier.
Capital: George Town.
Official language: English[2].
Official religion: none.
Monetary unit: Cayman Islands dollar (CI$); valuation (Sept. 1, 2011) CI$1.00 = U.S.$1.22 = £0.75.

Area and population

Islands	area sq mi	area sq km	population 2010 census[3]
Grand Cayman[4]	76	197	52,601
Cayman Brac[5]	15	39	2,277[6] (Cayman Brac and Little Cayman)
Little Cayman[5]	11	28	
TOTAL	102[7]	264[7]	54,878

Demography

Population (2011): 56,000.
Density (2011)[8]: persons per sq mi 602.2, persons per sq km 232.4.
Urban-rural (2009): urban 100%; rural 0%.
Sex distribution (2008): male 49.58%; female 50.42%.
Age breakdown (2007): under 15, 17.2%; 15–29, 20.3%; 30–44, 32.9%; 45–59, 18.7%; 60 and over, 10.9%.
Population projection: (2020) 60,000; (2030) 63,000.
Doubling time: 65 years.
Place of birth (2008): Cayman Islands 39.5%; Jamaica 24.8%; U.S. 5.2%; U.K. 4.9%; Honduras 4.6%; Philippines 4.2%; other 16.8%.[9]
Religious affiliation (2007): Protestant 62.6%, of which Church of God 25.5%, Presbyterian/United Church 9.2%, Seventh-day Adventist 8.4%; Roman Catholic 12.6%; independent Christian 5.7%; Hindu 1.0%; Muslim 0.8%; nonreligious 6.1%; other/unknown 11.2%.
Major urban areas (2010): George Town 27,704; West Bay 11,269; Bodden Town 10,341; Cayman Brac has 4 small settlements.

Vital statistics

Birth rate per 1,000 population (2006–08): 13.9 (world avg. 20.3).
Death rate per 1,000 population (2006–08): 3.1 (world avg. 8.5).
Natural increase rate per 1,000 population (2006–08): 10.8 (world avg. 11.8).
Total fertility rate (avg. births per childbearing woman; 2007): 1.89.
Marriage/divorce rates per 1,000 population (2007): 9.1[10]/3.0.
Life expectancy at birth (2007): male 77.6 years; female 82.9 years.
Major causes of death per 100,000 population (2004): diseases of the circulatory system 86.8, of which ischemic heart disease 25.9; malignant neoplasms (cancers) 72.1; pneumonia 27.7; accidents 22.2; diabetes mellitus 18.5.

National economy

Budget (2009). Revenue: CI$470,600,000 (taxes on goods and services 50.1%, of which financial services licenses 27.1%, work permit fees 7.8%; import duties 30.2%; nontax revenue 11.6%; other taxes 8.1%). Expenditures: CI$552,000,000 (current expenditure 82.3%; development expenditures/net lending 17.7%).
Public debt (2010): U.S.$721,500,000.
Production (metric tons except as noted). Agriculture, forestry, fishing (2009): bananas 189, citrus fruit 47, pumpkins, squash, and gourds 45, guavas and mangoes 36, yams 29, natural honey 10, avocados 9; livestock (number of live animals) 2,154 goats, 2,061 cattle; roundwood, n.a.; fisheries production 125 (from aquaculture, none). Mining and quarrying: crushed stone for local use. Manufacturing: industries include fish and turtle processing, handicrafts, and small-boat building. Energy production (consumption): electricity (kW-hr; 2009) 608,800,000[11] (559,800,000[11]); coal (metric tons; 2006) none (none); crude petroleum (barrels; 2007) none (none); petroleum products (metric tons; 2007) none (174,000); natural gas (cu m; 2007) none (none).
Gross national income (at current market prices; 2009): U.S.$2,912,000,000 (U.S.$53,036 per capita).

Structure of gross domestic product and labour force

	2008 in value U.S.$'000,000	2008 % of total value	2007 labour force	2007 % of labour force
Agriculture, forestry, fishing	10.9	0.4	639	1.8
Mining and quarrying	98.8 (with Public utilities)	3.5 (with Public utilities)	46	0.1
Public utilities			504	1.4
Manufacturing	47.1	1.7	658	1.8
Construction	269.8	9.5	5,646	15.5
Trade, hotels, restaurants	653.7	23.2	7,118	19.5
Transportation and communications	305.2	10.8	2,004	5.5
Finance, real estate, insurance[12]	1,390.8 (Finance through Services)	49.3 (Finance through Services)	7,532	20.6
International business[12]			…	…
Pub. admin., defense			2,509	6.9
Services[12]			7,627	20.9
Other	46.2	1.6	2,193[13]	6.0[13]
TOTAL	2,822.5	100.0	36,476	100.0

Population economically active (2009): total 36,100[14]; activity rate of total population 68.3% (participation rates: ages 15–64 [2007] 87.2%; female 49.0%; unemployed 6.0%).

Price index (2005 = 100)

	2004	2005	2006	2007	2008	2009	2010
Consumer price index	93.1	100.0	100.8	104.5	108.8	107.4	110.6

Household income and expenditure. Average household size (2008) 2.5; average annual income per household (1999) CI$52,400 (U.S.$62,880); sources of income (1999): wages and salaries 76.2%, self-employment 13.4%, transfers 1.2%; expenditure (2008)[15]: housing and energy 39.4%, transportation 9.6%, food 8.0%, communication 7.0%, household furnishings 5.6%, recreation/culture 4.0%.
Selected balance of payments data. Receipts from (U.S.$'000,000): tourism (2009) 486; cruise ship visitors (mostly day-trip participants; 2009) 1,520,400; remittances, n.a.; foreign direct investment (FDI; 2008–10 avg.) 16,507. Disbursements for (U.S.$'000,000): tourism (2009) 102; remittances (2009) 97.3; FDI (2008–10 avg.) 9,417.
Land use as % of total land area (2009): in temporary crops or left fallow 0.8%, in permanent crops 2.1%, in pasture 8.3%, forest area 52.9%.

Foreign trade[16]

Balance of trade (current prices)

	2005	2006	2007	2008	2009	2010
CI$'000,000	–926.9	–847.2	–837.9	–862.6	–719.9	–677.3
% of total	90.4%	95.2%	95.0%	96.9%	95.7%	96.9%

Imports (2008): CI$876,500,000 (refined petroleum 15.2%; food 10.9%; road vehicles 6.3%; refractory lime 5.3%; beverages 3.7%; remainder [significantly unspecified] 58.6%). *Major import sources* (2008): U.S. 74.5%; Netherlands Antilles 15.8%; Jamaica 0.7%; Japan 0.5%.
Exports (2007): CI$21,500,000 (reexports 59.4%; domestic exports [including rum, other manufactured consumer goods, turtle products, fish, and cut flowers] 40.6%). *Major export destinations* (2008): U.S. 85.5%; U.K. 9.4%; Jamaica 5.1%.

Transport and communications

Transport. Railroads: none. Roads (2002): total length 488 mi, 785 km (paved 100%). Vehicles (2007): passenger cars 25,636; trucks and buses 7,030. Air transport (2007)[17]: passengers arriving 479,800, passengers departing 489,700; freight loaded 498 metric tons, freight unloaded 3,486 metric tons.

Communications

Medium	date	number in '000s	units per 1,000 persons	Medium	date	number in '000s	units per 1,000 persons
Televisions	…	…	…	PCs	…	…	…
Telephones				Dailies	2009	18[18]	328[18]
Cellular	2010	100[19]	1,777[19]	Internet users	2009	24	428
Landline	2010	37	664	Broadband	2010	19[19]	335[19]

Education and health

Educational attainment (2007). Percentage of population age 15 and over having: no formal schooling 0.6%; primary education 4.4%; incomplete secondary 20.8%; complete secondary 28.7%; post-secondary 21.7%; university 18.6%; other/unknown 5.2%. *Literacy:* n.a.

Education (2007–08)

	teachers	students	student/ teacher ratio	enrollment rate (%)
Primary (age 5–10)	309	3,736	12.1	85
Secondary/Voc. (age 11–16)	361	3,198	8.9	81
Tertiary	34	912	26.8	36 (age 17–21)

Health: physicians (2008) 156 (1 per 359 persons); hospital beds (2008) 119 (1 per 471 persons); infant mortality rate per 1,000 live births (2007) 7.3; undernourished population, n.a.

Military

Total active duty personnel: none; defense is the responsibility of the United Kingdom.

[1]Includes three members appointed by the governor. [2]Per constitution effective Nov. 6, 2009. [3]Preliminary. [4]Grand Cayman has no local government structure. [5]Cayman Brac and Little Cayman together are administered by a district commissioner appointed by the governor. [6]Includes *c.* 150 people on Little Cayman. [7]Area includes 9 sq mi (23 sq km) of inland water. [8]Density based on land area. [9]In 2009 the population was 56% Caymanian citizens and 44% non-Caymanian. [10]Excludes marriages in which both the bride and groom are visitors. [11]Grand Cayman only. [12]The Cayman Islands is the world's largest centre for offshore banking, with 278 licensed banks, including 260 offshore (only) banking facilities, in 2008. In that year the assets of Cayman Islands banks exceeded U.S.$1,700,000,000,000. Trust management assets equal or exceed banking assets. Also of great importance to the economy are the captive insurance, mutual fund, and ship registration sectors. [13]Includes 1,395 unemployed and 798 not adequately defined. [14]Includes 18,165 Caymanian and 17,935 non-Caymanian. [15]Weights of consumer price index components. [16]Imports c.i.f.; exports f.o.b. [17]Combined total for Grand Cayman and Cayman Brac airports. [18]Circulation. [19]Subscribers.

Internet resources for further information:
- **Economics and Statistics Office http://www.eso.ky**
- **Cayman Islands Government http://www.gov.ky**

Central African Republic

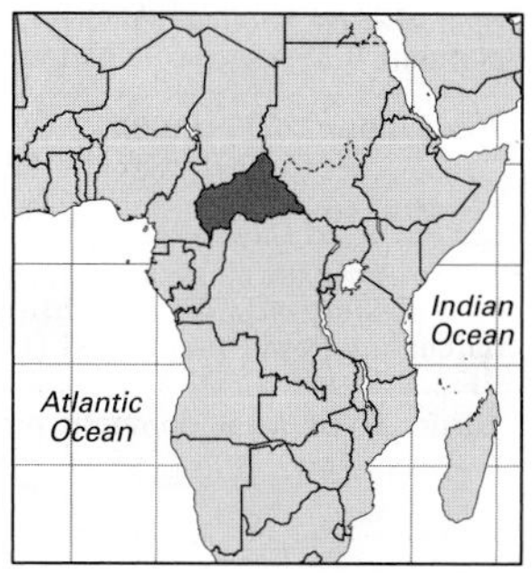

Official name: République Centrafricaine (Central African Republic).
Form of government: multiparty republic with one legislative body (National Assembly [105]).
Head of state: President.
Head of government: Prime Minister.
Capital: Bangui.
Official languages: French; Sango.
Official religion: none.
Monetary unit: CFA franc (CFAF); valuation (Sept. 1, 2011) 1 U.S.$ = CFAF 460.31; 1 £ = CFAF 743.83.

Area and population

Prefectures	area sq km	population 2003 census	Prefectures	area sq km	population 2003 census
Bamingui-Bangoran	58,200	43,229	Ombella-M'poko	31,835	356,725
Basse-Kotto	17,604	249,150	Ouaka	49,900	276,710
Haut-Mbomou	55,530	57,602	Ouham	50,250	369,220
Haute-Kotto	86,650	90,316	Ouham-Pendé	32,100	430,506
Kemo	17,204	118,420	Sangha-Mbaéré	19,412	101,074
Lobaye	19,235	246,875	Vakaga	46,500	52,255
Mambéré-Kadéï	30,203	364,795			
Mbomou	61,150	164,009	**Autonomous commune**		
Nana-Gribizi	19,996	117,816	Bangui	67	622,771
Nana-Mambéré	26,600	233,666	TOTAL	622,436	3,895,139

Demography

Population (2011): 4,950,000.
Density (2011): persons per sq mi 20.6, persons per sq km 8.0.
Urban-rural (2009): urban 38.7%; rural 61.3%.
Sex distribution (2009): male 49.41%; female 50.59%.
Age breakdown (2009): under 15, 41.2%; 15–29, 28.4%; 30–44, 16.4%; 45–59, 8.4%; 60–74, 4.4%; 75–84, 1.1%; 85 and over, 0.1%.
Population projection: (2020) 5,991,000; (2030) 7,325,000.
Doubling time: 33 years.
Ethnolinguistic composition (2004): Gbaya (Baya) *c.* 33%; Banda *c.* 27%; Mandjia *c.* 13%; Sara *c.* 10%; Mbum *c.* 7%; Ngbaka *c.* 4%; other *c.* 6%.
Religious affiliation (2005): Protestant/independent Christian *c.* 51%[1]; Roman Catholic *c.* 29%[1]; traditional beliefs *c.* 10%; Muslim *c.* 10%[1].
Major urban localities (2003): Bangui 622,771; Bimbo 124,176; Berbérati 76,918; Carnot 45,421; Bambari 41,356.

Vital statistics

Birth rate per 1,000 population (2009): 37.1 (world avg. 20.3).
Death rate per 1,000 population (2009): 15.6 (world avg. 8.5).
Natural increase rate per 1,000 population (2009): 21.5 (world avg. 11.8).
Total fertility rate (avg. births per childbearing woman; 2009): 4.73.
Life expectancy at birth (2009): male 48.0 years; female 50.5 years.
Adult population (ages 15–49) *living with HIV* (2009): 4.7%[2] (world avg. 0.8%).
Major causes of death per 100,000 population (2002): HIV/AIDS-related *c.* 604; lower respiratory infections *c.* 184; malaria *c.* 158; diarrheal diseases *c.* 105.

National economy

Budget (2006). Revenue: CFAF 176,300,000,000 (grants 58.4%; taxes 34.3%, of which taxes on goods and services 24.3%; nontax revenue 7.3%). Expenditures: CFAF 107,200,000,000 (current expenditure 58.3%; development expenditure 41.7%).
Public debt (external, outstanding; 2009): U.S.$250,000,000.
Production (metric tons except as noted). Agriculture, forestry, fishing (2009): cassava 642,897, yams 415,860, peanuts (groundnuts) 162,691, corn (maize) 151,168, bananas 115,287, taro 113,667, sugarcane 95,000, plantains 85,000, sesame seeds 50,008, natural honey (2008) 14,000, seed cotton 7,468, coffee 3,600; livestock (number of live animals) 4,150,000 goats, 4,045,000 cattle, 800,000 pigs, 1,400,000 beehives; roundwood (2010) 2,841,000 cu m, of which fuelwood 70%; fisheries production 15,000 (from aquaculture, negligible). Mining and quarrying (2009): diamonds 311,779 carats[3]. Manufacturing (2004): aluminum sheets 184,100; soap 1,800; cigarettes 16,000,000 packets; logs and sawn wood 630,900 cu m; beer (2006) 123,100 hectolitres; soft drinks (2003) 38,400 hectolitres; other manufactures include footwear, textiles, and bicycles. Energy production (consumption): electricity (kW-hr; 2007) 160,000,000 (160,000,000); coal, none (none); crude petroleum, none (none); petroleum products (metric tons; 2007) none (83,000); natural gas, none (none).
Household income and expenditure. Average household size (2004) 5.3; average annual income per household (1988) CFAF 91,985 (U.S.$435); sources of income: n.a.; expenditure (1991)[4]: food 70.5%, clothing 8.5%, energy 7.3%.
Population economically active (2008)[5]: total 2,019,000; activity rate of total population 46.5% (participation rates: ages 15–64, 79.1%; female 46.6%; unemployed, n.a.).

Price index (2005 = 100)

	2004	2005	2006	2007	2008	2009	2010
Consumer price index	97.2	100.0	106.7	107.7	117.7	121.8	123.6

Gross national income (GNI; 2010): U.S.$2,067,000,000 (U.S.$460 per capita); purchasing power parity GNI (U.S.$760 per capita).

Structure of gross domestic product and labour force

	2008 in value U.S.$'000	2008 % of total value	1988 labour force	1988 % of labour force
Agriculture, fishing, forestry	1,038,556	51.5	1,113,900	80.4
Mining }	71,523	3.5	15,400	1.1
Public utilities }			1,500	0.1
Manufacturing	146,414	7.3	22,400	1.6
Construction	52,830	2.6	7,000	0.5
Transp. and commun.	56,619	2.8	1,500	0.1
Trade, hotels, restaurants	291,631	14.5	118,000	8.5
Finance, real estate }	249,849	12.4	15,600	1.1
Services }				
Pub. admin., defense }			91,700	6.6
Other	108,132[6]	5.4[6]	—	—
TOTAL	2,015,554	100.0	1,387,000	100.0

Selected balance of payments data. Receipts from (U.S.$'000,000): tourism (2009) 4.5; remittances, n.a.; foreign direct investment (2008–10 avg.) 77; official development assistance (2009) 237. Disbursements for (U.S.$'000,000): tourism (2009) 52; remittances, n.a.
Land use as % of total land area (2007): in temporary crops or left fallow 3.1%, in permanent crops 0.1%, in pasture 5.1%, forest area 36.4%.

Foreign trade[7]

Balance of trade (current prices)

	2003	2004	2005	2006	2007	2008
CFAF '000,000,000	+6.1	–9.2	–24.8	–23.5	–33.9	–68.2
% of total	4.3%	6.1%	15.5%	12.5%	16.6%	34.0%

Imports (2005): CFAF 98,300,000,000 (refined petroleum 16.7%; logs and sawn wood 14.8%; food products 13.6%, of which cereals 6.6%; machinery and apparatus 8.6%; road vehicles 8.3%). *Major import sources* (2007): France 16.6%; Netherlands 13.0%; Cameroon 9.7%; U.S. 6.3%.
Exports (2008): CFAF 68,200,000,000 (wood and wood products 51.1%; diamonds 33.5%; coffee 1.7%; cotton 1.4%). *Major export destinations* (2007): Belgium 22.7%; Indonesia 19.3%; Italy 7.7%; France 7.1%; Spain 6.9%.

Transport and communications

Transport. Railroads: none. Roads (2005): total length 6,200 mi, 10,000 km (paved *c.* 7%)[8]. Vehicles (2007): passenger cars 1,225; trucks and buses 58. Air transport (2003): passenger arrivals 19,250[9], passenger departures 19,107[9]; metric ton-km cargo 7,000,000.

Communications

Medium	date	number in '000s	units per 1,000 persons	Medium	date	number in '000s	units per 1,000 persons
Televisions	2004	24	6.1	PCs	2006	13	3.0
Telephones				Dailies	2009	5[10]	1.1[10]
Cellular	2010	1,020[11]	232[11]	Internet users	2009	23	5.1
Landline	2010	12	2.7	Broadband	2010	—	—

Education and health

Educational attainment (1994–95)[12]. Percentage of population age 25 and over having: no formal schooling 54.1%; at least some primary education 30.5%; at least some secondary education 14.4%; unknown 1.0%. *Literacy* (2007): total population age 15 and over literate 56.6%; males literate 67.6%; females literate 46.4%.

Education (2008–09)

	teachers	students	student/teacher ratio	enrollment rate (%)
Primary (age 6–11)	6,427	608,075	94.6	67
Secondary/Voc. (age 12–18)	1,166	93,341	80.1	10
Tertiary	340	10,427	30.7	2 (age 19–23)

Health: physicians (2004) 331 (1 per 11,867 persons); hospital beds (2006) 5,118 (1 per 833 persons); infant mortality rate per 1,000 live births (2009) 103.8; undernourished population (2004–06) 1,700,000 (41% of total population based on the consumption of a minimum daily requirement of 1,730 calories).

Military

Total active duty personnel (November 2010): 2,150 (army 93.0%, air force 7.0%)[13]. *Military expenditure as percentage of GDP* (2009): 1.8%; per capita expenditure U.S.$8.

[1]Adherents may also incorporate traditional beliefs. [2]Statistically derived midpoint of range. [3]Official figure; a roughly equal amount was smuggled out of the country. [4]Weights of consumer price index components. [5]ILO estimates. [6]Taxes less subsidies. [7]Imports f.o.b. in balance of trade and c.i.f. in commodities and trading partners. [8]National roads only; much of the 9,700 mi (15,600 km) local road network is unusable. [9]Bangui airport only. [10]Circulation. [11]Subscribers. [12]Based on demographic and health survey of 9,414 people. [13]UN peacekeeping troops were withdrawn at the end of 2010.

Internet resource for further information:
- **Statistics, Economic Studies, and Social Division http://www.stat-centrafrique.com**

Chad

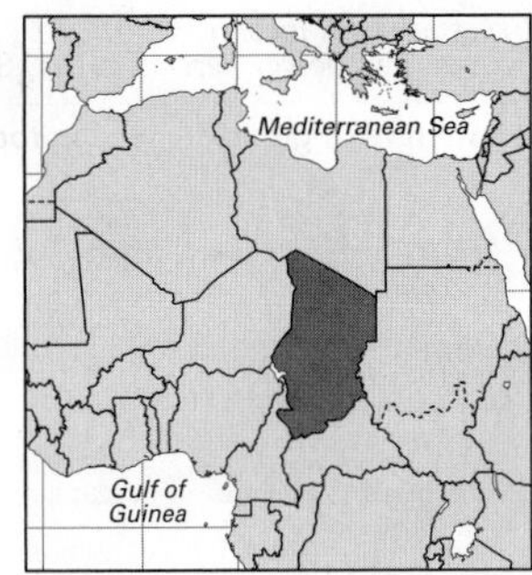

Official name: Jumhūriyyah Tshad (Arabic); République du Tchad (French) (Republic of Chad).
Form of government: unitary republic with one legislative body (National Assembly [188]).
Head of state: President.
Head of government: Prime Minister.
Capital: N'Djamena.
Official languages: Arabic; French.
Official religion: none.
Monetary unit: CFA franc (CFAF); valuation (Sept. 1, 2011) 1 U.S.$ = CFAF 460.31; 1 £ = CFAF 743.83.

Area and population

Regions	area sq km	population 2009 census[1]	Regions	area sq km	population 2009 census[1]
Bahr el Gazel	53,000	260,865	Mayo-Kébbi Ouest	14,000	565,087
Batha	88,000	527,031	Moyen-Chari	41,000	598,284
Bourkou	241,000	97,251	Ouaddaï	30,000	731,679
Chari-Baguirmi	46,000	621,785	Salamat	66,000	308,605
Ennedi	211,000	173,606	Sila	37,000	289,776
Guéra	62,000	553,795	Tandjilé	17,000	682,817
Hadjer-Lamis	29,000	562,957	Tibesti	130,000	21,970
Kanem	75,000	354,603	Wadi Fira (Biltine)	51,000	494,933
Lac	23,000	451,369			
Logone Occidental	9,000	683,293	**City**		
Logone Oriental	24,000	796,453	N'Djamena	1,000	993,492
Mandoul	17,000	637,086	OTHER UNCOUNTED[2]	—	98,191
Mayo-Kébbi Est	19,000	769,178	TOTAL	1,284,000	11,274,106[3]

Demography

Population (2011): 12,018,000.
Density (2011): persons per sq mi 24.3, persons per sq km 9.4.
Urban-rural (2009): urban 21.7%; rural 78.3%.
Sex distribution (2009): male 49.30%; female 50.70%.
Age breakdown (2007): under 15, 47.3%; 15–29, 26.4%; 30–44, 13.7%; 45–59, 8.0%; 60–74, 3.8%; 75–84, 0.7%; 85 and over, 0.1%.
Population projection: (2020) 15,087,000; (2030) 19,225,000.
Doubling time: 27 years.
Ethnolinguistic composition (1993): Sara 27.7%; Sudanic Arab 12.3%; Mayo-Kébbi peoples 11.5%; Kanem-Bornu peoples 9.0%; Ouaddaï peoples 8.7%; Hadjeray (Hadjaraï) 6.7%; Tangale (Tandjilé) peoples 6.5%; Gorane peoples 6.3%; Fitri-Batha peoples 4.7%; Fulani (Peul) 2.4%; other 4.2%.
Religious affiliation (2005): Muslim 57.0%; traditional beliefs 18.8%; Protestant 10.5%; other (significantly Roman Catholic and nonreligious) 13.7%.
Major cities (2009): N'Djamena 993,492; Moundou 132,411; Sarh 99,099; Abéché (2000) 63,165; Kelo (2000) 36,643; Pala (2000) 31,281.

Vital statistics

Birth rate per 1,000 population (2007): 42.4 (world avg. 20.3).
Death rate per 1,000 population (2007): 16.7 (world avg. 8.5).
Total fertility rate (avg. births per childbearing woman; 2007): 5.56.
Life expectancy at birth (2007): male 46.2 years; female 48.3 years.
Adult population (ages 15–49) *living with HIV* (2009): 3.4%[4] (world avg. 0.8%).
Major causes of death per 100,000 population (2002): lower respiratory infections *c.* 226; HIV/AIDS-related *c.* 204; malaria *c.* 181; diarrheal diseases *c.* 124.

National economy

Budget (2007). Revenue: CFAF 764,900,000,000 (petroleum revenue 73.6%, of which taxes on profits 55.7%, royalties and dividends 17.3%; nonpetroleum tax revenue 24.7%; other 1.7%). Expenditures: CFAF 709,300,000,000 (current expenditure 65.4%; development expenditure 34.6%).
Production (metric tons except as noted). Agriculture, forestry, fishing (2009): millet 708,965, sorghum 600,963, yams 519,860, peanuts (groundnuts) 413,062, cassava 230,000, corn (maize) 209,030, cow's milk 192,564, rice 130,700, cattle meat 104,340, sesame seed 35,000, gum arabic (2007) 26,900, goat meat 25,500, cotton lint 20,000; livestock (number of live animals) 7,245,230 cattle, 6,438,570 goats, 2,955,550 sheep, 1,391,050 camels; roundwood (2010) 7,709,988 cu m, of which fuelwood 90%; fisheries production 40,000 (from aquaculture, none). Mining and quarrying (2009): aggregate (gravel) 350,000; natron 12,000. Manufacturing (2004–05): cotton fibre 88,158; refined sugar 51,823; woven cotton fabrics (2000) 1,000,000 metres; carbonated beverages 104,205 hectolitres; beer 76,485 hectolitres; edible oil (2003–04) 74,514 hectolitres; cigarettes 41,873,000 packs. Energy production (consumption): electricity (kW-hr; 2007) 105,000,000 (105,000,000); coal, none (none); crude petroleum (barrels; 2009) 43,600,000 ([2007] 406,000); petroleum products (metric tons; 2007) none (65,000); natural gas, none (none).
Household income and expenditure. Average household size (2004) 5.0; sources of income: n.a.; expenditure (2005)[5]: food and nonalcoholic beverages 46.2%, housing and energy 13.3%, clothing and footwear 10.9%, transportation 6.4%, hotels and cafés 4.6%.
Selected balance of payments data. Receipts from (U.S.$'000,000): tourism (2005) 14; remittances, n.a.; foreign direct investment (2008–10 avg.) 492; official development assistance (2009) 561. Disbursements for (U.S.$'000,000): tourism (2002) 80; remittances, n.a.

Population economically active (2008)[6]: total 4,190,000; activity rate of total population 38.4% (participation rates: ages 15–64, 71.1%; female 47.9%).

Price index (2005 = 100)

	2003	2004	2005	2006	2007	2008	2009
Consumer price index	97.9	92.7	100.0	108.0	98.3	108.5	119.3

Public debt (external, outstanding; 2009): U.S.$1,711,000,000.
Gross national income (GNI; 2010): U.S.$6,929,000,000 (U.S.$600 per capita); purchasing power parity GNI (U.S.$1,180 per capita).

Structure of gross domestic product and labour force

	2007 in value CFAF '000,000,000	2007 % of total value	1993 labour force	1993 % of labour force
Agriculture	700.7	20.9	1,904,248	83.1
Mining	1,390.9	41.5		
Manufacturing	200.3	6.0	33,670	1.4
Construction	37.6	1.1	10,885	0.5
Public utilities	10.3	0.3	2,026	0.1
Transp. and commun.	55.3	1.7	13,252	0.6
Trade, hotels	417.9	12.5	211,812	9.2
Finance, real estate	…	…	1,071	—
Pub. admin., defense	288.9	8.6	61,875	2.7
Services	172.5	5.1	45,453	2.0
Other	78.4[7]	2.3[7]	9,271	0.4
TOTAL	3,352.8	100.0	2,291,577[8]	100.0

Land use as % of total land area (2007): in temporary crops or left fallow 3.4%, in permanent crops 0.02%, in pasture 35.7%, forest area 9.3%.

Foreign trade

Balance of trade (current prices)

	2003	2004	2005	2006	2007	2008
CFAF '000,000,000	–104.0	+657.3	+1,157.7	+1,077.2	+1,017.3	+1,020.1
% of total	13.0%	39.5%	53.6%	43.3%	40.6%	36.2%

Imports (2008): CFAF 898,000,000,000 (petroleum sector 34.1%, nonpetroleum private sector 32.2%, public sector 20.4%). *Major import sources* (2007): France 20.4%; Cameroon 16.1%; U.S. 10.9%; China 10.0%; Germany 7.5%.
Exports (2008): CFAF 1,918,100,000,000 (crude petroleum 88.5%, live cattle 6.4%, cotton 1.6%). *Major export destinations* (2007): U.S. 89.5%; Japan 3.7%; China 3.4%.

Transport and communications

Transport. Railroads: none. Roads (2006): total length 24,855 mi, 40,000 km (paved 2%). Vehicles (2006): passenger cars 18,867; trucks and buses 28,152. Air transport: [9].

Communications

Medium	date	number in '000s	units per 1,000 persons	Medium	date	number in '000s	units per 1,000 persons
Televisions	2004	55	5.9	PCs	2006	19	2.0
Telephones				Dailies	2009	—	—
Cellular	2010	2,614[10]	233[10]	Internet users	2009	188	17
Landline	2010	51	4.6	Broadband	2010	0.2[10]	—

Education and health

Educational attainment (2003)[11]. Percentage of population age 25 and over having: no formal schooling 74.5%; primary education 17.4%; secondary education 6.8%; higher education 1.3%. *Literacy* (2007): percentage of total population age 15 and over literate 53.7%; males 61.5%; females 46.3%.

Education (2007–08)

	teachers	students	student/teacher ratio	enrollment rate (%)
Primary (age 6–11)	23,938	1,495,961	62.5	61[12]
Secondary/Voc. (age 12–18)	9,555[13]	314,470[13]	32.9[13]	10[12]
Tertiary	1,306[14]	18,990	9.5[14]	2 (age 19–23)

Health: physicians (2004) 345 (1 per 26,370 persons); hospital beds (2005) 3,760 (1 per 2,500 persons); infant mortality rate per 1,000 live births (2007) 102.1; undernourished population (2005–07) 3,800,000 (37% of total population based on the consumption of a minimum daily requirement of 1,740 calories).

Military

Total active duty personnel (November 2010): 25,350 (army 78.9%, air force 1.4%, other 19.7%)[15]. *Military expenditure as percentage of GDP* (2008): 1.8%; per capita expenditure U.S.$14.

[1]Preliminary. [2]Includes an estimated 94,011 people in Sila and 4,180 people in Tibesti. [3]Includes 387,815 nomads and 291,233 refugees mostly from Sudan. [4]Statistically derived midpoint of range. [5]Weights of consumer price index components; N'Djamena only. [6]ILO estimates. [7]Taxes less subsidies. [8]Official census total; summed total equals 2,293,563. [9]Data unavailable for Toumaï Air Tchad, the national flag carrier. [10]Subscribers. [11]Based on the 2003 Chad Demographic and Health Survey, comprising 27,879 people in 5,369 households, about 80% of which were in rural areas. [12]2002–03. [13]2006–07. [14]2004–05. [15]UN peacekeeping troops withdrew at the end of 2010.

Internet resources for further information:

- **National Institute of Statistics and Economic and Demographic Studies http://www.inseed-tchad.org**
- **La Banque de France: La Zone Franc http://www.banque-france.fr/fr/eurosys/zonefr/zonefr.htm**

Chile

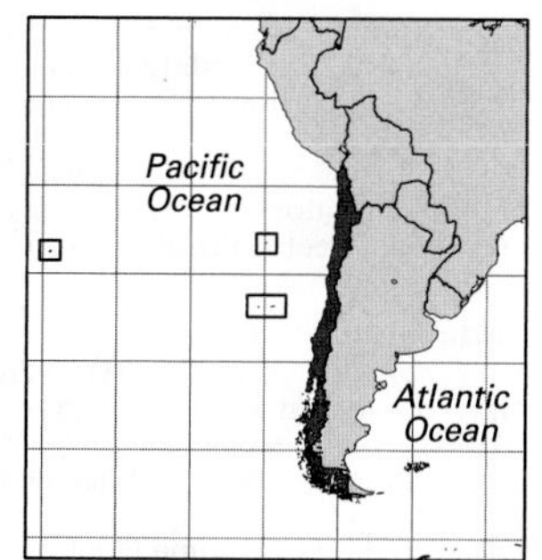

Official name: República de Chile (Republic of Chile).
Form of government: multiparty republic with two legislative houses (Senate [38]; Chamber of Deputies [120]).
Head of state and government: President.
Capital: Santiago[1].
Official language: Spanish.
Official religion: none.
Monetary unit: peso (Ch$); valuation (Sept. 1, 2011) 1 U.S.$ = Ch$460.40; 1 £ = Ch$743.98.

Area and population

Regions	area sq km	population 2009 estimate[2]	Regions	area sq km	population 2009 estimate[2]
Aisén del General Carlos Ibáñez del Campo	108,494	103,700	Los Lagos	48,584	825,800
Antofagasta	126,049	568,400	Los Ríos[3]	18,430	378,200
Araucanía	31,842	962,100	Magallanes y Antártica Chilena	132,291[4]	158,100[5]
Arica y Parinacota[3]	16,873	186,100	Maule	30,296	999,700
Atacama	75,176	278,500	Región Metropolitana	15,403	6,814,600
Bío-Bío	37,069	2,023,000	Tarapacá	42,226	307,400
Coquimbo	40,580	708,400	Valparaíso	16,396	1,739,900
Libertador General Bernardo O'Higgins	16,387	874,800	TOTAL	756,096[4]	16,928,900[6]

Demography

Population (2011): 17,270,000.
Density (2011): persons per sq mi 59.2, persons per sq km 22.8.
Urban-rural (2009): urban 86.9%; rural 13.1%.
Sex distribution (2008): male 49.52%; female 50.48%.
Age breakdown (2008): under 15, 23.6%; 15–29, 24.9%; 30–44, 21.2%; 45–59, 17.5%; 60–74, 9.5%; 75–84, 2.7%; 85 and over, 0.6%.
Population projection: (2020) 18,540,000; (2030) 19,536,000.
Ethnic composition (2002): mestizo *c.* 72%; white *c.* 22%; Amerindian *c.* 5%, of which Araucanian (Mapuche) *c.* 4%; other *c.* 1%.
Religious affiliation (2002)[7]: Roman Catholic 70.0%; Protestant/independent Christian 15.1%; atheist/nonreligious 8.3%; other 6.6%.
Major cities/urban agglomerations (2002): Santiago 200,792[8]/5,428,590[9]; Valparaíso–Viña del Mar (263,499; 286,931)/803,683; Concepción 212,003/666,381; La Serena–Coquimbo (147,815; 148,434)/296,253; Antofagasta 285,255/285,255.

Vital statistics

Birth rate per 1,000 population (2009): 14.6 (world avg. 20.3).
Death rate per 1,000 population (2009): 5.8 (world avg. 8.5).
Total fertility rate (avg. births per childbearing woman; 2009): 1.92.
Marriage/divorce rates per 1,000 population (2006): 3.5/0.2.
Life expectancy at birth (2009): male 74.1 years; female 80.8 years.
Major causes of death per 100,000 population (2006): diseases of the circulatory system 149.1; malignant neoplasms (cancers) 128.7; accidents and violence 48.6; diseases of the respiratory system 47.6.

National economy

Budget (2008). Revenue: Ch$22,353,000,000,000 (tax revenue 78.5%, nontax revenue 18.5%, other 3.0%). Expenditures: Ch$18,399,000,000,000 (social protection 29.1%, education 18.8%, health 16.1%, transportation 9.4%).
Public debt (external, outstanding; 2008): U.S.$9,282,000,000.
Population economically active (2008): total 7,285,100; activity rate of total population 43.3% (participation rates: ages 15–64, 62.6%; female 37.6%; unemployed [2010–11] 8.1%).

Price and earnings indexes (2005 = 100)

	2004	2005	2006	2007	2008	2009	2010
Consumer price index[10]	97.0	100.0	103.4	107.9	117.4	119.1	...
Hourly earnings index	95.3	100.0	105.4	113.1	122.7	130.6	135.3

Production (metric tons except as noted). Agriculture, forestry, fishing (2009): grapes 2,500,000, corn (maize) 1,345,650, wheat 1,145,290, apples 1,090,000, sugar beets 1,042,420, potatoes 924,555, tomatoes 850,000, peaches and nectarines 388,000, avocados 328,000, plums/sloes 296,000, onions 295,204, kiwi fruit 227,000, cherries 56,000; livestock (number of live animals) 3,950,000 sheep, 3,900,000 cattle, 2,724,620 pigs, 487,070 beehives; roundwood (2010) 51,498,917 cu m, of which fuelwood 29%; fisheries production 4,702,902 (from aquaculture 19%); aquatic plants production 456,225 (from aquaculture 19%). Mining (2009): copper 5,390,000[11]; iron ore 5,006,000[11]; molybdenum 34,925[11]; lithium carbonate 25,154; iodine 17,399; silver 1,301[11]; gold 40,834 kg[11]. Manufacturing (value added in U.S.$'000,000; 2006): nonferrous base metals 26,784; refined petroleum 6,245; base chemicals 5,337; food products 5,309; paper and paper products 2,027; beverages 1,857. Energy production (consumption): electricity (kW-hr; 2010–11) 56,742,000,000 ([2007] 60,137,000,000); hard coal (metric tons; 2010–11) 576,000 ([2007] 5,721,000); crude petroleum (barrels; 2010–11) 878,200 ([2007] 78,310,000); petroleum products (metric tons; 2007) 10,452,000 (15,195,000); natural gas (cu m; 2010–11) 1,122,174,100 ([2007] 4,191,000,000).
Land use as % of total land area (2007): in temporary crops 1.0%, left fallow 0.6%, in permanent crops 0.6%, in pasture 19.0%, forest area 21.8%.

Gross national income (GNI; 2010): U.S.$170,284,000,000 (U.S.$9,940 per capita); purchasing power parity GNI (U.S.$13,890 per capita).

Structure of gross domestic product and labour force

	2008 in value U.S.$'000,000	% of total value	labour force	% of labour force
Agriculture, fishing	6,769	4.0	789,700	10.8
Mining }	38,530	22.7	99,600	1.4
Public utilities }			38,200	0.5
Manufacturing	23,342	13.8	865,400	11.9
Construction	10,846	6.4	583,600	8.0
Transp. and commun.	12,956	7.6	561,500	7.7
Trade, hotels, restaurants	14,751	8.7	1,330,700	18.3
Finance, real estate }	53,199	31.4	626,500	8.6
Pub. admin., defense }			1,845,300	25.3
Services }				
Other	9,180[12]	5.4[12]	544,600[13]	7.5[13]
TOTAL	169,573	100.0	7,285,100	100.0

Household income and expenditure (2008). Average household size 3.4; average annual income per household Ch$6,968,400 (U.S.$13,338); sources of income: salaries and wages 54.6%, rent, transfers, other 38.3%, self-employment 7.1%; expenditure: n.a.
Selected balance of payments data. Receipts from (U.S.$'000,000): tourism (2009) 1,568; remittances (2010) 5; foreign direct investment (FDI; 2008–10 avg.) 14,373; official development assistance (2009) 80. Disbursements for (U.S.$'000,000): tourism (2009) 1,625; remittances (2009) 6; FDI (2008–10 avg.) 8,282.

Foreign trade[14]

Balance of trade (current prices)

	2004	2005	2006	2007	2008	2009
U.S.$'000,000	+7,727	+8,532	+20,274	+20,502	+10,912	+12,055
% of total	13.5%	11.5%	20.9%	17.9%	8.6%	13.1%

Imports (2008): U.S.$58,173,000,000 (petroleum 29.4%; machinery and apparatus 20.4%; chemicals and chemical products 11.2%; road vehicles 9.0%; food 6.5%). *Major import sources:* U.S. 19.9%; China 12.0%; Brazil 9.1%; Argentina 8.6%; South Korea 5.8%.
Exports (2008): U.S.$69,085,000,000 (refined copper 30.3%; copper ore 18.6%; food products 14.0%, of which fruits 4.0%, fish 3.9%; other base metal ores 4.5%; pulp and waste paper 3.8%). *Major export destinations:* China 14.3%; U.S. 11.3%; Japan 10.5%; Netherlands 6.1%; Brazil 6.0%.

Transport and communications

Transport. Railroads (2008): route length 3,406 mi, 5,481 km; passenger-km 759,000,000; metric ton-km cargo 4,293,000,000. Roads (2003): total length 50,023 mi, 80,505 km (paved 22%). Vehicles (2008): passenger cars 1,840,024; trucks and buses 863,468. Air transport (2010–11): passenger-km 20,846,000,000; metric ton-km cargo 1,424,757,000.

Communications

Medium	date	number in '000s	units per 1,000 persons	Medium	date	number in '000s	units per 1,000 persons
Televisions	2004	4,305	268	PCs	2006	2,277	141
Telephones				Dailies	2009	581[15]	35[15]
Cellular	2010	19,852[16]	1,160[16]	Internet users	2009	5,767	340
Landline	2010	3,458	202	Broadband	2010	1,789[16]	105[16]

Education and health

Educational attainment (2002). Percentage of population age 25 and over having: no formal schooling/other 5.4%; incomplete primary education 24.6%; complete primary 8.7%; secondary 43.9%; higher technical 4.9%; university 12.5%. *Literacy* (2006): total population age 15 and over literate 96.4%.

Education (2006–07)

	teachers	students	student/ teacher ratio	enrollment rate (%)
Primary (age 6–11)	66,862	1,679,017	25.1	94
Secondary/Voc. (age 12–17)	67,970	1,611,631	23.7	85
Tertiary	54,649	753,398	13.8	52 (age 18–22)

Health: physicians (2008) 22,247 (1 per 740 persons); hospital beds (2007) 37,797 (1 per 431 persons); infant mortality rate (2009) 7.7; undernourished population (2004–06) less than 5.0% of total population based on the consumption of a minimum daily requirement of 1,880 calories.

Military

Total active duty personnel (November 2010): 59,059 (army 59.3%, navy 27.6%, air force 13.1%). *Military expenditure as percentage of GDP* (2009): 3.3%[17]; per capita expenditure U.S.$315[17].

[1]Legislative bodies meet in Valparaíso. [2]Official projection based on 2002 census. [3]Created in March 2007. [4]Excludes the 1,250,000 sq km (480,000 sq mi) section of Antarctica claimed by Chile and "inland" (actually tidal) water areas. [5]Includes 130 people (in 2005) in Chilean-claimed Antarctica. [6]Detail does not add to total given because of rounding. [7]For population age 15 years and older. [8]1 of 32 communes constituting Santiago province (4,656,690). [9]Extends beyond Santiago province within the Región Metropolitana. [10]Capital city only. [11]Metal content. [12]Import duties and VAT less imputed bank service charges. [13]Unemployed. [14]Exports f.o.b.; imports c.i.f. [15]Circulation. [16]Subscribers. [17]Includes military pensions and funding for the paramilitary and the Copper Stabilisation Fund.

Internet resources for further information:
- **Instituto Nacional de Estadísticas http://www.ine.cl**
- **Banco Central de Chile http://www.bcentral.cl/eng**

China

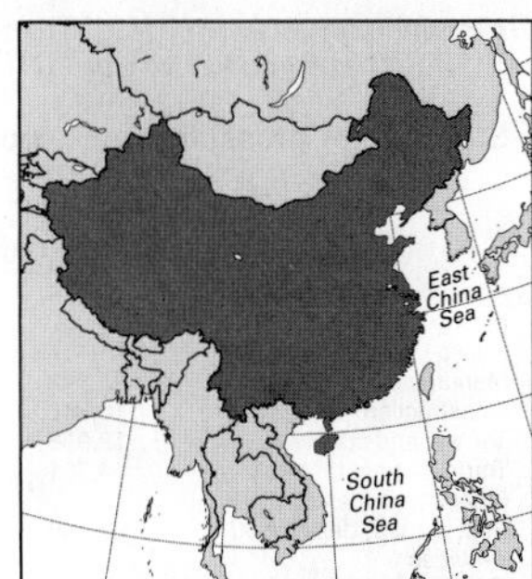

Official name: Zhonghua Renmin Gongheguo (People's Republic of China).
Form of government: single-party people's republic with one legislative house (National People's Congress [3,000[1]]).
Head of state: President.
Head of government: Premier.
Capital: Beijing (Peking).
Official language: Mandarin Chinese.
Official religion: none.
Monetary unit: renminbi (yuan) (Y); valuation (Sept. 1, 2011) 1 U.S.$ = Y 6.38; 1 £ = Y 10.31.

Area and population[2]

		area[3]		population
Provinces[5]	Capitals[5]	sq mi	sq km	2010 census[4]
Anhui (Anhwei)	Hefei	54,000	139,900	59,500,510
Fujian (Fukien)	Fuzhou	47,500	123,100	36,894,216
Gansu (Kansu)	Lanzhou	141,500	366,500	25,575,254
Guangdong (Kwangtung)	Guangzhou (Canton)	76,100	197,100	104,303,132
Guizhou (Kweichow)	Guiyang	67,200	174,000	34,746,468
Hainan	Haikou	13,200	34,300	8,671,518
Hebei (Hopeh)	Shijiazhuang	78,200	202,700	71,854,202
Heilongjiang (Heilungkiang)	Harbin	179,000	463,600	38,312,224
Henan (Honan)	Zhengzhou	64,500	167,000	94,023,567
Hubei (Hupeh)	Wuhan	72,400	187,500	57,237,740
Hunan	Changsha	81,300	210,500	65,683,722
Jiangsu (Kiangsu)	Nanjing (Nanking)	39,600	102,600	78,659,903
Jiangxi (Kiangsi)	Nanchang	63,600	164,800	44,567,475
Jilin (Kirin)	Changchun	72,200	187,000	27,462,297
Liaoning (Liaoning)	Shenyang	58,300	151,000	43,746,323
Qinghai (Tsinghai)	Xining	278,400	721,000	5,626,722
Shaanxi (Shensi)	Xi'an (Sian)	75,600	195,800	37,327,378
Shandong (Shantung)	Jinan	59,200	153,300	95,793,065
Shanxi (Shansi)	Taiyuan	60,700	157,100	35,712,111
Sichuan (Szechwan)	Chengdu	188,000	487,000	80,418,200
Yunnan	Kunming	168,400	436,200	45,966,239
Zhejiang (Chekiang)	Hangzhou	39,300	101,800	54,426,891
Autonomous regions[5]				
Guangxi Zhuang (Kwangsi Chuang)	Nanning	85,100	220,400	46,026,629
Inner Mongolia (Nei Mongol)	Hohhot	454,600	1,177,500	24,706,321
Ningxia Hui (Ningsia Hui)	Yinchuan	25,600	66,400	6,301,350
Tibet (Xizang)	Lhasa	471,700	1,221,600	3,002,166
Xinjiang Uygur (Sinkiang Uighur)	Ürümqi (Urumchi)	635,900	1,646,900	21,813,334
Municipalities[5]				
Beijing (Peking)	—	6,500	16,800	19,612,368
Chongqing (Chungking)	—	31,700	82,000	28,846,170
Shanghai	—	2,400	6,200	23,019,148
Tianjin (Tientsin)	—	4,400	11,300	12,938,224
TOTAL		3,696,100	9,572,900	1,339,724,852[6]

Demography

Population (2011): 1,342,274,000.
Density (2011): persons per sq mi 363.2, persons per sq km 140.2.
Urban-rural (2010[7]): urban 46.6%; rural 53.4%.
Sex distribution (2010[7]): male 51.43%; female 48.57%.
Age breakdown (2008)[8]: under 15, 17.3%; 15–29, 21.2%; 30–44, 25.9%; 45–59, 21.6%; 60–74, 10.6%; 75–84, 2.9%; 85 and over, 0.5%.
Population projection: (2020) 1,384,047,000; (2030) 1,389,315,000.
Ethnic composition (2005)[9]: Han (Chinese) 90.95%; Zhuang 1.37%; Manchu 0.82%; Yi 0.79%; Hui 0.77%; Miao 0.75%; Uighur 0.74%; Tujia 0.65%; Tibetan 0.57%; Mongolian 0.49%; Dong 0.28%; Buyei 0.26%; Yao 0.24%; Korean 0.14%; Bai 0.14%; Hani 0.12%; Li 0.11%; Kazakh 0.09%; Tai 0.08%; other 0.64%.
Religious affiliation (2005): nonreligious 39.2%; Chinese folk-religionist 28.7%; Christian 10.0%, of which unregistered Protestant 7.7%[3], registered Protestant 1.2%[3], unregistered Roman Catholic 0.5%[3], registered Roman Catholic 0.4%[3]; Buddhist 8.4%; atheist 7.8%; traditional beliefs 4.4%; Muslim 1.5%.
Major urban agglomerations (2009)[10]: Shanghai 16,344,000; Beijing 12,214,000; Chongqing 9,348,000; Shenzhen 8,847,000; Guangzhou 8,735,000; Tianjin 7,759,000; Wuhan 7,582,000; Dongguan 5,219,000; Shenyang 5,074,000; Foshan 4,876,000; Chengdu 4,869,000; Xi'an 4,704,000; Nanjing 4,404,000; Harbin 4,224,000; Hangzhou 3,813,000; Changchun 3,504,000; Shantou 3,475,000; Qingdao 3,268,000; Dalian 3,252,000; Jinan 3,186,000; Taiyuan 3,084,000; Kunming 3,062,000; Zhengzhou 2,914,000; Fuzhou 2,698,000; Nanchang 2,648,000; Wuxi 2,631,000; Wenzhou 2,558,000; Shijiazhuang 2,426,000.
Households[8]. Average family household size 3.2, of which urban family households 3.0[9], rural family households 3.3[9]; 1 person 8.9%, 2 persons 24.6%, 3 persons 30.3%, 4 persons 21.0%, 5 persons 10.0%, 6 persons 3.7%, 7 persons 1.0%, 8 persons 0.3%, 9 or more persons 0.2%.
Mobility (2008)[8]. Population residing in registered enumeration area 90.6%; population not residing in registered enumeration area 9.4%.

Vital statistics

Birth rate per 1,000 population (2009): 12.1 (world avg. 20.3).
Death rate per 1,000 population (2009): 7.1 (world avg. 8.5).
Natural increase rate per 1,000 population (2009): 5.0 (world avg. 11.8).
Total fertility rate (avg. births per childbearing woman; 2009): 1.53.
Marriage/divorce rates per 1,000 population (2008): 8.3/1.7.
Life expectancy at birth (2009): male 72.4 years; female 76.6 years.
Adult population (ages 15–49) *living with HIV* (2009): 0.1%[11] (world avg. 0.8%).
Major causes of death per 100,000 population (2006): malignant neoplasms (cancers) 136.5; cerebrovascular diseases 100.3; heart diseases 80.1; diseases of the respiratory system 78.1; accidents and poisoning 40.1; endocrine, nutritional, and metabolic diseases 17[3]; diseases of the digestive system 12[3].

Social indicators

Educational attainment (2008)[8]. Percentage of population age 6 and over having: no formal schooling 7.5%; incomplete/complete primary education 31.2%; some secondary 40.9%; complete secondary 13.7%; some postsecondary through advanced degree 6.7%.

Distribution of income (2005)

percentage of household income by decile						
1 (lowest)	2	3–4	5–6	7–8	9	10 (highest)
2.4	3.3	9.8	14.7	22.0	16.4	31.4

Quality of working life. Average workweek (November 2007; hours actually worked): 45.5 hours. Annual rate per 100,000 workers for (2008): death in mining, industrial, or commercial enterprises 2.82. Death toll from work accidents (2008) 91,172.
Access to services. Percentage of population having access to electricity (2005) 99.4%. Percentage of urban/rural population with improved water supply (2003) 99.2%/80.2%, of which tap water 95.8%/34.0%, deep wells with hand pump 2.3%/34.0%. Sewage system (1999): total (urban, rural) households with flush apparatus 20.7% (50.0%, 4.3%), with pit latrines 69.3% (33.6%, 86.7%), with no latrine 5.3% (7.8%, 4.1%).
Social participation. Eligible voters participating in last national election: not applicable; members are indirectly elected. Trade union membership in total labour force (2006): 169,942,200 (*c.* 22%). Percentage of population who consider themselves religious (2005–06) 31.4%.
Social deviance. Annual reported arrest rate per 100,000 population (2008) for: theft 256.6; robbery 20.9; fraud 20.7; injury 12.1; rape 2.3; homicide 1.1; abducting women/children 0.2%.
Material well-being. Number of durable goods owned per 100 households (urban/rural; 2009[7]): automobiles (8.8/n.a.); washing machines 94.6/49.1; refrigerators 93.6/30.2; colour televisions 132.9/99.2; computers 59.3/5.4; air conditioners 100.3/9.8; cameras 39.1/4.4; dishwashers 0.8/n.a.; microwave ovens 54.6/n.a.

National economy

Gross national income (GNI; 2010): U.S.$5,700,018,000,000 (U.S.$4,260 per capita); purchasing power parity GNI (U.S.$7,570 per capita).

Structure of gross domestic product and labour force

	2007		2009[7]	
	in value Y '000,000,000	% of total value	labour force ('000)	% of labour force
Agriculture, forestry, fishing	2,863	11.1	306,540	38.7
Mining	1,346	5.2		
Manufacturing	8,747	34.0		
Public utilities	961	3.7	211,090	26.6
Construction	1,426	5.6		
Transp. and commun.	1,481	5.8		
Trade, hotels	2,441	9.5		
Finance/real estate	2,938	11.4	257,170	32.5
Information services	600	2.3		
Pub. admin. / Services / Other	2,928	11.4		
Other			17,630[12]	2.2[12]
TOTAL	25,731	100.0	792,430	100.0

Budget (2008)[13]. Revenue: Y 6,133,035,000,000 (tax revenue 88.4%, of which VAT 29.3%, corporate income taxes 18.2%, business tax 12.4%, individual income tax 6.1%; nontax revenue 11.6%). Expenditures: Y 6,259,266,000,000 (general administration 15.7%; education 14.4%; social security 10.9%; manufacturing/trade/finance 9.9%; agriculture/forestry/water conservancy 7.3%; defense 6.7%; public security 6.5%; health 4.4%).
Public debt (external, outstanding; 2009): U.S.$93,125,000,000.
Production (metric tons except as noted). Agriculture, forestry, fishing (2009): grains—rice 196,681,170, corn (maize) 164,107,560, wheat 115,115,364, barley 2,318,000; oilseeds—soybeans 14,981,221, peanuts (groundnuts) 14,764,841, rapeseed 13,657,012, sunflower seeds 1,955,640; fruits and nuts—watermelons 65,002,319, apples 31,684,445, citrus 23,088,471, pears 14,416,450, cantaloupes 12,224,801, persimmons 2,871,202; other—sugarcane 116,251,272, sweet potatoes 76,772,636, potatoes 73,281,890, tomatoes 45,365,543, cabbage 30,215,327, eggplants 25,912,524, onions 21,046,969, seed cotton 19,131,000, garlic 17,967,857, spinach 17,550,148, chilies and peppers 14,520,301, asparagus 6,502,479, mushrooms and truffles 4,680,726, tobacco leaves 3,067,928, tea 1,375,780, silkworm cocoons 317,157; livestock (number of live animals) 450,880,000 pigs, 152,499,101 goats, 128,557,213 sheep, 84,116,951 cattle, 23,279,162 water buffalo, 4,702,670,000 chickens, 769,427,000 ducks; roundwood (2010) 285,519,411 cu m, of which fuelwood 67%; fisheries production (2009) 49,702,864 (from aquaculture 70%); aquatic plants production (2009) 10,772,075 (from aquaculture 97%). Mining and quarrying (2008; by world rank): metal content of mine output—iron ore 270,000,000 (1), zinc 3,200,000 (1), manganese (2007) 2,000,000 (3), lead 1,500,000 (1), copper 960,000 (4), antimony 180,000 (1), tin 129,000 (1), tungsten 43,500 (1), silver 2,800 (3), gold 285 (1); metal ores—bauxite 35,000,000 (2), vanadium 20,000 (1); nonmetals—salt 59,520,000 (1), phosphate rock 15,200,000 (1), magnesite 10,000,000 (1), barite 4,600,000 (1), fluorspar

3,250,000 (1), talc 2,200,000 (1), asbestos 280,000 (2), celestite 200,000 (1). Distribution of industrial production (percentage of total value added by source of funding; 2007) from: domestic sources 68.5%, of which private enterprises 23.2%, limited liability corporations 22.3%, shareholding corporations 9.9%, state-owned enterprises 9.0%, collectives 2.5%; foreign sources 21.0%; Hong Kong–, Macau-, or Taiwan-based enterprises 10.5%. Retail trade (percentage of total sales by sector; 2007): domestically funded enterprises 88.0%, of which limited liability corporations 29.6%, private enterprises 26.6%, shareholding corporations 20.1%, state-owned enterprises 6.9%, collectives 2.2%; foreign-funded enterprises 8.1%; Hong Kong–, Macau-, or Taiwan-based enterprises 3.9%.

Manufacturing and mining enterprises (2007)

	no. of enterprises	no. of employees	value added (Y '000,000)
Manufacturing			
Iron and steel (base)	7,161	3,044,300	900,714
Telecommunications equipment, computers, other electronics	11,220	5,879,200	792,457
Industrial chemicals, paints, soaps	22,981	3,802,800	734,042
Transport equipment	14,091	4,085,900	697,448
Electrical machinery/apparatus	19,322	4,491,500	605,378
General purpose machinery	26,757	4,207,100	510,754
Textiles	27,914	6,262,600	491,392
Cement, bricks, ceramics, other related products	24,278	4,484,100	484,919
Food processing	18,140	2,648,000	464,245
Nonferrous metals (base)	6,701	1,562,700	447,761
Refined petroleum, coke, nuclear fuel	2,149	806,400	309,698
Special purpose machinery	13,409	2,565,100	306,736
Fabricated metal products	18,008	2,734,800	301,041
Tobacco products	150	186,100	291,882
Medicines and pharmaceuticals	5,748	1,373,400	228,660
Clothing and footwear	14,770	4,141,900	226,511
Plastics	15,376	2,240,500	213,714
Beverages	4,422	1,010,200	188,366
Food manufactures	6,644	1,350,300	186,156
Paper and paper products	8,376	1,380,300	174,305
Leather and fur products	7,452	2,569,800	148,039
Professional, scientific, and measuring equipment	4,526	1,069,700	116,325
Sawn wood; products of wood, bamboo, and rattan (excl. furniture)	7,852	1,061,800	103,029
Mining			
Petroleum and natural gas	184	906,700	645,083
Coal	7,537	4,637,000	469,633
Nonferrous metals	2,183	551,100	97,332
Ferrous metals	2,899	491,400	92,878
Nonmetals	3,004	466,200	51,724

Energy production (consumption): electricity (kW-hr; 2009) 3,714,650,000,000 (3,697,300,000,000); hard coal (metric tons; 2008) 2,610,000,000 ([2007] 2,514,000,000); lignite (metric tons; 2008) 110,000,000 (n.a.); crude petroleum (barrels; 2009) 1,383,000,000 (2,785,000,000); petroleum products (metric tons; 2007) 253,977,000 (273,857,000); natural gas (cu m; 2009) 85,170,000,000 (88,700,000,000).

Financial aggregates[14]

	2005	2006	2007	2008	2009	2010
Exchange rate, Y per:						
U.S. dollar	8.07	7.81	7.30	6.83	6.83	6.62
£	13.90	15.33	14.62	9.96	11.06	10.36
SDR	11.53	11.75	11.54	10.53	10.71	10.20
International reserves (U.S.$)						
Total (excl. gold; '000,000)	821,514	1,068,493	1,530,282	1,949,260	2,416,044	2,866,079
SDRs ('000,000)	1,251	1,068	1,192	1,199	12,510	12,344
Reserve pos. in IMF ('000,000)	1,391	1,081	840	2,031	4,382	6,397
Foreign exchange ('000,000)	818,872	1,066,344	1,528,249	1,946,030	2,399,152	2,847,338
Gold ('000,000 fine troy oz)	…	19.3	19.3	19.3	33.9	33.9
% world reserves	…	2.0	2.0	2.0	3.5	3.5
Interest and prices						
Central bank discount (%)	3.33	3.33	3.33	2.79	2.79	3.25
Balance of payments (U.S.$'000,000)						
Balance of visible trade, of which:	+134,189	+217,746	+315,381	+360,682	+249,510	+254,180
Imports, f.o.b.	–628,295	–751,936	–904,618	–1,073,919	–954,287	–1,327,238
Exports, f.o.b.	762,484	969,682	1,220,000	1,434,601	1,203,797	1,581,417
Balance of invisibles	+26,629	+35,522	+56,452	+75,425	+47,632	+51,194
Balance of payments, current account	+160,818	+253,268	+371,833	+436,107	+297,142	+305,374

Population economically active (2008): total 783,855,000[15]; activity rate of total population 58.6%[15] (participation rates: ages 15–64, 79.8%[15]; female 44.7%[15]; registered unemployed in urban areas [2009] 4.3%; urban unemployed including migrants, up to 9%; rural unemployment is substantial).

Price and earnings indexes (2005 = 100)

	2004	2005	2006	2007	2008	2009	2010
Consumer price index	98.3	100.0	101.5	106.4	112.7	111.9	118.1
Monthly earnings index[16]	89.1	100.0	114.0	132.5	153.5	…	…

Household income and expenditure. Average annual per capita disposable income of household (2009): rural households Y 5,153 (U.S.$754), urban households Y 17,175 (U.S.$2,514). Sources of income (2008): rural households—income from household businesses 51.2%, wages and salaries 38.9%, transfers 6.8%, property 3.1%; urban households—wages and salaries 66.2%, transfers 23.0%, business income 8.5%, property 2.3%. Expenditure (2008): rural (urban) households—food 43.7% (37.9%), housing and energy 18.5% (10.2%), education and recreation 8.6% (12.1%), transportation and communications 9.8% (12.6%), clothing 5.8% (10.4%), health and personal effects 6.7% (7.0%), household furnishings and operation 4.8% (6.2%).

Selected balance of payments data. Receipts from (U.S.$'000,000): tourism (2009) 39,675; remittances (2010) 51,300; foreign direct investment (FDI; 2008–10 avg.) 103,016; official development assistance (2009) 1,132. Disbursements for (U.S.$'000,000): tourism (2009) 43,702; remittances (2008) 5,737; FDI (2008–10 avg.) 58,893.

Land use as % of total land area (2009): in temporary crops or left fallow 10.3%, in permanent crops 1.5%, in pasture 42.9%, forest area 21.9%.

Foreign trade[17]

Balance of trade (current prices)

	2004	2005	2006	2007	2008	2009
U.S.$'000,000	+32,097	+102,000	+177,475	+261,820	+298,131	+197,611
% of total	2.8%	7.2%	10.1%	12.0%	11.6%	9.0%

Imports (2008): U.S.$1,132,562,000,000 (machinery and apparatus 35.5%, of which electronic integrated circuits and micro-assemblies 11.4%, computers and office machines 4.1%; mineral fuels 14.9%, of which crude petroleum 11.4%; chemicals and chemical products 10.5%, of which organic chemicals 3.4%, plastics in primary forms 3.4%; metal ore and metal scrap 8.8%, of which iron ore 5.4%; optical instruments and apparatus 4.3%). *Major import sources:* Japan 13.3%; South Korea 9.9%; Taiwan 9.1%; China free trade zones 8.2%; United States 7.2%; Germany 4.9%; Australia 3.3%; Malaysia 2.8%; Saudi Arabia 2.7%; Brazil 2.6%.

Exports (2008): U.S.$1,430,693,000,000 (machinery and apparatus 42.3%, of which computers/office machines/parts 12.4%, electrical machinery and electronics 10.7%, telecommunications equipment and parts 8.1%; wearing apparel and accessories 8.4%; chemicals and chemical products 5.5%; iron and steel 5.0%; textile yarn, fabrics, and made-up articles 4.6%). *Major export destinations:* United States 17.7%; Hong Kong 13.3%; Japan 8.1%; South Korea 5.2%; Germany 4.2%; Netherlands 3.2%; United Kingdom 2.5%; Singapore 2.3%; Russia 2.3%; India 2.2%.

Transport and communications

Transport. Railroads: route length (2008) 48,364 mi, 77,834 km; (2009) passenger-km 787,890,000,000; (2009) metric ton-km cargo 2,523,920,000,000. Roads (2007[7]): total length 2,317,834 mi, 3,730,200 km (paved [2005] 44%); (2009) passenger-km 1,345,070,000,000; (2009) metric ton-km cargo 3,638,350,000,000. Vehicles (2007): passenger cars 29,616,499; trucks and buses 12,884,000. Air transport (2009): passenger-km 337,490,000,000; metric ton-km cargo 12,630,000,000. Inland waterways (2009): passenger-km 6,910,000,000; metric ton-km cargo 5,743,990,000,000.

Communications

Medium	date	number in '000s	units per 1,000 persons	Medium	date	number in '000s	units per 1,000 persons
Televisions	2003	493,902	381	PCs	2007	75,118	57
Telephones				Dailies	2009	109,000[18]	82[18]
Cellular	2010	859,003[19]	640[19]	Internet users	2009	384,000	285
Landline	2010	294,383	220	Broadband	2010	126,337[19]	94[19]

Education and health

Literacy (2008)[8]: total population age 15 and over literate 92.2%; males literate 96.0%; females literate 88.5%.

Education (2007–08)

	teachers	students	student/ teacher ratio	enrollment rate (%)
Primary (age 7–11)	6,035,510	105,950,505	17.6	…
Secondary/Voc. (age 12–17)	6,343,783	101,448,265	16.0	…
Tertiary	1,594,702	26,691,696	16.7	23 (age 18–22)

Health (2010[7]): physicians[20] 2,160,000 (1 per 618 persons); hospital beds 3,960,000 (1 per 337 persons); infant mortality rate (2009) 17.0; undernourished population (2005–07) 130,400,000 (10% of total population based on the consumption of a minimum daily requirement of 1,900 calories).

Military

Total active duty personnel (November 2010): 2,285,000[21] (army 70.0%, navy 11.2%, air force 14.4%, strategic missile forces 4.4%); paramilitary 660,000; reserve *c.* 510,000. *Military expenditure as percentage of GDP* (2009): 1.4%[22]; per capita expenditure U.S.$53[22].

[1]Statutory number; includes 36 seats allotted to Hong Kong and 12 to Macau. [2]Data for Taiwan, Quemoy and Matsu (island groups of Fujian province administered by Taiwan), Hong Kong, and Macau are excluded; in January 2011 Tajikistan agreed to cede to China *c.* 386 sq mi (1,000 sq km), also excluded here. [3]Estimate(s). [4]Preliminary. [5]Preferred names in all instances are based on Pinyin transliteration (except for Inner Mongolia and Tibet, which are current English-language conventional names). [6]Total includes 2,300,000 military personnel and a population of 4,649,985 with "difficult to define" permanent residence. [7]January 1. [8]Based on 2008 national sample survey (about 0.9% of the total population). [9]Based on 2005 national sample survey (about 1.0% of the total population). [10]Per United Nations *World Urbanization Prospects: The 2009 Revision.* [11]Statistically derived midpoint of range. [12]Includes 8,860,000 registered unemployed; remainder mostly activities not defined. [13]For combined central and local governments. [14]End of period. [15]ILO estimate. [16]Manufacturing only. [17]Imports c.i.f.; exports f.o.b. [18]Circulation. [19]Subscribers. [20]Includes assistant doctors. [21]Of which UN peacekeepers deployed abroad 1,946. [22]Official defense budget at market exchange rates.

Internet resource for further information:

- **National Bureau of Statistics of China http://www.stats.gov.cn/english**

Colombia

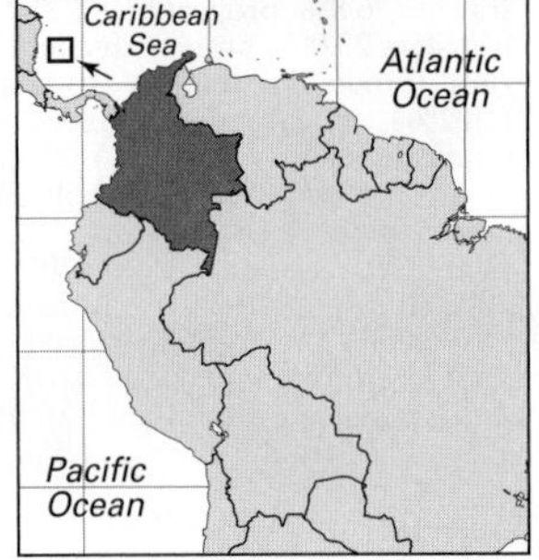

Official name: República de Colombia (Republic of Colombia).
Form of government: unitary, multiparty republic with two legislative houses (Senate [102]; House of Representatives [166]).
Head of state and government: President.
Capital: Bogotá.
Official language: Spanish.
Official religion: none[1].
Monetary unit: peso (Col$); valuation (Sept. 1, 2011) 1 U.S.$ = Col$1,778; 1 £ = Col$2,873.

Population (2007 estimate)

Departments	population	Departments	population	Departments	population
Amazonas	68,519	Cundinamarca	2,355,408	San Andrés y Providencia	72,923
Antioquia	5,831,851	Guainía	36,381	Santander	1,975,963
Arauca	238,605	Guaviare	98,189	Sucre	792,377
Atlántico	2,227,713	Huila	1,038,061	Tolima	1,371,253
Bolívar	1,924,139	La Guajira	715,175	Valle del Cauca	4,257,741
Boyacá	1,265,198	Magdalena	1,180,703	Vaupés	39,231
Caldas	973,226	Meta	817,857	Vichada	60,463
Caquetá	427,634	Nariño	1,578,877		
Casanare	306,510	Norte de Santander	1,267,028		
Cauca	1,285,794	Putumayo	319,804	**Capital District**	
Cesar	929,096	Quindío	542,752	Bogotá	7,050,133
Chocó	467,374	Risaralda	911,239	TOTAL	43,941,792
Córdoba	1,514,575				

Demography

Area: 440,831 sq mi, 1,141,748 sq km.
Population (2011): 44,726,000[2].
Density (2011): persons per sq mi 101.5, persons per sq km 39.2.
Urban-rural (2009): urban 74.8%; rural 25.2%.
Sex distribution (2008): male 49.41%; female 50.59%.
Age breakdown (2008): under 15, 28.3%; 15–29, 26.3%; 30–44, 21.8%; 45–59, 15.1%; 60–74, 6.5%; 75–84, 1.7%; 85 and over, 0.3%.
Population projection: (2020) 49,085,000; (2030) 52,965,000.
Ethnic composition (2006): mestizo *c.* 58%; white *c.* 20%; mulatto *c.* 14%; black *c.* 4%; black-Amerindian *c.* 3%; Amerindian *c.* 1%.
Religious affiliation (2007): Roman Catholic *c.* 80.0%; Protestant/independent Christian *c.* 13.5%; Mormon *c.* 0.3%; nonreligious *c.* 2.0%; other *c.* 4.2%.
Major cities (2009): Bogotá 7,243,698; Medellín 2,281,085; Cali 2,183,042; Barranquilla 1,174,971; Cartagena 888,012; Cúcuta 591,530.

Vital statistics

Birth rate per 1,000 population (2008): 18.4 (world avg. 20.3).
Death rate per 1,000 population (2008): 5.2 (world avg. 8.5).
Natural increase rate per 1,000 population (2008): 13.2 (world avg. 11.8).
Total fertility rate (avg. births per childbearing woman; 2007): 2.20.
Life expectancy at birth (2007): male 68.4 years; female 76.2 years.
Major causes of death per 100,000 population (2005)[3]: diseases of the circulatory system 164.4; malignant neoplasms (cancers) 90.4; violence and suicides 70.1; diseases of the respiratory system 56.9; accidents 31.6.
Adult population (ages 15–49) *living with HIV* (2009): 0.5% (world avg. 0.8%).

National economy

Budget (2007). Revenue: Col$103,986,000,000,000 (tax revenue 56.4%, of which taxes on goods and services 26.1%, income taxes 16.7%; nontax revenue 39.3%; other 4.3%). Expenditures: Col$110,014,000,000,000 (interest on debt 25.1%; other 74.9%).
Population economically active (2008): total 19,671,400; activity rate 45.5% (participation rates: ages 12–55, 63.3%; female 42.0%; unemployed [June 2009–May 2010] 12.1%).

Price and earnings indexes (2005 = 100)

	2004	2005	2006	2007	2008	2009	2010
Consumer price index	95.2	100.0	104.3	110.1	117.8	122.7	125.5
Monthly earnings index	92.2	100.0	100.6	97.1	…	…	…

Production (metric tons except as noted). Agriculture, forestry, fishing (2009): sugarcane 38,500,000, cow's milk 7,545,140, plantains 3,011,780, rice 2,985,220, cassava 2,202,210, bananas 2,020,390, corn (maize) 1,636,640, coffee 887,661, pineapples 427,766, yams 297,350, avocados 165,175;[4] livestock (number of live animals) 27,359,300 cattle, 3,400,000 sheep, 2,505,580 horses; roundwood (2010) 11,216,000 cu m, of which fuelwood 79%; fisheries production 191,933 (from aquaculture 44%). Mining and quarrying (2009): nickel (metal content) 90,000; gold 47,800 kg; emeralds 2,900,000 carats. Manufacturing (value added in U.S.$'000,000; 2005): processed food 3,471; petroleum products 2,873; medicines, fertilizers, soaps 1,956; beverages 1,813; iron and steel 1,120; cement, bricks, and ceramics 1,042; plastics 858; clothing 836.[5] Energy production (consumption): electricity (kW-hr; 2008) 51,015,000,000 (38,821,000,000); hard coal (metric tons; 2009) 89,148,000 ([2007] 4,480,000); crude petroleum (barrels; 2010) 286,700,000 ([2009] 101,105,000); petroleum products (metric tons; 2007) 12,884,000 (8,848,000); natural gas (cu m; 2009) 13,066,000,000 (10,842,000,000).
Land use as % of total land area (2009): in temporary crops or left fallow 1.6%, in permanent crops 1.4%, in pasture 35.3%, forest area 54.6%.
Gross national income (GNI; 2010): U.S.$255,290,000,000 (U.S.$5,510 per capita); purchasing power parity GNI (U.S.$9,000 per capita).

Structure of gross domestic product and labour force

	2007			
	in value Col$'000,000	% of total value	labour force[6]	% of labour force[6]
Agriculture, forestry	33,349	8.1	3,341,900	16.4
Mining	16,402	4.0	108,300	0.5
Manufacturing	69,279	16.8	2,444,500	12.0
Construction	28,835	7.0	916,900	4.5
Public utilities	11,576	2.8	88,700	0.5
Transp. and commun.	32,839	8.0	1,491,800	7.3
Trade, hotels	47,573	11.5	4,563,100	22.4
Finance, real estate	64,864	15.7	1,301,600	6.4
Pub. admin., defense	26,415	6.4	3,894,900	19.1
Services	45,630	11.0		
Other	35,881	8.7	2,213,500[7]	10.9[7]
TOTAL	412,643	100.0	20,365,200	100.0

Public debt (external, outstanding; 2010): U.S.$35,364,000,000.
Household income and expenditure. Average household size (March 2004) 3.8; sources of income (2002): wages 42.6%, self-employment 38.9%; expenditure[8] (2006): food and nonalcoholic beverages 27.8%, housing and energy 13.4%, transportation 12.8%, household furnishings 5.7%, health 4.9%, hotel and café expenditures 4.5%, alcohol and tobacco 3.9%.
Selected balance of payments data. Receipts from (U.S.$'000,000): tourism (2009) 1,999; remittances (2010) 3,942; foreign direct investment (FDI; 2008–10 avg.) 8,164; official development assistance (2009) 1,060. Disbursements for (U.S.$'000,000): tourism (2009) 1,752; remittances (2009) 92; FDI (2008–10 avg.) 3,949.

Foreign trade[9]

Balance of trade (current prices)

	2005	2006	2007	2008	2009	2010
U.S.$'000,000	–13.8	–1,771.4	–2,905.7	–2,042.9	–44.7	–863
% of total	0.0%	3.5%	4.6%	2.6%	0.1%	1.1%

Imports (2008): U.S.$39,668,800,000 (machinery and apparatus 25.9%; chemicals and chemical products 18.7%; road vehicles 9.0%; food 8.4%; iron and steel 6.3%). *Major import sources:* U.S. 29.2%; China 11.5%; Mexico 7.9%; Brazil 5.9%; Germany 3.9%.
Exports (2008): U.S.$37,625,900,000 (crude petroleum 24.7%; food 13.1%, of which coffee 5.1%; coal 12.2%; chemicals and chemical products 7.8%; refined petroleum 7.3%; iron and steel 3.3%). *Major export destinations:* U.S. 38.0%; Venezuela 16.2%; Ecuador 4.0%; Switzerland 2.5%; Peru 2.3%.

Transport and communications

Transport. Railroads (2008): route length[10] 825 mi, 1,327 km; passenger-km (2004) 25,000,000; metric ton-km cargo (2005) 8,236,000,000. Roads (2006): total length 102,077 mi, 164,278 km (paved [2000] 23%); passenger-km (2005) 157,000,000[11]; metric ton-km cargo (2005) 38,199,000,000. Vehicles (2007): cars 1,674,441; trucks and buses 1,213,050. Air transport (2009): passenger-km 11,724,000,000; metric ton-km cargo 145,044,000.

Communications

Medium	date	number in '000s	units per 1,000 persons	Medium	date	number in '000s	units per 1,000 persons
Televisions	2004	11,358	268	PCs	2007	3,513	80
Telephones				Dailies	2009	1,200[12]	27[12]
Cellular	2010	43,405[13]	938[13]	Internet users	2009	20,789	455
Landline	2010	6,809	147	Broadband	2010	2,622[13]	57[13]

Education and health

Educational attainment (2005)[14]. Percentage of population age 25 and over having: no schooling/unknown 10.2%; primary education 40.1%; secondary 34.2%; higher 15.5%. *Literacy* (2007): population age 15 and over literate 92.7%; males literate 92.4%; females literate 92.8%.

Education (2007–08)

	teachers	students	student/ teacher ratio	enrollment rate (%)
Primary (age 6–10)	179,806	5,285,523	29.4	90
Secondary/Voc. (age 11–16)	186,121	4,772,189	25.6	71
Tertiary	87,397[15]	1,372,674[16]	15.0[16]	35 (age 17–21)

Health: physicians (2006) 51,095 (1 per 849 persons); hospital beds (2004) 50,824 (1 per 833 persons); infant mortality rate (2007) 20.1; undernourished population (2004–06) 4,300,000 (10% of total population based on the consumption of a minimum daily requirement of 1,790 calories).

Military

Total active duty personnel (November 2010): 283,004[17] (army 83.3%, navy 11.7%, air force 4.9%); paramilitary 158,824. *Military expenditure as percentage of GDP* (2009): 4.1%[18]; per capita expenditure U.S.$207[18].

[1]The 1973 concordat with the Vatican declares that Roman Catholicism is of fundamental importance to the Colombian community. [2]Includes 2.7 million to 4.4 million internally displaced persons. [3]Projected rates based on about 79% of total deaths. [4]Also major producer of cut flowers (particularly roses and carnations). [5]In 2008 Colombia ranked first in the world in coca production; 430 metric tons of cocaine were produced. [6]Third quarter; includes ages 10 and over; excludes military. [7]Unemployed. [8]Actually household consumption. [9]Imports c.i.f.; exports f.o.b. [10]Operable or rehabilitated lines only. [11]Buses only. [12]Circulation of daily newspapers. [13]Subscribers. [14]Based on the 2005 Colombia Demographic and Health Survey, comprising 117,205 people. [15]2005–06. [16]2006–07. [17]Includes 310 unaccounted for. [18]Includes paramilitary.

Internet resource for further information:
- **National Administration Department of Statistics http://www.dane.gov.co**

Comoros[1]

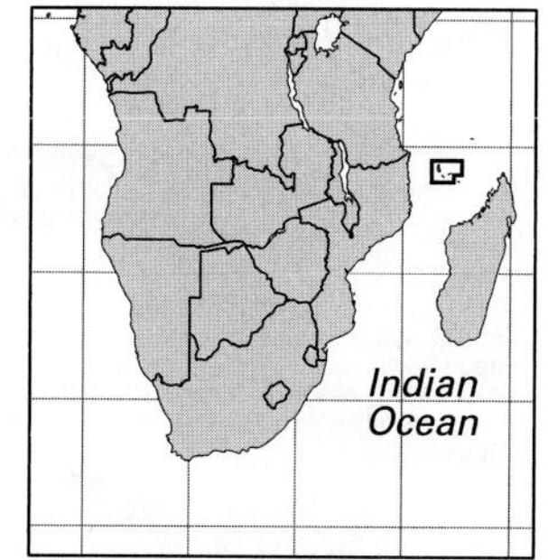

Official names: Udzima wa Komori (Comorian); Jumhūrīyat al-Qamar al-Muttaḥidah (Arabic); Union des Comores (French); (Union of the Comoros)[2].
Form of government: republic[3] with one legislative house (Assembly of the Union [33[4]]).
Head of state and government: President assisted by Vice Presidents.
Capital: Moroni.
Official languages[2]: Comorian (Shikomor); Arabic; French.
Official religion: Islam.
Monetary unit: Comorian franc (CF); valuation (Sept. 1, 2011) 1 U.S.$ = CF 345.23; 1 £ = CF 557.87.

Area and population

		area		population
Autonomous islands	Capitals	sq mi	sq km	2003 census[5]
Mwali (Mohéli)	Fomboni	112	290	35,751
Ngazidja (Grande Comore)	Moroni	443	1,148	296,177
Ndzuwani (Anjouan)	Mutsamudu	164	424	243,732
TOTAL		719	1,862	575,660

Demography

Population (2011): 754,000[6].
Density (2011): persons per sq mi 1,048.7, persons per sq km 404.9.
Urban-rural (2009): urban 28.1%; rural 71.9%.
Sex distribution (2006): male 49.61%; female 50.39%.
Age breakdown (2006): under 15, 42.7%; 15–29, 26.6%; 30–44, 17.8%; 45–59, 8.2%; 60–74, 3.9%; 75 and over, 0.8%.
Population projection: (2020) 933,000; (2030) 1,160,000.
Doubling time: 28 years.
Ethnic composition (2000): Comorian (a mixture of Bantu, Arab, Malay, and Malagasy peoples) 97.1%; Makua 1.6%; French 0.4%; other 0.9%.
Religious affiliation (2005): Muslim (nearly all Sunnī) 98.4%; other 1.6%.
Major cities (2002): Moroni (2007) 46,000; Mutsamudu 21,558; Domoni 13,254; Fomboni 13,053; Tsémbéhou 10,552.

Vital statistics

Birth rate per 1,000 population (2009): 31.9 (world avg. 20.3).
Death rate per 1,000 population (2009): 6.5 (world avg. 8.5).
Natural increase rate per 1,000 population (2009): 25.4 (world avg. 11.8).
Total fertility rate (avg. births per childbearing woman; 2009): 3.9.
Life expectancy at birth (2006): male 60.0 years; female 64.7 years.
Major causes of death per 100,000 population (2002): infectious and parasitic diseases 261.6, of which malaria 65.0, diarrheal diseases 52.0, measles 49.8; diseases of the circulatory system 118.9; accidents and injuries 68.1; perinatal conditions 59.2; malignant neoplasms (cancers) 46.9.

National economy

Budget (2007). Revenue: CF 33,945,000,000 (tax revenue 49.1%, of which taxes on international trade 17.6%, taxes on goods and services 11.5%; grants 37.7%; nontax revenue 13.2%). Expenditures: CF 37,314,000,000 (current expenditures 72.5%, of which interest on debt 2.2%; development expenditures 27.5%).
Public debt (external, outstanding; 2010): U.S.$213,000,000.
Production (metric tons except as noted). Agriculture, forestry, fishing (2009): coconuts 79,779, cassava 60,414, bananas 53,972, rice 20,465, taro 9,385, corn (maize) 5,123, yams 3,935, cloves 2,658, vanilla 65, ylang-ylang essence (2010) 45; other export crops grown in small quantities include coffee, cinnamon, and tuberoses; livestock (number of live animals) 118,000 goats, 50,000 cattle, 23,000 sheep; roundwood (2010) 283,400, of which fuelwood 91%; fisheries production 20,450 (from aquaculture, none). Mining and quarrying: sand, gravel, and crushed stone from coral mining for local construction. Manufacturing: products of small-scale industries include processed vanilla and ylang-ylang, cement, handicrafts, soaps, soft drinks, woodwork, and clothing. Energy production (consumption): electricity (kW-hr; 2007) 50,000,000 (50,000,000); coal, none (none); crude petroleum, none (none); petroleum products (metric tons; 2007) none (40,000); natural gas, none (none).
Population economically active (2008): total 324,000[7]; activity rate of total population 49.0%[7] (participation rates: ages 15–64, 83.5%[7]; female 46.3%[7]; unemployed [2005] 13.3%).

Price index (2005 = 100)

	2004	2005	2006	2007	2008	2009	2010
Consumer price index	98.0	100.0	104.5	109.3	114.6	119.8	122.3

Household income and expenditure. Average household size (2004) 5.8; average annual income per household (2004) CF 699,000[8] (U.S.$1,764); sources of income (2004)[8]: wages/self-employment 36.9%, value ascribed to self-produced food 27.7%, value ascribed to principal dwelling 23.9%; expenditure (1999)[9]: food, beverages, and tobacco products 68.0%, housing and energy 15.5%, clothing and footwear 4.7%, education 4.2%.

Gross national income (GNI; 2010): U.S.$550,000,000 (U.S.$820 per capita); purchasing power parity GNI (U.S.$1,180 per capita).

Structure of gross domestic product and labour force

	2009		2004	
	in value CF '000,000	% of total value	labour force[10]	% of labour force[10]
Agriculture, fishing	78,610	43.1	270,000	71.8
Mining	...	...		
Manufacturing	7,289	4.0		
Construction	10,007	5.5		
Public utilities	4,182	2.3		
Transportation and communications	9,918	5.4	106,000	28.2
Trade, restaurants, hotels	45,442	24.9		
Finance, insurance, real estate	7,776	4.3		
Public admin., defense	22,765	12.5		
Services	932	0.5		
Other	–4,491[11]	–2.5[11]		
TOTAL	182,430	100.0	376,000	100.0

Selected balance of payments data. Receipts from (U.S.$'000,000): tourism (2006) 27; remittances (2010) 11; foreign direct investment (2008–10 avg.) 9[12]; official development assistance (2009) 51. Disbursements for (U.S.$'000,000): tourism (2006) 11; remittances, n.a.
Land use as % of total land area (2009): in temporary crops or left fallow 42.9%, in permanent crops 32.2%, in pasture 8.1%, forest area 1.8%.

Foreign trade

Balance of trade (current prices)

	2005	2006	2007	2008
CF '000,000,000	–30.9	–34.3	–40.0	–56.0
% of total	73.1%	76.7%	77.2%	90.1%

Imports (2008): CF 59,040,000,000 (petroleum products 16.3%, road vehicles 7.8%, rice 7.5%, meat/fish 5.0%, cement 4.3%, iron and steel 2.4%, other 56.7%). *Major import sources:* France *c.* 14%; China *c.* 13%; India *c.* 11%; U.A.E. *c.* 10%; Italy *c.* 6%.
Exports (2008): CF 3,063,000,000 (ylang-ylang 26.6%, vanilla 21.3%, cloves 20.1%). *Major export destinations:* France *c.* 29%; Turkey *c.* 16%; Greece *c.* 12%; Brazil *c.* 10%; Algeria *c.* 8%.

Transport and communications

Transport. Railroads: none. Roads (2004): total length 493 mi, 793 km (paved 70%). Vehicles (2007): passenger cars 19,245; trucks and buses 1,790[13]. Air transport (2001): passengers arriving/departing Moroni 108,000.

Communications

Medium	date	number in '000s	units per 1,000 persons	Medium	date	number in '000s	units per 1,000 persons
Televisions	2002	13	23	PCs	2004	5.0	6.3
Telephones				Dailies	2005	[14]	[14]
Cellular	2010	165[15]	225[15]	Internet users	2009	24	36
Landline	2010	21	29	Broadband	2010	—	—

Education and health

Educational attainment (1996)[16]. Percentage of population age 25 and over having: no formal schooling 72.7%[17]; primary education 11.0%[17]; secondary 15.1%; unknown 1.2%. *Literacy* (2008): total population age 15 and over literate 73.6%; males literate 79.3%; females literate 67.8%.

Education (2004–05)

	teachers	students	student/ teacher ratio	enrollment rate (%)
Primary (age 6–11)	3,050	106,700	35.0	55[18]
Secondary/Voc. (age 12–18)	3,138	43,349	13.8	...
Tertiary[19]	130	1,779	13.7	2 (age 19–23)

Health: physicians (2004) 48 (1 per 12,417 persons); hospital beds (1995) 1,450[12] (1 per 342[12] persons); infant mortality rate per 1,000 live births (2006) 72.9; undernourished population (2005–07) 400,000[20] (46% of total population based on the consumption of a minimum daily requirement of 1,760 calories).

Military

Total active duty personnel (2008): the 1,100-member national army is not necessarily accepted by each of the islands; each island also has its own armed security. France provides training for military personnel. *Military expenditure as percentage of GDP* (2005): *c.* 3.5%; per capita expenditure U.S.$21.

[1]Excludes Mayotte, an overseas possession of France, unless otherwise indicated. [2]3 languages are official per 2001 constitution. [3]A constitutional referendum effective from May 23, 2009, returned greater powers to the central government. [4]Includes 9 indirectly elected seats. [5]Preliminary. [6]Excludes Comorians living abroad in France or Mayotte (about 150,000 people). [7]ILO Employment Trends Unit estimate. [8]Includes both monetary and nonmonetary income. [9]Weights of consumer price index components. [10]FAO estimate. [11]Less imputed bank service charge. [12]Estimated figure. [13]Excludes buses. [14]Circulation data unavailable for the one daily newspaper. [15]Subscribers. [16]Based on sample survey of 4,881 persons on all three islands. [17]Basic education may also be received through Qurʾanic schools. [18]1999–2000. [19]2003–04. [20]Includes Mayotte.

Internet resource for further information:
- **Central Bank of the Comoros**
  http://www.banque-comores.km

Congo, Democratic Republic of the

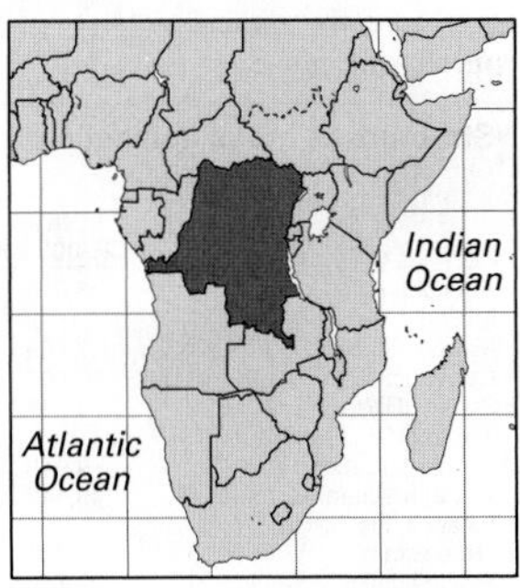

Official name: République Democratique du Congo (Democratic Republic of the Congo).
Form of government: unitary multiparty republic with two legislative bodies (Senate [108]; National Assembly [500]).
Head of state and government: President assisted by Prime Minister.
Capital: Kinshasa.
Official language: French[1].
Official religion: none.
Monetary unit: Congo franc (FC); valuation (Sept. 1, 2011) 1 U.S.$ = FC 920.59; 1 £ = FC 1,488.[2]

Area and population

		area		population
Provinces[3]	**Capitals**	sq mi	sq km	1998 estimate
Bandundu	Bandundu	114,154	295,658	5,201,000
Bas-Congo	Matadi	20,819	53,920	2,835,000
Equateur	Mbandaka	155,712	403,292	4,820,000
Kasai-Occidental	Kananga	59,746	154,742	3,337,000
Kasai-Oriental	Mbuji-Mayi	65,754	170,302	3,830,000
Katanga	Lubumbashi	191,845	496,877	4,125,000
Maniema	Kindu	51,062	132,250	1,246,787
Nord-Kivu	Goma	22,967	59,483	3,564,434
Orientale	Kisangani	194,302	503,239	5,566,000
Sud-Kivu	Bukavu	25,147	65,130	2,837,779
City				
Kinshasa	—	3,847	9,965	4,787,000
TOTAL		905,355[4]	2,344,858[4]	42,150,000

Demography

Population (2011): 67,758,000.
Density (2011): persons per sq mi 74.8, persons per sq km 28.9.
Urban-rural (2009): urban 34.6%; rural 65.4%.
Sex distribution (2009): male 49.71%; female 50.29%.
Age breakdown (2005): under 15, 47.2%; 15–29, 27.1%; 30–44, 14.2%; 45–59, 7.4%; 60–74, 3.4%; 75–84, 0.6%; 85 and over, 0.1%.
Population projection: (2020) 89,250,000; (2030) 108,872,000.
Doubling time: 23 years.
Ethnic composition (1983): Luba 18.0%; Kongo 16.1%; Mongo 13.5%; Rwanda 10.3%; Azande 6.1%; Bangi and Ngale 5.8%; Rundi 3.8%; Teke 2.7%; Boa 2.3%; Chokwe 1.8%; Lugbara 1.6%; Banda 1.4%; other 16.6%.
Religious affiliation (2004): Roman Catholic *c.* 50%; Protestant *c.* 20%; Kimbanguist (indigenous Christian) *c.* 10%; Muslim *c.* 10%; traditional beliefs and syncretic sects *c.* 10%.
Major urban areas (2009): Kinshasa 8,754,000; Lubumbashi 1,543,000; Mbuji-Mayi 1,488,000; Kananga 878,000; Kisangani 812,000; Bukavu (2004) 471,789.

Vital statistics

Birth rate per 1,000 population (2009): 42.6 (world avg. 20.3).
Death rate per 1,000 population (2009): 11.6 (world avg. 8.5).
Natural increase rate per 1,000 population (2009): 31.0 (world avg. 11.8).
Total fertility rate (avg. births per childbearing woman; 2009): 6.20.
Life expectancy at birth (2009): male 52.6 years; female 56.2 years.
Adult population (ages 15–49) *living with HIV* (2009): 1.2–1.6% (world avg. 0.8%).
Major causes of death per 100,000 population (2002): diarrheal diseases *c.* 219; HIV/AIDS-related *c.* 217; lower respiratory infections *c.* 211; malaria *c.* 191; war and violence *c.* 107.

National economy

Budget (2008). Revenue: FC 1,326,800,000,000 (customs and excise taxes 25.8%, taxes on goods and services 21.3%, income and profit taxes 19.1%, grants 9.2%, other revenue 24.6%). Expenditures: FC 1,478,700,000,000 (wages and salaries 30.6%, goods and services 18.8%, transfers and subsidies 15.3%, interest payments 13.8%).
Public debt (external, outstanding; 2009): U.S.$10,788,000,000.
Production (metric tons except as noted). Agriculture, forestry, fishing (2009): cassava 15,000,000, sugarcane 1,550,000, plantains 1,200,000, corn (maize) 1,200,000, peanuts (groundnuts) 367,000, rice 320,000, bananas 315,000, papayas 220,000, mangoes 210,000, oranges 180,000, dried beans 115,000, game meat 89,000, avocados 65,000, melonseed 51,000; livestock (number of live animals) 4,100,000 goats, 965,000 pigs; roundwood (2010) 79,933,134 cu m, of which fuelwood 94%; fisheries production 238,970 (from aquaculture 1%). Mining and quarrying (2009): copper 309,181[5]; cobalt 56,258[5]; tin 10,000[5]; silver (2008) 34,083 kg; gold 3,500 kg; diamonds 18,275,000 carats[6]. Manufacturing (2008): cement 443,550; flour 199,000; steel 113,000; sugar 96,000; paints 41,000; printed fabrics (2007) 5,616,000 sq m; cigarettes 3,536,000,000 cartons; shoes 21,814,000 pairs; beer 3,040,000 hectolitres; soft drinks 1,400,000 hectolitres. Energy production (consumption): electricity (kW-hr; 2009) 7,665,000,000 ([2008] 6,036,000,000); hard coal (metric tons; 2009) 141,000 ([2007] 183,000); crude petroleum (barrels; 2009) 9,382,000 ([2007] negligible); petroleum products (metric tons; 2007) none (432,000); natural gas, none (none).
Gross national income (GNI; 2010): U.S.$11,951,000,000 (U.S.$180 per capita); purchasing power parity GNI (U.S.$310 per capita).

Structure of gross domestic product and labour force

	2008		2006	
	in value FC '000,000	% of total value	labour force	% of labour force
Agriculture	2,574,000	39.4	15,099,000	60.4
Mining	951,000	14.6		
Manufacturing	353,000	5.4		
Construction	352,000	5.4		
Public utilities	133,000	2.0		
Transp. and commun.	289,000	4.4	9,913,000	39.6
Trade, restaurants	1,146,000	17.6		
Pub. admin., defense	330,000	5.1		
Finance and services	273,000	4.2		
Other	125,000[7]	1.9[7]		
TOTAL	6,526,000	100.0	25,012,000	100.0

Household income and expenditure: n.a.
Population economically active (2008)[8]: total 24,046,000; activity rate 37.4% (participation rates: ages 15–64, 71.9%; female 40.6%; unemployed, n.a.).

Price index (2005 = 100)

	2002	2003	2004	2005	2006	2007	2008
Consumer price index	70.2	79.3	82.4	100.0	113.1	132.2	155.1

Selected balance of payments data. Receipts from (U.S.$'000,000): tourism (2005) 1.0; remittances, n.a.; foreign direct investment (FDI; 2008–10 avg.) 1,776; official development assistance (2009) 2,354. Disbursements for (U.S.$'000,000): tourism (1997) 7.0; remittances, n.a.; FDI (2008–10 avg.) 32.
Land use as % of total land area (2009): in temporary crops or left fallow (2007) 3.0%, in permanent crops 0.3%, in pasture 6.6%, forest area 68.1%.

Foreign trade

Balance of trade (current prices)

	2003	2004	2005	2006	2007	2008
U.S.$'000,000	+117	+60	–402	+39	+886	–125
% of total	4.6%	1.7%	8.8%	6.7%	7.8%	0.9%

Imports (2007): U.S.$5,257,000,000 (aid-related imports 14.1%, other imports 85.9%). *Major import sources* (2008): South Africa 28.4%; Belgium 9.9%; Zambia 7.1%; Zimbabwe 6.0%; China 5.9%.
Exports (2007): U.S.$6,143,000,000 (cobalt 37.8%, copper 32.4%, diamonds 13.9%, crude petroleum 10.3%, coffee 0.8%). *Major export destinations* (2008): China 47.3%; Belgium 15.4%; Finland 9.6%; U.S. 8.1%; Zambia 4.4%.

Transport and communications

Transport. Railroads (2008): length 2,490 mi, 4,007 km[9]; passenger-km (2006) 167,000,000; metric ton-km cargo (2003) 506,010,000. Roads (2004): total length 95,378 mi, 153,497 km (paved *c.* 2%). Vehicles (1999): passenger cars 172,600; trucks and buses 34,600. Air transport (1999): passenger-km 263,000,000; metric ton-km cargo 39,000,000.

Communications

Medium	date	number in '000s	units per 1,000 persons	Medium	date	number in '000s	units per 1,000 persons
Televisions	2003	146	2.7	PCs	2007	...	...
Telephones				Dailies	2009	50[10]	0.8[10]
Cellular	2010	11,355[11]	172[11]	Internet users	2009	365	5.5
Landline	2010	42	0.6	Broadband	2010	8.7[11]	0.1[11]

Education and health

Educational attainment: n.a. *Literacy* (2008): percentage of total population age 15 and over literate 66.6%; males literate 77.5%; females literate 56.1%.

Education (2007–08)

	teachers	students	student/ teacher ratio	enrollment rate (%)
Primary (age 6–11)	255,594	9,973,365	39.0	...
Secondary/Voc. (age 12–17)	188,808	3,129,488	16.6	...
Tertiary	20,112	306,400	15.2	5 (age 18–22)

Health: physicians (2004) 5,827 (1 per 9,585 persons); hospital beds, n.a.; infant mortality rate per 1,000 live births (2005) 116.5; undernourished population (2004–06) 43,900,000 (75% of total population based on the consumption of a minimum daily requirement of 1,750 calories).

Military

Total active duty personnel (November 2010): *c.* 150,000 (army *c.* 79.8%, central staff *c.* 9.3%, republican guard *c.* 4.7%, air force *c.* 1.7%, navy *c.* 4.5%); UN peacekeepers (July 2011): 18,997 troops, 1,241 police. *Military expenditure as percentage of GDP* (2009): 1.1%; per capita expenditure U.S.$2.

[1]National languages are Kongo, Lingala, Swahili, and Tshiluba. [2]Most transactions are conducted outside of the banking system and often with U.S. dollars. [3]The scheduled reorganization into 25 provinces and 1 city (Kinshasa) as of late 2011 had not taken place. [4]Total area per more recent survey is 905,568 sq mi (2,345,410 sq km); the land part totals 875,525 sq mi (2,267,600 sq km). [5]Mine output, metal content. [6]Mostly artisanally mined; 20% of diamonds are of gem quality. [7]Import duties. [8]ILO estimates. [9]Generally serves mining centres; mostly in poor condition. [10]Circulation. [11]Subscribers.

Internet resource for further information:
- **Central Bank of the Democratic Republic of the Congo http://www.bcc.cd**

Congo, Republic of the

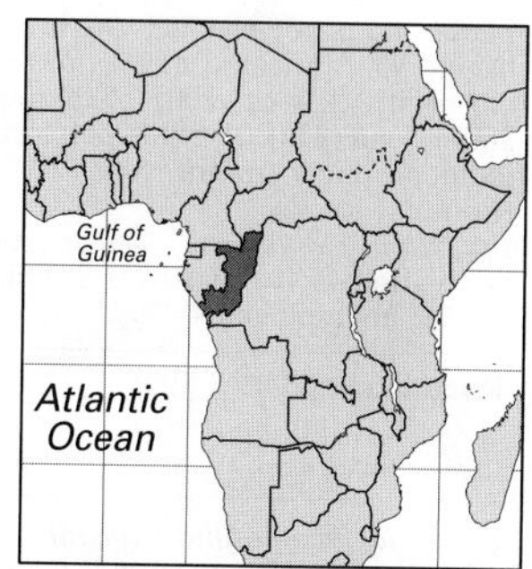

Official name: République du Congo (Republic of the Congo).
Form of government: republic with two legislative houses (Senate [72[1]]; National Assembly [137]).
Head of state and government: President.[2]
Capital: Brazzaville.
Official language: French[3].
Official religion: none.
Monetary unit: CFA franc (CFAF); valuation (Sept. 1, 2011) 1 U.S.$ = CFAF 460.31; 1 £ = CFAF 743.83.

Area and population

Regions	Capitals	area sq mi	area sq km	population 2007 census[4]
Bouenza	Madingou	4,733	12,258	237,496
Cuvette	Owando	18,861	48,850	156,136
Cuvette-Ouest	Ewo	10,039	26,000	73,011
Kouilou	Pointe-Noire	5,270	13,650	92,006
Lékoumou	Sibiti	8,089	20,950	96,424
Likouala	Impfondo	25,500	66,044	154,154
Niari	Dolisie	10,007	25,918	134,256
Plateaux	Djambala	14,826	38,400	174,617
Pool	Kinkala	13,110	33,955	236,616
Sangha	Ouesso	21,542	55,795	57,632
Communes				
Brazzaville	—	39	100	1,375,237
Dolisie	—	7	18	83,802
Mossendjo	—	2	5	13,239
Nkayi	—	3	8	71,623
Ouesso	—	2	5	28,202
Pointe-Noire	—	17	44	711,128
TOTAL		132,047	342,000	3,695,579

Demography

Population (2011): 3,920,000.
Density (2011): persons per sq mi 29.7, persons per sq km 11.5.
Urban-rural (2007): urban 61.0%; rural 39.0%.
Sex distribution (2008): male 49.72%; female 50.28%.
Age breakdown (2008): under 15, 46.1%; 15–29, 27.4%; 30–44, 14.8%; 45–59, 7.4%; 60–74, 3.4%; 75–84, 0.8%; 85 and over, 0.1%.
Population projection: (2020) 4,749,000; (2030) 5,856,000.
Doubling time: 24 years.
Ethnic composition (2000): Kongo 21.2%; Yombe 11.5%; Teke 10.7%; Kougni 8.0%; Mboshi 5.4%; Ngala 4.2%; Sundi 4.0%; other 35.0%.
Religious affiliation (2005): Roman Catholic *c.* 49%; independent Christian *c.* 13%; Protestant *c.* 11%; Muslim *c.* 2%; other (mostly traditional beliefs and nonreligious) *c.* 25%.
Major cities (2010): Brazzaville 1,408,150; Pointe-Noire 829,134; Dolisie 128,032; Nkayi (2007) 71,623; Ouesso (2007) 28,202.

Vital statistics

Birth rate per 1,000 population (2008): 41.8 (world avg. 20.3).
Death rate per 1,000 population (2008): 12.3 (world avg. 8.5).
Natural increase rate per 1,000 population (2008): 29.5 (world avg. 11.8).
Total fertility rate (avg. births per childbearing woman; 2008): 5.92.
Life expectancy at birth (2008): male 52.5 years; female 55.0 years.
Adult population (ages 15–49) *living with HIV* (2009): 3.4% (world avg. 0.8%).

National economy

Budget (2008). Revenue: CFAF 2,465,900,000,000 (petroleum revenue 85.9%, nonpetroleum receipts 13.4%, grants 0.7%). Expenditures: CFAF 1,227,500,000,000 (current expenditure 63.8%, capital expenditure 36.2%).
Public debt (external, outstanding; 2009): U.S.$4,785,000,000.
Household income and expenditure. Average household size (2000) 5.9.
Gross national income (GNI; 2010): U.S.$8,698,000,000 (U.S.$2,310 per capita); purchasing power parity GNI (U.S.$3,280 per capita).

Structure of gross domestic product and labour force

	2008 in value CFAF '000,000,000	2008 % of total value	2010 labour force	2010 % of labour force
Agriculture, forestry, fishing	199.9	4.2	487,000	32.0
Petroleum, mining	3,173.6	66.7		
Manufacturing	193.7	4.1		
Construction	143.7	3.0		
Public utilities	25.4	0.5		
Trade	270.1	5.7		
Transp. and commun.	210.5	4.4	1,037,000	68.0
Finance, real estate; Pub. admin., defense; Services	465.5	9.8		
Other	77.1[5]	1.6[5]		
TOTAL	4,759.5	100.0	1,524,000	100.0

Production (metric tons except as noted). Agriculture, forestry, fishing (2009): cassava 1,261,380, sugarcane 600,000, oil palm fruit 90,000, bananas 81,232, plantains 67,992, mangoes/guavas 27,827, peanuts (groundnuts) 23,000, yams 15,403, coffee 3,600; livestock (number of live animals) 295,000 goats, 115,000 cattle, 100,000 sheep; roundwood (2010) 3,746,291 cu m, of which fuelwood 35%; fisheries production 61,277 (from aquaculture, negligible). Mining and quarrying (2009): diamonds 68,000 carats[6]; gold 100 kg. Manufacturing (2004): residual fuel oil 437,000[7]; gas–diesel oils 141,000[7]; motor gasoline 63,000[7]; kerosene 55,000[7]; refined sugar 31,000; cigarettes 750,000,000 units; beer 674,000 hectolitres; soft drinks 436,000 hectolitres. Energy production (consumption): electricity (kW-hr; 2007) 407,000,000 (856,000,000); coal, none (none); crude petroleum (barrels; 2009) 100,200,000 ([2007] 5,610,000); petroleum products (metric tons; 2007) 717,000 (389,000); natural gas (cu m; 2007) 21,100,000 (21,100,000).
Population economically active (2008)[8]: total 1,554,000; activity rate of total population 43.0% (participation rates: ages 15–64, 72.9%; female 43.4%; unemployed, n.a.).

Price index (2005 = 100)

	2004	2005	2006	2007	2008	2009	2010
Consumer price index	97.0	100.0	106.5	109.4	117.4	123.3	...

Selected balance of payments data. Receipts from (U.S.$'000,000): tourism (2007) 54; remittances (2010) 13; foreign direct investment (2008–10 avg.) 2,461; official development assistance (2009) 283. Disbursements for (U.S.$'000,000): tourism (2007) 168; remittances (2008) 102.
Land use as % of total land area (2007): in temporary crops or left fallow 1.4%, in permanent crops 0.1%, in pasture 29.3%, forest area 65.7%.

Foreign trade

Balance of trade (current prices)

	2003	2004	2005	2006	2007	2008
CFAF '000,000,000	+1,074	+1,074	+1,817	+2,125	+1,487	+2,289
% of total	52.7%	48.2%	57.0%	50.2%	38.0%	47.7%

Imports (2007): CFAF 1,214,000,000,000 (nonpetroleum sector 62.5%, petroleum sector 37.5%). *Major import sources* (2008): France 22.2%; China 18.7%; India 6.0%; U.S. 5.6%; Italy 5.2%.
Exports (2007): CFAF 2,701,000,000,000 (crude petroleum 90.1%, wood and wood products 4.6%, petroleum products 2.5%). *Major export destinations* (2008): U.S. 42.1%; China 30.1%; France 5.6%.

Transport and communications

Transport. Railroads (2006): route length 488 mi, 795 km; passenger-km 167,000,000; metric ton-km cargo 264,000,000. Roads (2004): total length 10,805 mi, 17,289 km (paved 5%). Vehicles (2007): passenger cars 56,000; trucks and buses 36,500. Air transport (2003): passenger-km 31,000,000; metric ton-km cargo, n.a.

Communications

Medium	date	number in '000s	units per 1,000 persons	Medium	date	number in '000s	units per 1,000 persons
Televisions	2002	40	12	PCs	2006	17	5.0
Telephones				Dailies	2009	8[9]	2.1[9]
Cellular	2010	3,799[10]	940[10]	Internet users	2009	245	66
Landline	2010	9.8	2.4	Broadband	2010	0.1[10]	—

Education and health

Educational attainment (2005). Percentage of population ages 15–49 having[11]: no formal schooling 5.6%; primary education 28.1%; lower secondary 47.2%; upper secondary/higher 19.1%. *Literacy* (2007): total population age 15 and over literate 86.8%; males literate 92.1%; females literate 81.7%.

Education (2007–08)

	teachers	students	student/ teacher ratio	enrollment rate (%)
Primary (age 6–11)	12,124	628,081	51.8	59[12]
Secondary/Voc. (age 12–18)	6,965[13]	232,026[13]	33.3[13]	...
Tertiary[14]	894	12,456	13.9	4 (age 19–23)

Health: physicians (2005) 549[15] (1 per 6,386 persons); hospital beds (2007) 3,325[15] (1 per 1,117 persons); infant mortality rate per 1,000 live births (2008) 81.7; undernourished population (2004–06) 700,000 (21% of total population based on the consumption of a minimum daily requirement of 1,800 calories).

Military

Total active duty personnel (November 2010): 10,000 (army 80.0%, navy 8.0%, air force 12.0%). *Military expenditure as percentage of GDP* (2009): 1.4%; per capita expenditure U.S.$35.

[1]Statutory number. [2]The post of prime minister, an extraconstitutional creation from January 2005, was abolished on Sept. 15, 2009. [3]"Functional" national languages are Lingala and Monokutuba. [4]Preliminary. [5]Indirect taxes. [6]Reported figure; the Republic of the Congo was formerly a major illegal transshipment conduit for diamonds from nearby countries and was expelled from the Kimberley Process between 2004 and 2007. [7]2007. [8]ILO estimates. [9]Circulation. [10]Subscribers. [11]Survey of 9,975 persons only (including 7,051 females and 2,924 males). [12]2005–06. [13]2003–04. [14]2002–03. [15]Public sector only.

Internet resources for further information:

- **La Banque de France: La Zone Franc http://www.banque-france.fr/fr/eurosys/zonefr/zonefr.htm**
- **Republique du Congo: Centre National de la Statistique et des Etudes Economiques http://www.cnsee.org**

Costa Rica

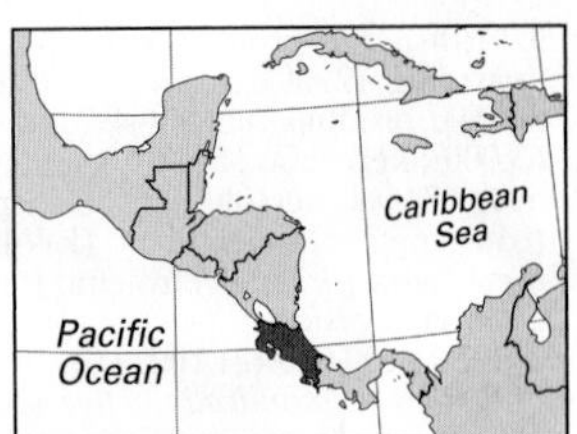

Official name: República de Costa Rica (Republic of Costa Rica).
Form of government: unitary multiparty republic with one legislative house (Legislative Assembly [57]).
Head of state and government: President.
Capital: San José.
Official language: Spanish.
Official religion: Roman Catholicism.
Monetary unit: Costa Rican colón (₡); valuation (Sept. 1, 2011) 1 U.S.$ = ₡513.99; 1 £ = ₡830.58.

Area and population		area		population
				2009[1]
Provinces	**Capitals**	sq mi	sq km	estimate
Alajuela	Alajuela	3,766	9,753	838,508
Cartago	Cartago	1,207	3,125	497,940
Guanacaste	Liberia	3,915	10,141	310,696
Heredia	Heredia	1,026	2,657	411,271
Limón	Limón	3,547	9,188	408,738
Puntarenas	Puntarenas	4,354	11,277	424,082
San José	San José	1,915	4,959	1,547,760
TOTAL		19,730	51,100	4,438,995

Demography

Population (2011): 4,577,000.
Density (2011): persons per sq mi 232.0, persons per sq km 89.6.
Urban-rural (2009): urban 63.9%; rural 36.1%.
Sex distribution (2006): male 50.76%; female 49.24%.
Age breakdown (2009): under 15, 25.5%; 15–29, 28.0%; 30–44, 22.0%; 45–59, 15.5%; 60–74, 6.8%; 75–84, 1.8%; 85 and over, 0.4%.
Population projection: (2020) 5,098,000; (2030) 5,571,000.
Doubling time: 55 years.
Ethnic composition (2000): white 77.0%; mestizo 17.0%; black/mulatto 3.0%; East Asian (mostly Chinese) 2.0%; Amerindian 1.0%.
Religious affiliation (2004): Roman Catholic (practicing) *c.* 47%; Roman Catholic (nonpracticing) *c.* 25%; Evangelical Protestant *c.* 13%; nonreligious *c.* 10%; other *c.* 5%.
Major cities (2009): San José 356,174[2] (urban agglomeration 1,461,000[3]); Limón 65,600[4]; Alajuela 50,989[4]; San Francisco 48,036[4]; Liberia 42,400[4]; Puntarenas 38,100[4].

Vital statistics

Birth rate per 1,000 population (2009): 16.6 (world avg. 20.3); within marriage (2007) 40.1%; outside of marriage (2007) 59.9%.
Death rate per 1,000 population (2009): 4.1 (world avg. 8.5).
Natural increase rate per 1,000 population (2009): 12.1 (world avg. 11.8).
Total fertility rate (avg. births per childbearing woman; 2009): 1.95.
Marriage/divorce rates per 1,000 population: (2007) 5.8/(1998) 2.2.
Life expectancy at birth (2009): male 76.8 years; female 81.8 years.
Major causes of death per 100,000 population (2003): diseases of the circulatory system 105.0; communicable diseases 92.3; malignant neoplasms (cancers) 78.1; accidents and violence 46.0.

National economy

Budget (2007). Revenue: ₡2,106,400,000,000 (taxes on goods and services 59.1%, income tax 25.2%, taxes on international trade 7.9%, social contributions 1.8%, grants 1.0%). Expenditures: ₡2,025,500,000,000 (education 31.8%, interest on debt 20.7%, social protection 16.0%, public order 11.4%, transportation 10.7%, health 2.5%).
Public debt (external, outstanding; 2009): U.S.$3,190,000,000.
Gross national income (GNI; 2010): U.S.$30,518,000,000 (U.S.$6,580 per capita); purchasing power parity GNI (U.S.$10,880).

Structure of gross domestic product and labour force	2009		2008	
	in value ₡'000,000	% of total value	labour force	% of labour force
Agriculture, forestry, fishing	1,069,408	6.4	241,632	11.7
Mining	29,729	0.2	2,167	0.1
Manufacturing	2,870,103	17.1	239,538	11.6
Construction	911,101	5.4	152,445	7.4
Public utilities	300,568	1.8	27,953	1.4
Transp. and commun.	1,519,643	9.1	143,045	6.9
Trade, restaurants	2,844,879	16.9	477,917	23.2
Finance, real estate	1,522,581	9.1	190,920	9.3
Public administration	719,358	4.3	93,762	4.6
Services	4,256,297	24.4	377,311	18.3
Other	744,377[5]	4.4[5]	112,923[6]	5.5[6]
TOTAL	16,788,044	100.0[7]	2,059,613	100.0

Production (metric tons except as noted). Agriculture, forestry, fishing (2009): sugarcane 4,100,000, bananas 2,365,470, pineapples 1,870,121, cow's milk 916,657, oil palm fruit 897,750, cassava 451,700, oranges 350,000, rice 256,460, green coffee 91,627, papayas 61,657; livestock (number of live animals) 1,287,100 cattle, 440,000 pigs, 22,100,000 chickens; roundwood (2010) 4,681,194 cu m, of which fuelwood 72%; fisheries production 46,475 (from aquaculture 53%). Mining and quarrying (2008): limestone 270,000; gold 198 kg. Manufacturing (value added in U.S.$'000,000; 2003): food products 734; beverages 188; paints, soaps, and pharmaceuticals 169; plastic products 121; paper and paper products 96; bricks, tiles, and cement 95; printing and publishing 95; fabricated metal products 74. Energy production (consumption): electricity (kW-hr; 2007) 9,050,000,000 (9,213,000,000); coal (metric tons; 2007) none (21,000); crude petroleum (barrels; 2007) none (5,454,000); petroleum products (metric tons; 2007) 713,000 (2,308,000); natural gas, none (none).
Population economically active (2008): total 2,059,613; activity rate of total population 45.4% (participation rates: ages 12–59 [2005] 60.8%; female [2005] 36.2%; unemployed 4.9%).

Price index (2005 = 100)	2004	2005	2006	2007	2008	2009	2010
Consumer price index	87.9	100.0	111.5	121.9	138.3	149.1	157.5

Household income and expenditure (2004–05). Average household size 3.7; average annual household income ₡4,225,680 (U.S.$9,214); sources of income: wages and salaries 67.9%, rent 11.0%, transfers 10.9%, self-employment 8.1%; expenditure: food, beverages, and tobacco 21.9%, housing and energy 19.3%, transportation 14.8%, recreation and culture 7.9%, wearing apparel 6.9%.
Selected balance of payments data. Receipts from (U.S.$'000,000): tourism (2009) 1,799; remittances (2010) 557; foreign direct investment (FDI; 2008–10 avg.) 1,613; official development assistance (2009) 109. Disbursements for (U.S.$'000,000): tourism (2009) 368; remittances (2009) 239; FDI (2008–10 avg.) 7.
Land use as % of total land area (2009): in temporary crops or left fallow 3.9%, in permanent crops 5.9%, in pasture 25.5%, forest area 50.6%[8].

Foreign trade[9]

Balance of trade (current prices)	2004	2005	2006	2007	2008	2009
U.S.$'000,000	–2,050	–2,023	–3,816	–3,830	–5,545	–2,617
% of total	14.7%	12.4%	20.8%	17.7%	22.1%	13.0%

Imports (2008): U.S.$15,289,000,000 (machinery and apparatus 29.1%, of which electronic integrated circuits/micro-assemblies 9.6%; chemicals and chemical products 14.7%; petroleum 13.9%; base and fabricated metals 9.5%; food 7.0%). *Major import sources:* U.S. 38.2%; Mexico 6.2%; China 5.7%; Japan 5.4%; Venezuela 4.5%.
Exports (2008): U.S.$9,744,000,000 (food products 29.4%, of which bananas 7.3%, pineapples 5.9%, coffee 3.5%; parts for office machines/computers 10.8%; electronic integrated circuits/micro-assemblies 10.7%; medical/surgical instruments 6.3%; medicines 3.3%). *Major export destinations:* U.S. 38.2%; China 6.3%; Netherlands 5.1%; Nicaragua 4.1%; Hong Kong 4.0%.

Transport and communications

Transport. Railroads (2007): 278 km[10]; passenger-km 870,000; metric ton-km cargo 230,000. Roads (2007): total length 22,789 mi, 36,654 km (paved 26%); passenger-km 27,000,000; metric ton-km cargo, n.a. Vehicles (2007): passenger cars 538,384; trucks and buses 151,933. Air transport (2005)[11]: passenger-km 2,284,000,000; metric ton-km cargo 10,351,000.

Communications			units				units
Medium	date	number in '000s	per 1,000 persons	**Medium**	date	number in '000s	per 1,000 persons
Televisions	2004	1,068	257	PCs	2005	1,000	233
Telephones				Dailies	2009	272[12]	81[12]
Cellular	2010	3,035[13]	651[13]	Internet users	2009	1,579	345
Landline	2010	1,482	318	Broadband	2010	288[13]	62[13]

Education and health

Educational attainment (2004). Percentage of population age 5 and over having: no formal schooling 9.9%; incomplete primary education 23.3%; complete primary 24.5%; incomplete secondary 18.2%; complete secondary 8.5%; higher 12.7%; other/unknown 2.9%. *Literacy* (2008): total population age 15 and over literate 96.0%; males literate 95.7%; females literate 96.2%.

Education (2007–08)	teachers	students	student/ teacher ratio	enrollment rate (%)
Primary (age 6–11)	28,186	534,816	19.0	...
Secondary/Voc. (age 12–16)	24,347	380,813	15.6	64[14]
Tertiary	4,494[15]	110,717[16]	17.7[15]	25[16] (age 17–21)

Health: physicians (2004) 6,600 (1 per 644 persons); hospital beds (2003) 5,908 (1 per 714 persons); infant mortality rate per 1,000 live births (2009) 8.8; undernourished population (2005–07) less than 5.0% of total population.

Military

Paramilitary expenditure as percentage of GDP (2009): 0.6%; per capita expenditure U.S.$40. The army was officially abolished in 1948. Paramilitary (police) forces had 9,800 members in November 2010.

[1]June 30. [2]Population of San José canton. [3]2009 estimate of UN *World Urbanization Prospects: The 2009 Revision.* [4]Urban population of commune. [5]Taxes less subsidies and imputed bank service charges. [6]Includes 101,905 unemployed. [7]Detail does not add to total given because of rounding. [8]Forest area overlaps with other categories. [9]Imports c.i.f.; exports f.o.b. [10]Limited service on part of route is primarily for tourist trains. [11]Lacsa (Costa Rican Airlines) only. [12]Circulation of daily newspapers. [13]Subscribers. [14]2006–07. [15]2002–03. [16]2004–05.

Internet resources for further information:
- **Central Bank of Costa Rica http://www.bccr.fi.cr**
- **National Institute of Statistics and the Census http://www.inec.go.cr**

Côte d'Ivoire

Official name: République de Côte d'Ivoire (Republic of Côte d'Ivoire [Ivory Coast]).
Form of government: republic with one legislative house (National Assembly [225[1]]).
Head of state and government: President assisted by Prime Minister.
Capital: Yamoussoukro.
De facto capital: Abidjan.
Official language: French.
Official religion: none.
Monetary unit: CFA franc (CFAF); valuation (Sept. 1, 2011) 1 U.S.$ = CFAF 460.31; 1 £ = CFAF 743.83.

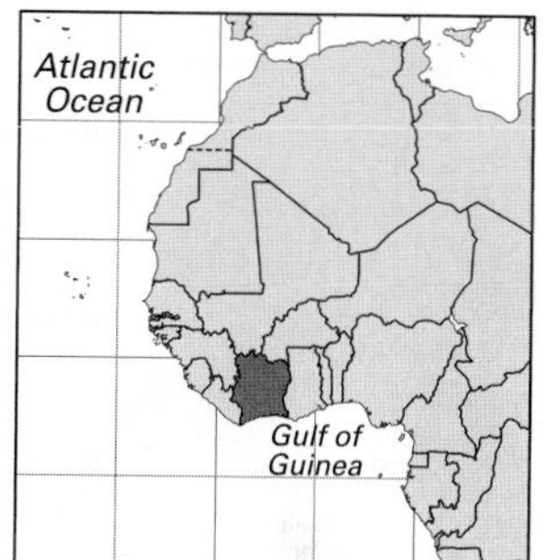

Area and population

Regions	area sq km	population 2002 estimate	Regions	area sq km	population 2002 estimate
Agnebi	9,080	720,900	Moyen-Cavally	14,150	443,200
Bafing	8,720	178,400	Moyen-Comoé	6,900	488,200
Bas-Sassandra	25,800	443,200	N'zi-Comoé	19,560	909,800
Denguélé	20,600	277,000	Savanes	40,323	1,215,100
Dix-huit Montagnes	16,600	1,125,800	Sud-Bandama	10,650	826,300
Fromager	6,900	679,900	Sud-Comoé	6,250	536,500
Haut-Sassandra	15,200	1,186,600	Vallée du Bandama	28,530	1,335,500
Lacs	8,940	597,500	Worodougou	21,900	400,200
Lagunes	14,200	4,210,200	Zanzan	38,000	839,000
Marahoué	8,500	651,700	TOTAL	320,803	17,065,000

Demography

Population (2011): 21,504,000.
Density (2011): persons per sq mi 173.6, persons per sq km 67.0.
Urban-rural (2008): urban 49.0%; rural 51.0%.
Sex distribution (2007): male 50.75%; female 49.25%.
Age breakdown (2007): under 15, 41.2%; 15–29, 29.2%; 30–44, 16.5%; 45–59, 8.4%; 60–74, 3.9%; 75–84, 0.6%; 85 and over, 0.2%.
Population projection: (2020) 25,504,000; (2030) 29,724,000.
Ethnolinguistic composition (1998)[2]: Akan 42.1%; Mande 26.5%; other 31.4%.
Religious affiliation (2005): traditional beliefs *c.* 37%; Christian *c.* 32%, of which Roman Catholic *c.* 17%, Protestant *c.* 8%, independent Christian *c.* 7%; Muslim *c.* 28%; other *c.* 3%.
Major cities (2009): Abidjan 4,009,000[3]; Yamoussoukro 808,000[3]; Bouaké 642,700; Daloa 241,020; Korhogo (2003) 115,000.

Vital statistics

Birth rate per 1,000 population (2009): 36.7 (world avg. 20.3).
Death rate per 1,000 population (2009): 13.3 (world avg. 8.5).
Total fertility rate (avg. births per childbearing woman; 2007): 4.33.
Life expectancy at birth (2009): male 50.7 years; female 54.1 years.
Adult population (ages 15–49) *living with HIV* (2009): 3.4%[4] (world avg. 0.8%).
Major causes of death per 100,000 population (2002): HIV/AIDS-related *c.* 299; malaria *c.* 153; lower respiratory infections *c.* 132; diarrheal diseases *c.* 102; perinatal conditions *c.* 92.

National economy

Budget (2008). Revenue: CFAF 2,156,200,000,000 (tax revenue 76.0%, nontax revenue 15.7%, grants 8.3%). Expenditures: CFAF 2,217,200,000,000 (current expenditure 84.8%, capital expenditure 14.4%, net lending 0.8%).
Public debt (external, outstanding; 2009): U.S.$10,979,000,000.
Production (metric tons except as noted). Agriculture, forestry, fishing (2009): yams 6,900,000, cassava 2,900,000, plantains 1,660,220, sugarcane 1,630,000, oil palm fruit 1,300,000, cacao beans 1,221,600, rice 680,000, corn (maize) 680,000, bananas 399,000, cashew nuts 246,000, pineapples 177,000, coffee 150,000, okra 115,000, natural rubber 114,000, kola nuts 58,000, shea nuts 25,400; livestock (number of live animals) 1,630,000 sheep, 1,540,000 cattle, 1,280,000 goats; roundwood (2010) 10,358,000 cu m, of which fuelwood 86%; fisheries production 49,290 (from aquaculture 3%). Mining and quarrying (2009): manganese 177,000; gold 6,947 kg; diamonds (2008) 300,000 carats[5]. Manufacturing (value added in CFAF '000,000,000; 1997): food 156.6, of which cocoa and chocolate 72.4, vegetable oils 62.7; chemicals 60.2; wood products 55.9; refined petroleum 46.0; textiles 37.9. Energy production (consumption): electricity (kW-hr; 2007) 5,631,000,000 (4,859,000,000); coal, none (none); crude petroleum (barrels; 2009) 21,100,000 ([2007] 26,600,000); petroleum products (metric tons; 2007) 3,200,000 (931,000); natural gas (cu m; 2007) 1,200,000,000 (1,200,000,000).
Population economically active (2008)[6]: total 8,126,000; activity rate of total population 39.5% (participation rates: ages 15–64, 67.3%; female 36.7%; unemployed 15.7%).

Price index (2005 = 100)

	2004	2005	2006	2007	2008	2009	2010
Consumer price index	96.3	100.0	102.5	104.4	111.0	112.1	114.0

Household income and expenditure. Average household size (2004) 8.0; expenditure (1996)[7]: food 32.2%, housing and energy 13.9%, hotels and restaurants 12.3%, transportation 9.6%, clothing 7.4%, household equipment 5.7%.
Selected balance of payments data. Receipts from (U.S.$'000,000): tourism (2007) 104; remittances (2010) 177; foreign direct investment (2008–10 avg.) 415; official development assistance (2009) 2,366. Disbursements for (U.S.$'000,000): tourism (2007) 396; remittances (2008) 20.
Gross national income (GNI; 2010): U.S.$22,976,000,000 (U.S.$1,070 per capita); purchasing power parity GNI (U.S.$1,650 per capita).

Structure of gross domestic product and labour force

	2008		2006	
	in value CFAF '000,000,000	% of total value	labour force	% of labour force
Agriculture	2,415.4	23.2	3,303,000	42.6
Mining	564.1	5.4		
Manufacturing	1,542.3	14.8		
Public utilities	119.0	1.1		
Construction	239.7	2.3		
Transp. and commun.	733.9	7.1		
Trade, restaurants	952.2	9.1	4,446,000	57.4
Finance, real estate	445.0	4.3		
Public admin., defense	1,086.5	10.4		
Services	1,585.3	15.2		
Other	733.9[8]	7.1[8]		
TOTAL	10,417.3	100.0	7,749,000	100.0

Land use as % of total land area (2007): in temporary crops or left fallow 8.8%, in permanent crops 13.2%, in pasture 41.5%, forest area 32.8%.

Foreign trade[9]

Balance of trade (current prices)

	2004	2005	2006	2007	2008
U.S.$'000,000	+1,864	+1,383	+2,327	+1,385	+1,895
% of total	16.5%	10.5%	16.7%	9.4%	10.7%

Imports (2008): U.S.$7,884,000,000 (crude petroleum 33.9%; food products 17.5%, of which rice 5.9%, fish 5.0%; machinery and apparatus 11.3%; road vehicles 5.1%). *Major import sources:* Nigeria 29.3%; France 12.7%; China 6.9%; Thailand 4.5%; Venezuela 3.6%.
Exports (2008): U.S.$9,779,000,000 (cocoa [all forms] 27.0%; refined petroleum 20.8%; crude petroleum 15.6%; natural rubber 5.1%; toiletries/soaps 2.6%; rough/sawn wood 2.3%). *Major export destinations:* France 13.9%; Neth. 11.3%; U.S. 9.7%; Germany 7.1%; Nigeria 6.4%.

Transport and communications

Transport. Railroads: route length (2006) 395 mi, 636 km[10]; (2001) passenger-km 182,000,000[11]; (2001) metric ton-km cargo 699,000,000[11]. Roads (2004): total length 49,710 mi, 80,000 km (paved 8%). Vehicles: passenger cars (2002) 114,000; trucks and buses (2001) 54,900. Air transport: [12].

Communications

Medium	date	number in '000s	units per 1,000 persons	Medium	date	number in '000s	units per 1,000 persons
Televisions	2004	880	52	PCs	2004	262	16
Telephones				Dailies	2009	200[13]	9.7[13]
Cellular	2010	14,910[14]	755[14]	Internet users	2009	968	46
Landline	2010	223	11	Broadband	2010	7.9[14]	0.4[14]

Education and health

Educational attainment (1998–99)[15]. Percentage of population age 25 and over having: no formal schooling 62.3%; primary education 19.4%; secondary 14.3%; higher 3.3%; unknown 0.7%. *Literacy* (2007): percentage of population age 15 and over literate 55.5%; males 65.1%; females 45.5%.

Education (2007–08)

	teachers	students	student/ teacher ratio	enrollment rate (%)
Primary (age 6–11)	56,248	2,356,240	41.9	55[16]
Secondary/Voc. (age 12–18)	...	736,649[17]	...	20[17]
Tertiary	...	156,772[18]	...	...

Health: physicians (2004) 2,081 (1 per 8,143 persons); hospital beds (2006) 7,731 (1 per 2,500 persons); infant mortality rate per 1,000 live births (2009) 96.7; undernourished population (2004–06) 2,500,000 (14% of total population based on the consumption of a minimum daily requirement of 1,780 calories).

Military

Total active duty personnel (November 2010): 17,050 (army 38.1%, navy 5.3%, air force 4.1%, presidential guard 7.9%, gendarmerie[19] 44.6%). *Military expenditure as percentage of GDP* (2009): 1.5%; per capita expenditure U.S.$17.[20]

[1]Statutory number; no elections between December 2000 and April 2011. [2]Local population only (in 1998 foreigners constituted 26% of the population). [3]Urban agglomeration. [4]Statistically derived midpoint of range. [5]Annual UN sanctions on rough diamond exports have been imposed from November 2004 to May 2012. [6]ILO estimates. [7]Weights of consumer price index components. [8]Indirect taxes less imputed bank service charges. [9]Imports c.i.f.; exports f.o.b. [10]Côte d'Ivoire part of Abidjan to Ouagadougou, Burkina Faso, railway. [11]Data for entire length of Abidjan–Ouagadougou railway. [12]Data unavailable for Air Ivoire, the national airline. [13]Circulation. [14]Subscribers. [15]Based on sample survey of 4,572 persons (38% urban, 62% rural). [16]2002–03. [17]2001–02. [18]2006–07. [19]The gendarmerie or the national police force reinforces the army. [20]Peacekeeping troops: UN (August 2011) 8,974; French (November 2010) 780.

Internet resources for further information:
- **La Banque de France: La Zone Franc http://www.banque-france.fr/fr/eurosys/zonefr/zonefr.htm**
- **Institut National de la Statistique http://www.ins.ci**

Croatia

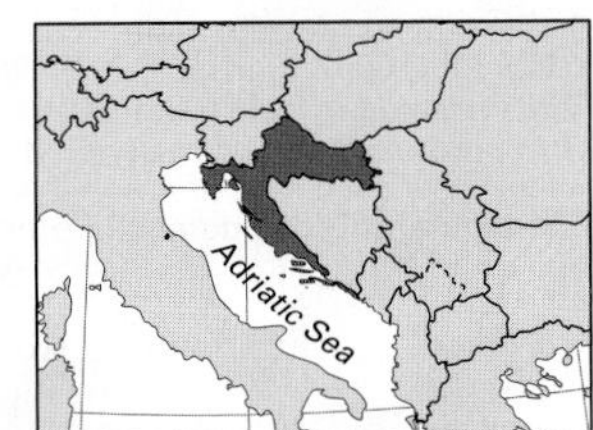

Official name: Republika Hrvatska (Republic of Croatia).
Form of government: multiparty republic with one legislative house (Croatian Parliament [153]).
Head of state: President.
Head of government: Prime Minister.
Capital: Zagreb.
Official language: Croatian.
Official religion: none[1].
Monetary unit: kuna (kn; plural kune); valuation (Sept. 1, 2011) 1 U.S.$ = kn 5.25; 1 £ = kn 8.49.

Area and population

Counties	area sq km	population 2011 census[2]	Counties	area sq km	population 2011 census[2]
Bjelovar-Bilogora	2,640	119,743	Sisak-Moslavina	4,468	172,977
Dubrovnik-Neretva	1,781	122,783	Slavonski Brod-Posavina	2,030	158,559
Istra (Istria)	2,813	208,440	Split-Dalmatia	4,540	455,242
Karlovac	3,626	128,749	Varaždin	1,262	176,046
Koprivnica-Križevci	1,748	115,582	Virovitica-Podravina	2,024	84,586
Krapina-Zagorje	1,229	133,064	Vukovar-Srijem	2,454	180,117
Lika-Senj	5,353	51,022	Zadar	3,646	170,398
Medimurje	729	114,414	Zagreb	3,060	317,642
Osijek-Baranja	4,155	304,899	**City**		
Požega-Slavonia	1,823	78,031	Zagreb	641	792,875
Primorje-Gorski kotar	3,588	296,123	TOTAL	56,594	4,290,612
Šibenik-Knin	2,984	109,320			

Demography

Population (2011): 4,287,000.
Density (2011): persons per sq mi 196.4, persons per sq km 75.8.
Urban-rural (2008): urban 57.3%; rural 42.7%.
Sex distribution (2009): male 48.23%; female 51.77%.
Age breakdown (2009): under 15, 15.3%; 15–29, 19.4%; 30–44, 20.6%; 45–59, 21.9%; 60–74, 15.4%; 75 and over, 7.4%.
Population projection: (2020) 4,206,000; (2030) 4,083,000.
Ethnic composition (2001): Croat 89.6%; Serb 4.5%; Bosniak 0.5%; Italian 0.4%; Hungarian 0.4%; other 4.6%.
Religious affiliation (2001): Christian 92.6%, of which Roman Catholic 87.8%, Eastern Orthodox 4.4%; Muslim 1.3%; nonreligious/atheist and other 6.1%.
Major cities (2011): Zagreb 686,568; Split 165,893; Rijeka 127,498; Osijek 83,496; Zadar 70,674.

Vital statistics

Birth rate per 1,000 population (2009): 10.1 (world avg. 20.3); within marriage (2008) 88.5%; outside of marriage (2008) 11.5%.
Death rate per 1,000 population (2009): 11.8 (world avg. 8.5).
Total fertility rate (avg. births per childbearing woman; 2008): 1.47.
Marriage/divorce rates per 1,000 population (2009): 5.1/1.1.
Life expectancy at birth (2009): male 72.9 years; female 79.6 years.
Major causes of death per 100,000 population (2008): diseases of the circulatory system 591.6; malignant neoplasms (cancers) 299.5; accidents, violence, and poisoning 68.4; diseases of the digestive system 54.9.

National economy

Budget (2008). Revenue: kn 115,772,655,000 (tax revenue 60.1%, of which VAT 35.7%, excise taxes 10.3%, corporate taxes 9.1%; social security contributions 35.2%; nontax revenue 4.7%). Expenditures: kn 115,292,426,000 (social security and welfare 45.6%; compensation of employees 26.0%; goods and services 7.0%; other 21.4%).
Public debt (external; October 2009): U.S.$59,400,000,000.
Population economically active (2008): total 1,784,800; activity rate 42.2% (participation rates: ages 15–64, 63.2%; female 45.5%; unemployed [July 2009–June 2010] 16.5%).

Price and earnings indexes (2005 = 100)

	2004	2005	2006	2007	2008	2009	2010
Consumer price index	96.8	100.0	103.2	106.2	112.6	115.3	116.5
Annual earnings index	95.4	100.0	105.2	110.6	118.3	121.4	122.1

Production (metric tons except as noted). Agriculture, forestry, fishing (2009): corn (maize) 2,182,521, sugar beets 1,217,041, wheat 936,076, potatoes 270,251, barley 243,609, grapes 206,437, apples 93,355, sunflower seeds 82,098, rapeseed 80,424, olives 32,592, tobacco leaves 13,348, poppy seeds 3,349; livestock (number of live animals) 1,250,000 pigs, 619,000 sheep, 447,000 cattle; roundwood (2010) 4,477,000 cu m, of which fuelwood 24%; fisheries production 69,121 (from aquaculture 19%). Mining and quarrying (2008): ceramic clay 300,000; ornamental stone 1,000,000 sq m. Manufacturing (value added in kn '000,000; 2007): food products, beverages, and tobacco 10,248; base and fabricated metals 3,982; electrical equipment and machinery 3,756; bricks, cement, and ceramics 3,581; coke, refined petroleum products, and nuclear fuel 3,106. Energy production (consumption): electricity (kW-hr; 2009–10) 14,105,000,000 ([2008] 18,000,000,000); coal (metric tons; 2007) none (1,081,000); crude petroleum (barrels; 2009–10) 5,682,200 ([2009] 38,690,000); petroleum products (metric tons; 2008) 4,300,000 ([2007] 4,675,000); natural gas (cu m; 2009–10) 2,429,568,000 ([2009] 3,205,000,000).

Gross national income (GNI; 2010): U.S.$60,965,000,000 (U.S.$13,760 per capita); purchasing power parity GNI (U.S.$18,710 per capita).

Structure of gross domestic product and labour force

	2009			
	in value kn '000,000	% of total value	labour force	% of labour force
Agriculture, forestry, hunting, fishing	19,512	5.9	69,560	3.9
Mining and quarrying	55,549	16.7	8,841	0.5
Manufacturing			272,812	15.5
Public utilities			38,340	2.2
Construction	23,189	7.0	140,661	8.0
Transp. and commun.	24,216	7.3	114,024	6.5
Trade, restaurants	44,540	13.4	329,223	18.7
Finance, real estate	70,847	21.3	152,597	8.7
Pub. admin., defense	52,241	15.7	113,466	6.4
Services			257,746	14.6
Other	42,970[3]	12.9[3]	264,688[4]	15.0[4]
TOTAL	333,063[5]	100.0[5]	1,761,958	100.0

Household income and expenditure (2005). Average household size (2001) 3.0; average annual income per household kn 69,180 (U.S.$11,629); sources: wages 51.0%, pensions 17.9%, self-employment 16.5%; expenditure (2009): food and nonalcoholic beverages 32.1%, housing and energy 14.4%, transportation 11.0%, clothing and footwear 7.3%, recreation and culture 6.0%.
Selected balance of payments data. Receipts from (U.S.$'000,000): tourism (2009) 9,000; remittances (2010) 1,513; foreign direct investment (FDI; 2008–10 avg.) 3,224; official development assistance (2009) 169. Disbursements for (U.S.$'000,000): tourism (2009) 1,013; remittances (2009) 99; FDI (2008–10 avg.) 819.
Land use as % of total land area (2009): in temporary crops 14.6%, left fallow 0.2%, in permanent crops 1.6%, in pasture 6.8%, forest area 34.2%.

Foreign trade[6]

Balance of trade (current prices)

	2004	2005	2006	2007	2008	2009
U.S.$'000,000	–8,565	–9,788	–11,126	–13,469	–16,603	–10,729
% of total	34.7%	35.8%	34.9%	35.3%	37.0%	33.9%

Imports (2008): U.S.$30,727,000,000 (machinery and apparatus 18.8%, petroleum 13.2%, base and fabricated metals 10.7%, road vehicles/parts 8.6%, food 7.1%). *Major import sources:* Italy 17.1%; Germany 13.4%; Russia 10.4%; China 6.1%; Slovenia 5.6%.
Exports (2008): U.S.$14,124,000,000 (machinery and apparatus 18.2%, mineral fuels 12.9%, ships and boats [particularly tankers] 11.5%, chemicals and chemical products 9.9%, food 7.4%). *Major export destinations:* Italy 19.1%; Bos.-Her. 15.4%; Germany 10.7%; Slovenia 7.8%; Austria 5.8%.

Transport and communications

Transport. Railroads (2009): route length 1,691 mi, 2,722 km; passenger-km 1,835,000,000; metric ton-km cargo 2,641,000,000. Roads (2009): total length 18,233 mi, 29,343 km (paved 91%); passenger-km (2006) 28,500,000,000[7]; metric ton-km cargo (2009) 9,429,000,000. Vehicles (2010[8]): passenger cars 1,522,851; trucks and buses 165,625. Air transport (2009): passenger-km 1,636,000,000; metric ton-km cargo 2,621,000.

Communications

Medium	date	number in '000s	units per 1,000 persons	Medium	date	number in '000s	units per 1,000 persons
Televisions	2003	1,401	315	PCs	2004	842	191
Telephones				Dailies	2009	535[9]	121[9]
Cellular	2010	6,362[10]	1,445[10]	Internet users	2009	2,234	506
Landline	2010	1,866	424	Broadband	2010	804[10]	183[10]

Education and health

Educational attainment (2001). Percentage of population age 15 and over having: no schooling or unknown 3.5%; incomplete primary education 15.8%; primary 21.7%; secondary 47.1%; postsecondary and higher 11.9%. *Literacy* (2008): population age 15 and over literate 98.7%; males 99.5%; females 98.0%.

Education (2009–10)

	teachers	students	student/ teacher ratio	enrollment rate (%)
Primary (age 7–10)	11,746	167,452	14.3	90[11]
Secondary/Voc. (age 11–18)	44,341	374,182	8.4	88[11]
Tertiary	8,768[12]	134,188[12]	15.3[12]	44 (age 19–23)[11]

Health (2008): physicians 9,044 (1 per 490 persons); hospital beds 24,000 (1 per 185 persons); infant mortality rate per 1,000 live births (2009) 5.3; undernourished population (2005–07) less than 5.0% of total population based on the consumption of a minimum daily requirement of 1,980 calories.

Military

Total active duty personnel (November 2010): 18,600 (army 61.2%, navy 10.0%, air force 18.8%, joint staff 10.0%); reserve 21,000. *Military expenditure as percentage of GDP* (2009): 1.5%; per capita expenditure U.S.$230.

[1]However, the Roman Catholic Church receives state financial support through concordats with the Vatican. [2]Preliminary. [3]Taxes on products less subsidies. [4]Includes 263,174 unemployed. [5]Detail does not add to total given because of rounding. [6]Imports c.i.f.; exports f.o.b. [7]Passenger cars 25,000,000,000; buses 3,500,000,000. [8]June 30. [9]Circulation. [10]Subscribers. [11]2006–07. [12]2008–09.

Internet resources for further information:
- **Central Bureau of Statistics http://www.dzs.hr/default_e.htm**
- **Croatian National Bank http://www.hnb.hr/eindex.htm**

Cuba

Official name: República de Cuba (Republic of Cuba).
Form of government: unitary socialist republic with one legislative house (National Assembly of the People's Power [614]).
Head of state and government: President.
Capital: Havana.
Official language: Spanish.
Official religion: none.
Monetary unit: Cuban peso (CUP); valuation (Sept. 1, 2011) 1 U.S.$ = CUP 26.50[1]; 1 £ = CUP 41.62[1].

Area and population		area[2]		population
Provinces	**Capitals**	sq mi	sq km	2011[3] estimate
Artemisa	Artemisa	1,538	3,983	504,368
Camagüey	Camagüey	6,029	15,615	780,598
Ciego de Avila	Ciego de Avila	2,619	6,783	424,245
Cienfuegos	Cienfuegos	1,614	4,180	407,189
Granma	Bayamo	3,234	8,375	836,366
Guantánamo	Guantánamo	2,381	6,168	511,116
Holguín	Holguín	3,588	9,293	1,037,573
La Habana	Havana	278	721	2,135,498
Las Tunas	Las Tunas	2,544	6,588	538,062
Matanzas	Matanzas	4,557	11,803	692,536
Mayabeque	San José de las Lajas	1,455	3,768	381,176
Pinar del Río	Pinar del Río	3,430	8,885	592,042
Sancti Spíritus	Sancti Spíritus	2,601	6,737	465,674
Santiago de Cuba	Santiago de Cuba	2,377	6,156	1,047,963
Villa Clara	Santa Clara	3,248	8,412	800,335
Special municipality				
Isla de la Juventud	Nueva Gerona	934	2,419	86,420
TOTAL		42,427	109,886	11,241,161

Demography

Population (2011): 11,240,000.
Density (2011): persons per sq mi 264.9, persons per sq km 102.3.
Urban-rural (2009): urban 75.4%; rural 24.6%.
Sex distribution (2009): male 50.09%; female 49.91%.
Age breakdown (2009): under 15, 17.6%; 15–29, 20.4%; 30–44, 25.5%; 45–59, 19.3%; 60–74, 12.0%; 75–84, 3.7%; 85 and over, 1.5%.
Population projection: (2020) 11,190,000; (2030) 11,080,000.
Ethnic composition (1994): mixed 51.0%; white 37.0%; black 11.0%; other 1.0%.
Religious affiliation (2005): Roman Catholic *c.* 47%; Protestant *c.* 5%; nonreligious *c.* 22%; other *c.* 26%.[4]
Major cities (2011[3]): Havana 2,135,498; Santiago de Cuba 425,851; Camagüey 305,845; Holguín 277,050; Guantánamo 207,857; Santa Clara 205,812.

Vital statistics

Birth rate per 1,000 population (2009): 11.6 (world avg. 20.3).
Death rate per 1,000 population (2009): 7.7 (world avg. 8.5).
Total fertility rate (avg. births per childbearing woman; 2009): 1.70.
Marriage/divorce rates per 1,000 population (2008): 5.5/3.2.
Life expectancy at birth (2005–07): male 76.0 years; female 80.0 years.
Major causes of death per 100,000 population (2009): diseases of the circulatory system 197.8; malignant neoplasms (cancers) 189.7; cerebrovascular disease 83.7; influenza and pneumonia 47.3; accidents 42.6.

National economy

Budget (2008). Revenue: CUP 42,055,600,000 (tax revenue 61.5%; nontax revenue 38.5%). Expenditures: CUP 46,255,600,000 (current expenditure 90.3%, of which education 16.2%, health 15.5%, social security contributions 9.5%, public safety and defense 4.4%; capital expenditure 9.7%).
Public debt (December 2010): U.S.$19,750,000,000[5].
Production (metric tons except as noted). Agriculture, forestry, fishing (2009): sugarcane 14,900,000, tomatoes 750,000, cow's milk 600,300, rice 563,600, sweet potatoes 437,100, plantains 425,000, pumpkins, squash, and gourds 413,191, mangoes, mangosteens, and guavas 354,200, yams 334,716, oranges 261,000, tobacco leaves 25,200; livestock (number of live animals) 3,892,800 cattle, 2,584,100 sheep, 1,767,800 pigs, 30,818,000 chickens; roundwood (2010) 2,033,700 cu m, of which fuelwood 63%; fisheries production 65,108 (from aquaculture 56%). Mining and quarrying (2008): nickel (metal content) 67,265; cobalt (metal content) 3,175. Manufacturing (2009): cement 1,677,500; steel 269,000; cigarettes 13,100,000,000 units; colour televisions (2008) 94,200 units; beer 2,433,800 hectolitres; other alcoholic beverages (excluding wine) 1,000,500 hectolitres. Energy production (consumption): electricity (kW-hr; 2009) 17,709,100,000 (17,709,100,000); coal (metric tons; 2007) none (14,000); crude petroleum (barrels; 2007) 18,730,000 (31,100,000); petroleum products (metric tons; 2007) 2,020,000 (5,038,000); natural gas (cu m; 2007) 1,186,000,000 (1,186,000,000).
Population economically active (2008): total 5,027,900; activity rate 44.7% (participation rates: ages 17–64, 62.6%; female 38.0%; unemployed 1.6%).

Price and earnings indexes (2006 = 100)					
	2006	2007	2008	2009	2010
Consumer price index	100.0	107.1	108.8	107.6	109.1
Monthly earnings index	…	…	…	…	…

Gross national income (2009): U.S.$60,003,000,000 (U.S.$5,355 per capita).

Structure of gross domestic product and labour force	2009		2008	
	in value CUP '000[6]	% of total value[6]	labour force	% of labour force
Agriculture	1,981,200	4.3	919,100	18.3
Mining	273,900	0.6	26,700	0.5
Manufacturing	6,230,900	13.5	543,100	10.8
Public utilities	664,700	1.4	79,800	1.6
Construction	2,883,700	6.2	245,200	4.9
Transp. and commun.	4,186,200	9.0	301,400	6.0
Finance, real estate	2,620,800	5.7	123,000	2.4
Trade, hotels, and restaurants	10,540,600	22.8	610,200	12.1
Pub. admin., social security	1,805,600	3.9	2,099,700	41.8
Services	14,700,200	31.7		
Other	419,500	0.9	79,700[7]	1.6[7]
TOTAL	46,307,300	100.0	5,027,900	100.0

Household income and expenditure. Average household size (2002) 3.2.
Selected balance of payments data. Receipts from (U.S.$'000,000): tourism (2009) 1,926; remittances (2010) *c.* 900–1,400; foreign direct investment (2008–10 avg.) 45; official development assistance (2009) 116. Disbursements for (U.S.$'000,000): tourism, n.a.; remittances, n.a.
Land use as % of total land area (2009): in temporary crops 21.9%, left fallow 12.3%, in permanent crops 3.5%, in pasture 24.7%, forest area 26.6%.

Foreign trade[8]

Balance of trade (current prices)						
	2001	2002	2003	2004	2005	2006
U.S.$'000,000	–3,586	–2,755	–2,985	–3,278	–5,766	–7,193
% of total	51.9%	49.2%	47.1%	41.3%	55.4%	54.7%

Imports (2005): U.S.$8,084,000,000 (machinery and apparatus 19.3%; food 17.4%, of which cereals 7.3%; refined petroleum 14.5%; crude petroleum 10.5%; chemicals and chemical products 8.0%). *Major import sources* (2008): Venezuela 31.4%; China 10.4%; Spain 8.7%; U.S. 5.6%; Canada 4.6%.
Exports (2005): U.S.$2,318,000,000 (nickel oxide 46.3%; food 12.7%, of which raw cane sugar 7.1%; cigars/cheroots/cigarillos 9.8%; medicine 9.1%). *Major export destinations* (2008): Canada 20.9%; China 18.4%; Venezuela 11.3%; Neth. 7.8%; Spain 5.4%.

Transport and communications

Transport. Railroads (2005)[9]: route length 2,526 mi, 4,065 km; (2008) passenger-km 1,056,000,000; (2008) metric ton-km cargo 1,388,000,000. Roads (2000): total length 37,814 mi, 60,856 km (paved 49%); (2008) passenger-km 6,551,000,000[10, 11]; (2008) metric ton-km cargo 2,222,000,000. Vehicles (1998): passenger cars 172,574; trucks and buses 185,495. Air transport (2008)[12]: passenger-km 3,096,000,000; metric ton-km cargo 45,000,000.

Communications							
Medium	date	number in '000s	units per 1,000 persons	**Medium**	date	number in '000s	units per 1,000 persons
Televisions	2004	3,000	267	PCs	2005	377	33
Telephones				Dailies	2009	1,800[13]	160[13]
Cellular	2010	1,003[14]	89[14]	Internet users	2009	1,605	143
Landline	2010	1,164	103	Broadband	2010	3.7[14]	0.3[14]

Education and health

Educational attainment (2002). Percentage of population age 25 and over having: no formal schooling 14.1%; primary education 17.2%; secondary 26.6%; vocational/technical/teacher training 32.8%; university 9.3%. *Literacy* (2004): total population age 15 and over literate 96.9%; males 97.0%; females 96.8%.

Education (2008–09)	teachers	students	student/ teacher ratio	enrollment rate (%)
Primary (age 6–11)	92,016	868,477	9.4	99
Secondary/Voc. (age 12–17)	85,957	826,088	9.6	83
Tertiary	154,807	970,895	6.3	118 (age 18–23)

Health (2009): physicians 74,880 (1 per 150 persons); hospital beds 66,375 (1 per 169 persons); infant mortality rate per 1,000 live births 4.8; undernourished population (2005–07) less than 5.0% of total population based on the consumption of a minimum daily requirement of 1,900 calories.

Military

Total active duty personnel (November 2010): 49,000 (army 77.6%, navy 6.1%, air force 16.3%); reserve 39,000; paramilitary 1,120,000; U.S. military forces at Naval Base Guantanamo Bay (November 2010) 886. *Military expenditure as percentage of GDP* (2008): 4.0%; per capita expenditure U.S.$204[15].

[1]Domestic transactions only; the Cuban convertible peso (CUC) is used for international transactions—1 U.S.$ = CUC 1.00; 1 £ = CUC 1.62. [2]Areas of major landmasses are: island of Cuba 40,369 sq mi (104,556 sq km); Isla de la Juventud 851 sq mi (2,204 sq km); numerous adjacent cays (administratively a part of provinces or the Isla de la Juventud) 1,207 sq mi (3,126 sq km). [3]January 1. [4]Up to 70% of the population also practice Santería. [5]CIA estimate using the exchange rate of the Cuban convertible peso (CUC). [6]At constant 1997 prices. [7]Unemployed. [8]Imports c.i.f.; exports f.o.b. [9]Cuban Railways only; excludes railways linking sugar plantations to factories totaling 2,817 mi (4,533 km) in 2005. [10]Excludes tourism-related transport. [11]Buses and taxis only. [12]Cubana airline only. [13]Circulation. [14]Subscribers. [15]Using exchange rate of Cuban convertible peso.

Internet resources for further information:
- **Oficina Nacional de Estadísticas http://www.one.cu**
- **Naciones Unidas en Cuba http://www.onu.org.cu**

Curaçao

Official name: Land Curaçao (Dutch); Pais Kòrsou (Papiamentu); Curaçao (English).
Political status: autonomous state of the Netherlands with one legislative house (Staten/Parlamento di Kòrsou, or Parliament of Curaçao [21])[1].
Head of state: Dutch Monarch represented by Governor.
Head of government: Prime Minister.
Capital: Willemstad.
Official languages: Dutch; Papiamentu; English.
Official religion: none.
Monetary unit: Netherlands Antillean guilder (NAf.)[2]; valuation (Sept. 1, 2011) 1 U.S.$ = NAf. 1.79; 1 £ = NAf. 2.89.

Area and population

		area		population
Geographical areas/city	Principal settlements	sq mi	sq km	2001 census
far northwest part of island	Barber	...	...	6,783
near northwest part of island	Sint Michiel	...	...	16,428
Willemstad	—	...	...	93,599
east end of island	Montaña Abou	...	...	13,539
REMAINDER	—	—	—	278
TOTAL		171[3]	444[3]	130,627

Demography

Population (2011): 143,000.
Density (2011): persons per sq mi 836.3, persons per sq km 322.1.
Urban-rural (2010)[4]: urban 92.9%; rural 7.1%.
Sex distribution (2010[5]): male 45.86%; female 54.14%.
Age breakdown (2010[5]): under 15, 21.0%; 15–29, 18.3%; 30–44, 20.6%; 45–59, 22.5%; 60–74, 12.7%; 75–84, 3.8%; 85 and over, 1.1%.
Population projection: (2020) 149,000; (2030) 148,000.
Ethnic composition (2000)[4]: local black-other (Antillean Creole) 81.1%; Dutch 5.3%; Surinamese 2.9%; other (significantly West Indian black) 10.7%.
Religious affiliation (2001): Roman Catholic 80.1%; undefined Protestant 3.8%; Pentecostal 3.5%; Seventh-day Adventist 2.2%; Jewish 0.3%; nonreligious 4.6%; other 5.5%.
Major city and settlements (2001): Willemstad (2009) 123,000[6]; Sint Michiel 4,928; Montaña Abou 4,064; Tera Cora 3,515; Montaña Rey 3,425.

Vital statistics

Birth rate per 1,000 population (2009): 13.4 (world avg. 20.3); within marriage 56.8%; outside of marriage 43.2%.
Death rate per 1,000 population (2009): 7.8 (world avg. 8.5).
Natural increase rate per 1,000 population (2009): 5.6 (world avg. 11.8).
Total fertility rate (avg. births per childbearing woman; 2008): 2.20.
Marriage/divorce rates per 1,000 population (2009): 5.9/2.9.
Life expectancy at birth (2009): male 78.6 years; female 82.5 years.
Major causes of death per 100,000 population (2000)[4]: diseases of the circulatory system 267.6, of which cerebrovascular diseases 83.3; malignant neoplasms (cancers) 203.6; accidents and violence 45.4; communicable diseases 39.3.

National economy

Budget (2009)[7]. Revenue: NAf. 1,493,400,000 (tax revenues 53.5%, of which tax on wages 32.7%, tax on profits 14.9%; grants 40.1%; nontax revenue 6.4%). Expenditures: NAf. 1,096,100,000 (current expenditure 98.5%; capital expenditure 1.5%).
Public debt (external, outstanding; June 2010): U.S.$403,000,000.
Selected balance of payments data. Receipts from (U.S.$'000,000): tourism (2009) 361; remittances (2010) 32[4]; foreign direct investment (2008–10 avg.) 17[4]. Disbursements for (U.S.$'000,000): tourism (2009) 209; remittances (2009) 106[4]; foreign direct disinvestment (2008–10 avg.) –1.7[4].
Production (metric tons except as noted). Agriculture, forestry, fishing (2009): limited cultivation of aloe, sorghum, peanuts, tropical fruits[8], and vegetables; livestock (number of live animals)[4] 13,600 goats, 9,100 sheep, 140,000 chickens; roundwood 3,293 cu m[4], of which fuelwood 100%; fisheries production 16,698[4] (from aquaculture, negligible). Mining and quarrying (2009): salt, n.a. Manufacturing (2007): residual fuel oils 4,056,000; gas-diesel oil 2,350,000; jet fuel 783,000; also limited production of processed foods, paint, soap, and cigarettes. Energy production (consumption): electricity (kW-hr; 2010) 868,900,000 ([2008] 970,000,000[4]); coal, none (none); crude petroleum (barrels; 2009) none ([2007] 73,600,000); petroleum products (metric tons; 2009) 68,876,000 ([2007] 1,978,000[4]); natural gas, none (none).
Land use (2007)[4]: in temporary crops, left fallow, or in permanent crops *c.* 10%; in pasture, n.a.; forest area *c.* 2%.
Population economically active (2009): total 62,627; activity rate of total population 44.1% (participation rates: ages 15 and over, 57.5%; female, n.a.; unemployed 9.7%).

Price index (2005 = 100)

	2003	2004	2005	2006	2007	2008	2009
Consumer price index	94.7	96.1	100.0	103.1	106.2	113.5	115.5

Gross national income (at current market prices; 2006): U.S.$2,498,000,000 (U.S.$18,170 per capita).

Structure of gross domestic product and labour force

	2009		2008	
	in value NAf. '000,000	% of total value	labour force	% of labour force
Agriculture, fishing, mining	30.6	0.6	721	1.1
Manufacturing	368.3	7.2	3,936	6.3
Construction	252.1	4.9	4,691	7.4
Public utilities	197.9	3.8	796	1.3
Transp. and commun.	434.8	8.5	3,812	6.1
Trade, hotels	710.9	13.8	14,238	22.6
Finance, real estate	1,715.4	33.4	10,211	16.2
Pub. admin., defense	355.3	6.9	4,691	7.4
Services	675.7	13.1	13,292	21.1
Other	399.5[9]	7.8[9]	6,633[10]	10.5[10]
TOTAL	5,140.5[11]	100.0	63,021	100.0

Household income and expenditure. Average household size (2008) 2.6; average annual income per household, n.a.; sources of income, n.a.; expenditure (2006)[12]: transportation 18.2%, housing 18.1%, food 12.3%, energy and water 9.3%, household furnishings 7.2%, recreation/culture 5.2%.

Foreign trade[4, 13, 14]

Balance of trade (current prices)

	2005	2006	2007	2008
U.S.$'000,000	–803	–887	–1,036	–1,291
% of total	81.5%	77.4%	81.7%	81.5%

Imports (2008): U.S.$1,437,000,000 (machinery and apparatus 21.5%; food 16.9%; chemicals and chemical products 11.6%; road vehicles 8.9%). *Major import sources:* U.S. 39.4%; Neth. 23.1%; Panama 3.6%; Venezuela 3.6%.
Exports (2008): U.S.$146,000,000 (food 25.7%, of which cocoa powder with sugar 9.9%, raw cane sugar 4.9%; machinery and apparatus 14.7%; aircraft parts 12.9%; precious metal jewelry 7.3%; salt/sea water 4.2%). *Major export destinations:* Neth. 34.7%; U.S. 23.0%; Aruba 10.2%; unspecified 12.9%.

Transport and communications

Transport. Railroads: none. Roads (2004)[4]: total length 525 mi, 845 km (paved 51%). Vehicles (2010[5]): passenger cars 78,430; trucks and buses 16,045. Air transport: n.a.

Communications[4]

Medium	date	number in '000s	units per 1,000 persons	Medium	date	number in '000s	units per 1,000 persons
Televisions	2010	...	...	PCs	2010	...	...
Telephones				Dailies	2009	30[15]	150[15]
Cellular	2008	200[16]	1,007[16]	Internet users	2010	...	...
Landline	2010	90	449	Broadband	2010	...	...

Education and health

Educational attainment (2001). Percentage of population age 25 and over having: no formal schooling 1.0%; primary education 24.4%; lower secondary 44.5%; upper secondary 15.9%; higher 11.1%; unknown 3.1%. *Literacy* (2008)[4]: total population age 15 and over literate 96.3%; males literate 96.3%; females literate 96.3%.

Education (2006–07)

	teachers	students	student/ teacher ratio	enrollment rate (%)
Primary (age 6–11)	974	18,885	19.4	97[4]
Secondary/Voc. (age 12–17)	520	13,972	26.9	81[4]
Tertiary	40[17]	1,954[17]	48.9[17]	21[4] (age 18–22)

Health: physicians (2004) 225 (1 per 597 persons); hospital beds (2001) 1,121 (1 per 120 persons); infant mortality rate per 1,000 live births (2008) 6.1[4]; undernourished population (2004–06) less than 5.0% of total population[4] based on the consumption of a minimum daily requirement of 1,880 calories.

Military

Total active duty personnel (2010): n.a.; Dutch and local coast guard personnel are assisted by the U.S. coast guard.

[1]Per the national reorganization plan promulgated on Oct. 10, 2010; the former Netherlands Antilles was dissolved on this date. [2]The Netherlands Antillean guilder will be the joint transitional currency for both Curaçao and Sint Maarten until 2012 when it is expected to be replaced by the Caribbean guilder. [3]Includes the area (0.7 sq mi [1.7 sq km]) of the uninhabited islet of Klein Curaçao. [4]Data for the former Netherlands Antilles. [5]January 1. [6]Population of urban area. [7]Curaçao island budget (not central government budget for the former Netherlands Antilles). [8]Peels of laraha citrus (bitter orange) are used to produce curaçao liqueur. [9]Taxes less subsidies and less imputed bank service charges. [10]Includes 6,486 unemployed (10.3%). [11]Summed total; reported total equaled NAf. 5,138,600,000. [12]Weights of consumer price index components. [13]Imports c.i.f.; exports f.o.b. [14]Excludes important crude petroleum imports and (mostly to U.S.) refined petroleum exports; Venezuela has operated a refinery on Curaçao since 1985. [15]Circulation. [16]Subscribers. [17]Students and full-time teachers at the University of the Netherlands Antilles.

Internet resources for further information:

- **Centrale Bank van Curaçao en Sint Maarten http://www.centralbank.an**
- **Central Bureau of Statistics http://www.cbs.an**

Cyprus

Island of Cyprus

Area: 3,572 sq mi, 9,251 sq km.
Population (2011): 1,118,000[1].

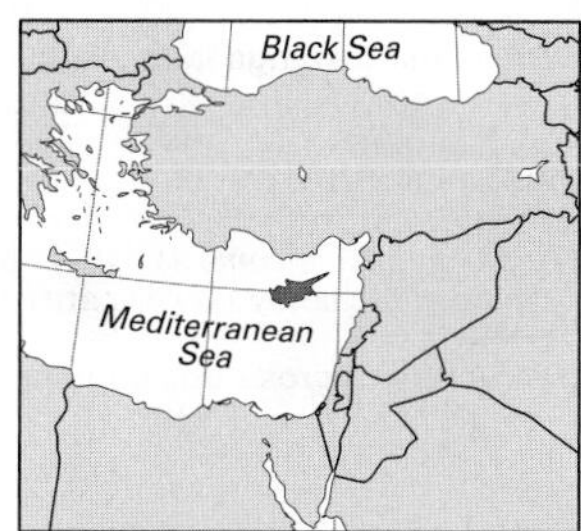

Two de facto states currently exist on the island of Cyprus: the Republic of Cyprus (ROC), predominantly Greek in character, occupying the southern two-thirds of the island, which is the original and still the internationally recognized de jure government of the whole island; and the Turkish Republic of Northern Cyprus (TRNC), proclaimed unilaterally Nov. 15, 1983, on territory originally secured for the Turkish Cypriot population by the July 20, 1974, intervention of Turkey. Only Turkey recognizes the TRNC. Provision of separate data below does not imply recognition of either state's claims but is necessitated by the lack of unified data.

Republic of Cyprus

Official name: Kipriakí Dhimokratía (Greek); Kıbrıs Cumhuriyeti (Turkish) (Republic of Cyprus).
Form of government: unitary multiparty republic with a unicameral legislature (House of Representatives [80[2]]).
Head of state and government: President.
Capital: Lefkosia (conventional Nicosia).
Official languages: Greek; Turkish.
Monetary unit: euro (€); valuation (Sept. 1, 2011) 1 U.S.$ = €0.70; 1 £ = €1.13[3].

Demography

Area[4]: 2,276 sq mi, 5,896 sq km.
Population (2011): 816,000[5].
Age breakdown (2008): under 15, 17.1%; 15–29, 23.9%; 30–44, 21.5%; 45–59, 19.7%; 60–74, 12.5%; 75 and over, 5.3%.
Ethnic composition (2000): Greek Cypriot 91.8%; Armenian 3.3%; Arab 2.9%, of which Lebanese 2.5%; British 1.4%; other 0.6%.
Religious affiliation (2001): Greek Orthodox 94.8%; Roman Catholic 2.1%, of which Maronite 0.6%; Anglican 1.0%; Muslim 0.6%; other 1.5%.
Urban areas (2008[6]): Lefkosia 231,800[7]; Limassol 183,000; Larnaca 81,700.

Vital statistics

Birth rate per 1,000 population (2008): 11.6 (world avg. 20.3).
Death rate per 1,000 population (2008): 6.5 (world avg. 8.5).
Natural increase rate per 1,000 population (2008): 5.1 (world avg. 11.8).
Total fertility rate (avg. births per childbearing woman; 2008): 1.46.
Life expectancy at birth (2006–07): male 78.3 years; female 81.9 years.

National economy

Budget (2009). Revenue: €6,088,400,000 (tax revenue 87.6%, of which VAT 24.8%; nontax revenue 10.9%; grants 1.5%). Expenditures: €7,108,727,000 (current expenditures 91.4%; development expenditures 8.6%).
Gross national income (2009): U.S.$23,121,000,000 (U.S.$29,000 per capita).

Structure of gross domestic product and labour force

	2008			
	in value €'000,000	% of total value	labour force	% of labour force
Agriculture, fishing	312.0	1.9	27,800	6.9
Mining	57.3	0.3	600	0.1
Manufacturing	1,132.7	6.7	37,100	9.2
Construction	1,405.0	8.3	38,600	9.5
Public utilities	339.3	2.0	1,800	0.4
Transp. and commun.	1,032.4	6.1	24,500	6.1
Trade, restaurants	2,971.5	17.5	106,800	26.4
Finance, insurance	4,119.0	24.3	41,500	10.3
Pub. admin., defense	1,503.4	8.9	27,800	6.9
Services	2,104.5	12.4	72,600	17.9
Other	1,971.4[8]	11.6[8]	25,700	6.3
TOTAL	16,948.5	100.0	404,800	100.0

Production. Agriculture/livestock (in '000 metric tons; 2009): cow's milk 148.5, potatoes 131.8, pork 58.2, grapes 27.5, chicken meat 26.4, olives 13.7. Manufacturing (value added in €'000,000; 2008): food products, beverages, and tobacco 439; cement, bricks, and ceramics 217; base metals and fabricated metal products 171; paper and paper products 111. Energy production (consumption): electricity (kW-hr; 2008) 4,993,000,000 (4,556,000,000).
Selected balance of payments data. Receipts from (U.S.$'000,000): tourism (2009) 2,188; remittances (2010) 148; foreign direct investment (FDI; 2008–10 avg.) 4,878. Disbursements for (U.S.$'000,000): tourism (2009) 1,275; remittances (2009) 409; FDI (2008–10 avg.) 4,471.
Land use as % of total land area (2009)[9]: in temporary crops 7.9%, left fallow 1.5%, in permanent crops 3.7%, in pasture 0.5%, forest area 18.7%.

Foreign trade[10]

Imports (2008): U.S.$10,849,000,000 (refined petroleum 18.7%, machinery and apparatus 14.6%, road vehicles 12.2%, food 9.9%). *Major import sources:* Greece 16.8%; Italy 10.5%; U.K. 8.7%; Germany 8.2%; Israel 8.0%.
Exports (2008): U.S.$1,717,000,000 (refined petroleum 19.8%, food 16.9%, medicine 9.2%, prostheses/body implants 6.1%, photosensitive semiconductor devices 5.2%, cigars/cigarettes 4.6%). *Major export destinations:* bunker and ships' stores 19.9%; Greece 18.8%; U.K. 10.2%; Germany 5.3%.

Transport and communications

Transport. Roads (2008): total length 7,656 mi, 12,321 km (paved 65%). Vehicles (2008): cars 443,517; trucks and buses 125,181. Air transport (2008): passenger-km 3,384,000,000; metric ton-km cargo 46,000,000.

Communications

Medium	date	number in '000s	units per 1,000 persons	Medium	date	number in '000s	units per 1,000 persons
Televisions	2003	276	384	PCs	2004	249	309
Telephones				Dailies	2009	100[9, 11]	93[9, 11]
Cellular	2010	1,034[9, 12]	937[9, 12]	Internet users	2009	434[9]	498[9]
Landline	2010	415[9]	376[9]	Broadband	2010	195[9, 12]	176[9, 12]

Education and health

Educational attainment (2008). Percentage of population age 20 and over having: no formal schooling/incomplete primary education 7%; complete primary 17%; secondary 46%; higher education 30%.
Health (2007): physicians 2,143 (1 per 366 persons); hospital beds 2,916 (1 per 269 persons); infant mortality rate per 1,000 live births (2008) 3.5.

Military

Total active duty personnel (November 2010): 10,000 (national guard 100%); Greek troops 950. *Military expenditure as percentage of GDP* (2008): 2.2%; per capita expenditure U.S.$674.

Internet resources for further information:
- **Central Bank of Cyprus http://www.centralbank.gov.cy**
- **Rep. of Cyprus Statistical Service http://www.pio.gov.cy/mof/cystat/statistics.nsf/index_en/index_en**

Turkish Republic of Northern Cyprus

Official name: Kuzey Kıbrıs Türk Cumhuriyeti (Turkish) (Turkish Republic of Northern Cyprus).
Capital: Lefkoşa (conventional Nicosia).
Official language: Turkish.
Monetary unit: new Turkish lira (YTL); valuation (Sept. 1, 2011) 1 U.S.$ = YTL 1.73; 1 £ = YTL 2.79; 1 YTL = 1,000,000 (old) TL.
Population (2011): 302,000[1] (Lefkoşa 49,237[13]; Mağusa [Famagusta] 34,803[13]; Girne [Kyrenia] 24,122[13]; Güzelyurt [Morphou] 12,425[13]).
Sex distribution (2006): male 53.99%; female 46.01%.
Ethnic composition (2006): Turkish Cypriot/Turkish 96.8%; other 3.2%.
Birth rate per 1,000 population (2008): 15.8 (world avg. 20.3).
Death rate per 1,000 population (2008): 6.8 (world avg. 8.5).
Total fertility rate (avg. births per childbearing woman; 2008) 1.80.

Structure of gross domestic product and labour force

	2008			
	in value YTL '000	% of total value	labour force[14]	% of labour force[14]
Agriculture and fishing	271,514	5.3	3,171	3.5
Mining	53,640	1.1	113	0.1
Manufacturing	194,636	3.8	7,171	7.9
Construction	399,647	7.8	10,491	11.5
Public utilities	261,169	5.1	860	0.9
Transp. and commun.	619,493	12.2	6,082	6.7
Trade, restaurants	632,637	12.4	22,066	24.2
Pub. admin.	1,154,441	22.7	14,854	16.3
Finance, real estate	549,665	10.8	6,642	7.3
Services	542,176	10.6	19,773	21.6
Other	414,929[15]	8.2[15]	—	—
TOTAL	5,093,947	100.0	91,223	100.0

Budget (2007). Revenue: YTL 1,912,021,000 (indirect taxes 29.4%, direct taxes 20.5%, foreign aid 14.8%, other 35.3%). Expenditures: YTL 2,125,064,000 (social transfers 39.8%, wages 35.6%, investments 10.7%, defense 5.6%).
Imports (2007): U.S.$1,539,200,000 (machinery and transport equipment 25.5%, food 10.6%). *Major import sources:* Turkey 67.9%; EU 16.1%.
Exports (2007): U.S.$83,700,000 (citrus fruits 27.1%, minerals 9.7%). *Major export destinations:* Turkey 58.4%; EU 13.2%.
Health (2008): physicians 557 (1 per 493 persons); hospital beds 1,211 (1 per 227 persons); infant mortality rate per 1,000 live births 14.3.

Internet resource for further information:
- **Turkish Republic of Northern Cyprus State Planning Organization http://www.devplan.org**

[1]Includes 160,000–170,000 immigrants (mostly from Turkey); excludes 2,791 British military in the Sovereign Base Areas (SBA) in the ROC and 842 UN peacekeeping troops. [2]Twenty-four seats reserved for Turkish Cypriots are not occupied. [3]The Cyprus pound (£C) was the former monetary unit; on Jan. 1, 2008, 1 £C = €1.71. [4]Area includes 99 sq mi (256 sq km) of British military SBA and *c.* 107 sq mi (*c.* 278 sq km) of the UN Buffer Zone. [5]Excludes British and UN military forces. [6]January 1. [7]ROC only. [8]Import duties and VAT less imputed bank service charges. [9]Island of Cyprus. [10]Imports c.i.f.; exports f.o.b. [11]Circulation. [12]Subscribers. [13]2006 census. [14]Employed only. [15]Import duties.

Czech Republic

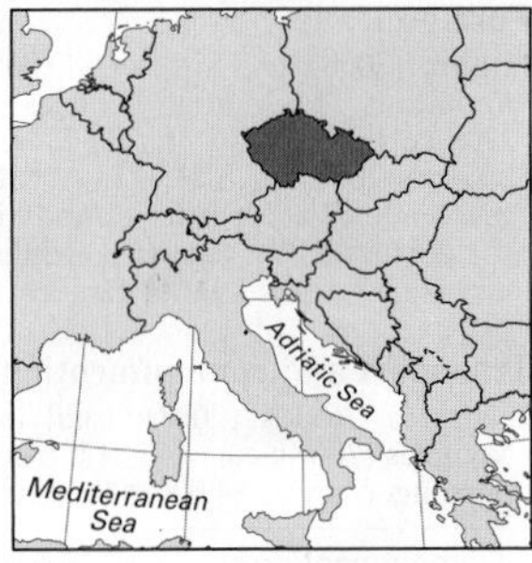

Official name: Česká republika (Czech Republic).
Form of government: unitary multiparty republic with two legislative houses (Senate [81]; Chamber of Deputies [200]).
Head of state: President.
Head of government: Prime Minister.
Capital: Prague.
Official language: Czech.
Official religion: none.
Monetary unit: koruna (Kč); valuation (Sept. 1, 2011) 1 U.S.$ = Kč 16.97; 1 £ = Kč 27.42.

Area and population

Regions	area sq km	population 2011[1] estimate	Regions	area sq km	population 2011[1] estimate
Central Bohemia	11,015	1,264,978	South Bohemia	10,057	638,706
Hradec Králové	4,759	554,803	South Moravia	7,195	1,154,654
Karlovy Vary	3,314	307,444	Ústí	5,335	836,045
Liberec	3,163	439,942	Vysočina	6,795	514,569
Moravia-Silesia	5,426	1,243,220	Zlín	3,964	590,361
Olomouc	5,267	641,681			
Pardubice	4,519	517,164	**Capital city**		
Plzeň	7,561	572,045	Prague (Praha)	496	1,257,158
			TOTAL	78,865[2]	10,532,770

Demography

Population (2011): 10,551,000.
Density (2011): persons per sq mi 346.5, persons per sq km 133.8.
Urban-rural (2009): urban 73.5%; rural 26.5%.
Sex distribution (2011[1]): male 49.07%; female 50.93%.
Age breakdown (2011[1]): under 15, 14.4%; 15–29, 19.2%; 30–44, 23.6%; 45–59, 20.2%; 60–74, 15.9%; 75–84, 5.2%; 85 and over, 1.5%.
Population projection: (2020) 10,781,000; (2030) 10,838,000.
Ethnic composition (2001): Czech 90.4%; Moravian 3.7%; Slovak 1.9%; Polish 0.5%; German 0.4%; Silesian 0.1%; Rom (Gypsy) 0.1%; other 2.9%.
Religious affiliation (2008): atheist *c.* 39%; Roman Catholic *c.* 33%; Protestant (mostly Lutheran) *c.* 3%; independent Catholic (Hussite Church of the Czech Republic) *c.* 1%; Muslim 0.1%; Jewish, negligible; nonreligious/other *c.* 24%.
Major cities (2011[1]): Prague 1,257,158; Brno 371,371; Ostrava 303,609; Plzeň 168,808; Liberec 101,865.

Vital statistics

Birth rate per 1,000 population (2010): 11.1 (world avg. 19.2); within marriage 59.7%; outside of marriage 40.3%.
Death rate per 1,000 population (2010): 10.1 (world avg. 8.2).
Total fertility rate (avg. births per childbearing woman; 2009): 1.49.
Marriage/divorce rates per 1,000 population (2010): 4.4/2.9.
Life expectancy at birth (2009): male 74.2 years; female 80.1 years.
Major causes of death per 100,000 population (2010): diseases of the circulatory system 508.8; malignant neoplasms (cancers) 267.9; diseases of the respiratory system 58.4; accidents, poisoning, and violence 57.1.

National economy

Budget (2008)[3]. Revenue: Kč 1,485,928,000,000 (tax revenue 85.9%, of which social security contributions 34.6%, taxes on goods and services 28.0%, taxes on income and profits 22.3%; nontax revenue 6.5%; grants 4.3%; other 3.3%). Expenditures: Kč 1,502,195,000,000 (social security and welfare 30.7%; health 14.6%; transportation and communications 12.2%; education 9.5%; general public services 7.2%; defense 2.9%).
Production (metric tons except as noted). Agriculture, forestry, fishing (2010): wheat 4,161,553, sugar beets 3,064,986, barley 1,584,456, rapeseed 1,042,418, corn (maize) 692,589, potatoes 665,176, sunflower seeds 57,358; livestock (number of live animals) 1,749,092 pigs, 1,343,686 cattle; roundwood 17,021,995 cu m, of which fuelwood 12%; fisheries production (2009) 24,183 (from aquaculture 83%). Mining and quarrying (2009): kaolin 2,886,000; feldspar 431,000. Manufacturing (value added in Kč '000,000; 2006): motor vehicles/parts 4,586; nonelectrical machinery/apparatus 3,648; fabricated/structural metal products 3,491; electrical machinery/apparatus 2,537; base metals 1,843; plastics 1,400; bricks, cement, and ceramics 1,071; electronic valves/telecommunications equipment/televisions 953; base chemicals 937. Energy production (consumption): electricity (kW-hr; 2010–11) 86,293,000,000 ([2007] 72,045,000,000); hard coal (metric tons; 2010–11) 11,893,000 ([2007] 4,141,000); lignite (metric tons; 2010–11) 31,244,000 ([2007] 54,200,000); crude petroleum (barrels; 2009) 4,004,000 ([2007] 50,700,000); petroleum products (metric tons; 2007) 5,351,000 (6,962,000); natural gas (cu m; 2010–11) 232,315,400 ([2007] 8,537,000,000).
Household income and expenditure (2010). Average household size 2.5; average annual money income per household (2004) Kč 295,011 (U.S.$11,479); sources of income (2009): wages and salaries 59.6%, transfer payments 23.3%, self-employment 14.0%, other 3.1%; expenditure: housing and energy 21.7%, food and nonalcoholic beverages 19.3%, transportation 10.7%, recreation and culture 10.2%, household furnishings 6.2%.
Land use as % of total land area (2007): in temporary crops 38.9%, left fallow 0.4%, in permanent crops 3.1%, in pasture 12.7%, forest area 34.3%.
Population economically active (2007): total 5,198,300; activity rate of total population 50.4% (participation rates: ages 15–64, 69.8%; female 43.6%; unemployed [April 2010–March 2011] 9.0%).

Price and earnings indexes (2005 = 100)

	2004	2005	2006	2007	2008	2009	2010
Consumer price index	98.2	100.0	102.5	105.5	112.2	113.4	115.0
Annual earnings index	95.0	100.0	102.9	110.3	119.0	123.0	125.3

Gross national income (GNI; 2010): U.S.$188,269,000,000 (U.S.$17,870 per capita); purchasing power parity GNI (U.S.$23,620 per capita).

Structure of gross domestic product and labour force

	2008 in value Kč '000,000	% of total value	labour force	% of labour force
Agriculture, forestry	77,416	2.1	166,000	3.2
Mining	47,429	1.3	56,000	1.1
Manufacturing	850,283	22.9	1,433,000	27.4
Construction	208,902	5.6	462,000	8.8
Public utilities	139,800	3.8	78,000	1.5
Transportation and communications	331,541	8.9	375,000	7.2
Trade, hotels	511,663	13.8	810,000	15.5
Finance, real estate	589,787	15.9	485,000	9.3
Pub. admin., defense	184,464	5.0	327,000	6.2
Services	377,309	10.2	812,000	15.5
Other	387,274[4]	10.5[4]	230,000[5]	4.4[5]
TOTAL	3,705,868	100.0	5,232,000[2]	100.0[2]

Public debt (external, outstanding; April 2011): U.S.$24,901,800,000.
Selected balance of payments data. Receipts from (U.S.$'000,000): tourism (2009) 6,477; remittances (2010) 1,263; foreign direct investment (FDI; 2008–10 avg.) 5,386. Disbursements for (U.S.$'000,000): tourism (2009) 4,077; remittances (2009) 2,562; FDI (2008–10 avg.) 2,325.

Foreign trade[6]

Balance of trade (current prices)

	2004	2005	2006	2007	2008	2009
U.S.$'000,000	–934	+1,681	+1,711	+4,078	+4,253	+7,973
% of total	0.7%	1.1%	0.9%	1.7%	1.5%	3.7%

Imports (2008): U.S.$141,834,000,000 (machinery and apparatus 31.9%; mineral fuels 10.4%; chemicals and chemical products 10.1%; road vehicles/parts 8.3%). *Major import sources:* Germany 26.7%; China 8.8%; Russia 6.4%; Poland 5.8%; Slovakia 5.6%.
Exports (2008): U.S.$146,087,000,000 (machinery and apparatus 36.0%, of which electrical machinery 9.0%, computers/office machines/parts 7.2%; motor vehicles/parts 15.6%; base/manufactured metals 10.9%; chemicals and chemical products 5.7%). *Major export destinations:* Germany 30.7%; Slovakia 9.2%; Poland 6.5%; France 5.3%; U.K. 4.8%.

Transport and communications

Transport. Railroads (2010): route length[1] 5,951 mi, 9,578 km; passenger-km (2008) 6,794,000,000; metric ton-km cargo 13,868,100,000. Roads (2007): total length 79,853 mi, 128,511 km (paved, virtually 100%); passenger-km 86,000,000,000[7]; metric ton-km cargo (2010) 51,832,000,000. Vehicles (2009[1]): passenger cars 4,423,370[8]; trucks and buses 663,596. Air transport (2010–11): passenger-km 5,874,000,000; metric ton-km cargo 17,396,000.

Communications

Medium	date	number in '000s	units per 1,000 persons	Medium	date	number in '000s	units per 1,000 persons
Televisions	2003	5,488	538	PCs	2004	5,100	500
Telephones				Dailies	2009	1,365[9]	130[9]
Cellular	2010	14,331[10]	1,366[10]	Internet users	2009	6,681	644
Landline	2010	2,198	210	Broadband	2010	1,538[10]	147[10]

Education and health

Educational attainment (2007). Percentage of population age 25–64 having: no formal schooling to lower secondary education 9%; upper secondary 76%; higher 14%; unknown 1%. *Literacy:* n.a.

Education (2008–09)

	teachers	students	student/ teacher ratio	enrollment rate (%)
Primary (age 6–10)	24,890	460,486	18.5	103
Secondary/Voc. (age 11–18)	77,855	868,328	11.2	95
Tertiary	22,549[11]	416,847	15.0[11]	61 (age 19–23)

Health (2010): physicians 38,818[1] (1 per 271 persons); hospital beds 62,992[1, 12] (1 per 167 persons); infant mortality rate per 1,000 live births 2.7; undernourished population (2004–06) less than 5.0% of total population based on the consumption of a minimum daily requirement of 1,990 calories.

Military

Total active duty personnel (November 2010): 23,441[13] (army 30.0%, air force 19.5%, unspecified 50.5%). *Military expenditure as percentage of GDP* (2009): 1.6%; per capita expenditure U.S.$304.

[1]January 1. [2]Detail does not add to total given because of rounding. [3]Consolidated general government. [4]Taxes less subsidies on products. [5]Unemployed. [6]Imports c.i.f.; exports f.o.b. [7]Passenger cars 70,000,000,000; buses 16,000,000,000. [8]Includes vans. [9]Circulation. [10]Subscribers. [11]2005–06. [12]Excludes beds at resorts with mineral springs. [13]Active only; civilian support totals 7,888.

Internet resources for further information:
- **Czech Statistical Office http://www.czso.cz**
- **Czech National Bank http://www.cnb.cz/en/index.html**

Denmark[1]

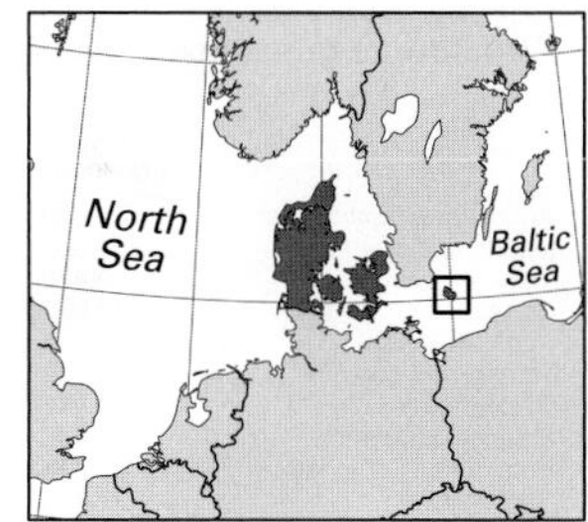

Official name: Kongeriget Danmark (Kingdom of Denmark).
Form of government: constitutional monarchy with one legislative house (Folketing [179]).
Head of state: Danish Monarch.
Head of government: Prime Minister.
Capital: Copenhagen.
Official language: Danish.
Official religion: Evangelical Lutheran.
Monetary unit: Danish krone (DKK; plural kroner); valuation (Sept. 1, 2011) 1 U.S.$ = DKK 5.23; 1 £ = DKK 8.45.

Area and population

		area		population
Regions	Capitals	sq mi	sq km	2011[2] estimate
Capital (Hovedstaden)	Hillerød	989	2,561	1,699,387
Central Jutland (Midtjylland)	Viborg	5,067	13,124	1,260,993
North Jutland (Nordjylland)	Ålborg	3,062	7,933	579,829
South Denmark (Syddanmark)	Vejle	4,713	12,206	1,200,656
Zealand (Sjælland)	Sorø	2,808	7,273	819,763
TOTAL		16,640[3]	43,098[3]	5,560,628

Demography

Population (2011): 5,574,000.
Density (2011): persons per sq mi 335.0, persons per sq km 129.3.
Urban-rural (2009[2]): urban 86.6%; rural 13.4%.
Sex distribution (2009[2]): male 49.57%; female 50.43%.
Age breakdown (2009[2]): under 15, 18.3%; 15–29, 17.6%; 30–44, 21.3%; 45–59, 20.0%; 60–74, 15.8%; 75–84, 5.0%; 85 and over, 2.0%.
Population projection: (2020) 5,688,000; (2030) 5,854,000.
Ethnic composition (2007[2])[4]: Danish 91.9%; Turkish 0.6%; German 0.5%; Iraqi 0.4%; Swedish 0.4%; Norwegian 0.3%; Bosnian 0.3%; other 5.6%.
Religious affiliation (2006): Evangelical Lutheran 83.0%; other Christian 1.3%; Muslim 3.7%; nonreligious 5.4%; atheist 1.5%; other 5.1%.
Major urban areas (2011[2]): Greater Copenhagen 1,199,224; Århus 249,709; Odense 167,615; Ålborg 103,545; Esbjerg 71,576.

Vital statistics

Birth rate per 1,000 population (2009): 11.4 (world avg. 20.3); within marriage (2008) 53.8%; outside of marriage (2008) 46.2%.
Death rate per 1,000 population (2009): 9.9 (world avg. 8.5).
Natural increase rate per 1,000 population (2009): 1.5 (world avg. 11.8).
Total fertility rate (avg. births per childbearing woman; 2009): 1.84.
Marriage/divorce rates per 1,000 population (2009): 6.0/2.7.
Life expectancy at birth (2008–09): male 76.5 years; female 80.8 years.
Major causes of death per 100,000 population (2005): diseases of the circulatory system 324.4; malignant neoplasms (cancers) 281.1; diseases of the respiratory system 96.6; mental disorders/diseases of the nervous system 71.1.

National economy

Budget (2007). Revenue: DKK 694,084,000,000 (taxes on income and profits 44.4%, taxes on goods and services 39.8%, other 15.8%). Expenditures: DKK 613,412,000,000 (social protection 35.1%, education 11.4%, economic affairs 5.8%, defense 4.3%, health 0.2%).
National debt (August 2010): U.S.$72,560,000,000.
Population economically active (2008): total 2,917,400[5]; activity rate of total population 53.3%[6] (participation rates: ages 16–64, 79.1%[5]; female 47.2%[5]; unemployed 2.1%).

Price and earnings indexes (2005 = 100)

	2004	2005	2006	2007	2008	2009	2010
Consumer price index	98.2	100.0	101.9	103.6	107.2	108.6	111.1
Hourly earnings index	97.2	100.0	103.1	107.0	111.8	115.2	117.9

Household income and expenditure. Average household size (2005) 2.2; average annual disposable income per household (2003) DKK 270,176 (U.S.$41,010); sources of gross income (2003): wages and salaries 63.8%, transfers 24.6%, property income 6.8%, self-employment 3.9%; expenditure (2003): housing 22.5%, transportation and communications 15.7%, food 11.1%, recreation and entertainment 11.1%, energy 7.5%.
Production (metric tons except as noted). Agriculture, forestry, fishing (2009): wheat 5,940,400, cow's milk 4,814,000, barley 3,393,800, sugar beets 1,898,200, potatoes 1,617,700, rapeseed 634,800, mushrooms and truffles 7,890; livestock (number of live animals) 12,369,145 pigs, 2,719,600 minks, 1,540,340 cattle; roundwood 2,786,000 cu m, of which fuelwood 40%; fisheries production 811,881 metric tons (from aquaculture 4%). Mining and quarrying (2008): sand and gravel 28,600,000 cu m; chalk 1,900,000 metric tons. Manufacturing (value added in U.S.$'000,000; 2006): nonelectrical machinery and apparatus 2,754; food products 2,743; printing and publishing 2,205; electrical machinery and apparatus 1,955; professional, scientific, and measuring equipment 1,805; plastics 1,698. Energy production (consumption): electricity (kW-hr; 2007) 39,154,000,000 (38,204,000,000); coal (metric tons; 2007) none (7,908,000); crude petroleum (barrels; 2007) 112,251,000 (57,417,000); petroleum products (metric tons; 2007) 7,582,000 (6,881,000); natural gas (cu m; 2007) 9,856,000,000 (4,842,000,000).

Gross national income (GNI; 2010): U.S.$328,252,000,000 (U.S.$58,980 per capita); purchasing power parity GNI (U.S.$40,140 per capita).

Structure of gross domestic product and labour force

	2008			
	in value DKK '000,000	% of total value	labour force[6]	% of labour force[6]
Agriculture, fishing	18,489	1.1	89,000	3.1
Mining	66,853	3.8		
Manufacturing	209,269	12.0	400,000	13.7
Construction	86,243	5.0	194,000	6.7
Public utilities	23,622	1.4	14,000	0.5
Transp. and commun.	128,823	7.4	174,000	6.0
Trade, restaurants	193,272	11.1	537,000	18.4
Finance, real estate	357,182	20.5	448,000	15.4
Pub. admin., defense	87,814	5.0	991,000	34.0
Services	306,960	17.6		
Other	261,188[7]	15.0[7]	70,000[8]	2.4[8]
TOTAL	1,739,716[3]	100.0[3]	2,917,000	100.0[3]

Selected balance of payments data. Receipts from (U.S.$'000,000): tourism (2009) 5,679; remittances (2010) 723; foreign direct investment (FDI; 2008–10 avg.) 1,122. Disbursements for (U.S.$'000,000): tourism (2008) 9,678; remittances (2009) 3,417; FDI (2008–10 avg.) 8,063.
Land use as % of total land area (2009): in temporary crops 43.9%, left fallow 0.8%, in permanent crops 0.1%, in pasture 17.3%, forest area 12.8%.

Foreign trade[9]

Balance of trade (current prices)

	2004	2005	2006	2007	2008	2009
U.S.$'000,000	+7,895	+8,150	+6,284	+4,414	+5,875	+9,645
% of total	5.6%	5.2%	3.6%	2.2%	2.6%	5.6%

Imports (2008): U.S.$109,785,000,000 (machinery and apparatus 23.0%; chemicals and chemical products 10.8%; food 9.9%; road vehicles 7.3%; petroleum 6.7%). *Major import sources:* Germany 21.2%; Sweden 14.0%; Netherlands 6.8%; China 5.9%; U.K. 5.1%.
Exports (2008): U.S.$115,660,000,000 (machinery and apparatus 22.4%, of which general industrial machinery 7.3%, power-generating machinery 4.6%; food 15.7%, of which meat 5.1% [including swine meat 3.3%]; petroleum 8.9%; medicine and pharmaceuticals 6.9%). *Major export destinations:* Germany 17.5%; Sweden 14.6%; U.K. 8.1%; Norway 6.1%; U.S. 5.6%.

Transport and communications

Transport. Railroads (2009[2]): route length 1,657 mi, 2,667 km; passenger-km (2008) 6,471,000,000; metric ton-km cargo (2008) 1,949,000,000. Roads (2009[2]): total length 45,565 mi, 73,331 km (paved 100%); passenger-km (2007) 71,339,000,000; metric ton-km cargo (2008) 19,480,000,000. Vehicles (2009[2]): passenger cars 2,099,090; trucks and buses 530,968. Air transport (2008)[10]: passenger-km 5,316,000,000; metric ton-km cargo (2007) 8,748,000.

Communications

Medium	date	number in '000s	units per 1,000 persons	Medium	date	number in '000s	units per 1,000 persons
Televisions	2003	5,264	977	PCs	2004	3,543	659
Telephones				Dailies	2009	1,058[11]	235[11]
Cellular	2010	6,905[12]	1,244[12]	Internet users	2009	4,751	868
Landline	2010	2,623	473	Broadband	2010	2,075[12]	374[12]

Education and health

Educational attainment (2004). Percentage of population age 25–69 having: completed lower secondary or not stated 30.3%; completed upper secondary or vocational 43.9%; undergraduate 19.6%; graduate 6.2%. *Literacy:* 100%.

Education (2006–07)

	teachers	students	student/ teacher ratio	enrollment rate (%)
Primary (age 7–12)	39,854[13]	415,793	9.9[13]	96
Secondary/Voc. (age 13–18)	43,921[13]	475,140	10.1[13]	90
Tertiary	...	232,194	...	67 (age 19–23)[14]

Health: physicians (2004) 19,450 (1 per 278 persons); hospital beds (2005) 20,487 (1 per 265 persons); infant mortality rate per 1,000 live births (2008) 4.0; undernourished population (2005–07) less than 5.0% of total population.

Military

Total active duty personnel (November 2010): 18,707[15] (army 53.1%, air force 18.0%, navy 15.8%, joint staff 13.1%). *Military expenditure as percentage of GDP* (2009): 1.4%; per capita expenditure U.S.$829.

[1]Data in this statistical presentation nearly always exclude the Faroe Islands and Greenland. [2]January 1. [3]Detail does not add to total given because of rounding. [4]Based on native land. [5]De jure population only. [6]Percentage of de jure population economically active based on total population. [7]Taxes less subsidies on products. [8]Includes 10,100 not adequately defined and 59,900 unemployed. [9]Imports c.i.f.; exports f.o.b. [10]Danish share of Scandinavian Airlines System. [11]Circulation. [12]Subscribers. [13]2000–01. [14]2005–06. [15]In addition, the home guard (reserves) number 53,507.

Internet resources for further information:
- **Statistics Denmark http://www.dst.dk/yearbook**
- **StatBank Denmark http://www.statbank.dk**

Djibouti

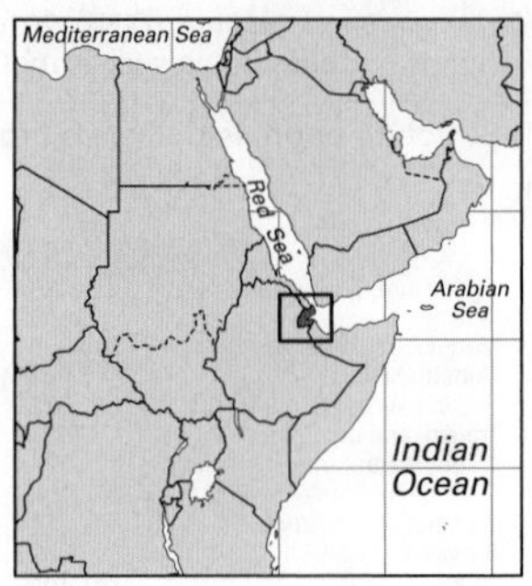

Official name: Jumhūrīyah Jībūtī (Arabic); République de Djibouti (French) (Republic of Djibouti).
Form of government: multiparty republic with one legislative house (National Assembly [65]).[1]
Head of state and government: President.
Capital: Djibouti.
Official languages: Arabic; French.
Official religion: Islam.
Monetary unit: Djibouti franc (FDJ); valuation (Sept. 1, 2011) 1 U.S.$ = FDJ 177.72[2]; 1 £ = FDJ 282.79.

Area and population

		area		population
				2009
Regions	**Capitals**	sq mi	sq km	census[3]
Ali Sabieh	Ali Sabieh	850	2,200	86,949
Arta	Arta	700	1,800	42,380
Dikhil	Dikhil	2,780	7,200	88,948
Obock	Obock	1,800	4,700	37,856
Tadjourah	Tadjourah	2,750	7,100	86,704
City				
Djibouti	—	75	200	475,322
TOTAL		8,960[4]	23,200	818,159

Demography

Population (2011): 840,000.
Density (2011): persons per sq mi 93.9, persons per sq km 36.2.
Urban-rural (2009): urban 70.6%; rural 29.4%.
Sex distribution (2008): male 46.60%; female 53.40%.
Age breakdown (2008): under 15, 37.0%; 15–29, 30.3%; 30–44, 18.1%; 45–59, 9.4%; 60–74, 4.3%; 75–84, 0.8%; 85 and over, 0.1%.
Population projection: (2020) 989,000; (2030) 1,172,000.
Doubling time: 39 years.
Ethnic composition (2000): Somali 46.0%; Afar 35.4%; Arab 11.0%; mixed African and European 3.0%; French 1.6%; other/unspecified 3.0%.
Religious affiliation (2000): Muslim (nearly all Sunnī) 94.1%; Christian 4.5%, of which Orthodox 3.0%, Roman Catholic 1.4%; nonreligious 1.3%; other 0.1%.
Major city and towns (2009)[5]: Djibouti 475,322; Ali Sabieh 37,939; Dikhil 24,886; Tadjourah 14,820; Arta 13,260.

Vital statistics

Birth rate per 1,000 population (2009): 26.3 (world avg. 20.3).
Death rate per 1,000 population (2009): 8.5 (world avg. 8.5).
Natural increase rate per 1,000 population (2009): 17.8 (world avg. 11.8).
Total fertility rate (avg. births per childbearing woman; 2009): 2.92.
Marriage/divorce rates per 1,000 population (1999): 8.9/2.8.
Life expectancy at birth (2009): male 57.9 years; female 62.8 years.
Major causes of death per 100,000 population (2002): communicable diseases 742; cardiovascular diseases 205; accidents, injuries, and violence 81; malignant neoplasms (cancers) 62; respiratory diseases 22.
Adult population (ages 15–49) *living with HIV* (2009): 2.5% (world avg. 0.8%).

National economy

Budget (2009). Revenue: FDJ 67,677,000,000 (tax revenue 67.7%; nontax revenue 16.6%; grants 15.7%). Expenditures: FDJ 69,812,000,000 (current expenditures 63.3%, of which wages and salaries 34.5%; capital expenditures 36.7%).
Public debt (external, 2009): U.S.$658,000,000.
Production (metric tons except as noted). Agriculture, forestry, fishing (2009): vegetables 30,332, cow's milk 9,093, camel's milk 6,373, cattle meat 6,050, lemons and limes 1,827, dry beans 1,674, tomatoes 1,153, mangoes and guavas 555, dry chilies and peppers 488; livestock (number of live animals) 512,000 goats, 466,000 sheep, 297,000 cattle, 70,000 camels; roundwood 349,480 cu m, of which fuelwood 100%; fisheries production 1,058 (from aquaculture, none). Mining and quarrying: mineral production limited to locally used construction materials such as basalt and salt (2009) 118,000. Manufacturing (value added in FDJ '000,000; 2000): beverages 1,030; animal products and hides 879; other food products 529; jewelry 160. Energy production (consumption): electricity (kW-hr; 2009) 343,000,000 (267,000,000); coal, none (none); crude petroleum, none (none); petroleum products (metric tons; 2007) none (139,000); natural gas, none (none); geothermal, wind, and solar resources are substantial but largely undeveloped.
Population economically active (2008): total 377,000[6]; activity rate of total population 44.4%[6] (participation rates: ages 15–64, 71.8%[6]; female 43.8%[6]; unemployed [2007] *c.* 59%).

Price index (2005 = 100)

	2004	2005	2006	2007	2008	2009	2010
Consumer price index	97.0	100.0	103.5	108.6	121.6	123.6	128.5

Household income and expenditure. Average household size (2004) 6.3; income per household: n.a.; sources of income: n.a.; expenditure (1999)[7]: food 36.2%, housing and energy 18.1%, tobacco and related products 14.4%, transportation 8.8%, household furnishings 7.7%.
Gross national income (GNI; 2009): U.S.$1,106,000,000 (U.S.$1,280 per capita); purchasing power parity GNI (U.S.$2,480 per capita).

Structure of gross domestic product and labour force

	2008		2010[8]	
	in value FDJ '000,000	% of total value	labour force	% of labour force
Agriculture, hunting, fishing	4,880	3.3	282,000	74.0
Mining and quarrying	1,369	0.9	99,000	26.0
Manufacturing	3,480	2.3		
Construction	11,277	7.6		
Public utilities	7,833	5.3		
Transp. and commun.	37,852	25.4		
Trade, hotels	21,817	14.6		
Finance, insurance	17,441	11.7		
Pub. admin., defense	22,548	15.1		
Services	2,458	1.7		
Other	18,040[9]	12.1[9]		
TOTAL	148,995	100.0	381,000	100.0

Selected balance of payments data. Receipts from (U.S.$'000,000): tourism (2009) 16.0; remittances (2010) 28; foreign direct investment (2008–10 avg.) 119; official development assistance (2009) 162. Disbursements for (U.S.$'000,000): tourism (2009) 5.8; remittances (2009) 5.
Land use as % of total land area (2009): in temporary crops, left fallow, or in permanent crops 0.1%, in pasture 73.3%, forest area 0.2%.

Foreign trade

Balance of trade (current prices)

	2004	2005	2006	2007	2008	2009
U.S.$'000,000	–223.4	–237.8	–280.5	–415.1	–505.3	–373.3
% of total	74.6%	75.1%	71.8%	78.1%	78.6%	70.7%

Imports (2007): U.S.$473,200,000 (top 20 agricultural imports *c.* 55%, of which palm oil *c.* 15%, refined sugar *c.* 9%, rice *c.* 5%; remainder *c.* 45%). *Major import sources* (2008): Saudi Arabia *c.* 21%; India *c.* 17%; China *c.* 11%; U.S. *c.* 6%; Malaysia *c.* 6%.
Exports (2007): U.S.$58,100,000 (camels *c.* 32%; raw sugar *c.* 27%; cattle *c.* 26%; rice *c.* 6%). *Major export destinations* (2008): Somalia *c.* 80%; U.A.E. *c.* 4%; Yemen *c.* 4%.

Transport and communications

Transport. Railroads (2008): length 62 mi, 100 km[10, 11]; passenger-km (1999) 81,000,000; metric ton-km cargo (2002) 201,000,000. Roads (2002): total length 1,796 mi, 2,890 km (paved 13%); passenger-km (2009) n.a.; metric ton-km cargo (2009) n.a. Vehicles (2002): passenger cars 15,700; trucks and buses 3,200. Air transport (2005): passenger arrivals and departures 219,119; metric tons of freight loaded and unloaded 10,973.

Communications

Medium	date	number in '000s	units per 1,000 persons	Medium	date	number in '000s	units per 1,000 persons
Televisions	2005	53	70	PCs	2008	31	38
Telephones				Dailies	2009	5.0[12]	6.1[12]
Cellular	2010	166[13]	186[13]	Internet users	2009	26	30
Landline	2010	19	21	Broadband	2010	8.1[13]	9.1[13]

Education and health

Educational attainment: n.a. *Literacy* (2007): percentage of population age 15 and over literate 72.2%; males literate 81.2%; females literate 63.8%.

Education (2007–08)

	teachers	students	student/ teacher ratio	enrollment rate (%)
Primary (age 6–11)	1,657	56,395	34.0	41
Secondary/Voc. (age 12–18)	1,201	41,159	34.3	22
Tertiary[14]	121	2,192	18.1	3 (age 19–23)

Health (2007): physicians[15] 85 (1 per 9,274 persons); hospital beds[15] 1,220 (1 per 646 persons); infant mortality rate per 1,000 live births (2009) 58.3; undernourished population (2004–06) 210,000 (31% of total population based on the consumption of a minimum daily requirement of 1,820 calories).

Military

Total active duty personnel (November 2010): 10,450 (army 76.6%, navy 1.9%, air force 2.4%, gendarmerie 19.1%); paramilitary 2,500. Foreign troops (2010): French 1,501; U.S. 1,285. *Military expenditure as percentage of GDP* (2008): 1.4%; per capita expenditure U.S.$18.

[1]Constitutional amendments adopted in April 2010 call for a new Senate, yet to be established, in addition to the existing National Assembly, forming a bicameral parliament. [2]Pegged rate of Djibouti franc to U.S.$. [3]Preliminary. [4]Detail does not add to total given because of rounding. [5]All populations include military and paramilitary personnel and refugees/homeless persons. [6]ILO estimate. [7]Weights of consumer price index components for Djibouti city only. [8]Midyear estimates. [9]Indirect taxes. [10]Djibouti portion of 492 mi (791 km) Chemins de Fer Djibouto-Ethiopien linking Djibouti city and Addis Ababa, Ethiopia. [11]Djibouti city–Dire Dawa (Ethiopia) link only section of railway open in late 2009 due to railway rehabilitation under way nearer to Addis Ababa. [12]Circulation of daily newspapers. [13]Subscribers. [14]2006–07. [15]Public health institutions only.

Internet resources for further information:
- **Banque Centrale de Djibouti**
  http://www.banque-centrale.dj
- **Ministry of Finance**
  http://www.ministere-finances.dj

Dominica

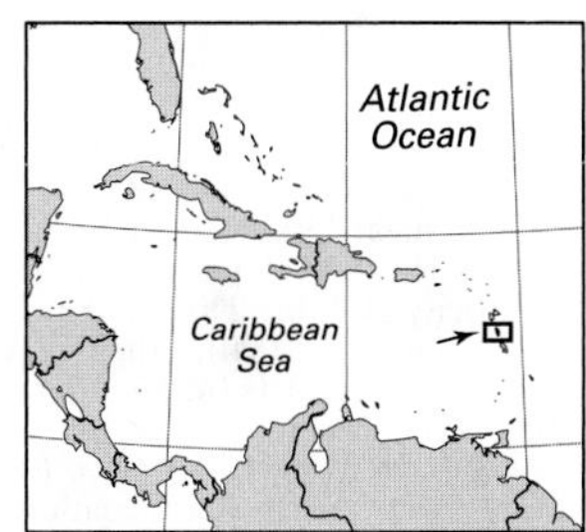

Official name: Commonwealth of Dominica.
Form of government: multiparty republic with one legislative house (House of Assembly [32[1]]).
Head of state: President.
Head of government: Prime Minister.
Capital: Roseau.
Official language: English.
Official religion: none.
Monetary unit: Eastern Caribbean dollar (EC$); valuation (Sept. 1, 2011) 1 U.S.$ = EC$2.70; 1 £ = EC$4.36.

Area and population	area		population
			2001
Parishes	sq mi	sq km	census
St. Andrew	69.3	179.6	10,240
St. David	49.0	126.8	6,758
St. George	20.7	53.5	19,825
St. John	22.5	58.5	5,327
St. Joseph	46.4	120.1	5,765
St. Luke	4.3	11.1	1,571
St. Mark	3.8	9.9	1,907
St. Patrick	32.6	84.4	8,383
St. Paul	26.0	67.4	8,397
St. Peter	10.7	27.7	1,452
TOTAL	285.3[2]	739.0[2]	69,625[3]

Demography

Population (2011): 72,500.
Density (2011)[2]: persons per sq mi 250.0, persons per sq km 96.5.
Urban-rural (2009): urban 67.2%; rural 32.8%.
Sex distribution (2006): male 50.34%; female 49.66%.
Age breakdown (2006): under 15, 26.1%; 15–29, 23.8%; 30–44, 27.4%; 45–59, 12.4%; 60–74, 7.0%; 75 and over, 3.3%.
Population projection: (2020) 75,000; (2030) 77,000.
Doubling time: 82 years.
Ethnic composition (2000): black 88.3%; mulatto 7.3%; black-Amerindian 1.7%; British expatriates 1.0%; Indo-Pakistani 1.0%; other 0.7%.
Religious affiliation (2001): Roman Catholic *c.* 61%; four largest Protestant groups (including Seventh-day Adventist, Pentecostal groups, and Methodist) *c.* 28%; nonreligious *c.* 6%; other *c.* 5%.
Major towns (2008): Roseau (2009) 13,600; Portsmouth 3,300; Marigot 2,700; Atkinson 2,300; Berekua 2,100.

Vital statistics

Birth rate per 1,000 population (2006): 15.3 (world avg. 20.3); within marriage (1991) 24.1%; outside of marriage (1991) 75.9%.
Death rate per 1,000 population (2006): 6.7 (world avg. 8.5).
Natural increase rate per 1,000 population (2006): 8.5 (world avg. 11.8).
Total fertility rate (avg. births per childbearing woman; 2006): 1.94.
Marriage/divorce rates per 1,000 population: (1999) 4.7/(1998) 0.9.
Life expectancy at birth (2006): male 72.0 years; female 77.9 years.
Major causes of death per 100,000 population (2008): diseases of the circulatory system 285.5, of which cerebrovascular diseases 100.7; malignant neoplasms (cancers) 133.8; diabetes mellitus 71.7; infectious and parasitic diseases 57.9; accidents, poisoning, and violence 22.1.

National economy

Budget (2009–10). Revenue: EC$467,700,000 (tax revenue 67.3%, grants 25.5%, nontax revenue 7.0%, capital revenue 0.2%). Expenditures: EC$468,800,000 (current expenditure 64.1%, capital expenditure 35.9%).
Public debt (external, outstanding; 2007): U.S.$290,000,000.
Gross national income (GNI; 2010): U.S.$367,000,000 (U.S.$4,960 per capita); purchasing power parity GNI (U.S.$8,580 per capita).

Structure of gross domestic product and labour force

	2008		2001	
	in value EC$'000,000	% of total value	labour force[4]	% of labour force[4]
Agriculture, fishing	118.8	12.3	5,218	18.7
Mining	7.9	0.8	164	0.6
Manufacturing	40.7	4.2	1,933	6.9
Construction	83.2	8.6	2,420	8.7
Public utilities	41.3	4.3	410	1.5
Transportation and communications	105.8	11.0	1,558	5.6
Trade, hotels, restaurants	128.1	13.3	5,120	18.4
Finance, real estate	115.1	11.9	1,144	4.1
Services	13.8	1.4	6,801	24.4
Pub. admin., defense	142.2	14.7		
Other	168.0[5]	17.4[5]	3,097[6]	11.1[6]
TOTAL	964.9	100.0[7]	27,865	100.0

Land use as % of total land area (2007): in temporary crops or left fallow 6.7%, in permanent crops 21.3%, in pasture 2.7%, forest area 60.7%.
Household income and expenditure. Average household size (2003) 3.0; income per household: n.a.; sources of income (2001)[8]: wages and salaries 68.2%, self-employment 24.4%, other 7.4%; expenditure (2001)[9]: food 32.9%, transportation and communications 19.4%, housing 11.2%, household furnishings 9.4%, clothing and footwear 8.2%, energy 5.9%.

Population economically active (2001)[4]: total 27,865; activity rate of total population 40.0% (participation rates: ages 15–64, 64.7%; female 38.9%; unemployed [2002] *c.* 25%).

Price index (2005 = 100)	2004	2005	2006	2007	2008	2009	2010
Consumer price index	98.3	100.0	102.6	105.9	112.6	112.7	116.3

Production (metric tons except as noted). Agriculture, forestry, fishing (2009): root crops 39,388 (of which taro 16,846, yams 13,283, yautia 5,228, sweet potatoes 2,690), bananas 21,136, grapefruit and pomelos 16,334, coconuts 8,925, oranges 7,307, plantains 5,049, sugarcane 4,800; livestock (number of live animals) 13,500 cattle, 9,700 goats, 7,600 sheep; roundwood (2010) 7,582 cu m, of which fuelwood 100%; fisheries production 790 (from aquaculture, negligible). Mining and quarrying: pumice, limestone, and sand and gravel are quarried primarily for local consumption. Manufacturing (2006): toilet and laundry soap 7,901; liquid disinfectant 1,861; toothpaste 1,376; crude coconut oil (2001) 855; other products include fruit juices, beer, garments, bottled spring water, and cardboard boxes. Energy production (consumption): electricity (kW-hr; 2007) 85,000,000 (85,000,000); coal, none (none); crude petroleum, none (none); petroleum products (metric tons; 2007) none (39,000); natural gas, none (none).
Selected balance of payments data. Receipts from (U.S.$'000,000): tourism (2009) 68; remittances (2005) 25; foreign direct investment (2008–10 avg.) 43; official development assistance (2009) 36. Disbursements for (U.S.$'000,000): tourism (2009) 10; remittances (2009) negligible.

Foreign trade[10]

Balance of trade (current prices)	2003	2004	2005	2006	2007	2008
U.S.$'000,000	−87.7	−103.8	−123.5	−125.4	−158.9	−192.4
% of total	52.7%	55.7%	59.6%	60.2%	68.3%	70.6%

Imports (2008): U.S.$232,400,000 (machinery and apparatus 17.8%; food 16.0%; refined petroleum 14.5%; chemicals and chemical products 8.7%; road vehicles 6.2%). *Major import sources:* U.S. 39.7%; Trinidad and Tobago 21.3%; U.K. 4.6%; Japan 4.3%; Canada 2.7%.
Exports (2008): U.S.$40,000,000 (food 37.3%, of which bananas 20.0%, roots and tubers 6.0%; soap 33.2%; pebbles/gravel/used cement aggregates 8.0%; paints and varnishes 7.0%). *Major export destinations:* Jamaica 16.3%; Antigua and Barbuda 15.3%; France (including overseas departments) 13.8%; U.K. 13.3%; Trinidad and Tobago 8.8%.

Transport and communications

Transport. Railroads: none. Roads (2002): total length 490 mi, 788 km (paved 50%). Vehicles (2005): passenger cars 10,000; trucks and buses 8,000. Air transport: n.a.

Communications

Medium	date	number in '000s	units per 1,000 persons	Medium	date	number in '000s	units per 1,000 persons
Televisions	2000	16	220	PCs	2004	13	182
Telephones				Dailies	2010	0	0
Cellular	2009	106[11]	1,591[11]	Internet users	2009	28	420
Landline	2010	16	229	Broadband	2010	32[11]	471[11]

Education and health

Educational attainment (2002). Percentage of population age 15 and over having: primary education 62%; secondary 31%; vocational/university 7%.
Literacy (2004): total population age 15 and over literate 88.0%.

Education (2007–08)	teachers	students	student/ teacher ratio	enrollment rate (%)
Primary (age 5–11)	500	8,369	16.7	72
Secondary/Voc. (age 12–16)	506	7,309	14.4	68
Tertiary	...[12]	229	...[12]	4 (age 17–21)

Health (2009): physicians 122 (1 per 589 persons); hospital beds 273 (1 per 263 persons); infant mortality rate per 1,000 live births 23.3; undernourished population (2004–06) less than 5.0% of total population based on the consumption of a minimum daily requirement of 1,870 calories.

Military

Total active duty personnel (2010): none[13].

[1]Includes 21 elective seats, 9 appointees of the president, the speaker (elected from outside of the House of Assembly membership as of the 2005 elections), and the attorney general serving ex officio. [2]Total area of Dominica per more recent survey is 290 sq mi (751 sq km). [3]The total population including institutionalized persons equals 71,474. [4]Excludes institutionalized population. [5]Taxes less imputed banking service charges and subsidies. [6]Includes 3,054 unemployed and 43 unclassified by economic activity. [7]Detail does not add to total given because of rounding. [8]For employed labour force only. [9]Weights of consumer price index components. [10]Imports c.i.f.; exports f.o.b. [11]Subscribers. [12]Data not available for Ross University School of Medicine in Dominica. [13]A 325-member police force includes a coast guard unit.

Internet resource for further information:
- **Eastern Caribbean Central Bank http://www.eccb-centralbank.org**

Dominican Republic

Official name: República Dominicana (Dominican Republic).
Form of government: multiparty republic with two legislative houses (Senate [32]; Chamber of Deputies [183]).[1]
Head of state and government: President.
Capital: Santo Domingo.
Official language: Spanish.
Official religion: none[2].
Monetary unit: Dominican peso (RD$); valuation (Sept. 1, 2011) 1 U.S.$ = RD$38.13; 1 £ = RD$61.61.

Area and population

Provinces	area sq km	population 2010 census[3]	Provinces	area sq km	population 2010 census[3]
Azua	2,532	222,175	Pedernales	2,077	29,917
Baoruco	1,283	94,210	Peravia	998	189,362
Barahona	1,739	186,239	Puerto Plata	1,857	328,195
Dajabón	1,021	58,954	Samaná	854	106,552
Duarte	1,605	290,375	San Cristóbal	1,265	557,270
El Seíbo (El Seybo)	1,786	79,091	San José de Ocoa	650	58,817
Elías Piña	1,424	61,743	San Juan	3,571	232,164
Espaillat	838	240,928	San Pedro de Macorís	1,255	300,207
Hato Mayor	1,329	83,527	Sánchez Ramírez	1,196	143,224
Hermanas Mirabal	440	90,863	Santiago	2,836	942,509
Independencia	2,008	53,063	Santiago Rodríguez	1,112	51,844
La Altagracia	3,010	268,314	Santo Domingo	1,296	2,359,327
La Romana	654	250,220	Valverde	823	159,170
La Vega	2,286	379,372			
María Trinidad Sánchez	1,271	133,347	**National District**		
Monseñor Nouel	992	169,826	Santo Domingo (city)	104	935,058
Monte Cristi	1,925	141,534	TOTAL	48,671[4, 5]	9,378,819[6]
Monte Plata	2,633	181,423			

Demography

Population (2011): 9,440,000.
Density (2011): persons per sq mi 502.3, persons per sq km 194.0.
Urban-rural (2009): urban 68.5%; rural 31.5%.
Sex distribution (2009): male 50.69%; female 49.31%.
Age breakdown (2009): under 15, 30.5%; 15–29, 26.8%; 30–44, 20.2%; 45–59, 13.5%; 60–74, 6.7%; 75–84, 1.9%; 85 and over, 0.4%.
Population projection: (2020) 10,456,000; (2030) 11,339,000.
Ethnic composition (2003)[7]: mulatto *c.* 73%; white *c.* 16%; black *c.* 11%.
Religious affiliation (2004): Roman Catholic 64.4%; other Christian 11.4%; nonreligious 22.5%; other 1.7%.
Major urban centres (2010): Santo Domingo 2,169,300; Santiago 574,900; San Pedro de Macorís 219,600; La Romana 215,600; San Cristóbal 163,100.

Vital statistics

Birth rate per 1,000 population (2009): 20.2 (world avg. 20.3).
Death rate per 1,000 population (2009): 4.3 (world avg. 8.5).
Total fertility rate (avg. births per childbearing woman; 2009): 2.51.
Marriage/divorce rates per 1,000 population (2008): 4.0/1.8.
Life expectancy at birth (2009): male 74.8 years; female 79.1 years.
Major causes of death per 100,000 population (2002): cardiovascular diseases 202.1; HIV/AIDS-related 98.9; malignant neoplasms (cancers) 76.6.

National economy

Budget (2008). Revenue: RD$329,826,000,000 (tax revenue 71.6%, of which taxes on goods and services 42.4%, income taxes 17.7%; loans 19.9%; non-tax revenue 3.2%; other 5.3%). Expenditures: RD$263,139,000,000 (current expenditure 65.2%; development expenditure 21.7%; debt payments 13.1%).
Public debt (external, outstanding; 2009): U.S.$7,714,000,000.
Gross national income (GNI; 2010): U.S.$49,662,000,000 (U.S.$4,860 per capita); purchasing power parity GNI (U.S.$8,700 per capita).

Structure of gross domestic product and labour force

	2009			
	in value RD$'000,000[8]	% of total value	labour force	% of labour force
Agriculture	26,354	7.7	538,382	12.6
Mining	768	0.2	11,256	0.3
Manufacturing	73,275	21.4	380,733	8.9
Construction	14,362	4.2	226,253	5.3
Public utilities	4,980	1.5	30,664	0.7
Transp. and commun.	76,525	22.3	277,717	6.5
Trade, restaurants	50,879	14.9	1,014,197	23.7
Pub. admin., defense	3,786	1.1	170,153	4.0
Finance, real estate	31,417	9.2	85,529	2.0
Services	27,729	8.1	900,603	21.1
Other	32,489[9]	9.5[9]	635,909[10]	14.9[10]
TOTAL	342,564	100.0[4]	4,271,396	100.0

Household income and expenditure (2007). Average household size (2002) 3.9; average annual household income RD$137,103 (U.S.$4,122); sources of income: wages and salaries 44.1%, self-employment 30.5%, transfers 16.4%; expenditure: food and nonalcoholic beverages 21.4%, transportation 17.3%, hotels and cafés 13.8%, housing and energy 10.0%, health 6.1%.
Production (metric tons except as noted). Agriculture, forestry, fishing (2009): sugarcane 4,716,170, cow's milk 649,857, bananas 589,500, rice 551,365, plantains 517,271, chicken meat 349,000, avocados 184,400, cattle meat 98,975, cocoa beans 50,200, tobacco 11,800; livestock (number of live animals) 2,652,600 cattle, 100,500,000 chickens; roundwood (2010) 913,633 cu m, of which fuelwood 99%; fisheries production 15,214 (from aquaculture 6%). Mining (2009): gypsum 175,000.[11] Manufacturing (2005): cement 2,779,000; refined sugar 139,203; beer 4,541,000 hectolitres; rum 499,000 hectolitres; cigarettes 165,015,000 packets of 20 units.[12] Energy production (consumption): electricity (kW-hr; 2007) 14,839,000,000 (14,839,000,000); coal (metric tons; 2007) none (728,000); crude petroleum (barrels; 2007) none (12,900,000); petroleum products (metric tons; 2007) 1,756,000 (5,317,000); natural gas (cu m; 2007) none (437,000,000).
Population economically active (2007): total 4,204,800; activity rate of total population 45.2% (participation rates: ages 15 and over, 64.3%; female 38.7%; unemployed [2009] 14.9%).

Price index (2005 = 100)

	2004	2005	2006	2007	2008	2009	2010
Consumer price index	96.0	100.0	107.6	114.2	126.3	128.2	136.3

Selected balance of payments data. Receipts from (U.S.$'000,000): tourism (2009) 4,051; remittances (2010) 3,369; foreign direct investment (2008–10 avg.) 2,220; official development assistance (2009) 120. Disbursements for (U.S.$'000,000): tourism (2009) 350; remittances (2009) 29.
Land use as % of total land area (2009): in temporary crops or left fallow 16.6%, in permanent crops 9.7%, in pasture 24.8%, forest area 40.8%.

Foreign trade[13]

Balance of trade (current prices)

	2004	2005	2006	2007	2008	2009
U.S.$'000,000	–1,839	–3,579	–5,464	–7,656	–10,768	–6,820
% of total	13.2%	22.2%	28.7%	38.2%	49.2%	38.4%

Imports (2008): U.S.$16,338,000,000 (machinery and apparatus 16.4%, refined petroleum 13.2%, food products 7.8%, crude petroleum 7.6%, road vehicles 6.4%). *Major import sources:* U.S. 40.3%; Venezuela 8.6%; China 8.0%; Mexico 5.3%; Colombia 4.6%.
Exports (2008): U.S.$5,570,000,000 (food 11.1%, apparel and clothing accessories 11.0%, medical/surgical instruments 9.0%, ferronickel 8.3%, tobacco [all forms] 7.2%, precious metal jewelry 6.3%, switches/fuses 5.4%). *Major export destinations:* U.S. 61.0%; Haiti 10.2%; Netherlands 3.2%; Spain 3.1%.

Transport and communications

Transport. Railroads (2006)[14]: route length 321 mi, 517 km. Roads (2002): total length 12,244 mi, 19,705 km (paved 51%). Vehicles (2008): passenger cars 630,815; trucks and buses 383,869. Air transport: (1999) passenger-km 4,900,000; (2003) metric ton-km cargo 200,000.

Communications

Medium	date	number in '000s	units per 1,000 persons	Medium	date	number in '000s	units per 1,000 persons
Televisions	2004	1,950	209	PCs	2007	331	35
Telephones				Dailies	2009	245[15]	24[15]
Cellular	2010	8,893[16]	896[16]	Internet users	2009	2,701	268
Landline	2010	1,010	102	Broadband	2010	362[16]	36[16]

Education and health

Educational attainment (2002). Percentage of population age 25 and older having: no formal education 1.7%; incomplete/complete primary education 53.1%; secondary 25.9%; undergraduate 15.9%; graduate 1.0%; unknown/other 2.4%. *Literacy* (2007): total population age 15 and over literate 89.1%.

Education (2007–08)

	teachers	students	student/ teacher ratio	enrollment rate (%)
Primary (age 6–11)	66,539	1,305,661	19.6	80
Secondary/Voc. (age 12–17)	37,164	868,017	23.4	58
Tertiary[17]	11,367	293,565	25.8	33 (age 18–22)

Health: physicians (2007) 14,479[18] (1 per 655 persons); hospital beds (2008) 9,566 (1 per 1,005 persons); infant mortality rate per 1,000 live births (2009) 24.1; undernourished population (2005–07) 2,100,000 (24% of total population based on the consumption of a minimum daily requirement of 1,840 calories).

Military

Total active duty personnel (November 2010): 24,500 (army 61.2%, navy 16.3%, air force 22.5%). *Military expenditure as percentage of GDP* (2009): 0.7%; per capita expenditure U.S.$33.

[1]New constitution promulgated on Jan. 26, 2010. [2]Roman Catholicism is the state religion per concordat with Vatican City. [3]Preliminary. [4]Detail does not add to total given because of rounding. [5]Mainland total is 48,512 sq km and offshore islands total is 159 sq km. [6]Reported total; summed total equals 9,378,820. [7]Significantly excludes data for Haitians (about 10% of the population). [8]At prices of 1991. [9]Taxes on products less subsidies and less imputed bank service charges. [10]Unemployed. [11]Nickel mining ended late 2008; extraction for gold to resume in late 2011. [12]Manufactured goods assembled in free zones include electronic components, clothing, and footwear. [13]Includes imports and exports of free zones. [14]Excludes railways operated by sugarcane growers only. [15]Circulation. [16]Subscribers. [17]2003–04. [18]Public sector only.

Internet resources for further information:
- **Banco Central de la República Dominicana http://www.bancentral.gov.do**
- **Oficina Nacional de Estadística http://www.one.gov.do**

East Timor (Timor-Leste[1])

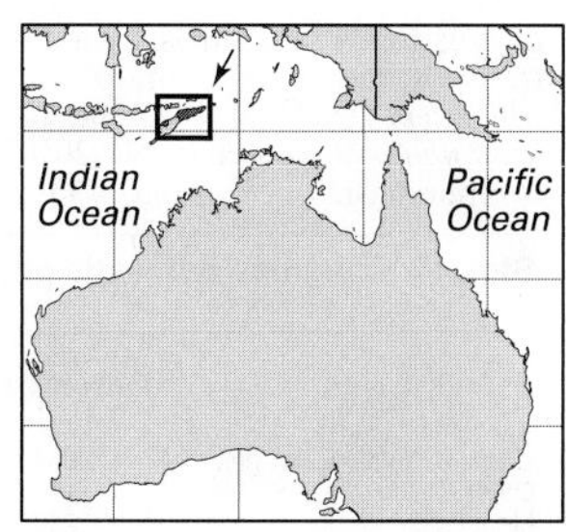

Official name: República Democrática de Timor-Leste (Portuguese); Repúblika Demokrátika Timor Lorosa'e (Tetum) (Democratic Republic of Timor-Leste [East Timor]).
Form of government: republic with one legislative body (National Parliament [65]).
Head of state: President.
Head of government: Prime Minister.
Capital: Dili.
Official languages: Portuguese; Tetum[2].
Official religion: none.
Monetary unit: dollar (U.S.$); valuation (Sept. 1, 2011) 1 U.S.$ = £0.62.

Area and population

Districts	Capitals	area sq mi	area sq km	population 2010 preliminary census
Aileu	Aileu	285	737	45,512
Ainaro	Ainaro	310	804	59,382
Ambeno (Ocussi) exclave	Pante Macassar	314	814	65,524
Baucau (Baukau)	Baucau	581	1,506	111,484
Bobonaro	Maliana	531	1,376	89,787
Covalima	Suai	464	1,203	60,063
Dili	Dili	142	367	234,331
Ermera	Ermera	297	768	114,635
Lautem	Los Palos	701	1,813	60,218
Liquiça	Liquiça	212	549	63,329
Manatuto	Manatuto	688	1,782	43,246
Manufahi	Same	511	1,323	48,894
Viqueque	Viqueque	725	1,877	70,177
TOTAL		5,760[3]	14,919	1,066,582

Demography

Population (2011): 1,092,000[4].
Density (2011): persons per sq mi 189.5, persons per sq km 73.2.
Urban-rural (2005): urban 7.8%; rural 92.2%.
Sex distribution (2009): male 50.76%; female 49.24%.
Age breakdown (2008): under 15, 45.0%; 15–29, 25.3%; 30–44, 15.1%; 45–59, 9.6%; 60–74, 4.0%; 75 and over, 1.0%.
Population projection: (2020) 1,424,000; (2030) 1,876,000.
Doubling time: 23 years.
Ethnic composition (1999): East Timorese *c.* 80%; other (nearly all Indonesian, and particularly West Timorese) *c.* 20%.
Religious affiliation (2005): Roman Catholic *c.* 98%[5]; Protestant *c.* 1%[6]; Muslim *c.* 1%[6].
Major urban areas (2004): Dili 151,026; Los Palos (Lospalos) 12,612; Same 9,966; Pante Macassar 9,754; Maliana 9,721.

Vital statistics

Birth rate per 1,000 population (2009): 40.3 (world avg. 20.3).
Death rate per 1,000 population (2009): 9.7 (world avg. 8.5).
Natural increase rate per 1,000 population (2009): 30.6 (world avg. 11.8).
Total fertility rate (avg. births per childbearing woman; 2009): 5.7.
Marriage/divorce rates per 1,000 population (1997–98): 0.4/0.1.
Life expectancy at birth (2006): male 64.0 years; female 68.7 years.
Major causes of death per 100,000 population (2002): communicable diseases 308; cardiovascular diseases 181; accidents 87; malignant neoplasms (cancers) 59; respiratory diseases 41.

National economy

Budget (2005–06). Revenue: U.S.$485,000,000 (oil and gas revenue 93.1%, of which taxes 74.8%, royalties 15.5%; domestic revenue 6.9%). Expenditures: U.S.$93,000,000 (current expenditure 71.3%; capital expenditure 16.9%; previous year spending 11.8%).
Public debt (external, outstanding): n.a.
Production (metric tons except as noted). Agriculture, forestry, fishing (2009): corn (maize) 134,715, rice 120,775, cassava 37,302, sweet potatoes 24,684, coconuts 16,905, coffee 15,893, peanuts (groundnuts) 3,921, candlenut (2001) 1,063, cinnamon 133; livestock (number of live animals) 388,000 pigs, 148,000 cattle, 102,500 buffalo, 20,000 beehives, 1,000,000 chickens; roundwood, n.a.; sandalwood exports were formerly more significant; fisheries production 3,177 (from aquaculture 2%); aquatic plants production 1,500 (from aquaculture 100%). Mining and quarrying (2006): commercial quantities of marble are exported. Manufacturing (2001): principally the production of textiles, garments, handicrafts, bottled water, and processed coffee. Energy production (consumption): electricity (kW-hr; 2007) 135,000,000 (135,000,000); coal, n.a. (n.a.); crude petroleum (barrels; 2007) 1,159,000 (negligible); petroleum products (metric tons; 2007) 6,745,000 (60,000); natural gas, n.a. (n.a.).
Population economically active (2008): total 427,000[7]; activity rate of total population 39%[7] (participation rates: ages 15–64, 73%[7]; female 41%[7]; unemployed [2000] *c.* 50%).

Price index (2005 = 100)

	2004	2005	2006	2007	2008	2009	2010
Consumer price index	98.9	100.0	103.9	114.6	125.0	125.9	134.4

Household income and expenditure. Average household size (2004) 4.7; average annual income per household, n.a.[8]; sources of income, n.a.; expenditure (2001)[9]: food 56.7%, housing 10.2%, clothing and footwear 8.9%, household furnishings 7.9%, alcohol and tobacco products 4.8%.
Gross national income (GNI; 2010): U.S.$1,497,000,000 (U.S.$1,280 per capita); purchasing power parity GNI (U.S.$2,060).

Structure of gross domestic product and labour force

	2004 in value U.S.$'000,000[10]	2004 % of total value[10]	2003 labour force	2003 % of labour force
Agriculture	107.1	31.6	340,000	81.3
Mining	2.8	0.8		
Manufacturing	12.5	3.7		
Public utilities	3.3	1.0		
Construction	31.9	9.4		
Transp. and commun.	31.8	9.4		
Trade, hotels	25.4	7.5	78,000	18.7
Finance, insurance	29.4	8.7		
Services	2.1	0.6		
Pub. admin., defense	92.7	27.3		
Other	—	—		
TOTAL	339.0	100.0	418,000	100.0

Selected balance of payments data. Receipts from (U.S.$'000,000): tourism, n.a.; remittances, n.a.; foreign direct investment (2008–10 avg.) negligible; official development assistance (2009) 217. Disbursements for (U.S.$'000,000): tourism, n.a.; remittances, n.a.
Land use as % of total land area (2007): in temporary crops or left fallow 11.4%, in permanent crops 4.6%, in pasture 10.1%, forest area 52.2%.

Foreign trade

Balance of trade (current prices)

	2004	2005	2006	2007	2008
U.S.$'000,000	–40.5	–65.7	–40.1	–187.0	–219.4
% of total	16.1%	43.0%	24.8%	83.0%	69.0%

Imports (2008): U.S.$268,583,000 (mineral fuels 26.5%, motor vehicles 16.3%, cereals 9.5%, electrical equipment 6.5%, machinery and parts 6.5%). *Major import sources:* Indonesia 42.5%; Singapore 17.1%; Australia 13.8%; Vietnam 7.0%; Japan 4.5%.
Exports (2008): U.S.$49,206,000 (domestic exports 26.2%, of which coffee 25.7%; reexports 73.8%). *Major export destinations*[11]: Germany 26.9%; U.S. 26.8%; Indonesia 16.6%; Singapore 10.0%; Portugal 6.4%; Japan 5.1%.

Transport and communications

Transport. Railroads: none. Roads (2005): total length 3,107 mi, 5,000 km (paved 50%). Vehicles (2008): passenger cars 1,159[12]; trucks and buses 457[12].

Communications

Medium	date	number in '000s	units per 1,000 persons	Medium	date	number in '000s	units per 1,000 persons
Televisions	2002[13]	...	...	PCs	2005	...	...
Telephones				Dailies	2009	3.0[14]	4.1[14]
Cellular	2010	601[15]	534[15]	Internet users	2009	2.1	1.9
Landline	2010	2.4	2.1	Broadband	2010	0.2[15]	0.2[15]

Education and health

Educational attainment (2002). Percentage of population age 15 and over having: no formal education 54.3%; some primary education 14.4%; complete primary 6.2%; lower secondary 10.4%; upper secondary and higher 14.7%.
Literacy (2005): percentage of population age 15 and over literate 49%; males literate 54%; females literate 45%.

Education (2008–09)

	teachers	students	student/ teacher ratio	enrollment rate (%)
Primary (age 6–11)	7,358	215,741	29.3	83
Secondary/Voc. (age 12–17)	3,916	85,849	21.9	23[16]
Tertiary	1,196	16,727	14.0	15 (age 18–22)[17]

Health: physicians (2009) 210 (1 per 5,310 persons); hospital beds (1999) 560 (1 per 1,277 persons); infant mortality rate per 1,000 live births (2008) 83.5; undernourished population (2004–06) 240,000 (23% of total population based on the consumption of a minimum daily requirement of 1,810[18] calories).

Military

Total active duty personnel (November 2010): 1,332 (army 93.8%, coastal patrol 6.2%). Foreign troops (November 2010): Australian 404; New Zealander 80.
Military expenditure as percentage of GDP: n.a.

[1]Timor-Leste is the preferred short-form name per the United Nations. [2]Indonesian and English are "working" languages. [3]Detail does not add to total given because of rounding. [4]Not based on 2010 preliminary census results. [5]Some vestiges of traditional beliefs are also practiced in conjunction with Roman Catholicism. [6]Most Protestants and Muslims left East Timor after 1999. [7]ILO estimate. [8]Minimum annual wage (1999) U.S.$276; average public administration wage (2003) U.S.$1,500. [9]Weights of consumer price index components for Dili only. [10]Figures do not include value added from petroleum (part of the GNI but not GDP), which in 2004 equaled U.S.$168,000,000. [11]Excludes reexports. [12]Registered vehicles only. [13]Locally produced television service commenced in May 2002. [14]Circulation of daily newspapers. [15]Subscribers. [16]2000–01. [17]2007–08. [18]Value for Indonesia used for East Timor.

Internet resources for further information:
- **Banking and Payments Authority of Timor-Leste http://www.bancocentral.tl/en**
- **Direcção Nacional de Estatística http://dne.mopf.gov.tl**

Ecuador

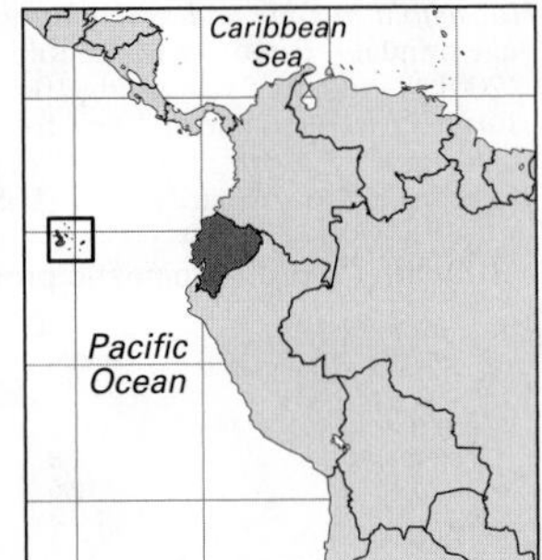

Official name: República del Ecuador (Republic of Ecuador).
Form of government: unitary multiparty republic with one acting legislative body (National Assembly [124][1]).
Head of state and government: President.
Capital: Quito.
Official language: Spanish[2].
Official religion: none.
Monetary unit: dollar (U.S.$); valuation (Sept. 1, 2011) 1 U.S.$ = £0.62.

Area and population

Regions Provinces	area sq km	population 2010 census	Regions Provinces	area sq km	population 2010 census
Amazonica	115,745	739,814	Sierra	63,516	6,449,355
Morona-Santiago	23,797	147,940	Azuay	7,995	712,127
Napo	12,484	103,697	Bolívar	3,926	183,641
Orellana	21,675	136,396	Cañar	3,142	225,184
Pastaza	29,325	83,933	Carchi	3,750	164,524
Sucumbíos	18,008	176,472	Chimborazo	6,470	458,581
Zamora-Chinchipe	10,456	91,376	Cotopaxi	5,984	409,205
Costa	68,324	7,236,822	Imbabura	4,615	398,244
El Oro	5,817	600,659	Loja	10,995	448,966
Esmeraldas	15,896	534,092	Pichincha	9,465	2,576,287
Guayas	16,803	3,645,483	Santo Domingo de los Tsáchilas	3,805	368,013
Los Ríos	7,151	778,115	Tungurahua	3,369	504,583
Manabí	18,894	1,369,780	NON-DELIMITED AREAS	775	32,384
Santa Elena	3,763	308,693	TOTAL	256,370	14,483,499
Insular	8,010	25,124			
Galápagos	8,010	25,124			

Demography

Population (2011): 14,650,000.
Density (2011): persons per sq mi 148.0, persons per sq km 57.1.
Urban-rural (2009): urban 66.3%; rural 33.7%.
Sex distribution (2010): male 49.56%; female 50.44%.
Age breakdown (2007): under 15, 32.1%; 15–29, 27.5%; 30–44, 19.5%; 45–59, 12.5%; 60–74, 6.1%; 75–84, 1.8%; 85 and over, 0.5%.
Doubling time: 68 years.
Population projection: (2020) 16,362,000; (2030) 17,900,000.
Ethnic composition (2010): mestizo 71.9%; Amerindian 14.4%; black 7.2%; white 6.1%; other 0.4%.
Religious affiliation (2005): Roman Catholic (practicing) *c.* 35%; Roman Catholic (non-practicing) *c.* 50%; other (significantly Evangelical Protestant) *c.* 15%.
Major cities (2010): Guayaquil 2,278,691; Quito 1,607,734; Cuenca 329,928; Santo Domingo de los Colorados 270,875; Machala 231,260.

Vital statistics

Birth rate per 1,000 population (2009): 15.4 (world avg. 20.3).
Death rate per 1,000 population (2009): 4.3 (world avg. 8.5).
Total fertility rate (avg. births per childbearing woman; 2008): 2.56.
Marriage/divorce rates per 1,000 population (2009): 5.5/1.2.
Life expectancy at birth (2008): male 72.2 years; female 78.1 years.
Major causes of death per 100,000 population (2009): diseases of the circulatory system 79.6; accidents and violence 45.2; malignant neoplasms (cancers) 38.6; diabetes mellitus 29.0; pneumonia and influenza 22.1; unspecified 140.3.

National economy

Budget (2009). Revenue: U.S.$11,583,000,000 (nonpetroleum revenue 80.2%, of which value-added tax 26.1%, income tax 21.7%, customs duties 8.0%; petroleum export revenue 19.8%). Expenditures: U.S.$14,218,000,000 (current expenditure 62.8%; capital expenditure 37.2%).
Production (metric tons except as noted). Agriculture, forestry, fishing (2009): sugarcane 8,473,140, bananas 7,637,320, oil palm fruit 2,100,000, rice 1,579,410, corn (maize) 811,385, plantains 549,388, cocoa beans 120,582, coffee 33,624, pyrethrum and dried flowers 105; livestock (live animals) 5,194,730 cattle, 1,860,000 sheep, 1,406,270 pigs, 110,000,000 chickens; roundwood (2010) 6,030,375 cu m, of which fuelwood 68%; fisheries production 696,763 (from aquaculture 31%). Mining and quarrying (2007): limestone 5,374,000; gold (2008) 800 kg. Manufacturing (value added in U.S.$'000,000; 2005): refined petroleum 1,885; food products 1,010; beverages 441; bricks, cement, and ceramics 254; printing and publishing 200; plastics 143. Energy production (consumption): electricity (kW-hr; 2007) 17,339,000,000 (18,161,000,000); coal, none (none); crude petroleum (barrels; 2009) 177,400,000 ([2007] 61,500,000); petroleum products (metric tons; 2007) 7,423,000 (7,999,000); natural gas (cu m; 2009) 1,246,000,000 ([2008] 255,000,000).
Population economically active (2006): total 4,204,800; activity rate of total population 45.2% (participation rates: ages 15–64, 69.6%; female 38.7%; unemployed [2009] 8.5%).

Price index (2005 = 100)

	2004	2005	2006	2007	2008	2009	2010
Consumer price index	97.6	100.0	103.0	105.4	114.2	120.1	124.4

Household income and expenditure (2003)[3]. Average household size (2008) 3.9; average annual income per household U.S.$8,161; sources of income: wages 47.0%, self-employment 25.6%, transfer payments 15.7%, rent 11.7%; expenditure: food, beverages, and tobacco 23.8%, housing and energy 19.1%, transportation and communications 12.9%, restaurants and hotels 10.4%.
Public debt (external, outstanding; July 2010): U.S.$7,903,000,000.
Gross national income (GNI; 2010): U.S.$62,102,000,000 (U.S.$4,510 per capita); purchasing power parity GNI (U.S.$9,270 per capita).

Structure of gross domestic product and labour force

	2008		2005	
	in value U.S.$'000,000	% of total value	labour force	% of labour force
Agriculture	3,478	6.4	324,600	7.7
Crude petroleum, nat. gas	9,867	18.2	10,700	0.3
Other mining	113	2.6		
Manufacturing	6,267[4]	9.2[4]	537,200	12.7
Construction	5,344	9.9	258,700	6.1
Public utilities	667	1.2	18,800	0.4
Transp. and commun.	3,307[5]	6.1[5]	280,100	6.6
Trade, restaurants, hotels	6,360[6]	11.7[6]	1,289,800	30.5
Finance, real estate	1,290[7]	2.4[7]	251,600	6.0
Pub. admin., defense	2,773	5.1	168,200	4.0
Services	13,828[8]	25.5[8]	752,100	17.8
Other	915	1.7	333,600[9]	7.9[9]
TOTAL	54,209	100.0	4,225,400	100.0

Selected balance of payments data. Receipts from (U.S.$'000,000): tourism (2009) 670; remittances (2010) 2,569; foreign direct investment (2008–10 avg.) 496; official development assistance (2009) 209. Disbursements for (U.S.$'000,000): tourism (2009) 549; remittances (2009) 81.
Land use as % of total land area (2009): in temporary crops 4.1%, left fallow 0.7%, in permanent crops 5.4%, in pasture 20.1%, forest area 40.5%.

Foreign trade

Balance of trade (current prices)

	2004	2005	2006	2007	2008	2009
U.S.$'000,000	+198	+551	+1,462	+1,261	+1,095	–310
% of total	1.3%	2.8%	6.1%	4.8%	3.0%	1.1%

Imports (2008): U.S.$17,415,000,000 (machinery and apparatus 21.2%, mineral fuels 18.7%, chemicals and chemical products 15.7%, road vehicles/parts 10.5%, iron and steel 7.6%, food 7.2%). *Major import sources:* U.S. 14.9%; China 12.2%; Colombia 9.5%; Japan 5.0%; Brazil 4.9%.
Exports (2008): U.S.$18,510,000,000 (crude petroleum 57.1%, bananas and plantains 8.9%, fish [all forms] 5.4%, refined petroleum 5.1%, shrimp 3.6%, cut flowers 3.1%). *Major export destinations:* U.S. 45.3%; Peru 9.2%; Chile 8.1%; Panama 4.8%; Colombia 4.2%.

Transport and communications

Transport (2007). Railroads: route length 600 mi, 965 km[10]; passenger-km 2,200,000; metric ton-km cargo, n.a. Roads: total length 27,135 mi, 43,670 km (paved 15%); passenger-km, n.a.; metric ton-km cargo 1,193,000,000. Vehicles: passenger cars 507,469; trucks and buses 334,405. Air transport: passenger-km 3,693,000,000; metric ton-km cargo 139,000,000.

Communications

Medium	date	number in '000s	units per 1,000 persons	Medium	date	number in '000s	units per 1,000 persons
Televisions	2004	3,298	253	PCs	2005	866	65
Telephones				Dailies	2009	705[11]	50[11]
Cellular	2010	14,781[12]	1,022[12]	Internet users	2009	2,052	151
Landline	2010	2,086	144	Broadband	2010	197[12]	14[12]

Education and health

Educational attainment (1995). Percentage of population age 25 and over having: no formal schooling/incomplete primary education 18.8%; complete primary/incomplete secondary 47.2%; complete secondary 16.1%; higher 17.9%.
Literacy (2007): total population age 15 and over literate 84.2%; males 87.3%; females 81.7%.

Education (2007–08)

	teachers	students	student/ teacher ratio	enrollment rate (%)
Primary (age 6–11)	90,430	2,040,617	22.6	97[13]
Secondary/Voc. (age 12–17)	85,099	1,247,316	14.7	62
Tertiary	26,910	534,522	19.9	42 (age 18–22)

Health: physicians (2008) 27,150 (1 per 508 persons); hospital beds (2007) 20,523 (1 per 663 persons); infant mortality rate (2009) 15.2; undernourished population (2005–07) 2,000,000 (15% of total population based on the consumption of a minimum daily requirement of 1,770 calories).

Military

Total active duty personnel (November 2010): 58,483 (army 79.5%, navy 12.4%, air force 8.1%). *Military expenditure as percentage of GDP* (2008): 2.0%; per capita expenditure U.S.$80.

[1]Permanent legislature reinstated with April 2009 elections. [2]Quechua and Shuar are also official languages for the indigenous peoples. [3]Based on a survey of urban households only. [4]Includes refined petroleum. [5]Transportation only. [6]Trade only. [7]Finance only. [8]Includes hotels, restaurants, communications, real estate, education, and health. [9]Unemployed. [10]176 mi (284 km) of the railway were operable in 2007. [11]Circulation. [12]Subscribers. [13]2006–07.

Internet resources for further information:
- **Instituto Nacional de Estadística y Censos http://www.inec.gov.ec**
- **Banco Central del Ecuador http://www.bce.fin.ec**

Egypt

Official name: Jumhūrīyyat Miṣr al-ʿArabīyyah (Arab Republic of Egypt).
Form of government: interim government led by military council.[1]
Head of state: President.
Head of government: Prime Minister.
Capital: Cairo.
Official language: Arabic.
Official religion: Islam.
Monetary unit: Egyptian pound (LE); valuation (Sept. 1, 2011) 1 U.S.$ = LE 5.95; 1 £ = LE 9.62.

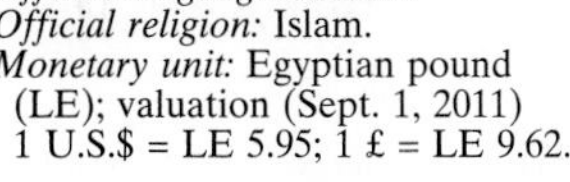

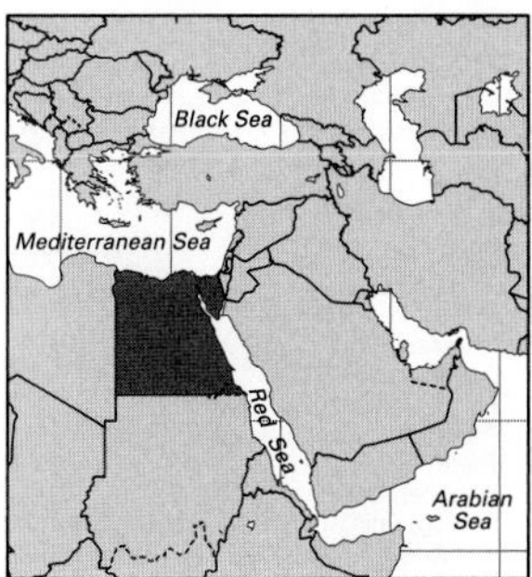

Area and population

Regions Governorates	area sq km	population 2010[2] estimate	Regions Governorates	area sq km	population 2010[2] estimate
Frontier			Upper Egypt		
Maṭrūḥ	212,112	352,885	Aswān	679	1,258,882
North Sinai	27,574	374,071	Asyūṭ	1,553	3,701,392
Red Sea	203,685	306,722	Banī Suwayf	...[3]	2,470,960
South Sinai	33,140	154,941	Al-Fayyūm	...[3]	2,721,478
Al-Wādī			Al-Jīzah (Giza)	100	3,326,444
al-Jadīd	376,505	199,810	Al-Minyā	...[3]	4,481,879
Lower Egypt			Qinā	1,851	3,209,982
Al-Buḥayrah	10,130	5,071,346	Sawhāj	1,547	4,004,613
Al-Daqahlīyah	3,471	5,338,831	"6 October"[4]	...[3]	2,780,921
Dumyāṭ	589	1,180,991	Urban		
Al-Gharbīyah	1,942	4,262,200	Alexandria	2,679	4,362,168
Al-Ismāʿīlīyah	1,442	1,029,136	Cairo	214	7,137,218
Kafr al-Shaykh	3,437	2,798,942	Ḥulwān[4]	7,500	1,831,505
Al-Minūfīyah	1,532	3,496,380	Luxor	55	484,132
Al-Qalyūbīyah	1,001	4,546,564	Port Said	72	604,451
Al-Sharqīyah	4,180	5,736,644	Suez	17,840	549,759
			REMAINDER	87,170[5]	
			TOTAL	1,002,000	77,775,247

Demography

Population (2011): 82,537,000[6].
Density (2011): persons per sq mi 213.3, persons per sq km 82.4.
Urban-rural (2009): urban 43.0%; rural 57.0%.
Sex distribution (2010[2]): male 51.13%; female 48.87%.
Age breakdown (2009): under 15, 31.7%; 15–29, 31.3%; 30–44, 18.5%; 45–59, 12.4%; 60–74, 5.1%; 75 and over, 1.0%.
Population projection: (2020) 94,810,000; (2030) 106,498,000.
Ethnic composition (2000): Egyptian Arab 84.1%; Sudanese Arab 5.5%; Arabized Berber 2.0%; Bedouin 2.0%; Rom (Gypsy) 1.6%; other 4.8%.
Religious affiliation (2000): Muslim 84.4%[7]; Christian 15.1%, of which Orthodox 13.6%, Protestant 0.8%, Roman Catholic 0.3%; nonreligious 0.5%.
Major cities ('000; 2006): Cairo 6,759 (11,893[8, 9]); Alexandria 4,085; Al-Jīzah 2,891; Shubrā al-Khaymah 1,026; Port Said 571; Suez 512.

Vital statistics

Birth rate per 1,000 population (2008–09): 25.0 (world avg. 20.3).
Death rate per 1,000 population (2008–09): 6.3 (world avg. 8.5).
Marriage/divorce rates per 1,000 population (2008): 8.1/0.8.
Total fertility rate (avg. births per childbearing woman; 2009): 2.80.
Life expectancy at birth (2009): male 70.2 years; female 74.8 years.

National economy

Budget (2009–10). Revenue: LE 297,639,000,000 (nontax revenue 41.4%, taxes on goods and services 22.5%, corporate taxes 20.2%). Expenditures: LE 391,050,000,000 (social protection 36.4%, wages and salaries 21.8%, interest on debt 16.0%, defense 6.0%).
Public debt (external; March 2011): U.S.$34,841,200,000.
Population economically active (2009): total 25,400,000; activity rate 30.4% (participation rates: ages 15–64, 51.2%; female 23.4%; unemployed [April 2009–March 2010] 9.3%).

Price index (2005 = 100)

	2004	2005	2006	2007	2008	2009	2010
Consumer price index	95.4	100.0	107.6	117.7	139.2	155.6	173.1

Production ('000; metric tons except as noted). Agriculture, forestry, fishing (2009): sugarcane 17,000, wheat 8,523, rice 7,500, corn (maize) 6,800, potatoes 4,000, oranges 2,200, grapes 1,550, dates 1,350, seed cotton 550, olives 500; livestock ('000; number of live animals) 5,500 sheep, 5,000 cattle, 4,550 goats, 110 camels; roundwood 17,665,000 cu m, of which fuelwood 98%; fisheries production 1,079,500 (from aquaculture 65%). Mining and quarrying (2009): phosphate rock 6,227; gypsum 456. Manufacturing (value added in LE '000,000; 2006): base metals 9,671; food products and beverages 9,244; chemicals and chemical products 8,568; cement, bricks, and ceramics 7,386; coke and refined petroleum products 6,854. Energy production (consumption): electricity ('000,000 kW-hr; 2009–10) 134,204 ([2008–09] 112,404); coal ('000 metric tons; 2009) 29 ([2010] 1,614); crude petroleum ('000 barrels; 2009–10) 211,121 ([2007] 193,050); petroleum products ('000 metric tons; 2007) 32,494 (32,810); natural gas ('000,000 cu m; 2009) 62,700 (42,500).
Land use as % of total land area (2009): in temporary crops or left fallow (2007) 3.0%, in permanent crops 0.8%, in pasture, n.a., forest area 0.1%.
Gross national income (GNI; 2010): U.S.$197,922,000,000 (U.S.$2,340 per capita); purchasing power parity GNI (U.S.$5,910 per capita).

Structure of gross domestic product and labour force

	2008–09		2008	
	in value LE '000,000[10]	% of total value[10]	labour force	% of labour force
Agriculture, forestry, fishing	135,464.6	13.7	7,116,000	28.9
Mining and quarrying	147,966.3	14.9	37,000	0.1
Manufacturing	164,523.3	16.6	2,567,000	10.4
Construction	44,026.0	4.4	2,268,000	9.2
Public utilities	16,020.4	1.6	297,000	1.2
Transp. and commun.	98,973.2[11]	10.0[11]	1,575,000	6.4
Trade, hotels	148,111.5	15.0	2,849,000	11.6
Finance, real estate	98,674.3	10.0	614,000	2.5
Pub. admin., defense	94,120.1	9.5	1,890,000	7.7
Services	42,332.1	4.3	3,268,000	13.2
Other	—	—	2,169,000[12]	8.8[12]
TOTAL	990,211.8	100.0	24,650,000	100.0

Household income and expenditure. Average household size (2006) 4.2.
Selected balance of payments data. Receipts from (U.S.$'000,000): tourism (2009) 10,755; remittances (2010) 7,681; foreign direct investment (FDI; 2008–10 avg.) 7,531; official development assistance (2009) 925. Disbursements for (U.S.$'000,000): tourism (2009) 2,538; remittances (2009) 255; FDI (2008–10 avg.) 1,222.

Foreign trade[13]

Balance of trade (current prices)

	2005	2006	2007	2008	2009	2010
U.S.$'000,000	–9,163	–7,028	–10,863	–22,528	–21,884	–26,485
% of total	30.1%	20.4%	25.1%	30.0%	32.2%	33.4%

Imports (2008): U.S.$52,752,000,000 (machinery and apparatus 18.2%; food products 12.3%, of which cereals 5.9%; chemicals and chemical products 12.0%; mineral fuels 10.9%; iron and steel 8.8%; road vehicles 5.6%). *Major import sources:* U.S. 10.8%; China 8.4%; Germany 6.2%; Saudi Arabia 5.9%; Italy 5.7%; Russia 4.3%.
Exports (2008): U.S.$26,224,000,000 (refined petroleum 18.9%; LNG 13.7%; food products 9.6%; crude petroleum 8.4%; organic chemicals/fertilizers/plastics 5.7%). *Major export destinations:* Italy 10.3%; India 6.3%; Spain 5.7%; Neth. 5.7%; bunkers and ships' stores 5.0%; U.S. 4.9%; Saudi Arabia 4.8%.

Transport and communications

Transport. Railroads (2007–08): length (2009) 3,418 mi, 5,500 km; passenger-km 63,840,000,000; metric ton-km cargo 4,790,000,000. Roads (2006): total length 61,933 mi, 99,672 km (paved 81%); passenger-km 145,576,000,000[14]; metric ton-km cargo 47,445,000,000. Vehicles (2007[2]): passenger cars 2,372,287; trucks and buses 1,541,986. Inland water (2008–09): Suez Canal, number of transits 19,354; metric ton cargo 811,400,000. Air transport (2009): passenger-km 16,325,000,000; metric ton-km cargo 176,858,000.

Communications

Medium	date	number in '000s	units per 1,000 persons	Medium	date	number in '000s	units per 1,000 persons
Televisions	2005	18,000	233	PCs	2008	3,261	40
Telephones				Dailies	2009	4,018[15]	48[15]
Cellular	2010	70,661[16]	871[16]	Internet users	2009	16,636	200
Landline	2010	9,618	119	Broadband	2010	1,477[16]	18[16]

Education and health

Educational attainment (2006). Percentage of population age 10 and over having: no formal schooling 41.6%; incomplete primary education/incomplete secondary 20.7%; complete secondary/some higher 28.1%; university 9.4%; advanced degree 0.2%. *Literacy* (2007): total population age 15 and over literate 72.0%; males 83.6%; females 60.7%.

Education (2008–09)

	teachers	students	student/ teacher ratio	enrollment rate (%)
Primary (age 6–11)	330,491	10,407,217	31.5	89[17]
Secondary/Voc. (age 12–17)	454,420	6,881,794	15.1	66[17]
Tertiary	79,774	2,345,407	29.4	28 (age 18–22)[17]

Health (2008–09): physicians 174,000 (1 per 471 persons); hospital beds 208,000 (1 per 394 persons); infant mortality rate 16.0; undernourished population (2004–06) less than 5.0% of total population based on the consumption of a minimum daily requirement of 1,840 calories.

Military

Total active duty personnel (November 2010): 468,500 (army 72.6%, navy 3.9%, air force [including air defense] 23.5%).[18] *Military expenditure as percentage of GDP* (2009): 2.2%; per capita expenditure U.S.$52.

[1]On Feb. 13, 2011, the Egypt Supreme Council of Armed Forces dissolved the National Assembly's two legislative houses. [2]January 1. [3]Area of new or newly delimited governorate unavailable in early 2010. [4]Officially created in April 2008. [5]Includes total area of undemarcated regions and inland water area. [6]Estimate of United Nations *World Population Prospects: The 2010 Revision*. [7]Nearly all Sunnī; Shīʿī make up less than 1% of population. [8]2007. [9]Urban agglomeration. [10]At factor cost. [11]Transportation includes earnings from traffic on the Suez Canal. [12]Includes 2,143,000 unemployed. [13]Imports c.i.f.; exports f.o.b. [14]Undefined; probably buses and taxis only. [15]Circulation. [16]Subscribers. [17]2007–08. [18]Foreign forces: 12-nation non-UN peacekeeping force in Sinai (2009) 1,662.

Internet resources for further information:
- **CAPMAS http://www.capmas.gov.eg**
- **Central Bank of Egypt http://www.cbe.org.eg**

El Salvador

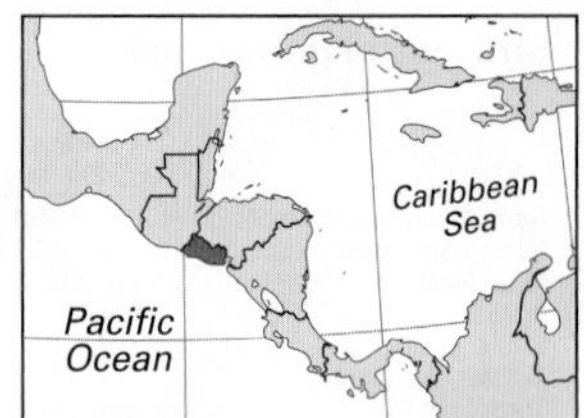

Official name: República de El Salvador (Republic of El Salvador).
Form of government: republic with one legislative house (Legislative Assembly [84]).
Head of state and government: President.
Capital: San Salvador.
Official language: Spanish.
Official religion: none[1].
Monetary unit: dollar (U.S.$)[2]; valuation (Sept. 1, 2011) 1 U.S.$ = £0.62.

Area and population

Departments	area sq km	population 2007 unadjusted census	Departments	area sq km	population 2007 unadjusted census
Ahuachapán	1,240	319,503	San Miguel	2,077	434,003
Cabañas	1,104	149,326	San Salvador	886	1,567,156
Chalatenango	2,017	192,788	San Vicente	1,184	161,645
Cuscatlán	756	231,480	Santa Ana	2,023	523,655
La Libertad	1,653	660,652	Sonsonate	1,225	438,960
La Paz	1,224	308,087	Usulután	2,130	344,235
La Unión	2,074	238,217	TOTAL	21,040	5,744,113
Morazán	1,447	174,406			

Demography

Population (2011): 6,072,000.
Density (2011): persons per sq mi 747.4, persons per sq km 288.6.
Urban-rural (2008): urban 64.8%; rural 35.2%.
Sex distribution (2009): male 48.30%; female 51.70%.
Age breakdown (2009): under 15, 32.5%; 15–29, 28.3%; 30–44, 18.7%; 45–59, 11.7%; 60–74, 6.4%; 75–84, 1.9%; 85 and over, 0.5%.
Population projection: (2020) 6,217,000; (2030) 6,340,000.
Doubling time: 53 years.
Ethnic composition (2000): mestizo 88.3%; Amerindian 9.1%, of which Pipil 4.0%; white 1.6%; other/unknown 1.0%.
Religious affiliation (2005): Roman Catholic *c.* 71%; independent Christian *c.* 11%; Protestant *c.* 10%; Jehovah's Witness *c.* 2%; other *c.* 6%.
Major cities (2007): San Salvador 316,090 (urban agglomeration 1,566,629); Soyapango 241,403[3]; Santa Ana 204,340; San Miguel 158,136; Mejicanos 140,751[3].

Vital statistics

Birth rate per 1,000 population (2009): 20.2 (world avg. 20.3); within marriage (*c.* 2003) 27%; outside of marriage (*c.* 2003) 73%.
Death rate per 1,000 population (2009): 6.9 (world avg. 8.5).
Natural increase rate per 1,000 population (2008): 13.3 (world avg. 11.8).
Total fertility rate (avg. births per childbearing woman; 2009): 2.20.
Marriage/divorce rates per 1,000 population (2008): 4.6/1.0.
Life expectancy at birth (2009): male 66.8 years; female 76.3 years.
Major causes of death per 100,000 population (2005): diseases of the circulatory system 92.8; homicide and suicide 62.7; malignant neoplasms (cancers) 57.1; diseases of the respiratory system 45.9; accidents 39.0.

National economy

Budget (2009). Revenue: U.S.$3,584,400,000 (tax revenue 72.8%, social security contributions 9.9%, nontax revenue 6.1%, grants 3.0%, other 8.2%). Expenditures: U.S.$4,385,500,000 (current expenditure 85.3%, capital expenditure 14.7%).
Public debt (external, outstanding; 2010): U.S.$6,131,000,000.
Production (metric tons except as noted). Agriculture, forestry, fishing (2009): sugarcane 5,736,060, corn (maize) 785,965, sorghum 163,698, plantains 96,493, mangoes/guavas 85,122, dry beans 80,110, bananas 78,053, coffee 76,591, papayas 71,226, lemons and limes 55,953; livestock (number of live animals) 1,342,510 cattle, 13,800,000 chickens; roundwood (2010) 4,904,555 cu m, of which fuelwood 86%; fisheries production 35,851 (from aquaculture 12%). Mining and quarrying (2008): limestone 1,200,000. Manufacturing (value added in U.S.$'000,000; 2008)[4]: food products 619, of which flour and bakery products 202, sugar products 157; maquiladora industries 238; textiles and wearing apparel 227; chemicals and chemical products 185; beverages 170. Energy production (consumption): electricity (kW-hr; 2007) 5,806,000,000 (5,837,000,000); coal, none (none); crude petroleum (barrels; 2007) none (7,030,000); petroleum products (metric tons; 2007) 927,000 (1,952,000); natural gas, none (none).
Household income and expenditure (2008). Average household size 4.0; average annual income per household U.S.$6,059; expenditure (June 2005)[5]: food, beverages, and tobacco 36.4%, housing and energy 16.8%, transportation and communications 10.2%, household furnishings 8.4%.
Land use as % of total land area (2007): in temporary crops 17.4%, left fallow 15.5%, in permanent crops 11.4%, in pasture 30.7%, forest area 13.9%.
Population economically active (2008): total 2,495,908; activity rate of total population 40.8% (participation rates: ages 16–64, 62.9%; female 41.3%; unemployed [2009] 7.3%).

Price index (2005 = 100)

	2004	2005	2006	2007	2008	2009	2010
Consumer price index	95.5	100.0	104.0	108.8	116.1	117.3	118.7

Gross national income (GNI; 2010): U.S.$20,820,000,000 (U.S.$3,360 per capita); purchasing power parity GNI (U.S.$6,390 per capita).

Structure of gross domestic product and labour force

	2008 in value U.S.$'000,000	2008 % of total value	2007 labour force	2007 % of labour force
Agriculture	2,693	12.2	435,800	16.9
Mining	86	0.4	3,700	0.1
Manufacturing	4,452	20.1	403,600	15.6
Construction	860	3.9	148,400	5.7
Public utilities	417	1.9	10,200	0.4
Transp. and commun.	1,992	9.0	103,200	4.0
Trade, restaurants	4,434	20.0	720,600	27.9
Finance, real estate	3,296	14.9	114,400	4.4
Public admin., defense	1,404	6.4	98,700	3.8
Services	1,595	7.2	380,100	14.7
Other	886[6]	4.0[6]	167,100[7]	6.5[7]
TOTAL	22,115	100.0	2,585,800	100.0

Selected balance of payments data. Receipts from (U.S.$'000,000): tourism (2009) 319; remittances (2010) 3,648; foreign direct investment (2008–10 avg.) 449; official development assistance (2009) 277. Disbursements for (U.S.$'000,000): tourism (2009) 187; remittances (2009) 19; foreign direct disinvestment (2008–10 avg.) –27.

Foreign trade[8]

Balance of trade (current prices)

	2004	2005	2006	2007	2008	2009
U.S.$'000,000	–3,024	–3,271	–3,957	–4,728	–5,205	–3,457
% of total	31.4%	32.4%	34.8%	37.2%	36.4%	31.3%

Imports (2008): U.S.$9,754,000,000 (petroleum 17.3%; chemicals and chemical products 15.4%; machinery and apparatus 13.1%; food 12.3%; fabrics 7.1%). *Major import sources:* U.S. 34.4%; Mexico 9.0%; Guatemala 8.5%; China 4.9%; Honduras 3.8%.
Exports (2008): U.S.$4,549,000,000 (apparel and clothing accessories 34.7%, of which T-shirts/athletic jerseys 19.1%; food 17.8%, of which coffee 5.7%; paper and paper products 3.8%). *Major export destinations:* U.S. 48.1%; Guatemala 13.6%; Honduras 13.0%; Nicaragua 5.5%; Costa Rica 3.7%.

Transport and communications

Transport. Railroads (2007)[9]: length 176 mi, 283 km. Roads (2002): total length 11,458 km (paved 23%). Vehicles (2007): passenger cars 283,787; trucks and buses 290,094. Air transport (2008)[10]: passenger-km 10,233,000,000; metric ton-km cargo 65,000,000.

Communications

Medium	date	number in '000s	units per 1,000 persons	Medium	date	number in '000s	units per 1,000 persons
Televisions	2004	1,560	233	PCs	2007	359	52
Telephones				Dailies	2009	280[11]	46[11]
Cellular	2010	7,700[12]	1,243[12]	Internet users	2009	889	144
Landline	2010	1,001	162	Broadband	2010	175[12]	28[12]

Education and health

Educational attainment (2004). Percentage of population over age 25 having: no formal schooling 22.0%; primary education: grades 1–3 19.1%, grades 4–6 19.9%; secondary: grades 7–9 13.9%, grades 10–12 14.6%; higher 10.5%.
Literacy (2008): total population age 16 and over literate 83.5%; males literate 86.6%; females literate 80.8%.

Education (2007–08)

	teachers	students	student/ teacher ratio	enrollment rate (%)
Primary (age 7–12)	30,474	993,795	32.6	94
Secondary/Voc. (age 13–18)	20,484	539,277	26.3	55
Tertiary	8,562	138,615	16.2	25 (age 19–23)

Health (2005): physicians 8,670 (1 per 794 persons); hospital beds 4,816 (1 per 1,429 persons); infant mortality rate per 1,000 live births (2008) 30.0; undernourished population (2004–06) 600,000 (10% of total population based on the consumption of a minimum daily requirement of 1,760 calories).

Military

Total active duty personnel (November 2010): 15,500 (army 89.4%, navy 4.5%, air force 6.1%); paramilitary 17,000. *Military expenditure as percentage of GDP* (2010): 5.2%; per capita expenditure U.S.$187.

[1]Roman Catholicism, although not official, enjoys special recognition in the constitution. [2]The U.S. dollar has been legal tender in El Salvador from Jan. 1, 2001. [3]Within San Salvador urban agglomeration. [4]At constant prices of 1990. [5]Weights of consumer price index components. [6]Import duties and VAT less imputed bank service charges. [7]Unemployed less 500 not adequately defined. [8]Imports c.i.f., exports f.o.b. (including assembled components for reexport). [9]All rail service was suspended from 2002; very limited passenger service was resumed in 2007. [10]TACA only (a regional airline of 5 independently owned Central American airlines headquartered in El Salvador). [11]Circulation. [12]Subscribers.

Internet resources for further information:
- **Banco Central de Reserva de El Salvador http://www.bcr.gob.sv**
- **Dirección General de Estadística y Censos http://www.digestyc.gob.sv**

Equatorial Guinea

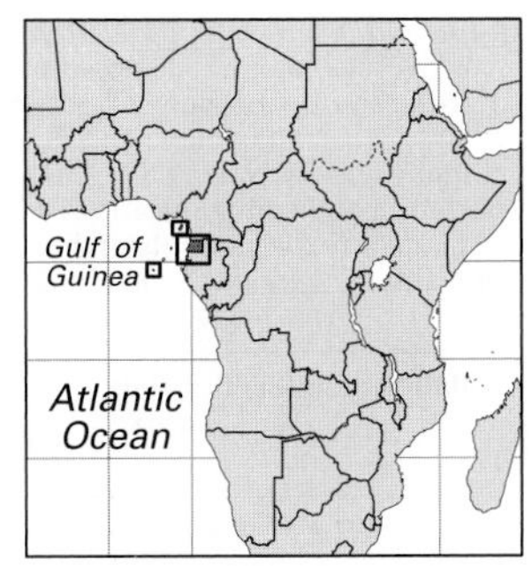

Official name: República de Guinea Ecuatorial (Spanish); République du Guinée Équatoriale (French) (Republic of Equatorial Guinea).
Form of government: republic with one legislative house (House of People's Representatives [100]).
Head of state and government: President assisted by the Prime Minister.
Capital: Malabo.
Official languages: Spanish; French.
Official religion: none.
Monetary unit: CFA franc (CFAF); valuation (Sept. 1, 2011) 1 U.S.$ = CFAF 460.31; 1 £ = CFAF 743.83.

Area and population

Regions / Provinces	Capitals	area sq mi	area sq km	population 2001 census
Insular		785[1]	2,034	265,470
Annobón	Palé	7	17	5,008
Bioko Norte	Malabo	300	776	231,428
Bioko Sur	Luba	479	1,241	29,034
Continental		10,045[1]	26,017	749,529
Centro-Sur	Evinayong	3,834	9,931	125,856
Kie-Ntem	Ebebiyin	1,522	3,943	167,279
Litoral[2]	Bata	2,573	6,665	298,414
Wele-Nzas	Mongomo	2,115	5,478	157,980
TOTAL		10,831[1]	28,051	1,014,999[3]

Demography

Population (2011): 720,000[4].
Density (2011): persons per sq mi 66.5, persons per sq km 25.7.
Urban-rural (2010): urban 39.7%; rural 60.3%.
Sex distribution (2008): male 49.57%; female 50.43%.
Age breakdown (2008): under 15, 42.0%; 15–29, 26.6%; 30–44, 16.6%; 45–59, 8.7%; 60–74, 5.0%; 75–84, 1.0%; 85 and over, 0.1%.
Population projection: (2020) 905,000[4]; (2030) 1,102,000[4].
Doubling time: 26 years.
Ethnic composition (2000): Fang 56.6%; migrant labourers from Nigeria 12.5%, of which Yoruba 8.0%, Igbo 4.0%; Bubi 10.0%; Seke 2.9%; Spaniard 2.8%; other 15.2%.
Religious affiliation (2000): Roman Catholic 79.9%; Sunnī Muslim 4.1%; independent Christian 3.7%; Protestant 3.2%; traditional beliefs 2.1%; nonreligious/atheist 4.9%; other 2.1%.
Major cities (2003): Malabo (2009) 128,000; Bata 66,800; Mbini 11,600; Ebebiyin 9,100; Luba 6,800.

Vital statistics

Birth rate per 1,000 population (2008): 37.1 (world avg. 20.3).
Death rate per 1,000 population (2008): 9.7 (world avg. 8.5).
Natural increase rate per 1,000 population (2008): 27.4 (world avg. 11.8).
Total fertility rate (avg. births per childbearing woman; 2008): 5.16.
Life expectancy at birth (2008): male 60.4 years; female 62.1 years.
Major causes of death per 100,000 population (2002): infectious and parasitic diseases 812.5, of which HIV/AIDS 274.3, malaria 178.4, diarrheal diseases 94.9, respiratory infections 89.5; diseases of the circulatory system 197.5; accidents, poisoning, and violence 124.3.
Adult population (ages 15–49) *living with HIV* (2009): 5.0% (world avg. 0.8%).

National economy

Budget (2009). Revenue: CFAF 2,368,100,000,000 (tax revenue 38.2%, of which corporate tax 33.2%; nontax revenue 61.8%, of which royalties 46.2%). Expenditures: CFAF 2,827,500,000,000 (current expenditure 12.2%, of which goods and services 5.5%, subsidies 4.0%; capital expenditure 87.8%).
Public debt (external, outstanding; 2009): U.S.$626,100,000.
Gross national income (GNI; 2010): U.S.$10,182,000,000 (U.S.$14,680 per capita); purchasing power parity GNI (U.S.$23,810 per capita).

Structure of gross domestic product and labour force

	2009 in value CFAF '000,000	2009 % of total value	2003 labour force	2003 % of labour force
Agriculture, fishing	134,000	2.3	141,000	69.1
Forestry	47,700	0.8		
Crude petroleum	3,393,800	58.8		
Manufacturing	775,000	13.4		
Construction	1,060,100	18.4		
Public utilities	54,100	0.9		
Transportation and communications	9,500	0.2	63,000	30.9
Trade, hotels	85,700	1.5		
Finance, real estate	34,700	0.6		
Pub. admin., defense	76,000	1.3		
Services	34,800	0.6		
Other	65,800[5]	1.2[5]		
TOTAL	5,771,200	100.0	204,000	100.0

Production (metric tons except as noted). Agriculture, forestry, fishing (2009): roots and tubers 203,636 (of which sweet potatoes 92,154, cassava 73,134), plantains 39,555, oil palm fruit 35,000, bananas 27,456, coconuts 6,129, coffee 2,700, cacao beans 1,200; livestock (number of live animals) 38,000 sheep, 9,100 goats, 6,300 pigs, 5,100 cattle; roundwood (2010) 824,465 cu m, of which fuelwood 23%; fisheries production 7,722 (from aquaculture, negligible). Mining and quarrying: gold (2009) 200 kg. Manufacturing (2004): methanol 1,027,300; processed timber 31,200 cu m. Energy production (consumption): electricity (kW-hr; 2007) 95,000,000 (95,000,000); coal, none (none); crude petroleum (barrels; 2009) 113,000,000 (negligible); petroleum products (metric tons; 2007) 4,592,000 (195,000); natural gas (cu m; 2009) 7,900,000,000 ([2007] 1,672,000,000).
Population economically active (2008): total 251,000[6]; activity rate of total population 38.1%[6] (participation rates: ages 15–64, 66.4%[6]; female 38.4%[6]; unemployed, n.a.).

Price index (2005 = 100)

	2004	2005	2006	2007	2008	2009	2010
Consumer price index	94.7	100.0	104.4	107.4	113.3	119.5	125.1

Household income and expenditure. Average household size, n.a.; income per household: n.a.; sources of income: n.a.; expenditure (2000)[7]: food and beverages 60.4%, clothing 14.7%, household furnishings 8.6%.
Land use as % of total land area (2009): in temporary crops or left fallow 4.7%, in permanent crops 2.5%, in pasture 3.7%, forest area 58.4%.
Selected balance of payments data. Receipts from (U.S.$'000,000): tourism (2005) 5; remittances, n.a.; foreign direct investment (2008–10 avg.) 512; official development assistance (2009) 32. Disbursements for (U.S.$'000,000): tourism, n.a.; remittances, n.a.

Foreign trade

Balance of trade (current prices)

	2003	2004	2005	2006	2007	2008
CFAF '000,000,000	+910	+1,600	+3,035	+3,235	+3,571	+4,699
% of total	38.8%	49.2%	68.7%	60.5%	57.4%	57.1%

Imports (2008): CFAF 1,767,000,000,000 (for petroleum sector 22.1%, for nonpetroleum sector 77.9%). *Major import sources:* China *c.* 18%; Spain *c.* 14%; U.S. *c.* 12%; France *c.* 11%; Côte d'Ivoire *c.* 8%.
Exports (2008): CFAF 6,466,000,000,000 (crude petroleum 78.1%, methanol 21.2%, timber 0.4%). *Major export destinations:* U.S. *c.* 23%; Spain *c.* 18%; China *c.* 15%; Taiwan *c.* 11%; France *c.* 8%.

Transport and communications

Transport. Railroads: none. Roads (2000): total length 1,790 mi, 2,880 km (paved, n.a.). Vehicles (2002): passenger cars 8,380; trucks and buses 6,618. Air transport: n.a.[8].

Communications

Medium	date	number in '000s	units per 1,000 persons	Medium	date	number in '000s	units per 1,000 persons
Televisions	2002	55	116	PCs	2004	7.0	3.3
Telephones				Dailies	2009	0[9]	0[9]
Cellular	2010	399[10]	570[10]	Internet users	2009	14	21
Landline	2010	14	19	Broadband	2010	1.2[10]	1.7[10]

Education and health

Educational attainment: n.a. *Literacy* (2008): percentage of total population age 15 and over literate 93.0%; males literate 96.9%; females literate 89.1%.

Education (1999–2000)

	teachers	students	student/ teacher ratio	enrollment rate (%)
Primary (age 7–11)	2,936[11]	81,099[11]	27.6[11]	66[12]
Secondary/Voc. (age 12–18)	894	21,173[13]	23.2	22[14]
Tertiary	206	1,003	3.9	3 (age 19–23)

Health: physicians (2004) 101 (1 per 5,020 persons); hospital beds (1998) 907 (1 per 472 persons); infant mortality rate per 1,000 live births (2008) 83.8; undernourished population, n.a.

Military

Total active duty personnel (November 2010): 1,320 (army 83.3%, navy 9.1%, air force 7.6%). *Military expenditure as percentage of GDP* (2008): 0.1%; per capita expenditure U.S.$18.

[1]Detail does not add to total given because of rounding. [2]Includes three islets in Corisco Bay. [3]Official government census figures; credible estimates are significantly lower. [4]Estimate of United Nations *World Population Prospects: The 2010 Revision*. [5]Import duties. [6]Estimate of the ILO Employment Trends Unit. [7]Weights of consumer price index components. [8]Data unavailable for Ecuato Guineana, the national airline. [9]Circulation. [10]Subscribers. [11]2006–07. [12]2002–03. [13]2001–02. [14]2000–01.

Internet resources for further information:

- **La Banque de France: La Zone Franc**
  http://www.banque-france.fr/fr/eurosys/zonefr/zonefr.htm
- **Government of the Republic of Equatorial Guinea: Statistics**
  http://www.guineaecuatorialpress.com/estadistica.php

Eritrea

Official name: State of Eritrea[1].
Form of government: transitional regime[2] with one interim legislative body ([transitional] National Assembly [150][3]).
Head of state and government: President.
Capital: Asmara.
Official language: none[4].
Official religion: none.
Monetary unit: nakfa (Nfa); valuation (Sept. 1, 2011) 1 U.S.$ = Nfa 15.00; 1 £ = Nfa 24.24.

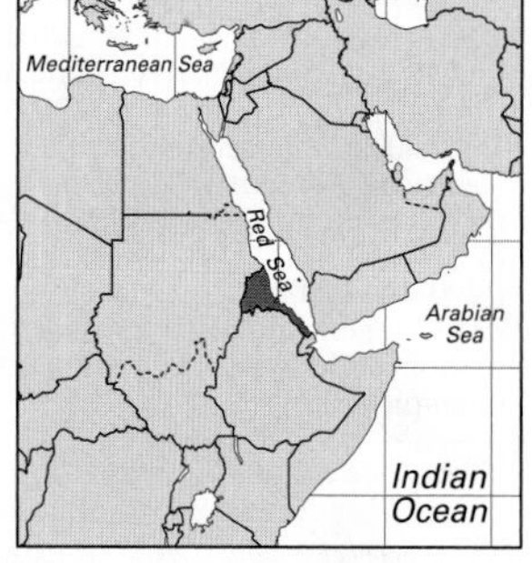

Area and population		area[5]		population
				2002
Regions	**Capitals**	sq mi	sq km	estimate
Anseba	Keren	8,960	23,200	580,700
Debub	Mendefera	3,090	8,000	1,018,000
Debub-Keih-Bahri (Southern Red Sea)	Assab (Aseb)	10,660	27,600	274,800
Gash-Barka	Barentu	12,820	33,200	747,200
Maekel	Asmara (Asmera)	500	1,300	727,800
Semien-Keih-Bahri (Northern Red Sea)	Massawa	10,730	27,800	569,000
TOTAL		46,760	121,100	3,917,500

Demography

Population (2011): 5,415,000.
Density (2011)[6]: persons per sq mi 115.8, persons per sq km 44.7.
Urban-rural (2009): urban 21.1%; rural 78.9%.
Sex distribution (2007): male 49.35%; female 50.65%.
Age breakdown (2007): under 15, 43.2%; 15–29, 27.6%; 30–44, 16.3%; 45–59, 7.5%; 60–74, 4.4%; 75–84, 0.9%; 85 and over, 0.1%.
Population projection: (2020) 6,848,000; (2030) 8,394,000.
Doubling time: 26 years.
Ethnolinguistic composition (2004): Tigrinya (Tigray) 50.0%; Tigré 31.4%; Afar 5.0%; Saho 5.0%; Beja 2.5%; Bilen 2.1%; other 4.0%.
Religious affiliation (2004): Muslim (virtually all Sunnī) *c.* 50%; Christian *c.* 48%, of which Eritrean Orthodox *c.* 40%, Roman Catholic *c.* 5%, Protestant *c.* 2%; traditional beliefs *c.* 2%.
Major cities (2003): Asmara (2009) 649,000[7]; Keren 57,000; Assab 28,000; Afabet 25,000; Massawa 25,000.

Vital statistics

Birth rate per 1,000 population (2007): 35.7 (world avg. 20.3).
Death rate per 1,000 population (2007): 8.8 (world avg. 8.5).
Natural increase rate per 1,000 population (2007): 26.9 (world avg. 11.8).
Total fertility rate (avg. births per childbearing woman; 2007): 4.96.
Life expectancy at birth (2007): male 59.0 years; female 63.0 years.
Major causes of death per 100,000 population (2002): infectious and parasitic diseases 459.1, of which HIV/AIDS 168.0, diarrheal diseases 64.8, malaria 61.4; diseases of the circulatory system 104.9; accidents, poisoning, and violence 74.6; malignant neoplasms (cancers) 42.8.

National economy

Budget (2008). Revenue: Nfa 4,457,000,000 (tax revenue 55.2%, of which direct taxes 38.6%, import duties 7.7%; nontax revenue 31.3%; grants 13.5%). Expenditures: Nfa 9,844,000,000 (current expenditure 70.1%; capital expenditure 23.7%; net lending 6.2%).
Gross national income (2009): U.S.$1,792,000,000 (U.S.$340 per capita).

Structure of gross domestic product and labour force				
	2008			
	in value U.S.$'000,000	% of total value	labour force[8]	% of labour force
Agriculture, fishing	333.1	22.6	1,087,000	77.0
Mining, Public utilities	18.6	1.2	324,000	23.0
Manufacturing	85.1	5.8		
Construction	165.7	11.2		
Transp. and commun.	165.0	11.2		
Trade, hotels	257.7	17.5		
Finance, Pub. admin., defense, Services	372.2	25.2		
Other	78.4	5.3		
TOTAL	1,475.8	100.0	1,411,000	100.0

Production (metric tons except as noted). Agriculture, forestry, fishing (2009): roots and tubers 71,524, barley 65,084, sorghum 59,188, wheat 26,142, pulses 24,402, millet 17,217, corn (maize) 16,652, chickpeas 6,570, sesame seeds 150; livestock (number of live animals) 2,260,250 sheep, 2,046,340 cattle, 1,740,000 goats, 338,584 camels; roundwood 2,606,177 cu m, of which fuelwood 99.9%; fisheries production 3,030 (from aquaculture, none). Mining and quarrying (2009): coral 60,000, basalt 45,000, granite 25,000. Manufacturing (value added in U.S.$'000,000; 2007): beverages 18; furniture/unspecified manufactures 9; textiles 7; food products 5; bricks, cement, and ceramics 3. Energy production (consumption): electricity (kW-hr; 2007) 288,000,000 (288,000,000); coal, none (none); crude petroleum, none (none); petroleum products (metric tons; 2007) none (181,000); natural gas, none (none).

Household income and expenditure (1996–97). Average household size (2004) 5.0; average annual disposable income per household Nfa 10,967 (U.S. $1,707); sources of income[9]: wages and salaries 34.0%, transfers 29.3%, rent 19.8%, self-employment 16.9%; expenditure[9]: food 36.2%, housing 30.2%, clothing and footwear 9.3%, energy 6.8%, household furnishings 4.6%, transportation and communications 4.1%.
Public debt (external, outstanding; 2009): U.S.$1,013,000,000.
Population economically active (2008): 2,057,000; activity rate of total population 41.7% (participation rates: ages 15–64, 72.7%; female 43.7%).

Inflation rate (2005 = 100)	2004	2005	2006	2007	2008	2009	2010
Inflation rate	88.9	100.0	115.1	124.4	144.3	177.3	190.0

Selected balance of payments data. Receipts from (U.S.$'000,000): tourism (2009) 26; remittances (2007) *c.* 225; foreign direct investment (2008–10 avg.) 19; official development assistance (2009) 145. Disbursements for (U.S.$'000,000): tourism, n.a.; remittances, n.a.
Land use as % of total land area (2007): in temporary crops or left fallow 6.4%, in permanent crops 0.02%, in pasture 68.3%, forest area 15.3%.

Foreign trade

Balance of trade (current prices)	2003	2004	2005	2006	2007	2008
U.S.$'000,000	–426	–449	–472	…	…	–513
% of total	97.0%	95.2%	95.6%	…	…	93.8%

Imports (2008): U.S.$530,000,000 (machinery and apparatus 24.9%; sugars/confectioneries 7.8%; cereals 7.4%; vehicles [excl. railway] 4.4%). *Major import sources* (2008): Saudi Arabia *c.* 21%; India *c.* 14%; Italy *c.* 13%; China *c.* 10%; U.S. *c.* 5%.
Exports (2008): U.S.$17,000,000 (vehicles [excl. railway] 26.9%; hides, skins, and leather 10.8%; oil seeds [particularly sesame] 7.8%; apparel 7.3%). *Major export destinations* (2008): India *c.* 25%; Italy *c.* 21%; Sudan *c.* 14%; China *c.* 13%; France *c.* 5%.

Transport and communications

Transport. Railroads (2007): route length 190 mi, 306 km[10]. Roads (2008): total length 2,492 mi, 4,010 km (paved 22%). Vehicles (1996): automobiles 5,940; trucks and buses, n.a. Air transport: n.a.

Communications							
Medium	date	number in '000s	units per 1,000 persons	**Medium**	date	number in '000s	units per 1,000 persons
Televisions	2004	250	58	PCs	2007	38	8
Telephones				Dailies	2009	—	—
Cellular	2010	185[11]	35[11]	Internet users	2009	250	49
Landline	2010	54	10	Broadband	2010	0.1[11]	—

Education and health

Educational attainment (2002)[12]. Percentage of population age 25 and over having: no formal education 66.4%, incomplete primary education 16.6%, complete primary 1.3%, incomplete secondary 5.8%, complete secondary 5.7%, higher 3.0%, unknown 1.2%. *Literacy* (2006): total population age 15 and over literate 61.4%; males 72.3%; females 50.7%.

Education (2007–08)	teachers	students	student/ teacher ratio	enrollment rate (%)
Primary (age 7–11)	6,626	314,034	47.4	39
Secondary/Voc. (age 12–18)	4,425[13]	229,079	49.3[13]	26
Tertiary[14]	620	9,949	16.0	2 (age 19–23)

Health: physicians (2004) 215 (1 per 20,791 persons); hospital beds (2006) 5,500 (1 per 833 persons); infant mortality rate per 1,000 live births (2007) 45.4; undernourished population (2004–06) 3,000,000 (66% of total population based on the consumption of a minimum daily requirement of 1,680 calories).

Military

Total active duty personnel (November 2010): 201,750 (army 99.1%, navy 0.7%, air force 0.2%). Mandate for the UN peacekeeping force along the Eritrean-Ethiopian border was terminated in July 2008. *Military expenditure as percentage of GDP* (2009): 4.1%; per capita expenditure U.S.$15.

[1]The name in Tigrinya, the most widely spoken local language, is Hagere Iertra. [2]New constitution ratified in May 1997 was not implemented in September 2010. [3]All seats indirectly elected; last elections were held in 1994. [4]The de facto "working" languages of government are Tigrinya, English, and Arabic. [5]Approximate figures. The published total area is 46,774 sq mi (121,144 sq km); water area is 7,776 sq mi (20,140 sq km). [6]Based on land area only. [7]Urban agglomeration. [8]Estimated employed only. [9]Data taken from a 1996–97 survey of the 12 largest urban centres in the country. [10]Out of use from 1978; 73 mi (118 km) section from Massawa to Asmara reopened in 2003. [11]Subscribers. [12]Based on household survey of 14,201 persons. [13]2006–07. [14]2008–09.

Internet resource for further information:
- **African Development Bank Group: Eritrea**
http://www.afdb.org/en/countries/east-africa/eritrea

Estonia

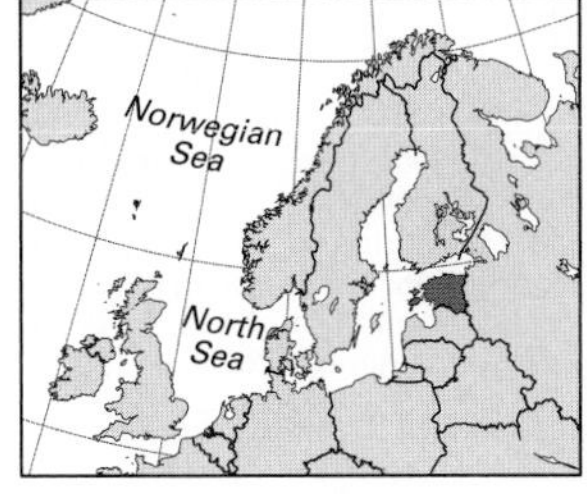

Official name: Eesti Vabariik (Republic of Estonia).
Form of government: unitary multiparty republic with a single legislative body (Riigikogu, or Parliament [101]).
Head of state: President.
Head of government: Prime Minister.
Capital: Tallinn.
Official language: Estonian.
Official religion: none.
Monetary unit: euro (€)[1]; valuation (Sept. 1, 2011) 1 U.S.$ = €0.70; 1 £ = €1.13.

Area and population

Counties	Capitals	area sq mi	area sq km	population 2010[2] estimate
Harju	Tallinn	1,673	4,333	526,505
Hiiu	Kärdla	395	1,023	10,032
Ida-Viru	Jõhvi	1,299	3,364	168,656
Järva	Paide	950	2,460	36,058
Jõgeva	Jõgeva	1,005	2,604	36,671
Lääne	Haapsalu	920	2,383	27,366
Lääne-Viru	Rakvere	1,401	3,628	66,996
Pärnu	Pärnu	1,856	4,807	88,428
Põlva	Põlva	836	2,165	30,889
Rapla	Rapla	1,151	2,980	36,620
Saare	Kuressaare	1,128	2,922	34,644
Tartu	Tartu	1,156	2,993	150,074
Valga	Valga	789	2,044	34,048
Viljandi	Viljandi	1,321	3,422	55,447
Võru	Võru	890	2,305	37,693
TOTAL		16,769[3, 4, 5]	43,432[3, 4, 5]	1,340,127

Demography

Population (2011): 1,340,000.
Density (2011)[6]: persons per sq mi 81.9, persons per sq km 31.6.
Urban-rural (2009[2]): urban 68.0%; rural 32.0%.
Sex distribution (2009[2]): male 46.05%; female 53.95%.
Age breakdown (2009): under 15, 14.9%; 15–29, 21.6%; 30–44, 19.9%; 45–59, 20.5%; 60–74, 15.3%; 75–84, 6.3%; 85 and over, 1.5%.
Population projection: (2020) 1,329,000; (2030) 1,296,000.
Ethnic composition (2009[2]): Estonian 68.7%; Russian 25.6%; Ukrainian 2.1%; Belarusian 1.2%; Finnish 0.8%; other 1.6%.
Religious affiliation (2000): Christian 63.5%, of which unaffiliated Christian 25.6%, Protestant (mostly Lutheran) 17.2%, Orthodox 16.5%, independent Christian 3.3%; nonreligious 25.1%; atheist 10.9%; other 0.5%.
Major cities (2010[2]): Tallinn 399,340; Tartu 103,284; Narva 65,881; Kohtla-Järve 44,492; Pärnu 44,083.

Vital statistics

Birth rate per 1,000 population (2008): 12.0 (world avg. 20.3); within marriage 40.9%; outside of marriage 59.1%.
Death rate per 1,000 population (2008): 12.4 (world avg. 8.5).
Total fertility rate (avg. births per childbearing woman; 2008): 1.66.
Marriage/divorce rates per 1,000 population (2008): 4.6/2.6.
Life expectancy at birth (2008): male 68.6 years; female 79.2 years.
Major causes of death per 100,000 population (2008): diseases of the circulatory system 676.8; malignant neoplasms (cancers) 264.3; accidents, poisoning, and violence 101.3; diseases of the digestive system 54.1.
Adult population (ages 15–49) *living with HIV* (2009): 1.2% (world avg. 0.8%).

National economy

Budget (2007). Revenue: EEK 69,209,800,000 (tax revenue 59.5%, of which taxes on goods and services 46.7%, taxes on income and profits 12.8%; social contributions 21.6%; grants/nontax revenue 18.9%). Expenditures: EEK 63,085,800,000 (social protection 31.4%; general administration 17.8%; economic affairs 13.1%; education 9.5%; health 7.1%; defense 5.0%).
Production (metric tons except as noted). Agriculture, forestry, fishing (2009): cow's milk 670,554, barley 376,945, wheat 342,520, potatoes 139,050, rapeseed 135,992, oats 86,504; livestock (number of live animals) 346,900 pigs, 237,900 cattle; roundwood 7,560,000 cu m, of which fuelwood 23%; fisheries production 98,100 (from aquaculture, negligible). Mining and quarrying (2008): oil shale 16,100,000; peat 706,000. Manufacturing (value added in U.S.$'000,000; 2007): wood products (excluding furniture) 266; sawn wood 164; furniture 163; food products 145; fabricated metal products (2006) 137; printing and publishing 83. Energy production (consumption): electricity (kW-hr; 2009) 8,736,000,000 ([2008] 7,913,000,000); hard coal (metric tons; 2007) none (130,000); lignite (metric tons; 2009) 14,928,000 ([2007] 16,810,000); crude petroleum, none (none); petroleum products (metric tons; 2009) none (975,000); natural gas (cu m; 2009) none (1,271,000,000).
Population economically active (2008): total 694,900; activity rate of total population 51.8% (participation rates: ages 15–64, 73.6%; female 49.5%; unemployed [April 2010–March 2011] 15.5%).

Price and earnings indexes (2005 = 100)

	2004	2005	2006	2007	2008	2009	2010
Consumer price index	96.1	100.0	104.4	111.3	122.9	122.8	126.4
Monthly earnings index	90.3	100.0	116.5	140.4	159.9	…	…

Household income and expenditure (2005). Average household size (2004) 2.5; average annual disposable income per household member EEK 41,176 (U.S.$3,272); sources of income: wages and salaries 66.1%, transfers 25.6%, self-employment 3.3%; expenditure: food and beverages 28.3%, transportation and communications 16.8%, housing 15.0%, recreation and culture 7.6%.
Public debt (external, outstanding; 2008): U.S.$918,000,000.
Gross national income (GNI; 2010): U.S.$19,247,000,000 (U.S.$14,360 per capita); purchasing power parity GNI (U.S.$19,500 per capita).

Structure of gross domestic product and labour force

	2008 in value EEK '000,000	% of total value	labour force	% of labour force
Agriculture, fishing, forestry, and hunting	5,757	2.3	25,500	3.7
Mining and quarrying	2,258	0.9	6,000	0.9
Manufacturing	37,092	14.9	138,500	19.9
Public utilities	6,009	2.4	8,900	1.3
Construction	18,393	7.4	79,900	11.5
Trade, restaurants	33,923	13.7	117,700	16.9
Transp. and commun.	22,662	9.1	55,700	8.0
Finance, real estate	53,163	21.4	62,300	9.0
Pub. admin., defense	14,110	5.7	38,400	5.5
Services	26,753	10.8	123,600	17.8
Other	28,031[7]	11.3[7]	38,400[8]	5.5[8]
TOTAL	248,149[3]	100.0[3]	694,900	100.0

Selected balance of payments data. Receipts from (U.S.$'000,000): tourism (2009) 1,090; remittances (2010) 342; foreign direct investment (FDI; 2008–10 avg.) 1,703. Disbursements for (U.S.$'000,000): tourism (2009) 606; remittances (2009) 81; FDI (2008–10 avg.) 932.
Land use as % of total land area (2009): in temporary crops 10.0%, left fallow 0.7%, in permanent crops 0.2%, in pasture 7.7%, forest area 52.5%.

Foreign trade[9]

Balance of trade (current prices)

	2005	2006	2007	2008	2009	2010
U.S.$'000,000	–2,454	–3,678	–4,926	–3,631	–914	–359.5
% of total	13.7%	16.1%	17.3%	11.7%	4.2%	1.4%

Imports (2008): U.S.$17,278,000,000 (machinery and apparatus 20.0%, refined petroleum 13.2%, chemicals/chemical products 9.9%, road vehicles 8.9%, food products 7.0%, iron and steel 5.7%). *Major import sources:* Germany 11.8%; Russia 10.1%; Finland 9.7%; Lithuania 6.4%; Sweden 6.3%.
Exports (2008): U.S.$13,695,000,000 (machinery and apparatus 20.0%, sawn wood/wood manufactures [incl. paper/furniture] 11.1%, refined petroleum 9.7%, road vehicles/parts 7.3%, electrical machinery/electronics 6.9%, food products 6.5%, telecommunications equipment 4.3%). *Major export destinations:* Finland 16.7%; Russia 15.1%; Sweden 12.6%; Latvia 9.1%; U.S. 5.7%.

Transport and communications

Transport. Railroads (2009[2]): route length 571 mi, 919 km; passenger-km (2010) 248,000,000; metric ton-km cargo (2010) 6,642,000,000. Roads (2008): total length 3,606 mi, 58,034 km (paved 29%); passenger-km (2006) 12,900,000,000[10]; metric ton-km cargo 8,279,000,000. Vehicles (2009[2]): passenger cars 551,830; trucks and buses 87,642. Air transport (2008): passenger-km 980,000,000; metric ton-km cargo 1,600,000.

Communications

Medium	date	number in '000s	units per 1,000 persons	Medium	date	number in '000s	units per 1,000 persons
Televisions	2003	686	507	PCs	2007	700	522
Telephones				Dailies	2009	227[11]	169[11]
Cellular	2010	1,653[12]	1,232[12]	Internet users	2009	970	724
Landline	2010	482	360	Broadband	2010	327[12]	243[12]

Education and health

Educational attainment (2007). Percentage of population ages 25–64 having: less than upper secondary education 11%; complete upper secondary 56%; higher 33%.

Education (2007–08)

	teachers	students	student/ teacher ratio	enrollment rate (%)
Primary (age 7–12)	6,141	74,629	12.2	94
Secondary/Voc. (age 13–18)	11,272	106,093	9.4	90
Tertiary	6,358[13]	68,168	10.7[13]	64 (age 19–23)

Health: physicians (2008[2]) 4,504 (1 per 298 persons); hospital beds (2008[2]) 7,473 (1 per 179 persons); infant mortality rate per 1,000 live births (2008) 5.0; undernourished population (2004–06) less than 5.0% of total population.

Military

Total active duty personnel (November 2009): 5,450[14] (army 88.1%, navy 7.3%, air force 4.6%). *Military expenditure as a percentage of GDP* (2009): 1.8%; per capita expenditure U.S.$265.

[1]The euro (€) replaced the kroon (EEK) on Jan. 1, 2011, at an exchange rate of €1 = EEK 15.65. [2]January 1. [3]Detail does not add to total given because of rounding. [4]Total includes 1,596 sq mi (4,133 sq km) of Baltic Sea Islands and the areas of small inland lakes. [5]The total area of Estonia including the Estonian portion of Lake Peipus (590 sq mi [1,529 sq km]), Lake Võrtsjärv, and Muuga harbour is 17,462 sq mi (45,227 sq km). [6]Based on land area of 16,367 sq mi (42,390 sq km). [7]Net taxes. [8]Unemployed. [9]Imports c.i.f.; exports f.o.b. [10]Passenger cars 10,000,000,000; buses 2,900,000,000. [11]Circulation. [12]Subscribers. [13]2005–06. [14]Other military groups include the Defence League (12,000) and the Reserve (30,000).

Internet resources for further information:
- **Statistical Office of Estonia http://www.stat.ee**
- **Bank of Estonia http://www.bankofestonia.info**

Ethiopia

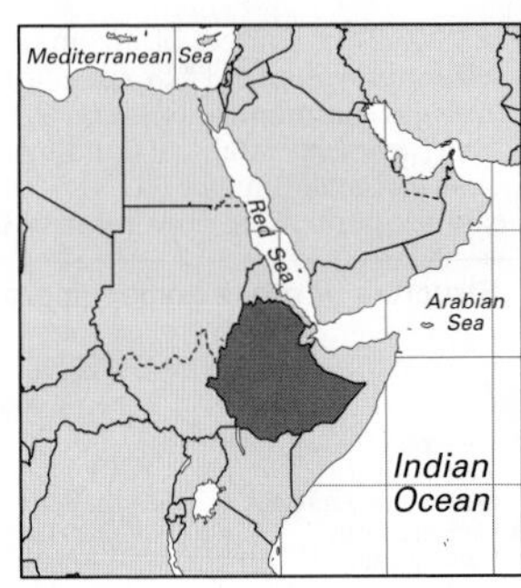

Official name: Federal Democratic Republic of Ethiopia.
Form of government: federal republic with two legislative houses (House of the Federation [135]; House of Peoples' Representatives [547]).
Head of state: President.
Head of government: Prime Minister.
Capital: Addis Ababa.
Official language: none[1].
Official religion: none.
Monetary unit: birr (Br); valuation (Sept. 1, 2011) 1 U.S.$ = Br 17.11; 1 £ = Br 27.66.

Area and population

Regional states	Capitals	area sq mi	area sq km	population 2007 census
Afar (Affar)	Asayita (Asaita)	27,820	72,053	1,390,273
Amhara (Amara)	Bahir Dar	59,733	154,709	17,221,976
Benishangul Gumuz	Asosa (Asossa)	19,575	50,699	784,345
Gambella	Gambella	11,499	29,783	307,096
Harari (Hareri)	Harar (Harer)	129	334	183,415
Oromia (Oromiya)	Addis Ababa	109,861	284,538	26,993,933
Somali (Sumale)	Jijiga	107,820[2]	279,252[2]	4,445,219
Southern Nations, Nationalities and Peoples' (SNNP)	Hawassa (Awasa)	40,725	105,476	14,929,548
Tigray	Mekele	32,711	84,722	4,316,988
Cities				
Addis Ababa	—	203	527	2,739,551
Dire Dawa	—	602	1,559	341,834
TOTAL		410,678	1,063,652	73,750,932[3]

Demography

Population (2011): 82,102,000.
Density (2011): persons per sq mi 199.9, persons per sq km 77.2.
Urban-rural (2007): urban 16.2%; rural 83.8%.
Sex distribution (2007): male 50.46%; female 49.54%.
Age breakdown (2007): under 15, 45.0%; 15–29, 28.3%; 30–44, 14.7%; 45–59, 7.2%; 60–74, 3.7%; 75–84, 0.8%; 85 and over, 0.3%.
Population projection: (2020) 104,677,000; (2030) 129,056,000.
Ethnic composition (2007): Oromo 34.5%; Amhara 26.9%; Somali 6.2%; Tigray 6.1%; Sidamo 4.0%; Gurage 2.5%; Welaita 2.3%; other 17.5%.
Religious affiliation (2007): Orthodox 43.5%; Muslim 33.9%; Protestant 18.6%; traditional beliefs 2.7%; Roman Catholic 0.7%; other 0.6%.
Major cities (2007): Addis Ababa 2,739,551; Dire Dawa 233,224; Adama (Nazret) 220,212; Mekele 215,914; Gonder 207,044; Hawassa 157,139.

Vital statistics

Birth rate per 1,000 population (2008): 44.0 (world avg. 20.3).
Death rate per 1,000 population (2008): 11.8 (world avg. 8.5).
Total fertility rate (avg. births per childbearing woman; 2008): 6.17.
Life expectancy at birth (2008): male 52.5 years; female 57.5 years.
Adult population (ages 15–49) *living with HIV* (2007): 2.1% (world avg. 0.8%).

National economy

Budget (2006–07). Revenue: Br 30,274,000,000 (tax revenue 57.3%, of which import duties 27.0%, income and profits tax 16.1%, sales tax 9.5%; grants 28.0%; nontax revenue 14.7%). Expenditures: Br 35,564,000,000 (capital expenditure 51.7%, of which economic development 32.0%; current expenditure 48.3%, of which education 13.8%, defense 8.4%).
Public debt (external, outstanding; 2009): U.S.$4,812,000,000.
Gross national income (GNI; 2010): U.S.$32,409,000,000 (U.S.$380 per capita); purchasing power parity GNI (U.S.$1,010 per capita).

Structure of gross domestic product and labour force

	2008–09 in value Br '000,000	2008–09 % of total value	1995[4] labour force	1995[4] % of labour force
Agriculture	160,491	47.8	21,605,317	87.8
Mining	1,270	0.4	16,540	0.1
Manufacturing	12,621	3.8	384,955	1.6
Construction	16,074	4.8	61,232	0.2
Public utilities	4,037	1.2	17,066	0.1
Transp. and commun.	12,719	3.8	103,154	0.4
Trade, hotels	56,744	16.9	935,937	3.8
Finance, real estate	29,111	8.7	19,451	0.1
Pub. admin., defense	10,320	3.1	1,252,224	5.1
Services	15,666	4.7		
Other	17,053[5]	5.1[5]	210,184[6]	0.9[6]
TOTAL	336,106	100.0[7]	24,606,060	100.0[7]

Production (metric tons except as noted). Agriculture, forestry, fishing (2009): roots and tubers 7,310,716, corn (maize) 3,897,160, wheat 3,075,640, teff (2008–09) 3,028,000, sorghum 2,971,270, barley 1,750,440, dry broad beans 610,845, chickpeas 312,080, coffee 265,469, sesame seeds 260,534, maté (2007) 260,000; leading producer of beeswax, honey, cut flowers, and khat; livestock (number of live animals) 50,884,000 cattle, 25,979,900 sheep, 21,960,700 goats, 8,076,024 horses, mules, and asses, 2,400,000 camels, (2000) 4,000 civets; roundwood (2010) 102,798,321 cu m, of which fuelwood 97%; fisheries production 17,072 (from aquaculture, negligible). Mining and quarrying (2008): rock salt 260,000; tantalum 37,000 kg; niobium 8,300 kg; gold 3,465 kg. Manufacturing (value added in U.S.$'000,000; 2007): food products 171; bricks, cement, and ceramics 153; beverages 139; textiles 37; tobacco products 32. Energy production (consumption): electricity (kW-hr; 2007–08) 3,530,280,000 ([2007] 3,503,000,000); crude petroleum (barrels; 2005) none (5,640,000); petroleum products (metric tons; 2007) n.a. (1,844,000).
Land use as % of total land area (2009): in temporary crops 11.9%, left fallow 0.6%, in permanent crops 1.0%, in pasture 21.4%, forest area 12.4%.
Population economically active (2008): total 38,149,000[8]; activity rate of total population 47.3%[8] (participation rates: ages 15–64, 85.9%[8]; female 47.1%[8]; unemployed [2005] 5.0%).

Price index (2005 = 100)

	2004	2005	2006	2007	2008	2009	2010
Consumer price index	89.6	100.0	112.3	131.7	190.1	206.1	223.0

Household income and expenditure (1999–2000). Average household size (2004) 5.3; sources of income[9]: self-employment 70.9% (of which agriculture-based 57.6%), wages and salaries 10.9%, salvaging 6.6%, rent 3.9%, other 7.7%; expenditure[9]: food and beverages 52.8%, housing and energy 14.4%, household operations 13.9%, clothing and footwear 7.9%.
Selected balance of payments data. Receipts from (U.S.$'000,000): tourism (2009) 329; remittances (2010) 225; foreign direct investment (2008–10 avg.) 171; official development assistance (2009) 3,820. Disbursements for (U.S.$'000,000): tourism (2009) 138; remittances (2009) 21.

Foreign trade[10]

Balance of trade (current prices)

	2003	2004	2005	2006	2007	2008
U.S.$'000,000	–1,399	–2,090	–2,784	–3,081	–3,871	–5,652
% of total	58.5%	60.6%	60.3%	60.1%	60.1%	64.5%

Imports (2008): U.S.$8,680,000,000 (refined petroleum 22.7%; machinery and apparatus 22.5%; food 10.8%, of which cereals 7.3%; road vehicles 5.9%; iron and steel 5.9%). *Major import sources:* China 20.2%; Saudi Arabia 14.2%; U.A.E. 8.4%; India 7.3%; Italy 5.8%.
Exports (2008): U.S.$1,602,000,000 (coffee 34.7%; sesame seeds 13.1%; legumes 7.3%; cut flowers 6.5%; gold 5.0%; live animals/meat 4.7%; leather 3.8%). *Major export destinations:* Germany 10.5%; Saudi Arabia 7.7%; Neth. 7.4%; U.S. 7.2%; Switzerland 6.2%; China 5.3%.

Transport and communications

Transport. Railroads (2007): route length 423 mi, 681 km[11]; passenger-km (2006–07) 28,200,000[12]; metric ton-km cargo, n.a. Roads (2007–08): total length 44,359 km (paved 14%); passenger-km (2006–07) 9,968,000,000; metric ton-km cargo, n.a. Vehicles (2007): passenger cars 70,893; trucks and buses 166,095. Air transport (2008): passenger-km 9,300,000,000; metric ton-km cargo 227,760,000.

Communications

Medium	date	number in '000s	units per 1,000 persons	Medium	date	number in '000s	units per 1,000 persons
Televisions	2003	547	7.9	PCs	2007	551	7.0
Telephones				Dailies	2009	92[13]	2.0[13]
Cellular	2010	6,517[14]	79[14]	Internet users	2009	445	5.4
Landline	2010	909	11	Broadband	2010	4.1[14]	—[14]

Education and health

Educational attainment (2000)[15]. Percentage of population age 15 and over having: no formal schooling 63.8%; incomplete primary education 21.6%; primary 2.6%; incomplete secondary 8.1%; secondary 2.5%; post-secondary 1.4%. *Literacy* (2007): total population age 15 and over literate 47.5%.

Education (2006–07)

	teachers	students	student/teacher ratio	enrollment rate (%)
Primary (age 7–12)	124,202[16]	12,174,719	66.6[16]	71
Secondary/Voc. (age 13–18)	...	3,430,129	...	24
Tertiary	8,355	210,456	25.2	3 (age 19–23)

Health (2004–05): physicians 1,077 (1 per 66,236 persons); hospital beds (2007–08) 13,145 (1 per 6,062 persons); infant mortality rate per 1,000 live births (2008) 82.6; undernourished population (2005–07) 31,600,000 (41% of total population based on the consumption of a minimum daily requirement of 1,680 calories).

Military

Total active duty personnel (November 2010): 138,000 (army 97.8%, air force 2.2%); mandate for the UN peacekeeping force along the Ethiopian-Eritrean border was terminated in July 2008. *Military expenditure as percentage of GDP* (2009): 1.1%; per capita expenditure U.S.$4.

[1]Amharic is the "working" language. [2]Estimate. [3]Includes special enumeration areas having a population of 96,754. [4]For ages 10 and up. [5]Taxes on products less imputed bank service charges. [6]First-time job seekers. [7]Detail does not add to total given because of rounding. [8]Estimate of the ILO Employment Trends Unit. [9]Based on the national Household Income and Expenditure Survey, comprising 17,332 households. [10]Imports f.o.b. in balance of trade and c.i.f. in commodities and trading partners. [11]Length of Ethiopian segment of Addis Ababa–Djibouti railroad; rehabilitation of railway was under way from 2007. [12]Includes Djibouti part of Addis Ababa–Djibouti railroad. [13]Circulation of daily newspapers. [14]Subscribers. [15]Based on the national Ethiopian Demographic and Health Survey, comprising 14,072 households. [16]2003–04.

Internet resources for further information:

- **Central Statistical Agency of Ethiopia http://www.csa.gov.et**
- **National Bank of Ethiopia http://www.nbe.gov.et**

Faroe Islands[1]

Official name: Føroyar (Faroese); Færøerne (Danish) (Faroe Islands).
Political status: self-governing overseas administrative division of Denmark with one legislative house (Løgting, or Parliament [33]).
Head of state: Danish Monarch.
Heads of government: High Commissioner (for Denmark); Prime Minister (for Faroe Islands).
Capital: Tórshavn (Thorshavn).
Official languages: Faroese; Danish.
Official religion: Faroese Lutheran[2].
Monetary unit: Danish krone[3] (DKK); valuation (Sept. 1, 2011) 1 U.S.$ = DKK 5.23; 1 £ = DKK 8.45.

Area and population

Regions[5]	Largest municipalities	area sq mi	area sq km	population 2011[4] estimate
Eysturoy	Runavík	110	286	10,839
Nordhoy (Northern)	Klaksvík	93	241	5,824
Sandoy	Skopun	48	125	1,358
Streymoy	Tórshavn	151	392	22,766
Sudhuroy	Tvøroyri	64	167	4,721
Vágar	Sørvágur	73	188	3,066
TOTAL		540[6]	1,399	48,574

Demography

Population (2011): 48,600.
Density (2011): persons per sq mi 90.0, persons per sq km 34.7.
Urban-rural (2011[4]): urban 41.0%; rural 59.0%.
Sex distribution (2011[4]): male 51.94%; female 48.06%.
Age breakdown (2011[4]): under 15, 21.7%; 15–29, 18.8%; 30–44, 19.4%; 45–59, 19.3%; 60–74, 13.9%; 75–84, 4.9%; 85 and over, 2.0%.
Population projection: (2020) 50,900; (2030) 53,800.
Ethnic composition (2000): Faroese 97.0%; Danish 2.5%; other Scandinavian 0.4%; other 0.1%.
Religious affiliation (2005): Protestant *c.* 91%, of which Lutheran *c.* 79%, Plymouth Brethren *c.* 10%; other (mostly nonreligious) *c.* 9%.
Major municipalities (2011[4]): Tórshavn 19,919; Klaksvík 4,817; Runavík 3,832; Eystur 1,977; Vága 1,940.

Vital statistics

Birth rate per 1,000 population (2010): 13.1 (world avg. 19.2); within marriage (1998) 62.0%; outside of marriage (1998) 38.0%.
Death rate per 1,000 population (2010): 7.2 (world avg. 8.2).
Natural increase rate per 1,000 population (2010): 5.9 (world avg. 11.0).
Total fertility rate (avg. births per childbearing woman; 2010): 2.47.
Marriage/divorce rates per 1,000 population (2010): 4.8/1.9.
Life expectancy at birth (2008): male 76.8 years; female 82.3 years.
Major causes of death per 100,000 population (2009): diseases of the circulatory system 262.8; malignant neoplasms (cancers) 193.5; diseases of the respiratory system 78.0; accidents, poisoning, and violence 49.3; diseases of the digestive system 24.6.

National economy

Budget (2009). Revenue: DKK 4,042,000,000 (tax revenue 84.3%, transfers from the Danish government 15.7%). Expenditures: DKK 4,544,000,000 (current expenditure 94.9%, development expenditure 5.1%).
Gross national income (at current market prices; 2009): U.S.$2,232,190,000 (U.S.$45,822 per capita).

Structure of gross domestic product and labour force

	2009 in value DKK '000,000[7]	2009 % of total value[7]	2008 labour force	2008 % of labour force
Agriculture	1,818[8]	17.8[8]	77	0.3
Mining	—	—	74	0.3
Fishing/fish processing	[8]	[8]	4,546	17.5
Manufacturing (excluding fish-related)	397	3.9	969	3.7
Construction	702	6.9	2,057	7.9
Public utilities	147	1.4	148	0.6
Transp. and commun.	898	8.8	1,951	7.5
Trade, hotels	1,079	10.6	3,828	14.7
Finance and real estate	1,692	16.6	1,759	6.8
Pub. admin., defense	669	6.6	9,202	35.4
Services	2,795	27.4	827	3.2
Other	—	—	572[9]	2.2[9]
TOTAL	10,198[6]	100.0	26,010	100.0[6]

Production (metric tons except as noted). Agriculture, forestry, fishing (2010): potatoes (2009) 1,500, other vegetables, grass, hay, and silage are produced; livestock (number of live animals; 2009) 68,000 sheep, 1,990 cattle; roundwood, n.a.; fisheries production 393,875 (including herring 87,576, mackerel 71,641, blue whiting 52,301, pollock 48,991, and cod 33,003; from aquaculture 10% [including salmon 37,221]). Pilot whales captured (2010) 1,107. Mining and quarrying: negligible[10]. Manufacturing: principally fish processing; also handicrafts, woolen textiles and clothing, and small ship repair. Energy production (consumption): electricity (kW-hr; 2010) 280,323,000 ([2008] 264,000,000); coal, none (none); crude petroleum, none (none); petroleum products (metric tons; 2009) none (216,551); natural gas, none (none).

Population economically active (2010): total 28,970; activity rate of total population 59.6% (participation rates: ages 15–74, 83.5%; female 45.7%; unemployed [August 2010–July 2011] 6.5%).

Price and earnings indexes (2005 = 100)

	2004	2005	2006	2007	2008	2009	2010
Consumer price index	96.7	100.0	101.5	105.1	111.7	110.5	111.0
Annual earnings index	95.1	100.0	106.7	114.0	111.4	105.9	...

Public debt (external, outstanding; January 2009): U.S.$511,448,000.
Household income and expenditure. Average household size: n.a.; average annual income per household: n.a.; sources of income: n.a.; expenditure (1998)[11]: food and beverages 25.1%, transportation and communications 17.7%, housing 12.5%, recreation 11.9%, energy 7.7%.
Selected balance of payments data. Receipts from (U.S.$'000,000): tourism (2005) *c.* 25; remittances (2003) 44; foreign direct investment (FDI), n.a. Disbursements for (U.S.$'000,000): tourism, n.a.; remittances (2008) 5; FDI, n.a.
Land use as % of total land area (2007): in temporary crops, left fallow, or in permanent crops 2.1%; in pasture, n.a.; forest area 0.1%.

Foreign trade[12]

Balance of trade (current prices)

	2005	2006	2007	2008	2009	2010
DKK '000,000	–904	–823	–1,466	–690	–101	–274
% of total	11.2%	9.6%	15.3%	7.4%	1.2%	3.0%

Imports (2008): DKK 5,013,000,000 (goods for household consumption 26.9%; fuels, lubricants, and electric current 21.0%; goods for the construction industry 10.9%; machinery and apparatus 10.0%; road vehicles 5.5%). *Major import sources* (2010): Denmark 34.2%; Norway 17.7%; Sweden 7.0%; Germany 6.3%; China 4.4%.
Exports (2008): DKK 4,323,000,000 (chilled and frozen fish 63.3%; ships/boats and related products 14.0%; salted fish 10.4%; dried, smoked, canned, and other conserved fish 8.1%). *Major export destinations* (2010): United Kingdom 16.3%; Germany 11.4%; Denmark 10.4%; France 8.9%; Norway 5.2%.

Transport and communications

Transport. Railroads: none. Roads (2007): total length 292 mi, 470 km (paved 99%); passenger-km, n.a.; metric ton-km cargo, n.a. Vehicles (2011[4]): passenger cars 19,897; trucks, vans, and buses 4,560. Air transport (2010)[13]: passenger-km 285,000,000; metric ton-km cargo (2010) n.a.

Communications

Medium	date	number in '000s	units per 1,000 persons	Medium	date	number in '000s	units per 1,000 persons
Televisions	2008	16[14]	304[14]	PCs	2007	...	...
Telephones				Dailies	2010	26[15]	544[15]
Cellular	2010	59[14]	1,221[14]	Internet users	2009	38	752
Landline	2010	20	414	Broadband	2010	16[14]	334[14]

Education and health

Educational attainment (2008). Percentage of population age 15–74 having: no formal schooling to complete primary education 30%; incomplete/complete secondary 45%; incomplete/complete higher 25%. *Literacy:* n.a.

Education (2005–06)

	teachers	students	student/ teacher ratio	enrollment rate (%)
Primary (age, n.a.)	...	5,567[16]	...	...
Secondary/Voc. (age, n.a.)	...	3,446[16]	...	...
Tertiary[17]	22	150	6.8	...

Health (2007): physicians 88 (1 per 549 persons); hospital beds 243 (1 per 199 persons); infant mortality rate per 1,000 live births 4.5; undernourished population, n.a.

Military

Defense responsibility lies with Denmark.

[1]English-language alternative spelling is Faeroe Islands. [2]Formally independent of the national Danish Lutheran church from July 2007. [3]The local currency, the Faroese króna (plural krónur), is equivalent to the Danish krone. Banknotes used are Faroese or Danish; coins are Danish. [4]January 1. [5]Represents the 5 main islands (with associated islets) and the northeasternmost (Northern) islands. Actual local administration is based on 34 municipalities. [6]Detail does not add to total given because of rounding. [7]At factor cost. [8]Agriculture includes Fishing/fish processing. [9]Includes 429 unemployed. [10]The maritime boundary demarcation agreement between the Shetland Islands (U.K.) and the Faroes in 1999 has allowed for the still unsuccessful exploration for deep-sea petroleum as of mid-2011. [11]Weights of consumer price index components. [12]Imports c.i.f.; exports f.o.b. [13]Atlantic Airways only. [14]Subscribers. [15]Circulation. [16]2002–03. [17]University of the Faroe Islands.

Internet resources for further information:
- **Statistics Faroe Islands**
  http://www.hagstova.fo
- **Governmental Bank of the Faroe Islands**
  http://landsbankin.fo/Default.asp
- **Danmarks Statistik**
  http://www.dst.dk/HomeUK.aspx

Fiji

Official name: Republic of the Fiji Islands[1, 2].
Form of government: interim regime[3,4]
Head of state: President.
Head of government: Prime Minister.
Capital: Suva.
Official languages: [2].
Official religion: none.
Monetary unit: Fiji dollar (F$); valuation (Sept. 1, 2011) 1 U.S.$ = F$1.73; 1 £ = F$2.80.

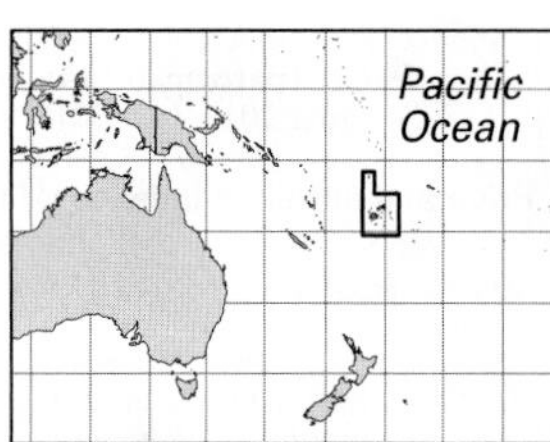

Area and population

Divisions Provinces	area sq km	population 2007 census	Divisions Provinces	area sq km	population 2007 census
Central	4,293[5]	342,389	Northern	6,199[6]	135,956
Naitasiri	1,666	160,759	Bua	1,379	14,176
Namosi	570	6,898	Cakaudrove	2,816	49,339
Rewa	272	100,791	Macuata	2,004	72,441
Serua	830	18,249	Western	6,360[5]	319,613
Tailevu	955	55,692	Ba	2,634	231,762
Eastern	1,376	37,311	Nadroga/Navosa	2,385	58,387
Kadavu	478	10,167	Ra	1,341	29,464
Lau	487	10,683	Fijian dependency		
Lomaiviti	411	16,461	Rotuma	46	2,002
			TOTAL	18,272[7]	837,271

Demography

Population (2011): 852,000.
Density (2011): persons per sq mi 120.8, persons per sq km 46.6.
Urban-rural (2009): urban 51.5%; rural 48.5%.
Sex distribution (2008): male 50.82%; female 49.18%.
Age breakdown (2008): under 15, 29.8%; 15–29, 27.5%; 30–44, 20.5%; 45–59, 14.6%; 60–74, 6.4%; 75–84, 1.1%; 85 and over, 0.1%.
Population projection: (2020) 890,000; (2030) 946,320.
Doubling time: 50 years.
Ethnic composition (2007): Fijian 56.8%; Indian 37.5%; other Pacific islanders 3.0%, of which Rotuman (Polynesian/other) 1.2%; European/part-European 1.7%; Chinese 0.6%; other 0.4%.
Religious affiliation (2007): Christian 64.4%, of which Methodist 34.6%, Roman Catholic 9.1%, Assemblies of God 5.7%; Hindu 27.9%; Muslim 6.3%; other 1.4%.
Major urban areas (2007): Nasinu 87,446[8]; Suva 85,691 (urban agglomeration 241,432); Lautoka 52,220; Nausori 47,604[8]; Nadi 42,284.

Vital statistics

Birth rate per 1,000 population (2008): 21.5 (world avg. 20.3).
Death rate per 1,000 population (2008): 7.4 (world avg. 8.5).
Natural increase rate per 1,000 population (2008): 14.1 (world avg. 11.8).
Total fertility rate (avg. births per childbearing woman; 2008): 2.81.
Marriage/divorce rates per 1,000 population (2004): 8.6/n.a.
Life expectancy at birth (2008): male 67.9 years; female 73.1 years.
Major causes of death per 100,000 population (2008): diseases of the circulatory system 250.9; endocrine, nutritional, and metabolic diseases 152.2; malignant neoplasms (cancers) 73.0; infectious and parasitic diseases 47.9; accidents and violence 45.4; diseases of the respiratory system 42.3.

National economy

Budget (2008). Revenue: F$1,455,000,000 (direct taxes 30.1%, VAT 27.6%, customs duties 22.8%, fees and fines 7.5%, other 12.0%). Expenditures: F$1,427,000,000 (current expenditure 81.5%, remainder 18.5%).
Public debt (external, outstanding; June 2010): U.S.$282,000,000.
Production (metric tons except as noted). Agriculture, forestry, fishing (2009): sugarcane 2,089,000, coconuts 150,000, taro 69,863, cow's milk 59,000, cassava 42,332, chicken meat 11,642, rice 11,637, cattle meat 8,358, ginger 3,041, yaqona (kava) 2,603; livestock (number of live animals) 312,000 cattle, 3,500,000 chickens; roundwood (2010) 482,205 cu m, of which fuelwood 8%; fisheries production 39,850 (from aquaculture, 1%). Mining and quarrying (2009–10[9]): gold 1,856 kg. Manufacturing (value added in U.S.$'000,000; 2004): food products 63; textiles and clothing 53; beverages 46; sawn wood and wood products including furniture 28. Energy production (consumption): electricity (kW-hr; 2007) 836,000,000 (837,000,000); coal (metric tons; 2007) none (1,000); crude petroleum, none (none); petroleum products (metric tons; 2007) none (452,000); natural gas, none (none).
Household income and expenditure. Average household size (2007) 4.7; average annual income per household (2002–03) F$12,753 (U.S.$6,176); sources of income (2002–03): wages and salaries 54.0%, self-employment 17.1%; expenditure (2005): food and nonalcoholic beverages 40.3%, transportation 16.2%, housing 9.9%, energy 9.2%.
Population economically active (2007): total 334,787; activity rate of total population 40.0% (participation rates: ages 15–64, 57.0%; female 33.9%; unemployed [2009] 8.6%).

Price index (2005 = 100)

	2004	2005	2006	2007	2008	2009	2010
Consumer price index	97.7	100.0	102.5	107.4	115.7	120.0	126.6

Gross national income (GNI; 2010): U.S.$3,085,000,000 (U.S.$3,610 per capita); purchasing power parity GNI (U.S.$4,490 per capita).

Structure of gross domestic product and labour force

	2008 in value F$'000,000[10]	2008 % of total value	2004 labour force[11]	2004 % of labour force[11]
Agriculture, fishing	619.6	14.1	89,523	28.3
Mining	7.9	0.2	3,222	1.0
Manufacturing	592.5	13.5	43,088	13.6
Construction	129.2	2.9	16,950	5.4
Public utilities	53.0	1.2	2,508	0.8
Transp. and commun.	626.6	14.3	22,551	7.1
Trade, hotels	725.7	16.6	66,043	20.9
Finance, real estate	879.6	20.1	10,220	3.2
Pub. admin., defense	284.2	6.5	61,936	19.6
Services	462.0	10.5		
TOTAL	4,380.3	100.0[7]	316,041	100.0[7]

Selected balance of payments data. Receipts from (U.S.$'000,000): tourism (2009) 422; remittances (2010) 183; foreign direct investment (2008–10 avg.) 199; official development assistance (2009) 71. Disbursements for (U.S.$'000,000): tourism (2009) 94; remittances (2009) 44.
Land use as % of total land area (2009): in temporary crops or left fallow 8.8%, in permanent crops 4.5%, in pasture 9.6%, forest area 55.3%.

Foreign trade[12, 13]

Balance of trade (current prices)

	2004	2005	2006	2007	2008	2009
F$'000,000	–1,029	–1,536	–1,945	–1,680	–2,130	–1,578
% of total	30.8%	39.3%	45.3%	41.0%	42.0%	39.1%

Imports (2008): F$3,601,000,000 (mineral fuels 33.9%, machinery and transport equipment 20.2%, food products 14.4%). *Major import sources:* Singapore 34.8%; Australia 19.7%; New Zealand 13.3%; U.S. 6.7%; China 4.3%.
Exports (2008): F$1,471,000,000 (reexports [mostly petroleum products] 33.2%, sugar 16.9%, fish 9.1%, mineral water [2007] 9.1%, clothing 6.9%, lumber 4.0%). *Major export destinations:* U.K. 14.9%; Australia 12.3%; U.S. 12.2%; other Pacific Islands 10.5%; New Zealand 5.6%.

Transport and communications

Transport. Railroads (2007)[14]: track length 370 mi, 595 km. Roads (2002): total length 2,140 mi, 3,440 km (paved 49%). Vehicles (2007): passenger cars 94,387; trucks and buses 50,218. Air transport (2008)[15]: passenger-km 3,809,000,000; metric ton-km cargo 75,000,000.

Communications

Medium	date	number in '000s	units per 1,000 persons	Medium	date	number in '000s	units per 1,000 persons
Televisions	2003	98	118	PCs	2004	44	52
Telephones				Dailies	2009	40[16]	48[16]
Cellular	2010	1,000[17]	1,162[17]	Internet users	2009	114	134
Landline	2010	137	159	Broadband	2010	16[17]	19[17]

Education and health

Educational attainment (1996). Percentage of population age 25 and over having: no formal schooling 4.4%; some education 22.3%; incomplete secondary 47.7%; complete secondary 17.0%; some higher 6.7%; university degree 1.9%. *Literacy* (2003): total population age 15 and over literate 93.7%; males 95.5%; females 91.9%.

Education (2007–08)

	teachers	students	student/ teacher ratio	enrollment rate (%)
Primary (age 6–11)	3,939	102,543	26.0	89
Secondary/Voc. (age 12–18)	5,265	98,561	18.7	79[18]
Tertiary	943	12,717[19]	...	15[19] (age 19–23)

Health (2008): physicians 352 (1 per 2,381 persons); hospital beds 1,743 (1 per 481 persons); infant mortality rate per 1,000 live births 13.1; undernourished population (2005–07) less than 5% of total population.

Military

Total active duty personnel (November 2010): 3,500 (army 91.4%, navy 8.6%, air force, none); reserve *c.* 6,000.[20] *Military expenditure as percentage of GDP* (2009): 1.9%; per capita expenditure U.S.$62.

[1]Fijian long/short-form names: Matanitu Tu-Vaka-i-koya ko Viti/Viti; Hindustani long-form name: Fiji Ripablik. [2]English, Fijian, and Hindustani (Fijian Hindi) had equal status per 1997 constitution. [3]Backed by the military from December 2006; the 1997 constitution was not formally abrogated until April 2009. [4]The people's charter, a precursor to a possible new constitution, was approved by the president in late December 2008. [5]Central and Western divisions together (10,653 sq km) comprise Viti Levu (10,429 sq km), Fiji's main island, and smaller nearby islands. [6]Northern division (6,199 sq km) is composed mostly of Fiji's second largest island, Vanua Levu (5,556 sq km). [7]Detail does not add to total given because of rounding. [8]Within Suva urban agglomeration. [9]For fiscal year ending August 31; Vatukuolamine only. [10]At constant prices of 2005. [11]Data for paid employees only who are 15 and over. [12]Imports c.i.f.; exports f.o.b. [13]All export data include reexports. [14]All privately owned sugarcane-related railways. [15]Air Pacific only. [16]Circulation. [17]Subscribers. [18]2005–06. [19]2004–05. [20]Peacekeepers abroad (both UN and non-UN) 570.

Internet resources for further information:
- **Fiji Islands Bureau of Statistics http://www.statsfiji.gov.fj**
- **Reserve Bank of Fiji http://www.reservebank.gov.fj**

Finland

Official names[1]: Suomen Tasavalta (Finnish); Republiken Finland (Swedish) (Republic of Finland).
Form of government: multiparty republic with one legislative house (Parliament [200]).
Head of state: President.
Head of government: Prime Minister.
Capital: Helsinki.
Official languages: none[1].
Official religion: none.
Monetary unit: euro (€); valuation (Sept. 1, 2011) 1 U.S.$ = €0.70; 1 £ = €1.13.

Area and population[2]

Regions	area sq km	population 2009[3] estimate
Finland, Central	16,707	271,747
Finland, Southwest	10,663	461,177
Kainuu	21,504	83,160
Kanta-Häme	5,200	173,041
Karelia, North	17,763	166,129
Karelia, South	5,613	134,448
Kymenlaakso	5,112	182,754
Lapland	92,664	183,963
Ostrobothnia	7,749	175,985
Ostrobothnia, Central	5,273	71,029
Ostrobothnia, North	35,236	386,144
Ostrobothnia, South	13,444	193,511
Päijät-Häme	5,127	200,847
Satakunta	7,957	227,652
Savo, North	16,771	248,423
Savo, South	13,986	156,632
Tampere Region	12,447	480,705
Uusimaa	6,395	1,408,020
Uusimaa, East	2,736	93,491
Autonomous Region		
Åland (Aland Islands)	1,553	27,456
TOTAL LAND AREA	303,899[4]	
FRESHWATER AREA	34,526	
TOTAL	338,424[4]	5,326,314

Demography

Population (2011): 5,387,000.
Density (2011)[5]: persons per sq mi 45.9, persons per sq km 17.7.
Urban-rural (2009): urban 84.8%; rural 15.2%.
Sex distribution (2009): male 49.06%; female 50.94%.
Age breakdown (2009): under 15, 16.6%; 15–29, 18.8%; 30–44, 18.8%; 45–59, 21.4%; 60–74, 16.4%; 75–84, 6.0%; 85 and over, 2.0%.
Population projection: (2020) 5,619,000; (2030) 5,833,000.
Linguistic composition (2009): Finnish 90.8%; Swedish 5.4%; Russian 0.9%; other 2.9%.
Religious affiliation (2009): Evangelical Lutheran 79.9%; nonreligious 17.7%; Finnish (Greek) Orthodox 1.1%; other 1.3%.
Major cities (2011[3]): Helsinki 588,549 (urban agglomeration [2007] 1,115,000); Espoo 247,970[6]; Tampere 213,217; Vantaa 200,055[6]; Turku 177,326.

Vital statistics

Birth rate per 1,000 population (2010): 11.4 (world avg. 19.2); within marriage 58.9%; outside of marriage 41.1%.
Death rate per 1,000 population (2010): 9.5 (world avg. 8.2).
Total fertility rate (avg. births per childbearing woman; 2010): 1.87.
Marriage/divorce rates per 1,000 population (2010): 5.6/2.6.
Life expectancy at birth (2009): male 76.5 years; female 83.2 years.
Major causes of death per 100,000 population (2008): cardiovascular disease 379.1; malignant neoplasms (cancers) 211.1; diseases of the nervous system 93.4; accidents and violence 70.1; diseases of the respiratory system 37.2.

National economy

Budget (2009). Revenue: €46,291,000,000 (tax revenue 80.6%, of which turnover taxes 33.0%, income and property taxes 30.9%, excise duties 11.1%; other 19.4%). Expenditures: €46,291,000,000 (social security and health 20.5%; education 13.2%; agriculture and forestry 6.1%; defense 6.0%).
Production (metric tons except as noted). Agriculture, forestry, fishing (2010): barley 1,340,200, oats 809,700, wheat 724,400, potatoes 659,100, sugar beets 542,100; livestock (number of live animals[7]) 1,366,900 pigs, 925,800 cattle, (2009) 193,000 reindeer; roundwood 50,951,529 cu m, of which fuelwood 10%; fisheries production (2009) 168,219 (from aquaculture 8%). Mining and quarrying (2009): talc 500,000; zinc (metal content) 56,415; copper (metal content) 13,000. Manufacturing (value added in €'000,000; 2010): electrical and optical equipment (largely telephone apparatus) 3,892; nonelectrical machinery and apparatus 3,492; paper and paper products 2,875; food and beverages 2,453; fabricated metal products 2,290; chemicals and chemical products 1,682; base metals 1,345. Energy production (consumption): electricity (kW-hr; 2010–11) 76,164,000,000 ([2007] 93,806,000,000); hard coal (metric tons; 2010–11) none (5,541,000); crude petroleum (barrels; 2008) none ([2007] 81,600,000); petroleum products (metric tons; 2007) 13,381,000 (10,656,000); natural gas (cu m; 2007) none (4,438,000,000).
Land use as % of total land area (2007): in temporary crops 4.5%, left fallow 0.8%, in permanent crops 0.03%, in pasture 2.3%, forest area 74.0%.
Population economically active (2008): total 2,725,600; activity rate of total population 51.3% (participation rates: ages 15–64, 76.1%; female 47.8%; unemployed [April 2010–March 2011] 8.2%).

Price and earnings indexes (2005 = 100)

	2004	2005	2006	2007	2008	2009	2010
Consumer price index	99.1	100.0	101.6	104.1	108.4	108.4	109.7
Hourly earnings index	96.2	100.0	102.6	106.6	112.3	115.7	117.2

Household income and expenditure (2004). Average household size 2.2; disposable income per household €31,706 (U.S.$39,367); sources of gross income (2003): wages and salaries 74.4%, rent 18.0%, self-employment 7.1%; expenditure (2008): housing and energy 24.9%, food and nonalcoholic beverages 12.4%, recreation and culture 11.9%, transportation 11.7%.
Gross national income (GNI; 2010): U.S.$252,958,000,000 (U.S.$47,170 per capita); purchasing power parity GNI (U.S.$37,180 per capita).

Structure of gross domestic product and labour force

	2007 in value U.S.$'000,000	2007 % of total value	2006 labour force	2006 % of labour force
Agriculture, fishing, forestry	6,021	2.5	114,000	4.3
Manufacturing	49,692	20.3	465,000	17.6
Mining and public utilities	5,436	2.2	...	...
Construction	12,338	5.1	162,000	6.1
Transp. and commun.	22,285	9.1	181,000	6.8
Trade, restaurants	25,671	10.5	381,000	14.4
Finance, real estate			336,000	12.7
Pub. admin., defense; Services	91,093	37.2	801,000	30.2
Other	32,156	13.1	208,000[8]	7.9[8]
TOTAL	244,692	100.0	2,648,000	100.0

Public debt (March 2010; central government only): U.S.$94,500,000,000.
Selected balance of payments data. Receipts from (U.S.$'000,000): tourism (2009) 2,814; remittances (2010) 872; foreign direct investment (FDI; 2008–10 avg.) 1,092. Disbursements for (U.S.$'000,000): tourism (2009) 4,373; remittances (2009) 436; FDI (2008–10 avg.) 7,171.

Foreign trade[9]

Balance of trade (current prices)

	2004	2005	2006	2007	2008	2009
€'000,000	+8,187	+5,426	+6,237	+6,073	+3,213	+1,753
% of total	9.1%	5.5%	5.3%	4.8%	2.5%	2.0%

Imports (2008): €62,938,000,000 (machinery and apparatus 25.8%, petroleum 13.3%, chemicals and chemical products 10.4%, road vehicles/parts 8.6%, base/fabricated metals 8.2%). *Major import sources:* Russia 16.3%; Germany 14.0%; Sweden 10.0%; China 7.0%; Neth. 4.1%.
Exports (2008): €66,151,000,000 (telecommunications equipment/parts 13.4%, paper and cardboard 11.4%, iron and steel 7.0%, specialized machinery for particular industries 6.7%, refined petroleum 6.5%, general industrial machinery 5.7%, road vehicles 4.9%). *Major export destinations:* Russia 11.6%; Sweden 10.1%; Germany 10.0%; U.S. 6.3%; U.K. 5.5%.

Transport and communications

Transport. Railroads (2009)[10]: route length 3,678 mi, 5,919 km; passenger-km 3,900,000,000; metric ton-km cargo 8,900,000,000. Roads (2009)[10]: total length 48,567 mi, 78,161 km (paved [2007] 65%); passenger-km (2008) 70,900,000,000[11]; metric ton-km cargo (2008) 29,856,000,000. Vehicles (2011[3]): passenger cars 2,877,484; trucks and buses 490,704. Air transport (2010–11): passenger-km 17,881,000,000; metric ton-km cargo 813,770,000.

Communications

Medium	date	number in '000s	units per 1,000 persons
Televisions	2003	3,540	679
Telephones			
Cellular	2010	8,390[13]	1,564[13]
Landline	2010	1,250	233
PCs	2007	2,644	500
Dailies	2009	2,049[12]	384[12]
Internet users	2009	4,481	841
Broadband	2010	1,559[13]	291[13]

Education and health

Educational attainment (2004[3]). Percentage of population age 25 and over having: incomplete upper-secondary education 35.6%; complete upper secondary or vocational 35.8%; higher 28.6%. *Literacy:* virtually 100%.

Education (2007–08)

	teachers	students	student/ teacher ratio	enrollment rate (%)
Primary (age 7–12)	24,830	357,403	14.4	96
Secondary/Voc. (age 13–18)	42,991	431,233	10.0	96
Tertiary	14,225	309,648	21.8	94 (age 19–23)

Health: physicians (2009) 19,500 (1 per 274 persons); hospital beds (2007) 36,095 (1 per 147 persons); infant mortality rate per 1,000 live births (2010) 2.3; undernourished population (2004–06) less than 5.0% of total population.

Military

Total active duty personnel (November 2010): 22,250 (army 71.9%, navy 15.7%, air force 12.4%); reserve 350,000. *Military expenditure as percentage of GDP* (2010): 1.5%; per capita expenditure U.S.$669.

[1]Finnish and Swedish are national (not official) languages. [2]Administrative changes from Jan. 1, 2010: the regions created in 1997 (as second-order administrative subdivisions except for Åland) replaced the 5 former provinces as first-order administrative subdivisions. [3]January 1. [4]Detail does not add to total given because of rounding. [5]Based on land area only. [6]Within Helsinki urban agglomeration. [7]From farms of 1 hectare and larger only. [8]Includes 204,000 unemployed persons not previously employed and 4,000 not adequately defined. [9]Imports c.i.f.; exports f.o.b. [10]Excludes Åland. [11]Passenger cars 63,400,000,000; buses 7,500,000,000. [12]Circulation. [13]Subscribers.

Internet resources for further information:
- **Statistics Finland http://www.stat.fi/index_en.html**
- **Bank of Finland http://www.suomenpankki.fi/en**

France[1]

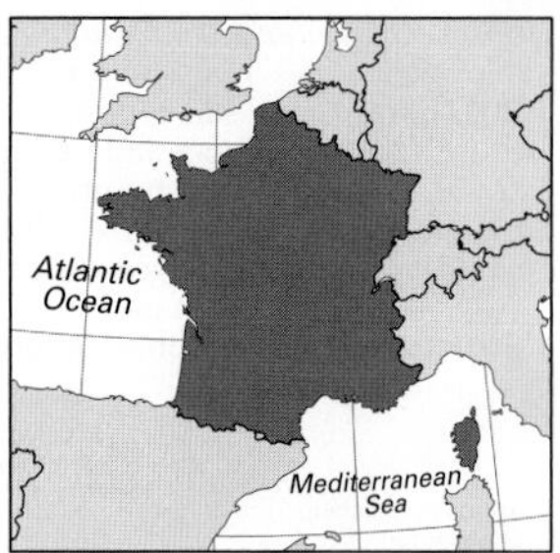

Official name: République Française (French Republic).
Form of government: republic with two legislative houses (Parliament; Senate [348], National Assembly [577]).
Head of state: President.
Head of government: Prime Minister.
Capital: Paris.
Official language: French.
Official religion: none.
Monetary unit: euro (€); valuation (Sept. 1, 2011) 1 U.S.$ = €0.70; 1 £ = €1.13.

Area and population

Regions / Departments	Capitals	area sq mi	area sq km	population 2008[2] estimate
Alsace	Strasbourg			1,837,500
Bas-Rhin	Strasbourg	1,836	4,755	1,091,000
Haut-Rhin	Colmar	1,361	3,525	746,500
Aquitaine	Bordeaux			3,175,500
Dordogne	Périgueux	3,498	9,060	408,500
Gironde	Bordeaux	3,861	10,000	1,422,500
Landes	Mont-de-Marsan	3,569	9,243	371,500
Lot-et-Garonne	Agen	2,070	5,361	326,000
Pyrénées-Atlantiques	Pau	2,952	7,645	647,000
Auvergne	Clermont-Ferrand			1,341,500
Allier	Moulins	2,834	7,340	342,500
Cantal	Aurillac	2,211	5,726	148,500
Haute-Loire	Le Puy-en-Velay	1,922	4,977	221,500
Puy-de-Dôme	Clermont-Ferrand	3,077	7,970	629,000
Basse-Normandie (Lower Normandy)	Caen			1,464,000
Calvados	Caen	2,142	5,548	676,000
Manche	Saint-Lô	2,293	5,938	496,000
Orne	Alençon	2,356	6,103	292,000
Bourgogne (Burgundy)	Dijon			1,636,000
Côte-d'Or	Dijon	3,383	8,763	520,500
Nièvre	Nevers	2,632	6,817	221,000
Saône-et-Loire	Mâcon	3,311	8,575	552,500
Yonne	Auxerre	2,868	7,427	342,000
Bretagne (Brittany)	Rennes			3,141,000
Côtes-d'Armor	Saint-Brieuc	2,656	6,878	579,000
Finistère	Quimper	2,600	6,733	888,500
Ille-et-Vilaine	Rennes	2,616	6,775	965,500
Morbihan	Vannes	2,634	6,823	708,000
Centre	Orléans			2,535,000
Cher	Bourges	2,793	7,235	314,500
Eure-et-Loir	Chartres	2,270	5,880	424,000
Indre	Châteauroux	2,622	6,791	232,500
Indre-et-Loire	Tours	2,366	6,127	585,500
Loir-et-Cher	Blois	2,449	6,343	327,500
Loiret	Orléans	2,616	6,775	651,000
Champagne-Ardenne	Châlons-en-Champagne			1,338,500
Ardennes	Charleville-Mézières	2,019	5,229	284,000
Aube	Troyes	2,318	6,004	302,000
Haute-Marne	Chaumont	2,398	6,211	186,500
Marne	Châlons-en-Champagne	3,151	8,162	566,000
Corse (Corsica)[3]	Ajaccio			303,000
Corse-du-Sud	Ajaccio	1,550	4,014	141,500
Haute-Corse	Bastia	1,802	4,666	161,500
Franche-Comté	Besançon			1,163,000
Doubs	Besançon	2,021	5,234	522,500
Haute-Saône	Vesoul	2,070	5,360	238,000
Jura	Lons-le-Saunier	1,930	4,999	259,500
Territoire de Belfort	Belfort	235	609	143,000
Haute-Normandie (Upper Normandy)	Rouen			1,819,500
Eure	Évreux	2,332	6,040	575,500
Seine-Maritime	Rouen	2,424	6,278	1,244,000
Île-de-France	Paris			11,672,500
Essonne	Évry	696	1,804	1,209,500
Hauts-de-Seine	Nanterre	68	176	1,557,500
Paris	Paris	40	105	2,199,500
Seine-et-Marne	Melun	2,284	5,915	1,301,500
Seine-Saint-Denis	Bobigny	91	236	1,517,000
Val-de-Marne	Créteil	95	245	1,311,500
Val-d'Oise	Cergy/Pontoise	481	1,246	1,167,000
Yvelines	Versailles	882	2,284	1,409,000
Languedoc-Roussillon	Montpellier			2,587,500
Aude	Carcassonne	2,370	6,139	349,500
Gard	Nîmes	2,260	5,853	696,500
Hérault	Montpellier	2,356	6,101	1,023,000
Lozère	Mende	1,995	5,167	77,000
Pyrénées-Orientales	Perpignan	1,589	4,116	441,500
Limousin	Limoges			739,000
Corrèze	Tulle	2,261	5,857	242,500
Creuse	Guéret	2,149	5,565	123,500
Haute-Vienne	Limoges	2,131	5,520	373,000
Lorraine	Metz			2,341,000
Meurthe-et-Moselle	Nancy	2,024	5,241	727,500
Meuse	Bar-le-Duc	2,400	6,216	194,000
Moselle	Metz	2,400	6,216	1,039,500
Vosges	Épinal	2,268	5,874	380,000
Midi-Pyrénées	Toulouse			2,837,500
Ariège	Foix	1,888	4,890	150,000
Aveyron	Rodez	3,373	8,736	275,500
Gers	Auch	2,416	6,257	184,500
Haute-Garonne	Toulouse	2,436	6,309	1,220,000
Haute-Pyrénées	Tarbes	1,724	4,464	229,000
Lot	Cahors	2,014	5,217	172,000
Tarn	Albi	2,223	5,758	372,000
Tarn-et-Garonne	Montauban	1,435	3,718	234,500
Nord-Pas-de-Calais	Lille			4,022,000
Nord	Lille	2,217	5,742	2,563,000
Pas-de-Calais	Arras	2,576	6,671	1,459,000

Area and population (continued)

Regions / Departments	Capitals	area sq mi	area sq km	population 2008[2] estimate
Pays de la Loire	Nantes			3,510,500
Loire-Atlantique	Nantes	2,631	6,815	1,259,000
Maine-et-Loire	Angers	2,767	7,166	775,000
Mayenne	Laval	1,998	5,175	302,000
Sarthe	Le Mans	2,396	6,206	559,500
Vendée	La Roche-sur-Yon	2,595	6,720	615,000
Picardie (Picardy)	Amiens			1,903,500
Aisne	Laon	2,845	7,369	537,500
Oise	Beauvais	2,263	5,860	799,500
Somme	Amiens	2,382	6,170	566,500
Poitou-Charentes	Poitiers			1,749,500
Charente	Angoulême	2,300	5,956	350,500
Charente-Maritime	La Rochelle	2,650	6,864	609,500
Deux-Sèvres	Niort	2,316	5,999	365,000
Vienne	Poitiers	2,699	6,990	424,500
Provence-Alpes–Côte d'Azur	Marseille			4,900,500
Alpes-de-Haute-Provence	Digne	2,674	6,925	157,500
Alpes-Maritimes	Nice	1,660	4,299	1,089,500
Bouches-du-Rhône	Marseille	1,964	5,087	1,973,000
Hautes-Alpes	Gap	2,142	5,549	133,500
Var	Toulon	2,306	5,973	1,005,000
Vaucluse	Avignon	1,377	3,567	542,000
Rhône-Alpes	Lyon			6,113,000
Ain	Bourg-en-Bresse	2,225	5,762	580,500
Ardèche	Privas	2,135	5,529	312,000
Drôme	Valence	2,521	6,530	477,500
Haute-Savoie	Annecy	1,694	4,388	715,000
Isère	Grenoble	2,869	7,431	1,188,500
Loire	Saint-Étienne	1,846	4,781	741,500
Rhône	Lyon	1,254	3,249	1,689,000
Savoie	Chambéry	2,327	6,028	409,000
TOTAL		210,026[4]	543,965[4]	62,131,000

Demography

Population (2011): 63,292,000[5].
Density (2011): persons per sq mi 301.4, persons per sq km 116.4.
Urban-rural (2009): urban 84.6%; rural 15.4%.
Sex distribution (2010[2]): male 48.43%; female 51.57%.
Age breakdown (2010[2]): under 15, 18.3%; 15–29, 18.8%; 30–44, 19.9%; 45–59, 20.1%; 60–74, 14.0%; 75–84, 6.4%; 85 and over, 2.5%.
Population projection: (2020) 66,071,000; (2030) 68,672,000.
Ethnic composition (2000): French 76.9%; Algerian and Moroccan Berber 2.2%; Italian 1.9%; Portuguese 1.5%; Moroccan Arab 1.5%; Fleming 1.4%; Algerian Arab 1.3%; Basque 1.3%; Jewish 1.2%; German 1.2%; Vietnamese 1.0%; Catalan 0.5%; other 8.1%.
Religious affiliation (2004): Roman Catholic 64.3%, of which practicing *c.* 8%; nonreligious/atheist *c.* 27%; Muslim 4.3%; Protestant 1.9%; Buddhist *c.* 1%; Jewish 0.6%; Jehovah's Witness 0.4%; Orthodox 0.2%; other 0.3%.
Major cities/urban agglomerations (2008): Paris 2,211,297/10,354,675; Marseille 851,420/1,560,343; Lyon 474,946/1,521,030; Lille 225,784/1,012,634; Nice 344,875/947,337; Toulouse 439,553/864,936; Bordeaux 235,891/832,605; Nantes 283,288/584,683; Toulon 166,733/559,421; Douai-Lens: Douai 42,413, Lens 36,120/509,953; Grenoble 156,659/495,429; Rouen 109,425/464,282; Strasbourg 272,116/450,375; Montpellier 252,998/383,972; Saint-Étienne 172,696/371,513; Tours 135,480/344,799; Valenciennes 42,656/333,920; Rennes 206,655/305,270; Metz 122,838/290,523; Nancy 106,361/286,733.
Households (2004). Average household size (2006) 2.31; 1 person 32.8%, 2 persons 32.5%, 3 persons 15.1%, 4 persons 12.8%, 5 persons or more 6.8%. Individual households 14,320,000 (56.0%); collective households 11,232,000 (44.0%).
Immigration: total immigrant population (2005[2]) *c.* 4,850,000; immigrants admitted (2002) 205,707, of which North African 30.7%, EU 20.8%, sub-Saharan African 15.2%, Asian 14.1%, other European 11.8%.

Vital statistics

Birth rate per 1,000 population (2009): 12.6 (world avg. 20.3); within marriage (2008) 47.5%; outside of marriage (2008) 52.5%.
Death rate per 1,000 population (2009): 8.6 (world avg. 8.5).
Total fertility rate (avg. births per childbearing woman; 2009): 1.98.
Marriage/divorce rates per 1,000 population: (2009) 4.0/(2008) 2.1.
Life expectancy at birth (2009): male 77.8 years; female 84.5 years.
Major causes of death per 100,000 population (2007): malignant neoplasms (cancers) 241.6; diseases of the circulatory system 237.9; accidents and violence 59.2; diseases of the respiratory system 51.7; diseases of the digestive system 37.1.
Adult population (ages 15–49) *living with HIV* (2009): 0.4% (world avg. 0.8%).

Social indicators

Educational attainment (2006). Percentage of population age 15 and over with no formal schooling through incomplete secondary education 45.5%, complete lower vocational 21.2%, complete secondary 13.3%, incomplete/complete higher 19.8%, unknown 0.2%.
Quality of working life. Legally worked week for full-time employees (2009) 35.0 hours. Rate of fatal injuries per 100,000 insured workers (2007): 3.4. Average days lost to labour stoppages per 1,000 workers (2008): 107. Trade union membership (2003): 1,900,000 (*c.* 8% of labour force).
Access to services (2004). Proportion of principal residences having: electricity 97.4%; indoor toilet 94.6%; indoor kitchen with sink 94.2%; hot water 60.3%; air conditioner 15.4%.
Social participation. Eligible voters participating in last (May 2007) national election: 84.0%. Population over 15 years of age participating in voluntary associations (2008): *c.* 16%. Percentage of population who "never" or "almost never" attend church services (2000) 60%; percentage of Roman Catholic population who attend Mass weekly (2003) 12%.

Social deviance. Offense rate per 100,000 population (2006) for: murder 1.5, rape 16.0, other assault 269.2; theft (including burglary and housebreaking) 3,403.8. Incidence per 100,000 in general population of: homicide (2001) 0.8; suicide (2001) 16.1.
Leisure (2007). Members of sports federations: 16,254,000, of which football (soccer) 2,321,000. Movie tickets sold: 178,000,000. Average daily hours of television viewing for population age 4 and over: 3.45.
Material well-being (2004). Households possessing: automobile (2007) 82%; colour television 95%; personal computer 45%; washing machine 92%; microwave 74%; dishwasher (2001) 39%.

National economy

Gross national income (GNI; 2010)[6]: U.S.$2,749,821,000,000 (U.S.$42,390 per capita); purchasing power parity GNI (U.S.$34,440 per capita).

Structure of gross domestic product and labour force

	2008			
	in value €'000,000	% of total value	labour force	% of labour force
Agriculture, forestry, fishing	35,000	1.8	789,100	2.8
Mining and quarrying	...	...	25,500	0.1
Manufacturing	203,800	10.5	3,877,200	13.9
Construction	117,100	6.0	1,860,000	6.6
Public utilities	37,400	1.9	201,200	0.7
Transp. and commun.	77,400	4.0	1,640,700	5.9
Trade, hotels	174,300	8.9	4,291,800	15.3
Finance, real estate	633,900	32.5	3,578,100	12.8
Pub. admin., defense	135,200	6.9	2,652,500	9.5
Services	338,300	17.4	6,795,300	24.3
Other	197,600[7]	10.1[7]	2,271,800[8]	8.1[8]
TOTAL	1,950,100[9]	100.0	27,983,500[9]	100.0

Budget (2007). Revenue: €369,600,000,000 (tax revenue 80.0%, of which taxes on goods and services 43.6%; social contributions 10.9%; grants 4.5%). Expenditures: €411,410,000,000 (social protection 20.0%; education 19.4%; economic affairs 13.8%; debt service 11.1%; defense 8.2%).
Public debt (2010): U.S.$2,003,150,000,000.
Production (metric tons except as noted). Agriculture, forestry, fishing (2009): wheat 38,332,200, sugar beets 35,066,600, cow's milk 23,341,000, corn (maize) 15,288,200, barley 12,875,800, potatoes 7,226,310, grapes 6,101,620, rapeseed 5,588,730, triticale 2,015,600, apples 1,953,600, sunflower seeds 1,713,290, goat's milk 623,460, tomatoes 603,296, oats 572,976, dry peas 546,846, cauliflower and broccoli 378,224, string beans 338,162, carrots and turnips 300,000, duck meat 235,985, apricots 190,382, leeks 171,250, chicory roots 163,975, spinach 130,580, mushrooms and truffles 117,934, flax fibre and tow 67,000, garlic 19,315; livestock (number of live animals) 19,199,300 cattle, 14,810,000 pigs, 7,715,200 sheep, 183,000,000 chickens, 24,300,000 ducks, 23,500,000 turkeys; roundwood (2010) 57,362,134 cu m, of which fuelwood 45%; fisheries production 645,098 (from aquaculture 36%); aquatic plants production 18,694 (from aquaculture, negligible). Mining and quarrying (2008): gypsum 3,500,000; crude talc 420,000; kaolin 300,000; gold[10] 1,500 kg. Manufacturing (value added in U.S.$'000,000; 2006): chemicals and chemical products 35,549; transportation equipment 33,822, of which motor vehicles 13,459, aircraft and spacecraft 9,499; fabricated metal products 27,754; food and food products 20,939; general purpose machinery 14,188; printing and publishing 13,651; electrical machinery and apparatus 11,262; medical, measuring, and testing appliances 10,592; plastic products 9,985; base metals 8,753; bricks, cement, and ceramics 8,414; electronics 8,127; special purpose machinery 7,294; textiles and wearing apparel 6,376; beverages 6,068; paper and paper products 5,189; furniture 4,503.

Financial aggregates[11]	2005	2006	2007	2008	2009	2010
Exchange rate, € per:						
U.S. dollar	0.85	0.76	0.68	0.72	0.69	0.75
£	1.46	1.49	1.36	1.01	1.13	1.17
SDR	1.21	1.14	1.07	1.07	1.09	1.15
International reserves (U.S.$)						
Total (excl. gold; '000,000)	27,753	42,652	45,710	33,617	46,633	55,800
SDRs ('000,000)	878	948	995	966	15,234	15,000
Reserve pos. in IMF ('000,000)	2,878	1,417	1,127	2,270	3,671	4,589
Foreign exchange	23,996	40,287	43,587	30,382	27,729	36,211
Gold ('000,000 fine troy oz)	90.85	87.44	83.69	80.13	78.30	78.30
% world reserves	10.3	11.2	11.5	12.0	12.4	8.0
Interest and prices						
Central bank discount (%)	...	...	...	...	...	...
Govt. bond yield (%)	3.41	3.80	4.30	4.23	3.65	3.12
Industrial share prices (2005 = 100)[12]	100.0	119.8	134.3	101.8	78.3	87.9
Balance of payments (U.S.$'000,000)						
Balance of visible trade	–27,840	–38,120	–56,810	–87,280	–59,940	–71,210
Imports, f.o.b.	–467,290	–522,890	–605,340	–692,600	–535,820	–588,360
Exports, f.o.b.	439,450	484,770	548,530	605,330	475,870	517,150
Balance of invisibles	+17,580	+25,130	+30,200	+37,400	+20,070	+26,710
Balance of payments, current account	–10,260	–12,990	–26,610	–49,880	–39,870	–44,500

Energy production (consumption): electricity (kW-hr; 2009) 518,123,000,000 ([2007] 513,027,000,000[13]); hard coal (metric tons; 2009) 147,000 (16,756,000); lignite (metric tons; 2007) negligible (51,000[13]); crude petroleum (barrels; 2009–10) 6,663,000 ([2009] 684,375,000); petroleum products (metric tons; 2007) 73,923,000[13] (72,997,000[13]); natural gas (cu m; 2008–09) 837,663,800 ([2009] 44,840,000,000).
Retail trade (value of sales in €'000,000; 2004): large food stores 162,600; large nonfood stores 136,400; auto repair shops 120,400; pharmacies and stores selling orthopedic equipment 32,600; shops selling bread, pastries, or meat 31,800; small food stores and boutiques 15,300.
Population economically active (2008): total 27,983,500; activity rate of total population 44.9% (participation rates: ages 15–64, 70.1%; female 47.5%; unemployed [July 2009–June 2010] 9.8%).

Price index (2005 = 100)	2004	2005	2006	2007	2008	2009	2010
Consumer price index	98.3	100.0	101.7	103.2	106.1	106.2	107.8

Household income and expenditure. Average household size (2006) 2.3; average disposable income per household (2004) €28,340 (U.S.$35,187); sources of income (2004): wages and salaries 66%, transfers 23%, self-employment 7%, other 4%; expenditure (2009): housing and energy 19.7%, transportation 10.9%, food and nonalcoholic beverages 10.4%, recreation and culture 7.0%, restaurants and hotels 4.7%, household furnishings 4.5%.
Selected balance of payments data. Receipts from (U.S.$'000,000): tourism (2009) 49,450; remittances (2010) 15,373; foreign direct investment (FDI; 2008–10 avg.) 44,039. Disbursements for (U.S.$'000,000): tourism (2009) 38,575; remittances (2009) 5,224; FDI (2008–10 avg.) 114,036.
Land use as % of total land area (2009): in temporary crops 26.5%, left fallow 1.3%, in permanent crops 1.9%, in pasture 23.8%, forest area 29.0%.

Foreign trade[14]

Balance of trade (current prices)	2004	2005	2006	2007	2008	2009
U.S.$'000,000	–4,850	–27,840	–38,120	–55,930	–86,880	–75,400
% of total	0.6%	3.1%	3.8%	4.9%	6.7%	7.6%

Imports (2008)[13]: U.S.$695,004,000,000 (machinery and apparatus 20.4%, of which electrical machinery/apparatus/parts 5.0%, general industrial machinery 4.1%; mineral fuels 16.9%, of which crude petroleum 8.6%, refined petroleum 3.7%; chemicals and chemical products 12.8%, of which medicines and pharmaceuticals 3.6%; road vehicles/parts 10.0%; apparel and clothing accessories 3.4%; iron and steel 3.4%). *Major import sources:* Germany 16.4%; Belgium 8.5%; Italy 8.1%; Spain 6.5%; China 6.5%; U.S. 5.5%; U.K. 4.8%; Neth. 4.1%; Russia 2.9%; Switzerland 2.3%.
Exports (2008)[13]: U.S.$594,505,000,000 (machinery and apparatus 24.9%, of which electrical machinery/apparatus/parts 5.9%; chemicals and chemical products 16.8%, of which medicines and pharmaceuticals 5.6%, perfumery and cosmetics 2.4%; road vehicles/parts 10.1%; food 8.2%; aircraft/parts 6.4%; mineral fuels 5.1%, of which petroleum 3.4%; iron and steel 3.9%; alcoholic beverages [mostly wine] 2.4%). *Major export destinations:* Germany 14.6%; Italy 8.8%; Spain 8.4%; U.K. 7.9%; Belgium 7.6%; U.S. 5.9%; Neth. 4.2%; Switzerland 3.0%; China 2.2%; Russia 1.7%.

Transport and communications

Transport. Railroads (2008): route length (in operation) 18,152 mi, 29,213 km; passenger-km (2009) 86,307,000,000; metric ton-km cargo 41,190,000,000. Roads (2007): total length 591,001 mi, 951,125 km (paved 100%); passenger-km (2006) 768,900,000,000; metric ton-km cargo 211,445,000,000. Vehicles (2007): passenger cars 30,700,000; trucks and buses 6,353,000. Air transport (2009–10)[15]: passenger-km 123,784,000,000; metric ton-km cargo (2009) 11,155,000,000.

Communications Medium	date	number in '000s	units per 1,000 persons	Medium	date	number in '000s	units per 1,000 persons
Televisions	2004	23,723	391	PCs	2007	40,400	652
Telephones				Dailies	2009	7,362[16]	118[16]
Cellular	2010	62,600[17]	997[17]	Internet users	2009	44,625	716
Landline	2010	35,200	561	Broadband	2010	21,300[17]	339[17]

Education and health

Education (2007–08)	teachers	students	student/ teacher ratio	enrollment rate (%)
Primary (age 6–10)	217,428	4,139,284	19.0	98
Secondary/Voc. (age 11–17)	480,564	5,899,298	12.3	98
Tertiary	110,441	2,164,538	19.6	55 (age 18–22)

Health (2008): physicians 213,821 (1 per 291 persons); hospital beds 440,656 (1 per 141 persons); infant mortality rate per 1,000 live births (2009) 3.6; undernourished population (2005–07) less than 5.0% of total population.

Military

Total active duty personnel (November 2010): 341,967[18] (army 38.2%, navy 11.8%, air force 15.4%, other staff 4.4%, gendarmerie 30.2%). *Military expenditure as percentage of GDP* (2008): 2.3%[6, 19]; per capita expenditure U.S.$1,047[6, 19].

[1]Since 2005 international and country sources are more likely to combine social and economic data for the four French overseas departments (FODs; that is, French Guiana, Guadeloupe, Martinique, and Réunion) with metropolitan France. *Britannica World Data* continues to compile separate pages for the four FODs and acknowledges that some data are without a doubt double-counted. Data for France are footnoted if taken from an international source that clearly cites the inclusion of the FODs. [2]January 1. [3]Commonly referred to as a region but officially a territorial collectivity with special status. [4]Area including four FODs equals 244,317 sq mi (632,777 sq km). [5]Excludes population of four FODs totaling 1,903,000 people in mid-2011. [6]Includes the overseas departments of French Guiana, Guadeloupe, Martinique, and Réunion. [7]Taxes on products less subsidies. [8]Includes 2,070,000 unemployed. [9]Detail does not add to total given because of rounding. [10]Metal content. [11]Data are end of year unless otherwise indicated. [12]Period average. [13]Includes Monaco. [14]Imports f.o.b. in balance of trade and c.i.f. in commodities and trading partners. [15]Air France only. [16]Circulation. [17]Subscribers. [18]About 22,000 troops are stationed outside of metropolitan France, including *c.* 3,750 in Afghanistan, *c.* 2,800 in Germany, and *c.* 1,700 in Djibouti. [19]Includes military pensions.

Internet resource for further information:
- **INSEE http://www.insee.fr/en**

French Guiana

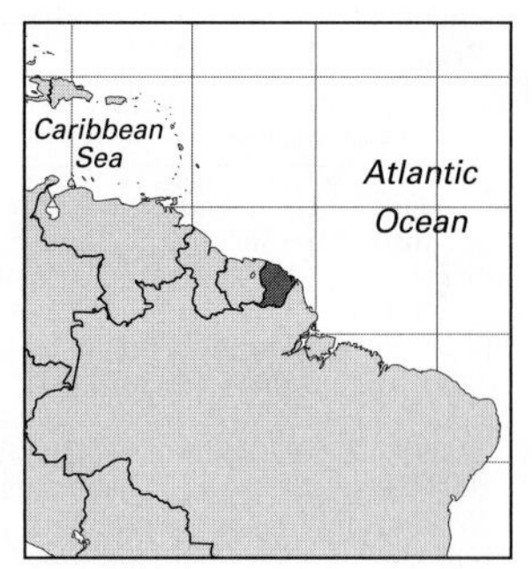

Official name: Département d'Outre-Mer de la Guyane française (Overseas Department of French Guiana).[1]
Political status: overseas department/overseas region of France with two legislative houses (General Council[2] [19]; Regional Council[3] [31]).
Head of state: President of France.
Heads of government: Prefect (for France); President of the General Council (for French Guiana); President of the Regional Council (for French Guiana).
Capital: Cayenne.
Official language: French.
Official religion: none.
Monetary unit: euro (€); valuation (Sept. 1, 2011) 1 U.S.$ = €0.70; 1 £ = €1.13.

Area and population

		area		population
Arrondissements	**Capitals**	sq mi	sq km	2008[4] estimate
Cayenne	Cayenne	17,727	45,913	153,352
Saint-Laurent-du-Maroni	Saint-Laurent-du-Maroni	14,526	37,621	65,914
TOTAL		32,253	83,534	219,266

Demography

Population (2011): 243,000.
Density (2011): persons per sq mi 7.5, persons per sq km 2.9.
Urban-rural (2009): urban 76.1%; rural 23.9%.
Sex distribution (2009[4]): male 49.51%; female 50.49%.
Age breakdown (2009[4]): under 15, 35.1%; 15–29, 23.6%; 30–44, 21.5%; 45–59, 13.5%; 60–74, 4.7%; 75 and over, 1.6%.
Population projection: (2020) 303,000; (2030) 374,000.
Doubling time: 29 years.
Ethnic composition (2000): Guianese Mulatto 37.9%; French 8.0%; Haitian 8.0%; Surinamese 6.0%; Antillean 5.0%; Chinese 5.0%; Brazilian 4.9%; East Indian 4.0%; other (other West Indian, Hmong, other South American) 21.2%.
Religious affiliation (2000): Christian 84.6%, of which Roman Catholic 80.0%, Protestant 3.9%; Chinese folk-religionist 3.6%; Spiritist 3.5%; nonreligious/atheist 3.0%; traditional beliefs 1.9%; Hindu 1.6%; Muslim 0.9%; other 0.9%.
Major cities (2008[4])[5]: Cayenne (2009) 62,000 (urban agglomeration 76,519); Saint-Laurent-du-Maroni 35,631; Kourou 25,934; Matoury 25,629[6]; Rémire-Montjoly 18,817[6].

Vital statistics

Birth rate per 1,000 population (2009): 26.9 (world avg. 20.3); within marriage 12.1%; outside of marriage 87.9%.
Death rate per 1,000 population (2009): 3.1 (world avg. 8.5).
Natural increase rate per 1,000 population (2009): 23.8 (world avg. 11.8).
Total fertility rate (avg. births per childbearing woman; 2009): 3.20.
Marriage/divorce rates per 1,000 population (2009): 2.7/0.9.
Life expectancy at birth (2009): male 72.8 years; female 80.1 years.
Major causes of death per 100,000 population (2008): diseases of the circulatory system 71.5; malignant neoplasms (cancers) 60.7; external causes 58.4; diseases of the digestive system 18.4; infectious and parasitic diseases 18.0.

National economy

Budget (2008)[7]. Revenue: €287,300,000 (current revenue 85.2%, of which tax revenue 59.4%, grants and subsidies 16.8%, other revenue 9.0%; capital revenue 14.8%). Expenditures: €272,800,000 (current expenditure 80.2%; capital expenditure 19.8%).
Production (metric tons except as noted). Agriculture, forestry, fishing (2009): cassava 28,624, rice (2010) 9,481, cabbages 4,317, tomatoes 4,036, sugarcane 4,000, taro 3,753, bananas 3,733, plantains 3,320, pineapples 2,967, lemons and limes 1,351; livestock (number of live animals) 20,000 pigs, 14,000 cattle; roundwood (2010) 215,254 cu m, of which fuelwood 57%; fisheries production 4,169 (from aquaculture 1%). Mining and quarrying (2009): clays 5,000; gold (metal content) 2,000 kg[8]. Manufacturing (2010): cement (2009) 62,000; rum 1,803 hectolitres; other products include finished wood products, leather goods, clothing, rosewood essence, yogurt, and beer. Number of launches from the Guiana Space Centre at Kourou (2010): 6[9]. Energy production (consumption): electricity (kW-hr; 2008) 763,000,000 ([2009] 722,000,000); coal, none (none); crude petroleum, none (none); petroleum products (metric tons; 2007) none (282,000); natural gas, none (none).
Household income and expenditure (2007). Average household size 3.5; income per household (2000) €30,542 (U.S.$28,139); sources of income: wages and salaries 81.5%, self-employment 6.3%; expenditure (2005)[10]: food and beverages 21.7%, housing and energy 20.8%, transportation and communications 15.4%, restaurants and hotels 7.9%, household furnishings 7.3%, clothing and footwear 6.4%.
Land use as % of total land area (2007): in temporary crops or left fallow 0.14%, in permanent crops 0.04%, in pasture 0.08%, forest area 91.5%.
Gross domestic product (at current market prices; 2008): U.S.$4,693,000,000 (U.S.$20,806 per capita).

Structure of gross domestic product and labour force

	2007		2002	
	in value €'000,000	% of total value	labour force[11]	% of labour force[11]
Agriculture, forestry, fishing	136	5.1	1,024	2.1
Mining			409	0.8
Manufacturing	221	8.2	1,053	2.1
Construction	239	8.9	2,583	5.2
Public utilities	63	2.3	644	1.3
Transp. and commun.	159	5.9	2,134	4.3
Trade, restaurants, hotels	259	9.6	4,815	9.8
Finance, real estate			830	1.7
Pub. admin., defense	1,672	62.0	9,758	19.8
Services			14,975	30.4
Other	–53	–2.0	11,095	22.5
TOTAL	2,696	100.0	49,320	100.0

Population economically active (2009): total 70,701; activity rate of total population 30.6% (participation rates [2008]: ages 15 and over, 50.9%; female 45.9%; unemployed [June 2010] 21.0%).

Price and earnings indexes (2005 = 100)[12]

	2003	2004	2005	2006	2007	2008	2009
Consumer price index	97.1	98.6	100.0	103.3	106.4	110.0	110.9
Monthly earnings index[13]	93.5	94.0	100.0	103.1	105.1	108.5	110.2

Selected balance of payments data. Receipts from (U.S.$'000,000): tourism (2007) 49; remittances, n.a.; foreign direct investment, n.a. Disbursements for (U.S.$'000,000): tourism, n.a.; remittances, n.a.

Foreign trade

Balance of trade (current prices)

	2005	2006	2007	2008	2009	2010
€'000,000	–641	–627	–779	–951	–825	–924
% of total	77.5%	71.8%	70.0%	82.6%	77.5%	74.5%

Imports (2009): €944,700,000 (machinery and apparatus 21.8%, food and agricultural products 16.4%, mineral fuels 15.7%, road vehicles 12.8%). *Major import sources:* France *c.* 37%; other EU *c.* 10%; Latin America *c.* 6%.
Exports (2009): €119,700,000 (motor vehicles/parts 28.1%, gold 21.1%, electrical machinery and electronics 20.9%, fish 5.3%, shrimp 5.3%, transport equipment 4.3%). *Major export destinations:* France *c.* 44%; other EU *c.* 25%.

Transport and communications

Transport. Railroads: none. Roads (2010[4]): total length 815 mi, 1,311 km (paved, n.a.). Vehicles (2001): passenger cars 32,900; trucks and buses 11,900. Air transport (2007)[14]: passenger-km 55,000,000; metric ton-km cargo, n.a.

Communications

Medium	date	number in '000s	units per 1,000 persons	Medium	date	number in '000s	units per 1,000 persons
Televisions	1998	37	202	PCs	2004	33	168
Telephones				Dailies	2009	15[15]	65[15]
Cellular	2009	218[16]	965[16]	Internet users	2009	58	257
Landline	2010	46	197	Broadband	2010	30[16]	134[16]

Education and health

Educational attainment (1999). Percentage of population age 20 and over having: no formal education through lower secondary education 57.3%; vocational 17.5%; upper secondary 9.3%; incomplete higher 5.6%; completed higher 6.7%; other 3.6%. *Literacy:* n.a.

Education (2008–09)

	teachers	students	student/ teacher ratio	enrollment rate (%)
Primary (age 6–11)	2,139[17]	40,178	...	...
Secondary/Voc. (age 12–18)[18]	2,129[17]	28,758	...	...
Tertiary	...	...	...	... (age 19–23)

Health (2009): physicians[4] 397 (1 per 560 persons); hospital beds (2010[4]) 792 (1 per 289 persons); infant mortality rate per 1,000 live births 10.4; undernourished population, n.a.

Military

Total active duty personnel (November 2010): French troops *c.* 1,600 (army [including the French Foreign Legion] *c.* 90%, navy *c.* 9%, air force, n.a., gendarmerie *c.* 1%).

[1]French Guiana is simultaneously administered as an overseas region (*région d'outre-mer*). [2]Assembly for overseas department. [3]Assembly for overseas region. [4]January 1. [5]Commune population. [6]Within Cayenne urban agglomeration. [7]Data are for budget managed by French Guiana's Regional Council. [8]Legal production only. [9]In 2004 the European Space Agency accounted for 26% of GDP and employed 8,300. [10]Weights of consumer price index components. [11]Employed only. [12]Indices based on end-of-year figures. [13]Based on minimum-level wage in public administration. [14]Air Guyane Express. [15]Circulation. [16]Subscribers. [17]2004–05. [18]Excludes vocational.

Internet resources for further information:
- **IEDOM Guyane: http://www.iedom.fr/guyane**
- **INSEE Guyane http://www.insee.fr/fr/regions/guyane**

French Polynesia

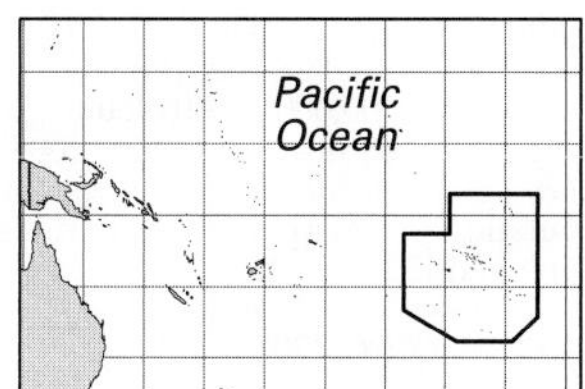

Official name: Pays d'Outre-Mer de la Polynésie Française (French) (Overseas Country of French Polynesia).[1]
Political status: overseas collectivity (France) with one legislative house (Assembly [57]).
Head of state: President of France.
Heads of government: High Commissioner (for France); President of the Government (for French Polynesia).
Capital: Papeete.
Official language: French.
Official religion: none.
Monetary unit: CFP franc (CFPF); valuation (Sept. 1, 2011) 1 U.S.$ = CFPF 83.74; 1 £ = CFPF 135.32.

Area and population

Administrative subdivisions/ Principal islands	area sq km	population 2007 census	Administrative subdivisions/ Principal islands	area sq km	population 2007 census
Îles Australes	148	6,304	Îles Sous le Vent	404	33,165
Îles du Vent	1,194	194,683	Bora-Bora		8,930
Moorea		16,208	Raiatea		12,008
Tahiti		178,173	Îles Tuamotu et Gambier	726	16,896
Îles Marquises	1,049	8,658	TOTAL	4,000[2]	259,706

Demography

Population (2011): 272,000.
Density (2011)[3]: persons per sq mi 200.1, persons per sq km 77.2.
Urban-rural (2009): urban 51.3%; rural 48.7%.
Sex distribution (2007): male 51.25%; female 48.75%.
Age breakdown (2007): under 15, 26.0%; 15–29, 26.6%; 30–44, 23.4%; 45–59, 15.3%; 60–74, 6.9%; 75 and over, 1.8%.
Population projection: (2020) 296,000; (2030) 316,000.
Ethnic composition (2000): Polynesian 58.4%, of which Tahitian 41.0%, Tuamotuan 8.5%; mixed European-Polynesian 17.0%; Han Chinese 11.3%; French 11.0%; other 2.3%.
Religious affiliation (2005): Protestant *c.* 36%, of which Maōhi Protestant Church (Presbyterian) *c.* 33%; Roman Catholic *c.* 31%; other Christian *c.* 11%, of which Mormon *c.* 6%; Chinese folk-religionist, nonreligious, and other *c.* 22%.
Major communes (2007): Faaa 29,781[4]; Papeete 26,050 (urban agglomeration 131,695[5]); Punaauia 25,399[4]; Pirae 14,551[4]; Nunue 4,927[6].

Vital statistics

Birth rate per 1,000 population (2009): 17.0 (world avg. 20.3); within marriage (2004) *c.* 26%; outside of marriage (2004) *c.* 74%.
Death rate per 1,000 population (2009): 4.3 (world avg. 8.5).
Total fertility rate (avg. births per childbearing woman; 2008): 2.18.
Marriage/divorce rates per 1,000 population (2009): 4.0/n.a.
Life expectancy at birth (2008): male 73.0 years; female 78.2 years.
Major causes of death per 100,000 population (2005): diseases of the circulatory system 123.0; malignant neoplasms (cancers) 114.4; diseases of the respiratory system 53.5; accidents and violence 52.7.

National economy

Budget (2009)[7]. Revenue: CFPF 140,567,000,000 (tax revenue 76.1%, loans 8.1%, nontax revenue 2.9%, other 12.9%). Expenditures: CFPF 140,567,000,000 (current expenditure 75.4%, capital expenditure 17.0%, debt service 7.6%).
Production (metric tons except as noted). Agriculture, forestry, fishing (2009): coconuts 97,100, cassava 3,640, pineapples 3,500, hen's eggs 2,740, *noni*[8] juice and puree (export production) 2,634, tomatoes 1,630, pig meat 1,220, cow's milk 1,200, vanilla 74; livestock (number of live animals) 31,000 pigs, 270,000 chickens; roundwood (2010) 5,380 cu m, of which fuelwood 81.4%; fisheries production 12,473 (from aquaculture, negligible); export production of black pearls (2010) 16,042 kg. Mining and quarrying: submerged phosphate deposits at Mataiva Atoll were not mined in 2009. Manufacturing (2009): copra 11,466; coconut oil 6,879; other manufactures include (2008) beer, dairy products, *monoï* oil (primarily refined coconut and sandalwood oils), printed cloth, and sandals. Energy production (consumption): electricity (kW-hr; 2008) 670,000,000 (623,000,000); coal, none (none); crude petroleum, none (none); petroleum products (metric tons; 2007) none (261,000); natural gas, none (none).
Population economically active (2007): total 107,926; activity rate of total population 41.6% (participation rates: ages 15 and over, 56.2%; female 41.0%; unemployed 11.7%).

Price index (2005 = 100)

	2004	2005	2006	2007	2008	2009	2010
Consumer price index	97.8	100.0	102.4	104.4	107.9	107.1	108.9

Selected balance of payments data. Receipts from (U.S.$'000,000): tourism (2009) 438; remittances (2010) 771; foreign direct investment (FDI; 2008–10 avg.) 17. Disbursements for (U.S.$'000,000): tourism (2009) 164; remittances (2009) 69; FDI (2008–10 avg.) 18.

Gross domestic product (2009): U.S.$4,535,000,000 (U.S.$17,084 per capita).

Structure of gross domestic product and labour force

	2008 in value U.S.$'000,000	2008 % of total value	2006 labour force[9]	2006 % of labour force[9]
Agriculture, fishing	128.2	2.7	2,808	4.1
Mining and quarrying	83.8	1.8	156	0.2
Public utilities			537[10]	0.8[10]
Manufacturing	290.5	6.1	4,645[10]	6.8[10]
Construction	279.1	5.9	5,961	8.8
Transp. and commun.	354.4	7.5	6,509	9.6
Trade, hotels	1,152.0	24.4	17,578	25.8
Finance, real estate			6,307	9.3
Services	2,508.4	53.1	8,469	12.4
Pub. admin., defense			15,070	22.2
Other	–71.9	–1.5	—	—
TOTAL	4,724.5	100.0	68,040	100.0

Public debt (external, outstanding): n.a.
Household income and expenditure. Average household size (2007) 3.8; average annual income per household, n.a.; sources of income: n.a.; expenditure (2000–01): food and beverages 21.9%, housing 19.2%, transportation 16.7%, hotel and café expenditures 7.7%, culture and recreation 6.9%, household furnishings 5.8%.
Land use as % of total land area (2009): in temporary crops or left fallow (2007) 0.8%, in permanent crops 6.0%, in pasture 5.5%, forest area 40.9%.

Foreign trade[11]

Balance of trade (current prices)

	2005	2006	2007	2008	2009	2010
CFPF '000,000	–143,400	–139,700	–144,000	–159,700	–134,600	–141,700
% of total	78.0%	81.6%	81.1%	83.1%	84.3%	83.6%

Imports (2008): CFPF 178,900,000,000 (food 17.7%; machinery and apparatus 17.3%; refined petroleum 13.8%; motor vehicles and parts 9.0%). *Major import sources:* France 30.1%; Singapore 14.2%; U.S. 9.9%; China 7.4%; New Zealand 6.2%.
Exports (2008): CFPF 16,500,000,000 (black cultured pearls 51.9%; aircraft/parts 12.3%; gold/silver/pearl jewelry 11.9%; fruit [particularly *noni*[8]] 2.9%; corals, shells 2.8%; fish 1.6%; vanilla 1.2%). *Major export destinations:* Hong Kong 41.4%; France 19.7%; Japan 14.2%; U.S. 8.1%; New Caledonia 2.9%.

Transport and communications

Transport. Railroads: none. Roads (2006): total length 390 mi, 792 km (paved 33%). Motor vehicles: n.a. Air transport (2007)[12]: passenger-km 4,356,000,000; metric ton-km cargo 106,000,000.

Communications

Medium	date	number in '000s	units per 1,000 persons	Medium	date	number in '000s	units per 1,000 persons
Televisions	2004	56	223	PCs	2005	28	109
Telephones				Dailies	2009	20[13]	75[13]
Cellular	2010	216[14]	797[14]	Internet users	2009	120	446
Landline	2010	55	203	Broadband	2010	32[14]	119[14]

Education and health

Educational attainment (2007). Percentage of population age 15 and over having: no formal schooling 4.4%; primary education 19.9%; lower secondary 20.8%; vocational 19.8%; upper secondary 18.7%; higher 16.4%. *Literacy:* virtually 100%.

Education (2006–07)

	teachers	students	student/ teacher ratio	enrollment rate (%)
Primary (age 6–10)	...	26,939	...	...
Secondary/Voc. (age 11–17)	...	33,193	...	...
Tertiary[15]	74	2,649	35.8	... (age 18–22)

Health: physicians (2009) 478 (1 per 559 persons); hospital beds (2007) 894 (1 per 290 persons); infant mortality rate per 1,000 live births (2008): 5.0; undernourished population (2004–06) less than 5.0% of total population.

Military

Total active duty personnel (November 2010): 1,350 French troops (army 47.4%, navy 52.6%, air force, n.a.).

[1]French Polynesia in Tahitian is Polynesia Farani; the Tahitian language provides the fundamental element of cultural identity per article 57 of the Statute of Autonomy. [2]Approximate total area including inland water; total land area is 3,521 sq km (1,359 sq mi). [3]Based on land area. [4]Part of Papeete urban agglomeration. [5]Preliminary census total. [6]Located on Bora-Bora, Nunue is the largest town not on the island of Tahiti. [7]Territorial budget only; excludes French grants and subsidies (CFPF 170,000,000,000 in 2007). [8]Fruit known locally as *nono;* also known as Indian mulberry. [9]Salaried employees only. [10]The manufacture of energy-generating products is included in Public utilities. [11]Imports c.i.f.; exports f.o.b. [12]Air Tahiti and Air Tahiti Nui only. [13]Circulation. [14]Subscribers. [15]University of French Polynesia only.

Internet resources for further information:
- **Institut de la Statistique de la Polynésie Française http://www.ispf.pf**
- **IEOM La Polynésie française: Rapport Annuel http://www.ieom.fr/ieom/**

Gabon

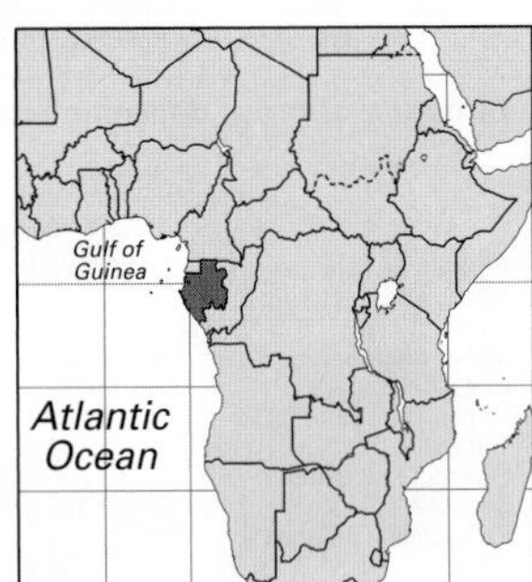

Official name: République Gabonaise (Gabonese Republic).
Form of government: unitary multiparty republic with a Parliament comprising two legislative houses (Senate [102]; National Assembly [120]).
Head of state: President.
Head of government: Prime Minister.
Capital: Libreville.
Official language: French.
Official religion: none.
Monetary unit: CFA franc (CFAF); valuation (Sept. 1, 2011) 1 U.S.$ = CFAF 460.31; 1 £ = CFAF 743.83.

Area and population

		area		population
				2003
Provinces	Capitals	sq mi	sq km	census[1]
Estuaire	Libreville	8,008	20,740	662,028
Haut-Ogooué	Franceville	14,111	36,547	228,471
Moyen-Ogooué	Lambaréné	7,156	18,535	60,990
Ngounié	Mouila	14,575	37,750	101,415
Nyanga	Tchibanga	8,218	21,285	50,297
Ogooué-Ivindo	Makokou	17,790	46,075	64,163
Ogooué-Lolo	Koulamoutou	9,799	25,380	64,534
Ogooué-Maritime	Port-Gentil	8,838	22,890	128,774
Woleu-Ntem	Oyem	14,851	38,465	157,013
TOTAL		103,347[2]	267,667	1,517,685

Demography

Population (2011): 1,534,000.
Density (2011): persons per sq mi 14.8, persons per sq km 5.7.
Urban-rural (2009): urban 85.6%; rural 14.4%.
Sex distribution (2007): male 49.67%; female 50.33%.
Age breakdown (2007): under 15, 42.1%; 15–29, 27.6%; 30–44, 15.5%; 45–59, 9.0%; 60–74, 4.5%; 75–84, 1.1%; 85 and over, 0.2%.
Population projection: (2020) 1,818,000; (2030) 2,146,000.
Doubling time: 29 years.
Ethnic composition (2000): Fang 28.6%; Punu 10.2%; Nzebi 8.9%; French 6.7%; Mpongwe 4.1%; Teke 4.0%; other 37.5%.
Religious affiliation (2005): Christian *c.* 73%[3], of which Roman Catholic *c.* 45%[3], Protestant/independent Christian *c.* 28%[3]; Muslim *c.* 12%[4]; traditional beliefs *c.* 10%; nonreligious *c.* 5%.
Major urban areas (2003): Libreville (2009) 619,000; Port-Gentil 116,200; Franceville 41,300; Lambaréné 9,000.

Vital statistics

Birth rate per 1,000 population (2007): 36.0 (world avg. 20.3).
Death rate per 1,000 population (2007): 12.4 (world avg. 8.5).
Natural increase rate per 1,000 population (2007): 23.6 (world avg. 11.8).
Total fertility rate (avg. births per childbearing woman; 2007): 4.71.
Life expectancy at birth (2007): male 52.8 years; female 55.2 years.
Major causes of death per 100,000 population (2002): HIV/AIDS-related *c.* 206; malaria *c.* 87; ischemic heart disease *c.* 76; cerebrovascular disease *c.* 65; measles *c.* 54.
Adult population (ages 15–49) *living with HIV* (2009): 5.2%[5] (world avg. 0.8%).

National economy

Budget (2008). Revenue: CFAF 2,078,100,000,000 (oil revenues 65.5%, other revenues 34.5%). Expenditures: CFAF 1,296,300,000,000 (current expenditure 69.9%, capital expenditure 30.1%).
Public debt (external, outstanding; 2009): U.S.$2,022,000,000.
Gross national income (GNI; 2010): U.S.$11,655,000,000 (U.S.$7,760 per capita); purchasing power parity GNI (U.S.$13,190 per capita).

Structure of gross domestic product and labour force

	2008		2006	
	in value CFAF '000,000	% of total value	labour force	% of labour force
Agriculture, forestry, fishing	268,400	3.8	193,000	30.4
Crude petroleum	3,728,000	53.0		
Other mining	283,600	4.0		
Manufacturing	285,300	4.1		
Construction	158,300	2.2		
Public utilities	53,100	0.7		
Transp. and commun.	321,000	4.6	442,000	69.6
Trade, restaurants	287,400	4.1		
Finance, real estate	60,800	0.9		
Services; Pub. admin., defense	1,236,400	17.6		
Other	350,500[6]	5.0[6]		
TOTAL	7,032,800	100.0	635,000	100.0

Production (metric tons except as noted). Agriculture, forestry, fishing (2009): cassava 306,897, plantains 288,095, sugarcane 240,000, yams 210,342, taro 71,131, corn (maize) 46,005, oil palm fruit 33,500, peanuts (groundnuts) 18,000, natural rubber 13,414; livestock (number of live animals) 215,000 pigs, 196,000 sheep, 3,200,000 chickens; roundwood (2010) 4,470,000 cu m, of which fuelwood 24%; fisheries production 30,124 (from aquaculture, negligible). Mining and quarrying (2009): manganese ore 1,992,000. Manufacturing (value added in CFAF '000,000,000; 2008): agricultural products 85.0; refined petroleum products 48.1; wood products 43.2. Energy production (consumption): electricity (kW-hr; 2008) 1,694,100,000 ([2007] 1,844,000,000); coal, none (none); crude petroleum (barrels; 2009) 87,100,000 ([2007] 6,000,000); petroleum products (metric tons; 2008) 732,340 ([2007] 552,000); natural gas (cu m; 2008) 187,000,000 ([2007] 156,000,000).
Population economically active (2008)[7]: total 687,000; activity rate of total population 47.4% (participation rates: ages 15–64, 76.9%; female 46.3%; unemployed [2010] *c.* 15%).

Price index (2005 = 100)

	2004	2005	2006	2007	2008	2009	2010
Consumer price index	96.4	100.0	98.6	103.6	109.0	111.1	112.7

Household income and expenditure (2008). Average household size (2004) 5.0; average annual income per household CFAF 1,978,000 (U.S.$4,183); sources of income: wages and salaries 63.3%, self-employment and rent 36.7%; expenditure: food 30.5%, beverages and tobacco 9.1%, communications 5.7%, clothing and footwear 5.6%, hotels and cafés 4.9%, transportation 4.7%, unspecified 22.8%.
Selected balance of payments data. Receipts from (U.S.$'000,000): tourism (2005) 9; remittances (2010) 10; foreign direct investment (FDI; 2008–10 avg.) 137; official development assistance (2009) 78. Disbursements for (U.S.$'000,000): tourism (2005) 274; remittances (2008) 186; FDI (2008–10 avg.) 88.
Land use as % of total land area (2007): in temporary crops or left fallow 1.3%, in permanent crops 0.7%, in pasture 18.1%; overall forest area (overlapping with other categories) 84.4%.

Foreign trade[8]

Balance of trade (current prices)

	2003	2004	2005	2006	2007	2008
CFAF '000,000,000	+1,509	+2,165	+2,152	+2,351	+2,575	+3,207
% of total	54.0%	60.2%	59.8%	59.0%	61.2%	63.0%

Imports (2008): CFAF 940,000,000,000 (petroleum sector 27.4%, mining sector 4.8%, forest sector 0.7%, remainder 67.1%). *Major import sources:* France 35.4%; Belgium/Luxembourg 13.8%; U.S. 7.4%; China 3.9%; Neth. 3.4%.
Exports (2008): CFAF 4,147,000,000,000 (petroleum 76.4%, manganese ore and concentrate 14.7%, wood [all forms] 5.3%). *Major export destinations:* U.S. 51.8%; China 13.2%; India 6.4%; France 6.0%; Neth. 3.6%.

Transport and communications

Transport. Railroads (2005): route length 506 mi, 814 km; (2003) passenger-km 86,000,000; (2003) metric ton-km cargo 2,998,000,000. Roads (2007): total length 5,700 mi, 9,170 km (paved 12%). Vehicles (2002): passenger cars 25,600; trucks and buses 17,000. Air transport: (2005) passenger-km 829,000,000; (2007) metric ton-km cargo 70,000,000.

Communications

Medium	date	number in '000s	units per 1,000 persons	Medium	date	number in '000s	units per 1,000 persons
Televisions	2004	220	173	PCs	2007	46	36
Telephones				Dailies	2009	20[9]	14[9]
Cellular	2010	1,610[10]	1,069[10]	Internet users	2009	99	67
Landline	2010	30	20	Broadband	2010	3.8[10]	2.5[10]

Education and health

Educational attainment (2000)[11]: no formal schooling 6.2%; incomplete primary and complete primary education 32.7%; lower secondary 41.3%; upper secondary 14.2%; higher 5.6%. *Literacy* (2007): total population age 15 and over literate 86.2%; males literate 90.2%; females literate 82.2%.

Education (2003–04)

	teachers	students	student/ teacher ratio	enrollment rate (%)
Primary (age 6–11)	7,807	281,371	36.0	80[12]
Secondary/Voc. (age 12–18)	...	105,191[13]	...	...
Tertiary	...	...	...	... (age 19–23)

Health (2008): physicians 271 (1 per 5,343 persons); hospital beds 3,724 (1 per 389 persons); infant mortality rate per 1,000 live births (2007) 53.5; undernourished population (2004–06) less than 5.0% of total population.

Military

Total active duty personnel (November 2010): 4,700 (army 68.1%, navy 10.6%, air force 21.3%); French troops (November 2010) *c.* 645. *Military expenditure as percentage of GDP* (2010): 1.9%; per capita expenditure U.S.$166.

[1]Results are disputed by international authorities. [2]Detail does not add to total given because of rounding. [3]Many also practice elements of traditional beliefs. [4]Mostly foreigners. [5]Statistically derived midpoint within range. [6]Royalties and import taxes. [7]ILO estimates. [8]Imports f.o.b. in balance of trade and commodities and c.i.f. in trading partners. [9]Circulation. [10]Subscribers. [11]Figures based on a national sample survey of people ages 15–59 from 6,203 households. [12]2000–01. [13]2001–02.

Internet resources for further information:

- **Direction Générale des Statistiques**
  http://www.stat-gabon.org/
- **La Banque de France: La Zone Franc**
  http://www.banque-france.fr/fr/eurosys/zonefr/zonefr.htm

Gambia, The

Official name: Republic of The Gambia.
Form of government: multiparty republic with one legislative house (National Assembly [53[1]]).
Head of state and government: President.
Capital: Banjul.
Official language: English.
Official religion: none.
Monetary unit: dalasi (D); valuation (Sept. 1, 2011) 1 U.S.$ = D 28.80; 1 £ = D 46.54.

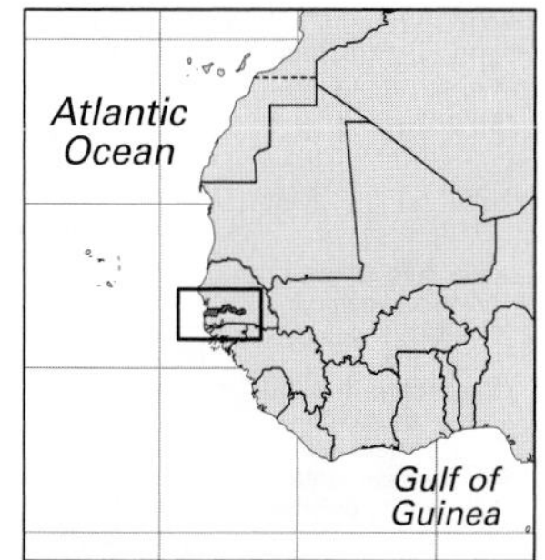

Area and population

Divisions	area sq km	population 2006 estimate	Municipal Council	area sq km	population 2006 estimate
Basse	2,048	217,014	Kanifing[2, 3]	76	358,133
Brikama	1,764	453,456			
Janjanbureh (Georgetown)	1,463	113,674	City Banjul[3]	12	33,131
Kerewan	2,199	178,072	SUBTOTAL	10,624	
Kuntaur	1,501	82,028	REMAINDER	1,008	
Mansakonko	1,561	74,420	TOTAL	11,632[4]	1,509,928

Demography

Population (2011): 1,776,000[5].
Density (2011): persons per sq mi 395.5, persons per sq km 152.7.
Urban-rural (2009): urban 57.4%; rural 42.6%.
Sex distribution (2007): male 49.92%; female 50.08%.
Age breakdown (2007): under 15, 44.1%; 15–29, 26.9%; 30–44, 15.6%; 45–59, 8.8%; 60–74, 3.8%; 75–84, 0.7%; 85 and over, 0.1%.
Population projection: (2020) 2,242,000; (2030) 2,818,000.
Doubling time: 27 years.
Ethnic composition (2003): Malinke *c.* 42%; Fulani *c.* 18%; Wolof *c.* 16%; Diola *c.* 10%; Soninke *c.* 9%; other *c.* 5%.
Religious affiliation (2005): Muslim *c.* 90%; Christian (mostly Roman Catholic) *c.* 9%; traditional beliefs/other *c.* 1%.
Major cities/urban areas (2006): Serekunda 335,700[2]; Brikama 80,700; Bakau 45,500[2]; Banjul 33,131 (Greater Banjul [2003] 523,589[3]); Farafenni 30,400.

Vital statistics

Birth rate per 1,000 population (2007): 39.0 (world avg. 20.3).
Death rate per 1,000 population (2007): 13.0 (world avg. 8.5).
Natural increase rate per 1,000 population (2007): 26.0 (world avg. 11.8).
Total fertility rate (avg. births per childbearing woman; 2007): 5.20.
Marriage/divorce rates per 1,000 population: n.a.
Life expectancy at birth (2006): male 52.3 years; female 56.0 years.
Major causes of death per 100,000 population (2002): infectious and parasitic diseases *c.* 404, of which malaria *c.* 94; cardiovascular diseases *c.* 172; lower respiratory infections *c.* 145; accidents *c.* 80.
Adult population (ages 15–49) *living with HIV* (2009): 2.0% (world avg. 0.8%).

National economy

Budget (2008). Revenue: D 4,142,000,000 (tax revenue 81.6%; nontax revenue 9.6%; grants 8.8%). Expenditures: D 4,627,000,000 (current expenditure 61.3%, of which wages and salaries 19.8%; capital expenditure 36.3%; net lending 2.4%).
Public debt (external, outstanding; 2009): U.S.$449,000,000.
Production (metric tons except as noted). Agriculture, forestry, fishing (2009): millet 144,870, peanuts (groundnuts) 121,950, paddy rice 79,000, corn (maize) 54,625, oil palm fruit 35,000, sorghum 31,880, fresh vegetables 9,330, cassava 7,370, pulses (mostly beans) 2,670; livestock (number of live animals) 432,000 cattle, 380,000 goats, 209,500 sheep; roundwood (2010) 797,200 cu m, of which fuelwood 86%; fisheries production 45,881 (from aquaculture, none). Mining and quarrying: sand, clay ([2007] 6,713), and gravel are excavated for local use. Manufacturing (value added in U.S.$; 1995): food products and beverages 6,000,000; textiles, clothing, and footwear 750,000; wood products 550,000. Energy production (consumption): electricity (kW-hr; 2008) 220,000,000 (205,000,000); coal, none (none); crude petroleum, none (none); petroleum products (metric tons; 2007) none (127,000); natural gas (cu m; 2007) none (2,306,000).
Population economically active (2008)[6]: total 743,000; activity rate of total population 44.8% (participation rates: ages 15–64, 77.8%; female 46.3%; unemployed, n.a.).

Price index (2005 = 100)

	2004	2005	2006	2007	2008	2009	2010
Consumer price index	95.4	100.0	102.1	107.5	112.3	117.4	123.4

Household income and expenditure. Average household size (2003) 8.6; income per household: n.a.; sources of income: n.a.; expenditure (1991)[7]: food and beverages 58.0%, clothing and footwear 17.5%, energy and water 5.4%, housing 5.1%, education, health, transportation and communications, recreation, and other 14.0%.
Land use as % of total land area (2009): in temporary crops or left fallow (2007) 34.8%, in permanent crops 0.6%, in pasture 26.0%, forest area 47.8%[8].
Gross national income (GNI; 2010): U.S.$770,000,000 (U.S.$440 per capita); purchasing power parity GNI (U.S.$1,270 per capita).

Structure of gross domestic product and labour force

	2008		1993	
	in value D '000,000	% of total value	labour force[9]	% of labour force[9]
Agriculture	5,590	24.3	181,752	52.6
Mining	374	1.6	398	0.1
Manufacturing	1,241	5.4	21,682	6.3
Construction	820	3.6	9,679	2.8
Public utilities	334	1.5	1,858	0.5
Transp. and commun.	2,231	9.7	14,203	4.1
Trade, hotels	6,824	29.7	54,728	15.8
Finance, real estate	2,543	11.1	2,415	0.7
Public administration	832	3.6	41,254	11.9
Services	953	4.1		
Other	1,237[10]	5.4[10]	17,412[11]	5.0[11]
TOTAL	22,978[12, 13]	100.0	345,381	100.0[13]

Selected balance of payments data. Receipts from (U.S.$'000,000): tourism (2009) 63; remittances (2010) 61; foreign direct investment (2008–10 avg.) 51; official development assistance (2009) 128. Disbursements for (U.S.$'000,000): tourism (2009) 9; remittances (2009) 3.

Foreign trade[14]

Balance of trade (current prices)

	2002	2003	2004	2005	2006	2007
U.S.$'000,000	–62.3	–50.0	–106.0	–142.5	–138.2	–171.5
% of total	18.6%	19.1%	35.4%	46.8%	45.1%	48.4%

Imports (2007): U.S.$262,900,000 (imports for domestic use 70.0%, of which petroleum products 10.8%; imports for reexport [principally to Senegal] 30.0%). *Major import sources:* Denmark *c.* 14%; U.S. *c.* 13%; China *c.* 11%; Germany *c.* 8%; U.K. *c.* 8%.
Exports (2007): U.S.$91,400,000 (reexports 86.3%; peanut [groundnut] oil 3.3%; peanuts [groundnuts] 2.7%; fish 2.0%). *Major export destinations:* reexports (principally to Senegal) 86.3%; domestic exports 13.7%, of which to Senegal 3.5%, to U.K. 2.7%, to France 1.9%.

Transport and communications

Transport. Railroads: none. Roads (2004): total length 2,325 mi, 3,742 km (paved 19%); passenger-km (2003) 16,100,000,000; metric ton-km cargo (2008) n.a. Vehicles (2007): passenger cars 8,815; trucks and buses 3,613. Air transport (2001)[15]: passenger arrivals 300,000, passenger departures 300,000; cargo loaded and unloaded 2,700 metric tons.

Communications

Medium	date	number in '000s	units per 1,000 persons	Medium	date	number in '000s	units per 1,000 persons
Televisions	2003	20	13	PCs	2007	53	33
Telephones				Dailies	2009	4[16]	2.3[16]
Cellular	2010	1,478[17]	855[17]	Internet users	2009	130	76
Landline	2010	49	28	Broadband	2010	0.4[17]	0.2[17]

Education and health

Educational attainment: n.a. *Literacy* (2009): total population age 15 and over literate 45.3%; males literate 56.7%; females literate 34.3%.

Education (2007–08)

	teachers	students	student/ teacher ratio	enrollment rate (%)
Primary (age 7–12)	6,429	220,931	34.4	69
Secondary/Voc. (age 13–18)	4,358	105,237	24.1	42
Tertiary[18]	134	1,530	11.4	1 (age 19–23)

Health: physicians (2003) 156 (1 per 9,769 persons); hospital beds (2005) 1,221 (1 per 1,250 persons); infant mortality rate per 1,000 live births (2008) 73.0; undernourished population (2004–06) 460,000 (29% of total population based on the consumption of a minimum daily requirement of 1,770 calories).

Military

Total active duty personnel (November 2010): 800[19] (army 100%). *Military expenditure as percentage of GDP* (2008): 2.2%; per capita expenditure U.S.$10.

[1]Includes 5 nonelective seats. [2]Kanifing includes the urban areas of Serekunda and Bakau. [3]Kanifing and Banjul make up most of Greater Banjul. [4]Includes national area near the mouth of the Gambia River not allocated by division. [5]Estimate of the United Nations *World Population Prospects: The 2010 Revision.* [6]ILO estimates. [7]Low-income population in Banjul and Kanifing only; weights of consumer price index components. [8]Forest area overlaps with other categories. [9]Based on census data excluding numerous unemployed. [10]Less imputed bank service charges. [11]Not adequately defined. [12]Reexports make up about 1/3 of The Gambia's GDP; goods imported into The Gambia under lower taxes are reexported (sometimes illegally) to nearby countries (particularly Senegal). [13]Detail does not add to total given because of rounding. [14]Imports c.i.f.; exports f.o.b. [15]Yumdum International Airport at Banjul. [16]Circulation. [17]Subscribers. [18]2003–04. [19]Of which deployed as UN peacekeepers in Sudan, 200.

Internet resources for further information:

- **Central Statistics Department**
  http://www.gambia.gm/Statistics/Statistics.htm
- **Central Bank of The Gambia**
  http://www.cbg.gm

Georgia

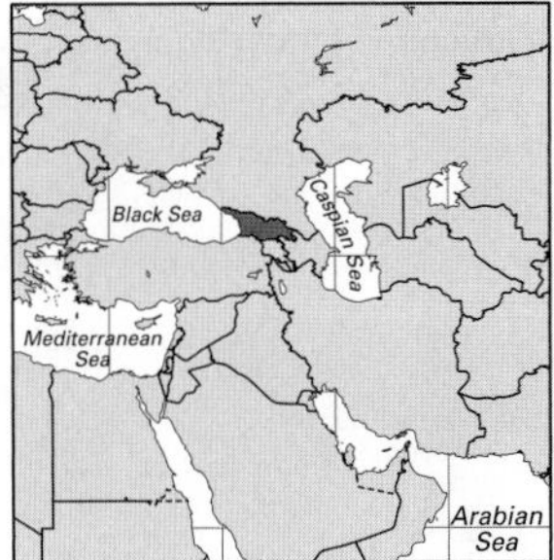

Official name: Sakartvelo (Georgia).
Form of government: unitary multiparty republic with a single legislative body (Parliament [150]).
Head of state and government: President, assisted by Prime Minister.
Capital: Tbilisi[1].
Official language: Georgian.
Official religion: none[2].
Monetary unit: Georgian lari (GEL); valuation (Sept. 1, 2011) 1 U.S.$ = GEL 1.66; 1 £ = GEL 2.68.

Area and population

Regions	area sq km	population 2011[3] estimate	City	area sq km	population 2011[3] estimate
Guria	2,032	140,300	Tbilisi (T'bilisi)	700[4]	1,162,400
Imereti	6,475	704,500	**Autonomous republic**		
Kakheti	11,311	406,200	Ajaria (Adjara)	2,880	390,600
Kvemo Kartli	6,072	505,700	**Autonomous republics/ disputed areas**[5]		
Mtskheta-Mtianeti	5,400[4]	109,300	Abkhazia	8,640	*242,862*[6]
Racha-Lechkhumi & Kvemo Svaneti	4,850[4]	47,300	South Ossetia[7]	3,900[4]	*55,000*[8]
Samegrelo & Zemo Svaneti	7,440	477,100	TOTAL	69,700[9]	4,469,200[10]
Samtskhe-Javakheti	6,413	212,800			
Shida Kartli	3,550[4]	313,000			

Demography

Population (2011): 4,474,000[10].
Density (2011)[10]: persons per sq mi 202.7, persons per sq km 78.3.
Urban-rural (2010[3])[10]: urban 53.0%; rural 47.0%.
Sex distribution (2010[3])[10]: male 47.54%; female 52.46%.
Age breakdown (2010[3])[10]: under 15, 17.1%; 15–29, 23.6%; 30–44, 20.7%; 45–59, 20.3%; 60–74, 12.3%; 75 and over, 6.0%.
Population projection[10]: (2020) 4,222,000; (2030) 3,890,000.
Ethnic composition (2002)[10]: Georgian 83.8%; Azerbaijani 6.5%; Armenian 5.7%; Russian 1.5%; Ossetian 0.9%; other 1.6%.
Religious affiliation (2005)[11]: Georgian Orthodox 54.8%; Sunnī Muslim 14.5%; Shīʿī Muslim 5.0%; Armenian Apostolic (Orthodox) 3.9%; Catholic 0.8%; Yazidi 0.4%; Protestant 0.4%; nonreligious 13.0%; other 7.2%.
Major cities (2010[3]): Tbilisi 1,122,300; Kutaisi 192,500; Batumi 123,500; Rustavi 119,500; Zugdidi 74,200.

Vital statistics

Birth rate per 1,000 population (2009)[10]: 14.5 (world avg. 20.3); within marriage 68.6%; outside of marriage 31.4%.
Death rate per 1,000 population (2009)[10]: 10.6 (world avg. 8.5).
Total fertility rate (avg. births per childbearing woman; 2008)[10]: 1.67.
Marriage/divorce rates per 1,000 population (2009)[10]: 7.2/0.9.
Life expectancy at birth (2009)[10]: male 69.2 years; female 77.7 years.
Major causes of death per 100,000 population (2009)[10]: diseases of the circulatory system 588.1; malignant neoplasms (cancers) 115.0; accidents, poisoning, and violence 37.0; diseases of the digestive system 27.1.

National economy

Budget (2007). Revenue: GEL 5,158,600,000 (tax revenue 72.4%, of which VAT 38.3%, social tax 14.0%, taxes on corporate profits 8.4%, excise tax 8.3%; nontax revenue 23.3%; grants 4.3%). Expenditures: GEL 5,237,100,000 (defense 28.6%; social security and welfare 14.8%; general public service 14.6%; public order 13.1%; education 7.3%).
Public debt (external, outstanding; June 2010): U.S.$2,862,500,000.
Population economically active (2009): total 1,991,800; activity rate of total population 45.4% (participation rates: ages 15 and over, 63.6%; female 46.2%; unemployed 16.9%).

Price and earnings indexes (2005 = 100)

	2004	2005	2006	2007	2008	2009	2010
Consumer price index	92.4	100.0	109.2	119.3	131.2	133.4	142.9
Monthly earnings index	76.7	100.0	136.1	180.3	261.9	...	...

Production (metric tons except as noted). Agriculture, forestry, fishing (2009): cow's milk 539,400, corn (maize) 291,000, potatoes 216,800, grapes 150,100, tangerines, mandarins, and clementines 90,500, apples 80,700, wheat 53,900, tomatoes 51,400, hazelnuts 21,800, tea 5,800; livestock (number of live animals) 1,027,500 cattle, 690,000 sheep; roundwood (2010) 838,006, of which fuelwood 87%; fisheries production 25,260 (from aquaculture 1%). Mining and quarrying (2009): manganese ore 350,000; gold 2,000 kg. Manufacturing (value added in GEL '000,000; 2008): base and fabricated metals 314.1; food products, beverages, and tobacco 241.1; cement, bricks, and ceramics 145.8; chemicals and chemical products 66.8; transportation equipment 62.7. Energy production (consumption): electricity (kW-hr; 2009) 8,303,000,000 (7,935,000,000); coal (metric tons; 2007) 14,000 (48,000); crude petroleum (barrels; 2009) 363,139 (4,745,000); petroleum products (metric tons; 2007) 13,000 (809,000); natural gas (cu m; 2009) 8,000,000 (1,730,000,000).
Household income and expenditure (2008). Average household size (2004) 3.7; average annual income per household GEL 5,407 (U.S.$3,835); sources of income: wages and salaries 36.9%, transfers 14.0%, remittances 13.9%, self-employment 11.7%, agricultural income 6.7%; expenditure: food, beverages, and tobacco 39.5%, energy 10.4%, transportation 8.8%, health 8.5%.

Gross national income (GNI; 2010)[10]: U.S.$11,976,000,000 (U.S.$2,700 per capita); purchasing power parity GNI (U.S.$4,980 per capita).

Structure of gross domestic product and labour force

	2009		2007	
	in value GEL '000,000	% of total value	labour force	% of labour force
Agriculture, forestry, fishing	1,488.4	8.3	910,500	46.3
Mining and quarrying	105.9	0.6	4,700	0.2
Manufacturing	1,793.1	10.0	82,700	4.2
Public utilities	463.7	2.6	18,200	0.9
Construction	949.3	5.3	71,200	3.6
Transp. and commun.	1,845.6	10.3	71,700	3.6
Trade, restaurants	2,587.9	14.4	186,800	9.5
Finance, real estate	1,620.4	9.0	52,000	2.6
Pub. admin., defense	2,457.6	13.7	64,300	3.3
Services	2,421.6	13.5	242,000	12.3
Other	2,215.2[12]	12.3[12]	261,200[13]	13.3[13]
TOTAL	17,948.6[14]	100.0	1,965,300	100.0[14]

Selected balance of payments data. Receipts from (U.S.$'000,000): tourism (2009) 470; remittances (2010) 808; foreign direct investment (2008–10 avg.) 924; official development assistance (2009) 908. Disbursements for (U.S.$'000,000): tourism (2009) 181; remittances (2009–10) 77.
Land use as % of total land area (2009): in temporary crops and left fallow 6.4%, in permanent crops 1.7%, in pasture 27.9%, forest area 39.5%.

Foreign trade[15]

Balance of trade (current prices)

	2004	2005	2006	2007	2008	2009
U.S.$'000,000	−1,199	−1,624	−2,742	−3,983	−4,559	−3,243
% of total	48.1%	48.4%	59.4%	61.8%	60.3%	58.8%

Imports (2008): U.S.$6,056,000,000 (machinery and apparatus 18.1%, refined petroleum 12.6%, food 12.2%, road vehicles 10.4%). *Major import sources* (2009): Turkey 18.0%; Ukraine 9.6%; Azerbaijan 8.6%; Germany 6.9%; Russia 6.6%.
Exports (2008): U.S.$1,497,000,000 (ferrosilico-manganese 15.4%, ferrous waste and scrap 8.6%, copper ore/concentrates 7.9%, motor vehicles 7.6%, food 7.0%, gold 6.7%, ammonium nitrate 6.6%, wine/grape brandy 5.5%). *Major export destinations* (2009): Turkey 19.9%; Azerbaijan 14.7%; Canada 10.3%; Armenia (2008) 8.2%; Ukraine 7.4%; Bulgaria 7.3%.

Transport and communications

Transport. Railroads (2008): 1,561 km; passenger-km 674,500,000; metric ton-km cargo 6,515,700,000. Roads (2007): 20,329 km (paved 94%); passenger-km (2008) 5,568,000,000[16]; metric ton-km cargo (2008) 601,000,000. Vehicles (2008): passenger cars 466,900; trucks and buses 105,100. Air transport (2008): passenger-km 485,700,000; metric ton-km cargo 1,900,000.

Communications

Medium	date	number in '000s	units per 1,000 persons	Medium	date	number in '000s	units per 1,000 persons
Televisions	2003	1,627	357	PCs	2008	1,191	272
Telephones				Dailies	2009	43[17]	9.8[17]
Cellular	2010	3,193[18]	734[18]	Internet users	2009	1,300	305
Landline	2010	597	137	Broadband	2010	222[18]	51[18]

Education and health

Educational attainment (2004). Percentage of population age 15 and over having: no formal education/unknown 1.6%; primary education 4.1%; incomplete secondary 10.5%; secondary 48.2%; incomplete higher 12.3%; higher 23.3%. *Literacy* (2008): virtually 100%.

Education (2007–08)

	teachers	students	student/ teacher ratio	enrollment rate (%)
Primary (age 6–11)	25,098	311,265	12.4	99
Secondary/Voc. (age 12–16)	40,919	305,388	7.5	82[19]
Tertiary	17,824	129,926	7.3	34 (age 17–21)

Health (2009): physicians 20,609 (1 per 213 persons); hospital beds 13,600 (1 per 322 persons); infant mortality rate per 1,000 live births[10] 14.9; undernourished population (2004–06) 550,000[11] (12% of total population based on the consumption of a minimum daily requirement of 1,920 calories).

Military

Total active duty personnel (November 2010): 20,655[20] (army 86.0%, national guard 7.6%, air force 6.4%).[21] *Military expenditure as percentage of GDP* (2008): 8.0%; per capita expenditure U.S.$235.

[1]Officially T'bilisi. [2]Special recognition is given to the Georgian Orthodox Church. [3]January 1. [4]Approximate areas. [5]On Aug. 26, 2008, Russia became the first country to recognize Abkhazia's and South Ossetia's independence from Georgia. [6]Preliminary 2011 Abkhazia census results. [7]Georgia claims as part of Shida Kartli region. [8]2010 rough estimate. [9]Reported total; summed total equals 69,663 sq km. Includes areas of Abkhazia and South Ossetia; total area excluding 2 autonomous republics/disputed areas equals 57,160 sq km (22,070 sq mi). [10]Excludes Abkhazia and South Ossetia. [11]Includes Abkhazia and South Ossetia. [12]Taxes on products less subsidies and less imputed bank service charges. [13]Including 261,000 unemployed. [14]Detail does not add to total given because of rounding. [15]Imports c.i.f.; exports f.o.b. [16]Buses only. [17]Circulation. [18]Subscribers. [19]2006–07. [20]Excluding 11,700 paramilitary troops, of which 5,400 Georgian Border Guard comprising the former navy and coast guard, which merged in 2009. [21]Russian troops in Abkhazia and South Ossetia (November 2010) *c.* 7,000.

Internet resources for further information:
- **National Bank of Georgia http://www.nbg.gov.ge**
- **National Statistics Office of Georgia http://www.geostat.ge**

Germany

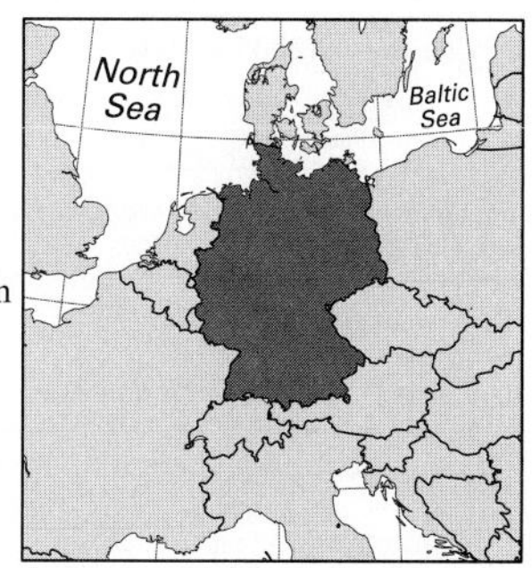

Official name: Bundesrepublik Deutschland (Federal Republic of Germany).
Form of government: federal multiparty republic with two legislative houses (Bundesrat, or Federal Council [69[1]]; German Bundestag, or Federal Assembly [622[2]]).
Head of state: President.
Head of government: Chancellor.
Capital: Berlin[3].
Official language: German.
Official religion: none.
Monetary unit: euro (€); valuation (Sept. 1, 2011) 1 U.S.$ = €0.70; 1 £ = €1.13.

Area and population

		area		population
Federal states[5]	**Capitals**	sq mi	sq km	2010[4] estimate
Baden-Württemberg	Stuttgart	13,804	35,751	10,744,921
Bavaria	Munich	27,240	70,552	12,510,331
Berlin	—	344	891	3,442,675
Brandenburg	Potsdam	11,382	29,480	2,511,525
Bremen	Bremen	156	404	661,716
Hamburg	Hamburg	292	755	1,774,224
Hesse	Wiesbaden	8,153	21,115	6,061,951
Lower Saxony	Hannover	18,388	47,625	7,928,815
Mecklenburg–West Pomerania	Schwerin	8,952	23,185	1,651,216
North Rhine–Westphalia	Düsseldorf	13,161	34,086	17,872,763
Rhineland-Palatinate	Mainz	7,665	19,853	4,012,675
Saarland	Saarbrücken	992	2,569	1,022,585
Saxony	Dresden	7,111	18,418	4,168,732
Saxony-Anhalt	Magdeburg	7,895	20,447	2,356,219
Schleswig-Holstein	Kiel	6,100	15,799	2,832,027
Thuringia	Erfurt	6,244	16,172	2,249,882
TOTAL		137,879	357,104[6]	81,802,257

Demography

Population (2011): 81,604,000.
Density (2011): persons per sq mi 591.6, persons per sq km 228.5.
Urban-rural (2008): urban 84.1%; rural 15.9%[7].
Population projection: (2020) 80,431,000; (2030) 78,922,000.
Major cities (2010[4]; *urban agglomerations*): Dortmund 581,308 (4,667,623[8]); Essen 576,259 (4,667,623[8]); Duisburg 491,931 (4,667,623[8]); Bochum 376,319 (4,667,623[8]); Berlin 3,442,675 (4,315,249); Hamburg 1,774,224 (2,604,336); Munich 1,330,440 (2,004,526); Frankfurt am Main 671,927 (1,930,178); Cologne 998,105 (1,896,786); Stuttgart 601,646 (1,785,972); Mannheim 311,969 (1,251,926); Düsseldorf 586,217 (1,219,908); Nuremberg (Nürnberg) 503,673 (1,051,781); Hannover 520,966 (970,766); Bonn 319,841 (886,703); Bremen 547,685 (852,351); Dresden 517,052 (784,952); Wuppertal 351,050 (761,506); Saarbrücken 175,810 (671,727); Leipzig 518,862 (646,740); Wiesbaden-Mainz 277,493, 197,778 (645,179); Aachen 258,380 (617,982); Karlsruhe 291,959 (612,038); Bielefeld 323,084 (590,977); Augsburg 263,646 (455,166); Chemnitz 243,089 (445,360); Hagen-Iserlohn 190,121, 95,232 (445,066); Freiburg im Breisgau 221,924 (395,698); Mönchengladbach 258,251 (366,842).

Other principal cities (2010[4])

	population		population		population
Braunschweig	247,400	Kiel	238,281	Oldenburg	161,334
Darmstadt	143,332	Krefeld	235,414	Osnabrück	163,514
Erfurt	203,830	Leverkusen	160,593	Paderborn	145,320
Gelsenkirchen[8]	259,744	Lübeck	209,818	Potsdam	154,606
Göttingen	121,457	Ludwigshafen		Recklingshausen[8]	119,050
Halle	232,323	am Rhein	163,340	Regensburg	134,218
Hamm	181,741	Magdeburg	230,456	Rostock	201,442
Heidelberg	146,466	Mülheim		Solingen	160,992
Heilbronn	122,415	an der Ruhr[8]	167,471	Ulm	122,087
Herne[8]	165,632	Münster	275,543	Wolfsburg	121,109
Ingolstadt	124,387	Neuss	151,280	Würzburg	133,195
Kassel	194,774	Oberhausen[8]	214,024		

Sex distribution (2010[4]): male 49.03%; female 50.97%.
Ethnic composition (by nationality; 2000): German 88.2%; Turkish 3.4% (including Kurdish 0.7%); Italian 1.0%; Greek 0.7%; Serb 0.6%; Russian 0.6%; Polish 0.4%; other 5.1%.
Households (2009). Number of households 40,188,000; average household size 2.0; 1 person 39.8%, more than 1 person 60.2%.
Age breakdown (2009[4]): under 15, 13.6%; 15–29, 17.5%; 30–44, 21.2%; 45–59, 22.2%; 60–74, 16.9%; 75–84, 6.4%; 85 and over, 2.2%.
Religious affiliation (2005): Protestant 35.0%, of which Lutheran/Reformed churches *c.* 34%; Roman Catholic 32.5%; Sunnī Muslim 4.3%; Orthodox 1.7%; New Apostolic (an independent Christian group) 0.5%; Buddhist 0.3%; Jewish 0.2%; nonreligious 18.0%; atheist 2.0%; other 5.5%.
Resident foreign population (2008[4]): 6,744,900 (8.2% of total population); *region/country of birth:* EU countries 34.7%, of which Italy 7.8%, Poland 5.7%, Greece 4.4%, Austria 2.6%; Turkey 25.4%; other Asian countries 12.1%; combined Serbia and Montenegro 4.9%; African countries 4.0%; Croatia 3.3%; Russia 2.8%; Bosnia and Herzegovina 2.3%; U.S. 1.5%; other 9.0%.
Population with immigrant background (2008): 14,800,000 (18% of total population).
Immigration/emigration trends (2009): foreigners arriving 721,000; emigrants (including many foreigners returning home) 734,000, of which Germans 155,000.

Vital statistics

Birth rate per 1,000 population (2009): 7.9 (world avg. 20.3); within marriage (2008) 68.2%; outside of marriage (2008) 31.8%.
Death rate per 1,000 population (2009): 10.2 (world avg. 8.5).
Natural increase rate per 1,000 population (2009): –2.3 (world avg. 11.8).
Total fertility rate (avg. births per childbearing woman; 2008): 1.37.
Marriage/divorce rates per 1,000 population: (2009) 4.6/(2008) 2.3.
Life expectancy at birth (2008): male 77.2 years; female 82.5 years.
Major causes of death per 100,000 population (2008): diseases of the circulatory system 434.4, of which ischemic heart disease 164.2, cerebrovascular disease 76.9, hypertensive diseases 37.8; malignant neoplasms (cancers) 263.0; diseases of the respiratory system 71.9; diseases of the digestive system 53.2; accidents and violence 38.4; diabetes mellitus 27.2; diseases of the genitourinary system 22.6; infectious and parasitic diseases 17.8.
Adult population (ages 15–49) *living with HIV* (2009): 0.1% (world avg. 0.8%).

Social indicators

Educational attainment (2007). Percentage of population age 25–64 having: no formal schooling through primary education 3%; lower secondary 13%; upper secondary 53%; post-secondary non-tertiary 7%; higher vocational 9%; university 14%; advanced degree 1%.
Quality of working life. Average workweek (2007): 38.4 hours. Annual rate per 100,000 workers (2007) for: injuries or accidents at work 2,803; deaths 2.16. Proportion of labour force insured for damages of income loss resulting from: injury, virtually 100%; permanent disability, virtually 100%; death, virtually 100%. Average days lost to labour stoppages per 1,000 workers (2008): 3.7.
Access to services. Proportion of dwellings (2002) having: electricity, virtually 100%; piped water supply, virtually 100%; flush sewage disposal (1993) 98.4%; public fire protection, virtually 100%.
Social participation. Eligible voters participating in last (September 2005) national election 77.7%. Trade union membership in total workforce (2009[4]): 6,441,045 (15.4%). Population "religious"/"deeply religious" (2007): in western Germany 78%/21%; in eastern Germany 36%/8%; 15% of Roman Catholics "regularly" attend religious services.
Social deviance (2006)[9]. Conviction rate per 100,000 population for: murder[10] and manslaughter 0.8; sexual abuse of children 3.1; rape 2.7; assault and battery 91.3; theft 195.3; fraud 132.4.
Leisure. Favourite sporting activities by total membership (2008)[11]: soccer 6,564,000; gymnastics 5,012,000; tennis 1,587,000; shooting 1,462,000; track and field 891,000; handball 848,000; alpine-related (not skiing) 783,000; horseback riding 758,000; sport fishing 653,000; ping-pong 615,000; skiing 606,000; swimming 575,000. Other leisure activities include using mobile devices/computers, going to the cinema, attending theatrical and musical performances, visiting museums, and taking part in package tours.
Material well-being (2008). Households possessing: automobile 77.1%; navigation system 20.7%; bicycle 79.5%; refrigerator 98.6%; freezer 52.4%; dishwasher 62.5%; microwave oven 69.6%; washing machine (2004) 95.5%; clothes dryer 38.5%; DVD player 69.1%; personal stationary computer 62.1%; personal mobile computer 34.7%; Internet access 64.4%; MP3 player 37.3%.

National economy

Budget (2007)[12]. Revenue: €1,064,730,000,000 (tax revenue 54.5%, of which individual income taxes 21.6%, general taxes on goods and services 15.6%, excise taxes 6.0%; social security contributions 37.6%; nontax revenue 7.5%; other 0.4%). Expenditures: €1,061,590,000,000 (social protection 45.7%; health 14.0%; education 9.1%; economic affairs 7.2%; public debt payments 6.3%; public order 3.5%; defense 2.4%).
Public debt (June 2010)[13]: U.S.$2,270,000,000,000.
Production (metric tons except as noted). Agriculture, forestry, fishing (2009): cereal grains 49,748,000 (of which wheat 25,190,300, barley 12,288,000, rye 4,270,000, triticale 2,514,000), cow's milk 27,938,000, sugar beets 25,919,000, potatoes 11,618,000, rapeseed 6,307,000, pig meat 5,265,000, grapes 1,456,000, cattle meat 1,143,000, apples 1,070,700, asparagus 98,200, gooseberries 42,000, hops 31,300; livestock (number of live animals) 26,887,000 pigs, 12,945,000 cattle, 118,000,000 chickens; roundwood (2010) 54,418,000 cu m, of which fuelwood 17%; fisheries production 290,300 (from aquaculture 14%). Mining and quarrying (2009): salt 18,393,000[14]; kaolin 4,514,000[14]; potash (potassium oxide content) 1,825,000[15]; bentonite 326,000; feldspar 160,000; barite 45,606.

Manufacturing enterprises (2005)

	no. of employees	wages as a % of avg. of all manufacturing wages	value added at factor values (U.S.$'000,000)[16]
Motor vehicles	516,461	144.7	56,071
General purpose machinery	506,461	113.1	45,036
Fabricated metal products	543,629	84.3	39,114
Special purpose machinery	472,082	107.5	38,937
Food products	735,803	55.5	35,346
Paints, soaps, pharmaceuticals	268,827	123.3	32,761
Motor vehicle parts	309,014	118.5	26,806
Components and control apparatus for electricity distribution	269,703	131.7	25,047
Medical equipment and instruments	283,349	90.8	22,178
Plastics	301,622	84.8	21,176
Electrical equipment and accessories (not electricity- or television-related)	217,618	102.9	17,337
Iron and steel	126,902	111.3	15,406
Structural metal products, tanks	221,576	82.2	15,152
Bricks, cement, ceramics	177,289	87.6	13,055
Publishing	190,104	81.1	12,259
Paper and paper products	143,919	97.6	12,224
Printing and printing-related services	160,339	87.9	10,889

Manufacturing enterprises (2005) (continued)

	no. of employees	wages as a % of avg. of all manufacturing wages	value added at factor values (U.S.$'000,000)[16]
Furniture	155,271	79.2	9,663
Sawn wood and wood products (excluding furniture)	109,970	69.2	8,271
Aircraft and spacecraft	72,976	162.0	8,065
Electronic valves and tubes and related products	72,621	117.6	7,808
Refined petroleum products	...	...	6,928
Base nonferrous metals	62,754	118.2	6,299
Television-, telecommunications/ sound equipment–related	...	...	5,796
Rubber products	75,390	99.7	5,782
Beverages	64,842	100.5	5,693
Casting of metals	69,306	99.2	5,443
Office and computing machinery	41,651	136.2	4,632

Energy production (consumption): electricity (kW-hr; 2010) 502,592,000,000 ([2008] 544,467,000,000); hard coal (metric tons; 2010) 12,800,000 ([2007] 70,100,000); lignite (metric tons; 2009) 169,700,000[17] ([2007] 180,500,000); crude petroleum (barrels; 2010) 34,560,000 ([2007] 801,900,000); petroleum products (metric tons; 2007) 102,550,000 (88,325,000); natural gas (cu m; 2010) 15,786,000,000 (124,096,000,000). In 2009 Germany was a world leader in the production of wind and solar power.

Gross national income (GNI; 2010): U.S.$3,537,180,000,000 (U.S.$43,330 per capita); purchasing power parity GNI (U.S.$38,170 per capita).

Structure of gross domestic product and labour force

	2008			
	in value €'000,000	% of total value	labour force	% of labour force
Agriculture	20,250	0.8	872,000	2.1
Mining	5,730	0.2	109,000	0.3
Manufacturing	516,990	20.7	8,516,000	20.3
Public utilities	49,540	2.0	346,000	0.8
Construction	95,230	3.8	2,521,000	6.0
Transp. and commun.	128,040	5.2	2,147,000	5.1
Trade, restaurants	269,390	10.8	6,749,000	16.1
Finance, real estate	659,160	26.4	5,473,000	13.1
Services	494,450	19.8	9,133,000	21.8
Pub. admin., defense			2,836,000	6.8
Other	257,020[18]	10.3[18]	3,173,000[19]	7.6[19]
TOTAL	2,495,800	100.0	41,875,000	100.0

Household income and expenditure. Average annual disposable income per household (2008) €34,824 (U.S.$51,009); sources of income (2003): wages and salaries 42.1%, transfers 24.6%, property income 9.0%, self-employment 4.8%, other 19.5%; expenditure (2006): housing and energy 24.4%, transportation 14.1%, food and nonalcoholic beverages 11.0%, recreation and culture 9.3%, household furnishings 6.9%, restaurants and hotels 5.4%, clothing and footwear 5.2%, health 4.8%.

Financial aggregates[20]

	2004	2005	2006	2007	2008	2009	2010
Exchange rate, € per:							
U.S. dollar	0.73	0.85	0.76	0.68	0.72	0.69	0.75
£	1.42	1.46	1.49	1.36	1.05	1.12	1.17
SDR	1.14	1.21	1.14	1.07	1.11	1.09	1.15
International reserves (U.S.$)							
Total (excl. gold; '000,000)	48,823	45,140	41,687	44,327	43,137	59,925	62,295
SDRs ('000,000)	2,061	1,892	2,010	2,162	2,198	19,101	18,769
Reserve pos. in IMF ('000,000)	6,863	3,483	1,958	1,396	2,382	3,896	6,169
Foreign exchange	39,899	39,765	37,719	40,768	38,557	36,928	37,356
Gold ('000,000 fine troy oz)	110.38	110.21	110.04	109.87	109.72	109.53	109.34
% world reserves	...	11.15	11.27	11.44	11.43	11.21	11.14
Interest and prices							
Central bank discount (%)	...	...	...	...	...	...	...
Govt. bond yield (%)	4.0	3.4	3.8	4.2	4.0	3.2	2.7
Share prices (2005 = 100)	86.0	100.0	125.4	155.8	121.3	92.2	111.1
Balance of payments (U.S.$'000,000,000)							
Balance of visible trade	+186.04	+193.14	+198.05	+270.75	+263.03	+188.50	+204.72
Imports, f.o.b.	–721.75	–790.00	–938.11	–1,083.52	–1,238.77	–972.49	–1,098.61
Exports, f.o.b.	907.79	983.14	1,136.16	1,354.26	1,501.80	1,160.99	1,303.33
Balance of invisibles	–58.04	–52.53	–15.38	–21.65	–34.92	+0.13	–16.35
Balance of payments, current account	+128.00	+140.61	+182.67	+249.10	+228.11	+188.63	+188.37

Selected service enterprises (2004)

	no. of enter-prises	no. of employees	annual turnover (€'000,000)
Transport, storage, and communication			
Air	409	53,002	11,765
Land, pipelines	58,329	656,597	55,747
Water	2,408	26,678	18,109
Transport support, travel agencies	22,258	501,724	87,973
Postal services, telecommunications	8,137	610,549	101,715
Real estate	175,620	383,122	94,487
Rental of equipment and goods	14,464	80,217	26,984
Computer-related activities	45,205	370,346	58,525
Research and development	4,185	87,840	6,820
Other business activities	323,742	3,057,849	191,162

Land use as % of total land area (2009): in temporary crops 26.8%, left fallow 0.7%, in permanent crops 0.6%, in pasture 13.6%, forest area 31.8%.

Population economically active (2008): total 41,875,000; activity rate of total population 51.0% (participation rates: ages 15–64, 76.0%; female 45.4%; unemployed [July 2010–June 2011] 7.4%).

Price index (2005 = 100)

	2004	2005	2006	2007	2008	2009	2010
Consumer price index	98.5	100.0	101.6	103.9	106.6	107.0	108.2

Selected balance of payments data. Receipts from (U.S.$'000,000): tourism (2009) 34,781; remittances (2010) 11,559; foreign direct investment (FDI; 2008–10 avg.) 29,326. Disbursements for (U.S.$'000,000): tourism (2009) 81,044; remittances (2009) 15,924; FDI (2008–10 avg.) 86,733.

Foreign trade[21]

Balance of trade (current prices)

	2005	2006	2007	2008	2009	2010
U.S.$'000,000	+197,456	+199,736	+267,822	+264,709	+194,512	+203,299
% of total	11.2%	9.8%	11.3%	10.0%	9.5%	8.7%

Imports (2008): U.S.$1,204,209,000,000 (machinery and equipment 21.7%, of which electrical machinery/parts 6.4%, general industrial machinery 3.7%; manufactured goods 13.6%, of which iron and steel 3.6%; mineral fuels 13.6%, of which crude petroleum 9.0%; road vehicles/parts 7.5%; food products 5.3%; medicines and pharmaceuticals 3.9%; special transactions 12.9%). *Major import sources:* Neth. 8.8%; France 8.2%; China 7.2%; U.S. 5.6%; Italy 5.6%; U.K. 5.4%; Belgium 4.9%; Russia 4.4%; Austria 4.0%; Switzerland 3.8%.

Exports (2008): U.S.$1,466,137,000,000 (machinery and equipment 27.9%, of which electrical machinery and electronic components 7.3%, general industrial machinery 7.3%, machinery specialized for particular industries 4.8%; transport equipment 18.3%, of which road vehicles/parts 15.5%; chemicals and chemical products 14.6%, of which medicines and pharmaceuticals 4.6%; manufactured goods 13.8%, of which base and fabricated metals 8.4%). *Major export destinations:* France 9.7%; U.S. 7.2%; U.K. 6.7%; Neth. 6.6%; Italy 6.4%; Austria 5.4%; Belgium 5.2%; Spain 4.4%; Switzerland 4.0%; Poland 4.0%.

Transport and communications

Transport. Railroads (2006): route length 25,606 mi, 41,209 km; (2008) passenger-km 60,663,000,000; (2008) metric ton-km cargo 115,652,000,000. Roads (2008): total length 400,316 mi, 644,248 km (paved, n.a.); (2006) passenger-km 935,200,000,000[22]; (2008) metric ton-km cargo 256,327,000,000. Vehicles (2008): passenger cars 41,183,594; trucks and buses 4,321,367. Air transport (2008)[23]: passenger-km 210,682,000,000; metric ton-km cargo 8,330,000,000. Inland Waterway (2008): passenger-km, n.a.; metric ton-km cargo 48,719,000,000.

Communications

Medium	date	number in '000s	units per 1,000 persons	Medium	date	number in '000s	units per 1,000 persons
Televisions	2003	55,758	675	PCs	2007	53,967	656
Telephones				Dailies	2009	19,746[24]	241[24]
Cellular	2010	104,560[25]	1,270[25]	Internet users	2009	65,124	793
Landline	2010	45,600	554	Broadband	2010	26,000[25]	316[25]

Education and health

Education (2007–08)

	teachers	students	student/ teacher ratio	enrollment rate (%)
Primary (age 6–9)	239,761	3,236,158	13.5	98[26]
Secondary/Voc. (age 10–18)	597,269	7,907,105	13.2	...
Tertiary	304,686	...	...	... (age 19–23)

Health (2008): physicians (2010) 325,945[27] (1 per 251 persons); hospital beds 504,051[28] (1 per 163 persons); infant mortality rate per 1,000 live births 4.0; undernourished population (2004–06) less than 5.0% of total population.

Military

Total active duty personnel (November 2010): 251,465 (army 41.9%, navy 7.6%, air force 17.7%, joint medical and support services 32.8%); reserve 40,396; German peacekeeping troops abroad (November 2010) *c.* 7,900, including *c.* 4,400 in Afghanistan, 1,355 in Kosovo; U.S. troops in Germany (November 2010) 53,130; British troops (November 2010) 18,230; French troops (November 2010) 2,800. *Military expenditure as percentage of GDP* (2009): 1.4%[29]; per capita expenditure U.S.$580[29].

[1]All seats appointed by local government. [2]Current number of seats; statutory number is 598. [3]Some ministries remain in Bonn. The federal supreme court meets in Karlsruhe. [4]January 1. [5]State names used in this table are English conventional. [6]Detail does not add to total given because of rounding. [7]Rural population is defined as being communes with 5,000 or less population. [8]Part of the Ruhrgebiet ("Ruhr region") urban agglomeration. [9]Excludes eastern Germany except for the former East Berlin. [10]Includes attempted murder. [11]Includes both active and passive membership. [12]General government budget (combined budgets of central, state, and local governments). [13]Includes debt of federal states. [14]World rank: 3. [15]World rank: 6. [16]2006. [17]World rank: 1. [18]Taxes less subsidies. [19]Includes 3,141,000 unemployed. [20]End-of-period figures. [21]Imports c.i.f.; exports f.o.b. [22]Passenger cars 869,000,000,000; buses 66,200,000,000. [23]Lufthansa, Air Berlin, Condor, and Hapag Lloyd only. [24]Circulation. [25]Subscribers. [26]2006–07. [27]Active physicians only. [28]Excludes rehabilitation facilities. [29]Includes military pensions.

Internet resource for further information:

- **Federal Statistical Office of Germany (in English) http://www.destatis.de/e_home.htm**

Ghana

Official name: Republic of Ghana.
Form of government: unitary multiparty republic with one legislative house (Parliament [230]).
Head of state and government: President.
Capital: Accra.
Official language: English.
Official religion: none.
Monetary unit: Ghana cedi (GH¢)[1]; valuation (Sept. 1, 2011) 1 U.S.$ = GH¢1.53; 1 £ = GH¢2.47.

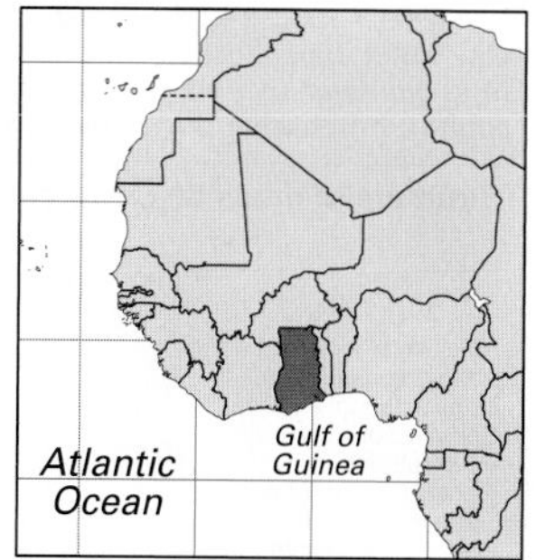

Area and population

		area		population
Regions	Capitals	sq mi	sq km	2010 census[2]
Ashanti	Kumasi	9,417	24,389	4,725,046
Brong-Ahafo	Sunyani	15,273	39,557	2,282,128
Central	Cape Coast	3,794	9,826	2,107,209
Eastern	Koforidua	7,461	19,323	2,596,013
Greater Accra	Accra	1,253	3,245	3,909,764
Northern	Tamale	27,175	70,384	2,468,557
Upper East	Bolgatanga	3,414	8,842	1,031,478
Upper West	Wa	7,134	18,476	677,763
Volta	Ho	7,942	20,570	2,099,876
Western	Sekondi-Takoradi	9,236	23,921	2,325,597
TOTAL		92,098[3]	238,533	24,223,431

Demography

Population (2011): 24,661,000.
Density (2011): persons per sq mi 267.8, persons per sq km 103.4.
Urban-rural (2009): urban 50.7%; rural 49.3%.
Sex distribution (2008): male 50.02%; female 49.98%.
Age breakdown (2008): under 15, 37.7%; 15–29, 29.4%; 30–44, 18.3%; 45–59, 9.5%; 60–74, 4.1%; 75–84, 0.9%; 85 and over, 0.1%.
Population projection: (2020) 29,998,000; (2030) 36,144,000.
Doubling time: 35 years.
Ethnic composition (2000): Akan 41.6%; Mossi 23.0%; Ewe 10.0%; Ga-Adangme 7.2%; Gurma 3.4%; Nzima 1.8%; Yoruba 1.6%; other 11.4%.
Religious affiliation (2005): Protestant 23.7%; traditional beliefs 21.5%; Sunnī Muslim 20.1%; independent Christian 15.9%; Roman Catholic 12.2%; other 6.6%.
Major urban agglomerations (2009): Accra 2,370,000; Kumasi 1,850,000; Tamale 447,300; Takoradi 308,300; Tema 175,700; Cape Coast 175,700.

Vital statistics

Birth rate per 1,000 population (2008): 29.4 (world avg. 20.3).
Death rate per 1,000 population (2008): 9.3 (world avg. 8.5).
Total fertility rate (avg. births per childbearing woman; 2008): 3.78.
Life expectancy at birth (2008): male 58.5 years; female 60.8 years.
Major causes of death per 100,000 population (2002): communicable diseases (excluding HIV/AIDS; significantly malaria) 458; cardiovascular diseases 159; HIV/AIDS 147; accidents and violence 83; malignant neoplasms 61.
Adult population (ages 15–49) *living with HIV* (2009): 1.8%[4] (world avg. 0.8%).

National economy

Budget (2009). Revenue: GH¢6,048,000,000 (tax revenue 74.2%, of which income tax 28.4%, VAT 21.0%, trade tax 12.6%, petroleum tax 5.7%; grants 18.2%; nontax revenue 7.6%). Expenditures: GH¢7,330,000,000 (current expenditure 66.9%, of which wages and salaries 33.8%, interest payments 14.1%, transfers 8.2%; capital expenditure 33.1%).
Public debt (external, outstanding; March 2011): U.S.$6,333,760,000.
Household income and expenditure (2006)[5]. Average household size 4.0; mean annual household income GH¢1,217 (U.S.$1,327); sources of income: income from agriculture 34.8%, wages and salaries 28.6%, other self-employment 24.5%, remittances 8.9%; expenditure: food and nonalcoholic beverages 43.2%, housing and energy 9.5%, education 8.9%, clothing 8.7%, transportation 7.3%.
Gross national income (GNI; 2010): U.S.$30,080,000,000 (U.S.$1,240 per capita); purchasing power parity GNI (U.S.$1,600 per capita).

Structure of gross domestic product and labour force

	2009		1999	
	in value GH¢'000,000	% of total value	labour force[6, 7]	% of labour force[6]
Agriculture, forestry, fishing	6,996	32.3	3,778,000	50.5
Mining, quarrying	1,389	6.4	48,000	0.6
Manufacturing	1,575	7.3	798,000	10.7
Construction	2,006	9.2	97,000	1.3
Public utilities	468	2.2	14,000	0.2
Transp. and commun.	1,098	5.1	150,000	2.0
Trade, hotels	1,590	7.3	1,257,000	16.8
Finance, real estate	1,076	5.0	52,000	0.7
Pub. admin., defense	2,771	12.8	673,000	9.0
Services	641	3.0		
Other	2,080[8]	9.6[8]	613,000[9]	8.2[9]
TOTAL	21,690	100.0[3]	7,480,000	100.0

Production (metric tons except as noted). Agriculture, forestry, fishing (2010): cassava 13,504,086, yams 5,960,486, plantains 3,537,734, oil palm fruit (2009) 2,103,600, corn (maize) 1,871,695, taro 1,354,799, cacao 632,037, peanuts (groundnuts) 530,887, oranges (2009) 528,798, rice 491,603, sorghum 324,422, cowpeas 219,257, millet 218,952, tomatoes (2009) 187,306; livestock (number of live animals; 2009) 4,625,000 goats, 3,642,000 sheep, 1,438,000 cattle; roundwood 37,863,781 cu m, of which fuelwood 97%; fisheries production (2009) 328,969 (from aquaculture 2%). Mining and quarrying (2009): bauxite 440,000; manganese (metal content) 350,000; gold 79,883 kg[10]; gem diamonds 376,000 carats. Manufacturing (value added in U.S.$'000,000; 2003): wood products 157; chemical products 115; food products 108; petroleum products 55; precious and nonferrous metal products (including gold) 47; plastic products 39. Energy production (consumption): electricity (kW-hr; 2007) 6,984,000,000 (7,170,000,000); coal, none (none); crude petroleum (barrels; 2009) 2,190,000 ([2007] 14,463,000); petroleum products (metric tons; 2007) 1,232,000 (2,065,000); natural gas, none (none).
Population economically active (2009): total 10,816,000; activity rate of total population 45.4% (participation rates: ages 15–64, 78.3%; female 49.0%; unemployed [2001] 20.3%).

Price and earnings indexes (2005 = 100)

	2004	2005	2006	2007	2008	2009	2010
Consumer price index	86.9	100.0	110.9	122.8	143.1	170.7	188.9
Daily earnings index[11]	82.9	100.0	118.5	140.7	166.7	196.3	...

Selected balance of payments data. Receipts from (U.S.$'000,000): tourism (2009) 968; remittances (2010) 119; foreign direct investment (FDI; 2008–10 avg.) 1,811; official development assistance (2009) 1,583. Disbursements for (U.S.$'000,000): tourism (2009) 584; remittances (2008) 6; FDI (2008–10 avg.) 8.
Land use as % of total land area (2007): in temporary crops or left fallow 18.0%, in permanent crops 10.5%, in pasture 36.7%, forest area 23.2%.

Foreign trade[12]

Balance of trade (current prices)

	2003	2004	2005	2006	2007	2008
U.S.$'000,000	−886	−1,623	−1,819	−1,715	−3,744	−5,025
% of total	16.0%	24.9%	22.9%	19.2%	34.6%	38.4%

Imports (2008): U.S.$9,058,000,000 (machinery and apparatus 22.5%; road vehicles 13.9%; food 12.9%, of which cereals 5.9%; crude petroleum 12.7%). *Major import sources:* China 11.7%; Nigeria 8.7%; U.S. 7.7%; Belgium 5.0%; U.K. 4.3%; India 4.3%.
Exports (2008): U.S.$4,033,000,000 (gold 45.0%; cocoa [all forms] 27.3%; sawn wood 3.6%; veneers, plywood 3.4%; cashews 3.0%). *Major export destinations:* South Africa 44.0%; Neth. 11.7%; India 5.3%; U.K. 3.7%; Malaysia 3.2%.

Transport and communications

Transport. Railroads (2006): route length 588 mi, 947 km[13]; (2004) passenger-km 80,000,000, metric ton-km cargo 216,000,000. Roads (2010): total length 57,610 km (paved 15%). Vehicles (2007): passenger cars 493,770; trucks and buses 279,492. Air transport[14]: (2004) passenger-km 363,000,000; (2003) metric ton-km cargo 17,000,000.

Communications

Medium	date	number in '000s	units per 1,000 persons	Medium	date	number in '000s	units per 1,000 persons
Televisions	2003	1,114	53	PCs	2004	112	5.2
Telephones				Dailies	2009	200[15]	8[15]
Cellular	2010	17,437[16]	715[16]	Internet users	2009	1,297	54
Landline	2010	278	11	Broadband	2010	50[16]	2.1[16]

Education and health

Educational attainment (2003)[17]. Percentage of population age 25 and over having: no formal schooling or unknown 41.8%; incomplete primary education 9.6%; primary 3.6%; incomplete secondary 35.0%; secondary 5.4%; higher 4.6%. *Literacy* (2009): total population age 15 and over literate 66.6%; males literate 72.8%; females literate 60.4%.

Education (2008–09)

	teachers	students	student/ teacher ratio	enrollment rate (%)
Primary (age 6–11)	110,508	3,659,116	33.1	76
Secondary/Voc. (age 12–17)	99,154	1,812,084	18.3	46
Tertiary	7,698	203,376	26.4	9 (age 18–22)

Health (2004): physicians 3,240 (1 per 6,631 persons); hospital beds 19,199 (1 per 1,124 persons); infant mortality rate (2009) 52.5; undernourished population (2004–06) 1,700,000 (8% of total population based on the consumption of a minimum daily requirement of 1,800 calories).

Military

Total active duty personnel (November 2010): 15,500[18] (army 74.2%, navy 12.9%, air force 12.9%). *Military expenditure as percentage of GDP* (2010): 0.7%; per capita expenditure U.S.$5.

[1]The Ghana cedi (GH¢) replaced the cedi (₵) on July 1, 2007, at a rate of 1 GH¢ = ₵10,000. [2]Provisional. [3]Detail does not add to total given because of rounding. [4]Statistically derived midpoint within range. [5]Based on the Ghana Living Standards Survey of 8,687 households. [6]Ages 15–64 only. [7]Derived figures calculated from percentages. [8]Indirect taxes. [9]Unemployed. [10]Legal production only. [11]Minimum daily wage. [12]Imports c.i.f.; exports f.o.b. [13]Of which about 391 mi, 630 km were operable. [14]Ghana Airways only, which subsequently ceased operations in July 2004. [15]Circulation. [16]Subscribers. [17]Based on the Ghana Demographic and Health Survey of 6,251 households. [18]Of which deployed UN peacekeepers 3,136.

Internet resources for further information:
- **Bank of Ghana http://www.bog.gov.gh**
- **Ghana Statistical Service http://www.statsghana.gov.gh**

Greece

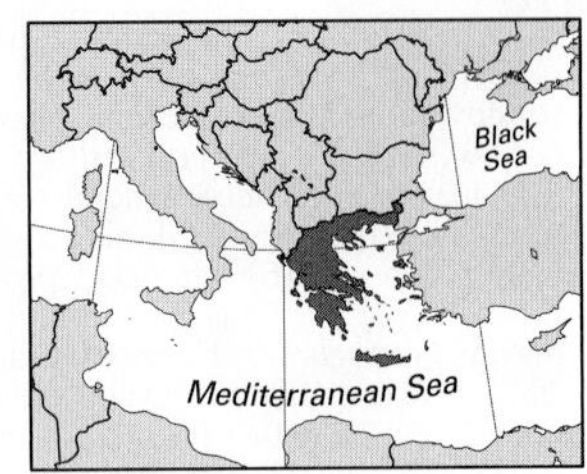

Official name: Ellinikí Dhimokratía (Hellenic Republic).
Form of government: unitary multiparty republic with one legislative house (Hellenic Parliament [300]).
Head of state: President.
Head of government: Prime Minister.
Capital: Athens.
Official language: Greek.
Official religion: [1].
Monetary unit: euro (€); valuation (Sept. 1, 2011) 1 U.S.$ = €0.70; 1 £ = €1.13.

Area and population

Regions[2]	area sq km	population 2008 estimate	Regions[2]	area sq km	population 2008 estimate
Insular			Epirus	9,203	351,786
Aegean Islands	9,122	506,483	Greater Athens	3,808	4,061,326
Crete	8,336	606,274	Macedonia	34,178	2,469,322
Ionian Islands	2,307	228,572	Peloponnese	21,379	1,114,636
Mainland			Thessaly	14,037	736,079
Central Greece			Thrace	8,578	366,541
and Euboea	21,010	772,766	TOTAL	131,957[3]	11,213,785

Demography

Population (2011): 11,372,000.
Density (2011): persons per sq mi 223.2, persons per sq km 86.2.
Urban-rural (2005): urban 60.4%; rural 39.6%.
Sex distribution (2006): male 49.51%; female 50.49%.
Age breakdown (2006): under 15, 14.3%; 15–29, 19.3%; 30–44, 22.9%; 45–59, 19.7%; 60–74, 15.8%; 75–84, 6.6%; 85 and over, 1.4%.
Population projection: (2020) 11,561,000; (2030) 11,613,000.
Ethnic composition (2000)[4]: Greek 90.4%; Macedonian 1.8%; Albanian 1.5%; Turkish 1.4%; Pomak 0.9%; Rom (Gypsy) 0.9%; other 3.1%.
Religious affiliation (2005)[5]: Orthodox *c.* 90%; Sunnī Muslim *c.* 5%; Roman Catholic *c.* 2%; other *c.* 3%.
Major cities (2001): Athens 745,514 (urban agglomeration 3,187,734); Thessaloníki 363,987 (urban agglomeration 800,764); Piraeus (Piraiévs) 175,697[6]; Pátrai 161,114; Peristérion 137,918[6]; Irákleio (Iráklion) 133,012.

Vital statistics

Birth rate per 1,000 population (2009): 10.7 (world avg. 20.3); within marriage (2008) 93.5%; outside of marriage (2008) 6.5%.
Death rate per 1,000 population (2009): 9.8 (world avg. 8.5).
Total fertility rate (avg. births per childbearing woman; 2008): 1.45.
Marriage/divorce rates per 1,000 population: (2009) 4.7/(2007) 1.2.
Life expectancy at birth (2008): male 77.2 years; female 82.2 years.
Major causes of death per 100,000 population (2006): diseases of the circulatory system 352.4; malignant neoplasms (cancers) 280.2; cerebrovascular diseases 186.1; diseases of the respiratory system 66.7; accidents, poisoning, and violence 38.4.

National economy

Budget (2007). Revenue: €89,100,000,000 (tax revenue 51.0%, of which VAT 28.8%, income taxes 19.2%; social contributions 35.7%; other revenue 13.3%). Expenditures: €95,398,000,000 (social benefits 41.1%; wages and salaries 23.8%; goods and services 10.5%; interest payments 10.4%).
Public debt (consolidated, general; 2010): U.S.$374,759,000,000.
Production (metric tons except as noted). Agriculture, forestry, fishing (2009): corn (maize) 2,352,000, olives (2008) 2,313,055, wheat 1,830,000, tomatoes 1,350,000, sugar beets 1,000,000, grapes 850,000, potatoes 848,000, oranges 800,000, peaches and nectarines 734,000, seed cotton 715,000, barley 280,000, apples 235,000, rice 205,000; livestock (number of live animals) 8,994,000 sheep, 4,178,000 goats, 1,340,000 beehives; roundwood (2010) 1,742,916 cu m, of which fuelwood 46%; fisheries production 205,299 (from aquaculture 59%). Mining and quarrying (2008): bauxite 2,176,300; nickel (metal content) 16,700; marble 150,000 cu m. Manufacturing (value added in U.S.$'000,000; 2005): food products and beverages *c.* 5,300; textiles *c.* 1,950; chemicals and chemical products *c.* 1,750; cement, bricks, and ceramics *c.* 1,600; refined petroleum and coal derivatives *c.* 1,500; wearing apparel *c.* 1,500; basic metals *c.* 1,450. Energy production (consumption): electricity (kW-hr; 2007) 63,496,000,000 (67,851,000,000); hard coal (metric tons; 2007) none (710,000); lignite (metric tons; 2007) 66,308,000 (66,373,000); crude petroleum (barrels; 2007) 535,000 (140,300,000); petroleum products (metric tons; 2007) 21,238,000 (18,907,000); natural gas (cu m; 2007) 26,000,000 (3,993,000,000).
Population economically active (2008): total 4,974,000; activity rate of total population 44.2% (participation rates: ages 15–64, 67.7%; female [2007] 40.9%; unemployed [January–March 2009] 9.3%).

Price and earnings indexes (2005 = 100)

	2004	2005	2006	2007	2008	2009	2010
Consumer price index	96.6	100.0	103.2	106.2	110.6	111.9	117.2
Monthly earnings index	98.4	100.0	102.1	105.6	108.1	113.8	110.7

Household income and expenditure (1998–99). Average household size (2004) 3.1; income per family Dr 6,429,000[7] (U.S.$21,390); sources of income: wages and salaries 21.8%, transfer payments 21.7%, income from agriculture, forestry, fishing 15.6%, self-employment 11.9%, other 29.0%; expenditure (2004–05): food 17.1%, transportation 12.6%, housing and energy 10.7%, café/hotel expenditures 9.6%, clothing and footwear 8.4%.
Gross national income (GNI; 2010): U.S.$308,596,000,000 (U.S.$27,240 per capita); purchasing power parity GNI (U.S.$27,360 per capita).

Structure of gross domestic product and labour force

	2008		2009	
	in value €'000,000	% of total value	labour force	% of labour force
Agriculture, forestry, fishing	7,803	3.3	520,000	10.5
Mining, quarrying	936	0.4	13,500	0.3
Manufacturing	23,361	9.8	529,000	10.7
Construction	10,173	4.3	367,700	7.4
Public utilities	5,652	2.4	59,300	1.2
Transp. and commun.	20,300	8.5	293,000	5.9
Trade, restaurants	52,590	22.0	1,116,900	22.6
Finance, real estate	38,680	16.2	429,100	8.7
Pub. admin., defense	18,174	7.6	372,800	7.5
Services	33,055	13.8	784,500	15.9
Other	28,417[8]	11.9[8]	462,300[9]	9.3[9]
TOTAL	239,141	100.0[3]	4,948,100	100.0

Selected balance of payments data. Receipts from (U.S.$'000,000): tourism (2009) 14,681; remittances (2009) 1,843; foreign direct investment (FDI; 2008–10 avg.) 3,041. Disbursements for (U.S.$'000,000): tourism (2009) 3,401; remittances (2008) 1,912; FDI (2008–10 avg.) 1,914.
Land use as % of total land area (2007): in temporary crops or left fallow 19.8%, in permanent crops 8.8%, in pasture 35.7%, forest area 29.6%.

Foreign trade[10]

Balance of trade (current prices)

	2005	2006	2007	2008	2009	2010
U.S.$'000,000	–37,460	–42,796	–52,595	–63,792	–43,943	–31,797
% of total	51.8%	50.5%	52.8%	55.6%	50.1%	49.4%

Imports (2008): U.S.$89,301,000,000 (mineral fuels 20.0%; machinery and apparatus 14.7%; food 8.6%; road vehicles/parts 7.7%; medicine and pharmaceuticals 6.0%; ships and tankers 3.8%). *Major import sources:* Germany 11.9%; Italy 11.4%; Russia 7.3%; China 5.5%; France 5.1%.
Exports (2008): U.S.$25,509,000,000 (food 15.6%, of which vegetables and fruit 7.7%; machinery and apparatus 10.6%; refined petroleum 10.1%; apparel 6.0%; iron and steel 5.6%; medicine 4.9%; aluminum 4.2%). *Major export destinations:* Italy 11.5%; Germany 10.5%; Bulgaria 7.1%; Cyprus 6.4%; U.S. 5.1%.

Transport and communications

Transport. Railroads (2008): route length 1,583 mi, 2,548 km; passenger-km (2007) 1,930,000,000; metric ton-km cargo (2007) 835,000,000. Roads (2005): total length 34,863 km (paved 93%); passenger-km (2006) 111,800,000,000; metric ton-km cargo (2008) 28,850,000,000. Vehicles (2007): passenger cars 4,798,530; trucks and buses 1,283,047. Air transport (2008): passenger-km 6,612,000,000; metric ton-km cargo 69,660,000.

Communications

Medium	date	number in '000s	units per 1,000 persons	Medium	date	number in '000s	units per 1,000 persons
Televisions	2003	6,152	558	PCs	2007	1,058	94
Telephones				Dailies	2009	1,100[11]	116[11]
Cellular	2010	12,293[12]	1,082[12]	Internet users	2009	4,971	445
Landline	2010	5,203	458	Broadband	2010	2,253[12]	198[12]

Education and health

Educational attainment (2001). Percentage of population age 25 and over having: no formal schooling 12.7%; primary education 34.3%; lower secondary 8.5%; upper secondary 25.7%; higher 18.8%. *Literacy* (2007): total population age 15 and over literate 97.1%; males 98.2%; females 96.0%.

Education (2005–06)

	teachers	students	student/ teacher ratio	enrollment rate (%)
Primary (age 6–11)	61,251	645,324	10.5	99
Secondary/Voc. (age 12–17)	86,024	704,515	8.2	92
Tertiary	28,863	653,003	22.6	95 (age 18–22)

Health (2006): physicians 21,038[13] (1 per 436 persons); hospital beds 44,307[13] (1 per 207 persons); infant mortality rate per 1,000 live births (2009) 3.4; undernourished population (2004–06) less than 5.0% of total population.

Military

Total active duty personnel (November 2010): 138,936 (army 56.7%, navy 14.4%, air force 20.5%, joint staff 8.4%); reserve 250,876; Greek troops in Cyprus (2010) 950; U.S. troops in Greece (2010) 346. *Military expenditure as percentage of GDP* (2009): 3.1%[14]; per capita expenditure U.S.$903[14].

[1]The autocephalous Greek Orthodox Church has special recognition per the constitution. [2]Traditional regions; local administration is based on 13 administrative regions and 1 autonomous self-governing monastic region (Mount Athos). [3]Detail does not add to total given because of rounding. [4]Unofficial source; government states there are no ethnic divisions in Greece. [5]Including non-citizen residents. [6]Within Athens urban agglomeration. [7]The drachma (Dr) was the former monetary unit; on Jan. 1, 2002, Dr 340.75 = €1. [8]Taxes less subsidies. [9]Unemployed. [10]Imports c.i.f.; exports f.o.b. [11]Circulation of daily newspapers. [12]Subscribers. [13]Public health institutions only. [14]Includes military pensions.

Internet resources for further information:

- **Bank of Greece http://www.bankofgreece.gr/Pages/en**
- **National Statistical Service of Greece http://www.statistics.gr**

Greenland

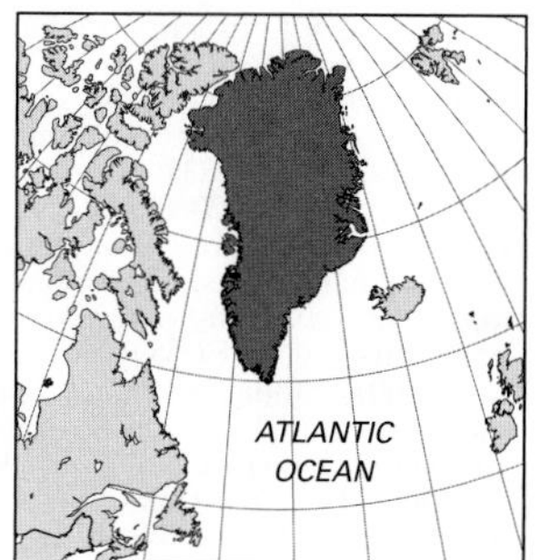

Official name: Kalaallit Nunaat (Greenlandic)[1] (Greenland).
Political status: self-governing overseas administrative division of Denmark with one legislative house (Parliament [31])[2].
Head of state: Danish Monarch.
Heads of government: High Commissioner (for Denmark); Prime Minister (for Greenland).
Capital: Nuuk.
Official language: Greenlandic.
Official religion: Evangelical Lutheran (Lutheran Church of Greenland).
Monetary unit: Danish krone (DKK); valuation (Sept. 1, 2011) 1 U.S.$ = DKK 5.23; 1 £ = DKK 8.45.

Area and population

Municipalities[4]	Administrative centre	area sq mi	area sq km	population 2011[3] estimate
Kujalleq	Qaqortoq	19,700	51,000	7,441
Qaasuitsup	Ilulissat	225,900	585,100	17,742
Qeqqata	Sisimiut	37,500	97,000	9,684
Sermersooq	Nuuk	222,100	575,300	21,559
Unincorporated areas				
Northeast Greenland National Park	—	331,100	857,600	—
Pituffik (Thule Air Base)	Pituffik	…	…	…[5]
TOTAL		836,300[6]	2,166,000[6]	56,615[7]

Demography

Population (2011): 56,700.
Density (2011)[8]: persons per sq mi 0.36, persons per sq km 0.14.
Urban-rural (2010[3]): urban (town) 84.1%; rural (settlement) 15.9%.
Sex distribution (2010[3]): male 53.03%; female 46.97%.
Age breakdown (2008[3]): under 15, 23.7%; 15–29, 22.1%; 30–44, 23.3%; 45–59, 20.4%; 60–74, 8.7%; 75 and over, 1.8%.
Population projection: (2020) 57,000; (2030) 58,000.
Doubling time: 75 years.
Ethnic composition (2010[3]): Inuit (Greenland Eskimo) 88%; Danish and others 12%.
Religious affiliation (2000): Protestant 69.2%, of which Evangelical Lutheran 64.2%, Pentecostal 2.8%; other Christian 27.4%; other/nonreligious 3.4%.
Major towns (2011[3]): Nuuk 15,862; Sisimiut 5,498; Ilulissat 4,606; Qaqortoq 3,230; Aasiaat 3,113.

Vital statistics

Birth rate per 1,000 population (2009): 15.9 (world avg. 20.3); within marriage (1993) 29.2%; outside of marriage (1993) 70.8%.
Death rate per 1,000 population (2009): 6.6 (world avg. 8.5).
Natural increase rate per 1,000 population (2009): 9.3 (world avg. 11.8).
Total fertility rate (avg. births per childbearing woman; 2009): 2.36.
Marriage/divorce rates per 1,000 population (1999): 4.5/n.a.
Life expectancy at birth (2008): male 66.6 years; female 71.6 years.
Major causes of death per 100,000 population (2006; 2 categories only): malignant neoplasms (cancers) *c.* 186; suicide *c.* 88.

National economy

Budget (general government; 2008). Revenue: DKK 8,847,000,000 (block grant from Danish government 45.2%, taxes on income and wealth 34.1%, import duties 6.2%, other 14.5%). Expenditures: DKK 8,756,000,000 (social welfare 25.9%, education 18.9%, health 12.7%, general administration 11.2%, economic affairs 11.0%, housing 4.4%, public order 3.6%).
Production (metric tons except as noted). Agriculture, forestry, fishing, other marine: locally grown broccoli, cauliflower, and cabbage sold commercially for the first time in 2007, potatoes also produced; roundwood, n.a.; fish catch (2009) 170,900 (of which prawn 116,700, Greenland halibut 30,700, Atlantic cod 10,300, lumpfish 6,600, crab 3,400); number of other marine catch (2009) narwhals 371, beluga whales 228, pilot whales 172, minke whales 165, porpoises 1,642, seals 98,008, walrus 127; livestock (number of live animals; 2009) 19,500 sheep, (2008) 2,500 tame reindeer, 150 horses; number of animals killed (2009) reindeer 10,620, musk ox 2,331, polar bear 124. Mining (2008): gold 1,518 kg. Manufacturing: principally fish and prawn processing, handicrafts, hides and skins, and ship repair. Energy production (consumption): electricity (kW-hr; 2009) 376,000,000 (213,000,000); coal, none (none); crude petroleum, none (none); petroleum products (metric tons; 2007) none (170,000); natural gas, none (none).
Tourism (2009): number of overnight stays at hotels 224,801, of which visitors from within Greenland 57,438, from Denmark 30,050, from the U.S. 5,718.
Land use as % of total land area (2009): in temporary crops or left fallow, negligible; in permanent crops, none; in pasture 0.6%; forest area, negligible (1.2 sq mi [2 sq km]).
Household income and expenditure. Average household size (2009[3]) 2.5; average disposable income per household (2008) DKK 260,014 (U.S.$48,869); sources of income: n.a.; expenditure (1994): food, beverages, and tobacco 41.6%, housing and energy 22.4%, transportation and communications 10.2%, recreation 6.4%.
Gross national income (2009): U.S.$1,857,000,000 (U.S.$32,960 per capita).

Structure of gross domestic product and labour force

	2007 in value U.S.$'000,000	2007 % of total value	2006 labour force[9]	2006 % of labour force[9]
Agriculture, fishing, hunting, trapping	92	4.2	1,456	5.0
Mining	57	2.6	160	0.5
Public utilities			420	1.4
Manufacturing	170	7.7	924	3.1
Construction	129	5.9	2,904	9.9
Transp. and commun.	103	4.7	2,582	8.8
Trade, restaurants	178	8.1	5,862	19.9
Finance, real estate	1,118	50.9	1,446	4.9
Public administration			13,718	46.5
Services				
Other	350[10]	15.9[10]	—	—
TOTAL	2,197	100.0	29,472	100.0

Population economically active (2009[3]): total 32,652; activity rate of total population 58.1% (participation rates: ages 15–62 [2004[3]] 83.5%; female [2006] 48.6%; unemployed[11] 7.1%).

Price index (2005 = 100)

	2004	2005	2006	2007	2008	2009	2010
Consumer price index	97.8	100.0	102.2	107.7	112.6	117.0	119.7

Public debt (2008): none[12].

Foreign trade

Balance of trade (current prices)

	2004	2005	2006	2007	2008	2009
DKK '000,000	−987	−1,165	−1,308	−1,323	−1,948	−1,745
% of total	17.8%	19.4%	21.8%	22.2%	28.3%	31.2%

Imports (2008): DKK 4,421,000,000 (mineral fuels [mostly refined petroleum] 26.9%, machinery and transport equipment 20.9%, food 16.8%, manufactured products 13.6%). *Major import sources:* Denmark 60.2%; Sweden 25.7%; Norway 2.4%; Germany 2.3%; China 1.2%.
Exports (2008): DKK 2,473,000,000 (prawn 50.8%, Greenland halibut 18.4%, cod 11.2%, gold 6.1%, crab 1.7%). *Major export destinations:* Denmark 85.2%; Canada 6.1%; U.K. 2.0%.

Transport and communications

Transport. Railroads: none. Roads (1998): total length[13] 93 mi, 150 km (paved 60%); passenger-km, n.a.; metric ton-km cargo, n.a. Vehicles (2008): passenger cars 5,125; trucks and buses 435. Air transport (2009)[14]: passenger-km 458,534,000; metric ton-km cargo 49,934,000.

Communications

Medium	date	number in '000s	units per 1,000 persons	Medium	date	number in '000s	units per 1,000 persons
Televisions	2002	…[15]	…[15]	PCs	2009	…	…
Telephones				Dailies	2009	—[16]	—[16]
Cellular	2010	57[17]	1,001[17]	Internet users	2009	36	628
Landline	2010	22	381	Broadband	2010	12[17]	210[17]

Education and health

Educational attainment (2002). Two-thirds of labour force has no formal education. *Literacy* (2001): total population age 15 and over literate: virtually 100%.

Education (2007–08)

	teachers	students	student/ teacher ratio	enrollment rate (%)
Primary	1,189	10,255	8.6	…
Secondary/Voc.	…	…	…	…
Tertiary[18]	29	230	7.9	…

Health: physicians (2005[3]) 91 (1 per 626 persons); hospital beds (2007) 227 (1 per 249 persons); infant mortality rate per 1,000 live births (2008) 9.6; undernourished population, n.a.

Military

Total active duty personnel. Denmark is responsible for Greenland's defense. Greenlanders are not liable for military service. U.S. air force personnel at Thule Air Base (June 2011): 135.

[1]Called Grønland in Danish, an official language of Greenland prior to June 21, 2009. [2]A referendum approved in November 2008 endorsed the gradual expansion of Greenland's autonomy from Denmark; the Greenland government assumed greater responsibility for local matters on June 21, 2009. [3]January 1. [4]New administrative structure from Jan. 1, 2009. [5]There were 135 U.S. military personnel in June 2011. [6]Surveyed ice-free area in 1996 was 158,475 sq mi (410,449 sq km) and permanent ice area was 677,855 sq mi (1,755,637 sq km), making the total surveyed area 836,330 sq mi (2,166,086 sq km). [7]Includes 189 in unknown municipality. [8]Population density calculated with reference to ice-free area only. [9]Employed persons only. [10]Includes taxes and import duties. [11]Town residents only. [12]But government-owned corporations have debt obligations in ships and buildings. [13]All short roads in towns; there are no roads between towns. [14]Air Greenland A/S only. [15]In 2002, 97% of households had a television. [16]There are no daily newspapers in Greenland. One paper is published twice a week, one weekly. [17]Subscribers. [18]2006–07; summed total for the University of Greenland and the Teacher Training School.

Internet resources for further information:
- **Statistics Greenland http://www.stat.gl/**
- **Danmarks Statistik Yearbook http://www.dst.dk/HomeUK/Statistics/ofs/Publications/Yearbook.aspx**

Grenada

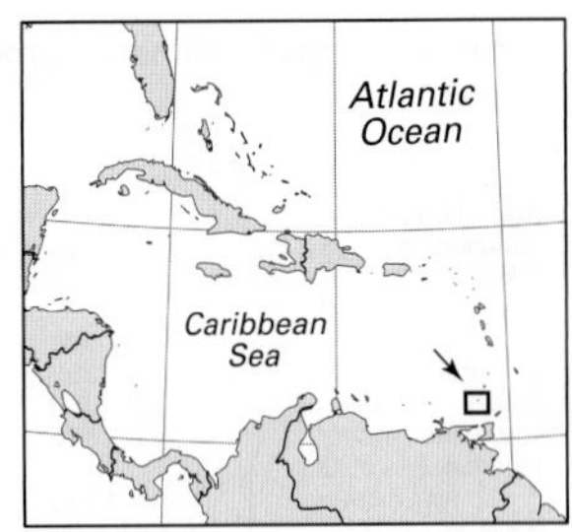

Official name: Grenada.
Form of government: constitutional monarchy with two legislative houses (Senate [13]; House of Representatives [15]).
Head of state: British Monarch represented by Governor-General.
Head of government: Prime Minister.
Capital: St. George's.
Official language: English.
Official religion: none.
Monetary unit: Eastern Caribbean dollar (EC$); valuation (Sept. 1, 2011) 1 U.S.$ = EC$2.70; 1 £ = EC$4.36.

Area and population

		area		population
Parishes[1]	**Principal towns**	sq mi	sq km	2001 census
St. Andrew	Grenville	38	99	24,749
St. David	St. David's	17	44	11,486
St. George	…	25[2]	65[2]	37,057[2]
St. John	Gouyave	14	35	8,591
St. Mark	Victoria	10	25	3,994
St. Patrick	Sauteurs	16	42	10,674
Town				
St. George's	—	[2]	[2]	[2, 3]
Grenadian dependencies[1]				
Carriacou	Hillsborough	10	26	6,081
Petite Martinique	…	3	8	
TOTAL		133	344	102,632

Demography

Population (2011): 108,000.
Density (2011): persons per sq mi 812.0, persons per sq km 314.0.
Urban-rural (2009): urban 30.9%; rural 69.1%.
Sex distribution (2008): male 51.96%; female 48.04%.
Age breakdown (2008): under 15, 32.4%; 15–29, 33.7%; 30–44, 21.6%; 45–59, 8.2%; 60–74, 3.1%; 75 and over, 1.0%.
Population projection: (2020) 113,000; (2030) 116,000.
Doubling time: 71 years.
Ethnic composition (2000): black 51.7%; mixed 40.0%; Indo-Pakistani 4.0%; white 0.9%; other 3.4%.
Religious affiliation (2005): Roman Catholic *c.* 41%; Protestant (of which significantly Anglican and Seventh-day Adventist) *c.* 30%; Rastafarian *c.* 5%; nonreligious/other *c.* 24%.
Major localities (2006): St. George's (2009) 5,200 (urban agglomeration [2007] 32,000); Gouyave 3,400; Grenville 2,500; Victoria 2,300.

Vital statistics

Birth rate per 1,000 population (2009): 19.5 (world avg. 20.3).
Death rate per 1,000 population (2009): 8.4 (world avg. 8.5).
Natural increase rate per 1,000 population (2009): 11.1 (world avg. 11.8).
Total fertility rate (avg. births per childbearing woman; 2009): 2.3.
Marriage/divorce rates per 1,000 population (2001): 5.0/1.1.
Life expectancy at birth (2009): male 74.0 years; female 77.1 years.
Major causes of death per 100,000 population (2008): diseases of the circulatory system 301.3, of which ischemic heart disease 73.4; malignant neoplasms (cancers) 142.9; diabetes mellitus 62.8; accidents, poisoning, and violence 41.5.

National economy

Budget (2009). Revenue: EC$431,100,000 (tax revenue 88.1%, of which tax on international trade 45.9%, income taxes 20.2%; grants 6.8%; nontax revenue 5.1%). Expenditures: EC$533,700,000 (current expenditure 78.1%, of which wages 35.8%, transfers 17.6%, debt service 8.5%; capital expenditure 21.9%).
Public debt (external, outstanding; 2009): U.S.$542,000,000.
Gross national income (GNI; 2010): U.S.$580,000,000 (U.S.$5,560 per capita); purchasing power parity GNI (U.S.$7,560 per capita).

Structure of gross domestic product and labour force

	2009		1998	
	in value EC$'000,000	% of total value	labour force	% of labour force
Agriculture	92.6	5.5	4,794	11.7
Quarrying	6.3	0.4	58	0.1
Manufacturing	58.7	3.5	2,579	6.3
Construction	102.0	6.0	5,163	12.6
Public utilities	95.7	5.7	505	1.2
Transp. and commun.	269.3	15.9	2,043	5.0
Trade, restaurants	181.2	10.7	8,298	20.2
Finance, real estate	197.1	11.7	1,312	3.2
Pub. admin., defense	274.2	16.2	1,879	4.6
Services	282.0	16.7	6,837	16.7
Other	132.6[4]	7.8[4]	7,547[5]	18.4[5]
TOTAL	1,691.7	100.0[6]	41,015	100.0

Production (metric tons except as noted). Agriculture, forestry, fishing (2009): sugarcane 7,200, coconuts 7,028, nutmeg 2,395[7], mangoes 2,274, grapefruit 1,772, avocados 1,610, bananas 1,412[7], oranges 1,071, plantains 758, plums 740, yams 664, pigeon peas 598, cacao 261[7], cinnamon 37, cloves 13; livestock (number of live animals) 13,200 sheep, 7,200 goats, 4,450 cattle, 2,650 pigs; roundwood, n.a.; fisheries production 2,615 (from aquaculture, none). Mining and quarrying: excavation of limestone, sand, and gravel for local use. Manufacturing (value of production in EC$'000; 1997): wheat flour 13,390; soft drinks 9,798; beer 7,072; animal feed 5,852; rum 5,497; toilet paper 4,237; malt 4,192; stout 3,835; cigarettes 1,053. Energy production (consumption): electricity (kW-hr; 2008) 169,568,000 ([2007] 171,000,000); coal, none (none); crude petroleum, none (none); petroleum products (metric tons; 2007) none (78,000); natural gas, none (none).
Household income and expenditure. Average household size (2003) 3.3; income per capita (2000) EC$8,922 (U.S.$3,400); sources of income: n.a.; expenditure (2001)[8]: food, beverages, and tobacco 38.6%, transportation and communications 15.7%, housing 10.2%, clothing and footwear 9.8%.
Population economically active (2004): total 37,000; activity rate of total population *c.* 35% (participation rates: ages 15–64 [1998] *c.* 78%; female [1998] 43.5%; unemployed [2008] 24.9%).

Price index (2005 = 100)

	2004	2005	2006	2007	2008	2009	2010
Consumer price index	94.2	100.0	101.7	109.2	114.8	112.1	118.6

Selected balance of payments data. Receipts from (U.S.$'000,000): tourism (2009) 99; remittances (2010) 59; foreign direct investment (2008–10 avg.) 111; official development assistance (2009) 48. Disbursements for (U.S.$'000,000): tourism (2010) 10; remittances (2009) 4.
Land use as % of total land area (2007): in temporary crops or left fallow 5.9%, in permanent crops 29.4%, in pasture 2.9%, forest area 12.1%.

Foreign trade[9]

Balance of trade (current prices)

	2004	2005	2006	2007	2008
U.S.$'000,000	–218.9	–306.4	–273.5	–331.7	–332.8
% of total	77.6%	84.7%	84.3%	83.2%	84.5%

Imports (2008): U.S.$363,300,000 (refined petroleum 18.6%; food 17.9%; machinery and apparatus 15.2%; road vehicles 5.3%; manufactures of metal 4.9%). *Major import sources:* U.S. 30.9%; Trinidad and Tobago 24.9%; Venezuela 7.0%; U.K. 4.4%; Japan 3.6%.
Exports (2008): U.S.$30,500,000 (food 57.0%, of which wheat flour 24.6%, spices [nearly all nutmeg and mace] 8.9%, tuna 8.5%, cocoa 7.5%; toilet paper 9.5%; general industrial machinery 4.5%; road vehicles 4.3%). *Major export destinations:* U.S. 16.4%; Dominica 16.4%; Saint Lucia 11.1%; Barbados 9.5%; St. Kitts and Nevis 8.5%.

Transport and communications

Transport. Railroads: none. Roads (2000): total length 700 mi, 1,127 km (paved 61%). Vehicles (2001): passenger cars 15,800; trucks and buses 4,200. Air transport: n.a.

Communications

Medium	date	number in '000s	units per 1,000 persons	Medium	date	number in '000s	units per 1,000 persons
Televisions	2001	38	375	PCs	2004	16	155
Telephones				Dailies	2010	—	—
Cellular	2010	122[10]	1,167[10]	Internet users	2009	25	241
Landline	2010	28	272	Broadband	2010	11[10]	102[10]

Education and health

Educational attainment (2001). Percentage of population age 18 and over having: no formal schooling or unknown 7.6%; primary education 65.1%; secondary 21.7%; higher 5.6%, of which university 1.5%. *Literacy* (2004): total population age 15 and over literate 98.0%.

Education (2008–09)

	teachers	students	student/ teacher ratio	enrollment rate (%)
Primary (age 5–11)	830	14,186	17.1	93[11]
Secondary/Voc. (age 12–16)	600	11,031	18.4	89[11]
Tertiary	…	6,689	…	53 (age 17–21)

Health (2009): physicians 81 (1 per 1,323 persons); hospital beds 257 (1 per 417 persons); infant mortality rate per 1,000 live births (2007) 11.0; undernourished population (2004–06) 24,000 (23% of total population based on the consumption of a minimum daily requirement of 1,840 calories).

Military

Total active duty personnel (2010): paramilitary and coast guard units only. *Military expenditure as percentage of GDP:* n.a.; per capita expenditure, n.a.

[1]Grenada does not have a local government system. [2]St. George local council includes St. George's town. [3]Preliminary 2001 census figure for St. George's town is 3,908. [4]Taxes on products less subsidies and less imputed bank service charges. [5]Includes 1,321 participants in activities not adequately defined and 6,226 unemployed. [6]Detail does not add to total given because of rounding. [7]Hurricanes Ivan and Emily, which struck Grenada in September 2004 and June 2005, respectively, destroyed much of the nutmeg and cacao fields as well as the banana crop; it is estimated that it will take a decade to regrow the nutmeg groves. [8]Weights of consumer price index components. [9]Imports c.i.f.; exports f.o.b. [10]Subscribers. [11]2007–08.

Internet resources for further information:
- **Eastern Caribbean Central Bank**
  http://www.eccb-centralbank.org
- **Caricom Statistics**
  http://www.caricomstats.org

Guadeloupe

Official name: Département d'Outre-Mer de la Guadeloupe (Overseas Department of Guadeloupe).[1, 2]
Political status: overseas department/overseas region (France) with two legislative houses (General Council[3] [40]; Regional Council[4] [41]).
Head of state: President of France.
Heads of government: Prefect (for France); President of the General Council (for Guadeloupe); President of the Regional Council (for Guadeloupe).
Capital: Basse-Terre.
Official language: French.
Official religion: none.
Monetary unit: euro (€); valuation (Sept. 1, 2011) 1 U.S.$ = €0.70; 1 £ = €1.13.

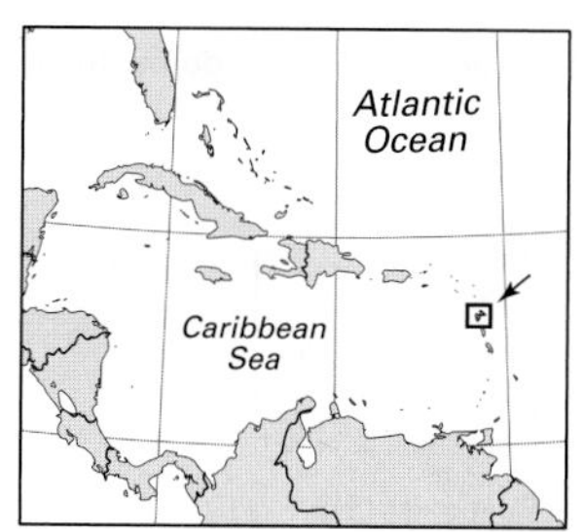

Area and population[5]

Arrondissements	Capitals	area sq mi	area sq km	population mid-2008 estimate[6]
Basse-Terre[7]	Basse-Terre	330	855	190,644
Pointe-à-Pitre[8]	Pointe-à-Pitre	299	775	211,140
TOTAL		629	1,630	401,784

Demography

Population (2011): 407,000[5].
Density (2011): persons per sq mi 647.1, persons per sq km 249.7.
Urban-rural (2009): urban 98.5%; rural 1.5%.
Sex distribution (2007[9]): male 47.00%; female 53.00%.
Age breakdown (2005): under 15, 23.1%; 15–29, 19.8%; 30–44, 22.6%; 45–59, 17.8%; 60–74, 10.3%; 75–84, 5.1%; 85 and over, 1.3%.
Population projection[5]: (2020) 421,000; (2030) 431,000.
Ethnic composition (2000): Creole (mulatto) 76.7%; black 10.0%; Guadeloupe mestizo (French–East Asian) 10.0%; white 2.0%; other 1.3%.
Religious affiliation (2000): Roman Catholic 86.4%; Protestant 4.5%; Jehovah's Witness 3.9%; nonreligious/atheist 3.1%; other 2.1%.
Major communes (2008)[6]: Les Abymes 59,270[10]; Baie-Mahault 29,503[10]; Le Gosier 26,895[10]; Pointe-à-Pitre 17,216 (urban agglomeration 255,059); Basse-Terre 12,173 (urban agglomeration 52,815).

Vital statistics

Birth rate per 1,000 population (2009): 13.2 (world avg. 20.3); within marriage (1999) 34.7%; outside of marriage (1999) 65.3%.
Death rate per 1,000 population (2009): 7.0 (world avg. 8.5).
Natural increase rate per 1,000 population (2009): 6.2 (world avg. 11.8).
Total fertility rate (avg. births per childbearing woman; 2009): 2.30.
Marriage/divorce rates per 1,000 population (2007): 3.6/2.0.
Life expectancy at birth (2007): male 76.2 years; female 83.3 years.
Major causes of death per 100,000 population (2006): diseases of the circulatory system 210.5, of which cerebrovascular disease 72.2, hypertensive diseases 31.4; malignant neoplasms (cancers) 178.1; accidents 43.8; diabetes mellitus 37.3; diseases of the digestive system 34.6.

National economy

Budget (2008)[11]. Revenue: €684,000,000 (grants and subsidies 44.5%, indirect taxes 33.3%, direct taxes 16.6%, loans 2.0%, other 3.6%). Expenditures: €624,100,000 (current expenditures 83.8%, development expenditures 16.2%).
Public debt: n.a.
Production (metric tons except as noted). Agriculture, forestry, fishing (2009): sugarcane 700,000, bananas 55,676, vegetables 40,479, roots and tubers 13,294, melons 8,106, pineapples 7,000, plantains 6,188, cattle meat 3,300; livestock (number of live animals) 75,000 cattle, 15,000 pigs, 300,000 chickens; roundwood (2010) 15,300 cu m, of which fuelwood 98%; fisheries production 10,012 (from aquaculture, negligible). Mining and quarrying (2008): pumice 210,000. Manufacturing (value added in €'000,000; 2006): food and agricultural products (including rum) 51; machinery and apparatus 43; other products include clothing, wooden furniture and posts, and metalware. Energy production (consumption): electricity (kW-hr; 2007) 1,227,000,000 (1,227,000,000); coal, none (none); crude petroleum, none (none); petroleum products (metric tons; 2007) none (668,000); natural gas, none (none).
Selected balance of payments data. Receipts from (U.S.$'000,000): tourism (2008) 384; remittances, n.a.; foreign direct investment, n.a. Disbursements for (U.S.$'000,000): tourism, n.a.; remittances, n.a.
Land use as % of total land area (2009): in temporary crops or left fallow 12.4%, in permanent crops 1.9%, in pasture 11.2%, forest area 38.3%.
Population economically active (2006): total 219,000; activity rate of total population 48.5% (participation rates: ages 15–59, 74.8%; female 50.5%; unemployed [2009] 23.5%).

Price index (2005 = 100)

	2004	2005	2006	2007	2008	2009	2010
Consumer price index	96.9	100.0	102.0	103.3	105.7	105.9	108.8

Gross domestic product (at current market prices; 2009): U.S.$11,336,000,000 (U.S.$25,243 per capita).

Structure of gross domestic product and labour force

	2007 in value €'000,000	2007 % of total value	2008 labour force[12]	2008 % of labour force[12]
Agriculture	241	3.0	2,375	2.0
Mining	...	...	...	...
Manufacturing	353	4.3	7,237	6.0
Public utilities	43	0.5	1,010	0.8
Construction	678	8.3	8,562	7.1
Transp. and commun.	273	3.4	7,748	6.5
Trade, hotels	986	12.1	24,608	20.6
Finance, real estate; Services }			46,275	38.7
Finance, real estate; Services; Pub. admin., defense }	5,189	63.7		
Pub. admin., defense			19,123	16.0
Other	384	4.7	2,735	2.3
TOTAL	8,147	100.0	119,673	100.0

Household income and expenditure (2006). Average household size 3.2[13]; disposable income per household (2000) €25,441 (U.S.$23,439); sources of income (2000): wages and salaries 81.5%, transfer payments 17.2%, property 1.3%; expenditure[14]: food and beverages 20.9%, energy 10.1%, housing 8.9%, clothing 7.8%, health 6.5%, transportation and communications 6.1%.

Foreign trade[15]

Balance of trade (current prices)

	2004	2005	2006	2007	2008	2009
€'000,000	–1,691	–2,000	–2,123	–2,192	–2,396	–1,659
% of total	85.8%	84.4%	85.0%	82.2%	85.4%	85.6%

Imports (2008): €2,601,000,000 (refined petroleum 18.5%, agricultural and food products 14.5%, machinery and apparatus 12.4%, road vehicles 12.2%, pharmaceuticals 5.4%). *Major import sources:* France (metropolitan) 52.1%; other EU countries 13.3%; Martinique 8.1%; U.S. 5.6%.
Exports (2008): €205,000,000 (refined petroleum 20.5%, sugar 13.3%, bananas 10.0%, rum 8.4%, base and fabricated metals 7.2%, electrical machinery and electronics 5.1%). *Major export destinations:* France (metropolitan) 38.5%; Martinique 21.5%; French Guiana 19.5%; other EU countries 6.8%.

Transport and communications

Transport. Railroads: none. Roads (2009): total length[16] 643 mi, 1,035 km (paved, n.a.). Vehicles (2001): passenger cars 117,700; trucks and buses 31,400. Air transport (2007): passenger-km[17] 3,794,000,000; metric ton-km cargo, n.a.

Communications

Medium	date	number in '000s	units per 1,000 persons	Medium	date	number in '000s	units per 1,000 persons
Televisions	2001	125	289	PCs	2005	90	200
Telephones				Dailies	2009	2[18]	4.9[18]
Cellular	2005	315[19]	710[19]	Internet users	2009	109	234
Landline	2010	256	555	Broadband	2010	...	...

Education and health

Educational attainment (2006). Percentage of population age 15 and over having: no formal education through incomplete secondary education 60.0%; complete lower vocational 15.7%; complete secondary 12.1%; incomplete/complete higher 12.2%. *Literacy:* n.a.

Education (2007–08)

	teachers	students	student/teacher ratio	enrollment rate (%)
Primary (age 6–10)	3,384[20]	38,189	...	...
Secondary/Voc. (age 11–17)	4,696[20]	53,153	...	...
Tertiary	...	8,718	...	... (age 18–22)

Health (2007[9]): physicians 1,014 (1 per 398 persons); hospital beds 1,513 (1 per 266 persons); infant mortality rate per 1,000 live births (2006) 9.0; undernourished population, n.a.

Military

Total active duty personnel (November 2010): French troops in West Indies (Guadeloupe and Martinique) *c.* 1,185 (army *c.* 61%, navy *c.* 38%, air force, n.a., gendarmerie *c.* 1%).

[1]On Feb. 22, 2007, Saint-Martin (the northern half of the island of St. Martin) and Saint-Barthélemy formally separated from Guadeloupe to become overseas collectivities of France. [2]Guadeloupe is simultaneously administered as an overseas region (*région d'outre-mer*). [3]Assembly for overseas department. [4]Assembly for overseas region. [5]Excludes Saint-Martin (2011 pop. 38,500) and Saint-Barthélemy (2011 pop. 9,000). [6]Actually totals for combined/assorted censuses taken over several years. [7]Comprises Basse-Terre 325 sq mi (842 sq km), pop. 187,782, and Îles des Saintes 5 sq mi (13 sq km), pop. 2,862. [8]Comprises Grande-Terre 230 sq mi (596 sq km), pop. 197,681; Marie-Galante 61 sq mi (158 sq km), pop. 11,872; La Désirade 8 sq mi (21 sq km), pop. 1,587; and the uninhabited Îles de la Petite-Terre. [9]January 1. [10]Within Pointe-à-Pitre urban agglomeration. [11]Departmental budget. [12]Employed workers only excluding the informal sector. [13]Including secondary residences; excluding vacant homes. [14]Weights of consumer price index components. [15]Imports c.i.f.; exports f.o.b. [16]National and departmental roads only. [17]Air Caraïbes only. [18]Circulation. [19]Subscribers. [20]2004–05.

Internet resources for further information:

- **INSEE Guadeloupe**
  http://www.insee.fr/fr/regions/guadeloupe
- **Region Guadeloupe**
  http://www.cr-guadeloupe.fr

Guam

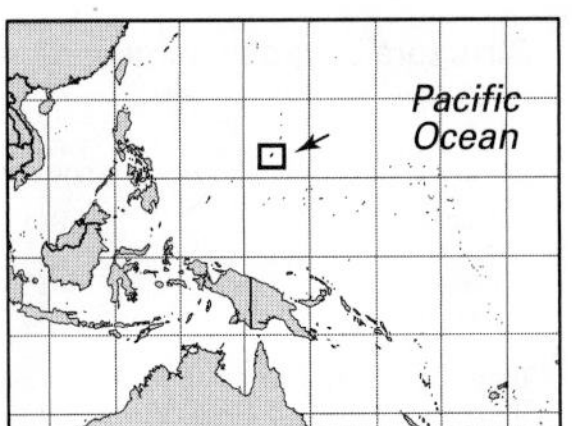

Official name: Guåhan (Chamorro); Territory of Guam (English).
Political status: self-governing, organized, unincorporated territory of the United States with one legislative house (Guam Legislature [15]).
Head of state: President of the United States.
Head of government: Governor.
Capital: Hagåtña (formerly Agana).
Official languages: Chamorro; English.
Official religion: none.
Monetary unit: United States dollar (U.S.$); valuation (Sept. 1, 2011) 1 U.S.$ = £0.62.

Area and population

Municipalities	land area sq km	population[1] 2010 census	Municipalities	land area sq km	population[1] 2010 census
Agat	29	4,917	Mongmong-Toto-Maite	5	6,825
Asan	16	2,137	Piti	18	1,454
Barrigada	23	8,875	Santa Rita	42	6,084
Chalan Pago-Ordot	16	6,822	Sinajana	3	2,592
Dededo	78	44,943	Talofofo	44	3,050
Hagåtña	3	1,051	Tamuning	16	19,685
Hagåtña Heights	3	3,808	Umatac	16	782
Inarajan	49	2,273	Yigo	91	20,539
Mangilao	26	15,191	Yona	52	6,480
Merizo	16	1,850	TOTAL	541[2]	159,358

Demography

Population (2011): 160,000.
Density (2011)[3]: persons per sq mi 765.6, persons per sq km 295.6.
Urban-rural (2009): urban 93.3%; rural 6.7%.
Sex distribution (2009): male 50.86%; female 49.14%.
Age breakdown (2009): under 15, 27.8%; 15–29, 23.5%; 30–44, 20.9%; 45–59, 17.1%; 60–74, 8.2%; 75 and over, 2.5%.
Population projection: (2020) 177,000; (2030) 195,000.
Doubling time: 52 years.
Ethnic composition (2007): Chamorro 41.4%; other Micronesian 10.3%; Filipino 29.3%; white 4.0%; other (mostly mixed race) 15.0%.
Religious affiliation (2005): Roman Catholic *c.* 72%; Protestant *c.* 12%; nonreligious/other *c.* 16%.
Major populated places (2000): Tamuning 10,833; Mangilao 7,794; Yigo 6,391; Astumbo 5,207; Hagåtña 1,122.

Vital statistics

Birth rate per 1,000 population (2010): 18.1 (world avg. 19.2); within marriage (2004) 42.8%; outside of marriage (2004) 57.2%.
Death rate per 1,000 population (2010): 4.6 (world avg. 8.2).
Natural increase rate per 1,000 population (2010): 13.5 (world avg. 11.0).
Total fertility rate (avg. births per childbearing woman; 2010): 2.52.
Marriage/divorce rates per 1,000 population: (2005) 13.2/(2004) 11.9.
Life expectancy at birth (2010): male 75.1 years; female 81.4 years.
Major causes of death per 100,000 population (2005): ischemic heart disease 130.8; malignant neoplasms (cancers) 57.1; cerebrovascular disease 38.3; accidents 27.7; diabetes mellitus 19.4; suicide 17.1.

National economy

Budget (2008). Revenue: U.S.$816,300,000 (taxes 62.0%, federal contributions 28.7%, other 9.3%). Expenditures: U.S.$880,600,000 (public education 27.5%, general administration 10.8%, public order 10.6%, health 8.7%, interest 2.0%).
Public debt (September 2008): U.S.$313,000,000.
Production (metric tons except as noted). Agriculture, forestry, fishing (2009): coconuts 59,378, roots and tubers 2,412, watermelons 2,383, bananas 441, tomatoes 257, string beans 110, oranges 66; livestock (number of live animals) 5,200 pigs, 200,000 chickens; roundwood, n.a.; fisheries production 624 (from aquaculture 22%). Mining and quarrying: sand and gravel. Manufacturing (value of sales in U.S.$'000; 2007): cement, bricks, and ceramics 72,811; food processing 23,244; printing and publishing 10,008; other industries include textiles/garments and boat building. Energy production (consumption): electricity (kW-hr; 2007) 1,879,000,000 (1,879,000,000); crude petroleum, none (none); petroleum products (metric tons; 2002) none (1,333,000); natural gas, none (none).
Household income and expenditure. Average household size (2008) 3.5; annual average (median) household income (2008) U.S.$45,786[4] (U.S.$37,741)[4]; sources of income: n.a.; expenditure (2007)[5]: health care 20.4%, household furnishings 15.7%, food and nonalcoholic beverages 14.7%, energy 11.3%, transportation 8.6%, clothing and footwear 6.7%, housing 5.3%.
Population economically active (2011[6]): total 74,950[7]; activity rate of total population *c.* 47% (participation rates: over age 15, 62.6%; female 38.7%; unemployed 13.3%).

Price index (2005 = 100)

	2003	2004	2005	2006	2007	2008	2009
Consumer price index	87.6	92.9	100.0	111.7	119.3	126.7	128.8

Gross domestic product (at current market prices; 2009): U.S.$4,491,000,000 (U.S.$24,446 per capita).

Structure of gross domestic product and labour force

	2007 in value U.S.$'000,000[8]	2007 % of total value	2009 labour force[7]	2009 % of labour force[7]
Agriculture			300	0.5
Manufacturing			1,720	2.6
Construction			6,210	9.3
Trade	*c.* 2,354	*c.* 55.0	13,520	20.3
Transp. and commun.			4,650[9]	7.0[9]
Finance			2,520[10]	3.8[10]
Pub. admin. (local)			11,490	17.2
Pub. admin., defense (federal)	*c.* 1,177	*c.* 27.5	3,750	5.6
Services (tourism-related)	*c.* 749	*c.* 17.5	15,940	23.9
Other	—	—	6,510[11]	9.8[11]
TOTAL	4,280	100.0	66,610	100.0

(The *c.* 2,354 and *c.* 55.0 values are bracketed for Agriculture through Pub. admin. (local).)

Selected balance of payments data. Receipts from (U.S.$'000,000): tourism (2005) 1,149 (of which significantly from Japanese tourists); remittances, n.a.; foreign direct investment, n.a. Disbursements for (U.S.$'000,000): tourism, n.a.; remittances, n.a.
Land use as % of total land area (2007): in temporary crops or left fallow *c.* 2%, in permanent crops *c.* 19%, in pasture *c.* 15%, forest area *c.* 48%.

Foreign trade

Balance of trade (current prices)[12]

	2002	2003	2004	2005	2006	2007
U.S.$'000,000	–340	–545	–547	–498	–448	–414
% of total	74%	83%	84%	83%	81%	69%

Imports (2008): U.S.$224,914,000[13] (food products and nonalcoholic beverages 29.7%, motor cars 17.2%, leather luggage and handbags 8.6%, perfumes 3.6%). *Major import sources:* significantly U.S. and Japan.
Exports (2008): U.S.$104,878,000 (motor cars 45.8%, fish 18.3%, precious metal jewelry 8.1%, perfumes 3.6%, leather luggage and handbags 3.4%, iron and steel 3.3%). *Major export destinations* (2008): U.S. 26.8%; remainder 73.2%.

Transport and communications

Transport. Railroads: none. Roads (2004): total length 550 mi, 885 km (paved 76%)[14]. Vehicles (2007): passenger cars 65,355; trucks and buses 25,439. Air transport (2008)[15]: passenger-km 3,908,000,000; metric ton-km cargo 81,000,000.

Communications

Medium	date	number in '000s	units per 1,000 persons	Medium	date	number in '000s	units per 1,000 persons
Televisions	1997	106	668	PCs	2008	...	...
Telephones				Dailies	2009	20[16]	109[16]
Cellular	2004	98[17]	594[17]	Internet users	2009	90	506
Landline	2010	66	364	Broadband	2010	3.0[17]	17[17]

Education and health

Educational attainment (2007). Percentage of population age 25 and over having: no formal schooling through incomplete secondary education 21.1%; completed secondary 56.7%; completed university 22.2%. *Literacy:* virtually 100%.

Education (2008–09)

	teachers	students	student/ teacher ratio	enrollment rate (%)
Primary (age 5–13)[18]	1,917[19]	27,715	14.5	...
Secondary/Voc. (age 14–17)	1,108[19]	12,160	10.9	...
Tertiary	...	8,837[20]	...	... (age 18–22)

Health: physicians (2007) 141[21] (1 per 1,256 persons); hospital beds (2007) 172 (1 per 1,029 persons); infant mortality rate per 1,000 live births (2010) 5.9; undernourished population, n.a.

Military

Total active duty U.S. personnel (November 2010): 2,982[22].

[1]Includes active-duty U.S. military personnel, U.S. Department of Defense employees, and dependents of both. [2]Detail does not add to total given because of rounding. [3]Based on land area; total area per most recent survey including area designated as inland water equals 217 sq mi (561 sq km). [4]Excludes all military, dependents of military, and nonresident aliens. [5]Weights of consumer price index components. [6]March. [7]Civilian labour force only, including unemployed. [8]Per U.S. Bureau of Economic Analysis. [9]Includes utilities. [10]Includes real estate. [11]Unemployed. [12]Includes (significantly petroleum) imports for transshipment to Micronesia. [13]Excludes some imports for transshipment. [14]Public roads only; 426 mi (685 km) of roads are private (including roads on federal government installations). [15]Continental Micronesia only. [16]Circulation. [17]Subscribers. [18]Includes kindergarten. [19]2005–06. [20]Combined total of Guam Community College and the University of Guam. [21]Includes military physicians licensed by the Guam public health office. [22]A 2006 agreement to move 8,000 U.S. Marines from Okinawa to Guam by 2014 was ratified by the Japanese Diet in May 2009.

Internet resource for further information:
- **Guam Bureau of Statistics and Plans http://www.bsp.guam.gov**

Guatemala

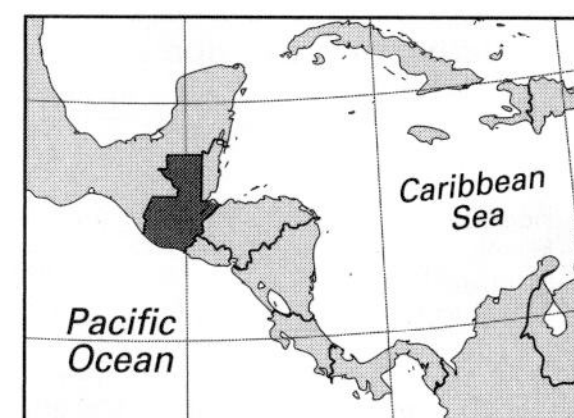

Official name: República de Guatemala (Republic of Guatemala).
Form of government: republic with one legislative house (Congress of the Republic [158]).
Head of state and government: President.
Capital: Guatemala City.
Official language: Spanish.
Official religion: none.
Monetary unit: quetzal (Q); valuation (Sept. 1, 2011) 1 U.S.$ = Q 7.84; 1 £ = Q 12.67.

Area and population

Departments	area sq km	population 2011[1] projection	Departments	area sq km	population 2011[1] projection
Alta Verapaz	9,569	1,112,800	Petén	33,635	638,300
Baja Verapaz	3,104	270,500	Quetzaltenango	2,098	789,400
Chimaltenango	1,960	613,000	Quiché	10,172	953,000
Chiquimula	2,361	370,900	Retalhuleu	1,844	304,200
El Progreso	1,910	158,100	Sacatepéquez	462	316,600
Escuintla	4,356	701,000	San Marcos	3,802	1,019,700
Guatemala	2,218	3,156,300	Santa Rosa	2,936	346,600
Huehuetenango	7,285	1,143,900	Sololá	1,050	437,100
Izabal	8,981	413,400	Suchitepéquez	2,409	516,500
Jalapa	2,050	318,400	Totonicapán	1,043	476,400
Jutiapa	3,199	436,100	Zacapa	2,673	221,600
			TOTAL	109,117	14,713,800

Demography

Population (2011): 14,729,000.
Density (2011): persons per sq mi 349.6, persons per sq km 135.0.
Urban-rural (2009): urban 48.9%; rural 51.1%.
Sex distribution (2011)[1]: male 48.76%; female 51.24%.
Age breakdown (2006): under 15, 41.5%; 15–29, 28.6%; 30–44, 14.7%; 45–59, 9.6%; 60–74, 4.4%; 75–84, 1.1%; 85 and over, 0.1%.
Population projection: (2020) 18,360,000; (2030) 22,700,000.
Doubling time: 32 years.
Ethnic composition (2002): mestizo 60.0%; Maya 39.3%, of which Quiché 11.3%, Kekchi 7.6%, Cakchiquel 7.4%, Mam 5.5%; other 0.7%.
Religious affiliation (2005): Roman Catholic *c.* 57%; Protestant/independent Christian *c.* 40%[2]; traditional Mayan religions *c.* 1%; other *c.* 2%.
Major cities (2002)[3]: Guatemala City (2009) 1,075,000; Mixco 277,400[4]; Villa Nueva 187,700[4]; Quetzaltenango 106,700; Escuintla 65,400.

Vital statistics

Birth rate per 1,000 population (2008): 27.0 (world avg. 20.3).
Death rate per 1,000 population (2008): 5.1 (world avg. 8.5).
Natural increase rate per 1,000 population (2008): 21.9 (world avg. 11.8).
Total fertility rate (avg. births per childbearing woman; 2007): 3.70.
Marriage/divorce rates per 1,000 population (2008): 3.8/0.2.
Life expectancy at birth (2007): male 66.7 years; female 73.8 years.
Major causes of death per 100,000 population (2004): diseases of the respiratory system 91.2, of which pneumonia 77.4; external causes 78.8, of which violence 27.5, accidents 20.6, unclassified 28.7; diseases of the circulatory system 64.6; malignant neoplasms (cancers) 51.2; infectious and parasitic diseases 45.0.

National economy

Budget (2008). Revenue: Q 35,448,000,000 (tax revenue 94.1%, of which taxes on goods and services 58.1%, corporate income taxes 24.7%; nontax revenue 2.8%; social contributions 2.1%; grants 1.0%). Expenditures: Q 40,133,000,000 (education 19.6%; general public services 18.5%; transport 12.6%; housing and communities 12.1%; public order 11.0%; health 7.4%; defense 2.3%).
Public debt (external, outstanding; 2010): U.S.$5,562,000,000.
Production (metric tons except as noted). Agriculture, forestry, fishing (2009): sugarcane 18,391,700, bananas 2,544,240, corn (maize) 1,686,890, oil palm fruit 1,233,300, coffee 249,275, plantains 203,560, hen's eggs 89,390, cardamom and nutmeg 24,000; livestock (number of live animals) 3,061,000 cattle, 2,676,500 pigs, 31,430,000 chickens; roundwood (2010) 18,138,800 cu m, of which fuelwood 97%; fisheries production 36,617 (from aquaculture 45%). Mining and quarrying (2009): zinc (2008; metal content) 14,000; silver 128,420 kg; gold 8,900 kg. Manufacturing (value added in Q '000,000; 2007): food products, beverages, and tobacco products 24,429; textiles, wearing apparel, and footwear 8,340; cement, bricks, and rubber or plastic products 4,284. Energy production (consumption): electricity (kW-hr; 2010) 7,914,000,000 ([2008] 7,108,000,000); coal (metric tons; 2007) none (660,000); crude petroleum (barrels; 2009) 4,933,000 ([2007] 620,000); petroleum products (metric tons; 2007) 26,000 (3,224,000); natural gas (cu m; 2009) 410,000 (none).
Household income and expenditure. Average household size (2002) 4.4; income per household (1989) Q 4,306 (U.S.$1,529); sources of income: n.a.; expenditure (2000)[5]: food and beverages 32.9%, household furnishings 14.7%, clothing 11.8%, recreation and culture 9.2%, health 7.3%.
Selected balance of payments data. Receipts from (U.S.$'000,000): tourism (2010) 985.6; remittances (2010) 4,130; foreign direct investment (FDI; 2008–10 avg.) 680; official development assistance (2009) 376. Disbursements for (U.S.$'000,000): tourism (2010) 698; remittances (2008) 23; FDI (2008–10 avg.) 22.

Gross national income (GNI; 2010): U.S.$39,345,000,000 (U.S.$2,740 per capita); purchasing power parity GNI (U.S.$4,610 per capita).

Structure of gross domestic product and labour force

	2007 in value Q '000,000	2007 % of total value	2006 labour force[6]	2006 % of labour force[6]
Agriculture	29,365	11.2	1,791,400	33.2
Mining	4,121	1.6	7,500	0.1
Manufacturing	47,972	18.4	854,800	15.9
Construction	13,433	5.1	354,900	6.6
Public utilities	6,392	2.5	12,400	0.2
Transp. and commun.	18,270	7.0	160,700	3.0
Trade	39,884	15.3	1,226,900[7]	22.8[7]
Finance, real estate	7,883	3.0	176,100	3.3
Pub. admin., defense	16,971	6.5	115,500	2.1
Services	63,731	24.4	690,400	12.8
Other	13,107[8]	5.0[8]	—	—
TOTAL	261,129	100.0	5,390,500[9]	100.0

Population economically active (2006): total 5,565,200; activity rate of total population 42.8% (participation rates: ages 15–64, 68.0%; female 38.1%; unemployed, n.a.).

Price index (2005 = 100)

	2004	2005	2006	2007	2008	2009	2010
Consumer price index	92.2	100.0	106.4	113.3	127.6	130.0	135.0

Land use as % of total land area (2009): in temporary crops or left fallow (2008) 12.4%, in permanent crops 8.8%, in pasture 18.2%, forest area 34.7%.

Foreign trade[10]

Balance of trade (current prices)

	2005	2006	2007	2008	2009	2010
U.S.$'000,000	–5,119	–6,342	–6,646	–6,785	–4,313	–5,370
% of total	32.2%	49.8%	32.5%	30.5%	23.0%	24.1%

Imports (2008): U.S.$14,522,000,000 (refined petroleum 17.1%; chemicals and chemical products 16.5%; machinery and apparatus 14.8%; food products 10.2%; road vehicles/parts 6.6%). *Major import sources:* U.S. 36.7%; Mexico 9.7%; China 5.8%; El Salvador 4.7%; Netherlands Antilles 3.2%.
Exports (2008): U.S.$7,737,000,000 (food products 32.1%, of which coffee 8.4%, raw sugar 4.9%, bananas 4.4%; apparel and clothing accessories 15.9%, of which women's outerwear 8.0%; crude petroleum 4.8%; toiletries and soaps 3.8%; silver 3.4%). *Major export destinations:* U.S. 39.4%; El Salvador 12.6%; Honduras 9.5%; Mexico 6.6%; Nicaragua 4.2%.

Transport and communications

Transport. Railroads (2007): route length 497 mi, 800 km[11]. Roads (2002): total length 8,727 mi, 14,044 km (paved 39%). Vehicles (2007): passenger cars 1,558,145[12]. Air transport (1999): passenger-km 342,000,000; metric ton-km cargo (2003) 200,000.

Communications

Medium	date	number in '000s	units per 1,000 persons	Medium	date	number in '000s	units per 1,000 persons
Televisions	2004	2,000	167	PCs	2005	262	21
Telephones				Dailies	2009	490[13]	35[13]
Cellular	2010	18,068[14]	1,256[14]	Internet users	2009	2,280	163
Landline	2010	1,499	104	Broadband	2010	259[14]	18.0[14]

Education and health

Educational attainment (2002). Percentage of heads of households having: no formal schooling 33.3%; incomplete/complete primary education 46.1%; incomplete/complete secondary 15.0%; higher 5.6%. *Literacy* (2008): total population age 15 and over literate 73.8%; males literate 79.5%; females literate 68.7%.

Education (2007–08)

	teachers	students	student/ teacher ratio	enrollment rate (%)
Primary (age 7–12)	84,980	2,500,575	29.4	95
Secondary/Voc. (age 13–17)	54,498	902,796	16.6	40
Tertiary[15]	3,843	233,885[16]	29.2	18 (age 18–22)

Health: physicians (2006[17]) 12,273 (1 per 1,049 persons); hospital beds (2005) 8,894 (1 per 1,429 persons); infant mortality rate (2006) 30.8; undernourished population (2004–06) 2,100,000 (16% of total population based on the consumption of a minimum daily requirement of 1,690 calories).

Military

Total active duty personnel (November 2010): 15,212 (army 88.4%, navy 5.9%, air force 5.7%); paramilitary 19,000. *Military expenditure as percentage of GDP* (2009): 0.4%; per capita expenditure U.S.$12.

[1]Official midyear projections. [2]Rough estimate; may also incorporate Mayan spiritual ritual. [3]Urban populations of *municipios*. [4]Within Guatemala department. [5]Weights of consumer price index components. [6]10 years and older; employed only. [7]Includes restaurants and hotels. [8]Taxes less subsidies and less imputed bank service charges. [9]Detail does not add to total given because of rounding. [10]Imports c.i.f.; exports f.o.b. [11]Last operating rail service was shut down in September 2007; no passenger service is available. [12]Includes trucks and buses. [13]Circulation. [14]Subscribers. [15]2005–06. [16]2006–07. [17]January 1.

Internet resources for further information:
- **Banco de Guatemala http://www.banguat.gob.gt**
- **Instituto Nacional de Estadística http://www.ine.gob.gt**

Guernsey[1]

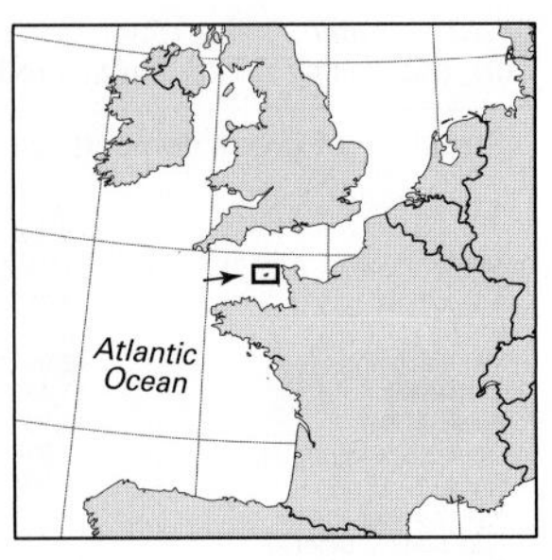

Official name: Bailiwick of Guernsey.
Political status: crown dependency (United Kingdom) with one legislative house (States of Deliberation [50[2, 3, 4]]).
Head of state: British Monarch represented by Lieutenant Governor.
Head of government: Chief Minister[5] assisted by the Policy Council.
Capital: St. Peter Port.
Official language: English.
Official religion: none.
Monetary unit: Guernsey pound[6]; valuation (Sept. 1, 2011) 1 Guernsey pound = U.S.$1.64.

Area and population

	area		population
	sq mi	sq km	2001 census
Parishes of Guernsey			
Castel	3.9	10.2	8,975
Forest	1.6	4.1	1,549
St. Andrew	1.7	4.5	2,409
St. Martin	2.8	7.3	6,267
St. Peter (St. Pierre du Bois)	2.4	6.2	2,188
St. Peter Port	2.5	6.4	16,488
St. Sampson	2.4	6.3	8,592
St. Saviour	2.5	6.4	2,696
Torteval	1.2	3.1	973
Vale	3.4	8.9	9,573
Dependencies of Guernsey			
Alderney	3.07	7.94	2,294
Brechou	0.12	0.30	0
Herm[7]	0.50	1.29	95
Jethou[7]	0.07	0.18	2
Lihou[7]	0.06	0.15	0
Little Sark	0.42	1.09	591
Sark (Great Sark)	1.62	4.19	
TOTAL (ROUNDED)	30.3	78.5	62,692

Demography

Population (2011)[8]: 65,300.
Density (2011)[8]: persons per sq mi 2,155.1, persons per sq km 831.8.
Urban-rural (2005)[8, 9]: urban 30.9%; rural 69.1%.
Sex distribution (2010): male 49.17%; female 50.83%.
Age breakdown (2010): under 15, 15.2%; 15–29, 19.2%; 30–44, 21.2%; 45–59, 21.5%; 60–74, 14.8%; 75–84, 5.7%; 85 and over, 2.4%.
Population projection[8]: (2020) 69,400; (2030) 72,200.
Population by place of birth (2001): Guernsey 64.3%; United Kingdom 27.4%; Portugal 1.9%; Jersey 0.7%; Ireland 0.7%; Alderney 0.2%; Sark 0.1%; other Europe 3.2%; other 1.5%.
Religious affiliation (2000)[8, 9]: Protestant 51.0%, of which Anglican 44.1%; unaffiliated Christian 20.1%; Roman Catholic 14.6%; nonreligious 12.4%; other 1.9%.
Major cities (2001)[10]: St. Peter Port 16,488; Vale 9,573; Castel 8,975; St. Sampson 8,592; St. Martin 6,267.

Vital statistics

Birth rate per 1,000 population (2010): 10.5 (world avg. 19.2); within marriage (2000) 65.2%; outside of marriage (2000) 34.8%.
Death rate per 1,000 population (2010): 8.2 (world avg. 8.2).
Natural increase rate per 1,000 population (2010): 2.3 (world avg. 11.0).
Total fertility rate (avg. births per childbearing woman; 2009): 1.53.
Marriage/divorce rates per 1,000 population (2000): 5.7/2.9.
Life expectancy at birth (2009): male 79.6 years; female 85.1 years.
Major causes of death per 100,000 population (2007): malignant neoplasms (cancers) *c.* 202; ischemic heart disease *c.* 70; other cardiovascular diseases *c.* 207.

National economy

Budget (2009). Revenue: £341,000,000 (income tax 80.1%, customs duties and excise taxes 8.5%, document duties 4.1%, property taxes 3.8%, company fees 1.8%, other 1.7%). Expenditures: £325,507,000 (health 32.9%, education 22.2%, social security and welfare 14.5%, law and order 9.1%).
Production (metric tons except as noted). Agriculture, forestry, fishing (value of exports in £'000; 2009): young plants 31,280, postal and cut flowers 7,790, edibles 3,460; livestock (number of live animals; 1999) 3,262 cattle; roundwood, n.a.; fisheries production (2009) 1,403 (from aquaculture, n.a.), of which crabs 622, bass 94, black bream 92, scallops 90, lobsters 67. Mining and quarrying: n.a. Manufacturing (2008): includes small-scale manufacturers of furniture, ceramics, confectionery, fabricated metals, and jewelry. Energy production (consumption): electricity (kW-hr; 2007) 158,000,000 ([2010–11] 375,000,000).
Population economically active (2011[11]): total 33,052; activity rate of total population 50.6% (participation rates: ages 15–64 [2001] 79.1%; female 45.5%[12]; unemployed [July 2010–June 2011] 1.4%).

Retail price index (June 2005 = 100)

	2005	2006	2007	2008	2009	2010	2011
Retail price index[11]	100.0	103.4	108.1	113.6	112.3	114.6	117.6

Gross national income (2010): U.S.$3,050,270,000 (U.S.$48,847 per capita).

Structure of gross domestic product and labour force

	2007		2011[11]	
	in value £'000	% of total value	labour force	% of labour force
Horticulture, fishing	23,241	1.4	506	1.5
Mining	—	—	—	—
Manufacturing	41,120	2.5	704	2.1
Construction	131,430	7.9	3,113	9.4
Public utilities	12,467	0.8	413	1.2
Transp. and commun.	74,864	4.5	2,074	6.3
Trade, hotels	200,862	12.1	6,513	19.7
Finance, real estate, insurance, international business	760,534	45.9	10,450	31.6
Pub. admin., defense	253,033	15.3	5,522	16.7
Services			3,270	9.9
Other	158,039[13]	9.6[13]	487[14]	1.5[14]
TOTAL	1,655,590	100.0	33,052	100.0[15]

Public debt (July 2010): none.
Household income and expenditure. Average household size (2001) 2.6; expenditure (2005–06): housing 33.8%, recreation and culture 13.9%, household furnishings and communications 11.4%, transportation 9.7%, food 9.7%, food away from home 4.8%, alcohol and tobacco products 4.5%, clothing and footwear 3.7%, energy 3.4%.
Selected balance of payments data. Receipts from (U.S.$'000,000): tourism (1996) 275 (total visitors [2010] 326,500); remittances, n.a.; foreign direct investment, n.a. Disbursements for (U.S.$'000,000): tourism, n.a.; remittances, n.a.
Land use as % of total land area (2007)[9]: in temporary crops or left fallow *c.* 18%; in permanent crops, n.a.; in pasture *c.* 20%, forest area *c.* 4%.

Foreign trade

Imports (2007): petroleum products are important. *Major import sources:* significantly United Kingdom.
Exports (2006)[16]: £46,910,000 (high-value young plants exported to final producers 74.5%; postal and cut flowers [particularly freesia, roses, and carnations] 18.5%; edibles [mostly niche crops] 7.0%). *Major export destinations:* mostly United Kingdom.

Transport and communications

Transport. Railroads: none. Roads (2009): n.a.[17]; passenger-km, n.a.; metric ton-km cargo, n.a. Vehicles (2009): passenger cars 61,747; trucks and buses 14,030. Air transport[18]: passenger-km (2009) 104,000,000; metric ton-km cargo (2008) 56,000.

Communications

Medium	date	number in '000s	units per 1,000 persons	Medium	date	number in '000s	units per 1,000 persons
Televisions	2007	...	...	PCs	2009	...	...
Telephones				Dailies	2008	16[19]	244[19]
Cellular	2005	43.8[20]	790[20]	Internet users	2009	48	735
Landline	2009	45	692	Broadband	2009	...	...

Education and health

Educational attainment: n.a. *Literacy* (2006): virtually 100%.

Education (2009–10)

	teachers	students	student/ teacher ratio	enrollment rate (%)
Primary (age 5–10)	...	4,406	...	...
Secondary/Voc. (age 11–16)	...	4,292	...	...
Tertiary	...	858[21]	...	... (age 17–21)

Health (2006): physicians 102 (1 per 625 persons); hospital beds *c.* 548 (1 per 116 persons); infant mortality rate per 1,000 live births (2009) 3.5; undernourished population, n.a.

Military

Total active duty personnel: the United Kingdom is responsible for defense.

[1]Data exclude Alderney and Sark unless otherwise noted. [2]The States of Deliberation was reorganized in 2004. [3]Includes 3 ex officio members (2 of whom have no voting rights) and 2 representatives from Alderney. [4]Alderney and Sark have their own parliaments. The States of Alderney has a president and 10 elected members; Sark's feudal system of government ended with elections to a 28-member assembly in December 2008. [5]The first Chief Minister was elected by the States of Deliberation in May 2004. [6]Equivalent in value to pound sterling (£); the Guernsey government issues both paper money and coins. [7]Islets that are directly administered by Guernsey. [8]Includes Alderney, Sark, and other dependencies. [9]Includes Jersey. [10]Populations of parishes. [11]June. [12]March 31. [13]Less pensions (£34,206,000) and adjustment to profit account (£1,405,000). [14]Includes 481 unemployed. [15]Detail does not add to total given because of rounding. [16]Horticultural exports only. [17]Roads are narrow and unsuitable for large commercial vehicles. [18]Aurigny Air Services Ltd. only. [19]Circulation of *Guernsey Press and Star*. [20]Subscribers. [21]Studying in the United Kingdom.

Internet resource for further information:
- **The States of Guernsey**
  http://www.gov.gg/ccm/portal

Guinea

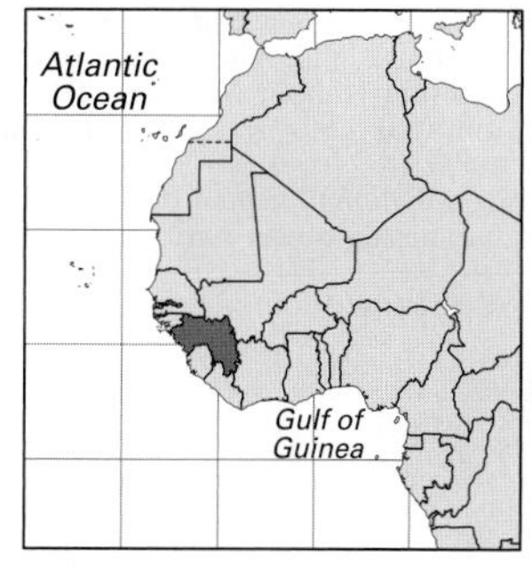

Official name: République de Guinée (Republic of Guinea).
Form of government: republic[1] with one advisory body (National Transition Council[2] [155]).
Head of state and government: President assisted by Prime Minister[1].
Capital: Conakry.
Official language: French.
Official religion: none.
Monetary unit: Guinean franc (FG); valuation (Sept. 1, 2011) 1 U.S.$ = FG 6,768; 1 £ = FG 10,936.

Area and population		area		population
Regions	Capitals	sq mi	sq km	1996 census
Boké	Boké	12,041	31,186	760,119
Faranah	Faranah	13,738	35,581	602,845
Kankan	Kankan	27,859	72,156	1,011,644
Kindia	Kindia	11,148	28,873	928,312
Labé	Labé	8,830	22,869	799,545
Mamou	Mamou	6,592	17,074	612,218
Nzérékoré	Nzérékoré	14,544	37,668	1,348,787
Special zone				
Conakry	Conakry	174	450	1,092,936
TOTAL		94,926	245,857	7,156,406

Demography

Population (2011): 10,222,000.
Density (2011): persons per sq mi 107.7, persons per sq km 41.6.
Urban-rural (2009): urban 34.9%; rural 65.1%.
Sex distribution (2008): male 50.00%; female 50.00%.
Age breakdown (2008): under 15, 42.9%; 15–29, 26.5%; 30–44, 16.0%; 45–59, 9.2%; 60–74, 4.4%; 75 and over, 1.0%.
Population projection: (2020) 12,765,000; (2030) 15,946,000.
Doubling time: 26 years.
Ethnic composition (2000): Fulani 38.3%; Malinke 25.6%; Susu 12.2%; Kpelle 5.2%; Kisi 4.8%; other 13.9%.
Religious affiliation (2005): Muslim (nearly all Sunnī) *c.* 85%[3]; Christian *c.* 8%[3]; traditional beliefs *c.* 7%.
Major cities: Conakry (2009) 1,597,000; Kankan (2004) 113,900; Labé (2001) 64,500; Kindia (2001) 56,000; Nzérékoré (2001) 55,000.

Vital statistics

Birth rate per 1,000 population (2008): 37.8 (world avg. 20.3).
Death rate per 1,000 population (2008): 11.3 (world avg. 8.5).
Natural increase rate per 1,000 population (2008): 26.5 (world avg. 11.8).
Total fertility rate (avg. births per childbearing woman; 2008): 5.25.
Marriage/divorce rates per 1,000 population: n.a./n.a.
Life expectancy at birth (2008): male 55.1 years; female 58.1 years.
Major causes of death per 100,000 population (2002): infectious and parasitic diseases 682; cardiovascular diseases 150; injuries and accidents 118; malignant neoplasms (cancers) 62; cerebrovascular diseases 52.
Adult population (ages 15–49) *living with HIV* (2009): 1.3%[4] (world avg. 0.8%).

National economy

Budget (2008). Revenue: FG 3,854,400,000,000 (tax revenue 81.9%, of which taxes on domestic production and trade 29.8%, mining sector revenue 22.0%, taxes on international trade 18.5%; nontax revenue 5.4%; grants 12.7%). Expenditures: FG 3,735,600,000,000 (current expenditure 65.2%, of which wages and salaries 23.0%, interest on debt 14.6%; capital expenditure 34.6%; net lending and restructuring 0.2%).
Public debt (external, outstanding; June 2011): U.S.$2,920,000,000.
Production (metric tons except as noted). Agriculture, forestry, fishing (2009): rice 1,499,000, cassava 989,326, oil palm fruit 830,000, corn (maize) 792,280, plantains 479,944, peanuts (groundnuts) 337,873, fonio 329,874, sugarcane 283,000, citrus fruits 244,002, sweet potatoes 194,498, bananas 179,602, mangoes 165,000, pineapples 108,000, coffee 22,500; livestock (number of live animals) 4,651,500 cattle, 1,800,000 goats, 1,500,000 sheep, 20,050,000 chickens; roundwood (2010) 12,552,398 cu m, of which fuelwood 95%; fisheries production 86,129 (from aquaculture, none). Mining and quarrying (2009–10): bauxite 15,749,630; gold 779,320 troy oz; diamonds 423,510 carats. Manufacturing (2009–10): cement 285,100; flour 45,720; paints 5,451. Energy production (consumption): electricity (kW-hr; 2009–10) 642,800,000 ([2007] 973,000,000); coal, none (none); crude petroleum, none (none); petroleum products (metric tons; 2007) none (394,000); natural gas (cu m; 2009–10) 83,460 ([2007] 102,500).
Selected balance of payments data. Receipts from (U.S.$'000,000): tourism (2009) 2.8; remittances (2010) 59; foreign direct investment (2008–10 avg.) 275; official development assistance (2009) 215. Disbursements for (U.S.$'000,000): tourism (2009) 13; remittances (2009) 56.
Population economically active (2008)[5]: total 4,720,000; activity rate of total population 48.0% (participation rates: ages 15 and over, 84.0%; female 46.8%; unemployed, n.a.).

Price index (2005 = 100)	2004	2005	2006	2007	2008	2009	2010
Consumer price index	76.1	100.0	134.7	165.5	197.4	205.0	236.8

Gross national income (GNI; 2010): U.S.$3,972,000,000 (U.S.$380 per capita); purchasing power parity GNI (U.S.$980 per capita).

Structure of gross domestic product and labour force	2008		1996	
	in value FG '000,000,000	% of total value	labour force	% of labour force
Agriculture, forestry, fishing	4,738.6	22.7	2,433,480	74.2
Mining	4,473.0	21.4	34,975	1.1
Manufacturing	1,329.6	6.4	90,885	2.8
Construction	2,054.1	9.8	60,526	1.9
Public utilities	77.0	0.4	4,690	0.1
Transp. and commun.	504.5	2.4	77,070	2.4
Trade, hotels	3,263.1	15.6	373,709	11.4
Finance, real estate	1,175.3	5.6	3,440	0.1
Pub. admin., defense	1,518.7	7.3	63,192	1.9
Services	...	...	132,045	4.0
Other	1,759.1[6]	8.4[6]	4,822	0.1
TOTAL	20,893.0	100.0	3,278,834	100.0

Household income and expenditure (1994–95). Average household size (2004) 6.6; average annual household income[7] FG 1,905,899 (U.S.$1,952); sources of income[7]: agriculture 49.3%, self-employment 22.2%, wages and salaries 15.7%; expenditure[7]: food 50.0%, housing 14.0%, health 12.3%, transportation and communications 8.4%, clothing 6.3%.
Land use as % of total land area (2009): in temporary crops or left fallow 11.6%, in permanent crops 2.8%, in pasture 43.5%, forest area 26.8%.

Foreign trade[8]

Balance of trade (current prices)	2004	2005	2006	2007	2008
U.S.$'000,000	–326.3	–852.1	–301.9	–222.5	–421.1
% of total	20.6%	34.9%	15.8%	9.5%	12.4%

Imports (2008): U.S.$1,907,900,000 (refined petroleum 32.8%; machinery and apparatus 21.5%, of which civil engineering equipment 7.5%; food 10.2%; road vehicles 6.6%). *Major import sources:* Neth. 20.6%; France 10.1%; U.K. 7.9%; China 6.7%; Belgium 5.2%.
Exports (2008): U.S.$1,486,800,000 (bauxite 40.1%; gold 32.0%; alumina 11.3%; printed matter 7.9%; natural rubber 1.6%). *Major export destinations:* France 24.5%; Switzerland 19.5%; Russia 10.6%; Spain 9.9%; Ireland 7.4%.

Transport and communications

Transport. Railroads (2008): route length 245 mi, 395 km[9]; passenger-km, n.a.; metric ton-km cargo (1993) 710,000,000. Roads (2009): total length 4,199 mi, 6,758 km[10] (paved 35%[10]). Vehicles (2003): passenger cars 47,524; trucks and buses 26,467. Air transport: n.a.

Communications Medium	date	number in '000s	units per 1,000 persons	Medium	date	number in '000s	units per 1,000 persons
Televisions	2004	140	16	PCs	2006	47	5.0
Telephones				Dailies	2009	25[11]	1.9[11]
Cellular	2010	4,000[12]	401[12]	Internet users	2009	90	9.5
Landline	2010	18	1.8	Broadband	2010	0.5[12]	0.1[12]

Education and health

Educational attainment of those age 25 and over having attended school (1999)[13]: none or unknown 81.4%; primary 7.8%; secondary 6.8%; higher 4.0%. *Literacy* (2008): percentage of total population age 15 and over literate 38.0%; males literate 49.6%; females literate 26.4%.

Education (2008–09)	teachers	students	student/ teacher ratio	enrollment rate (%)
Primary (age 7–12)	30,933	1,364,491	44.1	71
Secondary/Voc. (age 13–19)	15,941	530,705	33.3	28
Tertiary	2,163	80,222	37.1	9 (age 20–24)

Health: physicians (2006) 689 (1 per 13,660 persons); hospital beds (2005) 2,766 (1 per 3,333 persons); infant mortality rate per 1,000 live births (2008) 67.4; undernourished population (2005–07) 1,600,000 (17% of total population based on the consumption of a minimum daily requirement of 1,760 calories).

Military

Total active duty personnel (November 2010): 12,300 (army 69.1%, navy 3.3%, air force 6.5%, gendarmerie 8.1%, republican guard 13.0%). *Military expenditure as percentage of GDP* (2008): 1.0%; per capita expenditure U.S.$5.

[1]Per constitution promulgated on May 7, 2010. [2]The National Transition Council, an advisory body appointed in February 2010, is to be replaced by an elected legislative body in 2012 or thereafter. [3]Significantly influenced by traditional beliefs and rituals. [4]Statistically derived midpoint of range. [5]ILO estimates. [6]Indirect taxes and taxes on products less subsidies. [7]Based on the national Enquête Intégrale sur les Conditions de Vie des Ménages avec Module Budget et Consommation, comprising 4,416 households. [8]Imports c.i.f.; exports f.o.b. [9]Length of bauxite railways; other tracks are nonoperational. [10]Officially reported figure. [11]Circulation of daily newspapers, which are subject to rigorous government censorship. [12]Subscribers. [13]Based on the national Enquête Démographique et de Santé, comprising 5,090 households.

Internet resources for further information:
- **National Statistics Directorate**
  http://www.stat-guinee.org
- **Banque Centrale de la Republique de Guinée**
  http://www.bcrg-guinee.org

Guinea-Bissau

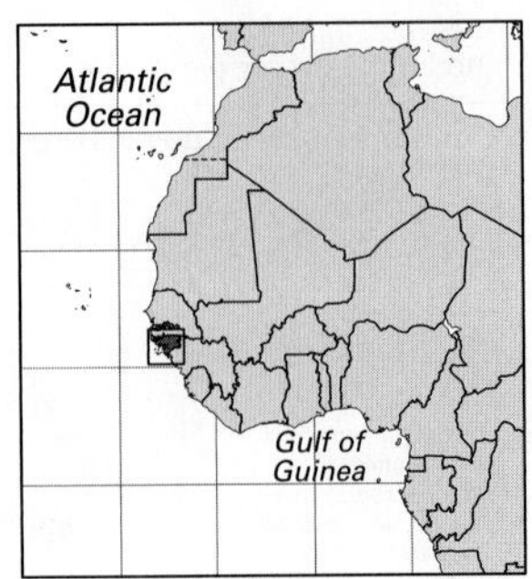

Official name: Républica da Guiné-Bissau (Republic of Guinea-Bissau).
Form of government: republic[1] with one legislative house (National People's Assembly [102[2]]).
Head of state and government: President assisted by the Prime Minister.
Capital: Bissau.
Official language: Portuguese.
Official religion: none.
Monetary unit: CFA franc (CFAF); valuation (Sept. 1, 2011) 1 U.S.$ = CFAF 460.31; 1 £ = CFAF 743.83.

Area and population

Regions	Chief towns	area sq mi	area sq km	population 2009 census
Bafatá	Bafatá	2,309	5,981	210,007
Biombo	Quinhámel	324	840	97,120
Bolama/Bijagós	Bolama	1,013	2,624	34,563
Cacheu	Cacheu	1,998	5,175	192,508
Gabú	Gabú	3,533	9,150	215,530
Oio	Bissorã	2,086	5,403	224,644
Quinara	Fulacunda	1,212	3,138	63,610
Tombali	Catió	1,443	3,736	94,939
Autonomous sector				
Bissau	—	30	78	387,909
TOTAL		13,948[3]	36,125[3]	1,520,830

Demography

Population (2011): 1,606,000.
Density (2011)[4]: persons per sq mi 147.9, persons per sq km 57.1.
Urban-rural (2009): urban 29.9%; rural 70.1%.
Sex distribution (2010): male 48.50%; female 51.50%.
Age breakdown (2005): under 15, 42.6%; 15–29, 25.7%; 30–44, 16.2%; 45–59, 10.0%; 60–74, 4.5%; 75–84, 0.9%; 85 and over, 0.1%.
Population projection: (2020) 1,935,000; (2030) 2,350,000.
Doubling time: 27 years.
Ethnic composition (2000): Balante 25.0%; Fulani (locally Fulakunda) 17.1%; Mandyako 12.0%; Malinke 10.0%; Guinean mestiço (Portuguese-black) 9.2%; Pepel 6.3%; nonindigenous Cape Verdean mulatto 1.0%; other 19.4%.
Religious affiliation (2005): traditional beliefs *c.* 49%; Muslim *c.* 42%; Christian/other *c.* 9%.
Major cities (2009): Bissau 387,909; Gabú 81,495; Bafatá 68,956; Bissorã 56,585; Bigene 51,412.

Vital statistics

Birth rate per 1,000 population (2010): 41.8 (world avg. 19.2).
Death rate per 1,000 population (2010): 16.0 (world avg. 8.2).
Natural increase rate per 1,000 population (2010): 25.8 (world avg. 11.0).
Total fertility rate (avg. births per childbearing woman; 2010): 5.10.
Marriage/divorce rates per 1,000 population: n.a./n.a.
Life expectancy at birth (2006): male 43.4 years; female 46.2 years.
Major causes of death per 100,000 population (2002): diseases of the circulatory system 165; HIV/AIDS 126; accidents, poisoning, and violence 114; malignant neoplasms (cancers) 66; chronic respiratory diseases 41.
Adult population (ages 15–49) *living with HIV* (2009): 2.5%[5] (world avg. 0.8%).

National economy

Budget (2011). Revenue: CFAF 80,900,000,000 (tax revenue 44.1%; grants 41.0%; nontax revenue 14.9%). Expenditures: CFAF 91,300,000,000 (current expenditures 57.9%, of which wages and salaries 24.5%; capital expenditures 42.1%).
Public debt (external, outstanding; 2009): U.S.$950,000,000.
Production (metric tons except as noted). Agriculture, forestry, fishing (2009): rice 150,000, oil palm fruit 80,000, cashew nuts 64,653, coconuts 46,326, cassava 45,000, plantains 44,032, peanuts (groundnuts) 31,793, millet 29,000, sorghum 20,000, corn (maize) 14,000, bananas 7,206; livestock (number of live animals) 620,000 cattle, 420,000 sheep, 415,970 goats; roundwood (2010) 553,910 cu m, of which fuelwood 76%; fisheries production 6,800 (from aquaculture, none). Mining and quarrying: small-scale production of clays, limestone, and granite. Manufacturing (2003): processed wood 11,000; bakery products 7,900; wood products 4,400; dried and smoked fish 3,800; soap 2,400; vegetable oils 37,000 hectolitres. Energy production (consumption): electricity (kW-hr; 2007) 70,000,000 (70,000,000); coal, none (none); crude petroleum, none (none); petroleum products (metric tons; 2007) none (93,000); natural gas, none (none).
Selected balance of payments data. Receipts from (U.S.$'000,000): tourism (2008) 38.2; remittances (2010) 27; foreign direct investment (2008–10 avg.) 9.7; official development assistance (2009) 146. Disbursements for (U.S.$'000,000): tourism (2008) 45.6; remittances (2009) 17.
Population economically active (2008)[6]: total 645,000; activity rate of total population 41.0% (participation rates: ages 15–64, 73.3%; female 42.5%; unemployed, n.a.).

Price index (2005 = 100)

	2004	2005	2006	2007	2008	2009	2010
Consumer price index	96.8	100.0	102.0	106.7	117.8	115.9	118.8

Household income and expenditure. Average household size (1996) 6.9; income per household: n.a.; sources of income: n.a.; expenditure (2001–02)[7, 8]: food and nonalcoholic beverages 59.7%, housing and energy 13.6%, clothing and footwear 7.6%, transport and communications 6.5%, household furnishings 4.4%.
Gross national income (GNI; 2010): U.S.$890,000,000[9] (U.S.$540 per capita); purchasing power parity GNI (U.S.$1,080 per capita).

Structure of gross domestic product and labour force

	2009 in value U.S.$'000,000	2009 % of total value	2011 labour force	2011 % of labour force
Agriculture, fishing	236.4	58.4	495,000	78.9
Mining / Public utilities	3.5	0.9	132,000	21.1
Manufacturing	32.3	8.0		
Construction	12.2	3.0		
Transportation and communications	11.2	2.8		
Trade, hotels	68.3	16.9		
Finance, services / Pub. admin., defense	34.5	8.5		
Other	6.0	1.5		
TOTAL	404.4	100.0	627,000	100.0

Land use as % of total land area (2007): in temporary crops or left fallow 10.7%, in permanent crops 8.9%, in pasture 38.4%, forest area 73.0%[10].

Foreign trade

Balance of trade (current prices)

	2005	2006	2007	2008	2009
CFAF '000,000,000	–8.6	–27.6	–29.2	–31.9	–37.5
% of total	8.3%	26.2%	22.2%	22.2%	25.0%

Imports (2008): CFAF 87,900,000,000 (agricultural products 32.1%, petroleum products 22.8%, machinery and apparatus 22.8%). *Major import sources:* Portugal *c.* 24%; Senegal *c.* 17%; India *c.* 11%; Pakistan *c.* 5%; France *c.* 5%.
Exports (2008): CFAF 56,000,000,000 (cashews 86.3%, fish and shrimp 4.5%). *Major export destinations:* India *c.* 64%; Nigeria *c.* 30%.

Transport and communications

Transport. Railroads: none. Roads (2003): total length 1,710 mi, 2,755 km (paved 28%). Vehicles (2002): passenger cars, trucks, and buses 1,985. Air transport (2003): passenger arrivals 17,834, passenger departures 18,528; cargo unloaded, n.a.; cargo loaded, n.a.

Communications

Medium	date	number in '000s	units per 1,000 persons	Medium	date	number in '000s	units per 1,000 persons
Televisions	2001	47	36	PCs	2007	2.9	2.0
Telephones				Dailies	2009	—	—
Cellular	2010	594[11]	392[11]	Internet users	2009	37	23
Landline	2010	5.0	3.3	Broadband	2010	—	—

Education and health

Educational attainment: n.a. *Literacy* (2008): total population age 15 and over literate 51.0%; males literate 66.1%; females literate 36.5%.

Education (2009–10)

	teachers	students	student/ teacher ratio	enrollment rate (%)
Primary (age 7–12)	6,000	360,000	60.0	52[12]
Secondary/Voc. (age 13–17)	1,800	72,000	40.0	10[12]
Tertiary[13]	25	3,689	147.6	3 (age 18–22)

Health (2010): physicians 157 (1 per 9,994 persons); hospital beds 2,040 (1 per 769 persons); infant mortality rate per 1,000 live births 103; undernourished population (2004–06) 440,000 (31% of total population based on the consumption of a minimum daily requirement of 1,720 calories).

Military

Total active duty personnel (November 2010): *c.* 4,458 (army *c.* 90%, navy *c.* 8%, air force *c.* 2%). *Military expenditure as percentage of GDP* (2009): 1.7%; per capita expenditure U.S.$9.

[1]A constitution adopted by the National People's Assembly in 2001 was not promulgated by October 2011. [2]Includes 2 unfilled seats reserved for citizens of Guinea-Bissau residing abroad. [3]Includes water area of about 3,089 sq mi (8,000 sq km). [4]Based on land area of 10,859 sq mi (28,125 sq km). [5]Statistically derived midpoint of range. [6]ILO estimates. [7]Bissau only. [8]Weights of consumer price index components. [9]Formal economy only; in 2010 much of Guinea-Bissau's income was derived from trafficking South American cocaine into Europe. [10]Forest area overlaps with other categories. [11]Subscribers. [12]1999–2000. [13]2005–06.

Internet resources for further information:
- **La Banque de France: La Zone Franc**
  http://www.banque-france.fr/fr/eurosys/zonefr/zonefr.htm
- **National Institute of Statistics**
  http://www.stat-guinebissau.com

Guyana

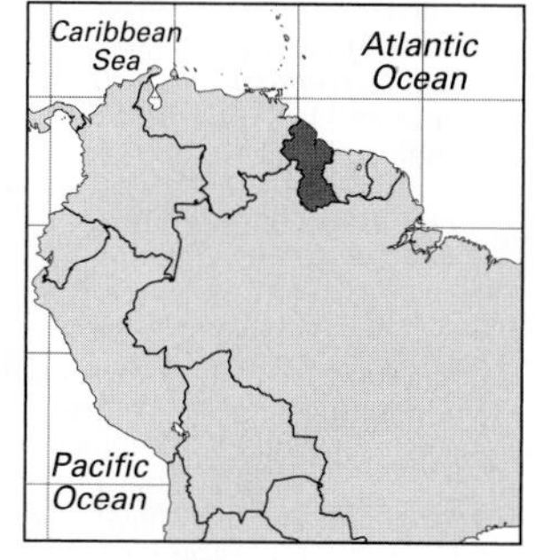

Official name: Co-operative Republic of Guyana.
Form of government: unitary multiparty republic with one legislative house (National Assembly [65[1]]).
Head of state and government: President.
Capital: Georgetown.
Official language: English.
Official religion: none.
Monetary unit: Guyanese dollar (G$); valuation (Sept. 1, 2011) 1 U.S.$ = G$200.70; 1 £ = G$324.32.

Area and population

Administrative regions		Capitals	area sq mi	area sq km	population 2002 census
Region 1	(Barima-Waini)	Mabaruma	7,853	20,339	24,275
Region 2	(Pomeroon-Supenaam)	Anna Regina	2,392	6,195	49,253
Region 3	(Essequibo Islands–West Demerara)	Vreed en Hoop	1,450	3,755	103,061
Region 4	(Demerara-Mahaica)	Paradise	862	2,232	310,320
Region 5	(Mahaica-Berbice)	Fort Wellington	1,618	4,190	52,428
Region 6	(East Berbice–Corentyne)	New Amsterdam	13,990	36,234	123,695
Region 7	(Cuyuni-Mazaruni)	Bartica	18,229	47,213	17,597
Region 8	(Potaro-Siparuni)	Mahdia	7,742	20,051	10,095
Region 9	(Upper Takutu–Upper Essequibo)	Lethem	22,297	57,750	19,387
Region 10	(Upper Demerara–Berbice)	Linden	6,579	17,040	41,112
TOTAL			83,012[2]	214,999[2]	751,223

Demography

Population (2011): 756,000.
Density (2011)[3]: persons per sq mi 9.9, persons per sq km 3.8.
Urban-rural (2005): urban 38.5%; rural 61.5%.
Sex distribution (2008): male 50.06%; female 49.94%.
Age breakdown (2005): under 15, 26.5%; 15–29, 29.7%; 30–44, 23.0%; 45–59, 13.3%; 60–74, 5.6%; 75 and over, 1.9%.
Population projection: (2020) 773,000; (2030) 795,000.
Doubling time: 67 years.
Ethnic composition (2002): East Indian 43.5%; black 30.2%; mixed race 16.7%; Amerindian 9.2%; other 0.4%.
Religious affiliation (2002): Christian 57.3%, of which Protestant/independent Christian 48.2% (including Anglican 6.9%), Roman Catholic 8.0%, Jehovah's Witness 1.1%; Hindu 28.4%; Muslim 7.2%; Rastafarian 0.5%; nonreligious 4.3%; other/unknown 2.3%.
Major urban areas (2006): Georgetown 236,900; Linden 44,900; New Amsterdam 35,700; Corriverton 12,700; Bartica 11,300.

Vital statistics

Birth rate per 1,000 population (2008): 18.5 (world avg. 20.3).
Death rate per 1,000 population (2008): 7.9 (world avg. 8.5).
Natural increase rate per 1,000 population (2008): 10.6 (world avg. 11.8).
Total fertility rate (avg. births per childbearing woman; 2008): 2.60.
Marriage/divorce rates per 1,000 population (2006): 6.1/n.a.
Life expectancy at birth (2005): male 62.9 years; female 68.3 years.
Major causes of death per 100,000 population (2006): diseases of the circulatory system 194.2; homicide/violence/suicide 59.6; diabetes mellitus 58.0; malignant neoplasms (cancers) 48.6; accidents 39.6; HIV/AIDS-related 39.2.
Adult population (ages 15–49) *living with HIV* (2009): 1.2%[4] (world avg. 0.8%).

National economy

Budget (2008). Revenue: G$99,513,000,000 (current revenue 82.9%, of which VAT 24.1%, company income tax 18.7%, excise tax 13.2%, personal income tax 12.7%; grants 13.7%; other 3.4%). Expenditures: G$105,838,000,000 (current expenditure 59.5%; development expenditure 40.5%).
Production (metric tons except as noted). Agriculture, forestry, fishing (2009): sugarcane 2,766,500, rice 553,500, coconuts 50,947, roots and tubers 37,044, cassava (manioc) 17,972, bananas 6,385, pumpkins, squash, and gourds 6,210, oranges 5,717, mangoes 3,428, natural gums 500; livestock (number of live animals) 130,000 sheep, 110,000 cattle, 19,900,000 chickens; roundwood (2010) 1,309,005 cu m, of which fuelwood 65%; fisheries production 44,114 (from aquaculture, negligible), of which shrimp or prawns 17,581. Mining and quarrying (2008): bauxite 1,995,000; gold 8,131 kg; diamonds 169,000 carats. Manufacturing (2008): flour 35,700; margarine 1,528; rum 142,000 hectolitres; beer and stout 84,000 hectolitres; soft drinks 3,966,000 cases; pharmaceuticals 20,400,000 tablets. Energy production (consumption): electricity (kW-hr; 2007) 867,000,000 (867,000,000); coal, none (none); crude petroleum, none (none); petroleum products (metric tons; 2007) none (491,000); natural gas, none (none).
Population economically active (2008): total 342,000[5]; activity rate of total population 44.8%[5] (participation rates: ages 15–64, 68.0%[5]; female 34.5%[5]; unemployed [2002] 11.7%).

Price index (2005 = 100)

	2004	2005	2006	2007	2008	2009	2010
Consumer price index	93.5	100.0	106.6	119.7	129.4	133.2	135.9

Gross national income (GNI; 2010): U.S.$2,491,000,000 (U.S.$3,270 per capita); purchasing power parity GNI (U.S.$3,530 per capita).

Structure of gross domestic product and labour force

	2009 in value G$'000,000	2009 % of total value	2002 labour force	2002 % of labour force
Sugar	14,328	5.6	51,200	18.8
Other agriculture	25,928	10.1		
Fishing, forestry	15,310	6.0		
Mining	22,701	8.9	9,500	3.5
Manufacturing	6,880	2.7	30,600	11.3
Public utilities			2,300	0.8
Construction	26,946	10.5	16,200	6.0
Transp. and commun.	13,133	5.1	17,000	6.3
Trade	13,925	5.4	43,500	16.0
Finance, real estate	19,191	7.5	10,500	3.9
Pub. admin., defense	39,178	15.3	15,100	5.6
Services	4,736	1.9	34,600	12.7
Other	53,565[6]	20.9[6]	41,300[7]	15.2[7]
TOTAL	255,823[8]	100.0[8]	271,800	100.0[8]

Public debt (external, outstanding; 2010): U.S.$1,043,000,000.
Household income and expenditure. Average household size (2002) 4.1.
Selected balance of payments data. Receipts from (U.S.$'000,000): tourism (2008) 59; remittances (2010) 308; foreign direct investment (2008–10 avg.) 170; official development assistance (2009) 173. Disbursements for (U.S.$'000,000): tourism (2008) 52; remittances (2009) 77.
Land use as % of total land area (2009): in temporary crops or left fallow 2.1%, in permanent crops 0.1%, in pasture 6.2%, forest area 77.2%.

Foreign trade[9]

Balance of trade (current prices)

	2003	2004	2005	2006	2007	2008
U.S.$'000,000	–84.7	–92.8	–239.4	–325.5	–244.1	–582.7
% of total	9.1%	7.9%	18.2%	24.7%	13.5%	25.9%

Imports (2008): U.S.$1,417,000,000 (refined petroleum 34.2%, machinery and apparatus 16.2%, food 11.2%, chemicals and chemical products 9.7%). *Major import sources:* Trinidad and Tobago 29.0%; U.S. 26.6%; Netherlands Antilles 6.5%; Venezuela 5.6%; China 5.4%.
Exports (2008): U.S.$834,300,000 (gold 22.7%, bauxite 22.3%, raw cane sugar 13.9%, rice 13.0%, shrimp 4.7%, sawn wood 4.1%, diamonds 3.5%). *Major export destinations:* Canada 22.5%; U.S. 17.5%; U.K. 13.5%; Ukraine 5.4%; Jamaica 4.8%.

Transport and communications

Transport. Railroads (2008): none. Roads (2000): total length 4,952 mi, 7,970 km (paved 7%). Vehicles (2008): passenger cars 44,739; trucks and buses 28,112. Air transport: passenger-km (2000) 299,000,000; metric ton-km cargo (2003) 200,000.

Communications

Medium	date	number in '000s	units per 1,000 persons	Medium	date	number in '000s	units per 1,000 persons
Televisions	2003	125	169	PCs	2005	29	39
Telephones				Dailies	2009	30[10]	52[10]
Cellular	2010	555[11]	736[11]	Internet users	2009	220	289
Landline	2010	150	199	Broadband	2010	12[11]	16[11]

Education and health

Educational attainment (2002). Percentage of population age 15 and over having: no formal schooling 3.0%; primary education 26.0%; secondary 62.1%; post-secondary 3.7%; higher 4.8%; other 0.4%. *Literacy* (2005): total population age 15 and over literate 99.0%; males literate 99.2%; females literate 98.7%.

Education (2007–08)

	teachers	students	student/ teacher ratio	enrollment rate (%)
Primary (age 6–11)	4,204	107,456	25.6	95
Secondary/Voc. (age 12–16)	3,574	74,673	20.9	...
Tertiary	816	7,306	9.0	12 (age 17–21)

Health: physicians (2005) 323 (1 per 2,325 persons); hospital beds (2004–05) 1,887 (1 per 401 persons); infant mortality rate per 1,000 live births (2005) 33.3; undernourished population (2005–07) 100,000 (7% of total population based on the consumption of a minimum daily requirement of 1,840 calories).

Military

Total active duty personnel (November 2010): 1,100 (army 81.8%, navy 9.1%, air force 9.1%); paramilitary 1,500. *Military expenditure as percentage of GDP* (2008): 5.6%; per capita expenditure U.S.$87.

[1]Excludes 3 nonelected ministers, one nonelected parliamentary secretary, and the speaker. [2]Includes inland water area equaling *c.* 7,000 sq mi (*c.* 18,000 sq km). [3]Based on land area only. [4]Statistically derived midpoint within range. [5]Estimate of the ILO Employment Trends Unit. [6]Indirect taxes less subsidies. [7]Includes 32,100 unemployed. [8]Detail does not add to total given because of rounding. [9]Imports c.i.f.; exports f.o.b. [10]Circulation of daily newspapers. [11]Subscribers.

Internet resources for further information:
- **Bank of Guyana http://www.bankofguyana.org.gy**
- **Bureau of Statistics http://www.statisticsguyana.gov.gy**

Haiti

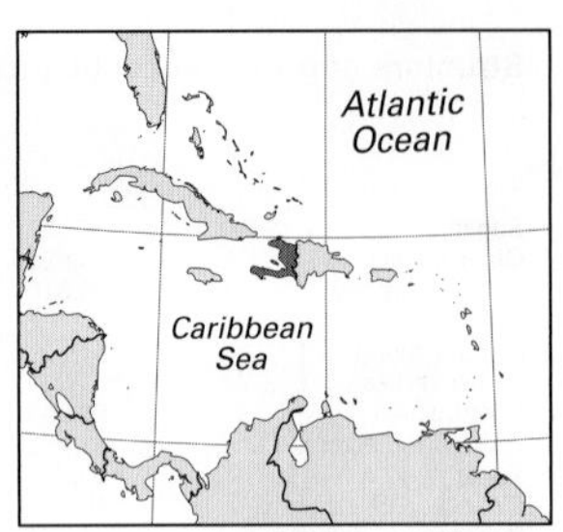

Official name: Repiblik d' Ayiti (Haitian Creole); République d'Haïti (French) (Republic of Haiti).
Form of government: republic with two legislative houses (Senate [30]; Chamber of Deputies [99]).
Head of state: President.
Head of government: Prime Minister.
Capital: Port-au-Prince.
Official languages: Haitian Creole; French.
Official religions: [1].
Monetary unit: gourde (G); valuation (Sept. 1, 2011) 1 U.S.$ = G 40.35; 1 £ = G 65.20.

Area and population

		area		population
				2009
Departments	**Capitals**	sq mi	sq km	estimate
Artibonite	Gonaïves	1,924	4,984	1,571,020
Centre	Hinche	1,419	3,675	678,626
Grand'Anse	Jérémie	807	2,091	425,878
Nippes	Miragoâne	471	1,219	311,497
Nord	Cap-Haïtien	813	2,106	970,495
Nord-Est	Fort-Liberté	697	1,805	358,277
Nord-Ouest	Port-de-Paix	840	2,176	662,777
Ouest	Port-au-Prince	1,864	4,827	3,664,620
Sud	Les Cayes	1,079	2,794	704,760
Sud-Est	Jacmel	781	2,023	575,293
TOTAL		10,695[2]	27,700[2]	9,923,243

Demography

Population (2011): 9,720,000[3].
Density (2011): persons per sq mi 908.8, persons per sq km 350.9.
Urban-rural (2007): urban 40.1%; rural 59.9%.
Sex distribution (2007): male 49.47%; female 50.53%.
Age breakdown (2007): under 15, 38.4%; 15–29, 28.6%; 30–44, 17.4%; 45–59, 9.7%; 60–74, 4.8%; 75–84, 1.0%; 85 and over, 0.1%.
Population projection: (2020) 10,693,000; (2030) 11,784,000.
Ethnic composition (2000): black 94.2%; mulatto 5.4%; other 0.4%.
Religious affiliation (2003): Roman Catholic 54.7%[4]; Protestant/independent Christian 28.5%, of which Baptist 15.4%, Pentecostal 7.9%; voodoo 2.1%; nonreligious 10.2%; other/unknown 4.5%.
Major cities (2009): Port-au-Prince 875,978 (metropolitan area [March 2010] *c.* 1,700,000); Carrefour 430,250[5]; Delmas 359,451[5]; Pétionville 271,175[5]; Cité Soleil 241,055[5]; Gonaïves 228,725; Cap-Haïtien 155,505.

Vital statistics

Birth rate per 1,000 population (2007): 27.9 (world avg. 20.3).
Death rate per 1,000 population (2007): 9.2 (world avg. 8.5).
Total fertility rate (avg. births per childbearing woman; 2007): 3.50.
Life expectancy at birth (2007): male 59.1 years; female 62.8 years.
Major causes of death per 100,000 population (2003)[6]: diseases of the circulatory system *c.* 175; infectious and parasitic diseases *c.* 157; pneumonia and influenza *c.* 41; malignant neoplasms (cancers) *c.* 37; malnutrition *c.* 31.
Adult population (ages 15–49) *living with HIV* (2009): 1.9%[7] (world avg. 0.8%).

National economy

Budget (2008–09). Revenue: U.S.$1,206,000,000 (grants 40.8%, domestic taxes 40.1%, customs duties 18.2%, other 0.9%)[8]. Expenditures: U.S.$1,536,000,000 (current expenditure 52.2%, capital expenditure 47.8%).
Public debt (external, outstanding; March 2010): U.S.$1,467,000,000.
Gross national income (GNI; 2010): U.S.$6,464,000,000 (U.S.$650 per capita); purchasing power parity GNI (U.S.$1,110 per capita).

Structure of gross domestic product and labour force

	2007–08		2003	
	in value G '000,000[9]	% of total value	labour force[10]	% of labour force[10]
Agriculture, fishing	3,204	23.4	...	45.7
Mining	16	0.1	...	0.3
Manufacturing	1,029	7.5	...	6.5
Construction	1,085	7.9	...	2.7
Public utilities	52	0.4	...	0.2
Transp. and commun.	967	7.1	...	2.1
Trade, restaurants	3,868	28.2	...	29.2
Finance, real estate	1,653	12.1	...	1.6
Services Pub. admin., defense	1,514	11.0	...	11.7
Other	313[11]	2.3[11]	...	...
TOTAL	13,701	100.0	...	100.0

Production (metric tons except as noted). Agriculture, forestry, fishing (2009): sugarcane 1,110,000, cassava (manioc) 467,643, yams 306,654, bananas 284,298, sweet potatoes 271,601, mangoes/mangosteens/guavas 244,607, plantains 229,010, rice 128,250, dry beans 77,599, coffee 47,667, avocados 44,280, cattle meat 42,000, cacao 8,814; livestock (number of live animals) 1,455,000 cattle, 1,001,000 pigs; roundwood (2010) 2,271,686 cu m, of which fuelwood 89%; fisheries production 8,382 (from aquaculture 1%). Mining and quarrying (2009): sand 2,000,000 cu m. Manufacturing (export value in U.S.$'000; 2009–10): reassembled manufactures (mostly wearing apparel) 191,620; essential oils (mostly vetiver) 4,960; not reassembled clothing/textiles 2,931. Energy production (consumption): electricity (kW-hr; 2007) 469,000,000 (469,000,000); crude petroleum, none (none); petroleum products (metric tons; 2007) none (732,000).
Population economically active (2008): total 4,377,000[12]; activity rate of total population 44.3%[12] (participation rates: ages 15–64, 70.4%[12]; female 42.8%[12]; unemployed[13]).

Price index (2005 = 100)

	2004	2005	2006	2007	2008	2009	2010
Consumer price index	86.4	100.0	113.1	122.7	141.8	141.7	149.8

Household income and expenditure. Average household size (2003) 4.6; sources of income (2001): self-employment 37%, transfers 25%, wages 20%, self-consumption 11%; expenditure (1996)[14]: food/beverages/tobacco 49.4%, housing/energy 9.1%, transportation 8.7%, clothing/footwear 8.5%.
Selected balance of payments data. Receipts from (U.S.$'000,000): tourism (2009) 315; remittances (2010) 1,499; foreign direct investment (2008–10 avg.) 72; official development assistance (2009) 1,120. Disbursements for (U.S.$'000,000): tourism (2009) 63; remittances (2009) 135.
Land use as % of total land area (2009): in temporary crops or left fallow 38.1%, in permanent crops 10.9%, in pasture 17.8%, forest area 3.7%.

Foreign trade[15]

Balance of trade (current prices)

	2004	2005	2006	2007	2008	2009
U.S.$'000,000	–832.8	–849.6	–1,112.1	–1,096.0	–1,617.6	–1,445.2
% of total	52.4%	48.1%	52.1%	51.2%	62.3%	56.8%

Imports (2009): U.S.$2,142,800,000 (diverse manufactured goods 27.5%, food 22.6%, mineral fuels 17.9%, machinery and transport equipment 9.2%). *Major import sources* (2008): U.S. *c.* 34%; Dominican Republic *c.* 23%; Netherlands Antilles *c.* 11%; China *c.* 5%.
Exports (2009): U.S.$550,400,000 (reassembled manufactures [mostly wearing apparel] 89.3%, mangoes 1.9%, essential oils [mostly vetiver] 1.8%, cacao 1.4%). *Major export destinations* (2008): U.S. *c.* 70%; Dominican Republic *c.* 9%; Canada *c.* 3%.

Transport and communications

Transport. Railroad: none. Roads (2000): total length 2,585 mi, 4,160 km (paved 24%). Vehicles (1999): passenger cars 93,000; trucks and buses 61,600.

Communications

Medium	date	number in '000s	units per 1,000 persons	Medium	date	number in '000s	units per 1,000 persons
Televisions	2003	60	7.2	PCs	2007	499	52
Telephones				Dailies	2009	20[16]	2.2[16]
Cellular	2010	4,000[17]	400[17]	Internet users	2009	1,000	100
Landline	2010	50	5.0	Broadband	2010	—	—

Education and health

Educational attainment (2000). Percentage of population age 25 and over having: no formal schooling or unknown 46.1%; incomplete primary education 28.9%; primary 5.3%; incomplete secondary 15.6%; secondary 1.8%; higher 2.3%. *Literacy* (2008): total population age 15 and over literate 53%[18].

Education (2005–06)

	teachers	students	student/ teacher ratio	enrollment rate (%)
Primary (age 6–11)	...	...	...	...
Secondary/Voc. (age 12–18)	...	...	...	...
Tertiary	920[19]	12,482[19]	13.6[19]	... (age 19–23)

Health: physicians (1999) 1,910 (1 per 4,000 persons); hospital beds (2000) 6,431 (1 per 1,234 persons); infant mortality rate per 1,000 live births (2007) 71.0; undernourished population (2005–07) 5,500,000 (57% of total population based on the consumption of a minimum daily requirement of 1,860 calories).

Military

Total active duty personnel: [20, 21].

[1]Roman Catholicism has special recognition per concordat with the Vatican; Vodou (Voodoo) became officially sanctioned per governmental decree of April 2003. [2]Approximate figure. Includes four offshore islands totaling about 382 sq mi (989 sq km) in area; excludes the 2.1 sq mi (5.4 sq km) Navassa (Navase) Island, which is administered by the U.S. but also claimed by Haiti. [3]Roughly 223,000 people were killed in the January 2010 earthquake; 1.3 million people were displaced in September 2010. [4]About 80% of all Roman Catholics also practice voodoo. [5]Within Port-au-Prince metropolitan area. [6]Projected rates based on *c.* 9% of total deaths. [7]Statistically derived midpoint within range. [8]Donor pledges in response to 2010 earthquake (for 2009–10): humanitarian aid U.S.$3,047,000,000; recovery and reconstruction assistance U.S.$3,407,000,000. [9]At prices of 1986–87. [10]Based on national survey. [11]Import duties less imputed bank service charges. [12]ILO estimate. [13]Unofficial estimate (2009) is *c.* 70%. [14]Weights of consumer price index components. [15]Imports f.o.b. in balance of trade and c.i.f. in commodities and trading partners. [16]Circulation. [17]Subscribers. [18]Haiti uses Haitian Creole literacy rate rather than French literacy rate. [19]Combined figures for the State University and Quisqueya University. [20]The Haitian army was disbanded in 1995. The national police force had 2,000 personnel in late 2009. [21]UN peacekeepers (July 2011): 8,728 troops, 3,524 police.

Internet resources for further information:
- **IHSI http://www.ihsi.ht**
- **Banque de la République d'Haïti http://www.brh.net**

Honduras

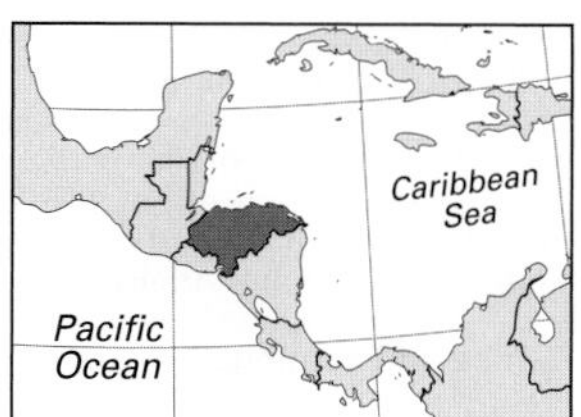

Official name: República de Honduras (Republic of Honduras).
Form of government: multiparty republic[1] with one legislative house (National Congress [128]).
Head of state and government: President.
Capital: Tegucigalpa.
Official language: Spanish.
Official religion: none.
Monetary unit: lempira (L); valuation (Sept. 1, 2011) 1 U.S.$ = L 18.83; 1 £ = L 30.43.

Area and population

Departments	Administrative centres	area sq mi	area sq km	population 2001 census
Atlántida	La Ceiba	1,688	4,372	344,099
Choluteca	Choluteca	1,515	3,923	390,805
Colón	Trujillo	1,683	4,360	246,708
Comayagua	Comayagua	3,185	8,249	352,881
Copán	Santa Rosa de Copán	1,978	5,124	288,766
Cortés	San Pedro Sula	1,252	3,242	1,202,510
El Paraíso	Yuscarán	2,892	7,489	350,054
Francisco Morazán	Tegucigalpa	3,328	8,619	1,180,676
Gracias a Dios	Puerto Lempira	6,563	16,997	67,384
Intibucá	La Esperanza	1,206	3,123	179,862
Islas de la Bahía	Roatán	91	236	38,073
La Paz	La Paz	975	2,525	156,560
Lempira	Gracias	1,632	4,228	250,067
Ocotepeque	Nueva Ocotepeque	629	1,630	108,029
Olancho	Juticalpa	9,230	23,905	419,561
Santa Bárbara	Santa Bárbara	1,940	5,024	342,054
Valle	Nacaome	643	1,665	151,841
Yoro	Yoro	3,004	7,781	465,414
TOTAL		43,433[2]	112,492	6,535,344

Demography

Population (2011): 7,755,000.
Density (2011): persons per sq mi 178.6, persons per sq km 68.9.
Urban-rural (2009): urban 50.8%; rural 49.2%.
Sex distribution (2008): male 49.95%; female 50.05%.
Age breakdown (2005): under 15, 40.5%; 15–29, 29.2%; 30–44, 16.7%; 45–59, 8.6%; 60–74, 3.9%; 75 and over, 1.1%.
Population projection: (2020) 9,179,000; (2030) 10,657,000.
Ethnic composition (2000): mestizo 86.6%; Amerindian 5.5%; black (including Black Carib) 4.3%; white 2.3%; other 1.3%.
Religious affiliation (2002): Roman Catholic *c.* 63%; Evangelical Protestant *c.* 23%; other *c.* 14%.
Major cities (2009): Tegucigalpa 990,600; San Pedro Sula 646,300; Choloma 223,900; La Ceiba 172,900; El Progreso 122,000.

Vital statistics

Birth rate per 1,000 population (2009): 27.0 (world avg. 20.3).
Death rate per 1,000 population (2009): 5.0 (world avg. 8.5).
Total fertility rate (avg. births per childbearing woman; 2009): 3.2.
Marriage/divorce rates per 1,000 population (2000–02): 1.0/n.a.
Life expectancy at birth (2009): male 70.1 years; female 74.9 years.
Major causes of death (percent of total; 2000–02): diseases of the circulatory system 23.6%; accidents and violence 21.3%; malignant neoplasms (cancers) 12.2%; diseases of the respiratory system 10.9%.

National economy

Budget (2008). Revenue: L 52,343,000,000 (tax revenue 80.5%; nontax revenue 8.5%; grants 11.0%). Expenditures: L 58,650,000,000 (current expenditure 78.7%, of which wages and salaries 41.8%; capital expenditure 21.3%).
Public debt (external, outstanding; December 2010): U.S.$3,748,000,000.
Production (metric tons except as noted). Agriculture, forestry, fishing (2009): sugarcane 6,203,136, oil palm fruit 1,526,000, bananas 690,625, corn (maize) 587,235, oranges 270,096, cantaloupes 229,912, coffee 205,800, pineapples 135,186, plantains 71,484; livestock (number of live animals) 2,697,581 cattle, 424,819 pigs, 38,645,000 chickens; roundwood (2010) 9,119,185 cu m, of which fuelwood 94%; fisheries production 40,160 (from aquaculture 72%). Mining and quarrying (2007): zinc (metal content) 38,000; gypsum (2008) 5,500; silver 50,000 kg; gold 4,100 kg. Manufacturing (value added in L '000,000; 2008): food, beverages, and tobacco 21,997; textiles and wearing apparel 15,624; fabricated metal products 4,905. Energy production (consumption): electricity (kW-hr; 2008) 6,589,300,000 (6,589,300,000); coal (metric tons; 2007) none (201,000); crude petroleum, none (none); petroleum products (metric tons; 2007) none (2,476,000).
Selected balance of payments data. Receipts from (U.S.$'000,000): tourism (2009) 611; remittances (2010) 2,649; foreign direct investment (2008–10 avg.) 775; official development assistance (2009) 457. Disbursements for (U.S.$'000,000): tourism (2009) 296; remittances (2009) 12; foreign direct disinvestment (2008–10 avg.) –0.3.
Population economically active (2006): total 2,811,800; activity rate of total population 40.0% (participation rates: ages 15 and over, 60.0%; female 34.7%; officially unemployed [2008] 3.5%).

Price and earnings indexes (2005 = 100)

	2004	2005	2006	2007	2008	2009	2010
Consumer price index	91.9	100.0	105.5	112.9	125.8	132.7	138.9
Earnings index[3]	94.5	100.0	105.1	108.0	108.2	...	...

Gross national income (GNI; 2010): U.S.$14,302,000,000 (U.S.$1,880 per capita); purchasing power parity GNI (U.S.$3,730 per capita).

Structure of gross domestic product and labour force

	2009 in value L '000,000	% of total value	labour force	% of labour force
Agriculture	31,192	11.5	1,161,800	37.1
Mining, quarrying	1,990	0.7	8,100	0.3
Manufacturing	46,674	17.3	411,500	13.1
Construction	15,943	5.9	205,800	6.6
Public utilities	3,348	1.2	11,800	0.4
Transp. and commun.	19,959	7.4	104,500	3.3
Trade, hotels	42,691	15.8	692,800	22.1
Finance, real estate	45,138	16.7	95,400	3.0
Public admin., defense	19,257	7.1	}	
Services	38,517	14.2	} 443,700[5]	14.2[5]
Other	5,834[4]	2.2[4]	}	
TOTAL	270,543	100.0	3,135,400	100.0[2]

Household income and expenditure (2004). Average household size (2006) 4.8; average annual income per household L 85,860 (U.S.$4,716); sources of income: wages and salaries *c.* 51%, self-employment *c.* 34%, remittances *c.* 8%, other *c.* 7%; expenditure (December 1999)[6]: food and nonalcoholic beverages 32%, housing and energy 19%, transportation 9%, clothing 8%.
Land use as % of total land area (2009): in temporary crops or left fallow 9.1%, in permanent crops 3.7%, in pasture 15.7%, forest area 47.5%.

Foreign trade[7, 8]

Balance of trade (current prices)

	2003	2004	2005	2006	2007	2008
U.S.$'000,000	–1,020	–1,293	–1,497	–2,027	–3,104	–4,052
% of total	12.0%	12.5%	12.9%	16.1%	21.2%	23.9%

Imports (2008): U.S.$11,170,000,000 (goods for reassembly 21.0%, of which textiles 16.7%; mineral fuels 17.8%; machinery and apparatus 14.3%; chemicals and chemical products 13.9%; food products 11.8%). *Major import sources:* U.S. 48.8%; Guatemala 7.2%; El Salvador 5.8%; Mexico 4.5%; Panama 3.4%.
Exports (2008): U.S.$6,199,000,000 (reassembled goods 57.4%, of which garments incl. knitwear 44.8%; coffee 10.1%; bananas 6.2%; palm oil 3.0%). *Major export destinations:* U.S. 61.2%; El Salvador 8.2%; Nicaragua 7.3%; Guatemala 3.3%; Mexico 2.9%.

Transport and communications

Transport. Railroads (2008): serviceable lines 47 mi, 75 km; most tracks are out of use but not dismantled. Roads (2008): total length 8,848 mi, 14,239 km (paved 22%). Vehicles (2008): passenger cars 224,628; trucks and buses 490,956. Air transport: n.a.[9]

Communications

Medium	date	number in '000s	units per 1,000 persons	Medium	date	number in '000s	units per 1,000 persons
Televisions	2004	1,000	143	PCs	2007	143	20
Telephones				Dailies	2009	190[10]	39[10]
Cellular	2010	9,505[11]	1,251[11]	Internet users	2009	732	98
Landline	2010	670	88	Broadband	2010	76[11]	10[11]

Education and health

Educational attainment (2005–06)[12]. Percentage of population age 25 and over having: no formal schooling/unknown 16.7%; incomplete primary education 37.0%; complete primary 22.7%; secondary 17.6%; higher 6.0%. *Literacy* (2007): total population age 15 and over literate 83.1%; males literate 82.4%; females literate 83.7%.

Education (2007–08)

	teachers	students	student/ teacher ratio	enrollment rate (%)
Primary (age 6–11)	38,283	1,276,495	33.3	97
Secondary/Voc. (age 12–16)	18,155	566,938	31.2	...
Tertiary	5,262	147,740	28.1	19 (age 17–21)

Health: physicians (2006) 5,977 (1 per 1,176 persons); hospital beds (2008) 6,929 (1 per 1,056 persons); infant mortality rate (2007) 20.0; undernourished population (2005–07) 900,000 (12% of total population based on the consumption of a minimum daily requirement of 1,720 calories).

Military

Total active duty personnel (November 2010): 12,000 (army 69.2%, navy 11.7%, air force 19.1%); reserve 60,000; U.S. troops (June 2011) 358. *Military expenditure as percentage of GDP* (2009): 0.7%; per capita expenditure U.S.$14.

[1]An interim regime supported by the military held power from June 28, 2009, to Jan. 27, 2010, when a democratically elected president was installed. [2]Detail does not add to total given because of rounding. [3]Minimum wage. [4]Taxes and import duties less imputed bank service charges. [5]Includes official unemployment figures; unofficial estimates of unemployment are significantly higher. [6]Weights of consumer price index components. [7]Import figures are f.o.b. in balance of trade and c.i.f. in commodities and trading partners. [8]All figures include goods reassembled for export. [9]Honduras did not have a national airline in 2009. [10]Circulation of daily newspapers. [11]Subscribers. [12]Based on the Encuesta Nacional de Demografía y Salud 2005–06.

Internet resources for further information:
- **Banco Central de Honduras http://www.bch.hn**
- **Instituto Nacional de Estadística http://www.ine.gob.hn**

Hong Kong

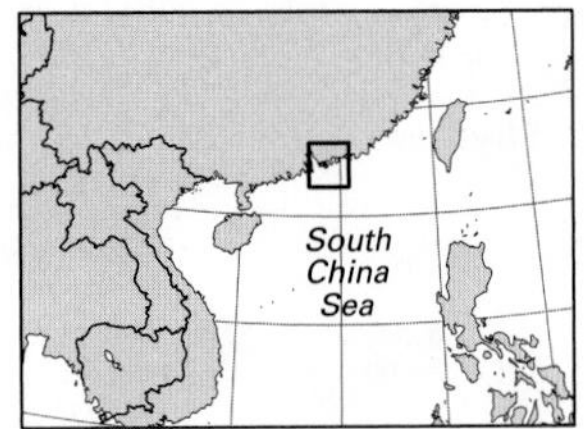

Official name: Xianggang Tebie Xingzhengqu (Chinese); Hong Kong Special Administrative Region (English).
Political status: special administrative region of China with one legislative house (Legislative Council [60[1]]).
Head of state: President of China.
Head of government: Chief Executive.
Government offices: [2].
Official languages: Chinese; English.
Official religion: none.
Monetary unit: Hong Kong dollar (HK$); valuation (Sept. 1, 2011) 1 U.S.$ = HK$7.78; 1 £ = HK$12.58.

Area and population

Geographic areas[3]	area sq mi	area sq km	population 2010 estimate
Hong Kong Island	31	81	1,310,800
Kowloon	18	47	2,090,800
New Territories (mainland)	289	748	3,533,000
New Territories (islands[4])	88	228	157,600
marine	—	—	1,800
TOTAL	426	1,104	7,094,000

Demography

Population (2011): 7,125,000.
Density (2011): persons per sq mi 16,725, persons per sq km 6,454.
Urban-rural (2009): urban 100.0%.
Sex distribution (2011[5]): male 46.74%; female 53.26%.
Age breakdown (2011[5]): under 15, 11.9%; 15–29, 20.2%; 30–44, 24.0%; 45–59, 25.4%; 60–74, 12.0%; 75–84, 4.8%; 85 and over, 1.7%.
Population projection: (2020) 7,803,000; (2030) 8,483,000.
Ethnic composition (2006): Chinese 95.0%; Filipino 1.6%; Indonesian 1.3%; assorted Caucasian 0.5%; Indian 0.3%; Nepalese 0.2%; other 1.1%.
Religious affiliation (2002): nonreligious/non-practitioner of religion *c.* 57%; Protestant *c.* 4.5%; Roman Catholic *c.* 3.5%; Muslim *c.* 1.5%; remainder (mostly Buddhist, Taoist, or Confucianist) 33.5%.
Major built-up areas (2010): Kowloon 2,090,800; Victoria 1,019,800; Tuen Mun 492,900; Sha Tin 434,800; Tseung Kwan O 354,500.

Vital statistics

Birth rate per 1,000 population (2010): 12.5 (world avg. 19.2).
Death rate per 1,000 population (2010): 5.9 (world avg. 8.2).
Total fertility rate (avg. births per childbearing woman; 2008): 1.06.
Marriage/divorce rates per 1,000 population: (2010) 7.4/(2009) 2.7.
Life expectancy at birth (2010): male 80.0 years; female 85.9 years.
Major causes of death per 100,000 population (2010): malignant neoplasms (cancers) 185.0; diseases of the circulatory system 142.3; pneumonia 81.0; accidents, poisoning, and violence 25.6.

National economy

Budget (2007–08). Revenue: HK$358,465,000,000 (earnings and profits taxes 37.3%, indirect taxes 26.9%, capital revenue 22.9%, other 12.9%). Expenditures: HK$252,400,000,000 (education 21.3%, social welfare 13.8%, health 13.3%, police 11.1%, housing 5.7%, economic services 5.3%).
Gross national income (GNI; 2009): U.S.$231,658,000,000 (U.S.$32,900 per capita); purchasing power parity GNI (U.S.$47,300 per capita).

Structure of gross domestic product and labour force

	2008			
	in value HK$'000,000	% of total value	labour force	% of labour force
Agriculture	824	0.1	11,003	0.3
Mining	96	—	—	—
Manufacturing	38,710	2.3	168,710	4.6
Construction	47,922	2.9	278,738	7.6
Public utilities	38,421	2.3	11,003	0.3
Transp. and commun.	120,647	7.2	385,098	10.5
Trade	442,454	26.4	1,224,978	33.4
Finance, insurance, and real estate	418,389	25.0	612,489	16.7
Pub. admin., defense, and services	279,909	16.7	975,581	26.6
Other	265,425[6]	15.8[6]	…	…
TOTAL	1,675,171[7]	100.0[7]	3,667,600	100.0

Production (metric tons except as noted). Agriculture, forestry, fishing (2008): vegetables 16,400, fruits 1,395, eggs 2,894,000 units, cut flowers are also produced; livestock (number of live animals) 87,240 pigs, 4,664,000 chickens; roundwood, n.a.; fisheries production (2009) 163,784 (from aquaculture 3%). Quarrying (2006): stone/aggregates 6,000,000. Manufacturing (value added in HK$'000,000; 2007): publishing and printed materials 13,689; food 6,346; transport equipment 4,203; textiles 3,222; wearing apparel 2,211; chemicals and chemical products 2,080; electronic parts and components 1,817; machinery and apparatus 1,688. Energy production (consumption): electricity (kW-hr; 2010–11) 38,355,000,000 ([2010] 41,863,000,000); hard coal (metric tons; 2010) none (10,324,000); crude petroleum, none (none); petroleum products (metric tons; 2007) none (3,482,000); natural gas (cu m; 2007) none (2,006,000,000).

Selected balance of payments data. Receipts from (U.S.$'000,000): tourism (2009) 16,020; remittances (2010) 369; foreign direct investment (FDI; 2008–10 avg.) 60,306. Disbursements for (U.S.$'000,000): tourism (2009) 15,960; remittances (2009) 402; FDI (2008–10 avg.) 63,550.
Population economically active (2010): total 3,676,000[8]; activity rate of total population 52.0% (participation rates: ages 15–64, 69.4%; female 47.0%; unemployed [June–August 2011] 3.5%).

Price and earnings indexes (2005 = 100)

	2004	2005	2006	2007	2008	2009	2010
Consumer price index	99.1	100.0	102.1	104.1	108.5	109.2	111.8
Average earnings index[9]	99.9	100.0	103.3	106.1	111.2	108.9	110.1

Public debt (external, outstanding; 2007[5]): U.S.$1,673,000,000.
Household income and expenditure (2001). Average household size (2010) 2.9; median annual income per household HK$224,500 (U.S.$28,800); sources of income: n.a.; expenditure: housing and energy 22.2%, clothing and footwear 15.2%, food and nonalcoholic beverages 13.5%, household furnishings 12.6%, transportation 11.0%.
Land use as % of total land area (2000): in temporary and permanent crops 5.4%, in pasture 29.3%[10]; overall forest area 18.0%.

Foreign trade[11]

Balance of trade (current prices)

	2004	2005	2006	2007	2008	2009
U.S.$'000,000,000	–7.4	–8.0	–13.1	–20.7	–22.7	–28.8
% of total	1.4%	1.4%	2.0%	2.9%	3.0%	4.3%

Imports (2008): U.S.$392,962,000,000 (machinery and apparatus 51.9%, of which electronic integrated circuits/microassemblies 13.2%, telecommunications equipment/parts 10.6%, computers/office machines/parts 9.0%; garments 4.7%; video games/toys/sporting goods 3.6%; diamonds 3.1%; food 3.0%). *Major import sources:* China 46.1%; Japan 10.0%; Singapore 6.4%; Taiwan 6.3%; U.S. 5.0%.
Exports (2008): U.S.$370,242,000,000 (machinery and apparatus 54.4%, of which telecommunications equipment/parts 13.4%, electronic integrated circuits/microassemblies 11.7%, computers/office machines/parts 10.0%; garments 7.5%; video games/toys/sporting goods 4.2%). *Major export destinations:* China 48.2%; U.S. 12.5%; Japan 4.3%; Germany 3.3%; U.K. 2.9%.

Transport and communications

Transport. Railroads (2009): route length 130 mi, 210 km[12]; passenger-km 4,731,000,000[13]; metric ton-km cargo, n.a. Roads (2010): total length 1,287 mi, 2,071 km (paved 100%). Vehicles (2010): passenger cars 433,000; trucks and buses 128,000. Air transport (2010–11): passenger-km 84,892,000,000; metric ton-km cargo 7,302,415,000.

Communications

Medium	date	number in '000s	units per 1,000 persons	Medium	date	number in '000s	units per 1,000 persons
Televisions	2003	3,467	507	PCs	2007	4,751	686
Telephones				Dailies	2009	2,200[14]	355[14]
Cellular	2010	13,416[15]	1,902[15]	Internet users	2009	4,300	612
Landline	2010	4,345	616	Broadband	2010	2,127[15]	302[15]

Education and health

Educational attainment (2010). Percentage of population age 15 and over having: no formal schooling 5.4%; primary education 16.9%; secondary 52.2%; nondegree higher 7.3%; higher degree 18.2%. *Literacy* (2002): total population age 15 and over literate 93.5%; males literate 96.9%; females literate 89.6%.

Education (2008–09)

	teachers	students	student/ teacher ratio	enrollment rate (%)
Primary (age 6–11)	23,278	369,047	15.9	94
Secondary/Voc. (age 12–18)	30,334[16]	511,872	17.8[16]	75
Tertiary	…	254,273	…	57 (age 19–23)

Health (2010): physicians 12,722[17, 18] (1 per 556 persons); hospital beds 35,339 (1 per 200 persons); infant mortality rate per 1,000 live births 1.6; undernourished population, n.a.

Military

Total active duty personnel (November 2009): *c.* 5,000 troops of Chinese military (including elements of army, navy, and air force); Hong Kong residents are exempted from military service.

[1]Thirty seats are directly elected by ordinary voters, and the remaining 30 are elected by special interest groups. [2]On Hong Kong Island in historic capital area of Victoria. [3]The 18 districts of Hong Kong have no administrative function. District councils advise the government on local matters. [4]Primarily Lantau. [5]January 1. [6]Includes ownership of premises and taxes on production and imports. [7]Detail does not add to total given because of statistical discrepancy. [8]Does not include unemployed not previously employed. [9]Manufacturing sector only. [10]Represents grassland that may not be grazed. [11]Imports are c.i.f., exports f.o.b. [12]Excludes 36 km of light rail and 16 km of tramway. [13]Data for Kowloon–Canton Railway part of MTR (Mass Transit Railway). [14]Circulation of daily newspapers. [15]Subscribers. [16]2006–07. [17]Registered personnel; all may not be present and working in the country. [18]There were an additional 9,188 practitioners of traditional Chinese medicine in Hong Kong in 2010.

Internet resources for further information:
- **Census and Statistics Department http://www.censtatd.gov.hk**
- **Hong Kong Monetary Authority http://www.hkma.gov.hk**

Hungary

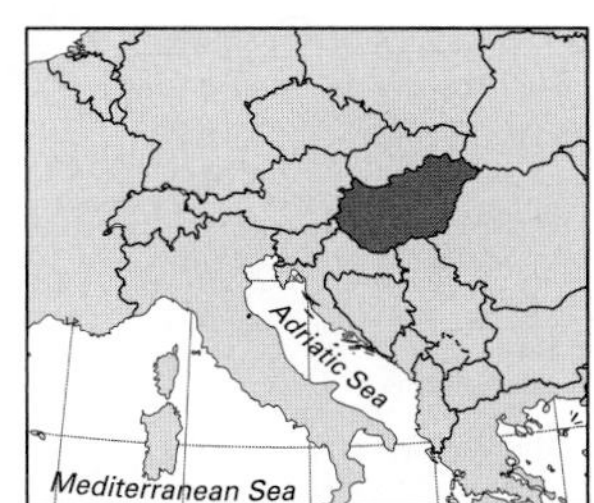

Official name: Magyarország (Hungary).
Form of government: unitary multiparty republic with one legislative house (National Assembly [386]).
Head of state: President.
Head of government: Prime Minister.
Capital: Budapest.
Official language: Hungarian.
Official religion: none.
Monetary unit: forint (Ft); valuation (Sept. 1, 2011) 1 U.S.$ = Ft 192.15; 1 £ = Ft 310.51.

Area and population

		area		population
Counties	Capitals	sq mi	sq km	2010[1] estimate
Bács-Kiskun	Kecskemét	3,261	8,445	528,418
Baranya	Pécs	1,710	4,430	393,758
Békés	Bekéscsaba	2,174	5,631	366,556
Borsod-Abaúj-Zemplén	Miskolc	2,798	7,247	692,771
Csongrád	Szeged	1,646	4,263	423,240
Fejér	Székesfehérvár	1,683	4,359	427,416
Győr-Moson-Sopron	Győr	1,579	4,089	448,435
Hajdú-Bihar	Debrecen	2,398	6,211	541,298
Heves	Eger	1,404	3,637	311,454
Jász-Nagykun-Szolnok	Szolnok	2,155	5,582	390,775
Komárom-Esztergom	Tatabánya	875	2,265	312,431
Nógrád	Salgótarján	982	2,544	204,917
Pest	Budapest[2]	2,468	6,393	1,229,880
Somogy	Kaposvár	2,331	6,036	320,578
Szabolcs-Szatmár-Bereg	Nyíregyháza	2,292	5,937	560,429
Tolna	Szekszárd	1,430	3,703	233,650
Vas	Szombathely	1,288	3,336	259,364
Veszprém	Veszprém	1,781	4,613	358,807
Zala	Zalaegerszeg	1,461	3,784	288,591
Capital city				
Budapest[2]		203	525	1,721,556
TOTAL		35,919	93,030	10,014,324

Demography

Population (2011): 9,972,000.
Density (2011): persons per sq mi 277.6, persons per sq km 107.2.
Urban-rural (2009): urban 67.7%; rural 32.3%.
Sex distribution (2010[1]): male 47.50%; female 52.50%.
Age breakdown (2009[1]): under 15, 14.9%; 15–29, 19.8%; 30–44, 22.4%; 45–59, 20.8%; 60–74, 14.9%; 75–84, 5.7%; 85 and over, 1.5%.
Population projection: (2020) 9,829,000; (2030) 9,648,000.
Ethnic composition (2000): Hungarian 84.4%; Rom 5.3%; Ruthenian 2.9%; German 2.4%; Romanian 1.0%; Slovak 0.9%; Jewish 0.6%; other 2.5%.
Religious affiliation (2001): Roman Catholic 51.9%; Reformed 15.9%; Lutheran 3.0%; Greek Catholic 2.6%; Jewish 0.1%; nonreligious 14.5%; other/unknown 12.0%.
Major cities (2010[1]): Budapest 1,721,556; Debrecen 207,270; Szeged 169,713; Miskolc 169,226; Pécs 157,680.

Vital statistics

Birth rate per 1,000 population (2009): 9.6 (world avg. 20.3); within marriage 59.2%; outside of marriage 40.8%.
Death rate per 1,000 population (2009): 13.0 (world avg. 8.5).
Total fertility rate (avg. births per childbearing woman; 2009): 1.33.
Marriage/divorce rates per 1,000 population (2009): 3.7/2.4.
Life expectancy at birth (2009): male 70.1 years; female 77.9 years.
Major causes of death per 100,000 population (2008): diseases of the circulatory system 645.0; malignant neoplasms (cancers) 326.5; diseases of the digestive system 84.4; accidents, poisoning, and violence 73.3.

National economy

Budget (2006). Revenue: Ft 8,653,000,000,000 (social security contributions 34.6%, taxes on goods and services 34.0%, personal income taxes 13.2%). Expenditures: Ft 10,710,700,000,000 (social protection 38.0%, economic affairs 12.5%, health 11.6%, public debt 8.6%, education 8.6%, defense 3.1%).
Public debt (2010[1]): U.S.$116,800,000,000.
Production (metric tons except as noted). Agriculture, forestry, fishing (2009): corn (maize) 7,528,380, wheat 4,419,160, cow's milk 1,748,470, sunflower seeds 1,256,190, barley 1,063,880, sugar beets 737,014, rapeseed 579,365, apples 575,368, Hungarian red paprika (2006) 32,633; livestock (number of live animals) 3,383,000 pigs, 1,236,000 sheep, 701,000 cattle; roundwood (2010) 5,740,275 cu m, of which fuelwood 52%; fisheries production 21,191 (from aquaculture 70%). Mining and quarrying (2009): bauxite 317,000. Manufacturing (value added in U.S.$'000,000; 2006): transportation equipment 2,976; chemical products 2,247; electrical machinery and apparatus 2,153; electronics 1,910. Energy production (consumption): electricity ('000,000 kW-hr; 2009–10) 30,056 ([2008] 37,400); hard coal ('000 metric tons; 2007) none (1,965); lignite ('000 metric tons; 2009) 9,905 ([2007] 10,088); crude petroleum ('000 barrels; 2009) 4,937 (57,743); petroleum products ('000 metric tons; 2007) 6,418 (6,485); natural gas ('000,000 cu m; 2009) 5,758 (11,320).
Selected balance of payments data. Receipts from (U.S.$'000,000): tourism (2009) 5,712; remittances (2010) 2,514; foreign direct investment (FDI; 2008–10 avg.) 3,935. Disbursements for (U.S.$'000,000): tourism (2009) 3,638; remittances (2009) 1,338; FDI (2008–10 avg.) 2,452.
Land use as % of total land area (2009): in temporary crops 46.9%, left fallow 3.7%, in permanent crops 2.1%, in pasture 11.1%, forest area 22.3%.

Population economically active (2009): total 4,202,600; activity rate of total population 41.9% (participation rates: ages 15–64, 61.6%; female 45.8%; unemployed [July 2009–June 2010] 11.0%).

Price and earnings indexes (2005 = 100)

	2004	2005	2006	2007	2008	2009	2010
Consumer price index	96.6	100.0	103.9	112.1	118.9	123.9	130.0
Annual earnings index	91.9	100.0	107.8	111.0	117.8	122.8	134.6

Gross national income (GNI; 2010): U.S.$129,923,000,000 (U.S.$12,990 per capita); purchasing power parity GNI (U.S.$19,280 per capita).

Structure of gross domestic product and labour force

	2009			
	in value Ft '000,000	% of total value	labour force	% of labour force
Agriculture, forestry, fishing	730,253	2.8	175,800	4.2
Mining and quarrying	54,905	0.2	8,500	0.2
Public utilities	749,184	2.9	84,100	2.0
Manufacturing	4,710,845	18.1	794,600	18.9
Construction	976,749	3.7	293,300	7.0
Transp. and commun.	1,735,593	6.7	345,300	8.2
Trade, restaurants	2,909,425	11.2	702,000	16.7
Finance, real estate	5,185,718	19.9	369,800	8.8
Public administration	1,975,058	7.6	304,700	7.2
Services	3,041,402	11.7	617,100	14.7
Other	3,985,195[3]	15.3[3]	507,400[4]	12.1[4]
TOTAL	26,054,327	100.0[5]	4,202,600	100.0

Household income and expenditure. Average household size (2009[1]) 2.3; income per household[6] (2001) Ft 2,898,000 (U.S.$10,300); sources of income (2007): wages 52.1%, transfers 28.8%, self-employment 11.7%; expenditure (2008): transportation and communications 19.5%, housing and energy 19.3%, food and nonalcoholic beverages 17.5%.

Foreign trade[7]

Balance of trade (current prices)

	2005	2006	2007	2008	2009	2010
U.S.$'000,000	–3,648	–2,923	–69	–574	+5,299	+7,337
% of total	2.8%	1.9%	0.0%	0.3%	3.3%	4.0%

Imports (2008): U.S.$108,785,000,000 (electrical machinery/electronic devices 12.9%; nonelectrical machinery 12.2%; mineral fuels 8.5%; telecommunications equipment 8.4%; road vehicles 8.1%). *Major import sources:* Germany 25.5%; Russia 9.3%; Austria 6.2%; China 5.6%; Neth. 4.5%.
Exports (2008): U.S.$108,211,000,000 (machinery and apparatus 46.1%, of which telecommunications equipment 11.6%, electrical machinery 9.6%; road vehicles/parts 10.8%; food 6.0%). *Major export destinations:* Germany 26.7%; Italy 5.3%; Romania 5.3%; Austria 4.9%; Slovakia 4.7%.

Transport and communications

Transport. Railroads (2009): route length (2008) 5,006 mi, 8,057 km; passenger-km 8,073,000,000; metric ton-km cargo 7,663,000,000. Roads (2008): total length 99,455 mi, 160,057 km (paved 44%); passenger-km (2006) 64,900,000,000[8]; metric ton-km cargo (2009) 35,373,000,000. Vehicles (2010[1]): passenger cars 3,013,719; trucks and buses 437,136. Air transport (2009)[9]: passenger-km 3,654,000,000; metric ton-km cargo 9,000,000.

Communications

Medium	date	number in '000s	units per 1,000 persons	Medium	date	number in '000s	units per 1,000 persons
Televisions	2003	4,810	475	PCs	2007	2,574	256
Telephones				Dailies	2009	1,239[10]	124[10]
Cellular	2010	12,012[11]	1,203[11]	Internet users	2009	6,176	618
Landline	2010	2,977	298	Broadband	2010	1,956[11]	196[11]

Education and health

Educational attainment (2008). Population age 25–64 having: no formal schooling through primary education 2%; lower-secondary 19%; upper secondary/higher vocational 60%; university 18%; unknown 1%.

Education (2007–08)

	teachers	students	student/ teacher ratio	enrollment rate (%)
Primary (age 7–10)	37,844	394,246	10.4	90
Secondary/Voc. (age 11–18)	90,423	924,414	10.2	91
Tertiary	23,634	413,715	17.5	65 (age 19–23)

Health (2008): physicians 31,024 (1 per 324 persons); hospital beds 70,714 (1 per 142 persons); infant mortality rate per 1,000 live births (2009) 5.1; undernourished population (2004–06) n.a.

Military

Total active duty personnel (November 2009): 29,626 (army 34.1%, air force 19.6%, joint staff 46.3%); paramilitary 12,000; reserves 44,000. *Military expenditure as percentage of GDP* (2009): 1.1%; per capita expenditure U.S.$148.

[1]January 1. [2]Budapest acts as the capital of Pest county even though it is administratively not part of Pest county. [3]Taxes less subsidies on products. [4]Includes 420,700 unemployed. [5]Detail does not add to total given because of rounding. [6]Adjusted disposable income including government transfers. [7]Imports c.i.f.; exports f.o.b. [8]Passenger cars 47,000,000,000; buses 17,900,000,000. [9]Malév Hungarian Airlines only. [10]Circulation of daily newspapers. [11]Subscribers.

Internet resource for further information:
- **Hungarian Central Statistical Office http://portal.ksh.hu**

Iceland

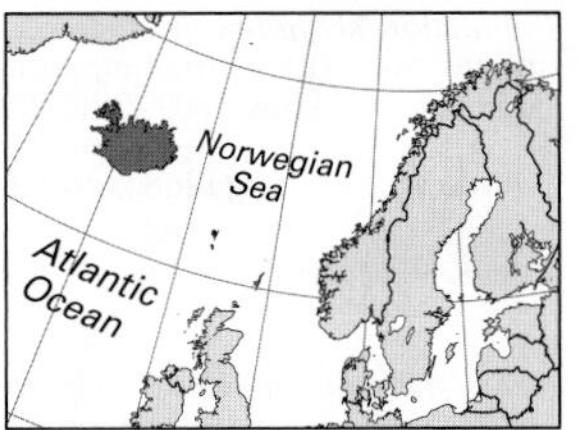

Official name: Lýdhveldidh Ísland (Republic of Iceland).
Form of government: unitary multiparty republic with one legislative house (Althingi, or Parliament [63]).
Head of state: President.
Head of government: Prime Minister.
Capital: Reykjavík.
Official language: Icelandic.
Official religion: Evangelical Lutheran.
Monetary unit: króna (ISK); valuation (Sept. 1, 2011) 1 U.S.$ = ISK 114.32; 1 £ = ISK 184.73.

Area and population

		area		population
Geographic regions[2]	**Principal centres**	sq mi	sq km	2011[1] estimate
Capital region[3]	Reykjavík	410	1,062	202,341
East	Egilsstadhir	8,773	22,721	12,306
Northeast	Akureyri	8,482	21,968	29,006
Northwest	Saudhárkrókur	4,918	12,737	7,393
South	Selfoss	9,469	24,526	23,802
Southwest	Keflavík	320	829	21,088
West	Borgarnes	3,689	9,554	15,379
Westfjords	Ísafjördhur	3,633	9,409	7,137
REMAINDER	—	75	194	0
TOTAL		39,769	103,000	318,452

Demography

Population (2011): 319,000.
Density (2011)[4]: persons per sq mi 34.7, persons per sq km 13.4.
Urban-rural (2008[1]): urban 93.1%; rural 6.9%.
Sex distribution (2010): male 50.26%; female 49.74%.
Age breakdown (2010): under 15, 20.9%; 15–29, 22.1%; 30–44, 20.6%; 45–59, 19.4%; 60–74, 11.2%; 75–84, 4.3%; 85 and over, 1.5%.
Population projection: (2020) 341,000; (2030) 372,000.
Ethnic composition (2009[1])[5]: Icelandic 92.4%; European 6.4%, of which Polish 3.4%, Nordic 0.5%; Asian 0.7%; other 0.5%.
Religious affiliation (2010): Evangelical Lutheran 79.2%; Roman Catholic 3.0%; other Christian 6.9%; nonreligious/other 10.9%.
Major cities (2011[1]): Reykjavík 118,898 (urban area 202,131); Kópavogur 30,779[6]; Hafnarfjördhur 26,099[6]; Akureyri 17,754; Gardhabær 10,909[6].

Vital statistics

Birth rate per 1,000 population (2009): 15.7 (world avg. 20.3); within marriage 35.9%; outside of marriage 64.1%.
Death rate per 1,000 population (2009): 6.3 (world avg. 8.5).
Natural increase rate per 1,000 population (2009): 9.4 (world avg. 11.8).
Total fertility rate (avg. births per childbearing woman; 2009): 2.22.
Marriage/divorce rates per 1,000 population (2009): 4.6/1.7.
Life expectancy at birth (2009): male 79.7 years; female 83.3 years.
Major causes of death per 100,000 population (2009): diseases of the circulatory system 228.3; malignant neoplasms (cancers) 176.0; diseases of the respiratory system 54.8; diseases of the nervous system 51.4; accidents 36.9.

National economy

Budget (2007). Revenue: ISK 454,588,000,000 (tax revenue 78.4%, of which VAT 42.9%, individual income tax 31.5%; nontax revenue 21.6%). Expenditures: ISK 403,199,000,000 (social security and health 48.8%; education 10.6%; social affairs 9.4%; interest payment 6.9%).
Production (metric tons except as noted). Agriculture, forestry, fishing (2009): cow's milk 125,569, potatoes 9,500, hen's eggs 3,024, tomatoes 1,481, cucumbers 1,452, greasy wool 787, hay 2,105,238 cu m; livestock (number of live animals) 469,429 sheep, 73,498 cattle, 39,065 mink; roundwood, n.a.; fisheries production (value in ISK '000,000; 2010): 132,979, of which cod 44,582, haddock 15,236, redfish 12,016, saithe 8,480, Norwegian spring-spawning herring 7,980, blue whiting 3,265; fisheries production by tonnage (2010) 1,063,467 (from aquaculture, negligible). Mining and quarrying (2007): pumice 95,000. Manufacturing (value of sales in ISK '000,000; 2008): base metals (nearly all aluminum and ferrosilicon) 196,547; preserved and processed fish 162,252; other food products and beverages 72,049; cement, bricks, and ceramics 17,742; fabricated metal products 14,992. Energy production (consumption): electricity (kW-hr; 2008) 16,468,000,000 (16,468,000,000); coal (metric tons; 2007) none (138,000); crude petroleum, none (none); petroleum products (metric tons; 2008) none (849,000); natural gas, none (none).
Selected balance of payments data. Receipts from (U.S.$'000,000): tourism (2009) 555; remittances (2010) 24; foreign direct investment (2008–10 avg.) 1,650. Disbursements for (U.S.$'000,000): tourism (2009) 533; remittances (2009) 34; foreign direct disinvestment (2008–10 avg.) –1,288.
Population economically active (2007): total 181,500; activity rate of total population 58.3% (participation rates: ages 16–64, 87.7%; female 45.5%; unemployed [April–June 2009] 9.1%).

Price and earnings indexes (2005 = 100)

	2004	2005	2006	2007	2008	2009	2010
Consumer price index	96.2	100.0	106.7	112.1	126.3	141.4	149.1
Annual earnings index	93.3	100.0	109.8	119.2	129.1	133.8	139.9

Gross national income (GNI; 2010): U.S.$10,787,000,000 (U.S.$33,870 per capita); purchasing power parity GNI (U.S.$28,630 per capita).

Structure of gross domestic product and labour force

	2008		2007	
	in value ISK '000,000,000	% of total value	labour force	% of labour force
Agriculture	18.2	1.2	6,000	3.3
Fishing	62.4	4.2	4,500	2.5
Mining, quarrying	1.3	0.1	19,200	10.6
Manufacturing	144.2	9.8		
Construction	136.4	9.2	15,700	8.7
Public utilities	59.8	4.1	1,700	0.9
Transp. and commun.	100.1	6.8	11,100	6.1
Trade, restaurants	146.8	9.9	31,600	17.4
Finance, real estate	343.0	23.2	25,900	14.3
Services	287.1	19.5	52,100	28.7
Public administration			8,900	4.9
Other	177.2[7]	12.0[7]	4,800[8]	2.6[8]
TOTAL	1,476.5	100.0	181,500	100.0

Public debt (December 2008): U.S.$9,906,000,000.
Household income and expenditure. Average household size (2006) 2.5; annual employment income per household (2008) ISK 3,673,000 (U.S.$41,600); sources of income (2001): wages and salaries 78.6%, pension 10.3%, self-employment 2.0%, other 9.1%; expenditure (2005–07): housing and energy 25.7%, transportation and communications 20.6%, recreation, education, and culture 13.3%, food 11.8%, household furnishings 6.6%.
Land use as % of total land area (2009): in temporary crops, left fallow, or in permanent crops 0.07%; in pasture 22.7%; forest area 0.3%.

Foreign trade[9]

Balance of trade (current prices)

	2004	2005	2006	2007	2008	2009
ISK '000,000	–37,787	–94,539	–158,461	–92,145	–6,665	+87,192
% of total	8.5%	19.6%	24.6%	13.1%	0.7%	9.6%

Imports (2008): ISK 542,279,000,000 (machinery and apparatus 21.3%, refined petroleum 11.2%, alumina 10.3%, road vehicles 7.1%, food products 7.0%, aircraft/parts 3.5%). *Major import sources:* Norway 11.2%; Germany 10.3%; Sweden 9.0%; U.S. 8.0%; Denmark 7.3%; China 6.6%.
Exports (2008): ISK 470,997,000,000 (aluminum 39.0%, fresh fish 21.7%, dried/salted fish 8.0%, aircraft 6.1%, fish foodstuff for animals 3.0%, ferrosilicon 2.5%). *Major export destinations:* Netherlands 34.4%; U.K. 11.6%; Germany 11.3%; U.S. 5.6%; Japan 4.4%.

Transport and communications

Transport. Railroads: none. Roads (2009[1]): total length 7,996 mi, 12,869 km (paved 34%[10]); passenger-km (2006) 5,600,000,000[11]; metric ton-km cargo, n.a. Vehicles (2009[1]): passenger cars 209,740; trucks and buses 33,774. Air transport (2008): passenger-km 3,861,000,000[12]; metric ton-km cargo 143,000,000[13].

Communications

Medium	date	number in '000s	units per 1,000 persons	Medium	date	number in '000s	units per 1,000 persons
Televisions	2004	101	345	PCs	2005	142	481
Telephones				Dailies	2009	50[14]	199[14]
Cellular	2010	348[15]	1,087[15]	Internet users	2009	302	935
Landline	2010	204	637	Broadband	2010	111[15]	347[15]

Education and health

Educational attainment (2007): Percentage of population ages 25–64 having: primary education 3%; lower secondary 33%; upper secondary 23%; post-secondary non-tertiary 11%; higher vocational 4%; university 25%; advanced degree 1%. *Literacy:* virtually 100%.

Education (2005–06)

	teachers	students	student/ teacher ratio	enrollment rate (%)
Primary (age 6–12)	2,903	30,421	10.5	98
Secondary/Voc. (age 13–19)	3,144	33,900	10.8	90
Tertiary	1,865	15,721	8.4	73 (age 20–24)

Health: physicians (2009) 1,190 (1 per 268 persons); hospital beds (2002) 2,162 (1 per 133 persons); infant mortality rate per 1,000 live births (2008) 2.5; undernourished population (2005–07) less than 5.0% of total population.

Military

Total active duty personnel (November 2010): 130 coast guard (paramilitary) personnel; Iceland has no military.[16] *Coast guard expenditure as percentage of GDP* (2008): 0.3%; per capita expenditure U.S.$140.

[1]January 1. [2]Actual local administration is based on 78 municipalities. [3]Includes municipalities adjacent to Reykjavík. [4]Population density calculated with reference to 9,191 sq mi (23,805 sq km) area free of glaciers (covering 4,603 sq mi [11,922 sq km]), lava fields or wasteland (covering 24,918 sq mi [64,538 sq km]), and lakes (covering 1,064 sq mi [2,757 sq km]). [5]By citizenship. [6]Within Reykjavík urban area. [7]Taxes on products less subsidies. [8]Includes 4,200 unemployed. [9]Imports f.o.b. in balance of trade and c.i.f. in commodities and trading partners. [10]Includes oil-gravelled roads. [11]Passenger cars 5,000,000,000; buses 600,000,000. [12]Icelandair and Air Iceland. [13]Icelandair only. [14]Circulation of daily newspapers. [15]Subscribers. [16]NATO members (from July 2007) police Icelandic airspace.

Internet resources for further information:
- **Statistics Iceland http://www.statice.is**
- **Central Bank of Iceland http://www.sedlabanki.is**

India

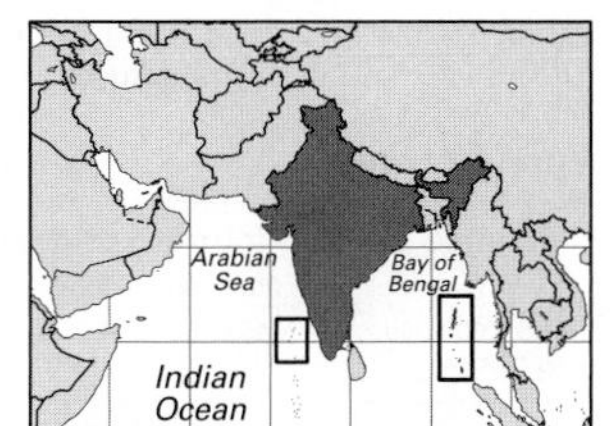

Official name: Bharat (Hindi); Republic of India (English).
Form of government: multiparty federal republic with two legislative houses (Council of States [245[1]]; House of the People [545[2]]).
Head of state: President.
Head of government: Prime Minister.
Capital: New Delhi.
Official languages: Hindi; English.
Official religion: none.
Monetary unit: Indian rupee (Re, plural Rs[3]); valuation (Sept. 1, 2011) 1 U.S.$ = Rs 46.05; 1 £ = Rs 74.41.

Area and population

		area		population
States	Capitals	sq mi	sq km	2011 census[4]
Andhra Pradesh	Hyderabad	106,204	275,068	84,665,533
Arunachal Pradesh	Itanagar	32,333	83,743	1,382,611
Assam	Dispur	30,285	78,438	31,169,272
Bihar	Patna	38,301	99,200	103,804,637
Chhattisgarh	Raipur	52,199	135,194	25,540,196
Goa	Panaji	1,429	3,702	1,457,723
Gujarat	Gandhinagar	75,685	196,024	60,383,628
Haryana	Chandigarh	17,070	44,212	25,353,081
Himachal Pradesh	Shimla	21,495	55,673	6,856,509
Jammu and Kashmir	Srinagar	39,146	101,387	12,548,926
Jharkhand	Ranchi	28,833	74,677	32,966,238
Karnataka	Bangalore (Bengaluru)	74,051	191,791	61,130,704
Kerala	Thiruvananthapuram (Trivandrum)	15,005	38,863	33,387,677
Madhya Pradesh	Bhopal	119,016	308,252	72,597,565
Maharashtra	Mumbai (Bombay)	118,800	307,690	112,372,972
Manipur	Imphal	8,621	22,327	2,721,756
Meghalaya	Shillong	8,660	22,429	2,964,007
Mizoram	Aizawl	8,139	21,081	1,091,014
Nagaland	Kohima	6,401	16,579	1,980,602
Orissa (Odisha)	Bhubaneshwar	60,119	155,707	41,947,358
Punjab	Chandigarh	19,445	50,362	27,704,236
Rajasthan	Jaipur	132,139	342,239	68,621,012
Sikkim	Gangtok	2,740	7,096	607,688
Tamil Nadu	Chennai (Madras)	50,216	130,058	72,138,958
Tripura	Agartala	4,049	10,486	3,671,032
Uttar Pradesh	Lucknow	93,933	243,286	199,581,477
Uttarakhand	Dehra Dun	19,739	51,125	10,116,752
West Bengal	Kolkata (Calcutta)	34,267	88,752	91,347,736
Union Territories				
Andaman and Nicobar Islands	Port Blair	3,185	8,249	379,944
Chandigarh	Chandigarh	44	114	1,054,686
Dadra and Nagar Haveli	Silvassa	190	491	342,853
Daman and Diu	Daman	43	112	242,911
Lakshadweep	Kavaratti	12	32	64,429
Puducherry (Pondicherry)	Puducherry (Pondicherry)	190	492	1,244,464
National Capital Territory				
Delhi	Delhi	573	1,483	16,753,235
TOTAL		1,222,559[5, 6]	3,166,414[5]	1,210,193,422

Demography

Population (2011): 1,216,728,000.
Density (2011)[5]: persons per sq mi 995.2, persons per sq km 384.3.
Urban-rural (2011): urban 31.2%; rural 68.8%.
Sex distribution (2011): male 51.54%; female 48.46%.
Age breakdown (2008): under 15, 30.9%; 15–29, 26.9%; 30–44, 21.2%; 45–59, 13.1%; 60–74, 6.4%; 75–84, 1.3%; 85 and over, 0.2%.
Population projection: (2020) 1,360,935,000; (2030) 1,494,946,000.
Major cities (2009; *urban agglomerations,* 2010): Delhi 12,260,000 (22,157,000); Mumbai (Bombay) 13,920,000 (20,041,000); Kolkata (Calcutta) 5,080,000 (15,552,000); Chennai (Madras) 4,590,000 (7,547,000); Bangalore (Bengaluru) 5,310,000 (7,218,000); Hyderabad 4,030,000 (6,751,000); Ahmadabad 3,910,000 (5,717,000); Pune (Poona) 3,340,000 (5,002,000); Surat 3,230,000 (4,168,000); Kanpur 3,140,000 (3,364,000); Jaipur 3,100,000 (3,131,000); Lucknow 2,690,000 (2,873,000); Nagpur 2,400,000 (2,607,000); Patna 1,810,000 (2,321,000); Indore 1,810,000 (2,173,000); Vadodara 1,306,227[7] (1,872,000); Bhopal 1,750,000 (1,843,000); Coimbatore 930,882[7] (1,807,000); Ludhiana 1,700,000 (1,760,000); New Delhi[8] 302,363[7].

Other principal cities (2001)

	population		population		population
Agra	1,275,134	Kalyan-Dombivali[10]	1,193,512	Srinagar	898,440
Allahabad	975,393	Madurai	928,869	Thane (Thana)[10]	1,262,551
Amritsar	966,862	Meerut	1,068,772	Thiruvananthapuram (Trivandrum)	744,983
Chandigarh	808,515	Mysuru (Mysore)	755,379	Tiruchirappalli	752,066
Faridabad	1,055,938	Nashik (Nasik)	1,077,236	Varanasi (Benares)	1,091,918
Ghaziabad	968,256	Pimpri-Chinchwad[11]	1,012,472	Vijayawada	851,282
Guwahati	809,895	Rajkot	967,476	Vishakhapatnam	982,904
Gwalior	827,026	Ranchi	847,093		
Howrah (Haora)[9]	1,007,532	Shambajinagar (Aurangabad)	873,311		
Hubli-Dharwad	786,195	Sholapur (Solapur)	872,478		
Jabalpur	932,484				
Jodhpur	851,051				

Linguistic composition (2001)[12]: Hindi 41.03%; Bengali 8.11%; Telugu 7.19%; Marathi 6.99%; Tamil 5.91%; Urdu 5.01%; Gujarati 4.48%; Kannada 3.69%; Malayalam 3.21%; Oriya (Odia) 3.21%; Punjabi 2.83%; Assamese 1.28%; Maithili 1.18%; Bhili/Bhilodi 0.93%[13]; Santhali 0.63%; Kashmiri 0.54%; Nepali 0.28%; Gondi 0.26%[13]; Sindhi 0.25%; Konkani 0.24%; Dogri 0.22%; Khandeshi 0.20%[13]; Tulu 0.17%[13]; Kurukh/Oraon 0.17%[13]; Manipuri 0.14%; Bodo 0.13%; Khasi 0.11%[13]; Mundari 0.10%[13]; Ho 0.10%[13]; Sanskrit 0.0013%; other *c.* 1.41%. Hindi (roughly 66%) and English (roughly 33%) are also spoken as lingua francas.
Castes/tribes (2001): number of Scheduled Castes (formerly referred to as "Untouchables") 166,635,700; number of Scheduled Tribes (aboriginal peoples) 84,326,240.
Religious affiliation (2005): Hindu 72.04%; Muslim 12.26%, of which Sunnī 8.06%, Shīʿī 4.20%; Christian 6.81%, of which Independent 3.23%, Protestant 1.74%, Roman Catholic 1.62%, Orthodox 0.22%; traditional beliefs 3.83%; Sikh 1.87%; Buddhist 0.67%; Jain 0.51%; Bahāʾī 0.17%; Zoroastrian (Parsi) 0.02%[14]; nonreligious 1.22%; atheist 0.17%; remainder 0.43%.
Households (2001). Total number of households 193,579,954. Average household size 5.3. Type of household: permanent 51.8%; semipermanent 30.0%; temporary 18.2%. Average number of rooms per household 2.2; 1 room 38.4%, 2 rooms 30.0%, 3 rooms 14.3%, 4 rooms 7.5%, 5 rooms 2.9%, 6 or more rooms 3.7%, unspecified number of rooms 3.2%.

Vital statistics

Birth rate per 1,000 population (2008): 22.8 (world avg. 20.3).
Death rate per 1,000 population (2008): 8.2 (world avg. 8.5).
Natural increase rate per 1,000 population (2008): 14.6 (world avg. 11.8).
Total fertility rate (avg. births per childbearing woman; 2008): 2.80.
Life expectancy at birth (2008): male 63.0 years; female 67.0 years.
Major causes of death per 100,000 population (2002): infectious and parasitic diseases 420, of which HIV/AIDS 34; diseases of the circulatory system 268, of which ischemic heart disease 146; accidents, homicide, and other violence 100; malignant neoplasms (cancers) 71; chronic respiratory diseases 58.
Adult population (ages 15–49) *living with HIV* (2009): 0.3% (world avg. 0.8%).

Social indicators

Educational attainment (2001). Percentage of population age 25 and over having: no formal schooling 48.1%; incomplete primary education 9.0%; complete primary 22.1%; secondary 13.7%; higher 7.1%.

Distribution of expenditure (2004–05)

percentage of household expenditure by decile/quintile

1	2	3	4	5	6	7	8	9	10 (highest)
3.6	4.5	—11.3—		—14.9—		—20.4—		14.2	31.1

Quality of working life. Average workweek (2006): 46.9[15]. Rate of fatal injuries per 100,000 employees (2006) 38[15]. Agricultural workers in servitude ("debt bondage") to creditors (early 1990s) 10–20%. Children ages 5–14 working as child labourers (2003): 35,000,000 (14% of age group). Percentage of population living below the poverty line (official estimate; 2009–10): 37.2%.
Access to services (2005–06)[16]. Percentage of total (urban, rural) households having access to: electricity for lighting purposes 67.9% (93.1%, 55.7%), kerosene for lighting purposes (2001) 36.9% (8.3%, 46.6%), water closets 24.3% (50.8%, 11.4%), pit latrines 7.9% (7.0%, 8.6%), no latrines 55.3% (16.8%, 74.0%), closed drainage for waste water (2001) 12.5% (34.5%, 3.9%), open drainage for waste water (2001) 33.9% (43.4%, 30.3%), no drainage for waste water (2001) 53.6% (22.1%, 65.8%). Type of fuel used for cooking in households: firewood 54.4% (23.0%, 69.6%), LPG (liquefied petroleum gas) 24.7% (58.7%, 8.2%), dung 10.6% (2.8%, 14.4%), kerosene 3.2% (8.2%, 0.8%), coal 1.9% (4.3%, 0.8%). Source of drinking water: hand pump or tube well 42.8% (21.3%, 53.2%), piped water 24.5% (50.7%, 11.8%), well 9.3% (2.9%, 12.4%), river, canal, spring, public tank, pond, or lake 1.5% (0.8%, 1.8%).
Social participation. Eligible voters participating in April/May 2009 national election: 63.2%. Trade union membership (2002) 24,601,589[17].
Social deviance (2008)[18]. Offense rate per 100,000 population for: theft 27.8; cruelty by husband 7.1; riots 5.8; molestation of women 3.5; murder 2.9; kidnapping/abduction 2.7, of which women/girls 2.0; rape 1.9; robbery 1.8; dowry deaths 0.7; dacoity (gang robbery) 0.4. Rate of suicide per 100,000 population (2007): 10.5.
Material well-being (2005–06)[16]. Total (urban, rural) households possessing: television receivers 44.2% (73.2%, 30.1%), scooters, motorcycles, or mopeds 17.2% (30.5%, 10.8%), cars, jeeps, or vans 2.7% (6.1%, 1.0%). Households availing banking services (2001) 35.5% (49.5%, 30.1%). Agricultural households with access to credit (2008) 48.6%

National economy

Gross national income (GNI; 2010): U.S.$1,566,636,000,000 (U.S.$1,340 per capita); purchasing power parity GNI (U.S.$3,560 per capita).

Structure of gross domestic product and labour force

	2008–09		1999–2000	
	in value Rs '000,000,000	% of total value	labour force	% of labour force
Agriculture, forestry, fishing	8,618	17.5	190,940,000	52.6
Mining and quarrying	1,254	2.5	2,260,000	0.6
Manufacturing	7,804	15.8	40,790,000	11.2
Construction	4,370	8.9	14,950,000	4.1
Public utilities	795	1.6	1,150,000	0.3
Transp. and commun. } Trade, restaurants, hotels }	12,467	25.3	13,650,000	3.8
			37,540,000	10.3
Finance, real estate	6,912	14.0	4,620,000	1.3
Pub. admin., defense } Services }	7,112	14.4	30,840,000	8.5
			…	…
Other			26,580,000[19]	7.3[19]
TOTAL	49,332	100.0	363,330,000[6]	100.0

Budget (2008–09). Revenue: Rs 9,009,530,000,000 (tax revenue 51.7%, of which corporate taxes 18.3%, income tax 10.0%, excise taxes 9.8%; capital revenue 37.6%; nontax revenue 10.7%). Expenditures: Rs 9,009,530,000,000 (current expenditure 89.2%, of which public debt payments 21.4%, subsidies 14.3%, defense 8.2%; capital expenditure 10.8%).

Public debt (external, outstanding; 2009): U.S.$76,531,000,000.

Production (in '000 metric tons except as noted). Agriculture, forestry, fishing (2009): sugarcane 285,029, cereals 248,810 (of which rice 133,700, wheat 80,680, corn [maize] 16,680, millet 8,810, sorghum 7,250), vegetables 91,613 (of which dry onions 13,900, tomatoes 11,149, eggplants 10,378, okra 4,528, garlic 1,070), fruits 70,395 (of which bananas 26,997, mangoes 13,557[20], papayas 3,912, lemons and limes 2,572), water buffalo milk 62,860, cow's milk 45,140, potatoes 34,391, soybeans 10,050, rapeseed 7,201, chickpeas 7,060, peanuts (groundnuts) 5,510, cotton lint 3,794, hen's eggs 3,200, pigeon peas 2,270, jute 1,926, chilies and peppers 1,300, castor oil seed 1,098, sunflower seed 900, natural rubber (2008) 819, tea 800, sesame seed 657, tobacco 620, ginger 380, safflower seed 189, anise, badian, fennel, and coriander 177; livestock (number of live animals) 172,451,000 cattle, 126,009,000 goats, 106,630,000 water buffalo, 65,717,000 sheep; roundwood (2010) 331,737,424 cu m, of which fuelwood 93%; fisheries production 7,845 (from aquaculture 48%). Mining and quarrying (2009): iron ore 157,000[21, 22]; bauxite 14,000[23]; chromite 3,800[24]; barite 1,200[24]; manganese 980[21]; zinc 365[21]; lead 92[21]; copper 31[21]; mica 1.8; silver 95,000 kg; gem diamonds 14,000 carats.

Manufacturing enterprises (2005)

	no. of persons engaged	annual wages per employee (U.S.$)	annual value added (U.S.$'000,000)
Refined petroleum products	54,546	5,346	10,408
Iron and steel	430,053	3,070	8,785
Pharmaceuticals, paints, and soaps	596,764	2,223	7,059
Base chemicals	201,454	3,543	5,731
Textiles (spun and woven only)	1,028,045	1,319	4,313
Motor vehicles	84,856	5,132	3,915
Bricks, cement, ceramics	524,267	1,187	3,261
Food products (vegetable-, pulse-, or seed-based)	690,553	1,091	2,672
General purpose machinery	219,562	2,823	2,339
Base nonferrous metals	81,106	2,020	2,176
Parts of motor vehicles	253,003	2,318	2,138
Special purpose machinery	214,521	2,670	1,959
Electrical motors, generators, and transformers	83,209	3,214	1,347
Wearing apparel	540,231	1,133	1,343
Cigarettes, other tobacco products	473,608	472	1,268
Fabricated metal products	239,824	1,606	1,238
Paper and paper products	177,696	1,745	1,224
Plastics	198,276	1,373	1,174
Structural metal products	132,902	1,971	1,063

Energy production (consumption): electricity (kW-hr; 2009) 756,422,000,000 ([2007] 818,245,000,000); hard coal (metric tons; 2009) 521,371,000 ([2007–08] 502,660,000); lignite (metric tons; 2009) 35,727,000 ([2007–08] 34,657,000); crude petroleum (barrels; 2009) 247,200,000 ([2007–08] 1,186,382,800); petroleum products (metric tons; 2008–09) 149,519,000 ([2007–08] 140,697,000); natural gas (cu m; 2009) 38,653,000,000 (51,282,000,000).

Financial aggregates[25]

	2004	2005	2006	2007	2008	2009	2010
Exchange rate, Rs per:							
U.S. dollar	43.59	45.07	44.25	39.42	48.46	46.68	44.81
£	84.18	77.59	86.85	78.97	70.64	75.59	70.15
SDR	67.69	64.41	66.56	62.29	74.63	73.18	69.10
International reserves (U.S.$)							
Total (excl. gold; '000,000)	126,593	131,924	170,738	266,988	247,419	265,182	275,277
SDRs ('000,000)	5	4	1	3	3	5,169	5,078
Reserve pos. in IMF ('000,000)	1,424	902	550	432	813	1,430	2,385
Foreign exchange ('000,000)	125,164	131,018	170,187	266,553	246,603	258,583	267,814
Gold ('000,000 fine troy oz)	11.502	11.502	11.502	11.502	11.502	17.932	17.932
% world reserves	1.3	1.2	1.2	1.2	1.2	1.8	1.8
Interest and prices							
Central bank discount (%)	6.00	6.00	6.00	6.00	6.00	6.00	6.00
Advance (prime) rate (%)	10.9	10.8	11.2	13.0	13.3	12.2	...
Industrial share prices (2005 = 100)	75.4	100.0	155.0	216.3	207.7	194.3	252.3
Balance of payments (U.S.$'000,000)							
Balance of visible trade	–17,600	–32,517	–42,804	–54,827	–93,142	–79,665	–97,934
Imports, f.o.b.	–95,539	–134,692	–166,572	–208,611	–291,740	–247,883	–323,435
Exports, f.o.b.	77,939	102,175	123,768	153,784	198,598	168,219	225,502
Balance of invisibles	+18,380	+22,233	+33,505	+46,751	+62,170	+53,743	+46,153
Balance of payments, current account	+780	–10,284	–9,299	–8,076	–30,972	–25,922	–51,781

Population economically active (2008)[26]: total 466,270,000; activity rate of total population 39.5% (participation rates: ages 15–64, 61.0%; female 27.8%; unemployed [2009] 10.7%).

Price index (2005 = 100)

	2004	2005	2006	2007	2008	2009	2010
Consumer price index	95.9	100.0	105.8	112.5	121.9	135.2	151.4

Selected balance of payments data. Receipts from (U.S.$'000,000): tourism (2009) 11,136; remittances (2010) 53,131; foreign direct investment (FDI; 2008–10 avg.) 34,278; official development assistance (2009) 2,393. Disbursements for (U.S.$'000,000): tourism (2009) 9,310; remittances (2009) 4,000; FDI (2008–10 avg.) 16,651.

Household income and expenditure. Average household size (2005–06)[16] 4.7; sources of income: n.a.; expenditure (2003): food and nonalcoholic beverages 50.0%, housing and energy 11.2%, clothing and footwear 7.8%, health 6.7%, transportation 4.1%, tobacco and intoxicants 2.3%.

Land use as % of total land area (2009): in temporary crops or left fallow (2007) 53.4%, in permanent crops 3.9%, in pasture 3.5%, forest area 23.0%.

Foreign trade

Balance of trade (current prices)

	2005–06	2006–07	2007–08	2008–09	2009–10	2010–11
U.S.$'000,000	–46,075	–59,321	–88,535	–116,034	–109,621	–98,173
% of total	18.3%	19.0%	21.4%	24.1%	23.5%	16.2%

Imports (2008–09): U.S.$303,696,000,000 (crude and refined petroleum 30.8%; electronics 7.7%; nonelectrical machinery and apparatus 7.1%; gold 6.8%; precious stones/semiprecious stones/pearls 5.5%; transport equipment 4.4%; manufactured fertilizers 3.9%; coal/coke 3.3%; iron and steel 3.1%). *Major import sources:* China 10.6%; U.A.E. 7.6%; Saudi Arabia 6.4%; U.S. 6.1%; Iran 4.0%; Germany 3.9%; Switzerland 3.8%; Australia 3.6%; Kuwait 3.1%; South Korea 2.8%.

Exports (2008–09): U.S.$185,295,000,000 (gems and jewelry [significantly diamonds] 15.1%; refined petroleum products 14.9%; textiles and wearing apparel 10.8%, of which ready-made garments 5.9%; food, beverages, and tobacco 9.5%; chemicals and chemical products 8.4%; transportation equipment 6.0%; machinery and apparatus 5.9%; fabricated metal products 4.1%; electronic goods 3.7%; iron and steel 3.1%). *Major export destinations:* U.A.E. 12.9%; U.S. 11.3%; China 5.0%; Singapore 4.4%; U.K. 3.6%; Hong Kong 3.6%; Netherlands 3.4%; Germany 3.4%; Saudi Arabia 2.7%; Belgium 2.4%.

Transport and communications

Transport. Railroads (2007): route length 39,225 mi, 63,126 km; (2008–09) passenger-km 733,000,000,000; (2008–09) metric ton-km cargo 512,000,000,000. Roads (2004): total length 2,251,000 mi, 3,622,000 km (paved 49%). Vehicles (2006): passenger cars 11,526,000; trucks and buses 5,428,000. Air transport (2008–09): passenger-km 75,932,000,000; metric ton-km cargo 1,071,000,000.

Communications

Medium	date	number in '000s	units per 1,000 persons	Medium	date	number in '000s	units per 1,000 persons
Televisions	2003	88,876	83	PCs	2007	38,434	33
Telephones				Dailies	2009	109,900[27]	95[27]
Cellular	2010	752,190[28]	614[28]	Internet users	2009	61,300	51
Landline	2010	35,090	29	Broadband	2010	10,990[28]	9.0[28]

Education and health

Literacy (2007): percentage of total population age 15 and over literate 66.0%; males literate 76.9%; females literate 54.5%.

Education (2006–07)

	teachers	students	student/ teacher ratio	enrollment rate (%)
Primary (age 6–10)	3,387,905[29]	140,357,454	40.2[29]	90
Secondary/Voc. (age 11–17)	2,586,211[29]	96,049,060	32.7[29]	...
Tertiary	538,769[29]	14,862,962	18.6[29]	13 (age 18–22)

Health (2008): physicians[30, 31] 696,700 (1 per 1,696 persons); hospital beds[30, 31] 482,500 (1 per 2,449 persons); infant mortality rate per 1,000 live births 54.0; undernourished population (2004–06) 251,500,000 (22% of total population based on the consumption of a minimum daily requirement of 1,770 calories).

Military

Total active duty personnel (November 2010): 1,325,000 (army 85.3%, navy 4.4%, air force 9.6%, coast guard 0.7%); paramilitary 1,300,586; reserve 1,155,000. *Military expenditure as percentage of GDP* (2009): 3.1%; per capita expenditure U.S.$31.

[1]Includes 12 members appointed by the President. [2]Includes 2 Anglo-Indians appointed by the President. [3]The first symbol for the rupee was announced in July 2010; it should be adopted internationally by mid-2012. [4]Populations are provisional results of census. [5]Excludes 46,660 sq mi (120,849 sq km) of territory in the Kashmir region claimed by India as part of Jammu and Kashmir state but administered by Pakistan or China; inland water constitutes 9.6% of total area of India. [6]Detail does not add to total given because of rounding. [7]2001 census. [8]Within Delhi urban agglomeration. [9]Within Kolkata urban agglomeration. [10]Within Mumbai urban agglomeration. [11]Within Pune urban agglomeration. [12]Data are for the 22 scheduled ("officially recognized") languages of India (including associated languages/dialects of each of the 22) unless otherwise footnoted. [13]Nonscheduled ("not officially recognized") language. [14]2000 estimate. [15]Data apply to the workers employed in the "organized sector" only (27.3 million in 2006–07, of which 18.0 million were employed in the public sector and 9.3 million were employed in the private sector); few legal protections exist for the more than 370 million workers in the "unorganized sector." [16]2005–06 data based on the National Family Health Survey 2005–06, comprising 515,507 people in 109,041 households. [17]Registered with Ministry of Labour only. [18]Crimes reported to National Crime Records Bureau by police authorities of state governments. [19]Unemployed. [20]Includes mangosteens and guavas. [21]Metal content. [22]World rank: 4. [23]World rank: 6. [24]World rank: 2. [25]End-of-period. [26]ILO estimates. [27]Circulation of daily newspapers. [28]Subscribers. [29]2003–04. [30]Government hospitals only. [31]January 1.

Internet resources for further information:

- **Reserve Bank of India http://www.rbi.org.in**
- **Ministry of Statistics and Programme Implementation http://mospi.nic.in**

Indonesia

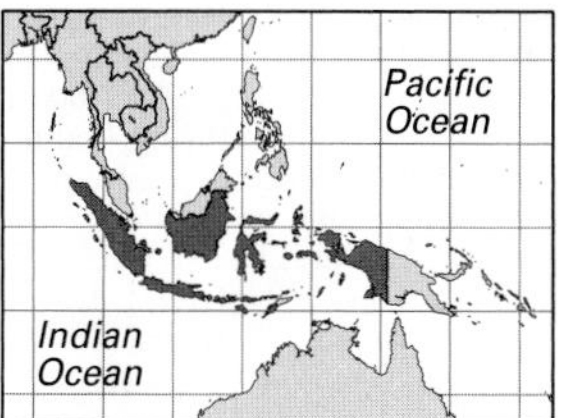

Official name: Republik Indonesia (Republic of Indonesia).
Form of government: multiparty republic with two legislative houses (Regional Representatives Council[1] [128]; House of Representatives [560]).
Head of state and government: President.
Capital: Jakarta.
Official language: Indonesian.
Official religion: monotheism.
Monetary unit: rupiah (Rp); valuation (Sept. 1, 2011) 1 U.S.$ = Rp 8,533; 1 £ = Rp 13,789.

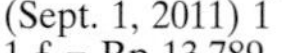

Area and population

Island(s) Provinces	area sq km	population 2010 census[2]
Bali and the Lesser Sunda Islands	73,071	13,067,599
Bali	5,780	3,891,428
East Nusa Tenggara	48,718	4,679,316
West Nusa Tenggara	18,573	4,496,855
Celebes (Sulawesi)[3]	188,522	17,359,398
Central Sulawesi	61,841	2,633,420
Gorontalo	11,257	1,038,585
North Sulawesi	13,852	2,265,937
South Sulawesi	46,717	8,032,551
Southeast Sulawesi	38,068	2,230,569
West Sulawesi	16,787	1,158,336
Java[3]	129,438	136,563,142
Banten	9,663	10,644,030
Central Java	32,800	32,380,687
East Java	47,800	37,476,011
Jakarta[4]	664	9,588,198
West Java	35,378	43,021,826
Yogyakarta[5]	3,133	3,452,390

Island(s) Provinces	area sq km	population 2010 census[2]
Kalimantan[3, 6]	544,150	13,772,543
Central Kalimantan	153,565	2,202,599
East Kalimantan	204,534	3,550,586
South Kalimantan	38,744	3,626,119
West Kalimantan	147,307	4,393,239
Maluku[7] & Papua[3]	494,957	6,179,734
Maluku	46,914	1,531,402
North Maluku	31,983	1,035,478
Papua	319,036	2,851,999
West Papua[8]	97,024	760,855
Sumatra[3]	480,793	50,613,947
Aceh[9]	57,956	4,486,570
Bangka-Belitung	16,424	1,223,048
Bengkulu	19,919	1,713,393
Jambi	50,058	3,088,618
Lampung	34,624	7,596,115
North Sumatra	72,981	12,985,075
Riau	87,024	5,543,031
Riau Islands	8,202	1,685,698
South Sumatra	91,592	7,446,401
West Sumatra	42,013	4,845,998
TOTAL	1,910,931	237,556,363

Demography

Population (2011): 241,343,000.
Density (2011): persons per sq mi 327.1, persons per sq km 126.3.
Urban-rural (2009): urban 44.0%; rural 56.0%.
Sex distribution (2009): male 50.01%; female 49.99%.
Age breakdown (2009): under 15, 27.0%; 15–29, 27.2%; 30–44, 23.3%; 45–59, 14.7%; 60–74, 6.1%; 75 and over, 1.7%.
Population projection: (2020) 261,802,000; (2030) 278,843,000.
Ethnic composition (2000): Javanese 36.4%; Sundanese 13.7%; Malay 9.4%; Madurese 7.2%; Han Chinese 4.0%; Minangkabau 3.6%; other 25.7%.
Religious affiliation (2005): Muslim (excluding syncretists) 55.8%; Neo-religionists (syncretists) 21.2%; Christian 13.2%; Hindu 3.2%; traditional beliefs 2.6%; nonreligious 1.8%; other 2.2%.
Major urban agglomerations (2010): Jakarta 9,588,198; Surabaya 2,765,908; Bandung 2,417,584; Bekasi 2,378,211; Medan 2,109,339.

Vital statistics

Birth rate per 1,000 population (2006): 20.1 (world avg. 20.3).
Death rate per 1,000 population (2006): 6.3 (world avg. 8.5).
Total fertility rate (avg. births per childbearing woman; 2007): 2.17.
Life expectancy at birth (2006): male 67.4 years; female 72.4 years.
Adult population (ages 15–49) *living with HIV* (2007): 0.2% (world avg. 0.8%).

National economy

Budget (2009). Revenue: Rp 984,787,000,000,000 (tax revenue 73.7%, of which income tax 36.3%, VAT 25.3%; nontax revenue 26.3%, of which revenue from natural resources 17.6%). Expenditures: Rp 716,376,000,000,000 (subsidies 23.3%; personnel expenditures 20.0%; interest payment 14.2%).
Public debt (external, outstanding; 2009): U.S.$65,323,000,000.
Population economically active (2008): total 111,947,265; activity rate 49.2% (participation rates: over age 15, 67.2%; unemployed 8.4%).

Price index (2005 = 100)

	2004	2005	2006	2007	2008	2009	2010
Consumer price index	90.5	100.0	113.1	123.4	137.0	140.9	150.6

Household income and expenditure. Average household size (2008) 4.0.
Production (metric tons except as noted). Agriculture, forestry, fishing (2009): oil palm fruit 86,000,000, rice 64,398,890, sugarcane 26,500,000, cassava 22,039,148, coconuts 21,565,700, natural rubber 2,789,850, cocoa beans 800,000, cloves 81,000, cinnamon 67,209; livestock (number of live animals) 15,768,500 goats, 12,859,000 cattle, 10,199,500 sheep; roundwood (2010) 98,694,921 cu m, of which fuelwood 63%; fisheries production 6,832,789 (from aquaculture 25%); aquatic plants production 2,965,896 (from aquaculture 99%). Mining and quarrying (2008): bauxite 1,152,000; copper[10] 651,000; nickel[10] 192,600; tin[10] 53,228; silver 226,051 kg; gold 64,390 kg. Manufacturing (value added in U.S.$'000,000; 2006): food products 8,542; textiles and wearing apparel 6,208; chemicals and chemical products 5,977; transport equipment 5,515; tobacco products 5,397; paper products 3,353. Energy production (consumption): electricity (kW-hr; 2007) 142,236,000,000 (142,236,000,000); hard coal (metric tons; 2009[11]) 145,076,000 ([2007] 38,354,000); lignite (metric tons; 2007) 34,516,000 (30,238,000); crude petroleum (barrels; 2009[11]) 259,103,000 ([2007] 337,029,000); petroleum products (metric tons; 2007) 40,411,000 (53,524,000); natural gas (cu m; 2009[11]) 63,610,000,000 ([2007] 31,990,000,000).
Gross national income (GNI; 2010): U.S.$599,148,000,000 (U.S.$2,580 per capita); purchasing power parity GNI (U.S.$4,300 per capita).

Structure of gross domestic product and labour force

	2008			
	in value Rp '000,000,000	% of total value	labour force	% of labour force
Agriculture, fishing, forestry	713,291	14.4	41,331,706	36.9
Mining	543,364	11.0	1,070,540	1.0
Manufacturing	1,380,731	27.9	12,549,376	11.2
Public utilities	40,847	0.8	201,114	0.2
Construction	419,322	8.4	5,438,965	4.9
Transp. and commun.	312,454	6.3	6,179,503	5.5
Trade, hotels	692,119	14.0	21,221,744	19.0
Finance, real estate	368,130	7.4	1,459,985	1.3
Public admin., defense	257,548	5.2	13,099,817	11.6
Services	226,223	4.6		
Other	—	—	9,394,515[12]	8.4[12]
TOTAL	4,954,029	100.0	111,947,265	100.0

Selected balance of payments data. Receipts from (U.S.$'000,000): tourism (2009) 6,318; remittances (2010) 7,250; foreign direct investment (FDI; 2008–10 avg.) 9,166; official development assistance (2009) 1,049. Disbursements for (U.S.$'000,000): tourism (2009) 5,165; remittances (2009) 2,702; FDI (2008–10 avg.) 3,604.
Land use as % of total land area (2009): in temporary crops or left fallow 13.0%, in permanent crops 10.5%, in pasture 6.1%, forest area 52.5%.

Foreign trade[13]

Balance of trade (current prices)

	2004	2005	2006	2007	2008	2009
U.S.$'000,000	+25,058	+27,959	+39,733	+39,627	+7,776	+27,053
% of total	21.2%	19.5%	24.5%	21.0%	4.7%	12.8%

Imports (2008): U.S.$129,244,000,000 (machinery and apparatus 25.3%, petroleum 23.5%, chemicals and chemical products 12.3%, iron and steel 6.9%, food 6.1%, road vehicles 5.1%). *Major import sources:* Singapore 16.9%; China 11.8%; Japan 11.7%; Malaysia 6.9%; U.S. 6.1%.
Exports (2008): U.S.$137,020,000,000 (machinery and apparatus 9.9%, natural gas 9.5%, crude petroleum 9.1%, palm oil 9.0%, coal 7.7%, food 5.8%, apparel 4.6%, natural rubber 4.4%, copper [all forms] 3.9%). *Major export destinations:* Japan 20.2%; U.S. 9.5%; Singapore 9.4%; China 8.5%; South Korea 6.7%.

Transport and communications

Transport. Railroads (2007): route length 2,984 mi, 4,803 km; passenger-km (2008) 16,800,000,000; metric ton-km cargo 4,425,000,000. Roads (2007): length 246,287 mi, 396,362 km (paved 56%). Vehicles (2008): passenger cars 9,859,926; trucks and buses 7,729,844. Air transport (2008)[14]: passenger-km 17,677,000,000; metric ton-km cargo 275,000,000.

Communications

Medium	date	number in '000s	units per 1,000 persons
Televisions	2003	33,255	153
Telephones			
Cellular	2010	220,000[16]	917[16]
Landline	2010	37,960	158
PCs	2005	3,285	15
Dailies	2009	5,728[15]	25[15]
Internet users	2009	20,000	87
Broadband	2010	1,900[16]	7.9[16]

Education and health

Educational attainment (2002–03). Percentage of population ages 15–64 having: no schooling or incomplete primary education 19.3%; primary and some secondary 57.2%; complete secondary 19.3%; higher 4.2%. *Literacy* (2008): total population age 15 and over literate 92.2%; males 95.4%; females 89.1%.

Education (2007–08)

	teachers	students	student/ teacher ratio	enrollment rate (%)
Primary (age 7–12)	1,687,371	29,498,266	17.5	96
Secondary/Voc. (age 13–18)	1,531,383	18,314,900	12.0	68
Tertiary	286,127	4,419,577	15.4	21 (age 19–23)

Health: physicians (2003) 29,499 (1 per 7,368 persons); hospital beds (2001) 124,834 (1 per 1,697 persons); infant mortality rate (2008) 26.8; undernourished population (2005–07) 29,900,000 (13% of total population based on the consumption of a minimum daily requirement of 1,810 calories).

Military

Total active duty personnel (November 2010): 302,000 (army 77.2%, navy 14.9%, air force 7.9%); reserve 400,000. *Military expenditure as percentage of GDP* (2009): 0.6%; per capita expenditure U.S.$15.

[1]Has limited legislative authority. [2]Preliminary. [3]Includes area and population of nearby islands. [4]Special capital district. [5]Special district. [6]Kalimantan is the name of the Indonesian part of the island of Borneo. [7]Conventionally the Moluccas. [8]The final status of West Papua (the westernmost part of Papua known as West Irian Jaya prior to April 2007) was unresolved. [9]Autonomous province. [10]Metal content. [11]January–September only. [12]Unemployed. [13]Imports c.i.f.; exports f.o.b. [14]Garuda Indonesia only. [15]Circulation. [16]Subscribers.

Internet resource for further information:
- **Statistics Indonesia http://www.bps.go.id**

Iran

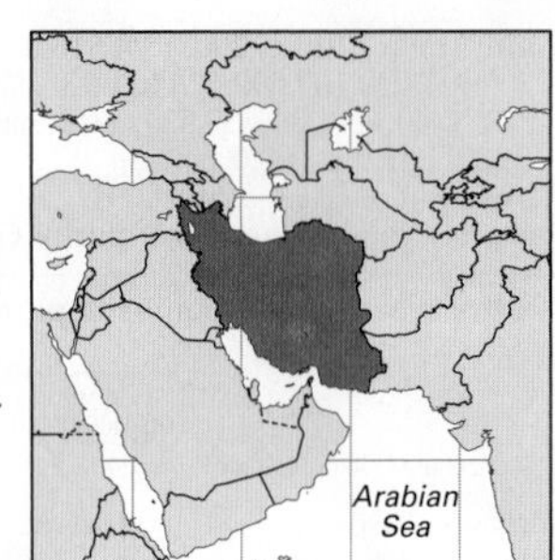

Official name: Jomhūrī-ye Eslāmī-ye Īrān (Islamic Republic of Iran).
Form of government: unitary Islamic republic with one legislative house (Islamic Consultative Assembly [290[1]]).
Supreme political/religious authority: Leader.
Head of state and government: President.
Capital: Tehrān.
Official language: Farsī (Persian).
Official religion: Islam.
Monetary unit: rial (Rls); valuation (Sept. 1, 2011) 1 U.S.$ = Rls 10,600; 1 £ = Rls 17,129.

Area and population

Provinces	area sq km	population 2010 estimate	Provinces	area sq km	population 2010 estimate
Ardabīl	17,800	1,242,956	Khorāsān-e Shomālī	28,434	838,781
Āzārbāyjān-e Gharbī	37,411	3,016,301	Khūzestān	64,055	4,471,488
Āzārbāyjān-e Sharqī	45,650	3,691,270	Kohgīlūyeh va Būyer Aḥmad	15,504	669,140
Būshehr	22,743	943,535	Kordestān	29,137	1,467,585
Chahār Maḥāll va Bakhtīārī	16,332	892,909	Lorestān	28,294	1,758,226
Eṣfahān	107,029	4,804,458	Markazi	29,127	1,392,435
Fārs	122,608	4,528,514	Māzandarān	23,842	3,037,336
Gilan	14,042	2,453,469	Qazvīn	15,567	1,212,464
Golestān	20,367	1,687,086	Qom	11,526	1,127,713
Hamadān	19,368	1,699,588	Semnān	97,491	624,482
Hormozgān	70,697	1,558,878	Sīstān va Balūchestān	181,785	2,733,205
Ilām	20,133	566,332	Tehrān[2]	18,814	14,795,116
Kermān	180,726	2,947,346	Yazd	129,285	1,065,893
Kermānshāh	24,998	1,905,793	Zanjān	21,773	983,369
Khorāsān-e Jonūbī	95,385	676,794	TOTAL	1,628,750[3]	74,733,230[4]
Khorāsān-e Razavī	118,854	5,940,766			

Demography

Population (2011): 75,276,000.
Density (2011)[5]: persons per sq mi 118.3, persons per sq km 45.7.
Urban-rural (2009–10): urban 71.77%; rural 28.23%.
Sex distribution (2009–10): male 50.79%; female 49.21%.
Age breakdown (2006–07): under 15, 25.1%; 15–29, 35.4%; 30–44, 20.6%; 45–59, 11.6%; 60–74, 5.4%; 75–84, 1.6%; 85 and over, 0.3%.
Population projection: (2020) 81,722,000; (2030) 85,145,000.
Ethnic composition (2000): Persian 34.9%; Azerbaijani 15.9%; Kurd 13.0%; Lurī 7.2%; Gīlaki 5.1%; Mazāndarānī 5.1%; Afghan 2.8%; other 16.0%.
Religious affiliation (2005): Muslim 98.2% (Shīʿī 86.1%, Sunnī 10.1%, other 2.0%); Bahāʾī 0.5%; Christian 0.4%; Zoroastrian 0.1%; other 0.8%.
Major cities (2007): Tehrān 7,873,000; Mashhad 2,469,000; Eṣfahān 1,628,000; Karaj 1,423,000; Tabrīz 1,413,000; Shīrāz 1,240,000.

Vital statistics

Birth rate per 1,000 population (2008): 18.6 (world avg. 20.3).
Death rate per 1,000 population (2008): 5.9 (world avg. 8.5).
Total fertility rate (avg. births per childbearing woman; 2008): 1.90.
Marriage/divorce rates per 1,000 population (2006–07): 11.0/1.3.
Life expectancy at birth (2008): male 71.7 years; female 73.6 years.
Major causes of death (2008): [6].

National economy

Budget (2008–09). Revenue: Rls 948,745,000,000,000 (petroleum and natural gas revenue 73.5%; taxes 19.0%, of which taxes on income and profits 11.8%; other 7.5%). Expenditures: Rls 923,015,000,000,000 (current expenditure 65.8%; development expenditures 26.3%; other 7.9%).
Public debt (external, outstanding; 2009): U.S.$7,524,000,000.
Gross national income (GNI; 2009): U.S.$330,619,000,000 (U.S.$4,530 per capita); purchasing power parity GNI (U.S.$11,490 per capita).

Structure of gross domestic product and labour force

	2007–08		2008	
	in value Rls '000,000,000	% of total value	labour force	% of labour force
Agriculture, forestry, fishing	268,002	10.2	4,344,000	19.0
Petroleum	709,021	27.0	128,000	0.6
Other mining	19,142	0.7		
Manufacturing	276,876	10.6	3,512,000	15.3
Construction	131,470	5.0	2,791,000	12.2
Public utilities	30,148	1.1	180,000	0.8
Transportation and communications	191,497	7.3	2,067,000	9.0
Trade, restaurants	280,590	10.7	3,192,000	14.0
Finance, real estate	504,997	19.3	805,000	3.5
Pub. admin., defense	221,743	8.5	1,332,000	5.8
Services	73,498	2.8	2,130,000	9.3
Other	–83,807[7]	–3.2[7]	2,411,000[8]	10.5[8]
TOTAL	2,623,177	100.0	22,892,000	100.0

Production (metric tons except as noted). Agriculture, forestry, fishing (2009): wheat 13,484,500, cow's milk 6,620,240, potatoes 4,107,630, watermelons 3,074,580, oranges 2,713,240, apples 2,431,990, rice 2,253,420, grapes 1,876,850, chicken meat 1,674,220, dates 1,088,040, apricots 397,749, pistachios 255,000, cherries 225,000, almonds 128,464; livestock (number of live animals) 53,800,000 sheep, 25,500,000 goats, 8,120,000 cattle, 152,000 camels; roundwood (2010) 886,000 cu m, of which fuelwood 8%; fisheries production 599,476 (from aquaculture 30%). Mining and quarrying (2008): gypsum 12,000,000; iron ore 12,000,000[9]; copper ore 248,000[9]; chromite 180,000; zinc 150,000[9]. Manufacturing (value added in U.S.$'000,000; 2005): base metals 3,032; motor vehicles and parts 2,850; refined petroleum products 2,210; cement, bricks, and ceramics 2,158. Energy production (consumption): electricity (kW-hr; 2008–09) 215,800,000,000 (162,000,000,000); coal (metric tons; 2008) 2,000,000 ([2007] 1,973,000); crude petroleum (barrels; 2009–10) 1,281,715,000 ([2009] 660,285,000); petroleum products (metric tons; 2007) 76,343,000 (70,023,000); natural gas (cu m; 2009) 116,300,000,000 (119,000,000,000).
Population economically active (2008): total 22,892,000; activity rate of total population 31.9% (participation rates: ages 10 and over, 42.0%; female 17.7%; unemployed [2009] 11.8%).

Price and earnings indexes (2004–05 = 100)

	2004–05	2005–06	2006–07	2007–08	2008–09	2009–10
Consumer price index	100.0	110.4	123.5	146.2	183.3	203.1
Monthly earnings index[10]	100.0	118.8	140.7	171.7	206.0	247.2

Household income and expenditure (2006–07). Average household size 4.1; annual average income per urban household Rls 65,509,108 (U.S.$6,822); sources of urban income: wages 35.4%, self-employment 25.9%; expenditure: housing and energy 29.5%, food, beverages, and tobacco 22.6%, transportation/communications 15.3%, health 7.9%.
Selected balance of payments data. Receipts from (U.S.$'000,000): tourism (2009) 2,012; remittances (2010) 1,181; foreign direct investment (FDI; 2008–10 avg.) 2,749; official development assistance (2009) 93. Disbursements for (U.S.$'000,000): tourism (2009) 9,108; FDI (2008–10 avg.) 361.
Land use as % of total land area (2009): in temporary crops 7.9%, left fallow 2.7%, in permanent crops 1.1%, in pasture 18.1%, forest area 6.8%.

Foreign trade

Balance of trade (current prices)

	2003–04	2004–05	2005–06	2006–07	2007–08	2008–09
U.S.$'000,000	+4,430	+5,073	+21,143	+26,204	+39,427	+32,039
% of total	7.0%	6.1%	19.6%	20.8%	25.3%	18.9%

Imports (2005–06): U.S.$40,969,000,000 (nonelectrical machinery 23.5%, base metals 13.8%, road vehicles 13.0%, chemical products 10.7%). *Major import sources* (2008): U.A.E. *c.* 19%; China *c.* 13%; Germany *c.* 9%; South Korea *c.* 7%.
Exports (2008–09): U.S.$100,571,000,000 (petroleum/natural gas 85.2%, organic chemicals 3.1%, plastics 1.4%, pistachios 0.7%, handwoven carpets 0.4%). *Major export destinations* (2008): China *c.* 15%; Japan *c.* 14%; India *c.* 9%; South Korea *c.* 6%; Turkey *c.* 6%.

Transport and communications

Transport. Railroads (2008–09): route length 5,407 mi, 8,702 km; passenger-km 14,100,000,000; metric ton-km cargo 20,500,000,000. Roads (2006–07): length 45,118 mi, 72,611 km (paved 92%). Vehicles (2006–07): passenger cars 920,136; trucks and buses 184,629. Air transport (2009–10): passenger-km 8,005,000,000; metric ton-km cargo 66,723,000.

Communications

Medium	date	number in '000s	units per 1,000 persons	Medium	date	number in '000s	units per 1,000 persons
Televisions	2003	11,566	173	PCs	2007	7,678	106
Telephones				Dailies	2009	1,600[11]	22[11]
Cellular	2010	67,500[12]	913[12]	Internet users	2009	27,915	376
Landline	2010	26,849	363	Broadband	2010	500[12]	6.8[12]

Education and health

Educational attainment: n.a. *Literacy* (2008): total population age 15 and over literate 82.3%; males literate 87.3%; females literate 77.2%.

Education (2007–08)

	teachers	students	student/teacher ratio	enrollment rate (%)
Primary (age 6–10)	350,525	7,027,775	20.0	94[13]
Secondary/Voc. (age 11–17)	409,699[14]	8,187,132	20.3[14]	75
Tertiary	143,503	3,391,852	23.6	36 (age 18–22)

Health (2008): physicians 63,924 (1 per 1,124 persons); hospital beds 99,118 (1 per 725 persons); infant mortality rate per 1,000 live births 21.8; undernourished population (2005–07) less than 5.0% of total population.

Military

Total active duty personnel (November 2010): 523,000 (army 66.9%, revolutionary guard corps 23.9%, navy 3.5%, air force 5.7%). *Military expenditure as percentage of GDP* (2008): 2.8%[15]; per capita expenditure U.S.$131[15].

[1]Includes seats reserved for Christians (3), of which Armenian 2; Jews (1); and Zoroastrians (1). [2]Includes Alborz, which split from Tehrān in June 2010. [3]Reported total of land area only (summed land area total equals 1,628,777 sq km); estimated total area is 1,648,200 sq km; Iran reported a total area of 1,873,959 sq km in September 2011. [4]Detail does not add to total given because of statistical discrepancy. [5]Based on estimated total area. [6]Per official announcement by deputy health minister: road accidents, heart disease, depression/suicide, addiction. [7]Less imputed bank service charges. [8]Includes 2,392,000 unemployed. [9]Metal content. [10]Minimum wage. [11]Circulation. [12]Subscribers. [13]2005–06. [14]2006–07. [15]Excludes defense industry funding.

Internet resources for further information:
- **Statistical Centre of Iran http://www.amar.org.ir**
- **Central Bank of Iran http://www.cbi.ir/default_en.aspx**

Iraq

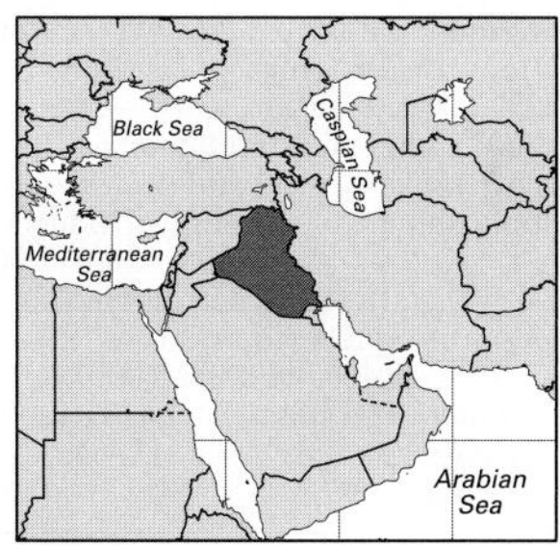

Official name: Al-Jumhūrīyah al-ʿIrāqīyah (Republic of Iraq).
Form of government: multiparty republic with one legislative house (Council of Representatives of Iraq [325[1]]).
Head of state: President.
Head of government: Prime Minister.
Capital: Baghdad.
Official languages: Arabic; Kurdish.
Official religion: Islam.
Monetary unit: Iraqi dinar (ID); valuation (Sept. 1, 2011) 1 U.S.$ = ID 1,884; 1 £ = ID 1,166.

Area and population

Governorates	Capitals	area sq mi	area sq km	population 2009 estimate
Al-Anbār	Al-Ramādī	53,208	137,808	1,451,600
Bābil	Al-Ḥillah	2,163	5,603	1,727,000
Baghdād	Baghdad	1,572	4,071	7,180,900
Al-Baṣrah	Al-Baṣrah	7,363	19,070	2,555,500
Dhī Qār	Al-Nāṣirīyah	4,981	12,900	1,846,800
Diyālā[2]	Baʿqūbah	6,828	17,685	1,370,500
Karbalāʾ	Karbalāʾ	1,944	5,034	1,003,500
Maysān	Al-ʿAmārah	6,205	16,072	1,009,600
Al-Muthannā	Al-Samāwah	19,977	51,740	719,800
Al-Najaf	Al-Najaf	11,129	28,824	1,180,700
Nīnawā[2]	Mosul	14,410	37,323	3,237,900
Al-Qādisiyah	Al-Dīwānīyah	3,148	8,153	1,121,800
Ṣalāḥ al-Dīn	Tikrīt	9,407	24,363	1,259,300
Al-Taʾmīm[2]	Kirkūk	3,737	9,679	1,290,000
Wāsiṭ	Al-Kūt	6,623	17,153	1,158,000
Region				
Kurdistan Region (in part)	Arbīl	14,923	38,650	3,992,000
TOTAL		167,618	434,128	32,105,000[3]

Demography

Population (2011): 32,665,000[4].
Density (2011): persons per sq mi 194.9, persons per sq km 75.2.
Urban-rural (2009): urban 66.3%; rural 33.7%.
Sex distribution (2007): male 50.35%; female 49.65%.
Age breakdown (2007): under 15, 39.4%; 15–29, 29.8%; 30–44, 18.4%; 45–59, 7.9%; 60–74, 3.3%; 75–84, 1.0%; 85 and over, 0.2%.
Population projection: (2020) 42,684,000; (2030) 55,257,000.
Doubling time: 27 years.
Ethnic composition (2000): Arab 64.7%; Kurd 23.0%; Turkmen/Azerbaijani 6.8%; other 5.5%.
Religious affiliation (2000): Shīʿī Muslim 62.0%; Sunnī Muslim 34.0%; Christian (primarily Chaldean rite and Syrian rite Catholic and Nestorian) 3.2%; other (primarily Yazīdī syncretist) 0.8%.
Major urban agglomerations (2009): Baghdad 6,250,000; Mosul 1,450,000; Al-Baṣrah 1,200,000; Arbīl 925,000; Kirkūk 900,000.

Vital statistics

Birth rate per 1,000 population (2008): 30.7 (world avg. 20.3).
Death rate per 1,000 population (2008): 5.1 (world avg. 8.5).
Natural increase rate per 1,000 population (2008): 25.6 (world avg. 11.8).
Total fertility rate (avg. births per childbearing woman; 2008): 3.97.
Marriage/divorce rates per 1,000 population: (2008) 8.1/(1997) 1.3.
Life expectancy at birth (2008): male 68.3 years; female 71.0 years.
Major causes of death per 100,000 population (2002): communicable diseases 377; diseases of the circulatory system 187; accidents and violence 115; malignant neoplasms (cancers) 54.

National economy

Budget (2007). Revenue: ID 58,714,000,000,000 (crude oil export revenue 80.3%, oil-related public enterprises 9.8%, grants 4.9%, other 5.0%). Expenditures: ID 48,153,000,000,000 (current expenditure 79.6%, development expenditure 20.4%).
Production (metric tons except as noted). Agriculture, forestry, fishing (2009): wheat 1,700,400, tomatoes 913,493, dates 507,002, barley 501,508, cucumbers/gherkins 420,945, eggplants 396,155, watermelons 326,742, grapes 194,731, okra 152,751, fava beans 144,327, cattle meat 47,493; livestock (number of live animals) 7,800,000 sheep, 1,600,000 cattle; roundwood (2010) 177,000 cu m, of which fuelwood 67%; fisheries production 53,237 (from aquaculture 35%). Mining and quarrying (2008): salt 109,000. Manufacturing (2008): gasoline 17,228,000 barrels; distillate fuels 30,551,000 barrels; residual fuels 76,577,000 barrels. Energy production (consumption): electricity (kW-hr; 2007) 33,183,000,000 (34,538,000,000); coal, none (none); crude petroleum (barrels; 2008) 884,000,000 ([2007] 146,315,000); petroleum products (metric tons; 2008) 25,940,000 ([2007] 25,773,000); natural gas (cu m; 2007) 1,422,000,000 (1,422,000,000).
Household income and expenditure (2004). Average household size 6.4; median annual household income ID 2,230,000 (U.S.$1,517); sources of income: n.a.; expenditure (1993)[5]: food 63.2%, housing 11.5%, clothing 9.7%.
Land use as % of total land area (2009): in temporary crops or left fallow 10.4%, in permanent crops 0.6%, in pasture 9.2%, forest area 1.9%.
Population economically active (2008)[6]: total 7,303,000; activity rate of total population 24.3% (participation rates: ages 15–64, 43.2%; female 16.1%; unemployed [UN estimate; 2009] 18%).

Price index (2005 = 100)

	2004	2005	2006	2007	2008	2009	2010
Consumer price index	73.0	100.0	153.2	137.8	155.3	165.9	170.7

Public debt (external, outstanding; 2010): U.S.$45,090,000,000.
Gross national income (GNI; 2010): U.S.$74,885,000,000 (U.S.$2,320 per capita); purchasing power parity GNI (U.S.$3,320 per capita).

Structure of gross domestic product and labour force

	2008 in value ID '000,000,000	% of total value	labour force[7]	% of labour force[7]
Agriculture	5,717	3.7	1,781,600	23.4
Mining	86,867	55.7	32,400	0.4
Manufacturing	2,332	1.5	369,400	4.9
Public utilities	1,308	0.8	161,600	2.1
Construction	5,973	3.8	823,500	10.8
Transp. and commun.	12,031	7.7	608,100	8.0
Trade, hotels	10,078	6.5	1,229,800	16.2
Finance, real estate	12,970	8.3	55,900	0.8
Pub. admin., defense	19,394	12.4	1,003,300	13.2
Services			1,523,500	20.0
Other	–688[8]	–0.4[8]	17,000	0.2
TOTAL	155,982	100.0	7,606,100	100.0

Selected balance of payments data. Receipts from (U.S.$'000,000): tourism, n.a.; remittances (2009) 71; foreign direct investment (FDI; 2008–10 avg.) 1,578; official development assistance (2009) 2,791. Disbursements for (U.S.$'000,000): tourism, n.a.; remittances (2008) 781; FDI (2008–10 avg.) 67.

Foreign trade

Balance of trade (current prices)

	2003	2004	2005	2006	2007	2008
U.S.$'000,000	...	...	+3,695	+9,637	+20,031	+28,230
% of total	...	...	8.5%	18.7%	33.9%	28.5%

Imports (2008): U.S.$35,496,000,000 (machinery and transport equipment 38.5%, assorted manufactured goods 27.2%, mineral fuels and lubricants 9.8%, oils and fats 6.4%). *Major import sources:* Syria *c.* 26%; Turkey *c.* 20%; U.S. *c.* 11%; China *c.* 6%; Jordan *c.* 6%.
Exports (2008): U.S.$63,726,000,000 (crude petroleum 97.1%, refined petroleum 2.4%, remainder 0.5%). *Major export destinations:* U.S. *c.* 39%; India *c.* 12%; Italy *c.* 10%; South Korea *c.* 7%.

Transport and communications

Transport. Railroads (2010): route length 1,412 mi, 2,272 km[9]; passenger-km (2005) 2,000,000; metric ton-km cargo (2005) 73,000,000. Roads (2002): total length 28,303 mi, 45,550 km (paved 84%). Vehicles (2006): passenger cars 784,794; trucks and buses 1,457,474. Air transport: [10].

Communications

Medium	date	number in '000s	units per 1,000 persons	Medium	date	number in '000s	units per 1,000 persons
Televisions	2001	472	19	PCs	2007	...	...
Telephones				Dailies	2009	...	...
Cellular	2010	24,000[11]	758[11]	Internet users	2009	325	10.0
Landline	2010	1,600	51	Broadband	2010	0.1[11]	—[11]

Education and health

Educational attainment (2004)[12]. Percentage of population age 25 and over having: no formal schooling 28%; incomplete primary education 12%; primary 36%; secondary 9%; higher 15%. *Literacy* (2008): total population age 15 and over literate 77.6%; males 86.0%; females 69.2%.

Education (2004–05)

	teachers	students	student/ teacher ratio	enrollment rate (%)
Primary (age 6–11)	215,795	4,430,267	20.5	87
Secondary/Voc. (age 12–17)	93,219	1,751,164	18.8	40
Tertiary	19,231	424,908	22.1	16 (age 18–22)

Health (2008): physicians 16,000[13] (1 per 1,901 persons); hospital beds (2003) 34,505 (1 per 778 persons); infant mortality rate per 1,000 live births 46.2; undernourished population, n.a.

Military

Total active duty personnel (November 2010): 245,782 (army 96.8%, navy 1.1%, air force 2.1%); U.S. forces (June 2011): 91,700[14]. *Military expenditure as percentage of GDP:* n.a.

[1]Includes 8 seats reserved for minorities. [2]Kurdistan Region has de facto authority in part. [3]Detail does not add to total given because of rounding. [4]Including about 750,000 Iraqi refugees in Syria, 500,000 Iraqi refugees in Jordan, and 500,000 Iraqi refugees elsewhere; about 1.5 million Iraqis were internally displaced in January 2010. [5]Weights of consumer price index components. [6]ILO estimates. [7]Employed only; per Labor Force Survey. [8]Imputed bank service charges. [9]Some lines were not operational in early 2010. [10]Data unavailable for Iraqi Airways, the national airline. [11]Subscribers. [12]Based on the Iraq Living Conditions Survey, which comprised 21,668 households and was conducted between March and August 2004. [13]End of 2008 estimate. [14]All U.S. forces were scheduled to withdraw by the end of 2011.

Internet resources for further information:
- **Central Bank of Iraq http://www.cbi.iq**
- **Central Organization for Statistics http://cosit.gov.iq/english**

Ireland

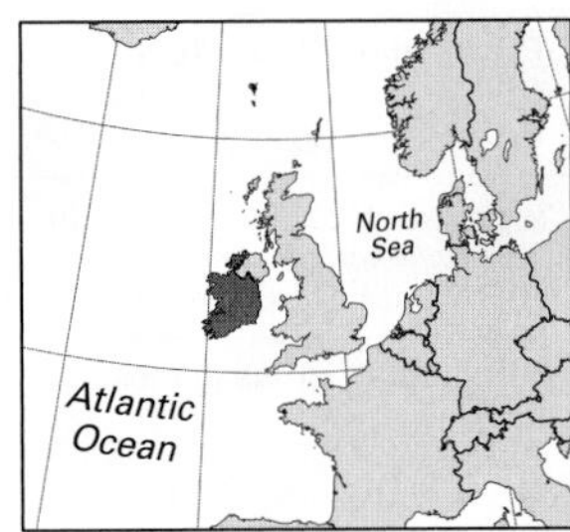

Official name: Éire (Irish); Ireland[1] (English).
Form of government: unitary multiparty republic with two legislative houses (Senate [60[2]]; House of Representatives [166]).
Head of state: President.
Head of government: Prime Minister.
Capital: Dublin.
Official languages: Irish; English.
Official religion: none.
Monetary unit: euro (€); valuation (Sept. 1, 2011) 1 U.S.$ = €0.70; 1 £ = €1.13[3].

Area and population

Provinces Counties/Cities	area sq km	population 2011 census	Provinces Counties/Cities	area sq km	population 2011 census
Connaught (Connacht)	17,711	542,039	South Dublin	224	265,174
Galway	6,098	175,127	Westmeath	1,840	85,961
Galway (city)	51	75,414	Wexford	2,367	145,273
Leitrim	1,590	31,778	Wicklow	2,027	136,448
Mayo	5,586	130,552	Munster	24,674	1,243,726
Roscommon	2,548	63,898	Clare	3,450	116,885
Sligo	1,838	65,270	Cork	7,460	399,216
Leinster	19,801[4]	2,501,208	Cork (city)	40	118,912
Carlow	897	54,532	Kerry	4,807	145,048
Dublin (city)	118	525,383	Limerick	2,735	134,527
Dun Laoghaire-Rathdown	126	206,995	Limerick (city)	21	56,779
Fingal	455	273,051	North Tipperary	2,046	70,219
Kildare	1,695	209,955	South Tipperary	2,258	88,433
Kilkenny	2,073	95,360	Waterford	1,816	66,960
Laoighis	1,720	80,458	Waterford (city)	41	46,747
Longford	1,091	38,970	Ulster (part of)	8,088	294,296
Louth	826	122,808	Cavan	1,932	72,874
Meath	2,342	184,034	Donegal	4,861	160,927
Offaly	2,001	76,806	Monaghan	1,295	60,495
			TOTAL	70,273[4]	4,581,269

Demography

Population (2011): 4,606,000.
Density (2011): persons per sq mi 169.8, persons per sq km 65.5.
Urban-rural (2005): urban 60.5%; rural 39.5%.
Sex distribution (2011[5]): male 49.52%; female 50.48%.
Age breakdown (2008): under 15, 20.6%; 15–29, 23.4%; 30–44, 23.1%; 45–59, 17.5%; 60–74, 10.6%; 75–84, 3.6%; 85 and over, 1.2%.
Population projection: (2020) 5,065,000; (2030) 5,460,000.
Ethnic composition (2000): Irish 95.0%; British 1.7%, of which English 1.4%; Ulster Irish 1.0%; U.S. white 0.8%; other 1.5%.
Religious affiliation (2006): Roman Catholic 86.8%; Church of Ireland (Anglican) 3.0%; other Christian 2.7%; nonreligious 4.4%; other 3.1%.
Major cities (2011): Dublin 525,383 (urban agglomeration 1,186,159); Cork 118,912; Galway 75,414; Limerick 56,779; Waterford 46,747.

Vital statistics

Birth rate per 1,000 population (2010): 16.9 (world avg. 19.2); within marriage (2008) 66.9%; outside of marriage (2008) 33.1%.
Death rate per 1,000 population (2010): 6.5 (world avg. 8.2).
Marriage/divorce rates per 1,000 population: (2009) 4.8/(2007) 0.8.
Total fertility rate (avg. births per childbearing woman; 2008): 2.10.
Life expectancy at birth (2008): male 77.5 years; female 82.3 years.
Major causes of death per 100,000 population (2008): diseases of the circulatory system 223.5; malignant neoplasms (cancers) 185.5; diseases of the respiratory system 77.7; accidents and violence 37.6.

National economy

Budget (2005). Revenue: €39,849,000,000 (VAT 30.3%, income taxes 28.3%, corporate taxes 13.5%). Expenditures: €33,496,000,000 (current expenditure 88.4%, capital expenditure 11.6%).
Public debt (consolidated, general; 2010): U.S.$147,186,000,000.
Gross national income (GNI; 2010): U.S.$182,474,000,000 (U.S.$40,990 per capita); purchasing power parity GNI (U.S.$32,740 per capita).

Structure of gross domestic product and labour force

	2005		2008	
	in value €'000,000	% of total value	labour force[6]	% of labour force[6]
Agriculture	2,955	1.8	114,800	5.4
Mining	497	0.3		
Manufacturing	34,893	21.7	287,300	13.6
Public utilities	1,667	1.0		
Construction	14,256	8.8	241,400	11.4
Transp. and commun.	7,549	4.7	164,000	7.8
Trade, hotels	16,881	10.5	432,700	20.5
Finance, real estate	35,850	22.2	221,700	10.5
Pub. admin., defense	6,418	4.0	102,700	4.9
Services	21,265	13.2	443,400	21.0
Other	18,932[7]	11.7[7]	104,700[8]	5.0[8]
TOTAL	161,163	100.0[4]	2,112,800[4]	100.0[4]

Production (metric tons except as noted). Agriculture, forestry, fishing (2009): cow's milk 5,147,000, barley 1,167,000, wheat 674,100, cattle meat 514,200, potatoes 361,300, oats 146,100, mushrooms[9] 57,747, wool 13,711; livestock (number of live animals) 6,716,100 cattle, 4,778,000 sheep, 1,468,200 pigs; roundwood (2010) 2,607,000 cu m, of which fuelwood 7%; fisheries production 316,295 (from aquaculture 15%). Mining and quarrying (2009): zinc ore 357,000[10]; lead ore 43,000[10]. Manufacturing (gross value added in €'000,000; 2007): chemicals and chemical products 13,158; food, beverages, and tobacco 7,188; electrical and optical equipment 6,842; paper products, printing, and publishing 4,035. Energy production (consumption): electricity (kW-hr; 2009) 25,537,000,000 ([2008] 25,677,000,000); coal (metric tons; 2009) none (2,319,000); crude petroleum (barrels; 2010) none ([2007] 24,841,000); petroleum products (metric tons; 2007) 3,245,000 (7,432,000); natural gas (cu m; 2010) 396,400,000 (5,663,000,000); peat (metric tons; 2009) 4,300,000 (n.a.).
Population economically active (2008): total 2,236,000; activity rate 50.6% (participation rates: ages 15–64, 71.9%; female 43.2%; unemployed [2010] 13.7%).

Price and earnings indexes (2005 = 100)

	2004	2005	2006	2007	2008	2009	2010
Consumer price index	97.6	100.0	103.9	109.0	113.4	108.3	107.3
Weekly earnings index	93.3	100.0	101.7	107.6	105.4	106.4	107.4

Household income and expenditure. Average household size (2006) 2.8; average annual disposable income per household (1999–2000) £Ir 22,589 (U.S.$28,800); expenditure (2004): housing and energy 20.7%, food, beverages, and tobacco 14.9%, hotels and restaurants 14.2%, transportation and communications 14.0%.
Selected balance of payments data. Receipts from (U.S.$'000,000): tourism (2009) 4,894; remittances (2010) 601; foreign direct investment (FDI; 2008–10 avg.) 11,946. Disbursements for (U.S.$'000,000): tourism (2009) 8,773; remittances (2009) 1,988; FDI (2008–10 avg.) 21,122.
Land use as % of total land area (2009): in temporary crops or left fallow (2007) 5.5%, in permanent crops 0.04%, in pasture 45.0%, forest area 10.6%.

Foreign trade[11]

Balance of trade (current prices)

	2005	2006	2007	2008	2009	2010
€'000,000	+32,505	+16,858	+27,069	+29,728	+39,178	+43,518
% of total	22.6%	11.2%	17.8%	21.0%	30.3%	32.3%

Imports (2008): €57,840,000,000 (machinery and apparatus 25.3%, of which computers/office machines/parts 11.8%; mineral fuels 11.5%; food 8.1%; road vehicles 5.6%; medicines and pharmaceuticals 5.0%). *Major import sources:* U.K. 33.4%; U.S. 11.7%; Germany 8.1%; China 6.8%; Neth. 5.0%.
Exports (2008): €86,735,000,000 (organic chemicals 20.6%; medicinal and pharmaceutical products 19.3%; computers/office machines/parts 10.8%; food 8.2%; essential oils used in food/drink 5.6%). *Major export destinations:* U.S. 19.3%; U.K. 18.4%; Belgium 14.2%; Germany 7.1%; France 5.8%.

Transport and communications

Transport. Railroads (2008): route length (2007) 1,163 mi, 1,872 km; passenger-km 1,976,000,000; metric ton-km cargo 103,000,000. Roads (2003): length 60,026 mi, 96,602 km (paved 100%); passenger-km (2006) 34,900,000,000; metric ton-km cargo (2008) 17,402,000,000. Vehicles (2007): passenger cars 1,882,901; trucks and buses 345,874[12]. Air transport (2008)[13]: passenger-km 78,700,000,000; metric ton-km cargo 142,000,000.

Communications

Medium	date	number in '000s	units per 1,000 persons	Medium	date	number in '000s	units per 1,000 persons
Televisions	2002	2,707	694	PCs	2007	2,536	582
Telephones				Dailies	2009	767[14]	218[14]
Cellular	2010	4,702[15]	1,052[15]	Internet users	2009	3,043	674
Landline	2010	2,078	461	Broadband	2010	1,020[15]	228[15]

Education and health

Educational attainment (2006). Percentage of population ages 15–64 having: no formal schooling/primary education 15.1%; some/complete secondary 46.5%; postsecondary certificate 9.4%; some higher 9.5%; complete higher 16.8%; unknown 2.7%.

Education (2007–08)

	teachers	students	student/teacher ratio	enrollment rate (%)
Primary (age 4–11)	30,697	486,921	15.9	97
Secondary/Voc. (age 12–16)	29,729[16]	318,382	10.5[16]	88
Tertiary	13,975	178,518	12.8	58 (age 17–21)

Health: physicians (2004) 11,141 (1 per 365 persons); hospital beds (2006) 12,051[17] (1 per 352 persons); infant mortality rate per 1,000 live births (2010) 3.9; undernourished population (2004–06) less than 5.0% of total population.

Military

Total active duty personnel (November 2010): 10,460 (army 81.3%, navy 10.6%, air force 8.1%); reserve 14,875. *Military expenditure as percentage of GDP* (2009): 0.6%; per capita expenditure U.S.$304.

[1]As provided by the constitution. [2]Includes 11 nonelective seats. [3]The Irish pound was the former monetary unit; on Jan. 1, 2002, 1 £Ir = €1.27. [4]Detail does not add to total given because of rounding. [5]April 10. [6]Ages 15 and over, employed only. [7]Taxes less subsidies plus minuscule statistical discrepancy. [8]Unspecified. [9]Includes truffles. [10]Metal content. [11]Imports c.i.f.; exports f.o.b. [12]Excludes buses. [13]Ryanair Aer Lingus and Aer Arann only. [14]Circulation. [15]Subscribers. [16]2005–06. [17]Publicly funded acute hospitals only.

Internet resources for further information:
- **Central Statistics Office (Ireland) http://www.cso.ie**
- **Central Bank of Ireland http://www.centralbank.ie**

Isle of Man

Official name: Isle of Man[1].
Political status: crown dependency (United Kingdom) with two legislative bodies[2] (Legislative Council [11[3]]; House of Keys [24]).
Head of state: British Monarch represented by Lieutenant-Governor.
Head of government: Chief Minister assisted by the Council of Ministers.
Capital: Douglas.
Official language: English[4].
Official religion: none.
Monetary unit: Manx pound (£M)[5]; valuation (Sept. 1, 2011) 1 £M = U.S.$1.62.

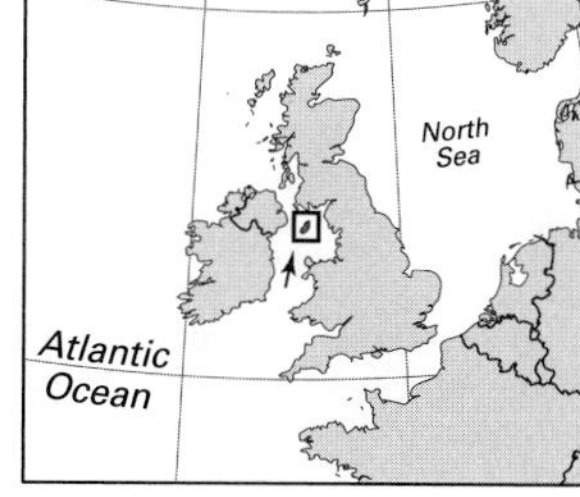

Area and population

	area	population		area	population
		2006			2006
	sq km	census		sq km	census
Towns			**Parishes** (cont.)		
Castletown	2.3	3,109	Ballaugh	23.6	1,042
Douglas	10.1	26,218	Braddan	42.6	3,151
Peel	1.7	4,280	Bride	21.7	418
Ramsey	3.7	7,309	German	45.3	995
			Jurby	17.7	659
Villages			Lezayre	62.3	1,237
Laxey	2.4	1,768	Lonan	35.2	1,563
Onchan	24.7	9,172	Malew	47.1	2,304
Port Erin	2.6	3,575	Marown	26.7	2,086
Port St. Mary	1.4	1,913	Maughold	34.5	950
			Michael	33.9	1,640
Parishes			Patrick	42.2	1,294
Andreas	31.1	1,381	Rushen	24.6	1,591
Arbory	17.7	1,723	Santon	16.9	680
			TOTAL	572.0[6]	80,058

Demography

Population (2011): 84,700.
Density (2011): persons per sq mi 383.5, persons per sq km 148.1.
Urban-rural (2006): urban 71.6%; rural 28.4%.
Sex distribution (2006): male 49.37%; female 50.63%.
Age breakdown (2006): under 15, 16.9%; 15–29, 17.2%; 30–44, 22.0%; 45–59, 21.1%; 60–74, 14.4%; 75–84, 6.0%; 85 and over, 2.4%.
Population projection: (2020) 90,500; (2030) 93,900.
Population by place of birth (2006): Isle of Man 47.6%; United Kingdom 43.9%, of which England 37.2%, Scotland 3.4%, Northern Ireland 2.1%, Wales 1.2%; Ireland 2.1%; other Europe 2.0%; other 4.4%.
Religious affiliation (2000): Christian 63.7%, of which Anglican 40.5%, Methodist 9.9%, Roman Catholic 8.2%; other (mostly nonreligious) 36.3%.
Major towns (2006): Douglas 26,218; Onchan 9,172; Ramsey 7,309; Peel 4,280; Port Erin 3,575.

Vital statistics

Birth rate per 1,000 population (2010): 12.2 (world avg. 19.2); within marriage (2006) 62.1%; outside of marriage (2006) 37.9%.
Death rate per 1,000 population (2010): 9.6 (world avg. 8.2).
Natural increase rate per 1,000 population (2010): 2.6 (world avg. 11.0).
Total fertility rate (avg. births per childbearing woman; 2006): 1.65.
Marriage/divorce rates per 1,000 population: (2006) 5.3/(2003) 4.4.
Life expectancy at birth (2006): male 75.3 years; female 81.2 years.
Major causes of death per 100,000 population (2005): diseases of the circulatory system 347.5, of which ischemic heart diseases 123.4, cerebrovascular disease 86.9; malignant neoplasms (cancers) 246.7; diseases of the respiratory system 146.0; diseases of the digestive system 35.2; accidents 26.4.

National economy

Budget (2009–10). Revenue: £569,587,000 (customs duties and excise taxes 65.5%, income taxes 32.7%, nontax revenue 1.8%). Expenditures: £572,397,000 (health and social security 44.6%, education 18.2%, transportation 6.6%, home affairs 6.5%, local government/environment 4.6%, tourism and recreation 4.5%).
Production. Agriculture, forestry, fishing: main crops include hay, oats, barley, wheat, potatoes, and orchard crops; livestock (number of live animals; 2010) 137,102 sheep, 32,160 cattle, 580 pigs; roundwood, n.a.; fish catch (value of principal catch in £; 2010): scallops 2,138,574, queen scallops 985,999, crab 458,837, lobster (2008) 441,000; fisheries production by tonnage (2010) 4,608 metric tons (from aquaculture, none). Mining and quarrying: sand, gravel, and limestone. Manufacturing (value added in £; 2006–07): electrical and nonelectrical machinery/apparatus, textiles, other 121,700,000; food and beverages 24,400,000. Energy production (consumption): electricity (kW-hr; 2010) n.a. (382,800,000); crude petroleum, none (n.a.); petroleum products, n.a. (n.a.); natural gas, none (n.a.).
Household income and expenditure. Average household size (2006) 2.4; average annual income per household (2006–07) £36,624 (U.S.$70,648); sources of income (2006–07): wages and salaries 72.1%, interest/private pensions 11.3%, transfer payments 11.0%, self-employment 2.1%, other 3.5%; expenditure (January 2008)[7]: recreation and culture 22.2%, housing and energy 15.5%, food and nonalcoholic beverages 13.1%, transportation 12.0%, restaurants and hotels 8.1%, household furnishings 5.7%.
Gross national income (at current market prices; 2008–09): U.S.$5,509,000,000 (U.S.$67,471 per capita).

Structure of gross domestic product and labour force

	2008–09		2006	
	in value £'000[8]	% of total value[8]	labour force	% of labour force
Agriculture, fishing	23,818	0.8	642	1.5
Mining	15,380	0.5 }	2,248	5.4
Manufacturing	146,343	4.6 }		
Construction	173,721	5.5	3,374	8.1
Public utilities	40,701	1.3	603	1.4
Transp. and commun.	216,341	6.8	3,171	7.6
Trade, hotels	187,743	5.9	6,809[9]	16.3[9]
Finance, real estate, insurance	1,205,081[10]	38.0[10] }	11,143	26.7
International business	399,027[10]	12.6[10] }		
Pub. admin., defense	130,406	4.1	2,898	6.9
Services	625,992	19.7	9,876	23.6
Other	5,591[11]	0.2[11]	1,029	2.5
TOTAL	3,170,143[12]	100.0	41,793	100.0

Public debt: n.a.
Population economically active (2006): total 41,793; activity rate of total population 52.2% (participation rates: ages 16–64, 79.9%; female 45.8%; unemployed [December 2010] 1.9%).

Price and earnings indexes (2005 = 100)

	2004	2005	2006	2007	2008	2009	2010
Retail price index	96.0	100.0	103.0	107.1	112.6	113.3	119.0
Weekly earnings index	99.1	100.0	109.6	112.7	116.2	116.8	120.7

Selected balance of payments data. Receipts from (U.S.$'000,000): tourism (2010) 140; remittances, n.a.; foreign direct investment (FDI) n.a. Disbursements for (U.S.$'000,000): tourism, n.a.; remittances, n.a.; FDI, n.a.
Land use as % of total land area (2007): in temporary crops, left fallow, or in permanent crops *c.* 12%, in pasture *c.* 33%, forest area *c.* 6%.

Foreign trade[13]

Imports: n.a. *Major import sources:* mostly the United Kingdom.
Exports: traditional exports including scallops, herring, beef, lambs, and tweeds are of declining importance; light manufacturing is encouraged. *Major export destinations:* mostly the United Kingdom.

Transport and communications

Transport. Railroads (2008): route length 39 mi, 63 km[14]. Roads (2006): total length 500 mi, 800 km (paved virtually 100%). Vehicles (2003): passenger cars 50,596; trucks and buses 11,637. Air transport: n.a.

Communications

Medium	date	number in '000s	units per 1,000 persons	Medium	date	number in '000s	units per 1,000 persons
Televisions	2000	29	355	PCs	2009	...	...
Telephones				Dailies	2010	0	0
Cellular	2010	...	...	Internet users	2010	...	...
Landline	2010	...	...	Broadband	2010	...	...

Education and health

Educational attainment: n.a. *Literacy:* n.a.

Education (2008–09)

	teachers	students	student/teacher ratio	enrollment rate (%)
Primary (age 5–10)	...	5,139	...	...
Secondary/Voc. (age 11–17)	...	5,574	...	...
Tertiary	...	1,429[15]	...	... (age 18–22)

Health (2009): physicians 85 (1 per 977 persons); hospital beds 330[16] (1 per 252 persons); infant mortality rate per 1,000 live births (2006) 5.0; undernourished population, n.a.

Military

Total active duty personnel: [17].

[1]Ellan Vannin in Manx Gaelic. [2]Collective name is Tynwald. [3]Includes 3 ex officio seats. [4]Manx Gaelic has limited official recognition. [5]Equivalent in value to pound sterling (£); the Isle of Man government issues both paper money and coins. [6]220.9 sq mi. [7]Weights of consumer price index components. [8]At factor cost. [9]Includes entertainment and catering. [10]The Isle of Man is an international finance centre with 33 licensed banks, 159 authorized insurers, and 23,476 registered companies at the end of 2010; more than U.S.$77,692,000,000 was deposited in the island at the end of 2010. [11]Ownership of dwellings and nonprofit surpluses less imputed bank service charges. [12]Detail does not add to total given because of rounding. [13]Because of the customs union between the Isle of Man and the U.K. since 1980, there are no customs controls on the movement of goods between the Isle of Man and the U.K. [14]Length of three tourist (novel) railways operating in summer. [15]Includes Isle of Man College and students studying abroad; excludes Isle of Man International Business School. [16]Total for Noble's Hospital. [17]The United Kingdom is responsible for defense.

Internet resources for further information:

- **Isle of Man Government: Economic Affairs**
  http://www.gov.im/treasury/economic
- **Isle of Man Finance**
  http://www.gov.im/iomfinance

Israel

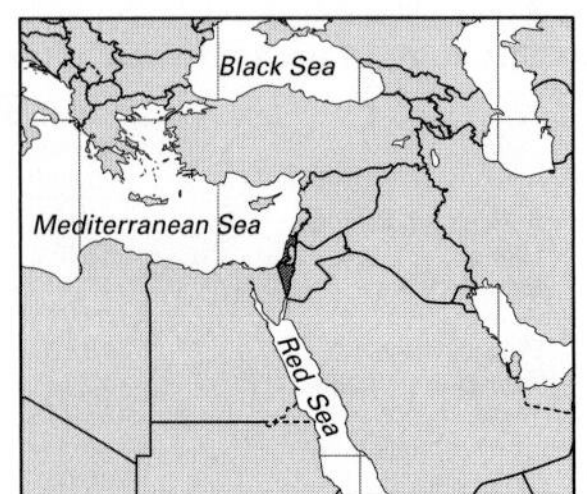

Official name: Medinat Yisra'el (Hebrew); Dawlat Isrā'īl (Arabic) (State of Israel).
Form of government: multiparty republic with one legislative house (Knesset [120]).
Head of state: President.
Head of government: Prime Minister.
Capital (proclaimed): Jerusalem; international recognition of its capital status has largely been withheld.
Official languages: Hebrew; Arabic.
Official religion: none.
Monetary unit: new Israeli sheqel (NIS); valuation (Sept. 1, 2011) 1 U.S.$ = NIS 3.58; 1 £ = NIS 5.79.

Area and population

		area[1]		population
Districts	**Capitals**	sq mi	sq km	2011[2] estimate
Central (Ha Merkaz)	Ramla	500	1,294	1,854,900
Haifa (Ḥefa)	Haifa	334	866	913,000
Jerusalem (Yerushalayim)	Jerusalem	252	653	945,000
Northern (Ha Ẕafon)	Tiberias	1,727	4,473	1,279,200
Southern (Ha Darom)	Beersheba	5,477	14,185	1,106,900
Tel Aviv	Tel Aviv–Yafo	66	172	1,285,000
TOTAL		8,357[3]	21,643	7,384,000[4]

Demography

Population (2011): 7,431,000[5].
Density (2011)[5]: persons per sq mi 889.2, persons per sq km 343.3.
Urban-rural (2011[2]): urban 91.6%; rural 8.4%.
Sex distribution (2010): male 49.47%; female 50.53%.
Age breakdown (2010): under 15, 28.0%; 15–29, 22.9%; 30–44, 19.7%; 45–59, 15.2%; 60–74, 9.5%; 75–84, 3.4%; 85 and over, 1.3%.
Population projection[5]: (2020) 8,569,000; (2030) 9,707,000.
Ethnic composition (2011[2]): Jewish 75.4%; Arab 20.5%; other 4.1%.
Religious affiliation (2011[2]): Jewish 75.4%; Muslim 17.2%; Christian 2.0%; Druze 1.7%; other 3.7%.
Major cities (2011[2]): Jerusalem 788,100; Tel Aviv–Yafo 404,300 (metro area 3,350,400); Haifa 268,200 (metro area 1,048,900); Rishon LeẔiyyon 231,000; Beersheba 195,400 (metro area 558,500).

Vital statistics

Birth rate per 1,000 population (2010): 21.8 (world avg. 19.2); within marriage 95.9%[6]; outside of marriage 4.1%[6].
Death rate per 1,000 population (2010): 5.2 (world avg. 8.2).
Total fertility rate (avg. births per childbearing woman; 2010): 3.03.
Marriage/divorce rates per 1,000 population (2009): 6.5/1.8.
Life expectancy at birth (2010): male 79.7 years; female 83.4 years.
Major causes of death per 100,000 population (2009): diseases of the circulatory system 132.7; malignant neoplasms (cancers) 132.6; diseases of the respiratory system 39.2; diabetes mellitus 31.8.

National economy

Budget (2009). Revenue: NIS 328,145,000,000 (tax revenue 53.1%, of which income tax 21.7%, VAT 21.1%; internal loans 27.6%; external loans and grants 6.1%). Expenditures: NIS 331,416,000,000 (debt repayment 25.1%; defense 17.1%; education 11.7%; interest 10.2%; social affairs 9.5%).
Public debt (December 2010): U.S.$170,554,000,000.
Gross national income (GNI; 2010): U.S.$207,193,000,000 (U.S.$27,340 per capita); purchasing power parity GNI (U.S.$27,800 per capita).

Structure of gross domestic product and labour force

	2008			
	in value NIS '000,000	% of total value	labour force	% of labour force
Agriculture	11,422	1.6	47,900	1.6
Mining }	111,625	15.6	…	…
Manufacturing }			432,000	14.6
Construction	32,301	4.5	150,700	5.1
Public utilities	12,728	1.8	19,900	0.7
Transp. and commun.	49,324	6.9	174,500	5.9
Trade, hotels	71,023	9.9	507,800	17.2
Finance, real estate	178,595	25.0	488,100	16.5
Public admin., defense	117,102[7]	16.4[7]	130,600	4.4
Services	83,992	11.8	802,200	27.1
Other	46,226[8]	6.5[8]	203,400	6.9
TOTAL	714,338	100.0	2,957,100	100.0

Production (metric tons except as noted). Agriculture, forestry, fishing (2010): potatoes 548,700, tomatoes 446,600, carrots 234,300[9], grapefruit 204,400[10], chilies and green peppers 202,000, grapes 144,300, apples 131,500, avocados 73,200, peaches 65,800, almonds 7,800; livestock (number of live animals) 430,000 cattle, 42,599,000 chickens; roundwood 27,000 cu m, of which fuelwood 8%; fisheries production (2009) 22,401 (from aquaculture 87%). Mining and quarrying (2009): potash 2,100,000, bromine 128,000, magnesium metal 29,000, diamonds 382,000 carats[11]. Manufacturing (gross value added in NIS '000,000; 2008): chemical products (including refined petroleum products) 20,644; medical, measuring, and testing appliances 11,532; electronics and telecommunications equipment 10,428; food products 9,365; fabricated metal products 8,605; transportation equipment 5,594. Energy production (consumption): electricity (kW-hr; 2010) 58,194,000,000 ([2007] 53,010,000,000); hard coal (metric tons; 2008) none (12,882,000); lignite (metric tons; 2007) 429,000 (429,000); crude petroleum (barrels; 2009) 14,000 ([2007] 74,200,000); petroleum products (metric tons; 2006) 10,687,000 (11,572,000); natural gas (cu m; 2010) 3,220,550,000 ([2008] 1,189,000,000).
Population economically active (2010): total 3,147,100; activity rate 41.3% (participation rates: ages 15 and over, 57.3%; female 47.1%; unemployed [July 2010–June 2011] 6.2%).

Price and earnings indexes (2005 = 100)

	2004	2005	2006	2007	2008	2009	2010
Consumer price index	98.7	100.0	102.1	102.6	107.4	110.9	113.9
Daily earnings index	97.3	100.0	104.6	109.2	112.8	117.3	122.0

Household income and expenditure (2009). Average household size (2010) 3.4; gross annual income per household NIS 162,936 (U.S.$42,897); sources of income: salaries and wages 66.1%, self-employment 10.4%; expenditure: housing 24.4%, transport and communications 19.1%, food and beverages 16.4%, education and entertainment 13.9%, household operations and energy 9.7%.
Selected balance of payments data. Receipts from (U.S.$'000,000): tourism (2009) 3,741; remittances (2010) 1,379; foreign direct investment (FDI; 2008–10 avg.) 6,822. Disbursements for (U.S.$'000,000): tourism (2009) 2,909; remittances (2009) 3,283; FDI (2008–10 avg.) 5,622.
Land use as % of total land area (2007): in temporary crops 9.9%, left fallow 4.3%, in permanent crops 3.2%, in pasture 5.8%, forest area 8.0%.

Foreign trade[12]

Balance of trade (current prices)

	2004	2005	2006	2007	2008	2009
U.S.$'000,000	–2,349	–2,262	–1,042	–2,528	–3,833	–5,091
% of total	3.0%	2.6%	1.1%	2.3%	3.0%	5.7%

Imports (2008): U.S.$65,170,000,000 (machinery and apparatus 19.7%; crude petroleum 16.7%; diamonds 14.3%; chemicals and chemical products 10.9%; road vehicles 6.4%; food 5.4%). *Major import sources:* U.S. 12.3%; Belgium 6.5%; China 6.5%; Switzerland 6.1%; Germany 6.0%; unspecified 17.0%.
Exports (2008): U.S.$61,337,000,000 (polished diamonds 25.3%; chemicals and chemical products 25.2%, of which medicines 7.4%; machinery and apparatus 19.5%, of which electrical machinery/electronics 6.2%; rough diamonds 6.3%). *Major export destinations:* U.S. 32.6%; Belgium 7.5%; Hong Kong 6.8%; India 3.8%; Netherlands 3.3%.

Transport and communications

Transport. Railroads (2010–11): route length (2009) 606 mi, 975 km; passenger-km 1,970,400,000; metric ton-km cargo 1,047,500. Roads (2011[2]): total length 11,477 mi, 18,470 km (paved 100%). Vehicles (2011[2]): passenger cars 2,002,774; trucks and buses 378,253. Air transport (2010)[13]: passenger-km 18,438,000,000; metric ton-km cargo 557,000,000.

Communications

Medium	date	number in '000s	units per 1,000 persons	Medium	date	number in '000s	units per 1,000 persons
Televisions	2003	2,136	330	PCs	2004	5,037	734
Telephones				Dailies	2009	700[14]	94[14]
Cellular	2010	9,875[15]	1,331[15]	Internet users	2009	3,700	516
Landline	2010	3,276	442	Broadband	2010	1,865[15]	251[15]

Education and health

Educational attainment (2007). Percentage of population age 25–64 having: no formal schooling/unknown 1%; primary 12%; secondary 44%; postsecondary, vocational, and higher 43%. *Literacy* (2004): total population age 15 and over literate 97.1%; males literate 98.5%; females literate 95.9%.

Education (2010–11)

	teachers	students	student/ teacher ratio	enrollment rate (%)[16]
Primary (age 6–11)	71,876	899,611	12.5	97
Secondary/Voc. (age 12–17)	71,126	630,626	8.9	86
Tertiary	…	251,800[17]	…	63 (age 18–22)

Health (2010): physicians 26,700[18] (1 per 274 persons); hospital beds (2011[2]) 42,625[19] (1 per 175 persons); infant mortality rate per 1,000 live births 3.7.

Military

Total active duty personnel (November 2010): 176,500 (army 75.3%, navy 5.4%, air force 19.3%); reserve 565,000. *Military expenditure as percentage of GDP* (2010): 7.1%; per capita expenditure U.S.$2,132.

[1]Excludes the West Bank (2,183 sq mi [5,655 sq km]), the Gaza Strip (141 sq mi [365 sq km]), the Sea of Galilee (63 sq mi [164 sq km]), and the Dead Sea (102 sq mi [265 sq km]); includes the Golan Heights (446 sq mi [1,154 sq km]) and East Jerusalem (27 sq mi [70 sq km]). [2]January 1. [3]Detail does not add to total given because of rounding. [4]Includes the population of the Golan Heights and East Jerusalem; excludes the Jewish population of the West Bank. [5]Excludes January 2011 estimate of Jewish population of the West Bank (311,100). [6]Jewish women only. [7]Includes community services. [8]Taxes on products less imputed bank service charges and statistical discrepancy. [9]Includes turnips. [10]Includes pomelos. [11]Imported diamonds cut in Israel. [12]Imports c.i.f.; exports f.o.b. [13]El Al only. [14]Circulation. [15]Subscribers. [16]2008–09. [17]Universities, academic colleges, and colleges of education only. [18]Up to age 65. [19]Includes beds in old-age homes and kibbutzim.

Internet resources for further information:

- **Central Bureau of Statistics http://www.cbs.gov.il/engindex.htm**
- **Bank of Israel http://www.bankisrael.gov.il/firsteng.htm**

Italy

Official name: Repubblica Italiana (Italian Republic).
Form of government: republic with two legislative houses (Senate [321[1]]; Chamber of Deputies [630]).
Head of state: President.
Head of government: Prime Minister.
Capital: Rome.
Official language: Italian.[2]
Official religion: none.
Monetary unit: euro (€); valuation (Sept. 1, 2011) 1 U.S.$ = €0.70;
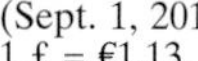
1 £ = €1.13.

Area and population

Regions Provinces[5]	Capitals	area[3] sq mi	area[3] sq km	population 2011[4] estimate
Abruzzo (Abruzzi)	L'Aquila	4,156	10,763	1,342,366
Chieti	Chieti	999	2,587	397,123
L'Aquila	L'Aquila	1,944	5,034	309,820
Pescara	Pescara	473	1,225	323,184
Teramo	Teramo	752	1,948	312,239
Basilicata	Potenza	3,859	9,995	587,517
Matera	Matera	1,331	3,447	203,726
Potenza	Potenza	2,527	6,545	383,791
Calabria	Catanzaro	5,823	15,081	2,011,395
Catanzaro	Catanzaro	924	2,392	368,597
Cosenza	Cosenza	2,568	6,650	734,656
Crotone	Crotone	662	1,716	174,605
Reggio di Calabria	Reggio di Calabria	1,229	3,183	566,977
Vibo Valentia	Vibo Valentia	440	1,139	166,560
Campania	Naples	5,247	13,590	5,834,056
Avellino	Avellino	1,078	2,792	439,137
Benevento	Benevento	800	2,071	287,874
Caserta	Caserta	1,019	2,639	916,467
Napoli	Naples	452	1,171	3,080,873
Salerno	Salerno	1,900	4,922	1,109,705
Emilia-Romagna	Bologna	8,539	22,117	4,432,418
Bologna	Bologna	1,429	3,702	991,924
Ferrara	Ferrara	1,016	2,632	359,994
Forlì-Cesena	Forlì	969	2,510	395,489
Modena	Modena	1,039	2,690	700,913
Parma	Parma	1,332	3,449	442,120
Piacenza	Piacenza	1,000	2,589	289,875
Ravenna	Ravenna	718	1,859	392,458
Reggio nell'Emilia	Reggio nell'Emilia	885	2,292	530,343
Rimini	Rimini	154	400	329,302
Lazio	Rome	6,655	17,236	5,728,688
Frosinone	Frosinone	1,251	3,239	498,167
Latina	Latina	869	2,251	555,692
Rieti	Rieti	1,061	2,749	160,467
Roma	Rome	2,066	5,352	4,194,068
Viterbo	Viterbo	1,395	3,612	320,294
Liguria	Genoa	2,093	5,422	1,616,788
Genova	Genoa	709	1,836	882,718
Imperia	Imperia	446	1,155	222,648
La Spezia	La Spezia	341	882	223,516
Savona	Savona	596	1,545	287,906
Lombardy[5]	Milan	9,213	23,863	9,917,714
Bergamo	Bergamo	1,051	2,722	1,098,740
Brescia	Brescia	1,846	4,782	1,256,025
Como	Como	497	1,288	594,988
Cremona	Cremona	684	1,771	363,606
Lecco	Lecco	315	816	340,167
Lodi	Lodi	302	783	227,655
Mantova	Mantova	903	2,339	415,442
Milano[5]	Milan	765	1,980	4,006,330
Pavia	Pavia	1,145	2,965	548,307
Sondrio	Sondrio	1,240	3,212	183,169
Varese	Varese	463	1,199	883,285
Marche[5]	Ancona	3,743	9,694	1,565,335
Ancona	Ancona	749	1,940	481,028
Ascoli Piceno[5]	Ascoli Piceno	806	2,087	391,982
Macerata	Macerata	1,071	2,774	325,362
Pesaro e Urbino	Pesaro	1,117	2,892	366,963
Molise	Campobasso	1,713	4,438	319,780
Campobasso	Campobasso	1,123	2,909	231,086
Isernia	Isernia	590	1,529	88,694
Piedmont	Turin	9,808	25,402	4,457,335
Alessandria	Alessandria	1,375	3,560	440,613
Asti	Asti	583	1,511	221,687
Biella	Biella	352	913	185,768
Cuneo	Cuneo	2,665	6,903	592,303
Novara	Novara	530	1,373	371,802
Torino	Turin	2,637	6,830	2,302,353
Verbano-Cusio-Ossola	Verbania	858	2,221	163,247
Vercelli	Vercelli	806	2,088	179,562
Puglia[5]	Bari	7,474	19,358	4,091,259
Bari[5]	Bari	1,980	5,129	1,651,569
Brindisi	Brindisi	710	1,838	403,229
Foggia[5]	Foggia	2,774	7,185	640,836
Lecce	Lecce	1,065	2,759	815,597
Taranto	Taranto	941	2,437	580,028
Tuscany	Florence	8,878	22,993	3,749,813
Arezzo	Arezzo	1,248	3,232	349,651
Firenze	Florence	1,365	3,536	998,098
Grosseto	Grosseto	1,739	4,504	228,157
Livorno	Livorno	468	1,213	342,955
Lucca	Lucca	684	1,773	393,795
Massa-Carrara	Massa	447	1,157	203,901
Pisa	Pisa	945	2,448	417,782
Pistoia	Pistoia	373	965	293,061
Prato	Prato	133	344	249,775
Siena	Siena	1,475	3,821	272,638
Umbria	Perugia	3,265	8,456	906,486
Perugia	Perugia	2,446	6,334	671,821
Terni	Terni	819	2,122	234,665

Area and population (continued)

Regions Provinces[5]	Capitals	area[3] sq mi	area[3] sq km	population 2011[4] estimate
Veneto	Venice	7,104	18,399	4,937,854
Belluno	Belluno	1,420	3,678	213,474
Padova	Padova	827	2,142	934,216
Rovigo	Rovigo	691	1,789	247,884
Treviso	Treviso	956	2,477	888,249
Venezia	Venice	950	2,460	863,133
Verona	Verona	1,195	3,096	920,158
Vicenza	Vicenza	1,051	2,722	870,740
Autonomous regions Provinces				
Friuli-Venezia Giulia	Trieste	3,034	7,858	1,235,808
Gorizia	Gorizia	180	467	142,407
Pordenone	Pordenone	878	2,273	315,323
Trieste	Trieste	82	212	236,556
Udine	Udine	1,889	4,893	541,522
Sardinia	Cagliari	9,301	24,090	1,675,411
Cagliari	Cagliari	1,764	4,570	563,180
Carbonia-Iglesias	Carbonia, Iglesias	577	1,495	129,840
Medio Campidano	Sanluri, Villacidro	585	1,516	102,409
Nuoro	Nuoro	1,519	3,934	160,677
Ogliastra	Lanusei; Tortolì	716	1,854	57,965
Olbia-Tempio	Olbia	1,312	3,399	157,859
Oristano	Oristano	1,174	3,040	166,244
Sassari	Sassari	1,653	4,282	337,237
Sicily	Palermo	9,927	25,711	5,051,075
Agrigento	Agrigento	1,175	3,042	454,002
Caltanissetta	Caltanissetta	822	2,128	271,729
Catania	Catania	1,371	3,552	1,090,101
Enna	Enna	989	2,562	172,485
Messina	Messina	1,254	3,248	653,737
Palermo	Palermo	1,927	4,992	1,249,577
Ragusa	Ragusa	623	1,614	318,549
Siracusa	Siracusa	814	2,109	404,271
Trapani	Trapani	951	2,462	436,624
Trentino–Alto Adige (Trentino-Südtirol)	Trento (Trient)	5,254	13,607	1,037,114
Bolzano (Bozen)	Bolzano (Bozen)	2,857	7,400	507,657
Trento	Trento (Trient)	2,401	6,218	529,457
Valle d'Aosta (Vallée d'Aoste)	Aosta (Aoste)	1,260	3,263	128,230
TOTAL		116,346	301,336	60,626,442

Demography

Population (2011): 60,769,000.
Density (2011): persons per sq mi 522.3, persons per sq km 201.7.
Urban-rural (2005): urban 67.6%; rural 32.4%.
Sex distribution (2009[4]): male 48.55%; female 51.45%.
Age breakdown (2008[4]): under 15, 14.1%; 15–29, 16.3%; 30–44, 23.8%; 45–59, 20.1%; 60–74, 16.1%; 75–84, 7.2%; 85 and over, 2.4%.
Population projection: (2020) 62,468,000; (2030) 63,583,000.
Ethnolinguistic composition (2000): Italian 96.0%; North African Arab 0.9%; Italo-Albanian 0.8%; Albanian 0.5%; German 0.4%; Austrian 0.4%; other 1.0%.
Religious affiliation (2005): Roman Catholic *c.* 83%, of which practicing *c.* 28%; Muslim *c.* 2%; nonreligious/atheist *c.* 14%; other *c.* 1%.
Major cities/urban agglomerations (2011[4]/2007): Rome 2,761,477 (3,339,000); Milan 1,324,110 (2,945,000); Naples 959,574 (2,250,000); Turin 907,563 (1,652,000); Palermo 655,875 (863,000); Genoa 607,906; Bologna 380,181; Florence 371,282; Bari 320,475; Catania 293,458; Venice 270,884; Verona 263,964; Messina 242,503; Padua 214,198; Trieste 205,535; Brescia 193,879; Taranto 191,810; Prato 188,011; Parma 186,690; Reggio di Calabria 186,547; Modena 184,663.
Households. Average household size (2008[4]) 2.4; composition of households (2001): 1 person 24.9%, 2 persons 27.1%, 3 persons 21.6%, 4 persons 19.0%, 5 or more persons 7.4%. Family households (2001): 21,810,676, of which couple with children 41.5%, single family 24.9%, couple without children 20.8%, mother with children 7.3%, father with children 1.6%.
Immigration (2008[4]): resident foreigners 3,432,651, of which from EU countries 17.7%, other Europe 23.0%, North African countries 15.2%, other Africa 6.6%, Asian countries 7.7%, other/not stated 29.8%.

Vital statistics

Birth rate per 1,000 population (2009): 9.5 (world avg. 20.3); within marriage (2007) 79.3%; outside of marriage (2007) 20.7%.
Death rate per 1,000 population (2009): 9.8 (world avg. 8.5).
Natural increase rate per 1,000 population (2009): –0.3 (world avg. 11.8).
Total fertility rate (avg. births per childbearing woman; 2007): 1.37.
Marriage/divorce rates per 1,000 population: (2009) 4.0/(2007) 0.8.
Life expectancy at birth (2009): male 78.9 years; female 84.1 years.
Major causes of death per 100,000 population (2006): diseases of the circulatory system 373.4; malignant neoplasms (cancers) 286.2; diseases of the respiratory system 60.7; diseases of the digestive system 39.2.
Adult population (ages 15–49) *living with HIV* (2009): 0.3%[6] (world avg. 0.8%).

Social indicators

Educational attainment (2007). Percentage of population ages 25 to 64 having: no formal schooling through primary education 15%; lower secondary 33%; upper secondary 37%; university 13%; other 2%.
Quality of working life. Average workweek (2008): 34.6 hours. Annual rate per 100,000 workers (2008) for: nonfatal injury 2,445; fatal injury 4. Number of working days lost to labour stoppages per 1,000 workers (2007): 52.6.
Material well-being. Rate per 100 households possessing (2008): mobile phone 88.5; personal computer 50.1; Internet access 42.0; satellite dish 30.7.
Transport used for work per 100 employees (includes double-counting; 2008): car 75.7%, walking 11.1%, bus 4.9%, motorcycle/motorbike 4.6%, bicycle 3.1%, train 2.9%, underground 2.5%, other 2.9%.

Social participation. Eligible voters participating in last national election (June 2011): 57%. Trade union membership in total workforce (2004): *c.* 30%.
Social deviance (2007). Offense rate per 100,000 population for: murder/manslaughter 4.6; rape 8.2; theft 2,756; battery 132.2; robbery 86.2.
Access to services (2002). Nearly 100% of dwellings have access to electricity, a safe water supply, and toilet facilities.
Leisure (2006). Favourite leisure activities (attendance per 100 people age 6 and over): cinema 48.9; museum/art exhibition 27.7; sporting events 27.3; discotheque 24.8; archaeological sites/monuments 21.1.

National economy

Gross national income (GNI; 2010): U.S.$2,125,845,000,000 (U.S.$35,090 per capita); purchasing power parity GNI (U.S.$31,090 per capita).

Structure of gross domestic product and labour force

	2009		2008	
	in value €'000,000	% of total value	labour force	% of labour force
Agriculture	25,084	1.6	895,000	3.6
Mining	4,865	0.3	36,000	0.1
Manufacturing	220,602	14.5	4,805,000	19.1
Construction	85,932	5.7	1,970,000	7.9
Public utilities	31,327	2.1	144,000	0.6
Transportation and communications	99,599	6.5	1,294,000	5.2
Trade, hotels	203,946	13.4	4,719,000	18.8
Finance, real estate	393,893	25.9	3,271,000	13.0
Pub. admin., defense	93,207	6.1	1,436,000	5.7
Services	209,271	13.8	4,798,000	19.1
Other	153,144[7]	10.1[7]	1,728,000[8]	6.9[8]
TOTAL	1,520,870	100.0	25,096,000	100.0

Budget (2006)[9]. Revenue: €672,610,000,000 (taxes on goods and services 27.6%, social security contributions 27.6%, individual income taxes 24.4%, nontax revenue 6.7%, taxes on corporations 6.4%). Expenditures: €722,750,000,000 (social protection 37.2%, health 14.4%, economic affairs 12.0%, public debt 9.5%, education 9.2%, defense 2.8%).
Public debt (May 2009): U.S.$2,137,581,000,000.

Financial aggregates

	2005	2006	2007	2008	2009	2010
Exchange rate, € per[10]:						
U.S. dollar	0.85	0.76	0.68	0.72	0.69	0.75
£	1.46	1.49	1.36	1.03	1.08	1.17
SDR	1.21	1.14	1.07	1.11	1.09	1.15
International reserves (U.S.$)[10]						
Total (excl. gold; '000,000)	25,515	25,662	28,385	37,088	45,770	47,684
SDRs ('000,000)	229	272	331	261	9,414	9,549
Reserve pos. in IMF ('000,000)	1,758	977	735	1,520	1,835	2,457
Foreign exchange ('000,000)	23,528	24,413	27,319	35,306	34,521	35,678
Gold ('000,000 fine troy oz)	78.83	78.83	78.83	78.83	78.83	78.83
% world reserves	8.1	8.1	8.2	8.3	8.1	8.0
Interest and prices						
Central bank discount (%)	…	…	…	…	…	…
Govt. bond yield (%)	3.56	4.05	4.49	4.68	4.31	4.04
Share prices[11] (2005 = 100)	100.0	115.7	127.0	88.1	63.0	66.9
Balance of payments (U.S.$'000,000)						
Balance of visible trade	+564	−12,511	+4,581	−2,841	+1,458	−27,278
Imports, f.o.b.	−371,814	−430,585	−496,700	−547,921	−405,998	−475,652
Exports, f.o.b.	372,378	418,074	501,281	545,081	407,456	448,374
Balance of invisibles	−30,277	−35,534	−56,155	−63,411	−42,463	−43,951
Balance of payments, current account	−29,713	−48,045	−51,574	−66,252	−41,005	−71,229

Energy production (consumption): electricity (kW-hr; 2008) 316,719,000,000 ([2007] 360,171,000,000); coal (metric tons; 2007) 158,000 (25,118,000); crude petroleum (barrels; 2008) 36,400,000 ([2007] 680,004,000); petroleum products (metric tons; 2007) 91,714,000 (75,191,000); natural gas (cu m; 2008) 9,103,000,000 ([2007] 84,927,000,000).
Production (metric tons except as noted). Agriculture, forestry, fishing (2009): cow's milk 12,219,500, grapes 8,242,500, corn (maize) 7,877,700, tomatoes 6,877,400, wheat 6,341,000, sugar beets 3,307,700, olives 3,286,600, oranges 2,359,400, apples 2,313,600, potatoes 1,753,200, peaches and nectarines 1,692,500, pig meat 1,462,000, cattle meat 887,700, pears 847,500, artichokes 486,600, kiwi fruit 436,300, hazelnuts 104,900; livestock (number of live animals) 9,252,400 pigs, 8,175,200 sheep, 6,446,700 cattle, 120,000,000 chickens; roundwood (2010) 7,254,327 cu m, of which fuelwood 67%; fisheries production 415,316 (from aquaculture 39%). Mining and quarrying (2008): limestone 32,900,000; feldspar 4,700,000 [world rank: 2]; marble and travertine 4,600,000; pozzolana 4,000,000 [world rank: 2]. Manufacturing (value added in U.S.$'000,000; 2005): fabricated metal products 34,849; food products 21,119; general purpose machinery 19,782; paints, soaps, pharmaceuticals 14,945; special purpose machinery 13,548; bricks, cement, ceramics 12,684; printing and publishing 10,567; plastic products 9,205; textiles 9,063; motor vehicles and parts 8,533; wearing apparel 8,317; furniture 8,195; iron and steel 7,298; footwear and leather products 6,643.
Population economically active (2008): total 25,096,600; activity rate of total population 42.2% (participation rates: ages 15–64, 63.0%; female 40.7%; unemployed [2009] 7.8%).

Price and earnings indexes (2005 = 100)

	2004	2005	2006	2007	2008	2009	2010
Consumer price index	98.0	100.0	102.1	103.9	107.4	108.2	109.9
Earnings index	97.1	100.0	103.2	106.1	108.3	111.6	114.0

Selected balance of payments data. Receipts from (U.S.$'000,000): tourism (2009) 40,311; remittances (2010) 5,258; foreign direct investment (FDI; 2008–10 avg.) 6,242. Disbursements for (U.S.$'000,000): tourism (2009) 27,864; remittances (2009) 12,986; FDI (2008–10 avg.) 36,426.

Household income and expenditure. Average household size (2008[4]) 2.4; average annual disposable income per household (2008) €19,342 (U.S.$28,332); sources of income (1996): salaries and wages 38.8%, property income and self-employment 38.5%, transfer payments 22.0%; expenditure (2007[4]): housing and energy 31.4%, food and beverages 18.8%, transportation and communications 16.7%, clothing 6.3%, leisure 5.4%.
Land use as % of total land area (2009): in temporary crops 21.7%, left fallow 1.6%, in permanent crops 8.9%, in pasture 15.0%, forest area 30.8%.

Foreign trade[12]

Balance of trade (current prices)

	2004	2005	2006	2007	2008	2009
U.S.$'000,000	−1,724	−11,879	−25,412	−11,619	−16,887	−4,058
% of total	0.2%	1.6%	3.0%	1.1%	1.5%	0.7%

Imports (2008): U.S.$553,962,000,000 (machinery and apparatus 15.9%, of which nonelectrical machinery 7.7%; chemicals and chemical products 12.2%; crude petroleum 10.6%; road vehicles/parts 9.5%; food 6.5%; iron and steel 5.9%). *Major import sources:* Germany 15.7%; France 8.5%; China 6.3%; Netherlands 5.1%; Spain 3.9%; Belgium 3.8%; Libya 3.8%; U.S. 3.1%; Switzerland 3.0%; U.K. 2.9%.
Exports (2008): U.S.$537,075,000,000 (nonelectrical machinery and apparatus 21.0%, of which general industrial machinery 10.2%, specialized machinery for particular industries 6.3%; chemicals and chemical products 9.9%; road vehicles/parts 7.7%; iron and steel 5.4%; electrical machinery and apparatus 5.1%; food 4.9%; apparel and clothing accessories 4.7%; manufactures of metals 4.4%; refined petroleum 3.9%; furniture 2.6%; footwear 2.1%). *Major export destinations:* Germany 12.7%; France 11.1%; Spain 6.5%; U.S. 6.3%; U.K. 5.2%; Switzerland 4.0%; Russia 2.9%; Belgium 2.6%; Poland 2.6%; Austria 2.3%.

Transport and communications

Transport. Railroads (2008): route length 10,163 mi, 16,356 km; passenger-km 45,767,000,000; metric ton-km cargo 20,118,000,000. Roads (2005): total length 303,040 mi, 487,700 km (paved 100%); passenger-km (2006) 795,700,000,000[13]; metric ton-km cargo (2007) 179,411,000,000. Vehicles (2007): passenger cars 35,680,000; trucks and buses 4,534,020. Air transport (2008)[14]: passenger-km 39,421,000,000; metric ton-km cargo 1,231,000,000.

Communications

Medium	date	number in '000s	units per 1,000 persons	Medium	date	number in '000s	units per 1,000 persons
Televisions	2001	28,153	494	PCs	2007	21,791	367
Telephones				Dailies	2009	4,842[15]	94[15]
Cellular	2010	82,000[16]	1,354[16]	Internet users	2009	29,236	488
Landline	2010	21,600	356	Broadband	2010	13,400[16]	221[16]

Education and health

Literacy (2007): total population age 15 and over literate 98.9%; males literate 99.1%; females literate 98.6%.

Education (2005–06)

	teachers	students	student/ teacher ratio	enrollment rate (%)
Primary (age 6–10)	264,378	2,790,254	10.6	99
Secondary/Voc. (age 11–18)	426,822	4,531,571	10.6	94
Tertiary	99,595	2,029,023	20.4	67 (age 19–23)

Health: physicians (2006) 215,000 (1 per 274 persons); hospital beds (2005) 234,428 (1 per 250 persons); infant mortality rate per 1,000 live births (2007) 3.8; undernourished population (2005–07) less than 5.0% of total population.

Military

Total active duty personnel (November 2010): 292,576 (army 36.1%, navy 11.6%, air force 14.7%, carabinieri 37.6%); U.S. military forces (June 2011) 10,771. *Military expenditure as percentage of GDP* (2008): 1.3%[17]; per capita expenditure U.S.$516.

[1]Included 6 nonelective seats in May 2011 (4 presidential appointees and 2 former presidents serving ex officio). [2]In addition, German is locally official in the region of Trentino–Alto Adige and French is locally official in the region of Valle d'Aosta. [3]Region areas are based on an end-of-2002 survey; province areas are based on an older survey and therefore may not sum to the region area. [4]January 1. [5]Three new provinces were formally established in June 2009. Monza and Brianza province was created from part of Milano province, Lombardy region; Fermo from part of Ascoli Piceno province, Marche region; and Barletta-Andria-Trani from parts of Bari and Foggia provinces, Puglia region. [6]Statistically derived midpoint within range. [7]Taxes less subsidies. [8]Includes 1,692,000 unemployed. [9]According to the general government budget; for Italy this is the central government budget and some of the local government budget. [10]End of year. [11]Yearly average. [12]Imports c.i.f.; exports f.o.b. [13]Passenger cars 693,000,000,000; buses 102,700,000,000. [14]Air One, Alitalia, Livingston S.P.A., and Meridiana airlines only. [15]Circulation of daily newspapers. [16]Subscribers. [17]Includes military pensions.

Internet resources for further information:

- **National Statistical Institute http://www.istat.it**
- **Banca d'Italia http://www.bancaditalia.it**

Jamaica

Official name: Jamaica.
Form of government: constitutional monarchy with two legislative houses (Senate [21[1]]; House of Representatives [60]).
Head of state: British Monarch represented by Governor-General.
Head of government: Prime Minister.
Capital: Kingston.
Official language: English.
Official religion: none.
Monetary unit: Jamaican dollar (J$); valuation (Sept. 1, 2011) 1 U.S.$ = J$85.68; 1 £ = J$138.45.

Area and population

Parishes	Capitals	area sq mi	area sq km	population 2011[2] estimate
Clarendon	May Pen	462	1,196	247,751
Hanover	Lucea	174	450	70,276
Kingston	[3]	9	22	[3]
Manchester	Mandeville	320	830	191,875
Portland	Port Antonio	314	814	82,656
Saint Andrew	[3]	166	431	669,512[3]
Saint Ann	Saint Ann's Bay	468	1,213	174,281
Saint Catherine	Spanish Town	460	1,192	500,942
Saint Elizabeth	Black River	468	1,212	151,887
Saint James	Montego Bay	230	595	185,334
Saint Mary	Port Maria	236	611	114,889
Saint Thomas	Morant Bay	287	743	94,716
Trelawny	Falmouth	338	875	75,996
Westmoreland	Savanna-la-Mar	312	807	145,712
TOTAL		4,244	10,991	2,705,827

Demography

Population (2011): 2,709,000.
Density (2011): persons per sq mi 638.3, persons per sq km 246.5.
Urban-rural (2009): urban 52.0%; rural 48.0%.
Sex distribution (2009[2]): male 49.28%; female 50.72%.
Age breakdown (2009[2]): under 15, 27.9%; 15–29, 25.0%; 30–44, 23.8%; 45–59, 12.4%; 60–74, 7.1%; 75 and over, 3.8%.
Population projection: (2020) 2,787,000; (2030) 2,800,000.
Doubling time: 67 years.
Ethnic composition (2001): black 91.6%; mixed race 6.2%; East Indian 0.9%; Chinese 0.2%; white 0.2%; other/unknown 0.9%.
Religious affiliation (2001): Protestant 61.2%, of which Church of God 23.8%[4], Seventh-day Adventist 10.8%, Pentecostal 9.5%; Roman Catholic 2.6%; other Christian 1.7%; Rastafarian 0.9%; nonreligious 20.9%; other 12.7%.
Major cities (2006): Kingston (2011[2]) 668,645[5]; Spanish Town 148,800; Portmore 103,900; Montego Bay 82,700; Mandeville 47,700; May Pen 44,800.

Vital statistics

Birth rate per 1,000 population (2009): 16.3 (world avg. 20.3).
Death rate per 1,000 population (2009): 6.5 (world avg. 8.5).
Natural increase rate per 1,000 population (2009): 9.8 (world avg. 11.8).
Total fertility rate (avg. births per childbearing woman; 2008): 2.30.
Marriage/divorce rates per 1,000 population (2009): 7.9/0.7.
Life expectancy at birth (2009): male 71.3 years; female 77.1 years.
Major causes of death per 100,000 population (2002): circulatory diseases 321, of which cerebrovascular disease 135; malignant neoplasms (cancers) 130; communicable diseases 106; diabetes 81.
Adult population (ages 15–49) *living with HIV* (2009): 1.7%[6] (world avg. 0.8%).

National economy

Budget (2009–10). Revenue: J$300,193,300,000 (tax revenue 88.6%, nontax revenue 7.0%, grants and other revenue 4.4%). Expenditures: J$421,458,500,000 (interest 44.8%, wages and salaries 30.0%, capital expenditures 8.2%).
Production (metric tons except as noted). Agriculture, forestry, fishing (2009): sugarcane 1,968,000, goat's milk 203,353, oranges 173,436, coconuts 163,002, chicken meat 106,363, bananas 89,312, pumpkins, squash, and gourds 40,801, dry chilies and peppers 10,565, coffee 3,064; livestock (number of live animals) 440,000 goats, 14,100,000 chickens; roundwood (2010) 825,626 cu m, of which fuelwood 66%; fisheries production 19,002 (from aquaculture 32%). Mining and quarrying (2008): bauxite 14,697,000; alumina 3,991,000; limestone (2007) 2,950,000; gypsum 238,000. Manufacturing (2008): cement 724,600,000; animal feeds (2005) 367,600; sugar 140,000; flour 132,561; molasses 62,654; beer 859,870 hectolitres; rum [and other distilled spirits] 265,349 hectolitres; cigarettes (2005) 724,313,000 units. Energy production (consumption): electricity (kW-hr; 2007) 7,782,000,000 (7,782,000,000); hard coal (metric tons; 2007) none (36,000); crude petroleum (barrels; 2007) none (6,267,000); petroleum products (metric tons; 2007) 838,000 (4,418,000); natural gas, none (none).
Land use as % of total land area (2009): in temporary crops or left fallow 11.1%, in permanent crops 9.2%, in pasture 21.1%, forest area 31.2%.
Population economically active (2010[7]): total 1,242,000; activity rate of total population 46.0% (participation rates: ages 14 and over, 62.0%; female 45.1%; unemployed 11.4%).

Price index (2005 = 100)

	2004	2005	2006	2007	2008	2009	2010
Consumer price index	86.9	100.0	108.4	118.6	144.7	158.6	178.7

Gross national income (GNI; 2010): U.S.$12,892,000,000 (U.S.$4,750 per capita); purchasing power parity GNI (U.S.$7,430 per capita).

Structure of gross domestic product and labour force

	2009 in value J$'000,000	% of total value	labour force[8]	% of labour force[8]
Agriculture	58,768.1	5.4	232,900	16.6
Mining	8,955.8	0.8	6,400	0.5
Manufacturing	86,367.5	8.0	85,200	6.1
Construction	76,496.5	7.1	116,500	8.3
Public utilities	37,916.0	3.5	8,500	0.6
Transp. and commun.	101,204.4	9.3	79,300	5.6
Trade, hotels	233,407.2	21.5	330,400	23.5
Finance, real estate	199,881.0	18.5	77,800	5.5
Pub. admin., defense	133,291.7	12.3	55,600	4.0
Services	61,418.5	5.7	240,700	17.1
Other	85,741.6[9]	7.9[9]	171,700[10]	12.2[10]
TOTAL	1,083,448.3	100.0	1,405,000	100.0

Public debt (external, outstanding; April 2010): U.S.$7,729,300,000.
Household income and expenditure. Average household size (2004) 3.5; average annual income per household: n.a.; expenditure (2006)[11]: food and nonalcoholic beverages 37.5%, housing/energy 12.8%, transportation 12.8%, restaurants and hotels 6.2%, household furnishings 4.9%.
Selected balance of payments data. Receipts from (U.S.$'000,000): tourism (2009) 1,925; remittances (2010) 2,011; foreign direct investment (FDI; 2008–10 avg.) 726; official development assistance (2009) 150. Disbursements for (U.S.$'000,000): tourism (2009) 216; remittances (2009–10) 270; FDI (2008–10 avg.) 68.

Foreign trade[12]

Balance of trade (current prices)

	2004	2005	2006	2007	2008	2009
U.S.$'000,000	–1,944	–2,581	–2,943	–3,841	–5,047	–3,123
% of total	37.8%	43.7%	40.8%	44.8%	50.2%	53.0%

Imports (2008): U.S.$8,465,000,000 (refined petroleum 29.5%; chemicals and chemical products 11.5%; food 10.5%; machinery and apparatus 10.2%; crude petroleum 10.2%). *Major import sources:* U.S. 39.4%; Trinidad and Tobago 17.5%; Venezuela 11.6%; China 3.8%; Brazil 2.6%.
Exports (2008): U.S.$2,439,000,000 (alumina 50.5%; refined petroleum 17.9%; food 10.6%, of which raw sugar 4.3%, coffee 1.1%; undenatured ethyl alcohol 6.2%; rum 1.8%; beer 1.4%). *Major export destinations:* U.S. 40.3%; Canada 10.6%; U.K. 9.2%; Neth. 7.8%; France 5.6%.

Transport and communications

Transport. Railroads (2008): route length 27 mi, 43 km[13]. Roads (2007): total length 13,745 mi, 22,121 km (paved [2005] 74%). Vehicles: passenger cars (2006) 373,742; trucks and buses (2004) 128,239. Air transport (2008)[14]: passenger-km 3,027,000,000; metric ton-km cargo 12,400,000.

Communications

Medium	date	number in '000s	units per 1,000 persons	Medium	date	number in '000s	units per 1,000 persons
Televisions	2003	1,006	374	PCs	2005	179	68
Telephones				Dailies	2009	115[15]	43[15]
Cellular	2010	3,103[16]	1,132[16]	Internet users	2009	1,581	582
Landline	2010	263	96	Broadband	2010	117[16]	43[16]

Education and health

Educational attainment (2001). Percentage of population age 15 and over having: no formal schooling 0.9%; primary education 25.5%; secondary 55.5%; higher 12.3%, of which university 4.2%; unknown 5.8%. *Literacy* (2008): population age 15 and over literate 85.9%; males 80.6%; females 90.8%.

Education (2004–05)

	teachers	students	student/ teacher ratio	enrollment rate (%)
Primary (age 6–11)	11,793	326,411	27.7	90
Secondary/Voc. (age 12–16)	13,336	246,332	18.5	78
Tertiary[17]	2,006	45,770	22.8	19 (age 17–21)

Health: physicians (2005) 2,253 (1 per 1,176 persons); hospital beds (2006) 5,326 (1 per 500 persons); infant mortality rate per 1,000 live births (2009) 16.7; undernourished population (2005–07) 100,000 (5% of total population based on the consumption of a minimum daily requirement of 1,860 calories).

Military

Total active duty personnel (November 2010): 2,830 (army 88.3%, coast guard 6.7%, air force 5.0%). *Military expenditure as percentage of GDP* (2009): 0.7%; per capita expenditure U.S.$33.

[1]All seats appointed by Governor-General. [2]January 1. [3]The parishes of Kingston and Saint Andrew are jointly administered from the Half Way Tree section of Saint Andrew. [4]Includes numerous denominations. [5]Urban population of the amalgamated Kingston and St. Andrew parishes. [6]Statistically derived midpoint of range. [7]April. [8]October. [9]Taxes on products less subsidies and less imputed bank service charges. [10]Includes 25,900 not adequately defined and 145,800 unemployed. [11]Weights of consumer price index components. [12]Imports f.o.b. in balance of trade and c.i.f. in commodities and trading partners. [13]Only operable railway transported bauxite. [14]Air Jamaica. [15]Circulation. [16]Subscribers. [17]2002–03.

Internet resources for further information:

- **Statistical Institute of Jamaica http://www.statinja.gov.jm**
- **Bank of Jamaica http://www.boj.org.jm**

Japan

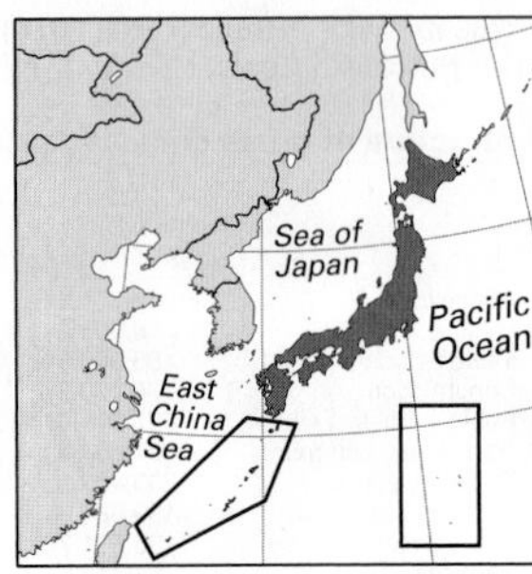

Official name: Nihon, or Nippon (Japan).
Form of government: constitutional monarchy with a national Diet consisting of two legislative houses (House of Councillors [242]; House of Representatives [480]).
Symbol of state: Emperor.
Head of government: Prime Minister.
Capital: Tokyo.
Official language: Japanese.
Official religion: none.
Monetary unit: yen (¥); valuation (Sept. 1, 2011) 1 U.S.$ = ¥76.98; 1 £ = ¥124.40.

Area and population

Regions Prefectures	Capitals	area sq mi	area sq km	population 2010[1] census
Chūbu		25,786	66,786	21,714,995
Aichi	Nagoya	1,991	5,156	7,408,499
Fukui	Fukui	1,617	4,189	806,470
Gifu	Gifu	4,092	10,598	2,081,147
Ishikawa	Kanazawa	1,616	4,185	1,170,040
Nagano	Nagano	5,245	13,585	2,152,736
Niigata	Niigata	4,858	12,582	2,374,922
Shizuoka	Shizuoka	3,003	7,779	3,765,044
Toyama	Toyama	1,640	4,247	1,093,365
Yamanashi	Kōfu	1,724	4,465	862,772
Chūgoku		12,322	31,913	7,561,899
Hiroshima	Hiroshima	3,273	8,477	2,860,769
Okayama	Okayama	2,746	7,112	1,944,986
Shimane	Matsue	2,590	6,707	716,354
Tottori	Tottori	1,354	3,507	588,418
Yamaguchi	Yamaguchi	2,359	6,110	1,451,372
Hokkaidō		32,221	83,453	5,507,456
Hokkaidō	Sapporo	32,221	83,453	5,507,456
Kantō		12,522	32,432	42,607,376
Chiba	Chiba	1,991	5,156	6,217,119
Gumma	Maebashi	2,457	6,363	2,008,170
Ibaraki	Mito	2,354	6,096	2,968,865
Kanagawa	Yokohama	932	2,415	9,049,500
Saitama	Saitama	1,466	3,797	7,194,957
Tochigi	Utsunomiya	2,474	6,408	2,007,014
Tokyo-to	Tokyo	848	2,197	13,161,751
Kinki		12,783	33,108	22,755,030
Hyōgo	Kōbe	3,240	8,392	5,589,177
Kyōto-fu	Kyōto	1,781	4,613	2,636,704
Mie	Tsu	2,230	5,776	1,854,742
Nara	Nara	1,425	3,691	1,399,978
Ōsaka-fu	Ōsaka	731	1,893	8,862,896
Shiga	Ōtsu	1,551	4,017	1,410,272
Wakayama	Wakayama	1,825	4,726	1,001,261
Kyūshū		17,157	44,436	14,596,977
Fukuoka	Fukuoka	1,919	4,971	5,072,804
Kagoshima	Kagoshima	3,547	9,187	1,706,428
Kumamoto	Kumamoto	2,859	7,404	1,817,410
Miyazaki	Miyazaki	2,986	7,734	1,135,120
Nagasaki	Nagasaki	1,580	4,092	1,426,594
Ōita	Ōita	2,447	6,338	1,196,409
Okinawa	Naha	877	2,271	1,392,503
Saga	Saga	942	2,439	849,709
Shikoku		7,259	18,802	3,977,205
Ehime	Matsuyama	2,192	5,676	1,430,957
Kagawa	Takamatsu	724	1,876	995,779
Kōchi	Kōchi	2,743	7,105	764,596
Tokushima	Tokushima	1,600	4,145	785,873
Tohoku		25,825	66,886	9,335,088
Akita	Akita	4,483	11,612	1,085,878
Aomori	Aomori	3,709	9,606	1,373,164
Fukushima	Fukushima	5,321	13,782	2,028,752
Iwate	Morioka	5,899	15,278	1,330,530
Miyagi	Sendai	2,813	7,285	2,347,975
Yamagata	Yamagata	3,600	9,323	1,168,789
TOTAL		145,898[2]	377,873[2]	128,056,026

Demography

Population (2011): 127,937,000.
Density (2011): persons per sq mi 876.9, persons per sq km 338.6.
Urban-rural (2009): urban 66.6%; rural 33.4%.
Sex distribution (2010[3]): male 48.69%; female 51.31%.
Age breakdown (2010[3]): under 15, 13.3%; 15–29, 15.9%; 30–44, 20.9%; 45–59, 19.1%; 60–74, 19.7%; 75–84, 8.1%; 85 and over, 3.0%.
Population projection: (2020) 126,360,000; (2030) 121,717,000.
Composition by nationality (2006): Japanese 98.4%; Korean 0.5%; Chinese 0.4%; Brazilian 0.2%; other 0.5%.
Immigration/Emigration (2007[4]): permanent immigrants/registered aliens in Japan 2,152,973, from Taiwan, Hong Kong, Macau, and China 28.2%, from North and South Korea 27.6%, from Brazil 14.7%, from the Philippines 9.4%, from Peru 2.8%, from the U.S. 2.4%, from Thailand 1.9%, from Vietnam 1.7%, other 11.3%. Japanese nationals living abroad 1,085,671, in the U.S. 34.5%, in China 11.8%, in the U.K. 5.9%, in Australia 5.8%, in Brazil 5.7%, in Canada 4.4%, in Thailand 3.9%, other 28.0%. Permanent expatriates (including those with dual nationality) 339,774, of which living in the U.S. 37.4%, in Brazil 17.6%, in Australia 9.0%, in Canada 8.8%.
Major cities (2010[3]): Tokyo 8,843,000; Yokohama 3,681,000; Ōsaka 2,668,000; Nagoya 2,259,000; Sapporo 1,910,000; Kōbe 1,538,000; Kyōto 1,464,000; Fukuoka 1,461,000; Kawasaki 1,420,000; Saitama 1,229,100; Hiroshima 1,173,000; Sendai 1,037,000.
Major metropolitan areas (2009): Tokyo 36,507,000; Ōsaka-Kōbe 11,325,000; Nagoya 3,257,000; Fukuoka–Kita-Kyūshū 2,809,000; Sapporo 2,673,000; Sendai 2,362,000; Hiroshima 2,079,000; Kyōto 1,805,000.

Other principal cities (2010[1])

	population		population		population
Akita	323,363	Kawagoe	342,714	Ōita	473,955
Amagasaki	453,608	Kawaguchi	500,311	Okayama	709,622
Asahikawa	347,275	Kita-Kyūshū	977,288	Okazaki	372,472
Chiba	962,130	Kōchi	343,416	Ōtsu	337,629
Fujisawa	409,734	Koriyama	338,772	Sagamihara	717,561
Fukuyama	461,471	Koshigaya	326,423	Sakai	842,134
Funabashi	609,081	Kumamoto	734,294	Shizuoka	716,328
Gifu	413,239	Kurashiki	475,421	Suita	355,567
Hachiōji	579,799	Kurume	302,323	Takamatsu	419,291
Hamamatsu	800,912	Machida	426,827	Takasaki	371,352
Higashi-Ōsaka	509,632	Maebashi	340,390	Takatsuki	357,423
Himeji	536,338	Matsudo	484,639	Tokorozawa	341,900
Hirakata	407,997	Matsuyama	517,088	Toyama	421,890
Ichikawa	474,926	Miyazaki	400,352	Toyohashi	376,861
Ichinomiya	375,621	Nagano	381,533	Toyonaka	389,359
Iwaki	342,198	Nagasaki	443,469	Toyota	421,552
Kagoshima	605,940	Naha	315,765	Utsunomiya	511,296
Kanazawa	462,478	Nara	366,528	Wakayama	369,400
Kashiwa	404,079	Niigata	812,192	Yokkaichi	307,807
Kasugai	305,662	Nishinomiya	482,790	Yokosuka	418,448

Religious affiliation (2003): Shintō and related beliefs 84.2%[5]; Buddhism and related beliefs 73.6%[5]; Christian 1.7%; Muslim 0.1%; other 7.8%.
Households (2007). Total households (2009) 48,013,000; average household size (2010[3]) 3.1; composition of households 1 person 28.2%, 2 persons 28.0%, 3 persons 18.5%, 4 persons 16.2%, 5 persons 6.1%, 6 or more persons 3.0%. Family households (2009) 32,823,000 (68.4%); nonfamily 15,189,000 (31.6%).

Type of household (2008)

Total number of occupied dwelling units: 49,598,300

	number of dwellings	percentage of total
by kind of dwelling		
exclusively for living	48,281,000	97.3
mixed use	1,523,600[6]	3.3[6]
combined with nondwelling	81,400[6]	0.2[6]
detached house	27,450,000	55.3
apartment building	20,684,000	41.7
tenement (substandard or overcrowded building)	1,330,000	2.7
other	134,000	0.3
by legal tenure of householder		
owned	30,316,000	61.1
rented	17,770,000	35.8
other	1,512,300	3.1
by kind of amenities		
flush toilet	45,008,500	90.7
bathroom	47,386,200	95.5
by year of construction		
1950 and earlier	1,858,300	3.7
1951–70	5,052,400	10.2
1971–80	8,969,000	18.1
1981–90	9,957,600	20.1
1991–2000	11,582,800	23.3
2001–2008 (Sept.)	8,624,100	17.4
not reported/unknown	3,554,100	7.2

Mobility (2009). Percentage of total population moving: within a prefecture 1.9%; between prefectures 2.2%.

Vital statistics

Birth rate per 1,000 population (2009): 8.5 (world avg. 20.3).
Death rate per 1,000 population (2009): 9.1 (world avg. 8.5).
Natural increase rate per 1,000 population (2009): –0.6 (world avg. 11.8).
Total fertility rate (avg. births per childbearing woman; 2009): 1.37.
Marriage/divorce rates per 1,000 population (2009): 5.6 (average age at first marriage, men 30.4 years; women 28.6 years)/2.0.
Life expectancy at birth (2009): male 79.6 years; female 86.4 years.
Major causes of death per 100,000 population (2009): malignant neoplasms (cancers) 269.8; heart disease 141.7; cerebrovascular disease 95.9; pneumonia 87.8; accidents 29.6; suicide 24.1; renal failure 17.8; diseases of the liver 12.5; pulmonary disease 12.0; diabetes mellitus 11.0.

Social indicators

Educational attainment (2008). Percentage of population ages 25–64 having: no formal schooling through upper secondary education 57%; higher vocational 19%; university 24%.

Distribution of income (2000)

percentage of average household income by quintile

1	2	3	4	5 (highest)
11.2	15.3	18.8	23.0	31.7

Quality of working life. Average hours worked per week (2010[7]): 40.6. Annual rate of deaths/nonfatal injuries per 100,000 workers (2008): 1.9/177.5. Proportion of labour force insured for damages or income loss resulting from injury, permanent disability, and death (2005): 53.1%. Average man-days lost to labour stoppages per 1,000 workdays (2006): 1.8. Average duration of journey to work (2008): 27.8 minutes.
Access to services (2004). Proportion of households having access to: safe public water supply 96.9%; public sewage system *c.* 68%.
Social participation. Eligible voters participating in last national election (August 2009): 69%. Adult population working as volunteers at least once

in the year (2006) 26.2%. Trade union membership in total workforce (2008): 15.8%.

Social deviance (2009). Offense rate per 100,000 population for: homicide 0.9; robbery 3.5; larceny and theft 101.9. Incidence in general population of: alcoholism per 100,000 population, n.a.; drug and substance abuse (2005) 0.1. Rate of suicide per 100,000 population: 24.1.

Leisure/use of personal time

Discretionary daily activities (2006)
(Population age 10 years and over)

	weekly average hrs./min.
Total discretionary daily time	6:23
of which	
Hobbies and amusements	0:45
Sports	0:15
Learning (except schoolwork)	0:12
Social activities	0:22
Radio, television, newspapers, and magazines	2:24
Rest and relaxation	1:25
Other activities	1:00

Favourite sports according to the rates of participation (2007): males—jogging/marathon 24.9%, bowling 24.1%, fishing 16.4%, baseball 15.9%, gymnastics 14.5%, swimming in pool 13.5%; females—gymnastics 24.1%, bowling 21.4%, jogging/marathon 16.5%, swimming in pool 14.5%, aerobics 7.8%, badminton 7.4%.

Favourite amusements according to the rates of participation (2007): males—lotteries 40.7%, karaoke 40.3%, home video games 32.2%; females—karaoke 37.8%, lotteries 36.1%, card games 28.5%.

Favourite hobbies according to the rates of participation (2007): average for both sexes—personal computer–related activities *c.* 37%, listening to music *c.* 34%, gardening *c.* 28%.

Favourite excursions according to the rates of participation (2007): average for both sexes—taking part in domestic sightseeing tours *c.* 52%, going for a drive *c.* 46%, visiting zoos, museums, aquariums, or botanical gardens *c.* 38%, visiting amusement parks *c.* 26%, picnicking/hiking *c.* 24%.

Material well-being (2007). Households possessing: automobile (2003–04) 81.6%; air conditioner (2002) 87.2%; personal computer 85.0%.

National economy

Gross national income (GNI; 2010): U.S.$5,369,116,000,000 (U.S.$42,150 per capita); purchasing power parity GNI (U.S.$34,790 per capita).

Structure of gross domestic product and labour force

	2008		2010[8]	
	in value ¥'000,000,000	% of total value	labour force	% of labour force
Agriculture, forestry, fishing	7,372.3	1.5	2,500,000	3.8
Mining and quarrying	407.8	0.1	…	…
Manufacturing	100,279.3	19.8	10,310,000	15.6
Construction	30,923.8	6.1	4,960,000	7.5
Public utilities	9,007.7	1.8	…	…
Transportation and communications	34,001.1	6.7	5,390,000	8.1
Trade, hotels	69,617.1	13.8	14,400,000	21.8
Finance, real estate	91,200.7	18.1	2,910,000	4.4
Pub. admin., defense	48,220.1	9.5	2,170,000	3.3
Services	124,867.6	24.7	18,880,000	28.5
Other	–10,785.4[9]	–2.1[9]	4,620,000[10]	7.0[10]
TOTAL	505,111.9[11]	100.0	66,150,000[11]	100.0

Budget (2009–10)[12]. Revenue: ¥92,299,000,000,000 (government bonds 48.0%, income tax 13.7%, VAT 10.4%, corporate taxes 6.4%, other 21.5%). Expenditures: ¥92,299,000,000,000 (social security 29.5%, debt service 22.4%, public works 6.3%, education and science 6.1%, national defense 5.2%).

Financial aggregates

	2004	2005	2006	2007	2008	2009	2010
Exchange rate[4], ¥ per:							
U.S. dollar	104.12	117.97	118.95	114.00	90.75	92.06	81.45
£	201.09	203.12	233.49	228.39	132.30	149.08	127.51
SDR	161.70	168.61	178.95	180.15	139.78	144.32	125.44
International reserves (U.S.$)							
Total (excl. gold; '000,000)	833,891	834,275	879,682	952,784	1,009,365	1,022,236	1,061,490
SDRs ('000,000)	2,839	2,584	2,812	3,033	3,032	20,968	20,626
Reserve pos. in IMF ('000,000)	6,789	2,877	1,934	1,395	2,658	4,313	4,608
Foreign exchange ('000,000)	824,264	828,813	874,936	948,356	1,003,674	996,955	1,036,256
Gold ('000,000 fine troy oz)	24.60	24.60	24.60	24.60	24.60	24.60	24.60
% world reserves	…	…	2.5	2.6	2.6	2.5	2.5
Interest and prices							
Central bank discount (%)[4]	0.10	0.10	0.40	0.75	0.30	0.30	0.30
Govt. bond yield (%)	1.50	1.36	1.73	1.65	1.45	1.34	1.15
Share prices (2005 = 100)	88.1	100.0	128.2	131.1	93.5	68.4	69.8
Balance of payments (U.S.$'000,000,000)							
Balance of visible trade	+132.13	+93.96	+81.30	+104.75	+38.13	+43.63	+90.97
Imports, f.o.b.	–406.87	–473.61	–534.51	–573.34	–708.34	–501.65	–639.10
Exports, f.o.b.	539.00	567.57	615.81	678.09	746.47	545.28	730.08
Balance of invisibles	+39.93	+71.82	+89.22	+105.74	+118.50	+98.56	+104.78
Balance of payments, current account	+172.06	+165.78	+170.52	+210.49	+156.63	+142.19	+195.75

Household income and expenditure. Average household size (2010[8])[13] 3.1; average annual disposable income per household (2009) ¥5,134,800 (U.S.$55,668); sources of income (1994): wages and salaries 59.0%, transfer payments 20.5%, self-employment 12.8%, other 7.7%; expenditure (2010[8])[13]: food 23.8%, transportation and communications 14.5%, culture and recreation 11.7%, housing 6.9%, fuel, light, and water charges 6.8%, medical care 3.8%, furniture and household utensils 3.8%, clothing and footwear 3.0%, education 2.6%.

Public debt (June 2011): U.S.$11,687,100,000,000.

Population economically active (2010[8]): total 66,150,000; activity rate of total population 52.0% (participation rates: ages 15–64, 74.3%; female 42.1%; unemployed [August 2011] 4.3%).

Price and earnings indexes (2005 = 100)

	2004	2005	2006	2007	2008	2009	2010
Consumer price index	100.3	100.0	100.2	100.3	101.7	100.3	99.6
Monthly earnings index	99.4	100.0	100.6	102.3	101.4	98.9	99.8

Retail and wholesale trade (2004)

	no. of establish-ments	avg. no. of em-ployees	annual sales (¥'000,000,000)
Retail trade	1,238,296	7,767,000	133,285
Food and beverages	444,693	3,154,000	41,434
Grocery	38,536	855,000	17,099
Liquors	60,194	177,000	3,330
General merchandise	5,555	541,000	16,897
Department stores	1,982	517,000	16,392
Motor vehicles and bicycles	87,009	542,000	16,189
Furniture and home furnishings	115,135	517,000	11,371
Apparel and accessories	177,881	698,000	11,009
Gasoline service stations	62,557	400,000	10,937
Books and stationery	54,338	636,000	4,745
Wholesale trade	375,378	3,805,000	405,646
Machinery and equipment	89,913	1,018,000	98,795
Motor vehicles and parts	18,078	180,000	15,109
General machinery except electrical	33,075	308,000	24,043
General merchandise	1,245	38,000	49,031
Farm, livestock, and fishery products	39,520	406,000	42,628
Food and beverages	45,069	482,000	43,819
Building materials	84,063	712,000	87,387
Minerals and metals	17,063	185,000	40,962
Chemicals	15,191	151,000	20,940
Textiles, apparel, and accessories	30,322	307,000	18,898
Drugs and toilet goods	18,709	245,000	22,023

Production (metric tons except as noted). Agriculture, forestry, fishing (2009): rice 10,592,500, cow's milk 7,909,490, sugar beets 3,649,000, hen's eggs 2,505,000, potatoes 2,398,000, sugarcane 1,515,000, chicken meat 1,394,480, pig meat 1,309,770, cabbages 1,300,000, dry onions 1,154,000, sweet potatoes 1,026,000, tangerines and mandarin oranges 1,018,000, apples 845,600, tomatoes 716,900, wheat 674,200, cucumbers 620,200, carrots and turnips 620,000, green onions 570,000, lettuce 535,000, cattle meat 517,020, pears 351,500, eggplant 349,200, spinach 288,000, persimmons 258,000, pumpkins 235,000, soybeans 229,900, grapes 210,000, yams 190,000, strawberries 184,700, taro 182,000, peaches and nectarines 150,700, chilies 142,700, apricots 115,200, tea 86,000, mushrooms 64,140, ginger 52,000, string beans 48,000, kiwi 35,000, chestnuts 21,700, garlic 20,500, cherries 18,000; cut flowers (number of flowers [2010]) 4,366,000; livestock (number of live animals) 9,899,000 pigs, 4,423,000 cattle, 285,349,000 chickens; roundwood (2010) 16,710,801 cu m, of which fuelwood 0.5%; fisheries production (2010)[14, 15] 4,672,000, of which mackerel 420,000, bonito 274,000, pollack 235,000, squid 225,000, tuna 171,000 (from aquaculture [including aquatic plants] 20% [of which laver 302,000, oysters 149,000, yellowtail 139,000, wakame (seaweed) 13,000, pearls 21,000]); whales caught (2009–10) 507. Mining and quarrying (2009): limestone 132,350,000; gypsum 5,800,000 (world rank: 6); dolomite 3,122,000; silica (industrial sand and gravel) 2,856,000 (world rank: 9); pyrophyllite 340,000; magnesium 13,000; iodine 9,600 (world rank: 2); gold 7,708 kg; silver 1,500 kg.

Manufacturing enterprises (2005)

	avg. no. of persons engaged	annual wages as a % of avg. of all mfg. wages	value added (U.S.$'000,000)
Food products	1,067,940	60.5	80,059
Paints, soaps, and pharmaceuticals	203,164	148.4	65,407
Motor vehicle parts	533,865	142.9	61,424
Special purpose machinery	481,666	101.0	58,629
Motor vehicles	157,138	220.1	56,461
Iron and steel	136,210	167.6	47,941
General purpose machinery	376,192	117.2	45,210
Plastics	393,660	79.3	39,458
Fabricated metal products (not structural)	433,195	77.8	39,340
Electronic valves and tubes	247,858	148.4	37,958
Television and radio receivers, sound or video equipment	268,461	128.0	36,464
Base chemicals	105,820	174.1	33,896
Printing	328,159	76.0	29,260
Publishing	…	…	…
Structural metal products	259,709	66.5	24,878
Bricks, cement, and ceramics	220,148	63.8	24,306
Paper and paper products	197,817	90.7	23,363
Medical appliances and instruments	155,601	117.2	19,779
Beverages	64,097	97.0	18,609
Office machines and computers	118,012	142.7	15,170
Domestic appliances	83,741	115.5	12,493
Rubber products	108,272	108.8	11,985
Electricity distribution and control apparatus	114,290	107.8	10,216

Energy production (consumption): electricity (kW-hr; 2009–10) 924,330,-000,000 (906,680,000,000); coal (metric tons; 2008) 1,300,000[16] ([2007] 186,983,000); crude petroleum (barrels; 2009–10) 5,778,080 ([2009] 1,552,-630,500); petroleum products (metric tons; 2007) 171,212,000 (170,147,000); natural gas (cu m; 2009–10) 3,549,000,000 (94,000,000,000). Composition of energy supply by source (2007): crude oil and petroleum products 43.9%; coal 22.1%; natural gas 17.9%; nuclear power 10.2%; hydroelectric power 2.8%; other, including solar and geothermal power, 3.1%.

Selected balance of payments data. Receipts from (U.S.$'000,000): tourism (2009) 10,329; remittances (2010) 1,911; foreign direct investment (FDI; 2008–10 avg.) 11,705. Disbursements for (U.S.$'000,000): tourism (2009) 25,199; remittances (2009) 4,069; FDI (2008–10 avg.) 86,327.

Land use as % of total land area (2009): in temporary crops or left fallow 10.1%, in permanent crops 0.9%, in pasture (2007) 1.7%, forest area 68.5%.

Foreign trade[17]

Balance of trade (current prices)

	2005	2006	2007	2008	2009	2010
¥'000,000,000	+8,810	+8,213	+11,077	+2,059	+2,805	+6,782
% of total	7.2%	5.7%	7.1%	1.3%	2.7%	5.3%

Imports (2008): ¥78,815,000,000,000 (mineral fuels 35.1%, of which crude petroleum 20.4%, LNG 5.9%, coal 3.9%, refined petroleum 3.1%; machinery and apparatus 17.9%, of which nonelectrical machinery/apparatus/parts 4.6%, office machines/computers/parts 3.2%, microcircuits and transistors 3.1%; chemicals and chemical products 7.2%; food 7.0%; metal ores and metal scrap [particularly iron and copper] 4.4%; apparel and clothing accessories 3.4%; nonferrous base metals [particularly aluminum and platinum-group] 3.1%; road vehicles 2.1%). *Major import sources:* China 18.8%; U.S. 10.4%; Saudi Arabia 6.7%; U.A.E. 6.2%; Australia 6.2%; Indonesia 4.3%; South Korea 3.9%; Qatar 3.5%; Malaysia 3.0%; unspecified Asia (probably Taiwan) 2.9%.

Exports (2008): ¥80,766,000,000,000 (machinery and apparatus 37.2%, of which machinery specialized for particular industries 6.4%, microcircuits, transistors, photosensitive devices 5.7%, general industrial machinery 5.5%, telecommunications, sound recording, and reproducing equipment 4.4%, power-generating machinery 3.8%, office machines/computers/parts 3.1%; road vehicles 21.8%, of which passenger cars 14.8%, parts for road vehicles 3.9%; chemicals and chemical products 8.8%; iron and steel 5.6%; professional, scientific, and controlling instruments 2.8%). *Major export destinations:* U.S. 17.8%; China 16.0%; South Korea 7.6%; unspecified Asia (probably Taiwan) 5.9%; Hong Kong 5.2%; Thailand 3.8%; Germany 3.4%; Singapore 3.1%; Netherlands 2.7%; Australia 2.2%.

Trade by commodity group (2007)

	imports		exports	
SITC group	U.S.$'000,000	%	U.S.$'000,000	%
00 Food and live animals	45,475	7.3	…	…
01 Beverages and tobacco	5,852	0.9	…	…
02 Crude materials, excluding fuels	49,539	8.0	8,953	1.3
03 Mineral fuels, lubricants, and related materials	172,785	27.8	9,280	1.3
04 Animal and vegetable oils, fats, and waxes	…	…	…	…
05 Chemicals and related products, n.e.s.	45,521	7.3	65,191	9.1
06 Basic manufactures	60,475	9.7	83,628	11.7
07 Machinery and transport equipment	150,712	24.2	451,952	63.3
08 Miscellaneous manufactured articles	79,539	12.8	52,492	7.3
09 Goods not classified by kind/remainder	12,345	2.0	42,831	6.0
TOTAL	622,243	100.0	714,327	100.0

Direction of trade (2007)

	imports		exports	
	U.S.$'000,000	%	U.S.$'000,000	%
Africa	14,768	2.4	11,492	1.6
Asia	383,453	61.6	374,138	52.4
Eastern Asia	176,592	28.4	247,800	34.7
Southeastern Asia	87,134	14.0	87,168	12.2
Western Asia	101,513	16.3	28,345	4.0
Australia	31,252	5.0	14,203	2.0
Europe (excl. Russia)	72,021	11.6	108,971	15.2
Russia	10,563	1.7	10,770	1.5
North America	82,464	13.2	156,223	21.9
Latin America and Caribbean	22,797	3.7	33,266	4.7
REMAINDER	4,925	0.8	5,264	0.7
TOTAL	622,243	100.0	714,327	100.0

Transport and communications

Transport. Railroads (2008): route length (2009) 16,426 mi, 26,435 km; passengers carried 22,976,000; passenger-km 404,590,000,000; metric ton-km cargo 22,260,000,000. Roads (2008): total length 747,991 mi, 1,203,777 km (paved 80%); passenger-km 905,910,000,000[18]; metric ton-km cargo 346,420,000,000. Vehicles (2010[19]): passenger cars 58,005,000; trucks and buses 15,751,000. Air transport (2009–10): passengers carried (2009) 99,300,000; passenger-km 124,865,000,000; metric ton-km cargo 7,398,519,000.

Distribution of traffic (2008)

	cargo carried ('000,000 tons)	% of national total	passengers carried ('000,000)	% of national total
Road	4,718	91.7	66,774	74.2
Rail (intercity)	46	0.9	22,976	25.6
Inland water	379	7.4	99	0.1
Air	1	0.0	91	0.1
TOTAL	5,144	100.0	89,940	100.0

Urban transport (2000)[20]: passengers carried 57,719,000, of which by rail 34,020,000, by road 19,466,000, by subway 4,233,000.

Communications

Medium	date	number in '000s	units per 1,000 persons	Medium	date	number in '000s	units per 1,000 persons
Televisions	2003	107,527	842	PCs	2005	86,389	675
Telephones				Dailies	2009	50,353[21]	395[21]
Cellular	2010	120,709[22]	954[22]	Internet users	2009	99,144	780
Landline	2010	40,419	319	Broadband	2010	34,055[22]	269[22]

Radio and television broadcasting (2007): total radio stations 1,703, of which commercial 807; total television stations 15,386, of which commercial 8,115. Commercial broadcasting hours (by percentage of programs): reports—radio 12.7%, television 19.9%; education—radio 2.3%, television 12.4%; culture—radio 12.6%, television 25.1%; entertainment—radio 69.8%, television 36.2%. Advertisements (daily average): radio 137, television 500.

Other communications media (2008–09)

	titles		titles
Print (2007–08)		**Cinema (2008)**	
Books (new)	78,013	Feature films	806
of which		Domestic	418
Social sciences	16,196	Foreign	388
Fiction	12,759		
Arts	10,921		traffic ('000)
Engineering	8,623		
Natural sciences	6,563	**Post**	
History	5,131	Postal offices	24,539
Philosophy	3,933	Mail	20,114,000[11]
Magazines/journals (2006–07)	4,511	Domestic	20,054,000
Weekly	133	International	59,800
Monthly	2,620	Parcels	2,806,200
		Domestic	2,804,700
		International	1,500

Education and health

Literacy: total population age 15 and over literate, virtually 100%.

Education (2007–08)

	teachers	students	student/ teacher ratio	enrollment rate (%)
Primary (age 6–11)	391,967	7,166,285	18.3	100
Secondary/Voc. (age 12–17)	607,062	7,355,678	12.1	98
Tertiary	516,232	3,938,632	7.6	58 (age 18–22)

Health (2008): physicians 283,915 (1 per 450 persons); dentists 98,063 (1 per 1,302 persons); nurses and assistant nurses 1,252,224 (1 per 102 persons); pharmacists 249,251 (1 per 512 persons); midwives 27,789 (1 per 4,595 persons); hospital beds 1,609,403 (1 per 79 persons); infant mortality rate per 1,000 live births (2009) 2.4; undernourished population (2004–06) less than 5.0% of total population.

Military

Total active duty personnel (November 2010): 247,746 (army 61.2%, navy 18.4%, air force 19.0%, central staff 1.4%); reserve 56,379. U.S. troops (November 2010) 35,598[23]. *Military expenditure as percentage of GDP* (2009): 1.0%; per capita expenditure U.S.$399.

[1]October 1. [2]Region areas do not sum to total given because of particular excluded inland water areas; total area in 2010 per *Statistical Handbook of Japan 2011* equals 145,927 sq mi (377,950 sq km). [3]August 1. [4]End of year. [5]Many Japanese practice both Shintōism and Buddhism. [6]2003. [7]July. [8]August. [9]Statistical discrepancy and import duties less imputed bank service charges and less consumption taxes for gross capital formation. [10]Includes 1,250,000 not adequately defined and 3,370,000 unemployed. [11]Detail does not add to total given because of rounding. [12]Budgeted funds for General Account. [13]Households with two or more persons. [14]Fisheries production (2009) 4,633,927 (from aquaculture 17%); aquatic plants production (2009) 560,626 (from aquaculture 81%). [15]Excludes production in Iwate, Miyagi, and Fukushima prefectures. [16]All major coal mines were closed by 2002 but 8 smaller mines were still operational in 2008. [17]Imports c.i.f.; exports f.o.b. [18]Passenger cars 769,080,000,000; trucks and buses 136,830,000,000. [19]June 1. [20]Tokyo, Nagoya, and Ōsaka metropolis traffic range only. [21]Circulation of daily newspapers. [22]Subscribers. [23]Includes 2,860 troops deployed in Afghanistan and Iraq as of June 2010.

Internet resources for further information:

- **Bank of Japan http://www.boj.or.jp/en/index.htm**
- **Statistics Bureau and Statistical Research and Training Institute http://www.stat.go.jp/english/index.htm**

Jersey

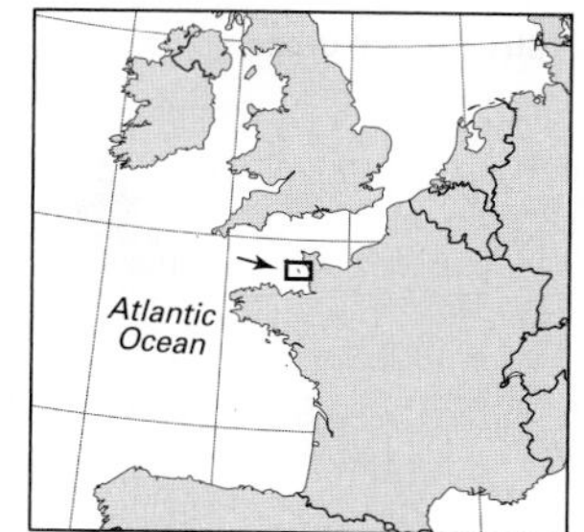

Official name: Bailiwick of Jersey.
Political status: crown dependency (United Kingdom) with one legislative house (Assembly of the States of Jersey [58[1]]).
Head of state: British Monarch represented by Lieutenant Governor.
Head of government: Chief Minister[2] assisted by the Council of Ministers.
Capital: Saint Helier.
Official language: English[3].
Official religion: none.
Monetary unit: Jersey pound (£J); valuation (Sept. 1, 2011) 1 Jersey pound = U.S.$1.62; at par with the British pound.

Area and population

Parishes	area sq mi	area sq km	population 2001 census
Grouville	3.0	7.8	4,702
St. Brelade	4.9	12.8	10,134
St. Clement	1.6	4.2	8,196
St. Helier	4.1	10.6	28,310
St. John	3.4	8.7	2,618
St. Lawrence	3.7	9.5	4,702
St. Martin	3.8	9.9	3,628
St. Mary	2.5	6.5	1,591
St. Ouen	5.8	15.0	3,803
St. Peter	4.5	11.6	4,293
St. Saviour	3.6	9.3	12,491
Trinity	4.7	12.3	2,718
TOTAL	45.6	118.2	87,186

Demography

Population (2011): 94,100.
Density (2011): persons per sq mi 2,063, persons per sq km 796.0.
Urban-rural (2009)[4]: urban 31.3%; rural 68.7%.
Sex distribution (2009): male 49.03%; female 50.97%.
Age breakdown (2009): under 15, 17.0%; 15–29, 21.1%; 30–44, 20.3%; 45–59, 21.3%; 60–74, 13.6%; 75–84, 4.8%; 85 and over, 1.9%.
Population projection: (2020) 99,000; (2030) 102,000.
Population by place of birth (2010)[5]: Jersey *c.* 47%; United Kingdom, Guernsey, or Isle of Man *c.* 41%; Portugal *c.* 4%; Poland *c.* 1%; other *c.* 7%.
Religious affiliation (2000)[4]: Christian 86.0%, of which Anglican 44.1%, Roman Catholic 14.6%, other Protestant 6.9%, unaffiliated Christian 20.1%; nonreligious/atheist 13.4%; other 0.6%.
Major towns (2001)[6]: St. Helier 28,310; St. Saviour 12,491; St. Brelade 10,134.

Vital statistics

Birth rate per 1,000 population (2010): 11.5 (world avg. 19.2).
Death rate per 1,000 population (2010): 8.6 (world avg. 8.2).
Natural increase rate per 1,000 population (2010): 2.9 (world avg. 11.0).
Total fertility rate (avg. births per childbearing woman; 2008): 1.57.
Marriage/divorce rates per 1,000 population: (2007) 6.5/(2001) 3.2.
Life expectancy at birth (2008): male 77.1 years; female 82.3 years.
Major causes of death per 100,000 population (2004–08 avg.): diseases of the circulatory system *c.* 270; malignant neoplasms (cancers) *c.* 223; diseases of the respiratory system *c.* 100; diseases of the digestive system *c.* 33.

National economy

Budget (2009). Revenue: £J 674,000,000 (income tax 75.2%, import duties 7.6%, VAT 7.0%, stamp duties 3.6%, other 6.6%). Expenditures: £J 666,954,000 (current expenditure 93.1%, capital expenditure 6.9%).
Production. Agriculture, forestry, fishing (value of export crops in £J '000; 2010): potatoes 31,450, tomatoes (2008) 3,400, narcissus 876, zucchini 584, narcissus bulbs 340, lilies 161, cauliflower 96; livestock (number of live animals; 2010) 5,204 cattle (of which 2,970 dairy heifers), 853 horses, 20,560 chickens; roundwood, n.a.; fisheries production (metric tons; 2009) 2,261 (including brown crabs 361, scallops 361, lobsters 177, spider crabs 177; from aquaculture 45% [including oysters 903]). Mining and quarrying: n.a. Manufacturing: light industry, mainly electrical goods, textiles, and clothing. Energy production (consumption): electricity (kW-hr; 2008) 38,390,600 (651,821,000); crude petroleum, none (n.a.); petroleum products (metric tons; 2008) n.a. (102,586); natural gas, none (n.a.).
Gross national income (2009): U.S.$5,757,000,000 (*c.* U.S.$62,474 per capita).

Structure of gross value added[7] and labour force

	2009 in value £J '000,000	2009 % of total value	2009 labour force	2009 % of labour force
Agriculture, fishing	62	1.7	2,210	3.9
Mining and quarrying	...	... }	5,240	9.1
Construction	226	6.3 }		
Manufacturing	53	1.5	1,360	2.4
Public utilities	37	1.0	530	0.9
Transp. and commun.	167	4.6	2,810[8]	4.9[8]
Trade, hotels, restaurants	378	10.4	14,540	25.4
Finance, real estate, services[9, 10]	1,859	51.3	22,810	39.9
Pub. admin., defense	304	8.4	6,750	11.8
Other	535[11]	14.8[11]	960[12]	1.7[12]
TOTAL	3,621	100.0	57,210	100.0

Household income and expenditure (2009–10). Average household size (2007) 2.3; average/median annual gross household income £J 44,720 (U.S.$70,876)/£J 34,684 (U.S.$54,970); sources of income: n.a.; expenditure: housing and energy 28.3%, transportation 13.0%, recreation 11.9%, food 10.2%, restaurants and hotels 7.1%, household furnishings 6.2%.
Population economically active (2008): total 54,210; activity rate of total population *c.* 59% (participation rates: ages 15–64 [male], 15–59 [female] *c.* 85%; female *c.* 48%; unemployed [June 2011] 2.2%).

Price and earnings indexes (2005 = 100)

	2004	2005	2006	2007	2008	2009	2010
Consumer price index[13]	96.5	100.0	102.9	107.3	113.4	113.0	116.2
Weekly earnings index	96.2	100.0	103.8	109.4	113.2	116.6	117.9

Public debt: none.
Selected balance of payments data. Receipts from (U.S.$'000,000): tourism (2010) 356; remittances, n.a.; foreign direct investment (FDI) n.a. Disbursements for (U.S.$'000,000): tourism, n.a.; remittances, n.a.; FDI, n.a.
Land use as % of total land area (2007)[4]: in temporary crops or left fallow *c.* 18%; in permanent crops, n.a.; in pasture *c.* 20%; forest area *c.* 4%.

Foreign trade

Imports: [14]. *Major import sources* (2010): significantly the United Kingdom.
Exports: [14]; agricultural exports (2010) £J 34,555,766 (potatoes 91.0%; greenhouse tomatoes, n.a.; flowers 3.0%; zucchini 1.7%; flower bulbs 1.0%). *Major export destinations* (2010): significantly the United Kingdom.

Transport and communications

Transport. Railroads: none. Roads (1995): total length 346 mi, 557 km (paved 100%). Vehicles (2002): passenger cars 74,007; trucks and buses 12,957. Air transport (2010): 720,249 passenger arrivals.

Communications

Medium	date	number in '000s	units per 1,000 persons	Medium	date	number in '000s	units per 1,000 persons
Televisions	2006[15]	...	...	PCs	2006[16]	...	...
Telephones				Dailies	2008	20[17]	220[17]
Cellular	2006	102[18]	1,148[18]	Internet users	2009	29	320
Landline	2010	74	793	Broadband	2010	...	...

Education and health

Educational attainment (2008)[19]. Percentage of male population (ages 16–64), female population (ages 16–59) having: no formal degree/unknown *c.* 20%; primary education, n.a.; secondary *c.* 55%; higher *c.* 25%. *Literacy* (2008): virtually 100%.

Education (2010)

	teachers	students	student/ teacher ratio	enrollment rate (%)
Primary (age 5–10)	...	6,896	...	...
Secondary/Voc. (age 11–16)	...	6,365	...	...
Tertiary	...	...	...	... (age 17–21)

Health (2010): physicians (2001) 174 (1 per 500 persons); hospital beds 433[20] (1 per 215 persons); infant mortality rate per 1,000 live births 3.6; undernourished population, n.a.

Military

Total active duty personnel: none; defense is the responsibility of the United Kingdom.

[1]Includes 53 elected officials and 5 ex officio members (4 of the 5 ex officio members have no voting rights). [2]The first chief minister of Jersey was elected in December 2005. [3]Until the 1960s French was an official language of Jersey and is still used by the court and legal professions; Jerriais, a Norman-French dialect, is spoken by a small number of residents. [4]Includes Guernsey. [5]Based on the Jersey Annual Social Survey 2010. [6]Population of parishes. [7]Gross value added total includes subsidies but excludes taxes. [8]Includes storage. [9]Includes trust and funds management, legal support, and accountancy. [10]In 2010 Jersey was an international finance centre with 45 banks and 1,327 administered investment funds; about U.S.$258,600,000,000 was deposited in the banks. [11]Rental income. [12]Unemployed. [13]June. [14]Customs ceased recording imports and exports as of 1980. [15]In 2006 98% of households had a television. [16]In 2006 76% of households had a computer. [17]Circulation of the *Jersey Evening Post*. [18]Subscribers. [19]Based on the Jersey Annual Social Survey 2008. [20]The main hospital (Jersey General Hospital) only.

Internet resource for further information:

- **States of Jersey: Statistics http://www.gov.je/statistics**

Jordan

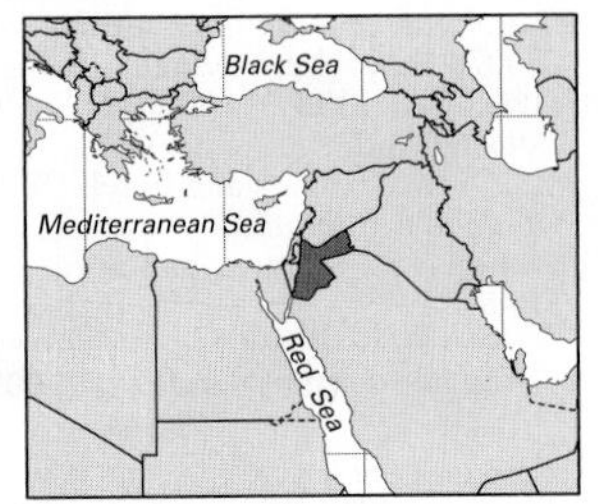

Official name: Al-Mamlakah al-Urduniyyah al-Hāshimiyyah (Hashemite Kingdom of Jordan).
Form of government: constitutional monarchy with two legislative houses (Senate [60[1]]; House of Representatives [120[2]]).
Head of state and government: King assisted by Prime Minister.
Capital: Amman.
Official language: Arabic.
Official religion: Islam.
Monetary unit: Jordanian dinar (JD); valuation (Sept. 1, 2011) JD 1.00 = U.S.$1.41 = £0.87.

Area and population

		area		population
Governorates	Capitals	sq mi	sq km	2011[3] estimate
ʿAjlūn	ʿAjlūn	162	420	140,600
ʿAmmān	Amman	2,926	7,579	2,367,000
Al-ʿAqabah	Al-ʿAqabah	2,664	6,900	133,200
Al-Balqāʾ	Al-Salṭ	432	1,119	409,500
Irbid	Irbid	607	1,572	1,088,100
Jarash	Jarash	158	410	183,400
Al-Karak	Al-Karak	1,349	3,495	238,400
Maʿān	Maʿān	12,677	32,832	116,200
Mādabā	Mādabā	363	940	152,900
Al-Mafraq	Al-Mafraq	10,248	26,541	287,300
Al-Ṭafīlah	Al-Ṭafīlah	853	2,209	85,600
Al-Zarqāʾ	Al-Zarqāʾ	1,838	4,761	910,800
TOTAL		34,277	88,778	6,113,000

Demography

Population (2011): 6,180,000[4].
Density (2011): persons per sq mi 180.3, persons per sq km 69.6.
Urban-rural (2009): urban 78.5%; rural 21.5%.
Sex distribution (2008): male 51.05%; female 48.95%.
Age breakdown (2005): under 15, 37.2%; 15–29, 28.9%; 30–44, 20.7%; 45–59, 8.2%; 60–74, 4.2%; 75–84, 0.7%; 85 and over, 0.1%.
Population projection: (2020) 6,931,000; (2030) 8,201,000.
Doubling time: 32 years.
Ethnic composition (2000): Arab 97.8%, of which Jordanian 32.4%, Palestinian 32.2%, Iraqi 14.0%, Bedouin 12.8%; Circassian 1.2%; other 1.0%.
Religious affiliation (2005): Sunnī Muslim *c.* 95%; Christian *c.* 3%; other (mostly Shīʿī Muslim and Druze) *c.* 2%.
Major cities (2004): Amman (2009) 1,088,000; Al-Zarqāʾ 395,227; Irbid 250,645; Al-Ruṣayfah 227,735; Al-Quwaysimah 135,500; Wādī al-Sīr 122,032.

Vital statistics

Birth rate per 1,000 population (2008): 29.1 (world avg. 20.3).
Death rate per 1,000 population (2008): 7.0 (world avg. 8.5).
Total fertility rate (avg. births per childbearing woman; 2008): 3.50.
Marriage/divorce rates per 1,000 population (2008): 10.4/2.2.
Life expectancy at birth (2008): male 71.6 years; female 74.4 years.

National economy

Budget (2007). Revenue: JD 3,971,500,000 (tax revenue 75.4%, of which taxes on goods and services 39.5%, taxes on corporations 10.0%, customs duties 9.3%, property taxes 7.7%; nontax revenue 15.5%; grants 8.6%). Expenditures: JD 4,540,100,000 (social protection 28.0%; defense 16.7%; education 13.9%; public order 8.8%; economic affairs 7.6%; health 7.1%; public debt 7.1%).
Public debt (external, outstanding; 2009): U.S.$5,445,000,000.
Production (metric tons except as noted). Agriculture, forestry, fishing (2009): tomatoes 653,693, cow's milk 244,600, olives 140,719, cucumbers and gherkins 137,681, potatoes 118,705, eggplants 106,793, watermelons 106,323, cauliflower/broccoli 80,320, hen's eggs 45,900, green chilies and peppers 43,672; livestock (number of live animals) 2,070,940 sheep, 919,740 goats, 25,000,000 chickens; roundwood (2010) 297,839 cu m, of which fuelwood 99%; fisheries production 1,009 (from aquaculture 44%). Mining and quarrying (2009): phosphate ore 5,152,900; potash (crude salts) 1,122,700; bromine (2008) 106,000. Manufacturing (value added in U.S.$'000,000; 2007): bricks, cement, and ceramics 472; food products 295; wearing apparel 273; tobacco products 265; base chemicals 182; iron and steel 156. Energy production (consumption): electricity (kW-hr; 2008) 12,682,000,000 ([2007] 12,870,000,000); coal, none (none); crude petroleum (barrels; 2008) 15,604 ([2007] 29,500,000); petroleum products (metric tons; 2007) 3,821,000 (4,701,000); natural gas (cu m; 2008) 210,000,000 ([2007] 2,581,600,000).
Land use as % of total land area (2009): in temporary crops 1.6%, left fallow 0.7%, in permanent crops 0.9%, in pasture 8.4%, forest area 1.1%.
Population economically active (2008): total 1,983,000[5]; activity rate of total population 32.3%[5] (participation rates: ages 15–64, 52.3%[5]; female 22.8%[5]; unemployed 12.7%).

Price index (2005 = 100)

	2004	2005	2006	2007	2008	2009	2010
Consumer price index	96.6	100.0	106.3	112.0	128.7	127.8	134.2

Gross national income (GNI; 2010): U.S.$26,520,000,000 (U.S.$4,350 per capita); purchasing power parity GNI (U.S.$5,770 per capita).

Structure of gross domestic product and labour force

	2007		2003	
	in value JD '000,000	% of total value	labour force	% of labour force
Agriculture	312	2.8	39,000	3.0
Mining	312	2.8	14,000	1.1
Manufacturing	1,890	16.8	137,000	10.6
Construction	478	4.3	71,000	5.5
Public utilities	208	1.9	18,000	1.4
Transp. and commun.	1,510	13.5	110,000	8.5
Trade, hotels	1,016	9.1	224,000	17.3
Pub. admin., defense	1,673	14.9	184,000	14.2
Finance, real estate	2,198	19.6	59,000	4.5
Services	578	5.1	246,000	19.1
Other	1,050[6]	9.4[6]	191,000[7]	14.8[7]
TOTAL	11,225	100.0[8]	1,293,000	100.0

Selected balance of payments data. Receipts from (U.S.$'000,000): tourism (2009) 2,911; remittances (2010) 3,812; foreign direct investment (FDI; 2008–10 avg.) 2,321; official development assistance (2009) 761. Disbursements for (U.S.$'000,000): tourism (2009) 1,064; remittances (2009) 502; FDI (2008–10 avg.) 38.
Household income and expenditure. Average household size (2008) 5.4; income per household (2006) JD 6,220 (U.S.$8,770); sources of income (2006): wages and salaries 45.3%, transfer payments 21.7%, rent and property income 18.4%, self-employment 14.6%; expenditure (2006): food and beverages 33.0%, housing and energy 26.8%, transp. and commun. 15.8%, education 7.0%, clothing and footwear 5.0%, alcohol and tobacco 3.6%.

Foreign trade[9]

Balance of trade (current prices)

	2004	2005	2006	2007	2008	2009
U.S.$'000,000	–4,252	–6,176	–6,280	–7,831	–9,090	–8,002
% of total	35.3%	41.9%	37.8%	40.7%	36.9%	38.0%

Imports (2008): U.S.$16,872,000,000 (crude petroleum 16.1%; machinery and apparatus 16.0%; food 14.2%, of which cereals 5.7%; chemicals and chemical products 9.5%; road vehicles/parts 6.9%; iron and steel 5.1%). *Major import sources:* Saudi Arabia 21.6%; China 10.4%; Germany 6.0%; United States 4.6%; Egypt 4.3%.
Exports (2008): U.S.$7,782,000,000 (fertilizers [all types] 24.3%; apparel/accessories 13.4%; food products 10.8%, of which vegetables 5.1%; machinery and apparatus 10.7%; medicines 6.6%; inorganic chemicals 5.8%). *Major export destinations:* Iraq 16.5%; India 16.5%; U.S. 13.5%; free zones 8.5%; Saudi Arabia 7.0%; U.A.E. 4.7%.

Transport and communications

Transport. Railroads (2008): route length 314 mi, 506 km; (2006) passenger-km 600,000; (2006) metric ton-km cargo 400,000,000. Roads (2007): total length 4,827 mi, 7,768 km (paved 100%). Vehicles (2007): passenger cars 536,665; trucks and buses 248,058. Air transport (2008)[10]: passenger-km 7,669,000,000; metric ton-km cargo 197,000,000.

Communications

Medium	date	number in '000s	units per 1,000 persons	Medium	date	number in '000s	units per 1,000 persons
Televisions	2004	1,065	198	PCs	2007	383	67
Telephones				Dailies	2009	320[11]	47[11]
Cellular	2010	6,620[12]	1,070[12]	Internet users	2009	5,300	339
Landline	2010	485	78	Broadband	2010	1,969[12]	32[12]

Education and health

Educational attainment (2004). Percentage of population age 25 and over having: no formal schooling: illiterate 14.0%, literate 4.8%; primary/lower secondary education 36.6%; upper secondary 19.4%; some higher 25.1%, of which advanced degree 2.1%; unknown 0.1%. *Literacy* (2008): percentage of population age 15 and over literate 92.3%; males 95.9%; females 88.6%.

Education (2007–08)

	teachers	students	student/ teacher ratio	enrollment rate (%)
Primary (age 6–11)	39,441[13]	817,160	19.9[13]	89
Secondary/Voc. (age 12–17)	34,294[13]	700,342	17.9[13]	82
Tertiary	9,681	254,752	26.3	41 (age 18–22)

Health: physicians (2007) 15,280 (1 per 375 persons); hospital beds (2008) 11,200 (1 per 517 persons); infant mortality rate (2008) 19.0; undernourished population (2005–07) less than 5.0% of total population.

Military

Total active duty personnel (November 2010): 100,500 (army 84.6%, navy 0.5%, air force 14.9%). *Military expenditure as percentage of GDP* (2009): 11.0%; per capita expenditure U.S.$386.

[1]Appointed by the king. [2]Includes 9 seats reserved for Christians and 3 seats reserved for Circassians. [3]January 1. [4]Includes roughly 2.0 million registered Palestinian refugees of whom *c.* 350,000 reside in camps; excludes 500,000 Iraqi refugees. [5]ILO estimate. [6]Net taxes on products less imputed bank service charges. [7]Including 4,000 not adequately defined and 187,000 unemployed. [8]Detail does not add to total given because of rounding. [9]Imports c.i.f.; exports f.o.b. [10]Royal Jordanian and Jordan Aviation only. [11]Circulation of daily newspapers. [12]Subscribers. [13]2002–03.

Internet resources for further information:
- **Dept. of Statistics http://www.dos.gov.jo**
- **Central Bank of Jordan http://www.cbj.gov.jo**

Kazakhstan

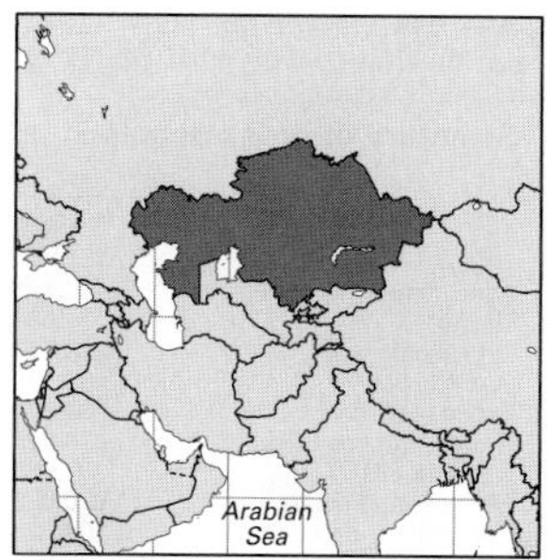

Official name: Qazaqstan Respūblīkasy (Kazakh); Respublika Kazakhstan (Russian) (Republic of Kazakhstan).
Form of government: unitary republic[1] with a Parliament consisting of two chambers (Senate [47[2]] and House of Representatives [107]).
Head of state and government: President assisted by Prime Minister.
Capital: Astana.
Official languages: Kazakh; Russian[3].
Official religion: none.
Monetary unit: tenge (T); valuation (Sept. 1, 2011) 1 U.S.$ = T 146.68; 1 £ = T 237.02.

Area and population

	area	population		area	population
		2010			2010
Provinces	sq km	estimate	**Provinces**	sq km	estimate
Almaty	224,000	1,852,400	Qostanay	196,000	881,900
Aqmola	146,200	733,100	Qyzylorda[4]	226,000	696,700
Aqtöbe	300,600	773,400	Shyghys Qazaqstan (Eastern Kazakhstan)	283,200	1,397,400
Atyraū	118,600	528,700	Soltüstik Qazaqstan (Northern Kazakhstan)	98,000	589,800
Batys Qazaqstan (Western Kazakhstan)	151,300	606,600	Zhambyl	144,300	1,041,200
Mangghystaū	165,600	517,300	**Cities**		
Ongtüstik Qazaqstan (Southern Kazakhstan)	117,300	2,550,200	Almaty	300	1,422,000
Pavlodar	124,800	745,800	Astana	700	685,900
Qaraghandy	428,000	1,350,000	TOTAL	2,724,900	16,372,400

Demography

Population (2011): 16,560,000.
Density (2011): persons per sq mi 15.7, persons per sq km 6.1.
Urban-rural (2009): urban 54.0%; rural 46.0%.
Sex distribution (2009): male 48.25%; female 51.75%.
Age breakdown (2010[5]): under 15, 24.3%; 15–29, 27.2%; 30–44, 21.0%; 45–59, 17.3%; 60–74, 7.7%; 75–84, 2.1%; 85 and over, 0.4%.
Population projection: (2020) 18,300,000; (2030) 19,534,000.
Ethnic composition (2009): Kazakh 63.1%; Russian 23.7%; Uzbek 2.8%; Ukrainian 2.1%; Uighur 1.4%; Tatar 1.3%; German 1.1%; other 4.5%.
Religious affiliation (2000): Muslim (mostly Sunnī) 42.7%; nonreligious 29.3%; Christian 16.7%, of which Orthodox 8.6%; atheist 10.9%; other 0.4%.
Major cities (2009): Almaty 1,365,105; Astana 639,311; Shymkent (Chimkent) 566,996; Qaraghandy (Karaganda) 465,634; Taraz 347,486.

Vital statistics

Birth rate per 1,000 population (2009): 22.5 (world avg. 20.3).
Death rate per 1,000 population (2009): 9.0 (world avg. 8.5).
Total fertility rate (avg. births per childbearing woman; 2008): 1.88.
Marriage/divorce rates per 1,000 population (2009): 8.8/2.5.
Life expectancy at birth (2009): male 63.6 years; female 73.6 years.
Major causes of death per 100,000 population (2009): diseases of the circulatory system 416.4; malignant neoplasms (cancers) 112.8; accidents, poisoning, and violence 108.4; diseases of the respiratory system 48.5.

National economy

Budget (2007). Revenue: T 2,895,975,900,000 (tax revenue 81.4%, transfers 8.9%, capital revenue 3.2%). Expenditures: T 2,678,280,300,000 (social security 18.8%, education 17.0%, health 11.2%, transportation and communications 10.8%, public order 9.0%).
Public debt (external, outstanding; June 2011): U.S.$6,829,800,000.
Population economically active (2009): total 8,457,900; activity rate of total population 52.6% (participation rates: ages 15–64 [2008] 78.2%; female 49.4%; unemployed [March 2010] 6.2%).

Price and earnings indexes (2005 = 100)

	2004	2005	2006	2007	2008	2009	2010
Consumer price index	93.0	100.0	108.6	120.3	140.9	151.2	162.0
Monthly earnings index	83.4	100.0	120.4	154.3	179.3	180.4	207.2

Production (metric tons except as noted). Agriculture, forestry, fishing (2009): wheat 17,052,000, cow's milk 5,267,000, potatoes 2,755,600, barley 2,519,000, tomatoes 592,000; livestock (number of live animals) 16,770,400 sheep and goats, 5,991,600 cattle, 148,300 camels; roundwood (2010) 345,000 cu m, of which fuelwood 79%; fisheries production 33,940 (from aquaculture 1%). Mining and quarrying (2007): iron ore 13,600,000; bauxite 4,800,000; chromite 3,687,200 (world rank: 2); copper (metal content) 405,000; zinc (metal content) 386,000; silver 800,000 kg; gold 22,000 kg. Manufacturing (value of production in T '000,000; 2008): base metals 1,408,325; food products 757,757; machinery and apparatus 297,501; coke, refined petroleum products, and nuclear fuel 235,309. Energy production (consumption): electricity (kW-hr; 2008–09) 77,556,000,000 ([2008] 80,603,000,000); hard coal (metric tons; 2008–09) 95,011,000 ([2007] 71,706,000); lignite (metric tons; 2008–09) 4,478,000 ([2007] 3,903,000); crude petroleum (barrels; 2008–09) 515,758,000 ([2008] 59,461,000); petroleum products (metric tons; 2007) 12,996,000 (10,284,000); natural gas (cu m; 2008) 11,273,000,000 (588,000,000).
Gross national income (GNI; 2010): U.S.$121,383,000,000 (U.S.$7,440 per capita); purchasing power parity GNI (U.S.$10,610 per capita).

Structure of gross domestic product and labour force

	2008			
	in value T '000,000,000	% of total value	labour force	% of labour force
Agriculture, forestry, and fishing	842	5.3	2,370,000	28.2
Mining and quarrying	3,004	18.8	200,000	2.4
Manufacturing	1,853	11.6	573,000	6.8
Public utilities	273	1.7	165,000	2.0
Construction	1,304	8.2	549,000	6.5
Transp. and commun.	1,623	10.2	589,000	7.0
Trade, hotels	2,112	13.3	1,253,000	14.9
Finance, real estate	3,280	20.6	474,200	5.6
Pub. admin., defense	268	1.7	353,000	4.2
Services	990	6.2	1,330,400	15.8
Other	388[6]	2.4[6]	558,100[7]	6.6[7]
TOTAL	15,937	100.0	8,415,100[8]	100.0

Household income and expenditure (2008). Average household size (2004) 3.8; sources of income: salaries/wages 77.4%, pensions 11.5%, agriculture 4.1%; expenditure: food and beverages 42.5%, clothing 10.6%, housing 10.4%.
Selected balance of payments data. Receipts from (U.S.$'000,000): tourism (2009) 963; remittances (2010) 132; foreign direct investment (FDI; 2008–10 avg.) 12,685. Disbursements for (U.S.$'000,000): tourism (2009) 1,131; remittances (2009) 3,138; FDI (2008–10 avg.) 4,043.
Land use as % of total land area (2009): in temporary crops or left fallow 8.7%, in permanent crops 0.03%, in pasture 68.5%, forest area 1.2%.

Foreign trade[9]

Balance of trade (current prices)

	2004	2005	2006	2007	2008	2009
U.S.$'000,000	+7,290	+10,497	+14,581	+14,999	+33,357	+15,430
% of total	22.4%	23.2%	23.6%	18.6%	30.6%	21.4%

Imports (2008): U.S.$37,815,000,000 (mineral fuels 14.4%; iron and steel 11.0%; general industrial machinery 10.0%; machinery specialized for particular industries 6.9%; road vehicles 6.4%; food 6.0%). *Major import sources:* Russia 36.4%; China 12.1%; Germany 6.8%; Ukraine 5.6%; U.S. 5.1%.
Exports (2008): U.S.$71,172,000,000 (crude petroleum 61.1%; iron and steel 8.3%; nonferrous metals 6.3%, of which refined copper 3.4%; metal ore and metal scrap 5.0%; food 4.0%, of which wheat 3.2%). *Major export destinations:* Italy 16.7%; Switzerland 15.9%; China 10.8%; Russia 8.7%; France 7.6%.

Transport and communications

Transport. Railroads (2008): route length 8,827 mi, 14,205 km; passenger-km 14,719,000,000; metric ton-km cargo 214,900,000,000. Roads (2008): total length 58,160 mi, 93,600 km (paved 90%); passenger-km 106,878,000,000[10]; metric ton-km cargo 63,500,000,000. Vehicles (2008[5]): passenger cars 2,183,131; trucks and buses 442,566. Air transport (2008): passenger-km 5,495,000,000; metric ton-km cargo 70,000,000.

Communications

Medium	date	number in '000s	units per 1,000 persons	Medium	date	number in '000s	units per 1,000 persons
Televisions	2003	5,106	338	PCs	2005	...	...
Telephones				Dailies	2009	320[11]	20[11]
Cellular	2010	19,769[12]	1,070[12]	Internet users	2009	5,300	339
Landline	2010	4,011	250	Broadband	2010	847[12]	53[12]

Education and health

Educational attainment (1999). Population age 25 and over having: no formal schooling/some primary education 9.1%; primary education 23.1%; secondary/some postsecondary 57.8%; higher 10.0%. *Literacy* (2008): percentage of total population age 15 and over literate 99.7%; males 99.8%; females 99.5%.

Education (2008–09)

	teachers	students	student/ teacher ratio	enrollment rate (%)
Primary (age 6–9)	57,962	950,976	16.4	89
Secondary/Voc. (age 10–17)	179,237	1,740,549	9.7	89
Tertiary	37,814	635,241	16.8	41 (age 18–22)

Health (2008): physicians 58,945 (1 per 266 persons); hospital beds 120,840 (1 per 130 persons); infant mortality rate per 1,000 live births (2009) 18.2; undernourished population (2005–07) less than 5.0% of total population based on the consumption of a minimum daily requirement of 1,910 calories.

Military

Total active duty personnel (November 2010): 49,000 (army 61.2%, navy 6.1%, air force 24.5%, Ministry of Defense staff 8.2%). *Military expenditure as percentage of GDP* (2009): 1.3%; per capita expenditure U.S.$84.

[1]No election since independence in 1991 has been deemed free and fair by international standards. [2]Includes 15 nonelective seats. [3]Russian has official equal status per article 7.2 of the constitution. [4]Includes an area of 6,700 sq km (2,600 sq mi) enclosing the Bayqongyr (Baykonur) space launch facilities and the city of Bayqongyr (formerly Leninsk) leased to Russia in 1995 until 2050. The estimated 70,000 residents of Bayqongyr are excluded from the Qyzylorda population total. [5]January 1. [6]Taxes on products less imputed bank service charges. [7]Includes 558,000 unemployed and 100 undefined. [8]Detail does not add to total given because of rounding. [9]Imports c.i.f.; exports f.o.b. [10]Passenger cars only. [11]Circulation of daily newspapers. [12]Subscribers.

Internet resources for further information:
- **National Bank of Kazakhstan http://www.nationalbank.kz**
- **Agency of Statistics of Kazakhstan http://www.eng.stat.kz**

Kenya

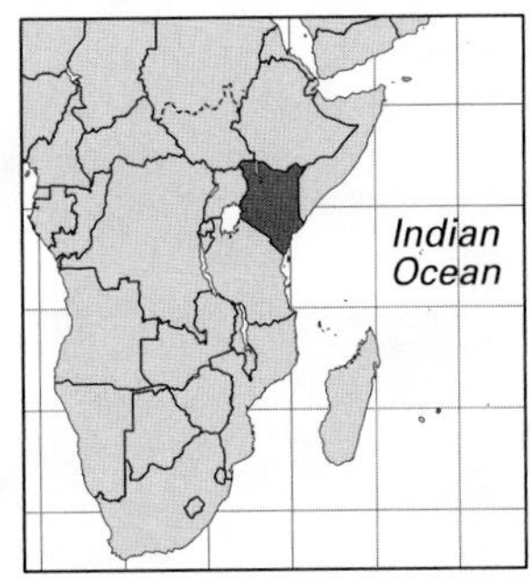

Official name: Jamhuri ya Kenya (Swahili); Republic of Kenya (English).
Form of government: unitary multiparty republic with one legislative house[1] (National Assembly [224[2]]).
Head of state and government: President assisted by the Prime Minister[3].
Capital: Nairobi.
Official languages: Swahili; English.
Official religion: none.
Monetary unit: Kenyan shilling (K Sh); valuation (Sept. 1, 2011) 1 U.S.$ = K Sh 94.05; 1 £ = K Sh 151.98.

Area and population

Provinces	Provincial headquarters	area sq mi	area sq km	population 2009 census
Central	Nyeri	5,087	13,176	4,383,743
Coast	Mombasa	32,279	83,603	3,325,307
Eastern	Embu	61,734	159,891	5,668,123
North Eastern	Garissa	48,997	126,902	2,310,757
Nyanza	Kisumu	6,240	16,162	5,442,711
Rift Valley	Nakuru	67,131	173,868	10,006,805
Western	Kakamega	3,228	8,360	4,334,282
Special area				
Nairobi	—	264	684	3,138,369
TOTAL		224,961[4]	582,646	38,610,097

Demography

Population (2011): 40,770,000.
Density (2011): persons per sq mi 181.2, persons per sq km 70.0.
Urban-rural (2009): urban 32.3%; rural 67.7%.
Sex distribution (2009): male 49.71%; female 50.29%.
Age breakdown (2006): under 15, 43.1%; 15–29, 30.2%; 30–44, 15.2%; 45–59, 7.0%; 60–74, 3.5%; 75 and over, 1.0%.
Population projection: (2020) 48,786,000; (2030) 55,536,000.
Doubling time: 25 years.
Ethnic composition (2004): Kikuyu *c.* 21%; Luhya *c.* 14%; Luo *c.* 13%; Kalenjin *c.* 11%; Kamba *c.* 11%; Gusii *c.* 6%; Meru *c.* 5%; other *c.* 19%.
Religious affiliation (2009): Protestant/independent Christian 59.5%; Roman Catholic 23.5%; Muslim 11.2%; nonreligious 2.4%; traditional beliefs 1.7%; other 1.7%.
Major cities (2006): Nairobi (2009) 3,138,369; Mombasa (2009) 939,370; Nakuru 266,500; Eldoret 227,800; Kisumu 220,000; Ruiru 120,900; Thika 102,300.

Vital statistics

Birth rate per 1,000 population (2009): 38.4 (world avg. 20.3).
Death rate per 1,000 population (2009): 11.3 (world avg. 8.5).
Natural increase rate per 1,000 population (2009): 27.1 (world avg. 11.8).
Total fertility rate (avg. births per childbearing woman; 2009): 4.9.
Life expectancy at birth (2006): male 54.3 years; female 54.2 years.
Adult population (ages 15–49) *living with HIV* (2009): 6.3%[5] (world avg. 0.8%).

National economy

Budget (2008–09). Revenue: K Sh 511,355,000,000 (tax revenue 85.5%, of which income and profit taxes 39.9%, VAT 24.8%, excise tax 13.7%; nontax revenue 11.0%; grants 3.5%). Expenditures: K Sh 621,909,000,000 (current expenditure 74.3%, of which interest payments 8.4%; development expenditure 25.7%).
Production (metric tons except as noted). Agriculture, forestry, fishing (2009): sugarcane 5,610,702, cow's milk 4,070,000, corn (maize) 2,439,000, sweet potatoes 930,784, plantains 843,465, bananas 843,465, cassava 819,967, cabbages and other brassicas 627,828, tomatoes 526,922, dry beans 465,363, potatoes 400,000, cattle meat 375,000, tea 314,100, pineapples 257,623, wheat 129,200, coffee 57,000, pigeon peas 46,474, supplier of cut flowers for EU; livestock (number of live animals) 12,490,100 cattle, 9,903,300 sheep; roundwood (2010) 26,071,454 cu m, of which fuelwood 95%; fisheries production 144,290 (from aquaculture 3%). Mining and quarrying (2009): soda ash 404,904; salt 24,145; fluorspar 15,667[6]; tourmaline 5,600 kg; ruby 3,600 kg. Manufacturing (value added in U.S.$'000,000; 2006): food products 473; coke oven products (nearly all soda ash) 268; glass and glass products 244; beverages 175; iron and steel 106. Energy production (consumption): electricity (kW-hr; 2008) 5,694,000,000 (5,301,000,000); coal (metric tons; 2007) none (110,000); crude petroleum (barrels; 2007) none (11,700,000); petroleum products (metric tons; 2007) 1,579,000 (3,193,000); natural gas, none (none).
Household income and expenditure. Average household size (2009) 4.4; average annual income per household: n.a.; sources of income: n.a.; expenditure (2005): food and beverages *c.* 44%, transportation *c.* 9%, housing and energy *c.* 8%, cafés and hotels *c.* 5%, clothing and footwear *c.* 3%, unspecified *c.* 22%.
Population economically active (2008): total 18,181,000[7]; activity rate of total population 46.9%[7] (participation rates: ages 15–64, 83.2%[7]; female 46.5%[7]; unemployed 40%).

Price index (2005 = 100)

	2004	2005	2006	2007	2008	2009	2010
Consumer price index	90.7	100.0	114.5	125.6	158.6	173.2	180.1

Gross national income (GNI; 2010): U.S.$31,880,000,000 (U.S.$780 per capita); purchasing power parity GNI (U.S.$1,610 per capita).

Structure of gross domestic product and labour force

	2008 in value K Sh '000,000	2008 % of total value	2006 labour force	2006 % of labour force
Agriculture	499,421	23.8	334,600[8]	3.9[8]
Mining	14,630	0.7	6,000[8]	0.1[8]
Manufacturing	223,353	10.6	253,800[8]	2.9[8]
Construction	80,135	3.8	79,900[8]	0.9[8]
Public utilities	30,805	1.5	19,500[8]	0.2[8]
Transp. and commun.	214,983	10.2	132,900[8]	1.5[8]
Trade, hotels	234,535	11.2	185,900[8]	2.2[8]
Finance, real estate	206,029	9.8	90,400[8]	1.0[8]
Pub. admin., defense	104,828	5.0	755,400[8]	8.7[8]
Services	263,306	12.5		
Other	227,774[9]	10.8[9]	6,814,900[10]	78.6[10]
TOTAL	2,099,798[4]	100.0[4]	8,673,300	100.0

Public debt (external, outstanding; 2009): U.S.$6,543,000,000.
Selected balance of payments data. Receipts from (U.S.$'000,000): tourism (2009) 690; remittances (2009) 1,686; foreign direct investment (FDI; 2008–10 avg.) 123; official development assistance (2009) 1,788. Disbursements for (U.S.$'000,000): tourism (2009) 234; remittances (2008) 16; FDI (2008–10 avg.) 36.
Land use as % of total land area (2007): in temporary crops or left fallow 9.1%, in permanent crops 0.9%, in pasture 37.4%, forest area 6.1%.

Foreign trade[11]

Balance of trade (current prices)

	2004	2005	2006	2007	2008	2009
K Sh '000,000	–148,209	–220,763	–278,969	–330,525	–423,829	–443,148
% of total	25.8%	31.2%	36.0%	37.6%	38.0%	39.1%

Imports (2008): K Sh 769,766,000,000 (machinery and apparatus 18.4%, refined petroleum 15.9%, chemicals and chemical products 13.1%, crude petroleum 10.6%, road vehicles 7.3%, food 6.2%). *Major import sources:* U.A.E. 14.9%; India 11.8%; China 8.4%; South Africa 6.1%; Japan 5.8%.
Exports (2008): K Sh 345,937,000,000 (tea 18.6%, cut flowers 8.9%, vegetables 5.5%, apparel/accessories 5.1%, inorganic chemicals 4.4%, petroleum 3.8%, coffee 2.9%). *Major export destinations:* Uganda 12.3%; U.K. 11.0%; Tanzania 8.5%; Neth. 7.6%; U.S. 6.0%.

Transport and communications

Transport. Railroads (2005): route length (2008) 1,817 mi, 2,924 km; passenger-km 489,000,000; metric ton-km cargo 1,358,000,000. Roads (2004): total length 39,311 mi, 63,265 km (paved 14%). Vehicles (2007): passenger cars 562,376; trucks and buses 230,976. Air transport (2008)[12]: passenger-km 8,829,000,000; metric ton-km cargo 238,451,000.

Communications

Medium	date	number in '000s	units per 1,000 persons	Medium	date	number in '000s	units per 1,000 persons
Televisions	2000	758	25	PCs	2007	529	14
Telephones				Dailies	2009	310[13]	14[13]
Cellular	2010	24,969[14]	616[14]	Internet users	2009	3,996	100
Landline	2010	460	11	Broadband	2010	4.3[14]	0.1[14]

Education and health

Educational attainment (1998–99). Percentage of population age 6 and over having: no formal schooling 16.4%; primary education 59.0%; secondary 19.7%; university 1.1%; other/unknown 3.8%. *Literacy* (2008): total population over age 15 literate 86.5%; males literate 90.3%; females literate 82.8%.

Education (2007–08)

	teachers	students	student/ teacher ratio	enrollment rate (%)
Primary (age 6–11)	147,596	6,868,810	46.5	82
Secondary/Voc. (age 12–17)	103,956	3,106,919	29.9	49
Tertiary	...	167,983[15]	...	4[15] (age 18–22)

Health: physicians (2007) 6,271 (1 per 5,886 persons); hospital beds (2006) 51,481 (1 per 714 persons); infant mortality rate per 1,000 live births (2006) 59.0; undernourished population (2004–06) 10,800,000 (30% of total population based on the consumption of a minimum daily requirement of 1,750 calories).

Military

Total active duty personnel (November 2010): 24,120 (army 82.9%, navy 6.7%, air force 10.4%). *Military expenditure as percentage of GDP* (2009): 1.8%; per capita expenditure U.S.$17.

[1]A new constitution promulgated Aug. 27, 2010, provides for the establishment of a 68-seat Senate; elections are expected in 2012. [2]Includes 12 nonelective seats and 2 ex officio members. [3]The 2010 constitution abolishes the post of Prime Minister effective from the 2012 presidential election. [4]Detail does not add to total given because of rounding. [5]Statistically derived midpoint of range. [6]Kenya Fluorspar Company shut down operations in June 2009. [7]ILO estimate. [8]Formally employed only. [9]Taxes less subsidies and less imputed bank service charges. [10]Includes informally employed, small-scale farmers and pastoralists, unemployed, self-employed, and unpaid family workers. [11]Imports c.i.f.; exports f.o.b. [12]Kenya Airways and African Express. [13]Circulation. [14]Subscribers. [15]2008–09.

Internet resources for further information:
- **Central Bank of Kenya http://www.centralbank.go.ke**
- **Central Bureau of Statistics http://www.knbs.or.ke**

Kiribati

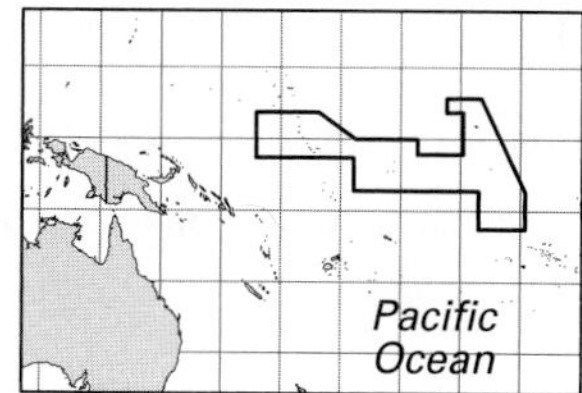

Official name: Republic of Kiribati.[1]
Form of government: unitary republic with a unicameral legislature (House of Assembly [46[2]]).
Head of state and government: President.
Seats of government: islet villages of Bairiki (executive), Ambo (legislative), Betio (judicial) on South Tarawa.
Official language: English.
Official religion: none.
Monetary unit: Australian dollar ($A); valuation (Sept. 1, 2011) 1 U.S.$ = $A 0.93; 1 £ = $A 1.50.

Area and population

Island/Atoll Groups Islands/Atolls[4]	area[3] sq km	population 2005 census	Island/Atoll Groups Islands/Atolls[4]	area[3] sq km	population 2005 census
Gilbert Group (Kiribati)	285.5[5]	83,683	Tamana	4.7	875
Abaiang	17.5	5,502	Tarawa, North	15.3	5,678
Abemama	27.4	3,404	Tarawa, South	15.8	40,311
Aranuka	11.6	1,158	Line and Phoenix Group	525.0[5]	8,850
Arorae	9.5	1,256	Northern Line	431.7	8,809
Banaba[6]	6.3	301	Kiritimati (Christmas)	388.4	5,115
Beru	17.7	2,169	Tabuaeran (Fanning)	33.7	2,539
Butaritari	13.5	3,280	Teraina (Washington)	9.6	1,155
Kuria	15.5	1,082	Southern Line[7] and Phoenix Group[8]	93.4	41
Maiana	16.7	1,908	Kanton (Canton) in Phoenix Group	9.2	41
Makin	7.9	2,385	TOTAL	810.5	92,533
Marakei	14.1	2,741			
Nikunau	19.1	1,912			
Nonouti	19.9	3,179			
Onotoa	15.6	1,644			
Tabiteuea, North	25.8	3,600			
Tabiteuea, South	11.9	1,298			

Demography

Population (2011): 101,000.
Density (2011)[9]: persons per sq mi 360.7, persons per sq km 139.1.
Urban-rural (2009): urban 43.9%; rural 56.1%.
Sex distribution (2011): male 49.64%; female 50.36%.
Age breakdown (2009): under 15, 35.2%; 15–29, 29.3%; 30–44, 18.3%; 45–59, 11.5%; 60–74, 4.6%; 75–84, 1.0%; 85 and over, 0.1%.
Population projection: (2020) 116,000; (2030) 132,000.
Ethnic composition (2000): Micronesian 98.8%; Polynesian 0.7%; European 0.2%; other 0.3%.
Religious affiliation (2005): Roman Catholic 55.3%; Kiribati Protestant (Congregational) 35.7%; Mormon 3.1%; Bahā'ī 2.2%; other/nonreligious 3.7%.
Major villages (2005)[10]: Betio 12,509; Bikenibeu 6,170; Teaoraereke 3,939; Bairiki 2,766.

Vital statistics

Birth rate per 1,000 population (2009): 23.8 (world avg. 20.3).
Death rate per 1,000 population (2009): 7.6 (world avg. 8.5).
Natural increase rate per 1,000 population (2009): 16.2 (world avg. 11.8).
Total fertility rate (avg. births per childbearing woman; 2009): 3.00.
Life expectancy at birth (2009): male 61.3 years; female 66.1 years.
Major causes of death per 100,000 population (2005): diseases of the circulatory system 90.7; infectious and parasitic diseases 75.6; perinatal conditions 68.0; diseases of the respiratory system 67.0; diseases of the digestive system 59.4; endocrine and metabolic disorders 52.9; unspecified 137.2.

National economy

Budget (2008). Revenue: $A 161,700,000 (grants 57.5%, fishing license fees 19.9%, tax revenue 18.4%, other 4.2%). Expenditures: $A 183,000,000 (development expenditure 50.9%, current expenditure 49.1%).
Public debt (external, outstanding; December 2009): U.S.$9,900,000.
Production (metric tons except as noted). Agriculture, forestry, fishing (2009): coconuts 131,351, roots and tubers 7,914 (of which taro 2,189), bananas 7,325, vegetables 6,233; livestock (number of live animals) 12,600 pigs, 480,000 chickens; roundwood (2010) 2,876 cu m, of which fuelwood 100%; fisheries production 40,231 (from aquaculture, negligible); aquatic plants (all seaweed) production 1,788 (from aquaculture 100%). Mining and quarrying: small amounts of salt. Manufacturing: copra (6,240 metric tons produced in 2009), processed fish, clothing, and handicrafts. Energy production (consumption): electricity (kW-hr; 2010) 21,600,000 (17,600,000); petroleum products (metric tons; 2007) none (11,000).
Selected balance of payments data. Receipts from (U.S.$'000,000): tourism (2001) 3.2; remittances (2010) 9; foreign direct investment (FDI; 2008–10 avg.) 3.3; official development assistance (2009) 27. Disbursements for (U.S.$'000,000): tourism (1999) 2.0; remittances, n.a.; FDI (2008–10 avg.) negligible.
Population economically active (2005): total 36,969; activity rate of total population 38.8% (participation rates: over age 15, 63.4%; female 45.9%; unemployed 6.1%).

Price index (2005 = 100)

	2003	2004	2005	2006	2007	2008	2009
Consumer price index[11]	101.3	100.3	100.0	98.6	102.7	113.9	123.4

Gross national income (GNI; 2010): U.S.$200,000,000 (U.S.$2,010 per capita); purchasing power parity GNI (U.S.$3,510 per capita).

Structure of gross domestic product and labour force

	2010		2005	
	in value $A '000	% of total value	labour force	% of labour force
Agriculture, fishing	36,022	23.3	22,518[12]	60.9[12]
Mining	46	—	...	...
Manufacturing	7,906	5.1	305	0.8
Construction	2,276	1.5	511	1.4
Public utilities	1,469	1.0	293	0.8
Transp. and commun.	16,619	10.8	1,473	4.0
Trade, hotels	10,741	7.0	1,873	5.1
Finance	9,817	6.4	356	1.0
Pub. admin., defense	25,047	16.2	6,953	18.8
Services	38,208[13]	24.7[13]	433	1.2
Other	6,233[14]	4.0[14]	2,254[15]	6.1[15]
TOTAL	154,382[5]	100.0	36,969	100.0[5]

Household income and expenditure (2006)[16]. Average household size 6.3; average annual household income U.S.$8,745; sources of income: wages 35.4%, rent 13.9%, agriculture 10.9%, remittances 9.6%; expenditure: food 46.8%, housing 16.7%, household operations 15.1%, transportation 6.6%.
Land use as % of total land area (2007): in temporary crops or left fallow *c.* 2%; in permanent crops *c.* 43%; in pasture, none; forest area *c.* 3%.

Foreign trade

Balance of trade (current prices)

	2004	2005	2006	2007	2008	2009	2010
$A '000,000	–77.4	–93.3	–78.3	–70.5	–77.8	–78.0	–74.2
% of total	92.0%	87.2%	90.2%	72.5%	79.0%	82.8%	86.8%

Imports (2005): $A 96,900,000 (food 29.6%, of which rice 10.7%, meat 6.4%; refined petroleum 16.8%; machinery and apparatus 14.6%, of which starting equipment/generators 6.2%; road vehicles 5.7%). *Major import sources* (2010): Japan 29.7%; Fiji 28.2%; Australia 17.5%; China 10.6%; United States 8.7%.
Exports (2007): $A 11,655,000 (domestic exports 81.0%, of which crude coconut oil 45.7%, copra/copra cake 14.4%, fish 10.7%, handicrafts 8.3%, seaweed 1.9%; reexports 19.0%). *Major export destinations* (2010): Thailand 28.1%; Ecuador 21.9%; Japan 16.2%; South Korea 15.1%; Indonesia 8.6%.

Transport and communications

Transport. Roads (2000): total length 416 mi, 670 km (paved, n.a.). Vehicles (2008): passenger cars 9,600; trucks and buses 4,480. Air transport: n.a.[17]

Communications

Medium	date	number in '000s	units per 1,000 persons	Medium	date	number in '000s	units per 1,000 persons
Televisions	2005	1.0	11	PCs	2005	1	11
Telephones				Dailies	2010	0	0
Cellular	2010	10[18]	101[18]	Internet users	2009	2.0	20
Landline	2010	4.1	41	Broadband	2010	0.9[18]	9.0[18]

Education and health

Educational attainment (2005). Percentage of population age 5 and over having: no schooling/unknown 9.2%; primary education 40.3%; secondary 47.6%; higher 2.9%. *Literacy* (2005): population age 15 and over literate 91.0%; males literate, n.a.; females literate, n.a.

Education (2007–08)

	teachers	students	student/ teacher ratio	enrollment rate (%)
Primary (age 6–11)	645	16,123	25.0	97[19]
Secondary/Voc. (age 12–17)	664	11,583	17.4	68[20]
Tertiary[21]	5	300	60.0	... (age 18–22)

Health: physicians (2006) 30 (1 per 3,120 persons); hospital beds (2008) 174 (1 per 556 persons); infant mortality rate per 1,000 live births (2009) 41.4; undernourished population (2004–06) 5,000 (5% of total population based on the consumption of a minimum daily requirement of 1,760 calories).

Military

Total active duty personnel (November 2010): none; defense assistance is provided by Australia and New Zealand.

[1]Ribaberikin Kiribati in Gilbertese (also known as I-Kiribati). [2]Includes two nonelective members. [3]Includes uninhabited islands in Southern Line and Phoenix Group. [4]Administratively Kiribati has six district councils; in addition, each of the 21 inhabited islands have their own island councils. [5]Detail does not add to total given because of rounding. [6]Banaba is actually an isolated island to the west of the Gilbert Group. [7]Includes Caroline (Millennium), Malden, Starbuck, Vostok, and Flint islands. Total area is *c.* 64 sq km. [8]Includes Birnie, Enderbury, McKean, Manra, Nikumaroro, Orona, Rawaki (Phoenix), and Kanton (Canton) islands. Total area is *c.* 29 sq km. [9]Based on inhabited island areas (280 sq mi [726 sq km]) only. [10]All on South Tarawa. [11]Urban Tarawa only. [12]Includes 21,582 persons engaged in "village work" (subsistence agriculture or fishing). [13]Includes real estate. [14]Indirect taxes less imputed bank service charges and less subsidies. [15]Unemployed. [16]Based on the 2006 Household Income and Expenditure Survey, comprising 1,161 households. [17]Air Kiribati operates scheduled services to outer islands. [18]Subscribers. [19]2001–02. [20]2004–05. [21]2006–07; Kiribati campus, University of the South Pacific.

Internet resources for further information:
- **Key Indicators for Asia and the Pacific http://www.adb.org/Documents/Books/Key_Indicators/2011**
- **Kiribati Statistics Office http://www.spc.int/prism/Country/KI/Stats**

Korea, North

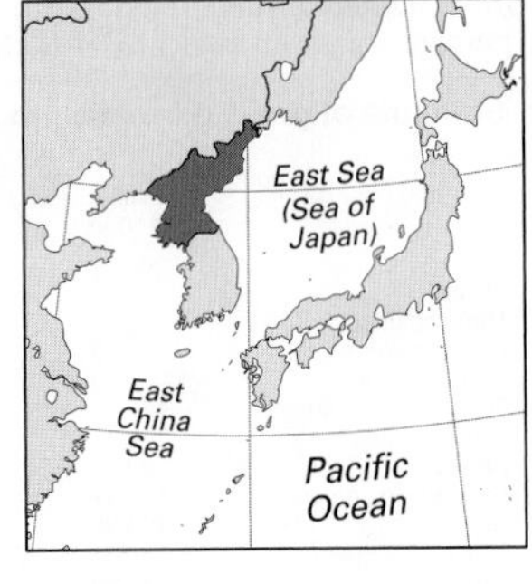

Official name: Chosŏn Minjujuŭi In'min Konghwaguk (Democratic People's Republic of Korea).
Form of government: unitary single-party republic with one legislative house (Supreme People's Assembly [687]).
Head of state and government: Supreme Leader[1]/Chairman of the National Defense Commission.
Capital: P'yŏngyang.
Official language: Korean.
Official religion: none.
Monetary unit: ([new] North Korean) won (W); valuation (Sept. 1, 2011) 1 U.S.$ = 1.30 [new] won[2]; 1 £ = 2.10 [new] won[2].

Area and population

		area		population
Provinces	**Capitals**	sq mi	sq km	2008 census
Chagang-do	Kanggye	6,551	16,968	1,299,830
Kangwŏn-do	Wŏnsan	4,306[3]	11,152[3]	1,477,582[3]
North Hamgyŏng (Hamgyŏng-pukdo)	Ch'ŏngjin	6,784[4]	17,570[4]	2,327,362[4]
North Hwanghae (Hwanghae-pukdo)	Sariwŏn	3,576[5]	9,262[5]	2,113,672[5]
North P'yŏngan (P'yŏngan-pukdo)	Sinŭiju	4,707	12,191	2,728,662
South Hamgyŏng (Hamgyŏng-namdo)	Hamhŭng	7,324	18,970	3,066,013
South Hwanghae (Hwanghae-namdo)	Haeju	3,090	8,002	2,310,485
South P'yŏngan (P'yŏngan-namdo)	P'yŏngsŏng	4,761	12,330	4,051,696
Yanggang-do	Hyesan	5,528	14,317	719,269
Special districts				
Kaesŏng (industrial region)	...	[5]	[5]	[5]
Kŭmgang-san (tourist region)	...	[3]	[3]	[3]
Special cities				
P'yŏngyang	—	772	2,000	3,255,288
Rasŏn (Nasŏn)	—	[4]	[4]	[4]
MILITARY CAMPS	—	...	...	702,372
TOTAL		47,399	122,762	24,052,231

Demography

Population (2011): 24,336,000.
Density (2011): persons per sq mi 513.4, persons per sq km 198.2.
Urban-rural (2005): urban 61.6%; rural 38.4%.
Sex distribution (2008): male 48.73%; female 51.27%.
Age breakdown (2007): under 15, 22.1%; 15–29, 23.6%; 30–44, 25.6%; 45–59, 15.5%; 60–74, 11.0%; 75–84, 2.0%; 85 and over, 0.2%.
Population projection: (2020) 25,241,000; (2030) 26,063,000.
Ethnic composition (1999): Korean 99.8%; Chinese 0.2%.
Religious affiliation (2005): mostly nonreligious/atheist; autonomous religious activities almost nonexistent.
Major cities (2008): P'yŏngyang 2,581,076; Hamhŭng 703,610; Ch'ŏngjin 614,892; Sinŭiju 334,031; Wŏnsan 328,467; Namp'o 310,531.

Vital statistics

Birth rate per 1,000 population (2009): 14.8 (world avg. 20.3).
Death rate per 1,000 population (2009): 10.4 (world avg. 8.5).
Natural increase rate per 1,000 population (2009): 4.4 (world avg. 11.8).
Total fertility rate (avg. births per childbearing woman; 2009): 1.96.
Marriage/divorce rates per 1,000 population (1987): 9.3/0.2.
Life expectancy at birth (2009): male 61.2 years; female 66.5 years.
Major causes of death per 100,000 population (2002): diseases of the circulatory system 288; malignant neoplasms (cancers) 90; diseases of the respiratory system 62; injuries, violence, and accidents 62.

National economy

Budget (1999). Revenue: 19,801,000,000 [old] won (turnover tax and profits from state enterprises). Expenditures: 20,018,200,000 [old] won (1994; national economy 67.8%, social and cultural affairs 19.0%, defense 11.6%).
Public debt (external, outstanding; 2001): U.S.$12,500,000,000.
Population economically active (2008)[6]: total 12,174,000; activity rate of total population 51.1% (participation rates: ages 15–64, 70.8%; female 42.6%; unemployed, n.a.).
Production (metric tons except as noted). Agriculture, forestry, fishing (2009): rice 2,336,000, corn (maize) 1,705,000, potatoes 1,560,000, cabbages 751,001, apples 719,682, sweet potatoes 390,000, soybeans 350,000, dry beans 216,305, wheat 169,000, hen's eggs 158,243, peaches and nectarines 147,095, pears 137,900, rabbit meat 133,900, green onions 116,104, garlic 101,347, cow's milk 95,188, tobacco 80,324, pumpkins, squash, and gourds 77,785, cucumbers and gherkins 71,620, tomatoes 69,466, barley 63,000; livestock (number of live animals) 3,570,000 goats, 2,150,000 pigs, 576,000 cattle, 165,000 sheep; roundwood (2010) 7,448,867 cu m, of which fuelwood 80%; fisheries production 269,050 (from aquaculture 24%); aquatic plants production 444,300 (from aquaculture 100%). Mining and quarrying (2008): iron ore (metal content) 1,488,000; phosphate rock 300,000; magnesite 150,000; zinc (metal content) 70,000; sulfur 42,000; lead (metal content) 13,000; copper (metal content) 12,000; silver 20; gold 2,000 kg. Manufacturing (2007): cement 6,415,000; coke 2,000,000; crude steel 1,279,000; pig iron 900,000; fertilizers 479,000; synthetic fibres 30,000; textile fabrics (2004) 100,000,000 sq m; automobiles 4,700 vehicles. Energy production (consumption): electricity (kW-hr; 2007) 25,460,000,000 ([2006] 22,436,000,000); hard coal (metric tons; 2007) 25,060,000 (20,267,000); lignite (metric tons; 2007) 7,000,000 (6,478,000); crude petroleum (barrels; 2007) none (3,218,000); petroleum products (metric tons; 2007) 422,000 (838,000); natural gas, none (none).
Household income and expenditure. Average household size (1999) 4.6.
Gross national income (2009): U.S.$22,027,000,000 (U.S.$942 per capita).

Structure of gross domestic product and labour force

	2007		2004	
	in value U.S.$'000,000	% of total value	labour force	% of labour force
Agriculture	3,688	25.0	3,202,000	27.2
Mining / Public utilities	2,066	14.0	8,549,000 (Mining through Other)	72.8 (Mining through Other)
Manufacturing	2,803	19.0		
Construction	1,372	9.3		
Transp. and commun. / Trade / Finance / Pub. admin., defense / Services	4,819	32.7		
Other	5	—		
TOTAL	14,753	100.0	11,751,000	100.0

Selected balance of payments data. Receipts from (U.S.$'000,000): tourism, n.a.; remittances, n.a.; foreign direct investment (2008–10 avg.) 28; official development assistance (2009) 67. Disbursements for (U.S.$'000,000): tourism, n.a.; remittances, n.a.
Land use as % of total land area (2009): in temporary crops or left fallow 22.0%, in permanent crops 1.7%, in pasture 0.4%, forest area 48.1%.

Foreign trade

Balance of trade (current prices)

	2003	2004	2005	2006	2007	2008
U.S.$'000,000	−837	−817	−1,380	−1,102	−1,104	−1,512
% of total	35.0%	28.6%	34.0%	36.8%	37.5%	26.8%

Imports (2008): U.S.$3,574,000,000 ([2002] food, beverages, and other agricultural products 19.3%, mineral fuels and lubricants 15.5%, machinery and apparatus 15.4%, textiles and clothing 10.4%[7]). *Major import sources* (2008): China *c.* 57%; South Korea *c.* 25%; Russia *c.* 3%; Singapore *c.* 3%.
Exports (2008): U.S.$2,062,000,000 ([2002] live animals and agricultural products 39.3%, textiles and wearing apparel 16.7%, machinery and apparatus 11.6%, mineral fuels and lubricants 9.5%[7]). *Major export destinations* (2008): China *c.* 42%; South Korea *c.* 38%; India *c.* 5%.

Transport and communications

Transport. Railroads (2007): route length 2,796 mi, 4,500 km[8]; passenger-km 3,400,000,000[9]; metric ton-km cargo 9,100,000,000[9]. Roads (2007): total length 16,033 mi, 25,802 km (paved [2006] 3%). Vehicles (1990): passenger cars 248,000. Air transport: passenger-km (2005) 42,000,000; metric ton-km cargo (2007) 2,000,000.

Communications

Medium	date	number in '000s	units per 1,000 persons	Medium	date	number in '000s	units per 1,000 persons
Televisions	2003	3,563	160	PCs	2007	...	...
Telephones				Dailies	2009	4,500[10]	252[10]
Cellular	2010[11]	432[12]	18[12]	Internet users	2009	—	—
Landline	2010	1,180	49	Broadband	2010	—	—

Education and health

Educational attainment (2009[13]). Percentage of population age 15–64 having: primary education 43.9%; secondary 52.9%; vocational 1.2%; tertiary or higher 1.2%; other 0.9%. *Literacy* (2007): 99%.

Education (2000)

	teachers	students	student/ teacher ratio	enrollment rate (%)
Primary (age 6–9)	...	1,609,865	...	...
Secondary/Voc. (age 10–15)	...	2,181,524	...	...
Tertiary	...	...	...	... (age 16–20)

Health: physicians (2003) 74,597 (1 per 299 persons); hospital beds, n.a.; infant mortality rate per 1,000 live births (2009) 51.3; undernourished population (2005–07) 7,800,000 (33% of total population based on the consumption of a minimum daily requirement of 1,860 calories).

Military

Total active duty personnel (November 2010): 1,190,000 (army 85.7%, navy 5.0%, air force 9.3%); reserve 600,000; paramilitary 189,000; paramilitary reserve 5,700,000. *Military expenditure as percentage of GNP* (2004): 8.1%; per capita expenditure U.S.$80.

[1]Per constitutional revision of April 2009. [2]Currency revalued on Dec. 1, 2009; as of this date, 100 ([old] North Korean) won = 1 ([new] North Korean) won. The approximate value of the [new] won on the black market at the beginning of February 2010 was about 1 U.S.$ = 530 [new] won; 1 £ = 807 [new] won. [3]Kangwŏn-do includes Kŭmgang-san special district. [4]North Hamgyŏng includes Rasŏn. [5]North Hwanghae includes Kaesŏng special district. [6]ILO estimates. [7]Data for commodities (imports U.S.$1,525,400,000; exports U.S.$735,000,000) exclude trade with South Korea. [8]Estimate figure excludes some narrow-gauge railways. [9]At last report; year unknown. [10]Circulation of daily newspapers. [11]The ban on cellular phones, which began in 2004, was lifted in 2008, and service began in January 2009. [12]Subscribers. [13]Based on a survey of North Korean refugees in China; residents of the northeast provinces and lower-income classes are overrepresented.

Internet resource for further information:

- **Ministry of Unification**
  http://eng.unikorea.go.kr

Korea, South

Official name: Taehan Min'guk (Republic of Korea).
Form of government: unitary multiparty republic with one legislative house (National Assembly [299]).
Head of state and government: President assisted by Prime Minister.
Capital: Seoul.
Official language: Korean.
Official religion: none.
Monetary unit: (South Korean) won (W); valuation (Sept. 1, 2011) 1 U.S.$ = W 1,061; 1 £ = W 1,715.

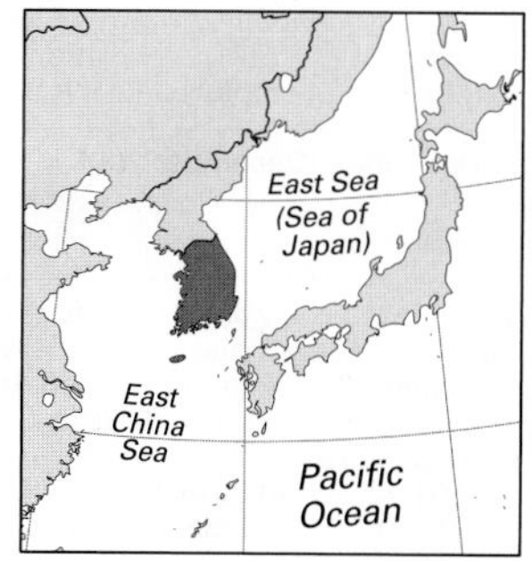

Area and population

Provinces	area sq km	population 2010 census[1]	Metropolitan cities	area sq km	population 2010 census[1]
Cheju[2]	1,849	531,905	Inch'ŏn	1,002	2,662,509
Kangwŏn	16,613	1,471,513	Kwangju	501	1,475,745
Kyŏnggi	10,132	11,379,459	Pusan	765	3,414,950
North Chŏlla	8,055	1,777,220	Sŏul (Seoul; special city)	605	9,794,304
North Ch'ungch'ŏng	7,432	1,512,157	Taegu	884	2,446,418
North Kyŏngsang	19,026	2,600,032	Taejŏn	540	1,501,859
South Chŏlla	12,095	1,741,499	Ulsan	1,057	1,082,567
South Ch'ungch'ŏng	8,600	2,028,002	TOTAL	99,678	48,580,293
South Kyŏngsang	10,522	3,160,154			

Demography

Population (2011): 48,755,000.
Density (2011): persons per sq mi 1,266.8, persons per sq km 489.1.
Urban-rural (2009): urban 82.7%; rural 17.3%.
Sex distribution (2008): male 50.23%; female 49.77%.
Age breakdown (2005): under 15, 18.6%; 15–29, 22.5%; 30–44, 26.0%; 45–59, 19.2%; 60–74, 10.7%; 75–84, 2.5%; 85 and over, 0.5%.
Population projection: (2020) 50,127,000; (2030) 50,655,000.
Ethnic composition (2000): Korean 97.7%; Japanese 2.0%; U.S. white 0.1%; Han Chinese 0.1%; other 0.1%.
Religious affiliation (2005): Christian *c.* 43%, of which Protestant *c.* 17%, independent Christian *c.* 16%, Roman Catholic *c.* 9%; traditional beliefs *c.* 15%; Buddhist *c.* 14%; New Religionist *c.* 14%; Confucianist *c.* 10%; other *c.* 4%.
Major cities (2010): Seoul 9,794,304; Pusan 3,414,950; Inch'ŏn 2,662,509; Taegu 2,446,418; Taejŏn 1,501,859.

Vital statistics

Birth rate per 1,000 population (2009): 9.1 (world avg. 20.3).
Death rate per 1,000 population (2009): 5.0 (world avg. 8.5).
Total fertility rate (avg. births per childbearing woman; 2009): 1.15.
Marriage/divorce rates per 1,000 population (2009): 6.3/2.5.
Life expectancy at birth (2008): male 76.5 years; female 83.3 years.
Major causes of death per 100,000 population (2009): malignant neoplasms (cancers) 142.2; cerebrovascular diseases 52.7; diseases of the heart 45.5.

National economy

Budget (2008). Revenue: W 178,649,200,000,000 (tax revenue 93.7%, of which income tax 42.3%, VAT 24.5%; nontax revenue 6.3%). Expenditures: W 170,762,900,000,000 (public services 25.1%; education 20.9%; defense 14.7%; health 0.4%).
Production (metric tons except as noted). Agriculture, forestry, fishing (2009): rice 7,023,000, cabbages 3,100,000, cow's milk 2,222,000, onions 1,200,000, pig meat 999,467, tangerines, mandarins, satsumas 620,000, hen's eggs 566,000, persimmons 450,000, garlic 380,000, strawberries 203,227, chestnuts 73,000; livestock (number of live animals) 9,584,900 pigs, 3,079,350 cattle, 138,768,000 chickens; roundwood (2010) 5,652,595 cu m, of which fuelwood 44%; fisheries production 2,329,675 (from aquaculture 20%); aquatic plants production 869,502 (from aquaculture 99%). Mining and quarrying (2008): feldspar 344,257; zinc (metal content) 3,672[3]; cadmium 3,090[4]; silver (metal content) 1,462 kg[3]. Manufacturing (value added in U.S.$'000,000; 2006): televisions, radios, telecommunications equipment, and electronic parts 70,085; transportation equipment 52,349, of which automobiles 20,987, automobile parts 16,175, ship and boat construction 12,771; machinery and apparatus 30,704; chemicals and chemical products 27,076; iron and steel 20,064; food and food products 19,928; fabricated metal products 19,172; textiles and wearing apparel 16,913; refined petroleum products 12,161. Energy production (consumption): electricity (kW-hr; 2008–09) 425,174,000,000 ([2008] 385,100,000,000); hard coal (metric tons; 2008–09) 2,604,000 ([2007] 88,558,000); lignite (metric tons; 2007) none (3,486,000); crude petroleum (barrels; 2006) 329,850 (868,150,000); petroleum products (metric tons; 2008) 102,023,000 (54,754,000); natural gas (cu m; 2007) 380,000,000 (37,150,000,000).
Household income and expenditure (2008). Average household size 2.9; annual income per household W 39,618,000 (U.S.$31,477); sources of income: wages 64.5%, self-employment 22.4%, transfers 7.9%; expenditure: transportation and communications 19.4%, food and beverages 15.2%, hotels and restaurants 6.1%.
Selected balance of payments data. Receipts from (U.S.$'000,000): tourism (2009) 9,442; remittances (2010) 2,744; foreign direct investment (FDI; 2008–10 avg.) 7,594. Disbursements for (U.S.$'000,000): tourism (2009) 13,330; remittances (2009) 3,120; FDI (2008–10 avg.) 18,893.
Gross national income (GNI; 2010): U.S.$972,299,000,000 (U.S.$19,890 per capita); purchasing power parity GNI (U.S.$29,010 per capita).

Structure of gross domestic product and labour force

	2007 in value W '000,000,000	2007 % of total value	2009 labour force	2009 % of labour force
Agriculture, forestry, and fishing	23,982	2.7	1,788,000	7.3
Mining and quarrying	2,839	0.3	23,000	0.1
Manufacturing	223,324	24.8	3,761,000	15.3
Construction	71,118	7.9	1,681,000	6.9
Public utilities	18,051	2.0	2,741,000	11.2
Transp. and commun.	57,451	6.4		
Trade, hotels	74,351	8.2	5,495,000	22.4
Finance, real estate	173,077	19.2	8,131,000	33.1
Pub. admin., defense	51,422	5.7		
Services	104,689	11.6		
Other	100,885[5]	11.2[5]	905,000[6]	3.7[6]
TOTAL	901,189	100.0	24,525,000	100.0

Public debt (June 2010): U.S.$255,287,000,000.
Population economically active (2009): total 24,525,000; activity rate 50.7% (participation rates: ages 15 and older 61.1%; female 41.3%; unemployed [October 2009–September 2010] 3.7%).

Price and earnings indexes (2005 = 100)

	2004	2005	2006	2007	2008	2009	2010
Consumer price index	97.3	100.0	102.2	104.8	109.7	112.8	116.1
Monthly earnings index	92.5	100.0	105.7	112.6	116.4	118.6	129.2

Land use as % of total land area (2009): in temporary crops 16.0%, left fallow 0.4%, in permanent crops 2.1%, in pasture 0.6%, forest area 64.1%.

Foreign trade[7]

Balance of trade (current prices)

	2004	2005	2006	2007	2008	2009
U.S.$'000,000	+29,382	+23,181	+16,082	+14,643	−13,267	+38,771
% of total	6.1%	4.2%	2.5%	2.0%	1.5%	5.7%

Imports (2008): U.S.$435,274,737,000 (mineral fuels 32.7%, of which crude petroleum 24.1%, natural gas 5.7%; machinery and apparatus 23.5%, of which electrical machinery 11.2%; chemicals and chemical products 8.4%; iron and steel 7.7%). *Major import sources:* China 17.7%; Japan 14.0%; U.S. 8.8%; Saudi Arabia 7.8%; U.A.E. 4.4%.
Exports (2008): U.S.$422,007,328,000 (machinery and apparatus 34.0%, of which telecommunications equipment 11.7%, electrical equipment 11.7%; transportation equipment 21.4%; chemicals and chemical products 10.1%; crude and refined petroleum 9.1%; professional and scientific equipment 6.0%). *Major export destinations:* China 21.7%; U.S. 11.0%; Japan 6.8%; Hong Kong 4.9%; Singapore 3.9%.

Transport and communications

Transport. Railroads (2008): length 2,101 mi, 3,381 km; passenger-km 54,997,000,000; metric ton-km cargo 11,566,000,000. Roads (2008): total length 64,019 mi, 103,029 km (paved 78%); passenger-km (2006) 97,854,000,000; metric ton-km cargo (2006) 12,545,000,000. Vehicles (2008): passenger cars 12,408,000; trucks and buses 4,260,000. Air transport (2008)[8]: passenger-km 79,575,000,000; metric ton-km cargo 12,235,000,000.

Communications

Medium	date	number in '000s	units per 1,000 persons	Medium	date	number in '000s	units per 1,000 persons
Televisions	2004	22,915	477	PCs	2007	27,736	578
Telephones				Dailies	2009	12,800[9]	261[9]
Cellular	2010	50,767[10]	1,054[10]	Internet users	2009	39,440	816
Landline	2010	28,543	592	Broadband	2010	17,650[10]	366[10]

Education and health

Educational attainment (2008). Percentage of population age 15 and older having: no formal schooling through lower secondary education 31.7%; upper secondary/higher vocational 39.2%; college 9.1%; university 20.0%. *Literacy* (2002): total population age 15 and over literate 97.9%; males 99.2%; females 96.6%.

Education (2007–08)

	teachers	students	student/ teacher ratio	enrollment rate (%)
Primary (age 6–11)	152,891	3,679,629	24.1	99
Secondary/Voc. (age 12–17)	219,288	3,958,781	18.1	95
Tertiary	208,262	3,204,310	15.4	98 (age 18–22)

Health: physicians (2008) 95,013 (1 per 507 persons); hospital beds (2006) 417,387 (1 per 114 persons); infant mortality rate (2009) 3.2; undernourished population (2005–07) less than 5.0% of total population based on the consumption of a minimum daily requirement of 1,900 calories.

Military

Total active duty personnel (November 2010): 655,000 (army 79.7%, navy 10.4%, air force 9.9%); reserve 4,500,000; [11]. *Military expenditure as percentage of GDP* (2009): 2.8%; per capita expenditure U.S.$507.

[1]Excludes usual residents who were abroad on census date. [2]Specifically a special autonomous province. [3]Excluding smelted metals. [4]Smelted only. [5]Taxes on products less subsidies. [6]Unemployed. [7]Imports c.i.f.; exports f.o.b. [8]Korean Air and Asiana Airlines. [9]Circulation of daily newspapers. [10]Subscribers. [11]U.S. troops (2010) 25,374.

Internet resource for further information:
- **Statistics Korea http://kostat.go.kr**

Kosovo

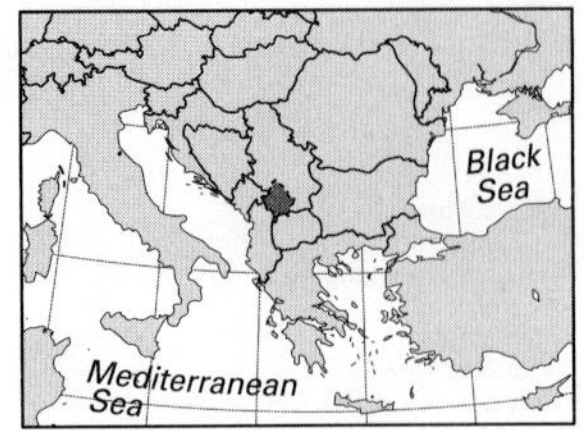

Official name: Republika e Kosovës (Albanian); Republika Kosovo (Serbian) (Republic of Kosovo)[1].
Form of government/Political status: multiparty transitional republic[2] with one legislative body (Assembly of Kosovo [120[3]]).
International authority: UN Interim Administrator[4].
Head of state: President.
Head of government: Prime Minister.
Capital: Pristina.
Official languages: Albanian; Serbian.
Official religion: none.
Monetary unit: euro (€); valuation (Sept. 1, 2011) 1 U.S.$ = €0.70; 1 £ = €1.13.[5]

Area and population

Regions[7]	area sq km	population 2008[6] estimate	Regions[7]	area sq km	population 2008[6] estimate
Ferizaj	1,022	181,501	Pejë	1,367	287,883
Gjakovë	1,237	118,423	Prishtinë (Pristina)	2,165	676,723
Gjilan	1,333	218,982	Prizren	1,730	401,335
Mitrovicë (Mitrovica)	2,053	268,292	TOTAL	10,908[8]	2,153,139

Demography

Population (2011): 1,826,000[9].
Density (2011): persons per sq mi 433.5, persons per sq km 167.4.
Urban-rural (2006): urban 37%; rural 63%.
Sex distribution (2009): male 50.50%; female 49.50%.
Age breakdown (2009): under 15, 28.2%; 15–64, 64.0%; 65 and over, 7.8%.
Population projection: (2020) 1,933,000[9]; (2030) 2,066,000[9].
Doubling time: 48 years.
Ethnic composition (2008): Albanian 92.0%; Serb 5.3%; other 2.7%.
Religious affiliation (2006): Muslim (including nominal population) *c.* 91%; Orthodox *c.* 5.5%; Roman Catholic *c.* 3%; Protestant *c.* 0.5%.
Major cities (2010[6]): Pristina 197,000; Prizren 131,000; Ferizaj 88,400; Gjakovë 81,000; Pejë 78,600; Mitrovicë (Mitrovica) 76,000.

Vital statistics

Birth rate per 1,000 population (2010): 18.6 (world avg. 19.2); within marriage 59.7%; outside of marriage 40.3%.
Death rate per 1,000 population (2010): 4.0 (world avg. 8.2).
Natural increase rate per 1,000 population (2010): 14.6 (world avg. 11.0).
Total fertility rate (avg. births per childbearing woman; 2003): 3.0.
Marriage/divorce rates per 1,000 population (2010): 10.1/0.9.
Life expectancy at birth (2004)[10]: male 69.8 years; female 71.4 years.
Major causes of death per 100,000 population (2007): diseases of the circulatory system *c.* 143; malignant neoplasms (cancers) *c.* 32; perinatal conditions *c.* 14; accidents *c.* 8; unspecified *c.* 145.

National economy

Budget (2009). Revenue: €1,146,700,000 (tax revenue 71.1%, of which border taxes [including customs duties and VAT] 55.3%, domestic taxes [mostly income and corporate taxes] 15.8%; nontax revenue 24.7%; other 4.2%). Expenditures: €1,232,400,000 (current expenditure 67.5%; capital expenditure 32.5%).
Public debt (external, outstanding; 2009): U.S.$359,000,000.
Production (metric tons except as noted). Agriculture, forestry, fishing (2008): wheat 293,064, hay 216,515, potatoes 103,958, corn (maize) 68,424, peppers 51,274, tomatoes 20,587, cabbage 19,041, onions 15,987, apples 12,612, plums 10,901, grapes 8,601; livestock (number of live animals) 341,608 cattle, 161,353 sheep, 2,046,925 chickens, 43,297 beehives; roundwood 457,983 cu m, of which fuelwood 99%; fisheries production, n.a. Mining and quarrying (2010): lead 7,660[11]; zinc 6,450[11]; limestone 2,606,047 cu m. Manufacturing (2010): cement, bricks, and tiles for reconstruction of housing; food; beverages. Energy production (consumption): electricity (kW-hr; 2010–11) 5,609,200,000 (3,577,000,000); hard coal, none (none); lignite (metric tons; 2010–11) 8,532,600 (8,598,000); crude petroleum, none (none); petroleum products, none (n.a.); natural gas, none (none).
Gross national income (at current market prices; 2009): U.S.$5,981,000,000 (U.S.$3,300 per capita).

Structure of gross domestic product and labour force

	2007 in value €'000,000	2007 % of total value	2006[12] labour force	2006[12] % of labour force
Agriculture	413.6	12.0	81,100	11.9
Mining	25.2	0.7	5,700	0.8
Manufacturing }	384.8	11.2	27,700	4.1
Public utilities }			13,600	2.0
Construction	342.4	10.0	30,700	4.5
Trade, hotels	349.2	10.2	72,800	10.7
Transp. and commun.	122.7	3.6	14,000	2.1
Finance, real estate	574.9	16.7	13,300	2.0
Pub. admin., defense	454.3	13.2	24,600	3.6
Services	182.3	5.3	91,300	13.4
Other	584.2[13]	17.0[13]	305,200[14]	44.9[14]
TOTAL	3,433.6	100.0[8]	680,000	100.0

Population economically active (2007): total *c.* 633,000[12]; activity rate of total population *c.* 30% (participation rates: ages 15–64 *c.* 47%; female *c.* 28%[12]; unofficially unemployed [2009] 45.4%).

Price index (December 2005 = 100)

	2004	2005	2006	2007	2008	2009	2010
Consumer price index	101.4	100.0	100.6	105.0	114.8	112.1	116.0

Household income and expenditure (2010). Average household size 5.8; sources of income: wages and salaries 54%, self-employment 16%, remittances 10%, pensions 9%; expenditure: food and nonalcoholic beverages 35.4%, housing 33.1%, transportation 5.9%, clothing 5.6%, alcohol and tobacco 3.6%.
Selected balance of payments data. Receipts from (U.S.$'000,000): tourism (2008) 42; remittances (2009) 702; foreign direct investment (FDI; 2007–09 avg.) 510; official development assistance (2009) 788. Disbursements for (U.S.$'000,000): tourism (2008) 82; remittances (2006) 126; FDI (2006–08 avg.) 15.
Land use as % of total land area (2007): in temporary crops 12.2%, left fallow 2.0%, in permanent crops 0.5%, in pasture 9.1%, forest area 41.3%.

Foreign trade[15]

Balance of trade (current prices)

	2005	2006	2007	2008	2009	2010
€'000,000	–1,101.2	–1,195.1	–1,411.1	–1,732.0	–1,770.2	–1,845.5
% of total	90.7%	83.7%	81.0%	81.6%	84.3%	75.8%

Imports (2010): €2,139,534,000 ([2008] food and live animals 24.6%, mineral fuels 20.1%, machinery and apparatus 12.2%, base metals 9.3%, chemicals and chemical products 7.2%, transportation equipment 6.7%). *Major import sources:* Macedonia 14.8%; Germany 12.9%; Serbia 12.2%; Turkey 7.0%; China 6.3%.
Exports (2010): €294,031,000 ([2008] iron and steel [all forms] 63.3%[16], food products 11.0%, mineral fuels 9.1%). *Major export destinations:* Italy 27.2%; India 15.0%; Albania 11.0%; Macedonia 8.9%; Switzerland 6.0%.

Transport and communications

Transport. Railroads (2006): route length[17] (2009) 207 mi, 333 km; passenger-km 317,320; metric ton-km cargo 82,459. Roads (2009): total length 1,196 mi, 1,925 km (paved 87%). Vehicles (2007[6]): passenger cars 146,744; trucks and buses 20,850. Air transport (2009)[18]: passenger arrivals 578,451; passenger departures 613,527.

Communications

Medium	date	number in '000s	units per 1,000 persons	Medium	date	number in '000s	units per 1,000 persons
Televisions	2005	...	...	PCs	2007	...	...
Telephones				Dailies	2009	32[19]	18[19]
Cellular	2009	1,220[20]	676[20]	Internet users	2008	377	209
Landline	2009	76	42	Broadband	2009	115[20]	64[20]

Education and health

Educational attainment (2009). Percentage of population age 15 and over having: less than complete secondary education 53.0%; complete secondary 37.8%; higher 9.2%. *Literacy* (2004): total population age 15 and over literate 94.1%; males literate 97.3%; females literate 91.3%.

Education (2009–10)

	teachers	students	student/teacher ratio	enrollment rate (%)
Primary (age 6–15)[21]	17,393	307,090	17.7	...
Secondary/Voc. (age 16–19)[22]	5,565	104,900	18.8	...
Tertiary	1,015	37,839	37.3	... (age 20–24)

Health (2009): physicians 2,006 (1 per 900 persons); hospital beds[23] 3,764 (1 per 480 persons); infant mortality rate per 1,000 live births (2010) 8.1.

Military

Total active duty personnel (October 2011): NATO-led Kosovo Force 6,240 troops[24]; local Albanian paramilitary (Kosovo Security Force; March 2010) 2,500.

[1]Alternate short-form names in Albanian include Kosova and Kosovë. [2]Independence was declared Feb. 17, 2008, and the new constitution became effective on June 15, 2008. Serbia continued to claim Kosovo as an integral part despite a ruling by the International Court of Justice in July 2010 supporting Kosovo's independence. [3]20 seats are reserved for minority communities. [4]Assisted by the EU special envoy from February 2008. A 2,000-member EU mission to Kosovo (headed by the special envoy) is expected to eventually replace the UN as international administrative authority. [5]Kosovo uses the euro as its official currency even though it is not a member of the EU. The Serb-populated area of Kosovo uses the Serbian dinar. [6]January 1. [7]Statistical/planning regions; actual local government is based on 30 municipalities. [8]Detail does not add to total given because of rounding. [9]Estimate of U.S. Bureau of the Census International Database (December 2008 update). [10]Albanian population only. [11]Metal content. [12]Ages 15–64 only. [13]Taxes on products less very small statistical discrepancy. [14]Unemployed. [15]Imports c.i.f.; exports f.o.b. [16]Nearly all scrap metal. [17]Of which 40% functional in 2009. [18]Pristina airport only. [19]Circulation. [20]Subscribers. [21]Includes lower secondary. [22]Excludes lower secondary. [23]Excluding Family Medicine Center of Kosovo. [24]Troops providing security and stability from 30 nations including 8 non-NATO nations.

Internet resources for further information:

- **Statistical Office of Kosovo**
  http://esk.rks-gov.net/eng
- **Central Bank of the Republic of Kosovo**
  http://www.bqk-kos.org/

Kuwait

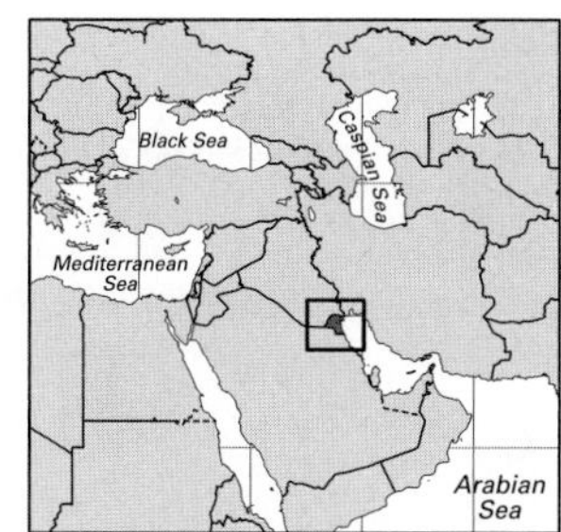

Official name: Dawlat al-Kuwayt (State of Kuwait).
Form of government: constitutional monarchy with one legislative body (National Assembly [50[1]]).
Head of state and government: Emir assisted by the Prime Minister.
Capital: Kuwait (city).
Official language: Arabic.
Official religion: Islam.
Monetary unit: Kuwaiti dinar (KD); valuation (Sept. 1, 2011) 1 KD = U.S.$3.67 = £2.27.

Area and population

Governorates	Capitals	area sq mi	area sq km	population 2011[2] estimate
Al-Aḥmadī	Al-Aḥmadī	1,977	5,120	682,582
Al-ʿĀṣimah	Kuwait (city) (Al-Kuwayt)	77	200	509,692
Al-Farwānīyah	Al-Farwānīyah	73	190	935,900
Ḥawallī	Ḥawallī	31	80	769,752
Al-Jahrāʾ	Al-Jahrāʾ	4,336	11,230	454,836
Mubārak al-Kabīr	...	39	100	223,912
Islands[3]	—	347	900	...
TOTAL		6,880	17,818[4]	3,582,054[5]

Demography

Population (2011): 3,650,000.
Density (2011): persons per sq mi 530.5, persons per sq km 204.8.
Urban-rural (2005): urban 98.3%; rural 1.7%.
Sex distribution (2007): male 59.34%; female 40.66%.
Age breakdown (2005): under 15, 24.3%; 15–29, 26.8%; 30–44, 34.2%; 45–59, 11.6%; 60–74, 2.7%; 75–84, 0.3%; 85 and over, 0.1%.
Population projection: (2020) 4,423,000; (2030) 5,228,000.
Doubling time: 36 years.
Ethnic composition (2005): Arab 57%, of which Kuwaiti 35%; Bedouin 4%; non-Arab (primarily Asian) 39%.
Religious affiliation (2005)[6]: Muslim 74%, of which Sunnī 59%, Shīʿī 15%; Christian 13%, of which Roman Catholic 9%; Hindu 10%; Buddhist 3%.
Major cities (2011[2]): Qalīb al-Shuyūkh 265,984; Al-Sālimīyah 238,577; Ḥawallī 171,804; Kuwait (city) 56,234 (urban agglomeration [2007] 2,063,000).

Vital statistics

Birth rate per 1,000 population (2008): 21.9 (world avg. 20.3).
Death rate per 1,000 population (2008): 2.3 (world avg. 8.5).
Natural increase rate per 1,000 population (2008): 19.6 (world avg. 11.8).
Total fertility rate (avg. births per childbearing woman; 2008): 2.81.
Marriage/divorce rates per 1,000 population (2007): 5.5/2.1.
Life expectancy at birth (2008): male 76.4 years; female 78.7 years.
Major causes of death per 100,000 population (2006): circulatory diseases 94.5; accidents and violence 36.4; malignant neoplasms (cancers) 29.1; respiratory diseases 11.7; endocrine, nutritional, and metabolic diseases 8.6.

National economy

Budget (2006–07). Revenue: KD 15,509,300,000 (oil revenue 93.6%, assorted taxes 1.9%). Expenditures: KD 12,568,700,000 (social security and welfare 29.1%, general public administration 15.8%, oil/electricity 13.4%, defense 10.3%, education 10.1%, health 5.3%).
Public debt (external, outstanding; 2010): U.S.$7,092,000,000.
Gross national income (2009): U.S.$120,816,000,000 (U.S.$40,474 per capita).

Structure of gross domestic product and labour force

	2008 in value KD '000,000	2008 % of total value	2007 labour force	2007 % of labour force
Agriculture	71.9	0.2	35,600	1.7
Mining	47.4	0.1	6,300	0.3
Oil and natural gas	23,608.1	59.3		
Manufacturing	2,222.4[7]	5.6[7]	115,100	5.5
Construction	589.7	1.5	169,500	8.1
Public utilities	325.6	0.8	12,600	0.6
Transp. and commun.	2,179.2	5.5	62,800	3.0
Trade, hotels	1,377.1	3.5	311,800	14.9
Finance, real estate	5,972.1	15.0	100,400	4.8
Pub. admin., defense Services	4,870.1	12.2	973,000	46.5
Other	–1,476.2[8]	–3.7[8]	305,400[9]	14.6[9]
TOTAL	39,787.4	100.0	2,092,500	100.0

Production (metric tons except as noted). Agriculture, forestry, fishing (2009): tomatoes 62,000, cucumbers and gherkins 44,000, potatoes 25,229, hen's eggs 22,807, eggplants 21,000, dates 15,787, chilies and peppers 8,948; livestock (number of live animals) 900,000 sheep, 145,000 goats, 31,500 cattle, 5,800 camels; roundwood (2010) 18,079 cu m, of which fuelwood 100%; fisheries production 4,733 (from aquaculture 8%). Mining and quarrying (2009): sulfur 830,000; lime 45,000. Manufacturing (value added in KD '000,000; 2006): refined petroleum products 829; basic chemicals 230; bricks, cement, tiles 98; food products 57; structural metal products 51; wearing apparel 40. Energy production (consumption): electricity (kW-hr; 2007) 48,753,000,000 (48,753,000,000); coal, none (none); crude petroleum (barrels; 2008) 979,300,000 ([2007] 346,800,000); petroleum products (metric tons; 2007) 38,667,000 (11,765,000); natural gas (cu m; 2007) 13,305,000,000 (13,305,000,000).
Population economically active (2007): total 2,092,509, of which Kuwaiti 15.5%, non-Kuwaiti 84.5%; activity rate of total population 61.6% (participation rates: ages 15–64 [2005] 70.8%[10]; female [2005] 25.2%[10]; unemployed [2006] 4.0%[11]).

Price index (2005 = 100)

	2004	2005	2006	2007	2008	2009	2010
Consumer price index	96.0	100.0	103.0	108.7	120.2	125.0	130.0

Household income and expenditure. Average Kuwaiti household size (2004) 4.8; average non-Kuwaiti household size (2004) 5.0; sources of income, n.a.; expenditure (2000)[12]: housing and energy 26.8%, food 18.3%, transportation and communications 16.1%, household furnishings 14.7%, clothing and footwear 8.9%.
Selected balance of payments data. Receipts from (U.S.$'000,000): tourism (2009) 248; remittances, n.a.; foreign direct investment (FDI; 2008–10 avg.) 396. Disbursements for (U.S.$'000,000): tourism (2009) 7,441; remittances (2009) 9,912; FDI (2008–10 avg.) 6,599.
Land use as % of total land area (2009): in temporary crops or left fallow 0.6%, in permanent crops 0.2%, in pasture 7.6%, forest area 0.3%.

Foreign trade[13]

Balance of trade (current prices)

	2003	2004	2005	2006	2007	2008
KD '000,000	+2,888	+4,705	+8,488	+11,252	+11,742	+16,774
% of total	30.6%	38.7%	47.9%	52.9%	49.2%	55.6%

Imports (2007): KD 6,069,000,000 (machinery and apparatus 26.6%, road vehicles 15.1%, food 11.5%, iron and steel 9.3%). *Major import sources* (2008): U.S. *c.* 12%; Japan *c.* 9%; Germany *c.* 8%; China *c.* 8%; Saudi Arabia *c.* 7%.
Exports (2007): KD 17,811,000,000 (crude petroleum 61.6%, refined petroleum 29.8%, liquefied propane and butane 3.1%, polyethylene 1.7%). *Major export destinations* (2008): Japan *c.* 19%; South Korea *c.* 15%; India *c.* 11%; Taiwan *c.* 10%; U.S. *c.* 9%.

Transport and communications

Transport. Railroads: none. Roads (2008): total length 3,941 mi, 6,342 km (paved [2004] 85%). Vehicles (2009): passenger cars 1,098,251; trucks and buses 225,474. Air transport (2008)[14]: passenger-km 7,447,000,000; metric ton-km cargo 280,346,000.

Communications

Medium	date	number in '000s	units per 1,000 persons	Medium	date	number in '000s	units per 1,000 persons
Televisions	2004	1,040	392	PCs	2007	779	237
Telephones				Dailies	2009	961[15]	485[15]
Cellular	2010	4,400[16]	1,608[16]	Internet users	2009	1,100	369
Landline	2010	566	207	Broadband	2010	46[16]	17[16]

Education and health

Educational attainment (2005). Percentage of population age 10 and over having: no formal schooling: illiterate 6.2%, literate 37.9%; primary education 12.7%; lower secondary 20.8%; upper secondary 11.7%; some higher 4.1%; completed undergraduate 6.6%. *Literacy* (2007): total population age 15 and over literate 94.5%; males literate 95.2%; females literate 93.1%.

Education (2007–08)

	teachers	students	student/ teacher ratio	enrollment rate (%)
Primary (age 6–10)	22,895	208,608	9.1	88
Secondary/Voc. (age 11–17)	27,496	249,784	9.1	80
Tertiary[17]	1,986	37,521	18.9	18 (age 18–22)

Health (2006): physicians 4,775 (1 per 646 persons); hospital beds 5,760 (1 per 535 persons); infant mortality rate per 1,000 live births (2008) 9.2; undernourished population (2005–07) 100,000 (5.0% of total population based on the consumption of a minimum daily requirement of 1,950 calories).

Military

Total active duty personnel (November 2010): 15,500 (army 71.0%, navy/coast guard 12.9%, air force 16.1%); reserve 23,700; U.S. troops for Iraqi support (May 2009) *c.* 15,000[18]. *Military expenditure as percentage of GDP* (2009): 5.4%; per capita expenditure U.S.$1,932.

[1]Excludes 15 cabinet ministers not elected to National Assembly serving ex officio. [2]January 1. [3]Includes Būbiyān Island 333 sq mi (863 sq km) and Warbah Island 14 sq mi (37 sq km). [4]Detail does not add to total given because of rounding. [5]Includes 5,380 inhabitants with unknown residence. [6]Includes noncitizens. [7]Manufacturing includes oil products. [8]Import duties less imputed bank and insurance service charges. [9]Unclassified. [10]2005 census data are based on only about one-half of the non-Kuwaiti population economically active. [11]Kuwaiti nationals only. [12]Weights of consumer price index components. [13]Imports c.i.f.; exports f.o.b. [14]Kuwait Airways. [15]Circulation of daily newspapers. [16]Subscribers. [17]2005–06. [18]U.S. troops were scheduled to withdraw from Iraq by the end of 2011; some troops were expected to remain in Kuwait as a backup force in 2012.

Internet resources for further information:
- **Central Bank of Kuwait http://www.cbk.gov.kw**
- **Central Statistical Office http://www.cso.gov.kw**

Kyrgyzstan

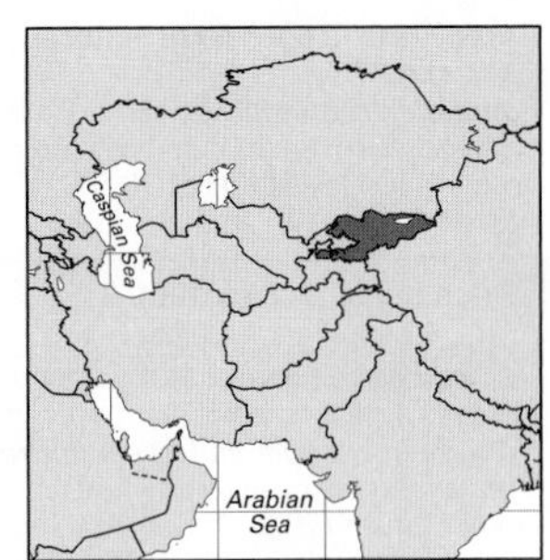

Official name: Kyrgyz Respublikasy (Kyrgyz); Respublika Kirgizstan (Russian) (Kyrgyz Republic).
Form of government: interim regime[1] with one legislative house (Jogorku Kenesh, or Supreme Council [120]).
Head of state and government: President (interim)[1].
Capital: Bishkek.
Official languages: Kyrgyz; Russian.
Official religion: none.
Monetary unit: Kyrgyzstan som (KGS); valuation (Sept. 1, 2011) 1 U.S.$ = KGS 44.70; 1 £ = KGS 72.24.

Area and population

		area		population
				2009
Provinces	**Capitals**	sq mi	sq km	census
Batken	Batken	6,564	17,000	380,300
Chüy	Bishkek[2]	7,795	20,189	790,500
Jalal-Abad	Jalal-Abad	12,991	33,648	938,600
Naryn	Naryn	17,453	45,202	245,300
Osh	Osh	11,251	29,139	1,000,000
Talas	Talas	4,419	11,446	219,600
Ysyk-Köl	Ysyk-Köl	16,658	43,144	425,100
City Districts				
Bishkek[2]	—	49	127	865,100
Osh		19	50	243,200
TOTAL		77,199	199,945	5,107,700[3]

Demography

Population (2011): 5,168,000.
Density (2011): persons per sq mi 66.9, persons per sq km 25.8.
Urban-rural (2009): urban 35.3%; rural 64.7%.
Sex distribution (2009): male 48.73%; female 51.27%.
Age breakdown (2005): under 15, 31.3%; 15–29, 29.3%; 30–44, 19.9%; 45–59, 12.2%; 60–74, 5.2%; 75–84, 1.9%; 85 and over, 0.2%.
Population projection: (2020) 5,755,000; (2030) 6,382,000.
Doubling time: 41 years.
Ethnic composition (2008[4]): Kyrgyz 69.2%; Uzbek 14.5%; Russian 8.7%; Hui 1.2%; Uighur 1.0%; other 5.4%.
Religious affiliation (2000): Muslim (mostly Sunnī) 60.8%; Christian 10.4%, of which Russian Orthodox 7.7%; nonreligious 21.6%; atheist 6.3%; other 0.9%.
Major cities (2009[5]): Bishkek 865,100; Osh 243,200; Jalal-Abad 92,100; Karakol 63,700; Tokmok 53,100.

Vital statistics

Birth rate per 1,000 population (2008): 24.1 (world avg. 20.3); within marriage (1994) 83.2%; outside of marriage (1994) 16.8%.
Death rate per 1,000 population (2008): 7.1 (world avg. 8.5).
Total fertility rate (avg. births per childbearing woman; 2008): 2.80.
Marriage/divorce rates per 1,000 population: (2008) 8.4/(2006) 1.3.
Life expectancy at birth (2008): male 64.6 years; female 72.7 years.
Major causes of death per 100,000 population (2007): diseases of the circulatory system 363.9; diseases of the respiratory system 70.9; malignant neoplasms (cancers) 58.4; diseases of the digestive system 54.5; accidents 49.7.

National economy

Budget (2008). Revenue: KGS 45,479,000,000 (tax revenue 79.0%, of which VAT 36.4%, customs duties 10.2%, personal income tax 8.6%; nontax revenue 17.9%; grants 3.1%). Expenditures: KGS 36,944,000,000 (education 26.0%; general administration 18.3%; defense/public order 14.8%; social security 12.6%; health 11.8%).
Public debt (external, outstanding; 2011[6]): U.S.$2,769,900,000.
Population economically active (2008): total 2,379,900; activity rate of total population 46.5% (participation rates: ages 15–64 [2006] 70.4%; female 43.0%; unemployed [2010] 9.3%).

Price and earnings indexes (2005 = 100)

	2004	2005	2006	2007	2008	2009	2010
Consumer price index	95.8	100.0	105.6	116.3	144.8	154.8	167.1
Average earnings index	85.8	100.0	119.0	155.0	211.3	243.5	278.2

Production (metric tons except as noted). Agriculture, forestry, fishing (2009): potatoes 1,393,140, cow's milk 1,273,540, wheat 1,056,660, corn (maize) 486,636, tomatoes 194,161, apples 146,000, sunflower seeds 57,510, garlic 32,024, tobacco leaves 12,005; livestock (number of live animals) 3,605,790 sheep, 1,224,600 cattle, 362,433 horses; roundwood (2010) 27,300 cu m, of which fuelwood 66%; fisheries production 143 (from aquaculture 93%). Mining and quarrying (2009): mercury 250; gold 16,950 kg. Manufacturing (value of production in KGS '000,000; 2009): base metals and fabricated metal products 47,340; food, beverages, and tobacco products 13,933; cement, bricks, and ceramics 5,256; textiles and wearing apparel 4,498. Energy production (consumption): electricity (kW-hr; 2009) 9,983,000,000[7] ([2007] 13,858,000,000); hard coal (metric tons; 2009) 54,000[7] ([2007] 839,000); lignite (metric tons; 2009) 441,000[7] ([2007] 468,000); crude petroleum (barrels; 2009) 458,737[7] ([2007] 923,290); petroleum products (metric tons; 2007) 121,000 (624,000); natural gas (cu m; 2009) 13,710,445[7] ([2008] 750,000,000).
Household income and expenditure. Average household size (2004) 4.3; income per capita of household (2003) KGS 9,270 (U.S.$212); sources of income (1999): wages and salaries 29.2%, self-employment 25.6%, other 45.2%; expenditure (2005): food and nonalcoholic beverages 46.4%, transport 10.4%, alcohol, tobacco products, and narcotics 9.5%, clothing and footwear 9.0%, housing and energy 8.0%, household furnishings 3.4%.
Gross national income (GNI; 2009): U.S.$4,701,000,000 (U.S.$880 per capita); purchasing power parity GNI (U.S.$2,180 per capita).

Structure of gross domestic product and labour force

	2009		2008	
	in value KGS '000,000	% of total value	labour force	% of labour force
Agriculture, forestry, fishing	43,372.8	22.1	743,000	31.2
Mining and quarrying	1,232.7	0.6	13,300	0.6
Manufacturing	24,577.0	12.5	178,000	7.5
Public utilities	3,334.0	1.7	37,800	1.6
Construction	11,235.3	5.7	221,900	9.3
Transp. and commun.	17,931.0	9.1	133,800	5.6
Trade, hotels	34,900.2	17.8	385,600	16.2
Finance, real estate	9,573.9	4.9	61,900	2.6
Public admin., defense	12,322.3	6.3	101,700	4.3
Services	16,083.9	8.2	307,400	12.9
Other	21,860.0[8]	11.1[8]	195,600[9]	8.2[9]
TOTAL	196,423.1	100.0	2,379,900[10]	100.0

Selected balance of payments data. Receipts from (U.S.$'000,000): tourism (2009) 459; remittances (2010) 1,037; foreign direct investment (2008–10 avg.) 267; official development assistance (2009) 315. Disbursements for (U.S.$'000,000): tourism (2009) 265; remittances (2009) 188.
Land use as % of total land area (2009): in temporary crops or left fallow (2007) 6.7%, in permanent crops 0.4%, in pasture 48.3%, forest area 4.9%.

Foreign trade[11]

Balance of trade (current prices)

	2005	2006	2007	2008	2009	2010
U.S.$'000,000	–435.8	–924.1	–1,282.8	–2,454.7	–1,795.6	–1,734.2
% of total	24.5%	36.8%	36.1%	43.1%	43.2%	36.8%

Imports (2007): U.S.$2,417,000,000 (refined petroleum 25.2%, machinery and apparatus 14.4%, food products 11.6%, chemicals and chemical products 10.6%, road vehicles/parts 4.8%). *Major import sources* (2009): Russia 37.2%; China 18.9%; Kazakhstan 10.9%; Uzbekistan 3.8%; U.S. 3.6%.
Exports (2007): U.S.$1,134,200,000 (refined petroleum 20.8%, gold 19.8%, machinery and apparatus 6.2%, women's/girls' outerwear 5.5%, vegetables 4.2%, glass 3.5%, portland cement 3.5%). *Major export destinations* (2009): Switzerland 31.7%; Russia 13.4%; Uzbekistan 11.9%; Kazakhstan 9.7%; U.A.E. 7.2%.

Transport and communications

Transport. Railroads (2008): route length 292 mi, 470 km; passenger-km 90,200,000; metric ton-km cargo 945,500,000. Roads (2007): total length 21,127 mi, 34,000 km (paved, n.a.); passenger-km 6,468,000,000; metric ton-km cargo 902,000,000. Vehicles (2007): passenger cars 229,735; trucks and buses, n.a. Air transport (2009–10): passenger-km 484,000,000; metric ton-km cargo 2,160,000.

Communications

Medium	date	number in '000s	units per 1,000 persons	Medium	date	number in '000s	units per 1,000 persons
Televisions	2004	955	185	PCs	2007	99	19
Telephones				Dailies	2009	65[12]	13[12]
Cellular	2010	4,900[13]	919[13]	Internet users	2009	2,194	400
Landline	2010	502	94	Broadband	2010	15.4[13]	2.9[13]

Education and health

Educational attainment (1999). Percentage of population age 15 and over having: primary education 6.3%; some secondary 18.3%; completed secondary 50.0%; some postsecondary 14.9%; higher 10.5%. *Literacy* (2008): total population age 15 and over literate, virtually 100%.

Education (2007–08)

	teachers	students	student/ teacher ratio	enrollment rate (%)
Primary (age 7–10)	16,524	399,833	24.2	84
Secondary/Voc. (age 11–17)	52,614[14]	696,833	13.6[14]	80
Tertiary	17,810	296,267	16.6	52 (age 18–22)

Health (2007): physicians 12,395 (1 per 408 persons); hospital beds 26,345 (1 per 192 persons); infant mortality rate per 1,000 live births 30.6; undernourished population (2004–06) less than 5.0% of total population based on the consumption of a minimum daily requirement of 1,880 calories.

Military

Total active duty personnel (November 2010): 10,900 (army 78.0%, air force 22.0%)[15]. *Military expenditure as percentage of GDP* (2009): 0.5%; per capita expenditure U.S.$5.

[1]Interim regime from April 7, 2010; new constitution approved June 27, 2010. [2]Bishkek is the capital of Chüy province, even though it is not part of the province. [3]De facto population; de jure population including residents temporarily abroad equals 5,362,800. [4]January 1. [5]March. [6]June 30. [7]Excludes November production. [8]Taxes on products. [9]Unemployed. [10]Detail does not add to total given because of rounding. [11]Imports c.i.f.; exports f.o.b. [12]Circulation of daily newspapers. [13]Subscribers. [14]2006–07. [15]Russian troops (November 2010) *c.* 500.

Internet resource for further information:

- **National Bank of Kyrgyz Republic http://www.nbkr.kg**

Laos

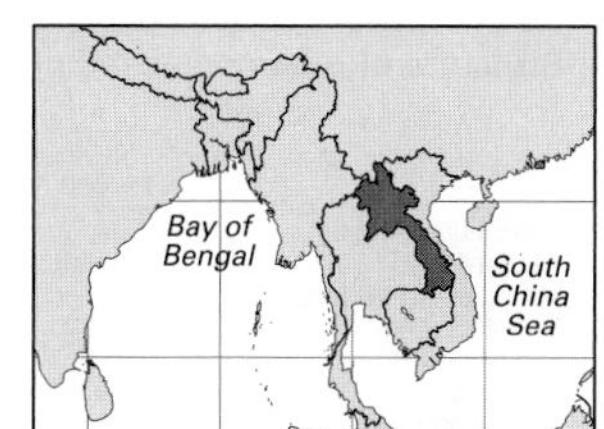

Official name: Sathalanalat Paxathipatai Paxaxôn Lao (Lao People's Democratic Republic).
Form of government: unitary single-party people's republic with one legislative house (National Assembly [132]).
Head of state: President.
Head of government: Prime Minister.
Capital: Vientiane (Viangchan).
Official language: Lao.
Official religion: none.
Monetary unit: kip (KN); valuation (Sept. 1, 2011) 1 U.S.$ = KN 7,986; 1 £ = KN 12,905.

Area and population

Provinces	area sq km	population 2009 estimate	Provinces	area sq km	population 2009 estimate
Attapu	10,320	124,000	Savannakhét	21,774	891,000
Bokèo	6,196	162,000	Viangchan	18,526	467,000
Bolikhamxai	14,863	256,000	Xaignabouli	16,389	367,000
Champasak	15,415	644,000	Xékong	7,665	95,000
Houaphan	16,500	310,000	Xiangkhoang	20,386	264,000
Khammouan	16,315	368,000			
Louangnamtha	9,325	160,000	**Municipality**		
Louangphrabang	16,875	440,000	Vientiane		
Oudomxay	15,370	293,000	(Viangchan)	3,920	754,000
Phôngsali	16,270	174,000	TOTAL	236,800	6,128,000[1]
Salavan	10,691	358,000			

Demography

Population (2011): 6,392,000.
Density (2011): persons per sq mi 69.9, persons per sq km 27.0.
Urban-rural (2009): urban 32.0%; rural 68.0%.
Sex distribution (2009): male 49.90%; female 50.10%.
Age breakdown (2009): under 15, 37.8%; 15–29, 29.3%; 30–44, 17.4%; 45–59, 10.0%; 60–74, 4.4%; 75–84, 1.0%; 85 and over, 0.1%.
Population projection: (2020) 7,170,000; (2030) 7,892,000.
Doubling time: 30 years.
Ethnic composition (2005): Lao 54.6%; Khmou 10.9%[2]; Hmong 8.0%; Tai 3.8%[3]; Phu Tai (Phouthay) 3.3%[3]; Lue 2.2%[3]; Katang 2.1%[2]; Makong 2.1%[2]; other 13.0%.
Religious affiliation (2005): traditional beliefs *c.* 49%; Buddhist *c.* 43%; Christian *c.* 2%; nonreligious/other *c.* 6%.
Major cities (2003): Vientiane 194,200 (urban agglomeration [2009] 799,000); Savannakhét 58,200; Pakxé 50,100; Xam Nua 40,700; Muang Khammouan 27,300; Louangphrabang 26,400.

Vital statistics

Birth rate per 1,000 population (2009): 27.2 (world avg. 20.3).
Death rate per 1,000 population (2009): 8.4 (world avg. 8.5).
Natural increase rate per 1,000 population (2009): 18.8 (world avg. 11.8).
Total fertility rate (avg. births per childbearing woman; 2009): 3.32.
Life expectancy at birth (2009): male 59.8 years; female 63.5 years.
Major causes of death per 100,000 population (2002): communicable diseases 673; cardiovascular diseases 210; injuries, accidents, and violence 112; malignant neoplasms (cancers) 73; chronic respiratory diseases 58.

National economy

Budget (2008–09). Revenue: KN 8,065,000,000,000 (tax revenue 78.6%, of which excise tax 17.8%, turnover tax 16.7%, tax on mining sector 12.6%, import duties 10.3%; nontax revenue 12.1%; grants 9.3%). Expenditures: KN 9,783,000,000,000 (current expenditure 58.3%; capital expenditure 36.5%).
Public debt (external, outstanding; 2009): U.S.$2,923,000,000.
Population economically active (2008): total 3,000,000[4]; activity rate of total population 48.3%[4] (participation rates: ages 15–64, 81.0%[4]; female 50.5%[4]; unofficially unemployed, n.a.).

Price index (2005 = 100)

	2004	2005	2006	2007	2008	2009	2010
Consumer price index	93.3	100.0	106.8	111.6	120.1	120.2	127.4

Production (metric tons except as noted). Agriculture, forestry, fishing (2009): rice 3,144,800, corn (maize) 848,745, sugarcane 433,500, cassava 152,590, sweet potatoes 127,708, watermelons 114,780, pig meat 61,716, bananas 61,203, coffee 46,035, pineapples 45,780, oranges 38,150, peanuts (groundnuts) 29,309, nutmeg, mace, and cardamom 3,982, natural rubber (hectares; 2006) 11,778; livestock (number of live animals) 2,947,000 pigs, 1,426,000 cattle, 1,178,000 water buffalo, 22,521,000 chickens; roundwood (2010) 6,163,665 cu m, of which fuelwood 96%; fisheries production 105,001 (from aquaculture 71%). Mining and quarrying (2008): gypsum 775,000; limestone 750,000; copper (metal content) 100,000; tin (metal content) 700; gold 4,300 kg. Manufacturing (2009): nails 2,312,500; plastic products 7,750; plywood 1,009,000 sheets; bricks 269,000,000 units; cigarettes 136,600,000 packs; garments 51,375,000 pieces; beer 1,391,300 hectolitres. Energy production (consumption): electricity (kW-hr; 2008) 3,705,000,000 ([2006] 1,021,000,000); hard coal (metric tons; 2008) 392,000 ([2006] 305,000); lignite (metric tons; 2006) 319,000 (96,000); crude petroleum, none (none); petroleum products (metric tons; 2006) none (133,000); natural gas, none (none).
Gross national income (GNI; 2010): U.S.$6,469,000,000 (U.S.$1,010 per capita); purchasing power parity GNI (U.S.$2,300 per capita).

Structure of gross domestic product and labour force

	2009 in value KN '000,000,000	2009 % of total value	2003 labour force[5]	2003 % of labour force[5]
Agriculture	14,511	30.5	2,150,000	78.5
Mining	3,289	6.9		
Manufacturing	4,833	10.2		
Construction	2,265	4.8		
Public utilities	1,281	2.7		
Transp. and commun.	2,310	4.9		
Trade, hotels	9,664	20.3	589,000	21.5
Finance, real estate	3,114	6.5		
Pub. admin., defense	3,472	7.3		
Services	817	1.7		
Other	2,006[6]	4.2[6]		
TOTAL	47,562	100.0	2,739,000	100.0

Household income and expenditure. Average household size (2005) 5.9; average annual income per household (1995) KN 3,710 (U.S.$371); sources of income: n.a.; expenditure (2002–03)[7]: food and nonalcoholic beverages 37.0%, transportation and communications 16.5%, housing 12.1%, household furnishings 5.7%, energy 5.7%.
Selected balance of payments data. Receipts from (U.S.$'000,000): tourism (2009) 268; remittances (2010) 41; foreign direct investment (2008–10 avg.) 299; official development assistance (2009) 420. Disbursements for (U.S.$'000,000): tourism (2009) 83; remittances (2008) 1.0.
Land use as % of total land area (2009): in temporary crops or left fallow 5.9%, in permanent crops 0.5%, in pasture 3.8%, forest area 68.6%.

Foreign trade[8]

Balance of trade (current prices)

	2003	2004	2005	2006	2007	2008
U.S.$'000,000	–314.2	–520.4	–573.6	–456.7	–835.4	–1,177.5
% of total	25.0%	32.7%	29.2%	16.8%	24.0%	26.4%

Imports (2008): U.S.$2,816,100,000 (capital goods 41.6%, petroleum 15.0%, materials for garment assembly 5.1%). *Major import sources:* Thailand 68.6%; China 11.3%; Vietnam 4.7%; South Korea 2.5%; Japan 2.5%.
Exports (2008): U.S.$1,638,600,000 (copper 37.9%, garments 11.6%, timber 8.0%, gold 7.3%, electricity 7.2%). *Major export destinations:* Thailand 34.7%; Vietnam 13.2%; China 8.6%; South Korea 4.5%; U.K. 3.3%.

Transport and communications

Transport. Railroads: none. Roads (2009): total length 24,586 mi, 39,568 km (paved 14%). Vehicles (2007): passenger cars 12,822; trucks and buses 115,395. Air transport (2009): passenger-km 368,500,000; metric ton-km cargo 200,000.

Communications

Medium	date	number in '000s	units per 1,000 persons	Medium	date	number in '000s	units per 1,000 persons
Televisions	2003	321	59	PCs	2007	110	18
Telephones				Dailies	2009	10[9]	1.6[9]
Cellular	2010	4,003[10]	646[10]	Internet users	2009	300	48
Landline	2010	103	17	Broadband	2010	12[10]	1.9[10]

Education and health

Educational attainment (2005). Percentage of population age 25 and over having: no formal schooling 32.8%; incomplete primary education 21.6%; complete primary 18.2%; lower secondary 11.4%; upper secondary 6.2%; higher 9.8%. *Literacy* (2005): total population age 15 and over literate 72.7%; males literate 82.5%; females literate 63.2%.

Education (2007–08)

	teachers	students	student/ teacher ratio	enrollment rate (%)
Primary (age 6–10)	29,541	900,817	30.5	82
Secondary/Voc. (age 11–16)	18,117	412,375	22.8	36[11]
Tertiary	3,042	89,457	29.4	13 (age 17–21)

Health: physicians (2005) 5,000 (1 per 1,129 persons); hospital beds (2009) 6,425[12] (1 per 956 persons); infant mortality rate per 1,000 live births (2009) 62.9; undernourished population (2005–07) 1,400,000 (23% of total population based on the consumption of a minimum daily requirement of 1,690 calories).

Military

Total active duty personnel (November 2010): 29,100 (army 88.0%, air force 12.0%); paramilitary 100,000. *Military expenditure as percentage of GDP* (2008): 0.3%; per capita expenditure U.S.$3.

[1]Detail does not add to total given because of rounding. [2]A principal ethnic group of the Lao-Theung (Mon-Khmer) peoples. [3]A principal ethnic group of the Lao-Tai (tribal Tai) peoples. [4]ILO estimate. [5]Excludes registered unemployed. [6]Taxes/import duties less imputed bank service charges. [7]Per an expenditure and consumption survey of 8,100 households. [8]Imports c.i.f.; exports f.o.b. [9]Circulation of daily newspapers. [10]Subscribers. [11]2006–07. [12]Includes 2,076 beds in dispensaries.

Internet resources for further information:
- **National Statistics Centre http://www.nsc.gov.la**
- **Bank of the Lao PDR http://www.bol.gov.la**

Latvia

Official name: Latvijas Republika (Republic of Latvia).
Form of government: unitary multiparty republic with a single legislative body (Parliament, or Saeima [100]).
Head of state: President.
Head of government: Prime Minister.
Capital: Riga.
Official language: Latvian.
Official religion: none.
Monetary unit: lats (Ls; plural lati); valuation (Sept. 1, 2011) 1 Ls = U.S.$2.01 = £1.24.

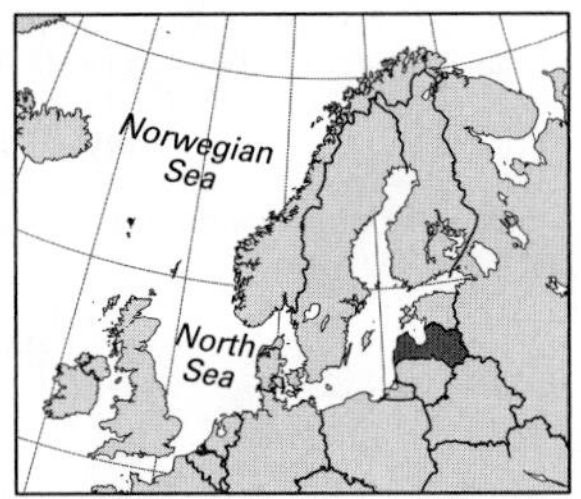

Area and population[1]

Planning region	area sq km	population 2011[2] estimate	Planning region	area sq km	population 2011[2] estimate
Kurzeme	13,601	296,529	Riga	307	700,107
Cities			**City**		
Liepāja	61	83,061	Riga	307	700,107
Ventspils	55	42,371	Vidzeme	15,258	231,067
Amalgamated Municipalities (17)	13,485	171,097	**City**		
Latgale	14,547	335,013	Valmiera	18	27,038
Cities			**Amalgamated Municipalities** (25)	15,240	204,029
Daugavpils	72	102,870	Zemgale	10,742	277,265
Rēzekne	18	34,522	**Cities**		
Amalgamated Municipalities (19)	14,457	197,621	Jēkabpils	26	26,159
Pierīga	10,134	389,660	Jelgava	60	64,279
City			**Amalgamated Municipalities** (20)	10,656	186,827
Jūrmala	100	55,767	TOTAL	64,589	2,229,641
Amalgamated Municipalities (28)	10,034	333,893			

Demography

Population (2011): 2,217,000.
Density (2011): persons per sq mi 88.9, persons per sq km 34.3.
Urban-rural (2011[2]): urban 67.5%; rural 32.5%.
Sex distribution (2011[2]): male 46.17%; female 53.83%.
Age breakdown (2011[2]): under 15, 13.7%; 15–29, 21.7%; 30–44, 20.9%; 45–59, 20.8%; 60–74, 15.3%; 75–84, 6.0%; 85 and over, 1.6%.
Population projection: (2020) 2,143,000; (2030) 2,048,000.
Ethnic composition (2011[2]): Latvian 59.5%; Russian 27.4%; Belarusian 3.5%; Ukrainian 2.5%; Polish 2.3%; Lithuanian 1.3%; Jewish 0.4%; other 3.1%.
Religious affiliation (2005): Orthodox *c.* 29%, of which Russian *c.* 16%; Roman Catholic *c.* 19%; Lutheran *c.* 14%; nonreligious *c.* 26%; atheist/other *c.* 12%.
Major cities (2011[2]): Riga 700,107; Daugavpils 102,870; Liepāja 83,061; Jelgava 64,279; Jūrmala 55,767.

Vital statistics

Birth rate per 1,000 population (2010): 8.6 (world avg. 19.2); within marriage 55.9%; outside of marriage 44.1%.
Death rate per 1,000 population (2010): 13.4 (world avg. 8.2).
Total fertility rate (avg. births per childbearing woman; 2010): 1.18.
Marriage/divorce rates per 1,000 population (2010): 4.1/2.2.
Life expectancy at birth (2010): male 68.8 years; female 78.4 years.
Major causes of death per 100,000 population (2010): diseases of the circulatory system 728.2; malignant neoplasms (cancers) 273.6; accidents, poisoning, and violence 93.6; diseases of the digestive system 46.7.

National economy

Budget (2009)[3]. Revenue: Ls 4,589,000,000 (indirect taxes 29.7%, social security contributions 22.1%, personal income taxes 15.7%, nontax revenue 14.7%, EU grants 12.2%, other taxes 5.6%). Expenditures: Ls 6,279,000,000 (current expenditure 91.3%, capital expenditure 8.7%).
Production (metric tons except as noted). Agriculture, forestry, fishing (2010): wheat 973,000, potatoes 484,000, rapeseed 226,300, barley 184,000, rye 69,400, cabbages (2009) 61,856[4]; livestock (number of live animals) 390,000 pigs, 379,000 cattle; roundwood 12,965,072 cu m, of which fuelwood 11%; fisheries production 165,400 (from aquaculture 1%). Mining and quarrying (2009): peat 1,163,803; limestone (2008) 515,900; gypsum 230,000. Manufacturing (value added in Ls '000,000; 2009): food products 276.4; wood products (excluding furniture) 222.3; printing and publishing 87.1; fabricated metal products 84.3; chemicals and chemical products 75.0; furniture 60.0. Energy production (consumption): electricity (kW-hr; 2010–11) 6,574,000,000 ([2008–09] 7,276,000,000); coal (metric tons; 2010–11) none (160,000); crude petroleum, none (none); petroleum products (metric tons; 2010–11) none (1,235,000); natural gas (cu m; 2010–11) none (1,767,000,000).
Household income and expenditure (2009). Average household size (2011[2]) 2.5; annual disposable income per household Ls 6,586 (U.S.$13,292); sources of income[5]: wages and salaries 68.7%, pensions and transfers 29.1%, other 2.2%; expenditure (2010): food, beverages, and tobacco 31.8%, transportation and communications 17.0%, housing and energy 16.3%, recreation and culture 7.0%, clothing and footwear 5.9%, health 5.8%.
Selected balance of payments data. Receipts from (U.S.$'000,000): tourism (2009) 723; remittances (2010) 643; foreign direct investment (FDI; 2008–10 avg.) 568. Disbursements for (U.S.$'000,000): tourism (2009) 799; remittances (2009) 46; FDI (2008–10 avg.) 66.
Gross national income (GNI; 2010): U.S.$26,056,000,000 (U.S.$11,620 per capita); purchasing power parity GNI (U.S.$16,360 per capita).

Structure of gross domestic product and labour force

	2009 in value Ls '000,000	2009 % of total value	2008 labour force	2008 % of labour force
Agriculture, forestry, and fishing	388.4	3.0	89,100	7.3
Mining and quarrying	56.1	0.4	2,800	0.2
Manufacturing	1,171.4	8.9	171,000	14.1
Public utilities	425.8	3.3	21,300	1.8
Construction	780.9	6.0	125,500	10.3
Transp. and commun.	1,341.9	10.3	105,800	8.7
Trade, restaurants	1,955.6	14.9	217,000	17.9
Finance, real estate	3,076.2	23.5	97,700	8.0
Pub. admin., defense	980.7	7.5	86,600	7.1
Services	1,611.5	12.3	202,500	16.7
Other	1,294.3[6]	9.9[6]	96,500[7]	7.9[7]
TOTAL	13,082.8	100.0	1,215,800	100.0

Public debt (central government; June 2011): U.S.$8,907,000,000.
Population economically active (2010): total 1,157,000; activity rate of total population 51.7% (participation rates: ages 15–74, 65.3%; female 49.8%; unemployed [July 2010–June 2011] 16.9%).

Price and earnings indexes (2005 = 100)

	2004	2005	2006	2007	2008	2009	2010
Consumer price index	93.7	100.0	106.5	117.3	135.4	140.1	138.6
Annual earnings index	86.3	100.0	121.5	158.3	190.5	185.8	186.9

Land use as % of total land area (2007): in temporary crops 19.1%, left fallow 1.0%, in permanent crops 0.2%, in pasture 10.3%, forest area 47.6%.

Foreign trade[8]

Balance of trade (current prices)

	2005	2006	2007	2008	2009	2010
Ls '000,000	–1,979	–3,085	–3,740	–3,099	–1,108	–1,217
% of total	25.5%	31.9%	31.6%	25.9%	13.3%	11.5%

Imports (2010): Ls 5,911,949,000 (machinery and apparatus 16.4%, food products 16.3%, mineral fuels 15.4%, chemicals and chemical products 11.2%, base and fabricated metals 10.2%, transportation equipment 7.2%). *Major import sources:* Lithuania 17.1%; Germany 11.5%; Russia 10.0%; Poland 7.9%; Estonia 7.2%.
Exports (2010): Ls 4,694,885,000 (wood and wood products 19.0%, food products 17.9%, base and fabricated metals 13.8%, machinery and apparatus 13.0%, chemicals and chemical products 7.4%, transportation equipment 6.0%). *Major export destinations:* Lithuania 16.2%; Estonia 13.5%; Russia 10.6%; Germany 8.7%; Sweden 6.3%.

Transport and communications

Transport. Railroads (2010–11): length (2009[2]) 1,406 mi, 2,263 km; passenger-km 594,100,000; metric ton-km cargo 19,082,800,000. Roads: total length (2009[2]) 31,876 mi, 51,300 km (paved 39%); (2006) passenger-km 18,800,000,000[9]; (2010–11) metric ton-km cargo 11,499,500,000. Vehicles (2011[10]): passenger cars 612,878; trucks and buses 76,343. Air transport (2008): passenger-km 3,498,000,000; metric ton-km cargo 15,000,000.

Communications

Medium	date	number in '000s	units per 1,000 persons	Medium	date	number in '000s	units per 1,000 persons
Televisions	2003	1,992	857	PCs	2005	566	245
Telephones				Dailies	2009	220[11]	192[11]
Cellular	2010	2,306[12]	1,024[12]	Internet users	2009	1,503	668
Landline	2010	532	236	Broadband	2010	435[12]	193[12]

Education and health

Educational attainment (2007). Percentage of population age 15–74 having: none/unknown through complete primary education 26.1%; secondary 25.5%; vocational 30.1%; higher 18.3%. *Literacy* (2009): virtually 100%.

Education (2008–09)

	teachers	students	student/ teacher ratio	enrollment rate (%)
Primary (age 7–12)	10,934	114,236	10.4	93
Secondary/Voc. (age 13–18)	18,396	158,325	8.6	84
Tertiary	7,731	125,360	16.2	67 (age 19–23)

Health (2011[2]): physicians 7,951 (1 per 279 persons); hospital beds 11,920 (1 per 186 persons); infant mortality rate per 1,000 live births (2010) 5.7; undernourished population (2004–06) less than 5.0% of total population based on the consumption of a minimum daily requirement of 1,930 calories.

Military

Total active duty personnel (November 2010): 5,745 (army 18.4%, navy 10.2%, air force 5.6%, joint staff 55.7%, national guard 10.1%); reserve 10,866. *Military expenditure as percentage of GDP* (2010): 1.1%; per capita expenditure U.S.$112.

[1]New administrative scheme from July 2009. [2]January 1. [3]General government. [4]Includes other brassicas. [5]Per household member. [6]Indirect taxes less subsidies. [7]Includes 91,600 unemployed. [8]Imports c.i.f.; exports f.o.b. [9]Passenger cars 16,000,000,000; buses 2,800,000,000. [10]July 1. [11]Circulation. [12]Subscribers.

Internet resources for further information:
- **Bank of Latvia http://www.bank.lv/en**
- **Central Statistical Bureau of Latvia http://www.csb.gov.lv/en**

Lebanon

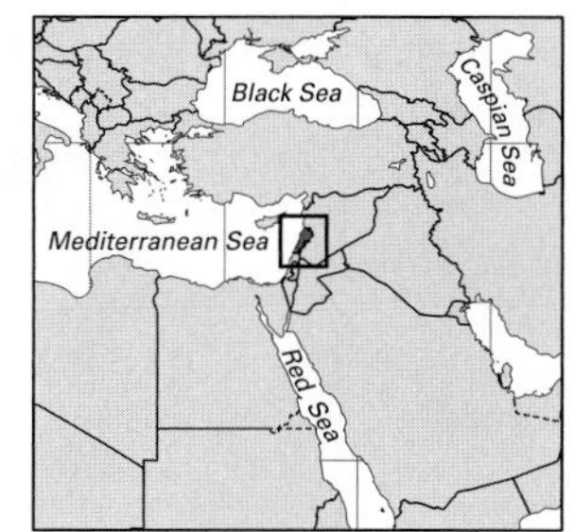

Official name: Al-Jumhūrīyah al-Lubnānīyah (Lebanese Republic).
Form of government: unitary multiparty republic with one legislative house (National Assembly [128][1]).
Head of state: President.
Head of government: Prime Minister.
Capital: Beirut.
Official language: Arabic[2].
Official religion: none.
Monetary unit: Lebanese pound (LBP); valuation (Sept. 1, 2011) 1 U.S.$ = LBP 1,507[3]; 1 £ = LBP 2,431.

Area and population

Provinces	Capitals	area sq mi	area sq km	population 2007 estimate
ʻAkkār[4]	Halba	304	788	[5]
Baalbek-Hermel[4]	Baalbek	1,091	2,825	[6]
Beirut (Bayrūt)	Beirut (Bayrūt)	8	20	361,366
Al-Biqāʻ (Bekaa)	Zahlah	516	1,336	489,865[6]
Mount Lebanon	Bʻabdā	760	1,969	1,484,475
Al-Nabaṭīyah	Al-Nabaṭīyah	424	1,098	[7]
North Lebanon	Tripoli (Ṭarābulus)	477	1,236	763,712[5]
South Lebanon	Sidon (Ṣaydā)	359	930	659,718[7]
WATER AREA		66	170	—
REMAINDER		31	80	
TOTAL		4,036	10,452	3,759,136

Demography

Population (2011): 4,143,000[8].
Density (2011): persons per sq mi 1,027, persons per sq km 396.4.
Urban-rural (2005): urban 86.6%; rural 13.4%.
Sex distribution (2008): male 48.97%; female 51.03%.
Age breakdown (2005): under 15, 27.6%; 15–29, 27.1%; 30–44, 21.7%; 45–59, 13.6%; 60–74, 7.7%; 75–84, 2.0%; 85 and over, 0.3%.
Population projection: (2020) 4,243,000; (2030) 4,335,000.
Ethnic composition (2000): Arab 84.5%, of which Lebanese 71.2%, Palestinian 12.1%; Armenian 6.8%; Kurd 6.1%; other 2.6%.
Religious affiliation (*c.* 2005): Muslim *c.* 56%, of which Shīʻī *c.* 28%, Sunnī *c.* 28%; Maronite (Eastern-rite Roman Catholic) *c.* 22%; Greek Orthodox *c.* 8%; Druze *c.* 5%; Greek Catholic *c.* 4%; other *c.* 5%.
Major cities (2003): Beirut (2007) 361,400 (urban agglomeration [2007] 1,846,000); Tripoli 212,900; Sidon 149,000; Tyre (Ṣūr) 117,100; Al-Nabaṭīyah 89,400.

Vital statistics

Birth rate per 1,000 population (2009): 21.4 (world avg. 20.3).
Death rate per 1,000 population (2009): 5.3 (world avg. 8.5).
Natural increase rate per 1,000 population (2009): 16.1 (world avg. 11.8).
Total fertility rate (avg. births per childbearing woman; 2007): 2.21.
Marriage/divorce rates per 1,000 population (2009): 9.6/1.4.
Life expectancy at birth (2007): male 69.9 years; female 74.2 years.
Major causes of death per 100,000 population (2002): cardiovascular diseases 305; injuries, accidents, and violence 87; malignant neoplasms (cancers) 67; communicable diseases 64; chronic respiratory diseases 33.

National economy

Budget (2007). Revenue: LBP 8,390,000,000,000 (tax revenue 66.7%, of which taxes on goods and services 34.8%, customs duties 6.7%; nontax revenue 26.5%; grants 5.9%; social contributions 0.9%). Expenditures: LBP 12,599,000,000,000 (public debt 37.3%; fuel/electricity 11.2%; defense 9.2%; social protection 7.5%; education 6.9%; health 2.2%).
Public debt (external, outstanding; August 2011): U.S.$21,276,000,000.
Gross national income (GNI; 2010): U.S.$38,374,000,000 (U.S.$9,020 per capita); purchasing power parity GNI (U.S.$14,170 per capita).

Structure of gross domestic product and labour force

	2007 in value LBP '000,000,000	2007 % of total value	2001 labour force	2001 % of labour force
Agriculture	2,348	6.2	320,000	20.0
Mining, Manufacturing	3,579	9.5	1,120,000	70.0
Construction	4,052	10.7		
Public utilities	–507	–1.3		
Transp. and commun.	3,118	8.3		
Trade, hotels	10,092	26.7		
Finance, real estate	7,349	19.5		
Services	6,856	18.2		
Pub. admin., defense	3,553	9.4	160,000	10.0
Other	–2,682[9]	–7.1[9]	—	—
TOTAL	37,758	100.0[10]	1,600,000	100.0

Production (metric tons except as noted). Agriculture, forestry, fishing (2009): potatoes 515,000, tomatoes 308,000, oranges 230,000, cucumbers and gherkins 132,000, apples 126,500, grapes 120,000, lemons and limes 115,000, olives 83,500, cherries 34,662, almonds 30,500; livestock (number of live animals) 450,000 goats, 330,000 sheep, 77,000 cattle, 37,500,000 chickens; roundwood (2010) 86,048 cu m, of which fuelwood 92%; fisheries production 4,614 (from aquaculture 17%). Mining and quarrying (2008): [11]. Manufacturing (value added in U.S.$'000,000; 1998): food and food products 345; cement, bricks, and ceramics 212; wood and wood products 188; fabricated metal products 185; paints, soaps, and pharmaceuticals 94; wearing apparel 91. Energy production (consumption): electricity (kW-hr; 2008) 11,188,000,000 (11,142,000,000); coal (metric tons; 2007) none (200,000); crude petroleum, none (none); petroleum products (metric tons; 2007) none (3,382,000); natural gas, none (none).
Population economically active (2007): total 1,228,800; activity rate of total population 32.7% (participation rates: ages 15–64, 47.6%; female 25.0%; unemployed 9.2%).

Price index (December 2005 = 100)

	2004	2005	2006	2007	2008	2009	2010
Consumer price index[12]	102.7	100.0	105.6	115.4	121.7	125.9	128.0

Household income and expenditure. Average household size (2004) 4.3; sources of income: n.a.; expenditure (2007)[13]: food and nonalcoholic beverages 19.9%, housing 16.2%, transportation 12.3%, energy 9.5%, education 7.7%, health 6.8%, clothing 6.5%.
Selected balance of payments data. Receipts from (U.S.$'000,000): tourism (2009) 6,774; remittances (2010) 8,409; foreign direct investment (FDI; 2008–10 avg.) 4,697; official development assistance (2009) 641. Disbursements for (U.S.$'000,000): tourism (2009) 4,012; remittances (2009) 5,749; FDI (2008–10 avg.) 896.
Land use as % of total land area (2009): in temporary crops or left fallow 14.2%, in permanent crops 14.0%, in pasture 39.1%, forest area 13.4%.

Foreign trade

Balance of trade (current prices)

	2004	2005	2006	2007	2008	2009
U.S.$'000,000	–6,708	–6,467	–6,613	–8,005	–12,659	–12,761
% of total	64.2%	60.0%	59.3%	55.6%	64.5%	64.7%

Imports (2008): U.S.$16,137,000,000 (mineral products [significantly petroleum] 26.5%, food and live animals 13.2%, transportation equipment 10.6%, electrical equipment 10.5%). *Major import sources:* U.S. 11.5%; China 8.6%; France 8.3%; Italy 6.9%; Germany 6.4%; Turkey 4.3%.
Exports (2008): U.S.$3,478,000,000 (precious metal jewelry and stones [significantly gold and diamonds] 16.5%, electrical equipment 15.4%, base and fabricated metals [significantly scrap] 15.2%, chemicals and chemical products 12.5%). *Major export destinations:* U.A.E. 10.0%; Switzerland 9.5%; Iraq 7.7%; Syria 6.4%; Saudi Arabia 6.0%; Turkey 5.9%.

Transport and communications

Transport. Railroads: [14]. Roads (2005): total length 4,330 mi, 6,970 km[15] (paved, n.a.). Vehicles: n.a. Air transport (2008)[16]: passenger-km 2,748,000,000; metric ton-km cargo 38,524,000.

Communications

Medium	date	number in '000s	units per 1,000 persons	Medium	date	number in '000s	units per 1,000 persons
Televisions	2004	1,269	320	PCs	2007	433	104
Telephones				Dailies	2009	259[17]	87[17]
Cellular	2010	2,875[18]	680[18]	Internet users	2009	1,000	237
Landline	2010	888	210	Broadband	2010	200[18]	47[18]

Education and health

Educational attainment (2004). Percentage of population age 4 and over having: no formal education or unknown 13.7%; incomplete primary education 3.2%; primary 54.2%; secondary/vocational 15.5%; upper vocational 1.7%; higher 11.7%. *Literacy* (2005): total population age 15 and over literate 88.3%; males literate 93.6%; females literate 83.4%.

Education (2008–09)

	teachers	students	student/ teacher ratio	enrollment rate (%)
Primary (age 6–11)	33,302	464,442	13.9	90
Secondary/Voc. (age 12–17)	42,492	391,087	9.2	75
Tertiary	24,302	199,656	8.2	53 (age 18–22)

Health: physicians (2008) 10,234 (1 per 405 persons); hospital beds (2006) 12,037 (1 per 343 persons); infant mortality rate (2005) 23.6; undernourished population (2005–07) less than 5.0% of total population.

Military

Total active duty personnel (November 2010): 59,100 (army 96.4%, navy 1.9%, air force 1.7%); estimated strength of Hezbollah (November 2009) 2,000. UN peacekeeping troops (August 2011) 12,056. *Military expenditure as percentage of GDP* (2009): 3.0%; per capita expenditure U.S.$216.

[1]By law one-half of the membership is Christian and one-half Muslim/Druze. [2]A law determines French usage per article 11 of the constitution. In 2004 *c.* 20% of the population spoke French in their daily lives. [3]Rounded pegged rate. [4]Created in 2003; not officially implemented by parliamentary decree by November 2011. [5]North Lebanon includes ʻAkkār. [6]Al-Biqāʻ (Bekaa) includes Baalbek-Hermel. [7]South Lebanon includes Al-Nabaṭīyah. [8]Includes about 455,000 registered Palestinian refugees, of whom about 225,000 live in refugee camps. [9]Taxes less imputed bank service charges. [10]Detail does not add to total given because of rounding. [11]Lebanon has between 300 and 400 rock and sand quarries (many of which are unlicensed). [12]As of December. [13]Weights of consumer price index components. [14]The 249 mi (401 km) network was unusable in 2010. [15]Roads were severely damaged and nearly all bridges destroyed by the Israeli military offensive against Hezbollah militants in 2006. [16]Middle East Airlines. [17]Circulation of daily newspapers. [18]Subscribers.

Internet resources for further information:

- **Central Administration for Statistics http://www.cas.gov.lb**
- **Central Bank of Lebanon http://www.bdl.gov.lb**

Lesotho

Official name: Musa oa Lesotho (Sotho); Kingdom of Lesotho (English).
Form of government: constitutional monarchy with two legislative houses (Senate [33 nonelected seats]; National Assembly [120]).
Head of state: King.
Head of government: Prime Minister.
Capital: Maseru.
Official languages: Sotho; English.
Official religion: Christianity.
Monetary unit: loti (plural maloti [M]); valuation (Sept. 1, 2011) 1 U.S.$ = M 7.01; 1 £ = M 11.32[1].

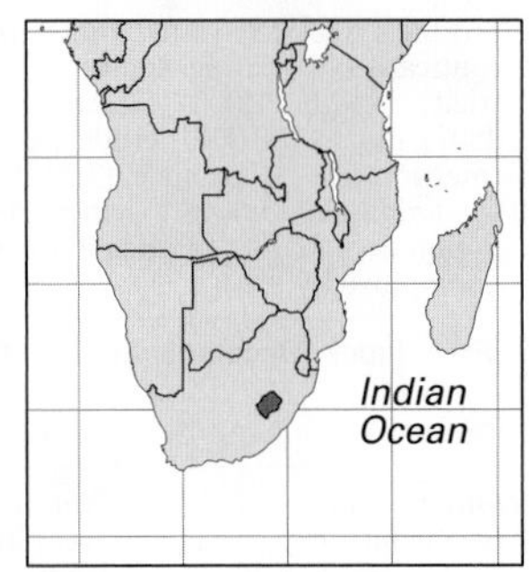

Area and population		area		population
				2006
District Councils[2]	**Capitals**	sq mi	sq km	census[3, 4]
Berea	Teyateyaneng	858	2,222	250,006
Botha-Bothe	Botha-Bothe	682	1,767	110,320
Leribe	Hlotse	1,092	2,828	293,369
Mafeteng	Mafeteng	818	2,119	192,621
Maseru	Maseru	1,652	4,279	431,998
Mohale's Hoek	Mohale's Hoek	1,363	3,530	176,928
Mokhotlong	Mokhotlong	1,573	4,075	97,713
Qacha's Nek	Qacha's Nek	907	2,349	69,749
Quthing	Quthing	1,126	2,916	124,048
Thaba-Tseka	Thaba-Tseka	1,649	4,270	129,881
TOTAL		11,720	30,355	1,876,633

Demography

Population (2011): 1,925,000[5].
Density (2011): persons per sq mi 164.2, persons per sq km 63.4.
Urban-rural (2006)[4]: urban 22.8%; rural 77.2%.
Sex distribution (2006)[4]: male 48.64%; female 51.36%.
Age breakdown (2006)[4]: under 15, 33.9%; 15–29, 32.5%; 30–44, 15.9%; 45–59, 10.0%; 60–74, 5.6%; 75–84, 1.5%; 85 and over, 0.6%.
Population projection[5]: (2020) 1,969,000; (2030) 1,952,000.
Doubling time: 67 years.
Ethnic composition (2000): Sotho 80.3%; Zulu 14.4%; other 5.3%.
Religious affiliation (2000): Christian 91.0%, of which Roman Catholic 37.5%, unaffiliated Christian 23.9%, Protestant (mostly Reformed and Anglican) 17.7%, independent Christian 11.8%; traditional beliefs 7.7%; other 1.3%.
Major urban centres (2006): Maseru 197,907; Teyateyaneng 61,475; Mafeteng 32,148; Maputsoe 30,800; Mohale's Hoek 28,310.

Vital statistics

Birth rate per 1,000 population (2009): 27.5 (world avg. 20.3).
Death rate per 1,000 population (2009): 17.1 (world avg. 8.5).
Total fertility rate (avg. births per childbearing woman; 2009): 3.07.
Marriage/divorce rates per 1,000 population (2009): 1.4/0.1.
Life expectancy at birth (2009): male 48.6 years; female 48.5 years.
Adult population (ages 15–49) *living with HIV* (2009): 23.6%[6] (world avg. 0.8%).
Major causes of death per 100,000 population (2002): HIV/AIDS-related *c.* 1,624; cardiovascular diseases *c.* 205; lower respiratory infections *c.* 89; diarrheal diseases *c.* 84.

National economy

Budget (2008–09). Revenue: M 8,818,100,000 (tax revenue 88.0%, of which customs receipts 55.6%, VAT 11.2%, income tax 9.6%; nontax revenue 9.5%; grants 2.5%). Expenditures: M 6,462,200,000 (wages and salaries 36.0%; grants 11.9%; social benefits 3.5%; transfers 3.2%; debt service 1.8%).
Public debt (external; December 2010): U.S.$747,000,000.
Production (metric tons except as noted). Agriculture, forestry, fishing (2009): potatoes 83,871, corn (maize) 57,126, cow's milk 33,835, sorghum 10,151, wheat 7,420, game meat 4,723, wool (greasy) 3,900, dry beans 3,452; livestock (number of live animals) 1,401,430 sheep, 1,009,300 goats, 616,496 cattle, 83,705 pigs, 75,060 horses; roundwood (2010) 2,083,979 cu m, of which fuelwood 100%; fisheries production 153 (from aquaculture 71%). Mining and quarrying (2009): diamonds 450,000 carats. Manufacturing (value added in M '000,000; 2008): textiles and clothing 393.7; food and beverages 64.8; leather and footwear 29.4. Energy production (consumption): electricity (kW-hr; 2008) 200,000,000 (236,000,000); coal, none (none); crude petroleum, none (none); petroleum products (metric tons; 2003) none (100,000); natural gas, none (none).
Population economically active (2008): total 788,541; activity rate of total population 38.5% (participation rates: ages 15 and older, 63.5%; female 55.3%; unemployed 22.7%).

Price and earnings indexes (2005 = 100)							
	2004	2005	2006	2007	2008	2009	2010
Consumer price index	96.7	100.0	106.0	114.6	126.8	135.9	140.8
Monthly earnings index[7]	96.6	100.0	103.6	112.2	120.7	124.2	...

Household income and expenditure (2002–03)[8]. Average household size (2004) 4.1; sources of income: wages and salaries 40.3%, agriculture 25.4%, remittances 10.7%; expenditure (2010[9])[10]: food 37.0%, clothing and footwear 17.5%, transportation and communications 10.4%, household furnishings 9.4%, energy 6.1%.
Gross national income (GNI; 2010): U.S.$2,248,000,000 (U.S.$1,080 per capita); purchasing power parity GNI (U.S.$1,910 per capita).

Structure of gross domestic product and labour force	2008		1996	
	in value M '000,000	% of total value	labour force	% of labour force
Agriculture, forestry, fishing	789	6.7	105,250	18.4
Mining and quarrying	764	6.5	102,037[11]	17.8[11]
Manufacturing	2,015	17.1	21,087	3.7
Construction	575	4.9	19,202	3.4
Public utilities	497	4.2	2,486	0.4
Transp. and commun.	593	5.0	14,690	2.6
Trade, hotels	1,591	13.5	14,891	2.6
Finance, real estate	1,958	16.6	3,829	0.7
Pub. admin., defense	1,153	9.8	130,684	22.8
Services	1,238	10.5		
Other	605[12]	5.1[12]	158,908[13]	27.7[13]
TOTAL	11,778	100.0[14]	573,064[15]	100.0[14, 15]

Selected balance of payments data. Receipts from (U.S.$'000,000): tourism (2009) 40; remittances (2010) 525; foreign direct investment (2008–10 avg.) 53; official development assistance (2009) 123. Disbursements for (U.S.$'000,000): tourism (2009) 14; remittances (2009) 13.
Land use as % of total land area (2007): in temporary crops or left fallow 9.9%, in permanent crops 0.1%, in pasture 65.9%, forest area 0.3%.

Foreign trade[16]

Balance of trade (current prices)							
	2004	2005	2006	2007	2008	2009	2010
M '000,000	–4,729	–4,830	–5,460	–6,824	–9,274	–10,458	–10,250
% of total	34.1%	36.9%	36.8%	38.6%	38.9%	46.3%	46.7%

Imports (2008): M 13,237,230,000 ([2006] assorted manufactured goods *c.* 40%; food *c.* 24%; chemicals and chemical products *c.* 13%; machinery and transport equipment *c.* 13%). *Major import sources* (2007): other Southern African Customs Union (SACU) countries 85.4%; Taiwan 4.9%; Hong Kong 4.2%.
Exports (2008): M 7,256,070,000 (textiles and wearing apparel 50.4%; diamonds 24.0%; machinery and transportation equipment 14.0%; food, beverages, and tobacco 6.6%). *Major export destinations* (2007): U.S. 59.7%; other SACU countries 19.0%; Belgium 17.0%.

Transport and communications

Transport. Railroads (2008): route length 1.6 mi, 2.6 km[17]. Roads (2007): total length 1,473 mi, 2,371 km (paved 38%); passenger-km, n.a.; metric ton-km cargo, n.a. Vehicles (2002): passenger cars 4,800; trucks and buses 13,000. Air transport (2009): n.a.[18]

Communications			units				units
Medium	date	number in '000s	per 1,000 persons	**Medium**	date	number in '000s	per 1,000 persons
Televisions	2003	80	41	PCs	2005	1	0.5
Telephones				Dailies	2009	0	0
Cellular	2010	699[19]	322[19]	Internet users	2009	77	37
Landline	2010	39	18	Broadband	2010	0.4[19]	0.2[19]

Education and health

Educational attainment (2004)[20]. Percentage of population age 25 and over having: no formal education/unknown 18%; incomplete primary education 44%; complete primary 15%; secondary 20%; vocational and higher 3%. *Literacy* (2008): total population age 15 and over literate 89.5%; males literate 82.6%; females literate 95.1%.

Education (2007–08)	teachers	students	student/ teacher ratio	enrollment rate (%)
Primary (age 6–12)	11,285	395,089	35.0	73[21]
Secondary/Voc. (age 13–17)	4,102	98,580	24.0	25[21]
Tertiary[22]	638	8,500	13.3	4 (age 18–22)

Health: physicians (2007) 127 (1 per 15,093 persons); hospital beds (2006) 2,618 (1 per 769 persons); infant mortality rate per 1,000 live births (2009) 57.8; undernourished population (2004–06) 290,000 (15% of total population based on the consumption of a minimum daily requirement of 1,770 calories).

Military

Total active duty personnel (November 2010): 2,000 (army 100%). *Military expenditure as percentage of GDP* (2009): 3.3%; per capita expenditure U.S.$28.

[1]The loti is pegged to the South African rand at 1 to 1; the rand is accepted as legal tender within Lesotho. [2]New effective local government system introduced in 2005. [3]Final. [4]De jure figure including usual residents abroad (significantly absentee miners working in South Africa). [5]Estimate of the U.S. Bureau of the Census International Database (December 2009 update). [6]Statistically derived midpoint of range. [7]Minimum wage. [8]Data for 2002–03 based on the Household Budget Survey comprising 5,992 households. [9]March. [10]Weights of consumer price index components. [11]Includes 94,190 mine workers in South Africa; the average number of mine workers in South Africa in 2007 equaled 50,100. [12]Indirect taxes less subsidies and less imputed bank service charges. [13]Includes 101,599 not adequately defined and military personnel and 57,309 unemployed, not previously employed. [14]Detail does not add to total given because of rounding. [15]Includes 132,609 workers outside Lesotho (nearly all in South Africa). [16]Imports c.i.f.; exports f.o.b. [17]Length of link to South African rail network. [18]Lesotho has no domestic airline. [19]Subscribers. [20]Based on 2004 Lesotho Demographic and Health Survey of 32,747 people. [21]2006–07. [22]2005–06.

Internet resources for further information:
- **Central Bank of Lesotho http://www.centralbank.org.ls**
- **Lesotho Bureau of Statistics http://www.bos.gov.ls**

Liberia

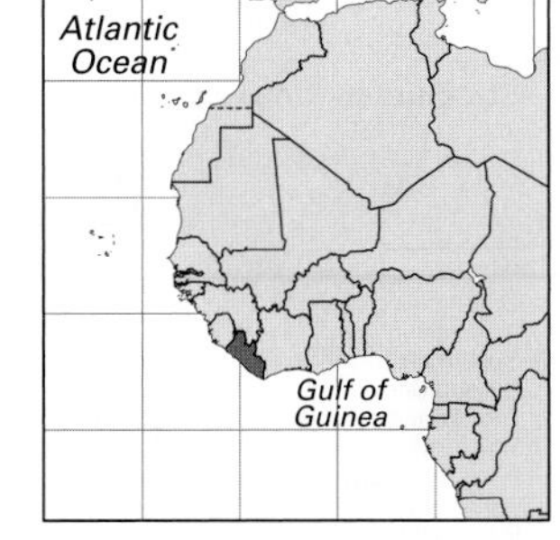

Official name: Republic of Liberia.
Form of government: multiparty republic with two legislative bodies (Liberian Senate [30]; House of Representatives [73]).
Head of state and government: President.
Capital: Monrovia.
Official language: English.
Official religion: none.
Monetary unit: Liberian dollar (L$); valuation (Sept. 1, 2011) 1 U.S.$ = L$72.00; 1 £ = L$116.35.

Area and population

		area		population
				2008
Counties	Capitals	sq mi	sq km	census[1]
Bomi	Tubmanburg	746	1,932	84,119
Bong	Gbarnga	3,380	8,754	333,481
Gbarpolu	Bopulu	3,843	9,953	83,388
Grand Bassa	Buchanan	3,017	7,814	221,693
Grand Cape Mount	Robertsport	1,846	4,781	127,076
Grand Gedeh	Zwedru	4,191	10,854	125,258
Grand Kru	Barclayville	1,504	3,895	57,913
Lofa	Voinjama	3,854	9,982	276,863
Margibi	Kakata	1,039	2,691	209,923
Maryland	Harper	887	2,297	135,938
Montserrado	Bensonville	726	1,880	1,118,241
Nimba	Sanniquellie	4,460	11,551	462,026
River Cess	River Cess	2,183	5,654	71,509
River Gee	Fish Town	1,974	5,113	66,789
Sinoe	Greenville	3,770	9,764	102,391
TOTAL		37,420	96,917[2]	3,476,608

Demography

Population (2011): 3,953,000.
Density (2011): persons per sq mi 105.6, persons per sq km 40.8.
Urban-rural (2009): urban 47.4%; rural 52.6%.
Sex distribution (2008): male 50.05%; female 49.95%.
Age breakdown (2008): under 15, 41.9%; 15–29, 29.1%; 30–44, 16.7%; 45–59, 7.4%; 60–74, 3.4%; 75–84, 1.0%; 85 and over, 0.5%.
Population projection: (2020) 4,945,000; (2030) 6,254,000.
Doubling time: 32 years.
Ethnic composition (2008): Kpelle 20.3%; Bassa 13.4%; Grebo 10.0%; Gio (Dan) 8.0%; Mano 7.9%; Kru 6.0%; Loma (Lorma) 5.1%; Kissi 4.8%; Gola 4.4%; Krahn 4.0%; Vai 4.0%; other 12.1%.
Religious affiliation (2008): Christian 85.6%; Muslim 12.2%; traditional beliefs 0.6%; other religion 0.2%; no religion 1.4%.
Major urban areas (2008): Monrovia 1,010,970; Ganta 41,106; Buchanan 34,270; Gbarnga 34,046; Kakata 33,945.

Vital statistics

Birth rate per 1,000 population (2008): 38.7 (world avg. 20.3).
Death rate per 1,000 population (2008): 11.1 (world avg. 8.5).
Natural increase rate per 1,000 population (2008): 27.6 (world avg. 11.8).
Total fertility rate (avg. births per childbearing woman; 2009): 5.30.
Life expectancy at birth (2008): male 54.3 years; female 57.3 years.
Adult population (ages 15–49) *living with HIV* (2009): 1.5% (world avg. 0.8%).

National economy

Budget (2007). Revenue: L$10,222,400,000 (customs and excise duties 44.3%, direct taxes 32.1%, indirect taxes 12.6%, maritime revenue 7.6%, petroleum sales tax 2.4%, other 1.0%). Expenditures: L$9,498,000,000 (general administration 41.5%, social and community services 19.8%, economic services 6.9%, other 31.8%).
Public debt (external, outstanding; June 2009): U.S.$1,782,000,000.
Population economically active (2009): total 1,455,000; activity rate 37.0% (participation rates: ages 15–64 [2006] 70.7%[3]; female 40.2%; unemployed [2007] *c.* 80%).

Price index (2005 = 100)

	2004	2005	2006	2007	2008	2009	2010
Consumer price index	93.5	100.0	107.2	119.4	140.3	151.2	162.9

Production (metric tons except as noted). Agriculture, forestry, fishing (2009): cassava 493,706, rice 292,983, sugarcane 265,000, oil palm fruit 183,000, bananas 166,298, natural rubber 59,500, plantains 47,334, taro 26,724, sweet potatoes 19,963, yams 18,010, game meat 7,146, peanuts (groundnuts) 4,800, cacao beans 4,600, coffee 1,800; livestock (number of live animals) 310,500 goats, 252,150 sheep, 230,060 pigs, 6,500,000 chickens; roundwood (2010) 7,170,676 cu m, of which fuelwood 94%; fisheries production 8,016 (from aquaculture, negligible). Mining and quarrying (2008): diamonds 60,536 carats; gold 624 kg. Manufacturing (value of sales in L$'000; 2007): cement 1,308,767; beer 1,023,734; carbonated beverages 429,776; mattresses 200,391; paints and varnishes 41,313; candles 32,163. International maritime licensing (registration fees earned; 2007): more than U.S.$12,000,000. Energy production (consumption): electricity (kW-hr; 2007) 353,000,000 (353,000,000); coal, none (none); crude petroleum, none (none); petroleum products (metric tons; 2007) none (194,000); natural gas, none (none).
Household income and expenditure. Average household size (2008) 5.1; income per household: n.a.; sources of income: n.a.; expenditure (2005)[4]: food 45.2%, housing and energy 12.0%, clothing 7.8%, transportation 6.1%, household furnishings 5.3%, restaurants and hotels 4.6%.
Gross national income (GNI; 2010): U.S.$782,000,000 (U.S.$190 per capita); purchasing power parity GNI (U.S.$330 per capita).

Structure of gross domestic product and labour force

	2008			
	in value U.S.$'000,000[5]	% of total value	labour force[6]	% of labour force[6]
Agriculture	182.5	36.0	176,326	59.7
Rubber	31.2	6.2		
Forestry	97.5	19.2		
Mining	0.8	0.2	2,508	0.8
Manufacturing	64.3	12.7	2,785	0.9
Construction	16.1	3.2	4,300	1.5
Public utilities	3.8	0.7	...	...
Transp. and commun.	34.8	6.9	11,178	3.8
Trade, hotels	36.7	7.2	18,928	6.4
Finance	11.9	2.3	18,321	6.2
Pub. admin., defense	11.3	2.2	47,681	16.2
Services	16.2	3.2	13,327	4.5
TOTAL	507.1	100.0	295,354[7]	100.0

Selected balance of payments data. Receipts from (U.S.$'000,000): tourism, n.a.; remittances (2010) 27; foreign direct investment (FDI; 2008–10 avg.) 287; official development assistance (2009) 505. Disbursements for (U.S.$'000,000): tourism, n.a.; remittances (2009[8]) 123; FDI (2008–10 avg.) 19.
Land use as % of total land area (2009): in temporary crops or left fallow 4.2%, in permanent crops 2.2%, in pasture 20.8%, forest area 45.3%.

Foreign trade

Balance of trade (current prices)

	2004	2005	2006	2007	2008	2009[8]
U.S.$'000,000	−233	−179	−309	−301	−571	−417
% of total	52.9%	40.5%	49.5%	42.9%	54.1%	58.5%

Imports (2009): U.S.$565,000,000[8] (food 28.7%, of which rice 11.3%; machinery and transport equipment 23.0%; assorted manufactures 15.2%; petroleum products 13.1%). *Major import sources* (2008): South Korea *c.* 27%; Singapore *c.* 25%; Japan *c.* 12%; China *c.* 11%.
Exports (2009): U.S.$148,000,000[8] (rubber 62.4%; gold 6.5%; diamonds 5.0%; cocoa beans/coffee 2.4%; logs 1.5%; other [mostly scrap metals] 22.2%). *Major export destinations* (2008): India *c.* 21%; U.S. *c.* 19%; Poland *c.* 15%; Germany *c.* 11%; Belgium *c.* 7%.

Transport and communications

Transport. Railroads: none[9]. Roads (2007): total length, n.a. Vehicles (2007): passenger cars 7,428; trucks and buses 3,326. Air transport: n.a.[10]

Communications

Medium	date	number in '000s	units per 1,000 persons	Medium	date	number in '000s	units per 1,000 persons
Televisions	2001	69	25	PCs	2007	...	...
Telephones				Dailies	2009	50[11]	14[11]
Cellular	2010	1,571[12]	393[12]	Internet users	2009	20	5.1
Landline	2010	5.9	1.5	Broadband	2010	0.2[12]	—[12]

Education and health

Educational attainment (2008). Percentage of population age 25 and over having: no formal schooling 55.3%; incomplete primary education 7.5%; complete primary 3.3%; incomplete secondary 16.2%; complete secondary 11.3%; vocational 1.2%; higher 5.2%. *Literacy* (2008): total population age 15 and over literate 54.0%; males literate 65.6%; females literate 42.6%.

Education (2007–08)

	teachers	students	student/ teacher ratio	enrollment rate (%)
Primary (age 6–11)	22,610	539,887	23.9	75[13]
Secondary/Voc. (age 12–17)	12,794	158,242	12.4	20[13]
Tertiary[14]	443	6,120	13.8	17[13] (age 18–22)

Health: physicians (2009) 122 (1 per 32,418 persons); hospital beds (2001) 2,751 (1 per 1,075 persons); infant mortality rate per 1,000 live births (2009) 78.1; undernourished population (2005–07) 1,200,000 (33% of total population based on the consumption of a minimum daily requirement of 1,730 calories).

Military

Total active duty personnel (November 2010): 2,050; UN peacekeeping troops (August 2011) 9,138. *Military expenditure as percentage of GDP:* n.a.

[1]Final results. [2]Detail does not add to total given because of rounding. [3]ILO estimate. [4]Weights of consumer price index components. [5]At constant prices of 1992. [6]Formal employment only. [7]Excludes informal sector employment equaling 487,000 and an unknown number of unofficially unemployed. [8]Excludes December. [9]No railway lines were operational in early 2009. [10]Liberia had no domestic airline in 2009. [11]Circulation of daily newspapers. [12]Subscribers. [13]1999–2000. [14]University of Liberia, two Monrovia-based colleges, and a Kakata-based college only.

Internet resource for further information:
- **Central Bank of Liberia**
http://www.cbl.org.lr

Libya

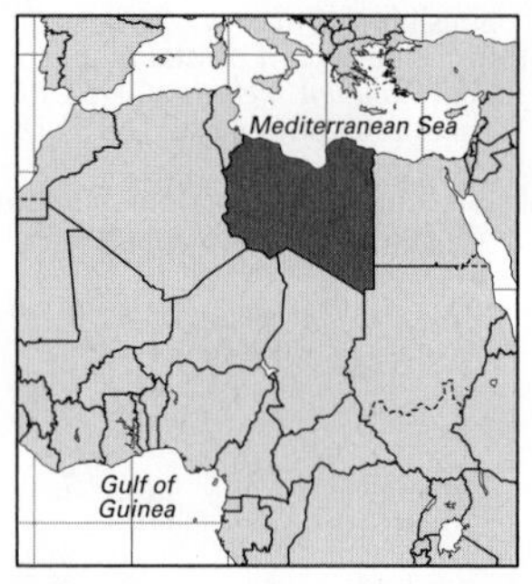

Official name: Al-Jumhūriyyah al-Lībiyyah (The Libyan Republic).
Form of government: interim government led by Transitional National Council.
Head of state: Chairman of the Transitional National Council[1].
Head of government: Head of the Executive Board of the Transitional National Council[1].
Capital: Tripoli[2].
Official language: Arabic.
Official religion: Islam.
Monetary unit: Libyan dinar (LD); valuation (Sept. 1, 2011) 1 U.S.$ = LD 1.20; 1 £ = LD 1.94.

Area and population

Municipalities	area sq km	population 2006 census	Municipalities	area sq km	population 2006 census
Banghāzī	11,372	670,797	Miṣrātah	29,172	550,938
Al-Buṭnān	84,996	159,536	Nālūt	67,191	93,224
Darnah	31,511	163,351	Al-Nuqāṭ al-Khams	6,089	287,662
Ghāt	68,482	23,518	Sabhā	17,066	212,694
Al-Jabal al-Akhḍar	11,429	203,156	Surt	86,399	193,720
Al-Jabal al-Gharbī	76,717	304,159	Tripoli (Ṭarābulus)	835	1,065,405
Al-Jifārah	2,666	453,198	Wādī al-Ḥayāt	31,485	76,858
Al-Jufrah	139,038	...	Wādī al-Shāṭī	90,244	...
Al-Kufrah	433,611	50,104	Al-Wāḥāt	108,523	177,047
Al-Marj	13,515	185,848	Al-Zāwiyah	2,753	290,993
Al-Marqab	6,796	432,202	TOTAL	1,676,198	5,673,031[3]
Marzūq	356,308	78,621			

Demography

Population (2011): 6,423,000[4].
Density (2011): persons per sq mi 9.9, persons per sq km 3.8.
Urban-rural (2009): urban 77.7%; rural 22.3%.
Sex distribution (2009): male 51.21%; female 48.79%.
Age breakdown (2009): under 15, 33.0%; 15–29, 28.6%; 30–44, 21.9%; 45–59, 10.1%; 60–74, 4.7%; 75–84, 1.4%; 85 and over, 0.3%.
Population projection[4]: (2020) 7,083,000; (2030) 7,783,000.
Doubling time: 33 years.
Ethnic composition (2000): Arab 87.1%, of which Libyan 57.2%, Bedouin 13.8%, Egyptian 7.7%, Sudanese 3.5%, Tunisian 2.9%; Amazigh (Berber) 6.8%, of which Arabized 4.2%; other 6.1%.
Religious affiliation (2000): Muslim (nearly all Sunnī) 96.1%; Orthodox 1.9%; Roman Catholic 0.8%; other 1.2%.
Major cities/urban agglomerations (2006/2007): Tripoli (Ṭarābulus) 1,065,405/ 2,189,000; Banghāzī 670,797/(2005) 1,113,000; Miṣrātah (2003) 121,669.

Vital statistics

Birth rate per 1,000 population (2009): 25.1 (world avg. 20.3).
Death rate per 1,000 population (2009): 3.4 (world avg. 8.5).
Natural increase rate per 1,000 population (2009): 21.7 (world avg. 11.8).
Total fertility rate (avg. births per childbearing woman; 2009): 3.08.
Marriage/divorce rates per 1,000 population (2002): 6.0/0.3.
Life expectancy at birth (2009): male 75.0 years; female 79.7 years.
Major causes of death per 100,000 population (2002): diseases of the circulatory system 185, of which ischemic heart disease 98; infectious and parasitic diseases 72; malignant neoplasms (cancers) 44; accidents, injuries, and violence 43; chronic respiratory diseases 16.

National economy

Budget (2008). Revenue: LD 72,741,200,000 (oil revenues 88.6%, other 11.4%). Expenditures: LD 44,115,000,000 (development expenditures 65.5%, administrative expenditures 26.9%).
Production (metric tons except as noted). Agriculture, forestry, fishing (2009): potatoes 311,330, watermelons 220,000, dry onions 201,970, tomatoes 200,000, olives 170,890, dates 160,100, wheat 100,000, almonds 25,000; livestock (number of live animals) 6,500,000 sheep, 2,500,000 goats, 185,000 cattle, 50,000 camels, 27,000,000 chickens; roundwood (2010) 1,054,950 cu m, of which fuelwood 89%; fisheries production 52,350 (from aquaculture 0.5%). Mining and quarrying (2009): gypsum 300,000; lime 260,000; salt 40,000. Manufacturing (value of production in LD '000,000; 1996): base metals 212; electrical equipment 208; petrochemicals 175; food products 79; cement and other building materials 68. Energy production (consumption): electricity (kW-hr; 2008) 26,947,000,000 (22,886,000,000); coal (metric tons; 2007) none (n.a.); crude petroleum (barrels; 2009) 592,500,000 ([2007] 114,806,000); petroleum products (metric tons; 2009) 16,201,000 ([2008] 10,244,000); natural gas (cu m; 2009) 15,300,000,000 ([2007] 6,307,000,000).
Land use as % of total land area (2009): in temporary crops or left fallow (2007) 1.0%, in permanent crops 0.2%, in pasture 7.7%, forest area 0.1%.
Population economically active (2008): total 2,295,000[5]; activity rate of total population 36.5%[5] (participation rates: ages 15–64, 54.3%[5]; female 21.9%[5]; unemployed [2004] 30.0%).

Price index (2005 = 100)

	2004	2005	2006	2007	2008	2009	2010
Consumer price index	97.4	100.0	101.5	107.8	119.0	121.9	...

Gross national income (GNI; 2009): U.S.$77,185,000,000 (U.S.$12,020 per capita); purchasing power parity GNI (U.S.$16,430 per capita).

Structure of gross domestic product and labour force

	2008 in value LD '000,000	2008 % of total value	2007 labour force	2007 % of labour force
Agriculture	2,021	1.9	135,700	7.6
Petroleum and natural gas[6]	70,681	67.8	32,800	1.8
Other mining			23,700	1.3
Manufacturing[7]	4,747	4.6	141,800	7.9
Construction	5,995	5.7	42,400	2.4
Public utilities	1,256	1.2	56,400	3.1
Transp. and commun.	3,884	3.7	140,800	7.8
Trade, hotels	3,950	3.8	195,100	10.9
Finance, insurance, real estate	6,805	6.5	41,200	2.3
Pub. admin., defense	6,671	6.4	290,400	16.2
Services	364	0.3	694,200	38.7
Other	−2,059[8]	−2.0[8]	—	—
TOTAL	104,313[9]	100.0[9]	1,794,500	100.0

Public debt (external outstanding; 2005): U.S.$3,900,000,000.
Selected balance of payments data. Receipts from (U.S.$'000,000): tourism (2009) 50; remittances (2010) 16; foreign direct investment (FDI; 2008–10 avg.) 3,539; official development assistance (2009) 39. Disbursements for (U.S.$'000,000): tourism (2009) 1,587; remittances (2009) 1,000; FDI (2008–10 avg.) 2,778.
Household income and expenditure. Average household size (2006) 5.9; income per household: n.a.; sources of income: n.a.; expenditure (2003)[10]: food and beverages 36.6%, housing 23.3%, transportation 11.2%, clothing and footwear 7.3%, education/culture/entertainment 6.4%.

Foreign trade

Balance of trade (current prices)

	2004	2005	2006	2007	2008	2009
U.S.$'000,000	+8,657	+17,675	+24,254	+29,269	+40,292	+15,053
% of total	33.1%	47.4%	50.0%	43.8%	48.2%	25.5%

Imports (2007): U.S.$17,401,000,000 (petroleum sector 17.7%, remainder 82.3%). *Major import sources* (2008): Italy *c.* 22%; China *c.* 9%; Germany *c.* 9%; Turkey *c.* 6%; Tunisia *c.* 6%.
Exports (2007): U.S.$44,523,000,000 (hydrocarbons [mostly crude petroleum] 97.5%, remainder 2.5%). *Major export destinations* (2008): Italy *c.* 38%; Germany *c.* 12%; Spain *c.* 7%; France *c.* 7%; U.S. *c.* 6%.

Transport and communications

Transport. Railroads: none.[11] Roads (2000): total length 51,100 mi, 83,200 km (paved 57%). Vehicles (2007): passenger cars 1,338,165; trucks and buses 401,838. Air transport (2008): passenger-km 1,260,000,000[12]; metric ton-km cargo, n.a.

Communications

Medium	date	number in '000s	units per 1,000 persons	Medium	date	number in '000s	units per 1,000 persons
Televisions	2000	717	133	PCs	2005	130	21
Telephones				Dailies	2009	100[13]	24[13]
Cellular	2010	10,900[14]	1,715[14]	Internet users	2009	354	55
Landline	2010	1,228	193	Broadband	2010	73[14]	11.5[14]

Education and health

Educational attainment: n.a. *Literacy* (2006): percentage of total population age 15 and over literate 88.1%; males literate 93.0%; females literate 83.1%.

Education (2002–03)

	teachers	students	student/ teacher ratio	enrollment rate (%)
Primary (age 6–11)	...	755,338[15]	...	...
Secondary/Voc. (age 12–18)	...	732,614[15]	...	...
Tertiary	15,711	375,028	23.8	56 (age 19–23)

Health: physicians (2004) 7,405 (1 per 775 persons); hospital beds (2002) 21,400 (1 per 256 persons); infant mortality rate per 1,000 live births (2009) 267; undernourished population (2004–06) less than 5.0% of total population.

Military

Total active duty personnel (November 2010): 76,000 (army 65.8%, navy 10.5%, air force 23.7%). *Military expenditure as percentage of GDP* (2009): 2.8%; per capita expenditure U.S.$266.

[1]Interim position. [2]Tripoli was made the capital in the early 1970s. [3]Final census results include 349,040 foreigners. [4]Per United Nations *World Population Prospects: The 2010 Revision.* [5]ILO estimate. [6]Includes refined petroleum. [7]Excludes refined petroleum. [8]Taxes less subsidies and less imputed bank service charges. [9]Detail does not add to total given because of rounding. [10]Weights of consumer price index components. [11]A Mediterranean coast rail line is to be built from the Egyptian border to the Tunisian border; the 554 km Surt-to-Banghāzī section was under way in 2010. [12]Afriqiyah Airways only. [13]Circulation of daily newspapers. [14]Subscribers. [15]2005–06.

Internet resource for further information:
- **Central Bank of Libya http://www.cbl.gov.ly/en**

Liechtenstein

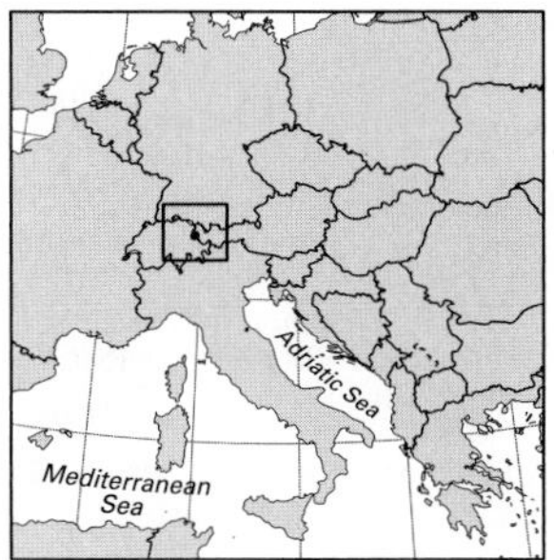

Official name: Fürstentum Liechtenstein (Principality of Liechtenstein).
Form of government: constitutional monarchy with one legislative house (Diet [25]).
Head of state: Prince[1].
Head of government: Head of the Government (Prime Minister).
Capital: Vaduz.
Official language: German.
Official religion: [2].
Monetary unit: Swiss franc (CHF); valuation (Sept. 1, 2011) 1 U.S.$ = CHF 0.80; 1 £ = CHF 1.29.

Area and population

Regions / Communes	area sq mi	area sq km	population 2010[3] estimate
Oberland (Upland)			23,254
Balzers	7.6	19.7	4,517
Planken	2.0	5.3	422
Schaan	10.4	26.9	5,791
Triesen	10.2	26.5	4,807
Triesenberg	11.5	29.7	2,509
Vaduz	6.7	17.3	5,208
Unterland (Lowland)			12,650
Eschen	4.0	10.4	4,196
Gamprin	2.4	6.2	1,584
Mauren	2.9	7.5	3,887
Ruggell	2.9	7.4	1,965
Schellenberg	1.4	3.6	1,018
TOTAL	62.0	160.5	35,904

Demography

Population (2011): 36,300.
Density (2011): persons per sq mi 585.3, persons per sq km 226.1.
Urban-rural (2009): urban 13.9%; rural 86.1%.
Sex distribution (2009[3]): male 49.43%; female 50.57%.
Age breakdown (2009[3]): under 15, 16.4%; 15–29, 18.5%; 30–44, 23.3%; 45–59, 22.8%; 60–74, 13.7%; 75–84, 3.9%; 85 and over, 1.4%.
Population projection: (2020) 39,000; (2030) 41,500.
Ethnic composition (2009[3]): Liechtensteiner 66.9%; Swiss 10.0%; Austrian 5.7%; German 3.5%; Italian 3.3%; other 10.6%.
Religious affiliation (2002): Christian 83.9%, of which Roman Catholic 76.0%, Protestant 7.0%, Orthodox 0.8%; Muslim 4.1%; nonreligious/other/unknown 12.0%.
Major towns (2010[3]): Schaan 5,791; Vaduz 5,208; Triesen 4,807; Balzers 4,517; Eschen 4,196.

Vital statistics

Birth rate per 1,000 population (2008): 9.9 (world avg. 20.3); within marriage 86.0%; outside of marriage 14.0%.
Death rate per 1,000 population (2008): 5.8 (world avg. 8.5).
Natural increase rate per 1,000 population (2008): 4.1 (world avg. 11.8).
Total fertility rate (avg. births per childbearing woman; 2008): 1.40.
Marriage/divorce rates per 1,000 population (2008): 5.8/2.8.
Life expectancy at birth (2006): male 78.9 years; female 83.1 years.
Major causes of death per 100,000 population (2009): diseases of the circulatory system *c.* 109; malignant neoplasms (cancers) *c.* 81; diseases of the respiratory system *c.* 36; accidents, violence, and suicide *c.* 11.

National economy

Budget (2008). Revenue: CHF 1,140,000,000 (current revenue 96.8%, of which taxes and duties 71.4%, revenues from assets 20.0%, fees 3.6%; capital revenue 3.2%). Expenditures: CHF 1,268,100,000 (current expenditure 91.3%; capital expenditure 8.7%).
Public debt (2011): none.
Tourism (2009): 54,389 tourist arrivals; receipts from visitors, n.a.
Selected balance of payments data: n.a.
Population economically active (2009[3]): total 16,387[4]; activity rate of total population 45.8% (participation rates: age 15 and over, 55.1%; female [2004[3]] 41.4%; unemployed [2008] 1.6%).

Price index (2005 = 100)

	2003	2004	2005	2006	2007	2008	2009
Consumer price index[5]	97.8	98.9	100.0	101.1	101.8	104.3	103.8

Household income and expenditure. Average household size (2003) 2.5.
Production (metric tons except as noted). Agriculture, forestry, fishing (2008): cow's milk 11,500; grapes 200; significantly market gardening, other crops include potatoes, corn (maize), and apples; livestock (number of live animals; 2009) 6,078 cattle, 3,963 sheep, 1,811 pigs; roundwood (2009) 25,000 cu m, of which fuelwood 52%; fisheries production, n.a. Mining and quarrying: n.a. Manufacturing (2007): small-scale precision manufacturing includes optical lenses, electron microscopes, electronic equipment, dentures, and high-vacuum pumps; metal manufacturing, construction machinery, and ceramics are important; dairy products and wine are also produced. Energy production (consumption): electricity (kW-hr; 2007) 72,273,000 ([2009] 377,600,000); crude petroleum, none (none); coal (metric tons; 2008) none (n.a.); petroleum products (metric tons; 2004) none (50,000); natural gas, none (none).
Gross national income (GNI; 2008): U.S.$4,307,000,000 (U.S.$121,509 per capita).

Structure of gross domestic product and labour force

	2008 in value U.S.$'000,000	2008 % of total value	2007[3] labour force	2007[3] % of labour force
Agriculture, forestry	60	1.2	398	1.3
Mining	113	2.2	45	0.1
Public utilities			207	0.7
Manufacturing	1,064	21.2	10,813	34.8
Construction	287	5.7	2,504	8.0
Transportation and communications	341	6.8	1,123	3.6
Trade, public accommodation	818	16.3	3,216	10.3
Finance, insurance, real estate	2,513	50.0	5,177	16.7
Consulting, trust management			2,390	7.7
Pub. admin., defense			1,479	4.8
Services			3,722	12.0
Other	–168	–3.4	—	—
TOTAL	5,028	100.0	31,074[6]	100.0

Land use as % of total land area (2007): in temporary crops, left fallow, or in permanent crops *c.* 25%; in pasture *c.* 13%; forest area *c.* 43%.

Foreign trade[7, 8]

Balance of trade (current prices)

	2004	2005	2006	2007	2008	2009
CHF '000,000	+1,323	+1,318	+1,440	+1,766	+1,784	+1,157
% of total	26.0%	25.7%	25.0%	26.8%	26.6%	23.1%

Imports (2009): CHF 1,924,000,000 (machinery and electronic goods 36.6%, fabricated metals/iron and steel 23.5%, chemical and rubber products 8.8%, nonmetallic mineral products 6.7%). *Major import sources:* Germany 41.1%; Austria 35.0%; Italy 4.2%; U.S. 2.0%; Poland 1.8%.
Exports (2009): CHF 3,081,000,000 (machinery and electronic goods 41.6%, fabricated metals/precision tools 18.7%, food and beverages 9.3%, transport equipment/parts 9.2%, glass and ceramic products [including lead crystal and specialized dental products] 6.5%). *Major export destinations:* Germany 23.6%; U.S. 11.3%; Austria 11.0%; France 10.1%; Italy 6.5%.

Transport and communications

Transport. Railroads (2009): route length 5.6 mi, 9 km; passenger-km, n.a.; metric ton-km cargo 328,000,000. Roads (2009): total length 235 mi, 380 km (paved 100%). Vehicles (2009): passenger cars 25,909; trucks and buses 8,105[9]. Air transport: the nearest scheduled airport service is through Zürich, Switzerland.

Communications

Medium	date	number in '000s	units per 1,000 persons	Medium	date	number in '000s	units per 1,000 persons
Televisions	2002	17	510	PCs	2005	...	...
Telephones				Dailies	2009	20[10]	559[10]
Cellular	2010	36[11]	985[11]	Internet users	2009	23	641
Landline	2010	20	544	Broadband	2010	23[11]	638[11]

Education and health

Educational attainment (2000)[12]. Percentage of population age 25 and over having: incomplete compulsory education (schooling to age 16) 3.0%; complete compulsory 22.9%; lower vocational 44.5%; higher vocational, teacher training 13.8%; university 6.6%; unknown 9.2%. *Literacy:* virtually 100%.

Education (2007–08)

	teachers	students	student/ teacher ratio	enrollment rate (%)
Primary (age 6–10)	332	2,158	6.5	90
Secondary/Voc. (age 11–17)	326	3,213	9.9	83
Tertiary	...	800	...	37 (age 18–22)

Health: physicians (2008) 62[13] (1 per 572 persons); hospital beds (1997) 108 (1 per 288 persons); infant mortality rate per 1,000 live births (2006) 5.5; undernourished population, n.a.

Military

Total active duty personnel: none; Liechtenstein has had no standing army since 1868; defense is the responsibility of Switzerland. *Military expenditure as percentage of GDP:* none.

[1]In August 2004 the prince turned over most official day-to-day responsibilities to his son but did not rescind the role of head of state. [2]The designation of "state church" for Roman Catholicism per article 37 of the constitution was under review in 2010. [3]January 1. [4]Residents employed within Liechtenstein only (including 10,794 Liechtensteiners resident in Liechtenstein and 5,593 other nationalities resident in Liechtenstein); 17,028 inward commuters are excluded along with 1,371 outward commuters. [5]Figures are derived from statistics for Switzerland. [6]Residents employed within Liechtenstein only plus inward commuters. [7]Excludes trade with Switzerland and transshipments through Switzerland. [8]Liechtenstein has formed a customs union with Switzerland since 1923. [9]Includes vans, motorcycles, and tractors. [10]Circulation. [11]Subscribers. [12]Based on 14,211 Liechtensteiners and 8,855 foreigners. [13]Practicing physicians only.

Internet resource for further information:
- **Liechtenstein Office of Economic Affairs**
http://www.llv.li

Lithuania

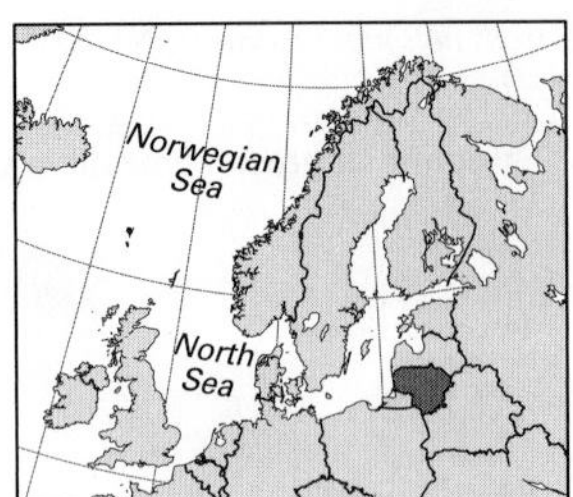

Official name: Lietuvos Respublika (Republic of Lithuania).
Form of government: unitary multiparty republic with single legislative body (Seimas, or Parliament [141]).
Head of state: President.
Head of government: Prime Minister.
Capital: Vilnius.
Official language: Lithuanian.
Official religion: none.
Monetary unit: litas (LTL); valuation (Sept. 1, 2011) 1 U.S.$ = LTL 2.42; 1 £ = LTL 3.92.

Area and population

Counties	Capitals	area sq mi	area sq km	population 2011[1] estimate
Alytus	Alytus	2,095	5,425	167,261
Kaunas	Kaunas	3,123	8,089	647,609
Klaipėda	Klaipėda	2,011	5,209	366,902
Marijampolė	Marijampolė	1,723	4,463	173,695
Panevėžys	Panevėžys	3,043	7,881	270,783
Šiauliai	Šiauliai	3,297	8,540	329,119
Tauragė	Tauragė	1,703	4,411	120,704
Telšiai	Telšiai	1,680	4,350	166,323
Utena	Utena	2,780	7,201	163,353
Vilnius	Vilnius	3,757	9,731	838,852
TOTAL		25,212	65,300	3,244,601

Demography

Population (2011): 3,218,000.
Density (2011): persons per sq mi 127.6, persons per sq km 49.3.
Urban-rural (2009[1]): urban 66.9%; rural 33.1%.
Sex distribution (2009[1]): male 46.55%; female 53.45%.
Age breakdown (2009[1]): under 15, 15.1%; 15–29, 22.7%; 30–44, 21.1%; 45–59, 20.4%; 60–74, 13.8%; 75–84, 5.7%; 85 and over, 1.2%.
Population projection: (2020) 3,101,000; (2030) 2,982,000.
Ethnic composition (2009[1]): Lithuanian 84.1%; Polish 6.1%; Russian 4.9%; Belarusian 1.1%; Ukrainian 0.6%; Jewish 0.1%; other/unknown 3.1%.
Religious affiliation (2007): Roman Catholic 80.2%; Orthodox 4.9%, of which Old Believers 0.8%; Lutheran/Reformed 0.8%; other Christian *c.* 3%; Jewish 0.1%; Muslim 0.1%; nonreligious/other 10.9%.
Major cities (2011[1]): Vilnius 542,932; Kaunas 336,912; Klaipėda 177,812; Šiauliai 120,969; Panevėžys 109,028; Alytus 63,642.

Vital statistics

Birth rate per 1,000 population (2009): 11.0 (world avg. 20.3); within marriage 72.1%; outside of marriage 27.9%.
Death rate per 1,000 population (2009): 12.6 (world avg. 8.5).
Natural increase rate per 1,000 population (2009): –1.6 (world avg. 11.8).
Total fertility rate (avg. births per childbearing woman; 2009): 1.55.
Marriage/divorce rates per 1,000 population (2009): 6.2/2.8.
Life expectancy at birth (2009): male 67.5 years; female 78.6 years.
Major causes of death per 100,000 population (2009): diseases of the circulatory system 697.8; malignant neoplasms (cancers) 203.3; diseases of the digestive system 55.6; diseases of the respiratory system 39.1.

National economy

Budget (2007). Revenue: LTL 30,067,000,000 (tax revenue 58.4%, of which tax on goods and services 36.8%, individual income tax 13.0%; social security contributions 30.4%; grants 5.8%; nontax revenue 5.4%). Expenditures: LTL 30,933,000,000 (social security and welfare 33.1%; general administration 23.7%; health 11.4%; economic affairs 11.1%; education 6.9%; defense 5.8%).
Gross national income (GNI; 2010): U.S.$37,838,000,000 (U.S.$11,400 per capita); purchasing power parity GNI (U.S.$17,880 per capita).

Structure of gross national product and labour force

	2008 in value LTL '000,000	% of total value	labour force	% of labour force
Agriculture, forestry	4,500	4.0	119,800	7.4
Mining	400	0.4	4,100	0.3
Manufacturing	18,600	16.7	260,400	16.1
Construction	10,000	9.0	166,500	10.3
Public utilities	3,200	2.9	35,500	2.2
Transp. and commun.	12,700	11.4	120,800	7.5
Trade, restaurants	18,000	16.1	309,000	19.1
Finance, real estate	15,600	14.0	118,200	7.3
Pub. admin., defense	6,400	5.7	83,100	5.2
Services	10,500	9.4	302,700	18.8
Other	11,600	10.4	94,300[2]	5.8[2]
TOTAL	111,500	100.0	1,614,300[3]	100.0

Production (metric tons except as noted). Agriculture, forestry, fishing (2009): wheat 2,100,200, cow's milk 1,786,949, barley 858,200, sugar beets 682,000, potatoes 662,500, triticale 426,000, rapeseed 415,800, rye 207,900, cabbages 121,124, carrots and turnips 63,716, apples 53,259, hen's eggs 47,820, mushrooms and truffles 14,056; livestock (number of live animals) 897,100 pigs, 770,900 cattle; roundwood (2010) 7,097,064 cu m, of which fuelwood 27%; fisheries production 176,114 (from aquaculture 2%). Mining and quarrying (2007): sand and gravel 9,181,600; cement 1,105,365; clays 384,850; peat 306,500. Manufacturing (value added in U.S.$'000,000; 2007): food and beverages 868, of which dairy products 242; wood products 636, of which furniture 324; bricks, tiles, and ceramics 275; wearing apparel 215; plastics 196; refined petroleum 125. Energy production (consumption): electricity (kW-hr; 2008) 13,101,000,000 ([2007] 12,635,000,000); coal (metric tons; 2007) none (379,000); crude petroleum (barrels; 2008) 938,000 ([2007] 34,800,000); petroleum products (metric tons; 2007) 5,612,000 (3,304,000); natural gas (cu m; 2007) none (3,447,000,000).
Public debt (December 2009): U.S.$8,043,000,000.
Population economically active (2009): total 1,641,000; activity rate of total population 49.1% (participation rates: ages 15–64, 69.8%; female 53.2%; registered unemployed 13.7%).

Price and earnings indexes (2005 = 100)

	2004	2005	2006	2007	2008	2009	2010
Consumer price index	97.4	100.0	103.7	109.7	121.7	127.1	128.8
Annual earnings index	93.1	100.0	116.9	141.6	166.6	160.8	160.4

Household income and expenditure (2008). Average household size 2.4; average annual per capita disposable household income LTL 11,748 (U.S.$4,984); sources of income: wages and salaries 61.6%, transfers 24.3%, self-employment 10.4%; expenditure: food and nonalcoholic beverages 34.8%, housing and energy 12.6%, transportation 9.8%, clothing and footwear 8.5%, hotels and cafés 5.5%, household furnishings 5.0%.
Selected balance of payments data. Receipts from (U.S.$'000,000): tourism (2009) 1,092; remittances (2010) 1,543; foreign direct investment (FDI; 2008–10 avg.) 949. Disbursements for (U.S.$'000,000): tourism (2009) 1,131; remittances (2009) 620; FDI (2008–10 avg.) 227.
Land use as % of total land area (2009): in temporary crops 23.4%, left fallow 1.7%, in permanent crops 0.4%, in pasture 17.4%, forest area 34.3%.

Foreign trade[4]

Balance of trade (current prices)

	2004	2005	2006	2007	2008	2009
U.S.$'000,000	–3,077	–3,634	–5,253	–7,283	–7,525	–1,777
% of total	14.2%	13.1%	15.7%	17.5%	13.7%	5.1%

Imports (2008): U.S.$31,295,000,000 (mineral fuels 27.7%, of which crude petroleum 21.4%; machinery and apparatus 14.6%; chemicals and chemical products 11.3%; road vehicles 9.9%). *Major import sources:* Russia 30.1%; Germany 11.8%; Poland 10.0%; Latvia 5.2%; Italy 3.5%.
Exports (2008): U.S.$23,770,000,000 (refined petroleum 22.8%; food 13.3%; machinery and apparatus 10.5%; road vehicles/parts 6.7%; fertilizers 6.4%; furniture/parts 4.0%; apparel/clothing accessories 3.3%). *Major export destinations:* Russia 16.0%; Latvia 11.6%; Germany 7.2%; Poland 5.8%; Estonia 5.7%.

Transport and communications

Transport. Railroads (2009[1]): route length 1,097 mi, 1,765 km[5]; passenger-km (2008) 397,000,000; metric ton-km cargo (2008) 14,747,000,000. Roads (2009[1]): total length 50,350 mi, 81,030 km (paved 88%); passenger-km (2006) 42,700,000,000[6]; metric ton-km cargo (2008) 20,417,000,000. Vehicles (2008): passenger cars 1,671,065; trucks and buses 142,557. Air transport (2008)[7]: passenger-km 1,502,000,000; metric ton-km cargo 1,300,000.

Communications

Medium	date	number in '000s	units per 1,000 persons	Medium	date	number in '000s	units per 1,000 persons
Televisions	2004	1,785	519	PCs	2007	618	183
Telephones				Dailies	2009	574[8]	172[8]
Cellular	2010	4,891[9]	1,472[9]	Internet users	2009	1,964	598
Landline	2010	734	221	Broadband	2010	684[9]	206[9]

Education and health

Educational attainment (2005). Percentage of population age 15 and over having: no schooling through complete primary education 14.7%; lower secondary 18.0%; higher secondary 28.2%; vocational/technical 19.3%; higher 19.8%. *Literacy* (2008): total population age 15 and over literate 99.7%.

Education (2007–08)

	teachers	students	student/ teacher ratio	enrollment rate (%)
Primary (age 7–10)	10,441	135,719	13.0	92
Secondary/Voc. (age 11–18)	41,142	376,683	9.2	92
Tertiary	14,934	204,767	13.7	77 (age 19–23)

Health (2009[1]): physicians 13,403 (1 per 250 persons); hospital beds 27,362 (1 per 122 persons); infant mortality rate per 1,000 live births (2009) 4.9; undernourished population (2005–07) less than 5.0% of total population based on the consumption of a minimum daily requirement of 1,930 calories.

Military

Total active duty personnel (November 2010): 10,640 (army 77.1%, navy 5.0%, air force 9.2%, joint support/training and command 8.7%); reserve 6,700; paramilitary 14,600. *Military expenditure as percentage of GDP* (2009): 1.2%; per capita expenditure U.S.$150.

[1]January 1. [2]Unemployed. [3]Detail does not add to total given because of rounding. [4]Imports c.i.f.; exports f.o.b. [5]Operated lines only. [6]Passenger cars 39,000,000,000; buses 3,700,000,000. [7]FlyLAL only (operations suspended January 2009). [8]Circulation of daily newspapers. [9]Subscribers.

Internet resources for further information:
- **Lithuanian Department of Statistics http://www.stat.gov.lt**
- **Bank of Lithuania http://www.lb.lt**

Luxembourg

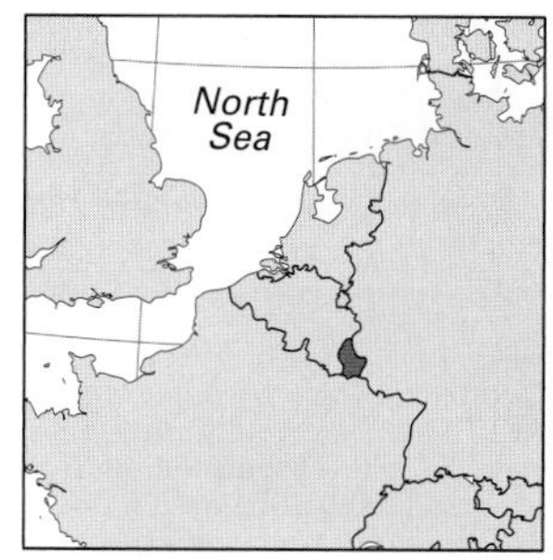

Official names[1]: Groussherzogtum Lëtzebuerg (Luxembourgish); Grand-Duché de Luxembourg (French); Grossherzogtum Luxemburg (German) (Grand Duchy of Luxembourg).
Form of government: constitutional monarchy with one legislative body (Chamber of Deputies [60])[2].
Head of state: Grand Duke.
Head of government: Prime Minister.
Capital: Luxembourg.
Official languages: [1].
Official religion: none.
Monetary unit: € (euro); valuation (Sept. 1, 2011) 1 U.S.$ = €0.70; 1 £ = €1.13.

Area and population

		area		population
Districts	Administrative centres	sq mi	sq km	2011[3] estimate
Diekirch	Diekirch	447	1,157	78,404
Grevenmacher	Grevenmacher	203	525	61,424
Luxembourg	Luxembourg	349	904	372,012
TOTAL		999	2,586	511,840

Demography

Population (2011): 517,000.
Density (2011): persons per sq mi 517.3, persons per sq km 199.8.
Urban-rural (2010): urban 85.2%; rural 14.8%.
Sex distribution (2011[3]): male 49.75%; female 50.25%.
Age breakdown (2011[3]): under 15, 17.6%; 15–29, 18.8%; 30–44, 23.5%; 45–59, 21.1%; 60–74, 12.4%; 75–84, 5.1%; 85 and over, 1.5%.
Population projection: (2020) 580,000; (2030) 642,000.
Ethnic composition (nationality; 2011[3]): Luxembourger 56.8%; Portuguese 15.9%; French 6.1%; Italian 3.5%; Belgian 3.3%; German 2.3%; other 12.1%.
Religious affiliation (2005): Roman Catholic (including non-practicing) *c.* 90%; Protestant *c.* 3%; Muslim *c.* 2%; Orthodox *c.* 1%; other *c.* 4%.
Major communes/urban agglomerations (2011[3]): Luxembourg 94,034/136,816; Esch-sur-Alzette 30,630/75,697; Pétange 15,971/23,399; Differdange 21,869[4]; Dudelange 18,657.

Vital statistics

Birth rate per 1,000 population (2010): 11.6 (world avg. 19.2); within marriage (2009) 67.9%; outside of marriage (2009) 32.1%.
Death rate per 1,000 population (2010): 7.5 (world avg. 8.2).
Total fertility rate (avg. births per childbearing woman; 2010): 1.63.
Marriage/divorce rates per 1,000 population (2010): 3.5/2.2.
Life expectancy at birth (2007): male 77.6 years; female 82.7 years.
Major causes of death per 100,000 population (2008): diseases of the circulatory system 196.8; malignant neoplasms (cancers) 154.3; accidents, poisoning, and violence 43.5; diseases of the respiratory system 39.8.

National economy

Budget (2010)[5]. Revenue: €16,445,900,000 (indirect taxes 33.7%, social contributions 28.9%, direct taxes 28.8%). Expenditures: €17,155,800,000 (social benefits 47.7%, development expenditure 9.8%).
Public debt (2007): negligible.
Gross national income (GNI; 2010): U.S.$40,281,000,000 (U.S.$79,510 per capita); purchasing power parity GNI (U.S.$63,850 per capita).

Structure of gross domestic product and labour force

	2008			
	in value €'000,000	% of total value	labour force	% of labour force
Agriculture	119.8	0.3	5,200	1.5
Mining	37.4	0.1	300	0.1
Manufacturing	3,090.9	7.9	35,700	10.0
Construction	1,951.7	5.0	38,300	10.7
Public utilities	379.4	1.0	1,700	0.5
Transp. and commun.	3,224.5	8.2	28,500	7.9
Trade, restaurants	3,924.7	10.0	60,800	17.0
Finance[6], insurance	10,306.2	26.2	41,200	11.5
Real estate	7,111.5	18.1	60,000	16.7
Pub. admin., defense	1,724.1	4.4	17,800	5.0
Services	3,686.1	9.4	59,200	16.5
Other	3,790.4[7]	9.6[7]	9,900[8]	2.8[8]
TOTAL	39,348.4[9]	100.0[9]	358,600[10]	100.0[9]

Production (metric tons except as noted). Agriculture, forestry, fishing (2010): wheat 83,474, barley 43,003, triticale 25,523, potatoes 19,531, grapes (2009) 16,900, rapeseed 15,895, apples (2009) 10,190, rye 5,188, oats 4,789; livestock (number of live animals; 2009) 196,470 cattle, 80,217 pigs; roundwood 274,946 cu m, of which fuelwood 6%; fisheries production, n.a. Mining and quarrying (2009): limited quantities of dolomite, limestone, and slate. Manufacturing (value added in €'000,000; 2010): base and fabricated metals 528.6; rubber and plastic products 362.3; agricultural and food products 265.2; nonelectrical machinery and apparatus 219.3; cement, bricks, and ceramics 176.5; electrical machinery and electronics 148.6; chemicals and chemical products 135.4. Energy production (consumption): electricity (kW-hr; 2010–11) 4,669,000,000 ([2007] 7,962,000,000); coal (metric tons; 2007) none (109,000); crude petroleum, none (none); petroleum products (metric tons; 2007) none (2,410,000); natural gas (cu m; 2007) none (1,403,300,000).
Population economically active (2010): total 221,000[11]; activity rate of total population 43.7% (participation rates: ages 15–64, 65.2%; female [2008] 43.5%; unemployed [August 2010–July 2011] 6.1%).

Price index (2005 = 100)

	2004	2005	2006	2007	2008	2009	2010
Consumer price index	97.6	100.0	102.7	105.0	108.6	109.0	111.5

Household income and expenditure (2009). Average household size (2005) 2.5; income per household €61,008 (U.S.$87,438); sources of income (1992): wages and salaries 67.1%, transfer payments 28.1%, self-employment 4.8%; expenditure: housing and energy 34.4%, transportation and communications 16.1%, food, beverages, and tobacco 10.2%, hotels and restaurants 7.7%, entertainment and culture 7.4%, clothing and footwear 6.2%.
Selected balance of payments data. Receipts from (U.S.$'000,000): tourism (2009) 4,180; remittances (2010) 1,724; foreign direct investment (FDI; 2008–10 avg.) 20,110. Disbursements for (U.S.$'000,000): tourism (2009) 3,650; remittances (2009) 10,556; FDI (2008–10 avg.) 15,730.
Land use as % of total land area (2007): in temporary crops or left fallow 23.6%, in permanent crops 0.8%, in pasture 26.3%, forest area 33.5%.

Foreign trade[12]

Balance of trade (current prices)

	2005	2006	2007	2008	2009	2010
€'000,000	–3,868	–4,337	–4,462	–5,531	–4,442	–4,884
% of total	15.8%	16.1%	15.8%	18.9%	19.5%	18.6%

Imports (2010): €15,567,400,000 (base and fabricated metals 16.7%, transportation equipment 15.5%, machinery and apparatus 14.4%, mineral fuels 12.9%, agricultural and food products 11.3%, chemicals and chemical products 10.3%). *Major import sources:* Belgium 35.9%; Germany 29.7%; France 13.6%; Netherlands 5.9%; Italy 2.5%.
Exports (2010): €10,683,900,000 (base and fabricated metals 46.0%, machinery and apparatus 16.4%, agricultural and food products 11.7%, chemicals and chemical products 8.0%, transportation equipment 7.6%). *Major export destinations:* Germany 28.9%; France 16.4%; Belgium 12.6%; Netherlands 5.2%; Italy 4.9%.

Transport and communications

Transport. Railroads (2010): route length 275 km; passenger-km 347,000,000; metric ton-km cargo (2008) 294,000,000. Roads (2011[3]): total length 1,801 mi, 2,899 km (paved 100%); passenger-km (2006) 7,800,000,000; metric ton-km cargo (2010) 8,658,000,000. Vehicles (2011[3]): passenger cars 337,239; trucks and buses 31,794. Air transport (2010)[13]: passenger-km 1,471,000,000; metric ton-km cargo, negligible.

Communications

Medium	date	number in '000s	units per 1,000 persons	Medium	date	number in '000s	units per 1,000 persons
Televisions	2003	70	156	PCs	2006	318	673
Telephones				Dailies	2009	113[14]	282[14]
Cellular	2010	727[15]	1,433[15]	Internet users	2009	425	873
Landline	2010	272	537	Broadband	2010	167[15]	328[15]

Education and health

Educational attainment (2009). Percentage of population age 25–64 having: no formal schooling through primary education 9%; lower secondary 14%; upper secondary/higher vocational 42%; higher 35%. *Literacy* (2010): virtually 100% literate.

Education (2009–10)

	teachers	students	student/ teacher ratio	enrollment rate (%)
Primary (age 6–11)	3,511	32,312	9.2	96[16]
Secondary/Voc. (age 12–18)	4,096	37,941	9.3	84[16]
Tertiary[17]	...	4,729	...	... (age 19–23)

Health (2009): physicians 1,350 (1 per 369 persons); hospital beds 2,721 (1 per 183 persons); infant mortality rate per 1,000 live births (2010) 3.4; undernourished population (2004–06) less than 5.0% of total population.

Military

Total active duty personnel (November 2010): 900 (army 100%). *Military expenditure as percentage of GDP* (2009): 0.5%; per capita expenditure U.S.$500.

[1]Luxembourgish is the national language; German and French are both languages of administration. [2]In addition, the 22-member Council of State (a 21-member body of unelected citizens appointed by the Grand Duke plus the hereditary Grand Duke) serves in an advisory capacity to the government. [3]January 1. [4]Within Esch-sur-Alzette urban agglomeration. [5]General government (consolidated) budget figures. [6]In early 2011 total banking assets (at 146 banks) exceeded U.S.$1,026,190,000,000. [7]Taxes less subsidies. [8]Unemployed. [9]Detail does not add to total given because of rounding. [10]In 2008 included *c.* 201,500 Luxembourgers, *c.* 11,000 resident foreigners, and *c.* 146,100 workers from neighbouring countries; excludes Luxembourgers working abroad. [11]Luxembourgers and resident foreigners only, includes Luxembourgers working abroad. [12]Imports c.i.f.; exports f.o.b. [13]Luxair only. [14]Circulation. [15]Subscribers. [16]2007–08. [17]2008–09.

Internet resources for further information:
- **Central Bank of Luxembourg http://www.bcl.lu/en**
- **Le Portail des Statistiques du Luxembourg http://www.statistiques.public.lu/fr**

Macau

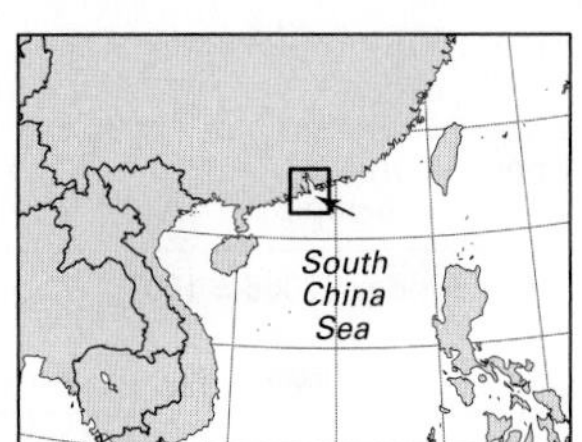

Official name: Aomen Tebie Xingzhengqu (Chinese); Região Administrativa Especial de Macau (Portuguese) (Macau Special Administrative Region).
Political status: special administrative region (China) with one legislative house (Legislative Assembly [29[1]]).
Head of state: President of China.
Head of government: Chief Executive.
Capital: Macau.
Official languages: Chinese; Portuguese.
Official religion: none.
Monetary unit: pataca (MOP)[2]; valuation (Sept. 1, 2011) 1 U.S.$ = MOP 8.02; 1 £ = MOP 12.96.

Area and population

	area		population
Geographic areas	sq mi	sq km	2011[3] estimate
Macau peninsula	3.6	9.3	470,600
islands (formerly separate)	5.6	14.4	80,200
Coloane	3.0	7.6	3,500
Taipa	2.6	6.8	76,700
CoTai[4] reclamation area	2.2	5.8	—
Hengqin island (part)[5]	0.4	1.1	—
marine	—	—	1,600
TOTAL	11.8	30.6	552,300[6]

Demography

Population (2011): 561,000.
Density (2011): persons per sq mi 47,542, persons per sq km 18,333.
Urban-rural (2008): urban, virtually 100%.
Sex distribution (2010[3]): male 49.07%; female 50.93%.
Age breakdown (2010[3]): under 15, 12.8%; 15–29, 24.9%; 30–44, 24.6%; 45–59, 25.8%; 60–74, 8.1%; 75 and over, 3.8%.
Population projection: (2020) 662,000; (2030) 751,000.
Ethnic composition by place of birth (2006): mainland China 47.1%; Macau 42.5%; Hong Kong 3.7%; Philippines 2.0%; Portugal 0.3%; other 4.4%.
Religious affiliation (2006): Buddhist *c.* 80%; Roman Catholic *c.* 4%; Protestant *c.* 1%; other/nonreligious *c.* 15%.
Major city (2011[3]): Macau 470,600.

Vital statistics

Birth rate per 1,000 population (2009): 8.8 (world avg. 20.3); within marriage (2004) 82.7%; outside of marriage (2004) 17.3%.
Death rate per 1,000 population (2009): 3.1 (world avg. 8.5).
Natural increase rate per 1,000 population (2009): 5.7 (world avg. 11.8).
Total fertility rate (avg. births per childbearing woman; 2007): 0.90.
Marriage/divorce rates per 1,000 population (2009): 5.6/1.4.
Life expectancy at birth (2006–09): male 79.4 years; female 85.2 years.
Major causes of death per 100,000 population (2009): malignant neoplasms (cancers) 101.3; diseases of the circulatory system 81.1; diseases of the respiratory system 41.5; accidents, poisoning, and violence 20.6; endocrine, nutritional, and metabolic diseases 17.6.

National economy

Budget (2009). Revenue: MOP 57,641,000,000 (revenue from gambling tax 76.9%, other 23.1%). Expenditures: MOP 33,825,000,000 (current expenditure 87.6%, capital expenditure 12.4%).
Land use as % of total land area (2009): "green area" 26.1%.
Gross national income (at current market prices; 2009): U.S.$19,911,000,000 (U.S.$37,012 per capita).

Structure of gross domestic product and labour force

	2008		2009	
	in value MOP '000,000	% of total value	labour force	% of labour force
Agriculture, fishing	…	…	1,100	0.3
Mining, quarrying	…	…		
Manufacturing	2,525	2.0	17,000	5.2
Construction	16,112	12.6	32,700	9.9
Public utilities	1,397	1.1	1,000	0.3
Transportation and communications	3,993	3.1	16,700	5.1
Trade, hotels	15,528	12.1	85,200	25.9
Finance, real estate	29,176	22.8	33,100	10.1
Public administration	6,921	5.4	20,300	6.2
Services	9,491	7.4	47,800	14.5
Gaming activities	47,554	37.2	62,700	19.0
Other	–4,798[7]	–3.7[7]	11,700[8]	3.6[8]
TOTAL	127,899	100.0	329,200[6, 9]	100.0[6]

Production (metric tons except as noted). Agriculture, forestry, fishing (2009): small production of chicken eggs, pig meat, and vegetables; roundwood, n.a.; fisheries production 1,500 (from aquaculture, none). Quarrying: n.a. Manufacturing (value added in MOP '000,000; 2008): wearing apparel 905; food and beverages 259; textiles 234; publishing and printing 186. Energy production (consumption): electricity (kW-hr; 2009) 1,466,000,000 ([2007] 3,203,000,000); coal, none (none); crude petroleum, none (none); petroleum products (metric tons; 2007) none (505,000); natural gas (cu m; 2009) none (93,000,000).

Public debt (2010): n.a.
Population economically active (2009): total 329,200[9]; activity rate of total population 60.7% (participation rates: ages 20–64, 81.6%; female 48.0%; unemployed 3.6%).

Price and earnings indexes (2005 = 100)

	2004	2005	2006	2007	2008	2009	2010
Consumer price index	95.9	100.0	105.2	111.0	120.6	122.0	125.4
Monthly earnings index	89.5	100.0	116.2	135.3	…	…	…

Selected balance of payments data. Receipts from (U.S.$'000,000): tourism (2009) 17,886; remittances (2010) 835; foreign direct investment (2008–10 avg.) 2,640. Disbursements for (U.S.$'000,000)[10]: tourism (2009) 510; remittances (2009) 707; foreign direct disinvestment (2008–10 avg.) –360.
Household income and expenditure. Average household size (2010) 2.8; average annual income per household (2007–08) MOP 303,000 (U.S.$37,743); sources of income: n.a.; expenditure (2008–09)[10]: food and nonalcoholic beverages 32.8%, housing (rent) 16.9%, transportation 7.9%, clothing and footwear 6.8%, energy 5.9%, recreation and culture 5.9%.

Foreign trade[11]

Balance of trade (current prices)

	2004	2005	2006	2007	2008	2009
U.S.$'000,000	–666	–2,040	–2,679	–3,502	–3,882	–3,661
% of total	10.6%	29.2%	34.4%	40.8%	49.3%	65.6%

Imports (2008): U.S.$5,880,000,000 (machinery and apparatus 18.6%; apparel and clothing accessories 14.8%; mineral fuels 12.1%; food 6.6%; beverages and tobacco 4.9%). *Major import sources:* China 35.9%; Hong Kong 9.3%; Japan 7.7%; United States 5.7%; France 4.8%.
Exports (2008): U.S.$1,998,000,000 (apparel and clothing accessories 52.7%, of which outerwear 32.2%; machinery and apparatus 10.5%; refined petroleum 9.6%; yarn and fabric 5.4%). *Major export destinations:* U.S. 39.9%; Hong Kong 19.7%; China 12.3%; Germany 4.0%.

Transport and communications

Transport. Railroads: none. Roads (2009): total length 257 mi, 413 km (paved 100%). Vehicles: passenger cars (2009) 86,784; trucks and buses (2008) 5,649. Air transport (2008)[12]: passenger-km 2,586,000,000; metric ton-km cargo 98,000,000.

Communications

Medium	date	number in '000s	units per 1,000 persons	Medium	date	number in '000s	units per 1,000 persons
Televisions	2003	130	292	PCs	2005	160	338
Telephones				Dailies	2009	190[13]	349[13]
Cellular	2010	1,122[14]	2,064[14]	Internet users	2009	281	522
Landline	2010	168	308	Broadband	2010	131[14]	241[14]

Education and health

Educational attainment (2006). Population age 25 and over having: no formal schooling 6.2%; incomplete primary education 10.7%; completed primary 22.5%; incomplete secondary 24.9%; completed secondary 21.4%; higher technical 1.7%; university 12.6%. *Literacy* (2006): percentage of population age 15 and over literate 93.5%.

Education (2008–09)

	teachers	students	student/ teacher ratio	enrollment rate (%)
Primary (age 6–11)	1,585	27,483	17.3	87
Secondary/Voc. (age 12–17)	2,294	39,328	17.1	76
Tertiary[15]	1,826	25,407	13.9	57 (age 18–22)

Health (2009): physicians 1,283 (1 per 424 persons); hospital beds 1,109 (1 per 491 persons); infant mortality rate per 1,000 live births 2.1; undernourished population, n.a.

Military

Total active duty personnel (2007): up to 500 Chinese troops within Macau; another 500 troops are stationed in nearby Zhuhai, China. Macau residents are prohibited from entering military service. *Military expenditure as percentage of GDP:* n.a.

[1]Includes 12 directly elected seats, 7 seats appointed by the chief executive, and 10 seats appointed by business and special-interest groups. [2]Pegged to the Hong Kong dollar at a rate of 1 HK$ = MOP 1.03. [3]January 1. [4]Name of landfilled casino and tourism district linking Coloane and Taipa. [5]A small part of eastern Hengqin island, China (adjacent to Macau), was ceded to Macau in June 2009 for construction of a new university campus. [6]Detail does not add to total given because of rounding. [7]Statistical discrepancy less imputed bank service charges. [8]Unemployed. [9]Nonresidents constituted *c.* 23% of the workforce in 2009. [10]Weights of consumer price index components. [11]Imports c.i.f.; exports f.o.b. [12]Air Macau only. [13]Circulation. [14]Subscribers. [15]2007–08.

Internet resources for further information:
- **Macau Statistics and Census Service http://www.dsec.gov.mo**
- **Monetary Authority of Macao http://www.amcm.gov.mo**

Macedonia

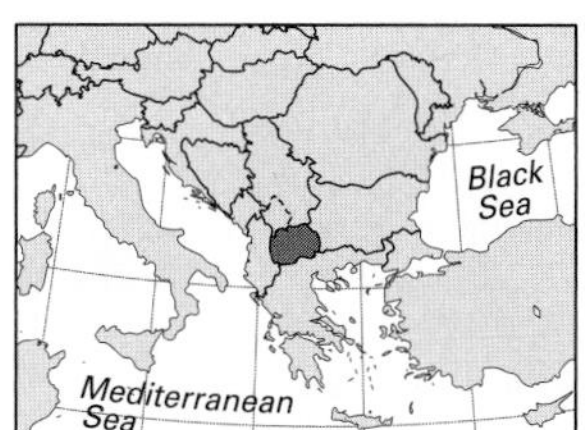

Official name[1]: Republika Makedonija (Macedonian); Republika e Maqedonisë (Albanian) (Republic of Macedonia).
Form of government: unitary multiparty republic with a unicameral legislature (Sobranie, or Assembly [123]).
Head of state: President.
Head of government: Prime Minister.
Capital: Skopje.
Official languages: Macedonian; Albanian.
Official religion: none.
Monetary unit: denar (MKD); valuation (Sept. 1, 2011) 1 U.S.$ = MKD 43.08; 1 £ = MKD 69.62.

Area and population

Statistical regions[3]	Principal municipalities	area sq mi	area sq km	population 2010[2] estimate
East	Štip	1,617	4,188	179,846
North-East	Kumanovo	890	2,306	174,876
Pelagonia	Bitola	1,822	4,719	234,320
Polog	Tetovo	957	2,479	314,194
Skopje	[4]	702	1,818	601,057
South-East	Strumica	1,058	2,741	172,693
South-West	Ohrid	1,266	3,280	221,899
Vardar	Veles	1,292	3,346	153,837
"non-statistical areas"	—	323	836	—
TOTAL		9,928[5]	25,713	2,052,722

Demography

Population (2011): 2,060,000.
Density (2011): persons per sq mi 207.5, persons per sq km 80.1.
Urban-rural (2009): urban 59.2%; rural 40.8%.
Sex distribution (2010[2]): male 50.12%; female 49.88%.
Age breakdown (2010[2]): under 15, 17.7%; 15–29, 23.5%; 30–44, 22.0%; 45–59, 20.2%; 60–74, 12.3%; 75–84, 3.7%; 85 and over, 0.6%.
Population projection: (2020) 2,070,000; (2030) 2,040,000.
Ethnic composition (2002): Macedonian 64.2%; Albanian 25.2%; Turkish 3.9%; Rom (Gypsy) 2.7%; Serbian 1.8%; Bosniac 0.8%; other 1.4%.
Religious affiliation (2005): Orthodox *c.* 65%[6]; Sunnī Muslim *c.* 32%[6]; Roman Catholic *c.* 1%; other (mostly Protestant) *c.* 2%.
Major city/municipalities (2009[2]): Skopje (city) 486,600; Bitola 73,300; Kumanovo 71,700; Prilep 66,000; Tetovo 54,500.

Vital statistics

Birth rate per 1,000 population (2009): 11.6 (world avg. 20.3); within marriage (2008) 87.8%; outside of marriage (2008) 12.2%.
Death rate per 1,000 population (2009): 9.3 (world avg. 8.5).
Total fertility rate (avg. births per childbearing woman; 2009): 1.50.
Marriage/divorce rates per 1,000 population (2009): 7.3/0.6.
Life expectancy at birth (2007): male 71.1 years; female 75.9 years.
Major causes of death per 100,000 population (2005): diseases of the circulatory system 527.7; malignant neoplasms (cancers) 157.6; accidents, violence, and poisoning 35.4; endocrine, nutrition, and immunity disorders 34.2; ill-defined conditions 65.6.

National economy

Budget (2009). Revenue: MKD 128,498,000,000 (tax revenue 85.5%, of which social contributions 30.2%, VAT 27.4%, excise taxes 11.3%, income and profit taxes 10.2%; nontax revenue 12.8%; other 1.7%). Expenditure: MKD 139,393,000,000 (current expenditure 90.4%, of which transfers 60.7%, wages and salaries 16.3%, interest 1.8%; capital expenditure 9.6%).
Production (metric tons except as noted). Agriculture, forestry, fishing (2009): wheat 271,117, grapes 253,456, potatoes 207,152, green chilies and peppers 154,771, apples 106,356, tobacco leaves 24,122; livestock (number of live animals) 455,356 sheep, 252,521 cattle; roundwood (2010) 639,000 cu m, of which fuelwood 83%; fisheries production 1,799 (from aquaculture 92%). Mining and quarrying (2009): gypsum 154,550; lead (metal content) 52,000; zinc (metal content) 32,000; copper (metal content) 7,600. Manufacturing (value added in U.S.$'000,000; 2007): base metals 333; textiles and wearing apparel 221; food and beverages 211; cement, bricks, and glass products 111; chemical products 84; refined petroleum 72; tobacco products 50. Energy production (consumption): electricity (kW-hr; 2009–10) 7,326,000,000 ([2009] 7,797,000,000); hard coal (metric tons; 2007) none (12,000); lignite (metric tons; 2009–10) 7,326,000 ([2007] 6,956,000); crude petroleum (barrels; 2009) none (7,300,000); petroleum products (metric tons; 2008) 1,036,000 ([2007] 1,009,000); natural gas (cu m; 2009) none (80,000,000).
Selected balance of payments data. Receipts from (U.S.$'000,000): tourism (2009) 218; remittances (2010) 414; foreign direct investment (2008–10 avg.) 360; official development assistance (2009) 193. Disbursements for (U.S.$'000,000): tourism (2009) 100; remittances (2009) 26.
Population economically active (2008): total 919,400; activity rate 44.9% (participation rates: ages 15–64, 63.5%; female 38.9%; unemployed [April 2010–March 2011] 31.4%).

Price and earnings indexes (2005 = 100)

	2004	2005	2006	2007	2008	2009	2010
Consumer price index	99.8	100.0	103.3	107.0	114.7	114.4	116.8
Monthly earnings index	97.5	100.0	107.3	115.8	127.7	158.4	163.1

Household income and expenditure. Average household size (2002) 3.6; income per household (2000) U.S.$3,798; sources of income (2000): wages and salaries 54.2%, transfers 22.6%, other 23.2%; expenditure (2008): food and nonalcoholic beverages 39.4%, transportation and communications 12.2%, housing and energy 10.4%, clothing and footwear 6.3%.
Gross national income (GNI; 2010): U.S.$9,319,000,000 (U.S.$4,520 per capita); purchasing power parity GNI (U.S.$10,830 per capita).

Structure of gross domestic product and labour force

	2008			
	in value MKD '000,000	% of total value	labour force	% of labour force
Agriculture, forestry, fishing	41,341	10.0	119,800	13.0
Mining and quarrying	4,350	1.1	6,700	0.7
Manufacturing	70,634	17.2	129,000	14.0
Construction	20,258	4.9	39,400	4.3
Public utilities	11,159	2.7	15,500	1.7
Transp. and commun.	33,143	8.0	37,700	4.1
Trade, hotels	56,222	13.7	105,700	11.5
Finance, real estate	28,539	6.9	24,000	2.6
Pub. admin., defense	26,677	6.5	42,200	4.6
Services	36,592	8.9	89,000	9.7
Other	82,812[7]	20.1[7]	310,400[8]	33.8[8]
TOTAL	411,728[5]	100.0	919,400	100.0

Public debt (external, outstanding; March 2010): U.S.$1,059,950,000.
Land use as % of total land area (2009): in temporary crops or left fallow 16.7%, in permanent crops 1.4%, in pasture 22.1%, forest area 39.4%.

Foreign trade[9]

Balance of trade (current prices)

	2005	2006	2007	2008	2009	2010
U.S.$'000,000	–1,187	–1,355	–1,875	–2,923	–2,341	–2,159
% of total	22.5%	22.0%	22.1%	27.2%	30.3%	24.7%

Imports (2008): U.S.$6,852,000,000 (machinery and apparatus 14.3%; crude petroleum 12.3%; iron and steel 11.1%; food 9.1%; road vehicles 6.5%; fabrics 5.9%; electricity 5.1%). *Major import sources:* Russia 13.6%; Germany 9.5%; Serbia 7.8%; Greece 7.5%; Italy 5.6%.
Exports (2007): U.S.$3,356,000,000 (iron and steel 37.6%, of which ferronickel 15.8%, flat-rolled products 13.6%; clothing and accessories 18.9%, of which female outerwear 9.6%; food 7.4%; refined petroleum 4.7%; metal ore/metal scrap 3.8%). *Major export destinations:* Serbia 19.1%; Germany 14.4%; Greece 12.5%; Italy 10.3%; Bulgaria 7.2%.

Transport and communications

Transport. Railroads (2009–10): route length (2009) 434 mi, 699 km; passenger-km 152,300,000; metric ton-km cargo 534,200,000. Roads (2009): length 8,535 mi, 13,736 km (paved [2000] 58%); passenger-km (2006) 6,300,000,000[10]; metric ton-km cargo (2009–10) 4,482,000,000. Vehicles (2009[2]): passenger cars 263,112; trucks and buses 31,150. Air transport (2008)[11]: passenger-km 237,000,000; metric ton-km cargo, none.

Communications

Medium	date	number in '000s	units per 1,000 persons	Medium	date	number in '000s	units per 1,000 persons
Televisions	2003	507	250	PCs	2007	756	370
Telephones				Dailies	2009	160[12]	78[12]
Cellular	2010	2,153[13]	1,045[13]	Internet users	2009	1,057	518
Landline	2010	413	201	Broadband	2010	257[13]	125[13]

Education and health

Educational attainment (2002). Percentage of population age 15 and over having: less than full primary education 18.1%; primary 35.0%; secondary 36.9%; postsecondary and higher 10.0%. *Literacy* (2008): total population age 15 and over literate 97.0%; males literate 98.6%; females literate 95.4%.

Education (2007–08)

	teachers	students	student/ teacher ratio	enrollment rate (%)
Primary (age 7–10)[14]	5,519	100,911	18.3	87
Secondary/Voc. (age 11–18)	15,577	203,853	13.1	82[15]
Tertiary	3,506	65,504	18.7	40 (age 19–23)

Health (2007): physicians 5,052 (1 per 405 persons); hospital beds 9,326 (1 per 219 persons); infant mortality rate per 1,000 live births (2009) 11.7; undernourished population (2004–06) less than 5.0% of the total population based on the consumption of a minimum daily requirement of 1,950 calories.

Military

Total active duty personnel (November 2010): 8,000 (joint operational command 100%); paramilitary 7,600. *Military expenditure as percentage of GDP* (2009): 1.7%; per capita expenditure U.S.$78.

[1]Member of the United Nations under the name The Former Yugoslav Republic of Macedonia (FYROM). [2]January 1. [3]Actual first-order administration is based on 84 municipalities. [4]Includes the 10 municipalities forming (at least in part) the city of Skopje. [5]Detail does not add to total given because of rounding. [6]Includes nominal practitioners. [7]Rent, VAT, and import duties less subsidies. [8]Unemployed. [9]Imports c.i.f.; exports f.o.b. [10]Passenger cars 5,000,000,000; buses 1,300,000,000. [11]MAT–Macedonian Airlines. [12]Circulation of daily newspapers. [13]Subscribers. [14]2006–07. [15]2004–05.

Internet resources for further information:
- **National Bank of the Republic of Macedonia http://www.nbrm.mk**
- **State Statistical Office http://www.stat.gov.mk**

Madagascar

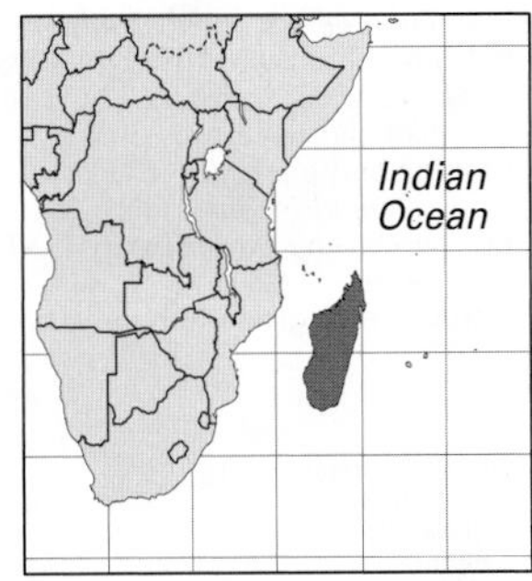

Official name: [1].
Form of government: transitional regime[2].
Heads of state and government: President of High Authority of Transition assisted by Prime Minister.
Capital: Antananarivo.
Official languages: Malagasy; French[3]; English[3].
Official religion: none.
Monetary unit: ariary (MGA); valuation (Sept. 1, 2011) 1 U.S.$ = MGA 1,972; 1 £ = MGA 3,187.

Population (2004 estimate)

Regions[4]	population	Regions[4]	population	Regions[4]	population
Alaotra Mangoro	877,700	Atsinanana	1,117,100	Melaky	175,500
Amoron'i Mania	693,200	Betsiboka	236,500	Menabe	390,800
Analamanga	2,811,500	Boeny	543,200	Sava	805,300
Analanjirofo	860,800	Bongolava	326,600	Sofia	940,800
Androy	476,600	Diana	485,800	Vakinankaratra	1,589,800
Anosy	544,200	Haute Matsiatra	1,128,900	Vatovavy Fitovinany	1,097,700
Atsimo-Andrefana	1,018,500	Ihorombe	189,200		
Atsimo-Atsinanana	621,200	Itasy	643,000	TOTAL	17,573,900

Demography

Area: 226,658 sq mi, 587,041 sq km.
Population (2011): 21,307,000.
Density (2011): persons per sq mi 94.0, persons per sq km 36.3.
Urban-rural (2009): urban 29.8%; rural 70.2%.
Sex distribution (2007): male 49.80%; female 50.20%.
Age breakdown (2006): under 15, 44.1%; 15–29, 27.1%; 30–44, 15.7%; 45–59, 8.4%; 60–74, 3.7%; 75–84, 0.9%; 85 and over, 0.1%.
Population projection: (2020) 27,366,000; (2030) 35,333,000.
Doubling time: 23 years.
Ethnic composition (2000): Malagasy 95.9%, of which Merina 24.0%, Betsimisaraka 13.4%, Betsileo 11.3%, Tsimihety 7.0%, Sakalava 5.9%; Makua 1.1%; French 0.6%; Comorian 0.5%; Reunionese 0.4%; other 1.5%.
Religious affiliation (2005): traditional beliefs *c.* 42%; Protestant (significantly Lutheran) *c.* 27%; Roman Catholic *c.* 20%; Sunnī Muslim *c.* 2%; other *c.* 9%.
Major cities (2001): Antananarivo 1,403,449; Toamasina 179,045; Antsirabe 160,356; Fianarantsoa 144,225; Mahajanga 135,660.

Vital statistics

Birth rate per 1,000 population (2006): 38.8 (world avg. 20.3).
Death rate per 1,000 population (2006): 8.7 (world avg. 8.5).
Natural increase rate per 1,000 population (2006): 30.1 (world avg. 11.8).
Total fertility rate (avg. births per childbearing woman; 2008–09): 4.8[5].
Life expectancy at birth (2006): male 59.9 years; female 63.7 years.

National economy

Budget (2008). Revenue: MGA 2,685,400,000,000 (tax revenue 77.7%, grants 20.4%, nontax revenue 1.9%). Expenditures: MGA 2,998,700,000,000 (current expenditure 58.5%, capital expenditure 41.5%).
Public debt (external, outstanding; 2009): U.S.$1,846,000,000.
Production (metric tons except as noted). Agriculture, forestry, fishing (2009): paddy rice 4,005,250, cassava 2,701,860, sugarcane 2,600,000, sweet potatoes 886,790, cow's milk 555,000, corn (maize) 370,000, vegetables/melons 357,610, bananas 281,550, taro 239,900, mangoes 221,290[6], potatoes 219,700, cattle meat 150,450, coffee 65,000, cloves (whole and stem) 7,600, vanilla 2,830; livestock (number of live animals) 9,700,000 cattle, 1,360,000 pigs; roundwood (2010) 13,377,330 cu m, of which fuelwood 98%; fisheries production 137,399 (from aquaculture 4%). Mining and quarrying (2009): ilmenite 240,000; chromite ore 43,000; tourmalines 43,000 kg[7]; sapphires 2,100 kg[7]; gold 70 kg (illegally smuggled, *c.* 1,500 kg). Manufacturing (value added in MGA '000,000,000[8]; 2009): beverages 13.0; food products 12.3; fabricated/base metals 3.6; tobacco products 3.3. Energy production (consumption): electricity (kW-hr; 2008) 1,110,000,000 (1,032,000,000); coal (metric tons; 2009) none (10,000); crude petroleum (barrels; 2008) 14,000 ([2007] 5,000,000); petroleum products (metric tons; 2007) negligible (682,000); natural gas, none (none).
Population economically active (2005): total 9,844,100; activity rate of total population 52.8% (participation rates: ages 15–64, 88.1%; female 49.6%; unemployed 2.8%).

Price index (2005 = 100)

	2004	2005	2006	2007	2008	2009	2010
Consumer price index	84.4	100.0	110.8	122.2	133.5	145.4	158.9

Selected balance of payments data. Receipts from (U.S.$'000,000): tourism (2009) 308; remittances (2010) n.a.; foreign direct investment (2008–10 avg.) 1,031; official development assistance (2009) 445. Disbursements for (U.S.$'000,000): tourism (2009) 123; remittances (2009) n.a.
Household income and expenditure. Average household size (2008–09) 4.7[5]; expenditure (2000)[9]: food, beverages, and tobacco 50.1%, housing and energy 18.2%, transportation 8.0%, clothing 7.0%, household furnishings 4.6%.
Gross national income (GNI; 2010): U.S.$8,820,000,000 (U.S.$440 per capita); purchasing power parity GNI (U.S.$980 per capita).

Structure of gross domestic product and labour force

	2009		2005	
	in value MGA '000,000,000[8]	% of total value	labour force	% of labour force
Agriculture, fishing	186.2	31.3	7,844,300	79.7
Mining	1.5	0.3	18,800	0.2
Manufacturing	55.9	9.4	267,500	2.7
Public utilities	8.6	1.4	27,500	0.3
Construction	25.9	4.4	13,000	0.1
Transp. and commun.	98.2	16.5	86,300	0.9
Trade, hotels	61.7	10.4	534,400	5.4
Finance	15.2	2.6	4,100	—
Services	65.1	10.9	572,100	5.8
Pub. admin., defense	27.0	4.5	202,400	2.1
Other	49.6[10]	8.3[10]	273,700[11]	2.8[11]
TOTAL	595.1[12]	100.0	9,844,100	100.0

Land use as % of total land area (2009): in temporary crops or left fallow (2007) 5.1%, in permanent crops 1.0%, in pasture 64.1%, forest area 21.7%.

Foreign trade[13]

Balance of trade (current prices)

	2004	2005	2006	2007	2008	2009
U.S.$'000,000	–680.7	–850.0	–752.1	–1,102.2	–2,179.4	–2,063.4
% of total	26.0%	33.7%	27.2%	29.1%	39.5%	48.5%

Imports (2008): U.S.$3,845,900,000 (machinery and apparatus 23.0%, of which machinery specialized for particular industries 6.3%; fabrics/yarn 13.6%; refined petroleum 12.8%; food 7.8%; iron and steel 7.1%; road vehicles 6.0%). *Major import sources:* China 21.0%; France 8.9%; Bahrain 8.0%; South Africa 6.1%; U.S. 5.0%.
Exports (2008): U.S.$1,666,500,000 (apparel/clothing accessories 53.2%, of which pants/shorts 27.1%; food/spices 19.4%, of which shrimp 6.6%, vanilla 3.0%, fish 2.0%, cloves 1.8%; refined petroleum 5.4%; aircraft/parts 4.2%; chromium ore 2.0%; precious/semiprecious stones 0.5%[7]). *Major export destinations:* France 45.1%; U.S. 21.9%; Germany 6.5%; China 3.1%; Italy 2.4%.

Transport and communications

Transport. Railroads: route length (2008) 500 mi, 804 km; passenger-km (2007) 26,000,000; metric ton-km cargo (2007) 77,000,000. Roads (2000): total length 30,968 mi, 49,827 km (paved 12%). Vehicles (2008): passenger cars 146,273; trucks and buses 364,613. Air transport: passenger-km (2008) 1,042,000,000[14]; metric ton-km cargo (2007) 24,000,000.

Communications

Medium	date	number in '000s	units per 1,000 persons	Medium	date	number in '000s	units per 1,000 persons
Televisions	2002	410	25	PCs	2005	102	5.5
Telephones				Dailies	2009	115[15]	5.9[15]
Cellular	2010	8,242[16]	398[16]	Internet users	2009	320	16
Landline	2010	172	8.3	Broadband	2010	4.9[16]	0.2[16]

Education and health

Educational attainment (2003–04)[17]. Percentage of population age 25–59 (male) and 25–49 (female) having: no formal schooling 20.4%; incomplete primary education 33.6%; complete primary 13.2%; incomplete secondary 23.0%; complete secondary 6.4%; higher 3.4%. *Literacy* (2008–09)[5]: percentage of literate population ages 15–49, 76.0%; males 78.5%; females 74.7%.

Education (2007–08)

	teachers	students	student/ teacher ratio	enrollment rate (%)
Primary (age 6–10)	85,257	4,020,322	47.2	98[18]
Secondary/Voc. (age 11–17)	35,343	945,245	26.7	24
Tertiary	3,527	62,069	17.6	3 (age 18–22)

Health (2004): physicians 1,861 (1 per 9,998 persons); hospital beds 9,303 (1 per 2,000 persons); infant mortality rate per 1,000 live births (2008–09) 48[5]; undernourished population (2004–06) 6,600,000 (35% of total population based on the consumption of a minimum daily requirement of 1,760 calories).

Military

Total active duty personnel (November 2010): 13,500 (army 92.6%, navy 3.7%, air force 3.7%); paramilitary 8,100. *Military expenditure as percentage of GDP* (2009): 1.0%; per capita expenditure U.S.$4.

[1]Repoblikan'i Madagasikara (Malagasy); République de Madagascar (French); Republic of Madagascar (English). [2]From March 2009; two transitional bodies were appointed by the president in October 2010—the Higher Transitional Council (90) and the Transitional Parliament (256). [3]Per decisions of High Constitutional Court. [4]The 22 regions were promoted to first-order subdivisions effective October 2009. [5]Based on a demographic and health survey of 17,857 households (17,375 females and 8,586 males). [6]Includes mangosteens and guavas. [7]A ban on all gemstone exports was in place between March 2008 and July 2009. [8]At constant prices of 1984. [9]Weights of consumer price index components. [10]Indirect taxes less imputed bank charges. [11]Unemployed. [12]Detail does not add to total given because of rounding. [13]Imports c.i.f.; exports f.o.b. [14]Air Madagascar only. [15]Circulation. [16]Subscribers. [17]Based on demographic survey of 6,629 persons (5,029 females, 1,600 males). [18]2006–07.

Internet resource for further information:
- **Institut National de la Statistique http://www.instat.mg**

Malawi

Official name: Republic of Malawi[1,2].
Form of government: multiparty republic with one legislative house (National Assembly [193]).
Head of state and government: President.
Capital: Lilongwe[3].
Official language: [1].
Official religion: none.
Monetary unit: Malawian kwacha (MK); valuation (Sept. 1, 2011) 1 U.S.$ = MK 165.34; 1 £ = MK 267.18.

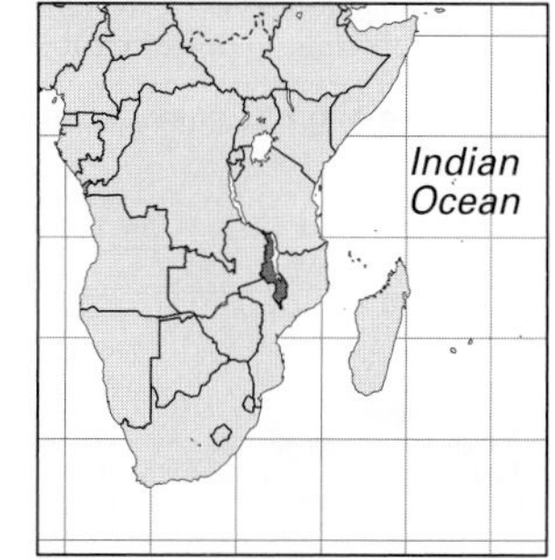

Area and population

Regions Districts/Cities	area sq km	population 2008 census[4]	Regions Districts/Cities	area sq km	population 2008 census[4]
Central	35,592	5,510,195	Southern	31,753	5,858,035
Dedza	3,624	624,445	Balaka	2,193	317,324
Dowa	3,041	558,470	Blantyre (rural)	1,792	340,728
Kasungu	7,878	627,467	Blantyre (city)	220	661,256
Lilongwe (rural)	5,703	1,230,834	Chikwawa	4,755	434,648
Lilongwe (city)	456	674,448	Chiradzulu	767	288,546
Mchinji	3,356	456,516	Machinga	3,771	490,579
Nkhota kota	4,259	303,659	Mangochi	6,273	797,061
Ntcheu	3,424	471,589	Mulanje	2,056	521,391
Ntchisi	1,655	224,872	Mwanza	826	92,947
Salima	2,196	337,895	Neno	1,469	107,317
Northern	26,931	1,708,930	Nsanje	1,942	238,103
Chitipa	4,288	178,904	Phalombe	1,394	313,129
Karonga	3,355	269,890	Thyolo	1,715	587,053
Likoma	18	10,414	Zomba (rural)	2,541	579,639
Mzimba	10,382	727,931	Zomba (city)	39	88,314
Mzuzu (city)	48	133,968	TOTAL LAND AREA	94,276	
Nkhata Bay	4,071	215,789	INLAND WATER	24,208	
Rumphi	4,769	172,034	TOTAL	118,484	13,077,160

Demography

Population (2011): 15,381,000[5].
Density (2011)[6]: persons per sq mi 422.6, persons per sq km 163.1.
Urban-rural (2008): urban 15.3%; rural 84.7%.
Sex distribution (2008): male 48.63%; female 51.37%.
Age breakdown (2008): under 15, 45.9%; 15–29, 27.7%; 30–44, 14.5%; 45–59, 6.7%; 60–74, 3.4%; 75–84, 1.2%; 85 and over, 0.6%.
Population projection: (2020) 20,677,000; (2030) 28,174,000.
Doubling time: 26 years.
Tribal composition (2008): Chewa 32.6%; Lomwe 17.6%; Yao 13.5%; Ngoni 11.5%; Tumbuka 8.8%; Nyanja 5.8%; Sena 3.6%; other 6.6%.
Religious affiliation (2005): Protestant/independent Christian *c.* 55%; Roman Catholic *c.* 20%; Muslim *c.* 20%; traditional beliefs *c.* 3%; other *c.* 2%.
Major cities (2008): Lilongwe 674,448; Blantyre 661,256; Mzuzu 133,968; Zomba 88,314; Karonga 40,334.

Vital statistics

Birth rate per 1,000 population (2009): 39.7 (world avg. 20.3).
Death rate per 1,000 population (2009): 11.8 (world avg. 8.5).
Total fertility rate (avg. births per childbearing woman; 2008): 5.67.
Life expectancy at birth (2008): male 48.4 years; female 49.5 years.
Adult population (ages 15–49) *living with HIV* (2009): 11.0%[7] (world avg. 0.8%).
Major causes of death per 100,000 population (2002): HIV/AIDS-related *c.* 729; lower respiratory infections *c.* 244; cardiovascular diseases *c.* 175; malaria *c.* 169; diarrheal diseases *c.* 164.

National economy

Budget (2008–09). Revenue: MK 187,402,000,000 (tax revenue 62.4%, of which VAT 21.0%, excises 9.7%, corporate tax 8.1%; grants 29.3%; nontax revenue 6.9%; remainder 1.4%). Expenditures: MK 223,502,000,000 (current expenditure 82.0%; capital expenditure 18.0%).
Public debt (external, outstanding; March 2009): U.S.$664,000,000.
Production (metric tons except as noted). Agriculture, forestry, fishing (2009): cassava 3,874,710, corn (maize) 3,767,410, sugarcane 2,500,000, plantains 351,812, bananas 337,860, peanuts (groundnuts) 282,054, tobacco leaves 208,155, pigeon peas 206,021, dry beans 171,420, mangoes, mangosteens, and guavas 82,659, seed cotton 72,664, tea 52,559, sunflower seeds 8,089; livestock (number of live animals) 3,547,200 goats, 1,627,200 pigs, 1,031,000 cattle; roundwood (2010) 5,868,068 cu m, of which fuelwood 91%; fisheries production 70,945 (from aquaculture 2%). Mining and quarrying (2008): limestone 74,000; gemstones (including rubies and sapphires) 3,710 kg. Manufacturing (value added in U.S.$'000,000; 2001): food products 62; beverages 28; chemicals and chemical products 11; wearing apparel 7. Energy production (consumption): electricity (kW-hr; 2007) 1,637,000,000 (1,620,000,000); hard coal (metric tons; 2007) 58,550 (61,000); petroleum products (metric tons; 2007) none (257,000).
Land use as % of total land area (2009): in temporary crops or left fallow 38.2%, in permanent crops 1.3%, in pasture 19.6%, forest area 34.7%.
Population economically active (2008): total 6,109,000[8]; activity rate 41.1%[8] (participation rates: ages 15–64, 76.1%[8]; female 49.9%[8]; unemployed, n.a.).

Price index (2005 = 100)

	2004	2005	2006	2007	2008	2009	2010
Consumer price index	86.6	100.0	114.0	123.0	133.8	145.0	155.8

Household income and expenditure. Average household size (2008) 4.6; average annual household income MK 50,904 (U.S.$467)[9]; expenditure[9]: food 55.6%, housing and energy 20.6%, transportation and communications 6.6%, clothing and footwear 4.3%.
Gross national income (GNI; 2010): U.S.$4,886,000,000 (U.S.$330 per capita); purchasing power parity GNI (U.S.$850 per capita).

Structure of gross domestic product and labour force

	2009		1998	
	in value MK '000,000[10]	% of total value[10]	labour force	% of labour force
Agriculture	150,900	34.1	3,765,827	83.6
Mining	4,046	0.9	2,499	0.1
Manufacturing	33,979	7.7	118,483	2.6
Construction	20,205	4.6	73,402	1.6
Public utilities	6,317	1.4	7,319	0.2
Transp. and commun.	31,483	7.1	32,623	0.7
Trade, hotels	68,475	15.5	257,389	5.7
Finance, real estate	46,666	10.6	13,957	0.3
Public administration	12,464	2.8	101,433	2.2
Services	52,860	12.0	85,996	1.9
Other	14,661[11]	3.3[11]	50,362	1.1
TOTAL	442,056	100.0	4,509,290	100.0

Selected balance of payments data. Receipts from (U.S.$'000,000): tourism (2007) 27; remittances (2009) 1.0; foreign direct investment (2008–10 avg.) 70; official development assistance (2009) 772. Disbursements for (U.S.$'000,000): tourism (2007) 73; remittances (2008) 1.0.

Foreign trade[12]

Balance of trade (current prices)

	2003	2004	2005	2006	2007	2008
MK '000,000	–24,400	–33,889	–58,850	–69,734	–42,151	–65,981
% of total	22.4%	23.7%	32.8%	32.1%	15.9%	22.0%

Imports (2008): MK 309,664,000,000 (machinery and apparatus 18.7%, of which tractors 7.9%; fertilizers 16.7%; refined petroleum 9.2%; road vehicles 8.2%; food 6.2%). *Major import sources:* South Africa 26.6%; Mozambique 20.3%; Tanzania 5.8%; Switzerland 5.3%; U.A.E. 5.0%.
Exports (2008): MK 123,517,000,000 (unmanufactured tobacco 67.1%; raw sugar 5.8%; tea 4.2%; apparel/clothing accessories 2.9%; cotton 2.5%). *Major export destinations:* Belgium 13.0%; South Africa 10.1%; U.K. 8.9%; Neth. 5.9%; U.S. 5.7%.

Transport and communications

Transport. Railroads (2008): route length 495 mi, 797 km; passenger-km 54,000,000; metric ton-km cargo 51,000,000. Roads (2003): total length 9,600 mi, 15,451 km (paved 45%). Vehicles (2001): passenger cars 22,500; trucks and buses 57,600. Air transport (2007)[13]: passenger-km 165,000,000; metric ton-km cargo, n.a.

Communications

Medium	date	number in '000s	units per 1,000 persons	Medium	date	number in '000s	units per 1,000 persons
Televisions	2003	65	5.2	PCs	2007	28	2.0
Telephones				Dailies	2009	22[14]	2.8[14]
Cellular	2010	3,038[15]	204[15]	Internet users	2009	716	47
Landline	2010	160	11	Broadband	2010	5.1[15]	0.3[15]

Education and health

Educational attainment (2004)[16]. Percentage of population age 25 and over having: no formal education/unknown 33.5%; incomplete primary education 24.2%; complete primary 27.9%; secondary and university 14.4%. *Literacy* (2007): total population age 15 and over literate 65.9%; males literate 78.1%; females literate 53.9%.

Education (2006–07)

	teachers	students	student/ teacher ratio	enrollment rate (%)
Primary (age 6–11)	...	2,943,248	...	87
Secondary/Voc. (age 12–17)	11,360[17]	574,003	45.6[17]	24
Tertiary	861	6,458	7.5	[18] (age 18–22)

Health: physicians (2008) 260 (1 per 56,246 persons); hospital beds (2007) 15,658 (1 per 909 persons); infant mortality rate (2008) 88.1; undernourished population (2005–07) 3,900,000 (28% of total population based on the consumption of a minimum daily requirement of 1,720 calories).

Military

Total active duty personnel (November 2010): 5,300 (army 100%). *Military expenditure as percentage of GDP* (2008): 1.5%; per capita expenditure U.S.$3.

[1]No official language is stated in the constitution. English is the official language of instruction. [2]Dziko la Malaŵi in Chewa, the principal national language. [3]Judiciary meets in Blantyre. [4]Final de facto results. [5]Estimate of *UN World Population Prospects* (2010 revision). [6]Based on land area. [7]Statistically derived midpoint of range. [8]ILO estimate. [9]Based on the Malawi Integrated Household Survey 2004–05, comprising 10,777 households. [10]At constant prices of 2005. [11]Taxes less subsidies and less imputed bank service charges. [12]Imports f.o.b. in balance of trade and c.i.f. in commodities and trading partners. [13]Air Malawi only. [14]Circulation. [15]Subscribers. [16]Based on the Malawi Demographic and Household Survey 2004, comprising 13,664 households. [17]2001–02. [18]Less than 0.5.

Internet resources for further information:
- **National Statistical Office of Malawi http://www.nso.malawi.net**
- **Reserve Bank of Malawi http://www.rbm.mw**

Malaysia

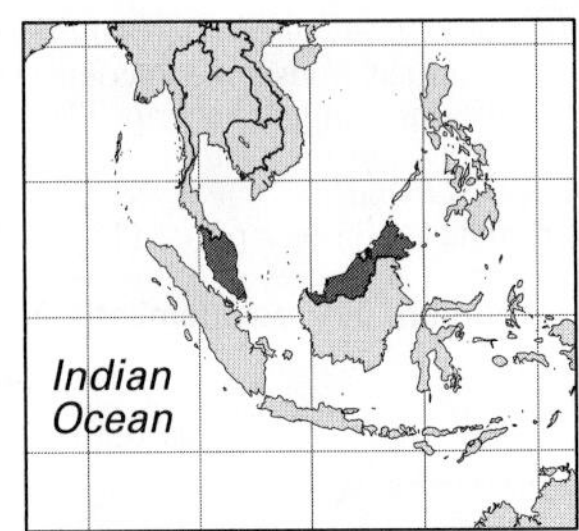

Official name: Malaysia.
Form of government: federal constitutional monarchy with two legislative houses (Senate [70[1]]; House of Representatives [222]).
Head of state: Paramount Ruler.
Head of government: Prime Minister.
Capital: Kuala Lumpur[2].
Administrative centre: Putrajaya[3].
Official language: Malay.
Official religion: Islam.
Monetary unit: ringgit (RM); valuation (Sept. 1, 2011) 1 U.S.$ = RM 2.98; 1 £ = RM 4.82.

Area and population

Regions / States	Capitals	area sq mi	area sq km	population 2010 census
East Malaysia				
Sabah	Kota Kinabalu	28,429	73,631	3,206,742
Sarawak	Kuching	48,050	124,450	2,471,140
West Malaysia (Peninsular Malaysia)				
Johor	Johor Bahru	7,417	19,210	3,348,283
Kedah	Alor Setar	3,668	9,500	1,947,651
Kelantan	Kota Baharu	5,830	15,099	1,539,601
Melaka	Melaka	642	1,664	821,110
Negeri Sembilan	Seremban	2,581	6,686	1,021,064
Pahang	Kuantan	13,952	36,137	1,500,817
Perak	Ipoh	8,122	21,035	2,352,743
Perlis	Kangar	317	821	231,541
Pulau Pinang	George Town	405	1,048	1,561,383
Selangor	Shah Alam	3,131	8,108	5,462,141
Terengganu	Kuala Terengganu	5,033	13,035	1,035,977
Federal Territories				
Kuala Lumpur	—	94	243	1,674,621
Labuan[4]	—	35	91	86,908
Putrajaya	—	18	46	72,413
TOTAL		127,724	330,804	28,334,135

Demography

Population (2011): 28,161,000.
Density (2011): persons per sq mi 220.5, persons per sq km 85.1.
Urban-rural (2009): urban 71.3%; rural 28.7%.
Sex distribution (2010): male 50.88%; female 49.12%.
Age breakdown (2009): under 15, 30.2%; 15–29, 26.1%; 30–44, 21.7%; 45–59, 14.7%; 60–74, 5.8%; 75 and over, 1.5%.
Population projection: (2020) 32,221,000; (2030) 36,402,000.
Ethnic composition (2009): Malay 50.9%; other indigenous 11.1%; Chinese 22.7%; Indian 6.9%; other citizen 1.2%; noncitizen 7.2%.
Religious affiliation (2000): Muslim 60.4%; Buddhist 19.2%; Christian 9.1%; Hindu 6.3%; Chinese folk religionist 2.6%; animist 0.8%; other 1.6%.
Major cities (2009): Kuala Lumpur 1,493,000; Klang 1,071,000; Johor Bahru 958,000; Subang Jaya 954,300[5, 6]; Ipoh 692,200[6]; Putrajaya 55,000[6].

Vital statistics

Birth rate per 1,000 population (2009): 21.8 (world avg. 20.3).
Death rate per 1,000 population (2009): 4.9 (world avg. 8.5).
Total fertility rate (avg. births per childbearing woman; 2009): 2.74.
Life expectancy at birth (2010): male 71.7 years; female 76.6 years.
Major causes of death per 100,000 population (2002): diseases of the circulatory system 149; infectious and parasitic diseases 101; malignant neoplasms (cancers) 83; accidents and violence 43; chronic respiratory diseases 40.

National economy

Budget (2008). Revenue: RM 159,793,000,000 (tax revenue 70.7%, of which corporate taxes 23.6%, taxes on petroleum 15.1%, income tax 9.4%; nontax revenue 29.3%). Expenditures: RM 196,346,000,000 (current expenditure 78.2%, of which wages and salaries 20.9%; development expenditure 21.8%).
Population economically active (2009): total 11,315,300; activity rate 40.7% (participation rates: ages 15–64 [2008] 62.6%; female [2008] 35.8%; unemployed [April 2009–March 2010] 3.5%).

Price index (2005 = 100)

	2004	2005	2006	2007	2008	2009	2010
Consumer price index	97.1	100.0	103.6	105.7	111.5	112.1	114.0

Production (metric tons except as noted). Agriculture, forestry, fishing (2009): oil palm fruit 84,842,000, rice 2,510,000, natural rubber 857,019, sugarcane 700,000, bananas 625,000, coconuts 459,640, cacao beans 18,152; livestock (number of live animals) 2,050,000 pigs, 800,000 cattle; roundwood (2010) 22,984,176 cu m, of which fuelwood 12%; fisheries production 1,729,034 (from aquaculture 19%); aquatic plants production 138,857 (from aquaculture 100%). Mining and quarrying (2008–09): iron ore 1,023,434; tin (metal content) 2,646; gold 2,427 kg. Manufacturing (value added in RM '000,000; 2008): petroleum products 122,000; food products 107,700; electrical machinery and electronics 84,200; chemical products 60,000; office, accounting, and computing machinery 49,900. Energy production (consumption): electricity (kW-hr; 2008–09) 103,734,200,000 (92,662,100,000); coal (metric tons; 2008–09) 1,433,341 ([2007] 12,289,000); crude petroleum (barrels; 2009–10) 240,034,400 ([2007] 198,200,000); petroleum products (metric tons; 2008–09) 23,380,000 ([2007] 25,752,000); natural gas (cu m; 2008–09) 56,794,675,000 ([2007] 32,900,000,000).

Gross national income (GNI; 2010): U.S.$220,417,000,000 (U.S.$7,900 per capita); purchasing power parity GNI (U.S.$14,360 per capita).

Structure of gross domestic product and labour force

	2008 in value RM '000,000	% of total value	labour force	% of labour force
Agriculture, forestry, and fishing	76,219	10.3	1,487,700	13.5
Mining and quarrying	127,277	17.2	54,500	0.5
Manufacturing	195,027	26.3	1,944,700	17.6
Construction	19,519	2.6	998,000	9.1
Public utilities	17,345	2.3	60,500	0.6
Transp. and commun.	45,608	6.2	583,400	5.3
Trade, hotels	97,785	13.2	2,513,000	22.8
Finance, real estate	87,135	11.8	829,200	7.5
Pub. admin., defense	54,337	7.3	751,100	6.8
Services	33,026	4.5	1,437,400	13.0
Other	–12,555[7]	–1.7[7]	368,500[8]	3.3[8]
TOTAL	740,721[9]	100.0	11,028,100[9]	100.0

Public debt (external, outstanding; 2009): U.S.$21,364,000,000.
Household income and expenditure. Average household size (2008) 4.4; gross income per household (2004) RM 39,000 (U.S.$10,263); expenditure (2005)[10]: food and nonalcoholic beverages 31.4%, housing and energy 21.4%, transportation 15.9%.
Selected balance of payments data. Receipts from (U.S.$'000,000): tourism (2009) 15,798; remittances (2009) 1,900; foreign direct investment (FDI; 2008–10 avg.) 5,901. Disbursements for (U.S.$'000,000): tourism (2009) 6,508; remittances (2009) 6,800; FDI (2008–10 avg.) 12,074.
Land use as % of total land area (2007): in temporary crops or left fallow 5.5%, in permanent crops 17.6%, in pasture 0.9%, forest area 62.7%.

Foreign trade[11]

Balance of trade (current prices)

	2004	2005	2006	2007	2008	2009
U.S.$'000,000	+21,483	+27,334	+29,542	+29,295	+42,644	+33,770
% of total	9.3%	10.7%	10.1%	9.1%	12.0%	12.0%

Imports (2008): U.S.$156,202,000,000 (machinery and apparatus 37.5%, mineral fuels 10.9%, base and fabricated metals 9.8%, food 5.4%). *Major import sources:* China 12.8%; Japan 12.5%; Singapore 10.9%; U.S. 10.8%.
Exports (2008): U.S.$198,846,000,000 (computers/office machines/parts 12.8%, petroleum 11.2%, electrical machinery/parts 10.0%, palm oil 6.4%, LNG 6.1%). *Major export destinations:* Singapore 14.7%; U.S. 12.5%; Japan 10.8%; China 9.5%; Thailand 4.8%.

Transport and communications

Transport. Railroads (2008–09): route length (2008) 1,149 mi, 1,849 km; passenger-km 1,466,892,000; metric ton-km cargo 1,267,935,000. Roads (2006): total length 56,002 mi, 90,127 km (paved 79%). Vehicles (2008): passenger cars 8,056,999; trucks and buses 973,293. Air transport (2008–09): passenger-km 32,297,000,000; metric ton-km cargo 2,142,483,000.

Communications

Medium	date	number in '000s	units per 1,000 persons	Medium	date	number in '000s	units per 1,000 persons
Televisions	2003	5,480	222	PCs	2006	6,106	234
Telephones				Dailies	2009	2,595[12]	93[12]
Cellular	2010	34,456[13]	1,213[13]	Internet users	2009	15,824	576
Landline	2010	4,573	161	Broadband	2010	2,079[13]	73[13]

Education and health

Educational attainment (2002). Percentage of population age 25–64 having: no formal schooling/unknown 8.4%; primary education 28.7%; lower secondary 20.7%; upper secondary 31.1%; higher 11.1%. *Literacy* (2008): total population age 15 and over literate 92.1%; males 94.3%; females 89.8%.

Education (2008–09)

	teachers	students	student/ teacher ratio	enrollment rate (%)
Primary (age 6–11)	210,912	3,154,090	15.0	96[14]
Secondary/Voc. (age 12–18)	159,019	2,310,660	14.5	68[14]
Tertiary[14]	42,335	805,136	19.0	32 (age 19–23)

Health (2008): physicians 25,102 (1 per 1,076 persons); hospital beds (2007) 47,784 (1 per 556 persons); infant mortality rate 6.7; undernourished population (2004–06) less than 5.0% of total population based on the consumption of a minimum daily requirement of 1,810 calories.

Military

Total active duty personnel (November 2010): 109,000 (army 73.4%, navy 12.8%, air force 13.8%); paramilitary 24,600. *Military expenditure as percentage of GDP* (2009): 2.0%; per capita expenditure U.S.$139.

[1]Includes 44 appointees of the Paramount Ruler; the remaining 26 are indirectly elected. [2]Location of the first royal palace and both houses of parliament. [3]Location of the second royal palace, the prime minister's office, and the supreme court. [4]Geographically within East Malaysia. [5]Conurbation contiguous with Kuala Lumpur. [6]2006. [7]Net of import duties less imputed bank service charges. [8]Unemployed. [9]Detail does not add to total given because of rounding. [10]Weights of consumer price index components. [11]Imports c.i.f.; exports f.o.b. [12]Circulation of daily newspapers. [13]Subscribers. [14]2006–07.

Internet resources for further information:
- **Department of Statistics http://www.statistics.gov.my**
- **Central Bank of Malaysia http://www.bnm.gov.my**

Maldives

Official name: Dhivehi Raajjeyge Jumhooriyyaa (Republic of Maldives).
Form of government: multiparty republic[1] with one legislative house (People's Majlis [77]).
Head of state and government: President.
Capital: Male[2].
Official language: Dhivehi (Maldivian).
Official religion: Islam.
Monetary unit: rufiyaa (Rf); valuation (Sept. 1, 2011) 1 U.S.$ = Rf 15.37; 1 £ = Rf 24.84.

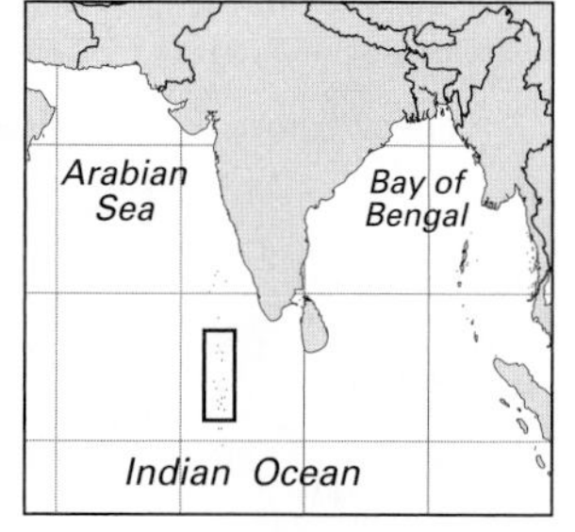

Area and population

		area[3]		population
				2006
Provinces[4, 5]	**Administrative seat**	sq mi	sq km	census
Upper North	...	15.29	39.61	41,672
North	...	8.50	22.01	43,539
North Central	...	3.92	10.16	31,202
Central	...	2.15	5.56	13,442
South Central	...	6.88	17.83	20,483
Upper South	...	4.06	10.52	19,275
South	...	5.26	13.61	25,662
Capital island				
Male[2]	Male[2]	0.76	1.97	103,693
SUBTOTAL	—	46.82	121.27	298,968[6]
REMAINDER[7]	—	68.24	176.73	—
TOTAL	—	115.06	298.00	298,968[6]

Demography

Population (2011): 325,000[7].
Density (2011)[8]: persons per sq mi 6,944, persons per sq km 2,681.
Urban-rural (2006): urban 34.7%; rural 65.3%.
Sex distribution (2010): male 50.58%; female 49.42%.
Age breakdown (2006): under 15, 31.1%; 15–29, 33.2%; 30–44, 18.3%; 45–59, 9.2%; 60–74, 5.2%; 75–84, 1.1%; 85 and over, 0.2%; unknown 1.7%.
Population projection[7]: (2020) 375,000; (2030) 422,000.
Doubling time: 53 years.
Ethnic composition (2000)[7]: Maldivian 98.5%; Sinhalese 0.7%; other 0.8%.
Religious affiliation: virtually 100% Sunnī Muslim[9].
Major localities (2006): Male[2] 92,555; Hithadhoo 9,465; Fuvammulah 7,636; Kulhudhuffushi 6,998; Villingili 6,956.

Vital statistics

Birth rate per 1,000 population (2010): 16.8 (world avg. 19.2).
Death rate per 1,000 population (2010): 3.6 (world avg. 8.2).
Total fertility rate (avg. births per childbearing woman; 2010): 1.80.
Marriage/divorce rates per 1,000 population (2009): 20.2/8.2.
Life expectancy at birth (2009): male 72.5 years; female 74.2 years.
Major causes of death per 100,000 population (2005): external causes 227.1; diseases of the circulatory system 19.9; diseases of the respiratory system 15.8; malignant neoplasms (cancers) 12.3.

National economy

Budget (2010). Revenue: Rf 7,040,900,000 (tax revenue 49.5%, of which import duties 28.3%; nontax revenue 47.3%, of which resort lease rent 24.7%; grants 2.8%; other 0.4%). Expenditures: Rf 10,906,600,000 (general administration 23.1%; education 15.6%; police/security 11.8%; community programs 11.3%; social security and welfare 11.1%; health 8.4%; defense 5.4%).
Production (metric tons except as noted). Agriculture, forestry, fishing (2009): vegetables 28,156, bananas 4,340, nuts 2,100, coconuts 271; roundwood (2010) 15,182 cu m, of which fuelwood 100%; fisheries production 116,902, of which skipjack tuna 66,179, yellowfin tuna 20,919 (from aquaculture, none). Mining and quarrying: coral for construction materials. Manufacturing: details, n.a.; however, major industries have included boat building and repairing, coir yarn and mat weaving, coconut and fish processing, lacquerwork, garment manufacturing, and handicrafts. Energy production (consumption): electricity (kW-hr; 2010) 182,000,000 (196,000,000); petroleum products (metric tons; 2007) none (293,000).
Selected balance of payments data. Receipts from (U.S.$'000,000): tourism (2010) 714; remittances (2010) 3; foreign direct investment (2008–10 avg.) 137; official development assistance (2009) 33. Disbursements for (U.S.$'000,000): tourism (2009) 97; remittances (2009) 116.
Population economically active (2006): total 128,836; activity rate of total population 43.1% (participation rates: ages 15–64, 65.8%; female 41.3%; unemployed [2010] 14.5%[10]).

Price index (2005 = 100)

	2004	2005	2006	2007	2008	2009	2010
Consumer price index	98.7	100.0	103.5	111.1	124.7	129.7	135.8

Household income and expenditure. Average household size (2006) 6.5; average annual income per household (2002–03)[11] Rf 188,743 (U.S.$14,746); sources of income (2002–03)[11]: self-employment 34.5%, wages and salaries 31.5%, rent 13.4%; expenditure (2004)[12]: food, beverages, and tobacco 33.3%, housing and energy 19.5%, clothing and footwear 6.0%, communications 5.8%, health 5.4%.
Gross national income (GNI; 2010): U.S.$1,340,000,000 (U.S.$4,270 per capita); purchasing power parity GNI (U.S.$5,480 per capita).

Structure of gross domestic product and labour force

	2010		2006	
	in value Rf '000[13]	% of total value	labour force	% of labour force
Agriculture, fishing	525,200	4.9	12,624	9.8
Mining	52,600	0.5	339	0.3
Manufacturing	700,100	6.6	19,259	14.9
Public utilities	499,700	4.7	1,229	1.0
Construction	502,900	4.7	5,930	4.6
Transp. and commun.	2,118,700	19.9	7,098	5.5
Trade	409,500	3.8	23,801	18.5
Tourism (resorts)	2,983,700	28.0	...	...
Finance, real estate	1,187,700	11.1	1,738	1.3
Pub. admin., defense	1,930,100	18.1	15,949	12.4
Services	163,500	1.5	17,302	13.4
Other	–409,800[14]	–3.8[14]	23,567[15]	18.3[15]
TOTAL	10,664,000[16]	100.0	128,836	100.0

Public debt (external, outstanding; April 2011): U.S.$661,600,000.
Land use as % of total land area (2007): in temporary crops or left fallow *c.* 13%, in permanent crops *c.* 27%, in pasture *c.* 3%, forest area *c.* 3%.

Foreign trade[17, 18]

Balance of trade (current prices)

	2005	2006	2007	2008	2009	2010
U.S.$'000,000	–583.3	–701.3	–868.3	–1,056.4	–798.3	–895.2
% of total	64.3%	60.9%	65.6%	61.5%	70.3%	69.1%

Imports (2010): U.S.$1,095,100,000 (refined petroleum products 23.0%, of which diesel fuel 18.2%; food products 21.5%; goods for construction 10.2%; transport equipment and parts 6.2%). *Major import sources:* U.A.E. 18.8%; Singapore 17.9%; India 11.5%; Malaysia 7.1%; Sri Lanka 5.8%.
Exports (2010): U.S.$199,900,000 (reexports [mostly jet fuel] 63.0%; fish 35.3%, of which fresh yellowfin tuna 14.1%, fresh skipjack tuna 9.2%, dried fish 6.6%). *Major export destinations*[19]: Thailand 31.4%; Sri Lanka 20.6%; France 11.1%; U.K. 10.1%; India 3.7%.

Transport and communications

Transport. Railroads: none. Roads: total length, n.a. Vehicles (2008): passenger cars 3,917; trucks and buses 2,314. Air transport (2007): passenger-km 27,000,000[20]; metric ton-km cargo, n.a.

Communications

Medium	date	number in '000s	units per 1,000 persons	Medium	date	number in '000s	units per 1,000 persons
Televisions	2003	41	144	PCs	2005	45	152
Telephones				Dailies	2009	21[21]	68[21]
Cellular	2010	494[22]	1,565[22]	Internet users	2009	88	284
Landline	2010	48	152	Broadband	2010	16[22]	49[22]

Education and health

Educational attainment (2006). Population age 6 and over 267,283; percentage with bachelor's degree 0.6%, master's degree 0.3%. *Literacy* (2006): total population age 15 and over literate 93.5%; males literate 92.5%; females literate 94.5%.

Education (2008–09)

	teachers	students	student/teacher ratio	enrollment rate (%)
Primary (age 6–12)	3,524	44,530	12.6	96
Secondary/Voc. (age 13–17)	3,432	29,040	8.5	71
Tertiary[23]	138	6,898	50.0	... (age 18–22)

Health (2009): physicians 535 (1 per 588 persons); hospital beds (2008) 785 (1 per 395 persons); infant mortality rate per 1,000 live births 11.0; undernourished population (2004–06) 24,000 (7% of total population based on the consumption of a minimum daily requirement of 1,770 calories).

Military

Total active duty personnel (2006): 2,000-member paramilitary incorporates coast guard duties. *Paramilitary expenditure as percentage of GDP* (2008): 4.9%; per capita expenditure U.S.$139.

[1]New constitution ratified on Aug. 7, 2008; first multiparty election held in October 2008. [2]Also spelled Maale or Male'. [3]Area data by province for inhabited islands only. [4]Per administrative reorganization beginning in March 2009. [5]Administratively ordered from uppermost north to lowermost south. [6]Excludes (in 2009) *c.* 80,000 legal foreign workers and *c.* 20,000 undocumented workers. Most foreign workers are Indian or Bangladeshi. [7]Includes areas of uninhabited islands, 88 resort islands, and 34 industrial islands. [8]Based on areas of inhabited islets only. [9]The only non-Sunnī are Shīʿī members of the Indian trading community and non-Muslim workers who serve alcohol on the resort islands. [10]Includes workers not actively seeking employment. [11]Data taken from the Household Income and Expenditure Survey 2002–03, comprising 834 households in both Male and outer atolls. [12]Weights of consumer price index components. [13]At constant prices of 1995. [14]Less imputed bank service charges. [15]Includes 18,605 unemployed. [16]Detail does not add to total given because of rounding. [17]Imports c.i.f.; exports f.o.b. [18]Exports include reexports unless otherwise footnoted. [19]Domestic exports only. [20]Trans Maldivian Airways; operates seaplanes to resort islands. [21]Circulation. [22]Subscribers. [23]2003; Maldives College of Higher Education.

Internet resources for further information:

- **Ministry of Planning and National Development http://www.planning.gov.mv/en**
- **Maldives Monetary Authority http://www.mma.gov.mv**

Mali

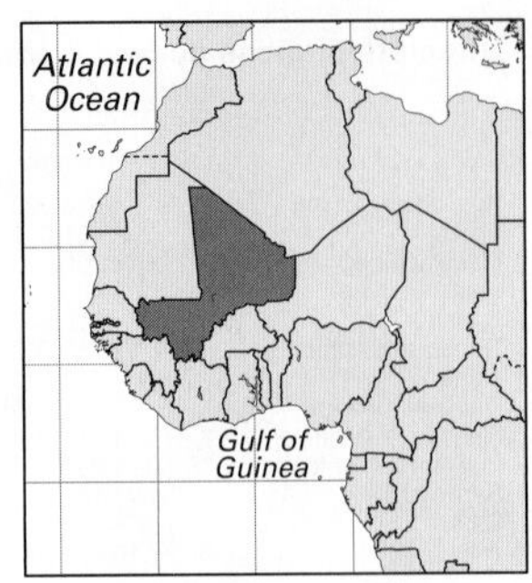

Official name: République du Mali (Republic of Mali).
Form of government: multiparty republic with one legislative house (National Assembly [147]).
Head of state: President.
Head of government: Prime Minister.
Capital: Bamako.
Official language: French.
Official religion: none.
Monetary unit: CFA franc (CFAF); valuation (Sept. 1, 2011) 1 U.S.$ = CFAF 460.31; 1 £ = CFAF 743.83.

Area and population

		area		population
Regions	**Capitals**	sq mi	sq km	2009 census[1]
Gao	Gao	65,858	170,572	544,120
Kayes	Kayes	46,233	119,743	1,996,812
Kidal	Kidal	58,467	151,430	67,638
Koulikoro	Koulikoro	37,007	95,848	2,418,305
Mopti	Mopti	30,509	79,017	2,037,330
Ségou	Ségou	25,028	64,821	2,336,255
Sikasso	Sikasso	27,135	70,280	2,625,919
Tombouctou	Tombouctou (Timbuktu)	191,743	496,611	681,691
District				
Bamako	Bamako	97	252	1,809,106
TOTAL		482,077	1,248,574	14,517,176

Demography

Population (2011): 15,525,000.
Density (2011): persons per sq mi 32.2, persons per sq km 12.4.
Urban-rural (2008): urban 32.4%; rural 67.6%.
Sex distribution (2009)[1]: male 49.62%; female 50.38%.
Age breakdown (2008): under 15, 47.7%; 15–29, 26.1%; 30–44, 13.7%; 45–59, 7.8%; 60–74, 3.9%; 75–84, 0.7%; 85 and over, 0.1%.
Population projection: (2020) 20,128,000; (2030) 26,251,000.
Doubling time: 26 years.
Ethnic composition (2000): Bambara 30.6%; Senufo 10.5%; Fula Macina (Niafunke) 9.6%; Soninke 7.4%; Tuareg 7.0%; Maninka 6.6%; Songhai 6.3%; Dogon 4.3%; Bobo 3.5%; other 14.2%.
Religious affiliation (2005): Muslim (nearly all Sunnī) *c.* 90%; Christian (mostly Roman Catholic) *c.* 5%; traditional beliefs/nonreligious *c.* 5%.
Major cities (2009)[1]: Bamako 1,809,106; Sikasso 225,753[2]; Kalabancoro 166,722[2, 3]; Koutiala 137,919[2]; Ségou 130,690[2]; Kayes 127,368[2].

Vital statistics

Birth rate per 1,000 population (2009): 42.3 (world avg. 20.3).
Death rate per 1,000 population (2009): 15.4 (world avg. 8.5).
Natural increase rate per 1,000 population (2009): 26.9 (world avg. 11.8).
Total fertility rate (avg. births per childbearing woman; 2009): 5.40.
Life expectancy at birth (2008): male 49.9 years; female 53.0 years.
Major causes of death per 100,000 population (2002): infectious and parasitic diseases 1,487, of which HIV/AIDS 97; diseases of the circulatory system 135; accidents and injuries 120; malignant neoplasms (cancers) 54; chronic respiratory diseases 36.

National economy

Budget (2009). Revenue: CFAF 896,500,000,000 (tax revenue 69.7%, grants 19.1%, nontax revenue 3.2%, other 8.0%). Expenditures: CFAF 1,018,600,000,000 (current expenditure 53.9%, capital expenditure 36.9%, other 9.2%).
Public debt (external, outstanding; 2009): U.S.$2,592,000,000.
Selected balance of payments data. Receipts from (U.S.$'000,000): tourism (2008) 275; remittances (2010) 414; foreign direct investment (2008–10 avg.) 146; official development assistance (2009) 985. Disbursements for (U.S.$'000,000): tourism (2008) 147; remittances (2009) 105.
Population economically active (2004): total 2,598,200[4]; activity rate of total population *c.* 23% (participation rates: ages 15–64, 51.1%; female 42.5%; officially unemployed 8.8%).

Price index (2005 = 100)

	2004	2005	2006	2007	2008	2009	2010
Consumer price index	94.0	100.0	101.5	103.0	112.4	114.9	116.2

Production (metric tons except as noted). Agriculture, forestry, fishing (2009): rice 1,950,810, corn (maize) 1,476,990, sorghum 1,465,620, millet 1,390,410, peanuts (groundnuts) 334,698, seed cotton 236,000, karite nuts 232,149, cattle meat 164,628, sheep meat 48,819; livestock (number of live animals) 10,657,900 goats, 10,174,000 sheep, 8,737,500 cattle, 1,767,000 asses, 1,150,000 camels; roundwood (2010) 5,676,920 cu m, of which fuelwood 93%; fisheries production 100,796 (from aquaculture 1%). Mining and quarrying (2009): salt 6,000; gold 42,364 kg[5]. Manufacturing (2005): raw sugar 35,000; cigarettes 330,000,000 units; soft drinks 419,000 hectolitres; beer 149,000 hectolitres. Energy production (consumption): electricity (kW-hr; 2007) 495,000,000 (495,000,000); crude petroleum, none (none); petroleum products (metric tons; 2007) none (189,000); natural gas, none (none).
Household income and expenditure. Average household size (2009) 6.1; average annual income per household: n.a.; expenditure: n.a.

Gross national income (GNI; 2010): U.S.$9,146,000,000 (U.S.$600 per capita); purchasing power parity GNI (U.S.$1,020 per capita).

Structure of gross domestic product and labour force

	2008		2004	
	in value CFAF '000,000	% of total value	labour force[4]	% of labour force
Agriculture, fishing	1,302,120	33.8	984,600	37.9
Mining	236,394	6.1	11,400	0.4
Manufacturing	195,145	5.1	272,500	10.5
Construction	199,682	5.2	102,100	3.9
Public utilities	74,662	1.9	5,100	0.2
Transp. and commun.	228,567	5.9	55,300	2.1
Trade, hotels	579,794	15.1	675,700	26.0
Finance, real estate	292,767	7.6	8,400	0.3
Pub. admin., defense	345,430	9.0	39,900	1.5
Services	...	...	214,000	8.2
Other	396,277[6]	10.3[6]	229,200[7]	8.8[7]
TOTAL	3,850,838	100.0	2,598,200	100.0[8]

Land use as % of total land area (2009): in temporary crops 4.1%, left fallow 0.8%, in permanent crops 0.01%, in pasture 28.7%, forest area 10.3%.

Foreign trade[9]

Balance of trade (current prices)

	2003	2004	2005	2006	2007	2008
U.S.$'000,000	–343.0	–376.9	–468.5	–293.7	–744.2	–1,420.6
% of total	15.6%	16.0%	17.9%	8.8%	20.5%	27.0%

Imports (2008): U.S.$3,338,900,000 (refined petroleum 20.9%, machinery and apparatus 19.2%, food products 9.6%, road vehicles 6.6%, portland cement 4.7%, fertilizers 4.4%). *Major import sources:* Senegal 17.2%; France 13.9%; Côte d'Ivoire 10.4%; China 10.2%; U.S. 6.6%.
Exports (2008): U.S.$1,918,300,000 (gold 74.9%, raw cotton 10.6%, livestock 5.9%). *Major export destinations:* South Africa 72.5%; Senegal 6.8%; Côte d'Ivoire 2.6%; Switzerland 2.6%; China 1.8%.

Transport and communications

Transport. Railroads (2007): route length 368 mi, 593 km[10]; (2005) passenger-km, less than 500,000; (2005) metric ton-km cargo 334,000,000. Roads (2005): total length 11,751 mi, 18,912 km (paved 19%). Vehicles (2007): passenger cars 86,967; trucks and buses 26,759. Air transport: n.a.

Communications

Medium	date	number in '000s	units per 1,000 persons	Medium	date	number in '000s	units per 1,000 persons
Televisions	2004	400	36	PCs	2007	98	8.0
Telephones				Dailies	2009	40[11]	2.7[11]
Cellular	2010	7,326[12]	477[12]	Internet users	2009	250	19
Landline	2010	114	7.4	Broadband	2010	2.3[12]	0.2[12]

Education and health

Educational attainment (2001)[13]. Population age 25 and over having: no formal schooling/unknown 82.1%; incomplete primary education 7.7%; complete primary 2.0%; secondary 6.5%; higher 1.7%. *Literacy* (2007): percentage of total population age 15 and over literate 23.3%; males literate 31.4%; females literate 16.0%.

Education (2008–09)

	teachers	students	student/ teacher ratio	enrollment rate (%)
Primary (age 7–12)	38,413	1,926,242	50.1	73
Secondary/Voc. (age 13–18)	25,990	686,071	26.4	29[14]
Tertiary	...	76,667	...	5 (age 19–23)

Health: physicians (2004) 1,053 (1 per 10,566 persons); hospital beds (2001) 1,664 (1 per 6,203 persons); infant mortality rate per 1,000 live births (2008) 118.1; undernourished population (2005–07) 1,500,000 (12% of total population based on the consumption of a minimum daily requirement of 1,720 calories).

Military

Total active duty personnel (November 2010): 7,350 (army 100%). *Military expenditure as percentage of GDP* (2008): 2.1%; per capita expenditure U.S.$12.

[1]Preliminary. [2]Population of commune. [3]Adjacent to Bamako. [4]Per 2004 Malian labour force survey; the 2004 population economically active estimate of the ILO Employment Trends Unit is 5,322,000. [5]Excludes artisanal production (*c.* 4,500 kg annually). [6]Net taxes on products less imputed bank service charges. [7]Includes 227,500 unemployed. [8]Detail does not add to total given because of rounding. [9]Imports c.i.f.; exports f.o.b. [10]Mali section of Transrail SA (Dakar, Senegal–Bamako railway). [11]Circulation. [12]Subscribers. [13]Based on the Mali Demographic and Health Survey 2001, comprising 64,116 people in 12,331 households. [14]2007–08.

Internet resources for further information:
- **Institut National de la Statistique**
  http://www.instat.gov.ml
- **La Banque de France: La Zone Franc**
  http://www.banque-france.fr/fr/eurosys/zonefr/zonefr.htm

Malta

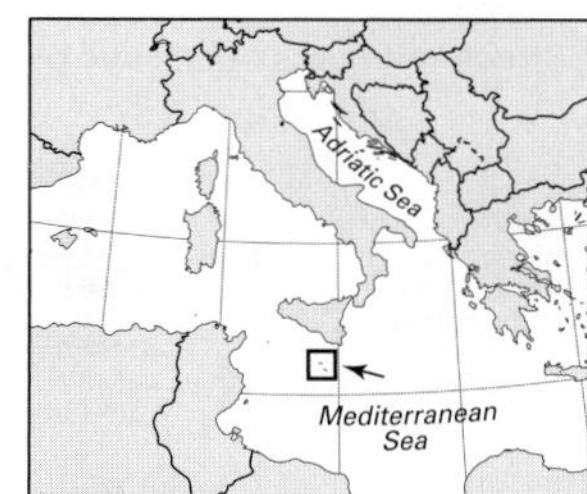

Official name: Repubblika ta' Malta (Maltese); Republic of Malta (English).
Form of government: unitary multiparty republic with one legislative house (Kamra tad-Deputati, or House of Representatives [69[1]]).
Head of state: President.
Head of government: Prime Minister.
Capital: Valletta.
Official languages: Maltese; English.
Official religion: Roman Catholicism.
Monetary unit: euro (€); valuation (Sept. 1, 2011) 1 U.S.$ = €0.70; 1 £ = €1.13.[2]

Area and population

Islands Statistical districts[4]	Largest localities	area sq mi	area sq km	population 2010[3] estimate
Comino	—	1.1	2.8	[5]
Gozo	Rabat	25.9	67.1	31,295
Malta		94.9[6]	245.7[6]	381,675
Northern District	Mosta	28.5	73.7	59,369
Northern Harbour	Birkirkara	9.3	24.0	121,450
South Eastern District	Żejtun	19.4	50.2	61,212
Southern Harbour	Żabbar	10.1	26.2	81,800
Western District	Żebbuġ	28.0	72.5	57,844
TOTAL		121.9	315.6	412,970

Demography

Population (2011): 419,000.
Density (2011): persons per sq mi 3,437, persons per sq km 1,328.
Urban-rural (2009): urban 94.4%; rural 5.6%.
Sex distribution (2010[3]): male 49.74%; female 50.26%.
Age breakdown (2010[3]): under 15, 15.6%; 15–29, 21.5%; 30–44, 19.8%; 45–59, 21.1%; 60–74, 15.7%; 75–84, 4.9%; 85 and over, 1.4%.
Population projection: (2020) 429,000; (2030) 432,000.
Ethnic composition (2005): Maltese 97.0%; other European 2.3%, of which British 1.2%; other 0.7%.
Religious affiliation (2004): Roman Catholic *c.* 95%, of which practicing *c.* 63%; other Christian *c.* 0.5%; Muslim *c.* 0.7%; nonreligious/atheist *c.* 2%; other *c.* 1.8%.
Major localities (2010[3]): Birkirkara 22,492; Mosta 19,155; Qormi 16,730; Żabbar 14,981; Valletta 6,221 (urban agglomeration 81,800).

Vital statistics

Birth rate per 1,000 population (2009): 10.0 (world avg. 20.3); within marriage 72.6%; outside of marriage 27.4%.
Death rate per 1,000 population (2009): 7.8 (world avg. 8.5).
Total fertility rate (avg. births per childbearing woman; 2009): 1.40.
Marriage/divorce rates per 1,000 population (2009): 5.7/[7].
Life expectancy at birth (2009): male 77.7 years; female 82.2 years.
Major causes of death per 100,000 population (2009): diseases of the circulatory system 302.0; malignant neoplasms (cancers) 206.2; diseases of the respiratory system 73.3; endocrine, nutritional, and metabolic diseases 39.7.

National economy

Budget (2009). Revenue: €2,370,770,000 (income tax 31.2%; social security contributions 22.2%; VAT 19.2%; customs duties and excise taxes 7.4%; other 20.0%). Expenditures: €2,667,791,000 (recurrent expenditures 82.6%, of which social security 24.8%; capital expenditure 17.4%).
Public debt (June 2010): U.S.$5,102,770,000.
Production (metric tons except where noted). Agriculture, forestry, fishing (2009): cow's milk 39,455, tomatoes 11,566, potatoes 10,069, wheat 9,050, onions 7,645, cauliflower and broccoli 5,425, grapes 4,821, garlic 659; livestock (number of live animals) 65,511 pigs, 17,777 cattle, 12,843 sheep; roundwood, n.a.; fisheries production 4,142 (from aquaculture 62%). Mining and quarrying (2009): salt 6,000; limestone[8] 1,200,000 cu m. Manufacturing (value added in U.S.$'000,000; 2005): electronic products 153; food products 109; printing and publishing 99; textiles and wearing apparel 88; beverages 61. Energy production (consumption): electricity (kW-hr; 2008) 2,173,000,000 (1,841,000,000); coal, none (none); crude petroleum, none (none); petroleum products (metric tons; 2007) none (887,000); natural gas, none (none).
Population economically active (2009): total 173,894; activity rate of total population 42.1% (participation rates: ages 15–64 [2006] 59.1%; female 33.6%; unemployed [April 2009–March 2010] 7.1%).

Price index (2005 = 100)

	2004	2005	2006	2007	2008	2009	2010
Consumer price index	97.1	100.0	102.8	104.1	108.5	110.8	112.4

Household income and expenditure (2008). Average household size 2.9; average annual disposable income per household €20,695 (U.S.$29,170); sources of income: wages and salaries 65.5%, interest and dividends 21.7%, self-employment 5.1%; expenditure: food and nonalcoholic beverages 22.4%, transportation 13.8%, household furnishings 8.9%, recreation and culture 8.5%, housing and energy 8.4%, clothing and footwear 7.1%, restaurants and hotels 7.1%.
Land use as % of total land area (2009): in temporary crops *c.* 23%; left fallow *c.* 2%; in permanent crops *c.* 4%; in pasture, n.a.; forest area *c.* 1%.

Gross national income (GNI; 2008): U.S.$8,028,000,000 (U.S.$19,512 per capita); purchasing power parity GNI (U.S.$22,640).

Structure of gross domestic product and labour force

	2009 in value €'000,000	% of total value	labour force	% of labour force
Agriculture, forestry, fishing	95.9	1.7	2,545	1.5
Manufacturing	669.8	11.7	24,467	14.1
Mining and quarrying	16.3	0.3	669	0.4
Construction	168.0	2.9	11,705	6.7
Public utilities	88.4	1.6	3,554	2.1
Transp. and commun.	427.5	7.5	13,608	7.8
Trade, hotels	748.4	13.1	38,330	22.0
Finance, real estate	1,189.3	20.8	18,163	10.5
Pub. admin., defense	349.0	6.1	14,499	8.3
Services	1,182.0	20.7	34,316	19.7
Other	776.8[9]	13.6[9]	12,044[10]	6.9[10]
TOTAL	5,711.6[11]	100.0	173,894[11]	100.0

Selected balance of payments data. Receipts from (U.S.$'000,000): tourism (2009) 914; remittances (2010) 46; foreign direct investment (FDI; 2008–10 avg.) 882. Disbursements for (U.S.$'000,000): tourism (2009) 444; remittances (2009) 53; FDI (2008–10 avg.) 175.

Foreign trade[12]

Balance of trade (current prices)

	2005	2006	2007	2008	2009	2010
€'000,000	–1,158	–1,231	–1,293	–1,561	–1,485	–1,474
% of total	22.8%	21.4%	22.0%	27.2%	30.8%	25.0%

Imports (2008): U.S.$5,017,000,000 (machinery and apparatus 28.7%, of which electronic integrated circuits and micro-assemblies 13.9%; refined petroleum 16.0%; food 12.1%; chemicals and chemical products 9.8%). *Major import sources:* Italy 26.4%; U.K. 12.7%; France 7.7%; Germany 7.6%; Singapore 5.9%.
Exports (2008): U.S.$2,980,000,000 (machinery and apparatus 55.6%, of which semiconductor devices 41.0%; medicines 8.3%; food 6.3%, of which fish 3.2%; printed matter 4.9%; children's toys 3.2%; professional/scientific equipment 2.8%). *Major export destinations:* Singapore 13.6%; Germany 13.0%; France 11.6%; U.S. 9.0%; U.K. 8.2%.

Transport and communications

Transport. Railroads: none. Roads (2004): total length 1,924 mi, 3,096 km (paved 88%); passenger-km (2006) 2,500,000,000[13]; metric ton-km cargo (2009) n.a. Vehicles (2010[14]): passenger cars 237,517; trucks and buses 49,925. Air transport (2009)[15, 16]: passenger-km 2,204,000,000; metric ton-km cargo 7,000,000.

Communications

Medium	date	number in '000s	units per 1,000 persons	Medium	date	number in '000s	units per 1,000 persons
Televisions	2009	139[17]	336[17]	PCs	2005	67	166
Telephones				Dailies	2009	100[18]	242[18]
Cellular	2010	455[19]	1,093[19]	Internet users	2009	241	589
Landline	2010	247	594	Broadband	2010	115[19]	275[19]

Education and health

Educational attainment (2010[20]). Percentage of population age 15 and over having: no formal schooling 1.1%; primary education 25.6%; secondary 45.7%; some postsecondary 16.9%; higher 10.7%. *Literacy* (2005): total population age 10 and over literate 92.8%; males literate 91.7%; females literate 93.9%.

Education (2007–08)

	teachers	students	student/ teacher ratio	enrollment rate (%)
Primary (age 5–10)	3,203	26,771	8.4	91[21]
Secondary/Voc. (age 11–17)	4,373	37,780	8.6	82[21]
Tertiary	968	9,472	9.8	33 (age 18–22)[21]

Health (2009): physicians 1,257 (1 per 329 persons); hospital beds 1,993 (1 per 207 persons); infant mortality rate per 1,000 live births 5.3; undernourished population (2004–06) less than 5.0% of total population.

Military

Total active duty personnel (November 2010): 1,954 (armed forces includes air and marine elements); Italian military (November 2010) 35 troops. *Military expenditure as percentage of GDP* (2009): 0.7%; per capita expenditure U.S.$140.

[1]Current number as of March 2008 elections; statutory number equals 65. [2]The Maltese lira (Lm) was the former monetary unit; on Jan. 1, 2008, 1 Lm = €2.33. [3]January 1. [4]Actual local administration in 2009 was based on 68 local councils grouped into 3 regions. [5]Apart from the occupants of one hotel, Comino is uninhabited. [6]Detail does not add to total given because statistical district data are based on older survey. [7]Divorce was legalized in mid-2011. [8]Mostly golden limestone or globigerina limestone. [9]Indirect taxes less subsidies. [10]Unemployed. [11]Detail does not add to total given because of rounding. [12]Imports c.i.f.; exports f.o.b. [13]Passenger cars 2,000,000,000; buses 500,000,000. [14]October 1. [15]Air Malta only. [16]Scheduled flights only. [17]Cable television subscribers. [18]Circulation of daily newspapers. [19]Subscribers. [20]July 1. [21]2006–07.

Internet resources for further information:
- **National Statistics Office http://www.nso.gov.mt**
- **Central Bank of Malta http://www.centralbankmalta.org**

Marshall Islands

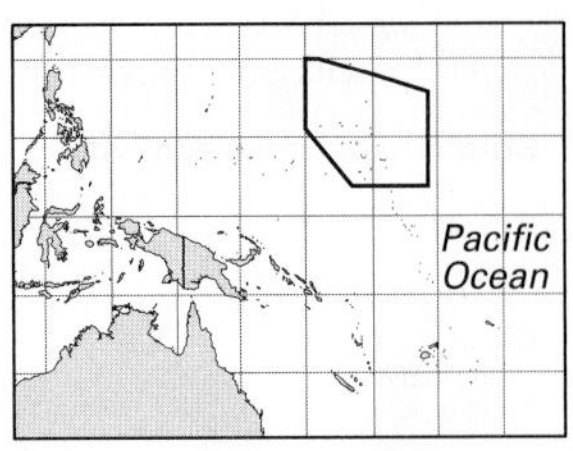

Official name: Majol (Marshallese); (Republic of the Marshall Islands).
Form of government: unitary republic with one legislative house[1] (Nitijela, or Parliament [33]).
Head of state and government: President.
Capital: Majuro[2].
Official language: Marshallese[3].
Official religion: none.
Monetary unit: U.S. dollar (U.S.$); valuation (Sept. 1, 2011) 1 U.S.$ = £0.62.

Area and population

Atolls/Islands[4]	area sq km	population 1999 census	Atolls/Islands[4]	area sq km	population 1999 census
Ailinglaplap	14.69	1,959	Majuro	9.71	23,682
Ailuk	5.36	514	Maloelap	9.82	856
Arno	12.95	2,069	Mejit	1.86	416
Aur	5.62	537	Mili	15.93	1,032
Bikini	6.01	13	Namorik	2.77	772
Ebon	5.75	902	Namu	6.27	903
Enewetak	5.85	853	Rongelap	7.95	19
Jabat	0.57	95	Ujae	1.86	440
Jaluit	11.34	1,669	Ujelang	1.74	0
Kili	0.93	774	Utirik	2.43	433
Kwajalein	16.39	10,903	Wotho	4.33	145
Lae	1.45	322	Wotje	8.18	866
Lib	0.93	147	Other atolls	10.46	0
Likiep	10.26	527	TOTAL	181.43[5, 6]	50,848

Demography

Population (2011): 55,000.
Density (2011): persons per sq mi 785.2, persons per sq km 303.1.
Urban-rural (2008): urban 68.0%; rural 32.0%.
Sex distribution (2008): male 50.99%; female 49.01%.
Age breakdown (2008): under 15, 38.5%; 15–29, 29.6%; 30–44, 16.8%; 45–59, 10.5%; 60–74, 3.6%; 75–84, 0.8%; 85 and over, 0.2%.
Population projection: (2020) 59,000; (2030) 62,000.
Ethnic composition (2006)[7]: Marshallese 92.1%; other Pacific Islanders 1.0%; East Asians 0.5%; U.S. white 0.3%; other 6.1%.
Religious affiliation (1999): Protestant 85.0%, of which United Church of Christ 54.8%, Assemblies of God 25.8%; Roman Catholic 8.4%; Mormon 2.1%; nonreligious 1.5%; other/unknown 3.0%.
Major towns (1999): Majuro[2] (2004) 20,800; Ebeye (in Kwajalein Atoll) 9,345; Laura (in Majuro Atoll) 2,256; Ajeltake (in Majuro Atoll) 1,170; Enewetak 823.

Vital statistics

Birth rate per 1,000 population (2008): 31.5 (world avg. 20.3).
Death rate per 1,000 population (2008): 4.6 (world avg. 8.5).
Total fertility rate (avg. births per childbearing woman; 2008): 3.68.
Life expectancy at birth (2008): male 68.9 years; female 73.0 years.
Major causes of death per 100,000 population (2007–08; registered deaths only): sepsis/septicemia 83.7; malignant neoplasms (cancers) 41.3; pneumonia 26.3; myocardial infarction 24.2.

National economy

Budget (2007). Revenue: U.S.$98,900,000 (U.S. government grants 63.6%; tax revenue 25.0%, of which income tax 11.0%, import duties 8.9%; nontax revenue 11.4%). Expenditures: U.S.$99,900,000 (current expenditure 79.0%; capital expenditure 21.0%).
Public debt (external, outstanding; 2009): U.S.$89,900,000.
Production (metric tons except as noted). Agriculture, forestry, fishing (2002–03): coconuts (2009) 27,511, copra (2008) 6,515, breadfruit 4,536, bananas 161, pandanus 114, taro 108; livestock (number of live animals) 12,900 pigs, 86,000 chickens; roundwood, n.a.; fisheries production (2009) 46,933, of which skipjack 40,344 (from aquaculture, none); black pearls harvested (2010) 1,300. Mining and quarrying: for local construction only. Manufacturing (2008): copra 6,515; coconut oil and processed fish are important products; the manufacture of handicrafts and personal items (clothing, mats, boats, etc.) by individuals is also significant. Energy production (consumption): electricity (kW-hr; 2007) 108,000,000 (108,000,000); coal, none (none); petroleum products (metric tons; 2007) none (32,000).
Population economically active (2007): total 15,100; activity rate of total population 28.3% (participation rates: ages 15–64, 51.1%; female 34.1%; unemployed [2008] 30.9%).

Price and earnings indexes (2005 = 100)

	2003	2004	2005	2006	2007	2008	2009
Consumer price index	93.6	95.7	100.0	104.3	107.6	126.5	127.2
Annual earnings index[8]	88.3	93.1	100.0	101.8	100.9	…	…

Household income and expenditure. Average household size (2007)[9] 7.2; average annual income per household (2005)[7] U.S.$17,482; sources of income (2002)[10]: wages and salaries 89.3%, rent and investments 2.4%, social security 2.2%; expenditure (2006)[11]: food 46.7%, housing and energy 15.9%, transportation 12.3%, apparel 6.1%, education and communication 4.4%.
Gross national income (2010): U.S.$187,000,000 (U.S.$2,990 per capita).

Structure of gross domestic product and labour force

	2008 in value U.S.$'000	2008 % of total value	2007–08 labour force[12]	2007–08 % of labour force[12]
Agriculture, fishing	16,056.2	9.7	492	4.9
Mining and quarrying	} 12,596.6	} 7.6	—	—
Manufacturing			58	0.6
Public utilities			286	2.8
Construction	18,154.3	10.9	706	7.0
Transp. and commun.	8,548.2	5.1	655	6.5
Trade, restaurants, hotels	28,081.8	16.9	2,131	21.1
Finance, insurance, real estate	} 76,764.0	} 46.2	430	4.3
Public administration			3,485	34.4
Services			791	7.8
Other	5,815.7	3.5	1,084	10.7
TOTAL	166,016.8	100.0[6]	10,117[6]	100.0[6]

Selected balance of payments data. Receipts from (U.S.$'000,000): tourism (2009) 2.7; remittances (2005) 0.4; foreign direct investment (2008–10 avg.) 8; official development assistance (2009) 59. Disbursements for (U.S.$'000,000): tourism (2006) 0.4; remittances, n.a.[13].
Land use as % of total land area (2009): in temporary crops or left fallow *c.* 11%, in permanent crops *c.* 44%, in pasture *c.* 17%, forest area *c.* 70%[14].

Foreign trade[15]

Balance of trade (current prices)

	2004	2005	2006	2007	2008	2009
U.S.$'000,000	−59.9	−68.5	−74.6	−73.8	−74.9	−71.0
% of total	67.8%	64.2%	79.4%	73.1%	70.1%	71.7%

Imports (2000): U.S.$54,700,000 (mineral fuels and lubricants 37.3%, machinery and transport equipment 15.0%, beverages and tobacco 11.0%). *Major import sources* (2006): U.S. 45.8%; Australia 8.5%; Japan 8.1%; New Zealand 3.3%; Philippines 3.1%.
Exports (2006): U.S.$20,283,000 (frozen fish 44.5%, reexports of diesel fuel 41.2%, crude coconut oil 9.9%, remainder 4.4%). *Major export destinations* (2009): mostly the U.S.

Transport and communications

Transport. Roads (2007): 47 mi, 75 km[16]. Vehicles (2004): passenger cars 1,694; trucks and buses 602. Air transport (2007)[17]: passenger-km 26,600,000; metric ton-km cargo 300,000.

Communications

Medium	date	number in '000s	units per 1,000 persons	Medium	date	number in '000s	units per 1,000 persons
Televisions	2008	…	…	PCs	2005	4.6	88
Telephones				Dailies	2008	0	0
Cellular	2010	3.8[18]	70[18]	Internet users	2009	2.2	36
Landline	2010	4.4	81	Broadband	2009	—	—

Education and health

Educational attainment (2006)[7]. Percentage of population age 25 and over having: no formal schooling 2.1%; elementary education 28.0%; secondary 55.8%; some higher 7.9%; undergraduate degree 5.1%; advanced degree 1.1%. *Literacy* (2007)[9]: total population age 15 and over literate 95.2%; males literate 95.0%; females literate 95.3%.

Education (2002–03)

	teachers	students	student/ teacher ratio	enrollment rate (%)
Primary (age 6–11)	526	8,393[19]	16.9	90
Secondary/Voc. (age 12–17)	387	5,901[19]	16.7	74
Tertiary	49	919	18.8	17 (age 18–22)

Health (2008): physicians 38 (1 per 1,401 persons); hospital beds (2004) 140 (1 per 411 persons); infant mortality rate 26.4; undernourished population, n.a.

Military

The United States provides for the defense of the Republic of the Marshall Islands under the 1984 and 2003 compacts of free association; number of U.S. troops (June 2011) 15.[20]

[1]In addition, the Council of Iroij (Council of Chiefs), a 12-member body of tribal chiefs, serves in an advisory capacity. [2]Local name of town is DUD (an acronym for Delap [Woja], Uliga, and Djarrit [Rita]—three small islands now merged by landfill). [3]Language of the Nitijela, or Parliament. [4]Four districts centred at Majuro, Ebeye, Wotje, and Jaluit make up the local government structure. [5]Land area only; excludes lagoon area of 11,673 sq km (4,507 sq mi). [6]Detail does not add to total given because of rounding. [7]Based on the Marshall Islands 2006 Community Survey, comprising 9,491 respondents in 1,205 households. [8]Data are for fiscal year. [9]Based on the 2007 Demographic and Health Survey comprising 1,106 households. [10]Based on the 2002 Household Income and Expenditure Survey, comprising 5,074 respondents in 657 households. [11]Weights of consumer price index components. [12]Employed only. [13]Labour income of Marshallese at Kwajalein (2003–04) U.S.$17,600,000. [14]Forest area overlaps with other categories. [15]Imports f.o.b. in balance of trade; c.i.f. in commodities and trading partners. [16]Length of paved roads on Majuro and Kwajalein; other roads are coral surfaced. [17]Air Marshall Islands only. [18]Subscribers. [19]2004–05. [20]The U.S. Army's premier ballistic missile test site is at Kwajalein.

Internet resources for further information:
- **Economic Policy-Planning and Statistics Office http://www.spc.int/prism/country/mh/stats**
- **Republic of the Marshall Islands: Documents http://marshall.wetserver.net**

Martinique

Official name: Département d'Outre-Mer de la Martinique (Overseas Department of Martinique).[1]
Political status: overseas department/ overseas region (France) with two legislative houses (General Council[2] [45]; Regional Council[3] [41]).
Head of state: President of France.
Heads of government: Prefect (for France); President of the General Council (for Martinique); President of the Regional Council (for Martinique).
Capital: Fort-de-France.
Official language: French.
Official religion: none.
Monetary unit: euro (€); valuation (Sept. 1, 2011) 1 U.S.$ = €0.70; 1 £ = €1.13.

Area and population

		area		population
Arrondissements	Capitals	sq mi	sq km	2008[4] estimate
Fort-de-France	Fort-de-France	66	171	167,113
La Trinité	La Trinité	131	338	86,343
Le Marin	Le Marin	158	409	120,454
Saint-Pierre	Saint-Pierre	81	210	23,783
TOTAL		436	1,128	397,693

Demography

Population (2011): 401,000.
Density (2011): persons per sq mi 920.0, persons per sq km 355.5.
Urban-rural (2009): urban 89.1%; rural 10.9%.
Sex distribution (2005[4]): male 47.01%; female 52.99%.
Age breakdown (2005): under 15, 21.6%; 15–29, 18.4%; 30–44, 23.4%; 45–59, 18.9%; 60–74, 11.6%; 75–84, 4.3%; 85 and over, 1.8%.
Population projection: (2020) 415,000; (2030) 423,000.
Ethnic composition (2000): mixed race (black/white/Asian) 93.4%; French (metropolitan and Martinique white) 3.0%; East Indian 1.9%; other 1.7%.
Religious affiliation (2000): Roman Catholic 86.0%; Protestant 5.6% (mostly Seventh-day Adventist); other Christian 5.4%; other 3.0%.
Major communes (2007[4]): Fort-de-France 89,794 (urban agglomeration 132,980); Le Lamentin 39,442; Le Robert 24,068; Schœlcher 21,510.

Vital statistics

Birth rate per 1,000 population (2009): 12.3 (world avg. 20.3); within marriage (2008) 27.5%; outside of marriage (2008) 72.5%.
Death rate per 1,000 population (2009): 7.9 (world avg. 8.5).
Total fertility rate (avg. births per childbearing woman; 2009): 1.90.
Marriage/divorce rates per 1,000 population: (2008) 3.9/(2007) 1.6.
Life expectancy at birth (2009): male 76.8 years; female 82.5 years.
Major causes of death per 100,000 population (2005): diseases of the circulatory system 181.8; malignant neoplasms (cancers) 167.9; accidents, poisoning, and violence 51.5; metabolic and nutritional disorders 42.2; diseases of the nervous system 36.4; diseases of the respiratory system 34.6.

National economy

Budget (2006)[5]. Revenue: €285,000,000 (tax revenue 46.5%, grants and subsidies from France 34.6%, loans 18.6%). Expenditures: €285,000,000 (current expenditure 46.7%, capital expenditure 53.3%).
Public debt: n.a.
Production (metric tons except as noted). Agriculture, forestry, fishing (2009): sugarcane 210,000, bananas 150,000, pineapples 18,000, plantains 13,180, tomatoes 7,000, lettuce[6] 7,000, cucumbers and gherkins 4,860; livestock (number of live animals) 21,000 cattle, 15,000 pigs, 15,000 sheep, 8,000 goats; roundwood (2010) 12,410 cu m, of which fuelwood 81%; fisheries production 6,310 (from aquaculture 2%). Mining and quarrying (2009): salt 200,000, pumice 130,000. Manufacturing (2008): cement 263,700; gas-diesel oils 179,000[7]; motor gasoline 164,000[7]; kerosene 143,000[7]; sugar 4,700; rum 74,500 hectolitres; other products include clothing, fabricated metals, and yawls and sails. Energy production (consumption): electricity (kW-hr; 2009) 1,550,000,000 ([2007] 1,225,000,000); coal, none (none); crude petroleum (barrels; 2007) none (5,849,340); petroleum products (metric tons; 2007) 830,000 ([2009–10] 583,600); natural gas, none (none).
Household income and expenditure. Average household size (2006) 2.6; average annual disposable income per household, n.a.; sources of income (2000): wages and salaries 54.7%, inheritance or endowment 14.0%, self-employment 12.7%, other 18.6%; expenditure (2006): food and beverages 18.1%, transportation and communications 17.8%, housing and energy 15.5%, household durable goods 10.1%, clothing and footwear 8.9%.
Population economically active (2009): total 164,493; activity rate of total population 41.0% (participation rates: ages 15–64, 62.5%; female 52.2%; unemployed 22.0%).

Price index (2005 = 100)

	2004	2005	2006	2007	2008	2009	2010
Consumer price index	97.6	100.0	102.4	104.9	107.7	107.1	108.6

Gross domestic product (2007): U.S.$10,847,000,000 (U.S.$26,953 per capita).

Structure of gross domestic product and labour force

	2004		2005[4, 8]	
	in value €'000,000	% of total value	labour force	% of labour force
Agriculture, forestry, fishing	174	2.6	8,922	5.9
Mining and quarrying	...	...	4,998	3.3
Manufacturing	372	5.5		
Construction	399	5.9	6,044	4.0
Public utilities	146	2.1	1,163	0.8
Transp. and commun.	218	3.2	5,939	3.9
Trade, restaurants, hotels	1,082	15.9	19,693	13.0
Finance, real estate, insurance	1,962	28.8	8,003	5.3
Pub. admin., defense	2,108	31.0	22,390	14.8
Services			36,247	23.9
Other	339[9]	5.0[9]	38,020[10]	25.1[10]
TOTAL	6,800	100.0	151,419	100.0

Selected balance of payments data. Receipts from (U.S.$'000,000): tourism (2007) 299; remittances, n.a.; foreign direct investment (FDI) n.a. Disbursements for (U.S.$'000,000): tourism, n.a.; remittances, n.a.; FDI, n.a.
Land use as % of total land area (2009): in temporary crops (2007) *c.* 8%, left fallow *c.* 2%, in permanent crops *c.* 6%, in pasture *c.* 9%, forest area *c.* 46%.

Foreign trade

Balance of trade (current prices)

	2005	2006	2007	2008	2009	2010
€'000,000	–1,923	–2,016	–2,191	–2,399	–1,756	–2,205
% of total	71.8%	67.3%	76.5%	76.6%	76.7%	76.7%

Imports (2008): €2,766,000,000 (mineral fuels 21.6%, food and agricultural products 14.2%, machinery and apparatus 12.0%, automobiles/parts 11.6%). *Major import sources:* metropolitan France 54.9%; U.K. 11.8%; U.S. 7.2%; Aruba 2.8%; Germany 2.6%.
Exports (2008): €367,000,000 (refined petroleum 58.0%, agricultural products [significantly bananas] 11.7%, beverages [significantly rum] 11.7%). *Major export destinations:* Guadeloupe 57.2%; metropolitan France 24.5%; French Guiana 10.4%; U.S. 2.5%.

Transport and communications

Transport. Railroads: none. Roads (2008): total length, more than 1,243 mi, 2,000 km (paved, n.a.). Vehicles (2008[4]): passenger cars 204,917; trucks and buses 35,943. Air transport (2009): passengers 1,608,000; cargo 11,336 metric tons.

Communications

Medium	date	number in '000s	units per 1,000 persons	Medium	date	number in '000s	units per 1,000 persons
Televisions	2001	66	169	PCs	2004	82	208
Telephones				Dailies	2009	65[11]	162[11]
Cellular	2004	295[12]	748[12]	Internet users	2009	170	420
Landline	2010	172	424	Broadband	2010	6.0[12]	14.8[12]

Education and health

Educational attainment (2006). Percentage of population age 15 and over having: unknown, or no formal education through lower secondary education 57.8%; complete lower vocational 16.8%; complete secondary 11.7%; incomplete higher 6.7%; complete higher 7.0%. *Literacy* (2005): percentage of total population age 15 and over literate 98.0%; males literate 97.6%; females literate 98.3%.

Education (2008–09)

	teachers	students	student/ teacher ratio	enrollment rate (%)
Primary (age 6–11)	3,018	29,929	9.9	...
Secondary/Voc. (age 12–18)	4,390	40,264	9.2	...
Tertiary	...	8,985[13]	...	... (age 19–23)

Health: physicians (2008) 1,035 (1 per 386 persons); hospital beds (2007[4]) 1,505 (1 per 263 persons); infant mortality rate per 1,000 live births (2009) 6.5; undernourished population, n.a.

Military

Total active duty personnel (November 2009): French troops in West Indies (Martinique and Guadeloupe) *c.* 1,825 (army *c.* 42%, navy *c.* 25%, air force, n.a., gendarmerie *c.* 33%).

[1]Martinique is simultaneously administered as an overseas region (*région d'outre-mer*). [2]Assembly for overseas department. [3]Assembly for overseas region. [4]January 1. [5]Budget for region. [6]Includes chicory. [7]2006. [8]Salaried employees only. [9]Import duties less subsidies and less imputed financial service charges. [10]Unemployed. [11]Circulation of daily newspapers. [12]Subscribers. [13]2007–08.

Internet resources for further information:
- **INSEE: Martinique**
  http://www.insee.fr/fr/regions/martinique
- **IEDOM: Martinique**
  http://www.iedom.fr/martinique

Mauritania

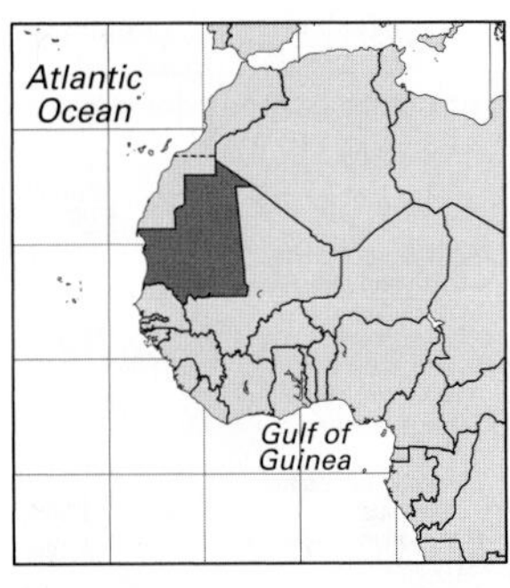

Official name: Al-Jumhūriyyah al-Islāmiyyah al-Mūrītāniyyah (Arabic) (Islamic Republic of Mauritania).
Form of government: republic[1] with two legislative houses (Senate [56[2]]; National Assembly [95]).
Head of state and government: President assisted by the Prime Minister.
Capital: Nouakchott.
Official language: Arabic[3].
Official religion: Islam.
Monetary unit: ouguiya (UM); valuation (Sept. 1, 2011) 1 U.S.$ = UM 279.98; 1 £ = UM 452.43.

Area and population

		area		population
Regions	Capitals	sq mi	sq km	2007 estimate[4]
El-ʾAçâba	Kiffa	14,100	36,600	284,629
Adrar	Atar	83,100	215,300	72,991
Brakna	Aleg	13,000	33,800	282,168
Dakhlet Nouadhibou	Nouadhibou	8,600	22,300	113,500
Gorgol	Kaédi	5,300	13,600	281,503
Guidimaka	Sélibaby	4,000	10,300	204,663
Hodh ech-Chargui	Néma	70,600	182,700	336,857
Hodh el-Gharbi	ʿAyoûn el-ʾAtroûs	20,600	53,400	249,768
Inchiri	Akjoujt	18,100	46,800	10,005
Tagant	Tidjikdja	36,800	95,200	81,692
Tiris Zemmour	Zouérate	97,600	252,900	52,471
Trarza	Rosso	25,800	66,800	291,820
Capital District				
Nouakchott	Nouakchott	400	1,000	813,200
TOTAL		398,000	1,030,700	3,075,267

Demography

Population (2011): 3,282,000.
Density (2011): persons per sq mi 8.2, persons per sq km 3.2.
Urban-rural (2009): urban 41.2%; rural 58.8%.
Sex distribution (2008): male 48.16%; female 51.84%.
Age breakdown (2008): under 15, 41.2%; 15–29, 28.0%; 30–44, 16.4%; 45–59, 9.1%; 60–74, 4.3%; 75–84, 0.9%; 85 and over, 0.1%.
Population projection: (2020) 4,005,000; (2030) 4,851,000.
Doubling time: 24 years.
Ethnic composition (2003)[5]: black African-Arab-Berber (Black Moor) 40%; Arab-Berber (White Moor) 30%; black African (mostly Wolof, Tukulor, Soninke, and Fulani) 30%.
Religious affiliation (2000): Sunnī Muslim 99.1%; traditional beliefs 0.5%; Christian 0.3%; other 0.1%.
Major cities: Nouakchott (2009) 709,000; Nouadhibou (2005) 94,700; Rosso (2000) 48,922; Boghé (2000) 37,531; Adel Bagrou (2000) 36,007.

Vital statistics

Birth rate per 1,000 population (2008): 34.6 (world avg. 20.3).
Death rate per 1,000 population (2008): 9.3 (world avg. 8.5).
Marriage/divorce rates per 1,000 population (2005): n.a./n.a.
Total fertility rate (avg. births per childbearing woman; 2008): 4.52.
Life expectancy at birth (2008): male 57.9 years; female 62.2 years.
Major causes of death per 100,000 population (2002): cardiovascular diseases 178; malignant neoplasms (cancers) 71; diseases of the respiratory system 44; diseases of the digestive system 26.

National economy

Budget (2009). Revenue: UM 188,500,000,000 (tax revenue 56.6%, of which taxes on goods and services 28.5%, income taxes 18.4%, import taxes 7.5%; nontax revenue 40.2%, of which fishing royalties 21.8%; grants 3.2%). Expenditures: UM 242,900,000,000 (current expenditure 76.9%, of which goods and services 21.3%, wages and salaries 31.7%; capital expenditure 23.1%).
Public debt (external, outstanding; 2009): U.S.$1,851,000,000.
Production (metric tons except as noted). Agriculture, forestry, fishing (2009): cow's milk 142,327, goat's milk 120,066, rice 99,300, sorghum 90,259, camel meat 22,500, dates 20,000, corn (maize) 12,497, peas 11,608, cowpeas 10,277; livestock (number of live animals) 8,860,000 sheep, 5,600,000 goats, 1,700,000 cattle, 1,495,000 camels; roundwood (2010) 1,794,052 cu m, of which fuelwood 99.8%; fisheries production 178,541, of which octopuses 15,992 (from aquaculture, none). Mining and quarrying (gross weight; 2009–10): iron ore 11,365,000; gypsum 53,550; copper (2008) 33,073. Manufacturing (value added in U.S.$'000,000; 1997): food, beverages, and tobacco products 5.2; machinery, transport equipment, and fabricated metals 3.8; bricks, tiles, and cement 1.6. Energy production (consumption): electricity (kW-hr; 2009–10) 492,000,000 ([2009] 347,000,000); coal (metric tons; 2004) none (7,000); crude petroleum (barrels; 2009–10)[6] 3,354,900 ([2007] negligible); petroleum products (metric tons; 2007) none (562,000).
Population economically active (2008)[7]: total 1,353,000; activity rate of total population 44.3% (participation rates: over age 15, 69.9%; female 41.7%; unemployed [2005] 32.5%).

Price index (2005 = 100)

	2004	2005	2006	2007	2008	2009	2010
Consumer price index	89.2	100.0	106.2	113.9	122.3	125.0	132.9

Household income and expenditure. Average household size (2004) 5.8; expenditure (2002–03)[8]: food and beverages 53.1%, housing and energy 13.7%, transportation and communications 12.1%, household furnishings 6.3%.
Gross national income (GNI; 2010): U.S.$3,571,000,000 (U.S.$1,060 per capita); purchasing power parity GNI (U.S.$2,000 per capita).

Structure of gross domestic product and labour force

	2008		2000	
	in value UM '000,000	% of total value	labour force	% of labour force
Agriculture, livestock, fishing	146,990	17.2	314,306	48.2
Mining	187,159	21.9	5,769	0.9
Crude petroleum	57,219	6.7	...	...
Manufacturing }	29,615	3.5	30,156	4.6
Public utilities }			2,837	0.4
Construction	42,180	4.9	15,562	2.4
Transp. and commun.	36,309	4.2	17,916	2.8
Trade, restaurants }	85,293	10.0	108,532	16.7
Finance }			2,011	0.3
Services	82,535	9.7 }	98,720	15.1
Pub. admin., defense	111,969	13.1 }		
Other	75,549[9]	8.8[9]	55,958[10]	8.6[10]
TOTAL	854,818	100.0	651,767	100.0

Selected balance of payments data. Receipts from (U.S.$'000,000): tourism (2005) 11; remittances (2009) 2; foreign direct investment (2008–10 avg.) 105; official development assistance (2009) 287. Disbursements for (U.S.$'000,000): tourism (1999) 55; remittances, n.a.
Land use as % of total land area (2009): in temporary crops or left fallow 0.4%, in permanent crops 0.01%, in pasture 38.1%, forest area 0.2%.

Foreign trade[11]

Balance of trade (current prices)

	2004	2005	2006	2007	2008	2009[12]
U.S.$'000,000	–904.8	–785.6	...	–76.7	–10.5	–59.7
% of total	51.0%	41.4%	...	2.8%	0.3%	2.1%

Imports (2008): U.S.$1,637,600,000 (refined petroleum 33.3%, machinery and apparatus 13.0%, road vehicles 6.6%, wheat 6.6%, milk/cream 4.6%, rice 4.5%). *Major import sources:* France 16.3%; Russia 11.2%; Neth. 7.7%; Belgium 6.1%; China 4.9%.
Exports (2008): U.S.$1,627,100,000 (iron ore 47.5%, crude petroleum 20.1%, fish 11.3%, copper ore 7.8%, gold 7.4%). *Major export destinations:* France 16.3%; Germany 8.2%; China 7.8%; Switz. 7.4%; Italy 7.3%.

Transport and communications

Transport. Railroads (2008): route length 452 mi, 728 km; passenger-km (2005) *c.* 10,000,000; metric ton-km cargo 7,565,000,000. Roads (2007): total length 6,876 mi, 11,066 km (paved 27%). Vehicles (2001): passenger cars 12,200; trucks and buses 18,200. Air transport: passenger-km (2005) 60,000,000; metric ton-km cargo (2007) less than 500,000.

Communications

Medium	date	number in '000s	units per 1,000 persons	Medium	date	number in '000s	units per 1,000 persons
Televisions	2003	123	44	PCs	2005	42	14
Telephones				Dailies	2009	9[13]	2.9[13]
Cellular	2010	2,745[14]	793[14]	Internet users	2009	75	23
Landline	2010	72	21	Broadband	2010	6.6[14]	1.9[14]

Education and health

Educational attainment (2000). Percentage of population age 6 and over having: no formal schooling 43.9%; no formal schooling but literate 2.5%; Islamic schooling 18.4%; primary education 23.2%; lower secondary 5.3%; upper secondary 4.6%; higher technical 0.4%; higher 1.7%. *Literacy* (2008): percentage of total population age 15 and over literate 56.8%; males literate 64.1%; females literate 49.5%.

Education (2005–06)

	teachers	students	student/ teacher ratio	enrollment rate (%)
Primary (age 6–11)[15]	11,379	483,776	42.5	80
Secondary/Voc. (age 12–17)	3,777	98,946	26.2	16
Tertiary	353	10,157	28.8	4 (age 18–22)

Health: physicians (2008) 458 (1 per 6,212 persons); hospital beds (2006) 1,826 (1 per 1,667 persons); infant mortality rate per 1,000 live births (2008) 64.9; undernourished population (2005–07) 200,000 (7% of total population based on the consumption of a minimum daily requirement of 1,790 calories).

Military

Total active duty personnel (November 2010): 15,870 (army 94.5%, navy 3.9%, air force 1.6%). *Military expenditure as percentage of GDP* (2008): 0.7%; per capita expenditure U.S.$7.

[1]In actuality a military-backed regime with a democratically elected president. [2]Three of which are appointed by the 53 elected senators. [3]The 1991 constitution named Arabic as the official language and the following as national languages: Arabic, Fula, Soninke, and Wolof. [4]Mid-year official projection based on 2000 census. [5]Estimated figures. [6]Offshore crude petroleum production began in February 2006. [7]ILO estimates. [8]Weights of consumer price index components. [9]Indirect taxes. [10]Not adequately defined. [11]Imports c.i.f.; exports f.o.b. [12]Import data for 2009 are f.o.b. [13]Circulation of daily newspapers. [14]Subscribers. [15]2006–07.

Internet resources for further information:
- **Office National de Statistique http://www.ons.mr**
- **Central Bank of Mauritania http://www.bcm.mr**

Mauritius

Official name: Republic of Mauritius.
Form of government: republic with one legislative house (National Assembly [69[1]]).
Head of state: President.
Head of government: Prime Minister.
Capital: Port Louis.
Official language: English[2].
Official religion: none.
Monetary unit: Mauritian rupee (Mau Re; plural Mau Rs); valuation (Sept. 1, 2011) 1 U.S.$ = Mau Rs 27.90; 1 £ = Mau Rs 45.09.

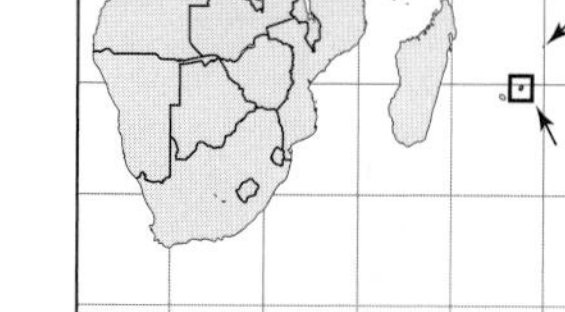

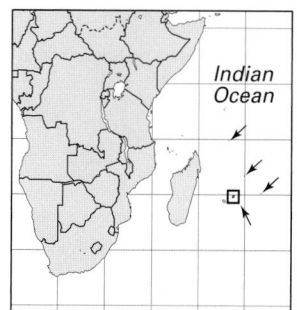

Area and population

Island / Non-administrative districts[3]	Principal centres	area sq mi	area sq km	population 2010 estimate
Mauritius		720	1,865[4]	1,243,084
Black River	Tamarin	100	259	75,974
Flacq	Centre de Flacq	115	298	139,958
Grand Port	Mahébourg	100	260	115,377
Moka	Moka	89	231	81,182
Pamplemousses	Pamplemousses	69	179	137,879
Plaines Wilhems	Beau Bassin–Rose Hill	78	203	384,434
Port Louis	Port Louis	17	43	128,851
Rivière du Rempart	Poudre d'Or	57	148	108,999
Savanne	Souillac	95	245	70,430
Mauritian dependencies				
Agalega[5]	…	27	70	289[6]
Cargados Carajos Shoals (Saint Brandon)[5]	—	0.4	1	0[6]
Rodrigues	Port Mathurin	40	104	37,840
TOTAL		788[4]	2,040	1,281,213

Demography

Population (2011): 1,288,000.
Density (2011): persons per sq mi 1,635, persons per sq km 631.
Urban-rural (2011[7]): urban 41.6%; rural 58.4%.
Sex distribution (2011[7]): male 49.30%; female 50.70%.
Age breakdown (2010): under 15, 21.6%; 15–29, 23.9%; 30–44, 23.3%; 45–59, 20.0%; 60–74, 8.4%; 75–84, 2.2%; 85 and over, 0.6%.
Population projection: (2020) 1,366,000; (2030) 1,419,000.
Ethnic composition (2000): Indo-Pakistani 67.0%; Creole (mixed Caucasian, Indo-Pakistani, and African) 27.4%; Chinese 3.0%; other 2.6%.
Religious affiliation (2000)[8]: Hindu 49.6%; Christian 32.2%, of which Roman Catholic 23.6%; Muslim 16.6%; Buddhist 0.4%; other 1.2%.
Major municipalities (2010[7]): Port Louis 148,756; Beau Bassin–Rose Hill 110,459; Vacoas-Phoenix 107,899; Curepipe 84,337; Quatre Bornes 81,594.

Vital statistics

Birth rate per 1,000 population (2010): 11.7 (world avg. 19.2).
Death rate per 1,000 population (2010): 7.1 (world avg. 8.2).
Total fertility rate (avg. births per childbearing woman; 2010): 1.50.
Marriage/divorce rates per 1,000 population (2010): 16.5/2.9.
Life expectancy at birth (2010): male 69.6 years; female 76.8 years.
Major causes of death per 100,000 population (2010): diseases of the circulatory system 236.6; endocrine, nutritional, and metabolic disorders 173.9; neoplasms 82.3; diseases of the respiratory system 58.6.

National economy

Budget (2010). Revenue: Mau Rs 65,479,500,000 (tax revenue 84.3%, of which taxes on goods and services 52.9%, corporate income tax 12.9%; nontax revenue 11.1%; grants 3.1%; social contributions 1.5%). Expenditures: Mau Rs 75,059,300,000 (general public services 29.1%; social security 21.0%; education 13.4%; health 10.3%; police/paramilitary 8.2%).
Public debt (external, outstanding; 2010): U.S.$893,000,000.
Gross national income (GNI; 2010): U.S.$9,925,000,000 (U.S.$7,740 per capita); purchasing power parity GNI (U.S.$13,670 per capita).

Structure of gross domestic product and labour force

	2010 in value Mau Rs '000,000	2010 % of total value	2008 labour force	2008 % of labour force
Agriculture	10,369	3.6	46,100	8.2
Mining	92	—	500	0.1
Manufacturing	47,888	16.5	102,200	18.3
Construction	18,260	6.3	57,700	10.3
Public utilities	6,569	2.3	3,700	0.7
Transp. and commun.	27,308	9.4	38,300	6.8
Trade, hotels	50,453	17.4	108,700	19.4
Finance, real estate	62,484	21.6	39,800	7.1
Pub. admin., defense	17,286	6.0	34,000	6.1
Services	34,027	11.7	85,900	15.4
Other	15,174[9]	5.2[9]	42,500[10]	7.6[10]
TOTAL	289,910	100.0	559,400	100.0

Production (metric tons except as noted). Agriculture, forestry, fishing (2010): sugarcane 4,365,852, potatoes 17,000, pumpkins/squash/gourds (2009) 17,119, bananas 11,007, tomatoes 10,907, pineapples 6,288, onions 5,875, tea 1,467, ginger 1,356; livestock (number of live animals; 2009) 13,650,000 chickens; roundwood 14,920 cu m, of which fuelwood 43%; fisheries production (2009) 8,113 (from aquaculture 5%). Mining (2009): sand 87,506. Manufacturing (value added in Mau Rs '000,000; 2009)[11]: wearing apparel 11,965; food products 10,935; beverages and tobacco products 6,074; cement, bricks, and ceramics 3,467; textiles 2,249; fabricated metal products 2,023. Energy production (consumption): electricity (kW-hr; 2010–11) 2,443,000,000 ([2007] 2,465,000,000); coal (metric tons; 2007) none (573,000); petroleum products (metric tons; 2007) none (770,000).
Population economically active (2010): total 581,300; activity rate of total population 45.4% (participation rates: ages 16–64, 59.8%; female 37.7%; unemployed [April 2010–March 2011] 7.7%).

Price index (2005 = 100)

	2004	2005	2006	2007	2008	2009	2010
Consumer price index	95.3	100.0	108.9	118.5	130.1	133.4	137.2

Household income and expenditure (2006–07). Average household size 3.7; annual income per household Mau Rs 228,996 (U.S.$7,047); sources of income (2001–02): wages and salaries 69.8%, self-employment 17.6%, other 12.6%; expenditure: food and nonalcoholic beverages 28.6%, transportation 14.7%, housing/energy 13.1%, alcohol/tobacco 9.2%, household furnishings 6.4%.
Selected balance of payments data. Receipts from (U.S.$'000,000): tourism (2010) 1,249; remittances (2010) 220; foreign direct investment (FDI; 2008–10 avg.) 357; official development assistance (2009) 156. Disbursements for (U.S.$'000,000): tourism (2009) 354; remittances (2009) 12; FDI (2008–10 avg.) 73.
Land use as % of total land area (2007): in temporary crops or left fallow *c.* 44%, in permanent crops *c.* 2%, in pasture *c.* 3%, forest area *c.* 18%.

Foreign trade[12]

Balance of trade (current prices)

	2004	2005	2006	2007	2008	2009
U.S.$'000,000	–980	–1,156	–1,470	–1,847	–2,268	–1,769
% of total	20.8%	22.4%	25.3%	31.0%	32.1%	31.3%

Imports (2008): U.S.$4,670,000,000 (refined petroleum 18.1%; food 18.0%, of which fish 5.7%; machinery and apparatus 14.5%; base and fabricated metals 6.0%; road vehicles 4.7%; fabrics/yarn 4.2%). *Major import sources:* India 23.9%; China 11.5%; South Africa 8.1%; France 7.8%; Japan 4.1%.
Exports (2008): U.S.$2,402,000,000 (apparel/clothing accessories 35.2%, of which T-shirts 15.2%, men's/boys' shirts 7.3%; food 27.1%, of which raw sugar 12.1%, tuna 8.9%; telecommunications equipment 3.4%). *Major export destinations:* U.K. 29.5%; France 14.7%; bunkers and ships' stores 13.1%; U.S. 5.8%; Madagascar 5.1%.

Transport and communications

Transport. Railroads: none. Roads (2010)[13]: total length 1,292 mi, 2,080 km (paved 98%). Vehicles (2011[7]): passenger cars 175,634; trucks and buses 41,945. Air transport (2010–11): passenger-km 6,515,000,000; metric ton-km cargo 180,415,000.

Communications

Medium	date	number in '000s	units per 1,000 persons	Medium	date	number in '000s	units per 1,000 persons
Televisions	2010	315	242	PCs	2006	220	176
Telephones				Dailies	2009	105[14]	82[14]
Cellular	2010	1,191[15]	917[15]	Internet users	2010	284[15]	221[15]
Landline	2010	388	298	Broadband	2010	82[15]	63[15]

Education and health

Educational attainment (2000). Percentage of population age 25 and over having: no formal education 12.3%; primary 44.1%; lower secondary 23.2%; upper secondary/some higher 17.3%; complete higher 2.6%; unknown 0.5%.
Literacy (2009): percentage of total population age 15 and over literate 87.9%; males literate 90.6%; females literate 85.3%.

Education (2010–11)

	teachers	students	student/ teacher ratio	enrollment rate (%)
Primary (age 5–10)	5,627	116,068	20.6	94[16]
Secondary/Voc. (age 11–17)	8,507	122,559	14.4	80[17]
Tertiary	…	25,578[18]	…	26[18] (age 18–22)

Health (2011[7]): physicians 1,500 (1 per 859 persons); hospital beds 3,419 (1 per 377 persons); infant mortality rate per 1,000 live births (2010) 12.5; undernourished population (2004–06) 70,000 (6% of total population based on the consumption of a minimum daily requirement of 1,870 calories).

Military

Total active duty personnel (November 2010): none; a 2,000-person paramilitary force includes a 500-person coast guard unit. *Paramilitary expenditure as percentage of GDP* (2009): 0.5%; per capita expenditure U.S.$32.

[1]Includes 7 appointed members. [2]French is not official but may be used to address the speaker of the National Assembly. [3]The island of Mauritius is administratively divided between 5 municipalities and 4 district councils; detail is unavailable. [4]Detail does not add to total given because of rounding. [5]Administered directly from Port Louis. [6]As of 2000 census. [7]January 1. [8]Includes Rodrigues; Rodrigues is 91% Roman Catholic. [9]Taxes less subsidies and less imputed bank service charges. [10]Includes 2,100 not adequately defined and 40,400 unemployed. [11]Establishments employing 10 or more persons only. [12]Imports c.i.f.; exports f.o.b. [13]Island of Mauritius only. [14]Circulation. [15]Subscribers. [16]2008–09. [17]2004–05. [18]2007–08.

Internet resources for further information:
- **Statistics Mauritius http://www.gov.mu/portal/site/cso**
- **Bank of Mauritius http://bom.intnet.mu**

Mayotte

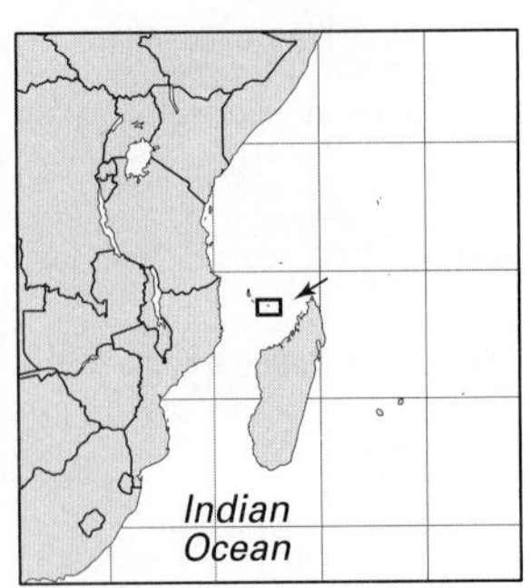

Official name: Département d'Outre-Mer de Mayotte[1] (Overseas Department of Mayotte).[2]
Political status: overseas department of France[3] with one legislative house (General Council [19]).
Head of state: President of France.
Head of government: Prefect (for France); President of the General Council (for Mayotte).
Capital: Mamoudzou.
Official language: French.
Official religion: none.
Monetary unit: euro (€); valuation (Sept. 1, 2011) 1 U.S.$ = €0.70; 1 £ = €1.13.

Area and population		area		population
Islands				2007
Communes	**Capitals**	sq mi	sq km	census
Grande Terre				
Acoua	Acoua	4.9	12.6	4,622
Bandraboua	Bandraboua	12.5	32.4	9,013
Bandrele	Bandrele	14.1	36.5	6,838
Boueni	Boueni	5.4	14.1	5,296
Chiconi	Chiconi	3.2	8.3	6,412
Chirongui	Chirongui	11.3	29.3	6,605
Dembeni	Dembeni	15.0	38.8	10,141
Kani-Keli	Kani-Keli	7.9	20.5	4,527
Koungou	Koungou	11.0	28.4	19,831
Mamoudzou	Mamoudzou	16.2	41.9	53,022
M'tsangamouji	M'tsangamouji	8.4	21.8	5,028
M'tzamboro	M'tzamboro	5.3	13.7	6,917
Ouangani	Ouangani	7.3	19.0	6,577
Sada	Sada	4.3	11.2	8,007
Tsingoni	Tsingoni	13.4	34.8	9,200
Petite Terre				
Dzaoudzi	Dzaoudzi	2.6	6.7	15,339
Pamandzi	Pamandzi	1.7	4.3	9,077
TOTAL		144.5	374.2[4]	186,452[5]

Demography

Population (2011): 210,000.
Density (2011): persons per sq mi 1,453, persons per sq km 561.2.
Urban-rural: n.a.
Sex distribution (2007): male 49.04%; female 50.96%.
Age breakdown (2006): under 15, 45.9%; 15–29, 24.6%; 30–44, 18.1%; 45–59, 8.4%; 60–74, 2.5%; 75–84, 0.4%; 85 and over, 0.1%.
Population projection: (2020) 265,000; (2030) 324,000.
Doubling time: 21 years.
Ethnic composition (2000): Comorian[6] 92.3%; Swahili 3.2%; white (French) 1.8%; Makua 1.0%; other 1.7%.
Religious affiliation (2000): Sunnī Muslim 96.5%; Christian, principally Roman Catholic, 2.2%; other 1.3%.
Major villages/communes (2007): Mamoudzou 6,186/53,022; Koungou 6,710/19,831; village of Labattoir 15,067/commune of Dzaoudzi 15,339; Pamandzi 9,077/9,077.

Vital statistics

Birth rate per 1,000 population (2006): 41.0 (world avg. 20.3).
Death rate per 1,000 population (2006): 7.7 (world avg. 8.5).
Natural increase rate per 1,000 population (2006): 33.3 (world avg. 11.8).
Total fertility rate (avg. births per childbearing woman; 2006): 5.79.
Life expectancy at birth (2006): male 59.6; female 64.0.

National economy

Budget (2005)[7]. Revenue: €269,400,000 (current revenue 81.0%, of which taxes including customs duties 44.8%; development revenue 19.0%). Expenditures: €252,000,000 (current expenditure 78.9%; development expenditure 21.1%).
Production (metric tons except as noted). Agriculture, forestry, fishing (2010): ylang-ylang 2,900 kg[8], vanilla, negligible[8], bananas, coconuts, and mangoes are also cultivated; livestock (number of live animals; 2003) 22,800 goats, 17,200 cattle; roundwood, n.a.; fisheries production (2009) 15,256 (from aquaculture 1%). Mining and quarrying: negligible. Manufacturing: mostly processing of agricultural products, housing construction materials, printing and publishing, and textiles/clothing. Energy production (consumption): electricity (kW-hr; 2008) 190,000,000 ([2009–10] 230,262,000); petroleum products, none (n.a.).
Land use as % of total land area (2009): in temporary crops or left fallow *c.* 19%; in permanent crops *c.* 35%; in pasture, n.a.; forest area *c.* 37%.
Selected balance of payments data. Receipts from (U.S.$'000,000): tourism (2006) 20; remittances, n.a.; foreign direct investment (2005–06 avg.) 3; official development assistance (2009) 544. Disbursements for (U.S.$'000,000): tourism, n.a.; remittances, n.a.
Population economically active (2007): total 51,524; activity rate of total population 27.6% (participation rates: ages 15–60 [2002] 50.0%; female 41.6%; unemployed [2008] *c.* 26%).

Price and earnings indexes (December 2006 = 100)							
	2004	2005	2006	2007	2008	2009	2010
Consumer price index	...	...	100.0	103.3	108.5	109.5	112.4
Hourly earnings index[9]	84.8	83.3	100.0	117.0	131.3	141.9	151.4

Gross national income (2002): U.S.$444,000,000 (U.S.$2,780 per capita).

Structure of value added[10] and labour force	2005		2007	
	in value €'000	% of total value	labour force[11]	% of labour force[11]
Agriculture, forestry, and fishing	1,000	0.4	3,204	6.2
Mining	...	...	...	...
Manufacturing } Public utilities }	38,000	16.7	...	...
			...	...
Construction	37,000	16.3	3,024	5.9
Transp. and commun.	19,000	8.4	5,043[12]	9.8[12]
Trade, restaurants	62,000	27.3	3,763	7.3
Finance, insurance	18,000	7.9	...	...
Pub. admin., defense }	61,000	26.9	6,535	12.7
Services }			14,536	28.2
Other	–9,000	–4.0	15,419[13]	29.9[13]
TOTAL	227,000	100.0[4]	51,524	100.0

Public debt: n.a.
Household income and expenditure. Average household size (2007) 4.3; average annual income per household (2005) €9,337 (U.S.$11,612); sources of income (2005): wages and salaries *c.* 79%, transfers *c.* 9%, self-employment *c.* 9%; expenditure (2005)[14]: food and beverages 25.9%, transportation 14.9%, housing 9.5%, clothing and footwear 7.4%, energy 6.4%, recreation and culture 6.2%, household furnishings 6.2%.

Foreign trade

Balance of trade (current prices)[15, 16]						
	2005	2006	2007	2008	2009	2010
€'000,000	–214	–247	–330	–371	–350	–431
% of total	95.5%	95.4%	96.0%	97.3%	96.9%	95.4%

Imports (2008): €376,163,000[16] (food products 23.5%; machinery and apparatus 22.1%; transport equipment 14.4%; base and fabricated metals 9.5%). *Major import sources:* metropolitan France 41.8%; China 7.7%; Germany 5.1%; Italy 4.1%.
Exports (2008): €5,339,000 (reexports 77.6%; domestic exports 22.4%, of which ylang-ylang 11.4%, farm-grown fish 11.0%). *Major export destinations:* metropolitan France 45.5%; Comoros 16.4%; Réunion 10.0%; India 9.6%; Singapore 9.2%.

Transport and communications

Transport. Railroads: none. Roads (2006): total length 144 mi, 232 km (paved 100%). Vehicles (2004): passenger cars 2,279; trucks and buses 1,453. Air transport (2008): passenger arrivals and departures 263,332; cargo unloaded and loaded 1,604 metric tons.

Communications			units				units
Medium	date	number in '000s	per 1,000 persons	**Medium**	date	number in '000s	per 1,000 persons
Televisions	2005	...	...	PCs	2007	...	...
Telephones				Dailies	2007	0	0
Cellular	2004	48[17]	283[17]	Internet users	2010	...	...
Landline	2010	10	49	Broadband	2010	...	...

Education and health

Educational attainment (2002). Percentage of population age 15 and over having: no formal education 37.6%; participating in formal education 17.8%; primary education 20.8%; lower secondary 13.4%; upper secondary 6.3%; higher 4.1%. *Literacy:* n.a.

Education (2006–07)	teachers	students	student/ teacher ratio	enrollment rate (%)
Primary (age 6–10)	2,274	31,333	13.8	...
Secondary/Voc. (age 11–15)	1,718[18]	24,733	...	...
Tertiary	—	—[19]	—	— (age 16–20)

Health (2006): physicians 120 (1 per 1,587 persons); hospital beds 245 (1 per 780 persons); infant mortality rate per 1,000 live births 61.2; undernourished population, n.a.

Military

Total active duty personnel (November 2010): *c.* 875 French troops in Mayotte and Réunion (army *c.* 99%; navy, n.a.; air force, n.a.; gendarmerie *c.* 1%).

[1]Mahoré or Maore in Shimaoré, the local Swahili-based language. [2]Formerly a departmental collectivity, Mayotte became an overseas department of France in March 2011. [3]Mayotte has been claimed by Comoros since Comoros's unilateral declaration of independence in 1975. Comoros represents Mayotte in the UN. [4]Detail does not add to total given because of rounding. [5]Including illegal residents (40.7% of total population; mostly Comorians from adjacent islands but also Malagasy and continental Africans). [6]About 1/3 of all Comorians (a mixture of Bantu, Arab, and Malagasy peoples) are recent arrivals from other nearby Comorian islands. [7]Mayotte is largely dependent on French aid. [8]Export production only. [9]Minimum wage. [10]For 555 larger enterprises only. [11]14 years and over. [12]Includes real estate. [13]Includes 13,614 unemployed. [14]Based on a household budget survey. [15]Based on rounded data. [16]Excludes imports of mineral fuels (totaling €56,000,000 in 2008). [17]Subscribers. [18]Excludes vocational. [19]2,345 students study in metropolitan France or Réunion.

Internet resources for further information:
- **IEDOM: Agence de Mayotte**
  http://www.iedom.fr/mayotte/publications-77
- **INSEE: Mayotte**
  http://www.insee.fr/fr/regions/mayotte

Mexico

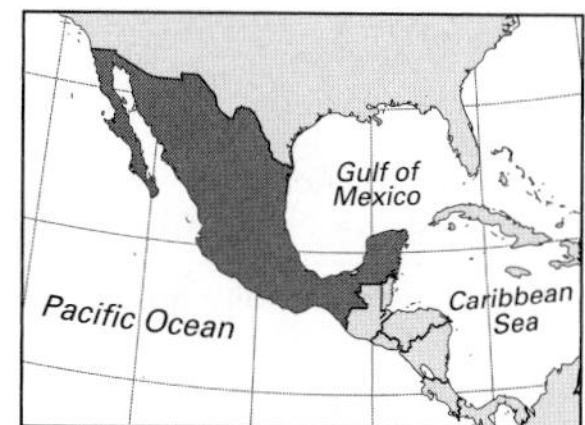

Official name: Estados Unidos Mexicanos (United Mexican States).
Form of government: federal republic with two legislative houses (Senate [128]; Chamber of Deputies [500]).
Head of state and government: President.
Capital: Mexico City.
Official language: Spanish.
Official religion: none.
Monetary unit: Mexican peso (Mex$); valuation (Sept. 1, 2011) 1 U.S.$ = Mex$12.25; 1 £ = Mex$19.80.

Area and population

		area		population
States	**Capitals**	sq mi	sq km	2010 census
Aguascalientes	Aguascalientes	2,112	5,471	1,184,996
Baja California	Mexicali	26,997	69,921	3,155,070
Baja California Sur	La Paz	28,369	73,475	637,026
Campeche	Campeche	19,619	50,812	822,441
Chiapas	Tuxtla Gutiérrez	28,653	74,211	4,796,580
Chihuahua	Chihuahua	94,571	244,938	3,406,465
Coahuila de Zaragoza	Saltillo	57,908	149,982	2,748,391
Colima	Colima	2,004	5,191	650,555
Durango	Durango	47,560	123,181	1,632,934
Guanajuato	Guanajuato	11,773	30,491	5,486,372
Guerrero	Chilpancingo	24,819	64,281	3,388,768
Hidalgo	Pachuca	8,036	20,813	2,665,018
Jalisco	Guadalajara	31,211	80,836	7,350,682
México	Toluca	8,245	21,355	15,175,862
Michoacán de Ocampo	Morelia	23,138	59,928	4,351,037
Morelos	Cuernavaca	1,911	4,950	1,777,227
Nayarit	Tepic	10,417	26,979	1,084,979
Nuevo León	Monterrey	25,067	64,924	4,653,458
Oaxaca	Oaxaca	36,275	93,952	3,801,962
Puebla	Puebla	13,090	33,902	5,779,829
Querétaro de Arteaga	Querétaro	4,420	11,449	1,827,937
Quintana Roo	Chetumal	19,387	50,212	1,325,578
San Luis Potosí	San Luis Potosí	24,351	63,068	2,585,518
Sinaloa	Culiacán	22,521	58,328	2,767,761
Sonora	Hermosillo	70,291	182,052	2,662,480
Tabasco	Villahermosa	9,756	25,267	2,238,603
Tamaulipas	Ciudad Victoria	30,650	79,384	3,268,554
Tlaxcala	Tlaxcala	1,551	4,016	1,169,936
Veracruz-Llave	Jalapa (Xalapa)	27,683	71,699	7,643,194
Yucatán	Mérida	14,827	38,402	1,955,577
Zacatecas	Zacatecas	28,283	73,252	1,490,668
Federal District				
Distrito Federal	—	571	1,479	8,851,080
CONTINENTAL AREA		756,066[1]	1,958,201[1]	
LAND		736,950	1,908,690	
WATER		19,116	49,511	
INSULAR AREA[2]		1,980	5,127	
TOTAL		758,450[3]	1,964,375[3]	112,336,538

Demography

Population (2011): 114,492,000.
Density (2011): persons per sq mi 151.0, persons per sq km 58.3.
Urban-rural (2010): urban 77.8%; rural 22.2%.
Sex distribution (2010): male 48.83%; female 51.17%.
Age breakdown (2010): under 15, 29.1%; 15–29, 26.2%; 30–44, 21.8%; 45–59, 13.9%; 60–74, 6.4%; 75–89, 2.4%; 90 and over, 0.2%.
Population projection: (2020) 125,792,000; (2030) 135,251,000.
Doubling time: 54 years.
Ethnic composition (2000): mestizo 64.3%; Amerindian 18.0%, of which detribalized 10.5%; Mexican white 15.0%; Arab 1.0%; Mexican black 0.5%; Spaniard 0.3%; U.S. white 0.2%; other 0.7%.
Religious affiliation (2000): Christian 96.3%, of which Roman Catholic 87.0%, Protestant 3.2%, independent Christian 2.7%, unaffiliated Christian 1.4%, other Christian (mostly Mormon and Jehovah's Witness) 2.0%; Muslim 0.3%; nonreligious 3.1%; other 0.3%.
Major cities/metropolitan areas (2010): Mexico City 8,555,272 (20,116,842); Ecatepec 1,655,015[4]; Guadalajara 1,495,182 (4,434,878); Puebla 1,434,062 (2,668,437); Juárez 1,321,004 (1,332,131); Tijuana 1,300,983 (1,751,430); León 1,238,962 (1,609,504); Zapopan 1,142,483[5]; Monterrey 1,135,512 (4,089,962); Ciudad Netzahualcóyotl 1,104,585[4]; Chihuahua 809,232 (852,533); Naucalpan 792,211[4]; Mérida 777,615 (973,046); San Luis Potosí 722,772 (1,040,443); Aguascalientes 722,250 (932,369); Hermosillo 715,061; Saltillo 709,671 (823,128); Mexicali 689,775 (936,826); Culiacán 675,773; Guadelupe 673,616[6]; Acapulco 673,479; Tlalnepantla 653,410[4]; Cancun 628,306 (677,379); Querétaro 626,495 (1,097,025); Chimalhuacán 612,383; other cities with an urban agglomeration of more than one million include: Torreon 608,836 (1,215,817) and Toluca 489,333 (1,846,116).
Households (2010). Total households 28,614,991; distribution by size (2005): 1 person 7.3%, 2 persons 14.0%, 3 persons 18.2%, 4 persons 22.8%, 5 persons 17.4%, 6 persons 9.5%, 7 or more persons 10.8%.
Migration. Legal Mexican immigrants entering the U.S. in 2004: 173,664; total number of illegal Mexican immigrants in U.S. (2006) 6,600,000.

Vital statistics

Birth rate per 1,000 population (2010): 17.8 (world avg. 19.2); within marriage (*c.* 2003) 62%; outside of marriage (*c.* 2003) 38%.
Death rate per 1,000 population (2010): 5.0 (world avg. 8.2).
Natural increase rate per 1,000 population (2009): 13.1 (world avg. 11.8).
Total fertility rate (avg. births per childbearing woman; 2008): 2.10.
Marriage/divorce rates per 1,000 population (2008): 5.5/0.8.
Life expectancy at birth (2008): male 74.0 years; female 78.8 years.
Major causes of death per 100,000 population (2007): diseases of the circulatory system 103.8; endocrine, metabolic, and nutritional disorders 80.9; malignant neoplasms (cancers) 65.0; accidents and violence 52.0; diseases of the digestive system 46.9; diseases of the respiratory system 41.3.
Adult population (ages 15–49) *living with HIV* (2009): 0.3%[7] (world avg. 0.8%).

Social indicators

Educational attainment (2005). Percentage of population age 15 and over having: no formal schooling 8.4%; incomplete primary education 14.3%; complete primary 17.6%; incomplete/complete secondary 25.2%; vocational/professional 31.3%; advanced university (masters or doctorate degree) 0.7%; other/unknown 2.5%.
Access to services (2005). Proportion of dwellings having: electricity 96.6%; piped water supply 87.8%; piped sewage 84.8%.

Distribution of income (2008)

percentage of household income by decile

1	2	3	4	5	6	7	8	9	10 (highest)
1.7	2.9	3.9	4.9	6.0	7.4	9.2	11.7	16.1	36.2

Material well-being. Percentage of households possessing (2005): television 91.0%, refrigerator 79.0%, washing machine 62.7%, computer 19.6%.
Quality of working life (2008). Average workweek 44.5 hours. Annual rate per 100,000 insured workers for: injury 3,569; death 10. Labour stoppages: 21, involving 13,242 workers.
Social participation. Eligible voters participating in last national election (July 2009): 47.8%. Trade union membership in total workforce (2000): formal sector only, less than 20%; both formal and informal sectors, *c.* 17%. Practicing religious population (1995–97): percentage of adult population attending church services at least once per week 46%.
Social deviance (2007). Formally registered offense rate per 100,000 population for: murder 6.2; property damage 14.5; rape 4.3; battery 30.2; robbery 69.3; illegal narcotics possession 16.0; fraud 4.4; squatting 3.3; breaking and entering 2.5. Incidence per 100,000 in general population of: alcoholism (2000) 7.6; suicide 4.2.

National economy

Gross national income (GNI; 2010): U.S.$1,012,316,000,000 (U.S.$9,330 per capita); purchasing power parity GNI (U.S.$15,010 per capita).

Structure of gross domestic product and labour force

	2008			
	in value Mex$'000,000	% of total value	labour force	% of labour force
Agriculture, forestry, and fishing	444,765	3.7	5,758,500	12.7
Mining and quarrying	1,114,706	9.2	183,200	0.4
Manufacturing	2,219,380	18.3	7,228,100	15.9
Construction	846,299	7.0	3,641,200	8.0
Public utilities	192,498	1.6	206,200	0.4
Transp. and commun.	1,157,265	9.6	2,034,400	4.5
Trade, hotels	2,094,039	17.3	12,811,100	28.2
Finance, real estate	2,023,278	16.7	2,595,000	5.7
Pub. admin., defense }	1,911,234	15.8	2,172,000	4.8
Services }			6,903,800	15.2
Other	107,091[8]	0.9[8]	1,926,500[9]	4.2[9]
TOTAL	12,110,555	100.0[10]	45,460,000	100.0

Budget (2008). Revenue: Mex$2,857,100,000,000 (nontax revenue 36.9%; tax revenue 34.8%, of which income tax 21.3%; other revenue, from PEMEX state oil company 12.6%, other state-owned organizations or companies 15.7%). Expenditures: Mex$2,865,300,000,000 (current expenditure 58.3%; extra-budgetary expenditure 23.2%; capital expenditure 18.5%).
Public debt (external, outstanding; 2009): U.S.$99,374,000,000.
Production (metric tons except as noted). Agriculture, forestry, fishing (2009): sugarcane 49,492,700, corn (maize) 20,142,800, cow's milk 10,549,000, sorghum 6,108,090, oranges 4,193,480, wheat 4,116,160, chicken meat 2,626,490, tomatoes 2,591,400, bananas 2,232,360, lemons and limes 1,987,450, chilies and green peppers 1,941,560, cattle meat 1,704,990, guavas and mangoes 1,509,270, potatoes 1,501,230, avocados 1,230,970, dry onions 1,195,820, dry beans 1,041,350, blue agave (2006) *c.* 778,000, papayas 707,347, pineapples 685,000, grapefruit and pomelos 395,000, coffee (green) 252,000, strawberries 233,040, nuts (2008) 168,688, vanilla 520; livestock (number of live animals) 32,000,000 cattle, 15,200,000 pigs, 8,900,000 goats, 7,800,000 sheep, 6,350,000 horses, 510,000,000 chickens; roundwood (2010) 45,177,445 cu m, of which fuelwood 86%; fisheries production 1,768,063 (from aquaculture 9%); aquatic plants production 5,152 (from aquaculture, none). Mining and quarrying (2009): fluorspar 1,046,000 [world rank: 2]; silver 3,553,840 kg[11] [world rank: 2]; bismuth 850[11] [world rank: 3]; strontium 36,130 [world rank: 3]; lead 143,840[11] [world rank: 5]; cadmium 1,510[11] [world rank: 6]; gypsum 5,756,940 [world rank: 6]; zinc 489,770[11] [world rank: 7]; iron ore 11,677,000[11]; sulfur 1,814,000; copper 227,750[11]; gold 51,390 kg[11]. Manufacturing (value added in Mex$'000,000; 2007): food and beverages 994,797; transportation equipment 146,839, of which motor vehicles 84,137, motor vehicle parts 58,470; mineral fuels 130,233, of which refined petroleum products 121,740; chemicals and chemical products 125,629, of which pharmaceutical products 58,561; basic metals 74,005; bricks, cement, and ceramics 66,932; electrical machinery and equipment 28,962; paper and paper products 28,773; fabricated metal products 26,355; rubber and plastic products 25,690; textiles and

wearing apparel 23,195; nonelectrical machinery and apparatus 21,529; electronics 6,442; printing and publishing 6,085; wood and wood products 5,780.

Selected economic activities (2003)

	no. of establish-ments	no. of employees	yearly wage as a % of avg. of all wages	value added (Mex$'000,000)
Manufacturing	328,178	4,198,579	130.8	927,987
Services				
Transportation, storage	41,899	634,940	158.1	124,561
Mass media	7,586	244,679	340.7	166,901
Finance, insurance	10,417	275,830	358.4	285,715
Real estate, rental	45,579	179,146	52.2	38,967
Professional, scientific, and technical	68,589	472,348	109.8	65,479
Sanitation, waste management	43,152	815,388	129.2	90,233
Education	30,891	517,958	118.6	53,846
Health, social assistance	102,940	355,169	46.2	22,700
Recreation	31,790	143,589	53.1	11,340
Hotel, restaurant	277,436	1,218,262	35.2	64,700
Trade				
Wholesale	86,997	962,143	113.3	261,546
Retail	1,493,590	4,035,223	35.2	318,648
Mining	3,077	122,640	255.2	432,764
Electricity, gas, water	2,437	221,335	279.5	168,941
Construction	13,444	652,387	59.7	60,542

Energy production (consumption): electricity (kW-hr; 2009) 286,739,000,000 ([2007] 256,281,000,000); hard coal (metric tons; 2008–09) 10,679,000 ([2007] 2,513,000); lignite (metric tons; 2007) 10,456,000 (14,972,000); crude petroleum (barrels; 2008–09) 913,369,200 ([2007] 505,356,000); petroleum products (metric tons; 2007) 80,186,000 (94,352,000); natural gas (cu m; 2008–09) 74,360,122,000 ([2007] 53,139,915,000).

Household income and expenditure (2008). Average household size 4.0; average annual income per household Mex$38,263 (U.S.$2,805); sources of income: wages and salaries 47.9%, nonmonetary income 19.1%, self-employment 14.7%, transfers 9.6%; expenditure: food and nonalcoholic beverages 22.1%, transportation and communications 12.2%, housing/energy 6.6%, education 6.3%, household furnishings 4.0%, clothing and footwear 3.5%, health 2.1%.

Population economically active (2008): total 45,460,000; activity rate of total population 42.6% (participation rates: ages 15–64, 63.6%; female 37.7%; unemployed [September 2010] 5.7%).

Price and earnings indexes (2005 = 100)

	2004	2005	2006	2007	2008	2009	2010
Consumer price index	96.2	100.0	103.6	107.7	113.3	119.3	124.2
Monthly earnings index	99.2	100.0	101.4	98.8	99.6	99.0	98.2

Financial aggregates

	2004	2005	2006	2007	2008	2009	2010
Exchange rate[12], Mex$ per:							
U.S. dollar	11.26	10.78	10.88	10.87	13.54	13.06	12.36
£	21.75	18.56	21.36	21.78	19.74	21.15	19.34
SDR	17.49	15.40	16.37	17.17	20.85	20.47	19.03
International reserves (U.S.$)							
Total (excl. gold; '000,000)	64,141	74,054	76,271	87,109	95,126	99,589	120,264
SDRs ('000,000)	465	445	482	466	519	4,525	4,325
Reserve pos. in IMF ('000,000)	898	594	340	334	613	961	1,057
Foreign exchange ('000,000)	62,778	73,015	75,448	86,309	93,994	94,103	114,883
Gold ('000,000 fine troy oz)	0.14	0.11	0.09	0.12	0.20	0.28	0.23
% world reserves	0.02	0.01	0.01	0.01	0.02	0.03	0.02
Interest and prices							
Treasury bill rate	6.82	9.20	7.19	7.19	7.68	5.43	4.40
Balance of payments (U.S.$'000,000)							
Balance of visible trade,	–8,811	–7,587	–6,133	–10,074	–17,261	–4,681	–3,009
of which:							
Imports, f.o.b.	–196,810	–221,820	–256,058	–281,949	–308,603	–234,385	–301,482
Exports, f.o.b.	187,999	214,233	249,925	271,875	291,343	229,704	298,473
Balance of invisibles	+3,558	+2,492	+1,631	+1,209	+908	–1,685	–2,631
Balance of payments, current account	–5,253	–5,095	–4,502	–8,865	–16,353	–6,366	–5,640

Selected balance of payments data. Receipts from (U.S.$'000,000): tourism (2010) 11,872, of which border shoppers only 1,970; remittances (2010) 21,997; foreign direct investment (FDI; 2008–10 avg.) 20,103; official development assistance (2009) 185. Disbursements for (U.S.$'000,000): tourism (2010) 7,283, of which border shoppers only 3,068; remittances, n.a.; FDI (2008–10 avg.) 7,507.

Land use as % of total land area (2009): in temporary crops or left fallow (2007) 12.6%, in permanent crops 1.4%, in pasture 38.6%, forest area 33.4%.

Foreign trade

Balance of trade (current prices)

	2005	2006	2007	2008	2009	2010
U.S.$'000,000	–7,524	–5,689	–11,209	–18,734	–4,702	–3,344
% of total	1.7%	1.1%	2.0%	3.1%	1.0%	0.6%

Imports (2008): U.S.$308,583,000,000 (machinery and apparatus 35.6%, of which electrical machinery/apparatus/parts 11.6%, telecommunications equipment/parts 7.3%, general industrial machinery 5.3%, road vehicles/parts 8.5%; base and fabricated metals 8.4%; refined petroleum 6.8%; food 5.3%; plastics [all forms/articles] 5.2%). *Major import sources:* U.S. 49.2%; China 11.2%; Japan 5.3%; South Korea 4.4%; Germany 4.1%; Canada 3.1%; Taiwan 2.2%; Brazil 1.7%; Italy 1.7%; Malaysia 1.5%.

Exports (2008): U.S.$291,265,000,000 (machinery and apparatus 37.4%, of which electrical machinery/apparatus/parts 10.4%, television receivers 7.7%, telecommunications equipment/parts 6.9%; crude petroleum 14.9%; road vehicles/parts 14.6%; base and fabricated metals 5.6%; food 4.3%). *Major export destinations:* U.S. 80.3%; Canada 2.4%; Germany 1.7%; Spain 1.5%; Brazil 1.2%; Colombia 1.0%; Neth. 0.9%; Venezuela 0.8%.

Trade by commodity group (2006)

	imports		exports	
SITC group	U.S.$'000,000	%	U.S.$'000,000	%
00 Food and live animals	12,007	4.7	10,342	4.1
01 Beverages and tobacco	13	13	3,021	1.2
02 Crude materials, excluding fuels	7,418	2.9	3,548	1.4
03 Mineral fuels, lubricants, and related materials	14,471	5.7	38,636	15.5
04 Animal and vegetable oils, fats, and waxes	13	13	14	14
05 Chemicals and related products, n.e.s.	27,525	10.7	8,832	3.5
06 Basic manufactures	40,532	15.8	20,838	8.3
07 Machinery and transport equipment	122,105	47.7	135,168	54.1
08 Miscellaneous manufactured articles	27,153	10.6	27,701	11.1
09 Goods not classified by kind	3,455	1.3	14	14
TOTAL	256,086	100.0	249,961	100.0

Direction of trade (2005)

	imports		exports	
	U.S.$'000,000	%	U.S.$'000,000	%
Western Hemisphere	137,680	62.2	198,708	93.0
United States	118,262	53.4	183,052	85.7
Latin America and the Caribbean	13,255	6.0	11,426	5.3
Canada	6,163	2.8	4,230	2.0
Europe	28,371	12.8	9,462	4.4
EU	25,963	11.7	9,166	4.3
Other Europe	2,408	1.1	296	0.1
Asia	53,426	24.1[10]	4,760	2.2
Japan	13,023	5.9	1,471	0.7
China	17,631	8.0	1,134	0.5
Other Asia	22,772	10.3	2,155	1.0
Africa	570	0.3	343	0.2
Other	1,222	0.6	438	0.2
TOTAL	221,270[10]	100.0	213,711	100.0

Transport and communications

Transport. Railroads (2008): route length 16,604 mi, 26,722 km; passenger-km 147,000,000; metric ton-km cargo 78,872,000,000. Roads (2008): total length 223,912 mi, 360,352 km (paved 35%); passenger-km (2007) 449,917,000,000[15]; metric ton-km cargo (2007) 222,391,000,000. Vehicles (2007): passenger cars 17,533,245; trucks and buses 8,152,942. Air transport (2008): passenger-km 28,514,000,000; metric ton-km cargo 223,958,000.

Communications

Medium	date	number in '000s	units per 1,000 persons	Medium	date	number in '000s	units per 1,000 persons
Televisions	2003	29,400	282	PCs	2006	14,578	139
Telephones				Dailies	2009	4,800[16]	61[16]
Cellular	2010	91,363[17]	806[17]	Internet users	2009	28,439	260
Landline	2010	19,892	175	Broadband	2010	11,325[17]	100[17]

Education and health

Literacy (2008): total population age 15 and over literate 92.9%; males literate 94.6%; females literate 91.5%.

Education (2007–08)

	teachers	students	student/teacher ratio	enrollment rate (%)
Primary (age 6–11)	524,517	14,699,146	28.0	98
Secondary/Voc. (age 12–17)	635,518	11,444,055	18.3	72
Tertiary	285,958	2,623,367	9.2	27 (age 18–22)

Health: physicians[18] (2007) 171,193 (1 per 618 persons); hospital beds[18] (2008) 84,813 (1 per 1,258 persons); infant mortality rate (2009) 14.7; undernourished population (2004–06) less than 5.0% of total population based on the consumption of a minimum daily requirement of 1,850 calories.

Military

Total active duty personnel (November 2010): 280,250 (army 75.6%, navy 20.2%, air force 4.2%); paramilitary 51,500. *Military expenditure as percentage of GDP* (2009): 0.5%[19]; per capita expenditure U.S.$43[19].

[1]Continental area per more recent survey equals 756,470 sq mi (1,959,248 sq km). [2]Uninhabited (nearly all Pacific) islands directly administered by federal government. [3]Total area based on more recent survey figure for continental area. [4]Within Mexico City urban agglomeration. [5]Within Guadalajara urban agglomeration. [6]Within Monterrey urban agglomeration. [7]Statistically derived midpoint within range. [8]Indirect taxes less subsidies and less imputed bank service charges. [9]Includes 1,593,300 unemployed. [10]Detail does not add to total given because of rounding. [11]Metal content. [12]End of year. [13]Together categories 01 and 04 equal U.S.$1,420,000,000 and 0.6%. [14]Together categories 04 and 09 equal U.S.$1,875,000,000 and 0.8%. [15]Buses only. [16]Circulation. [17]Subscribers. [18]Public health institutions only. [19]Excludes paramilitary expenditures.

Internet resources for further information:

- **National Institute of Statistics, Geography, and Informatics http://www.inegi.org.mx**
- **Banco de México http://www.banxico.org.mx**

Micronesia, Federated States of

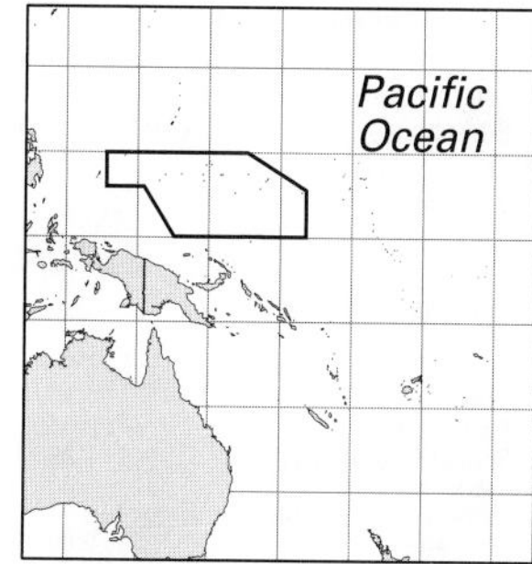

Official name: Federated States of Micronesia.
Form of government: federal nonparty republic in free association with the United States with one legislative house (Congress [14]).
Head of state and government: President.
Capital: Palikir, on Pohnpei.
Official language: English[1].
Official religion: none.
Monetary unit: U.S. dollar (U.S.$); valuation (Sept. 1, 2011) 1 U.S.$ = £0.62.

Area and population

States		area		population
Major Islands	Capitals	sq mi	sq km	2010 preliminary census
Chuuk (Truk)	Weno	49.2	127.4	48,651
Chuuk Islands		…	…	…
Kosrae	Lelu (Tofol)	42.3	109.6	6,616
Kosrae Island		42.3	109.6	…
Pohnpei (Ponape)	Kolonia	133.3	345.2	35,981
Pohnpei Island		129.0	334.1	…
Yap	Colonia	45.8	118.6	11,376
Yap Islands[2]		38.7	100.2	…
TOTAL		270.6	700.9[3]	102,624

Demography

Population (2011): 102,000.
Density (2011): persons per sq mi 376.9, persons per sq km 145.5.
Urban-rural (2009): urban 22.5%; rural 77.5%.
Sex distribution (2009): male 49.90%; female 50.10%.
Age breakdown (2009): under 15, 34.9%; 15–29, 29.4%; 30–44, 18.2%; 45–59, 12.6%; 60–74, 4.0%; 75 and over, 0.9%.
Population projection: (2020) 100,000; (2030) 103,000.
Doubling time: 38 years.
Ethnic composition (2000): Chuukese/Mortlockese 33.6%; Pohnpeian 24.9%; Yapese 10.6%; Kosraean 5.2%; U.S. white 4.5%; Asian 1.3%; other 19.9%.
Religious affiliation (2005): Roman Catholic *c.* 50%; Protestant *c.* 47%; other *c.* 3%.
Major towns (2010): Weno, in Chuuk state 13,700; Palikir, on Pohnpei 6,640; Kolonia, on Pohnpei 6,068; Colonia, on Yap 3,130; Lelu, on Kosrae 2,160.

Vital statistics

Birth rate per 1,000 population (2009): 23.1 (world avg. 20.3); within marriage (2006) 83.2%; outside of marriage (2006) 16.8%.
Death rate per 1,000 population (2009): 4.5 (world avg. 8.5).
Marriage/divorce rates per 1,000 population (2009): n.a./n.a.
Total fertility rate (avg. births per childbearing woman; 2009): 2.89.
Life expectancy at birth (2009): male 69.1 years; female 72.9 years.
Major causes of death per 100,000 population (2006): diseases of the endocrine system 49.9; diseases of the respiratory system 45.4; diseases of the circulatory system 40.8; infectious and parasitic diseases 27.2; malignant neoplasms (cancers) 13.6.

National economy

Budget (2007–08; for consolidated general government). Revenue: U.S.$149,800,000 (external grants 63.0%; tax revenue 19.6%; nontax revenue 17.4%, of which fishing access revenue 11.3%). Expenditures: U.S.$154,200,000 (current expenditures 91.8%; capital expenditure 8.2%).
Public debt (external, outstanding; September 2009): U.S.$82,700,000.
Population economically active (2000): total 37,414; activity rate of total population 35.0% (participation rates: ages 15–64, 60.7%; female 42.9%; unemployed 22.0%).

Price and earnings indexes (2005 = 100)

	2004	2005	2006	2007	2008	2009	2010
Consumer price index	96.0	100.0	104.3	108.2	115.5	124.4	128.7
Earnings index[4]	98.2	100.0	102.0	102.4	105.7	…	…

Production (metric tons except as noted). Agriculture, forestry, fishing (2009): coconuts 41,016, cassava 8,276, sweet potatoes 2,947, bananas 2,651, plantains 326, betel nuts (2005) 228, kava (*sakau*) n.a.; livestock (number of live animals) 33,000 pigs, 14,000 cattle, 4,100 goats; roundwood (2010) 2,406 cu m, of which fuelwood 100%; fisheries production 27,706, of which 16,784 skipjack tuna (from aquaculture, negligible)[5]. Mining and quarrying: quarrying of sand and aggregate for local construction only. Manufacturing: copra and coconut oil are traditionally important products; the manufacture of handicrafts and personal items (garments, mats, boats, etc.) is also important. Energy production (consumption): electricity (kW-hr; 2007) 67,289,000 (n.a.); coal, none (none); crude petroleum, none (none); petroleum products, none (n.a.); natural gas, none (none).
Household income and expenditure (2005). Average household size 6.9; annual median income per household U.S.$12,390; sources of income: wages and salaries 47.2%, rent 10.3%, self-employment 9.1%, transfers and remittances 6.9%; expenditure: food 39.4%, housing 17.4%, transportation and communications 9.3%, energy 5.1%, household furnishings 4.1%, clothing and footwear 3.7%, alcohol, tobacco, kava (*sakau*), and betel nut 3.5%.
Gross national income (GNI; 2010): U.S.$300,000,000 (U.S.$2,700 per capita); purchasing power parity GNI (U.S.$3,420 per capita).

Structure of gross domestic product and labour force

	2008		2000	
	in value U.S.$'000,000	% of total value	labour force	% of labour force
Agriculture and fishing[6]	42.8	18.0	15,216	40.7
Public utilities	3.3	1.4	360	1.0
Mining				
Manufacturing	3.2	1.3	1,164	3.1
Construction	2.3	1.0	781	2.1
Transp. and commun.	10.5	4.4	806	2.1
Trade, hotels	53.8	22.6	2,540	6.8
Finance			726	1.9
Services	108.2	45.5	1,445	3.9
Public administration			6,137	16.4
Other	13.7[7]	5.8[7]	8,239[8]	22.0[8]
TOTAL	237.8	100.0	37,414	100.0

Selected balance of payments data. Receipts from (U.S.$'000,000): tourism (2006) 18; remittances (2005) 6.0; foreign direct investment (2008–10 avg.) 8; official development assistance (2009) 121. Disbursements for (U.S.$'000,000): tourism (2006) 5.7; remittances, n.a.
Land use as % of total land area (2009): in temporary crops or left fallow *c.* 3%, in permanent crops *c.* 24%, in pasture *c.* 4%, forest area *c.* 92%[9].

Foreign trade[10]

Balance of trade (current prices)

	2002	2003	2004	2005	2006	2007
U.S.$'000,000	–89.8	–99.7	–118.7	–117.2	–129.1	–126.5
% of total	75.7%	73.3%	80.9%	82.0%	87.9%	79.7%

Imports (2007): U.S.$142,659,000 (food and beverages 29.8%, mineral fuels 22.1%, machinery and apparatus 14.4%, transport equipment 6.0%, chemicals and chemical products 5.4%). *Major import sources* (2007): U.S. 41.2%; Singapore 8.7%; Japan 8.5%; Hong Kong 6.3%; Australia 4.1%.
Exports (2007): U.S.$16,190,000 (tuna 69.9%, betel nuts 13.7%, reef fish 5.2%, cooked food 4.9%, kava 2.6%). *Major export destinations* (2007): Guam 22.5%; U.S. (mainland only) 17.2%; Northern Marianas 4.3%; Japan 4.1%; unspecified 51.2%.

Transport and communications

Transport. Railroads: none. Roads (2000): total length 149 mi, 240 km (paved 18%). Vehicles (2007): passenger cars 3,916; trucks and buses 3,849. Air transport (2009): n.a.

Communications

Medium	date	number in '000s	units per 1,000 persons	Medium	date	number in '000s	units per 1,000 persons
Televisions	2004	2.8	26	PCs	2005	6.0	55
Telephones				Dailies	2009	0	0
Cellular	2010	28[11]	248[11]	Internet users	2009	17	154
Landline	2010	8.5	76	Broadband	2010	1.0[11]	9.0[11]

Education and health

Educational attainment (2000). Percentage of population age 25 and over having: no formal schooling/unknown 13.4%; primary education 37.0%; some secondary 18.3%; secondary 12.9%; some college 18.4%. *Literacy* (2000): total population age 10 and over literate 92.4%; males literate 92.9%; females literate 91.9%.

Education (2006–07)

	teachers	students	student/ teacher ratio	enrollment rate (%)
Primary (age 6–11)	1,113	18,512	16.6	…
Secondary/Voc. (age 12–17)	829	14,742	17.8	…
Tertiary	103	5,883	57.1	14[12] (age 18–22)

Health: physicians (2005) 62 (1 per 1,774 persons); hospital beds (2006) 365 (1 per 301 persons); infant mortality rate per 1,000 live births (2009) 26.1; undernourished population, n.a.

Military

External security is provided by the United States per Compact of Free Association amended in 2004.

[1]English is the language of the Congress per article 9, section 19, of the constitution. [2]Yap Islands is the collective name of Yap Island and its immediately adjacent islands linked by common coral reef. The population of Yap Island at the 2000 census was 4,916. [3]Detail does not add to total given because of rounding. [4]Fiscal year. [5]Foreign fishing in the Exclusive Economic Zone (200-mile limit; 2007): 111,512 metric tons, of which Taiwanese 53,767 metric tons, Japanese 32,431 metric tons. [6]Includes subsistence farming and fishing. [7]Indirect taxes. [8]Unemployed. [9]Forest area overlaps with other categories. [10]Imports c.i.f.; exports f.o.b. [11]Subscribers. [12]1999–2000.

Internet resources for further information:
- **Division of Statistics**
  http://www.spc.int/prism/country/fm/stats
- **Asian Development Bank: Key Indicators for Asia and the Pacific 2011**
  http://www.adb.org/documents/books/key_indicators/2011

Moldova

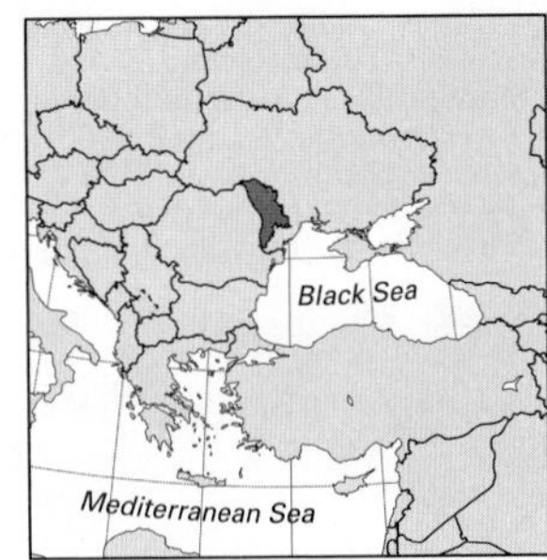

Official name: Republica Moldova (Republic of Moldova).
Form of government: unitary parliamentary republic with a single legislative body (Parliament [101]).
Head of state: President.
Head of government: Prime Minister.
Capital: Chişinău.
Official language: [1].
Official religion: none.
Monetary unit: Moldovan leu (plural lei); valuation (Sept. 1, 2011) 1 U.S.$ = 11.30 Moldovan lei; 1 £ = 18.26 Moldovan lei[2].

Population (2011[3] estimate)

Districts	population	Districts	population	Districts	population
Anenii-Noi	82,100	Floreşti	86,400	Străşeni	88,600
Basarabeasca	28,500	Glodeni	59,200	Taraclia	42,300
Briceni	75,200	Hînceşti	118,200	Teleneşti	69,500
Cahul	119,300	Ialoveni	98,800	Ungheni	110,700
Călăraşi	73,500	Leova	51,700	**Municipalities**	
Cantemir	61,000	Nisporeni	64,600	Bălţi	127,800
Căuşeni	89,400	Ocniţa	54,800	Chişinău	759,800
Cimişlia	59,400	Orhei	115,300	**Autonomous Region**	
Criuleni	72,300	Rezina	50,000	Găgăuzia	156,700
Donduşeni	43,900	Rîşcani	67,100	**Disputed Territory[4]**	
Drochia	85,200	Sîngerei	86,700	Transdniestria	
Dubăsari (rural)	35,100	Şoldăneşti	41,200	(Stînga Nistrului)	518,000
Edineţ	81,200	Soroca	99,000	TOTAL	3,931,100[5]
Făleşti	88,800	Ştefan-Vodă	69,800		

Demography

Area: 13,067 sq mi, 33,843 sq km[6].
Population (2011): 3,927,000[5, 7].
Density (2011)[5, 7]: persons per sq mi 300.5, persons per sq km 116.0.
Urban-rural (2010[3])[8]: urban 39.8%; rural 60.2%.
Sex distribution (2010[3])[8]: male 48.22%; female 51.78%.
Age breakdown (2009[3])[8, 9]: under 15, 17.1%; 15–29, 27.4%; 30–44, 20.5%; 45–59, 21.3%; 60–74, 9.8%; 75–84, 3.3%; 85 and over, 0.6%.
Population projection[5, 7]: (2020) 3,713,000; (2030) 3,480,000.
Ethnic composition (2004)[8, 10]: Moldovan 75.8%; Ukrainian 8.4%; Russian 5.9%; Gagauz 4.4%; Rom (Gypsy) 2.2%; Bulgarian 1.9%; other 1.4%.
Religious affiliation (2005): Moldovan Orthodox 31.8%; Bessarabian Orthodox 16.1%; Russian Orthodox 15.4%; Sunnī Muslim 5.5%; Protestant 1.7%; Jewish 0.6%; nonreligious 19.9%; other 9.0%.
Major cities (2011[3]): Chişinău 632,100; Tiraspol 147,800[11]; Bălţi 122,900; Bender (Tighina) 93,300[11]; Rybnitsa (Rîbniţa) 49,400[11].

Vital statistics

Birth rate per 1,000 population (2009): 11.4 (world avg. 20.3); within marriage (2008) 77.7%; outside of marriage (2008) 22.3%.
Death rate per 1,000 population (2009): 11.8 (world avg. 8.5).
Total fertility rate (avg. births per childbearing woman; 2008): 1.28.
Marriage/divorce rates per 1,000 population (2009): 7.5/3.3.
Life expectancy at birth (2009): male 65.3 years; female 73.4 years.
Major causes of death per 100,000 population (2009)[8]: diseases of the circulatory system 663.2; malignant neoplasms (cancers) 160.5; diseases of the digestive system 115.5; accidents, poisoning, and violence 97.0.

National economy

Budget (2008)[12]. Revenue: 25,517,000,000 Moldovan lei (tax revenue 84.5%, of which VAT 44.5%, social insurance 21.3%; nontax revenue 4.1%; unspecified 11.4%). Expenditures: 26,147,000,000 Moldovan lei (social assistance 30.2%; education 19.8%; health care 13.0%; public order/defense 7.8%).
Public debt (external, outstanding; June 2011): U.S.$1,174,000,000.
Production (metric tons except as noted). Agriculture, forestry, fishing (2009): corn (maize) 1,141,000, wheat 737,000, grapes 685,000, cow's milk 540,200, sugar beets 337,000, sunflower seeds 284,000, potatoes 261,000, apples 210,000, sour cherries 21,000; livestock (number of live animals) 762,000 sheep, 284,000 pigs, 218,000 cattle; roundwood (2010) 3,518,000 cu m, of which fuelwood 88%; fisheries production 6,307 (from aquaculture 75%). Mining and quarrying (2007): gypsum 846,400. Manufacturing (value of production in '000,000 Moldovan lei; 2008)[8]: food products 8,703, of which meat products 1,468, dairy products 1,192, processed fruits/vegetables 1,148; beverages 3,078, of which wine 2,210; rubber and plastic products 1,034. Energy production (consumption): electricity (kW-hr; 2007) 1,103,000,000 (4,037,000,000); coal (metric tons; 2007) none (130,000); crude petroleum (barrels; 2007) 58,600 (58,600); petroleum products (metric tons; 2007) none (629,000); natural gas (cu m; 2007) none (1,133,000,000).
Land use as % of total land area (2009): in temporary crops 54.4%, left fallow 0.9%, in permanent crops 9.2%, in pasture 10.8%, forest area 11.6%.
Population economically active (2008)[8, 13]: total 1,302,800; activity rate of total population *c.* 36% (participation rates: ages 15–64 *c.* 49%; female 49.4%; unemployed 3.8%).

Price and earnings indexes (2005 = 100)

	2004	2005	2006	2007	2008	2009	2010
Consumer price index	89.3	100.0	112.8	126.7	142.9	142.8	153.4
Earnings index	83.7	100.0	128.7	156.6	191.8	208.4	225.4

Gross national income (GNI; 2010)[8]: U.S.$6,456,000,000 (U.S.$1,810 per capita); purchasing power parity GNI (U.S.$3,340 per capita).

Structure of gross domestic product and labour force

	2009[8]		2008[8]	
	in value '000,000 Moldovan lei	% of total value	labour force	% of labour force
Agriculture	5,063	8.4	392,000	37.7
Mining	216	0.4	4,000	0.1
Manufacturing	6,305	10.5	142,200	9.3
Public utilities	1,296	2.2	23,900	1.8
Construction	2,058	3.4	87,400	3.6
Transp. and commun.	7,396	12.3	73,100	5.0
Trade, hotels	8,609	14.3	214,500	12.9
Finance, real estate	9,213	15.3	48,500	3.0
Pub. admin., defense	2,897	4.8	70,400	4.3
Services	8,401	14.0	223,800	15.0
Other	8,589[14]	14.3[14]	59,900	7.4
TOTAL	60,043	100.0[15]	1,339,700	100.0[15]

Household income and expenditure. Average household size (2004) 3.2; annual average income per household (2002) U.S.$1,200; sources of income (2008): wages and salaries 42.9%, remittances 19.1%, self-employment 18.0%, social benefits 14.9%; expenditure (2008): food and drink 42.1%, housing and energy 21.1%, clothing and footwear 12.7%, transportation and communications 9.8%, health 5.6%.
Selected balance of payments data. Receipts from (U.S.$'000,000): tourism (2009) 168; remittances (2010) 1,306; foreign direct investment (2008–10 avg.) 347; official development assistance (2009) 245. Disbursements for (U.S.$'000,000): tourism (2009) 243; remittances (2009) 103.

Foreign trade[16]

Balance of trade (current prices)

	2004	2005	2006	2007	2008	2009
U.S.$'000,000	–783	–1,201	–1,642	–2,348	–3,307	–1,981
% of total	28.4%	35.5%	34.6%	46.7%	51.0%	43.3%

Imports (2008): U.S.$4,899,000,000 (mineral fuels 22.5%; machinery and apparatus 14.9%; chemicals and chemical products 11.5%; food 8.8%; road vehicles 7.3%). *Major import sources:* Ukraine 17.1%; Russia 13.6%; Romania 12.1%; Germany 7.4%; China 6.6%.
Exports (2008): U.S.$1,592,000,000 (apparel/clothing accessories 16.8%, of which outerwear 12.3%; food 15.6%; wine 9.7%; oilseeds/vegetable oils 8.2%; insulated wire/cable 6.3%). *Major export destinations:* Romania 21.1%; Russia 19.7%; Italy 10.5%; Ukraine 9.0%; Belarus 5.8%.

Transport and communications

Transport. Railroads (2008): route length 719 mi, 1,157 km; passenger-km 486,000,000; metric ton-km cargo 2,878,000,000. Roads (2008): total length 5,805 mi, 9,343 km (paved 94%); passenger-km 2,688,000,000[17]; metric ton-km cargo 2,012,000,000. Vehicles (2007): passenger cars 338,944; trucks and buses 115,962. Air transport (2008): passenger-km 638,000,000; metric ton-km cargo 1,200,000.

Communications

Medium	date	number in '000s	units per 1,000 persons	Medium	date	number in '000s	units per 1,000 persons
Televisions	2003	1,300	327	PCs	2005	348	83
Telephones				Dailies	2009	400[18]	111[18]
Cellular	2010	3,165[19]	886[19]	Internet users	2009	1,295	360
Landline	2010	1,161	325	Broadband	2010	269[19]	75[19]

Education and health

Literacy (2007): total population age 15 and over literate 99.2%.

Education (2008–09)[8]

	teachers	students	student/ teacher ratio	enrollment rate (%)
Primary (age 7–10)	9,231	145,369	15.7	88
Secondary/Voc. (age 11–17)	29,186	326,608	11.2	80
Tertiary	7,698	135,147	17.6	38 (age 18–22)

Health (2009): physicians[8] 12,783 (1 per 279 persons); hospital beds[8] 21,938 (1 per 162 persons); infant mortality rate 12.1; undernourished population (2005–07) less than 5% of total population based on the consumption of a minimum daily requirement of 1,930 calories.

Military

Total active duty personnel (November 2010): 5,354 (army 60.3%, air force 15.4%, logistic support 24.3%); reserve 57,971. Russian troops in Transdniestria (November 2010) *c.* 1,500. *Military expenditure as percentage of GDP* (2009): 0.4%; per capita expenditure U.S.$6.

[1]Moldovan, a form of Romanian, is the state (official) language per article 13 of the constitution. [2]The Transdniestrian ruble is the official currency of Transdniestria. [3]January 1. [4]Breakaway area from 1991 also known as Transnistria or Pridnestrovye. [5]Excludes Moldovans abroad. [6]Of which Transdniestria 1,607 sq mi, 4,163 sq km. [7]Includes Transdniestria. [8]Excludes Transdniestria. [9]Includes Moldovans abroad. [10]Transdniestria ethnic composition (2004): Moldovan 31.9%; Russian 30.4%; Ukrainian 28.8%; other 8.9%. [11]Within Transdniestria. [12]Consolidated ("national public") budget. [13]Excludes unemployed previously employed. [14]Taxes less imputed bank service charges. [15]Detail does not add to total given because of rounding. [16]Imports c.i.f.; exports f.o.b. [17]Buses and taxis only. [18]Circulation. [19]Subscribers.

Internet resources for further information:
- **National Bureau of Statistics http://www.statistica.md**
- **National Bank of Moldova http://www.bnm.md**

Monaco

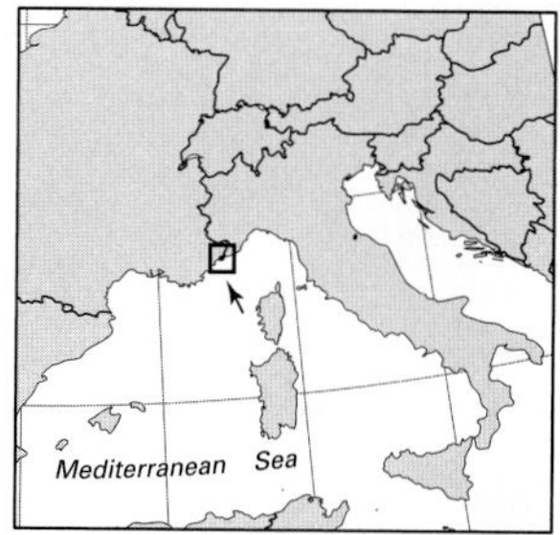

Official name: Principauté de Monaco (Principality of Monaco).
Form of government: constitutional monarchy with one legislative body (National Council [24]).
Head of state: Prince.
Head of government[1]: Minister of State assisted by the Council of Government.
Capital: [2].
Official language: French.
Official religion: Roman Catholicism.
Monetary unit: euro (€)[3]; valuation (Sept. 1, 2011) 1 U.S.$ = €0.70; 1 £ = €1.13.

Area and population

Quarters[2]	Capitals[2]	area sq mi	area sq km	population 2008 census
Condamine	—	0.24	0.62	11,946
Fontvieille	—	0.13	0.33	3,602
Monaco-Ville	—	0.07	0.19	975
Monte-Carlo	—	0.34	0.88	14,586
TOTAL		0.78	2.02	31,109[4]

Demography

Population (2011): 36,000.
Density (2011): persons per sq mi 46,154, persons per sq km 17,822.
Urban-rural (2008): urban 100%.
Sex distribution (2008): male 47.94%; female 52.06%.
Age breakdown (2008): under 15, 12.8%; 15–29, 12.7%; 30–44, 19.2%; 45–59, 21.8%; 60–74, 19.1%; 75–84, 7.9%; 85 and over, 4.2%; unknown 2.3%.
Population projection: (2020) 36,000; (2030) 38,000.
Doubling time: 58 years.
Ethnic composition (2008): French 28.4%; Monegasque 21.6%; Italian 18.7%; British 7.5%; Belgian 2.8%; Swiss 2.5%; German 2.5%; U.S. 1.0%; other 15.0% (including Asian countries *c.* 2.5%, African countries *c.* 2.2%).
Religious affiliation (2000): Christian 93.2%, of which Roman Catholic 89.3%; Jewish 1.7%; nonreligious and other 5.1%.

Vital statistics

Birth rate per 1,000 population (2010): 27.3 (world avg. 19.2); within marriage (2005) 61.4%; outside of marriage (2005) 38.6%.
Death rate per 1,000 population (2010): 15.2 (world avg. 8.2).
Natural increase rate per 1,000 population (2008): 12.0 (world avg. 11.8).
Total fertility rate (avg. births per childbearing woman; 2007): 1.75.
Marriage/divorce rates per 1,000 population (2005): 4.8/2.1.
Life expectancy at birth (2007): male 76.0 years; female 83.9 years.
Major causes of death per 100,000 population: n.a.; however, principal causes are those of a developed country with an older population.

National economy

Budget (2007). Revenue: €845,600,700 (taxes on commerce 47.4%[5], property taxes 12.9%, state-run monopolies 10.0%, customs duties 3.1%). Expenditures: €843,119,681 (current expenditure 65.1%, capital expenditure 34.9%).
Public debt: n.a.
Production. Agriculture, forestry, fishing: some horticulture and greenhouse cultivation; no agriculture as such; roundwood, n.a.; fisheries production (2009; metric tons) 1 (from aquaculture, none). Mining and quarrying: none. Manufacturing (value of sales in €'000; 2007): chemicals, cosmetics, perfumery, and pharmaceuticals 364,077; plastic products 266,366; light electronics and precision instruments 86,113; textiles 41,982; paper and card manufactures 41,470. Energy production (consumption): electricity (kW-hr; 2001) n.a. (475,000,000 [imported from France]); coal, none (n.a.); crude petroleum, none (n.a.); natural gas, none (n.a.).
Gross national income (2009): U.S.$6,109,000,000[6] (U.S.$186,175 per capita).

Structure of gross domestic product and labour force

	2006 in value €'000,000[7]	2006 % of total value	2007 labour force	2007 % of labour force
Agriculture, forestry, fishing	…	…	29	—
Mining and quarrying	…	…	2	—
Manufacturing	216.6	6.5	3,535	8.0
Public utilities } Construction }	236.7	7.1	139	0.3
			3,560	8.0
Transp. and commun.	194.5	5.9	2,463	5.5
Trade, hotels	786.1	23.8	12,476	28.1
Finance, real estate	1,248.4	37.8	13,717	30.8
Public administration	221.1	6.7	256	0.6
Services } Other }	402.8	12.2	8,305	18.7
			…	…
TOTAL	3,306.2	100.0	44,482[8]	100.0

Population economically active (2005): total 40,289; activity rate of total population 58.4% (participation rates: ages 17–64 [2000] 61.1%; female 41.4%; unemployed [2000] 3.6%).

Price index (2005 = 100)

	2004	2005	2006	2007	2008	2009	2010
Consumer price index[9]	98.3	100.0	101.7	103.2	106.1	106.2	107.8

Household income and expenditure. Average household size (2008) 2.1; average annual income per household: n.a.; sources of income: n.a.; expenditure: n.a.
Selected balance of payments data. Receipts from (U.S.$'000,000): tourism (2010) n.a., 2,535 hotel rooms, 817,011 overnight visitors; remittances (2010) n.a.; foreign direct investment, n.a. Disbursements for (U.S.$'000,000): tourism (2010) n.a.; remittances (2009) n.a.
Land use as % of total land area (2000): public gardens *c.* 20%.

Foreign trade[10]

Balance of trade (current prices)

	2003	2004	2005	2006	2007	2008	2009
€'000,000	+188	+17	−128	−73	−16	+11	+73
% of total	18.4%	1.5%	8.9%	5.1%	1.0%	1.0%	7.7%

Imports (2008): €548,753,494 (nonelectrical machinery and apparatus 40.2%; pharmaceuticals, perfumes, clothing, and publishing 19.2%; rubber and plastic products, glass, construction materials, organic chemicals, and paper products 15.7%; food products 7.4%; products of the automobile industry 7.0%).
Major import sources: China 34.9%; Italy 18.6%; Japan 8.5%; U.K. 7.1%; Belgium 5.3%.
Exports (2008): €560,147,354 (rubber and plastic products, glass, construction materials, organic chemicals, and paper products 39.9%; products of the automobile industry 12.7%; pharmaceuticals, perfumes, clothing, and publishing 12.2%; nonelectrical machinery and apparatus 12.1%; food products 9.6%).
Major export destinations: Germany 10.7%; Italy 8.4%; Spain 7.9%; U.K. 6.6%; Lithuania 5.2%; unspecified 26.0%.

Transport and communications

Transport. Railroads (2007): length 1.1 mi, 1.7 km[11]; passenger-km 6,700,000; metric ton-km cargo, n.a. Roads (2007): total length 48 mi, 77 km (paved 100%). Vehicles (1997): passenger cars 21,120; trucks and buses 2,770. Air transport: [12]; passenger-km (2005) 5,000,000; metric ton-km cargo, n.a.

Communications

Medium	date	number in '000s	units per 1,000 persons	Medium	date	number in '000s	units per 1,000 persons
Televisions	2004	25	758	PCs	2005	…	…
Telephones				Dailies	2005	0	0
Cellular	2010	26[13]	743[13]	Internet users	2009	23	701
Landline	2010	34	964	Broadband	2010	15[13]	419[13]

Education and health

Educational attainment (2000). Percentage of population age 17 and over having: primary/lower secondary education 24.7%; upper secondary 27.6%; vocational 12.7%; university 35.0%. *Literacy:* virtually 100%.

Education (2007–08)

	teachers	students	student/ teacher ratio	enrollment rate (%)
Primary (age 6–10)	133[14]	1,852	13.7[14]	…
Secondary/Voc. (age 11–17)	519	3,015	5.8	…
Tertiary[15]	…	…	…	… (age 18–22)

Health (2002): physicians 156 (1 per 207 persons); hospital beds 521 (1 per 62 persons); infant mortality rate per 1,000 live births (2007) 5.2; undernourished population, n.a.

Military

Defense responsibility lies with France according to the terms of the Versailles Treaty of 1919.

[1]Under the authority of the prince. [2]The principality is a single administrative unit, and no separate area within it is distinguished as capital. [3]Monaco uses the euro as its official currency, even though it is not a member of the EU. [4]Unadjusted figure; adjusted census total equals 35,352. [5]On hotels, banks, and the industrial sector. [6]Per United Nations National Accounts Main Aggregates Database. [7]At constant prices of 2000. [8]Includes *c.* 30,000 French workers. [9]The index is for France. [10]Excludes trade with France; Monaco has participated in a customs union with France since 1963. [11]Operated by the French state railway. [12]Fixed-wing service is provided at Nice, France; helicopter service is available at Fontvieille. [13]Subscribers. [14]2004–05. [15]Most Monegasque students undertake higher education in France.

Internet resource for further information:

- **La Principauté de Monaco http://www.gouv.mc**

Mongolia

Official name: Mongol Uls (Mongolia).
Form of government: unitary multiparty republic with one legislative house (State Great Hural [76]).
Head of state: President.
Head of government: Prime Minister.
Capital: Ulaanbaatar (Ulan Bator).
Official language: Khalkha Mongolian.
Official religion: none.
Monetary unit: tugrik (Tug); valuation (Sept. 1, 2011) 1 U.S.$ = Tug 1,248; 1 £ = Tug 2,017.

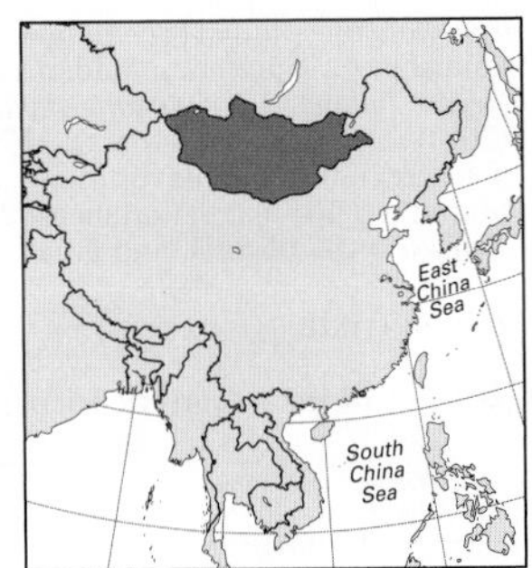

Area and population

Provinces	area[1] sq km	population 2010[2] estimate	Provinces	area[1] sq km	population 2010[2] estimate
Arhangay	55,300	89,331	Hovd	76,100	82,628
Bayan-Ölgiy	45,700	93,017	Hövsgöl	100,600	125,274
Bayanhongor	116,000	80,848	Ömnögovĭ (South Gobi)	165,400	50,681
Bulgan	48,700	58,834	Orhon	840	91,212
Darhan-Uul	3,280	91,358	Övörhangay	62,900	111,977
Dornod (Eastern)	123,600	73,892	Selenge	41,200	100,202
Dornogovĭ (East Gobi)	109,500	57,733	Sühbaatar	82,300	54,363
Dundgovĭ (Central Gobi)	74,700	47,622	Töv (Central)	74,000	87,210
Dzavhan	82,500	74,906	Uvs	69,600	77,408
Govĭ-Altay	141,400	55,426	**Autonomous municipality**		
Govĭ-Sümber	5,540	14,135	Ulaanbaatar	4,700	1,106,719
Hentiy	80,300	70,179	TOTAL	1,564,160	2,694,955

Demography

Population (2011): 2,765,000.
Density (2011): persons per sq mi 4.6, persons per sq km 1.8.
Urban-rural (2010): urban 63.3%; rural 36.7%.
Sex distribution (2010): male 48.61%; female 51.39%.
Age breakdown (2009): under 15, 25.6%; 15–29, 31.7%; 30–44, 23.4%; 45–59, 13.4%; 60–74, 4.6%; 75–84, 1.1%; 85 and over, 0.2%.
Population projection: (2020) 3,150,000; (2030) 3,485,000.
Ethnic composition (2000): Khalkha Mongol 81.5%; Kazakh 4.3%; Dörbed Mongol 2.8%; Bayad 2.1%; Buryat Mongol 1.7%; Dariganga Mongol 1.3%; Zakhchin 1.3%; Tuvan (Uriankhai) 1.1%; other 3.9%.
Religious affiliation (2005): traditional beliefs (shamanism) *c.* 32%; Buddhist (Lamaism) *c.* 23%; Muslim *c.* 5%; Christian *c.* 1%; nonreligious *c.* 30%; atheist/other *c.* 9%.
Major cities (2010): Ulaanbaatar (Ulan Bator; 2011[2]) 1,161,800; Erdenet 83,379; Darhan 74,738; Choybalsan 38,537; Mörön 35,789.

Vital statistics

Birth rate per 1,000 population (2009): 25.1 (world avg. 20.3); within marriage (2001) 82.2%; outside of marriage (2001) 17.8%.
Death rate per 1,000 population (2009): 5.7 (world avg. 8.5).
Total fertility rate (avg. births per childbearing woman; 2008): 2.60.
Marriage/divorce rates per 1,000 population: (2008) 12.4[3]/(2007) 0.7.
Life expectancy at birth (2008): male 63.7 years; female 71.0 years.
Major causes of death per 100,000 population (2008): diseases of the circulatory system 205.5; malignant neoplasms (cancers) 118.0; accidents and violence 93.3; diseases of the digestive system 52.7; diseases of the respiratory system 24.0.

National economy

Budget (2010). Revenue: Tug 2,451,137,800,000 (tax revenue 78.8%, of which VAT 23.6%, corporate taxes 15.9%, excises 11.0%; nontax revenue 11.8%; grants and transfers 9.4%). Expenditures: Tug 2,376,197,400,000 (wages and salaries 24.9%; debt service 19.9%; subsidies and transfers 19.8%).
Population economically active (2010): total 1,072,000; activity rate of total population 39.0% (participation rates: ages 16–59, 61.6%; female [2008] 51.0%; unemployed 3.6%[4]).

Price index (2005 = 100)

	2004	2005	2006	2007	2008	2009	2010
Consumer price index	88.7	100.0	105.1	114.6	143.3	152.3	167.8

Production (metric tons except as noted). Agriculture, forestry, fishing (2010): hay 1,132,314, wheat 345,458, potatoes 167,956, vegetables 82,266; livestock (number of live animals) 14,480,400 sheep, 13,883,200 goats, 2,176,000 cattle, 1,920,300 horses, 269,600 camels; roundwood 808,216 cu m, of which fuelwood 94%; fisheries production (2009) 90 (from aquaculture, none). Mining and quarrying (2010): iron ore 3,203,200; copper[5] 357,100; fluorspar 140,700; zinc[5] 112,600; molybdenum[5] 4,677; gold 6,037 kg[6]. Manufacturing (value added in U.S.$'000,000; 2008): beverages 50; food products 41; textiles and wearing apparel 38; base metals 32; bricks, cement, and ceramics 23. Energy production (consumption): electricity (kW-hr; 2010) 3,654,200 (3,376,000); hard coal (metric tons; 2007) 1,506,000 (1,506,000); lignite (metric tons; 2007) 7,732,000 (4,464,000); crude petroleum (barrels; 2010) 2,181,400 (6,205,000); petroleum products (metric tons; 2007) none (781,000); natural gas, none (none).
Gross national income (GNI; 2010): U.S.$5,106,000,000 (U.S.$1,890 per capita); purchasing power parity GNI (U.S.$3,700 per capita).

Structure of gross domestic product and labour force

	2009 in value Tug '000,000,000	2009 % of total value	2008 labour force	2008 % of labour force
Agriculture, forestry, fishing	1,284.8	21.2	377,600	35.2
Mining and quarrying	1,338.0	22.1	46,500	4.3
Manufacturing	254.3	4.2	47,500	4.4
Construction	49.4	0.8	66,800	6.2
Public utilities	144.2	2.4	30,100	2.8
Transp. and commun.	644.6	10.6	46,300	4.3
Trade, hotels	398.2	6.6	204,200	19.1
Finance, real estate	722.8	11.9	31,800	3.0
Public admin., defense	270.1	4.5	50,900	4.8
Services	513.7	8.5	140,000	13.1
Other	435.7[7]	7.2[7]	29,800[8]	2.8[8]
TOTAL	6,055.8	100.0	1,071,600[9]	100.0

Public debt (external; 2009): U.S.$1,860,000,000.
Household income and expenditure (2005). Average household size (2011[2]) 3.7; annual income per household Tug 1,629,600 (U.S.$1,350); sources of income: wages 35.2%, self-employment 31.3%, transfer payments 10.6%, other 22.9%; expenditure[10]: food and nonalcoholic beverages 42.2%, housing and energy 10.5%, clothing and footwear 10.1%, transportation 9.5%, education 5.4%.
Selected balance of payments data. Receipts from (U.S.$'000,000): tourism (2010) 244; remittances (2010) 211; foreign direct investment (FDI; 2008–10 avg.) 1,053; official development assistance (2009) 372. Disbursements for (U.S.$'000,000): tourism (2010) 259; remittances (2009) 83; FDI (2008–10 avg.) 41.
Land use as % of total land area (2007): in temporary crops 0.5%; left fallow 0.1%; in permanent crops, negligible; in pasture 74.1%; forest area 6.5%.

Foreign trade

Balance of trade (current prices)

	2005	2006	2007	2008	2009	2010
U.S.$'000,000	–113.4	+107.0	–114.3	–710.0	–252.3	–378.7
% of total	5.1%	3.6%	2.9%	12.3%	6.3%	6.1%

Imports (2010): U.S.$3,277,886,100 (refined petroleum products 23.2%, machinery and apparatus 20.9%, transportation equipment 19.4%, food products 11.8%). *Major import sources:* Russia 33.3%; China 30.5%; Japan 6.0%; South Korea 5.6%; U.S. 4.9%.
Exports (2010): U.S.$2,899,188,400 (coal 30.3%, copper ore/concentrate 27.3%, iron ore 8.7%, wool/fine animal hair 6.2%, gold 6.2%, crude petroleum 5.3%, zinc concentrate 4.6%). *Major export destinations:* China 84.9%; Canada 4.9%; Russia 2.7%; U.K. 2.3%; Italy 1.1%.

Transport and communications

Transport. Railroads (2010): route length 1,186 mi, 1,908 km; passenger-km 1,215,600,000; metric ton-km cargo 10,268,300,000. Roads (2010): total length 30,602 mi, 49,249 km (paved 6%); passenger-km 1,480,200,000; metric ton-km cargo 1,834,000,000. Vehicles (2010): passenger cars 172,125; trucks and buses 78,843. Air transport (2010–11): passenger-km 756,000,000; metric ton-km cargo 4,521,000.

Communications

Medium	date	number in '000s	units per 1,000 persons	Medium	date	number in '000s	units per 1,000 persons
Televisions	2009	490	181	PCs	2008	665	250
Telephones				Dailies	2009	49[11]	18[11]
Cellular	2010	2,511[12]	911[12]	Internet users	2009	350	131
Landline	2010	193	70	Broadband	2010	64[12]	23[12]

Education and health

Educational attainment (2000). Percentage of population age 10 and over having: no formal education 11.6%; primary education 23.5%; secondary 46.1%; vocational secondary 11.2%; higher 7.6%. *Literacy* (2009): percentage of total population age 15 and over literate 97.5%; males 97.1%; females 97.9%.

Education (2008–09)

	teachers	students	student/ teacher ratio	enrollment rate (%)
Primary (age 7–11)	8,320	252,604	30.4	90
Secondary/Voc. (age 12–17)	16,605[13]	305,791	19.8[13]	82
Tertiary	8,554	162,217	19.0	53 (age 18–22)

Health (2010): physicians 7,497 (1 per 366 persons); hospital beds (2009) 15,988 (1 per 169 persons); infant mortality rate per 1,000 live births 19.4; undernourished population (2004–06) 750,000 (29% of total population based on the consumption of a minimum daily requirement of 1,840 calories).

Military

Total active duty personnel (November 2010): 10,000 (army 89.0%, air force 8.0%, other 3.0%); reserve 137,000. *Military expenditure as percentage of GDP* (2009): 0.9%; per capita expenditure U.S.$14.

[1]Rounded figures. [2]January 1. [3]In 2006 the government implemented a "newly married couple" program to promote marriage. [4]Registered figure. [5]Metal content. [6]Excludes gold contained in copper concentrate. [7]Net taxes on products less imputed bank service charges. [8]Unemployed. [9]Detail does not add to total given because of rounding. [10]Weights of consumer price index components. [11]Circulation of daily newspapers. [12]Subscribers. [13]2006–07.

Internet resources for further information:
- **National Statistical Office of Mongolia http://www.nso.mn/v3/index2.php**
- **Bank of Mongolia http://www.mongolbank.mn**

Montenegro

Official name: Crna Gora (Montenegro).
Form of government: multiparty republic with one legislative house (Parliament [81[1]]).
Head of state: President.
Head of government: Prime Minister.
Capital: Podgorica; Cetinje is the Old Royal Capital.
Official language: Montenegrin[2].
Official religion: none.
Monetary unit: euro (€)[3]; valuation (Sept. 1, 2011) 1 U.S.$ = €0.70; 1 £ = €1.13.

Area and population

Municipalities	area sq km	population 2011 census[4]	Municipalities	area sq km	population 2011 census[4]
Andrijevica	283	5,071	Nikšić	2,065	72,443
Bar	598	42,048	Plav	486	13,108
Berane	717	33,970	Pljevlja	1,346	30,786
Bijelo Polje	924	46,051	Plužine	854	3,246
Budva	122	19,218	Podgorica	1,441	185,937
Cetinje	910	16,657	Rožaje	432	22,964
Danilovgrad	501	18,472	Šavnik	553	2,070
Herceg Novi	235	30,864	Tivat	46	14,031
Kolašin	897	8,380	Ulcinj	255	19,921
Kotor	335	22,601	Žabljak	445	3,569
Mojkovac	367	8,622	TOTAL	13,812	620,029

Demography

Population (2011): 620,000.
Density (2011): persons per sq mi 116.3, persons per sq km 44.9.
Urban-rural (2011): urban 63.2%; rural 36.8%.
Sex distribution (2011): male 49.39%; female 50.61%.
Age breakdown (2011): under 15, 19.2%; 15–29, 21.4%; 30–44, 20.5%; 45–59, 20.6%; 60–74, 13.1%; 75–84, 4.4%; 85 and over, 0.8%.
Population projection: (2020) 624,000; (2030) 622,000.
Ethnic composition (2011): Montenegrin 45.0%; Serb 28.7%; Bosniak/Muslim 12.0%; Albanian 4.9%; undeclared 4.9%; other 4.5%.
Religious affiliation (2011): Orthodox 72.1%; Muslim 19.1%; Roman Catholic 3.4%; other 5.4%.
Major settlements (2011): Podgorica 151,312; Nikšić 57,278; Pljevlja 19,327; Bijelo Polje (2003) 15,883; Cetinje 13,991; Bar 13,586.

Vital statistics

Birth rate per 1,000 population (2010): 12.0 (world avg. 19.2); within marriage (2008) 82.6%; outside of marriage (2008) 17.4%.
Death rate per 1,000 population (2010): 9.1 (world avg. 8.2).
Natural increase rate per 1,000 population (2010): 2.9 (world avg. 11.0).
Total fertility rate (avg. births per childbearing woman; 2009): 1.9.
Marriage/divorce rates per 1,000 population (2010): 5.9/0.8.
Life expectancy at birth (2008): male 71.2 years; female 76.1 years.
Major causes of death per 100,000 population (2008): diseases of the circulatory system 490.6; malignant neoplasms (cancers) 146.3; diseases of the respiratory system 39.6; injuries, accidents, and violence 36.7, of which suicide 20.0; ill-defined conditions 125.0.

National economy

Budget (2006). Revenue: €582,258,287 (tax revenue 85.8%, of which VAT 44.5%, income tax 12.5%, excise tax 12.4%, taxes on international trade 9.7%; nontax revenue 14.2%). Expenditures: €579,780,129 (wages and salaries 27.4%; transfers 20.7%; debt service 20.0%).
Production (metric tons except as noted). Agriculture, forestry, fishing (2009): potatoes 156,380, cow's milk 149,500, cabbages 50,060, watermelons 42,700, grapes 38,640, tomatoes 22,090, chilies and peppers 18,180, plums 10,240, corn (maize) 10,000, apples 8,100, sheep's milk 7,500, oranges 7,430, cattle meat 4,760, figs 4,600, peaches[5] 3,800, cherries 2,250, olives 1,600; livestock (number of live animals) 199,764 sheep, 100,835 cattle, 12,377 pigs; roundwood (2010) 346,000 cu m, of which fuelwood 43%; fisheries production 2,980 (from aquaculture 23%). Mining and quarrying (2010): bauxite 61,205; sea salt 11,200. Manufacturing (2008): base metals and fabricated metal products (mostly of aluminum) 697,563; food products 88,590; chemicals and chemical products 14,766; paper products, publishing, and printing 3,709; wood and wood products 68,989 cu m. Energy production (consumption): electricity (kW-hr; 2009) 2,760,000,000 (2,232,000,000[6]); hard coal (metric tons; 2009) none (none[6]); lignite (metric tons; 2010) 1,937,847 ([2009] 17,000[6]); crude petroleum (barrels; 2007) none (n.a.); petroleum products, n.a. (n.a.); natural gas (cu m; 2009) none (n.a.).
Land use as % of total land area (2009): in temporary crops 2.4%, left fallow 1.0%, in permanent crops 1.2%, in pasture 24.2%, forest area 40.4%.
Population economically active (2008): total 266,700; activity rate 51.9% (participation rates: over age 15 [2007] 52.9%; female 43.4%; unemployed [April 2010–March 2011] 16.8%).

Price index (2005 = 100)

	2005	2006	2007	2008	2009	2010
Consumer price index	100.0	102.9	107.4	116.8	120.9	121.6

Gross national income (GNI; 2010): U.S.$4,183,000,000 (U.S.$6,690 per capita); purchasing power parity GNI (U.S.$12,710 per capita).

Structure of gross domestic product and labour force

	2008 in value €'000,000	2008 % of total value	2007 labour force	2007 % of labour force
Agriculture, forestry, fishing	230.5	7.5	17,600	6.5
Mining and quarrying	37.4	1.2	23,900	8.9
Manufacturing	166.5	5.4		
Construction	190.8	6.2	8,300	3.1
Public utilities	129.1	4.2	6,100	2.3
Transp. and commun.	288.9	9.4	22,900	8.5
Trade, hotels	515.2	16.7	60,700	22.5
Finance, real estate	371.0	12.0	9,200	3.4
Pub. admin., defense	269.1	8.7	20,400	7.6
Services	278.1	9.0	48,200	17.9
Other	609.0[7]	19.7[7]	52,100[8]	19.3[8]
TOTAL	3,085.6	100.0	269,500[9]	100.0

Public debt (external, outstanding; December 2008): U.S.$670,400,000.
Household income and expenditure (2008)[10]. Average household size 3.4; average annual income per household €7,284 (U.S.$10,669); sources of income: wages and salaries 61.4%, pension benefits 22.7%, agriculture 5.4%; expenditure: food and nonalcoholic beverages 35.2%, transportation 12.3%, housing and energy 12.0%, clothing and footwear 7.6%, communications 5.6%, household furnishings 5.6%.
Selected balance of payments data. Receipts from (U.S.$'000,000): tourism (2009) 659; remittances (2010) n.a.; foreign direct investment (FDI; 2008–10 avg.) 1,082; official development assistance (2009) 75. Disbursements for (U.S.$'000,000): tourism (2009) 49; remittances (2009) n.a.; FDI (2008–10 avg.) 61.

Foreign trade[11]

Balance of trade (current prices)

	2005	2006	2007	2008	2009	2010
€'000,000	–673.5	–1,016.3	–1,618.4	–2,113.5	–1,377.2	–1,326.9
% of total	47.7%	53.5%	64.0%	71.7%	71.3%	66.8%

Imports (2007): €2,134,377,900 (mineral fuels 11.6%, automobiles 11.4%, nonelectrical machinery and apparatus 9.0%, electrical machinery and apparatus 8.8%, base and fabricated metals 7.1%). *Major import sources* (2008): Serbia 33.2%; Italy 7.6%; Greece 7.3%; Croatia 6.7%; Bos.-Her. 6.5%.
Exports (2007): €599,020,700,000 (aluminum and aluminum products 47.0%, base metals 11.9%, beverages and tobacco 8.9%, mineral fuels 8.1%). *Major export destinations* (2008): Italy 30.1%; Serbia 24.9%; Greece 12.3%; Slovenia 8.6%; Bos.-Her. 5.1%.

Transport and communications

Transport. Railroads (2010): route length 155 mi, 250 km; passenger-km 91,000,000; metric ton-km cargo 151,000,000. Roads (2010): total length 4,824 mi, 7,763 km (paved 69%); passenger-km 81,000,000; metric ton-km cargo 167,000,000. Vehicles (2010): passenger cars 164,653; buses 1,140. Air transport (2008): passenger-km 348,000,000[12]; metric ton-km cargo, n.a.

Communications

Medium	date	number in '000s	units per 1,000 persons	Medium	date	number in '000s	units per 1,000 persons
Televisions	2008	...	...	PCs	2007	...	...
Telephones				Dailies	2009	62[13]	98[13]
Cellular	2010	1,170[14]	1,853[14]	Internet users	2009	280	449
Landline	2010	170	268	Broadband	2010	52[14]	83[14]

Education and health

Educational attainment (2005). Percentage of population age 15 and over having: no formal education 3.2%; incomplete primary education 6.8%; complete primary 22.5%; secondary 55.0%; higher 12.5%. *Literacy* (2003): total population age 15 and over literate 97.6%; males literate 99.6%; females literate 95.7%.

Education (2008–09)

	teachers	students	student/ teacher ratio	enrollment rate (%)
Primary (age 6–14)	5,039	74,130	14.7	...
Secondary/Voc. (age 15–18)	2,243	31,274	13.9	...
Tertiary	1,405	20,490	14.6	... (age 19–23)

Health (2009): physicians 1,346 (1 per 469 persons); hospital beds 3,922 (1 per 161 persons); infant mortality rate per 1,000 live births 5.7; undernourished population, n.a.

Military

Total active duty personnel (November 2010): 3,127 (army 80.0%, navy 12.8%, air force 7.2%); paramilitary 10,100. *Military expenditure as percentage of GDP* (2009): 1.4%; per capita expenditure U.S.$92.

[1]Four seats reserved for Albanians. [2]Serbian, Bosnian, Albanian, and Croatian can also be used as official languages per article 13 of the constitution. [3]Montenegro uses the euro as its official currency, even though it is not a member of the EU. [4]First results revised. [5]Includes nectarines. [6]Industrial consumption only. [7]Taxes on products less imputed bank service charges and less subsidies. [8]Unemployed. [9]Detail does not add to total given because of rounding. [10]Based on the 2008 Household Budget Survey. [11]Imports c.i.f.; exports f.o.b. [12]Montenegro Airlines. [13]Circulation of daily newspapers. [14]Subscribers.

Internet resources for further information:
- **Central Bank of Montenegro http://www.cb-mn.org/eng**
- **Statistical Office of the Republic of Montenegro http://www.monstat.org**

Morocco

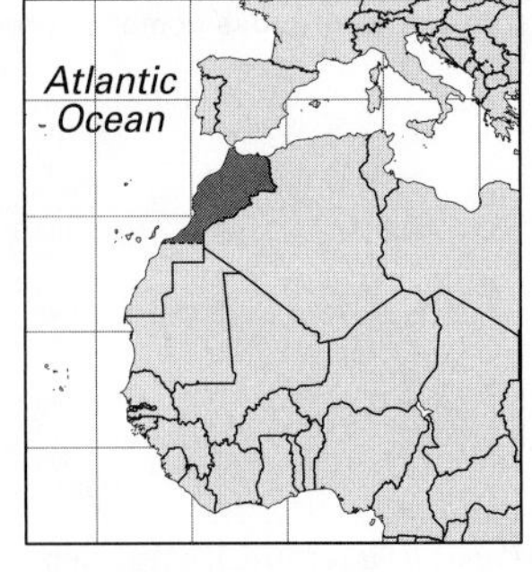

Official name: Al-Mamlakah al-Maghribiyyah (Kingdom of Morocco).
Form of government: constitutional monarchy with two legislative houses (House of Councillors [270[1]]; House of Representatives [395]).
Head of state: King.
Head of government: Prime Minister[2].
Capital: Rabat.
Official languages: Arabic; Tamazight[2].
Official religion: Islam.
Monetary unit: Moroccan dirham (DH); valuation (Sept. 1, 2011) 1 U.S.$ = DH 7.94; 1 £ = DH 12.83.

Area and population[3]

Regions	area sq km	population 2007 estimate	Regions	area sq km	population 2007 estimate
Chaouia-Ouardigha	16,845	1,685,000	Meknès-Tafilalet	60,407	2,191,000
Doukkala-Abda	13,285	2,020,000	Oriental	80,579	1,955,000
Fès-Boulemane	20,008	1,637,000	Oued Eddahab-Lagouira[6]	*120,000*	*135,000*
Gharb-Chrarda-Beni Hssen	8,936	1,912,000	Rabat-Salé-Zemmour-Zaër	10,226	2,500,000
Grand Casablanca	1,026	3,718,000	Souss-Massa-Drâa	73,207	3,244,000
Guelmim-Es Smara[4]	*130,500*	*491,000*	Tadla-Azilal	17,209	1,472,000
Laâyoune-Bojador-Sakia El-Hamra[5]	*76,300*	*284,000*	Tanger-Tétouan	12,745	2,586,000
Marrakech-Tensift-Al Haouz	31,881	3,187,000	Taza-Al Hoceima-Taounate	24,157	1,830,000
			TOTAL	694,420[7]	30,847,000

Demography

Area[3]: 268,117 sq mi, 694,420 sq km.
Population (2011)[3]: 32,476,000[8].
Density (2011)[3]: persons per sq mi 121.1, persons per sq km 46.8.
Urban-rural (2009)[9]: urban 57.6%; rural 42.4%.
Sex distribution (2008)[9]: male 49.28%; female 50.72%.
Age breakdown (2008)[9]: under 15, 29.1%; 15–29, 28.6%; 30–44, 21.0%; 45–59, 13.1%; 60–74, 6.0%; 75–84, 1.8%; 85 and over, 0.4%.
Population projection[3]: (2020) 35,608,000; (2030) 38,708,000.
Ethnic composition (2000): Amazigh (Berber) *c.* 45%, of which Arabized *c.* 24%; Arab *c.* 44%; Moors originally from Mauritania *c.* 10%; other *c.* 1%.
Religious affiliation (2004): Muslim more than 99% (including Sunnī *c.* 97%; Shīʿī *c.* 2%); other less than 1%.
Major urban agglomerations (2009): Casablanca 3,245,000; Rabat (incl. Salé) 1,770,000; Fès 1,044,000; Marrakech 909,000; Tangier 768,000.

Vital statistics

Birth rate per 1,000 population (2009): 19.2 (world avg. 20.3).
Death rate per 1,000 population (2009): 5.7 (world avg. 8.5).
Total fertility rate (avg. births per childbearing woman; 2009): 2.2.
Life expectancy at birth (2009): male 71.6 years; female 74.2 years.
Major causes of death per 100,000 population (2002): diseases of the circulatory system 201, of which ischemic heart disease 100; infectious and parasitic diseases 120; malignant neoplasms (cancers) 41; accidents and injuries 40.

National economy

Budget (2009). Revenue: DH 196,726,000,000 (indirect taxes 41.5%, direct taxes 37.6%, nontax revenue 7.5%, customs duties 6.0%, other 7.4%). Expenditures: DH 221,141,000,000 (current expenditure 75.0%, capital expenditure 17.3%, other 7.7%).
Public debt (external, outstanding; December 2009): U.S.$10,018,000,000.
Household income and expenditure. Average household size (2004) 5.3; expenditure (2006)[10]: food and nonalcoholic beverages 39.3%, housing and energy 14.8%, transportation 11.4%, health 5.5%, education 3.9%.
Population economically active (2008): total 11,458,500; activity rate 36.7% (participation rates: ages 15–59, 53.9%; female 27.2%; unemployed [July 2009–June 2010] 9.3%).
Production (metric tons except as noted). Agriculture, forestry, fishing (2009): wheat 6,400,000, barley 3,800,000, cow's milk 1,750,000, potatoes 1,500,000, tomatoes 1,300,000, oranges 1,200,000, olives 770,000, chicken meat 446,424, apples 400,000, string beans 182,180, almonds 104,115; livestock (number of live animals) 17,475,500 sheep, 2,861,200 cattle; roundwood (2010) 761,000 cu m, of which fuelwood 35%; fisheries production 1,163,457 (from aquaculture, negligible)[11]. Mining and quarrying (2008): phosphate rock 25,000,000; barite 660,000; zinc 96,900[12]; fluorspar 80,000; lead 33,500[12]; cobalt 1,711[12]; silver 230,000 kg[13]. Manufacturing (value added in U.S.$'000,000; 2007): food products 1,512; bricks, cement, and ceramics 1,105; base chemicals 925; tobacco products 871; wearing apparel 774. Energy production (consumption): electricity (kW-hr; 2009) 20,195,000,000 ([2007] 26,313,000,000); coal (metric tons; 2007) none (6,027,000); crude petroleum (barrels; 2008) 250,000 ([2007] 46,800,000); petroleum products (metric tons; 2007) 5,213,000 (7,760,000); natural gas (cu m; 2008) 36,000,000 ([2007] 648,000,000).
Selected balance of payments data. Receipts from (U.S.$'000,000): tourism (2009) 6,625; remittances (2010) 6,452; foreign direct investment (FDI; 2008–10 avg.) 1,914; official development assistance (2009) 912. Disbursements for (U.S.$'000,000): tourism (2009) 1,106; remittances (2009) 61; FDI (2008–10 avg.) 510.
Gross national income (GNI; 2009)[3]: U.S.$94,053,000,000 (U.S.$2,850 per capita); purchasing power parity GNI (U.S.$4,560 per capita).

Structure of gross domestic product and labour force

	2008		2006	
	in value DH '000,000	% of total value	labour force	% of labour force
Agriculture, forestry, fishing	90,690	13.2	4,303,300	39.1
Mining and quarrying	45,121	6.6		
Manufacturing	87,959	12.8	1,224,700	11.1
Public utilities	16,123	2.3		
Construction	38,663	5.6	789,600	7.2
Transp. and commun.	45,262	6.6	394,700	3.6
Trade, hotels	86,875	12.6	1,402,600	12.8
Pub. admin., defense	54,000	7.8	508,900	4.6
Finance, real estate; Services	154,939	22.5	1,292,800	11.8
Other	69,211[14]	10.0[14]	1,073,400[15]	9.8[15]
TOTAL	688,843	100.0	10,990,000	100.0

Land use as % of total land area (2009): in temporary crops 13.6%, left fallow 4.5%, in permanent crops 2.2%, in pasture 47.1%, forest area 11.4%.

Foreign trade[16]

Balance of trade (current prices)

	2004	2005	2006	2007	2008	2009
DH '000,000	–70,025	–85,115	–98,575	–132,613	–170,626	–153,188
% of total	28.5%	30.0%	31.5%	36.9%	35.2%	41.1%

Imports (2008): DH 327,995,000,000 (mineral fuels 22.3%, of which crude petroleum 9.4%; machinery and apparatus 19.9%; food 9.4%; road vehicles 6.9%). *Major import sources:* France 15.0%; Spain 11.2%; Italy 6.7%; Saudi Arabia 6.7%; China 5.7%.
Exports (2008)[17]: DH 157,369,000,000 (fertilizers [all kinds] 18.4%; inorganic chemicals 14.8%; outerwear 11.7%; fish/shrimp/octopuses 7.9%; insulated wire/cable 7.3%; vegetables/fruit/nuts 7.2%; petroleum 4.2%). *Major export destinations:* France 20.2%; Spain 17.9%; India 6.8%; Brazil 4.8%; Italy 4.7%.

Transport and communications

Transport. Railroads (2007): route length 1,185 mi, 1,907 km; (2008) passenger-km 3,836,000,000; (2008) metric ton-km cargo 4,985,000,000. Roads (2008): total length 36,199 mi, 58,256 km (paved 68%); passenger-km, n.a.; metric ton-km cargo 794,000,000. Vehicles (2007): passenger cars 1,644,523; trucks and buses 548,175. Air transport (2008)[18]: passenger-km 13,146,000,000; metric ton-km cargo 55,477,000.

Communications

Medium	date	number in '000s	units per 1,000 persons	Medium	date	number in '000s	units per 1,000 persons
Televisions	2004	5,010	164	PCs	2007	1,115	36
Telephones				Dailies	2009	340[19]	11[19]
Cellular	2010	31,982[20]	1,001[20]	Internet users	2009	10,300	322
Landline	2010	3,749[21]	117[21]	Broadband	2010	499[20]	16[20]

Education and health

Educational attainment (2004). Percentage of population age 10 and over having: no formal education through incomplete primary education 45.5%; complete primary 40.8%; secondary 8.7%; higher 5.0%. *Literacy* (2009): total population over age 15 literate *c.* 56%; males *c.* 69%; females *c.* 44%.

Education (2008–09)

	teachers	students	student/ teacher ratio	enrollment rate (%)
Primary (age 6–11)	144,722	3,850,994	26.6	90
Secondary/Voc. (age 12–17)	100,367[22]	2,173,454	18.7[22]	35[23]
Tertiary	19,598	418,833	21.4	13 (age 18–22)

Health (2009): physicians 19,703 (1 per 1,612 persons); hospital beds 35,888 (1 per 885 persons); infant mortality rate (2008) 17.0; undernourished population[3] (2005–07) less than 5.0% of total population.

Military

Total active duty personnel (November 2010): 195,800 (army 89.4%, navy 4.0%, air force 6.6%). *Military expenditure as percentage of GDP* (2009): 3.4%; per capita expenditure U.S.$101.

[1]All seats indirectly elected. [2]Per constitutional reforms adopted by referendum in July 2011. [3]Includes Western Sahara, annexure of Morocco whose political status has been unresolved since 1991; Western Sahara area: 252,120 sq km, 97,344 sq mi; Western Sahara population (2011 est.) 507,000. [4]About 50% of the land area of Guelmim-Es Smara is located within Western Sahara. [5]About 83% of the land area of Laâyoune-Bojador-Sakia El-Hamra is located within Western Sahara. [6]The entire area of Oued Eddahab-Lagouira is located within Western Sahara. [7]Total includes gross rounding of Western Sahara areas. [8]Estimates of U.S. Bureau of the Census International Database (June/December 2009 updates). [9]Excludes Western Sahara. [10]Weights of consumer price index components. [11]Roughly 60% of Morocco's fisheries production comes from Atlantic waters off of Western Sahara. [12]Metal content. [13]Including smelter bullion. [14]Import taxes and duties less subsidies. [15]Including 1,062,000 unemployed. [16]Imports c.i.f.; exports f.o.b. [17]Cannabis is an important illegal export; Morocco was the world's number 2 producer in 2009. [18]Royal Air Maroc and Atlas Blue airlines only. [19]Circulation. [20]Subscribers. [21]Includes fixed wireless. [22]2003–04. [23]2002–03.

Internet resources for further information:

- **Haut-Commissariat au Plan http://www.hcp.ma**
- **Bank al-Maghrib http://www.bkam.ma**

Mozambique

Official name: República de Moçambique (Republic of Mozambique).
Form of government: multiparty republic with a single legislative house (Assembly of the Republic [250]).
Head of state and government: President.
Capital: Maputo.
Official language: Portuguese.
Official religion: none.
Monetary unit: (new) metical (MTn; plural meticais)[1]; valuation (Sept. 1, 2011) 1 U.S.$ = MTn 26.65; 1 £ = MTn 43.07.

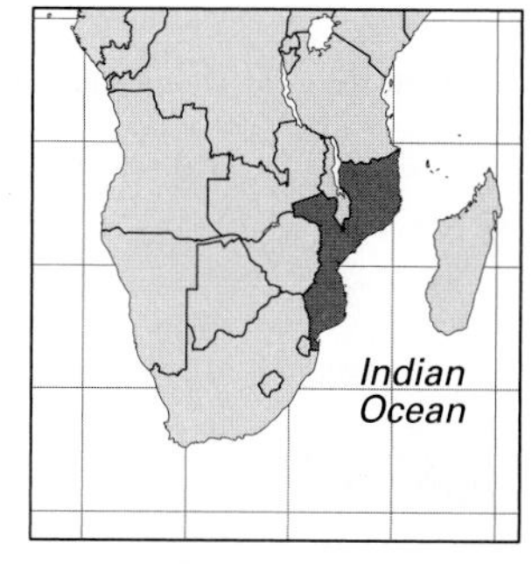

Area and population

		area		population
Provinces	**Capitals**	sq mi	sq km	2009 official estimate
Cabo Delgado	Pemba	31,902	82,625	1,698,000
Gaza	Xai-Xai	29,231	75,709	1,277,000
Inhambane	Inhambane	26,492	68,615	1,354,000
Manica	Chimoio	23,808	61,661	1,551,000
Maputo	Maputo	10,061	26,058	1,329,000
Nampula	Nampula	31,508	81,606	4,301,000
Niassa	Lichinga	49,828	129,056	1,309,000
Sofala	Beira	26,262	68,018	1,769,000
Tete	Tete	38,890	100,724	1,966,000
Zambézia	Quelimane	40,544	105,008	4,102,000
City				
Maputo	—	116	300	1,145,000
TOTAL		308,642	799,380	21,803,000[2]

Demography

Population (2011): 22,949,000.
Density (2011): persons per sq mi 74.4, persons per sq km 28.7.
Urban-rural (2011): urban 37.6%; rural 62.4%.
Sex distribution (2009): male 48.16%; female 51.84%.
Age breakdown (2009): under 15, 45.5%; 15–29, 26.7%; 30–44, 15.3%; 45–59, 7.8%; 60–74, 3.6%; 75 and over, 1.1%.
Population projection: (2020) 28,603,000; (2030) 36,622,000.
Doubling time: 31 years.
Ethnic composition (2000): Makuana 15.3%; Makua 14.5%; Tsonga 8.6%; Sena 8.0%; Lomwe 7.1%; Tswa 5.7%; Chwabo 5.5%; other 35.3%.
Religious affiliation (2005): traditional beliefs *c.* 46%; Christian *c.* 37%, of which Roman Catholic *c.* 19%, Protestant *c.* 11%; Muslim *c.* 9%; other *c.* 8%.
Major cities (2009): Maputo 1,120,200 (urban agglomeration 1,589,000); Matola 729,500; Nampula 515,300; Beira 442,000; Chimoio 253,300; Quelimane 200,800.

Vital statistics

Birth rate per 1,000 population (2009): 38.3 (world avg. 20.3).
Death rate per 1,000 population (2009): 15.7 (world avg. 8.5).
Natural increase rate per 1,000 population (2009): 22.6 (world avg. 11.8).
Total fertility rate (avg. births per childbearing woman; 2006): 5.35.
Life expectancy at birth (2009): male 49.6 years; female 53.8 years.
Adult population (ages 15–49) *living with HIV* (2009): 11.5%[3] (world avg. 0.8%).

National economy

Budget (2008). Revenue: MTn 69,107,000,000 (tax revenue 47.3%, grants 45.4%, nontax revenue 7.3%). Expenditures: MTn 83,220,000,000 (capital expenditures 48.6%, current expenditures 45.5%, net lending 5.9%).
Public debt (external, outstanding; 2008): U.S.$2,788,000,000.
Production (metric tons except as noted). Agriculture, forestry, fishing (2009): cassava 5,672,370, sugarcane 2,451,170, corn (maize) 1,437,040, sweet potatoes 838,410, coconuts 270,000, sorghum 214,800, pulses 166,940, bananas 109,310, rice 104,290, tobacco 75,660, peanuts (groundnuts) 68,000, cashews 67,850, castor oil seed 37,490; livestock (number of live animals) 4,324,760 goats, 1,266,350 pigs, 1,240,340 cattle, 18,000,000 chickens; roundwood (2010) 18,028,000 cu m, of which fuelwood 93%; fisheries production 68,291 (from aquaculture 1%). Mining and quarrying (2009): ilmenite concentrate 551,695; bauxite 3,612; tantalite 113,000 kg; garnet 2,648 kg; gold 511 kg[4]. Manufacturing (value added in MT '000,000,000; 2003): aluminum 19,067; beverages 4,773; food products 2,577; tobacco 581; chemicals and chemical products 297. Energy production (consumption): electricity (kW-hr; 2008) 14,975,000,000 (10,175,000,000); hard coal (metric tons; 2009) 26,300 (22,700); crude petroleum, none (none); petroleum products (metric tons; 2007) none (599,000); natural gas (cu m; 2009) 2,803,000,000 (113,268,000).
Household income and expenditure. Average household size (2004) 4.2; income per household: n.a.; sources of income (1992–93)[5]: wages and salaries 51.6%, self-employment 12.5%, barter 11.5%, private farming 7.7%; expenditure (1998)[5]: food, beverages, and tobacco 63.5%, firewood and furniture 17.0%, transportation and communications 4.6%, clothing and footwear 4.6%.
Population economically active (2008): total 10,750,000[6]; activity rate 48.0%[6] (participation rates: ages 15–64, 86.1%[6]; female 52.1%[6]; unemployed, n.a.).

Price index (2005 = 100)

	2004	2005	2006	2007	2008	2009	2010
Consumer price index	93.3	100.0	113.2	122.5	135.1	139.5	157.2

Gross national income (GNI; 2010): U.S.$10,344,000,000 (U.S.$440 per capita); purchasing power parity GNI (U.S.$920 per capita).

Structure of gross domestic product and labour force

	2008		2002	
	in value MTn '000,000	% of total value	labour force	% of labour force
Agriculture	67,231	28.0	7,837,000	80.8
Mining	3,350	1.4		
Manufacturing	30,906	12.9		
Construction	6,633	2.8		
Public utilities	11,322	4.7		
Transp. and commun.	22,237	9.3	1,859,000	19.2
Finance, real estate	22,852	9.5		
Trade, hotels	37,085	15.5		
Pub. admin., defense	8,518	3.6		
Services	16,219	6.8		
Other	13,423[7]	5.6[7]	...	...
TOTAL	239,775[8]	100.0[8]	9,696,000	100.0

Selected balance of payments data. Receipts from (U.S.$'000,000): tourism (2009) 196; remittances (2010) 118; foreign direct investment (2008–10 avg.) 789; official development assistance (2009) 2,013. Disbursements for (U.S.$'000,000): tourism (2009) 212; remittances (2009) 63.
Land use as % of total land area (2009): in temporary crops or left fallow (2007) 5.7%, in permanent crops 0.3%, in pasture 56.0%, forest area 49.9%.

Foreign trade[9]

Balance of trade (current prices)

	2005	2006	2007	2008	2009	2010
U.S.$'000,000	–625	–488	–638	–1,355	–1,400	–1,350
% of total	14.9%	9.3%	11.7%	20.3%	22.8%	17.4%

Imports (2008): U.S.$4,008,000,000 (refined petroleum 16.2%; machinery and apparatus 13.9%; food 10.7%, of which cereals 6.9%; road vehicles 9.9%; unspecified 16.8%). *Major import sources:* South Africa 29.1%; Netherlands 17.4%; Bahrain 6.7%; U.S. 4.0%; China 3.9%.
Exports (2008): U.S.$2,653,000,000 (aluminum 54.7%; electricity 8.5%; unmanufactured tobacco 7.3%; food 5.6%). *Major export destinations:* Netherlands 55.6%; South Africa 10.0%; Zimbabwe 3.0%; China 1.9%; Spain 1.9%.

Transport and communications

Transport. Railroads (2008): route length 1,821 mi, 2,931 km; passenger-km (2006) 342,000,000; metric ton-km cargo (2006) 775,000,000. Roads (2006): total length 11,063 mi, 17,805 km (paved 29%). Vehicles (2001): passenger cars 81,600; trucks and buses 76,000. Air transport (2008)[10]: passenger-km 502,000,000; metric ton-km cargo 6,700,000.

Communications

Medium	date	number in '000s	units per 1,000 persons	Medium	date	number in '000s	units per 1,000 persons
Televisions	2003	391	20	PCs	2005	283	14
Telephones				Dailies	2009	18[11]	1.5[11]
Cellular	2010	7,224[12]	309[12]	Internet users	2009	613	27
Landline	2010	88	3.8	Broadband	2010	15[12]	0.6[12]

Education and health

Educational attainment (1997). Percentage of population age 15 and over having: no formal schooling 78.4%; primary education 18.4%; secondary 2.0%; technical 0.4%; higher 0.2%; other/unknown 0.6%. *Literacy* (2008): percentage of total population age 15 and over literate 54.0%; males literate 69.5%; females literate 40.1%.

Education (2008–09)

	teachers	students	student/ teacher ratio	enrollment rate (%)
Primary (age 6–12)	82,753	5,076,283	61.3	82
Secondary/Voc. (age 13–17)	15,730	595,555	37.9	9
Tertiary[13]	3,009	28,298	9.4	1 (age 18–22)

Health: physicians (2003) 635 (1 per 30,525 persons); hospital beds (2003) 16,493 (1 per 1,175 persons); infant mortality rate per 1,000 live births (2009) 89.9; undernourished population (2004–06) 7,500,000 (37% of total population based on the consumption of a minimum daily requirement of 1,800 calories).

Military

Total active duty personnel (November 2010): 11,200 (army 89.3%, navy 1.8%, air force 8.9%). *Military expenditure as percentage of GDP* (2009): 0.9%; per capita expenditure U.S.$4.

[1]The (new) metical (MTn) replaced the (old) metical (MT) on July 1, 2006, at a rate of 1 MTn = MT 1,000. [2]Reported total; the summed total equals 21,801,000. [3]Statistically derived midpoint of range. [4]Official figures; unofficial artisanal production is 600–900 kg per year. [5]Weights of consumer price index components. [6]Estimate of the ILO Employment Trends Unit. [7]Taxes less subsidies and less imputed bank service charges. [8]Detail does not add to total given because of rounding. [9]Imports c.i.f.; exports f.o.b. [10]LAM (Linhas Aéreas de Moçambique) only. [11]Circulation of daily newspapers. [12]Subscribers. [13]2004–05.

Internet resources for further information:
- **Instituto Nacional de Estatística http://www.ine.gov.mz**
- **Banco de Moçambique http://www.bancomoc.mz**

Myanmar (Burma)

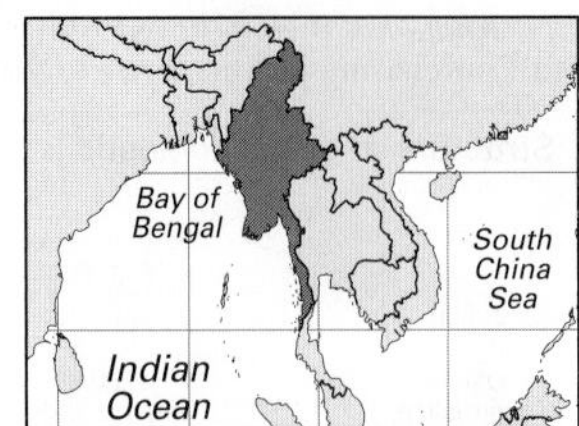

Official name: Pyihtaungsu Thamada Myanmar Naingngandaw (Republic of the Union of Myanmar)[1, 2].
Form of government: constitutional republic[1] with two legislative houses (House of Nationalities [224[3, 4]]; House of Representatives [440[3, 5]].
Head of state and government: President assisted by Vice Presidents.
Capital: Nay Pyi Taw (Naypyidaw).
Official language: Myanmar (Burmese).
Official religion: none[6].
Monetary unit: Myanmar kyat (K); valuation[7] (Sept. 1, 2011) 1 U.S.$ = K 6.41; 1 £ = K 10.36.

Area and population

	area	population		area	population
	sq km	2002 estimate		sq km	2002 estimate
Divisions			**States**		
Ayeyarwady			Chin	36,019	495,000
(Irrawaddy)	35,138	7,184,000	Kachin	89,041	1,364,000
Bago (Pegu)	39,404	5,327,000	Kayah	11,733	293,000
Magway			Kayin (Karen)	30,383	1,575,000
(Magwe)	44,820	4,873,000	Mon	12,297	2,672,000
Mandalay	37,024	7,246,000	Rakhine (Arakan)	36,778	2,915,000
Sagaing	94,625	5,655,000	Shan	155,801	5,061,000
Tanintharyi					
(Tenasserim)	43,343	1,455,000	**Union territory**[8]		
Yangôn	10,171	6,056,000	Nay Pyi Taw	...	...
			TOTAL	676,577	52,171,000

Demography

Population (2011): 54,000,000.
Density (2011): persons per sq mi 206.7, persons per sq km 79.8.
Urban-rural (2008): urban 32.6%; rural 67.4%.
Sex distribution (2008): male 49.49%; female 50.51%.
Age breakdown (2008): under 15, 25.7%; 15–29, 28.6%; 30–44, 23.4%; 45–59, 14.3%; 60–74, 6.2%; 75–89, 1.7%; 90 and over, 0.1%.
Population projection[9]: (2020) 59,126,000; (2030) 64,103,000.
Ethnic composition (2000): Burman 55.9%; Karen 9.5%; Shan 6.5%; Han Chinese 2.5%; Mon 2.3%; Yangbye 2.2%; Kachin 1.5%; other 19.6%.
Religious affiliation (2005): Buddhist *c.* 74%; Protestant *c.* 6%; Muslim *c.* 3%; Hindu *c.* 2%; traditional beliefs *c.* 11%; other *c.* 4%.
Major urban agglomerations (2007): Yangon (Rangoon) 4,088,000; Mandalay 961,000; Nay Pyi Taw (Naypyidaw) 930,000; Mawlamyine (Moulmein) 405,800[10]; Pathein (Bassein) 215,600[10]; Bago (Pegu) 200,900[10].

Vital statistics

Birth rate per 1,000 population (2009): 19.8 (world avg. 20.3).
Death rate per 1,000 population (2009): 8.3 (world avg. 8.5).
Total fertility rate (avg. births per childbearing woman; 2009): 2.32.
Life expectancy at birth (2009): male 61.9 years; female 66.6 years.
Major causes of death per 100,000 population (2002): infectious and parasitic diseases 477; cardiovascular diseases 258; injuries, accidents, and violence 92; malignant neoplasms (cancers) 74; chronic respiratory diseases 57.
Adult population (ages 15–49) *living with HIV* (2009): 0.6% (world avg. 0.8%).

National economy

Budget (2005–06). Revenue: K 819,534,000,000 (tax revenue 58.2%, of which taxes on goods and services 30.7%, taxes on individual income 25.2%; nontax revenue 41.8%). Expenditures: K 1,008,785,000,000 (economic affairs 34.3%, of which transport 19.7%; defense 19.6%; education 6.8%.
Public debt (external, outstanding; 2009): U.S.$6,320,000,000.
Production (metric tons except as noted). Agriculture, forestry, fishing (2009): rice 32,682,000, sugarcane 8,500,000, dry beans 3,000,000, peanuts (groundnuts) 1,362,070, corn (maize) 1,226,000, onions 1,050,000, sesame seeds 867,000, plantains 825,000, sunflower seeds 767,000, pigeon peas 765,000, coconuts 420,393, garlic 200,000; livestock (number of live animals) 13,000,000 cattle, 7,800,000 pigs, 125,000,000 chickens; roundwood (2010) 42,548,000 cu m, of which fuelwood 90%; fisheries production 3,545,036 (from aquaculture 22%). Mining and quarrying (2008–09): copper (2008; metal content) 6,900; jade 32,311,589 kg; rubies 1,751,355 carats; sapphires 1,313,723 carats; spinel 339,894 carats. Manufacturing (value added in U.S.$'000,000; 2003): nonelectrical machinery and apparatus 728; transportation equipment 483; fabricated metal products 254; food products, n.a.; cement (2008–09) 702,419 metric tons. Energy production (consumption): electricity (kW-hr; 2009–10) 5,850,000,000 (4,936,000,000); hard coal (metric tons; 2007) 1,075,000 (163,000); lignite (metric tons; 2007) 414,000 (113,000); crude petroleum (barrels; 2008–09) 7,058,000 ([2007] 6,121,000); petroleum products (metric tons; 2007) 807,000 (1,671,000); natural gas (cu m; 2009–10) 11,579,000,000 ([2007] 3,653,100,000).
Selected balance of payments data. Receipts from (U.S.$'000,000): tourism (2006) 46; remittances (2009) 148; foreign direct investment (2008–10 avg.) 770; official development assistance (2009) 357. Disbursements for (U.S.$'000,000): tourism (2006) 37; remittances (2008) 32.
Household income and expenditure. Average household size (2004) 5.0; average annual income per household: n.a.; sources of income: n.a.; expenditure (2001): food and nonalcoholic beverages 70.4%, fuel and lighting 6.6%, transportation 3.3%, clothing and footwear 2.4%.

Gross national income (2009): U.S.$18,989,000,000 (U.S.$380 per capita).

Structure of gross domestic product and labour force

	2009–10		1997–98	
	in value K '000,000,000	% of total value	labour force[11]	% of labour force[11]
Agriculture	12,889	38.2	12,093,000	65.9
Mining	328	1.0	121,000	0.7
Manufacturing	6,135	18.2	1,666,000	9.1
Construction	1,518	4.5	400,000	2.2
Public utilities	251	0.7	26,000	0.1
Transp. and commun.	4,568	13.5	495,000	2.7
Trade	6,890	20.4	1,781,000	9.7
Finance	23	0.1	1,485,000	8.1
Public administration	549	1.6		
Services, other	610	1.8	270,000	1.5
TOTAL	33,761	100.0	18,337,000	100.0

Population economically active (2008; ILO estimates): total 28,361,000; activity rate of total population 57.6% (participation rates: ages 15–64, 79.3%; female 45.5%; official unemployed 4.9%).

Price index (2005 = 100)

	2003	2004	2005	2006	2007	2008	2009
Consumer price index	87.5	91.4	100.0	120.0	162.0	205.4	208.5

Land use as % of total land area (2007): in temporary crops 15.7%, left fallow 0.5%, in permanent crops 1.7%, in pasture 0.5%, forest area 47.9%.

Foreign trade[12]

Balance of trade (current prices)

	2004–05	2005–06	2006–07	2007–08	2008–09	2009–10
K '000,000	+5,359	+9,132	+13,191	+16,878	+12,154	+18,452
% of total	19.1%	28.4%	28.1%	31.4%	19.6%	28.8%

Imports (2008–09): K 24,874,000,000 (nonelectrical machinery and transport equipment 29.1%; refined petroleum 12.8%; base and fabricated metals 7.3%; vegetable oils 6.5%). *Major import sources:* China 26.4%; Singapore 23.0%; Thailand 8.6%; Malaysia 7.9%; Indonesia 4.6%.
Exports (2008–09): K 37,028,000,000 (natural gas 33.3%; pulses [mostly beans] 12.1%; hardwood 6.9%, of which teak 2.7%; garments 4.1%; rice 3.9%; unspecified [including gemstones] 33.3%). *Major export destinations:* Thailand 38.7%; Singapore 12.5%; India 11.9%; Hong Kong 9.8%; China 9.1%.

Transport and communications

Transport. Railroads (2008–09): route length (2009) 3,126 mi, 5,031 km; passenger-km 5,466,155,000; metric ton-km cargo 883,650,000. Roads (2005): total length 16,800 mi, 27,000 km (paved 12%). Vehicles (2009): passenger cars 249,048; trucks and buses 79,987. Air transport (2008): passenger-km 166,000,000[13]; metric ton-km cargo (2007) 3,000,000. Inland waterway (2008–09): passenger-km 2,475,000,000; metric ton-km cargo 974,000,000.

Communications

Medium	date	number in '000s	units per 1,000 persons	Medium	date	number in '000s	units per 1,000 persons
Televisions	2004	373	8.1	PCs	2005	400	8.6
Telephones				Dailies	2009	420[14]	12[14]
Cellular	2009	448[15]	9.0[15]	Internet users	2009	110	2.2
Landline	2009	812	16	Broadband	2009	15[15]	0.3[15]

Education and health

Educational attainment: n.a. *Literacy* (2008): total population age 15 and over literate 89.2%; males literate 94.7%; females literate 91.9%.

Education (2007–08)

	teachers	students	student/ teacher ratio	enrollment rate (%)
Primary (age 5–9)	177,331	5,109,630	28.8	...
Secondary/Voc. (age 10–15)	82,001	2,828,868	34.5	49
Tertiary[16]	10,669	507,660	47.6	11 (age 16–20)

Health (2004–05): physicians 17,564 (1 per 2,660 persons); hospital beds 34,654 (1 per 1,350 persons); infant mortality rate (2009) 52.3; undernourished population (2004–06) 8,300,000 (17% of total population based on the consumption of a minimum daily requirement of 1,800 calories).

Military

Total active duty personnel (November 2010): 406,000 (army 92.4%, navy 3.9%, air force 3.7%). *Military expenditure as percentage of GDP* (2008): n.a.

[1]The military-backed constitution approved by referendum in May 2008 entered into force in March 2011, when the new 2-chamber union parliament convened for the first time. [2]Official long-form name of the country per the constitution effective on Jan. 31, 2011. [3]Statutory number. [4]Includes 56 nonelected seats. [5]Includes 110 nonelected seats. [6]The government promotes Theravada Buddhism over other religions. [7]The kyat is not freely traded internationally; the unofficial (but tolerated) black market rate in September 2010 was 1 U.S.$ = K 975. [8]Per the 2008 constitution effective Jan. 31, 2011. [9]Estimate from U.S. Census Bureau International Database (December 2009 update). [10]City population; 2004. [11]Employed only. [12]Imports c.i.f.; exports f.o.b.; for fiscal year April 1 through March 31. [13]Myanmar Airways only. [14]Circulation. [15]Subscribers. [16]2006–07.

Internet resources for further information:

- **Key Indicators for Asia and the Pacific http://www.adb.org/documents/books/key_indicators/2010**
- **Central Statistical Organization http://www.csostat.gov.mm**

Namibia

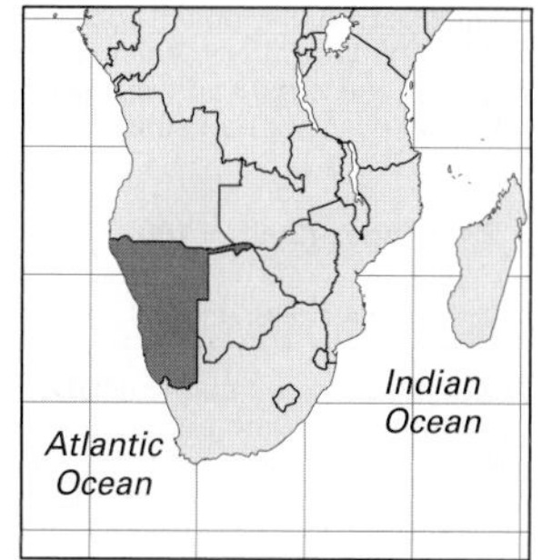

Official name: Republic of Namibia.
Form of government: republic with two legislative houses (National Council [26]; National Assembly [72[1]]).
Head of state and government: President.
Capital: Windhoek.
Official language: English.
Official religion: none.
Monetary unit: Namibian dollar (N$); valuation (Sept. 1, 2011) 1 U.S.$ = N$7.01; 1 £ = N$11.32.

Area and population

		area		population
Regions	**Capitals**	sq mi	sq km	2001 census
Caprivi	Katima Mulilo	5,609	14,528	79,826
Erongo	Swakopmund	24,548	63,579	107,663
Hardap	Mariental	42,336	109,651	68,249
Karas	Keetmanshoop	62,245	161,215	69,329
Kavango	Rundu	18,712	48,463	202,694
Khomas	Windhoek	14,288	37,007	250,262
Kunene	Opuwo	44,515	115,293	68,735
Ohangwena	Eenhana/Oshikango	4,132	10,703	228,384
Omaheke	Gobabis	32,669	84,612	68,039
Omusati	Outapi	10,260	26,573	228,842
Oshana	Oshakati	3,341	8,653	161,916
Oshikoto	Tsumeb	14,924	38,653	161,007
Otjozondjupa	Otjiwarongo/Grootfontein	40,612	105,185	135,384
TOTAL		318,193[2]	824,116[2]	1,830,330

Demography

Population (2011): 2,324,000.
Density (2011): persons per sq mi 7.3, persons per sq km 2.8.
Urban-rural (2009): urban 37.4%; rural 62.6%.
Sex distribution (2006): male 50.13%; female 49.87%.
Age breakdown (2006): under 15, 38.0%; 15–29, 31.5%; 30–44, 15.7%; 45–59, 9.2%; 60–74, 4.5%; 75–84, 0.9%; 85 and over, 0.2%.
Population projection: (2020) 2,672,000; (2030) 3,042,000.
Ethnic composition (2000): Ovambo 34.4%; mixed race (black/white) 14.5%; Kavango 9.1%; Afrikaner 8.1%; San (Bushmen) and Bergdama 7.0%; Herero 5.5%; Nama 4.4%; Kwambi 3.7%; German 2.8%; other 10.5%.
Religious affiliation (2000): Protestant (mostly Lutheran) 49.3%; Roman Catholic 17.7%; unaffiliated Christian 14.1%; independent Christian 10.8%; traditional beliefs 6.0%; other 2.1%.
Major urban localities (2009): Windhoek 306,100; Rundu 76,300; Walvis Bay 64,000; Oshakati 38,600; Swakopmund 32,400; Grootfontein 28,200.

Vital statistics

Birth rate per 1,000 population (2009): 27.1 (world avg. 20.3).
Death rate per 1,000 population (2009): 8.4 (world avg. 8.5).
Total fertility rate (avg. births per childbearing woman; 2006): 3.06.
Life expectancy at birth (2006): male 44.5 years; female 42.3 years.
Adult population (ages 15–49) *living with HIV* (2009): 13.1%[3] (world avg. 0.8%).

National economy

Budget (2008–09). Revenue: N$23,447,000,000 (tax revenue 90.5%, of which customs duties and excises 36.3%, VAT 17.5%, companies' income taxes 13.9%; nontax revenue 9.1%; grants 0.4%). Expenditures: N$21,946,000,000 (current expenditure 77.3%; capital expenditure 22.7%).
Public debt (external, outstanding; June 2010): U.S.$572,000,000[4].
Production (metric tons except as noted). Agriculture, forestry, fishing (2009): roots and tubers 293,876, cow's milk 111,700, cattle meat 59,808, corn (maize) 57,320, millet 37,301, grapes 18,788, sheep meat 14,308; livestock (number of live animals) 2,700,000 sheep, 2,500,000 cattle, 2,000,000 goats; roundwood (2010) 816,623 cu m, of which fuelwood 100%; fisheries production 369,976 (from aquaculture, negligible). Mining and quarrying (2009): salt 781,800; fluorspar 80,857; zinc (metal content) 47,000; lead (metal content) 20,000; copper (metal content; 2008) 7,471; uranium oxide 5,375[5]; silver 30,000 kg; gold 2,022 kg; diamonds 1,192,000 carats[6]. Manufacturing (value added in N$'000,000; 2009): food products and beverages 5,532 (of which fish processing 1,123, meat processing 227); other manufactures, which include fur products (from Karakul sheep), textiles, carved wood products, and refined metals 4,989. Energy production (consumption): electricity (kW-hr; 2007) 1,694,000,000 (3,699,000,000); coal (metric tons; 2007) none (77,000); crude petroleum, none (none); petroleum products (metric tons; 2007) none (916,000); natural gas, none (none).
Household income and expenditure (2003–04). Average household size[7] 4.9; average annual income per household[7] N$43,520 (U.S.$6,554); sources of income[7]: wages and salaries 46.4%, farming 29.6%, transfers 10.2%, self-employment 7.1%; expenditure (2006): food and nonalcoholic beverages 44.0%, housing and energy 15.1%, clothing and footwear 4.4%, remainder 36.5%.
Selected balance of payments data. Receipts from (U.S.$'000,000): tourism (2009) 363; remittances (2010) 15; foreign direct investment (2008–10 avg.) 698; official development assistance (2009) 326. Disbursements for (U.S.$'000,000): tourism (2009) 109; remittances (2009) 16.
Population economically active (2008): total 760,000[8]; activity rate of total population 35.7%[8] (participation rates: ages 15–64, 58.5%[8]; female 46.7%[8]; unofficially unemployed [September 2010] 35–51%).

Price index (2005 = 100)

	2004	2005	2006	2007	2008	2009	2010
Consumer price index	97.8	100.0	105.1	112.1	123.7	134.6	140.6

Gross national income (GNI; 2010): U.S.$10,286,000,000 (U.S.$4,650 per capita); purchasing power parity GNI (U.S.$6,580 per capita).

Structure of gross domestic product and labour force

	2009		2000	
	in value N$'000,000	% of total value	labour force	% of labour force
Agriculture, fishing	6,709	8.6	134,259	20.6
Mining	8,104	10.4	3,868	0.6
Manufacturing	10,521	13.5	22,922	3.5
Construction	2,883	3.7	21,788	3.3
Public utilities	1,934	2.5	4,193	0.7
Transp. and commun.	3,715	4.8	14,308	2.2
Trade, hotels	10,146	13.0	46,579	7.1
Finance, real estate	9,254	11.8	44,251	6.8
Services	11,289	14.4	112,172	17.2
Pub. admin., defense	8,088	10.3	24,419	3.7
Other	5,526[9]	7.1[9]	223,726[10]	34.3[10]
TOTAL	78,169	100.0[2]	652,483[2]	100.0

Land use as % of total land area (2009): in temporary crops or left fallow 1.0%; in permanent crops, negligible; in pasture 46.2%; forest area 8.9%.

Foreign trade[11]

Balance of trade (current prices)

	2004	2005	2006	2007	2008
U.S.$'000,000	+24.2	–11.9	+577.4	+14.3	+40.7
% of total	0.5%	0.2%	9.4%	0.2%	0.4%

Imports (2008): U.S.$4,688,600,000 (machinery and apparatus 17.5%; refined petroleum 12.8%; road vehicles 12.7%; food 10.8%; manufactures of metal 5.7%). *Major import sources:* South Africa 67.8%; U.K. 8.0%; India 3.5%; Neth. 3.4%; China 3.3%.
Exports (2008): U.S.$4,729,300,000 (food 18.0%, of which fish 10.4%, meat 3.6%; metal ores 17.8%, of which uranium 15.7%; printed matter 17.1%; diamonds 16.5%; zinc metal 6.0%). *Major export destinations:* South Africa 31.8%; U.K. 15.0%; Angola 8.6%; Canada 7.1%; U.S. 5.5%.

Transport and communications

Transport. Railroads: route length (2007) 1,634 mi, 2,629 km; passenger-km (2003) *c.* 50,000,000; metric ton-km cargo (2003–04) 1,247,400,000. Roads (2004): total length 26,245 mi, 42,237 km (paved 13%); passenger-km (2001) 73,000,000; metric ton-km cargo (2001) 555,000,000. Vehicles (2008): passenger cars 107,825; trucks and buses 119,806. Air transport[12]: passenger-km (2007) 1,710,000,000; metric ton-km cargo (2005) 60,429,000.

Communications

Medium	date	number in '000s	units per 1,000 persons	Medium	date	number in '000s	units per 1,000 persons
Televisions	2003	509	259	PCs	2007	504	240
Telephones				Dailies	2009	55[13]	25[13]
Cellular	2010	1,535[14]	672[14]	Internet users	2009	127	59
Landline	2010	152	67	Broadband	2010	9.6[14]	4.2[14]

Education and health

Educational attainment (2000)[15]. Percentage of population age 25 and over having: no formal schooling/unknown 26.5%; incomplete primary education 25.5%; complete primary 8.0%; incomplete secondary 24.9%; complete secondary 11.4%; higher 3.7%. *Literacy* (2009): total population age 15 and over literate 88.2%; males literate 88.7%; females literate 87.7%.

Education (2007–08)

	teachers	students	student/ teacher ratio	enrollment rate (%)
Primary (age 7–13)[16]	13,516	406,920	30.1	89
Secondary/Voc. (age 14–18)	6,695	163,873	24.5	54[17]
Tertiary	1,204	19,707	16.4	9 (age 19–23)

Health: physicians (2004) 598 (1 per 3,201 persons); hospital beds (2006) 6,759 (1 per 303 persons); infant mortality rate (2006) 48.1; undernourished population (2005–07) 400,000 (19% of total population based on the consumption of a minimum daily requirement of 1,790 calories).

Military

Total active duty personnel (November 2010): 9,200 (army 97.8%, navy 2.2%). *Military expenditure as percentage of GDP* (2009): 2.6%; per capita expenditure U.S.$145.

[1]Excludes 6 nonvoting members appointed by the president. [2]Detail does not add to total given because of rounding. [3]Statistically derived midpoint of range. [4]Combined foreign debt of central government and parastatals. [5]World rank no. 4. [6]World rank no. 8 in the production of all (both gem and industrial) diamonds. [7]Based on the National Household Income and Expenditure Survey 2003/04, comprising 10,920 households. [8]ILO estimate. [9]Taxes less imputed bank service charges and less subsidies. [10]Includes 220,634 unemployed. [11]Imports c.i.f.; exports f.o.b. [12]Air Namibia only. [13]Circulation. [14]Subscribers. [15]Based on the Namibia Demographic and Health Survey 2000, comprising 6,392 households. [16]2008–09. [17]2006–07.

Internet resources for further information:
- **Bank of Namibia http://www.bon.com.na**
- **Namibia Central Bureau of Statistics http://www.cbs.gov.na**

Nauru

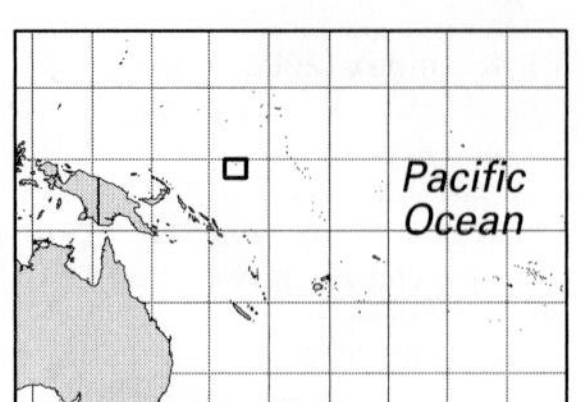

Official name: Naoero (Nauruan[1]) (Republic of Nauru).
Form of government: republic with one legislative house (Parliament [18]).
Head of state and government: President.
Capital: [2].
Official language: none[1].
Official religion: none.
Monetary unit: Australian dollar ($A); valuation (Sept. 1, 2011) 1 U.S.$ = $A 0.93; 1 £ = $A 1.50.

Area and population

	area		population
Districts	sq mi	sq km	2006 survey[3]
Aiwo	0.4	1.1	1,285
Anabar	0.6	1.5	473
Anetan	0.4	1.0	351
Anibare	1.2	3.1	116
Baitsi	0.5	1.2	657
Boe	0.2	0.5	825
Buada	1.0	2.6	657
Denigomodu	0.3	0.9	1,577[4]
Ewa	0.5	1.2	723
Ijuw	0.4	1.1	347
Meneng	1.2	3.1	1,509
Nibok	0.6	1.6	671
Uaboe	0.3	0.8	143
Yaren	0.6	1.5	635
TOTAL	8.2	21.2	9,968[5]

Demography

Population (2011): 9,300.
Density (2011): persons per sq mi 1,134, persons per sq km 438.7.
Urban-rural (2010): urban 100%.
Sex distribution (2010): male 50.79%; female 49.21%.
Age breakdown (2005): under 15, 37.5%; 15–29, 29.5%; 30–44, 17.8%; 45–59, 11.8%; 60–74, 3.1%; 75 and over, 0.3%.
Population projection: (2020) 9,800; (2030) 10,300.
Doubling time: 33 years.
Ethnic composition (2006): Nauruan 95.8%; Kiribertese (Gilbertese) 1.5%; Asian 1.4%; other Pacific Islanders 0.3%; other/unknown 1.0%.
Religious affiliation (2005): Protestant *c.* 49%, of which Congregational *c.* 29%; Roman Catholic *c.* 24%; Chinese folk-religionist *c.* 10%; other *c.* 17%.
Major cities: none; population of Yaren urban area (2007) 4,616.

Vital statistics

Birth rate per 1,000 population (2009): 29.8 (world avg. 20.3).
Death rate per 1,000 population (2009): 9.0 (world avg. 8.5).
Natural increase rate per 1,000 population (2009): 20.8 (world avg. 11.8).
Total fertility rate (avg. births per childbearing woman; 2007): 3.4[6].
Marriage/divorce rates per 1,000 population: n.a.
Life expectancy at birth (2008): male 52.5 years; female 58.2 years.
Major causes of death per 100,000 population (2008): diseases of the circulatory system 391; endocrine nutritional and metabolic diseases 98; diseases of the respiratory system 65; malignant neoplasms (cancers) 43.

National economy

Budget (2007). Revenue: $A 17,751,000 (grants 38.2%, property income 35.3%, sales of goods and services 13.1%, other taxes 13.4%). Expenditures: $A 21,-769,000.
Total public and private debt (July 2007): U.S.$854,000,000.
Gross national income (at current market prices; 2009): U.S.$54,338,800 (U.S.$5,322 per capita).

Distribution of gross domestic product and labour force

	2008–09		1997	
	in value $A '000,000	% of total value	labour force[7, 8, 9]	% of labour force[7, 8, 9]
Agriculture, fishing	2.8	4.0	...	...
Mining (phosphate)	10.2	14.7	528	24.7
Public utilities	5.8	8.3		
Manufacturing	17.3	24.9	...	...
Construction	2.3	3.3	...	...
Transportation and communications	6.4	9.2	...	...
Trade, hotels	6.7	9.5	137	6.4
Finance	2.9	4.2	33	1.6
Pub. admin.	4.9	7.1	1,238	58.0
Services	10.3	14.8	...	...
Other			198	9.3
TOTAL	69.5[10]	100.0	2,134	100.0

Production (metric tons except as noted). Agriculture, forestry, fishing (2009): coconuts 2,179, vegetables 463, tropical fruit 356, coffee, almonds, figs, and pandanus (screw pine) are also cultivated, but most foodstuffs and beverages (including water) are imported; livestock (number of live animals) 3,000 pigs, (2008) 5,000 chickens; roundwood, none; fisheries production 220 (from aquaculture, none). Mining and quarrying (2007): phosphate rock (gross weight including basic slag and guano) 45,000[11]. Manufacturing: none; virtually all consumer manufactures are imported. Energy production (consumption): electricity (kW-hr; 2007) 35,000,000 (35,000,000); coal, none (none); crude petroleum, none (none); petroleum products (metric tons; 2007) none (47,000); natural gas, none (none).
Population economically active (2002): 3,280[8]; activity rate of total population 32.6% (participation rates: over age 15, 76.7%; female 45.5%; unemployed [2006] 26.7%).

Price index (2005 = 100)

	2002	2003	2004	2005	2006	2007	2008
Consumer price index	92.5	95.4	97.7	100.0	103.2	106.2	111.0

Household income and expenditure (2006). Average household size 6.5; average annual income per household $A 9,550 (U.S.$7,199); sources of income: wages and salaries 68.7%, gifts 6.2%, imputed rent 5.4%, other 19.7%; expenditure: food and nonalcoholic beverages 52.1%, housing/energy/household furnishings 17.0%, gifts 8.8%, transportation 7.6%.
Selected balance of payments data. Receipts from (U.S.$'000,000): tourism, n.a.; remittances, n.a.; foreign direct investment (2008–10 avg.) 1.0; official development assistance (2009) 24. Disbursements for (U.S.$'000,000): tourism, n.a.; remittances, n.a.
Land use as % of total land area (2007): in temporary crops, n.a.; in permanent crops, n.a.; in pasture, n.a.; forest area, n.a.

Foreign trade

Balance of trade (current prices)

	2003–04	2004–05	2005–06
$A '000,000	–26.2	–26.5	–30.8
% of total	74.4%	94.3%	91.1%

Imports (2005–06): $A 32,300,000 (unspecified [mostly personal material needs] 100.0%). *Major import sources* (2005): South Korea *c.* 48%; Australia *c.* 36%; U.S. *c.* 6%; Germany *c.* 5%.
Exports (2005–06): $A 1,500,000 (phosphate, virtually 100%[11, 12]). *Major export destinations* (2005): South Korea *c.* 30%; Canada *c.* 24%; other *c.* 46%.

Transport and communications

Transport. Railroads (2008): route length 3.2 mi[13], 5.2 km[13]; passenger traffic, n.a.; metric ton-km cargo, n.a. Roads (2008): total length 10 mi[14], 16 km[14] (paved 100%). Vehicles: n.a. Air transport (2006): passenger-km 376,000,000; metric ton-km cargo 37,000,000[15].

Communications

Medium	date	number in '000s	units per 1,000 persons	Medium	date	number in '000s	units per 1,000 persons
Televisions	2002	0.8	77	PCs	2007	...	...
Telephones				Dailies	2009	0	0
Cellular	2010	6.2[16]	605[16]	Internet users	2009	...	...
Landline	2010	[17]	[17]	Broadband	2010	0.4[16]	39[16]

Education and health

Educational attainment (2007). Percentage of population age 15–49 and over having: incomplete/complete primary education 4%; incomplete secondary 71%; complete secondary 17%; more than secondary 8%. *Literacy* (2007): total population age 15 to 49 literate *c.* 98%; males literate 96.1%; females literate 99.3%.

Education (2007–08)

	teachers	students	student/ teacher ratio	enrollment rate (%)
Primary (age 6–11)	56	1,254	22.4	...
Secondary/Voc. (age 12–17)	57	816	14.3	...
Tertiary	—	—	—	... (age 18–22)

Health (2008): physicians 10 (1 per 957 persons); hospital beds 51 (1 per 188 persons); infant mortality rate per 1,000 live births (2003–07) 37.9[6]; undernourished population, n.a.

Military

Total active duty personnel (2010): Nauru does not have any military establishment. The defense is assured by Australia, but no formal agreement exists.

[1]Nauruan is the national language; English is the language of business and government. [2]No official capital; government offices are located in Yaren district. [3]Based on 2006 Nauru Household Income and Expenditure Survey. [4]Includes housing complex for foreign workers. The majority of foreign mine workers were repatriated to Kiribati and Tuvalu in 2006. [5]Reported total; summed total equals 9,969. [6]Based on 2007 Republic of Nauru Demographic and Health Survey. [7]Employed only. [8]Nauruan only. [9]Most non-Nauruans are phosphate industry contract workers. [10]Detail does not add to total given because of rounding. [11]Phosphate extraction, the backbone of the Nauruan economy, halted in 2003 but resumed in 2006. Expect phosphate extraction for the next 5 years (on the surface) to 20 years (from the subsurface) using processing refurbishments. [12]Coral gravel, a by-product of phosphate extraction, was exported in 2008. [13]Serves the phosphate workings. [14]Length of paved road circling Nauru. [15]Includes weight of passengers and mail. [16]Subscribers. [17]Landlines were decommissioned in Nauru by 2010.

Internet resources for further information:

- **Nauru Bureau of Statistics**
  http://www.spc.int/prism/country/nr/stats
- **Asian Development Bank Nauru Page**
  http://beta.adb.org/countries/nauru/main

Nepal

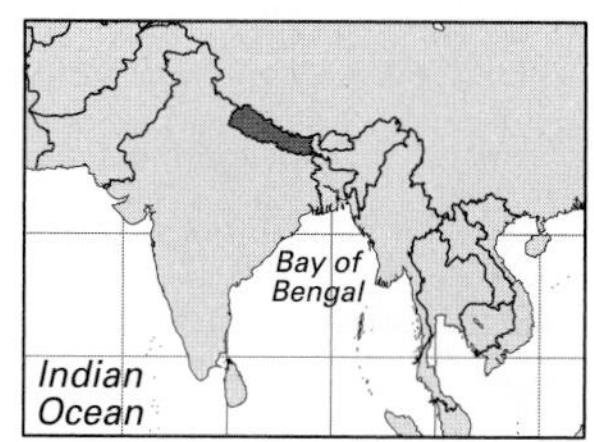

Official name: Sanghiya Loktantrik Ganatantra Nepal (Federal Democratic Republic of Nepal).
Form of government: multiparty republic with interim legislature (Constituent Assembly [601[1]])[2].
Head of state: President.
Head of government: Prime Minister.
Capital: Kathmandu.
Official language: Nepali.
Official religion: none.
Monetary unit: Nepalese rupee (NRs); valuation (Sept. 1, 2011) 1 U.S.$ = NRs 73.68; 1 £ = NRs 119.06.

Area and population

Development regions	Principal centres	area sq mi	area sq km	population 2011 census[3]
Eastern	Dhankuta	10,987	28,456	5,834,182
Central	Kathmandu	10,583	27,410	9,713,702
Western	Pokhara	11,351	29,398	4,945,190
Mid-western	Birendranagar	16,362	42,378	3,584,386
Far-western	Dipayal	7,544	19,539	2,543,349
TOTAL		56,827	147,181	26,620,809

Demography

Population (2011): 26,629,000.
Density (2011): persons per sq mi 468.6, persons per sq km 180.9.
Urban-rural (2006): urban 16.7%; rural 83.3%.
Sex distribution (2007): male 50.10%; female 49.90%.
Age breakdown (2005): under 15, 39.0%; 15–29, 27.9%; 30–44, 17.2%; 45–59, 10.2%; 60–74, 4.7%; 75–84, 0.9%; 85 and over, 0.1%.
Population projection: (2020) 30,759,000; (2030) 34,939,000.
Doubling time: 33 years.
Ethnic composition (2000): Nepalese 55.8%; Maithili 10.8%; Bhojpuri 7.9%; Tharu 4.4%; Tamang 3.6%; Newar 3.0%; Awadhi 2.7%; Magar 2.5%; Gurkha 1.7%; other 7.6%.
Religious affiliation (2001): Hindu 80.6%; Buddhist 10.7%; Muslim 4.2%; Kirat (local traditional belief) 3.6%; Christian 0.5%; other 0.4%.
Major cities (2001): Kathmandu 671,846; Biratnagar 166,674; Lalitpur 162,991; Pokhara 156,312; Birganj 112,484.

Vital statistics

Birth rate per 1,000 population (2008): 27.7 (world avg. 20.3).
Death rate per 1,000 population (2008): 8.3 (world avg. 8.5).
Natural increase rate per 1,000 population (2008): 19.4 (world avg. 11.8).
Total fertility rate (avg. births per childbearing woman; 2007): 3.10.
Life expectancy at birth (2008): male 63.6 years; female 64.5 years.
Major causes of death per 100,000 population (2002): infectious and parasitic diseases 472; diseases of the circulatory system 203, of which ischemic heart disease 95; accidents and injuries 86; malignant neoplasms (cancers) 63.

National economy

Budget (2007–08). Revenue: NRs 104,865,300,000 (tax revenue 81.1%, of which VAT 28.4%, customs duties 20.1%, corporate income tax 12.6%; nontax revenue 18.9%). Expenditures: NRs 151,969,500,000 (current expenditures 64.6%, of which education 16.8%, defense 6.7%, health 6.1%; capital expenditures 35.4%).
Production (metric tons except as noted). Agriculture, forestry, fishing (2009): rice 4,523,690, potatoes 2,424,048, sugarcane 2,354,412, corn (maize) 1,930,669, wheat 1,343,862, buffalo milk 1,031,500, millet 292,683, ginger 174,268, tangerines 172,058, buffalo meat 156,629, lentils 147,725, mustard seed 135,494, nutmeg 9,774; livestock (number of live animals) 8,473,082 goats, 7,175,198 cattle, 4,680,486 buffalo; roundwood (2010) 13,814,715 cu m, of which fuelwood 91%; fisheries production 48,230 (from aquaculture 55%). Mining and quarrying (2009): limestone 822,000; talc 9,000; marble 22,000 sq m. Manufacturing (value added in U.S.$'000,000; 2002): food products 83; textiles and wearing apparel 73; tobacco products 55; beverages 49; paints, soaps, and pharmaceuticals 42. Energy production (consumption): electricity (kW-hr; 2009) 2,853,000,000 (2,705,000,000); coal (metric tons; 2007) 9,000 (439,000); crude petroleum, none (none); petroleum products (metric tons; 2007) none (664,000); natural gas, none (none).
Gross national income (GNI; 2010): U.S.$14,529,000,000 (U.S.$490 per capita); purchasing power parity GNI (U.S.$1,200 per capita).

Structure of gross domestic product and labour force

	2009–10 in value NRs '000,000	2009–10 % of total value	2008 labour force[4]	2008 % of labour force[4]
Agriculture	372,560	31.5	8,704,000	73.9
Mining	5,782	0.5	27,000	0.2
Manufacturing	69,349	5.9	773,000	6.6
Construction	73,684	6.2	367,000	3.1
Public utilities	16,597	1.4	109,000	0.9
Transp. and commun.	108,394	9.2	198,000	1.7
Trade, restaurants, hotels	173,710	14.7	889,000	7.5
Finance, real estate	136,842	11.6	103,000	0.9
Pub. admin., defense	22,053	1.9	109,000	0.9
Services	131,333	11.1	494,000	4.2
Other	72,375[5]	6.1[5]	6,000	0.1
TOTAL	1,182,680[6]	100.0[6]	11,779,000	100.0

Population economically active (2008): total 12,929,000[7]; activity rate of total population 44.9%[7] (participation rates: ages 15–64, 73.7%[7]; female 45.4%[7]; unofficially unemployed [2004] c. 42%).

Price index (2005 = 100)

	2004	2005	2006	2007	2008	2009	2010
Consumer price index	93.6	100.0	107.6	114.1	126.6	141.3	155.4

Public debt (external, outstanding; 2009): U.S.$3,563,000,000.
Household income and expenditure (2005–06)[8]. Average household size (2011) 4.70; income per household NRs 328,692 (U.S.$4,439); sources of income: self-employment 29.5%, wages and salaries 28.1%, remittances 16.1%, real estate 10.2%; expenditure: food and beverages 38.9%, housing and energy 24.3%, recreation and culture 8.7%, education 7.6%, clothing and footwear 5.1%.
Selected balance of payments data. Receipts from (U.S.$'000,000): tourism (2009) 371; remittances (2010) 3,507; foreign direct investment (2008–10 avg.) 26; official development assistance (2009) 855. Disbursements for (U.S.$'000,000): tourism (2009) 434; remittances (2009) 12.
Land use as % of total land area (2009): in temporary crops 16.6%, left fallow 0.1%, in permanent crops 0.8%, in pasture 12.1%, forest area 25.4%.

Foreign trade[9]

Balance of trade (current prices)

	2003–04	2004–05	2005–06	2006–07	2007–08	2008–09
NRs '000,000	–82,366	–90,768	–113,546	–135,311	–162,671	–217,324
% of total	43.3%	43.6%	48.5%	53.3%	57.8%	61.8%

Imports (2008–09): NRs 284,571,000,000 (petroleum products 14.5%, machinery and apparatus 8.7%, transport equipment 7.6%, gold 5.8%, medicine 3.4%, unspecified 25.4%). *Major import sources* (2008): India c. 55%; China c. 13%; Singapore c. 2%.
Exports (2008–09): NRs 67,247,000,000 (textiles/thread/yarn 12.2%, pulses 9.9%, ready-made garments 9.7%, woolen carpets 8.4%, zinc sheets 4.2%, pashmina 2.4%, unspecified 25.1%). *Major export destinations* (2008): India c. 55%; U.S. c. 10%; Bangladesh c. 9%; Germany c. 5%.

Transport and communications

Transport. Railroads (2008): route length 33 mi, 53 km[10]; passenger-km (2006) 51,000,000; metric ton-km cargo (2006) 700,000. Roads (2007): total length 11,049 mi, 17,782 km (paved 30%). Vehicles (2007): passenger cars 93,266; trucks and buses 64,959. Air transport: passenger-km (2005) 873,000,000; metric ton-km cargo (2007) 8,000,000.

Communications

Medium	date	number in '000s	units per 1,000 persons	Medium	date	number in '000s	units per 1,000 persons
Televisions	2003	249	9.6	PCs	2005	132	4.9
Telephones				Dailies	2009	700[11]	39[11]
Cellular	2010	9,196[12]	307[12]	Internet users	2009	626	21
Landline	2010	842	28	Broadband	2010	114[12]	3.8[12]

Education and health

Educational attainment (2005–06)[8]. Percentage of population having: unknown through literate 15.4%; primary education 22.0%; secondary 44.0%; higher 18.6%. *Literacy* (2008): total population age 15 and over literate 57.9%; males literate 71.1%; females literate 45.4%.

Education (2008–09)

	teachers	students	student/ teacher ratio	enrollment rate (%)
Primary (age 5–9)	143,574	4,782,313	33.3	76[13]
Secondary/Voc. (age 10–16)[14]	56,294	2,305,166	40.9	...
Tertiary	...	289,262	...	6[15] (age 17–21)

Health (2006): physicians[16] 1,259 (1 per 21,737 persons); hospital beds 9,881 (1 per 2,801 persons); infant mortality rate per 1,000 live births (2007) 48.0; undernourished population (2005–07) 4,500,000 (16% of total population based on the consumption of a minimum daily requirement of 1,760 calories).

Military

Total active duty personnel (November 2010): 95,753[17] (army 100%). *Military expenditure as percentage of GDP* (2009): 4.2%; per capita expenditure U.S.$7.

[1]Includes 26 nonelected seats. [2]An interim constitution was promulgated Jan. 15, 2007; in November 2011 the Constituent Assembly's timetable to write a new permanent constitution was extended by six months. [3]Preliminary. [4]Employed only; excludes 2,100,000 workers ages 5–14. [5]Indirect taxes less imputed bank service charges and less subsidies. [6]Detail does not add to total given because of rounding. [7]Estimate of the ILO Employment Trends Unit. [8]Based on the Household Budget Survey 2005–06. [9]Imports c.i.f.; exports f.o.b. [10]20 mi (32 km) operational in 2008. [11]Circulation of daily newspapers. [12]Subscribers. [13]2006–07. [14]2007–08. [15]2003–04. [16]Public health system only. [17]Of which deployed as UN peacekeepers 4,080.

Internet resources for further information:
- **Central Bank of Nepal http://www.nrb.org.np**
- **Central Bureau of Statistics http://www.cbs.gov.np**

Netherlands

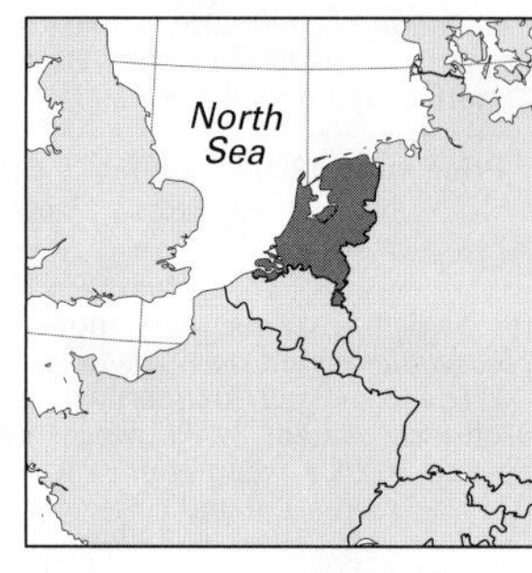

Official name: Koninkrijk der Nederlanden (Kingdom of the Netherlands).
Form of government: constitutional monarchy with a parliament (States General) comprising two chambers (Senate [75]; House of Representatives [150]).
Head of state: Monarch.
Head of government: Prime Minister.
Capital: Amsterdam.
Seat of government: The Hague.
Official language: Dutch[1].
Official religion: none.
Monetary unit: euro (€); valuation (Sept. 1, 2011) 1 U.S.$ = €0.70; 1 £ = €1.13.

Area and population

Provinces	area sq km	population 2010[2] estimate	Provinces	area sq km	population 2010[2] estimate
Drenthe	2,680	490,981	Noord-Holland	4,092	2,669,084
Flevoland	2,412	387,881	Overijssel	3,421	1,130,345
Friesland	5,741	646,305	Utrecht	1,449	1,220,910
Gelderland	5,137	1,998,936	Zeeland	2,934	381,409
Groningen	2,968	576,668	Zuid-Holland	3,403	3,505,611
Limburg	2,209	1,122,701	**Other admin.**[3]	322	18,012
Noord-Brabant	5,082	2,444,158	TOTAL	41,850	16,593,001

Demography

Population (2011): 16,683,000.
Density (2011)[4]: persons per sq mi 1,279, persons per sq km 493.8.
Urban-rural (2010): urban 82.9%; rural 17.1%.
Sex distribution (2011[2]): male 49.49%; female 50.51%.
Age breakdown (2011[2]): under 15, 17.5%; 15–29, 18.3%; 30–44, 20.5%; 45–59, 21.5%; 60–74, 15.2%; 75–84, 5.2%; 85 and over, 1.8%.
Population projection: (2020) 17,224,000; (2030) 17,630,000.
Ethnic composition (by place of origin[5]; 2011[2]): Netherlander 79.8%; from EU countries 5.5%; Indonesian 2.3%; Turkish 2.3%; German 2.3%; Surinamese 2.1%; Moroccan 2.1%; Netherlands Antillean/Aruban 0.8%; other 2.8%.
Religious affiliation (2004): Roman Catholic *c.* 30%; Reformed/Lutheran tradition *c.* 20%; Muslim *c.* 6%; nonreligious/atheist *c.* 40%; other *c.* 4%.
Major urban agglomerations (2011[2]): Amsterdam 1,525,081; Rotterdam 1,168,758; The Hague 1,026,469; Utrecht 634,957; Haarlem 414,364.

Vital statistics

Birth rate per 1,000 population (2010): 11.1 (world avg. 19.2); within marriage 58.9%; outside of marriage 41.1%.
Death rate per 1,000 population (2010): 8.2 (world avg. 8.2).
Total fertility rate (avg. births per childbearing woman; 2010): 1.8.
Marriage/divorce rates per 1,000 population (2009): 4.4[6]/1.9.
Life expectancy at birth (2010): male 78.8 years; female 82.7 years.
Major causes of death per 100,000 population (2010): malignant neoplasms (cancers) 254.3; diseases of the circulatory system 236.8; diseases of the respiratory system 78.1; accidents, poisoning, and violence 34.5.

National economy

Budget (2007). Revenue: €261,628,000,000 (social security contributions 31.3%; indirect taxes 28.3%; direct taxes 26.0%; nontax revenue 7.3%; sales tax 7.1%). Expenditures: €259,526,000,000 (current expenditure 92.3%, of which social security and welfare 45.3%; development expenditure 7.7%).
Production (metric tons except as noted). Agriculture, forestry, fishing (2010): potatoes 6,843,529, sugar beets 5,280,433, wheat 1,369,553, onions 1,252,294, tomatoes 815,000, carrots 481,000, cucumbers 430,000, peppers 365,000, apples 338,000, pears 274,000, mushrooms 220,000, corn (maize) 196,903, leeks 100,000, flowering bulbs and tubers (2009) 239,750 acres (97,000 hectares), of which tulips 29,660 acres (12,000 hectares), cut flowers/plants under glass 7,415 acres (3,000 hectares); livestock (number of live animals) 12,254,972 pigs, 3,975,194 cattle, 1,129,500 sheep; roundwood 1,080,593 cu m, of which fuelwood 27%; fisheries production (2009) 437,703 (from aquaculture 13%). Mining: limestone, n.a. Manufacturing (value added in €'000,000; 2008): food, beverages, and tobacco 16,198; petroleum products 8,094; base chemicals and man-made fibres 7,975; machinery and equipment 7,084; fabricated metal products 6,129; printing and publishing 5,946. Energy production (consumption): electricity (kW-hr; 2010–11) 113,265,000,000 (119,604,000,000); coal (metric tons; 2008) none ([2007] 13,503,000); crude petroleum (barrels; 2010–11) 7,487,040 ([2010] 368,285,000); petroleum products (metric tons; 2007) 55,574,000 (23,517,000); natural gas (cu m; 2010–11) 80,449,000,000 (48,379,000,000).
Land use as % of total land area (2007): in temporary crops or left fallow 31.4%, in permanent crops 1.0%, in pasture 24.3%, forest area 10.9%.
Population economically active (2010): total 8,761,000; activity rate of total population 52.7% (participation rates: ages 15 and older, 65.1%; female 46.0%; unemployed [October 2010–September 2011] 5.22%).

Price and earnings indexes (2005 = 100)

	2004	2005	2006	2007	2008	2009	2010
Consumer price index	98.3	100.0	101.1	102.8	105.3	106.6	107.9
Hourly earnings index	99.1	100.0	101.8	103.4	107.3	110.3	111.7

Gross national income (GNI; 2010): U.S.$826,491,000,000 (U.S.$49,720 per capita); purchasing power parity GNI (U.S.$42,590 per capita).

Structure of gross domestic product and labour force

	2008			
	in value €'000,000	% of total value	labour force[7]	% of labour force[7]
Agriculture, forestry, fishing	9,414	1.6	228,000	2.6
Mining and quarrying	21,579	3.6	11,000	0.1
Manufacturing	71,767	12.1	973,000	11.2
Construction	30,570	5.1	509,000	5.9
Public utilities	10,779	1.8	40,000	0.5
Transp. and commun.	35,007	5.9	512,000	5.9
Trade, hotels	75,857	12.7	1,523,000	17.5
Finance, real estate	149,658	25.1	1,344,000	15.4
Pub. admin., defense	58,675	9.9	541,000	6.2
Services	65,692	11.0	2,297,000	26.4
Other	66,885[8]	11.2[8]	723,000[9]	8.3[9]
TOTAL	595,883	100.0	8,701,000	100.0

Public debt (December 2008): U.S.$392,000,000,000.
Selected balance of payments data. Receipts from (U.S.$'000,000): tourism (2009) 13,346; remittances (2010) 4,079; foreign direct investment (FDI; 2008–10 avg.) 7,317. Disbursements for (U.S.$'000,000): tourism (2009) 20,757; remittances (2009) 8,142; FDI (2008–10 avg.) 42,105.
Household income and expenditure (2010). Average household size[2] 2.22; disposable income per household €35,380 (U.S.$46,884); sources of income (2003): wages 70.8%, transfers 25.3%, other 3.9%; expenditure: housing and energy 22.1%, transportation 14.5%, food and nonalcoholic beverages 11.2%.

Foreign trade[10]

Balance of trade (current prices)

	2004	2005	2006	2007	2008	2009
€'000,000	+27,413	+31,455	+32,724	+40,495	+34,761	+33,904
% of total	5.7%	5.9%	5.4%	6.2%	4.9%	5.8%

Imports (2008): €337,893,000,000 (machinery and apparatus 22.7%, of which office machines/computers/parts 7.7%; chemicals and chemical products 10.7%; crude petroleum 8.5%; food products 7.2%; refined petroleum 5.3%; road vehicles 5.0%). *Major import sources:* Germany 19.2%; Belgium 10.1%; U.S. 8.1%; China 7.4%; U.K. 6.3%.
Exports (2008): €372,654,000,000 (machinery and apparatus 22.9%, of which office machines/computers/parts 7.2%; chemicals and chemical products 13.4%; food 10.1%; refined petroleum 9.7%; bulbs/plants/flowers 1.7%). *Major export destinations:* Germany 24.5%; Belgium 11.6%; U.K. 9.1%; France 8.7%; Italy 5.3%.

Transport and communications

Transport. Railroads (2010[2]): route length 1,872 mi, 3,013 km; passenger-km (2009) 16,315,000,000; metric ton-km cargo (2007) 6,984,000,000. Roads (2010[2]): total length 85,343 mi, 137,347 km (paved 91%); passenger-km (2006) 160,000,000,000[11]; metric ton-km cargo 78,159,000,000. Vehicles (2010[2]): passenger cars 7,622,000; trucks and buses 1,094,000. Air transport (2008)[12]: passenger-km 88,774,000,000; metric ton-km cargo 4,646,000,000.

Communications

Medium	date	number in '000s	units per 1,000 persons	Medium	date	number in '000s	units per 1,000 persons
Televisions	2003	10,514	648	PCs	2007	14,934	912
Telephones				Dailies	2009	3,530[13]	213[13]
Cellular	2010	19,310[14]	1,162[14]	Internet users	2009	14,872	896
Landline	2010	7,169	432	Broadband	2010	6,308[14]	380[14]

Education and health

Educational attainment (2009). Percentage of population age 25 and older having: no formal schooling through lower secondary education 34.1%; upper secondary 34.4%; higher vocational 3.5%; university 28.0%.

Education (2008–09)

	teachers	students	student/ teacher ratio	enrollment rate (%)
Primary (age 6–11)	...	1,659,000[15]	...	99
Secondary/Voc. (age 12–17)	109,140	1,459,000[15]	13.4	88
Tertiary	50,029	618,502	12.4	63 (age 18–22)

Health: physicians (2008) 47,138 (1 per 349 persons); hospital beds (2009) 76,980 (1 per 215 persons); infant mortality rate (2010) 3.7.

Military

Total active duty personnel (November 2010): 37,368 (army 55.8%, navy 22.7%, air force 21.5%); military constabulary 5,911[16]. *Military expenditure as percentage of GDP* (2010): 1.4%; per capita expenditure U.S.$680.

[1]Frisian is officially recognized in Friesland but not legally codified by the national government. [2]January 1. [3]Refers to the special municipalities of Bonaire, Saba, and Sint Eustatius, which collectively are called the Caribbean Netherlands. [4]Based on land area. [5]Including second generation. [6]Includes same-sex marriages. [7]Ages 15 and over; per Labour Force Survey. [8]Taxes less imputed bank service charges and less subsidies. [9]Includes 479,000 unclassified and 244,000 unemployed. [10]Imports c.i.f.; exports f.o.b. [11]Passenger cars 148,000,000,000; buses 12,000,000,000. [12]KLM and Transavia only. [13]Circulation. [14]Subscribers. [15]2009–10. [16]U.S. troops (2010) 477.

Internet resources for further information:
- **Statistics Netherlands http://www.cbs.nl**
- **Netherlands Bank http://www.dnb.nl/en/home/index.jsp**

New Caledonia

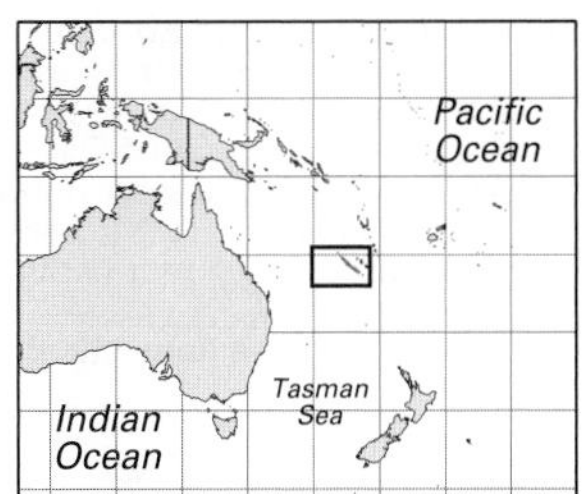

Official name: Territoire des Nouvelle-Calédonie et Dépendances (Territory of New Caledonia and Dependencies)[1].
Political status[2]: unique collectivity (France) with one legislative house (Congress[3] [54]).
Head of state: President of France.
Heads of government: High Commissioner (for France); President of the Government (for New Caledonia).
Capital: Nouméa.
Official language: none[4].
Official religion: none.
Monetary unit: CFP franc (CFPF); valuation (Sept. 1, 2011) 1 U.S.$ = CFPF 83.74; 1 £ = CFPF 135.32.

Area and population

Provinces Island(s)	Capitals	area sq mi	area sq km	population 2009 preliminary census
Loyauté (Loyalty)	Wé	765	1,981	17,436
Lifou		466	1,207	8,627
Maré		248	642	5,417
Ouvéa		51	132	3,392
Nord (Northern)	Koné	3,305	8,561	45,137
Bélep, Îles		27	70	895
New Caledonia (part)		3,278	8,491	44,242
Sud (Southern)	Nouméa	3,102	8,033	183,007
New Caledonia (part)		3,043	7,881	181,038
Pins, Île des		59	152	1,969
TOTAL		7,172	18,575	245,580

Demography

Population (2011): 255,000.
Density (2011): persons per sq mi 35.6, persons per sq km 13.7.
Urban-rural (2005): urban 63.7%; rural 36.3%.
Sex distribution (2008[5]): male 50.42%; female 49.58%.
Age breakdown (2008[5]): under 15, 26.7%; 15–29, 24.1%; 30–44, 22.8%; 45–59, 15.7%; 60–74, 8.2%; 75–84, 2.0%; 85 and over, 0.5%.
Population projection: (2020) 289,000; (2030) 323,000.
Doubling time: 60 years.
Ethnic composition (1996): Melanesian 45.3%, of which local (Kanak) 44.1%, Vanuatuan 1.2%; European 34.1%; Wallisian or Futunan 9.0%; Indonesian 2.6%; Tahitian 2.6%; Vietnamese 1.4%; other 5.0%.
Religious affiliation (2000): Roman Catholic 54.2%; Protestant 14.0%; unaffiliated/other Christian 18.8%; Muslim 2.7%; nonreligious 5.8%; other 4.5%.
Major communes (2009): Nouméa 97,579 (urban agglomeration 163,723); Mont-Dore 25,683[6]; Dumbéa 24,103[6]; Païta 16,358[6]; Koné 5,199.

Vital statistics

Birth rate per 1,000 population (2009): 16.7 (world avg. 20.3); within marriage (2007) 30.8%; outside of marriage (2007) 69.2%.
Death rate per 1,000 population (2009): 5.0 (world avg. 8.5).
Total fertility rate (avg. births per childbearing woman; 2007): 2.20.
Marriage/divorce rates per 1,000 population: (2009) 3.8/(2005) 1.5.
Life expectancy at birth (2007): male 71.8 years; female 80.3 years.
Major causes of death per 100,000 population (2007): malignant neoplasms (cancers) 132.0; diseases of the circulatory system 117.5; poisonings and violence 72.6; diseases of the respiratory system 49.1; accidents 25.6.

National economy

Budget (2008). Revenue: CFPF 163,834,000,000 (direct taxes 36.3%, indirect taxes 29.1%, subsidies 4.3%, other 30.3%). Expenditures: CFPF 184,661,000,000 (current expenditure 93.3%, development expenditure 6.7%).
Public debt: n.a.
Production (metric tons except as noted). Agriculture, forestry, fishing (2009): coconuts 16,506, yams 10,316, vegetables 6,435, cattle meat 3,181, sweet potatoes 2,641, cassava 2,394, pig meat 2,252, hen's eggs 2,159, potatoes 1,488, bananas 1,145; livestock (number of live animals) 90,000 cattle, 37,000 pigs, 600,000 chickens, 2,000 beehives; roundwood (2010) 26,518 cu m, of which fuelwood 45%; fisheries production 5,465, of which tuna 2,593, shrimp 1,860[7] (from aquaculture 35%). Mining and quarrying (2009): nickel ore 6,400,000, of which nickel content 92,500; cobalt 1,000 (recovered). Manufacturing (metric tons; 2008): cement (2007) 134,000; ferronickel (metal content) 38,548; nickel matte (metal content) 13,564; other manufactures include beer, copra cake, and soap. Energy production (consumption): electricity (kW-hr; 2009) 1,944,000,000 (1,820,000,000); coal (metric tons; 2007) none (244,000); petroleum products (metric tons; 2007) none (697,000).
Land use as % of total land area (2009): in temporary crops or left fallow 0.4%, in permanent crops 0.3%, in pasture 13.1%, forest area 45.9%.
Population economically active (2004): total 96,406; activity rate of total population 41.8% (participation rates: over age 14, 57.1%; female [1996] 39.7%; registered unemployed [July 2008–June 2009] 6.8%).

Price index (December 2005 = 100)

	2004	2005	2006	2007	2008	2009	2010
Consumer price index[8]	97.5	100.0	101.5	103.3	107.1	107.3	110.1

Gross national income (2009): U.S.$9,283,000,000 (U.S.$37,124 per capita).

Structure of gross domestic product and labour force

	2004		2009	
	in value CFPF '000,000	% of total value	labour force[9]	% of labour force[9]
Agriculture, fishing	10,105	1.8	2,258	2.7
Mining	55,336	9.8	1,241	1.5
Public utilities	9,392	1.7	829	1.0
Manufacturing	29,530	5.2	8,389	10.2
Construction	46,496	8.2	8,415	10.2
Transp. and commun.	39,517	7.0	4,269	5.2
Trade, hotels	76,720	13.6	13,192	16.0
Finance, real estate	69,048	12.2	8,351	10.1
Pub. admin., defense	99,253	17.5	24,477	29.6
Services	84,662	15.0	11,162	13.5
Other	45,469[10]	8.0[10]	...	...
TOTAL	565,528	100.0	82,583	100.0

Household income and expenditure. Average household size (2004) 3.6; average annual income per household, n.a.; sources of income (2008): wages and salaries 67.1%, transfer payments 18.3%, self-employment 9.6%, other 5.0%; expenditure (2008): housing and energy 30.8%, food and beverages 19.5%, transportation 19.1%.
Selected balance of payments data. Receipts from (U.S.$'000,000): tourism (2009) 141; remittances (2010) 638; foreign direct investment (FDI; 2008–10 avg.) 1,274. Disbursements for (U.S.$'000,000): tourism (2009) 170; remittances (2009) 66; FDI (2008–10 avg.) 67.

Foreign trade[11]

Balance of trade (current prices)

	2004	2005	2006	2007	2008	2009
U.S.$'000,000	–627.0	–659.7	–862.3	–779.5	–1,636.5	–673.2
% of total	23.7%	22.8%	27.5%	19.1%	33.4%	26.0%

Imports (2008): U.S.$3,268,600,000 (mineral fuels 18.6%, of which refined petroleum 16.4%; machinery and apparatus 18.4%; road vehicles 12.7%; food 9.0%; chemicals and chemical products 7.0%). *Major import sources:* France 26.1%; Singapore 16.9%; Australia 10.0%; China 6.0%; Germany 4.7%.
Exports (2008): U.S.$1,632,100,000 (ferronickel 49.4%; nickel matte 31.9%; nickel ore and concentrate 13.7%; shrimp 1.2%). *Major export destinations:* France 33.2%; Japan 17.0%; Taiwan 10.7%; Spain 7.1%; Australia 5.8%.

Transport and communications

Transport. Railroads: none. Roads (2005): total length 3,061 mi, 4,926 km (paved 47%). Vehicles: passenger cars (2005) 105,159; trucks and buses, n.a. Air transport (2008)[12]: passenger-km 1,498,000,000; metric ton-km cargo 26,127,000.

Communications

Medium	date	number in '000s	units per 1,000 persons	Medium	date	number in '000s	units per 1,000 persons
Televisions	2004	115	498	PCs	2007	...	...
Telephones				Dailies	2009	26[13]	156[13]
Cellular	2010	221[14]	880[14]	Internet users	2009	85	340
Landline	2010	72	288	Broadband	2010	38[14]	152[14]

Education and health

Educational attainment (2004). Percentage of population age 25 and over having: no formal schooling through some primary education 38.1%; primary 9.5%; lower secondary 6.4%; upper secondary 11.8%; vocational 19.8%; higher 14.4%. *Literacy* (2002): total population age 15 and over literate 91.0%; males literate 92.0%; females literate 90.0%.

Education (2009)

	teachers	students	student/ teacher ratio	enrollment rate (%)
Primary (age 6–10)	1,966	36,502	18.6	...
Secondary/Voc. (age 11–17)	2,763	32,463	11.7	...
Tertiary	111[15]	3,735	26.4[15]	... (age 18–22)

Health: physicians (2008) 550 (1 per 448 persons); hospital beds (2007) 696 (1 per 348 persons); infant mortality rate per 1,000 live births (2008) 6.1; undernourished population (2005–07) *c.* 20,000 (9% of total population based on the consumption of a minimum daily requirement of 1,880 calories).

Military

Total active duty personnel (November 2010): *c.* 1,240 French troops (army *c.* 58%, navy *c.* 41%, air force, n.a., gendarmerie *c.* 1%).

[1]Locally known as Kanaky. [2]The Nouméa Accord granting New Caledonia limited autonomy was signed in May 1998; future referenda concerning possible independence are to be held between 2014 and 2018. [3]Operates in association with 3 provincial assemblies. [4]Kanak languages and French have special recognition per Nouméa Accord. [5]January 1. [6]Within Nouméa urban agglomeration. [7]All from aquaculture. [8]As of December. [9]Employed only. [10]Taxes and subsidies less imputed bank service charges. [11]Imports c.i.f.; exports f.o.b. [12]Air Calédonie International only. [13]Circulation of daily newspapers. [14]Subscribers. [15]2005.

Internet resources for further information:

- **L'Institut d'Emission d'Outre-Mer**
  http://www.ieom.fr
- **Institut de la statistique et des études économiques Nouvelle-Calédonie**
  http://www.isee.nc

New Zealand

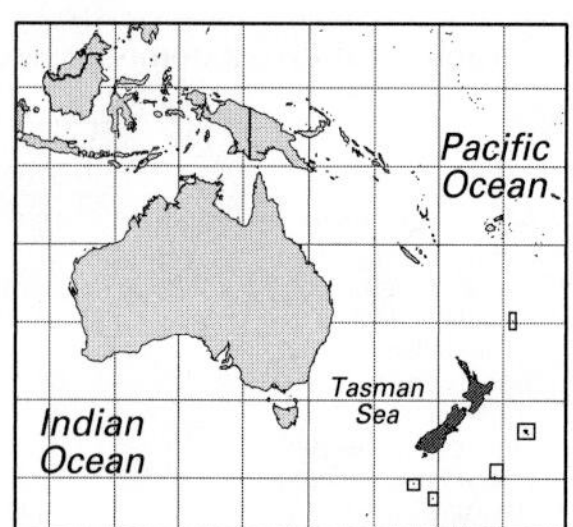

Official name: New Zealand (English); Aotearoa (Maori).
Form of government: constitutional monarchy with one legislative house (House of Representatives [121[1]]).
Head of state: British Monarch, represented by Governor-General.
Head of government: Prime Minister.
Capital: Wellington.
Official languages: English; Maori; New Zealand Sign Language[2].
Official religion: none.
Monetary unit: New Zealand dollar (NZ$); valuation (Sept. 1, 2011) 1 U.S.$ = NZ$1.18; 1 £ = NZ$1.90.

Area and population

Islands / Regional Councils/ Unitary Council	area sq km	population 2010[3] estimate	Islands / Regional Councils/ Unitary Council	area sq km	population 2010[3] estimate
North Island[4]	116,219	3,329,000	South Island[4, 5]	152,229[6]	1,038,100
Auckland[7]	6,059	1,459,700	Canterbury	44,638	565,700
Bay of Plenty	12,277	275,100	Marlborough (district)[8]	10,781	45,300
Gisborne (district)[8]	8,355	46,600	Nelson (city)[8]	444	45,500
Hawke's Bay	14,111	154,800	Otago	31,241	207,400
Manawatu-Wanganui	22,206	231,500	Southland[5]	32,079	94,200
Northland	13,789	157,400	Tasman (district)[8]	9,771	47,300
Taranaki	7,257	109,100	West Coast	23,276	32,700
Waikato	24,025	411,500	offshore islands[9]	2,244	700
Wellington	8,140	483,300	TOTAL	270,692	4,367,800

Demography

Population (2011): 4,407,000.
Density (2011): persons per sq mi 42.2, persons per sq km 16.2.
Urban-rural (2010): urban 86.0%; rural 14.0%.
Sex distribution (2010): male 49.10%; female 50.90%.
Age breakdown (2009): under 15, 20.7%; 15–29, 21.0%; 30–44, 20.6%; 45–59, 19.8%; 60–74, 12.1%; 75–84, 4.3%; 85 and over, 1.5%.
Population projection: (2020) 4,758,000; (2030) 5,085,000.
Ethnic composition (2006): European 67.6%, of which NZ European 59.1%; Maori (local Polynesian) 14.6%; Asian 9.2%, of which Chinese 3.7%; other Pacific peoples (mostly other Polynesian) 6.9%; other 1.7%.
Religious affiliation (2006): Christian 51.1%, of which Anglican 13.3%, Roman Catholic 12.2%, Presbyterian 9.2%, Maori Christian 1.6%; Hindu 1.6%; Buddhist 1.3%; Muslim 1.0%; nonreligious 31.1%; unknown/other 13.9%.
Major urban areas (2010): Auckland 1,354,900; Christchurch 390,300; Wellington 389,700; Hamilton 203,400; Napier-Hastings 124,400.

Vital statistics

Birth rate per 1,000 population (2010): 14.6 (world avg. 19.2); within marriage (2009) 51.5%; outside of marriage (2009) 48.5%.
Death rate per 1,000 population (2010): 6.5 (world avg. 8.2).
Total fertility rate (avg. births per childbearing woman; 2008): 2.18.
Marriage/divorce rates per 1,000 population (2010): 4.8/2.0.
Life expectancy at birth (2009): male 78.8 years; female 82.7 years.
Major causes of death per 100,000 population (2006): diseases of the circulatory system 258.9, of which ischemic heart disease 141.2, cerebrovascular disease 63.8; malignant neoplasms (cancers) 191.0; diseases of the respiratory system 57.0.

National economy

Budget (2007). Revenue: NZ$65,859,000,000 (tax revenue 85.3%, of which individual income taxes 41.3%; nontax revenue 14.5%; social contributions 0.2%). Expenditures: NZ$60,247,000,000 (social protection 33.9%; education 16.7%; health 16.7%; defense 3.2%).
Public debt (June 2009): U.S.$25,500,000,000.
Production (metric tons except as noted). Agriculture, forestry, fishing (2009): cow's milk 15,400,000, cattle meat 637,030, potatoes 490,000, sheep meat 478,380, kiwifruit 390,000, apples 357,000, grapes 210,500, green onions[10] 203,000, wool 179,240; livestock (number of live animals) 32,383,600 sheep, 9,961,500 cattle; roundwood (2010) 20,210,000 cu m, of which fuelwood, none; fisheries production 542,874 (from aquaculture 19%). Mining and quarrying (2009): iron sand 585,000; gold 13,442 kg[11]; silver 14,264 kg[11]. Manufacturing (value added in U.S.$'000,000; 2007): food products 5,053; structural metal products 1,359; publishing 1,131; general purpose machinery 1,106; sawn/planed wood 988. Energy production (consumption): electricity (kW-hr; 2010–11) 43,261,000,000 ([2008] 39,020,000,000); hard coal (metric tons; 2009) 5,228,000 ([2007] 185,000); lignite (metric tons; 2009) 316,400 ([2007] 2,897,000); crude petroleum (barrels; 2010) 19,400,000 ([2007] 33,600,000); petroleum products (metric tons; 2007–08) 5,187,000 ([2007] 6,086,000); natural gas (cu m; 2010) 4,474,000,000 (4,474,000,000).
Land use as % of total land area (2009): in temporary crops or left fallow (2007) 3.2%, in permanent crops 0.3%, in pasture 41.6%, forest area 31.4%.
Population economically active (2008): total 2,283,200; activity rate 53.5% (participation rates: ages 15–64, 77.5%; female 46.8%; unemployed[12] 6.7%).

Price index (2005 = 100)

	2004	2005	2006	2007	2008	2009	2010
Consumer price index	96.9	100.0	103.2	105.8	109.9	112.0	115.3

Household income and expenditure. Average household size (2007) 2.8; average annual income per household (2008–09) NZ$78,876 (U.S.$47,245); sources of income (2008–09): wages and salaries 72.9%, transfers/pensions 11.3%, self-employment 5.7%; expenditure (2006–07): housing and energy 23.4%, food 16.3%, transportation 14.2%, recreation and culture 10.1%.
Gross national income (GNI; 2009–10): U.S.$115,816,000,000 (U.S.$26,754 per capita); purchasing power parity GNI ([2008] U.S.$25,090 per capita).

Structure of gross domestic product and labour force

	2008–09		2007	
	in value NZ$'000,000[13]	% of total value	labour force	% of labour force
Agriculture, forestry	9,645	7.2	154,400	6.9
Mining			5,100	0.2
Public utilities	2,522	1.9	8,800	0.4
Manufacturing	17,612	13.2	274,400	12.3
Construction	6,010	4.5	183,100	8.2
Transp. and commun.	14,334	10.7	115,400	5.2
Trade, hotels	20,015	15.0	485,700	21.7
Finance, real estate	36,793	27.6	320,400	14.3
Pub. admin., defense	6,673	5.0	136,100	6.1
Services	15,947	11.9	461,700	20.7
Other	3,935	2.9	90,300	4.0
TOTAL	133,486	100.0[6]	2,235,400	100.0

Selected balance of payments data. Receipts from (U.S.$'000,000): tourism (2009) 4,396; remittances (2010) 845; foreign direct investment (FDI; 2008–10 avg.) 1,289. Disbursements for (U.S.$'000,000): tourism (2009) 2,559; remittances (2009) 871; FDI (2008–10 avg.) 248.

Foreign trade[14]

Balance of trade (current prices)

	2005	2006	2007	2008	2009	2010
U.S.$'000,000	–4,489	–4,015	–3,959	–3,789	–633	+774
% of total	9.4%	8.3%	6.8%	5.8%	1.3%	1.3%

Imports (2008): U.S.$34,367,000,000 (machinery and apparatus 21.3%; road vehicles 9.8%; crude petroleum 9.7%; food 7.5%; refined petroleum 7.3%). *Major import sources:* Australia 18.0%; China 13.3%; U.S. 9.5%; Japan 8.2%; Singapore 4.6%.
Exports (2008): U.S.$30,578,000,000 (food 47.0%, of which meat 12.3%, milk/cream 11.3%, vegetables/fruits 4.9%, butter 4.0%; wood/paper [all forms] 7.8%; machinery and apparatus 6.9%; crude petroleum 6.5%). *Major export destinations:* Australia 23.3%; U.S. 10.2%; Japan 8.4%; China 5.9%; U.K. 3.9%.

Transport and communications

Transport. Railroads (2008): route length 2,565 mi, 4,128 km; passenger-km, n.a.; metric ton-km cargo (2008–09) 3,962,000,000. Roads (2008): total length 58,288 mi, 93,805 km (paved 66%); passenger-km (2007) 40,000,000,000[15]; metric ton-km cargo (2008) 19,538,000,000. Vehicles (2009[16]): passenger cars 2,789,676; trucks and buses 570,557. Air transport (2008)[17]: passenger-km 27,539,000,000; metric ton-km cargo 851,000,000.

Communications

Medium	date	number in '000s	units per 1,000 persons	Medium	date	number in '000s	units per 1,000 persons
Televisions	2004	2,338	576	PCs	2005	2,077	507
Telephones				Dailies	2009	632[18]	146[18]
Cellular	2010	5,020[19, 20]	1,149[19]	Internet users	2009	3,600	844
Landline	2010	1,870[20]	428	Broadband	2010	1,089[19, 21]	249[19]

Education and health

Educational attainment (2007). Percentage of population age 15 and over having: no formal schooling/incomplete primary education 26.8%; primary 9.0%; vocational 29.8%; secondary 15.0%; higher 19.4%. *Literacy* (2006): 89%.

Education (2007–08)

	teachers	students	student/ teacher ratio	enrollment rate (%)
Primary (age 5–10)	22,730	348,160	15.3	99
Secondary/Voc. (age 11–17)	35,504	514,563	14.5	91[22]
Tertiary	13,767	244,355	17.7	78 (age 18–22)

Health: physicians (2007) 9,757 (1 per 433 persons); hospital beds (2002) 23,825 (1 per 165 persons); infant mortality rate per 1,000 live births (2009) 4.6; undernourished population (2004–06) less than 5.0% of total population.

Military

Total active duty personnel (November 2010): 9,673 (army 50.7%, navy 22.3%, air force 27.0%); reserve 2,314. *Military expenditure as percentage of GDP* (2009): 1.2%; per capita expenditure U.S.$315.

[1]Statutory number is 120 seats; actual current number is 121 seats. [2]Became official Aug. 10, 2006. [3]Midyear. [4]Includes nearby islands, islets, or water areas that are within regional councils. [5]Includes Stewart Island (Rakiura). Stewart Island's area is 1,681 sq km. [6]Detail does not add to total given because of rounding. [7]Functions under a new local government structure (as a unitary council) from Nov. 1, 2010. [8]A unitary authority that is administered by a city council or district council with regional powers. [9]Distant islands including Chatham Islands regional council (area: 963 sq km, pop. 700). [10]Includes shallots. [11]Mine output, metal content. [12]April 2010–March 2011. [13]At constant prices of 1995/96. [14]Imports c.i.f.; exports f.o.b. [15]Passenger cars/vans/pickup trucks 37,000,000,000; buses/heavy trucks 3,000,000,000. [16]January 1. [17]Air New Zealand only. [18]Circulation. [19]Subscribers. [20]June. [21]December. [22]2001–02.

Internet resource for further information:
- **Statistics New Zealand/Tatauranga Aotearoa http://www.stats.govt.nz**

Nicaragua

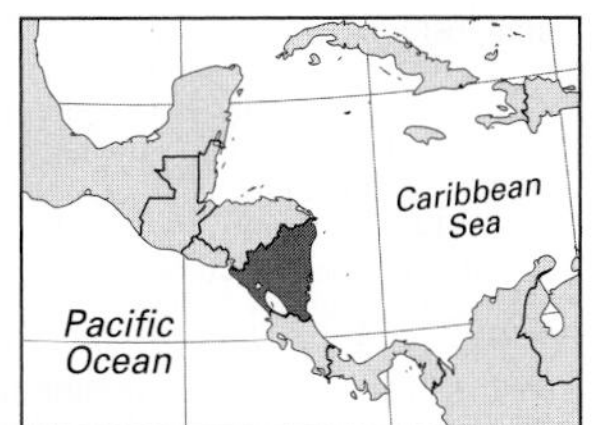

Official name: República de Nicaragua (Republic of Nicaragua).
Form of government: unitary multiparty republic with one legislative house (National Assembly [92[1]]).
Head of state and government: President.
Capital: Managua.
Official language: Spanish.
Official religion: none.
Monetary unit: córdoba (C$); valuation (Sept. 1, 2011) 1 U.S.$ = C$22.61; 1 £ = C$36.53.

Area and population

Departments	Capitals	area[2] sq mi	area[2] sq km	population 2008 estimate
Boaco	Boaco	1,613	4,177	164,700
Carazo	Jinotepe	417	1,081	176,107
Chinandega	Chinandega	1,862	4,822	409,987
Chontales	Juigalpa	2,502	6,481	171,654
Estelí	Estelí	861	2,230	216,462
Granada	Granada	402	1,040	189,344
Jinotega	Jinotega	3,561	9,222	376,129
León	León	1,984	5,138	392,096
Madriz	Somoto	659	1,708	146,477
Managua	Managua	1,338	3,465	1,365,315
Masaya	Masaya	236	611	326,452
Matagalpa	Matagalpa	2,627	6,804	507,335
Nueva Segovia	Ocotal	1,348	3,491	229,950
Río San Juan	San Carlos	2,912	7,541	105,747
Rivas	Rivas	835	2,162	167,141
Autonomous regions				
North Atlantic	Puerto Cabezas	12,782	33,106	382,498
South Atlantic	Bluefields	10,525	27,260	341,472
TOTAL LAND AREA		46,464	120,340[3]	
INLAND WATER		3,874	10,034	
TOTAL		50,337[3]	130,373[3]	5,668,866

Demography

Population (2011): 5,870,000.
Density (2011)[4]: persons per sq mi 126.3, persons per sq km 48.8.
Urban-rural (2005): urban 55.9%; rural 44.1%.
Sex distribution (2008): male 50.03%; female 49.97%.
Age breakdown (2008): under 15, 34.6%; 15–29, 31.3%; 30–44, 19.3%; 45–59, 9.8%; 60–74, 3.1%; 75–84, 0.9%; 85 and over, 1.0%.
Population projection: (2020) 6,603,000; (2030) 7,240,000.
Doubling time: 36 years.
Ethnic composition (2000): mestizo (Spanish/Indian) 63.1%; white 14.0%; black 8.0%; multiple ethnicities 5.0%; other 9.9%.
Religious affiliation (2005): Roman Catholic 58.5%; Protestant/independent Christian 23.2%, of which Evangelical 21.6%, Moravian 1.6%; nonreligious 15.7%; other 2.6%.
Major cities (2005)[5]: Managua 908,892; León 139,433; Chinandega 95,614; Masaya 92,598; Estelí 90,294.

Vital statistics

Birth rate per 1,000 population (2008): 23.7 (world avg. 20.3).
Death rate per 1,000 population (2008): 4.3 (world avg. 8.5).
Natural increase rate per 1,000 population (2008): 19.4 (world avg. 11.8).
Total fertility rate (avg. births per childbearing woman; 2008): 2.63.
Marriage/divorce rates per 1,000 population (2006): 4.2/1.1.
Life expectancy at birth (2008): male 69.1 years; female 73.4 years.
Major causes of death per 100,000 population (2002)[6]: diseases of the circulatory system 131.0; accidents, injuries, and violence 69.3; malignant neoplasms 60.6; communicable diseases 49.0; diabetes mellitus 28.1.

National economy

Budget (2008). Revenue: U.S.$1,209,700,000 (tax revenue 92.6%, of which taxes on goods and services 32.7%, taxes on international trade 30.0%, tax on income and profits 29.8%; nontax revenue 7.4%). Expenditures: U.S.$1,641,600,000 (education 20.7%; health 14.4%; economic services 14.4%; defense and public order 11.4%).
Public debt (external, outstanding; 2009): U.S.$2,461,000,000.
Production (metric tons except as noted). Agriculture, forestry, fishing (2009): sugarcane 4,690,390, cow's milk 747,809, corn (maize) 522,024, rice 334,516, dry beans 213,464, peanuts (groundnuts) 167,371, coffee 91,131, oranges 89,221, plantains 60,089, pineapples 53,532, bananas 46,595; livestock (number of live animals) 3,600,000 cattle, 268,000 horses; roundwood (2010) 6,117,718 cu m, of which fuelwood 99%; fisheries production 54,801, of which lobster 3,643 (from aquaculture 35%). Mining and quarrying (2009): gold 1,337 kg. Manufacturing (value added in C$'000,000; 2003[7]): food 1,917; textiles and wearing apparel 969; beverages 713; wood products (including furniture) 503. Energy production (consumption): electricity (kW-hr; 2008) 3,313,400,000 (2,193,900,000); coal, none (none); crude petroleum (barrels; 2007) none (5,996,000); petroleum products (metric tons; 2007) 787,000 (1,417,000); natural gas, none (none).
Household income and expenditure. Average household size (2005) 4.9; expenditure (1999)[8]: food and beverages 41.8%, education 9.8%, housing 9.8%, transportation 8.5%.
Population economically active (2009): total 2,282,700; activity rate of total population 39.7% (participation rates: ages 10 and over, 51.8%; female [2005] 35.2%; officially unemployed 8.2%).

Price index (2005 = 100)

	2004	2005	2006	2007	2008	2009	2010
Consumer price index	91.2	100.0	109.1	121.3	145.3	150.7	158.9

Gross national income (GNI; 2010): U.S.$6,282,000,000 (U.S.$1,080 per capita); purchasing power parity GNI (U.S.$2,610 per capita).

Structure of gross domestic product and labour force

	2009 in value C$'000,000	% of total value	labour force	% of labour force
Agriculture, forestry	21,003.5	16.8	600,807	26.3
Mining	1,433.9	1.1	5,723	0.3
Manufacturing	22,085.9	17.7	274,617	12.0
Construction	5,893.6	4.7	99,411	4.4
Public utilities	3,257.5	2.6	10,948	0.5
Transp. and commun.	6,835.2	5.5	86,644	3.8
Trade, restaurants	17,713.3	14.2	486,012	21.3
Finance, real estate	15,713.2	12.6	82,653	3.6
Pub. admin., defense	15,750.5	12.6	449,662	19.7
Services	8,263.2	6.6		
Other	7,118.8[9]	5.7[9]	186,223[10]	8.2[10]
TOTAL	125,068.6	100.0[3]	2,282,700	100.0[3]

Selected balance of payments data. Receipts from (U.S.$'000,000): tourism (2009) 346; remittances (2010) 820; foreign direct investment (FDI; 2008–10 avg.) 523; official development assistance (2009) 774. Disbursements for (U.S.$'000,000): tourism (2009) 147; remittances, n.a.; FDI (2008–10 avg.) 15.
Land use as % of total land area (2009): in temporary crops or left fallow 15.8%, in permanent crops 1.9%, in pasture 25.1%, forest area 26.5%.

Foreign trade[11]

Balance of trade (current prices)

	2004	2005	2006	2007	2008	2009
U.S.$'000,000	–1,266	–1,520	–1,724	–2,073	–2,434	–1,832
% of total	45.6%	47.0%	45.6%	46.5%	45.3%	39.7%

Imports (2007): U.S.$3,538,000,000 (petroleum 21.6%, machinery and apparatus 14.9%, food 12.3%, road vehicles 6.9%, medicines 5.8%). *Major import sources:* U.S. 23.0%; Mexico 13.1%; Costa Rica 8.6%; China 7.9%; Guatemala 6.1%.
Exports (2007): U.S.$1,195,000,000 (coffee 15.8%, bovine meat 15.0%, milk/cream/cheese 7.8%, raw sugar 6.1%, crustaceans 5.9%, gold 5.4%, vegetables 4.7%, peanuts [groundnuts] 4.7%). *Major export destinations:* U.S. 31.2%; El Salvador 14.1%; Honduras 9.3%; Costa Rica 7.3%; Canada 5.8%.

Transport and communications

Transport. Railroads: [12]. Roads (2007): total length 12,634 mi, 20,333 km (paved 10%). Vehicles (2007): passenger cars 101,899; trucks and buses 187,526. Air transport: passenger-km (2000) 72,200,000; metric ton-km cargo (2007) 200,000.

Communications

Medium	date	number in '000s	units per 1,000 persons	Medium	date	number in '000s	units per 1,000 persons
Televisions	2003	648	123	PCs	2005	220	43
Telephones				Dailies	2009	170[13]	44[13]
Cellular	2010	3,771[14]	651[14]	Internet users	2009	200	35
Landline	2010	258	45	Broadband	2010	48[14]	8.2[14]

Education and health

Educational attainment (2005). Percentage of population age 10 and over having: no formal schooling 20.1%; 1–3 years 16.6%; 4–6 years 27.0%; 7–9 years 16.1%; 10–12 years 10.5%; vocational 2.3%; incomplete university 2.6%; complete university 4.4%; unknown 0.4%. *Literacy* (2005): total population age 15 and over literate 78.0%; males literate 78.1%; females literate 77.9%.

Education (2007–08)

	teachers	students	student/ teacher ratio	enrollment rate (%)
Primary (age 6–11)	32,349	944,341	29.2	92
Secondary/Voc. (age 12–16)	16,164	462,198	28.6	45
Tertiary	...	103,577[15]	...	18[15] (age 17–21)

Health (2008): physicians 3,776 (1 per 1,501 persons); hospital beds 4,971 (1 per 1,140 persons); infant mortality rate (2005) 26.4; undernourished population (2005–07) 1,100,000 (19% of total population based on the consumption of a minimum daily requirement of 1,770 calories).

Military

Total active duty personnel (November 2010): 12,000 (army 83.3%, navy 6.7%, air force 10.0%). *Military expenditure as percentage of GDP* (2009): 0.6%; per capita expenditure U.S.$7.

[1]Includes the runner-up in the presidential election and the immediate past president. [2]Lakes and lagoons are excluded from the areas of departments and autonomous regions. [3]Detail does not add to total given because of rounding. [4]Based on land area. [5]Populations of urban area of *municipios*. [6]Estimates. [7]At prices of 1994. [8]Weights of consumer price index components. [9]Taxes less imputed bank service charges. [10]Unemployed. [11]Imports f.o.b. in balance of trade and c.i.f. in commodities and trading partners. [12]Public railroad service ended in 1994; private rail service ended in 2001. [13]Circulation. [14]Subscribers. [15]2002–03.

Internet resources for further information:
- **Central Bank of Nicaragua http://www.bcn.gob.ni**
- **Instituto Nacional de Estadísticas y Censos http://www.inide.gob.ni**

Niger

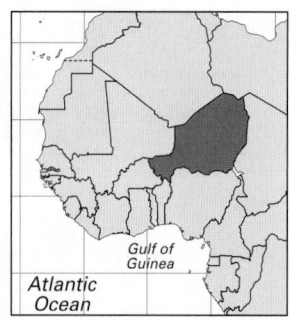

Official name: République du Niger (Republic of Niger).
Form of government: republic with one legislative house (National Assembly [113])[1].
Head of state: President of Supreme Council for the Restoration of Democracy[1, 2].
Head of government: Prime Minister.
Capital: Niamey.
Official language: French.
Official religion: none.
Monetary unit: CFA franc (CFAF); valuation (Sept. 1, 2011) 1 U.S.$ = CFAF 460.31; 1 £ = CFAF 743.83.

Area and population

		area		population
				2010
Regions	**Capitals**	sq mi	sq km	estimate
Agadez	Agadez	257,839	667,799	487,313
Diffa	Diffa	60,582	156,906	473,563
Dosso	Dosso	13,067	33,844	2,016,690
Maradi	Maradi	16,138	41,796	3,021,169
Tahoua	Tahoua	43,773	113,371	2,658,099
Tillabéri	Tillabéri	37,549	97,251	2,500,454
Zinder	Zinder	60,146	155,778	2,824,468
City				
Niamey	Niamey	155	402	1,222,066
TOTAL		489,200[3]	1,267,000[3]	15,203,822

Demography

Population (2011): 16,469,000[4].
Density (2011): persons per sq mi 33.7, persons per sq km 13.0.
Urban-rural (2009): urban 19.8%; rural 80.2%.
Sex distribution (2008): male 50.02%; female 49.98%.
Age breakdown (2008): under 15, 49.6%; 15–29, 25.6%; 30–44, 13.7%; 45–59, 7.2%; 60–74, 3.3%; 75 and over, 0.6%.
Population projection[4]: (2020) 22,749,000; (2030) 31,946,000.
Doubling time: 19 years.
Ethnolinguistic composition (2001): Hausa 55.4%; Zarma-Songhai-Dendi 21.0%; Tuareg 9.3%; Fulani (Peul) 8.5%; Kanuri 4.7%; other 1.1%.
Religious affiliation (2005): Muslim *c.* 90%, of which Sunnī *c.* 85%, Shīʿī *c.* 5%; traditional beliefs *c.* 9%; other *c.* 1%.
Major cities (2001): Niamey 707,951 (urban agglomeration [2009] 1,004,000); Zinder 170,575; Maradi 148,017; Agadez 78,289; Tahoua 73,002.

Vital statistics

Birth rate per 1,000 population (2008): 52.2 (world avg. 20.3).
Death rate per 1,000 population (2008): 15.2 (world avg. 8.5).
Natural increase rate per 1,000 population (2008): 37.0 (world avg. 11.8).
Total fertility rate (avg. births per childbearing woman; 2008): 7.83.
Marriage/divorce rates per 1,000 population (2008): n.a./n.a.
Life expectancy at birth (2008): male 51.0 years; female 53.4 years.
Major causes of death per 100,000 population (2002): infectious and parasitic diseases (significantly malaria, meningitis, pneumonia, and diarrhea) 1,697; diseases of the circulatory system 121; malignant neoplasms (cancers) 50; diseases of the respiratory system 34.

National economy

Budget (2009–10). Revenue: CFAF 485,500,000,000 (tax revenue 71.3%; external aid and grants 24.5%; nontax revenue 3.5%; other 0.7%). Expenditures: CFAF 567,700,000,000 (current expenditures 52.6%, of which wages and salaries 16.9%; capital expenditures 47.4%).
Public debt (external, outstanding; 2009): U.S.$909,000,000.
Selected balance of payments data. Receipts from (U.S.$'000,000): tourism (2008) 79; remittances (2010) 88; foreign direct investment (FDI; 2008–10 avg.) 751; official development assistance (2009) 470. Disbursements for (U.S.$'000,000): tourism (2008) 68; remittances (2009) 22; FDI (2008–10 avg.) 16.
Gross national income (GNI; 2010): U.S.$5,689,000,000 (U.S.$360 per capita); purchasing power parity GNI (U.S.$700 per capita).

Structure of gross domestic product and labour force

	2008			
	in value CFAF '000,000	% of total value	labour force[5, 6]	% of labour force[5, 6]
Agriculture, forestry, fishing	1,010,389	43.3	72,000	2.0
Mining and quarrying	106,358	4.6	29,000	0.8
Manufacturing	116,925	5.0	907,000	25.7
Construction	57,028	2.4	421,000	11.9
Public utilities	29,745	1.3	79,000	2.2
Transp. and commun.	148,234	6.4	342,000	9.7
Trade, hotels	322,528	13.8	704,000	19.9
Finance, real estate	...	...	205,000	5.8
Pub. admin., defense	194,288	8.3	...	...
Services	194,454	8.3	775,000	21.9
Other	153,149[7]	6.6[7]		
TOTAL	2,333,098	100.0	3,535,000[3]	100.0[3]

Production (metric tons except as noted). Agriculture, forestry, fishing (2009): millet 2,677,855, cowpeas 1,550,000, sorghum 738,660, cow's milk 458,451, dry onions 384,309, peanuts (groundnuts) 253,497, cattle meat 238,577, mangoes, mangosteens, and guavas 170,572, camel's milk 96,814, sesame seeds 75,632, goat meat 56,709, tomatoes 56,054; livestock (number of live animals) 13,147,200 goats, 10,548,000 sheep, 9,261,640 cattle, 1,654,380 camels; roundwood (2010) 3,558,000 cu m, of which fuelwood 80%; fisheries production 29,954 (from aquaculture, negligible). Mining and quarrying (2009): limestone 146,000; uranium 3,243; salt 1,300; gold (metal content) 1,852 kg. Manufacturing (value added in CFAF '000,000; 2008): food and food products 6,797; paper products, printing, and publishing 2,604; soaps and other chemical products 1,625; wood products and furniture 1,557; textiles 412. Energy production (consumption): electricity (kW-hr; 2009) 254,714,000[8] ([2007] 593,000,000); hard coal (metric tons; 2009) 225,072 ([2007] 185,000); crude petroleum, none[9] (none); petroleum products (metric tons; 2007) none (161,000); natural gas, none (none).
Population economically active (2006): total 6,139,000; activity rate of total population 42.6% (participation rates: over age 15, 83.5%; female 41.9%; registered unemployed, n.a.).

Price index (2005 = 100)

	2004	2005	2006	2007	2008	2009	2010
Consumer price index	92.8	100.0	100.0	100.1	111.4	116.2	117.1

Household income and expenditure. Average household size (2004) 6.2; income per household: n.a.; expenditure (2005)[10]: food, beverages, and tobacco products 53.7%, housing and rent 10.3%, transportation 9.9%, clothing and footwear 5.3%, health 4.6%.
Land use as % of total land area (2009): in temporary crops or left fallow 11.8%, in permanent crops 0.01%, in pasture 22.7%, forest area 1.0%.

Foreign trade

Balance of trade (current prices)

	2004	2005	2006	2007	2008	2009
CFAF '000,000	−202,411	−196,552	−273,612	−201,909	−185,193	−454,749
% of total	44.2%	37.4%	48.7%	32.0%	22.6%	47.6%

Imports (2008): CFAF 501,605,000,000 (food and food products 25.1%; petroleum products 15.5%; machinery and equipment 15.1%; chemicals and chemical products 14.9%; transportation equipment 6.8%). *Major import sources:* France 13.7%; China 13.3%; Netherlands 7.6%; U.S. 7.4%; Nigeria 4.9%.
Exports (2008): CFAF 316,412,000,000 (uranium 62.6%; livestock 23.7%, of which cattle 9.5%; gold 5.6%; onions 4.2%). *Major export destinations:* France 36.8%; Nigeria 25.0%; U.S. 14.2%; Japan 10.4%; Switzerland 5.6%.

Transport and communications

Transport. Railroads: none. Roads (2008): total length 11,774 mi, 18,949 km (paved 21%). Vehicles (2007): passenger cars 75,697; trucks and buses 20,978. Air transport (2007)[11]: passenger arrivals 64,904, passenger departures 60,297; cargo unloaded 1,394 metric tons, cargo loaded 149 metric tons.

Communications

Medium	date	number in '000s	units per 1,000 persons	Medium	date	number in '000s	units per 1,000 persons
Televisions	2004	150	13	PCs	2005	10	0.8
Telephones				Dailies	2009	4[12]	0.1[12]
Cellular	2010	3,806[13]	245[13]	Internet users	2009	116	7.6
Landline	2010	84	5.4	Broadband	2010	3.7[13]	0.2[13]

Education and health

Educational attainment (2006)[10, 14]. Percentage of population age 25 and over having: no formal schooling/unknown 86.2%; incomplete primary education 6.9%; complete primary 1.0%; incomplete secondary 3.7%; complete secondary 0.4%; higher 0.9%. *Literacy* (2007–08): total population age 15 and over literate 29.0%; males literate 42.8%; females literate 17.1%.

Education (2008–09)

	teachers	students	student/ teacher ratio	enrollment rate (%)
Primary (age 7–12)	40,021	1,554,102	38.8	54
Secondary/Voc. (age 13–19)	9,289	256,555	27.6	9[15]
Tertiary	1,176	15,992	13.6	1 (age 20–24)

Health: physicians (2008) 427[16] (1 per 34,548 persons); hospital beds (2007) 2,934 (1 per 4,845 persons); infant mortality rate (2009) 81; undernourished population (2005–07) 2,700,000 (20% of total population based on the consumption of a minimum daily requirement of 1,720 calories).

Military

Total active duty personnel (November 2010): 5,300 (army 98.1%, air force 1.9%); paramilitary 5,400. *Military expenditure as percentage of GDP* (2008): 1.1%; per capita expenditure U.S.$4.

[1]Per military coup of Feb. 18, 2010; constitutional transition to civilian rule took place on April 7, 2011. [2]Assisted by Prime Minister. [3]Detail does not add to total given because of rounding. [4]Estimate of the U.S. Bureau of the Census International Database (December 2008 update). [5]Excluding nomadic population. [6]January 1. [7]Import taxes and duties. [8]SONICHAR and Nigelec electricity companies only. [9]Crude petroleum production was expected to begin in 2011. [10]Niamey only. [11]Niamey airport. [12]Circulation of *Le Sahel Quotidien* only. [13]Subscribers. [14]Based on a 2006 demographic and health survey of 14,945 persons age 25 and over. [15]2006–07. [16]Public health institutions only.

Internet resources for further information:

- **Institut National de la Statistique**
  http://www.stat-niger.org
- **La Banque de France: La Zone Franc**
  http://www.banque-france.fr/fr/eurosys/zonefr/zonefr.htm

Nigeria

Official name: Federal Republic of Nigeria.
Form of government: federal republic with two legislatures (Senate [109]; House of Representatives [360]).
Head of state and government: President.
Capital: Abuja.
Official language: English.
Official religion: none.
Monetary unit: Nigerian naira (₦); valuation (Sept. 1, 2011) 1 U.S.$ = ₦154.70; 1 £ = ₦249.99.

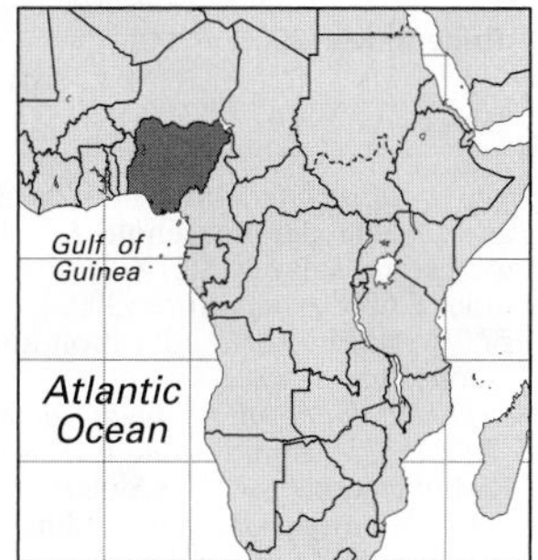

Area and population

States	area sq km	population 2006 census	States	area sq km	population 2006 census
Abia	6,320	2,845,380	Kebbi	36,800	3,256,541
Adamawa	36,917	3,178,950	Kogi	29,833	3,314,043
Akwa Ibom	7,081	3,902,051	Kwara	36,825	2,365,353
Anambra	4,844	4,177,828	Lagos	3,345	9,113,605
Bauchi	45,837	4,653,066	Nassarawa	27,117	1,869,377
Bayelsa	10,773	1,704,515	Niger	76,363	3,954,772
Benue	34,059	4,253,641	Ogun	16,762	3,751,140
Borno	70,898	4,171,104	Ondo	14,606	3,460,877
Cross River	20,156[1]	2,892,988[1]	Osun	9,251	3,416,959
Delta	17,698	4,112,445	Oyo	28,454	5,580,894
Ebonyi	5,670	2,176,947	Plateau	30,913	3,206,531
Edo	17,802	3,233,366	Rivers	11,077	5,198,716
Ekiti	6,353	2,398,957	Sokoto	25,973	3,702,676
Enugu	7,161	3,267,837	Taraba	54,473	2,294,800
Gombe	18,768	2,365,040	Yobe	45,502	2,321,339
Imo	5,530	3,927,563	Zamfara	39,762	3,278,873
Jigawa	23,154	4,361,002			
Kaduna	46,053	6,113,503	**Federal Capital Territory**		
Kano	20,131	9,401,288			
Katsina	24,192	5,801,584	Abuja	7,315	1,406,239
			TOTAL	923,768[1]	140,431,790

Demography

Population (2011): 162,471,000.
Density (2011): persons per sq mi 445.5, persons per sq km 175.9.
Urban-rural (2009): urban 49.1%; rural 50.9%.
Sex distribution (2006): male 50.80%; female 49.20%.
Age breakdown (2005): under 15, 43.1%; 15–29, 28.2%; 30–44, 15.3%; 45–59, 8.6%; 60–74, 4.0%; 75–84, 0.7%; 85 and over, 0.1%.
Population projection: (2020) 203,869,000; (2030) 257,815,000.
Ethnic composition (2000): Yoruba 17.5%; Hausa 17.2%; Igbo (Ibo) 13.3%; Fulani 10.7%; Ibibio 4.1%; Kanuri 3.6%; Egba 2.9%; Tiv 2.6%; Igbira 1.1%; Nupe 1.0%; Edo 1.0%; Ijo 0.8%; detribalized 0.9%; other 23.3%.
Religious affiliation (2003): Muslim (predominantly Sunnī) 50.5%; Christian 48.2%, of which Protestant 15.0%, Roman Catholic 13.7%, other (mostly independent Christian) 19.5%; other 1.3%.
Major urban agglomerations (2007): Lagos 9,466,000; Kano 3,140,000; Ibadan 2,628,000; Abuja 1,576,000; Kaduna 1,442,000; Benin City 1,190,000.

Vital statistics

Birth rate per 1,000 population (2009): 39.3 (world avg. 20.3).
Death rate per 1,000 population (2009): 16.2 (world avg. 8.5).
Total fertility rate (avg. births per childbearing woman; 2009): 5.20.
Life expectancy at birth (2007): male 46.4 years; female 47.3 years.
Adult population (ages 15–49) *living with HIV* (2009): 3.6%[2] (world avg. 0.8%).
Major causes of death per 100,000 population (2002): HIV/AIDS *c.* 258; respiratory infections *c.* 182; malaria *c.* 181; cardiovascular diseases *c.* 167.

National economy

Budget (2008)[3]. Revenue: ₦2,411,000,000,000 (petroleum revenue 83.3%, of which tax on profits and royalties 39.8%; nonpetroleum revenue 16.7%, of which companies' income tax 6.3%). Expenditures: ₦2,451,000,000,000 (current expenditure 65.3%; capital expenditure 34.7%).
Production (metric tons except as noted). Agriculture, forestry, fishing (2009): cassava 36,804,300, yams 29,092,000, oil palm fruit 8,500,000, corn (maize) 7,338,840, sorghum 5,270,790, millet 4,884,890, taro 4,459,650, rice 3,402,590, peanuts (groundnuts) 2,969,260, plantains 2,910,680, sweet potatoes 2,746,820, cowpeas 2,369,580, okra 826,170, cashews 580,760, melon seeds 502,320, karite nuts (shea nuts) 441,560, cocoa beans 370,000, ginger 152,110; livestock 55,145,400 goats, 34,687,300 sheep, 16,400,000 cattle; roundwood (2010) 72,211,234 cu m, of which fuelwood 87%; fisheries production 751,006 (from aquaculture 20%). Mining and quarrying (2010): limestone 4,300,000; marble (2009) 190,000. Manufacturing (value added in ₦'000,000; 2008): refined petroleum 44,297; cement 18,036; other unspecified (particularly food, beverages, and textiles) 543,259. Energy production (consumption): electricity (kW-hr; 2008) 20,130,000,000 (18,141,000,000); coal (metric tons; 2007) 530,000 (8,000); crude petroleum (barrels; 2010) 896,000,000 ([2007] 19,200,000); petroleum products (metric tons; 2007) 2,319,000 (9,234,000); natural gas (cu m; 2007) 46,046,000,000 (10,677,000,000).
Household income and expenditure. Avg. household size (2005) 4.7; expenditures (2003)[4]: food 63.8%, housing/energy 18.1%, transportation 4.2%.
Land use as % of total land area (2009): in temporary crops or left fallow (2007) 40.1%, in permanent crops 3.3%, in pasture 41.2%, forest area 10.4%.
Gross national income (GNI; 2010): U.S.$186,406,000,000 (U.S.$1,180 per capita); purchasing power parity GNI (U.S.$2,160 per capita).

Structure of gross domestic product and labour force

	2009 in value ₦'000,000,000	2009 % of total value	2005 labour force	2005 % of labour force
Agriculture, fishing	9,194	35.5	37,487,000	58.6
Crude petroleum/mining	7,362	28.5	89,000	0.1
Manufacturing	559	2.2	1,173,000	1.8
Construction	348	1.3	353,000	0.6
Public utilities	116	0.4	551,000	0.9
Transp. and commun.	764	3.0	537,000	0.8
Trade, hotels	4,182	16.2	259,000	0.4
Finance, real estate	1,587	6.1	441,000	0.7
Pub. admin., defense	407	1.6	6,547,000	10.3
Services	197	0.8	16,496,000	25.8
Other	1,148[5]	4.4[5]	—	—
TOTAL	25,864	100.0	63,932,000[6]	100.0

Public debt (external, outstanding; 2009): U.S.$4,938,000,000.
Population economically active (2008): total 48,613,000[7]; activity rate 32.1%[7] (participation rates: ages 15–64, 57.1%[7]; female 34.9%[7]; unofficially unemployed [2007] *c.* 60%).

Price index (2005 = 100)

	2004	2005	2006	2007	2008	2009	2010
Consumer price index	84.8	100.0	108.2	114.1	127.3	142.0	161.4

Selected balance of payments data. Receipts from (U.S.$'000,000): tourism (2009) 602; remittances (2010) 10,045; foreign direct investment (FDI; 2008–10 avg.) 7,666; official development assistance (2009) 1,659. Disbursements for (U.S.$'000,000): tourism (2009) 4,084; remittances (2009) 66; FDI (2008–10 avg.) 1,174.

Foreign trade

Balance of trade (current prices)

	2003	2004	2005	2006	2007	2008
₦'000,000	+583	+1,439	+3,474	+3,077	+3,771	+4,504
% of total	16.2%	30.5%	31.5%	26.6%	30.2%	31.1%

Imports (2008): ₦4,991,000,000,000 (basic manufactures 33.0%, chemicals and chemical products 25.0%, machinery and transport equipment 22.0%, food and live animals 6.0%). *Major import sources*[8]: U.S. 14.4%; China 10.5%; France 9.4%; U.K. 7.9%; Netherlands 7.4%.
Exports (2008): ₦9,495,000,000,000 (crude petroleum 92.2%, other petroleum sector 6.8%, cocoa beans 0.3%). *Major export destinations*[9]: U.S. 23.0%; Spain 9.3%; China 6.0%; Brazil 5.0%; Italy 4.1%.

Transport and communications

Transport. Railroads (2005): length (2007) 3,505 km; passenger-km 75,170,000; metric ton-km cargo 18,027,000. Roads (2004): total length 120,000 mi, 193,200 km (paved 15%). Vehicles (2007): passenger cars 4,560,000. Air transport (2008): passenger-km 2,136,000,000; metric ton-km cargo 7,368,000.

Communications

Medium	date	number in '000s	units per 1,000 persons	Medium	date	number in '000s	units per 1,000 persons
Televisions	2003	8,393	64	PCs	2007	1,182	8.0
Telephones				Dailies	2009	480[10]	5.5[10]
Cellular	2010	87,298[11]	510[11]	Internet users	2009	43,982	284
Landline	2010	1,050	6.6	Broadband	2010	99[11]	0.6[11]

Education and health

Educational attainment (2003)[12]. Percentage of population age 25 and over having: no formal schooling/unknown 50.4%; primary education 20.4%; secondary 20.1%; higher 9.1%. *Literacy* (2008): total population age 15 and over literate 60.1%; males literate 71.5%; females literate 48.8%.

Education (2006–07)

	teachers	students	student/teacher ratio	enrollment rate (%)
Primary (age 6–11)	466,784	21,632,070	46.3	61
Secondary/Voc. (age 12–17)	213,366	6,068,160	28.4	26
Tertiary	37,031[13]	1,391,527[14]	34.8[13]	10[14] (age 18–22)

Health (2007): physicians 55,376 (1 per 2,602 persons); hospital beds (2005) 85,523 (1 per 1,609 persons); infant mortality rate per 1,000 live births (2007) 109.0; undernourished population (2004–06) 11,300,000 (8% of total population based on the consumption of a minimum daily requirement of 1,750 calories).

Military

Total active duty personnel (November 2010): 80,000 (army 77.5%, navy 10.0%, air force 12.5%); paramilitary 82,000. *Military expenditure as percentage of GDP* (2009): 0.9%; per capita expenditure U.S.$9.

[1]Includes the area of Bakassi Peninsula, which was formally ceded by Nigeria to Cameroon in August 2006 and officially handed over in August 2008. [2]Statistically derived midpoint of range. [3]Federal budget only. [4]Weights of consumer price index components. [5]Indirect taxes less subsidies. [6]Detail does not add to total given because of rounding. [7]ILO estimate. [8]Nonpetroleum imports only (81.6% of all imports). [9]Crude petroleum exports only. [10]Circulation of daily newspapers. [11]Subscribers. [12]Based on the 2003 Nigeria Demographic and Health Survey of 35,173 people, about two-thirds of whom live in rural areas. [13]2003–04. [14]2004–05.

Internet resources for further information:

- **National Bureau of Statistics http://www.nigerianstat.gov.ng/**
- **Central Bank of Nigeria http://www.cenbank.org**

Northern Mariana Islands

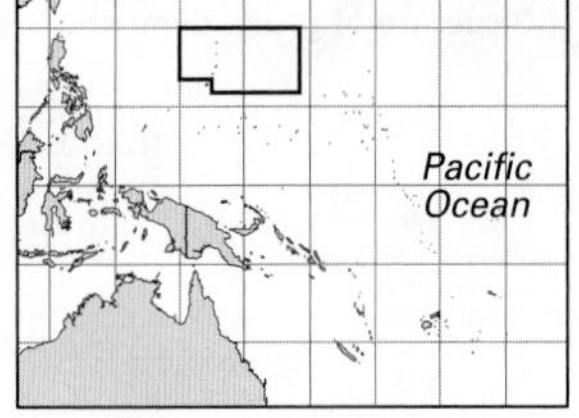

Official name: Commonwealth of the Northern Mariana Islands.
Political status: self-governing commonwealth in association with the United States, having two legislative houses (Senate [9]; House of Representatives [20])[1].
Head of state: President of the United States.
Head of government: Governor.
Seat of government: on Saipan[2].
Official languages: Chamorro; Carolinian; English.
Official religion: none.
Monetary unit: dollar (U.S.$); valuation (Sept. 1, 2011) 1 U.S.$ = £0.62.

Area and population

		area		population
Municipal councils	Major villages	sq mi	sq km	2005 estimate
Northern Islands[3]	...	55.3	143.2	[3]
Rota (island)	Songsong	32.8	85.0	2,490
Saipan (island)	San Antonio	46.5	120.4	60,608
Tinian[4]	San Jose	41.9	108.5	2,829
TOTAL		176.5[5]	457.1[5]	65,927

Demography

Population (2011): 46,100[6].
Density (2011): persons per sq mi 260.9, persons per sq km 100.7.
Urban-rural (2009): urban 90.8%; rural 9.2%.
Sex distribution (2009): male 48.05%; female 51.95%.
Age breakdown (2009): under 15, 26.0%; 15–29, 25.6%; 30–44, 23.0%; 45–59, 19.6%; 60–74, 5.0%; 75–84, 0.7%; 85 and over, 0.1%.
Population projection[6]: (2020) 48,900; (2030) 55,600.
Doubling time: 36 years.
Ethnic composition (2005)[7]: Asian 52.4%, of which Filipino 30.6%, Chinese 15.4%, Korean 2.3%; Pacific Islanders 37.2%, of which Chamorro 22.9%, Micronesian/Palauan 13.6%; white 1.7%; multiethnic 8.3%; other 0.4%.
Religious affiliation (2000): Christian 88.9%, of which Roman Catholic 72.7%, independent Christian 7.0%, Protestant 6.8%; Buddhist 5.3%; other 5.8%.
Major village groups (2005)[8]: Garapan 11,196; San Antonio 6,104; Susupe–Chalan Kanoa 5,911.

Vital statistics

Birth rate per 1,000 population (2009): 22.0 (world avg. 20.3).
Death rate per 1,000 population (2009): 3.1 (world avg. 8.5).
Total fertility rate (avg. births per childbearing woman; 2009): 2.24.
Life expectancy at birth (2010): male 74.3 years; female 79.7 years.
Major causes of death per 100,000 population (1998): heart diseases 51; malignant neoplasms (cancers) 40; cerebrovascular disease 22; perinatal conditions 20; accidents 18.

National economy

Budget (2009). Revenue: U.S.$154,690,000 (tax revenue 73.9%, of which corporate taxes 39.0%, income tax 15.8%, excise tax 11.6%; nontax revenue 26.1%). Expenditures: U.S.$168,120,000 (2001; health 20.4%, education 20.1%, general government 15.0%, social services 12.0%, public safety 9.3%).
Gross domestic product (2009): U.S.$716,000,000 (U.S.$13,907 per capita).

Structure of labour force

	2005 labour force	2005 % of labour force
Agriculture, forestry, and fishing	249	0.6
Mining and quarrying	173	0.4
Manufacturing (garments)	10,217	26.5
Manufacturing (other)	771	2.0
Construction	1,640	4.3
Public utilities	27	0.1
Transp. and commun.	885	2.3
Trade, restaurants, hotels	7,602	19.7
Finance, insurance, and real estate	821	2.1
Pub. admin., defense	3,153	8.2
Services	8,083	21.0
Other	4,912[9]	12.7
TOTAL	38,533[10]	100.0[11]

Production (metric tons except as noted). Agriculture, forestry, fishing (2007)[12]: sweet potatoes 352,300, taro 221,600, bananas 146,900, cucumbers 93,800, betel nuts 88,300, yams 67,700, papayas 50,700, eggplants 47,300, coconuts 42,900; livestock (number of live animals) 1,483 pigs, 1,395 cattle, 276 goats; roundwood, n.a.; fisheries production (2009) 142 (from aquaculture, none). Mining and quarrying: negligible amount of quarrying for building material. Manufacturing (value of sales in U.S.$'000,000; 2007): garments 160; bricks, tiles, and cement 9; printing and related activities 5; food products 4. Energy production (consumption): electricity, n.a. (n.a.); coal, none (none); crude petroleum, none (none); petroleum products, n.a. (n.a.); natural gas, none (none).
Population economically active (2005): total 38,533; activity rate of total population 58.4% (participation rates: ages 16 and over, 79.2%; female 54.0%; unemployed [2007] 4.6%).

Price index (2005 = 100)

	2003	2004	2005	2006	2007	2008	2009
Consumer price index	97.4	98.3	100.0	97.6	110.8	116.1	120.4

Household income and expenditure. Average household size (2005) 4.1; average income per household (2004) U.S.$25,172; sources of income (2004): wages and salaries 85.7%, transfer payments 9.3%, self-employment 2.4%, other 2.6%; expenditure (2003)[13]: transportation 33.5%, housing and energy 27.7%, food 19.0%, education and communications 5.7%, recreation 2.4%, medical care 2.4%.
Selected balance of payments data. Receipts from (U.S.$'000,000): tourism (2002) 225; remittances (2009–10) 66.4; foreign direct investment, n.a. Disbursements for (U.S.$'000,000): tourism, n.a.; remittances, n.a.
Public debt (external, outstanding): n.a.
Land use as % of total land area (2007): in temporary crops or left fallow *c.* 2%, in permanent crops *c.* 2%, in pasture *c.* 2%, forest area *c.* 72%.

Foreign trade

Balance of trade (current prices)

	2005	2006	2007	2008
U.S.$'000,000	–331.5	–291.7	–156.8	–113.1
% of total	93.7%	91.9%	86.1%	80.9%

Imports (2008): U.S.$126,400,000 (mineral fuels 44.7%; fabric 9.4%; articles of leather/travel goods 8.5%; food 7.7%; vehicles 5.5%). *Major import sources:* n.a.
Exports (2008): U.S.$13,300,000 (apparel and clothing accessories 53.7%; iron and steel 16.3%; fish, crustaceans, and mollusks 11.8%). *Major export destinations:* mostly to the United States.

Transport and communications

Transport. Railroads: none. Roads (2008): total length 333 mi, 536 km (paved, nearly 100%). Vehicles (2002): passenger cars 11,983; trucks and buses 4,858. Air transport (2008–09): passengers arriving 467,462; passengers departing 462,179.

Communications

Medium	date	number in '000s	units per 1,000 persons	Medium	date	number in '000s	units per 1,000 persons
Televisions	1999	4.1	59	PCs	2009	...	...
Telephones				Dailies	2009	6[14]	117[14]
Cellular	2004	20[15]	266[15]	Internet users	2009	...	...
Landline	2010	26	419	Broadband	2009	...	...

Education and health

Educational attainment (2005). Percentage of population age 25 and over having: no formal schooling 0.4%; incomplete/complete primary education 8.1%; some secondary 10.9%; completed secondary 43.4%; some postsecondary 21.3%; completed undergraduate 13.4%; advanced degree 2.5%. *Literacy* (2000): *c.* 100%.

Education (2002–03)

	teachers	students	student/ teacher ratio	enrollment rate (%)
Primary (age 6–11) / Secondary/Voc. (age 12–17)	717	12,880	18.0	...
Tertiary[16]	504	2,383	4.7	... (age 18–22)

Health (2009): physicians 38[17] (1 per 1,355 persons); hospital beds 86[17] (1 per 599 persons); infant mortality rate per 1,000 live births 6.0; undernourished population, n.a.

Military

The United States is responsible for military defense; in 2011 the Northern Island of Farallon de Medinilla continued to be used as a target range by the U.S. military.

[1]In November 2008 residents elected their first nonvoting delegate to the U.S. Congress. [2]Executive and legislative branches meet at Capital Hill; the judiciary meets at Susupe. [3]Comprises the islands of Agrihan, Pagan, and Alamagan, as well as seven other uninhabited islands; the Northern Islands are administered as part of Saipan municipal council because of the forced removal of the population owing to volcanic activity. [4]Comprises Tinian island and Aguijan island. [5]Area measured at high tide; at low tide, total dry land area is 184.0 sq mi (476.6 sq km). [6]Estimate of U.S. Bureau of the Census International Database (June 2009 update). [7]Includes aliens. [8]All villages are unincorporated census-designated places. [9]Includes 1,744 not adequately defined and 1,869 unemployed. [10]Of which ethnic Chamorro 16.6%, other (significantly Filipino and Chinese) 83.4%. [11]Detail does not add to total given because of rounding. [12]Crop data are harvested for sale only; in pounds. [13]Weights of consumer price index components. [14]Circulation of daily newspapers. [15]Subscribers. [16]Northern Marianas College; 2000–01. [17]Saipan Commonwealth Health Center only.

Internet resource for further information:
- **CNMI: Central Statistics Division**
http://commerce.gov.mp/divisions/central-statistics

Norway

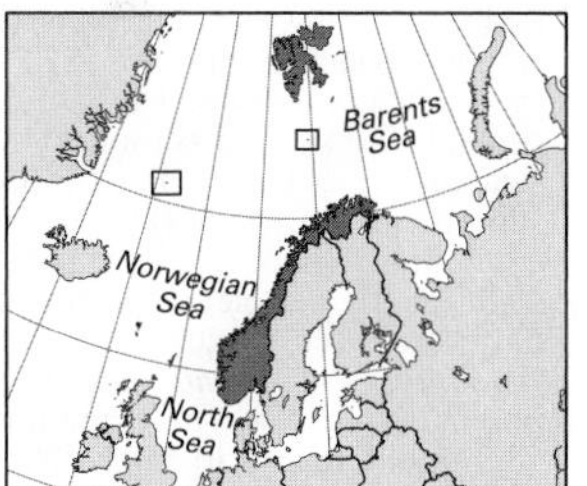

Official name: Kongeriket Norge (Kingdom of Norway).
Form of government: constitutional monarchy with one legislative house (Storting, or Parliament [169]).
Head of state: King.
Head of government: Prime Minister.
Capital: Oslo.
Official languages: Norwegian; Sami[1].
Official religion: Evangelical Lutheran.
Monetary unit: Norwegian krone (pl. kroner; NOK); valuation (Sept. 1, 2011) 1 U.S.$ = NOK 5.40; 1 £ = NOK 8.72.

Area and population

Mainland counties	area sq km	population 2011[2] estimate	Mainland counties	area sq km	population 2011[2] estimate
Akershus	4,918	545,653	Sør-Trøndelag	18,856	294,066
Aust-Agder	9,158	110,048	Telemark	15,299	169,185
Buskerud	14,911	261,110	Troms	25,870	157,554
Finnmark	48,616	73,417	Vest-Agder	7,276	172,408
Hedmark	27,400	191,622	Vestfold	2,224	233,705
Hordaland	15,440	484,240	SUBTOTAL	323,782[3]	4,920,305
Møre og Romsdal	15,114	253,904			
Nord-Trøndelag	22,415	132,140			
Nordland	38,460	237,280	**Overseas Arctic territories**		
Oppland	25,190	186,087			
Oslo	454	599,230	Jan Mayen	377[4]	[5]
Østfold	4,182	274,827	Svalbard	61,020[3, 4]	[5]
Rogaland	9,376	436,087	SUBTOTAL	61,397	—
Sogn og Fjordane	18,623	107,742	TOTAL	385,179	4,920,305

Demography

Population (2011): 4,953,000.
Density (2011)[6]: persons per sq mi 38.9, persons per sq km 15.0.
Urban-rural (2009): urban 78.8%; rural 21.2%.
Sex distribution (2010[2]): male 49.95%; female 50.05%.
Age breakdown (2010[2]): under 15, 18.9%; 15–29, 19.2%; 30–44, 21.5%; 45–59, 19.5%; 60–74, 13.6%; 75–84, 5.0%; 85 and over, 2.3%.
Population projection: (2020) 5,565,000; (2030) 6,096,000.
Ethnic composition (2010[2]): Norwegian (nonimmigrant) 83.0%; other 17.0%[7], of which from Europe 5.3%, Asia 4.1%, Africa 1.4%.
Religious affiliation (2004[2]): Evangelical Lutheran 85.7%; other Christian 4.5%; Muslim 1.8%; other/nonreligious 8.0%.
Major cities (2011[2])[8]: Oslo 599,230 (urban agglomeration [2008] 856,915); Bergen 260,392; Trondheim 173,486; Stavanger 126,021; Bærum 112,789.

Vital statistics

Birth rate per 1,000 population (2009): 12.8 (world avg. 20.3); within marriage 45.0%; outside of marriage 55.0%.
Death rate per 1,000 population (2009): 8.6 (world avg. 8.5).
Natural increase rate per 1,000 population (2009): 4.2 (world avg. 11.8).
Total fertility rate (avg. births per childbearing woman; 2009): 1.98.
Marriage/divorce rates per 1,000 population (2009): 5.1[9]/2.1.
Life expectancy at birth (2009): male 78.6 years; female 83.1 years.
Major causes of death per 100,000 population (2008): circulatory diseases 296.5; malignant neoplasms (cancers) 228.3; respiratory diseases 86.4.

National economy

Budget (2008). Revenue: NOK 1,157,580,000,000 (tax revenue 61.7%, nontax revenue 20.2%, social security 18.0%). Expenditures: NOK 1,162,040,000,000 (general public services 46.9%, social protection 27.1%, health 10.6%, education 3.4%, defense 3.4%, transportation 2.5%).
Public debt (June 2011): U.S.$117,750,000,000.
Production (metric tons except as noted). Agriculture, forestry, fishing (2009): barley 435,000, potatoes 332,700, oats 245,000, wheat 240,000; livestock (number of live animals) 2,289,860 sheep, 877,711 cattle, 839,346 pigs; roundwood (2010) 8,883,594 cu m, of which fuelwood 25%; fisheries production 3,486,277 (from aquaculture 28%). Mining and quarrying (2009): olivine sand 1,267,000; iron ore 896,000[10]; ilmenite concentrate 671,000. Manufacturing (value added in NOK '000,000; 2008): machinery and equipment 55,474; food products, beverages, and tobacco 34,589; ships and oil platforms 26,139; base metals 18,798; printing/publishing 17,010. Energy production (consumption): electricity (kW-hr; 2009) 138,348,000,000 ([2007] 114,453,000,000); coal (metric tons; 2009) 3,207,000 (1,270,000); crude petroleum (barrels; 2009) 735,938,000 ([2008] 80,362,000); petroleum products (metric tons; 2007) 22,414,000 (11,406,000); natural gas (cu m; 2009) 102,700,000,000 ([2007] 6,512,000,000).
Household income and expenditure. Average household size (2002) 2.2; average annual net income per household (2004) NOK 359,300 (U.S.$53,302); sources of income (2004): wages and salaries 63.3%, transfers 22.1%, self-employment 6.0%; expenditure (2007–09): housing 31.2%, transportation 16.3%, recreation and culture 12.5%, food 10.6%.
Population economically active (2008): total 2,591,000; activity rate of total population 53.2% (participation rates: ages 15–64, 78.2%; female 47.0%; unemployed [2009] 3.1%).

Price and earnings indexes (2005 = 100)

	2004	2005	2006	2007	2008	2009	2010
Consumer price index	98.5	100.0	102.3	103.1	107.0	109.3	111.9
Monthly earnings index	96.3	100.0	104.1	110.7	116.9	122.0	126.4

Gross national income (GNI; 2010): U.S.$416,905,000,000 (U.S.$85,380 per capita); purchasing power parity GNI (U.S.$57,130 per capita).

Structure of gross domestic product and labour force

	2009			
	in value NOK '000,000	% of total value	labour force	% of labour force
Agriculture, fishing	22,298	0.9	58,000	2.2
Mining	4,219	0.2	4,400	0.2
Crude petroleum and natural gas	505,182	21.1	42,400	1.6
Manufacturing	206,470	8.6	280,000	10.4
Construction	109,805	4.6	180,100	6.7
Public utilities	53,578	2.2	19,000	0.7
Transp. and commun.	134,078	5.6	204,500	7.6
Trade, hotels	209,756	8.7	447,900	16.6
Finance, real estate	331,741	13.8	370,400	13.8
Pub. admin., defense	106,066	4.4	162,900	6.0
Services	463,393	19.3	827,800	30.7
Other	254,086	10.6	94,700[11]	3.5[11]
TOTAL	2,400,672	100.0	2,692,100	100.0

Selected balance of payments data. Receipts from (U.S.$'000,000): tourism (2009) 4,082; remittances (2010) 692; foreign direct investment (FDI; 2008–10 avg.) 12,237. Disbursements for (U.S.$'000,000): tourism (2009) 12,366; remittances (2009) 4,147; FDI (2008–10 avg.) 22,269.
Land use as % of total land area (2009): in temporary crops 1.1%, left fallow 0.01%, in permanent crops 0.02%, in pasture 2.2%, forest area 32.7%.

Foreign trade[12]

Balance of trade (current prices)

	2004	2005	2006	2007	2008	2009
NOK '000,000	+226,591	+311,103	+371,188	+326,448	+444,487	+327,455
% of total	26.0%	30.3%	31.1%	25.8%	30.7%	27.7%

Imports (2008): NOK 501,972,000,000 (machinery and apparatus 25.2%, of which nonelectrical machinery and equipment 12.7%; base and fabricated metals 10.3%; road vehicles 9.0%; chemicals and chemical products 8.9%; food 5.4%). *Major import sources:* Sweden 14.3%; Germany 13.4%; Denmark 6.9%; China 6.5%; U.K. 6.0%.
Exports (2008): NOK 946,459,000,000 (crude petroleum 39.4%; natural gas 20.4%; machinery and apparatus 7.1%; refined petroleum 4.6%; aluminum 3.5%; fish 3.3%). *Major export destinations:* U.K. 26.9%; Germany 12.8%; Netherlands 10.3%; France 9.4%; Sweden 6.5%.

Transport and communications

Transport. Railroads (2009[2]): route length 4,114 km; passenger-km 3,040,000,000; metric ton-km cargo 3,359,000,000. Roads (2007): total length 92,920 km (paved 80%); passenger-km 60,316,000,000[13]; metric ton-km cargo 20,595,000,000. Vehicles: passenger cars (2009[2]) 2,197,193; trucks and buses (2007) 538,225. Air transport (2008)[14]: passenger-km 7,835,000,000; metric ton-km cargo 8,000,000.

Communications

Medium	date	number in '000s	units per 1,000 persons	Medium	date	number in '000s	units per 1,000 persons
Televisions	2003	7,110	1,557	PCs	2007	2,959	629
Telephones				Dailies	2009	2,061[15]	427[15]
Cellular	2010	5,525[16]	1,132[16]	Internet users	2009	4,431[17]	921[17]
Landline	2010	1,702	349	Broadband	2010	1,690[16]	346[16]

Education and health

Educational attainment (2007). Percentage of population age 16 and over having: primary and lower secondary education 29.6%; higher secondary 41.3%; higher 24.8%; unknown 4.3%. *Literacy* (2000): virtually 100% literate.

Education (2007–08)

	teachers	students	student/ teacher ratio	enrollment rate (%)
Primary (age 6–12)	41,161[18]	429,585	10.5[18]	99
Secondary/Voc. (age 13–18)	45,505[18]	423,598	8.8[18]	96
Tertiary	20,268	212,672	10.5	73 (age 19–23)

Health: physicians (2006) 17,523 (1 per 266 persons); hospital beds (2007) 22,882 (1 per 206 persons); infant mortality rate (2009) 3.1; undernourished population (2005–07) less than 5.0% of total population.

Military

Total active duty personnel (November 2010): 26,450 (army 33.6%, navy 14.2%, air force 21.0%, central support 29.3%, other 1.9%); reserve 45,250. *Military expenditure as percentage of GDP* (2008): 1.3%; per capita expenditure U.S.$1,172.

[1]Official locally. [2]January 1. [3]Includes area of freshwater lakes. [4]Includes area of glaciers. [5]Persons on Jan Mayen and Svalbard are normally registered as residents on the mainland. The population of Jan Mayen on July 1, 2009, was 24; the population of Svalbard on March 1, 2010, was 2,495, including Norwegian settlements 2,066, the Russian settlement 420, and the Polish settlement 9. [6]Population density calculated with reference to 329,847 sq km area free of mainland freshwater lakes (18,312 sq km), Svalbard freshwater lakes (395 sq km), Svalbard glaciers (36,500 sq km), and Jan Mayen glaciers (125 sq km). [7]Including 2nd generation immigrants. [8]Population of municipalities. [9]Includes same-sex marriages. [10]Metal content. [11]Includes 87,000 unemployed. [12]Imports c.i.f.; exports f.o.b. [13]Passenger cars 55,956,000,000; buses 4,360,000,000. [14]SAS (Norwegian part) and Widerøe only. [15]Circulation of daily newspapers. [16]Subscribers. [17]As reported in surveys. [18]2003–04.

Internet resource for further information:
- **Statistics Norway http://www.ssb.no/english**

Oman

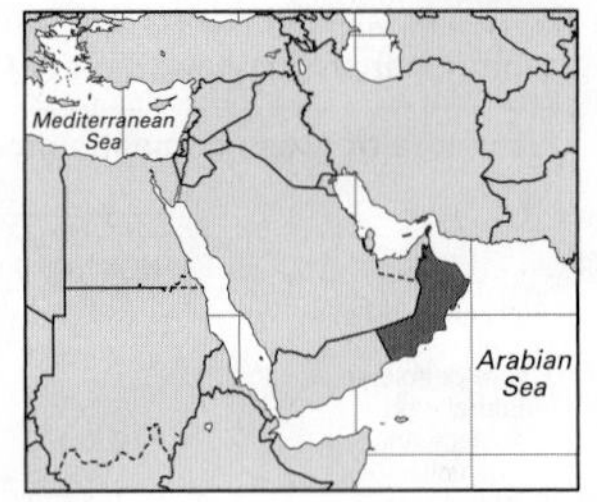

Official name: Salṭanat ʿUmān (Sultanate of Oman).
Form of government: monarchy with two advisory bodies (State Council [83[1]]; Consultative Council [84]).
Head of state and government: Sultan.
Capital: Muscat[2].
Official language: Arabic.
Official religion: Islam.
Monetary unit: rial Omani (RO); valuation (Sept. 1, 2011) 1 RO = U.S.$2.60 = £1.61.

Area and population		area[3]		population
				2010
Regions	**Capitals**	sq mi	sq km	census
Al-Bāṭinah	Al-Rustāq; Ṣuḥār	4,825	12,500	772,590
Al-Dākhilīyah	Nizwā	12,325	31,900	326,651
Al-Sharqīyah	Ibrā; Ṣūr	14,200	36,800	350,514
Al-Wusṭa	Haymā'; Ṣayy	30,775	79,700	42,111
Al-Ẓāhirah	ʿIbrī	14,100	36,500	151,664
Governorates				
Al-Buraymī	Al-Buraymī	2,900	7,500	72,917
Masqaṭ	Muscat (Masqaṭ)	1,350	3,500	775,878
Musandam	Khaṣab	700	1,800	31,425
Ẓufār (Dhofar)	Salālah	38,350	99,300	249,729
TOTAL		119,500[4]	309,500	2,773,479[5]

Demography

Population (2011): 2,810,000.
Density (2011): persons per sq mi 23.5, persons per sq km 9.1.
Urban-rural (2010): urban 73.0%; rural 27.0%.
Sex distribution (2010): male 58.1%; female 41.9%.
Age breakdown (2010): under 15, 27.8%; 15–29, 34.4%; 30–44, 24.3%; 45–59, 9.4%; 60–74, 3.2%; 75 and over, 0.9%.
Population projection: (2020) 3,244,000; (2030) 3,553,000.
Doubling time: 34 years.
Ethnic composition (2000): Omani Arab 48.1%; Indo-Pakistani 31.7%, of which Balochi 15.0%, Bengali 4.4%, Tamil 2.5%; other Arab 7.2%; Persian 2.8%; Zanzibari (blacks originally from Zanzibar) 2.5%; other 7.7%.
Religious affiliation (2005): Muslim *c.* 89%, of which Ibāḍiyah *c.* 75%, Sunnī *c.* 8%, Shīʿī *c.* 6%; Hindu *c.* 5%; Christian *c.* 5%; other *c.* 1%.
Major cities (2010): Al-Sīb 299,800; Bawshar 189,600[6]; Maṭraḥ 150,124[6]; Salālah 147,400; Ṣuḥār 128,500; Muscat 19,891 (urban agglomeration [2009] 634,000).

Vital statistics

Birth rate per 1,000 population (2010): 23.9 (world avg. 19.2).
Death rate per 1,000 population (2010): 3.5 (world avg. 8.2).
Marriage/divorce rates per 1,000 population (2009): 7.9/0.8.
Total fertility rate (avg. births per childbearing woman; 2010): 2.87.
Life expectancy at birth (2010): male 72.2 years; female 75.9 years.
Major causes of death per 100,000 population (2002): diseases of the circulatory system 126, of which ischemic heart disease 63; infectious and parasitic diseases 39; malignant neoplasms (cancers) 37; accidents and injuries 35; diabetes mellitus 17.

National economy

Budget (2010). Revenue: RO 7,915,400,000 (oil revenue 69.1%; nontax revenue 13.4%; natural gas revenue 11.8%; other tax revenue 5.7%). Expenditures: RO 7,963,800,000 (current expenditure 60.1%, of which defense 23.7%; capital expenditure 32.6%, of which oil-, gas-related 11.3%; other 7.3%).
Public debt (2010): U.S.$2,938,800,000.
Gross national income (GNI; 2009): U.S.$49,840,000,000 (U.S.$17,890 per capita); purchasing power parity GNI (U.S.$24,410 per capita).

Structure of gross national product and labour force	2009		2003	
	in value RO '000,000	% of total value	labour force[7]	% of labour force[7]
Agriculture, forestry, fishing	244.5	1.4	58,114	7.9
Oil and natural gas	7,261.5[8]	41.0[8]	20,115	2.7
Other mining	61.8	0.3		
Manufacturing	1,816.9[8]	10.3[8]	59,492	8.1
Construction	1,206.3	6.8	118,257	16.0
Public utilities	208.3	1.2	4,045	0.5
Transp. and commun.	1,086.0	6.1	27,674	3.8
Trade, restaurants, hotels	1,814.4	10.2	109,157	14.8
Finance, real estate	1,759.9	9.9	25,200	3.4
Pub. admin., defense	1,291.3	7.3	162,742	22.1
Services	1,380.6	7.8	137,420	18.7
Other	–400.4[9]	–2.3[9]	14,408	2.0
TOTAL	17,731.1	100.0	736,624	100.0

Household income and expenditure. Average household size (2003) 6.8; expenditure (2000)[10]: food and nonalcoholic beverages 29.9%, transportation/communications 22.2%, housing 15.3%, clothing/footwear 7.2%, energy 6.0%.
Production (metric tons except as noted). Agriculture, forestry, fishing (2009): dates 278,590, tomatoes 43,000, bananas 32,463, chilies 8,176, mangoes 6,500, okra 5,400; livestock (number of live animals; 2010) 1,719,100 goats, 388,600 sheep, 322,800 cattle, 129,600 camels; roundwood (2010) 37,603 cu m, of which fuelwood 100%; fisheries production 158,669 (from aquaculture, negligible). Mining and quarrying (2009): limestone 7,947,606; chromite (gross weight) 636,482; marble 587,892; copper (metal content) 1,500. Manufacturing (value added in U.S.$'000,000; 2007): petroleum products 1,686; cement, bricks, and ceramics 429; base chemicals 339; food products 213; structural metal products 91; iron and steel 87. Energy production (consumption): electricity (kW-hr; 2010) 19,844,000,000 ([2007] 14,443,000,000); coal, none (none); crude petroleum (barrels; 2010) 315,725,000 ([2008] 29,565,000); petroleum products (metric tons; 2007) 3,538,000 (3,603,000); natural gas (cu m; 2010) 33,259,000,000 (26,072,700,000).
Population economically active (2009): total 1,085,600; activity rate of total population 41.5% (participation rates: ages 15 and over, 55.7%; female 18.8%; unemployed [2004] 15%).

Price index (2005 = 100)	2004	2005	2006	2007	2008	2009	2010
Consumer price index	98.2	100.0	103.2	109.4	122.6	127.4	131.5

Selected balance of payments data. Receipts from (U.S.$'000,000): tourism (2009) 700; remittances (2010) 40; foreign direct investment (FDI; 2008–10 avg.) 2,015; official development assistance (2009) 212. Disbursements for (U.S.$'000,000): tourism (2009) 869; remittances (2009) 5,313; FDI (2008–10 avg.) 288.
Land use as % of total land area (2007): in temporary crops or left fallow 0.2%, in permanent crops 0.1%, in pasture 5.5%, forest area 0.01%.

Foreign trade[11]

Balance of trade (current prices)	2004	2005	2006	2007	2008	2009
RO '000,000	+1,721	+3,793	+4,103	+3,137	+5,689	+3,917
% of total	20.2%	35.8%	33.1%	20.3%	24.4%	22.2%

Imports (2008): RO 8,814,500,000 (motor vehicles and parts 25.1%, of which cars 16.6%; machinery and apparatus 22.4%; food and live animals 9.3%; iron and steel 9.2%). *Major import sources:* U.A.E. 27.2%; Japan 15.6%; U.S. 5.7%; China 4.6%; India 4.5%.
Exports (2008): RO 14,503,000,000 (crude petroleum 58.0%; LNG 11.0%; refined petroleum 7.1%; chemicals and chemical products 3.4%). *Major export destinations:* China 29.3%; U.A.E. 10.9%; Japan 10.6%; South Korea 9.6%; Thailand 6.8%.

Transport and communications

Transport. Railroads: none. Roads (2011[12]): total length 36,384 mi, 58,554 km (paved 48%). Vehicles (2007): passenger cars 453,362; trucks and buses 139,728. Air transport (2010)[13]: passenger-km 6,960,000,000; metric ton-km cargo 107,000,000.

Communications			units				units
Medium	date	number in '000s	per 1,000 persons	**Medium**	date	number in '000s	per 1,000 persons
Televisions	2003	1,557	633	PCs	2007	460	183
Telephones				Dailies	2009	274[14]	94[14]
Cellular	2010	4,606[15]	1,655[15]	Internet users	2009	1,237	435
Landline	2010	284	102	Broadband	2010	53[15]	19[15]

Education and health

Educational attainment (2008). Percentage of population age 25 and over having: no formal schooling through incomplete primary education 33.7%; complete primary 12.4%; lower secondary 12.5%; higher secondary/technical 27.4%; higher 14.0%. *Literacy* (2008): percentage of total population age 15 and over literate 86.7%; males literate 90.0%; females literate 80.9%.

Education (2008–09)	teachers	students	student/ teacher ratio	enrollment rate (%)
Primary (age 6–11)	25,578	302,037	11.8	77
Secondary/Voc. (age 12–17)	21,768	321,670	14.8	82
Tertiary	5,027	75,313	15.0	26 (age 18–22)

Health (2010): physicians 5,862 (1 per 455 persons); hospital beds 5,757 (1 per 464 persons); infant mortality rate per 1,000 live births 16.0; undernourished population, n.a.

Military

Total active duty personnel (November 2010): 42,600 (army 58.7%, navy 9.9%, air force 11.7%, royal household 15.0%, foreign forces serving within Omani military command 4.7%).[16] *Military expenditure as percentage of GDP* (2009): 7.5%; per capita expenditure U.S.$1,427.

[1]All appointed by sultan; extent of authority is unclear in 2011. [2]Many ministries are located in adjacent Bawshar. [3]Approximate; no comprehensive survey of surface area has ever been carried out in Oman. [4]Summed total equals 119,525 sq mi. [5]Official census results include 816,143 expatriates. [6]Within Muscat urban agglomeration. [7]Employed only; includes 424,178 expatriate workers and 312,446 Omani workers. [8]Oil and natural gas excludes petroleum products; Manufacturing includes petroleum products. [9]Taxes less subsidies and less imputed bank service charges. [10]Weights of consumer price index components. [11]Imports c.i.f.; exports f.o.b. [12]January 1. [13]Oman Air only. [14]Circulation. [15]Subscribers. [16]Foreign troops (2010): U.K. 80.

Internet resources for further information:
- **Ministry of National Economy http://www.moneoman.gov.om**
- **Central Bank of Oman http://www.cbo.gov.om**

Pakistan

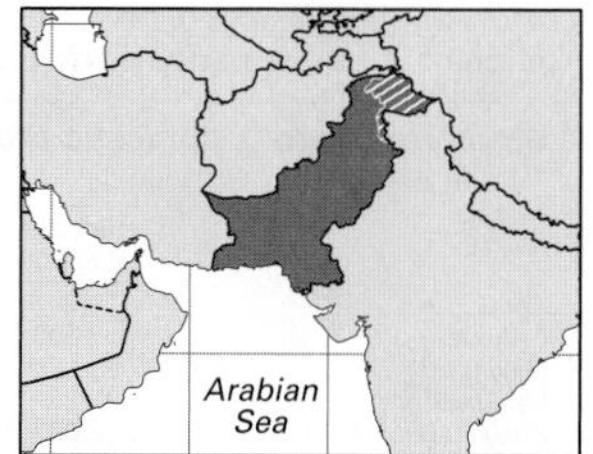

Official name: Islamic Republic of Pakistan.
Form of government: federal republic with two legislative houses (Senate [100]; National Assembly [342]).
Head of state: President.
Head of government: Prime Minister.
Capital: Islamabad.
Official language: [1].
Official religion: Islam.
Monetary unit: Pakistani rupee (PKR); valuation (Sept. 1, 2011) 1 U.S.$ = PKR 87.25; 1 £ = PKR 140.99.

Area and population

		area[2]		population
Provinces	**Capitals**	sq mi	sq km	2009 estimate[3]
Balochistan	Quetta	134,051	347,190	8,713,000
Khyber-Pakhtunkhwa	Peshawar	28,773	74,521	23,383,000
Punjab	Lahore	79,284	205,345	93,568,000
Sindh (Sind)	Karachi	54,407	140,914	40,028,000
Federally Administered Tribal Areas	admin. centre is Peshawar	10,509	27,220	4,093,000
Federal Capital Area				
Islamabad	—	350	906	1,049,000
TOTAL		307,374	796,096	170,834,000

Demography

Population (2011): 187,343,000[4].
Density (2011)[5]: persons per sq mi 550.2, persons per sq km 212.4.
Urban-rural (2009): urban 35.6%; rural 64.4%.
Sex distribution (2009): male 51.65%; female 48.35%.
Age breakdown (2005): under 15, 37.2%; 15–29, 29.9%; 30–44, 16.8%; 45–59, 10.2%; 60–74, 4.7%; 75–84, 1.0%; 85 and over, 0.2%.
Population projection[4]: (2020) 213,719,000; (2030) 242,862,000.
Ethnic composition (2000): Punjabi 52.6%; Pashtun 13.2%; Sindhi 11.7%; Urdu-speaking *muhajirs* 7.5%; Balochi 4.3%; other 10.7%.
Religious affiliation (2000): Muslim 96.1%[6]; Christian 2.5%; Hindu 1.2%; others (including Ahmadiyah) 0.2%.
Major urban agglomerations (2010[7]): Karachi 13,125,000; Lahore 7,132,000; Faisalabad 2,849,000; Rawalpindi 2,026,000; Multan 1,659,000; Gujranwala 1,652,000; Hyderabad 1,590,000; Peshawar 1,422,000; Islamabad 856,000.

Vital statistics

Birth rate per 1,000 population (2009): 28.4 (world avg. 20.3).
Death rate per 1,000 population (2009): 7.6 (world avg. 8.5).
Total fertility rate (avg. births per childbearing woman; 2009): 3.90.
Life expectancy at birth (2009): male 66.5 years; female 67.2 years.
Major causes of death per 100,000 population (2003): childhood diseases 126.7; infectious and parasitic diseases 104.0; diseases of the circulatory system 96.4; diseases of the respiratory system 67.0; accidents and violence 42.6.

National economy

Budget (2008–09). Revenue: PKR 1,679,239,000,000 (tax revenue 74.5%, of which income/corporate profits 28.4%, sales tax 28.1%, customs 6.7%; nontax revenue 25.5%). Expenditures: PKR 1,974,461,000,000 (current expenditure 75.6%, of which general public service 47.1%, defense 15.0%, economic affairs 10.2%; capital expenditure 24.4%).
Public debt (external, outstanding; June 2010): U.S.$42,115,000,000.
Production (metric tons except as noted). Agriculture, forestry, fishing (2009): sugarcane 50,045,000, wheat 24,033,000, buffalo's milk 21,622,000, cow's milk 11,985,000, rice 10,324,500, seed cotton 6,338,000, corn (maize) 3,261,500, potatoes 2,941,300, mangoes 1,728,000, onions 1,704,100, oranges 1,492,400, chickpeas 740,500, dates 735,276; livestock (number of live animals) 58,279,000 goats, 33,030,000 cattle, 29,883,000 buffalo, 27,432,000 sheep, 957,000 camels; roundwood (2010) 32,483,016 cu m, of which fuelwood 91%; fisheries production (2009) 684,461 (from aquaculture 20%). Mining and quarrying (2009–10): limestone 37,104,000; rock salt 1,944,000; gypsum 854,000; kaolin 23,000. Manufacturing (value added in U.S.$'000,000; 2006): textiles and wearing apparel 4,241; food and food products 2,527; chemicals and chemical products 2,124; cement, bricks, and ceramics 1,154; transportation equipment 955; refined petroleum and coke 859. Energy production (consumption) in '000: electricity (kW-hr; 2009) 91,843,000 (70,371,000); coal (metric tons; 2009–10) 3,493 ([2009] 8,390); crude petroleum (barrels; 2009–10) 24,000 ([2009] 134,332); petroleum products (metric tons; 2007) 10,363 (18,406); natural gas (cu m; 2009–10) 41,993,900 ([2009] 35,765,000).
Land use as % of total land area (2009): in temporary crops or left fallow 26.5%, in permanent crops 1.1%, in pasture 6.5%, forest area 2.2%.
Population economically active (2008): total 51,784,000[8]; activity rate of total population 29.0% (participation rates: ages 15–64, 53.6%; female 21.2%; officially unemployed [2009–10] 5.5%).

Price index (2005 = 100)

	2004	2005	2006	2007	2008	2009	2010
Consumer price index	91.7	100.0	107.9	116.1	139.7	158.7	180.8

Gross national income (GNI; 2010): U.S.$182,537,000,000 (U.S.$1,050 per capita); purchasing power parity GNI (U.S.$2,780 per capita).

Structure of gross domestic product and labour force

	2009–10		2008	
	in value PKR '000,000	% of total value	labour force[8]	% of labour force[8]
Agriculture, forestry, fishing	3,016,565	20.6	21,919,000	42.3
Mining, quarrying	346,256	2.4	57,000	0.1
Manufacturing	2,369,029	16.1	6,377,000	12.3
Construction	308,425	2.1	3,088,000	6.0
Public utilities	246,086	1.7	343,000	0.7
Transp. and commun.	1,894,188	12.9	2,681,000	5.2
Trade, hotels	2,391,058	16.3	7,178,000	13.9
Finance, real estate	1,013,309	6.9	692,000	1.3
Pub. admin., defense	794,439	5.4	6,706,000	12.9
Services	1,464,134	10.0		
Other	824,939[9]	5.6[9]	2,743,000[10]	5.3[10]
TOTAL	14,668,428	100.0	51,784,000	100.0

Selected balance of payments data. Receipts from (U.S.$'000,000): tourism (2009) 269; remittances (2010) 9,683; foreign direct investment (FDI; 2008–10 avg.) 3,264; official development assistance (2009) 2,781. Disbursements for (U.S.$'000,000): tourism (2009) 685; remittances (2009) 8; FDI (2008–10 avg.) 55.
Household income and expenditure (2007–08). Average household size 6.6; income per household PKR 173,472 (U.S.$2,817); sources of income: wages and salaries 39.6%, self-employment 29.1%, real estate 13.6%; expenditure: food and beverages 44.2%, housing and energy 22.7%, transportation and communications 6.2%, clothing and footwear 5.5%.

Foreign trade[11]

Balance of trade (current prices)

	2004	2005	2006	2007	2008	2009
U.S.$'000,000	–3,396	–6,341	–9,647	–10,587	–16,769	–10,440
% of total	11.3%	17.0%	22.1%	22.5%	28.2%	22.6%

Imports (2008): U.S.$42,327,000,000 (machinery and apparatus 18.2%; refined petroleum 16.9%; chemicals and chemical products 14.0%; crude petroleum 13.9%; food 6.5%). *Major import sources* (2009): China 14.3%; Saudi Arabia 12.2%; U.A.E. 11.3%; Kuwait 5.5%; U.S. 4.8%.
Exports (2008): U.S.$20,279,000,000 (apparel and accessories 19.3%, of which men's/boys' outerwear 8.6%; rice 12.0%; woven cotton fabrics 10.9%; bed linen 9.0%; refined petroleum 5.7%). *Major export destinations* (2009): U.S. 16.1%; U.A.E. 11.7%; Afghanistan 8.6%; U.K. 4.5%; China 4.2%.

Transport and communications

Transport. Railroads (2007–08): route length (2008) 4,829 mi, 7,771 km; passenger-km 24,731,000,000; metric ton-km cargo 6,187,000,000. Roads (2008): total length 160,958 mi, 259,038 km (paved 68%); passenger-km (2005) 263,788,000,000; metric ton-km cargo (2005) 149,249,000,000. Vehicles (2008): passenger cars 1,583,883; trucks and buses 393,650. Air transport (2009)[12]: passenger-km 13,891,000,000; metric ton-km cargo 270,000,000.

Communications

Medium	date	number in '000s	units per 1,000 persons	Medium	date	number in '000s	units per 1,000 persons
Televisions	2008[7]	9,940	56	PCs	2005	803	5.2
Telephones				Dailies	2009	6,100[13]	34[13]
Cellular	2010	102,777[14]	592[14]	Internet users	2009	20,350	113
Landline	2010	3,419	20	Broadband	2010	532[14]	3.1[14]

Education and health

Educational attainment: n.a. *Literacy* (2009–10): total population age 10 and over literate 60%; males literate 73%; females literate 46%.

Education (2008–09)

	teachers	students	student/ teacher ratio	enrollment rate (%)
Primary (age 5–9)	465,334	18,468,096	39.7	74[15]
Secondary/Voc. (age 10–16)	197,082[16]	9,432,977	41.9[16]	33
Tertiary	63,421	1,226,004	19.3	6 (age 17–21)

Health: physicians (2010[17]) 139,555 (1 per 1,300 persons); hospital beds (2009[17]) 103,708 (1 per 1,721 persons); infant mortality rate (2009–10) 73.5; undernourished population (2005–07) 43,400,400[18] (26% of total population based on the consumption of a minimum daily requirement of 1,750 calories).

Military

Total active duty personnel (November 2010): 617,000 (army 89.1%, navy 3.6%, air force 7.3%); paramilitary 304,000. *Military expenditure as percentage of GDP* (2008): 3.0%; per capita expenditure U.S.$26.

[1]English may be used for official purposes. Urdu is the national (not yet official) language as of mid-2010. [2]Excludes 33,125 sq mi (85,793 sq km) area of Pakistani-administered Jammu and Kashmir (comprising both Azad Kashmir [AK; 5,134 sq mi (13,297 sq km)] and Gilgit-Baltistan [GB; 27,991 sq mi (72,496 sq km)]); GB name changed from Northern Areas in August 2009. [3]Excludes Afghan refugees and the populations of AK (2009; 3,890,000) and GB (2009; 1,009,000). [4]Per U.S. Bureau of the Census International Database (June 2010 update) including Afghan refugees and AK and GB. [5]Includes AK and GB. [6]Mostly Sunnī, with Shīʿī constituting about 17% of total population. [7]July 1. [8]Excludes armed forces. [9]Indirect taxes less subsidies. [10]Includes 49,000 inadequately defined and 2,694,000 unemployed. [11]Imports f.o.b. in balance of trade and c.i.f. in commodities and trading partners. [12]Pakistan International Airlines only. [13]Circulation of daily newspapers. [14]Subscribers. [15]2009–10. [16]2003–04. [17]January 1. [18]Excludes Azad Kashmir and Northern Areas.

Internet resources for further information:
- **Statistics Division: Government of Pakistan http://www.statpak.gov.pk**
- **State Bank of Pakistan http://www.sbp.org.pk**

Palau

Official name: Beluu er a Belau (Palauan); Republic of Palau (English).
Form of government: republic with two legislative houses (Senate [13]; House of Delegates [16]).
Head of state and government: President.
Capital: Melekeok, on Babelthuap[1].
Official languages: Palauan; English.
Official religion: none.
Monetary unit: U.S. dollar (U.S.$); valuation (Sept. 1, 2011) 1 U.S.$ = £0.62.

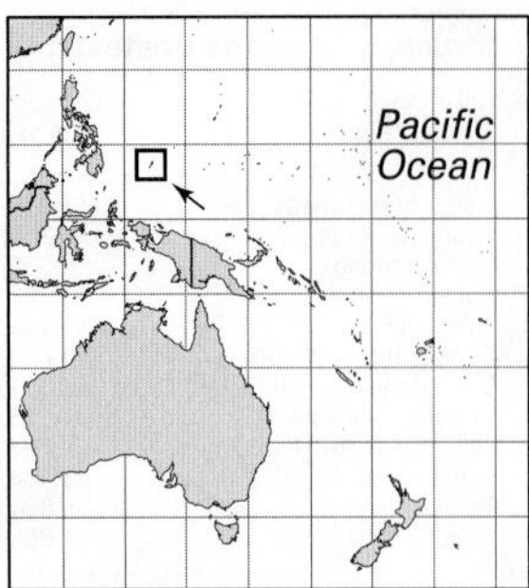

Area and population

	area		population
			2005
States	sq mi	sq km	census
Aimeliik[2]	20	52	270
Airai[2]	17	44	2,723
Angaur	3	8	320
Hatohobei	1	3	44
Kayangel	1	3	188
Koror	7	18	12,676
Melekeok[2]	11	28	391
Ngaraard[2]	14	36	581
Ngarchelong[2]	4	10	488
Ngardmau[2]	18	47	166
Ngaremlengui[2]	25	65	317
Ngatpang[2]	18	47	464
Ngchesar[2]	16	41	254
Ngiwal[2]	10	26	223
Peleliu	5	13	702
Sonsorol	1	3	100
Other			
Rock Islands	18	47	—
TOTAL	188[3]	488[3]	19,907

Demography

Population (2011): 20,600.
Density (2011): persons per sq mi 109.6, persons per sq km 42.2.
Urban-rural (2009): urban 81.6%; rural 19.4%.
Sex distribution (2007): male 53.53%; female 46.47%.
Age breakdown (2007): under 15, 24.1%; 15–29, 22.8%; 30–44, 28.0%; 45–59, 16.8%; 60–74, 5.3%; 75–84, 2.4%; 85 and over, 0.6%.
Population projection: (2020) 22,000; (2030) 23,000.
Ethnic composition (2005)[4]: Palauan (Micronesian/Malay/Melanesian admixture) 65.2%; Asian 30.3%, of which Filipino 21.6%, Vietnamese 2.3%; other Micronesian 3.1%; white 1.1%; other 0.3%.
Religious affiliation (2005)[4]: Roman Catholic 51.0%; Protestant 26.7%; Modekngei (marginal Christian sect) 8.9%; other Christian 1.8%; other 11.6%.
Major towns (2005): Koror 10,743; Meyuns 1,153; Kloulklubed 680.

Vital statistics

Birth rate per 1,000 population (2007): 12.4 (world avg. 20.3).
Death rate per 1,000 population (2007): 7.9 (world avg. 8.5).
Natural increase rate per 1,000 population (2007): 4.5 (world avg. 11.8).
Marriage/divorce rates per 1,000 population (2006): n.a./n.a.
Total fertility rate (avg. births per childbearing woman; 2007): 2.00.
Life expectancy at birth (2008): male 66.3 years; female 72.1 years.
Major causes of death per 100,000 population (2002): diseases of the circulatory system 244, of which ischemic heart disease 82, cerebrovascular disease 78; infectious and parasitic diseases 138; malignant neoplasms (cancers) 61; diseases of the respiratory system 45; injuries and accidents 34.

National economy

Budget (2008–09). Revenue: U.S.$81,300,000 (grants 53.5%, of which part of U.S. Compact of Free Association assistance 15.8%; tax revenue 36.5%; nontax revenue 7.9%; other 2.1%).[5, 6] Expenditures: U.S.$95,000,000 (current expenditure 77.6%; capital expenditure 22.4%).
Production (metric tons except as noted). Agriculture, forestry, fishing (2008): principally coconuts, root crops, bananas, pig meat, chicken meat, and hen's eggs; livestock (number of live animals) pigs, n.a., chickens, n.a.; roundwood, n.a.; fisheries production (2009) 1,012 (from aquaculture 2%). Mining and quarrying: n.a. Manufacturing: includes handicrafts and small items. Energy production (consumption): electricity (kW-hr; 2007) 154,000,000 (154,000,000); coal, none (none); crude petroleum, none (none); petroleum products (metric tons; 2007) none (68,000); natural gas, none (none).
Selected balance of payments data. Receipts from (U.S.$'000,000): tourism (2007–08) 117; remittances (2010) n.a.; foreign direct investment (2008–10 avg.) 2; official development assistance (2009) 35. Disbursements for (U.S.$'000,000): tourism (2006) 1.4; remittances (2009) n.a.
Land use as % of total land area (2009): in temporary crops or left fallow (2007) *c.* 2%, in permanent crops *c.* 4%, in pasture *c.* 4%, forest area *c.* 88%[7].
Population economically active (2005): total 10,203; activity rate of total population 51.3% (participation rates: over age 15, 69.1%; female 39.1%; unemployed 4.2%).

Price index (2005 = 100)

	2003	2004	2005	2006	2007	2008	2009
Consumer price index	91.7	96.2	100.0	104.5	107.8	120.8	122.6

Gross national income (GNI; 2010): U.S.$133,000,000 (U.S.$6,460 per capita); purchasing power parity GNI (U.S.$10,760 per capita).

Structure of gross domestic product and labour force

	2007		2005	
	in value U.S.$'000	% of total value	labour force[8]	% of labour force[8]
Agriculture	2,097	1.3	451	4.4
Fisheries	3,500	2.1	310	3.0
Mining	180	0.1	...	...
Manufacturing	822	0.5	259	2.5
Public utilities	7,027	4.3	[9]	[9]
Construction	25,099	15.3	1,365	13.4
Transportation and communications	12,655	7.7	769[9]	7.5[9]
Trade, hotels	50,382	30.7	1,670	16.4
Finance, real estate	13,337	8.1	182	1.8
Public administration, defense	32,340	19.7	1,734	17.0
Services	12,568	7.6	3,037	29.8
Other	4,280[10]	2.6[10]	426[11]	4.2[11]
TOTAL	164,289[3]	100.0	10,203	100.0

Public debt (gross external debt; 2006–07): U.S.$22,857,000.
Household income and expenditure. Average household size (2005) 3.9; annual average income per household (2006) U.S.$19,759; sources of income (2006): wages and salaries 57.8%, imputed rent 18.2%, social security 9.6%, customs 3.9%, other 10.5%; expenditure (2006): imputed rent 18.6%, housing and energy 16.9%, food 16.4%, transportation 10.8%, health, personal care, and education 6.0%, cash gifts given 4.4%, alcohol, tobacco, and betel nut 3.4%, other 23.5%.

Foreign trade

Balance of trade (current prices)

	2003–04	2004–05	2005–06	2006–07	2007–08	2008–09
U.S.$'000	−101,398	−91,765	−101,690	−81,206	−118,500	−91,700
% of total	89.6%	85.7%	78.9%	80.1%	83.4%	79.5%

Imports (2006–07): U.S.$91,287,000 (mineral fuels and lubricants 37.5%, machinery and transport equipment 17.6%, beverages and tobacco products 14.9%, food and live animals 9.4%, chemicals and chemical products 8.7%). *Major import sources* (2006–07): U.S. 33.2%; Singapore 24.8%; Guam 11.2%; Japan 9.6%; Philippines 7.6%; Taiwan 5.9%.
Exports (2006–07): U.S.$10,081,000 (mostly high-grade tuna and garments). *Major export destinations* (2008): mostly Japan; far less significantly the Philippines and South Korea.

Transport and communications

Transport. Railroads: none. Roads (2007): total length 91 mi, 146 km (paved, n.a.). Vehicles (2004): passenger cars and trucks 7,247. Air transport (2003): passenger arrivals 80,017, passenger departures 78,608.

Communications

Medium	date	number in '000s	units per 1,000 persons	Medium	date	number in '000s	units per 1,000 persons
Televisions	1997	11	606	PCs	2007	...	...
Telephones				Dailies	2009	0	0
Cellular	2010	15[12]	709[12]	Internet users	2009	...	...
Landline	2010	7.0	341	Broadband	2010	0.2[12]	11.4[12]

Education and health

Educational attainment (2005). Percentage of population age 25 and over having: no formal schooling 1.9%; incomplete primary education 9.0%; complete primary 3.9%; incomplete secondary 14.9%; complete secondary 42.2%; some postsecondary 10.0%; vocational 4.1%; higher 14.0%. *Literacy* (2005): total population age 15 and over literate 99.7%; males literate 99.6%; females literate 99.8%.

Education (2004–05)

	teachers	students	student/ teacher ratio	enrollment rate (%)
Primary (age 6–10)	153	1,913	12.5	96[13]
Secondary/Voc. (age 11–17)	126[13]	2,282	15.1[13]	...
Tertiary	34[14]	650[14]	19.1[14]	38[15] (age 18–22)

Health: physicians (2006) 26 (1 per 771 persons); hospital beds (2004) 135 (1 per 147 persons); infant mortality rate per 1,000 live births (2007) 7.2; undernourished population, n.a.

Military

The United States is responsible for the external security of Palau, as specified in the renewed Compact of Free Association of September 2010.

[1]Formal transfer of capital to Melekeok on Babelthuap from Koror took place Oct. 1, 2006. [2]State on Babelthuap island. [3]Detail does not add to total given because of rounding. [4]Population age 18 and over only. [5]Aid payments since 1994 from the U.S. per the Compact of Free Association have greatly benefited Palau. [6]The licensing of fishing vessels from the U.S., Japan, Taiwan, and China is a source of revenue. [7]Forest area overlaps with other categories. [8]Foreign workers constituted 73% of the paid workforce in 2008. [9]Transportation and communications includes Public utilities. [10]Import duties less imputed bank service charges. [11]Unemployed. [12]Subscribers. [13]1999–2000. [14]2007–08; Palau Community College. [15]2001–02.

Internet resource for further information:
- **Palau Office of Planning and Statistics http://www.palaugov.net/stats**

Panama

Official name: República de Panamá (Republic of Panama).
Form of government: multiparty republic with one legislative house (National Assembly [71]).
Head of state and government: President.
Capital: Panama City.
Official language: Spanish.
Official religion: none.
Monetary unit: balboa (B); valuation (Sept. 1, 2011) 1 U.S.$ = B 1.00; 1 £ = B 1.62.

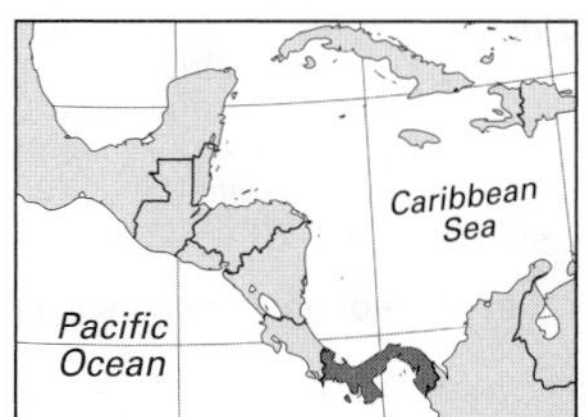

Area and population

Provinces	Capitals	area sq mi	area sq km	population 2010 census
Bocas del Toro	Bocas del Toro	1,798	4,657	125,461
Chiriquí	David	2,506	6,491	416,873
Coclé	Penonomé	1,910	4,947	233,708
Colón	Colón	1,767	4,576	241,928
Darién	La Palma	4,592	11,893	48,378
Herrera	Chitré	912	2,362	109,955
Los Santos	Las Tablas	1,471	3,809	89,592
Panamá	Panama City	4,359	11,289	1,713,070
Veraguas	Santiago	4,088	10,588	226,991
Indigenous districts				
Emberá	Unión Chocoe	1,696	4,394	10,001
Kuna Yala (San Blas)	El Porvenir	910	2,358	33,109
Ngöbe Buglé	Llano Tugri	2,631	6,814	156,747
TOTAL		28,640	74,177[1]	3,405,813

Demography

Population (2011): 3,643,000.
Density (2011): persons per sq mi 127.2, persons per sq km 49.1.
Urban-rural (2010): urban 74.8%; rural 25.2%.
Sex distribution (2010): male 50.28%; female 49.72%.
Age breakdown (2010): under 15, 29.2%; 15–29, 24.9%; 30–44, 21.1%; 45–59, 14.2%; 60–74, 7.6%; 75–84, 2.2%; 85 and over, 0.8%.
Population projection: (2020) 4,138,000; (2030) 4,622,000.
Ethnic composition (2000): mestizo 58.1%; black and mulatto 14.0%; white 8.6%; Amerindian 6.7%; Asian 5.5%; other 7.1%.
Religious affiliation (2008): Roman Catholic (including nominal) *c.* 75%; Protestant/independent Christian *c.* 20%; Mormon *c.* 1%; Jewish *c.* 0.3%; Muslim *c.* 0.3%; other *c.* 3.4%.
Major cities/districts (2010): Panama City 430,299/880,691 (urban agglomeration 1,378,000); San Miguelito 315,019[2]; Arraiján 41,041/220,779; Colón 34,655/206,553; La Chorrera 62,803/161,470; David 82,907/144,858.

Vital statistics

Birth rate per 1,000 population (2008): 20.3 (world avg. 20.3); within marriage (2006) 17.3%; outside of marriage (2006) 82.7%.
Death rate per 1,000 population (2008): 4.5 (world avg. 8.5).
Natural increase rate per 1,000 population (2008): 15.8 (world avg. 11.8).
Total fertility rate (avg. births per childbearing woman; 2007): 2.62.
Marriage/divorce rates per 1,000 population (2008): 3.4/0.9.
Life expectancy at birth (2007): male 73.7 years; female 79.5 years.
Major causes of death per 100,000 population (2008): diseases of the circulatory system 127.8; malignant neoplasms (cancers) 77.6; accidents and violence 56.7; diseases of the respiratory system 46.8.

National economy

Budget (2007). Revenue: B 4,433,000,000 (tax revenue 48.1%, of which indirect taxes 22.5%, income taxes 22.2%; nontax revenue 32.9%, of which revenue from Panama Canal 10.5%; capital revenue 16.9%). Expenditures: B 4,432,000,000 (current expenditure 78.1%, of which debt servicing 30.7%, education 14.4%, health 13.5%, public order 5.6%; development expenditure 21.9%).
Production (metric tons except as noted). Agriculture, forestry, fishing (2009): sugarcane 1,913,850, bananas 320,540, rice 241,530, cow's milk 195,000, plantains 99,280, corn (maize) 85,540, watermelons 79,660, oil palm fruit 75,000, pineapples 56,300, canteloupes and other melons 43,890, coffee 12,960, papayas 7,800, yautia 5,280; livestock (number of live animals) 1,614,100 cattle, 272,700 pigs, 190,000 horses; roundwood (2010) 1,312,585 cu m, of which fuelwood 87%; fisheries production 228,509 (from aquaculture 3%). Mining and quarrying (2009): limestone 270,000; gold (metal content) 800 kg. Manufacturing (value added in B '000,000; 2006): food and food products 468; beverages 167; cement, bricks, and ceramics 82; printing and publishing 64; structural metal products 61. Energy production (consumption): electricity (kW-hr; 2009) 6,397,150,000 (5,859,630,000); coal, none (none); crude petroleum, none (none); petroleum products (metric tons; 2007) none (1,997,000); natural gas, none (none).
Land use as % of total land area (2009): in temporary crops or left fallow (2007) 7.4%, in permanent crops 2.0%, in pasture 20.6%, forest area 43.9%.
Population economically active (2008): total 1,416,600; activity rate of total population 43.8% (participation rates: ages 15–64, 68.7%; female 38.1%; unemployed [October 2009] 6.6%).

Price index (2005 = 100)

	2004	2005	2006	2007	2008	2009	2010
Consumer price index	96.9	100.0	102.1	106.4	115.7	118.5	122.6

Household income and expenditure. Average household size (2010) 3.2; average annual income per household (1997–98) B 12,180 (U.S.$12,180); sources of income, n.a.; expenditure (2001): food *c.* 22%, energy *c.* 18%, health care *c.* 14%, education *c.* 4%, other *c.* 42%.
Gross national income (GNI; 2010): U.S.$24,531,000,000 (U.S.$6,990 per capita); purchasing power parity GNI (U.S.$12,940 per capita).

Structure of gross domestic product and labour force

	2008 in value B '000,000[3]	% of total value[3]	labour force[4]	% of labour force[4]
Agriculture, fishing	1,120	6.0	185,600	13.1
Mining	254	1.4	3,300	0.2
Manufacturing	1,168	6.3	114,100	8.1
Construction	1,101	5.9	136,700	9.6
Public utilities	514	2.9	6,900	0.5
Transp. and commun.	3,965	21.4	100,900	7.1
Trade, restaurants	3,178	17.1	329,400	23.3
Finance, real estate	4,184	22.5	100,100	7.1
Pub. admin.	1,321	7.1	78,700	5.6
Services	915	4.9	278,000	19.6
Other	838[5]	4.5[5]	82,900[6]	5.8[6]
TOTAL	18,558	100.0	1,416,600	100.0

Public debt (external, outstanding; 2009): U.S.$11,282,000,000.
Selected balance of payments data (2009). Receipts from (U.S.$'000,000): tourism 1,483; remittances (2010) 204; foreign direct investment (FDI; 2008–10 avg.) 2,110; official development assistance 66. Disbursements for (U.S.$'000,000): tourism 338; remittances 229; FDI (2008–10 avg.) 2,269.

Foreign trade[7, 8]

Balance of trade (current prices)

	2005	2006	2007	2008	2009	2010
U.S.$'000,000	–3,190	–3,796	–5,743	–7,866	–6,980	–8,420
% of total	62.3%	65.0%	71.8%	77.5%	81.0%	85.3%

Imports (2008): U.S.$9,023,000,000 (refined petroleum 19.9%, machinery and apparatus 19.8%, road vehicles 9.9%, food 9.2%, iron and steel 5.5%). *Major import sources:* U.S. 29.7%; free zones 24.8%; Costa Rica 5.1%; China 5.0%; Japan 4.3%.
Exports (2008): U.S.$1,145,000,000 (fish 29.3% [including tuna 8.4%], melons and papayas 18.8%, bananas 8.6%, crustaceans and mollusks 7.2%, metal scrap 4.7%). *Major export destinations:* U.S. 39.2%; Neth. 10.7%; Costa Rica 5.8%; Sweden 5.5%; U.K. 5.4%.

Transport and communications

Transport. Railroads (2007)[9]: route length 48 mi, 77 km; passenger-km (2005) 44,734,000,000; metric ton-km cargo (2005) 138,104,000,000. Roads (2008): total length 8,530 mi, 13,727 km (paved 38%). Vehicles (2007): passenger cars 436,205; trucks and buses 194,615. Panama Canal traffic (2008–09): number of transits 12,849; net tonnage transiting 201,191,000 metric tons. Air transport (2008)[10]: passenger-km 9,316,000,000; metric ton-km cargo (2007) 36,400,000.

Communications

Medium	date	number in '000s	units per 1,000 persons	Medium	date	number in '000s	units per 1,000 persons
Televisions	2004	620	195	PCs	2007	154	46
Telephones				Dailies	2009	230[11]	70[11]
Cellular	2010	6,496[12]	1,847[12]	Internet users	2009	960	278
Landline	2010	553	157	Broadband	2010	276[12]	78[12]

Education and health

Educational attainment (2000). Percentage of population age 25 and over having: no formal schooling 8.9%; primary 36.4%; secondary 33.9%; undergraduate 14.4%; graduate 1.5%; other/unknown 4.9%. *Literacy* (2008): total population age 15 and over literate 93.5%; males literate 94.1%; females literate 92.8%.

Education (2007–08)

	teachers	students	student/ teacher ratio	enrollment rate (%)
Primary (age 6–11)	18,364	445,107	24.2	98
Secondary/Voc. (age 12–17)	17,337	266,760	15.4	66
Tertiary	13,464	134,290	10.0	45 (age 18–22)

Health (2007): physicians 4,524 (1 per 739 persons); hospital beds 7,689 (1 per 435 persons); infant mortality rate per 1,000 live births (2008) 12.8; undernourished population (2004–06) 550,000 (17% of total population based on the consumption of a minimum daily requirement of 1,790 calories).

Military

Total active duty personnel (November 2010): none[13]. *Paramilitary expenditure as percentage of GDP* (2009): 1.1%; per capita expenditure U.S.$80.

[1]Detail does not add to total given because of rounding. [2]District adjacent to Panama City within Panama City urban agglomeration. [3]At prices of 1996. [4]Ages 15 and over. [5]Taxes and import duties less imputed bank service charges and less subsidies. [6]Unemployed. [7]Imports c.i.f.; exports f.o.b. [8]Excludes trade passing through Colón Free Zone (2010 imports c.i.f. U.S.$10,228,000,000; 2010 reexports f.o.b. U.S.$11,396,000,000, of which chemicals and chemical products 32.4%, garments 20.0%, machinery and apparatus 18.2%, footwear/hats/other apparel accessories 9.8%). [9]All data for Panama Canal Railway. [10]COPA only. [11]Circulation of daily newspapers. [12]Subscribers. [13]Military abolished 1990; 12,000-member paramilitary includes air and maritime units.

Internet resource for further information:

- **Instituto Nacional de Estadística y Censo http://www.contraloria.gob.pa/inec**

Papua New Guinea

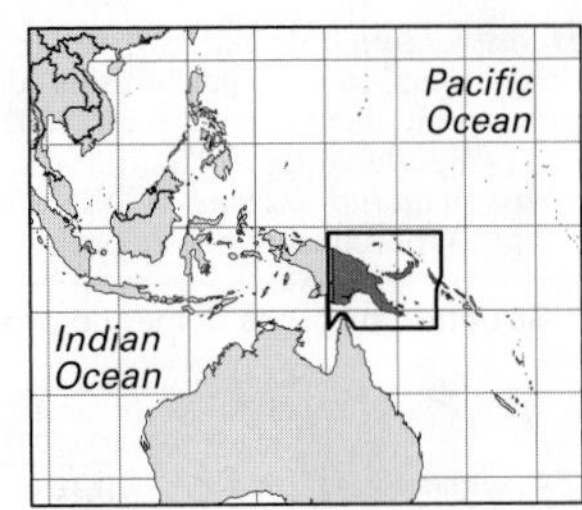

Official names[1]: Independent State of Papua New Guinea.
Form of government: constitutional monarchy with one legislative house (National Parliament [109]).
Head of state: British Monarch represented by Governor-General.
Head of government: Prime Minister.
Capital: Port Moresby.
Official languages: English; Hiri Motu; Tok Pisin.
Official religion: none.
Monetary unit: kina (K); valuation (Sept. 1, 2011) 1 U.S.$ = K 2.24; 1 £ = K 3.62.

Area and population

Regions / Provinces	area sq km	population 2000 census	Regions / Provinces	area sq km	population 2000 census
Highlands	62,400	1,973,996	East Sepik	42,800	343,181
Eastern Highlands	11,200	432,972	Madang	29,000	365,106
Enga	12,800	295,031	Morobe	34,500	539,404
Simbu (Chimbu)	6,100	259,703	Sandaun (West Sepik)	36,300	185,741
Southern Highlands	23,800	546,265	Papua (Southern Coastal)	200,340	1,041,820
Western Highlands	8,500	440,025	Central	29,500	183,983
Islands	57,500	741,538	Gulf	34,500	106,898
Bougainville (autonomous region)[2]	9,300	175,160	Milne Bay	14,000	210,412
East New Britain	15,500	220,133	National Capital District	240	254,158
Manus	2,100	43,387	Oro (Northern)	22,800	133,065
New Ireland	9,600	118,350	Western	99,300	153,304
West New Britain	21,000	184,508	TOTAL	462,840	5,190,786[3]
Momase (Northern Coastal)	142,600	1,433,432			

Demography

Population (2011): 6,188,000.
Density (2011): persons per sq mi 34.6, persons per sq km 13.3.
Urban-rural (2008): urban 12.0%; rural 88.0%.
Sex distribution (2008): male 51.49%; female 48.51%.
Age breakdown (2008): under 15, 37.7%; 15–29, 27.2%; 30–44, 19.4%; 45–59, 10.3%; 60–74, 4.5%; 75–84, 0.8%; 85 and over, 0.1%.
Population projection: (2020) 7,259,000; (2030) 8,359,000.
Ethnic composition (1983)[4]: New Guinea Papuan 84.0%; New Guinea Melanesian 15.0%; other 1.0%.
Religious affiliation (2005): Protestant/independent Christian 44%; Roman Catholic 22%; traditional beliefs 34%[5].
Major cities (2009): Port Moresby 307,600; Lae 73,000; Arawa (on Bougainville) 39,700; Mount Hagen 39,000; Popondetta 37,800; Kokopo (on New Britain) 33,000.

Vital statistics

Birth rate per 1,000 population (2008): 29.3 (world avg. 20.3).
Death rate per 1,000 population (2008): 9.6 (world avg. 8.5).
Total fertility rate (avg. births per childbearing woman; 2008): 3.7.
Life expectancy at birth (2008): male 55.0 years; female 60.0 years.
Major causes of death per 100,000 population (2002): infectious and parasitic diseases *c.* 249; cardiovascular diseases *c.* 153; perinatal conditions *c.* 85; respiratory infections *c.* 65; accidents *c.* 53.

National economy

Budget (2009). Revenue: K 6,651,000,000 (tax revenue 74.8%, of which personal income taxes 18.7%, company taxes 16.9%; grants 13.2%; nontax revenue 11.5%; other 0.5%). Expenditures: K 6,688,000,000 (current expenditure 62.3%; capital expenditure 35.1%; reappropriation to trust account 2.6%).
Public debt (external, outstanding; June 2010): U.S.$904,000,000.
Production (metric tons except as noted). Agriculture, forestry, fishing (2009): fruit 2,324,492 (of which bananas 1,187,020), oil palm fruit 1,730,000, coconuts 930,000, sweet potatoes 534,085, taro 313,814, game meat 301,813, yams 262,153, green corn (maize) 225,608, berries 133,632, coffee 60,240, cacao 51,000; livestock (number of live animals) 1,800,000 pigs; roundwood (2010) 8,573,000 cu m, of which fuelwood 65%; fisheries production 229,817 (from aquaculture, negligible). Mining and quarrying (2009): copper (metal content) 166,700; gold 63,600 kg; silver 50,000 kg. Manufacturing (value of exports in K '000,000; 2008–09): palm oil 788.8; refined petroleum products 486.5; forest products 367.9; coconut oil 99.8; copra 28.8. Energy production (consumption): electricity (kW-hr; 2008) 2,970,000,000 (2,760,000,000); coal none (none); crude petroleum (barrels; 2009) 12,700,000 ([2008] 12,000,000); petroleum products (metric tons; 2007) 574,000 (800,000); natural gas (cu m; 2008) 414,000,000 (497,000,000).
Land use as % of total land area (2009): in temporary crops or left fallow 0.6%, in permanent crops 1.5%, in pasture 0.4%, forest area 63.7%.
Population economically active (2008)[6]: total 2,853,000; activity rate 43.4% (participation rates: ages 15–64, 73.2%; female 48.9%; unemployed, n.a.).

Price index (2005 = 100)

	2004	2005	2006	2007	2008	2009	2010
Consumer price index	98.3	100.0	102.4	103.3	114.4	122.3	129.7

Household income and expenditure. Average household size, n.a.; sources of income: n.a.; expenditure (2003)[7]: transportation and communication 28.6%, alcohol/tobacco/narcotics 21.6%, food and nonalcoholic beverages 17.7%, household furnishings 14.3%, clothing/footwear 11.2%, housing/energy 6.6%.
Gross national income (GNI; 2010): U.S.$8,935,000,000 (U.S.$1,300 per capita); purchasing power parity GNI (U.S.$2,390 per capita).

Structure of gross domestic product and labour force

	2008 in value K '000,000	2008 % of total value	2000 labour force	2000 % of labour force
Agriculture, forestry, fishing	7,500	34.8	1,696,271	70.3
Mining and quarrying	5,414	25.1	9,282	0.4
Manufacturing	1,278	5.9	25,557	1.1
Construction	2,241	10.4	48,312	2.0
Public utilities	361	1.7	2,208	0.1
Transp. and commun.	440	2.0	24,513	1.0
Trade, hotels	1,368	6.4	357,581	14.8
Finance, real estate	648	3.0	31,129	1.3
Pub. admin., defense	1,804	8.4	32,043	1.3
Services			86,391	3.6
Other	500[8]	2.3[8]	100,070	4.1
TOTAL	21,554	100.0	2,413,357	100.0

Selected balance of payments data. Receipts from (U.S.$'000,000): tourism (2009) 1.2; remittances (2010) 15; foreign direct investment (FDI; 2008–10 avg.) 141; official development assistance (2009) 414. Disbursements for (U.S.$'000,000): tourism (2009) 29; remittances (2008) 135.

Foreign trade[9]

Balance of trade (current prices)

	2004	2005	2006	2007	2008	2009
K '000,000	+3,734	+5,559	+6,767	+6,282	+7,196	+4,192
% of total	28.4%	37.1%	35.8%	28.7%	29.8%	20.9%

Imports (2004): K 5,050,000,000 (nonelectrical machinery 18.4%; refined petroleum 16.6%; food products 15.1%, of which cereals 7.8%; chemicals and chemical products 8.2%; fabricated metals 6.4%; road vehicles 6.4%). *Major import sources* (2008): Australia 42.0%; U.S. 22.7%; Singapore 11.3%; Japan 4.7%; China 3.5%.
Exports (2009): K 12,080,000,000 (gold 44.9%; copper 16.8%; crude petroleum 13.6%; palm oil 5.9%; coffee 3.8%; logs 3.6%; refined petroleum 3.1%; cocoa 2.8%). *Major export destinations* (2008): Australia 44.3%; Japan 13.3%; Philippines 7.8%; Germany 4.8%; South Korea 4.7%.

Transport and communications

Transport. Railroads: none. Roads (2000): total length 12,179 mi, 19,600 km[10] (paved 4%). Vehicles (2007): passenger cars 38,173; trucks and buses 17,894. Air transport (2007)[11]: passenger-km 864,000,000; metric ton-km cargo 20,800,000.

Communications

Medium	date	number in '000s	units per 1,000 persons	Medium	date	number in '000s	units per 1,000 persons
Televisions	2003	130	22	PCs	2005	391	64
Telephones				Dailies	2009	53[12]	8.9[12]
Cellular	2010	1,909[13]	278[13]	Internet users	2009	125	21
Landline	2010	121	18	Broadband	2010	6.1[13]	0.9[13]

Education and health

Educational attainment (1990). Percentage of population age 25 and over having: no formal schooling 82.6%; some primary education 8.2%; completed primary 5.0%; some secondary 4.2%. *Literacy* (2008): total population age 15 and over literate 59.6%; males literate 63.6%; females literate 55.6%.

Education (2005–06)

	teachers	students	student/ teacher ratio	enrollment rate (%)
Primary (age 7–12)	14,860	532,250	35.8	...
Secondary/Voc. (age 13–18)	...	...	...	...
Tertiary	930[14]	9,095[14]	9.8[14]	2[15] (age 19–23)

Health: physicians (2008) 333 (1 per 17,466 persons); hospital beds (2000) 14,516 (1 per 371 persons); infant mortality rate (2008) 60.0.

Military

Total active duty personnel (November 2010): 3,100 (army 80.6%, maritime element [coastal patrol] 12.9%, air force 6.5%). *Military expenditure as percentage of GDP* (2008): 0.6%; per capita expenditure U.S.$6.

[1]Gau Hedinarai ai Papua-Matamata Guinea (Hiri Motu); Papua-Niugini (Tok Pisin). [2]Bougainville formally attained autonomy within Papua New Guinea (PNG) on June 15, 2005. A referendum on possible future independence is to be held between 2014 and 2019. [3]Unadjusted total; census total adjusted for undercount equals *c.* 5,398,000. [4]PNG has about 1,200 ethnic communities, more than half of which number less than 1,000 people. New Guinea Papuans are predominantly descendants of original arrivals; New Guinea Melanesians are more racially mixed with other Pacific peoples. [5]According to the 2000 census PNG is 96% Christian. In actuality, many citizens combine Christian faith with some traditional indigenous practices. [6]ILO estimates. [7]Based on 6 categories with available data. [8]Import duties less imputed bank service charges and less subsidies. [9]Imports f.o.b. in balance of trade and trading partners and c.i.f. in commodities. [10]Port Moresby is not connected by road to other major population centres. Air and sea travel are therefore of particular importance. [11]Air Niugini only. [12]Circulation. [13]Subscribers. [14]Data for five of the six universities only. [15]1998–99.

Internet resources for further information:
- **Bank of Papua New Guinea http://www.bankpng.gov.pg**
- **National Statistical Office of Papua New Guinea http://www.nso.gov.pg**

Paraguay

Official name: República del Paraguay (Spanish); Tetã Paraguáype (Guaraní) (Republic of Paraguay).
Form of government: multiparty republic with two legislative houses (Chamber of Senators [45[1]]; Chamber of Deputies [80]).
Head of state and government: President.
Capital: Asunción.
Official languages: Spanish; Guaraní.
Official religion: none[2].
Monetary unit: guaraní (plural guaranies; ₲); valuation (Sept. 1, 2011) 1 U.S.$ = ₲3,900; 1 £ = ₲6,302.

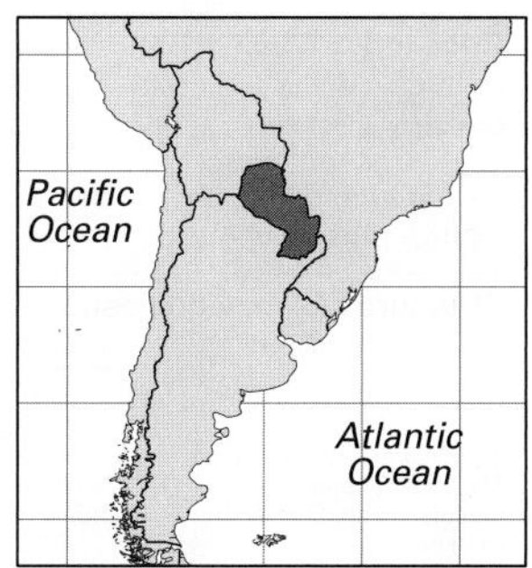

Area and population

Departments	area sq km	population 2009 estimate	Departments	area sq km	population 2009 estimate
Alto Paraguay	82,349	11,413	Itapúa	16,525	529,358
Alto Paraná	14,895	736,942	Misiones	9,556	115,851
Amambay	12,933	124,848	Ñeembucú	12,147	83,504
Boquerón	91,669	56,164	Paraguarí	8,705	239,050
Caaguazú	11,474	478,612	Presidente Hayes	72,907	101,656
Caazapá	9,496	150,910	San Pedro	20,002	355,115
Canindeyú	14,667	179,656			
Central	2,465	1,998,994	**Capital district**		
Concepción	18,051	190,322	Asunción	117	518,507
Cordillera	4,948	273,606	TOTAL	406,752	6,340,639[3]
Guairá	3,846	196,130			

Demography

Population (2011): 6,459,000.
Density (2011): persons per sq mi 41.1, persons per sq km 15.9.
Urban-rural (2010): urban 61.4%; rural 38.6%.
Sex distribution (2010): male 50.19%; female 49.81%.
Age breakdown (2010): under 15, 29.5%; 15–29, 28.9%; 30–44, 19.6%; 45–59, 13.4%; 60–74, 6.3%; 75–84, 1.8%; 85 and over, 0.5%.
Population projection: (2020) 7,192,000; (2030) 7,974,000.
Ethnic composition (2000): mixed (white/Amerindian) 85.6%; white 9.3%, of which German 4.4%, Latin American 3.4%; Amerindian 1.8%; other 3.3%.
Religious affiliation (2002): Roman Catholic 89.6%; Protestant (including all Evangelicals) 6.2%; other Christian 1.1%; nonreligious/atheist 1.1%; traditional beliefs 0.6%; other/unknown 1.4%.
Major urban areas (2002)[4]: Asunción (2008) 518,792 (urban agglomeration [2010] 2,030,000); Ciudad del Este 222,274; San Lorenzo 204,356[5]; Luque 170,986[5]; Capiatá 154,274[5].

Vital statistics

Birth rate per 1,000 population (2010): 17.7 (world avg. 19.2).
Death rate per 1,000 population (2010): 4.6 (world avg. 8.2).
Total fertility rate (avg. births per childbearing woman; 2010): 2.16.
Marriage/divorce rates per 1,000 population (2008): 3.0[6]/n.a.
Life expectancy at birth (2010): male 73.4 years; female 78.7 years.
Major causes of death per 100,000 population (2008): diseases of the circulatory system 158.5, of which cerebrovascular diseases 54.1; malignant neoplasms (cancers) 83.5; accidents, poisoning, and violence 74.0; diabetes mellitus 40.7.

National economy

Budget (2008–09). Revenue: ₲13,907,000,000,000 (tax revenue 66.2%, of which VAT 32.0%, corporate taxes 15.8%; nontax revenue including grants 33.8%). Expenditures: ₲13,862,000,000,000 (current expenditure 76.5%, of which wages and salaries 43.9%; capital expenditure 23.5%).
Public debt (external, outstanding; March 2011): U.S.$2,288,900,000.
Population economically active (2010): total 2,885,000; activity rate 45.2% (participation rates: ages 15 and over, 67.3%; female 38.4%; unemployed 6.9%).

Price and earnings indexes (2005 = 100)

	2004	2005	2006	2007	2008	2009	2010
Consumer price index	93.6	100.0	109.6	118.5	130.5	133.9	140.1
Earnings index	88.4	100.0	116.4	132.9	146.5	156.2	171.9

Household income and expenditure. Average household size (2009) 4.2.
Production (metric tons except as noted). Agriculture, forestry, fishing (2009): sugarcane 4,800,000, soybeans 3,855,000, cassava 2,610,000, corn (maize) 1,857,840, wheat 1,066,800, oranges 226,090, rice 219,800, sunflower seeds 194,000, oil palm fruit 152,000, maté 76,730, sesame seeds 65,000, dry beans 42,980, mangoes 29,700; livestock (number of live animals) 11,643,390 cattle, 1,200,000 pigs, 18,000,000 chickens; roundwood (2010) 10,510,004 cu m, of which fuelwood 62%; fisheries production 3,800 (from aquaculture 55%). Mining and quarrying (2009): dimension stone 70,000; kaolin 66,000. Manufacturing (value added in ₲'000,000,000; 2010): food products 4,404; beverages and tobacco products 1,751; textiles and wearing apparel 1,030; cement, bricks, and ceramics 776; wood and wood products 463; machinery and apparatus 445; chemicals and chemical products 401; paper and paper products 398. Energy production (consumption): electricity (kW-hr; 2007) 53,715,000,000 (8,588,000,000); coal, none (none); crude petroleum (barrels; 2007) none (negligible); petroleum products (metric tons; 2007) negligible (1,250,000); natural gas, none (none).

Gross national income (GNI; 2010): U.S.$19,008,000,000 (U.S.$2,940 per capita); purchasing power parity GNI (U.S.$5,430 per capita).

Structure of gross domestic product and labour force

	2009 in value ₲'000,000,000	2009 % of total value	2008 labour force	2008 % of labour force
Agriculture, forestry, fishing	13,657.7	19.3	745,200	25.0
Mining and quarrying	105.7	0.2	6,600	0.2
Manufacturing	9,186.7	13.0	340,200	11.4
Construction	4,625.1	6.6	174,100	5.8
Public utilities	1,084.6	1.5	10,800	0.4
Transp. and commun.	5,164.4	7.3	118,400	4.0
Trade, hotels, restaurants	13,524.0	19.1	673,800	22.6
Finance, real estate	5,113.3	7.2	120,800	4.1
Pub. admin., defense	7,205.7	10.2	620,000	20.8
Services	4,118.9	5.8		
Other	6,919.2[7]	9.8[7]	171,200[8]	5.7[8]
TOTAL	70,705.3	100.0	2,981,100	100.0

Selected balance of payments data. Receipts from (U.S.$'000,000): tourism (2009) 227; remittances (2010) 573; foreign direct investment (FDI; 2008–10 avg.) 316; official development assistance (2009) 148. Disbursements for (U.S.$'000,000): tourism (2009) 188; remittances (2009) n.a.; FDI (2008–10 avg.) 4.
Land use as % of total land area (2007): in temporary crops or left fallow 10.8%, in permanent crops 0.2%, in pasture 40.3%, forest area 45.6%.

Foreign trade[9, 10]

Balance of trade (current prices)

	2004	2005	2006	2007	2008	2009
U.S.$'000,000	–1,472	–2,027	–2,955	–3,096	–4,587	–3,773
% of total	31.2%	37.5%	45.2%	36.1%	34.3%	37.3%

Imports (2010): U.S.$9,399,843,000 (machinery and apparatus 30.3%; refined petroleum products 11.4%; transportation equipment 10.6%; chemicals and chemical products 7.3%; food products, beverages, and tobacco 7.1%). *Major import sources* (2009): China 30.1%; Brazil 23.3%; Argentina 16.0%; Venezuela 5.1%; Japan 4.9%.
Exports (2010): U.S.$4,533,777,000[9] (soybeans 35.1%; meat products 20.3%; cereals 12.1%; flour 7.7%; soybean oil 6.1%). *Major export destinations:* Uruguay 22.0%; Brazil 14.6%; Argentina 11.9%; other 51.5%.

Transport and communications

Transport. Railroads (2008): route length 22 mi, 36 km[11]; passenger-km, n.a.; (2002) metric ton-km cargo 1,000,000. Roads (2000): total length 18,330 mi, 29,500 km (paved 51%). Vehicles (2008): passenger cars 266,662; trucks 247,671. Air transport (2007)[12]: passenger-km 700,000,000; metric ton-km cargo, n.a.

Communications

Medium	date	number in '000s	units per 1,000 persons	Medium	date	number in '000s	units per 1,000 persons
Televisions	2004	1,300	224	PCs	2005	460	78
Telephones				Dailies	2010	133[13]	21[13]
Cellular	2010	5,915[14]	916[14]	Internet users	2009	1,000	158
Landline	2010	405	63	Broadband	2010	39[14]	6.1[14]

Education and health

Educational attainment (2007). Percentage of population age 25 and over having: no formal schooling 5.2%; incomplete primary education 28.3%; complete primary 29.6%; secondary 28.2%; higher 8.7%. *Literacy* (2010): percentage of total population age 15 and over literate 95.3%; males 95.9%; females 93.6%.

Education (2008–09)

	teachers	students	student/teacher ratio	enrollment rate (%)
Primary (age 6–11)	32,998[15]	852,168	26.5[15]	85
Secondary/Voc. (age 12–17)	34,341[15]	549,482	15.8[15]	60
Tertiary	...	236,194	...	37 (age 18–22)

Health (2009): physicians[16] 5,114 (1 per 1,213 persons); hospital beds 6,108 (1 per 1,030 persons); infant mortality rate per 1,000 live births (2010) 23.8; undernourished population (2004–06) 700,000 (12% of total population based on the consumption of a minimum daily requirement of 1,810 calories).

Military

Total active duty personnel (November 2010): 10,650 (army 71.4%, navy 18.3%, air force 10.3%); paramilitary 14,800; reserve 164,500. *Military expenditure as percentage of GDP* (2010): 0.8%; per capita expenditure U.S.$22.

[1]Excludes former presidents serving as senators-for-life but having no voting power. [2]Roman Catholicism, although not official, enjoys special recognition in the constitution. [3]Detail does not add to total given because of statistical discrepancy. [4]Unadjusted final census figures. [5]Within Asunción urban agglomeration. [6]Civil registry records only. [7]Taxes on products. [8]Includes 170,600 unemployed and 600 unclassified. [9]Electricity exports are excluded; contracted value of electricity sold (2006): to Brazil U.S.$210,000,000; to Argentina, n.a. In September 2009 Brazil agreed to pay Paraguay U.S.$360,000,000 annually for electricity from the shared Itaipú hydroelectric dam. [10]Imports c.i.f. in balance of trade and f.o.b. in commodities and trading partners. [11]30-km tourist train and 6-km link to the Argentine railways. [12]Transportes Aéreos del Mercosur only. [13]Circulation. [14]Subscribers. [15]2007–08. [16]January 1.

Internet resources for further information:
- **Banco Central del Paraguay http://www.bcp.gov.py**
- **Dirección General de Estadística, Encuestas, y Censos http://www.dgeec.gov.py**

Peru

Official name: República del Perú (Spanish) (Republic of Peru).
Form of government: unitary multiparty republic with one legislative house (Congress of the Republic [130]).
Head of state and government: President, assisted by Prime Minister.
Capital: Lima.
Official languages: Spanish; Quechua (locally); Aymara (locally).
Official religion: none[1].
Monetary unit: nuevo sol (S/.); valuation (Sept. 1, 2011) 1 U.S.$ = S/. 2.73; 1 £ = S/. 4.41.

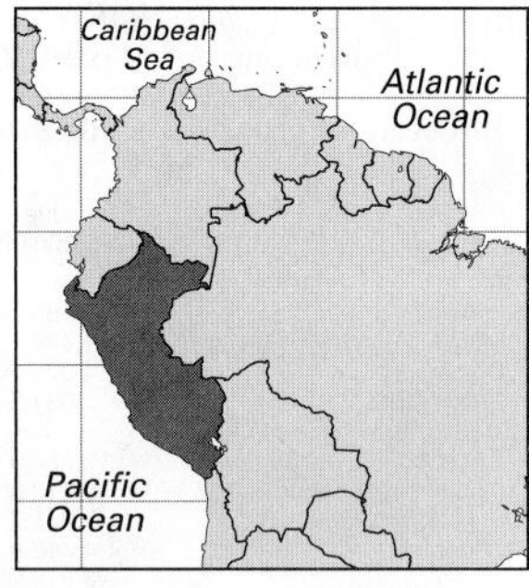

Area and population

Departments	area sq km	population 2007 census	Departments	area sq km	population 2007 census
Amazonas	39,249	375,993	Lambayeque	14,231	1,112,868
Ancash	35,826	1,063,459	Lima	34,802	8,445,211
Apurímac	20,896	404,190	Loreto	368,852	891,732
Arequipa	63,345	1,152,303	Madre de Dios	85,183	109,555
Ayacucho	43,814	612,489	Moquegua	15,734	161,533
Cajamarca	33,247	1,387,809	Pasco	25,320	280,449
Callao	147	876,877	Piura	35,892	1,676,315
Cusco	71,892	1,171,403	Puno	71,999[2]	1,268,441
Huancavelica	22,131	454,797	San Martin	51,253	728,808
Huánuco	36,938	762,223	Tacna	16,076	288,781
Ica	21,328	711,932	Tumbes	4,669	200,306
Junín	44,410	1,232,611	Ucayali	102,411	432,159
La Libertad	25,570	1,617,050	TOTAL	1,285,216[2, 3]	27,419,294[4]

Demography

Population (2011): 29,249,000.
Density (2011): persons per sq mi 58.9, persons per sq km 22.8.
Urban-rural (2007): urban 75.9%; rural 24.1%.
Sex distribution (2007): male 49.68%; female 50.32%.
Age breakdown (2007): under 15, 30.5%; 15–29, 27.5%; 30–44, 20.4%; 45–59, 12.5%; 60–74, 6.4%; 75–84, 2.0%; 85 and over, 0.7%.
Population projection: (2020) 31,915,000; (2030) 34,444,000.
Doubling time: 50 years.
Ethnic composition (2000): Quechua 47.0%; mestizo 31.9%; white 12.0%; Aymara 5.4%; Japanese 0.5%; other 3.2%.
Religious affiliation (2005): Roman Catholic *c.* 85%, of which practicing weekly *c.* 15%; Protestant *c.* 7%; independent Christian *c.* 4%; other *c.* 4%.
Major cities (2007): metropolitan Lima 8,472,935; Arequipa 784,651; Trujillo 682,834; Chiclayo 524,442; Piura 377,496; Iquitos 370,962; Cusco 348,935.

Vital statistics

Birth rate per 1,000 population (2007): 20.2 (world avg. 20.3).
Death rate per 1,000 population (2007): 6.2 (world avg. 8.5).
Marriage/divorce rates per 1,000 population (2008): 3.3/n.a.
Total fertility rate (avg. births per childbearing woman; 2007): 2.46.
Life expectancy at birth (2007): male 68.3 years; female 72.0 years.
Major causes of death per 100,000 population (2002): diseases of the circulatory system 113; malignant neoplasms (cancers) 112; accidents, poisoning, and violence 60; diseases of the respiratory system 27; diabetes mellitus 14.

National economy

Budget (2008). Revenue: S/. 68,352,000,000 (tax revenue 85.2%, of which VAT 46.2%, taxes on income and profits 35.3%; nontax revenue 14.8%). Expenditures: S/. 60,073,000,000 (current expenditure 76.9%; capital expenditure 14.6%; debt service 8.5%).
Production (metric tons except as noted). Agriculture, forestry, fishing (2009): sugarcane 10,100,100, potatoes 3,716,700, rice 2,989,590, plantains 1,854,240, chicken meat 966,350, asparagus 313,880, coffee 255,016, quinoa 39,998; livestock (number of live animals) 14,137,700 sheep, 5,459,440 cattle, 5,000,000 llamas/alpacas/others; roundwood (2010) 8,690,000 cu m, of which fuelwood 84%; fisheries production 6,958,769 (from aquaculture 1%). Mining and quarrying (2009): iron ore 4,490,000[5]; zinc 1,509,129[5]; copper 1,118,643[5]; lead 302,412[5]; molybdenum 12,295[5]; silver 3,854[5]; gold 156,089 kg. Manufacturing (value in U.S.$'000,000; 2007): food products 4,066; wearing apparel 1,326; paints, soaps, pharmaceuticals 1,233; cement, bricks, and ceramics 1,081; refined petroleum products 862; base metals 802; structural/fabricated metal products 752.[6] Energy production (consumption): electricity (kW-hr; 2009) 32,676,000,000 ([2008] 29,260,000,000); coal (metric tons; 2008) 188,000 (1,341,000); crude petroleum (barrels; 2009) 57,600,000 ([2007] 67,600,000); petroleum products (metric tons; 2007) 9,612,000 (6,570,000); natural gas (cu m; 2009) 3,483,000,000 (3,483,000,000).
Household income and expenditure. Average household size (2005) 4.3; sources of income: n.a.; expenditure: n.a.
Selected balance of payments data. Receipts from (U.S.$'000,000): tourism (2009) 2,046; remittances (2010) 2,543; foreign direct investment (FDI; 2008–10 avg.) 6,609; official development assistance (2009) 442. Disbursements for (U.S.$'000,000): tourism (2009) 1,086; remittances (2009) 85; FDI (2008–10 avg.) 450.
Population economically active (2008): total 13,312,000[7]; activity rate of total population 46.2%[7] (participation rates: ages 15–64, 69.4%[7]; female 43.3%[7]; officially unemployed[8] [July 2009–June 2010] 8.1%).

Price index (2005 = 100)

	2004	2005	2006	2007	2008	2009	2010
Consumer price index	98.4	100.0	102.0	103.8	109.8	113.0	114.8

Gross national income (GNI; 2010): U.S.$138,978,000,000 (U.S.$4,710 per capita); purchasing power parity GNI (U.S.$8,940 per capita).

Structure of gross domestic product and labour force

	2007		2008	
	in value S/. '000,000	% of total value	labour force[9]	% of labour force[9]
Agriculture, forestry, fishing	20,403	6.1	769,700	7.7
Mining and quarrying	38,413	11.5	98,800	1.0
Manufacturing	48,811	14.5	1,316,600	13.1
Construction	20,395	6.1	512,000	5.1
Public utilities	6,011	1.8	35,800	0.3
Transp. and commun.	28,622	8.5	907,000	9.0
Trade, hotels	53,859	16.0	2,831,600	28.2
Finance, real estate	41,842	12.5	578,700	5.8
Pub. admin., defense	22,194	6.6	423,200	4.2
Services	26,853	8.0	1,972,100	19.6
Other	28,327[10]	8.4[10]	604,900[11]	6.0[11]
TOTAL	335,730	100.0	10,050,400	100.0

Public debt (external, outstanding; 2009): U.S.$20,791,000,000.
Land use as % of total land area (2009): in temporary crops or left fallow 2.9%, in permanent crops 0.6%, in pasture 13.3%, forest area 53.2%.

Foreign trade[12]

Balance of trade (current prices)

	2004	2005	2006	2007	2008	2009
U.S.$'000,000	+2,997	+5,284	+8,933	+8,301	+3,157	+5,879
% of total	13.2%	17.9%	23.1%	17.5%	5.3%	12.3%

Imports (2007): U.S.$20,494,000,000 (machinery and apparatus 23.0%; chemicals and chemical products 14.6%; crude petroleum 13.4%; food 8.4%; base and fabricated metals 8.3%). *Major import sources:* U.S. 17.7%; China 12.1%; Brazil 9.2%; Ecuador 7.4%; Argentina 5.5%.
Exports (2008): U.S.$31,163,000,000 (ores/concentrates 27.7%, of which copper 15.7%, zinc 4.1%, molybdenum 3.5%; gold 17.8%; food 14.4%, of which fish meal 4.6%; petroleum 9.1%; refined copper 8.7%; apparel/clothing accessories 5.2%). *Major export destinations:* U.S. 18.6%; China 12.0%; Switzerland 10.9%; Canada 6.3%; Japan 5.9%.

Transport and communications

Transport. Railroads: route length (2009) 1,158 mi, 1,864 km; passenger-km (2007) 1,694,000,000; metric ton-km cargo (2007) 1,267,000,000. Roads (2006): total length 49,080 mi, 78,986 km (paved 14%). Vehicles (2007): passenger cars 917,110; trucks and buses 525,277. Air transport (2008): passenger-km 8,724,000,000; metric ton-km cargo 222,000,000.

Communications

Medium	date	number in '000s	units per 1,000 persons	Medium	date	number in '000s	units per 1,000 persons
Televisions	2002	4,592	172	PCs	2005	2,800	103
Telephones				Dailies	2009	...	...
Cellular	2010	29,115[13]	1,001[13]	Internet users	2009	8,085	277
Landline	2010	3,160	109	Broadband	2010	912[13]	31[13]

Education and health

Educational attainment (2008). Percentage of population age 25 and over having: no formal schooling 9.3%; incomplete primary education 18.3%; complete primary 19.4%; incomplete secondary 6.0%; complete secondary 28.6%; higher 18.2%; other/unknown 0.2%. *Literacy* (2007): total population age 15 and over literate 89.6%; males 94.9%; females 84.6%.

Education (2007–08)

	teachers	students	student/ teacher ratio	enrollment rate (%)
Primary (age 6–11)	184,641	3,854,764	20.9	94
Secondary/Voc. (age 12–16)	160,669	2,566,702	16.0	75
Tertiary	56,070[14]	952,437[15]	14.8[14]	34[15] (age 17–21)

Health: physicians (2007) 41,788 (1 per 672 persons); hospital beds (2008) 42,800 (1 per 667 persons); infant mortality rate (2007) 30.5; undernourished population (2005–07) 4,300,000 (15% of total population based on the consumption of a minimum daily requirement of 1,780 calories).

Military

Total active duty personnel (November 2010): 115,000 (army 64.3%, navy 20.9%, air force 14.8%); paramilitary 77,000; reserve 188,000. *Military expenditure as percentage of GDP* (2009): 1.1%; per capita expenditure U.S.$54.

[1]The state recognizes Roman Catholicism as an important element in the historical and cultural development of Peru. [2]Includes the 4,996 sq km area of the Peruvian part of Lake Titicaca. [3]Detail does not add to total given because of rounding. [4]Unadjusted figure; adjusted census total equals 28,220,764. [5]Metal content. [6]In 2008 Peru ranked second in the world in coca production; 302 metric tons of cocaine were produced. [7]ILO estimate. [8]Metropolitan Lima only. [9]Excludes rural areas. [10]Import duties and other taxes. [11]Unemployed. [12]Imports f.o.b. in balance of trade and c.i.f. in commodities and trading partners. [13]Subscribers. [14]2001–02. [15]2005–06.

Internet resources for further information:
- **Instituto Nacional de Estadística e Informática http://www.inei.gob.pe**
- **Banco Central de Reserva del Peru http://www.bcrp.gob.pe**

Philippines

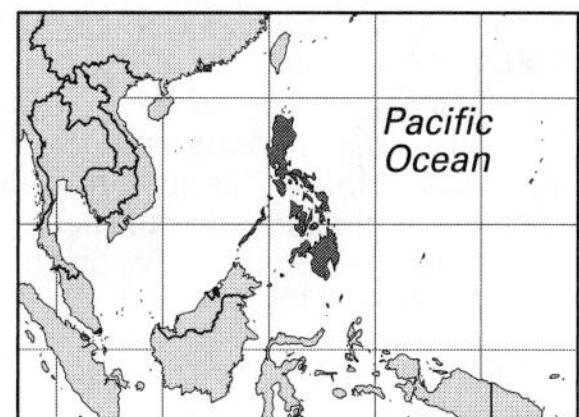

Official name: Republika ng Pilipinas (Filipino); Republic of the Philippines (English).
Form of government: unitary republic with two legislative houses (Senate [24]; House of Representatives [280]).
Head of state and head of government: President.
Capital: Manila[1].
Official languages: Filipino; English.
Official religion: none.
Monetary unit: piso[2] (₱); valuation (Sept. 1, 2011) 1 U.S.$ = ₱ 42.24; 1 £ = ₱ 68.26.

Area and population

Regions	area sq km	population 2007 census	Regions	area sq km	population 2007 census
Autonomous Region in Muslim Mindanao (ARMM)	19,196	4,120,795	Davao	27,172	4,156,653
Bicol	18,035	5,109,798	Eastern Visayas	21,988	3,912,936
Cagayan Valley	30,149	3,051,487	Ilocos	12,821	4,545,906
Calabarzon	16,052	11,743,110	Mimaropa	29,199	2,559,791
Caraga	19,324	2,293,480	National Capital	633	11,553,427
Central Luzon	19,579	9,720,982	Northern Mindanao	15,617	3,952,437
Central Visayas	15,582	6,398,628	Soccsksargen	15,890	3,829,081
Cordillera Administrative	16,745	1,520,743	Western Visayas	20,158	6,843,643
			Zamboanga Peninsula	18,154	3,230,094
			TOTAL	316,294[3, 4]	88,574,614[5]

Demography

Population (2011): 95,849,000.
Density (2011)[6]: persons per sq mi 784.9, persons per sq km 303.0.
Urban-rural (2009): urban 48.7%; rural 51.3%.
Sex distribution (2005): male 50.38%; female 49.62%.
Age breakdown (2005): under 15, 35.6%; 15–29, 28.4%; 30–44, 18.8%; 45–59, 11.2%; 60–74, 4.9%; 75–84, 1.0%; 85 and over, 0.1%.
Population projection: (2020) 110,966,000; (2030) 127,731,000.
Ethnic composition (2000): Tagalog 20.9%; Visayan (Cebu) 19.0%; Ilocano 11.1%; Hiligaynon (Visaya) 9.4%; Waray-Waray (Binisaya) 4.7%; Central Bikol (Naga) 4.6%; Filipino mestizo 3.5%; Pampango 3.1%; other 23.7%.
Religious affiliation (2005): Roman Catholic 64.9%; independent Christian 17.7%[7]; Muslim 5.1%; Protestant 5.0%; traditional beliefs 2.2%; other 5.1%.
Major cities (2007): Quezon City 2,679,450[8]; Manila 1,660,714; Caloocan 1,378,856[8]; Davao 1,363,337; Cebu City 798,809.

Vital statistics

Birth rate per 1,000 population (2009): 24.0 (world avg. 20.3).
Death rate per 1,000 population (2009): 4.8 (world avg. 8.5).
Total fertility rate (avg. births per childbearing woman; 2006): 3.20.
Life expectancy at birth (2009): male 70.0 years; female 74.0 years.
Marriage/divorce rates per 1,000 population (2007): 5.5/[9].
Major causes of death per 100,000 population (2004): circulatory diseases 148.4; respiratory diseases 61.8; malignant neoplasms (cancers) 49.0; accidents and violence 41.3; tuberculosis 31.3.

National economy

Budget (2009). Revenue: ₱ 1,123,200,000,000 (tax revenue 87.4%, nontax revenues and grants 12.6%). Expenditures: ₱ 1,426,000,000,000 (general public services 18.4%, education 15.6%, transportation and communications 10.9%, social security and welfare 6.3%, defense 4.6%, health 2.7%).
Public debt (external, outstanding; March 2010): U.S.$39,393,000,000.
Production (metric tons except as noted). Agriculture, forestry, fishing (2009): sugarcane 22,932,819, rice 16,266,417, coconuts 15,667,565, bananas 9,013,986, corn (maize) 7,034,033, pineapples 2,198,497, cassava 2,043,719, natural rubber 390,962; livestock (number of live animals) 13,596,000 pigs, 4,222,000 goats, 3,321,000 buffalo; roundwood (2010) 16,266,718 cu m, of which fuelwood 77%; fisheries production 3,339,851 (from aquaculture 22%); aquatic plants production 1,740,429 (from aquaculture, virtually 100%). Mining and quarrying (2008): nickel 83,895[10]; copper 21,235[10]; chromite 15,268; gold 35,568 kg[10]. Manufacturing (value added in U.S.$'000,000; 2003): petroleum products 1,980; electronic products 1,696; food products 1,338; paints/soaps/pharmaceuticals 983; beverages 813; motor vehicles 559. Energy production (consumption): electricity (kW-hr; 2009) 61,379,000,000 (49,658,000,000); hard coal (metric tons; 2007) 2,558,000 (7,783,000); lignite (metric tons; 2007) 3,000 (3,000); crude petroleum (barrels; 2007) 174,840 (73,775,200); petroleum products (metric tons; 2007) 9,377,000 (12,057,000); natural gas (cu m; 2009) 2,940,000,000 (2,940,000,000).
Household income and expenditure. Average household size (2007) 4.8; income per family (2006) ₱ 173,000 (U.S.$3,371); sources of income (2000): wages 52.1%, self-employment 25.1%, receipts from abroad 11.1%; expenditure (2006): food and nonalcoholic beverages 47.2%, housing 12.7%, transportation and communications 8.2%, energy 7.6%.
Selected balance of payments data. Receipts from (U.S.$'000,000): tourism (2009) 2,329; remittances (2009) 19,688; foreign direct investment (FDI; 2008–10 avg.) 1,740; official development assistance (2008) 61. Disbursements for (U.S.$'000,000): tourism (2009) 2,989; remittances (2009) 58; FDI (2008–10 avg.) 368.
Gross national income (GNI; 2010): U.S.$192,238,000,000 (U.S.$2,050 per capita); purchasing power parity GNI (U.S.$3,930 per capita).

Structure of gross domestic product and labour force

	2009 in value ₱ '000,000	2009 % of total value	2006 labour force	2006 % of labour force
Agriculture, forestry, fishing	773,540	14.1	11,841,000	32.7
Mining and quarrying	88,616	1.6	134,000	0.4
Manufacturing	1,058,155	19.4	3,070,000	8.5
Construction	296,056	5.4	1,691,000	4.7
Public utilities	190,585	3.5	114,000	0.3
Transp. and commun.	380,733	7.0	2,470,000	6.8
Trade, hotels, restaurants	793,215	14.5	7,270,000	20.1
Finance, real estate	654,943	12.0	1,153,000	3.2
Pub. admin., defense	412,846	7.5	1,552,000	4.3
Services	818,255	15.0	3,962,000	11.0
Others	—	—	2,908,000[11]	8.0[11]
TOTAL	5,466,944	100.0	36,165,000	100.0

Population economically active (2008): total 37,058,000; activity rate 41.0% (participation rates: ages 15–64, 65.5%; female 38.3%; unemployed [April 2009–March 2010] 7.4%).

Price index (2005 = 100)

	2004	2005	2006	2007	2008	2009	2010
Consumer price index	92.9	100.0	106.2	109.2	119.4	123.3	128.0

Land use as % of total land area (2007): in temporary crops or left fallow 17.1%, in permanent crops 16.4%, in pasture 5.0%, forest area 23.0%.

Foreign trade[12]

Balance of trade (current prices)

	2004	2005	2006	2007	2008	2009[13]
U.S.$'000,000	–6,422	–8,232	–6,668	–7,530	–11,342	–5,515
% of total	7.5%	9.1%	6.6%	6.9%	10.4%	6.8%

Imports (2008): U.S.$60,420,000,000 (electronic integrated circuits/parts 22.7%, petroleum 19.2%, food 9.7%, parts for office machines/computers 7.3%). *Major import sources:* U.S. 12.8%; Japan 11.8%; Singapore 10.3%; Saudi Arabia 8.5%; China 7.5%; Taiwan 6.7%.
Exports (2008): U.S.$49,078,000,000 (electronic integrated circuits/parts 22.7%, computers/office machines/parts 18.4%, food 4.8%, parts of road vehicles 4.2%, apparel 3.9%). *Major export destinations:* U.S. 16.7%; Japan 15.7%; China 11.1%; Hong Kong 10.2%; Netherlands 7.6%; Singapore 5.3%.

Transport and communications

Transport. Railroads (2009): route length 301 mi[14], 484 km[14]; passenger-km (2005) 20,000,000; metric ton-km cargo (2004) 76,000,000. Roads (2003): total length 124,297 mi, 200,037 km (paved 21%). Vehicles (2009): passenger cars 780,200; trucks and buses 2,210,500. Air transport (2009–10): passenger-km 18,982,000,000; metric ton-km cargo 321,281,000.

Communications

Medium	date	number in '000s	units per 1,000 persons	Medium	date	number in '000s	units per 1,000 persons
Televisions	2003	14,770	182	PCs	2006	6,097	70
Telephones				Dailies	2009	3,800[15]	41[15]
Cellular	2010	79,895[16]	857[16]	Internet users	2009	5,955	65
Landline	2010	6,783	73	Broadband	2010	1,722[16]	19[16]

Education and health

Educational attainment (2000). Percentage of population age 25 and over having: no formal schooling 3.8%; primary education 38.5%; incomplete secondary 12.5%; complete secondary 17.2%; technical 5.9%; incomplete undergraduate 11.8%; complete undergraduate 7.3%; graduate 0.7%; unknown 2.3%. *Literacy* (2008): total population age 15 and over literate 93.6%.

Education (2006–07)

	teachers	students	student/ teacher ratio	enrollment rate (%)
Primary (age 6–11)	390,432	13,145,210	33.7	92[17]
Secondary/Voc. (age 12–15)	181,193	6,365,985	35.1	61[17]
Tertiary	112,941[18]	2,651,466[17]	21.3[18]	29[17] (age 16–20)

Health: physicians (2005) 98,210 (1 per 865 persons); hospital beds (2008) 94,199 (1 per 959 persons); infant mortality rate (2009) 22.0; undernourished population (2004–06) 12,700,000 (15% of total population based on the consumption of a minimum daily requirement of 1,750 calories).

Military

Total active duty personnel (November 2010): 125,000 (army 68.8%, navy 19.2%, air force 12.0%); reserve 131,000. *Military expenditure as percentage of GDP* (2009): 0.7%; per capita expenditure U.S.$13.

[1]Other government offices and ministries are located in Quezon City and other Manila suburbs. [2]Piso in Filipino; peso in English and Spanish. [3]Sum of regional areas, including coastal water; actual reported total area is 300,000 sq km. [4]Land area excluding inland water is 298,170 sq km. [5]Reported total; summed total of 88,542,991 excludes 29,344 persons residing in a disputed area between the National Capital Region and Calabarzon and 2,279 Filipinos residing in embassies abroad. [6]Based on actual reported total area. [7]Includes indigenous Catholics and Protestants. [8]Within the National Capital Region. [9]Divorce was illegal in mid-2010. [10]Metal content. [11]Unemployed. [12]Imports c.i.f.; exports f.o.b. [13]Excludes December. [14]Operational length; total length equals 557 mi, 897 km. [15]Circulation of daily newspapers. [16]Subscribers. [17]2007–08. [18]2004–05.

Internet resources for further information:
- **National Statistics Office http://www.census.gov.ph**
- **Bangko Sentral ng Pilipinas http://www.bsp.gov.ph**

Poland

Official name: Rzeczpospolita Polska (Republic of Poland).
Form of government: unitary multiparty republic with two legislative houses (Senate [100]; Sejm [460]).
Head of state: President.
Head of government: Prime Minister.
Capital: Warsaw.
Official language: Polish.
Official religion: none[1].
Monetary unit: złoty (zł); valuation (Sept. 1, 2011) 1 U.S.$ = zł 2.92; 1 £ = zł 4.71.

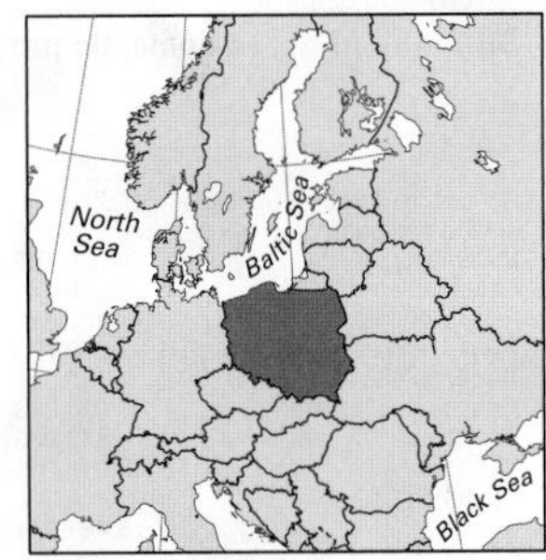

Area and population		area		population
				2010
Provinces	Capitals	sq mi	sq km	estimate
Dolnośląskie	Wrocław	7,702	19,947	2,877,840
Kujawsko-Pomorskie	Bydgoszcz/Toruń	6,939	17,972	2,069,543
Łódzkie	Łódź	7,034	18,219	2,534,357
Lubelskie	Lublin	9,700	25,122	2,151,895
Lubuskie	Gorzów Wielkopolski/ Zielona Góra	5,401	13,988	1,011,024
Małopolskie	Kraków	5,862	15,183	3,310,094
Mazowieckie	Warsaw (Warszawa)	13,729	35,558	5,242,911
Opolskie	Opole	3,634	9,412	1,028,585
Podkarpackie	Rzeszów	6,890	17,846	2,103,505
Podlaskie	Białystok	7,794	20,187	1,188,329
Pomorskie	Gdańsk	7,070	18,310	2,240,319
Śląskie	Katowice	4,762	12,333	4,635,882
Świętokrzyskie	Kielce	4,521	11,711	1,266,014
Warmińsko-Mazurskie	Olsztyn	9,333	24,173	1,427,241
Wielkopolskie	Poznań	11,516	29,826	3,419,426
Zachodniopomorskie	Szczecin	8,839	22,892	1,693,072
TOTAL		120,726	312,679	38,200,037

Demography

Population (2011): 38,216,000.
Density (2011): persons per sq mi 316.6, persons per sq km 122.2.
Urban-rural (2010): urban 60.9%; rural 39.1%.
Sex distribution (2010): male 48.28%; female 51.72%.
Age breakdown (2010): under 15, 15.0%; 15–29, 22.4%; 30–44, 21.4%; 45–59, 21.5%; 60–74, 13.2%; 75–84, 5.1%; 85 and over, 1.4%.
Population projection: (2020) 38,304,000; (2030) 38,763,000.
Ethnic composition (2000): Polish 90.0%; Ukrainian 4.0%; German 4.0%; Belarusian 0.5%; Kashubian 0.4%; other 1.1%.
Religious affiliation (end of 2007): Roman Catholic 88.6%; other Catholic 0.1%; Polish Orthodox 1.3%; Protestant 0.4%; Jehovah's Witness 0.3%; other (mostly nonreligious) 9.3%.
Major cities (2010): Warsaw 1,720,398; Kraków 756,183; Łódź 737,098; Wrocław 632,996; Poznań 551,627; Gdańsk 456,967; Szczecin 405,606.

Vital statistics

Birth rate per 1,000 population (2009): 10.9 (world avg. 20.3); within marriage 79.8%; outside of marriage 20.2%.
Death rate per 1,000 population (2009): 10.1 (world avg. 8.5).
Total fertility rate (avg. births per childbearing woman; 2009): 1.40.
Marriage/divorce rates per 1,000 population (2009): 6.6/1.7.
Life expectancy at birth (2010): male 72.1 years; female 80.6 years.
Major causes of death per 100,000 population (2008): diseases of the circulatory system 453.7; malignant neoplasms (cancers) 244.2; diseases of the respiratory system 50.6; diseases of the digestive system 44.8%.

National economy

Budget (2008). Revenue: zł 253,547,000,000 (VAT 40.1%, excise tax 19.9%, income tax 15.2%, corporate taxes 10.7%). Expenditures: zł 277,893,000,000 (social security and welfare 29.6%, public debt 9.0%, national defense 5.0%, education 4.8%, public safety 4.5%).
Public debt (external, outstanding; August 2010): U.S.$62,182,000,000.
Gross national income (GNI; 2010): U.S.$474,045,000,000 (U.S.$12,420 per capita); purchasing power parity GNI (U.S.$19,020 per capita).

Structure of gross domestic product and labour force	2007		2008	
	in value zł '000,000	% of total value	labour force	% of labour force
Agriculture, forestry, fishing	44,553	3.8	2,120,000	12.3
Mining	23,171	2.0	225,000	1.3
Manufacturing	194,763	16.6	2,992,000	17.4
Public utilities	34,292	2.9	334,000	2.0
Construction	73,459	6.2	1,360,000	7.9
Transp. and commun.	72,188	6.1	1,190,000	6.9
Trade, restaurants, hotels	200,663	17.1	2,635,000	15.3
Finance, real estate	195,808	16.6	1,381,000	8.0
Pub. admin., defense	59,624	5.1	1,013,000	5.9
Services	130,921	11.1	2,567,000	14.9
Other	147,295[2]	12.5[2]	1,385,000[3]	8.1[3]
TOTAL	1,176,737	100.0	17,202,000	100.0

Production (metric tons except as noted). Agriculture, forestry, fishing (2009): cow's milk 12,447,000, sugar beets 10,849,000, wheat 9,790,000, potatoes 9,703,000, triticale 5,234,000, mixed grain 3,884,100, rye 3,713,000, apples 2,626,000, rapeseed 2,497,000, cabbage 1,337,000[4], strawberries 198,900, currants 196,500, sour cherries 189,000, mushrooms 180,000[5]; livestock (number of live animals) 14,279,000 pigs, 5,700,000 cattle, 1,450,000 beehives; roundwood (2010) 35,377,800 cu m, of which fuelwood 12%; fisheries production 260,396 (from aquaculture 14%). Mining and quarrying (2009): feldspar 550,000; copper (metal content of ore) 498,960; silver (metal content of concentrate) 1,206. Manufacturing (value of sales in zł '000,000; 2009): food products 145,417; transportation equipment 95,728; fabricated/structural metal products 55,145; refined petroleum/coke 48,325; rubber and plastic products 46,379. Energy production (consumption): electricity ('000,000 kW-hr; 2010–11[6]) 116,410 ([2008] 132,000); hard coal ('000 metric tons; 2010–11[7]) 76,329 ([2007] 85,336); lignite ('000 metric tons; 2010–11[6]) 58,679 ([2007] 57,529); crude petroleum (barrels; 2010) 4,712,000 ([2007] 146,800,000); petroleum products (metric tons; 2007) 17,501,000 (21,261,000); natural gas (cu m; 2010–11[7]) 4,387,000,000 ([2010] 17,188,000,000).
Population economically active (2008): total 17,202,000; activity rate of total population 45.1% (participation rates: ages 15–64, 64.4%; female 45.2%; unemployed [July 2010–June 2011] 9.4%).

Price and earnings indexes (2005 = 100)	2004	2005	2006	2007	2008	2009	2010
Consumer price index	97.9	100.0	101.1	103.5	108.0	112.2	115.2
Annual earnings index	96.9	100.0	105.2	114.4	125.5	131.6	138.2

Household income and expenditure (2008). Average household size 2.9; average per capita disposable annual income zł 12,079 (U.S.$4,110); sources of income: wages 53.6%, transfers 28.6%, self-employment 8.8%; expenditure: food, beverages, and tobacco 28.2%, housing and energy 18.9%, transportation 10.1%, recreation and culture 7.9%.
Selected balance of payments data. Receipts from (U.S.$'000,000): tourism (2009) 9,011; remittances (2010) 7,889; foreign direct investment (FDI; 2008–10 avg.) 12,739. Disbursements for (U.S.$'000,000): tourism (2009) 7,327; remittances (2009) 1,328; FDI (2008–10 avg.) 4,778.
Land use as % of total land area (2009): in temporary crops 39.5%, left fallow 1.7%, in permanent crops 1.3%, in pasture 10.5%, forest area 30.6%.

Foreign trade[8]

Balance of trade (current prices)	2005	2006	2007	2008	2009	2010
zł '000,000	–37,438	–50,251	–64,695	–86,480	–40,142	–53,844
% of total	6.1%	6.8%	7.8%	9.8%	4.5%	5.4%

Imports (2008): zł 497,028,300,000 (electrical equipment 13.2%, chemical products 13.0%, mineral fuels 11.2%, transportation equipment 11.2%, machinery and apparatus 11.0%, base and fabricated metals 10.9%). *Major import sources:* Germany 23.0%; Russia 9.8%; China 8.0%; Italy 6.5%; France 4.7%.
Exports (2008): zł 405,383,100,000 (transportation equipment 17.4%, base and fabricated metals 12.9%, electrical equipment 12.4%, machinery and apparatus 12.3%, food products 10.1%, chemical products 5.9%, furniture 5.7%). *Major export destinations:* Germany 25.1%; France 6.2%; Italy 6.0%; U.K. 5.8%; Czech Republic 5.7%.

Transport and communications

Transport. Railroads (2009): route length 12,549 mi[9], 20,196 km[9]; passenger-km 18,671,000,000; metric ton-km cargo 43,455,000,000. Roads: total length (2008[9, 10]) 238,047 mi, 383,100 km (paved 68%); passenger-km (2008) 247,100,000,000[11]; metric ton-km cargo (2009) 191,484,000,000. Vehicles (2010[9]): passenger cars 16,495,000; trucks and buses 2,892,000. Air transport (2009): passenger-km 7,428,000,000; metric ton-km cargo 85,000,000.

Communications			units				units
Medium	date	number in '000s	per 1,000 persons	Medium	date	number in '000s	per 1,000 persons
Televisions	2009[9]	7,091[12]	186[12]	PCs	2004	7,362	191
Telephones				Dailies	2009	3,168[13]	83[13]
Cellular	2010	46,000[12]	1,202[12]	Internet users	2009	22,451	590
Landline	2010	9,451	247	Broadband	2010	5,044[12]	132[12]

Education and health

Educational attainment (2008). Percentage of population age 25 and over having: no formal schooling 0.3%; incomplete primary education 1.1%; complete primary 19.7%; incomplete/complete secondary 58.2%; higher vocational 3.2%; university 17.5%. *Literacy* (2008): 99.5%.

Education (2007–08)	teachers	students	student/ teacher ratio	enrollment rate (%)
Primary (age 7–12)	238,917	2,375,205	9.9	95
Secondary/Voc. (age 13–18)	279,408	3,085,019	11.0	93
Tertiary	100,500	2,165,980	21.6	69 (age 19–23)

Health (2009): physicians (2008) 78,229[9] (1 per 487 persons); hospital beds[9] 212,428 (1 per 180 persons); infant mortality rate per 1,000 live births 5.5.

Military

Total active duty personnel (November 2010): 100,000[14] (army 47.3%, navy 8.0%, air force 17.5%, special forces 1.6%, joint staff 25.6%); paramilitary 21,400. *Military expenditure as percentage of GDP* (2009): 1.7%; per capita expenditure U.S.$191.

[1]Roman Catholicism has special recognition per 1997 concordat with Vatican City. [2]Taxes less subsidies. [3]Includes 1,355,000 unemployed. [4]Includes other brassicas. [5]Includes truffles. [6]July–June. [7]June–May. [8]Imports c.i.f.; exports f.o.b. [9]January 1. [10]Public roads only. [11]Passenger cars 219,000,000,000; buses 28,100,000,000. [12]Subscribers. [13]Circulation of daily newspapers. [14]Of which deployed abroad 2,417.

Internet resource for further information:
- **Central Statistical Office http://www.stat.gov.pl/english**

Portugal

Official name: República Portuguesa (Portuguese Republic).
Form of government: republic with one legislative house (Assembly of the Republic [230]).
Head of state: President.
Head of government: Prime Minister.
Capital: Lisbon.
Official language: Portuguese.
Official religion: none[1].
Monetary unit: euro (€); valuation (Sept. 1, 2011) 1 U.S.$ = €0.70; 1 £ = €1.13.

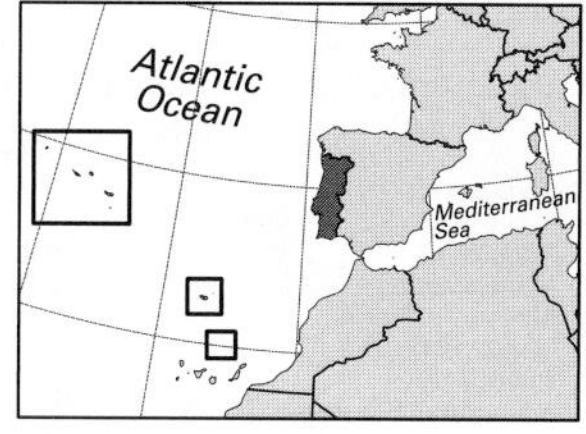

Area and population

		area		population
Continental Portugal[2]		sq mi	sq km	2011 census[3]
Regions	**Principal cities**			10,041,813
Alentejo	Évora	12,182	31,551	758,739
Algarve	Faro	1,929	4,996	450,484
Centro	Coimbra	10,888	28,200	2,327,026
Lisboa (Lisbon)	Lisbon	1,135	2,940	2,815,851
Norte	Porto	8,218	21,284	3,689,713
Insular Portugal				
Autonomous regions				514,040
Açores (Azores)	Ponta Delgado	897	2,322	246,102
Madeira	Funchal	309	801	267,938
TOTAL		35,558	92,094	10,555,853

Demography

Population (2011): 10,555,000.
Density (2011): persons per sq mi 296.8, persons per sq km 114.6.
Urban-rural (2009): urban 60.1%; rural 39.9%.
Sex distribution (2011): male 47.86%; female 52.14%.
Age breakdown (2005): under 15, 15.7%; 15–29, 20.4%; 30–44, 22.6%; 45–59, 19.2%; 60–74, 14.8%; 75–84, 5.9%; 85 and over, 1.4%.
Population projection: (2020) 10,508,000; (2030) 10,197,000.
Ethnic composition (2000): Portuguese 91.9%; mixed race people from Angola, Mozambique, and Cape Verde 1.6%; Brazilian 1.4%; Marrano 1.2%; other European 1.2%; Han Chinese 0.9%; other 1.8%.
Religious affiliation (2000): Christian 92.4%, of which Roman Catholic 87.4%, independent Christian 2.7%, Protestant 1.3%, other Christian 1.0%; nonreligious/atheist 6.5%; Buddhist 0.6%; other 0.5%.
Major cities (2011): Lisbon 545,245 (urban agglomeration 2,815,851); Villa Nova de Gaia 302,092; Porto 237,559 (urban agglomeration [2009] 1,344,000); Braga 181,819; Amadora 175,558.

Vital statistics

Birth rate per 1,000 population (2009): 9.4 (world avg. 20.3); within marriage 61.9%; outside of marriage 38.1%.
Death rate per 1,000 population (2009): 9.8 (world avg. 8.5).
Natural increase rate per 1,000 population (2009): –0.4 (world avg. 11.8).
Total fertility rate (avg. births per childbearing woman; 2008): 1.37.
Marriage/divorce rates per 1,000 population (2009): 3.8/2.5.
Life expectancy at birth (2008): male 75.5 years; female 81.7 years.
Major causes of death per 100,000 population (2005): diseases of the circulatory system 348.1; malignant neoplasms (cancers) 215.4; diseases of the respiratory system 107.1; diseases of the digestive system 44.0.

National economy

Budget (2005). Revenue: €56,498,000,000 (tax revenue 56.2%, of which taxes on goods and services 33.7%, income taxes 20.3%; social contributions 32.9%). Expenditures: €65,096,000,000 (social protection 35.6%, education 16.1%, health 15.9%, public order 4.5%, defense 3.2%).
Public debt (2010): U.S.$216,300,000,000.
Production (metric tons except as noted). Agriculture, forestry, fishing (2009): cow's milk 1,938,921, tomatoes 1,346,702, corn (maize) 593,500, potatoes 519,300, grapes 487,800, olives 362,600, pig meat 305,406, chicken meat 288,041, apples 280,078, oranges 201,592, cork (2008) 165,000, chestnuts 20,752; livestock (number of live animals) 3,144,600 sheep, 2,339,700 pigs, 1,438,700 cattle, 39,000,000 chickens; roundwood (2010) 9,648,360 cu m, of which fuelwood 6%; fisheries production 206,707 (from aquaculture 3%). Mining and quarrying (2009): marble (2008) 578,000; kaolin 270,450; copper (metal content) 86,500; tungsten (metal content) 823. Manufacturing (value added in U.S.$'000,000; 2003): food products 2,148; cement, tiles, and ceramics 1,611; fabricated metals 1,536; wearing apparel 1,527; printing and publishing 1,225; textiles 1,131. Energy production (consumption): electricity (kW-hr; 2009–10) 41,642,000,000 ([2007] 54,741,000,000); coal (metric tons; 2007) none (4,742,000); crude petroleum (barrels; 2007) none (90,613,000); petroleum products (metric tons; 2007) 10,960,000 (10,468,000); natural gas (cu m; 2007) none (4,540,000,000).
Population economically active (2009): total 5,583,000; activity rate of total population 52.5% (participation rates: ages 15–64, 73.7%; female 47.2%; unemployed [June 2010] 10.6%).

Price index (2005 = 100)

	2004	2005	2006	2007	2008	2009	2010
Consumer price index	97.8	100.0	102.7	105.6	108.4	107.5	109.0

Gross national income (GNI; 2010): U.S.$232,590,000,000 (U.S.$21,860 per capita); purchasing power parity GNI (U.S.$24,710 per capita).

Structure of gross domestic product and labour force

	2006		2008	
	in value €'000,000	% of total value	labour force	% of labour force
Agriculture, fishing	3,716	2.4	595,600	10.6
Mining	21,083	13.6	18,000	0.3
Manufacturing			916,900	16.3
Construction	8,488	5.5	553,600	9.8
Public utilities	3,779	2.4	32,400	0.6
Trade, hotels	23,854	15.4	1,096,700	19.5
Finance, real estate	19,731	12.7	432,400	7.7
Transp. and commun.	8,762	5.6	224,900	4.0
Services	44,655	28.7	985,500	17.5
Pub. admin., defense			341,900	6.1
Other	21,221[4]	13.7[4]	427,100[5]	7.6[5]
TOTAL	155,289	100.0	5,624,900[6]	100.0

Household income and expenditure. Average household size (2004) 3.0; average annual household net income (2005) €22,136 (U.S.$17,780); sources of income (2005): wages and salaries 48.7%, nonmonetary income 19.2%, pensions/retirement benefits 18.0%, self-employment 9.1%; expenditure (2005–06): housing and energy 26.6%, food and nonalcoholic beverages 15.5%, transportation 12.9%, restaurants and hotels 10.8%, health 6.1%, clothing and footwear 4.1%.
Selected balance of payments data. Receipts from (U.S.$'000,000): tourism (2009) 9,707; remittances (2010) 3,585; foreign direct investment (2008–10 avg.) 2,941. Disbursements for (U.S.$'000,000): tourism (2009) 3,776; remittances (2009) 1,460; foreign direct disinvestment (2008–10 avg.) –1,684.
Land use as % of total land area (2009): in temporary crops 8.8%, left fallow 3.5%, in permanent crops 8.5%, in pasture 19.5%, forest area 37.7%.

Foreign trade[7]

Balance of trade (current prices)

	2004	2005	2006	2007	2008	2009
€'000,000	–13,011	–17,066	–18,095	–18,971	–23,324	–18,989
% of total	19.7%	24.8%	21.0%	20.6%	23.4%	23.4%

Imports (2008): €61,515,000,000 (machinery and apparatus 18.0%, chemicals and chemical products 10.4%, crude petroleum 9.9%, food 9.8%, road vehicles 9.7%). *Major import sources:* Spain 28.9%; Germany 11.5%; France 8.0%; Italy 4.9%; Netherlands 4.3%.
Exports (2008): €38,191,000,000 (machinery and apparatus 18.0%, road vehicles/parts 11.2%, base and fabricated metals 7.7%, apparel/clothing accessories 6.0%, food 5.7%, refined petroleum 4.5%, footwear 3.3%, cork manufactures 1.8%, wine 1.5%). *Major export destinations:* Spain 25.2%; Germany 12.3%; France 10.9%; Angola 6.0%; U.K. 5.2%.

Transport and communications

Transport. Railroads (2009): route length 1,763 mi, 2,838 km; passenger-km (2008) 3,816,000,000; metric ton-km cargo (2008) 2,549,000,000. Roads (2007): total length 47,722 mi, 76,802 km (paved, n.a.); passenger-km (2006) 83,100,000,000[8]; metric ton-km cargo (2008) 39,091,000,000. Vehicles (2006): passenger cars 5,234,477; trucks and buses 148,706. Air transport (2010): passenger-km 26,004,000,000; metric ton-km cargo 370,368,000.

Communications

Medium	date	number in '000s	units per 1,000 persons	Medium	date	number in '000s	units per 1,000 persons
Televisions	2003	4,312	413	PCs	2007	1,823	172
Telephones				Dailies	2009	533[9]	50[9]
Cellular	2010	15,195[10]	1,423[10]	Internet users	2009	5,169	483
Landline	2010	4,485	420	Broadband	2010	2,075[10]	194[10]

Education and health

Educational attainment (2007). Percentage of population age 25 and older having: no formal schooling through complete primary 64%; complete lower secondary 13%; complete upper secondary 11%; higher 12%. *Literacy* (2008): total population age 15 and over literate 94.6%.

Education (2007–08)

	teachers	students	student/ teacher ratio	enrollment rate (%)
Primary (age 6–11)	66,956	754,142	11.3	99
Secondary/Voc. (age 12–17)	95,296	691,701	10.6	88[11]
Tertiary	35,178	376,917	10.7	60 (age 18–22)

Health (2008): physicians 38,932 (1 per 280 persons); hospital beds 35,762 (1 per 294 persons); infant mortality rate per 1,000 live births 3.3; undernourished population (2005–07) less than 5.0% of total population.

Military

Total active duty personnel (November 2010): 44,340 (army 60.2%, navy 23.8%, air force 16.0%); paramilitary 47,700; reserve 210,900; U.S. troops (November 2010) 705[12]. *Military expenditure as percentage of GDP* (2008): 1.5%[13]; per capita expenditure U.S.$350[13].

[1]A 2004 concordat with the Vatican acknowledges the special role of the Roman Catholic Church in Portugal. [2]For statistical classification only; the actual first order administration of continental Portugal is based on 18 districts. [3]Preliminary. [4]Taxes less statistical discrepancy. [5]Unemployed. [6]Detail does not add to total given because of rounding. [7]Imports c.i.f.; exports f.o.b. [8]Passenger cars 72,000,000,000; buses 11,100,000,000. [9]Circulation of daily newspapers. [10]Subscribers. [11]2006–07. [12]Mostly air force personnel stationed at Lajes, Azores. [13]Including military pensions.

Internet resources for further information:
- **Instituto Nacional de Estatística http://www.ine.pt**
- **Banco de Portugal http://www.bportugal.pt**

Puerto Rico

Official name: Estado Libre Asociado de Puerto Rico (Spanish); Commonwealth of Puerto Rico (English).
Political status: self-governing commonwealth in association with the United States, having two legislative houses (Senate [27[1]]; House of Representatives [51[1]]).
Head of state: President of the U.S.
Head of government: Governor.
Capital: San Juan.
Official languages: Spanish; English.
Monetary unit: U.S. dollar (U.S.$); valuation (Sept. 1, 2011) 1 £ = U.S.$1.62.

Population (2010 census)

Municipalities	population	Municipalities	population	Municipalities	population
Adjuntas	19,483	Fajardo	36,993	Naguabo	26,720
Aguada	41,959	Florida	12,680	Naranjito	30,402
Aguadilla	60,949	Guánica	19,427	Orocovis	23,423
Agunas Buenas	28,659	Guayama	45,362	Patillas	19,277
Aibonito	25,900	Guayanilla	21,581	Peñuelas	24,282
Añasco	29,261	Guaynabo	97,924	Ponce	166,327
Arecibo	96,440	Gurabo	45,369	Quebradillas	25,919
Arroyo	19,575	Hatillo	41,953	Rincón	15,200
Barceloneta	24,816	Hormigueros	17,250	Río Grande	54,304
Barranquitas	30,318	Humacao	58,466	Sabana Grande	25,265
Bayamón	208,116	Isabela	45,631	Salinas	31,078
Cabo Rojo	50,917	Jayuya	16,642	San Germán	35,527
Caguas	142,893	Juana Díaz	50,747	San Juan	395,326
Camuy	35,159	Juncos	40,290	San Lorenzo	41,058
Canóvanas	47,648	Lajas	25,753	San Sebastián	42,430
Carolina	176,762	Lares	30,753	Santa Isabel	23,274
Cataño	28,140	Las Marías	9,881	Toa Alta	74,066
Cayey	48,119	Las Piedras	38,675	Toa Baja	89,609
Ceiba	13,631	Loíza	30,060	Trujillo Alto	74,842
Ciales	18,782	Luquillo	20,068	Utuado	33,149
Cidra	43,480	Manatí	44,113	Vega Alta	39,951
Coamo	40,512	Maricao	6,276	Vega Baja	59,662
Comerío	20,778	Maunabo	12,225	Vieques (island)	9,301
Corozal	37,142	Mayagüez	89,080	Villalba	26,073
Culebra (island)	1,818	Moca	40,109	Yabucoa	37,941
Dorado	38,165	Morovis	32,610	Yauco	42,043
				TOTAL	3,725,789

Demography

Area: 3,515 sq mi, 9,104 sq km.
Population (2011): 3,716,000.
Density (2011): persons per sq mi 1,057, persons per sq km 408.2.
Urban-rural (2005): urban 97.6%; rural 2.4%.
Sex distribution (2009): male 47.98%; female 52.02%.
Age breakdown (2009): under 15, 19.8%; 15–29, 21.5%; 30–44, 20.2%; 45–59, 18.8%; 60–74, 13.5%; 75–84, 4.4%; 85 and over, 1.8%.
Population projection: (2020) 3,714,000; (2030) 3,721,000.
Ethnic composition (2000): local white 72.1%; black 15.0%; mixed black/white 10.0%; U.S. white 2.2%; other 0.7%.
Religious affiliation (2000): Roman Catholic *c.* 74%; Protestant *c.* 13%; independent Christian *c.* 6%; Jehovah's Witness *c.* 2%; nonreligious/atheist *c.* 2%; Spiritist *c.* 1%; other *c.* 2%.
Major metropolitan areas (2010): San Juan 2,478,905; Aguadilla 306,292; Ponce 243,147; San Germán 137,462; Yauco 107,333; Mayagüez 106,330.

Vital statistics

Birth rate per 1,000 population (2009): 11.6 (world avg. 20.3).
Death rate per 1,000 population (2009): 7.4 (world avg. 8.5).
Total fertility rate (avg. births per childbearing woman; 2009): 1.62.
Marriage/divorce rates per 1,000 population: (2005) 6.0/(2006) 3.9[2].
Life expectancy at birth (2009): male 75.5 years; female 82.8 years.
Major causes of death per 100,000 population (2005): circulatory diseases 213.2; malignant neoplasms (cancers) 123.7; respiratory diseases 76.1; diabetes mellitus 71.3; infectious and parasitic diseases 41.5.

National economy

Budget (2006–07). Revenue: U.S.$14,988,600,000 (income taxes 42.6%, federal grants 34.5%, excise taxes 9.8%, charges for services 5.1%). Expenditures: U.S.$17,158,000,000 (education 25.6%, public housing/welfare 17.8%, general government services 14.8%, health 11.4%, public safety 10.9%, interest on debt 4.7%).
Public debt (June 2009): U.S.$61,790,000,000.
Production (in metric tons except as noted). Agriculture, forestry, fishing (2009): cow's milk 378,600, plantains 69,942, bananas 56,539, chicken meat 50,002, tomatoes 22,090, oranges 18,139, pig meat 11,498, cattle meat 10,200, coffee 7,523; livestock (number of live animals) 380,000 cattle, 50,000 pigs, 13,200,000 chickens; roundwood, n.a.; fisheries production 1,752 (from aquaculture 3%). Mining (2006): crushed stone 8,790,000. Manufacturing (value added in U.S.$'000,000; 2004): chemical products (nearly all drugs and medicine) 20,276; nonelectrical machinery 3,271; professional and scientific equipment 3,211; electrical machinery 1,754; nonalcoholic beverages 1,594. Energy production (consumption): electricity (kW-hr; 2007) 23,720,000,000 (23,720,000,000); coal (metric tons; 2006) none (1,499,000); crude petroleum (barrels; 2008) none ([2005] 70,800,000); petroleum products, n.a. (n.a.); natural gas (cu m; 2007) none (736,000,000).

Gross national income (2009): U.S.$64,123,000,000 (U.S.$16,105 per capita).

Structure of gross domestic product and labour force

	2008		2006	
	in value U.S.$'000,000	% of total value	labour force	% of labour force
Agriculture	385.9	0.4	22,000	1.5
Manufacturing	38,457.7	41.2	136,000	9.6
Mining }	1,991.4	2.1	1,000	0.1
Construction }			87,000	6.1
Public utilities }	6,019.5	6.5	16,000	1.1
Transp. and commun. }			43,000	3.0
Trade	11,810.8	12.7	271,000	19.1
Finance, real estate	16,391.1	17.6	47,000	3.3
Pub. admin., defense	8,762.2	9.4	278,000	19.6
Services	8,866.5	9.5	354,000	24.9
Other	577.8	0.6	165,000[3]	11.6[3]
TOTAL	93,262.9	100.0	1,420,000	100.0[4]

Population economically active (2005): total 1,410,000[5]; activity rate of total population 36.0%[5] (participation rates: ages 16–64, 56.1%[5]; female 43.7%[5]; unemployed [September 2010] 16.3%).

Price index (2005 = 100)

	2004	2005	2006	2007	2008	2009	2010
Consumer price index	87.8	100.0	114.6	122.4	128.8	129.2	132.3

Household income and expenditure (2009). Average family size 3.2; average annual income per family U.S.$47,697; sources of income: wages and salaries 44.1%, transfers 34.2%, rent 11.4%, self-employment 5.8%, other 4.5%; expenditure: health care 17.0%, housing 16.5%, food and nonalcoholic beverages 15.4%, household furnishings 12.6%, transportation 9.9%.
Selected balance of payments data. Receipts from (U.S.$'000,000): tourism (2009) 3,473; remittances, n.a.; foreign direct investment (2008–10 avg.) n.a. Disbursements for (U.S.$'000,000): tourism (2009) 1,106; remittances, n.a.
Land use as % of total land area (2009): in temporary crops or left fallow 6.8%, in permanent crops 4.5%, in pasture 10.1%, forest area 61.2%.

Foreign trade

Balance of trade (current prices)

	2003–04	2004–05	2005–06	2006–07	2007–08	2008–09
U.S.$'000,000	+16,183	+17,638	+17,488	+14,745	+19,025	+20,156
% of total	17.2%	18.5%	17.0%	14.0%	17.5%	19.9%

Imports (2007–08): U.S.$44,928,000,000 (imports for pharmaceutical industry 33.5%, petroleum and coal products 11.5%, base chemicals 7.3%, computers/electronics 6.6%, food 5.8%). *Major import sources* (2008–09): U.S. 46.9%; U.S. Virgin Islands 4.0%; remainder 49.1%.
Exports (2007–08): U.S.$63,954,000,000 (pharmaceuticals and medicine 66.0%, food 7.0%, computers/electronics 6.4%). *Major export destinations* (2008–09): U.S. 71.6%; U.S. Virgin Islands 0.2%; remainder 28.2%.

Transport and communications

Transport. Railroads: [6]. Roads (2008): total length 16,576 mi, 26,676 km (paved 99%). Vehicles (2007): passenger cars 2,421,055; trucks and buses 110,144. Air transport (2006): passenger arrivals and departures 11,450,700; cargo loaded and unloaded 352,396 metric tons.

Communications

Medium	date	number in '000s	units per 1,000 persons	Medium	date	number in '000s	units per 1,000 persons
Televisions	2000	1,290	338	PCs	2007	…	…
Telephones				Dailies	2009	456[7]	143[7]
Cellular	2010	2,934[8]	783[8]	Internet users	2009	1,000	251
Landline	2010	892	238	Broadband	2010	552[8]	147[8]

Education and health

Educational attainment (2000). Percentage of population age 25 and over having: no formal schooling to lower secondary education 25.4%; some upper secondary to some higher 56.3%; undergraduate or graduate degree 18.3%.
Literacy (2002): total population age 15 and over literate 94.1%.

Education (2005–06)[9]

	teachers	students	student/ teacher ratio	enrollment rate (%)
Primary (age 5–12) } Secondary/Voc. (age 13–18) }	42,036	563,490	13.4	…
Tertiary	…	67,990	…	… (age 19–23)

Health: physicians (2001) 7,623 (1 per 504 persons); hospital beds (2002) 12,351 (1 per 312 persons); infant mortality rate (2009) 7.9.

Military

Total active duty U.S. personnel (June 2011): 190[10].

[1]Minimum number of seats per constitution; minority parties may have additional representation. [2]Data are probably for local population only. [3]Unemployed. [4]Detail does not add to total given because of rounding. [5]Excludes armed forces. [6]Remnants of the former railway system are conserved for tourism purposes. [7]Circulation of daily newspapers. [8]Subscribers. [9]Public schools only. [10]Puerto Rican paramilitary forces (national guard; 2008): 11,000.

Internet resources for further information:

- **Junta de Planificación http://www.jp.gobierno.pr**
- **Government Development Bank for Puerto Rico http://www.gdb-pur.com**

Qatar

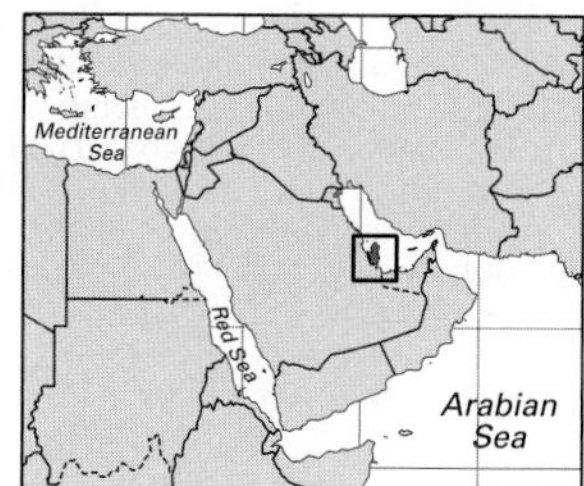

Official name: Dawlat Qaṭar (State of Qatar).
Form of government: constitutional emirate with one advisory body (Advisory Council [35[1]]).
Head of state and government: Emir assisted by Prime Minister.
Capital: Ḍoha.
Official language: Arabic.
Official religion: Islam.
Monetary unit: Qatari riyal (QR); valuation (Sept. 1, 2011) 1 U.S.$ = QR 3.64; 1 £ = QR 5.88.

Area and population

		area		population
Municipalities	**Capitals**	sq mi	sq km	2010 final census
Al-Ḍaʿāyin	...	91	236	43,176
Al-Dawḥah (Ḍoha)	—	90	234	796,947
Al-Khawr and Al-Dhakhīrah	Al-Khawr	599	1,551	193,983
Al-Rayyān	Al-Rayyān	2,246	5,818	455,623
Al-Shamāl	Madīnat al-Shamāl	348	902	7,975
Umm Ṣalāl	Umm Ṣalāl Muḥammad	120	310	60,509
Al-Wakrah	Al-Wakrah	973	2,520	141,222
TOTAL		4,468[2]	11,571	1,699,435

Demography

Population (2011): 1,624,000.
Density (2011): persons per sq mi 363.6, persons per sq km 140.4.
Urban-rural (2010): urban 95.8%; rural 4.2%.
Sex distribution (2010): male 75.73%; female 24.27%.
Age breakdown (2010): under 15, 13.7%; 15–29, 31.3%; 30–44, 40.2%; 45–59, 13.1%; 60–74, 1.5%; 75 and over, 0.2%.
Population projection: (2020) 1,986,000; (2030) 2,141,000.
Doubling time: 68 years.
Ethnic composition (2008): Arab *c.* 40%, of which Qatari *c.* 20%; Indian *c.* 20%; Nepali *c.* 13%; Filipino *c.* 10%; Pakistani *c.* 7%; Sri Lankan *c.* 5%; U.S. *c.* 0.5%; other *c.* 4.5%.
Religious affiliation (2000): Muslim *c.* 83%, of which Sunnī *c.* 73%, Shīʿī *c.* 10%; Christian *c.* 10%, of which Roman Catholic *c.* 6%; Hindu *c.* 3%; Buddhist *c.* 2%; nonreligious *c.* 2%.
Major cities (2010): Al-Dawḥah (Ḍoha) 521,283; Al-Rayyān 392,428; Al-Dhakhīrah 128,574; Al-Khawr 80,220; Al-Wakrah 79,457.

Vital statistics

Birth rate per 1,000 population (2010): 11.5 (world avg. 19.2).
Death rate per 1,000 population (2010): 1.2 (world avg. 8.2).
Total fertility rate (avg. births per childbearing woman; 2010): 2.04.
Marriage/divorce rates per 1,000 population (2010): 1.8/0.7.
Life expectancy at birth (2010): male 78.1 years; female 77.3 years.
Major causes of death per 100,000 population (2010): accidents, poisoning, and violence 23.7; diseases of the circulatory system 17.9; neoplasms 12.6; endocrine, metabolic, and nutritional disorders 7.4; diseases of the respiratory system 4.5; diseases of the digestive system 3.1.

National economy

Budget (2010–11). Revenue: QR 155,907,000,000 (oil and natural gas revenue 62.1%; investment income 23.2%; other 14.7%). Expenditures: QR 142,370,000,000 (current expenditure 68.9%, of which wages and salaries 16.2%, debt service 3.9%; development expenditure 31.1%).
Production (metric tons except as noted). Agriculture, forestry, fishing (2009): dates 21,600, tomatoes 11,900, barley 6,692, pumpkins 4,100, dry onions 3,900, eggplants 3,050, corn (maize) 1,350, chilies and peppers 875, okra 600, figs 322; livestock (number of live animals) 148,000 sheep, 140,000 goats, 34,000 camels, 7,500 cattle; roundwood (2010) 4,933 cu m, of which fuelwood 100%; fisheries production 14,100 (from aquaculture, negligible). Mining and quarrying (2009): limestone 1,100,000; gypsum 135,000; sand and gravel and clay are also produced. Manufacturing (value added in QR '000,000; 2008): chemicals and chemical products 11,632; cement, bricks, and ceramics 7,496; refined petroleum products 7,029; base metals 4,599; fabricated metal products 1,633. Energy production (consumption): electricity (kW-hr; 2008) 16,136,000,000 ([2007] 16,079,000,000); coal, none (none); crude petroleum (barrels; 2010–11) 263,345,500 ([2009] 51,830,000); petroleum products (metric tons; 2007) 6,393,000 (3,990,000); natural gas (cu m; 2010) 96,335,000,000 ([2008] 20,200,000,000).
Household income and expenditure (2007). Average household size (2010) 5.3; average income per household[3] QR 497,796 (U.S.$136,615); sources of income[3]: wages and salaries 56.7%, self-employment 33.0%, transfers 6.0%; expenditure[3]: housing and energy 29.3%, transportation 13.8%, food, beverages, and tobacco 11.2%, household furnishings 9.9%, clothing and footwear 6.2%, culture and entertainment 4.6%, education 3.7%.
Population economically active (2010): total 1,275,971; activity rate of total population 75.1% (participation rates: ages 15 and over, 87.0%; female 12.3%; unemployed 0.4%).

Price index (2005 = 100)

	2004	2005	2006	2007	2008	2009	2010
Consumer price index	91.9	100.0	111.8	127.2	146.4	139.3	135.9

Gross national income (2009): U.S.$100,081,000,000 (U.S.$71,008 per capita).

Structure of gross domestic product and labour force

	2010			
	in value QR '000,000	% of total value	labour force	% of labour force
Agriculture, fishing	534	0.1	17,116	1.3
Oil, natural gas sector, other mining	239,745	51.7	85,735	6.7
Manufacturing	49,185[4]	10.6[4]	100,665	7.9
Construction	24,144	5.2	506,437	39.7
Public utilities	2,070	0.5	4,996	0.4
Transp. and commun.	18,275	4.0	43,150	3.4
Trade, hotels	32,310	7.0	171,966	13.5
Finance, real estate	62,119	13.4	78,649	6.2
Pub. admin., defense	35,814	7.7	72,220	5.7
Services	10,246	2.2	188,854	14.8
Other	–10,953[5]	–2.4[5]	6,183[6]	0.5[6]
TOTAL	463,489	100.0	1,275,971[7]	100.0[2]

Public debt (external, outstanding; April 2011): U.S.$19,287,400,000.
Selected balance of payments data. Receipts from (U.S.$'000,000): tourism (2006) 874; remittances, n.a.; foreign direct investment (FDI; 2008–10 avg.) 5,813. Disbursements for (U.S.$'000,000): tourism (2006) 3,751; remittances (2010) 7,906; FDI (2008–10 avg.) 6,492.
Land use as % of total land area (2007): in temporary crops or left fallow 1.6%, in permanent crops 0.3%, in pasture 4.3%, forest area, negligible.

Foreign trade[8]

Balance of trade (current prices)

	2003	2004	2005	2006	2007	2008
U.S.$'000,000	+8,485	+12,681	+15,702	+17,611	+18,591	+27,012
% of total	46.4%	51.4%	43.8%	34.9%	28.4%	32.6%

Imports (2008): U.S.$27,900,000,000 (machinery and apparatus 37.2%, of which general industrial machinery 13.1%, insulated wire/cable 4.4%; iron and steel 12.7%; road vehicles 12.2%; manufactures of metal 5.9%; chemicals and chemical products 5.6%; food 5.1%). *Major import sources:* Japan 9.6%; U.S. 9.0%; Germany 8.4%; Italy 7.4%; China 7.2%; U.A.E. 6.6%.
Exports (2008): U.S.$54,912,000,000 (crude petroleum 46.9%; liquefied natural gas 29.4%; liquefied gaseous hydrocarbons 11.6%; refined petroleum 3.3%; polyethylene 2.5%). *Major export destinations:* Japan 34.3%; South Korea 21.8%; Singapore 11.7%; India 5.2%; Thailand 3.7%.

Transport and communications

Transport. Railroads: none. Roads (2006): total length 4,840 mi, 7,790 km (paved, n.a.). Vehicles (2007): passenger cars 605,699[9]. Air transport (2010–11)[10]: passenger-km 56,526,000,000; metric ton-km cargo 3,347,006,000.

Communications

Medium	date	number in '000s	units per 1,000 persons	Medium	date	number in '000s	units per 1,000 persons
Televisions	2004	315	412	PCs	2006	157	156
Telephones				Dailies	2009	120[11]	81[11]
Cellular	2010	2,329[12]	1,324[12]	Internet users	2009	399	283
Landline	2010	298	170	Broadband	2010	161[12]	92[12]

Education and health

Educational attainment (2010). Percentage of population age 15 and over having: no formal education/unknown 27.2%, of which illiterate 3.7%; primary education 21.2%; preparatory (lower secondary) 12.2%; vocational 1.6%; secondary 20.0%; postsecondary 17.8%. *Literacy* (2009): total population age 15 and over literate 94.7%; males literate 95.1%; females literate 92.9%.

Education (2009–10)

	teachers	students	student/ teacher ratio	enrollment rate (%)
Primary (age 6–11)	7,374	88,723	12.0	92
Secondary/Voc. (age 12–17)	6,938	68,924	9.9	83
Tertiary	1,602	13,846	8.6	10 (age 18–22)

Health (2009): physicians 5,217 (1 per 285 persons); hospital beds 2,017 (1 per 738 persons); infant mortality rate per 1,000 live births (2010) 6.8; undernourished population, n.a.

Military

Total active duty personnel (November 2010): 11,800 (army 72.0%, navy 15.3%, air force 12.7%); U.S. troops (November 2010) 531. *Military expenditure as percentage of GDP* (2009): 2.5%; per capita expenditure U.S.$1,680.

[1]All seats are appointed by the emir. [2]Detail does not add to total given because of rounding. [3]Qatari households only. [4]Excludes oil- and natural gas–related manufacturing. [5]Import duties less imputed bank service charges. [6]Including 4,519 unemployed. [7]Of which Qatari 74,087. [8]Imports c.i.f.; exports f.o.b. [9]Includes trucks and buses. [10]Data for international flights only. [11]Circulation of daily newspapers. [12]Subscribers.

Internet resources for further information:
- **Qatar Statistics Authority http://www.qsa.gov.qa/eng**
- **Qatar Central Bank http://www.qcb.gov.qa**

Réunion

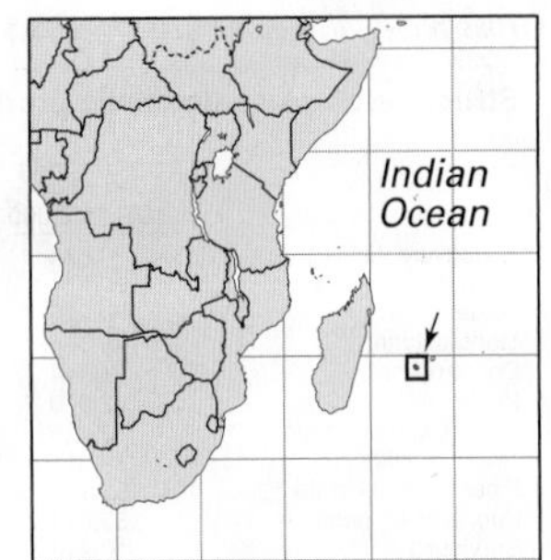

Official name: Département d'Outre-Mer de la Réunion (Overseas Department of Réunion).[1]
Political status: overseas department/overseas region (France) with two legislative houses (General Council[2] [49]; Regional Council[3] [45]).
Head of state: President of France.
Heads of government: Prefect (for France); President of General Council (for Réunion); President of Regional Council (for Réunion).
Capital: Saint-Denis.
Official language: French.
Official religion: none.
Monetary unit: euro (€); valuation (Sept. 1, 2011) 1 U.S.$ = €0.70; 1 £ = €1.13.

Area and population

		area		population
				2008[4]
Arrondissements	**Capitals**	sq mi	sq km	estimate
Saint-Benoît	Saint-Benoît	284	736	117,205
Saint-Denis	Saint-Denis	111	288	197,464
Saint-Paul	Saint-Paul	208	537	207,004
Saint-Pierre	Saint-Pierre	364	943	286,577
TOTAL		973[5, 6]	2,520[5, 6]	808,250

Demography

Population (2011): 852,000.
Density (2011): persons per sq mi 875.6, persons per sq km 338.1.
Urban-rural (2009): urban 93.7%; rural 6.3%.
Sex distribution (2006[4]): male 48.49%; female 51.51%.
Age breakdown (2005): under 15, 27.0%; 15–29, 23.6%; 30–44, 24.1%; 45–59, 15.0%; 60–74, 7.5%; 75–84, 2.3%; 85 and over, 0.5%.
Population projection: (2020) 933,000; (2030) 1,003,000.
Doubling time: 53 years.
Ethnic composition (2000): mixed race (black-white-South Asian) 42.6%; local white 25.6%; South Asian 23.0%, of which Tamil 20.0%; Chinese 3.4%; East African 3.4%; Malagasy 1.4%; other 0.6%.
Religious affiliation (2000): Christian 87.8%, of which Roman Catholic 81.8%, Pentecostal 4.2%; Hindu 4.5%; Muslim 4.2%; nonreligious 1.7%; other 1.8%.
Major urban agglomerations (2008[4]): Saint-Denis 175,053; Saint-Paul 170,085; Saint-Pierre 154,295; Saint-André 52,956.

Vital statistics

Birth rate per 1,000 population (2008): 18.4 (world avg. 20.3); within marriage 30.5%; outside of marriage 69.5%.
Death rate per 1,000 population (2008): 5.1 (world avg. 8.5).
Natural increase rate per 1,000 population (2008): 13.2 (world avg. 11.8).
Total fertility rate (avg. births per childbearing woman; 2006): 2.44.
Marriage/divorce rates per 1,000 population (2008): 3.9/1.7.
Life expectancy at birth (2006): male 73.2 years; female 80.9 years.
Major causes of death per 100,000 population (2006): diseases of the circulatory system 163.1; malignant neoplasms (cancers) 112.5; infectious and parasitic diseases 33.0; diseases of the respiratory system 32.5; accidents 31.2; diabetes mellitus 29.4.

National economy

Budget (2009)[7]. Revenue: €1,404,900,000 (receipts from French central government and local administrative bodies 66.2%; indirect and direct taxes 26.1%; other subsidies 3.6%; other 4.1%). Expenditures: €1,404,900,000 (social welfare 58.5%; general services 20.4%; other 21.1%).
Public debt (external, outstanding): n.a.
Gross domestic product (2009): U.S.$20,033,000,000 (U.S.$24,340 per capita).

Structure of gross domestic product and labour force

	2005			
	in value €'000,000	% of total value	labour force[4, 8]	% of labour force[4, 8]
Agriculture, fishing	202	1.7	7,562	3.7
Manufacturing, mining }	789	6.6	7,365	3.6
Public utilities }			1,550	0.7
Construction	860	7.1	11,835	5.8
Transp. and commun.	720	6.0	9,169	4.5
Trade	1,098[9]	9.1[9]	29,976	14.6
Finance, real estate, business services	643	5.3	18,562	9.0
Pub. admin., defense	1,377	11.4	40,984	19.9
Services	5,661[9]	46.9[9]	55,474	27.0
Other	711[10]	5.9[10]	23,013[11]	11.2[11]
TOTAL	12,061	100.0	205,490	100.0

Production (metric tons except as noted). Agriculture, forestry, fishing (2009): sugarcane 1,907,600, pineapples 16,980, chicken meat 15,000, pig meat 13,950, tomatoes 11,530, corn (maize) 11,200, bananas 8,689, citrus fruit 6,225, lettuce 4,508[12], lychees (2010) 3,447, duck meat 3,287, dry chilies and peppers 865, vanilla (2010) 13, geranium essence (2008) 2,074 kg; livestock (number of live animals) 80,672 pigs, 33,154 cattle, 15,000,000 chickens, 520,000 ducks; roundwood (2010) 36,100 cu m, of which fuelwood 86%; fisheries production 3,144 (from aquaculture 5%). Mining and quarrying: gravel and sand for local use. Manufacturing (value added in €'000,000; 2006): food and beverages 172; construction materials (mostly cement) 98; printing and publishing 50; base and fabricated metals 26. Energy production (consumption): electricity (kW-hr; 2008) 2,546,000,000 ([2007] 1,792,000,000); petroleum products (metric tons; 2007) none (770,000).
Population economically active (2009): total 323,900; activity rate of total population 39.4% (participation rates: ages 15–64, 60.5%; female 46.1%; unemployed 27.2%).

Price index (2005 = 100)

	2004	2005	2006	2007	2008	2009	2010
Consumer price index	97.9	100.0	102.6	104.0	107.0	107.6	108.9

Household income and expenditure. Average household size (2006) 3.0; average annual income per capita of household (2003) €11,446 (U.S.$14,456); sources of income (1997): wages and salaries and self-employment 41.8%, transfer payments 41.3%, other 16.9%; expenditure (2001): housing and energy 24.0%, transportation and communications 20.0%, food and beverages 17.0%, recreation and culture 10.0%.
Selected balance of payments data. Receipts from (U.S.$'000,000): tourism (2009) 425; remittances, n.a.; foreign direct investment (FDI) n.a. Disbursements for (U.S.$'000,000): tourism, n.a.; remittances, n.a.; FDI, n.a.
Land use as % of total land area (2009): in temporary crops 12.4%, left fallow 0.3%, in permanent crops 1.2%, in pasture 4.6%, forest area 35.0%.

Foreign trade

Balance of trade (current prices)

	2004	2005	2006	2007	2008	2009
€'000,000	–3,050	–3,427	–3,674	–3,747	–4,255	–3,930
% of total	85.9%	86.7%	88.5%	87.4%	89.1%	88.9%

Imports (2009): €4,176,800,000 (machinery and equipment 21.0%; food and agricultural products 17.4%; transport equipment 11.1%; mineral fuels 9.5%). *Major import sources:* France *c.* 54%; other EU *c.* 11%; U.S. *c.* 7%; Singapore *c.* 7%; China *c.* 6%.
Exports (2009): €246,500,000 (food products 62.1%, of which sugar 29.0%, fish 18.8%, beverages [mostly rum] 6.9%; machinery and apparatus 12.7%; transportation equipment and parts 8.2%). *Major export destinations:* France *c.* 42%; other EU *c.* 14%; Mayotte *c.* 8%; Madagascar *c.* 7%; Hong Kong *c.* 4%.

Transport and communications

Transport. Railroads: [13]. Roads (2001): total length 754 mi, 1,214 km (paved [1991] 79%). Vehicles (2005): passenger cars 339,000; trucks and buses 64,000. Air transport (2007)[14]: passenger-km 3,456,000,000; metric ton-km cargo 48,000,000.

Communications

Medium	date	number in '000s	units per 1,000 persons	Medium	date	number in '000s	units per 1,000 persons
Televisions	2002	138	185	PCs	2004	278	351
Telephones				Dailies	2009	70[15]	85[15]
Cellular	2004	579[16]	753[16]	Internet users	2009	300	363
Landline	2010	481	568	Broadband	2009	185[16]	224[16]

Education and health

Educational attainment (2006). Percentage of population age 15 and over having: no formal schooling through incomplete secondary education 64.2%; complete lower vocational 14.2%; complete secondary 10.1%; some/complete higher 11.5%. *Literacy* (2003): total population age 15 and over literate 88.9%; males literate 87.0%; females literate 90.8%.

Education (2007–08)

	teachers	students	student/teacher ratio	enrollment rate (%)
Primary[17]	6,866	122,517	17.8	…
Secondary/Voc.	9,178	101,467	11.1	…
Tertiary[18]	498	10,348	20.8	…

Health: physicians (2010[4]) 2,104 (1 per 394 persons); hospital beds (2009[4]) 2,790 (1 per 293 persons); infant mortality rate per 1,000 live births (2007) 6.1; undernourished population, n.a.

Military

Total active duty personnel (November 2010): *c.* 875 French troops in Réunion and Mayotte (army *c.* 99%, navy, n.a., air force, n.a., gendarmerie *c.* 1%).

[1]Réunion is simultaneously administered as an overseas region (*région d'outre-mer*). [2]Assembly for overseas department. [3]Assembly for overseas region. [4]January 1. [5]Reported total; summed total equals 967 sq mi (2,504 sq km). [6]Excludes the French overseas territory of French Southern and Antarctic Lands, which is administered from Réunion. [7]Departmental budget. [8]Employed only. [9]Trade excludes restaurants and hotels, and Services includes restaurants and hotels. [10]Taxes less subsidies and less imputed bank service charges. [11]Non-salaried employees. [12]Includes chicory. [13]No public railways; railways in use are for sugar industry. [14]Air Austral only. [15]Circulation. [16]Subscribers. [17]Includes pre-primary. [18]Université de la Réunion only.

Internet resources for further information:

- **INSEE: Réunion**
  http://www.insee.fr/fr/regions/reunion
- **Institut d'Émission des Departements d'Outre-Mer**
  http://www.iedom.fr

Romania

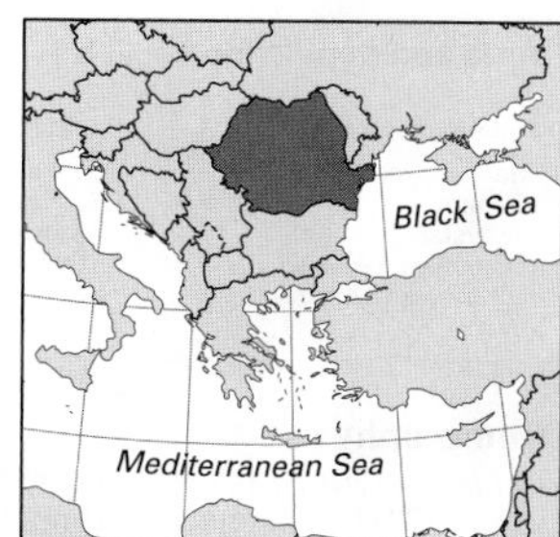

Official name: România (Romania).
Form of government: unitary republic with two legislative houses (Senate [137]; Chamber of Deputies [334[1]]).
Head of state: President.
Head of government: Prime Minister.
Capital: Bucharest.
Official language: Romanian.
Official religion: none.
Monetary unit: (new) leu[2] (RON; plural [new] lei); valuation (Sept. 1, 2011) 1 U.S.$ = RON 2.97; 1 £ = RON 4.80.

Population

Counties	population 2009[3] estimate	Counties	population 2009[3] estimate	Counties	population 2009[3] estimate
Alba	374,535	Dâmbovița	531,011	Prahova	817,092
Arad	457,306	Dolj	707,629	Sălaj	242,472
Argeş	642,359	Galați	611,040	Satu Mare	365,508
Bacău	718,165	Giurgiu	282,322	Sibiu	424,855
Bihor	593,606	Gorj	378,310	Suceava	707,588
Bistrița-Năsăud	317,346	Harghita	325,345	Teleorman	405,070
Botoșani	451,193	Hunedoara	466,586	Timiș	676,360
Brăila	361,414	Ialomița	288,472	Tulcea	248,367
Brașov	596,853	Iași	823,388	Vâlcea	408,518
Buzău	483,988	Ilfov	308,726	Vaslui	452,816
Călărași	313,460	Maramureș	511,946	Vrancea	391,641
Caraș-Severin	324,236	Mehedinți	294,364		
Cluj	690,590	Mureș	581,628	**Municipality**	
Constanța	721,896	Neamț	564,471	Bucharest	1,944,367
Covasna	222,846	Olt	468,931	TOTAL	21,498,616

Demography

Area: 92,043 sq mi, 238,391 sq km.
Population (2011): 21,393,000.
Density (2011): persons per sq mi 232.4, persons per sq km 89.7.
Urban-rural (2010[3]): urban 55.1%; rural 44.9%.
Sex distribution (2010[3]): male 48.70%; female 51.30%.
Age breakdown (2009[3]): under 15, 15.2%; 15–29, 22.0%; 30–44, 23.3%; 45–59, 19.8%; 60–74, 13.5%; 75–84, 5.2%; 85 and over, 1.0%.
Population projection: (2020) 20,930,000; (2030) 20,251,000.
Ethnic composition (2002): Romanian 89.5%; Hungarian 6.6%; Rom (Gypsy) 2.5%; Ukrainian 0.3%; German 0.3%; other 0.8%.
Religious affiliation (2002): Romanian Orthodox 86.7%; Protestant 6.3%; Roman Catholic 4.7%; Greek Catholic 0.9%; Muslim 0.3%; other 1.1%.
Major cities (2009[3]): Bucharest 1,944,367; Timişoara 311,586; Iași 308,843; Cluj-Napoca 306,474; Constanța 302,171.

Vital statistics

Birth rate per 1,000 population (2009): 10.4 (world avg. 20.3); within marriage (2008) 72.6%; outside of marriage (2008) 27.4%.
Death rate per 1,000 population (2009): 12.0 (world avg. 8.5).
Total fertility rate (avg. births per childbearing woman; 2009): 1.26.
Marriage/divorce rates per 1,000 population (2009): 6.3/1.5.
Life expectancy at birth (2009): male 69.7 years; female 77.1 years.
Major causes of death per 100,000 population (2004): diseases of the circulatory system 739.0; malignant neoplasms (cancers) 204.1; diseases of the digestive system 70.2; accidents and violence 62.5.

National economy

Budget (2007). Revenue: RON 106,905,000,000 (social security contributions 37.5%, taxes on goods and services 30.4%, nontax revenue 11.7%, corporate taxes 11.3%). Expenditures: RON 116,445,000,000 (social protection 35.8%, health 13.2%, education 7.1%, transport 7.1%, defense 3.4%).
Public debt (external, outstanding; August 2011): U.S.$14,367,700,000.
Population economically active (2008): total 9,944,700; activity rate 46.2% (participation rates: ages 15–64, 62.9%; female 44.4%; unemployed[4] [August 2010–July 2011] 6.2%).

Price and earnings indexes (2005 = 100)

	2004	2005	2006	2007	2008	2009	2010
Consumer price index	91.8	100.0	106.6	111.7	120.5	127.2	135.0
Annual earnings index	80.8	100.0	116.8	141.3	173.7	187.2	190.6

Household income and expenditure (2008). Average household size (2003) 2.8; average annual income per household RON 25,580 (U.S.$9,040); sources of income: wages and salaries 62.7%, transfers 26.0%; expenditure: food and nonalcoholic beverages 40.9%, housing and energy 15.6%, clothing and footwear 6.7%, alcohol and tobacco 6.5%.
Production (metric tons except as noted). Agriculture, forestry, fishing (2009): corn (maize) 7,973,258, cow's milk 5,208,712, wheat 5,202,526, potatoes 4,003,980, barley 1,182,062, sunflower seed 1,098,047, grapes 990,232, tomatoes 755,596, sheep's milk 600,444, plums and sloes 533,691, apples 517,491; livestock (number of live animals) 8,882,000 sheep, 6,174,000 pigs, 2,684,000 cattle, 84,373,000 chickens; roundwood (2010) 14,333,265 cu m, of which fuelwood 26%; fisheries production 17,151 (from aquaculture 77%). Mining (2009): copper 1,000[5]; zinc (2007) 1,000[5]; lead (2007) 800[5]. Manufacturing (value added in U.S.$'000,000; 2006): food products 1,333; wearing apparel 1,257; transportation equipment 978; fabricated metal products 923; cement, bricks, and ceramics 920; base metals 800; nonelectrical machinery 795; chemical products 736. Energy production (consumption): electricity (kW-hr) 62,430,000,000[6] (11,043,000,000[7]); hard coal (metric tons) 1,948,000[8] (2,950,000[9]); lignite (metric tons) 31,743,000[6] (31,941,000[10]); crude petroleum (barrels) 33,250,000[10] (98,861,500[9]); petroleum products (metric tons) 12,985,000[10] (8,867,000[9]); natural gas (cu m) 9,390,000,000[6] ([2010] 12,842,000,000).
Gross national income (GNI; 2010): U.S.$168,208,000,000 (U.S.$7,840 per capita); purchasing power parity GNI (U.S.$14,050 per capita).

Structure of gross domestic product and labour force

	2008			
	in value RON '000,000	% of total value	labour force	% of labour force
Agriculture, forestry, fishing	32,566.4	6.5	2,689,900	27.1
Mining and quarrying	115,192.2	22.9	107,200	1.1
Public utilities			161,400	1.6
Manufacturing			1,929,800	19.4
Construction	52,893.9	10.5	746,400	7.5
Transp. and commun.	117,224.3	23.3	508,500	5.1
Trade, hotels			1,332,400	13.4
Finance, real estate	63,657.0	12.6	408,700	4.1
Pub. admin.	68,335.1	13.5	476,100	4.8
Services			1,004,400	10.1
Other	54,089.8	10.7	579,900[11]	5.8[11]
TOTAL	503,958.7	100.0	9,944,700	100.0

Selected balance of payments data. Receipts from (U.S.$'000,000): tourism (2009) 1,228; remittances (2010) 4,409; foreign direct investment (FDI; 2008–10 avg.) 7,443. Disbursements for (U.S.$'000,000): tourism (2009) 1,473; remittances (2009) 310; FDI (2008–10 avg.) 128.
Land use as % of total land area (2009): in temporary crops 30.7%, left fallow 3.9%, in permanent crops 1.6%, in pasture 19.0%, forest area 28.4%.

Foreign trade[12]

Balance of trade (current prices)

	2005	2006	2007	2008	2009	2010
U.S.$'000,000	–12,733	–18,770	–29,682	–33,426	–13,635	–12,593
% of total	18.7%	22.5%	26.9%	25.2%	14.4%	11.3%

Imports (2008): U.S.$82,965,000,000 (machinery and apparatus 23.2%; mineral fuels 12.6%, of which crude petroleum 7.2%; road vehicles/parts 11.2%; chemicals and chemical products 10.6%; food 5.7%; iron and steel 5.6%). *Major import sources:* Germany 16.4%; Italy 11.4%; Hungary 7.4%; Russia 6.0%; France 5.7%.
Exports (2008): U.S.$49,539,000,000 (machinery and apparatus 23.4%, of which electrical machinery/parts 10.8%; base and fabricated metals 12.0%, of which iron and steel 7.3%; road vehicles/parts 8.2%; refined petroleum 7.9%; apparel 7.8%). *Major export destinations:* Germany 16.5%; Italy 15.5%; France 7.3%; Turkey 6.6%; Hungary 5.1%.

Transport and communications

Transport. Railroads (2008): route length 6,703 mi, 10,788 km; passenger-km 6,877,000,000; metric ton-km cargo 15,236,000,000. Roads (2004): total length 123,539 mi, 198,817 km (paved 30%); passenger-km (2006) 71,700,000,000[13]; metric ton-km cargo (2008) 56,386,000,000. Vehicles (2008): cars 4,027,000; trucks and buses 687,000. Air transport (2008–09): passenger-km 3,835,000,000; metric ton-km cargo 5,466,000,000.

Communications

Medium	date	number in '000s	units per 1,000 persons	Medium	date	number in '000s	units per 1,000 persons
Televisions	2006	5,478[14]	254[14]	PCs	2007	4,137	192
Telephones				Dailies	2009	1,241[15]	58[15]
Cellular	2010	24,640[14]	1,147[14]	Internet users	2009	7,787	366
Landline	2010	4,500	209	Broadband	2010	3,000[14]	140[14]

Education and health

Educational attainment (2008). Percentage of population age 25 and over having: no formal schooling 2.2%; primary education 11.5%; lower secondary 21.6%; upper secondary/vocational 49.4%; higher vocational 4.2%; tertiary 11.1%. *Literacy* (2008): total population age 15 and over literate 97.6%.

Education (2007–08)

	teachers	students	student/ teacher ratio	enrollment rate (%)
Primary (age 7–10)	54,550	865,175	15.9	90
Secondary/Voc. (age 11–18)	151,981	1,934,151	12.7	73
Tertiary	31,964	1,056,622	33.1	66 (age 19–23)

Health (2009): physicians 50,415 (1 per 428 persons); hospital beds 138,915 (1 per 156 persons); infant mortality rate per 1,000 live births 11.5; undernourished population (2004–06) less than 5.0% of total population based on the consumption of a minimum daily requirement of 1,970 calories.

Military

Total active duty personnel (November 2010): 71,745 (army 59.3%, navy 10.2%, air force 11.7%, joint staff 18.8%); paramilitary 79,900. *Military expenditure as percentage of GDP* (2009): 1.4%; per capita expenditure U.S.$104.

[1]Includes 18 elective seats for ethnic minorities. [2]The leu was redenominated on July 1, 2005. As of that date 10,000 (old) lei (ROL) = 1 (new) leu (RON). [3]January 1. [4]Registered. [5]Metal content of mine output. [6]July 2010–June 2011. [7]2010. [8]2009–10. [9]2007. [10]2008–09. [11]Includes 4,400 not adequately defined and 575,500 unemployed. [12]Imports c.i.f.; exports f.o.b. [13]Passenger cars 60,000,000,000; buses (interurban only) 11,700,000,000. [14]Subscribers. [15]Circulation of daily newspapers.

Internet resource for further information:
- **National Institute of Statistics http://www.insse.ro/cms/rw/pages/index.en.do**

Russia

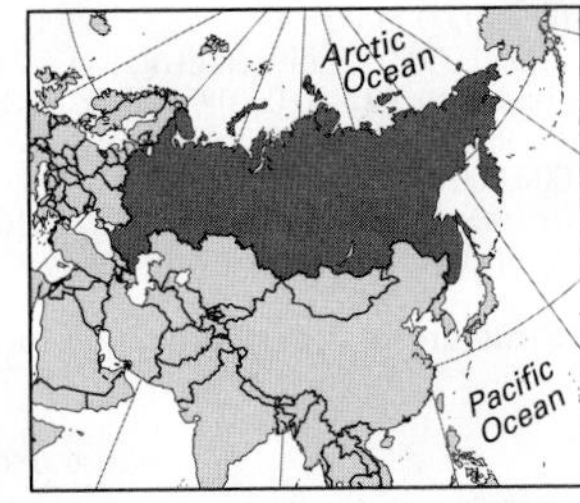

Official name: Rossiyskaya Federatsiya (Russian Federation).
Form of government: federal multiparty republic with a bicameral legislative body (Federal Assembly comprising the Federation Council [178[1]] and the State Duma [450]).
Head of state: President.
Head of government: Prime Minister.
Capital: Moscow.
Official language: Russian.
Official religion: none.
Monetary unit: ruble (RUB); valuation (Sept. 1, 2011) 1 U.S.$ = RUB 29.01; 1 £ = RUB 46.87.

Area and population

Federal districts	Capitals	area[2] sq mi	area[2] sq km	population 2010 census[3]
Central	Moscow (Moskva)	251,000	650,200	38,438,639
Belgorod (region)	Belgorod	10,500	27,100	1,532,670
Bryansk (region)	Bryansk	13,500	34,900	1,278,087
Ivanovo (region)	Ivanovo	8,300	21,400	1,062,629
Kaluga (region)	Kaluga	11,500	29,800	1,011,608
Kostroma (region)	Kostroma	23,200	60,200	667,477
Kursk (region)	Kursk	11,600	30,000	1,126,504
Lipetsk (region)	Lipetsk	9,300	24,000	1,172,818
Moscow (city)		400	1,100	11,514,330
Moskva (Moscow; region)	Moscow (Moskva)	17,700	45,800	7,092,941
Oryol (region)	Oryol	9,500	24,700	787,163
Ryazan (region)	Ryazan	15,300	39,600	1,154,231
Smolensk (region)	Smolensk	19,200	49,800	985,481
Tambov (region)	Tambov	13,300	34,500	1,092,396
Tula (region)	Tula	9,900	25,700	1,553,874
Tver (region)	Tver	32,500	84,100	1,353,550
Vladimir (region)	Vladimir	11,200	29,100	1,444,606
Voronezh (region)	Voronezh	20,100	52,200	2,335,789
Yaroslavl (region)	Yaroslavl	14,000	36,200	1,272,485
Far East	Khabarovsk	2,382,000	6,169,300[4]	6,291,908
Amur (region)	Blagoveshchensk	139,700	361,900	829,204
Chukotka (autonomous district)	Anadyr	278,600	721,500	50,530
Kamchatka (territory)[5]	Petropavlovsk-Kamchatsky	179,300	464,300	321,764
Khabarovsk (territory)	Khabarovsk	304,100	787,600	1,344,271
Magadan (region)	Magadan	178,600	462,500	156,956
Primorye (territory)	Vladivostok	63,600	164,700	1,956,426
Sakha (republic)	Yakutsk	1,190,500	3,083,500	958,291
Sakhalin (region)	Yuzhno-Sakhalinsk	33,600	87,100	497,899
Yevrey (autonomous region)	Birobidzhan	14,000	36,300	176,567
North Caucasus[6]	Pyatigorsk	65,800	170,500	9,496,791
Chechnya (republic)	Grozny	6,000	15,600	1,269,095
Dagestan (republic)	Makhachkala	19,400	50,300	2,977,419
Ingushetiya (republic)	Magas	1,400	3,600	412,997
Kabardino-Balkariya (republic)	Nalchik	4,800	12,500	859,802
Karachayevo-Cherkesiya (republic)	Cherkessk	5,500	14,300	478,517
Severnaya Osetiya–Alaniya (North Ossetia; republic)	Vladikavkaz	3,100	8,000	712,877
Stavropol (territory)	Stavropol	25,600	66,200	2,786,084
Northwest	St. Petersburg	651,400[4]	1,687,000[4]	13,583,806
Arkhangelsk (region)[7]	Arkhangelsk	159,500	413,100	1,228,056
Kaliningrad (region)	Kaliningrad	5,800	15,100	941,474
Kareliya (Karelia; republic)	Petrozavodsk	69,700	180,500	645,205
Komi (republic)	Syktyukar	160,900	416,800	901,642
Leningrad (region)	St. Petersburg	32,400	83,900	1,712,690
Murmansk (region)	Murmansk	55,900	144,900	796,117
Nenets (autonomous district)[7]	Naryan-Mar	68,300	176,800	42,628[8]
Novgorod (region)	Novgorod	21,000	54,500	634,135
Pskov (region)	Pskov	21,400	55,400	673,451
St. Petersburg (city)		500	1,400	4,848,742
Vologda (region)	Vologda	55,800	144,500	1,202,294
Siberia	Novosibirsk	1,986,500	5,145,000[4]	19,254,315
Altay (republic)	Gorno-Altaysk	35,900	92,900	206,195
Altay (territory)	Barnaul	64,900	168,000	2,419,379
Buryatiya (republic)	Ulan-Ude	135,600	351,300	972,658
Irkutsk (region)[9]	Irkutsk	299,200	774,800	2,428,696
Kemerovo (region)	Kemerovo	36,900	95,700	2,763,481
Khakasiya (republic)	Abakan	23,800	61,600	532,319
Krasnoyarsk (territory)[10]	Krasnoyarsk	913,800	2,366,800	2,828,207
Novosibirsk (region)	Novosibirsk	68,600	177,800	2,665,853
Omsk (region)	Omsk	54,500	141,100	1,977,450
Tomsk (region)	Tomsk	121,400	314,400	1,045,541
Tyva (republic)	Kyzyl	65,100	168,600	307,925
Zabaykalye (territory)[11]	Chita	166,800	431,900	1,106,611
Southern	Rostov-na-Donu	162,500	420,800[4]	13,856,692
Adygeya (republic)	Maykop	3,000	7,800	440,388
Astrakhan (region)	Astrakhan	18,900	49,000	1,010,679
Kalmykiya (republic)	Elista	28,800	74,700	289,464
Krasnodar (territory)	Krasnodar	29,200	75,500	5,225,826
Rostov (region)	Rostov-na-Donu	39,000	101,000	4,279,179
Volgograd (region)	Volgograd	43,600	112,900	2,611,156
Urals	Yekaterinburg	702,100	1,818,500	12,082,698
Chelyabinsk (region)	Chelyabinsk	34,200	88,500	3,478,620
Kurgan (region)	Kurgan	27,600	71,500	910,832
Sverdlovsk (region)	Yekaterinburg	75,000	194,300	4,298,030
Tyumen (region)[12]	Tyumen	565,300	1,464,200	3,395,216[13]
Volga	Nizhny Novgorod	400,400	1,037,000[4]	29,900,359
Bashkortostan (republic)	Ufa	55,200	142,900	4,072,102
Chuvashiya (republic)	Cheboksary	7,100	18,300	1,251,599
Kirov (region)	Kirov	46,500	120,400	1,341,265
Mari El (republic)	Yoshkar-Ola	9,000	23,400	696,357
Mordoviya (republic)	Saransk	10,100	26,100	834,819
Nizhegorod (region)	Nizhny Novgorod	29,600	76,600	3,310,562
Orenburg (region)	Orenburg	47,800	123,700	2,032,915
Penza (region)	Penza	16,700	43,400	1,386,178
Perm (territory)[14]	Perm	61,800	160,200	2,635,849
Samara (region)	Samara	20,700	53,600	3,215,661
Saratov (region)	Saratov	39,100	101,200	2,521,759
Tatarstan (republic)	Kazan	26,200	67,800	3,786,358
Udmurtiya (republic)	Izhevsk	16,200	42,100	1,522,761
Ulyanovsk (Simbirsk; region)	Ulyanovsk	14,400	37,200	1,292,174
TOTAL		6,601,700	17,098,200[4]	142,905,208

Demography

Population (2011): 141,707,000.
Density (2011): persons per sq mi 21.5, persons per sq km 8.3.
Urban-rural (2010): urban 73.7%; rural 26.3%.
Sex distribution (2010): male 46.33%; female 53.67%.
Age breakdown (2008): under 15, 14.8%; 15–29, 24.0%; 30–44, 21.1%; 45–59, 22.8%; 60–74, 11.8%; 75–84, 4.7%; 85 and over, 0.8%.
Population projection: (2020) 141,000,000; (2030) 136,000,000.
Ethnic composition (2002): Russian 79.82%; Tatar 3.83%; Ukrainian 2.03%; Bashkir 1.15%; Chuvash 1.13%; Chechen 0.94%; Armenian 0.78%; Mordvin 0.58%; Belarusian 0.56%; Avar 0.52%; Kazakh 0.45%; Udmurt 0.44%; Azerbaijani 0.43%; Mari 0.42%; German 0.41%; Kabardinian 0.36%; Ossetian 0.35%; Dargin 0.35%; Buryat 0.31%; Sakha 0.31%; other 4.83%.
Religious affiliation (2005): Christian 58.4%, of which Russian Orthodox 53.1%, Roman Catholic 1.0%, Ukrainian Orthodox 0.9%, Protestant 0.9%; Muslim 8.2%[15, 16]; traditional beliefs 0.8%; Jewish 0.6%; nonreligious 25.8%; atheist 5.0%; other 1.2%.
Major cities (2010): Moscow 11,514,330; St. Petersburg 4,848,742; Novosibirsk 1,473,737; Yekaterinburg 1,350,136; Nizhny Novgorod 1,250,615; Samara 1,164,896; Omsk 1,153,971; Kazan 1,143,546; Chelyabinsk 1,130,273; Rostov-na-Donu 1,089,851; Ufa 1,062,300; Volgograd 1,021,244; Perm 991,500.

Other principal cities (2010[17])

	population		population		population
Astrakhan	520,662	Lipetsk	508,124	Tomsk	522,940
Barnaul	612,091	Naberezhnye Chelny	513,242	Tula	501,129
Irkutsk	587,225	Novokuznetsk	547,885	Tyumen	581,758
Izhevsk	628,116	Orenburg	546,987	Ulyanovsk	613,793
Kemerovo	532,884	Penza	517,137	Vladivostok	592,069
Khabarovsk	577,668	Ryazan	525,062	Volgograd	1,021,244
Krasnodar	744,933	Saratov	837,831	Voronezh	889,989
Krasnoyarsk	973,891	Tolyatti	719,514	Yaroslavl	591,486

Migration (2009): immigrants 279,907; emigrants 32,458.
Refugees (2008[18]): 159,500, of which from Afghanistan 84,500, Georgia 45,000.
Households. Total households (2004) 51,209,000; average household size (2006) 2.7; distribution by size (2002)[19]: 1 person 22.3%; 2 persons 27.6%; 3 persons 23.8%; 4 persons 17.0%; 5 persons 5.7%; 6 or more persons 3.6%.

Vital statistics

Birth rate per 1,000 population (2010): 12.5 (world avg. 19.2); within marriage (2008) 73.1%; outside of marriage (2008) 26.9%.
Death rate per 1,000 population (2010): 14.2 (world avg. 8.2).
Natural increase rate per 1,000 population (2010): –1.7 (world avg. 11.0).
Total fertility rate (avg. births per childbearing woman; 2009): 1.53.
Marriage/divorce rates per 1,000 population (2010): 8.5/4.5.
Life expectancy at birth (2009): male 62.8 years; female 74.7 years.
Major causes of death per 100,000 population (2009): diseases of the circulatory system 797; malignant neoplasms (cancers) 206; accidents, poisoning, and violence 150, of which suicide 26, transport accidents 21, homicide 15, alcohol poisoning 12, drowning 7; diseases of the digestive system 62; diseases of the respiratory system 55; infectious and parasitic diseases 23.
Adult population (ages 15–49) *living with HIV* (2009): 1.0%[20] (world avg. 0.8%).

Social indicators

Educational attainment (2002). Percentage of population age 15 and over having: no formal schooling 2.1%; primary education 7.7%; some secondary 18.1%; complete secondary/basic vocational 53.0%; incomplete higher 3.1%; complete higher 16.0%, of which advanced degrees 0.3%. *Literacy* (2008) 99.5%.
Quality of working life (2009). Average workweek (2004): 40 hours. Annual rate per 100,000 workers of: injury or accident 210; industrial illness (2008) 15.0; death 9.0.
Material well-being (2009[18]). Number of items possessed per 100 households: refrigerators/freezers 121; washing machines 100; VCRs 60; personal computers 47; passenger cars 44; "musical centres" 38.
Social participation. Eligible voters participating in last national election (2008): 69.7%. Trade union membership in total workforce (2003) *c.* 45%[21].
Degree of poverty (2009). Total number of people lacking subsistence-level monetary income: 18,500,000 (13.1% of total population).
Social deviance. Offense rate per 100,000 population (2009) for: murder and attempted murder 12.5; rape and attempted rape 3.8; serious injury 30.4; burglary 144.5; drug abuse 168.4; robbery 21.2; theft 837.8. Number of terrorist attacks (2009) 15.

National economy

Budget (2009)[22]. Revenue: RUB 13,599,700,000,000 (tax revenue 59.8%, of which VAT 15.1%, individual income tax 12.2%, tax on corporate profits 9.3%; nontax revenue 26.0%; unknown 14.2%). Expenditures: RUB 16,048,300,000,000 (social welfare 29.4%; national economy 17.3%;

education 11.1%; health/sports 10.3%; public security 7.8%; defense 7.4%).
Public debt (external, outstanding; June 2011): U.S.$35,120,000,000.
Gross national income (GNI; 2010): U.S.$1,404,179,000,000 (U.S.$9,910 per capita); purchasing power parity GNI (U.S.$19,190 per capita).

Structure of gross domestic product and labour force

	2008		2007	
	in value RUB '000,000	% of total value	labour force	% of labour force
Agriculture, forestry, fishing	1,771,800	4.3	6,347,000	8.4
Mining	3,353,600	8.1	1,324,000	1.8
Manufacturing	6,295,500	15.2	12,324,000	16.4
Public utilities	1,076,600	2.6	2,017,000	2.7
Construction	2,336,800	5.6	4,933,000	6.6
Transp. and commun.	3,398,300	8.2	6,573,000	8.7
Trade, restaurants, hotels	7,876,000	19.0	12,440,000	16.6
Finance, real estate	5,692,300	13.7	5,659,000	7.5
Services	2,729,400	6.6	14,052,000	18.7
Pub. admin., defense	1,811,200	4.4	4,903,000	6.5
Other	5,198,900[23]	12.5[23]	4,588,000[24]	6.1[24]
TOTAL	41,540,400	100.0[4]	75,159,000[4]	100.0

Production (metric tons except as noted). Agriculture, forestry, fishing (2009): wheat 61,740,000, cow's milk 32,326,000, potatoes 31,134,000, sugar beets 24,892,000, barley 17,881,000[25], sunflower seeds 6,454,000[25], oats 5,401,000[25], rye 4,333,000[25], corn (maize) 3,963,000, cabbages 3,312,000[26], tomatoes 2,170,000, cattle meat 1,741,000, dry onions 1,602,000, apples 1,596,000, cucumbers 1,133,000[27], currants 314,000[25], garlic 227,300, raspberries 120,000[25], gooseberries 47,000[25]; livestock (number of live animals) 21,038,000 cattle, 19,602,000 sheep, 16,162,000 pigs, 366,300,000 chickens; roundwood (2010) 173,000,000 cu m, of which fuelwood 23%; fisheries production 3,942,700 (from aquaculture 3%); aquatic plants production 6,567 (from aquaculture 1%). Mining and quarrying (2008): nickel 266,807[28] [world rank: 1]; mica 100,000 [world rank: 1]; platinum-group metals 123,200 kg [world rank: 2], of which palladium 87,700 kg [world rank: 1]; gem diamonds 21,925,000 carats [world rank: 2]; vanadium 14,500[28] [world rank: 3]; industrial diamonds 15,000,000 carats [world rank: 3]; cobalt 6,200[28] [world rank: 4]; iron ore 57,800,000[28] [world rank: 5]; copper ore 750,000[28] [world rank: 6]; gold 176,347 kg [world rank: 6]; molybdenum 3,600[28] [world rank: 9]. Manufacturing (value added in U.S.$'000,000; 2007): refined petroleum products 36,216; nonferrous base metals 19,848; iron and steel 19,399; food products 17,159; base chemicals 12,636; beverages 7,663; general purpose machinery 7,445; motor vehicles/parts 6,426; special purpose machinery 4,619; cement, bricks, and ceramics 4,400; rubber products 4,305; paints, soaps, and pharmaceuticals 3,665; publishing 3,391; medical appliances and instruments 3,372; structural metal products 3,236; paper and paper products 3,167.

Financial aggregates

	2005	2006	2007	2008	2009	2010
Exchange rate[29], RUB per:						
U.S. dollar	28.78	26.33	24.55	29.38	30.24	30.48
£	49.56	51.69	49.18	42.83	48.98	47.71
SDR	41.14	39.61	38.79	45.25	47.41	46.94
International reserves (U.S.$)						
Total (excl. gold; '000,000)	175,891	295,568	466,750	411,750	416,649	443,586
SDRs ('000,000)	5.6	7.1	0.8	0.8	8,897	8,744
Reserve pos. in IMF ('000,000)	195.9	283.3	373.9	1,053.4	1,927	1,893
Foreign exchange ('000,000)	175,690	295,277	466,376	410,695	405,825	432,949
Gold ('000,000 fine troy oz)	12.44	12.91	14.48	16.71	20.87	25.36
% world reserves	1.4	1.5	1.5	1.7	2.1	2.6
Balance of payments (U.S.$'000,000)						
Balance of visible trade	+118,364	+139,269	+130,915	+179,742	+111,585	+151,681
Imports, f.o.b.	–125,434	–164,281	–223,486	–291,861	–191,803	–248,738
Exports, f.o.b.	243,798	303,550	354,401	471,603	303,388	400,419
Balance of invisibles	–33,762	–44,583	–53,147	–76,212	–62,980	–81,082
Balance of payments, current account	+84,602	+94,686	+77,768	+103,530	+48,605	+70,599

Energy production (consumption): electricity (kW-hr; 2010–11[30]) 1,043,397,000,000 ([2010] 162,165,000,000); hard coal (metric tons; 2010–11[30]) 250,600,000 ([2007] 142,034,000); lignite (metric tons; 2010–11[30]) 73,600,000 ([2007] 70,147,000); crude petroleum (barrels; 2009) 3,466,000,000 ([2007] 1,538,000,000); petroleum products (metric tons; 2007) 204,013,000 (103,182,000); natural gas (cu m; 2010–11[30]) 481,541,000,000 (495,000,000).
Population economically active (2008): total 75,756,000; activity rate of total population 53.4% (participation rates: ages 15–64, 73.3%; female 48.9%; unemployed [July 2010–June 2011] 7.0%).

Price and earnings indexes (2005 = 100)

	2004	2005	2006	2007	2008	2009	2010
Consumer price index	88.7	100.0	109.7	119.6	136.4	152.3	162.8
Annual earnings index	88.3	100.0	119.2	143.4	165.4	172.6	186.9

Land use as % of total land area (2009): in temporary crops or left fallow (2007) 7.4%, in permanent crops 0.1%, in pasture 5.6%, forest area 49.4%.
Household income and expenditure. Average household size (2006) 2.7; income per household: n.a.; sources of monetary income (2009): wages 69.6%[31], transfers 14.5%, self-employment 9.6%, property income 4.3%, other 2.0%; expenditure (2009): food 30.5%, transportation 13.4%, housing and energy 10.8%, clothing and footwear 10.4%, recreation and culture 7.3%, household furnishings 7.0%, communications 3.8%, hotels and restaurants 3.4%.
Selected balance of payments data. Receipts from (U.S.$'000,000): tourism (2009) 9,297; remittances (2010) 5,477; foreign direct investment (FDI; 2008–10 avg.) 50,899. Disbursements for (U.S.$'000,000): tourism (2009) 20,763; remittances (2009) 18,613; FDI (2008–10 avg.) 50,319.

Foreign trade[32, 33]

Balance of trade (current prices)

	2005	2006	2007	2008	2009	2010
U.S.$'000,000	+142,744	+163,437	+152,540	+200,943	+130,970	+155,641
% of total	42.0%	37.2%	27.6%	27.3%	27.7%	26.4%

Imports (2008): U.S.$267,051,000,000 (machinery and apparatus 28.6%, of which machinery specialized for particular industries 6.2%, general industrial machinery/parts 6.1%, electrical machinery/electronics/parts 5.2%, telecommunications equipment/television receivers/video recorders 5.2%; road vehicles/parts 17.7%, of which passenger cars 11.3%; chemicals and chemical products 10.1%; food 9.7%; base and fabricated metals 6.4%). *Major import sources:* China 13.0%; Germany 12.8%; Japan 7.0%; Ukraine 6.1%; U.S. 5.2%; Italy 4.1%; Belarus 4.0%; South Korea 3.9%; France 3.8%; U.K. 2.9%.
Exports (2008): U.S.$467,994,000,000 (mineral fuels 65.7%, of which crude petroleum 32.4%, refined petroleum 16.8%, natural gas [in gaseous state] 14.2%, coal/coke 1.8%; iron and steel 6.1%, of which ingots/semifinished products 2.3%; chemicals and chemical products 4.8%, of which fertilizers 2.5%; nonferrous base metals 4.0%, of which aluminum 1.8%; machinery and apparatus 2.2%; food 1.4%; unspecified special transactions 8.2%). *Major export destinations:* Netherlands 12.2%; Italy 9.0%; Germany 7.1%; Turkey 5.9%; Belarus 5.1%; Ukraine 5.0%; China 4.5%; Poland 4.3%; Finland 3.4%; U.K. 3.2%.

Transport and communications

Transport. Railroads: length (2010[18])[34] 53,438 mi, 86,000 km; (2009) passenger-km 151,500,000,000; (2009) metric ton-km cargo 1,865,000,000,000. Roads (2010[18]): total length 610,185 mi, 982,000 km (paved 79%); (2009) passenger-km 106,900,000,000[35]; (2009) metric ton-km cargo 180,000,000,000. Vehicles (2007): passenger cars 29,249,000; trucks and buses 5,591,000. Air transport (2009): passenger-km 112,500,000,000; metric ton-km cargo 3,600,000,000. Inland waterways (2009): passenger-km 800,000,000; metric ton-km cargo 53,000,000,000.

Communications

Medium	date	number in '000s	units per 1,000 persons	Medium	date	number in '000s	units per 1,000 persons
Televisions	2003	50,599	351	PCs	2005	17,400	121
Telephones				Dailies	2007	1,150[36]	9.5[36]
Cellular	2010	237,690[37]	1,667[37]	Internet users	2009	59,700	424
Landline	2010	44,959	315	Broadband	2010	15,700[37]	110[37]

Education and health

Education (2007–08)

	teachers	students	student/ teacher ratio	enrollment rate (%)
Primary (age 7–10)	284,789	4,968,710	17.4	...
Secondary/Voc. (age 11–17)	1,183,126	10,087,007	8.5	...
Tertiary	691,693	9,446,408	13.7	77 (age 18–22)

Health: physicians (2009[18]) 704,000 (1 per 202 persons); hospital beds (2009[18]) 1,398,000 (1 per 102 persons); infant mortality rate per 1,000 live births (2010) 7.5; undernourished population (2004–06) 3,900,000 (less than 5% of total population based on the consumption of a minimum daily requirement of 1,950 calories).

Military

Total active duty personnel (November 2010): 1,046,000 (army 34.4%, airborne 3.3%, navy 15.4%, air force 15.3%, strategic deterrent forces 7.7%, command and support 23.9%); reserve 20,000,000; paramilitary 449,000; troops abroad 30,606, of which in Ukraine 13,000, in Tajikistan 5,000, in Georgia 7,000, in Armenia 3,214. *Military expenditure as percentage of GDP* (2009): 4.6%; per capita expenditure U.S.$403.

[1]Statutory number per Inter-Parliamentary Union Web site. [2]Area figures given are as of Jan. 1, 2009; a new national cadastral system came into effect on March 1, 2008. [3]Preliminary results. [4]Detail does not add to total given because of rounding. [5]Kamchatka (region) and Koryak (autonomous district) merged on July 1, 2007, to form Kamchatka (territory). [6]New federal district created in January 2010. [7]Most administrative functions of Nenets have been assumed by Arkhangelsk. [8]Population is included in the total population for the Arkhangelsk region. [9]Includes Ust–Orda Buryat (autonomous district) from Jan. 1, 2008. [10]Krasnoyarsk (territory) formally absorbed Evenk and Taymyr autonomous districts on Jan. 1, 2007. [11]Chita (region) and Agin Buryat (autonomous district) merged on March 3, 2008, to form Zabaykalye (territory). [12]Most administrative functions of Khanty-Mansi and Yamalo-Nenets autonomous districts have been assumed by Tyumen. [13]Includes the population of the autonomous districts of Khanty-Mansi (206,500 sq mi [534,800 sq km]) and Yamalo-Nenets (297,000 sq mi [769,300 sq km]). [14]On Dec. 1, 2005, Komi-Permyak (autonomous district) merged with Perm (region) to form Perm (territory). [15]Muslim population may be as high as 16%. [16]Shīʿī make up *c.* 8% of all Muslims. [17]Per preliminary 2010 census results. [18]January 1. [19]Excludes collective households (1.6% of all Russians live in collective households). [20]Statistically derived midpoint of range. [21]Mostly based on a claimed membership of 28,000,000 in the Federation of Independent Trade Unions of Russia, the successor to the former labour movement. [22]Data are for consolidated (federal and local) governments. [23]Net taxes on products less imputed bank service charges. [24]Unemployed. [25]World's leading producer. [26]Includes other brassicas. [27]Includes gherkins. [28]Metal content. [29]End of period. [30]June 2010–May 2011. [31]Includes unreported wages and salaries. [32]Imports c.i.f.; exports f.o.b. [33]Based on data published by the UN *International Trade Statistics Yearbook (2009, 2010)*. [34]Commercially operated public railway tracks only. [35]Buses only. [36]Circulation. [37]Subscribers.

Internet resources for further information:
- **Federal State Statistics Service http://www.gks.ru/eng/default.asp**
- **Central Bank of the Russian Federation http://www.cbr.ru/eng**

Rwanda

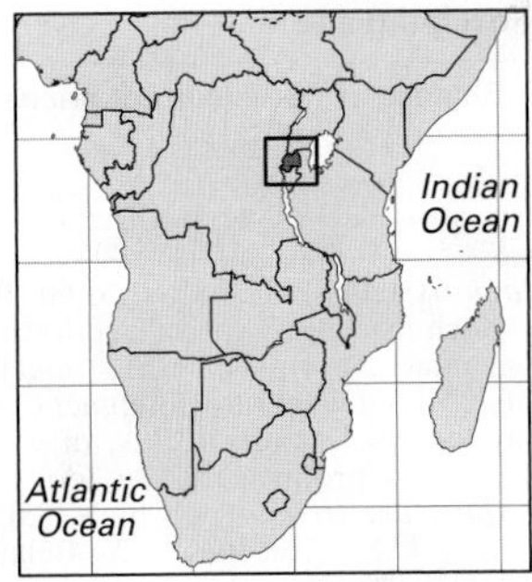

Official name: Repubulika y'u Rwanda (Rwanda); République Rwandaise (French); Republic of Rwanda (English).
Form of government: multiparty republic with two legislative houses (Senate [26]; Chamber of Deputies [80]).
Head of state and government: President assisted by Prime Minister.
Capital: Kigali.
Official languages: Rwanda; French; English.
Official religion: none.
Monetary unit: Rwandan franc (RF); valuation (Sept. 1, 2011) 1 U.S.$ = RF 599.42; 1 £ = RF 968.64.

Area and population[1]

		area		population
Provinces	**Principal cities**	sq mi	sq km	2002 census
Est (Eastern)	Rwamagana	3,560[2]	9,220[2]	1,640,000[2]
Kigali	Kigali	280[2]	720[2]	745,000[2]
Nord (Northern)	Ruhengeri	1,430[2]	3,700[2]	1,740,000[2]
Ouest (Western)	Gisenyi	2,197	5,689	1,940,888
Sud (Southern)	Gitarama	2,312	5,987	2,072,131
SUBTOTAL		9,774[3]	25,314[3]	—
SUBTOTAL (Rwandan part of Lake Kivu)		411	1,065	—
TOTAL		10,185	26,379	8,128,553[3]

Demography

Population (2011): 10,943,000.
Density (2011)[4]: persons per sq mi 1,120, persons per sq km 432.3.
Urban-rural (2009): urban 18.6%; rural 81.4%.
Sex distribution (2009): male 49.77%; female 50.23%.
Age breakdown (2009): under 15, 42.7%; 15–29, 28.9%; 30–44, 16.3%; 45–59, 8.3%; 60–74, 3.0%; 75–84, 0.7%; 85 and over, 0.1%.
Population projection: (2020) 14,042,000; (2030) 17,579,000.
Doubling time: 25 years.
Ethnic composition (2002): Hutu 85%; Tutsi 14%; Twa 1%.
Religious affiliation (2005): Roman Catholic *c.* 44%; Protestant *c.* 25%; Muslim *c.* 13%; other *c.* 18%[5].
Major cities (2002): Kigali (2010) 939,000[6]; Gitarama 84,669; Butare 77,449; Ruhengeri 71,511; Gisenyi 67,766.

Vital statistics

Birth rate per 1,000 population (2009): 38.1 (world avg. 20.3).
Death rate per 1,000 population (2008): 10.6 (world avg. 8.5).
Marriage/divorce rates per 1,000 population: n.a./n.a.
Total fertility rate (avg. births per childbearing woman; 2009): 5.12.
Life expectancy at birth (2009): male 55.4 years; female 58.1 years.
Adult population (ages 15–49) *living with HIV* (2009): 2.9%[7] (world avg. 0.8%).

National economy

Budget (2009). Revenue: RF 727,900,000,000 (grants 47.7%; taxes on goods and services 25.4%; income taxes 18.7%; import and export duties 5.9%; nontax revenue 2.3%). Expenditures: RF 754,300,000,000 (current expenditures 56.3%, of which wages and salaries 12.9%; capital expenditure 39.1%; net lending 4.6%).
Public debt (external, outstanding; 2010): U.S.$766,590,000.
Production (metric tons except as noted). Agriculture, forestry, fishing (2009): plantains 2,981,800, potatoes 1,287,400, cassava 980,000, sweet potatoes 801,376, dry beans 326,532, corn (maize) 285,505, sorghum 174,499, taro 136,849, avocados 80,000, coffee 28,000, tea 20,000, pyrethrum 1,000; livestock (number of live animals) 1,736,210 goats, 1,548,520 cattle, 470,000 sheep, 310,833 pigs; roundwood (2010) 3,076,927 cu m, of which fuelwood 61%; fisheries production (2009) 9,438 (from aquaculture 4%). Mining and quarrying (2009): cassiterite (tin content) 850; tungsten (wolframite content) 700; niobium 130,000 kg; tantalum 104,000 kg. Manufacturing (value added in RF '000,000; 2009): food products 80,500; beverages and tobacco products 55,600; cement, bricks, and ceramics 14,600; furniture and unspecified products 12,200; textiles and wearing apparel 9,900. Energy production (consumption): electricity (kW-hr; 2009–10) 275,000,000 ([2008] 277,205,023); coal, none (none); crude petroleum, none (none); petroleum products (metric tons; 2007) none (164,000); natural gas (cu m; 2008) 2,000,000 ([2007] 615,048).
Population economically active (2008): total 4,813,000[8]; activity rate of total population 49.5%[8] (participation rates: ages 15–64, 86.9%[8]; female 52.8%[8]; officially unemployed [2005–06] 1.2%).

Price index (2005 = 100)

	2004	2005	2006	2007	2008	2009	2010
Consumer price index	91.7	100.0	108.9	118.8	137.1	151.3	154.8

Land use as % of total land area (2009): in temporary crops or left fallow 52.7%, in permanent crops 11.3%, in pasture 17.0%, forest area 17.2%.
Household income and expenditure. Average household size (2008) 4.3; average annual income per household: n.a.; sources of income: n.a.; expenditure (2003)[9]: food and nonalcoholic beverages 37.1%, housing and energy 15.8%, transportation 9.9%, household furnishings 7.6%, health 7.1%.

Gross national income (GNI; 2010): U.S.$5,537,000,000 (U.S.$540 per capita); purchasing power parity GNI (U.S.$1,180 per capita).

Structure of gross domestic product and labour force

	2009		2002	
	in value RF '000,000,000	% of total value	labour force	% of labour force
Agriculture, forestry, fishing	1,012.3	33.8	2,951,492	86.2
Mining and quarrying	15.7	0.5	5,274	0.2
Manufacturing	190.2	6.3	43,053	1.3
Construction	218.8	7.3	42,180	1.2
Public utilities	5.7	0.2	2,482	0.1
Transp. and commun.	223.4	7.5	30,255	0.9
Trade, hotels, restaurants	448.7	15.0	94,175	2.8
Finance, real estate	350.6	11.7	10,920	0.3
Pub. admin., defense	128.0	4.3	25,668	0.7
Services	214.0	7.2	155,980	4.6
Other	184.7[10]	6.2[10]	56,568	1.7
TOTAL	2,992.1	100.0	3,418,047	100.0

Selected balance of payments data. Receipts from (U.S.$'000,000): tourism (2009) 174; remittances (2010) 92; foreign direct investment (FDI; 2008–10 avg.) 88; official development assistance (2009) 934. Disbursements for (U.S.$'000,000): tourism (2009) 72; remittances (2009) 71; FDI (2008–10 avg.) n.a.

Foreign trade[11]

Balance of trade (current prices)

	2004	2005	2006	2007	2008	2009
U.S.$'000,000	–186.1	–268.2	–419.3	–513.4	–747.3	–1,034.2
% of total	48.7%	47.7%	60.4%	58.3%	48.4%	72.8%

Imports (2008): U.S.$1,145,600,000 (machinery and apparatus 24.9%, road vehicles 11.1%, iron and steel 8.0%, refined petroleum 6.5%, food products 6.4%). *Major import sources* (2008): Kenya 16.0%; Uganda 14.5%; U.A.E. 8.4%; China 8.4%; South Africa 6.6%.
Exports (2009): U.S.$192,800,000 (tea 25.0%, coffee 19.3%, cassiterite [major ore of tin] 14.8%, columbite/tantalite 10.5%, tungsten 3.0%). *Major export destinations* (2008): Kenya 31.9%; Belgium 16.6%; Democratic Republic of the Congo 12.7%; Hong Kong 6.5%; Swaziland 5.1%.

Transport and communications

Transport. Railroads: none. Roads (2004): total length 8,704 mi, 14,008 km (paved 19%); passenger-km (2009) n.a.; metric ton-km cargo (2009) n.a. Vehicles (2009[12]): passenger cars 21,350; trucks and buses 16,470. Air transport (2008)[13]: passengers embarked and disembarked 253,431; cargo loaded and unloaded 6,023 metric tons.

Communications

Medium	date	number in '000s	units per 1,000 persons	Medium	date	number in '000s	units per 1,000 persons
Televisions	2004	70	7.4	PCs	2007	28	3.0
Telephones				Dailies	2009	10[14]	1.0[14]
Cellular	2010	3,549[15]	334[15]	Internet users	2009	450	45
Landline	2010	40	3.7	Broadband	2010	2.6[15]	0.2[15]

Education and health

Educational attainment (2005)[16]. Percentage of population age 15–49 having: no formal education/unknown 21.4%; primary education 68.2%; secondary 9.6%; higher 0.8%. *Literacy* (2008): percentage of total population age 15 and over literate 70.3%; males literate 74.8%; females literate 66.1%.

Education (2008–09)

	teachers	students	student/ teacher ratio	enrollment rate (%)
Primary (age 7–12)	33,158	2,264,672	68.3	94[17]
Secondary/Voc. (age 13–18)	16,105[17]	346,518	17.9[17]	14[17]
Tertiary	1,231	55,213	44.9	5 (age 19–23)

Health (2008): physicians 571 (1 per 17,025 persons); hospital beds 15,771 (1 per 616 persons); infant mortality rate per 1,000 live births (2009) 67.2; undernourished population (2005–07) 3,100,000 (34% of total population based on the consumption of a minimum daily requirement of 1,710 calories).

Military

Total active duty personnel (November 2010): 33,000[18] (army 97.0%, air force 3.0%). *Military expenditure as percentage of GDP* (2008): 1.8%; per capita expenditure U.S.$7.

[1]The new administrative structure went into effect at the beginning of 2006. [2]Estimate. [3]Detail does not add to total given because of some estimated data. [4]Based on area excluding Rwandan part of Lake Kivu. [5]Many small usually Christian-linked schismatic religious groups have proliferated since the 1994 genocide. [6]Population of urban agglomeration. [7]Statistically derived midpoint of range. [8]ILO estimate. [9]Weights of consumer price index components. [10]Taxes on products less imputed bank service charges. [11]Imports c.i.f.; exports f.o.b. [12]January 1. [13]Data unavailable for RwandAir, the national airline. [14]Circulation of daily newspapers. [15]Subscribers. [16]Based on the 2005 Rwanda Demographic and Health Survey, of which 15,735 people in 10,272 households were age 15–49. [17]2007–08. [18]Of which deployed as UN peacekeepers 3,513.

Internet resources for further information:
- **National Institute of Statistics http://www.statistics.gov.rw**
- **National Bank of Rwanda http://www.bnr.rw**

Saint Kitts and Nevis

Official name: Federation of Saint Kitts and Nevis[1].
Form of government: federated constitutional monarchy with one legislative house (National Assembly [15[2]]).
Head of state: British Monarch represented by Governor-General.
Head of government: Prime Minister.
Capital: Basseterre.
Official language: English.
Official religion: none.
Monetary unit: Eastern Caribbean dollar (EC$); valuation (Sept. 1, 2011) 1 U.S.$ = EC$2.70; 1 £ = EC$4.36.

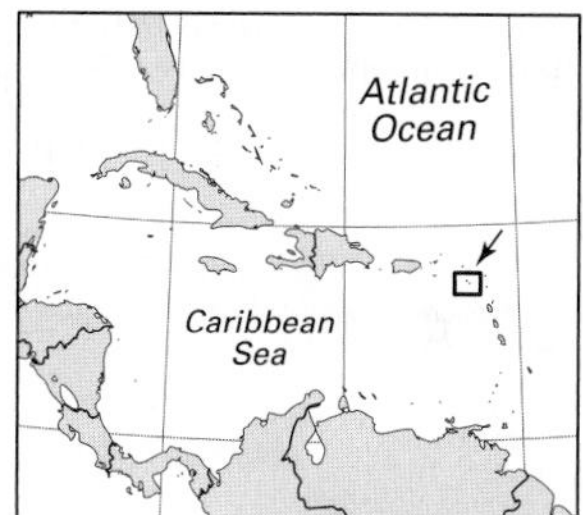

Area and population		area		population
				2001
Islands	Capitals	sq mi	sq km	census[3]
Nevis[4]	Charlestown	36.0	93.2	11,181
St. Kitts (St. Christopher)	Basseterre	68.0	176.2	34,703
TOTAL		104.0	269.4	45,884

Demography

Population (2011): 50,300.
Density (2011): persons per sq mi 483.8, persons per sq km 186.8.
Urban-rural (2010): urban 32.7%; rural 67.3%.
Sex distribution (2008): male 49.70%; female 50.30%.
Age breakdown (2008): under 15, 26.7%; 15–29, 25.9%; 30–44, 19.8%; 45–59, 17.3%; 60–74, 6.3%; 75–84, 2.9%; 85 and over, 1.1%.
Population projection: (2020) 53,800; (2030) 56,600.
Doubling time: 96 years.
Ethnic composition (2000): black 90.4%; mulatto 5.0%; Indo-Pakistani 3.0%; white 1.0%; other/unspecified 0.6%.
Religious affiliation (2005): Protestant *c.* 75%, of which Anglican *c.* 24%, Methodist *c.* 23%; Roman Catholic *c.* 11%; other *c.* 14%.
Major towns (2006): Basseterre (on St. Kitts; 2009) 12,847; Charlestown (on Nevis) 1,500; St. Paul's (on St. Kitts) 1,200.

Vital statistics

Birth rate per 1,000 population (2010): 14.2 (world avg. 19.2).
Death rate per 1,000 population (2010): 7.1 (world avg. 8.2).
Total fertility rate (avg. births per childbearing woman; 2009): 2.30.
Marriage/divorce rates per 1,000 population: (2001) 7.1/(2002) 0.5.
Life expectancy at birth (2009): male 70.3 years; female 76.3 years.
Major causes of death per 100,000 population (2008): diseases of the circulatory system 256.8, of which cerebrovascular diseases 93.8; malignant neoplasms (cancers) 120.3; diabetes mellitus 97.8; accidents, violence, and poisoning 85.6.

National economy

Budget (2008). Revenue: EC$641,200,000 (tax revenue 64.9%, of which taxes on international trade 30.3%, taxes on income and profits 20.5%, taxes on domestic goods and services 13.1%; nontax revenue 18.4%; grants 8.4%; other 8.3%). Expenditures: EC$634,400,000 (current expenditure 87.8%, of which interest payments 20.6%; development expenditure 12.2%).
Production (metric tons except as noted). Agriculture, forestry, fishing (2009): sugarcane 110,000, coconuts 930, potatoes 250, sweet potatoes 200, carrots and turnips 170, tomatoes 130, pineapples 70; livestock (number of live animals) 9,000 goats, 7,500 cattle, 7,000 sheep, 6,000 pigs, 80,000 chickens; roundwood, n.a.; fisheries production 450 (from aquaculture, none). Mining and quarrying: excavation of sand and crushed stone for local use. Manufacturing (2003): raw sugar 22,000[5]; carbonated beverages (2002) 32,000 hectolitres; beer (2002) 20,000 hectolitres; other manufactures include electronic components, garments, and cement. Energy production (consumption): electricity (kW-hr; 2009) 223,390,000 ([2007] 137,000,000); coal, none (none); crude petroleum, none (none); petroleum products (metric tons; 2007) none (81,000); natural gas, none (none).
Gross national income (GNI; 2010): U.S.$499,000,000 (U.S.$9,980 per capita); purchasing power parity GNI (U.S.$13,170 per capita).

Structure of gross domestic product and labour force	2008		1994	
	in value EC$'000,000	% of total value	labour force[6]	% of labour force[6]
Agriculture, fishing	34.6	2.2	2,439[7]	14.7[7]
Mining	2.7	0.2	29	0.2
Manufacturing	110.6	7.2	1,290[8]	7.8[8]
Construction	188.2	12.2	1,745	10.5
Public utilities	30.0	1.9	416	2.5
Transp. and commun.	216.1	14.0	534	3.2
Trade, restaurants	266.4	17.3	3,367	20.3
Finance, real estate	254.8	16.6	3,708[9]	22.3[9]
Pub. admin., defense	228.8	14.9	2,738	16.5
Services	59.7	3.9	[9]	[9]
Other	147.5[10]	9.6[10]	342	2.1
TOTAL	1,539.4	100.0	16,608	100.0[11]

Household income and expenditure. Average household size (2001) 2.9; average annual income per wage earner (2006) EC$24,216 (U.S.$8,969); sources of income: n.a.; expenditure (2001)[12]: food, beverages, and tobacco 28.8%, education 19.3%, health 14.1%, housing 13.0%, clothing and footwear 9.3%, fuel and light 4.4%, household furnishings 3.7%, transportation 2.1%, other 5.3%.
Public debt (external, outstanding; December 2010): U.S.$252,400,000.
Population economically active (1995): total 18,170; activity rate of total population 41.7% (participation rates [1991]: ages 15–64, 70.5%; female 44.4%[6]; unemployed [2006] 5.1%).

Price index (2005 = 100)	2004	2005	2006	2007	2008	2009	2010
Consumer price index	94.3	100.0	107.9	110.1	118.5	117.6	118.6

Selected balance of payments data. Receipts from (U.S.$'000,000): tourism (2010) 84; remittances (2010) 44; foreign direct investment (2008–10 avg.) 141; official development assistance (2009) 6. Disbursements for (U.S.$'000,000): tourism (2009) 13; remittances (2009) 6.
Land use as % of total land area (2007): in temporary crops, left fallow, or in permanent crops *c.* 15%; in pasture *c.* 4%; forest area *c.* 20%.

Foreign trade[13]

Balance of trade (current prices)	2002	2003	2004	2005	2006	2007
U.S.$'000,000	–118.6	–121.0	–106.3	–135.1	–166.8	–183.6
% of total	50.2%	52.6%	49.4%	57.4%	61.9%	61.8%

Imports (2008): U.S.$324,800,000 (base and fabricated metals 17.8%; machinery and apparatus 16.4%; food products and live animals 15.0%; refined petroleum 6.9%; chemicals and chemical products 6.5%; road vehicles 6.2%). *Major import sources:* United States 61.0%; Trinidad and Tobago 11.5%; United Kingdom 4.5%; Japan 3.0%; Canada 2.1%.
Exports (2008): U.S.$51,800,000 (machinery and apparatus 79.7%, of which electrical equipment 45.9%; food products, live animals, beverages, and tobacco 8.9%; publishing and printing 3.7%). *Major export destinations:* United States 83.6%; United Kingdom 4.4%; Netherlands Antilles 2.3%; Antigua and Barbuda 1.5%.

Transport and communications

Transport. Railroads (2005)[14]: route length 31 mi, 50 km. Roads (2002): total length 238 mi, 383 km (paved 43%). Vehicles (2004): passenger cars 9,000; trucks and buses 3,000. Air transport (2001)[15]: passenger arrivals 135,237, passenger departures 134,937; cargo handled 1,802.

Communications			units				units
Medium	date	number in '000s	per 1,000 persons	Medium	date	number in '000s	per 1,000 persons
Televisions	2001	11	239	PCs	2004	11	226
Telephones				Dailies	2009	2[16]	40[16]
Cellular	2010	85[17]	1,614[17]	Internet users	2009	17	329
Landline	2010	21	393	Broadband	2010	13[17]	250[17]

Education and health

Educational attainment (1991). Percentage of population age 25 and over having: no formal schooling 1.6%; primary education 45.9%; secondary 38.4%; higher 8.9%; other or not stated 5.2%. *Literacy* (2004): total population age 15 and over literate 97.8%.

Education (2009–10)	teachers	students	student/ teacher ratio	enrollment rate (%)
Primary (age 5–11)	443	6,225	14.1	83
Secondary/Voc. (age 12–16)	465	4,308	9.3	88
Tertiary	80[18]	600[18]	7.5[18]	18[19] (age 17–21)

Health: physicians (2005) 62 (1 per 796 persons); hospital beds (2009) 297 (1 per 167 persons); infant mortality rate per 1,000 live births (2008) 14.3; undernourished population (2004–06) 7,000 (15% of total population based on the consumption of a minimum daily requirement of 1,850 calories).

Military

Total active duty personnel (2010): the defense force includes coast guard and police units. *Military expenditure as percentage of GDP:* n.a.

[1]The Federation of Saint Christopher and Nevis is the alternate official long-form name. [2]Includes 3 appointed seats and 1 ex officio seat for the attorney general (if not elected); in addition, a speaker may be appointed from outside of the National Assembly. [3]Preliminary figures. [4]Nevis has full internal self-government. The Nevis legislature is subordinate to the National Assembly only with regard to external affairs and defense. [5]Sugar production ended in July 2005. [6]Employed persons only. [7]Includes sugar manufacturing. [8]Excludes sugar manufacturing. [9]Finance, real estate includes Services. [10]Taxes less subsidies and less imputed bank service charges. [11]Detail does not add to total given because of rounding. [12]Weights of consumer price index components. [13]Imports f.o.b. in balance of trade and c.i.f. in commodities and trading partners. [14]Former railway of the sugar industry is now used for tourist purposes. [15]Saint Kitts airport only. [16]Circulation of daily newspapers. [17]Subscribers. [18]Data for Medical University of the Americas at Charlestown, Nevis; 2004–05. [19]2007–08.

Internet resources for further information:
- **Official Web site of the Government of St. Kitts & Nevis http://www.gov.kn**
- **Eastern Caribbean Central Bank http://www.eccb-centralbank.org**

Saint Lucia

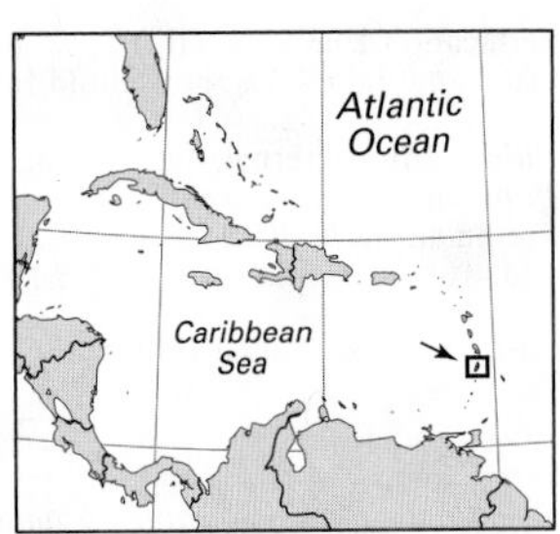

Official name: Saint Lucia.
Form of government: constitutional monarchy with a Parliament consisting of two legislative chambers (Senate [11[1]]; House of Assembly [18[2]]).
Head of state: British Monarch represented by Governor-General.
Head of government: Prime Minister.
Capital: Castries.
Official language: English.
Official religion: none.
Monetary unit: Eastern Caribbean dollar (EC$); valuation (Sept. 1, 2011) 1 U.S.$ = EC$2.70; 1 £ = EC$4.36.

Area and population

Districts	Capitals	area sq mi	area sq km	population 2010 census[3]
Anse-la-Raye	Anse-la-Raye	18	47	6,247
Canaries	Canaries			2,044
Castries	Castries	31	79	65,656
Choiseul	Choiseul	12	31	6,098
Dennery	Dennery	27	70	12,599
Gros Islet	Gros Islet	39	101	25,210
Laborie	Laborie	15	38	6,701
Micoud	Micoud	30	78	16,284
Soufrière	Soufrière	19	51	8,472
Vieux Fort	Vieux Fort	17	44	16,284
TOTAL		238[4]	617[4]	165,595

Demography

Population (2011): 167,000.
Density (2011): persons per sq mi 701.7, persons per sq km 270.7.
Urban-rural (2009): urban 27.9%; rural 72.1%.
Sex distribution (2009): male 49.00%; female 51.00%.
Age breakdown (2009): under 15, 25.9%; 15–29, 29.0%; 30–44, 21.6%; 45–59, 14.2%; 60–74, 6.5%; 75 and over, 2.8%.
Population projection: (2020) 181,000; (2030) 191,000.
Doubling time: more than 100 years.
Ethnic composition (2000): black 50%; mulatto 44%; East Indian 3%; white 1%; other 2%.
Religious affiliation (2001): Roman Catholic 67.5%; Protestant 22.0%, of which Seventh-day Adventist 8.4%, Pentecostal 5.6%; Rastafarian 2.1%; nonreligious 4.5%; other/unknown 3.9%.
Major towns (2006): Castries 65,000; Vieux Fort 4,600; Micoud 3,400; Dennery 2,900; Soufrière 2,900.

Vital statistics

Birth rate per 1,000 population (2009): 13.6 (world avg. 20.3); within marriage 14.0%; outside of marriage 86.0%.
Death rate per 1,000 population (2009): 7.4 (world avg. 8.5).
Natural increase rate per 1,000 population (2009): 6.2 (world avg. 11.8).
Total fertility rate (avg. births per childbearing woman; 2009): 2.0.
Marriage/divorce rates per 1,000 population (2009): 3.5/1.0.
Life expectancy at birth (2009): male 72.1 years; female 75.9 years.
Major causes of death per 100,000 population (2005): diseases of the circulatory system 228.8; malignant neoplasms (cancers) 109.8; diseases of the respiratory system 63.7; accidents and violence 51.6; infectious and parasitic diseases 47.9.

National economy

Budget (2008–09). Revenue: EC$815,950,000 (tax revenue 90.3%, of which consumption taxes 17.5%, corporate taxes 13.9%, import duties 12.7%, income tax 9.3%; nontax revenue 6.4%; grants 3.3%). Expenditures: EC$959,100,000 (current expenditures 67.8%, of which wages and salaries 31.8%, interest payments 9.5%; capital expenditures 32.2%).
Production (metric tons except as noted). Agriculture, forestry, fishing (2009): bananas 45,000, coconuts 12,148, roots and tubers 4,438, plantains 1,500, pepper 190, cocoa beans 46, ginger 14; livestock (number of live animals) 20,000 pigs, 11,000 cattle, 10,000 sheep, 9,500 goats; roundwood, n.a.; fisheries production (2010) 1,800, of which tuna 613, dolphin 352 (from aquaculture, none). Mining and quarrying: excavation of sand for local construction and pumice. Manufacturing (value of production in EC$'000; 2009): food, beverages (significantly alcoholic beverages), and tobacco products 79,929; electrical products 37,394; paper products and cardboard boxes 27,175; fabricated metal products 9,617; chemicals and chemical products 6,561; coconut oil 2,152. Energy production (consumption): electricity (kW-hr; 2009) 363,351,000 (363,351,000); coal, none (none); crude petroleum, none (none); petroleum products (metric tons; 2007) none (124,000); natural gas, none (none).
Population economically active (2007): total 85,260; activity rate of total population 49.8% (participation rates: ages 15 and over [2004] 68.6%; female 46.6%; unemployed 14.6%).

Price index (2005 = 100)

	2004	2005	2006	2007	2008	2009	2010
Consumer price index	96.2	100.0	102.3	105.5	113.1	114.1	116.2

Household income and expenditure. Average household size (2001) 3.2; income per household: n.a.; sources of income: n.a.; expenditure: n.a.

Gross national income (GNI; 2010): U.S.$865,000,000 (U.S.$4,970 per capita); purchasing power parity GNI (U.S.$8,520 per capita).

Structure of gross domestic product and labour force

	2008 in value EC$'000,000	2008 % of total value	2007 labour force	2007 % of labour force
Agriculture, forestry, fishing	103.3	4.8	8,270	9.7
Mining and quarrying	7.2	0.3	...	...
Manufacturing	126.9	5.8	4,160	4.9
Construction	142.0	6.5	8,940	10.5
Public utilities	110.1	5.1	420	0.5
Transportation and communications	448.1	20.6	4,370	5.1
Trade, restaurants	592.2	27.3	20,080	23.6
Finance, real estate	449.2	20.7	4,040	4.7
Pub. admin., defense	323.7	14.9	12,200	14.3
Services	67.3	3.1	5,530	6.5
Other	–198.6[5]	–9.1[5]	17,250[6]	20.2[6]
TOTAL	2,171.5[7]	100.0	85,260	100.0

Public debt (external, outstanding; December 2010): U.S.$393,859,000.
Selected balance of payments data. Receipts from (U.S.$'000,000): tourism (2009) 296; remittances (2010) 30; foreign direct investment (2008–10 avg.) 135; official development assistance (2009) 41. Disbursements for (U.S.$'000,000): tourism (2009) 41; remittances (2009) 4.
Land use as % of total land area (2009): in temporary crops or left fallow *c.* 5%, in permanent crops *c.* 11%, in pasture *c.* 2%, forest area *c.* 47%.

Foreign trade[8]

Balance of trade (current prices)

	2003	2004	2005	2006	2007	2008
U.S.$'000,000	–345.2	–341.8	–421.6	–498.7	–561.4	–491.7
% of total	73.4%	68.2%	76.7%	72.7%	84.2%	60.0%

Imports (2008): U.S.$655,700,000 (refined petroleum 24.0%, food 16.6%, machinery and apparatus 10.2%, road vehicles 9.2%, chemicals and chemical products 6.2%). *Major import sources:* United States 42.6%; Trinidad and Tobago 23.8%; Japan 4.3%; United Kingdom 4.1%; Barbados 3.5%.
Exports (2008): U.S.$164,000,000 (refined petroleum 19.0%, machinery and apparatus 14.0%, bananas 13.3%, beer 8.2%, precious metal jewelry 6.5%). *Major export destinations:* United States 34.0%; Trinidad and Tobago 23.2%; United Kingdom 15.1%; Barbados 8.5%; St. Vincent and the Grenadines 3.9%.

Transport and communications

Transport. Railroads: none. Roads (2002): total length 750 mi, 1,210 km (paved 5%). Vehicles (2008): passenger cars 38,504; trucks and buses 11,577. Air transport (2008)[9]: passenger arrivals and departures 872,032; cargo unloaded and loaded 3,363 metric tons.

Communications

Medium	date	number in '000s	units per 1,000 persons	Medium	date	number in '000s	units per 1,000 persons
Televisions	2001	46	291	PCs	2004	26	173
Telephones				Dailies	2009	0	0
Cellular	2010	179[10]	1,029[10]	Internet users	2009	143	830
Landline	2010	41	236	Broadband	2010	19[10]	107[10]

Education and health

Educational attainment (2007). Percentage of population age 15 and over having: no formal schooling 4.5%; incomplete primary education 5.6%; complete primary 43.1%; secondary 32.0%; higher vocational 7.1%; university 3.4%; other/unknown 4.3%. *Literacy* (2004): 94.8%.

Education (2008–09)

	teachers	students	student/ teacher ratio	enrollment rate (%)
Primary (age 5–11)	951	19,287	20.3	99[11]
Secondary/Voc. (age 12–16)	952	15,753	16.5	76[12]
Tertiary[12]	206	1,628	7.9	10 (age 17–21)

Health (2008): physicians (2005) 83 (1 per 1,983 persons); hospital beds 470 (1 per 374 persons); infant mortality rate per 1,000 live births (2009) 19.1; undernourished population (2005–07) 13,000 (8% of total population based on the consumption of a minimum daily requirement of 1,860 calories).

Military

Total active duty personnel (2009): [13].

[1]17 seats are directly elected. [2]Represents elected seats only; the speaker may be elected from outside the House of Assembly. [3]Preliminary. [4]Total includes the uninhabited 30 sq mi (78 sq km) Central Forest Reserve. [5]Taxes on products less subsidies and less imputed bank service charges. [6]Includes 12,480 unemployed and 4,770 inadequately defined. [7]Detail does not add to total given because of rounding. [8]Imports c.i.f.; exports f.o.b. [9]Combined data for both Castries and Vieux Fort airports. [10]Subscribers. [11]2006–07. [12]2005–06. [13]The police force includes a specially trained paramilitary unit and a coast guard unit.

Internet resources for further information:
- **Saint Lucian Government Statistics Department http://www.stats.gov.lc**
- **Eastern Caribbean Central Bank http://www.eccb-centralbank.org**

Saint Vincent and the Grenadines

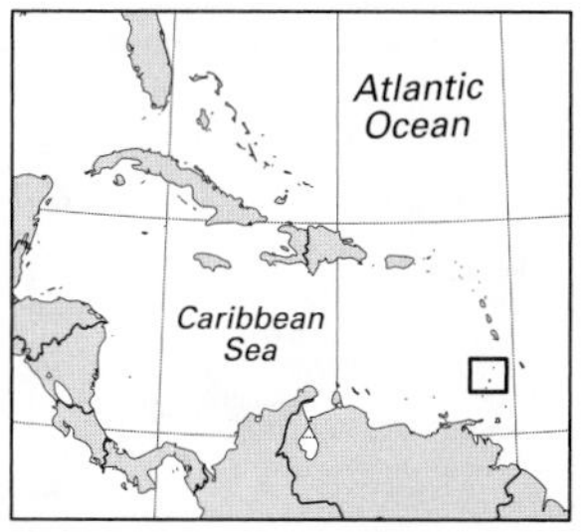

Official name: Saint Vincent and the Grenadines.
Form of government: constitutional monarchy with one legislative house (House of Assembly [22[1]]).
Head of state: British Monarch represented by Governor-General.
Head of government: Prime Minister.
Capital: Kingstown.
Official language: English.
Official religion: none.
Monetary unit: Eastern Caribbean dollar (EC$); valuation (Sept. 1, 2011) 1 U.S.$ = EC$2.70; 1 £ = EC$4.36.

Area and population

Census Divisions[3]	area sq mi	area sq km	population 2004[2] estimate
Island of Saint Vincent			
Barrouallie	14.2	36.8	5,142
Bridgetown	7.2	18.6	6,381
Calliaqua	11.8	30.6	21,376
Chateaubelair	30.9	80.0	5,725
Colonarie	13.4	34.7	7,052
Georgetown	22.2	57.5	6,576
Kingstown (city)	1.9	4.9	13,044
Kingstown (suburbs)	6.4	16.6	12,263
Layou	11.1	28.7	5,966
Marriaqua	9.4	24.3	7,770
Sandy Bay	5.3	13.7	2,640
Saint Vincent Grenadines			
Northern Grenadines	9.0	23.3	5,316
Southern Grenadines	7.5	19.4	3,380
TOTAL	150.3	389.3[4]	102,631

Demography

Population (2011): 101,000.
Density (2011): persons per sq mi 672.0, persons per sq km 259.4.
Urban-rural (2009): urban 48.6%; rural 51.4%.
Sex distribution (2009): male 50.67%; female 49.33%.
Age breakdown (2009): under 15, 25.9%; 15–29, 25.8%; 30–44, 21.7%; 45–59, 15.9%; 60–74, 7.4%; 75–84, 2.6%; 85 and over, 0.7%.
Population projection: (2020) 101,000; (2030) 101,000.
Doubling time: 89 years.
Ethnic composition (2000): black 65.1%; mixed black-white 19.9%; Indo-Pakistani 5.5%; British 3.0%; black-Amerindian 2.0%; other 4.5%.
Religious affiliation (2000): Protestant 47.0%; unaffiliated Christian 20.3%; independent Christian 11.7%; Roman Catholic 8.8%; Hindu 3.4%; Spiritist 1.8%; Muslim 1.5%; nonreligious 2.3%; other 3.2%.
Major cities (2006): Kingstown (2009) 28,000[5]; Georgetown 1,700; Byera 1,400; Port Elizabeth (on Bequia in the Northern Grenadines) 850.

Vital statistics

Birth rate per 1,000 population (2009): 15.3 (world avg. 20.3); within marriage (2003) 15.6%; outside of marriage (2003) 84.4%.
Death rate per 1,000 population (2009): 6.9 (world avg. 8.5).
Total fertility rate (avg. births per childbearing woman; 2009): 1.98.
Marriage/divorce rates per 1,000 population (2005): 5.6/0.9.
Life expectancy at birth (2009): male 71.8 years; female 75.5 years.
Major causes of death per 100,000 population (2008): diseases of the circulatory system 310.7, of which ischemic heart disease 132.9, cerebrovascular disease 82.5; malignant neoplasms (cancers) 104.5; communicable diseases 72.4; accidents, injuries, and violence 51.3; diabetes mellitus 14.7.

National economy

Budget (2009). Revenue: EC$522,500,000 (tax revenue 81.9%, of which VAT 27.3%, tax on international trade 16.4%, income tax 11.1%, corporate taxes 8.6%; grants 11.2%; nontax revenue 6.9%). Expenditures: EC$571,500,000 (current expenditure 81.5%, of which wages and salaries 37.1%, transfers 20.9%; development expenditure 18.5%).
Production (metric tons except as noted). Agriculture, forestry, fishing (2009): bananas 53,000, sugarcane 22,000, roots and tubers (significantly eddoes and dasheens[6]) 20,397, coconuts 5,000, plantains 2,400, mangoes, mangosteens, and guavas 1,819, oranges 1,700, apples 1,572, pig meat 557, nutmegs 172, soursops and papayas are also grown; livestock (number of live animals) 13,500 sheep, 9,300 pigs, 7,500 goats, 5,200 cattle; roundwood (2010) 7,502 cu m, of which fuelwood 100%; fisheries production 3,977 (from aquaculture, none). Mining and quarrying: sand and gravel for local use. Manufacturing (value added in EC$'000,000; 2000): beverages and tobacco products 17.4; food 15.6; paper products and publishing 3.6; textiles, clothing, and footwear 3.3. Energy production (consumption): electricity (kW-hr; 2008) 139,000,000 ([2007] 135,000,000); coal, none (none); crude petroleum, none (none); petroleum products (metric tons; 2007) none (65,000); natural gas, none (none).
Selected balance of payments data. Receipts from (U.S.$'000,000): tourism (2009) 90; remittances (2010) 33; foreign direct investment (2008–10 avg.) 119; official development assistance (2009) 31. Disbursements for (U.S.$'000,000): tourism (2009) 18; remittances (2009) 7.
Gross national income (GNI; 2010): U.S.$530,000,000 (U.S.$4,850 per capita); purchasing power parity GNI (U.S.$8,260 per capita).

Structure of gross domestic product and labour force

	2009 in value EC$'000	2009 % of total value	2001 labour force	2001 % of labour force
Agriculture, forestry, fishing	95,370	6.1	5,303	12.1
Mining and quarrying	2,870	0.2	104	0.2
Manufacturing	52,950	3.4	2,444	5.6
Construction	183,370	11.6	3,659	8.4
Public utilities	73,860	4.7	596	1.4
Transp. and commun.	248,520	15.8	2,594	5.9
Trade, restaurants	282,710	18.0	8,271	18.9
Finance, real estate	156,430	9.9	1,905	4.3
Pub. admin., defense	266,130	16.9	2,151	4.9
Services	28,220	1.8	6,045	13.8
Other	182,750[7]	11.6[7]	10,707[8]	24.5[8]
TOTAL	1,573,180	100.0	43,779	100.0

Population economically active (2008)[9]: total 53,000; activity rate of total population 48.6% (participation rates: ages 15–64, 73.2%; female 41.5%; unemployed [2001] 21%).

Price index (2005 = 100)

	2004	2005	2006	2007	2008	2009	2010
Consumer price index	96.4	100.0	103.0	110.2	121.3	121.8	123.6

Public debt (external, outstanding; December 2010): U.S.$290,900,000.
Household income and expenditure. Average household size, n.a.; income per household: n.a.; sources of income: n.a.; expenditure (2001)[10]: food and beverages 53.6%, housing and energy 12.8%, clothing and footwear 8.9%, transportation and communications 6.9%.
Land use as % of total land area (2009): in temporary crops or left fallow *c.* 13%, in permanent crops *c.* 8%, in pasture *c.* 5%, forest area *c.* 68%.

Foreign trade[11]

Balance of trade (current prices)

	2003	2004	2005	2006	2007	2008
U.S.$'000,000	–163.0	–188.6	–200.5	–233.2	–279.0	–321.0
% of total	68.1%	72.0%	71.5%	75.4%	74.5%	75.5%

Imports (2008): U.S.$373,200,000 (machinery and apparatus 23.1%; food and beverages 22.6%; refined petroleum 12.5%). *Major import sources:* U.S. 37.0%; Trinidad and Tobago 21.7%; U.K. 5.9%; Venezuela 3.3%; Japan 2.8%.
Exports (2008): U.S.$52,200,000 (food 61.7%, of which bananas 15.9%, wheat flour 15.1%, rice 12.1%, roots and tubers 7.1%; machinery and apparatus 23.0%, of which telecommunications equipment 10.7%). *Major export destinations:* Grenada 18.2%; Trinidad and Tobago 17.4%; St. Lucia 14.8%; Barbados 10.7%; U.K. 9.0%.

Transport and communications

Transport. Railroads: none. Roads (2004): total length 515 mi, 829 km (paved *c.* 70%); passenger-km (2009) n.a.; metric ton-km cargo (2009) n.a. Vehicles (2008): passenger cars 9,247; trucks and buses 13,019. Air transport: passenger arrivals (2006) 106,466; passenger departures (2003) 137,899.

Communications

Medium	date	number in '000s	units per 1,000 persons	Medium	date	number in '000s	units per 1,000 persons
Televisions	2000	50	446	PCs	2005	16	152
Telephones				Dailies	2007	...[12]	...[12]
Cellular	2010	132[13]	1,205[13]	Internet users	2009	76	696
Landline	2010	22	199	Broadband	2010	13[13]	114[13]

Education and health

Educational attainment (2001). Percentage of employed population having: no formal schooling 0.4%; primary education 55.6%; secondary 27.3%; higher vocational 15.1%; university 0.3%; other/unknown 1.3%. *Literacy* (2004): total population age 15 and over literate 88.1%.

Education (2008–09)

	teachers	students	student/ teacher ratio	enrollment rate (%)
Primary (age 5–11)	879	14,909	17.0	95
Secondary/Voc. (age 12–16)	886	11,704	13.2	90
Tertiary	...	...	...	... (age 17–21)

Health (2009): physicians 61 (1 per 1,654 persons); hospital beds (2008) 280 (1 per 375 persons); infant mortality rate per 1,000 live births 15.1; undernourished population (2005–07) 5,000 (5% of total population based on the consumption of a minimum daily requirement of 1,860 calories).

Military

Total active duty personnel (2010): no regular military forces; the paramilitary includes coast guard and police units.

[1]Includes 8 nonelective seats (including 1 seat for the attorney-general and 1 seat for the speaker serving ex officio). [2]January 1. [3]For statistical purposes and the election of legislative representatives only. [4]Detail does not add to total given because of rounding. [5]Population of urban agglomeration. [6]Varieties of taro roots. [7]Indirect taxes less subsidies and less imputed bank service charges. [8]Includes 9,258 unemployed. [9]Estimates of the ILO. [10]Based on weights of consumer price index components. [11]Imports c.i.f.; exports f.o.b. [12]No data for one daily newspaper. [13]Subscribers.

Internet resources for further information:
- **Eastern Caribbean Central Bank http://www.eccb-centralbank.org**
- **Official Website of St. Vincent and the Grenadines http://www.gov.vc**

Samoa

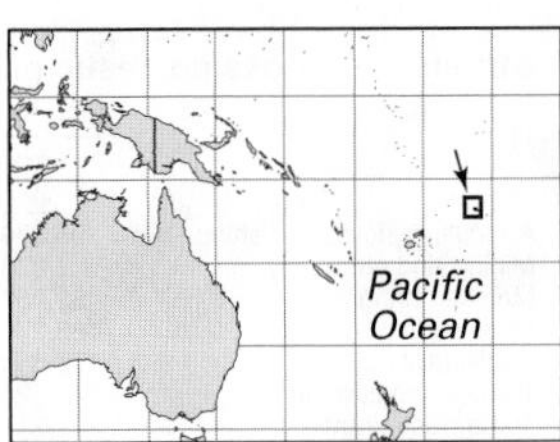

Official name: Malo Sa'oloto Tuto'atasi o Samoa (Samoan); Independent State of Samoa (English).
Form of government: mix of parliamentary democracy and Samoan customs with one legislative house (Legislative Assembly [49[1]]).
Head of state: Head of State.
Head of government: Prime Minister.
Capital: Apia.
Official languages: Samoan; English.
Official religion: none.
Monetary unit: tala (SAT); valuation (Sept. 1, 2011) 1 U.S.$ = SAT 2.23; 1 £ = SAT 3.61.

Area and population

Islands / Statistical regions	Largest towns	area sq mi	area sq km	population 2006 final census
Savai'i	Matavai	654	1,694	43,142
Upolu	Apia	421	1,091	137,599
Apia urban area		23	60	37,708
North West Upolu		97	251	56,122
Upolu (remainder)[2]		301	780	43,769
TOTAL		1,075	2,785	180,741

Demography

Population (2011): 184,000.
Density (2011): persons per sq mi 171.2, persons per sq km 66.1.
Urban-rural (2009): urban 20.4%; rural 79.6%.
Sex distribution (2008): male 51.46%; female 48.54%.
Age breakdown (2008): under 15, 37.3%; 15–29, 26.3%; 30–44, 18.2%; 45–59, 11.1%; 60–74, 5.3%; 75–84, 1.6%; 85 and over, 0.2%.
Population projection: (2020) 188,000; (2030) 198,000.
Doubling time: 30 years.
Ethnic composition (2006): Samoan (Polynesian) 92.6%; Euronesian (European and Polynesian) 7.0%; European and U.S. white 0.4%.
Religious affiliation (2006): Congregational 33.8%; Roman Catholic 19.6%; Methodist 14.3%; Mormon 13.3%; Assemblies of God 6.9%; other Christian 9.8%; other/unknown 2.3%.
Major towns (2006)[3]: Apia 37,237 (urban agglomeration 60,702); Vaitele 6,294[4]; Faleasi'u 3,548; Vailele 3,174[4]; Le'auva'a 3,015.

Vital statistics

Birth rate per 1,000 population (2008): 25.5 (world avg. 20.3).
Death rate per 1,000 population (2008): 5.5 (world avg. 8.5).
Natural increase rate per 1,000 population (2008): 20.0 (world avg. 11.8).
Total fertility rate (avg. births per childbearing woman; 2008): 3.8.
Marriage/divorce rates per 1,000 population: (2008) 5.8/(2005) 0.2.
Life expectancy at birth (2008): male 68.8 years; female 74.6 years.
Major causes of death per 100,000 population (2005–06): diseases of the circulatory system 56.3, of which hypertensive diseases 21.1; diabetes mellitus 24.9; malignant neoplasms (cancers) 22.2; accidents/injuries 21.7.

National economy

Budget (2008–09). Revenue: SAT 492,000,000 (tax revenue 66.0%, grants 22.5%, nontax revenue 11.5%). Expenditures: SAT 551,000,000 (current expenditure 64.7%, development expenditure 33.0%, net lending 2.3%).
Production (metric tons except as noted). Agriculture, forestry, fishing (2009): coconuts 155,060, bananas 29,044, taro 20,248, pig meat 4,001, pineapples 4,000, mangoes 3,792, avocados 1,150, cattle meat 1,100, honey 217, noni[5], n.a.; livestock (number of live animals) 202,000 pigs, 30,000 cattle; roundwood (2010) 75,700 cu m, of which fuelwood 92%; fisheries production 3,977 (from aquaculture, negligible). Mining and quarrying: n.a. Manufacturing (value of manufactured exports in SAT '000; 2006–07): ignition wiring sets, n.a.; beer 3,520; noni[5] juice 3,130; coconut cream 2,130. Energy production (consumption): electricity (kW-hr; 2009) 108,000,000 ([2008] 99,900,000); coal, none (none); crude petroleum, none (none); petroleum products (metric tons; 2007) none (52,000); natural gas, none (none).
Household income and expenditure. Average household size (2004) 7.2; average annual income per household (2008) SAT 36,088[6] (U.S.$13,648[6]); sources of income (2008): wages and salaries/self-employment 49.1%, gifts 13.5%, own produce consumed 12.5%, remittances 10.8%, other 14.1%; expenditure (2008)[7]: food, alcohol, and tobacco products 39.1%, miscellaneous goods and services 23.5%[8], household furnishings and operation 15.4%, transportation 7.6%.
Land use as % of total land area (2009): in temporary crops or left fallow 8.8%, in permanent crops 13.8%, in pasture 1.1%, forest area 60.4%.
Population economically active (2008)[9]: total 62,000; activity rate of total population *c.* 35% (participation rates: ages 15–64, *c.* 63%; female *c.* 31%; unemployed [2006] 1.1%).

Price index (2005 = 100)

	2004	2005	2006	2007	2008	2009	2010
Consumer price index	98.2	100.0	103.7	109.5	122.1	129.9	130.9

Gross national income (GNI; 2010): U.S.$524,000,000 (U.S.$2,930 per capita); purchasing power parity GNI (U.S.$4,300 per capita).

Structure of gross domestic product and labour force

	2009 in value SAT '000,000	2009 % of total value	2006 labour force	2006 % of labour force
Agriculture, fishing	169	11.8	19,099	34.9
Mining	…	…	10,548[10]	19.3[10]
Manufacturing	122	8.5		
Construction	183	12.8	2,476	4.5
Public utilities	72	5.0	872	1.6
Transp. and commun.	201	14.1	3,255	6.0
Trade, hotels, restaurants	338	23.7	5,965	10.9
Finance, real estate	172	12.0	1,439	2.6
Pub. admin., defense	128	9.0	2,706	5.0
Services	62	4.4	6,923	12.7
Other	–18[11]	–1.3[11]	1,356[12]	2.5[12]
TOTAL	1,429	100.0	54,639	100.0

Public debt (external, outstanding; 2009): U.S.$235,500,000.
Selected balance of payments data. Receipts from (U.S.$'000,000): tourism (2009) 116; remittances (2010) 143; foreign direct investment (2008–10 avg.) 7; official development assistance (2009) 77. Disbursements for (U.S.$'000,000): tourism (2009) 11; remittances (2007) 13.

Foreign trade[13]

Balance of trade (current prices)

	2004	2005	2006	2007	2008
U.S.$'000,000	–124.7	–151.4	–210.0	–168.1	–215.9
% of total	42.3%	46.5%	61.7%	46.3%	60.0%

Imports (2008): U.S.$287,900,000 (food 23.8%, of which meat 7.7%, cereals 6.0%; refined petroleum 22.8%; machinery and apparatus 6.7%; manufactures of metal 5.0%; unspecified 16.4%). *Major import sources:* Australia 25.6%; New Zealand 22.8%; U.S. 12.4%; China 7.4%; Singapore 7.4%.
Exports (2008): U.S.$72,000,000 (ignition wiring sets 80.1%; tuna 6.8%; beer 1.8%; fruit juice [mostly noni[5]] 1.7%; coconut oil 1.4%). *Major export destinations:* Australia 81.7%; New Zealand 10.1%; American Samoa 3.6%; U.S. 1.9%.

Transport and communications

Transport. Railroads: none. Roads (2001): total length 1,452 mi, 2,337 km (paved 14%). Vehicles (2005): passenger cars 5,924; trucks and buses 4,894. Air transport (2005): passenger-km 368,000,000; metric ton-km cargo, n.a.

Communications

Medium	date	number in '000s	units per 1,000 persons	Medium	date	number in '000s	units per 1,000 persons
Televisions	2003	27	152	PCs	2005	4.0	22
Telephones				Dailies	2009	5[14]	101[14]
Cellular	2010	167[15]	914[15]	Internet users	2009	9.0	50
Landline	2010	35	193	Broadband	2010	0.2[15]	1.1[15]

Education and health

Educational attainment (2002). Percentage of population age 25 and over having: no formal schooling 1.8%; incomplete/complete primary education 32.4%; incomplete/complete secondary 55.4%; higher 10.4%. *Literacy* (2008): total population over age 15 literate 98.7%; males literate 99.0%; females literate 98.5%.

Education (2008–09)

	teachers	students	student/teacher ratio	enrollment rate (%)
Primary (age 5–10)	936	29,663	31.7	93
Secondary/Voc. (age 11–17)	1,206	25,429	21.1	71
Tertiary[16]	140	1,179	8.4	7 (age 18–23)

Health (2005): physicians 50 (1 per 3,570 persons); hospital beds 219 (1 per 831 persons); infant mortality rate per 1,000 live births (2006) 20.4; undernourished population (2005–07) less than 5.0% of total population based on the consumption of a minimum daily requirement of 1,800 calories.

Military

No military forces are maintained; informal defense ties exist with New Zealand, and Australia assists with maritime surveillance training.

[1]47 seats are reserved for ethnic Samoans. [2]Includes Manono and Apolima islands. [3]Preliminary census. [4]Within Apia urban agglomeration. [5]Fruit known locally as *nonu;* also known as Indian mulberry. [6]Includes estimated value of agricultural products consumed by grower. [7]Weights of consumer price index components. [8]Includes 7.0% as contribution/donation to church, village, and school. [9]ILO estimates. [10]Includes handicrafts. [11]Less imputed bank service charges. [12]Includes 711 unemployed (1.3% of labour force). [13]Imports c.i.f.; exports f.o.b. [14]Circulation for one of two daily newspapers. [15]Subscribers. [16]2000–01.

Internet resources for further information:
- **Central Bank of Samoa http://www.cbs.gov.ws**
- **Secretariat of the Pacific Community http://www.spc.int/**

San Marino

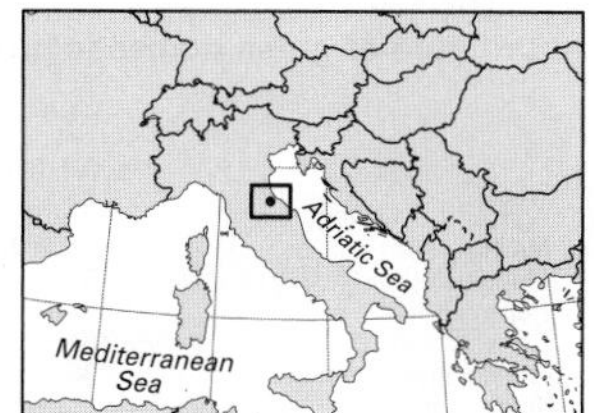

Official name: Repubblica di San Marino (Republic of San Marino).
Form of government: unitary multiparty republic with one legislative house (Great and General Council [60]).
Heads of state and government: Captains-Regent (2).
Capital: San Marino.
Official language: Italian.
Official religion: none.
Monetary unit: euro (€)[1]; valuation (Sept. 1, 2011) 1 U.S.$ = €0.70; 1 £ = €1.13.

Area and population

Municipalities	Capitals	area sq mi	area sq km	population 2011[2] estimate
Acquaviva	Acquaviva	1.88	4.86	2,051
Borgo Maggiore	Borgo Maggiore	3.48	9.01	6,377
Chiesanuova	Chiesanuova	2.11	5.46	1,059
Città (San Marino)	San Marino	2.74	7.09	4,296
Domagnano	Domagnano	2.56	6.62	3,122
Faetano	Faetano	2.99	7.75	1,176
Fiorentino	Fiorentino	2.53	6.57	2,502
Montegiardino	Montegiardino	1.28	3.31	911
Serravalle	Serravalle	4.07	10.53	10,394
TOTAL		23.63[3]	61.20	31,888

Demography

Population (2011): 32,000.
Density (2011): persons per sq mi 1,354, persons per sq km 522.8.
Urban-rural (2010): urban 93.8%; rural 6.2%.
Sex distribution (2011[2]): male 49.09%; female 50.91%.
Age breakdown (2009): under 15, 15.4%; 15–29, 14.2%; 30–44, 25.5%; 45–59, 21.8%; 60–74, 14.7%; 75–84, 6.0%; 85 and over, 2.4%.
Population projection: (2020) 32,900; (2030) 33,900.
Ethnic composition (2011[2]): Sammarinese 84.7%; Italian 13.4%; other 1.9%.
Religious affiliation (2000): Roman Catholic 88.7%; other Christian 3.5%; nonreligious 5.1%; other 2.7%.
Major municipalities (2011[2]): Serravalle 10,394; Borgo Maggiore 6,377; San Marino 4,296.

Vital statistics

Birth rate per 1,000 population (2010): 10.6 (world avg. 19.2); within marriage 70.7%; outside of marriage 29.3%.
Death rate per 1,000 population (2010): 7.0 (world avg. 8.2).
Total fertility rate (avg. births per childbearing woman; 2009): 1.50.
Marriage/divorce rates per 1,000 population (2010): 7.3/1.9.
Life expectancy at birth (2010): male 80.9 years; female 86.0 years.
Major causes of death per 100,000 population (2010): diseases of the circulatory system 363.6, of which cerebrovascular diseases 88.5; malignant neoplasms (cancers) 208.6; pneumonia 28.5; accidents, violence, and suicide 9.5.

National economy

Budget (2005). Revenue: €504,800,000 (VAT 23.6%, social contributions 21.3%, income tax 20.2%). Expenditures: €433,100,000 (wages and salaries 35.4%, social benefits 30.5%).
Public debt (2003): U.S.$52,900,000.
Tourism: number of visitor arrivals (2010–11) 1,997,424; receipts from visitors, n.a.; expenditures by nationals abroad, n.a.
Remittances: n.a.
Population economically active (2010): total 22,714; activity rate of total population 71.8% (participation rates: ages 15–64 [2002] 72.1%[4]; female 40.7%; unemployed [September 2010–August 2011] 3.8%).

Price and earnings indexes (2003 = 100)

	2004	2005	2006	2007	2008	2009	2010
Consumer price index	101.4	103.1	105.3	107.9	112.6	115.0	118.0
Annual earnings index	100.7	103.0	106.2	108.6	...	...	...

Household income and expenditure. Average household size (2010)[5] 2.3; income per household: n.a.; sources of income: n.a.; expenditure (2006)[5]: food and beverages 21.3%, housing 15.3%, transportation 10.6%, vacation and recreation 10.4%, restaurants 10.2%, clothing and footwear 5.6%, energy 5.4%, household furnishings 4.4%.
Production (metric tons except as noted). Agriculture, forestry, fishing: small amounts of wheat, grapes, and barley; livestock (number of live animals; 2005) 991 cattle, 91 sheep, 32 pigs. Quarrying: building stone is an important export product. Manufacturing (2008): processed meats 232,398 kg, of which beef 226,870 kg, pork 3,650 kg; cheese (2005) 56,610 kg; butter (2005) 8,110 kg; milk 1,542,262 litres; yogurt (2004) 10,314 litres; other major products include electrical appliances, musical instruments, printing ink, paint, cosmetics, furniture, floor tiles, gold and silver jewelry, clothing, and postage stamps. Energy production (consumption): all electrical power is imported via electrical grid from Italy (kW-hr; consumption [2008] 249,713,050); coal, none (n.a.); crude petroleum, none (none); petroleum products, none (n.a.); natural gas (cu m; 2008) none (55,133,260).
Gross national income (GNI; 2009): U.S.$1,572,000,000 (U.S.$50,670 per capita); purchasing power parity GNI, n.a.

Structure of gross domestic product and labour force

	2009 in value U.S.$'000,000	2009 % of total value	2008 labour force	2008 % of labour force
Agriculture, forestry, fishing	1.1	0.1	76	0.3
Manufacturing	367.0	33.3	6,398	28.2
Construction	65.0	5.9	1,716	7.6
Public utilities	...	...	...	...
Mining and quarrying	...	...	...	...
Transp. and commun.	26.4	2.4	615	2.7
Trade, hotels	148.8	13.5	3,731	16.4
Finance and insurance	194.0	17.6	4,064	17.9
Services	149.9	13.6	1,365	6.0
Pub. admin., defense	149.8	13.6	4,030	17.8
Other	...	...	713[6]	3.1[6]
TOTAL	1,102.0	100.0	22,708	100.0

Land use as % of total land area (2007): in temporary crops, left fallow, or in permanent crops *c.* 17%; in pasture, n.a.; forest area *c.* 2%.

Foreign trade[7]

Balance of trade (current prices)[8]

	2003	2004	2005	2006	2007	2008
U.S.$'000,000	–95	–54	–51	–4	+42	+298
% of total	2.3%	1.1%	1.0%	0.1%	0.6%	3.7%

Imports (2008): U.S.$3,929,000,000[8] (manufactured goods of all kinds, petroleum products, natural gas, electricity, and gold). *Major import sources* (2008): Italy 83.2%; China 3.9%; Germany 1.8%; Netherlands 1.8%.
Exports (2008): U.S.$4,227,000,000[8] (goods include electronics, postage stamps, leather products, ceramics, wine, wood products, and building stone). *Major export destinations* (2008): Italy 90.1%; France 1.3%; Russia 1.2%.

Transport and communications

Transport. Railroads: none (nearest rail terminal is at Rimini, Italy, 17 mi [27 km] northeast). Roads (2006): total length *c.* 137 mi, *c.* 220 km (paved, n.a.). Vehicles (2008): passenger cars 34,025; trucks and buses 6,370. Air transport: a heliport provides passenger and cargo service between San Marino and Rimini, Italy, during the summer months.

Communications

Medium	date	number in '000s	units per 1,000 persons	Medium	date	number in '000s	units per 1,000 persons
Televisions	2003	25	893	PCs	2003	23	819
Telephones				Dailies	2009	6[9]	191[9]
Cellular	2010	24[10]	761[10]	Internet users	2009	17	542
Landline	2010	22	688	Broadband	2010	10[10]	320[10]

Education and health

Educational attainment (2007). Percentage of population age 15 and over having: basic literacy or primary education 55.3%; secondary or vocational 34.5%; higher degree 10.2%. *Literacy* (2001): total population age 15 and over literate 98.7%; males literate 98.9%; females literate 98.4%.

Education (2009–10)

	teachers	students	student/ teacher ratio	enrollment rate (%)
Primary (age 6–10)	244	1,577	6.5	92[11]
Secondary/Voc. (age 11–18)	161	2,334	14.5	...
Tertiary[12]	...	43	...	... (age 19–23)

Health (2002): physicians 117 (1 per 230 persons); hospital beds 134 (1 per 191 persons); infant mortality rate per 1,000 live births (2010) 3.0; undernourished population, n.a.

Military

Total active duty personnel (2011): [13]. *Military expenditure as percentage of GDP:* n.a.

[1]San Marino uses the euro as its official currency even though it is not a member of the EU. [2]January 1. [3]Detail does not add to total given because of rounding. [4]Percentage includes cross-border workers. [5]Data is for families. [6]Unemployed. [7]A customs union with Italy has existed since 1862. [8]Estimated data. [9]Circulation. [10]Subscribers. [11]2008–09. [12]Excludes 832 university students enrolled abroad. [13]Defense is the responsibility of Italy; a small voluntary military force performs ceremonial duties and provides limited assistance to police.

Internet resource for further information:

- **Office of Economic Planning: Data Processing and Statistics http://www.statistica.sm**

Sao Tome and Principe

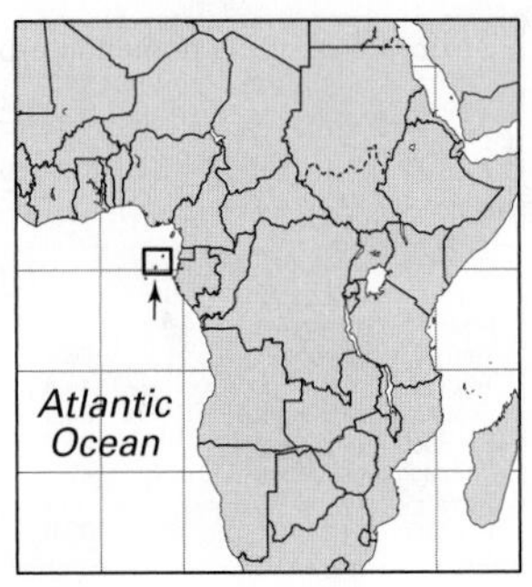

Official name: República Democrática de São Tomé e Príncipe (Democratic Republic of Sao Tome and Principe).
Form of government: multiparty republic with one legislative house (National Assembly [55]).
Head of state: President.
Head of government: Prime Minister.
Capital: São Tomé.
Official language: Portuguese.
Official religion: none.
Monetary unit: dobra (Db)[1]; valuation (Sept. 1, 2011) 1 U.S.$ = Db 17,140; 1 £ = Db 27,697.

Area and population

Islands	Capitals	area sq mi	area sq km	population 2006 estimate
São Tomé		332	859	145,175
Districts				
Água-Grande	São Tomé	7	17	56,492
Cantagalo	Santana	46	119	14,681
Caué	São João Angolares	103	267	6,324
Lembá	Neves	88	229	11,759
Lobata	Guadalupe	41	105	17,251
Mé-Zóchi	Trindade	47	122	38,668
Príncipe		55	142	6,737
Autonomous Region				
Príncipe	Santo António	55	142	6,737
TOTAL		386[2]	1,001	151,912

Demography

Population (2011): 169,000.
Density (2011): persons per sq mi 437.8, persons per sq km 168.8.
Urban-rural (2008): urban 60.8%; rural 39.2%.
Sex distribution (2009): male 49.85%, female 50.15%.
Age breakdown (2009): under 15, 45.0%; 15–29, 27.4%; 30–44, 15.3%; 45–59, 7.6%; 60–74, 3.4%; 75–84, 1.1%; 85 and over, 0.2%.
Population projection: (2020) 200,000; (2030) 235,000.
Doubling time: 23 years.
Ethnic composition (2000): black-white admixture 79.5%; Fang 10.0%; Angolares (descendants of former Angolan slaves) 7.6%; Portuguese 1.9%; other 1.0%.
Religious affiliation (2005): Roman Catholic *c.* 80%; Protestant *c.* 15%; Muslim *c.* 3%; other *c.* 2%.
Major urban areas (2001): São Tomé 49,957; Neves 6,635; Santana 6,228; Trindade 6,049; Santo António (on Príncipe) 1,010.

Vital statistics

Birth rate per 1,000 population (2009): 39.9 (world avg. 20.3).
Death rate per 1,000 population (2009): 8.7 (world avg. 8.5).
Natural increase rate per 1,000 population (2009): 31.2 (world avg. 11.8).
Total fertility rate (avg. births per childbearing woman; 2009): 5.31.
Marriage/divorce rates per 1,000 population (2003): 2.2/n.a.
Life expectancy at birth (2009): male 61.2 years; female 63.5 years.
Major causes of death per 100,000 population (2002): infectious and parasitic diseases 253.7, of which malaria 52.7; diseases of the circulatory system 198.6; accidents and injuries 74.3; malignant neoplasms 69.0; iron-deficiency anemia 50.2.

National economy

Budget (2008). Revenue: Db 1,216,000,000,000 (grants 62.9%, tax revenue 33.8%, nontax revenue 3.3%). Expenditures: Db 841,000,000,000 (current expenditure 67.7%, capital expenditure 26.0%, other 6.3%).
Public debt (external, outstanding; June 2011): U.S.$168,140,000.
Production (metric tons except as noted). Agriculture, forestry, fishing (2009): taro 35,066, bananas 30,744, coconuts 25,643, oil palm fruit 15,000, vegetables 9,268, cassava 8,311, corn (maize) 4,182, cacao 2,500, yams 2,339; livestock (number of live animals) 420,000 chickens; roundwood (2010) 115,377 cu m, of which fuelwood 92%; fisheries production 4,250 (from aquaculture, none). Mining and quarrying (2008): limestone 1,000,000; clay 77,000. Manufacturing (2009): small processing plants produce beer, soft drinks, soap, and textiles. Energy production (consumption): electricity (kW-hr; 2007) 43,000,000 (43,000,000); coal, none (none); crude petroleum, none[3] (none); petroleum products (metric tons; 2007) none (42,000); natural gas, none (none).
Household income and expenditure. Average household size (2004) 5.5; income per household: n.a.; sources of income: n.a.; expenditure (1995)[4]: food, beverages, and tobacco 71.9%, housing and energy 10.2%, transportation and communications 6.4%, clothing and footwear 5.3%, household durable goods 2.8%.
Population economically active (2006): total 53,266; activity rate of total population 35.1% (participation rates: ages 15–64, 59.5%[5]; female 41.6%; unemployed, n.a.).

Price index (December 2005 = 100)

	2004	2005	2006	2007	2008	2009
Consumer price index[6]	85.3	100.0	124.6	158.9	198.3	230.2

Gross national income (GNI; 2010): U.S.$199,000,000 (U.S.$1,200 per capita); purchasing power parity GNI (U.S.$1,910 per capita).

Structure of gross domestic product and labour force

	2008 in value Db '000,000	2008 % of total value	2001 labour force[7]	2001 % of labour force[7]
Agriculture, fishing	387,100	16.4	13,518	31.5
Mining	1,500	0.1	...	...
Manufacturing	54,000	2.3	2,893	6.7
Public utilities	12,700	0.5		
Construction	151,300	6.4	4,403	10.2
Transp. and commun.	208,500	8.9	792	1.8
Trade, hotels	209,600	8.9	8,787	20.5
Finance, real estate	26,500	1.1	...	...
Pub. admin., defense	529,400	22.5	3,307	7.7
Services			9,237	21.5
Other	774,300[8]	32.9[8]	...	...
TOTAL	2,354,900	100.0	42,937	100.0[2]

Selected balance of payments data. Receipts from (U.S.$'000,000): tourism (2009) 8.3; remittances (2010) 2; foreign direct investment (FDI; 2008–10 avg.) 17; official development assistance (2009) 31. Disbursements for (U.S.$'000,000): tourism (2007) 0.1; remittances (2009) 1; FDI (2008–10 avg.) 5.
Land use as % of total land area (2009): in temporary crops or left fallow *c.* 10%, in permanent crops *c.* 47%, in pasture *c.* 1%, forest area *c.* 28%.

Foreign trade

Balance of trade (current prices)

	2004	2005	2006	2007	2008	2009
U.S.$'000,000	–37.8	–46.3	–67.0	–75.2	–108.5	–31.1
% of total	84.3%	87.2%	89.8%	90.5%	90.6%	82.7%

Imports (2009): U.S.$34,312,000 (food products 35.9%, mineral fuels 13.4%, machinery and equipment 13.0%, beverages 8.3%, transportation equipment 7.8%). *Major import sources:* Portugal 48.2%; Brazil 14.6%; Angola 12.7%; Japan 10.8%.
Exports (2009): U.S.$3,240,000 (cocoa beans 98.3%, coconuts 0.6%, remainder 1.1%). *Major export destinations:* Netherlands 34.7%; Portugal 29.3%; Belgium 19.2%; remainder 16.8%.

Transport and communications

Transport. Railroads: none. Roads (2002): total length 239 mi, 384 km (paved 71%). Vehicles (2007): passenger cars 305; trucks and buses 37. Air transport (2005): passenger-km 18,000,000; short ton-km cargo, n.a.

Communications

Medium	date	number in '000s	units per 1,000 persons	Medium	date	number in '000s	units per 1,000 persons
Televisions	2003	19	128	PCs	2005	6.0	38
Telephones				Dailies	2009	[9]	[9]
Cellular	2010	103[10]	620[10]	Internet users	2009	27	164
Landline	2010	7.7	46	Broadband	2010	0.6[10]	3.5[10]

Education and health

Educational attainment (2001). Percentage of population age 25 and over having: no formal schooling 0.3%; primary education 41.4%; lower secondary 25.0%; upper secondary/vocational 8.8%; higher 1.9%; unknown 22.6%.
Literacy (2008): total population age 15 and over literate 88.3%; males literate 93.5%; females literate 83.3%.

Education (2009–10)

	teachers	students	student/teacher ratio	enrollment rate (%)
Primary (age 7–12)	1,265	33,982	26.9	99
Secondary/Voc. (age 13–17)	373[11]	10,045	21.7[11]	32[12]
Tertiary	...	766	...	4 (age 18–22)

Health: physicians (2006) 58 (1 per 2,621 persons); hospital beds (2003) 474 (1 per 313 persons); infant mortality rate per 1,000 live births (2009) 56.0; undernourished population (2005–07) less than 5.0% of total population based on the consumption of a minimum daily requirement of 1,690 calories.

Military

Total active duty personnel (2005): 460 (army/coast guard 65.2%; presidential guard 34.8%). *Military expenditure as percentage of GDP* (2005): 1.2%; per capita expenditure U.S.$4.

[1]The dobra was pegged to the euro (€) from January 2010 at a rate of 24,500 dobras = €1. [2]Detail does not add to total given because of rounding. [3]Licenses for petroleum exploration in an offshore area shared by Sao Tome and Principe and Nigeria were awarded in March 2006; no crude petroleum was extracted from this area as of mid-2011. [4]Weights of consumer price index components. [5]ILO estimate for 2006. [6]As of December. [7]Employed only. [8]Taxes on products. [9]No print dailies. [10]Subscribers. [11]2004–05. [12]2006–07.

Internet resources for further information:
- **Instituto Nacional de Estatística http://www.ine.st**
- **Banco Central de São Tomé e Príncipe http://www.bcstp.st**

Saudi Arabia

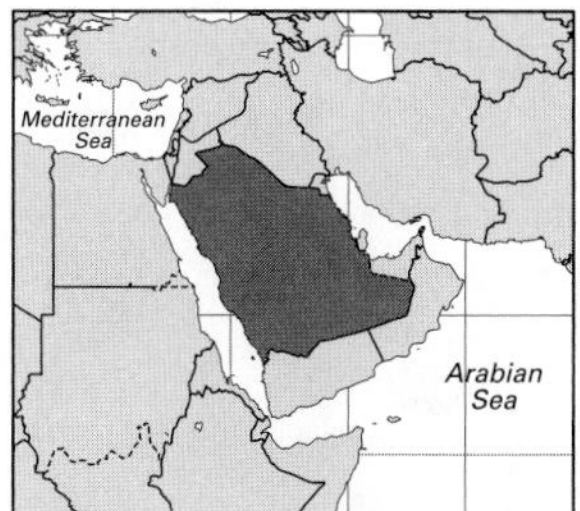

Official name: Al-Mamlakah al-ʿArabiyyah al-Suʿūdiyyah (Kingdom of Saudi Arabia).
Form of government: monarchy[1].
Head of state and government: King.
Capital: Riyadh.
Official language: Arabic.
Official religion: Islam.
Monetary unit: Saudi riyal (SR); valuation (Sept. 1, 2011) 1 U.S.$ = SR 3.75; 1 £ = SR 6.06.

Area and population

		area		population
Administrative Regions	Capitals	sq mi	sq km	2010 census[2]
ʿAsīr	Abha	29,611	76,693	1,913,392
Al-Bāḥah	Al-Bāḥah	3,830	9,921	411,888
Ḥāʾil	Ḥāʾil	40,111	103,887	597,144
Al-Ḥudūd al-Shamālīyah (Northern Borders)	ʿArʿar	43,165	111,797	320,524
Al-Jawf	Sakākah	38,692	100,212	440,009
Jīzān	Jīzān	4,506	11,671	1,365,110
Al-Madīnah	Medina (Al-Madīnah)	58,684	151,990	1,777,933
Makkah	Mecca (Makkah)	59,123	153,128	6,915,006
Najrān	Najrān	57,727	149,511	505,652
Al-Qaṣīm	Buraydah	22,412	58,046	1,215,858
Al-Riyāḍ	Riyadh (Al-Riyāḍ)	156,078	404,240	6,777,146
Al-Sharqīyah (Eastern Province)	Al-Dammām	259,662	672,522	4,105,780
Tabūk	Tabūk	56,399	146,072	791,535
TOTAL		830,000	2,149,690	27,136,977

Demography

Population (2011): 28,572,000[3].
Density (2011): persons per sq mi 34.4, persons per sq km 13.3.
Urban-rural (2009): urban 81.9%; rural 18.1%.
Sex distribution (2010): male 56.4%; female 43.6%.
Age breakdown (2009): under 15, 30.8%; 15–29, 30.7%; 30–44, 24.3%; 45–59, 9.8%; 60–74, 3.5%; 75–84, 0.8%; 85 and over, 0.1%.
Population projection: (2020) 32,626,000; (2030) 37,010,000.
Doubling time: 44 years.
Ethnic composition (2005): Saudi Arab *c.* 74%; expatriates *c.* 26%, of which Indian *c.* 5%, Bangladeshi *c.* 3.5%, Pakistani *c.* 3.5%, Filipino *c.* 3%, Egyptian *c.* 3%, Palestinian *c.* 1%, other *c.* 7%.
Religious affiliation (2000): Muslim *c.* 94%, of which Sunnī *c.* 84%, Shīʿī *c.* 10%; Christian *c.* 3.5%, of which Roman Catholic *c.* 3%; Hindu *c.* 1%; nonreligious/other *c.* 1.5%.
Major cities (2010)[4]: Riyadh 5,188,286; Jiddah 3,430,697; Mecca 1,534,731; Medina 1,100,093; Al-Dammām 903,312.

Vital statistics

Birth rate per 1,000 population (2009): 20.0 (world avg. 20.3).
Death rate per 1,000 population (2009): 3.4 (world avg. 8.5).
Marriage/divorce rates per 1,000 population (2007): 4.8/1.0.
Total fertility rate (avg. births per childbearing woman; 2009): 2.46.
Life expectancy at birth (2009): male 71.7 years; female 75.6 years.
Major causes of death per 100,000 population (2002): diseases of the circulatory system 144, of which ischemic heart disease 69; accidents and violence 66; malignant neoplasms (cancers) 44; diabetes mellitus 20.

National economy

Budget (2009). Revenue: SR 509,805,000,000 (oil revenues 85.2%). Expenditures: SR 596,434,000,000 (current expenditures 69.8%, capital expenditures 30.2%).
National debt (public only; end of 2008): *c.* U.S.$62,649,000,000.
Production (metric tons except as noted). Agriculture, forestry, fishing (2009): cow's milk 1,292,000, dates 1,052,000, wheat 1,000,000, chicken meat 570,000, tomatoes 536,000, potatoes 480,000, cucumbers 281,000, sorghum 210,000, grapes 181,000, hen's eggs 171,000, corn (maize) 160,000; livestock (number of live animals) 8,000,000 sheep, 4,300,000 goats, 421,000 cattle, 260,000 camels; roundwood (2010) 240,054 cu m, of which fuelwood 100%; fisheries production 95,061 (from aquaculture 27%). Mining and quarrying (2009): gypsum 2,100,000; silver 9,500 kg; gold 5,500 kg. Manufacturing (value added in U.S.$'000,000; 2006): industrial chemicals 6,207; food products 4,447; glass products 2,078; refined petroleum (1998) 1,806; electronics 1,785; fabricated metal products 1,298; rubber products 1,150. Energy production (consumption): electricity (kW-hr; 2009) 194,390,000,000 ([2008] 174,476,000,000); coal, none (none); crude petroleum (barrels; 2010–11) 3,052,900,000 ([2008] 838,400,000); petroleum products (metric tons; 2007) 113,753,000 (71,727,000); natural gas (cu m; 2010) 87,669,000,000 (87,669,000,000).
Land use as % of total land area (2009): in temporary crops or left fallow (2007) 1.6%, in permanent crops 0.1%, in pasture 79.1%, forest area 0.5%.
Population economically active (2009): total 8,611,001, of which 4,286,515 Saudi workers and 4,324,486 foreign nationals; activity rate of total population 34.0% (participation rates: ages 15–64, 51.5%; female 14.9%; unemployed 5.4%).

Price index (2005 = 100)

	2004	2005	2006	2007	2008	2009	2010
Consumer price index	99.3	100.0	102.2	106.5	117.0	122.9	129.5

Gross national income (2008): U.S.$471,692,446,000 (U.S.$18,718 per capita).

Structure of gross domestic product and labour force

	2009			
	in value SR '000,000	% of total value	labour force	% of labour force
Agriculture, forestry, fishing	41,419	2.9	331,072	3.8
Petroleum and natural gas[5]	610,100	43.3	86,601	1.0
Other mining	3,590	0.3		
Manufacturing[6]	146,673	10.4	527,891	6.1
Construction	71,092	5.1	964,663	11.2
Public utilities	13,722	1.0	85,384	1.0
Transp. and commun.	56,858	4.0	375,082	4.4
Trade, hotels	85,261	6.1	1,645,986	19.1
Finance, real estate	126,965	9.0	410,030	4.8
Pub. admin., defense	225,857	16.0	1,540,098	17.9
Services	33,989	2.4	2,181,185	25.3
Other	–6,402[7]	–0.5[7]	463,009[8]	5.4[8]
TOTAL	1,409,124	100.0	8,611,001[9]	100.0[9]

Household income and expenditure. Average household size (2006) 6.0; income per household: n.a.; sources of income: n.a.; expenditure (2006–07): food and nonalcoholic beverages 17.4%, housing and energy 17.0%, transportation 8.3%, household furnishings 7.3%.
Selected balance of payments data. Receipts from (U.S.$'000,000): tourism (2009) 5,964; remittances (2010) 238; foreign direct investment (FDI; 2008–10 avg.) 32,785. Disbursements for (U.S.$'000,000): tourism (2009) 18,814; remittances (2009) 25,969; FDI (2008–10 avg.) 3,194.

Foreign trade[10]

Balance of trade (current prices)

	2005	2006	2007	2008	2009	2010
SR '000,000,000	+454.2	+529.9	+536.3	+743.7	+362.8	+541.0
% of total	50.5%	50.3%	44.2%	46.3%	33.6%	40.3%

Imports (2008): SR 431,753,000,000 (machinery and apparatus 27.2%; transport equipment 18.0%; base and fabricated metals 15.3%; food and live animals 14.4%; chemicals and chemical products 12.3%). *Major import sources:* U.S. 13.7%; China 11.0%; Japan 8.2%; Germany 7.4%; South Korea 4.5%.
Exports (2008): SR 1,175,354,000,000 (crude petroleum 78.8%; refined petroleum products 10.8%; other mineral fuels [mostly natural gas] 5.3%). *Major export destinations:* U.S. 16.3%; Japan 15.2%; China 8.9%; South Korea 8.6%; India 7.3%.

Transport and communications

Transport. Railroads (2007): route length (2009) 884 mi, 1,423 km; passenger-km 343,000,000; metric ton-km cargo 1,257,000,000. Roads (2008): total length 114,285 mi, 183,925 km (paved 29%). Vehicles (2005): passenger cars 3,206,000; trucks and buses 1,240,973. Air transport (2008)[11]: passenger-km 31,444,000,000; metric ton-km cargo 1,404,000,000.

Communications

Medium	date	number in '000s	units per 1,000 persons	Medium	date	number in '000s	units per 1,000 persons
Televisions	2004	6,576	292	PCs	2005	8,184	354
Telephones				Dailies	2009	1,878[12]	74[12]
Cellular	2010	51,564[13]	1,879[13]	Internet users	2009	9,800	381
Landline	2010	4,166	152	Broadband	2010	1,497[13]	55[13]

Education and health

Educational attainment (2007). Percentage of Saudi ([2000] non-Saudi) population age 10 and over who: are illiterate 13.7% (12.1%), are literate/have primary education 34.0% (40.6%), have some/completed secondary 42.1% (36.0%), have at least begun university 10.2% (11.3%). *Literacy* (2008): percentage of total population age 15 and over literate 85.5%; males literate 89.5%; females literate 80.2%.

Education (2008–09)

	teachers	students	student/ teacher ratio	enrollment rate (%)
Primary (age 6–11)	284,750	3,255,243	11.4	86
Secondary/Voc. (age 12–17)	264,141	2,989,910	11.3	73[14]
Tertiary	39,406	757,770	19.2	33 (age 18–22)

Health (2007): physicians 47,919 (1 per 506 persons); hospital beds 53,519 (1 per 453 persons); infant mortality rate per 1,000 live births 17.9; undernourished population (2004–06) less than 5.0% of total population based on the consumption of a minimum daily requirement of 1,850 calories.

Military

Total active duty personnel (November 2010): 233,500 (army 32.1%, navy 5.8%, air force 8.6%, air defense forces 6.8%, industrial security force 3.9%, national guard 42.8%). U.S. troops 258. *Military expenditure as percentage of GDP* (2009): 11.0%[15]; per capita expenditure U.S.$1,578[15].

[1]Additionally, the Consultative Council (consisting of 150 appointed members) acts as an advisory body. [2]Preliminary results. [3]Expatriates constituted 31% of total population in 2010. [4]Urban agglomerations. [5]Excludes refined petroleum. [6]Includes refined petroleum. [7]Import duties less imputed bank service charges. [8]Unemployed. [9]Includes 4,324,486 (50.2%) foreign workers. [10]Imports c.i.f.; exports f.o.b. [11]Saudi Arabian Airlines only. [12]Circulation of daily newspapers. [13]Subscribers. [14]2006–07. [15]Defense and security budget.

Internet resources for further information:
- **Ministry of Economy and Planning http://www.mep.gov.sa**
- **Saudi Arabian Monetary Agency http://www.sama.gov.sa**

Senegal

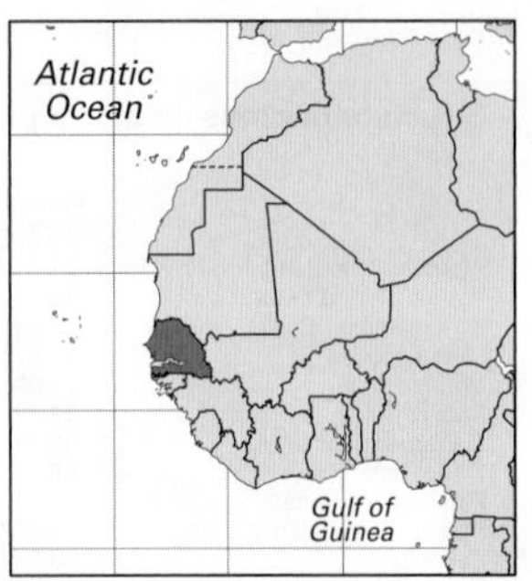

Official name: République du Sénégal (Republic of Senegal).
Form of government: multiparty republic with two legislative houses (Senate[1] [100[2]]; National Assembly [150]).
Head of state and government: President assisted by Prime Minister.
Capital: Dakar.
Official language: French.
Official religion: none.
Monetary unit: CFA franc (CFAF); valuation (Sept. 1, 2011) 1 U.S.$ = CFAF 460.31; 1 £ = CFAF 743.83.

Area and population

	area	population		area	population
		2010[3]			2010[3]
Regions	sq km	estimate	**Regions**	sq km	estimate
Dakar	550	2,680,852	Matam	25,083	552,978
Diourbel	4,359	1,369,198	Saint-Louis	19,044	863,553
Fatick	6,685	625,708	Sédhiou[4]	7,293	424,629
Kaffrine[4]	11,853	479,858	Tambacounda	42,706	629,064
Kaolack	5,407	804,186	Thiès	6,601	1,501,675
Kédougou[4]	16,896	121,584	Ziguinchor	7,339	479,860
Kolda	13,718	567,788	TOTAL	196,722	11,894,343
Louga	29,188	793,410			

Demography

Population (2011): 12,644,000[5].
Density (2011): persons per sq mi 166.5, persons per sq km 64.3.
Urban-rural (2009): urban 42.6%; rural 57.4%.
Sex distribution (2009): male 48.37%; female 51.63%.
Age breakdown (2009): under 15, 43.8%; 15–29, 28.6%; 30–44, 15.2%; 45–59, 8.0%; 60–74, 3.5%; 75–84, 0.8%; 85 and over, 0.1%.
Population projection: (2020) 15,736,000; (2030) 19,485,000.
Doubling time: 26 years.
Ethnic composition (2000): Wolof 34.6%; Peul (Fulani) and Tukulor 27.1%; Serer 12.0%; Malinke (Mandingo) 9.7%; other 16.6%.
Religious affiliation (2005): Muslim *c.* 94%[6] (including Shīʿī *c.* 5%); Christian (mostly Roman Catholic) *c.* 4%; other *c.* 2%.
Major cities (2008[3]): Dakar 2,243,400[7]; Touba 529,200; Thiès 263,500; Kaolack 186,000; Mbour 181,800; Saint-Louis 171,300; Rufisque 162,100.

Vital statistics

Birth rate per 1,000 population (2009): 38.0 (world avg. 20.3).
Death rate per 1,000 population (2009): 10.6 (world avg. 8.5).
Total fertility rate (avg. births per childbearing woman; 2009): 4.95.
Life expectancy at birth (2009): male 57.1 years; female 60.9 years.
Major causes of death per 100,000 population (2002): infectious and parasitic diseases *c.* 385, of which malaria *c.* 134; respiratory infections *c.* 165; cardiovascular diseases *c.* 119; perinatal conditions *c.* 91; accidents *c.* 81.

National economy

Budget (2008). Revenue: CFAF 1,350,900,000,000 (tax revenue 86.0%, grants 10.5%, nontax revenue 3.5%). Expenditures: CFAF 1,678,561,000,000 (current expenditures 67.1%, development expenditure 32.9%).
Production (metric tons except as noted). Agriculture, forestry, fishing (2009): peanuts (groundnuts) 1,032,651, sugarcane 836,000, millet 810,121, paddy rice 502,104, corn (maize) 328,644, cassava 265,533, sorghum 224,956, watermelons 190,582, dry cow peas 86,625, oil palm fruit 71,000; livestock (number of live animals) 5,400,000 sheep, 4,591,300 goats, 3,300,000 cattle, 522,486 horses; roundwood 6,190,367 cu m, of which fuelwood 87%; fisheries production 459,303 (from aquaculture, negligible). Mining and quarrying (2008): calcium phosphate (crude rock) 645,000. Manufacturing (value added in U.S.$'000,000; 2002): food and food products 108; industrial chemicals 70; cement, bricks, and ceramics 31; paints, soaps, and pharmaceuticals 21; beverages 11. Energy production (consumption): electricity (kW-hr; 2009) 2,491,000,000 ([2007] 2,305,000,000); coal (metric tons; 2007) none (301,000); crude petroleum (barrels; 2007) none (5,263,000); petroleum products (metric tons; 2007) 684,000 (967,000); natural gas (cu m; 2007) 10,430,000 (10,430,000).
Population economically active (2008; ILO estimates): total 5,242,000; activity rate of total population 42.9% (participation rates: ages 15–64, 77.4%; female 43.2%; unemployed [2005] *c.* 40%).

Price index (2005 = 100)

	2004	2005	2006	2007	2008	2009	2010
Consumer price index	98.3	100.0	102.1	108.1	114.3	113.1	114.5

Household income and expenditure. Average household size (2005) 8.7; sources of income (1997–2000)[8]: agricultural 45%, other 55%; expenditure (2005): food and nonalcoholic beverages 54.8%, household furnishings 6.9%, housing and energy 6.3%, communications 6.0%, transportation 4.3%.
Selected balance of payments data. Receipts from (U.S.$'000,000): tourism (2008) 543; remittances (2009) 1,276; foreign direct investment (FDI; 2008–10 avg.) 239; official development assistance (2009) 1,022. Disbursements for (U.S.$'000,000): tourism (2008) 276; remittances (2008) 143; FDI (2008–10 avg.) 59.
Gross national income (GNI; 2010): U.S.$13,533,000,000 (U.S.$1,050 per capita); purchasing power parity GNI (U.S.$1,850 per capita).

Structure of gross domestic product and labour force

	2009		2006	
	in value CFAF '000,000	% of total value	labour force	% of labour force
Agriculture, fishing	820,740	13.7	1,063,400	30.4
Mining	56,353	0.9	14,100	0.4
Manufacturing	736,204	12.3	245,400	7.0
Public utilities	146,318	2.4	21,800	0.6
Construction	288,900	4.8	186,600	5.3
Transp. and commun.	618,757	10.3	141,700	4.1
Trade, hotels	976,484	16.3	814,500	23.2
Finance, real estate	537,564	9.0	16,700	0.5
Services	442,559	7.4	157,700	4.5
Pub. admin., defense	681,632	11.4		
Other	679,766[9]	11.4[9]	842,400[10]	24.0[10]
TOTAL	5,985,277	100.0[11]	3,504,300	100.0

Public debt (external, outstanding; 2009): U.S.$2,961,000,000.
Land use as % of total land area (2007): in temporary crops or left fallow 15.5%, in permanent crops 0.3%, in pasture 29.1%, forest area 44.6%.

Foreign trade[12]

Balance of trade (current prices)

	2003	2004	2005	2006	2007	2008
U.S.$'000,000	–1,244	–1,523	–2,027	–2,179	–3,325	–4,357
% of total	35.0%	36.7%	40.8%	42.2%	51.8%	50.1%

Imports (2008): U.S.$6,528,000,000 (mineral fuels 27.7%, of which refined petroleum 13.3%, crude petroleum 11.8%; food 21.3%, of which rice 9.9%; machinery and apparatus 14.6%; base and fabricated metals 6.5%). *Major import sources:* France 17.2%; Nigeria 11.9%; Thailand 6.8%; China 6.0%; U.K. 4.5%.
Exports (2008): U.S.$2,171,000,000 (refined petroleum 33.6%; food 15.6%, of which fish 6.5%; phosphoric acid [and related products] 10.1%; portland cement 5.6%; iron and steel 4.3%). *Major export destinations:* Mali 23.3%; bunker and ships' stores 18.0%; India 11.6%; France 7.5%; The Gambia 4.2%.

Transport and communications

Transport. Railroads (2008): route length 563 mi, 906 km; (2004) passenger-km 122,000,000; (2004) metric ton-km cargo 358,000,000. Roads (2008): total length 8,894 mi, 14,314 km (paved 33%). Vehicles (2008): passenger cars 205,704; trucks and buses 72,777. Air transport (2007)[13]: passenger-km 1,096,000,000; metric ton-km cargo, n.a.

Communications

Medium	date	number in '000s	units per 1,000 persons	Medium	date	number in '000s	units per 1,000 persons
Televisions	2003	869	77	PCs	2005	250	21
Telephones				Dailies	2009	198[14]	25[14]
Cellular	2010	8,344[15]	671[15]	Internet users	2009	923	74
Landline	2010	342	28	Broadband	2010	79[15]	6.3[15]

Education and health

Educational attainment (2005)[16]. Percentage of population age 25 and over having: no formal schooling 68.2%; incomplete primary education 13.0%; complete primary 3.7%; incomplete secondary 9.5%; complete secondary 1.4%; higher 2.4%; unknown 1.8%. *Literacy* (2007): percentage of total population age 15 and over literate 44.0%; males literate 53.4%; females literate 34.9%.

Education (2008–09)

	teachers	students	student/ teacher ratio	enrollment rate (%)
Primary (age 7–12)	47,685	1,652,585	34.7	73
Secondary/Voc. (age 13–19)	15,394[17]	582,101[18]	26.4[17]	20[19]
Tertiary	...	94,371	...	8 (age 20–24)

Health: physicians (2005) 693 (1 per 17,115 persons); hospital beds (1998) 3,582 (1 per 2,500 persons); infant mortality rate (2009) 58.9; undernourished population (2004–06) 2,900,000 (25% of total population based on the consumption of a minimum daily requirement of 1,770 calories).

Military

Total active duty personnel (November 2010): 13,620[20] (army 87.4%, navy 7.0%, air force 5.6%); French troops (November 2010) 531[21]. *Military expenditure as percentage of GDP* (2008): 1.7%; per capita expenditure U.S.$18.

[1]Originally created in 1999, abolished in 2001, and reinstated in August 2007. [2]Includes 65 appointees of president. [3]January 1. [4]Officially created in 2008. [5]Estimate of United States Bureau of the Census International Database (June 2010 update). [6]Most citizens practice a syncretic form of Islam. [7]Includes communes of Pikine (2004; pop. 815,378) and Guédiawaye (2004; pop. 274,014), adjacent to Dakar commune (2004; pop. 1,009,256). [8]Approximate figures for span of years. [9]Taxes on products less imputed bank service charges. [10]Includes 484,000 not adequately defined and 351,400 unemployed. [11]Detail does not add to total given because of rounding. [12]Imports c.i.f.; exports f.o.b. [13]Air Sénégal International only. [14]Circulation. [15]Subscribers. [16]Based on the 2005 Senegal Demographic and Health Survey, of which 22,795 people were age 25 and over. [17]2004–05. [18]2007–08. [19]2005–06. [20]Of which deployed as UN peacekeepers 1,386. [21]In June 2010 France closed its military bases in Senegal and began withdrawing all but 300 of its troops based there.

Internet resources for further information:
- **Agence Nationale de la Statistique et de la Démographie http://www.ansd.sn**
- **La Banque de France: La Zone Franc http://www.banque-france.fr/fr/eurosys/zonefr/zonefr.htm**

Serbia[1]

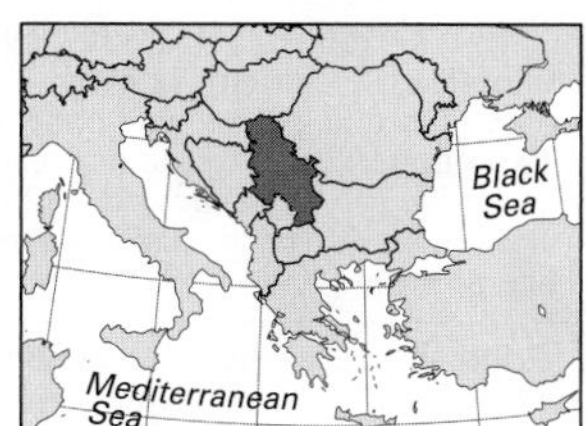

Official name: Republika Srbija (Republic of Serbia).
Form of government: republic with National Assembly (250).
Head of state: President.
Head of government: Prime Minister.
Capital: Belgrade.
Official language: Serbian.
Official religion: none.
Monetary unit: Serbian dinar (CSD); valuation (Sept. 1, 2011) 1 U.S.$ = CSD 70.48; 1 £ = CSD 113.88.

Area and population

Administrative divisions	area sq km	population 2010[2] estimate	Administrative divisions	area sq km	population 2010[2] estimate
Central Serbia	55,962	5,333,851	Raška	3,918	299,689
Districts			Šumadija	2,387	288,151
Bor	3,507	130,557	Toplica	2,231	93,513
Braničevo	3,865	187,341	Zaječar	3,623	122,605
Grad Beograd			Zlatibor	6,140	294,400
(City of Belgrade)[3]	3,224	1,639,505	Vojvodina	21,536	1,957,585
Jablanica	2,769	224,776	**Districts**		
Kolubara	2,474	178,464	Central Banat	3,256	191,031
Mačva	3,268	307,904	North Bačka	1,784	190,919
Moravica	3,016	213,939	North Banat	2,329	151,982
Nišava	2,729	372,670	South Bačka	4,016	608,725
Pčinja	3,520	227,554	South Banat	4,245	298,400
Pirot	2,761	94,575	Srem	3,486	323,197
Podunavlje	1,248	201,908	West Bačka	2,420	193,331
Pomoravlje	2,614	214,260	TOTAL	77,498	7,291,436
Rasina	2,668	242,040			

Demography

Population (2011): 7,262,000.
Density (2011): persons per sq mi 242.7, persons per sq km 93.7.
Urban-rural (2009): urban 55.7%; rural 44.3%.
Sex distribution (2009): male 48.63%; female 51.37%.
Age breakdown (2007): under 15, 15.8%; 15–29, 19.7%; 30–44, 20.4%; 45–59, 22.4%; 60–74, 14.9%; 75–84, 5.9%; 85 and over, 0.9%.
Population projection: (2020) 6,961,000; (2030) 6,623,000.
Ethnic composition (2002): Serb 82.9%; Hungarian 3.9%; Bosniak 1.8%; Rom (Gypsy) 1.4%; Yugoslav 1.1%; Croat 0.9%; Montenegrin 0.9%; other 7.1%.
Religious affiliation (2002): Orthodox 85.0%; Roman Catholic 5.5%; Muslim 3.2%; Protestant 1.1%; other/unknown 5.2%.
Major cities (2010): Belgrade (municipality) 1,639,505; Novi Sad 330,527; Niš 255,699; Kragujevac 174,229; Leskovac 147,959.

Vital statistics

Birth rate per 1,000 population (2009): 9.6 (world avg. 20.3); within marriage 76.8%; outside of marriage 23.2%.
Death rate per 1,000 population (2009): 14.2 (world avg. 8.5).
Total fertility rate (avg. births per childbearing woman; 2009): 1.40.
Marriage/divorce rates per 1,000 population (2009): 5.0/1.1.
Life expectancy at birth (2009): male 71.1 years; female 76.4 years.
Major causes of death per 100,000 population (2009): diseases of the circulatory system 777.9; malignant neoplasms (cancers) 292.5; diseases of the respiratory system 57.4; accidents, poisoning, and violence 51.1.

National economy

Budget (2009). Revenue: CSD 1,140,000,000,000 (tax revenue 87.6%, of which social contributions 28.2%, VAT 26.1%; nontax revenue 12.4%). Expenditures: CSD 1,274,000,000,000 (current expenditure 91.2%, of which transfers 49.6%, wages and salaries 24.0%; capital expenditure 7.2%; other 1.6%).
Population economically active (2009): total 3,119,419; activity rate of total population 41.4% (participation rates: ages 15 and older, 49.1%; female 44.1%; unemployed [September 2009–August 2010] 28.8%).

Price and earnings indexes (2005 = 100)

	2004	2005	2006	2007	2008	2009	2010
Consumer price index	86.1	100.0	111.7	118.9	133.6	144.5	153.3
Monthly earnings index	80.6	100.0	124.4	151.9	179.0	...	...

Land use as % of total land area (2009)[4]: in temporary crops 35.3%, left fallow 2.4%, in permanent crops 3.4%, in pasture 16.7%, forest area 30.5%.
Production (metric tons except as noted). Agriculture, forestry, fishing (2009)[4]: corn (maize) 6,396,262, sugar beets 2,797,596, wheat 2,067,555, cow's milk 1,509,000, plums 662,631, grapes 431,306, raspberries 86,961; livestock (number of live animals) 3,631,000 pigs, 1,504,000 sheep, 302,000 beehives; roundwood (2010) 7,636,000 cu m, of which fuelwood 81%; fisheries production 11,286 (from aquaculture 66%). Mining and quarrying (2009): copper 19,000[5]; silver 4,000[5]; selenium 7,500 kg. Manufacturing (value added in CSD '000,000; 2008): food and beverages 50,864; rubber and plastic products 10,865; cement, bricks, and ceramics 10,789; printing and publishing 10,219. Energy production (consumption): electricity (kW-hr; 2009) 36,000,000,000 (33,400,000,000); hard coal (metric tons; 2009) 69,000 (134,116); lignite (metric tons; 2009) 38,491,114 ([2007] 37,359,000); crude petroleum (barrels; 2009) 4,916,116 ([2007] 24,271,700); petroleum products (metric tons; 2008) 2,470,000 ([2007] 3,474,000); natural gas (cu m; 2009) 291,399,000 ([2008] 2,610,000,000).
Gross national income (GNI; 2010): U.S.$42,394,000,000 (U.S.$5,820 per capita); purchasing power parity GNI (U.S.$11,230 per capita).

Structure of gross domestic product and labour force

	2008 in value CSD '000,000	2008 % of total value	2009 labour force	2009 % of labour force
Agriculture, forestry, fishing	246,735.6	9.1	625,317	20.0
Mining and quarrying	33,424.6	1.2	26,814	0.8
Manufacturing	403,049.1	14.8	451,281	14.5
Construction	128,091.2	4.7	136,779	4.4
Public utilities	86,070.1	3.2	46,959	1.5
Transp. and commun.	203,516.4	7.5	149,496	4.8
Trade, hotels	332,284.1	12.2	445,020	14.3
Finance, real estate	499,331.4	18.3	146,662	4.7
Pub. admin., defense	91,878.8	3.4	128,792	4.1
Services	326,577.5	12.0	458,220	14.7
Other	371,502.5[6]	13.6[6]	504,080[7]	16.2[7]
TOTAL	2,722,461.3	100.0	3,119,419[8]	100.0

Public debt (external, outstanding; August 2010): U.S.$10,616,000,000.
Household income and expenditure (2009). Average household size 3.0; average annual income per household CSD 540,960 (U.S.$8,012); sources of income: wages and salaries 48.4%, transfers 32.8%; expenditure: food and nonalcoholic beverages 41.3%, housing and energy 16.1%, transportation 9.0%.
Selected balance of payments data. Receipts from (U.S.$'000,000): tourism (2009) 857; remittances (2010) 4,896; foreign direct investment (FDI; 2008–10 avg.) 2,081; official development assistance (2009) 608. Disbursements for (U.S.$'000,000): tourism (2009) 959; remittances (2009) 91; FDI (2008–10 avg.) 175.

Foreign trade[9]

Balance of trade (current prices)

	2004	2005	2006	2007	2008	2009
U.S.$'000,000	–7,230	–5,980	–6,744	–9,729	–11,903	–7,217
% of total	50.6%	40.0%	34.4%	35.5%	35.2%	30.3%

Imports (2008): U.S.$22,875,000,000 (mineral fuels 20.4%, of which petroleum 12.6%; machinery and apparatus 18.4%; chemical products 13.8%; base and fabricated metals 11.0%; road vehicles 8.1%). *Major import sources:* Russia 15.3%; Germany 11.8%; Italy 9.5%; China 7.5%; Hungary 3.6%.
Exports (2008): U.S.$10,972,000,000 (base and fabricated metals 23.9%, of which iron and steel 13.2%, copper 3.8%; food 13.5%; machinery and apparatus 13.1%). *Major export destinations:* Bosnia and Herzegovina 12.2%; Montenegro 11.7%; Germany 10.4%; Italy 10.3%; Russia 5.0%.

Transport and communications

Transport. Railroads (2009–10): route length (2010[10]) 2,367 mi, 3,809 km; passenger-km 522,000,000; metric ton-km cargo 3,316,000,000. Roads (2009–10): total length (2009) 24,358 mi, 39,200 km (paved 65%); passenger-km 4,516,000,000; metric ton-km cargo 1,385,000,000. Vehicles (2010[10]): passenger cars 1,654,826; trucks and buses 180,702. Air transport (2009–10): passenger-km 1,110,000,000; metric ton-km cargo 2,650,000.

Communications

Medium	date	number in '000s	units per 1,000 persons	Medium	date	number in '000s	units per 1,000 persons
Televisions	2007	...	...	PCs	2008	1,896	258
Telephones				Dailies	2009	1,052[11]	144[11]
Cellular	2010	9,915[12]	1,292[12]	Internet users	2009	4,107	417
Landline	2010	3,110	405	Broadband	2010	652[12]	85[12]

Education and health

Educational attainment (2002). Percentage of population age 15 and over having: no formal education/unknown 7.8%; incomplete primary education 16.2%; complete primary 23.9%; secondary 41.1%; higher 11.0%. *Literacy* (2008): percentage of total population age 15 and over literate 97.6%.

Education (2008–09)

	teachers	students	student/ teacher ratio	enrollment rate (%)
Primary (age 7–10)	17,449	282,395	16.2	94
Secondary/Voc. (age 11–18)	60,202	603,825	10.0	90
Tertiary	14,628	235,940	16.1	50 (age 19–23)

Health (2009): physicians 20,825[13] (1 per 352 persons); hospital beds 41,020[13] (1 per 178 persons); infant mortality rate 7.0; undernourished population (2006–08) less than 5.0%[4] of total population based on the consumption of a minimum daily requirement of 1,960 calories.

Military

Total active duty personnel (November 2010): 29,125 (army 42.1%, air force 14.6%, training command 21.3%, ministry of defense 22.0%). *Military expenditure as percentage of GDP* (2009) 2.2%; per capita expenditure U.S.$145.

[1]Excludes Kosovo, a disputed transitional republic that declared its independence from Serbia on Feb. 17, 2008, unless otherwise indicated. [2]June 30. [3]Comprises 17 municipalities. [4]Includes Kosovo. [5]Metal content. [6]Taxes less subsidies and less imputed bank service charges. [7]Includes 502,982 unemployed. [8]Detail does not add to total given because of rounding. [9]Imports c.i.f.; exports f.o.b. [10]January 1. [11]Circulation of daily newspapers. [12]Subscribers. [13]Public health only.

Internet resources for further information:

- **National Bank of Serbia**
  http://www.nbs.rs/internet/english/index.html
- **Statistical Office of the Republic of Serbia**
  http://webrzs.stat.gov.rs/WebSite

Seychelles

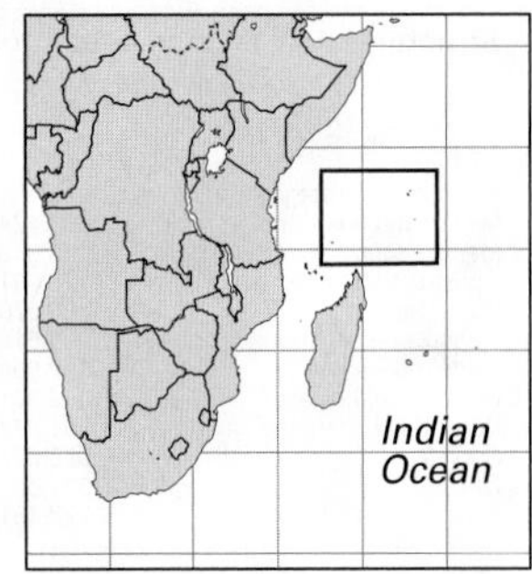

Official name: Repiblik Sesel (Creole); République des Seychelles (French); Republic of Seychelles (English).
Form of government: multiparty republic with one legislative house (National Assembly [31]).
Head of state and government: President.
Capital: Victoria.
Official languages: none[1].
Official religion: none.
Monetary unit: Seychelles rupee (roupi; SR); valuation (Sept. 1, 2011) 1 U.S.$ = SR 12.22; 1 £ = SR 19.75.

Area and population

Island Groups/ Islands[2]	area sq km	population 2002 census	Island Groups/ Islands[2]	area sq km	population 2002 census
Inner (granitic) Islands	243.4	81,007	Inner (coralline) Islands	2.1	115
La Digue	9.8	2,104	Outer (coralline)		
Fregate	2.0	208	Islands	206.2	633
Mahé	154.2	69,065	Aldabra Group	152.6	—
Les Mamelles	4.2	2,391	Amirantes Group	6.6	115
Praslin	37.9	7,103	Coetivy	8.9	252
Silhouette	19.9	136	Farquhar Group	11.3	169
remainder	15.4	—	remainder	26.8	97
			TOTAL	451.7	81,755[3]

Demography

Population (2011): 92,000.
Density (2011): persons per sq mi 527.5, persons per sq km 203.7.
Urban-rural (2009): urban 54.8%; rural 45.2%.
Sex distribution (2010): male 51.58%; female 48.42%.
Age breakdown (2010): under 15, 22.4%; 15–29, 25.0%; 30–44, 25.1%; 45–59, 17.2%; 60–74, 7.0%; 75–84, 2.5%; 85 and over, 0.8%.
Population projection: (2020) 95,000; (2030) 97,000.
Doubling time: 68 years.
Ethnic composition (2000): Seychellois Creole (mixture of Asian, African, and European) 93.2%; British 3.0%; French 1.8%; Chinese 0.5%; Indian 0.3%; other unspecified 1.2%.
Religious affiliation (2002): Roman Catholic 82.3%; Anglican 6.4%; other Christian 4.5%; Hindu 2.1%; Muslim 1.1%; other 2.1%; unknown 1.5%.
Major towns (2010): Victoria 26,450; Anse Royale 4,168.

Vital statistics

Birth rate per 1,000 population (2009): 18.1 (world avg. 20.3); within marriage 20.3%; outside of marriage 79.7%.
Death rate per 1,000 population (2009): 7.8 (world avg. 8.5).
Natural increase rate per 1,000 population (2009): 10.3 (world avg. 11.8).
Total fertility rate (avg. births per childbearing woman; 2009): 2.38.
Marriage/divorce rates per 1,000 population (2009): 5.2[4]/1.7.
Life expectancy at birth (2008): male 67.7 years; female 78.9 years.
Major causes of death per 100,000 population (2006): diseases of the circulatory system 279.0; malignant neoplasms (cancers) 121.7; diseases of the respiratory system 88.7; diseases of the digestive system 37.8.

National economy

Budget (2007). Revenue: SR 2,487,300,000 (tax revenue 64.7%, of which taxes on goods and services 37.2%, taxes on international trade 13.0%; social contributions 18.1%; grants 0.7%; other 16.5%). Expenditures: SR 2,854,900,000 (social protection 21.5%; public debt interest charges 14.5%; education 9.9%; health 7.0%; public order 4.8%; defense 3.9%).
Public debt (2009): U.S.$274,000,000.
Gross national income (GNI; 2010): U.S.$845,000,000 (U.S.$9,490 per capita); purchasing power parity GNI (U.S.$20,470 per capita).

Structure of gross domestic product and labour force

	2008			
	in value SR '000,000	% of total value	labour force[5]	% of labour force[5]
Agriculture, fishing	209	2.4	953	2.3
Mining, quarrying	...	...	18	—
Manufacturing	750	8.6	4,170	10.1
Construction	499	5.7	5,726	13.9
Public utilities	93	1.1	1,013	2.5
Trade, hotels	2,157	24.6	8,808	21.3
Transportation and communications	1,460	16.7	4,242	10.3
Pub. admin., defense	850	9.7	6,039	14.6
Finance, real estate	1,047	12.0	2,852	6.9
Services	547	6.2	7,521	18.2
Other	1,144[6]	13.1[6]	—	—
TOTAL	8,756	100.0[7]	41,342	100.0[7]

Production (metric tons except as noted). Agriculture, forestry, fishing (2009): assorted vegetables 2,210, bananas 1,730, coconuts 1,400, hen's eggs 1,210, tea 63, cinnamon 63, copra (2008) 28; livestock (number of live animals) 5,200 goats, 5,180 pigs, 370,000 chickens; roundwood (2010) 12,840 cu m, of which fuelwood 25%; fisheries production 81,489 (from aquaculture 0.4%). Mining and quarrying (2010): granite 150. Manufacturing (2006): canned tuna 40,222; fish meal 14,821; copra 253; soft drinks 92,250 hectolitres; beer and stout 67,300 hectolitres; mineral water 60,270 hectolitres; fruit juices 30,950 hectolitres; cigarettes 19,000,000 units. Energy production (consumption): electricity (kW-hr; 2009) 276,000,000 (239,000,000); coal, none (none); crude petroleum, none (none); petroleum products (metric tons; 2007) none (203,000); natural gas, none (none).
Population economically active (2002): total 43,859; activity rate of total population 53.6% (participation rates: ages 15–64, 80.1%; female [1997] 47.6%; unemployed [2006] 2.6%).

Price and earnings indexes (2005 = 100)

	2004	2005	2006	2007	2008	2009	2010
Consumer price index	99.1	100.0	99.6	104.9	143.8	189.4	184.8
Monthly earnings index	98.9	100.0	105.0	107.1	123.9	158.9	...

Selected balance of payments data. Receipts from (U.S.$'000,000): tourism (2009) 208; remittances (2010) 14; foreign direct investment (FDI; 2008–10 avg.) 274; official development assistance (2009) 23. Disbursements for (U.S.$'000,000): tourism (2009) 32; remittances (2009) 24; FDI (2008–10 avg.) 8.
Household income and expenditure (2006–07). Average household size 3.7; average annual income per household SR 77,064 (U.S.$11,174); sources of income: wages and salaries 76%, pension and social security 14%, self-employment 7%, remittances 1%; expenditure[8]: housing and energy 30.8%, food and nonalcoholic beverages 21.2%, transportation and communications 13.1%, alcoholic beverages 10.3%, household furnishings 4.5%, recreation 3.4%.
Land use as % of total land area (2009): in temporary crops or left fallow (2007) *c.* 2%; in permanent crops *c.* 4%; in pasture, n.a.; forest area *c.* 88%.

Foreign trade[9]

Balance of trade (current prices)

	2005	2006	2007	2008	2009	2010
SR '000,000	–1,843	–2,084	–3,344	–5,890	–5,598	–3,016
% of total	33.0%	33.2%	40.9%	42.0%	34.2%	23.8%

Imports (2007): SR 5,728,000,000 (mineral fuels 25.1%; machinery and apparatus 22.4%; food 19.5%, of which marine products 11.9%; transportation equipment 4.1%; iron and steel 3.4%). *Major import sources:* Saudi Arabia 24.8%; Germany 9.5%; Singapore 8.5%; France 7.8%; Spain 6.6%.
Exports (2007): SR 2,435,000,000 (domestic exports 55.3%, of which canned tuna 50.6%, fish meal 1.2%, medicine and medical appliances 1.2%; reexports 44.7%, of which petroleum products to ships and aircraft 43.1%). *Major export destinations*[10]: United Kingdom 40.1%; France 34.7%; Italy 10.0%; Germany 3.2%; unspecified 9.0%.

Transport and communications

Transport. Railroads: none. Roads (2007): total length 316 mi, 508 km (paved 96%). Vehicles (2007): passenger cars 7,662; trucks and buses 2,715. Air transport (2008)[11]: passenger-km 1,091,000,000; metric ton-km cargo 38,000,000.

Communications

Medium	date	number in '000s	units per 1,000 persons	Medium	date	number in '000s	units per 1,000 persons
Televisions	2003	22	266	PCs	2005	16	193
Telephones				Dailies	2009	5[12]	75[12]
Cellular	2010	118[13]	1,359[13]	Internet users	2009	34	404
Landline	2010	22	255	Broadband	2010	6.3[13]	73[13]

Education and health

Educational attainment (2003). Percentage of population age 12 and over having: less than primary or primary education 23.2%; secondary 73.4%; higher 3.4%. *Literacy* (2008): total population age 15 and over literate 91.8%; males literate 91.4%; females literate 92.3%.

Education (2008–09)

	teachers	students	student/ teacher ratio	enrollment rate (%)
Primary (age 6–11)	624	8,624	13.8	94
Secondary/Voc. (age 12–16)	596	7,487	12.6	97
Tertiary	—	—	—	... (age 17–21)

Health (2008): physicians 70 (1 per 1,243 persons); hospital beds 341 (1 per 255 persons); infant mortality rate per 1,000 live births (2009) 10.8; undernourished population (2004–06) 7,000 (8% of total population based on the consumption of a minimum daily requirement of 1,740 calories).

Military

Total active duty personnel (November 2010): 200 (army 100%)[14]. *Military expenditure as percentage of GDP* (2009): 0.7%; per capita expenditure U.S.$67.

[1]Creole, English, and French are all national languages per constitution. [2]The Seychelles are administratively divided into 26 districts and geographically split among 47 Inner (granitic) Islands, 2 Inner (coralline) Islands, and 70 Outer (coralline) Islands. [3]Final 2010 census results put total population at 90,945; individual island totals not available as of Nov. 1, 2011. [4]Residents only; marriage rate including visitors is 13.7. [5]Formally employed only. [6]Import duties less subsidies and less imputed bank service charges. [7]Detail does not add to total given because of rounding. [8]Weights of consumer price index components. [9]Imports c.i.f.; exports f.o.b. [10]Domestic exports only. [11]Air Seychelles only. [12]Circulation of daily newspapers. [13]Subscribers. [14]Excludes the 450-member paramilitary, which includes both the coast guard and national guard.

Internet resources for further information:
- **Seychelles in Figures http://www.nsb.gov.sc**
- **Central Bank of Seychelles http://www.cbs.sc**

Sierra Leone

Official name: Republic of Sierra Leone.
Form of government: republic with one legislative body (Parliament [124[1]]).
Head of state and government: President.
Capital: Freetown.
Official language: English.
Official religion: none.
Monetary unit: leone (Le); valuation (Sept. 1, 2011) 1 U.S.$ = Le 4,405; 1 £ = Le 7,118.

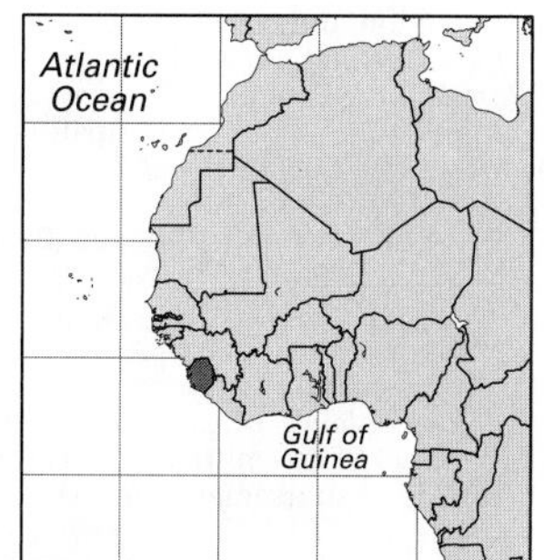

Area and population

Provinces/Area Local Councils	area sq km	population 2004 census	Provinces/Area Local Councils	area sq km	population 2004 census
Eastern Province	15,553	1,191,539	Tonkolili (district)	7,003	347,197
Kailahun (district)	3,859	358,190	Southern Province	19,694	1,092,657
Kenema (district)	6,053	369,546	Bo (district)	5,219	313,711
Kenema (town)		128,402	Bo (town)		149,957
Koidu (town)	5,641	80,025	Bonthe (district)	3,458	129,947
Kono (district)		255,376	Bonthe (town)	10	9,740
Northern Province	35,936	1,745,553	Moyamba (district)	6,902	260,910
Bombali (district)	7,985	325,550	Pujehun (district)	4,105	228,392
Kambia (district)	3,108	270,462	Western Area	557	947,122
Koinadugu (district)	12,121	265,758	Freetown (rural area)	544	174,249
Makeni (town)		82,840	Freetown (city)	13	772,873
Port Loko (district)	5,719	453,746	TOTAL	71,740	4,976,871

Demography

Population (2011): 5,997,000.
Density (2011): persons per sq mi 216.5, persons per sq km 83.6.
Urban-rural (2010): urban 38.4%; rural 61.6%.
Sex distribution (2010): male 48.70%; female 51.30%.
Age breakdown (2008): under 15, 41.7%; 15–29, 27.4%; 30–44, 17.2%; 45–59, 8.1%; 60–74, 4.7%; 75–84, 0.8%; 85 and over, 0.1%.
Population projection: (2020) 7,178,000; (2030) 8,532,000.
Doubling time: 24 years.
Ethnic composition (2000): Mende 26.0%; Temne 24.6%; Limba 7.1%; Kuranko 5.5%; Kono 4.2%; Fulani 3.8%; Bullom-Sherbro 3.5%; other 25.3%.
Religious affiliation (2005): Muslim *c.* 65%[2]; Christian *c.* 25%[2]; traditional beliefs/other *c.* 10%.
Major city/towns (2006): Freetown (urban agglomeration; 2010) 900,847; Bo 181,800; Kenema 148,800; Makeni 90,400; Koidu 87,300.

Vital statistics

Birth rate per 1,000 population (2010): 38.8 (world avg. 19.2).
Death rate per 1,000 population (2010): 12.0 (world avg. 8.2).
Marriage/divorce rates per 1,000 population (2010): n.a./n.a.
Total fertility rate (avg. births per childbearing woman; 2010): 4.97.
Life expectancy at birth (2010): male 53.3 years; female 58.2 years.
Major causes of death per 100,000 population (2002): infectious and parasitic diseases 1,343.0, of which diarrheal diseases 270.8, malaria 198.7, HIV/AIDS 116.5; accidents, injuries, and violence 215.2; diseases of the circulatory system 180.5; malignant neoplasms (cancers) 75.6.
Adult population (ages 15–49) *living with HIV* (2009): 1.6%[3] (world avg. 0.8%).

National economy

Budget (2010). Revenue: Le 1,475,000,000,000 (grants 35.9%; import duties 14.6%; income tax 10.0%; excise duties on petroleum products 9.3%; nontax revenue 7.3%). Expenditures: Le 2,389,000,000,000 (current expenditures 74.1%, of which wages and salaries 21.2%; capital expenditures 25.9%).
Public debt (external, outstanding; June 2011): U.S.$639,100,000.
Gross national income (GNI; 2010): U.S.$2,009,000,000 (U.S.$340 per capita); purchasing power parity GNI (U.S.$830 per capita).

Structure of gross domestic product and labour force

	2010 in value Le '000,000	2010 % of total value	2011 labour force	2011 % of labour force
Agriculture, forestry, fishing	4,904,308	57.4	1,340,000[4]	59.5[4]
Mining and quarrying	142,111	1.7	911,000[5]	40.5[5]
Manufacturing, handicrafts	156,869	1.8		
Construction	119,354	1.4		
Public utilities	24,833	0.3		
Transp. and commun.	560,867	6.6		
Trade, hotels	680,114	8.0		
Finance, real estate	396,264	4.6		
Pub. admin., defense	279,729	3.3		
Services	861,604	10.1		
Other	413,341[6]	4.8[6]		
TOTAL	8,539,392[7]	100.0	2,251,000	100.0

Production (metric tons except as noted). Agriculture, forestry, fishing (2009): rice 784,737, cassava 349,618, oil palm fruit 195,000, peanuts (groundnuts) 75,053, plantains 43,521, green coffee 18,948, tomatoes 15,687, cacao beans 10,000, mangoes, mangosteens, and guavas 7,761, kola nuts 4,508; livestock (number of live animals) 540,000 goats, 470,000 sheep, 415,000 horses, 350,000 cattle, 7,800,000 chickens; roundwood (2010) 5,667,310 cu m, of which fuelwood 98%; fisheries production 200,040 (from aquaculture, negligible). Mining and quarrying (2010–11): bauxite 1,316,380; rutile 64,690; ilmenite 12,580; diamonds 397,660 carats; gold 215 kg. Manufacturing (2010–11): soap 337,560; cement 311,840; refined petroleum products (2007) 166,000; paint 229,550 gallons; soft drinks 1,932,910 crates; beer and stout 854,010 cartons. Energy production (consumption): electricity (kW-hr; 2010–11) 173,025,000 ([2010] 85,175,000); coal, none (none); crude petroleum (barrels; 2007) none (1,994,000); petroleum products (metric tons; 2007) 166,000 (301,000); natural gas, none (none).
Household income and expenditure (2003–04). Average household size (2008) 5.9; average annual income per household Le 4,369,000[8] (U.S.$1,731); sources of income, n.a.; expenditure: food and nonalcoholic beverages 40.6%, housing and energy 14.5%, health 13.6%, clothing and footwear 7.7%, transportation 4.8%, household furnishings 4.3%.
Population economically active (2010): total 2,141,000; activity rate of total population 36.5% (participation rates: ages 15–64 [2009] 68.8%; female 51.3%; unemployed [2007] unofficially 65%).

Price index (2006 = 100)

	2004	2005	2006	2007	2008	2009	2010
Consumer price index	81.5	91.3	100.0	111.6	128.2	140.1	163.4

Selected balance of payments data. Receipts from (U.S.$'000,000): tourism (2009) 25; remittances (2010) 48; foreign direct investment (FDI; 2008–10 avg.) 58; official development assistance (2009) 437. Disbursements for (U.S.$'000,000): tourism (2009) 13; remittances (2009) 3; FDI (2008–10 avg.) 1.7.
Land use as % of total land area (2007): in temporary crops or left fallow 12.6%, in permanent crops 1.1%, in pasture 30.7%, forest area 37.9%.

Foreign trade[9]

Balance of trade (current prices)

	2003	2004	2005	2006	2007	2008
Le '000,000	–490,166	–400,959	–538,275	–513,189	–599,782	–948,541
% of total	53.0%	34.9%	37.0%	28.6%	29.0%	42.5%

Imports (2010): U.S.$770,037,500 (machinery and apparatus 32.3%; mineral fuels 22.3%; food products 13.6%; chemicals and chemical products 5.7%). *Major import sources* (2008): China *c.* 10%; U.S. *c.* 8%; Belgium *c.* 7%; U.K. *c.* 7%; Côte d'Ivoire *c.* 6%.
Exports (2010): U.S.$317,780,700 (diamonds 33.3%; rutile 11.9%; cacao 10.9%; bauxite 9.1%; reexports 6.9%; gold, n.a.; ilmenite, n.a.). *Major export destinations:* Belgium *c.* 39%; U.S. *c.* 22%; India *c.* 7%; France *c.* 5%.

Transport and communications

Transport. Railroads (2010)[10]: length 52 mi, 84 km. Roads (2002): total length 7,020 mi, 11,300 km (paved 8%). Vehicles (2008): passenger cars 16,528; trucks and buses 17,038. Air transport (2006): passenger-km 101,000,000; metric ton-km cargo 10,000,000.

Communications

Medium	date	number in '000s	units per 1,000 persons	Medium	date	number in '000s	units per 1,000 persons
Televisions	2007	65	12	PCs	1999	0.1	...
Telephones				Dailies	2009	22[11]	3.9[11]
Cellular	2010	2,000[12]	341[12]	Internet users	2009	15	2.6
Landline	2010	14	2.4	Broadband	2010	...	...

Education and health

Educational attainment (2008)[13]. Percentage of population age 25 and over having: no formal schooling 72.6%; incomplete/complete primary education 8.2%; incomplete/complete secondary 13.5%; incomplete/complete higher 4.0%; unknown 1.7%. *Literacy* (2009): total population age 15 and over literate 40.9%; males literate 52.7%; females literate 30.1%.

Education (2006–07)

	teachers	students	student/ teacher ratio	enrollment rate (%)
Primary (age 6–11)	30,239	1,322,205	43.7	...
Secondary/Voc. (age 12–17)	10,024	239,579	23.9	25
Tertiary[14]	1,198	9,041	7.5	2 (age 18–22)

Health (2010): physicians (2008) 78 (1 per 71,949 persons); hospital beds 1,174 (1 per 5,000 persons); infant mortality rate per 1,000 live births 80.2; undernourished population (2004–06) 2,500,000 (46% of total population based on the consumption of a minimum daily requirement of 1,750 calories).

Military

Total active duty personnel (November 2010): *c.* 10,500 (total armed forces 100%). *Military expenditure as percentage of GDP* (2010): 0.7%; per capita expenditure U.S.$2.

[1]Includes 12 paramount chiefs elected to represent each of the provincial districts. [2]Often mixed with traditional beliefs. [3]Statistically derived midpoint of range. [4]Represents crop farming. [5]Represents trade and repairs. [6]Indirect taxes less subsidies and less imputed bank service charges. [7]Detail does not add to total given because of rounding. [8]Includes estimated value for income in kind. [9]Imports c.i.f.; exports f.o.b. [10]Private iron-ore railway was being rehabilitated in 2010. [11]Circulation of daily newspapers. [12]Subscribers. [13]Based on demographic survey of 8,741 females and 7,306 males. [14]2001–02.

Internet resources for further information:

- **Statistics Sierra Leone**
  http://www.statistics.sl
- **Bank of Sierra Leone**
  http://www.bsl.gov.sl

Singapore

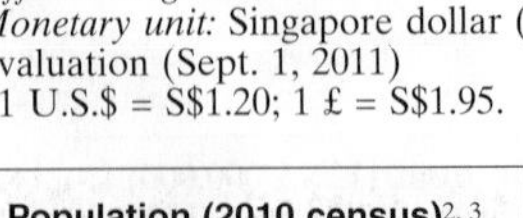

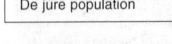

Official name: Xinjiapo Gongheguo (Mandarin Chinese); Republik Singapura (Malay); Cingkappur Kudiyarasu (Tamil); Republic of Singapore (English).
Form of government: unitary multiparty republic with one legislative house (Parliament [99[1]]).
Head of state: President.
Head of state government: Prime Minister.
Capital: Singapore.
Official languages: Mandarin Chinese; Malay; Tamil; English.
Official religion: none.
Monetary unit: Singapore dollar (S$); valuation (Sept. 1, 2011) 1 U.S.$ = S$1.20; 1 £ = S$1.95.

Population (2010 census)[2, 3]	
De facto population	5,076,700[4]
De jure population	3,771,700[5]

Demography

Area: 274.2 sq mi, 710.3 sq km.
Population (2011): 5,182,000.
Density (2011): persons per sq mi 18,899, persons per sq km 7,296.
Urban-rural: urban 100%.
Sex distribution (2010)[6]: male 49.34%; female 50.66%.
Age breakdown (2010)[6]: under 15, 17.3%; 15–29, 20.8%; 30–44, 24.6%; 45–59, 23.2%; 60–74, 10.5%; 75–84, 2.8%; 85 and over, 0.8%.
Population projection: (2020) 6,143,000; (2030) 7,145,000.
Ethnic composition (2010)[6]: Chinese 74.1%; Malay 13.4%; Indian 9.2%; other 3.3%.
Religious affiliation (2000)[6]: Buddhist/Taoist/Chinese folk-religionist 51.0%; Muslim 14.9%; Christian 14.6%; Hindu 4.0%; traditional beliefs 0.6%; nonreligious 14.9%.

Vital statistics

Birth rate per 1,000 population (2009)[6]: 9.9 (world avg. 20.3).
Death rate per 1,000 population (2009)[6]: 4.3 (world avg. 8.5).
Natural increase rate per 1,000 population (2009)[6]: 5.6 (world avg. 11.8).
Total fertility rate (avg. births per childbearing woman; 2009)[6]: 1.22.
Marriage/divorce rates per 1,000 population (2009)[7]: 4.4/1.2.
Life expectancy at birth (2009)[6]: male 79.0 years; female 83.7 years.
Major causes of death per 100,000 population (2009)[7]: diseases of the circulatory system 112.5; malignant neoplasms (cancers) 101.5; diseases of the respiratory system 63.9; diseases of the genitourinary system 17.3; accidents 8.8.

National economy

Budget (2009). Revenue: S$37,872,100,000 (tax revenue 93.1%, of which taxes on corporate income 25.1%, personal income taxes 19.3%, taxes on goods and services 17.5%; nontax revenue 6.9%). Expenditures: S$40,482,900,000 (security and external relations 35.6%; education 20.2%; transport 11.2%; health 8.2%; trade and industry 7.1%).
Public debt (December 2010): U.S.$241,500,000,000.
Production (metric tons except as noted). Agriculture, forestry, fishing (2009): hen's eggs 19,991, vegetables 19,584, orchids (15% of the world market) and other ornamental plants are cultivated for export; livestock (number of live animals) 260,000 pigs, 3,200,000 chickens, 750,000 ducks; roundwood, n.a.; fisheries production 5,688 (from aquaculture 63%)[8]. Quarrying: limestone, n.a. Manufacturing (value added in S$'000,000; 2009): electronic products and components 13,453; pharmaceuticals 7,827; transport equipment 5,927; nonelectrical machinery and equipment 4,845; fabricated metal products 2,187; precision and medical equipment 2,027. Energy production (consumption): electricity (kW-hr; 2009) 41,796,000,000 ([2008] 37,110,000,000); coal (metric tons; 2007) none (negligible); crude petroleum (barrels; 2009) none ([2008] 327,000,000); petroleum products (metric tons; 2007) 36,417,000 (8,119,000); natural gas (cu m; 2009) none (9,656,000,000).
Gross national income (GNI; 2010): U.S.$210,323,000,000 (U.S.$40,920 per capita); purchasing power parity GNI (U.S.$54,700 per capita).

Structure of gross domestic product and labour force

	2009		2008	
	in value S$'000,000	% of total value	labour force[6, 9]	% of labour force[6]
Agriculture, quarrying	107.6	0.1	22,800[10]	1.2[10]
Manufacturing	48,910.2	18.5	311,900	16.2
Construction	13,585.0	5.1	105,500	5.5
Public utilities	3,537.8	1.3	...	...
Transp. and commun.[11]	31,983.4	12.1	269,400	14.0
Trade, hotels	49,907.7	18.8	389,500	20.2
Finance, real estate	77,446.3	29.2	361,100	18.7
Pub. admin., defense, services	25,700.9	9.7	391,900	20.3
Other	13,879.0[12]	5.2[12]	76,200[13]	3.9[13]
TOTAL	265,057.9	100.0	1,928,300	100.0

Household income and expenditure (2008). Average household size 3.5; average annual income per household S$85,080 (U.S.$62,455); sources of income (2003): wages and salaries 82.5%, self-employment 12.3%, other 5.2%; expenditure (2009)[14]: housing and energy 19.7%, transportation 14.4%, recreation and culture 9.3%, food and nonalcoholic beverages 7.7%, health 7.4%, restaurants 7.2%.
Population economically active (2008): total 1,928,300[6, 9]; activity rate of total population 52.9%[6] (participation rates: ages 15–64, 71.7%[6]; female 43.3%[6]; unemployed [2009; incl./excl. temporary residents] 3.2%/4.5%).

Price and earnings indexes (2005 = 100)

	2004	2005	2006	2007	2008	2009	2010
Consumer price index	99.6	100.0	101.0	103.1	109.9	110.5	113.6
Monthly earnings index	96.7	100.0	103.2	109.6	115.5	112.4	118.7

Selected balance of payments data. Receipts from (U.S.$'000,000): tourism (2010) 14,957; remittances, n.a.; foreign direct investment (FDI; 2008–10 avg.) 20,835. Disbursements for (U.S.$'000,000): tourism (2010) 17,721; remittances, n.a.; FDI (2008–10 avg.) 12,649.
Land use as % of total land area (2009): in temporary crops or left fallow 0.7%; in permanent crops 0.3%; in pasture, n.a.; forest area 3.3%.

Foreign trade[15]

Balance of trade (current prices)

	2004	2005	2006	2007	2008	2009
S$'000,000	+58,721	+49,341	+52,635	+54,607	+25,869	+34,819
% of total	9.6%	6.9%	6.5%	6.5%	2.8%	7.8%

Imports (2009): S$356,299,000,000 (crude and refined petroleum 24.0%, nonelectronic machinery and equipment 19.8%, integrated circuits/parts 15.5%, base and fabricated metals 5.1%, personal computers/parts 4.5%). *Major import sources:* Malaysia 11.6%; U.S. 11.6%; China 10.5%; Japan 7.6%; Indonesia 5.8%; South Korea 5.7%.
Exports (2009): S$391,118,000,000 (integrated circuits/parts 20.4%, crude and refined petroleum 19.9%, nonelectronic machinery and equipment 15.5%, personal computers/parts 6.3%, organic chemicals 4.7%). *Major export destinations:* Hong Kong 11.6%; Malaysia 11.5%; Indonesia 9.7%; China 9.7%; U.S. 6.5%; South Korea 4.7%.

Transport and communications

Transport. Railroads (2009): route length 24 mi, 39 km[16]. Roads (2010[17])[18]: total length 2,085 mi, 3,356 km (paved 100%). Vehicles (2010[17]): passenger cars 604,073; trucks and buses 174,230. Air transport (2008)[19]: passenger-km 96,855,000,000; metric ton-km cargo 7,517,000,000.

Communications

Medium	date	number in '000s	units per 1,000 persons	Medium	date	number in '000s	units per 1,000 persons
Televisions	2008	583[20]	120[20]	PCs	2007	3,409	743
Telephones				Dailies	2009	1,020[21]	205[21]
Cellular	2010	7,307[20]	1,437[20]	Internet users	2009	3,658	772
Landline	2010	1,984	390	Broadband	2010	1,257[20]	247[20]

Education and health

Educational attainment (2005)[6]. Percentage of population age 15 and over[22] having: no schooling 16.4%; primary education 22.0%; lower secondary 21.3%; upper secondary 15.1%; technical 8.2%; university 17.0%. *Literacy* (2008)[7]: 94.5%; males literate 97.4%; females literate 91.6%.

Education (2007–08)

	teachers	students	student/ teacher ratio	enrollment rate (%)
Primary (age 6–11)	15,525	299,704	19.3	...
Secondary/Voc. (age 12–15)	14,128	231,144	16.4	...
Tertiary[23]	15,160	198,634	13.1	... (age 16–20)

Health (2009): physicians 7,733[24] (1 per 645 persons); hospital beds 11,663 (1 per 428 persons); infant mortality rate per 1,000 live births[6] 2.2; undernourished population, n.a.

Military

Total active duty personnel (November 2010): 72,500 (army 69.0%, navy 12.4%, air force 18.6%); reserve 312,500; paramilitary 44,000. *Military expenditure as percentage of GDP* (2009): 4.8%; per capita expenditure U.S.$1,661.

[1]Includes 12 nonelective seats. [2]July 1 preliminary. [3]Singapore does not have a local government structure. Five community development councils established in 2001 manage a variety of social services. [4]The de facto population figure (as of the 2010 census) includes citizens (3,230,700), noncitizens with permanent residency status (541,000), and temporary residents (1,305,000). [5]The de jure population figure excludes temporary residents. [6]Based on de jure population. [7]Based on de facto population. [8]Aquarium fish farming is also an important economic pursuit; Singapore produces roughly 30% of the world's ornamental fish. [9]Total labour force including temporary residents equals 2,939,000. [10]Includes not adequately defined. [11]Includes storage and information services. [12]Taxes on products. [13]Unemployed. [14]Domestic expenditures of de jure population. [15]Imports c.i.f.; exports f.o.b. [16]Length of Singapore portion of Singapore–to–Kuala Lumpur, Malaysia, railway. [17]January 1. [18]Public roads only. [19]Singapore Airlines and Silkair only. [20]Subscribers. [21]Circulation. [22]Nonstudent population only. [23]2008–09. [24]Excluding physicians not in active practice.

Internet resources for further information:
- **Statistics Singapore http://www.singstat.gov.sg**
- **Ministry of Trade and Industry http://app.mti.gov.sg**

Sint Maarten[1]

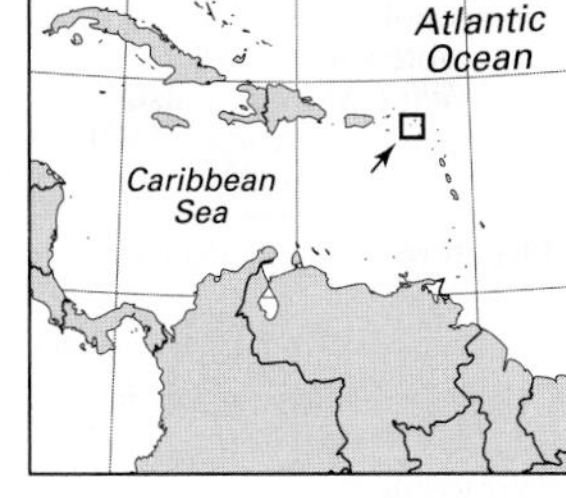

Official name: Land Sint Maarten (Dutch); Country of Sint Maarten (English).
Political status: autonomous state of the Netherlands with one legislative house (Parliament [15])[2].
Head of state: Dutch Monarch represented by Governor.
Head of government: Prime Minister.
Capital: Philipsburg.
Official languages: Dutch; English.
Official religion: none.
Monetary unit: Netherlands Antillean guilder (NAf.)[3]; valuation (Sept. 1, 2011) 1 U.S.$ = NAf. 1.79; 1 £ = NAf. 2.89[4].

Demography

Area: 13 sq mi, 34 sq km.
Population (2011): 38,300.
Density (2011): persons per sq mi 2,946, persons per sq km 1,126.
Sex distribution (2010[5]): male 47.98%; female 52.02%.
Age breakdown (2010[5]): under 15, 23.4%; 15–29, 19.0%; 30–44, 28.3%; 45–59, 22.1%; 60–74, 6.1%; 75–84, 0.8%; 85 and over, 0.3%.
Population projection: (2020) 40,800; (2030) 42,600.
Ethnic composition: n.a.
Religious affiliation (2001): Christian 82.9%, of which Roman Catholic 39.8%, Pentecostal 11.6%, Methodist 11.5%; nonreligious 6.7%; other/undefined 10.4%.
Major settlements (2001): Lower Prince's Quarter 8,123; Cul de Sac 7,880; Cole Bay 6,046; Upper Prince's Quarter 4,021; Philipsburg 1,227.

Vital statistics

Birth rate per 1,000 population (2009): 12.5 (world avg. 20.3).
Death rate per 1,000 population (2009): 3.1 (world avg. 8.5).
Total fertility rate (avg. births per childbearing woman; 2009): 1.7.
Life expectancy at birth (2009): male 73.1 years; female 78.2 years.

National economy

Tourism (2008): receipts from visitors U.S.$663,000,000; expenditures by nationals abroad U.S.$88,000,000.[6]
Production (metric tons except as noted). Agriculture, forestry, fishing (2009): n.a. Mining and quarrying (2009): n.a. Manufacturing (2009): n.a. Energy production (consumption): electricity (kW-hr; 2007) 344,600,000 (n.a.).
Gross domestic product (at current market prices; 2009): U.S.$793,400,000 (U.S.$20,267 per capita).

Structure of gross domestic product (current prices)

	2009		2007	
	in value NAf. '000,000	% of total value	labour force	% of labour force
Agriculture, Mining	6.1	0.4	191	0.8
Manufacturing	34.8	2.5	595	2.6
Construction	137.6	9.7	2,170	9.4
Trade and hotels	323.7	22.8	6,952	29.9
Public utilities	78.3	5.5	311	1.3
Transp. and commun.	145.4	10.2	1,857	8.0
Finance, real estate	385.1	27.1	2,908	12.5
Pub. admin., defense	77.8	5.5	1,606	6.9
Services	140.4	9.9	3,922	16.9
Other	91.0[7]	6.4[7]	2,705[8]	11.7[8]
TOTAL	1,420.2	100.0	23,217	100.0

Population economically active (2009): total 24,344; activity rate of total population 59.5% (participation rates: over age 15, 76.9%; female 48.5%; unemployed 12.2%).
Household income and expenditure. Average household size (2008[5]) 2.5; average annual income per household: n.a.; sources of income: n.a.; expenditure: n.a.
Land use as % of total land area (2009): in temporary crops or left fallow *c.* 10%; in permanent crops, none; in pasture, n.a.; forest area, n.a.

Transport and communications

Transport: [9].

[1]The 34 sq mi (87 sq km) island of Saint Martin has a 2011 estimated population of 76,800; administratively, the island is split between the French-governed Saint-Martin (Saint Martin) to the north and the Dutch-governed Sint Maarten to the south. [2]According to the national reorganization plan promulgated for Sint Maarten on Oct. 10, 2010; the former Netherlands Antilles was dissolved on this date. [3]The Netherlands Antillean guilder will be the joint transitional currency for both Sint Maarten and Curaçao until 2012, when it is replaced by the Caribbean guilder. [4]U.S.$ are accepted. [5]January 1. [6]Tourists arriving by cruise ship (2009): French side of island 13,383; Dutch side of island 1,215,146. Yacht slips in marinas (2009): French side of island 780; Dutch side of island 397. [7]Taxes less subsidies and less imputed bank service charges. [8]Includes 2,446 unemployed (10.5%). [9]Passenger arrivals (2009): Aeroport de Saint-Martin Grand-Case 192,891; Princess Juliana International Airport (Dutch side of the island) 440,185.

Internet resources for further information:
- **Central Bureau of Statistics**
  http://www.cbs.an
- **Centrale Bank van Curaçao en Sint Maarten**
  http://www.central bank.an

Saint-Martin (Saint Martin)[1]

Official name: Collectivité Départementale de Saint-Martin (French) (Departmental Collectivity of Saint Martin).
Political status: overseas collectivity[2] (France) with one legislative house (Territorial Council [23]).
Head of state: President of France.
Heads of government: Deputy Prefect (for France); President of the Territorial Council (for Saint-Martin).
Capital: Marigot.
Official language: French.
Official religion: none.
Monetary unit: euro (€); valuation (Sept. 1, 2011) 1 U.S.$ = €0.70; 1 £ = €1.13.

Demography

Area: 21 sq mi, 54 sq km.
Population (2011): 38,500.
Density (2011): persons per sq mi 1,833, persons per sq km 713.0.
Sex distribution (2006): male 48.47%; female 51.53%.
Age breakdown (2006): under 15, 27.8%; 15–29, 20.5%; 30–44, 27.3%; 45–59, 17.2%; 60–74, 5.6%; 75–84, 1.1%; 85 and over, 0.5%.
Population projection: (2020) 42,000; (2030) 44,100.
Ethnic composition (2007): residents of Saint-Martin (mostly black/white admixture) *c.* 62%; Haitian *c.* 18%; from the Dominican Republic or Dominica *c.* 8%; European/North American *c.* 8%; other *c.* 4%.
Religious affiliation: n.a.
Major settlements (2008[4]): Marigot 3,403; Grand-Case, n.a.; Quartier d'Orléans, n.a.

Vital statistics

Birth rate per 1,000 population (2008): 26.3 (world avg. 20.3).
Death rate per 1,000 population (2008): 3.1 (world avg. 8.5).
Total fertility rate (avg. births per childbearing woman): n.a.
Life expectancy at birth: n.a.

National economy

Tourism (2009): receipts from visitors, n.a.; expenditures by nationals abroad, n.a.
Production (metric tons except as noted). Agriculture, forestry, fishing (2009): n.a. Mining and quarrying (2009): n.a. Manufacturing (2009): n.a. Energy production (consumption): electricity (kW-hr; 2010) 197,300,000 (n.a.).
Gross domestic product (at current market prices; 1999): U.S.$450,000,000 (U.S.$14,665 per capita).

Structure of gross domestic product (current prices)

	1999		2009	
	in value €'000,000	% of total value	labour force	% of labour force
Agriculture	2.2	0.5	69	0.4
Mining	...	...	...	...
Manufacturing	18.7	4.2	742	4.4
Construction	47.8	10.8	1,198	7.1
Public utilities	4.8	1.1	...	...
Trade and hotels	73.9	16.8	6,611 (Trade and hotels; Transp. and commun.; Finance, real estate)	39.2
Transp. and commun.	20.9	4.7		
Finance, real estate	123.3	28.0		
Pub. admin., defense	19.8	4.5	2,733 (Pub. admin., defense; Services)	16.2
Services	129.7	29.4		
Other	—	—	5,503[6]	32.7[6]
TOTAL	441.1	100.0	16,856[7]	100.0

Population economically active (2008): total 17,311; activity rate of total population 46.8% (participation rates: ages 15–64, 71.4%; female 50.3%; unemployed 25.5%).
Land use: n.a.

Transport and communications

Transport: [8].

[1]The 34 sq mi (87 sq km) island of Saint Martin has a 2011 estimated population of 76,800; administratively, the island is split between the French-governed Saint-Martin (Saint Martin) to the north and the Dutch-governed Sint Maarten to the south. [2]From July 2007. [3]U.S.$ are accepted. [4]January 1. [5]Tourists arriving by cruise ship: French side of island 13,383; Dutch side of island 1,215,146. Yacht slips in marinas: French side of island 780; Dutch side of island 397. [6]Includes 1,392 (8.3%) inadequately defined and 4,111 (24.4%) unemployed. [7]Tourism employs 85% of the labour force. [8]Passenger arrivals (2009): Aeroport de Saint-Martin Grand-Case 192,891; Princess Juliana International Airport (Dutch side of the island) 440,185.

Internet resource for further information:
- **IEDOM Saint-Martin Rapport annuel 2010**
  http://www.iedom.fr/saint-martin

Slovakia

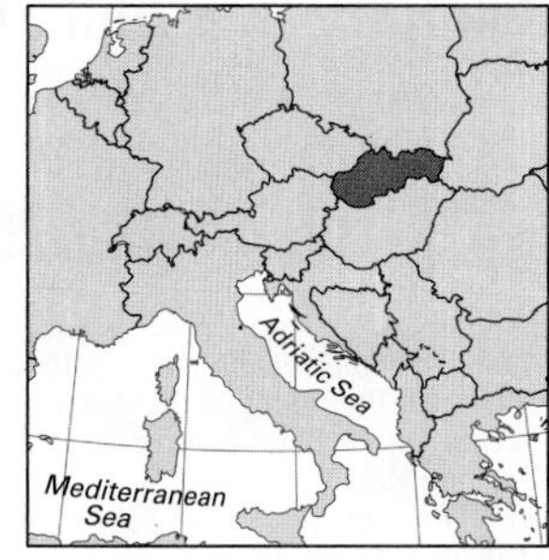

Official name: Slovenská republika (Slovak Republic).
Form of government: unitary multiparty republic with one legislative house (National Council [150]).
Head of state: President.
Head of government: Prime Minister.
Capital: Bratislava.
Official language: Slovak.
Official religion: none.
Monetary unit: euro (€)[1]; valuation (Sept. 1, 2011) 1 U.S.$ = €0.70; 1 £ = €1.13.

Area and population

Regions	Capitals	area sq mi	area sq km	population 2011[2] estimate
Banská Bystrica	Banská Bystrica	3,651	9,455	652,218
Bratislava	Bratislava	793	2,053	628,686
Košice	Košice	2,607	6,753	780,000
Nitra	Nitra	2,449	6,343	704,752
Prešov	Prešov	3,472	8,993	809,443
Trenčín	Trenčín	1,738	4,501	598,819
Trnava	Trnava	1,601	4,148	563,081
Žilina	Žilina	2,621	6,788	698,274
TOTAL		18,932	49,034	5,435,273

Demography

Population (2011): 5,440,000.
Density (2011): persons per sq mi 287.3, persons per sq km 110.9.
Urban-rural (2006): urban 55.4%; rural 44.6%.
Sex distribution (2011[2]): male 48.61%; female 51.39%.
Age breakdown (2008): under 15, 16.3%; 15–29, 24.0%; 30–44, 22.2%; 45–59, 21.1%; 60–74, 11.4%; 75–84, 4.0%; 85 and over, 1.0%.
Population projection: (2020) 5,514,000; (2030) 5,590,000.
Ethnic composition (2001): Slovak 85.8%; Hungarian 9.7%; Rom (Gypsy) 1.7%; Czech 0.8%; Ruthenian and Ukrainian 0.7%; other 1.3%.
Religious affiliation (2001): Roman Catholic 68.9%; Protestant 9.2%, of which Lutheran 6.9%, Reformed Christian 2.0%; Greek Catholic 4.1%; Eastern Orthodox 0.9%; nonreligious 13.0%; other/unknown 3.9%.
Major cities (2010[2]): Bratislava 431,061; Košice 233,880; Prešov 91,193; Žilina 85,252; Nitra 83,692; Banská Bystrica 79,990.

Vital statistics

Birth rate per 1,000 population (2009): 11.6 (world avg. 20.3); within marriage (2008) 69.9%; outside of marriage (2008) 30.1%.
Death rate per 1,000 population (2009): 9.8 (world avg. 8.5).
Natural increase rate per 1,000 population (2009): 1.8 (world avg. 11.8).
Total fertility rate (avg. births per childbearing woman; 2009): 1.41.
Marriage/divorce rates per 1,000 population: (2009) 4.9/(2008) 2.3.
Life expectancy at birth (2008): male 70.9 years; female 78.7 years.
Major causes of death per 100,000 population (2005): diseases of the circulatory system 540.7; malignant neoplasms (cancers) 220.4; accidents and violence 58.1; diseases of the respiratory system 57.8.

National economy

Budget (2007)[3]. Revenue: Sk 546,660,000,000 (tax revenue 47.9%, of which taxes on goods and services 35.6%; social security contributions 39.8%; nontax revenue 10.9%; grants 1.4%). Expenditures: Sk 580,610,000,000 (social protection 33.0%; health 20.0%; general administration 18.9%; economic affairs 11.8%; police 5.9%; defense 4.5%; education 3.7%).
Production (metric tons except as noted). Agriculture, forestry, fishing (2009): wheat 1,537,910, corn (maize) 988,053, cow's milk 957,327, sugar beets 898,807, barley 675,475, rapeseed 386,691, potatoes 216,123, sunflower seeds 187,238, pig meat 88,432, rye 56,932; livestock (number of live animals) 740,862 pigs, 483,810 cattle; roundwood (2010) 13,939,063 cu m, of which fuelwood 3%; fisheries production 2,584 (from aquaculture 32%). Mining and quarrying (2009): magnesite 800,000; kaolin 44,000; barite 13,000. Manufacturing (value added in U.S.$'000,000; 2006): fabricated metal products 1,200; nonelectrical machinery and apparatus 1,165; motor vehicles/parts 1,000; electrical/electronic machinery and apparatus 850; food and beverages 805; base metals (mostly iron and steel and to a lesser extent aluminum) 795. Energy production (consumption): electricity (kW-hr; 2010–11[4]) 27,107,000,000 ([2010] 13,445,000,000); hard coal (metric tons; 2007) none (5,021,000); lignite (metric tons; 2010–11[4]) 2,333,000 ([2007] 2,935,000); crude petroleum (barrels; 2007) 170,000 (43,650,000); petroleum products (metric tons; 2007) 5,707,000 (3,084,000); natural gas (cu m; 2010) 113,000,000 (6,258,000,000).
Population economically active (2008): total 2,691,200; activity rate of total population 49.8% (participation rates: ages 15–64, 68.9%; female 44.7%; unemployed [July 2010–June 2011] 13.8%).

Price and earnings indexes (2005 = 100)

	2004	2005	2006	2007	2008	2009	2010
Consumer price index	97.4	100.0	104.5	107.4	112.3	114.1	115.2
Annual earnings index	91.6	100.0	108.6	116.7	126.2	130.0	131.0

Household income and expenditure. Average household size (2003) 2.9; average annual gross income per household (2003) Sk 288,388 (U.S.$7,842); sources of income (2003): wages and salaries 73.9%, transfers 19.6%, self-employment 4.7%; expenditure (2006): housing and energy 26.3%, food and nonalcoholic beverages 17.9%, transportation 8.7%, recreation and culture 8.6%, hotels and restaurants 7.8%.
Public debt (external, outstanding; December 2008): U.S.$10,313,000,000.
Gross national income (GNI; 2010): U.S.$88,051,000,000 (U.S.$16,220 per capita); purchasing power parity GNI (U.S.$23,140 per capita).

Structure of gross domestic product and labour force

	2009 in value €'000,000	2009 % of total value	2008 labour force[5]	2008 % of labour force[5]
Agriculture	1,494	2.4	98,000	3.6
Mining	353	0.6	14,200	0.5
Manufacturing	11,067	17.5	647,600	24.1
Public utilities	3,276	5.2	42,100	1.6
Construction	5,076	8.0	256,700	9.5
Transp. and commun.	4,254	6.7	177,700	6.6
Trade, restaurants	9,724	15.4	406,500	15.1
Finance, real estate	12,598	19.9	213,100	7.9
Pub. admin., defense	9,704	15.3	167,100	6.2
Services			410,000	15.2
Other	5,784[6]	9.1[6]	258,300[7]	9.6[7]
TOTAL	63,332[8]	100.0[8]	2,691,300	100.0[8]

Selected balance of payments data. Receipts from (U.S.$'000,000): tourism (2009) 2,341; remittances (2010) 1,696; foreign direct investment (FDI; 2008–10 avg.) 1,721. Disbursements for (U.S.$'000,000): tourism (2009) 2,098; remittances (2009) 134; FDI (2008–10 avg.) 430.
Land use as % of total land area (2009): in temporary crops 27.2%, left fallow 0.3%, in permanent crops 0.5%, in pasture 10.9%, forest area 40.2%.

Foreign trade

Balance of trade (current prices)

	2005	2006	2007	2008	2009	2010
U.S.$'000,000	–2,374	–3,072	–1,172	–2,423	+393	–1,230
% of total	3.6%	3.6%	1.0%	1.7%	0.4%	0.9%

Imports (2008): U.S.$72,612,000,000 (machinery and apparatus 29.2%, of which telecommunications equipment/televisions/parts 10.5%; road vehicles/parts 13.2%; mineral fuels 12.8%; base and fabricated metals 10.3%; chemicals and chemical products 8.7%). *Major import sources:* Germany 19.8%; Czech Republic 11.4%; Russia 10.7%; South Korea 5.8%; China 5.7%.
Exports (2008): U.S.$70,189,000,000 (machinery and apparatus 31.2%, of which colour television receivers 12.0%; road vehicles/parts 22.0%, of which passenger cars 15.5%; base and fabricated metals 12.4%, of which iron and steel 7.3%; refined petroleum 4.7%). *Major export destinations:* Germany 20.2%; Czech Republic 13.1%; France 6.8%; Poland 6.6%; Hungary 6.2%.

Transport and communications

Transport. Railroads (2009[2]): route length 2,251 mi, 3,623 km; passenger-km (2008) 2,296,000,000; metric ton-km cargo 9,280,000,000. Roads (2006): total length 27,197 mi, 43,770 km (paved 87%); passenger-km (2006) 33,700,000,000; metric ton-km cargo (2008) 29,094,000,000. Vehicles (2009[2]): passenger cars 1,544,888; trucks and buses 257,430. Air transport (2008)[9]: passenger-km 3,733,000,000; metric ton-km cargo, none.

Communications

Medium	date	number in '000s	units per 1,000 persons	Medium	date	number in '000s	units per 1,000 persons
Televisions	2004	2,285	425	PCs	2007	2,774	514
Telephones				Dailies	2009	434[10]	94[10]
Cellular	2010	5,925[11]	1,085[11]	Internet users	2009	4,064	752
Landline	2010	1,099	201	Broadband	2010	877[11]	161[11]

Education and health

Educational attainment (2007). Percentage of population age 25–64 having: primary education 1%; lower secondary 12%; upper secondary 73%; higher vocational 1%; university 13%. *Literacy* (2007): total population age 15 and over literate nearly 100%.

Education (2007–08)

	teachers	students	student/teacher ratio	enrollment rate (%)
Primary (age 6–9)	13,529	224,769	16.6	92[12]
Secondary/Voc. (age 10–18)	46,989	591,482	12.6	...
Tertiary	12,284	229,477	18.7	54 (age 19–23)

Health: physicians (2006) 17,031 (1 per 317 persons); hospital beds (2007) 36,426 (1 per 148 persons); infant mortality rate per 1,000 live births (2009) 5.7; undernourished population (2004–06) less than 5.0% of total population.

Military

Total active duty personnel (November 2010): 16,531 (army 44.3%, air force 25.4%, headquarters staff 8.8%, support/training 21.5%). *Military expenditure as percentage of GDP* (2009): 1.2%; per capita expenditure U.S.$203.

[1]The euro (€) replaced the Slovak koruna (Sk) on Jan. 1, 2009, at an exchange rate of €1 = Sk 30.13. [2]January 1. [3]Central government only. [4]July 2010–June 2011. [5]Excludes persons on child-care leave and conscripts. [6]Taxes less subsidies. [7]Including 256,000 unemployed. [8]Detail does not add to total given because of rounding. [9]SkyEurope airlines only; operations suspended September 2009. [10]Circulation. [11]Subscribers. [12]2004–05.

Internet resources for further information:
- **National Bank of Slovakia http://www.nbs.sk**
- **Statistical Office of the Slovak Republic http://portal.statistics.sk**

Slovenia

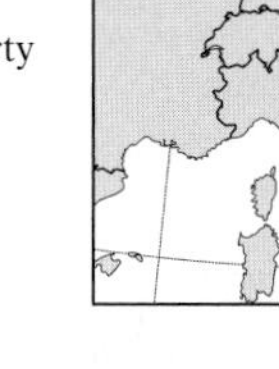

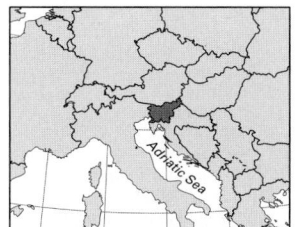

Official name: Republika Slovenija (Republic of Slovenia).
Form of government: unitary multiparty republic with two legislative houses (National Council [40]; National Assembly [90]).
Head of state: President.
Head of government: Prime Minister.
Capital: Ljubljana.
Official language: Slovene.
Official religion: none.
Monetary unit: euro (€); valuation (Sept. 1, 2011) 1 U.S.$ = €0.70; 1 £ = €1.13[1].

Area and population

Statistical regions[3]	Principal cities	area sq mi	area sq km	population 2011[2] estimate
Gorenjska	Kranj	825	2,137	203,427
Goriška	Nova Gorica	898	2,325	119,146
Jugovzhodna Slovenija	Novo mesto	653	1,690	142,483
Koroška	Ravne na Koroškem	401	1,041	72,494
Notranjsko-kraška	Postojna	562	1,456	52,287
Obalno-kraška	Koper	403	1,044	110,760
Osrednjeslovenska	Ljubljana	1,367	3,540	533,213
Podravska	Maribor	838	2,170	323,119
Pomurska	Murska Sobota	516	1,337	119,145
Savinjska	Celje	920	2,384	259,726
Spodnjeposavska	Krško	342	885	70,167
Zasavska	Trbovlje	102	264	44,222
TOTAL		7,827	20,273	2,050,189

Demography

Population (2011): 2,052,000.
Density (2011): persons per sq mi 262.1, persons per sq km 101.2.
Urban-rural (2009): urban 49.6%; rural 50.4%.
Sex distribution (2011[2]): male 49.49%; female 50.51%.
Age breakdown (2010[2]): under 15, 14.0%; 15–29, 18.9%; 30–44, 22.6%; 45–59, 22.5%; 60–74, 14.5%; 75–84, 5.9%; 85 and over, 1.6%.
Population projection: (2020) 2,140,000; (2030) 2,163,000.
Ethnic composition (2002)[4]: Slovene 91.2%; Serb 2.2%; Croat 2.0%; Bosniak (ethnic Muslim) 1.8%; other 2.8%.
Religious affiliation (2002): Roman Catholic 57.8%; Muslim 2.4%; Orthodox 2.3%; Protestant 0.8%; nonreligious/atheist 10.2%; other/unknown 26.5%.
Major cities (2011[2]): Ljubljana 272,220; Maribor 95,171; Celje 37,520; Kranj 36,874; Velenje 25,456.

Vital statistics

Birth rate per 1,000 population (2010): 10.9 (world avg. 19.2); within marriage 44.3%; outside of marriage 55.7%.
Death rate per 1,000 population (2010): 9.1 (world avg. 8.2).
Total fertility rate (avg. births per childbearing woman; 2010): 1.57.
Marriage/divorce rates per 1,000 population (2010): 3.2/1.2.
Life expectancy at birth (2009): male 76.0 years; female 82.8 years.
Major causes of death per 100,000 population (2010): diseases of the circulatory system 357.7; neoplasms 287.2; accidents, poisoning, and violence 73.9; diseases of the digestive system 56.2.

National economy

Budget (2010–11)[5]. Revenue: €15,347,000,000 (tax revenue 86.2%, of which social security contributions 34.4%, taxes on goods and services 31.9%, income tax 13.4%; nontax revenue 5.7%; other [including grants] 8.1%). Expenditures: €16,890,000,000 (current expenditures 88.0%; capital expenditures 12.0%).
Production (metric tons except as noted). Agriculture, forestry, fishing (2010): corn (maize) 311,000, wheat 153,400, grapes 109,100, potatoes 101,700, apples 95,622[6], peaches and nectarines 9,950[6], pears 9,862[6], cherries 3,951[6], walnuts 2,956[6], hops 2,669[6]; livestock (number of live animals) 470,000 cattle, 396,000 pigs, 42,000 beehives[6]; roundwood 2,945,347 cu m, of which fuelwood 37%; fisheries production (2009) 2,339 (from aquaculture 56%). Mining and quarrying (2009): sand and gravel 19,000,000. Manufacturing (value added in U.S.$'000,000; 2007): pharmaceuticals, paints, and soaps 1,168; nonelectrical machinery 1,100; fabricated metal products 1,024; electrical machinery 618; food products 562; motor vehicles/parts 521; plastics products 400. Energy production (consumption): electricity (kW-hr; 2010–11) 16,125,000,000 ([2010] 12,084,000,000); hard coal (metric tons; 2010) 419,000 (851,000); lignite (metric tons; 2010–11) 4,108,000 ([2010] 4,051,000); crude petroleum (barrels; 2010) 1,484 (n.a.); petroleum products (metric tons; 2007) 5,707,000 (3,084,000); natural gas (cu m; 2010–11) 6,432,000 ([2010] 1,059,000,000).
Population economically active (2010): total 1,042,000; activity rate 50.8% (participation rates: ages 15 and over, 59.2%; female 46.0%; unemployed [July 2010–June 2011] 7.7%).

Price and earnings indexes (2005 = 100)

	2004	2005	2006	2007	2008	2009	2010
Consumer price index	97.6	100.0	102.5	106.2	112.2	113.1	115.2
Earnings index	96.5	100.0	104.8	111.0	120.2	124.4	129.2

Gross national income (GNI; 2010): U.S.$49,276,000,000 (U.S.$23,860 per capita); purchasing power parity GNI (U.S.$26,970 per capita).

Structure of gross domestic product and labour force

	2010 in value €'000,000	% of total value	labour force	% of labour force
Agriculture, forestry, fishing	767	2.2	80,000	7.7
Mining and quarrying	135	0.4	4,000	0.4
Manufacturing	5,967	16.8	231,000	22.2
Construction	1,969	5.6	56,000	5.4
Public utilities	1,157	3.3	17,000	1.6
Transp. and commun.	3,033	8.6	86,000	8.3
Trade, restaurants	4,568	12.9	164,000	15.7
Finance, real estate	6,834	19.3	97,000	9.3
Pub. admin., defense	2,044	5.8	59,000	5.7
Services	4,350	12.3	169,000	16.2
Other	4,593[7]	13.0[7]	78,000[8]	7.5[8]
TOTAL	35,416[9]	100.0[9]	1,042,000[9]	100.0

Public debt (July 2011): U.S.$14,556,500,000.
Household income and expenditure (2006). Average household size (2010) 2.5; average annual income per household SIT 4,104,896[1] (U.S.$21,542); sources of income: wages and salaries 57.6%, transfers 28.9%, self-employment 5.5%; expenditure (2009): housing and energy 29.2%, food and nonalcoholic beverages 14.5%, transportation 13.6%, recreation and culture 8.7%.
Selected balance of payments data. Receipts from (U.S.$'000,000): tourism (2009) 2,518; remittances (2010) 297; foreign direct investment (FDI; 2008–10 avg.) 733. Disbursements for (U.S.$'000,000): tourism (2009) 1,355; remittances (2009) 191; FDI (2008–10 avg.) 569.
Land use as % of total land area (2007): in temporary crops 7.6%, left fallow 0.1%, in permanent crops 1.3%, in pasture 15.8%, forest area 63.3%.

Foreign trade[10]

Balance of trade (current prices)

	2004	2005	2006	2007	2008	2009
U.S.$'000,000	–1,692	–1,730	–2,029	–2,928	–4,733	–1,436
% of total	5.1%	4.6%	4.6%	5.2%	7.5%	3.1%

Imports (2010): €19,881,000,000 (machinery and apparatus 14.8%; base and fabricated metals 10.3%; motor vehicles 10.1%; petroleum products 9.2%; chemicals and chemical products 5.7%). *Major import sources:* Germany 18.4%; Italy 17.8%; Austria 12.1%; France 5.5%; Hungary 4.0%.
Exports (2010): €18,243,000,000 (machinery and apparatus 19.6%, of which electrical machinery 11.0%; motor vehicles 14.1%; pharmaceutical products 8.8%; base and fabricated metals 8.2%; cement, bricks, and ceramics 3.1%). *Major export destinations:* Germany 19.8%; Italy 12.2%; Austria 8.2%; France 8.1%; Croatia 6.7%.

Transport and communications

Transport. Railroads (2010): route length 763 mi, 1,228 km; passenger-km 813,000,000; metric ton-km cargo 3,421,000,000. Roads (2010): total length 24,266 mi, 39,052 km (paved 100%); (2008) passenger-km 23,900,000,000[11]; metric ton-km cargo 15,931,000,000. Vehicles (2011[2]): passenger cars 1,061,646; trucks and buses 86,507. Air transport (2010): passenger-km 1,226,000,000; metric ton-km cargo 1,537,000.

Communications

Medium	date	number in '000s	units per 1,000 persons	Medium	date	number in '000s	units per 1,000 persons
Televisions	2005	559	279	PCs	2007	850	425
Telephones				Dailies	2009	297[12]	145[12]
Cellular	2010	2,122[13]	1,046[13]	Internet users	2009	1,299	643
Landline	2010	914	450	Broadband	2010	495[13]	244[13]

Education and health

Educational attainment (2009). Percentage of population age 25 and over having: no formal schooling through complete primary education 4.4%; lower secondary 18.3%; upper secondary 56.6%; higher 20.7%. *Literacy* (2009): virtually 100%.

Education (2008–09)

	teachers	students	student/ teacher ratio	enrollment rate (%)
Primary (age 6–10)	6,243	107,104	17.2	97
Secondary/Voc. (age 11–18)	15,501	142,349	9.2	92
Tertiary	6,259	114,391	18.3	87 (age 19–23)

Health (2009): physicians 4,915 (1 per 416 persons); hospital beds 9,389 (1 per 218 persons); infant mortality rate (2010) 2.5; undernourished population (2004–06) 60,000 (less than 5% of total population based on the consumption of a minimum daily requirement of 1,960 calories).

Military

Total active duty personnel (November 2010): 7,600 (army 100%). *Military expenditure as percentage of GNP* (2010): 1.4%; per capita expenditure U.S.$328.

[1]The Slovenian tolar (SIT) was the former monetary unit; on Jan. 1, 2007, SIT 239.64 = €1. [2]January 1. [3]Actual first-order administration is based on 210 municipalities. [4]Prorating 8.9% of population not responding to census questionnaire. [5]Data for general government. [6]2009. [7]Net taxes on products. [8]Includes 74,000 unemployed and 4,000 not distributed. [9]Detail does not add to total given because of rounding. [10]Imports c.i.f.; exports f.o.b. [11]Passenger cars 23,000,000,000; buses 900,000,000. [12]Circulation. [13]Subscribers.

Internet resources for further information:
- **Statistical Office of the Republic of Slovenia http://www.stat.si/eng/index.asp**
- **Bank of Slovenia http://www.bsi.si/en**

Solomon Islands

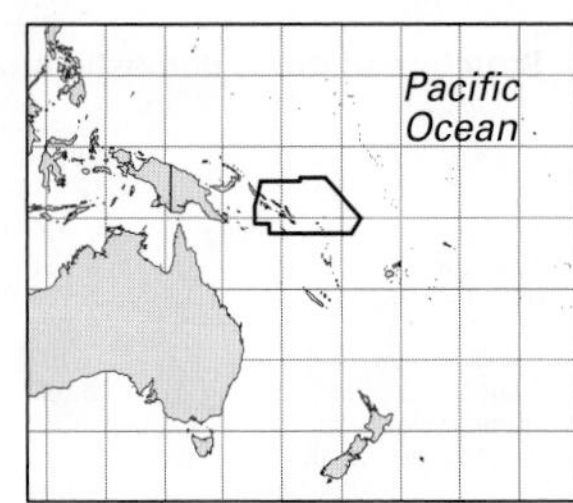

Official name: Solomon Islands.
Form of government: constitutional monarchy with one legislative house (National Parliament [50]).
Head of state: British Monarch represented by Governor-General.
Head of government: Prime Minister.
Capital: Honiara.
Official language: English.
Official religion: none.
Monetary unit: Solomon Islands dollar (SI$); valuation (Sept. 1, 2011) 1 U.S.$ = SI$7.46; 1 £ = SI$12.10.

Area and population

Provinces	Capitals	area sq mi	area sq km	population 2009 estimates
Central Islands	Tulagi	237	615	26,051
Choiseul	Taro	1,482	3,837	26,379
Guadalcanal	Honiara	2,060	5,336	93,613
Isabel	Buala	1,597	4,136	26,158
Makira-Ulawa	Kirakira	1,231	3,188	40,419
Malaita	Auki	1,631	4,225	137,596
Rennell and Bellona	Tigoa	259	671	3,041
Temotu	Santa Cruz	334	865	21,362
Western	Gizo	2,114	5,475	76,649
Capital Territory				
Honiara	—	9	22	64,602
TOTAL		10,954	28,370	515,870

Demography

Population (2011): 535,000.
Density (2011): persons per sq mi 48.8, persons per sq km 18.9.
Urban-rural (2009): urban 18.2%; rural 81.8%.
Sex distribution (2009): male 51.26%; female 48.74%.
Age breakdown (2009): under 15, 38.8%; 15–29, 28.0%; 30–44, 18.9%; 45–59, 8.7%; 60–74, 4.3%; 75–84, 1.1%; 85 and over, 0.2%.
Population projection: (2020) 665,000; (2030) 817,000.
Doubling time: 28 years.
Ethnic composition (2002): Melanesian 93.0%; Polynesian 4.0%; Micronesian 1.5%; other 1.5%.
Religious affiliation (2005): Protestant *c.* 70%, of which Anglican *c.* 32%, Adventist *c.* 10%; Roman Catholic *c.* 18%; traditional beliefs *c.* 5%; other *c.* 7%.
Major towns (2009): Honiara (on Guadalcanal) 64,609; Auki (on Malaita) 5,105; Gizo (in the New Georgia Islands) 3,547; Buala (on Santa Isabel) 971.

Vital statistics

Birth rate per 1,000 population (2009): 29.3 (world avg. 20.3).
Death rate per 1,000 population (2009): 4.0 (world avg. 8.5).
Natural increase rate per 1,000 population (2009): 25.3 (world avg. 11.8).
Total fertility rate (avg. births per childbearing woman; 2009): 3.76.
Marriage/divorce rates per 1,000 population (2006): n.a./n.a.
Life expectancy at birth (2009): male 71.1 years; female 76.4 years.
Major causes of death per 100,000 population (2002): diseases of the circulatory system 157, of which cerebrovascular diseases 47, ischemic heart disease 46; respiratory diseases 45; malignant neoplasms (cancers) 43; about 20% of the population has malaria, one of the world's highest rates.

National economy

Budget (2009). Revenue: SI$1,704,800,000 (tax revenue 76.7%, of which VAT 21.5%, corporate tax 13.0%, logging duties 9.7%, import duties 7.5%; nontax revenue 10.6%; grants 12.7%). Expenditures: SI$1,701,600,000 (current expenditure 83.9%; capital expenditure 16.1%).
Public debt (external, outstanding; December 2010): U.S.$119,900,000.
Gross national income (GNI; 2010): U.S.$552,000,000 (U.S.$1,030 per capita); purchasing power parity GNI (U.S.$2,210 per capita).

Structure of gross domestic product and labour force

	2006 in value SI$'000,000	2006 % of total value	2004 labour force[1]	2004 % of labour force[1]
Agriculture, forestry, fishing	1,217.4	35.0	14,938	28.7
Mining	1.7	—	1,476	2.8
Manufacturing	165.5	4.8		
Construction	18.8	0.5	1,397	2.7
Public utilities	44.6	1.3	469	0.9
Transportation and communications	322.2	9.3	1,246	2.4
Trade, hotels	477.9	13.8	3,274	6.3
Finance, real estate	492.6	14.2	806	1.5
Pub. admin., defense	238.1	6.9	6,758	13.0
Services	435.8	12.5	21,757	41.7
Other	60.5[2]	1.7[2]	...	...
TOTAL	3,475.3[3]	100.0	52,121	100.0

Household income and expenditure (2005–06)[4]. Average household size (2009) 5.5; average annual income per household U.S.$3,129; sources of income: home production[5] 36.9%, wages and salaries 26.6%, transfers 8.8%, self-employment 7.8%; expenditure: food 53.5%, housing 15.8%, transportation 6.8%, education 3.8%.

Population economically active (2008)[6]: total 113,000; activity rate of total population 22.1% (participation rates: ages 15 and over, 35.9%; female 31.0%; unemployed [2003] 15.2%).

Price index (2005 = 100)

	2004	2005	2006	2007	2008	2009	2010
Consumer price index	93.2	100.0	111.2	119.7	140.5	150.5	151.9

Production (metric tons except as noted). Agriculture, forestry, fishing (2009): coconuts 384,000, oil palm fruit 190,000, sweet potatoes 80,391, taro 48,449, yams 27,061, cacao beans 4,671; livestock (number of live animals) 54,000 pigs, 14,500 cattle, 235,000 chickens; roundwood (2010) 1,555,081 cu m, of which fuelwood 8%; fisheries production 27,938 (from aquaculture, negligible); aquatic plants production 150 (from aquaculture 100%). Mining and quarrying (2005): gold 10 kg[7]. Manufacturing (2009): vegetable oils and fats (2002) 50,000, palm oil 23,204, copra 21,973, cocoa 4,671, coconut oil 634. Energy production (consumption): electricity (kW-hr; 2009) 75,000,000 (71,000,000); coal, none (none); petroleum products (metric tons; 2007) none (62,000); natural gas, none (none).
Selected balance of payments data. Receipts from (U.S.$'000,000): tourism (2009) 44; remittances (2010) 3; foreign direct investment (FDI; 2008–10 avg.) 151; official development assistance (2009) 206. Disbursements for (U.S.$'000,000): tourism (2009) 32; remittances (2009) 4; FDI (2008–10 avg.) 3.
Land use as % of total land area (2009): in temporary crops or left fallow 0.6%, in permanent crops 2.1%, in pasture 0.3%, forest area 79.3%.

Foreign trade[8]

Balance of trade (current prices)

	2003	2004	2005	2006	2007	2008
U.S.$'000,000	−27.2	−35.7	−68.4	−110.7	−126.5	−130.2
% of total	17.0%	17.2%	32.7%	31.3%	28.5%	25.2%

Imports (2008): U.S.$323,400,000 (mineral fuels 26.1%, machinery and transport equipment 24.3%, food 19.7%, chemicals and chemical products 6.8%). *Major import sources* (2007): Australia 31.2%; Singapore 27.1%; Japan 8.2%; Malaysia 5.8%; Papua New Guinea 5.7%.
Exports (2008): U.S.$193,200,000 (logs 57.1%, copra 11.3%, palm oil 10.7%, fish 7.8%, cacao beans 4.6%, sawn wood 3.4%, gold[7] 1.4%). *Major export destinations* (2007): China 46.6%; Thailand 7.2%; Philippines 7.1%; Dem. Rep. of the Congo 6.1%; Japan 4.8%.

Transport and communications

Transport. Railroads: none. Roads (2007): total length 932 mi, 1,500 km (paved 3%). Vehicles (1993): passenger cars 2,052; trucks and buses 2,574. Air transport (2007)[9]: passenger-km 94,200,000; metric ton-km cargo 700,000.

Communications

Medium	date	number in '000s	units per 1,000 persons	Medium	date	number in '000s	units per 1,000 persons
Televisions	2004	5.3	11	PCs	2005	22	47
Telephones				Dailies	2009	5[10]	9.6[10]
Cellular	2010	30[11]	56[11]	Internet users	2009	10	19
Landline	2010	8.4	16	Broadband	2010	2[11]	3.7[11]

Education and health

Educational attainment (2009). Percentage of population age 12 and over having: no schooling/unknown 18.9%; primary education 56.8%; secondary 18.9%; vocational 1.0%; higher 4.4%. *Literacy* (2009): total population age 15 and over literate 84.1%; males literate 88.9%; females literate 79.2%.

Education (2007)

	teachers	students	student/ teacher ratio	enrollment rate (%)
Primary (age 6–11)	...	83,232	...	81
Secondary/Voc. (age 12–18)	...	27,332	...	30
Tertiary	...	...	...	... (age 19–23)

Health (2005): physicians 89 (1 per 5,293 persons); hospital beds 691 (1 per 682 persons); infant mortality rate per 1,000 live births (2009) 19.0; undernourished population (2006–08) 100,000 (11% of total population based on the consumption of a minimum daily requirement of 1,730 calories).

Military

Total active duty personnel (2009): no military (police force only); peacekeepers (November 2010) from Australia 80, from Tonga 34, from New Zealand 5.

[1]Persons employed in the monetary sector only. [2]Taxes on products less subsidies and less imputed bank charges. [3]Detail does not add to total given because of rounding. [4]Based on the Household Income and Expenditure Survey 2005–06 comprising 3,822 households. [5]Mostly food preparations and handicrafts. [6]ILO estimates. [7]Although small-scale artisanal production continued, production at the country's only gold mine was suspended from 2000 because of lawlessness, but it resumed in 2007. [8]Imports c.i.f.; exports f.o.b. [9]Solomon Airlines only. [10]Circulation of daily newspapers. [11]Subscribers.

Internet resources for further information:
- **Central Bank of Solomon Islands**
  http://www.cbsi.com.sb
- **Solomon Islands National Statistics Office**
  http://www.spc.int/prism/country/sb/stats

Somalia[1]

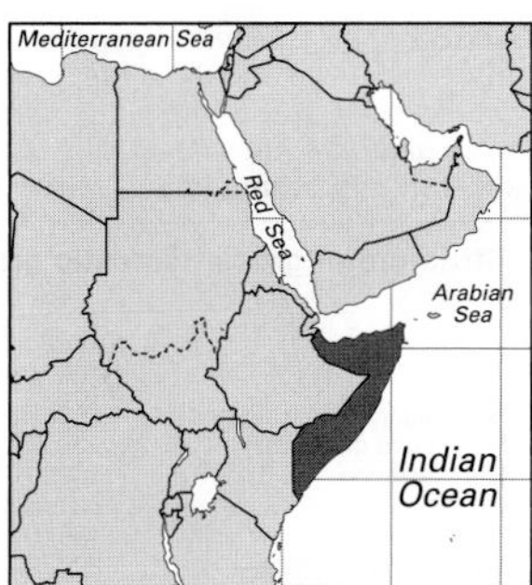

Official name: Soomaaliya (Somali) (Somalia).
Form of government: transitional regime[2] with one legislative body (Transitional Federal Assembly [TFA; 550[3]]).
Head of state and government: President assisted by Prime Minister[2].
Capital: Mogadishu.
Official languages: Somali; Arabic.
Official religion: Islam.
Monetary unit: Somali shilling (Shilin Soomaali; So.Sh.); valuation[4, 5].

Area and population

Historic Administrative Regions	Principal cities	area sq mi	area sq km	population 2010 estimate
Awdal[6]	Borama	8,253	21,374	...
Bakool	Xudur	10,410	26,962	...
Banaadir	Mogadishu (Muqdisho)	143	370	...
Bari[7]	Boosaaso	27,061	70,088	...
Bay	Baidoa (Baydhaba)	13,574	35,156	...
Galguduud	Dhuusamarreeb	17,809	46,126	...
Gedo[8]	Garbahaarey	23,316	60,389	...
Hiiraan	Belet Weyne	12,166	31,510	...
Juba Dhexe[8]	Bu'aale	3,798	9,836	...
Juba Hoose[8]	Kismayo	16,555	42,876	...
Mudug[9]	Gaalkacyo	28,160	72,933	...
Nugaal[7]	Garoowe	10,108	26,180	...
Sanaag[10]	Ceerigaabo	20,608	53,374	...
Shabelle Dhexe	Jowhar	8,750	22,663	...
Shabelle Hoose	Marka	9,763	25,285	...
Sool[10]	Laas Caanood (Las Anod)	9,666	25,036	...
Togdheer[10]	Burao (Burco)	14,928	38,663	...
Woqooyi Galbeed[6]	Hargeysa	11,134	28,836	...
TOTAL		246,201[11]	637,657	9,331,000[12]

Demography

Population (2011): 9,926,000.
Density (2011): persons per sq mi 40.3, persons per sq km 15.6.
Urban-rural (2009): urban 37.0%; rural 63.0%.
Sex distribution (2009): male 49.89%; female 50.11%.
Age breakdown (2009): under 15, 45.0%; 15–29, 25.7%; 30–44, 16.9%; 45–59, 8.6%; 60–74, 3.1%; 75–84, 0.6%; 85 and over, 0.1%.
Population projection: (2020) 11,757,000; (2030) 15,041,000.
Doubling time: 25 years.
Ethnic composition (2000): Somali 92.4%; Arab 2.2%; Afar 1.3%; other 4.1%.
Religious affiliation (2005): Muslim (nearly all Sunnī) *c.* 99%; other *c.* 1%.
Major cities (2008): Mogadishu (2009) 1,353,000[13]; Hargeysa (in Somaliland) 436,232[14]; Burao (in Somaliland) 151,451[14]; Belet Weyne 108,125[14]; Boosaaso (in Puntland) 108,016[14].

Vital statistics

Birth rate per 1,000 population (2009): 43.7 (world avg. 20.3).
Death rate per 1,000 population (2009): 15.6 (world avg. 8.5).
Total fertility rate (avg. births per childbearing woman; 2009): 6.52.
Life expectancy at birth (2008): male 47.8 years; female 51.3 years.
Major causes of death as percentage of all deaths (2001–02): sickness 61.1%; old age 19.0%; accidents 11.0%, of which land mines 3.6%; war-related 4.3%; pregnancy/childbirth-related 4.0%.

National economy

Budget: n.a. UN assistance (2007): U.S.$175,000,000, of which food aid U.S.$50,000,000.
Public debt (external, outstanding; 2009): U.S.$1,987,000,000.
Production (metric tons except as noted). Agriculture, forestry, fishing (2009): camel's milk 1,005,940, sheep's milk 465,710, cow's milk 452,150, goat's milk 394,870, sugarcane 215,000, corn (maize) 111,840, sorghum 86,080, cassava 82,570, sesame seed 64,450, camel meat 44,200, goat meat 42,250, bananas 40,940, dry beans 20,100, coconuts 17,780, rice 16,500, dates 11,870, oranges 8,600, lemons and limes 8,480; other tree/bush products include khat, frankincense, and myrrh; livestock (number of live animals) 13,100,000 sheep, 12,700,000 goats, 7,000,000 camels, 5,350,000 cattle; roundwood (2010) 12,273,423 cu m, of which fuelwood 99%; fisheries production 30,000 (from aquaculture, none). Mining and quarrying (2010): small quantities of gemstones (including garnet and opal) and salt. Manufacturing: small manufacturers produce textiles, handicrafts, and processed meat. Energy production (consumption): electricity (kW-hr; 2008) 315,000,000 (293,000,000); coal, none (none); crude petroleum (barrels; 2007) none (1,319,400); petroleum products (metric tons; 2007) 177,000 (193,000); natural gas, none (none).
Population economically active (2009): total 3,631,000; activity rate of total population 39.8% (participation rates: ages 15 and over [2007] 71.1%; female 39.1%; unemployed, n.a.).

Price index (2005 = 100)

	2004	2005	2006	2007	2008	2009	2010
Consumer price index	...	100.0	...	...	...	...	...

Land use as % of total land area (2009): in temporary crops or left fallow (2007) 1.6%, in permanent crops 0.04%, in pasture 68.5%, forest area 10.9%.

Gross national income (2008): U.S.$2,570,000,000 (U.S.$288 per capita).

Structure of gross domestic product and labour force

	2008 in value U.S.$'000,000	2008 % of total value	2010 labour force	2010 % of labour force
Agriculture, livestock	1,657	62.3	2,447,000	65.6
Mining and quarrying; Public utilities	18	0.7		
Manufacturing	68	2.5	1,284,000	34.4
Construction	116	4.4		
Transp. and commun.	266	10.0		
Trade, restaurants	293	11.0		
Finance, real estate; Pub. admin., defense; Services	339	12.7		
Other	–97	–3.6		
TOTAL	2,660	100.0	3,731,000	100.0

Selected balance of payments data. Receipts from (U.S.$'000,000): tourism, n.a.; remittances (2008) 2,000; foreign direct investment (2008–10 avg.) 102; official development assistance (2009) 662. Disbursements for (U.S.$'000,000): tourism, n.a.; remittances, n.a.
Household income and expenditure (2001–02). Average household size 5.8; income per household U.S.$226; sources of income: self-employment 50%, remittances 22.5%, wages 14%, rent/aid 13.5%; expenditure: n.a.

Foreign trade

Balance of trade (current prices)

	2002	2003	2004	2005	2006	2007
U.S.$'000,000	–245	–324	–388	–422	–494	–494
% of total	48.5%	60.0%	49.5%	45.9%	45.3%	45.3%

Imports (2007): U.S.$793,000,000 (agricultural products 48.1%, of which sugar [all forms] 12.3%, cereals 12.0%, vegetable/animal oils 6.6%; unspecified 51.9%). *Major import sources* (2008): Djibouti *c.* 30%; India *c.* 8%; Kenya *c.* 8%; U.S. *c.* 6%; Oman *c.* 6%.
Exports (2007): U.S.$299,000,000 (goats 12.0%; sheep 6.4%; cattle 5.5%; other agricultural products 1.4%; unspecified 74.7%). *Major export destinations* (2008): U.A.E. *c.* 57%; Yemen *c.* 21%; Saudi Arabia *c.* 4%.

Transport and communications

Transport. Railroads: none. Roads (2009): total length 13,732 mi, 22,100 km (paved 12%); passenger-km, n.a.; metric ton-km cargo, n.a. Vehicles (2002): passenger cars 12,700; trucks and buses 10,400. Air transport (2003)[15]: passenger arrivals 50,096, passenger departures 41,979; cargo unloaded 3,817 metric tons, cargo loaded 152 metric tons.

Communications

Medium	date	number in '000s	units per 1,000 persons	Medium	date	number in '000s	units per 1,000 persons
Televisions	2003	108	14	PCs	2007	79	9.0
Telephones				Dailies	2009	22[16]	2.4[16]
Cellular	2010	648[17]	70[17]	Internet users	2009	106	12
Landline	2010	100	11	Broadband	2010	—	—

Education and health

Educational attainment: n.a. *Literacy* (2002): percentage of total population age 15 and over literate 19.2%; males literate 25.1%; females literate 13.1%.

Education (2006–07)

	teachers	students	student/ teacher ratio	enrollment rate (%)
Primary	12,870	457,132	35.5	...
Secondary/Voc.	4,504	86,929	19.3	...
Tertiary	...	...	...	...

Health: physicians (2006) 300 (1 per 28,333 persons); hospital beds, n.a.; infant mortality rate per 1,000 live births (2009) 109.2; undernourished population, n.a.

Military

Total active duty personnel: no national army from 1991[18, 19]. *Military expenditure as percentage of GDP:* n.a.

[1]Proclamation of the "Republic of Somaliland" in May 1991 on territory corresponding to the former British Somaliland (which unified with the former Italian Trust Territory of Somalia to form Somalia in 1960) had not received international recognition as of December 2011. This entity represented about a quarter of Somalia's territory. [2]"Transitional government" from October 2004 controlled very little of Somalia in August 2011. [3]Planned number; TFA met in Baidoa from February 2006 to January 2009—some government officials met in Djibouti thereafter. [4]The So.Sh. had limited availability and circulation in 2009; 1 U.S.$ = *c.* 34,000 So.Sh. (1 £ = *c.* 66,000 So.Sh.) at the "black market" rate of May 2008. [5]Somaliland's sole legal tender from 1995 is the Somaliland shilling; in January 2009 1 U.S.$ = 7,500 Somaliland shillings. [6]Part of "Republic of Somaliland" from 1991. [7]Part of "autonomous region" of Puntland from 1998. [8]Part of the newly created (2011) semiautonomous region of Jubaland, with an estimated population of 1.3 million. [9]Administered (in part) as part of Puntland. [10]Administration disputed (at least in part) between Puntland and Somaliland. [11]Detail does not add to total given because of rounding. [12]Estimate of United Nations *World Population Prospects: The 2010 Revision,* including Somaliland. [13]Urban agglomeration. [14]Estimate of www.world-gazetteer.com. [15]Four Somaliland airports only. [16]Circulation of daily newspapers. [17]Subscribers. [18]Ethiopian forces backing the transitional government intermittently fought Islamist forces from December 2006 into 2010. [19]AU peacekeeping troops (November 2010) 7,250.

Internet resource for further information:
- **UNDP in Somalia http://www.so.undp.org**

South Africa

Official name: Republic of South Africa (English).
Form of government: multiparty republic with two legislative houses (National Council of Provinces [90]; National Assembly [400]).
Head of state and government: President.
Capitals (de facto): Pretoria[1] (executive); Bloemfontein[2] (judicial); Cape Town (legislative).
Official languages: [3].
Official religion: none.
Monetary unit: rand (R); valuation (Sept. 1, 2011) 1 U.S.$ = R 7.01; 1 £ = R 11.32.

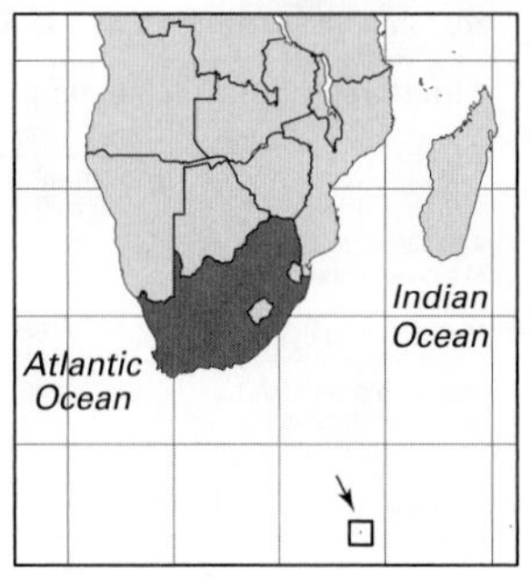

Area and population

Provinces	Capitals	area sq mi	area sq km	population 2010 estimate[4]
Eastern Cape	Bisho	65,238	168,966	6,829,958
Free State	Bloemfontein	50,126	129,825	2,759,644
Gauteng	Johannesburg	6,389	16,548	11,328,203
KwaZulu-Natal	Pietermaritzburg	36,433	94,361	10,819,130
Limpopo	Polokwane	48,554	125,755	5,554,657
Mpumalanga	Nelspruit	29,535	76,495	3,657,181
North West	Mafikeng	41,125	106,512	3,253,390
Northern Cape	Kimberley	143,973	372,889	1,096,731
Western Cape	Cape Town	49,986	129,462	5,287,863
TOTAL		471,359	1,220,813	50,586,757

Demography

Population (2011): 50,587,000.
Density (2011): persons per sq mi 107.3, persons per sq km 41.4.
Urban-rural (2010): urban 61.70%; rural 38.30%.
Sex distribution (2011)[4]: male 48.46%; female 51.54%.
Age breakdown (2011)[4]: under 15, 31.3%; 15–29, 29.0%; 30–44, 20.3%; 45–59, 11.8%; 60–74, 6.0%; 75 and over, 1.6%.
Population projection: (2020) 52,798,000; (2030) 54,945,000.
Ethnic composition (2009): black 79.3%, of which Zulu *c.* 24%, Xhosa *c.* 18%, Pedi *c.* 9%, Tswana *c.* 8%, Sotho *c.* 8%, Tsonga *c.* 4%, Swazi *c.* 3%, other black *c.* 5%; white 9.1%; mixed white/black 9.0%; Asian/other 2.6%.
Religious affiliation (2005): independent Christian 37.1%, of which Zion Christian 9.5%; Protestant 26.1%; traditional beliefs 8.9%; Roman Catholic 6.7%; Muslim 2.5%; Hindu 2.4%; nonreligious 3.0%; other/unknown 13.3%.
Major urban agglomerations (2010): Johannesburg 3,670,000; Cape Town 3,405,000; Ekurhuleni (East Rand) 3,202,000; eThekwini (Durban[5]) 2,879,000; Tshwane (Pretoria[1]) 1,429,000.

Vital statistics

Birth rate per 1,000 population (2011): 21.0 (world avg. 19.2).
Death rate per 1,000 population (2011): 11.7 (world avg. 8.2).
Marriage/divorce rates per 1,000 population (2009): 3.8/0.6.
Total fertility rate (avg. births per childbearing woman; 2011): 2.35.
Life expectancy at birth (2011): male 54.9 years; female 59.1 years.
Adult population (ages 15–49) *living with HIV* (2010): 17.3% (world avg. 0.8%).
Major causes of death per 100,000 population (2007): infectious and parasitic diseases 316; circulatory diseases 210; respiratory diseases 172; accidents and injuries 112; malignant neoplasms (cancers) 72.

National economy

Budget (2010–11). Revenue: R 666,562,700,000 (income tax 34.2%, VAT 27.2%, corporate taxes 22.4%). Expenditures: R 809,923,300,000 (transfer to provinces 32.7%, police and defense 13.6%, debt payments 8.2%, education 4.1%, transportation 3.7%).
Production (metric tons except as noted). Agriculture, forestry, fishing (2009): sugarcane 20,500,000, corn (maize) 12,050,000, wheat 1,958,000, potatoes 1,819,250, grapes 1,703,540, oranges 1,445,300, sunflower seeds 801,000, apples 702,284; livestock (number of live animals) 24,989,000 sheep, 13,761,200 cattle, 65,000 beehives; roundwood (2010) 30,887,580 cu m, of which fuelwood 39%; fisheries production 514,596 (from aquaculture, negligible); aquatic plants production 13,681 (from aquaculture 14%). Mining and quarrying (value of sales in R '000,000,000; 2010): platinum-group metals 73.8; coal 69.4; gold 53.1; iron ore 43.4; rough diamond production 8,868,400 carats. Manufacturing (value of sales in R '000,000; 2010): food products and beverages 248,529; transport equipment 161,651; chemicals 129,957; refined petroleum 95,580; base metals 94,330; fabricated metals 71,012. Energy production (consumption): electricity (kW-hr; 2010–11) 262,100,000,000 (240,068,000,000); coal (metric tons; 2010–11) 253,844,000 ([2007] 183,591,000[6]); crude petroleum (barrels; 2007) 7,528,000[6] (148,510,000[6]); petroleum products (metric tons; 2007) 21,996,000[6] (19,834,000[6]); natural gas (cu m; 2007) 1,917,000,000[6] (4,492,000,000[6]).
Land use as % of total land area (2007): in temporary crops or left fallow 11.9%, in permanent crops 0.8%, in pasture 69.1%, forest area 7.6%.
Population economically active (2011)[4]: total 17,663,000; activity rate of total population 34.9% (participation rates: ages 15–64, 54.5%; female 45.4%; unemployed [July 2010–June 2011] 25.0%).

Price index (2005 = 100)

	2004	2005	2006	2007	2008	2009	2010
Consumer price index	96.7	100.0	104.6	112.1	125.0	133.9	139.6

Household income and expenditure. Average household size (2004) 4.0; expenditure (2010): food, beverages, and tobacco 26.4%, transportation and communications 13.1%, housing 12.3%, health 6.1%.
Gross national income (GNI; 2010): U.S.$304,591,000,000 (U.S.$6,100 per capita); purchasing power parity GNI (U.S.$10,280 per capita).

Structure of gross domestic product and labour force

	2010 in value R '000,000	2010 % of total value	2009 labour force	2009 % of labour force
Agriculture, forestry, fishing	59,543	2.2	679,000	3.9
Mining and quarrying	230,402	8.7	312,000	1.8
Manufacturing	352,176	13.2	1,805,000	10.4
Construction	91,353	3.4	1,096,000	6.3
Public utilities	66,812	2.5	93,000	0.5
Transp. and commun.	220,039	8.3	740,000	4.3
Trade, hotels	335,562	12.6	2,927,000	16.8
Finance, real estate	511,332	19.2	1,719,000	9.9
Pub. admin., defense	385,417	14.5	3,841,000	22.1
Services	152,747	5.7		
Other	258,886[7]	9.7[7]	4,171,000[8]	24.0[8]
TOTAL	2,664,269	100.0	17,383,000	100.0

Public debt (external, outstanding; 2009): U.S.$15,063,000,000.
Selected balance of payments data. Receipts from (U.S.$'000,000): tourism (2009) 7,624; remittances (2010) 1,008; foreign direct investment (2008–10 avg.) 5,308; official development assistance (2009) 1,075. Disbursements for (U.S.$'000,000): tourism (2009) 4,151; remittances (2009) 1,158; foreign direct disinvestment (2008–10 avg.) –511.

Foreign trade

Balance of trade (current prices)

	2004	2005	2006	2007	2008	2009
R '000,000	–1,234	–6,367	–40,872	–40,531	–64,046	+2,300
% of total	0.2%	0.9%	4.7%	3.8%	4.6%	0.2%

Imports (2008): R 723,624,000,000 (machinery and apparatus 25.7%, crude petroleum 17.1%, chemicals and chemical products 9.8%, road vehicles 7.0%). *Major import sources:* Germany 11.3%; China 11.3%; U.S. 8.0%; Saudi Arabia 6.3%; Japan 5.6%.
Exports (2008): R 659,578,000,000 (platinum-group metals 12.3%, iron and steel 11.1%, road vehicles 9.4%, gold 7.4%, coal 5.9%, food 5.2%, pumps/compressors 4.0%, iron ore 3.0%, diamonds 2.9%, aluminum 2.6%, manganese ore 2.4%). *Major export destinations*[9]: Japan 11.0%; U.S. 10.8%; Germany 7.8%; U.K. 6.6%; China 5.8%.

Transport and communications

Transport. Railroads: route length (2009) 13,410 mi, 21,582 km; (2006–07) passenger-km 13,500,000,000[10]; (2007) metric ton-km cargo 129,000,000,000. Roads (2002): total length 224,997 mi, 362,099 km (paved 20%); (2007) passenger-km, n.a.; (2007) metric ton-km cargo 245,000,000,000. Vehicles (2008[11]): passenger cars 5,160,844; trucks and buses 2,442,324. Air transport (2009): passenger-km 25,548,000,000; metric ton-km cargo 648,996,000.

Communications

Medium	date	number in '000s	units per 1,000 persons	Medium	date	number in '000s	units per 1,000 persons
Televisions	2003	9,134	199	PCs	2005	3,966	85
Telephones				Dailies	2009	1,596[12]	32[12]
Cellular	2010	50,372[13]	1,005[13]	Internet users	2009	4,420	88
Landline	2010	4,225	84	Broadband	2010	743[13]	15[13]

Education and health

Educational attainment (2009). Percentage of population age 25 and over having: no formal schooling through incomplete primary education 23.6%; complete primary 6.0%; complete secondary 58.6%; vocational/higher 11.8%.
Literacy (2008): total population age 15 and over literate 89.0%.

Education (2008–09)

	teachers	students	student/ teacher ratio	enrollment rate (%)
Primary (age 7–13)	232,160	7,128,500	30.7	87[14]
Secondary/Voc. (age 14–18)	187,162	4,687,958	25.0	72[14]
Tertiary[15]	16,320	837,779	51.3	... (age 19–23)

Health (2007): physicians 362,725 (1 per 133 persons); hospital beds 1,591,154 (1 per 30 persons); infant mortality rate (2011) 37.9; undernourished population (2004–06) less than 5.0% of total population.

Military

Total active duty personnel (November 2010): 62,082 (army 59.8%, navy 10.1%, air force 17.2%, military health service 12.9%). *Military expenditure as percentage of GDP* (2010): 1.1%; per capita expenditure U.S.$83.

[1]Name of larger municipality including Pretoria is Tshwane. [2]Name of larger municipality including Bloemfontein is Mangaung. [3]Afrikaans; English; Ndebele; Pedi (North Sotho); Sotho (South Sotho); Swati (Swazi); Tsonga; Tswana (West Sotho); Venda; Xhosa; Zulu. [4]Official South African mid-year estimate. [5]Within eThekwini municipality. [6]Includes Botswana, Lesotho, Namibia, and Swaziland. [7]Taxes on products less subsidies on products. [8]Includes 4,167,000 unemployed. [9]Excluding gold exports. [10]Nearly all commuter service rail for 5 largest metropolitan regions only. [11]January 1. [12]Circulation of daily newspapers. [13]Subscribers. [14]2006–07. [15]Data for public institutions only.

Internet resources for further information:
- **South African Reserve Bank http://www.resbank.co.za**
- **Statistics South Africa http://www.statssa.gov.za**

Spain

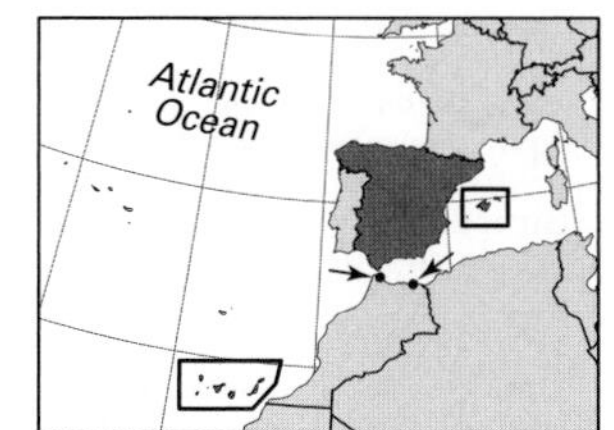

Official name: Reino de España (Kingdom of Spain).
Form of government: constitutional monarchy with two legislative houses (Senate [264[1]]; Congress of Deputies [350]).
Head of state: King.
Head of government: Prime Minister.
Capital: Madrid.
Official language: Castilian Spanish[2].
Official religion: none.
Monetary unit: euro (€); valuation (Sept. 1, 2011) 1 U.S.$ = €0.70; 1 £ = €1.13.

Area and population

Autonomous communities	area sq km	population 2011[3] estimate	Autonomous communities	area sq km	population 2011[3] estimate
Andalusia	87,597	8,415,490	Galicia	29,574	2,794,516
Aragon	47,721	1,345,132	La Rioja	5,045	322,621
Asturias	10,604	1,081,348	Madrid	8,028	6,481,514
Balearic Islands	4,992	1,112,712	Murcia	11,313	1,469,721
Basque Country	7,235	2,183,615	Navarra	10,390	641,293
Canary Islands	7,447	2,125,256	Valencia	23,255	5,111,767
Cantabria	5,321	592,560			
Castile–La Mancha	79,462	2,113,506	**Autonomous cities**		
Castile-León	94,226	2,555,742	Ceuta	19	82,159
Catalonia	32,113	7,535,251	Melilla	13	78,476
Extremadura	41,634	1,108,140	TOTAL	505,991[4]	47,150,819

Demography

Population (2011): 47,215,000.
Density (2011): persons per sq mi 241.7, persons per sq km 93.3.
Urban-rural (2009): urban 77.2%; rural 22.8%.
Sex distribution (2008): male 49.38%; female 50.62%.
Age breakdown (2008): under 15, 14.7%; 15–29, 18.9%; 30–44, 25.4%; 45–59, 19.2%; 60–74, 13.4%; 75–84, 6.3%; 85 and over, 2.1%.
Population projection: (2020) 49,034,000; (2030) 51,079,000.
Ethnic composition (2000): Spaniard 44.9%; Catalonian 28.0%; Galician 8.2%; Basque 5.5%; Aragonese 5.0%; Rom (Gypsy) 2.0%; other 6.4%[5].
Religious affiliation (2006): Roman Catholic *c.* 77%, of which practicing weekly *c.* 19%; Muslim *c.* 2.5%; Protestant *c.* 1%; other (mostly nonreligious) *c.* 19.5%.
Major cities (2010): Madrid 3,273,049 (urban agglomeration [2007] 5,764,000); Barcelona 1,619,337 (urban agglomeration [2007] 5,057,000); Valencia 809,267; Sevilla 704,198; Zaragoza 675,121.

Vital statistics

Birth rate per 1,000 population (2009): 10.7 (world avg. 20.3); within marriage (2008) 67.9%; outside of marriage (2008) 32.1%.
Death rate per 1,000 population (2009): 8.4 (world avg. 8.5).
Marriage/divorce rates per 1,000 population (2009): 3.8/2.2.
Total fertility rate (avg. births per childbearing woman; 2009): 1.40.
Life expectancy at birth (2008): male 79.1 years; female 85.2 years.
Major causes of death per 100,000 population (2006): diseases of the circulatory system 265.1; malignant neoplasms (cancers) 223.2; diseases of the respiratory system 86.7; diseases of the digestive system 42.5.
Adult population (ages 15–49) *living with HIV* (2009): 0.4%[6] (world avg. 0.8%).

National economy

Budget (2007). Revenue: €297,701,000,000 (tax revenue 49.1%, social contributions 45.6%, grants 1.9%, other 3.4%). Expenditures: €270,293,000,000 (social protection 45.3%, debt service 4.9%, public safety 4.1%, defense 4.0%, health 1.6%, education 0.6%).
Public debt (June 2010): U.S.$2,166,000,000,000.
Gross national income (GNI; 2010): U.S.$1,464,894,000,000 (U.S.$31,650 per capita); purchasing power parity GNI (U.S.$31,550 per capita).

Structure of gross domestic product and labour force

	2009 in value €'000,000	2009 % of total value	2007 labour force	2007 % of labour force
Agriculture, forestry, fishing	25,955	2.5	925,500	4.2
Mining and quarrying	121,917	11.6	60,100	0.3
Manufacturing			3,089,800	13.9
Public utilities	28,208	2.7	111,900	0.5
Construction	105,522	10.0	2,697,300	12.2
Transp. and commun.	...	...	1,177,100	5.3
Trade, hotels	...	...	4,579,100	20.6
Finance, real estate	540,133	51.3	2,517,100	11.3
Services	157,964	15.0	3,957,700	17.8
Pub. admin., defense			1,238,400	5.6
Other	74,215[7]	7.0[7]	1,836,000[8]	8.3[8]
TOTAL	1,053,914	100.0[4]	22,189,900[4]	100.0

Production (metric tons except as noted). Agriculture, forestry, fishing (2009): olives 7,923,000, barley 7,348,500, grapes 5,573,400, wheat 4,723,900, tomatoes 4,603,600, sugar beets 4,153,900, oranges 2,617,700, potatoes 2,459,800, tangerines, mandarins, and clementines 2,026,200, chilies and peppers 1,011,700, sunflower seeds 876,400, almonds 282,100, strawberries 263,700; livestock (number of live animals) 26,289,600 pigs, 19,718,200 sheep, 6,020,200 cattle, 2,425,000 beehives; roundwood (2010) 15,648,323 cu m, of which fuelwood 16%; fisheries production 1,171,435 (from aquaculture 23%). Mining and quarrying (2009): slate 1,200,000; sepiolite 700,007; fluorspar 122,408; gold 3,400 kg. Manufacturing (value added in U.S.$'000,000; 2006): food products 17,818; chemicals and chemical products 13,734; cement, bricks, and ceramics 13,109; motor vehicles and parts 11,647; fabricated metal products 10,271; printing and publishing 8,124. Energy production (consumption): electricity (kW-hr; 2007–08) 303,278,000,000 (279,709,000,000); hard coal (metric tons; 2007) 10,995,000 (36,281,000); lignite (metric tons; 2007) 6,016,000 (6,016,000); crude petroleum (barrels; 2007–08) 1,133,400 (453,309,900); petroleum products (metric tons; 2007–08) 55,886,000 ([2007] 60,987,000); natural gas (cu m; 2007–08) 15,447,500 (39,414,926,000).
Population economically active (2009): total 23,037,500; activity rate of total population 50.1% (participation rates: ages 16–64 [2007] 72.6%; female 43.8%; unemployed 18.0%).

Price and earnings indexes (2005 = 100)

	2004	2005	2006	2007	2008	2009	2010
Consumer price index	96.7	100.0	103.5	106.4	110.7	110.3	112.4
Earnings index	96.6	100.0	104.3	108.7	113.5	119.8	120.6

Selected balance of payments data. Receipts from (U.S.$'000,000): tourism (2008) 61,978; remittances (2010) 10,510; foreign direct investment (FDI; 2008–10 avg.) 36,892. Disbursements for (U.S.$'000,000): tourism (2008) 20,363; remittances (2009) 12,646; FDI (2008–10 avg.) 35,351.
Household income and expenditure (2005). Average household size 2.9; average annual net income per household (2007) €26,010 (U.S.$35,600); expenditure: housing 26.5%, food 17.8%, household expenses 7.5%, clothing/footwear 6.5%.
Land use as % of total land area (2009): in temporary crops or left fallow 25.1%, in permanent crops 9.5%, in pasture 21.0%, forest area 36.1%.

Foreign trade[9]

Balance of trade (current prices)

	2004	2005	2006	2007	2008	2009
€'000,000	–60,670	–77,813	–89,687	–98,952	–95,235	–50,182
% of total	17.2%	20.2%	20.9%	21.4%	20.0%	13.7%

Imports (2008): €285,866,000,000 (machinery and apparatus 19.9%; petroleum 14.5%; road vehicles and parts 11.3%; base and fabricated metals 7.4%; food 7.2%). *Major import sources:* Germany 13.9%; France 11.1%; Italy 7.7%; China 7.2%; U.K. 4.6%.
Exports (2008): €190,631,000,000 (road vehicles and parts 19.2%; machinery and apparatus 14.6%; food 11.3%, of which fruits and vegetables 5.6%; base and fabricated metals 10.1%). *Major export destinations:* France 18.2%; Germany 10.5%; Portugal 8.8%; Italy 8.0%; U.K. 7.1%.

Transport and communications

Transport. Railroads (2008): route length 9,500 mi, 15,288 km; passenger-km 22,794,600,000; metric ton-km cargo 10,839,100,000. Roads (2006): length 423,292 mi, 681,224 km (paved 100%); passenger-km (2006) 390,400,000,000; metric ton-km cargo (2008) 238,654,000,000. Vehicles (2008): cars 21,440,700; trucks, vans, and buses 5,273,000. Air transport (2007–08): passenger-km 81,252,000,000; metric ton-km cargo 1,169,204,000.

Communications

Medium	date	number in '000s	units per 1,000 persons	Medium	date	number in '000s	units per 1,000 persons
Televisions	2003	24,228	564	PCs	2007	17,646	393
Telephones				Dailies	2009	3,915[10]	99[10]
Cellular	2010	51,493[11]	1,118[11]	Internet users	2009	28,118	626
Landline	2010	19,904	432	Broadband	2010	10,579[11]	230[11]

Education and health

Educational attainment (2007). Percentage of population age 16 and over having: no formal schooling through incomplete primary education 11.6%; complete primary 20.9%; secondary 44.4%; undergraduate degree 14.2%; graduate degree 8.9%. *Literacy* (2008): total population age 15 and over literate 97.6%; males 98.4%; females 96.9%.

Education (2007–08)

	teachers	students	student/teacher ratio	enrollment rate (%)
Primary (age 6–11)	211,320	2,625,414	12.4	100
Secondary/Voc. (age 12–17)	284,084	3,069,321	10.8	95
Tertiary	145,673	1,781,019	12.2	71 (age 18–22)

Health (2009[3]): physicians 213,977 (1 per 214 persons); hospital beds (2008[3]) 160,292 (1 per 283 persons); infant mortality rate (2008) 3.5; undernourished population (2006–08) less than 5.0% of total population.

Military

Total active duty personnel (November 2010): 142,212 (army 54.9%, navy 15.2%, air force 14.9%, joint 15.0%); reserve 319,000.[12] *Military expenditure as percentage of GDP* (2009): 0.8%; per capita expenditure U.S.$254.

[1]Includes 56 indirectly elected seats. [2]The constitution states that "Castilian is the Spanish official language of the State," but that "all other Spanish languages (including Euskera [Basque], Catalan, and Galician) will also be official in the corresponding autonomous communities." [3]January 1. [4]Detail does not add to total given because of rounding. [5]Foreign residents (2009): 5.6 million, of which Romanian 14%, Moroccan 13%, Ecuadorian 7%, U.K. 7%. [6]Statistically derived midpoint within range. [7]Taxes less subsidies. [8]Includes 1,833,900 unemployed. [9]Imports c.i.f.; exports f.o.b. [10]Circulation of daily newspapers. [11]Subscribers. [12]U.S. troops (June 2011) 1,483.

Internet resources for further information:
- **Banco de España http://www.bde.es**
- **National Institute of Statistics http://www.ine.es/en/welcome_en.htm**

Sri Lanka

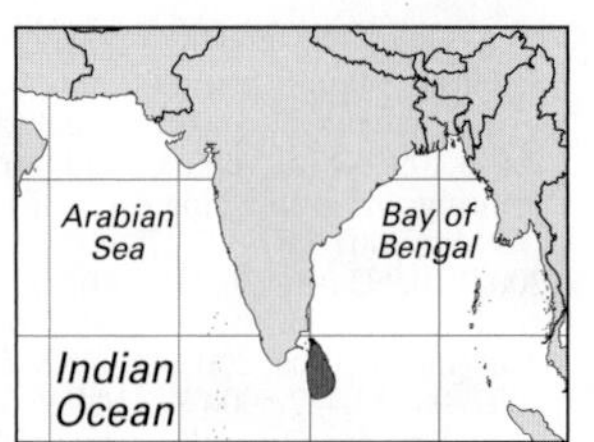

Official name: Sri Lanka Prajatantrika Samajavadi Janarajaya (Sinhala); Ilangai Jananayaka Socialisa Kudiarasu (Tamil) (Democratic Socialist Republic of Sri Lanka).
Form of government: unitary multiparty republic with one legislative house (Parliament [225]).
Head of state and government: President assisted by Prime Minister.
Capitals: Colombo (executive and judicial); Sri Jayewardenepura Kotte (Colombo suburb; legislative).
Official languages: Sinhala; Tamil[1].
Official religion: none[2].
Monetary unit: Sri Lankan rupee (LKR); valuation (Sept. 1, 2011) 1 U.S.$ = LKR 109.99; 1 £ = LKR 177.74.

Area and population

Districts	area sq km	population 2010 estimate	Districts	area sq km	population 2010 estimate
Ampara	4,415	644,000	Kurunegala	4,816	1,563,000
Anuradhapura	7,179	830,000	Mannar	1,996	104,000
Badulla	2,861	886,000	Matale	1,993	497,000
Batticaloa	2,854	543,000	Matara	1,283	839,000
Colombo	699	2,553,000	Monaragala	5,639	440,000
Galle	1,652	1,084,000	Mullaitivu	2,617	148,000
Gampaha	1,387	2,177,000	Nuwara Eliya	1,741	761,000
Hambantota	2,609	571,000	Polonnaruwa	3,293	410,000
Jaffna	1,025	611,000	Puttalam	3,072	779,000
Kalutara	1,598	1,135,000	Ratnapura	3,275	1,125,000
Kandy	1,940	1,431,000	Trincomalee	2,727	374,000
Kegalle	1,693	818,000	Vavuniya	1,967	174,000
Kilinochchi	1,279	156,000	TOTAL	65,610	20,653,000

Demography

Population (2011): 21,045,000.
Density (2011): persons per sq mi 830.8, persons per sq km 320.8.
Urban-rural (2009): urban 14.3%; rural 85.7%.
Sex distribution (2009): male 49.62%; female 50.38%.
Age breakdown (2009): under 15, 26.3%; 15–29, 27.0%; 30–44, 22.0%; 45–59, 15.4%; 60–74, 7.1%; 75 and over, 2.2%.
Population projection: (2020) 22,344,000; (2030) 23,094,000.
Ethnic composition (2001): Sinhalese 81.9%; Tamil 9.4%; Sri Lankan Moor 8.0%; other 0.7%.
Religious affiliation (2005): Buddhist *c.* 70%; Hindu *c.* 15%; Christian (mostly Roman Catholic) *c.* 8%; Muslim (nearly all Sunnī) *c.* 7%.
Major cities (2009): Colombo 681,000 (greater Colombo [2004] 2,490,300); Dehiwala–Mount Lavinia (2007) 219,827[3]; Moratuwa (2007) 185,668[3]; Jaffna (2007) 151,612; Negombo (2007) 150,364; Sri Jayewardenepura Kotte 123,000[3].

Vital statistics

Birth rate per 1,000 population (2009): 18.4 (world avg. 20.3).
Death rate per 1,000 population (2009): 5.9 (world avg. 8.5).
Marriage/divorce rates per 1,000 population (2009): 9.5/n.a.
Total fertility rate (avg. births per childbearing woman; 2009): 2.30.
Life expectancy at birth (2009): male 70.6 years; female 78.1 years.
Major causes of death per 100,000 population (2002): diseases of the circulatory system 252; malignant neoplasms (cancers) 101; diseases of the respiratory system 82; injuries, accidents, and violence 81.

National economy

Budget (2009). Revenue: LKR 887,632,000,000 (tax revenue 86.9%, of which VAT 30.9%, excises 14.5%; nontax revenue 11.0%; foreign grants 2.1%). Expenditures: LKR 1,760,939,000,000 (debt service 27.0%; transfers 15.1%; wages and salaries 10.5%).
Household income and expenditure (2009–10)[4]. Average household size 4.0; average annual income per household LKR 425,940 (U.S.$3,719); sources of income (2006–07): wages 35.8%, nonmonetary income 14.0%, agriculture 12.1%; expenditure: food and nonalcoholic beverages 39.8%, housing 10.9%, transportation and communication 10.0%, health 5.2%, energy 3.9%.
Selected balance of payments data. Receipts from (U.S.$'000,000): tourism (2009) 350; remittances (2010) 4,110; foreign direct investment (FDI; 2008–10 avg.) 545; official development assistance (2009) 704. Disbursements for (U.S.$'000,000): tourism (2009) 411; remittances (2009) 435; FDI (2008–10 avg.) 43.
Production (metric tons except as noted). Agriculture, forestry, fishing (2009): rice 3,652,000, coconuts 2,099,000, sugarcane 919,530, plantains 511,680, tea 290,000, cassava 277,850, natural rubber 136,000, peppercorns 25,300, cinnamon 14,600, ginger 10,780, sesame seeds 8,530, cloves 3,790; livestock (number of live animals) 1,136,860 cattle, 377,460 goats, 371,790 buffalo; roundwood (2010) 5,894,453 cu m, of which fuelwood 89%; fisheries production 363,243 (from aquaculture 2%). Mining and quarrying (2009): kaolin 10,000; graphite 7,000; sapphires 600,000 carats; rubies 50,000 carats; diamonds, n.a. Manufacturing (value added in LKR '000,000; 2009): food, beverages, and tobacco 397,244; textiles and apparel 155,409; rubber and plastic products 63,749; coal and refined petroleum products 44,882. Energy production (consumption): electricity (kW-hr; 2009) 9,882,000,000 (8,441,000,000); coal (metric tons; 2007) none (68,000); crude petroleum (barrels; 2007) none (13,978,000); petroleum products (metric tons; 2009) 1,895,000 (3,811,000).
Gross national income (GNI; 2010): U.S.$46,738,000,000 (U.S.$2,290 per capita); purchasing power parity GNI (U.S.$5,070 per capita).

Structure of gross domestic product and labour force

2009	in value LKR '000,000	% of total value	labour force	% of labour force
Agriculture, forestry, fishing	607,788	12.6	2,475,921	30.7
Mining and quarrying	79,204	1.6		
Public utilities	113,118	2.3	562,234	7.0
Construction	366,248	7.6		
Manufacturing	875,562	18.1	1,348,084	16.7
Transp. and commun.	606,345	12.6	445,111	5.5
Trade, hotels, restaurants	968,882	20.1	1,118,737	13.8
Finance, real estate	658,753	13.7	226,660	2.8
Pub. admin., defense	445,543	9.2	524,390	6.5
Services	103,642	2.2	692,088	8.6
Other	—	—	680,443[5]	8.4[5]
TOTAL	4,825,085	100.0	8,073,668	100.0

Public debt (external, outstanding; April 2011): U.S.$18,948,000,000.
Population economically active (2009): total 8,073,668; activity rate 39.9% (participation rates: ages 15 and over, 54.1%; female 35.8%; unemployed [July 2009–June 2010] 5.4%).

Price and earnings indexes (2005 = 100)

	2004	2005	2006	2007	2008	2009	2010
Consumer price index	89.6	100.0	110.0	127.4	156.1	161.5	171.1
Minimum wage index	91.5	100.0	102.6	119.3	149.7	153.8	217.9

Land use as % of total land area (2009): in temporary crops or left fallow 19.1%, in permanent crops 15.5%, in pasture 7.0%, forest area 29.9%.

Foreign trade[6]

Balance of trade (current prices)

	2004	2005	2006	2007	2008	2009
LKR '000,000	–227,171	–253,083	–350,110	–404,703	–561,029	–358,707
% of total	16.3%	16.5%	19.6%	19.4%	23.5%	18.1%

Imports (2008): LKR 1,476,495,000,000 (refined petroleum 12.0%; food 12.0%; machinery and apparatus 11.9%; yarn and fabrics 11.0%; crude petroleum 9.7%; base and fabricated metals 6.5%). *Major import sources:* India 20.8%; Singapore 11.7%; Iran 8.7%; China 8.1%; Hong Kong 5.1%.
Exports (2008): LKR 915,466,000,000 (garments and clothing accessories 40.9%; tea 14.9%; precious gemstones 5.9%, of which diamonds 3.7%; rubber tires 4.0%; fish 1.7%; parts of aircraft 1.6%; natural rubber 1.3%). *Major export destinations:* U.S. 22.5%; U.K. 13.1%; Germany 5.5%; Italy 5.3%; India 5.3%.

Transport and communications

Transport. Railroads (2009): route length (2008) 900 mi, 1,449 km; passenger-km 4,572,000,000; metric ton-km cargo 114,000,000. Roads (2009): total length 57,108 mi, 91,907 km (paved [2003] 81%); passenger-km 15,131,000,000[7]; metric ton-km cargo, n.a. Vehicles (2010[8]): passenger cars 387,210; trucks and buses 667,930. Air transport (2009–10): passenger-km 8,906,000,000; metric ton-km cargo 313,000,000.

Communications

Medium	date	number in '000s	units per 1,000 persons	Medium	date	number in '000s	units per 1,000 persons
Televisions	2007	2,823	142	PCs	2005	734	35
Telephones				Dailies	2009	590[9]	29[9]
Cellular	2010	17,359[10]	832[10]	Internet users	2009	1,777	88
Landline	2010	3,579	172	Broadband	2010	214[10]	10[10]

Education and health

Educational attainment: n.a. *Literacy* (2009): percentage of population age 10 and over literate 91.4%; males literate 92.8%; females literate 90.0%.

Education (2008–09)

	teachers	students	student/ teacher ratio	enrollment rate (%)
Primary (age 5–9)[11]	69,436	1,631,430	23.5	99
Secondary/Voc. (age 10–17)[12]	119,491	2,332,326	19.5	...
Tertiary	4,738	65,558	13.8	... (age 18–22)

Health (2009): physicians 13,633 (1 per 1,484 persons); hospital beds 68,897 (1 per 294 persons); infant mortality rate 15.0; undernourished population (2006–08) 3,900,000 (20% of total population based on the consumption of a minimum daily requirement of 1,800 calories).

Military

Total active duty personnel (November 2010): 160,900 (army 73.3%, navy 9.3%, air force 17.4%). *Military expenditure as percentage of GDP* (2009): 3.5%; per capita expenditure U.S.$78.

[1]English has official status as "the link language" between Sinhala and Tamil. [2]Buddhism has special recognition. [3]Within greater Colombo. [4]Excludes 7 districts in northern and eastern Sri Lanka. [5]Includes 209,189 unclassified and 471,254 unemployed. [6]Imports c.i.f.; exports f.o.b. [7]Buses only. [8]January 1. [9]Circulation of daily newspapers. [10]Subscribers. [11]2007–08. [12]2003–04.

Internet resources for further information:
- **Central Bank of Sri Lanka http://www.cbsl.gov.lk**
- **Department of Census and Statistics http://www.statistics.gov.lk**

Sudan[1, 2]

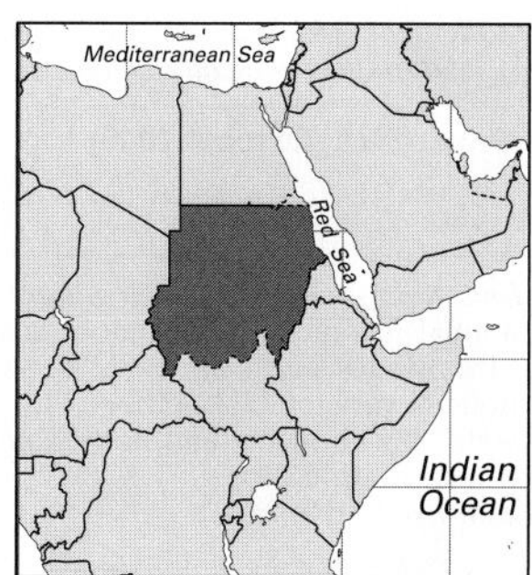

Official name: Jumhūriyyat al-Sūdān (Republic of the Sudan).
Form of government: military-backed interim regime with Council of States (32[3]); National Assembly (354)[4].
Head of state and government: President assisted by Vice Presidents.
Capital: Khartoum[5].
Official languages: Arabic[6]; English[6].
Official religion: [7].
Monetary unit: Sudanese pound (SDG); valuation (Sept. 1, 2011) 1 U.S.$ = SDG 2.68; 1 £ = SDG 4.33.[8]

Area and population[9]

States	area sq km	population 2008 census[10]	States	area sq km	population 2008 census[10]
Blue Nile	45,844	832,112	Kordofan, Southern[12]	158,355	1,406,404
Darfur, Northern[11]	296,420	2,113,626	Nile	122,123	1,120,441
Darfur, Southern[11]	127,300	4,093,594	Northern	348,765	699,065
Darfur, Western[11]	79,460	1,308,225	al-Qaḍārif	75,263	1,348,378
al-Jazīrah	23,373	3,575,280	Red Sea	218,887	1,396,110
Kassala	36,710	1,789,806	Sinnār	37,844	1,285,058
Khartoum	22,142	5,274,321	White Nile	30,411	1,730,588
Kordofan, Northern	221,900	2,920,992	TOTAL	1,844,797	30,894,000[13]

Demography

Population (2011): 36,787,000[14].
Density (2011): persons per sq mi 51.6, persons per sq km 19.9.
Urban-rural (2009): urban 39.4%; rural 60.6%.
Sex distribution (2009): male 50.18%; female 49.82%.
Age breakdown (2009): under 15, 42.7%; 15–29, 28.3%; 30–44, 16.4%; 45–59, 8.2%; 60–74, 3.8%; 75–84, 0.5%; 85 and over, 0.1%.
Population projection: (2020) 45,975,000; (2030) 57,168,000.
Ethnic composition (2003): black *c.* 52%; Arab *c.* 39%; Beja *c.* 6%; foreigners *c.* 2%; other *c.* 1%.
Religious affiliation (2005): Sunnī Muslim 68.4%; traditional beliefs 10.8%; Roman Catholic 9.5%; Protestant 8.8%, of which Anglican 5.4%; other 2.5%.
Major cities (2008): Omdurman 1,849,659; Khartoum 1,410,858[15]; Khartoum North 1,012,211; Nyala 492,984; Port Sudan 394,561.

Vital statistics

Birth rate per 1,000 population (2009): 37.0 (world avg. 20.3).
Death rate per 1,000 population (2009): 12.0 (world avg. 8.5).
Total fertility rate (avg. births per childbearing woman; 2009): 5.02.
Life expectancy at birth (2009): male 52.5 years; female 54.9 years.
Major causes of death per 100,000 population (2002): ischemic heart disease 81; malaria 63; HIV/AIDS 58; diarrheal diseases 55; measles 49.
Adult population (ages 15–49) *living with HIV* (2009): 1.1% (world avg. 0.8%).

National economy

Budget (2008). Revenue: SDG 26,424,000,000 (nontax revenue 68.8%, of which export receipts for crude petroleum 52.3%; tax revenue 29.0%, of which taxes on goods and services 18.0%; grants 2.2%). Expenditures: SDG 24,331,-000,000 (federal government 52.5%; transfers to: Southern Sudan 25.3%; northern states 22.2%).
Public debt (external, outstanding; 2009): U.S.$12,998,000,000.
Gross national income (GNI; 2010): U.S.$55,277,000,000 (U.S.$1,270 per capita); purchasing power parity GNI (U.S.$2,020 per capita).

Structure of gross domestic product and labour force

	2008 in value SDG '000,000,000	2008 % of total value	2004 labour force[16]	2004 % of labour force[16]
Agriculture	3,748	29.3	7,925,000	57.4
Petroleum	1,979	15.5		
other Mining	27	0.2		
Manufacturing	973	7.6		
Construction	524	4.1		
Public utilities	224	1.8		
Transp. and commun.	1,505	11.8	5,881,000	42.6
Trade, hotels	1,838	14.4		
Finance, real estate	817	6.4		
Pub. admin., defense	668	5.2		
Services	250	2.0		
Other	222[17]	1.7[17]		
TOTAL	12,775	100.0	13,806,000	100.0

Production (metric tons except as noted). Agriculture, forestry, fishing (2009): sugarcane 7,526,700, cow's milk 5,328,000, sorghum 4,192,000, goat's milk 1,475,000, peanuts (groundnuts) 942,000, wheat 641,700, millet 630,000, tomatoes 453,000, cattle meat 340,000, dates 339,300, sesame seeds 318,000, okra 249,000, seed cotton 169,000, gum arabic (2010) 30,200; livestock (number of live animals; 2010) 52,079,000 sheep, 43,441,000 goats, 41,761,000 cattle, 4,623,000 camels; roundwood (2010) 20,720,350 cu m, of which fuelwood 90%; fisheries production 73,890 (from aquaculture 3%). Mining and quarrying (2009): marble 1,600[18] cu m; gold (metal content) 1,922 kg. Manufacturing (2008): diesel (2006) 1,817,000; flour 1,360,000; benzene 1,083,700; sugar 733,000; cement 340,000; soap 70,000; animal hides and skins 4,500,000 units. Energy production (consumption): electricity (kW-hr; 2010) 7,653,000,000 (6,026,000,000); crude petroleum (barrels; 2009) 173,500,000 ([2007] 38,000,000); petroleum products (metric tons; 2008) 4,374,000 ([2007] 3,568,000); natural gas, none (none).
Population economically active (2008)[19]: total 13,087,000; activity rate of total population 31.7% (participation rates: ages 15–64, 53.2%; female 29.5%).

Price index (2005 = 100)

	2004	2005	2006	2007	2008	2009	2010
Consumer price index	92.2	100.0	107.2	115.7	132.3	147.2	166.3

Household income and expenditure. Average household size (2004) 6.2.
Selected balance of payments data. Receipts from (U.S.$'000,000): tourism (2009) 299; remittances (2010) 3,240; foreign direct investment (FDI; 2008–10 avg.) 2,294; official development assistance (2009) 2,289. Disbursements for (U.S.$'000,000): tourism (2009) 868; remittances (2007) 2; FDI (2008–10 avg.) 67.
Land use as % of total land area (2009): in temporary crops 7.6%, left fallow 0.8%, in permanent crops 0.1%, in pasture 49.0%, forest area 29.5%.

Foreign trade[20]

Balance of trade (current prices)

	2005	2006	2007	2008	2009	2010
U.S.$'000,000	–1,940	–2,417	+104	+2,319	–1,434	+1,359
% of total	16.7%	17.6%	0.6%	11.0%	7.5%	6.3%

Imports (2010): U.S.$10,045,000,000 (machinery and equipment 23.4%, manufactured goods 20.3%, transport equipment 12.2%, wheat and wheat flour 9.7%, petroleum products 4.3%). *Major import sources:* China 20.7%; Saudi Arabia 9.4%; U.A.E. 5.8%; Romania 5.6%; Japan 4.7%; India 4.7%.
Exports (2010): U.S.$11,404,000,000 (crude petroleum 82.5%, gold 8.9%, sesame seeds 1.5%, livestock 1.2%, cotton 0.4%, gum arabic 0.2%). *Major export destinations:* China 72.6%; U.A.E. 11.5%; Japan 4.3%; Singapore 1.7%.

Transport and communications

Transport. Railroads (2008): route length 3,623 mi, 5,831 km; passenger-km 52,000,000; metric ton-km cargo 919,000,000. Roads (2000): total length 7,394 mi, 11,900 km (paved 36%). Vehicles (2002): passenger cars 47,300; trucks and buses 62,500. Air transport (2008): passenger-km 992,000,000; metric ton-km cargo 46,000,000.

Communications

Medium	date	number in '000s	units per 1,000 persons	Medium	date	number in '000s	units per 1,000 persons
Televisions	2003	12,886	352	PCs	2007	4,528	112
Telephones				Dailies	2009	96[21]	2.2[21]
Cellular	2010	17,654[22]	405[22]	Internet users	2009	4,200	99
Landline	2010	375	8.6	Broadband	2010	165[22]	3.8[22]

Education and health

Educational attainment: n.a. *Literacy* (2008): total population age 15 and over literate 69.3%; males 79.0%; females 59.6%.

Education (2008–09)

	teachers	students	student/ teacher ratio	enrollment rate (%)
Primary (age 6–11)	123,633	4,744,468	38.4	41[23]
Secondary/Voc. (age 12–16)	82,665	1,837,456	22.2	...
Tertiary	4,486[24]	508,233[25]	45.5[24]	6[24] (age 17–21)

Health (2008): physicians 8,642 (1 per 4,823 persons); hospital beds 29,114 (1 per 1,432 persons); infant mortality rate (2009) 74.4; undernourished population (2004–06) 7,500,000 (20% of total population based on the consumption of a minimum daily requirement of 1,770 calories).

Military

Total active duty personnel (November 2010): 109,300 (army 96.1%, navy 1.2%, air force 2.7%)[26]; paramilitary 17,500. *Military expenditure as percentage of GDP* (2009): 1.3%; per capita expenditure U.S.$16.

[1]Alternately known as The Sudan. [2]Data prior to 2011 include the newly created South Sudan unless otherwise noted. [3]Includes 2 observers from Abyei Area Council, who do not have voting rights. [4]Comprehensive peace agreement ending 21-year-long war in southern Sudan signed Jan. 9, 2005; interim constitution from July 9, 2005, to be effective for 6 years. [5]Council of States meets in Khartoum; National Assembly meets in Omdurman; Juba is an alternating seat of "the interim power-sharing government." [6]Official working language per 2005 interim constitution. [7]Islamic law and custom are applicable to Muslims only. [8]The Sudanese pound (SDG) replaced the Sudanese dinar (SDD) on Jan. 10, 2007; 1 SDG = 100 SDD. [9]Excludes South Sudan. [10]Preliminary. [11]The creation of two additional states, Central and Eastern Darfur, was approved in 2011, but they were not yet operational in December. [12]Includes disputed Abyei area. [13]4.9 million Sudanese internally displaced in January 2010 and an estimated 285,500 were refugees in eastern Chad. [14]Estimate of U.S. Bureau of the Census (June 2010 update). [15]Population of 2008 urban agglomeration (including Omdurman and Khartoum North) is 8.0 million including 1.2 to 1.5 million internally displaced persons. [16]FAO estimate. [17]Import duties. [18]2008 revised reported figure. [19]Estimates of ILO. [20]Imports c.i.f.; exports f.o.b. [21]Circulation of daily newspapers. [22]Subscribers. [23]2006–07. [24]1999–2000. [25]2007–08. [26]Foreign troops (t), police (p; September 2011): Darfur—African Union/UN hybrid peacekeeping force (t) 17,763, (p) 5,159.

Internet resources for further information:
- **Central Bank of Sudan http://www.cbos.gov.sd**
- **Central Bureau of Statistics http://cbs.gov.sd**

Sudan, South

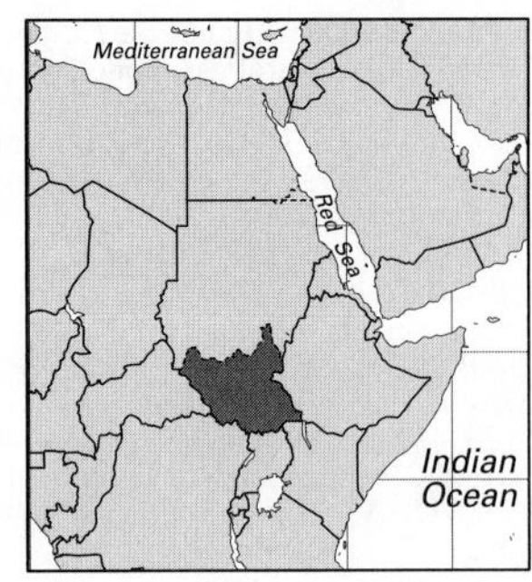

Official name: The Republic of South Sudan.
Form of government: republic with two legislative bodies (National Legislative Assembly [332[1]]; Council of States [50[2]]).
Head of state and government: President.
Capital: Juba.[3]
Official language: English[4].
Official religion: none.
Monetary unit: South Sudan pound (n.a.)[5, 6]; valuation (n.a.).

Area and population

		area		population
States	**Capitals**	sq mi	sq km	2010 estimate
Central Equatoria	Juba	16,615	43,033	1,199,805
Eastern Equatoria	Torit	28,368	73,472	965,819
Jonglei	Bor	47,329	122,581	1,448,158
Lakes	Rumbek	16,832	43,595	790,972
Northern Bahr el Ghazal	Aweil	11,793	30,543	831,014
Unity	Bentiu	14,609	37,837	650,715
Upper Nile	Malakal	29,839	77,283	1,015,392
Warab (Warrap)	Kuajok	17,593	45,567	1,049,891
Western Bahr el Ghazal	Wau	35,165	91,076	360,145
Western Equatoria	Yambio	30,634	79,343	661,696
TOTAL		248,777	644,330	8,973,607

Demography

Population (2011): 9,150,000.
Density (2011): persons per sq mi 36.8, persons per sq km 14.2.
Urban-rural (2011): urban 17%; rural 83%.
Sex distribution (2008): male 51.90%; female 48.10%.
Age breakdown (2008): under 15, 44.4%; 15–29, 27.7%; 30–44, 16.5%; 45–59, 7.3%; 60–74, 3.1%; 75–84, 0.7%; 85 and over, 0.3%.
Population projection: (2020) 11,433,000; (2030) 14,217,000.
Ethnic composition (2008): Dinka *c.* 38%; Nuer *c.* 17%; Zande *c.* 10%; Bari *c.* 10%; Shilluk/Anywa *c.* 10%; Arab *c.* 4%; other *c.* 11%.
Religious affiliation (2010): Christian, roughly 60%[7]; remainder, roughly 40%[8].
Major towns (2008)[9]: Yei 111,268; Yambio 105,881; Juba 82,346; Aweil 59,217; Bentiu 41,328; Wau, n.a.; Malakal, n.a.

Vital statistics

Birth rate per 1,000 population: n.a. (world avg. 20.3).
Death rate per 1,000 population: n.a. (world avg. 8.5).
Natural increase rate per 1,000 population: n.a. (world avg. 11.8).
Total fertility rate (avg. births per childbearing woman; 2009): 6.79.
Marriage/divorce rates per 1,000 population: n.a.
Life expectancy at birth (2009): 42 years.
Major causes of death per 100,000 population: n.a.

National economy

Budget (2009). Revenue: SDG 6,276,000,000 (oil-sharing revenue with Khartoum governmental authority [including arrears and Abyei oil share] 65.7%; grants 32.4%; personal income tax 1.4%; customs/VAT/other 0.5%). Expenditures: SDG 6,271,000,000 (current expenditure 51.5%; capital expenditure 16.0%; other expenditures per grants 32.5%).
Selected balance of payments data. Receipts from (U.S.$'000,000): tourism, n.a.; remittances, n.a.; foreign direct investment (FDI), n.a.; official development assistance, n.a. Disbursements for (U.S.$'000,000): tourism, n.a.; remittances, n.a.; FDI, n.a.
Production (metric tons except as noted). Agriculture, forestry, fishing (2010): cereals (mostly sorghum [also corn (maize), millet, and rice]) 695,000, other crops include cassava, peanuts (groundnuts), sweet potatoes, okra, cowpeas, tomatoes, and onions; livestock (number of live animals) 14,000,000 goats, 13,000,000 sheep, 11,000,000 cattle; roundwood (2009) 20,720,000 cu m[10], of which fuelwood 90%[10]; fisheries production, n.a. Mining and quarrying (2010): negligible except for oil extraction. Manufacturing (2010): beer and soft drink production began in 2010; other limited production includes roofing tiles. Energy production (consumption): electricity, n.a. (n.a.); coal, none (none); crude petroleum (barrels; 2009) 147,000,000 (n.a.); petroleum products, n.a. (n.a.); natural gas, none (none).
Gross national income (at current market prices; 2007): U.S.$718,000,000 (U.S.$90 per capita).

Origin of gross domestic product (current prices)

	in value '000,000	% of total value	labour force	% of labour force
Agriculture	...	...	...	...[11]
Mining	...	...	...	...
Manufacturing	...	...	...	...
Construction	...	...	...	...
Trade	...	...	...	...
Public utilities	...	...	...	...
Transp. and commun.	...	...	...	...
Finance	...	...	...	...
Pub. admin., defense	...	...	...	...
Services	...	...	...	...
Other	...	...	...	...
TOTAL	...	...	...	...

Public debt (external, outstanding): n.a.
Population economically active: n.a.

Price index (October 2009)

	2009	2010[12]
Consumer price index[13]	100.0	106.5

Household income and expenditure. Average household size (2008) 7; average annual income per household, n.a.; sources of income: agriculture/livestock 41%, wages and salaries 22%, selling firewood/charcoal 15%, selling alcoholic beverages 11%, other 11%; expenditure (2009): food 79%, energy and water 6%, housing and household furnishings 4%, health 3%, clothing 3%, transportation 2%.
Land use (2010): n.a.[14]

Foreign trade

Balance of trade (current prices)

	2005	2006	2007	2008	2009	2010
U.S.$'000,000	...	...	...	...	...	...
% of total	...	...	...	...	...	...

Imports (2009): n.a. *Major import sources:* n.a.
Exports (2009): nearly all crude petroleum. *Major export destinations:* n.a.

Transport and communications

Transport. Railroads (2010): route length 151 mi, 243 km[15]; passenger-km, none; metric ton-km cargo, n.a. Roads (paved only; 2010): total length 31 mi, 50 km[16]. Vehicles: passenger cars, n.a.; trucks and buses, n.a. Air transport: n.a.[17]

Communications

Medium	date	number in '000s	units per 1,000 persons	Medium	date	number in '000s	units per 1,000 persons
Televisions	2009	...	...	PCs	2009	...	...
Telephones				Dailies	2009	—	—
Cellular	2009	...	...	Internet users	2009	...	...
Landline	2009	...	...	Broadband	2009	...	...

Education and health

Educational attainment: n.a. *Literacy* (2009): total population age 15 and over literate *c.* 27%; males literate *c.* 40%; females literate *c.* 16%.

Education (2009)

	teachers	students	student/ teacher ratio	enrollment rate (%)
Primary (age 6–13)	...	1,380,580	52	48
Secondary/Voc. (age 14–17)	...	44,027		
Tertiary[18]	...	1,200	...	... (age 18–22)

Health (2010): physicians 34[19] (1 per 262,000 persons); hospital beds, n.a.; infant mortality rate per 1,000 live births (2009) 102; undernourished population (2009) 4,090,000 (47% of total population based on the consumption of a minimum daily requirement of 1,717 calories).

Military

Total active duty personnel: [20]; UN peacekeeping personnel (September 2011): troops 5,109; police 374. *Military expenditure as percentage of GDP:* n.a.

[1]Includes 66 members appointed by various political parties; the remainder is composed of 170 former Southern Sudan Legislative Assembly members and 96 former members of the Sudanese National Assembly. [2]Includes 30 members appointed by the president; the remainder are former members of the Council of States of Sudan. [3]The transferring of the capital to Ramciel was approved in late 2011 to be implemented in phases. [4]English is the official working language of South Sudan; according to the constitution "all indigenous languages are national languages and shall be respected, developed, and promoted." [5]The South Sudan pound was entered into circulation on July 18, 2011; it replaced the Sudanese pound (SDG) as the official currency. [6]The U.S. dollar along with the currencies of Kenya, Ethiopia, and Uganda circulate in South Sudan when available. [7]Significantly Roman Catholic, Anglican, and Presbyterian. [8]Traditional believers outnumber Muslims. [9]Limited to places designated as towns in 2008 census. [10]Combined production total for Sudan/South Sudan; most roundwood by far is harvested from South Sudan. [11]Primary source of livelihood of 78% of households. [12]October. [13]Juba only. [14]A significant part of South Sudan forms the world's largest contiguous swamp. [15]Approximate length of the South Sudan portion of the 446 km Babanusa, Sudan–Wau, South Sudan railway; this freight railway reopened in 2010. [16]More than 317 mi (510 km) of roads linking Juba to state capitals were rehabilitated between 2005 and 2011. [17]Transport is mainly undertaken by barges on the White Nile River and its tributaries. [18]University of Juba only. [19]South Sudanese doctors practicing in South Sudan; foreign doctors are excluded from the total. [20]Estimated strength of local paramilitary is unknown.

Internet resource for further information:
- **The Republic of South Sudan National Bureau of Statistics http://ssnbs.org**

Suriname

Official name: Republiek Suriname (Republic of Suriname).
Form of government: multiparty republic with one legislative house (National Assembly [51]).
Head of state and government: President.
Capital: Paramaribo.
Official language: Dutch.
Official religion: none.
Monetary unit: Suriname dollar (SRD)[1]; valuation (Sept. 1, 2011) 1 U.S.$ = SRD 3.30; 1 £ = SRD 5.33.

Area and population

Districts	Capitals	area sq mi	area sq km	population 2004 census
Brokopondo	Brokopondo	2,843	7,364	14,215
Commewijne	Nieuw Amsterdam	908	2,353	24,649
Coronie	Totness	1,507	3,902	2,887
Marowijne	Albina	1,786	4,627	16,642
Nickerie	Nieuw Nickerie	2,067	5,353	36,639
Para	Onverwacht	2,082	5,393	18,749
Saramacca	Groningen	1,404	3,636	15,980
Sipaliwini	[2]	50,412	130,567	34,136
Wanica	Lelydorp	171	443	85,986
Town district				
Paramaribo	Paramaribo	70	182	242,946
TOTAL		63,251[3, 4]	163,820[3]	492,829

Demography

Population (2011): 529,000.
Density (2011): persons per sq mi 8.4, persons per sq km 3.2.
Urban-rural (2009): urban 68.9%; rural 31.1%.
Sex distribution (2006): male 49.71%; female 50.29%.
Age breakdown (2006): under 15, 28.5%; 15–29, 26.8%; 30–44, 24.3%; 45–59, 12.0%; 60–74, 6.2%; 75 and over, 2.2%.
Population projection: (2020) 569,000; (2030) 602,000.
Doubling time: 64 years.
Ethnic composition (2004): Indo-Pakistani ("Hindustani") 27.4%; Suriname Creole ("Afro-Surinamese") 17.7%; Maroon (descendants of runaway slaves living in the interior) 14.7%; Javanese ("Indonesian") 14.6%; mixed race 12.5%; Amerindian *c.* 1.5%; other/unknown *c.* 11.6%.
Religious affiliation (2004): Christian (mostly Roman Catholic and Moravian) 40.7%; Hindu 19.9%; Muslim 13.5%; nonreligious 4.4%; traditional beliefs 3.3%; other 2.5%; unknown 15.7%.
Major city/towns (2004): Paramaribo 242,946; Nieuw Nickerie 13,842; Nieuw Amsterdam 5,489.

Vital statistics

Birth rate per 1,000 population (2009): 18.7 (world avg. 20.3).
Death rate per 1,000 population (2009): 7.5 (world avg. 8.5).
Natural increase rate per 1,000 population (2009): 11.2 (world avg. 11.8).
Total fertility rate (avg. births per childbearing woman; 2009): 2.37.
Marriage/divorce rates per 1,000 population (2007): 4.2/1.3.
Life expectancy at birth (2009): male 65.7 years; female 72.9 years.
Major causes of death per 100,000 population (2002): diseases of the circulatory system 265; communicable diseases 172; malignant neoplasms (cancers) 87; injuries 76; diabetes mellitus 32.

National economy

Budget (2007). Revenue: SRD 2,002,000,000 (tax revenue 79.1%, of which corporate taxes 22.0%, taxes on international trade 21.5%, income tax 15.4%; nontax revenue 16.0%; grants 4.9%). Expenditures: SRD 1,806,500,000 (current expenditures 87.5%, of which wages and salaries 37.6%, transfers 12.0%, interest 5.2%; capital expenditures 12.5%).
Public debt (external, outstanding; 2007): U.S.$161,100,000.
Production (metric tons except as noted). Agriculture, forestry, fishing (2009): rice 195,000, sugarcane 120,000, bananas 91,997, oranges 12,939, plantains 9,002, coconuts 6,192, cassava 2,761; livestock (number of live animals) 50,000 cattle, 27,127 pigs, 5,300,000 chickens; roundwood (2010) 254,947 cu m, of which fuelwood 18%; fisheries production 25,872 (from aquaculture, negligible). Mining and quarrying (2010): bauxite 4,000,000; alumina 1,083,000; gold 12,286 kg[5]. Manufacturing (2007): residual fuel oils 360,000; cement (2004) 65,000; distillate fuel oil 41,000; beer (2008) 21,000; coconut oil 870. Energy production (consumption): electricity (kW-hr; 2007) 1,618,000,000 (1,618,000,000); coal, none (none); crude petroleum (barrels; 2007) 4,100,000 (3,480,000); petroleum products (metric tons; 2007) 401,000 (624,000); natural gas, none (none).
Land use as % of total land area (2009): in temporary crops or left fallow 0.4%, in permanent crops 0.04%, in pasture 0.1%, forest area 94.7%.
Population economically active (2008): total 189,000[6]; activity rate of total population 36.7%[6] (participation rates: ages 15–64, 56.5%[6]; female 36.5%[6]; unemployed [2007] 11.0%).

Price index (2005 = 100)

	2004	2005	2006	2007	2008	2009	2010
Consumer price index	91.0	100.0	111.3	118.4	135.8	135.7	145.1

Gross national income (2009): U.S.$2,976,000,000 (U.S.$5,726 per capita).

Structure of gross domestic product and labour force

	2006 in value SRD '000,000	2006 % of total value	2004 labour force	2004 % of labour force
Agriculture, forestry, fishing	272,799	4.7	12,593	7.3
Mining and quarrying	687,804	11.9	9,308	5.4
Manufacturing	749,826	12.9	10,971	6.3
Construction	176,858	3.1	14,031	8.1
Public utilities	274,092	4.7	1,659	1.0
Transp. and commun.	459,316	7.9	8,711	5.0
Trade, hotels	633,094	10.9	29,845	17.2
Finance, real estate	600,206	10.3	9,073	5.2
Pub. admin., defense	553,809	9.5	27,995	16.2
Services	66,952	1.2	25,063	14.5
Informal sector[7]	808,561	13.9	…	…
Other	519,148[8]	9.0[8]	23,881[9]	13.8[9]
TOTAL	5,802,465	100.0	173,130	100.0

Household income and expenditure (2004). Average household size 4.0; average disposable income per household SRD 32,150 (U.S.$11,760); sources of income: n.a.; expenditure (2000)[10]: food and beverages 40.0%, housing, energy, and household furnishings 23.6%, clothing and footwear 11.0%.
Selected balance of payments data. Receipts from (U.S.$'000,000): tourism (2009) 64; remittances (2010) 4; foreign direct investment (2008–10 avg.) 180; official development assistance (2009) 157. Disbursements for (U.S.$'000,000): tourism (2009) 32; remittances (2009) 8.

Foreign trade[11]

Balance of trade (current prices)

	2004	2005	2006	2007	2008
U.S.$'000,000	+67.8	–52.5	+161.5	+314.8	+439.1
% of total	4.4%	2.6%	7.4%	13.1%	14.4%

Imports (2008): U.S.$1,304,000,000 (machinery and apparatus 14.6%, refined petroleum 14.6%, road vehicles 10.0%, food products 7.9%, unspecified 24.8%). *Major import sources* (2008): U.S. 24.0%; Trinidad and Tobago 20.6%; Netherlands 20.0%; China 8.0%; Japan 4.5%.
Exports (2007): U.S.$1,541,000,000 (alumina 41.9%, gold 31.7%, crude petroleum 7.0%, shrimp and fish 6.4%, rice 1.2%). *Major export destinations* (2007): Canada 23.0%; Norway 14.4%; U.S. 12.1%; Trinidad and Tobago 7.2%; France 5.4%; unspecified 29.3%.

Transport and communications

Transport. Railroads (2009): none[12]. Roads (2003): total length 2,674 mi, 4,304 km (paved 26%). Vehicles (2006): passenger cars 81,778; trucks and buses 28,774. Air transport (2008)[13]: passenger-km 958,323,000; metric ton-km cargo 25,794,000.

Communications

Medium	date	number in '000s	units per 1,000 persons	Medium	date	number in '000s	units per 1,000 persons
Televisions	2003	118	243	PCs	2001	20	45
Telephones				Dailies	2009	55[14]	157[14]
Cellular	2010	890[15]	1,696[15]	Internet users	2009	163	314
Landline	2010	85	162	Broadband	2010	16[15]	30[15]

Education and health

Educational attainment: n.a. *Literacy* (2008): total population age 15 and over literate 90.7%; males literate 93.0%; females literate 88.4%.

Education (2006–07)

	teachers	students	student/ teacher ratio	enrollment rate (%)
Primary (age 6–11)	4,913	65,020	13.2	94
Secondary/Voc. (age 12–18)	3,373	47,235	14.0	68[16]
Tertiary[17]	550	5,186	9.4	12 (age 19–23)

Health: physicians (2008) 460 (1 per 1,120 persons); hospital beds (2005) 1,797 (1 per 278 persons); infant mortality rate per 1,000 live births (2009) 21.6; undernourished population (2006–08) 100,000 (15% of total population based on the consumption of a minimum daily requirement of 1,870 calories).

Military

Total active duty personnel (November 2010): 1,840[18] (army 76.1%, navy 13.0%, air force 10.9%). *Military expenditure as percentage of GDP* (2008): 1.3%; per capita expenditure U.S.$60.

[1]The Suriname dollar (SRD) replaced the Suriname guilder (SRG) on Jan. 1, 2004, at a rate of 1 SRD = SRG 1,000. [2]No capital; administered from Paramaribo. [3]Area excludes 6,809 sq mi (17,635 sq km) of territory disputed with Guyana. [4]Detail does not add to total given because of rounding. [5]Recorded production; unrecorded production may be as high as 30,000 kg. [6]Estimate of the ILO Employment Trends Unit. [7]Smuggling or unregulated activities in such areas as gold mining and tree removal. [8]Indirect taxes less subsidies and less imputed bank service charges. [9]Includes 16,425 unemployed. [10]Weights of consumer price index components. [11]Imports c.i.f.; exports f.o.b. [12]75-km railway for bauxite ore transport was unused. [13]Surinam Airways only. [14]Circulation of daily newspapers. [15]Subscribers. [16]2004–05. [17]2001–02. [18]All services are part of the army.

Internet resource for further information:
- **General Bureau of Statistics http://www.statistics-suriname.org**

Swaziland

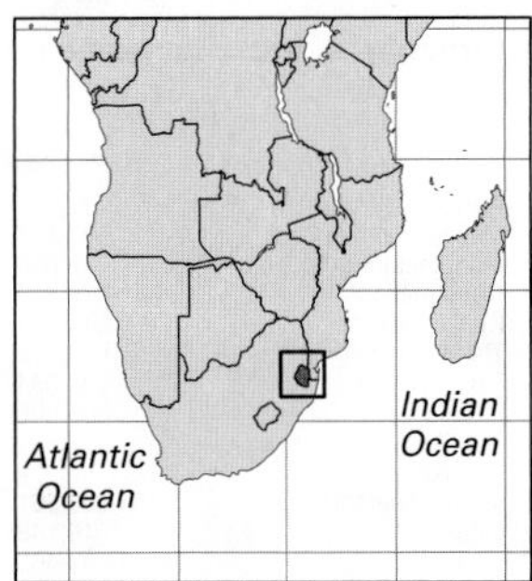

Official name: Umbuso weSwatini (Swati); Kingdom of Swaziland (English).
Form of government: monarchy[1] with two legislative houses (Senate [30[2]]; House of Assembly [66[3]]).
Head of state and government: King, assisted by Prime Minister.
Capitals: Mbabane (administrative and judicial); Lobamba (legislative)[4].
Official languages: Swati (Swazi); English.
Official religion: none.
Monetary unit: lilangeni[5] (plural emalangeni [E]); valuation (Sept. 1, 2011) 1 U.S.$ = E 7.01; 1 £ = E 11.32.

Area and population		area		population
				2007
Districts	**Capitals**	sq mi	sq km	census
Hhohho	Mbabane	1,378	3,569	282,734
Lubombo	Siteki	2,296	5,947	207,731
Manzini	Manzini	1,571	4,068	319,530
Shiselweni	Nhlangano	1,459	3,780	208,454
TOTAL		6,704	17,364	1,018,449

Demography

Population (2011): 1,203,000.
Density (2011): persons per sq mi 179.4, persons per sq km 69.3.
Urban-rural (2010): urban 21.4%; rural 78.6%.
Sex distribution (2008): male 49.60%; female 50.40%.
Age breakdown (2008): under 15, 38.9%; 15–29, 31.5%; 30–44, 15.8%; 45–59, 8.6%; 60–74, 4.2%; 75–84, 0.9%; 85 and over, 0.1%.
Population projection: (2020) 1,341,000; (2030) 1,462,000.
Ethnic composition (2000): Swazi 82.3%; Zulu 9.6%; Tsonga 2.3%; Afrikaner 1.4%; mixed (black-white) 1.0%; other 3.4%.
Religious affiliation (2006): Protestant *c.* 35%; syncretistic Christianity/traditional beliefs *c.* 30%; Roman Catholic *c.* 25%; Muslim *c.* 1%; other (including Bahā'ī and Mormon) *c.* 9%.
Major towns (2006): Manzini (urban agglomeration) 115,200; Mbabane (2009) 73,815; Lobamba 11,000; Big Bend 10,400; Malkerns 10,000.

Vital statistics

Birth rate per 1,000 population (2010): 29.2 (world avg. 19.2).
Death rate per 1,000 population (2010): 15.1 (world avg. 8.2).
Total fertility rate (avg. births per childbearing woman; 2010): 3.19.
Life expectancy at birth (2010): male 48.1 years; female 47.8 years.
Adult population (ages 15–49) *living with HIV* (2009): 25.9%[6] (world avg. 0.8%).
Major causes of death per 100,000 population (2002): infectious and parasitic diseases *c.* 1,846, of which HIV/AIDS-related *c.* 1,560, tuberculosis *c.* 94; cardiovascular diseases *c.* 138; respiratory infections *c.* 126; malignant neoplasms (cancers) *c.* 71.

National economy

Budget (2010–11). Revenue: E 7,260,400,000 (receipts from Customs Union of Southern Africa 36.2%, income tax 19.2%, sales taxes 16.2%, corporate taxes 11.3%, grants 7.3%). Expenditures: E 10,347,400,000 (general administration 20.7%, education 20.2%, police/defense 16.1%, health 12.4%, transportation and communications 10.4%, agriculture 5.2%).
Public debt (external; March 2011): U.S.$354,467,000[7].
Gross national income (GNI; 2010): U.S.$3,119,000,000 (U.S.$2,600 per capita); purchasing power parity GNI (U.S.$4,890 per capita).

Structure of gross domestic product and labour force	2008		2005	
	in value E '000,000	% of total value	labour force[8]	% of labour force[8]
Agriculture	1,460	5.9	42,455[9]	12.8[9]
Mining	52	0.2	1,283	0.4
Manufacturing	7,816	31.3	20,272	6.1
Construction	551	2.2	5,115	1.5
Public utilities	175	0.7	859	0.3
Transp. and commun.	1,363	5.5	3,007	0.9
Trade, hotels	2,007	8.0	11,454	3.5
Finance, real estate	1,850	7.4	6,430	1.9
Pub. admin., defense	3,358	13.5	27,228	8.2
Services	306	1.2		
Other	6,009[10]	24.1[10]	213,697[11]	64.4[11]
TOTAL	24,947	100.0	331,800	100.0

Population economically active (2010): total 477,000; activity rate of total population 40.2% (participation rates: ages 15–64, 70.6%; female 50.1%; unemployed [2007] 40.6%).

Price index (2005 = 100)	2004	2005	2006	2007	2008	2009	2010
Consumer price index	95.4	100.0	105.3	113.8	128.2	137.8	144.0

Land use as % of total land area (2007): in temporary crops or left fallow 10.3%, in permanent crops 0.8%, in pasture 66.9%, forest area 32.0%[12].

Production (metric tons except as noted). Agriculture, forestry, fishing (2009): sugarcane 5,000,000, corn (maize) 60,765, oranges 38,960, grapefruit and pomelos 33,008, pineapples 16,841, bananas 5,403, tomatoes 4,080, peanuts (groundnuts) 3,699, seed cotton 1,115, almonds 769; livestock (number of live animals) 585,000 cattle, 276,000 goats, 3,200,000 chickens; roundwood (2010) 1,375,398 cu m, of which fuelwood 76%; fisheries production 143 (from aquaculture 51%). Mining and quarrying (2010): ferrovanadium (2009) 500; crushed stone 304,844 cu m. Manufacturing (value of exports in E '000,000; 2010–11): apparel and clothing accessories (2002) 1,483.4; sugar 969.3; wood furniture (2002) 100.9; preserved fruit (significantly pineapples) 80.0; unbleached wood pulp, n.a. Energy production (consumption): electricity (kW-hr; 2010) 288,100,000 (1,018,600,000); hard coal (metric tons; 2010) 145,903 ([2007] 223,000); crude petroleum, none (none); petroleum products, none (n.a.); natural gas, none (none).
Household income and expenditure. Average household size (2007) 4.7; average annual income per household (2002) *c.* U.S.$1,540; sources of income: n.a.; expenditure (1996)[13]: food 24.5%, housing 15.9%, household furnishings and operation 13.2%, clothing and footwear 11.0%, transportation and communications 8.2%, education 6.1%.
Selected balance of payments data. Receipts from (U.S.$'000,000): tourism (2009) 40; remittances (2010) 118; foreign direct investment (FDI; 2008–10 avg.) 88; official development assistance (2009) 58. Disbursements for (U.S.$'000,000): tourism (2009) 72; remittances (2008) 8; FDI (2008–10 avg.) 3.

Foreign trade[14]

Balance of trade (current prices)	2003	2004	2005	2006	2007
U.S.$'000,000	+299.3	+400.2	–84.2	+222.7	–81.9
% of total	9.5%	10.0%	2.6%	7.8%	3.6%

Imports (2007): U.S.$1,164,200,000 (food products 18.2%, of which cereals/flour 7.6%; chemicals and chemical products 13.6%; refined petroleum 13.4%; machinery and apparatus 12.5%; road vehicles/parts 6.5%). *Major import sources:* South Africa 92.9%; Namibia 2.2%; Lesotho 1.4%.
Exports (2007): U.S.$1,082,300,000 (essential oils for food/drink industries 29.4%; food 21.0%, of which raw sugar 14.1%; silicates 19.9%; apparel/clothing accessories 4.4%; organic chemicals 4.3%; rough/sawn wood 4.2%). *Major export destinations:* South Africa 45.2%; Botswana 31.6%; U.K. 14.2%; U.S. 3.2%.

Transport and communications

Transport. Railroads (2010): route length 185 mi, 297 km; passenger-km, n.a.[15]; metric ton-km cargo (2006) 730,000,000. Roads (2002): total length 2,233 mi, 3,594 km (paved 30%). Vehicles (2008[16]): passenger cars 52,223; trucks and buses 49,902. Air transport: n.a.[17]

Communications Medium	date	number in '000s	units per 1,000 persons	Medium	date	number in '000s	units per 1,000 persons
Televisions	2003	38	34	PCs	2006	47	37
Telephones				Dailies	2009	25[18]	37[18]
Cellular	2010	733[19]	618[19]	Internet users	2009	90	76
Landline	2010	44	37	Broadband	2010	1.6[19]	1.4[19]

Education and health

Educational attainment (2006–07)[20]. Percentage of population age 25 and over having: no formal schooling 22.3%; incomplete primary education 23.9%; complete primary 10.1%; incomplete/complete secondary 33.6%; higher 8.9%; unknown 1.2%. *Literacy* (2009): total population age 15 and over literate 86.9%; males literate 87.8%; females literate 86.2%.

Education (2009–10)	teachers	students	student/ teacher ratio	enrollment rate (%)
Primary (age 6–12)	7,462	241,237	32.3	86
Secondary/Voc. (age 13–17)	4,883	88,787	18.2	33
Tertiary[21]	462	5,692	12.3	4 (age 18–22)

Health: physicians (2004) 171 (1 per 7,240 persons); hospital beds (2006) 2,688 (1 per 476 persons); infant mortality rate per 1,000 live births (2010) 66.7; undernourished population (2004–06) 230,000 (18% of total population based on the consumption of a minimum daily requirement of 1,790 calories).

Military

Total active duty personnel (2006): *c.* 3,000 troops. *Military expenditure as percentage of GDP* (2004): 1.8%; per capita expenditure U.S.$39.

[1]Controversial constitution became effective by royal decree on Feb. 8, 2006. [2]Includes 20 nonelective seats. [3]Includes 10 nonelective seats and one ex officio seat (the speaker, who may be designated from outside the House of Assembly). [4]Lozitha and Ludzidzini, royal residences close to Lobamba, have national symbolic significance. [5]The lilangeni is pegged to the South African rand at 1 to 1; the rand is accepted as legal tender within Swaziland. [6]Statistically derived midpoint of range. [7]Includes public short-term external debt. [8]Rough estimates. [9]Includes informally employed. [10]Indirect taxes less imputed bank service charges and less subsidies. [11]Includes unemployed. [12]Forest area overlaps with other categories. [13]Weights of consumer price index components. [14]Imports c.i.f.; exports f.o.b. [15]Passenger service is for tourists and private charter only. [16]January 1. [17]Data unavailable for Swaziland Airlink, the national carrier. [18]Circulation of daily newspapers. [19]Subscribers. [20]Based on 4,457 individuals age 25 or over in the Swaziland Demographic and Health Survey 2006–07. [21]2005–06.

Internet resources for further information:
- **Central Bank of Swaziland http://www.centralbank.org.sz**
- **Swaziland Government http://www.gov.sz**

Sweden

Official name: Konungariket Sverige (Kingdom of Sweden).
Form of government: constitutional monarchy with one legislative house (Riksdagen, or Parliament [349]).
Head of state: King.
Head of government: Prime Minister.
Capital: Stockholm.
Official language: Swedish.
Official religion: none.
Monetary unit: Swedish krona (SEK); valuation (Sept. 1, 2011) 1 U.S.$ = SEK 6.39; 1 £ = SEK 10.33.

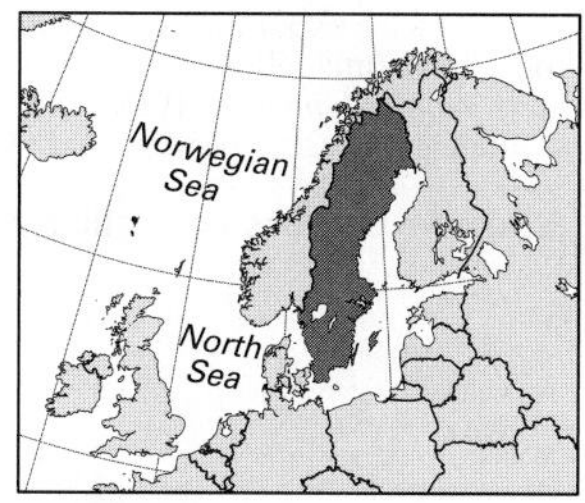

Area and population

Counties	area sq km	population 2011[1] estimate	Counties	area sq km	population 2011[1] estimate
Blekinge	3,055	153,227	Skåne	11,369	1,243,329
Dalarna	30,405	277,047	Södermanland	7,064	270,738
Gävleborg	19,756	276,508	Stockholm	7,169	2,054,343
Gotland	3,184	57,269	Uppsala	8,640	335,882
Halland	5,719	299,484	Värmland	21,923	273,265
Jämtland	54,100	126,691	Västerbotten	59,284	259,286
Jönköping	11,754	336,866	Västernorrland	23,107	242,625
Kalmar	11,694	233,536	Västmanland	5,690	252,756
Kronoberg	9,430	183,940	Västra Götaland	28,944	1,580,297
Norrbotten	106,012	248,609	OTHER UNDISTRIBUTED	22	
Örebro	9,685	280,230	TOTAL	450,295[2]	9,415,570
Östergötland	12,289	429,642			

Demography

Population (2011): 9,451,000.
Density (2011)[3]: persons per sq mi 59.7, persons per sq km 23.0.
Urban-rural (2009): urban 84.6%; rural 15.4%.
Sex distribution (2009[1]): male 49.74%; female 50.26%.
Age breakdown (2009[1]): under 15, 16.7%; 15–29, 19.3%; 30–44, 20.4%; 45–59, 19.1%; 60–74, 15.9%; 75–89, 7.8%; 90 and over, 0.8%.
Population projection: (2020) 9,956,000; (2030) 10,321,000.
Ethnic composition (2009[1])[4]: Swedish 86.2%; other European 7.9%, of which Finnish 1.9%; Asian 3.9%, of which Iraqi 1.2%; other 2.0%.
Religious affiliation (2005): Church of Sweden (including nonpracticing) *c.* 77%; other Protestant *c.* 4.5%; Muslim *c.* 4%; Roman Catholic *c.* 1.5%; Orthodox *c.* 1%; other *c.* 12%.
Major cities (2009[1]): Stockholm 810,120; Göteborg 500,197; Malmö 286,535; Uppsala 190,668; Linköping 141,863.

Vital statistics

Birth rate per 1,000 population (2011[1]): 12.3 (world avg. 19.2); within marriage (2008) 45.4%; outside of marriage (2008) 54.6%.
Death rate per 1,000 population (2011[1]): 9.6 (world avg. 8.2).
Total fertility rate (avg. births per childbearing woman; 2009): 1.94.
Marriage/divorce rates per 1,000 population (2009)[5]: 5.2/2.4.
Life expectancy at birth (2009): male 79.4 years; female 83.4 years.
Major causes of death per 100,000 population (2007): diseases of the circulatory system 415.2, of which ischemic heart disease 183.8; malignant neoplasms (cancers) 247.5; diseases of the respiratory system 62.3.

National economy

Budget (2007). Revenue: SEK 857,200,000,000 (current revenue 95.2%, of which tax revenue 87.7%; capital revenue 2.1%; other 2.7%). Expenditures: SEK 768,604,000,000 (social insurance 37.6%; defense 6.0%; health 5.9%; education 5.7%; debt service 5.4%).
Production (metric tons except as noted). Agriculture, forestry, fishing (2009): cow's milk 2,974,000, sugar beets 2,405,800, wheat 2,284,000, barley 1,676,600, potatoes 854,300, oats 750,000, rapeseed 298,400, pig meat 260,700, triticale 255,400, blueberries 2,600; livestock (number of live animals) 1,538,280 cattle, 1,528,740 pigs, 540,490 sheep, (2006) 254,893 reindeer; roundwood (2010) 70,200,000 cu m, of which fuelwood 8%; fisheries production 211,953 (from aquaculture 4%). Mining and quarrying (2009): iron ore 11,300,000[6]; zinc 192,538[6]; copper 46,019[6]; silver 290,000 kg[6]. Manufacturing (value added in SEK '000,000[7]; 2007): electrical machinery, telecommunications equipment, and electronics 243,346; transportation equipment 81,295; nonelectrical machinery 70,506; chemicals and chemical products 63,716; paper and paper products 46,860; fabricated metal products 44,637; food, beverages, and tobacco 36,518; base metals 26,466. Energy production (consumption): electricity (kW-hr; 2010–11[8]) 143,232,000,000 ([2008] 159,114,000,000); coal (metric tons; 2007) none (3,192,000); crude petroleum (barrels; 2008) none (128,417,950); petroleum products (metric tons; 2007) 15,329,000 (10,491,000); natural gas (cu m; 2008) none (913,000,000).
Household income and expenditure (2009). Average household size 2.1; average annual disposable income per household (2008) SEK 325,200 (U.S.$49,339); sources of gross income (2004): wages and salaries 60.2%, transfer payments 30.7%, self-employment 2.8%; expenditure: housing and energy 25.4%, recreation and culture 19.4%, transportation 15.4%, food and nonalcoholic beverages 13.6%, household furnishings 5.8%.
Selected balance of payments data. Receipts from (U.S.$'000,000): tourism (2009) 10,275; remittances (2010) 690; foreign direct investment (FDI; 2008–10 avg.) 17,473. Disbursements for (U.S.$'000,000): tourism (2009) 11,856; remittances (2009) 757; FDI (2008–10 avg.) 29,168.
Gross national income (GNI; 2010): U.S.$469,002,000,000 (U.S.$49,930 per capita); purchasing power parity GNI (U.S.$39,600 per capita).

Structure of gross domestic product and labour force

	2009 in value SEK '000,000	2009 % of total value	2008 labour force	2008 % of labour force
Agriculture, forestry, fishing	40,616	1.3	101,000	2.1
Mining and quarrying	12,046	0.4	9,000	0.2
Manufacturing	445,240	14.6	655,000	13.4
Public utilities	88,391	2.9	24,000	0.5
Construction	137,501	4.5	306,000	6.2
Transp. and commun.	165,685	5.4	275,000	5.6
Trade, hotels	364,840	11.9	711,000	14.5
Finance, real estate	656,172	21.5	791,000	16.2
Pub. admin., defense	564,916	18.5	261,000	5.3
Services	189,810	6.2	1,455,000	29.7
Other	391,839[9]	12.8[9]	310,000[10]	6.3[10]
TOTAL	3,057,056	100.0	4,898,000	100.0

Population economically active (2010[11]): total 4,939,000; activity rate of total population 52.6% (participation rates: ages 15–74, 70.2%; female [2008] 47.4%; unemployed [September 2011] 6.8%).

Price and earnings indexes (2005 = 100)

	2004	2005	2006	2007	2008	2009	2010
Consumer price index	99.5	100.0	101.4	103.6	107.2	106.6	107.9
Hourly earnings index	97.1	100.0	103.0	106.6	111.0	113.3	117.0

Public debt (2010): U.S.$158,124,000,000.
Land use as % of total land area (2009): in temporary crops (2007) 6.4%, left fallow 0.4%, in permanent crops 0.02%, in pasture 1.1%, forest area 68.7%.

Foreign trade[12]

Balance of trade (current prices)

	2005	2006	2007	2008	2009	2010
SEK '000,000	+143,500	+149,900	+105,200	+96,500	+83,900	+71,100
% of total	7.9%	7.4%	4.8%	4.2%	4.4%	3.2%

Imports (2008): SEK 1,103,048,000,000 (machinery and apparatus 24.5%, crude petroleum 12.5%, chemicals and chemical products 10.8%, base and fabricated metals 9.6%, road vehicles/parts 9.4%). *Major import sources* (2009): Germany 17.9%; Denmark 9.0%; Norway 9.0%; Netherlands 6.5%; U.K. 5.7%; Finland 5.2%.
Exports (2008): SEK 1,211,818,000,000 (machinery and apparatus 27.2%, road vehicles/parts 10.8%, refined petroleum 6.3%, iron and steel 5.9%, paper and cardboard 5.8%, medicines and pharmaceuticals 5.0%). *Major export destinations* (2009): Norway 10.6%; Germany 10.2%; U.K. 7.4%; Denmark 7.3%; Finland 6.4%; U.S. 6.4%.

Transport and communications

Transport. Railroads (2008): length 7,228 mi, 11,633 km; passenger-km 11,017,000,000; metric ton-km cargo 23,243,000,000. Roads (2010[1]): total length 361,053 mi, 581,059 km[13] (paved [2007] 32%); passenger-km (2006) 105,700,000,000[14]; metric ton-km cargo (2008) 31,336,000,000. Vehicles (2010[1]): passenger cars 4,300,752; trucks and buses 528,000. Air transport (2008)[15]: passenger-km 6,339,000,000; metric ton-km cargo 2,200,000.

Communications

Medium	date	number in '000s	units per 1,000 persons	Medium	date	number in '000s	units per 1,000 persons
Televisions	2003	8,645	965	PCs	2005	7,548	836
Telephones				Dailies	2009	3,205[16]	345[16]
Cellular	2010	10,650[17]	1,135[17]	Internet users	2009	8,398	908
Landline	2010	5,014	535	Broadband	2010	2,963[17]	316[17]

Education and health

Educational attainment (2008). Percentage of population age 16–74 having: incomplete or complete primary education 7.6%; lower secondary 15.0%; upper secondary 44.5%; vocational and higher 30.9%; unknown 2.0%.

Education (2007–08)

	teachers	students	student/ teacher ratio	enrollment rate (%)
Primary (age 7–12)	61,220	584,726	9.6	95
Secondary/Voc. (age 13–18)	78,978	764,264	9.7	99
Tertiary	36,569	406,879	11.1	71 (age 19–23)

Health (2008): physicians 29,100 (1 per 317 persons); hospital beds 25,889 (1 per 356 persons); infant mortality rate per 1,000 live births (2009) 2.5; undernourished population (2004–06) less than 5.0% of total population.

Military

Total active duty personnel (November 2010): 21,070 (army 34.8%, navy 16.2%, air force 17.9%, staff 31.1%); reserve 200,000; paramilitary 800. *Military expenditure as percentage of GDP* (2009): 1.3%[18]; per capita expenditure U.S.$570[18].

[1]January 1. [2]Land area equals 410,335 sq km; inland water area equals 39,960 sq km. [3]Density based on land area only. [4]Foreign-born persons or those with both parents born abroad are identified by country of origin. [5]From May 1, 2009, includes same-sex marriages. [6]Metal content. [7]At constant prices of 2000. [8]July 2010–June 2011. [9]Taxes less subsidies. [10]Includes 305,000 unemployed. [11]October. [12]Imports c.i.f.; exports f.o.b. [13]Of which open to the public 137,237 mi (220,862 km) in 2010. [14]Passenger cars 97,000,000,000; buses 8,700,000,000. [15]Swedish part of SAS, Malmö Aviation, Skyways, City Airline, and Golden Air only. [16]Circulation. [17]Subscribers. [18]Excluding civil defense.

Internet resources for further information:
- **Statistics Sweden http://www.scb.se**
- **Sveriges Riksbank http://www.riksbank.com**

Switzerland

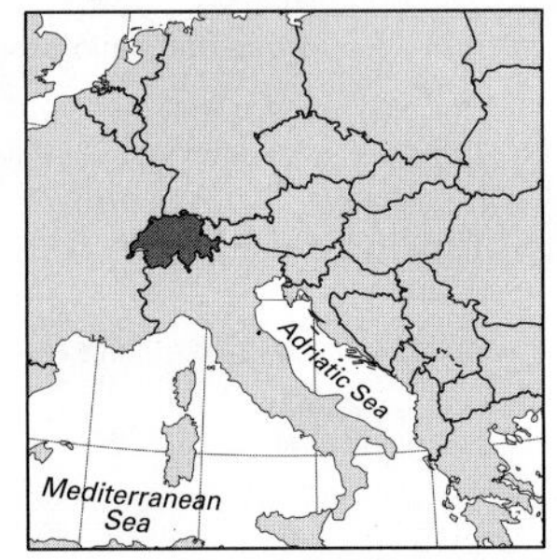

Official name: Swiss Confederation[1].
Form of government: federal state with two legislative houses (Council of States [46]; National Council [200]).
Head of state and government: President of the Federal Council.
Capital: Bern[2].
Official languages: French; German; Italian; Romansh (locally).
Official religion: none.
Monetary unit: Swiss franc (CHF); valuation (Sept. 1, 2011) 1 U.S.$ = CHF 0.80; 1 £ = CHF 1.29.

Area and population

Cantons	area sq km	population 2010 census[3]	Cantons	area sq km	population 2010 census[3]
Aargau	1,404	611,466	Nidwalden	276	41,024
Appenzell Ausser-Rhoden	243	53,017	Obwalden	491	35,585
Appenzell Inner-Rhoden	173	15,688	Sankt Gallen	2,026	478,907
Basel-Landschaft	518	274,404	Schaffhausen	298	76,356
Basel-Stadt	37	184,950	Schwyz	908	146,730
Bern	5,959	979,802	Solothurn	791	255,284
Fribourg	1,671	278,493	Thurgau	991	248,444
Genève	282	457,715	Ticino	2,812	333,753
Glarus	685	38,608	Uri	1,077	35,422
Graubünden	7,105	192,621	Valais	5,224	312,684
Jura	839	70,032	Vaud	3,212	713,281
Luzern	1,493	377,610	Zug	239	113,105
Neuchâtel	803	172,085	Zürich	1,729	1,373,068
			TOTAL	41,285[4]	7,870,134

Demography

Population (2011): 7,913,000.
Density (2011): persons per sq mi 496.4, persons per sq km 191.7.
Urban-rural (2009[5]): urban 73.6%; rural 26.4%.
Sex distribution (2010[3]): male 49.26%; female 50.74%.
Age breakdown (2009[5]): under 15, 15.3%; 15–29, 18.4%; 30–44, 22.7%; 45–59, 21.1%; 60–74, 14.5%; 75–84, 5.7%; 85 and over, 2.3%.
Population projection: (2020) 8,402,000; (2030) 8,761,000.
National composition (2008[5]): Swiss 78.9%; Italian 3.8%; German 2.7%; Serb/Montenegrin 2.5%; Portuguese 2.4%; Turkish 1.0%; other 8.7%.
Religious affiliation (2000): Roman Catholic 41.8%; Protestant 33.0%; Muslim 4.3%; Orthodox 1.8%; Jewish 0.2%; nonreligious 11.1%; other 7.8%.
Major urban agglomerations (2010[3]): Zürich 1,373,068; Geneva 526,442; Basel 497,725; Bern 353,255; Lausanne 336,364; Luzern 209,796.

Vital statistics

Birth rate per 1,000 population (2009): 10.1 (world avg. 20.3); within marriage 82.1%; outside of marriage 17.9%.
Death rate per 1,000 population (2009): 8.1 (world avg. 8.5).
Total fertility rate (avg. births per childbearing woman; 2009): 1.50.
Marriage/divorce rates per 1,000 population (2009): 5.4/2.5.
Life expectancy at birth (2009): male 79.8 years; female 84.4 years.
Major causes of death per 100,000 population (2007): diseases of the circulatory system 299.5; malignant neoplasms (cancers) 212.2; diseases of the respiratory system 49.4; mental and behavioral disorders 41.2.

National economy

Budget (2007)[6]. Revenue: CHF 165,097,000,000 (tax revenue 59.1%, of which taxes on income and wealth 39.6%; nontax revenue 22.2%; social security obligations 18.7%). Expenditures: CHF 170,738,000,000 (social security/welfare 35.2%; education 16.2%; health 11.3%; transport 8.4%; defense 2.9%).
Production (metric tons except as noted). Agriculture, forestry, fishing (2009): cow's milk 4,073,100, sugar beets 1,719,710, potatoes 517,000, apples 252,086, pig meat 237,633, cattle meat 141,650, grapes 141,002, pears 73,884, lettuce 70,543[7]; livestock (number of live animals) 1,597,480 cattle, 1,557,200 pigs; roundwood (2010) 4,920,037 cu m, of which fuelwood 30%; fisheries production 2,931 (from aquaculture 42%). Mining (2009): salt 435,000. Manufacturing (value added in CHF '000,000; 2008): chemicals/chemical products/refined petroleum 21,163; professional and scientific equipment/watches 16,006; nonelectrical machinery and apparatus 13,877; fabricated/structural metal products 10,074; food products, beverages, and tobacco 9,203.[8, 9] Energy production (consumption): electricity (kW-hr; 2008) 64,380,000,000 (58,930,000,000); coal (metric tons; 2007) none (258,000); crude petroleum (barrels; 2009) none ([2007] 34,300,000); petroleum products (metric tons; 2007) 4,695,000 (9,691,000); natural gas (cu m; 2009) none (3,284,000,000).
Population economically active (2008): total 4,375,000; activity rate of total population *c.* 57% (participation rates: ages 15–64, 82.3%; female 46.2%; unemployed [August 2009–July 2010] 4.0%).

Price index (2005 = 100)

	2004	2005	2006	2007	2008	2009	2010
Consumer price index	98.8	100.0	101.1	101.8	104.3	103.8	104.5

Household income and expenditure (2008). Average household size 2.2; average annual disposable income per household CHF 77,580 (U.S.$71,628); sources of income: wages and salaries 66.5%, transfers 18.1%, self-employment 10.0%; expenditure: housing and energy 28.8%, transportation 14.0%, food and nonalcoholic beverages 12.4%.
Gross national income (GNI; 2010): U.S.$548,012,000,000 (U.S.$70,350 per capita); purchasing power parity GNI (U.S.$49,180 per capita).

Structure of gross domestic product and labour force

	2008 in value CHF '000,000	2008 % of total value	2007 labour force	2007 % of labour force
Agriculture, forestry, fishing	6,506	1.2	160,000	3.7
Mining	792	0.1	5,000	0.1
Manufacturing	103,430	19.0	684,000	15.7
Public utilities	10,087	1.9	24,000	0.5
Construction	27,810	5.1	297,000	6.8
Transp. and commun.	39,521	7.3	253,000	5.8
Trade, restaurants	74,182	13.6	806,000	18.4
Finance, insurance[10]	121,140	22.3	672,000	15.4
Pub. admin., defense	52,856	9.7	158,000	3.6
Services	77,007	14.1	837,000	19.2
Other	30,865[11]	5.7[11]	473,000	10.8
TOTAL	544,196	100.0	4,369,000	100.0

Public debt (general government; 2010): U.S.$193,152,000,000.
Selected balance of payments data. Receipts from (U.S.$'000,000): tourism (2009) 13,816; remittances (2010) 2,632; foreign direct investment (FDI; 2008–10 avg.) 11,851. Disbursements for (U.S.$'000,000): tourism (2009) 10,628; remittances (2009) 19,562; FDI (2008–10 avg.) 38,936.
Land use as % of total land area (2009): in temporary crops 6.9%, left fallow 0.1%, in permanent crops 0.6%, in pasture 30.6%, forest area 30.9%.

Foreign trade[12]

Balance of trade (current prices)

	2004	2005	2006	2007	2008	2009
U.S.$'000,000	+7,041	+4,356	+6,457	+10,898	+17,099	+18,530
% of total	5.1%	1.7%	2.2%	3.2%	4.5%	5.9%

Imports (2008): U.S.$183,516,000,000 (machinery and apparatus 18.9%; medicine and pharmaceuticals 9.7%; base and fabricated metals 9.6%; road vehicles 6.7%; petroleum 6.3%; organic chemicals 5.0%). *Major import sources:* Germany 33.3%; Italy 11.0%; France 9.4%; U.S. 5.8%; Neth. 4.6%.
Exports (2008): U.S.$200,615,000,000 (medicine and pharmaceuticals 22.0%, of which vaccines/related products 7.0%; machinery and apparatus 21.5%; wrist watches 7.3%; base and fabricated metals 6.9%; organic chemicals 5.9%). *Major export destinations:* Germany 19.7%; U.S. 9.6%; Italy 8.7%; France 8.6%; U.K. 5.1%.

Transport and communications

Transport. Railroads (2008): route length 3,037 mi, 4,888 km; passenger-km 18,028,000,000; metric ton-km cargo 12,265,000,000. Roads (2008): total length 44,338 mi, 71,355 km (paved 100%); passenger-km (2006) 93,000,000,000[13]; metric ton-km cargo (2008) 11,307,000,000. Vehicles (2008): passenger cars 3,989,811; trucks and buses 344,354. Air transport (2010): passenger-km 42,552,000,000; metric ton-km cargo 1,282,500,000.

Communications

Medium	date	number in '000s	units per 1,000 persons	Medium	date	number in '000s	units per 1,000 persons
Televisions	2004	4,300	576	PCs	2007	6,977	918
Telephones				Dailies	2009	2,126[14]	275[14]
Cellular	2009	9,255[15]	1,223[15]	Internet users	2009	5,480	724
Landline	2010	4,488	586	Broadband	2010	2,925[15]	382[15]

Education and health

Educational attainment (2007). Percentage of population age 25 and over having: no formal schooling to primary education 4.1%; lower secondary 2.0%; upper secondary 63.8%; higher vocational 2.6%; university 27.5%.

Education (2007–08)

	teachers	students	student/ teacher ratio	enrollment rate (%)
Primary (age 7–12)	...	505,382	...	94
Secondary/Voc. (age 13–19)	...	598,957	...	85
Tertiary	33,797	224,469	6.6	49 (age 20–24)

Health: physicians (2008) 15,294[16] (1 per 500 persons); hospital beds (2008) 39,764 (1 per 192 persons); infant mortality rate per 1,000 live births (2009) 4.3; undernourished population (2006–08) less than 5.0% of total population.

Military

Total active duty personnel (November 2010): 25,620[17]. *Military expenditure as percentage of GDP* (2009): 0.9%; per capita expenditure U.S.$571.

[1]Official long-form name in French is Confédération Suisse; in German, Schweizerische Eidgenossenschaft; in Italian, Confederazione Svizzera; in Romansh, Confederaziun Svizra. [2]The federal supreme court is located in Lausanne. [3]Preliminary census results, December 31. [4]Detail does not add to total given because of rounding. [5]January 1. [6]Combines federal, cantonal, and communal budgets. [7]Includes chicory. [8]Polished diamond exports (2006): U.S.$661,000,000. [9]40% of the world's gold was refined in Switzerland in 2008. [10]Includes consulting services. [11]Taxes less subsidies. [12]Imports c.i.f.; exports f.o.b. [13]Passenger cars 87,000,000,000; buses 6,000,000,000. [14]Circulation. [15]Subscribers. [16]Practicing physicians only. [17]Reserve 171,891; civil defense (not part of armed forces) 80,000.

Internet resources for further information:
- **Swiss National Bank http://www.snb.ch/en**
- **Swiss Federal Statistical Office http://www.bfs.admin.ch**

Syria

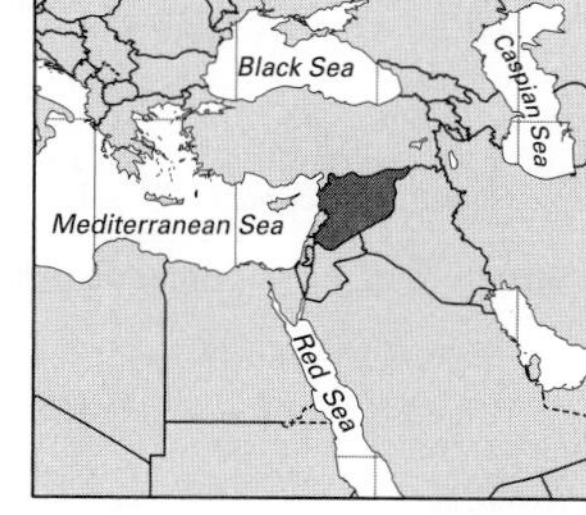

Official name: Al-Jumhūriyyah al-ʿArabiyyah al-Sūriyyah (Syrian Arab Republic).
Form of government: unitary multiparty republic with one legislative house (People's Assembly [250]).
Head of state and government: President.
Capital: Damascus.
Official language: Arabic.
Official religion: none[1].
Monetary unit: Syrian pound (S.P); valuation (Sept. 1, 2011) 1 U.S.$ = S.P 47.37; 1 £ = S.P 76.55.

Area and population

Governorates	area sq km	population 2011[2] estimate	Governorates	area sq km	population 2011[2] estimate
Darʿā	3,730	998,000	Al-Lādhiqīyah (Latakia)	2,297	991,000
Dayr al-Zawr	33,060	1,202,000	Al-Qunayṭirah	1,861[3]	87,000
Dimashq (Damascus)	18,032	2,744,000	Al-Raqqah	19,616	921,000
Ḥalab (Aleppo)	18,500	4,744,000	Al-Suwaydā'	5,550	364,000
Ḥamāh	8,883	1,593,000	Ṭarṭūs	1,892	785,000
Al-Ḥasakah	23,334	1,477,000	**Municipality**		
Ḥimṣ (Homs)	42,223	1,763,000	Damascus	105	1,733,000
Idlib	6,097	1,464,000	TOTAL	185,180[3]	20,866,000

Demography

Population (2011): 20,766,000[4, 5].
Density (2011): persons per sq mi 290.4, persons per sq km 112.1.
Urban-rural (2010): urban 53.5%; rural 46.5%.
Sex distribution (2010): male 51.11%; female 48.89%.
Age breakdown (2009): under 15, 36.4%; 15–29, 30.7%; 30–44, 18.1%; 45–59, 9.4%; 60–74, 4.1%; 75–84, 1.1%; 85 and over, 0.2%.
Population projection: (2020) 24,079,000; (2030) 27,859,000.
Ethnic composition (2000): Syrian Arab 74.9%; Bedouin Arab 7.4%; Kurd 7.3%; Palestinian Arab 3.9%; Armenian 2.7%; other 3.8%.
Religious affiliation (2000): Muslim *c.* 86%, of which Sunnī *c.* 74%, ʿAlawite (Shīʿī) *c.* 11%; Christian *c.* 8%, of which Orthodox *c.* 5%, Roman Catholic *c.* 2%; Druze *c.* 3%; nonreligious/atheist *c.* 3%.
Major cities (2009): Aleppo 3,087,000[6]; Damascus 2,597,000[6]; Ḥimṣ (Homs) 1,328,000[6]; Ḥamāh 897,000[6]; Latakia (2004) 424,392.

Vital statistics

Birth rate per 1,000 population (2009): 25.0 (world avg. 20.3).
Death rate per 1,000 population (2009): 3.7 (world avg. 8.5).
Total fertility rate (avg. births per childbearing woman; 2009): 3.12.
Marriage/divorce rates per 1,000 population (2009)[7]: 12.0/1.5.
Life expectancy at birth (2009): male 71.9 years; female 76.7 years.
Major causes of death per 100,000 population (2002): diseases of the circulatory system 156, of which ischemic heart disease 64, cerebrovascular disease 44; malignant neoplasms (cancers) 56; accidents, injuries 38.

National economy

Budget (2009). Revenue: S.P 533,000,000,000 (nonpetroleum tax on income and profits 55.6%, nonpetroleum nontax revenues 23.5%, petroleum royalties and taxes 20.9%). Expenditures: S.P 666,400,000,000 (current expenditures 62.4%, capital expenditures 37.6%).
Public debt (external, outstanding; 2009): U.S.$4,480,000,000.
Gross national income (GNI; 2010): U.S.$57,003,000,000 (U.S.$2,640 per capita); purchasing power parity GNI (U.S.$4,870 per capita).

Structure of gross domestic product and labour force

	2009 in value S.P '000,000	2009 % of total value	2007 labour force[8]	2007 % of labour force[8]
Agriculture	530,588.5	21.1	946,500	17.5
Mining	} 789,043.5	} 31.4	34,700	0.6
Manufacturing			633,100	11.7
Public utilities			33,500	0.6
Construction	86,506.5	3.4	735,900	13.7
Transp. and commun.	253,685.0	10.1	352,200	6.5
Trade, restaurants, hotels	427,122.5	17.0	783,100	14.5
Finance, real estate	151,973.0	6.0	132,400	2.5
Pub. admin.	245,478.5	9.8	648,500	12.0
Services	57,331.5	2.3	646,200	12.0
Other	−28,771.0[9]	−1.1[9]	454,700[10]	8.4[10]
TOTAL	2,512,958.0	100.0	5,400,800	100.0

Production (metric tons except as noted). Agriculture, forestry, fishing (2009): wheat 3,701,784, tomatoes 1,165,611, olives 885,952, barley 845,669, sugar beets 732,706, potatoes 709,601, oranges 689,751, seed cotton 652,058, apples 360,978, grapes 358,000, eggplants 147,041, almonds 97,002, cherries 76,055, pistachios 61,484; livestock (number of live animals) 21,700,000 sheep, 1,508,030 goats, 1,084,540 cattle, 32,494 camels; roundwood (2010) 66,962 cu m, of which fuelwood 41%; fisheries production 15,304 (from aquaculture 57%). Mining and quarrying (2009): phosphate rock 2,466,000; gypsum 403,000. Manufacturing (value added in S.P '000,000; 2007): textiles and clothing 35,953; food, beverages, and tobacco 28,975; fabricated metals 20,003; cement, bricks, and tiles 14,186. Energy production (consumption): electricity (kW-hr; 2008) 41,170,000,000 (41,170,000,000); coal, none (none); crude petroleum (barrels; 2009) 146,146,000 (91,980,000); petroleum products (metric tons; 2008) 11,159,000 ([2007] 17,399,000); natural gas (cu m; 2009) 6,040,000,000 (6,180,000,000).
Population economically active (2008): total 5,442,399; activity rate of total population 25.5% (participation rates: ages 15 and over, 44.4%; female 16.3%; unemployed [June 2010] 8.4%).

Price index (2005 = 100)

	2004	2005	2006	2007	2008	2009	2010
Consumer price index	93.2	100.0	110.0	114.3	132.3	136.2	142.2

Household income and expenditure. Average household size (2004) 5.2; income per household: n.a.; sources of income (2003–04)[11]: wages 49.2%, self-employment 39.8%; expenditure: n.a.
Selected balance of payments data. Receipts from (U.S.$'000,000): tourism (2009) 3,757; remittances (2010) 1,487; foreign direct investment (FDI; 2008–10 avg.) 1,427; official development assistance (2009) 245. Disbursements for (U.S.$'000,000): tourism (2009) 882; remittances (2009) 212; FDI (2008–10 avg.) negligible.
Land use as % of total land area (2009): in temporary crops 18.2%, left fallow 7.2%, in permanent crops 5.4%, in pasture 50.3%, forest area 2.6%.

Foreign trade[12]

Balance of trade (current prices)

	2003	2004	2005	2006	2007	2008
U.S.$'000,000	+620	−1,666	−1,448	−569	−3,109	−3,725
% of total	5.7%	13.4%	10.1%	2.5%	11.9%	11.5%

Imports (2007): U.S.$14,655,000,000 (refined petroleum 29.5%; iron and steel 10.5%; food 10.1%; machinery and apparatus 9.5%; road vehicles 6.6%; plastics 5.9%). *Major import sources:* Russia 9.8%; China 8.0%; Italy 6.9%; Ukraine 5.8%; Saudi Arabia 5.7%; Malta 5.0%.
Exports (2007): U.S.$11,546,000,000 (crude petroleum 34.5%; food 17.3%, of which vegetables 4.5%; apparel 7.9%; yarn and fabrics 7.0%; refined petroleum 6.5%; machinery and apparatus 4.9%). *Major export destinations:* Italy 23.7%; France 11.5%; Saudi Arabia 10.6%; Iraq 5.6%; Turkey 5.2%.

Transport and communications

Transport. Railroads (2008): length 1,760 mi, 2,833 km; passenger-km 1,120,021,000; metric ton-km cargo 2,370,473,000. Roads (2008): total length 40,378 mi, 64,983 km (paved 91%); passenger-km, n.a.; metric ton-km cargo, n.a. Vehicles (2008): passenger cars 551,858; trucks and buses 607,932. Air transport (2008)[13]: passenger-km 2,448,000,000; metric ton-km cargo 10,800,000.

Communications

Medium	date	number in '000s	units per 1,000 persons	Medium	date	number in '000s	units per 1,000 persons
Televisions	2006	3,750	194	PCs	2007	1,844	90
Telephones				Dailies	2009	379[14]	17[14]
Cellular	2010	11,696[15]	573[15]	Internet users	2009	4,469	204
Landline	2010	4,069	199	Broadband	2010	67[15]	3.3[15]

Education and health

Educational attainment (2003–04)[11]. Percentage of population having: no formal education (illiterate) 14.3%; no formal education (literate) 9.9%; primary education 45.8%; secondary 22.5%; incomplete higher 3.9%; higher 3.6%. *Literacy* (2008): percentage of population age 15 and over literate 83.6%; males literate 90.0%; females literate 77.2%.

Education (2007–08)

	teachers	students	student/ teacher ratio	enrollment rate (%)
Primary (age 6–9)	132,099	2,383,223[16]	17.8	95[17]
Secondary/Voc. (age 10–17)	180,703	2,664,335[16]	14.5	68[16]
Tertiary[18, 19]	8,084	279,614	34.6	... (age 18–22)

Health (2008): physicians 29,473 (1 per 724 persons); hospital beds 30,210 (1 per 706 persons); infant mortality rate per 1,000 live births (2009) 16.7; undernourished population (2004–06) less than 5.0% of total population based on the consumption of a minimum daily requirement of 1,800 calories.

Military

Total active duty personnel (November 2010): 295,000 (army 74.6%, navy 1.7%, air force 10.2%, air defense 13.5%); reserve 314,000; paramilitary 108,000. UN peacekeeping troops in Golan Heights (September 2011) 1,038. *Military expenditure as percentage of GDP* (2009): 4.2%; per capita expenditure U.S.$111.

[1]Islam is required to be the religion of the head of state and is the basis of the legal system. [2]January 1. [3]Includes 1,176 sq km (454 sq mi) of territory in the Golan Heights recognized internationally as part of Syria but occupied by Israel or UN peacekeepers. [4]Includes roughly 1,005,000 Iraqi refugees and 460,000 long-term Palestinian refugees in January 2011. [5]Estimate of United Nations *World Population Prospects: The 2010 Revision.* [6]Urban agglomeration. [7]Syrian Arabs only. [8]Labour force survey of Syrian population only, age 15 years and over. [9]Customs duties less imputed bank service charges. [10]Unemployed. [11]Based on the Household Income and Expenditure Survey with a survey population of 124,525. [12]Imports c.i.f.; exports f.o.b. [13]SyrianAir only. [14]Circulation of daily newspapers. [15]Subscribers. [16]2008–09. [17]2001–02. [18]2006–07. [19]Excluding private universities.

Internet resources for further information:
- **Central Bureau of Statistics http://www.cbssyr.org/index-EN.htm**
- **Central Bank of Syria http://www.banquecentrale.gov.sy**

Taiwan

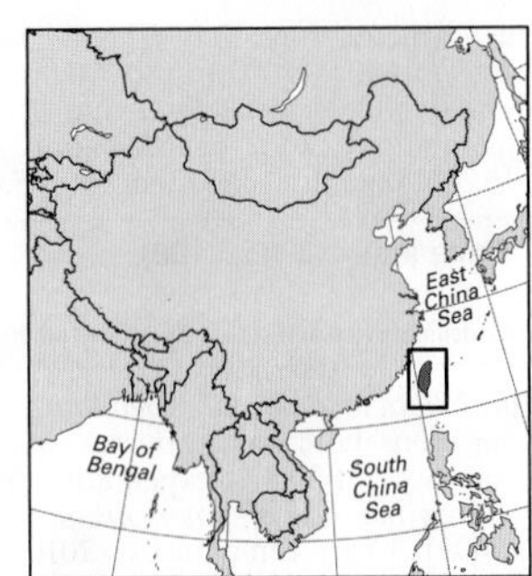

Official name: Chung-hua Min-kuo (Republic of China).
Form of government: multiparty republic with one legislative body (Legislative Yuan [113[1]]).
Head of state: President.
Head of government: Premier.
Seat of government: Taipei.
Official language: Mandarin Chinese.
Official religion: none.
Monetary unit: New Taiwan dollar (NT$); valuation (Sept. 1, 2011) 1 U.S.$ = NT$28.95; 1 £ = NT$46.79.

Area and population

	area (sq km)	population (2010[2] estimate)
Taiwan area		
Counties		
Chang-hua	1,074	1,312,467
Chia-i	1,902	547,716
Hsin-chu	1,428	510,882
Hua-lien	4,629	340,964
I-lan	2,144	461,625
Miao-li	1,820	561,744
Nan-t'ou	4,106	530,824
P'eng-hu	127	96,210
P'ing-tung	2,776	882,640
T'ai-tung	3,515	232,497
T'ao-yüan	1,221	1,978,782
Yün-lin	1,291	722,795
Special municipalities		
Hsin-pei[3]	2,053	3,873,653
Kao-hsiung[3]	2,947	2,770,887
T'ai-chung[3]	2,214	2,635,761
T'ai-nan[3]	2,192	1,875,406
Taipei	272	2,607,428
Municipalities		
Chi-lung	133	388,321
Chia-i	60	273,861
Hsin-chu	104	411,587
Non-Taiwan area		
Counties		
Kinmen (Quemoy)	152	93,803
Lienchiang (Matsu)	29	9,919
TOTAL	36,190[4, 5]	23,119,772

Demography

Population (2011): 23,190,000.
Density (2011): persons per sq mi 1,660, persons per sq km 640.8.
Urban-rural (2005): urban 81%; rural 19%.
Sex distribution (2011[2]): male 50.23%; female 49.77%.
Age breakdown (2011[2]): under 15, 15.7%; 15–29, 21.9%; 30–44, 24.5%; 45–59, 22.7%; 60–74, 10.4%; 75–84, 3.7%; 85 and over, 1.1%.
Population projection: (2020) 23,434,000; (2030) 23,249,000.
Ethnic composition (2003): Taiwanese *c.* 84%; mainland Chinese *c.* 14%; indigenous tribal peoples *c.* 2%, of which Ami 0.6%.
Religious affiliation (2002): Buddhism 23.8%; Taoism 19.7%; Christian 4.5%, of which Protestant 2.6%, Roman Catholic 1.3%; I-kuan Tao (syncretistic religion) 3.7%; other (mostly Chinese folk-religionist or non-religious) 48.3%.
Major cities/metropolitan areas (2008[2]): Taipei 2,629,269 (urban agglomeration 6,698,319); Kao-hsiung 1,520,555; T'ai-chung 1,055,898; T'ai-nan 764,658; T'ao-yüan 391,822.

Vital statistics

Birth rate per 1,000 population (2010): 7.2 (world avg. 19.2); within marriage 95.5%; outside of marriage 4.5%.
Death rate per 1,000 population (2010): 6.3 (world avg. 8.2).
Total fertility rate (avg. births per childbearing woman; 2010): 0.90.
Marriage/divorce rates per 1,000 population (2010): 6.0/2.5.
Life expectancy at birth (2010): male 76.2 years; female 82.7 years.
Major causes of death per 100,000 population (2010): malignant neoplasms (cancers) 177.4; heart disease 67.7; cerebrovascular diseases 43.8; pneumonia 38.5; diabetes mellitus 35.5; accidents 28.8.

National economy

Budget (2010; general government). Revenue: NT$2,115,497,000,000 (tax revenue 74.0%; income from public enterprises 13.5%; fees 4.6%). Expenditures: NT$2,566,825,000,000 (education, science, and culture 21.6%; economic development 20.1%; social welfare 16.2%; general administration 14.3%; defense 11.2%).
Public debt (external, outstanding; March 2011): U.S.$7,464,000,000.
Population economically active (2010)[6]: total 11,070,000; activity rate of total population 48.1% (participation rates: ages 15 and over, 58.1%; female 43.6%; unemployed 5.2%).

Price and earnings indexes (2005 = 100)

	2004	2005	2006	2007	2008	2009	2010
Consumer price index	97.7	100.0	100.6	102.4	106.0	105.1	106.1
Monthly earnings index[7]	97.1	100.0	101.3	103.1	103.0	93.5	101.3

Selected balance of payments data. Receipts from (U.S.$'000,000): tourism (2010) 8,719; remittances (2006) 355; foreign direct investment (FDI; 2008–10 avg.) 3,576. Disbursements for (U.S.$'000,000): tourism (2009) 7,800; remittances (2006) 1,370; FDI (2008–10 avg.) 10,290.
Production (metric tons except as noted). Agriculture, forestry, fishing (2010): rice 1,451,011, pineapples 420,172, bamboo shoots 292,209, pears 174,858, betel nuts 131,737, grapes 102,831, tea 17,467, shiitake mushrooms 4,540; livestock (number of live animals; 2006) 7,068,621 pigs, 134,793 cattle; roundwood 19,468 cu m, of which fuelwood 2%; fisheries production 1,167,081 (from aquaculture 27%); aquatic plants production (2009) 4,596 (from aquaculture 95%). Mining and quarrying (2010): marble 25,118,000. Manufacturing (value added in NT$'000,000,000; 2006): electronic parts and components 610; base metals 288; base chemicals 230; refined petroleum/coal products 206; computers, telecommunications, video electronics 191; nonelectrical machinery and equipment 164. Energy production (consumption): electricity (kW-hr; 2010) 247,045,000,000 (237,559,000,000); coal (metric tons; 2010) none (58,294,000); crude petroleum (barrels; 2010) 283,000 (321,365,300); natural gas (cu m; 2010) 290,000,000 ([2007] 11,298,000,000).
Gross national income (2010): U.S.$476,891,000,000 (U.S.$20,602 per capita).

Structure of gross domestic product and labour force

	2010			
	in value NT$'000,000	% of total value	labour force[6]	% of labour force[6]
Agriculture, forestry, fishing	214,622	1.6	550,000	5.0
Mining, quarrying	63,001	0.5	4,000	—
Manufacturing	3,573,474	26.3	2,861,000	25.9
Construction	377,341	2.8	797,000	7.2
Public utilities	248,972	1.8	107,000	1.0
Transp. and commun.	886,813	6.5	612,000	5.5
Trade, restaurants	2,742,067	20.2	2,474,000	22.4
Finance, real estate	2,034,852	15.0	503,000	4.5
Pub. admin., defense	987,197	7.3	389,000	3.5
Services	2,072,386	15.0	2,196,000	19.8
Other	402,752[8]	3.0[8]	577,000[9]	5.2[9]
TOTAL	13,603,477	100.0	11,070,000	100.0

Household income and expenditure (2010). Average household size 2.9; average annual income per household NT$1,071,938 (U.S.$36,461); sources of income: wages and salaries 57.7%, transfers 18.0%, self-employment 13.6%; expenditure: housing and energy 24.6%, food, beverages, and tobacco 16.6%, health care 14.4%, transportation and communication 12.5%.
Land use as % of total land area (2008): in temporary crops, left fallow, or in permanent crops 22.7%; in pasture, n.a.; forest area 58.1%.

Foreign trade[10]

Balance of trade (current prices)

	2005	2006	2007	2008	2009	2010
U.S.$'000,000	+15,818	+21,319	+27,425	+15,181	+29,304	+23,365
% of total	4.2%	5.0%	5.9%	3.1%	7.8%	4.4%

Imports (2009): U.S.$174,371,000,000 (machinery and apparatus 33.8%, of which electronic goods/parts 17.9%; mineral fuels 22.6%; chemicals and chemical products 11.7%). *Major import sources:* Japan 20.8%; China 14.0%; U.S. 10.4%; South Korea 6.0%; Saudi Arabia 5.0%.
Exports (2009): U.S.$203,675,000,000 (machinery and electronic goods 46.7%; base and fabricated metals 9.5%; plastics and rubber products 8.1%; precision instruments, watches, and musical instruments 7.9%). *Major export destinations:* China 26.6%; Hong Kong 14.5%; U.S. 11.6%; Japan 7.1%; Singapore 4.2%.

Transport and communications

Transport. Railroads (2010): route length 1,580 km[11]; passenger-km 20,931,000,000; metric ton-km cargo 873,000,000. Roads (2010): total length (2009) 25,771 mi, 41,475 km (paved 99%); passenger-km 15,843,000,000; metric ton-km cargo 29,632,000,000. Vehicles (2010): passenger cars 5,803,000; trucks and buses 1,023,000. Air transport (2010)[12]: passenger-km 60,038,000,000; metric ton-km cargo 11,866,000,000.

Communications

Medium	date	number in '000s	units per 1,000 persons	Medium	date	number in '000s	units per 1,000 persons
Televisions	1999	9,200	418	PCs	2005	13,098	575
Telephones				Dailies	2009	3,700[13]	193[13]
Cellular	2010	27,840[14]	1,199[14]	Internet users	2009	16,130	698
Landline	2010	16,434	708	Broadband	2010	5,265[14]	227[14]

Education and health

Educational attainment (2010). Percentage of population age 25 and over having: no formal schooling 3.8%; primary education 18.0%; vocational/secondary 43.8%; higher 34.4%. *Literacy* (2007): population age 15 and over literate 97.6%.

Education (2009–10)

	teachers	students	student/ teacher ratio	enrollment rate (%)[15]
Primary (age 6–11)	99,541	1,519,456	15.3	99
Secondary/Voc. (age 12–17)	104,064[16]	1,320,444[16]	12.7[16]	95
Tertiary	50,684	1,343,603	26.5	64 (age 18–21)

Health (2011[2]): physicians 44,252 (1 per 523 persons); hospital beds 158,922 (1 per 146 persons); infant mortality rate per 1,000 live births (2010) 4.2.

Military

Total active duty personnel (November 2010): 290,000 (army 69.0%, navy 15.5%, air force 15.5%); reserve 1,657,000. *Military expenditure as percentage of GDP* (2010): 2.1%; per capita expenditure U.S.$402.

[1]Includes 6 elected seats reserved for aboriginal peoples. [2]January 1. [3]One of four special municipalities created on Dec. 25, 2010. [4]Total area per most recent survey is 36,191 sq km (13,973 sq mi). [5]Detail does not add to total given because of rounding. [6]Civilian persons only. [7]Manufacturing. [8]Import duties plus VAT and plus statistical discrepancy. [9]Unemployed. [10]Imports c.i.f.; exports f.o.b. [11]Includes 345 km high-speed rail link between Taipei and Kao-hsiung. [12]China Airlines, EVA, Mandarin Airlines, TransAsia Airways, and Uni Air. [13]Circulation of daily newspapers. [14]Subscribers. [15]2007–08. [16]2008–09.

Internet resource for further information:
- **Statistical Bureau of the Republic of China http://eng.stat.gov.tw**

Tajikistan

Official name: Jumhurii Tojikiston (Republic of Tajikistan).
Form of government: republic with two legislative houses (National Assembly [34[1]]; Assembly of Representatives [63]).
Head of state: President.
Head of government: Prime Minister.
Capital: Dushanbe.
Official language: Tajik.
Official religion: none.
Monetary unit: somoni (TJS); valuation (Sept. 1, 2011) 1 U.S.$ = TJS 4.75; 1 £ = TJS 7.68.

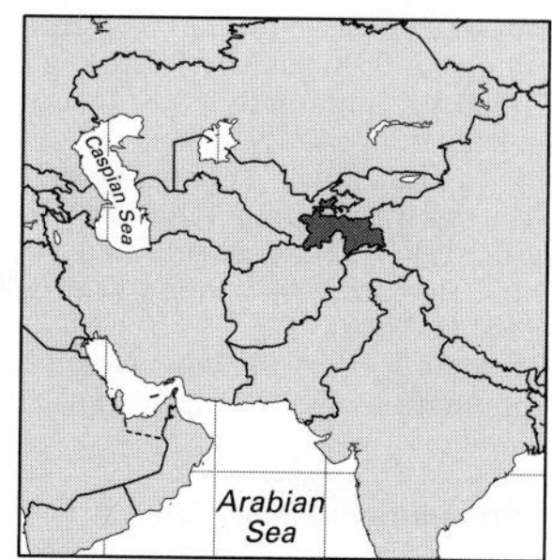

Area and population

		area		population
Provinces	**Capitals**	sq mi	sq km	2010[2] estimate
Khatlon	Kurgan-Tyube	9,600	24,800	2,724,500
Sughd	Khujand	9,800	25,400	2,215,700
Autonomous province				
Kŭhistoni Badakhshon (Gorno-Badakhshan)	Khorugh	24,800	64,200	220,000
City				
Dushanbe	—	40	100	709,600
No provincial administration	—	11,050	28,600	1,694,800
TOTAL		55,300[3]	143,100	7,564,600[4]

Demography

Population (2011): 7,681,000.
Density (2011): persons per sq mi 138.9, persons per sq km 53.7.
Urban-rural (2010): urban 26.5%; rural 73.5%.
Sex distribution (2009): male 50.15%; female 49.85%.
Age breakdown (2007): under 15, 35.0%; 15–29, 31.5%; 30–44, 18.8%; 45–59, 9.7%; 60–74, 3.8%; 75 and over, 1.2%.
Population projection: (2020) 8,761,000; (2030) 9,922,000.
Doubling time: 35 years.
Ethnic composition (2000): Tajik 80.0%; Uzbek 15.3%; Russian 1.1%; Tatar 0.3%; other 3.3%.
Religious affiliation (2005): Sunnī Muslim *c.* 78%; Shīʿī Muslim *c.* 6%; nonreligious *c.* 12%; other (mostly Christian) *c.* 4%.
Major cities (2010)[5]: Dushanbe 724,000; Khujand 162,000; Kulyab 95,000; Kurgan-Tyube 75,000; Istaravshan (Ura-Tyube) 55,000.

Vital statistics

Birth rate per 1,000 population (2007): 27.3 (world avg. 20.3).
Death rate per 1,000 population (2007): 7.0 (world avg. 8.5).
Natural increase rate per 1,000 population (2010): 20.5 (world avg. 11.0).
Total fertility rate (avg. births per childbearing woman; 2007): 3.09.
Marriage/divorce rates per 1,000 population (2010): 13.3/0.8.
Life expectancy at birth (2009): male 70.5 years; female 75.3 years.
Major causes of death per 100,000 population (2005)[6]: diseases of the circulatory system *c.* 344, of which ischemic heart disease *c.* 133, hypertensive diseases *c.* 83; diseases of the respiratory system *c.* 64; malignant neoplasms (cancers) *c.* 51; diseases of the digestive system *c.* 33; accidents *c.* 31.

National economy

Budget (2009). Revenue: TJS 4,175,000,000 (tax revenue 87.3%; grants 7.6%; nontax revenue 5.1%). Expenditures: TJS 5,643,000,000 (economic services 31.1%; education 17.8%; social security/welfare 12.7%; health 6.0%; defense, n.a.).
Production (metric tons except as noted). Agriculture, forestry, fishing (2009): wheat 905,000, potatoes 690,900, cow's milk 574,000, tomatoes 310,000, dry onions 272,000, grapes 138,700, cotton lint 95,000, sheep meat 33,400; livestock (number of live animals) 2,579,000 sheep, 1,799,500 cattle, 1,568,000 goats; roundwood (2010) 90,000, of which fuelwood 100%; fisheries production 401 (from aquaculture 64%). Mining and quarrying (2009): antimony (metal content) 2,000; silver 4,500 kg; gold 1,361 kg. Manufacturing (value of production in TJS '000,000[7]; 2007): nonferrous metals (nearly all aluminum) 585,103; food 301,156; textiles 209,375; grain mill products 94,649. Energy production (consumption): electricity (kW-hr; 2008) 15,970,000,000 (13,990,000,000); hard coal (metric tons; 2008) 216,000 ([2007] 158,000); lignite (metric tons; 2009) 34,500 ([2007] 15,000); crude petroleum (barrels; 2009) 189,000 ([2007] 153,000); petroleum products (metric tons; 2007) none (1,718,000); natural gas (cu m; 2009) 22,000,000 ([2008] 510,000,000).
Population economically active (2008): total 2,217,000; activity rate of total population 30.1% (participation rates: ages 15–64 [2004] 66.5%; female [2004] 41.7%; officially unemployed [2010] 2.4%).

Price and earnings indexes (2005 = 100)

	2004	2005	2006	2007	2008	2009	2010
Consumer price index	93.4	100.0	110.0	124.4	149.9	159.5	169.7
Monthly earnings index	73.9	100.0	139.1	195.3	277.0	344.3	...

Selected balance of payments data. Receipts from (U.S.$'000,000): tourism (2009) 2.4; remittances (2010) 2,032; foreign direct investment (2008–10 avg.) 146; official development assistance (2009) 409. Disbursements for (U.S.$'000,000): tourism (2009) 5.8; remittances (2009) 124.

Gross national income (GNI; 2010): U.S.$5,512,000,000 (U.S.$780 per capita); purchasing power parity GNI (U.S.$2,060 per capita).

Structure of gross domestic product and labour force

	2008		2007	
	in value TJS '000,000[8]	% of total value	labour force	% of labour force
Agriculture	3,518	19.9	1,430,000	65.0
Mining, Public utilities, Manufacturing	2,516	14.2	114,000	5.2
Construction	1,833	10.4	63,000	2.9
Transp. and commun.	1,782	10.1	62,000	2.8
Trade, hotels	3,573	20.2	115,000	5.2
Finance, real estate	343	1.9	...	...
Pub. admin., defense	407	2.3	34,000	1.5
Services	1,674	9.5	332,000	15.1
Other	2,061[9]	11.6[9]	51,700[10]	2.3[10]
TOTAL	17,707	100.0[3]	2,201,000[3]	100.0

Public debt (external, outstanding; 2009): U.S.$1,603,000,000.
Household income and expenditure (2007). Average household size (2004) 5.2; average disposable income per household (2005) TJS 3,462 (U.S.$1,111); sources of income: wages and salaries 42.3%, self-employment 22.1%, transfers 3.8%; expenditure: food 58.4%, household furnishings 9.4%, clothing 9.4%, transportation and communications 7.0%.
Land use as % of total land area (2009): in temporary crops or left fallow (2007) 5.1%, in permanent crops 1.0%, in pasture 27.7%, forest area 2.9%.

Foreign trade[11]

Balance of trade (current prices)

	2005	2006	2007	2008	2009	2010
U.S.$'000,000	–421	–324	–987	–1,863	–1,559	–1,463
% of total	18.8%	10.4%	25.2%	39.9%	43.6%	38.0%

Imports (2009): U.S.$2,569,000,000 (petroleum products 12.6%, alumina 11.3%, wheat and flour 6.8%, electricity 3.0%, natural gas 2.0%, unspecified 64.3%). *Major import sources* (2008): China 25.9%; Russia 24.8%; Kazakhstan 10.6%; Uzbekistan 6.8%; Turkey 5.4%.
Exports (2009): U.S.$1,010,000,000 (aluminum 58.5%, cotton fibre 9.9%, electricity 6.3%, unspecified 25.3%). *Major export destinations* (2008): Israel 39.6%; Turkey 8.7%; Russia 7.6%; Italy 7.4%; Norway 7.2%.

Transport and communications

Transport. Railroads (2009): route length 423 mi, 680 km; passenger-km (2005) 46,000,000; metric ton-km cargo (2005) 1,066,000,000. Roads (2002): total length *c.* 18,600 mi, *c.* 30,000 km (paved, n.a.); passenger-km (2009) 7,912,000,000; metric ton-km cargo (2009) 4,366,000,000. Vehicles (2007): passenger cars 192,973; trucks and buses 64,324. Air transport: passenger-km (2005) 942,000,000; metric ton-km cargo (2007) 2,000,000.

Communications

Medium	date	number in '000s	units per 1,000 persons	Medium	date	number in '000s	units per 1,000 persons
Televisions	2003	2,350	357	PCs	2007	87	13
Telephones				Dailies	2007	217[12]	32[12]
Cellular	2010	5,941[13]	864[13]	Internet users	2009	700	101
Landline	2010	368	54	Broadband	2010	4.7[13]	0.7[13]

Education and health

Educational attainment (2000). Percentage of population age 25 and over having: no formal schooling 0.8%; incomplete primary education 2.1%; complete primary 4.7%; lower secondary 13.5%; upper secondary 59.1%; higher vocational 9.2%; university 10.6%. *Literacy* (2008): percentage of total population age 15 and over literate 99.7%.

Education (2007–08)

	teachers	students	student/ teacher ratio	enrollment rate (%)
Primary (age 7–10)	30,530	692,247	22.7	97
Secondary/Voc. (age 11–17)	61,585	1,019,250	16.6	83
Tertiary[14]	8,798	157,452	17.9	20 (age 18–22)

Health (2008): physicians 12,900 (1 per 529 persons); hospital beds 35,900 (1 per 190 persons); infant mortality rate per 1,000 live births (2007) 43.6; undernourished population (2004–06) 1,700,000 (26% of total population based on the consumption of a minimum daily requirement of 1,830 calories).

Military

Total active duty personnel (November 2010): 8,800 (army 83%, air force 17%); paramilitary 7,500; Russian troops (2010) 5,000. *Military expenditure as percentage of GDP* (2009): 1.0%; per capita expenditure U.S.$7.

[1]Includes 8 members appointed by the President and 1 seat reserved for the outgoing president. [2]January 1. [3]Detail does not add to total given because of rounding. [4]Official estimate including at least 1 million Tajik workers abroad (particularly in Russia). [5]Per preliminary census results. [6]Projected rates based on about 66% of total deaths. [7]At constant prices of 1998. [8]At constant prices of 1995. [9]Indirect taxes less subsidies. [10]Unemployed. [11]Imports c.i.f.; exports f.o.b. [12]Circulation. [13]Subscribers. [14]2008–09.

Internet resources for further information:
- **State Committee on Statistics http://www.stat.tj/english/home.htm**
- **National Bank of Tajikistan http://nbt.tj**

Tanzania

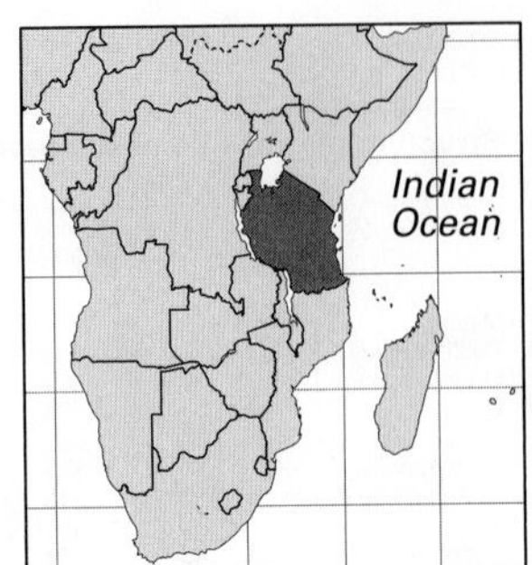

Official name: Jamhuri ya Muungano wa Tanzania (Swahili); United Republic of Tanzania (English).
Form of government: unitary multiparty republic with one legislative house (National Assembly [357[1]]).
Head of state and government: President.
Capital: Dar es Salaam (acting)[2].
Official languages: Swahili; English.
Official religion: none.
Monetary unit: Tanzanian shilling (TZS); valuation (Sept. 1, 2011) 1 U.S.$ = TZS 1,620; 1 £ = TZS 2,617.

Area and population

Administrative regions	area sq km	population 2010 estimate	Administrative regions	area sq km	population 2010 estimate
Mainland Tanzania (Tanganyika)			Rukwa	68,635	1,503,000
Arusha	36,486	1,665,000	Ruvuma	63,498	1,375,000
Dar es Salaam	1,393	3,118,000	Shinyanga	50,781	3,842,000
Dodoma	41,311	2,112,000	Singida	49,341	1,367,000
Iringa	56,864	1,737,000	Tabora	76,151	2,349,000
Kagera	28,388	2,564,000	Tanga	26,808	1,967,000
Kigoma	37,037	1,814,000	**Autonomous territory**		
Kilimanjaro	13,309	1,636,000	Zanzibar[3]		
Lindi	66,046	924,000	Pemba	906	501,000
Manyara	45,820	1,388,000	Unguja (Zanzibar)	1,554	773,000
Mara	19,566	1,823,000	TOTAL LAND AREA	883,749	
Mbeya	60,350	2,662,000	INLAND WATER	59,050	
Morogoro	70,799	2,115,000	TOTAL	942,799[4]	43,188,000
Mtwara	16,707	1,324,000			
Mwanza	19,592	3,566,000			
Pwani (Coast)	32,407	1,063,000			

Demography

Population (2011): 45,030,000.
Density (2011)[5]: persons per sq mi 123.7, persons per sq km 51.0.
Urban-rural (2008): urban 25.6%; rural 74.4%.
Sex distribution (2006): male 49.46%; female 50.54%.
Age breakdown (2006): under 15, 44.3%; 15–29, 29.1%; 30–44, 14.6%; 45–59, 7.6%; 60–74, 3.6%; 75–84, 0.7%; 85 and over, 0.1%.
Population projection: (2020) 57,899,000; (2030) 75,803,000.
Ethnolinguistic composition (2000): 130 different Bantu tribes 95%, of which Sukuma 9.5%, Hehe and Bena 4.5%, Gogo 4.4%, Haya 4.2%, Nyamwezi 3.6%, Makonde 3.3%, Chagga 3.0%, Ha 2.9%; other 5%.
Religious affiliation (2005): Muslim *c.* 35%, of which Sunnī *c.* 30%, Shīʿī *c.* 5%; Christian *c.* 35%; other (significantly traditional beliefs) *c.* 30%; Zanzibar only is 99% Muslim.
Major urban areas (2006): Dar es Salaam 2,805,500; Mwanza 458,100; Zanzibar (Unguja) 422,300; Arusha 362,900; Mbeya 304,200; Dodoma 188,200.

Vital statistics

Birth rate per 1,000 population (2009): 34.3 (world avg. 20.3).
Death rate per 1,000 population (2009): 12.6 (world avg. 8.5).
Total fertility rate (avg. births per childbearing woman; 2009): 4.46.
Life expectancy at birth (2009): male 50.6 years; female 53.5 years.
Adult population (ages 15–49) *living with HIV* (2009): 5.6% (world avg. 0.8%).

National economy

Budget (2006–07). Revenue: TZS 3,691,247,900,000 (tax revenue 68.5%, of which excise tax 27.6%, income tax 19.4%; nontax revenue 5.7%; grants 25%). Expenditures: TZS 4,474,680,900,000 (current expenditure 70.1%, of which interest payments on debt 4.8%; capital expenditure 29.9%).
Gross national income (GNI; 2010): U.S.$23,366,000,000[6] (U.S.$530[6] per capita); purchasing power parity GNI (U.S.$1,420[6] per capita).

Structure of gross domestic product and labour force

	2007		2006	
	in value TZS '000,000[6]	% of total value[6]	labour force[7]	% of labour force[7]
Agriculture, fishing	5,690,446	27.2	13,394,700	74.6
Mining	742,932	3.5	104,900	0.6
Manufacturing	1,625,504	7.8	565,100	3.1
Construction	1,641,741	7.8	211,500	1.2
Public utilities	420,880	2.0	17,000	0.1
Transp. and commun.	1,373,976	6.6	258,100	1.4
Trade, restaurants	2,976,228	14.2	1,950,200	10.9
Finance, real estate	2,327,107	11.1	99,500	0.6
Pub. admin., defense	1,652,556	7.9	184,700	1.0
Services	746,757	3.6	1,158,800	6.5
Other	1,750,278[8]	8.4[8]		
TOTAL	20,948,405	100.0[9]	17,944,600[9]	100.0

Public debt (external, outstanding; 2009): U.S.$4,637,000,000.
Production (metric tons except as noted). Agriculture, forestry, fishing (2009): cassava 5,916,000, corn (maize) 3,324,200, sweet potatoes 1,381,120, rice 1,334,000, sorghum 709,000, coconuts 577,099, peanuts (groundnuts) 385,480, seed cotton 250,000, coffee 68,577, tobacco leaves 55,400, tea 32,000, cloves 7,518; livestock (number of live animals) 19,100,000 cattle, 12,550,000 goats, 3,550,000 sheep; roundwood (2010) 24,901,785 cu m, of which fuelwood 91%; fisheries production 315,024 (from aquaculture, negligible). Mining and quarrying (2009): gold 39,112 kg; garnets 3,300 kg; tanzanites 2,500 kg; rubies 1,500 kg; diamonds 181,874 carats. Manufacturing (2005): cement 1,281,000; wheat flour 347,296; sugar 202,200; soft drinks 36,566,355 hectolitres; *konyagi* (a Tanzanian liquor) 41,050 hectolitres; cigarettes 4,308,000,000 units. Energy production (consumption): electricity (kW-hr; 2007) 4,175,000,000 (4,232,000,000); coal (metric tons; 2007) 85,000 (85,000); petroleum products (metric tons; 2007) none (1,316,000); natural gas (cu m; 2007) 531,000,000 (531,000,000).
Population economically active (2006): total 18,821,500; activity rate of total population 46.9% (participation rates: ages 10 and over, 69.1%; female 51.3%; officially unemployed 4.3%).

Price index (2005 = 100)

	2004	2005	2006	2007	2008	2009	2010
Consumer price index	95.2	100.0	107.3	114.8	126.6	142.0	150.8

Household income and expenditure (2007)[6]. Average household size 4.8; annual income per household TZS 2,267,000 (U.S.$1,820); sources of income: agricultural income 59.4%, wages and salaries 17.8%, self-employment 12.6%, remittances 3.0%; expenditure: food 64.1%, other nondurable goods 26.7%, education 1.8%, health 1.8%.
Selected balance of payments data. Receipts from (U.S.$'000,000): tourism (2009) 1,160; remittances (2010) 25; foreign direct investment (2008–10 avg.) 675; official development assistance (2009) 2,934. Disbursements for (U.S.$'000,000): tourism (2009) 766; remittances (2009) 54.
Land use as % of total land area (2009): in temporary crops or left fallow 11.3%, in permanent crops 1.7%, in pasture 27.1%, forest area 38.2%.

Foreign trade[10]

Balance of trade (current prices)

	2004	2005	2006	2007	2008	2009
TZS '000,000,000	–1,366	–1,829	–3,158	–4,706	–5,268	–5,186
% of total	30.0%	32.5%	42.0%	51.5%	45.1%	45.4%

Imports (2007): TZS 7,369,000,000,000 (refined petroleum 29.4%, machinery and apparatus 18.2%, chemicals and chemical products 11.5%, road vehicles 8.5%, food 6.5%). *Major import sources* (2008): U.A.E. 12.4%; India 11.9%; South Africa 11.0%; China 9.9%; Singapore 6.1%.
Exports (2007): TZS 2,663,000,000,000 (gold [and much less significantly copper and silver] 35.8%, fish 7.1%, coffee 5.3%, tobacco 4.5%, cotton fibre/worn clothing 4.5%). *Major export destinations* (2008): Switzerland 20.8%; Kenya 8.6%; South Africa 8.5%; China 8.2%; India 6.3%.

Transport and communications

Transport. Railroads (2006): length 1,690 mi, 2,720 km; passenger-km (2003) 1,305,000,000; metric ton-km cargo (2003) 4,461,000,000. Roads (2008): length 49,021 mi, 78,892 km (paved 6%). Vehicles (2007): passenger cars 80,913; trucks and buses 393,005. Air transport (2008)[11]: passenger-km 414,000,000; metric ton-km 1,600,000.

Communications

Medium	date	number in '000s	units per 1,000 persons	Medium	date	number in '000s	units per 1,000 persons
Televisions	2003	1,500	41	PCs	2005	356	9.3
Telephones				Dailies	2009	167[12]	4.1[12]
Cellular	2010	20,984[13]	468[13]	Internet users	2009	676	16
Landline	2010	175	3.9	Broadband	2010	3.2[13]	0.1[13]

Education and health

Educational attainment (2002). Percentage of population age 25 and over having: no formal schooling 49.4%; primary education 44.0%; secondary 5.5%; postsecondary 0.9%; other 0.2%. *Literacy* (2008): percentage of population age 15 and over literate 72.6%; males 79.0%; females 66.3%.

Education (2005–06)[6]

	teachers	students	student/ teacher ratio	enrollment rate (%)
Primary (age 7–13)	151,882	7,959,884	52.4	98
Secondary/Voc. (age 14–19)	...	...	...	...
Tertiary[14]	2,735	51,080	18.7	1 (age 20–24)

Health (2002): physicians 822 (1 per 42,085 persons); hospital beds 36,853 (1 per 939 persons); infant mortality rate (2009) 69.3; undernourished population (2006–08) 13,900,000 (34% of total population based on the consumption of a minimum daily requirement of 1,730 calories).

Military

Total active duty personnel (November 2010): 27,000 (army 85.2%, navy 3.7%, air force 11.1%); reserve 80,000. *Military expenditure as percentage of GDP* (2008): 0.9%; per capita expenditure U.S.$5.

[1]Includes 107 indirectly elected seats (102 for women, 5 for Zanzibar), 10 seats appointed by the President, and a seat for the Attorney General serving ex officio. [2]Only the legislature meets in Dodoma, the longtime planned capital. [3]Has local internal government structure; Unguja (Zanzibar) island has 3 administrative regions, Pemba island has 2. [4]A recent survey indicates a total area of 945,090 sq km (364,901 sq mi). [5]Based on land area only. [6]Mainland Tanzania only. [7]Employed only. [8]Net taxes less imputed bank service charge. [9]Detail does not add to total given because of rounding. [10]Imports c.i.f.; exports f.o.b. [11]Air Tanzania and Precision Air. [12]Circulation of daily newspapers. [13]Subscribers. [14]2004–05.

Internet resources for further information:
- **Bank of Tanzania http://www.bot-tz.org**
- **National Bureau of Statistics http://www.nbs.go.tz**

Thailand

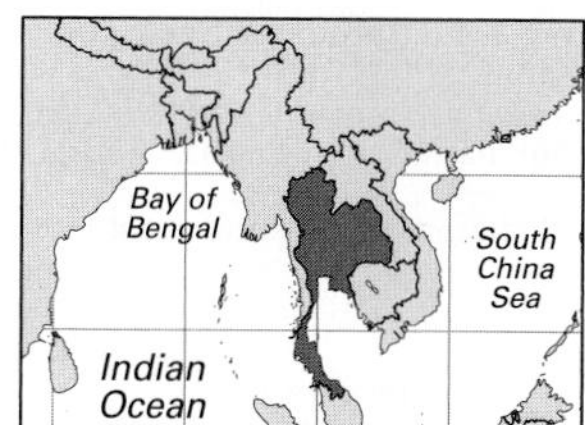

Official name: Ratcha Anachak Thai (Kingdom of Thailand).
Form of government: constitutional monarchy with two legislative houses (Senate [150[1]]; House of Representatives [500]).
Head of state: King.
Head of government: Prime Minister.
Capital: Bangkok.
Official language: Thai.
Official religion: none.
Monetary unit: baht (THB); valuation (Sept. 1, 2011) 1 U.S.$ = THB 29.98; 1 £ = THB 48.44.

Area and population

Regions[2]	Principal cities	area sq mi	area sq km	population 2010 census[3]
Bangkok and vicinities	Bangkok	2,997	7,762	14,565,547
Eastern	Chon Buri	14,094	36,503	5,163,868
Northeastern	Udon Thani	65,195	168,855	18,808,011
Northern	Chiang Mai	65,500	169,644	11,432,488
Southern	Surat Thani	27,303	70,715	8,841,364
Sub-central	Saraburi	6,407	16,594	3,109,531
Western	Ratchaburi	16,621	43,047	3,558,644
TOTAL		198,117	513,120	65,479,453

Demography

Population (2011): 65,856,000.
Density (2011): persons per sq mi 332.4, persons per sq km 128.3.
Urban-rural (2009): urban 33.6%; rural 66.4%.
Sex distribution (2010): male 49.08%; female 50.92%.
Age breakdown (2008): under 15, 21.2%; 15–29, 23.9%; 30–44, 24.5%; 45–59, 18.2%; 60–74, 9.2%; 75–89, 2.9%; 90 and over, 0.1%.
Population projection: (2020) 68,728,000; (2030) 70,438,000.
Ethnic composition (2000): Tai peoples 81.4%, of which Thai (Siamese) 34.9%, Lao 26.5%; Han Chinese 10.6%; Malay 3.7%; Khmer 1.9%; other 2.4%.
Religious affiliation (2005): Buddhist *c.* 83%; Muslim (nearly all Sunnī) *c.* 9%; traditional beliefs *c.* 2.5%; nonreligious *c.* 2%; other (significantly Christian) *c.* 3.5%.
Major cities (2000): Bangkok (2009) 6,902,000; Samut Prakan 378,741; Nonthaburi 291,555; Udon Thani 222,425; Nakhon Ratchasima 204,641.

Vital statistics

Birth rate per 1,000 population (2008): 13.6 (world avg. 20.3).
Death rate per 1,000 population (2008): 7.1 (world avg. 8.5).
Total fertility rate (avg. births per childbearing woman; 2008): 1.64.
Marriage/divorce rates per 1,000 population (2006): 5.5/1.5.
Life expectancy at birth (2008): male 70.5 years; female 75.3 years.
Major causes of death per 100,000 population (2002): infectious and parasitic diseases *c.* 170, of which HIV/AIDS-related *c.* 91; cardiovascular diseases *c.* 135; malignant neoplasms (cancers) *c.* 97; accidents *c.* 52.
Adult population (ages 15–49) *living with HIV* (2009): 1.3% (world avg. 0.8%).

National economy

Budget (2008). Revenue: THB 1,839,600,000,000 (tax revenue 89.9%, of which VAT 27.4%, corporate taxes 25.0%, excise tax 15.1%, income tax 11.1%; nontax revenue 10.1%). Expenditures: THB 1,633,300,000,000 (current expenditure 79.9%; capital expenditure 20.1%).
Production (metric tons except as noted). Agriculture, forestry, fishing (2009): sugarcane 66,816,446, rice 31,462,886, cassava 30,088,024, oil palm fruit 8,162,379, corn (maize) 4,616,119, natural rubber 3,090,280, mangoes[4] 2,469,814, pineapples 1,894,862, bananas 1,528,082, coconuts 1,380,980, dry chilies and peppers 170,125; livestock (number of live animals) 7,480,530 pigs, 6,700,000 cattle, 228,207,000 chickens; roundwood (2010) 28,098,094 cu m, of which fuelwood 69%; fisheries production 3,137,682 (from aquaculture 45%). Mining and quarrying (2009): gypsum 8,500,000; dolomite 1,200,000; feldspar 600,000; zinc (metal content) 34,000; gemstones (significantly rubies and sapphires) 30,000 carats; silver 15,300 kg; gold 5,400 kg. Manufacturing (value added in U.S.$'000,000; 2006): motor vehicles 3,408; textiles and wearing apparel 3,329; electronics 2,238; food products 1,311; tobacco products 812; office machines and computers 469; electrical machinery and parts 303. Energy production (consumption): electricity (kW-hr; 2008) 138,986,000,000 (131,637,000,000); hard coal (metric tons; 2007) none (14,051,000); lignite (metric tons; 2009) 16,400,000 ([2007] 18,121,000); crude petroleum (barrels; 2010–11[5]) 79,900,000 ([2008] 340,545,000); petroleum products (metric tons; 2007) 44,753,000 (36,570,000); natural gas (cu m; 2010–11[6]) 31,033,000,000 ([2010] 45,080,000,000).
Land use as % of total land area (2009): in temporary crops or left fallow (2007) 29.8%, in permanent crops 7.2%, in pasture 1.6%, forest area 37.1%.
Population economically active (2009): total 38,426,800; activity rate of total population 57.7% (participation rates: ages 15–59 (2008[7]) 79.3%; female 45.7%; unemployed [August 2011] 0.7%).

Price and earnings indexes (2005 = 100)

	2004	2005	2006	2007	2008	2009	2010
Consumer price index	95.7	100.0	104.6	107.0	112.8	111.8	115.5
Monthly earnings index[8]	95.7	100.0	108.3	109.2	…	…	…

Gross national income (GNI; 2010): U.S.$286,676,000,000 (U.S.$4,210 per capita); purchasing power parity GNI (U.S.$8,240 per capita).

Structure of gross domestic product and labour force

	2008 in value THB '000,000	% of total value	labour force[7]	% of labour force[7]
Agriculture, forestry, fishing	1,056,838	11.6	16,067,000	41.9
Mining and quarrying	314,823	3.5	55,000	0.1
Manufacturing	3,169,629	34.9	5,231,400	13.6
Construction	260,717	2.9	2,012,100	5.3
Public utilities	262,123	2.9	103,100	0.3
Transp. and commun.	643,244	7.1	1,090,500	2.9
Trade, hotels	1,720,694	19.0	7,988,100	20.8
Services	680,095	7.5	2,834,300	7.4
Finance, real estate	566,891	6.2	1,113,200	2.9
Pub. admin., defense	400,439	4.4	1,303,300	3.4
Other	—	—	546,700[9]	1.4[9]
TOTAL	9,075,493	100.0	38,344,700	100.0

Public debt (external, outstanding; 2009): U.S.$11,185,000,000.
Household income and expenditure (2007). Average household size 4.6; average annual income per household THB 223,920 (U.S.$7,522); sources of income: wages and salaries 39.9%, self-employment 31.7%, nonmonetary income 14.5%, transfers 9.9%; expenditure: food and nonalcoholic beverages 31.0%, transportation and communications 21.6%, housing, energy, and household furnishings 20.1%.
Selected balance of payments data. Receipts from (U.S.$'000,000): tourism (2009) 15,665; remittances (2010) 1,816; foreign direct investment (FDI; 2008–10 avg.) 6,412. Disbursements for (U.S.$'000,000): tourism (2009) 4,343; remittances, n.a.; FDI (2008–10 avg.) 4,430.

Foreign trade[10]

Balance of trade (current prices)

	2005	2006	2007	2008	2009	2010
THB '000,000,000	–315.3	+74.9	+431.9	–94.9	+591.9	+337.0
% of total	3.4%	0.8%	4.2%	0.8%	6.0%	2.8%

Imports (2008): THB 5,946,311,060,000 (mineral fuels 20.7%, of which crude petroleum 16.2%; chemicals and chemical products 10.1%; electronic parts 8.5%; electrical machinery 8.3%; iron and steel 7.6%; nonelectrical machinery and equipment 6.5%; fabricated metal products 5.7%). *Major import sources:* Japan 18.8%; China 11.3%; U.S. 6.4%; U.A.E. 6.2%; Malaysia 5.4%.
Exports (2008): THB 5,851,371,140,000 (computers and parts 9.4%; transportation equipment 9.4%; agricultural products 9.0%; integrated circuits and parts 8.7%; electrical machinery and apparatus 6.8%; refined petroleum products 5.4%; nonelectrical machinery and equipment 4.9%). *Major export destinations:* U.S. 11.4%; Japan 11.3%; China 9.1%; Singapore 5.7%; Hong Kong 5.7%; Malaysia 5.6%.

Transport and communications

Transport. Railroads (2008): route length 2,530 mi, 4,071 km; passenger-km 8,570,000,000; metric ton-km cargo 3,139,000,000. Roads (2007): total length 32,024 mi, 51,538 km (paved 99%). Vehicles (2007): passenger cars 3,560,222; trucks and buses 3,615,153. Air transport (2008)[11]: passenger-km 58,108,000,000; metric ton-km cargo 2,292,000,000.

Communications

Medium	date	number in '000s	units per 1,000 persons	Medium	date	number in '000s	units per 1,000 persons
Televisions	2003	17,971	289	PCs	2007	4,039	62
Telephones				Dailies	2009	7,500[12]	113[12]
Cellular	2010	69,683[13]	1,008[13]	Internet users	2009	17,486	258
Landline	2010	7,009	101	Broadband	2010	2,673[13]	39[13]

Education and health

Educational attainment (2007). Percentage of employed population having: no formal schooling 4.9%; incomplete primary education 32.4%; complete primary 21.2%; lower secondary 29.6%; upper secondary/higher 11.4%; other/unknown 0.5%. *Literacy* (2007): population age 15 and over literate 94.1%; males literate 95.9%; females literate 92.6%.

Education (2008–09)

	teachers	students	student/ teacher ratio	enrollment rate (%)
Primary (age 6–11)	347,959	5,564,622	16.0	94[14]
Secondary/Voc. (age 12–17)	222,799	4,728,761	21.2	72
Tertiary	75,642	2,430,047	32.1	45 (age 18–22)

Health (2005): physicians 19,546 (1 per 3,287 persons); hospital beds 134,016 (1 per 470 persons); infant mortality rate (2008) 18.1; undernourished population (2004–06) 10,700,000 (17% of total population based on the consumption of a minimum daily requirement of 1,850 calories).

Military

Total active duty personnel (November 2010): 305,860 (army 62.1%, navy 22.9%, air force 15.0%); reserve 200,000; paramilitary 113,700. *Military expenditure as percentage of GDP* (2009): 1.8%; per capita expenditure U.S.$74.

[1]Includes 73 indirectly elected seats chosen by the Senate Selection Commission. [2]Actual local administration is based on 76 provinces and one administrative unit (Bangkok). [3]Preliminary results. [4]Includes mangosteens and guavas. [5]June–May. [6]July–June. [7]Third quarter. [8]Manufacturing only. [9]Includes 450,900 unemployed. [10]Imports c.i.f.; exports f.o.b. [11]Thai Airways and Bangkok Airlines. [12]Circulation of daily newspapers. [13]Subscribers. [14]2006–07.

Internet resources for further information:
- **National Statistical Office http://www.nso.go.th/index-1.html**
- **Bank of Thailand http://www.bot.or.th**

Togo

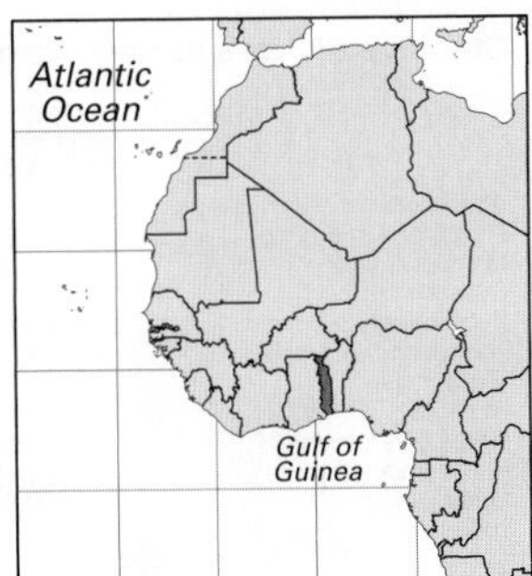

Official name: République Togolaise (Togolese Republic).
Form of government: multiparty republic with one legislative body (National Assembly [81]).
Head of state and government: President assisted by Prime Minister.
Capital: Lomé.
Official language: French.
Official religion: none.
Monetary unit: CFA franc (CFAF); valuation (Sept. 1, 2011) 1 U.S.$ = CFAF 460.31; 1 £ = CFAF 743.83.

Population

Regions Prefectures	population 2010 census[1]	Regions Prefectures	population 2010 census[1]
Centrale	577,629	Plateaux	1,278,566
Blitta	129,030	Agou	79,247
Sotouboua	148,282	Akébou	57,172
Tchamba	122,352	Amou	98,338
Tchaoudjo	177,965	Anié	88,867
Kara	721,504	Danyi	36,018
Assoli	48,191	Est-Mono	113,855
Bassar	112,871	Haho	232,928
Binah	65,469	Kloto	125,724
Dankpen	122,209	Kpélé	70,241
Doufelgou	73,734	Moyen-Mono	72,156
Kéran	87,736	Ogou	208,981
Kozah	211,294	Wawa	95,039
Maritime	2,398,915	Savanes	776,710
Avé	93,181	Cinkassé	74,494
Bas-Mono	83,163	Kpendjal	145,109
Golfe[2]	1,432,453	Oti	178,135
Lacs	160,991	Tandjouaré	110,721
Vo	195,245	Tône	268,251
Yoto	157,426	TOTAL	5,753,324
Zio	276,456		

Demography

Area: 21,853 sq mi, 56,600 sq km.
Population (2011): 5,830,000.
Density (2011): persons per sq mi 266.8, persons per sq km 103.0.
Urban-rural (2010): urban 37.4%; rural 62.6%.
Sex distribution (2010): male 48.65%; female 51.35%.
Age breakdown (2008): under 15, 41.6%; 15–29, 30.0%; 30–44, 15.9%; 45–59, 8.1%; 60–74, 3.6%; 75–84, 0.7%; 85 and over, 0.1%.
Population projection: (2020) 6,963,000; (2030) 8,234,413.
Ethnic composition (2000): Ewe 22.2%; Kabre 13.4%; Wachi 10.0%; Mina 5.6%; Kotokoli 5.6%; Bimoba 5.2%; Losso 4.0%; Gurma 3.4%; Lamba 3.2%; Adja 3.0%; other 24.4%.
Religious affiliation (2004): Christian 47.2%, of which Roman Catholic 27.8%, Protestant 9.5%, independent and other Christian 9.9%; traditional beliefs 33.0%; Muslim 13.7%; nonreligious 4.9%; other 1.2%.
Major cities (2010): Lomé 750,757 (urban agglomeration 1,348,619); Kara 89,439; Sokodé 88,557; Kpalimé 69,531; Atakpamé 62,531.

Vital statistics

Birth rate per 1,000 population (2009): 32.4 (world avg. 20.3).
Death rate per 1,000 population (2009): 8.0 (world avg. 8.5).
Total fertility rate (avg. births per childbearing woman; 2008): 4.85.
Life expectancy at birth (2008): male 57.0 years; female 61.6 years.
Adult population (ages 15–49) *living with HIV* (2009): 3.2%[3] (world avg. 0.8%).
Major causes of death per 100,000 population (2002): infectious and parasitic diseases *c.* 572, of which HIV/AIDS-related *c.* 220, malaria *c.* 136; lower respiratory infections *c.* 180; perinatal conditions *c.* 86.

National economy

Budget (2008). Revenue: CFAF 249,900,000,000 (tax revenue 84.5%, of which taxes on international trade 66.5%; grants 11.7%; nontax revenue 3.8%). Expenditures: CFAF 253,300,000,000 (current expenditure 80.2%; capital expenditure 19.8%).
Population economically active (2008): total 2,866,000[4]; activity rate of total population 44.4%[4] (participation rates: ages 15–64, 75.4%[4]; female 43.3%[4]; unemployed [2004] *c.* 32%).

Price index (2005 = 100)

	2004	2005	2006	2007	2008	2009	2010
Consumer price index	93.6	100.0	102.2	103.2	112.2	114.4	116.5

Production (metric tons except as noted). Agriculture, forestry, fishing (2009): cassava 776,715, corn (maize) 651,738, yams 560,584, sorghum 231,660, cacao beans 105,000, rice 69,721, dry beans 57,348, peanuts (groundnuts) 37,000, coffee 8,400; livestock (number of live animals) 2,054,250 sheep, 1,517,250 goats; roundwood (2010) 4,590,000 cu m, of which fuelwood 96%; fisheries production 27,132 (from aquaculture, negligible). Mining and quarrying (2009): limestone 1,704,280; phosphate rock (gross weight) 726,000; diamonds 125 carats. Manufacturing (value added in CFAF '000,000; 2006): food products, beverages, and tobacco manufactures 33,800; bricks, cement, and ceramics 19,300; base and fabricated metals 10,800; wood and wood products 7,300. Energy production (consumption): electricity (kW-hr; 2007) 196,000,000 (710,000,000); coal, none (none); crude petroleum, none (none); petroleum products (metric tons; 2007) none (298,000); natural gas, none (none).
Gross national income (GNI; 2010): U.S.$2,957,000,000 (U.S.$440 per capita); purchasing power parity GNI (U.S.$790 per capita).

Structure of gross domestic product and labour force

	2009 in value CFAF '000,000,000	2009 % of total value	2003 labour force	2003 % of labour force
Agriculture, forestry, fishing	640.3	42.7	1,210,000	57.9
Mining	45.0	3.0		
Manufacturing	126.6	8.5		
Construction	67.3	4.5		
Public utilities	39.5	2.6		
Transp. and commun.	75.0	5.0	881,000	42.1
Trade, hotels	114.4	7.6		
Finance, real estate	135.3	9.0		
Pub. admin., defense	107.6	7.2		
Services	29.7	2.0		
Other	117.2[5]	7.8[5]		
TOTAL	1,498.0[6]	100.0[6]	2,091,000	100.0

Public debt (external, outstanding; 2009): U.S.$1,502,000,000.
Household income and expenditure. Average household size (2004) 6.0; expenditure (2004)[7]: food products 36.1%, hotels and restaurants 12.9%, housing and energy 12.4%, transportation 8.5%, clothing and footwear 6.0%.
Selected balance of payments data. Receipts from (U.S.$'000,000): tourism (2008) 40; remittances (2010) 336; foreign direct investment (2008–10 avg.) 38; official development assistance (2009) 499. Disbursements for (U.S.$'000,000): tourism (2008) 19; remittances (2009) 58.
Land use as % of total land area (2009): in temporary crops or left fallow 40.4%, in permanent crops 3.3%, in pasture 18.4%, forest area 5.6%.

Foreign trade[8]

Balance of trade (current prices)

	2002	2003	2004	2005	2006	2007
U.S.$'000,000	–154.7	–73.8	–167.9	–232.7	...	–507.1
% of total	23.6%	6.9%	17.7%	24.4%	...	47.5%

Imports (2007): U.S.$787,100,000 (refined petroleum 26.7%; food 10.6%, of which cereals 5.2%; machinery and apparatus 9.4%; cement clinker 7.9%; medicinal and pharmaceutical products 6.2%). *Major import sources:* France 19.2%; China 15.8%; Netherlands 11.1%; U.S. 4.2%; Belgium 3.7%.
Exports (2007): U.S.$280,000,000 (portland cement 24.1%; cement clinker 19.6%; iron and steel 12.5%; crude fertilizer 11.2%; food 9.5%; cotton 8.9%). *Major export destinations:* Niger 12.7%; Benin 10.9%; India 9.8%; Burkina Faso 9.8%; Mali 7.1%; unspecified zones 19.7%.

Transport and communications

Transport. Railroads (2007): route length 364 km[9]; passenger-km, none; metric ton-km cargo (2001) 440,000,000. Roads (2001): total length 4,660 mi, 7,500 km (paved 24%). Vehicles (2007): passenger cars 10,611; trucks and buses 2,412. Air transport (2007): passenger-km, n.a.; metric ton-km cargo, n.a.

Communications

Medium	date	number in '000s	units per 1,000 persons	Medium	date	number in '000s	units per 1,000 persons
Televisions	2004	650	107	PCs	2007	171	30
Telephones				Dailies	2009	5[10]	1.4[10]
Cellular	2010	2,452[11]	407[11]	Internet users	2009	356	54
Landline	2010	214	36	Broadband	2010	5.4[11]	0.2[11]

Education and health

Educational attainment (1998)[12]. Percentage of population age 25 and over having: no formal education 56.3%; primary education 24.5%; secondary and higher 18.3%; unknown 0.9%. *Literacy* (2008): total population age 15 and over literate 64.9%; males 76.6%; females 53.7%.

Education (2006–07)

	teachers	students	student/ teacher ratio	enrollment rate (%)
Primary (age 6–11)[13]	28,153	1,163,902	41.3	94
Secondary/Voc. (age 12–18)	11,518	408,964	35.5	22[14]
Tertiary	51	32,502	637.3	5 (age 19–23)

Health: physicians (2004) 225 (1 per 23,364 persons); hospital beds (2005) 4,862 (1 per 1,111 persons); infant mortality rate (2008) 58.2; undernourished population (2006–08) 1,900,000 (30% of total population based on the consumption of a minimum daily requirement of 1,770 calories).

Military

Total active duty personnel (November 2010): 8,550 (army 94.7%, navy 2.3%, air force 3.0%). *Military expenditure as percentage of GDP* (2009): 2.2%; per capita expenditure U.S.$11.

[1]Preliminary. [2]Golfe prefecture includes Lomé commune. [3]Statistically derived midpoint of range. [4]ILO estimate. [5]Import duties and taxes. [6]Detail does not add to total given because of rounding. [7]Weights of consumer price index components. [8]Imports c.i.f.; exports f.o.b. [9]Length of 3 operational lines. [10]Circulation of daily newspapers. [11]Subscribers. [12]Based on the 1998 Togo Demographic and Health Survey, of which 14,075 respondents were age 25 and over. [13]2008–09. [14]1999–2000.

Internet resources for further information:
- **Banque Centrale des Etats de l'Afrique de l'Ouest http://www.bceao.int**
- **DGSCN-Togo http://www.stat-togo.org**

Tonga

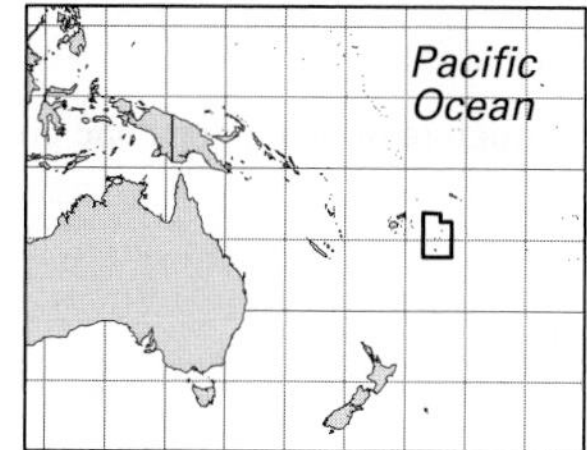

Official name: Fakatuʻi ʻo Tonga (Tongan); Kingdom of Tonga (English).
Form of government: hereditary constitutional monarchy with one legislative house (Legislative Assembly [28[1]]).
Head of state: King[2].
Head of government: Prime Minister.
Capital: Nukuʻalofa.
Official languages: Tongan; English.
Official religion: none.
Monetary unit: paʻanga (T$); valuation (Sept. 1, 2011) 1 U.S.$ = T$1.62; 1 £ = T$2.61.

Area and population

Divisions[3]	Principal towns	area sq mi	area sq km	population 2006 census
ʻEua[4]	ʻOhonua	34	87	5,206
Haʻapai[5]	Pangai	42	109	7,570
Niuas	Hihifo	28	72	1,665
Tongatapu[4]	Nukuʻalofa	101	261	72,045
Vavaʻu[5]	Neiafu	47	121	15,505
UNINHABITED ISLANDS		26[6]	68[6]	—
TOTAL LAND AREA		277[7]	718	
INLAND WATER		12	30	
TOTAL		289	748	101,991

Demography

Population (2011): 104,000.
Density (2010)[8]: persons per sq mi 359.0, persons per sq km 138.7.
Urban-rural (2006): urban 23.2%; rural 76.8%.
Sex distribution (2007): male 51.09%; female 48.91%.
Age breakdown (2006): under 15, 38.2%; 15–29, 26.3%; 30–44, 17.2%; 45–59, 10.1%; 60–74, 6.1%; 75–84, 1.7%; 85 and over, 0.4%.
Population projection: (2020) 106,000; (2030) 112,000.
Doubling time: 36 years.
Ethnic composition (2006): Tongan 96.6%; Tongan/other 1.6%; white 0.6%; Chinese 0.4%; other 0.8%.
Religious affiliation (2006): Protestant 64.9%, of which Methodist-related denominations 55.9%; Mormon 16.8%; Roman Catholic 15.6%; Bahāʼī 0.7%; unknown 1.4%; other 0.6%.
Major towns (2009): Nukuʻalofa (on Tongatapu) 24,200; Muʻa (on Tongatapu) 5,100; Neiafu (on Vavaʻu) 4,000; Haveloloto (on Tongatapu) 3,500; Pangai (in the Haʻapai Group) 1,600.

Vital statistics

Birth rate per 1,000 population (2008): 25.3 (world avg. 20.3).
Death rate per 1,000 population (2008): 5.7 (world avg. 8.5).
Natural increase rate per 1,000 population (2008): 19.6 (world avg. 11.8).
Total fertility rate (avg. births per childbearing woman; 2008): 3.76.
Marriage/divorce rates per 1,000 population (2004): 6.6[9]/1.1.
Life expectancy at birth (2008): male 72.4 years; female 74.4 years.
Major causes of death per 100,000 population (2004)[10]: circulatory diseases 150.5; malignant neoplasms (cancers) 71.8; endocrine, nutritional, and metabolic disorders 51.8; respiratory diseases 39.9.

National economy

Budget (2008–09). Revenue: T$200,294,000 (tax revenue 64.5%, grants 22.7%, nontax revenue 12.8%). Expenditures: T$185,329,000 (current expenditure 96.7%, development expenditure 3.3%).
Public debt (external, outstanding; June 2010): U.S.$117,500,000[11].
Gross national income (GNI; 2010): U.S.$353,000,000 (U.S.$3,380 per capita); purchasing power parity GNI (U.S.$4,630 per capita).

Structure of gross domestic product and labour force

	2008–09 in value T$'000	2008–09 % of total value	2003 labour force	2003 % of labour force
Agriculture, fishing	110,700	17.1	10,990	30.1
Mining	1,900	0.3	60	0.2
Manufacturing	45,600	7.0	8,540	23.4
Construction	39,200	6.1	1,440	3.9
Public utilities	18,300	2.8	530	1.5
Transp. and commun.	26,100	4.0	1,580	4.3
Trade, restaurants	82,500	12.7	3,570	9.8
Finance, real estate	63,800	9.8	760	2.1
Pub. admin., defense	79,200	12.2	2,590	7.1
Services	114,400	17.6	4,500	12.4
Other	67,600[12]	10.4[12]	1,890[13]	5.2[13]
TOTAL	649,500[7]	100.0	36,450	100.0

Production (metric tons except as noted). Agriculture, forestry, fishing (2009): coconuts 59,200, pumpkins, squash, and gourds 21,251, cassava 6,690, taro 4,184, yams 3,974, lemons and limes 2,833, pig meat 1,561, vanilla 263; livestock (number of live animals) 81,200 pigs, 11,300 cattle, 330,000 chickens; roundwood (2010) 4,142 cu m, of which fuelwood 52%; fisheries production 2,038 (from aquaculture, negligible). Mining and quarrying: coral and sand for local use. Manufacturing (value of production in T$'000; 2005): food products and beverages 19,722; bricks, cement, and ceramics 4,109; chemicals and chemical products 2,044; printing and publishing 1,313; furniture 1,310; fabricated metal products 1,193. Energy production (consumption): electricity (kW-hr; 2008) 55,000,000 ([2009–10] 42,800,000); crude petroleum, none (none); petroleum products (metric tons; 2007) none (57,000).
Population economically active (2008)[14]: total 42,000; activity rate *c.* 40% (participation rates: ages 15–64 *c.* 66%; female *c.* 40%; unemployed, n.a.).

Price index (2005 = 100)

	2004	2005	2006	2007	2008	2009	2010
Consumer price index	92.3	100.0	106.4	112.7	124.5	126.2	130.7

Household income and expenditure (2009). Average household size (2006) 5.8; average annual income per household T$16,692 (U.S.$8,204); sources of income: wages and salaries 43.5%, remittances 20.9%, sales of own agricultural products, fish, or handicrafts 18.8%; expenditure: food and nonalcoholic beverages 50.6%, transportation 11.0%, housing and energy 10.1%, household furnishings 4.4%, communications 3.9%, alcoholic beverages, kava, and tobacco 3.7%.
Selected balance of payments data. Receipts from (U.S.$'000,000): tourism (2008) 19.5; remittances (2009) 96; foreign direct investment (FDI; 2008–10 avg.) 12; official development assistance (2008) 26. Disbursements for (U.S.$'000,000): tourism (2008) 25.1; remittances (2009) 14; FDI (2007–09 avg.) 2.
Land use as % of total land area (2007): in temporary crops or left fallow *c.* 21%, in permanent crops *c.* 17%, in pasture *c.* 6%, forest area *c.* 5%.

Foreign trade[15]

Balance of trade (current prices)

	2004–05	2005–06	2006–07	2007–08	2008–09
T$'000,000	–197.5	–208.5	–235.8	–290.9	–294.2
% of total	78.4%	81.0%	88.2%	90.0%	90.7%

Imports (2008–09): T$309,300,000 (food and beverages 30.0%; refined petroleum 18.4%; machinery and transport equipment 18.4%). *Major import sources:* New Zealand 26.5%; Fiji 13.1%; U.S. 11.6%; Australia 10.8%.
Exports (2008–09): T$15,100,000 (fish 27.8%; root crops 20.5%; squash, none; other agricultural products [incl. kava] 23.8%). *Major export destinations:* New Zealand 36.2%; U.S. 17.1%; Japan 13.2%; Australia 11.8%.

Transport and communications

Transport. Railroads: none. Roads (2000): total length 423 mi, 680 km (paved 27%). Vehicles (2004): passenger cars 7,705; trucks and buses 5,297. Air transport (2004): passenger-km 19,000,000; metric ton-km cargo, n.a.

Communications

Medium	date	number in '000s	units per 1,000 persons	Medium	date	number in '000s	units per 1,000 persons
Televisions	2003	7.1	70	PCs	2005	5.0	50
Telephones				Dailies	2009	0	0
Cellular	2010	54[16]	522[16]	Internet users	2009	8.4	81
Landline	2010	31	298	Broadband	2010	1.0[16]	9.6[16]

Education and health

Educational attainment (2006). Percentage of population age 25 and over having: no formal schooling 1.5%; primary education 29.5%; lower secondary 46.7%; upper secondary 11.0%; higher 11.0%, of which university 3.6%; other 0.3%. *Literacy* (2007): 99.2%.

Education (2005–06)

	teachers	students	student/ teacher ratio	enrollment rate (%)
Primary (age 5–10)	760	16,941	22.3	99
Secondary/Voc. (age 11–16)	1,012[17]	13,938	14.4[17]	66
Tertiary[18]	...	657	...	6 (age 17–21)

Health (2007): physicians 58[19] (1 per 1,762 persons); hospital beds 266 (1 per 384 persons); infant mortality rate per 1,000 live births (2007) 11.8; undernourished population, n.a.

Military

Total active duty personnel (2009): 500-member force includes air and coast guard elements. Tonga has defense cooperation agreements with both Australia and New Zealand. *Military expenditure as percentage of GDP* (2005): 1.1%; per capita expenditure U.S.$26.

[1]Includes 17 directly elected seats and 9 nobles elected by the hereditary nobles of Tonga, as well as 2 cabinet members who are not elected. [2]The king voluntarily ceded much of his power in July 2008. [3]Divisions have no administrative functions; 3 island councils constitute the local administrative framework (including a combined islands council for ʻEua, Niuas, and Tongatapu. [4]ʻEua and Tongatapu together constitute Tongatapu island group. [5]Also the name of an island group. [6]Estimated figure. [7]Detail does not add to total given because of rounding. [8]Based on land area. [9]Marriages on Tongatapu only. [10]Deaths occurring in hospitals only. [11]Includes short-term debt. [12]Indirect taxes less subsidies and less imputed bank service charges. [13]Unemployed. [14]ILO estimates. [15]Imports c.i.f.; exports f.o.b. [16]Subscribers. [17]2001–02. [18]2003–04. [19]Government doctors only.

Internet resources for further information:
- **Tonga Department of Statistics**
  http://www.spc.int/prism/Country/TO/stats
- **National Reserve Bank of Tonga**
  http://www.reservebank.to

Trinidad and Tobago

Official name: Republic of Trinidad and Tobago.
Form of government: multiparty republic with two legislative houses (Senate [31[1]]; House of Representatives [42]).
Head of state: President.
Head of government: Prime Minister.
Capital: Port of Spain.
Official language: English.
Official religion: none.
Monetary unit: Trinidad and Tobago dollar (TT$); valuation (Sept. 1, 2011) 1 U.S.$ = TT$6.39; 1 £ = TT$10.33.

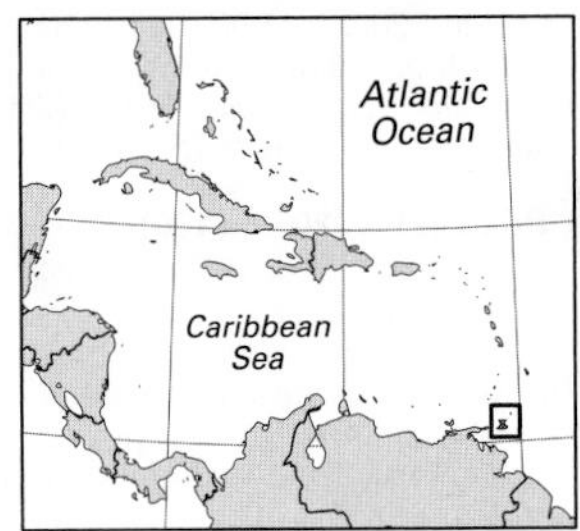

Area and population

	area	population		area	population
	sq km	2000 census		sq km	2000 census
Trinidad	4,852	1,208,282	**City corporations**		
Regional corporations			Port of Spain	13	49,031
Couva/Tabaquite/ Talparo	720	162,779	San Fernando	19	55,419
Diego Martin	128	105,720	**Borough corporations**		
Mayaro/Rio Claro	853	33,480	Arima	11	32,278
Penal/Debe	247	83,609	Chaguanas	60	67,433
Princes Town	621	91,947	Point Fortin	24	19,056
San Juan/Laventille	220	157,295	**Tobago**[2]	303	54,084
Sangre Grande	899	64,343	TOTAL	5,155	1,262,366
Siparia	510	81,917			
Tunapuna/Piarco	527	203,975			

Demography

Population (2011): 1,325,000.
Density (2011): persons per sq mi 665.9, persons per sq km 257.1.
Urban-rural (2010): urban 13.9%; rural 86.1%.
Sex distribution (2007): male 50.59%; female 49.41%.
Age breakdown (2010): under 15, 20.3%; 15–29, 27.8%; 30–44, 22.1%; 45–59, 18.2%; 60–74, 8.0%; 75 and over, 3.6%.
Population projection: (2020) 1,354,000; (2030) 1,335,000.
Ethnic composition (2000): black 39.2%; East Indian 38.6%; mixed 16.3%; Chinese 1.6%; white 1.0%; other/not stated 3.3%.
Religious affiliation (2005): Roman Catholic *c.* 29%; Hindu *c.* 24%; Protestant *c.* 19%; independent and other Christian *c.* 7%; Muslim *c.* 7%; nonreligious *c.* 2%; other/unknown *c.* 12%.
Major cities/built-up areas (2006): Chaguanas 73,100; San Juan 57,100[3]; San Fernando 56,600; Port of Spain 49,800 (greater Port of Spain [2004] 264,000); Arima 35,600[3].

Vital statistics

Birth rate per 1,000 population (2010): 14.9 (world avg. 19.2).
Death rate per 1,000 population (2010): 8.1 (world avg. 8.2).
Total fertility rate (avg. births per childbearing woman; 2010): 1.70.
Marriage/divorce rates per 1,000 population (2002): 5.8/1.2.
Life expectancy at birth (2007): male 67.6 years; female 73.5 years.
Major causes of death per 100,000 population (2006): diseases of the circulatory system 256.5, of which ischemic heart disease 118.8; malignant neoplasms (cancers) 99.8; diabetes mellitus 99.1; accidents, poisoning, and violence 77.2.
Adult population (ages 15–49) *living with HIV* (2009): 1.5%[4] (world avg. 0.8%).

National economy

Budget (2010). Revenue: TT$43,211,900,000 (taxes on oil/natural gas corporations 34.1%, nonoil company taxes 15.3%, VAT 13.8%, income taxes 10.4%, nontax revenue 8.1%). Expenditures: TT$43,520,100,000 (current expenditures 86.2%, development expenditures and net lending 13.8%).
Public debt (external, outstanding; June 2011): U.S.$1,675,800,000.
Production (metric tons except as noted). Agriculture, forestry, fishing (2009): sugarcane 810,000, coconuts 14,578, pineapples 7,819, taro 7,063, bananas 6,903, plantains 4,372, yautia (cocoyams) 1,635, cacao beans 600; livestock (number of live animals) 61,430 goats, 47,000 pigs, 28,500,000 chickens; roundwood (2010) 80,135 cu m, of which fuelwood 41%; fisheries production 13,868 (from aquaculture, negligible). Mining and quarrying (2009): limestone 850,000; natural asphalt 16,200. Manufacturing (value added in U.S.$'000,000; 2006): chemicals and chemical products 1,393; refined petroleum products 1,289; food products 200; iron and steel 148; beverages 124; cement, bricks, and ceramics 108; tobacco products 71. Energy production (consumption): electricity (kW-hr; 2009) 7,873,300,000 ([2007] 7,662,000,000); coal, none (none); crude petroleum (barrels; 2010–11) 31,565,300 ([2007] 60,700,000); petroleum products (metric tons; 2007) 8,029,000 (1,016,000); natural gas (cu m; 2010–11) 44,184,900,000 ([2007] 16,108,000,000).
Land use as % of total land area (2007): in temporary crops or left fallow 4.9%, in permanent crops 4.3%, in pasture 1.4%, forest area 43.9%.
Population economically active (2010): total 608,400; activity rate of total population 46.2% (participation rates: ages 15 and over, 61.0%; female 41.0%; unemployed 6.4%).

Price index (2005 = 100)

	2004	2005	2006	2007	2008	2009	2010
Consumer price index	93.6	100.0	108.3	116.9	130.9	140.1	154.8

Gross national income (GNI; 2010): U.S.$20,664,000,000 (U.S.$15,380 per capita); purchasing power parity GNI (U.S.$24,000 per capita).

Structure of gross domestic product and labour force

	2010		2006	
	in value TT$'000,000	% of total value	labour force	% of labour force
Agriculture, forestry, fishing	740.8	0.6	25,700	4.1
Petroleum, natural gas, other mining	46,296.2	35.7	20,400	3.2
Manufacturing	6,905.1	5.3	55,500	8.9
Construction	12,815.2	9.9	104,500	16.7
Public utilities	1,697.7	1.3		
Transp. and commun.	7,705.3	5.9	42,700	6.8
Trade, hotels	18,743.4	14.5	106,600	17.1
Finance, real estate	14,927.0	11.5	48,100	7.7
Pub. admin., defense	13,247.2	10.2	181,000	29.0
Services	5,378.6	4.1		
Other	1,296.7[5]	1.0[5]	40,600[6]	6.5[6]
TOTAL	129,753.2	100.0	625,200[7]	100.0

Household income and expenditure. Average household size (2004) 3.8; average income per household[8] TT$53,015 (U.S.$8,484); expenditure (2003): housing 20.4%, food and nonalcoholic beverages 18.0%, transportation 16.7%, recreation and culture 8.5%, energy 5.8%.
Selected balance of payments data. Receipts from (U.S.$'000,000): tourism (2008) 397; remittances (2010) 109; official development assistance (2009) 7; foreign direct investment (FDI; 2008–10 avg.) 1,353. Disbursements for (U.S.$'000,000): tourism (2008) 75; remittances, n.a.; FDI (2008–10 avg.) 233.

Foreign trade[9]

Balance of trade (current prices)

	2005	2006	2007	2008	2009	2010
TT$'000,000	+24,679	+48,364	+36,054	+56,710	+13,772	+29,844
% of total	25.6%	37.1%	27.2%	32.0%	13.5%	26.5%

Imports (2010): TT$41,283,000,000 (mineral fuels 33.3%; machinery and apparatus 25.9%, of which transportation equipment 9.0%; food products, beverages, and tobacco 11.0%; chemicals and chemical products 7.6%). *Major import sources:* United States 27.7%; Gabon 12.9%; Colombia 9.5%; Brazil 7.2%; Canada 2.8%.
Exports (2010): TT$71,126,500,000 (crude and refined petroleum 43.0%; chemicals and chemical products 21.4%; liquefied natural gas 18.5%; iron and steel 5.0%; machinery and apparatus 3.2%). *Major export destinations:* United States 46.9%; Jamaica 6.4%; Barbados 3.3%; Suriname 2.6%; Colombia 2.5%.

Transport and communications

Transport. Railroads: none. Roads (2000): total length 5,170 mi, 8,320 km (paved 51%). Vehicles (2005): passenger cars 320,000; trucks and buses 71,000. Air transport (2008)[10]: passenger-km 2,285,000,000; metric ton-km cargo 19,696,000.

Communications

Medium	date	number in '000s	units per 1,000 persons	Medium	date	number in '000s	units per 1,000 persons
Televisions	2003	461	359	PCs	2007	172	132
Telephones				Dailies	2009	140[11]	142[11]
Cellular	2010	1,894[12]	1,412[12]	Internet users	2009	485	362
Landline	2010	293	219	Broadband	2010	145[12]	108[12]

Education and health

Educational attainment (2009). Percentage of population age 25 and over having: no formal schooling/unknown 1.9%; primary education 38.8%; secondary 15.6%; vocational 34.1%; university 9.6%. *Literacy* (2010): total population age 15 and over literate 99.1%; males 99.4%; females 98.8%.

Education (2007–08)

	teachers	students	student/ teacher ratio	enrollment rate (%)
Primary (age 5–11)	7,628	130,880	17.2	92
Secondary/Voc. (age 12–16)	7,045	95,275	13.5	74
Tertiary[13]	1,800	16,920	9.4	11 (age 17–21)

Health (2009): physicians 1,992 (1 per 658 persons); hospital beds 3,585 (1 per 365 persons); infant mortality rate per 1,000 live births (2010) 11.1; undernourished population (2004–06) 120,000 (10% of total population based on the consumption of a minimum daily requirement of 1,900 calories).

Military

Total active duty personnel (November 2010): 4,063 (army 73.8%, coast guard 26.2%). *Military expenditure as percentage of GDP* (2010): 0.8%; per capita expenditure U.S.$131.

[1]All seats are nonelected. [2]Semiautonomous island. [3]Within greater Port of Spain. [4]Statistically derived midpoint of range. [5]Net of VAT less imputed bank service charges. [6]Includes 39,000 unemployed. [7]Detail does not add to total given because of rounding. [8]Approximately 2002; exact date of information is unknown. [9]Imports c.i.f.; exports f.o.b. [10]Caribbean Airlines. [11]Circulation of daily newspapers. [12]Subscribers. [13]2004–05.

Internet resources for further information:
- **Central Bank of Trinidad and Tobago http://www.central-bank.org.tt**
- **Central Statistical Office http://www.cso.gov.tt**

Tunisia

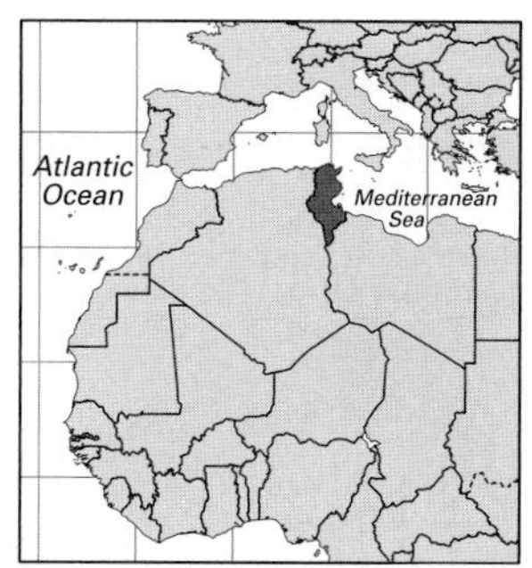

Official name: Al-Jumhūriyyah al-Tūnisiyyah (Tunisian Republic).
Form of government: interim regime[1] with one interim legislative house[2] (Constituent Assembly [217]).
Head of state: President.
Head of government: Prime Minister.
Capital: Tunis.
Official language: Arabic.
Official religion: Islam.
Monetary unit: dinar (TND); valuation (Sept. 1, 2011) 1 U.S.$ = TND 1.38; 1 £ = TND 2.23.

Area and population

Governorates	area sq km	population 2010 estimate	Governorates	area sq km	population 2010 estimate
Al-Ariānah	498	498,000	Al-Qayrawān	6,712	559,700
Bājah	3,558	306,200	Qibilī	22,084	150,700
Banzart	3,685	546,600	Ṣafāqis	7,545	931,000
Bin ʿArūs	761	577,500	Sīdī Bū Zayd	6,994	412,500
Jundūbah	3,102	423,200	Siliānah	4,631	234,000
Al-Kāf	4,965	256,600	Sūsah	2,621	611,800
Madanīn	8,588	455,900	Tatāuīn	38,889	146,200
Al-Mahdīyah	2,966	396,300	Tawzar	4,719	103,500
Manūbah	1,060	368,700	Tūnis	346	1,000,300
Al-Munastīr	1,019	515,300	Zaghwān	2,768	170,500
Nābul	2,788	752,800	INTERMITTENT SALT LAKES	9,080	—
Qābis	7,175	361,500	TOTAL	163,610	10,549,100[3]
Qafṣah	8,990	338,100			
Al-Qaṣrayn	8,066	432,300			

Demography

Population (2011): 10,594,000[4].
Density (2011)[5]: persons per sq mi 177.6, persons per sq km 68.6.
Urban-rural (2009): urban 66.9%; rural 33.1%.
Sex distribution (2008): male 50.30%; female 49.70%.
Age breakdown (2005): under 15, 25.9%; 15–29, 30.1%; 30–44, 22.1%; 45–59, 13.2%; 60–74, 6.6%; 75–84, 1.8%; 85 and over, 0.3%.
Population projection: (2020) 11,518,000; (2030) 12,212,000.
Ethnic composition (2000): Tunisian Arab 67.2%; Bedouin Arab 26.6%; Algerian Arab 2.4%; Amazigh (Berber) 1.4%; other 2.4%.
Religious affiliation (2005): Muslim *c.* 99%, of which Sunnī *c.* 97%; other *c.* 1%.
Major cities (2004): Tunis (2009) 759,000; Ṣafāqis 265,131; Al-Ariānah 240,749[6]; Sūsah 173,047; Ettadhamen 118,487[6].

Vital statistics

Birth rate per 1,000 population (2008–09): 15.3 (world avg. 20.3).
Death rate per 1,000 population (2008–09): 4.3 (world avg. 8.5).
Total fertility rate (avg. births per childbearing woman; 2009): 2.05.
Marriage/divorce rates per 1,000 population: (2008–09) 5.2/(1999) 0.1.
Life expectancy at birth (2009): male 72.5 years; female 76.5 years.
Major causes of death per 100,000 population (2002): cardiovascular diseases 267; accidents, injuries, and violence 62; malignant neoplasms (cancers) 57.

National economy

Budget (2007). Revenue: TND 13,880,700,000 (tax revenue 68.6%, of which VAT 19.2%, income tax 9.8%; grants and loans 17.5%; nontax revenue 13.9%). Expenditures: TND 15,089,000,000 (social services 40.9%; debt service 26.0%; economic services 17.4%).
Production (metric tons except as noted). Agriculture, forestry, fishing (2009): wheat 1,653,600, cow's milk 1,048,000, tomatoes 1,000,000, barley 850,000, olives 750,000, green chilies and peppers 296,000, oranges 170,000, dates 145,000, grapes 110,000, almonds 60,000; livestock (live animals) 7,361,620 sheep, 1,454,640 goats, 679,080 cattle, 235,000 camels; roundwood (2010) 2,395,284 cu m, of which fuelwood 91%; fisheries production 102,069 (from aquaculture 4%). Mining and quarrying (2008–09): phosphate rock 8,017,200; iron ore 178,900. Manufacturing (value added in TND '000,000; 2008): crude and refined petroleum and natural gas 4,033; electrical machinery 2,144; textiles, leather, and clothing 2,133; chemicals and chemical products 1,706; food products 1,563. Energy production (consumption): electricity (kW-hr; 2009–10) 14,306,000,000 ([2008–09] 11,861,200,000); coal (metric tons; 2009) none (none); crude petroleum (barrels; 2009–10) 29,395,000 ([2008–09] 12,739,100); petroleum products (metric tons; 2008–09) 1,710,800 (3,336,900); natural gas (cu m; 2009–10) 2,397,000,000 ([2009] 4,842,200,000).
Household income and expenditure (2005). Average household size (2009) 4.2; income per household TND 8,211 (U.S.$6,329); expenditure: food and beverages 34.8%, housing and energy 22.8%, transportation 10.7%, health and personal care 10.3%, household furnishings 8.8%.
Population economically active (2009): total 3,689,200; activity rate of total population 35.9% (participation rates: age 15 and over [2007] 46.8%; female 24.8%; unemployed 13.3%).

Price and earnings indexes (2005 = 100)

	2004	2005	2006	2007	2008	2009	2010
Consumer price index	98.0	100.0	104.5	108.1	113.4	117.4	122.6
Hourly earnings index[7]	...	100.0	102.9	106.5	111.5	...	...

Gross national income (GNI; 2010): U.S.$42,826,000,000 (U.S.$4,070 per capita); purchasing power parity GNI (U.S.$8,140 per capita).

Structure of gross domestic product and labour force

	2008 in value TND '000	2008 % of total value	2007 labour force	2007 % of labour force
Agriculture, forestry, fishing	4,884,300	9.6	570,700	15.9
Mining and quarrying	554,900	1.1	1,002,700	27.9
Public utilities	4,743,800[8]	9.3[8]		
Manufacturing	9,425,600	18.5		
Construction	2,728,800	5.4		
Transp. and commun.	5,709,900	11.2	1,511,700	42.1
Trade, hotels	7,412,100	14.5		
Finance, real estate	6,221,300	12.2		
Pub. admin., defense	5,327,700	10.5		
Services	1,079,700	2.1		
Other	2,866,500[9]	5.6[9]	508,100[10]	14.1[10]
TOTAL	50,954,600	100.0	3,593,200	100.0

Public debt (external, outstanding; June 2009): U.S.$14,673,200,000.
Selected balance of payments data. Receipts from (U.S.$'000,000): tourism (2009) 2,773; remittances (2010) 1,970; foreign direct investment (FDI; 2008–10 avg.) 1,986; official development assistance (2009) 474. Disbursements for (U.S.$'000,000): tourism (2009) 415; remittances (2009) 13; FDI (2008–10 avg.) 64.
Land use as % of total land area (2009): in temporary crops or left fallow 17.4%, in permanent crops 14.3%, in pasture 31.2%, forest area 6.1%.

Foreign trade[11]

Balance of trade (current prices)

	2004	2005	2006	2007	2008	2009
TND '000,000	–3,781	–3,498	–4,446	–5,029	–6,568	–6,230
% of total	13.2%	11.3%	12.5%	11.5%	12.2%	13.8%

Imports (2009): TND 25,692,000,000 (textiles and wearing apparel 14.7%; machinery and apparatus 12.6%; road vehicles 7.2%; refined petroleum 6.6%; base and fabricated metals 6.3%; plastics [incl. articles] 4.7%). *Major import sources:* France 20.1%; Italy 16.4%; Germany 8.8%; China 5.0%; Spain 4.5%.
Exports (2009): TND 19,462,000,000 (apparel [incl. knitwear] 21.4%; petroleum 13.6%; phosphate products [mostly fertilizers] 7.0%; electrical wires/cables 7.0%; footwear/leather goods 4.0%; olive oil 2.7%). *Major export destinations:* France 29.7%; Italy 21.0%; Germany 8.8%; Libya 5.8%; U.K. 4.8%.

Transport and communications

Transport. Railroads (2009): route length (2008) 1,347 mi, 2,167 km; passenger-km 1,364,000,000[12]; metric ton-km cargo 1,669,000,000[12]. Roads (2004): total length 11,950 mi, 19,232 km (paved 66%). Vehicles (2007): passenger cars 746,695; trucks and buses 310,621. Air transport (2009): passenger-km 3,228,000,000; metric ton-km cargo 14,040,000.

Communications

Medium	date	number in '000s	units per 1,000 persons	Medium	date	number in '000s	units per 1,000 persons
Televisions	2006	2,300	231	PCs	2008	997	98
Telephones				Dailies	2009	399[13]	39[13]
Cellular	2010	11,114[14]	1,060[14]	Internet users	2009	3,500	341
Landline	2010	1,290	123	Broadband	2010	482[14]	46[14]

Education and health

Educational attainment (2005). Percentage of population age 10 and over having: no formal schooling 22.0%; primary education 36.5%; secondary 33.1%; higher 8.4%. *Literacy* (2008): total population age 10 and over literate 77.6%; males literate 86.4%; females literate 71.0%.

Education (2007–08)

	teachers	students	student/ teacher ratio	enrollment rate (%)
Primary (age 6–11)	59,977	1,036,445	17.3	98
Secondary/Voc. (age 12–18)	82,981	1,259,240	15.2	71
Tertiary	18,608	350,828	18.9	34 (age 19–23)

Health (2008): physicians 11,533 (1 per 882 persons); hospital beds 18,851 (1 per 539 persons); infant mortality rate per 1,000 live births (2009) 17.8; undernourished population (2006–08) less than 5.0% of total population based on the consumption of a minimum daily requirement of 1,860 calories.

Military

Total active duty personnel (November 2010): 35,800 (army 75.4%, navy 13.4%, air force 11.2%). *Military expenditure as percentage of GDP* (2008): 1.3%; per capita expenditure U.S.$53.

[1]From Jan. 14, 2011. [2]From Oct. 23, 2011, elections. [3]Detail does not add to total given because of rounding. [4]Estimate of United Nations *World Population Prospects: The 2010 Revision*. [5]Excluding area of intermittent salt lakes. [6]Within Tunis urban agglomeration. [7]Minimum wage for 40-hour workweek. [8]Includes the extraction and refining of petroleum and natural gas. [9]Indirect taxes less subsidies and less imputed bank service charges. [10]Unemployed. [11]Imports c.i.f.; exports f.o.b. [12]Excludes December. [13]Circulation of six top daily newspapers only. [14]Subscribers.

Internet resources for further information:
- **Central Bank of Tunisia http://www.bct.gov.tn**
- **National Statistics Institute http://www.ins.nat.tn**

Turkey

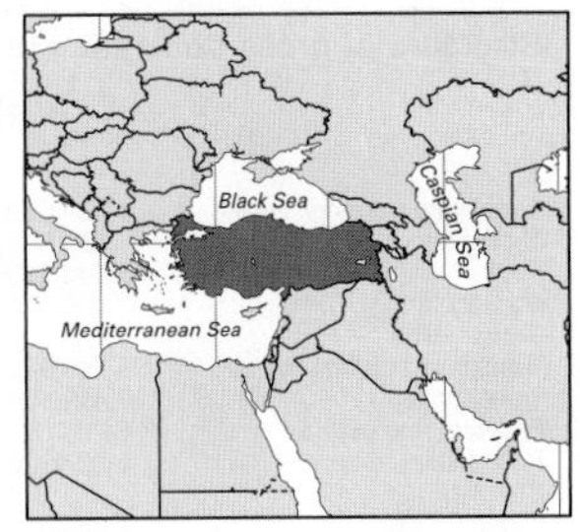

Official name: Türkiye Cumhuriyeti (Republic of Turkey).
Form of government: multiparty republic with one legislative house (Grand National Assembly of Turkey [550]).
Head of state: President.
Head of government: Prime Minister.
Capital: Ankara.
Official language: Turkish.
Official religion: none.
Monetary unit: Turkish lira[1] (TL); valuation (Sept. 1, 2011) 1 U.S.$ = TL 1.73; 1 £ = TL 2.79.

Area and population

Geographic regions[3]	area sq km	population 2010[2] estimate[4]	Geographic regions[3]	area sq km	population 2010[2] estimate[4]
Aegean	90,251	9,517,153	Black Sea, East	35,163	2,526,619
Anatolia, Central	91,809	3,831,373	Black Sea, West	73,840	4,512,288
Anatolia, Central East	82,948	3,638,401	Istanbul	5,313	12,915,158
Anatolia, North East	71,003	2,198,061	Marmara, East	49,383	6,701,343
Anatolia, South East	76,938	7,462,893	Marmara, West	42,989	3,129,772
Anatolia, West	75,362	6,875,349	Mediterranean	90,348	9,252,902
			TOTAL	785,347	72,561,312

Demography

Population (2011): 74,306,000.
Density (2011): persons per sq mi 245.0, persons per sq km 94.6.
Urban-rural (2009): urban 69.2%; rural 30.8%.
Sex distribution (2011[2]): male 50.25%; female 49.75%.
Age breakdown (2011[2]): under 15, 25.6%; 15–29, 25.8%; 30–44, 22.2%; 45–59, 15.8%; 60–74, 7.8%; 75–84, 2.4%; 85 and over, 0.4%.
Population projection: (2020) 82,172,000; (2030) 88,188,000.
Ethnic composition (2000): Turk 65.1%; Kurd 18.9%; Crimean Tatar 7.2%; Arab 1.8%; Azerbaijani 1.0%; Yoruk 1.0%; other 5.0%.
Religious affiliation (2005): Muslim *c.* 97.5%, of which Sunnī *c.* 82.5%, Shīʿī (mostly nonorthodox Alevi) *c.* 15.0%; nonreligious *c.* 2.0%; other[5] *c.* 0.5%.
Major cities (2011[2]): Istanbul 12,946,730; Ankara 4,223,398; İzmir 2,774,103; Bursa 1,667,321; Adana 1,584,053; Gaziantep 1,324,520.

Vital statistics

Birth rate per 1,000 population (2009): 17.3 (world avg. 20.3).
Death rate per 1,000 population (2009): 6.4 (world avg. 8.5).
Total fertility rate (avg. births per childbearing woman; 2009): 2.12.
Marriage/divorce rates per 1,000 population (2009): 8.2/1.6.
Life expectancy at birth (2009): male 71.5 years; female 76.1 years.
Major causes of death per 100,000 population (2008): diseases of the circulatory system 144.2; malignant neoplasms (cancers) 46.7; accidents 8.4; infectious and parasitic diseases 5.9.

National economy

Budget (2007). Revenue: YTL 218,858,000,000 (tax revenue 72.1%, of which taxes on goods and services 42.2%, individual income taxes 16.2%; nontax revenue 27.4%; grants 0.5%). Expenditures: YTL 206,965,000,000 (public debt transactions 24.1%; remainder 75.9%).
Production (in '000 metric tons except as noted). Agriculture, forestry, fishing (2009): wheat 20,600, sugar beets 17,275, cow's milk 11,583, tomatoes 10,746, barley 7,300, potatoes 4,398, grapes 4,265, corn (maize) 4,250, watermelons 3,810, apples 2,782, dry onions 1,850, cucumbers and gherkins 1,735, seed cotton 1,725, oranges 1,690, olives 1,291, sunflower seeds 1,057, apricots 695, chickpeas 563, hazelnuts 500, cherries 418, figs 244, walnuts 177, garlic 105; livestock (number of live animals) 23,974,600 sheep, 10,859,900 cattle, 146,986 angora goats, 244,280,000 chickens, 5,339,220 beehives; roundwood (2010) 20,554,000 cu m, of which fuelwood 24%; fisheries production 623 (from aquaculture 25%). Mining (2009): refined borates 1,000; magnesite 861; chromite (2007) 466; copper ore (metal content) 105; marble 2,715,600 cu m; silver 352,000 kg. Manufacturing (value added in U.S.$'000,000; 2005)[6]: food products 8,800; telecommunications equipment, electronics 7,450; chemicals and chemical products 7,400; base metals 7,000; motor vehicles and parts 6,500; textiles 6,100. Energy production (consumption): electricity (kW-hr; 2009–10) 205,316,000,000 ([2009] 161,947,528,000); hard coal (metric tons; 2009–10) 3,856,000 ([2007] 25,350,000); lignite (metric tons; 2009–10) 74,286,000 ([2007] 72,827,000); crude petroleum (barrels; 2009–10) 18,235,820 ([2009] 211,517,500); petroleum products (metric tons; 2009) 14,070,424 ([2007] 24,744,000); natural gas (cu m; 2009) 1,014,000,000 (35,070,000,000).
Population economically active (2009): total 24,748,000; activity rate of total population 34.4% (participation rates: ages 15–64 [2008] 50.6%; female 27.7%; unemployed [July 2010–June 2011] 10.8%).

Price and earnings indexes (2005 = 100)

	2004	2005	2006	2007	2008	2009	2010
Consumer price index	90.8	100.0	110.5	120.2	132.7	141.0	153.1
Annual earnings index[7]	...	100.0	108.7	117.5	127.7	139.2	152.6

Household income and expenditure (2008). Average household size 4.0; average annual income per household (2007) YTL 15,102 (U.S.$12,822); sources of income: wages and salaries 41.9%, self-employment 22.4%, transfers 22.2%; expenditure: housing 29.1%, food and nonalcoholic beverages 22.6%, transportation 14.1%, household furnishings 5.8%.

Gross national income (GNI; 2010): U.S.$719,404,000,000 (U.S.$9,500 per capita); purchasing power parity GNI (U.S.$14,580 per capita).

Structure of gross domestic product and labour force

	2009			
	in value YTL '000	% of total value	labour force	% of labour force
Agriculture, forestry, fishing	78,397,837	8.2	5,254,000	21.2
Mining and quarrying	14,235,361	1.5	103,000	0.4
Manufacturing	142,704,498	15.0	3,949,000	16.0
Construction	36,594,333	3.8	1,249,000	5.0
Public utilities	22,800,876	2.4	78,000	0.3
Transp. and commun.	127,027,822	13.3	1,081,000	4.4
Trade, hotels	126,287,247	13.2	4,542,000	18.3
Finance, real estate	209,817,997	22.0	1,339,000	5.4
Pub. admin., defense	41,356,310	4.3	3,682,000	14.9
Services	66,642,687	7.0		
Other	88,108,893[8]	9.2[8]	3,478,000[9]	14.1[9]
TOTAL	953,973,862[10]	100.0[10]	24,748,000[10]	100.0

Public debt[11] (external, outstanding; June 2010): U.S.$76,645,000,000.
Selected balance of payments data. Receipts from (U.S.$'000,000): tourism (2009) 21,250; remittances (2010) 892; foreign direct investment (FDI; 2008–10 avg.) 12,329; official development assistance (2009) 1,362. Disbursements for (U.S.$'000,000): tourism (2009) 4,147; remittances (2009) 141; FDI (2008–10 avg.) 1,961.
Land use as % of total land area (2009): in temporary crops 22.0%, left fallow 5.6%, in permanent crops 3.8%, in pasture 19.0%, forest area 14.6%.

Foreign trade[12]

Balance of trade (current prices)

	2005	2006	2007	2008	2009	2010
U.S.$'000,000	–43,298	–54,041	–62,791	–69,937	–38,785	–71,661
% of total	22.8%	24.0%	22.6%	20.9%	16.0%	23.9%

Imports (2008): U.S.$201,961,000,000 (machinery and apparatus 18.0%; petroleum 13.4%; base and fabricated metals 11.3%; road vehicles/parts 6.1%). *Major import sources:* Russia 15.5%; Germany 9.3%; China 7.8%; U.S. 5.9%; Italy 5.5%; France 4.5%.
Exports (2008): U.S.$132,002,000,000 (base and fabricated metals 18.0%, of which iron and steel 12.8%; machinery and apparatus 13.8%; road vehicles 13.6%; apparel 8.8%; petroleum 5.4%; vegetables/fruits/nuts 4.0%). *Major export destinations:* Germany 9.8%; U.K. 6.2%; U.A.E. 6.0%; Italy 5.9%; France 5.0%; Russia 4.9%.

Transport and communications

Transport. Railroads (2008): route length 5,405 mi, 8,699 km; passenger-km 5,134,000,000; metric ton-km cargo 10,459,000,000. Roads (2008): total length 218,751 mi, 352,046 km (paved 89%); passenger-km 206,098,000,000; metric ton-km cargo 181,935,000,000. Vehicles (2009): passenger cars 7,093,964; trucks and buses 3,517,339. Air transport (2008)[13]: passenger-km 51,183,000,000; metric ton-km cargo 533,501,000.

Communications

Medium	date	number in '000s	units per 1,000 persons	Medium	date	number in '000s	units per 1,000 persons
Televisions	2002	29,440	424	PCs	2007	4,207	60
Telephones				Dailies	2009	4,719[14]	66[14]
Cellular	2010	61,770[15]	849[15]	Internet users	2009	27,233	364
Landline	2010	16,202	223	Broadband	2010	7,096[15]	98[15]

Education and health

Educational attainment (2007). Percentage of population age 25–64 having: no formal schooling through primary education 61%; lower secondary 10%; upper secondary 18%; university 11%. *Literacy* (2009): total population age 6 and over literate 92.4%; males literate 97.0%; females literate 87.9%.

Education (2009–10)

	teachers	students	student/ teacher ratio	enrollment rate (%)
Primary (age 6–11)	485,677	10,916,643	22.5	95[16]
Secondary/Voc. (age 12–16)	206,862	4,240,139	20.5	74[16]
Tertiary	100,504[17]	2,757,828[17]	27.4[17]	38[16] (age 17–21)

Health (2008): physicians 113,151 (1 per 628 persons); hospital beds 188,065 (1 per 378 persons); infant mortality rate per 1,000 live births (2009) 15.3; undernourished population (2004–06) less than 5.0% of total population based on the consumption of a minimum daily requirement of 1,920 calories.

Military

Total active duty personnel (November 2010): 510,600 (army 78.7%, navy 9.5%, air force 11.8%)[18, 19]; paramilitary 102,200. *Military expenditure as percentage of GDP* (2009): 1.8%[20]; per capita expenditure U.S.$151[20].

[1]The New Turkish lira (YTL) was removed from circulation on Jan. 1, 2010, to be replaced by the Turkish lira (TL). [2]January 1. [3]Administratively divided into 81 provinces as of 2011. [4]Based on an address-based registration system. [5]Mostly Christian. [6]Rounded figures. [7]Minimum wage. [8]Taxes less subsidies and less imputed bank service charges. [9]Unemployed. [10]Detail does not add to total given because of rounding. [11]General government. [12]Imports c.i.f.; exports f.o.b. [13]Atlasjet, Turkish, Pegasus, and Onur airlines only. [14]Circulation of daily newspapers. [15]Subscribers. [16]2007–08. [17]2008–09. [18]Turkish troops in Turkish Republic of Northern Cyprus (November 2010) *c.* 36,000. [19]U.S. troops in Turkey 1,560. [20]Includes coast guard and gendarmerie.

Internet resources for further information:
- **Central Bank of Turkey http://www.tcmb.gov.tr/yeni/eng**
- **Turkish Statistical Institute http://www.turkstat.gov.tr/Start.do**

Turkmenistan

Official name: Türkmenistan (Turkmenistan).
Form of government[1]: unitary single-party[2] republic with one legislative body (Mejlis, or Assembly [125]).
Head of state and government: President.
Capital: Ashgabat.
Official language: Turkmen.
Official religion: none.
Monetary unit: (new) manat (TMT)[3]; valuation (Sept. 1, 2011) 1 U.S.$ = TMT 2.85[4]; 1 £ = TMT 4.60.

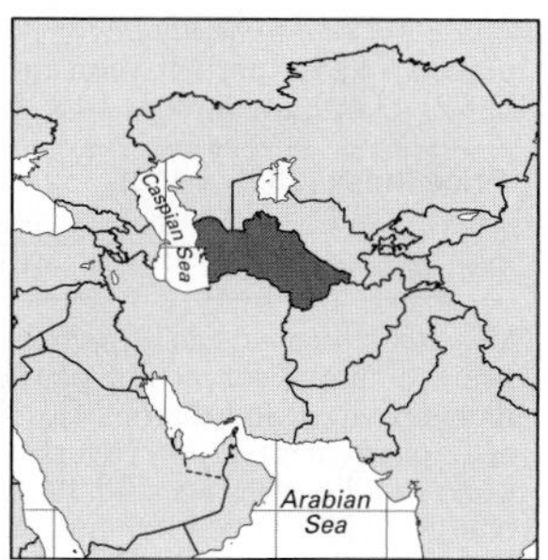

Area and population

Provinces	Capitals	area sq mi	area sq km	population 2005 estimate
Ahal	Ashgabat	37,514	97,160	939,700
Balkan	Balkanabat	53,772	139,270	553,500
Daşoguz	Daşoguz	28,352	73,430	1,370,400
Lebap	Türkmenabat (Chärjew)	36,189	93,730	1,334,500
Mary	Mary	33,649	87,150	1,480,400
City				
Ashgabat	—	181	470	871,500
TOTAL		189,657	491,210	6,550,000

Demography

Population (2011): 4,998,000[5].
Density (2011): persons per sq mi 26.4, persons per sq km 10.2.
Urban-rural (2008): urban 48.2%; rural 51.8%.
Sex distribution (2005): male 49.24%; female 50.76%.
Age breakdown (2005): under 15, 31.8%; 15–29, 30.0%; 30–44, 20.6%; 45–59, 11.4%; 60–74, 4.6%; 75–84, 1.4%; 85 and over, 0.2%.
Population projection[5]: (2020) 5,529,000; (2030) 6,027,000.
Doubling time: 50 years.
Ethnic composition (2003): Turkmen *c.* 85%; Uzbek *c.* 5%; Russian *c.* 4%; other *c.* 6%.
Religious affiliation (2000): Muslim (mostly Sunnī) 87.2%; Russian Orthodox 1.7%; nonreligious 9.0%; other 2.1%.
Major cities (2004): Ashgabat (2007) 744,000; Türkmenabat 256,000; Daşoguz 210,000; Mary 159,000; Balkanabat 139,000.

Vital statistics

Birth rate per 1,000 population (2009): 21.7 (world avg. 20.3); within marriage (1998) 96.2%; outside of marriage (1998) 3.8%.
Death rate per 1,000 population (2009): 7.6 (world avg. 8.5).
Natural increase rate per 1,000 population (2009): 14.1 (world avg. 11.8).
Total fertility rate (avg. births per childbearing woman; 2008): 2.48.
Marriage/divorce rates per 1,000 population: (1998) 5.4/(1994) 1.5.
Life expectancy at birth (2009): male 61.1 years; female 69.2 years.
Major causes of death per 100,000 population (2002): cardiovascular diseases 462.1, of which ischemic heart diseases 243.4, hypertensive heart disease 105.7; lower respiratory infections 77.6; infectious and parasitic diseases 65.6; malignant neoplasms (cancers) 60.9.

National economy

Budget (2006)[6]. Revenue: TMM 22,474,000,000,000 (tax revenue 93.8%, non-tax revenue 6.2%). Expenditures: TMM 16,631,000,000,000 (current expenditure 94.2%, development expenditure 5.8%).
Public debt (external, outstanding; 2009): U.S.$463,000,000.
Production (metric tons except as noted). Agriculture, forestry, fishing (2009): wheat 2,957,940, cow's milk 2,145,900, seed cotton 667,000, tomatoes 327,000, potatoes 246,700, grapes 230,000, cattle meat 140,004, sheep meat 127,950, wool 37,500; livestock (number of live animals) 13,512,900 sheep, 2,153,900 cattle; roundwood (2010) 10,000 cu m, of which fuelwood 100%; fisheries production 15,016 (from aquaculture, negligible). Mining and quarrying (2007): iodine 270,000, salt 5,200, gypsum 3,300. Manufacturing (2004): distillate fuel (gas-diesel oil) 2,511,000; residual fuel oils 1,745,000; motor spirits (gasoline) 1,265,000; wheat flour (2003) 503,000; cement 450,000. Energy production (consumption): electricity (kW-hr; 2007) 14,880,000,000 (13,420,000,000); coal, none (none); crude petroleum (barrels; 2007) 65,700,000 (40,200,000); petroleum products (metric tons; 2007) 7,212,000 (3,929,000); natural gas (cu m; 2007) 66,881,000,000 (15,983,000,000).
Household income and expenditure. Average household size (2002) 5.7; income per household: n.a.; sources of income (1998): wages and salaries 70.6%, pensions and grants 20.9%, self-employment (mainly agricultural income) 2.3%, nonwage income of workers 1.1%; expenditure (1998): food 45.2%, clothing and footwear 16.8%, furniture 13.3%, transportation 7.6%, health 7.0%.
Population economically active (2008): total 2,557,000[7]; activity rate of total population 50.7%[7] (participation rates: ages 15–64, 70.9%[7]; female 46.7%[7]; unofficially unemployed, n.a.).

Price index (2005 = 100)

	2004	2005	2006	2007	2008	2009	2010
Consumer price index	90.4	100.0	110.5	120.0	130.7	130.9	136.9

Gross national income (GNI; 2010): U.S.$19,159,000,000 (U.S.$3,700 per capita); purchasing power parity GNI (U.S.$7,160 per capita).

Structure of gross domestic product and labour force

	2008 in value U.S.$'000,000	2008 % of total value	1998 labour force	1998 % of labour force
Agriculture	1,846.6	22.6	892,400	48.5
Mining / Manufacturing	3,069.2 (incl. Public utilities)	37.6 (incl. Public utilities)	226,800	12.3
Public utilities			48,300	2.6
Construction	353.8	4.3	108,200	5.9
Transp. and commun.	259.7	3.2	90,700	4.9
Trade, hotels	169.2	2.1	115,800	6.4
Finance			12,600	0.7
Public administration, defense	2,470.7 (Finance, Public administration, Services, Other)	30.2	28,800	1.6
Services			284,900	15.5
Other			30,200	1.6
TOTAL	8,169.2	100.0	1,838,700	100.0

Selected balance of payments data. Receipts from (U.S.$'000,000): tourism, n.a.; remittances (2006) 4[8]; foreign direct investment (2008–10 avg.) 2,409; official development assistance (2009) 40. Disbursements for (U.S.$'000,000): tourism, n.a.; remittances (2006) 1[8].
Land use as % of total land area (2009): in temporary crops or left fallow 3.9%, in permanent crops 0.1%, in pasture 65.3%, forest area 8.8%.

Foreign trade[9]

Balance of trade (current prices)

	2002	2003	2004	2005	2006	2007
U.S.$'000,000	+1,030	+886	+705	+1,997	+4,598	+5,216
% of total	21.9%	14.7%	10.1%	25.3%	47.3%	41.2%

Imports (2006): U.S.$2,668,000,000 (machinery and transport equipment 42.6%, basic manufactures 28.0%, chemicals and chemical products 9.0%, food products 7.1%). *Major import sources* (2008): Turkey *c.* 15%; China *c.* 15%; U.A.E. *c.* 14%; Russia *c.* 12%; Ukraine *c.* 7%; Iran *c.* 7%.
Exports (2005–06): U.S.$4,113,000,000 (natural gas 55.8%, petroleum [all forms] 24.7%, textile yarn 3.9%, ships/boats/floating structures 2.1%). *Major export destinations* (2008): Ukraine *c.* 40%; Iran *c.* 16%; Poland *c.* 9%; Hungary *c.* 8%.

Transport and communications

Transport. Railroads (2006): length 1,852 mi, 2,980 km; passenger-km (1999) 701,000,000; metric ton-km cargo (2002) 7,476,000,000. Roads (2001): total length 22,000 km (paved 82%). Vehicles (2007[10]): passenger cars 226,800; trucks and buses, n.a. Air transport: passenger-km (2005) 1,905,000,000; metric ton-km cargo (2007) 11,000,000.

Communications

Medium	date	number in '000s	units per 1,000 persons	Medium	date	number in '000s	units per 1,000 persons
Televisions	2003	855	182	PCs	2005	348	72
Telephones				Dailies	2009	56[11]	16[11]
Cellular	2010	3,198[12]	634[12]	Internet users	2009	80	16
Landline	2010	520	103	Broadband	2010	0.7[12]	0.1[12]

Education and health

Educational attainment (2000)[13]. Percentage of population age 25 and over having: no formal schooling 3.0%; incomplete primary to complete standard secondary education 60.1%; vocational secondary 23.5%; higher 13.2%; unknown 0.2%. *Literacy* (2007): total population age 15 and over literate 99.5%; males literate 99.7%; females literate 99.3%.

Education (2006–07)

	teachers	students	student/ teacher ratio	enrollment rate (%)
Primary (age 7–9)	...	...	...	...
Secondary/Voc. (age 10–15)	...	...	...	...
Tertiary	...	...	...	... (age 16–20)

Health (2006): physicians 12,210 (1 per 387 persons); hospital beds 20,296 (1 per 233 persons); infant mortality rate per 1,000 live births (2007) 45.0; undernourished population (2006–08) 300,000 (7% of total population based on the consumption of a minimum daily requirement of 1,880 calories).

Military

Total active duty personnel (November 2010): 22,000 (army 84.1%, navy 2.3%, air force 13.6%). *Military expenditure as percentage of GDP* (2008): 0.7%; per capita expenditure U.S.$17.

[1]New constitution adopted on Sept. 26, 2008. [2]Single party in practice if not in principle. [3]The manat was redenominated on Jan. 1, 2009. As of this date 1 (new) manat (TMT) = 5,000 (old) manat (TMM). [4]Stabilized rate from the beginning of 2009. [5]Estimate of U.S. Bureau of the Census International Database (December 2008 update); official Turkmen estimates are significantly higher. [6]Budget statistics are unreliable because the government spends large amounts of extra-budgetary funds. [7]Estimate of the ILO Employment Trends Unit. [8]2nd quarter only; from/to Russia only. [9]Imports c.i.f.; exports f.o.b. [10]January 1. [11]Circulation of daily newspapers. [12]Subscribers. [13]Based on 2000 Turkmenistan Demographic and Health Survey of 13,566 people age 25 and over.

Internet resource for further information:
- **Asia Development Bank: Turkmenistan http://beta.adb.org/countries/turkmenistan/main**

Tuvalu

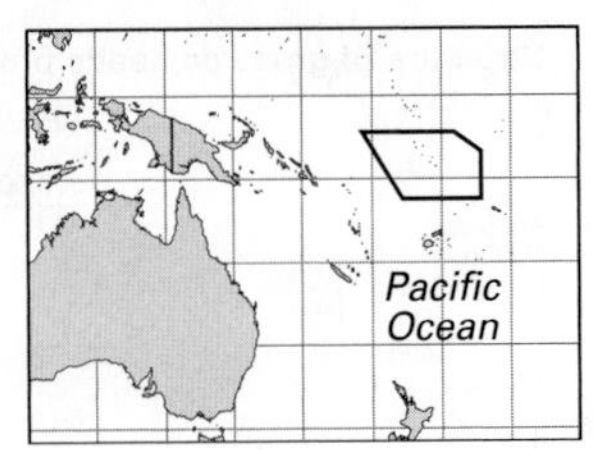

Official name: Tuvalu.
Form of government: constitutional monarchy with one legislative house (Parliament [15]).
Head of state: British Monarch, represented by Governor-General.
Head of government: Prime Minister.
Capital: government offices are at Vaiaku, Fongafale (Funafuti) islet, of Funafuti atoll.
Official language: none.
Official religion: none.
Monetary units: Tuvaluan dollar = Australian dollar ($T = $A)[1]; valuation (Sept. 1, 2011) 1 U.S.$ = $A 0.93; 1 £ = $A 1.50.

Area and population

Atolls/Islands[2]	Principal villages	area sq mi	area sq km	population 2002 census
Funafuti	Alapi	1.08	2.79	4,492
Nanumaga	Tonga	1.07	2.78	589
Nanumea	...	1.49	3.87	664
Niulakita	...	0.16	0.42	35
Niutao	Teava	0.98	2.53	663
Nui	...	1.09	2.83	548
Nukufetau	Aulotu	1.15	2.99	586
Nukulaelae	...	0.70	1.82	393
Vaitupu	Motufoua	2.16	5.60	1,591
TOTAL		9.90[3, 4]	25.63[3]	9,561

Demography

Population (2011): 11,200.
Density (2011): persons per sq mi 1,132, persons per sq km 437.2.
Urban-rural (2010): urban 50.4%; rural 49.6%.
Sex distribution (2010): male 49.17%; female 50.83%.
Age breakdown (2010): under 15, 31.1%; 15–29, 28.8%; 30–44, 15.5%; 45–59, 16.4%; 60–74, 6.4%; 75–84, 1.5%; 85 and over, 0.3%.
Population projection: (2020) 11,800; (2030) 12,500.
Doubling time: 52 years.
Ethnic composition (2004–05)[5]: Tuvaluan (Polynesian) 95.1%; mixed (Tuvaluan/other) 3.4%; I-Kiribati 1.1%; other 0.4%.
Religious affiliation (2002): Christian 97.0%, of which Church of Tuvalu (Congregational) 91.0%, Seventh-day Adventist 2.0%, Roman Catholic 1.0%; Bahā'ī 1.9%; other 1.1%.
Major urban area (2010): Vaiaku (on Fongafale islet) 5,100.

Vital statistics

Birth rate per 1,000 population (2010): 23.0 (world avg. 19.2); within marriage (2005) 92.7%; outside of marriage (2005) 7.3%.
Death rate per 1,000 population (2010): 9.4 (world avg. 8.2).
Total fertility rate (avg. births per childbearing woman; 2010): 3.14.
Marriage/divorce rates per 1,000 population (2010): n.a./n.a.
Life expectancy at birth (2010): male 62.4 years; female 66.5 years.
Major causes of death per 100,000 population (2007): cardiac arrest 82.9; diabetes mellitus 51.8; pneumonia 41.5; hypertension 31.1; congestive heart failure 31.1; cerebrovascular diseases 20.7.

National economy

Budget (2008). Revenue: $A 45,357,000 (grants[6] 63.0%; nontax revenue[7] 22.1%; tax revenue 14.9%). Expenditures: $A 42,936,000 (current expenditure, n.a.; development expenditure, n.a.).
Public debt (external; 2010): U.S.$11,000,000.
Gross national income (2009): U.S.$27,294,800 (U.S.$2,749 per capita).

Structure of gross domestic product and labour force

	2008		2002	
	in value U.S.$'000	% of total value	labour force[8]	% of labour force[8]
Agriculture, fishing	5,798	18.2	1,259[9]	36.4[9]
Manufacturing, handicrafts	1,186	3.7		
Mining	1,971	6.2	...	...
Public utilities			435	12.6
Construction	1,611	5.1		
Transp. and commun.	3,886	12.2	178	5.1
Trade, hotels, and restaurants	4,418	13.9	198	5.7
Finance, real estate	16,042	50.5	395	11.4
Pub. admin., defense			712	20.6
Services				
Other	–3,139[10]	–9.9[10]	286[11]	8.3[11]
TOTAL	31,773	100.0[4]	3,463	100.0[4]

Production (metric tons except as noted). Agriculture, forestry, fishing (2009): coconuts 1,700, vegetables 543, tropical fruit 435 (of which bananas 354), roots and tubers 145; livestock (number of live animals) 13,600 pigs, 45,000 chickens, (2008) 15,000 ducks; roundwood, n.a.; fisheries production 4,198 (from aquaculture, none). Mining and quarrying: n.a. Manufacturing (2010): limited to small-scale production of coconut-based products (including soaps) and handicrafts. Energy production (consumption): electricity (kW-hr; 2006) n.a. (4,235,100); coal, none (none); crude petroleum, none (none); petroleum products, n.a. (n.a.); natural gas, none (none).

Population economically active (2004): total 4,302[8]; activity rate of total population 44.8% (participation rates: ages 15 and over [2002] 58.2%; female [2002] 43.4%; unemployed 16.3%).

Price index (2005 = 100)

	2002	2003	2004	2005	2006	2007	2008
Consumer price index	91.2	94.3	96.8	100.0	100.9	101.4	102.5

Household income and expenditure (2004–05). Average household size 5.3; average annual net income per household $A 13,007 (U.S.$9,746); sources of income: wages and salaries 47.0%, rents, interest, bonuses, and other 28.7%, self-employment 12.1%, overseas remittances 9.1%; expenditure: food and nonalcoholic beverages 48.9%, housing 18.8%, household furnishings and energy 12.2%, education, health, and recreation 9.5%, transportation 6.3%, alcohol and tobacco 2.6%.
Selected balance of payments data. Receipts from (U.S.$'000,000): tourism, n.a.; remittances (2008) *c.* 0.7; foreign direct investment (2008–10 avg.) 2.0; official development assistance (2009) 18. Disbursements for (U.S.$'000,000): tourism, n.a.; remittances, n.a.
Land use as % of total land area (2007): in temporary crops, n.a.; left fallow, n.a.; in permanent crops *c.* 67%; in pasture, n.a.; forest area *c.* 33%.

Foreign trade[12]

Balance of trade (current prices)

	2002	2003	2004	2005	2006	2007
$A '000	–20,086	–23,896	–15,317	–16,828	–17,773	–18,277
% of total	97.3%	98.8%	97.7%	99.1%	98.6%	98.8%

Imports (2007): $A 18,386,120 (food products [including live animals] 30.2%; mineral fuels 16.1%, of which diesel fuel 9.1%; telecommunications equipment 4.4%; clothing 4.1%; base and fabricated metals 3.9%; wood products 3.4%). *Major import sources* (2008): Fiji 23.8%; Australia 18.3%; New Zealand 17.2%; Japan 16.3%.
Exports (2007): $A 109,413 ([2005] precision instruments 18.6%; machinery and apparatus 17.4%; base and fabricated metals 15.4%; wood and wood products 12.5%; transportation equipment 11.6%). *Major export destinations:* Fiji 93.1%; El Salvador 4.6%; New Zealand 2.2%; U.K. 0.1%.

Transport and communications

Transport. Railroads: none. Roads (2010): total length 5 mi, 8 km[13]. Vehicles (2007): passenger cars 15; trucks and buses 2. Air transport: n.a.

Communications

Medium	date	number in '000s	units per 1,000 persons	Medium	date	number in '000s	units per 1,000 persons
Televisions	2007	0.3	33	PCs	2007	...	...
Telephones				Dailies	2010	—[14]	—[14]
Cellular	2010	2.5[15]	254[15]	Internet users	2008	4.2	433
Landline	2010	1.6	165	Broadband	2010	0.3[15]	33[15]

Education and health

Educational attainment (2004–05)[5]. Percentage of population age 15 and over having: no formal education/unknown 8.8%; primary education 52.4%; secondary 29.8%; higher 9.0%. *Literacy* (2004): total population literate 95%.

Education (2003–04)

	teachers	students	student/teacher ratio	enrollment rate (%)
Primary (age 6–11)	73	1,460[16]	19.2	...
Secondary/Voc. (age 12–17)	...	912[17]	...	...
Tertiary[18]	...	...	...	... (age 18–22)

Health: physicians (2009) 12 (1 per 924 persons); hospital beds (2001) 56 (1 per 170 persons); infant mortality rate per 1,000 live births (2010) 35.5; undernourished population, n.a.

Military

Total active duty personnel (November 2010): none; Tuvalu has nonformal security arrangements with Australia and New Zealand.

[1]Transactions over $A 1 are conducted in $A only. [2]Local government councils have been established on all true atolls and isolated reef islands. [3]Another survey puts the area at 9.4 sq mi (24.4 sq km). [4]Detail does not add to total given because of rounding. [5]Based on the 2004–05 Household Income and Expenditure Survey, comprising 459 households. [6]Includes distributions of the Tuvalu Trust Fund significantly funded by the governments of Australia, New Zealand, and the U.K. [7]May include remittances from phosphate miners in Nauru and seafarers on foreign ships, rentals of fishing resources to Japan, Taiwan, and the U.S., and the leasing of the country's Internet domain "tv." [8]Total number of wage earners, unpaid workers, and subsistence workers all over age 15. [9]Excludes non-handicraft manufacturing. [10]Indirect taxes less subsidies and less imputed bank service charges. [11]Includes 60 not adequately defined and 226 unemployed. [12]Imports c.i.f.; exports f.o.b. [13]Length of impacted-coral roads; tracks also exist. [14]One newspaper is published fortnightly and one is published quarterly. [15]Subscribers. [16]2005–06. [17]2000–01. [18]Data unavailable for University of the South Pacific, Tuvalu Centre; degrees require completion in Fiji.

Internet resource for further information:
- **Central Statistics Division**
  http://www.spc.int/prism/country/tv/stats

Uganda

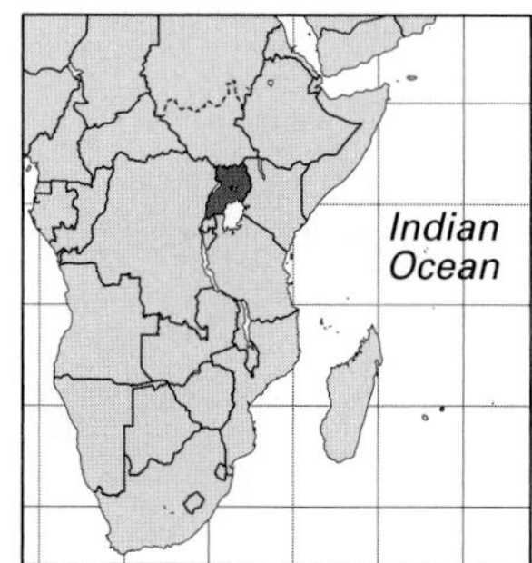

Official name: Jamhuri ya Uganda (Swahili); Republic of Uganda (English).
Form of government: multiparty republic with one legislative house (Parliament [375[1]]).
Head of state and government: President assisted by the Prime Minister.
Capital: Kampala.
Official languages: English; Swahili.
Official religion: none.
Monetary unit: Ugandan shilling (UGX); valuation (Sept. 1, 2011) 1 U.S.$ = UGX 2,820; 1 £ = UGX 4,557.

Area and population

		area		population
Geographic regions[2]	Principal cities	sq mi	sq km	2009[3] estimate
Central	Kampala	23,708	61,403	7,958,600
Eastern	Jinja	15,243	39,479	7,960,500
Northern	Gulu	32,970	85,392	7,003,100
Western	Mbarara	21,343	55,277	7,739,200
TOTAL		93,263[4, 5]	241,551[5]	30,661,400

Demography

Population (2011): 34,509,000[6].
Density (2011)[7]: persons per sq mi 447.3, persons per sq km 172.7.
Urban-rural (2009[3]): urban 14.8%; rural 85.2%.
Sex distribution (2009[3]): male 48.71%; female 51.29%.
Age breakdown (2009[3]): under 15, 50.2%; 15–29, 27.2%; 30–44, 13.9%; 45–59, 6.3%; 60–74, 2.1%; 75 and over, 0.3%.
Population projection[6]: (2020) 45,424,000; (2030) 59,846,000.
Ethnolinguistic composition (2002): Ganda 17.3%; Nkole 9.8%; Soga 8.6%; Kiga 7.0%; Teso 6.6%; Lango 6.2%; Acholi 4.8%; Gisu 4.7%.
Religious affiliation (2002): Christian 85.3%, of which Roman Catholic 41.9%, Anglican 35.9%, Pentecostal 4.6%, Seventh-day Adventist 1.5%; Muslim 12.1%; traditional beliefs 1.0%; nonreligious 0.9%; other 0.7%.
Major cities (2009[3]): Kampala 1,533,600; Kira 164,700; Gulu 146,600; Lira 102,200; Mbale 86,200.

Vital statistics

Birth rate per 1,000 population (2009): 45.8 (world avg. 20.3).
Death rate per 1,000 population (2009): 12.3 (world avg. 8.5).
Natural increase rate per 1,000 population (2009): 33.5 (world avg. 11.8).
Total fertility rate (avg. births per childbearing woman; 2008): 6.81.
Life expectancy at birth (2008): male 51.3 years; female 53.4 years.
Adult population (ages 15–49) *living with HIV* (2009): 6.5%[8] (world avg. 0.8%).

National economy

Budget (2009). Revenue: UGX 5,395,900,000,000 (tax revenue 75.6%; grants 20.6%; nontax revenue 3.8%). Expenditures: UGX 6,303,600,000,000 (current expenditures 65.1%, of which salaries and wages 19.7%; capital expenditures 31.6%).
Public debt (external, outstanding; June 2010): U.S.$2,343,370,000.
Production (metric tons except as noted). Agriculture, forestry, fishing (2009): plantains 9,512,000, cassava 5,179,000, sweet potatoes 2,766,000, sugarcane 2,350,000, corn (maize) 1,272,000, millet 841,000, cow's milk 809,025, potatoes 689,000, sorghum 497,000, beans (dry) 452,000, coffee (green) 195,871, sesame seed 178,000, cattle meat 106,500, pigeon peas 91,000, cowpeas 84,000, tea 48,663, tobacco 18,846, vanilla 48; livestock (number of live animals) 8,778,600 goats, 7,620,000 cattle, 2,252,000 pigs, 1,800,000 sheep, 28,305,000 chickens; roundwood (2010) 42,535,470 cu m, of which fuelwood 92%; fisheries production 476,654 (from aquaculture 16%). Mining and quarrying (2009): cobalt 660; columbite-tantalite (ore and concentrate) 275 kg. Manufacturing (value added in U.S.$'000,000; 2002): food and food products 109; chemicals and chemical products 59; beverages 53; fabricated metal products 17; tobacco and tobacco products 15; textiles and wearing apparel 15. Energy production (consumption): electricity (kW-hr; 2008) 2,176,000,000 (1,958,000,000); crude petroleum (barrels; 2008) none (4,745,000); petroleum products (metric tons; 2007) none (920,000).
Gross national income (GNI; 2010): U.S.$16,553,000,000 (U.S.$490 per capita); purchasing power parity GNI (U.S.$1,230 per capita).

Structure of gross domestic product and labour force

	2008–09		2003	
	in value UGX '000,000	% of total value	labour force	% of labour force
Agriculture, forestry, fishing	7,055,000	23.7	6,361,600	66.2
Mining and quarrying	85,000	0.3	27,800	0.3
Manufacturing	2,238,000	7.5	564,900	5.9
Construction	3,661,000	12.3	120,400	1.2
Public utilities	1,230,000	4.1	9,300	0.1
Transp. and commun.	2,028,000	6.8	175,900	1.8
Trade, hotels	4,884,000	16.4	1,315,000	13.7
Pub. admin., defense	875,000	2.9	74,100	0.8
Finance, real estate	3,374,000	11.3	37,000	0.4
Services	2,665,000	8.9	574,200	6.0
Other	1,729,000[9]	5.8[9]	346,000[10]	3.6[10]
TOTAL	29,824,000	100.0	9,606,000[4]	100.0

Population economically active (2009): total 14,376,000; activity rate of total population 43.9% (participation rates: ages 15 and older [2005–06] 81.6%; female 47.8%; officially unemployed [2005–06] 1.9%).

Price and earnings indexes (2005 = 100)

	2004	2005	2006	2007	2008	2009	2010
Consumer price index	92.2	100.0	107.3	113.9	127.2	144.2	150.0
Monthly earnings index[11]	...		97.0	113.8	135.7	156.2	200.8

Household income and expenditure (2005–06)[12]. Average household size 5.2; income per household UGX 2,050,692 (U.S.$1,126); sources of income: subsistence farming 49.2%, wages and salaries 20.8%, transfers 4.9%; expenditure[13]: food, beverages, and tobacco 31.9%, rent, energy, and services 14.8%, education 14.7%, transportation and communications 12.8%, household durable goods and furnishings 4.5%, clothing and footwear 4.4%.
Selected balance of payments data. Receipts from (U.S.$'000,000): tourism (2009) 667; remittances (2010) 839; foreign direct investment (2008–10 avg.) 798; official development assistance (2009) 1,786. Disbursements for (U.S.$'000,000): tourism (2009) 179; remittances (2009) 463.
Land use as % of total land area (2009): in temporary crops or left fallow 33.0%, in permanent crops 11.3%, in pasture 25.6%, forest area 15.4%.

Foreign trade[14]

Balance of trade (current prices)

	2004	2005	2006	2007	2008	2009
U.S.$'000,000	–1,061.1	–1,241.3	–1,595.1	–2,158.7	–2,801.6	–2,690.0
% of total	44.4%	43.3%	45.3%	44.7%	44.8%	46.2%

Imports (2008): U.S.$4,525,859,000 (refined petroleum 18.5%; chemicals and chemical products 14.1%; food and food products 11.7%, of which cereals 3.8%; electrical machinery 11.4%; nonelectrical machinery 8.5%; transportation equipment 7.8%; base metals 7.4%). *Major import sources:* U.A.E. 11.4%; Kenya 11.3%; India 10.4%; China 8.1%; South Africa 6.7%.
Exports (2008): U.S.$1,724,300,000 (food products and beverages 49.6%, of which coffee 23.4%, fresh fish 7.2%; base metals 6.2%; electrical machinery 5.1%; cement, bricks, and ceramics 5.0%; tobacco and tobacco products 4.0%). *Major export destinations:* Sudan 14.3%; Kenya 9.5%; Switzerland 9.0%; Rwanda 7.9%; U.A.E. 7.4%; Dem. Rep. of the Congo 7.2%.

Transport and communications

Transport. Railroads (2008): route length 773 mi, 1,244 km; passenger-km (2009)[15]; metric ton-km cargo (2005) 185,559,000. Roads (2008)[16]: total length 6,813 mi, 10,965 km (paved 28%). Vehicles (2008): passenger cars 90,856; trucks and buses 137,290. Air transport: passenger-km (2005) 302,000,000; metric ton-km cargo (2007) 34,000,000.

Communications

Medium	date	number in '000s	units per 1,000 persons	Medium	date	number in '000s	units per 1,000 persons
Televisions	2003	450	17	PCs	2005	300	10
Telephones				Dailies	2009	100[17]	3.1[17]
Cellular	2010	12,828[18]	384[18]	Internet users	2009	3,200	98
Landline	2010	327	9.8	Broadband	2010	20[18]	0.6[18]

Education and health

Educational attainment (2005–06)[12]. Percentage of population age 15 and over having: no formal schooling/unknown 20.0%; incomplete primary education 43.3%; complete primary 14.1%; incomplete secondary 18.1%; complete secondary (some higher) 1.1%; complete higher (including vocational) 3.4%. *Literacy* (2008): population age 15 and over literate 74.6%; males literate 82.4%; females literate 66.8%.

Education (2009)

	teachers	students	student/ teacher ratio	enrollment rate (%)
Primary (age 6–12)	168,376	8,297,774	49.3	98
Secondary/Voc. (age 13–18)	70,425	1,277,543	18.1	22[19]
Tertiary[19]	3,581	107,728	30.1	4 (age 19–23)

Health: physicians (2004) 2,209 (1 per 11,947 persons); hospital beds (2006) 32,617 (1 per 909 persons); infant mortality rate (2008) 66.0; undernourished population (2006–08) 6,700,000 (22% of total population based on the consumption of a minimum daily requirement of 1,710 calories).

Military

Total active duty personnel (November 2010): 45,000 (army/air force 100%); Ugandan peacekeeping troops in Somalia (November 2010): 4,250. *Military expenditure as percentage of GDP* (2008): 1.4%; per capita expenditure U.S.$7.

[1]Excludes ex officio members appointed by the president; ex officio members do not have any voting rights. [2]Actual local administration in May 2010 was based on 115 districts. [3]July 1. [4]Detail does not add to total given because of rounding. [5]Includes water and swamp area of 16,117 sq mi (41,743 sq km); Uganda's portion of Lake Victoria comprises 11,954 sq mi (30,960 sq km). [6]Estimate of United Nations *World Population Prospects: The 2010 Revision*. [7]Based on land area only. [8]Statistically derived midpoint of range. [9]Indirect taxes less imputed bank service charges. [10]Unemployed. [11]Manufacturing only. [12]Based on the Uganda National Household Survey 2005–06, comprising approximately 7,400 households. [13]Weights of consumer price index components. [14]Imports c.i.f.; exports f.o.b. [15]Suspended passenger service from 1997 was to be reintroduced in October 2009. [16]National roads only. [17]Circulation of daily newspapers. [18]Subscribers. [19]2008.

Internet resources for further information:

- **Bank of Uganda http://www.bou.or.ug**
- **Uganda Bureau of Statistics http://www.ubos.org**

Ukraine

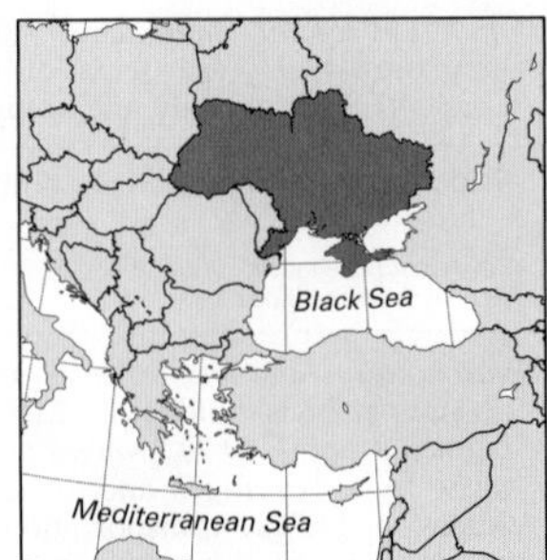

Official name: Ukrayina (Ukraine).
Form of government: unitary multiparty republic with a single legislative body (Verkhovna Rada[1] [450]).
Head of state: President.
Head of government: Prime Minister.
Capital: Kiev (Kyiv).
Official language: Ukrainian.
Official religion: none.
Monetary unit: hryvnya (UAH); (Sept. 1, 2011) 1 U.S.$ = UAH 8.01; 1 £ = UAH 12.94.

Area and population

Regions	area sq km	population 2011[2] estimate	Regions	area sq km	population 2011[2] estimate
Cherkasy	20,900	1,285,384	Sumy	23,834	1,161,544
Chernihiv	31,865	1,098,209	Ternopil	13,823	1,084,127
Chernivtsi	8,097	904,277	Vinnytsya	26,513	1,641,201
Dnipropetrovsk	31,974	3,336,504	Volyn	20,144	1,037,149
Donetsk	26,517	4,433,011	Zakarpattya (Transcarpathia)	12,777	1,247,350
Ivano-Frankivsk	13,928	1,379,766	Zaporizhzhya	27,180	1,801,315
Kharkiv	31,415	2,755,108	Zhytomyr	29,832	1,279,008
Kherson	28,461	1,088,237	**Autonomous republic**		
Khmelnytsky	20,645	1,326,926	Krym (Crimea)	26,081	1,963,514
Kirovohrad	24,588	1,009,987	**Cities**		
Kyiv (Kiev)	28,131	1,717,649	Kiev (Kyiv)	839	2,799,199
Luhansk	26,684	2,291,271	Sevastopol	864	380,821
Lviv	21,833	2,544,748	TOTAL	603,628	45,778,534
Mykolayiv	24,598	1,183,282			
Odesa (Odessa)	33,310	2,388,670			
Poltava	28,748	1,487,751			
Rivne	20,047	1,152,526			

Demography

Population (2011): 45,672,000.
Density (2011): persons per sq mi 195.5, persons per sq km 75.7.
Urban-rural (2011[2]): urban 68.7%; rural 31.3%.
Sex distribution (2011[2]): male 46.05%; female 53.95%.
Age breakdown (2010[2]): under 15, 14.2%; 15–29, 22.5%; 30–44, 21.0%; 45–59, 21.6%; 60 and over, 20.7%.
Population projection: (2020) 43,494,000; (2030) 40,936,000.
Ethnic composition (2001): Ukrainian 77.8%; Russian 17.3%; Belarusian 0.6%; Moldovan 0.5%; Crimean Tatar 0.5%; other 3.3%.
Religious affiliation (2004): Ukrainian Orthodox, of which "Kiev patriarchy" 19%, "no particular patriarchy" 16%, "Moscow patriarchy" 9%, Ukrainian Autocephalous Orthodox 2%; Ukrainian Catholic 6%; Protestant 2%; Latin Catholic 2%; Muslim 1%; Jewish 0.5%; nonreligious/atheist/other 42.5%.
Major cities (2011[2]): Kiev 2,799,199; Kharkiv 1,446,500; Odesa (Odessa) 1,009,145; Dnipropetrovsk 1,004,853; Donetsk 962,049.

Vital statistics

Birth rate per 1,000 population (2010): 10.8 (world avg. 19.2).
Death rate per 1,000 population (2010): 15.2 (world avg. 8.2).
Total fertility rate (avg. births per childbearing woman; 2007): 1.30.
Marriage/divorce rates per 1,000 population (2010): 6.7/2.7.
Life expectancy at birth (2007): male 62.5 years; female 74.2 years.
Major causes of death per 100,000 population (2004): diseases of the circulatory system 998.4; malignant neoplasms (cancers) 192.4; accidents 96.7.
Adult population (ages 15–49) *living with HIV* (2009): 1.1% (world avg. 0.8%).

National economy

Budget (2008). Revenue: UAH 229,597,600,000 (tax revenue 73.8%, of which VAT 40.1%, tax on profits 20.7%; nontax revenue 19.9%; grants 3.4%; other 2.9%). Expenditures: UAH 241,490,100,000 (public services 33.4%; social protection 22.0%; education and health 12.4%; fuel and energy 6.4%).
Production (metric tons except as noted). Agriculture, forestry, fishing (2009): wheat 20,886,400, potatoes 19,666,100, barley 11,833,100, cow's milk 11,363,500, corn (maize) 10,486,300, sugar beets 10,067,500, sunflower seeds 6,360,600, tomatoes 2,040,800, rapeseed 1,873,300, cabbages 1,509,300[3], chicken meat 894,200, pumpkins/squash 559,900, sour cherries 70,000; livestock (number of live animals) 6,526,000 pigs, 5,079,000 cattle, 158,800,000 chickens; roundwood (2010) 16,884,300 cu m, of which fuelwood 56%; fisheries production 237,256 (from aquaculture 10%). Mining and quarrying (2008): iron ore 77,320,000[4]; ilmenite concentrate 520,000; manganese 492,000[5]. Manufacturing (value of sales in UAH '000,000,000; 2007): base and fabricated metals 157.5; food, beverages, and tobacco products 110.0; coke and refined petroleum 52.5; transport equipment 47.0; chemicals and chemical products 31.0. Energy production (consumption): electricity ('000,000 kW-hr; 2009–10) 182,000 ([2007] 187,080); coal (metric tons; 2009–10) 53,970,000[6] ([2007] 68,205,000[6]); crude petroleum (barrels; 2009–10) 27,172,000 ([2007] 97,005,000); petroleum products (metric tons; 2007) 13,505,000 (13,178,000); natural gas ('000,000 cu m; 2009–10) 17,650 ([2007] 65,366).
Household income and expenditure (2007). Average household size 2.6; average annual disposable income per household UAH 25,819 (U.S.$5,113); sources of income: wages and salaries 44.0%, transfers 37.4%[7]; expenditures: food and nonalcoholic beverages 57.1%, housing and energy 12.1%, clothing and footwear 6.6%.
Population economically active (2010): total 22,051,600[2]; activity rate of total population 48.2%[2] (participation rates: ages 15–70, 65.6%[2]; female [2009] 48.1%[2]; unemployed 8.1%).

Price index (2005 = 100)

	2004	2005	2006	2007	2008	2009	2010
Consumer price index	88.1	100.0	109.1	119.1	149.1	172.8	189.0

Gross national income (GNI; 2010): U.S.$137,917,000,000 (U.S.$3,010 per capita); purchasing power parity GNI (U.S.$6,580 per capita).

Structure of gross domestic product and labour force

	2008			
	in value UAH '000,000	% of total value	labour force	% of labour force
Agriculture	64,297	6.8	3,322,100	14.8
Mining	49,714	5.2	} 3,871,400	} 17.3
Manufacturing	179,644	18.9		
Public utilities	29,583	3.1		
Construction	34,741	3.7	1,043,400	4.6
Transp. and commun.	91,193	9.6	1,465,800	6.5
Trade, restaurants	130,205	13.7	4,744,400	21.2
Finance, real estate	} 284,353	} 29.9	1,545,300	6.9
Pub. admin., defense			1,067,500	4.8
Services			3,912,400	17.5
Other	86,134[8]	9.1[8]	1,425,100[9]	6.4[9]
TOTAL	949,864	100.0	22,397,400	100.0

Public debt (external; April 2008): U.S.$15,100,000,000.
Selected balance of payments data. Receipts from (U.S.$'000,000): tourism (2009) 4,349; remittances (2009) 4,972; foreign direct investment (FDI; 2008–10 avg.) 7,408; official development assistance (2009) 668. Disbursements for (U.S.$'000,000): tourism (2009) 3,751; FDI (2008–10 avg.) 636.
Land use as % of total land area (2007): in temporary crops 53.2%, left fallow 2.8%, in permanent crops 1.6%, in pasture 13.7%, forest area 16.6%.

Foreign trade[10]

Balance of trade (current prices)

	2004	2005	2006	2007	2008	2009
U.S.$'000,000	+3,669	–1,908	–6,671	–11,322	–18,496	–5,703
% of total	6.0%	2.7%	8.0%	10.3%	12.1%	6.7%

Imports (2008): U.S.$85,448,000,000 (machinery and apparatus 16.3%; road vehicles/parts 12.8%; petroleum 12.5%; chemical products 11.3%; natural gas [in gaseous state] 11.0%). *Major import sources:* Russia 22.7%; Germany 8.4%; Turkmenistan 6.6%; China 6.6%; Poland 5.0%.
Exports (2008): U.S.$66,952,000,000 (iron and steel 38.0%, of which ingots 12.9%, flat-rolled products 9.1%; machinery and apparatus 9.6%; cereals 6.1%; metal ore/metal scrap 4.4%; petroleum 4.1%). *Major export destinations:* Russia 23.5%; Turkey 6.9%; Italy 4.3%; Poland 3.5%; Belarus 3.1%.

Transport and communications

Transport. Railroads (2008): route length 13,480 mi, 21,700 km; passenger-km 53,225,000,000; metric ton-km cargo 257,007,000,000. Roads (2008): total length 105,320 mi, 169,500 km (paved 98%); passenger-km 61,300,000,000[11]; metric ton-km cargo 54,900,000,000. Vehicles (2009[2]): passenger cars 6,393,900; trucks and buses 1,164,200. Air transport (2008): passenger-km 10,800,000,000; metric ton-km cargo 400,000,000.

Communications

Medium	date	number in '000s	units per 1,000 persons	Medium	date	number in '000s	units per 1,000 persons
Telephones				Dailies	2009	2,864[12]	62[12]
Cellular	2010	53,929[13]	1,187[13]	Internet users	2009	15,300	335
Landline	2010	12,941	285	Broadband	2010	3,661[13]	81[13]

Education and health

Educational attainment (2001). Percentage of population age 25 and over having: no formal schooling 0.7%; incomplete primary education 2.8%; complete primary/incomplete secondary 22.7%; complete secondary 35.9%; incomplete higher 21.7%; complete higher 16.2%. *Literacy* (2008): 99.7%.

Education (2008–09)

	teachers	students	student/ teacher ratio	enrollment rate (%)
Primary (age 6–9)	98,310	1,531,943	15.6	89
Secondary/Voc. (age 10–17)	350,716[14]	3,288,557	10.6[14]	85
Tertiary[15]	200,535	2,847,713	14.3	79 (age 18–22)

Health (2009): physicians 225,000 (1 per 205 persons); hospital beds 431,000 (1 per 107 persons); infant mortality rate per 1,000 live births (2010) 9.1; undernourished population (2004–06) less than 5.0% of total population based on the consumption of a minimum daily requirement of 1,940 calories.

Military

Total active duty personnel (November 2010): 129,925 (army 54.5%, air force/air defense 34.8%, navy 10.7%); reserve 1,000,000. Russian naval forces at Sevastopol (November 2010) *c.* 13,000. *Military expenditure as percentage of GDP* (2010): 1.0%; per capita expenditure U.S.$32.

[1]Translated as Supreme Council. [2]January 1. [3]Includes other brassicas. [4]2009–10; gross weight. [5]Metal content. [6]Includes negligible (less than 1%) production/consumption of lignite. [7]Includes pensions, scholarships, subsidies, and remittances. [8]Net indirect taxes and taxes on production less subsidies and less imputed bank service charges. [9]Unemployed. [10]Imports c.i.f.; exports f.o.b. [11]Buses only. [12]Circulation of daily newspapers. [13]Subscribers. [14]2006–07. [15]2007–08.

Internet resource for further information:
- **State Statistics Committee of Ukraine http://www.ukrstat.gov.ua**

United Arab Emirates

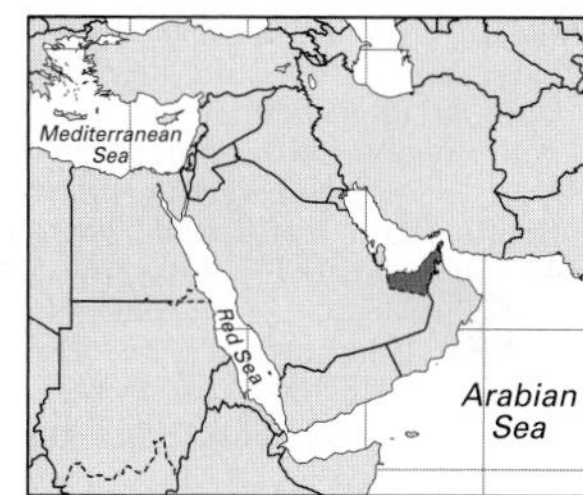

Official name: Al-Imārāt al-ʿArabīyah al-Muttaḥidah (United Arab Emirates).
Form of government: federation of seven emirates with one advisory body (Federal National Council [40[1]]).
Head of state: President.
Head of government: Prime Minister.
Capital: Abu Dhabi.
Official language: Arabic.
Official religion: Islam.
Monetary unit: dirham (AED); valuation (Sept. 1, 2011) 1 U.S.$ = AED 3.67; 1 £ = AED 5.94.

Area and population

Emirates	Capitals	area[2] sq mi	area[2] sq km	population 2008 estimate
Abū Ẓaby (Abu Dhabi)	Abu Dhabi	28,210	73,060	1,559,000
ʿAjmān (Ajman)	ʿAjmān	100	260	237,000
Dubayy (Dubai)	Dubai	1,510	3,900	1,596,000
Al-Fujayrah (Fujairah)	Al-Fujayrah	500	1,300	143,000
Ra's al-Khaymah	Ra's al-Khaymah	660	1,700	231,000
Al-Shāriqah (Sharjah)	Sharjah	1,000	2,600	946,000
Umm al-Qaywayn	Umm al-Qaywayn	300	780	53,000
TOTAL		32,280	83,600	4,765,000

Demography

Population (2011): 7,891,000[3].
Density (2011): persons per sq mi 244.5, persons per sq km 94.4.
Urban-rural (2008): urban 80.0%; rural 20.0%.
Sex distribution (2008): male 68.96%; female 31.04%.
Age breakdown (2008): under 15, 19.1%; 15–29, 32.3%; 30–44, 36.6%; 45–59, 10.5%; 60–74, 1.2%; 75 and over, 0.3%.
Population projection: (2020) 9,174,000; (2030) 10,489,000.
Doubling time: 51 years.
Ethnic composition (2009): Asian Indian *c.* 29%; Pakistani *c.* 21%; U.A.E. Arab *c.* 15%; Bangladeshi *c.* 8%; other Asian *c.* 17%; other *c.* 10%.
Religious affiliation (2005): Muslim *c.* 62% (mostly Sunnī); Hindu *c.* 21%; Christian *c.* 9%; Buddhist *c.* 4%; other *c.* 4%.
Major cities (2006): Dubai 1,354,980; Sharjah 685,000; Abu Dhabi 630,000; Al-ʿAyn 350,000; ʿAjmān 202,244; Ra's al-Khaymah 113,347.

Vital statistics

Birth rate per 1,000 population (2007): 16.1 (world avg. 20.3).
Death rate per 1,000 population (2007): 2.2 (world avg. 8.5).
Natural increase rate per 1,000 population (2007): 13.9 (world avg. 11.8).
Total fertility rate (avg. births per childbearing woman; 2007): 2.43.
Marriage/divorce rates per 1,000 population (2008): 3.2/0.8.
Life expectancy at birth (2007): male 73.2 years; female 78.3 years.
Major causes of death per 100,000 population (2002): cardiovascular diseases 119.6, of which ischemic heart disease 55.9; accidents 61.9; malignant neoplasms (cancers) 34.1; infectious and parasitic diseases 17.6.

National economy

Budget (2008). Revenue: AED 292,600,000,000 (royalties on hydrocarbons 74.3%; investment income 6.3%; other 19.4%). Expenditures: AED 289,000,000,000 (current expenditure 68.1%; loans, net equity, and foreign grants 18.9%; development expenditure 13.0%).
Gross national income (2009): U.S.$251,717,000,000 (U.S.$54,738 per capita).

Structure of gross domestic product and labour force

	2008 in value AED '000,000	2008 % of total value	2007 labour force	2007 % of labour force
Agriculture	8,852	0.9	225,499	7.3
Crude petroleum[4]	344,132	36.8	38,783	1.3
Quarrying	1,668	0.2	6,418	0.2
Manufacturing	113,245	12.1	393,173	12.7
Construction	69,218	7.4	624,242	20.2
Public utilities	13,579	1.5	39,958	1.3
Transp. and commun.	46,973	5.0	190,133	6.1
Trade, hotels	162,948	17.4	723,117	23.3
Finance, real estate	141,145	15.1	127,176	4.1
Pub. admin., defense	37,857	4.1	334,207	10.8
Services	16,404	1.8	393,942	12.7
Other	–21,759[5]	–2.3[5]	—	—
TOTAL	934,262	100.0	3,096,646[6]	100.0

Public debt (December 2010): U.S.$151,800,000,000.
Production (metric tons except as noted). Agriculture, forestry, fishing (2009): dates 759,000, tomatoes 205,000, camel's milk 40,356, goat meat 36,800, chicken meat 33,434, hen's eggs 25,500, pumpkins and squash 20,772, camel meat 18,053, cucumbers and gherkins 17,500, mangoes, mangosteens, and guavas 11,000; livestock (number of live animals) 1,710,000 goats, 620,000 sheep, 380,000 camels, 15,500,000 chickens; roundwood, n.a.; fisheries production 77,705 (from aquaculture, negligible). Mining and quarrying (2009): lime 120,000; gypsum 40,000. Manufacturing (2007): cement 15,000,000; aluminum 890,000; steel 90,000; refined/unrefined gold U.S.$19,000,000,000[7]; worked/unworked diamonds U.S.$11,230,000,000[7]. Energy production (consumption): electricity (kW-hr; 2007) 76,532,000,000 (74,717,000,000); coal, none (none); crude petroleum (barrels; 2008) 978,600,000 ([2007] 124,400,000); petroleum products (metric tons; 2007) 20,927,000 (10,553,000); natural gas (cu m; 2008) 50,200,000,000 ([2007] 38,900,000,000).

Population economically active (2008): total 1,923,214; activity rate of total population 54.9% (participation rates: ages 15–64, 73.3%; female 20.4%; unemployed 4.0%).

Price index (2005 = 100)

	2002	2003	2004	2005	2006	2007	2008
Consumer price index	86.9	89.6	94.2	100.0	109.2	121.4	136.4

Household income and expenditure (2007–08). Average household size 5.1; average annual income per household AED 218,983 (U.S.$59,628)[8]; sources of income: n.a.; expenditure: housing and energy 39.4%, food and beverages 14.2%.
Selected balance of payments data. Receipts from (U.S.$'000,000): tourism (2008) 7,162; remittances (2010) n.a.; foreign direct investment (FDI; 2008–10 avg.) 7,225. Disbursements for (U.S.$'000,000): tourism (2008) 13,288; remittances (2007) *c.* 5,000; FDI (2008–10 avg.) 6,853.
Land use as % of total land area (2009): in temporary crops or left fallow 0.8%, in permanent crops 2.4%, in pasture 3.6%, forest area 3.8%.

Foreign trade[9]

Balance of trade (current prices)

	2003	2004	2005	2006	2007	2008
U.S.$'000,000	+15,061	+18,566	+34,639	+44,641	+29,633	+34,514
% of total	12.6%	11.4%	17.6%	31.8%	10.4%	9.0%

Imports (2008): U.S.$175,486,000,000 (machinery and apparatus 18.7%, base and fabricated metals 15.4%, road vehicles 9.8%, gold 8.4%, food 5.1%, unset diamonds 4.2%). *Major import sources:* China *c.* 13%; India *c.* 12%; U.S. *c.* 9%; Germany *c.* 6%; Japan *c.* 6%.
Exports (2008): U.S.$210,000,000,000 (crude petroleum 38.3%, refined petroleum 10.9%, gold [not jewelry] 4.3%, unset diamonds 3.2%, road vehicles/parts 3.0%, platinum-group metals 1.9%, unspecified 26.6%). *Major export destinations:* Japan *c.* 27%; South Korea *c.* 11%; India *c.* 11%; Iran *c.* 8%; Thailand *c.* 6%.

Transport and communications

Transport. Railroads: none[10]. Roads (2008): total length, n.a. (paved roads only, 4,080 km). Vehicles (2007): passenger cars 1,279,098; trucks and buses 48,205. Air transport (2008)[11]: passenger-km 131,960,000,000; metric ton-km cargo 7,318,000,000.

Communications

Medium	date	number in '000s	units per 1,000 persons	Medium	date	number in '000s	units per 1,000 persons
Televisions	2004	843	216	PCs	2006	1,396	330
Telephones				Dailies	2009	1,027[12]	269[12]
Cellular	2010	10,926[13]	1,455[13]	Internet users	2009	3,778	822
Landline	2010	1,480	197	Broadband	2010	787[13]	105[13]

Education and health

Educational attainment (2005). Percentage of population age 10 and over having: no formal schooling (illiterate/unknown) 9.4%, (literate) 13.9%; primary education 14.6%; incomplete/complete secondary 43.7%; postsecondary 4.0%; undergraduate 12.8%; graduate 1.6%. *Literacy* (2007): total population age 10 and over literate 90.4%; males literate 90.9%; females literate 89.2%.

Education (2008–09)

	teachers	students	student/ teacher ratio	enrollment rate (%)
Primary (age 6–10)	19,503	304,250	15.6	90
Secondary/Voc. (age 11–17)	26,895	322,470	12.0	83
Tertiary[14]	4,710	77,428	16.4	25 (age 18–22)

Health (2007): physicians 8,662 (1 per 518 persons); hospital beds 8,348 (1 per 538 persons); infant mortality rate per 1,000 live births 7.8; undernourished population (2006–08) less than 5.0% of total population.

Military

Total active duty personnel (November 2010): 51,000 (army 86.3%, navy 4.9%, air force 8.8%)[15]. *Military expenditure as percentage of GDP* (2009): 6.3%; per capita expenditure U.S.$3,247.

[1]Twenty seats are appointed by the rulers of the 7 emirates and 20 seats are indirectly elected. [2]Approximate figures; border/territorial disputes exist with Saudi Arabia/Iran, respectively. [3]Estimate of United Nations *World Population Prospects: The 2010 Revision.* [4]Includes natural gas. [5]Less imputed bank service charges. [6]Detail does not add to total given because of rounding. [7]Total import/export trade value. The U.A.E. has 3 gold refineries. [8]Average annual income: for citizen households AED 437,257 (U.S.$119,063), for noncitizen households AED 180,892 (U.S.$49,256). [9]Imports c.i.f.; exports f.o.b. [10]A national railway company was formally established in October 2009. [11]Emirates, Etihad Airways, and Air Arabia only. [12]Circulation of daily newspapers. [13]Subscribers. [14]2007–08. [15]U.S. troops (June 2011) 140; French military base for up to 500 troops officially opened in May 2009.

Internet resources for further information:

- **United Arab Emirates National Media Council**
  http://uaeinteract.com
- **Central Bank of the United Arab Emirates**
  http://www.centralbank.ae
- **United Arab Emirates National Bureau of Statistics**
  http://www.uaestatistics.gov.ae

United Kingdom

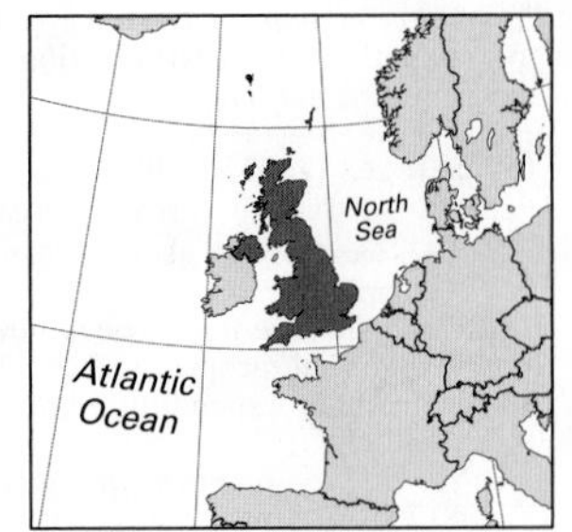

Official name: United Kingdom of Great Britain and Northern Ireland.
Form of government: constitutional monarchy with two legislative houses (House of Lords [733[1]]; House of Commons [650]).
Head of state: Sovereign.
Head of government: Prime Minister.
Capital: London.
Official languages: English; both English and Scots Gaelic in Scotland; both English and Welsh in Wales.
Official religion: [2].
Monetary unit: pound sterling (£); valuation (Sept. 1, 2011) 1 £ = U.S.$1.62; 1 U.S.$ = £0.62.

Population (2010 estimate)

Countries	population
England	52,234,000[3]
Counties	
Buckinghamshire	498,100
Cambridgeshire	616,300
Cumbria	494,400
Derbyshire	763,700
Devon	749,900
Dorset	404,800
East Sussex	515,500
Essex	1,413,000
Gloucestershire	593,500
Hampshire	1,296,800
Hertfordshire	1,107,500
Kent	1,427,400
Lancashire	1,169,300
Leicestershire	648,700
Lincolnshire	703,000
Norfolk	862,300
North Yorkshire	599,700
Northamptonshire	687,300
Nottinghamshire	779,900
Oxfordshire	648,700
Somerset	525,200
Staffordshire	831,300
Suffolk	719,500
Surrey	1,127,300
Warwickshire	536,000
West Sussex	799,700
Worcestershire	557,400
Unitary Authorities	
Bath and NE Somerset	179,700
Bedford[4]	160,800
Blackburn with Darwen	140,000
Blackpool	140,000
Bournemouth	168,100
Bracknell Forest	116,500
Brighton and Hove	258,800
Bristol	441,300
Central Bedfordshire[4]	255,200
Cheshire East[4]	363,800
Cheshire West & Chester[4]	327,300
Cornwall[4]	535,300
Darlington	100,800
Derby	246,900
Durham[4]	510,800
East Riding of Yorkshire	338,700
Halton	119,300
Hartlepool	91,300
Herefordshire	179,300
Isle of Wight	140,500
Isles of Scilly	2,100
Kingston upon Hull	263,900
Leicester	306,600
Luton	198,800
Medway	256,700
Middlesborough	142,400
Milton Keynes	241,500
North-east Lincolnshire	157,300
North Lincolnshire	161,300
North Somerset	212,200
Northumberland[4]	312,000
Nottingham	306,700
Peterborough	173,400
Plymouth	258,700
Poole	142,100
Portsmouth	207,100
Reading	154,200
Redcar and Cleveland	137,400
Rutland	38,600
Shropshire[4]	293,400
Slough	131,100
South Gloucestershire	264,800
Southampton	239,700
Southend-on-Sea	165,300
Stockton-on-Tees	192,400
Stoke-on-Trent	240,100
Swindon	201,800
Telford and Wrekin	162,600
Thurrock	159,700
Torbay	134,300
Warrington	198,900
West Berkshire	154,000
Wiltshire[4]	459,800
Windsor and Maidenhead	146,100
Wokingham	163,200
York	202,400
Metropolitan Counties/Greater London	
Greater London	7,825,200
Greater Manchester	2,629,400
Merseyside	1,353,400
South Yorkshire	1,328,300
Tyne and Wear	1,119,500
West Midlands	2,655,100
West Yorkshire	2,249,500
Wales	3,006,400[3]
Unitary Districts	
Blaenau Gwent	68,400
Bridgend	134,600
Caerphilly	173,100
Cardiff	341,100
Carmarthenshire	180,700
Ceredigion	76,900
Conwy	110,900
Denbighshire	96,700
Flintshire	149,700
Gwynedd	119,000
Isle of Anglesey	68,600
Merthyr Tydfil	55,700
Monmouthshire	88,100
Neath and Port Talbot	137,400
Newport	141,300
Pembrokeshire	117,100
Powys	131,300
Rhondda, Cynon, Taff	234,300
Swansea	232,500
Torfaen	90,500
The Vale of Glamorgan	125,000
Wrexham	133,600
Scotland	5,222,100[3]
Unitary Districts	
Aberdeen City	217,100
Aberdeenshire	245,800
Angus	110,600
Argyll and Bute	89,200
Clackmannanshire	50,600
Dumfries and Galloway	148,200
Dundee City	144,300
East Ayrshire	120,200
East Dumbartonshire	104,600
East Lothian	97,500
East Renfrewshire	89,500
Edinburgh, City of	486,100
Eilean Siar[5]	26,200
Falkirk	153,300
Fife	365,000
Glasgow City	592,800
Highland	221,600
Inverclyde	79,800
Midlothian	81,100
Moray	87,700
North Ayrshire	135,200
North Lanarkshire	326,400
Orkney Islands	20,100
Perth and Kinross	147,800
Renfrewshire	170,300
Scottish Borders	112,900
Shetland Islands	22,400
South Ayrshire	111,400
South Lanarkshire	311,900
Stirling	89,900
West Dumbartonshire	90,600
West Lothian	172,100
Northern Ireland	1,799,400
Districts	
Antrim	54,100
Ards	78,200
Armagh	59,400
Ballymena	63,500
Ballymoney	30,600
Banbridge	48,000
Belfast	268,700
Carrickfergus	40,200
Castlereagh	67,000
Coleraine	56,800
Cookstown	36,700
Craigavon	93,600
Derry	109,800
Down	70,800
Dungannon	57,700
Fermanagh	63,100
Larne	31,700
Limvady	33,600
Lisburn	117,800
Magherafelt	44,700
Moyle	17,000
Newry and Mourne	99,900
Newtownabbey	83,600
North Down	79,900
Omagh	52,900
Strabane	40,100
TOTAL	62,262,000[3]

Demography

Population (2011): 62,675,000.
Area[6]: 93,851 sq mi, 243,073 sq km, of which England 50,302 sq mi, 130,281 sq km; Wales 8,005 sq mi, 20,732 sq km; Scotland 30,087 sq mi, 77,925 sq km; Northern Ireland 5,457 sq mi, 14,135 sq km.
Density (2011): persons per sq mi 667.8, persons per sq km 257.8.
Urban-rural (2009): urban 79.5%; rural 20.5%.
Sex distribution (2009): male 49.16%; female 50.84%.
Age breakdown (2009): under 15, 17.5%; 15–29, 20.0%; 30–44, 20.8%; 45–59, 19.3%; 60–74, 14.6%; 75–84, 5.6%; 85 and over, 2.2%.
Population projection: (2020) 66,542,000; (2030) 70,493,000.
Ethnic composition (2007): white 86.8%, of which British 81.6%; Asian 5.3%, of which Indian 2.0%, Pakistani 1.6%, Bangladeshi 0.6%, Chinese 0.4%; black 2.5%, of which from Africa 1.3%, from the Caribbean 1.1%; mixed race 1.1%; other 1.5%; unknown 2.8%.
Religious affiliation (2001): Christian 71.8%, of which Anglican-identified 29%, other Protestant-identified (significantly Presbyterian) 14%, Roman Catholic-identified 10%; Muslim 2.8%; Hindu 1.0%; Sikh 0.6%; Jewish 0.5%; nonreligious 15.0%; other 0.5%; unknown 7.8%.
Major cities/urban agglomerations (2008/2009): London 7,619,800/8,615,000; Birmingham 1,010,400/2,296,000; Manchester 465,900/2,247,000; Leeds 477,600/1,541,000[7]; Glasgow 637,000/1,166,000; Newcastle upon Tyne 200,200/888,000; Liverpool 464,200/816,000; Bristol 465,500; Sheffield 458,100; Edinburgh 452,200; Leicester 348,000; Kingston upon Hull 320,100; Bradford 315,100; Coventry 312,500; Cardiff 310,800; Nottingham 273,300; Belfast 268,400; Stoke-on-Trent 258,600; Plymouth 256,000; Southampton 252,700.
Mobility (2001). Population living in the same residence as 2000, 88.6%; different residence, same country/region (of the U.K.) 8.6%; different residence, different country/region (of the U.K.) 2.1%; from outside the U.K. 0.7%.
Households (2007)[8]. Average household size (2007–08) 2.4; 1 person 29%, 2 persons 35%, 3 persons 16%, 4 persons 13%, 5 or more persons 7%.
Immigration (2008): permanent residents 590,000, from Bangladesh, India, Pakistan, and Sri Lanka 13.6%; Australia 4.9%; United States 4.7%; South Africa 3.4%; Canada 1.7%; New Zealand 1.5%; other 70.2%, of which EU 38.0%.

Vital statistics

Birth rate per 1,000 population (2009): 12.8 (world avg. 20.3); within marriage 53.7%; outside of marriage 46.3%.
Death rate per 1,000 population (2009): 9.1 (world avg. 8.5).
Total fertility rate (avg. births per childbearing woman; 2009): 1.94.
Marriage/divorce rates per 1,000 population (2008): 4.4/2.2.
Life expectancy at birth (2008): male 77.7 years; female 81.9 years.
Major causes of death per 100,000 population (2008): diseases of the circulatory system 312.6, of which ischemic heart disease 143.7, cerebrovascular diseases 86.6; malignant neoplasms (cancers) 261.8; diseases of the respiratory system 132.4, of which pneumonia 52.6; diseases of the digestive system 48.5; accidents 23.0; diseases of the genitourinary system 22.1; diabetes mellitus 10.5; suicide and intentional self-harm 6.9; homicide and assault 0.8.
Adult population (ages 15–49) *living with HIV* (2009): 0.2% (world avg. 0.8%).

Social indicators

Educational attainment (2008). Percentage of population age 25–64 having: unknown through lower secondary education 13%; upper secondary 54%; higher 33%, of which at least some university 23%.

Distribution of disposable income (2006–07)

percentage of household income by quintile				
1	2	3	4	5 (highest)
7.4	11.7	16.6	23.3	41.0

Quality of working life. Average full-time workweek (hours; 2009): male 38.5, female 33.7. Annual rate per 100,000 workers for (2008–09): injury or accident 502.3; death 0.5. Proportion of labour force (employed persons) insured for damages or income loss resulting from (2004): injury 100%; permanent disability 100%; death 100%. Average days lost to labour stoppages per 1,000 employee workdays (2008): 28.
Social participation. Eligible voters participating in last national election (May 2010): 65.1%. Population age 16 and over participating in voluntary work (2001)[8]: 39%. Trade union membership in total workforce (2008–09) 26%. Percentage of population attending weekly church services (2001) 8%.
Social deviance (2009–10)[9]. Offense rate per 100,000 population for: theft and handling stolen goods 2,796; violence against a person 1,590; criminal damage 1,472; burglary 986; drug offenses 429; fraud and forgery 278; robbery 137; sex offenses 99.
Leisure (2009). Favourite leisure activities: watching television, videos, and DVDs, listening to the radio, watching sporting events, and attending the cinema; the common free-time activity outside of the home is a visit to the pub; favourite sporting activities: for men—walking, golf, snooker, and billiards, for women—walking, swimming, fitness classes, and yoga.
Material well-being (2008). Households possessing: automobile 74%, of which two cars 25%, three cars 6%; refrigerator/freezer 97%; washing machine 96%; central heating 95%; digital, cable, or satellite television receiver (2009) 89%; computer 72%; Internet connection (2009) 70%; dishwasher 38%.

National economy

Budget (2008–09). Revenue: £534,000,000,000 (income tax 27.7%; production and import taxes 24.4%, of which VAT 14.7%; social security contributions 18.3%; corporate taxes 8.1%). Expenditures: £583,300,000,000 (social protection 34.9%; health 18.9%; education 14.2%; defense 6.3%; public order 5.8%).
Public debt (July 2011): U.S.$1,920,772,000,000.
Production (metric tons except as noted). Agriculture, forestry, fishing (2009): wheat 14,379,000, cow's milk 13,236,500, sugar beets 8,330,000, barley 6,769,000, potatoes 6,423,000, rapeseed 1,951,000, cattle meat 850,000, oats 757,000, carrots 671,000, onions 376,000, apples 243,000, greasy wool 65,393, mushrooms and truffles 45,000; livestock (number of live animals) 32,038,100 sheep, 9,901,000 cattle, 4,601,000 pigs; roundwood (2010) 9,662,160 cu m, of which fuelwood 14%; fisheries production 770,086 (from aquaculture 23%). Mining and quarrying (2009): sand and gravel 65,800,000; rock salt 2,000,000; slate 1,100,000[10]; china clay (kaolin) 1,060,000; potash 600,000. Manufacturing (value added in £'000,000; 2007): food, beverages, and tobacco 22,587; paper products, printing, and publishing 19,831; chemicals and chemical products 19,508; electrical and optical equipment 17,358; base and fabricated metals 17,064; transportation equipment 15,770; rubber and plastic products 7,188; bricks, cement, and ceramics 5,700.

Gross national income (GNI; 2010): U.S.$2,399,292,000,000 (U.S.$38,540 per capita); purchasing power parity GNI (U.S.$36,580 per capita).

Structure of gross domestic product and labour force

	2007		2008	
	in value £'000,000	% of total value	labour force[11]	% of labour force[11]
Agriculture, forestry, fishing	9,302	0.7	433,000	1.4
Mining and quarrying	32,196	2.3	127,000	0.4
Manufacturing	154,918	11.1	3,547,000	11.4
Construction	80,148	5.7	2,380,000	7.7
Public utilities	21,086	1.5	199,000	0.6
Transp. and commun.	86,854	6.2	1,963,000	6.3
Trade, hotels, restaurants	176,193	12.6	5,599,000	18.0
Finance, real estate	397,852	28.4	4,881,000	15.7
Pub. admin., defense	63,084	4.5	2,092,000	6.7
Services	224,102	16.0	8,153,000	26.2
Other	153,147[12]	11.0[12]	1,745,000[13]	5.6[13]
TOTAL	1,398,882	100.0	31,118,000[3]	100.0

Energy production (consumption): electricity (kW-hr; 2009–10) 338,870,000,000 ([2008] 350,505,000,000); hard coal (metric tons; 2009–10) 17,182,000 (46,878,000); crude petroleum (barrels; 2009–10) 444,528,000 ([2009] 609,185,000); petroleum products (metric tons; 2008) 80,435,000 (70,249,000); natural gas (cu m; 2009–10) 68,040,175,000 ([2009] 101,205,250,000).

Financial aggregates

	2005	2006	2007	2008	2009	2010
Exchange rate (end of year)						
U.S. dollar per £	1.72	1.96	2.00	1.46	1.62	1.57
SDRs per £	1.20	1.30	1.27	0.95	1.03	1.02
International reserves (U.S.$)						
Total (excl. gold; '000,000,000)	38.47	40.70	48.96	44.35	55.70	68.34
SDRs ('000,000,000)	0.29	0.40	0.36	0.45	14.34	14.12
Reserve pos. in IMF ('000,000)	2.33	1.41	1.10	2.35	3.33	4.89
Foreign exchange	35.85	38.89	47.50	41.55	38.03	49.33
Gold ('000,000 fine troy oz)	9.99	9.97	9.98	9.98	9.98	9.98
% world reserves	1.0	1.0	1.0	1.0	1.0	1.0
Interest and prices						
Central bank discount (%)	…	…	…	…	…	…
Govt. bond yield (%) long term	4.46	4.37	5.04	4.58	3.65	3.61
Balance of payments (U.S.$'000,000,000,000)						
Balance of visible trade	−124.72	−140.66	−179.74	−173.46	−127.77	−152.93
Imports, f.o.b.	−509.04	−588.25	−622.02	−641.60	−483.94	−563.15
Exports, f.o.b.	384.32	447.59	442.28	468.14	356.17	410.22
Balance of invisibles	+65.31	+58.70	+108.66	+132.30	+104.12	+81.33
Balance of payments, current account	−59.41	−81.96	−71.08	−41.16	−23.65	−71.60

Manufacturing enterprises (2004)

	no. of employees	annual wages as a % of avg. of all wages	annual value added (U.S.$'000,000)
Food products	414,711	81.3	31,474
Fabricated metals	329,390	87.4	21,204
Paints, soaps, pharmaceuticals	162,921	133.7	21,011
Publishing	162,710	117.9	16,385
Motor vehicles, trailers, parts	202,398	112.7	16,141
General purpose machinery	173,197	103.6	12,644
Printing	156,611	94.5	12,007
Aircraft and spacecraft	100,477	139.6	11,734
Plastics	181,799	89.0	11,645
Medical, measuring, testing appliances	100,797	110.1	9,323
Bricks, cement, ceramics	92,879	93.6	8,052
Base chemicals	59,165	145.0	7,706
Beverages	51,069	131.8	7,270
Special purpose machinery	96,563	110.4	7,232
Furniture	117,267	78.9	6,311
Paper and paper products	81,171	104.8	5,983

Retail trade and service enterprises (2001)

	no. of enterprises	no. of employees	weekly wage as a % of all wages	annual turnover (£'000,000)
Food, beverages, and tobacco	27,074	993,000	…	85,534
of which				
meats	8,485	46,000	…	2,216
Household goods,	23,553	319,000	…	29,151
of which				
electronics, appliances	7,157	101,000	…	10,821
furniture	10,592	119,000	…	8,784
Clothing and footwear	17,869	446,000	…	25,963
Pharmaceuticals and cosmetics	6,915	110,000	…	9,543
Business services,	534,956	4,273,000	…	265,631
of which				
real estate	30,779	79,000	…	32,779
Transp. and commun.	81,154	1,621,000	…	181,669
Hotels, restaurants	118,988	1,792,000	…	49,902
Social services,	35,622	1,026	…	16,233
of which				
health	9,683	453,000	…	7,575

Population economically active (2009[11]): total 31,374,000; activity rate of total population 50.8% (participation rates: ages 16 and over, 63.4%; female 45.9%; unemployed [April 2009–March 2010] 7.8%).

Price and earnings indexes (2005 = 100)

	2004	2005	2006	2007	2008	2009	2010
Consumer price index	98.0	100.0	102.3	104.7	108.5	110.8	114.5
Monthly earnings index	95.6	100.0	104.7	109.8	113.7	113.6	116.2

Household income and expenditure (2007–08). Average household size 2.4; average annual disposable income per household £27,769 (U.S.$56,834); sources of income: wages and salaries 66.8%, social security benefits 12.4%, income from self-employment 9.3%, transfers 6.8%; expenditure (2009): housing and energy 22.7%, transportation 14.8%, recreation and culture 11.3%, restaurants and hotels 10.6%, food and nonalcoholic beverages 9.3%, clothing and footwear 5.4%, household furnishings 5.2%, alcoholic beverages and tobacco products 3.5%, communications 2.1%, health 1.6%, education 1.4%.

Selected balance of payments data. Receipts from (U.S.$'000,000): tourism (2009) 30,498; remittances (2010) 7,703; foreign direct investment (FDI; 2008–10 avg.) 69,512. Disbursements for (U.S.$'000,000): tourism (2009) 50,559; remittances (2009) 3,670; FDI (2008–10 avg.) 72,152.

Land use as % of total land area (2009): in temporary crops 18.9%, left fallow 1.0%, in permanent crops 0.2%, in pasture 51.6%, forest area 11.9%.

Foreign trade[14]

Balance of trade (current prices)

	2004	2005	2006	2007	2008	2009
U.S.$'000,000	−111,490	−124,730	−140,660	−179,740	−173,930	−127,620
% of total	13.8%	14.0%	13.6%	16.9%	15.7%	15.2%

Imports (2008): U.S.$631,804,000,000 (machinery and apparatus 22.0%, of which telecommunications equipment, televisions, sound recording equipment 4.5%, electrical machinery/apparatus/parts 4.4%, office machines/computers/parts 4.1%; mineral fuels 12.9%, of which petroleum 9.7%; chemicals and chemical products 10.8%, of which medicine and pharmaceuticals 3.3%; road vehicles 10.0%; food 7.5%; base and fabricated metals 5.9%; apparel and clothing accessories 3.9%). *Major import sources:* Germany 13.0%; U.S. 8.7%; China 7.9%; Neth. 7.3%; France 6.9%; Norway 5.9%; Belgium 4.6%; Italy 4.1%; Ireland 3.5%; Spain 3.0%.

Exports (2008): U.S.$455,596,000,000 (machinery and apparatus 23.0%, of which engines/motors/parts 5.0%, electrical machinery/apparatus/parts 4.2%, general industrial machinery 4.1%; chemicals and chemical products 16.4%, of which medicines 5.9%, organic chemicals 3.1%; mineral fuels 13.2%, of which crude petroleum 6.6%, refined petroleum 5.2%; road vehicles 9.1%, of which cars 6.2%; base and fabricated metals 7.6%; professional, scientific, and controlling instruments 2.6%; diamonds 1.9%; whiskey 1.3%; works of art/antiques 1.1%). *Major export destinations:* U.S. 14.1%; Germany 11.5%; Neth. 7.7%; Ireland 7.5%; France 7.5%; Belgium 5.1%; Spain 4.0%; Italy 3.7%; Sweden 2.0%; China 2.0%.

Transport and communications

Transport. Railroads (2009): route length (2008) 10,224 mi, 16,454 km; passenger-km 52,765,000,000; metric ton-km cargo 21,168,000,000. Roads (2009): total length (2007) 260,981 mi, 420,009 km (paved 100%); passenger-km[8] 727,000,000,000[15]; metric ton-km cargo 139,536,000,000. Vehicles (2010)[8]: passenger cars 28,681,400; trucks and buses 3,928,300. Air transport (2009): passenger-km 297,000,000,000; metric ton-km cargo 6,851,000,000.

Communications

Medium	date	number in '000s	units per 1,000 persons	Medium	date	number in '000s	units per 1,000 persons
Televisions	2003	56,576	950	PCs	2006	48,591	802
Telephones				Dailies	2009	14,009[16]	227[16]
Cellular	2010	80,799[17]	1,303[17]	Internet users	2009	51,444	836
Landline	2010	33,320	537	Broadband	2010	19,468[17]	314[17]

Education and health

Literacy (2006): total population literate, about 99%.

Education (2007–08)

	teachers	students	student/ teacher ratio	enrollment rate (%)
Primary (age 5–10)	244,391	4,465,021	18.3	100
Secondary/Voc. (age 11–17)	375,385	5,356,450	14.3	93
Tertiary	134,170	2,329,494	17.4	57 (age 18–22)

Health (2009): physicians 156,995[18] (1 per 363[18] persons); hospital beds (2008–09) 206,900 (1 per 298 persons); infant mortality rate per 1,000 live births 4.6; undernourished population (2006–08) less than 5.0% of total population.

Military

Total active duty personnel (November 2010): 178,470 (army 57.5%, navy 19.9%, air force 22.6%); reserve 82,274. U.K. troops deployed abroad (November 2010) *c.* 35,000, of which in Germany *c.* 18,500, in Afghanistan *c.* 9,500, in Cyprus 2,861, in the Falkland Islands 1,520; U.S. troops in the U.K. (June 2011) 9,436. *Military expenditure as percentage of GDP* (2008): 2.3%; per capita expenditure U.S.$988.

[1]Active members as of September 2011 including 92 hereditary peers, 616 life peers, and 25 archbishops and bishops. [2]Church of England "established" (protected by the state but not "official"); Church of Scotland "national" (exclusive jurisdiction in spiritual matters per Church of Scotland Act 1921); no established church in Northern Ireland or Wales. [3]Detail does not add to total given because of rounding. [4]One of nine new unitary authorities formally established in April 2009. [5]Formerly Western Isles. [6]Total area as of 2001 census. [7]West Yorkshire urban agglomeration. [8]Great Britain (England, Scotland, and Wales) only. [9]England and Wales only. [10]Includes fill. [11]Second quarter. [12]VAT and other taxes less subsidies. [13]Includes 1,643,000 unemployed. [14]Imports f.o.b. in balance of trade and c.i.f. in commodities and trading partners. [15]Passenger cars 680,000,000,000; buses 37,000,000,000; other 10,000,000,000. [16]Circulation of daily newspapers. [17]Subscribers. [18]England and Scotland only.

Internet resource for further information:

- **Office for National Statistics http://www.ons.gov.uk/ons/index.html**

United States

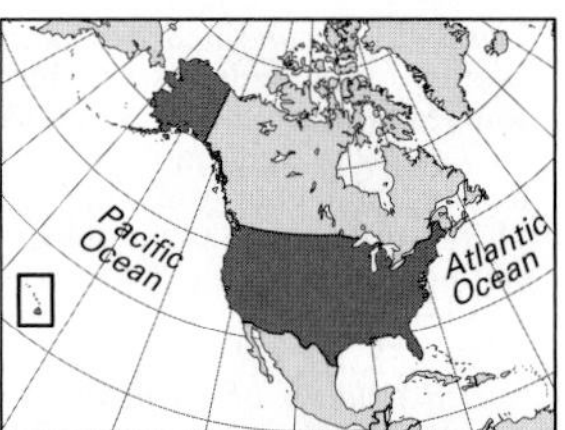

Official name: United States of America.
Form of government: federal republic with two legislative houses (Senate [100]; House of Representatives [435[1]]).
Head of state and government: President.
Capital: Washington, D.C.
Official language: none.
Official religion: none.
Monetary unit: dollar (U.S.$); valuation (Sept. 1, 2011) 1 U.S.$ = €0.70; 1 U.S.$ = £0.62.

Area and population

States	Capitals	area[2] sq mi	area[2] sq km	population 2010[3, 4] census
Alabama	Montgomery	51,701	133,905	4,779,736
Alaska	Juneau	590,693	1,529,888	710,231
Arizona	Phoenix	113,991	295,235	6,392,017
Arkansas	Little Rock	53,179	137,733	2,915,918
California	Sacramento	158,608	410,793	37,253,956
Colorado	Denver	104,095	269,605	5,029,196
Connecticut	Hartford	5,004	12,960	3,574,097
Delaware	Dover	2,023	5,240	897,934
Florida	Tallahassee	58,976	152,747	18,801,310
Georgia	Atlanta	58,921	152,605	9,687,653
Hawaii	Honolulu	6,468	16,752	1,360,301
Idaho	Boise	83,569	216,443	1,567,582
Illinois	Springfield	57,916	150,002	12,830,632
Indiana	Indianapolis	36,417	94,320	6,483,802
Iowa	Des Moines	56,273	145,746	3,046,355
Kansas	Topeka	82,278	213,099	2,853,118
Kentucky	Frankfort	40,411	104,664	4,339,367
Louisiana	Baton Rouge	47,632	123,366	4,533,372
Maine	Augusta	33,123	85,788	1,328,361
Maryland	Annapolis	10,441	27,042	5,773,552
Massachusetts	Boston	8,262	21,398	6,547,629
Michigan	Lansing	96,713	250,486	9,883,640
Minnesota	St. Paul	86,935	225,161	5,303,925
Mississippi	Jackson	47,692	123,522	2,967,297
Missouri	Jefferson City	69,703	180,530	5,988,927
Montana	Helena	147,039	380,829	989,415
Nebraska	Lincoln	77,349	200,333	1,826,341
Nevada	Carson City	110,572	286,380	2,700,551
New Hampshire	Concord	9,280	24,035	1,316,470
New Jersey	Trenton	7,812	20,233	8,791,894
New Mexico	Santa Fe	121,590	314,917	2,059,179
New York	Albany	53,095	137,515	19,378,102
North Carolina	Raleigh	52,663	136,397	9,535,483
North Dakota	Bismarck	70,698	183,107	672,591
Ohio	Columbus	44,825	116,096	11,536,504
Oklahoma	Oklahoma City	69,899	181,038	3,751,351
Oregon	Salem	97,048	251,353	3,831,074
Pennsylvania	Harrisburg	46,055	119,282	12,702,379
Rhode Island	Providence	1,221	3,162	1,052,567
South Carolina	Columbia	31,114	80,585	4,625,364
South Dakota	Pierre	77,116	199,730	814,180
Tennessee	Nashville	42,145	109,155	6,346,105
Texas	Austin	266,833	691,094	25,145,561
Utah	Salt Lake City	84,897	219,882	2,763,885
Vermont	Montpelier	9,617	24,908	625,741
Virginia	Richmond	40,599	105,151	8,001,024
Washington	Olympia	68,095	176,365	6,724,540
West Virginia	Charleston	24,230	62,755	1,852,994
Wisconsin	Madison	65,496	169,634	5,686,986
Wyoming	Cheyenne	97,812	253,332	563,626
District				
District of Columbia	—	68	176	601,723
TOTAL		3,678,190[5]	9,526,468[5]	308,745,538

Demography

Population (2011): 313,387,000[6].
Density (2011)[7]: persons per sq mi 88.7, persons per sq km 34.3.
Urban-rural (2010): urban 83.5%; rural 16.5%.
Sex distribution (2010): male 49.16%; female 50.84%.
Age breakdown (2010): under 15, 19.8%; 15–29, 21.0%; 30–44, 19.8%; 45–59, 20.9%; 60–74, 12.5%; 75–84, 4.2%; 85 and over, 1.8%.
Population projection: (2020) 339,393,000; (2030) 368,459,000.
Population by race and Hispanic[8] origin (2010): non-Hispanic white 63.7%; Hispanic 16.3%; non-Hispanic black 12.6%; Asian and Pacific Islander 4.9%; American Indian and Eskimo 0.9%; other 1.6%.
Religious affiliation (2005): Christian 83.3%, of which independent Christian 23.2%, Roman Catholic 19.6%, Protestant (including Anglican) 18.9%, unaffiliated Christian 16.5%, Orthodox 1.8%, other Christian (primarily Mormon and Jehovah's Witness) 3.3%; Jewish 1.9%; Muslim 1.6%; Buddhist 0.9%; New Religionists 0.5%; Hindu 0.4%; traditional beliefs 0.4%; Bahāʾī 0.3%; Sikh 0.1%; nonreligious 9.8%; atheist 0.5%; other 0.3%.
Mobility (2005). Reported gross % of population living in the same residence as in 2004: *c.* 86%; different residence, same county *c.* 8%; different county, same state *c.* 3%; different state *c.* 3%; moved from abroad *c.* 1%.
Households (2010). Total households 117,538,000 (married-couple families 58,410,000 [49.7%]). Average household size 2.6; 1 person 26.7%, 2 persons 33.6%, 3 persons 15.9%, 4 persons 13.7%, 5 or more persons 10.1%. Family households: 78,833,000 (67.1%); nonfamily 38,705,000 (32.9%), of which 1-person 81.1%.
Place of birth (2010): native-born 266,674,000 (87.6%); foreign-born 37,606,000 (12.4%), of which (2004) Mexico 10,011,000, the Philippines 1,222,000, China and Hong Kong 1,067,000, India 1,007,000, Cuba 952,000, Vietnam 863,000, El Salvador 765,000, South Korea 701,000.

Components of population change (2000–09)

States	net change in population[9]	percentage change	births	deaths	net domestic/ international migration
Alabama	261,326	5.9	566,363	427,844	136,452
Alaska	71,542	11.4	97,287	28,894	–724
Arizona	1,465,171	28.6	875,726	411,488	986,764
Arkansas	216,064	8.1	361,135	258,324	112,923
California	3,090,016	9.1	5,058,440	2,179,958	306,925
Colorado	722,733	16.8	641,107	272,191	357,683
Connecticut	112,681	3.3	388,331	271,426	16,608
Delaware	101,565	13.0	106,409	66,314	66,047
Florida	2,555,130	16.0	2,046,244	1,566,658	2,034,234
Georgia	1,642,430	20.1	1,301,426	616,981	849,133
Hawaii	83,640	6.9	168,965	83,575	5,843
Idaho	251,846	19.5	211,735	95,443	134,462
Illinois	490,751	4.0	1,681,839	960,627	–228,888
Indiana	342,593	5.6	810,225	512,148	71,633
Iowa	81,476	2.8	361,766	255,370	–15,876
Kansas	129,936	4.8	370,672	225,837	–17,574
Kentucky	271,825	6.7	519,005	370,888	126,831
Louisiana	23,104	0.5	595,844	382,645	–285,765
Maine	43,386	3.4	128,319	116,170	38,804
Maryland	402,934	7.6	698,269	405,035	95,290
Massachusetts	244,468	3.9	729,448	508,747	–31,623
Michigan	31,235	0.3	1,196,297	802,544	–372,082
Minnesota	346,722	7.0	654,294	348,464	62,426
Mississippi	107,330	3.8	403,008	263,192	–18,973
Missouri	390,896	7.0	726,153	507,227	105,461
Montana	72,799	8.1	108,579	77,395	42,980
Nebraska	85,354	5.0	241,832	139,626	–9,156
Nevada	644,825	32.3	333,232	165,152	485,443
New Hampshire	88,784	7.2	135,471	92,897	53,460
New Jersey	293,361	3.5	1,038,937	664,523	–60,000
New Mexico	190,630	10.5	265,766	136,175	70,558
New York	564,642	3.0	2,323,103	1,417,221	–846,993
North Carolina	1,334,478	16.6	1,143,251	685,324	889,589
North Dakota	4,649	0.7	76,697	53,637	–15,217
Ohio	189,495	1.7	1,389,016	999,895	–247,751
Oklahoma	236,412	6.9	481,766	325,299	92,977
Oregon	404,220	11.8	433,972	284,372	274,031
Pennsylvania	323,696	2.6	1,350,244	1,183,448	136,359
Rhode Island	4,894	0.5	115,762	89,989	–14,632
South Carolina	549,410	13.7	537,443	355,877	376,441
South Dakota	57,548	7.6	105,163	64,270	13,367
Tennessee	606,978	10.2	754,589	525,554	356,078
Texas	3,930,484	18.8	3,568,617	1,444,493	1,781,785
Utah	551,368	24.7	479,519	124,262	118,543
Vermont	12,939	2.1	59,886	47,266	3,877
Virginia	803,542	11.4	957,904	532,166	375,639
Washington	770,052	13.1	772,324	424,029	440,988
West Virginia	11,433	0.6	192,926	193,308	21,653
Wisconsin	291,066	5.4	654,879	429,869	59,904
Wyoming	50,487	10.2	65,633	38,277	25,660
District					
District of Columbia	27,602	4.8	73,986	50,911	–17,427
TOTAL/RATE	25,581,948	9.1	38,358,804	22,483,225	8,944,170

Principal metropolitan statistical areas/cities (2010)

Metropolitan statistical area	population	Largest city proper	population
New York-Northern New Jersey-Long Island	18,897,109	New York	8,175,133
Los Angeles-Long Beach-Santa Ana	12,828,837	Los Angeles	3,792,621
Chicago-Joliet-Naperville	9,461,105	Chicago	2,695,598
Dallas-Fort Worth-Arlington	6,371,773	Dallas	1,197,816
Philadelphia-Camden-Wilmington	5,965,343	Philadelphia	1,526,006
Houston-Sugar Land-Baytown	5,946,800	Houston	2,099,451
Washington-Arlington-Alexandria	5,582,170	Washington	601,723
Miami-Fort Lauderdale-Pompano Beach	5,565,635	Miami	399,457
Atlanta-Sandy Springs-Marietta	5,268,860	Atlanta	420,003
Boston-Cambridge-Quincy	4,552,402	Boston	617,594
San Francisco-Oakland-Fremont	4,335,391	San Francisco	805,235
Detroit-Warren-Livonia	4,296,250	Detroit	713,777
Riverside-San Bernardino-Ontario	4,224,851	Riverside	303,871
Phoenix-Mesa-Glendale	4,192,887	Phoenix	1,445,632
Seattle-Tacoma-Bellevue	3,439,809	Seattle	608,660
Minneapolis-St. Paul-Bloomington	3,279,833	Minneapolis	382,578
San Diego-Carlsbad-San Marcos	3,095,313	San Diego	1,307,402
St. Louis	2,812,896	St. Louis	319,294
Tampa-St. Petersburg-Clearwater	2,783,243	Tampa	335,709
Baltimore-Towson	2,710,489	Baltimore	620,961
Denver-Aurora-Broomfield	2,543,482	Denver	600,158
Pittsburgh	2,356,285	Pittsburgh	305,704
Portland-Vancouver-Hillsboro	2,226,009	Portland	583,776
Sacramento-Arden-Arcade-Roseville	2,149,127	Sacramento	466,488
San Antonio-New Braunfels	2,142,508	San Antonio	1,327,407
Orlando-Kissimmee	2,134,411	Orlando	238,300
Cincinnati-Middletown	2,130,151	Cincinnati	296,943
Cleveland-Elyria-Mentor	2,077,240	Cleveland	396,815
Kansas City	2,035,334	Kansas City, Mo.	459,787
Las Vegas-Paradise	1,951,269	Las Vegas	583,756
San Jose-Sunnyvale-Santa Clara	1,836,911	San Jose	945,942
Columbus, Ohio	1,836,536	Columbus	787,033
Charlotte-Gastonia-Concord	1,758,038	Charlotte	731,424
Indianapolis-Carmel	1,756,241	Indianapolis	820,445
Austin-Round Rock-San Marcos	1,716,289	Austin	790,390
Virginia Beach-Norfolk-Newport News	1,671,683	Virginia Beach	437,994
Providence-New Bedford-Fall River	1,600,852	Providence	178,042
Nashville-Davidson-Murfreesboro	1,589,934	Nashville	601,222
Milwaukee-Waukesha-West Allis	1,555,908	Milwaukee	594,833
Jacksonville	1,345,596	Jacksonville	821,784
Memphis	1,316,100	Memphis	646,889
Louisville-Jefferson County	1,283,566	Louisville	597,337
Richmond	1,258,251	Richmond	204,214
Oklahoma City	1,252,987	Oklahoma City	579,999
Hartford-West Hartford-East Hartford	1,212,381	Hartford	124,775
New Orleans-Metairie-Kenner	1,167,764	New Orleans	343,829
Buffalo-Niagara Falls	1,135,509	Buffalo	261,310
Raleigh-Cary	1,130,490	Raleigh	403,892
Birmingham-Hoover	1,128,047	Birmingham	212,237
Salt Lake City	1,124,197	Salt Lake City	186,440
Rochester, New York	1,054,323	Rochester, N.Y.	210,565
Tucson	980,263	Tucson	520,116

Immigration (2010): permanent immigrants admitted 1,042,625, from Mexico 13.3%, China 6.8%, India 6.6%, the Philippines 5.6%, Dominican Republic 5.2%, Cuba 3.2%, Vietnam 2.9%, Haiti 2.2%, Colombia 2.1%, South Korea 2.1%, Iraq 1.9%, Jamaica 1.9%, El Salvador 1.8%, Pakistan 1.8%, other 42.6%. Refugees (end of 2009) 275,461. Asylum seekers (end of 2009) 63,803.

Vital statistics

Birth rate per 1,000 population (2009): 13.5 (world avg. 20.3); within marriage (2008) 59.4%; outside of marriage (2008) 40.6%.
Death rate per 1,000 population (2009): 7.9 (world avg. 8.5).
Natural increase rate per 1,000 population (2009): 5.6 (world avg. 11.8).
Marriage rate per 1,000 population (2009): 6.8; median age at first marriage: men 28.1 years, women 25.9 years.
Divorce rate per 1,000 population (2009): 3.4.
Total fertility rate (avg. births per childbearing woman; 2008): 2.09.
Life expectancy at birth (2007): male 75.4 years, of which white male 75.9 years, black male 70.0 years; female 80.4 years, of which white female 80.8 years, black female 76.8 years.

Vital statistics (2010)

States	live births	birth rate per 1,000 population	death rate per 1,000 population[10]	infant mortality rate per 1,000 live births[11]	abortion rate per 1,000 live births[12]	life expectancy[13]
Alabama	60,053	12.6	10.2	9.9	188	74.6
Alaska	11,466	16.1	5.1	6.5	180	76.7
Arizona	88,905	13.9	7.0	6.8	202	77.5
Arkansas	38,539	13.2	10.3	7.7	120	75.1
California	509,968	13.7	6.4	5.2	379	78.3
Colorado	66,344	13.2	6.3	6.1	234	78.4
Connecticut	39,441	11.0	8.2	6.6	402	78.4
Delaware	11,342	12.6	8.7	7.5	442	76.6
Florida	214,552	11.4	9.3	7.1	408	77.5
Georgia	133,915	13.8	7.2	8.0	233	75.3
Hawaii	18,985	14.0	7.4	6.5	298	79.8
Idaho	23,194	14.8	7.2	6.8	78	78.0
Illinois	165,194	12.9	8.0	6.7	356	76.7
Indiana	83,939	12.9	8.9	7.6	143	76.2
Iowa	38,715	12.7	9.5	5.5	162	78.5
Kansas	40,640	14.2	8.9	7.9	261	77.5
Kentucky	55,790	12.9	9.7	6.7	69	75.3
Louisiana	62,383	13.8	9.3	9.2	187	74.4
Maine	12,967	9.8	9.5	6.3	196	77.6
Maryland	73,776	12.8	7.8	8.0	501	76.3
Massachusetts	72,757	11.1	8.2	4.9	355	78.4
Michigan	114,523	11.6	8.8	7.9	318	76.5
Minnesota	68,605	12.9	7.4	5.6	196	79.1
Mississippi	40,033	13.5	9.9	10.0	73	73.7
Missouri	76,756	12.8	9.6	7.5	107	76.2
Montana	12,060	12.2	9.2	6.4	185	77.3
Nebraska	25,916	14.2	8.7	6.8	123	78.3
Nevada	35,862	13.3	8.0	6.4	363	75.9
New Hampshire	12,867	9.8	7.8	5.4	220	78.5
New Jersey	109,249	12.4	8.1	5.2	538	77.5
New Mexico	27,769	13.5	8.1	6.3	216	77.3
New York	241,711	12.5	7.6	5.6	633	77.9
North Carolina	122,267	12.8	8.4	8.5	280	75.8
North Dakota	9,100	13.5	9.2	7.5	147	78.7
Ohio	139,137	12.1	9.6	7.7	235	76.4
Oklahoma	53,234	14.2	10.2	8.5	134	75.3
Oregon	45,535	11.9	8.4	5.8	287	77.9
Pennsylvania	142,325	11.2	10.2	7.6	235	76.8
Rhode Island	11,149	10.6	9.3	7.4	417	78.2
South Carolina	58,293	12.6	9.0	8.6	123	74.9
South Dakota	11,809	14.5	8.8	6.4	69	78.0
Tennessee	79,485	12.5	9.5	8.3	222	75.0
Texas	386,096	15.4	6.8	6.3	222	76.7
Utah	52,232	18.9	5.1	5.1	70	78.7
Vermont	6,223	9.9	8.4	5.1	230	78.2
Virginia	102,972	12.9	7.6	7.8	254	76.9
Washington	86,530	12.9	7.4	4.8	281	78.2
West Virginia	20,471	11.0	11.9	7.5	113	75.0
Wisconsin	68,483	12.0	8.3	6.5	138	78.1
Wyoming	7,555	13.4	7.9	7.4	97	77.1
District						
District of Columbia	9,167	15.2	9.3	13.1	916	72.6
TOTAL/RATE	4,000,279	13.0	8.1	6.8	373	77.0

Major causes of death per 100,000 population (2007): cardiovascular diseases 266.4, of which ischemic heart disease 133.9, cerebrovascular diseases 44.4, atherosclerosis 2.7; malignant neoplasms (cancers) 185.7; diseases of the respiratory system 77.0, of which pneumonia 17.4; accidents and adverse effects 38.8, of which motor-vehicle accidents 14.3; diabetes mellitus 23.5; kidney disease 15.3; suicide 11.0; chronic liver disease and cirrhosis 9.5; AIDS (2006) 4.0.
Adult population (ages 15–49) *living with HIV* (2009): 0.6% (world avg. 0.8%).
Morbidity rates of infectious diseases per 100,000 population (2007): chlamydia 367.4; gonorrhea 118.0; salmonellosis 15.9; syphilis 13.6; chicken pox 13.3; AIDS 12.4; lyme disease 9.1; shigellosis 6.6; pertussis 3.5; hepatitis B (serum) 1.5; hepatitis A (infectious) 1.0.

Social indicators

Educational attainment (2008). Percentage of population age 25 and over having: unknown/primary and incomplete secondary 13.4%; secondary 31.2%; some postsecondary 26.0%; 4-year higher degree 19.1%; advanced degree 10.3%. Number of earned degrees (2007): associate's degree 728,114; bachelor's degree 1,524,092; master's degree 604,607; doctor's degree 60,616; first-professional degrees (in fields such as medicine, theology, and law) 90,064.

Distribution of income (2007)

percentage of disposable family income by quintile

1	2	3	4	5 (highest)
3.4	8.7	14.8	23.4	49.7

Quality of working life (2009). Average workweek (2010): 42.2 hours. Annual death rate per 100,000 workers: 2.8; leading causes of occupational deaths: transportation incidents 39%, assaults/violent acts 18%, falls 15%, struck by object 16%. Annual occupational injury rate per 100,000 workers: 3.9. Average duration of journey to work: 25.1 minutes (private automobile 86.1%, of which drive alone 76.1%, carpool 10.0%; take public transportation 5.0%; walk 2.9%; work at home 4.3%; other 1.7%). Rate per 1,000 employed workers of discouraged workers (unemployed no longer seeking work; 2006): 3.1.
Access to services (2009). Proportion of occupied dwellings having access to: electricity 100.0%; safe public water supply 99.4%; public sewage collection 79.3%; septic tanks 20.5%.
Social participation (2008). Eligible voters participating in last presidential election: 61.6%. Population age 16 and over volunteering for an organization 26.4%; median annual hours 52. Trade-union membership in total workforce 12.4%.
Social deviance (2009). Offense rate per 100,000 population for: murder 5.0; rape 28.7; robbery 133.0; aggravated assault 262.8; motor-vehicle theft 258.8; burglary and housebreaking 716.3; larceny-theft 2,060.9; drug-abuse violation (2007) 495.5; drunkenness (2007) 149.5. Estimated drug and substance users (population age 12 and over): cigarettes 24.2%; binge alcohol[14] 23.3%; marijuana and hashish 5.8%. Rate per 100,000 population of suicide (2007): 11.5.
Leisure (2008). Favourite leisure activities (percentage of total population age 18 and over that undertook activity at least once in the previous year): attending a movie 53.3%, dining out 50.2%, reading books 40.9%, entertaining friends or relatives at home 40.1%, barbecuing 33.9%.
Material well-being (2009). Occupied dwellings with householder possessing: automobiles, trucks, or vans 92.2%, 1 car with or without trucks or vans 46.9%, 2 cars 25.1%, only trucks and vans 12.4%, no cars, trucks, or vans 7.8%, 3 or more cars 8.1%; television receiver 98.2%; telephone 97.8%; air conditioner 88.8%; video 90.2%[12]; washing machine 77.9%; clothes dryer 75.8%; cable television 79.9%; personal computers 61.8%[15]; Internet connections 71.1%; broadband Internet (2010) 68.2%.

Households with computers and Internet access

States	computers (%) (2003)	Internet (%) (2010)
Alabama	53.9	60.0
Alaska	72.7	78.7
Arizona	64.3	75.5
Arkansas	50.0	58.8
California	66.3	75.9
Colorado	70.0	74.8
Connecticut	69.2	76.5
Delaware	64.3	71.7
Florida	61.0	72.0
Georgia	60.6	70.4
Hawaii	63.3	71.1
Idaho	69.2	75.5
Illinois	60.0	70.7
Indiana	59.6	61.3
Iowa	64.7	70.7
Kansas	63.8	76.4
Kentucky	58.1	61.3
Louisiana	52.3	62.8
Maine	67.8	73.4
Maryland	66.0	76.3
Massachusetts	64.1	77.5
Michigan	59.9	69.8
Minnesota	67.9	73.7
Mississippi	48.3	57.7
Missouri	60.7	67.8
Montana	59.5	65.5
Nebraska	66.1	71.3
Nevada	61.3	76.6
New Hampshire	71.5	81.0
New Jersey	65.5	74.8
New Mexico	53.9	62.6
New York	60.0	71.1
North Carolina	57.7	68.4
North Dakota	61.2	73.1
Ohio	58.8	67.5
Oklahoma	55.4	66.2
Oregon	67.0	78.3
Pennsylvania	60.2	70.2
Rhode Island	62.3	72.1
South Carolina	54.9	63.8
South Dakota	62.1	69.0
Tennessee	56.7	63.3
Texas	59.0	69.5
Utah	74.1	82.3
Vermont	65.5	74.7
Virginia	66.8	73.0
Washington	71.4	79.7
West Virginia	55.0	65.1
Wisconsin	63.8	73.7
Wyoming	65.4	74.4
District		
District of Columbia	59.5	73.4
U.S. RATE	61.8	71.1

National economy

Budget (2010). Revenue: U.S.$2,165,100,000,000 (individual income tax 43.2%, social-insurance taxes and contributions 40.5%, corporation income tax 7.2%, excise taxes 3.4%, other 5.7%). Expenditures: U.S.$3,720,700,000,000 (social security and medicare 31.7%, defense 19.3%, health 10.0%, interest on debt 5.0%).
Total outstanding national debt (November 2011): U.S.$15,110,499,000,000, of which debt held by the public U.S.$10,389,958,000,000, intragovernment holdings U.S.$4,720,541,000,000.
Gross national income (GNI; 2010): U.S.$14,600,828,000,000 (U.S.$47,140 per capita); purchasing power parity GNI (U.S.$47,020 per capita).

Structure of gross domestic product and labour force

	2008			
	in value U.S.$'000,000,000	% of total value	labour force[16]	% of labour force[16]
Agriculture, forestry, fishing	157.7	1.1	2,168,000	1.4
Mining and quarrying	325.3	2.3	819,000	0.5
Manufacturing	1,637.7	11.5	15,904,000	10.3
Construction	581.5	4.1	10,974,000	7.1
Public utilities	306.0	2.1	1,225,000	0.8
Transp. and commun.	1,036.9	7.3	6,501,000	4.2
Trade, hotels, restaurants	2,100.5	14.7	30,380,000	19.7
Finance, real estate	2,848.4	20.0	25,768,000	16.7
Public administration, defense	1,840.0	12.9	6,763,000	4.4
Services	3,430.7	24.0	44,860,000	29.1
Other	—	—	8,924,000[17]	5.8[17]
TOTAL	14,264.7	100.0	154,286,000	100.0

Components of gross domestic product (2008)

States	gross domestic product by state (U.S.$'000,000,000)	personal income (U.S.$'000,000,000)	disposable personal income (U.S.$'000,000,000)	per capita disposable personal income (U.S.$)
Alabama	170.0	156.8	143.4	30,297
Alaska	47.9	29.7	27.5	39,458
Arizona	248.9	214.2	202.9	29,391
Arkansas	98.3	89.3	84.7	28,270
California	1,846.8	1,569.4	1,409.9	37,041
Colorado	248.6	209.3	189.6	37,039
Connecticut	216.2	196.9	168.6	46,775
Delaware	61.8	35.7	31.5	35,880
Florida	744.1	716.1	669.5	34,880
Georgia	397.8	329.1	306.0	30,082
Hawaii	63.8	52.2	48.8	35,939
Idaho	52.7	49.0	45.3	28,638
Illinois	633.7	547.0	488.8	37,298
Indiana	254.9	217.5	199.2	30,437
Iowa	135.7	110.1	102.4	32,919
Kansas	122.7	106.4	99.8	33,642
Kentucky	156.4	135.9	123.9	28,424
Louisiana	222.2	160.0	152.2	32,651
Maine	49.7	46.6	43.1	31,593
Maryland	273.3	270.9	237.6	41,325
Massachusetts	365.0	329.7	286.4	43,134
Michigan	382.5	353.1	315.9	31,719
Minnesota	262.8	223.3	197.4	37,300
Mississippi	91.8	86.9	83.0	27,077
Missouri	237.8	208.3	195.0	31,339
Montana	35.9	33.1	30.5	30,627
Nebraska	83.3	67.3	64.1	33,678
Nevada	131.2	104.9	94.9	35,768
New Hampshire	60.0	56.4	51.7	38,304
New Jersey	474.9	442.1	386.0	43,921
New Mexico	79.9	63.7	60.7	28,922
New York	1,144.5	937.0	785.8	40,254
North Carolina	400.2	317.6	292.0	30,311
North Dakota	31.2	25.2	24.0	35,824
Ohio	471.5	407.9	369.5	31,370
Oklahoma	146.4	134.4	120.6	33,143
Oregon	161.6	136.3	122.0	31,643
Pennsylvania	553.3	501.2	447.3	35,413
Rhode Island	47.4	43.1	39.1	36,336
South Carolina	156.4	142.8	134.3	28,556
South Dakota	37.0	30.1	28.9	34,216
Tennessee	252.1	213.4	201.6	31,327
Texas	1,223.5	938.4	872.5	34,850
Utah	109.8	82.9	79.3	26,641
Vermont	25.4	24.2	21.7	34,634
Virginia	397.0	333.1	305.4	37,194
Washington	322.8	277.4	259.9	38,009
West Virginia	61.7	55.9	51.4	27,926
Wisconsin	240.4	210.0	188.1	32,835
Wyoming	35.3	26.5	24.0	43,607
District				
District of Columbia	97.2	38.5	35.2	56,245
TOTAL/AVERAGE	14,165.6[5]	12,086.5[5]	10,942.8[5]	34,949

Production. Agriculture, forestry, fishing (value of production in U.S.$'000,000 except as noted; 2010): corn (maize) 66,650, soybeans 38,915, hay 14,401, wheat 12,992, cotton 7,318, potatoes 3,489, grapes 3,472, rice 3,041, lettuce 2,499, almonds 2,294[18], apples 2,247, strawberries 2,245, oranges 1,935, tobacco 1,499[18], tomatoes 1,391, sugar beets 1,290[10], sorghum 1,242[18], mushrooms 964[10], barley 916[18], peanuts (groundnuts) 835[18], sugarcane 814[10], walnuts 739[18], peppers 685[18], cottonseed 666[18], broccoli 649, blueberries 641, carrots 627, peaches 615, pistachios 593[18], cherries 506[18], watermelons 461, sunflowers 445, pecans 417[18], sweet potatoes 410[18], lemons 381, cabbage 378, pears 334, cantaloupe 314, onions 105; livestock (number of live animals; 2010) 92,600,000 cattle, 64,600,000 pigs, (2009) 9,500,000 horses, 5,600,000 sheep, (2009) 2,100,000,000 chickens; roundwood (2009) 344,834,676 cu m, of which fuelwood 12% (coniferous 200,471,339 cu m, non-coniferous 144,363,337 cu m); fisheries production (2009) 4,702,125 metric tons (from aquaculture 10%); aquatic plants production 8,207 (from aquaculture, none). Metals mining (metal content in metric tons unless otherwise noted; 2009): beryllium 120 (world rank: 1); molybdenum 50,000 (world rank: 2); copper 1,190,000 (world rank: 3); lead 400,000 (world rank: 3); gold 210,000 kg (world rank: 3); palladium 12,500 kg (world rank: 3); zinc 690,000 (world rank: 5); platinum 3,800 kg (world rank: 5); silver 1,230,000 kg (world rank: 8); iron 26,000,000 (world rank: 10). Nonmetals mining (metric tons unless otherwise noted; 2009): diatomite 790,000 (world rank: 1); bromine 235,000[10] (world rank: 1); boron 1,150,000[19] (world rank: 2); perlite 380,000 (world rank: 2); kyanite 80,000 (world rank: 2); barite 380,000 (world rank: 3); vermiculite 110,000 (world rank: 3); silicon 140,000 (world rank: 6); feldspar 530,000 (world rank: 8). Quarrying (metric tons unless otherwise noted; 2009): salt 46,000,000 (world rank: 2); phosphate rock 27,200,000 (world rank: 2); lime 15,000,000 (world rank: 2); gypsum 9,400,000 (world rank: 4). Manufacturing (value added in U.S.$'000,000; 2009): chemicals and chemical products 328,871, of which pharmaceuticals and medicine 140,568; food and food products 258,615; transportation equipment 229,642, of which aerospace products and parts 99,173, motor vehicle parts 51,570, motor vehicles 41,968; computer and electronic products 193,242, of which semiconductors and electronics 58,361, computers and related components 25,974, communications equipment 24,941; fabricated metal products 146,876; nonelectrical machinery 133,057; plastic and rubber products 82,295; petroleum and coal 78,559; paper and paper products 76,531; beverages and tobacco products 70,959; navigational, measuring, medical, and scientific equipment 58,361; printing and publishing 50,502; general electrical equipment 50,498; cement, bricks, and glass 48,900; base metals 48,170. Construction (completed; 2010): private U.S.$508,240,000,000, of which nonresidential U.S.$266,550,000,000, residential U.S.$241,690,000,000; public U.S.$306,293,000,000.

Energy consumption by source and by state (2009)

('000,000,000,000 Btu)

States	petroleum	natural gas[20]	coal	hydroelectric power	nuclear electric power
Alabama	593	474	631	122	415
Alaska	258	344	15	13	0.0
Arizona	540	377	413	63	321
Arkansas	349	248	264	41	159
California	3,590	2,391	52	272	332
Colorado	480	530	350	18	0.0
Connecticut	353	188	26	5	174
Delaware	95	52	34	0.0	0.0
Florida	1,683	1,082	582	2	305
Georgia	1,062	475	723	32	331
Hawaii	234	2.7	19	0.8	0.0
Idaho	154	87	8.4	102	0.0
Illinois	1,282	958	1,015	1.3	999
Indiana	792	514	1,365	4.9	0.0
Iowa	423	317	445	9.5	49
Kansas	393	289	356	0.1	92
Kentucky	680	214	937	32	0.0
Louisiana	1,385	1,300	253	12	176
Maine	206	73	1.7	34	0.0
Maryland	545	205	267	18	152
Massachusetts	595	409	92	12	56
Michigan	861	747	736	13	229
Minnesota	626	406	329	6.6	130
Mississippi	415	371	142	0.0	115
Missouri	677	267	766	18	107
Montana	175	76	173	93	0.0
Nebraska	215	165	84	4.2	99
Nevada	250	284	84	24	0.0
New Hampshire	163	62	33	16	92
New Jersey	1,111	639	60	0.3	359
New Mexico	252	247	306	2.6	0.0
New York	1,465	1,166	156	268	455
North Carolina	871	251	679	50	427
North Dakota	129	58	423	14	0.0
Ohio	1,205	769	1,267	5	159
Oklahoma	501	678	373	35	0.0
Oregon	373	255	33	322	0.0
Pennsylvania	1,318	834	1,224	26	809
Rhode Island	100	95	[21]	—	0.0
South Carolina	561	197	372	23	546
South Dakota	120	66	38	43	0.0
Tennessee	778	223	478	100	282
Texas	5,512	3,462	1,498	10	434
Utah	271	224	365	8.2	0.0
Vermont	85	9	[21]	14	56
Virginia	864	331	335	14	295
Washington	777	319	84	711	69
West Virginia	218	114	743	10	0.0
Wisconsin	552	393	426	13	133
Wyoming	166	146	474	9.4	0.0
District					
District of Columbia	20	34	0.3	0.0	0.0
TOTAL	36,321[5]	23,414[5]	19,693[5]	2,650[5]	8,356[5]

Energy production (consumption): electricity (kW-hr; 2007) 4,348,856,000,000 (4,380,109,000,000); hard coal (metric tons; 2007) 506,351,000 (497,391,000); lignite (metric tons; 2007) 546,406,000 (529,393,000); crude petroleum (barrels; 2007) 1,847,000,000 (5,752,000,000); petroleum products (metric tons; 2007) 813,796,000 (830,757,000); natural gas (cu m; 2007) 542,920,000,000 (655,310,000,000). Domestic production of energy by source (2010): natural gas 29.5%, coal 29.4%, crude petroleum 15.6%, nuclear power 11.3%, renewable energy 10.7%, other 3.5%.

Household income and expenditure (2007). Average household size 2.6; median annual income per household U.S.$50,233, of which median Asian (including Hispanic) household U.S.$65,876, median white (including Hispanic) household U.S.$52,034, median non-Hispanic household[19] U.S.$52,423, median Hispanic[8] household U.S.$38,679, median black (including Hispanic) household U.S.$34,091; sources of personal income: wages and salaries 79.8%, transfer payments 10.1%, self-employment 5.5%, other 4.6%; consumption expenditure: housing 20.2%, transportation 17.6%, insurance and pension 10.7%, fuel and utilities 7.0%, food at home 7.0%, health 5.7%, recreation 5.7%, food away from home 5.4%, wearing apparel 3.8%, alcoholic beverages and tobacco products 1.6%, other 15.3%.

Financial aggregates

	2005	2006	2007	2008	2009	2010	2011[22]
Exchange rate, U.S.$ per:							
£[23]	1.82	1.84	2.00	1.85	1.56	1.55	1.61
SDR[23]	1.48	1.47	1.53	1.58	1.54	1.53	1.59
International reserves (U.S.$)[24]							
Total (excl. gold; '000,000,000)	54.08	54.85	59.52	66.61	119.72	121.39	138.66
SDRs ('000,000,000)	8.21	8.87	9.48	9.34	57.81	56.82	57.18
Reserve pos. in IMF ('000,000,000)	8.04	5.04	4.24	7.68	11.39	12.49	26.85
Foreign exchange ('000,000,000)	37.84	40.94	45.80	49.58	50.52	52.08	54.63

Financial aggregates (continued)

	2005	2006	2007	2008	2009	2010	2011[22]
Gold ('000,000 fine troy oz)	261.55	261.50	261.50	261.50	261.50	261.50	261.50
% world reserves	29.76	30.14	30.67	27.39	26.9	26.6	26.5
Interest and prices							
Central bank discount (%)[24]	5.16	6.25	4.83	0.86	0.50	0.75	0.75
Govt. bond yield (%)[23]	4.29	4.79	4.63	3.67	3.25	3.21	3.00
Industrial share prices[23] (2005 = 100)	100.0	108.2	124.9	106.7	84.2	101.1	118.6
Balance of payments (U.S.$'000,000,000)							
Balance of visible trade	−777.80	−832.90	−815.84	−827.14	−503.53	−642.36	…
Imports, f.o.b.	−1,693.31	−1,876.05	−1,983.88	−2,138.65	−1,576.46	−1,935.58	…
Exports, f.o.b.	915.51	1,043.15	1,168.05	1,311.51	1,072.93	1,293.22	…
Balance of invisibles	+32.02	+32.28	+105.54	+150.00	+126.98	+171.46	…
Balance of payments, current account	−745.78	−800.62	−710.30	−677.14	−376.55	−470.90	…

Median household income[25]

States	2007 (in current U.S.$)	2008 (in current U.S.$)	2009 (in current U.S.$)
Alabama	40,554	42,666	40,489
Alaska	64,333	68,460	66,953
Arizona	49,889	50,958	48,745
Arkansas	38,134	38,815	37,823
California	59,948	61,021	58,931
Colorado	55,212	56,993	55,430
Connecticut	65,967	68,595	67,034
Delaware	54,610	57,989	56,860
Florida	47,804	47,778	44,736
Georgia	49,136	50,861	47,590
Hawaii	63,746	67,214	64,098
Idaho	46,253	47,576	44,926
Illinois	54,124	56,235	53,966
Indiana	47,448	47,966	45,424
Iowa	47,292	48,980	48,044
Kansas	47,451	50,177	47,817
Kentucky	40,267	41,538	40,072
Louisiana	40,926	43,733	42,492
Maine	45,888	46,581	45,734
Maryland	68,080	70,545	69,272
Massachusetts	62,365	65,401	64,081
Michigan	47,950	48,591	45,255
Minnesota	55,802	57,288	55,616
Mississippi	36,338	37,790	36,646
Missouri	45,114	46,867	45,229
Montana	43,531	43,654	42,322
Nebraska	47,085	49,693	47,357
Nevada	55,062	56,361	53,341
New Hampshire	62,369	63,731	60,567
New Jersey	67,035	70,378	68,342
New Mexico	41,452	43,508	43,028
New York	53,514	56,033	54,659
North Carolina	44,670	46,549	43,674
North Dakota	43,753	45,685	47,827
Ohio	46,597	47,988	45,395
Oklahoma	41,567	42,822	41,664
Oregon	48,730	50,169	48,457
Pennsylvania	48,576	50,713	49,520
Rhode Island	53,568	55,701	54,119
South Carolina	43,329	44,625	42,442
South Dakota	43,424	46,032	45,043
Tennessee	42,367	43,614	41,725
Texas	47,548	50,043	48,259
Utah	55,109	56,633	55,117
Vermont	49,907	52,104	51,618
Virginia	59,562	61,233	59,330
Washington	55,591	58,078	56,548
West Virginia	37,060	37,989	37,435
Wisconsin	50,578	52,094	49,993
Wyoming	51,731	53,207	52,664
District			
District of Columbia	54,317	57,936	59,290
U.S. AVERAGE	50,740	52,029	50,221

Home ownership rates

States	percent 2000	percent 2010	States	percent 2000	percent 2010
Alabama	73.2	73.2	Nevada	64.0	59.7
Alaska	66.4	65.7	New Hampshire	69.2	74.9
Arizona	68.0	66.6	New Jersey	66.2	66.5
Arkansas	68.9	67.9	New Mexico	73.7	68.6
California	57.1	56.1	New York	53.4	54.5
Colorado	68.3	68.5	North Carolina	71.1	69.5
Connecticut	70.0	70.8	North Dakota	70.7	67.1
Delaware	72.0	74.7	Ohio	71.3	69.7
Florida	68.4	69.3	Oklahoma	72.7	69.2
Georgia	69.8	67.1	Oregon	65.3	66.3
Hawaii	55.2	56.1	Pennsylvania	74.7	72.2
Idaho	70.5	72.4	Rhode Island	61.5	62.8
Illinois	67.9	68.8	South Carolina	76.5	74.8
Indiana	74.9	71.2	South Dakota	71.2	70.6
Iowa	75.2	71.1	Tennessee	70.9	71.0
Kansas	69.3	67.4	Texas	63.8	65.3
Kentucky	73.4	70.3	Utah	72.7	72.5
Louisiana	68.1	70.4	Vermont	68.7	73.6
Maine	76.5	73.8	Virginia	73.9	68.7
Maryland	69.9	68.9	Washington	63.6	64.4
Massachusetts	59.9	65.3	West Virginia	75.9	79.0
Michigan	77.2	74.5	Wisconsin	71.8	71.0
Minnesota	76.1	72.6	Wyoming	71.0	73.4
Mississippi	75.2	74.8	**District**		
Missouri	74.2	71.2	District of Columbia	41.9	45.6
Montana	70.2	68.1	U.S. RATE	67.4	66.9
Nebraska	70.2	70.4			

Selected household characteristics (2010). Total number of households 117,538,000, of which (family households by race) white including Hispanic 81.2%, black including Hispanic 12.5%, other 6.3%—Hispanic of any race 11.3%; (by tenure; 2008) owned 78,825,000 (67.3%), rented 36,761,000 (31.4%), other 1,595,000 (1.4%); family households 78,833,000, of which married couple 74.1%, female householder 18.8%, male householder 7.1%; nonfamily households 38,705,000, of which female living alone 45.7%, male living alone 36.7%, other 17.6%.

Population economically active (December 2009): total 153,059,000 (civilian population only); activity rate of total population 49.6% (participation rates: ages 16–64, 64.6%; female [2007] 46.5%; unemployed 10.0%).

Price and earnings indexes (2005 = 100)

	2004	2005	2006	2007	2008	2009	2010
Consumer price index	96.7	100.0	103.2	106.2	110.2	109.9	111.7
Hourly earnings index[26]	97.5	100.0	101.5	104.3	107.2	110.2	112.4

Selected balance of payments data. Receipts from (U.S.$'000,000): tourism (2009) 121,131; remittances (2009) 2,941; foreign direct investment (FDI; 2008–10 avg.) 229,169. Disbursements for (U.S.$'000,000): tourism (2009) 105,202; remittances (2009) 48,308; FDI (2008–10 avg.) 306,629. Number of foreign visitors (2009) 54,884,184 (17,964,454 from Canada, 13,164,000 from Mexico, 10,978,668 from Western Europe); number of nationals traveling abroad (2009) 61,500,000 (19,500,000 to Mexico, 11,700,000 to Canada, 10,635,000 to Europe).

Land use as % of total land area (2007): in temporary crops or left fallow 18.6%, in permanent crops 0.3%, in pasture 26.0%, forest area 33.1%.

Foreign trade

Balance of trade (current prices)

	2004	2005	2006	2007	2008	2009
U.S.$'000,000,000	−668.4	−787.1	−843.5	−826.9	−800.0	−517.0
% of total	29.2%	30.5%	29.3%	26.4%	23.5%	19.8%

Imports (2008): U.S.$2,100,141,200,000 (crude and refined petroleum 21.1%; motor vehicles 9.1%; chemicals and chemical products 8.4%; telecommunications equipment 6.3%; electrical machinery 5.4%; computers and office equipment 4.6%; wearing apparel 3.8%; industrial machinery 3.2%; food and beverages 3.2%). *Major import sources:* China 16.1%; Canada 16.0%; Mexico 10.3%; Japan 6.6%; Germany 4.6%; United Kingdom 2.8%; Saudi Arabia 2.6%; Venezuela 2.4%; South Korea 2.3%; France 2.1%; Nigeria 1.8%; Taiwan 1.7%.

Exports (2008): U.S.$1,300,135,700,000 (chemicals and chemical products 13.8%; motor vehicles and parts 8.2%; electrical machinery 8.1%; agricultural commodities 6.6%; other transportation equipment 6.0%; mineral fuels 5.9%; crude materials [inedible] 5.9%; power-generating machinery 4.5%; general industrial machinery 4.5%; specialized industrial machinery 4.3%; scientific and precision equipment 3.9%; computers and office equipment 3.5%; telecommunications equipment 3.2%). *Major export destinations:* Canada 20.1%; Mexico 11.7%; China 5.5%; Japan 5.1%; Germany 4.2%; United Kingdom 4.1%; Netherlands 3.1%; South Korea 2.7%; Brazil 2.5%; France 2.2%; Singapore 2.2%; Taiwan 1.9%.

Direction of trade (2007)

	imports U.S.$'000,000	imports %	exports U.S.$'000,000	exports %
Africa	89,141	4.4	17,795	1.5
Nigeria	33,741	1.7	2,787	0.2
South Africa	9,291	0.5	5,518	0.4
Americas	672,132	33.3	492,147	42.3
Brazil	27,193	1.3	24,628	2.1
Canada	317,604	15.7	248,437	21.3
Caribbean countries	19,546	1.0	18,392	1.6
Central America	15,864	0.8	20,296	1.8
Mexico	212,889	10.6	136,541	11.7
Venezuela	41,011	2.0	10,200	0.9
Asia	824,250	40.9	342,978	29.5
China	340,118	16.9	65,238	5.6
Taiwan	39,853	2.0	26,359	2.3
Japan	149,423	7.4	62,665	5.4
Saudi Arabia	37,165	1.8	10,399	0.9
Singapore	18,692	0.9	26,285	2.3
South Korea	49,319	2.4	34,703	3.0
Europe	419,147	20.8	286,860	24.7
France	42,498	2.1	27,820	2.4
Germany	96,640	4.8	49,652	4.3
Italy	36,471	1.8	14,174	1.2
Netherlands	19,140	0.9	32,986	2.8
United Kingdom	58,096	2.9	50,296	4.3
Oceania	12,678	0.6	22,328	1.9
Australia	8,971	0.4	19,207	1.7
TOTAL	2,017,358[5]	100.0	1,162,533[5]	100.0[5]

Transport and communications

Transport. Railroads (2008): route length 125,541 mi, 202,039 km, of which Amtrak operates 21,178 mi, 34,083 km; passenger-km 9,943,000,000; metric ton-km cargo 2,523,786,000,000. Roads (2009): total length 4,050,717 mi, 6,518,997 km (paved [2008] 67%); length of expressways (2009) 46,718 mi, 75,186 km; passenger-km 7,874,329,000,000[27]; metric ton-km cargo (2006) 1,885,576,000,000. Vehicles (2009): passenger cars 134,880,000; trucks and buses 111,403,000. Merchant marine (2006)[28]: vessels (1,000 gross tons and over) 625; total deadweight tonnage 10,172,000. Navigable channels (2008) 25,320 mi, 40,749 km; oil pipeline length (2009) 172,048 mi, 276,884 km; gas pipeline[29] (2009) 1,540,000 mi, 2,478,000 km. Air transport (2008): passenger-km 1,270,512,000,000; metric ton-km cargo 39,213,000,000. Certified route passenger/cargo air carriers (2005) 80; operating revenue (U.S.$'000,000; 2007) 173,104; operating expenses (U.S.$'000,000; 2007) 163,894. Inland waterway (2008): passenger-km, n.a.; metric ton-km cargo 837,697,000,000.

Communications

Medium	date	number in '000s	units per 1,000 persons	Medium	date	number in '000s	units per 1,000 persons
Televisions	2003	260,000	893	PCs	2005	223,810	755
Telephones				Dailies	2009	46,278[30]	192[30]
Cellular	2010	278,900[31]	899[31]	Internet users	2009	239,894	762
Landline	2010	151,171	487	Broadband	2010	85,723[31]	276[31]

Education and health

Literacy (2003): percentage of population age 16 and over: "illiterate" (able to perform no more than the most simple literacy skills—14% of population [or 30,000,000 people]); "basically literate" (able to perform simple and everyday literacy activities—29% of population [or 63,000,000 people]); "intermediately and proficiently literate" (able to perform moderately challenging to complex literacy activities—57% of population [or 123,000,000 people]). An additional 6,500,000 people were not interviewed for this 2003 survey because they did not speak English or had cognitive or mental disabilities.

Education (2007–08)

	teachers	students	student/ teacher ratio	enrollment rate (%)
Primary (age 6–11)	1,802,647	24,676,574	13.7	92
Secondary/Voc. (age 12–17)	1,717,576	24,692,888	14.4	88
Tertiary	1,371,390	18,248,124	13.3	83 (age 18–22)

High school and college graduates (2009)

	Percent age 25 and over	
States	high school	college
Alabama	82.1	22.0
Alaska	91.4	26.6
Arizona	84.2	25.6
Arkansas	82.4	18.9
California	80.6	29.9
Colorado	89.3	35.9
Connecticut	88.6	35.6
Delaware	87.4	28.7
Florida	85.3	25.3
Georgia	83.9	27.5
Hawaii	90.4	29.6
Idaho	88.4	23.9
Illinois	86.4	30.6
Indiana	86.6	22.5
Iowa	90.5	25.1
Kansas	89.7	29.5
Kentucky	81.7	21.0
Louisiana	82.2	21.4
Maine	90.2	26.9
Maryland	88.2	35.7
Massachusetts	89.0	38.2
Michigan	87.9	24.6
Minnesota	91.5	31.5
Mississippi	80.4	19.6
Missouri	86.8	25.2
Montana	90.8	27.4
Nebraska	89.6	27.4
Nevada	83.9	21.8
New Hampshire	91.3	32.0
New Jersey	87.4	34.5
New Mexico	82.8	25.3
New York	84.7	32.4
North Carolina	84.3	26.5
North Dakota	90.1	25.8
Ohio	87.6	24.1
Oklahoma	85.6	22.7
Oregon	89.1	29.2
Pennsylvania	87.9	26.4
Rhode Island	84.7	30.5
South Carolina	83.6	24.3
South Dakota	89.9	25.1
Tennessee	83.1	23.0
Texas	79.9	25.5
Utah	90.4	28.5
Vermont	91.0	33.1
Virginia	86.6	34.0
Washington	89.7	31.0
West Virginia	82.8	17.3
Wisconsin	89.8	25.7
Wyoming	91.8	23.8
District		
District of Columbia	87.1	48.5
U.S. RATE	85.3	27.9

Food (2007): daily per capita caloric intake 3,748 (vegetable products 72.6%, animal products 27.4%); 178% of FAO recommended minimum requirement. Per capita consumption of major food groups (kilograms annually): milk 253.8; fresh vegetables 127.6; cereal products 111.6; fresh fruits 111.0; red meat 72.1; potatoes 55.6; poultry products 50.7; fats and oil 34.8; sugar 32.7; fish and shellfish 24.1; undernourished population (2004–06) less than 5.0% of total population.

Health (2009): doctors of medicine 972,400[32] (1 per 315 persons), of which office-based practice 560,400—male 70.4%, female 29.6% (including specialties in internal medicine 16.7%, general and family practice 9.9%, pediatrics 8.0%, obstetrics and gynecology 4.4%, anesthesiology 4.4%, psychiatry 4.2%, general surgery 3.9%, emergency medicine 3.3%, diagnostic radiology 2.6%, orthopedic surgery 2.6%, cardiovascular diseases 2.3%, pathology 2.0%, ophthalmology 1.9%); doctors of osteopathy (2010) 70,480; nurses (2009) 2,583,770 (1 per 119 persons); dentists (2007) 184,000 (1 per 1,639 persons); hospital beds (2009) 944,000 (1 per 325 persons), of which nonfederal 95.2% (community hospitals 85.4%, psychiatric 8.1%, long-term general and special 1.7%), federal 4.8%; infant mortality rate per 1,000 live births (2009) 6.3.

Active physicians and nurses (2009)

	physicians		nurses	
States	number	per 100,000 population	number	per 100,000 population
Alabama	10,265	218	42,880	912
Alaska	1,574	225	5,010	717
Arizona	14,051	213	38,570	585
Arkansas	5,902	204	23,050	798
California	100,131	271	233,030	630
Colorado	13,047	260	41,750	831
Connecticut	13,370	380	35,790	1,017
Delaware	2,177	246	10,220	1,155
Florida	46,645	252	150,940	814
Georgia	21,269	216	65,370	665
Hawaii	4,800	371	8,930	689
Idaho	2,649	171	10,540	682
Illinois	36,528	283	116,340	901
Indiana	13,938	217	57,880	901
Iowa	5,696	189	30,750	1,022
Kansas	6,436	228	26,320	934
Kentucky	10,076	234	43,250	1,003
Louisiana	11,974	267	39,560	881
Maine	3,663	278	14,410	1,093
Maryland	24,118	423	51,620	906
Massachusetts	31,252	474	83,060	1,260
Michigan	25,697	258	84,620	849
Minnesota	15,620	297	57,560	1,093
Mississippi	5,281	179	28,030	950
Missouri	14,789	247	62,130	1,038
Montana	2,138	219	8,340	855
Nebraska	4,511	251	18,930	1,054
Nevada	4,967	188	16,100	609
New Hampshire	3,828	289	13,330	1,006
New Jersey	27,433	315	74,730	858
New Mexico	4,877	243	12,340	614
New York	77,042	394	165,730	848
North Carolina	24,072	257	88,190	940
North Dakota	1,617	250	6,260	968
Ohio	31,315	271	117,870	1,021
Oklahoma	6,467	175	27,340	742
Oregon	10,753	281	30,730	803
Pennsylvania	38,676	307	129,810	1,030
Rhode Island	4,020	382	11,630	1,104
South Carolina	10,403	228	38,020	834
South Dakota	1,818	224	10,530	1,296
Tennessee	16,754	266	61,980	984
Texas	53,546	216	168,020	678
Utah	5,903	212	17,670	635
Vermont	2,313	372	5,680	914
Virginia	21,931	278	60,230	764
Washington	18,090	271	54,260	814
West Virginia	4,295	236	17,340	953
Wisconsin	14,816	262	53,510	946
Wyoming	1,020	187	4,700	864
District				
District of Columbia	4,900	817	8,890	1,483
U.S. TOTAL	838,453[33]	273	2,583,770[5]	842

Military

Total active duty personnel (November 2010): 1,563,996 (army 40.9%, navy 21.5%, air force 21.8%, marines 13.0%, coast guard 2.8%). *Total reserve duty personnel*[34] (November 2010): 871,240 (army 55.5%, navy 11.8%, air force 19.6%, marines 12.2%, coast guard 0.9%). *Military expenditure as percentage of GDP* (2010): 4.9%; per capita expenditure U.S.$2,299. *Major overseas deployment* (March 2011): 305,315, of which in support of Operation New Dawn (in and around Iraq) *c.* 30%, in support of Operation Enduring Freedom (in and around Afghanistan) *c.* 36%, remainder *c.* 34%. *Foreign military sales deliveries* (September 2008–September 2010): U.S.$37,873,000,000, of which to Saudi Arabia 11.1%, to Israel 8.0%, to Egypt 6.9%, to Japan 6.0%, to Australia 5.8%, to Greece 5.4%, to Taiwan 5.2%, to South Korea 5.0%, to Iraq 4.6%, to Pakistan 4.3%.

[1]Excludes 5 nonvoting delegates from the District of Columbia, the U.S. Virgin Islands, American Samoa, the Northern Mariana Islands, and Guam and a nonvoting resident commissioner from Puerto Rico. [2]Total area (excluding 43,185 sq mi [111,849 sq km] of coastal water and 74,575 sq mi [193,148 sq km] of territorial water) equals 3,678,190 sq mi (9,526,468 sq km), of which land area equals 3,531,822 sq mi (9,147,377 sq km), inland water area equals 86,409 sq mi (223,798 sq km), and Great Lakes water area equals 59,959 sq mi (155,293 sq km). [3]Excluding military abroad. [4]April 1. [5]Detail does not add to total given because of rounding. [6]Includes 1,042,523 living overseas. [7]Based on land area only. [8]Persons of Hispanic origin may be of any race. [9]Net change in population does not include a usual small residual population that is not accounted for under births less deaths in conjunction with net domestic/international migration. [10]2008. [11]2007. [12]2005. [13]2000. [14]Drinking 5 or more drinks on the same occasion on at least one day in the past 30 days per survey. [15]2003. [16]Excludes military personnel overseas. [17]Unemployed. [18]2009. [19]2006. [20]Includes supplemental gaseous fuels. [21]Less than 0.7 trillion Btu. [22]July 1. [23]Period average. [24]End of year, except 2009. [25]In 2007 current dollars in conjunction with annually revised U.S. Bureau of Labor Statistics experimental Consumer Price Index (or CPI-U-RS deflator). [26]Manufacturing only. [27]Passenger cars (including light trucks and vans) 7,336,925,000,000; buses 507,800,000,000; other 29,604,000,000. [28]Excluding foreign-flagged U.S.-domiciled vessels. [29]Excludes service pipelines. [30]Circulation of daily newspapers. [31]Subscribers. [32]Includes Puerto Rico and other U.S. dependencies. [33]Excludes doctors of osteopathy, physicians with unknown addresses, and inactive physicians. [34]Includes national guard.

Internet resources for further information:

- **U.S. Census Bureau**
  http://www.census.gov
- **Statistical Abstract of the United States**
  http://www.census.gov/prod/www/abs/statab2011_2015.html

Uruguay

Official name: República Oriental del Uruguay (Oriental Republic of Uruguay).
Form of government: republic with two legislative houses (Senate [31[1]]; House of Representatives [99]).
Head of state and government: President.
Capital: Montevideo.
Official language: Spanish.
Official religion: none.
Monetary unit: peso uruguayo (UYU); valuation (Sept. 1, 2011) 1 U.S.$ = UYU 18.50; 1 £ = UYU 29.90.

Area and population

Departments	area sq km	population 2010 estimate	Departments	area sq km	population 2010 estimate
Artigas	11,928	79,270	Río Negro	9,282	56,513
Canelones	4,536	525,980	Rivera	9,370	112,084
Cerro Largo	13,648	90,883	Rocha	10,551	70,374
Colonia	6,106	120,894	Salto	14,163	128,669
Durazno	11,643	62,155	San José	4,992	110,714
Flores	5,144	25,726	Soriano	9,008	88,449
Florida	10,417	70,811	Tacuarembó	15,438	96,783
Lavalleja	10,016	61,994	Treinta y Tres	9,529	49,497
Maldonado	4,793	152,523	TOTAL LAND AREA	175,016	
Montevideo	530	1,336,878	OTHER AREAS[2]	2,863	
Paysandú	13,922	116,387	TOTAL	177,879	3,356,584

Demography

Population (2011): 3,380,000[3].
Density (2011): persons per sq mi 49.2, persons per sq km 19.0.
Urban-rural (2010): urban 92.5%; rural 7.5%.
Sex distribution (2010): male 48.31%; female 51.69%.
Age breakdown (2010): under 15, 22.5%; 15–29, 22.8%; 30–44, 19.7%; 45–59, 17.0%; 60–74, 11.5%; 75–84, 4.9%; 85 and over, 1.6%.
Population projection: (2020) 3,495,000[3]; (2030) 3,601,000[3].
Ethnic composition (2006): white (mostly Spanish, Italian, or mixed Spanish-Italian) 87.4%; black/part-black 8.4%; Amerindian/part-Amerindian 3.0%; other/unknown 1.2%.
Religious affiliation (2004): Roman Catholic *c.* 54%; Protestant *c.* 11%; Mormon *c.* 3%; Jewish 0.8%; nonreligious/atheist *c.* 26%; other 5.2%.
Major cities (2004): Montevideo (urban agglomeration; 2010) 1,635,000; Salto 99,072; Paysandú 73,272; Las Piedras 69,222; Rivera 64,426.

Vital statistics

Birth rate per 1,000 population (2010): 14.2 (world avg. 19.2); within marriage (2002) 42.9%; outside of marriage (2002) 57.1%.
Death rate per 1,000 population (2010): 9.4 (world avg. 8.2).
Total fertility rate (avg. births per childbearing woman; 2010): 1.99.
Marriage/divorce rates per 1,000 population: (2009) 3.3/(2004) 4.3.
Life expectancy at birth (2010): male 72.7 years; female 79.9 years.
Major causes of death per 100,000 population (2004): diseases of the circulatory system 350.4, of which cerebrovascular disease 121.5, ischemic heart disease 91.9; malignant neoplasms (cancers) 241.9; accidents and violence 56.9.

National economy

Budget (2006). Revenue: UYU 111,321,000,000 (taxes on goods and services 59.1%; corporate taxes 12.3%; property taxes 7.1%; nontax revenue 6.7%; individual income taxes 5.6%). Expenditures: UYU 117,225,000,000 (social security and welfare 27.6%; government transfers including debt servicing 20.7%; public administration 13.9%; education 12.3%; health 7.4%).
Production (metric tons except as noted). Agriculture, forestry, fishing (2009): wheat 1,844,420, rice 1,287,200, soybeans 1,028,600, barley 464,071, corn (maize) 269,800, oranges 130,100, potatoes 102,287, tangerines 92,777, grapes 87,498, apples 58,775, sunflower seeds 50,600, wool (2008) 45,000, lemons and limes 41,993, honey (2008) 15,500; livestock (number of live animals) 12,490,000 cattle, 8,662,000 sheep, 497,647 beehives; roundwood (2010) 8,400,000 cu m, of which fuelwood 26%; fisheries production 81,502 (from aquaculture, negligible). Mining and quarrying (2009): limestone 1,200,000; clays 82,200; gold 1,690 kg. Manufacturing (value added in UYU '000,000; 2010): food and beverages 41,074; chemicals and chemical products 13,950; paper and paper products 13,403; machinery and apparatus 11,597; wood and wood products 8,970; textiles/hides/leather goods 5,161. Energy production (consumption): electricity (kW-hr; 2007) 9,424,000,000 (9,217,000,000); coal (metric tons; 2007) none (2,000); crude petroleum (barrels; 2007) none (11,970,000); petroleum products (metric tons; 2007) 1,552,000 (1,764,000); natural gas (cu m; 2007) none (102,000,000).
Household income and expenditure. Avg. household size (2007) 2.9; avg. annual income per household (2007) UYU 235,746 (U.S.$10,044); expenditure (2005–06)[4]: housing 26.0%, food and nonalcoholic beverages 19.5%, health 12.1%, transportation 10.9%, recreation and culture 6.5%.
Population economically active (2010): total 1,665,000; activity rate 49.6% (participation rates: ages 15 and over, 62.7%; female 45.6%; unemployed 6.8%).

Price and earnings indexes (2005 = 100)

	2004	2005	2006	2007	2008	2009	2010
Consumer price index	95.5	100.0	106.4	115.0	124.1	132.9	141.8
Annual earnings index	95.6	100.0	104.3	109.2	113.1	121.3	125.4

Gross national income (GNI; 2010): U.S.$35,557,000,000 (U.S.$10,590 per capita); purchasing power parity GNI (U.S.$13,890 per capita).

Structure of gross domestic product and labour force

	2010		2007	
	in value UYU '000,000	% of total value	labour force[5]	% of labour force[5]
Agriculture, forestry, fishing	66,702	8.3	163,300	10.0
Mining and quarrying	2,688	0.3		
Manufacturing	105,798	13.1	219,900	13.5
Public utilities	25,558	3.2		
Construction	58,170	7.2	102,100	6.3
Transp. and commun.	54,272	6.7	83,900	5.1
Trade, hotels	116,215	14.4	319,200	19.6
Finance, real estate	151,346	18.7	114,400	7.0
Pub. admin., defense	41,560	5.1	94,400	5.8
Services	102,603	12.7	384,900	23.6
Other	82,773[6]	10.3[6]	149,300[7]	9.1[7]
TOTAL	807,685	100.0	1,631,400	100.0

Public debt (external, outstanding; 2009): U.S.$10,955,000,000.
Selected balance of payments data. Receipts from (U.S.$'000,000): tourism (2009) 1,312; remittances (2010) 104; foreign direct investment (FDI; 2008–10 avg.) 2,018; official development assistance (2009) 51. Disbursements for (U.S.$'000,000): tourism (2009) 336; remittances (2009) 6; FDI (2008–10 avg.) 4.7.
Land use as % of total land area (2007): in temporary crops or left fallow 7.7%, in permanent crops 0.2%, in pasture 76.0%, forest area 8.8%.

Foreign trade[8]

Balance of trade (current prices)

	2004	2005	2006	2007	2008	2009
U.S.$'000,000	−183	−474	−804	−1,241	−2,984	−792
% of total	3.0%	6.5%	9.2%	12.2%	20.1%	6.8%

Imports (2008): U.S.$8,933,000,000 (machinery and apparatus 17.1%; chemicals and chemical products 16.9%; crude petroleum 16.8%; refined petroleum 10.0%; road vehicles 7.2%; food 6.6%). *Major import sources:* Argentina 25.2%; Brazil 18.1%; China 10.2%; Russia 10.0%; Venezuela 6.3%.
Exports (2008): U.S.$5,949,000,000 (beef 20.1%; cereals 13.3%, of which rice 7.5%; milk/butter/cheese 7.2%; wood chips or particles/rough wood 6.3%; soybeans 5.5%; leather 4.2%; petroleum 3.1%; wool 2.9%). *Major export destinations:* Brazil 16.6%; free zones 9.6%; Argentina 8.5%; Russia 5.6%; Spain 4.0%; Venezuela 4.0%.

Transport and communications

Transport. Railroads (2008): route length 1,288 mi, 2,073 km[9]; passenger-km 21,000,000; metric ton-km cargo 294,000,000. Roads (2007): length 16,398 km (paved 22%). Vehicles (2009): passenger cars 606,660; trucks and buses 100,214. Air transport (2008)[10]: passenger-km 809,094,000; metric ton-km cargo, none.

Communications

Medium	date	number in '000s	units per 1,000 persons	Medium	date	number in '000s	units per 1,000 persons
Televisions	2003	838	252	PCs	2005	450	135
Telephones				Dailies	2009	145[11]	43[11]
Cellular	2010	4,437[12]	1,317[12]	Internet users	2009	1,855	552
Landline	2010	962	286	Broadband	2010	368[12]	109[12]

Education and health

Educational attainment (2009). Percentage of population age 25 and over having: no formal schooling 1.5%; incomplete primary education 12.5%; complete primary 36.2%; complete secondary 34.8%; vocational 5.3%; complete higher 9.7%. *Literacy* (2010): population age 15 and over literate 98.3%; males 97.9%; females 98.7%.

Education (2008–09)

	teachers	students	student/teacher ratio	enrollment rate (%)
Primary (age 6–11)	24,931	348,691	14.0	99
Secondary/Voc. (age 12–17)	23,216	271,722	11.7	70[13]
Tertiary	14,920	161,459	10.8	63 (age 18–22)

Health (2010): physicians 15,049 (1 per 223 persons); hospital beds 6,130 (1 per 548 persons); infant mortality rate per 1,000 live births (2009) 9.6; undernourished population (2004–06) less than 5.0% of total population based on the consumption of a minimum daily requirement of 1,870 calories.

Military

Total active duty personnel (November 2010): 24,621 (army 65.9%, navy/coast guard 22.0%, air force 12.1%). *Military expenditure as percentage of GDP* (2010): 1.0%; per capita expenditure U.S.$128.

[1]Includes the vice president, who serves as ex officio presiding officer. [2]Includes the Uruguayan part of the Uruguay River, with islands (633 sq km), Río Negro reservoirs (1,199 sq km), and the Uruguayan part of Laguna Merín (1,031 sq km); excludes the Uruguayan part of the Río de la Plata (15,240 sq km) and a contested area with Brazil (237 sq km). [3]Estimate of United Nations *World Population Prospects: The 2010 Revision*. [4]Average for 3-member households only. [5]Excludes military conscripts. [6]Taxes less subsidies and less imputed bank service charges. [7]Unemployed. [8]Imports c.i.f.; exports f.o.b. [9]Of which 1,020 mi (1,641 km) were operational in 2008. [10]PLUNA only. [11]Circulation of daily newspapers. [12]Subscribers. [13]2007–08.

Internet resources for further information:
- **Instituto Nacional de Estadística—Uruguay http://www.ine.gub.uy**
- **Banco Central del Uruguay http://www.bcu.gub.uy**

Uzbekistan

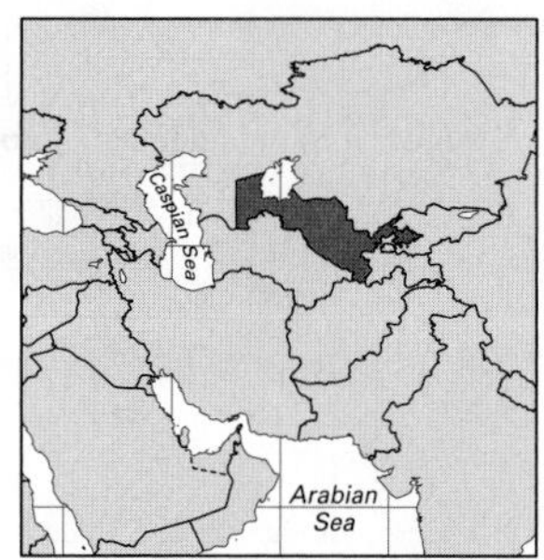

Official name: Òzbekiston Respublikasi (Republic of Uzbekistan).
Form of government: republic[1] with two legislative bodies (Senate [100[2]]; Legislative Chamber [150[3]]).
Head of state and government: President assisted by Prime Minister.
Capital: Tashkent (Toshkent).
Official language: Uzbek.
Official religion: none.
Monetary unit: sum (UZS); valuation (Sept. 1, 2011) 1 U.S.$ = UZS 1,734; 1 £ = UZS 2,802.

Area and population

Provinces	area sq km	population 2009 estimate	Provinces	area sq km	population 2009 estimate
Andijon	4,303	2,524,600	Toshkent (Tashkent)	15,258	4,789,500[4]
Buxoro (Bukhara)	41,937	1,600,700	Xorazm	6,464	1,546,200
Fargona	7,005	3,048,700			
Jizzax	21,179	1,107,800	**City**		
Namangan	7,181	2,238,100	Tashkent	327	[4]
Navoiy	109,375	845,300			
Qashqadaryo	28,568	2,589,600	**Autonomous republic**		
Samarqand (Samarkand)	16,773	3,090,700			
Sirdaryo	4,276	708,400	Qoraqalpoghiston	161,358	1,623,100
Surxondaryo	20,099	2,054,400	TOTAL	444,103	27,767,100

Demography

Population (2011): 28,129,000[5].
Density (2011): persons per sq mi 164.0, persons per sq km 63.3.
Urban-rural (2010): urban 51.5%; rural 48.5%.
Sex distribution (2006): male 49.56%; female 50.44%.
Age breakdown (2006): under 15, 32.9%; 15–29, 30.3%; 30–44, 19.6%; 45–59, 11.2%; 60–74, 4.3%; 75 and over, 1.7%.
Population projection: (2020) 30,565,000; (2030) 32,855,000.
Ethnic composition (2000): Uzbek 78.3%; Tajik 4.7%; Kazakh 4.1%; Tatar 3.3%; Russian 2.5%; Karakalpak 2.1%; other 5.0%.
Religious affiliation (2000): Muslim (mostly Sunnī) 76.2%; Russian Orthodox 0.8%; Jewish 0.2%; nonreligious 18.1%; other 4.7%.
Major cities (2007): Tashkent 1,959,190; Namangan 446,237; Andijon 321,622; Samarkand 312,863; Bukhara 249,037; Nukus 240,734.

Vital statistics

Birth rate per 1,000 population (2009): 23.3 (world avg. 20.3).
Death rate per 1,000 population (2009): 4.7 (world avg. 8.5).
Total fertility rate (avg. births per childbearing woman; 2006): 2.91.
Marriage/divorce rates per 1,000 population (2009): 10.0/0.6.
Life expectancy at birth (2006): male 61.2 years; female 68.1 years.
Major causes of death per 100,000 population (2005): diseases of the circulatory system 297.5; diseases of the respiratory system 41.5; accidents, poisoning, and violence 37.0; cancers 35.6; diseases of the digestive system 31.7.

National economy

Budget (2006)[6]. Revenue: UZS 6,406,000,000,000 (taxes on income and profits 20.2%, VAT 17.3%, taxes on property and resources 12.2%, excise taxes 10.2%). Expenditures: UZS 6,331,000,000,000 (health and education 34.4%, social security 27.0%, national economy 9.0%, centralized investments 8.1%).
Household income and expenditure. Average household size (2004) 5.6; income per household (1995) UZS 35,165 (U.S.$1,040); sources of income (2006): self-employment and rent 55.1%, wages and salaries 29.8%, transfers 15.1%; expenditure (1995): food and beverages 71%, clothing and footwear 14%, recreation 6%, household durables 4%, housing 3%.
Production (metric tons except as noted). Agriculture, forestry, fishing (2009): wheat 6,637,700, cow's milk 5,732,400, seed cotton 3,419,800, tomatoes 2,110,000, potatoes 1,524,500, watermelons 1,071,000, carrots and turnips 995,000, grapes 899,600, dry onions 795,000, apples 635,000, cabbages 486,000, cucumbers 350,000, apricots 290,000, cherries 67,000, raw silk (2008) 1,200; livestock (number of live animals) 11,405,000 sheep, 8,024,800 cattle, 2,154,400 goats, 17,000 camels, 29,100,000 chickens; roundwood (2010) 30,000 cu m, of which fuelwood 73%; fisheries production 9,469 (from aquaculture 36%). Mining and quarrying (2009): copper (metal content) 100,000; uranium (metal content) 2,400; gold 85,000 kg. Manufacturing (value of production in UZS '000,000,000; 2006): nonferrous metals 2,705; mineral fuels 2,487; machinery and metalworking products 1,986; food and food products 1,699; chemicals and chemical products 715; iron and steel 328. Energy production (consumption): electricity (kW-hr; 2009) 50,000,000,000 ([2007] 48,869,000,000); lignite (metric tons; 2007) 3,282,000 (3,201,000); crude petroleum (barrels; 2007) 23,249,000 (23,249,000); petroleum products (metric tons; 2007) 4,548,000 (4,331,000); natural gas (cu m; 2007) 63,131,000,000 (49,961,000,000).
Population economically active (2008): total 12,208,000[7]; activity rate of total population 44.9%[7] (participation rates: ages 15–64, 67.7%[7]; female 45.9%[7]; unemployed [official rate] 0.2%).

Price index (2005 = 100)

	2005	2006	2007	2008	2009
Consumer price index	100.0	114.2	128.2	144.5	162.6

Gross national income (GNI; 2010): U.S.$36,086,000,000 (U.S.$1,280 per capita); purchasing power parity GNI (U.S.$3,090 per capita).

Structure of gross domestic product and labour force

	2008 in value UZS '000,000	2008 % of total value	2000 labour force	2000 % of labour force
Agriculture, fishing	7,974,300	23.6	3,083,000	34.3
Manufacturing, mining, and public utilities	7,523,800	22.3	1,145,000	12.7
Construction	1,745,800	5.2	676,000	7.5
Transp. and commun.	3,807,000	11.3	382,000	4.3
Trade, hotels	3,165,000	9.4	754,000	8.4
Finance, real estate / Pub. admin., defense / Services	6,228,600	18.4	2,042,000	22.7
Other	3,345,200[8]	9.9[8]	901,000[9]	10.0[9]
TOTAL	33,789,600[10]	100.0[10]	8,983,000	100.0[10]

Public debt (external, outstanding; 2009): U.S.$3,238,000,000.
Selected balance of payments data. Receipts from (U.S.$'000,000): tourism (2008) 64; remittances (2005) 790; foreign direct investment (2008–10 avg.) 748; official development assistance (2009) 190. Disbursements for (U.S.$'000,000): tourism (2009) n.a.; remittances (2009) n.a.
Land use as % of total land area (2009): in temporary crops or left fallow (2007) 10.1%, in permanent crops 0.8%, in pasture 51.7%, forest area 7.8%.

Foreign trade[11]

Balance of trade (current prices)

	2005	2006	2007	2008	2009	2010
U.S.$'000,000	+1,317.5	+1,608.2	+3,755.9	+4,068.8	+2,333.0	+4,244.8
% of total	13.9%	14.4%	26.4%	21.3%	11.0%	19.4%

Imports (2008): U.S.$7,504,100,000 (machinery and apparatus 53.3%; chemicals and chemical products 13.0%; food products 8.1%; base and fabricated metals 6.8%). *Major import sources:* Russia 24.8%; China 13.8%; South Korea 12.9%; Ukraine 8.3%; Kazakhstan 6.0%.
Exports (2008): U.S.$11,572,900,000 (energy products [including natural gas and crude petroleum] 25.2%; gold [2007] *c.* 20%; cotton fibre 9.2%; machinery and apparatus 7.5%; selected base metals [incl. copper, zinc, and silver] 7.0%; uranium, n.a.). *Major export destinations:* Russia 17.2%; Switzerland 8.9%; Ukraine 8.5%; Turkey 4.6%; Iran 4.6%; Afghanistan 4.6%.

Transport and communications

Transport. Railroads (2008): route length (2007) 2,265 mi, 3,645 km; passenger-km 2,500,000,000; metric ton-km cargo 23,400,000,000. Roads (2005): total length 52,400 mi, 84,400 km (paved 85%); passenger-km (2008) 55,800,000,000[12]; metric ton-km cargo (2008) 21,300,000,000. Vehicles: n.a. Air transport (2008): passenger-km 5,600,000,000; metric ton-km cargo 83,300,000.

Communications

Medium	date	number in '000s	units per 1,000 persons	Medium	date	number in '000s	units per 1,000 persons
Televisions	2003	7,232	280	PCs	2006	...	...
Telephones				Dailies	2009	30[13]	1.5[13]
Cellular	2010	20,952[14]	763[14]	Internet users	2009	4,689	171
Landline	2010	1,863	68	Broadband	2010	89[14]	3.2[14]

Education and health

Educational attainment (2002)[15]. Percentage of population age 25 and over having: no formal education/unknown 2.5%; incomplete primary education 9.0%; primary 7.3%; secondary 66.0%; higher 15.2%. *Literacy* (2008): percentage of total population age 15 and over literate 99.2%.

Education (2008–09)

	teachers	students	student/ teacher ratio	enrollment rate (%)
Primary (age 7–10)	116,603	1,995,747	17.1	87
Secondary/Voc. (age 11–17)	367,224	4,506,226	12.3	92
Tertiary	23,842	300,782	12.6	10 (age 18–22)

Health (2005): physicians 70,159 (1 per 371 persons); hospital beds 135,143 (1 per 193 persons); infant mortality rate per 1,000 live births (2009) 11.9; undernourished population (2004–06) 3,400,000 (13% of total population based on the consumption of a minimum daily requirement of 1,870 calories).

Military

Total active duty personnel (November 2010): 67,000 (army 74.6%, air force 25.4%); paramilitary 20,000; German troops 163. *Military expenditure as percentage of GDP* (2009): 2.4%; per capita expenditure U.S.$28.

[1]In actuality an authoritarian regime; recent executive elections and referenda have not been deemed free or fair by international observers. [2]Includes 84 indirectly elected seats and 16 appointed seats. [3]Includes 15 indirectly elected seats. [4]Toshkent province includes Tashkent city. [5]Estimate of U.S. Bureau of the Census International Data Base (June 2008 update). [6]General government consolidated budget. [7]ILO estimate. [8]Indirect taxes less subsidies. [9]Includes 863,000 persons on forced leave and 38,000 unemployed. [10]Detail does not add to total given because of rounding. [11]Imports c.i.f.; exports f.o.b. [12]Total of passenger cars and buses. [13]Circulation of daily newspapers. [14]Subscribers. [15]Based on the 2002 Uzbekistan Health Examination Survey, of which 9,624 respondents were age 25 and over.

Internet resources for further information:
- **UNDP Uzbekistan in Figures http://statistics.design.uz**
- **State Committee on Statistics http://www.stat.uz/en**

Vanuatu

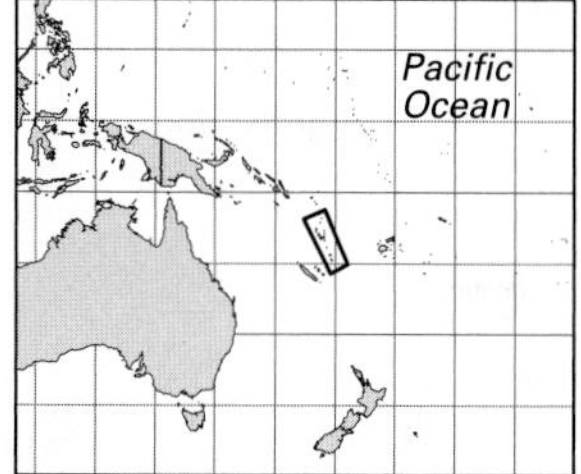

Official name: Ripablik blong Vanuatu (Bislama); République de Vanuatu (French); Republic of Vanuatu (English).
Form of government: republic with a single legislative house (Parliament [52]).
Head of state: President.
Head of government: Prime Minister.
Capital: Port-Vila.
Official languages: Bislama; French; English.
Official religion: none.
Monetary unit: vatu (Vt); valuation (Sept. 1, 2011) 1 U.S.$ = Vt 90.88; 1 £ = Vt 146.85.

Area and population

		area		population
Provinces	Capitals	sq mi	sq km	2009 census
Malampa	Lakatoro	1,073	2,779	36,722
Penama	Longana	463	1,198	30,819
Sanma	Luganville	1,640	4,248	45,860
Shefa	Port-Vila	562	1,455	78,723
Tafea	Isangel	628	1,628	32,540
Torba	Sola	341	882	9,359
TOTAL		4,707	12,190	234,023

Demography

Population (2011): 251,000.
Density (2011): persons per sq mi 53.4, persons per sq km 20.6.
Urban-rural (2010): urban 25.6%; rural 74.4%.
Sex distribution (2011[1]): male 50.96%; female 49.04%.
Age breakdown (2005): under 15, 40.1%; 15–29, 27.7%; 30–44, 17.5%; 45–59, 9.7%; 60–74, 4.1%; 75 and over, 0.9%.
Population projection: (2020) 321,000; (2030) 396,000.
Doubling time: 27 years.
Ethnic composition (1999): Ni-Vanuatu (Melanesian) 98.7%; European and other Pacific Islanders 1.3%.
Religious affiliation (2009): Protestant *c.* 70%, of which Presbyterian *c.* 28%, Anglican *c.* 15%, Adventist *c.* 12%; Roman Catholic *c.* 12%; traditional beliefs (John Frum cargo cult) *c.* 4%; other *c.* 14%.
Major towns (2009): Port-Vila (on Éfaté) 44,040; Luganville (on Espiritu Santo) 13,167; Norsup (on Malakula; 2006) 3,000; Isangel (on Tanna; 2006) 1,500.

Vital statistics

Birth rate per 1,000 population (2011[1]): 31.1 (world avg. 19.2).
Death rate per 1,000 population (2011[1]): 5.3 (world avg. 8.2).
Total fertility rate (avg. births per childbearing woman; 2011[1]): 2.39.
Marriage/divorce rates per 1,000 population: n.a./n.a.
Life expectancy at birth (2011[1]): male 63.0 years; female 66.4 years.
Major causes of death per 100,000 population (2002): cardiovascular diseases 194.5; infectious and parasitic diseases 112.6; diseases of the respiratory system 65.3; malignant neoplasms (cancers) 50.3; diseases of the digestive system 26.1.

National economy

Budget (2009–10). Revenue: Vt 17,209,000,000 (tax revenue 62.3%, of which VAT 24.5%, import duties 19.6%; grants 29.4%; nontax revenue 8.3%). Expenditures: Vt 18,754,000,000 (current expenditure 71.4%, of which salaries and wages 39.0%, subsidies and transfers 8.6%; development expenditure 28.6%).
Production (metric tons except as noted). Agriculture, forestry, fishing (2009): coconuts 309,000, roots and tubers 46,000, copra (2010) 36,066, bananas 18,310, peanuts (groundnuts) 2,550, corn (maize) 846, kava (2004) 825, cacao beans (2010) 155; livestock (number of live animals) 170,000 cattle, 89,000 pigs, 19,000 goats, 800,000 chickens; roundwood (2010) 119,000 cu m, of which fuelwood 76%; fisheries production 144,600 (from aquaculture, negligible). Mining and quarrying: small quantities of coral-reef limestone, crushed stone, sand, and gravel. Manufacturing (value added in Vt '000,000; 1995): food, beverages, and tobacco 645; wood products 423; fabricated metal products 377; paper products 125; chemical, rubber, plastic, and nonmetallic products 84; textiles, clothing, and leather 54. Energy production (consumption): electricity (kW-hr; 2010) 57,000,000 (57,000,000); coal, none (none); crude petroleum, none (none); petroleum products (metric tons; 2007) none (34,000); natural gas, none (none).
Land use as % of total land area (2007): in temporary crops or left fallow 1.6%, in permanent crops 7.0%, in pasture 3.4%, forest area 36.1%.
Population economically active (2008)[2]: total 119,000; activity rate of total population 50.9% (participation rates: ages 15–64, 83.2%; female 47.1%; unemployed, n.a.).

Price index (2005 = 100)

	2004	2005	2006	2007	2008	2009	2010
Consumer price index	98.8	100.0	102.0	106.1	111.2	115.9	119.2

Gross national income (GNI; 2010): U.S.$662,000,000 (U.S.$2,760 per capita); purchasing power parity GNI (U.S.$4,450 per capita).

Structure of gross domestic product and labour force

	2009		1999	
	in value Vt '000,000	% of total value	labour force	% of labour force
Agriculture, forestry, fishing	12,425	19.7	58,690[3]	76.8[3]
Mining and quarrying	26	0.1	3	—
Manufacturing	1,915	3.0	810	1.1
Construction	3,162	5.0	1,494	2.0
Public utilities	1,125	1.8	107	0.1
Transportation and communications	6,847	10.9	1,570	2.1
Trade, restaurants	9,392	14.9	4,070	5.3
Finance, real estate	4,623	7.3	738	1.0
Pub. admin., defense	8,140	12.9	2,513	3.3
Services	10,071	16.0	5,117	6.7
Other	5,298[4]	8.4[4]	1,258[5]	1.6[5]
TOTAL	63,024	100.0	76,370	100.0

Public debt (external, outstanding; January 2010): U.S.$98,800,000.
Household income and expenditure (2006). Average household size (2009) 5.3; income per household Vt 728,532 (U.S.$6,585); sources of income: wages and salaries 35.1%, own-account production[6] 27.7%, agriculture, fishing, and handicrafts 26.2%; expenditure: own-account production[6] 31.3%, food 22.8%, tobacco and alcohol 10.4%, housing and energy 8.6%, household furnishings 6.1%, transportation 5.5%.
Selected balance of payments data. Receipts from (U.S.$'000,000): tourism (2007) 119; remittances (2010) 7.0; foreign direct investment (FDI; 2008–10 avg.) 38; official development assistance (2009) 103. Disbursements for (U.S.$'000,000): tourism (2007) 11; remittances (2007) 3.0; FDI (2008–10 avg.) 1.0.

Foreign trade[7]

Balance of trade (current prices)

	2005	2006	2007	2008	2009	2010
Vt '000,000	–12,190	–15,590	–17,550	–25,885	–21,571	–22,807
% of total	59.6%	78.3%	74.3%	74.8%	63.8%	70.8%

Imports (2010): Vt 27,512,000,000 (machinery and transportation equipment 26.4%; food and live animals 19.1%; basic manufactures 13.9%; mineral fuels 13.2%; chemicals and chemical products 10.6%). *Major import sources:* Australia 31.0%; New Zealand 13.5%; Singapore 12.6%; Fiji 7.8%; Japan 3.7%.
Exports (2010): Vt 4,705,000,000 (domestic exports 95.5%, of which coconut oil 19.9%, copra 12.3%, kava 10.8%, beef 10.5%, cocoa 8.1%; reexports 4.5%). *Major export destinations* (2007): Philippines 14.0%; New Caledonia 9.7%; Fiji 6.7%; Japan 5.4%; Singapore 5.4%; unspecified 26.8%.

Transport and communications

Transport. Railroads: none. Roads (2009): total length 665 mi, 1,070 km (paved 24%). Vehicles (2002): passenger cars 8,200; trucks and buses 2,100. Air transport (2008)[8]: passenger-km 457,518,000; metric ton-km cargo 1,714,000.

Communications

Medium	date	number in '000s	units per 1,000 persons	Medium	date	number in '000s	units per 1,000 persons
Televisions	2004	2.7	13	PCs	2005	3.0	14
Telephones				Dailies	2009	3[9]	12[9]
Cellular	2010	285[10]	1,191[10]	Internet users	2009	17	71
Landline	2010	5.0	21	Broadband	2010	0.5[10]	2.1[10]

Education and health

Educational attainment (1999). Percentage of population age 15 and over having: no formal schooling 18.0%; incomplete primary education 20.6%; completed primary 35.5%; some secondary 12.2%; completed secondary 8.5%; higher 5.2%, of which university 1.3%. *Literacy* (2010): total population age 15 and over literate 84.8%; males literate 85.7%; females literate 83.9%.

Education (2009–10)

	teachers	students	student/ teacher ratio	enrollment rate (%)
Primary (age 6–11)	1,931	41,384	21.4	99[11]
Secondary/Voc. (age 12–18)	883[12]	20,256	13.9[12]	47
Tertiary	36[12]	955[13]	24.9[12]	5[13] (age 19–23)

Health (2008): physicians 26 (1 per 9,000 persons); hospital beds 383 (1 per 592 persons); infant mortality rate per 1,000 live births (2011[1]) 56.9; undernourished population (2004–06) 12,000 (6% of total population based on the consumption of a minimum daily requirement of 1,720 calories).

Military

Total active duty personnel (2010): none; Australia and New Zealand assist paramilitary forces through defense assistance programs.

[1]Midyear estimate. [2]ILO estimates. [3]Mostly not stated, which are significantly subsistence workers. [4]Taxes less subsidies and less imputed bank service charges. [5]Unemployed. [6]Production of goods and services that are retained by their producers for their own final consumption. [7]Imports c.i.f.; exports f.o.b. [8]Air Vanuatu only. [9]Circulation of daily newspapers. [10]Subscribers. [11]2004–05. [12]2001–02. [13]2003–04.

Internet resources for further information:
- **Vanuatu National Statistics Office http://www.vnso.gov.vu**
- **Reserve Bank of Vanuatu http://www.rbv.gov.vu**

Venezuela

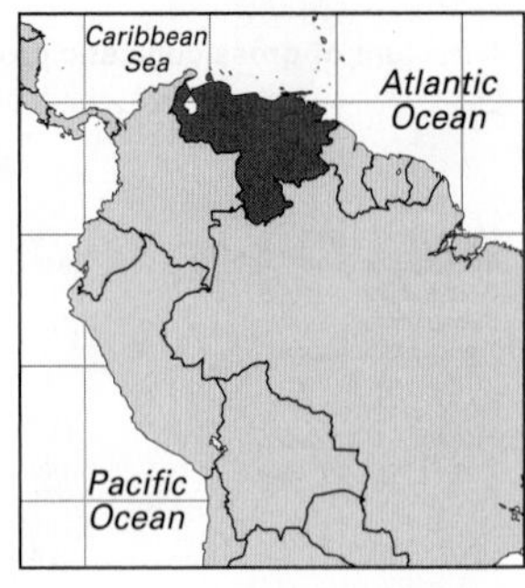

Official name: República Bolivariana de Venezuela (Bolivarian Republic of Venezuela).
Form of government: federal multiparty republic with a unicameral legislature (National Assembly [165[1]]).
Head of state and government: President.
Capital: Caracas.
Official language: Spanish[2].
Official religion: none.
Monetary unit: bolívar[3] (plural bolívares; VEF); valuation (Sept. 1, 2011) 1 U.S.$ = VEF 4.29; 1 £ = VEF 6.94[4].

Area and population

States	area sq km	population 2009 estimate[5]	States	area sq km	population 2009 estimate[5]
Amazonas	180,145	149,800	Nueva Esparta	1,150	450,100
Anzoátegui	43,300	1,526,400	Portuguesa	15,200	907,700
Apure	76,500	497,100	Sucre	11,800	945,600
Aragua	7,014	1,712,600	Táchira	11,100	1,220,500
Barinas	35,200	789,000	Trujillo	7,400	738,400
Bolívar	238,000	1,592,100	Vargas	1,497	337,800
Carabobo	4,650	2,296,900	Yaracuy	7,100	622,000
Cojedes	14,800	312,300	Zulia	63,100	3,754,200
Delta Amacuro	40,200	159,800			
Falcón	24,800	933,800	**Other federal entities**		
Guárico	64,986	773,900	Dependencias		
Lara	19,800	1,852,900	Federales	120	1,820
Mérida	11,300	876,000	Distrito Capital	433	2,097,400
Miranda	7,950	2,945,500			
Monagas	28,900	890,700	TOTAL	916,445	28,384,100[6]

Demography

Population (2011): 29,437,000.
Density (2011): persons per sq mi 83.2, persons per sq km 32.1.
Urban-rural (2009): urban 93.7%; rural 6.3%.
Sex distribution (2007): male 50.19%; female 49.81%.
Age breakdown (2006): under 15, 32.1%; 15–29, 26.9%; 30–44, 20.5%; 45–59, 13.2%; 60–74, 5.5%; 75–84, 1.5%; 85 and over, 0.3%.
Population projection: (2020) 33,340,000; (2030) 37,040,000.
Ethnic composition (2000): mestizo 63.7%; local white 20.0%; local black 10.0%; other white 3.3%; Amerindian 1.3%; other 1.7%.
Religious affiliation (2005): Roman Catholic 84.5%; Protestant 4.0%; nonreligious/other 11.5%.
Major cities/urban agglomerations (2009/2007): Caracas 2,097,400 (2,985,000); Maracaibo 1,891,800 (2,072,000); Valencia 1,408,400 (1,770,000); Barquisimeto 1,018,900 (1,116,000); Ciudad Guayana 789,500.

Vital statistics

Birth rate per 1,000 population (2008): 21.3 (world avg. 20.3).
Death rate per 1,000 population (2008): 5.1 (world avg. 8.5).
Total fertility rate (avg. births per childbearing woman; 2008): 2.55.
Marriage/divorce rates per 1,000 population (2008): 3.4/1.0.
Life expectancy at birth (2007): male 70.7 years; female 76.6 years.
Major causes of death per 100,000 population (2002): cardiovascular diseases 137.4, of which ischemic heart disease 71.2; malignant neoplasms (cancers) 67.8; violence/suicide 43.3; accidents 40.6; infectious/parasitic diseases 31.7.

National economy

Budget (2006). Revenue: VEB 117,326,000,000,000 (petroleum income 52.9%, of which royalties 37.5%, taxes 13.0%; nonpetroleum income 47.1%, of which VAT 22.4%). Expenditures: VEB 117,255,000,000,000 (current expenditure 75.0%; development expenditure 22.8%; other 2.2%).
Production (metric tons except as noted). Agriculture, forestry, fishing (2009): sugarcane 9,500,000, corn (maize) 2,800,000, cow's milk 2,200,000, rice 1,330,000, chicken meat 800,000, plantains 480,000, oranges 380,000, sorghum 370,000, pineapples 360,000, dry onions 270,000, rabbit meat 240,000, watermelons 180,000, taro 80,000, coffee 70,000; livestock (number of live animals) 16,900,000 cattle, 115,000,000 chickens; roundwood (2010) 6,358,625 cu m, of which fuelwood 63%; fisheries production 310,423 (from aquaculture 5%). Mining and quarrying (2010): iron ore (metal content) 15,200,000; bauxite 5,500,000; phosphate rock (gross weight) 400,000; gold 12,000 kg; gem diamonds 45,000 carats. Manufacturing (value added in VEB '000,000,000; 2004): food products 8,122; iron and steel 3,022; refined petroleum 2,890; soaps, paints, and pharmaceuticals 1,835; base chemicals 1,582; printing and publishing 1,580; fabricated metals 1,465; nonferrous base metals 1,377. Energy production (consumption): electricity (kW-hr; 2009) 123,391,000,000 ([2008] 84,715,000,000); coal (metric tons; 2010) 7,500,000 ([2007] 62,000); crude petroleum (barrels; 2010) 985,500,000 ([2007] 364,000,000); petroleum products (metric tons; 2007) 57,307,000 (33,050,000); natural gas (cu m; 2010) 28,000,000,000 ([2007] 24,362,000,000).
Selected balance of payments data. Receipts from (U.S.$'000,000): tourism (2009) 788; remittances (2010) 137; foreign direct disinvestment (2008–10 avg.) –1,387; official development assistance (2009) 67. Disbursements for (U.S.$'000,000): tourism (2009) 1,568; remittances (2009) 581; foreign direct investment (2008–10 avg.) 1,832.
Household income and expenditure. Average household size (2005) 4.5; average annual household income (2006) VEB 13,848,000 (U.S.$6,450)[7]; expenditure (2002): food and nonalcoholic beverages 27.3%, housing and energy 13.5%, transport 10.5%, expenditures in cafés and hotels 9.0%.

Gross national income (GNI; 2010): U.S.$334,113,000,000 (U.S.$11,590 per capita); purchasing power parity GNI (U.S.$11,950 per capita).

Structure of gross domestic product and labour force

	2009		2008	
	in value VEB '000,000,000[8]	% of total value[8]	labour force	% of labour force
Agriculture	...	...	1,005,900	7.9
Petroleum and natural gas	6,471.4[9]	11.6[9]	106,800	0.8
Mining	307.4	0.5		
Manufacturing	8,633.9[10]	15.4[10]	1,416,400	11.1
Construction	3,890.8	6.9	1,153,700	9.1
Public utilities	1,292.9	2.3	54,700	0.4
Transp. and commun.	5,092.5	9.1	1,042,500	8.2
Trade, hotels	5,687.7	10.2	2,808,900	22.1
Finance, real estate	7,877.3	14.1	614,000	4.8
Pub. admin., defense	6,610.7	11.8	3,633,800	28.5
Services	3,292.8	5.9		
Other	6,865.2	12.3	899,400[11]	7.1[11]
TOTAL	56,022.7[12]	100.0[12]	12,736,100	100.0

Public debt (external, outstanding; 2009): U.S.$35,184,000,000.
Population economically active (2008): total 12,736,100; activity rate 45.7% (participation rates: ages 15–64, 68.5%; female 39.0%; unemployed 6.9%).

Price index (2005 = 100)

	2004	2005	2006	2007	2008	2009	2010
Consumer price index	86.2	100.0	113.7	134.9	177.3	228.0	294.3

Land use as % of total land area (2009): in temporary crops or left fallow (2007) 3.0%, in permanent crops 0.7%, in pasture 20.4%, forest area 52.8%.

Foreign trade

Balance of trade (current prices)

	2005	2006	2007	2008	2009	2010
U.S.$'000,000	+33,873	+35,018	+27,104	+50,045	+20,689	+35,045
% of total	43.7%	36.4%	24.4%	35.7%	21.9%	36.3%

Imports (2008): U.S.$45,128,000,000 (machinery and apparatus 31.7%, food 14.4%, chemicals and chemical products 13.8%, base and fabricated metals 7.5%, road vehicles 6.4%). *Major import sources:* U.S. 26.4%; Colombia 15.0%; China 9.4%; Brazil 9.0%; Mexico 4.6%.
Exports (2008): U.S.$83,288,000,000 (crude petroleum 93.5%, iron and steel 1.9%, aluminum 1.1%, organic chemicals 0.4%, coal 0.3%). *Major export destinations:* U.S. 40.4%; Latin America 24.8%; Neth. Antilles 20.2%.

Transport and communications

Transport. Railroads: route length (2009) 806 km; metric ton-km cargo (2004) 22,000,000. Roads (2004): total length 59,800 mi, 96,200 km (paved 34%). Vehicles (2007): passenger cars 2,952,129; trucks and buses 1,091,883. Air transport (2007): passenger-km 941,000,000[13]; metric ton-km cargo 2,000,000.

Communications

Medium	date	number in '000s	units per 1,000 persons	Medium	date	number in '000s	units per 1,000 persons
Televisions	2004	5,000	201	PCs	2005	2,475	98
Telephones				Dailies	2009	1,810[14]	97[14]
Cellular	2010	27,880[15]	962[15]	Internet users	2009	8,847	310
Landline	2010	7,083	244	Broadband	2010	1,557[15]	54[15]

Education and health

Educational attainment (2003). Percentage of head-of-household population[16] having: no formal schooling 10.2%; primary education or less 38.5%; some secondary 36.9%; completed secondary/higher 14.4%. *Literacy* (2007): 95.2%.

Education (2007–08)

	teachers	students	student/ teacher ratio	enrollment rate (%)
Primary (age 6–11)	212,425	3,439,199	16.2	90
Secondary/Voc. (age 12–16)	217,516	2,224,214	10.2	69
Tertiary	122,525	2,109,331	17.2	79 (age 17–21)

Health (2003): physicians 35,756 (1 per 722 persons); hospital beds 74,866 (1 per 345 persons); infant mortality rate (2008) 15.8; undernourished population (2004–06) 3,100,000 (12% of total population based on the consumption of a minimum daily requirement of 1,830 calories).

Military

Total active duty personnel (November 2010): 115,000 (army 54.8%, navy 15.2%, air force 10.0%, national guard 20.0%). *Military expenditure as percentage of GDP* (2009): 1.0%; per capita expenditure U.S.$116.

[1]Includes 3 seats reserved for indigenous residents. [2]Indigenous Indian languages are also official. [3]The bolívar was redenominated on Jan. 1, 2008; as of this date 1,000 (old) bolívares (VEB) = 1 (new) bolívar or "bolívar fuerte" (VEF). [4]The black market rate of the "bolívar fuerte" (VEF) in March 2010 was about 1 U.S.$ = VEF 6.80. [5]Official projection based on 2001 census. [6]Reported total; summed total is 28,384,320. [7]At official exchange rate; excludes top 2.4% of all households by income. [8]At prices of 1997. [9]Includes refined petroleum. [10]Excludes refined petroleum. [11]Includes 872,900 unemployed. [12]Detail does not add to total given because of rounding. [13]Aeropostal airlines only. [14]Circulation of daily newspapers. [15]Subscribers. [16]Data based on survey of 5,528,902 heads of households.

Internet resources for further information:
- **Banco Central de Venezuela http://www.bcv.org.ve/EnglishVersion**
- **Instituto Nacional de Estadística http://www.ine.gov.ve**

Vietnam

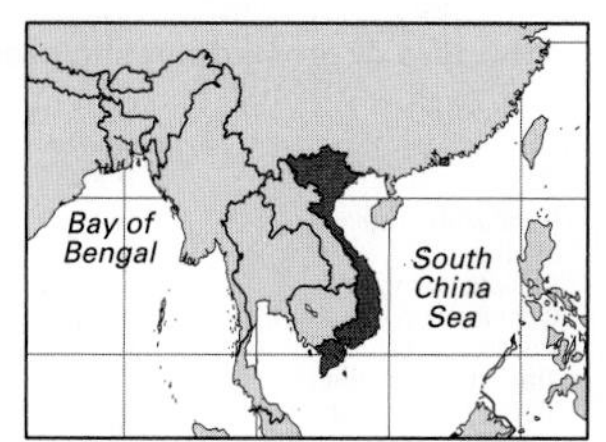

Official name: Cong Hoa Xa Hoi Chu Nghia Viet Nam (Socialist Republic of Vietnam).
Form of government: socialist republic with one legislative house (National Assembly [500]).
Head of state: President.
Head of government: Prime Minister.
Capital: Hanoi.
Official language: Vietnamese.
Official religion: none.
Monetary unit: dong (VND); valuation (Sept. 1, 2011) 1 U.S.$ = VND 20,832; 1 £ = VND 33,664.

Area and population

Economic regions[1]	Principal cities	area sq mi	area sq km	population 2009 census
Central Highlands	Buon Ma Thuot	21,104	54,660	5,115,135
Mekong River Delta	Long Xuyen	15,678	40,605	17,191,470
North Central Coast	Hue	19,904	51,552	10,070,311
North East	Thai Nguyen	24,720	64,025	9,476,498
North West	Hoa Binh	14,492	37,534	2,722,080
Red River Delta	Hanoi	5,738	14,862	18,439,299
South Central Coast	Da Nang	12,806	33,166	7,032,827
South East	Ho Chi Minh City	13,440	34,808	15,799,377
TOTAL		127,882	331,212	85,846,997

Demography

Population (2011): 88,145,000.
Density (2011): persons per sq mi 689.2, persons per sq km 266.1.
Urban-rural (2009): urban 29.6%; rural 70.4%.
Sex distribution (2009): male 49.52%; female 50.48%.
Age breakdown (2008): under 15, 26.6%; 15–29, 29.8%; 30–44, 22.2%; 45–59, 13.8%; 60–74, 5.3%; 75–84, 1.9%; 85 and over, 0.4%.
Population projection: (2020) 96,883,000; (2030) 104,325,000.
Ethnic composition (2003): Vietnamese 85.7%; Tho (Tay) 2.0%; Thai 1.8%; Muong 1.5%; Khmer 1.4%; Nung 1.1%; Hoa 1.1%; Miao (Hmong) 1.1%; Dao 0.8%; other 3.5%.
Religious affiliation (2005): Buddhist *c.* 48%; New-Religionist (mostly Cao Dai and Hoa Hao) *c.* 11%; traditional beliefs *c.* 10%; Roman Catholic *c.* 7%; Protestant *c.* 1%; nonreligious/atheist *c.* 20%; other *c.* 3%.
Major cities (2009): Ho Chi Minh City 5,968,384; Hanoi 2,644,536; Haiphong 846,191; Da Nang 770,911.

Vital statistics

Birth rate per 1,000 population (2009): 17.6 (world avg. 20.3).
Death rate per 1,000 population (2009): 6.8 (world avg. 8.5).
Marriage/divorce rates per 1,000 population (2002): 12.1/0.5.
Total fertility rate (avg. births per childbearing woman; 2009): 2.03.
Life expectancy at birth (2009): male 70.2 years; female 75.6 years.
Adult population (ages 15–49) *living with HIV* (2009): 0.4% (world avg. 0.8%).
Major causes of death per 100,000 population (2002): diseases of the circulatory system 200.7; infectious and parasitic diseases 93.6; malignant neoplasms (cancers) 80.4; diseases of the respiratory system 64.3.

National economy

Budget (2008). Revenue: VND 323,000,000,000,000 (tax revenue 89.0%, of which oil related 20.3%, non-oil related 68.7%; nontax revenue 9.9%; grants 1.1%). Expenditures: VND 364,000,000,000,000 (current expenditure 72.6%; capital expenditure 27.4%).
Public debt (external, outstanding; 2009): U.S.$23,403,000,000.
Gross national income (GNI; 2010): U.S.$96,899,000,000 (U.S.$1,100 per capita); purchasing power parity GNI (U.S.$2,910 per capita).

Structure of gross domestic product and labour force

	2009 in value VND '000,000,000	2009 % of total value	2008 labour force[2]	2008 % of labour force[2]
Agriculture, fishing	326,505	22.1	23,634,700	52.6
Mining	131,968	8.9	431,200	1.0
Public utilities	47,644	3.2	224,600	0.5
Manufacturing	311,848	21.1	6,306,200	14.0
Construction	95,696	6.5	2,394,000	5.3
Transp. and commun.	67,100	4.5	1,221,700	2.7
Trade, restaurants	269,563	18.3	6,202,800	13.8
Finance, real estate	80,958	5.5	471,600	1.1
Pub. admin., defense	40,992	2.8	866,900	1.9
Services, other	105,441	7.1	3,162,100	7.1
TOTAL	1,477,717[3]	100.0	44,915,800	100.0

Production (metric tons except as noted). Agriculture, forestry, fishing (2009): rice 38,895,500, sugarcane 15,246,400, cassava 8,556,900, corn (maize) 4,381,800, pig meat 2,908,500, bananas 1,532,400, sweet potatoes 1,207,600, coffee (green) 1,176,000, coconuts 1,128,500, cashews 958,000, natural rubber 723,700, oranges 600,000, groundnuts (peanuts) 525,100, pineapples 460,000, tea 185,700, black pepper 98,300[4], cinnamon 13,965; livestock (number of live animals) 27,627,700 pigs, 6,103,300 cattle, 2,886,600 buffalo, 84,060,000 ducks; roundwood (2010) 27,850,000 cu m, of which fuelwood 79%; fisheries production 4,799,300 (from aquaculture 53%); aquatic plants production 33,600 (from aquaculture 100%). Mining and quarrying (2009): phosphate rock 1,896,000[5]; kaolin 650,000; barite 70,000; zinc 45,600[6]; tin 5,400[6]. Manufacturing (value of production in VND '000,000,000,000; 2004): food and beverages 156.1; cement, bricks, and pottery 46.2; paints, soaps, and pharmaceuticals 43.9; transport equipment (excluding motor vehicles) 38.6; fabricated metal products 35.0; leather products/footwear 33.5; wearing apparel 32.6. Energy production (consumption): electricity (kW-hr) 95,900,000,000[7] ([2008] 62,603,000,000); hard coal (metric tons) 45,328,000[7] ([2007] 16,250,000); crude petroleum (barrels) 105,460,000[7] ([2007] negligible); petroleum products (metric tons; 2007) 281,000,000 (12,523,000); natural gas (cu m) 9,186,000,000[7] ([2007] 6,514,000,000).
Population economically active (2008): total 46,045,000; activity rate of total population 52.9% (participation rates: ages 15–64, 77.4%; female 48.7%; unemployed [2009] 2.9%).

Price index (2005 = 100)

	2004	2005	2006	2007	2008	2009	2010
Consumer price index	92.4	100.0	107.4	116.3	143.2	153.3	166.9

Household income and expenditure (2004). Average household size 3.8[8]; average annual income per household (1997–98)[9] VND 15,494,000 (U.S.$1,165); sources of income: wages and salaries 32.7%, self-employment 27.0%, agriculture 22.6%; expenditure: food, beverages, and tobacco 53.5%, transportation and communications 10.8%, household furnishings 9.1%, health 7.0%, education 6.3%.
Selected balance of payments data. Receipts from (U.S.$'000,000): tourism (2009) 3,050; remittances (2010) 8,000; foreign direct investment (FDI; 2008–10 avg.) 8,451; official development assistance (2009) 3,744. Disbursements for (U.S.$'000,000): tourism (2009) 1,100; FDI (2008–10 avg.) 618.
Land use as % of total land area (2009): in temporary crops or left fallow 20.1%, in permanent crops 10.8%, in pasture 2.1%, forest area 44.0%.

Foreign trade[10]

Balance of trade (current prices)

	2005	2006	2007	2008	2009	2010
U.S.$'000,000	–4,319	–5,189	–14,121	–18,029	–12,853	–12,121
% of total	6.2%	6.1%	12.7%	12.6%	10.1%	7.8%

Imports (2007): U.S.$62,765,000,000 (machinery and apparatus 23.8%; chemicals and chemical products 13.3%; refined petroleum 12.8%; iron and steel 9.3%; yarn and fabrics 7.3%). *Major import sources:* China 20.3%; Singapore 12.1%; Taiwan 11.1%; Japan 9.9%; South Korea 8.5%; Thailand 6.0%.
Exports (2007): U.S.$48,561,000,000 (crude petroleum 17.5%; apparel 14.6%; machinery and apparatus 10.4%; footwear 8.4%, of which sports footwear 3.6%; fish/crustaceans/mollusks 7.7%; furniture/parts 4.9%; coffee 3.9%; rice 3.1%; natural rubber 2.7%). *Major export destinations:* U.S. 20.8%; Japan 12.5%; Australia 7.8%; China 7.5%; Singapore 4.6%.

Transport and communications

Transport. Railroads (2005): route length 1,615 mi, 2,600 km; passenger-km (2008) 4,560,000,000; metric ton-km cargo (2008) 4,028,000,000. Roads (2007): total length 99,475 mi, 160,089 km (paved 51%). Vehicles (2007): passenger cars 1,146,312; trucks and buses, n.a. Air transport (2008): passenger-km 16,116,000,000; metric ton-km cargo 295,764,000. Inland waterway (2008): passenger-km, n.a.; metric ton-km cargo 22,680,000,000.

Communications

Medium	date	number in '000s	units per 1,000 persons	Medium	date	number in '000s	units per 1,000 persons
Televisions	2003	15,938	197	PCs	2007	8,306	96
Telephones				Dailies	2009	4,000[11]	46[11]
Cellular	2010	154,000[12]	1,753[12]	Internet users	2009	24,000	273
Landline	2010	16,400	187	Broadband	2010	3,631[12]	41[12]

Education and health

Educational attainment (1999). Percentage of population age 18 and over having: no formal education 9.0%; primary education 29.2%; lower secondary 32.5%; upper secondary 24.9%; incomplete/complete higher 4.3%; advanced degree 0.1%. *Literacy* (2008): percentage of population age 15 and over literate 93.6%; males 96.1%; females 91.3%.

Education (2008–09)

	teachers	students	student/teacher ratio	enrollment rate (%)
Primary (age 6–10)	345,505	6,745,016	19.5	94[13]
Secondary/Voc. (age 11–17)	461,663[14]	9,543,007[14]	20.7[14]	62[13]
Tertiary	61,190	1,774,321	29.0	10[13] (age 18–22)

Health (2008): physicians 57,300 (1 per 1,579 persons); hospital beds 219,800 (1 per 410 persons); infant mortality rate per 1,000 live births (2009) 16.0; undernourished population (2004–06) 11,200,000 (13% of total population based on the consumption of a minimum daily requirement of 1,800 calories).

Military

Total active duty personnel (November 2010): 482,000 (army 85.5%, navy 8.3%, air force 6.2%); paramilitary 40,000. *Military expenditure as percentage of GDP* (2009): 2.2%; per capita expenditure U.S.$34.

[1]Eight economic regions are divided into 58 provinces and 5 municipalities. [2]Employed only; ages 15 and over. [3]Detail does not add to total given because of rounding. [4]2008. [5]Gross weight. [6]Metal content. [7]July 2010–June 2011. [8]2009. [9]Based on a survey of about 6,000 urban and rural households. [10]Imports c.i.f.; exports f.o.b. [11]Circulation of daily newspapers. [12]Subscribers. [13]2000–01. [14]2007–08.

Internet resource for further information:
- **General Statistics Office of Vietnam http://www.gso.gov.vn**

Virgin Islands (U.S.)

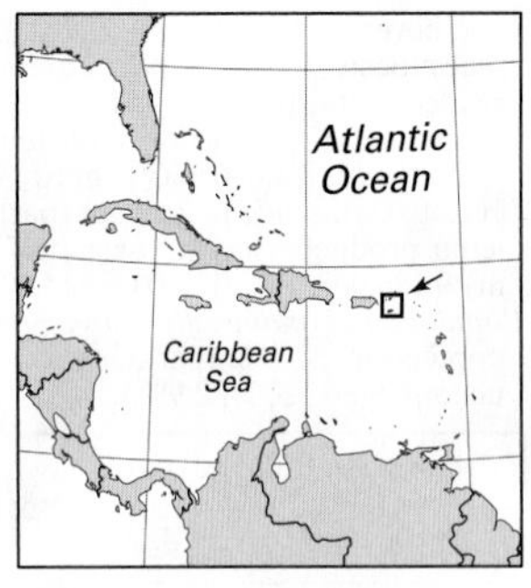

Official name: United States Virgin Islands.
Political status: organized unincorporated territory of the United States with one legislative house (Legislature [15]).
Head of state: President of the United States.
Head of government: Governor.
Capital: Charlotte Amalie.
Official language: English.
Official religion: none.
Monetary unit: U.S. dollar (U.S.$); valuation (Sept. 1, 2011) 1 U.S.$ = £0.62.

Area and population		area		population
				2009
Islands[1]	**Principal towns**	sq mi	sq km	estimate
St. Croix	Christiansted	84	218	57,351
St. John	Cruz Bay[2]	20	52	4,522
St. Thomas	Charlotte Amalie	32	83	55,138
TOTAL		136	353	117,011

Demography

Population (2011): 119,000.
Density (2011): persons per sq mi 877.4, persons per sq km 338.0.
Urban-rural (2010): urban 95.4%; rural 4.6%.
Sex distribution (2010): male 47.28%; female 52.72%.
Age breakdown (2010): under 15, 19.9%; 15–29, 19.1%; 30–44, 18.2%; 45–59, 21.4%; 60–74, 16.3%; 75–84, 4.0%; 85 and over, 1.1%.
Population projection: (2020) 117,000; (2030) 113,000.
Ethnic composition (2006): non-Hispanic black 70.6%; non-Hispanic white 11.3%; Hispanic black 5.6%; Hispanic white 1.7%; other Hispanic 6.6%; Asian 1.1%; other 3.1%.[3]
Religious affiliation (2000): Christian 96.3%, of which Protestant 51.0% (including Anglican 13.0%), Roman Catholic 27.5%, independent Christian 12.2%; nonreligious 2.2%; other 1.5%.
Major towns (2000): Charlotte Amalie 11,004 (urban agglomeration 18,914); Christiansted 2,637; Frederiksted 732.

Vital statistics

Birth rate per 1,000 population (2010): 11.5 (world avg. 19.2); within marriage (1998) 30.2%[4]; outside of marriage (1998) 69.8%.
Death rate per 1,000 population (2010): 7.0 (world avg. 8.2).
Total fertility rate (avg. births per childbearing woman; 2010): 1.81.
Marriage/divorce rates per 1,000 population: (2004) 35.8[5]/(2003) 3.9.
Life expectancy at birth (2010): male 76.1 years; female 82.4 years.
Major causes of death per 100,000 population (2007): diseases of the circulatory system 251.5, of which ischemic heart disease 134.9, cerebrovascular diseases 36.5; malignant neoplasms (cancers) 105.7; accidents, poisoning, and violence 79.3; diabetes mellitus 41.0; communicable diseases 33.7.

National economy

Budget. Revenue (2009): n.a.; direct federal expenditures U.S.$876,000,000, rum excise tax returned to U.S.V.I. government U.S.$106,800,000. Expenditures (proposed; 2009): U.S.$837,000,000.
Public debt (2005–06): U.S.$1,150,000,000.
Production. Agriculture, forestry, fishing (value of sales in U.S.$'000; 2002): ornamental plants and other nursery products 799, livestock and livestock products 775 (notably cattle and calves and hogs and pigs), vegetables 340 (notably tomatoes and cucumbers), fruits and nuts 131 (notably mangoes, bananas, papayas, and avocados); livestock (number of live animals; 2009) 8,100 cattle, 4,100 goats, 3,250 sheep, 2,650 hogs and pigs, 40,000 chickens; roundwood, n.a.; fisheries production (2009) 1,130 metric tons (from aquaculture 1%). Mining and quarrying: sand and crushed stone for local use. Manufacturing (U.S.$'000[6]; 2002): beverages and tobacco products 44,766; stone, clay, and glass products 32,939; computer and electronic products 22,875; chemicals and chemical products 16,989. Energy production (consumption): electricity (kW-hr; 2008) 843,600,000 (784,500,000); coal (metric tons; 2002) none (290,000); crude petroleum (barrels; 2010) 6,365,600 (31,025,000); petroleum products (metric tons; 2002) 18,801,000 (1,588,000); natural gas, none (none).
Household income and expenditure (2004). Average household size 2.5; average annual income per household U.S.$37,201; sources of income (1999): wages and salaries 73.9%, transfers 10.0%, self-employment 8.8%, interest, dividends, and rents 5.7%; expenditures (2001)[7]: housing 38.8%, food and beverages 12.5%, transportation 11.1%, education and communications 7.1%, health 5.8%.
Population economically active (2009)[8]: total 52,275; activity rate of total population 44.7% (participation rates: over age 15 [2008] 53.1%; female [2008] 52.7%; unemployed [2010] 8.1%).

Price and earnings indexes (2005 = 100)							
	2003	2004	2005	2006	2007	2008	2009
Consumer price index	95.2	97.6	100.0	103.0	108.0	115.7	...
Annual earnings index[9]	92.8	95.7	100.0	105.9	109.4	110.8	111.7

Gross territorial product (at current market prices; 2007): U.S.$4,580,000,000 (U.S.$39,915 per capita).

Structure of gross domestic product and labour force	2003		2009	
	in value U.S.$'000,000	% of total value	labour force[8]	% of labour force[8]
Agriculture, fishing	...	...	...	...
Mining	...	...	[10]	[10]
Manufacturing	189	7.5	2,220	4.2
Construction	142	5.6	2,179[10]	4.2[10]
Public utilities	...	...	1,613	3.1
Transp. and commun.	...	...		
Trade, hotels, restaurants, leisure	648	25.7	13,682	26.2
Services	555	22.0	9,984	19.1
Finance, insurance, real estate	...	...	2,458	4.7
Pub. admin., defense	584	23.2	13,000	24.9
Other	404	16.0	7,139[11]	13.7[11]
TOTAL	2,522[12]	100.0[12]	52,275	100.0[13]

Selected balance of payments data. Receipts from (U.S.$'000,000): tourism (2009) 1,468; remittances, n.a.; foreign direct investment, n.a. Disbursements for (U.S.$'000,000): tourism, n.a.; remittances, n.a.
Land use as % of total land area (2007): in temporary crops or left fallow *c.* 3%, in permanent crops *c.* 3%, in pasture *c.* 6%, forest area *c.* 26%.

Foreign trade

Balance of trade (current prices)						
	2004	2005	2006	2007	2008	2009
U.S.$'000,000	+359.8	+233.0	+11.8	+710.8	–611.9	–561.6
% of total	2.3%	1.1%	0.5%	2.8%	1.7%	2.8%

Imports (2009): U.S.$10,289,900,000 (foreign crude petroleum 68.9%, other [significantly manufactured goods] 31.1%). *Major import sources:* United States 11.1%; other countries (mostly Venezuela) 88.9%.
Exports (2009): U.S.$9,728,300,000 (refined petroleum to U.S. 85.6%, unspecified [significantly rum and watches] 14.4%). *Major export destinations:* United States 87.3%; other countries 12.7%.

Transport and communications

Transport. Railroads: none. Roads (2008): total length 783 mi, 1,260 km (paved [2007] 95%). Vehicles (total registered vehicles; 2008–09): 75,951. Cruise ships (2010): passenger arrivals 1,858,946. Air transport (2010): passenger arrivals 691,559; passenger-km 17,000,000[14]; metric ton-km cargo, none.

Communications			units				units
Medium	date	number in '000s	per 1,000 persons	**Medium**	date	number in '000s	per 1,000 persons
Televisions	2000	65	594	PCs	2005	3.0	26.9
Telephones				Dailies	2009	9[15]	77[15]
Cellular	2005	80[16]	713[16]	Internet users	2009	30	274
Landline	2010	76	695	Broadband	2010	9.1[16]	83[16]

Education and health

Educational attainment (2004). Percentage of population age 25 and over having: no formal schooling 0.5%; incomplete primary to incomplete secondary 39.1%; complete secondary 29.8%; some higher 11.9%; undergraduate 13.8%; advanced degree 4.9%. *Literacy:* n.a.

Education (2002)	teachers	students	student/ teacher ratio	enrollment rate (%)
Primary (age 5–12)[17]	750	9,475	12.6	...
Secondary (age 12–18)[17]	772	8,329	10.8	...
Tertiary[18]	107	2,392	22.4	... (age 19–23)

Health: physicians (2006) 167 (1 per 681 persons); hospital beds (2005) 320[19] (1 per 350 persons); infant mortality rate per 1,000 live births (2010) 7.4; undernourished population, n.a.

Military

Total active duty personnel (2010): no domestic military force is maintained; the United States is responsible for defense and external security.

[1]May be administered by officials assigned by the governor. [2]Census-designated place. [3]*Birthplace* (2004): U.S. Virgin Islands 45.4%; other Caribbean 34.9%, of which St. Kitts and Nevis 6.9%, Dominica 5.9%, Antigua and Barbuda 4.8%; mainland U.S. 11.3%; Puerto Rico 5.4%; other 3.0%. [4]Percentage of births within marriage may be an underestimation due to the common practice of consensual marriage. [5]Includes numerous marriages by visitors. [6]Figures are for value of sales. [7]Weights of consumer price index components. [8]Age 16 and over. [9]Average gross pay. [10]Construction includes Mining. [11]Includes 3,998 unemployed. [12]Tourism in 2003 accounted for more than 60% of gross domestic product. [13]Detail does not add to total given because of rounding. [14]Seaborne Airlines. [15]Circulation of daily newspapers. [16]Subscribers. [17]Public schools only. [18]2005. [19]Main hospitals on St. Thomas and St. Croix only.

Internet resources for further information:
- **Pacific Web**
  http://www.pacificweb.org
- **Bureau of Economic Research**
  http://www.usviber.org

Yemen

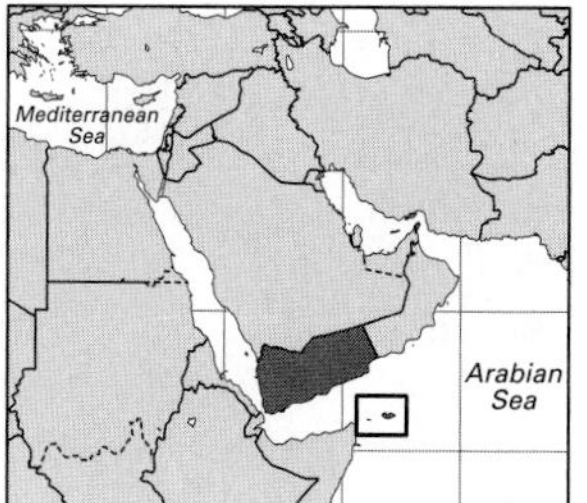

Official name: Al-Jumhūriyyah al-Yamaniyyah (Republic of Yemen).
Form of government: multiparty republic with two legislative houses (Consultative Council [111[1]]; House of Representatives [301]).
Head of state: President.
Head of government: Prime Minister.
Capital: Sanaa.
Official language: Arabic.
Official religion: Islam.
Monetary unit: Yemeni rial (YR); valuation (Sept. 1, 2011) 1 U.S.$ = YR 213.80; 1 £ = YR 345.49.

Area and population

	area[2]	population		area[2]	population
Governorates	sq km	2009 estimate	**Governorates**	sq km	2009 estimate
Abyān	23,897	497,231	Al-Mahrah	93,907	101,701
ʿAdan (Aden)	6,863	684,322	Al-Maḥwīt	2,545	564,067
ʿAmrān	9,261	1,002,099	Maʾrib	15,201	271,855
Al-Bayḍāʾ	10,757	656,811	Raymah	2,241	448,550
Al-Ḍāliʿ	3,448	537,243	Ṣaʿdah	13,343	791,823
Dhamār	8,296	1,514,297	Ṣanʿāʾ (Sanaa)	16,394	1,048,310
Ḥaḍramawt	193,582	1,181,863	Shabwah	39,134	536,594
Ḥajjah	8,882	1,683,554	Taʿizz	12,631	2,727,186
Al-Ḥudaydah	15,657	2,470,703			
Ibb	6,160	2,422,013	**Capital City**		
Al-Jawf	28,930	503,151	Sanaa[3]	292	2,022,867
Laḥij	16,655	825,794	TOTAL	528,076	22,492,035[4]

Demography

Population (2011): 24,800,000.
Density (2011): persons per sq mi 121.6, persons per sq km 47.0.
Urban-rural (2009): urban 31.2%; rural 68.8%.
Sex distribution (2009): male 50.79%; female 49.21%.
Age breakdown (2009): under 15, 43.9%; 15–29, 29.8%; 30–44, 14.4%; 45–59, 7.9%; 60–74, 3.2%; 75–84, 0.7%; 85 and over, 0.1%.
Population projection: (2020) 32,232,000; (2030) 41,342,000.
Doubling time: 23 years.
Ethnic composition (2000): Arab 92.8%; Somali 3.7%; black 1.1%; Indo-Pakistani 1.0%; other 1.4%.
Religious affiliation (2005): Muslim nearly 100%, of which Sunnī *c.* 58%, Shīʿī *c.* 42%.
Major cities (2004): Sanaa (2009) 2,022,867; Aden 588,938; Taʿizz 466,968; Al-Ḥudaydah 409,994; Ibb 212,992.

Vital statistics

Birth rate per 1,000 population (2009): 35.3 (world avg. 20.3).
Death rate per 1,000 population (2009): 7.5 (world avg. 8.5).
Total fertility rate (avg. births per childbearing woman; 2009): 5.00.
Life expectancy at birth (2009): male 61.0 years; female 65.1 years.
Major causes of death per 100,000 population (2002): cardiovascular diseases *c.* 184, of which ischemic heart disease *c.* 84; infectious and parasitic diseases *c.* 171, of which diarrheal diseases *c.* 99; lower respiratory infections *c.* 126; perinatal conditions *c.* 90; accidents *c.* 77.

National economy

Budget (2009). Revenue: YR 1,276,600,000,000 (oil revenue 58.3%, tax revenue 31.8%, nontax revenue 8.3%, grants 1.6%). Expenditures: YR 1,843,900,000,000 (transfers and subsidies 30.8%, wages and salaries 30.3%, interest on debt 6.9%).
Public debt (external, outstanding; October 2011): U.S.$6,197,200,000.
Population economically active (2009): total 5,434,425; activity rate of total population 23.7% (participation rates: ages 15 and older, 42.2%; female 11.6%; unemployed 14.6%).

Price index (2005 = 100)

	2004	2005	2006	2007	2008	2009	2010
Consumer price index	89.4	100.0	110.8	119.6	142.3	150.0	166.8

Production (metric tons except as noted). Agriculture, forestry, fishing (2009): mangoes 404,573, sorghum 311,504, alfalfa 300,909, potatoes 278,022, tomatoes 251,269, wheat 222,129, onions 215,500, khat (qat) 173,856[5], bananas 132,418, grapes 129,385, oranges 112,502, dates 56,760, chickpeas 50,567, sesame seed 24,285, camel's milk 19,040, coffee 18,924; livestock (number of live animals) 9,087,000 sheep, 8,883,000 goats, 1,567,000 cattle, 384,000 camels; roundwood (2010) 424,823 cu m, of which fuelwood 100%; fisheries production 127,132 (from aquaculture, none). Mining and quarrying (2009): gypsum 100,000; salt 65,000. Manufacturing (gross value added in YR '000,000; 2009): food and beverages 141,263; cement, bricks, and ceramics 74,928; fabricated metal products 61,382; tobacco products 46,433; refined petroleum products 34,529; plastic products 32,754; wearing apparel, textiles, and leather 32,701; wood and wood products 20,512; furniture 20,447. Energy production (consumption): electricity (kW-hr; 2009) 6,748,930,000 (4,644,000,000); coal, none (none); crude petroleum (barrels; 2009) 103,700,000 (56,575,000); petroleum products (metric tons; 2008) 3,307,000 ([2007] 5,560,000); natural gas (cu m; 2009) 30,000,000,000[6].
Gross national income (GNI; 2009): U.S.$25,026,000,000 (U.S.$1,060 per capita); purchasing power parity GNI (U.S.$2,340 per capita).

Structure of gross domestic product and labour force

	2009		2005–06	
	in value YR '000,000	% of total value	labour force	% of labour force
Agriculture, forestry, fishing[5]	732,577	12.1	1,406,099	28.4
Crude petrol., natural gas	1,120,678	18.5	14,959	0.3
Mining and quarrying	12,243	0.2		
Manufacturing	493,974[7]	8.1[7]	222,138	4.5
Public utilities	44,247	0.7	18,773	0.4
Construction	271,808	4.5	485,864	9.8
Transp. and commun.	794,965	13.1	239,477	4.8
Trade, restaurants, hotels	1,305,709	21.5	724,868	14.7
Finance, real estate	568,666	9.4	39,907	0.8
Pub. admin., defense	364,823	6.0	453,532	9.2
Services	303,273	5.0	402,816	8.2
Other	56,634[8]	0.9[8]	936,328[9]	18.9[9]
TOTAL	6,069,598[4]	100.0	4,944,763[4]	100.0

Household income and expenditure. Average household size (2009) 7.1; income per household (1998) YR 29,035 (U.S.$217); expenditures (2005–06): food and nonalcoholic beverages 38.5%, housing 14.6%, tobacco and khat (qat) 14.2%, health 11.6%, transportation and communications 10.8%.
Selected balance of payments data. Receipts from (U.S.$'000,000): tourism (2009) 496; remittances (2010) 1,240; foreign direct investment (FDI; 2008–10 avg.) 452; official development assistance (2009) 500. Disbursements for (U.S.$'000,000): tourism (2009) 214; remittances (2009) 337; FDI (2008–10 avg.) 67.
Land use as % of total land area (2009): in temporary crops or left fallow 2.2%, in permanent crops 0.5%, in pasture 41.7%, forest area 1.0%.

Foreign trade[10]

Balance of trade (current prices)

	2005	2006	2007	2008	2009	2010
YR '000,000	+44,036	+114,370	–440,038	–591,777	–593,508	–263,508
% of total	2.1%	4.6%	14.9%	16.3%	18.9%	6.6%

Imports (2008): YR 2,087,876,317,000 (crude and refined petroleum 29.1%; food and live animals 22.3%, of which grains 13.2%; transportation equipment 7.0%; base and fabricated metals 6.5%; chemicals and chemical products 6.4%). *Major import sources:* U.A.E. 28.9%; China 7.0%; Saudi Arabia 6.7%; Kuwait 6.4%; India 3.9%.
Exports (2008): YR 1,519,162,467,000 (refined petroleum products 77.3%; crude petroleum 9.9%; food and live animals 5.0%, of which fish 2.6%; transportation equipment 1.9%; chemicals and chemical products 1.7%). *Major export destinations:* China 31.1%; Thailand 23.8%; U.A.E. 9.5%; India 8.0%; South Korea 6.3%.

Transport and communications

Transport. Railroads: none. Roads (2007): total length 44,304 mi, 71,300 km (paved 9%). Vehicles (2004): passenger cars 522,437; trucks and buses 506,766. Air transport (2007)[11]: passenger-km 3,041,000,000; metric ton-km cargo 37,000,000.

Communications

Medium	date	number in '000s	units per 1,000 persons	Medium	date	number in '000s	units per 1,000 persons
Televisions	2003	6,780	359	PCs	2006	587	28
Telephones				Dailies	2009	170[12]	7.4[12]
Cellular	2010	11,085[13]	461[13]	Internet users	2009	2,349	100
Landline	2010	1,046	44	Broadband	2010	79[13]	3.3[13]

Education and health

Educational attainment (2005–06). Percentage of population age 10 and over having: no formal schooling/unknown 42.3%; reading and writing ability 33.6%; primary education 13.1%; secondary 8.7%; higher 2.3%. *Literacy* (2008): percentage of total population age 15 and over literate 60.9%; males literate 78.9%; females literate 42.8%.

Education (2007–08)

	teachers	students	student/ teacher ratio	enrollment rate (%)
Primary (age 6–11)	110,127[14]	3,282,457	22.4[14]	73
Secondary/Voc. (age 12–17)	55,862[15]	1,455,206	24.6[15]	37
Tertiary	8,919[16]	256,125[16]	28.7[16]	10[17] (age 18–22)

Health (2009): physicians 6,468 (1 per 3,541 persons); hospital beds 16,095 (1 per 1,423 persons); infant mortality rate 58.4; undernourished population (2004–06) 6,700,000 (32% of total population based on the consumption of a minimum daily requirement of 1,690 calories).

Military

Total active duty personnel (November 2010): 66,700 (army 90.0%, navy 2.5%, air force/air defense 7.5%); paramilitary 71,200. *Military expenditure as percentage of GDP* (2009): 6.8%; per capita expenditure U.S.$68.

[1]All appointed by president. [2]Approximate figures. [3]Regarded as a governorate for administrative purposes. [4]Detail does not add to total given because of rounding. [5]Khat's (or qat's) agricultural contribution to GDP is about 2.4% of total GDP; khat cultivation employs nearly 15% of the labour force. [6]Virtually all natural gas was flared or reinjected for field pressure maintenance. [7]Includes petroleum refining. [8]Import duties. [9]Includes 795,316 unemployed. [10]Imports c.i.f.; exports f.o.b. [11]Yemenia airlines only. [12]Circulation of daily newspapers. [13]Subscribers. [14]1999–2000. [15]2002–03. [16]2008–09. [17]2006–07.

Internet resources for further information:
- **Central Bank of Yemen http://www.centralbank.gov.ye**
- **Central Statistical Organisation http://www.cso-yemen.org**

Zambia

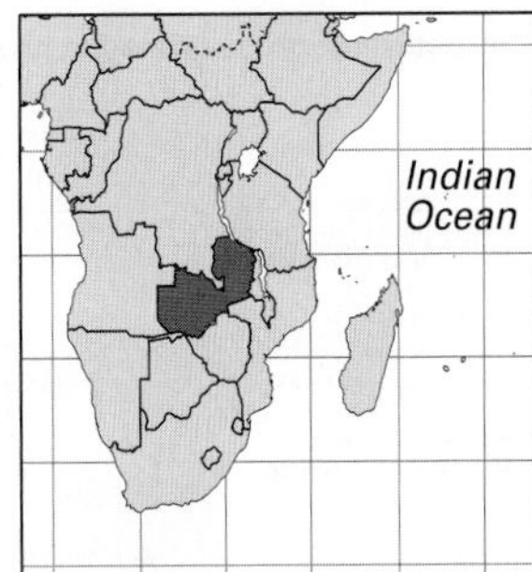

Official name: Republic of Zambia.
Form of government: multiparty republic with one legislative house (National Assembly [158[1]]).
Head of state and government: President.
Capital: Lusaka.
Official language: English.
Official religion: none[2].
Monetary unit: Zambian kwacha (K); valuation (Sept. 1, 2011) 1 U.S.$ = K 4,960; 1 £ = K 8,015.

Area and population

		area		population
				2010
Provinces	**Capitals**	sq mi	sq km	census[3]
Central	Kabwe	36,446	94,394	1,267,803
Copperbelt	Ndola	12,096	31,328	1,958,623
Eastern	Chipata	26,682	69,106	1,707,731
Luapula	Mansa	19,524	50,567	958,976
Lusaka	Lusaka	8,454	21,896	2,198,996
North-Western	Solwezi	48,582	125,827	706,462
Northern	Kasama	57,076	147,826	1,759,600
Southern	Livingstone	32,928	85,283	1,606,793
Western	Mongu	48,798	126,386	881,524
TOTAL		290,585[4]	752,612[4]	13,046,508

Demography

Population (2011): 13,306,000.
Density (2011): persons per sq mi 45.8, persons per sq km 17.7.
Urban-rural (2010): urban 35.7%; rural 64.3%.
Sex distribution (2009): male 50.03%; female 49.97%.
Age breakdown (2009): under 15, 46.6%; 15–29, 28.5%; 30–44, 14.3%; 45–59, 6.7%; 60–74, 3.2%; 75–84, 0.6%; 85 and over, 0.1%.
Population projection: (2020) 17,340,000; (2030) 22,547,000.
Doubling time: 23 years.
Ethnic composition (2000): Bemba 21.5%; Tonga 11.3%; Lozi 5.2%; Nsenga 5.1%; Tumbuka 4.3%; Ngoni 3.8%; Chewa 2.9%; other 45.9%.
Religious affiliation (2000): Christian 82.4%, of which Roman Catholic 29.7%, Protestant (including Anglican) 28.2%, independent Christian 15.2%, unaffiliated Christian 5.5%; traditional beliefs 14.3%; Bahāʾī 1.8%; Muslim 1.1%[5]; other 0.4%.
Major cities (2010): Lusaka 1,742,979; Kitwe 504,194; Ndola 455,194; Kabwe 202,914; Chingola 179,658.

Vital statistics

Birth rate per 1,000 population (2009): 44.6 (world avg. 20.3).
Death rate per 1,000 population (2009): 13.3 (world avg. 8.5).
Natural increase rate per 1,000 population (2009): 31.3 (world avg. 11.8).
Marriage/divorce rates per 1,000 population (2005): n.a./n.a.
Total fertility rate (avg. births per childbearing woman; 2009): 6.07.
Life expectancy at birth (2009): male 50.0 years; female 52.2 years.
Major causes of death by overall percentage (2004): fever/malaria 21.7%, diarrhea 11.8%, tuberculosis 10.4%, cough/chest infection 9.6%, abdominal pain 5.2%, lack of blood/anemia 5.1%.
Adult population (ages 15–49) *living with HIV* (2009): 13.5% (world avg. 0.8%).

National economy

Budget (June 2009). Revenue: K 6,441,000,000,000 (tax revenue 69.4%, of which income tax 36.7%, VAT 17.0%; grants 27.7%; nontax revenue 2.9%). Expenditures: K 7,469,000,000,000 (current expenditure 81.1%, of which wages and salaries 32.7%, goods and services 24.5%; capital expenditure 16.3%).
Production (metric tons except as noted). Agriculture, forestry, fishing (2009): sugarcane 2,500,000, corn (maize) 1,887,010, cassava 900,000, wheat 195,456, seed cotton 159,363, peanuts (groundnuts) 120,564, sweet potatoes 100,000, tobacco 75,335, sunflower seeds 8,000, fresh-cut flowers (value of sales; 2000) U.S.$21,000,000; livestock (number of live animals) 2,850,000 cattle, 2,000,000 goats, 340,000 pigs, 30,000,000 chickens; roundwood (2010) 10,303,029 cu m, of which fuelwood 87%; fisheries production 93,221 (from aquaculture 9%). Mining and quarrying (2009): copper (metal content) 697,000; cobalt (metal content) 2,300; amethyst 1,400,000 kg; emeralds 2,500 kg. Manufacturing (2005): cement 435,000; refined copper 399,000; vegetable oils (2001) 11,800; refined cobalt 5,422. Energy production (consumption): electricity (kW-hr; 2007) 9,853,000,000 (9,585,000,000); hard coal (metric tons; 2007) 276,000 (182,000); crude petroleum (barrels; 2007) none (4,794,000); petroleum products (metric tons; 2007) 590,000 (604,000); natural gas, none (none).
Household income and expenditure. Average household size (2007) 4.9; average annual income per household (2004) K 6,024,360 (U.S.$1,261); expenditure (1993–94)[6]: food, beverages, and tobacco 57.1%, transportation and communications 9.6%, housing and energy 8.5%, household furnishings 8.2%.
Selected balance of payments data. Receipts from (U.S.$'000,000): tourism (2009) 98; remittances (2010) 44; foreign direct investment (2008–10 avg.) 892; official development assistance (2009) 1,269. Disbursements for (U.S.$'000,000): tourism (2009) 39; remittances (2009) 66.
Population economically active (2008): total 4,689,000; activity rate of total population 37.2% (participation rates: ages 15–64, 69.5%; female 43.7%; unemployed [2006] 14.0%).

Price index (2005 = 100)

	2004	2005	2006	2007	2008	2009	2010
Consumer price index	84.5	100.0	109.0	120.6	135.7	153.8	166.9

Gross national income (GNI; 2010): U.S.$13,816,000,000 (U.S.$1,070 per capita); purchasing power parity GNI (U.S.$1,370 per capita).

Structure of gross domestic product and labour force

	2008		2000	
	in value K '000,000,000	% of total value	labour force	% of labour force
Agriculture, forestry, fishing	10,709	19.6	2,014,000	62.5
Mining	2,280	4.2	36,500	1.1
Manufacturing	5,273[7]	9.7[7]	77,500	2.4
Construction	8,516	15.6	36,800	1.1
Public utilities	1,525	2.8	11,000	0.3
Transp. and commun.	2,492	4.6	53,700	1.7
Trade, hotels	9,635	17.7	190,400	5.9
Finance, real estate	7,362	13.5	29,200	0.9
Pub. admin., defense	1,325	2.4	363,400	11.3
Services	4,183	7.7		
Other	1,205[8]	2.2[8]	409,800[9]	12.7[9]
TOTAL	54,505	100.0	3,222,200[4]	100.0[4]

Public debt (external, outstanding; 2009): U.S.$1,210,000,000.
Land use as % of total land area (2009): in temporary crops or left fallow 4.5%, in permanent crops 0.1%, in pasture 26.9%, forest area 66.8%.

Foreign trade[10]

Balance of trade (current prices)

	2003	2004	2005	2006	2007	2008
U.S.$'000,000	–306	+118	+86	+1,293	+899	+402
% of total	20.7%	3.3%	2.0%	19.7%	11.1%	4.2%

Imports (2008): U.S.$5,061,000,000 (machinery and apparatus 22.8%, petroleum 15.6%, base and fabricated metals 9.7%, road vehicles 9.4%, copper ore/concentrate 8.4%, fertilizers [all kinds] 6.1%). *Major import sources:* South Africa 42.6%; Dem. Rep. of the Congo 10.6%; Kuwait 10.2%; China 4.5%; India 3.8%.
Exports (2008): U.S.$5,099,000,000 (copper metal 64.2%, copper ore/concentrate 13.5%, cobalt 5.8%, food 3.9%). *Major export destinations:* Switzerland 49.8%; South Africa 10.4%; Egypt 7.5%; Dem. Rep. of the Congo 5.6%; China 5.6%.

Transport and communications

Transport. Railroads (*c.* 2003): route length (2007)[11] 1,340 mi, 2,157 km; passenger-km *c.* 150,000,000; metric ton-km cargo *c.* 530,000,000. Roads (2001): total length 56,818 mi, 91,440 km (paved 22%). Vehicles (2008): passenger cars 172,670; trucks and buses 91,835. Air transport (2007): passenger-km 60,000,000[12]; metric ton-km cargo, less than 500,000.

Communications

Medium	date	number in '000s	units per 1,000 persons	Medium	date	number in '000s	units per 1,000 persons
Televisions	2003	551	51	PCs	2005	131	11
Telephones				Dailies	2009	80[13]	6.1[13]
Cellular	2010	4,947[14]	378[14]	Internet users	2009	817	63
Landline	2010	90	6.9	Broadband	2010	11[14]	0.8[14]

Education and health

Educational attainment (2001–02)[15]. Percentage of population age 15 and over having: no formal schooling 14.4%; some primary education 33.4%; completed primary 19.7%; some secondary 22.0%; completed secondary 5.9%; higher 4.3%; unknown 0.3%. *Literacy* (2009): population age 15 and over literate 70.7%; males literate 80.6%; females literate 61.0%.

Education (2009)

	teachers	students	student/ teacher ratio	enrollment rate (%)
Primary (age 7–13)	48,075[16]	2,840,540	60.5[16]	91
Secondary/Voc. (age 14–18)	29,148[16]	707,744	23.2[16]	46
Tertiary	…	24,553[17]	…	2[17] (age 19–23)

Health: physicians (2004) 1,264 (1 per 8,672 persons); hospital beds (2004) 21,924 (1 per 500 persons); infant mortality rate (2009) 70.2; undernourished population (2006–08) 5,400,000 (44% of total population based on the consumption of a minimum daily requirement of 1,720 calories).

Military

Total active duty personnel (November 2010): 15,100 (army 89.4%; navy, none; air force 10.6%). *Military expenditure as percentage of GDP* (2009): 1.8%; per capita expenditure U.S.$18.

[1]Statutory number (including 8 nonelective seats). [2]Zambia is a Christian nation per the preamble of a constitutional amendment. [3]Preliminary. [4]Detail does not add to total given because of rounding. [5]3 to 4% in 2005. [6]Weights of consumer price index components. [7]Manufacturing includes the smelting of copper. [8]Taxes less imputed bank service charges. [9]Unemployed. [10]Imports f.o.b. in balance of trade and c.i.f. in commodities and trading partners. [11]Includes 554 mi (891 km) of the Tanzania-Zambia Railway Authority. [12]Zambian Airways. [13]Circulation of daily newspapers. [14]Subscribers. [15]Based on a sample survey of 19,531 persons. [16]2008. [17]2000.

Internet resources for further information:
- **Zambia Central Statistical Office http://www.zamstats.gov.zm**
- **Bank of Zambia http://www.boz.zm**

Zimbabwe

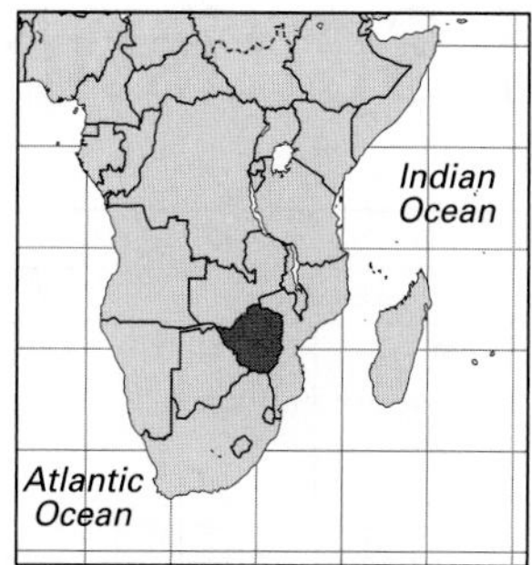

Official name: Republic of Zimbabwe.
Form of government: transitional regime with two legislative houses (Senate [100[1]]; House of Assembly [214[2]]).
Heads of state and government: President/Prime Minister/Cabinet[3].
Capital: Harare.
Official language: English.
Official religion: none.
Monetary unit: [4, 5].

Area and population

		area		population
Provinces	Capitals	sq mi	sq km	2002 preliminary census
Bulawayo	—	185	479	676,787
Harare	—	337	872	1,903,510
Manicaland	Mutare	14,077	36,459	1,566,889
Mashonaland Central	Bindura	10,945	28,347	998,265
Mashonaland East	Marondera	12,444	32,230	1,125,355
Mashonaland West	Chinhoyi	22,178	57,441	1,222,583
Masvingo	Masvingo	21,840	56,566	1,318,705
Matabeleland North	Lupane	28,967	75,025	701,359
Matabeleland South	Gwanda	20,916	54,172	654,879
Midlands	Gweru	18,983	49,166	1,466,331
TOTAL		150,872	390,757	11,634,663

Demography

Population (2011): 12,084,000[6].
Density (2011): persons per sq mi 80.1, persons per sq km 30.9.
Urban-rural (2010): urban 38.3%; rural 61.7%.
Sex distribution (2010): male 47.26%; female 52.74%.
Age breakdown (2010): under 15, 43.9%; 15–29, 28.7%; 30–44, 13.8%; 45–59, 7.9%; 60–74, 4.2%; 75–84, 1.2%; 85 and over, 0.3%.
Population projection: (2020) 15,832,000; (2030) 18,820,000.
Ethnic composition (2003): Shona 71%; Ndebele 16%; other African 11%; white 1%; mixed race/Asian 1%.
Religious affiliation (2005): African independent Christian *c.* 38%; traditional beliefs *c.* 25%; Protestant *c.* 14%; Roman Catholic *c.* 8%; Muslim *c.* 1%; other (mostly unaffiliated Christian) *c.* 14%.
Major cities (2002): Harare (urban agglomeration; 2010) 1,631,594; Bulawayo 676,787; Chitungwiza 321,782; Mutare 170,106; Gweru 141,260.

Vital statistics

Birth rate per 1,000 population (2010): 31.6 (world avg. 19.2).
Death rate per 1,000 population (2010): 14.9 (world avg. 8.2).
Total fertility rate (avg. births per childbearing woman; 2010): 3.66.
Life expectancy at birth (2010): male 48.0 years; female 47.1 years.
Adult population (ages 15–49) *living with HIV* (2009): 14.3% (world avg. 0.8%).
Major causes of death per 100,000 population (2002): HIV/AIDS-related *c.* 1,406; cardiovascular diseases *c.* 142; lower respiratory infections *c.* 84; tuberculosis *c.* 55; malignant neoplasms (cancers) *c.* 54.

National economy

Budget (2009). Revenue: U.S.$933,600,000 (tax revenue 94.5%, of which VAT 39.3%, income tax 23.7%; nontax revenue 5.5%). Expenditures: U.S.$920,-900,000 (current expenditures 87.3%; capital expenditure 4.9%).
Public debt (external, outstanding; January 2011): U.S.$3,493,000,000.
Population economically active (2008): total 5,836,000; activity rate of total population 46.8% (participation rates: ages 15–64 [2003] 74.0%; female 43.2%; unemployed [2009] *c.* 95%).

Price index (2002 = 100)

	2002	2003	2004	2005	2006	2007	2008
Consumer price index	100.0	575.0	2,150	8,675	103,750	25,432,300	...[7]

Production (metric tons except as noted). Agriculture, forestry, fishing (2009): sugarcane 3,100,000, corn (maize) 700,000, seed cotton 236,000, cassava 216,149, soybeans 110,000, bananas 102,352, oranges 96,504, tobacco 96,367, peanuts (groundnuts) 92,850, sorghum 70,000, tea 20,862, sunflower seeds 10,000, jute 3,277, coffee (green) 1,740; livestock (number of live animals) 5,030,000 cattle, 2,894,600 goats, 630,000 pigs, 380,000 sheep; roundwood (2010) 9,396,476 cu m, of which fuelwood 92%; fisheries production 13,152 (from aquaculture 20%). Mining and quarrying (2009): chromite 193,673; nickel[8] 4,858; copper[8] 3,572; cobalt[8] 74; platinum-group metals (palladium, platinum, rhodium, ruthenium, and iridium) 14,600 kg; gold 4,965 kg; diamonds 963,502 carats[9]. Manufacturing (value added in U.S.$'000,000; 1998): beverages 171; foodstuffs 148; textiles 99; iron and steel 86; fabricated metal products 64; cement, bricks, and tiles 63; tobacco products 51. Energy production (consumption): electricity (kW-hr; 2008) 8,890,000,000 (10,890,000,-000); coal (metric tons; 2007) 3,237,000 (3,306,000); crude petroleum, none (none); petroleum products (metric tons; 2007) none (599,000).
Household income and expenditure. Average household size (2004) 4.5; expenditure (2001)[10]: food and nonalcoholic beverages 31.9%, housing and energy 16.2%, household furnishings 15.1%, transportation 9.8%.
Land use as % of total land area (2007): in temporary crops or left fallow 8.3%, in permanent crops 0.3%, in pasture 31.3%, forest area 43.7%.
Gross national income (2010): U.S.$5,841,000,000 (U.S.$460 per capita).

Structure of gross domestic product and labour force

	2008		2002	
	in value Z$'000,000,000,000	% of total value	labour force	% of labour force
Agriculture, forestry, fishing	351,723	22.4	2,800,000	56.4
Mining and quarrying	99,668	6.4	50,000	1.0
Manufacturing	103,044	6.6	378,000	7.6
Construction	13,623	0.9	106,000	2.1
Public utilities	113,993	7.3	10,000	0.2
Transp. and commun.	154,989	9.9	102,000	2.1
Trade, restaurants	384,243	24.5	333,000	6.7
Finance, real estate	69,965	4.5	121,000	2.4
Services	139,494	8.9	578,000	11.7
Pub. admin., defense	22,172	1.4		
Other	113,318[11]	7.2[11]	485,000[12]	9.8[12]
TOTAL	1,566,233[13]	100.0	4,963,000	100.0

Selected balance of payments data. Receipts from (U.S.$'000,000): tourism (2009) 314; remittances, n.a.; foreign direct investment (FDI; 2008–10 avg.) 87; official development assistance (2009) 737. Disbursements for (U.S.$'000,-000): tourism (1998) 131; remittances, n.a.; FDI (2008–10 avg.) 14.

Foreign trade[14]

Balance of trade (current prices)

	2002	2003	2004	2005	2006	2007
U.S.$'000,000	−139	...	−278	−679	−3,851	−284
% of total	29.1%	...	6.7%	19.6%	42.8%	4.1%

Imports (2007): U.S.$3,594,400,000 (refined petroleum products 15.7%; chemicals and chemical products 12.6%; transportation equipment 9.3%; food and live animals 7.9%; base metals 4.7%). *Major import sources:* South Africa 42.8%; Botswana 11.4%; China 5.7%; Mozambique 4.8%; Malawi 4.8%.
Exports (2007)[9]: U.S.$3,310,200,000 (base metals 18.8%, of which iron and steel 12.6%, nickel 5.9%; machinery and apparatus 10.7%, of which transportation equipment 5.4%; food and live animals 8.6%; beverages and tobacco 8.4%; textile fibres 4.0%). *Major export destinations:* South Africa 37.4%; Mozambique 13.0%; U.K. 7.4%; Botswana 6.1%; Netherlands 4.6%.

Transport and communications

Transport. Railroads (2010): route length 2,129 mi, 3,427 km; passenger-km, n.a.; metric ton-km cargo (2007) 1,580,000,000. Roads (2002): total length 60,439 mi, 97,267 km (paved 19%). Vehicles: passenger cars (2002) 570,866; trucks and buses (2007) 202,361. Air transport (2008)[15]: passenger-km 882,000; metric ton-km cargo 17,000,000.

Communications

Medium	date	number in '000s	units per 1,000 persons	Medium	date	number in '000s	units per 1,000 persons
Televisions	2004	610	50	PCs	2007	1,257	101
Telephones				Dailies	2009	40[16]	3.2[16]
Cellular	2010	7,700[17]	613[17]	Internet users	2009	1,422	114
Landline	2010	379	30	Broadband	2010	33[17]	2.6[17]

Education and health

Educational attainment (2005–06)[18]. Percentage of population age 25 and over having: no formal schooling/unknown 13.6%; incomplete primary education 32.8%; complete primary 5.1%; secondary 43.2%; vocational/higher 5.3%.
Literacy (2009): percentage of total population age 15 and over literate 91.9%; males literate 94.7%; females literate 89.4%.

Education (2006)

	teachers	students	student/ teacher ratio	enrollment rate (%)
Primary (age 6–12)	64,001	2,445,520	38.2	90
Secondary/Voc. (age 13–18)	33,964[19]	831,488	22.3[19]	38
Tertiary[20]	4,081	94,611	23.2	6 (age 19–23)

Health: physicians (2004) 2,086 (1 per 5,792 persons); hospital beds (2006) 37,377 (1 per 333 persons); infant mortality rate (2010) 30.9; undernourished population (2004–06) 5,100,000 (39% of total population based on the consumption of a minimum daily requirement of 1,800 calories).

Military

Total active duty personnel (November 2010): 29,000 (army 86.2%, air force 13.8%). *Military expenditure as percentage of GDP* (2010): 1.8%; per capita expenditure U.S.$8.

[1]Includes 5 presidential appointees, 16 traditional chiefs, 10 provincial governors, and 9 others. [2]Includes 4 ex officio members. [3]Historic pact for the sharing of executive authority (Constitutional Amendment 19) entered into force Feb. 13, 2009. [4]The use of the Zimbabwe dollar (Z$) as legal currency was suspended indefinitely on April 12, 2009, because of long-term hyperinflation. [5]Multiple foreign currencies (including the U.S. dollar and South African rand) became legal tender in January 2009. [6]Includes 3 million Zimbabweans living outside of the country, many of whom are in South Africa. [7]Official year-on-year inflation rate in July 2008 was 231,000,000%; private sector estimates placed it at 80,000,000,000% or higher. Lack of commodities in shops and multiple price changes per day make precise calculation of CPI virtually impossible. [8]Metal content. [9]In November 2011, the Kimberley Process cleared sanctions on Zimbabwe, in place since 2009, that had prohibited the country from exporting diamonds. [10]Weights of consumer price index components. [11]Indirect taxes less imputed bank service charges. [12]Includes 298,000 unemployed. [13]Detail does not add to total given because of rounding. [14]Imports c.i.f.; exports f.o.b. [15]Air Zimbabwe. [16]Circulation of daily newspapers. [17]Subscribers. [18]Based on the 2005–06 Zimbabwe Demographic and Household Survey, comprising 16,082 people. [19]2003. [20]2009–10.

Internet resource for further information:
- **Reserve Bank of Zimbabwe www.rbz.co.zw**

Comparative National Statistics

World and regional summaries

region/bloc	area and population, 2011						gross national income						labour force, 2010[2]		
	area		population			population projection, 2030	total ('000,000 U.S.$), 2010	GNI per capita (U.S.$), 2010	% agricul-ture, 2000	% industry, 2000	% ser-vices, 2000	avg. annual growth rate, 2000–08[1]	total ('000)	% male	% female
	square miles	square kilometres	total	per sq mi	per sq km										
World	52,437,924	135,813,396	6,938,985,800	132.3	51.1	8,303,862,900	61,710,049	8,872	4	28	68	3.2	3,223,919	60.1	39.9
Africa	11,649,228	30,171,372	1,050,581,000	90.2	34.8	1,542,693,000	1,601,459	1,767	16	30	53	4.8	397,596	57.5	42.5
Central Africa	2,553,531	6,613,615	130,760,000	51.2	19.8	201,547,000	150,000	1,160	17	36	21	5.8	49,788	52.1	47.9
East Africa	2,441,964	6,324,657	326,333,000	133.6	51.6	520,111,000	192,048	597	28	17	54	4.4	148,503	51.5	48.5
North Africa	3,252,437	8,423,779	222,906,000	68.5	26.5	293,779,000	625,157	2,934	16	33	51	5.3	70,051	75.3	24.7
Southern Africa	1,032,582	2,674,378	58,072,000	56.2	21.7	64,003,000	333,877	9,456	3	28	68	4.2	21,481	56.8	43.2
West Africa	2,368,714	6,134,943	312,510,000	131.9	50.9	463,253,000	300,377	978	31	30	38	4.1	107,773	57.0	43.0
Americas	16,295,700	42,205,672	936,177,400	57.5	22.2	1,137,316,100	20,211,570	22,358	2	23	75	2.8	458,052	56.9	43.1
Anglo-America[4]	8,369,737	21,677,520	347,962,100	41.6	16.1	405,714,100	16,033,789	46,700	1	22	76	1.8	176,863	53.8	46.2
Canada	3,855,103	9,984,670	34,447,000	8.9	3.5	39,901,000	1,422,977[5]	42,170[5]	3	27	70	1.1	18,930	52.9	47.1
United States	3,678,190	9,526,468	313,387,000	85.2	32.9	365,683,000	14,600,828	47,140	1	22	77	2.4	157,933	53.9	46.1
Latin America	7,925,963	20,528,152	588,215,300	74.2	28.7	731,602,000	4,177,781	7,919	7	29	64	3.9	281,189	58.8	41.2
Caribbean	90,202	233,620	40,787,800	452.2	174.6	87,418,500	260,873	6,305	5	33	56	4.0	18,053	58.1	41.9
Central America	201,261	521,264	42,968,000	213.5	82.4	57,572,000	137,086	3,201	17	21	63	4.6	17,610	62.4	37.6
Mexico	758,450	1,964,375	114,492,000	151.0	58.3	135,251,000	1,012,316	9,330	4	27	69	2.7	49,605	63.5	36.5
South America	6,876,050	17,808,893	389,967,500	56.7	21.9	451,360,500	2,767,506	8,208	8	30	63	4.3	195,921	57.4	42.6
Andean Group	2,105,975	5,454,456	145,420,000	69.1	26.7	175,276,000	978,753	6,738	9	32	59	4.9	70,562	58.1	41.9
Brazil	3,287,612	8,514,877	192,813,000	58.7	22.6	216,410,000	1,380,392	9,390	8	31	60	3.6	101,601	56.4	43.6
Other South America	1,482,463	3,839,560	51,734,500	34.9	13.5	59,674,500	408,361	7,867	5	24	70	4.3	23,758	59.6	40.4
Asia	12,296,185	31,846,885	4,174,999,000	339.5	131.1	4,827,986,000	19,056,903	4,642	8	35	57	6.6	1,985,732	62.5	37.5
Eastern Asia	4,546,232	11,774,732	1,576,943,000	346.9	133.9	1,623,718,000	12,787,043	8,135	4	36	59	5.8	911,827	55.6	44.4
China	3,696,100	9,572,900	1,342,274,000	363.2	140.2	1,389,315,000	5,700,018	4,260	18	49	33	10.4	801,588	55.4	44.6
Japan	145,927	377,950	127,937,000	876.7	338.5	121,717,000	5,369,116	42,150	2	33	66	1.6	66,191	57.6	42.4
South Korea	38,486	99,678	48,755,000	1,266.8	489.1	50,655,000	972,299	19,890	6	49	45	4.5	24,264	58.7	41.3
Other Eastern Asia	665,719	1,724,204	57,977,000	87.1	33.6	62,031,000	745,610	12,919	1	22	73	6.5	19,784	52.7	47.3
South Asia	1,969,205	5,100,220	1,622,088,000	823.7	318.0	2,008,334,000	1,930,472	1,220	28	23	48	6.7	638,021	72.9	27.1
India	1,222,559	3,166,414	1,216,728,000	995.2	384.3	1,494,946,000	1,566,636	1,340	28	24	48	7.9	472,580	74.7	25.3
Pakistan	340,499	881,889	187,343,000	550.2	212.4	242,862,000	182,537	1,050	24	18	58	5.4	59,739	79.3	20.7
Other South Asia	406,147	1,051,917	218,017,000	536.8	207.3	270,526,000	181,299	753	35	28	36	6.7	105,702	61.3	38.7
Southeast Asia	1,738,183	4,501,872	601,144,000	345.9	133.5	717,161,000	1,653,888	2,803	21	30	49	7.1	302,270	57.6	42.4
Southwest Asia	4,042,565	10,470,061	374,824,000	92.7	35.8	478,773,000	2,685,500	7,500	10	36	52	6.9	133,614	72.0	28.0
Central Asia	1,545,715	4,003,258	62,536,000	40.5	15.6	74,720,000	186,841	3,022	16	25	58	8.7	27,892	56.5	43.5
Gulf Cooperation Council	993,420	2,572,936	45,872,000	46.2	17.8	60,036,000	920,596	24,960	4	51	45	6.7	19,083	84.3	15.7
Iran	636,374	1,648,200	75,276,000	118.3	45.7	85,145,000	355,804	4,795	21	30	50	5.9	25,226	82.1	17.9
Other Southwest Asia	867,056	2,245,667	191,140,000	220.5	85.1	258,872,000	1,222,259	6,282	11	28	57	6.5	61,413	71.1	28.9
Europe	8,905,139	23,064,078	740,914,300	83.2	32.1	750,785,500	19,738,398	26,769	3	27	70	3.7	364,198	54.2	45.8
European Union (EU)	1,534,644	3,974,710	473,619,000	308.6	119.2	496,630,000	16,844,358	35,577	2	27	71	2.3	229,245	55.4	44.6
France	210,026	543,965	63,278,000	301.3	116.3	68,672,000	2,749,821	42,390	3	22	75	1.8	28,918	52.9	47.1
Germany	137,879	357,104	81,604,000	591.9	228.5	78,922,000	3,537,180	43,330	1	31	68	1.2	42,465	54.4	45.6
Italy	116,346	301,336	60,769,000	522.3	201.7	63,583,000	2,125,847	35,090	3	31	67	1.0	25,151	59.7	40.3
Spain	195,364	505,991	47,215,000	241.7	93.3	51,079,000	1,462,894	31,650	3	24	73	3.3	23,235	55.7	44.3
United Kingdom	93,851	243,073	62,675,000	667.8	257.8	70,493,000	2,399,292	38,540	1	26	73	2.5	31,707	54.1	45.9
Other EU	781,178	2,023,241	158,078,000	202.4	78.1	163,881,000	4,569,324	29,017	3	25	72	4.0	77,769	55.9	44.1
Other Western Europe[6]	205,532	532,324	13,697,300	66.6	25.7	15,777,500	918,418	75,818	2	29	67	2.2	7,225	53.7	46.3
Eastern Europe	7,164,963	18,557,044	253,598,000	35.4	13.7	238,378,000	1,975,622	7,764	7	32	61	6.5	127,728	52.0	48.0
Russia	6,601,700	17,098,200	142,707,000	21.6	8.4	136,374,000	1,404,179	9,910	7	35	59	6.7	76,185	51.2	48.8
Ukraine	233,062	603,628	45,672,000	196.0	75.7	40,936,000	137,917	3,010	11	30	59	7.2	22,999	50.7	49.3
Other Eastern Europe	330,201	855,216	65,219,000	197.5	76.3	61,068,000	433,526	6,446	7	30	62	5.7	28,544	55.1	44.9
Oceania	3,291,672	8,525,389	36,314,100	11.0	4.3	45,082,300	1,101,719	31,358	4	21	74	3.2	18,341	54.5	45.5
Australia	2,973,952	7,702,501	22,651,000	7.6	2.9	27,896,000	957,529[5]	43,770[5]	3	22	76	3.3	11,822	54.7	45.3
Pacific Ocean Islands	317,720	822,888	13,663,100	43.0	16.6	17,186,300	144,190	10,791	9	21	64	3.0	6,519	54.0	46.0

[1]Average annual growth rate of gross domestic product. [2]Estimates of the ILO Employment Trends Unit. [3]Refers only to the outstanding long-term external public and publicly guaranteed debt of the 114 developing countries that report under the World Bank's Debtor Reporting System (DRS). [4]Anglo-America includes Canada, the United States, Greenland, Bermuda, and St. Pierre and Miquelon. [5]2009.

Africa

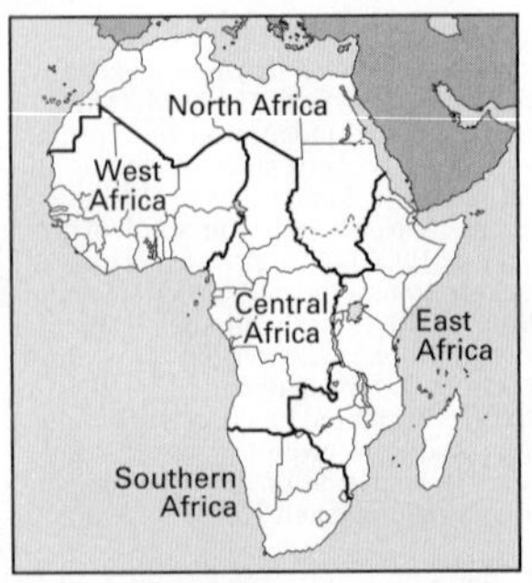

Americas

Asia

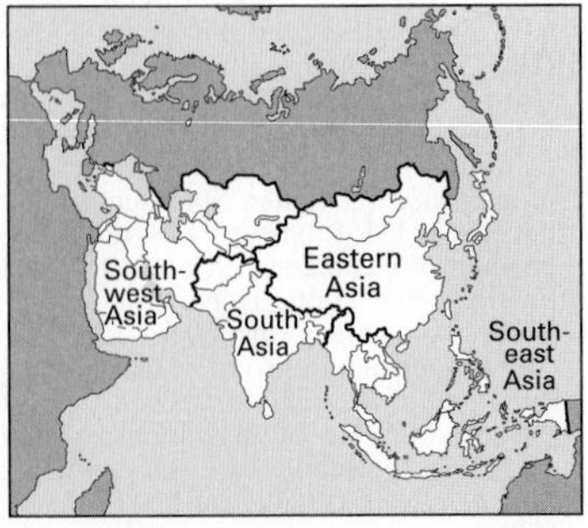

economic indicators							social indicators								region/bloc
pop. per 1,000 ha of arable land, 2002	electricity consumption (kW-hr per capita), 2004	trade ('000,000 U.S.$), 2001–03			debt ('000,000 U.S.$), 2008[3]		life expectancy (years), 2005		health			food (% FAO recommended minimum), 2004	literacy (%) (latest)		
		imports (c.i.f.)	exports (f.o.b.)	balance	total	% of GNI	male	female	pop. per doctor (latest)	infant mortality per 1,000 births, 2005	pop. having safe water (%), 2000		male	female	
4,387	2,717	6,930,434	6,744,616	−185,818	1,363,576	9.1	66.0	70.0	730	38.3	82	118	87.2	80.3	World
4,434	607	128,896	140,874	+11,978	188,226	14.5	51.8	53.8	2,560	78.4	64	103	72.2	53.8	Africa
4,365	137	8,854	16,653	+7,799	35,563	35.6	49.8	50.2	12,890	96.1	46	80	76.5	55.4	Central Africa
5,667	179	19,575	9,904	−9,671	26,573	19.9	46.9	48.2	13,620	86.7	50	86	72.5	54.9	East Africa
4,591	1,006	39,602	41,639	+2,037	77,115	15.1	67.2	71.0	890	39.2	87	125	77.1	58.5	North Africa
3,161	4,818	38,442	36,089	−2,353	14,569	4.8	47.8	51.2	1,610	55.1	85	119	89.3	88.1	Southern Africa
3,876	147	22,423	36,590	+14,167	34,406	13.4	47.7	49.7	6,260	94.3	65	109	63.3	42.3	West Africa
2,328	6,753	2,138,514	1,595,412	−543,102	408,702	10.8	71.5	77.6	520	17.1	91	129	93.1	91.9	Americas
1,441	14,647	1,528,316	976,367	−551,949	—	—	75.0	80.4	370	6.2	100	140	95.7	95.3	Anglo-America[4]
686	18,408	222,241	252,418	+30,177	—	—	76.7	83.6	540	4.8	100	136	96.6	96.6	Canada
1,637	14,240	1,305,092	723,609	−581,483	—	—	74.8	80.1	360	6.4	100	141	95.7	95.3	United States
3,692	2,056	610,198	619,045	+8,847	408,702	10.8	69.4	76.0	690	23.6	86	123	91.6	89.9	Latin America
7,532	1,946	134,133	113,899	−20,234	15,574	25.4	67.5	71.6	380	29.4	79	118	83.1	82.8	Caribbean
6,969	853	25,355	11,344	−14,011	27,370	22.4	67.9	73.7	950	21.4	88	106	84.0	79.4	Central America
4,153	2,190	168,651	160,670	−7,981	113,955	10.7	72.7	77.6	810	12.6	88	134	94.6	91.5	Mexico
3,253	2,160	120,755	158,917	+38,162	251,803	9.9	68.9	76.2	710	26.3	86	122	92.4	91.4	South America
9,110	1,790	56,520	68,915	+12,395	99,461	12.5	69.4	75.6	830	23.5	86	108	94.3	90.9	Andean Group
2,986	2,340	49,735	60,632	+10,897	73,623	5.2	67.7	75.9	770	30.7	87	132	89.8	90.2	Brazil
1,358	2,484	14,500	29,640	+15,140	78,719	24.0	72.1	79.4	410	17.5	82	120	97.3	97.1	Other South America
7,318	1,565	1,799,979	2,028,586	+228,607	561,163	7.4	67.2	70.3	970	39.6	81	116	87.4	81.1	Asia
9,736	2,525	1,179,486	1,321,391	+141,905	90,936	2.5	71.2	75.0	610	22.3	78	121	97.1	91.5	Eastern Asia
9,005	1,684	295,170	325,596	+30,426	89,283	2.4	70.4	73.7	620	25.2	75	123	96.7	90.5	China
28,837	8,459	383,452	471,996	+88,544	—	—	78.6	85.6	530	2.7	97	110	100.0	100.0	Japan
28,282	7,716	149,572	160,855	+11,283	—	—	71.7	79.3	740	6.4	92	123	99.2	96.6	South Korea
6,672	4,276	351,292	362,945	+11,653	1,653	37.1	71.7	77.3	500	13.8	94	93	97.3	90.8	Other Eastern Asia
6,864	546	91,054	75,813	−15,241	153,411	10.2	63.3	64.6	2,100	60.5	85	108	73.9	67.3	South Asia
6,490	618	61,118	52,471	−8,647	76,904	6.3	63.6	65.2	1,920	56.3	84	112	77.2	75.2	India
6,805	564	13,013	11,910	−1,103	39,359	24.2	64.7	65.5	1,840	76.2	90	100	66.8	40.0	Pakistan
9,923	157	16,923	11,432	−5,491	37,148	30.9	60.4	60.5	5,080	71.0	85	97	63.2	49.5	Other South Asia
8,406	862	353,337	410,291	+56,954	183,226	16.0	66.8	71.9	3,120	33.9	78	123	94.5	89.5	Southeast Asia
3,508	2,845	176,101	221,090	+44,989	133,590	10.5	67.3	71.9	610	35.5	85	118	93.0	82.5	Southwest Asia
1,876	2,678	12,654	15,806	+3,152	8,978	6.2	61.0	68.9	330	54.0	82	99	99.6	99.2	Central Asia
8,843	8,580	79,974	121,229	+41,255	—	—	73.4	77.5	620	12.7	95	117	90.3	83.5	Gulf Cooperation Council
4,455	2,460	20,336	28,356	+8,020	8,902	2.6	68.6	71.4	1,200	41.6	92	131	88.7	80.3	Iran
3,868	1,908	63,138	55,700	−7,438	115,710	14.8	67.6	71.9	690	31.6	82	119	93.2	77.8	Other Southwest Asia
2,534	6,440	2,932,353	3,068,534	+136,181	204,421	8.6	71.0	79.1	300	7.2	98	130	99.1	98.0	Europe
4,422	6,936	2,667,945	2,727,170	+59,225	51,013	9.8	75.5	81.8	290	4.8	100	137	99.4	99.0	European Union (EU)
3,223	8,231	362,398	357,881	−4,517	—	—	76.7	83.8	330	3.6	100	142	98.9	98.7	France
6,997	7,442	601,761	748,531	+146,770	—	—	75.8	82.0	290	4.1	100	131	100.0	100.0	Germany
6,935	6,029	242,744	251,003	+8,259	—	—	77.6	83.2	180	5.9	100	151	99.1	98.5	Italy
3,054	6,412	165,920	125,872	−40,048	—	—	76.7	83.2	240	4.4	99	138	98.4	96.9	Spain
10,296	6,756	399,478	320,057	−79,421	—	—	75.9	81.0	720	5.1	100	137	100.0	100.0	United Kingdom
3,436	6,722	895,644	923,825	+28,181	51,013	9.8	73.6	80.3	320	5.2	100	133	99.5	98.9	Other EU
9,474	15,621	125,857	153,411	+27,554	—	—	78.5	83.5	480	3.8	100	131	100.0	100.0	Other Western Europe[6]
1,427	5,060	138,550	187,954	+49,404	153,408	8.2	62.3	73.8	290	11.7	95	119	98.5	96.2	Eastern Europe
1,177	6,425	52,410	125,960	+73,550	103,246	7.6	59.9	73.3	240	11.5	99	117	99.7	99.4	Russia
1,481	3,727	16,976	17,927	+951	10,726	7.2	62.2	74.0	330	10.0	98	120	99.8	99.6	Ukraine
2,496	3,083	69,164	44,066	−25,098	39,436	11.3	67.3	74.7	370	13.4	84	121	95.1	86.9	Other Eastern Europe
564	8,660	91,999	85,427	−6,572	1,064	16.3	74.5	79.4	480	14.7	87	117	92.5	90.8	Oceania
407	11,849	69,260	66,366	−2,894	—	—	78.5	83.3	400	4.7	100	116	100.0	100.0	Australia
1,498	3,741	22,738	19,061	−3,677	1,064	16.3	68.3	73.3	770	30.1	67	118	80.1	75.6	Pacific Ocean Islands

[6]Other Western Europe includes Andorra, Faroe Islands, Gibraltar, Guernsey, Iceland, Isle of Man, Jersey, Liechtenstein, Monaco, Norway, San Marino, and Switzerland.

Europe

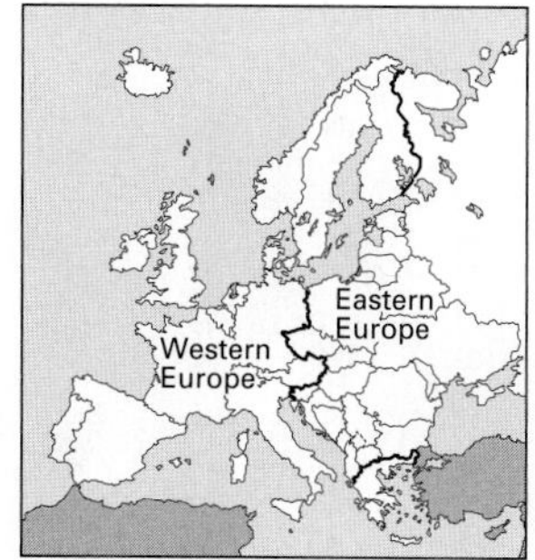

Eastern Europe

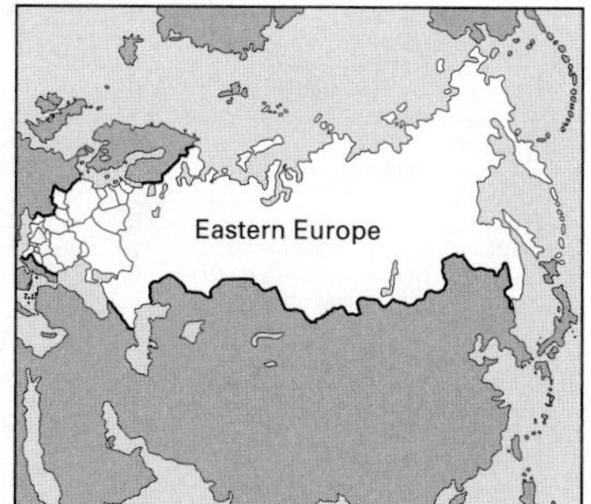

Oceania

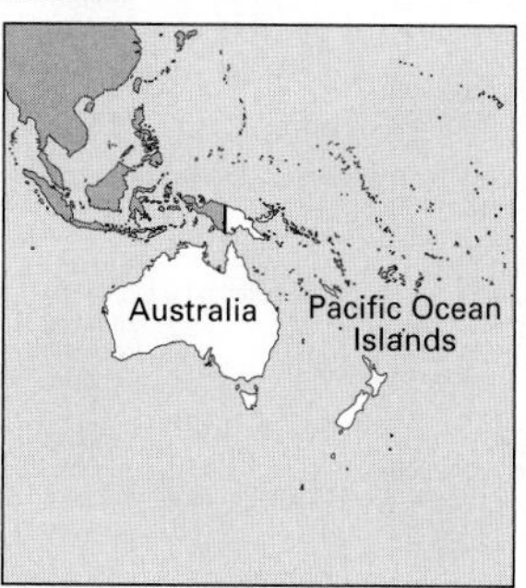

Government and international organizations

This table summarizes principal facts about the governments of the countries of the world, their branches and organs, the topmost layers of local government constituting each country's chief administrative subdivisions, and the participation of their central governments in the principal intergovernmental organizations of the world.

In this table "date of independence" may refer to a variety of circumstances. In the case of the newest countries, those that attained full independence after World War II, the date given is usually just what is implied by the heading—the date when the country, within its present borders, attained full sovereignty over both its internal and external affairs. In the case of longer established countries, the choice of a single date may be somewhat more complicated, and grounds for the use of several different dates often exist. The reader should refer to appropriate Britannica articles on national histories and relevant historical acts.

The date of the current, or last, constitution is in some ways a less complicated question, but governments sometimes do not, upon taking power, either adhere to existing constitutional forms or trouble to terminate the previous document and legitimize themselves by the installation of new constitutional forms. Often, however, the desire to legitimize extraconstitutional political activity by associating it with existing forms of long precedent leads to partial or incomplete modification, suspension, or abrogation of a constitution, so that the actual day-to-day conduct of government may be largely unrelated to the provisions of a constitution still theoretically in force.

The characterizations adopted under "type of government" represent a compromise between the forms provided for by the national constitution and the more pragmatic language that a political scientist might adopt to describe these same systems. For an explanation of the application of these terms in the Britannica World Data, *see* the Glossary at page 525.

The positions denoted by the terms "head of state" and "head of government" are usually those identified with those functions by the constitution. The duties of the head of state may range from largely ceremonial responsibilities, with little or no authority over the day-to-day conduct of government, to complete executive authority as the effective head of government. In certain countries, an individual outside the constitutional structure may exercise the powers of both positions.

Membership in the legislative house(s) of each country as given here includes all elected or appointed members, as well as ex officio members (those who by virtue of some other office or title are members of the body), whether voting or nonvoting. The legislature of a country with a unicameral system is shown as the upper house in this table.

The number of administrative subdivisions for each country is listed down to the second level. In some instances, planning or statistical subdivisions may be substituted when administrative subdivisions do not exist.

Government and international organizations

country	date of independence[a]	date of current or last constitution[b]	type of government	executive branch[c]		legislative branch[d]		admin. subdivisions		seaward claims	
				head of state	head of government	upper house (members)	lower house (members)	first-order (number)	second-order (number)	territorial (nautical miles)	fishing/economic (nautical miles)
Afghanistan	Aug. 19, 1919	Jan. 26, 2004	Islamic republic	—president—		102	249	34	364	—	—
Albania	Nov. 28, 1912	Nov. 28, 1998	republic	president	prime minister	140	—	12	36	12	[2]
Algeria	July 5, 1962	Nov. 12, 2008[3]	republic	—president[4]—		144	389	48	553	12	[5]
American Samoa	—	July 1, 1967	territory (U.S.)	U.S. president	governor	18	20[6]	—	5[7]	12	200
Andorra	Dec. 6, 1288	May 4, 1993	parl. coprincipality	[8]	head of govt.	28	—	7	…	—	—
Angola	Nov. 11, 1975	Feb. 5, 2010	republic	—president—		220	—	18	164	12	200
Antigua and Barbuda	Nov. 1, 1981	Nov. 1, 1981	constitutional monarchy	British monarch	prime minister	17	17[9]	17	—	12[10]	200[10]
Argentina	July 9, 1816	Aug. 24, 1994[11]	federal republic	—president—		72	257	24	376[12]	12	200
Armenia	Sept. 23, 1991	Nov. 27, 2005[13]	republic	president	prime minister	131	—	11	926	—	—
Aruba	—	Jan. 1, 1986	autonomous state (Neth.)	Dutch monarch	[14]	21	—	…	…	12	200
Australia	Jan. 1, 1901	Jan. 1, 1901	federal parl. state[16]	British monarch	prime minister	76	150	8	563[17]	12	200
Austria	Oct. 30, 1918	Oct. 1, 1920[18]	federal state	president	chancellor	62	183	9	99	—	—
Azerbaijan	Aug. 30, 1991	March 18, 2009[19]	republic	—president[4]—		125	—	80	…	…	…
Bahamas, The	July 10, 1973	July 10, 1973	constitutional monarchy	British monarch	prime minister	16	41	33[20]	…	12[10]	200[10]
Bahrain	Aug. 15, 1971	Feb. 14, 2002	constitutional monarchy	monarch	prime minister	40	40	5	…	12	…
Bangladesh	March 26, 1971	Dec. 16, 1972	republic	president	prime minister	345	—	7	64	12	200
Barbados	Nov. 30, 1966	Nov. 30, 1966	constitutional monarchy	British monarch	prime minister	21	30	—	—	12	200[21]
Belarus	Aug. 25, 1991	Nov. 27, 1996[22]	republic	—president[4]—		64[23]	110	7	118	—	—
Belgium	Oct. 4, 1830	July 14, 1993[24]	fed. const. monarchy	monarch	prime minister	71[25]	150	[26]	10	12	[27]
Belize	Sept. 21, 1981	Sept. 21, 1981	constitutional monarchy	British monarch	prime minister	12[28]	31[28]	[29]	…	12[30]	200
Benin	Aug. 1, 1960	Dec. 2, 1990	republic	—president—		83	—	12	77	200	200
Bermuda	—	June 8, 1968	overseas territory (U.K.)	British monarch	[31]	11	36	11	—	12	200
Bhutan	March 24, 1910	July 18, 2008	constitutional monarchy	monarch	prime minister	25	47	20	47	—	—
Bolivia	Aug. 6, 1825	Feb. 7, 2009	republic	—president—		36	130	9	…	—	—
Bosnia and Herzegovina	March 3, 1992	Dec. 14, 1995[32]	emerging fed. republic	[33]	chairman CM	15	42	3	10	…	…
Botswana	Sept. 30, 1966	Sept. 30, 1966	republic	—president—		35[34]	63	9	7[35]	—	—
Brazil	Sept. 7, 1822	Oct. 5, 1988[18]	federal republic	—president—		81	513	27	5,565	12	200
Brunei	Jan. 1, 1984	Sept. 29, 1959[36]	monarchy (sultanate)	—sultan—		33[34]	—	4	38	12	200
Bulgaria	Oct. 5, 1908	July 12, 1991	republic	president	prime minister	240	—	28	264	12	200
Burkina Faso	Aug. 5, 1960	June 11, 1991	republic	president	prime minister	111	—	13	45	—	—
Burundi	July 1, 1962	March 18, 2005	republic	—president[37]—		41	106	17	117	—	—
Cambodia	Nov. 9, 1953	March 4, 1999[38]	constitutional monarchy	king	prime minister	61	123	24	185	12	200
Cameroon	Jan. 1, 1960	Jan. 18, 1996	republic	president	prime minister	180	—	10	58	12	[2, 39]
Canada	July 1, 1867	April 17, 1982	federal parl. state[16]	Canadian GG[40]	prime minister	105[23]	308	13	…	12	200
Cape Verde	July 5, 1975	Sept. 25, 1992	republic	president	prime minister	72	—	22	32	12[10]	200[10]
Cayman Islands	—	Nov. 6, 2009	overseas territory (U.K.)	British monarch	[31]	20[41]	—	…	1	…	…
Central African Republic	Aug. 13, 1960	Dec. 27, 2004	republic	president	prime minister	105	—	17	71	—	—
Chad	Aug. 11, 1960	April 14, 1996	republic	president	prime minister	188	—	22	62	—	—
Chile	Sept. 18, 1810	Sept. 17, 2005[38]	republic	—president—		38	120	15	54	12	200
China	1523 BC	Dec. 4, 1982	people's republic	president	premier SC	3,000[23]	—	31	333	12	200
Colombia	July 20, 1810	July 6, 1991	republic	—president—		102	166	33	1,102	12	200
Comoros	July 6, 1975	May 23, 2009	republic	—president[37]—		33	—	3	4	12[10]	200[10]
Congo, Dem. Rep. of the	June 30, 1960	Feb. 18, 2006	republic	—president[4]—		108	500	26[42]	…	12	200
Congo, Rep. of the	Aug. 15, 1960	Aug. 10, 2002	republic	—president—		72[23]	137	16	84	12	200
Costa Rica	Sept. 15, 1821	Nov. 9, 1949	republic	—president—		57	—	7	81	12	200
Côte d'Ivoire	Aug. 7, 1960	July 23, 2000	republic	—president[4]—		255[23]	—	19	…	12	200
Croatia	June 25, 1991	Dec. 22, 1990	republic	president	prime minister	153	—	21	…	12	[44]
Cuba	May 20, 1902	Feb. 24, 1976	socialist republic	—president—		614	—	15	168	12	200
Curaçao	—	Oct. 20, 2010	autonomous state (Neth.)	Dutch monarch	[14]	21	—	…	…	12	12
Cyprus[46]	Aug. 16, 1960	Aug. 16, 1960	republic	—president—		56[47]	—	…	…	12	…
Czech Republic	Jan. 1, 1993	Jan. 1, 1993	republic	president	prime minister	81	200	14	76	—	—
Denmark	*c.* 800	June 5, 1953	constitutional monarchy	monarch	prime minister	179	—	5	98	12	[48]
Djibouti	June 27, 1977	Sept. 15, 1992	republic	—president—		65	—	6	…	12	200
Dominica	Nov. 3, 1978	Nov. 3, 1978	republic	president	prime minister	32	—	…	41[49]	12	200
Dominican Republic	Feb. 27, 1844	Jan. 26, 2010	republic	—president—		32	183	32	153	12[10]	200[10]
East Timor	May 20, 2002	May 20, 2002	republic	president	prime minister	65	—	13	65	12	200
Ecuador	May 24, 1822	Oct. 20, 2008	republic	—president—		124	—	24	226	200[50]	…
Egypt	Feb. 28, 1922	*Sept. 11, 1971*	interim military regime	—president[4]—		(264[34])	(518)	29	254	12	[51]
El Salvador	Jan. 30, 1841	Dec. 20, 1983	republic	—president—		84	—	14	262	200	200
Equatorial Guinea	Oct. 12, 1968	Nov. 17, 1991	republic	—president[4]—		100	—	7	30	12	200
Eritrea	May 24, 1993	[52]	transitional regime	—president—		150	—	6	…	12	[53]
Estonia	Feb. 24, 1918	July 3, 1992	republic	president	prime minister	101	—	15	226	12[54]	[54]

Finally, in the second half of the table are listed the memberships each country maintains in the principal international intergovernmental organizations of the world. This part of the table may also be utilized to provide a complete membership list for each of these organizations as of Dec. 15, 2011.

Notes for the column headings

a. The date may also be either that of the organization of the present form of government or the inception of the present administrative structure (federation, confederation, union, etc.).
b. Constitutions whose dates are in italic type had been wholly or substantially suspended, abolished, or not made effective as of late 2011.
c. For abbreviations used in this column see the list on this page.
d. When a legislative body has been adjourned or otherwise suspended, figures in parentheses indicate the number of members in the legislative body as provided for in constitution or law.
e. 15 nations with judicial representation in ICJ in 2011.
f. 19 nations with judicial representation in the ICC in 2011 (the ICC entered into force in July 2002; 120 countries had ratified or acceded to the ICC statute by December 2011).
g. The European Union (EU) is the 20th member of the G-20.

International organizations, conventions

AC	Arctic Council
ACP	African, Caribbean, and Pacific (Cotonou Agreement) states
ADB	Asian Development Bank
APEC	Asia-Pacific Economic Co-operation
ASEAN	Association of Southeast Asian Nations
ATs	Antarctic Treaty signatories
AU	African Union
CARICOM	Caribbean Community and Common Market
ECOWAS	Economic Community of West African States
EU	The European Union
FAO	Food and Agriculture Org.
FZ	The Franc Zone
G-20	Group of Twenty
GECF	Gas Exporting Countries Forum
I-ADB	Inter-American Development Bank
IAEA	International Atomic Energy Agency
IBRD	International Bank for Reconstruction and Development
ICC	International Criminal Court
ICJ	International Court of Justice
IDA	International Development Association
IDB	Islamic Development Bank
ILO	International Labour Org.
IMF	International Monetary Fund
IMO	International Maritime Org.
ITU	International Telecommunication Union
LAS	League of Arab States (Arab League)
OAS	Organization of American States
OPEC	Organization of the Petroleum Exporting Countries
PC	Pacific Community
SCO	Shanghai Cooperation Org.
UNCTAD	United Nations Conference on Trade and Development
UNESCO	United Nations Educational, Scientific and Cultural Org.
UNIDO	United Nations Industrial Development Org.
WHO	World Health Org.
WTO	World Trade Org.

Abbreviations used in the executive-branch column

CM	Council of Ministers
FC	Federal Council
GC	General Council
GG	Governor-General
HAT	High Authority of Transition
NDC	National Defense Commission
Pc	Policy Council
SC	State Council
SSC	State Supreme Council
TNC	Transitional National Council

membership in international organizations																																					country
United Nations (date of admission)	UN organ★ and affiliated intergovernmental organizations																regional multipurpose																		economic		
	UNCTAD	ICJ★e	FAO	IAEA	IBRD	IDA	ILO	IMF	IMO	ITU	UNESCO	UNIDO	WHO	WTO	ICCf	The Commonwealth	AC	ASEAN	ATs	AU	EU	G-20g	SCO	LAS	OAS	PC	ACP	ADB	APEC	CARICOM	ECOWAS	FZ	I-ADB	IDB	OPEC	GECF	
1946	•		•	•	•	•	•	•		•	•	•	•	1														•						•			Afghanistan
1955	•		•	•	•	•	•	•	•	•	•	•	•	•											1									•			Albania
1962	•		•	•	•	•	•	•	•	•	•	•	•	1						•				•	1									•	•	•	Algeria
—										•																•											American Samoa
1993	•		•							•	•		•	1																							Andorra
1976	•		•	•	•	•	•	•	•	•	•	•	•	•						•					1		•								•		Angola
1981	•		•		•		•	•	•	•	•		•	•		•									•		•			•							Antigua and Barbuda
1945	•		•	•	•	•	•	•	•	•	•	•	•	•	•				•			•			•								•				Argentina
1992	•		•	•	•	•	•	•		•	•	•	•	•											1			•									Armenia
—							•	•		•	15																										Aruba
1945	•		•	•	•	•	•	•	•	•	•		•	•		•			•			•				•		•	•								Australia
1955	•		•	•	•	•	•	•	•	•	•	•	•	•					•		•				1			•					•				Austria
1992	•		•	•	•	•	•	•	•	•	•	•	•	1											1			•						•			Azerbaijan
1973	•		•		•	•	•	•	•	•	•	•	•	1		•									•		•			•			•				Bahamas, The
1971	•		•	•	•		•	•	•	•	•	•	•	•										•										•			Bahrain
1974	•		•	•	•	•	•	•	•	•	•	•	•	•		•												•						•			Bangladesh
1966	•		•		•	•	•	•	•	•	•	•	•	•		•									•		•			•			•				Barbados
1945	•		•	•	•		•	•		•	•	•	•	1					•																		Belarus
1945	•		•	•	•	•	•	•	•	•	•	•	•	•	•				•		•				1			•					•				Belgium
1981	•		•	•	•	•	•	•	•	•	•	•	•	•		•									•		•			•			•				Belize
1960	•		•	•	•	•	•	•	•	•	•	•	•	•						•					1		•				•	•		•			Benin
—										•																				15							Bermuda
1971	•		•		•	•		•		•	•	•	•	1														•									Bhutan
1945	•		•	•	•	•	•	•	•	•	•	•	•	•	•										•								•			•	Bolivia
1992	•		•	•	•	•	•	•	•	•	•	•	•	1											1												Bosnia and Herzegovina
1966	•		•	•	•	•	•	•		•	•	•	•	•	•	•				•							•										Botswana
1945	•	•	•	•	•	•	•	•	•	•	•	•	•	•	•				•			•		1	•								•				Brazil
1984	•				•		•	•	•	•	•		•	•		•		•										•	•					•			Brunei
1955	•		•	•	•		•	•	•	•	•	•	•	•	•				•		•				1												Bulgaria
1960	•		•	•	•	•	•	•		•	•	•	•	•						•							•				•	•		•			Burkina Faso
1962	•		•	•	•	•	•	•		•	•	•	•	•						•							•										Burundi
1955	•		•	•	•	•	•	•	•	•	•	•	•	•				•										•									Cambodia
1960	•		•	•	•	•	•	•	•	•	•	•	•	•		•				•							•					•		•			Cameroon
1945	•		•	•	•	•	•	•	•	•	•		•	•		•	•		•			•			•			•	•				•				Canada
1975	•		•	•	•	•	•	•	•	•	•	•	•	•						•							•				•						Cape Verde
—										•	15																			15							Cayman Islands
1960	•		•	•	•	•	•	•		•	•	•	•	•						•							•					•					Central African Republic
1960	•		•	•	•	•	•	•		•	•	•	•	•						•							•				1	•		•			Chad
1945	•		•	•	•	•	•	•	•	•	•	•	•	•					•						•				•				•				Chile
1945	•	•	•	•	•	•	•	•	•	•	•	•	•	•					•			•	•		1			•	•				•				China
1945	•		•	•	•	•	•	•	•	•	•	•	•	•					•						•								•				Colombia
1975	•		•		•	•	•	•	•	•	•	•	•	1						•				•			•					•		•			Comoros
1960	•		•	•	•	•	•	•	•	•	•	•	•	•						•							•										Congo, Dem. Rep. of the
1960	•		•	•	•	•	•	•	•	•	•	•	•	•						•							•					•					Congo, Rep. of the
1945	•		•	•	•	•	•	•	•	•	•	•	•	•	•										•								•				Costa Rica
1960	•		•	•	•	•	•	•	•	•	•	•	•	•						•							•				43	•		•			Côte d'Ivoire
1992	•		•	•	•	•	•	•	•	•	•	•	•	•											1								•				Croatia
1945	•		•	•			•		•	•	•	•	•	•					•						45		•										Cuba
—								•			15																										Curaçao
1960	•		•	•	•	•	•	•	•	•	•	•	•	•		•					•				1												Cyprus[46]
1993	•		•	•	•	•	•	•	•	•	•	•	•	•					•		•				1												Czech Republic
1945	•		•	•	•	•	•	•	•	•	•	•	•	•			•		•		•				1			•					•				Denmark
1977	•		•		•	•	•	•	•	•	•	•	•	•						•				•			•							•			Djibouti
1978	•		•	•	•	•	•	•	•	•	•	•	•	•		•									•		•			•							Dominica
1945	•		•	•	•	•	•	•	•	•	•	•	•	•											•		•						•				Dominican Republic
2002	•		•		•	•	•	•	•	•	•	•	•					1									•	•									East Timor
1945	•		•	•	•	•	•	•	•	•	•	•	•	•					•						•								•		•		Ecuador
1945	•		•	•	•	•	•	•	•	•	•	•	•	•						•				•	1									•		•	Egypt
1945	•		•	•	•	•	•	•	•	•	•	•	•	•											•								•				El Salvador
1968	•		•		•	•	•	•	•	•	•	•	•	1						•					1		•					•				•	Equatorial Guinea
1993	•		•	•	•	•	•	•	•	•	•	•	•							•				1			•										Eritrea
1991	•		•	•	•	•	•	•	•	•	•		•	•					•		•				1												Estonia

Government and international organizations (continued)

country	date of independence[a]	date of current or last constitution[b]	type of government	executive branch[c]: head of state	executive branch[c]: head of government	legislative branch[d]: upper house (members)	legislative branch[d]: lower house (members)	admin. subdivisions: first-order (number)	admin. subdivisions: second-order (number)	seaward claims: territorial (nautical miles)	seaward claims: fishing/economic (nautical miles)
Ethiopia	c. 1000 BC	Aug. 22, 1995	federal republic	president	prime minister	135	547	11	68	—	—
Faroe Islands	—	April 1, 1948	[55]	Danish monarch	[56]	33	—	34	—	12	200
Fiji	Oct. 10, 1970	July 27, 1998[57]	interim regime	president	prime minister	(32)	(71)	4	15	12[10]	200[10]
Finland	Dec. 6, 1917	March 1, 2000	republic	president	prime minister	200	—	20	86[58]	12[54]	[54]
France	August 843	Oct. 4, 1958[18]	republic	president	prime minister	348	577	22[59]	96[59]	12	200
French Guiana	—	Feb. 28, 1983	[60]	French president	[61]	19[62]	31[63]	2	22	12	200
French Polynesia	—	Feb. 27, 2004	overseas collectivity (Fr.)	French president	[64]	57	—	5	48	12	200
Gabon	Aug. 17, 1960	March 26, 1991	republic	president	prime minister	102	120	9	49	12	200
Gambia, The	Feb. 18, 1965	Jan. 16, 1997	republic	—president—		53	—	8	39	12	200
Gaza Strip	—	May 4, 1994[65]	interim authority[66]	…	…	…	…	…	…	…	…
Georgia	April 9, 1991	Feb. 6, 2004	republic	—president[4]—		150	—	11[68]	[69]	12	…
Germany	May 5, 1955	May 23, 1949	federal republic	president	chancellor	69	622	16	22	12[48]	[27]
Ghana	March 6, 1957	Jan. 7, 1993	republic	—president—		230	—	10	138	12	200
Greece	Feb. 3, 1830	April 17, 2001[70]	republic	president	prime minister	300	—	14	325	6/10	[2]
Greenland	—	June 21, 2009[71]	[55]	Danish monarch	[56]	31	—	4	17/5[72]	12	200
Grenada	Feb. 7, 1974	Feb. 7, 1974	constitutional monarchy	British monarch	prime minister	13	15	—	—	12[10]	200[10]
Guadeloupe	—	Feb. 28, 1983	[60]	French president	[61]	40[62]	41[63]	2	32	12	200
Guam	—	Aug. 1, 1950	territory (U.S.)	U.S. president	governor	15	—	19	—	12	200
Guatemala	Sept. 15, 1821	Jan. 14, 1986	republic	—president—		158	—	22	333	12	200
Guernsey	—	Jan. 1, 1949[18]	crown dependency (U.K.)	British monarch[73]	chief minister Pc	47[74]	—	1	2	3	12
Guinea	Oct. 2, 1958	May 7, 2010	republic	—president[4]—		155[34]	—	8	33	12	200
Guinea-Bissau	Sept. 10, 1974	—	republic	—president[4]—		102	—	9	37	12	200
Guyana	May 26, 1966	Oct. 6, 1980	republic	—president—		65[75]	—	10	…	12	200
Haiti	Jan. 1, 1804	March 29, 1987	republic	president	prime minister	30	99	10	41	12	200
Honduras	Nov. 5, 1838	Jan. 20, 1982	republic	—president—		128	—	18	298	12	200
Hong Kong	—	July 1, 1997	[76]	Chinese president	chief executive	60	—	18	—	…	…
Hungary	Nov. 16, 1918	Aug. 20, 1949[77]	republic	president	prime minister	386	—	20	328[78]	—	—
Iceland	June 17, 1944	June 17, 1944	republic	president	prime minister	63	—	76	—	12	200
India	Aug. 15, 1947	Jan. 26, 1950	federal republic	president	prime minister	245	545	35	626	12	200
Indonesia	Aug. 17, 1945	Aug. 17, 1945	republic	—president—		132[34]	560	33	349/91[79]	12[10]	200[10]
Iran	Oct. 7, 1906	Dec. 2–3, 1979	Islamic republic	—president[80]—		290	—	30	336	12	[48]
Iraq	Oct. 3, 1932	Oct. 15, 2005	republic	president	prime minister	325	—	…	…	12	…
Ireland	Dec. 6, 1921	Dec. 29, 1937	republic	president	prime minister	60	166	34	…	12	200
Isle of Man	—	[81]	crown dependency (U.K.)	British monarch[73]	chief minister CM	11	24	24	—	12[82]	…
Israel	May 14, 1948	June 1950[18]	republic	president	prime minister	120	—	6	15	12	[2]
Italy	March 17, 1861	Jan. 1, 1948	republic	president	prime minister	321	630	20	110	12	[83]
Jamaica	Aug. 6, 1962	Aug. 6, 1962	constitutional monarchy	British monarch	prime minister	21	60	13	—	12[10]	200[10]
Japan	c. 660 BC	May 3, 1947	constitutional monarchy	[84]	prime minister	242	480	47	784[85]	12[86]	200
Jersey	—	Jan. 1, 1949[18]	crown dependency (U.K.)	British monarch[73]	chief minister CM	58	—	…	—	12	…
Jordan	May 25, 1946	Jan. 8, 1952	constitutional monarchy	—king[4]—		60	120	12	52	3	[2]
Kazakhstan	Dec. 16, 1991	Sept. 6, 1995	republic	—president[4]—		47	107	16	175	—	—
Kenya	Dec. 12, 1963	Aug. 27, 2010	republic	—president[4]—		224	—	8	68	12	200
Kiribati	July 12, 1979	July 12, 1979	republic	—president—		46	—	6	…	12[10]	200[10]
Korea, North	Sept. 9, 1948	Sept. 5, 1998	socialist republic	—supreme leader/chairman NDC—		687	—	13	173	12	200
Korea, South	Aug. 15, 1948	Feb. 25, 1988	republic	—president[4]—		299	—	16	165[87]	12	200
Kosovo	Feb. 17, 2008	June 15, 2008	transitional republic	[88]	prime minister	120	—	30	—	—	—
Kuwait	June 19, 1961	Nov. 16, 1962	const. mon. (emirate)	—emir[4]—		65[89]	—	6	72	12	[2]
Kyrgyzstan	Aug. 31, 1991	June 27, 2010	interim regime	—president (interim)—		120	—	9	41	—	—
Laos	Oct. 23, 1953	Aug. 15, 1991	people's republic	president	prime minister	132	—	17	139	—	—
Latvia	Nov. 18, 1918	Nov. 7, 1922	republic	president	prime minister	100	—	118[90]	…	12	[48]
Lebanon	Nov. 26, 1941	Sept. 21, 1990	republic	president	prime minister	128	—	8	25	12	[44]
Lesotho	Oct. 4, 1966	April 2, 1993	constitutional monarchy	king	prime minister	33[34]	120	10	129	—	—
Liberia	July 26, 1847	Jan. 6, 1986	republic	—president—		30	73	15	136	200	[2]
Libya	Dec. 24, 1951	—	interim regime	chairman TNC	[91]	—	—	22	…	12	[27]
Liechtenstein	July 12, 1806	March 16, 2003	constitutional monarchy	prince	head of govt.	25	—	11	—	—	—
Lithuania	Feb. 16, 1918	Nov. 6, 1992	republic	president	prime minister	141	—	10	60	12	[48]
Luxembourg	May 10, 1867	Oct. 17, 1868	constitutional monarchy	grand duke	prime minister	22[34, 92]	60	3	116	—	—
Macau	—	Dec. 20, 1999	[76]	Chinese president	chief executive	29	—	…	…	…	…
Macedonia	Nov. 17, 1991	Nov. 20, 2001	republic	president	prime minister	123	—	84	…	—	—
Madagascar	June 26, 1960	Nov. 23, 2010	transitional regime	—president HAT[4]—		[93]	[93]	22	119	12	200
Malawi	July 6, 1964	May 18, 1994	republic	—president—		193	—	32	…	—	—
Malaysia	Aug. 31, 1957	Aug. 31, 1957	fed. const. monarchy	paramount ruler	prime minister	70	222	16	140	12	200
Maldives	July 26, 1965	Aug. 7, 2008	republic	—president—		77	—	8	…	12[10]	200[10]
Mali	Sept. 22, 1960	Feb. 25, 1992	republic	president	prime minister	147	—	9	49	—	—
Malta	Sept. 21, 1964	Dec. 13, 1974	republic	president	prime minister	69	—	68	—	12	25
Marshall Islands	Dec. 22, 1990	May 1, 1979	republic	—president—		12[34]	33	4	…	12[10]	200[10]
Martinique	—	Feb. 28, 1983	[60]	French president	[61]	45[62]	41[63]	4	34	12	200
Mauritania	Nov. 28, 1960	July 21, 1991	republic	—president[4]—		56	95	13	44	12	200
Mauritius	March 12, 1968	March 12, 1992	republic	president	prime minister	69	—	[94]	…	12[10]	200[10]
Mayotte	—	July 11, 2001	overseas dept. (Fr.)	French president	president GC	19	—	17	—	12	200
Mexico	Sept. 16, 1810	Feb. 5, 1917	federal republic	—president—		128	500	32	2,438	12	200
Micronesia	Dec. 22, 1990	Jan. 1, 1981	federal republic	—president—		14	—	4	74	12	200
Moldova	Aug. 27, 1991	Aug. 27, 1994	parliamentary republic	president	prime minister	101	—	35/1	…	—	—
Monaco	Feb. 2, 1861	April 12, 2002[38]	constitutional monarchy	prince	min. of state[95]	24	—	—	—	12	[2]
Mongolia	Feb. 12, 1992	Feb. 12, 1992	republic	president	prime minister	76	—	22	329	—	—
Montenegro	June 3, 2006	Oct. 22, 2007	republic	president	prime minister	81	—	21	—	…	…
Morocco	March 2, 1956	Oct. 7, 1996	constitutional monarchy	king	prime minister	270	395	16[96]	62[96]	12	200
Mozambique	June 25, 1975	Nov. 16, 2004	republic	—president—		250	—	11	128	12	200
Myanmar (Burma)	Jan. 4, 1948	March 1, 2011[97]	constitutional republic	—president[37]—		224[23]	440[23]	15	65	12	200
Namibia	March 21, 1990	March 21, 1990	republic	—president—		26	72	13	102	12	200
Nauru	Jan. 31, 1968	Jan. 31, 1968	republic	—president—		18	—	—	—	12	200
Nepal	Nov. 13, 1769	Jan. 15, 2007[99]	republic	president	prime minister	601	—	14	75	—	—
Netherlands	March 30, 1814	Feb. 17, 1983	constitutional monarchy	monarch	prime minister	75	150	12	430	12	[27]
New Caledonia	—	March 19, 2003	unique collectivity (Fr.)	French president	[64]	54	—	3	33	12	200
New Zealand	Sept. 26, 1907	June 30, 1852[18]	constitutional monarchy	British monarch	prime minister	122	—	17	…	12	200
Nicaragua	April 30, 1838	Jan. 9, 1987	republic	—president—		92	—	17	153	12	200
Niger	Aug. 3, 1960	October 2010	republic	president	prime minister	113	—	8	36	—	—

membership in international organizations	UN organ★ and affiliated intergovernmental organizations															regional multipurpose																		economic		country
United Nations (date of admission)	UNCTAD	ICJ★[e]	FAO	IAEA	IBRD	IDA	ILO	IMF	IMO	ITU	UNESCO	UNIDO	WHO	WTO	ICC[f]	The Commonwealth	AC	ASEAN	ATs	AU	EU	G-20[g]	SCO	LAS	OAS	PC	ACP	ADB	APEC	CARICOM	ECOWAS	FZ	I-ADB	IDB	OPEC	GECF	
1945	●		●	●	●	●	●	●	●	●	●	●	●	1						●							●										Ethiopia
—			15						15	●	15						●																				Faroe Islands
1970	●		●		●	●	●	●	●	●	●	●	●	●		43										●	●	●									Fiji
1955	●		●	●	●		●	●	●	●	●	●	●	●	●		●		●		●				1			●					●				Finland
1945	●	●	●	●	●	●	●	●	●	●	●	●	●	●	●		1		●		●	●			1	●		●				●	●				France
—										●																						●					French Guiana
—										●																●						●					French Polynesia
1960	●		●	●	●	●	●	●	●	●	●	●	●	●						●							●					●		●			Gabon
1965	●		●		●	●	●	●	●	●	●	●	●	●		●				●							●				●			●			Gambia, The
—										●67	●67													●67										●67			Gaza Strip
1992	●		●	●	●	●	●	●	●	●	●	●	●	●											1			●									Georgia
1973	●	●	●	●	●	●	●	●	●	●	●	●	●	●	●		1		●		●	●			1			●					●				Germany
1957	●		●	●	●	●	●	●	●	●	●	●	●	●	●	●				●					1		●				●						Ghana
1945	●		●	●	●	●	●	●	●	●	●	●	●	●					●		●				1												Greece
—										●							●																				Greenland
1974	●		●		●	●	●	●	●	●	●	●	●	●		●									●		●			●							Grenada
—										●																						●					Guadeloupe
—										●																●											Guam
1945	●		●	●	●	●	●	●	●	●	●	●	●	●					●						●								●				Guatemala
—										●																											Guernsey
1958	●		●		●	●	●	●	●	●	●	●	●	●						●							●				●			●			Guinea
1974	●		●		●	●	●	●	●	●	●	●	●	●						●							●				●	●		●			Guinea-Bissau
1966	●		●		●	●	●	●	●	●	●	●	●	●		●									●		●			●			●				Guyana
1945	●		●	●	●	●	●	●	●	●	●	●	●	●											●		●			●			●				Haiti
1945	●		●	●	●	●	●	●	●	●	●	●	●	●											●								●				Honduras
—								●	15	●				●														●	●								Hong Kong
1955	●		●	●	●	●	●	●	●	●	●	●	●	●					●		●				1												Hungary
1946	●		●	●	●	●	●	●	●	●	●		●	●			●								1												Iceland
1945	●		●	●	●	●	●	●	●	●	●	●	●	●		●			●			●	1	1	1			●									India
1950	●		●	●	●	●	●	●	●	●	●	●	●	●				●				●						●	●					●			Indonesia
1945	●		●	●	●	●	●	●	●	●	●	●	●	1									1											●	●	●	Iran
1945	●		●	●	●	●	●	●	●	●	●	●	●	1										●										●	●		Iraq
1955	●		●	●	●	●	●	●	●	●	●	●	●	●							●				1			●									Ireland
—																																					Isle of Man
1949	●		●	●	●	●	●	●	●	●	●	●	●	●											1								●				Israel
1955	●		●	●	●	●	●	●	●	●	●	●	●	●	●				●		●	●			1			●					●				Italy
1962	●		●	●	●		●	●	●	●	●	●	●	●		●									●		●			●			●				Jamaica
1956	●	●	●	●	●	●	●	●	●	●	●	●	●	●	●				●			●			1			●	●				●				Japan
—										●																											Jersey
1955	●	●	●	●	●	●	●	●	●	●	●	●	●	●										●										●			Jordan
1992	●		●	●	●	●	●	●	●	●	●	●	●	1									●		1			●						●		1	Kazakhstan
1963	●		●	●	●	●	●	●	●	●	●	●	●	●	●	●				●							●										Kenya
1999	●		●		●	●	●	●	●	●	●		●			●										●	●	●									Kiribati
1991	●		●						●	●	●	●	●						●																		Korea, North
1991	●		●	●	●	●	●	●	●	●	●	●	●	●	●				●			●			1			●	●				●				Korea, South
—					●	●		●		●																											Kosovo
1963	●		●	●	●	●	●	●	●	●	●	●	●	●										●										●	●		Kuwait
1992	●		●	●	●	●	●	●		●	●	●	●	●									●					●						●			Kyrgyzstan
1955	●		●	●	●	●	●	●		●	●	●	●	1				●										●									Laos
1991	●		●	●	●	●	●	●	●	●	●		●	●	●						●				1												Latvia
1945	●		●	●	●	●	●	●	●	●	●	●	●	1										●	1									●			Lebanon
1966	●		●	●	●	●	●	●		●	●	●	●	●		●				●							●										Lesotho
1945	●		●	●	●	●	●	●	●	●	●	●	●	1						●							●				●						Liberia
1955	●		●	●	●	●	●	●	●	●	●	●	●	1						●				●										●	●	●	Libya
1990	●			●						●				●																							Liechtenstein
1991	●		●	●	●		●	●	●	●	●	●	●	●							●				1												Lithuania
1945	●		●	●	●	●	●	●	●	●	●	●	●	●							●				1			●									Luxembourg
—								●	15	●	15			●																							Macau
1993	●		●	●	●	●	●	●	●	●	●	●	●	●											1												Macedonia
1960	●		●	●	●	●	●	●	●	●	●	●	●	●						43							●										Madagascar
1964	●		●	●	●	●	●	●	●	●	●	●	●	●		●				●							●										Malawi
1957	●		●	●	●	●	●	●	●	●	●	●	●	●		●		●	●									●	●					●			Malaysia
1965	●		●		●	●	●	●	●	●	●	●	●	●		●												●						●			Maldives
1960	●		●	●	●	●	●	●		●	●	●	●	●	●					●							●				●	●		●			Mali
1964	●		●	●	●		●	●	●	●	●	●	●	●		●					●				1												Malta
1991	●		●	●	●	●	●	●	●	●	●		●													●	●	●									Marshall Islands
—										●																						●					Martinique
1961	●		●	●	●	●	●	●	●	●	●	●	●	●						43				●			●							●			Mauritania
1968	●		●	●	●	●	●	●	●	●	●	●	●	●		●				●							●										Mauritius
—										●																						●					Mayotte
1945	●	●	●	●	●	●	●	●	●	●	●	●	●	●								●			●				●				●				Mexico
1991	●		●		●	●		●		●	●		●													●	●	●									Micronesia
1992	●		●	●	●	●	●	●	●	●	●	●	●	●																							Moldova
1993	●		●	●					●	●	●	●	●						●						1							●					Monaco
1961	●		●	●	●	●	●	●	●	●	●	●	●	●									1					●									Mongolia
2006	●		●	●	●	●	●	●	●	●	●	●	●	1																							Montenegro
1956	●	●	●	●	●	●	●	●	●	●	●	●	●	●										●	1									●			Morocco
1975	●		●	●	●	●	●	●	●	●	●	●	●	●		●				●							●							●			Mozambique
1948	●		●	●	●	●	●	●	●	●	●	●	●	●				●										●									Myanmar (Burma)
1990	●		●	●	●		●	●	●	●	●	●	●	●		●				●							●										Namibia
1999	●		●							●	●		●			98										●	●	●									Nauru
1955	●		●	●	●	●	●	●	●	●	●	●	●	●														●									Nepal
1945	●		●	●	●	●	●	●	●	●	●	●	●	●			1		●		●				1			●					●			1	Netherlands
—										●																●						●					New Caledonia
1945	●	●	●	●	●	●	●	●	●	●	●	●	●	●		●			●							●		●	●								New Zealand
1945	●		●	●	●	●	●	●	●	●	●	●	●	●											●								●				Nicaragua
1960	●		●	●	●	●	●	●		●	●	●	●	●						●							●				●	●		●			Niger

Government and international organizations (continued)

country	date of independence[a]	date of current or last constitution[b]	type of government	executive branch[c]		legislative branch[d]		admin. subdivisions		seaward claims	
				head of state	head of government	upper house (members)	lower house (members)	first-order (number)	second-order (number)	territorial (nautical miles)	fishing/economic (nautical miles)
Nigeria	Oct. 1, 1960	May 5, 1999	federal republic	—president—		109	360	37	774	12	200[39]
Northern Mariana Is.	—	Jan. 9, 1978	commonwealth (U.S.)	U.S. president	governor	9	20	3	—	12	200
Norway	June 7, 1905	May 17, 1814	constitutional monarchy	king	prime minister	169	—	19	430	12[100]	200[100, 101]
Oman	Dec. 20, 1951	Nov. 6, 1996[102]	monarchy (sultanate)	—sultan—		83[34]	84[34]	9	61	12	200
Pakistan	Aug. 14, 1947	Aug. 14, 1973	republic	president	prime minister	100	342	6[103]	...	12	200
Palau	Oct. 1, 1994	Jan. 1, 1981	republic	—president—		13	16	16	—	12	200
Panama	Nov. 3, 1903	Oct. 27, 2004[38]	republic	—president—		71	—	12	75	12	200
Papua New Guinea	Sept. 16, 1975	Sept. 16, 1975	constitutional monarchy	British monarch	prime minister	109	—	20	87	12[10]	200[10]
Paraguay	May 14, 1811	June 22, 1992	republic	—president—		45[104]	80	18	229	—	—
Peru	July 28, 1821	Dec. 31, 1993	republic	—president[4]—		130	—	25	195	200	200
Philippines	July 4, 1946	Feb. 11, 1987	republic	—president—		24	280	17	80	[105]	200[10]
Poland	Nov. 10, 1918	Oct. 17, 1997	republic	president	prime minister	100	460	16	314	12	[48]
Portugal	c. 1140	April 25, 1976	republic	president	prime minister	230[106]	—	20	308	12	200
Puerto Rico	—	July 25, 1952	commonwealth (U.S.)	U.S. president	governor	27[23]	51	—	78	12	200
Qatar	Sept. 3, 1971	June 9, 2005	constitutional emirate	—emir[4]—		35[34]	—	7	—	12	[48]
Réunion	—	Feb. 28, 1983	[60]	French president	[61]	49[62]	45[63]	4	24	12	200
Romania	May 21, 1877	Oct. 29, 2003	republic	president	prime minister	137	334	42	320	12	200
Russia	Dec. 8, 1991	Dec. 24, 1993	federal republic	president	prime minister	178[23]	450	8	83	12	200
Rwanda	July 1, 1962	June 4, 2003	republic	—president[4]—		26	80	5	30	—	—
St. Kitts and Nevis	Sept. 19, 1983	Sept. 19, 1983	constitutional monarchy	British monarch	prime minister	15	—	1	—	12	200
St. Lucia	Feb. 22, 1979	Feb. 22, 1979	constitutional monarchy	British monarch	prime minister	11	17[9]	...	...	12	200
St. Vincent	Oct. 27, 1979	Oct. 27, 1979	constitutional monarchy	British monarch	prime minister	21[9]	—	—	—	12[10]	200[10]
Samoa	Jan. 1, 1962	Oct. 28, 1960	[107]	head of state	prime minister	49	—	11	—	12	200
San Marino	855	Oct. 8, 1600	republic	—captains-regent (2)—		60	—	9	—	—	—
Sao Tome and Principe	July 12, 1975	Sept. 10, 1990	republic	president	prime minister	55	—	7	—	12[10]	200[10]
Saudi Arabia	Sept. 23, 1932	[108]	monarchy	—king—		150[34]	—	13	178	12	[2]
Senegal	Aug. 20, 1960	Jan. 22, 2001	republic	—president[4]—		100	150	14	46	12[27]	200[27]
Serbia	June 5, 2006	Nov. 8, 2006	republic	president	prime minister	250	—	1	25	—	—
Seychelles	June 29, 1976	June 21, 1993	republic	—president—		31	—	25	—	12[10]	200[10]
Sierra Leone	April 27, 1961	Oct. 1, 1991	republic	—president—		124	—	19	...	12	200
Singapore	Aug. 9, 1965	June 3, 1959[19]	republic	president	prime minister	99	—	—	—	12	[2]
Sint Maarten	—	Oct. 20, 2010	autonomous state (Neth.)	Dutch monarch	[14]	15	—	...	...	...	...
Slovakia	Jan. 1, 1993	Jan. 1, 1993	republic	president	prime minister	150	—	8	79	—	—
Slovenia	June 25, 1991	Dec. 23, 1991	republic	president	prime minister	40	90	210	—	12[109]	[109]
Solomon Islands	July 7, 1978	July 7, 1978	constitutional monarchy	British monarch	prime minister	50	—	10	...	12[10]	200[10]
Somalia	July 1, 1960	March 12, 2004[110]	transitional regime	—president[4, 111]—		550[112]	—	...	...	200	200
South Africa	May 31, 1910	June 30, 1997	republic	—president—		90	400	9	283	12	200
Spain	1492	Dec. 29, 1978	constitutional monarchy	king	prime minister	264[23]	350	19	50	12	[113]
Sri Lanka	Feb. 4, 1948	Sept. 7, 1978	republic	—president[4]—		225	—	[114]	25	12	200
Sudan	Jan. 1, 1956	July 9, 2005[99]	interim regime	—president[37]—		32	354	15[115]	25	12	[2]
Sudan, South	July 9, 2011	July 7, 2011	republic	—president—		50	332	10	—	—	—
Suriname	Nov. 25, 1975	Nov. 25, 1987	republic	—president—		51	—	10	...	12	200
Swaziland	Sept. 6, 1968	Feb. 8, 2006	monarchy	—king[4]—		30[34]	66[34]	4	55	—	—
Sweden	before 836	Jan. 1, 1975	constitutional monarchy	king	prime minister	349	—	21	290	12	[109]
Switzerland	Sept. 22, 1499	Jan. 1, 2000	federal state	—president FC—		46	200	26	2,596[116]	—	—
Syria	April 17, 1946	March 14, 1973	republic	—president—		250	—	14	60	12	200
Taiwan	—	Dec. 25, 1947[18]	republic	president	premier	113	—	1	25	12	200
Tajikistan	Sept. 9, 1991	Nov. 6, 1994	republic	president	prime minister	34[117]	63	4	58	—	—
Tanzania	Dec. 9, 1961	April 25, 1977	republic	—president—		357	—	1	26	12	200
Thailand	1350	Aug. 24, 2007	constitutional monarchy	king	prime minister	150	500	76	878	12	200
Togo	April 27, 1960	Sept. 27, 1992	republic	—president[4]—		81	—	31	...	30	200
Tonga	June 4, 1970	Nov. 4, 1875	constitutional monarchy	king	prime minister	26[9]	—	3	...	12	200
Trinidad and Tobago	Aug. 31, 1962	July 27, 1976	republic	president	prime minister	31	42	15	...	12[10]	200[10]
Tunisia	March 20, 1956	June 1, 2002[38]	interim regime	president	prime minister	217	—	24	246	12	[109]
Turkey	Oct. 29, 1923	Nov. 7, 1982	republic	president	prime minister	550	—	81	923	[118]	200[119]
Turkmenistan	Oct. 27, 1991	Sept. 26, 2008	republic	—president—		125	—	6	48/13[120]	—	—
Tuvalu	Oct. 1, 1978	Oct. 1, 1986	constitutional monarchy	British monarch	prime minister	15	—	9	—	12[10]	200[10]
Uganda	Oct. 9, 1962	Oct. 8, 1995	republic	—president[4]—		375	—	115	...	—	—
Ukraine	Aug. 24, 1991	June 28, 1996	republic	president	prime minister	450	—	27	490	12	200
United Arab Emirates	Dec. 2, 1971	Dec. 2, 1971	federation of emirates	president	prime minister	40[34]	—	7	...	12	200
United Kingdom	Dec. 6, 1921	[121]	constitutional monarchy	monarch	prime minister	733	650	3	474	12[82]	200
United States	July 4, 1776	March 4, 1789	federal republic	—president—		100	435	51	3,135[122]	12	200
Uruguay	Aug. 25, 1828	Feb. 15, 1967	republic	—president—		31[123]	99	19	...	12	200
Uzbekistan	Aug. 31, 1991	Dec. 8, 1992	republic	—president[4]—		100	150	14	157	—	—
Vanuatu	July 30, 1980	July 30, 1980	republic	president	prime minister	52	—	6	3/62[124]	12[10]	200[10]
Venezuela	July 5, 1811	Dec. 20, 1999	federal republic	—president—		165	—	25	335	12	200
Vietnam	Sept. 2, 1945	April 15, 1992	socialist republic	president	prime minister	500	—	8	63	12	200
Virgin Islands (U.S.)	—	July 22, 1954	territory (U.S.)	U.S. president	governor	15	—	—	3	12	200
West Bank	—	May 4, 1994[65]	interim authority	president[125]	prime minister[125]	132	—	16[126]	...	—	—
Western Sahara	—	—	annexure of Morocco	—	—	—	—	...	...	12	200
Yemen	December 1918	Sept. 29, 1994	republic	president	prime minister	111[34]	301	21	333	12	200
Zambia	Oct. 24, 1964	May 28, 1996	republic	—president—		158	—	9	72	—	—
Zimbabwe	April 18, 1980	April 18, 1980	transitional regime	—president/prime minister/cabinet[128]—		100	214	10	...	—	—

[1]Observer. [2]Territorial sea claim. [3]Fifth significant revision of Nov. 22, 1976, constitution. [4]Assisted by the prime minister. [5]Varies between 32 and 52 nautical miles. [6]Excludes nonvoting delegate from Swains Island. [7]Comprises 3 districts and 2 islands. [8]President of France and Bishop of Urgell, Spain. [9]Excludes possible ex officio members. [10]Measured from claimed archipelagic baselines. [11]Promulgation date of significant amendments to July 9, 1853, constitution. [12]Represents the number of departments (including 2 "claimed only" departments in Tierra del Fuego province). [13]Date of referendum adopting significant amendments to 1995 constitution. [14]Executive responsibilities divided between (for the Netherlands) the governor and (locally) the prime minister. [15]Associate member. [16]Formally a constitutional monarchy. [17]Number of local councils, the generic local administrative body. [18]Evolving body of constitutional law. [19]Date of referendum approving significant constitutional amendments. [20]Represents 32 districts and directly administered New Providence Island. [21]Seaward claims between Barbados and Trinidad and Tobago defined mostly by equidistant line. [22]Per nondemocratic national referendum of Nov. 24, 1996, amending the constitution. [23]Statutory number of seats. [24]Federal state formally created per revision to constitution. [25]Excludes children of the monarch serving ex officio from age 18. [26]3 autonomous regions/3 linguistic communities. [27]Defined by coordinates of points. [28]Excludes speaker who may be designated from outside of the legislative house. [29]6 districts; 8 town boards. [30]3 nautical miles from the mouth of the Sarstoon River (southern boundary with Guatemala) to Ranguana Caye. [31]Executive responsibilities divided between (for the U.K.) the governor and (locally) the premier. [32]Date of international treaty confirming the existence of a single state; the treaty included a constitution now in force. [33]Tripartite presidency under the final authority of the international high representative/EU special representative. [34]Body with limited or no legislative authority. [35]Represents number of town/township councils. [36]Emergency powers since 1962. [37]Assisted by vice presidents. [38]Date significant amendments were adopted. [39]Cameroon-Nigeria maritime boundary over oil fields delimited in 2007. [40]Governor-general can exercise all the powers of the reigning monarch of the Commonwealth. [41]Includes 2 appointees by governor. [42]Implementation pending in late 2011. [43]Suspended membership. [44]Defined by geographical coordinates. [45]Suspension of Cuba from 1962 revoked in June 2009, but Cuba rejects membership. [46]Republic of Cyprus only. [47]24 seats reserved for Turkish Cypriots are not occupied. [48]National legislation in possible conjunction with a median (equidistant) line delimits maritime boundaries with adjacent states. [49]3 municipal councils, the Carib Council, and 37 village councils. [50]Around the Galápagos Islands and the marine area directly west of mainland Ecuador toward the Galápagos Islands only. [51]Limits of economic zones between Egypt and Cyprus were defined by agreement in 2003. [52]Constitution adopted in May 1997 had not been implemented by December 2011. [53]Partially delimited by Eritrean-Yemeni arbitration. [54]Defined by coordinates in some parts of the Gulf of Finland. [55]Overseas administrative division (Denmark). [56]Executive responsibilities divided between (for Denmark) the high commissioner and (locally) the prime minister. [57]The People's Charter, a precursor to a possible new constitution, was approved by the president in December 2008. [58]Excluding Åland. [59]Metropolitan France only. [60]Overseas department/overseas region (France). [61]Executive responsibilities divided among (for France) the prefect and (locally) the president of the General Council and the president of the Regional Council. [62]Assembly for overseas department. [63]Assembly for

membership in international organizations

	UN organ★ and affiliated intergovernmental organizations																regional multipurpose																		economic		
United Nations (date of admission)	UNCTAD	ICJ★[e]	FAO	IAEA	IBRD	IDA	ILO	IMF	IMO	ITU	UNESCO	UNIDO	WHO	WTO	ICC[f]	The Commonwealth	AC	ASEAN	ATs	AU	EU	G-20[g]	SCO	LAS	OAS	PC	ACP	ADB	APEC	CARICOM	ECOWAS	FZ	I-ADB	IDB	OPEC	GECF	country
1960	•		•	•	•	•	•	•	•	•	•	•	•	•		•				•					1		•				•			•	•	•	Nigeria
—										•																•											Northern Mariana Is.
1945	•		•	•	•	•	•	•	•	•	•	•	•	•			•		•						1			•					•			1	Norway
1971	•		•	•	•	•	•	•	•	•	•	•	•	•										•										•			Oman
1947	•		•	•	•	•	•	•	•	•	•	•	•	•		•							1		1			•						•			Pakistan
1994	•		•	•	•	•		•	•	•	•		•													•	•	•									Palau
1945	•		•	•	•	•	•	•	•	•	•	•	•	•											•								•				Panama
1975	•		•	•	•	•	•	•	•	•	•	•	•	•		•		1	•							•	•	•	•								Papua New Guinea
1945	•		•	•	•	•	•	•	•	•	•	•	•	•											•								•				Paraguay
1945	•		•	•	•	•	•	•	•	•	•	•	•	•					•						•				•				•				Peru
1945	•		•	•	•	•	•	•	•	•	•	•	•	•				•							1			•	•								Philippines
1945	•		•	•	•	•	•	•	•	•	•	•	•	•			1		•		•				1												Poland
1955	•		•	•	•	•	•	•	•	•	•	•	•	•					•		•				1			•					•				Portugal
—										•			15																								Puerto Rico
1971	•		•	•	•		•	•	•	•	•	•	•	•										•	1									•	•	•	Qatar
—										•																						•					Réunion
1955	•		•	•	•		•	•	•	•	•	•	•	•					•		•				1												Romania
1991	•	•	•	•	•	•	•	•	•	•	•	•	•	1			•		•			•	•		1				•							•	Russia
1962	•		•	•	•	•	•	•		•	•	•	•	•		•				•							•										Rwanda
1983	•		•		•	•	•	•	•	•	•	•	•	•		•									•		•			•							St. Kitts and Nevis
1979	•		•		•	•	•	•	•	•	•	•	•	•		•									•		•			•							St. Lucia
1980	•		•		•	•	•	•	•	•	•	•	•	•		•									•		•			•							St. Vincent
1976	•		•		•	•	•	•	•	•	•	•	•	1		•										•	•	•									Samoa
1992	•		•		•		•	•	•	•	•	•	•																								San Marino
1975	•		•		•	•	•	•	•	•	•	•	•	1						•							•										Sao Tome and Principe
1945	•		•	•	•	•	•	•	•	•	•	•	•	•								•		•	1									•	•		Saudi Arabia
1960	•		•	•	•	•	•	•	•	•	•	•	•	•						•							•				•	•		•			Senegal
1945	•		•	•	•	•	•	•	•	•	•	•	•	1											1												Serbia
1976	•		•	•	•		•	•	•	•	•	•	•	1		•				•							•										Seychelles
1961	•	•	•	•	•	•	•	•	•	•	•	•	•	•		•				•							•				•			•			Sierra Leone
1965	•			•	•	•	•	•	•	•	•		•	•		•		•										•	•								Singapore
—								•			15																										Sint Maarten
1993	•	•	•	•	•	•	•	•	•	•	•	•	•	•					•		•				1												Slovakia
1992	•		•	•	•	•	•	•	•	•	•	•	•	•							•				1								•				Slovenia
1978	•		•		•	•	•	•	•	•	•		•	•		•										•	•	•									Solomon Islands
1960	•	•	•		•	•	•	•	•	•	•	•	•							•				•			•							•			Somalia
1945	•		•	•	•	•	•	•	•	•	•	•	•	•		•			•	•		•					•										South Africa
1955	•		•	•	•	•	•	•	•	•	•	•	•	•			1		•		•				1			•					•				Spain
1955	•		•	•	•	•	•	•	•	•	•	•	•	•		•									1			•									Sri Lanka
1956	•		•	•	•	•	•	•	•	•	•	•	•	1						•				•			•							•			Sudan
2011	•										•		•							•																	Sudan, South
1975	•		•		•		•	•	•	•	•	•	•	•											•		•			•			•	•			Suriname
1968	•		•		•	•	•	•		•	•	•	•	•		•				•							•										Swaziland
1946	•		•	•	•	•	•	•	•	•	•	•	•	•			•		•		•				1			•					•				Sweden
2002	•		•	•	•	•	•	•	•	•	•	•	•	•					•						1			•					•				Switzerland
1945	•		•	•	•	•	•	•	•	•	•	•	•	1										43										•			Syria
—										•				•														•	•								Taiwan
1992	•		•	•	•	•	•	•		•	•	•	•	1									•					•						•			Tajikistan
1961	•		•	•	•	•	•	•	•	•	•	•	•	•		•				•							•										Tanzania
1946	•		•	•	•	•	•	•	•	•	•	•	•	•				•							1			•	•								Thailand
1960	•		•	•	•	•	•	•	•	•	•	•	•	•						•							•				•	•		•			Togo
1999	•		•	•	•	•		•	•	•	•	•	•	•		•										•	•	•									Tonga
1962	•		•		•	•	•	•	•	•	•	•	•	•		•									•		•			•			•			•	Trinidad and Tobago
1956	•		•	•	•	•	•	•	•	•	•	•	•	•						•				•	1									•			Tunisia
1945	•		•	•	•	•	•	•	•	•	•	•	•	•					•			•			1			•						•			Turkey
1992	•		•		•		•	•	•	•	•	•	•															•						•			Turkmenistan
2000	•		•		•		•	•	•	•	•	•	•			•										•	•	•									Tuvalu
1962	•		•	•	•	•	•	•	•	•	•	•	•	•	•	•				•							•							•			Uganda
1945	•		•	•	•	•	•	•	•	•	•	•	•	•					•						1												Ukraine
1971	•		•	•	•	•	•	•	•	•	•	•	•	•										•										•	•		United Arab Emirates
1945	•	•	•	•	•	•	•	•	•	•	•	•	•	•	•	•	1		•		•	•			1			•					•				United Kingdom
1945	•	•	•	•	•	•	•	•	•	•	•		•	•			•		•			•			•	•		•	•				•				United States
1945	•		•	•	•		•	•	•	•	•	•	•	•					•						•								•				Uruguay
1992	•		•	•	•	•	•	•		•	•	•	•	1									•					•						•			Uzbekistan
1981	•		•		•	•	•	•	•	•	•	•	•	1		•									1	•	•	•									Vanuatu
1945	•		•	•	•		•	•	•	•	•	•	•	•					•					1	•								•		•	•	Venezuela
1977	•		•	•	•	•	•	•	•	•	•	•	•	•				•										•	•								Vietnam
—										•																											Virgin Islands (U.S.)
—										•[67]	•[67]													•[67]										•[67]			West Bank
—																				127																	Western Sahara
1947	•		•	•	•	•	•	•	•	•	•	•	•	1										•	1									•			Yemen
1964	•		•	•	•	•	•	•		•	•	•	•	•		•				•							•										Zambia
1980	•		•	•	•	•	•	43	•	•	•	•	•	•						•							•										Zimbabwe

overseas region. [64]Executive responsibilities divided between (for France) the high commissioner and (locally) the president of the government. [65]Date of agreement providing for Palestinian self-rule. [66]Controlled by Hamas from June 14, 2007. [67]As Palestine. [68]Excludes Abkhazia and South Ossetia. [69]69 local councils/7 city governments. [70]Date significant constitutional amendments were concluded. [71]Date Greenland officially gained greater autonomy from Denmark with the implementation of the official law of self-governance. [72]17 towns/5 settlements. [73]Represented by the lieutenant governor. [74]2 members have no voting rights. [75]Excludes 3 nonelected ministers, one nonelected parliamentary secretary, and the speaker. [76]Special administrative region (China). [77]Has been significantly amended. [78]Number of towns. [79]Number of regencies (349) and cities (91). [80]Shares coexecutive authority with spiritual leader. [81]Based on evolving body of statutes and common law in both the United Kingdom and the Isle of Man. [82]Median line boundary between the Isle of Man and the United Kingdom. [83]Where determined, the outer limit is determined by reference to a median line. [84]The emperor is symbol of state. [85]Number of cities in 2008. [86]3 nautical miles in 3 straits and 2 channels. [87]Number of cities and counties. [88]President under the final authority of the UN interim administrator/EU special envoy. [89]Includes 15 ex officio members. [90]9 cities/109 amalgamated municipalities. [91]Head of the Executive Board of the Transitional National Council. [92]Includes the one child of the grand duke having the title hereditary grand duke. [93]Two transitional bodies—the Higher Transitional Council (90) and the Transitional Congress (256)—were appointed by the president in October 2010. [94]Includes 5 municipalities, 4 districts, and 1 autonomous region. [95]Under prince's authority. [96]Includes Western Sahara annexure. [97]Effective date of military-backed constitution. [98]Special member. [99]Interim constitution. [100]Includes Jan Mayen and Svalbard. [101]Delimitation treaties in place for Jan Mayen (with Denmark and Iceland) and Svalbard (with Russia). [102]Basic law promulgated by sultan. [103]Excludes Azad Kashmir and Gilgit-Baltistan. [104]Excludes former presidents serving as senators-for-life. [105]Rectangle defined by coordinates; claim extends beyond 12 mi. [106]Includes four members representing Portuguese citizens living abroad. [107]Mix of parliamentary democracy and Samoan customs. [108]Royal decrees from March 1, 1992, created first written rules of governance. [109]National legislation delimits maritime boundaries with adjacent states. [110]Approval date of federal transitional charter. [111]No effective central government in December 2011. [112]Planned number. [113]200 km in the Atlantic Ocean; defined by geographical coordinates in the Mediterranean Sea. [114]7 functioning provincial councils in 2011. [115]The creation of two new states—Central Darfur and East Darfur—was announced by the government, but they were not yet operational in December 2011. [116]Number of municipalities. [117]Includes seat for outgoing president. [118]6 nautical miles in the Aegean Sea; 12 nautical miles in the Black Sea. [119]In the Black Sea only. [120]48 districts/13 cities. [121]Based on evolving body of statutes and common law. [122]Includes counties, parishes, independent cities, boroughs, and census areas as of early 2007. [123]Includes the vice president of Uruguay serving ex officio. [124]3 municipalities/62 area councils. [125]Of Palestinian Authority. [126]Including the Gaza Strip. [127]Membership held by the Saharawi Arab Democratic Republic. [128]Shared executive authority from Feb. 13, 2009.

Area and population

This table provides the area and particular populations for each of the countries of the world and for all but the smallest political dependencies having a permanent civilian population. The data represent the latest published and unpublished data for both the surveyed area of the countries and their populations, the latter as of a single recent year (2011), as of a recent census to provide the fullest comparison of certain demographic measures that are not always available between successive national censuses, and as of decade population estimates over a seventy year (1960–2030) span. The 2011 midyear estimates (as a population estimate by decade) are based on a combination of national sources (both print and online), the United Nations *World Population Prospects: The 2010 Revision,* the U.S. Bureau of the Census International Data Base, databases of other international organizations, and *Encyclopædia Britannica*'s own estimates.

One principal point to bear in mind when studying these statistics is that all of them, whatever degree of precision may be implied by the exactness of the numbers, are estimates—all of varying, and some of suspect, accuracy—even when they *contain* a very full enumeration. The United States—which has a long tradition both of census taking and of the use of the most sophisticated analytical tools in processing the data—is unable to determine within 1.4% (the estimated 2000 undercount) its total population nationally. And that is an *average* underenumeration. In states and larger cities, where enumeration of particular populations, including illegal, is more difficult, the accuracy of the enumerated count may be off as much as 3.1% at a state level (in New Mexico, for instance) and by a greater percent for a single city. The high accuracy attained by census operations in China may approach 0.25% of rigorously maintained civil population registers. Other national census operations not so based, however, are inherently less accurate. For example, Ethiopia's first-ever census in 1984 resulted in figures that were 30% or more above prevailing estimates. An undercount of 2–8% is more typical, but even census operations offering results of 30% or more above or below prevailing estimates can still represent well-founded benchmarks from which future planning may proceed. The editors have tried to take account of the range of variation and accuracy in published data, but it is difficult to establish a value for many sources of inaccuracy unless some country or agency has made a conscientious effort to establish both the relative accuracy (precision) of its estimate and the absolute magnitude of the quantity it is trying to measure—for example, the number of people in Cambodia who died at the hands of the Khmer Rouge. If a figure of 2,000,000 is adopted, what is its accuracy: ± 1%, 10%, 50%? Are the original data documentary or evidentiary, complete or incomplete, analytically biased or unbiased, in good agreement with other published data?

Many similar problems exist and in endless variations: What is the extent of eastern European immigration to western Europe in search of jobs? And how many of these migrants have returned to their home countries in the recent past? How many registered and unregistered refugees from Afghanistan, Sudan, or Iraq are there in surrounding countries? How many undocumented aliens are there in the United Kingdom, Japan, or the United States? How many Tamils have left Sri Lanka as a result of civil unrest in their homeland? How many Amerindians exist (remain, preserving their original language and a mode of life unassimilated by the larger national culture) in the countries of South America?

Area and population

country	area			population (latest estimate)					population (recent census)				
	square miles	square kilometres	rank	total midyear 2011	rank	density per sq mi	density per sq km	% annual growth rate 2006–11	census year	total	male (%)	female (%)	urban (%)
Afghanistan	252,072	652,864	41	26,442,000	46	104.9	40.5	1.9	2008–09	23,511,400	51.1[1]	48.9[1]	22.7[1]
Albania	11,082	28,703	143	3,196,000	136	288.4	111.3	0.3	2001	3,069,275	49.9	50.1	42.7
Algeria	919,595	2,381,741	11	36,649,000	35	39.9	15.4	1.9	2008	34,452,759[2]	50.5[2]	49.5[2]	65.9[3]
American Samoa	77	200	210	66,700	207	862.9	333.2	1.1	2010	55,519	50.7[5]	49.3[5]	92.0[5]
Andorra	179	464	195	85,600	204	478.2	184.5	1.4	2010[6, 7]	84,082	52.1	47.9	90.3
Angola	481,354	1,246,700	24	19,618,000	59	40.8	15.7	2.9	1970	5,673,046	52.1	47.9	14.2
Antigua and Barbuda	171	442	199	91,400	203	536.0	206.9	1.6	2001	76,886	47.0	53.0	37.1[8]
Argentina	1,073,520	2,780,403	8	40,365,000	32	37.6	14.5	1.0	2010	40,117,096	48.7	51.3	88.3[8]
Armenia	11,484	29,743	142	3,100,000	137	270.0	104.2	0.2	2001	3,002,594[10]	46.9	53.1	64.8
Aruba	75	193	211	102,000	197	1,360.0	528.5	1.0	2010	101,484	47.5	52.5	50.5[11]
Australia	2,973,952	7,702,501	6	22,651,000	52	7.6	2.9	1.8	2006	19,855,288[12]	49.4	50.6	88.2[13]
Austria	32,386	83,879	114	8,419,000	93	260.0	100.4	0.4	2001	8,032,926	48.4	51.6	66.8
Azerbaijan	33,436	86,600[14]	113	9,150,000	90	273.9	105.7	1.2	2009	8,922,300[15]	49.5[16]	51.5[16]	54.1[16]
Bahamas, The	5,382	13,939	160	360,000	179	66.9	25.8	1.5	2010	353,658[15]	48.3	51.7	83.9[3]
Bahrain	292	757	186	1,325,000	155	4,537.7	1,750.3	6.6	2010	1,234,571	62.2	37.8	88.5[3]
Bangladesh	56,977	147,570	94	142,875,000	8	2,507.6	968.2	1.3	2011	142,319,000	50.1	49.9	27.6[3]
Barbados	166	430	200	277,000	183	1,668.7	644.2	0.2	2000	268,792	48.1	51.9	50.0[11]
Belarus	80,153	207,595	86	9,472,000	86	118.1	45.6	–0.4	2009	9,503,807	46.5	53.5	74.3
Belgium	11,787	30,528	140	10,971,000	76	930.8	359.4	0.8	2008[6, 7]	10,666,866	49.0	51.0	97.4[3]
Belize	8,867	22,965	151	322,000	181	36.3	14.0	2.7	2010	312,698	50.5	49.5	44.4
Benin	44,310	114,763	102	9,100,000	91	205.4	79.3	2.9	2002	6,769,914	48.5	51.5	38.9
Bermuda	21	54	217	65,300	208	3,185.3	1,229.8	0.3	2010	65,069	48.0[19]	52.0[19]	100.0
Bhutan	14,824	38,394	136	701,000	167	47.3	18.3	1.6	2005	634,982	52.5	47.5	30.9
Bolivia	424,164	1,098,581	27	10,088,000	82	23.8	9.2	1.6	2001	8,274,325	49.8	50.2	62.4
Bosnia and Herzegovina	19,772	51,209	128	3,843,000	129	194.4	75.0	–0.0	1991	4,377,033	49.9	50.1	39.6
Botswana	224,607	581,730	48	2,033,000	146	9.1	3.5	1.9	2011	2,038,228[9, 10]	50.0[4]	50.0[4]	60.4[3]
Brazil	3,287,612	8,514,877	5	192,813,000	5	58.6	22.6	1.2	2010	190,732,694[9]	49.0[9]	51.0[9]	84.3[9]
Brunei	2,226	5,765	170	422,000	175	189.6	73.2	2.0	2001	332,844	50.8	49.2	75.2[3]
Bulgaria	42,858	111,002	104	7,333,000	99	171.1	66.1	–0.8	2011	7,351,234	48.4[16]	51.6[16]	71.4[16]
Burkina Faso	104,543	270,764	74	16,968,000	61	159.6	61.6	3.0	2006	14,017,262	48.3	51.7	22.7
Burundi	10,740	27,816	146	8,575,000	92	798.4	308.3	2.8	2008	8,036,618[15]	48.9	51.1	10.7[3]
Cambodia	69,898	181,035	90	14,702,000	68	210.3	81.2	1.7	2008	13,395,862	48.6	51.4	19.5
Cameroon	183,920	476,350	54	20,073,000	58	109.1	42.1	2.5	2005	17,463,836	49.4	50.6	58.2[25]
Canada	3,855,103	9,984,670	2	34,447,000	37	8.9	3.4	0.6	2006	31,612,897[12]	49.0[12]	51.0[12]	80.1[13]
Cape Verde	1,557	4,033	173	498,000	174	319.8	123.5	1.2	2010	491,875	49.5	50.5	61.8
Cayman Islands	102	264	209	56,000	211	549.0	212.1	3.0	2010	54,878[9, 27]	49.4[19]	50.6[19]	100.0[3]
Central African Republic	240,324	622,436	44	4,950,000	119	20.6	8.0	2.2	2003	3,895,139	49.8	50.2	37.9
Chad	495,755	1,284,000	21	12,018,000	73	24.2	9.4	3.4	2009	11,175,915[15, 29]	49.3	50.7	21.7
Chile	291,930	756,096	38	17,270,000	60	59.2	22.8	1.0	2002	15,116,435	49.3	50.7	86.6
China	3,696,100	9,572,900	3	1,342,274,000	1	363.2	140.2	0.5	2010	1,339,724,852	51.4	48.6	46.6
Colombia	440,831	1,141,748	26	44,726,000	30	101.5	39.2	1.2	2005	42,090,502	49.1	50.9	75.0
Comoros	719	1,862	179	754,000	165	1,048.7	404.9	2.7	2003	575,660	49.6	50.4	27.9
Congo, Dem. Rep. of the	905,568	2,345,410	11	67,758,000	19	74.8	28.9	2.8	1984	29,671,407	49.2	50.8	32.1[13]
Congo, Rep. of the	132,047	342,000	65	3,920,000	128	29.7	11.5	1.1	2007[31]	3,697,490	49.3	50.7	61.8
Costa Rica	19,730	51,100	129	4,577,000	121	232.0	89.6	1.4	2000	3,929,248	49.9	50.1	59.0
Côte d'Ivoire	123,863	320,803	69	21,504,000	53	173.6	67.0	2.2	1998	15,366,672	51.0	49.0	43.6[11]
Croatia	21,851	56,594	127	4,287,000	124	196.2	75.8	–0.3	2011	4,290,612	48.2[3]	51.8[3]	57.3[4]
Cuba	42,427	109,886	105	11,240,000	75	264.9	102.3	–0.0	2002	11,177,743	50.1	49.9	75.9
Curaçao	171[32]	444[32]	198	143,000	193	836.3	322.1	0.8	2001	130,627	45.9[16]	54.1[16]	92.9[7]
Cyprus[33]	3,572	9,251	168	1,118,000	159	313.0	120.9	1.7	2001[34]	689,565	49.1	50.9	68.8
Czech Republic	30,450	78,865	117	10,551,000	80	346.5	133.8	0.6	2001	10,230,060	48.7	51.3	74.6
Denmark	16,640	43,098	133	5,574,000	111	335.0	129.3	0.5	2008[6]	5,475,791	49.5	50.5	86.3
Djibouti	8,960	23,200	150	840,000	163	93.8	36.2	1.3	2009	818,159[15]	46.6[4]	53.4[4]	70.6
Dominica	290	751	187	72,500	206	250.0	96.5	0.4	2001	71,239	51.0	49.0	71.4[8]
Dominican Republic	18,792	48,671	131	9,440,000	88	502.3	194.0	1.1	2010[9]	9,378,819	50.2	49.8	68.5[3]
East Timor	5,760	14,919	159	1,092,000	160	189.6	73.2	2.4	2010[9]	1,066,582	50.7	49.3	7.8[13]

Still, much information is accurate, well founded, and updated regularly. The sources of these data are censuses; national population registers (cumulated periodically); registration of migration, births, deaths, and so on; sample surveys to establish demographic conditions; and the like.

The statistics provided for area and population by country are ranked, and the population densities based on those values are also provided. The population densities, for purposes of comparison within this table, are calculated on the bases of the 2011 midyear population estimate as shown and of total area of the country. Elsewhere in individual country presentations the reader may find densities calculated on more specific population figures and more specialized area bases: land area for Finland (because of its many lakes) or ice-free area for Greenland (most of which is ice cap). The data in this section conclude with the estimated average annual growth rate for the country (including both natural growth and net migration) during the five-year period 2006–2011.

In the section containing census data, information supplied includes the census total (more often de facto, the population actually present, rather than de jure, the population legally resident, who might be anywhere); the male-female breakdown; the proportion that is urban (often according to the country's own definition); and finally an analysis of the age structure of the population by 15-year age groups. This last analysis may be particularly useful in distinguishing the type of population being recorded—young, fast-growing nations show a high proportion of people under 30 (many countries in sub-Saharan Africa have about 40% of their population under 15 years), while other nations (for example, the United States) exhibit quite uniform proportions.

Finally, a section is provided giving the population of each country at 10-year intervals from 1960 to 2030 based on sources cited earlier. The projections for 2020 and 2030 represent the best fit of available data through late summer 2011. The evidence of the last 40 years with respect to similar estimates published about 1970, however, shows how cloudy is the glass through which these numbers are read. In 1970 no respectable Western analyst would have imagined proposing that mainland China could achieve the degree of birth control that it has since then. Or in 2000 who would have thought that Spain's population would increase by about 6,000,000 people by 2010, nearly all of which was due to heightened immigration. Repeatedly assorted social, economic, political, and biological factors affect the 222 countries' population projections, and thus the difficulty facing the prospective compiler of such projections should be appreciated.

Specific data about the vital rates affecting the data in this table may be found in great detail in both the country statistical profiles in the "Countries, Dependencies, and Territories" section and in the *Vital statistics, marriage, family* table, beginning at page 798.

Percentages in this table for male and female population will always total 100.0, but percentages by age group may not, for reasons such as nonresponse on census forms, "don't know" responses (which are common in countries with poor birth registration systems), and the like.

age distribution (%)						population (by decade, '000s)								country
0–14	15–29	30–44	45–59	60–74	75 and over	1960	1970	1980	1990	2000	2010	2020 projection	2030 projection	
46.1[1]	24.3[1]	14.7[1]	9.3[1]	5.6[1]		9,829	12,431	15,044	13,449	21,259	26,290	32,478	38,527	Afghanistan
29.3	24.1	21.2	14.2	8.7	2.5	1,611	2,136	2,671	3,289	3,068	3,195	3,276	3,273	Albania
26.3[4]	32.0[4]	22.2[4]	12.3[4]	5.3[4]	1.9[4]	10,800	13,746	18,811	25,299	30,534	35,949	41,003	44,365	Algeria
35.4[5]	25.7[5]	19.7[5]	13.1[5]	5.1[5]	1.0[5]	20	27	32	47	58	66	75	84	American Samoa
14.5	17.3	28.6	22.0	11.1	6.5	8	20	34	53	66	85	98	112	Andorra
41.7	23.2	17.0	7.4	3.8	1.0	5,012	6,083	7,854	10,661	14,280	19,082	24,780	30,801	Angola
26.4[9]	25.4[9]	23.9[9]	13.9[9]	10.4[9]		55	66	69	64	76	90	99	107	Antigua and Barbuda
25.5	24.8	20.2	15.2	9.8	4.5	20,685	24,003	28,154	32,498	36,939	39,960	43,448	46,326	Argentina
24.8	24.9	21.8	13.6	12.1	2.8	1,867	2,518	3,096	3,545	3,076	3,092	3,146	3,105	Armenia
20.7	17.8	21.8	24.2	11.6	3.9	57	61	60	63	91	102	106	107	Aruba
19.8	20.1	21.9	20.1	11.7	6.4	10,315	12,552	14,471	17,065	19,153	22,272	25,355	27,896	Australia
16.9	18.6	24.9	18.6	13.8	7.2	7,047	7,467	7,549	7,678	8,012	8,390	8,722	9,018	Austria
22.6[17]	29.6[17]	21.9[17]	17.7[17]	8.2[17]		3,894	5,172	6,161	7,212	8,074	9,048	10,080	10,647	Azerbaijan
26.5	24.3	24.2	16.2	7.0	1.8	110	170	210	256	304	355	398	431	Bahamas, The
20.1	29.8	32.3	14.3	2.8	0.7	149	210	334	503	629	1,248	1,491	1,635	Bahrain
35.9[8]	31.5[8]	17.6[8]	9.9[8]	4.0[8]	1.1[8]	54,593	67,331	87,937	111,437	136,681	140,987	158,789	172,657	Bangladesh
21.8	22.5	24.4	16.0	15.3		232	239	252	263	269	276	282	284	Barbados
14.8	22.7	21.1	22.5	12.7	6.2	8,190	9,040	9,650	10,186	9,972	9,499	9,193	8,798	Belarus
16.7[18]	18.3[18]	20.9[18]	21.1[18]	14.4[18]	8.6[18]	9,153	9,690	9,859	9,967	10,251	10,883	11,639	12,253	Belgium
35.6	64.4					90	120	146	189	250	314	379	442	Belize
46.8	47.7			5.5		2,420	2,850	3,611	4,773	6,519	8,850	11,523	14,630	Benin
18.5[4]	18.0[4]	20.1[4]	24.1[4]	13.3[4]	6.0[4]	44	53	55	58	63	65	66	66	Bermuda
33.1[20]	32.0[20]	17.5[20]	10.4[20]	5.5[20]	1.5[20]	212	309	446	615	606	697	809	887	Bhutan
38.6	27.4	17.0	10.0	5.2	1.8	3,355	4,217	5,353	6,658	8,307	9,930	11,591	13,391	Bolivia
23.5[21]	26.3[21]	22.6[21]	16.9[21]	8.9[21]	2.7[21]	3,180	3,564	3,914	4,308	3,781	3,843	3,739	3,560	Bosnia and Herzegovina
35.3[4]	32.9[4]	17.4[4]	9.0[4]	3.9[4]	1.5[4]	524	693	996	1,382	1,758	1,994	2,290	2,602	Botswana
29.6[22]	28.2[22]	21.1[22]	12.5[22]	6.5[22]	2.1[22]	72,742	95,989	118,563	146,593	169,427	190,571	207,143	216,410	Brazil
30.3	29.0	26.2	10.2	4.3		82	130	193	253	325	414	483	542	Brunei
15.0[23]	21.3[23]	20.4[23]	20.9[23]	16.1[23]	6.3[23]	7,867	8,490	8,862	8,718	7,973	7,389	6,897	6,359	Bulgaria
46.4[24]	26.2[24]	14.3[24]	7.6[24]	3.8[24]	1.2[24]	4,882	5,807	7,212	9,324	12,294	16,469	22,150	29,112	Burkina Faso
41.4[13]	30.8[13]	14.7[13]	8.7[13]	3.5[13]	0.9[13]	2,940	3,513	4,130	5,602	6,374	8,383	10,057	11,441	Burundi
33.7	31.5	17.0	11.4	4.9	1.5	5,761	7,394	6,889	9,368	12,351	14,454	16,927	19,031	Cambodia
41.7[13]	28.9[13]	15.4[13]	8.6[13]	4.3[13]	1.1[13]	5,409	6,842	9,110	12,181	15,678	19,661	24,193	28,902	Cameroon
16.9[26]	20.2[26]	21.6[26]	22.0[26]	12.3[26]	7.0[26]	17,909	21,717	24,516	27,701	30,667	34,109	37,211	39,901	Canada
31.6	31.8	17.9	11.0	4.3	3.4	211	274	300	348	437	492	541	585	Cape Verde
17.2[5]	20.3[5]	32.9[5]	18.7[5]	10.9[5]		8	10	17	26	40	54	60	63	Cayman Islands
42.8[28]	27.9[28]	15.3[28]	7.8[28]	4.9[28]	1.3[28]	1,467	1,839	2,349	3,085	3,980	4,845	5,991	7,325	Central African Republic
46.0	26.9	14.3	8.1	3.9	0.8	2,954	3,656	4,554	6,011	8,222	11,707	15,087	19,225	Chad
25.7	24.3	23.6	15.0	8.3	3.1	7,652	9,578	11,179	13,188	15,420	17,114	18,540	19,536	Chile
17.3[30]	21.2[30]	25.9[30]	21.6[30]	10.6[30]	3.4[30]	658,270	814,623	983,171	1,145,195	1,262,600	1,337,900	1,384,047	1,389,315	China
30.8[13]	27.2[13]	21.3[13]	13.3[13]	5.5[13]	1.9[13]	15,953	21,430	26,631	33,147	38,910	44,205	49,085	52,965	Colombia
38.5[13]	30.5[13]	17.4[13]	8.9[13]	3.7[13]	1.0[13]	193	238	329	438	562	735	933	1,160	Comoros
47.2[13]	27.1[13]	14.2[13]	7.4[13]	3.4[13]	0.7[13]	15,368	20,267	27,019	36,406	49,626	65,966	85,054	105,956	Congo, Dem. Rep. of the
38.6	28.9	19.2	8.5	3.8	1.0	1,014	1,335	1,798	2,389	3,136	3,866	4,749	5,856	Congo, Rep. of the
31.9	27.1	21.7	11.4	5.7	2.2	1,277	1,780	2,316	3,057	3,929	4,516	5,098	5,571	Costa Rica
42.9	29.6	16.4	7.2	3.9		3,576	5,579	8,593	12,491	16,885	21,059	25,504	29,724	Côte d'Ivoire
15.3[3]	19.4[3]	20.6[3]	21.9[3]	15.4[3]	7.4[3]	4,036	4,205	4,383	4,508	4,453	4,301	4,206	4,083	Croatia
20.5	21.2	27.0	16.6	10.2	4.5	7,077	8,603	9,694	10,662	11,146	11,242	11,190	11,080	Cuba
21.0	18.3	20.6	22.5	12.7	4.9	124	145	148	145	134	143	143	136	Curaçao
21.6	22.4	22.1	17.8	11.2	4.9	579	627	658	751	906	1,092	1,221	1,304	Cyprus[33]
16.3	23.5	20.1	21.8	12.8	5.5	9,539	9,805	10,326	10,363	10,273	10,517	10,781	10,838	Czech Republic
18.4	17.7	21.6	20.0	15.4	6.9	4,585	4,938	5,107	5,135	5,330	5,544	5,688	5,854	Denmark
37.0[4]	30.3[4]	18.1[4]	9.4[4]	4.3[4]	0.9[4]	85	162	340	562	732	829	989	1,172	Djibouti
32.7	28.4	17.2	9.5	12.2		60	70	74	70	71	72	75	77	Dominica
30.5	26.8	20.2	13.5	6.7	2.3	3,294	4,502	5,808	7,179	8,554	9,335	10,456	11,339	Dominican Republic
43.2	24.7	17.0	9.4	4.5	1.2	509	598	557	746	847	1,066	1,424	1,876	East Timor

Area and population (continued)

country	area			population (latest estimate)					population (recent census)				
	square miles	square kilo-metres	rank	total midyear 2011	rank	density per sq mi	density per sq km	% annual growth rate 2006–11	census year	total	male (%)	female (%)	urban (%)
Ecuador	98,985	256,370	77	14,650,000	69	148.0	57.1	2.0	2010	14,483,499	49.6	50.4	66.3[3]
Egypt	386,874	1,002,000	30	82,537,000	14	213.3	82.4	1.8	2006	72,798,031	51.1	48.9	42.6
El Salvador	8,124	21,040	153	6,072,000	107	747.4	288.6	0.3	2007	5,744,113	47.3	52.7	62.7
Equatorial Guinea	10,831	28,051	145	720,000	166	66.5	25.7	2.8	2002	1,014,999	49.4	50.6	45.2[11]
Eritrea	46,774	121,144	100	5,415,000	113	115.8	44.7	3.1	1984	2,703,998	49.9	50.1	15.1
Estonia	17,462	45,227	132	1,340,000	154	76.7	29.6	−0.0	2000	1,370,052	46.1	53.9	69.2
Ethiopia	410,678	1,063,652	28	82,102,000	15	200.2	77.2	2.6	2007	73,750,932	50.5	49.5	16.2
Faroe Islands	540	1,399	181	48,600	214	90.0	34.7	0.2	2010[6, 7]	48,650	52.0	48.0	41.0[3]
Fiji	7,055	18,272	156	852,000	162	120.8	46.6	0.5	2007	837,271	50.7	49.3	50.7
Finland	130,666	338,424	66	5,387,000	114	41.2	15.9	0.5	2008[6, 7]	5,300,484	49.0	51.0	84.8[3]
France[35]	210,026	543,965	49	63,278,000	21	301.3	116.3	0.5	2008[36]	62,134,866[37]	48.4	51.6	84.6[3]
French Guiana	32,253	83,534	116	243,000	187	7.5	2.9	3.0	2008[36]	219,266[37]	49.5[3]	50.5[3]	76.1[3]
French Polynesia	1,544	4,000	174	272,000	184	176.2	68.0	1.2	2007	259,706	51.2	48.8	51.3[3]
Gabon	103,347	267,667	76	1,534,000	153	14.8	5.7	1.9	2003	1,269,000[38]	49.7[5]	50.3[5]	85.6[3]
Gambia, The	4,491	11,632	163	1,776,000	149	395.5	152.7	2.8	2003	1,364,507	49.6	50.4	26.1[28]
Gaza Strip	141	365	203	1,574,000	152	11,163.1	4,312.3	3.1	2007	1,416,539	50.7	49.3	...
Georgia	26,911[39]	69,700[39]	122	4,474,000[40]	122	202.7[40]	78.3[40]	0.3	2002	4,371,535[41]	47.2	52.8	52.3
Germany	137,879	357,104	64	81,604,000	16	591.9	228.5	−0.2	2007[6, 7]	82,314,906	49.0	51.0	73.4[13]
Ghana	92,098	238,533	82	24,661,000	48	267.8	103.4	2.4	2010	24,223,431[10]	48.7	51.3	50.7[3]
Greece	50,949	131,957	97	11,372,000	74	223.2	86.2	0.4	2011	10,787,690[38]	49.2	50.8	61.4[16]
Greenland	836,330	2,166,086	12	56,700	210	0.07	0.03	−0.1	2008[6, 7]	56,462	52.9	47.1	82.2[28]
Grenada	133	344	205	108,000	195	812.0	314.0	0.6	2001	103,137	49.2	50.8	38.4
Guadeloupe[43]	629	1,630	180	407,000	177	647.1	249.7	0.3	2008[36]	401,784[37]	46.8	53.2	98.5[3]
Guam	217	561	193	160,000	192	765.6[45]	295.6[45]	0.3	2010	159,358	50.9[3]	49.1[3]	93.3[3]
Guatemala	42,130	109,117	106	14,729,000	67	349.6	135.0	2.5	2002	11,237,196	48.9	51.1	46.1
Guernsey	30	78	215	65,300	209	2,176.7	837.2	0.4	2001	59,807[47]	48.7	51.3	28.9[8, 48]
Guinea	94,926	245,857	79	10,222,000	81	107.7	41.6	2.1	1996	7,165,750	48.8	51.2	26.0
Guinea-Bissau	13,948	36,125	138	1,606,000	151	115.1	44.5	2.4	2009	1,520,830	48.8	51.2	29.9[3]
Guyana	83,012	214,999	85	756,000	164	9.1	3.5	0.2	2002	751,223	50.1	49.9	28.4
Haiti	10,695	27,700	147	9,720,000	85	908.8	350.9	0.8	2003	8,373,750	48.2	51.8	40.8
Honduras	43,433	112,492	103	7,755,000	96	178.6	68.9	2.0	2001	6,535,344	49.4	50.6	44.8
Hong Kong	426	1,104	183	7,125,000	101	16,725.4	6,453.8	0.8	2006	6,864,346	47.7	52.3	100.0
Hungary	35,919	93,030	110	9,972,000	83	277.6	107.2	−0.2	2001	10,198,315	47.6	52.4	64.3
Iceland	39,769	103,000	107	319,000	182	8.0	3.1	0.9	2008[6, 7]	313,376	50.9	49.1	93.1
India	1,222,559	3,166,414	7	1,216,728,000	2	995.2	384.3	1.7	2011	1,210,193,422	51.5	48.5	31.2
Indonesia	737,815	1,910,931	15	241,343,000	4	327.1	126.3	1.4	2010	237,641,326	50.3	49.7	49.8
Iran	636,374	1,648,200	18	75,276,000	17	119.0	45.9	1.5	2006	70,495,782[15]	50.9	49.1	68.5
Iraq	167,618	434,128	59	32,665,000[49]	38	194.9	75.2	3.0	1997	21,941,050	49.7	50.3	67.9
Ireland	27,133	70,273	121	4,606,000	120	169.8	65.5	1.6	2011	4,581,269[10, 38]	49.5	50.5	60.5[13]
Isle of Man	221	572	192	84,700	205	383.3	148.1	1.0	2006	80,058	49.4	50.6	71.6
Israel[50]	8,357[51]	21,643[51]	152	7,431,000	98	889.2	343.3	1.7	2008[31]	7,412,180[52]	49.5[16]	50.5[16]	91.6[7, 17]
Italy	116,346	301,336	72	60,769,000	23	522.3	201.7	0.6	2001	56,995,744	48.4	51.6	67.3
Jamaica	4,244	10,991	165	2,709,000	140	638.3	246.5	0.3	2001	2,607,632	49.2	50.8	52.0
Japan	145,927	377,950	63	127,937,000	10	876.7	338.5	0.0	2010	128,057,352	48.7	51.3	66.6[3]
Jersey	46	118	214	94,100	201	2,045.7	797.5	1.1	2001	87,186	48.7	51.3	28.9[8, 48]
Jordan	34,277	88,778	112	6,180,000	106	180.3	69.6	2.2	2004	5,103,639	51.5	48.5	78.3
Kazakhstan	1,052,090	2,724,900	9	16,560,000	63	15.7	6.1	1.6	2009	16,009,597	48.3	51.7	54.0
Kenya	224,961	582,646	47	40,770,000	31	181.2	70.0	3.0	2009	38,610,097[15]	49.7	50.3	32.3
Kiribati	313	811	185	101,000	199	322.7	124.5	1.6	2005	92,533	49.3	50.7	47.5[13]
Korea, North	47,399	122,762	99	24,336,000	49	513.4	198.2	0.5	2008	24,052,231	48.7	51.3	61.6[13]
Korea, South	38,486	99,678	108	48,755,000	26	1,266.8	489.1	0.5	2010	48,580,293	50.3	49.7	82.7[3]
Kosovo	4,212	10,908	166	1,826,000	148	433.5	167.4	0.5	2011	1,733,872	50.4	49.6	...
Kuwait	6,880	17,818	157	3,650,000	131	530.5	204.8	3.4	2005	2,213,403[55]	59.2	40.8	98.3[13]
Kyrgyzstan	77,199	199,945	87	5,168,000	116	66.9	25.8	0.5	2009	5,107,700	48.7	51.3	35.3
Laos	91,429	236,800	84	6,392,000	104	69.9	27.0	2.2	2005	5,621,982	49.8	50.2	27.1
Latvia	24,938	64,589	125	2,217,000	143	88.9	34.3	−0.6	2000	2,377,383	46.1	53.9	68.1
Lebanon	4,036	10,452	167	4,143,000	125	1,026.5	396.4	1.5	1997	4,005,025[56]	50.2[56]	49.8[56]	86.6[13]
Lesotho	11,720	30,355	141	1,925,000	147	164.2	63.4	0.1	2006[31]	1,876,633	48.6	51.4	22.8
Liberia	37,420	96,917	109	3,953,000	126	105.6	40.8	3.5	2008	3,476,608	50.0	50.0	47.0
Libya	647,184	1,676,198	17	6,423,000	103	9.9	3.8	1.7	2006	5,673,031	51.9	48.1	77.0[13]
Liechtenstein	62	160	213	36,300	217	585.5	226.9	0.7	2008[6, 7]	35,356	49.3	50.7	14.3[13]
Lithuania	25,212	65,300	124	3,218,000	135	127.6	49.3	−1.0	2001	3,483,972	46.8	53.2	66.9
Luxembourg	999	2,586	176	517,000	172	517.5	200.0	1.8	2001	439,539	49.3	50.7	91.9[8]
Macau	11.8	30.6	219	561,000	169	47,542.4	18,333.3	2.4	2006	502,113	48.8	51.2	100.0
Macedonia	9,928	25,713	149	2,060,000	144	207.5	80.1	0.2	2002	2,022,547	50.2	49.8	59.5[28]
Madagascar	226,658	587,041	46	21,307,000	55	94.0	36.3	3.0	1993	12,238,914	49.7	50.3	22.9
Malawi	45,747	118,484	101	15,381,000	66	336.2	129.8	3.1	2008	13,077,160	48.6	51.4	15.3
Malaysia	127,724	330,804	68	28,161,000	43	220.5	85.1	2.2	2010	27,565,821	50.9	49.1	71.3[3]
Maldives	115	298	207	325,000[57]	180	2,826.1	1,090.6	1.6	2006	298,968[58]	50.7	49.3	34.7
Mali	482,077	1,248,574	23	15,525,000	65	32.2	12.4	3.0	2009	14,517,176[15]	49.6	50.4	35.1[3]
Malta	122	316	206	419,000	176	3,434.4	1,326.0	0.6	2005	404,962	49.6	50.4	95.3[13]
Marshall Islands	70	181	212	55,000	212	785.7	303.9	0.7	1999	50,848	51.2	48.8	65.2
Martinique	436	1,128	182	401,000	178	919.7	355.5	0.2	2008[36]	397,693[37]	47.0[13]	53.0[13]	89.1[3]
Mauritania	398,000	1,030,700	29	3,282,000	134	8.2	3.2	2.4	2000	2,508,159	49.5	50.5	57.7[11]
Mauritius	788	2,040	178	1,288,000	157	1,634.5	631.4	0.6	2000[31]	1,179,137	49.5	50.5	42.7[11]
Mayotte	144	374	202	210,000	188	1,458.3	561.5	3.1	2007	186,387	49.0	51.0	...
Mexico	758,450	1,964,375	14	114,492,000	11	151.0	58.3	1.8	2010	112,336,538	48.8	51.2	76.0[13]
Micronesia	271	701	190	102,000	198	376.4	145.5	−0.4	2010	102,624	50.7	49.3[17]	28.3[11]
Moldova	13,067	33,843	139	3,927,000	127	300.5	116.0	−0.2	2004	3,383,332[61]	48.1	51.9	61.4
Monaco	0.78	2.02	222	36,000	218	46,153.8	17,821.8	0.4	2008	35,352	47.9	52.1	100.0
Mongolia	603,909	1,564,116	19	2,765,000	139	4.6	1.8	1.3	2010	2,754,685[15]	48.6	51.4	63.3
Montenegro	5,333	13,812	161	620,000	168	116.3	44.9	−0.0	2011	620,029[15]	49.4	50.6	56.1[28]
Morocco[65]	170,773	442,300	58	31,968,000	39	187.2	72.3	1.1	2004	29,680,069[66, 67]	49.3[67]	50.7[67]	55.1[67]
Mozambique	308,642	799,380	36	22,949,000	51	74.4	28.7	2.3	2007	20,530,714[15]	47.7[9]	52.3[9]	34.5[13]
Myanmar (Burma)	261,228	676,577	40	54,000,000	24	206.7	79.8	1.1	1983	35,307,913	49.6	50.4	24.0
Namibia	318,193	824,116	35	2,324,000	142	7.3	2.8	1.9	2001	1,830,330	48.5	51.5	33.0

age distribution (%)						population (by decade, '000s)								country
0–14	15–29	30–44	45–59	60–74	75 and over	1960	1970	1980	1990	2000	2010	2020 projection	2030 projection	
32.1[5]	27.5[5]	19.5[5]	12.5[5]	6.1[5]	2.3[5]	4,439	5,972	7,958	10,261	12,345	14,367	16,362	17,900	Ecuador
31.8	—48.2—		13.7	—6.3—		27,903	35,575	44,952	56,843	67,648	81,121	94,810	106,498	Egypt
33.9	26.9	18.5	11.3	6.5	2.9	2,582	3,604	4,570	5,110	5,850	6,052	6,217	6,340	El Salvador
42.0[5]	26.6[5]	16.6[5]	8.7[5]	5.0[5]	1.1[5]	252	291	221	374	520	700	905	1,102	Equatorial Guinea
46.1	23.0	15.9	8.9	4.4	1.6	1,424	1,847	2,469	3,158	3,668	5,254	6,848	8,394	Eritrea
18.1	21.4	20.8	18.6	15.6	5.5	1,216	1,365	1,473	1,568	1,371	1,341	1,329	1,296	Estonia
45.0	28.3	14.7	7.2	3.7	1.1	22,553	28,959	35,426	48,333	65,578	79,456	104,677	129,056	Ethiopia
21.9	19.1	19.8	19.1	13.3	6.8	34	39	43	48	46	49	51	54	Faroe Islands
29.0	27.9	21.1	14.5	6.1	1.4	393	521	635	728	812	847	890	946	Fiji
16.9	18.7	19.3	22.0	15.3	7.8	4,430	4,606	4,799	4,986	5,176	5,363	5,619	5,833	Finland
18.3[7, 16]	18.8[7, 16]	19.9[7, 16]	20.1[7, 16]	14.0[7, 16]	8.9[7, 16]	45,689	50,763	53,880	56,708	59,048	62,954	66,071	68,672	France[35]
35.1[3]	23.6[3]	21.5[3]	13.5[3]	4.7[3]	1.6[3]	32	49	68	117	165	236	303	374	French Guiana
26.0	26.6	23.4	15.3	6.9	1.8	79	111	151	195	238	269	296	316	French Polynesia
42.1[5]	27.6[5]	15.5[5]	9.0[5]	4.5[5]	1.3[5]	486	530	683	929	1,235	1,505	1,818	2,146	Gabon
44.9[28]	26.4[28]	15.5[28]	8.8[28]	3.6[28]	0.8[28]	352	485	652	951	1,357	1,755	2,174	2,554	Gambia, The
45.0[5]	28.9[5]	14.9[5]	7.3[5]	2.9[5]	1.0[5]	308	343	456	646	1,130	1,604	2,121	2,565	Gaza Strip
21.0	22.8	21.9	15.6	14.6	4.1	4,159[42]	4,707[42]	5,073[42]	5,439[42]	4,418[40]	4,460[40]	4,222[40]	3,890[40]	Georgia
13.9	17.6	22.4	21.1	16.7	8.3	73,147	78,069	78,397	79,753	82,260	81,703	80,431	78,922	Germany
37.7[4]	29.4[4]	18.3[4]	9.5[4]	4.1[4]	1.0[4]	6,958	8,789	11,011	15,408	19,030	24,086	29,998	36,144	Ghana
14.3[26]	19.3[26]	22.9[26]	19.7[26]	15.8[26]	8.0[26]	8,333	8,793	9,643	10,161	10,987	11,327	11,561	11,613	Greece
23.8	22.1	23.3	20.4	—10.4—		33	46	50	56	56	57	57	58	Greenland
35.1	28.1	17.6	9.0	—10.2—		90	95	90	94	102	108	113	116	Grenada
22.5	18.0	21.9	19.9	11.8	5.9	266[44]	310[44]	318[44]	355[44]	388	405	421	431	Guadeloupe[43]
27.8[3]	23.5[3]	20.9[3]	17.1[3]	8.2[3]	2.5[3]	67	85	107	134	155	159	177	195	Guam
43.6[46]	27.4[46]	14.4[46]	9.4[46]	4.1[46]	1.1[46]	4,159	5,448	7,036	8,923	11,237	14,376	18,361	22,700	Guatemala
17.2	18.8	23.2	20.0	13.4	7.4	45	51	53	61	62	65	69	72	Guernsey
42.9[4]	26.5[4]	16.0[4]	9.2[4]	4.4[4]	1.0[4]	3,541	4,154	4,407	5,759	8,344	9,982	12,765	15,946	Guinea
40.8[3]	28.3[3]	16.7[3]	9.2[3]	4.2[3]	0.8[3]	593	603	835	1,017	1,241	1,569	1,935	2,350	Guinea-Bissau
26.5[13]	29.7[13]	23.0[13]	13.3[13]	5.6[13]	1.9[13]	560	721	777	725	733	754	773	795	Guyana
42.7[28]	29.3[28]	14.2[28]	8.2[28]	4.5[28]	1.1[28]	3,697	4,541	5,508	6,798	8,413	9,649	10,693	11,784	Haiti
42.2[8]	29.1[8]	15.1[8]	8.3[8]	4.1[8]	1.2[8]	2,000	2,688	3,628	4,889	6,218	7,601	9,179	10,657	Honduras
13.7	20.6	26.2	23.5	10.4	5.6	3,076	3,958	5,054	5,794	6,665	7,068	7,803	8,483	Hong Kong
16.6	22.2	19.8	21.0	14.3	6.1	9,961	10,301	10,709	10,374	10,211	10,000	9,829	9,648	Hungary
21.0	22.3	21.4	19.2	10.4	5.7	176	204	228	255	281	318	341	372	Iceland
30.9[4]	26.9[4]	21.2[4]	13.1[4]	6.4[4]	1.5[4]	447,844	553,874	700,059	873,785	1,053,898	1,197,123	1,360,935	1,494,946	India
28.9	26.1	23.1	14.3	6.0	1.6	91,947	118,362	150,820	184,346	213,395	237,920	261,802	278,843	Indonesia
25.1	35.4	20.6	11.6	5.4	1.9	21,999	28,662	38,577	54,871	65,342	74,733	81,722	85,145	Iran
39.4[5]	29.8[5]	18.4[5]	7.9[5]	3.3[5]	1.2[5]	7,380	10,022	13,744	17,374	23,857	31,672	42,684	55,257	Iraq
20.4[26]	23.7[26]	23.0[26]	17.6[26]	10.5[26]	4.8[26]	2,832	2,950	3,401	3,506	3,790	4,471	5,065	5,460	Ireland
16.9	17.2	22.0	21.1	14.4	8.4	48	53	64	69	76	84	90	94	Isle of Man
28.0[16]	22.9[16]	19.7[16]	15.2[16]	9.5[16]	4.7[16]	2,090	2,850	3,746	4,500	6,015	7,316	8,569	9,707	Israel[50]
14.1[8]	18.9[8]	23.8[8]	19.0[8]	16.0[8]	8.2[8]	49,519	53,325	56,221	56,832	57,646	60,482	62,468	63,583	Italy
32.4	25.9	20.6	11.0	6.8	3.3	1,629	1,869	2,132	2,365	2,582	2,702	2,787	2,800	Jamaica
13.3[16]	15.9[16]	20.9[16]	19.1[16]	19.7[16]	11.1[16]	92,501	103,710	115,915	122,251	125,720	127,450	126,360	121,717	Japan
16.9	18.4	25.9	19.7	12.6	6.5	63	69	76	84	87	93	99	102	Jersey
38.2	30.1	18.6	8.0	4.2	0.9	895	1,667	2,299	3,416	4,798	6,046	6,931	8,201	Jordan
24.3[16]	27.2[16]	21.0[16]	17.3[16]	7.7[16]	2.5[16]	9,982	13,106	15,000	16,775	14,884	16,315	18,301	19,534	Kazakhstan
42.9	—53.6[53]—			—3.5[54]—		8,157	11,247	16,331	23,361	30,606	39,586	48,786	55,336	Kenya
36.9	28.3	18.7	10.7	4.5	0.9	33	44	55	72	84	100	116	132	Kiribati
21.6[4]	23.8[4]	25.2[4]	15.8[4]	11.2[4]	2.4[4]	10,946	14,247	17,239	20,143	22,859	24,249	25,241	26,063	Korea, North
18.6[13]	22.5[13]	26.0[13]	19.2[13]	10.7[13]	3.0[13]	25,074	31,443	37,460	42,980	46,059	48,491	50,127	50,655	Korea, South
37.4	28.8	16.5	10.3	5.3	1.7	947	1,219	1,521	1,862	1,700	1,815	1,933	2,066	Kosovo
25.0	29.0	31.2	11.8	—3.0—		292	748	1,370	2,131	2,236	3,567	4,423	5,228	Kuwait
31.3[13]	29.3[13]	19.9[13]	12.2[13]	5.2[13]	2.1[13]	2,173	2,964	3,627	4,395	4,883	5,141	5,755	6,382	Kyrgyzstan
39.4	28.3	17.0	9.5	4.4	1.4	2,130	2,691	3,235	4,192	5,245	6,259	7,170	7,892	Laos
18.1	21.2	21.4	18.3	15.7	5.3	2,132	2,366	2,513	2,664	2,373	2,239	2,143	2,048	Latvia
28.0[56]	30.0[56]	19.8[56]	12.4[56]	—9.8[56]—		1,786	2,383	2,899	3,440	3,791	4,125	4,243	4,335	Lebanon
33.9	32.5	15.9	10.0	5.6	2.1	859	1,067	1,359	1,703	1,916	1,920	1,969	1,952	Lesotho
41.9	29.1	16.7	7.4	3.4	1.5	1,116	1,440	1,923	2,127	2,847	3,823	4,945	6,254	Liberia
30.3[13]	31.9[13]	21.0[13]	10.8[13]	4.9[13]	1.1[13]	1,349	1,994	3,063	4,334	5,231	6,355	7,083	7,783	Libya
16.8	19.9	22.5	22.6	13.1	5.1	16	21	25	29	33	36	39	41	Liechtenstein
19.5	21.2	22.8	17.2	14.2	5.1	2,765	3,138	3,436	3,698	3,500	3,292	3,101	2,982	Lithuania
18.9	18.6	25.5	18.4	12.9	5.7	314	339	364	381	435	507	577	638	Luxembourg
15.2	25.6	26.3	23.0	6.6	3.3	173	254	252	372	431	545	662	751	Macau
21.1	23.8	22.0	18.1	11.7	3.3	1,392	1,568	1,795	1,909	2,009	2,055	2,070	2,040	Macedonia
44.7	27.7	15.6	7.2	3.9	0.9	5,104	6,549	8,609	11,281	15,364	20,714	27,366	35,333	Madagascar
45.9	27.7	14.5	6.7	3.4	1.8	3,525	4,531	6,240	9,381	11,229	14,901	20,677	28,174	Malawi
30.2[3]	26.1[3]	21.7[3]	14.7[3]	5.8[3]	1.5[3]	8,428	10,910	13,460	17,882	22,198	27,558	32,221	36,402	Malaysia
31.1[59]	33.2[59]	18.3[59]	9.2[59]	5.2[59]	1.3[59]	99	121	158	216	272	320	375	422	Maldives
47.6[3]	26.2[3]	13.8[3]	7.7[3]	3.9[3]	0.8[3]	4,495	5,546	6,822	8,327	11,259	15,064	20,128	26,251	Mali
17.2	21.7	19.7	22.3	13.5	5.6	313	304	327	368	397	416	429	432	Malta
42.9	28.7	16.7	8.2	2.6	0.9	15	22	31	44	51	54	59	62	Marshall Islands
22.0	21.0	24.4	16.0	11.1	5.5	282	325	326	360	384	402	415	423	Martinique
43.9	27.0	15.9	7.7	4.3	1.2	1,117	1,289	1,545	1,925	2,501	3,205	4,005	4,851	Mauritania
25.2	26.0	24.8	14.9	6.8	2.3	662	829	966	1,059	1,187	1,282	1,366	1,419	Mauritius
41.2[60]	28.5[60]	17.8[60]	7.7[60]	3.8[60]	1.1[60]	25	35	52	89	147	203	265	324	Mayotte
29.1[16]	26.2[16]	21.8[16]	13.9[16]	6.4[16]	2.6[16]	38,419	51,868	68,776	84,307	99,960	112,437	125,792	135,251	Mexico
40.3	28.4	16.9	9.1	3.9	1.4	45	61	73	96	107	102	99	103	Micronesia
19.1[62]	26.3[62]	20.9[62]	19.1[62]	—14.3[62]—		3,004	3,595	4,010	4,364	4,223	3,935	3,713	3,480	Moldova
12.8[63]	12.7[63]	19.2[63]	21.8[63]	19.1[63]	12.1[63]	21	24	27	30	35	35	36	38	Monaco
35.8	30.2	20.5	8.3	—5.2—		931	1,248	1,663	2,086	2,389	2,747	3,150	3,485	Mongolia
20.6[64]	23.1[64]	20.5[64]	18.2[64]	12.8[64]	3.9[64]	467	519	576	609	633	631	636	633	Montenegro
31.3[67]	28.9[67]	20.1[67]	11.7[67]	6.0[67]	2.0[67]	12,423	15,909	19,487	24,000	28,113	31,627	34,956	37,887	Morocco[65]
44.7[5]	26.4[5]	15.6[5]	8.8[5]	3.8[5]	0.7[5]	7,472	9,304	12,103	12,989	17,996	22,417	28,603	36,622	Mozambique
38.6	28.7	15.5	10.9	5.2	1.1	22,839	27,393	33,336	40,464	47,439	53,414	59,126	64,103	Myanmar (Burma)
42.7[8]	28.6[8]	15.5[8]	7.9[8]	3.9[8]	1.4[8]	603	780	1,013	1,415	1,896	2,283	2,672	3,042	Namibia

Area and population (continued)

country	area			population (latest estimate)					population (recent census)				
	square miles	square kilo-metres	rank	total midyear 2011	rank	density per sq mi	density per sq km	% annual growth rate 2006–11	census year	total	male (%)	female (%)	urban (%)
Nauru	8.2	21.2	221	9,300	222	1,134.1	438.7	–0.5	2002	10,065	51.0	49.0	100.0
Nepal	56,827	147,181	95	26,629,000	45	468.6	180.9	1.4	2011	26,620,809[15]	49.9[68]	50.1[68]	14.2[68]
Netherlands	16,040	41,543	134	16,683,000	62	1,040.1	401.6	0.4	2001	15,985,538	49.5	50.5	89.6[8]
New Caledonia	7,172	18,575	155	255,000	185	35.6	13.7	1.6	2009	245,580	50.4[4]	49.6[4]	63.7[13]
New Zealand	104,515	270,692	75	4,407,000	123	42.2	16.3	1.0	2006	4,143,282	48.8	51.2	86.2[13]
Nicaragua	50,337	130,373	98	5,870,000	109	116.6	45.0	1.3	2005	5,142,098	49.3	50.7	55.9
Niger	489,191	1,267,000	22	16,469,000	64	33.7	13.0	3.8	2001	11,060,291	49.9	50.1	16.3
Nigeria	356,669	923,768	32	162,471,000	7	455.5	175.9	2.5	2006	140,431,790	50.8	49.2	48.2[13]
Northern Mariana Islands	176	457	196	46,100	215	261.9	100.9	–5.4	2000	69,221	46.2	53.8	90.1
Norway	148,718[69]	385,179[69]	62	4,953,000	118	33.3	12.9	1.2	2001	4,520,947	49.6	50.4	76.5
Oman	119,500	309,500	71	2,810,000	138	23.5	9.1	2.4	2010	2,773,479	58.1	41.9	71.5
Pakistan[70]	340,499	881,889	34	187,343,000	6	550.2	212.4	1.7	1998[71]	130,579,571	52.0	48.0	33.3
Palau	188	488	194	20,600	220	109.6	42.2	0.6	2005	19,907	53.7	46.3	70.0[13]
Panama	28,640	74,177	119	3,643,000	132	127.2	49.1	2.4	2010	3,405,813	50.3	49.7	74.1[3]
Papua New Guinea	178,704	462,840	55	6,188,000	105	34.6	13.4	2.1	2000	5,130,365	51.9	48.1	13.2[11]
Paraguay	157,048	406,752	60	6,459,000	102	41.1	15.9	1.4	2002	5,163,198	50.4	49.6	56.7
Peru	496,225	1,285,216	20	29,249,000	41	58.9	22.8	1.1	2007	28,220,764	49.7	50.3	75.9
Philippines	115,831	300,000	73	95,849,000	12	827.5	319.5	2.0	2007	88,548,366	50.4[22]	49.6[22]	58.5[11]
Poland	120,726	312,679	70	38,216,000	33	316.6	122.2	0.0	2002	38,230,100	48.4	51.6	61.8
Portugal	35,558	92,094	111	10,555,000	79	296.8	114.6	–0.1	2011	10,555,853[15, 31]	47.9	52.1	60.9[3]
Puerto Rico	3,515	9,104	169	3,716,000	130	1,057.2	408.2	–0.2	2010	3,725,789	48.0[3]	52.0[3]	94.6[11]
Qatar	4,468	11,571	164	1,624,000	150	363.5	140.4	10.1	2010	1,699,435	75.7	24.3	100.0[4]
Réunion	973	2,520	177	852,000	161	875.6	338.1	1.6	2006	781,962[31]	48.5	51.5	93.7[3]
Romania	92,043	238,391	83	21,393,000	54	232.4	89.7	–0.2	2002	21,680,974	48.7	51.3	52.7
Russia	6,601,700	17,098,200	1	142,707,000	9	21.6	8.3	0.0	2010	142,905,208	46.3	53.7	73.7
Rwanda	10,185	26,379	148	10,943,000	77	1,074.4	414.8	3.0	2002	8,128,553	47.7	52.3	16.9
St. Kitts and Nevis	104	269	208	50,300	213	483.7	187.0	0.8	2001	46,111	49.7	50.3	34.2[8]
St. Lucia	238	617	191	167,000	191	701.7	270.7	1.1	2010	165,595[15, 31]	49.8	50.2	38.0[8]
St. Vincent and the Grenadines	150	389	201	101,000	200	673.3	259.6	–0.0	2001	109,022	50.9	49.1	44.8[11]
Samoa	1,075	2,785	175	184,000	189	171.2	66.1	0.4	2006	180,741	51.8	48.2	20.9
San Marino	24	61	216	32,000	219	1,333.3	524.6	1.2	2010[6, 7]	31,632	49.1	50.9	96.0[13]
Sao Tome and Principe	386	1,001	184	169,000	190	437.8	168.8	1.7	2001	137,599	49.6	50.4	47.7[8]
Saudi Arabia	830,000	2,149,690	13	28,572,000	42	34.4	13.3	4.0	2010	27,136,977	50.9	49.1	87.7[28]
Senegal	75,955	196,722	88	12,644,000	71	166.5	64.3	2.6	2002	9,855,338	49.2	50.8	40.7
Serbia[72]	29,922	77,498	118	7,262,000	100	242.7	93.7	–0.4	2011	7,565,761[15]	48.6[3]	51.4[3]	55.7[3]
Seychelles	174	452	197	92,000	202	528.7	203.5	1.3	2010	90,945	51.6	48.4	64.6[8]
Sierra Leone	27,699	71,740	120	5,997,000	108	216.5	83.6	2.4	2004	4,976,871	48.6	51.4	38.8[28]
Singapore	274	710	189	5,182,000[73]	115	18,912.4	7,298.6	3.3	2010[6, 31]	3,771,721	49.3	50.7	100.0
Sint Maarten	13	34	218	38,300	216	2,946.2	1,126.5	–0.0	2001	30,594	48.0	52.0	...
Slovakia	18,932	49,034	130	5,440,000	112	287.3	110.9	0.2	2001	5,379,455	48.6	51.4	55.0
Slovenia	7,827	20,273	154	2,052,000	145	262.2	101.2	0.4	2011[6]	2,050,189	49.5	50.5	49.6[3]
Solomon Islands	10,954	28,370	144	535,000	170	48.8	18.9	2.3	2009	515,870	51.3	48.7	19.7
Somalia	246,201	637,657	43	9,926,000	84	40.3	15.6	2.0	1975	4,089,203	50.1	49.9	25.4
South Africa	471,359	1,220,813	25	50,587,000	25	107.3	41.4	1.1	2001	44,819,778	47.8	52.2	57.7[8]
Spain	195,364	505,991	52	47,215,000	27	241.7	93.3	1.0	2001	40,847,371	49.0	51.0	77.8[8]
Sri Lanka	25,332	65,610	123	21,045,000	56	830.8	320.8	1.0	2001	16,864,544[74]	49.5[74]	50.5[74]	14.6[74]
Sudan[76]	712,280[77]	1,844,797[77]	16	36,787,000[77]	34	51.6[77]	19.9[77]	3.0[77]	2008	39,154,490[15]	51.3	48.7	37.6[26]
Sudan, South	248,777	644,330	42	9,150,000	90	36.8	14.2	3.7	2008	8,260,490	51.9	48.1	17.0[17]
Suriname	63,251	163,820	92	529,000	171	8.4	3.2	0.9	2004	492,829	50.3	49.7	76.1[28]
Swaziland	6,704	17,364	158	1,203,000	158	179.4	69.3	1.5	2007	1,018,449	47.3	52.7	22.1
Sweden	173,860	450,295	56	9,451,000	87	54.4	21.0	0.8	2008[6, 7]	9,182,927	49.7	50.3	84.6[3]
Switzerland	15,940	41,285	135	7,913,000	94	496.4	191.7	1.0	2000[78]	7,288,010	49.0	51.0	68.0
Syria	71,498	185,180	89	20,766,000[79]	57	290.4	112.1	1.9	2004	17,920,844	51.1	48.9	50.6[13]
Taiwan	13,973	36,191	137	23,190,000	50	1,659.6	640.8	0.3	2010[31]	23,162,123	50.2[17]	49.8[17]	81.0[13]
Tajikistan	55,300	143,100	96	7,681,000	97	138.9	53.7	2.0	2010	7,565,000	50.2[3]	49.8[3]	26.5
Tanzania	364,901	945,090	31	45,030,000	30	123.4	47.6	3.0	2002	34,569,232	48.9	51.1	23.0
Thailand	198,117	513,120	51	65,856,000	20	332.4	128.3	1.0	2010	65,479,453	49.1	50.9	33.6[3]
Togo	21,853	56,600	126	5,830,000	110	266.8	103.0	2.1	2010	5,753,324	48.7	51.3	37.4[16]
Tonga	289	748	188	104,000	196	359.9	139.0	0.4	2006	101,991	50.8	49.2	23.2
Trinidad and Tobago	1,990	5,155	172	1,325,000	156	665.8	257.0	0.4	2000	1,262,366	50.1	49.9	74.1[11]
Tunisia	63,170	163,610	93	10,594,000	78	167.7	64.8	1.1	2004	9,910,872	50.1	49.9	64.9
Turkey	303,224	785,347	37	74,306,000	18	245.1	94.6	1.4	2011[7]	73,722,988[6]	50.3	49.7	69.2[3]
Turkmenistan	189,657	491,210	53	4,998,000	117	26.4	10.2	1.2	1995	4,483,251	49.6	50.4	46.0
Tuvalu	9.9	25.6	220	11,200	221	1,131.3	437.5	0.5	2002	9,561	49.5	50.5	47.0
Uganda	93,263	241,551	81	34,509,000	36	370.0	142.9	3.3	2002	24,442,084	48.8	51.2	12.3
Ukraine	233,062	603,628	45	45,672,000	28	196.0	75.7	–0.6	2001[31]	48,457,102	46.3	53.7	67.2
United Arab Emirates	32,280	83,600	115	7,891,000	95	244.5	94.4	11.0	2005	4,106,427	68.3	31.7	76.7[13]
United Kingdom	93,851	243,073	80	62,675,000	22	667.8	257.8	0.7	2001	58,789,194	48.6	51.4	89.5[8]
United States	3,678,190[80]	9,526,468[80]	4	313,387,000	3	85.2	32.9	0.9	2010	308,745,538[81]	49.2	50.8	83.5
Uruguay	68,679	177,879	91	3,380,000	133	49.2	19.0	0.3	2004[31]	3,241,003	48.3	51.7	91.8
Uzbekistan	171,469	444,103	57	28,129,000	44	164.0	63.3	1.0	1989	19,905,158	49.3	50.7	40.7
Vanuatu	4,707	12,190	162	251,000	186	53.3	20.6	3.0	2009	234,023	50.9	49.1	24.4
Venezuela	353,841	916,445	33	29,437,000	40	83.2	32.1	1.6	2001	23,054,210	49.5	50.5	87.2[8]
Vietnam	127,882	331,212	67	88,145,000	13	689.3	266.1	1.2	2009	85,846,997	49.5	50.5	29.6
Virgin Islands (U.S.)	136	352	204	119,000	194	875.0	338.1	1.0	2010	106,405	47.3	52.8	95.4
West Bank[84]	2,183	5,655	171	2,551,000[85]	141	1,168.6	451.1	2.4	2007	2,345,107	50.7	49.3	71.6[86]
Western Sahara	97,344	252,120	78	507,000	173	5.2	2.0	3.3	...	...	...	...	...
Yemen	203,891	528,076	50	24,800,000	47	121.6	47.0	3.6	2004	19,685,161	51.0	49.0	28.6
Zambia	290,585	752,612	39	13,306,000	70	45.8	17.7	2.8	2010	13,046,508[15]	50.0[3]	50.0[3]	35.7
Zimbabwe	150,872	390,757	61	12,084,000	72	80.1	30.9	0.9	2002	11,631,657	48.4	51.6	35.0

[1]Official estimate excluding nomads. [2]Preliminary figure; excludes nomads and other non-household residents. [3]2009 estimate. [4]2008 estimate. [5]2007 estimate. [6]Register-based census. [7]Beginning of year. [8]2001 estimate. [9]Based on preliminary census figures. [10]De facto population. [11]2000. [12]Unadjusted for undercount. [13]2005 estimate. [14]Rounded reported total. [15]Preliminary figure. [16]2010. [17]2011. [18]Excludes Brussels capital region. [19]Excludes institutionalized population. [20]Excludes temporary residents. [21]1991 estimate. [22]Based on 2000 census. [23]Beginning of 2002, estimate based on 2001 census. [24]Excludes a part of 0.5% unknown. [25]2010 official estimate based on 2005 census. [26]2006 estimate. [27]Includes institutionalized population. [28]2003 estimate. [29]Excludes a few census zones without official counts. [30]Based on 2008 national sample survey (about 1.0% of total population). [31]Data are for de jure population. [32]Includes the 0.7 sq mi (1.7 sq km) area of the uninhabited islet of Klein Curaçao [33]Data are for the island of Cyprus (except census information). [34]Republic of Cyprus only. [35]Metropolitan France only; overseas departments and territories are excluded. [36]Since 2004, based on annual census survey. [37]Computed from survey results of several years. [38]Provisional results. [39]Area of Georgia excluding Abkhazia and South Ossetia is 22,070 sq mi (57,160 sq km). [40]Excludes Abkhazia and South Ossetia. [41]Excludes about 230,000 people in Abkhazia and South Ossetia. [42]Includes Abkhazia and South Ossetia. [43]Excludes Saint-Martin and Saint-Barthélemy. [44]Includes Saint-Martin and Saint-Barthélemy. [45]Based on the land area of 209 sq mi (541 sq km) only. [46]2002. [47]Excludes Alderney and Sark. [48]Combined percentage for Guernsey and Jersey. [49]Includes nearly 1.7 million refugees in neighbouring countries. [50]Population figures (unless otherwise indicated) exclude Israelis in the West Bank. [51]Excludes the West Bank and the Gaza Strip. [52]Includes Israelis in the West Bank and the Gaza Strip. [53]Ages 15–64 only. [54]Ages 65 and over. [55]Census data are more narrowly defined than country estimates with particular

age distribution (%)						population (by decade, '000s)								country
0–14	15–29	30–44	45–59	60–74	75 and over	1960	1970	1980	1990	2000	2010	2020 projection	2030 projection	
38.5	27.7	21.0	10.2	2.2	0.4	4	7	8	9	10	9	10	10	Nauru
39.3[68]	27.0[68]	17.1[68]	10.1[68]	5.2[68]	1.3[68]	10,035	11,919	14,665	18,918	24,818	26,260	30,759	34,939	Nepal
18.6	18.8	24.3	20.0	12.2	6.1	11,494	13,020	14,150	14,952	15,926	16,602	17,224	17,630	Netherlands
26.7[4]	24.1[4]	22.8[4]	15.7[4]	8.2[4]	2.5[4]	79	112	139	169	211	249	289	323	New Caledonia
21.1	20.5	22.0	19.4	11.4	5.6	2,377	2,820	3,144	3,452	3,860	4,368	4,758	5,085	New Zealand
37.6	29.9	17.1	9.3	4.3	1.8	1,775	2,400	3,250	4,138	5,101	5,788	6,603	7,240	Nicaragua
47.5	25.0	16.2	6.8	3.3	1.2	3,913	4,841	6,093	7,842	10,951	15,878	22,749	31,946	Niger
42.1[26]	28.1[26]	16.3[26]	8.7[26]	4.0[26]	0.8[26]	45,148	56,467	74,523	97,338	124,842	158,259	193,252	226,651	Nigeria
22.5	31.9	32.2	10.7	2.3	0.4	9	12	17	44	70	48	49	56	Northern Mariana Islands
18.9[16]	19.2[16]	21.5[16]	19.5[16]	13.6[16]	7.3[16]	3,583	3,877	4,086	4,241	4,491	4,888	5,565	6,096	Norway
33.8	32.3	20.8	8.9	3.2	1.0	601	783	1,185	1,794	2,432	2,743	3,244	3,533	Oman
43.2	26.9	15.6	8.8	4.3	1.2	51,719	67,491	85,219	118,816	152,429	184,405	213,719	242,862	Pakistan[70]
24.1	21.7	28.7	17.3	5.7	2.5	9	12	13	15	19	21	22	23	Palau
29.2	24.9	21.1	14.2	7.6	3.0	1,136	1,524	1,982	2,474	3,005	3,585	4,138	4,622	Panama
40.0	28.5	18.6	8.8	3.5	0.6	1,718	2,214	2,846	3,683	4,813	6,065	7,259	8,359	Papua New Guinea
37.1	27.3	17.9	10.6	5.1	2.0	1,910	2,477	3,172	4,200	5,418	6,376	7,192	7,974	Paraguay
30.5	27.5	20.4	12.5	6.4	2.7	9,931	13,193	17,295	21,565	25,797	28,948	31,915	34,444	Peru
37.0[22]	27.6[22]	19.1[22]	10.3[22]	4.7[22]	1.3[22]	27,057	36,567	48,112	62,427	76,759	93,932	110,966	127,731	Philippines
18.2	24.4	20.4	20.0	12.1	4.9	29,561	32,526	35,578	38,031	38,259	38,187	38,304	38,763	Poland
16.0[31, 68]	22.2[31, 68]	21.8[31, 68]	18.3[31, 68]	14.9[31, 68]	6.8[31, 68]	9,037	9,044	9,778	9,923	10,235	10,637	10,508	10,197	Portugal
19.8[3]	21.5[3]	20.2[3]	18.8[3]	13.5[3]	6.2[3]	2,358	2,722	3,210	3,537	3,807	3,724	3,714	3,721	Puerto Rico
13.7	31.3	40.2	13.1	1.5	0.2	45	111	229	467	591	1,674	1,986	2,141	Qatar
27.0[13]	23.6[13]	24.1[13]	15.0[13]	7.5[13]	2.8[13]	338	447	507	601	723	839	933	1,003	Réunion
17.6	23.4	21.0	18.7	14.4	4.9	18,407	20,253	22,201	23,207	22,072	21,444	20,941	20,153	Romania
14.8[4]	24.0[4]	21.1[4]	22.8[4]	11.8[4]	5.5[4]	119,906	130,392	138,655	148,244	146,758	141,777	140,966	136,374	Russia
43.8	30.1	14.7	7.1	3.3	1.0	2,771	3,749	5,179	7,110	8,098	10,624	14,042	17,579	Rwanda
30.7[11]	26.5[11]	21.1[11]	10.8[11]	—10.9[11]—		51	46	44	42	46	50	54	57	St. Kitts and Nevis
24.1	25.9	22.2	15.9	8.1	3.8	90	104	118	138	157	166	181	191	St. Lucia
31.8[11]	28.0[11]	20.6[11]	11.2[11]	6.5[11]	1.9[11]	81	88	98	107	108	101	101	101	St. Vincent and the Grenadines
39.3	24.6	18.2	11.0	5.2	1.7	110	142	155	161	175	183	188	198	Samoa
15.0	14.9	26.4	21.5	14.1	8.1	15	19	21	24	27	32	33	34	San Marino
42.1	30.3	14.5	6.9	4.7	1.5	64	74	95	116	141	165	200	235	Sao Tome and Principe
34.3	28.6	23.8	9.1	3.2	1.0	4,718	6,109	10,022	16,061	21,312	27,346	32,626	37,010	Saudi Arabia
42.4	28.5	15.8	8.6	3.9	0.8	3,270	4,318	5,611	7,348	9,469	12,323	15,736	19,485	Senegal
15.8[5]	19.7[5]	20.4[5]	22.4[5]	14.9[5]	6.8[5]	6,659	7,248	7,588	7,786	7,604	7,291	6,961	6,623	Serbia[72]
22.4	25.0	25.0	17.2	7.1	3.3	41	52	63	71	79	91	95	97	Seychelles
41.7	27.1	16.7	8.0	4.3	2.2	2,187	2,593	3,162	3,982	4,143	5,868	7,178	8,532	Sierra Leone
17.3	20.8	24.6	23.2	10.5	3.6	1,634[73]	2,074[73]	2,415[73]	3,017[73]	3,919[73]	5,086[73]	5,597[73]	5,978[73]	Singapore
23.4	19.0	28.3	22.1	6.1	1.1	2,705	6,481	12,414	29,286	30,520	37,994	40,785	42,552	Sint Maarten
18.9	25.1	21.5	18.9	11.0	4.6	4,145	4,528	4,976	5,256	5,401	5,431	5,514	5,590	Slovakia
14.0[16]	18.9[16]	22.6[16]	22.5[16]	14.5[16]	7.5[16]	1,580	1,670	1,832	1,927	1,985	2,049	2,140	2,163	Slovenia
38.8	28.0	18.9	8.7	4.3	1.3	118	160	229	310	415	523	665	817	Solomon Islands
45.6	24.9	15.5	7.4	—5.4—		2,956	3,667	5,794	6,692	7,501	9,768	11,757	15,041	Somalia
32.0	29.5	20.2	11.0	5.5	1.8	17,396	22,502	29,075	36,745	44,872	49,991	52,798	54,945	South Africa
14.5	22.4	23.7	17.8	14.2	7.4	30,641	33,876	37,488	39,351	40,589	47,085	49,034	51,079	Spain
26.0[75]	27.5[75]	22.3[75]	14.5[75]	7.3[75]	2.4[75]	10,020	12,555	15,083	17,337	18,745	20,860	22,344	23,094	Sri Lanka
42.6	27.7	16.8	7.7	3.8	1.4	10,589	13,788	19,482	25,888	34,109	43,940	56,292	69,996	Sudan[76]
44.4	27.7	16.5	7.3	3.1	1.0	—	—	—	—	5,897	8,920	11,433	14,217	Sudan, South
30.0	26.2	22.7	12.5	6.6	2.0	290	372	366	407	467	525	569	602	Suriname
39.5	31.5	15.2	8.2	4.2	1.4	349	446	603	863	1,064	1,186	1,341	1,462	Swaziland
16.8	19.0	20.6	19.3	15.6	8.7	7,498	8,042	8,310	8,559	8,872	9,378	9,956	10,321	Sweden
15.3[3]	18.4[3]	22.7[3]	21.1[3]	14.5[3]	8.0[3]	5,328	6,181	6,319	6,712	7,184	7,824	8,385	8,732	Switzerland
39.5	30.2	16.9	8.5	—4.9—		4,533	6,258	8,752	12,500	16,471	22,198	24,744	28,224	Syria
15.7[17]	21.9[17]	24.5[17]	22.7[17]	10.4[17]	4.8[17]	10,668	14,583	17,642	20,279	22,185	23,148	23,434	23,249	Taiwan
35.0[5]	31.5[5]	18.8[5]	9.7[5]	3.8[5]	1.2[5]	2,082	2,942	3,953	5,303	6,181	7,531	8,761	9,922	Tajikistan
44.3	27.7	15.3	7.1	4.1	1.5	10,127	14,011	18,468	24,341	32,389	43,790	57,899	75,803	Tanzania
21.2[4]	23.9[4]	24.5[4]	18.2[4]	9.2[4]	3.0[4]	27,513	37,091	47,026	55,197	60,988	63,961	68,728	70,438	Thailand
41.6[4]	30.0[4]	15.9[4]	8.1[4]	3.6[4]	0.8[4]	1,578	2,097	2,667	3,666	4,629	5,709	6,963	8,234	Togo
38.2	26.3	17.2	10.1	6.1	2.1	65	80	92	96	99	103	106	112	Tonga
20.3[16]	27.8[16]	22.1[16]	18.2[16]	8.0[16]	3.6[16]	828	941	1,082	1,235	1,263	1,318	1,354	1,335	Trinidad and Tobago
26.6	29.6	21.3	13.1	7.0	2.4	4,221	5,127	6,457	8,215	9,456	10,481	11,518	12,212	Tunisia
25.6	25.8	22.2	15.8	7.8	2.8	27,506	35,321	44,439	55,120	64,252	73,136	82,172	88,188	Turkey
31.8[13]	30.0[13]	20.6[13]	11.4[13]	4.6[13]	1.6[13]	1,585	2,181	2,875	3,658	4,385	4,941	5,529	6,027	Turkmenistan
36.2	21.2	20.2	13.8	6.8	1.8	5	6	8	9	9	11	12	12	Tuvalu
49.3	27.3	13.4	5.6	3.3	1.1	6,788	9,446	12,662	17,700	24,213	33,425	45,424	59,846	Uganda
14.2[17]	22.5[17]	21.0[17]	21.6[17]	—20.7[17]—		42,783	47,317	50,034	51,892	49,176	45,860	43,494	40,936	Ukraine
19.5	32.4	36.1	10.5	—1.5—		90	232	1,016	1,809	3,033	7,512	9,174	10,489	United Arab Emirates
18.9	18.8	22.6	18.9	13.3	7.5	52,372	55,632	56,330	57,237	58,886	62,262	66,542	70,493	United Kingdom
19.8	21.0	19.8	20.9	12.5	6.0	180,671	204,879	227,726	249,806	282,385	310,497	339,393	368,459	United States
23.9	22.9	19.5	16.0	11.8	5.9	2,538	2,809	2,915	3,109	3,319	3,369	3,495	3,601	Uruguay
40.8	28.4	15.0	9.3	4.7	1.8	8,531	11,940	15,994	20,530	25,042	27,866	30,565	32,855	Uzbekistan
38.8	19.4[82]	—35.8[83]—		—6.0—		64	86	117	149	189	240	309	370	Vanuatu
33.1	27.5	20.7	11.7	5.1	1.9	7,562	10,681	15,036	19,685	24,348	28,980	33,340	37,040	Venezuela
26.1[3]	29.6[3]	22.2[3]	14.4[3]	5.3[3]	2.4[3]	31,656	42,577	53,715	67,258	77,450	87,115	96,883	104,325	Vietnam
19.9	19.1	18.2	21.4	16.3	5.1	33	63	97	102	109	106	105	102	Virgin Islands (U.S.)
38.8[5, 87]	29.0[5, 87]	18.4[5, 87]	8.6[5, 87]	3.9[5, 87]	1.3[5, 87]	…	608[88]	733[88]	1,011[88]	2,175[88]	2,811[88]	3,352[88]	3,878[88]	West Bank[84]
…	…	…	…	…	…	28	89	124	217	336	492	652	821	Western Sahara
45.6	29.5	12.8	6.9	3.8	1.4	5,872	7,098	9,133	12,416	17,723	23,939	32,232	41,342	Yemen
46.6[3]	28.5[3]	14.3[3]	6.7[3]	3.2[3]	0.7[3]	3,254	4,248	5,643	7,858	10,345	13,460	18,065	23,491	Zambia
40.0[46]	32.3[46]	15.2[46]	7.4[46]	4.0[46]	1.1[46]	4,011	5,515	7,170	10,156	11,820	11,652	15,832	18,820	Zimbabwe

regard to the number of non-Kuwaitis. [56]Derived figures from sample survey. [57]Excludes *c.* 80,000 legal foreign workers and *c.* 20,000 undocumented foreign workers in 2011. [58]Excludes foreign workers. [59]Excludes a part of 1.7% unknown. [60]Estimate based on population pyramid of 2007 census. [61]Excludes Transdniestria. [62]Excludes a part of 0.3% unknown. [63]Excludes a part of 2.3% unknown. [64]Excludes a part of 0.9% unknown. [65]Excludes Western Sahara, an annexure of Morocco, unless otherwise indicated. [66]Base for data; actual final census figure is 29,891,708. [67]Includes Western Sahara. [68]Based on 2001 census. [69]Includes Svalbard and Jan Mayen. [70]Includes Azad Kashmir, Gilgit-Baltistan, and Afghan refugees unless otherwise indicated. [71]Excludes Azad Kashmir, Gilgit-Baltistan, and Afghan refugees. [72]Excludes the disputed transitional republic of Kosovo. [73]De facto population including temporary nonresident workers. [74]Excludes 7 districts experiencing civil war whose 2001 estimated population equaled 1,867,711. [75]2001 estimate for entire country. [76]Includes the newly administered South Sudan unless otherwise indicated. [77]Does not include South Sudan. [78]Includes resident aliens; excludes seasonal workers. [79]Does not include some 1,500,000 Iraqi and Palestinian refugees. [80]Includes inland water area of 86,409 sq mi (223,798 sq km) and Great Lakes water area of 59,959 sq mi (155,293 sq km); excludes coastal water area of 43,185 sq mi (111,849 sq km) and territorial water area of 74,575 sq mi (193,148 sq km). [81]Does not include armed forces overseas, which total 1,042,523. [82]Ages 15–24 only. [83]Ages 25–59. [84]Excludes East Jerusalem. [85]Includes 310,000 Israeli Jews in the West Bank. [86]2005 estimate for both the West Bank and the Gaza Strip. [87]Excludes Israeli Jews in the West Bank. [88]Includes Israeli Jews in the West Bank.

Major cities and national capitals

The following table lists the principal cities or municipalities (those exceeding 105,500 in population) of the countries of the world, together with figures for each national capital or seat of government (indicated by a ★), regardless of size.

Most of the populations given refer to a so-called city proper, that is, a legally defined, incorporated, or chartered area defined by administrative boundaries and by national or state law. In some instances, where cities proper do not exist or are not strictly demarcated, populations of locally defined urban areas may be used. In a few cases, data refer to the municipality, or commune, similar to the medieval city-state in that the city is governed together with its immediately adjoining, economically dependent areas, whether urban or rural in nature. Some countries define no other demographic or legal entities within such communes or municipalities, but many identify a centre, seat, head (*cabecera*), or locality that corresponds to the most densely populated, compact, contiguous core of the municipality. Figures referring to municipalities or communes may be given (identified by the abbreviation "MU"), even though the country itself may define a smaller, more closely knit city proper.

Populations for urban agglomerations as defined by the United Nations are occasionally inset beneath the populations of cities proper. Specifically that is when the urban agglomeration populations are at least three times the size of cities proper.

For certain countries, more than one form of the name of the city is given, usually to permit recognition of recent place-name changes or of *forms* of the place-name likely to be encountered in press stories if the title of the city's entry in the *Encyclopædia Britannica* is spelled according to a different romanization or spelling policy.

Chinese names for China are usually given in their Pinyin spelling, the official Chinese system encountered in official documents and maps. For Taiwan, the Wade-Giles spelling of place-names is used.

Sources for this data were often national censuses and statistical abstracts of the countries concerned, supplemented by Internet sources.

Internet sources for further information:

- City Population: http://www.citypopulation.de/cities.html
- World Urbanization Prospects: http://esa.un.org/unup

Major cities and national capitals

country city	population
Afghanistan (2009 est.)	
Herāt	395,400
Jalālābād	188,300
★ Kabul	
agglomeration	2,938,300
Kandahār (Qandahār)	363,100
Kondoz	129,500
Mazār-e Sharīf	333,800
Albania (2010 est.)	
★ Tiranë	540,000
Algeria (2008)	
Aïn Beïda	118,662
★ Algiers	2,800,000[1]
Annaba	257,359
Baraki	116,375
Batna	290,645
Béchar	165,627
Bejaïa	177,988
Birel Djir	152,151
Biskra (Beskra)	205,608
Blida (el-Boulaida)	163,586
Bordj Bou Arreridj	168,346
Bordj el Kiffan	151,950
Bou Saâda	125,573
Constantine (Qacentina)	448,374
Djasr Kasentina	133,247
Djelfa	289,226
Ech-Cheliff (el-Asnam)	178,616
El Bouni	125,265
El Eulma	155,038
El Khroub	179,033
El-Oued	134,699
Guelma	120,847
Jijel	134,839
Khenchela	108,580
Laghouat	144,747
Maghnia	114,634
Mascara	108,857
Médéa	138,355
Mostaganem	145,696
M'Sila	156,647
Oran (Wahran)	770,000[1]
Relizane	130,094
Saïda	128,413
Sétif (Stif)	288,461
Sidi bel Abbès	212,935
Skikda	163,618
Souk Ahras	155,259
Tébessa (Tbessa)	196,537
Tiaret	201,263
Tizi Ouzou	135,088
Tlemcen (Tilimsen)	140,158
Wargla (Ouargla)	133,024
American Samoa (2000)	
★ Fagatogo (legislative and judicial)	2,096[2]
★ Utulei (executive)	807[2]
Andorra (2010 est.)	
★ Andorra la Vella	20,526
Angola (2004 est.)	
Huambo	173,600
★ Luanda	2,783,000
Antigua and Barbuda (2005 est.)	
★ Saint John's	31,000
Argentina (2010)	
Almirante Brown	552,902
Avellaneda	342,677
Bahía Blanca	301,572
Belén de Escobar	213,619
Berazategui	324,244
★ Buenos Aires	2,890,151
agglomeration	15,625,084
Caseros	336,467[3]
Catamarca	159,703
Colón	225,151
Concordia	170,033
Córdoba	1,329,604
Corrientes	358,223
Escalante	186,583
Esteban Echeverría	300,959
Ezeiza	163,722
Florencio Varela	426,005
Formosa	234,354
General Pueyrredón	618,989
General San Martín (Buenos Aires)	414,196
General San Martín (Córdoba)	127,454
Godoy Cruz	191,903
Hurlingham	181,241
Ituzaingo	167,824
José Carlos Paz	265,981
La Plata	654,324
La Rioja	180,995
Lanús	459,263
Las Heras	203,666
Lomas de Zamora	616,279
Los Polvorines	290,691[3]
Luján	106,273
Malvinas Argentinas	322,375
Mar del Plata	541,733[3]
Mendoza	115,041
Merlo	528,494
Moreno	452,505
Morón	321,109
Neuquén	201,868[3]
Olavarría	111,708
Paraná	339,930
Pilar	299,077
Posadas	324,756
Punilla	178,401
Quilmes	582,943
Rawson	131,313
Resistencia	274,490[3]
Río Cuarto	246,393
Rosario	1,193,605
Salta	536,113
San Fernando (Buenos Aires)	163,240
San Fernando (Chaco)	390,874
San Isidro	292,878
San Justo (Córdoba)	206,307
San Justo (La Matanza)	1,775,816
San Luis	153,322[3]
San Miguel	276,190
San Miguel de Tucumán	548,866
San Nicolás de los Arroyos	145,857
San Salvador de Jujuy	231,229[3]
Santa Fe	368,668[3]
Santiago del Estero	267,125
Tandil	123,871
Tercero Arriba	109,554
Tigre	376,381
Tres de Febrero	340,071
Vicente López	269,420
Villa Nueva	223,365[3]
Zárate	114,269
Armenia (2010 est.)	
Gyumri (Kumayri; Leninakan)	146,272
★ Yerevan	1,116,600
Aruba (2010)	
★ Oranjestad	28,294
Australia (2006)[4]	
Adelaide (S.Aus.)	1,040,719
Brisbane (Queens.)	1,676,389
★ Canberra (A.C.T.)–Queanbeyan (N.S.W.)	356,120
Geelong (Vic.)	137,220
Gold Coast (Queens.)–Tweed Heads (N.S.W.)	454,436
Gosford (N.S.W.)	282,726
Hobart (Tas.)	128,577
Melbourne (Vic.)	3,371,888
Newcastle (N.S.W.)	288,732
Perth (W.Aus.)	1,256,035
Sunshine Coast (Queens.)	184,662
Sydney (N.S.W.)	3,641,422
Townsville (Queens.)	128,808
Wollongong (N.S.W.)	234,482
Austria (2011 est.)	
Graz	261,540
Innsbruck	120,147
Linz	189,367
Salzburg	148,078
★ Vienna	1,714,142
Azerbaijan (2010 est.)	
★ Baku (Baky)	2,064,900
Gəncə (Gyandzha)	314,600
Sumqayıt (Sumgait)	312,000
Bahamas, The (2010)	
★ Nassau	248,948
Bahrain (2007 est.)	
★ Manama	157,000
Bangladesh (2001; MU)	
Barisal	210,374[5]
Bogra	154,807
Brahmanbaria	129,278
Chittagong	2,579,107[5]
Comilla	166,519[6]
★ Dhaka (Dacca)	7,000,940[5]
Dinajpur	157,914
Gazipur	122,801
Jamalpur	120,955
Jessore	176,655
Kadamrasul	128,561
Khulna	855,650[5]
Kotwali	285,308
Mymensingh	227,204
Naogaon	124,046
Narayanganj	241,393
Narsingdi	124,204
Nawabganj (Nowabgonj)	152,223
Pabna	116,305
Rajshahi	472,775[5]
Rangpur	241,310
Saidpur	112,609
Savar	127,540
Sirajganj	128,144
Sylhet	463,198[5]
Tangail	128,785
Tongi	352,900[6]
Barbados (2000)	
★ Bridgetown	5,996
agglomeration	112,000[7]
Belarus (2010)	
Babruysk	215,092
Baranavichy	168,240
Barysaw	147,381
Brest	309,764
Homyel	482,652
Hrodna	327,540
Mahilyow	358,279
Mazyr	108,792
★ Minsk	1,836,808
Orsha	117,225
Pinsk	130,355
Vitsyebsk	347,928
Belgium (2010 est.)	
Antwerp	483,505
Brugge (Bruges)	116,741
★ Brussels	157,673
agglomeration	1,089,538
Charleroi	202,598
Ghent	243,366
Liège (Luik)	192,504
Namur	108,950
Schaerbeek	121,232
Belize (2010)	
★ Belmopan	13,351
Benin (2004 est.)	
Abomey	126,800
★ Cotonou (de facto)	815,000[7]
Djougou	206,500
Parakou	227,900
★ Porto-Novo (official)	276,000[7]
Bermuda (2000; MU)	
★ Hamilton	969
St. George	1,752
Bhutan (2005)	
★ Thimphu	79,185
Bolivia (2008 est.)	
Cochabamba	603,300
El Alto	890,500
★ La Paz (administrative)	835,300
Oruro	216,700
Potosí	152,000
Sacaba	141,500
Santa Cruz	1,506,200
★ Sucre (judicial)	265,300
Tarija	182,700
Bosnia and Herzegovina (2010 est.)	
Banja Luka	198,000[6]
Mostar	111,364
★ Sarajevo	392,000[7]
Tuzla	131,718
Zenica	127,105
Botswana (2011)[8]	
★ Gaborone	227,333
Brazil (2010; MU)	
Abaetetuba	141,100
Águas Lindas de Goiás	159,378
Alagoinhas	141,949
Alvorada	195,673
Americana	210,638
Ananindeua	471,980
Anápolis	334,613
Angra dos Reis	169,511
Aparecida de Goiânia	455,657
Apucarana	120,919
Aracaju	571,149
Araçatuba	181,579
Araguaína	150,484
Araguari	109,801
Arapiraca	214,006
Araraquara	208,662
Araras	118,843
Araruama	112,008
Araucária	119,123
Atibaia	126,603
Bage	116,794
Balneário de Camboriú	108,089
Barbacena	126,284
Barra Mansa	177,813
Barreiras	137,427
Barretos	112,101
Barueri	240,749
Bauru	343,937
Belém	1,393,399
Belford Roxo	469,332
Belo Horizonte	2,375,151
Bento Gonçalves	107,278
Betim	378,089
Birigui	108,728
Blumenau	309,011
Boa Vista	284,313
Botucatu	127,328
Bragança	113,227
Bragança Paulista	146,744
★ Brasília	2,570,160
Brusque	105,503
Cabo de Santo Agostinho	185,025
Cabo Frio	186,227
Cachoeirinha	118,278
Cachoeiro de Itapemirim	189,889
Camaçari	242,970
Camaragibe	144,466
Cametá	120,896
Campina Grande	385,213
Campinas	1,080,113
Campo Grande	786,797
Campo Largo	112,377
Campos dos Goytacazes	463,731
Canoas	323,827
Carapicuíba	369,584
Cariacica	348,738
Caruaru	314,912
Cascavel	286,205
Castanhal	173,149
Catanduva	112,820
Caucaia	325,441
Caxias	155,129
Caxias do Sul	435,564
Chapecó	183,530
Codó	118,038
Colatina	111,788
Colombo	212,967
Conselheiro Lafaiete	116,512
Contagem	603,442
Cotia	201,150
Crato	121,428

country city	population
Criciúma	192,308
Cubatão	118,720
Cuiabá	551,098
Curitiba	1,751,907
Diadema	386,089
Divinópolis	213,016
Dourados	196,035
Duque de Caxias	855,048
Embu	240,230
Feira de Santana	556,642
Ferraz de Vasconcelos	168,306
Florianópolis	421,240
Fortaleza	2,452,185
Foz do Iguaçu	256,088
Franca	318,640
Francisco Morato	154,472
Franco da Rocha	131,604
Garanhuns	129,408
Goiânia	1,302,001
Governador Valadares	263,689
Gravataí	255,660
Guarapuava	167,328
Guaratinguetá	112,072
Guarujá	290,752
Guarulhos	1,221,979
Hortolândia	192,692
Ibirité	158,954
Ilhéus	184,236
Imperatriz	247,505
Indaiatuba	201,619
Ipatinga	239,468
Itabira	109,783
Itaboraí	218,008
Itabuna	204,667
Itajaí	183,373
Itapecerica da Serra	152,614
Itapetininga	144,377
Itapevi	200,769
Itapipoca	116,065
Itaquaquecetuba	321,770
Itu	154,147
Jaboatão dos Guararapes	644,620
Jacareí	211,214
Jandira	108,344
Jaraguá do Sul	143,123
Jaú	131,040
Jequié	151,895
Ji-Paraná	116,610
João Pessoa	723,515
Joinville	515,288
Juàzeiro	197,965
Juàzeiro do Norte	249,939
Juiz de Fora	516,247
Jundiaí	370,126
Lages	156,727
Lauro de Freitas	163,449
Limeira	276,022
Linhares	141,306
Londrina	506,701
Luziânia	174,531
Macaé	206,728
Macapá	398,204
Maceió	932,748
Magé	227,322
Manaus	1,802,014
Marabá	233,669
Maracanaú	209,057
Maranguape	113,561
Maricá	127,461
Marília	216,745
Maringá	357,077
Marituba	108,246
Mauá	417,064
Mesquita	168,376
Mogi das Cruzes	387,779
Mogi Guaçu	137,245
Montes Claros	361,915
Mossoró	259,815
Natal	803,739
Nilópolis	157,425
Niterói	487,562
Nossa Senhora do Socorro	160,827
Nova Friburgo	182,082
Nova Iguaçu	796,257
Novo Hamburgo	238,940
Olinda	377,779
Osasco	666,740
Palhoça	137,334
Palmas	228,332
Paranaguá	140,469
Parauapebas	153,908
Parnaíba	145,705
Parnamirim	202,456
Passo Fundo	184,826
Passos	106,290
Patos de Minas	138,710
Paulista	300,466
Paulo Afonso	108,396
Pelotas	328,275
Petrolina	293,962
Petrópolis	295,917
Pindamonhangaba	146,995
Pinhais	117,008
Piracicaba	364,571
Poá	106,013
Poços de Caldas	152,435
Ponta Grossa	311,611
Porto Alegre	1,409,351
Porto Seguro	126,929
Porto Sinop	113,099
Porto Velho	428,527
Pouso Alegre	130,615
Praia Grande	262,051
Presidente Prudente	207,610
Queimados	137,962
Recife	1,537,704
Resende	119,769
Ribeirão das Neves	296,317
Ribeirão Pires	113,068
Ribeirão Preto	604,682
Rio Branco	336,038
Rio Claro	186,253
Rio das Ostras	105,676
Rio de Janeiro	6,320,446
Rio Grande	197,228
Rio Verde	176,424
Rondonópolis	195,476
Sabará	126,269
Salto	105,516
Salvador	2,675,656
Santa Bárbara d'Oeste	180,009
Santa Cruz do Sul	118,374
Santa Luzia	202,942
Santa Maria	261,031
Santa Rita	120,310
Santana de Parnaiba	108,813
Santarém	294,580
Santo André	676,407
Santos	419,400
São Bernardo do Campo	765,463
São Caetano do Sul	149,263
São Carlos	221,950
São Gonçalo	999,728
São João de Meriti	458,673
São José	209,804
São José de Ribamar	163,045
São José do Rio Prêto	408,258
São José dos Campos	629,921
São José dos Pinhais	264,210
São Leopoldo	214,087
São Luís	1,014,837
São Mateus	109,028
São Paulo	11,253,503
São Vicente	332,445
Sapucaia do Sul	130,957
Serra	409,267
Sertãozinho	110,074
Sete Lagoas	214,152
Simões Filho	118,047
Sobral	188,233
Sorocaba	586,625
Sumaré	241,311
Susano (Suzano)	262,480
Taboão da Serra	244,528
Tatuí	107,326
Taubaté	278,686
Teixeira de Freitas	138,341
Teófilo Otoni	134,745
Teresina	814,230
Teresópolis	163,746
Timon	155,460
Toledo	119,313
Uberaba	295,988
Uberlândia	604,013
Uruguaiana	125,435
Valinhos	106,793
Valparaíso de Goiás	132,982
Varginha	123,081
Várzea Grande	252,596
Várzea Paulista	107,089
Viamão	239,384
Vila Velha	414,586
Vitória	327,801
Vitória da Conquista	306,866
Vitória de Santo Antão	129,974
Volta Redonda	257,803
Votorantim	108,809
Brunei (2008 est.)	
★ Bandar Seri Begawan	32,331
Bulgaria (2011)	
Burgas	200,271
Pleven	106,954
Plovdiv	338,153
Ruse	149,642
★ Sofia	1,202,761
Stara Zagora	138,272
Varna	334,870
Burkina Faso (2006)	
Bobo Dioulasso	489,967
★ Ouagadougou	1,475,233
Burundi (2007 est.)	
★ Bujumbura	429,000
Cambodia (2008; MU)	
★ Phnom Penh	1,242,992
Cameroon (2005)	
Bafoussam	239,287
Bamenda	269,530
Bertoua	252,866[9]
Douala	2,125,000[7]
Edéa	234,072[9]
Foumban	252,886[9]
Garoua	235,996
Kumba	144,268
Loum	199,808[9]
Maroua	201,371
Mbouda	125,288[9]
Ngaoundéré	152,698
★ Yaoundé	1,801,000[7]
Canada (2006)	
Abbotsford (B.C.)	123,864
Barrie (Ont.)	128,430
Brampton (Ont.)	433,806
Burlington (Ont.)	164,415
Burnaby (B.C.)	202,799
Calgary (Alta.)	988,193
Cambridge (Ont.)	120,371
Chatham-Kent (Ont.)	108,177
Coquitlam (B.C.)	114,565
Edmonton (Alta.)	730,372
Gatineau (Que.)	242,124
Greater Sudbury (Ont.)	157,857
Guelph (Ont.)	114,943
Halifax (N.S.)	372,679
Hamilton (Ont.)	504,559
Kelowna (B.C.)	106,707
Kingston (Ont.)	117,207
Kitchener (Ont.)	204,668
Langley (B.C.)	117,332
Laval (Que.)	368,709
Levis (Que.)	130,006
London (Ont.)	352,395
Longueuil (Que.)	229,330
Markham (Ont.)	261,573
Mississauga (Ont.)	668,549
Montreal (Que.)	1,620,693
North Vancouver (B.C.)	127,727
Oakville (Ont.)	165,613
Oshawa (Ont.)	141,590
★ Ottawa (Ont.)	812,129
Quebec (Que.)	491,142
Regina (Sask.)	179,246
Richmond (B.C.)	174,461
Richmond Hill (Ont.)	162,704
Saanich (B.C.)	108,265
Saguenay (Que.)	143,692
Saint Catharines (Ont.)	131,989
Saskatoon (Sask.)	202,340
Sherbrooke (Que.)	147,427
Surrey (B.C.)	394,976
Thunder Bay (Ont.)	109,140
Toronto (Ont.)	2,503,281
Trois-Rivières (Que.)	126,323
Vancouver (B.C.)	578,041
Vaughan (Ont.)	238,866
Whitby (Ont.)	111,184
Windsor (Ont.)	216,473
Winnipeg (Man.)	633,451
Cape Verde (2010; MU)	
★ Praia	131,719
Cayman Islands (2010)[10]	
★ George Town	27,704
Central African Republic (2003)	
★ Bangui	622,771
Bimbo	124,176
Chad (2009)[8]	
Moundou	132,411
★ N'Djamena	993,492
Chile (2002)	
Antofagasta	285,255
Arica	175,441
Calama	126,135
Chillán	165,528
Concepción	212,003
Copiapó	125,983
Coquimbo	148,434
Iquique	164,396
La Serena	147,815
Los Ángeles	117,972
Osorno	132,245
Puente Alto	492,603
Puerto Montt	153,118
Punta Arenas	116,005
Quilpué	126,893
Rancagua	206,971
San Bernardo	237,708
★ Santiago	200,792
(administrative) agglomeration	5,428,590
Talca	189,505
Talcahuano	161,692
Temuco	227,086
Valdívia	127,750
★ Valparaíso (legislative)	263,499
Viña del Mar	286,931
China (2006 est.)	
Acheng	246,305
Aksu	341,558
Altay	146,075
Anda	190,345
Ankang	206,484
Anning	144,308
Anqing	453,390
Anqiu	264,968
Anshan	1,293,028
Anshun	213,215
Anyang	679,184
Baicheng	289,506
Baise	125,613
Baishan	269,456
Baiyin	299,427
Baoding	885,303
Baoji	526,212
Baoshan	121,597
Baotou	1,194,613
Bazhong	226,793
Bazhou	205,366
Bei'an	279,140
Beihai	264,633
★ Beijing (Peking)	8,580,376
Beiliu	132,511
Beining	109,285
Beipiao	209,064
Bengbu	623,945
Benxi	846,740
Bijie	159,022
Binzhou	438,125
Bole	148,971
Botou	111,817
Bozhou	179,291
Cangzhou	465,214
Cenxi	129,675
Changchun	2,455,899
Changde	486,659
Changge	116,540
Changji	279,745
Changle	123,136
Changning	148,773
Changsha	1,731,937
Changshu	478,748
Changyi	191,387
Changzhi	526,219
Changzhou	1,103,856
Chaohu	210,158
Chaoyang (*Liaoning*)	329,823
Chaozhou	343,641
Chengde	343,359
Chengdu	3,582,019
Chenzhou	315,828
Chibi	159,633
Chifeng	513,922
Chizhou	131,967
Chongqing (Chungking)	4,776,027
Chongzhou	164,130
Chuxiong	144,137
Chuzhou	231,408
Cixi	160,813
Conghua	224,324
Da'an	154,874
Dafeng	212,869
Dali	209,507
Dalian	2,407,345
Dandong	597,930
Dangyang	124,522
Danjiangkou	204,199
Danyang	203,631
Danzhou	391,076
Daqing	976,188
Dashiqiao	196,968
Datong	1,105,121
Daye	907,212
Dazhou	225,983
Dehui	147,329
Dengfeng	154,781
Dengzhou	155,387
Dexing	118,356
Deyang	303,731
Dezhou	409,050
Diaobingshan	176,824
Dingzhou	218,575
Dongfang	106,903
Donggang	127,204
Dongguan	667,350
Dongtai	433,382
Dongyang	130,965
Dongying	628,428
Dujiangyan	169,588
Dunhua	265,263
Duyun	169,325
Emeishan	137,193
Enping	177,373
Enshi	194,597
Ezhou	369,619
Fangchenggang	135,706
Feicheng	224,202
Fengcheng (*Guangdong*)	178,659
Fengcheng (*Jiangxi*)	303,573
Foshan	3,544,802
Fu'an	161,715
Fuding	194,435
Fujin	180,494
Fuqing	194,669
Fushun	1,264,685
Fuxin	691,815
Fuyang (*Anhui*)	428,969
Fuyang (*Zhejiang*)	119,651
Fuzhou (*Fujian*)	1,457,626
Fuzhou (*Jiangxi*)	301,516
Gaizhou	180,093
Ganzhou	361,913
Gao'an	182,600
Gaobeidian	119,305
Gaomi	242,814
Gaoyao	107,541
Gaoyou	213,257
Gaozhou	477,258
Gejiu	216,476
Genhe	167,133
Gongyi	149,368
Gongzhuling	333,997
Guang'an	211,990
Guanghan	135,286
Guangshui	159,882
Guangyuan	300,669
Guangzhou (Canton)	6,172,839
Guigang	241,205
Guilin	573,828
Guiping	165,318
Guixi	118,138
Guiyang	1,475,927
Gujiao	135,580
Haicheng	289,645
Haikou	864,879
Hailin	261,250
Hailun	168,241
Haimen	176,688
Haining	223,418
Haiyang	203,012
Hami	284,336
Hancheng	126,508
Hanchuan	210,611
Handan	1,221,916
Hangzhou	2,455,584
Hanzhong	247,119
Haocheng	204,732
Harbin	3,075,326
Hebi	349,719
Hechi	113,679
Hechuan	279,068
Hefei	1,502,782
Hegang	611,852
Heihe	134,925
Helong	129,386
Hengshui	256,039
Hengyang	677,157
Heshan	150,077
Heyuan	290,515
Heze	678,852
Hezhou	152,664
Hohhot	825,911
Honghu	175,784
Hongjiang	126,420
Hotan	108,346
Houma	122,717
Huadian	204,069
Huai'an	1,113,658
Huaibei	674,224
Huaihua	235,946
Huainan	932,210
Huanggang	371,918
Huanghua	131,422

Major cities and national capitals (continued)

country city	population
Huangshan	182,252
Huangshi	627,976
Huazhou	245,549
Huichun	145,968
Huixian	495,743
Huizhou	1,144,654
Hulin	190,313
Huludao	509,989
Huozhou	109,769
Huzhou	401,586
Jiamusi	599,275
Ji'an (*Jiangxi*)	233,062
Jiande	122,618
Jiangdu	316,194
Jiangjin	373,233
Jiangmen	1,338,280
Jiangyan	270,508
Jiangyin	484,088
Jiangyou	239,267
Jian'ou	159,533
Jianyang (*Fujian*)	121,060
Jianyang (*Sichuan*)	195,231
Jiaohe	176,182
Jiaonan	367,838
Jiaozhou	282,820
Jiaozuo	637,722
Jiaxing	363,201
Jiayuguan	152,067
Jieshou	109,103
Jieyang	666,079
Jilin	1,263,884
Jimo	429,357
Jinan	2,726,435
Jinchang	149,664
Jincheng	242,177
Jingdezhen	357,211
Jinghong	153,880
Jingjiang	281,291
Jingmen	363,060
Jingzhou	636,801
Jinhua	313,574
Jining (*Inner Mongolia*)	235,985
Jining (*Shandong*)	542,390
Jinjiang	365,341
Jinshi	143,129
Jintan	231,891
Jinzhong	280,520
Jinzhou	721,515
Jishou	145,965
Jiujiang	462,766
Jiuquan	148,825
Jiutai	184,083
Jixi	740,470
Jiyuan	195,329
Jurong	199,411
Kaifeng	591,303
Kaili	171,050
Kaiping	250,314
Kaiyuan (*Liaoning*)	140,410
Kaiyuan (*Yunnan*)	108,680
Karamay	248,797
Kashgar (Kashi)	246,524
Korla	278,682
Kuitun	280,325
Kunming	1,700,210
Kunshan	364,771
Laibin	158,094
Laiwu	494,638
Laixi	311,493
Laiyang	295,036
Laizhou	374,670
Langfang	445,234
Langzhong	183,080
Lanxi	118,983
Lanzhou	1,708,168
Laohekou	290,909
Lechang	256,361
Leiyang	191,760
Leizhou	291,232
Leling	171,068
Lengshuijiang	249,478
Leping	180,408
Leqing	118,805
Leshan	440,545
Lhasa	156,096
Lianjiang	348,528
Lianyuan	159,296
Lianyungang	594,504
Liaocheng	588,956
Liaoyang	597,386
Liaoyuan	387,813
Liling	159,015
Lin'an	105,907
Linfen	341,543
Lingbao	118,137
Lingwu	110,344
Lingyuan	148,960
Linhai	144,095
Linhe	242,918
Linjiang	114,067
Linqing	293,078
Linxia	111,810
Linxiang	118,541
Linyi	1,389,193
Linzhou	164,221
Lishui	126,857
Liu'an	322,505
Liupanshui	420,414
Liuyang	143,881
Liuzhou	871,634
Liyang	269,881
Longhai	144,552
Longjing	141,025
Longkou	298,836
Longyan	305,289
Loudi	420,793
Lufeng	630,220
Luoding	369,735
Luohe	436,325
Luoyang	1,065,137
Luzhou	443,988
Ma'anshan	494,259
Macheng	279,728
Manzhouli	160,003
Maoming	1,213,554
Meihekou	261,024
Meishan	275,736
Meizhou	307,352
Mianyang	593,745
Miluo	533,030
Mingguang	113,114
Mishan	185,421
Mudanjiang	649,244
Muling	134,450
Nan'an	376,038
Nanchang	1,613,244
Nanchong	575,520
Nanjing (Nanking)	4,105,366
Nankang	122,275
Nanning	1,277,300
Nanping	263,564
Nantong	853,309
Nanyang	527,638
Nehe	134,327
Neijiang	340,533
Ning'an	145,153
Ningbo	1,214,361
Ningde	118,326
Ordos	162,317
Panjin	519,103
Panshi	174,937
Panzhihua	524,505
Penglai	171,433
Pengzhou	188,787
Pingdingshan	727,576
Pingdu	423,536
Pinghu	154,957
Pingliang	148,844
Pingxiang	416,036
Pizhou	422,364
Pulandian	217,005
Puning	636,665
Putian	397,965
Puyang	386,847
Qian'an	105,566
Qianjiang	300,077
Qidong	187,285
Qingdao	2,654,340
Qingyuan	544,389
Qingzhen	109,808
Qingzhou	300,477
Qinhuangdao	776,320
Qinzhou	196,687
Qionghai	140,757
Qionglai	191,590
Qiqihar (Tsitsihar)	1,115,061
Qitaihe	352,274
Qixia	152,530
Quanzhou	611,078
Quhu	189,938
Qujing	239,050
Quzhou	194,700
Renqiu	285,306
Rizhao	580,395
Rongcheng	318,841
Rugao	428,445
Rui'an	191,197
Ruijin	107,263
Rushan	156,901
Ruzhou	109,693
Sanhe	153,692
Sanmenxia	220,533
Sanming	211,055
Sanya	256,169
Shanghai	11,283,714
Shangluo	155,907
Shangqiu	848,548
Shangrao	202,606
Shangyu	193,603
Shangzhi	251,570
Shantou	4,840,520
Shanwei	464,857
Shaoguan	907,139
Shaowu	133,965
Shaoxing	459,022
Shaoyang	375,370
Shengzhou	137,737
Shenyang	4,101,197
Shenzhen	1,819,322
Shihezi	513,559
Shijiazhuang	2,241,451
Shishi	111,591
Shishou	140,472
Shiyan	467,641
Shizuishan	350,577
Shouguang	480,336
Shuangcheng	169,972
Shuangliao	169,096
Shuangyashan	453,427
Shulan	199,954
Shuozhou	172,979
Sihui	140,339
Siping	544,052
Songyuan	319,212
Songzi	145,358
Suihua	288,371
Suining	347,642
Suizhou	323,847
Suqian	1,091,692
Suzhou (*Anhui*)	382,043
Suzhou (*Jiangsu*)	1,416,234
Tai'an	698,165
Taicang	197,954
Taishan	272,125
Taixing	384,741
Taiyuan	2,162,014
Taizhou (*Jiangsu*)	587,903
Taizhou (*Zhejiang*)	295,293
Tangshan	1,658,162
Taonan	156,529
Tengzhou	370,233
Tianchang	154,800
Tianjin (Tientsin)	5,332,140
Tianmen	227,090
Tianshui	590,347
Tieli	279,452
Tieling	342,492
Tongchuan	385,874
Tonghua	397,373
Tongliao	432,834
Tongling	352,239
Tongren	123,000
Tongxiang	148,422
Tongzhou	410,215
Tumen	105,948
Ulanhot	222,120
Ürümqi	1,504,252
Wafangdian	328,609
Weifang	975,298
Weihai	452,163
Weihui	118,583
Weinan	250,162
Wenchang	117,529
Wendeng	249,530
Wenling	181,915
Wenzhou	633,577
Wuchang	235,005
Wuchuan	289,546
Wudalianchi	204,287
Wuhai	431,062
Wuhan	8,001,541
Wuhu	727,872
Wujiang	242,979
Wuwei	207,358
Wuxi	2,095,304
Wuxue	242,773
Wuzhong	166,667
Wuzhou	281,459
Xiamen (Amoy)	961,758
Xi'an (Sian)	3,094,267
Xiangcheng	187,748
Xiangfan	945,883
Xiangtan	576,399
Xiangxiang	120,411
Xianning	246,290
Xiantao	406,881
Xianyang	591,067
Xiaogan	893,043
Xiaoyi	191,622
Xichang	195,291
Xilinhot	133,966
Xingcheng	130,735
Xinghua	315,555
Xingning	317,541
Xingping	117,709
Xingtai	563,575
Xingyang	110,403
Xingyi	131,526
Xining	692,472
Xinji	201,055
Xinle	117,333
Xinmi	180,917
Xinmin	140,652
Xintai	393,179
Xinxiang	694,874
Xinyang	439,411
Xinyi (*Guangdong*)	343,557
Xinyi (*Jiangsu*)	203,318
Xinyu	311,911
Xinzheng	164,933
Xinzhou	178,576
Xuancheng	158,852
Xuanwei	135,515
Xuchang	391,592
Xuzhou	1,536,501
Ya'an	141,612
Yakeshi	373,618
Yan'an	196,049
Yancheng	765,388
Yangchun	222,727
Yangjiang	634,958
Yangquan	515,913
Yangzhou	790,596
Yanji	374,350
Yantai	1,258,082
Yanzhou	194,747
Yibin	343,888
Yichang	694,635
Yicheng	228,046
Yichun (*Heilongjiang*)	786,418
Yichun (*Jiangxi*)	248,608
Yidu	114,784
Yima	128,165
Yinchuan	663,655
Yingcheng	267,803
Yingde	215,272
Yingkou	651,479
Yingtan	132,394
Yining	285,809
Yiwu	203,884
Yixing	576,716
Yiyang	333,667
Yizheng	207,820
Yong'an	172,056
Yongcheng	174,616
Yongchuan	268,924
Yongzhou	287,382
Yuanjiang	145,554
Yuanping	118,418
Yucheng	164,893
Yueyang	855,823
Yulin (*Guangxi*)	209,299
Yulin (*Shaanxi*)	157,510
Yuncheng	211,913
Yunfu	284,710
Yushu	189,095
Yuxi	135,105
Yuyao	169,255
Yuzhou	189,469
Zaoyang	351,838
Zaozhuang	762,948
Zengcheng	317,008
Zhalantin	165,999
Zhangjiagang	396,375
Zhangjiajie	121,289
Zhangjiakou	719,798
Zhangqiu	264,007
Zhangshu	154,944
Zhangye	179,269
Zhangzhou	338,205
Zhanjiang	1,433,366
Zhaodong	279,327
Zhaoqing	483,933
Zhaotong	114,884
Zhaoyuan	197,464
Zhengzhou	1,883,232
Zhenjiang	594,310
Zhijiang	134,729
Zhongshan	721,082
Zhongwei	128,084
Zhongxiang	214,682
Zhoukou	231,563
Zhoushan	266,665
Zhuanghe	182,082
Zhucheng	362,201
Zhuhai	895,994
Zhuji	146,566
Zhumadian	248,580
Zhuozhou	187,142
Zhuzhou	602,625
Zibo	1,426,551
Zigong	596,938
Zixing	127,588
Ziyang	184,976
Zoucheng	389,027
Zunyi	411,829
Colombia (2009)	
Apartado	127,678
Armenia	279,500
Barrancabermeja	172,384
Barranquilla	1,174,971
Bello	394,433
★ Bogotá	7,243,698
Bucaramanga	516,005
Buenaventura	320,541
Cali	2,183,042
Cartagena	888,012
Cartago	125,416
Cúcuta	591,530
Dos Quebradas	178,200
Envigado	184,408
Florencia	132,613
Floridablanca	249,753
Girón	134,567
Ibagué	491,071
Itagüí	226,713
Manizales	360,020
Medellín	2,281,085
Montería	308,136
Neiva	307,508
Palmira	234,574
Pasto	333,123
Pereira	381,153
Popayán	235,785
Riohacha	168,001
Santa Marta	417,514
Sincelejo	234,886
Soacha	439,004
Soledad	519,624
Tuluá	169,531
Tunja	160,726
Valledupar	338,761
Villavicencio	397,559
Comoros (2007 est.)	
★ Moroni	46,000
Congo, Dem. Rep. of the (2004 est.; MU)	
Bandundu	117,197
Boma	171,552
Bukavu	471,789
Bunia	230,625
Butembo	165,333
Gandajka	120,170
Gemena	113,879
Goma	249,862
Isiro	147,524
Kabinda	126,723
Kamina	115,626
Kananga	720,362[11]
Kikwit	294,210
★ Kinshasa	7,273,947[11]
Kisangani	682,599
Kolwezi	456,446
Likasi	367,219
Lubumbashi	1,283,380[11]
Matadi	245,862
Mbanadaka	262,814
Mbuji-Mayi	1,213,726[11]
Mwene-Ditu	170,786
Tshikapa	366,503
Uvira	235,136
Congo, Rep. of the (2010 est.)	
★ Brazzaville	1,408,150
Dolisie	128,032
Pointe-Noire	829,134
Costa Rica (2009 est.; MU)	
★ San José	356,174[12]
Côte d'Ivoire (1998)	
★ Abidjan	4,007,000[7]
Bouaké	642,700[7]
Daloa	241,020[7]
Gagnoa	107,124
Korhogo	142,093
Man	116,657
San Pédro	131,800
Yamoussoukro	155,803
Croatia (2011)[13]	
Rijeka	127,498
Split	165,893
★ Zagreb	686,568
Cuba (2010[14])	
Bayamo	147,638
Camagüey	305,701
Ciego de Avila	110,085
Cienfuegos	143,894
Guantánamo	207,974
★ Havana	2,141,993
Holguín	277,261
Las Tunas	153,128
Matanzas	132,678
Pinar del Río	137,320
Santa Clara	206,379
Santiago de Cuba	426,840
Curaçao (2009)	
Willemstad	123,000
Cyprus (2006 est.)	
★ Lefkosia (Nicosia)	47,832[15]
agglomeration	228,400[15]

country city	population
Czech Republic (2011 est.)	
Brno	371,371
Ostrava	303,609
Plzeň	168,808
★ Prague	1,257,158
Denmark (2011[14])	
Århus	249,709
★ Copenhagen	1,199,224
Odense	167,615
Djibouti (2009)	
★ Djibouti	353,801
Dominica (2004 est.)	
★ Roseau	20,200
Dominican Republic (2009 est.; MU)	
Bajos de Haina	138,270
Baní	172,458
Boca Chica	118,029
Bonao	145,098
Higüey	201,773
La Romana	148,499
La Vega	268,277
Los Alcarrizos	241,045
Moca	180,173
Puerto Plata	153,791
San Cristóbal	268,033
San Francisco de Macorís	183,822
San Juan de la Maguana	138,265
San Pedro de Macorís	226,745
Santiago	737,043
★ Santo Domingo	2,138,000
East Timor (2010 est.)	
★ Dili	193,563
Ecuador (2003)	
Ambato	169,103
Cuenca	303,994
Eloy Alfaro	183,731
Guayaquil	2,634,000[7, 11]
Ibarra	118,116
Loja	129,429
Machala	217,266
Manta	193,232
Milagro	119,420
Portoviejo	194,916
Quevedo	128,068
★ Quito	1,801,000[7, 11]
Riobamba	140,558
Santo Domingo	211,689
Egypt (2006)	
Al-Ahrām	130,267
Al-ʿArīsh	137,944
Al-Fayyūm	315,940
Al-Ghurdaqah	160,901
Al-Ismāʿīlīyah	293,184
Al-Jīzah (Giza)	2,891,275
Al-Maḥallah al-Kubrā	442,958
Al-Manṣūrah	439,348
Al-Minyā	236,043
Al-Suways (Suez)	500,000
Al-Uqṣur (Luxor)	202,232
Al-Zaqāzīq	302,840
Alexandria	4,084,672
Aswān	266,013
Asyūṭ	389,307
Banhā	157,701
Banī Suwayf	193,048
Bilbays	137,182
Būr Saʿīd (Port Said)	570,603
★ Cairo	6,758,581
Damanhūr	244,043
Disūq	106,827
Dumyāt	206,664
Hulwān	649,571
Kafr al-Dawwar	114,030
Kafr al-Shaykh	147,393
Mallawī	139,929
Marza	120,539
Mīt Ghamr	116,593
Qalyūb	107,303
Qinā	201,191
Sawhāj	190,132
Shibīn al-Kawm	177,112
Shubrā al-Khaymah	1,025,569
Ṭanṭā	422,854
El Salvador (2007; MU)	
Ahuachapán	110,511
Apopa	131,286[16]
Delgado	120,200[16]
Mejicanos	140,751[16]
Nueva San Salvador	108,840
San Miguel	218,410
★ San Salvador	316,090
Santa Ana	245,421
Santa Tecla	121,908
Soyapango	241,403[16]
Equatorial Guinea (2009 est.)	
★ Malabo	128,000
Eritrea (2009 est.)	
★ Asmara	649,000
Estonia (2011 est.)	
★ Tallinn	400,292
Ethiopia (2007)	
★ Addis Ababa	2,739,551
Awasa	157,139
Bahir Dar	155,428
Dese	120,095
Dire Dawa	233,224
Gonder	207,044
Jijiga	125,876
Jima	120,960
Mekele	215,914
Nazret	220,212
Faroe Islands (2011 est.; MU)	
★ Tórshavn	12,333
Fiji (2007)	
Nasinu	87,446
★ Suva	85,691
Finland (2010 est.; MU)	
Espoo	247,970
★ Helsinki	588,549
Jyväskylä	130,816
Oulu	141,671
Tampere	213,217
Turku	177,326
Vantaa	200,055
France (2008)	
Aix-en-Provence	142,743
Amiens	134,381
Angers	148,405
Besançon	117,599
Bordeaux	235,891
Boulogne-Billancourt	112,233
Brest	142,097
Caen	109,899
Clermont-Ferrand	139,006
Dijon	151,576
Grenoble	156,659
Le Havre	178,769
Le Mans	143,547
Lille	225,784
Limoges	140,138
Lyon	474,946
Marseille	851,420
Metz	122,838
Montpellier	252,998
Mulhouse	111,860
Nancy	106,361
Nantes	283,288
Nice	344,875
Nîmes	140,267
Orléans	113,257
★ Paris	2,211,297
agglomeration	10,142,977[17]
Perpignan	116,676
Reims	181,468
Rennes	206,655
Rouen	109,425
Saint-Étienne	172,696
Strasbourg	272,116
Toulon	166,733
Toulouse	439,553
Tours	135,480
Villeurbanne	141,106
French Guiana (2008)	
★ Cayenne	57,643
French Polynesia (2008)	
★ Papeete	26,004
Gabon (2007 est.)	
★ Libreville	576,000
Gambia, The (2009 est.)	
★ Banjul	34,828[18]
agglomeration	436,000
Gaza Strip (2010 est.)	
★ Gaza (Ghazzah; acting administrative centre)	521,053
Jabālyah	181,423
Khān Yūnus	194,157
Rafah	170,144
Georgia (2010 est.)	
Bat'umi (Batumi)	123,500
K'ut'aisi (Kutaisi)	192,500
Rust'avi (Rustavi)	119,500
★ Tbilisi	1,122,300
Germany (2010[14])	
Aachen	258,380
Augsburg	263,646
Bergisch Gladbach	105,699
★ Berlin	3,442,675
Bielefeld	323,084
Bochum	376,319
Bonn	319,841
Bottrop	117,241
Braunschweig	247,400
Bremen	547,685
Bremerhaven	114,031
Chemnitz	243,089
Cologne (Köln)	998,105
Darmstadt	143,332
Dortmund	581,308
Dresden	517,052
Duisburg	491,931
Düsseldorf	586,217
Erfurt	203,830
Erlangen	105,554
Essen	576,259
Frankfurt am Main	671,927
Freiburg im Breisgau	221,924
Fürth	114,044
Gelsenkirchen	259,744
Göttingen	121,457
Hagen	190,121
Halle	232,323
Hamburg	1,774,224
Hamm	181,741
Hannover	520,966
Heidelberg	146,466
Heilbronn	122,415
Herne	165,632
Ingolstadt	124,387
Karlsruhe	291,959
Kassel	194,774
Kiel	238,281
Koblenz	106,445
Krefeld	235,414
Leipzig	518,862
Leverkusen	160,593
Lübeck	209,818
Ludwigshafen	163,340
Magdeburg	230,456
Mainz	197,778
Mannheim	311,969
Moers	105,929
Mönchengladbach	258,251
Mülheim an der Ruhr	167,471
Munich (München)	1,330,440
Münster	275,543
Neuss	151,280
Nürnberg	503,673
Oberhausen	214,024
Offenbach am Main	118,770
Oldenburg	161,334
Osnabrück	163,514
Paderborn	145,320
Pforzheim	119,781
Potsdam	154,606
Recklinghausen	119,050
Regensburg	134,218
Remscheid	111,422
Reutlingen	112,132
Rostock	201,442
Saarbrücken	175,810
Solingen	160,992
Stuttgart	601,646
Ulm	122,801
Wiesbaden	277,493
Wolfsburg	121,109
Wuppertal	351,050
Würzburg	133,195
Ghana (2002 est.)	
★ Accra	2,121,000[6]
Kumasi	627,600
Obuasi	122,600
Tamale	269,200
Tema	237,700
Greece (2011; MU)	
Akharnaí	107,500
★ Athens	655,780
agglomeration	3,158,400
Ioánnina	111,740
Iráklion	173,450
Khaniá	108,310
Lárissa	163,380
Nikaia	105,230
Pátrai (Patras)	214,580
Peristérion	138,920[19]
Piraiévs (Piraeus)	163,910[19]
Rhodes	115,290
Thessaloníki	322,240
Vólos	144,420
Greenland (2011[14] est.)	
★ Nuuk (Godthåb)	15,862
Grenada (2007 est.)	
★ Saint George's	4,300[9]
agglomeration	32,000
Guadeloupe (2008)	
★ Basse-Terre	12,173
agglomeration	45,123
Guam (2010)	
★ Hagåtña (Agana)	1,051
agglomeration	149,000[6]
Guatemala (2002)	
★ Guatemala City	1,024,000[6]
Mixco	403,689
Quetzaltenango	127,569
Villa Nueva	355,901
Guernsey (2001)	
★ St. Peter Port	16,488
Guinea (2007 est.)	
★ Conakry	1,494,000
Kankan	113,900[9]
Guinea-Bissau (2009)	
★ Bissau	387,909
Guyana (2002)	
★ Georgetown	35,440
Haiti (2009)	
Cap-Haïtien	155,505
Carrefour	430,250
Cité Soleil	241,055
Delmas	359,451
Gonaïves	228,725
Pétionville	271,175
★ Port-au-Prince	875,978
agglomeration	2,296,386
Saint-Marc	122,747
Honduras (2009 est.)	
Choloma	223,900
El Progreso	122,000
La Ceiba	172,900
San Pedro Sula	646,300
★ Tegucigalpa	990,600
Hong Kong (2008 est.)	
★ Hong Kong	6,977,700[20]
Hungary (2010[14] est.)	
★ Budapest	1,721,556
Debrecen	207,270
Győr	130,478
Kecskemét	112,233
Miskolc	169,226
Nyíregyháza	117,832
Pécs	157,680
Szeged	169,713
Iceland (2011[14] est.)	
★ Reykjavík	118,061
agglomeration	202,131
India (2001)	
Abohar	124,339
Adilabad	109,529
Adityapur	119,233
Adoni	157,305
Agartala	189,998
Agra	1,275,134
Ahmadabad	3,520,085
Ahmadnagar	307,615
Aizawl	228,280
Ajmer	485,575
Akola	400,520
Alandur	146,287
Alappuzha (Alleppey)	177,029
Aligarh	669,087
Allahabad (Prayag Raj)	975,393
Alwar	260,593
Ambala	139,279
Ambala Sadar	106,568
Ambarnath	203,804
Ambattur	310,967
Amravati	549,510
Amritsar	966,862
Amroha	165,129
Anand	130,685
Anantapur	218,808
Ara (Arrah)	203,380
Asansol	475,439
Ashoknagar Kalyangarh	111,607
Aurangabad	873,311
Avadi	229,403
Bahadurgarh	119,846
Baharampur	160,143
Bahraich	168,323
Baidyabati	108,229
Baleshwar	106,082
Bally	260,906
Balurghat	135,737
Banda	134,839
Bangalore	4,301,326
Bankura	128,781
Baranagar (Barahanagar)	250,768
Barasat	231,521
Barddhaman (Burdwan)	285,602
Bareilly	718,395
Barrackpore (Barrackpur)	144,391
Basirhat	113,159
Basti	107,601
Batala	125,677
Bathinda (Bhatinda)	217,256
Beawar	123,759
Belgaum	399,653
Bellary	316,766
Bettiah	116,670
Bhadravati	160,662
Bhadreswar	106,071
Bhagalpur	340,767
Bhalswa Jahangir Pur	152,339
Bharatpur	204,587
Bharuch (Broach)	148,140
Bhatpara	442,385
Bhavnagar	511,085
Bhilainagar	556,336
Bhilwara	280,128
Bhimavaram	137,409
Bhind	153,752
Bhiwandi	598,741
Bhiwani	169,531
Bhopal	1,437,354
Bhubaneshwar	648,032
Bhusawal	172,372
Bid (Bhir)	138,196
Bidar	172,877
Bidhan Nagar	164,221
Bihar Sharif (Bihar)	232,071
Bijapur	228,175
Bikaner	529,690
Bilaspur	275,694
Bokaro (Bokaro Steel City)	393,805
Bommanahalli	201,652
Brahmapur	307,792
Budaun	148,029
Bulandshahr	176,425
Burhanpur	193,725
Byatarayanapura	181,744
Chandannagar	162,187
Chandigarh	808,515
Chandrapur	289,450
Chapra	179,190
Chennai (Madras)	4,343,645
Chhindwara	122,247
Chitradurga	122,702
Chittoor	152,654
Coimbatore	930,882
Cuddalore	158,634
Cuddapah	126,505
Cuttack	534,654
Dallo Pura	132,621
Damoh	112,185
Darbhanga	267,348
Darjiling	107,197
Dasarahalli	264,940
Davanagere	364,523
Dehra Dun	426,674
Dehri	119,057
Delhi	9,879,172
Delhi Cantonment	124,917
Deoli	119,468
Dewas	231,672
Dhanbad	199,258
Dhule (Dhulia)	341,755
Dibrugarh	121,893
Dinapur Nizamat	131,176
Dindigul	196,955
Durg	232,517
Durgapur	493,405
Eluru	190,062
Erode	150,541
Etah	107,110
Etawah	210,453
Faizabad	144,705
Faridabad	1,055,938

Major cities and national capitals (continued)

country city	population
Farrukhabad-cum-Fatehgarh	228,333
Fatehpur	152,078
Fīrozabad	279,102
Gadag-Betigeri	154,982
Gajuwaka	259,180
Gandhidham	151,693
Gandhinagar	195,985
Ganganagar	210,713
Gaya	385,432
Ghatlodiya	106,684
Ghaziabad	968,256
Godhra	121,879
Gonda	120,301
Gondia	120,902
Gorakhpur	622,701
Gudivada	113,054
Gulbarga	422,569
Guna	137,175
Guntakal	117,103
Guntur	514,461
Gurgaon	172,955
Guwahati (Gauhati)	809,895
Gwalior	827,026
Habra	127,602
Hajipur	119,412
Haldia	170,673
Haldwani-cum-Kathgodam	129,015
Halisahar	124,510
Hanumangarh	129,556
Haora (Howrah)	1,007,532
Hapur	211,983
Hardoi	112,486
Haridwar (Hardwar)	175,340
Hassan	116,574
Hathras	123,244
Hazaribag	127,269
Hindupur	125,074
Hisar (Hissar)	256,689
Hoshiarpur	149,668
Hospet	164,240
Hubli-Dharwad	786,195
Hugli (Hooghly-Chinsurah)	170,206
Hyderabad	3,637,483
Ichalkaranji	257,610
Imphal	221,492
Indore	1,474,968
Ingraj Bazar (English Bazar)	161,456
Jabalpur	932,484
Jaipur	2,322,575
Jalandhar (Jullundur)	714,077
Jalgaon	368,618
Jalna	235,795
Jammu	369,959
Jamnagar	443,518
Jamshedpur	573,096
Jamuria	129,484
Jaunpur	160,055
Jhansi	383,644
Jind	135,855
Jodhpur	851,051
Junagadh	168,515
Kaithal	117,285
Kakinada	296,329
Kalyan-Dombivali	1,193,512
Kamarhati	314,507
Kanchipuram	153,140
Kanchrapara	126,191
Kanpur	2,551,337
Kapra	159,002
Karawal Nagar	148,624
Karimnagar	205,653
Karnal	207,640
Katihar	175,199
Khammam	159,544
Khandwa	172,242
Kharagpur	188,761
Khardaha	116,470
Kirari Suleman Nagar	154,633
Kishangarh	116,222
Kochi (Cochin)	595,575
Kolar	113,907
Kolhapur	493,167
Kolkata (Calcutta)	4,580,546
Kollam (Quilon)	361,560
Korba	315,690
Kota	694,316
Kozhikode (Calicut)	436,556
Krishnanagar	139,110
Krishnarajapura	186,210
Kukatpalle	292,289
Kulti-Barakar (Kulti)	289,903
Kumbakonam	139,954
Kurnool	269,122
Lakhimpur	121,486
Lalbahadur Nagar (L.B. Nagar)	268,689
Lalitpur	111,892
Latur	299,985
Loni	120,945
Lucknow	2,185,927
Ludhiana	1,398,467
Machilipatnam (Masulipatam)	179,353
Madhyamgram	155,451
Madurai	928,869
Mahadevapura	135,794
Mahbubnagar	130,986
Maheshtala	385,266
Malegaon	409,403
Malerkotla	107,009
Malkajgiri	193,863
Mandsaur	116,505
Mandya	131,179
Mangalore	399,565
Mango	166,125
Mathura	302,770
Maunath Bhanjan	212,657
Medinipur (Midnapore)	149,769
Meerut	1,068,772
Mira-Bhayandar	520,388
Mirzapur-cum-Vindhyachal	205,053
Modinagar	113,218
Moga	125,573
Moradabad	641,583
Morena	150,959
Morvi	145,719
Mumbai (Bombay)	11,978,450
Munger (Monghyr)	188,050
Murwara (Katni)	187,029
Muzaffarnagar	316,729
Muzaffarpur	305,525
Mysore	755,379
Nabadwip	115,016
Nadiad	192,913
Nagaon	107,667
Nagercoil	208,179
Nagpur	2,052,066
Naihati	215,303
Nala Sopara (Nalasopara)	184,538
Nalgonda	110,286
Nanded-Waghala	430,733
Nandyal	152,676
Nangloi Jat	150,948
Nashik (Nasik)	1,077,236
Navghar-Manikpur	116,723
Navi Mumbai (New Mumbai)	704,002
Navsari	134,017
Neemuch	107,663
Nellore	378,428
★ New Delhi	302,363
Neyveli	127,552
Nizamabad	288,722
Noida	305,058
North Barrackpore	123,668
North Dum Dum	220,042
Ongole	150,471
Orai	139,318
Ozhukarai	217,707
Palakkad	130,767
Palanpur	110,419
Pali	187,641
Pallavaram	144,623
Panchkula	140,925
Panihati	348,438
Panipat	261,740
Parbhani	259,329
Patan	112,219
Pathankot	157,925
Patiala	303,151
Patna	1,366,444
Pilibhit	124,245
Pimpri-Chinchwad	1,012,472
Pondicherry	220,865
Porbandar	133,051
Proddatur	150,309
Pudukkottai	109,217
Puna	119,092
Pune	2,538,473
Puri	157,837
Purnia (Purnea)	171,687
Puruliya	113,806
Quthbullapur	231,108
Rae Bareli	169,333
Raichur	207,421
Raiganj	165,212
Raigarh	111,154
Raipur	605,747
Raj Nandgaon	143,770
Rajahmundry	315,251
Rajapalaiyam	122,307
Rajarhat Gopalpur	271,811
Rajendranagar	143,240
Rajkot	967,476
Rajpur Sonarpur	336,707
Ramagundam	236,600
Rampur	281,494
Ranchi	847,093
Raniganj	111,116
Ratlam	222,202
Raurkela	224,987
Raurkela Township	206,693
Rewa	183,274
Rishra	113,305
Robertson Pet	141,424
Rohtak	286,807
S.A.S. Nagar (Mohali)	123,484
Sagar	232,133
Saharanpur	455,754
Saharsa	125,167
Salem	696,760
Sambalpur	153,643
Sambhal	182,478
Sangli-Miraj	436,781
Santipur (Shantipur)	138,235
Sasaram	131,172
Satara	108,048
Satna	225,464
Secunderabad	206,102
Serampore	197,857
Serilingampalle	153,364
Shahjahanpur	296,662
Shambajinagar (Aurangābād)	873,311
Shiliguri (Siliguri)	472,374
Shillong	132,867
Shimla	142,555
Shimoga	274,352
Shivpuri	146,892
Sholapur (Solapur)	872,478
Sikandarabad (Secundarabad) Cantonment	206,102
Sikar	185,323
Silchar	142,199
Singrauli	185,190
Sirsa	160,735
Sitapur	151,908
Siwan	109,919
Sonipat (Sonepat)	214,974
South Dum Dum	392,444
Srikakulam	109,905
Srinagar	898,440
Sultan Pur Majra	164,426
Surat	2,433,835
Surendranagar Dudhrej	156,161
Tambaram	137,933
Tenali	153,756
Thane (Thana)	1,262,551
Thanesar	119,687
Thanjavur	215,314
Thiruvananthapuram (Trivandrum)	744,983
Thoothukkudi (Tuticorin)	216,054
Thrissur (Trissur)	317,526
Tiruchchirappalli	752,066
Tirunelveli	411,831
Tirupati	228,202
Tirupper (Tiruppur)	344,543
Tiruvannamalai	130,567
Tiruvottiyur	212,281
Titagarh	124,213
Tonk	135,689
Tumkur	248,929
Udaipur	389,438
Udupi	113,112
Ujjain	430,427
Ulhasnagar	473,731
Uluberia	202,135
Unnao	144,662
Uppal Kalan	117,217
Uttarpara-Kotrung	150,363
Vadodara (Baroda)	1,306,227
Varanasi (Benares)	1,091,918
Vejalpur	113,445
Vellore	177,230
Veraval	141,357
Vidisha	125,453
Vijayawada	851,282
Virar	118,928
Vishakhapatnam	982,904
Vizianagaram	174,651
Warangal	530,636
Wardha	111,118
Yamunanagar	189,696
Yavatmal (Yeotmal)	120,676
Indonesia (2010)[21]	
Ambon	331,254
Balikpapan	557,579
Banda Aceh	223,446
Bandar Lampung	881,801
Bandung	2,394,873
Banjar	175,157
Banjarbaru	199,627
Banjarmasin	625,481
Batam	944,285
Batu	190,184
Baubau	136,991
Bekasi	2,334,871
Bengkulu	308,544
Bima	142,579
Binjai	246,154
Bitung	187,652
Blitar	131,968
Bogor	950,334
Bontang	143,683
Bukittinggi	111,312
Cilacap	206,928[22]
Cilegon-Merak	374,559
Cimahi	541,177
Ciomas	187,379[23]
Ciparay	111,467[23]
Ciputat	363,489[22]
Cirebon	296,389
Denpasar	788,589
Depok (*West Java*)	1,738,570
Depok (*Yogyakarta*)	106,825[23]
Dumai	253,803
Gorontalo	180,127
Gunungsitoli	126,202
★ Jakarta	9,586,705
Jambi	531,857
Jayapura	256,705
Jember	218,529[23]
Karawang (Krawang)	145,041[23]
Kediri	268,507
Kendari	289,966
Kotamobagu	107,459
Kupang	336,239
Langsa	148,945
Lhokseumawe	171,163
Lubukinggau	201,308
Madiun	170,964
Magelang	118,227
Malang	820,243
Manado	410,481
Mataram	402,843
Medan	2,097,610
Mojokerto	120,196
Padang	833,562
Padangsidempuan	191,531
Palangkaraya	220,962
Palembang	1,455,284
Palopo	147,932
Palu	336,532
Pangkalpinang	174,758
Parepare	129,262
Pasuruan	186,262
Payakumbuh	116,825
Pekalongan	281,434
Pekanbaru	897,767
Pemalang	152,667[22]
Pematangsiantar	234,698
Perabumulih	161,984
Percut	129,036[23]
Pondokgede	263,152[23]
Pontianak	554,764
Probolinggo	217,062
Purwokerto	215,195[22]
Salatiga	170,332
Samarinda	727,500
Semarang	1,555,984
Serang	577,785
Singkawang	186,462
Sorong	190,625
Sukabumi	298,681
Surabaya	2,765,487
Surakarta	499,337
Tangerang	1,798,601
Tanjungbalai	154,445
Tanjungpinang	187,359
Tarakan	193,370
Tasikmalaya	635,464
Tebingtinggi	145,248
Tegal	239,559
Ternate	185,705
Ujung Pandang	1,294,000[7]
Waru	124,282[23]
Yogyakarta	388,627
Iran (2006)	
Ābādān	219,772
Ahvāz	1,040,000[7]
Āmol	199,698
Andīmeshk	120,177
Arāk	446,760
Ardabīl	418,262
Bābol	201,335
Bandar ʿAbbās	379,301
Bandar-e-Anzali	110,643
Bandar-e Būshehr (Būshehr)	169,966
Bandar-e-Māhshahr	111,448
Bīrjand	166,138
Bojnūrd	176,726
Borūjerd	229,541
Būkān	150,703
Dezfūl	235,819
Emāmshahr (Shāhrūd)	132,379
Eṣfahān (Isfahan)	1,704,000[7]
Golestan	231,905
Gonbad-e Kavus	129,167
Gorgān	274,438
Hamadān	479,640
Īlām	160,355
Islāmshahr (Eslāmshahr)	357,389
Karaj	1,531,000[7]
Kāshān	253,509
Kermān	515,114
Kermānshāh (Bākhtarān)	825,000[7]
Khomeynīshahr	223,071
Khorramābād	333,945
Khorramshahr	125,859
Khvoy (Khoy)	181,465
Mahābād	135,780
Malārd	228,713
Malāyer	156,289
Māndoāb	114,153
Marāgheh	149,929
Marv Dasht	124,530
Mashhad (Meshed)	2,592,000[7]
Masjed-e Soleymān	108,682
Najafābād	208,647
Neyshābūr	208,860
Orūmīyeh	583,255
Qā'emshahr	174,768
Qarchak	174,006
Qazvīn	355,338
Qods	230,147
Qom	1,021,000[7]
Rasht	557,366
Sabzevār	214,582
Sanandaj	316,862
Saqqez	133,331
Sārī	261,293
Sāveh	180,548
Semnān	126,780
Shāhīnshahr	127,412
Shahr-e Kord	131,612
Shahreza	109,601
Shahriyar	189,421
Shāhrūd	132,379
Shīrāz	1,279,000[7]
Sīrjān	170,916
Tabrīz	1,459,000[7]
★ Tehrān	7,190,000[7]
Varāmīn	208,996
Yazd	432,194
Zābol	136,956
Zāhedān	567,449
Zanjān	349,713
Iraq (2003 est.)	
Al-ʿAmārah	325,000
Al-Baṣrah	905,000[7]
Al-Fallūjah	284,500[9]
Al-Ḥillah	350,000
Al-Kūfah	123,500[9]
Al-Kūt	300,000
Al-Najaf	500,000
Al-Nāṣirīyah	400,000
Al-Ramādī	300,000
Al-Samāwah	125,000
Al-Sulaymānīyah	806,000[7]
Al-Zubayr	180,900[9]
★ Baghdad	5,751,000[7]
Baʿqūbah	160,000
Dīwanīyah	300,000
Irbīl	981,000[7]
Karbalāʾ	475,000
Kirkūk	750,000
Mosul	1,402,000[7]
Sāmarrā	125,000
Tall ʿAfar	167,800[9]
Ireland (2006)	
Cork	119,418[24]
★ Dublin	506,211[24]
agglomeration	1,045,769
Isle of Man (2009)	
★ Douglas	26,000
Israel (2010[14] est.)	
Ashdod	206,400
Ashqelon	111,900
Bat Yam	130,000
Beersheba (Beʾer Shevaʿ)	194,300
Bene Beraq	154,400
Haifa (Ḥefa)	265,600
Ḥolon	184,700
★ Jerusalem (Yerushalayim, Al-Quds)	773,000
Netanya	183,200
Petaḥ Tiqwa	209,600
Ramat Gan	145,000

country city	population
Rehovot	112,700
Rishon LeẔiyyon	228,200
Tel Aviv–Yafo	403,700
Italy (2011[14] est.)	
Bari	320,475
Bergamo	119,551
Bologna	380,181
Brescia	193,879
Cagliari	156,488
Catania	293,458
Ferrara	135,369
Florence (Firenze)	371,282
Foggia	152,747
Forlì	118,167
Genoa (Genova)	607,906
Giugliano in Campania	117,963
Latina	119,804
Livorno	161,131
Messina	242,503
Milan (Milano)	1,324,110
Modena	184,663
Monza	122,712
Naples (Napoli)	959,574
Padua (Padova)	214,198
Palermo	655,875
Parma	186,690
Perugia	168,169
Pescara	123,077
Prato	188,011
Ravenna	158,739
Reggio di Calabria	186,547
Reggio nell'Emilia	170,086
Rimini	143,321
★ Rome (Roma)	2,761,477
Salerno	139,019
Sassari	130,658
Syracuse (Siracusa)	123,850
Taranto	191,810
Terni	113,324
Trento	116,298
Trieste	205,535
Turin (Torino)	907,563
Venice (Venezia)	270,884
Verona	263,964
Vicenza	115,927
Jamaica (2006 est.)	
★ Kingston	96,052[25]
agglomeration	585,300
Spanish Town	148,800
Japan (2010)[10]	
Abiko	134,047
Ageo	223,882
Aizuwakamatsu	126,125
Akashi	290,993
Akishima	112,286
Akita	323,363
Amagasaki	453,608
Anjō	178,738
Aomori	299,429
Asahikawa	347,275
Asaka	129,654
Ashikaga	154,462
Atsugi	224,426
Beppu	127,345[5]
Chiba	962,130
Chigasaki	235,140
Chikusei	108,518
Chōfu	223,609
Daitō	125,847[5]
Ebetsu	123,751
Ebina	127,720
Fuchu	255,453
Fuji	254,049
Fujieda	142,183
Fujimi	106,746
Fujimino	105,812
Fujinomiya	131,996
Fujisawa	409,734
Fukaya	144,555
Fukui	266,831
Fukuoka	1,463,826
Fukushima	292,280
Fukuyama	461,471
Funabashi	609,081
Gifu	413,239
Habikino	118,281[5]
Hachinohe	237,473
Hachiōji	579,799
Hadano	170,154
Hakodate	279,110
Hakusan	110,462
Hamamatsu	800,912
Handa	118,829
Hatsukaichi	115,184[5]
Higashi-Hiroshima	190,043
Higashi-Kurume	116,572
Higashi-Murayama	153,365
Higashi-Ōsaka	509,632
Higashiomi	115,472
Hikone	111,915
Himeji	536,338
Hino	179,464
Hirakata	407,997
Hiratsuka	260,776
Hirosaki	183,534
Hiroshima	1,174,209
Hitachi	193,129
Hitachinaka	157,012
Hōfu	116,393[5]
Ibaraki	274,832
Ichihara	279,601
Ichikawa	474,926
Ichinomiya	375,621
Ichinoseki	118,602
Iizuka	132,208[5]
Ikoma	115,359[5]
Imabari	166,532
Inazawa	136,415
Iruma	149,879
Isahaya	142,635[5]
Ise	130,228
Isesaki	207,199
Ishinomaki	160,704
Itami	196,160
Iwaki	342,198
Iwakuni	146,885[5]
Iwata	168,616
Izumi	185,017
Izumo	146,115[5]
Joetsu	203,869
Kadoma	130,026[5]
Kagoshima	605,940
Kakamigahara	145,615
Kakegawa	116,373
Kakogawa	266,889
Kamagaya	107,833
Kamakura	174,354
Kanazawa	462,478
Kanoya	105,673[5]
Karatsu	129,194[5]
Kariya	145,744
Kashihara	124,679[5]
Kashiwa	404,179
Kasuga	107,845[5]
Kasugai	305,662
Kasukabe	237,178
Kawachinagano	114,428[5]
Kawagoe	342,714
Kawaguchi	500,311
Kawanishi	156,476
Kawasaki	1,425,678
Kirishima	127,726[5]
Kiryū	121,720
Kisarazu	129,291
Kishiwada	199,172
Kitakyūshū	977,288
Kitami	125,628
Kobe	1,544,873
Kochi	343,416
Kodaira	187,039
Kofu	198,838
Koga	142,973
Koganei	118,888
Kokubunji	120,733
Komaki	147,059
Komatsu	108,439
Kōnosu	119,629
Koriyama	338,772
Koshigaya	326,423
Kuki	154,335
Kumagaya	203,192
Kumamoto	734,294
Kurashiki	475,421
Kure	239,553
Kurume	302,323
Kusatsu	130,854
Kushiro	181,206
Kuwana	140,281
Kyōto	1,474,473
Machida	426,827
Maebashi	340,390
Marugame	110,550[5]
Matsubara	125,274[5]
Matsudo	484,639
Matsue	193,331
Matsumoto	243,070
Matsusaka	168,146
Matsuyama	517,088
Matsuzaka	168,146
Minōh	127,757[5]
Misato	131,418
Mishima	111,823
Mitaka	186,028
Mito	268,818
Miyakonojō	169,633
Miyazaki	400,352
Moriguchi	146,294[5]
Morioka	298,572
Musashino	138,813
Nagano	381,533
Nagaoka	282,719
Nagareyama	163,994
Nagasaki	443,469
Nagoya	2,263,907
Naha	315,765
Nara	366,528
Narashino	164,421
Narita	128,944
Nasushiobara	117,706
Neyagawa	238,244
Niigata	812,192
Niihama	123,329[5]
Niiza	158,765
Nishinomiya	482,790
Nishio	106,829
Nishitokyo	196,494
Nobeoka	132,480[5]
Noda	155,446
Numazu	202,283
Obihiro	167,860
Odawara	198,373
Ōgaki	161,146
Ōita	473,955
Okayama	709,622
Okazaki	372,472
Okinawa	128,421[5]
Ōme	139,232
Ōmuta	127,474[5]
Onomichi	148,085[5]
Ōsaka	2,666,371
Osaki	135,127
Oshū	124,756
Ōta	216,444
Ōtaru	131,970
Ōtsu	337,629
Oyama	164,437
Saga	237,501
Sagamihara	717,561
Saijo	112,543[5]
Saitama	1,222,910
Sakai	842,134
Sakata	111,170
Sakura	172,167
Sanda	113,600[5]
Sano	121,259
Sapporo	1,914,434
Sasebo	261,146
Sayama	155,738
Sendai	1,045,903
Seto	132,240
Shimonoseki	280,987
Shizuoka	716,328
Shūnan	150,299[5]
Sōka	244,062
Suita	355,567
Suzuka	199,184
Tachikawa	179,503
Tajimi	112,635
Takamatsu	419,291
Takaoka	176,109
Takarazuka	225,587
Takasaki	371,352
Takatsuki	357,423
Tama	147,541
Toda	123,017
Tōkai	107,704
Tokorozawa	341,900
Tokushima	264,764
★ Tokyo	8,949,447
Tomakomai	173,406
Tondabayashi	122,205[5]
Toride	109,625
Tottori	197,391
Toyama	421,890
Toyohashi	376,861
Toyokawa	181,822
Toyonaka	389,359
Toyota	421,552
Tsu	285,728
Tsuchiura	143,023
Tsukuba	214,660
Tsuruoka	136,627
Tsuyama	109,493[5]
Ube	173,678
Ueda	159,604
Uji	189,609
Urasoe	108,052[5]
Urayasu	164,878
Uruma	114,087[5]
Utsunomiya	511,296
Wakayama	369,400
Yachiyo	189,789
Yaizu	143,229
Yamagata	254,084
Yamaguchi	196,643
Yamato	228,180
Yao	268,652
Yatsushiro	134,491[5]
Yokkaichi	307,807
Yokohama	3,689,603
Yokosuka	418,448
Yonago	149,140[5]
Zama	129,265
Jersey (2001)	
★ St. Helier	28,310
Jordan (2004)	
Al-Quwaysimah	135,500
Al-Ruṣayfah	227,735
Al-Zarqāʾ	395,227
★ Amman	1,036,330
Irbid	250,645
Tilāʿ al-ʿAlī	113,197
Wādī al-Sīr	122,032
Kazakhstan (2010 est.)	
Almaty (Alma-Ata)	1,404,329
Aqtaū (Aktau; Shevchenko)	156,440
Aqtöbe (Aktyubinsk)	277,442
★ Astana (Aqmola; Tselinograd)	684,018
Atyraū (Guryev)	174,726
Ekibastuz	122,747
Kökshetaū (Kokchetav)	133,459
Oral (Uralsk)	216,467
Öskemen (Ust-Kamenogorsk)	288,660
Pavlodar	311,218
Petropavl (Petropavlovsk)	194,290
Qaraghandy (Karaganda)	471,730
Qostanay (Kustanay)	212,617
Qyzylord (Kzyl-Orda)	174,348
Rūdny	112,006
Semey (Semipalatinsk)	288,608
Shymkent (Shimkent; Chimkent)	579,544
Taldykorgan (Taldy-Kurgan)	119,375
Taraz (Auliye-Ata; Dzhambul)	352,536
Temirtaū	166,614
Kenya (2006 est.)	
Eldoret	227,800
Kisumu	220,000
Mombasa	823,500
★ Nairobi	2,864,700
Nakuru	266,500
Ruiru	120,900
Kiribati (2005)	
★ Ambo (legislative)	1,688
★ Bairiki (executive; agglomeration)	2,766
★ Betio (judicial)	12,509
Korea, North (2008)	
Anju	167,646
Ch'ŏngjin	614,892
Haeju	241,599
Hamhŭng-Hungnam	703,610
Hŭich'ŏn	136,093
Hyesan	174,015
Kaech'ŏn	262,389
Kaesŏng	192,578
Kanggye	251,971
Kimch'aek (Songjin)	155,284
Kusŏng	155,181
Namp'o	310,531
P'yŏngsŏng	236,583
★ P'yŏngyang	2,581,076
Rasŏn	158,337
Sariwŏn	271,434
Sinp'o	130,951
Sinŭiju	334,031
Sunch'ŏn	250,738
Tanch'ŏn	240,873
Tŏkch'ŏn	210,571
Wŏnsan	328,467
Korea, South (2010)	
Andong	166,197
Ansan	728,775
Ansŏng	179,782
Anyang	602,122
Asan	278,676
Ch'angwŏn	509,801[7]
Chech'ŏn	134,698
Cheju (Jeju)	401,192
Chinhae	171,421[7]
Chinju	337,896
Ch'ŏnan	574,623
Chŏng-ŭp	110,352
Ch'ŏngju	666,924
Chŏnju	649,728
Ch'unch'ŏn	276,232
Ch'ungju	203,212
Hanam	138,829
Hwasŏng	488,758
Ich'ŏn	195,175
Iksan (Iri)	296,366
Inch'ŏn (Incheon)	2,662,509
Kangnŭng	218,471
Kimch'ŏn	127,889
Kimhae	494,510
Kimp'o	224,350
Kŏje	231,271
Kongju	122,153
Koyang	905,076
Kumi	402,607
Kunp'o	278,083
Kunsan	260,546
Kuri	185,550
Kwangju (*Gwangju*)	1,475,745
Kwangju (*Kyŏnggi*)	228,747
Kwangmyŏng	329,010
Kwangyang	137,810
Kyŏngju	256,150
Kyŏngsan	266,036
Masan	414,771[7]
Mokp'o	249,960
Namyangju	529,898
Nonsan	119,222
Osan	183,890
P'aju	328,128
Pocheon	140,997
P'ohang	511,390
Puch'ŏn	853,039
Pusan (Busan)	3,414,950
P'yŏngt'aek	388,508
Sach'ŏn	107,524
★ Seoul (Sŏul)	9,794,304
Shihŭng	407,090
Sŏgwip'o	130,713
Sŏngnam	949,964
Sŏsan	156,843
Sunch'ŏn	258,670
Suwŏn	1,071,913
Taegu	2,446,418
Taejŏn	1,501,859
Tongyŏng	129,366
Ŭijŏngbu	417,412
Ŭiwang	144,501
Ulsan	1,082,567
Wŏnju	311,449
Yangju	187,911
Yangsan	252,507
Yongin	856,765
Yŏngju	108,888
Yŏsu	269,937
Kosovo (2011; MU)[10]	
★ Pristina	198,214
Prizren	178,112
Kuwait (2010 est.)	
Al-Sālimīyah	238,577
Ḥawallī	171,804
★ Kuwait (Al-Kuwayt)	56,234
agglomeration	2,305,000
Qalīb al-Shuyūkh	265,984
Kyrgyzstan (2009 est.)	
★ Bishkek	822,000
Osh	233,800
Laos (2009 est.)	
★ Vientiane (Viangchan)	194,200
agglomeration	745,000[6]
Latvia (2009 est.)	
★ Rīga	713,019
Lebanon (2003 est.)	
★ Beirut (Bayrūt)	1,909,000[7]
Sidon	149,000
Tripoli (Ṭarābulus)	212,900
Tyre (Ṣūr)	117,100
Lesotho (2007 est.)	
★ Maseru	210,000
Liberia (2008)	
★ Monrovia	1,010,970
Libya (2005 est.; MU)	
Banghāzī	685,367
Miṣrātah	354,823
★ Tripoli (Ṭarābulus)	1,095,000[7]
agglomeration	2,189,000[6]
Liechtenstein (2011[14])	
★ Vaduz	5,214
Lithuania (2011[14])	
Kaunas	321,200
Klaipėda	161,300
Šiauliai	113,100
★ Vilnius	539,000
Luxembourg (2011[14] est.)	
★ Luxembourg	94,034

Major cities and national capitals (continued)

country city	population
Macau (2011[14])	
★ Macau	470,600
Macedonia (2010[14] est.; MU)	
Kumanovo	107,211
★ Skopje (Skopije)	530,258
Madagascar (2001 est.)	
★ Antananarivo	1,879,000[1]
Antsirabe	160,356
Fianarantsoa	144,225
Mahajanga	135,660
Toamasina	179,045
Malawi (2008)	
★ Blantyre (judicial)	661,256
★ Lilongwe (executive; legislative)	674,448
Mzuzu	133,968
Malaysia (2000)	
Alor Setar	186,433
George Town (Pinang)	181,380
Ipoh	536,832
Johor Bahru	642,944
Klang	626,699
Kluang	134,150
Kota Baharu	251,801
Kota Kinabalu	306,920
★ Kuala Lumpur	1,305,792
Kuala Terengganu	255,109
Kuantan	288,727
Kuching	422,240
Miri	169,005
Petaling Jaya	432,619
★ Putrajaya (partly completed in 2007)	...
Sandakan	276,791
Selayang Baru	174,628
Seremban	290,709
Shah Alam	314,440
Sibu	167,427
Sungai Petani	174,962
Taiping	199,489
Tawau	213,745
Maldives (2006)	
★ Male	103,693
Mali (2009)[8]	
★ Bamako	1,809,106
Kalaban Koro	166,722
Kati	114,983
Kayes	127,368
Mopti	114,296
Ségou	130,690
Sikasso	225,753
Malta (2010[14] est.)	
★ Valletta	6,221
agglomeration	81,204[5]
Marshall Is. (2004 est.)	
★ Majuro	20,800
Martinique (2009 est.; MU)	
★ Fort-de-France	89,000
Mauritania (2009 est.)	
★ Nouakchott	709,000
Mauritius (2008 est.)	
Beau Bassin–Rose Hill	109,949
★ Port Louis	149,054
Vacoas-Phoenix	107,175
Mayotte (2007; MU)	
★ Mamoudzou	53,022
Mexico (2010)	
Acapulco	673,479
Aguascalientes	722,250
Boca del Río	126,507
Buenavista	206,081
Campeche	220,389
Cancún	628,306
Celaya	340,387
Chalco	168,720
Chetumal	151,243
Chicoloapan de Juárez	172,919
Chihuahua	809,232
Chilpancingo	187,251
Chimalhuacán	612,383
Ciudad Acuña (Acuña)	134,233
Ciudad Apodaca (Apodaca)	467,157
Ciudad Benito Juárez	151,893
Ciudad del Carmen	169,466
Ciudad Delicias	118,071
Ciudad Madero	197,216
Ciudad Obregón	298,625
Ciudad Valles	124,644
Ciudad Victoria (Victoria)	305,155
Coacalco	277,959
Coatzacoalcos	235,983
Colima	137,383
Córdoba	140,896
Cuauhtémoc	114,007
Cuautitlán	108,449
Cuautitlán Izcalli	484,573
Cuautla	154,358
Cuernavaca	338,650
Culiacán	675,773
Durango	518,709
Ecatepec	1,655,015
Ensenada	279,765
Fresnillo	120,944
General Escobedo	352,444
Gómez Palacio	257,352
Guadalajara	1,495,182
Guadalupe (NLN)	673,616
Guadalupe (ZAC)	124,623
Guaymas	113,082
Hermosillo	715,061
Iguala	118,468
Irapuato	380,941
Ixtapaluca	322,271
Jiutepec	162,427
Juárez (Ciudad Juárez)	1,321,004
La Paz	215,178
León	1,238,962
López Mateos	489,160
Los Mochis	256,613
Los Reyes la Paz	232,211[22]
Manzanillo	130,035
Matamoros	449,815
Mazatlán	381,583
Mérida	777,615
Metepec	164,182[22]
Mexicali	689,775
★ Mexico City	8,851,080
Minatitlán	112,046
Miramar	118,614
Monclova	215,271
Monterrey	1,135,512
Morelia	597,511
Naucalpan	792,211
Navojoa	113,836
Nezahualcóyotl	1,104,585
Nogales	212,533
Nuevo Laredo	373,725
Oaxaca	255,029
Ojo de Agua	242,272
Orizaba	120,844
Pachuca	256,584
Piedras Negras	150,178
Playa del Carmen	149,923
Poza Rica de Hidalgo	185,242
Puebla	1,434,062
Puerta Vallarta	203,342
Querétaro	626,495
Reynosa	589,466
Salamanca	160,169
Saltillo	709,671
San Cristóbal de las Casas	158,027
San Juan del Rio	138,878
San Luis Potosí	722,772
San Luis Río Colorado	158,089
San Nicolás de los Garza	443,273
San Pablo de las Salinas	189,453
San Pedro Garza García	122,627
Santa Catarina	268,347
Soledad de Graciano Sanchez	255,015
Tampico	297,284
Tapachula	202,672
Tehuacán	248,716
Tepic	332,863
Tijuana	1,300,983
Tláhuac	305,076
Tlalnepantla	653,410
Tlaquepaque	575,942
Toluca	489,333
Tonalá	408,759
Torreón	608,836
Tuxtla Gutiérrez	537,102
Uruapan	264,439
Veracruz	428,323
Villa de Alvarez	117,600
Villa Nicolás Romero	281,799
Villahermosa	353,577
Xalapa (Jalapa Enríquez)	424,755
Xico	356,352
Zacatecas	129,011
Zamora de Hidalgo	141,627
Zapopan	1,142,483
Micronesia, Federated States of (2010 est.; MU)	
★ Palikir	6,640
Moldova (2011[14] est.)	
Bălţi (Beltsy)	144,000
★ Chişinău (Kishinyov)	664,700
Tiraspol	147,312
Monaco (2010)	
★ Monaco	35,881
Mongolia (2008 est.)	
★ Ulaanbaatar (Ulan Bator)	1,031,200
Montenegro (2010)[13]	
★ Cetinje (capital)	16,657
★ Podgorica (administrative centre)	185,937
Morocco (2004)	
Agadir	678,596
Beni-Mellal	163,286
Casablanca	2,933,684
El Jadida	144,440
Fès	946,815
Kenitra	359,142
Khouribga	166,397
Ksar el-Kebir	107,380
Larache	107,371
Marrakech	823,154
Meknès	536,232
Mohammedia	188,619
Nador	126,207
Oujda	400,738
★ Rabat	1,622,860[26]
Safi	284,750
Tangier	669,685
Taza	139,686
Tétouan	320,539
Mozambique (2007)	
Beira	431,583
Chimoio	237,497
Gurue	145,466
Lichinga	142,331
★ Maputo	1,589,000[7]
Matola	793,000[1]
Maxixe	108,824
Mocuba	168,736
Nacala[27]	206,449
Nampula	471,717
Pemba	138,716
Quelimane	193,343
Tete	155,870
Xai-Xai	115,752
Myanmar (Burma) (2004 est.)	
Bassein (Pathein)	215,600
Henzada	122,700
Lashio	133,600
Mandalay	1,009,000[7]
Maymyo	113,900
Meiktila	161,000
Mergui	148,200
Monywa	163,400
Moulmein (Mawlamyine)	405,800
Myingyan	128,600
★ Naypyidaw[28]	992,000[7]
Pakokku	112,500
Pegu (Bago)	200,900
Pyay (Prome, Pye)	131,200
Sittwe (Akyab)	161,400
Taunggyi	151,400
Tavoy (Dawei)	139,900
Yangôn (Rangoon)	4,350,000[7]
Namibia (2009 est.)	
★ Windhoek	342,000
Nauru (2006)	
★ Yaren	635
Nepal (2001; MU)	
Biratnagar	166,674
Birganj	112,484
★ Kathmandu	671,846
Lalitpur (Patan)	162,991
Pokhara	156,312
Netherlands (2011 est.; MU)	
Almere	191,493
Amersfoort	147,044
★ Amsterdam (capital)	784,317
Apeldoorn	156,428
Arnhem	148,358
Breda	174,938
Dordrecht	118,910
Ede	108,271
Eindhoven	216,211
Emmen	109,175
Enschede	157,295
Groningen	190,350
Haarlem	150,912
Haarlemmermeer	143,519
Leiden	117,865
Maastricht	119,494
Nijmegen	164,438
Rotterdam	611,880
's-Hertogenbosch	141,238
★ The Hague (seat of government)	497,128
Tilburg	206,134
Utrecht	312,787
Zaanstad	147,270
Zoetermeer	121,991
Zwolle	120,698
Netherlands Antilles (2009 est.)	
★ Willemstad	123,000
New Caledonia (2009; MU)	
★ Nouméa	97,579
New Zealand (2010)[11]	
Auckland	1,354,900
Christchurch	390,300
Dunedin	116,600
Hamilton	203,400
Manukau	375,600
Napier	124,400
North Shore	229,000
Tauranga	120,000
Waitakere	208,100
★ Wellington	389,700
Nicaragua (2005)	
Chinandega	121,793
Estelí	112,084
León	174,051
★ Managua	937,489
Masaya	139,582
Matagalpa	133,416
Niger (2001)	
Maradi	148,017
★ Niamey	1,004,000[7]
Zinder	170,575
Nigeria (2006)	
Aba	785,000[1]
Abeokuta	449,088
★ Abuja	1,857,000[7]
Ado-Ekiti	313,690
Akure	491,033
Awka	301,846
Bauchi	493,730
Benin City	1,302,000[1]
Bida	185,553
Calabar	375,196
Ede	159,307
Effon-Alaiye	219,745[22]
Enugu	717,291
Gboko	361,325
Gombe	266,844
Gusau	383,712
Ibadan	2,837,000[1]
Ife	643,582
Ijebu-Ode	157,161
Ikare	143,537[22]
Ikire	154,031[22]
Ikorodu	527,917
Ikot Ekpene	141,408
Ilawe-Ekiti	143,821[22]
Ilesha	212,225
Ilorin	835,000[1]
Ise	113,951
Iseyin	255,619
Iwo	191,348
Jimeta	195,897[22]
Jos	802,000[1]
Kaduna	1,561,000[1]
Kano	3,395,000[1]
Katsina	318,132
Lagos	10,578,000[1]
agglomeration	10,203,000[7]
Maiduguri	970,000[1]
Makurdi	300,377
Minna	261,509[22]
Mubi	281,471
Nnewi	388,805
Ogbomosho	1,032,000[1]
Okene	325,623
Okpogho	145,311[22]
Ondo	364,960
Onitsha	263,109
Oshogbo	155,507
Owerri	403,425
Owo	222,262
Oyo	260,552
Port Harcourt	1,104,000[1]
Sango Otta	142,830[22]
Sapele	174,273
Shagamu	255,885
Sokoto	430,698
Suleja	215,075
Ugep	186,289[22]
Umuahia	362,192
Warri	564,657
Zaria	963,000[1]
Northern Mariana Is. (2000)	
★ Capital Hill (executive; legislative)	1,498
★ Saipan	48,220[1]
★ Susupe (judicial)	2,083
Norway (2011)	
Bærum	109,700[7]
Bergen	260,392
★ Oslo	599,230
Sandvika	112,789
Stavanger	126,021
Trondheim	173,486
Oman (2010)	
Al-Sīb	302,992
Al-Suwayq	111,711
Bawshar	192,235
ʿIbrī	116,416
Maṭraḥ	150,124
★ Muscat	27,216
agglomeration	775,878
Ṣalālah	172,570
Ṣuḥār	140,006
Pakistan (1998)	
Abbottabad	106,101[29]
Bahawalnagar	111,313
Bahawalpur	408,395[29]
Burewala	149,857
Chiniot	169,282
Dera Ghazi Khan	188,149
Faisalabad (Lyallpur)	2,849,000[29, 30]
Gojra	114,967
Gujranwala	1,652,000[29, 30]
Gujrat	251,792
Hafizabad	130,216
Hyderabad	1,590,000[29, 30]
★ Islamabad	832,000[7]
Jacobabad	137,773
Jhang Sadar	293,366
Jhelum	145,847
Kamoke	150,984
Karachi	13,125,000[29, 30]
Kasur	245,321
Khanewal	132,962
Khanpur	117,764
Kohat	125,271[31]
Lahore	7,132,000[29, 30]
Larkana	270,283
Mardan	245,926[31]
Mingaora	174,469
Mirpur Khas	184,465
Multan	1,659,000[29, 30]
Muridike	108,578
Muzaffargarh	121,641
Nawabshah	183,110
Okara	201,815
Pakpattan	107,791
Peshawar	1,422,000[29, 30]
Quetta	841,000[30]
Rahimyar Khan	233,537
Rawalpindi	2,026,000[29, 30]
Sadiqabad	141,509
Sahiwal	208,778
Sargodha	458,440[29]
Shekhupura	280,263
Shikarpur	133,259
Sialkot	421,502[29]
Sukkur	335,551
Wah	198,431[29]
Palau (2005)	
★ Koror (de facto)	12,000[7]
★ Melekeok (complex under construction)	391
Panama (2010)	
★ Panama City	430,229
San Miguelito	315,019[32]
Papua New Guinea (2004 est.)	
Lae	109,800

country city	population
★ Port Moresby (National Capital District)	299,000[6]
Paraguay (2002)	
★ Asunción	1,977,000[7]
Capiatá	154,274
Ciudad del Este	222,274
Fernando de la Mora	113,560
Lambaré	119,795
Luque	170,986
San Lorenzo	204,356
Peru (2007)	
Arequipa	789,000[30]
Ayacucho	151,019
Cajamarca	162,326
Chiclayo	524,442
Chimbote	334,568
Chincha Alta	153,599
Cusco	348,935
Huancayo	323,054
Huánuco	149,210
Ica	219,856
Iquitos	370,962
Juliaca	216,716
Lima	
agglomeration	8,769,000[7]
Ate	419,663[22]
Callao	389,579[22]
Carabayllo	180,293[22]
Chorrillos	262,595[22]
Comas	464,745[22]
El Agustino	165,425[22]
Independencia	197,308[22]
La Victoría	190,218[22]
★ Lima	289,855[22]
Los Olivos	286,549[22]
Puente Piedra	203,473[22]
Rímac	175,793[22]
San Juan de Lurigancho	812,656[22]
San Juan de Miraflores	335,237[22]
San Martin de Porras	525,155[22]
San Miguel	124,904[22]
Santa Anita	160,777[22]
Santiago de Surco	272,690[22]
Ventanilla	243,526[22]
Villa el Salvador	367,436[22]
Villa Maria del Triunfo	355,761[22]
Piura	377,496
Pucallpa	204,772
Puno	120,229
Sullana	181,954
Tacna	242,451
Tarapoto	117,184
Trujillo	682,834
Philippines (2007; MU)	
Angeles	314,493
Antipolo	633,971
Bacolod	499,497
Bacoor	441,197
Bago	159,933
Baguio	301,926
Baliuag	136,982
Batangas	187,225
Biñan	262,735
Binangonan	238,931
Cabanatuan	243,934
Cabuyao	205,376
Cagayan de Oro	553,966
Cainta	289,833
Calamba	360,281
Calbayog	130,321
Cebu	798,809
Cotabato	259,153
Dagupan	149,554
Dasmariñas	556,330
Davao	1,366,153
Dumaguete	116,392
General Mariano Alvarez	136,613
General Santos	529,542
General Trias	218,387
Iligan	308,046
Iloilo	418,710
Imus	253,158
Jolo	140,307
Kabankalan	165,294
Kalookan (Caloocan)	1,378,856
Lapu-Lapu	292,530
Las Piñas	532,330
Legazpi	179,481
Lipa	260,568
Lucena	236,390
Mabalacat	203,307
Makati	510,383
Malabon	363,681
Malolos	223,069
Mandaluyong	305,576
Mandaue	318,575
★ Manila	1,660,714
Metro Manila	11,100,000
Marawi	177,391
Marikina	424,610
Marilau	160,452
Meycauayan	196,569
Montalban	187,750
Muntinlupa	452,943
Naga	160,516
Navotas	245,344
Olongapo	227,270
Ormoc	177,524
Ozamis	112,150
Parañaque	552,660
Pasay	403,064
Pasig	617,301
Puerto Princesa	210,508
★ Quezon City	2,679,450
Roxas	147,738
Sagay	140,511
San Carlos	129,829
San Fernando	269,365
San Juan del Monte	125,338
San Mateo	184,860
San Pablo	237,259
San Pedro	281,808
Santa Maria	205,258
Santa Rosa	266,943
Tacloban	217,199
Taguig	613,343
Tagum	118,942
Talisay	179,359
Tanauan	142,537
Tanza	171,795
Tarlac	203,606
Taytay	262,485
Urdaneta	120,785
Valenzuela	568,928
Zamboanga	774,407
Poland (2009 est.)	
Białystok	294,153
Bielsko-Biała	175,677
Bydgoszcz	358,928
Bytom	183,829
Chorzów	113,314
Częstochowa	240,612
Dąbrowa Górnicza	128,315
Elbląg	126,439
Gdańsk	455,581
Gdynia	249,257
Gliwice	196,669
Gorzów Wielkopolski	125,157
Kalisz	107,140
Katowice	309,621
Kielce	205,094
Koszalin	107,146
Kraków	754,624
Łódź	747,152
Lublin	350,462
Olsztyn	176,142
Opole	126,203
Płock	126,709
Poznań	557,264
Radom	224,226
Ruda Śląska	143,930
Rybnik	141,177
Rzeszów	172,683
Sosnowiec	221,259
Szczecin	406,941
Tarnów	115,518
Toruń	206,013
Tychy	129,475
Wałbrzych	122,411
★ Warsaw (Warszawa)	1,709,781
Włocławek	118,042
Wrocław	632,162
Zabrze	188,401
Zielona Góra	117,557
Portugal (2011)[10]	
Almada	173,298
Amadora	175,558
Barcelos	120,492
Braga	181,819
Cascais	205,117
Coimbra	143,052
Funchal	112,015
Gondomar	168,205
Guimarães	158,108
Leiria	127,468
★ Lisbon	545,245
agglomeration	2,815,851
Loures	205,577
Maia	135,049
Matosinhos	174,931
Odivelas	143,755
Oeiras	172,063
Porto	237,559
Santa Maria de Feira	139,393
Seixal	157,981
Setúbal	120,791
Sintra	377,249
Vila Franca de Xira	136,510
Vila Nova de Famalicão	133,804
Vila Nova de Gaia	302,092
Puerto Rico (2010; MU)	
Bayamón	208,116
Caguas	142,893
Carolina	176,762
Ponce	166,327
★ San Juan	395,326
agglomeration	2,478,905
Qatar (2010)	
Al-Dhakhīrah	128,574
Al-Rayyān	392,428
★ Doha	521,283
Réunion (2009 est.)	
★ Saint-Denis	141,000
Romania (2009 est.)	
Arad	166,003
Bacău	177,087
Baia Mare	139,154
Botoşani	116,110
Brăila	212,501
Braşov	278,048
★ Bucharest	1,944,367
Buzău	132,210
Cluj-Napoca	306,474
Constanţa	302,171
Craiova	298,928
Drobeta-Turnu Severin	106,507
Galaţi	291,354
Iaşi	308,843
Oradea	204,477
Piatra Neamţ	107,504
Piteşti	166,893
Ploieşti	229,285
Râmnicu Vâlcea	110,901
Satu Mare	112,705
Sibiu	154,548
Suceava	106,934
Târgu Mureş	145,151
Timişoara	311,586
Russia (2010)[8]	
Abakan	165,183
Achinsk	109,156
Almetyevsk	141,309
Angarsk	233,765
Arkhangelsk	348,716
Armavir	188,897
Arzamas	106,367
Astrakhan	520,662
Balakovo	199,573
Balashikha	215,353
Barnaul	612,091
Bataisk	111,856
Belgorod	356,426
Berezniki	156,512
Biysk	210,055
Blagoveshchensk	214,397
Bratsk	246,348
Bryansk	415,640
Cheboksary	453,645
Chelyabinsk	1,130,273
Cherepovets	312,311
Cherkessk	121,439
Chita	323,964
Derbent	119,961
Dimitrovgrad	122,549
Dzerzhinsk	240,762
Elektrostal	155,324
Engels	202,401
Grozny (Dzhokhar)	271,596
Irkutsk	587,225
Ivanovo	409,277
Izhevsk	628,116
Kaliningrad	431,491
Kaluga	325,185
Kamensk-Uralsky	174,710
Kamyshin	119,924
Kazan	1,143,546
Kemerovo	532,884
Khabarovsk	577,668
Khasavyurt	133,929
Khimki	207,125
Kirov	473,668
Kislovodsk	128,502
Kolomna	144,642
Komsomolsk-na-Amure	263,906
Kopeisk	137,604
Korolyov (Kaliningrad)	183,452
Kostroma	268,617
Kovrov	145,492
Krasnodar	744,933
Krasnogorsk	116,738
Krasnoyarsk	973,891
Kurgan	333,640
Kursk	414,595
Kyzyl	109,906
Lipetsk	508,124
Lyubertsy	171,978
Magnitogorsk	408,401
Makhachkala	577,990
Maykop	144,246
Miass	151,812
★ Moscow	11,514,330
Murmansk	307,664
Murom	116,078
Mytishchi	173,341
Naberezhnye Chelny (Brezhnev)	513,242
Nakhodka	159,695
Nalchik	240,095
Nazran	134,280[5]
Nefteyugansk	123,276
Nevinnomyssk	118,351
Nikolo-Beryozovka (Neftekamsk)	121,757
Nizhnekamsk	234,108
Nizhnevartovsk	251,860
Nizhny Novgorod (Gorky)	1,250,615
Nizhny Tagil	361,883
Noginsk	115,776[5]
Norilsk	175,301
Novocheboksarsk	124,113
Novocherkassk	169,039
Novokuybyshevsk	108,449
Novokuznetsk	547,885
Novomoskovsk	131,227
Novorossiysk	241,788
Novoshakhtinsk	111,087
Novosibirsk	1,473,737
Noyabrsk	110,572
Odintsovo	139,021
Oktyabrsky	109,379
Omsk	1,153,971
Orekhovo-Zuyevo	120,620
Orenburg	546,987
Orsk	239,752
Oryol	317,854
Penza	517,137
Perm	991,530
Pervouralsk	124,555
Petropavlovsk-Kamchatsky	179,526
Petrozavodsk	263,540
Podolsk	187,956
Prokopyevsk	210,150
Pskov	203,281
Pyatigorsk	142,397
Rostov-na-Donu	1,089,851
Rubtsovsk	147,008
Ryazan	525,062
Rybinsk (Andropov)	200,771
Saint Petersburg (Leningrad)	4,848,742
Salavat	156,085
Samara (Kuybyshev)	1,164,896
Saransk	297,425
Saratov	837,831
Sergiev Posad (Zagorsk)	110,878
Serpukhov	126,496
Severodvinsk	192,265
Seversk	108,466
Shakhty	240,152
Shchyolkovo	110,380
Simbirsk (Ulyanovsk)	613,793
Smolensk	326,863
Sochi	343,285
Stary Oskol	221,163
Stavropol	398,266
Sterlitamak	273,432
Surgut	306,703
Syktyvkar	235,006
Syzran	178,773
Taganrog	257,692
Tambov	280,457
Tolyatti	719,514
Tomsk	522,940
Tula	501,129
Tver (Kalinin)	403,726
Tyumen	581,758
Ufa	1,062,300
Ulan-Ude	404,357
Ussuriysk	157,946
Veliky Novgorod	218,724
Vladikavkaz (Ordzhonikidze)	311,635
Vladimir	345,598
Vladivostok	592,069
Volgodonsk	170,621
Volgograd	1,021,244
Vologda	301,642
Volzhsky	314,436
Voronezh	889,989
Yakutsk	269,486
Yaroslavl	591,486
Yekaterinburg (Sverdlovsk)	1,350,136
Yelets	108,404
Yoshkar-Ola	248,688
Yuzhno-Sakhalinsk	181,727
Zelenograd	220,300[33]
Zheleznodorozhny	131,729
Zlatoust	174,985
Rwanda (2009 est.)	
★ Kigali	909,000
St. Kitts and Nevis (2009 est.)	
★ Basseterre	13,000
St. Lucia (2010)[10]	
★ Castries	4,173
agglomeration	22,111
St. Vincent and the Grenadines (2009 est.)	
★ Kingstown	28,000
Samoa (2009 est.)	
★ Apia	36,000
San Marino (2010 est.)	
★ San Marino	4,335
Sao Tome and Principe (2001)	
★ São Tomé	3,666
agglomeration	60,000[7]
Saudi Arabia (2010)[8]	
Abhā	236,157
Al-Dammām	903,312
Al-Ḥawīyah	148,151
Al-Hufūf[34]	660,788
Al-Jubayl	337,778
Al-Kharj	234,607
Al-Khubar	219,679
Al-Qaṭīf	118,327
Al-Qurayyāt	116,162
Al-Ṭā'if	579,970
Al-Thuqbah	238,066
ʿArʿar	167,057
Buraydah	467,410
Dhahran	120,521
Ḥafar al-Bāṭin	271,642
Ḥā'il	310,897
Jiddah	3,430,697
Jīzān	127,743
Khamīs Mushayṭ	430,828
Mecca (Makkah)	1,534,731
Medina (Al-Madīnah)	1,100,093
Najrān	298,288
★ Riyadh (Al-Riyāḍ)	5,188,286
Sakākā	150,257
Tabūk	512,629
ʿUnayzah	152,895
Yanbuʿ al-Baḥr	233,236
Senegal (2009 est.; MU)	
★ Dakar	2,344,829
Kaolack	190,927
Mbour	193,368
Rufisque	169,371
Saint-Louis	177,662
Thiès	273,218
Touba	529,200[6]
Ziguinchor	162,887
Serbia (2008)	
★ Belgrade	1,119,020
Kragujevac	145,360
Niš	172,944
Novi Sad	197,694
Seychelles (2010 est.)	
★ Victoria	25,507[11]
Sierra Leone (2004)	
Bo	167,144
★ Freetown	875,000[7]
Kenema	137,696
Singapore (2007 est.)	
★ Singapore	4,436,000
Sint Maarten (2001)	
★ Philipsburg	1,227
Slovakia (2009 est.)	
★ Bratislava	428,791
Košice	233,659

Major cities and national capitals (continued)

country city	population
Slovenia (2011[14] est.)	
★ Ljubljana	280,140
Solomon Islands (2009)	
★ Honiara	64,609
Somalia (2009 est.)	
★ Mogadishu	...
agglomeration	1,353,000
South Africa (2005 est.)[31, 35]	
Alberton	145,529
Benoni	359,491
Boksburg	256,639
Botshabelo	175,061
Brakpan	168,557
★ Cape Town (de facto legislative)	3,103,000
Carletonville	161,679
Durban	2,643,000
East London	258,000
Ekurhuleni	3,043,000
George	152,000
Johannesburg	3,288,000
Kimberley	185,000
Klerksdorp	192,000
Krugersdorp	289,717
Ladysmith	168,000
Mabopane	324,000
★ Mangaung (Bloemfontein; de facto judicial)	397,000
Mdantsane	180,006
Midrand	124,333
Newcastle	170,000
Nigel	172,000
Paarl	149,000
Pietermaritzburg	436,000
Pietersburg	178,000
Port Elizabeth	998,000
Potchefstroom	122,000
Rustenburg	170,000
Soshanguve	363,000
Soweto	1,080,317
Springs	158,166
Tembisa	277,656
★ Tshwane (Pretoria; de facto executive)	1,282,000
Uitenhage	188,978
Vanderbijlpark	249,192
Vereeniging	1,033,000
Verwoerdburg	112,701
Welkom	190,000
West Rand	549,000
Westonaria	112,069
Witbank	210,000
Spain (2007 est.)	
Albacete	170,475
Alcalá de Henares	204,120
Alcobendas	110,080
Alcorcón	168,299
Algeciras	116,417
Alicante (Alacant)	334,418
Almería	190,013
Badajoz	150,376
Badalona	218,886
Barcelona	1,619,337
Bilbao	353,187
Burgos	178,574
Cádiz	125,826
Cartagena	214,165
Castellón de la Plana (Castelló de la Plana)	180,690
Córdoba	328,547
Coruña, A (Coruña, La)	246,047
Donostia–San Sebastián	185,506
Dos Hermanas	125,086
Elche (Elx)	230,822
Fuenlabrada	198,973
Getafe	169,130
Gijón	277,198
Granada	239,154
Hospitalet (de Llobregat)	258,642
Huelva	149,310
Jaén	116,790
Jerez de la Frontera	208,896
Laguna, La	152,222
Leganés	187,227
León	134,012
Lleida (Lérida)	137,387
Logroño	152,650
★ Madrid	3,273,049
Málaga	568,507
Marbella	136,322
Mataró	122,905
Móstoles	206,015
Murcia	441,345
Ourense (Orense)	108,673
Oviedo	225,155
Palma (de Mallorca)	404,681
Palmas de Gran Canaria, Las	383,308
Pamplona (Iruña)	197,488
Parla	120,182
Reus	106,622
Sabadell	207,338
Salamanca	154,462
Santa Coloma de Gramanet	120,060
Santa Cruz de Tenerife	222,643
Santander	181,589
Sevilla (Seville)	704,198
Tarragona	140,184
Terrassa (Tarrasa)	212,724
Torrejón de Ardoz	118,441
Valencia (València)	809,267
Valladolid	315,522
Vigo	297,124
Vitoria-Gasteiz	238,247
Zaragoza (Saragossa)	675,121
Sri Lanka (2007 est.)	
★ Colombo (executive; judicial)	672,743
Dehiwala–Mount Lavinia	219,827
Jaffna	151,612
Kandy	121,286
Moratuwa	185,668
Negombo	150,364
★ Sri Jayawardenepura Kotte (legislative)	121,370
Sudan (2008)	
Al-Damāzīn	136,788
Al-Du'ayn	137,103
Al-Fāshir	217,827
Al-Junaynah	134,264
Al-Qaḍārif	269,395
Al-Ubayyiḍ	345,129
Aṭbarah	112,021
Kassalā	298,529
★ Khartoum (executive)	1,410,858
agglomeration	4,272,728
Khartoum North	1,012,211
Kūsti	213,080
Nyala	492,984
★ Omdurman (legislative)	1,849,659
Port Sudan	394,561
Rabak	123,890
Sannār	123,158
Wad Madanī	289,482
Sudan, South (2008)[8]	
★ Juba	230,195
Malakal	114,528
Wau	118,331
Yambio	105,881
Yei	111,268
Suriname (2009 est.)	
★ Paramaribo	259,000
Swaziland (2007 est.)	
★ Lobamba (legislative)	...
★ Lozitha (royal)	...
★ Ludzidzini (royal)	...
★ Mbabane (administrative)	78,000
Sweden (2010 est.; MU)	
Göteborg	513,751
Helsingborg	129,177
Jönköping	127,382
Linköping	146,416
Lund	110,488
Malmö	298,963
Norrköping	130,050
Örebro	135,460
★ Stockholm	847,073
Umeå	115,473
Uppsala	197,787
Västerås	137,207
Switzerland (2010[14] est.)	
Basel (Bâle)	166,173
★ Bern (Berne) (administrative)	123,466
Geneva (Genève)	185,958
★ Lausanne (judicial)	125,885
Zürich	368,677
Syria (2004 est.)	
Aleppo (Ḥalab)	1,975,200
Al-Ḥasakah	211,300
Al-Qāmishlī	210,300
Al-Raqqah	229,100
★ Damascus (Dimashq)	1,614,500
Dayr al-Zawr	239,800
Ḥamāh	366,800
Homs (Ḥims)	800,400
Jaramānah	192,800
Latakia (al-Ladhiqiyah)	468,700
Ṭarṭūs	162,300
Taiwan (2011[14] est.)	
Chang-hua	236,503
Chi-lung (Keelung)	384,134
Chia-i	272,390
Chu-pei	141,852
Chung-ho	414,356
Chung-li	369,770
Feng-shan	341,120
Feng-yüan	165,433
Hsi-chih	189,618
Hsin-chu	415,344
Hsin-chuang	402,204
Hsin-tien	296,411
Hua-lien	109,251
Kao-hsiung	1,529,947
Kuei-shan	137,996
Lu-chou	197,793
Lu-chu	142,120
Lung-t'an	115,166
Pa-te	176,868
Pan-ch'iao	554,596
P'ing-chen	207,457
P'ing-tung	211,027
San-chu'ung	389,968
Shu-lin	176,077
Ta-li	197,716
Ta-liao	108,984
T'ai-chung	1,082,299
T'ai-nan	772,273
T'ai-p'ing	172,965
T'ai-tung	108,870
★ Taipei (T'ai-pei)	2,618,772
Tan-shui	143,481
T'ao-yuan	406,851
Tou-liu	106,854
T'u-ch'eng	238,477
Yang-mei	150,926
Yüan-lin	125,476
Yung-ho	234,536
Yung-k'ang	216,748
Tajikistan (2010)[8]	
★ Dushanbe	724,000
Khujand (Khudzhand; Leninabad)	162,000
Tanzania (2002)[36]	
Arusha	270,485
★ Dar es Salaam (executive; judicial)	2,339,910
Dodoma (legislative)	150,604
Kigoma	131,792
Mbeya	232,596
Morogoro	209,058
Moshi	143,799
Mwanza	209,806
Tabora	127,887
Tanga	180,237
Zanzibar	205,870
Thailand (2000)	
★ Bangkok (Krung Thep)	6,355,144
Chiang Mai	174,438
Chon Buri	183,317
Hat Yai	187,920
Khlong Luang	106,326
Khon Kaen	141,202
Lampang	148,199
Nakhon Pathom	120,818
Nakhon Ratchasima	204,641
Nakhon Si Thammarat	118,729
Nonthaburi	291,555
Pak Kret	142,225
Phra Pradaeng	171,544
Rayong	106,737
Samut Prakan	378,741
Si Racha	141,410
Surat Thani	111,340
Thanya Buri	113,825
Ubon Ratchathani	106,602
Udon Thani	222,425
Togo (2010)[10]	
★ Lomé	750,757
Tonga (2006)	
★ Nuku'alofa	23,658
Trinidad and Tobago (2007 est.)	
★ Port of Spain	54,000
Tunisia (2004)	
Al-Qayrawān (Kairouan)	117,903
Aryānah	240,749
Bizerte (Banzart)	114,371
Ettadhamen	118,487
Qābis	116,323
Ṣafāqis (Sfax)	265,131
Sūsah	173,047
★ Tunis	728,453
Turkey (2010)[37]	
Adana	1,584,053
Adıyaman	202,735
Afyon	173,100
Aksaray	176,504
★ Ankara	4,223,398
Antakya (Hatay)	213,581
Antalya	928,229
Aydın	188,337
Balıkesir	265,747
Bandirma	116,319
Batman	325,020
Bolu	119,898
Bursa	1,667,321
Çanakkale	106,116
Ceyhan	105,879
Çorlu	215,293
Çorum	218,130
Denizli	498,643
Derince	121,040
Diyarbakır	843,460
Düzce	129,118
Edirne	138,793
Elaziğ	331,479
Erzurum	367,250
Eskişehir	629,609
Gaziantep	1,324,520
Gebze	526,287[38]
Gölcük	131,450
İçel (Mersin)	843,429
İnegöl	167,419
İskenderun	201,183
Isparta	222,556
Istanbul	12,946,730
İzmir	2,774,103
Kahramanmaraş (Maraş)	412,252
Karabük	108,710
Karaman	135,185
Kayseri	826,523
Kırıkkale	193,093
Kirşehir	108,628
Kızıltepe	135,145
Kocaeli (İzmit)	294,875
Konya	1,036,027
Körfez	128,750
Kütahya	235,685
Malatya	401,705
Manisa	316,973
Menemen	119,230
Nazilli	110,116
Niğde	109,724
Ordu	141,341
Osmaniye	198,836
Sakarya (Adapazarı)	414,537
Samsun	495,145
Siirt	127,174
Silivri	126,218
Sivas	318,488
Siverek	111,628
Sultanbeyli	272,758
Tarsus	238,276
Tekirdağ	141,439
Tokat	136,595
Torbalı	116,326
Trabzon	234,063
Turgutlu	117,632
Urfa (Şanlıurfa)	498,111
Uşak	180,414
Van	367,419
Zonguldak	109,081
Turkmenistan (2004)	
★ Ashgabat	637,000[7]
Balkanabat (Nebitdag)	139,000
Daşoguz	210,000
Mary	159,000
Türkmenabat (Chārjew)	256,000
Tuvalu (2009 est.)	
★ Funafuti	5,000
Uganda (2010)[30]	
Gulu	149,900
★ Kampala	1,597,900
Kira	172,300
Ukraine (2010[14] est.)	
Alchevsk	113,980
Berdyansk	117,517
Bila Tserkva	209,250
Cherkasy	287,713
Chernihiv	297,402
Chernivtsi	251,776
Dniprodzerzhynsk	244,272
Dnipropetrovsk	1,011,177
Donetsk	968,250
Horlivka	263,647
Ivano-Frankivsk	224,401
Kerch	147,269
Kharkiv	1,452,256
Kherson	304,613
Khmelnytskyy	261,397
Kirovohrad	236,097
Kramatorsk	167,850
Kremenchuk	227,611
Kryvyy Rih	670,397
★ Kyiv (Kiev)	2,785,131
Luhansk	434,869
Lutsk	210,775
Lviv	733,989
Lysychansk	106,557
Makiyivka	360,989
Mariupol	469,336
Melitopol	157,626
Mykolayiv	501,183
Nikopol	123,748
Odesa (Odessa)	1,010,326
Pavlohrad	111,069
Poltava	300,501
Rivne	249,582
Sevastopol	340,102
Simferopol	336,588
Slov'yansk	119,482
Sumy	272,326
Syeverodonetsk	111,487
Ternopil	217,577
Uzhhorod	116,456
Vinnytsya	369,214
Yevpatoriya	106,846
Zaporizhzhya	780,733
Zhytomyr	271,714
United Arab Emirates (2007 est.)	
★ Abu Dhabi	666,000[7]
'Ajmān	250,808
Al-'Ayn	444,331
Dubai	1,567,000[1]
Ra's al-Khaymah	121,626
Sharjah	809,000[1]
United Kingdom (2006 est.)	
England	
Barnsley	223,500
Birmingham	994,900
Blackburn with Darwen	141,200
Blackpool	142,700
Bolton	262,400
Bournemouth	161,200
Bracknell Forest	112,200
Bradford	493,100
Brighton and Hove	251,400
Bristol	410,500
Bury	182,900
Calderdale	198,500
Cambridge	117,900
Canterbury	146,200
Chester	119,700
Chichester	108,900
Coventry	306,600
Derby	236,300
Doncaster	290,300
Dudley	305,300
Exeter	119,600
Gateshead	190,500
Gloucester	113,200

[1]2010 estimate. [2]Eight villages, including Fagatogo and Utulei, are collectively known as Pago Pago (2001 agglomeration pop. 15,000). [3]2001. [4]Urban centre ("urban agglomeration") as defined by 2001 census. [5]2008 estimate. [6]2007 estimate. [7]2009 estimate. [8]Provisional census results. [9]2004 estimate. [10]Preliminary census results. [11]Urban agglomeration. [12]San José canton. [13]First census results. [14]January 1. [15]Excludes Lefkoşa (Turkish Nicosia), whose population per 2006 estimate was 49,237. [16]Within San Salvador metropolitan area. [17]2006 estimate. [18]2003 census. [19]Within Athens urban agglomeration. [20]Urban population; Hong Kong is 100% urban. [21]Urban population (may or may not be city proper; not urban agglomeration). [22]2005 estimate. [23]1990 census.

country city	population
Halton	119,500
Kingston upon Hull	256,200
Kirklees	398,200
Knowsley	151,300
Lancaster	143,000
Leeds	750,200
Leicester	289,700
Liverpool	436,100
★ London (Greater London)	7,517,700[39]
Luton	186,800
Manchester	452,000
Milton Keynes	224,800
Newcastle upon Tyne	270,500
North Tyneside	195,000
Norwich	129,500
Nottingham	286,400
Oldham	219,600
Oxford	149,100
Peterborough	163,300
Plymouth	248,100
Poole	136,900
Portsmouth	196,400
Preston	132,000
Reading	142,800
Rochdale	206,500
Rotherham	253,300
St. Albans	131,300
St. Helens	177,600
Salford	218,000
Sandwell	287,600
Sefton	277,400
Sheffield	525,000
Slough	119,500
Solihull	203,000
South Tyneside	151,000
Southampton	228,600
Southend	159,900
Stockport	280,600
Stockton-on-Tees	189,100
Stoke-on-Trent	239,700
Sunderland	280,600
Swindon	186,600
Tameside	214,400
Thurrock	148,900
Torbay	133,200
Trafford	211,800
Wakefield	321,200
Walsall	254,500
Warrington	194,000
Wigan	305,500
Winchester	110,000
Windsor and Maidenhead	138,800
Wirral	311,200
Wolverhampton	236,600
York	191,800
Northern Ireland[40]	
Belfast	268,100
Derry (Londonderry)	107,300
Lisburn	111,500
Scotland	
Aberdeen	206,880
Dundee	142,170
Edinburgh	463,510
Glasgow	580,690
Wales	
Cardiff	317,500
Conwy	111,300
Neath Port Talbot	137,100
Newport	140,100
Rhondda, Cynon, Taff	233,900
Swansea	227,100
Wrexham	131,000
United States (2010)	
Abilene (*Texas*)	117,063
Akron (*Ohio*)	199,110
Albuquerque (*N.M.*)	545,852
Alexandria (*Va.*)	139,966
Allentown (*Pa.*)	118,032
Amarillo (*Texas*)	190,695
Anaheim (*Calif.*)	336,265
Anchorage (*Alaska*)	291,826
Ann Arbor (*Mich.*)	113,934
Arlington (*Texas*)	365,438
Arlington (*Va.*)[41]	207,627
Arvada (*Colo.*)	106,433
Athens (*Ga.*)	115,452
Atlanta (*Ga.*)	420,003
Augusta (*Ga.*)	195,844
Aurora (*Colo.*)	325,078
Aurora (*Ill.*)	197,899
Austin (*Texas*)	790,390
Bakersfield (*Calif.*)	347,483
Baltimore (*Md.*)	620,961
Baton Rouge (*La.*)	229,493
Beaumont (*Texas*)	118,296
Bellevue (*Wash.*)	122,363
Berkeley (*Calif.*)	112,580
Birmingham (*Ala.*)	212,237
Boise (*Idaho*)	205,671
Boston (*Mass.*)	617,594
Bridgeport (*Conn.*)	144,229
Brownsville (*Texas*)	175,023
Buffalo (*N.Y.*)	261,310
Cape Coral (*Fla.*)	154,305
Carrollton (*Texas*)	119,097
Cary (*N.C.*)	135,234
Cedar Rapids (*Iowa*)	126,326
Chandler (*Ariz.*)	236,123
Charleston (*S.C.*)	120,083
Charlotte (*N.C.*)	731,424
Chattanooga (*Tenn.*)	167,674
Chesapeake (*Va.*)	222,209
Chicago (*Ill.*)	2,695,598
Chula Vista (*Calif.*)	243,916
Cincinnati (*Ohio*)	296,943
Clarksville (*Tenn.*)	132,929
Clearwater (*Fla.*)	107,685
Cleveland (*Ohio*)	396,815
Colorado Springs (*Colo.*)	416,427
Columbia (*Mo.*)	108,500
Columbia (*S.C.*)	129,272
Columbus (*Ga.*)	189,885
Columbus (*Ohio*)	787,033
Concord (*Calif.*)	122,067
Coral Springs (*Fla.*)	121,096
Corona (*Calif.*)	152,374
Corpus Christi (*Texas*)	305,215
Costa Mesa (*Calif.*)	109,960
Dallas (*Texas*)	1,197,816
Dayton (*Ohio*)	141,527
Denton (*Texas*)	113,383
Denver (*Colo.*)	600,158
Des Moines (*Iowa*)	203,433
Detroit (*Mich.*)	713,777
Downey (*Calif.*)	111,772
Durham (*N.C.*)	228,330
East Los Angeles (*Calif.*)[41]	126,496
El Monte (*Calif.*)	113,475
El Paso (*Texas*)	649,121
Elgin (*Ill.*)	108,188
Elizabeth (*N.J.*)	124,969
Elk Grove (*Calif.*)	153,015
Enterprise (*Nev.*)[41]	108,481
Escondido (*Calif.*)	143,911
Eugene (*Ore.*)	156,185
Evansville (*Ind.*)	117,429
Fargo (*N.D.*)	105,549
Fayetteville (*N.C.*)	200,564
Fontana (*Calif.*)	196,069
Fort Collins (*Colo.*)	143,986
Fort Lauderdale (*Fla.*)	165,521
Fort Wayne (*Ind.*)	253,691
Fort Worth (*Texas*)	741,206
Fremont (*Calif.*)	214,089
Fresno (*Calif.*)	494,665
Frisco (*Texas*)	116,989
Fullerton (*Calif.*)	135,161
Gainesville (*Fla.*)	124,354
Garden Grove (*Calif.*)	170,883
Garland (*Texas*)	226,876
Gilbert (*Ariz.*)	208,453
Glendale (*Ariz.*)	226,721
Glendale (*Calif.*)	191,719
Grand Prairie (*Texas*)	175,396
Grand Rapids (*Mich.*)	188,040
Greensboro (*N.C.*)	269,666
Gresham (*Ore.*)	105,594
Hampton (*Va.*)	137,436
Hartford (*Conn.*)	124,775
Hayward (*Calif.*)	144,186
Henderson (*Nev.*)	257,729
Hialeah (*Fla.*)	224,669
Hollywood (*Fla.*)	140,768
Honolulu (*Hawaii*)	337,256
Houston (*Texas*)	2,099,451
Huntington Beach (*Calif.*)	189,992
Huntsville (*Ala.*)	180,105
Independence (*Mo.*)	116,830
Indianapolis (*Ind.*)	820,445
Inglewood (*Calif.*)	109,673
Irvine (*Calif.*)	212,375
Irving (*Texas*)	216,290
Jackson (*Miss.*)	173,514
Jacksonville (*Fla.*)	821,784
Jersey City (*N.J.*)	247,597
Joliet (*Ill.*)	147,433
Kansas City (*Kan.*)	145,786
Kansas City (*Mo.*)	459,787
Killeen (*Texas*)	127,921
Knoxville (*Tenn.*)	178,874
Lafayette (*La.*)	120,623
Lakewood (*Colo.*)	142,980
Lancaster (*Calif.*)	156,633
Lansing (*Mich.*)	114,297
Laredo (*Texas*)	236,091
Las Vegas (*Nev.*)	583,756
Lexington (*Ky.*)	295,803
Lincoln (*Neb.*)	258,379
Little Rock (*Ark.*)	193,524
Long Beach (*Calif.*)	462,257
Los Angeles (*Calif.*)	3,792,621
Louisville (*Ky.*)	597,337
Lowell (*Mass.*)	106,519
Lubbock (*Texas*)	229,573
McAllen (*Texas*)	129,877
McKinney (*Texas*)	131,117
Madison (*Wis.*)	233,209
Manchester (*N.H.*)	109,565
Memphis (*Tenn.*)	646,889
Mesa (*Ariz.*)	439,041
Mesquite (*Texas*)	139,824
Metairie (*La.*)[41]	138,481
Miami (*Fla.*)	399,457
Miami Gardens (*Fla.*)	107,167
Midland (*Texas*)	111,147
Milwaukee (*Wis.*)	594,833
Minneapolis (*Minn.*)	382,578
Miramar (*Fla.*)	122,041
Mobile (*Ala.*)	195,111
Modesto (*Calif.*)	201,165
Montgomery (*Ala.*)	205,764
Moreno Valley (*Calif.*)	193,365
Murfreesboro (*Tenn.*)	108,755
Naperville (*Ill.*)	141,853
Nashville (*Tenn.*)	601,222
New Haven (*Conn.*)	129,779
New Orleans (*La.*)	343,829
New York City (*N.Y.*)	8,175,133
Newark (*N.J.*)	277,140
Newport News (*Va.*)	180,719
Norfolk (*Va.*)	242,803
Norman (*Okla.*)	110,925
North Las Vegas (*Nev.*)	216,961
Norwalk (*Calif.*)	105,549
Oakland (*Calif.*)	390,724
Oceanside (*Calif.*)	167,086
Oklahoma City (*Okla.*)	579,999
Olathe (*Kan.*)	125,872
Omaha (*Neb.*)	408,958
Ontario (*Calif.*)	163,924
Orange (*Calif.*)	136,416
Orlando (*Fla.*)	238,300
Overland Park (*Kan.*)	173,372
Oxnard (*Calif.*)	197,899
Palmdale (*Calif.*)	152,750
Paradise (*Nev.*)[41]	223,167
Pasadena (*Calif.*)	137,122
Pasadena (*Texas*)	149,043
Paterson (*N.J.*)	146,199
Pembroke Pines (*Fla.*)	154,750
Peoria (*Ariz.*)	154,065
Peoria (*Ill.*)	115,007
Philadelphia (*Pa.*)	1,526,006
Phoenix (*Ariz.*)	1,445,632
Pittsburgh (*Pa.*)	305,704
Plano (*Texas*)	259,841
Pomona (*Calif.*)	149,058
Port St. Lucie (*Fla.*)	164,603
Portland (*Ore.*)	583,776
Providence (*R.I.*)	178,042
Provo (*Utah*)	112,488
Pueblo (*Colo.*)	106,595
Raleigh (*N.C.*)	403,892
Rancho Cucamonga (*Calif.*)	165,269
Reno (*Nev.*)	225,221
Richmond (*Va.*)	204,214
Riverside (*Calif.*)	303,871
Rochester (*Minn.*)	106,769
Rochester (*N.Y.*)	210,565
Rockford (*Ill.*)	152,871
Roseville (*Calif.*)	118,788
Sacramento (*Calif.*)	466,488
St. Louis (*Mo.*)	319,294
St. Paul (*Minn.*)	285,068
St. Petersburg (*Fla.*)	244,769
Salem (*Ore.*)	154,637
Salinas (*Calif.*)	150,441
Salt Lake City (*Utah*)	186,440
San Antonio (*Texas*)	1,327,407
San Bernardino (*Calif.*)	209,924
San Buenaventura (Ventura) (*Calif.*)	106,433
San Diego (*Calif.*)	1,307,402
San Francisco (*Calif.*)	805,235
San Jose (*Calif.*)	945,942
Santa Ana (*Calif.*)	324,528
Santa Clara (*Calif.*)	116,468
Santa Clarita (*Calif.*)	176,320
Santa Rosa (*Calif.*)	167,815
Savannah (*Ga.*)	136,286
Scottsdale (*Ariz.*)	217,385
Seattle (*Wash.*)	608,660
Shreveport (*La.*)	199,311
Simi Valley (*Calif.*)	124,237
Sioux Falls (*S.D.*)	153,888
Spokane (*Wash.*)	208,916
Spring Valley (*Nev.*)[41]	178,395
Springfield (*Ill.*)	116,250
Springfield (*Mass.*)	153,060
Springfield (*Mo.*)	159,498
Stamford (*Conn.*)	122,643
Sterling Heights (*Mich.*)	129,699
Stockton (*Calif.*)	291,707
Sunnyvale (*Calif.*)	140,081
Sunrise Manor (*Nev.*)[41]	189,372
Surprise (*Ariz.*)	117,517
Syracuse (*N.Y.*)	145,170
Tacoma (*Wash.*)	198,397
Tallahassee (*Fla.*)	181,376
Tampa (*Fla.*)	335,709
Tempe (*Ariz.*)	161,719
Thornton (*Colo.*)	118,772
Thousand Oaks (*Calif.*)	126,683
Toledo (*Ohio*)	287,208
Topeka (*Kan.*)	127,473
Torrance (*Calif.*)	145,438
Tucson (*Ariz.*)	520,116
Tulsa (*Okla.*)	391,906
Vallejo (*Calif.*)	115,942
Vancouver (*Wash.*)	161,791
Victorville (*Calif.*)	115,903
Virginia Beach (*Va.*)	437,994
Visalia (*Calif.*)	124,442
Waco (*Texas*)	124,805
Warren (*Mich.*)	134,056
★ Washington, D.C.	601,723
Waterbury (*Conn.*)	110,366
West Covina (*Calif.*)	106,098
West Valley City (*Utah*)	129,480
Westminster (*Colo.*)	106,114
Wichita (*Kan.*)	382,368
Wilmington (*N.C.*)	106,476
Winston-Salem (*N.C.*)	229,617
Worcester (*Mass.*)	181,045
Yonkers (*N.Y.*)	195,976
Uruguay (2009 est.)	
★ Montevideo	1,633,000
Uzbekistan (2006[14] est.)	
Andijon (Andizhan)	356,800
Angren	131,000
Buxoro (Bukhara)	241,300
Chirchiq (Chirchik)	140,700
Farghona (Fergana)	188,100
Jizzakh (Dzhizak)	139,200
Margilon (Margilan)	168,000
Namangan	415,000
Nawoiy (Navoi)	121,200
Nuqus (Nukus)	259,700
Olmaliq (Almalyk)	117,700
Qarshi (Karshi)	217,400
Qoqon (Kokand)	207,300
Samarqand (Samarkand)	364,200
★ Tashkent (Toshkent)	2,201,000[7]
Termiz	122,700
Urganch (Urgench)	140,700
Vanuatu (2009)	
★ Vila	44,040
Venezuela (2001)	
Acarigua	137,000
Barcelona	328,000
Barinas	229,000
Barquisimeto	811,000
Baruta	192,000
Cabimas	210,000
★ Caracas	1,836,000
Carúpano	112,000
Catia la Mar	112,000
Ciudad Bolívar	287,000
Ciudad Guayana	629,000
Ciudad Ojeda	114,000
Coro	159,000
Cumaná	263,000
El Tigre	146,000
Guacara	142,000
Guanare	111,000
Guarenas	186,000
Guatire	129,000
Los Teques	175,000
Maracaibo	1,609,000
Maracay	394,000
Maturín	325,000
Mérida	196,000
Petare	369,000
Puerto Cabello	154,000
Puerto La Cruz	199,000
Punto Fijo	117,000
San Cristóbal	234,000
Santa Teresa	125,000
Turmero	306,000
Valencia	1,196,000
Valera	113,000
Vietnam (2009)	
Bac Lieu	109,529
Bien Hoa	652,646
Buon Me Thuot	211,891
Ca Mau	129,896
Cam Pha	168,196
Can Tho	731,545
Da Lat	184,755
Da Nang	770,911
Hai Duong	170,420
Haiphong	769,739
★ Hanoi	2,316,772
Ho Chi Minh City (Saigon)	5,880,615
Hong Gai	201,990
Hue	302,983
Long Xuyen	245,699
My Tho	130,081
Nam Dinh	193,768
Nha Trang	292,693
Phan Rang–Tháp Chàm	152,906
Phan Thiet	189,619
Pleiku (Play Cu)	162,051
Qui Nhon	255,463
Rach Gia	210,784
Soc Trang	136,018
Thai Binh	106,915
Thai Nguyen	199,732
Thanh Hoa	147,559
Thu Dau Mot	187,379
Tuy Hoa	122,838
Vinh	215,577
Vung Tau	282,415
Virgin Islands (U.S.) (2010)	
★ Charlotte Amalie	10,354
West Bank (2007 est.)	
Hebron (Al-Khalīl)	163,146
Nābulus	126,132
★ Rām Allāh (Ramallah) (administrative centre)	27,460
Western Sahara (2007 est.; MU)	
Laayoune (El Aaiún)	200,000
Yemen (2004)	
Aden	588,938
Al-Ḥudaydah	409,994
Al-Mukallā	182,478
Dhamār	146,346
Ibb	212,992
★ Ṣanʿāʾ	1,707,531
Taʿizz	466,968
Zambia (2010)[10]	
Chingola	210,073
Kabwe	202,914
Kitwe	522,092
Luanshya	153,117
★ Lusaka	1,742,979
Mufulira	161,601
Ndola	455,194
Zimbabwe (2002)	
Bulawayo	676,787
Chitungwiza	321,782
Epworth	113,884
Gweru	137,000
★ Harare	1,606,000[7]
Mutare	170,106

[24]County borough population. [25]2001 census. [26]Includes Salé and Temera. [27]Includes Maiaia, Mutivaze, and Muanona. [28]Officially proclaimed capital March 27, 2006. [29]Includes cantonment(s). [30]Projection. [31]A new municipal system was created in 2005. [32]Urban district adjacent to Panama City. [33]2006. [34]Includes Al-Mubarraz. [35]Urban population. [36]Urban localities. [37]Registered population. [38]Includes Çayirova and Darıca. [39]Borough counties, not listed separately, constitute Greater London. [40]Cities and borough councils of Northern Ireland with more than 100,000 population. [41]Unincorporated place.

Language

This table presents estimated data on the principal language communities of the countries of the world. The countries, and the principal languages (occasionally, language families) represented in each, are listed alphabetically. A bullet (●) indicates those languages that are official in each country. The sum of the estimates equals the 2003 population of the country given in the "Area and population" table.

The estimates represent, so far as national data collection systems permit, the distribution of mother tongues (a mother tongue being the language spoken first and, usually, most fluently by an individual). Many countries do not collect any official data whatever on language use, and published estimates not based on census or survey data usually span a substantial range of uncertainty. The editors have adopted the best-founded distribution in the published literature (indicating uncertainty by the degree of rounding shown) but have also adjusted or interpolated using data not part of the base estimate(s). Such adjustments have not been made to account for large-scale refugee movements, as these are of a temporary nature.

A variety of approaches have been used to approximate mother-tongue distribution when census data were unavailable. Some countries collect data on ethnic or "national" groups only; for such countries ethnic distribution often had to be assumed to conform roughly to the distribution of language communities. This approach, however, should be viewed with caution, because a minority population is not always free to educate its children in its own language and because better economic opportunities often draw minority group members into the majority-language community. For some countries, a given individual may be visible in national statistics only as a passport-holder of a foreign country, however long he may remain resident. Such persons, often guest workers, have sometimes had to be assumed to be speakers of the principal language of their home country. For other countries, the language mosaic may be so complex, the language communities so minute in size, scholarly study so inadequate, or the census base so obsolete that it was possible only to assign percentages to entire groups, or families, of related languages, despite their mutual unintelligibility (Papuan and Melanesian languages in Papua New Guinea, for instance). For some countries in the Americas, so few speakers of any single indigenous language remain that it was necessary to combine these groups as *Amerindian* so as to give a fair impression of their aggregate size within their respective countries.

No systematic attempt has been made to account for populations that may legitimately be described as bilingual, unless the country itself collects data on that basis, as does Bolivia or the Comoros, for example. Where a nonindigenous official or excolonial language constitutes a lingua franca of the country, however, speakers of the language as a second tongue are shown in italics, even though very few may speak it as a mother tongue. Lingua franca figures that are both italicized and indented are not included in population totals. No comprehensive effort has been made to distinguish between dialect communities *usually* classified as belonging to the same language, though such distinctions were possible for some countries—*e.g.*, between French and Occitan (the dialect of southern France) or among the various dialects of Chinese.

In giving the names of Bantu languages, grammatical particles specific to a language's autonym (name for itself) have been omitted (the form *Rwanda* is used here, for example, rather than *kinyaRwanda* and *Tswana* instead of *seTswana*). Parenthetical alternatives are given for a number of languages that differ markedly from the name of the people speaking them (such as Kurukh, spoken by the Oraon tribes of India) or that may be combined with other groups sometimes distinguishable in national data but appearing here under the name of the largest member—*e.g.*, "Tamil (and other Indian languages)" combining data on South Asian Indian populations in Singapore. The term *creole* as used here refers to distinguishable dialectal communities related to a national, official, or former colonial language (such as the French creole that survives in Mauritius from the end of French rule in 1810).

Internet resources for further information:

- *Ethnologue* (14th ed.; Summer Institute of Linguistics) http://www.ethnologue.com
- Joshua Project 2000—People's List (Christian interfaith missionary database identifying some 2,000 ethnolinguistic groups) http://www.ad2000.org/peoples/index.htm
- U.S. Census Bureau: http://www.census.gov/ftp/pub/ipc/www/idbconf.html (especially tables 57 and 59)

Language

Major languages by country	Number of speakers
Afghanistan[1]	
Indo-Aryan languages	
Pashai	178,000
Iranian languages	
Balochi	266,000
● Dari (Persian)	
Chahar Aimak	810,000
Hazara	2,530,000
Tajik	5,859,000
Nuristani group	222,000
Pamir group	178,000
● Pashto	15,046,000
Turkic languages	
Turkmen	555,000
Uzbek	2,530,000
Other	544,000
Albania[1]	
● Albanian	3,102,000
Greek	59,000
Macedonian	4,600
Other	900
Algeria	
● Arabic	27,346,000
Berber	4,454,000
English	...
French	*6,243,000*
American Samoa	
● English	1,900
English (lingua franca)	*60,000*
● Samoan	56,000
Tongan	1,900
Other	1,900
Andorra[2]	
● Catalan (Andorran)	22,000
French	5,000
Portuguese	7,000
Spanish	29,000
Other	4,000
Angola[1]	
Ambo (Ovambo)	255,000
Chokwe	457,000
Herero	74,000
Kongo	1,423,000
Luchazi	255,000
Luimbe-Nkangala	584,000
Lunda	127,000
Luvale (Lwena)	382,000
Mbunda	127,000
Mbundu	2,325,000
Nyaneka-Nkhumbi	584,000
Ovimbundu (Umbundu)	4,003,000
● Portuguese	*3,822,000*
Other	170,000
Antigua and Barbuda	
● English	*76,800*
English/English Creole	72,000
Other	4,200
Argentina	
Amerindian languages	109,000
Italian	647,000
● Spanish	35,682,000
Other	408,000
Armenia	
● Armenian	2,853,000
Azerbaijani (Azeri)	80,000
Other	128,000
Aruba	
● Dutch	4,800
English	8,700
Papiamento	71,500
Spanish	6,800
Other	1,000
Australia	
Aboriginal languages	53,000
Arabic	194,000
Cantonese	227,000
Dutch	48,000
● English	16,141,000
English (lingua franca)	*19,189,000*
French	47,000
German	115,000
Greek	310,000
Hungarian	31,000
Indonesian Malay	31,000
Italian	439,000
Macedonian	82,000
Maltese	53,000
Mandarin	105,000
Pilipino (Filipino)	81,000
Polish	73,000
Portuguese	28,000
Russian	36,000
Serbo-Croatian	122,000
Spanish	104,000
Turkish	51,000
Vietnamese	160,000
Other/not stated	1,352,000
Austria	
Czech	19,000
● German	7,409,000
Hungarian	34,000
Polish	19,000
Romanian	17,000
Serbo-Croatian	175,000
Slovene	30,000
Turkish	122,000
Other	229,000
Azerbaijan	
Armenian	163,000
● Azerbaijani (Azeri)	7,326,000
Lezgi (Lezgian)	184,000
Russian	249,000
Other	317,000
Bahamas, The	
● English	...
English/English Creole	282,000
French (Haitian) Creole	32,000
Bahrain[2]	
● Arabic	459,000
English	...
Other	215,000
Bangladesh[1]	
● Bengali	130,078,000
Chakma	496,000
English	*3,503,000*
Garo	124,000
Khasi	103,000
Marma (Magh)	258,000
Mro	41,000
Santhali	93,000
Tripuri	93,000
Other	1,824,000
Barbados	
Bajan (English Creole)	259,000
● English	...
Other	13,000
Belarus	
● Belarusian	6,488,000
Polish	49,000
● Russian	3,155,000
Ukrainian	129,000
Other	59,000
Belgium[2, 3]	
Arabic	161,000
● Dutch (Flemish; Netherlandic)	6,128,000
● French (Walloon)	3,376,000
● German	101,000
Italian	252,000
Spanish	50,000
Turkish	91,000
Other	181,000
Belize	
● English	136,000
English Creole (lingua franca)	*202,000*
Garifuna (Black Carib)	18,000
German	4,300
Mayan languages	26,000
Spanish	85,000
Spanish (lingua franca)	*149,000*
Benin[1]	
Adja	782,000
Aizo (Ouidah)	606,000
Bariba	606,000
Dendi	154,000
Djougou	209,000
Fon	2,799,000
● French	*661,000*
Fula (Fulani)	397,000
Somba (Ditamari)	463,000
Yoruba (Nago)	859,000
Other	165,000
Bermuda	
● English	64,000
Portuguese	*6,100*
Bhutan[1]	
Assamese	104,000
● Dzongkha (Bhutia)	343,000
Nepali (Hindi)	239,000
Bolivia	
● Aymara	278,000
Guaraní	10,000
● Quechua	700,000
● Spanish	3,583,000
Spanish-Amerindian (multilingual),	3,943,000
of which	
Spanish-Aymara	*1,699,000*
Spanish-Guaraní	*31,000*
Spanish-Quechua	*2,224,000*
Other	72,000
Bosnia and Herzegovina[1]	
● Bosnian	1,637,000
● Croatian	630,000
● Serbian	1,153,000
Other	300,000
Botswana[1]	
● English (lingua franca)	*665,000*
Khoekhoe (Hottentot)	41,000
Ndebele	21,000
San (Bushman)	58,000
Shona	207,000
Tswana	1,255,000
Tswana (lingua franca)	*1,330,000*
Other	81,000
Brazil[1]	
Amerindian languages	183,000
German	978,000
Italian	752,000
Japanese	677,000
● Portuguese	174,226,000
Other	1,655,000
Brunei	
Chinese	32,000
English	10,400
English-Chinese	7,300
● Malay	159,000
Malay-Chinese	3,100
Malay-Chinese-English	13,500
Malay-English	101,000
Other	18,700
Bulgaria[1]	
● Bulgarian	6,480,000
Macedonian	191,000
Romany	286,000
Turkish	734,000
Other	95,000
Burkina Faso[4]	
Dogon	44,000
French	44,000
● French (lingua franca)	*5,419,000*
Fula (Fulani)	1,272,000
Gur (Voltaic) languages	
Bwamu	288,000
Gouin (Cerma)	77,000
Grusi (Gurunsi) group	
Ko	22,000
Lyele	321,000
Nuni	155,000
Sissala	11,000
Lobi	254,000
Moore (Mossi) group	
Dagara	409,100
Gurma	752,000
Kusaal	22,000
Moore (Mossi)	6,636,000
Senufo group	
Minianka	—
Senufo	188,000
Kru languages	
Seme (Siamou)	22,000
Mande languages	
Bobo	299,000
Busansi (Bisa)	476,000
Dyula (Jula)	343,000
Marka	221,000
Samo	310,000
Tamashek (Tuareg)	122,000
Other	940,000
Burundi[1]	
● French	*285,000*
● Rundi	3,015,000
Hutu	2,542,000

Major languages by country	Number of speakers
Tutsi	447,000
Twa	31,000
Other[5]	61,000
Cambodia[1]	
Cham	308,000
Chinese	403,000
● Khmer	11,629,000
Vietnamese	722,000
Other[6]	64,000
Cameroon[1]	
Chadic languages	
Buwal	307,000
Hausa	194,000
Kotoko	174,000
Mandara (Wandala)	889,000
Masana (Masa)	623,000
● English	*7,868,000*
● French	*4,700,000*
Niger-Congo languages	
Adamawa-Ubangi languages	
Chamba	378,000
Gbaya (Baya)	194,000
Mbum	204,000
Atlantic languages	
Fula (Fulani)	1,512,000
Benue-Congo languages	
Bamileke (Medumba)-Widikum (Mogha-mo)-Bamum (Mum)	2,922,000
Basa (Bassa)	174,000
Duala	1,717,000
Fang (Pangwe)-Beti-Bulu	3,096,000
Ibibio (Efik)	20,000
Igbo	82,000
Jukun	102,000
Lundu	429,000
Maka	777,000
Tikar	1,165,000
Tiv	409,000
Wute	51,000
Saharan languages	
Kanuri	51,000
Semitic languages	
Arabic	153,000
Other	123,000
Canada	
● English	18,703,000
● French	7,349,000
English-French	119,000
English-other	276,000
French-other	40,000
English-French-other	10,000
Arabic	164,000
Chinese	793,000
Cree	85,000
Dutch	148,000
Eskimo (Inuktitut) languages	30,000
German	499,000
Greek	135,000
Italian	537,000
Pilipino (Filipino)	149,000
Polish	236,000
Portuguese	234,000
Punjābī	224,000
Spanish	236,000
Ukrainian	180,000
Vietnamese	118,000
Other	1,327,000
Cape Verde	
Crioulo (Portuguese Creole)	438,000
● Portuguese	...
Central African Republic	
Banda	858,000
● French	*942,000*
Gbaya (Baya)	869,000
Mandjia	544,000
Mbum	230,000
Ngbaka	283,000
Nzakara	63,000
● Sango (lingua franca)	*3,244,000*
Sara	241,000
Zande (Azande)	73,000
Other	523,000
Chad[1]	
● Arabic	1,140,000
Bagirmi	143,000
Fitri-Batha	428,000
● French	*2,774,000*
Fula (Fulani)	230,000
Gorane	581,000
Hadjarai	614,000
Kanem-Bornu	833,000
Lac-Iro	55,000
Mayo-Kebbi	1,063,000
Ouaddai	811,000
Sara	2,554,000
Tandjile	603,000
Other	197,000
Chile[1]	
Araucanian (Mapuche)	1,421,000
Aymara	81,000
Rapa Nui	35,000
● Spanish	13,740,000
China[1]	
Achang	31,000
Bulang (Blang)	92,000
Ch'iang (Qiang)	225,000
Chinese (Han)	1,185,204,000
Cantonese (Yüeh [Yue])	*51,093,000*
Hakka	*28,612,000*
Hsiang (Xiang)	*39,853,000*
Kan (Gan)	*22,481,000*
● Mandarin	*918,652,000*
Min	*39,853,000*
Wu	*84,814,000*
Ching-p'o (Jingpo)	133,000
Chuang (Zhuang)	17,607,000
Daghur (Daur)	133,000
Evenk (Ewenki)	31,000
Gelo	501,000
Hani (Woni)	1,431,000
Hui	9,772,000
Kazak	1,267,000
Korean	2,187,000
Kyrgyz	164,000
Lahu	470,000
Li	1,267,000
Lisu	654,000
Manchu	11,169,000
Maonan	82,000
Miao	8,410,000
Mongol	5,467,000
Mulam	184,000
Na-hsi (Naxi)	317,000
Nu	31,000
Pai (Bai)	1,809,000
Pumi	31,000
Puyi (Chung-chia)	2,892,000
Salar	102,000
She	715,000
Shui	388,000
Sibo (Xibe)	194,000
Tai (Dai)	1,165,000
Tajik	41,000
Tibetan	5,222,000
Tu (Monguor)	215,000
T'u-chia (Tujia)	6,489,000
Tung (Dong)	2,861,000
Tung-hsiang (Dongxiang)	429,000
Uighur	8,206,000
Wa (Va)	399,000
Yao	2,422,000
Yi	7,470,000
Other	1,012,000
Colombia[1]	
Amerindian languages	352,000
Arawakan	39,000
Cariban	29,000
Chibchan	176,000
Other	107,000
English Creole	49,000
● Spanish	40,910,000
Comoros	
● Arabic	...
● Comorian	374,000
Comorian-French	65,000
Comorian-Malagasy	28,000
Comorian-Arabic	8,600
Comorian-Swahili	2,600
Comorian-French-other	20,000
● French	*104,000*
Other	2,600
Congo, Dem. Rep. of the[1]	
Boa	1,239,000
Chokwe	965,000
English	...
● French	*4,062,000*
Kongo	8,470,000
Kongo (lingua franca)	*16,250,000*
Lingala (lingua franca)	*36,562,000*
Luba	9,486,000
Lugbara	853,000
Mongo	7,109,000
Ngala and Bangi	3,047,000
Rundi	2,031,000
Rwanda	5,423,000
Swahili (lingua franca)	*25,390,000*
Teke	1,442,000
Zande (Azande)	3,219,000
Other	9,486,000
Congo, Rep. of the[1]	
Bobangi	39,000
● French	*1,960,000*
Kongo	1,908,000
Kota	39,000
Lingala (lingua franca)	...
Maka	65,000
Mbete	183,000
Mboshi	431,000
Monokutuba (lingua franca)	*2,221,000*
Punu	118,000
Sango	105,000
Teke	640,000
Other	196,000
Costa Rica	
Chibchan languages	12,500
Bribrí	8,000
Cabécar	4,600
Chinese	8,000
English Creole	83,000
● Spanish	4,044,000
Other	11,000
Côte d'Ivoire[1]	
Akan (including Baule and Anyi)	4,996,000
● French	*8,326,000*
Gur ([Voltaic] including Senufo and Lobi)	1,946,000
Kru (including Bete)	1,748,000
Malinke (including Dyula and Bambara)	1,905,000
Southern Mande (including Dan and Guro)	1,280,000
Other (non-Ivoirian population)	4,756,000
Croatia	
● Croatian	4,252,000
Other	176,000
Cuba	
● Spanish	11,295,000
Cyprus (island)[1]	
● Greek	685,000
● Turkish	203,000
Other	32,000
Czech Republic[1]	
Bulgarian	3,000
● Czech	8,282,000
German	48,000
Greek	3,000
Hungarian	20,000
Moravian	1,313,000
Polish	60,000
Romanian	1,000
Romany	33,000
Russian	5,000
Ruthenian	2,000
Silesian	44,000
Slovak	312,000
Ukrainian	8,000
Other	70,000
Denmark[2]	
Arabic	39,000
● Danish	5,102,000
English	20,000
German	26,000
South Slavic languages	39,000
Turkish	47,000
Other	120,000
Djibouti[1]	
Afar	162,000
● Arabic	51,000
● French	*71,000*
Somali	203,000
Gadaboursi	...
Issa	...
Issaq	...
Other	41,000
Dominica	
● English	...
English Creole	69,700
French Creole	*63,000*
Dominican Republic	
French (Haitian) Creole	176,000
● Spanish	8,540,000
East Timor	
Portuguese	80,000
Tetum (Tetun)	608,000
Other	310,000
Ecuador	
Quechuan (and other Amerindian languages)	915,000
● Spanish	12,088,000
Egypt[1]	
● Arabic	67,367,000
Other	818,000
El Salvador	
● Spanish	6,515,000
Equatorial Guinea[1]	
Bubi	51,000
Fang	401,000
● French	...
Krio (English Creole)	...
● Spanish	...
Other	41,000
Eritrea	
Cushitic languages	
Afar	180,000
Bilin	130,000
Hadareb (Beja)	160,000
Saho	120,000
Nilotic languages	
Kunama	110,000
Nara	90,000
Semitic languages	
Arabic (Rashaida)	10,000
Tigré	1,310,000
Tigrinya	2,031,000
Estonia[1]	
Belarusian	20,000
● Estonian	883,000
Finnish	12,000
Russian	380,000
Ukrainian	34,000
Other	25,000
Ethiopia[1]	
Afar	1,205,000
Agew (Awngi)	607,000
Amharic	18,668,000
Berta	149,000
Gedeo	548,000
Gumuz	129,000
Gurage	2,708,000
Hadya–Libida	1,085,000
Kaffa	717,000
Kambata	797,000
Kimant	199,000
Oromo (Oromifa)	20,291,000
Sidamo	2,161,000
Somali	3,973,000
Tigrinya	3,764,000
Walaita	3,883,000
Other	5,705,000
Faroe Islands	
● Danish	...
● Faroese	48,000
Fiji[1]	
● English	*172,000*
Fijian	420,000
Hindi	361,000
Other	45,000
Finland	
Finnish	4,820,000
Russian	26,000
Sami (Lapp)	2,000
Swedish	295,000
Other	68,000
France	
Arabic[7]	1,514,000
English[7]	81,000
● French[7, 8, 9]	55,974,000
Basque	*102,000*
Breton	*813,000*
Catalan (Rousillonais)	*264,000*
Corsican	*81,000*
Dutch (Flemish)	*91,000*
German (Alsatian)	*1,016,000*
Occitan	*711,000*
Italian[7]	264,000
Polish[7]	51,000
Portuguese[7]	691,000
Spanish[7]	224,000
Turkish[7]	213,000
Other[7]	762,000
French Guiana	
Amerindian languages	3,200
● French	...
French/French Creoles	167,000
Other	7,600
French Polynesia[10]	
Chinese	13,600
● French	197,000
Polynesian languages	271,000
Tahitian	...
Other	48,000
Gabon[1]	
Fang	476,000
● French	*1,108,000*
Kota	44,000
Mbete	188,000
Mpongwe (Myene)	199,000
Punu, Sira, Nzebi	222,000
Teke	22,000
Other	177,000
Gambia, The[1]	
● English	...
Gambians	
Aku (Krio)	8,300
Atlantic languages	
Diola (Jola)	131,000
Fula (Fulani)	230,000
Manjak	23,000
Serer	34,000
Wolof	179,000
Mande languages	
Bambara	10,000
Malinke	486,000
Soninke	109,000
Other	18,000
non-Gambians	196,000
Gaza Strip	
Arabic	1,297,000
Hebrew	6,800
Georgia	
Abkhaz	88,000
Armenian	343,000
Azerbaijani (Azeri)	274,000
● Georgian (Kartuli)	3,514,000
Ossetian	118,000
Russian	441,000
Other	157,000
Germany[2]	
● German	75,429,000
Greek	362,000
Italian	613,000
Kurdish	*402,000*
Polish	281,000
South Slavic languages	1,196,000
Turkish	2,120,000
Other	2,603,000
Ghana[1]	
Akan	10,732,000
● English	*1,436,000*
Ewe	2,431,000
Ga-Adangme	1,593,000
Gurma	681,000
Hausa (lingua franca)	*12,262,000*
Mole-Dagbani (Moore)	3,238,000
Yoruba	272,000
Other	1,520,000
Greece	
● Greek	10,834,000
Turkish	104,000
Other	63,000
Greenland[2]	
● Danish	7,100
● Greenlandic	50,000
Grenada	
● English	...
English/English Creole	102,000
Guadeloupe	
● French	...
French/French Creole	414,000
Other	21,000
Guam	
Asian languages	10,800
● Chamorro	34,000
● English	59,000
English (lingua franca)	*153,000*
Philippine languages	34,000
Other Pacific Island languages	10,500
Guatemala	
Garífuna (Black Carib)	26,000
Mayan languages	3,416,000
Cakchiquel	873,000
Kekchí	471,000
Mam	265,000
Quiché	985,000
● Spanish	6,311,000
Guernsey	
● English	63,000
Norman French	...
Guinea[1]	
Atlantic languages	
Basari-Konyagi	102,000
Fula (Fulani)	3,269,000
Kissi	511,000
Other	261,000
● French	*795,000*
Mande languages	
Kpelle	397,000
Loma	193,000
Malinke	1,964,000
Susu	931,000
Yalunka	250,000
Other	590,000
Other	11,400
Guinea-Bissau[1]	
Balante	411,000
Crioulo (Portuguese Creole)	*601,000*
Ejamat	32,000
French	*137,000*
Fula (Fulani)	295,000
Malinke	179,000
Mandyako	148,000
Mankanya	53,000
Pepel	137,000
● Portuguese	*148,000*
Other	106,000
Guyana	
Amerindian languages	
Arawakan	11,000
Cariban	17,000
● English	...
English/English Creoles	750,000

Language (continued)

Major languages by country	Number of speakers
Haiti	
● French	*1,535,000*
● Haitian (French) Creole	7,528,000
Honduras	
English Creole	13,000
Garifuna (Black Carib)	86,000
Miskito	12,000
● Spanish	6,611,000
Other	82,000
Hong Kong	
Chinese	
● Cantonese	6,059,000
Cantonese (lingua franca)	*6,549,000*
Chiu Chau	98,000
Fukien (Min)	130,000
Hakka	114,000
Putonghua (Mandarin)	76,000
Putonghua (lingua franca)	*1,239,000*
Sze Yap	27,000
● English	151,000
English (lingua franca)	*2,156,000*
Japanese	14,000
Pilipino (Filipino)	7,000
Other	164,000
Hungary	
German	40,000
● Hungarian	9,984,000
Romanian	10,000
Romany	51,000
Serbo-Croatian	20,000
Slovak	10,000
Other	20,000
Iceland[2]	
● Icelandic	278,000
Other	12,000
India	
Afro-Asiatic languages	
Arabic	32,000
Austroasiatic languages	
Ho	1,198,000
Kharia	284,000
Khasi	1,146,000
Korku	589,000
Munda	526,000
Mundari	1,083,000
Santhali	6,568,000
Savara (Sora)	347,000
Other Austroasiatic	200,000
Dravidian languages	
Gondi	2,680,000
Kannada	41,239,000
Khond	273,000
Koya	336,000
Kui	809,000
Kurukh (Oraon)	1,797,000
Malayalam	38,254,000
Tamil	66,745,000
Telugu	83,129,000
Tulu	1,955,000
Other Dravidian	694,000
English	221,000
● English (lingua franca)	*202,831,000*
Indo-Iranian (Indo-Aryan) languages	
Assamese	16,468,000
Bengali	87,638,000
Bhili (Bhilodi)	7,020,000
Barel	*586,000*
Bhilali	*586,000*
Gujarati	51,212,000
Halabi	673,000
● Hindi	424,684,000
Awadhi	*610,000*
Baghelkhandi	*1,745,000*
Bagri	*746,000*
Banjari	*1,114,000*
Bhojpuri	*29,090,000*
Bundelkhandi	*2,091,000*
Chhattisgarhi	*13,336,000*
Dhundhari	*1,219,000*
Garhwali	*2,354,000*
Harauti	*1,555,000*
Haryanvi	*452,000*
Hindi	*293,936,000*
Kangri	*620,000*
Khortha (Khotta)	*1,324,000*
Kumauni	*2,165,000*
Lamani (Banjari)	*2,585,000*
Magahi (Magadhi)	*13,305,000*
Maithili	*9,784,000*
Malvi	*3,741,000*
Mandeali	*557,000*
Marwari	*5,885,000*
Mewari	*2,659,000*
Nagpuri	*977,000*
Nimadi	*1,787,000*
Pahari	*2,743,000*
Rajasthani	*16,784,000*
Sadani (Sadri)	*1,976,000*
Surgujia	*1,314,000*
Surjapuri	*462,000*
Other Hindi dialects	*7,766,000*
Hindi (lingua franca)	*703,078,000*
Kashmiri	4,960,000
Khandeshi	1,230,000
Konkani	2,218,000
Lahnda	32,000
Marathi	78,673,000
Nepali (Gorkhali)	2,617,000
Oriya	35,333,000
Punjabi	29,437,000
Sanskrit	63,000
Sindhi	2,669,000
Kachchhi	*715,000*
Urdu	54,659,000
Sino-Tibetan languages	
Adi	200,000
Angami	126,000
Ao	221,000
Bodo/Boro	1,534,000
Dimasa	116,000
Garo	851,000
Karbi/Makir	462,000
Konyak	179,000
Lotha	105,000
Lushai (Mizo)	683,000
Manipuri (Meithei)	1,597,000
Miri/Mishing	494,000
Nissi/Dafla	221,000
Rabha	179,000
Sema	210,000
Tangkhul	126,000
Thado	137,000
Tripuri	872,000
Kokbarak	*652,000*
Other Sino-Tibetan languages	1,902,000
Other	5,560,000
Indonesia	
Balinese	3,655,000
Banjarese	3,844,000
Batak	4,884,000
Buginese	4,842,000
● Indonesian (Malay)	26,627,000
Javanese	86,697,000
Madurese	9,516,000
Minangkabau	5,189,000
Sundanese	34,673,000
Other	39,956,000
Iran[1]	
Armenian	317,000
Iranian languages	
Bakhtyari (Luri)	1,110,000
Balochi	1,511,000
● Farsi (Persian)	30,232,000
Farsi (lingua franca)	*54,843,000*
Gilaki	3,498,000
Kurdish	6,044,000
Luri	2,864,000
Mazandarani	2,388,000
Other	1,437,000
Semitic languages	
Arabic	1,427,000
Other	159,000
Turkic languages	
Afshari	750,000
Azerbaijani (Azeri)	11,138,000
Qashqa'i	845,000
Shahsavani	402,000
Turkish (mostly Pishagchi, Bayat, and Qajar)	476,000
Turkmen	1,036,000
Other	137,000
Other	486,000
Iraq[1]	
● Arabic	19,026,000
Assyrian	207,000
Azerbaijani (Azeri)	424,000
Kurdish	4,678,000
Persian	207,000
Other	141,000
Ireland	
● English	3,751,000
● Irish[11]	62,000
Irish	*1,571,000*
Isle of Man	
● English	77,000
Israel[12]	
● Arabic	1,165,000
● Hebrew	4,079,000
Russian	583,000
Other	646,000
Italy[1]	
Albanian	117,000
Catalan	29,000
French	302,000
German	302,000
Greek	39,000
● Italian	52,956,000
Rhaetian	722,000
Friulian	702,000
Ladin	20,000
Romany	107,000
Sardinian	1,492,000
Slovene	117,000
Other	127,000
Jamaica	
● English	...
English/English Creoles	2,492,000
Hindī and other Indian languages	51,000
Other	101,000
Japan[2]	
Ainu[1]	15,000
Chinese	241,000
English	80,000
● Japanese	126,406,000
Korean	663,000
Philippine languages	90,000
Other	50,000
Jersey	
● English	82,200
French	...
Norman French	*5,500*
Jordan[1]	
● Arabic	5,287,000
Armenian	54,000
Kabardian (Circassian)	54,000
Kazakhstan[1]	
Azerbaijani (Azeri)	89,000
Belarusian	149,000
German	456,000
● Kazakh	6,800,000
Korean	89,000
Russian	5,135,000
Tatar	288,000
Uighur	169,000
Ukrainian	734,000
Uzbek	337,000
Other	545,000
Kenya[1]	
Arabic	83,000
Bantu languages	
Bajun (Rajun)	73,000
Basuba	125,000
Embu	375,000
Gusii (Kisii)	1,949,000
Kamba	3,565,000
Kikuyu	6,609,000
Kuria	188,000
Luhya	4,378,000
Mbere	125,000
Meru	1,731,000
Nyika (Mijikenda)	1,512,000
Pokomo	83,000
Swahili	10,000
● Swahili (lingua franca)	*20,849,000*
Taita	313,000
Cushitic languages	
Oromo languages	
Boran	146,000
Gabbra	63,000
Gurreh	167,000
Orma	63,000
Somali languages	
Degodia	198,000
Ogaden	52,000
Somali	323,000
● English (lingua franca)	*2,815,000*
Nilotic languages	
Kalenjin	3,409,000
Luo	4,034,000
Masai	500,000
Sambur	156,000
Teso	271,000
Turkana	427,000
Other	709,000
Kiribati[1]	
● English	*22,000*
Kiribati (Gilbertese)	87,000
Tuvaluan (Ellice)	500
Other	600
Korea, North[1]	
Chinese	31,000
● Korean	22,435,000
Korea, South[1]	
Chinese	51,000
● Korean	47,874,000
Kosovo[13]	
● Albanian	...
● Serbian	...
Kuwait	
● Arabic	1,900,000
Other	539,000
Kyrgyzstan[1]	
Azerbaijani (Azeri)	21,000
German	31,000
Kazakh	52,000
● Kyrgyz	3,021,000
● Russian	817,000
Tajik	41,000
Tatar	62,000
Ukrainian	83,000
Uzbek	714,000
Other	217,000
Laos[1]	
● Lao-Lum (Lao)	3,004,000
Lao-Soung (Miao [Hmong] and Man [Yao])	569,000
Lao-Tai (Tai)	733,000
Lao-Theung (Mon-Khmer)	1,301,000
Other[14]	52,000
Latvia[1]	
Belarusian	87,000
● Latvian	1,298,000
Lithuanian	29,000
Polish	48,000
Russian	755,000
Ukrainian	69,000
Other	39,000
Lebanon[1]	
● Arabic	3,468,000
Armenian	219,000
French	*896,000*
Other	42,000
Lesotho[1]	
● English	*429,000*
● Sotho	1,533,000
Zulu	270,000
Liberia[1]	
Atlantic (Mel) languages	
Gola	137,000
Kissi	137,000
● English	*661,000*
Krio (English Creole)	*2,939,000*
Kru languages	
Bassa	462,000
Belle	21,000
De (Dewoin, Dey)	11,000
Grebo	294,000
Krahn	126,000
Kru (Krumen)	241,000
Mande (Northern) languages	
Gbandi	95,000
Kpelle	640,000
Loma	189,000
Malinke (Mandingo)	168,000
Mende	21,000
Vai	116,000
Mande (Southern) languages	
Gio (Dan)	262,000
Mano	231,000
Other	168,000
Libya	
● Arabic	5,334,000
Berber	54,000
Other[15]	163,000
Liechtenstein[2]	
● German	30,000
Italian	1,100
Other	3,200
Lithuania[1]	
Belarusian	43,000
● Lithuanian	2,907,000
Polish	235,000
Russian	220,000
Ukrainian	23,000
Other	24,000
Luxembourg[2]	
Belgian	11,000
Dutch	2,800
English	3,500
French	13,500
German	7,800
Italian	14,200
Luxemburgian	197,000
Portuguese	182,200
Other	21,300
Macau	
Chinese	
● Cantonese (Yüeh [Yue])	381,000
Mandarin	5,000
Other Chinese languages	40,000
English	2,000
● Portuguese	10,000
Other	5,000
Macedonia[1]	
Albanian	470,000
● Macedonian	1,368,000
Romany	46,000
Serbian	41,000
Turkish	82,000
Vlach	9,000
Other	39,000
Madagascar[1]	
● French	*2,464,000*
Malagasy	16,435,000
● English	...
Other	171,000
Malawi[1]	
Chewa (Maravi)	6,802,000
● English	*606,000*
Lomwe	2,144,000
Ngoni	746,000
Yao	1,538,000
Other	393,000
Malaysia	
Bajau	163,000
Chinese	1,464,000
Chinese-others	824,000
Dusun	260,000
English	130,000
English-others	282,000
English (lingua franca)	*7,700,000*
Iban	597,000
Iban-others	98,000
● Malay	10,877,000
Malay-others	3,861,000
Tamil	976,000
Tamil-others	11,000
Other	5,683,000
Maldives	
● Divehi (Maldivian)	285,000
Mali[1]	
Afro-Asiatic languages	
Berber languages	
Tamashek (Tuareg)	848,000
Semitic languages	
Arabic (Mauri)	185,000
● French	*1,195,000*
Niger-Congo languages	
Atlantic languages	
Dogon	467,000
Fula (Fulani) and Tukulor	1,619,000
Gur (Voltaic) languages	
Bwa (Bobo)	283,000
Moore (Mossi)	44,000
Senufo and Minianka	1,391,000
Mande languages	
Bambara	3,705,000
Bambara (lingua franca)	*9,236,000*
Bobo Fing	11,000
Dyula (Jula)	337,000
Malinke, Khasonke, and Wasulunka	771,000
Samo (Duun)	76,000
Soninke	1,021,000
Nilo-Saharan languages	
Songhai	837,000
Other	33,000
Malta[1]	
● English	24,000
English (lingua franca)	*210,000*
● Maltese	354,000
Italian (lingua franca)	*89,000*
Other	15,000
Marshall Islands[2]	
● English	*56,000*
● Marshallese	55,000
Other	1,700
Martinique	
● French	...
French/French Creole	380,000
Other	13,300
Mauritania[1]	
● Arabic	...
French	*274,000*
Fula (Fulani)	30,000
Hassānīyah Arabic	2,199,000
Soninke	71,000
Tukulor	142,000
Wolof	182,000
Zenaga	30,000
Other	41,000
Mauritius	
Bhojpuri	233,000
Bhojpuri-other	26,000
Chinese	4,000
● English	2,000
French	42,000
French Creole	754,000
French Creole-other	108,000
Hindi	16,000
Marathi	8,000
Tamil	9,000
Telugu	7,000
Urdu	8,000
Other	3,000
Mayotte[16]	
● Arabic	...
● French	68,000
Mahorais (local dialect of Comorian Swahili)	140,000
Other Comorian Swahili dialects	62,000
Malagasy	54,000
Other	10,000
Mexico	
Amerindian languages	7,278,000
Amuzgo	50,000
Aztec (Nahuatl)	1,744,000

Major languages by country	Number of speakers
Chatino	49,000
Chinantec	159,000
Chocho	1,200
Chol	194,000
Chontal	53,000
Cora	20,000
Cuicatec	16,000
Huastec	180,000
Huave	17,000
Huichol	38,000
Kanjobal	11,000
Mame	11,000
Mayo	44,000
Mazahua	172,000
Mazatec	254,000
Mixe	139,000
Mixtec	538,000
Otomí	360,000
Popoluca	66,000
Purépecha (Tarasco)	143,000
Tarahumara	92,000
Tepehua	11,000
Tepehuan	31,000
Tlapanec	123,000
Tojolabal	46,000
Totonac	287,000
Trique	25,000
Tzeltal	344,000
Tzotzil	362,000
Yaqui	16,000
Yucatec (Mayan)	948,000
Zapotec	533,000
Zoque	64,000
Other	496,000
● Spanish	85,871,000
Spanish-Amerindian languages	*5,987,000*
Micronesia	
Chuukese (Trukese)/Mortlockese	56,000
English	1,500
Kosraean	7,700
Pohnpeian	28,000
Polynesian languages	1,600
Woleaian	4,700
Yapese	6,000
Other	1,400
Moldova	
Bulgarian	70,000
Gagauz	139,000
● Romanian (Moldovan)	2,646,000
Russian	985,000
Ukrainian	368,000
Other	60,000
Monaco[2]	
English	2,100
● French	13,600
Italian	5,200
Monegasque	5,200
Other	6,300
Mongolia[1]	
Bayad	49,000
Buryat	43,000
Darhat	18,000
Dariganga	35,000
Dörbet	68,000
Dzakhchin	27,000
Kazakh	147,000
● Khalkha (Mongolian)	1,962,000
Khalkha (lingua franca)	*2,232,000*
Ould	10,000
Torgut	13,000
Tuvan (Uryankhai)	25,000
Other	98,000
Montenegro[17]	
● Montenegrin	...
Morocco	
● Arabic	19,390,000
Berber	9,845,000
French	*11,905,000*
Other	600,000
Mozambique	
Bantu languages	
Chuabo	1,167,000
Lomwe	1,410,000
Makua	4,883,000
Sena	1,303,000
Tsonga (Changana)	2,120,000
Other Bantu languages	6,128,000
● Portuguese	1,206,000
Portuguese (lingua franca)	*7,363,000*
Other	350,000
Myanmar (Burma)[1]	
● Burmese	29,312,000
Burmese (lingua franca)	*34,017,000*
Chin	927,000
Kachin (Ching-p'o)	581,000
Karen	2,648,000
Kayah	173,000
Mon	1,029,000
Rakhine (Arakanese)	1,915,000
Shan	3,595,000
Other	2,332,000
Namibia	
Afrikaans	183,000
Caprivi	90,000
● English	15,000
English (lingua franca)	*370,000*
German	17,000
Herero	154,000
Kavango (Okavango)	187,000
Nama	240,000
Ovambo (Ambo [Kwanyama])	976,000
San (Bushman)	37,000
Tswana	8,700
Other	18,500
Nauru	
Chinese	1,100
English	1,000
English (lingua franca)	*11,000*
Kiribati (Gilbertese)	2,200
Nauruan	7,300
Tuvaluan (Ellice)	1,100
Nepal	
Austroasiatic (Munda) languages	
Santhali	39,000
English	*7,147,000*
Indo-Aryan languages	
Bengali	39,000
Bhojpuri	1,801,000
Dhanwar	29,000
Hindi	225,000
Hindi (Awadhi dialect)	490,000
Maithili	2,869,000
● Nepali (Eastern Pahari)	12,169,000
Rajbansi	108,000
Tharu	1,302,000
Urdu	264,000
Tibeto-Burman languages	
Bhutia (Sherpa)	157,000
Chepang	29,000
Gurung	294,000
Limbu	333,000
Magar	558,000
Newari	901,000
Rai and Kiranti	578,000
Tamang	1,185,000
Thakali	9,800
Thami	20,000
Other	773,000
Netherlands, The[2]	
Arabic	133,000
● Dutch	15,556,000
Dutch and Frisian	*613,000*
Turkish	105,000
Other	444,000
Netherlands Antilles	
● Dutch	...
English	14,000
Papiamento	145,000
Other	10,000
New Caledonia[1]	
● French	75,000
Indonesian	5,000
Melanesian languages	99,000
Polynesian languages	26,000
Vietnamese	3,100
Other	12,000
New Zealand	
● English	3,483,000
English-Māori	155,000
● Māori	15,000
Other	349,000
Nicaragua	
English Creole	31,000
Misumalpan languages	
Miskito	90,000
Sumo	9,000
● Spanish	5,350,000
Other	2,300
Niger[1]	
Atlantic languages	
Fula (Fulani)	1,106,000
Berber languages	
Tamashek (Tuareg)	1,185,000
Chadic languages	
Hausa	6,029,000
Hausa (lingua franca)	*8,016,000*
● French	*1,694,000*
Gur (Voltaic) languages	
Gurma	34,000
Saharan languages	
Kanuri	508,000
Teda (Tubu)	45,000
Semitic languages	
Arabic	34,000
Songhai and Zerma	2,416,000
Other	23,000
Nigeria[1]	
Arabic	305,000
Bura	1,932,000
Edo	4,271,000
● English/English Creole (lingua franca)	*56,943,000*
Fula (Fulani)	14,134,000
Hausa	26,743,000
Hausa (lingua franca)	*63,044,000*
Ibibio	7,016,000
Igbo (Ibo)	22,574,000
Ijo (Ijaw)	2,237,000
Kanuri	5,186,000
Nupe	1,525,000
Tiv	2,847,000
Yoruba	26,743,000
Other	9,762,000
Northern Mariana Islands	
● Carolinian	3,100
● Chamorro	16,000
Chinese	16,900
● English	8,000
English (lingua franca)	*66,000*
Philippine languages	17,600
Other Pacific Island languages	3,900
Other	6,700
Norway[2]	
Danish	18,000
English	24,000
● Norwegian	4,411,000
Swedish	13,000
Other	102,000
Oman	
● Arabic (Omani)	2,012,000
Other	609,000
Pakistan	
Balochi	4,484,000
Brahui	1,821,000
English (lingua franca)	*16,842,000*
Pashto	19,579,000
Punjabi	
Hindko	3,621,000
Punjabi	71,778,000
Sindhi	
Saraiki	14,642,000
Sindhi	17,537,000
● Urdu	11,326,000
Other	4,242,000
Palau	
Chinese	300
● English	600
English (lingua franca)	*20,000*
● Palauan	17,000
Philippine languages	2,000
Other	700
Panama	
Amerindian languages	
Bokotá	5,500
Chibchan	
Guaymí (Ngöbe Buglé)	166,000
Kuna	63,000
Teribe	3,000
Chocó	
Emberá	20,000
Wounaan	3,000
Arabic	18,000
Chinese	9,000
English	...
English Creoles	436,000
● Spanish	2,393,000
Papua New Guinea[1]	
● English	*159,000*
Melanesian languages	1,121,000
Motu	*181,000*
Papuan languages	4,349,000
Tok Pisin (English Creole)	*3,624,000*
Other	113,000
Paraguay	
German	51,000
● Guaraní	2,267,000
Guaraní-Spanish	2,739,000
Portuguese	174,000
● Spanish	369,000
Other	41,000
Peru	
Amerindian languages	
● Aymara	624,000
● Quechua	4,465,000
Other	190,000
● Spanish	21,657,000
Other	212,000
Philippines	
Aklanon	595,000
Bantoanon	74,000
Bicol	4,614,000
Bilaan	43,000
Bontoc	64,000
Butuanon	85,000
Cebuano	18,882,000
Chavacano	500,000
Chinese	74,000
Davaweno (Mansaka)	553,000
● English (lingua franca)	*42,207,000*
● Filipino	23,761,000
Hiligaynon	7,389,000
Ibaloi (Nabaloi)	138,000
Ibanag	298,000
Ifugao	223,000
Ilocano	7,559,000
Ilongot	117,000
Kalinga	138,000
Kankanai	308,000
Kinaray-a (Hamtikanon)	510,000
Maguindanao	1,180,000
Manobo	542,000
Maranao	1,031,000
Masbateño	564,000
Palawano	85,000
Pampango	2,424,000
Pangasinan	1,467,000
Romblon	255,000
Samal	510,000
Sambal	213,000
Subanon	330,000
Surigaonon	595,000
Tau Sug	936,000
Tboli	106,000
Tinggian	74,000
Tiruray	74,000
Waray-Waray	3,094,000
Yakan	160,000
Other	1,595,000
Poland	
Belarusian	190,000
German	500,000
● Polish	37,704,000
Ukrainian	230,000
Portugal[2]	
● Portuguese	10,079,000
Other	102,000
Puerto Rico	
● English	543,000
● Spanish	3,297,000
Other	39,000
Qatar[2]	
● Arabic	250,000
Other[18]	376,000
Réunion	
Chinese	21,000
Comorian	21,000
● French	*232,000*
French Creole	697,000
Malagasy	11,000
Tamil	*148,000*
Other	11,000
Romania[1]	
Bulgarian	8,000
Czech	4,000
German	64,000
Hungarian	1,427,000
Polish	4,000
● Romanian	19,346,000
Romany (Tigani)	540,000
Russian	43,000
Serbo-Croatian	26,000
Slovak	22,000
Tatar	22,000
Turkish	43,000
Ukrainian	64,000
Other	43,000
Russia[1]	
Adyghian	119,000
Armenian	713,000
Avar	604,000
Azerbaijani (Azeri)	336,000
Bashkir	1,375,000
Belarusian	972,000
Buryat	453,000
Chechen	898,000
Chuvash	1,722,000
Dargin	353,000
Georgian (Kartuli)	132,000
German	788,000
Ingush	253,000
Kabardian	367,000
Kalmyk	166,000
Karachay	150,000
Kazakh	569,000
Komi-Permyak	147,000
Komi-Zyryan	354,000
Kumyk	286,000
Lak	117,000
Lezgi (Lezgian)	295,000
Mari	66,000
Mordvin	723,000
Ossetian	463,000
Romanian	95,000
Romany	130,000
● Russian	118,000,000
Tabasaran	97,000
Tatar	5,519,000
Tuvan	198,000
Udmurt	713,000
Ukrainian	3,446,000
Uzbek	127,000
Yakut	441,000
Other	3,836,000
Rwanda	
● English	...
● French	*576,000*
● Rwanda	8,387,000
St. Kitts and Nevis	
● English	...
English/English Creole	46,400
St. Lucia	
● English	32,000
English/French Creole	130,000
St. Vincent and the Grenadines	
● English	...
English/English Creole	112,000
Other	1,000
Samoa	
● English	1,000
● Samoan	85,000
Samoan-English	93,000
San Marino[1]	
● Italian (Romagnolo)	29,000
São Tomé and Príncipe	
Crioulo (Portuguese Creole)	124,000
English	...
French	1,000
● Portuguese	...
Other	17,000
Saudi Arabia[1]	
● Arabic	22,809,000
Other	1,199,000
Senegal	
● French	*3,547,000*
Senegalese	
Bambara	91,000
Diola	497,000
Fula (Fulani)-Tukulor	2,199,000
Malinke (Mandingo)	375,000
Serer	1,267,000
Soninke	132,000
Wolof	4,865,000
Wolof (lingua franca)	*8,108,000*
Other	446,000
non-Senegalese	223,000
Serbia[19]	
Albanian	1,738,000
Hungarian	346,000
Macedonian	49,000
Romanian	40,000
Romany	148,000
● Serbian	7,920,000
Slovak	69,000
Vlach	20,000
Other	198,000
Seychelles	
English	3,000
English (lingua franca)	*29,000*
French	1,000
French (lingua franca)	*78,000*
Seselwa (French Creole)	75,000
Other	3,000
Sierra Leone[1]	
Atlantic languages	
Bullom-Sherbro	190,000
Fula (Fulani)	190,000
Kissi	114,000
Limba	418,000
Temne	1,578,000
● English	*475,000*
Krio (English Creole [lingua franca])	*4,182,000*
Mande languages	
Kono-Vai	257,000
Kuranko	171,000
Mende	1,720,000
Susu	76,000
Yalunka	171,000
Other	86,000
Singapore[1]	
Chinese	3,253,000
● English	*1,585,000*
● Malay	589,000
● Mandarin Chinese	*1,837,000*
● Tamil (and other Indian languages)	335,000
Other	56,000
Slovakia[1]	
Czech and Silesian	59,000
German	5,000
Hungarian	569,000
Polish	3,000
Romany	90,000

Language (continued)

Major languages by country	Number of speakers
Ruthenian (Rusyn) and Ukrainian	35,000
● Slovak	4,626,000
Other	15,000
Slovenia	
Hungarian	9,000
Serbo-Croatian	156,000
● Slovene	1,732,000
Other	74,000
Solomon Islands[1]	
● English	*9,000*
Melanesian languages	385,000
Papuan languages	39,000
Polynesian languages	16,000
Solomon Island Pidgin (English Creole)	*157,000*
Other	10,000
Somalia[1]	
● Arabic	...
English	...
● Somali	7,892,000
Other	133,000
South Africa	
● Afrikaans	5,961,000
● English	3,675,000
Nguni	
● Ndebele	717,000
● Swazi	1,210,000
● Xhosa	7,888,000
● Zulu	10,667,000
Sotho	
● North Sotho (Pedi)	4,213,000
● South Sotho	3,540,000
● Tswana (Western Sotho)	3,675,000
● Tsonga	1,972,000
● Venda	1,031,000
Other	224,000
Spain	
Basque (Euskera)	641,000
● Castilian Spanish	30,373,000
Catalan (Català)	6,886,000
Galician (Gallego)	2,604,000
Other	305,000
Sri Lanka	
English[20]	10,000
English-Sinhala	1,051,000
English-Sinhala-Tamil	684,000
English-Tamil	218,000
● Sinhala	11,510,000
Sinhala-Tamil	1,785,000
● Tamil	3,748,000
Other	60,000
Sudan, The[1]	
● Arabic	18,818,000
Arabic (lingua franca)	*22,816,000*
Bari	934,000
Beja	2,434,000
Dinka	4,400,000
● English	...
Fur	782,000
Lotuko	565,000
Nubian languages	3,086,000
Nuer	1,869,000
Shilluk	652,000
Zande (Azande)	1,032,000
Other	3,542,000
Suriname	
● Dutch	*111,000*
English/English Creole	*415,000*
Sranantonga	172,000
Sranantonga-other	172,000
Other (mostly Hindi, Javanese, and Saramacca)	91,000
Swaziland[1]	
● English	*50,000*
● Swazi (Swati)	976,000
Zulu	20,000
Other	81,000
Sweden[2]	
Arabic	69,000
Danish	41,000
English	32,000
Finnish	211,000
German	46,000
Iranian languages[1]	50,000
Norwegian	47,000
Polish	39,000
South Slavic languages[1]	117,000
Spanish	57,000
● Swedish	8,021,000
Turkish	29,000
Other	199,000
Switzerland	
● French	1,410,000
● German	4,669,000
● Italian	562,000
Romansch	41,000
Other	654,000
Syria[1]	
● Arabic	15,829,000
Kurdish	1,585,000
Other	173,000
Taiwan	
Austronesian languages	
Ami	140,000
Atayal	91,000
Bunun	43,000
Paiwan	69,000
Puyuma	10,000
Rukai	11,000
Saisiyat	6,000
Tsou	7,000
Yami	4,000
Chinese languages	
Hakka	2,481,000
● Mandarin	4,535,000
Min (South Fukien)	15,049,000
Other	122,000
Tajikistan	
Russian	633,000
● Tajik (Tojik)	4,066,000
Uzbek	1,515,000
Other	322,000
Tanzania[1]	
Chaga (Chagga), Pare	1,719,000
● English	*3,775,000*
Gogo	1,381,000
Ha	1,202,000
Haya	2,066,000
Hehet	2,414,000
Iramba	1,003,000
Luguru	1,719,000
Luo	288,000
Makonde	2,066,000
Masai	348,000
Ngoni	467,000
Nyakusa	1,898,000
Nyamwesi (Sukuma)	7,401,000
Shambala	1,500,000
● Swahili	3,100,000
Swahili (lingua franca)	*31,790,000*
Tatoga	258,000
Yao	854,000
Other	5,394,000
Thailand[1]	
Chinese	7,764,000
Karen	226,000
Malay	2,328,000
Mon-Khmer languages	
Khmer	810,000
Kuy	687,000
Other	226,000
Tai languages	
Lao	17,221,000
● Thai (Siamese)	33,662,000
Other	441,000
Other	656,000
Togo[1]	
Atlantic (Mel) languages	
Fula (Fulani)	74,000
Benue-Congo languages	
Ana (Ana-Ife)	136,000
Nago	14,000
Yoruba	11,000
Chadic languages	
Hausa	15,000
● French	*2,704,000*
Gur (Voltaic) languages	
Basari	95,000
Chakossi (Akan)	64,000
Chamba	53,000
Dye (Gangam)	51,000
Gurma	184,000
Kabre	748,000
Konkomba	77,000
Kotokoli (Tem)	313,000
Moba	292,000
Moore (Mossi)	14,000
Namba (Lamba)	166,000
Naudemba (Losso)	223,000
Tamberma	30,000
Yanga	16,000
Kwa languages	
Adele	11,000
Adja (Aja)	170,000
Ahlo	10,000
Akposo	145,000
Ane (Basila)	307,000
Anlo	4,300
Anyaga	11,000
Ewe	1,259,000
Fon	54,000
Hwe	6,500
Kebu	63,000
Kpessi	4,300
Peda-Hula (Pla)	22,000
Watyi (Ouatchi)	559,000
Other	229,000
Tonga	
● English	*31,000*
● Tongan	100,000
Other	2,000
Trinidad and Tobago	
● English	...
English Creole[21]	37,000
Hindi	45,000
Trinidad English	1,195,000
● Other	3,000
Tunisia	
● Arabic	6,911,000
Arabic-French	2,596,000
Arabic-French-English	309,000
Arabic-other	10,000
Other-no Arabic	31,000
Other	31,000
Turkey[1]	
Arabic	967,000
Kurdish[22]	7,482,000
● Turkish	61,825,000
Other	323,000
Turkmenistan[1]	
Armenian	37,000
Azerbaijani (Azeri)	40,000
Balochi	40,000
Kazakh	96,000
Russian	328,000
Tatar	40,000
● Turkmen	3,731,000
Ukrainian	25,000
Uzbek	446,000
Other	85,000
Tuvalu	
English	...
Kiribati (Gilbertese)	800
Tuvaluan (Ellice)	9,400
Uganda[1]	
Bantu languages	
Amba	98,000
Ganda (Luganda)	4,603,000
Gisu (Masaba)	1,145,000
Gwere	415,000
Kiga (Chiga)	2,127,000
Konjo	556,000
Nkole (Nyankole and Hororo)	2,727,000
Nyole	349,000
Nyoro	753,000
Ruli	109,000
Rundi	153,000
Rwanda	818,000
Samia	338,000
Soga	2,094,000
● Swahili	...
Swahili (lingua franca)	*8,944,000*
Toro	742,000
Central Sudanic languages	
Lugbara	1,200,000
Madi	196,000
Ndo	251,000
● English	*2,727,000*
Nilotic languages	
Acholi	1,124,000
Alur	600,000
Kakwa	131,000
Karamojong	535,000
Kumam	175,000
Lango	1,494,000
Padhola	382,000
Sebei (Kupsabiny)	164,000
Teso	1,527,000
Other (mostly Gujarati and Hindi)	633,000
Ukraine	
Belarusian	145,000
Bulgarian	154,000
Hungarian	145,000
Polish	29,000
Romanian	318,000
Russian	15,714,000
● Ukrainian	30,937,000
Other	414,000
United Arab Emirates[2]	
● Arabic	1,606,000
Other[16]	2,212,000
United Kingdom	
● English	57,559,000
Scots-Gaelic	79,000
Welsh	565,000
Other	961,000
United States	
Amharic	42,000
Arabic	683,000
Armenian	225,000
Bengali	53,000
Cajun	42,000
Chinese (including Formosan)	2,247,000
Czech	117,000
Danish	42,000
Dutch	180,000
English	239,407,000
English (lingua franca)	*282,724,000*
Finnish	64,000
French	2,150,000
French Creole (mostly Haitian)	233,000
German	1,537,000
Greek	406,000
Gujarati	262,000
Hebrew	217,000
Hindi (including Urdu)	645,000
Hungarian	131,000
Ilocano	53,000
Italian	1,121,000
Japanese	531,000
Korean	994,000
Kru (Gullah)	85,000
Lithuanian	74,000
Malayalam	42,000
Miao (Hmong)	187,000
Mon-Khmer (mostly Cambodian)	202,000
Navajo	198,000
Norwegian	106,000
Pennsylvania Dutch	106,000
Persian	347,000
Polish	742,000
Portuguese	627,000
Punjābī	64,000
Romanian	85,000
Russian	785,000
Samoan	42,000
Serbo-Croatian	260,000
Slovak	106,000
Spanish	31,230,000
Swedish	95,000
Syriac	42,000
Tagalog	1,361,000
Tai (including Laotian)	300,000
Turkish	53,000
Ukrainian	127,000
Vietnamese	1,122,000
Yiddish	199,000
Other	858,000
Uruguay	
● Spanish	3,235,700
Other	114,000
Uzbekistan[1]	
Kazakh	1,046,000
Russian	1,542,000
Tajik	1,232,000
Tatar	414,000
● Uzbek	19,429,000
Other	1,977,000
Vanuatu[23]	
● Bislama (English Creole)	116,000
● English	58,000
● French	29,000
Other	1,900
Venezuela	
Amerindian languages	
Goajiro	170,000
Warrau (Warao)	21,000
Other	160,000
● Spanish	24,795,000
Other	553,000
Vietnam[1]	
Bahnar	177,000
Cham	125,000
Chinese (Hoa)	1,142,000
French	*395,000*
Hre	125,000
Jarai	312,000
Khmer	1,132,000
Koho	114,000
Man (Mien, or Yao)	602,000
Miao (Meo, or Hmong)	716,000
Mnong	83,000
Muong	1,162,000
Nung	903,000
Rade (Rhadé)	249,000
Roglai	96,000
San Chay (Cao Lan)	146,000
San Diu	125,000
Sedang	125,000
Stieng	62,000
Tai	1,329,000
Tho (Tay)	1,515,000
● Vietnamese	70,972,000
Other	168,000
Virgin Islands (U.S.)	
● English	91,000
French	2,800
Spanish	15,000
Other	2,800
West Bank[24]	
Arabic	2,275,000
Hebrew	192,000
Western Sahara	
Arabic	262,000
Yemen[1]	
● Arabic	19,930,000
Other	80,000
Zambia[25]	
Bemba group	
Bemba	3,217,000
Bemba (lingua franca)	*5,643,000*
Bisa	124,000
Lala	260,000
Lamba	237,000
Other	451,000
● English	124,000
English (lingua franca)	*2,032,000*
Lozi (Barotse) group	
Lozi (Barotse)	688,000
Other	124,000
Mambwe group	
Lungu	79,000
Mambwe	124,000
Mwanga (Winawanga)	148,000
Other	11,000
North-Western group	
Kaonde	248,000
Lunda	214,000
Luvale (Luena)	192,000
Other	293,000
Nyanja (Maravi) group	
Chewa	621,000
Ngoni	181,000
Nsenga	463,000
Nyanja (Maravi)	847,000
Nyanja (lingua franca)	*2,822,000*
Other	68,000
Tonga (Ila-Tonga) group	
Ila	102,000
Lenje	169,000
Tonga	1,185,000
Other	135,000
Tumbuka group	
Senga	79,000
Tumbuka	316,000
Other	11,000
Other	102,000
Zimbabwe	
● English	258,000
English (lingua franca)	*5,477,000*
Ndebele (Nguni)	1,902,000
Nyanja	269,000
Shona	8,453,000
Other	837,000

[1]Figures given represent ethnolinguistic groups. [2]Data refer to nationality (usually resident aliens holding foreign passports). [3]Data are partly based on place of residence. [4]Majority of population speak Moore (language of the Mossi); Dyula is language of commerce. [5]Swahili also spoken. [6]English and French also spoken. [7]Based on "nationality" at 1982 census. [8]Includes naturalized citizens. [9]French is the universal language throughout France; traditional dialects and minority languages are retained regionally in the approximate numbers shown, however. [10]Data reflect multilingualism; 2000 population estimate is 233,000. [11]Refers to Irish speakers in Gaeltacht areas. [12]Includes the population of the Golan Heights and East Jerusalem; excludes the Israeli population in the West Bank and Gaza Strip. [13]Kosovo included in Serbia. [14]English and French also spoken. [15]English and Italian also spoken. [16]Data reflect ability to speak the language, not mother tongue; 2003 population estimate is 160,000. [17]Montenegro included in Serbia. [18]Mostly Pakistanis, Indians, and Iranians. [19]Includes Montenegro and Kosovo. [20]English has official status as the "link language" between Sinhala and Tamil. [21]Spoken on Tobago only. [22]Other estimates of the Kurdish population range from 6 percent to 20–25 percent. [23]Data reflect multilingualism; 2000 population is 190,000. [24]Excludes East Jerusalem. [25]Groups are officially defined geographic divisions; elements comprising them are named by language.

Religion

The following table presents statistics on religious affiliation for each of the countries of the world. An assessment was made for each country of the available data on distribution of religious communities within the total population; the best available figures, whether originating as census data, membership figures of the churches concerned, or estimates by external analysts in the absence of reliable local data, were applied as percentages to the estimated 2001 midyear population of the country to obtain the data shown below.

Several concepts govern the nature of the available data, each useful separately but none the basis of any standard of international practice in the collection of such data. The word "affiliation" was used above to describe the nature of the relationship joining the religious bodies named and the populations shown. This term implies some sort of formal, usually documentary, connection between the religion and the individual (a baptismal certificate, a child being assigned the religion of its parents on a census form, maintenance of one's name on the tax rolls of a state religion, etc.) but says nothing about the nature of the individual's personal religious practice, in that the individual may have lapsed, never been confirmed as an adult, joined another religion, or may have joined an organization that is formally atheist.

The user of these statistics should be careful to note that not only does the nature of the affiliation (with an organized religion) differ greatly from country to country, but the social context of religious practice does also. A country in which a single religion has long been predominant will often show more than 90% of its population to be *affiliated*, while in actual fact, no more than 10% may actually *practice* that religion on a regular basis. Such a situation often leads to undercounting of minority religions (where someone [head of household, communicant, child] is counted at all), blurring of distinctions seen to be significant elsewhere (a Hindu country may not distinguish Protestant [or even Christian] denominations; a Christian country may not distinguish among its Muslim or Buddhist citizens), or double-counting in countries where an individual may conscientiously practice more than one "religion" at a time.

Until 1989 communist countries had for long consciously attempted to ignore, suppress, or render invisible religious practice within their borders. Countries with large numbers of adherents of traditional, often animist, religions and belief systems usually have little or no formal methodology for defining the nature of local religious practice. On the other hand, countries with strong missionary traditions, or good census organizations, or few religious sensitivities may have very good, detailed, and meaningful data.

The most comprehensive works available are DAVID B. BARRETT (ed.), *World Christian Encyclopedia* (2001); and PETER BRIERLEY, *World Churches Handbook* (1997).

Religion

Religious affiliation	2001 population
Afghanistan	
Sunnī Muslim	23,090,000
Shīʿī Muslim	2,310,000
other	490,000
Albania	
Muslim	1,200,000
Roman Catholic	520,000
Albanian Orthodox	320,000
other	1,050,000
Algeria	
Sunnī Muslim	30,550,000
Ibāḍīyah Muslim	180,000
other	90,000
American Samoa	
Congregational	23,800
Roman Catholic	11,300
other	23,400
Andorra	
Roman Catholic	60,000
other	7,000
Angola	
Roman Catholic	6,440,000
Protestant	1,550,000
African Christian	710,000
other	1,660,000
Antigua and Barbuda	
Protestant	30,000
Anglican	23,000
Roman Catholic	8,000
other	10,000
Argentina	
Roman Catholic	29,920,000
Protestant	2,040,000
Muslim	730,000
Jewish	500,000
nonreligious	880,000
other	3,430,000
Armenia	
Armenian Apostolic (Orthodox)	2,454,000
other	1,353,000
Aruba	
Roman Catholic	80,000
other	18,000
Australia	
Roman Catholic	5,230,000
Anglican	4,260,000
Uniting Church	1,460,000
Presbyterian	740,000
other Protestant	1,400,000
Orthodox	540,000
nonreligious	3,220,000
other	2,510,000
Austria	
Roman Catholic	6,060,000
Protestant (mostly Lutheran)	430,000
atheist and nonreligious	690,000
other	890,000
Azerbaijan	
Shīʿī Muslim	5,299,000
Sunnī Muslim	2,271,000
other	535,000
Bahamas, The	
Protestant	135,000
Roman Catholic	50,000
Anglican	32,000
other	77,000
Bahrain	
Shīʿī Muslim	420,000
Sunnī Muslim	140,000
other	140,000
Bangladesh	
Muslim	112,660,000
Hindu	16,260,000
other	2,360,000
Barbados	
Anglican	89,000
Protestant	80,000
Roman Catholic	12,000
other	88,000
Belarus	
Belarusian Orthodox	3,151,000
Roman Catholic	1,772,000
other	5,062,000
Belgium	
Roman Catholic	8,310,000
nonreligious	600,000
other	1,360,000
Belize	
Roman Catholic	143,000
Protestant	67,000
Anglican	17,000
other	20,000
Benin	
Voodoo (traditional beliefs)	3,390,000
Roman Catholic	1,370,000
Muslim	1,320,000
other	500,000
Bermuda	
Anglican	23,700
Methodist	10,400
Roman Catholic	8,800
other	20,900
Bhutan	
Lamaistic Buddhist	510,000
Hindu	140,000
other	40,000
Bolivia	
Roman Catholic	7,540,000
Protestant	770,000
other	210,000
Bosnia and Herzegovina	
Sunnī Muslim	1,690,000
Serbian Orthodox	1,180,000
Roman Catholic	710,000
other	350,000
Botswana	
African Christian	490,000
Protestant	170,000
Roman Catholic	60,000
other (mostly traditional beliefs)	870,000
Brazil	
Roman Catholic (including syncretic Afro-Catholic cults having Spiritist beliefs and rituals)	124,470,000
Evangelical Protestant	39,850,000
other	7,800,000
Brunei	
Muslim	222,000
other	121,000
Bulgaria	
Bulgarian Orthodox	5,690,000
Muslim (mostly Sunnī)	940,000
other	1,320,000
Burkina Faso	
Muslim	5,960,000
traditional beliefs	4,180,000
Christian	2,040,000
other	80,000
Burundi	
Roman Catholic	4,050,000
nonreligious	1,160,000
other (mostly Protestant)	1,020,000
Cambodia	
Buddhist	10,780,000
Chinese folk-religionist	600,000
traditional beliefs	550,000
Muslim	290,000
other	500,000
Cameroon	
Roman Catholic	4,180,000
traditional beliefs	3,750,000
Muslim	3,350,000
Protestant	3,270,000
other	1,250,000
Canada	
Roman Catholic	14,010,000
Protestant	8,620,000
Anglican	2,490,000
Eastern Orthodox	440,000
Jewish	360,000
Muslim	290,000
Buddhist	190,000
Hindu	180,000
Sikh	170,000
nonreligious	3,880,000
other	380,000
Cape Verde	
Roman Catholic	370,000
other	35,000
Central African Republic	
Roman Catholic	660,000
Muslim	560,000
traditional beliefs	550,000
Protestant	520,000
other	1,290,000
Chad	
Muslim	4,690,000
Roman Catholic	1,770,000
Protestant	1,250,000
traditional beliefs	640,000
other	350,000
Chile	
Roman Catholic	11,810,000
Evangelical Protestant	1,910,000
other	1,690,000
China	
nonreligious	661,390,000
Chinese folk-religionist	256,260,000
atheist	152,990,000
Buddhist	108,110,000
Christian	76,540,000
Muslim	18,360,000
traditional beliefs	1,280,000
Colombia	
Roman Catholic	39,590,000
other	3,480,000
Comoros	
Sunnī Muslim	555,000
other	11,000
Congo, Dem. Rep. of the	
Roman Catholic	21,990,000
Protestant	16,950,000
African Christian	7,170,000
traditional beliefs	5,740,000
Muslim	750,000
other	1,040,000
Congo, Rep. of the	
Roman Catholic	1,430,000
Protestant	490,000
African Christian	360,000
other	610,000
Costa Rica	
Roman Catholic	3,380,000
Protestant	360,000
other	190,000
Côte d'Ivoire	
Muslim	6,340,000
Roman Catholic	3,400,000
traditional beliefs	2,790,000
nonreligious	2,220,000
Protestant	870,000
other	770,000
Croatia	
Roman Catholic	3,890,000
Serbian Orthodox	250,000
Sunnī Muslim	100,000
Protestant	30,000
other	130,000
Cuba	
Roman Catholic	4,420,000
Protestant	270,000
other (mostly Santeria)	6,500,000
Cyprus	
Greek Orthodox	630,000
Muslim (mostly Sunnī)	200,000
other (mostly Christian)	40,000
Czech Republic	
Roman Catholic	4,010,000
Evangelical Church of Czech Brethren	200,000
Czechoslovak Hussite	180,000
Silesian Evangelical	30,000
Eastern Orthodox	20,000
atheist and nonreligious	4,100,000
other	1,730,000
Denmark	
Evangelical Lutheran	4,600,000
Muslim	120,000
other	640,000
Djibouti	
Sunnī Muslim	434,000
other	27,000
Dominica	
Roman Catholic	50,000
Protestant	12,000
other	10,000
Dominican Republic	
Roman Catholic	7,110,000
Protestant	560,000
other	1,020,000
East Timor	
Roman Catholic	780,000
Protestant	50,000
Muslim	30,000
other	40,000
Ecuador	
Roman Catholic	11,910,000
Protestant	440,000
other	530,000
Egypt	
Sunnī Muslim	58,060,000
Coptic Orthodox[1]	6,520,000
other	660,000
El Salvador	
Roman Catholic	4,880,000
Protestant	1,070,000
other	290,000
Equatorial Guinea	
Roman Catholic	390,000
other	110,000
Eritrea	
Eritrean Orthodox	1,980,000
Muslim	1,920,000
other	400,000
Estonia	
Estonian Orthodox	277,000
Evangelical Lutheran	187,000
other	899,000

Religion (continued)

Religious affiliation	2001 population
Ethiopia	
Ethiopian Orthodox	33,110,000
other Christian	7,090,000
Muslim (mostly Sunnī)	21,710,000
traditional beliefs	3,180,000
other	820,000
Faroe Islands	
Evangelical Lutheran	38,000
other	9,000
Fiji	
Christian (mostly Methodist and Roman Catholic)	437,000
Hindu	316,000
Muslim	65,000
other	9,000
Finland	
Evangelical Lutheran	4,420,000
other	770,000
France	
Roman Catholic	38,690,000
nonreligious	9,230,000
Muslim	4,180,000
atheist	2,380,000
Protestant	720,000
Jewish	590,000
other	3,290,000
French Guiana	
Roman Catholic	91,000
other	77,000
French Polynesia	
Protestant	119,000
Roman Catholic	94,000
other	25,000
Gabon	
Roman Catholic	690,000
Protestant	220,000
African Christian	170,000
other	160,000
Gambia, The	
Muslim (mostly Sunnī)	1,340,000
other	70,000
Gaza Strip	
Muslim (mostly Sunnī)	1,190,000
other	20,000
Georgia	
Georgian Orthodox	1,828,000
Sunnī Muslim	549,000
Armenian Apostolic (Orthodox)	279,000
Russian Orthodox	133,000
other (mostly nonreligious)	2,200,000
Germany	
Protestant (mostly Evangelical Lutheran)	29,330,000
Roman Catholic	27,590,000
Muslim	3,660,000
atheist	1,800,000
other (mostly nonreligious)	20,020,000
Ghana	
traditional beliefs	4,860,000
Muslim	3,910,000
Protestant	3,310,000
African Christian	2,870,000
Roman Catholic	1,890,000
other	3,050,000
Greece	
Greek Orthodox	10,010,000
Muslim	360,000
other	500,000
Greenland	
Evangelical Lutheran	36,500
other	19,800
Grenada	
Roman Catholic	54,000
Anglican	14,000
other	34,000
Guadeloupe	
Roman Catholic	350,000
other	82,000
Guam	
Roman Catholic	118,000
Protestant	19,000
other	21,000
Guatemala	
Roman Catholic	8,880,000
Evangelical Protestant	2,540,000
other	270,000
Guernsey	
Anglican	42,000
other	22,000
Guinea	
Muslim	6,470,000
Christian	760,000
other	380,000
Guinea-Bissau	
traditional beliefs	590,000
Muslim	530,000
Christian	170,000
other	20,000
Guyana	
Hindu	264,000
Protestant	145,000
Roman Catholic	89,000
Muslim	70,000
Anglican	67,000
other	142,000
Haiti	
Roman Catholic	4,770,000
Protestant	1,590,000
other	610,000
Honduras	
Roman Catholic	5,740,000
Evangelical Protestant	690,000
other	200,000
Hong Kong	
Buddhist and Taoist	4,970,000
Protestant	290,000
Roman Catholic	280,000
other	1,200,000
Hungary	
Roman Catholic	6,120,000
Protestant	2,470,000
nonreligious	750,000
other	850,000
Iceland	
Evangelical Lutheran	260,000
other	20,000
India	
Hindu	759,350,000
Sunnī Muslim	92,380,000
traditional beliefs	34,930,000
Shīʿī Muslim	30,790,000
independent	30,750,000
Sikh	22,290,000
Protestant	15,130,000
Roman Catholic	13,940,000
Buddhist	7,290,000
Jain	4,160,000
atheist	1,670,000
Bahāʾī	1,190,000
Zoroastrian (Parsi)	210,000
nonreligious	12,910,000
other	3,000,000
Indonesia	
Muslim	185,060,000
Protestant	12,820,000
Roman Catholic	7,600,000
Hindu	3,880,000
Buddhist	2,190,000
other	660,000
Iran	
Shīʿī Muslim	57,180,000
Sunnī Muslim	3,460,000
Zoroastrian	1,780,000
Bahāʾī	430,000
Christian	340,000
other	250,000
Iraq	
Shīʿī Muslim	13,890,000
Sunnī Muslim	8,510,000
Christian	750,000
other	180,000
Ireland	
Roman Catholic	3,500,000
other	320,000
Isle of Man	
Anglican	30,000
Methodist	7,000
Roman Catholic	6,000
other	31,000
Israel	
Jewish[2]	4,960,000
Muslim (mostly Sunnī)	930,000
other	360,000
Italy	
Roman Catholic	46,260,000
nonreligious and atheist	9,600,000
Muslim	680,000
other	1,350,000
Jamaica	
Protestant	1,020,000
Roman Catholic	270,000
Anglican	100,000
other	1,230,000
Japan	
Shintoist[3]	118,270,000
Buddhist[3]	88,490,000
Christian	1,470,000
other	10,250,000
Jersey	
Anglican	55,000
Roman Catholic	21,000
other	14,000
Jordan	
Sunnī Muslim	4,800,000
Christian	210,000
other	120,000
Kazakhstan	
Muslim (mostly Sunnī)	6,988,000
Russian Orthodox	1,216,000
Protestant	318,000
other (mostly nonreligious)	6,345,000
Kenya	
Roman Catholic	6,780,000
African Christian	6,400,000
Protestant	6,170,000
traditional beliefs	3,540,000
Anglican	2,900,000
Muslim	2,240,000
Orthodox	720,000
other	2,030,000
Kiribati	
Roman Catholic	50,000
Congregational	36,000
other	9,000
Korea, North	
atheist and nonreligious	15,000,000
traditional beliefs	3,430,000
Ch'ŏndogyo	3,050,000
other	480,000
Korea, South	
nonreligious	23,490,000
Buddhist	11,040,000
Protestant	9,370,000
Roman Catholic	3,160,000
Confucian	230,000
Wonbulgyo	90,000
other	290,000
Kosovo	
Muslim	1,775,000
Orthodox	107,300
Roman Catholic	58,500
Protestant	10,000
Kuwait	
Sunnī Muslim	1,020,000
Shīʿī Muslim	680,000
other Muslim	230,000
other (mostly Christian and Hindu)	340,000
Kyrgyzstan	
Muslim (mostly Sunnī)	3,701,000
Russian Orthodox	276,000
other (mostly nonreligious)	958,000
Laos	
Buddhist	2,750,000
traditional beliefs	2,350,000
other	540,000
Latvia	
Roman Catholic	350,000
Evangelical Lutheran	345,000
Russian Orthodox	181,000
other (mostly nonreligious)	1,482,000
Lebanon	
Shīʿī Muslim	1,230,000
Sunnī Muslim	770,000
Maronite Catholic	690,000
Druze	260,000
Greek Orthodox	220,000
Armenian Apostolic (Orthodox)	190,000
Greek Catholic (Melchite)	170,000
other	110,000
Lesotho	
Roman Catholic	820,000
Protestant	280,000
African Christian	260,000
traditional beliefs	170,000
Anglican	100,000
other	550,000
Liberia	
traditional beliefs	1,390,000
Christian	1,270,000
Muslim	520,000
other	60,000
Libya	
Sunnī Muslim	5,040,000
other	200,000
Liechtenstein	
Roman Catholic	26,000
other	7,000
Lithuania	
Roman Catholic	2,660,000
Russian Orthodox	90,000
other (mostly nonreligious)	940,000
Luxembourg	
Roman Catholic	400,000
other	40,000
Macau	
nonreligious	271,000
Buddhist	75,000
other	100,000
Macedonia	
Serbian (Macedonian) Orthodox	1,210,000
Sunnī Muslim	580,000
other	260,000
Madagascar	
traditional beliefs	7,670,000
Roman Catholic	3,250,000
Protestant	3,630,000
other	1,420,000
Malawi	
Roman Catholic	2,600,000
Protestant	2,070,000
African Christian	1,770,000
Muslim	1,560,000
traditional beliefs	820,000
other	1,730,000
Malaysia	
Muslim	10,770,000
Chinese folk-religionist	5,450,000
Christian	1,880,000
Hindu	1,660,000
Buddhist	1,500,000
other	1,350,000
Maldives	
Sunnī Muslim	273,000
other	2,000
Mali	
Muslim	9,010,000
traditional beliefs	1,760,000
Christian	220,000
other	10,000
Malta	
Roman Catholic	363,000
other	21,000
Marshall Islands	
Protestant	32,800
Roman Catholic	3,700
other	15,700
Martinique	
Roman Catholic	336,000
other	52,000
Mauritania	
Sunnī Muslim	2,720,000
other	20,000
Mauritius	
Hindu	610,000
Roman Catholic	330,000
Muslim	190,000
other	70,000
Mayotte	
Sunnī Muslim	153,000
Christian	5,000
Mexico	
Roman Catholic	90,370,000
Protestant	3,820,000
other Christian	1,820,000
other (mostly nonreligious)	3,970,000
Micronesia	
Roman Catholic	63,600
Protestant	40,100
other	14,200
Moldova	
Romanian Orthodox	1,263,000
Russian (Moldovan) Orthodox	342,000
other (mostly nonreligious)	2,007,000
Monaco	
Roman Catholic	28,000
other	4,000
Mongolia	
Tantric Buddhist (Lamaist)	2,340,000
Muslim	100,000
Montenegro	
Orthodox	430,000
Muslim	129,000
Roman Catholic	25,000
other	31,000
Morocco	
Muslim (mostly Sunnī)	28,730,000
other	500,000
Mozambique	
traditional beliefs	9,750,000
Roman Catholic	3,060,000
Muslim	2,040,000
Protestant	1,720,000
African Christian	1,400,000
other	1,400,000
Myanmar (Burma)	
Buddhist	37,560,000
Christian	2,060,000
Muslim	1,610,000
traditional beliefs	480,000
Hindu	210,000
other	70,000
Namibia	
Protestant (mostly Lutheran)	850,000
Roman Catholic	320,000
African Christian	200,000
other	430,000
Nauru	
Protestant	6,100
Roman Catholic	3,300
other	2,700
Nepal	
Hindu	19,180,000
traditional beliefs	2,350,000
Buddhist	2,050,000
Muslim	970,000
Christian	600,000
other	140,000
Netherlands, The	
Roman Catholic	4,950,000
Dutch Reformed Church (NHK)	2,240,000
Reformed Churches	1,120,000
Muslim	720,000
nonreligious	6,550,000
other	400,000
Netherlands Antilles	
Roman Catholic	152,000
other	54,000
New Caledonia	
Roman Catholic	132,000
Protestant	31,300
other	52,200

Religious affiliation	2001 population
New Zealand	
Anglican	674,000
Roman Catholic	505,000
Presbyterian	489,000
Methodist	130,000
Baptist	57,000
Mormon	44,000
Ratana	39,000
nonreligious	954,000
other	969,000
Nicaragua	
Roman Catholic	3,590,000
Protestant	810,000
other (mostly nonreligious)	520,000
Niger	
Sunnī Muslim	9,390,000
traditional beliefs	900,000
other	70,000
Nigeria	
Muslim	55,600,000
traditional beliefs	12,500,000
Christian	58,100,000
other	500,000
Northern Mariana Islands	
Roman Catholic	53,600
other	19,700
Norway	
Evangelical Lutheran (Church of Norway)	3,990,000
other	530,000
Oman	
Ibāḍīyāh Muslim	1,840,000
Sunnī Muslim	350,000
Hindu	190,000
Christian	100,000
other	20,000
Pakistan	
Sunnī Muslim	113,950,000
Shīʿī Muslim	25,010,000
Christian	3,560,000
Hindu	1,730,000
other	370,000
Palau	
Roman Catholic	7,600
Modekne	5,200
Protestant	4,900
other	2,100
Panama	
Roman Catholic	2,330,000
Protestant	420,000
other	150,000
Papua New Guinea	
Protestant	3,180,000
Roman Catholic	1,500,000
Anglican	210,000
other	420,000
Paraguay	
Roman Catholic	4,990,000
Protestant	280,000
other	370,000
Peru	
Roman Catholic	23,170,000
Protestant	1,730,000
other (mostly nonreligious)	1,190,000
Philippines	
Roman Catholic	63,530,000
Protestant	4,160,000
Muslim	3,500,000
Aglipayan	2,010,000
Church of Christ (Iglesia ni Cristo)	1,790,000
other	1,620,000
Poland	
Roman Catholic	35,050,000
Polish Orthodox	550,000
other (mostly nonreligious)	3,050,000
Portugal	
Roman Catholic	9,520,000
other	810,000
Puerto Rico	
Roman Catholic	2,480,000
Protestant	1,080,000
other	270,000
Qatar	
Muslim (mostly Sunnī)	490,000
Christian	60,000
other	40,000
Réunion	
Roman Catholic	599,000
Hindu	33,000
other	102,000
Romania	
Romanian Orthodox	19,460,000
Roman Catholic	1,140,000
other	1,810,000
Russia	
Russian Orthodox	23,580,000
Muslim	10,980,000
Protestant	1,320,000
Jewish	590,000
other (mostly nonreligious)	107,960,000
Rwanda	
Roman Catholic	3,730,000
Protestant	1,530,000
traditional beliefs	660,000
Muslim	580,000
Anglican	570,000
other	260,000
St. Kitts and Nevis	
Anglican	10,000
Methodist	10,000
other	15,000
Pentecostal	7,000
other	12,000
St. Lucia	
Roman Catholic	125,000
Protestant	20,000
other	13,000
St. Vincent and the Grenadines	
Anglican	20,000
Pentecostal	17,000
Methodist	12,000
Roman Catholic	12,000
other	52,000
Samoa	
Mormon	46,200
Congregational	44,000
Roman Catholic	38,100
Methodist	21,800
other	29,100
San Marino	
Roman Catholic	24,000
other	3,000
São Tomé and Príncipe	
Roman Catholic	111,000
African Christian	16,000
other	20,000
Saudi Arabia	
Sunnī Muslim	20,490,000
Shīʿī Muslim	840,000
Christian	840,000
Hindu	250,000
other	330,000
Senegal	
Sunnī Muslim	9,010,000
traditional beliefs	640,000
Roman Catholic	480,000
other	160,000
Serbia	
Orthodox	6,576,000
Roman Catholic	426,000
Muslim	248,000
Protestant	85,000
other/unknown	402,000
Seychelles	
Roman Catholic	69,800
other	10,800
Sierra Leone	
Sunnī Muslim	2,490,000
traditional beliefs	2,190,000
Christian	620,000
other	130,000
Singapore	
Buddhist and Taoist	1,695,000
Muslim	495,000
Christian	485,000
Hindu	133,000
nonreligious	493,000
other	21,000
Slovakia	
Roman Catholic	3,270,000
Slovak Evangelical	340,000
other (mostly nonreligious)	1,800,000
Slovenia	
Roman Catholic	1,650,000
other	340,000
Solomon Islands	
Protestant	173,000
Anglican	149,000
Roman Catholic	83,000
other	75,000
Somalia	
Sunnī Muslim	7,364,000
other	125,000
South Africa	
Christian	36,220,000
independents	17,040,000
Protestant	13,860,000
Roman Catholic	3,090,000
traditional beliefs	3,660,000
Hindu	1,050,000
Muslim	1,050,000
Bahāʾī	260,000
Jewish	170,000
nonreligious	1,050,000
other	130,000
Spain	
Roman Catholic	36,920,000
Muslim	200,000
other (mostly nonreligious)	3,010,000
Sri Lanka	
Buddhist	13,270,000
Hindu	2,190,000
Muslim	1,750,000
Roman Catholic	1,300,000
other	900,000
Sudan, The	
Sunnī Muslim	25,360,000
Christian	6,020,000
traditional beliefs	4,300,000
other	390,000
Suriname	
Hindu	119,000
Roman Catholic	91,000
Muslim	85,000
Protestant	71,000
other	68,000
Swaziland	
African Christian	480,000
Protestant	160,000
traditional beliefs	120,000
other	340,000
Sweden	
Church of Sweden (Lutheran)	7,690,000
other	1,200,000
Switzerland	
Roman Catholic	3,330,000
Protestant	2,890,000
other	1,000,000
Syria	
Sunnī Muslim	12,380,000
Shīʿī Muslim	2,010,000
Christian	920,000
Druze	500,000
other	920,000
Taiwan	
nonreligious	10,670,000
Buddhist	5,100,000
Taoist	4,040,000
I Kuan Tao	990,000
Protestant	440,000
Roman Catholic	320,000
Tien Te Chiao	210,000
Tien Ti Chiao	190,000
Confucianism (Li)	150,000
Hsuan Yuan Chiao	140,000
Muslim	50,000
Shinto (Tenrikyo)	20,000
Bahāʾī	20,000
Tajikistan	
Sunnī Muslim	4,920,000
Shīʿī Muslim	310,000
Russian Orthodox	90,000
atheist	120,000
other (mostly nonreligious)	820,000
Tanzania	
Christian	18,260,000
Muslim	11,520,000
traditional beliefs	5,830,000
other	620,000
Thailand	
Buddhist	57,920,000
Muslim	2,850,000
Christian	440,000
other	40,000
Togo	
traditional beliefs	1,940,000
Roman Catholic	1,250,000
Sunnī Muslim	970,000
Protestant	530,000
other	450,000
Tonga	
Free Wesleyan	44,000
Roman Catholic	16,000
other	41,000
Trinidad and Tobago	
Roman Catholic	380,000
Hindu	308,000
Protestant	244,000
Anglican	142,000
Muslim	76,000
other	149,000
Tunisia	
Sunnī Muslim	9,720,000
other	104,000
Turkey	
Muslim (mostly Sunnī)	64,360,000
nonreligious	1,340,000
other	530,000
Turkmenistan	
Muslim (mostly Sunnī)	4,752,000
Russian Orthodox	129,000
other (mostly nonreligious)	581,000
Tuvalu	
Congregational	9,400
other	1,600
Uganda	
Roman Catholic	10,050,000
Anglican	9,450,000
Muslim (mostly Sunnī)	1,250,000
traditional beliefs	1,050,000
other	2,190,000
Ukraine	
Ukrainian Orthodox (Russian patriarchy)	9,491,000
Ukrainian Orthodox (Kiev patriarchy)	4,746,000
Ukrainian Autocephalous Orthodox	332,000
Ukrainian Catholic (Uniate)	3,417,000
Protestant	1,736,000
Roman Catholic	576,000
Jewish	423,000
other (mostly nonreligious)	28,044,000
United Arab Emirates	
Sunnī Muslim	2,490,000
Shīʿī Muslim	500,000
other	120,000
United Kingdom	
Christian	49,510,000
Anglican	26,140,000
Roman Catholic	5,590,000
Protestant	5,020,000
Eastern Orthodox	370,000
other Christian	12,390,000
Muslim	1,220,000
Hindu	440,000
Jewish	310,000
Sikh	240,000
other (mostly nonreligious and atheist)	8,240,000
United States	
Christian (professing)	242,011,000
Christian (affiliated)	196,929,000
independent	80,639,000
Protestant	66,287,000
Roman Catholic	59,542,000
Eastern Orthodox	5,915,000
Anglican	2,464,000
other Christian	10,348,000
multi-affiliated Christians	−28,266,000
Christian (unaffiliated)	45,082,000
non-Christian	44,056,000
nonreligious	25,745,000
Jewish	5,771,000
Muslim	4,242,000
Buddhist	2,515,000
atheist	1,181,000
Hindu	1,059,000
New-Religionist	832,000
Bahāʾī	773,000
Ethnic religionist	447,000
Sikh	240,000
Chinese folk-religionist	80,000
other	1,171,000
Uruguay	
Roman Catholic	2,590,000
Protestant	150,000
Mormon	50,000
Jewish	30,000
other	480,000
Uzbekistan	
Muslim (mostly Sunnī)	19,156,000
Russian Orthodox	195,000
other (mostly nonreligious)	5,804,000
Vanuatu	
Presbyterian	70,000
Roman Catholic	28,000
Anglican	27,000
other	69,000
Venezuela	
Roman Catholic	22,050,000
other	2,590,000
Vietnam	
Buddhist	53,290,000
Roman Catholic	6,180,000
New-Religionist	
Cao Dai	2,810,000
Hoa Hao	1,690,000
other	16,500,000
Virgin Islands (U.S.)	
Protestant	56,000
Roman Catholic	41,000
other	24,000
West Bank	
Muslim (mostly Sunnī)	1,860,000
Jewish[4]	230,000
Christian and other	180,000
Western Sahara	
Sunnī Muslim	250,000
other	1,000
Yemen	
Muslim (mostly Sunnī)	18,050,000
other	20,000
Zambia	
traditional beliefs	2,640,000
Protestant	2,240,000
Roman Catholic	1,650,000
other	3,240,000
Zimbabwe	
African Christian	4,580,000
traditional beliefs	3,430,000
Protestant	1,400,000
Roman Catholic	1,090,000
other	870,000

[1]Official 1986 census figure is 5.9 percent. [2]Includes the Golan Heights and East Jerusalem; excludes the West Bank and Gaza Strip. [3]Many Japanese practice both Shintoism and Buddhism. [4]Excludes East Jerusalem.

Vital statistics, marriage, family

This table provides some of the basic measures of the factors that influence the size, direction, and rates of population change within a country. The accuracy of these data depends on the effectiveness of each respective national system for registering vital and civil events (birth, death, marriage, etc.) and on the sophistication of the analysis that can be brought to bear upon the data so compiled.

Data on birth rates, for example, depend not only on the completeness of registration of births in a particular country but also on the conditions under which those data are collected: Do all births take place in a hospital? Are the births reported comparably in all parts of the country? Are the records of the births tabulated at a central location in a timely way with an effort to eliminate inconsistent reporting of birth events, perinatal mortality, etc.? Similar difficulties attach to death rates but with the added need to identify "cause of death." Even in a developed country such identifications are often left to nonmedical personnel, and in a developing country with, say, only one physician for every 10,000 population, there will be too few physicians to perform autopsies to assess accurately the cause of death after the fact and also too few to provide ongoing care at a level where records would permit inference about cause of death based on prior condition or diagnosis.

Calculating natural increase, which at its most basic is simply the difference between the birth and death rates, may be affected by the differing degrees of completeness of birth and death registration for a given country. The total fertility rate may be understood as the average number of children that would be borne per woman if all childbearing women lived to the end of their childbearing years and bore children at each age at the average rate for that age. Calculating a meaningful fertility rate requires analysis of changing age structure of the female population over time, changing mortality rates among mothers and their infants, and changing medical practice at births, each improvement of natural survivorship or medical support leading to greater numbers of live-born children and greater numbers of children who survive their first year (the basis for measurement of infant mortality, another basic indicator of demographic conditions and trends within a population).

As indicated above, data for causes of death are not only particularly difficult to obtain, since many countries are not well equipped to collect the data, but also difficult to assess, as their accuracy may be suspect and their meaning may be subject to varying interpretation. Take the case of a citizen of a less developed country who dies of what is clearly a lung infection: Was the death complicated by chronic malnutrition, itself complicated by a parasitic infestation, these last two together so weakening the subject that he died of an infection that he might have survived had his general health been better? Similarly, in a developed country: Someone may die from what is identified in an autopsy as a cerebrovascular accident, but if that accident occurred in a vascular system that was weakened by diabetes, what was the actual cause of death? Statistics on causes of death seek to identify the "underlying" cause (that which sets the final train of events leading to death in motion) but often must settle for the most proximate cause or symptom. Even this kind of analysis may be misleading for those charged with interpreting the data with a view to ordering health-care priorities for a particular country. The eight groups of causes of death utilized here include most, but not all, of the detailed causes classified by the World Health Organization and would not, thus, aggregate to the country's crude death rate for the same year. Among the lesser causes excluded by the present classification are: benign neoplasms; anemias; mental disorders; kidney and genitourinary diseases not classifi-

Vital statistics, marriage, family

country	vital rates						causes of death (rate per 100,000 population)								
	year	birth rate per 1,000 population	death rate per 1,000 population	infant mortality rate per 1,000 live births	rate of natural increase per 1,000 population	total fertility rate	year	infectious and parasitic diseases	malignant neoplasms (cancers)	endocrine and metabolic disorders	diseases of the nervous system	diseases of the circulatory system	diseases of the respiratory system	diseases of the digestive system	accidents, poisoning, and violence
Afghanistan	2006	46.6	20.3	160.2	26.3	6.69	...	...	...	...	...	...	...	...	...
Albania	2008	11.2	5.1	6.0	6.1	1.40	2008	2.0	85.9	1.9	4.8	294.0	15.7	8.8	31.1
Algeria	2007	17.1	4.6	29.8	12.5	1.86	2002	96.5	54.2	...	...	...	45.2	...	41.2
American Samoa	2007	21.6	4.0	11.8	17.6	3.16[2]	2004	...	59.3	39.0[3]	...	121.7	54.6	...	34.3
Andorra	2009	10.0	3.2	2.4[4]	6.8	1.33	2002–06	14.0[5]	108.2	20.0[5]	66.0[5]	100.6	28.5	18.2	27.7
Angola	2007	44.5	24.8	184.4	19.7	6.27	...	...	...	...	...	...	...	...	...
Antigua and Barbuda	2007	14.4	5.9	21.8	8.5	2.09	1999	11.3	118.0[6]	81.0[3, 6]	14.8	215[6]	93.0	28.4	52.0
Argentina	2007	18.3	7.5	12.1	10.8	2.39	2005	35.2	144.8	24.4[3]	15.5[5]	239.8	73.3[5]	30.9[5]	47.7
Armenia	2008	12.7	8.5	10.8	4.2	1.30[2]	2008	8.6	170.2	42.3	8.7[7]	423.0	55.4	47.0	40.9
Aruba	2008	11.6	5.0	6.0[8]	6.6	1.70	2007	28.7	147.3	28.3[5]	4.8[5]	149.2	26.4[5]	13.0[5]	40.2
Australia	2007–08	13.6	6.7	4.1	6.9	1.93	2006	8.6[6]	192.0	23.9[6]	23.7	220.6	52.5	21.7	37.9
Austria	2008	9.3	9.0	3.7	0.3	1.41	2008	7.8	245.0	52.8	28.2	387.4	49.5	36.5	50.6
Azerbaijan	2009	17.2	5.9	11.3	11.3	2.30[10]	2009	16.8[5]	78.3	17.2[5]	19.3[5]	363.9	26.2	66.5[5]	27.3
Bahamas, The	2006	13.9	5.3	16.3	8.6	2.18	2005	9.2[11]	90.1	29.4[3]	12.2[11]	184.2	31.0	29.3[11]	63.8
Bahrain	2008	15.4	2.2	8.3[10]	13.2	2.79	2003	11.9	23.1[12]	20.3[12]	5.9	40.0[12]	20.7	13.8	26.5
Bangladesh	2007	20.9	6.3	43.0	14.6	2.39	2004[13]	98.3	26.6	...	...	54.0[5]	90.5	...	35.7
Barbados	2007	12.9	8.1	13.0	4.8	1.68	2000	38.3	165.0[5]	70.0[4]	18.8	270.5[5]	46.6	25.2	29.3[5]
Belarus	2009	11.6	14.2	4.7	–2.6	1.42	2003	10.8	171.2	7.6	14.9	693.5	45.0	28.4	161.6
Belgium	2008	11.3	9.4	3.4	1.9	1.82	2004	25.4	256.2	5.6	61.8	338.8	107.6	42.3	77.4
Belize	2007	28.3	5.7	21.2	22.6	3.52	2000	39.1	107.2	42.4	9.6	248.8	50.0	18.8	77.0
Benin	2008	39.8	9.7	66.2	30.1	5.58	...	...	...	...	...	...	...	...	...
Bermuda	2008	12.8	6.9	4.9	5.9	2.00	2006	18.3	149.7	37.1[11]	16.1[11]	247.5	45.8	27.4[11]	30.6
Bhutan	2008	20.6	7.5	51.9	13.1	2.48	2006[15]	...	...	...	...	13.1	13.6	21.3	...
Bolivia	2009	26.9	7.4	43.2	19.5	3.26[12]	2000	140.6[5]	145.6[5]	...	...	370.3	...	...	109.7
Bosnia and Herzegovina	2008	8.9	8.9	6.8[10]	0.0	1.19	2008	7.2	175.3	40.7	11.9[16]	468.2	26.9	22.0	31.3
Botswana	2008	23.2	8.5	13.4	14.7	2.66	...	...	...	...	...	...	...	...	...
Brazil	2008	16.2	6.2	23.6	10.0	1.89	2002	26.2[11]	95.7	27.6	10.5[11]	204.1	52.0[11]	25.3[11]	79.2
Brunei	2008	16.1	2.7	7.0	13.4	1.70	2006	...	57.4	26.5[5]	...	91.9	29.5	...	21.4
Bulgaria	2009	10.7	14.2	9.0	–3.5	1.57	2009	7.7	226.0	26.2	12.6	939.3	54.7	43.1	45.0
Burkina Faso	2007	45.0	13.9	87.6	31.1	6.41	...	...	...	...	...	...	...	...	...
Burundi	2005	35.4	14.8	102.0	20.6	5.04	...	...	...	...	...	...	...	...	...
Cambodia	2008	25.7	8.2	56.6	17.5	3.08	...	...	...	...	...	...	...	...	...
Cameroon	2006	35.6	13.0	67.2	22.6	4.58	...	...	...	...	...	...	...	...	...
Canada	2007–08	11.0	7.2	5.4[17]	3.8	1.59[2]	2004	12.5	209.6	31.8	32.1	227.7	61.4	27.1	40.7
Cape Verde	2007	25.1	5.3	21.7	19.8	2.89	2007	35.0	54.5	...	...	136.3	46.8	...	42.5
Cayman Islands	2008	14.2	3.0	7.3	11.2	1.6	2000	...	99.5	...	...	136.8	24.9	...	34.8
Central African Republic	2007	33.5	18.3	83.7	15.2	4.32	...	...	...	...	...	...	...	...	...
Chad	2007	42.4	16.7	102.1	25.7	5.56	...	...	...	...	...	...	...	...	...
Chile	2009	14.6	5.8	7.7	8.8	1.92	2006	10.9	128.7	26.6	14.4	149.1	47.6	38.5	49.0
China	2008	12.1	7.1	22.9[10]	5.0	1.77[10]	2008[19]	16.7[6]	167.0	21.1	6.3	162.5[5]	73.0	17.6	40.1[2]
Colombia	2007	20.2	5.5	20.1	14.7	2.51	2005[22]	37.8[5]	90.4	20.0[5]	5.1[23]	164.4	56.9	17.0[23]	101.7
Comoros	2008	32.6	6.3	72.9[2]	26.3	5.03[2]	2002	261.6	46.9	...	...	118.9	...	...	68.1
Congo, Dem. Rep. of the	2007	43.4	11.9	116.5[17]	31.5	6.37	...	...	...	...	...	...	...	...	...
Congo, Rep. of the	2008	41.8	12.3	81.7	29.5	5.92	...	...	...	...	...	...	...	...	...
Costa Rica	2009	16.6	4.1	8.8	12.5	1.97[12]	2007	8.9	88.2	16.5	9.6	115.6	35.4	29.0	46.0[7]
Côte d'Ivoire	2009	36.7	13.6	96.7	23.1	4.33[10]	...	...	...	...	...	...	...	...	...
Croatia	2007	9.4	11.8	5.7[17]	–2.4	1.40	2006	8.5	286.0	25.5	15.4	576.8	56.2	52.3	62.0
Cuba	2009	11.6	7.7	4.8	3.9	1.70	2008	6.7[24]	189.0	18.2[3]	9.7[24]	306.5	81.6	26.4[24]	39.4
Cyprus	2008	11.6	6.5	3.5	5.1	1.46	2008	8.53	138.4	49.3	18.3	252.9	44.7	18.8	39.2
Czech Republic	2008	11.5	10.1	2.8	1.4	1.50	2008	8.9	268.3	21.2	12.3	501.3	55.0	45.5	58.4

able under the main groups; maternal deaths; diseases of the skin and musculoskeletal systems; congenital and perinatal conditions; and general senility and other ill-defined (ill-diagnosed) conditions, a kind of "other" category.

Expectation of life is probably the most accurate single measure of the quality of life in a given society. It summarizes in a single number all of the natural and social stresses that operate upon individuals in that society. The number may range from as few as 35 years of life in the least developed countries to as much as 85 years for women in the most developed nations. The lost potential in the years separating those two numbers is prodigious, regardless of how the loss arises—wars and civil violence, poor public health services, or poor individual health practice in matters of nutrition, exercise, stress management, and so on.

Data on marriages and marriage rates probably are less meaningful in terms of international comparisons than some of the measures mentioned above because the number, timing, and kinds of social relationships that substitute for marriage depend on many kinds of social variables—income, degree of social control, heterogeneity of the society (race, class, language communities), or level of development of civil administration (if one must travel for a day or more to obtain a legal civil ceremony, one may forgo it). Nevertheless, the data for a single country say specific things about local practice in terms of the age at which a man or woman typically marries, and the overall rate will at least define the number of legal civil marriages, though it cannot say anything about other, less formal arrangements (here the figure for children born within marriage in the next section may identify some of the societies in which economics or social constraints may operate to limit the number of marriages that are actually confirmed on civil registers). The available data usually include both first marriages and remarriages after annulment, divorce, widowhood, or the like.

The data for families provide information about the average size of a family unit (individuals related by blood or civil register) and the average number of children under a specified age (set here at 15 to provide a consistent measure of social minority internationally, though legal minority depends on the laws of each country). When well-defined family data are not collected as part of a country's national census or vital statistics surveys, data for households have been substituted on the assumption that most households worldwide represent families in some conventional sense. But increasing numbers of households worldwide are composed of unrelated individuals (unmarried heterosexual couples, aged [or younger] groups sharing limited [often fixed] incomes for reasons of economy, or homosexual couples). Such arrangements do not yet represent great numbers overall. Increasing numbers of census programs, however, even in developing countries, are making more adequate provision for distinguishing these nontraditional, often nonfamily households.

Internet resources for further information:

- World Health Organization Mortality Database (World) http://www3.who.int/whosis/mort/table1_process.cfm
- Pan American Health Organization (the Americas) http://www.paho.org
- National Center for Health Statistics (U.S.) http://www.cdc.gov/nchs
- U.S. Census Bureau: International Data Base (World) http://www.census.gov/ipc/www/idbprint.html

expectation of life at birth (latest year) male	female	nuptiality, family, and family planning: marriages year	total number	rate per 1,000 population	age at marriage (latest): groom (percent) 19 and under	20–29	30 and over	bride (percent) 19 and under	20–29	30 and over	families (F), households (H) (latest): families (households) total ('000)	size	children number under age 15	percent within marriage	induced abortions number	ratio per 100 live births	country
43.2	43.5	…	…	…	…	…	…	…	…	…	H 2,774	H 8.0	H 2.8[1]	…	…	…	Afghanistan
72.9	77.8	2007	22,426	7.0	1.2	66.4	32.4	28.5	62.7	8.8	F 729	F 4.2	F 1.6	…	9,030	27.2	Albania
71.9	75.2	2002	218,620	7.0	0.7	67.1	32.2	29.8	61.4	8.8	H 5,072	H 6.2	H 3.0	…	…	…	Algeria
72.5	79.8	2004	287	4.5	…	…	…	…	…	…	H 9	H 5.7	H 2.7	65.3	…	…	American Samoa
80.4	85.4	2009	265	3.2	…	…	…	…	…	…	…	H 2.8	…	…	…	…	Andorra
36.7	38.6	…	…	…	…	…	…	…	…	…	H 2,787	H 5.0	…	…	…	…	Angola
71.8	80.7	2007	1,863	21.7	1.2	38.4	60.4	2.8	53.1	44.1	H 24	H 3.1	H 1.2	25.7	…	…	Antigua and Barbuda
72.9	79.6	2003	129,049	3.4	5.6	71.5	22.9	26.0	58.6	15.4	H 10,106	H 3.6	H 1.0	67.5	…	…	Argentina
70.4	76.9	2008	18,465	5.7	0.9	72.3	26.8	16.9	73.3	9.8	H 841	H 4.5	H 1.8	64.5	10,487	28.0	Armenia
76.0	82.8	2007[9]	1,013	9.7	1.4	27.4	71.2	4.2	37.8	58.0	H 29	H 2.8	…	43.7	…	…	Aruba
79.2	84.0	2008	118,756	5.5	0.5	42.4	57.1	2.4	52.7	44.9	H 8,187	H 3.0	H 0.6	67.3	84,460	33.6	Australia
77.6	83.0	2008	35,223	4.2	0.6	29.8	69.6	2.6	43.0	54.0	H 3,337	H 2.3	H 0.5	61.2	2,380	3.0	Austria
70.9	76.1	2009	78,072	8.8	0.9	67.5	31.6	22.4	65.5	12.1	H 1,740	H 4.5	H 1.7	88.5	19,798	15.0	Azerbaijan
62.2	69.0	2008[9]	4,291	12.7	0.6	41.6	57.8	4.6	50.6	44.8	H 87	H 3.5	…	43.2	…	…	Bahamas, The
71.7	76.8	2008	4,981	4.5	1.6	66.9	31.5	20.5	64.4	15.1	H 109	H 5.9	H 2.2	100.0	1,749	12.9	Bahrain
65.5	67.9	1998	1,154,000	9.2	…	…	…	…	…	…	H 25,673	H 4.7	…	…	…	…	Bangladesh
71.2	75.8	2000	3,516	13.1	0.1	40.2	59.7	1.4	53.6	44.9	H 97	H 2.8	H 1.5	26.9	723	19.6	Barbados
64.7	76.5	2004	60,265	6.1	3.1	67.3	29.6	14.8	62.9	22.3	H 3,210	H 2.6[14]	H 0.8	79.9	71,700	80.6	Belarus
77.5	83.5	2007	45,561	4.3	0.5	51.3	48.2	3.1	61.2	35.7	F 4,319	F 2.4	F 0.5	58.0	15,595	13.9	Belgium
66.4	70.1	2003	1,713	6.3	7.1	56.4	36.5	24.9	51.5	23.6	H 55	H 4.4	H 2.2	40.3	990	15.1	Belize
57.4	59.8	…	…	…	…	…	…	…	…	…	H 1,068	H 5.6	…	…	…	…	Benin
77.0	83.5	2008[9]	721	11.2	—	23.2	86.9	0.2	34.4	65.5	H 28	H 2.3	H 0.5	64.2	92	11.0	Bermuda
64.8	66.4	…	…	…	…	…	…	…	…	…	H 147	H 5.0	…	…	…	…	Bhutan
63.9	68.2	2006	…	2.2	…	…	…	…	…	…	H 1,923	H 4.3	H 1.6	80.9	…	…	Bolivia
66.9	72.5	2007	23,494	6.8	1.2	60.0	38.8	13.5	63.8	22.7	H 1,203	H 3.4	H 1.1	35.8	…	…	Bosnia and Herzegovina
61.5	62.1	…	…	…	…	…	…	…	…	…	H 414	H 4.3	H 2.0	28.8	…	…	Botswana
69.3	76.8	2007	916,006	6.7	4.3	57.9	37.8	18.8	55.2	26.0	F 48,514	F 3.2	H 1.2	…	…	…	Brazil
76.6	79.8	2008	2,391	6.0	2.3	55.0	42.7	11.7	62.2	26.1	H 57	H 5.6	H 2.0	…	…	…	Brunei
69.5	76.6	2009	25,923	3.4	1.2	61.9	36.9	10.0	70.8	19.2	H 2,913	H 2.5	…	48.9	48,035	71.3	Bulgaria
55.8	57.5	…	…	…	…	…	…	…	…	…	H 1,759	H 5.9	…	…	…	…	Burkina Faso
47.8	50.5	…	…	…	…	…	…	…	…	…	H 1,398	H 5.6	…	…	…	…	Burundi
60.5	64.3	…	…	…	…	…	…	…	…	…	H 2,418	H 4.7	…	…	…	…	Cambodia
51.7	53.0	…	…	…	…	…	…	…	…	…	H 2,880	H 5.5	…	…	…	…	Cameroon
76.9	83.7	2004	146,377	4.7	0.7	43.4	55.9	2.5	52.9	44.6	H 12,021	H 2.5	H 0.6	62.0	103,768	30.9	Canada
68.3	73.6	1994	1,200	3.2	…	…	…	…	…	…	H 95	H 4.9	…	28.9	…	…	Cape Verde
77.6	82.9	2008[18]	487	8.7	…	…	…	…	…	…	…	H 2.6	…	…	…	…	Cayman Islands
43.9	44.1	…	…	…	…	…	…	…	…	…	H 646	H 5.3	…	…	…	…	Central African Republic
46.2	48.3	…	…	…	…	…	…	…	…	…	H 1,574	H 5.0	…	…	…	…	Chad
74.1	80.8	2006	58,155	3.5	2.6	58.0	39.4	10.5	62.2	27.3	H 4,141	H 3.5	…	65.7	…	…	Chile
71.3	74.8	2004	8,672,000	6.7	…	…	…	…	…	…	H[20] 371[21]	H 3.1	H 1.1	…	6,340,000	37.1	China
68.4	76.2	…	…	…	…	…	…	…	…	…	H 8,835	H 3.4	F 2.5	75.2	…	…	Colombia
60.0	64.7	…	…	…	…	…	…	…	…	…	H 94	H 5.8	…	…	…	…	Comoros
51.9	55.4	…	…	…	…	…	…	…	…	…	H 18,326	H 2.3	…	…	…	…	Congo, Dem. Rep. of the
52.5	55.0	…	…	…	…	…	…	…	…	…	H 326	H 5.9	H 2.0	…	…	…	Congo, Rep. of the
76.8	81.8	2008	25,034	5.6	3.5	48.9	47.5	13.5	51.8	34.7	H 960	H 3.7	…	40.1	…	…	Costa Rica
50.7	54.1	…	…	…	…	…	…	…	…	…	H 2,027	H 8.0	…	…	…	…	Côte d'Ivoire
72.4	79.6	2007	23,140	5.2	1.0	59.1	39.9	8.4	68.0	23.6	H 1,877	H 2.3	H 0.6	88.5	5,232	13.0	Croatia
76.0	80.0	2008	61,852	5.5	2.6	30.1	67.2	11.2	35.4	53.4	F 3,121	H 3.2	H 1.6	…	67,277	52.9	Cuba
78.3	81.9	2008	6,115	7.7	0.7	49.8	49.5	3.9	63.2	32.9	H 276	H 2.9	H 1.1	96.7	…	…	Cyprus
74.1	80.1	2008	52,457	5.0	0.3	39.5	60.2	1.6	56.5	41.9	H 3,828	H 2.5	…	63.7	25,760	21.5	Czech Republic

Vital statistics, marriage, family (continued)

country	vital rates						causes of death (rate per 100,000 population)								
	year	birth rate per 1,000 population	death rate per 1,000 population	infant mortality rate per 1,000 live births	rate of natural increase per 1,000 population	total fertility rate	year	infectious and parasitic diseases	malignant neoplasms (cancers)	endocrine and metabolic disorders	diseases of the nervous system	diseases of the circulatory system	diseases of the respiratory system	diseases of the digestive system	accidents, poisoning, and violence
Denmark	2009	11.4	9.9	4.2	1.5	1.78[17]	2008	12.9	278.9	31.3	29.0	269.5	100.8	49.1	43.5
Djibouti	2006	39.5	19.3	102.4	20.2	5.31	2002	...	62.0	...	...	...	22.0	...	81
Dominica	2006	15.3	6.7	13.7	8.6	1.94	1999	18.3	154.2	90.2	9.2	283.7	66.7	26.1	36.6
Dominican Republic	2008	11.9	3.3	29.0[2]	8.6	2.83[2]	1998	30.6	38.0	15.9	4.7	102.7	19.0	17.2	42.1
East Timor	2008	40.9	10.0	83.5	30.9	6.50	2002	...	59.0	...	...	...	41.0	...	87.0
Ecuador	2009[1]	15.4	4.3	15.2	11.1	2.56	2005	20.8	51.9	21.1[3]	8.0[11]	94.0	36.2[11]	22.6[11]	44.6
Egypt	2008–09	25.0	6.3	16.0[25]	18.7	2.83[2]	2000	32.3	25.7	11.5	5.4	230.3	49.5	48.6	26.3
El Salvador	2008	22.5	5.9	9.5[2]	16.6	3.16	1999	32.8	44.4	19.5	12.3	88.3	40.5	25.8	118
Equatorial Guinea	2008	37.1	9.7	83.8	27.4	5.16	2002	812.5	...	...	...	197.5	89.5	...	124.3
Eritrea	2006	34.3	9.6	46.3	24.7	5.08	2002	459.1	42.8	...	...	104.9	...	...	74.6
Estonia	2008	12.0	12.4	5.0	–0.4	1.66	2008	9.1	264.3	19.5	17.5	676.8	36.5	54.1	101.3
Ethiopia	2008	44.0	11.8	82.6	32.2	6.17	...	...	...	...	...	...	...	...	...
Faroe Islands	2008	13.6	7.7	4.5	5.9	2.50	2007	22.7	175.8	10.3	6.2	289.5	86.9	39.3	57.9
Fiji	2007	20.7	7.1	18.4	13.6	2.73[2]	2001	45.8	38.0	23.7	0.5	330.0	50.2	14.1	31.7
Finland	2008	11.2	9.2	2.6	2.0	1.85	2006	6.4	204.6	11.2	60.8	379.4	40.4	45.7	79.4
France	2008	12.9	8.6	3.6[17]	4.3	2.00	2005	16.2	243.4	31.5	43.1	245.0	57.3	37.9	58.5
French Guiana	2007	30.0	3.5	12.1[17]	26.5	3.90	2005	32.1	58.2	c. 16[23]	9.4	75.0	...	c. 16[23]	50.8
French Polynesia	2007	17.1	4.8	6.8	12.3	2.11	2002	12.0	103.0	16.0	11.0	113.0	46.0	13.0	54.0
Gabon	2006	36.2	12.3	54.5	23.9	4.74	2002	c. 404.0	...	...	...	...	...	...	c. 80.0
Gambia, The	2007	39.0	13.0	72.0	26.0	5.20	...	...	...	...	...	...	...	...	...
Gaza Strip	2005	40.0	3.9	22.9	36.1	5.91	...	...	...	...	...	...	...	...	...
Georgia	2008[27]	12.9	9.8	17.0[28]	3.1	1.67	2008[27]	8.4	106.3	14.4	6.5	629.1	28.2	28.7	46.5
Germany	2008	8.3	10.3	4.0	–2.0	1.38	2007	16.9	257.4	32.1	22.2	436.0	70.5	51.3	35.1[5]
Ghana	2008	29.4	9.3	52.5	20.1	3.78	2002	...	61.0	...	...	...	...	...	83.0
Greece	2008	10.3	9.5	3.5	0.8	1.45	2006	7.0	230.7	13.8	11.0	453.1	79.6	23.0	36.2
Greenland	2007	14.9	8.0	8.2	6.9	2.28	2006	64.9[29]	c. 186.0	3.9[30]	1.8[30]	187.5	51.8	5.7[30]	c. 88.0
Grenada	2008	18.1	8.2	11.0[10]	9.9	2.30	1996	18.3	178.0[5]	63.0[3]	11.2	413.0[5]	25.0[5]	18.3	43.8
Guadeloupe	2007	14.8	6.4	8.6[17]	8.4	2.10	2002	23.8[31]	148.3	31.5	...	207.5	32.1[31]	31.4[31]	75.6
Guam	2007	20.1	4.5	10.0	15.6	2.58[2]	2002	1.7	57.1[17]	19.4[3]	6.9	162.7	32.6	16.9	44.8[17]
Guatemala	2007	29.3	5.3	24.5[2]	24.0	3.70	1999	59.3	44.9	48.2	8.9	74.7	110.8	33.5	71.6
Guernsey	2007	10.4	8.3	4.5[12]	2.1	1.40	1996	5.3	c. 202[10]	15.9	15.9	441.1	150.0	49.4	24.7
Guinea	2008	37.8	11.3	67.4	26.5	5.25	2002	682	62	...	...	...	...	...	118
Guinea-Bissau	2005	37.6	16.7	107.2	20.9	4.93	...	...	...	...	...	...	...	...	...
Guyana	2008	18.5	7.9	33.3[17]	10.6	2.60	2006	41.4[31]	48.6	62.5	9.8[31]	194.0	20.7	21.4	99.0
Haiti	2007	27.9	9.2	71.0	18.7	3.50	2002	...	55.3	31.1	...	227.9	...	...	59.3
Honduras	2008	27.4	5.6	20.0[10]	21.8	3.20	...	...	...	...	...	...	...	...	...
Hong Kong	2008	11.3	6.0	1.8	5.3	1.06	2007	15.9	177.8	8.8	4.6	155.0	109.5	22.7	33.6[17]
Hungary	2008	9.9	13.0	5.6	–3.1	1.35	2005	5.0	303.5	39.3	16.8[5]	703.2	64.5	84.3	78.0
Iceland	2008	15.1	6.2	2.5	8.9	2.14	2008	6.6	178.2	11.0	49.5	221.1	57.6	18.2	39.1
India	2008	22.8	8.2	54.0	14.6	2.80	2002	420.0	71.0	...	...	268.0	58.0	...	100.0
Indonesia	2006	20.1	6.3	26.8[12]	13.8	2.41	...	...	...	...	...	...	...	...	...
Iran	2006–07	17.8	5.8	29.1[10]	12.0	1.83[10]	2002	67.0	65.0	18.0	29.0	232.0	23.0	41.0	104.0
Iraq	2008	30.7	5.1	46.2	25.6	3.97	2002	...	54.0	...	...	187.0	...	...	115.0
Ireland	2008	16.9	6.4	2.9[10]	10.5	2.03[10]	2008	4.1[17]	184.0	37.0[7]	8.5[7]	221.6	83.5[10]	24.0[17]	31.4
Isle of Man	2008	12.1	10.4	5.0[2]	1.7	1.65[2]	2005	—	246.7	14.3[7]	29.8[7]	374.5	146.0	35.2	26.4
Israel	2008	21.5	5.4	3.8	16.1	2.96	2007	15.0[7]	137.0	34.0[3]	7.0[7]	157.0	46.0	27.0[7]	26.0
Italy	2008	9.6	9.8	3.6[2]	–0.2	1.37[10]	2006	12.5	286.2	30.7[7]	24.1[7]	373.4	60.7	39.2	45.5[7]
Jamaica	2008	16.7	6.3	15.6	10.4	2.30	2002	12.0	130.0	81.0[3]	13.0	321.0	61.0	43.0	38.0
Japan	2008	8.6	8.8	2.6	–0.2	1.37	2005	14.5	303.6[10]	12.6[3]	8.2[5]	228.1	94.9	28.9	34.3[10]
Jersey	2008	10.6	8.1	5.8	2.5	1.57	2003–06	...	c. 233	...	...	c. 298	c. 122	c. 38	c. 38
Jordan	2008	31.0	3.3	19.0	27.7	3.50	...	...	...	...	...	...	...	...	...
Kazakhstan	2008	22.6	9.7	20.5	12.9	1.88	2007	32.7[7]	164.8	14.2[7]	16.3[7]	814.7	75.8	65.6[7]	155.4
Kenya	2006	39.7	11.5	59.0	28.2	4.91	...	...	...	...	...	...	...	...	...
Kiribati	2007	30.5	8.1	45.9	22.4	4.12	2005	73.5	...	51.4	...	88.1	65.1	57.7	...
Korea, North	2007	15.5	10.4	53.8	5.1	1.99	2002	...	90.0	...	...	288.0	62.0	...	62.0
Korea, South	2008	9.4	5.0	3.4	4.4	1.19	2004	10.7	139.5[12]	20.7[3, 12]	8.5	120.4	29.4	25.0	63.0
Kosovo	2008	16.0	3.2	9.7	12.8	3.0[7]	2007	1.6	26.9	2.8	1.2	120.4	6.8	3.1	6.1
Kuwait	2008	21.9	2.3	9.2	19.6	2.81	2008	6.1	28.0	7.5	2.3	99.9	11.5	5.6	34.1
Kyrgyzstan	2008	24.1	7.1	30.6[10]	17.0	2.69[17]	2006	7.6[5]	59.1	6.5[5]	11.8[5]	354.5	77.4	50.3	49.7
Laos	2008	34.5	11.0	79.5[17]	18.5	4.50	2002	...	73.0	...	...	210.0	58.0	...	112.0
Latvia	2008	10.6	13.7	6.7	–3.1	1.45[10]	2008	12.8[17]	261.7	11.0[17]	16.4[17]	728.7	40.3[17]	49.0	107.9
Lebanon	2008	20.2	5.0	23.6	15.2	2.21[10]	2002	...	67.0	...	...	305.0	33.0	...	87.0
Lesotho	2008	24.4	22.3	78.6	2.1	3.13	2002	...	...	...	...	c. 205	c. 89	...	...
Liberia	2007	43.8	22.2	149.7	21.6	5.94	...	...	...	...	...	...	...	...	...
Libya	2005	26.8	3.5	24.6	23.3	3.34	2002	72.0	44.0	...	...	185.0	16.0	...	43.0
Liechtenstein	2008	9.8	5.8	5.5[2]	4.0	1.47	2008	14.0	157.4	...	...	182.6	61.8	16.9	36.5
Lithuania	2008	10.5	13.1	4.9	–2.6	1.47	2008	16.1	246.8	9.8[5]	10.5[5]	694.2	50.2	75.9	64.1
Luxembourg	2008	11.3	7.3	1.8	4.0	1.60	2006	20.3	202.3	18.6	27.9	312.7	54.8	39.4	53.5
Macau	2008	8.5	3.2	3.2	5.4	0.90[10]	2008	7.0	100.2	20.6	2.2	89.2	44.1	12.0	24.5
Macedonia	2008	11.2	9.3	9.7	1.9	1.46[10]	2005	4.9	157.6	34.2	5.9	527.7	28.8	16.3	35.4
Madagascar	2006	38.8	8.7	58.5	30.1	5.29	...	...	...	...	...	...	...	...	...
Malawi	2008	42.1	14.9	88.1	27.2	5.67	...	...	...	...	...	...	...	...	...
Malaysia	2008	17.5	4.2	6.7	13.3	2.57	2002	101.0	83.0	...	...	149.0	40.0	...	43.0
Maldives	2008	22.0	3.0	11.0	19.0	2.1[2]	2005	...	12.3	...	...	19.9	15.8	23.0[5]	44.0[5]
Mali	2008	46.8	15.3	118.1	31.5	6.70	2002	1,487.0	54.0	...	...	135.0	36.0	...	120.0
Malta	2008	10.0	7.9	8.2	2.1	1.43	2008	3.6	207.8	40.1	23.6	309.4	72.4	28.7	33.1
Marshall Islands	2008	31.5	4.6	26.4	26.9	3.68	2003–04	83.7	41.3[25]	...	...	...	...	...	23.7
Martinique	2007	13.2	7.0	6.6	6.2	1.90	2005	52.3[5]	167.9	42.2	46.4	181.8	34.6	...	51.5
Mauritania	2008	34.6	9.3	64.9	25.3	4.52	2002	...	71.0	...	...	178.0	44.0	26.0	...
Mauritius	2008	12.9	7.1	14.4	5.8	1.58	2008	16.3	85.9	166.6	10.2	248.3	45.2	35.6	42.6
Mayotte	2006	41.0	7.7	61.2	33.3	5.79	...	...	...	...	...	...	...	...	...
Mexico	2008	19.1	4.8	15.2	14.3	2.10	2007	17.1	65.0	80.9	8.8	113.2	41.3	46.9	52.0
Micronesia	2007	25.5	5.5	37.5	20.0	2.68[2]	2003	40.0	57.1	54.4	...	116.1	55.3	...	86.8
Moldova	2008	10.9	11.8	12.1	–0.8	1.28	2008	20.0	157.5	8.3[5]	12.4	657.9	69.0	112.4	99.4
Monaco	2008	7.5[18]	6.5[18]	5.2	1.0[18]	1.75	...	...	...	...	...	...	...	...	...

expectation of life at birth (latest year)		nuptiality, family, and family planning															country
		marriages			age at marriage (latest)						families (F), households (H) (latest)						
					groom (percent)			bride (percent)			families (households)		children		induced abortions		
male	female	year	total number	rate per 1,000 population	19 and under	20–29	30 and over	19 and under	20–29	30 and over	total ('000)	size	number under age 15	percent within marriage	number	ratio per 100 live births	
76.5	80.8	2009	32,934	6.0	0.1	22.1	77.8	0.6	33.2	66.2	H 2,573	H 2.1	...	53.8	15,053	23.2	Denmark
51.8	54.1	2006	3,059	6.3	...	...	...	...	...	...	H 98	H 6.3	...	96.8	...	...	Djibouti
72.0	77.9	1999	339	4.7	—	37.0	63.0	2.7	56.2	41.1	H 19	H 3.0	H 2.2	24.1	...	...	Dominica
71.0	74.5	2008	38,310	4.0	...	...	...	...	...	...	H 2,195	H 3.9	...	32.8	31,068	17.3	Dominican Republic
64.0	68.7	1997–98	...	0.4	...	...	...	...	...	...	H 197	H 4.7	...	...	...	...	East Timor
71.7	77.6	2004	63,299	4.7	10.2	58.6	31.2	25.6	53.7	20.7	H 2,876	H 4.2[19]	...	67.9	...	...	Ecuador
71.0	74.0	2003	537,092	7.9	2.9	58.8	38.3	10.4	56.3	33.3	H 17,266	H 3.9	H 2.1	100.0	10[26]	...	Egypt
67.9	75.3	2002	25,996	4.0	3.9	50.7	45.4	13.4	52.9	33.7	H 1,529	H 4.0	...	27.0	...	...	El Salvador
60.4	62.1	...	...	...	...	...	...	...	...	...	...	H 4.5	...	...	...	...	Equatorial Guinea
57.4	60.7	...	...	...	...	...	...	...	...	...	H 792	H 5.0	...	...	...	...	Eritrea
67.6	79.2	2008	6,127	4.6	1.5	49.7	48.8	7.1	57.4	35.5	H 567	H 2.4	H 0.8	40.9	10,699	66.8	Estonia
52.5	57.5	1999	630,290	9.1	...	...	...	...	...	...	H 15,534	H 4.7	...	...	...	...	Ethiopia
76.8	82.3	2008	260	5.4	...	...	...	...	...	...	F 14	F 3.0	F 0.9	61.0	37	5.6	Faroe Islands
67.3	72.5	1998	8,058	10.1	...	...	...	...	...	...	H 421	H 4.7	F 2.5	82.7	...	...	Fiji
76.3	83.0	2008	31,014	5.8	0.9	37.5	61.6	2.7	46.7	50.6	F 1,444	H 2.2	...	59.3	11,091	19.2	Finland
77.6	84.4	2008	265,400	4.3	0.2	38.2	61.6	1.6	50.6	47.8	H 24,643	H 2.4	H 1.0	48.3	205,600	27.0	France
74.9	79.8	2003	524	2.9	0.8	25.6	73.6	4.8	41.6	53.6	H 33	H 3.3	H 1.2	14.0	388	16.8	French Guiana
71.9	77.1	2004	1,148	4.5	...	...	...	...	...	...	H 67	H 3.8	H 1.7	29.9	...	...	French Polynesia
53.2	55.8	...	...	...	...	...	...	...	...	...	H 260	H 5.0	...	...	...	...	Gabon
52.3	56.0	...	...	...	...	...	...	...	...	...	H 154	H 8.6	...	...	...	...	Gambia, The
70.7	73.3	...	...	...	...	...	...	...	...	...	...	...	...	...	...	...	Gaza Strip
69.3	79.0	2008[27]	31,414	7.2	3.7	57.3	38.9	16.9	62.7	20.4	H 1,225	H 3.7	H 1.1	65.7	22,062	39.0	Georgia
77.2	82.5	2008	377,055	4.6	0.4	29.8	69.8	2.1	44.0	53.9	H 40,076	H 2.1	H 0.3	68.2	114,484	16.8	Germany
58.5	60.8	...	...	...	...	...	...	...	...	...	H 4,463	H 4.9	H 2.2	...	...	...	Ghana
77.2	82.2	2008	53,500	4.8	0.6	31.9	67.5	2.8	52.0	45.2	H 3,600	H 3.1	H 0.7	93.5	12,289	12.1	Greece
66.4	73.6	1999	250	4.5	1.1	44.6	54.3	2.7	59.6	37.7	F 31	H 2.5	F 0.5	29.2	869	97.1	Greenland
67.1	70.5	2001	509	5.0	0.3	28.6	71.1	2.6	40.1	57.3	H 29	H 3.3	H 2.2	18.1	...	...	Grenada
76.0	82.2	2003	1,701	3.9	0.2	21.7	78.1	1.6	38.2	60.2	H 146	H 2.3	H 0.9	34.7	561	8.7	Guadeloupe
75.7	82.0	2005	2,245	13.3	3.0	55.5	41.5	9.2	59.3	31.5	H 44	H 3.8	H 1.3	42.8	...	...	Guam
66.7	73.8	2006	57,505	4.4	14.6	57.3	28.1	34.6	45.5	19.9	H 2,600	H 4.4	...	34.8	...	...	Guatemala
77.3	82.5	2000	343	5.7	...	...	...	...	...	...	H 21	H 2.6	H 0.5	65.2	...	...	Guernsey
55.1	58.1	...	...	...	...	...	...	...	...	...	H 1,161	H 6.6	...	...	...	...	Guinea
44.8	48.5	...	...	...	...	...	...	...	...	...	H 179	H 7.0	H 2.8	11.3	...	...	Guinea-Bissau
62.9	68.3	2006	...	6.1	...	...	...	...	...	...	H 196	H 4.1	H 2.1	...	...	...	Guyana
59.1	62.8	...	...	...	...	...	...	...	...	...	H 1,732	H 4.6	H 1.8	...	...	...	Haiti
67.2	73.9	...	...	...	...	...	...	...	...	...	H 1,520	H 4.8	H 2.8	...	...	...	Honduras
79.3	85.5	2007	47,453	6.8	0.4	31.2	68.5	1.7	52.9	45.3	H 2,247	H 3.0	...	94.5	15,880	31.9	Hong Kong
67.8	77.8	2008	40,105	4.0	0.9	53.0	46.1	4.2	67.8	26.5	F 4,104	H 2.6	F 0.8	60.5	44,089	44.5	Hungary
79.6	83.0	2007	1,797	5.7	0.1	28.5	71.4	0.4	40.9	58.7	H 104	H 2.5	H 1.3	35.9	955	19.8	Iceland
63.0	67.0	...	...	...	...	...	...	...	...	...	H 194,736	H 4.7[32]	H 2.4	...	723,142	2.8	India
67.4	72.4	2003	1,588,000	7.7	...	...	...	...	...	...	H 57,689	H 4.0	...	...	...	...	Indonesia
70.0	72.7	2004	602,347	8.9	...	...	...	...	...	...	H 14,456	H 4.1	H 2.2	100	...	...	Iran
68.3	71.0	2007	268,638	9.1	...	...	...	...	...	...	H 3,965	H 6.4	H 4.1	...	...	...	Iraq
76.8	81.6	2007	22,544	5.2	0.7	62.2	37.1	1.6	74.7	23.7	H 1,328	H 2.8	H 1.3	66.8	6,320	10.3	Ireland
75.3	81.2	2004	399	5.1	0.3	30.8	68.9	1.5	39.8	58.7	H 33,390	H 2.4	...	62.1	152	17.6	Isle of Man
79.1	83.0	2007	46,448	6.5	3.4	61.9	33.1	15.2	66.7	17.3	H 2,087	H 3.3	H 1.1	96.6	20,445	12.5	Israel
78.8	84.1	2007	250,360	4.2	0.4	47.6	52.0	3.3	41.2	55.5	F 21,488	F 2.5	F 0.5	79.3	124,118	22.1	Italy
71.9	75.4	2005	25,903	9.8	0.3	33.2	66.5	1.4	44.0	54.6	H 753	H 3.5	H 1.4	14.9	...	...	Jamaica
79.3	86.1	2008	726,000	5.8	1.2	50.4	48.4	2.8	62.5	34.7	H 47,043	H 2.6	...	99.0	301,673	27.2	Japan
77.1	82.3	2001	660	7.6	...	...	...	...	...	...	H 38	H 2.3	H 0.4	88.1	296	28.0	Jersey
71.6	74.4	2008	60,922	10.4	2.1	66.3	31.5	27.1	61.9	11.0	H 919	H 5.4	H 3.4	100	...	...	Jordan
63.6	73.6	2004	114,685	7.6	3.2	68.3	28.5	15.3	68.2	16.5	H 3,984	H 3.8	H 1.4	76.1	135,000	61.2	Kazakhstan
54.3	54.2	...	...	...	...	...	...	...	...	...	H 6,848	H 4.5	H 2.7	...	...	...	Kenya
59.4	65.7	...	...	...	...	...	...	...	...	...	H 13	H 6.3	H 2.5	...	...	...	Kiribati
60.6	65.8	...	...	...	...	...	...	...	...	...	H 5,887	H 4.6	H 1.7	...	...	...	Korea, North
76.5	83.3	2008	328,000	6.6	0.4	41.7	57.9	1.6	64.4	34.0	H 14,852	H 2.9	H 1.0	99.5	...	...	Korea, South
69.8[33]	71.4[33]	2008	17,950	8.3	1.7	51.7	46.6	12.7	60.2	27.1	...	H c. 6.5	...	...	...	...	Kosovo
76.4	78.7	2008	14,709	5.9	4.1	57.4	32.4	23.1	55.6	19.4	H 472	H 4.8	H 1.6	100.0	19[26]	...	Kuwait
63.6	72.2	2004	34,542	6.8	2.1	73.2	24.7	18.5	69.7	11.8	H 1,145	H 4.3	H 1.9	83.2	19,984	18.2	Kyrgyzstan
54.1	58.4	...	...	...	...	...	...	...	...	...	H 891	H 5.9	...	...	...	...	Laos
67.2	77.9	2005	12,544	5.5	1.2	54.9	43.9	6.1	61.7	32.2	H 907	H 2.5	H 0.8	56.9	13,723	67.5	Latvia
69.9	74.2	2008	37,593	9.0	...	...	...	...	...	...	H 889	H 4.3	H 2.2	...	...	...	Lebanon
41.0	39.3	2009	2,662	1.3	0.4	41.6	58.0	5.0	62.7	32.3	H 439	H 4.1	H 2.0	...	...	...	Lesotho
38.9	41.9	...	...	...	...	...	...	...	...	...	H 474	H 5.1	...	...	...	...	Liberia
74.3	78.8	2002	33,323	6.0	...	...	...	...	...	...	H 670	H 5.1	F 2.9	...	...	...	Libya
78.9	83.1	2008	402	11.3	—	54.5	44.5	0.0	66.3	29.2	H 14	H 2.5	H 0.7	86.0	...	...	Liechtenstein
66.3	77.6	2008	24,063	7.2	2.1	61.7	44.9	9.3	65.7	30.6	H 1,357	H 2.4	H 0.8	71.5	10,644	35.0	Lithuania
77.6	82.7	2008	1,917	3.9	0.2	30.8	69.0	1.2	43.5	55.3	H 172	H 2.5	H 0.5	69.8	...	...	Luxembourg
79.0	84.8	2008	2,778	5.0	1.2	53.4	45.4	2.8	71.1	26.1	H 177	H 3.0	H 0.9	82.7	...	...	Macau
71.1	75.9	2008	14,695	7.2	2.5	65.5	32.0	16.0	67.0	17.0	H 561	H 3.6	H 1.3	87.8	11,407	38.9	Macedonia
59.9	63.7	...	...	...	...	...	...	...	...	...	H 3,650	H 4.6	H 2.0	...	...	...	Madagascar
48.4	49.5	...	...	...	...	...	...	...	...	...	H 2,870	H 4.4	...	...	...	...	Malawi
72.1	76.8	2006	176,636	6.6	...	...	...	...	...	...	H 6,265	H 4.4	...	...	...	...	Malaysia
72.5	74.1	2007	5,821	19.1	13.7	58.2	29.1	...	...	...	H 43	H 6.5	...	...	...	...	Maldives
49.9	53.0	...	...	...	...	...	...	...	...	...	H 2,370	H 6.0	...	...	...	...	Mali
76.7	82.3	2008	2,482	6.0	0.2	52.9	46.6	1.0	66.6	32.2	H 132	H 2.9	H 1.2	74.6	47	1.2	Malta
68.9	73.0	...	...	...	...	...	...	...	...	...	H 8	H 7.9	...	...	...	...	Marshall Islands
76.2	84.5	2003	1,414	3.6	0.1	19.9	80.0	0.8	33.4	65.8	H 127	H 2.6	H 0.8	31.8	2,900	42.9	Martinique
57.9	62.2	...	...	...	...	...	...	...	...	...	H 487	H 5.8	...	...	...	...	Mauritania
69.2	76.0	2008	11,197	8.8	1.2	51.0	48.8	13.1	57.1	29.7	F 310	H 3.7	F 2.0	72.8	...	...	Mauritius
59.6	64.0	...	...	...	...	...	...	...	...	...	H 37	H 4.3	H 2.3	89.2	...	...	Mayotte
74.0	78.8	2007	595,209	5.6	11.1	58.6	30.2	25.3	53.6	21.0	H 26,714	H 4.0	H 2.0	62.0	3,486	0.1	Mexico
67.4	68.0	...	...	...	...	...	...	...	...	...	H 16	H 6.9	...	83.2	...	...	Micronesia
65.6	73.2	2008	26,666	7.5	2.1	68.9	29.0	14.5	67.1	18.4	H 1,318	H 3.2	H 1.1	77.7	17,965	46.9	Moldova
76.0	83.9	2004	171	5.2	...	...	...	...	...	...	H 14	H 2.1	H 0.3	61.4	...	...	Monaco

Vital statistics, marriage, family (continued)

country	vital rates						causes of death (rate per 100,000 population)								
	year	birth rate per 1,000 population	death rate per 1,000 population	infant mortality rate per 1,000 live births	rate of natural increase per 1,000 population	total fertility rate	year	infectious and parasitic diseases	malignant neoplasms (cancers)	endocrine and metabolic disorders	diseases of the nervous system	diseases of the circulatory system	diseases of the respiratory system	diseases of the digestive system	accidents, poisoning, and violence
Mongolia	2009	25.1	5.7	20.1	19.4	1.97[17]	2004	…	121.6	…	…	230.6	30.3	48.2	103.4
Montenegro	2008	13.1	9.1	7.5	4.0	1.80	2008	1.1	146.5	14.2	4.0	491.3	39.7	21.3	36.8
Morocco	2007–08	19.5	5.8	30.9	13.7	2.28	2002	120.0	41.0	…	…	201.0	23.0	…	40.0
Mozambique	2008	38.7	19.5	112.1[2]	19.2	5.35[2]	…	…	…	…	…	…	…	…	…
Myanmar (Burma)	2008	17.2	9.2	49.1	12.0	1.92	2002	477.0	74.0	…	…	258.0	57.0	…	92.0
Namibia	2008	25.5	12.5	48.1[2]	13.0	3.06[2]	…	…	…	…	…	…	…	…	…
Nauru	2009	29.8	9.0	37.9[34]	20.8	3.4[10]	2008	…	43.0	98.0	…	391.0	65.0	…	79.5[7]
Nepal	2008	27.7	8.3	48.0[2]	19.4	3.10[2]	2002	472.0	63.0	…	…	203.0	…	…	86.0
Netherlands	2008	11.2	8.2	3.8	3.0	1.80	2006	11.2[17]	241.8	27.5[17]	21.8[17]	255.4	84.1	33.2	32.8[17]
Netherlands Antilles	2008	13.8	7.3	6.1	6.5	2.06	1995[35]	16.7	149.0	61.7	9.9	71.6	40.8	21.4	47.6
New Caledonia	2008	16.1	4.7	6.1[10]	11.4	2.20[10]	2004	11.6	132.0[10]	13.8	12.1	117.5[10]	49.1[10]	13.9	91.4
New Zealand	2009	14.5	6.7	4.9	7.8	2.18	2000	4.6	193.3[2]	26.7	21.2	289.3	54.4	19.1	42.8
Nicaragua	2008	23.7	4.3	26.4	19.4	2.63	2000	15.0	31.9	17.4	5.9	66.9	18.4	16.6	39.4
Niger	2008	52.2	15.2	118.9	37.0	7.83	2002	1,697.0	50.0	…	…	121.0	34.0	…	…
Nigeria	2007	39.9	16.8	109.0	23.1	5.30	2002	c. 258[36]	…	…	…	c. 167	c. 182	…	…
Northern Mariana Islands	2008	22.8	3.0	6.1	19.8	2.30	2000[37]	…	…	…	…	…	…	…	30.8
Norway	2008	12.6	8.7	2.7	3.9	1.96	2007	17.7	231.3	24.3	29.5	310.2	90.1	26.1	50.7
Oman	2008	20.3	2.6	8.7	17.7	2.61	2002	39.0	37.0	17.0[3]	…	126.0	…	…	35.0
Pakistan	2007	25.6	6.8	75.2	18.8	3.13	2003	104.0	41.8	…	…	96.5	67.0	…	42.6
Palau	2007	12.4	7.9	7.2	4.5	2.00	2002	138.0	61.0	…	…	244.0	45.0	…	34.0
Panama	2008	20.3	4.5	12.8	15.8	2.62[10]	2008	35.3	75.2	26.5[3]	3.5	123.8	45.3	10.3	40.7
Papua New Guinea	2008	29.3	9.6	60.0	19.7	3.70	2002	c. 249	50.0	…	…	153.0	c. 65	…	c. 53
Paraguay	2007	25.0	5.6	32.4	19.4	3.30[17]	2007	15.7	54.3	30.6	4.7	96.8	23.0	14.4	41.7
Peru	2007	20.2	8.5	30.5	11.7	2.46	2002	…	112.0	14.0[3]	…	113.0	27.0	…	60.0
Philippines	2005	24.1	5.6	21.9[10]	18.5	3.41	2004	…	49.0	…	…	148.4	61.8	…	41.3
Poland	2008	10.9	10.0	5.6	0.9	1.39	2007	6.0	243.8	17.7	12.8	449.6	51.0	44.0	64.9
Portugal	2008	9.8	9.8	3.3	0.0	1.37	2008	19.7[5]	226.1	48.2[5]	19.6[5]	318.2	109.0	43.1	54.7[7]
Puerto Rico	2008	12.1	7.3	8.3	4.8	1.65	2005	41.5	123.7	71.3[3]	32.3[11]	213.2	76.1	40.9[11]	63.4[11]
Qatar	2008	11.9	1.3	7.7	10.6	2.80[17]	2008	2.1	12.1	7.0	2.2	19.5	5.3	3.2	30.0
Réunion	2007	18.7	5.0	6.1	13.7	2.45[2]	2005	…	118.8	30.4[3]	…	168.6	39.1	32.5	29.9
Romania	2008	10.3	11.8	11.0	–1.5	1.35	2004	13.5	204.1	10.5	8.7	739.0	63.5	70.2	62.5
Russia	2008	12.1	14.7	8.5	–2.6	1.51	2008	24.0	203.0	16.9[5]	20.2[5]	833.0	55.0	63.0	165.0
Rwanda	2008	42.4	14.5	62.0	27.9	5.5	…	…	…	…	…	…	…	…	…
St. Kitts and Nevis	2008	17.7	8.2	14.3	9.5	2.28	2005	28.3	89.1	77.0	26.3	269.4	38.5	28.4	28.4
St. Lucia	2008	13.7	7.6	25.2	6.1	2.20	2005	47.9	109.8	77.4[5]	13.9[24]	228.8	63.7	17.7[24]	51.6
St. Vincent and the Grenadines	2007	16.0	6.9	16.1	9.1	2.06	2003	49.0	114.2	115.2	7.1	252.4	42.2	20.4	34.5
Samoa	2006	27.3	4.0	20.4	23.3	4.2	2002	89.0	22.2[38]	24.9[3, 38]	8.0	56.3[38]	43.0	29.0	21.7[38]
San Marino	2009	11.2	6.1	2.9[12]	5.1	1.50	2009	…	251.0	…	…	346.4	22.2[39]	6.3[40]	22.2
Sao Tome and Principe	2008	31.8	7.4	43.9[2]	24.4	5.62[2]	2002	253.7	69.0	…	…	198.6	…	…	74.3
Saudi Arabia	2008	24.1	3.9	17.9[10]	20.2	3.10	2002	…	44.0	20.0	…	144.0	…	…	…
Senegal	2008	38.9	11.5	61.4[2]	27.4	5.0	2002	c. 385	…	…	…	c. 119[41]	c. 165	…	c. 81
Serbia[42]	2008	9.4	14.0	6.7	–4.6	1.40[10]	2006	6.1	284.9[12]	35.6	15.4	780.2[12]	53.6[12]	44.5	49.2
Seychelles	2009	18.1	7.8	10.8	10.3	2.38	2007	60.0	136.4	30.6[3]	15.3	222.3	89.4	47.0	249.3
Sierra Leone	2008	45.8	21.8	163.0[17]	24.0	6.49[17]	2002	1,343.0	75.6	…	…	180.5	…	…	215.2
Singapore[43]	2008	10.2	4.4	2.1	5.8	1.28	2008	5.9	105.0	11.4	1.5	119.7	61.8	7.8	20.8
Slovakia	2008	10.6	9.8	5.9	0.8	1.33	2005	4.3	220.3	14.2	12.7	540.5	57.8	51.7	58.1
Slovenia	2008	10.8	9.1	2.4	1.7	1.53	2008	7.1	284.9	15.6	13.8	357.8	56.6	58.8	74.9
Solomon Islands	2008	28.5	3.8	19.7	24.7	3.65	2002	…	43.0	…	…	157.0	45.0	…	…
Somalia	2005	45.0	16.0	110.1	29.0	6.45	…	…	…	…	…	…	…	…	…
South Africa	2005	23.2	14.2	45.7[44]	9.0	2.38[44]	2005	300.6	72.7	56.7	33.7	167.7	167.3	34.4	113.3
Spain	2008	11.3	8.4	4.0	2.9	1.46	2007	17.2	228.2	17.1	36.9	274.1	97.2	43.4	35.1
Sri Lanka	2008	18.8	5.9	11.0[2]	12.9	1.88	2002	…	101.0	…	…	252.0	82.0	…	81.0
Sudan	2006	35.3	15.2	96.8	20.1	4.79	…	…	…	…	…	…	…	…	…
Suriname	2006	17.6	5.5	20.8	12.1	2.05	2002	172.0	87.0	32.0[3]	…	265.0	…	…	76.0
Swaziland	2008	29.1	14.9	72.6	14.2	3.45	2002	c. 1,846	c. 71	…	…	…	c. 126	…	…
Sweden	2008	11.8	9.9	2.5	1.9	1.91	2001	12.4	247.5[10]	25.3	24.0	415.2[10]	62.3[10]	33.0	53.3
Switzerland	2008	10.1	8.0	4.0	2.1	1.48	2007	8.4	211.0	23.0[17]	37.1[17]	297.8	49.2	32.3[17]	49.8
Syria	2008	25.6	3.7	17.3	21.9	3.23	2002	…	56.0	…	…	156.0	…	…	38.0
Taiwan	2009	8.3	6.2	5.9[17]	2.1	1.05[12]	2008	…	168.9	34.9[3]	…	129.8	60.9	21.3	48.6
Tajikistan	2007	27.3	7.0	43.6	20.3	3.09	2004[47]	30.5[24]	58.2	6.8[24]	7.8[24]	363.7	78.7	35.9	37.0
Tanzania	2008	38.3	12.6	73.0[2]	25.7	4.93[2]	…	…	…	…	…	…	…	…	…
Thailand	2008	13.6	7.1	18.1	6.5	1.64	2000	c. 170[5]	c. 97[5]	13.0	17.3	c. 135[5, 41]	34.1	14.6	c. 52[5]
Togo	2008	36.7	9.1	58.2	27.6	4.85	2002	c. 572	…	…	…	…	c. 180	…	…
Tonga	2008	25.3	5.7	20.0[2]	19.6	3.76	2004[15]	26.7	71.3	51.5	9.9	149.6	39.6	19.8	34.7
Trinidad and Tobago	2008	14.1	7.7	32.2[10]	6.4[10]	1.73[10]	2002	52.8	99.9	109.0	15.0	278.7	36.5	30.9	52.9
Tunisia	2008	17.7	5.8	18.4	11.9	2.06	2002	…	57.0	…	…	267.0	…	…	62.0
Turkey	2008	17.7	3.0	17.0	14.7	2.10	2008	5.9	46.4	4.5	0.2	143.4	3.2	3.3	8.3
Turkmenistan	2008	21.8	8.2	55.2[2]	13.6	2.48	1998	65.6[5]	60.9[5]	9.2	5.8	462.1[5, 41]	77.6[5]	30.2	59.3
Tuvalu	2008	21.8	9.5	19.5[10]	12.3	3.70	2007	…	…	51.8[3]	…	35.0	7.0	…	…
Uganda	2008	48.2	12.3	66.0	35.9	6.81	…	…	…	…	…	…	…	…	…
Ukraine	2008	11.1	16.3	10.0	–5.2	1.30[10]	2005	36.6	193.2	7.2	14.1	1,037.6	59.4	67.3	32.2
United Arab Emirates	2007	16.1	2.2	7.8	13.9	2.43	2002	17.6	34.1	…	…	119.6	…	…	61.9
United Kingdom	2008	12.9	9.4	4.7	3.5	1.94	2007	8.6[7]	255.8	10.4[3]	28.1[7]	319.7	128.5	48.8	22.4
United States	2008	14.0	8.1	6.5	5.9	2.09[10]	2007	20.9[11]	185.7	23.5[3]	32.2[11]	266.4[41]	77.0	29.8[11]	38.8
Uruguay	2008	14.6	9.4	12.0[10]	5.2	2.02[10]	2004	20.2	221.2	31.3	40.0	319.5	93.5	35.3	53.4
Uzbekistan	2009	23.3	4.7	11.9	18.6	2.91[2]	2005	15.2[6]	35.6	29.5[6]	12.3[6]	297.5	41.5	31.7	37.0
Vanuatu	2008	31.1	5.5	55.2[17]	25.6	4.40	2002	112.6	50.3	…	…	194.5	65.3	26.1	…
Venezuela	2007	21.5	5.1	23.0[2]	16.4	2.58	2005	21.6	67.9	31.4	6.7	132.5	28.2	18.2	63.9
Vietnam	2008	18.1	6.0	23.0	12.1	2.02	2002	93.6	80.4	…	…	200.7	64.3	…	60.8
Virgin Islands (U.S.)	2007	12.6	6.4	7.9	6.2	1.91	2002	27.5	114.6	25.6	19.3[11]	15	19.3[11]	24.9[11]	31.6
West Bank	2005	32.4	4.0	19.6	28.4	4.40	…	…	…	…	…	…	…	…	…
Western Sahara	2005	41.2	12.6	75.7	28.6	5.94	…	…	…	…	…	…	…	…	…
Yemen	2008	36.2	7.7	61.5[17]	28.5	5.20	2002	c. 171	…	…	…	c. 184	c. 126	…	c. 77
Zambia	2008	38.8	18.5	90.4	20.3	5.39[2]	…	…	…	…	…	…	…	…	…
Zimbabwe	2008	31.6	17.3	33.9	14.3	3.72	1990	64.7	c. 54[5]	4.9	9.4	c. 142[5]	c. 84[5]	12.1	44.9

[1]Excludes nomadic tribes. [2]2006. [3]Diabetes mellitus only. [4]2006–07. [5]2002. [6]2004. [7]2003. [8]2003–05. [9]Includes nonresidential marriages. [10]2007. [11]2000. [12]2008. [13]Based on national sample registration system. [14]Based on a sample survey of 4,831 households. [15]Hospital-diagnosed deaths only. [16]Includes mental disorders. [17]2005. [18]Residents only. [19]Based on urban sample populations. [20]Based on 2008 national sample survey (a sampling fraction of 0.887%). [21]Millions of households. [22]Projected rates based on about 79% of total deaths. [23]1999. [24]2001. [25]2007–08. [26]Abortions performed abroad. [27]Excludes Abkhazia and South Ossetia. [28]Includes Abkhazia and South Ossetia. [29]1996–98. [30]1995. [31]1996. [32]Data based on the National Family Health Survey

expectation of life at birth (latest year)		nuptiality, family, and family planning															country
		marriages			age at marriage (latest)						families (F), households (H) (latest)						
					groom (percent)			bride (percent)			families (households)		children		induced abortions		
male	female	year	total number	rate per 1,000 population	19 and under	20–29	30 and over	19 and under	20–29	30 and over	total ('000)	size	number under age 15	percent within marriage	number	ratio per 100 live births	
61.6	67.8	2004	11,200	4.4	3.8	73.1	23.1	9.5	73.8	16.7	H 607	H 4.2	...	82.2	12,870	25.9	Mongolia
71.2	76.1	2008	3,445	5.5	1.1	52.9	46.0	11.3	64.9	23.8	H 184	H 3.3	...	...	1,699	20.5	Montenegro
71.4	73.9	...	...	...	...	...	...	...	...	...	H 6,234	H 5.0	H 2.5	...	...	...	Morocco
41.2	40.4	...	...	...	...	...	...	...	...	...	F 4,270	F 4.2	F 2.0	73.1	...	...	Mozambique
60.7	65.3	...	...	...	...	...	...	...	...	...	H 8,550	H 5.0	...	...	...	...	Myanmar (Burma)
44.5	42.3	...	...	...	...	...	...	...	...	...	H 396	H 4.9	...	...	...	...	Namibia
52.5	58.2	1995	57	5.3	...	...	...	...	...	...	H 2	H 6.5	H 2.6	...	...	...	Nauru
63.6	64.5	...	...	...	...	...	...	...	...	...	H 4,600	H 5.4	H 2.3	...	...	...	Nepal
78.4	82.4	2008	75,800	4.6	0.2	30.5	69.3	1.8	46.2	52.0	H 7,242	H 2.2	H 0.4	58.9	29,450	14.6	Netherlands
72.8	79.9	2006	1,104	5.8	...	...	...	...	...	...	H 76	H 2.6	H 2.1	51.6	...	...	Netherlands Antilles
71.8	80.3	2007	884	3.6	0.1	30.2	69.7	2.7	45.9	51.4	H 62	H 3.6	...	30.8	1,466	33.7	New Caledonia
78.4	82.4	2009	21,628	5.0	1.0	39.1	59.9	2.8	48.3	48.9	H 1,550	H 2.8	H 0.7	51.9	17,531	30.4	New Zealand
69.1	73.4	2003	20,411	3.9	...	...	...	...	...	...	H 1,044	H 4.9	...	...	...	...	Nicaragua
51.0	53.4	...	...	...	...	...	...	...	...	...	H 1,883	H 6.2	...	...	...	...	Niger
46.4	47.3	...	...	...	...	...	...	...	...	...	H 24,554	H 4.9	...	...	...	...	Nigeria
73.9	79.3	...	...	...	...	...	...	...	...	...	H 19	H 4.1	H 1.5	40.2	...	...	Northern Mariana Islands
78.3	83.0	2008	25,125	5.2	0.4	28.1	71.5	2.0	44.6	53.4	H 2,143	H 2.2	...	45.0	16,054	26.5	Norway
73.2	75.4	...	...	...	...	...	...	...	...	...	H 343	H 6.8	...	...	...	...	Oman
63.6	68.0	...	...	...	...	...	...	...	...	...	H 21,350	H 6.5	...	...	...	...	Pakistan
66.3	72.1	...	...	...	...	...	...	...	...	...	H 5	H 3.9	...	...	44	...	Palau
73.7	79.5	2008	11,508	3.4	1.2	41.0	57.8	6.1	49.8	44.1	H 770	H 4.1	H 1.5	17.3	11	0.02	Panama
55.0	60.0	...	...	...	...	...	...	...	...	...	H 1,138	H 4.8	...	...	...	...	Papua New Guinea
69.6	73.8	2007	19,726	3.2	3.1	61.0	35.8	20.7	57.0	22.1	H 1,368	H 4.3	H 1.9	40.0	4,020	...	Paraguay
68.3	72.0	2003	51,500	1.9	...	...	...	...	...	...	H 6,754	H 4.3	...	57.8	...	...	Peru
67.0	72.9	2006	492,666	5.7	3.3	63.6	33.1	13.5	65.4	21.1	F 15,967	H 4.8	F 2.4	93.9	2,315	...	Philippines
71.3	80.0	2008	257,700	6.8	1.3	73.3	25.4	7.2	77.6	15.2	H 13,337	H 2.8	...	80.1	199	0.06	Poland
75.5	81.7	2008	43,228	4.1	1.4	60.2	38.4	6.9	65.3	27.8	H 3,474	H 3.0	H 0.8	63.8	906	0.8	Portugal
74.8	82.3	2003	25,236	6.5	5.1	50.1	44.8	13.1	50.0	36.9	H 1,278	H 3.2	H 1.0	59.6	...	...	Puerto Rico
74.4	75.8	2008	3,235	2.2	1.7	62.3	36.0	14.8	66.7	18.4	H 100	H 7.4	...	...	172	1.3	Qatar
73.2	80.9	2003	3,212	4.2	0.5	39.9	59.6	4.5	53.1	42.4	H 250	H 3.0	...	32.0	4,385	29.7	Réunion
69.5	76.7	2008	149,400	6.9	1.1	66.8	32.1	15.3	65.2	19.5	H 7,320	H 2.8	...	72.6	224,807	106	Romania
61.7	74.2	2008	1,178,700	8.3	6.5	64.5	29.0	28.5	47.7	23.8	H 51,209	H 2.8	H 0.8	73.1	1,797,567	120	Russia
54.6	57.1	...	...	...	...	...	...	...	...	...	H 2,286	H 4.3	H 2.3	94.9	...	...	Rwanda
70.1	78.0	2001	325	7.1	9.8	42.5	47.7	15.6	50.8	33.6	H 23	H 2.9	H 1.4	19.2	...	...	St. Kitts and Nevis
72.0	75.8	2004	459	2.8	0.2	29.2	70.6	2.5	41.3	56.2	H 49	H 3.2	H 2.0	14.0	...	...	St. Lucia
71.4	75.0	2003	491	4.7	1.0	37.0	62.0	4.8	46.3	48.9	H 27	H 3.9	H 2.0	15.6	...	...	St. Vincent and the Grenadines
71.5	74.2	2001	821	4.6	1.2	45.3	53.5	8.6	56.3	35.1	H 25	H 7.2	...	43.5	...	...	Samoa
80.1	85.7	2009	238	7.2	—	24.4	75.2	0.4	27.3	35.2	H 14	H 2.3	H 0.4	74.8	...	...	San Marino
63.5	68.5	2003	...	2.2	...	...	...	...	...	...	H 26	H 5.5	...	...	...	...	Sao Tome and Principe
70.9	75.3	2003	98,343	4.1	...	...	...	...	...	...	H 4,208	H 6.0	...	100.0	5[26]	...	Saudi Arabia
55.0	57.7	...	...	...	...	...	...	...	...	...	H 1,157	H 8.7	...	...	...	...	Senegal
71.1	76.3	2008	38,285	5.2	1.1	52.3	46.4	8.9	62.1	28.5	H 2,521	H 3.0	...	76.7	26,645	34.1	Serbia[42]
68.4	78.0	2009[20]	450	5.2	0.9	38.7	60.4	3.8	48.0	48.2	H 23	H 3.7	H 1.9	20.3	446	29.8	Seychelles
40.1	43.5	...	...	...	...	...	...	...	...	...	H 860	H 6.0	...	...	...	...	Sierra Leone
78.4	83.2	2008	24,596	5.1	0.5	43.4	56.1	2.3	63.9	33.8	H 1,156	H 3.5	H 1.3	...	12,070	32.5	Singapore[43]
70.9	78.7	2005	26,149	4.9	2.6	64.8	32.6	8.4	73.4	18.2	H 2,100	H 2.9	...	69.9	15,307	28.5	Slovakia
75.4	82.3	2008	6,703	3.3	0.4	41.1	58.5	2.0	58.5	39.5	H 685	H 2.6	...	47.1	6,403	35.3	Slovenia
70.9	76.1	...	...	...	...	...	...	...	...	...	H 67	H 6.2	...	...	...	...	Solomon Islands
48.0	51.1	...	...	...	...	...	...	...	...	...	...	H 5.8	...	...	...	...	Somalia
53.5	57.2	2008	186,522	3.8	0.2	33.2	66.6	2.0	49.9	48.1	H 11,400	H 4.0	...	75.9	82,686	10.8	South Africa
79.1	85.2	2008	194,022	4.2	0.2	33.5	66.3	0.9	47.5	51.6	H 15,600	H 2.7	...	67.9	84,985	18.7	Spain
68.8	76.3	2008	198,578	9.8	1.3	64.3	34.4	16.7	67.1	16.2	H 4,450	H 4.1[45]	...	96.3	...	...	Sri Lanka
47.1	48.8	...	...	...	...	...	...	...	...	...	H 6,300	H 6.2	...	...	...	...	Sudan
70.3	75.8	2004	1,951	4.0	1.1	48.0	50.9	19.4	46.3	34.3	H 109	H 4.0	...	...	...	...	Suriname
47.8	48.2	...	...	...	...	...	...	...	...	...	H 169	H 4.6	...	...	...	...	Swaziland
79.1	83.2	2008	50,332	5.4	0.1	20.0	79.9	1.8	34.2	64.0	H 4,320	H 2.0	H 0.5	45.4	38,053	34.8	Sweden
79.7	84.4	2008	41,534	5.4	0.1	20.0	79.9	1.8	34.2	64.0	H 3,362	H 2.2	H 0.4	82.9	11,792	16.3	Switzerland
71.6	76.4	2008[46]	379,319	16.7	...	...	...	...	...	...	H 3,460	H 5.2	F 2.4	...	...	...	Syria
75.6	82.3	2009	117,099	5.1	1.5	62.3	36.2	6.0	77.7	16.3	H 7,806	H 3.0	H 1.0	95.6	42,282	14.9	Taiwan
61.6	67.8	2005	52,352	7.6	8.6	80.0	11.4	39.2	56.0	4.8	H 1,265	H 5.2	H 2.7	90.8	18,822	10.6	Tajikistan
48.5	50.9	...	...	...	...	...	...	...	...	...	H 7,150	H 4.8	H 2.3	...	...	...	Tanzania
70.5	75.3	2006	356,187	5.5	...	...	...	...	...	...	H 17,853	H 3.5	...	...	...	...	Thailand
57.0	61.6	...	...	...	...	...	...	...	...	...	H 812	H 6.0	...	...	...	...	Togo
72.4	74.4	2003	697	6.9	8.3	63.5	28.2	22.6	59.0	18.4	F 18	H 5.8	F 2.7	80.6	...	...	Tonga
67.6	73.5	2002	7,434	5.8	1.5	46.6	51.9	10.5	53.9	35.6	H 347	H 3.8	H 1.3	...	...	—	Trinidad and Tobago
72.4	76.3	2008	78,748	5.2	0.3	33.5	64.7	7.2	63.9	28.6	H 2,210	H 4.3	H 1.9	99.8	19,000	10.6	Tunisia
71.4	75.8	2008	641,973	9.0	2.8	71.5	24.9	24.6	59.8	13.1	H 15,071	H 4.1	...	...	...	...	Turkey
59.1	67.4	1998	25,000	5.4	3.0	87.4	9.6	16.1	77.1	6.8	H 850	H 5.7	H 2.4	96.2	32,000	28.8	Turkmenistan
66.4	71.0	...	...	...	...	...	...	...	...	...	H 1.8	H 5.3	H 2.2	92.1	...	...	Tuvalu
51.3	53.4	...	...	...	...	...	...	...	...	...	H 5,255	H 5.2	...	...	...	...	Uganda
62.5	74.2	2008	321,992	7.0	3.7	64.9	31.4	20.0	57.6	22.4	H 18,250	H 2.6	H 0.8	79.1	289,065	67.7	Ukraine
73.2	78.3	2004	12,794	2.9	...	...	...	...	...	...	H 661	H 5.1	...	...	66[26]	...	United Arab Emirates
77.6	81.7	2004	311,180	5.2	0.7	35.3	64.0	2.6	45.9	51.5	H 24,200	H 2.4	H 1.7	54.6	197,913	29.6	United Kingdom
75.2	80.4	2005	2,230,000	7.5	4.3	51.8	43.9	10.9	55.8	35.3	H 114,384	H 2.6	F 1.0	64.2	1,293,000	31.9	United States
72.4	79.7	2007	12,771	3.8	2.6	51.5	45.9	11.1	55.4	33.5	H 1,090	H 2.9	H 0.9	42.9	...	...	Uruguay
61.2	68.1	2009	277,600	10.0	5.2	84.9	9.9	36.7	57.8	5.5	H 4,640	H 5.6	H 2.4	95.8	54,900	10.4	Uzbekistan
65.6	69.0	...	...	...	...	...	...	...	...	...	H 46	H 5.3	H 2.2	...	113	2.4	Vanuatu
70.7	76.6	2004	74,103	2.8	5.8	56.2	38.0	19.3	55.4	25.3	H 6,080	H 4.5	H 2.2	47.0	...	...	Venezuela
69.0	74.2	2002	964,701	12.1	...	...	...	...	...	...	H 18,590	H 4.4	H 1.9	...	1,000,000	59.0	Vietnam
75.8	82.0	2001[9]	4,087	37.4	0.4	33.6	66.0	1.9	45.9	52.2	H 43	H 2.5	H 1.0	30.2	...	...	Virgin Islands (U.S.)
71.3	74.9	2004[48]	27,634	...	7.8	73.8	18.4	53.8	40.5	5.7	...	...	...	...	...	...	West Bank
48.7	51.3	...	...	...	...	...	...	...	...	...	...	...	...	...	...	...	Western Sahara
60.7	64.7	...	...	...	...	...	...	...	...	...	H 3,108	H 7.1	...	...	...	...	Yemen
38.0	38.2	...	...	...	...	...	...	...	...	...	H 2,116	H 5.1	H 2.1	...	...	...	Zambia
45.1	43.5	...	...	...	...	...	...	...	...	...	H 2,620	H 4.5	H 1.1	95.8	...	...	Zimbabwe

2005–06, comprising 515,507 people in 109,041 households. [33]Albanian population only. [34]2003–07; based on 2007 Republic of Nauru Demographic and Health Survey. [35]Includes Aruba. [36]HIV/AIDS. [37]Natural causes of death: 177.7 per 100,000 population. [38]2005–06. [39]Pneumonia only. [40]Liver disease only. [41]Cardiovascular disease only. [42]Excludes Kosovo. [43]Based on de jure population. [44]2009. [45]Excludes 7 districts in northern and eastern Sri Lanka. [46]Syrian Arabs only. [47]Projected rates based on about 56% of total deaths. [48]Includes Gaza Strip.

National product and accounts

This table furnishes, for most of the countries of the world, breakdowns of (1) gross national income (GNI)—its global and per capita values, and purchasing power parity (PPP), (2) growth rates (2000–05) and principal industrial and accounting components of gross domestic product (GDP), and (3) principal elements of each country's external public debt outstanding and balance of payments, including international goods trade, invisibles, and tourism payments.

Measures of national output. The two most commonly used measures of national output are GDP and GNI. Each of these measures represents an aggregate value of goods and services produced by a specific country. The GDP, the more basic of these, is a measure of the total value of goods and services produced entirely within a given country. The GNI, the more comprehensive value, is composed of both domestic production (GDP) and the net income from current (short-term) transactions with other countries. When the income received from other countries is greater than payments to them, a country's GNI is greater than its GDP. In theory, if all national accounts could be equilibrated, the global summation of GDP would equal GNI.

In the first section of the table, data are presented for the nominal GNI, the nominal GNI per capita, and the GNI purchasing power parity per capita. "Nominal" refers to value in current prices for the year indicated. Purchasing power parity (PPP) is an economic theory used to determine the number of units in a country's currency that are required to buy the same amount of goods and services in another country. PPP is expressed in a common currency, usually U.S. dollars, and as such it is often used to compare the standards of living between countries. PPPs per capita in this table are nearly always values calculated by the World Bank. Beside the GNI are given figures for annual growth of total and per capita "real" GDP ("real" figures being adjusted to eliminate the effect of recent inflation [most often] or, occasionally, of deflation between two given dates) along with average annual population growth rates for the same span of years. Values should be compared cautiously, as they are subject to a number of distortions, notably of exchange rate, but also of PPP and in the existence of elements of national production that do not enter the monetary economy in such a way as to be visible to fiscal authorities (*e.g.*, food, clothing, or housing produced and consumed within families or communal groups or services exchanged). "Real" GDP data in this section are taken from the World Bank *World Development Indicators* whereas population growth rates are based on EB calculations.

The internal structure of the national product. GDP/GNI values allow comparison of the relative size of national economies, but further information is provided when these aggregates are analyzed according to their industrial sectors of origin and component kinds of expenditure.

The distribution of GDP for ten industrial sectors, usually compiled from national sources, is aggregated into three major industrial groups:

1. The primary sector, composed of agriculture (including forestry and fishing) and mineral production (including fossil fuels).
2. The secondary sector, composed of manufacturing, construction, and public utilities.

National product and accounts

country	gross national income (GNI), 2010			gross domestic product (GDP), 2000–05			origin of gross domestic product (GDP) by economic sector, 2005 (%)										
	nominal ('000,000 U.S.$)	per capita		average annual growth rates, 2000–05			primary		secondary			tertiary					other
		nominal (U.S.$)	purchasing power parity (PPP; U.S.$)	real GDP (%)	population (%)	real GDP per capita (%)	agriculture	mining	manufacturing	construction	public utilities	transp., communications	trade	financial svcs.	other svcs.	government	
Afghanistan	8,309[1]	319[1]	700[2]	12.0	3.3	8.7	—38—		15	—9—		9	8	6	4	7	4
Albania	12,677	4,000	8,840	5.3	0.4	4.9	—21—		8[2]	13[2]	…	8[2]	20[2]	[2, 3]	10[2]	20[2, 3]	—
Algeria	157,939	4,460	8,130	5.2	1.5	3.7	8	45	5	—7—		—19—				9	7
American Samoa	334[4]	5,800[4]	…	…	…	…	…	…	…	…	…	…	…	…	…	…	…
Andorra	3,337[1]	44,960[1]	39,000[4]	…	…	…	…	…	…	…	…	…	…	…	…	…	…
Angola	75,150	3,960	5,430	9.9	2.5	7.4	8[5]	53[5]	4[5]	4[5]	—	—15[5]—		—14[5]—			2[5]
Antigua and Barbuda	939	10,610	15,380	3.8	0.9	2.9	3	1	2	14	3	17	17	14	6	14	9
Argentina	343,636	8,450	15,150	2.2	1.0	1.2	10[5]	6[5]	23[5]	3[5]	2[5]	8[5]	13[5]	15[5]	10[5]	5[5]	5[5]
Armenia	9,556	3,090	5,450	12.4	–0.4	12.8	23[2]	[7]	19[2, 7]	15[2]	4[2]	6[2]	11[2]	5[2]	7[2]	3[2]	7[2]
Aruba	2,244[1]	21,600[1]	22,500[4]	…	…	…	—	—	3[6]	6[6]	6[6]	9[6]	24[6]	26[6]	11[6]	12[6]	3[6]
Australia	957,529[8]	43,770[8]	38,210[8]	3.2	1.2	2.0	3[5]	2[5]	11[5]	6[5]	2[5]	8[5]	13[5]	27[5]	14[5]	4[5]	10[5]
Austria	391,511	46,710	39,410	1.5	0.4	1.1	3	—	18[2]	7[2]	2[2]	7[2]	16[2]	20[2]	13[2]	5[2]	10[2]
Azerbaijan	45,983	5,180	9,220	12.7	0.8	11.9	9	[7]	47[7]	10	1	9	7	—14—		3	—
Bahamas, The	6,077[1]	18,600[1]	21,500[1]	…	…	…	5[9]	8[9]	3[9]	2[9]	—[9]	10[9]	20[9]	…	…	…	…
Bahrain	15,229[1]	20,600[1]	18,770[4]	…	…	…	—	26	13	4	1	1	12	32	4	13	–6
Bangladesh	104,478	640	1,620	5.4	1.4	4.0	20[2]	1[2]	15[2]	8[2]	1[2]	11[2]	14[2]	10[2]	14[2]	3[2]	3[2]
Barbados	3,307[1]	11,300[1]	12,240[1]	3.5	0.3	3.2	3	1	6	5	3	5	24	16	5	13	19
Belarus	58,169	6,030	14,020	7.5	–0.5	8.0	10	[7]	31[7]	8	—	11	12	—28—			—
Belgium	493,526	45,420	37,840	1.5	0.3	1.2	1	—	15	4	2	8	13	25	15	6	11
Belize	1,288	3,740	5,970	4.0	3.1	0.9	12	1	8	4	3	11	20	16	7	10	8
Benin	6,945	750	1,510	4.0	2.9	1.1	33	—	8	4	1	8	17	—21—			8
Bermuda	5,056[1]	78,500[1]	…	…	…	…	1	[7]	8[7]	…	2	6	13	57	9	5	—
Bhutan	1,361	1,920	5,070	8.8	2.8	6.0	25[2]	1[2]	7[2]	19[2]	9[2]	8[2]	10[2]	6[2]	—12[2]—		3[2]
Bolivia	17,982	1,790	4,560	3.0	1.7	1.3	15[2]	10[2]	17[2]	3[2]	2[2]	11[2]	11[2]	12[2]	5[2]	9[2]	5[2]
Bosnia and Herzegovina	18,015	4,790	8,970	5.0	0.4	4.6	9[2]	2[2]	10[2]	4[2]	6[2]	9[2]	14[2]	6[2]	11[2]	10[2]	19[2]
Botswana	13,633	6,890	13,910	5.9	0.1	5.8	2	33	4	5	3	4	12	12	4	16	5
Brazil	1,830,392	9,390	10,920	2.2	1.5	0.7	9[5]	4[5]	22[5]	7[5]	3[5]	5[5]	7[5]	16[5]	14[5]	9[5]	4[5]
Brunei	11,481[1]	30,100[1]	…	…	…	…	1	49	12	3	1	9	3	9	1	12	—
Bulgaria	47,159	6,240	13,210	5.0	–0.6	5.6	8	[7]	17[7]	4	4	12	7	4	—29—		15
Burkina Faso	9,031	550	1,260	5.1	3.6	1.5	29[5]	1[5]	15[5]	4[5]	—[5]	6[5]	18[5]	—22[5]—			5[5]
Burundi	1,402	160	390	2.2	3.3	–1.1	32	1	12	5	—	5	—30—				15
Cambodia	10,686	760	2,040	8.9	1.7	7.2	32	—	18	6	1	7	13	7	9	2	5
Cameroon	23,169	1,160	2,190	3.7	2.2	1.5	20[2]	7[2]	18[2]	3[2]	1[2]	7[2]	20[2]	1[2]	—17[2]—		6[2]
Canada	1,422,977[8]	42,170[8]	37,590[8]	2.5	1.0	1.5	2	4	16	6	3	5	15	24	20	6	–1
Cape Verde	1,620	3,160	3,670	5.5	1.8	3.7	9	[7]	8[7]	9	—	19	21	9	2	12	11
Cayman Islands	1,443[1]	32,100[1]	…	…	…	…	—4—		2	10	—	11	23	—49—			1
Central African Republic	2,067	460	760	–1.4	1.3	–2.7	54[5]	7[5]	2[5]	4[5]	1[5]	4[5]	10[5]	—6[5]—		7[5]	5[5]
Chad	6,929	600	1,180	14.5	3.0	11.5	21	43	5	2	—	—13—		—8—		7	1
Chile	170,284	9,940	13,890	4.3	1.1	3.2	6[2]	8[2]	16[2]	8[2]	3[2]	8[2]	11[2]	20[2]	11[2]	4[2]	5[2]
China	5,700,018	4,260	7,570	9.6	0.6	9.0	14[5]	[7]	45[5, 7]	7[5]	—[5]	6[5]	8[5]	8[5]	9[5]	3[5]	—[5]
Colombia	255,290	5,510	9,000	3.5	1.6	1.9	12[2]	7[2]	14[2]	5[2]	5[2]	7[2]	11[2]	15[2]	—20[2]—		—[2]
Comoros	550	820	1,180	3.0	2.2	0.8	51	…	4	5	2	9	17	6	—	10	–4
Congo, Dem. Rep. of the	11,951	180	310	4.4	2.8	1.6	47[2]	10[2]	5[2]	4[2]	3[2]	4[2]	16[2]	—7[2]—		2[2]	2[2]
Congo, Rep. of the	8,698	2,310	3,280	3.9	3.0	0.9	6[2]	52[2]	6[2]	4[2]	1[2]	6[2]	9[2]	—7[2]—		7[2]	2[2]
Costa Rica	30,518	6,580	10,880	4.2	1.5	2.7	8	—	20	4	3	9	18	13	17	4	4
Côte d'Ivoire	22,976	1,070	1,650	–0.1	2.1	–2.1	23[2]	1[2]	16[2]	3[2]	2[2]	5[2]	14[2]	—28[2]—			8[2]
Croatia	60,965	13,760	18,710	4.7	0.3	4.4	6	—	20	6	—	8	15	15	—17—		13
Cuba	51,504[1]	4,600[1]	…	3.4	0.3	3.1	4	1	11	7	1	8	24	6	—36—		2
Curaçao	…	…	…	…	…	…	…	…	…	…	…	…	…	…	…	…	…
Cyprus[13]	18,191[1]	23,700[1]	21,480[4]	3.8	1.4	2.4	3	—	9	8	2	8	19	23	13	10	5
Czech Republic	188,269	17,870	23,620	3.5	–0.1	3.6	3	2	26	7	4	10	12	17	13	6	—
Denmark	328,252	58,960	40,140	1.2	0.3	0.9	2	3	11	5	2	8	11	20	18	5	15
Djibouti	1,106[8]	1,280[8]	2,480[8]	3.2	2.0	1.2	3	—	3	7	5	24	15	12	14	18	–1
Dominica	367	4,960	8,580	3.1	–0.7	4.8	15	1	7	7	5	10	13	12	1	16	13
Dominican Republic	49,662	4,860	8,700	2.8	1.5	1.3	11	1	13	10	2	19	19	7	7	7	4

3. The tertiary sector, which includes transportation and communications, trade (wholesale and retail, including restaurants and hotels), financial services (including banking, real estate, insurance, and business services), other services (community, social, and personal), and government services.

The category "other" contains adjustments such as import duties and bank service charges that are not distributed by sector.

There are three major domestic components of GDP expenditure: private consumption, government spending, and gross domestic investment. The fourth, nondomestic, component of GDP expenditure is net foreign trade; values are given for both exports (a positive value) and imports (a negative value, representing obligations to other countries). The sum of these five percentages, excluding statistical discrepancies and rounding, should be 100% of the GDP.

External public debt. Because the majority of the world's countries are in the less developed bloc, and because their principal financial concern is often external debt and its service, data are given for outstanding external public and publicly guaranteed long-term debt rather than for total public debt, which is the major concern in the developed countries. For comparability, the data are given in U.S. dollars. The data presented in the table come from the World Bank's *Global Development Finance* (annual).

Balance of payments (external account transactions). The external account records the sum (net) of all economic transactions of a current nature between one country and the rest of the world. The account shows a country's net of overseas receipts and obligations, including not only the trade of goods and merchandise but also such invisible items as services, interest and dividends, short- and long-term investments, tourism, transfers to or from overseas residents, etc. Each transaction gives rise either to a foreign claim for payment, recorded as a deficit (*e.g.*, from imports, capital outflows), or a foreign obligation to pay, recorded as a surplus (*e.g.*, from exports, capital inflows) or a domestic claim on another country. Any international transaction automatically creates a deficit in the balance of payments of one country and a surplus in that of another. Values are given in U.S. dollars for comparability. The data in this section are taken from *International Financial Statistics* (monthly) published by the International Monetary Fund.

Tourist trade. Net income or expenditure from tourism (in U.S. dollars for comparability) is often a significant element in a country's balance of payments. Receipts from foreign nationals reflect payments for goods and services from foreign currency resources by tourists in the given country. Expenditures by nationals abroad are also payments for goods and services, but in this case made by the residents of the given country as tourists abroad. The majority of the data in this section are compiled by the World Tourism Organization.

gross domestic product (GDP) by type of expenditure, 2006 (%)					external public debt outstanding (long-term, disbursed only), 2005						balance of payments, 2006 (current external transactions; '000,000 U.S.$)			tourist trade, 2009 ('000,000 U.S.$)		country
consumption		gross domestic invest-ment	foreign trade		total ('000,000 U.S.$)	creditors (%)		debt service			net transfers		current balance of payments	receipts from foreign nationals	expendi-tures by nationals abroad	
private	govern-ment		exports	imports		offi-cial	private	total ('000,000 U.S.$)	repayment (%)		goods, merchan-dise	invisibles				
									princi-pal	inter-est						
121	10	17	33	−81	8,000	…	…	…	…	…	…	…	…	…	…	Afghanistan
63	10	51	23	−47	1,375	93	7	66	62.1	37.9	−2,123	1,452	−670.9	1,827	1,585	Albania
29	12	32	50	−23	15,476	78.9	21.1	5,079	83.0	17.0	1,749	−1,723	25.8	267	456	Algeria
…	…	…	…	…	…	…	…	…	…	…	…	…	…	…	…	American Samoa
58	18	30	26	−32	…	…	…	…	…	…	…	…	…	…	…	Andorra
39	20	13	74	−47	9,428	33.8	66.2	2,183	88.9	11.1	15,756[4]	−10,618[4]	5,138[4]	534	133	Angola
36	20	54	61	−71	…	…	…	…	…	…	−358.0[6]	222.2[6]	−135.8[6]	304	54	Antigua and Barbuda
64	12	16	23	−15	61,952	32.8	67.2	3,232	48.3	51.7	13,976	−5,923	8,053	3,962	4,482	Argentina
72	11	29	22	−34	923	99.8	0.2	25.0	64.0	36.0	−902.7	815.4	−87.3	334	326	Armenia
52	27	33	63	−75	478.6	…	…	…	…	…	−52.6	−206.2	−258.8	1,295	305	Aruba
56	18	27	21	−22	…	…	…	…	…	…	−9,684	−31,460	−41,144	25,594	17,575	Australia
56	18	21	55	−50	…	…	…	…	…	…	641.0	9,618	10,259	19,176	10,817	Austria
36	8	32	70	−46	1,344	95.5	4.5	76.0	72.4	27.6	7,745	−4,037	3,708	350	374	Azerbaijan
68	14	33	46	−61	…	…	…	…	…	…	−852.0[4]	87.3	−764.7[4]	1,948	240	Bahamas, The
34	14	21	97	−67	…	…	…	…	…	…	3,137	−1,219	1,918	1,118	408	Bahrain
73	6	29	18	−26	17,938	97.1	2.9	754	73.6	26.4	−3,199[4]	3,023[4]	−176.2[4]	69	249	Bangladesh
67	20	19	50	−56	660	52.4	47.6	96.3	56.8	43.2	−1,086[4]	699.3[4]	−386.7[4]	1,068	71	Barbados
52	20	30	62	−64	783	72.3	27.7	215	82.3	17.7	−2,398	886	−1,512	369	588	Belarus
53	23	21	90	−87	…	…	…	…	…	…	3,915	3,940	7,855	9,967	17,923	Belgium
75	13	19	60	−67	970	32.2	67.8	226	69.0	31.0	−49.8	25.1	−24.7	256	41	Belize
76	12	21	19	−28	1,762	100.0	—	60	68.3	31.7	−273.5[2]	−43[2]	−316.5[2]	236[10]	64[10]	Benin
59	11	19	47	−36	…	…	…	…	…	…	…	…	…	368	295	Bermuda
49	22	54	40	−65	636.7	100.0	—	6.6	69.7	30.3	…	…	…	42	39	Bhutan
69	16	13	31	−28	4,564	99.5	0.5	284	64.8	35.2	481.0[4]	17.4[4]	498.4[4]	279	98	Bolivia
86	23	21	27	−57	2,560	93.9	6.1	108	50.9	49.1	−4,237	2,976	−1,261	681	236	Bosnia and Herzegovina
29	37	20	48	−34	438	97.3	2.7	50.1	77.2	22.8	1,604[4]	−135[4]	1,469[4]	452	230	Botswana
60	20	17	15	−12	94,497	27.0	73.0	16,053	57.2	42.8	46,115	−32,839	13,276	5,305	10,898	Brazil
25	22	13	71	−32	…	…	…	…	…	…	1,600[9]	−1,972[9]	−372[9]	254	477	Brunei
71	18	30	64	−83	4,587	66.2	33.8	2,099	83.9	16.1	−6,810	1,800	−5,010	4,273	1,755	Bulgaria
68	22	24	10	−24	1,920	100.0	—	41	61.0	39.0	−392.0[11]	11.2[11]	−380.8[11]	62[10]	63[10]	Burkina Faso
84	26	23	6	−39	1,228	99.8	0.2	39	69.2	30.8	−190.8	−134.3	−325.1	1.5	62	Burundi
92	0	19	69	−79	3,155	100.0	—	20	40.0	60.0	−1,056.1	718.6	−337.4	1,185	103	Cambodia
67	11	21	27	−26	5,521	98.1	1.9	548	67.0	33.0	307.7[5]	−982.9[5]	−675.2[5]	222	361	Cameroon
56	19	22	37	−34	…	…	…	…	…	…	45,146	−24,349	20,797	13,707	24,169	Canada
76	20	39	16	−52	482.3	100.0	—	31.8	79.9	20.1	−441.5	401.5	−40	292	136	Cape Verde
63	15	22	62	−61	207.5	…	…	…	…	…	…	…	…	486	102	Cayman Islands
98	7	6	12	−23	871	96.6	3.4	—	—	—	…	…	…	4.5	52	Central African Republic
24	23	24	56	−27	1,537	97.9	2.1	47	61.7	38.3	…	…	…	25[9]	80[9]	Chad
55	10	20	45	−31	9,096	12.2	87.8	1,925	76.2	23.8	2,078	3,178	5,256	1,568	1,625	Chile
36	13	43	41	−33	82,853	63.0	37.0	8,765	75.0	25.0	217,746	32,120	249,866	39,675	43,702	China
62	19	21	23	−24	22,491	46.7	53.3	6,589	70.9	29.1	322	−3,383	−3,061	1,999	1,752	Colombia
94	13	14	12	−33	259.3	100.0	—	3.9	66.7	33.3	…	…	…	…	10.8[1]	Comoros
87	8	17	31	−43	9,412	96.1	3.9	209	53.6	46.4	…	…	…	…	…	Congo, Dem. Rep. of the
24	8	25	91	−47	5,161	59.2	40.8	100	65.0	35.0	3,374	−2,471	903.2	54[12]	168[12]	Congo, Rep. of the
66	14	28	50	−57	3,470	41.3	58.7	484	75.2	24.8	−2,604	1,527	−1,077	1,799	368	Costa Rica
67	16	12	47	−42	9,007	73.8	26.2	164	73.2	26.8	3,151.9	−2,623	529.2	50[5]	192[5]	Côte d'Ivoire
55	20	27	46	−48	9,782	22.4	77.6	1,926	74.8	25.2	−10,511	7,336	−3,175	9,000	1,013	Croatia
51	39	9	15	−15	…	…	…	…	…	…	…	…	…	1,926	…	Cuba
…	…	…	…	…	…	…	…	…	…	…	…	…	…	361	209	Curaçao
66	18	21	50	−54	…	…	…	…	…	…	−5,023	3,944	−1,079	2,188	1,275	Cyprus[13]
49	22	26	74	−72	…	…	…	…	…	…	2,979	−7,565	−4,586	6,477	4,077	Czech Republic
48	25	22	53	−49	…	…	…	…	…	…	2,906	3,790	6,696	5,679[10]	9,678[10]	Denmark
62	29	20	42	−53	389	100.0	—	17.1	77.8	22.2	−280.5	181.4	−99.1	16.0	5.8	Djibouti
71	18	27	44	−60	231.5	70.1	29.9	16.5	67.9	32.1	−103.5[4]	21.9[4]	−81.6[4]	68	10	Dominica
75	10	24	33	−42	6,093	45.8	54.2	831	66.4	33.6	−4,750	3,964	−786.1	4,051	350	Dominican Republic

National product and accounts (continued)

country	gross national income (GNI), 2010			gross domestic product (GDP), 2000–05			origin of gross domestic product (GDP) by economic sector, 2005 (%)										
	nominal ('000,000 U.S.$)	per capita		average annual growth rates, 2000–05			primary		secondary			tertiary					other
		nominal (U.S.$)	purchasing power parity (PPP; U.S.$)	real GDP (%)	population (%)	real GDP per capita (%)	agriculture	mining	manufacturing	construction	public utilities	transp., communications	trade	financial svcs.	other svcs.	government	
East Timor	1,497	1,280	2,060	…	…	…	32[2]	1[2]	4[2]	9[2]	1[2]	9[2]	8[2]	9[2]	1[2]	27[2]	–1[2]
Ecuador	62,106	4,510	9,270	5.1	1.3	3.8	7	16	10	7	2	15	14	10	7	5	7
Egypt	197,922	2,340	5,910	3.7	1.8	1.9	14	[7]	32[7]	4	2	10	14	10	3	10	1
El Salvador	20,820	3,360	6,390	2.2	1.8	0.4	9[2]	1[2]	22[2]	4[2]	2[2]	10[2]	19[2]	16[2]	7[2]	7[2]	3[2]
Equatorial Guinea	10,182	14,680	23,810	18.6	2.3	16.3	3[2]	86[2]	5[2]	1[2]	—[2]	—[2]	1[2]	—[2]	1[2]	1[2]	2[2]
Eritrea	1,792	340	540	3.5	2.3	1.2	14[5]	1[5]	10[5]	10[5]	—[5]	12[5]	18[5]		— 27[5] —		8[5]
Estonia	19,247	14,360	19,500	7.5	–0.4	7.9	4	1	16	7	3	12	15	18	11	5	8
Ethiopia	32,409	380	1,010	4.2	2.5	1.7	48	1	5	5	2	5	14	9	7	5	–1
Faroe Islands	1,472[5]	30,680[5]	31,000[5]	2.4	1.1	1.3	22[11]	6[11]	3[11]	6[11]	2[11]	8[11]	11[11]	14[11]	4[11]	21[11]	3[11]
Fiji	3,085	3,610	4,490	3.1	0.9	2.2	14	1	13	5	3	17	20	12	— 18 —		–3
Finland	252,958	47,170	37,180	2.4	0.3	2.1	3[2]	—[2]	19[2]	5[2]	2[2]	9[2]	11[2]	18[2]	— 20[2] —		13[2]
France	2,749,821	42,390	34,440	1.5	0.6	0.9	2	—	12	6	2	3	9	31	18	7	10
French Guiana	1,610[2]	9,040[2]	…	…	…	…	5[6]	2[6]	10[6]	9[6]	1[6]	—[6]	15[6]	14[6]	28[6]	16[6]	—[6]
French Polynesia	5,643[1]	21,800[1]	17,500[1]	5.1	1.6	3.5	…	…	…	…	…	…	…	…	…	…	…
Gabon	11,655	7,760	13,190	1.7	1.7	0.0	6[2]	45[2]	5[2]	2[2]	1[2]	5[2]	6[2]	2[2]	13[2]	8[2]	7[2]
Gambia, The	770	440	1,270	3.7	2.9	0.8	30	—	5	6	1	18	16	5	3	7	9
Gaza Strip[14]	5,530[1]	1,400[1]	…	…	…	…	9	—	14	2	3	11	11		— 50 —		—
Georgia	11,976[15]	2,700[15]	4,980[15]	7.4	–0.7	8.1	15	[16]	16[16]	8	[16]	12	15	7	10	7	10
Germany	3,537,180	43,330	38,170	0.7	0.1	0.6	1[5]	[5, 16]	21[5, 16]	4[5]	[5, 16]	6[5]	11[5]	28[5]	23[5]	6[5]	—[5]
Ghana	30,080	1,240	1,600	5.1	2.2	2.9	37	5	9	8	3	5	7	4	3	11	8
Greece	308,596	27,240	27,360	4.4	0.3	4.1	5[2]	1[2]	10[2]	8[2]	2[2]	9[2]	19[2]	19[2]	— 20[2] —		7[2]
Greenland	1,618[1]	28,000[1]	…	…	…	…	…	…	…	…	…	…	…	…	…	…	…
Grenada	580	5,560	7,560	0.9	0.5	0.4	5	1	6	22	6	23	15	13	3	17	–11
Guadeloupe	9,136[1]	20,040[1]	…	…	…	…	7[9]	[9, 16]	8[9, 16]	7[9]	[9, 16]	7[9]	18[9]		— 52[9] —		1[9]
Guam	2,500[4, 17]	15,000[4, 17]	…	…	…	…	…	…	…	…	…	…	…	…	…	…	…
Guatemala	39,345	2,740	4,610	2.5	2.4	0.1	23	1	12	2	5	12	25	10	6	6	–2
Guernsey[18]	2,886[4]	45,370[4]	…	…	…	…	2	—	3	8	…			— 64 —			23
Guinea	3,972	380	980	2.9	2.2	0.7	23[2]	14[2]	4[2]	10[2]	1[2]	6[2]	— 24[2] —		7[2]	5[2]	6[2]
Guinea-Bissau	890	540	1,020	–0.5	2.0	–2.5	60	[16]	9[16]	3	[16]	3	17		— 8 —		—
Guyana	2,491	3,270	3,530	4.5	0.2	4.3	30	8	3	5	1	9	4	7	2	15	16
Haiti	6,464	650	1,110	–0.5	1.4	–1.9	25	—	8	8	1	6	26	12	— 11 —		3
Honduras	14,302	1,880	3,730	3.6	2.5	1.1	12	2	18	4	5	6	11	15	16	7	4
Hong Kong	231,658	32,900	47,300	4.3	0.8	3.5	—	—	3	3	3	10	28	22	— 17 —		14
Hungary	129,923	12,990	19,280	4.1	–0.3	4.4	4	—	19	4	3	7	11	19	13	8	12
Iceland	10,787	33,870	28,630	2.6	0.9	1.7	10[2]	—	10[2]	9[2]	3[2]	8[2]	13[2]	22[2]	— 25[2] —		3[2]
India	1,566,636	1,340	3,560	7.0	1.6	5.4	19	3	15	6	2	22	13		— 13 —		7
Indonesia	599,148	2,580	4,300	4.7	1.3	3.4	13	10	28	6	1	7	15	8	5	4	3
Iran	330,619[8]	4,530[8]	11,490[8]	5.8	0.9	4.9	11	25	11	4	2	7	11	16	3	10	—
Iraq	74,885	2,320	3,320	–11.4	2.9	–14.3	11	60	2	1	—	11	10	2	2	1	—
Ireland	182,474	40,990	32,740	5.2	1.8	3.4	2[5]	[5]	28[5]	7[5]	1[5]	5[5]	11[5]	19[5]	22[5]	4[5]	—[5]
Isle of Man	2,719[4]	34,000[4]	…	…	…	…	1	—	9	9	2	7	12	64	4	5	–4
Israel	207,193	27,340	27,800	1.9	1.8	0.1	2	—	13	4	2	7	9	23	13	17	10
Italy	2,125,845	35,090	31,090	0.6	0.4	0.2	2	—	16	5	2	7	14	24	13	6	11
Jamaica	12,892	4,750	7,430	1.8	0.9	0.9	5	4	13	10	4	11	20	12	7	11	3
Japan	5,369,116	42,150	34,790	1.4	0.2	1.2	2[2]	—	20[2]	6[2]	3[2]	7[2]	13[2]	18[2]	22[2]	9[2]	—[2]
Jersey	5,800[4]	66,000[4]	…	…	…	…	1	—	2	5	1	4	10	69	— 7 —		1
Jordan	26,520	4,350	5,570	6.1	2.2	3.9	2	2	17	4	2	14	7	16	5	16	15
Kazakhstan	121,383	7,440	10,610	10.1	0.2	9.9	6	[16]	33[16]	11	[16]	13	13		— 37 —		–13
Kenya	31,810	780	1,610	3.4	2.4	1.0	25	1	11	3	2	11	12	9	4	15	7
Kiribati	200	2,010	3,510	0.3	1.8	–1.5	6	—	1	5	1	6	13	12	— 48 —		8
Korea, North	25,600[1]	1,108[1]	…	…	…	…	27[2]	9[2]	19[2]	9[2]	4[2]	—	—	— 10[2] —		23[2]	–1[2]
Korea, South	972,299	19,890	29,010	4.6	0.5	4.1	3	—	25	8	2	6	8	14	14	11	9
Kosovo	5,981	3,300	…	…	…	…	…	…	…	…	…	…	…	…	…	…	…
Kuwait	111,464[1]	40,100[1]	…	7.3	4.9	2.4	—	54	7	2	1	5	5	14	— 13 —		–1
Kyrgyzstan	4,701	880	2,180	4.0	1.2	2.8	29	1	11	3	3	6	21	3	7	4	12
Laos	6,469	1,010	2,300	6.2	2.3	3.9	44	3	21	3	3	6	10	—	5	4	1
Latvia	26,056	11,620	16,360	7.9	–0.6	8.5	3	—	10	6	2	11	20	19	11	6	12
Lebanon	38,374	9,020	14,170	4.0	1.0	3.0	10[9]	—[9]	10[9]	2[9]	7[9]	3[9]	32[9]	18[9]	10[9]	8[9]	—[9]
Lesotho	2,248	1,080	1,910	2.9	–0.1	3.0	16	2	17	14	4	4	12	10	9	6	6
Liberia	782	190	330	–6.8	1.5	–8.3	64	—	12	2	1	7	6	3	1	3	–2
Libya	77,185[8]	12,020[8]	16,430[8]	5.3	2.0	3.3	3	73	1	3	1	3	5	2	5	3	1
Liechtenstein	2,893[1]	82,800[1]	…	…	…	…	7[2]	—[2]	40[2]	…	…	…	…	26[2]	— 26[2] —		1[2]
Lithuania	37,838	11,400	17,880	7.8	–0.5	8.3	5	1	19	7	4	11	17	11	9	5	11
Luxembourg	40,281	79,510	63,850	6.2	0.9	5.3	—	—	9	5	1	— 18 —		44	— 15 —		8
Macau	14,902[1]	31,200[1]	24,300[1]	6.7	1.8	4.9	—	—	6[5]	4[5]	3[5]	6[5]	12[5]	19[5]	9[5]	8[5]	33[5, 19]
Macedonia	9,319	4,520	10,830	1.7	0.2	1.5	11	—	16	5	4	8	15	11	9	7	14
Madagascar	8,820	440	980	2.0	2.8	–0.8	26[2]	[2, 20]		— 17[2, 20] —		15[2]	12[2]	1[2]	15[2]	6[2]	8[2]
Malawi	4,886	330	850	3.4	2.5	0.9	21	1	14	1	1	4	17	5	2	3	31
Malaysia	220,417	7,900	14,360	4.8	2.4	2.4	9	16	31	3	3	6	13	11	6	7	4
Maldives	1,340	4,270	5,480	7.5	1.6	5.9	9	1	7	5	4	16	4	12	20	14	6
Mali	9,146	600	1,020	5.9	2.5	3.4	37	10	6	6	2	5	16	6	— 6 —		6
Malta	5,899[1]	14,600[1]	21,000[1]	2.4	0.7	1.7	2	—	15	4	1	9	16	16	17	7	13
Marshall Islands	187	2,990	…	…	…	…	10	—	12	11	2	5	18		— 42 —		—
Martinique	5,780[5]	14,730[5]	…	…	…	…	…	…	…	…	…	…	…	…	…	…	…
Mauritania	3,571	1,060	2,000	4.0	3.0	1.0	21	14	5	— 8 —		5	12	— 12 —		13	10
Mauritius	9,925	7,740	13,670	4.0	1.0	3.0	5[2]	—[2]	18[2]	5[2]	2[2]	11[2]	18[2]	17[2]	3[2]	13[2]	8[2]
Mayotte	444[6]	2,780[6]	…	…	…	…	…	…	…	…	…	…	…	…	…	…	…
Mexico	1,012,316	9,330	15,010	1.9	1.4	0.5	3	1	16	5	1	9	19	12	— 23 —		11
Micronesia	300	2,700	3,420	0.3	1.1	–0.8	14[9]	—[9]	1[9]	9[9]	1[9]	12[9]	14[9]		— 49[9] —		–4[9]
Moldova	6,456[21]	1,810[21]	3,340[21]	7.1	–0.3	–7.4	18[2]	—[2]	14[2]	4[2]	2[2]	12[2]	11[2]		— 27[2] —		12[2]
Monaco	1,165[1]	35,700[1]	…	…	…	…	…	…	…	…	…	…	…	…	…	…	…
Mongolia	5,106	1,890	3,700	5.8	1.3	4.5	22	20	4	2	2	12	25		— 13 —		—
Montenegro	4,183	6,690	12,710	…	…	…	8	1	8	3	5	10	14	14	12	9	6
Morocco	94,053[22]	2,850[22]	4,560[22]	4.3	1.4	2.9	14	2	17	5	6	8	12	— 12 —		17	7
Mozambique	10,344	440	920	8.6	1.8	6.8	20	1	13	6	6	16	23	5	7	3	—

gross domestic product (GDP) by type of expenditure, 2006 (%)					external public debt outstanding (long-term, disbursed only), 2005						balance of payments, 2006 (current external transactions; '000,000 U.S.$)			tourist trade, 2009 ('000,000 U.S.$)		country
consumption		gross domestic investment	foreign trade		total ('000,000 U.S.$)	creditors (%)		debt service			net transfers		current balance of payments	receipts from foreign nationals	expenditures by nationals abroad	
private	government		exports	imports		official	private	total ('000,000 U.S.$)	repayment (%) principal	repayment (%) interest	goods, merchandise	invisibles				
68	50	19	3	–40	…	…	…	…	…	…	…	…	…	18.0	39.8	East Timor
64	11	24	34	–33	10,662	54.2	45.8	1,525	56.3	43.7	712[4]	–771[4]	–59[4]	670	549	Ecuador
75	13	20	28	–36	24,892	94.2	5.8	2,000	73.2	26.8	–8,438	11,073	2,635	10,755	2,538	Egypt
94	10	16	26	–46	4,760	59.3	40.7	521	42.8	57.2	–3,008[4]	2,222[4]	–786.5[4]	319	187	El Salvador
6	3	33	95	–38	223.9	93.2	6.8	3.9	76.9	23.1	…	…	…	…	…	Equatorial Guinea
82	37	18	5	–42	723	95.4	4.6	20.2	58.4	41.6	–434.6[6]	329.9[6]	–104.7[6]	26	…	Eritrea
53	16	38	84	–92	435	16.6	83.4	82.0	68.3	31.7	–2,739	293	–2,446	1,090	606	Estonia
80	12	20	15	–27	5,897	93.8	6.2	80.0	38.8	61.2	–3,081	1,295	–1,786	329	138	Ethiopia
…	…	…	…	…	…	…	…	…	…	…	…	…	…	…	…	Faroe Islands
78	16	20	56	–70	119.6	96.0	4.0	12.0	67.5	32.5	…	…	…	422	94	Fiji
51	22	21	45	–38	…	…	…	…	…	…	11,553	795	12,348	2,814	4,373	Finland
57	23	21	28	–29	…	…	…	…	…	…	–37,690	9,390	–28,300	49,450	38,575	France
…	…	…	…	…	…	…	…	…	…	…	…	…	…	49[12]	…	French Guiana
49	44	13	21	–27	…	…	…	…	…	…	…	…	…	438	164	French Polynesia
26	8	21	74	–30	3,582	93.7	6.3	82	53.7	46.3	2,856[2]	–1,932[2]	924.5[2]	94[4]	274[4]	Gabon
84	10	24	51	–70	626.4	100.0	—	25.9	63.3	36.7	–114.5[4]	64.1[4]	–50.4[4]	63	9	Gambia, The
98	31	24	12	–64	…	…	…	…	…	…	–2,366[2]	883[2]	–1,483[2]	56[2]	286[2]	Gaza Strip[14]
74	16	28	33	–51	1,494	99.9	0.1	103	77.7	22.3	–915.5	–327.5	–1,243	470	181	Georgia
59	19	18	45	–40	…	…	…	…	…	…	197,330	–49,510	147,820	34,781	81,044	Germany
76	14	27	35	–52	5,734	94.5	5.5	229	68.6	31.4	–2,543[4]	1,731[4]	–811.6[4]	968	584	Ghana
68	14	25	19	–27	…	…	…	…	…	…	–44,285	14,620	–29,665	14,681	3,381	Greece
32	54	30	24	–40	…	…	…	…	…	…	…	…	…	…	…	Greenland
68	17	50	39	–75	390	44.2	55.8	10.7	67.3	32.7	–241.1[4]	111.7[4]	–129.4[4]	99	10	Grenada
…	…	…	…	…	…	…	…	…	…	…	…	…	…	384[10]	…	Guadeloupe
…	…	…	…	…	…	…	…	…	…	…	…	…	…	…	…	Guam
86	9	20	26	–41	3,688	66.5	33.5	402	49.5	50.5	–5,044	3,452	–1,592	1,179	715	Guatemala
…	…	…	…	…	…	…	…	…	…	…	…	…	…	…	…	Guernsey[18]
85	4	22	26	–36	2,931	99.0	1.0	89	67.9	32.1	37.2[2]	–212[2]	–174.8[2]	2.8	13	Guinea
82	16	16	35	–50	671.3	100.0	—	29.4	70.7	29.3	–7.1[2]	–6.1[2]	–13.2[2]	38.2[10]	45.6[10]	Guinea-Bissau
65	25	46	80	–116	1,021	99.1	0.9	25	60.0	40.0	–174.3[4]	78.1[4]	–96.2[4]	59[10]	52[10]	Guyana
92	8	29	14	–43	1,276	100.0	—	52	63.5	36.5	–849.6[4]	903.7[4]	54.1[4]	315	63	Haiti
79	14	33	41	–66	4,152	98.6	1.4	200	68.5	31.5	–1,540[4]	1,454[4]	–85.6[4]	611	296	Honduras
58	8	22	206	–194	…	…	…	…	…	…	–14,033	34,608	20,575	16,020	15,960	Hong Kong
54	23	22	78	–77	21,216	11.9	88.1	4,215	80.0	20.0	–508	–5,704	–6,212	5,712	3,638	Hungary
60	24	30	34	–47	…	…	…	…	…	…	–2,239	–2,218	–4,457	555	533	Iceland
57	12	32	22	–23	80,281	63.5	36.5	17,140	72.1	27.9	–32,526[4]	24,691[4]	–7,835[4]	11,136	9,310	India
63	9	25	30	–26	72,335	81.6	18.4	7,193	73.7	22.7	22,323[4]	–21,394[4]	929[4]	6,318	5,165	Indonesia
46	12	28	37	–23	10,493	17.3	82.7	2,133	80.4	19.6	13,138[6]	–657[6]	12,481[6]	2,012	9,108	Iran
53	28	22	90	–93	…	…	…	…	…	…	…	…	…	516[12]	794[10]	Iraq
45	16	28	81	–69	…	…	…	…	…	…	34,165	–41,373	–7,208	4,894	8,773	Ireland
…	…	…	…	…	…	…	…	…	…	…	…	…	…	…	…	Isle of Man
55	27	17	45	–44	…	…	…	…	…	…	–3,564	10,405	6,841	3,741	2,909	Israel
59	20	21	28	–28	…	…	…	…	…	…	–11,690	–35,622	–47,312	40,311	27,864	Italy
72	15	31	40	–58	5,508	38.7	61.3	902	60.0	40.0	–2,581	1,502	–1,079	1,925	216	Jamaica
57	18	24	16	–15	…	…	…	…	…	…	81,300	89,220	170,520	10,329	25,199	Japan
…	…	…	…	…	…	…	…	…	…	…	…	…	…	…	…	Jersey
97	20	26	51	–94	6,878	93.6	6.4	501	68.1	31.9	–5,056	3,084	–1,972	2,911	1,064	Jordan
49	10	31	54	–44	2,184	81.8	18.2	1,236	88.2	11.8	14,642	–16,439	–1,797	963	1,131	Kazakhstan
80	16	18	23	–38	5,520	93.3	6.7	199	72.4	27.6	–2,168[4]	1,673[4]	–495[4]	690	234	Kenya
62	36	44	30	–72	…	…	…	…	…	…	…	…	…	…	…	Kiribati
…	…	…	…	…	12,500[6]	…	…	…	…	…	…	…	…	…	…	Korea, North
55	15	30	44	–44	…	…	…	…	…	…	29,214	–23,122	6,092	9,442	13,330	Korea, South
…	…	…	…	…	…	…	…	…	…	…	…	…	…	…	…	Kosovo
28	13	17	68	–26	…	…	…	…	…	…	44,288	6,708	50,996	248	7,441	Kuwait
97	19	21	39	–76	1,670	100.0	—	28	57.1	42.9	–981.5	564.3	–417.2	459	265	Kyrgyzstan
59	8	31	32	–29	1,971	100.0	—	49	71.4	28.6	–216.8[11]	134.4[11]	–82.4[11]	268	83	Laos
65	17	38	44	–64	1,318	25.6	74.4	157	61.1	38.9	–3,018	–1,262	–4,280	723	799	Latvia
82	15	22	16	–35	17,912	9.1	90.9	2,996	61.2	38.8	–5,755	4,271	–1,484	6,774	4,012	Lebanon
83	19	41	42	–85	647	91.7	8.3	53.8	74.5	25.5	–609.8[4]	566.2[4]	–43.6[4]	40	14	Lesotho
91	9	12	34	–47	1,115	82.2	17.8	—	—	—	…	…	…	…	…	Liberia
19	14	14	83	–31	3,900	…	…	…	…	…	17,675[4]	–2,730[4]	14,945[4]	50	1,587	Libya
60	11	22	54	–47	…	…	…	…	…	…	…	…	…	…	…	Liechtenstein
67	16	26	63	–72	1,511	29.7	70.3	873	91.5	8.5	–4,169	925	–3,244	1,092	1,131	Lithuania
39	17	19	180	–156	…	…	…	…	…	…	–4,290	8,677	4,387	4,180	3,650	Luxembourg
24	8	34	92	–58	…	…	…	…	…	…	–2,792	6,159	3,367	17,886	510	Macau
79	19	21	48	–66	1,613	73.2	26.8	122	66.4	33.6	–1,285	1,261	–23.7	218	100	Macedonia
83	8	22	27	–40	3,178	99.7	0.3	66	57.6	42.4	–592[4]	–33[4]	–625[4]	308	123	Madagascar
104	16	10	24	–55	3,040	99.4	0.6	79	64.6	35.4	–150.8[9]	–49.9[9]	–200.7[9]	27[12]	73[12]	Malawi
44	13	20	122	–99	22,449	29.1	70.9	5,974	79.5	20.5	36,827	–11,272	25,555	15,798	6,508	Malaysia
30	38	56	83	–106	307	70.8	29.2	32.9	73.6	26.4	–590.1	220.9	–369.2	608	97	Maldives
66	16	22	29	–33	2,843	100.0	—	70	67.1	32.9	–144.6[4]	–293.1[4]	–437.7[4]	275[10]	147[10]	Mali
67	22	21	72	–82	…	…	…	…	…	…	–1,222	810	–412	827	440	Malta
91	54	57	12	–114	…	…	…	…	…	…	…	…	…	2.7	0.4[1]	Marshall Islands
…	…	…	…	…	…	…	…	…	…	…	…	…	…	299[12]	306[11]	Martinique
59	17	29	55	–61	2,043	98.9	1.1	54	63.0	37.0	…	…	…	28[6]	55[6]	Mauritania
72	14	23	62	–72	731	69.4	30.6	211	85.8	14.2	–794.6[4]	454.7[4]	–339.9[4]	1,120	354	Mauritius
…	…	…	…	…	…	…	…	…	…	…	…	…	…	…	…	Mayotte
68	11	21	33	–34	108,786	17.6	82.4	21,647	68.7	31.3	–6,133	4,266	–1,867	11,275	7,132	Mexico
84	58	38	3	–84	…	…	…	…	…	…	…	…	…	18.3[1]	5.7[1]	Micronesia
95	18	34	47	–94	700	95.1	4.9	65	66.2	33.8	–1,591	1,187	–403.7	168	243	Moldova
57	23	21	28	–29	…	…	…	…	…	…	…	…	…	…	…	Monaco
29	27	41	81	–78	1,267	99.9	0.1	34	55.9	44.1	–28.8[4]	24.2[4]	–4.6[4]	235	210	Mongolia
74	28	16	39	–57	…	…	…	…	…	…	14.7[4]	–30.3[4]	–15.6[4]	659	49	Montenegro
61	17	30	33	–40	13,113	81.8	18.2	2,372	78.6	21.4	–8,204[4]	9,222[4]	1,018[4]	6,625	1,106	Morocco
61	12	25	42	–40	3,727	100.0	—	54	46.3	53.7	–267.7	–819.3	–1,087	196	212	Mozambique

National product and accounts (continued)

country	gross national income (GNI), 2010			gross domestic product (GDP), 2000–05			origin of gross domestic product (GDP) by economic sector, 2005 (%)										
	nominal ('000,000 U.S.$)	per capita		average annual growth rates, 2000–05			primary		secondary			tertiary					other
		nominal (U.S.$)	purchasing power parity (PPP; U.S.$)	real GDP (%)	popu-lation (%)	real GDP per capita (%)	agri-culture	mining	manu-factur-ing	con-struc-tion	public util-ities	transp., commu-nications	trade	finan-cial svcs.	other svcs.	govern-ment	
Myanmar (Burma)	13,611[1]	280[1]	…	9.2	1.0	8.2	51[2]	—	10[2]	4[2]	—[2]	10[2]	23[2]	1[2]	—— −1[2] ——		—[2]
Namibia	10,286	4,650	6,410	4.6	1.3	3.3	11	9	11	3	4	7	12	13	1	20	9
Nauru	79[1]	7,840[1]	…	…	…	…	10	4	1	8	…	15	13	—— 49 ——			—
Nepal	14,529	490	1,200	2.8	2.1	0.7	37	—	7	10	2	10	10	11	—— 9 ——		4
Netherlands	826,491	49,720	42,590	0.7	0.5	0.2	2	3	13	5	1	6	13	24	11	11	11
New Caledonia	4,743[1]	19,930[1]	15,000[5]	…	…	…	2[5]	10[5, 23]	6[5]	6[5]	[5, 23]	6[5]	23[5]	—— 48[5] ——			−1[5]
New Zealand	98,383[1]	23,770[1]	26,470[1]	3.7	1.2	2.5	7[2]	1[2]	15[2]	5[2]	2[2]	10[2]	16[2]	24[2]	12[2]	4[2]	4[2]
Nicaragua	6,282	1,080	2,610	3.0	2.0	1.0	17	1	17	6	2	6	13	12	7	11	8
Niger	5,689	360	700	3.7	3.0	0.7	41	2	6	3	1	7	13	8	3	10	6
Nigeria	186,406	1,180	2,160	5.9	2.3	3.6	30[2]	33[2]	4[2]	1[2]	—[2]	4[2]	15[2]	7[2]	2[2]	1[2]	3[2]
Northern Mariana Is.	1,000[4, 17]	13,400[4, 17]	…	…	…	…	…	…	…	…	…	…	…	…	…	…	…
Norway	416,905	85,380	57,130	2.0	0.6	1.4	1[1]	25[1]	8[1]	4[1]	2[1]	6[1]	8[1]	12[1]	18[1]	4[1]	12[1]
Oman	28,710[1]	11,280[1]	14,570[4]	3.0	1.6	1.4	3	49	9	3	3	3	11	6	7	7	−1
Pakistan	182,537	1,050	2,780	4.8	1.9	2.9	20	2	17	2	2	14	17	6	8	5	7
Palau	133	6,460	10,760	5.5	1.9	3.6	4	—	—	5	3	9	31	8	17	23	—
Panama	24,531	6,990	12,940	4.3	1.7	2.6	7	1	7	4	3	18	17	23	6	9	5
Papua New Guinea	8,935	1,300	2,390	1.6	2.1	−0.5	39[2]	21[2]	6[2]	8[2]	2[2]	2[2]	2[2]	6[2]	3[2]	10[2]	1[2]
Paraguay	19,008	2,940	5,430	2.6	2.2	0.4	21	—	14	5	2	8	21	6	6	9	8
Peru	138,978	4,710	8,940	4.3	1.5	2.8	7	9	15	5	2	8	16	16	6	7	9
Philippines	192,238	2,050	3,930	4.7	1.9	2.8	14	1	23	4	4	8	1	5	8	8	1
Poland	474,045	12,420	19,020	3.2	−0.2	3.4	4	2	16	5	3	7	17	—— 46 ——			—
Portugal	232,590	21,860	24,710	0.5	0.3	0.2	2[1]	—	14[1]	5[1]	2[1]	6[1]	15[1]	13[1]	—— 29[1] ——		14[1]
Puerto Rico	58,418[1]	14,700[1]	19,300[1]	0.5	0.5	0.0	1	—	40	2	—	7	13	17	16	2	2
Qatar	54,259[1]	66,100[1]	…	7.1	4.6	2.5	—	60	8	6	1	3	4	10	2	8	−2
Réunion	14,910[4, 17]	19,130[4, 17]	…	…	…	…	5[5]	[7]	4[5, 7]	7[5]	1[5]	6[5]	12[5]	—— 57[5] ——		13[5]	−5[5]
Romania	168,208	7,840	14,050	5.8	−0.4	6.2	13[2]	[16]	25[2, 16]	6[2]	[16]	10[2]	11[2]	14[2]	5[2]	5[2]	11[2]
Russia	1,404,179	9,910	19,190	6.2	−0.5	6.7	4[1]	9[1]	17[1]	5[1]	3[1]	8[1]	18[1]	12[1]	7[1]	6[1]	11[1]
Rwanda	5,537	540	1,180	5.1	2.1	3.0	45[2]	—	9[2]	8[2]	1[2]	7[2]	9[2]	3[2]	11[2]	7[2]	7[2]
St. Kitts	499	9,980	13,170	4.9	0.4	4.5	2	—	8	12	2[2]	13	17	17	4	16	9
St. Lucia	865	4,970	8,520	5.1	0.9	4.2	3	—	4	6	4	16	22	15	4	12	14
St. Vincent	530	4,850	8,260	4.9	0.5	4.4	7	—	5	10	5	16	18	9	3	16	11
Samoa	524	2,930	4,300	5.5	0.9	4.6	13	—	15	9	4	12	23	9	7	9	−1
San Marino	1,257[1]	41,040[1]	…	4.6	2.4	2.2	—	—	42[5]	7[5]	—	2[5]	9[5]	16[5]	—— 24[5] ——		—
Sao Tome and Principe	199	1,200	1,910	4.4	2.3	2.1	16[2]	—	4[2]	10[2]	—	—— 28[2] ——		11[2]	1[2]	30[2]	—
Saudi Arabia	365,786[1]	15,130[1]	13,600[8]	4.2	2.9	1.3	3	48	10	5	1	3	5	8	2	14	1
Senegal	13,533	1,050	1,850	4.7	2.5	2.2	14[2]	1[2]	14[2]	4[2]	2[2]	9[2]	18[2]	13[2]	7[2]	7[2]	11[2]
Serbia	42,394	5,820	11,230	5.1	−0.2	5.3	13	2	15	3	3	10	11	15	—— 11 ——		17
Seychelles	845	9,490	20,470	−1.0	0.4	−0.6	3	…	15	12	3	18	3	3	2	2	−1
Sierra Leone	2,009	340	830	13.7	1.9	11.8	48[5]	15[5]	3[5]	3[5]	—	7[5]	6[5]	7[5]	3[5]	4[5]	4[5]
Singapore	210,323	40,920	54,700	4.2	1.3	2.9	—	—	27	4	2	12	17	28	—— 11 ——		−1
Sint Maarten	…	…	…	…	…	…	…	…	…	…	…	…	…	…	…	…	…
Slovakia	88,051	16,220	23,140	4.9	−0.1	5.0	4[1]	—	20[1]	6[1]	5[1]	9[1]	17[1]	4[1]	9[1]	5[1]	21[1]
Slovenia	49,276	23,860	26,970	3.4	0.1	3.3	2	1	21	5	3	7	12	18	13	5	13
Solomon Islands	552	1,030	2,210	4.4	2.5	1.9	32[5]	—	4[5]	1[5]	4[5]	3[5]	18[5]	8[5]	—— 31[5] ——		−1[5]
Somalia	2,313[1]	270[1]	…	…	…	…	65[2]	—[2]	3[2]	6[2]	—[2]	7[2]	8[2]	—— 9[2] ——			2[2]
South Africa	304,591	6,100	10,280	3.7	1.0	2.7	2	6	17	2	2	9	13	19	13	6	11
Spain	1,462,894	31,650	31,550	3.1	1.8	1.3	3	2	14	10	1	—— 47 ——				13	11
Sri Lanka	46,738	2,290	5,070	4.2	0.9	3.3	12	2	20	7	2	12	24	9	4	9	−1
Sudan	55,277	1,270	2,020	6.1	1.9	4.2	46[5]	10[5]	8[5]	5[5]	…	—— 25[5] ——				6[5]	—
Sudan, South	…	…	…	…	…	…	…	…	…	…	…	…	…	…	…	…	…
Suriname	2,039[1]	4,480[1]	8,120[1]	…	…	…	5[1]	12[1]	13[1]	3[1]	5[1]	8[1]	11[1]	10[1]	1[1]	9[1]	23[1]
Swaziland	3,119	2,600	4,890	2.3	0.2	2.1	7[2]	—	21[2]	5[2]	1[2]	3[2]	6[2]	3[2]	2[2]	11[2]	41[2]
Sweden	469,002	49,930	39,600	2.3	0.3	2.0	1[1]	—	18[1]	4[1]	3[1]	6[1]	11[1]	20[1]	6[1]	18[1]	14[1]
Switzerland	548,012	70,350	49,180	0.9	0.8	0.1	1	—[16]	21[16]	6	[16]	—— 22 ——		25	—— 26 ——		−1
Syria	57,003	2,640	4,870	3.7	2.4	1.3	25[5]	19[5]	4[5]	3[5]	1[5]	13[5]	17[5]	3[5]	3[5]	10[5]	2[5]
Taiwan	333,422[2]	14,700[2]	…	…	…	…	2[2]	—	22[2]	2[2]	2[2]	7[2]	20[2]	11[2]	4[2]	12[2]	18[2]
Tajikistan	5,512	780	2,060	9.5	2.1	7.4	21	[16]	19[16]	4	[16]	6	22	1	4	2	11
Tanzania	23,366[24]	530[24]	1,420[24]	6.9	2.1	4.8	41[5]	2[5]	7[5]	5[5]	2[5]	4[5]	11[5]	5[5]	9[5]	8[5]	6[5]
Thailand	286,676	4,210	8,240	5.4	0.7	4.7	11[1]	3[1]	35[1]	3[1]	3[1]	7[1]	19[1]	6[1]	8[1]	5[1]	—
Togo	2,957	440	790	2.7	2.8	−0.1	40[5]	3[5]	7[5]	3[5]	4[5]	6[5]	11[5]	7[5]	—— 11[5] ——		8[5]
Tonga	353	3,380	4,630	2.4	0.1	2.3	21[2]	—	4[2]	8[2]	2[2]	7[2]	14[2]	13[2]	5[2]	11[2]	15[2]
Trinidad and Tobago	20,664	15,380	24,000	8.3	0.5	7.8	1[1]	45[1]	6[1]	8[1]	1[1]	5[1]	12[1]	12[1]	4[1]	7[1]	−1[1]
Tunisia	42,826	4,070	8,140	4.5	1.0	3.5	12	1	18	5	5	10	6	22	—	13	8
Turkey	719,404	9,500	14,580	5.2	1.3	3.9	10	1	21	4	3	15	21	9	4	10	2
Turkmenistan	19,159	3,700	7,160	6.0	1.4	4.6	24[5]	[16]	35[5, 16]	7[5]	[16]	6[5]	4[5]	—— 24[5] ——			—
Tuvalu	26[1]	2,440[1]	…	…	…	…	17[9]	1[9]	4[9]	5[9]	5[9]	13[9]	14[9]	15[9]	7[9]	27[9]	−8[9]
Uganda	16,553	490	1,230	5.6	3.2	2.4	29[1]	1[1]	8[1]	10[1]	1[1]	9[1]	13[1]	6[1]	11[1]	4[1]	8[1]
Ukraine	137,917	3,010	6,580	8.0	−0.9	8.9	9	4	20	4	3	11	13	—— 26 ——			10
United Arab Emirates	174,536[1]	41,080[1]	…	8.2	7.6	0.6	2	36	13	7	2	7	13	13	2	7	−2
United Kingdom	2,399,292	38,540	36,580	2.4	0.4	2.0	1[2]	3[2]	13[2]	6[2]	1[2]	7[2]	14[2]	28[2]	16[2]	5[2]	6[2]
United States	14,600,828	47,140	47,020	2.6	1.0	1.6	1[1]	2[1]	12[1]	5[1]	2[1]	3[1]	15[1]	25[1]	23[1]	12[1]	—
Uruguay	35,557	10,590	13,890	0.9	0.3	0.6	9[1]	—	23[1]	5[1]	4[1]	10[1]	13[1]	19[1]	9[1]	8[1]	—
Uzbekistan	36,086	1,280	3,090	5.3	1.5	3.8	25	[16]	21[16]	5	[16]	11	9	—— 18 ——			11
Vanuatu	662	2,760	4,450	2.9	2.0	0.9	15[5]	—	4[5]	3[5]	2[5]	13[5]	38[5]	14[5]	2[5]	15[5]	−6[5]
Venezuela	334,113	11,590	11,950	1.3	1.8	−0.5	[25]	15[1]	17[1]	7[1]	2[1]	4[1]	10[1, 25]	14[1]	5[1]	11[1]	15[1, 25]
Vietnam	96,899	1,100	2,910	7.5	1.3	6.2	21	11	21	6	3	4	17	6	8	3	—
Virgin Islands (U.S.)	3,080[1, 26]	27,300[1, 26]	…	…	…	…	…	…	…	…	…	…	…	…	…	…	…
West Bank[14]	…	…	…	…	…	…	…	…	…	…	…	…	…	…	…	…	…
Western Sahara	…	…	…	…	…	…	…	…	…	…	…	…	…	…	…	…	…
Yemen	25,026[8]	1,060[8]	2,340[8]	3.3	3.1	0.2	13	32	6	4	1	11	13	8	2	10	—
Zambia	13,816	1,070	1,370	4.7	2.2	2.5	21	3	11	11	3	4	21	15	5	3	3
Zimbabwe	5,841	460	1,940[4]	−5.9	0.7	−6.6	15	8	17	1	—	8	12	—— 39 ——			—

gross domestic product (GDP) by type of expenditure, 2006 (%)					external public debt outstanding (long-term, disbursed only), 2005						balance of payments, 2006 (current external transactions; '000,000 U.S.$)			tourist trade, 2009 ('000,000 U.S.$)		country
consumption		gross domestic investment	foreign trade		total ('000,000 U.S.$)	creditors (%)		debt service			net transfers		current balance of payments	receipts from foreign nationals	expenditures by nationals abroad	
private	government		exports	imports		official	private	total ('000,000 U.S.$)	repayment (%) principal	repayment (%) interest	goods, merchandise	invisibles				
85		15	0	0	5,196	84.4	15.6	91	89.0	11.0	927.9[2]	–816.4[2]	111.5[2]	46[1]	37[1]	Myanmar (Burma)
55	24	26	42	–47	…	…	…	…	…	…	–282.8[2]	855.4[2]	572.6[2]	363	109	Namibia
62	36	44	30	–72	…	…	…	…	…	…	…	…	…	…	…	Nauru
79	10	30	19	–38	3,217	99.9	0.1	115	73.9	26.1	–1,374[4]	1,375[4]	1.1[4]	371	434	Nepal
47	25	19	76	–67	…	…	…	…	…	…	47,972	9,476	57,448	12,408	20,757	Netherlands
56	33	24	15	–29	…	…	…	…	…	…	…	…	…	141	170	New Caledonia
60	19	24	28	–31	…	…	…	…	…	…	–2,118	–7,255	–9,373	4,396	2,559	New Zealand
80	20	29	30	–59	4,113	92.5	7.5	107	58.9	41.1	–1,444	589.6	–854.4	346	147	Nicaragua
73	18	23	19	–32	1,771	100.0	—	24	50.0	50.0	–153[2]	–77.9[2]	–230.9[2]	79[10]	68[10]	Niger
68	7	12	32	–19	20,342	89.3	10.7	8,817	43.9	56.1	30,781[4]	–6,579[4]	24,202[4]	602	4,084	Nigeria
…	…	…	…	…	…	…	…	…	…	…	…	…	…	…	…	Northern Mariana Is.
41	20	21	46	–27	…	…	…	…	…	…	59,721	–4,508	55,213	4,082	12,366	Norway
46	21	15	64	–45	842	100.0	—	473	89.0	11.0	10,663[4]	–5,946[4]	4,717[4]	700	871	Oman
82	6	20	17	–25	29,490	95.6	4.4	1,127	65.9	34.1	–9,702	2,907	–6,795	269	685	Pakistan
41	46	21	76	–84	…	…	…	…	…	…	…	…	…	90[1]	1.4[1]	Palau
66	10	21	36	–33	7,514	17.7	82.3	1,720	67.0	33.0	–1,801	1,423	–378.2	1,483	338	Panama
63	12	18	40	–33	1,266	96.0	4.0	152	75.0	25.0	1,753[4]	–1,330[4]	422.7[4]	1.2	29	Papua New Guinea
66	10	20	34	–30	2,264	79.6	20.4	301	68.7	31.3	–492.3[4]	469.9[4]	–22.4[4]	227	188	Paraguay
63	10	18	28	–19	22,222	60.8	39.2	4,218	67.4	32.6	8,853	–6,397	2,456	2,046	1,086	Peru
70	10	15	47	–42	35,233	52.9	47.1	5,693	58.9	41.1	–7,546[4]	9,884[4]	2,338[4]	2,329	2,444	Philippines
63	18	20	41	–42	35,094	26.9	73.1	8,760	88.7	11.3	–4,953	–3,020	–7,973	9,011	7,327	Poland
66	21	21	31	–39	…	…	…	…	…	…	–4,898	–13,383	–18,281	9,707	3,776	Portugal
56	12	15	80	–63	…	…	…	…	…	…	…	…	…	3,473	1,106	Puerto Rico
17	13	35	65	–30	…	…	…	…	…	…	…	…	…	874[1]	3,751[1]	Qatar
…	…	…	…	…	…	…	…	…	…	…	…	…	…	425	…	Réunion
67	20	24	34	–46	13,341	46.2	53.8	2,372	71.6	28.4	–14,836	2,000	–12,836	1,228	1,473	Romania
49	18	20	34	–21	75,359	46.0	54.0	28,326	81.6	18.4	139,234	–43,911	95,323	9,297	20,763	Russia
90	14	21	10	–35	1,420	100.0	—	20	55.0	45.0	–343	163	–180	174	72	Rwanda
57	18	46	45	–67	299.3	54.7	45.3	47.8	57.1	42.9	–135.8[4]	28.8[4]	–107[4]	83	13	St. Kitts
52	18	41	62	–73	248.9	64.6	35.4	27.2	52.2	47.8	–345.3[4]	162.7[4]	–182.6[4]	296	41	St. Lucia
68	20	32	48	–68	248.3	46.2	53.8	22.6	63.7	36.3	–169.7[4]	59.6[4]	–110.1[4]	90	18	St. Vincent
92	22	10	30	–54	177	100.0	—	6.1	73.8	26.2	–175.2[4]	150.7[4]	–24.5[4]	116	10.7	Samoa
35	14	57	181	–188	…	…	…	…	…	…	…	…	…	…	…	San Marino
79	45	68	31	–123	326.7	100.0	—	9.6	62.5	37.5	–22.9[9]	0.1[9]	–22.8[9]	8.3	0.1[12]	Sao Tome and Principe
27	20	19	65	–31	…	…	…	…	…	…	123,308[4]	–36,177[4]	87,131[4]	5,964	18,814	Saudi Arabia
75	17	26	27	–44	3,467	99.7	0.3	119	63.9	36.1	–986.4[2]	473.3[2]	–513.1[2]	543[10]	175[10]	Senegal
70	21	28	27	–46	7,972	86.5	13.5	303	16.8	83.2	…	…	…	866	959	Serbia
50	22	16	108	–96	401.7	57.1	42.9	48.2	77.6	22.4	–287.2	111.7	–175.5	208	32	Seychelles
91	15	17	16	–40	1,420	99.9	0.1	21	47.6	52.4	–176.6[4]	8.0[4]	–168.6[4]	25	13	Sierra Leone
40	11	18	253	–221	…	…	…	…	…	…	37,890[4]	–4,678[4]	33,212[4]	9,200	15,808	Singapore
…	…	…	…	…	…	…	…	…	…	…	…	…	…	616	81	Sint Maarten
57	18	29	80	–84	3,340	29.4	70.6	1,593	86.3	13.7	–649[5]	367[5]	–282[5]	2,341	2,098	Slovakia
55	19	26	69	–69	…	…	…	…	…	…	–1,419	460	–959	2,518	1,355	Slovenia
48	32	20	59	–59	148.1	99.7	0.3	7.5	77.3	22.7	…	…	…	44.1	31.7	Solomon Islands
72	9	20	0	–2	1,882	98.1	1.9	—	—	—	…	…	…	…	…	Somalia
64	20	19	28	–31	11,662	2.7	97.3	1,051	54.0	46.0	–6,175	–10,101	–16,276	7,624	4,151	South Africa
58	18	31	26	–32	…	…	…	…	…	…	–100,729	–5,615	–106,344	53,337	16,911	Spain
70	13	27	33	–44	9,812	94.1	5.9	285	70.9	29.1	–1,630[4]	–110[4]	–1,740[4]	350	411	Sri Lanka
57	17	24	27	–24	11,163	80.4	19.6	359	81.1	18.9	–1,448	–3,662	–5,110	299	868	Sudan
…	…	…	…	…	…	…	…	…	…	…	…	…	…	…	…	Sudan, South
18	5	85	54	–62	504.3	…	…	…	…	…	22.4[4]	–166[4]	–143.6[4]	64	32	Suriname
62	27	17	90	–97	450.5	85.4	14.6	40	53.3	46.7	73[4]	–27.1[4]	45.9[4]	40	72	Swaziland
48	27	18	51	–43	…	…	…	…	…	…	19,701[4]	3,942[4]	23,643[4]	10,275	11,856	Sweden
60	11	22	54	–47	…	…	…	…	…	…	4,663	58,831	63,494	13,816	10,628	Switzerland
65	13	19	40	–37	5,640	81.3	18.7	186	77.4	22.6	–1,940[4]	875[4]	–1,065[4]	3,757	882	Syria
83[2]	17[2]	27[2]	63[2]	–27[2]	…	…	…	…	…	…	16,128[2]	2,530[2]	18,658[2]	6,816	7,800	Taiwan
78	23	11	59	–72	785	98.7	1.3	47	83.9	16.1	–442.8	421.4	–21.4	2.4	5.8	Tajikistan
81	8	22	24	–35	6,183	98.4	1.6	66	42.4	57.6	–2,141	699	–1,442	1,160	766	Tanzania
56	12	28	74	–70	13,483	59.9	40.1	3,166	86.3	13.7	14,813	–11,583	3,230	15,665	4,343	Thailand
88	9	21	39	–56	1,469	100.0	—	5	60.0	40.0	–512.2[4]	972.9[4]	460.7[4]	40[10]	19[10]	Togo
117	13	11	21	–62	83.2	100.0	—	4.0	72.5	27.5	–55,247[9]	51,928[9]	–3,319[9]	19.1[10]	8.7[10]	Tonga
37	14	15	69	–35	1,197	47.7	52.3	340	71.5	28.5	1,509[2]	–62[2]	1,447[2]	397[10]	75[10]	Trinidad and Tobago
64	15	23	50	–52	12,982	64.9	35.1	1,747	66.1	33.9	–1,968[4]	1,665[4]	–303[4]	2,773	415	Tunisia
70	12	24	26	–32	62,580	19.9	80.1	12,686	65.5	34.5	–40,186	8,422	–31,764	21,250	4,147	Turkey
55	13	24	63	–55	912	71.2	28.8	226	84.1	15.9	…	…	…	…	…	Turkmenistan
91	54	56	13	–114	5[9]	…	…	…	…	…	…	…	…	…	…	Tuvalu
78	14	25	14	–32	4,250	99.4	0.6	133	75.2	24.8	–1,245	1,114	–130.8	667	179	Uganda
60	19	24	47	–50	10,458	49.0	51.0	1,779	68.4	31.6	–5,194	3,557	–1,637	3,576	3,330	Ukraine
40	8	24	82	–55	…	…	…	…	…	…	…	…	…	7,162[10]	13,288[10]	United Arab Emirates
64	22	18	30	–34	…	…	…	…	…	…	–153,850	65,750	–88,100	30,498	50,559	United Kingdom
70	16	20	11	–17	…	…	…	…	…	…	–832,250	–24,430	–856,670	121,131	79,222	United States
73	12	15	30	–30	7,866	40.7	59.3	1,487	73.0	27.0	–473.7	17.1	–456.6	1,312	336	Uruguay
53	17	23	39	–31	3,639	67.7	36.3	628	81.4	18.6	…	…	…	99	455[2]	Uzbekistan
61	23	20	43	–47	71.9[2]	100.0	—	1.8	61.1	38.9	–109.4	59.1	–50.3	119[12]	11[12]	Vanuatu
48	11	25	37	–21	29,317	10.8	89.2	4,256	49.2	50.8	32,984	–5,817	27,167	788	1,568	Venezuela
64	6	35	75	–79	16,513	87.3	12.7	784	58.9	41.1	–838[4]	1,055[4]	217[4]	3,050	1,100	Vietnam
…	…	…	…	…	…	…	…	…	…	…	…	…	…	1,468	…	Virgin Islands (U.S.)
…	…	…	…	…	…	…	…	…	…	…	…	…	…	…	…	West Bank[14]
…	…	…	…	…	…	…	…	…	…	…	…	…	…	…	…	Western Sahara
61	16	22	47	–45	4,717	99.3	0.7	148	62.8	37.2	2,256[4]	–1,041[4]	1,215[4]	496	214	Yemen
68	14	26	19	–27	4,085	90.6	9.4	114	71.1	28.9	–221[6]	–363.3[6]	–584.3[6]	98	39	Zambia
73	31	10	50	–64	3,222	86.7	13.3	22	86.3	13.7	…	…	…	314	…	Zimbabwe

[1]2006. [2]2004. [3]Government services include financial services. [4]2005. [5]2003. [6]2000. [7]Manufacturing includes mining. [8]2009. [9]2002. [10]2008. [11]2001. [12]2007. [13]Republic of Cyprus only. [14]Gaza Strip includes West Bank. [15]Excludes Abkhazia and South Ossetia. [16]Manufacturing includes mining and public utilities. [17]GDP. [18]Excludes Alderney and Sark. [19]Gaming activities. [20]Manufacturing includes mining, construction, and public utilities. [21]Excludes Transdniestria. [22]Includes former Spanish Sahara. [23]Mining includes public utilities. [24]Covers mainland Tanzania only. [25]Other includes agriculture and hotels and restaurants. [26]Gross territorial income.

Energy

This table provides data about the commercial energy supplies (reserves, production, consumption, and trade) of the various countries of the world, together with data about petroleum and gas pipeline networks and traffic. Most of the data and concepts used in this table are adapted from the United Nations' *Energy Statistics Yearbook*.

Electricity. Total installed electrical power capacity comprises the sum of the rated power capacities of all main and auxiliary generators in a country. "Total installed capacity" (kW) is multiplied by 8,760 hours per year to yield "Total production capacity" (kW-hr).

Production of electricity comprises the total gross production of electricity by publicly or privately owned enterprises and also that generated by industrial establishments for their own use, but it usually excludes consumption by the utility itself. Measured in millions of kilowatt-hours (kW-hr), annual production of electricity ranges generally between 50% and 60% of total production capacity. The data are further analyzed by type of generation: fossil fuels, hydroelectric power, and nuclear fuel.

The great majority of the world's electrical and other energy needs are met by the burning of fossil hydrocarbon solids, liquids, and gases, either for thermal generation of electricity or in internal combustion engines. Many renewable and nontraditional sources of energy are being developed worldwide (wood, biogenic gases and liquids, tidal, wave, and wind power, geothermal and photothermal [solar] energy, and so on), but collectively these sources are still negligible in the world's total energy consumption. For this reason only hydroelectric and nuclear generation are considered here separately with fossil fuels.

Trade in electrical energy refers to the transfer of generated electrical output via an international grid. Total electricity consumption (residential and nonresidential) is equal to total electricity requirements less transformation and distribution losses.

Coal. In this table, coal comprises all grades of anthracite, bituminous, subbituminous, and lignite that have acquired or may in the future, by reason of new technology or changed market prices, acquire an economic value. These types of coal may be differentiated according to heat content (density) and content of impurities. Most coal reserve data are based on proven recoverable reserves only, of all grades of coal. Exceptions are footnoted, with proven in-place reserves reported only when recoverable reserves are unknown. Production figures include deposits removed from both surface and underground workings as well as quantities used by the producers themselves or issued to the miners. Wastes recovered from mines or nearby preparation plants are excluded from production figures.

Energy

country	electricity												coal		
	installed capacity, 2004 ('000 kW)	production		power source, 2004			trade, 2004		consumption				reserves, 2005 ('000,000 metric tons)	pro-duction, 2004 ('000 metric tons)	con-sump-tion, 2004 ('000 metric tons)
		capacity, 2002 ('000,000 kW-hr)	amount, 2004 ('000,000 kW-hr)	fossil fuel (%)	hydro-power (%)	nuclear fuel (%)	exports ('000,000 kW-hr)	imports ('000,000 kW-hr)	amount, 2004 ('000,000 kW-hr)	per capita, 2004 (kW-hr)	resi-dential, latest (%)	non-resi-dential, latest (%)			
Afghanistan	323	5,790	779	27.6	72.4	—	—	100	879	38	…	…	66	34	34
Albania	1,684	16,574	5,559	1.7	98.3	—	274	477	5,762	1,847	…	…	794	109	118
Algeria	6,468	59,830	31,250	99.2	0.8	—	197	211	31,264	889	28.4	71.6	40	—	615
American Samoa	58	508	138	100.0	—	—	—	—	138	2,226	…	…	…	…	…
Andorra	…	…	…	…	…	…	—	—	…	…	…	…	…	…	…
Angola	665	4,030	2,339	25.1	74.9	—	—	—	2,339	205	…	…	…	…	…
Antigua and Barbuda	27	237	109	100.0	—	—	—	—	109	1,595	…	…	…	…	…
Argentina	30,599	244,089	100,260	64.6	32.0	3.4[1]	4,143	7,612	103,729	2,714	47.3	52.7	423	51	937
Armenia	3,341	29,162	6,030	30.4	33.1	36.5	1,012	260	5,278	1,744	…	…	…	—	—
Aruba	150	1,314	816	100.0	—	—	—	—	816	11,458	…	…	…	…	…
Australia	48,630	387,507	239,497	92.8	7.2	—	—	—	239,497	11,849	…	…	78,456	354,461	133,516
Austria	16,712	160,632	64,125	37.8	62.2	—[1]	13,548	16,629	67,208	8,256	…	…	16	235	5,480
Azerbaijan	5,476	47,216	21,643	87.2	12.8	—	1,008	2,373	23,008	2,770	…	…	…	…	—
Bahamas, The	401	3,513	2,087	100.0	—	—	—	—	2,087	6,964	…	…	…	…	…
Bahrain	1,709	11,966	8,448	100.0	—	—	—	—	8,448	11,932	…	…	…	…	…
Bangladesh	4,680	30,572	21,466	94.3	5.7	—	—	—	21,466	154	37.7	62.3	…	…	700
Barbados	210	1,454	895	100.0	—	—	—	—	895	3,304	78.4	21.6	…	…	…
Belarus	7,847	68,748	31,211	99.9	0.1	—	4,723	7,975	34,463	3,508	…	…	…	…	234
Belgium	14,305	137,716	85,643	42.7	1.9	55.4	6,790	14,567	93,420	8,988	…	…	…	147	8,391
Belize	52	377	169	51.9	48.1	—	—	25	194	707	71	29	…	…	…
Benin	122	491	81	98.8	1.2	—	—	578	659	81	64.1	35.9	…	…	…
Bermuda	160	1,279	661	100.0	—	—	—	—	661	10,179	…	…	…	…	…
Bhutan	457	3,171	1,952	—	100.0	—	1,470	18	500	229	…	…	…	51	65
Bolivia	1,353	11,160	4,542	64.5	35.5	—	—	5	4,547	493	49.0	51.0	0.9	…	…
Bosnia and Herzegovina	4,368	23,924	12,599	53.0	47.0	—	3,079	997	10,517	2,690	…	…	…	8,578	8,953
Botswana	132	[2]	[2]	[2]	[2]	[2]	[2]	[2]	[2]	[2]	26.3	73.7	40	[2]	[2]
Brazil	86,504	722,332	387,451	13.5	78.4	8.1	7	37,392	424,836	2,340	26.7	73.3	10,113	5,406	19,830
Brunei	860	4,459	3,236	100.0	—	—	—	—	3,236	8,842	53.7	46.3	…	…	…
Bulgaria	11,206	111,217	41,621	51.5	8.1	40.4	6,620	741	35,742	4,582	53.1	46.9	2,181	26,485	26,526
Burkina Faso	177	683	400	75.0	25.0	—	—	—	400	31	…	…	…	…	…
Burundi	58	385	136	1.5	98.5	—	—	34	169	22	73.8	26.2	…	…	…
Cambodia	37	307	130	73.1	26.9	—	—	—	130	10	…	…	…	…	…
Cameroon	902	7,927	4,110	4.6	95.4	—	—	—	4,110	256	…	…	…	[1]	[1]
Canada	118,094	990,896	598,514	29.5	59.4	11.1[3]	33,249	22,785	588,050	18,408	…	…	6,578	65,999	58,861
Cape Verde	7	61	220	100.0	—	—	—	—	220	529	…	…	…	…	…
Cayman Islands	…	…	400	…	…	…	—	—	372	…	…	…	…	…	…
Central African Republic	40	377	110	23.6	76.4	—	—	—	110	26	69.3	30.7	2.7	…	…
Chad	29	254	99	100.0	—	—	—	—	99	11	…	…	…	…	…
Chile	10,737	97,639	51,984	60.1	39.9	—	—	—	53,887	3,347	30	70	1,181	188	4,435
China	391,420	2,095,129	2,193,736	81.7	16.0	2.3	9,476	3,400	2,187,660	1,684	25.3	74.7	114,500	1,992,234	1,922,654
Colombia	13,653	120,783	50,291	23.7	76.3	—	1,682	48	48,657	1,074	70.9	29.1	6,611	53,693	3,144
Comoros	6	53	20	90.0	10.0	—	—	—	20	31	…	…	…	…	…
Congo, Dem. Rep. of the	2,502	28,120	6,852	0.3	99.7	—	1,456	6	5,402	92	…	…	88	108	153
Congo, Rep. of the	121	1,060	399	0.5	98.5	—	—	404	803	229	…	…	…	…	…
Costa Rica	1,939	16,177	8,210	21.0	79.0	—	440	202	7,972	1,876	71.1	28.9	…	…	…
Côte d'Ivoire	909	10,538	5,411	67.7	32.3	—	1,409	—	4,002	224	26.1	73.9	…	…	…
Croatia	3,792	34,436	13,295	47.0	53.0	—	1,633	5,298	16,960	3,818	68	32	39	—	1,189
Cuba	3,959	34,681	15,652	99.4	0.6	—	—	—	15,652	1,380	52.8	47.2	…	…	13
Cyprus	988	8,804	4,176	100.0	—	—	—	—	4,176	5,718	82.4	17.6	…	…	58
Czech Republic	16,193	134,308	84,333	65.7	3.0	31.3	25,493	9,776	68,616	6,720	…	…	5,552	64,076	57,290
Denmark	13,315	116,464	40,477	83.7	0.1	16.2[5]	11,545	8,873	37,605	6,967	…	…	…	—	7,327
Djibouti	90	771	200	100.0	—	—	—	—	200	260	…	…	…	…	…
Dominica	22	123	79	57.0	43.0	—	—	—	79	1,129	…	…	…	…	…
Dominican Republic	5,530	44,781	13,759	85.6	14.4	—	—	—	13,759	1,536	72.3	27.7	…	…	777
East Timor	…	…	300	100.0	…	…	—	—	300	254	…	…	…	…	…
Ecuador	3,463	28,321	11,702	20.8	79.2	—	—	1,542	13,344	1,024	56.8	43.2	24	…	…
Egypt	17,058	148,578	101,299	87.0	13.0	—	873	174	100,800	1,465	74.4	25.6	21	33	1,850
El Salvador	1,219	9,207	4,564	48.9	30.3	20.8[6]	84	488	4,946	732	67.4	32.6	…	…	…
Equatorial Guinea	18	158	27	88.9	11.1	—	—	—	27	52	…	…	…	…	…
Eritrea	88	1,507	283	100.0	—	—	—	—	283	67	…	…	…	…	…

Natural gas. This term refers to any combustible gas (usually chiefly methane) of natural origin from underground sources. The data for production cover, to the extent possible, gas obtained from gas fields, petroleum fields, or coal mines that is actually collected and marketed. (Much natural gas in Middle Eastern and North African oil fields is flared [burned] because it is often not economical to capture and market it.) Manufactured gas is generally a by-product of industrial operations such as refineries, gasworks, coke ovens, and blast furnaces. It is usually burned at the point of production and rarely enters the marketplace.

Crude petroleum. Crude petroleum is the liquid product obtained from oil wells; the term also includes shale oil, tar sand extract, and field or lease condensate. Production and consumption and consumption per capita data in the table refer, so far as possible, to the same year so that the relationship between national production and consumption patterns can be clearly seen; data are given in barrels.

Proven reserves are that oil remaining underground in known fields whose existence has been "proved" by the evaluation of nearby producing wells or by seismic tests in sedimentary strata known to contain crude petroleum, and that is judged recoverable within the limits of present technology and economic conditions (prices). The published proven reserve figures do not necessarily reflect the true reserves of a country, because government authorities or corporations often have political or economic motives for withholding or altering such data.

The estimated exhaustion rate of petroleum reserves is an extrapolated ratio of published proven reserves to the current rate of withdrawal/production. Present world published proven reserves will last about 40 to 45 years at the present rate of withdrawal, but there are large country-to-country variations above or below the average.

Data on petroleum and gas pipelines are provided because of the great importance to both domestic and international energy markets of this means of bringing these energy sources from their production or transportation points to refineries, intermediate consumption and distribution points, and final consumers. The pipeline length for petroleum includes the combined total length for both crude and refined petroleum pipelines, whereas the pipeline length for gas includes the combined total length for natural gas, condensate, and liquefied petroleum gas pipelines. The source for these data was the latest edition of the *CIA World Factbook*.

A secondary source reviewed in the overall compilation of this table was the Energy Information Administration website of the U.S. government.

natural gas					crude petroleum						pipelines (2006) length (km)		country
published proven reserves, 2007 ('000,000,000 cu m)	production		consumption		reserves		production, 2004 ('000,000 barrels)	consumption, 2004 ('000,000 barrels)	consumption per capita (barrels)	refining capacity, 2007 ('000 barrels per day)			
	natural gas, 2004 ('000,000 cu m)	manufactured gas, 2004 ('000,000 cu m)	natural gas, 2004 ('000,000 cu m)	natural gas per capita (cu m)	published proven, 2007 ('000,000 barrels)	years to exhaust proven reserves, 2004					petroleum	gas	
50	3	…	3	0.1	…	…	—	—	—	—	387	466	Afghanistan
2.0	16	9.8	16	5.2	165	190	2.8	2.8	0.9	25	207	339	Albania
4,580	81,291	11,266	21,173	602	12,270	15	471	146	4.1	450	6,496	8,953	Algeria
…	…	…	…	…	…	…	—	—	—	—	—	—	American Samoa
…	…	…	…	…	…	…	…	…	…	…	—	—	Andorra
57	730	80	730	64	8,000	24	366	11.5	1.0	39	867	357	Angola
…	…	…	…	…	…	…	—	—	—	—	—	—	Antigua and Barbuda
456	52,390	7,561	43,459	1,137	2,468	10	254	194	5.1	625	10,373	29,845	Argentina
176	…	…	1,289	426	…	…	—	—	—	—	—	2,002	Armenia
…	…	…	…	…	…	…	—	3.3	46.8	271	—	—	Aruba
2,520	39,954	4,767	28,399	1,405	4,015	9	203	252	12.5	702	4,408	32,109	Australia
16	2,142	1,627	9,792	1,203	50	11	6.9	60	7.3	209	812	2,722	Austria
850	4,995	314	9,702	1,168	7,000	62	113	46	5.6	399	2,436	3,190	Azerbaijan
…	…	…	…	…	…	…	—	—	—	—	—	—	Bahamas, The
92	7,030	510	7,030	9,930	125	2	68	93	131	255	52	20	Bahrain
436	13,339	67	13,339	95.8	28	89	—	10	0.1	33	—	2,604	Bangladesh
0.2	25	1.1	25	92.0	3.0	12	0.6	—	…	—	—	—	Barbados
2.8	255	944	19,817	2,017	198	15	13	135	13.8	493	4,007	5,223	Belarus
—	—	2,357	14,522	1,397	7	…	—	252	24.3	858	693	1,561	Belgium
…	…	…	…	…	…	…	—	—	—	—	—	—	Belize
1.1	…	…	…	…	8.0	50	0.1	—	—	—	—	—	Benin
…	…	…	…	…	…	…	—	—	—	—	—	—	Bermuda
…	…	…	…	…	…	…	—	—	—	—	—	—	Bhutan
680	9,544	479	1,734	188	440	27	15	11	1.2	47	4,064	4,907	Bolivia
…	…	…	366	94.0	…	…	—	—	—	—	174	—	Bosnia and Herzegovina
1.1	…	[2]	…	…	—	—	…	[2]	…	—	—	—	Botswana
306	9,603	12,952	16,762	92.3	11,773	17	548	623	3.4	1,908	9,967	12,254	Brazil
391	10,556	59	1,458	3,982	1,100	17	71	0.6	1.8	9	463	672	Brunei
5.7	353	729	3,301	423	15	67	0.2	39	5.0	115	495	2,505	Bulgaria
…	…	…	…	…	…	…	—	—	—	—	—	—	Burkina Faso
…	…	…	…	…	…	…	—	—	—	—	—	—	Burundi
…	…	…	…	…	…	…	—	—	—	—	—	—	Cambodia
110	…	32	…	…	400	8	48	14	0.9	42	1,107	79	Cameroon
1,641	180,093	32,757	93,277	2,920	179,210[4]	…	764	610	19.1	2,017	23,564[5]	74,980[5]	Canada
…	…	…	…	…	…	…	—	—	—	—	—	—	Cape Verde
—	—	—	—	—	—	—	—	—	—	—	—	—	Cayman Islands
…	…	…	…	…	…	…	—	—	—	—	—	—	Central African Republic
…	…	…	…	…	1,500	…	—	—	—	—	205	—	Chad
98	1,967	1,444	8,436	524	150	48	1.3	75	4.7	227	1,760	3,148	Chile
2,265	39,589	45,746	37,259	28.7	16,000	19	1,287	2,124	1.6	6,246	21,362	22,664	China
113	7,843	1,489	7,843	173	1,453	9	189	112	2.5	286	9,298	4,360	Colombia
…	…	…	…	…	…	…	—	—	—	—	—	—	Comoros
1.0	…	5.0	…	…	180	25	7.5	—	—	—	78	54	Congo, Dem. Rep. of the
91	141	5.8	141	40.1	1,600	18	84	5.5	1.7	21	744	93	Congo, Rep. of the
…	…	16	…	—	…	…	—	3.0	0.9	24	242	—	Costa Rica
28	1,016	124	1,016	56.9	100	29	9.5	26	1.5	65	112	349	Côte d'Ivoire
30	2,414	735	3,305	744	74	8	6.5	37	8.4	250	583	1,340	Croatia
71	704	191	704	62.1	558	36	21	31	2.8	301	230	49	Cuba
—	—	20	…	—	…	…	—	2.0	2.8	—	—	—	Cyprus
4.0	229	2,540	10,969	1,074	15	39	2.1	45	4.5	198	641	7,010	Czech Republic
72	10,124	632	5,524	1,023	1,277	9	148	62	11	176	626	3,943	Denmark
…	…	…	…	…	…	…	—	—	—	—	—	—	Djibouti
…	…	…	…	…	—	—	—	—	…	—	—	—	Dominica
—	…	39	0.7	0.6	…	…	—	16	1.8	48	104	—	Dominican Republic
…	…	2,568	…	…	…	…	1.0	—	—	—	—	—	East Timor
90	352	133	352	27.0	4,517	24	195	66	5.0	176	3,122	71	Ecuador
1,657	32,967	2,830	29,378	428	3,700	13	253	240	3.5	726	6,017	7,476	Egypt
—	…	34	…	—	…	…	—	7.1	1.0	22	—	—	El Salvador
37	480	…	480	927	1,100	20	55	2.6	5.0	—	31	98	Equatorial Guinea
…	…	…	…	…	…	…	—	—	—	15	—	—	Eritrea

Energy (continued)

country	electricity												coal		
	installed capacity, 2004 ('000 kW)	production		power source, 2004			trade, 2004		consumption				reserves, 2005 ('000,000 metric tons)	production, 2004 ('000 metric tons)	consumption, 2004 ('000 metric tons)
		capacity, 2002 ('000,000 kW-hr)	amount, 2004 ('000,000 kW-hr)	fossil fuel (%)	hydropower (%)	nuclear fuel (%)	exports ('000,000 kW-hr)	imports ('000,000 kW-hr)	amount, 2004 ('000,000 kW-hr)	per capita, 2004 (kW-hr)	residential, latest (%)	nonresidential, latest (%)			
Estonia	2,554	22,294	10,128	99.7	0.3	—	2,141	347	8,334	6,168	55.4	44.6	...	13,993	15,561
Ethiopia	726	4,765	2,547	1.0	99.0	—	—	—	2,547	36	35.65	64.45	...	...	...
Faroe Islands	87	815	290	69.0	31.0	—	—	—	290	6,215	...	...	...	...	...
Fiji	199	1,752	540	19.4	80.6	—	—	—	540	613	22	78	...	...	13
Finland	16,569	145,144	85,817	55.8	17.6	26.9[1]	6,797	11,677	90,687	17,374	...	...	...	...	8,082
France	112,151	1,018,919[7]	572,241[7]	10.1[7]	11.3[7]	78.6[7]	68,588[7]	6,548[7]	510,201[7]	8,231[7]	...	...	15	872[7]	20,820[7]
French Guiana	140	1,226	430	100.0	—	—	—	—	430	2,248	55.42	44.62	...	...	...
French Polynesia	133	964	485	81.0	19.0	—	—	—	485	1,821	...	...	...	...	...
Gabon	414	3,635	1,537	41.9	58.1	—	—	—	1,537	1,128	41.9	58.1	...	...	...
Gambia, The	29	254	151	100.0	—	—	—	—	151	96	...	...	...	...	...
Gaza Strip	...	...	...	...	...	...	...	...	...	...	...	...	...	...	...
Georgia	4,388	39,035	6,924	12.6	87.4	—	—	1,281	8,205	1,577	...	...	...	8	12
Germany	118,850	1,100,825	616,785	64.2	4.5	27.1[8]	50,808	48,187	614,164	7,442	...	...	6,739	211,077	249,280
Ghana	1,432	10,985	6,044	12.6	87.4	—	878	665	6,257	289	7.2	92.8	...	...	4
Greece	11,320	99,163	59,344	89.2	8.8	2.0[6]	2,034	4,854	62,164	5,630	...	...	3,900	70,041	71,631
Greenland	106	929	270	100.0	—	—	—	—	270	4,789	...	...	183	...	...
Grenada	32	237	157	100.0	—	—	—	—	157	1,963	72.9	27.1	...	...	...
Guadeloupe	423	3,679	1,165	100.0	—	—	—	—	1,165	2,621	...	...	...	...	...
Guam	552	3,504	1,589	100.0	—	—	—	—	1,589	9,587	...	...	...	...	...
Guatemala	2,009	13,254	7,009	65.3	34.7	—	464	41	6,586	532	67.3	32.7	...	...	481
Guernsey	...	...	...	...	...	...	...	...	...	...	...	...	...	...	...
Guinea	284	1,726	801	45.2	54.8	—	—	—	801	87	...	...	...	...	...
Guinea-Bissau	21	184	61	100.0	—	—	—	—	61	44	...	...	...	...	...
Guyana	313	2,707	835	100.0	—	—	—	—	835	1,080	...	...	...	...	...
Haiti	244	2,278	547	51.9	48.1	—	—	—	547	81	44.1	55.9	...	...	...
Honduras	1,044	7,989	4,877	51.9	48.1	—	—	357	5,234	730	69.5	30.5	...	...	174
Hong Kong	11,683	103,368	37,129	100.0	—	—	3,087	9,837	43,879	6,401	...	...	...	...	10,012
Hungary	8,272	74,670	33,708	64.0	0.6	35.4	3,056	10,524	41,176	4,070	65.5	34.5	3,357	11,242	13,472
Iceland	1,507	13,219	8,623	0.1	82.7	17.2[6]	—	—	8,623	29,430	...	...	...	...	104
India	131,434	1,105,862	665,873	84.0	12.7	2.6[9]	40	1,735	667,568	618	53.5	46.5	92,445	412,952	434,719
Indonesia	25,034	221,488	103,536	85.3	14.5	0.2[10]	—	—	103,536	476	46.9	...	4,968	119,700	14,167
Iran	34,310	310,104	164,481	93.5	6.5	—	—	—	164,481	2,460	...	...	419	1,246	1,707
Iraq	2,760	83,220	33,410	98.5	1.5	—	—	1,318	34,728	1,280	...	...	...	...	...
Ireland	5,163	47,646	25,627	93.4	4.0	2.6[6]	10	1,574	27,191	6,751	...	...	14	—	2,671
Isle of Man	...	...	...	...	...	...	...	...	337	4,610	...	...	...	...	...
Israel	9,981	87,924	49,025	100.0	—	—	1,459	—	47,566	6,924	61.6	38.4	...	439	13,314
Italy	71,355	751,398[11]	303,347[11]	81.1[11]	16.4[11]	2.5[6, 11]	791[11]	46,426[11]	348,982[11]	6,029[11]	...	...	34[11]	98[11]	24,289[11]
Jamaica	1,469	11,808	7,217	98.3	1.7	—	—	—	7,217	2,697	36.2	63.8	...	...	66
Japan	243,512	2,285,353	1,080,124	63.9	9.5	26.6[12]	—	—	1,080,124	8,459	...	...	359	—	180,807
Jersey	...	...	...	...	...	...	...	...	557	6,265	...	...	...	...	...
Jordan	1,789	15,663	8,967	99.4	0.6	—	1	826	9,792	1,638	66.1	33.9	...	...	...
Kazakhstan	17,157	165,476	68,942	88.0	12.0	—	7,403	5,234	64,773	4,320	...	...	31,279	89,945	63,950
Kenya	1,143	10,056	5,894	35.8	59.2	5.0[6]	—	84	5,978	179	38.8	61.2	...	...	108
Kiribati	3	26	10	100.0	—	—	—	—	10	99	...	...	...	...	...
Korea, North	9,500	83,220	21,974	43.1	56.9	—	—	—	21,974	968	...	...	600	30,140	30,006
Korea, South	58,779	522,219	371,011	63.1	1.6	35.3	—	—	371,011	7,716	41.8	58.2	80	3,191	84,926
Kosovo	...	...	...	...	...	...	...	...	...	...	...	...	...	...	...
Kuwait	9,392	82,274	41,256	100.0	—	—	—	—	41,256	15,423	93.3	6.7	...	...	...
Kyrgyzstan	3,720	32,386	15,145	6.9	93.1	—	3,382	54	11,817	2,320	25.4	...	812	461	1,436
Laos	691	2,488	1,295	3.5	96.5	—	750	217	762	126	...	...	...	290	290
Latvia	2,164	18,545	4,683	33.6	66.4	—	636	2,733	6,780	2,923	59.5	40.5	...	...	98
Lebanon	2,537	20,122	10,192	91.0	9.0	—	—	216	10,408	2,691	...	...	...	...	200
Lesotho	76	[2]	[2]	[2]	[2]	[2]	[2]	[2]	[2]	[2]	...	...	...	[2]	[2]
Liberia	253	2,926	330	100	—	—	—	—	330	118	...	...	...	...	...
Libya	4,710	41,260	20,202	100.0	—	—	—	—	20,202	3,147	...	...	...	...	4
Liechtenstein	[13]	[13]	[13]	[13]	[13]	[13]	[13]	[13]	[13]	[13]	...	...	...	...	[13]
Lithuania	5,772	57,536	19,274	16.7	4.9	78.4	11,488	4,293	12,079	3,505	...	...	...	...	264
Luxembourg	528	10,897	4,136	78.2	20.6	1.2[6]	3,132	6,506	7,510	16,348	...	...	...	...	129
Macau	489	3,478	1,973	100.0	—	—	—	151	2,124	4,564	87.2	12.8	...	...	...
Macedonia	1,526	13,087	6,665	77.8	22.2	—	—	1,176	7,841	3,863	...	...	...	7,245	7,551
Madagascar	227	1,997	990	35.4	64.6	—	—	—	990	56	31.7	68.3	...	...	10
Malawi	238	1,717	1,270	—	100.0	—	8	—	1,262	100	67.4	32.6	1.8	70	57
Malaysia	20,082	137,278	82,282	92.9	7.1	—	616	93	81,759	3,475	48.4	51.6	3.6	382	13,275
Maldives	49	385	160	100.0	—	—	—	—	160	539	...	...	...	...	...
Mali	280	999	455	47.3	52.7	—	—	—	455	41	99	1	...	...	...
Malta	570	4,511	2,216	100.0	—	—	—	—	2,216	5,542	...	...	...	...	326
Marshall Islands	...	...	...	...	...	...	—	—	...	...	...	...	...	...	...
Martinique	396	3,469	1,190	100.0	—	—	—	—	1,190	2,771	...	...	...	...	...
Mauritania	115	1,007	240	85.0	15.0	—	—	—	240	80	...	...	...	...	7
Mauritius	663	5,782	2,165	94.4	5.6	—	—	—	2,165	1,775	64.7	35.3	...	...	289
Mayotte	...	...	...	...	...	...	—	—	139	666	...	...	...	...	...
Mexico	49,553	414,339	224,077	75.8	19.5	2.8[14]	1,006	47	223,118	2,190	...	...	1,211	9,882	13,446
Micronesia	...	...	...	...	...	...	—	—	...	...	...	...	...	...	...
Moldova	2,954	8,953	3,617	98.4	1.6	—	424	3,361	6,554	1,554	...	...	...	...	186
Monaco	[7]	[7]	[7]	[7]	[7]	[7]	[7]	[7]	[7]	[7]	...	...	...	[7]	[7]
Mongolia	901	7,893	3,303	100.0	—	—	8	171	3,466	1,260	...	...	...	6,865	6,865
Montenegro[15]	...	...	...	...	...	...	...	...	...	...	...	...	...	...	...
Morocco	4,851	41,146	18,241	90.2	9.8	—	—	1,700	19,941	652	54.5	45.5	...	—	5,472
Mozambique	2,340	20,752	11,714	0.3	99.7	—	9,047	7,913	10,579	545	...	...	212	38	23
Myanmar (Burma)	1,930	13,850	6,437	63.8	36.2	—	—	—	6,437	129	75.5	24.5	1.8	1,013	185
Namibia	70	[2]	[2]	[2]	[2]	[2]	[2]	[2]	[2]	[2]	...	...	...	[2]	[2]
Nauru	10	88	32	100.0	—	—	—	—	32	2,498	...	...	...	...	...
Nepal	603	4,012	2,345	0.2	99.8	—	213	155	2,287	86	59.5	40.5	0.9	11	301
Netherlands, The	20,904	183,890	100,770	94.2	0.1	5.7[14]	5,188	21,405	116,987	7,196	...	...	497	...	13,560
Netherlands Antilles	210	1,840	1,065	100.0	—	—	—	—	1,065	4,885	...	...	...	...	...

natural gas: published proven reserves, 2007 ('000,000,000 cu m)	natural gas: production: natural gas, 2004 ('000,000 cu m)	natural gas: production: manufactured gas, 2004 ('000,000 cu m)	natural gas: consumption: natural gas, 2004 ('000,000 cu m)	natural gas: consumption: natural gas per capita (cu m)	crude petroleum: reserves: published proven, 2007 ('000,000 barrels)	crude petroleum: reserves: years to exhaust proven reserves, 2004	crude petroleum: production, 2004 ('000,000 barrels)	crude petroleum: consumption, 2004 ('000,000 barrels)	crude petroleum: consumption per capita (barrels)	crude petroleum: refining capacity, 2007 ('000 barrels per day)	pipelines (2006) length (km): petroleum	pipelines (2006) length (km): gas	country
...	...	117	923	658	—	—	—	—	—	—	—	859	Estonia
25	...	3.5	4.7	...	0.4	...	—	5.6	0.1	—	—	—	Ethiopia
...	...	...	...	...	...	...	—	—	—	—	—	—	Faroe Islands
...	...	...	...	—	...	...	—	—	—	—	—	—	Fiji
—	—	1,533	4,769	940	...	...	—	78	15.2	252	—	694	Finland
9.7	1,374[7]	8,847[7]	49,845[7]	804[7]	122	15	8.3	632[7]	10.2[7]	1,979	7,913[7]	14,588[7]	France
...	...	...	...	...	...	...	—	—	—	—	—	—	French Guiana
...	...	...	...	...	...	...	—	—	—	—	—	—	French Polynesia
28	126	32	126	92.4	2,000	32	78	5.3	3.9	17	1,354	272	Gabon
...	...	...	...	...	...	...	—	—	...	—	—	—	Gambia, The
...	...	...	...	...	...	...	...	...	...	...	—	—	Gaza Strip
8.5	12	—	1,077	207	35	51	0.7	0.3	0.1	—	1,010	1,349	Georgia
255	22,564	19,596	120,583	1,461	367	17	25	811	9.8	2,428	7,373	25,072	Germany
23	...	122	...	—	15	...	...	13	0.6	45	13	316	Ghana
1.0	34	1,300	2,658	241	5.0	8	0.8	134	12.1	413	94	1,166	Greece
...	...	...	...	...	...	...	—	—	—	—	—	—	Greenland
...	...	...	...	...	...	...	—	—	—	—	—	—	Grenada
...	...	...	...	...	...	...	—	—	—	—	—	—	Guadeloupe
...	...	...	...	—	...	...	—	—	—	—	—	—	Guam
3.1	—	—	—	—	83	79	7.3	2.2	0.2	...	480	—	Guatemala
...	...	...	...	...	...	...	...	...	...	...	—	—	Guernsey
...	...	...	...	...	...	...	—	—	—	—	—	—	Guinea
...	...	...	...	...	...	...	—	—	—	—	—	—	Guinea-Bissau
...	...	...	...	...	...	...	—	—	—	—	—	—	Guyana
...	...	...	...	...	...	...	—	—	—	—	—	—	Haiti
—	...	...	...	—	...	...	—	—	—	—	—	—	Honduras
—	—	695	2,132	311	...	...	—	—	—	—	—	—	Hong Kong
8.1	3,035	992	15,021	1,485	127	12	7.2	43	4.2	161	1,325	4,397	Hungary
—	...	...	...	...	...	...	—	—	—	—	—	—	Iceland
1,075	26,764	9,482	26,764	24.8	5,625	20	259	983	0.9	2,255	12,652	7,185	India
2,769	72,710	3,938	33,142	152	4,300	9	412	382	1.8	993	9,051	10,254	Indonesia
27,581	81,259	5,049	83,865	1,252	136,270	61	1,430	539	8.0	1,451	16,329	18,138	Iran
3,172	2,600	1,636	2,600	95.8	115,000	157	729	173	6.4	598	7,143	3,146	Iraq
9.9	805	184	4,263	1,058	—	—	—	21	5.3	71	—	1,728	Ireland
...	...	...	...	...	...	...	—	—	—	—	—	—	Isle of Man
36	1,125	621	1,125	164	2.0	—	—	79	11.5	220	703	193	Israel
164	12,966	7,964	80,638[11]	1,393[11]	600	16	37	629[11]	10.8[11]	2,324	1,136	17,589	Italy
—	...	11	...	—	...	...	—	5.4	2.0	36	—	—	Jamaica
40	5,228	34,398	81,950	642	59	14	2.1	1,466	11.5	4,672	170	8,015	Japan
...	...	...	...	...	...	...	...	...	—	—	—	—	Jersey
6.0	267	180	267	47.3	1.0	...	—	30	5.3	90	49	426	Jordan
2,832	22,104	2,683	16,472	1,099	30,000	21	374	90	6.0	345	11,433	11,677	Kazakhstan
—	...	76	...	—	...	...	—	15	0.4	86	894	—	Kenya
...	...	...	...	...	...	...	—	—	—	—	—	—	Kiribati
...	...	51	...	...	...	...	—	4.2	0.2	71	154	—	Korea, North
—	—	29,269	29,611	616	...	...	—	828	17.2	2,577	827	1,482	Korea, South
...	...	...	...	...	...	...	...	...	...	...	...	...	Kosovo
1,557	9,700	5,787	9,700	3,626	101,500	106	855	321	120	889	597	269	Kuwait
5.7	29	...	798	157	40	68	0.5	0.7	0.1	10	16	254	Kyrgyzstan
...	...	...	...	...	...	...	—	—	...	—	540	—	Laos
...	...	7	1,588	685	40	...	—	—	—	—	497	1,097	Latvia
—	...	...	...	...	...	...	—	—	—	—	—	43	Lebanon
—	...	[2]	...	...	...	...	...	[2]	—	—	—	—	Lesotho
—	...	...	...	...	...	...	—	—	—	15	—	—	Liberia
1,491	6,817	954	5,746	895	41,464	61	566	126	20	380	6,916	4,363	Libya
—	...	[13]	...	...	...	...	...	[13]	[13]	—	—	20	Liechtenstein
—	...	935	2,828	821	12	212	2.2	64	18.5	190	349	1,696	Lithuania
...	...	5	1,399	3,099	...	...	—	—	—	—	—	155	Luxembourg
...	...	...	...	...	...	...	—	—	—	—	—	—	Macau
...	...	23	2,731	647	...	...	—	6.0	0.3	50	120	268	Macedonia
—	...	7	...	...	...	...	—	3.5	0.2	15	—	—	Madagascar
...	...	...	...	—	...	...	—	—	—	—	—	—	Malawi
2,124	55,889	1,714	30,045	1,277	3,000	11	280	201	8.5	545	1,829	5,654	Malaysia
...	...	...	...	...	...	...	—	—	—	—	—	—	Maldives
...	...	...	...	...	...	...	—	—	—	—	—	—	Mali
—	...	...	...	...	...	...	—	—	—	—	—	—	Malta
...	...	...	...	...	...	...	—	—	—	—	—	—	Marshall Islands
—	...	32	...	...	...	...	—	4.4	10.2	17	—	—	Martinique
28	...	48	...	...	100	...	...	—	—	—	—	—	Mauritania
...	...	...	...	...	...	...	—	—	—	—	—	—	Mauritius
...	...	...	...	...	...	...	—	—	—	—	—	—	Mayotte
412	37,311	3,720	45,948	439	12,352	12	1,242	506	4.8	1,684	15,208	24,580	Mexico
...	...	...	...	...	...	...	...	...	...	...	—	—	Micronesia
...	...	...	2,408	571	...	...	—	—	—	—	—	606	Moldova
...	...	[7]	[7]	...	...	...	...	[7]	[7]	—	—	—	Monaco
...	...	...	...	...	...	...	—	—	—	—	—	—	Mongolia
...	...	...	...	...	...	...	...	...	...	...	...	...	Montenegro[15]
1.6	45	23	45	1.5	1.0	20	0.8	47	1.5	155	285	715	Morocco
127	1,182	...	2.8	0.1	...	...	—	—	—	—	294	918	Mozambique
283	7,184	57	1,455	29.1	50	7	7.1	7.5	0.1	57	558	2,224	Myanmar (Burma)
62	...	[2]	...	...	...	...	...	[2]	[2]	—	—	—	Namibia
...	...	...	...	...	...	...	—	—	—	—	—	—	Nauru
...	...	50	...	—	...	...	—	—	—	—	—	—	Nepal
1,416	90,520	15,231	54,009	3,332	100	5	14	348	21.4	1,222	1,294	7,310	Netherlands, The
—	...	138	...	...	...	...	—	80	366	320	—	—	Netherlands Antilles

Energy (continued)

country	electricity												coal		
	installed capacity, 2004 ('000 kW)	production		power source, 2004			trade, 2004		consumption				reserves, 2005 ('000,000 metric tons)	production, 2004 ('000 metric tons)	consumption, 2004 ('000 metric tons)
		capacity, 2002 ('000,000 kW-hr)	amount, 2004 ('000,000 kW-hr)	fossil fuel (%)	hydropower (%)	nuclear fuel (%)	exports ('000,000 kW-hr)	imports ('000,000 kW-hr)	amount, 2004 ('000,000 kW-hr)	per capita, 2004 (kW-hr)	residential, latest (%)	nonresidential, latest (%)			
New Caledonia	348	2,900	1,678	79.9	20.1	—	—	—	1,678	7,271	…	…	1.8	…	281
New Zealand	8,642	73,873	41,813	28.0	64.6	7.4[6]	—	—	41,813	10,238	…	…	571	5,156	3,774
Nicaragua	693	5,615	2,822	79.6	19.4	1.0[6]	22	23	2,823	525	70.7	29.3	…	…	…
Niger	105	920	247	100.0	—	—	—	220	467	40	56	44	70	178	178
Nigeria	5,898	51,518	20,224	65.8	34.2	—	—	—	20,224	157	…	…	244	3	3
Northern Mariana Islands	…	…	…	…	…	…	—	—	…	…	…	…	…	…	…
Norway	26,637	245,674	110,598	1.0	98.8	0.2[6]	15,254	3,828	122,024	26,657	…	…	5.4	2,904	904
Oman	3,336	24,966	11,499	100.0	—	—	—	—	11,499	5,079	…	…	…	…	…
Pakistan	20,360	152,923	85,699	66.8	30.0	3.2	—	—	85,699	564	72.3	27.7	3,055	4,587	7,894
Palau	62	543	171	85.4	14.6	—	—	—	171	8,543	…	…	…	…	…
Panama	1,555	11,817	5,860	35.5	64.5	—	207	78	5,731	1,807	79.5	20.5	…	—	—
Papua New Guinea	544	4,135	1,399	33.7	66.3	—	—	—	1,399	258	27.9	72.1	…	…	…
Paraguay	7,416	64,964	51,921	0.1	99.9	—	44,997	—	6,925	1,141	79	21	…	…	…
Peru	5,970	51,798	25,547	23.2	76.8	—	—	—	25,547	927	67.74	32.34	1,060	16	963
Philippines	15,125	110,849	55,957	66.2	15.4	18.4[6]	—	—	55,957	686	65.34	34.74	236	2,485	9,461
Poland	30,041	268,038	154,159	97.5	2.5	—	14,605	5,312	144,866	3,793	41.84	58.24	14,000	162,428	145,091
Portugal	11,024	98,480	45,105	75.5	22.5	2.0[6]	2,131	8,612	51,586	4,925	…	…	36	—	5,514
Puerto Rico	5,358	42,933	24,130	99.4	0.6	—	—	—	24,130	6,195	…	…	…	…	176
Qatar	2,670	19,771	13,233	100.0	—	—	—	—	13,233	19,840	74.9	25.1	…	…	…
Réunion	440	3,846	1,620	64.2	35.8	—	—	—	1,620	2,114	…	…	…	…	…
Romania	20,073	191,879	56,503	61.0	29.2	9.8	3,766	2,584	56,321	2,548	27.1	72.9	495	31,792	35,099
Russia	215,277	1,863,848	931,865	65.3	19.2	15.5	19,800	12,179	924,244	6,425	36.1	63.9	157,010	262,344	220,438
Rwanda	35	377	173	2.9	97.1	—	10	120	283	31	…	…	…	…	…
St. Kitts and Nevis	20	175	130	100.0	—	—	—	—	130	3,333	…	…	…	…	…
St. Lucia	57	613	309	100.0	—	—	—	—	309	1,879	…	…	…	…	…
St. Vincent and the Grenadines	24	201	110	72.7	27.3	—	—	—	110	939	…	…	…	…	…
Samoa	29	210	110	63.6	36.4	—	—	—	110	619	…	…	…	…	…
San Marino	[11]	[11]	[11]	[11]	[11]	[11]	[11]	[11]	[11]	[11]	…	…	…	[11]	…
São Tomé and Príncipe	10	53	18	44.4	55.6	—	—	—	18	99	…	…	…	…	…
Saudi Arabia	29,119	211,116	156,506	100.0	—	—	—	—	156,506	6,902	…	…	…	…	…
Senegal	239	2,094	2,351	87.5	12.5	—	—	—	2,351	206	16.7	83.3	…	…	…
Serbia[15]	9,315	103,184	38,489	69.0	31.0	—	1,318	1,032	38,203	3,530	…	…	16,591	41,157	41,441
Seychelles	95	815	220	100.0	—	—	—	—	220	2,716	24.3	75.7	…	…	…
Sierra Leone	132	1,139	85	100.0	—	—	—	—	85	15	…	…	…	…	…
Singapore	7,368	77,508	36,810	100.0	—	—	—	—	36,810	8,682	…	…	…	…	1
Slovakia	7,273	76,151	30,567	30.5	13.8	55.7	10,593	8,731	28,705	5,335	…	…	172	2,952	8,740
Slovenia	2,985	22,277	15,279	37.4	26.8	35.8	7,094	6,314	14,499	7,262	…	…	275	4,809	5,374
Solomon Islands	12	105	33	100.0	—	—	—	—	33	63	…	…	…	…	…
Somalia	80	701	286	100.0	—	—	—	—	286	29	…	…	…	…	…
South Africa	40,481	346,992[2]	247,777[2]	92.0[2]	2.8[2]	5.2[2]	13,329[2]	13,232[2]	247,680[2]	4,818[2]	28.5	71.5	48,750	244,062	180,287
Spain	60,978	529,157	280,007	59.4	12.3	28.3[16]	11,139	8,111	276,979	6,412	…	…	530	20,487	45,804
Sri Lanka	2,958	24,248	8,158	63.7	36.3	—	—	—	8,158	420	62.7	37.3	…	…	95
Sudan, The	755	6,631	3,883	72.8	27.2	—	—	—	3,883	116	…	…	…	…	…
Suriname	389	3,408	1,509	9.1	90.9	—	—	—	1,509	3,437	…	…	…	…	…
Swaziland	128	[2]	[2]	[2]	[2]	[2]	[2]	[2]	[2]	[2]	…	…	208	[2]	[2]
Sweden	33,317	294,765	151,727	8.7	40.0	50.7[17]	17,750	15,646	149,623	16,670	…	…	0.9	—	3,329
Switzerland	17,468[13]	157,408[13]	65,299[13]	4.3[13]	54.3[13]	41.4[13]	27,759[13]	27,056[13]	64,596[13]	8,669[13]	…	…	…	…	177[13]
Syria	6,470	56,502	32,077	86.8	13.2	—	—	—	32,077	1,784	…	…	…	…	…
Taiwan	33,290	34,598	181,245	75.5	3.6	20.9	—	—	167,478	7,406	32.4	67.6	0.9	…	…
Tajikistan	4,443	38,921	17,277	2.3	97.7	—	4,714	4,400	16,963	2,638	…	…	…	51	154
Tanzania	881	4,757	2,478	4.9	95.1	—	…	—	2,591	69	…	…	200	85	85
Thailand	24,805	258,481	125,727	95.2	4.8	—	372	3,388	128,743	2,020	58.3	41.7	1,354	20,060	28,085
Togo	28	333	262	38.9	61.1	—	—	348	810	102	…	…	…	…	…
Tonga	8	70	36	100.0	—	—	—	—	36	327	…	…	…	…	…
Trinidad and Tobago	1,416	12,413	6,430	100.0	—	—	—	—	6,430	4,921	35.3	64.7	…	…	…
Tunisia	2,932	21,331	13,067	98.8	1.2	—	28	—	13,039	1,313	54.1	45.9	…	…	1
Turkey	35,587	279,032	150,698	69.3	30.7	—[1]	1,144	463	150,017	2,122	…	…	4,186	46,379	64,450
Turkmenistan	3,106	34,427	11,470	100.0	—	—	1,654	—	9,816	2,060	…	…	…	…	…
Tuvalu	…	…	…	…	…	…	—	—	…	…	…	…	…	…	…
Uganda	303	2,356	1,896	—	100	—	170	—	1,726	63	…	…	…	…	…
Ukraine	52,408	462,659	182,167	45.7	6.5	47.8	7,529	2,203	186,831	3,727	…	…	34,153	59,670	65,179
United Arab Emirates	5,880	51,509	52,417	100.0	—	—	—	—	52,417	12,000	…	…	…	…	…
United Kingdom	76,187	674,730	395,853	77.4	1.9	20.7[12]	2,294	9,784	403,343	6,756	…	…	220	25,097	33,353
United States	942,178	8,040,594	4,174,481	79.1	8.2	12.7[3]	22,898	34,210	4,185,793	14,240	21.4	78.6	242,721	1,008,880	1,000,482
Uruguay	2,171	19,027	5,936	19.5	80.5	—	19	2,348	8,265	2,408	76	34	…	…	1
Uzbekistan	11,751	102,571	51,030	87.2	12.8	—	11,929	11,843	50,944	1,944	…	…	4,000	2,699	2,699
Vanuatu	12	105	44	100.0	—	—	—	—	44	206	…	…	…	…	…
Venezuela	20,577	180,255	98,482	29.0	71.0	—	—	—	98,482	3,770	23.8	76.2	479	6,748	—
Vietnam	9,029	44,054	46,029	38.3	59.9	1.8[6]	—	—	46,029	560	…	…	150	25,500	14,900
Virgin Islands (U.S.)	323	2,829	1,050	100.0	—	—	—	—	1,050	9,633	…	…	…	…	290
West Bank	…	…	…	…	…	…	…	1,929	1,929	513	…	…	…	…	1
Western Sahara	58	508	90	100.0	—	—	—	—	90	336	…	…	…	…	…
Yemen	997	7,096	4,337	100.0	—	—	—	—	4,337	208	…	…	…	…	…
Zambia	1,778	19,798	8,512	0.6	99.4	—	231	—	8,251	721	33	67	10	233	153
Zimbabwe	2,099	17,616	9,908	44.3	55.7	—	—	2,040	11,948	924	42.6	57.4	502	3,398	3,435

[1]In addition, geothermal equals 0.1%. [2]South Africa includes Botswana, Lesotho, Namibia, and Swaziland. [3]In addition, geothermal equals 2.1%. [4]Includes 173,936,000,000 of Canadian oil sands. [5]2005. [6]Geothermal. [7]France includes Monaco. [8]In addition, geothermal equals 4.2%. [9]In addition, geothermal equals 0.7%. [10]In addition, geothermal equals 0.2%. [11]Italy includes San Marino.

natural gas					crude petroleum								country
published proven reserves, 2007 ('000,000,000 cu m)	production		consumption		reserves		production, 2004 ('000,000 barrels)	consumption, 2004 ('000,000 barrels)	consumption per capita (barrels)	refining capacity, 2007 ('000 barrels per day)	pipelines (2006) length (km)		
	natural gas, 2004 ('000,000 cu m)	manufactured gas, 2004 ('000,000 cu m)	natural gas, 2004 ('000,000 cu m)	natural gas per capita (cu m)	published proven, 2007 ('000,000 barrels)	years to exhaust proven reserves, 2004					petroleum	gas	
…	…	…	…	…	…	…	—	—	—	—	—	—	New Caledonia
25	3,776	438	3,776	925	53	7	7.4	38	9.3	104	568	1,962	New Zealand
—	…	37	…	—	…	…	—	6.4	1.2	20	54	—	Nicaragua
…	…	…	…	—	…	…	—	—	—	—	—	—	Niger
5,151	22,388	167	9,668	75	36,220	33	899	38	0.3	439	7,795	3,063	Nigeria
…	…	…	…	…	…	…	—	—	—	—	—	—	Northern Mariana Islands
2,328	81,278	7,760	5,106	1,115	7,849	8	1,130	108	23.7	310	2,557	6,418	Norway
850	18,096	139	8,019	3,542	5,506	20	285	27	12.0	85	3,405	4,072	Oman
793	32,153	967	32,162	212	289	11	24	85	0.6	269	2,001	10,257	Pakistan
—	…	…	…	…	—	—	—	—	—	…	—	—	Palau
—	…	—	—	—	…	…	—	—	—	—	—	—	Panama
345	85	…	85	15.7	240	12	18	0.5	0.1	33	264	—	Papua New Guinea
—	…	…	…	…	…	…	—	0.5	0.1	8	—	—	Paraguay
247	1,409	1,328	1,409	51.2	930	8	34	60	2.2	193	1,767	1,667	Peru
99	2,479	559	2,479	30.4	139	22	0.1	75	0.9	333	240	565	Philippines
165	5,821	6,045	17,616	461	96	18	6.6	134	3.5	467	2,161	13,552	Poland
—	…	431	3,938	376	…	…	—	93	8.9	304	182	1,099	Portugal
—	…	101	679	175	…	…	0.3	85	21.7	110	—	—	Puerto Rico
25,783	41,155	2,865	16,872	25,296	15,207	47	269	34	50	200	844	1,639	Qatar
…	…	…	…	…	…	…	—	—	—	—	—	—	Réunion
63	12,114	2,474	16,269	749	600	18	41	94	4.3	517	2,427	3,508	Romania
47,573	514,548	28,480	350,223	2,435	60,000	18	3,199	1,372	9.5	5,341	85,941	156,407	Russia
57	0.2	—	0.2	…	…	…	—	—	—	—	—	—	Rwanda
…	…	…	…	…	…	…	—	—	—	—	—	—	St. Kitts and Nevis
…	…	…	…	…	…	…	—	—	—	—	—	—	St. Lucia
…	…	…	…	…	…	…	—	—	—	—	—	—	St. Vincent and the Grenadines
…	…	…	…	…	…	…	—	—	—	—	—	—	Samoa
…	…	…	[11]	…	…	…	…	[11]	[11]	—	—	—	San Marino
…	…	…	…	…	…	…	—	—	—	—	—	—	São Tomé and Príncipe
6,796	65,679	37,145	65,679	2,897	262,300	74	3,264	610	27	2,095	5,681	3,275	Saudi Arabia
—	13	20	13	1.1	…	…	—	8.6	0.8	27	—	43	Senegal
48	306	111	2,342	216	78	34	4.8	29	2.7	215	393	3,177	Serbia[15]
…	…	…	…	…	…	…	—	—	—	—	—	—	Seychelles
—	…	…	…	…	…	…	—	1.9	0.3	10	—	—	Sierra Leone
—	—	1,721	6,303	1,487	…	…	—	324	76	1,337	8	139	Singapore
14	169	1,625	6,555	1,218	9.0	24	0.3	42	7.8	115	416	6,769	Slovakia
5.7	5.2	7.0	1,071	537	7.0	…	—	—	—	14	11	2,526	Slovenia
…	…	…	…	—	…	…	—	—	—	—	—	—	Solomon Islands
5.7	…	…	…	…	…	…	—	—	…	—	—	—	Somalia
2.8	1,978	4,000	1,978	38.5	15	1	34	207	4.0	505	2,320	1,162	South Africa
2.5	356	4,359	28,942	670	150	8	1.9	449	10.4	1,272	4,069	7,962	Spain
—	…	74	…	—	—	—	—	16	0.8	50	—	—	Sri Lanka
85	…	353	…	…	5,000	5	110	28	0.8	122	5,543	156	Sudan, The
—	…	…	…	…	111	42	3.8	3.2	7.4	7	51	—	Suriname
…	…	…	…	…	…	…	…	[2]	—	—	—	—	Swaziland
—	…	1,836	1,054	117	…	…	—	150	16.8	434	—	798	Sweden
—	—	571[13]	3,310[13]	444[13]	…	…	—	37[13]	5.0[13]	132	101	1,831	Switzerland
241	6,860	334	6,860	382	2,500	18	159	85	4.7	240	2,000	2,764	Syria
84	850	…	850	37.6	4.0	4	2.8	352	15.3	1,220	—	686	Taiwan
5.7	32	…	563	87.6	12	111	0.1	0.1	…	—	38	549	Tajikistan
6.5	127	—	127	3.4	…	…	—	—	—	15	872	254	Tanzania
418	18,819	7,027	27,295	428	290	8	29	315	5.0	703	379	3,760	Thailand
—	…	…	…	…	…	…	—	—	—	—	—	—	Togo
…	…	…	…	…	…	…	—	—	…	—	—	—	Tonga
733	26,303	1,032	12,527	9,588	728	13	45	48	36.6	175	571	1,531	Trinidad and Tobago
65	2,070	76	3,278	330	400	12	25	12	1.2	34	1,578	2,945	Tunisia
8.5	708	3,174	23,373	331	300	17	16	186	2.8	714	3,543	4,621	Turkey
2,832	57,288	443	13,691	2,873	600	7	69	47	10	237	1,361	6,441	Turkmenistan
…	…	…	…	…	…	…	…	…	—	—	—	—	Tuvalu
…	…	…	…	…	…	…	—	—	—	—	—	—	Uganda
1,104	20,479	5,476	78,531	1,655	395	48	22	178	3.7	880	8,725	19,951	Ukraine
6,071	45,800	9,142	38,753	8,872	97,800	96	878	68	16	781	3,106	3,400	United Arab Emirates
481	113,935	14,275	115,230	1,930	3,875	6	653	616	10.3	1,877	9,538	22,205	United Kingdom
5,788	529,874	121,163	622,433	2,117	21,757	11	1,965	5,869	20	17,339	244,620[18]	548,665[18]	United States
—	—	161	111	32.3	…	…	—	15.4	4.5	50	160	257	Uruguay
1,841	57,288	285	54,369	2,074	594	11	32	32	1.2	222	868	9,594	Uzbekistan
…	…	…	…	…	…	…	—	—	—	—	—	—	Vanuatu
4,315	24,964	5,849	24,964	956	80,012	70	1,022	373	14	1,282	10,280	5,369	Venezuela
193	5,501	391	5,501	67.0	600	16	144	—	—	—	256	595	Vietnam
—	…	…	…	…	…	…	6	42	380	495	—	—	Virgin Islands (U.S.)
…	…	…	…	…	…	…	—	—	—	—	—	—	West Bank
…	…	…	…	…	…	…	—	—	—	—	—	—	Western Sahara
479	…	104	…	…	3,000	26	148	29	1.4	130	1,284	93	Yemen
—	…	19	…	—	…	…	—	3.0	0.3	24	771	—	Zambia
…	…	105	…	—	…	…	—	—	—	—	261	—	Zimbabwe

[12]In addition, geothermal equals 0.5%. [13]Switzerland includes Liechtenstein. [14]In addition, geothermal equals 1.9%. [15]Serbia includes Montenegro. [16]In addition, geothermal equals 5.6%. [17]In addition, geothermal equals 0.6%. [18]2003.

Communications

Virtually all the states of the world have a variety of communications media and services available to their citizens: book, periodical, and newspaper publishing (although only daily papers are included in this table); postal services; and telecommunications systems, that is, television broadcasting, telephones (fixed and mobile), personal computers (PCs), and access to the Internet (including broadband). Unfortunately, the availability of information about these services often runs behind the capabilities of the services themselves. Certain countries publish no official information; others publish data analyzed according to a variety of fiscal, calendar, religious, or other years; still others, while they possess such data almost simultaneously with the end of the business or calendar year, may not see them published except in company or parastatal reports of limited distribution. Even when such data are published in national statistical summaries, it may be only after a delay of up to several years.

The data also differ in their completeness and reliability. Book production data generally include all works published in separate bindings except advertising works, timetables, telephone directories, price lists, catalogs of businesses or exhibitions, musical scores, maps, atlases, and the like. The figures include government publications, school texts, theses, offprints, series works, and illustrated works, even those consisting principally of illustrations. Figures refer to works actually published during the year of survey, usually by a registered publisher, and deposited for copyright. A book is defined as a work of 49 or more pages; a work published simultaneously in more than one country is counted as having been published in each. A periodical is a publication issued at regular or stated intervals and, in UNESCO's usage, directed to the general public. Newspaper statistics are especially difficult to collect and compare. Newspapers continually are founded, cease publication, merge, or change frequency of publication. Data on circulation are often incomplete, slow to be aggregated at the national level, or regarded as proprietary. In some countries no daily newspaper exists.

Post office statistics are compiled mainly from the Universal Postal Union's annual summary *Statistique des services postaux.* Postal services, unlike the other media discussed earlier, tend most often to be operated by a single national service, to cover a country completely, and to record traf-

Communications

country	publishing (latest)							postal services				telecommunications	
	books		periodicals		daily newspapers			post offices, 2004				television (latest)	
	number of titles	number of copies ('000)	number of titles	number of copies ('000)	number	average circulation ('000)	circulation per 1,000 adult persons	number	persons per office	pieces of mail handled ('000,000)	pieces handled per person	receivers (all types; '000)	receivers per 1,000 persons
Afghanistan	2,795	3,741	...	...	12	32	1.7	410	69,693	2.4	0.03	312	14
Albania	381	5,710	143	3,477	21	70	25	563	5,527	7.6	1.8	989	318
Algeria	670	...	48	803	24	2,600	102	3,287	9,844	234	11	3,633	114
American Samoa	...	...	...	...	2	6	140	...	...	...	...	13	211
Andorra	57	...	...	...	2	27	380	...	...	...	...	36	461
Angola	22	419	...	...	5	42	5.8	55	281,637	0.7	0.05	582	52
Antigua and Barbuda	...	...	...	...	2	9	143	13	6,194	6.0	32	34	449
Argentina	9,850	39,663	...	...	182	1,129	37	5,689	6,745	393	9	12,500	323
Armenia	396[2]	20,212[2]	44	541	12	42	16	907	3,298	3.6	0.6	687	229
Aruba	...	...	...	...	13	54	651	4	17,100	12	94	20	218
Australia	10,835	...	...	...	49	2,482	143	3,844	5,188	5,727	261	14,371	722
Austria	25,358	...	2,792	...	16	2,305	325	1,999	4,088	2,054	252	2,570	315
Azerbaijan	542	2,643	49	801	24	120	19	1,311	6,373	7	1.2	2,570	315
Bahamas, The	...	...	...	...	4	39	170	62	5,141	26	46	77	247
Bahrain	40[2]	...	26	73	6	189	350	13	55,063	48	54	273	386
Bangladesh	...	...	...	...	37	1,500	15	9,995	13,928	290	2.1	11,531	85
Barbados	...	...	...	...	2	48	209	18	14,938	45	156	78	291
Belarus	3,809	59,073	155	3,765	10	1,796	119	3,784	2,593	876	51	3,809	386
Belgium	13,913	...	13,706	...	29	1,382	157	1,369	7,597	3,713[4]	346[4]	5,800	557
Belize	70	—	...	...	10	23.5	0.5	134[5]	1,720[5]	4.0[5]	12[5]	52	190
Benin	84[2]	42[2]	...	...	8	50	10	178	45,939	12	1.0	431	59
Bermuda	...	...	...	...	1	16	286	...	...	...	...	68	1,077
Bhutan	...	...	...	...	1	...	...	110	19,235	1.4	1.9	25	33
Bolivia	...	...	...	...	19	155	25	78	84,300	9.9[4]	0.7[4]	1,210	134
Bosnia and Herzegovina	...	...	...	...	7	190	48	245	15,957	29	13	950	248
Botswana	158[2]	...	14	177	2	11	805	181	9,773	39	22	78	44
Brazil	21,574[6]	104,397[6]	...	...	532	8,193	57	12,367	14,871	8,318	44	65,949	369
Brunei	45[2]	56[2]	15	132	2	41	144	32	11,428	10	26	215	648
Bulgaria	4,840	20,317	772	1,740	62	870	133	3,008	2,587	131	17	3,620	453
Burkina Faso	12[2]	14[2]	37	24	5	36	4.3	73	175,640	3.5	0.5	156	12
Burundi	...	...	...	...	1	20	4.1	32	227,557	16[1]	1.3[1]	280	37
Cambodia	...	...	...	...	6	58	5.9	79	174,660	3.7	0.2	103	8.0
Cameroon	...	...	...	...	3	75	6.7	377[5]	37,000[5]	6.1[5, 7]	0.4[5, 7]	720	43
Canada	19,900	...	1,400	37,108	100	4,117	147	...	...	...	...	22,384	707
Cape Verde	...	...	...	...	4	...	...	54[4]	7,780[4]	1.6[4]	2.1[4]	48	105
Cayman Islands	...	...	...	...	...	18	462	...	...	...	...	23	639
Central African Republic	...	...	...	...	6	5.0	1.9	24	166,082	...	...	24	6.1
Chad	...	...	...	...	1	2.0	0.2	42	224,951	10	0.6	55	5.9
Chile	2,469	4,095	417	3,450	59	581	44	710[4]	20,870[4]	343[4]	23[4]	4,305	268
China	130,613	7,240[8]	7,999	250,400	1,035	109,000[9]	99[9]	66,393	19,700	25,163	19	493,902	381
Colombia	1,481	11,314	...	...	24	1,200	37	1,996	22,500	97	2.0	11,358	268
Comoros	...	...	...	...	1	...	...	37[4]	17,800[4]	0.4[4]	0.3[4]	13	23
Congo, Dem. Rep. of the	64[2]	535[2]	...	...	8	50	1.4	497[4]	98,870[4]	...	...	146	2.7
Congo, Rep. of the	...	...	3	34	6	8	3.7	...	...	...	...	40	12
Costa Rica	963	...	...	...	7	272	81	149	28,544	26	6.2	1,068	257
Côte d'Ivoire	...	...	...	...	20	200	16	197	90,720	40	2.1	880	52
Croatia	1,718	...	352	6,357	12	535	141	1,158	3,920	367	65	1,401	315
Cuba	932	4,610	14	285	16	1,800	192	1,855[4]	5,990[4]	12[4]	1.1[4]	3,000	267
Curaçao[10]	...	...	...	...	3	30	171	15	12,058	24	132	71	390
Cyprus	930	1,776	39	338	8	100	155	1,111	743	71	69	278	384
Czech Republic	10,244	...	1,168	81,387	81	1,365	152	3,419	2,992	3,364	303	5,488	538
Denmark	12,352	...	157	6,930	34	1,058	235	996	5,436	1,389	257	5,264	977
Djibouti	...	...	7	6.0	—	—	—	11	70,828	0.9	0.4	53	114
Dominica	...	...	...	...	—	—	—	...	...	...	...	16	220
Dominican Republic	...	...	...	...	11	245	37	278	31,539	6.6	0.6	1,950	209
East Timor	...	...	...	...	2	3	4.1	5	177,367	0.1	0.1	...	...
Ecuador	12[2]	19[2]	199	...	36	705	70	315[4]	38,600[4]	13[4]	0.4[4]	3,298	253
Egypt	2,215	92,353	258	2,373	17	4,018	71	5,615	12,937	312	3.2	17,500	253
El Salvador	...	...	45	774	5	280	60	317	21,333	9	0.8	1,560	233
Equatorial Guinea	...	...	...	...	...	...	...	20	24,612	...	...	55	116

fic data according to broadly similar schemes (although the details of *classes* of mail handled may differ). Some countries do not enumerate domestic traffic or may record only international traffic requiring handling charges. Data on mail traffic includes the number of copies of newspapers and excludes advertising material and ordinary money orders.

Data for some kinds of telecommunications apparatus are relatively easy to collect; telephones, for example, must be installed, and service recorded so that it may be charged. But in most countries the other types of apparatus mentioned above may be purchased by anyone and used whenever desired. As a result, data on distribution and use of these types of apparatus may be collected in a variety of ways—on the basis of numbers of subscribers, licenses issued, periodic sample surveys, trade data, census or housing surveys, or private consumer surveys. Data on telephones refer to "main lines," or the lines connecting a subscriber's apparatus (fixed or mobile) to the public, switched net. The information provided for the number of PCs is estimated only. "Users" refers to the number of people with access to computers connected to the Internet.

The *Statistical Yearbook* of UNESCO contains extensive data on book, periodical, and newspaper publishing, and on television broadcasting that have been collected from standardized questionnaires. The quality and recency of its data, however, depend on the completion and timely return of each questionnaire by national authorities. The commercially published annual *World Radio TV Handbook* (Andrew G. Sennitt, editor) is a valuable source of information on broadcast media and has complete and timely coverage. It depends on data received from broadcasters, but, because some do not respond, local correspondents and monitors are used in many countries, and some unconfirmed or unofficial data are included as estimates. The statistics on telecommunications apparatus and computers are derived mainly from the UN-affiliated International Telecommunication Union's *World Telecommunication Development Report* (annual).

... Not available.

— None, nil, or not applicable.

telephones, 2010		cellular phones, 2010		personal computers, 2005		Internet users, 2009		broadband, 2010		country
main lines		cellular subscriptions ('000)	subscriptions per 1,000 persons	units ('000)	units per 1,000 persons	number ('000)	users per 1,000 persons	subscriptions ('000)	subscriptions per 1,000 persons	
('000)	per 1,000 persons									
140	4.5	13,000	414	...	...	1,000	36	1.5	—	Afghanistan
332	104	4,548	1,419	36[1]	12[1]	1,300	412	110	34	Albania
2,923	82	32,780	924	350	11	4,700	135	900	25	Algeria
10	152	2.2[1]	38[1]	...	...	...	...	...	...	American Samoa
38	450	65	772	...	...	67	785	25	289	Andorra
303	16	8,909	467	27[1]	1.9[1]	607	33	20	1.0	Angola
42	471	164	1,847	...	...	65	742	15	173	Antigua and Barbuda
10,000	247	57,300	1,418	3,000[1]	82[1]	12,244	304	3,862	96	Argentina
590	191	3,865	1,250	200[3]	66[3]	208	68	83	27	Armenia
35	326	132	1,226	...	...	24	225	19	179	Aruba
8,660	389	22,500	1,010	13,720[3]	689[3]	15,757	740	5,165	232	Australia
3,245	387	12,241	1,458	4,996	611	6,144	735	2,002	239	Austria
1,500	163	9,100	990	195	23	3,689	417	500	54	Azerbaijan
129	377	428	1,249	...	...	116	339	25	71	Bahamas, The
228	181	1,567	1,242	121[3]	164[3]	649	820	154	122	Bahrain
900	6.1	68,650	462	1,650[3]	11[3]	617	3.8	60	0.4	Bangladesh
138	503	350	1,281	40	149	188	737	56	206	Barbados
4,139	431	10,333	1,077	109[3]	11[3]	4,437	461	1,666	174	Belarus
4,640	433	12,154	1,135	3,627[3]	351[3]	8,113	762	3,373	315	Belgium
30	97	194	623	35[3]	127[3]	36	117	8.9	29	Belize
133	15	7,075	799	32	4.3	200	22	26	2.9	Benin
58	890	88	1,358	34[3]	535[3]	54	833	40	618	Bermuda
26	36	394	543	13	17	50	72	8.7	12	Bhutan
848	85	7,179	723	190[3]	23[3]	1,103	112	959	9.7	Bolivia
999	266	3,014	802	...	...	1,422	377	391	104	Bosnia and Herzegovina
137	69	2,363	1,178	80[3]	45[3]	120	62	12	6.0	Botswana
42,141	216	202,944	1,041	19,350[3]	107[3]	75,943	392	14,087	72	Brazil
80	200	435	1,091	31[3]	85[3]	319	798	22	54	Brunei
2,200	294	10,585	1,412	461[3]	59[3]	3,395	450	1,102	147	Bulgaria
144	8.7	5,708	347	31	2.4	178	11	14	0.8	Burkina Faso
33	3.9	1,151	137	34[3]	4.8[3]	65	7.8	0.2	—	Burundi
359	25	8,151	577	38[3]	2.6[3]	78	5.3	36	2.5	Cambodia
497	25	8,156	416	160[3]	9.8[3]	750	38	1.0	0.1	Cameroon
17,021	500	24,037	707	22,390[3]	705[3]	26,225	781	10,139	298	Canada
72	145	372	750	48[3]	10[3]	150	297	15	30	Cape Verde
37	664	100	1,777	...	...	24	428	19	335	Cayman Islands
12	2.7	1,020	232	11[3]	2.8[3]	23	5.1	...	...	Central African Republic
51	4.6	2,614	233	15[3]	1.7[3]	188	17	0.2	—	Chad
3,458	202	19,852	1,160	2,300	148	5,767	340	1,789	105	Chile
294,383	220	859,003	640	52,990[3]	40[3]	384,000	285	126,337	94	China
6,809	147	43,405	938	1,892	42	20,789	455	2,622	57	Colombia
21	29	165	225	5.0[3]	6.3[3]	24	36	—	—	Comoros
42	0.6	11,355	172	...	...	365	5.5	8.7	0.1	Congo, Dem. Rep. of the
10	2.4	3,799	940	17[3]	4.5[3]	245	67	0.1	—	Congo, Rep. of the
1,482	318	3,035	651	1,014[3]	239[3]	1,579	345	288	62	Costa Rica
223	11	14,910	755	262[3]	16[3]	968	46	7.9	0.4	Côte d'Ivoire
1,866	424	6,362	1,445	842[3]	191[3]	2,234	506	804	183	Croatia
1,164	103	1,003	89	377	34	1,605	143	3.7	0.3	Cuba
90	449	...	...	...	...	...	...	...	...	Curaçao[10]
415	376	1,034	937	249[3]	309[3]	434	498	195	176	Cyprus
2,198	210	14,331	1,366	2,450[3]	240[3]	6,681	644	1,538	147	Czech Republic
2,623	473	6,905	1,244	3,543[3]	659[3]	4,751	868	2,075	374	Denmark
19	21	166	186	21[3]	31[3]	26	30	8.1	9.1	Djibouti
16	229	106[11]	1,591[11]	9.0[3]	127[3]	28	420	32	471	Dominica
1,010	102	8,893	896	...	...	2,701	268	361	36	Dominican Republic
2.4	2.1	601	534	...	...	2.1	1.9	0.2	0.2	East Timor
2,086	144	14,781	1,022	514	39	2,052	151	197	14	Ecuador
9,618	119	70,661	871	2,800	38	16,636	200	1,477	18	Egypt
1,010	162	7,700	1,243	350	51	889	144	175	28	El Salvador
14	19	399	570	7.0[3]	14[3]	14	21	1.2	1.7	Equatorial Guinea

Communications (continued)

country	publishing (latest)							postal services				telecommunications	
	books		periodicals		daily newspapers			post offices, 2004				television (latest)	
	number of titles	number of copies ('000)	number of titles	number of copies ('000)	number	average circulation ('000)	circulation per 1,000 adult persons	number	persons per office	pieces of mail handled ('000,000)	pieces handled per person	receivers (all types; '000)	receivers per 1,000 persons
Eritrea	106	420	...	...	—	—	—	66	64,114	2.8	0.4	250	58
Estonia	2,628	6,662	517	2,323	11	227	199	545	2,450	110	54	686	507
Ethiopia	240	674	...	...	5	92	2.0	650	116,307	29	0.3	547	7.9
Faroe Islands	...	...	...	...	1	17	436	33	1,416	11	271	47	1,022
Fiji	401	2,256	...	...	3	40	61	169	4,975	30	31	98	118
Finland	13,104	...	5,711	...	53	2,049	462	1,311	3,993	1,859	506	3,540	679
France	34,766	1,041	2,672	120,018	85	7,362	146	16,947	3,556	19,658	326	23,723	391
French Guiana	...	...	...	...	1	15	106	...	...	...	...	37	202
French Polynesia	...	...	...	...	2	20	92	97[4]	2,370[4]	28[4]	102[4]	56	223
Gabon	...	...	...	...	1	20	23	60	22,706	6.6	3.7	220	173
Gambia, The	14[12]	10[12]	10	885	2	4	4.0	19	77,772	7.8	2.0	20	13
Gaza Strip[13]	...	...	...	...	...	...	...	...	...	...	...	...	...
Georgia	581[2]	834[2]	...	...	9	43	11	998	4,527	3,241	716	1,627	357
Germany	71,515	...	9,010	395,036	371	19,746	279	13,019	6,348	23,869	289	55,758	675
Ghana	28	648	121	774	7	200	13	721	30,048	125[14]	2.5[14]	1,114	53
Greece	4,225	...	...	...	32	1,100	116	2,200	5,045	734	54	6,152	558
Greenland	103	...	...	...	—	—	—	75	757	7.9	85	22[5]	393[5]
Grenada	...	...	4	89	—	—	—	53	1,929	8.9	51	38	375
Guadeloupe	...	...	...	...	1	2	5.8	...	...	...	...	125	289
Guam	...	...	...	...	1	20	155	...	...	...	...	106	646
Guatemala	...	...	...	...	6	490	61	436	28,199	34	2.1	2,000	167
Guernsey	...	...	...	...	...	...	...	12	5,000	56	642	...	...
Guinea	...	...	3	5.0	2	25	4.4	40	94,800	7.9[4]	0.4[4]	140	16
Guinea-Bissau	...	...	...	...	—	—	—	20	76,986	...	...	47	36
Guyana	42[2]	508[2]	...	...	3	30	52	71	10,567	15	13	125	169
Haiti	...	...	...	...	3	20	3.6	55	152,853	1.7	0.3	60	7.2
Honduras	22	80	...	...	6	190	39	...	...	...	...	1,000	143
Hong Kong	...	...	598	...	30	2,200	355	131	53,152	1,254[4]	175[4]	3,467	507
Hungary	9,193	53,194	1,203	14,927	32	1,239	125	2,824	3,585	2,202	135	4,810	475
Iceland	1,527	...	938	384	3	50	199	94	3,106	68	355	101	345
India	11,903	...	...	...	410	109,900	143	153,021[4]	6,240[4]	16,394[4]	16[4]	88,876	83
Indonesia	4,018[12]	8,103[12]	115	4,173	218	5,728	33	19,632	11,210	1,076	4.5	33,255	153
Iran	15,073	87,861	318	6,166	32	1,600	31	6,511	10,567	267	4.0	11,566	173
Iraq	...	...	...	...	11	...	...	278	100,924	69[4]	2.1[4]	472	19
Ireland	...	...	...	...	7	767	218	1,604	2,543	749	184	2,707	694
Isle of Man	...	...	...	...	...	...	...	31	2,475	49	651	29	355
Israel	2,310[15]	9,368[15]	...	...	34	700	134	661	9,986	764	116	2,136	335
Italy	35,236	278,821	9,951	80,469	94	4,842	94	13,855	4,189	6,661	115	28,153	494
Jamaica	...	...	...	...	3	115	61	603	4,377	71	26	1,006	374
Japan	56,221[2]	400,013[2]	2,926	...	107	50,353	458	24,678	5,184	28,016	219	107,527	842
Jersey	...	...	...	...	...	...	...	21	4,190	62[5]	468[5]	...	...
Jordan	511	2,673[2]	31	43	4	313	72	392	12,941	24	4.8	1,065	198
Kazakhstan	1,226	21,014	...	...	4	320	27	3,733	3,975	153	10.1	5,106	338
Kenya	300[2]	452	...	...	5	310	14	865	38,691	136	4.1	758	25
Kiribati	...	...	...	...	—	—	—	25[5]	3,200[5]	1.9[5]	1.2[5]	4	44
Korea, North	...	...	...	...	3	4,500	252	...	...	...	...	3,563	160
Korea, South	30,487[2]	142,804[2]	...	...	136	12,800	317	3,692	12,905	4,952	103	22,915	477
Kosovo	...	...	...	...	...	...	...	...	...	...	...	...	...
Kuwait	196[20]	6,107[20]	...	...	7	961	485	59	44,177	32	12	1,040	392
Kyrgyzstan	351	1,980	...	...	3	65	17	922	5,644	28	5.6	955	185
Laos	88[2]	995[2]	...	...	4	10	2.5	234	24,751	1.1	0.2	321	59
Latvia	1,965	7,734	213	1,660	22	220	113	968	2,395	116	50	1,992	857
Lebanon	...	...	...	...	15	259	87	200	17,701	13	3.4	1,269	320
Lesotho	...	...	...	...	6	14	8.0	153	11,751	2.6	1.1	80	41
Liberia	...	...	...	...	3	50	26	342[21]	8,260[21]	...	...	69	25
Libya	26	2,645	...	...	5	100	24	360	15,945	50	8.8	717	133
Liechtenstein	...	...	...	...	2	20	690	12	2,850	34	977	17	510
Lithuania	3,645	14,915	269	...	19	574	202	955	3,606	175	51	1,785	519
Luxembourg	681	...	508	...	6	113	282	105	4,211	220	485	70	156
Macau	67	99	16	...	10	190	404	18	25,401	27	58	130	292
Macedonia	892	2,496	74	347	13	160	96	320	6,345	28	14	507	250
Madagascar	119	296	55	108	9	115	10	617	29,356	26[4]	1.5[4]	410	25
Malawi	117[2, 23]	9,174[2, 23]	...	...	2	22	2.8	325	38,795	44[4]	3.4[4]	65	5.2
Malaysia	5,843	29,040	25	996	35	2,595	147	1,202	20,711	1,238	49	5,480	222
Maldives	...	...	...	...	3	21	68	216	1,487	1.4	4.8	41	144
Mali	14[2]	28[2]	...	...	4	40	6.1	124[4]	86,200[4]	3.4[4]	0.2[4]	400	36
Malta	404	...	359	...	4	100	295	51	7,839	57	143	222	553
Marshall Islands	...	...	...	...	—	—	—	...	...	...	...	...	...
Martinique	...	...	...	...	1	65	192	...	...	...	...	66	169
Mauritania	...	...	...	...	3	9	4.9	26	114,629	0.3	0.1	123	44
Mauritius	80	163	62	...	2	105	106	125	9,865	74	60	290	230
Mayotte	...	...	...	...	...	...	...	...	...	...	...	3.5[21]	30[21]
Mexico	...	...	158	13,097	299	4,800	61	8,002	13,209	698	6.6	29,400	282
Micronesia	...	...	...	...	—	—	—	...	...	...	...	2.8	26
Moldova	921	2,779	76	196	6	400	110	1,146	3,681	99	24	1,300	327
Monaco	41	722	3	38	—	—	—	...	...	...	...	25	758
Mongolia	285[2]	959[2]	45	6,361	6	49	22	385	6,790	20	8.1	220	88
Montenegro	...	...	...	...	...	62	110	...	...	...	...	...	...
Morocco	918	1,836	...	...	20	340	14	1,653	18,766	284	9.5	5,010	164
Mozambique	...	3,490	...	...	6	18	1.5	299	64,963	8.9	0.5	391	20
Myanmar (Burma)	3,660	4,038	...	...	8	420	12	1,331	37,569	...	...	373	8.1
Namibia	106	...	...	...	5	55	41	118	17,028	79	39	509	259
Nauru	...	...	...	...	—	—	—	1	10,100	...	...	0.8	77
Nepal	...	...	...	...	29	700	39	4,156[4]	5,260[4]	74	2.8	249	9.6
Netherlands	34,067	...	367	19,283	36	3,530	260	3,188	5,090	5,303[25]	326[25]	10,514	648

telephones, 2010		cellular phones, 2010		personal computers, 2005		Internet users, 2009		broadband, 2010		country
main lines ('000)	main lines per 1,000 persons	cellular subscriptions ('000)	subscriptions per 1,000 persons	units ('000)	units per 1,000 persons	number ('000)	users per 1,000 persons	subscriptions ('000)	subscriptions per 1,000 persons	
54	10	185	35	35	8.0	250	49	0.1	—	Eritrea
482	360	1,653	1,232	650	489	970	724	327	243	Estonia
910	11	6,517	79	225[3]	3.1[3]	445	5.4	4.1	—	Ethiopia
20	414	59	1,221	...	...	38	752	16	334	Faroe Islands
137	159	1,000	1,162	44[3]	52[3]	114	135	16	19	Fiji
1,250	233	8,390	1,564	2,515[3]	482[3]	4,481	841	1,559	291	Finland
35,200	561	62,600	997	35,000	579	44,625	716	21,300	339	France
46	197	218[11]	965[11]	...	...	58	257	...	...	French Guiana
55	203	216	797	78[3]	315[3]	120	446	32	119	French Polynesia
30	20	1,610	1,069	45	33	99	67	3.8	2.5	Gabon
49	28	1,478	855	23[3]	16[3]	130	76	0.4	0.2	Gambia, The
...	...	...	...	...	...	...	...	...	...	Gaza Strip[13]
597	137	3,193	734	192[3]	38[3]	1,300	305	222	51	Georgia
45,600	554	104,560	1,270	46,300[3]	561[3]	65,124	793	26,000	316	Germany
278	11	17,437	715	112[3]	5.2[3]	1,297	54	50	2.1	Ghana
5,203	458	12,293	1,082	986[3]	90[3]	4,971	445	2,253	198	Greece
22	381	57	1,001	...	...	36	628	12	210	Greenland
28	272	122	1,167	16[3]	155[3]	25	241	11	101	Grenada
256	555	350[3]	790[3]	100[3]	217[3]	109	234	...	...	Guadeloupe
66	364	33[1]	207[1]	...	...	90	506	3.0	17	Guam
1,499	104	18,068	1,256	231[3]	18[3]	2,280	163	259	18	Guatemala
45	...	32[1]	500[1]	...	...	48	...	...	...	Guernsey
18	1.8	4,000	401	44[3]	55[3]	95	9.4	0.5	0.1	Guinea
5.0	3.3	594	392	...	...	37	23	...	...	Guinea-Bissau
150	199	555	736	29	39	220	289	12	16	Guyana
50	5.0	4,000	400	...	...	1,000	100	...	...	Haiti
670	88	9,505	1,251	110[3]	16[3]	732	98	76	10	Honduras
4,345	616	13,416	1,902	4,172	593	4,300	612	2,127	302	Hong Kong
2,977	298	12,012	1,203	1,476[3]	150[3]	6,176	618	1,956	196	Hungary
204	637	348	1,087	142	483	302	935	111	347	Iceland
35,090	29	752,190	614	17,000	15	61,300	51	10,990	9.0	India
37,960	158	220,000	917	3,022[3]	14[3]	20,000	87	1,900	7.9	Indonesia
26,849	363	67,500	913	7,347[3]	105[3]	27,915	376	500	6.8	Iran
1,600	51	24,000	758	...	...	325	11	0.1	—	Iraq
2,078	465	4,702	1,052	2,011[3]	503[3]	3,043	674	1,020	228	Ireland
...	...	...	...	...	...	...	...	...	...	Isle of Man
3,276	442	9,875	1,331	5,037[3]	734[3]	3,700	516	1,865	251	Israel
21,600	357	82,000	1,354	18,150[3]	317[3]	29,236	488	13,400	221	Italy
263	319	3,103	1,132	166[3]	62[3]	1,581	582	117	43	Jamaica
40,419	319	120,709	954	69,200[3]	542[3]	99,144	768	34,055	269	Japan
74	...	61[16]	706[16]	...	...	30	...	...	...	Jersey
485	78	6,620	1,070	300[3]	53[3]	1,742	276	197	32	Jordan
4,011	250	19,769	1,234	...	...	5,300	339	847	53	Kazakhstan
460	11	24,969	616	441[3]	14[3]	3,996	100	4.3	0.1	Kenya
4.1	41	10	101	2.0[1]	23[1]	2.0	20	0.9	9.0	Kiribati
1,180	49	432	18	...	...	...	...	...	...	Korea, North
28,543	592	50,767	1,054	26,201[3]	545[3]	39,440	816	17,650	366	Korea, South
106[17]	49[17]	562[17]	258[17]	...	...	50[18]	24[18]	4.7[19]	2.3[19]	Kosovo
566	207	4,400	1,608	600	223	1,100	369	46	17	Kuwait
502	94	4,900	919	100	19	2,194	400	15	2.9	Kyrgyzstan
103	17	4,003	646	100	17	300	48	12	1.9	Laos
532	236	2,306	1,024	501[3]	219[3]	1,503	668	435	193	Latvia
888	210	2,875	680	409	115	1,000	237	200	47	Lebanon
39	18	699	322	...	...	77	37	0.4	0.2	Lesotho
5.9	1.5	1,571	393	...	...	20	5.1	0.2	—	Liberia
1,228	193	10,900	1,715	130[3]	23[3]	354	55	73	12	Libya
20	544	36	985	...	...	23	641	23	638	Liechtenstein
734	221	4,891	1,472	533[3]	155[3]	1,964	598	684	206	Lithuania
272	539	727	1,433	290	624	425	873	167	328	Luxembourg
168	308	1,122	2,064	130[3]	278[3]	281	522	131	241	Macau
413	201	2,153[22]	1,045[22]	160	79	1,057	518	257	125	Macedonia
172	8.3	8,242	398	91[3]	5.1[3]	320	16	4.9	0.2	Madagascar
160	11	3,038	204	25	1.9	716	47	5.1	0.3	Malawi
4,573	161	34,456	1,213	4,900[3]	197[3]	15,824	576	2,079	73	Malaysia
48	152	494	1,565	36[3]	109[3]	88	284	16	49	Maldives
114	7.4	7,326	477	45	4.0	250	19	2.3	0.2	Mali
247	594	455	1,093	67	166	241	589	115	275	Malta
4.4	81	3.8	70	5.0[3]	88[3]	2.2	36	...	...	Marshall Islands
172	424	349[3]	884[3]	52[1]	130[1]	170	420	6.0	15	Martinique
72	21	2,745	793	42[3]	14[3]	75	23	6.6	1.9	Mauritania
388	298	1,191	917	344[3]	279[3]	290	225	82	63	Mauritius
10	49	22[1]	151[1]	...	...	...	...	...	...	Mayotte
19,892	175	91,363	806	14,000	131	28,439	260	11,325	100	Mexico
8.5	76	28	248	...	...	17	154	1.0	9.0	Micronesia
1,161	325	3,165	886	112[3]	26[3]	1,295	359	269	75	Moldova
34	964	26	743	...	...	23	701	15	419	Monaco
193	70	2,511	911	340	128	350	131	64	23	Mongolia
170	268	1,170	1,853	...	...	280	449	52	83	Montenegro
3,749	117	31,982	1,001	740	24	10,300	322	499	16	Morocco
88	3.6	7,224	309	112[3]	5.9[3]	613	27	15	0.6	Mozambique
605	13	594	12	400	8.5	110	2.2	16	0.3	Myanmar (Burma)
152	67	1,535	672	220[3]	109[3]	128	59	9.6	4.2	Namibia
—[24]	—[24]	6.2	605	...	...	0.3[1]	26[1]	0.4	39	Nauru
842	28	9,196	307	118[3]	4.6[3]	626	21	114	3.8	Nepal
7,169	432	19,310	1,162	11,110[3]	685[3]	14,872	896	6,308	380	Netherlands

Communications (continued)

country	publishing (latest)							postal services				telecommunications	
	books		periodicals		daily newspapers			post offices, 2004				television (latest)	
	number of titles	number of copies ('000)	number of titles	number of copies ('000)	number	average circulation ('000)	circulation per 1,000 adult persons	number	persons per office	pieces of mail handled ('000,000)	pieces handled per person	receivers (all types; '000)	receivers per 1,000 persons
New Caledonia	...	...	...	...	1	26	156	54	4,308	14	61	115	498
New Zealand	...	...	126	3,991	23	632	187	1,021	3,907	...	...	2,338	576
Nicaragua	...	...	...	...	6	170	44	183[4]	26,300[4]	8.3[4]	1.2[4]	648	123
Niger	5[2]	11[2]	...	...	1	4	0.5	52	259,952	1.9	0.2	150	13
Nigeria	1,314	18,800	...	...	25	480	5.5	5,342	24,094	391[1]	2.0[1]	8,393	84
Northern Mariana Islands	...	...	...	...	...	6	81	...	...	...	...	4.1	59
Norway	6,900[15]	...	8,017	...	78	2,061	538	1,504	3,057	2,570	560	7,110	1,567
Oman	7[2]	21[2]	15	...	6	274	140	644	3,935	32	7.6	1,557	633
Pakistan	124	714	...	...	204	6,100	55	12,107	12,785	604	4.0	7,972	51
Palau	...	...	...	...	...	...	...	...	...	...	...	11	606
Panama	...	...	...	...	7	230	97	125	25,403	17	5.5	572	194
Papua New Guinea	122	...	...	...	2	53	14	...	...	...	...	130	22
Paraguay	152	...	...	...	4	115	26	264	22,792	4.6[4]	0.5[4]	1,300	224
Peru	612	1,836	...	...	73	4,250	154	1,947	14,156	21	0.7	4,592	172
Philippines	1,507[2]	14,718[2]	1,570	9,468	42	3,800[28]	60[28]	2,441	33,436	357	4.3	14,700	182
Poland	14,104	80,306	5,260	75,358	48	3,168	98	10,923	3,530	1,890	50	7,091	186
Portugal	7,868[6]	26,942[6]	984	10,208	16	533	60	3,026	3,451	1,950	186	4,312	413
Puerto Rico	...	...	...	...	5	456	143	...	...	...	...	1,290	338
Qatar	209[12]	2,205[12]	11	47	5	120	184	37	20,998	23	31	315	412
Réunion	69	...	...	...	3	70	127	...	...	...	...	138	185
Romania	7,199	38,374	987	...	51	1,241	66	6,821	3,195	402	19	8,340	381
Russia	36,237	421,387	2,751	387,832	485	15,300	105	40,140	3,585	4,634	34	50,599	351
Rwanda	...	...	15	101	1	10	1.7	19	467,493	2.5	0.3	70	7.4
St. Kitts and Nevis	...	...	10	44	1	2	69	7	6,027	3.1	66	11	239
St. Lucia	...	...	...	...	1	...	...	46	3,467	5.2	33	46	291
St. Vincent and the Grenadines	...	...	...	...	2	5.0	36	41[5]	2,680[5]	...	...	50	446
Samoa	...	...	...	...	2	...	...	38[1]	4,470[1]	0.9[1]	3.0[1]	27	152
San Marino	...	...	15	9	2	6.0	240	10[21]	3,000[21]	...	...	25	893
Sao Tome and Principe	...	...	...	...	1	...	...	9	16,996	0.3[4]	0.6[4]	19	128
Saudi Arabia	3,900[2]	14,493[2, 23]	471	...	12	1,878	106	1,421[4]	14,200[4]	1,246[4]	45[4]	6,576	292
Senegal	...	...	...	...	18	198	25	137	83,109	12	1.1	869	77
Serbia	5,367[29]	16,669[29]	395[29]	...	29[29]	1,052	168	1,653[29]	6,358[29]	209[29]	21[29]	2,980[29]	282[29]
Seychelles	...	...	...	...	1	5.0	75	5	15,982	3.6	44	22	266
Sierra Leone	...	...	...	...	8	22	4.1	...	...	...	...	63	13
Singapore	...	...	...	...	11	1,020	256	138	30,961	834	197	1,220	304
Sint Maarten	...	...	...	...	...	...	...	...	...	...	...	...	...
Slovakia	3,800	6,139	424	8,725	12	434	94	1,598	3,380	517	96	2,285	425
Slovenia	3,441	6,267	784	...	7	297	169	557	3,532	849	425	559	279
Solomon Islands	...	...	...	...	1	5	14	127[4]	3,150[4]	...	...	5.3	11
Somalia	...	...	...	...	8	22	4.1	...	...	...	...	108	14
South Africa	5,418	31,349	11	2,149	18	1,596	47	2,449[4]	17,200[4]	2,700	56	9,134	199
Spain	46,330	192,019	...	...	136	3,915	99	3,291	12,958	5,871	135	24,228	564
Sri Lanka	4,115	19,650	...	...	13	590	36	4,680	4,395	411	20	2,400	117
Sudan[30]	...	...	...	...	10	96	3.9	209	169,966	2.7	0.1	12,886	352
Sudan, South[30]	...	...	...	...	...	...	...	...	...	...	...	...	...
Suriname	47[2]	21[2]	...	...	3	55	157	42	10,630	...	...	118	243
Swaziland	...	...	...	...	2	25	37	51	20,280	14	14	38	34
Sweden	13,496	...	373	19,242	95	3,205	422	1,720[21]	5,140[21]	4,570[21]	503[21]	8,645	965
Switzerland	15,371	...	60	4,561	93	2,126	322	2,585	2,801	5,674	761	4,300	576
Syria	598	310[21]	30	192	4	379	29	604	30,765	16	0.9	3,093	178
Taiwan	...	...	...	...	30	3,700	193	9,976	2,270	5,973	264	9,200	418
Tajikistan	132[2]	997[2]	11	130	—	217	47	593	10,844	24	3.6	2,350	357
Tanzania	172[2]	364[2]	...	...	19	167	7.1	418	90,017	38	1.1	1,500	41
Thailand	8,142	...	1,522	...	34	7,500	142	4,478	14,224	1,491	24	17,971	289
Togo	...	...	...	...	1	5	1.4	55	108,880	5.0	0.9	650	107
Tonga	...	...	...	...	—	—	—	...	...	...	...	7.1	70
Trinidad and Tobago	26	30	...	...	4	140	142	245[4]	5,220[4]	...	...	461	359
Tunisia	720	6,000[23]	170	1,748	10	399	49	1,257	7,952	149	15	2,300	231
Turkey	6,546	...	3,554	...	81	4,719	85	4,381	16,485	925	13	29,440	424
Turkmenistan	450[2]	5,493[2]	...	...	2	56	16	190	25,084	91	19	855	182
Tuvalu	...	...	...	...	—	—	—	...	...	...	...	0.3	33
Uganda	288	2,229[15]	26	158	5	100	6.2	329	84,561	25	0.9	450	17
Ukraine	6,225	68,876	717	2,521	38	2,864	73	15,554	3,021	1,230	26	22,500	456
United Arab Emirates	293[23]	5,117[23]	80	922	6	1,027	269	356	12,035	164	38	843	216
United Kingdom	107,263	...	...	...	109	14,009	285	14,609	4,071	21,865	361	56,576	950
United States	68,175	...	11,593	...	1,457	46,278	192	37,159	7,950	206,649	703	260,000	893
Uruguay	934	1,970	...	...	4	145	54	1,409	1,245	18	5.4	838	252
Uzbekistan	1,003	30,914	81	684	5	30	1.5	2,961	8,851	77	3.0	7,232	280
Vanuatu	...	...	...	...	1	3	20	...	...	...	...	2.7	13
Venezuela	3,468[2]	7,420[2]	...	...	92	1,810	97	355	74,034	58	2.2	5,000	201
Vietnam	5,581	83,000	338	2,710	10	4,000	61	3,061	27,152	545	6.7	15,938	197
Virgin Islands (U.S.)	...	...	...	...	1	9	102	10	2,175	1.8	17	65	594
West Bank[13]	...	...	...	...	3	35	15	...	...	...	...	...	...
Western Sahara	...	...	...	...	1	...	...	...	...	...	...	6.0[21]	24[21]
Yemen	...	...	...	...	3	170	13	251	80,993	6.5	0.3	6,780	359
Zambia	...	...	...	...	3	80	12	195[4]	45,000[4]	20	1.8	551	51
Zimbabwe	232	...	28	680	3	40	6.3	1,162	11,133	137[4]	9.4[4]	610	50

telephones, 2010		cellular phones, 2010		personal computers, 2005		Internet users, 2009		broadband, 2010		country
main lines										
('000)	per 1,000 persons	cellular subscriptions ('000)	subscriptions per 1,000 persons	units ('000)	units per 1,000 persons	number ('000)	users per 1,000 persons	subscriptions ('000)	subscriptions per 1,000 persons	
72	288	221	880	...	...	85	340	38	152	New Caledonia
1,870	428	5,020	1,149	1,924[3]	493[3]	3,600	844	1,089	249	New Zealand
258	45	3,771	651	220	43	200	35	48	8.2	Nicaragua
84	5.4	3,806	245	10	0.7	116	7.6	3.7	0.2	Niger
1,050	6.6	87,298	551	867[3]	6.8[3]	43,982	284	99	0.6	Nigeria
26	419	21[18]	260[18]	...	...	10[3]	0.1[3]	...	...	Northern Mariana Islands
1,702	349	5,525	1,132	2,630[3]	578[3]	4,431	921	1,690	346	Norway
284	102	4,606	1,655	118[3]	40[3]	469[26]	168[26]	53	19	Oman
3,419	20	102,777	592	600[16]	4.2[16]	20,350[27]	113[27]	532	3.1	Pakistan
7.0	341	15	709	...	...	5.4[17]	270[17]	0.2	11	Palau
553	157	6,496	1,847	147	46	960	278	276	78	Panama
121	18	1,909	278	367[3]	63[3]	125	19	6.1	0.9	Papua New Guinea
405	63	5,915	916	460	75	1,000	158	39	6.1	Paraguay
3,160	109	29,115	1,001	2,800	100	8,085	277	912	31	Peru
6,783	73	79,896	857	3,684[3]	45[3]	5,955	65	1,722	19	Philippines
9,451	247	46,000	1,202	7,362[3]	191[3]	22,451	590	5,044	132	Poland
4,485	420	15,195	1,423	1,402[3]	139[3]	5,169	483	2,075	194	Portugal
892	238	2,934	783	...	...	1,000	251	552	147	Puerto Rico
298	170	2,329	1,324	133[3]	215[3]	399	283	161	92	Qatar
481	568	579[17]	750[17]	32[16]	45[16]	300	363	185[11]	224[11]	Réunion
4,500	209	24,640	1,147	2,450[3]	110[3]	7,787	366	3,000	140	Romania
44,959	315	237,689	1,663	17,400	121	59,700	424	15,700	110	Russia
40	3.7	3,549	334	...	...	450	45	2.6	0.2	Rwanda
21	393	85	1,614	11[3]	239[3]	17	329	13	250	St. Kitts and Nevis
41	236	179	1,029	26[3]	173[3]	143	830	19	107	St. Lucia
22	199	132	1,205	16[3]	132[3]	76	696	13	114	St. Vincent and the Grenadines
35	193	167	914	1[1]	6.7[1]	9.0	5.0	0.2	1.1	Samoa
22	688	24	761	...	...	17	542	10	320	San Marino
7.7	46	103	620	...	...	27	164	0.6	3.5	Sao Tome and Principe
4,166	152	51,564	1,879	8,476[3]	340[3]	9,800	381	1,497	55	Saudi Arabia
342	28	8,344	671	250	21	923	74	79	6.3	Senegal
3,110	405	9,915	1,292	389[3, 29]	37[3, 29]	4,107	417	652	85	Serbia
22	255	118	1,359	16	198	34	404	6.3	73	Seychelles
14	2.4	2,000	341	...	...	15	2.6	...	...	Sierra Leone
1,984	390	7,307	1,437	3,939[3]	913[3]	3,658	772	1,257	247	Singapore
...	...	...	...	...	...	...	...	...	...	Sint Maarten
1,099	201	5,925	1,085	1,929	357	4,064	752	877	161	Slovakia
816	914	2,122	1,046	808	411	1,299	643	495	244	Slovenia
8.4	16	30	56	22	46	10	19	2.0	3.7	Solomon Islands
100	11	648	70	6.2[1]	0.8[1]	106	12	...	...	Somalia
4,225	84	50,372	927	3,966	84	4,420	88	743	15	South Africa
19,904	432	51,493	1,118	12,000	281	28,118	626	10,579	230	Spain
3,579	172	17,359	832	530[3]	28[3]	1,776	88	214	10	Sri Lanka
375	8.6	17,654	405	3,250	90	4,200	9.9	165	3.8	Sudan[30]
...	...	...	...	...	...	...	...	...	...	Sudan, South[30]
85	162	890	1,696	19[3]	42[3]	163	314	16	30	Suriname
44	37	733	618	36[3]	33[3]	90	76	1.6	1.4	Swaziland
5,014	535	10,650	1,135	6,861[18]	761[18]	8,398	908	2,963	316	Sweden
4,488	586	9,255[11]	1,223[11]	6,430	862	5,480	724	2,925	382	Switzerland
4,069	199	11,696	573	800	42	3,935	180	67	3.3	Syria
16,434	708	27,840	1,199	11,924[3]	524[3]	16,130	698	5,265	227	Taiwan
368	54	5,941	864	...	...	700	101	4.7	0.7	Tajikistan
175	3.9	20,984	468	278[3]	7.4[3]	676	15	3.2	0.1	Tanzania
7,009	101	69,683	1,008	3,716[3]	59[3]	17,486	258	2,673	39	Thailand
214	36	2,452	407	185	30	356	54	5.4	0.9	Togo
31	298	54	522	5.0[3]	48[3]	8.4	81	1.0	9.6	Tonga
293	219	1,894	1,412	137[3]	105[3]	485	362	145	108	Trinidad and Tobago
1,290	123	11,114	1,060	568	56	3,500	341	482	46	Tunisia
16,202	223	61,770	849	3,703[3]	51[3]	26,410	353	7,096	98	Turkey
520	103	3,198	634	...	...	80	16	0.7	0.1	Turkmenistan
1.6	165	...	...	...	...	4.3	433	0.3	33	Tuvalu
327	9.8	12,828	384	250	8.7	3,200	98	20	0.6	Uganda
12,941	285	53,929	1,187	1,810	39	15,300	335	3,661	81	Ukraine
1,480	197	10,926	1,455	450[3]	120[3]	3,778	822	787	105	United Arab Emirates
33,320	537	80,799	1,303	35,890[3]	604[3]	51,442	836	19,468	314	United Kingdom
151,171	487	278,900	899	220,000[3]	741[3]	239,894	762	81,744	263	United States
962	286	4,437	1,317	430[3]	133[3]	1,855	552	383	114	Uruguay
1,864	68	20,952	763	...	...	4,689	171	89	3.2	Uzbekistan
5.0	21	285	1,191	3[3]	14[3]	17	71	0.3	1.3	Vanuatu
7,083	244	27,880	962	2,145[3]	82[3]	8,847	310	1,557	54	Venezuela
16,400	187	154,000	1,753	1,044[3]	13[3]	24,000	273	3,631	41	Vietnam
76	695	80[19]	718[19]	...	...	30	274	9.1	8.3	Virgin Islands (U.S.)
349[19]	94[19]	1,095[19]	296[19]	169[3]	46[3]	243[19]	66[19]	...	...	West Bank[13]
...	...	...	...	...	...	...	...	...	...	Western Sahara
1,046	44	11,085	461	300[3]	15[3]	420	18	79	3.3	Yemen
90	6.9	4,947	378	113[3]	10[3]	817	63	11	0.8	Zambia
379	30	7,500	597	1,200	101	1,422	114	33	2.6	Zimbabwe

[1]2002. [2]First editions only. [3]2004. [4]1998. [5]1997. [6]Including reprints. [7]Foreign dispatched and foreign received only. [8]Millions of copies. [9]Only free dailies. [10]Data for the former Netherlands Antilles. [11]2009. [12]School textbooks and government publications only. [13]West Bank includes Gaza Strip. [14]Foreign received only. [15]Excludes government publications and school textbooks. [16]2001. [17]2007. [18]2006. [19]2005. [20]Government publications only. [21]1996. [22]Active subscribers. [23]School textbooks only. [24]Fixed landlines have been decommissioned. [25]Domestic and foreign received only. [26]2008. [27]Includes mobile. [28]Only free dailies. [29]Includes Montenegro. [30]Sudan data includes South Sudan.

Social protection

This table summarizes three principal areas of social protective activity for the countries of the world: social security, crime and law enforcement, and military affairs. Because the administrative structure, financing, manning, and scope of institutions and programmed tasks in these fields vary so greatly from country to country, no well-accepted or well-documented body of statistical comparisons exists in international convention to permit objective assessment of any of these subjects, either from the perspective of a single country or internationally. The data provided within any single subject area do, however, represent the most consistent approach to problems of international comparison found in the published literature for that field.

The provision of social security programs to answer specific social needs, for example, is summarized simply in terms of the existence or nonexistence of a specific type of benefit program because of the great complexity of national programs in terms of eligibility, coverage, term, age limits, financing, payments, and so on. Activities connected with a particular type of benefit often take place at more than one governmental level, through more than one agency at the same level, or through a mixture of public and private institutions. The data shown here are summarized from the U.S. Social Security Administration's *Social Security Programs Throughout the World* (regional coverage; Africa 2009, Asia 2010, Europe 2010, The Americas 2009). A bullet symbol (•) indicates that a country has at least one program within the defined area (a circle [○] indicates data is for 2009); in some cases it may have several. A blank space indicates that no program existed providing the benefit shown; ellipses (...) indicate that no information was available as to whether a program existed.

Data given for social security expenditure as a percentage of total central governmental expenditure are taken from the International Monetary Fund's *Government Finance Statistics Yearbook*, which provides the most comparable analytic series on the consolidated accounts of central governments, governmentally administered social security funds, and independent national agencies, all usually separate accounting entities, through which these services may be provided in a given country.

Data on the finances of social security programs are taken in large part from the International Labour Office's *The Cost of Social Security* (triennial), supplemented by national data sources.

Figures for criminal offenses known to police, usually excluding civil offenses and minor traffic violations, are taken in part from Interpol's *International Crime Statistics* (annual) and a variety of national sources. Statistics are usually based on the number of offenses reported to police, not the number of offenders apprehended or tried in courts. Attempted offenses are counted as the offense that was attempted. A person identified as having committed multiple offenses is counted only under the most serious offense. Murder refers to all acts involving the voluntary taking of life, including infanticide, but excluding abortion, or involuntary acts such as those normally classified as manslaughter. Assault includes "serious," or aggravated, assault—that involving injury, endangering life, or perpetrated with the use of a dangerous instrument. Burglary involves theft from the premises of another; although Interpol statistics are reported as "breaking and entering," national data may not always distinguish cases of forcible entry. Automobile theft excludes brief use of a car without the owner's

Social protection

country	social security														
	programs available, 2009 or 2010					expenditures, latest	finances, latest								
							receipts					expenditures			
	old-age, invalidity, death[a]	sickness and maternity[b]	work injury[c]	unemployment[d]	family allowances[e]	(% of total central govt.)[f]	total ('000,000 natl. cur.)	insured persons (%)	employers (%)	government (%)	other (%)	total ('000,000 natl. cur.)	benefits (%)	administration (%)	other (%)
Afghanistan	●	●	●			4.5	...	...	...	...	...	...	...	...	...
Albania	●	●	●	●	●	9.7	967.0	—	—	88.8	11.2	1,440.0	99.5	— 0.5 —	
Algeria	○	○	○	○	○	...	27,700.0	...	...	...	...	28,748.0	61.8	30.6	7.6
American Samoa	●	...	...	...	...	...	...	...	...	...	...	13.0	100.0	—	—
Andorra	●	●	●			...	11,832.2	...	...	...	...	7,937.2	90.2	4.6	5.2
Angola	...	...	...	...	...	...	...	...	...	...	...	...	...	...	...
Antigua and Barbuda	○	○				...	13.0	29.2	48.7	—	22.1	4.2	66.1	33.9	—
Argentina	○	○	○	○	○	33.6	1,015,837.0	28.8	45.0	16.6	9.6	989,009.0	95.0	5.0	—
Armenia	●	●	●	●	●	28.1	...	...	...	...	...	...	...	...	...
Aruba		...	○	○	...	5	197.1	...	...	...	...	179.0	...	...	...
Australia	●	●	●	●	●	40.4	...	...	...	...	1.9	41,825	99.6	0.3	—
Austria	●	●	●	●	●	47.2	425,417.0	30.1	45.9	21.1	2.9	412,134.0	96.5	2.3	1.2
Azerbaijan	●	●	●	●	●	40.8	...	...	...	...	...	...	...	...	...
Bahamas, The	○	○	○	○		10.5	95.9	22.9	38.5	2.1	36.5	43.5	71.1	27.2	1.7
Bahrain	●		●	●		12.9	39.6	12.3	40.2	—	47.5	9.7	69.8	20.9	9.3
Bangladesh	7	●	●			9.7	73.6	12.4	37.5	2.4	47.7	34.1	94.0	6.0	—
Barbados	○	○	○	○		33.7	191.7	38.0	40.8	1.5	19.7	149.1	93.5	5.8	0.7
Belarus	●	●	●	●	●	41.8	3,199.0	—	—	93.2	6.8	3,199.0	100.0	—	—
Belgium	●	●	●	●	●	47.9	1,347,070.0	24.4	39.7	31.6	4.3	1,322,636.0	94.5	4.3	1.2
Belize	○	○	○			...	15.3	8.9	53.2	—	38.0	3.9	56.7	43.3	—
Benin	○	○	○		○	...	3,551.9	16.8	81.4	—	1.8	4,500.9	69.3	28.1	2.6
Bermuda	○	9	○			...	...	...	...	...	...	...	...	...	...
Bhutan	...	...	...	...	...	5.2	...	...	...	...	...	26.0	...	...	...
Bolivia	○	○	○		○	17.4	346.6	29.3	47.7	11.2	11.8	340.2	84.9	14.3	0.8
Bosnia and Herzegovina	●	●	●	●	●	38.9	...	...	...	...	...	...	...	...	...
Botswana	○[10]		○			1.1	—	...	...	...	...	65.0	...	...	...
Brazil	○	○	○	○	○	47.3	71,847.0	24.4	51.0	20.0	4.6	68,957.0	61.9	18.6	19.5
Brunei	●	...	●	...	...	...	...	...	...	...	...	39.5	...	...	...
Bulgaria	●	●	●	●	●	42.3	6,016.8	—	71.4	28.1	0.5	6,000.1	96.6	3.3	0.1
Burkina Faso	○	○	○		○	3.7	8,816.5	15.6	62.9	—	21.5	4,975.3	69.5	30.4	0.1
Burundi	○		○		○	13.9	1,991.5	31.6	47.6	—	20.8	1,563.9	74.8	16.8	8.4
Cambodia	...	...	○	...	○	7.8	...	...	...	...	...	...	...	...	...
Cameroon	○	○	○		○	0.5	41,331.8	13.1	64.8	—	22.1	41,332.0	70.6	28.8	0.6
Canada	○	○	○	○	○	42.1	130,306.6	9.9	15.6	64.4	10.1	115,764.2	96.9	2.5	0.6
Cape Verde	○	○	○		○	...	697.7	26.5	58.5	—	15.0	316.7	82.4	16.1	1.5
Cayman Islands	○	○	○		○	...	...	...	...	...	...	...	...	...	...
Central African Republic	○	○	○		○	...	3,604.0	8.4	76.0	—	15.6	3,247.0	64.6	32.9	2.5
Chad	○		○		○	...	1,172.8	12.6	77.6	—	9.8	634.5	43.0	51.4	5.6
Chile	○	○	○	○	○	25.4	1,186,056.0	32.8	2.7	37.9	26.6	798,770.0	83.9	14.7	1.4
China	●	●	●	●	●	22.4	57,446.2	—	99.4	—	0.6	54,654	98.4	0.6	1.0
Colombia	○	○	○	○	○	22.4	294,438.0	24.8	56.0	0.2	19.0	257,455.0	85.5	11.5	3.0
Comoros	...	...	...	...	...	...	40.7	100.0	—	—	—	54.3	17.4	62.3	20.3
Congo, Dem. Rep. of the	○		○		○	0.1	1,238.3	28.6	60.2	—	11.2	1,044.2	27.9	72.1	—
Congo, Rep. of the	○	○	○		○	3.3	15,272.8	12.1	80.2	—	7.7	7,256.7	66.6	21.3	12.1
Costa Rica	○	○	○		○	24.1	36,407.3	33.2	44.4	1.2	21.2	31,049.8	89.0	4.1	6.9
Côte d'Ivoire	○	○	○		○	10.5	27,288.4	19.3	75.4	—	5.3	20,593.5	100.0	—	—
Croatia	●	●	●	●	●	45.4	...	...	...	...	...	...	...	...	...
Cuba	○	○	○		○	...	2,284.8	—	37.4	62.6	—	2,284.8	96.7	—	3.3
Curaçao[5]			○	○		12.9	317.0	100.0	—	—	—	275.0	...	...	...
Cyprus[17]	●	●	●	●	●	30.2	217.5	24.7	40.3	17.3	17.7	117.7	98.4	1.6	—
Czech Republic	●	●	●	●	●	45.9	...	...	...	...	...	...	...	...	...
Denmark	●	●	●	●	●	17.6	225,965.6	4.3	5.0	88.2	2.5	218,258.2	97.0	3.0	—
Djibouti	...	...	...	...	...	...	1,352.2	...	...	...	...	1,115.7	...	...	...
Dominica	○	○	○			...	12.3	22.6	50.9	—	26.5	4.4	68.0	32.0	—
Dominican Republic	○	○	○		○	9.0	77.9	20.1	72.9	—	6.8	74.3	75.9	24.1	—

permission, "joyriding," and implies intent to deprive the owner of the vehicle permanently. Criminal offense data for certain countries refer to cases disposed of in court, rather than to complaints. Police manpower figures refer, for the most part, to full-time, paid professional staff, excluding clerical support and volunteer staff. Personnel in military service who perform police functions are presumed to be employed in their principal activity, military service.

The figures for military manpower refer to full-time, active-duty military service and exclude reserve, militia, paramilitary, and similar organizations. Because of the difficulties attached to the analysis of data on military manpower and budgets (including problems such as data withheld on national security grounds, or the publication of budgetary data specifically intended to hide actual expenditure, or the complexity of long-term financing of purchases of military matériel [how much was actually spent as opposed to what was committed, offset by nonmilitary transfers, etc.]), extensive use is made of the principal international analytic tools: publications such as those of the International Institute for Strategic Studies (*The Military Balance*) and the U.S. Arms Control and Disarmament Agency (*World Military Expenditures and Arms Transfers*), both annuals.

The data on military expenditures are from the SIPRI Military Expenditure Database, as well as from the IMF's *Government Finance Statistics Yearbook* and country statistical publications.

The following notes further define the column headings:

a. Programs providing cash payments for *each* of the three types of long-term benefit indicated to persons (1) exceeding a specified working age (usually 50–65, often 5 years earlier for women) who are qualified by a term of covered employment, (2) partially or fully incapacitated for their usual employment by injury or illness, and (3) qualified by their status as spouse, cohabitant, or dependent minor of a qualified person who dies.
b. Programs providing cash payments (jointly, or alternatively, medical services as well) to occupationally qualified persons for *both* of the short-term benefits indicated: (1) illness and (2) maternity.
c. Programs providing cash or medical services to employment-qualified persons who become temporarily or permanently incapacitated (fully or partially) by work-related injury or illness.
d. Programs providing term-limited cash compensation (usually 40–75% of average earnings) to persons qualified by previous employment (of six months minimum, typically) for periods of involuntary unemployment.
e. Programs providing cash payments to families or mothers to mitigate the cost of raising children and to encourage the formation of larger families.
f. Includes welfare.
g. A police officer is a full-time, paid professional, performing domestic security functions. Data include administrative staff but exclude clerical employees, volunteers, and members of paramilitary groups.
h. Includes all active-duty personnel, regular and conscript, performing national security functions. Excludes reserves, paramilitary forces, border patrols, and gendarmeries.

crime and law enforcement (latest)						military protection								country
offenses reported to the police per 100,000 population					population per police officer[g]	manpower, 2010[h]		expenditure, 2009				arms trade ('000,000 U.S.$)		
total	personal		property			total ('000)	per 1,000 population	total ('000,000 U.S.$)	per capita	% of central government expenditure (2005)	% of GDP or GNP	imports 1999	exports 2005	
	murder	assault	burglary	automobile theft										
...	...	...	...	...	...	136.1[1]	5.2	252	8.9	11.4	1.7	0	0	Afghanistan
168.8	26.2	5.8	10.7	14.1	550	14.3	4.5	248	78	5.3	2.0	30	0	Albania
178.0	0.7	67.6	13.7	1.7	840	147.0	4.0	5,280	149	12.6[2]	3.8	550	0	Algeria
3,006	8.0	494.0	588.0	6.0	460	[3]	[3]	—	—	—	—	...	...	American Samoa
2,616	0	16.7	515.2	110.6	220	—	—	...	...	...	...	...	...	Andorra
143.5	8.7	15.3	30.5	3.7	14[4]	107.0	5.5	3,170	171	41.1[2]	4.2	350	0	Angola
4,977	4.7	475.0	1,984.4	35.9	120	0.2	2.0	8.0	93	...	0.7	...	...	Antigua and Barbuda
631.0	6.0	68.2	43.0	117.1	1,270	73.1	1.8	2,350	58	3.0	0.8	90	0	Argentina
264.4	4.1	4.7	16.6	0.7	...	48.6	15.7	401	130	15.5	4.7	10	0	Armenia
5,461	1.2	180.0	451.3	202.5	...	[5]	[5]	—	—	—	—	...	...	Aruba
7,003	3.7	708.5	2,926.2	684.8	438	56.6	2.5	19,500	893	6.1	2.0	1,100	593[6]	Australia
6,095	1.4	3.0	944.0	34.7	470	25.9	3.1	2,110	252	2.1	0.8	30	318	Austria
176	4.2	2.4	10.3	0.4	...	66.9	7.3	1,500	170	11.1	3.5	10	0	Azerbaijan
4,870	27.1	61.5	1,560.2	415.7	125	0.9	2.5	49	143	3.0	0.7	...	...	Bahamas, The
1,390	1.6	0.5	380.1	207.6	180	8.2	6.2	742	635	14.2	3.6	70	0	Bahrain
90	2.8	4.3	4.3	1.1	2,560	157.1	1.1	1,020	6.5	9.9	1.1	80	0	Bangladesh
3,813	8.6	161.9	1,080.8	105.5	280	0.6	2.2	26	94	2.0[6]	0.7	0	0	Barbados
1,282.4	11.6	20.6	197.9	59.9	...	72.9	7.7	896[8]	93[8]	3.3	1.9[8]	0	310[2]	Belarus
8,478	5.3	535.8	2,031.3	376.5	640	37.9	3.5	5,620	521	2.7	1.5	350	318	Belgium
...	12.8	20.0	600.0	4.0	290	1.1	3.3	14	42	4.8[6]	1.0	0	0	Belize
297	5.1	102.0	4.6	0.6	3,250	4.8	0.5	101	11	5.0[6]	1.5	5	0	Benin
8,871	5.1	221.7	1,949.2	...	370	[3]	[3]	—	—	—	—	...	...	Bermuda
...	...	...	...	...	...	...	...	...	...	...	...	0	0	Bhutan
660	28.6	59.4	0.9	...	...	46.1	4.6	286	29	5.1	1.7	10	0	Bolivia
402	2.5	2.6	...	...	...	10.6	2.8	243	63	6.2	1.4	40	0	Bosnia and Herzegovina
8,281	12.7	431.9	1.9	73.1	750	9.0	4.4	375	188	3.9	3.2	40	0	Botswana
779.1	11.2	255.7	5.2	61.2	...	318.5	1.7	26,000	135	9.3	1.6	180	20[2]	Brazil
932.9	1.5	1.2	79.8	57.5	100	7.0	16.6	332	830	11.5[2]	3.2	20	0	Brunei
1,170.7	7.3	1.9	402.9	94.5	...	31.3	4.3	905	119	5.9	1.9	10	285	Bulgaria
9	0.4	1.7	—	—	...	11.2	0.7	110	7	6.7	1.3	0	0	Burkina Faso
156	9.7	10.8	2.0	0.2	...	20.0[11]	2.3	42	5	27.7	3.2	60	0	Burundi
...	...	...	...	...	1,980	124.3	8.5	275	19	24.1	2.5	5	0	Cambodia
78	0.4	1.2	1.2	5.1	1,170	14.1	0.7	344	18	9.5	1.5	5	0	Cameroon
8,121	4.0	140.3	1,044.4	529.4	8,640	65.7	1.9	19,600	581	6.5	1.5	1,000	500	Canada
...	...	...	...	...	110	1.2	2.4	9	18	...	0.6	5	0	Cape Verde
...	...	...	...	...	...	[3]	[3]	...	...	...	...	—	—	Cayman Islands
135	1.6	22.8	2.7	...	...	2.2	0.4	36	8	...	1.8	0	0	Central African Republic
...	...	...	...	...	990	25.4	2.1	142	14	...	2.1	10	0	Chad
1,366	4.5	84.8	488.0	12.9	470	59.1	3.4	5,040	304	6.8	3.1	100	10[2]	Chile
128	0.2	5.2	45.2	6.9	...	2,285.0	1.7	98,360	74	7.3	2.0	675	900	China
790	56.3	61.8	57.9	75.3	420	283.0	6.3	9,600	214	18.9	4.1	60	0	Colombia
...	...	...	...	...	960	[12]	[12]	...	...	...	...	...	...	Comoros
...	...	...	...	...	910	[13]	[13]	123	2	...	1.1	110	0	Congo, Dem. Rep. of the
32	1.5	4.7	0.2	0.2	870	10.0	2.6	134	36	9.5[14]	1.4	0	0	Congo, Rep. of the
868	5.3	11.1	232.4	23.1	480	—	—	...	...	...	...	0	0	Costa Rica
67	2.5	73.1	19.5	11.9	4,640	17.1[15]	0.8[15]	330	16	3.4[2]	1.4	0	0	Côte d'Ivoire
1,216	6.1	24.1	290.9	38.6	...	18.6	4.3	1,010	228	4.1	1.6	10	10	Croatia
...	...	...	...	...	650	49.0	4.4	1,700[16]	124[16]	...	3.8[16]	0	0	Cuba
...	...	...	...	...	...	[3]	[3]	—	—	—	—	...	...	Curaçao[5]
689	1.9	17.7	203.3	3.0	180	...	...	498	476	5.6	2.3	340	0	Cyprus[17]
4,142	2.6	71.7	831.4	263.0	...	23.4	2.2	3,130	297	4.6	1.6	220	109	Czech Republic
9,300	4.1	20.8	1,899	638.1	600	18.7	3.4	4,340	786	4.6	1.4	290	109	Denmark
252	4.2	124.2	45.0	0.5	...	10.5	12.4	13	15	...	1.2	0	0	Djibouti
9,567	7.9	682.4	1,736	77.6	300	[18]	[18]	...	...	...	...	...	...	Dominica
...	15.8	28.4	154.0	14.0	580	24.5	2.6	265	27	4.5[14]	0.6	20	0	Dominican Republic

Social protection (continued)

country	social security														
	programs available, 2009 or 2010					expenditures, latest (% of total central govt.)[f]	finances, latest								
							receipts					expenditures			
	old-age, invalidity, death[a]	sickness and maternity[b]	work injury[c]	unemployment[d]	family allowances[e]		total ('000,000 natl. cur.)	insured persons (%)	employers (%)	government (%)	other (%)	total ('000,000 natl. cur.)	benefits (%)	administration (%)	other (%)
East Timor	…	…	…	…	…	…	…	…	…	…	…	…	…	…	…
Ecuador	○	○	○	○		1.9	71,286.0	37.0	50.0	—	13.0	52,032.4	86.0	14.0	—
Egypt	○	○	○	○		11.2	2,443.5	22.8	41.0	2.0	34.2	1,685.6	93.4	6.6	—
El Salvador	○	○	○			13.5	465.3	27.1	51.7	—	21.2	368.3	78.1	21.9	—
Equatorial Guinea	○	○	○		○	…	141.0	7.1	92.9	—	—	134.0	49.3	50.7	—
Eritrea	…	…	…	…	…	…	…	…	…	…	…	…	…	…	…
Estonia	●	●	●		●	34.2	90.1	…	…	…	…	…	…	…	…
Ethiopia	○		○			7.3	190.9	32.8	65.3	—	1.9	153.7	98.3	1.7	—
Faroe Islands	●	…	…	…	●	…	…	…	…	…	…	…	…	…	…
Fiji	●		●			5.4	153.5	20.9	33.8	0.8	44.5	75.5	95.3	4.7	—
Finland	●	●	●	●	●	47.1	118,589.0	7.7	41.1	44.0	7.2	106,235	96.3	3.7	—
France	●	●	●	●	●	49.1	1,700,202.0	77.7	—	20.4	1.9	1,669,096.0	95.5	3.7	0.8
French Guiana	○	…	○	…	○	…	1,071.5	…	…	…	…	997.1	…	…	…
French Polynesia	●	…	●	…	●	…	19,268.0	…	…	…	…	17,832.0	…	…	…
Gabon	○	○	○		○	…	3,415.0	—	44.3	29.3	26.4	2,737.0	55.2	44.8	—
Gambia, The	○		○			1.0	—	…	…	…	…	5.6	…	…	…
Gaza Strip	…	…	…	…	…	—	…	…	…	…	…	…	…	…	…
Georgia	●	●	●		●	12.2	…	…	…	…	…	…	…	…	…
Germany	●	●	●	●	●	72.1	…	…	…	…	…	…	…	…	…
Ghana	○		○			4.7	17,920.8	21.1	52.9	—	26.0	4,147.7	13.3	64.0	22.7
Greece	●	●	●	●	●	10.4	1,314,421.0	24.9	38.4	30.8	5.9	1,349,693.0	92.5	7.5	—
Greenland	●	…	…	…	●	…	…	…	…	…	…	…	…	…	…
Grenada	○	○	○			8.6	24.1	20.1	60.3	3.2	16.3	13.5	93.1	6.9	—
Guadeloupe	○	…	…	…	○	…	2,607.3	…	…	…	…	5,883.4	…	…	…
Guam	○	…	…	…	○	…	…	…	…	…	…	7.3	…	…	…
Guatemala	○	○	○			7.0	348.5	29.1	54.8	—	16.1	279.7	82.7	14.6	2.7
Guernsey	●	●	●	●	●	…	103,560	—— 45.0 ——		40.7	14.3	85,468	94.8	5.2	…
Guinea	○	○	○		○	5.1	3,387.0	0.4	90.3	—	9.3	1,108.1	54.9	45.1	—
Guinea-Bissau	…	…	…	…	…	8.8	138.0	22.8	63.4	10.3	3.8	61.9	59.6	40.4	—
Guyana	○	○	○			…	1,070.8	…	…	…	…	1,373.7	…	…	…
Haiti	○		○			5.1	…	…	…	…	…	…	…	…	…
Honduras	○	○	○			…	166.2	23.9	40.8	3.3	32.0	76.8	84.6	15.4	—
Hong Kong	●	●	●	●	●	24.1	…	…	…	…	…	26,939	…	…	…
Hungary	●	●	●	●	●	40.4	798,000.0	—	—	—	—	737,000.0	—	—	—
Iceland	●	●	●	●	●	18.2	14,799	—	—	—	—	96,094	98.2	1.8	—
India	●	●	●	●		…	43,913.8	23.8	27.7	5.3	43.2	13,775.8	90.0	8.2	1.8
Indonesia	●		●			6.0	239,477.0	50.7	49.3	—	—	181,499.0	12.3	15.8	71.9
Iran	●	●	●	●	●	16.5	346,460.0	83.2	0.1	8.2	8.5	167,879.0	43.4	6.3	50.0
Iraq	…	…	…	…	…	…	…	…	…	…	…	…	…	…	…
Ireland	●	●	●	●	●	33.1	4,627.5	16.3	24.8	57.7	1.2	4,612.9	95.2	4.7	0.1
Isle of Man	●	●	●	●	●	…	…	…	…	…	…	14.4	…	…	…
Israel	●	●	●	●	●	22.1	13,851.1	31.1	27.7	35.0	6.2	13,593.3	81.7	15.4	2.9
Italy	●	●	●	●	●	43.0	278,383.0	16.5	51.4	30.0	2.1	100,251.0	89.3	2.0	8.7
Jamaica	○	○25	○		○	2.3	374.3	11.5	13.6	43.8	31.1	273.6	92.6	7.4	—
Japan	●	●	●	●	●	48.9	59,571,299.0	27.4	31.6	24.4	16.6	46,684,159.0	94.3	1.7	4.0
Jersey	●	●	●	●	●	9.5	60.9	—— 63.8 ——		23.4	12.8	52.8	…	…	…
Jordan	●		●			16.7	53.6	28.7	55.3	—	16.0	9.5	77.4	14.0	8.6
Kazakhstan	●	●	●	●	●	22.3	…	…	…	…	…	…	…	…	…
Kenya	○	9	○			2.7	4,262.0	18.2	13.7	10.0	58.1	1,857.8	53.8	46.1	0.1
Kiribati	●		●			…	…	…	…	…	…	…	…	…	…
Korea, North	…	…	…	…	…	…	…	…	…	…	…	…	…	…	…
Korea, South	●	9	●	●		13.7	7,425,400.0	—	62.2	—	—	9,656,600.0	…	…	…
Kosovo	…	…	…	…	…	…	…	…	…	…	…	…	…	…	…
Kuwait	●					9.2	445.8	7.1	13.2	54.3	25.4	206.5	97.0	3.0	—
Kyrgyzstan	●	●	●	●	●	11.6	…	…	…	…	…	…	…	…	…
Laos	●	●	●			…	…	…	…	…	…	…	…	…	…
Latvia	●	●	●	●	●	28.7	…	…	…	…	…	…	…	…	…
Lebanon	●	9	●		●	6.8	…	…	…	…	…	…	…	…	…
Lesotho	…	…	…	…	…	1.1	—	…	…	…	…	12.0	…	…	…
Liberia	○		○			…	2.9	—	69.0	13.8	17.2	2.6	54.4	45.6	—
Libya	○	○	○			…	314.3	21.6	25.4	50.2	2.8	260.0	77.5	19.5	3.0
Liechtenstein	●	●	●	●	●	…	…	…	…	…	…	…	…	…	…
Lithuania	●	●	●	●	●	34.2	…	…	…	…	…	24,981.7	…	…	…
Luxembourg	●	●	●	●	●	51.8	72,471.8	24.2	34.6	34.4	6.8	65,214.4	97.2	2.4	0.4
Macau	…	…	…	…	…	6.2	223.2	…	…	…	…	207.4	…	…	…
Macedonia	●	●	●	●	●	…	24,482	…	…	…	…	…	…	…	…
Madagascar	○	○	○		○	1.5	15,229.0	22.2	77.8	—	—	14,542.0	81.2	18.8	—
Malawi		9	○			…	—	…	…	…	…	5.4	…	…	…
Malaysia	●	9	●			5.8	7,958.7	20.7	40.2	—	39.1	2,826.5	97.0	3.0	—
Maldives	…	…	…	…	…	…	—	…	…	…	…	7.1	…	…	…
Mali	○	○	○		○	…	8,128.8	16.6	74.3	—	9.1	7,924.6	63.7	34.7	1.6
Malta	●	●	●	●	●	31.7	82.2	26.1	31.6	42.3	—	110.7	92.5	7.5	—
Marshall Islands	●	9				…	…	…	…	…	…	…	…	…	…
Martinique	○	…	…	…	○	…	3,913.1	…	…	…	…	8,429.6	…	…	…
Mauritania	○	○	○		○	…	808.4	1.5	90.4	—	8.1	735.2	63.5	31.2	5.3
Mauritius	○	9	○	○	○	23.5	1,733.5	2.9	47.9	31.7	17.5	1,072.7	95.2	3.0	1.8
Mayotte	…	…	…	…	…	…	…	…	…	…	…	…	…	…	…
Mexico	○	○	○	○	○	20.1	16,011,795.0	20.9	54.8	12.9	11.4	14,562,293.0	79.9	15.5	4.6
Micronesia	●					…	…	…	…	…	…	…	…	…	…
Moldova	●	●	●	●	●	36.8	…	…	…	…	…	…	…	…	…
Monaco	●	●	●	32	●	…	…	…	…	…	…	…	…	…	…
Mongolia	●	●	…	…	●	26.9	2,431.6	—	—	20.8	79.2	2,304.6	100.0	—	—
Montenegro	…	…	…	…	…	…	…	…	…	…	…	…	…	…	…
Morocco	○	○	○		○	11.2	4,660.5	20.6	47.5	12.9	19.0	3,040.7	94.8	5.0	0.2
Mozambique	…	…	…	…	…	…	228.2	—	86.2	13.7	0.1	145.0	100.0	—	—

crime and law enforcement (latest)						military protection								country
offenses reported to the police per 100,000 population					population per police officer[g]	manpower, 2010[h]		expenditure, 2009				arms trade ('000,000 U.S.$)		
total	personal		property			total ('000)	per 1,000 population	total ('000,000 U.S.$)	per capita	% of central government expenditure (2005)	% of GDP or GNP	imports 1999	exports 2005	
	murder	assault	burglary	automobile theft										
…	…	…	…	…	…	1.3[19]	1.2[19]	4[6]	5[6]	…	1.3[6]	…	…	East Timor
587	25.9	35.6	164.5	52.9	260	58.5	4.0	1,080	77	…	1.9	20	0	Ecuador
3,693	1.6	0.7	…	3.1	580	468.5	5.7	4,120	50	10.1[6]	2.2	700	0	Egypt
879	36.9	71.1	…	82.0	1,000	15.5	2.6	1,160	187	3.9	5.5	10	0	El Salvador
…	…	…	…	…	190	1.3	1.8	8	13	16.5[2]	0.1	0	0	Equatorial Guinea
161.9	2.7	10.3	5.8	…	…	201.8	39.8	78	15	51.1[2]	4.2	170	20[2]	Eritrea
3,565	13.8	28.3	1,659.2	169.8	…	5.5	4.1	356	266	4.5[2]	1.8	10	0	Estonia
258.3	6.5	77.8	1.4	1.4	…	138.0	1.7	408	5	16.5[6]	1.4	270	0	Ethiopia
…	…	…	…	…	…	[3]	[3]	—	—	—	—	…	…	Faroe Islands
2,370	2.9	44.1	427.9	44.4	407	3.5	4.1	51	60	6.0	1.7	0	0	Fiji
14,350	0.7	34.9	1,739.7	33.2	640	22.3	3.8	3,890	729	4.4	1.6	400	128	Finland
6,097	3.4	162.7	632.4	511.0	630	238.6	3.8	54,400	869	4.8	2.0	800	1,600	France
8,936	27.2	178.7	1,367.3	150.6	…	[3]	[3]	—	—	—	—	…	…	French Guiana
1,799	0.9	98.9	232.7	…	…	[3]	[3]	—	—	—	—	…	…	French Polynesia
114	1.4	17.9	2.3	7.5	1,290	4.7	3.1	250[20]	166[20]	8.1[14]	1.9[20]	0	0	Gabon
89	0.4	10.6	5.6	…	3,310	0.8	0.5	7	4	6.6	0.7	0	0	Gambia, The
4,355	…	…	…	…	…	—	—	…	…	…	…	…	…	Gaza Strip
286	4.7	99.5	21.1	0.8	…	20.7	4.6	537	122	19.1	5.0	10	30[2]	Georgia
7,682	3.5	139.6	1,377.4	114.3	…	251.5	3.1	47,500	579	3.6	1.4	1,300	2,027	Germany
…	2.2	418.9	1.5	…	620	15.5	0.6	113	5	10[6]	0.7	0	0	Ghana
3,641	3.0	68.2	356.8	166.5	380	138.9	12.2	10,100	894	5.6[14]	3.1	1,900	36	Greece
9,360	18.1	845.0	1,883.5	…	340	[3]	[3]	—	—	—	—	…	…	Greenland
8,543	7.8	98.9	582.2	…	230	…	…	…	…	…	…	…	…	Grenada
5,793	13.2	215.2	821.5	453.9	…	[3]	[3]	—	—	—	—	…	…	Guadeloupe
10,080	7.9	169.3	634.2	333.6	…	[3]	[3]	—	—	—	—	…	…	Guam
510	27.4	77.1	27.9	58.1	670	15.2	1.0	166	12	2.4	0.4	0	0	Guatemala
…	…	…	…	…	…	[3]	[3]	—	—	—	—	…	…	Guernsey
18.4	0.5	0.7	0.7	0.1	1,140	12.3	1.2	75	7	4.5[14]	1.6	0	0	Guinea
129	0.5	8.7	4.0	0.2	…	4.5	2.8	14	9	8.2	1.6	0	0	Guinea-Bissau
1,277	19.1	246.0	365.8	32.2	190	1.1	1.5	128[20]	166[20]	2.0[2]	5.8[20]	0	0	Guyana
701	…	…	…	…	400	[21]	[21]	15[16]	2[16]	…	0.4[16]	0	0	Haiti
392	154.0	44.4	4.3	25.8	1,040	12.0	1.5	111	15	2.6[2]	0.8	10	0	Honduras
1,122	1.0	117.1	133.4	15.3	221	[3]	[3]	—	—	—	—	…	…	Hong Kong
5,011	4.1	76.6	804.4	41.3	237	29.6	3.0	1,480	147	4.1	1.1	80	15	Hungary
31,332	0.7	15.8	920.3	…	940	—	—	—	—	—	—	10	0	Iceland
594	4.6	…	15.6	…	820	1,325.0	1.1	38,300	32	19.1	3.1	700	57	India
120.9	1.0	4.4	1.8	1.7	1,119	302.0	1.3	3,250	14	6.6	0.9	450	100[2]	Indonesia
77	0.5	47.7	…	…	…	523.0	6.9	8,640[22]	116[22]	13.0	2.6[22]	150	10[2]	Iran
197	7.1	34.7	…	…	140	245.8[23]	7.5[23]	4,100	133	…	6.2	5	0	Iraq
1,696	1.4	12.4	479.8	16.3	310	10.5	2.3	1,400	307	2.1	0.6	40	37	Ireland
2,867	0.7	12.3	921.4	60.6	…	[3]	[3]	—	—	—	—	—	—	Isle of Man
6,254	2.2	491.8	990.1	501.7	210	176.5	23.8	13,500[24]	1,894[24]	22.3	6.9[24]	2,400	2,600	Israel
4,214	4.4	46.4	…	537.0	680	184.6	3.0	30,500	506	4.8	1.4	700	1,034	Italy
1,871	37.2	511.4	135.7	7.2	430	2.8	1.0	62	23	1.8	0.5	10	0	Jamaica
1,773	1.0	16.0	206.0	34.0	480	247.7	1.9	51,100[8]	400[8]	2.6	1.0[8]	3,000	20[2]	Japan
…	…	…	…	…	…	[3]	[3]	—	—	—	—	…	…	Jersey
1,256	6.3	14.0	31.0	52.2	630	100.5	16.3	1,390	232	12.3	5.5	70	0	Jordan
932	15.9	…	…	3.4	…	49.0	3.0	1,350	85	4.7	1.3	160	10[2]	Kazakhstan
484	6.4	54.1	76.9	9.7	1,500	24.1	0.6	533	13	8.1[14]	1.8	5	0	Kenya
261	5.1	11.6	38.6	…	330	—	—	…	…	…	…	…	…	Kiribati
…	…	…	…	…	460	1,190.0	48.9	4,380	181	…	7.3[6]	30	140[2]	Korea, North
3,494	2.1	64.6	7.0	…	506	655.0	13.4	22,400[8]	463[8]	10.4	2.7[8]	2,200	420[14]	Korea, South
…	…	…	…	…	…	[26]	[26]	…	…	…	…	…	…	Kosovo
1,346	1.5	36.4	75.9	56.7	80	15.5	4.2	4,180	1,214	16.5	4.3	725	0	Kuwait
987	…	12.6	482.4	…	…	10.9	2.1	24	4	7.5[14]	0.5	0	0	Kyrgyzstan
…	…	…	…	…	280	29.1	4.6	14	2.2	10.4[14]	0.3	0	0	Laos
2,097	9.3	18.6	56.1	129.0	…	5.7	2.6	316	140	4.0	1.2	5	0	Latvia
3,063	5.5	209.7	78.0	30.0	530	59.1[27]	14.3[27]	1,430	338	9.8	4.1	10	0	Lebanon
2,357	50.4	156.9	250.4	30.8	1,130	2.0	1.0	54	26	5.0[14]	3.3	0	0	Lesotho
…	…	…	…	…	1,570	2.1[28]	0.5[28]	1.6	0.4	9.4[6]	—	0	0	Liberia
1,065	2.1	5.4	…	…	…	76.0	11.8	1,710	266	6.4[6]	2.8	20	30[2]	Libya
…	…	114.3	614.3	153.6	660	[29]	[29]	—	—	—	—	…	…	Liechtenstein
2,029	9.0	10.4	585.6	96.7	…	10.6	3.3	402	120	4.5	1.1	20	0	Lithuania
6,280	17.2	89.0	1,152.8	182.0	829	0.9	1.7	249	500	0.7	0.5	50	0	Luxembourg
1,698	5.4	34.0	250.5	26.6	…	[3]	[3]	…	…	…	…	…	…	Macau
1,102	5.4	26.9	…	44.7	…	8.0	3.9	159	77	6.4	1.7	20	0	Macedonia
112	0.6	12.0	0.7	0.1	2,900	13.5	0.6	90	5	5.0[14]	1.0	0	0	Madagascar
850	3.1	82.2	13.1	…	1,670	5.3	0.3	51	3	2.2[2]	1.1	0	0	Malawi
604	3.1	25.9	155.6	20.8	760	109.0	3.9	3,880	141	7.0	2.0	925	0	Malaysia
2,353	1.9	3.3	36.1	…	35,710	…	…	6[30]	20[30]	10.1	1.2[30]	…	…	Maldives
10.0	0.7	1.5	0.8	0.3	160	7.4	0.5	177	13	8.7[2]	2.0	0	0	Mali
1,841	3.0	35.2	1,079.2	243.9	230	2.0	4.7	59	140	2.2	0.7	0	0	Malta
2,273	…	…	…	…	400	[31]	[31]	—	—	—	—	…	…	Marshall Islands
6,305	5.8	184.9	641.2	192.8	…	[3]	[3]	—	—	—	—	…	…	Martinique
95.4	0.8	27.0	7.3	2.5	710	15.9	4.8	115	37	13.2	3.8	0	0	Mauritania
2,712	2.9	7.8	116.0	…	240	—	—	41	32	0.7	0.5	0	0	Mauritius
…	…	…	…	…	…	[3]	[3]	—	—	—	—	…	…	Mayotte
108	7.3	30.2	…	…	…	280.3	2.4	4,770	44	3.0[6]	0.5	160	30[2]	Mexico
…	…	…	…	…	…	[31]	[31]	—	—	—	—	…	…	Micronesia
957	9.9	11.1	50.4	15.6	…	5.3	1.4	20	6	1.3	0.4	0	20[2]	Moldova
3,430	—	46.7	106.7	70.0	…	—	—	…	…	…	…	…	…	Monaco
1,010	30.0	74.7	486.0	2.1	120	10.0	3.6	38	14	5.9[6]	0.9	0	0	Mongolia
…	…	…	…	…	…	3.1	5.0	57	90	…	1.4	…	…	Montenegro
366	1.4	6.7	…	…	840	195.8	6.1	3,060	98	13.5[2]	3.3	130	0	Morocco
166	4.2	9.2	45.9	…	…	11.2	0.5	84	4	9.1[2]	0.9	5	0	Mozambique

Social protection (continued)

country	social security: programs available, 2009 or 2010: old-age, invalidity, death[a]	sickness and maternity[b]	work injury[c]	unemployment[d]	family allowances[e]	expenditures, latest (% of total central govt.)[f]	finances, latest: receipts: total ('000,000 natl. cur.)	insured persons (%)	employers (%)	government (%)	other (%)	expenditures: total ('000,000 natl. cur.)	benefits (%)	administration (%)	other (%)
Myanmar (Burma)		●	●			2.3	44.3	19.9	59.6	18.5	2.0	35.9	51.5	15.6	32.9
Namibia	○	…	…	…	…	12.2	…	…	…	…	…	…	…	…	…
Nauru	○	○	○	…	○	…	…	…	…	…	…	…	…	…	…
Nepal	●	9	●			4.6	—	…	…	…	…	59.3	…	…	…
Netherlands	●	●		●	●	44.0	154,427.0	37.3	30.3	19.0	13.4	135,609.0	96.9	3.1	—
New Caledonia	…	…	…	…	○	…	15,834.0	…	…	…	…	14,598.0	…	…	…
New Zealand	●	●	●	●	●	32.9	14,266.0	1.0	4.7	92.5	1.8	14,372.3	95.6	2.8	1.6
Nicaragua	○	○	○		○	11.3	647,454.8	13.5	49.1	7.6	29.8	452,038.6	82.4	17.6	—
Niger	○	○	○		○	…	5,634.9	9.4	90.6	—	—	3,804.2	62.5	—	37.5
Nigeria	○		○			…	54.0	50.0	50.0	—	—	22.6	42.5	57.5	—
Northern Mariana Islands	○	…	…	…	…	…	…	…	…	…	…	…	…	…	…
Norway	●	●	●	●	●	43.0	158,105.0	18.3	31.4	46.6	3.7	131,578.2	98.7	1.3	—
Oman	●		●			3.5	—	…	…	…	…	…	…	…	…
Pakistan	●	●	●			…	9,321.4	1.3	8.0	84.3	6.4	8,092.0	97.4	1.2	1.4
Palau	●					…	…	…	…	…	…	…	…	…	…
Panama	○	○	○			23.1	496.7	31.0	39.5	7.1	22.4	452.8	94.0	4.8	1.2
Papua New Guinea	●	9	●			0.9	45.0	40.5	32.1	8.0	19.4	9.4	82.3	9.7	8.0
Paraguay	○	○	○			14.9	…	…	…	…	…	253,341	…	…	…
Peru	○	○	○			15.7	1,363,280.6	30.2	65.1	4.7	—	1,435,134.1	78.5	21.5	—
Philippines	●	●	●			2.1	19,213.6	22.2	32.3	—	45.5	7,878.3	87.3	12.3	—
Poland	●	●	●	●	●	45.3	11,572,248.0	2.1	70.2	25.1	2.6	11,452,165.0	98.8	1.2	—
Portugal	●	●	●	●	●	41.7	833,442.5	31.3	50.1	13.4	5.2	756,410.8	94.6	4.2	1.2
Puerto Rico	○	○	○	○	○	…	…	…	…	…	…	1,041.3	100.0	—	—
Qatar	…	…	…	…	…	…	80.0	—	—	100.0	—	80.0	100.0	—	—
Réunion	…	…	…	…	…	…	…	…	…	…	…	13,200.0	…	…	…
Romania	●	●	●	●	●	35.8	90,561.2	—	48.9	51.1	—	90,561.2	100.0	—	—
Russia	●	●	●	●	●	40.4	…	…	…	…	…	…	…	…	…
Rwanda	○		○			…	2,350.0	23.9	39.8	—	36.3	965.8	60.8	39.2	—
St. Kitts and Nevis	○	○	○			4.9	14.3	…	…	…	…	7.9	…	…	…
St. Lucia	○	○	○			…	14.6	28.6	28.6	—	42.8	3.4	61.4	38.6	—
St. Vincent and the Grenadines	○	○	○			8.8	—	…	…	…	…	—	…	…	…
Samoa	●	9	●			—	—	…	…	…	…	—	…	…	…
San Marino	●	●	●	●	●	30.1	51,673.0	12.0	48.7	36.1	3.2	46,179.0	95.7	3.7	0.6
Sao Tome and Principe	○	○	○			…	46.4	37.7	56.3	—	6.0	23.7	100.0	—	—
Saudi Arabia	●		●			…	1,761.4	26.8	73.2	—	—	4,292.9	100.0	—	—
Senegal	7	○	○		○	1.8	17,202.0	—	47.6	51.4	1.0	15,371.0	84.6	11.1	4.3
Serbia	●	●		●	●	50.9	…	…	…	…	…	…	…	…	…
Seychelles	○	9	○			14.2	69.1	30.1	60.2	—	9.7	42.7	69.6	4.9	25.5
Sierra Leone	○		○			…	…	…	…	…	…	153.0	100.0	—	—
Singapore	●	●	●			18.1	7,531.9	49.1	35.3	0.1	15.6	5,045.8	78.0	0.6	21.4
Sint Maarten[5]			○	○		12.9	317.0	100.0	—	—	—	275.0	…	…	…
Slovakia	●	●	●	●	●	49.6	74,205	…	…	…	…	87,916	…	…	…
Slovenia	●	●	●	●	●	44.2	…	…	…	…	…	…	…	…	…
Solomon Islands	●			●		…	20.9	27.8	41.1	—	31.1	17.4	89.7	10.3	—
Somalia			○			…	—	…	…	…	…	…	…	…	…
South Africa	○	9	○	○	○	2.2	2,034	—	100.0	—	—	2,260.0	…	…	…
Spain	●	●	●	●	●	46.6	8,320,972.0	15.9	53.9	27.9	2.3	8,038,090.0	94.3	2.6	3.1
Sri Lanka	●	9	●		●	20.4	15,399.9	22.0	24.4	29.1	24.5	5,819.0	98.5	1.3	0.2
Sudan	○		○			0.6	62.0	24.9	0.5	—	74.6	14.7	37.5	62.5	—
Sudan, South	…	…	…	…	…	…	…	…	…	…	…	…	…	…	…
Suriname	○	…	…	…	○	…	73.0	24.7	75.3	—	—	70.6	100.0	—	—
Swaziland	○		○			0.4	10.7	31.4	31.4	—	37.2	3.9	45.8	54.2	—
Sweden	●	●	●	●	●	46.9	446,909.7	2.8	37.9	50.8	8.5	439,997.3	93.7	3.3	3.0
Switzerland	●	●	●	●	●	47.8	45,800.1	45.6	22.6	25.9	5.9	41,745.7	91.5	3.0	5.5
Syria	●		●			5.3	3,147.9	30.4	60.9	…	5.6	1,455.9	95.7	4.2	0.1
Taiwan	●	●	●	●		13.8	…	…	…	…	…	…	…	…	…
Tajikistan	●	●	●	●	●	12.2	…	…	…	…	…	…	…	…	…
Tanzania	○	○	○			…	3,275.8	25.9	25.9	—	48.2	2,780.7	5.8	14.1	80.1
Thailand	●	●	●	●	●	7.8	654.0	—	60.2	—	39.8	260.0	88.2	11.8	—
Togo	○	9	○		○	…	10,162.0	8.1	61.5	—	30.4	5,844.0	77.5	22.5	—
Tonga	…	…	…	…	…	0.8	…	…	…	…	…	…	…	…	…
Trinidad and Tobago	○	○	○		○	19.3	584.9	12.0	24.1	39.7	24.2	438.4	85.6	11.1	3.3
Tunisia	○	○	○	○	○	21.2	325.3	36.9	63.1	—	—	358.3	…	…	…
Turkey	●	●	●	●		4.2	12,075,809.0	28.5	32.9	22.8	15.8	10,241,427.0	97.2	2.2	0.6
Turkmenistan	●	●	●	●		…	…	…	…	…	…	…	…	…	…
Tuvalu	○	…	…	…	…	…	…	…	…	…	…	0.1	67.6	32.4	—
Uganda	○		○			2.2	265.9	32.1	64.3	1.1	2.5	145.0	0.3	76.8	22.9
Ukraine	●	●	●	●	●	48.9	20,350.0	—	—	—	—	20,350.0	100.0	—	—
United Arab Emirates	…	…	…	…	…	3.2	182.2	17.3	6.2	0.5	76.0	182.2	100.0	…	…
United Kingdom	●	●	●	●	●	28.9	92,157.0	18.1	24.9	52.9	4.1	88,294.0	93.8	3.3	2.9
United States	○	○	○	○	○	42.2	804,909.0	25.5	33.9	28.8	11.8	627,653.0	95.5	3.3	1.2
Uruguay	○	38	○	○	○	38.1	535,507.0	31.4	37.3	26.0	5.3	548,591.0	93.6	5.4	1.0
Uzbekistan	●	●	●	●	●	…	…	…	…	…	…	…	…	…	…
Vanuatu	●					…	—	…	…	…	…	—	…	…	…
Venezuela	○	○	○	○	38	11.2	7,457.6	21.3	40.7	12.7	25.3	6,355.7	86.1	14.9	—
Vietnam	●	●	●	●		10.5	…	…	…	…	…	…	…	…	…
Virgin Islands (U.S.)	○	…	…	○	○	…	…	…	…	…	…	…	…	…	…
West Bank	…	…	…	…	…	…	…	…	…	…	…	…	…	…	…
Western Sahara	…	…	…	…	…	…	…	…	…	…	…	…	…	…	…
Yemen	●		●			10.5	—	…	…	…	…	—	…	…	…
Zambia	○	9	○			1.3	179.2	28.4	28.4	—	43.2	67.7	40.6	59.4	—
Zimbabwe	○	9	○			…	167.0	25.9	7.6	64.2	2.3	112.2	93.7	6.2	0.1

[1]As of October 2011 U.S. forces numbered 90,000, and NATO-sponsored security forces numbered 40,638. [2]1999. [3]Political dependency; defense is the responsibility of the administering country. [4]Includes civilian militia. [5]Includes Curaçao and Sint Maarten. [6]2003. [7]Old age benefits only. [8]Excludes expenditure on military pensions. [9]Medical care only. [10]Old age and orphan's benefits only. [11]Excludes 31,050 paramilitary forces. [12]Military defense is the responsibility of France. [13]As of November 2010 there were 144,000–159,000 active forces; as of October 2011 UN peacekeeping troops numbered 18,916. [14]2004. [15]As of October 2011 UN troops numbered 10,891. [16]2005. [17]Republic of Cyprus only. [18]No regular military forces; Commonwealth of Dominica Police Force. [19]UN forces of 1,236 military police were stationed in East Timor as of October 2011. [20]2010. [21]Haitian Army was disbanded in 1995, and a National Police Force was formed numbered at 2,000 in late 2009;

crime and law enforcement (latest)						military protection								country
offenses reported to the police per 100,000 population					population per police officer[g]	manpower, 2010[h]		expenditure, 2009				arms trade ('000,000 U.S.$)		
total	personal		property			total ('000)	per 1,000 population	total ('000,000 U.S.$)	per capita	% of central government expenditure (2005)	% of GDP or GNP	imports 1999	exports 2005	
	murder	assault	burglary	automobile theft										
64.5	1.9	26.9	0.1	0.1	650	406.0	7.5	1,900	39	21.5[14]	5.5	60	0	Myanmar (Burma)
2,006	26.3	533.6	602.0	65.8	...	9.2	4.0	311	147	8.4[14]	3.2	130	0	Namibia
...	25.0	400.0	100.0	...	110	—	—	...	...	...	...	...	...	Nauru
9	2.8	1.1	0.8	...	1,000	95.8	3.6	184	6	12.4	1.4	0	0	Nepal
7,808	10.9	242.8	3,100.4	239.0	510	37.4	2.2	12,100	732	3.6	1.5	775	1,461	Netherlands
...	...	...	...	...	...	[3]	[3]	—	—	—	—	...	...	New Caledonia
13,854	3.9	546.3	2,352.9	788.6	630	9.7	2.2	1,360	315	2.5	1.2	575	0	New Zealand
1,069	25.6	203.8	110.7	...	90[4]	12.0	2.0	40	7	2.9[2]	0.7	0	0	Nicaragua
99	0.9	16.6	1.0	0.7	2,350[33]	5.3	0.3	51	3	6.4[2]	1.0	0	0	Niger
312	...	...	...	...	1,140	80.0	0.5	1,500	10	8.1[2]	0.9	0	0	Nigeria
245	3.8	92.6	73.7	20.8	...	[3]	[3]	—	—	—	—	...	...	Northern Mariana Islands
9,769	2.3	66.1	95.0	465.8	660	26.5	5.3	6,200	1,284	4.6	1.6	480	382	Norway
331	1.5	1.8	...	14.9	430	42.6	15.2	4,020	1,413	35.3[6]	8.7	30	0	Oman
318	7.1	2.2	10.4	9.0	720	617.0	3.3	4,200	24	19.8	2.4	1,000	100	Pakistan
...	...	...	323.0	...	...	[31]	[31]	—	—	—	—	...	...	Palau
419	2.0	11.8	25.1	77.7	180	—	—	269	78	...	1.1	5	0	Panama
766	8.6	66.7	63	22.0	720	3.1	0.5	40	7	2.4[6]	0.5	0	0	Papua New Guinea
418	11.5	54.2	21.4	30.5	310	10.7	1.6	126	20	3.9[2]	0.9	10	0	Paraguay
218	3.2	24.1	7.8	3.6	730	115.0	3.9	1,030	36	12.3[2]	1.2	30	0	Peru
...	13.1	14.9	...	3.3	1,160	125.0	1.3	1,360	15	4.5	0.8	110	0	Philippines
2,901	2.8	79.2	936.8	185.0	370	100.0	2.6	7,300	191	3.5	1.7	40	361	Poland
661	3.1	1.5	115.3	40.4	660	43.3	4.1	3,710	348	3.3[14]	1.6	60	9	Portugal
2,339	16.2	101.8	412.4	1,521	380	[31]	[31]	—	—	—	—	...	...	Puerto Rico
1,079	2.1	7.1	34.1	11.5	...	11.8	7.3	2,500	1,505	9.6[14]	2.5	120	0	Qatar
2,097	7.8	123.1	181.3	137.9	220	[3]	[3]	—	—	—	—	...	...	Réunion
2,206	7.1	5.8	367.8	30.4	...	71.7	3.4	2,230	103	5.0[6]	1.4	200	36	Romania
20,514	21.3	32.6	669.1	25.6	...	1,046.0	7.3	57,200	403	34.6	4.6	470	6,126	Russia
...	45.1	114.3	...	0.3	4,650	33.0	3.0	113	11	22.7[2]	2.2	30	0	Rwanda
3,808	12.0	434.0	1,790	...	300	—	—	...	...	...	...	...	...	St. Kitts and Nevis
4,386	17.0	1,193.0	778.0	...	430	—	—	...	...	...	...	...	...	St. Lucia
3,977	10.3	986.9	...	...	250	—	—	...	...	...	...	...	...	St. Vincent and the Grenadines
...	...	...	...	...	...	[34]	[34]	—	—	—	—	...	...	Samoa
...	4.1	...	...	...	...	—	—	...	...	...	...	...	...	San Marino
558	4.0	...	...	...	400	—	—	0.6[30]	4[30]	1.3	1.2[30]	0	0	Sao Tome and Principe
149	0.5	0.2	...	45.4	280	233.5	8.2	41,300	1,631	14.4	11.0	7,700	0	Saudi Arabia
123	0.5	8.8	2.1	8.2	730	13.6	1.1	210	17	7.3[14]	1.6	0	0	Senegal
...	...	...	...	...	...	29.1	4.0	969	132	...	2.2	10	0	Serbia
5,361	3.7	43.4	378.0	40.9	120	0.2	2.1	6	68	3.8	0.7	...	...	Seychelles
...	...	...	...	...	600	10.5	1.8	12	2	13.5	0.6	10	0	Sierra Leone
783	1.0	2.4	40.1	55.2	230	72.5	14.0	7,830	1,581	28.8[14]	4.3	950	20[2]	Singapore
...	...	...	...	...	...	[3]	[3]	—	—	—	—	...	...	Sint Maarten[5]
1,740	2.4	204.6	504.3	142.4	...	16.5	3.0	1,350	249	4.5	1.5	20	62	Slovakia
3,138	3.6	20.7	427.3	25.6	...	7.6	3.7	793	389	3.1	1.6	10	0	Slovenia
...	...	...	...	...	620	—	—	...	...	...	...	0	0	Solomon Islands
144	1.5	8.0	31.2	...	540	[35]	[35]	...	...	...	...	20	0	Somalia
7,140.8	121.9	595.6	896.6	262.7	870	62.1	1.2	4,300	87	4.2[6]	1.5	50	410[6]	South Africa
4,449	2.7	23.4	562.8	343.3	580	142.2	3.0	16,900	343	4.3	1.1	750	521	Spain
280	8.2	10.8	54.7	...	860	160.9	7.6	1,480	73	10.5	3.5	40	0	Sri Lanka
...	10.2	46.3	66.6	4.7	740	109.3	2.6	502[16]	13[16]	27.5[6]	1.8[16]	10	0	Sudan
...	...	...	...	...	...	[36]	[36]	...	...	...	...	...	...	Sudan, South
17,819	7.6	1,824.4	...	...	...	1.8	3.5	22	43	11.0[14]	1.0	10	0	Suriname
3,962	18.1	471.7	706.8	54.1	610	—	—	49[14]	39[14]	4.6	1.8[14]	0	0	Swaziland
12,982	4.5	42.5	1,615.1	658.9	330	21.1	2.2	5,300	570	5.4	1.2	230	1,416	Sweden
7,030	2.7	73.3	1,065.9	1,065.5	640	3.7	0.5	4,070	526	8.1[14]	0.8	1,100	207	Switzerland
42	1.0	—	15.6	2.7	1,970	295.0	14.2	2,230	102	23.6[2]	4.2	210	0	Syria
799	8.2	...	...	124.9	720	290.0	12.5	9,500	412	10.3	2.5	2,600	20[2]	Taiwan
317	2.5	4.6	...	...	...	8.8	1.1	49	7	2.0[14]	1.0	0	0	Tajikistan
1,714	7.7	1.7	96.6	0.9	1,330	27.0	0.6	247	6	10.1[2]	1.2	5	0	Tanzania
351	7.7	25.4	9.9	3.3	530	305.9	4.6	4,730	72	1.6	1.8	330	0	Thailand
11	...	...	...	...	1,970	8.6	1.5	67	11	9.4[2]	2.1	0	0	Togo
2,727	1.0	108.5	541.7	14.8	330	[34]	[34]	2[14]	23[14]	...	1.0[14]	...	...	Tonga
1,170	9.7	31.0	452.7	80.6	280	4.0	3.1	167	128	2.2[6]	8.5	0	0	Trinidad and Tobago
1,419	1.2	165.1	60.1	10.2	340	35.8	3.4	532	51	5.0	1.2	10	0	Tunisia
547	3.9	120.0	...	28.9	1,570	510.6	6.9	10,900	151	6.7[6]	1.8	3,200	337	Turkey
...	...	...	...	...	...	22.0	4.4	303	62	16.0[2]	1.6	10	0	Turkmenistan
...	...	...	...	—	290	—	—	...	...	...	...	...	...	Tuvalu
316	9.9	54.8	19.3	8.3	1,090	45.0	1.3	293	9	8.9[6]	2.0	30	0	Uganda
1,115	10.0	14.7	224.3	7.6	...	129.9	2.8	1,410	31	4.5	1.2	10	500[6]	Ukraine
2,604.7	3.0	10.1	5.1	23.0	140	51.0	6.5	7,960	1,670	30.1[2]	3.6	950	0	United Arab Emirates
9,823[37]	2.8[37]	405.2[37]	1,832.7[37]	752.9[37]	350	178.5	2.8	59,100	955	6.0	2.7	2,600	12,985	United Kingdom
5,374	9.0	430.2	1,041.8	591.2	318	1,564.0	5.0	690,300	2,247	20.1	4.9	1,600	11,552	United States
3,002	7.7	162.5	52.3	130.1	170	24.6	7.3	495	147	5.2	1.6	10	0	Uruguay
328	3.2	3.0	33.2	2.3	...	67.0	2.4	780	28	5.3[2]	2.4	0	10[2]	Uzbekistan
...	...	...	...	...	450	—	—	...	...	...	...	...	...	Vanuatu
1,106	22.1	152.2	358.2	239.4	320	115.0	3.9	3,320	116	5.0	1.0	310	0	Venezuela
74	1.5	8.5	...	...	...	482.0	5.5	2,140	24	...	2.2	70	0	Vietnam
10,441	22.3	1,943.2	3,183.7	954	240	[31]	[31]	—	—	—	—	...	...	Virgin Islands (U.S.)
2,226	...	...	...	...	...	—	—	...	...	...	...	...	...	West Bank
...	...	...	...	...	...	[3]	[3]	—	—	—	—	...	...	Western Sahara
...	5.3	3.2	1.2	3.6	1,940	66.7	2.7	1,570	69	18.8[2]	6.3	30	0	Yemen
666	9.8	9.5	153.5	9.6	540	15.1	1.1	213	16	3.9[2]	1.7	0	0	Zambia
5,619	9.0	198.4	435.9	13.4	750	29.0	2.4	67	5	12.1[2]	1.4	10	0	Zimbabwe

in October 2011 there were 12,552 UN troops in Haiti. [22]Includes public order. [23]As of October 2011 U.S. forces numbered 39,000; complete withdrawal took place in December 2011. [24]Includes U.S. military aid of U.S.$2 billion annually. [25]Maternity benefits only. [26]As of December 2011 NATO-led Kosovo Force numbered 5,500 troops. [27]As of October 2011 UN peacekeeping troops numbered 12,488. [28]As of October 2011 there were 9,227 UN peacekeeping troops in Liberia. [29]Military defense is the responsibility of Switzerland. [30]2007. [31]Military defense is the responsibility of the United States. [32]Coverage provided through France's program. [33]Includes paramilitary forces. [34]Military defense is the responsibility of New Zealand. [35]Following the 1991 revolution, no national armed forces have yet been formed. [36]As of October 2011 UN peacekeeping troops numbered 5,484. [37]England and Wales. [38]Coverage is provided under other programs.

BIBLIOGRAPHY AND SOURCES

The following list indicates the principal documentary sources used in the compilation of *Britannica World Data.* It is by no means a complete list, either for international or for national sources, but is indicative more of the range of materials to which reference has been made in preparing this compilation.

While *Britannica World Data* has long been based primarily on print sources, many rare in North American library collections, the burgeoning resources of the Internet can be accessed from any appropriately equipped personal computer (PC). At this writing, more than 100 national statistical offices had Internet sites and there were also sites for central banks, national information offices, individual ministries, and the like.

Because of the relative ease of access to these sites for PC users, uniform resource locators (URLs) for mainly official sites have been added to both country statements (at the end, in boldface) and individual Comparative National Statistics tables (at the end of the headnote) when a source providing comparable international data existed. Many sites exist that are narrower in coverage or less official and that may also serve the reader (online newspapers; full texts of national constitutions; business and bank sites) but space permitted the listing of only the top national and intergovernmental sites. Sites that are wholly or predominantly in a language other than English are so identified.

International Statistical Sources

Christian Research. *World Churches Handbook* (1997).
Comité Monétaire de la Zone Franc. *La Zone Franc: Rapport* (annual).
Eastern Caribbean Central Bank. *Balance of Payments Statistics* (annual).
Europa Publications Ltd. *Africa South of the Sahara* (annual); *The Europa Year Book* (2 vol.; annual); *The Far East and Australasia* (annual); *The Middle East and North Africa* (annual).
Europe in Figures—Eurostat Yearbook.
Food and Agriculture Organization (FAO). *Trade Yearbook; Yearbook of Forest Products; State of the World's Forests 2003.*
Her Majesty's Stationery Office. *The Commonwealth Yearbook.*
Instituts d'Émission d'Outre-Mer et des Départements d'Outre-Mer (France). *Bulletin trimestriel; Rapport annuel.*
Inter-American Development Bank. *Economic and Social Progress in Latin America* (annual).
Inter-Parliamentary Union (IPU). *Chronicle of Parliamentary Elections and Developments* (annual).
International Air Transport Association. *World Air Transport Statistics* (annual).
International Civil Aviation Organization. *Civil Aviation Statistics of the World* (annual); *Digest of Statistics.*
International Institute for Strategic Studies. *The Military Balance* (annual).
International Monetary Fund (IMF). *Annual Report on Exchange Arrangements and Exchange Restrictions; Direction of Trade Statistics Yearbook; Government Finance Statistics Yearbook; International Financial Statistics* (monthly, with yearbook).
International Road Federation. *World Road Statistics* (annual).
International Telecommunication Union. *Yearbook of Statistics: Telecommunication Services* (annual).
Jane's Publishing Co., Ltd. *Jane's World Railways* (annual).
Keesing's Worldwide LLC. *Keesing's Record of World Events* (monthly except August).
Macmillan Press Ltd. *The Statesman's Year-Book.*
Middle East Economic Digest Ltd. *Middle East Economic Digest* (weekly).
Nordic Council of Ministers, *Nordic Statistical Yearbook* (annual).
Oceana Publications. *Constitutions of the Countries of the World; Constitutions of Dependencies and Territories.*
Oxford University Press. *World Christian Encyclopedia* (David B. Barrett, ed. [2001, 2 vol.]).
PennWell Publishing Co. *International Petroleum Encyclopedia* (annual).
René Moreux et Cie. *Marchés tropicaux & Méditerranéens* (weekly).
Routledge. *The Europa World of Learning,* 2 vols. (annual).
United Nations (UN). *Industrial Commodities Statistics Yearbook; Energy Statistics Yearbook; International Trade Statistics Yearbook* (2 vol.); *Monthly Bulletin of Statistics; Statistical Yearbook.*
United Nations Economic Commission for Latin America and the Caribbean (UNECLAC). *Economic Survey of Latin America and the Caribbean* (2 vol.; annual).
United Nations Economic and Social Commission for Asia and the Pacific (UNESCAP). *Statistical Yearbook for Asia and the Pacific.*
United Nations Economic and Social Commission for Western Asia (UNESCWA). *Demographic and Related Socio-Economic Data Sheets* (irreg.); *National Accounts Studies of the ESCWA Region* (irreg.); *The Population Situation in the ESCWA Region* (irreg.).
United Nations Industrial Development Organization (UNIDO). *International Yearbook of Industrial Statistics 2006.*
United States: Dept. of Health and Human Services, *Social Security Programs Throughout the World* (4 vol.; semiannual); Dept. of Interior, *Minerals Yearbook* (3 vol. in 6 parts); Dept. of State, *World Military Expenditure and Arms Transfers* (annual).
World Association of Newspapers. *World Press Trends* (annual).
The World Bank Group. *World Bank Atlas* (annual); *Global Development Finance* (2 vol.; annual); *World Development Report* (annual); *World Development Indicators* (annual).
World Tourism Organization. *Compendium of Tourism Statistics* (annual).

Internet Resources

African Development Bank (AfDB) http://www.afdb.org
AfDB Documents and Publications http://www.afdb.org/portal/page?_pageid=473,970659&_dad=portal&_schema=PORTAL
Air Transport World: World Airline Traffic Results 2006 http://www.atwonline.com/channels/data AirlineEconomics/World_Airline_Report_2006.pdf
Asian Development Bank (ADB) http://www.adb.org/statistics
Asian Development Bank: *Key Indicators* (Asia and Pacific) http://www.adb.org/documents/books/key_indicators
Australian Department of Foreign Affairs and Trade http://www.dfat.gov.au/geo
Bank for International Settlements, central banks list http://www.bis.org/cbanks.htm
Banque des Etats de l'Afrique Centrale http://www.beac.int
Caribbean Community (CARICOM) Secretariat Statistics http://www.caricomstats.org
Caribbean Development Bank (CDB) http://www.caribank.org
Central Intelligence Agency (CIA) World Factbook https://www.cia.gov/library/publications/the_world_factbook
City Population (World): Thomas Brinkhoff http://www.citypopulation.de/index.html
Constitution Finder http://confinder.richmond.edu/country.php
Eastern Caribbean Central Bank (ECCB) http://www.eccb-centralbank.org
Economic Community of West African States (ECOWAS) http://www.ecowas.int
ECOWAS Statistics http://www.ecostat.org
Election Guide http://www.electionguide.org
Energy Information Administration (EIA): International Energy Annual (IEA) http://www.eia.doe.gov/iea
European Central Bank (ECB) http://www.ecb.int/stats/html/index.en.html
EUROSTAT Panorama of Transport http://epp.eurostat.ec.europa.eu/cache/ITY_OFFPUB/KS-DA-09-001-EN.PDF
EUROSTAT Statistics in Focus http://epp.eurostat.cec.eu.int/
Europe in Figures—Eurostat Yearbook 2006–07 http://epp.eurostat.ec.europa.eu/
FAO statistics http://faostat.fao.org
GeoHive (World) http://geohive.com/default1.aspx
IMF publications http://www.imf.org/external/pubind.htm
International Household Survey Network: IHSN central survey catalog http://www.surveynetwork.org/home/?MI=activitiesLlvl2=catalog&lv3=surveys
International Development Statistics http://www.oecd.org/dac/stats/idsonline
International Labour Organization: LABORSTA database (World) http://laborsta.ilo.org
International Telecommunication Union (ITU) statistics http://www.itu.int/ITU-D/ict/statistics
IPU PARLINE Database http://www.ipu.org/parline-e/parlinesearch.asp
Law Library of Congress http://www.loc.gov/law/guide
Library of Congress Country Profiles http://lcweb2.loc.gov/frd/cs/profiles.html
National Geospatial-Intelligence Agency http://gnswww.nga.mil/geonames/GNS/index.jsp
Observatoire Économique et Statistique d'Afrique Sub Saharienne (AFRISTAT) http://www.afristat.org
OECD International Development Statistics (IDS) http://www.oecd.org/dac/stats/idsonline
OECD Key Transport Statistics http://www.internationaltransportforum.org/Pub/pdf/10KeyStat2009.pdf
Secretariat of the Pacific Community: Pacific Regional Information System (PRISM [Pacific]) http://www.spc.int/prism
Sénats du Monde http://www.senat.fr/senatsdumonde/pays.html
Statistical, Economic, and Social Research and Training Centre for Islamic Countries (SESRTCIC): Statistics http://www.sesrtcic.org/stat_database.php

Statoids http://www.statoids.com
Stockholm International Peace Research Institute (SIPRI): SIPRI Military Expenditure Database (World) http://first.sipri.org/contents/webmaster/databases
UNAIDS: Report on the Global AIDS Epidemic 2010 http://www.unaids.org/globalreport/Global_report.htm
UNCTAD Handbook of Statistics: Remittances http://stats.unctad.org/statistics/handbook
UNCTAD World Investment Report 2007 http://www.unctad.org/en/docs/wir2007overview_en.pdf
UNECLAC Statistical Yearbook for Latin America and the Caribbean 2006 http://www.eclac.cl
UNESCAP Asia-Pacific in Figures 2004 http://www.unescap.org/stat/data/apif
UNESCAP Statistical Indicators for Asia and the Pacific 2005 http://www.unescap.org/stat/data/statind/pdf/index.asp
UNESCAP Statistics Division Data Centre http://www.unescap.org/stat/data/statind/pdf
UNESCWA Statistical Abstract http://www.escwa.un.org/
UNIDO statistics http://www.unido.org
United Nations Children's Fund (UNICEF [World]) http://www.unicef.org
United Nations Conference on Trade and Development (UNCTAD) Handbook of Statistics 2006–07 http://www.unctad.org/Templates/Page.asp?intltemID=1890
United Nations Development Programme (UNDP): Human Development Reports (World) http://hdr.undp.org
United Nations Economic and Social Development: World Population Prospects http://esa.un.org/unpp
United Nations Economic and Social Development: World Urbanization Prospects http://esa.un.org/unup
United Nations Educational, Scientific, and Cultural Organization (UNESCO): Institute for Statistics database (World) http://www.uis.unesco.org
UNESCO education tables http://stats.uis.unesco.org
UNESCO Global Education Digest http://www.uis.unesco.org/TEMPLATE/pdf/ged/2006/GED2006.pdf
United Nations Peacekeeping http://www.un.org/Depts/dpko
United Nations Population Division: World Population Prospects: 2008 Revision Population Database http://esa.un.org/unpp/
United Nations Statistics Division: Demographic Yearbook http://unstats.un.org/unsd/demographic
United Nations Statistics Division: National Accounts Main Aggregates Database http://unstats.org/unsd/snaama/Introduction.asp
United Nations Statistics Division: Population and Vital Statistics Report http://unstats.un.org/unsd/seriesa/introduction.asp
U.S. Census Bureau: International Data Base (IDB) http://www.census.gov/ipc/www/idb
U.S. Census Bureau, statistical agencies list http://www.census.gov/main/www/stat_int.html
U.S. Department of State Background Notes http://www.state.gov/r/pa/ei/bgn
U.S. Department of State International Religious Freedom Report 2007 http://www.state.gov/g/drl/rls/irf
U.S. Department of the Interior: Office of Insular Affairs (OIA) http://www.doi.gov/oia/index.html
OIA Statistics http://www.pacificweb.org
U.S. Geological Survey (USGS) mineral information http://minerals.usgs.gov/minerals/pubs/country
U.S. Agency for International Development (USAID) Demographic and Health Surveys (DHS) http://www.measuredhs.com
Women and Men in CARICOM Member States http://www.caricomstats.org/pdmpub.html
World Association of Newspapers and News Publishers World Press Trends http://www.wan-press.org/worldpresstrends/home.php
The World Bank Group: World Bank Database (World) http://devdata.worldbank.org
World Bank remittances tables http://siteresources.worldbank.org/EXTGEP2006/Resources/RemittancesDataGEP2006.xls
The World Gazetteer (World) http://www.world-gazetteer.com
World Health Organization (WHO) http://www.who.int/en
WHO Global Burden of Disease Estimates (World) http://www.who.int/healthinfo/bodestimates/en/index.html
WHO Global Health Atlas (World) http://who.int/globalatlas
WHO Pan American Health Organization (PAHO) http://www.paho.org
PAHO Health Situation in the Americas: Basic Indicators http://www.paho.org/english/dd/ais/BI-brochure-2005.pdf
PAHO Health Statistics from the Americas 2006 http://www.paho.org/English/DD/AIS/HSA2006.htm
WHO Regional Office for Africa http://www.afro.who.int
WHO Regional Office for Europe http://www.euro.who.int
WHO Regional Office for the Eastern Mediterranean http://www.emro.who.int/index.asp
WHO Regional Office for South-East Asia http://www.searo.who.int
WHO Regional Office for the Western Pacific http://www.wpro.who.int
WHO Statistical Information System http://www.who.int/whosis/en
World Military Guide http://www.globalsecurity.org/military/world/index.html
World Statesmen http://www.worldstatesmen.org

National Statistical Sources

Afghanistan. *Afghanistan Statistical Yearbook; Islamic Republic of Afghanistan: Selected Issues and Statistical Appendix* (IMF Staff Country Report [2006]).

Albania. *Population and Housing Census 2001; Statistical Yearbook of Albania; Albania in Figures* (annual); *Albania: Selected Issues* (IMF Staff Country Report [2006]).

Algeria. Bank *Rapport annuel; Annuaire statistique* (irregular); *Recensement général de la population et de l'habitat, 1998; Algeria: Statistical Appendix* (IMF Staff Country Report [2007]).

American Samoa. *American Samoa at a Glance*; *Report on the State of the Island* (U.S. Department of the Interior [annual]); *2000 Census of Population and Housing* (U.S.); *American Samoa Statistical Yearbook.*

Andorra. *Anuari Estadístic* (annual); Andorra Economic Report; *Andorra in Figures* (annual).

Angola. National Bank *Indicadores* (annual); *Angola: Selected Issues and Statistical Appendix* (IMF Staff Country Report [2007]); *Perfil estatìstico de Angola* (annual).

Antigua. *Antigua and Barbuda: Statistical Appendix* (IMF Staff Country Report [2006]); *Statistical Yearbook; 2001 Population and Housing Census.*

Argentina. *Statistical Yearbook of the Argentine Republic; Censo nacional de población, hogares, y vivienda* 2001.

Armenia. *Statistical Yearbook of Armenia; Socio-Economic Situation of the Republic of Armenia* (annual); *Armenia: Selected Issues* (IMF Staff Country Report [2006]).

Aruba. *Statistical Yearbook;* Central Bank *Bulletin* (quarterly); Central Bank *Annual Report; Fourth Population and Housing Census October 14, 2000.*

Australia. *Australia at a Glance* (annual); *Monthly Summary of Statistics; Social Indicators* (annual); *Demographic Statistical Yearbook* (monthly); *Year Book Australia; 2006 Census of Population and Housing; Australian Social Trends,* 2007.

Austria. *Grosszählung 2001* (General Census 2001). *Sozialstatistische Daten* (irreg.); *Statistisches Jahrbuch für die Republik Österreich* (annual).

Azerbaijan. *Azerbaijan in Figures* (annual); *Statistical Yearbook of Azerbaijan.*

Bahamas, The. *Census of Population and Housing 2000; Statistical Abstract* (annual); *Quarterly Statistical Digest;* Central Bank of the Bahamas *Annual Report.*

Bahrain. *Statistical Abstract* (annual); *The Population, Housing, Buildings, and Establishments Census 2001; Bahrain in Figures* (annual).

Bangladesh. *Bangladesh Population Census, 2001; Statistical Yearbook of Bangladesh;* Central Bank *Annual Report.*

Barbados. *Barbados Economic Report* (annual); *Monthly Digest of Statistics; Annual Statistical Digest;* Central Bank *Annual Report; Barbados Population and Housing Census 2000.*

Belarus. *Statistical Yearbook of the Republic of Belarus; Population Census 2009; The Republic of Belarus in Figures* (annual); *Republic of Belarus: Statistical Appendix* (IMF Staff Country Report [2007]).

Belgium. *Annuaire statistique de la Belgique* (annual) *Recensement de la population et des logements au 1er oct. 2001; Statistical Bulletin* (quarterly).

Belize. *Abstract of Statistics* (annual); *Belize Economic Survey* (annual); Central Bank *Annual Report and Accounts; 2000 Population Census: Major Findings. Belize: Selected Issues and Statistical Appendix* (IMF Staff Country Report [2006]).

Benin. *Annuaire statistique* (annual); *Recensement général de la population et de l'habitation* (2002); *Rapports annuel de la Zone franc.*

Bermuda. *Bermuda Digest of Statistics* (annual); *Bermuda Facts and Figures* (annual); *The 2000 Census of Population and Housing; Quarterly Bulletin of Statistics.*

Bhutan. *Statistical Yearbook of Bhutan; Population and Housing Census of Bhutan 2005;* Royal Monetary Authority of Bhutan *Monthly Bulletin.*

Bolivia. *Anuario estadístico* (annual); *Censo de población y vivienda 2001; Compendio estadístico* (annual); *Bolivia: Selected Issues* (IMF Staff Country Report [2007]); *Estadísticas socioeconómicas* (annual); Banco Central de Bolivia Mensual Bulletin.

Bosnia and Herzegovina. Central Bank *Annual Report;* Central Bank *Bulletin* (quarterly). *Bosnia and Herzegovina: Selected Issues* (IMF Staff Country Report [2007]).

Botswana. *Statistical Bulletin* (quarterly); Bank *Annual Report; 2001 Population and Housing Census; Botswana: Statistical Appendix* (IMF Staff Country Report [2007]).

Brazil. *Anuário Estatístico do Brasil* (annual); *Censo Demográfico 2000.*

Brunei. *Brunei Statistical Yearbook; Brunei Darussalam Population and Housing Census 2001; Brunei Economic Bulletin* (quarterly); *Statistical Appendix* (IMF Staff Country Report [2006]).

Bulgaria. *Bulgaria 2005—Social-Economic Development; Prebroyavaneto na naselenìeto kŭm 01.03.2001 godina* (Census of Population of March 1, 2001); *Statistical Reference Book of the Republic of Bulgaria* (annual); *Bulgaria: Selected Issues and Statistical Appendix* (IMF Staff Country Report [2006]).

Burkina Faso. *Burkina Faso: Selected Issues and Statistical Appendix* (IMF Staff Country Report [2005]); *Recensement général de la population du 10 au 20 decembre 1996.*

Burundi. Banque de la Republique du Burundi *Rapport Annuel* (annual); *Annuaire statistique* (annual); *Recensement général de la population, 2005; Burundi: Selected Issues and Statistical Appendix* (IMF Staff Country Report [2006]).

Cambodia. *2008 Population Census of Cambodia; Cambodia: Selected Issues and Statistical Appendix* (IMF Staff Country Report [2006]); *Cambodia Statistical Yearbook.*

Cameroon. *Cameroon Statistical Yearbook; Cameroon: Statistical Appendix* (IMF Staff Country Report [2007]); *Recensement général des entreprises de 2009.*

Canada. *Canada Year Book* (biennial); *Census Canada 2006: Population; Canada at a Glance* (annual).

Cayman Islands. *Annual Economic Report 2006; Overseas Trade Report 2006; Labour Force Survey 2006.*

Cape Verde. Bank *Boletim de Estatísticas Mensal; Cape Verde: Statistical Appendix* (IMF Staff Country Report [2006]); *O Recenseamento Geral da População e Habitação 2000; Cabo Verde en numeros* (annual).

Central African Republic. *Annuaire statistique* (annual); *Central African Republic: Selected*

Issues and Statistical Appendix (IMF Staff Country Report [2004]); *Recensement géneral de la population 2003.*

Chad. *Bulletin Trimestriel de Conjecture* (quarterly); *Annuaire statistique* (annual); *Recensement general de la population et de l'habitat 2009; Chad: Statistical Appendix* (IMF Staff Country Report [2007]).

Chile. *Statistical Synthesis of Chile* (annual); Central Bank *Annual Report; Chile XVII censo nacional de población y VI de vivienda, 24 de abril 2002; Quarterly Economic Indicators; Compendio estadístico* (annual).

China, People's Republic of. *China Statistical Yearbook; 2000 Population Census of the People's Republic of China.*

Colombia. *Colombia estadística* (annual); *Censo 93 informacion de vivienda; Colombia: Selected Issues* (IMF Staff Country Report [2006]).

Comoros. Central Bank *Rapport Annuel* (annual); *Recensement général de la population et de l'habitat 15 septembre 2003; Union of the Comoros: Selected Issues and Statistical Appendix* (IMF Staff Country Report [2006]).

Congo, Dem. Rep. of the (Zaire). *Dem. Rep. of the Congo: Selected Issues and Statistical Appendix* (IMF Staff Country Report [2007]).

Congo, Rep. of the. *Annuaire statistique* (annual); *Recensement général de la population et de l'habitat de 1984; Republic of Congo: Selected Issues and Statistical Appendix* (IMF Staff Country Report [2007]).

Costa Rica. *Anuario estadístico* (annual); *Costa Rica at a Glance* (annual); *IX censo nacional de población y V de viviendas, 2000.*

Côte d'Ivoire. *Côte d'Ivoire: Statistical Appendix* (IMF Staff Country Report [2004]); *Recensement général de la population et de l'habitat 1998.*

Croatia. *Monthly Statistical Review; Census of Population, Households and Dwellings 31st March 2001; Statistical Yearbook. Republic of Croatia: Selected Issues* (IMF Staff Country Report [2007]).

Cuba. *Anuario estadístico* (annual); *Censo de población y viviendas, 2002.*

Curaçao. *Statistical Orientation Curaçao* (annual); *General Population and Housing Census 2001.*

Cyprus. Central Bank *Annual Report; Cyprus in Figures* (annual); *Census of Industrial Production* (annual); *Census of Population 2001; Economic Report* (annual); *Statistical Abstract* (annual).

Czech Republic. *Czech Republic in Figures* (annual); *Statistical Yearbook of the Czech Republic.*

Denmark. *Statistical Yearbook; Denmark in Figures* (annual).

Djibouti. *Recensement général de la population et de l'habitat de 2009; Annuaire statistique de Djibouti* (annual); Central Bank *Rapport Annuel* (annual).

Dominica. *Dominica: Statistical Appendix* (IMF Staff Country Report [2007]); *Population and Housing Census 2001; Statistical Digest* (irregular).

Dominican Republic. Central Bank *Informe de la Economía Dominicana* (annual); *Cifras Dominicanas* (irregular); *VIII censo nacional de población y vivienda, 2002.*

East Timor. National Census 2004; *Economic Bulletin* (quarterly); *Democratic Republic of Timor-Leste: Selected Issues and Statistical Appendix* (IMF Staff Country Report [2007]).

Ecuador. *Serie estadística* (quinquennial); *VI censo de población y V de vivienda 2001; Ecuador: Selected Issues* (IMF Staff Country Report [2006]).

Egypt. *Monthly Bulletin of Statistics; Statistical Indicators about Egypt; Census Population, Housing, and Establishment, 2006; Statistical Yearbook.*

El Salvador. *Annual Economic Indicators; Censos nacionales: V censo de población y IV de vivienda (1992); El Salvador en cifras* (annual).

Equatorial Guinea. *Censos nacionales, I de población y I de vivienda—2001; Republic of Equatorial Guinea: Selected Issues and Statistical Appendix* (IMF Staff Country Report [2006]).

Eritrea. *Eritrea: Selected Issues and Statistical Appendix* (IMF Staff Country Report [2003]).

Estonia. *Monthly Bulletin of Estonian Statistics; 2000 Population and Housing Census; Statistical Yearbook of Estonia; The 2006 National Statistics.*

Ethiopia. *2007 Population and Housing Census of Ethiopia; Ethiopia Statistical Abstract* (annual); National Bank of Ethiopia *Annual Report; The Federal Democratic Republic of Ethiopia: Selected Issues and Statistical Appendix* (IMF Staff Country Report [2007]); *Ethiopia Demographic and Health Survey 2005; The 2005 National Labour Force Survey.*

Faroe Islands. *Nordic Statistical Yearbook; Faroe Islands Information Memorandum* 2005; *Statistical Bulletin* (annual); *Faroe Islands in Figures* (annual).

Fiji. *Key Statistics* (quarterly); *Quarterly Review; Current Economic Statistics* (quarterly); *Fiji Facts and Figures* (annual); *2007 Census of the Population and Housing.*

Finland. *Economic Survey* (annual); *Population Census 2000 Handbook; Statistical Yearbook of Finland; Finland in Figures* (annual).

France. *Annuaire statistique de la France* (annual); *Données sociales* (triennial); *Tableaux de l'Economie Française* (annual).

French Guiana. *Chiffres clés 2005—Guyane; Recensement général de la population de 2006; Tableaux economiques regionaux: Guyane* (biennial).

French Polynesia. *Résultats du recensement général de la population de la Polynésie Française, 2002; Tableaux de l'economie polynesienne* (irreg.); *Polynésie Francaise en Bref* (annual); *Polynesia at a Glance* (annual); *Te avei'a: Bulletin d'information statistique* (monthly); *Année 2006 des Resultats Mediocres.*

Gabon. *Recensement général de la population et de l'habitat 1993; Situation économique, financière et sociale de la République Gabonaise* (annual).

Gambia, The. *National Population and Housing Census 2003; The Gambia: Selected Issues and Statistical Appendix* (IMF Staff Country Report [2007]); *Atlas of The Gambia; Quarterly Bulletin.*

Gaza Strip. *Judaea, Samaria, and Gaza Area Statistics Quarterly; Palestinian Statistical Abstract.*

Georgia. *First General National Census* (2002); *Statistical Yearbook of Georgia;* National Bank *Bulletin of Monetary and Banking Statistics* (annual).

Germany. *Statistisches Jahrbuch für die Bundesrepublik Deutschland* (annual); *Germany Facts and Trends.*

Ghana. *Ghana: Selected Issues* (IMF Staff Country Report [2007]); *Population Census of Ghana, 2000; Quarterly Economic Bulletin; Quarterly Digest of Statistics.*

Greece. *Recensement de la population et des habitations, 2001;* Bank *Annual Report;* Bank *Monthly Statistical Bulletin; Statistical Yearbook of Greece.*

Greenland. *Greenland in Figures* (annual); *Greenland* (statistical yearbook); *Grønlands befolk-ning* (Greenland Population [annual]).

Grenada. *Abstract of Statistics* (annual); *Grenada: Statistical Appendix* (IMF Staff Country Report [2005]); *2001 Population and Housing Census.*

Guadeloupe. *Guadeloupe en faits et chiffres* (annual); *Recensement général de la population de 1999: Guadeloupe; Tableaux economiques regionaux: Guadeloupe* (biennial); Institut d'emission des départements d'Outre Mer La Guadeloupe Rapport Annuel.

Guam. *Guam Annual Economic Review; Guam Statistical Yearbook; 2000 Census of Population and Housing (U.S.).*

Guatemala. *Boletin estadístico* (monthly); *Anuario estadística* (annual); *Instituto nacional de estadística censos nationales XI de población y VI de habitación 2002;* Banco de Guatemala *Annual Report.*

Guernsey. *Guernsey Census 2001; Statistical Digest* (annual); *States of Guernsey Facts and Figures* (annual); *Economic and Statistics Review* (annual).

Guinea. *Recensement général de la population et de l'habitat 1996; Guinea: Selected Issues and Statistical Appendix* (IMF Staff Country Report [2006]); Central Bank *Annual Report.*

Guinea-Bissau. *Guinea-Bissau: Selected Issues and Statistical Appendix* (IMF Staff Country Report [2006]); *Recenseamento Geral da População e da Habitação, 2009.*

Guyana. Bank *Annual Report and Statement of Accounts; Statistical Bulletin* (quarterly); *2002 Population and Housing Census; Guyana: Statistical Annex* (IMF Staff Country Report [2001]); *Tableaux Economique Regionaux de la Guyana* (biennial).

Haiti. Bank *Rapport Annuel* (annual); *Indicateurs Economiques et Financiers* (monthly); *Résultats préliminaires du 4ème recensement général de population et d'habitat* (August 2003); *Haiti: Selected Issues and Statistical Appendix* (IMF Staff Country Report [2007]).

Honduras. *Anuario estadístico* (annual); *Censo nacional de población y vivienda, 2001; Honduras en cifras* (annual).

Hong Kong. *Annual Digest of Statistics; Hong Kong in Figures* (annual); *Hong Kong* (annual); *Hong Kong 2001 Population Census; Hong Kong Social and Economic Trends* (biennial).

Hungary. *Statistical Yearbook of Hungary; 2001, Evi népszámlálás* (Census of Population 2001).

Iceland. *Statistical Yearbook of Iceland; Iceland in Figures* (annual).

India. *Statistical Pocket Book of India* (annual); *Monthly Abstract of Statistics; Census of India, 2001; Economic Survey* (annual); *Statistical Abstract* (annual).

Indonesia. Bank *Annual Report; Indonesia: An Official Handbook* (irreg.); *Hasil Sensus penduduk Indonesia, 2000* (Census of Population); *Statistical Yearbook of Indonesia; Indonesia: Selected Issues* (IMF Staff Country Report [2007]).

Iran. Central Bank *Annual Review; National Census of Population and Housing, October 2006; Iran Statistical Yearbook; Islamic Republic of Iran: Statistical Appendix* (IMF Staff Country Report [2007]).

Iraq. *Census of Population Oct. 1997; Central Bank of Iraq Annual Bulletin; Statistical Bulletin 2003* (special issue).

Ireland. *Census of Population of Ireland, 2006; National Income and Expenditure* (annual); *Statistical Yearbook of Ireland.*

Isle of Man. *Annual Report and Statistical Review; Census Report 2001; Isle of Man Digest of Economic and Social Statistics* (annual).

Israel. *Israel in Figures* (annual); *Monthly Bulletin of Statistics; 1995 Census of Population and Housing; Statistical Abstract* (annual).

Italy. *Italy in Figures* (annual); *Italian Statistical Yearbook; Monthly Statistical Bulletin; Statistica agrarie; Statistiche demografiche* (4 parts); *Statistiche dell'istruzione; 14o Censimento generale della popolazione e delle Abìtazioni 21 Ottobre 2001.*

Jamaica. Bank *Annual Report; Economic and Social Survey* (annual); *Statistical Abstract* (annual); *Statistical Digest* (monthly); *Statistical Yearbook of Jamaica; Population Census 2001; Jamaica: Selected Issues* (IMF Staff Country Report [2006]).

Japan. *Japan in Figures* (annual); *Japan Statistical Yearbook; Statistical Indicators on Social Life* (annual); *2005 Population Census of Japan.*

Jersey. *Report of the Census for 2001; Statistical Review* (annual); *Jersey in Figures* (annual).

Jordan. *Population and Housing Census 2004;* Central Bank *Annual Report; Statistical Yearbook; Jordan in Figures* (annual).

Kazakhstan. *Statistical Yearbook of Kazakhstan; 2009 Population Census.*

Kenya. *Kenya: Facts and Figures* (annual); *Economic Survey* (annual); *2009 Population and Housing Census;* Central Bank *Statistical Bulletin; Statistical Abstract* (annual).

Kiribati. *Annual Abstract of Statistics; Kiribati Population Census 2005.*

Korea, North. *Population Census 2008; North Korea: A Country Study* (1994); *The Population of North Korea* (1990); *Economic and Social Status of South and North Korea* (annual).

Korea, South. *Korea Statistical Yearbook; Social Indicators in Korea* (annual); *2005 Population and Housing Census.*

Kosovo. Central Bank *Monthly Statistics Bulletin; Agricultural Household Survey; Kosovo in Figures.*

Kuwait. Central Bank *Quarterly Statistical Bulletin; Annual Statistical Abstract; General Census of Population and Housing and Buildings 1995; Kuwait: Statistical Appendix* (IMF Staff Country Report [2006]).

Kyrgyzstan. *Kyrgyz Republic: Statistical Appendix* (IMF Staff Country Report [2005]); *Statistichesky Yezhegodnik Kyrgyzstana* (Statistical Yearbook of Kyrgyzstan); *Population Census 2009;* National Bank of the Kyrgyz Republic *Monthly Bulletin.*

Laos. *Lao People's Democratic Republic: Selected Issues and Statistical Appendix* (IMF Staff Country Report [2006]); *Statistics Yearbook 1975–2005; 2005 Population Census.*

Latvia. *Statistical Yearbook of Latvia; Latvijas Republikas 2000 Iedzivotāju Skaits* (2000 Census of Population of the Republic of Latvia).

Lebanon. Central Bank *Annual Report; Statistical Year Book 2000–2005; Lebanon: Selected Issues* (IMF Staff Country Report [2006]).

Lesotho. *Kingdom of Lesotho: Statistical Appendix* (IMF Staff Country Report [2006]); *Statistical Yearbook; 2006 Population Census;* Central Bank *Annual Report.*

Liberia. Central Bank *Annual Report; Financial Statistical Report; Economic Survey* (annual); *Liberia: Statistical Appendix* (IMF Staff Country Report [2006]).

Libya. *Libya Population Census, 2006; Socialist People's Libyan Arab Jamahiriya: Statistical Appendix* (IMF Staff Country Report [2007]).

Liechtenstein. *Statistisches Jahrbuch* (annual); *Volkszählung, 2000* (Census of Population); *Liechtenstein in Figures* (annual).

Lithuania. Central Bank *Monthly Bulletin; Gyventojų ir Bustų Surašymu Skypīus 2001* (Population and Housing Census 2001); *Statistical Yearbook of Lithuania; Lithuania in Figures* (annual).

Luxembourg. *Chiffres-clés de Luxembourg* (annual); *Annuaire statistique* (annual); *Bulletin du STATEC* (monthly); *Recensement général de la population du 15 février 2001.*

Macau. *Yearbook of Statistics; Monthly Bulletin of Statistics; Macao in Figures* (annual); *XIV Recenseamento Geral da População, 2006.*

Macedonia. *Population Census 2002; Former Yugoslav Republic of Macedonia: Selected Issues* (IMF Staff Country Report [2006]); *Statistical Yearbook of the Republic of Macedonia;* National Bank *Annual Report.*

Madagascar. *Republic of Madagascar: Selected Issues* (IMF Staff Country Report [2007]); *Recensement général de la population et de l'habitat, août 1993; Situation économique.*

Malawi. *Malawi in Figures* (annual); *Statistical Yearbook; Financial and Economic Review; 2008 Population and Housing Census; Malawi Statistical Yearbook; Malawi Yearbook; Malawi: Selected Issues and Statistical Appendix* (IMF Staff Country Report [2004]).

Malaysia. *Monthly Statistical Bulletin; Population and Housing Census of Malaysia 2000; Yearbook of Statistics; Malaysia: Statistical Appendix* (IMF Staff Country Report [2005]).

Maldives. *Population and Housing Census of Maldives 2006; Statistical Year Book of Maldives; Maldives at a Glance;* Maldives Monetary Authority *Annual Report.*

Mali. *Annuaire statistique du Mali* (annual); *Recensement general de la population et de l'habitat* (*du 1er au 14 apr 2009*); *Mali: Statistical Annex* (IMF Staff Country Report [2006]).

Malta. *Population and Housing Census 2005;* Central Bank *Quarterly Review; Annual Abstract of Statistics; Quarterly Digest of Statistics; Malta in Figures* (annual).

Marshall Islands. *Marshall Islands Statistical Yearbook; Report on the State of the Islands* (U.S. Department of the Interior [annual]); *Quarterly Bulletin of Statistics; Population and Housing Census 1999; Republic of Marshall Islands: Selected Issues and Statistical Appendix* (IMF Staff Country Report [2006]).

Martinique. *Martinique en Faits et Chiffres; Recensement de la population de 1999; Martinique; Tableaux economiques regionaux: Martinique* (biennial).

Mauritania. *Recensement général de la population et de l'habitat 2000; Annuaire Statistique* (annual); Central Bank *Annual Report; Islamic Republic of Mauritania: Statistical Appendix* (IMF Staff Country Report [2006]).

Mauritius. *Annual Digest of Statistics; 2000 Housing and Population Census of Mauritius; Mauritius in Figures* (annual); *Mauritius: Selected Issues and Statistical Appendix* (IMF Staff Country Report [2006]).

Mayotte. *Bulletin Trimestriel* (quarterly) and *Rapport Annuel* (Institut d'Emission, France; annual); *Recensement de la population de Mayotte: Juillet 2002.*

Mexico. *Anuario estadístico* (annual); *XII Censo general de población y vivienda, 2005; Anuario estadístico de los Estados Unidos Mexicanos* (annual).

Micronesia. *Federated States of Micronesia: Selected Issues and Statistical Appendix* (IMF Staff Country Report [2007]); *FSM Statistical Yearbook* (annual); *Population Census 2000.*

Moldova. National Bank *Annual Report; Republic of Moldova: Statistical Appendix* (IMF Staff Country Report [2006]); *Republica Moldova in Cifre* (annual); *Population Census 2004.*

Monaco. *Recensement général de la population 2008; Monaco en chiffres* (annual).

Mongolia. *Mongolian Statistical Yearbook* (annual); *Mongolia: Selected Issues and Statistical Appendix* (IMF Staff Country Report [2007]); *Monthly Bulletin of Statistics; 2000 Population and Housing Census of Mongolia.*

Montenegro. *Census of Population, Households, and Dwellings 2003; Statistical Yearbook; Montenegro in Figures;* Central Bank *Quarterly Report;* Chief Economist *Annual Report.*

Morocco. *Annuaire statistique du Maroc* (annual); *Le Maroc en Chiffres* (annual); Central Bank *Annual Report; Recensement général de la population et de l'habitat de 2004; Morocco in Figures* (annual).

Mozambique. *Statistical Yearbook; Republic of Mozambique: Selected Issues* (IMF Staff Country Report [2007]); *II Recenseamento Geral da População e habitação, 1997; Mozambique in Figures* (annual).

Myanmar (Burma). *Report to the Pyithu Hluttaw on the Financial, Social, and Economic Conditions for 20*** (annual); *Statistical Abstract* (irreg.); *1983 Population Census.*

Namibia. *2001 Population and Housing Census;* Bank of Namibia *Quarterly Bulletin; Statistical/Economic Review* (annual); *Namibia in Figures* (annual); *Namibia: Selected Issues and Statistical Appendix* (IMF Staff Country Report [2006]).

Nauru. *Population Profile* (irreg.); *2002 Population and Housing Census.*

Nepal. *Economic Survey* (annual); *Statistical Yearbook of Nepal; National Population Census 2001; Nepal: Selected Issues and Statistical Appendix* (IMF Staff Country Report [2006]); *Nepal Statistical Pocketbook* (annual).

Netherlands. *Statistical Yearbook of the Netherlands; Monthly Bulletin of Statistics.*

Netherlands Antilles. Central Bank *Quarterly Bulletin; Fourth Population and Housing Census Netherlands Antilles 2001; Statistical Yearbook of the Netherlands Antilles.*

New Caledonia. *Recensement de la population 2009; Tableaux bilan economique* (annual); *New Caledonia Facts and Figures* (annual).

New Zealand. *2006 New Zealand Census of Population and Dwellings; New Zealand Official Yearbook.*

Nicaragua. *VIII censo de población y IV vivienda 2005;* Banco Central de Nicaragua *Nicaragua en Cifras; Compendio Estadístico* (annual); *Nicaragua: Selected Issues* (IMF Staff Country Report [2006]).

Niger. *Annuaire statistique* (annual); *Niger: Selected Issues and Statistical Appendix* (IMF Staff Country Report [2007]); *2ème Recensement général de la population 2001.*

Nigeria. *Annual Abstract of Statistics; Nigeria: Selected Issues and Statistical Appendix* (IMF Staff Country Report [2005]); *National Population and Housing Census March 2006.*

Northern Mariana Islands. *CNMI Population Profile; Statistical Yearbook* (irregular); *Report on the State of the Islands* (U.S. Department of the Interior [annual]); *2000 Census of Population and Housing* (U.S.).

Norway. *Folke-og boligtelling 2001* (Population and Housing Census); *Industristatistikk* (annual); *Statistical Yearbook of Norway; Monthly Bulletin of Statistics.*

Oman. *General Census of Population, Housing, and Establishments* (2003); *Statistical Yearbook; Bank of Oman Annual Report.*

Pakistan. *Economic Survey* (annual); *Pakistan Statistical Yearbook; Population Census of Pakistan, 1998.*

Palau. *Statistical Yearbook; Census 2005; Republic of Palau: Selected Issues and Statistical Appendix* (IMF Staff Country Report [2006]).

Panama. *Indicadores económicos y sociales* (annual); *XI censo nacional de población y VII de vivienda 16 de mayo del 2010; Panama en cifras* (annual); *Panama: Selected Issues and Statistical Appendix* (IMF Staff Country Report [2006]).

Papua New Guinea. Bank *Quarterly Economic Bulletin; Papua New Guinea: Selected Issues and Statistical Appendix* (IMF Staff Country Report [2007]); *Summary of Statistics* (annual); *2000 National Population Census.*

Paraguay. *Informe Económico* (monthly); *Anuario estadístico del Paraguay* (annual); *Censo nacional de población y viviendas, 2002; Paraguay: Statistical Appendix* (IMF Staff Country Report [2003]).

Peru. *Peru en Cifras* (annual); *Censos nacionales; X de población: V de vivienda 2005; Compendio estadístico* (3 vol.; annual); *Informe estadístico* (annual); *Peru: Selected Issues* (IMF Staff Country Report [2006]).

Philippines. *The Philippines in Figures* (annual); *Philippine Statistical Yearbook; 2000 Census of Population and Housing.*

Poland. *Narodowy spis powszechny 2002* (National Population and Housing Census); *Statistical Bulletin* (monthly); *Statistical Yearbook of the Republic of Poland; Demographic Yearbook of Poland; Concise Statistical Yearbook.*

Portugal. *Anuário Estatístico* (annual); *XIV Recenseamento Geral da População: IV Recenseamento Geral da Habitação, 2001; Economic Bulletin* (quarterly).

Puerto Rico. *Puerto Rico in Figures* (annual); *Estadísticas socioeconomicas* (annual); *Informe económico al gobernador* (Economic Report to the Governor [annual]); *2000 Census of Population and Housing* (U.S.); Government Development Bank *Economic Indicators* (monthly).

Qatar. *Qatar in Figures* (annual); *Annual Statistical Abstract; Economic Survey of Qatar* (annual); *Qatar Year Book;* Central Bank *Annual Report; 2010 Census of Population, Housing and Establishments.*

Réunion. *La Réunion en Bref; Recensement général de la population de 1999; Tableau Economique de la Réunion* (biennial).

Romania. *Romanian Statistical Yearbook; Census of Population and Housing March 27, 2002; Romania in Figures* (annual).

Russia. *Russia in Figures* (annual); *Current Statistical Survey* (quarterly); *Russia* (annual pocket statistical handbook); *2002 All-Russian Population Census;* Russian Federation: *Selected Issues* (IMF Staff Country Report [2007]).

Rwanda. *Bulletin de Statistique: Supplement Annuel* (annual); National Bank *Annual Report; Recensement général de la population et de l'habitat 2002; Rwanda: Selected Issues and Statistical Appendix* (IMF Staff Country Report [2004]).

St. Kitts and Nevis. *Annual Digest of Statistics; St. Kitts and Nevis: Statistical Appendix* (IMF Staff Country Report [2007]); *2001 Population Census.*

St. Lucia. *Annual Statistical Digest; St. Lucia: Statistical Appendix* (IMF Staff Country Report [2006]); *2001 Population and Housing Census.*

St. Vincent and the Grenadines. *Digest of Statistics* (annual); *Population and Housing Census 2001; St. Vincent and the Grenadines: Statistical Appendix* (IMF Staff Country Report [2006]).

Samoa (Western Samoa). *Annual Statistical Abstract;* Central Bank *Quarterly Bulletin; Census of Population and Housing, 2006; Samoa: Selected Issues and Statistical Appendix* (IMF Staff Country Report [2007]).

San Marino. *Bollettino di Statistica* (quarterly); *Relazione Economico Statistica* (annual); *Annuario Statistico Demografico* (irreg.); *San*

Marino: Selected Issues and Statistical Appendix (IMF Staff Country Report [2004]).

Sao Tome and Principe. *1º Recenseamento Geral da População e da Habitação 2001; Democratic Republic of Sao Tome and Principe: Selected Issues and Statistical Appendix* (IMF Staff Country Report [2006]).

Saudi Arabia. *Saudi Arabian Monetary Agency: Annual Report; Saudi Arabia Population and Housing Census 2004.*

Senegal. *Recensement de la population et de l'habitat 2002; Situation économique du Senegal* (annual); *Senegal: Selected Issues* (IMF Staff Country Report [2007]).

Serbia. National Bank *Statistical Bulletin* (monthly); *Census of Population, Households, and Housing 2002; Monthly Statistical Review;* National Bank *Annual Report; Statistical Pocket Book* (annual); *Statistical Yearbook; Republic of Serbia: Selected Issues* (IMF Staff Country Report [2006]).

Seychelles. *Statistical Abstract* (annual); Central Bank *Annual Report; Seychelles in Figures* (annual); *National Population and Housing Census 2002.*

Sierra Leone. *Sierra Leone: Statistical Appendix* (IMF Staff Country Report [2007]); Bank *Annual Report; Annual Statistical Digest; Population and Housing Census 2004.*

Singapore. *Singapore in Figures* (annual); *Census of Population, 2000; Singapore Yearbook; Yearbook of Statistics Singapore; Economic Survey of Singapore* (annual); *Monthly Statistical Bulletin; Singapore: Selected Issues* (IMF Staff Country Report [2006]).

Sint Maarten. *Sint Maarten Economic Indicators.*

Slovakia. *Sčítanie Obyvatel'ov, Domov a Btov 2001* (Population and Housing Census 2001); *Statistical Yearbook of the Slovak Republic; Slovak Republic in Figures* (annual); *Slovak Republic: Selected Issues* (IMF Staff Country Report [2007]).

Slovenia. *Slovenija Popis 2002* (Slovenia Population Census 2002); *Slovenia in Figures* (annual); Bank *Annual Report; Statistical Yearbook of the Republic of Slovenia; Republic of Slovenia: Selected Issues* (IMF Staff Country Report [2007]).

Solomon Islands. *Solomon Islands 1999 Population Census;* Central Bank *Annual Report; Solomon Islands: Statistical Appendix* (IMF Staff Country Report [2007]).

Somalia. *Socio-Economic Survey 2002* (The World Bank Report No. 1, Somalia Watching Brief, 2003).

South Africa. Reserve Bank *Quarterly Report; The People of South Africa Population Census, 2001; Bulletin of Statistics* (quarterly); *Statistics in Brief; South Africa: Official Yearbook of the Republic of South Africa.*

Spain. *Spain in Figures* (annual); *Anuario estadístico* (annual); *Population and Housing Census 2001; Boletín mensual de estadística.*

Sri Lanka. *Census of Population and Housing, 2001; Sri Lanka Statistical Abstract* (irreg.); Central Bank *Annual Report; Statistical Pocketbook of the Democratic Socialist Republic of Sri Lanka* (annual); *Sri Lanka: Selected Issues* (IMF Staff Country Report [2006]).

Sudan. Central Bank *Annual Report; Fifth Population and Housing Census, 2008; Sudan Statistical Yearbook; Sudan in Figures* (annual); *Sudan: Statistical Appendix* (IMF Staff Country Report [2000]).

Sudan, South. *Statistical Yearbook of Southern Sudan* (annual); *Key Indicators for Southern Sudan.*

Suriname. *Population and Housing Census 2004; Statistisch Jaarboek van Suriname* (annual); *Suriname: Statistical Appendix* (IMF Staff Country Report [2006]).

Swaziland. *Annual Statistical Bulletin; Report on the 1997 Swaziland Population Census;* Central Bank *Annual Report; The Kingdom of Swaziland: Statistical Appendix* (IMF Staff Country Report [2006]).

Sweden. *Folk-och bostadsräkningen, 2005* (Population and Housing Census); *Statistisk årsbok för Sverige* (Statistical Yearbook of Sweden).

Switzerland. *Switzerland in Figures* (annual); *Monthly Statistical Bulletin; Recensement fédéral de la population, 2000; Statistical Yearbook of Switzerland—Statistical Data in a Nutshell* (English); *Statistical Data on Switzerland* (annual).

Syria. *General Census of Housing and Inhabitants, 1994; Statistical Abstract* (annual); Central Bank *Quarterly Bulletin.*

Taiwan. *Statistical Abstract* (annual); *Statistical Yearbook of the Republic of China; Taiwan Statistical Data Book* (annual); *1990 Census of Population and Housing; Monthly Bulletin of Statistics.*

Tajikistan. *General Population Census of the Republic of Tajikistan 2000; Republic of Tajikistan: Selected Issues and Statistical Appendix* (IMF Staff Country Report [2005]).

Tanzania. *Tanzania: Selected Issues and Statistical Annex* (IMF Staff Country Report [2004]); *Tanzania in Figures* (annual); *Tanzania Statistical Abstract* (irreg.); *2002 Population Census; Economic Bulletin* (quarterly).

Thailand. *Statistical Handbook of Thailand* (annual); *Statistical Yearbook; Population and Housing Census 2000; Thailand: Selected Issues* (IMF Staff Country Report [2007]).

Togo. *Annuaire statistique du Togo* (annual); *Recensement général de la population et de l'habitat 1993; Togo: Statistical Appendix* (IMF Staff Country Report [2007]).

Tonga. *Population Census, 2006; Tonga: Selected Issues and Statistical Appendix* (IMF Staff Country Report [2007]).

Trinidad and Tobago. Central Bank *Annual Economic Survey; 2000 Population and Housing Census; Trinidad and Tobago: Statistical Appendix* (IMF Staff Country Report [2007]); *Annual Statistical Digest.*

Tunisia. Central Bank *Annual Report;* Central Bank *Financial Statistics Bulletin; Annuaire statistique de la Tunisie* (annual); *Recensement général de la population et des logements, 2004; Tunisia: Selected Issues* (IMF Staff Country Report [2007]).

Turkey. *2000 Genel Nüfus Sayımı* (2000 Census of Population); Central Bank *Quarterly Bulletin; Statistical Yearbook of Turkey.*

Turkmenistan. *1995 Population and Housing Census of the Republic of Turkmenistan; Turkmenistan v tsifrakh* (Turkmenistan in Figures [annual]).

Tuvalu. *Tuvalu Country Profile 2003; Annual Statistical Report; 2002 Population and Housing Census; Statistical Report 2005.*

Uganda. *2002 National Population and Housing Census; Uganda: Selected Issues and Statistical Appendix* (IMF Staff Country Report [2005]); *Statistical Abstract* (annual).

Ukraine. National Bank *Annual Report; Perepys Naselennya 2001* (Population Census 2001); *Ukraine in Figures* (annual); *Statistical Yearbook of Ukraine.*

United Arab Emirates. *Statistical Yearbook* (Abu Dhabi); *Population, Housing, and Establishments Census 2005; United Arab Emirates: Statistical Appendix* (IMF Staff Country Report [2006]); Central Bank *Report* (annual); *UAE in Figures* (annual).

United Kingdom. *Annual Abstract of Statistics; Britain: An Official Handbook* (annual); *Census 2001; General Household Survey* series (annual); *Monthly Bulletin of Statistics.*

United States. *Agricultural Statistics* (annual); *Current Population Reports; Digest of Education Statistics* (annual); *Minerals Yearbook* (3 vol. in 6 parts); *Statistical Abstract* (annual); *U.S. Exports: SIC-Based Products* (annual); *U.S. Imports: SIC-Based Products* (annual); *Vital and Health Statistics* (series 1–20); *2000 Census of Population and Housing.*

Uruguay. *Uruguay en Cifras* (annual); Central Bank *Informe año; Anuario estadístico* (annual); *VIII Censo general de población IV de hogares y VI de viviendas, 2004; Uruguay: Selected Issues* (IMF Staff Country Report [2006]).

Uzbekistan. *Republic of Uzbekistan: Recent Economic Developments* (IMF Staff Country Report [2000]); *Uzbekistan in Figures* (annual).

Vanuatu. *2009 National Census of Population and Housing; Vanuatu Statistical Yearbook; Vanuatu: Selected Issues and Statistical Appendix* (IMF Staff Country Report [2005]); Reserve Bank *Quarterly Economic Review.*

Venezuela. *Venezuela en Cifras* (annual); *Anuario estadístico* (annual); *Censo general de la población y vivienda 2001; Encuesta de hogares por muestreo* (annual); *Encuesta industrial* (annual); Central Bank *Informe económico* (annual).

Vietnam. *Statistical Year-book; Tong Dieu Tra Dan So Viet Nam—2009* (Vietnam Population Census—2009); *Vietnam: Statistical Appendix* (IMF Staff Country Report [2006]); *Population and AIDS Indicator Survey 2005.*

Virgin Islands of the United States. *Statistical Digest* (irregular); *2000 Census of Population and Housing* (U.S.); *U.S. Virgin Islands Economic Indicators* (annual); *U.S. Virgin Islands Economic Review and Industry Outlook.*

West Bank. *Population, Housing and Establishment Census—1997; Palestinian Statistical Abstract.*

Western Sahara. *Recensement général de la population et de l'habitat* (2004 [Morocco]).

Yemen. *Population of Yemen: 2004 Census; Republic of Yemen: Statistical Appendix* (IMF Staff Country Report [2005]); Central Bank *Annual Report.*

Zambia. *Zambia: Selected Issues and Statistical Appendix* (IMF Staff Country Report [2006]); *2000 Census of Population, Housing, Agriculture.*

Zimbabwe. *Population Census 2002; Statistical Yearbook* (irreg.); *Zimbabwe: Selected Issues and Statistical Appendix* (IMF Staff Country Report [2005]).

Index

This index covers both *Britannica Book of the Year* (cumulative for 10 years) and *Britannica World Data*. Biographies and obituaries are cumulative for 5 years.

Entries of major article topics in the *Book of the Year* are cumulative for 10 years; an accompanying year in **dark type** gives the year the reference appears, and the accompanying page number in light type shows the page on which the reference appears. For example, "military affairs **12:**268; **11:**268; **10:**270; **09:**270; **08:**270; **07:**258; **06:**247; **05:**248; **04:**248; **03:**277" indicates that military affairs appeared every year from **2003** through **2012.** Other references that appear with a page number but without a year are references for the current yearbook.

Indented entries under a topic refer by page number to some other places in the yearbook text where the topic is discussed. Names of people covered in biographies and obituaries are usually followed by the abbreviation "(biog.)" or "(obit.)" with the year in **dark type** and a page number in light type, e.g., Musk, Elon (biog.) **12:**96, or Taylor, Elizabeth (obit.) **12:**160. In the rare case where a person has both a biography and an obituary, both words appear under the main entry and are alphabetized accordingly, e.g.:
Winehouse, Amy
 biography **09:**110
 obituary **12:**165
References to illustrations are by page number and are preceded by the abbreviation *il.*

The index uses word-by-word alphabetization (treating a word as one or more characters separated by a space from the next word). Please note that "St." is treated as "Saint." "Mc" is alphabetized as "Mc" rather than "Mac."

A

B

C

E

F

G

H

Dark-type numbers refer to the yearly edition where the reference appears, e.g., **12:**324 for the 2012 edition, page 324.

I

L

M

N

O

P

Q

R

S

T

U

V

W

X

Z

Index of Special Features in *Britannica Book of the Year,* 2003–2012

W9-DHH-032

INTRODUCTION TO

Financial Accounting

INTRODUCTION TO Financial Accounting

PAUL DANOS
EUGENE A. IMHOFF, JR.
Both of
University of Michigan

Homewood, IL 60430
Boston, MA 02116

To Our Families
Mary Ellen, Amanda, and Melissa
Barbara, Catherine, and Darren

Cover illustration: Rob Day

Sponsoring editor: Mike Reynolds
Developmental editor: Lynelle Morgenthaler
Project editor: Karen Smith
Production manager: Irene H. Sotiroff
Designers: Robyn Basquin and Lucy Lesiak
Artist: Jay Bensen
Compositor: Beacon Graphics Corporation
Typeface: 10/12 Times Roman
Printer: Von Hoffmann Press, Inc.

Library of Congress Cataloging-in-Publication Data

Danos, Paul
Introduction to financial accounting / Paul Danos, Eugene A. Imhoff, Jr.
p. cm.
ISBN 0-256-06187-4
1. Accounting. I. Imhoff, Eugene A. II. Title.
HF5635.D192 1992
657—dc20 90-32768
CIP

Printed in the United States of America
1 2 3 4 5 6 7 8 9 0 VH 7 6 5 4 3 2 1 0

Preface

This introductory financial accounting text has been developed with considerable attention being given to users of accounting information. We recognize that a wide variety of students take introductory financial accounting, including accounting majors, other business majors, and nonbusiness majors. The common thread running through all these students is their interest in knowing how to read and evaluate accounting information and in being prepared for more accounting education if they desire it. For those students going on to take additional accounting coursework, this text provides the foundation needed to be successful at the intermediate level. In addition, careful attention to the learning objectives designated at the start of each chapter will guide students in their development of a fundamental understanding of how to read and evaluate financial statements.

This text is based on the premise that accounting knowledge and business knowledge are inseparable. We, therefore, **emphasize business decisions** throughout the text. We show the students why accounting is so crucial to business, and how accounting is used as a basis for making business decisions.

Given that aiding in business decisions is the basic motivation for the study of accounting, we introduce topics in a business setting and follow through with examples that stress the strengths and weaknesses of particular accounting concepts and procedures used in those settings. Our goal is **to impart knowledge and appreciation of accounting concepts and methods.** To help achieve this goal, we have developed the text with the following guidelines:

1. **Get and keep the student's attention.** We believe interest is heightened by appealing to the student's natural entrepreneurial instincts through a **business decision orientation.** By demonstrating from the first chapter that accounting systems and data are integral to planning, financing, and controlling of business activities, we get the student's interest early and maintain it throughout the text. For example, in Chapter 5 students are introduced to credit sales and merchandise inventory accounting by way of a start-up business where accounting information is created in response to the needs of two young entrepreneurs. The student is taken from the planning phase all the way to the analysis of the initial operating results.

2. **Emphasize accounting outputs.** We believe that students develop a deeper understanding of accounting concepts and methods when they visualize the outputs of the accounting system. Such concepts as assets, liabilities, and revenue come alive and are, therefore, appreciated when viewed in their "natural setting," (i.e., as part of financial statements). We accomplish this by a **liberal use of real world disclosure examples.** We know that introductory students can be confused by complex real world examples, so in most chapters we integrate selected excerpts of published financial reports. The first page of most chapters illustrates some dimension of financial statements, condensed for simplicity. Within most chapters, excerpts from published financial statements are used to exemplify a concept or principle.

3. **Emphasize conceptual foundations.** We believe that the hardest task for the text author is to develop a clear and usable conceptual framework for the student. While this cannot be a word-for-word quote of official language, the text must lay the groundwork for a fundamental understanding of accounting concepts. We start the text with this philosophy. After introducing students to the general nature of accounting outputs, we give them a **thorough, nontechnical introduction to the concepts involved.** In Chapter 1, we show simple financial relationships and link them to the fundamental concepts that underlie accounting. In Chapter 2, we introduce the fundamentals of matching, recognition, and measurement and link them to the elements of financial statements. Concepts are continually developed and referenced throughout the text, and Chapter 15 provides a recap of these concepts by examining in greater detail the conceptual framework of accounting.

4. **Emphasize analysis.** As early as Chapter 4, students are given an introduction to simple financial statement analysis. Because the example used in the chapter is complete and self-contained, the student is able to understand simple cash flow analysis based on the transactions illustrated in the example. By comparing relative balances of cash to other assets, current to noncurrent assets, liabilities to equities, expenses to revenue, and so forth, students are given a good start in **appreciating the analytical uses of accounting outputs.** Although Chapter 15 contains a more complete discussion of financial statement analysis by means of a complete set of financial statements, learning to use and evaluate financial statements for business decisions is addressed throughout the text. Analysis techniques are integrated throughout the text to reinforce evaluation of accounting information at the same time as students are learning to develop accounting information.

5. **Utilize graphics.** We have found that graphics help students learn concepts. Although our use of graphical depictions far exceeds other texts, we employ them only when they enhance understanding. These illustrations have been developed as teaching aids over a long period. We made them as clear and informative as possible while striving for simplicity in presentation. For instance, the concept of debt-to-equity comparisons is shown in pie charts of balance sheets. Graphics

are used to help illustrate accounting processes, too, including depreciation, the accrual of interest over time, and the consolidate of two companies. Of course these are not substitutes for good conceptual discussion, but **graphics are effective as supplements to conceptual development.**

Using these basic guidelines, we have developed *Introduction to Financial Accounting* into what we believe to be a useful tool for imparting knowledge about the production and use of accounting information in business. The class testing of these text and problem materials, along with numerous comments and suggestions from colleagues around the country during the development stage, lead us to believe that those who elect to use this text in class will find that it is an oustanding aid to learning.

Key Features of This Text

We realize there are many well established introductory accounting textbooks. In many respects this book is similar to others that have already been used in the classroom. Most texts that survive in a competitive market are technically sound, up-to-date, and easy for students to comprehend with good problem materials. In addition to these important characteristics, we have developed a number of unique key features in this text that have been found to enhance learning. These key features include:

1. Introduction to the financial statements and their contents (Chapters 1 and 2) before introducing details of the accounting system (Chapters 3 and 4).
2. Introduction to important topics not covered in other texts—international accounting , ethics, and not-for-profit accounting, for example.
3. End-of-chapter lists of synonyms to enhance understanding of business terminology.
4. End-of-chapter glossaries of key terms.
5. Labels describing the nature of all end-of-chapter exercises, problems, and cases, which are tied in with chapter learning objectives.
6. Problem and case materials based on actual financial statements.
7. Labels on all journal entries to identify the nature of the journalized accounts (e.g., Cash (A) reminds the student cash is an asset account).
8. Graphic depictions to enhance learning.
9. Use of appendixes to cover numerous topics as optional components of a chapter for ease of inclusion or deletion as desired by adopters.
10. Use of informal "vignettes" depicting real people talking in natural language to introduce common problems and misunderstandings. Students are then given formal coverage of the resolution of the issues raised.

Immediate Introduction to Financial Statements. Students are introduced to the outputs of financial accounting in Chapters 1 and 2 where balance sheets, income statements, statements of cash flows, and retained earnings statements are illustrated and discussed. These two chapters demonstrate how business transactions from operating, financing, and investing activities are captured and reported in the financial statements. This is done before introducing students to the mechanics of debits and credits to give them a good perspective on the objectives of financial accounting and how these objectives are accomplished with financial statements. This approach has proven to be most successful in teaching students the basics of the accounting information system, since they gain an appreciation for what financial statements are and how they work (the "forest") before delving into the mechanics of the accounting system (the "trees").

Topics Not in Other Texts. This text is a comprehensive introduction to financial accounting and business decisions. We include chapters or appendixes on the following subjects:

- Ethics in accounting (Appendix A, end of text)
- International accounting (Appendix B, end of text)
- Accounting for price changes (Appendix C, end of text)
- Not-for-profit accounting (Appendix D, end of text)
- An introduction to methods for estimating inventories (Appendix 6B)
- Reporting LIFO inventories (Appendix 6C)
- Deferred income taxes (Appendix to Chapter 9)
- Partnership accounting (Appendix to Chapter 11)
- Earnings per share: primary and fully diluted (Appendix 12A)
- Consolidations and pooling of interests (Appendixes 12A and 12B)
- Conceptual framework of accounting (Chapter 15)
- References to income taxes, such as inventories and depreciation (throughout the text)

These subjects are covered at an introductory level so students can recognize their respective roles in the overall financial reporting process. At the same time, each subject is presented independently (with related end-of-chapter material clearly labeled), so that selected topics may be easily omitted at the discretion of the instructor.

End-of-Chapter Aids. Students are often confused when they encounter accounting terms that differ from those used in their textbook but that mean the same thing. Even the most common synonyms—such as using "earnings" in place of "net income"—can be troublesome to students learning the language of business. To facilitate this aspect of learning, we include a brief list of synonyms at the end of each chapter. We also include a list of key terms at the end of each chapter, along with their definitions as developed in that chapter. (Key terms are identified in boldface color in the body of each chapter.) Finally, we include a brief description of each exercise, problem, and case in order to explain the basic thrust of each end-of-chapter assignment. This facilitates the instructor's assignment selection process and also helps students identify similar assignments, should extra work be desired on a particular topic.

Actual Financial Statement Assignments. Since students need to relate textbook knowledge to the real world for successful learning to occur, we include end-of-chapter material based on actual financial statement examples. These problem and case materials are appropriately identified in the assignment descriptions and are particularly relevant for those seeking a stronger user orientation in the introductory financial accounting course.

Labeled Journal Entries. Introductory students are frequently puzzled by the nature of new account titles as they progress through their introductory (and intermediate) accounting texts. They often want to ask, "What is it?" not knowing the nature of a new account title when it is first encountered in a journal entry or ledger entry. Students need to link the effects of journal entries to changes in financial statements in order to enhance understanding. To facilitate this need, we identify the nature of each account used in journal entries throughout the text with symbols ("(A)" for asset, "(XA)" for contra asset, "(R)" for revenue, etc.). We have found that students learn the effects of transactions and the relationship between the financial statements more thoroughly when these labels and symbols are used.

Graphical Depictions. Visual aids to learning and understanding are more prevalent in most other business subjects than in accounting texts, yet many financial reports of corporations and articles in the financial and popular press use graphics to portray financial information. We have found that these graphics enhance learning and have used them as supplements to the text discussions, where they help communicate effectively and efficiently.

Course Topics and Structure. The inclusion of many subjects in the appendixes is designed to enhance the flexibility of this text. We have found many differences of opinion on what should be included in introductory financial accounting and what should be omitted. By identifying some topics where differences of opinion are more common and placing these in appendixes, we hope to accommodate all preferences. The text and end-of-chapter materials are all designed to make it easy to add or omit appendix material from assignments as desired.

Problem Assignments Solvable with Computerized Template Software. A large number of the exercises, problems, and cases in the text can be solved using *Spreadsheet Applications Template Software (SPATS)* developed by Will Garland of Coastal Carolina College. *SPATS* contains innovatively designed templates based on Lotus® 1-2-3® and includes a very effective tutorial for Lotus® 1-2-3®. The exercises, problems, and cases solvable with *SPATS* are identified in the margin of the text with the following symbol.

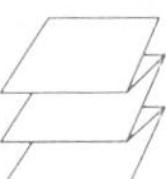

We believe that the nine key features, in combination with pedagogical foundations developed in the text and end-of-chapter assignments, will provide faculty and students with a user-friendly introductory financial accounting textbook.

Supplements

To supplement the text, the following items are included in our package.

- Solutions Manual
- Instructor's Resource Manual
- Test Bank
- Student Study Guide
- Computerized Problem Set
- Transparencies
- Practice Set
- Working Papers

Acknowledgments

We want to give special recognition to Karen Bird, who helped us with all aspects of the project. Her skill, dedication, and patience were immeasurable. Others to whom we are especially grateful are Debbie Chadwick, Cathy Imhoff, Darren Imhoff, Brenda Ostrowski, Lilly Somers, Janet Somers, and Rena Worley. Of valuable assistance in developing problem materials were Charles "Chip" Kemstine, Richard Jobes, Barbara Estevez, and Zack Homles.

We also want to acknowledge our project editor, Karen Smith, whose professionalism was superb throughout the project.

The following reviewers provided helpful comments:

Joseph H. Anthony
Michigan State University

Alvin A. Arens
Michigan State University

Jerry L. Arnold
University of Pennsylvania–Wharton

Francis A. Bird
University of Richmond

Louis S. Corsini
Boston College

Lane Daley
University of Minnesota

Charles J. Davis
California State University–Sacramento

Benjamin M. Doran
Iowa State University

Kenneth R. Ferris
Southern Methodist University

Elizabeth Jenkins
San Jose State University

Eugene J. Laughlin
Kansas State University

Elliot S. Levy
Bentley College

Alice Nichols
Florida State University

William D. Nichols
University of Notre Dame

Mohamed Onsi
Syracuse University

Ronald B. Pawliczek
Boston College

Mary Ellen Phillips
Oregon State University

Karen V. Pincus
University of Southern California–Los Angeles

Sharon L. Robinson
Frostburg State College

Ronald N. Savey
Western Washington University

Rudolph Schattke
University of Colorado–Boulder

Richard Simpson
University of Massachusetts–Amherst

Ken Stair
College of Lake County

Frederic M. Stiner
University of Delaware

Nancy O. Tang
Portland State University

Paul Danos
Eugene A. Imhoff, Jr.

Contents in Brief

Contents

PART 1

The Accounting Process

CHAPTER 1

The Accounting Environment and the Business Entity

LEARNING OBJECTIVES

After studying Chapter 1, you should understand:

1. The goals of accounting, p. 4.
2. How external and internal groups use accounting information, pp. 5-9.
3. The three forms of business entities — proprietorships, partnerships, and corporations, pp. 9-12.
4. The three basic categories of a balance sheet — assets, liabilities, and stockholders' equity, pp. 16-19.
5. How business transactions affect the balance sheet equation and the balance sheet, pp. 19-23.
6. The difference between the balance sheet, income statement, retained earnings statement, and statement of cash flows, pp. 24-27.
7. The organizations involved in accounting policymaking and how they serve the external, internal, and governmental user groups (Appendix), pp. 30-31.

Objective 1
The goals of accounting.

Accounting is a primary means of communicating in businesses, governments, and charitable and educational institutions—and among individuals. Almost every entity in our society is called on to develop and report on matters related to its financial status and performance, and accounting is a study of the concepts and techniques used in such reporting. In addition, because entities compete for economic resources, the successful manager must plan and control the activity of his or her entity in an effective manner, and accounting information is essential in those processes.

Accounting is a future-oriented enterprise in that the information generated by the accounting process is intended to be relevant for future decisions. Reports on past performance and current financial status are useful only as input to decisions about courses of action that will lead to future performance and status. Accounting is also intimately involved in sorting out the financial interests of the parties involved in all kinds of relationships. Taxing authorities are interested in past financial performance in order to assess and collect appropriate taxes. Stockholders want some indication of the potential for return on their investments. Workers and potential employees need financial information to make decisions about the viability of entities as employers. Decisions concerning rewards to managers are often based on past performance. The regulation of imports is often based on the financial information about the businesses in an industry. Decisions to open new plants, lay off workers, locate in foreign countries, and close banks and savings and loans are all based to some degree on financial information provided by the accounting system. The list goes on almost to infinity, encompassing all aspects of life from the personal finances of a student to the trillions of dollars involved in the federal budget.

The concepts and techniques covered in this text will give you a window into the basics of market-based economic systems, which are increasingly dominating the world. Information is the life's blood of such systems, and accounting information is one of the most fundamental and pervasive sources of information.

The first section in this chapter discusses the users of accounting and the forms of business entities. The chapter also introduces the balance sheet, a major financial statement that communicates an entity's financial position in terms of its resources and obligations. An appendix to this chapter discusses the organizations involved in accounting policymaking.

THE ACCOUNTING ENVIRONMENT

This section discusses (1) users of accounting information (including senders and receivers) and (2) forms of business entities. The goal of **accounting** is to communicate information about the economic activities and the economic states of entities in ways that are useful to decision makers. The accounting communication process involves individuals, businesses, and governments who, to some extent, can be both senders and receivers of financial information and regulators (policymakers) who determine what the standards for accounting information should be.

Users of Accounting Information

Users of accounting information can be classified into two broad groups (1) external users and (2) internal users, depending on the user's relationship to the reporting entity. These two groups need different kinds of accounting information

Objective 2
How external and internal groups use accounting information.

because each group makes different types of decisions. Although we have previously said that all kinds of entities report accounting information, our discussion will focus on profit-seeking business entities. Future references to the reporting entity will be made simply by using the terms *business* or *company.*

External Users. The **external users** of a company's accounting information include all individuals, businesses, and other entities that are not managers or officers of the company. This user group is sometimes called **outsiders** because, although they are interested in the business, they are not part of the company's management. External or outside users include potential and current owners, creditors, government units, and the general public. In large entities, owners are included in the external user group because they usually are not members of the company's management even though they have a voice in determining who management is. Bankers and bondholders, as the major creditor groups, are outsiders because they usually have no management functions.

In general, external users have limitations on their access to the financial records of the business. Under normal conditions, they have access to financial reports that are normally prepared according to a set of rules or guidelines known as **generally accepted accounting principles (GAAP),** which are discussed throughout the text. GAAP are widely accepted by companies preparing financial reports for external users. The process that generates these **financial statements** is called **financial accounting.** We will see that the financial accounting process, while culminating in financial statements, is used in all aspects of management.

The financial accounting process generates the financial statements used by outsiders, but it also is the source of much related information about the entity that is used by management. For instance, the financial statements show the total for receivables from customers and that number is, therefore, known to outsiders. The financial accounting system also keeps records on each individual customer, but that detailed information is available only to management. The same is true for the identification of the business's creditors, the age and costs of specific assets, and a great many other details management needs to run the business efficiently but are not usually needed by outsiders. In some cases, such as in merger negotiations or when applying for a loan, such detail is revealed. It is then generally made available to some outsiders along with the published financial statements.

Governmental Users. Governmental agencies use accounting information for various types of social, political, and economic decisions. Although **governmental users** are included in the external user group, in this textbook we view governmental users as a special class of external users. Generally, governmental agencies have some authority to require specific accounting information from businesses.

Two prominent governmental users of accounting reports are the **Internal Revenue Service (IRS)** and the **Securities and Exchange Commission (SEC).** The IRS requires special-purpose reports, tax returns, indicating the amount of income taxes owed by individuals and businesses. The goal of the IRS is to provide for government revenues according to tax laws and regulations. The SEC requires detailed quarterly and annual financial reports of all publicly owned companies for their files and to be made available to stockholders and the general public. The goal of the SEC's activities is to ensure that order is maintained in the financial markets.

The accounting environment related to governmental users is often highly specialized and relatively complicated. Banks, airlines, railroads, hospitals, utilities, shippers, and many other types of businesses make regular reports containing accounting information to various agencies of local, state, and/or federal governments who use it to regulate and tax the business.

Accounting environment facing external users. From the external user's viewpoint, the accounting environment consists of four main parties: **external users themselves, internal managers, independent auditors,** and **accounting policymakers.** External users **seek** accounting information in making business decisions; managers **provide** accounting information; independent auditors (certified public accountants) **report** on whether or not the financial reports are fairly presented in conformance to generally accepted accounting principles (GAAP) and accounting policymakers decide on the **nature** and **content** of financial reports by determining what constitutes GAAP.

Accounting policymakers weigh the costs and benefits of proposed reporting requirements for external users before issuing new requirements or revising old requirements. The ultimate goal of these policymakers is to develop GAAP that facilitate meaningful communication of relevant financial information between reporting entities and interested parties. Thus, accounting policymakers help the financial reporting process to run smoothly and fairly. The appendix at the end of this chapter identifies the various organizations that directly or indirectly affect the development of accounting policy.

Internal Users. Business managers are the **internal users** of accounting information. Managers are responsible for (1) designing an accounting information system that fits the needs of their particular business and (2) preparing all accounting information for both internal and external users.

The decisions made by internal users often require more detailed and timely information than that contained in standard financial reports to outsiders. This accounting information is usually referred to as **managerial accounting** information. Unlike financial accounting information, managerial accounting information need not comply with GAAP, the rules that govern external financial statements.

Managers who also own stock in the company they manage are in a unique position of being both internal and external users. Because they could profit from the more timely and detailed managerial accounting information available to insiders, managers of corporations are subject to certain rules and restrictions in dealings in the stocks of their own companies. Governmental agencies and stock exchanges carefully monitor the trading activities of insiders to guard against the misuse of information that is not available to the general public.

Accounting environment facing internal users. Managers are free to develop any accounting information that is necessary to satisfy their decision-making needs, constrained only by cost considerations and technological limitations. In other words, the development and use of managerial accounting information within the entity is not regulated by GAAP.

Managerial accounting helps managers to focus on problem situations and solutions, and managers must often use accounting information in conjunction with other information (i.e., the economic outlook for growth or technological changes in products) to make sound business decisions.

Most businesses share similar objectives which may be defined in terms of profits, providing a common purpose for the development of fairly standard managerial accounting procedures. It is not uncommon for different companies to have similar payroll systems, inventory control systems, and other accounting systems. Managerial accounting courses cover the concepts and techniques that have been developed to deal with common internal accounting problems.

What Information Is Relevant and Feasible? To illustrate the interplay of external users, managers, and auditors, consider a hypothetical case in which Mr. M (an inexperienced manager of a company) is negotiating for a loan from Ms. B (an inexperienced bank loan officer).

Ms. B: I am in the business of lending money and I really want you as a customer, but first I want you to provide the following information:

1. Financial statements showing the condition of your company and its performance over the last three years.
2. An evaluation of the credit ratings of all your customers.
3. Complete background reports on your employees.
4. A forecast of sales for the next five years.

Mr. M: I don't have all of that information and I believe that some of it is confidential. Anyway, all I have available are my financial statements, your item 1. The rest could be developed, but they are not required by GAAP.

Ms. B: O.K., give me your financial statements but they must be accompanied by a report from an independent auditor. After I have reviewed the statements, we will discuss the other items.

The above conversation illustrates some of the actual concerns that must be faced in the real world of business giving rise to a demand for standard financial information that are produced by managers and independently evaluated for fairness by an outside party.

Mr. M goes back to his office and calls a CPA, Ms. C, and relays to her the list of items the banker requested.

Ms. C, who is experienced in negotiations between borrowers and lenders and who makes fairness judgments about financial statements, states that item 1 is normally provided to banks in lending situations and that she, after checking the records of Mr. M's company, could make a statement about the fairness of presentations of the financial statements. Other items could also be provided by M's Company, such as a list of customers and a forecast, but because of the expense involved, the CPA is seldom called on to evaluate these less-standardized reports, which are not governed by GAAP. Ms. C also informs Ms. B that item 2 would be costly and perhaps impossible to obtain.

What Ms. C is suggesting is that if GAAP were applied by the company in this situation, then a standard set of financial information that could be evaluated by an independent party would result. Not all of the information desires of the banker will be met by the standardized, audited financial statements. In some cases, it may be too costly or inappropriate for borrowers to provide these additional data. In other cases, unaudited management information such as forecasts may also be provided. While unaudited information not included in the standardized financial statements may be developed if all parties can agree to it, such "special" information would not fall into the realm of GAAP. Opinions on financial statements by independent auditors, called *audit reports*, are often requested by banks and are a required part of all financial statements published by companies whose ownership shares (called *stock*) are publicly traded on the U.S. stock exchanges.

As stated earlier, management has access to all sorts of financial information about the entity, including all of the records and outputs of the accounting information system (depicted as circle A in Exhibit 1-1). Much of this information is private or insider information, that is not voluntarily revealed to outsiders. Some parties outside the business, such as a banker who is evaluating the company's

EXHIBIT 1-1

Relationships among the Information Sets

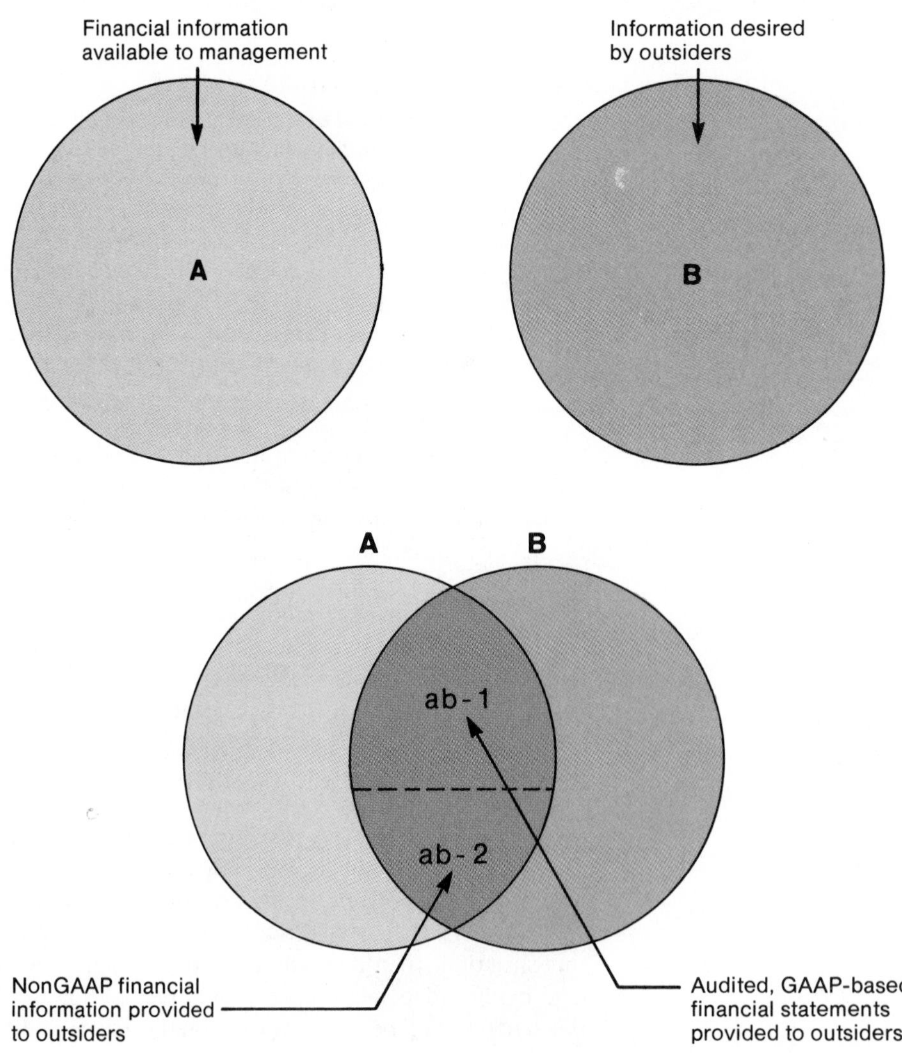

requests for a loan, may be desirous of all information that will aid in making the decision (depicted as circle B in Exhibit 1-1). A banker desires financial information such as historical and forecasted financial statements and perhaps other nonfinancial data such as the backgrounds and health of key employees.

A subset of all financial information available to management are the GAAP-based financial statements, which are the objects of audits by independent auditors and on which they express audit opinions (ab-1 in Exhibit 1-1). The audit opinion states whether or not the financial statements are fairly presented according to GAAP. Other non-GAAP financial information such as forecasts, budgets, and detailed schedules (ab-2 in Exhibit 1-1) may be provided to outsiders, but independent auditor involvement is not usually desired. The intersection of circles A and B, therefore, depict the financial information that an entity supplies to outsiders, only a portion of which (ab-1) is audited, GAAP-based financial statements.

Where does the outside party get the rest of the desired information? Some of it might be available from management such as reports on the history of key employees, and some might not be available such as the plans of competitors, or accurate estimates of inflation. Often estimates of such information can be acquired from analysts. For instance, a banker who lends money to a business may have access to economic projections and industry data, but there is always a residual uncertainty which remains in the realm of professional judgment and that creates a risk the bank must bear if it makes the loan. It also must be understood that even the formal, audited financial statements are not perfect reflections of the economic reality, and such imperfections can add to the risks of doing business.

In summary, not all financial information available to management is given to or desired by outside decision makers. Of that information requested, a portion is GAAP based and audited, and a portion is not. The future is uncertain, and though much accounting and other information is available, an element of risk will be borne by investors and creditors who buy stock and lend money. Of course, the returns they expect to earn on their investments or loans reflect relative riskiness; for example, government guaranteed bonds generally pay lower interest rates than bonds of corporations.

This textbook focuses most of its attention on financial accounting information for external and internal users — information that is communicated through GAAP-based standard financial statements. Exhibit 1-2 summarizes and compares the external, internal, and governmental user groups.

Forms of Business Entities

Objective 3
The three forms of business entities — proprietorships, partnerships, and corporations.

All business organizations use accounting information as a basis for making decisions. Based on their ownership structure, businesses are classified as *proprietorships, partnerships,* or *corporations*. Although the ownership structure of business organizations may differ, their accounting information processes are similar.

For accounting purposes, a **business entity** is an economic unit separate from its owners, and all business entities have some similar features. In other words, each business entity is viewed as a separate individual, and the accounting for a small business with only a few owners is remarkably similar in many respects to that of a business with thousands of owners. Of course, the scale and degree of complexity vary greatly.

EXHIBIT 1-2

Comparison of Accounting Information User Groups

	External Users		
	Nongovernment	**Government**	**Internal Users**
Who are they?	Investors and creditors, present and potential	Internal Revenue Service (IRS) Securities and Exchange Commission (SEC) Regulatory agencies	Company officers and employees who manage the business
What type of accounting is employed?	Financial accounting	Income tax accounting Other specialized accounting Regulatory reporting	Managerial accounting
What types of decisions do these users make?	Credit-granting decisions Investment decisions Mergers and acquisitions	Policy decisions concerning taxation and other economic consequences Assessing tax obligations Setting utility rates	Control of operating decisions: Investment decisions Product pricing decisions Salaries and bonuses for managers
What specific accounting information do they receive?	Financial statements published by the entity in periodic reports (including balance sheet, income statement, retained earnings statement, and statement of cash flows)	Special-purpose reports (such as income tax returns) Financial statements of public utilities, banks, etc.	All of those stated at left, plus budgets, cost reports, and many varied types of statements and records with specific details about business activity

By definition, then, an entity is the unit accounted for on the company's financial accounting reports; and for accounting purposes an entity is always viewed as separate from the owners of the business. This accounting concept of viewing the business as having an existence separate from its owners is known as the **business entity concept, separate entity concept,** or **entity concept.**

In this textbook we concentrate on profit-seeking business entities. Remember, however, that other types of organizations not operated for profit (churches, charities, municipalities, schools, and so on) also use accounting information and function as separate economic entities. Not-for-profit entities are discussed in Appendix D at the end of this text.

Proprietorships. A **proprietorship** is a business owned by one person. Usually proprietorships are small businesses that are managed by their owner, such as a restaurant or a small retail clothing store. However, many proprietors (sole owners) hire people to help manage their businesses.

Since accounting views all forms of businesses as separate entities, the business resources and activities of the proprietor (owner) must be kept separate from the owner's other resources and activities. For example, if you were the sole owner of a nightclub, a separate golf course business, and personal assets such as a home and car, you would probably have separate accounting records for each business, and you would not mix your golf course records or personal records with those of the nightclub's. However, the law does not view a proprietor's several businesses and personal assets as separate, and creditors could possibly claim any and all of the owned assets to cover the debts of any one entity. Thus, creditors of a proprietorship may claim the personal resources of the owner or those of other owned businesses. As a result, a proprietor is said to have **unlimited liability,** since the proprietor's obligation from one business or his/her personal affairs may exceed the resources of that one business. In a proprietorship the law focuses on the owner and what he/she owns, while accounting records and reports focus on each separate economic unit.

Partnerships. In a **partnership,** two or more persons share the ownership interest in a business. Many professionals, such as physicians, lawyers, and accountants, organize their practices as partnerships. Each partner has a specified percentage of ownership in the business that may differ from the interests of the other partners. For example, assume that Smith, Jones, and Colson are partners in a law firm, with Smith owning a 50% interest; Jones, a 30% interest; and Colson, a 20% interest. The partners use this ratio of partnership interest as the basis for sharing the profits and losses of their business, unless they agree to another sharing arrangement.

Like proprietorships, accounting views partnerships as entities separate from their owners. The Smith, Jones, and Colson law firm is the business entity and would be accounted for as such. However, **legally**, partnerships are like proprietorships in that the business is **not** viewed separately from its owners, and unlimited liability is conveyed to each of the partners. While some partnership agreements may limit one or more of the partner's liability, at least one partner must be personally liable for the debts of the partnership. Unlimited liability is a major disadvantage of both partnerships and proprietorships. Another unique feature of partnerships is that, in general, they dissolve when someone leaves the partnership or when someone new is admitted into the partnership. Later in this text we delve more deeply into partnership accounting.

Corporations. In a **corporation,** ownership interests are represented by shares of stock. Owners of corporate stock are called **stockholders** or **shareholders.** The shares of stock, called **capital stock** or **common stock,** represent a unit of ownership and may be sold or transferred to new owners at any time.

Corporations are unique in that they are viewed as separate entities for both accounting and legal purposes. Usually owners of corporate stock can sell shares without the approval of other stockholders; and in most cases, stock owners have **limited liability** in that the most they can lose in the corporation is the amount they originally invest.

A corporation is formed by filing for a corporate charter with the appropriate governmental unit in the state of incorporation. When the application is approved by the state, the corporation becomes a legal entity, ready to issue stock and conduct business in accordance with the terms of the approved corporate charter. The details of corporate accounting are covered in several succeeding chapters of this text.

BUSINESS FORMATION

In this section, we will see how all of the considerations discussed above affect the many decisions that have to be made before a business is organized.

Ann, Bill, and Connie are research scientists working for three different companies but with long-standing mutual interests since their college days. While they shared a dream of working together on space technology projects someday, each accepted a job with a different research-oriented organization after graduation. At their 10-year college reunion, they had long conversations discussing the exciting projects they could undertake and the feasibility of working jointly. Ann suggested that now was the time to fulfill their dream.

Ann: We can act as independent consultants, but share office space and expertise. If I have a problem on a project, I could call on one of you and vice versa.

Bill: How do we compensate each other for time spent on the other's project? Do we bill each other by the hour?

Connie: What happens if I expand and hire associates. My projects then could grow to such an extent that I could use up all of your time. Besides, some of the projects would have to have security clearance and I don't know if NASA would allow that kind of consultation.

Ann: Yes, and if one of us gets a patent, how do we share the glory and the profits?

Ann, Bill, and Connie are concerned about issues at the heart of the motivation for forming a business. As independent agents, Ann, Bill, and Connie could conceivably cooperate to their mutual advantage, but a formal business entity helps to solve the problems that are created when individual self-interest conflicts with the goal of coordinated effort. Obviously, Ann, Bill, and Connie feel that they would be better off sharing each others' expertise, but they are worried that if they operated as independent agents it would be difficult to achieve equitable sharing of efforts and rewards. Also, it would be difficult to control unique information and knowledge that springs from joint efforts. The answer to some of these concerns is found in a business entity. Listen as Ann, Bill, and Connie come to that conclusion themselves.

Connie: As much as I would like to maintain my independence, I can see that what we need is to form either a partnership or a corporation. That way, the company would be the contractor with the government and we could work on the things that each of us does best.

Bill: Wait, you know what a business is like. You've got to go through lawyers and red tape to form one and then you need accountants to keep track of everything. I don't know anything about accounting. What happens if one of us quits or dies? Also, to help us start the business, we probably would have to get bank loans and they would want financial statements. How would these loans affect my own savings if the company can't pay? How do we decide what our salaries are going to be?

Connie: Wait a minute. Forming a business solves our big problems. We can work together and share ideas and contract as a group. That's the main thing. So we need to learn some accounting and some principles of business. Look, we are rocket scientists for crying out loud. Business and accounting can't be that hard.

Connie is right. Forming a business solves some very important problems. The fact that millions of business entities exist tells us that many problems are solved this way and that the benefits often exceed the costs.

Accounting is designed to provide the information about a business needed by owners, managers, employees, government agencies, and others in order to make informed decisions. Some of these decisions are related to issues of equity among the various parties, such as systems of compensation and ownership interest.

Often, those who lend money to a business, called **creditors,** along with the owners who invest in the business, want to see accounting information that reveals the financial position of the company and the operating results, both of which accounting systems provide. All accounting information systems are not exactly the same, and they do not address all the information needs of outsiders (e.g., creditors) or the concerns expressed by Ann, Bill, and Connie automatically. However, with careful planning, accounting information can help to address the concerns of Ann, Bill, and Connie as well as the needs of creditors and other outside parties.

Choosing the Form of Business Organization

Ann, Bill, and Connie decide to take the plunge and form a business. However, Ann is worried.

Ann: Before we go any farther, I think we have to discuss the best way to organize. It seems to me that an equal partnership is the best; that way we all have equal incentives, but I don't really understand what a partnership means in terms of sharing profits and losses.

Bill: Maybe a corporation would be better. I heard that with a corporation our liability would be limited, whatever that means. I don't know whether a corporation or a partnership is best, but I'll tell you what I believe are the characteristics we want. We want a form of business where we can each invest different amounts, the business can continue if one of us leaves for any reason, and our personal assets can be protected from lawsuits that might result from our business activities.

Ann: And, where we are protected from lawsuits against one of us for something we may have done unrelated to the business, like an auto accident while on vacation.

Connie: Then, it seems to me that we want a corporate form of business, but doesn't that involve getting a state charter and that kind of thing? I think that a partnership would be best in that it would signal our customers that we take full responsibility for our actions and besides we can get professional insurance to cover any lawsuits. Also, I like the idea of having a say in who the other owners of the business are. I wouldn't want one of you to sell your shares to a stranger.

We can see that Ann, Bill, and Connie are discussing their major concerns about the form of a business organization—concerns that are valid for all types of businesses, from the smallest to the largest.

Exhibit 1-3 compares the three forms of business enterprises—proprietorships, partnerships, and corporations. Note again that legally, proprietorships and partnerships have unlimited owner liability, but accounting considers them as entities separate from their owners. Accounting also views corporations as separate entities, but they have the desirable feature of limiting owner liability. There are other factors besides those noted in Exhibit 1-3 which may need to be considered in selecting the form of business organization. For example, different forms of business may face different income tax laws. These other factors are considered in more detail in business law courses, income tax accounting courses, and other business courses. Also, not all of the concerns expressed by Ann, Bill, and Connie are addressed by the form of business. For example, their decision to form a corporation or a partnership does not resolve the compensation issue raised by Bill. Specific agreements would have to be made to resolve such issues.

The United States has more proprietorships than partnerships or corporations, but corporations own most of the business assets and generate most of the sales and income. Also, a corporation may have thousands of different owners, and the ownership may change daily as shares of the corporation's stock are bought and sold among owners through organized trading institutions called **stock exchanges.**

A corporation whose stock is traded by one or more stock exchanges (such as the New York Stock Exchange, American Stock Exchange, or Pacific Stock Exchange) is referred to as a **publicly held company** or **publicly traded company.**

EXHIBIT 1-3

Comparison of Forms of Business Entities

	Proprietorship	Partnership	Corporation
Ownership structure	Single owner	Multiple owners, with specified interest in business	Multiple owners with interest percentages represented by stock holdings
Requirements for transfer of ownership	Approval of proprietor	Usually approval of all partners	Sale of stock
For accounting purposes, the entity to be accounted for	Proprietorship (separate from the proprietor)	Partnership (separate from its partners)	Corporation (separate from its stockholders)
Legal liability from business activities	Unlimited; may result in personal loss	Unlimited; may result in personal loss	Limited to owners' investment in the business entity

Corporations whose stock is not publicly traded are referred to as **closely held** or **privately held companies.** An initial public offering (IPO) takes place when a privately held entity issues stock to the general public for the first time. This is called *going public*.

FINANCIAL STATEMENTS

Accounting information is communicated in many different types of statements and reports. However, as noted earlier in the discussion between Mr. M and the banker (Ms. B), external users of accounting data normally rely, to a large extent, on a standard set of financial statements. The standardized statements governed by GAAP include:

1. Balance sheet (or position statement)
2. Income statement (or earnings statement)
3. Retained earnings statement
4. Statement of cash flows

The remainder of this chapter will introduce you to the nature and purpose of each of these four statements. These four GAAP-governed standardized statements are what auditors must audit for publicly traded companies to comply with SEC regulations.

The Balance Sheet

The **balance sheet** is a "snapshot" of the business's financial position **at a specific date.** Exhibit 1-4 shows how the headings of balance sheets identify the name of the company (WAVO-FM Radio Station), the name of the statement

EXHIBIT 1-4

Corporation:

WAVO-FM Radio Station
Balance Sheet
December 31, 19xx

Assets		**Liabilities and Stockholders' Equity**	
Cash	$ 8,500	Liabilities:	
Accounts receivable	35,300	Accounts payable	$ 45,000
Equipment	44,500	Salaries payable	6,300
Building	160,000	Notes payable	120,000
Land	35,000	Total liabilities	$171,300
		Stockholders' equity:	
		Capital stock	$ 85,000
		Retained earnings	27,000
		Total stockholders' equity	$112,000
Total assets	$283,300	Total liabilities and stockholders' equity	$283,300

Objective 4
The three basic categories of a balance sheet— assets, liabilities, and stockholders' equity.

(Balance Sheet), and the specific date of the statement (December 31, 19xx). The following are the three basic categories of resources and obligations reported in a balance sheet:

1. **Assets.** Certain resources controlled by the business.
2. **Liabilities.** Claims by parties outside of the business.
3. **Stockholders' (owners') equity.** Claims by owners of the business.

Assets are defined as the **future economic benefits controlled by a particular business entity.** For example, cash held by a business is an asset that can be used to purchase other assets or pay for services. Land is an asset representing future economic benefits because land may provide a location to conduct future operations. Likewise, a factory or building and its furniture, machinery, and equipment are assets representing future benefits which will enable the business to operate and earn income (profits). Thus, assets are the pool of economic resources controlled by a business and used in its operations with the intent of generating a larger pool of economic resources.

Most businesses have obligations in the form of claims that outsiders can make on company assets. These obligations, or debts, are called **liabilities.** Liabilities require that a business transfer assets or something of value to other parties (usually individuals, businesses, and/or governments) in the future. Many different economic activities may result in liabilities, such as borrowing cash from a bank or buying goods or services on account (or on credit). Thus, we can think of liabilities as **the specific claims against the assets of a business entity that will require future outflows of assets or other value.**

Stockholders' (owners') equity is **the owners' claims to the net assets of a business entity.** We use "net asset" here because owners' claims have lower priority than creditors' claims. **Net assets** (assets minus liabilities) equal the owners' claims. These owners' claims are also equal to the sum of (1) the capital the owners originally invested in the business and (2) the net income from business operations that has been retained in the business since its beginning.

Exhibit 1-4 illustrates the stockholders' equity as it is reported in the balance sheet of a corporation—WAVO-FM. The term **stockholders' equity** (or shareholders' equity) is normally used for describing the owners' claims in the case of a corporation. The stockholders' equity section lists two items: capital stock, $85,000; and retained earnings, $27,000. The capital stock represents the capital invested by the owners (stockholders) in exchange for their ownership interest; and the retained earnings represents the income earned in all years by WAVO-FM Radio and retained in the business for future use. Both the capital stock and retained earnings represent the owners' claims to assets. Note that total assets of $283,300 minus total liabilities of $171,300 equals total stockholders' equity of $112,000.

Exhibit 1-5 illustrates how the owners' equity section would appear if WAVO-FM were structured as a proprietorship or a partnership. In the proprietorship example, Smith is the owner of WAVO-FM. His ownership claim of $112,000 is indicated under "Owner's equity" in the single item, "Smith, capital." In the partnership example, the WAVO-FM Radio Station is owned by three partners—Morgan, Dukes, and Beaver. The claims of the three owner-partners are listed separately under "Owners' equity" with a total also equaling $112,000.

EXHIBIT 1-5

Proprietorship and Partnership Forms of Ownership

Proprietorship:

WAVO-FM Radio Station
Balance Sheet
December 31, 19xx

Assets		**Liabilities and Owner's Equity**	
Cash	$ 8,500	Liabilities:	
Accounts receivable	35,300	Accounts payable	$ 45,000
Equipment	44,500	Salaries payable	6,300
Building	160,000	Notes payable	120,000
Land	35,000	Total liabilities	$171,300
		Owner's equity:	
		Smith, capital	112,000
		Total liabilities and	
Total assets	$283,300	owner's equity	$283,300

Partnership:

WAVO-FM Radio Station
Balance Sheet
December 31, 19xx

Assets		**Liabilities and Owners' Equity**	
Cash	$ 8,500	Liabilities:	
Accounts receivable	35,300	Accounts payable	$ 45,000
Equipment	44,500	Salaries payable	6,300
Building	160,000	Notes payable	120,000
Land	35,000	Total liabilities	$171,300
		Owners' equity:	
		Morgan, capital	$ 44,800
		Dukes, capital	33,600
		Beaver, capital	33,600
		Total owners' equity	$112,000
		Total liabilities and	
Total assets	$283,300	owners' equity	$283,300

The Balance Sheet Equation. From Exhibits 1-4 and 1-5, you can see that all the assets of a business entity are claimed by two major groups: (1) creditors who have specific claims against the business entity's assets; and (2) owners who have invested in the entity's assets and whose claims equal the total assets minus the creditors' claims. This relationship is expressed in the **balance sheet equation:**

Assets (A)	=	*Liabilities (L)*	+	*Owners' Equity (OE)*
Resources of the business entity **Examples:** • Cash • Inventory • Machinery • Buildings • Land	=	Claims of nonowners of the business entity **Examples:** • Accounts payable to suppliers • Loans payable to bank • Salaries payable to employees	+	Claims of owners of the business entity **Examples:** • Capital invested in the business • Profits earned by the business and kept in the business

For WAVO-FM as a corporation, this equation uses the term **stockholders' equity,** and is expressed as:

Assets (A)		=	*Liabilities (L)*		+	*Stockholders' Equity (SE)*	
$283,300		=	$171,300		+	$112,000	
Cash	$ 8,500		Accounts payable . .	$ 45,000		Capital	
Accounts receivable . .	35,300		Salaries payable . . .	6,300		stock. . . .	$ 85,000
Equipment.	44,500		Notes payable	120,000		Retained	
Building	160,000					earnings . .	27,000
Land	35,000						
	$283,300	=		$171,300	+		$112,000

The balance sheet equation applies to all balance sheets; but, since each business is different, the detailed elements (cash, equipment, inventory, and so on) shown in the balance sheet may differ. Also, just as with all algebraic equalities, the balance sheet equation can be manipulated to express different relationships, all of which are equally valid. For example, using the balance sheet numbers of WAVO-FM, the balance sheet equation can appear as:

1. Assets (A) = Liabilities (L) + Stockholders' Equity (SE)
$283,300 = $171,300 + $112,000

or

2. Assets (A) − Liabilities (L) = Stockholders' Equity (SE)
$283,300 − $171,300 = $112,000

or

3. Assets (A) − Stockholders' Equity (SE) = Liabilities (L)
$283,300 − $112,000 = $171,300

or

4. Assets (A) = Stockholders' Equity (SE) + Liabilities (L)
$283,300 = $112,000 + $171,300

or

5. Liabilities (L) + Stockholders' Equity (SE) = Assets (A)
$171,300 + $112,000 = $283,300

Since the balance sheet equation must always balance, given any two of the three components (A, L, and OE), you can compute the third component. For example, if a fire totally destroyed a business and all its records on June 3, 19xx, and if it were established that the owners' claims were $80,000 and creditors' claims (liabilities) were $200,000 on that date, then the assets appearing on the balance sheet before the loss must have been $280,000 (L + OE = A). Understanding the balance sheet equation is essential to understanding other financial statements and the entire accounting process.

Business Activity and the Balance Sheet. Business activities are the events that affect the assets, liabilities, and owners' equity of the business and its balance sheet. These events are called **accounting transactions.** Note that only business activities that affect the elements of the accounting equation are transactions. Business activities such as writing a memo or holding a business conference are not accounting transactions in themselves, although they may lead to future accounting events.

All accounting transactions can be classified as either (1) **financing**, (2) **investing**, or (3) **operating activities. Financing activities** are those accounting transactions related to creditors, debtors, and owners of the company, such as the borrowing and paying of loans and the sale of stock and payments to stockholders. **Investing activities** are related to the acquisition and disposal of assets for use in the business. **Operating activities** are those related to customers such as sales and payments to employees and other suppliers of goods and services. In Chapter 2, operating activities are introduced.

Objective 5
How business transactions affect the balance sheet equation and the balance sheet.

To illustrate how financing and investing activities affect the balance sheet, we return to our research scientists, Ann, Bill, and Connie, who are now entrepreneurs and who have decided to form Technotic Space Labs (TSL) as an equal partnership among the three. We will examine the first nine transactions of Technotic Space Labs (TSL)—a new partnership established to provide research for problems encountered with spacecraft. As you study these nine transactions, continually refer to Exhibit 1-6, which gives the transactions in a **spreadsheet analysis format.** Note that the balance sheet equality is maintained after the effect of each transaction is recorded on the spreadsheet.

Transaction 1: Financing—Partners Contribute Cash. On January 10, 19xx, Ann, Bill, and Connie formed the TSL partnership by each contributing $330,000. TSL begins its operations with the following balance sheet:

Technotic Space Labs
Balance Sheet
January 10, 19xx

Assets		Owners' Equity	
Cash	$990,000	A, capital	$330,000
		B, capital	330,000
		C, capital	330,000
Total assets	$990,000	Total owners' equity	$990,000

Note that both assets and owners' equity equal $990,000, and the balance sheet is in balance.

EXHIBIT 1-6

Spreadsheet Analysis of Balance Sheet Equation, Technotic Space Labs

Technotic Space Labs

	Assets					=	Liabilities		+ Owners' Equity
Transaction No.	*Cash*	*Note Receivable*	*Lab Equipment*	*Land*	*Lab*		*Accounts Payable*	*Notes Payable*	*Total Capital*
1	990,000								990,000
2	400,000							400,000	
3	−100,000			100,000					
4	−300,000				300,000				
5	− 6,000	6,000							
6			60,000				60,000		
7	−125,000		125,000						
8			− 2,000				− 2,000		
9	− 40,000						−40,000		
	819,000	6,000	183,000	100,000	300,000		18,000	400,000	990,000
	$1,408,000						$1,408,000		

Transactions 2 and 3: Financing—Borrowing from Bank; and Investing—Buying Land. On January 15, 19xx, TSL borrowed $400,000 from a bank (transaction 2). To do this, it gives the bank a note (promise to pay) stating that in five years TSL will repay the loan. On the same day, TSL uses $100,000 of the $400,000 to buy land for a building site (transaction 3). The bank note increased the asset cash by $400,000 and resulted in a note payable of $400,000—increasing both sides of the balance sheet to $1,390,000. The purchase of the land for $100,000 only affected the asset side of the balance sheet—cash decreased $100,000, and the new asset, land, $100,000, is added. The TSL balance sheet now appears as shown below:

Technotic Space Labs
Balance Sheet
January 15, 19xx

Assets		**Liabilities and Owners' Equity**	
Cash	$1,290,000	Liabilities:	
Land	100,000	Notes payable	$ 400,000
		Owners' equity:	
		A, capital	$ 330,000
		B, capital	330,000
		C, capital	330,000
		Total owners' equity	$ 990,000
Total assets	$1,390,000	Total liabilities and owners' equity	$1,390,000

Using the accounting equation to illustrate the balancing effect that transactions 1–3 have on the balance sheet, we have:

	Assets			=	Liabilities	+	Owners' Equity
Transaction No.	*Cash*		*Land*		*Notes Payable*		*Total Capital*
1	$ 990,000						$990,000
2	400,000				$400,000		
	$1,390,000				$400,000		$990,000
3	− 100,000		$100,000				
	$1,290,000	+	$100,000	=	$400,000	+	$990,000

Transaction 4: Investing—Building a Lab. The company hired a contractor to build a lab, which is completed at the end of October 19xx. On November 1, 19xx, it pays $300,000 to the contractor and takes title to the lab facility. The asset cash is reduced $300,000 (to $990,000), and the $300,000 is used to create the asset lab (or building). Many business transactions follow this pattern of decreasing one asset, cash in our example of TSL, and establishing a new asset, such as the lab built by TSL, or increasing an existing asset, for example, by adding an addition to the lab. These transactions do not change the total assets of the business—only the composition of the assets change.

After the November 1 transaction, the accounting equation and the three sections of the balance sheet are as follows:

Assets (A)		=	*Liabilities (L)*		+	*Owners' Equity (OE)*	
$1,390,000		=	$400,000		+	$990,000	
Cash	$ 990,000		Notes payable	$400,000		A, capital	$330,000
Land	100,000					B, capital	330,000
Lab	300,000					C, capital	330,000
	$1,390,000	=		$400,000	+		$990,000

Transaction 5: Investing—Partner Borrows from Partnership. On November 10, B borrowed $6,000 from the partnership agreeing to pay it back within 90 days. This transaction allows us to observe the separate entity concept. When one of the owners borrows money from the business, since the business is always viewed as a separate entity apart from its owners, the owners' equity, which is $990,000, is not affected. Instead, the asset cash is reduced by $6,000 and another asset, note receivable, is increased to show the claim of the business against one of its owners.

In the case of B, the note receivable represents the company's claim to receive cash from B in the future. Notes receivable could also result when customers acquire goods by promising to pay cash on some future date and sign a "note" to that effect. After the November 10 transaction, the effect on the balance sheet equation and the balance sheet is as follows:

Assets (A)		=	*Liabilities (L)*		+	*Owners' Equity (OE)*	
$1,390,000		=	$400,000		+	$990,000	
Cash	$ 984,000		Notes payable . . .	$400,000		A, capital	$330,000
Note receivable . .	6,000					B, capital	330,000
Land	100,000					C, capital	330,000
Lab	300,000						
	$1,390,000	=		$400,000	+		$990,000

Transaction 6: Investing—Acquire Lab Equipment. On November 20, TSL bought lab equipment amounting to $60,000 on open account from Duotech, Inc. This transaction differs from transactions 4 and 5 in that the balance sheet totals change—both assets and liabilities increase $60,000. Transaction 6 is similar to transaction 2 in that the financial size of the business seems to increase by adding more assets and liabilities to the balance sheet. Note, however, that the net assets and owners' equity remain at $990,000. Purchasing equipment on **open account**, called accounts payable, means that the seller gives the equipment to the company in exchange for its informal promise to pay for the supplies at a later date. **Buying on credit** is routine for companies with good credit ratings. Usually large businesses have purchasing agents who are authorized to buy items for the business on open account, thereby committing the business to pay for the purchases at a later date.

After transaction 6 is completed, the balance sheet equation and balance sheet totals are as follows:

Assets (A)		=	*Liabilities (L)*		+	*Owners' Equity (OE)*	
$1,450,000		=	$460,000		+	$990,000	
Cash	$ 984,000		Accounts payable . .	$ 60,000		A, capital	$330,000
Note receivable . .	6,000		Notes payable . . .	400,000		B, capital	330,000
Lab equipment. . .	60,000					C, capital	330,000
Land	100,000						
Lab	300,000						
	$1,450,000	=		$460,000	+		$990,000

Transactions 7, 8, and 9: Investing—Buying Equipment and Returning Equipment, and Paying a Debt. On December 3, TSL paid $125,000 for new equipment (transaction 7). Transaction 7 differs from transaction 6 in that TSL Labs used cash to pay for the equipment instead of credit. As a result, cash is decreased and equipment is increased for the cost of the lab equipment, $125,000.

On December 5, TSL Labs returned $2,000 of the lab equipment bought from Duotech, Inc., on November 20 because it was defective (transaction 8). Duotech gave TSL Labs a credit on account of $2,000. In this transaction, the balance sheet totals are again changed—assets and liabilities are decreased by $2,000. The return of the defective goods reduced both the asset lab equipment and the liability accounts payable by $2,000.

On December 27, TSL Labs paid $40,000 to Duotech (transaction 9). This transaction reduced assets and liabilities, thereby changing some of the balance sheet totals once again. The asset cash and the liability accounts payable are both reduced by $40,000 for the payment to Duotech for equipment purchased earlier on open account. TSL still owes Duotech $18,000 for equipment purchased on account as of the end of 19xx.

After transactions 7, 8, and 9 are completed, the balance sheet equation and balance sheet are:

Assets (A)		=	*Liabilities (L)*		+	*Owners' Equity (OE)*	
$1,408,000		=	$418,000		+	$990,000	
Cash	$ 819,000		Accounts payable	$ 18,000		A, capital	$330,000
Notes receivable	6,000		Notes payable	400,000		B, capital	330,000
Lab equipment	183,000					C, capital	330,000
Land	100,000						
Lab	300,000						
	$1,408,000	=		$418,000	+		$990,000

The balance sheet equality is maintained throughout the life of the business. A balance sheet such as the one shown below may be prepared at any time; and as long as all steps are performed to maintain the equality of the balance sheet equation, the balance sheet will balance; that is, assets will always equal liabilities plus owners' equity.

Technotic Space Labs
Balance Sheet
December 31, 19xx

Assets		**Liabilities and Owners' Equity**	
Cash	$ 819,000	Liabilities:	
Note receivable	6,000	Accounts payable	$ 18,000
Lab equipment	183,000	Notes payable	400,000
Land	100,000	Total liabilities	$ 418,000
Lab	300,000		
		Owners' equity:	
		A, capital	$ 330,000
		B, capital	330,000
		C, capital	330,000
		Total owners' equity	$ 990,000
Total assets	$1,408,000	Total liabilities and owners' equity	$1,408,000

Basic Financial Statements and Their Relationships

The **income statement,** also called the **statement of operations, earnings statement**, or **profit and loss statement**, reports the results of business operations for a period of time, such as one month, one quarter, or one year. These business operations involve business revenues and business expenses. **Revenues** represent measures of **increases** in owners' equity resulting from operating activities, while **expenses** represent measures of **decreases** in owners' equity resulting from operating activities. The excess of revenues over expenses represents **net income (net profit)** as follows:

Revenues − Expenses = Net Income

Although many consider the balance sheet to be the most fundamental financial statement, the income statement is also very important because it indicates the **profitability** of the business. As you will learn, if a company repeatedly shows a net loss, when expenses exceed revenues, the company will not be able to survive unless owners or creditors are willing to provide more resources.

The **retained earnings statement** explains the changes that occurred in the retained earnings portion of stockholders' equity during a period of time (one year, for example) due to business operations (net income) and payments made to owners in the form of **dividends** which are returns to stockholders for their investment in the business. As illustrated later in the chapter, retained earnings are only shown in statements prepared by corporations.

The **statement of cash flows** classifies the three major types of business activities—investing, financing, and operating—and shows where the cash came from during a period, how the cash was used, and the resulting cash balance. While, this statement is explained in greater detail in Chapter 14, the development and analysis of cash flows is covered throughout this textbook.

Objective 6
The difference between the balance sheet, income statement, retained earnings statement, and statement of cash flows.

To summarize the reporting characteristic of accounting, the balance sheet lists the financial position of the business as of a specific date, while the income statement, retained earnings statement, and statement of cash flows essentially explain how and why balance sheet amounts change from one date to another (e.g., from the beginning of the year to the end of the year). Most large businesses prepare these four financial statements, and they are the most common examples of standardized financial statements containing accounting measurements. However, businesses also use many other types of accounting reports.

Exhibit 1-7 shows the balance sheets, income statement, retained earnings statement, and statement of cash flows of the Hart Corporation as of December 31, 19x2, and 19x1. Since the balance sheets for the Hart Corporation are

EXHIBIT 1-7

Examples of the Four Standard Financial Statements

Balance Sheet:

Hart Corporation
Comparative Balance Sheets
December 31
(in thousands)

Assets	19x2	19x1	**Liabilities and Stockholders' Equity**	19x2	19x1
Cash	$ 7	$ 5	Liabilities:		
Accounts receivable	40	36	Accounts payable	$ 9	$ 8
Land	15	15	Notes payable	10	0
Buildings	35	35	Total liabilities	$ 19	$ 8
Equipment	22	0			
			Stockholders' equity:		
			Capital stock	$ 60	$60
			Retained earnings	40	23
			Total stockholders' equity	$100	$83
Total assets	$119	$91	Total liabilities and stockholders' equity	$119	$91

EXHIBIT 1-7 *(concluded)*

Income Statement:

Hart Corporation
Income Statement
For the Year Ended December 31, 19x2
(in thousands)

Revenues:		
Fees revenue	$140	
Other revenue	5	
Total revenues		$145
Less expenses:		
Salaries expense	$ 52	
Rent expense	15	
Other expenses	8	
Total expenses		75
Net income before taxes		$ 70
Income tax expense		23
Net income		$ 47

Retained Earnings Statement:

Hart Corporation
Retained Earnings Statement
For the Year Ended December 31, 19x2
(in thousands)

Retained earnings, January 1	$23
Add: Net income for the year	47
Total	$70
Less: Dividends	30
Retained earnings, December 31	$40

Statement of Cash Flows:

Hart Corporation
Statement of Cash Flows
For the Year Ended December 31, 19x2
(in thousands)

Operating activities:		
Cash from operations		$ 44
Investing activities:		
Cash for equipment purchase		(22)
Financing activities:		
Cash from issuance of note	$ 10	
Cash for dividends	(30)	(20)
Net increase in cash		$ 2

shown for more than one point in time, the statement is called **comparative balance sheets.**

In examining the financial statements illustrated in Exhibit 1-7, you should note several key relationships between the financial statements. The three change statements—income statement, retained earnings statement, and statement of cash flows—explain various changes that occurred in the balance sheet during 19x2, as follows:

Change Statement	*Net Amount of Change*	*Balance Sheet Changes Explained*
Income statement	+$47,000	$47,000 increase in the retained earnings element of stockholders' equity during 19x2 from operating activity.
Retained earnings statement	+$17,000	$17,000 increase in stockholders' equity from a combination of operating activities (+$47,000) and dividend payments to owners (−$30,000) during 19x2.
Statement of cash flows	+$2,000	$2,000 increase in cash during 19x2 from a combination of operating (+$44,000), investing (−$22,000), and financing (−$20,000) activities.

Exhibit 1-8 helps depict how the change statements are related to the changing balance sheet amounts. Note the following:

1. The result from the income statement, net income of $47,000, is included as an addition to the retained earnings in the retained earnings statement. Therefore, the change in the balance sheet item retained earnings is made to reflect the fact that operations were profitable.

2. Retained earnings are decreased by dividends of $30,000—the cash payments to the stockholders as their return for investing in the business. Dividends are viewed as distributions of net income. To the extent that dividends are less than net income, the business is said to have retained some portion of the income, hence the name **retained income** or **retained earnings.**

3. The focus of the income statement is on the **operations** of the business; the focus of the statement of cash flows is on the amount of cash provided or used by **operating**, **investing**, and **financing** activities; the focus of the retained earnings statement is on the link between the income statement and the balance sheet.

4. The income statement, retained earnings statement, and statement of cash flows all help explain changes in some of the balance sheet items from the end of 19x1 to the end of 19x2. Because these change statements are for a period of time, the time period is indicated in the headings of the statements, whereas the balance sheet has the date of the specific point in time it represents.

EXHIBIT 1-8

Relationship of the Change Statements to the Balance Sheet

*State at December 31, 19x1 (000s) Balance Sheet**			*Change Statements*[†] *(000s)*		*State at December 31, 19x2 (000s) Balance Sheet*	
Assets:			+ $2 on statement of cash flows		Assets:	
Cash	$ 5	→		→	Cash	$ 7
Other assets	86				Other assets	112
Total assets	$91				Total assets	$119
Liabilities	$ 8				Liabilities	$ 19
Stockholders' equity:					Stockholders' equity:	
Capital stock.	60				Capital stock	60
Retained earnings	23	→	+ $47 on income statement − $30 on retained earnings statement	→	Retained earnings	40
Total liabilities and stockholders' equity	$91				Total liabilities and stockholders' equity	$119

*Balance sheet shows the financial position or state of the entity at a specific point in time in terms of assets, liabilities, and stockholders' equity.

[†]1. Income statement—shows the revenues and expenses and net income or loss for the period.
2. Retained earnings statement—shows how net income and dividends affected retained earnings.
3. Statement of cash flows—shows how cash was affected by operating, investing, and financing activities.

SUMMARY

After studying this chapter, you should be aware of some of the complexities of the accounting environment. We divided the users of accounting information into two major groups: external users and internal users. Within these user groups, the focus was on external users, internal managers, independent auditors, accounting policymakers, and representatives of government—all playing the roles of either senders or receivers of accounting information.

We focused on business entities that produce accounting information: proprietorships, partnerships, and corporations. Through the use of financial statements, accounting information communicates in words and numbers the results of economic activities. While these financial statements are the primary source of accounting information for external users, we will see in later chapters that many decisions of internal users are also based on these statements.

The interrelationship of the four financial statements—balance sheet, income statement, statement of retained earnings, and statement of cash flows—was introduced. The balance sheet provides the financial position of the business as of a specific date, while the income statement, retained earnings statement, and statement of cash flows essentially explain how and why balance sheet amounts change from one date to another.

In this chapter we concentrated on the balance sheet and the balance sheet equation, which is the foundation of the accounting process. You learned the components of the balance sheet and how it communicates the financial position of the business. Financing and investing transactions, with the aid of a spreadsheet analysis, were examined in relation to the balance sheet equation and the balance sheet. The unbreakable rule of always maintaining the balance sheet equality of assets equaling liabilities plus owners' equity was repeatedly illustrated.

Accounting involves the process of providing information on economic activities that will be useful in the decision making of external and internal accounting information users. As you learn more about the strengths and weaknesses of accounting, you will gain a better understanding of why accounting is often called the *language of business.*

DEMONSTRATION EXERCISE

On April 1, 19xx, its first day of operations, the Gold Advertising Agency, Inc., had the following transactions:

a. Sold 100 shares of capital stock for $25,000 cash.
b. Purchased supplies to be used in the agency for $500 on account.
c. Paid the April and May rent of $4,800 in advance for office space.
d. Advanced J. J. Gold $5,000, accepting a note from J. J. Gold.
e. Purchased land for $10,000 cash and a $50,000 note.

Construct the end of the day (April 1, 19xx) balance sheet with the aid of the spreadsheet analysis format. (Refer to Exhibit 1-6.)

Solution:

Gold Advertising Agency, Inc.

	Assets					=	*Liabilities*	+	*Stockholders' Equity*
Date of Event	*Cash*	*Note Receivable*	*Supplies*	*Prepaid Rent*	*Land*		*Accounts Payable*	*Notes Payable*	*Capital Stock*
4/1/xx a.m.									
a.	25,000								25,000
b.			500				500		
c.	− 4,800			4,800					
d.	− 5,000	5,000							
e.	−10,000				60,000			50,000	
4/1/xx p.m.	5,200	5,000	500	4,800	60,000		500	50,000	25,000

Gold Advertising Agency, Inc.
Balance Sheet
April 1, 19xx

Assets		Liabilities and Stockholders' Equity	
Cash	$ 5,200	Liabilities:	
Note receivable	5,000	Accounts payable	$ 500
Supplies	500	Notes payable	50,000
Prepaid rent	4,800	Total liabilities	$50,500
Land	60,000	Stockholders' equity:	
		Capital stock	$25,000
		Total stockholders' equity	$25,000
Total assets	$75,500	Total liabilities and stockholders' equity	$75,500

APPENDIX

Organizations Involved in Policymaking

Objective 7
The organizations involved in accounting policymaking and how they serve the external, internal, and governmental user groups.

In accounting, as in other systems of our economy and society, organizations exist that perform important policy services for special groups of individuals. Exhibit 1A-1 lists eight accounting organizations and the accounting users they represent. Study this exhibit before reading the discussion that follows.

The **American Accounting Association (AAA)**, organized in the early 1900s, indirectly represents the interest of all parties in the accounting environment—external users, internal users, auditors, and policymakers. The AAA is made up primarily of university and college accounting educators, many with backgrounds in various aspects of accounting practice. Although the AAA cannot directly set policies, it provides indirect input to the policymaking processes of the Financial Accounting Standards Board (FASB) and other groups. Many members of the AAA hold influential positions, including one membership on the seven-member board of the FASB. In many direct and indirect ways, committees of the AAA have significantly influenced the development of accounting as we know it today.

The **American Institute of Certified Public Accountants (AICPA)** was originally organized in 1887 and has been the organization of practicing Certified Public Accountants (CPAs) since its beginning. An important function of the AICPA is to monitor the certification process of CPAs, which is conducted on a state-by-state basis. Upon completion of the CPA requirements, students of ac-

EXHIBIT 1A-1

Organizations Representing Accounting User Groups

Organization	*Users Represented*
American Accounting Association (AAA)	External users Internal users Policymakers Auditors
American Institute of Certified Public Accountants (AICPA)	Managers (internal users) Auditors Policymakers
Financial Executives Institute (FEI)	Managers (internal users)
Financial Accounting Standards Board (FASB)	Policymakers
Government Accounting Office (GAO) and other governmental agencies	Governmental users
Internal Revenue Service (IRS)	Governmental users
National Association of Accountants (NAA)	Managers (internal users)
Securities and Exchange Commission (SEC)	Policymakers Governmental users

counting are employed in (1) public accounting, which includes independent auditing, tax accounting, and consulting services; (2) private or industrial accounting; and (3) governmental and other not-for-profit accounting.

To guide auditors, the AICPA establishes **generally accepted auditing standards (GAAS)**—a set of rules and guidelines for auditing financial statements. In addition, the AICPA has been involved in establishing accounting policies that affect GAAP by defining the most appropriate accounting methods to be applied to certain special industries. These guidelines provide direction to both auditors and managers.

The AICPA provides its 250,000 members with a monthly publication, *The Journal of Accountancy.* This publication has been reporting current accounting events and issues of interest to CPAs since 1905.

The accounting organizations that specialize in representing the view of managers are the **Financial Executives Institute (FEI)** and the **National Association of Accountants (NAA).** The FEI is a national organization that includes in its membership the chief financial officers and other financial executives of many publicly traded corporations. The various committees of the FEI follow accounting developments and contact policymakers to express the position of its members. The NAA is also a national organization, and its membership consists of controllers, chief accounting officers, treasurers, accounting managers, and holders of other accounting-related positions. Both the FEI and the NAA have over 100,000 members each and publish monthly journals that report on current developments.

Accounting policymakers essentially look after the interests of the external users who are not otherwise represented by influential accounting organizations. In order of importance, the organizations that directly or indirectly influence policymaking by determining the nature and content of the financial statements of publicly traded companies are:

1. The Financial Accounting Standards Board (FASB).
2. The Securities and Exchange Commission (SEC).
3. The American Institute of Certified Public Accountants (AICPA).

The **Financial Accounting Standards Board (FASB)** is an independent, private organization that consists of seven full-time board members plus a full-time research staff. The board members are generally selected from backgrounds in auditing, corporate management, financial analysis, and education. The FASB is the primary organization responsible for establishing GAAP and setting accounting policy.

The **Securities and Exchange Commission (SEC)** is a branch of the federal government with legal authority to establish accounting policies for publicly traded companies. However, since 1939, the SEC has delegated the primary responsibility for policymaking to the private sector currently represented by the FASB. The SEC does influence the nature and content of GAAP, but the most significant accounting pronouncements are currently issued through the FASB.

Between 1939 and 1973, before the creation of the FASB, the AICPA had the primary responsibility for setting accounting policy. Today, as stated above, the AICPA defines appropriate methods for certain special industries and has primary responsibility for the development of generally accepted auditing standards (GAAS).

KEY TERMS

Accounting. An information process that communicates the results of economic activities and states in ways that are useful to decision makers.

Accounting transactions. Business activities or events that affect the assets, liabilities, and owners' equity of the business and its balance sheet.

Assets. Economic resources that a business owns or controls; future economic benefits controlled by a particular business entity as a result of past economic activities.

Balance sheet. Lists all of the company's assets, liabilities, and ownership interests at a specific point in time; also called position statement or statement of financial position. If the balance sheet contains data for more than one point in time, it is called a comparative balance sheet.

Balance sheet equation. Assets equal liabilities plus owners' equity.

Business entity. Economic unit separate from its owners; the business unit accounted for on the company's financial statements; viewed as separate from the owners of the business; also called the business entity, separate entity, or entity concept.

Capital stock. A unit of ownership in a corporation; also called common stock.

Closely held company. Corporation whose stock is not publicly traded; also called privately held company.

Comparative balance sheet. A balance sheet that shows information for more than one point in time.

Corporation. Business whose ownership interests are represented by shares of stock called common stock or capital stock; owners of stock (stockholders or shareholders) have limited liability.

Creditors. Those who lend money to the business.

Dividends. Payments to stockholders as a return on their investments. A distribution of the net income which reduces retained earnings.

Expenses. Measures of decreases in owners' equity resulting from operating activities.

External users. All individuals and other entities that are not managers employed by the business entity who have an interest in the company's financial affairs; also called outsiders.

Financial accounting. Accounting information provided to external users in the form of financial statements.

Financial statements. Standardized financial reports on the money measurements of a specific business entity.

Financing activities. Accounting transactions related to creditors, debtors, and owners of the company.

Generally accepted accounting principles (GAAP). A set of rules or guidelines used to prepare financial statements.

Governmental users. Governmental entities that often request specific accounting information they need, such as the Internal Revenue Service (IRS) and the Securities and Exchange Commission (SEC).

Income statement. Reports the results of business operations for a period of time such as a year; indicates the profitability of the business; also called statement of operations, earnings statement, or profit and loss statement.

Internal Revenue Service (IRS). A governmental agency that requires special-purpose reports indicating the amount of federal income taxes owed by the business.

Internal users. Managers of a business.

Investing activities. Accounting transactions related to the acquisition and disposal of long-term assets used in the business.

Liabilities. Claims by outsiders to receive cash or other assets from the business at some future date.

Managerial accounting. Accounting information used by internal managers to plan and operate the business.

Net assets. Assets minus liabilities; the owners' claims against the business.

Net income. Results when a business is able to sell its goods and/or services for more than they cost the company; also called net profit or earnings.

Open account. A purchase for credit rather than cash; also called buying on credit.

Operating activities. Accounting transactions related to customers and suppliers of products and services; transactions that are intended to affect income and are of interest to the business for income measurement purposes.

Owners' equity. The owners' claims to the net assets of a business entity; shown in the balance sheet of a proprietorship as owner's equity, of a partnership as owners' equity or partners' equity, and of a corporation as stockholders' equity.

Partnership. Noncorporate business owned by two or more owners.

Proprietorship. Noncorporate business owned by one person.

Publicly held company. Company (corporation) whose stock is traded by one or more stock exchanges; also called publicly traded company.

Retained earnings statement. Report explaining changes that occurred in retained earnings during a period of time (one year, for example) due to business operations and dividends payments made to owners.

Revenues. Measures of increases in owners' equity resulting from operating activities.

Securities and Exchange Commission (SEC). A governmental unit that regulates stock exchanges and corporations whose securities are traded thereon.

Spreadsheet analysis format. Tool used to show the effect of business transactions on the balance sheet equation.

Statement of cash flows. Classifies investing, financing, and operating activities—showing where the cash came from during a period, how the cash was used, and the resulting cash balance.

Stock exchanges. Organized trading institutions where shares of stock can be bought and sold.

Stockholders. Owners of corporate stock; also called shareholders.

Stockholders' equity. See owners' equity. Also called shareholders' equity.

APPENDIX KEY TERMS

American Accounting Association (AAA). Professional organization representing the interests of external users, internal users, auditors, and policymakers.

American Institute of Certified Public Accountants (AICPA). Professional organization of Certified Public Accountants (CPAs) representing auditors and other CPAs.

Financial Accounting Standards Board (FASB). Independent, private organization that is primarily responsible for establishing GAAP and setting accounting policy.

Financial Executives Institute (FEI). Professional organization representing the viewpoint of managers.

Generally accepted auditing standards (GAAS). A set of rules or guidelines for auditing financial statements.

National Association of Accountants (NAA). Professional organization representing managers.

SYNONYMS

Balance sheet; position statement; statement of financial position.

Balance sheet equation; accounting equation.

Business entity; business entity concept; separate entity concept; entity concept.

Capital stock; common stock.

Income; profit.

Income statement; statement of operations; earnings statement; profit and loss statement.

Merchandise; inventory.

Net income; net profit; earnings.

Open account; buying on credit.

Publicly held company; publicly traded company.

Retained earnings; retained income; retained surplus.

Stockholders; shareholders.

QUESTIONS

1. Define accounting.
2. Who are the external users of accounting?
3. Who are internal users?
4. Describe the responsibilities of internal users. What are the difficulties encountered in carrying out these responsibilities?
5. Name two of the governmental users of accounting.
6. What are the primary types of decisions involving accounting data made by external users?

7. What kinds of decisions involving accounting data are made by internal users?
8. What kinds of decisions involving accounting data are made by governmental users?
9. What are the three forms of businesses?
10. How do proprietorships differ from partnerships?
11. How do corporations differ from partnerships?
12. What is the difference between closely held companies and publicly traded companies?
13. What is a balance sheet?
14. What are the definitions of assets, liabilities, and owners' equity?
15. What is the balance sheet equation and why must it balance?
16. What are the primary examples of accounting reports?
17. Explain how the other financial statements relate to the balance sheet.
18. Describe the three categories into which all accounting transactions can be placed.
19. Describe two transactions that increase the total assets on the balance sheet.
20. Describe a transaction that does not change the total assets on the balance sheet.

APPENDIX QUESTIONS

21. What are the accounting organizations representing the interests of internal users?
22. What are the accounting organizations representing the interests of auditors?
23. What are the accounting organizations representing the interests of external users?
24. Who determines generally accepted accounting principles (GAAP)?
25. Who determines generally accepted auditing standards (GAAS)?
26. Your friend is a law student who is interested in learning about the legal structure of accounting. He wants to know who makes accounting rules that govern the financial reports of publicly owned companies. Also, he has noticed articles that refer to generally accepted accounting principles and would like to know what these are and who establishes these principles. Explain to your friend what you know about the answers to his questions.

EXERCISES

EXERCISE 1-1
L.O. 1, 2*

Accounting Users

1. The complex accounting environment consists of the following users:
   a. Senders and receivers.
   b. Investors, stockholders, bankers, and managers.
   c. Governmental, external, and internal.
   d. Internal and external.
2. Policymakers—
   a. Determine the accounting rules and procedures necessary to provide managers, external users, and auditors with meaningful information.
   b. Attempt to provide external users with as little information as possible.
   c. Include only the SEC and IRS.
   d. Report on the fairness of a company's financial reports.
3. Managerial accounting—
   a. Must follow GAAP.
   b. Provides more timely and detailed information than that provided to external users.

*L.O. refers to the learning objectives given at the beginning of each chapter.

c. Methods are identical no matter what purpose a company or an individual is pursuing.
d. All of the above.

4. Governmental users—
   a. Can be viewed as a special class of external users, since many governmental agencies have the power to require any specific accounting information they need.
   b. Include only the IRS and SEC.
   c. Operate in a relatively simple environment that is void of ambiguity.
   d. Request information for no specific purpose.

EXERCISE 1-2
L.O. 3

Forms of Business

1. In a proprietorship—
   a. One person is the owner.
   b. The owner has unlimited liability.
   c. The business is viewed as a separate entity by accountants.
   d. All of the above.
2. A partnership—
   a. Is owned by two or more individuals or entities with unlimited liability.
   b. Is viewed as the favorable form of business by manufacturing companies.
   c. Divides its income equally among partners no matter how the ownership interests are contributed.
   d. All of the above.
3. In a corporation—
   a. Ownership is represented by shares of stock.
   b. One or more individuals or entities can be the owners.
   c. Owners' liability is limited to the amount originally invested.
   d. All of the above.
4. In comparing legal views with accounting treatments—
   a. Corporations are viewed as separate entities for legal purposes only.
   b. Partnerships are viewed as separate entities for both legal and accounting purposes.
   c. Proprietorships are viewed as separate entities for accounting purposes but not for legal purposes.
   d. All of the above.

EXERCISE 1-3
L.O. 4

Characteristics of Accounting

1. In accounting, money amounts—
   a. Measure the economic resources or assets of the business.
   b. Measure the cash held by the business.
   c. Measure the net income or performance of the business.
   d. Help to communicate past, present, and future business activities.
   e. All of the above.
2. The change statements explain changes in a company's position from one date to another. The change statements include—
   a. Income statement, statement of cash flows, and retained earnings statement.
   b. Balance sheet, earnings statement, and statement of cash flows.
   c. Income statement, position statement, and statement of cash flows.
   d. Income statement, balance sheet, and retained earnings statement.

EXERCISE 1-4
L.O. 4, 6

Balance Sheet Preparation

Lawrence Pool Installation, Inc., has the following items on June 30, 19xx:

Accounts receivable	$27,000
Accounts payable	13,000
Cash	7,000
Capital stock	75,000
Equipment	85,000
Land	20,000
Notes payable	12,000
Salaries payable	15,000
Retained earnings	24,000

Required:
Prepare the June 30, 19xx, balance sheet.

EXERCISE 1-5
L.O. 4, 6

Balance Sheet Preparation

Carpet Cleaners, Inc., has the following items on September 30, 19xx:

Accounts receivable	$ 7,800
Accounts payable	5,890
Cash	15,400
Capital stock	25,000
Equipment	30,600
Notes payable	10,000
Retained earnings	11,105
Salaries payable	4,575
Supplies inventory	2,770

Required:
Prepare the September 30, 19xx, balance sheet.

EXERCISE 1-6
L.O. 4

Comparison of Different Forms of Owners' Equity

Net assets (assets less liabilities) for Blackford Lumber equal $81,375 on December 31, 19xx. Prepare the owners' equity section of the balance sheet for that date assuming:

1. The business is owned by John Blackford only.
2. The business is owned equally by brothers John and Rick Blackford and their sister Kate Merrill.
3. The business is incorporated and has capital stock of $50,000.

EXERCISE 1-7
L.O. 4, 6

Balance Sheet Equation and Balance Sheet Preparation

The following items make up the complete balance sheet of the Tres Hombres Company on June 30, 19xx:

Accounts receivable	$ 38,542
Accounts payable	21,856
Buildings and equipment	187,693
Cash	17,214
Inventory	49,047
Notes payable	105,356
Retained earnings	?
Salaries payable	25,070
Land	73,000
Capital stock	150,000

Required:
Prepare the June 30, 19xx, balance sheet.

EXERCISE 1-8
L.O. 4, 6

Balance Sheet Equation and Balance Sheet Preparation

The following items make up the complete balance sheet of the Python Company on September 30, 19xx:

Basko, capital	$205,000
Frich, capital	210,000
Wilson, capital	215,000
Accounts receivable	43,867
Notes payable	118,680
Cash	?
Machinery and equipment	197,542
Salaries payable	12,943
Land and building	347,108
Inventory	112,587
Income taxes payable	8,761
Accounts payable	13,056

Required:
1. Compute the September 30, 19xx, cash on hand.
2. Prepare the September 30, 19xx, balance sheet.

EXERCISE 1-9
L.O. 4, 6

Balance Sheet Equation

Assume that Gerry Lobo is the sole proprietor of a computer software business. His balance sheet on December 31, 19x1, was:

Software Styles
Balance Sheet
December 31, 19x1

Assets		Liabilities and Owner's Equity	
Cash	$ 2,000	Liabilities:	
Merchandise	8,000	Accounts payable	$ 7,000
Land	20,000	Notes payable	60,000
Building	48,000	Total liabilities	$67,000
		Owner's equity:	
		Lobo, capital	$11,000
		Total owner's equity	$11,000
Total assets	$78,000	Total liabilities and owner's equity	$78,000

On January 19, 19x2, a fire destroyed the facilities of Software Styles. The proprietor's capital account had not changed during January and had a balance of $11,000 at the date of the fire. At the date of the fire, the creditors said that the business owed them $10,000 for accounts payable and $60,000 for the note. Cash held by First National Bank in Lobo's checking account was $3,000 at the time of the fire. The insurance company agreed to pay for the lost assets. What was the amount of assets lost at the date of the fire? (Hint: Do not include land in the loss.)

EXERCISE 1-10
L.O. 4, 6

Balance Sheet Equation

1. If a company has total stockholders' equity of $8,900, then—
   a. A total of $8,900 in capital stock was issued by the company.
   b. The business has total assets of $8,900.
   c. Net income less dividends for the period was $8,900.
   d. Total assets exceed total liabilities by $8,900.
2. If assets are $4,000—
   a. Stockholders' equity must be $4,000.
   b. Liabilities must be $4,000.
   c. Stockholders' equity plus liabilities must be $4,000.
   d. None of the above.
3. When 5,000 shares of stock are issued for $10,000 cash at the start of a corporation—
   a. The stockholders are considered to be creditors of the corporation.
   b. All stockholders must own the same percentage interest in the corporation.
   c. The value of each share is $2 and may be sold back to the corporation at any time for that amount.
   d. The loss of the stockholders is limited to $10,000.
4. Assets of a business are:
   a. Things the business uses to operate.
   b. Future economic benefits controlled by the business as a result of past transactions.
   c. Things legally owned by a business that do not have a balance due remaining to be paid on them.
   d. Things provided by the owners of a business who hold stock.

5. The balance sheet equation may **not** be stated as:
   a. Liabilities = Assets − Owners' Equity.
   b. Owners' Equity + Liabilities = Assets.
   c. Assets − Liabilities = Owners' Equity.
   d. Assets = Liabilities − Owners' Equity.

EXERCISE 1-11
L.O. 5

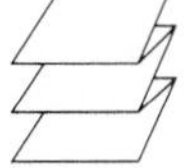

Balance Sheet Equation and Business Transactions

Analyze the following transactions and complete the form below by stating the amount of the increase or decrease and what component(s) of each balance sheet element is affected:

Example: Sold stock to three investors for $180,000.
a. Purchased office supplies for $600 cash.
b. Purchased land for $25,000 cash.
c. Borrowed $50,000 from the local bank.
d. Loaned a needy employee $20,000 cash.
e. Paid the insurance premium for the next 12 months, $12,000.
f. Purchased $1,000 of additional supplies on account.
g. Purchased a building for $100,000 cash.
h. Paid $300 to the supplies vendor and returned $500 of damaged supplies.

	Assets	=	*Liabilities*	+	*Stockholders' Equity*
Example:	+180,000 Cash				+180,000 Capital stock
a.					
b.					
c.					
d.					
e.					
f.					
g.					
h.					

Demonstrate that the balance sheet equation remains in balance.

APPENDIX EXERCISE

EXERCISE 1-12
L.O. 7

Policymaking Organizations

1. The set of rules and guidelines for auditing financial statements are:
   a. GAAP.
   b. GAAS.
   c. GAAP and GAAS.
   d. FASB and AICPA rules.
2. The policymaking organization with primary responsibility for establishing generally accepted accounting principles is:
   a. The Securities and Exchange Commission.
   b. The Internal Revenue Service.
   c. The Financial Accounting Standards Board.
   d. The American Institute of Certified Public Accountants.
3. The accounting organizations that exist to represent managers are:
   a. The Financial Accounting Standards Board and the American Accounting Association.
   b. The AICPA and the SEC.

c. The Internal Revenue Service and the Government Accounting Office.
d. The National Association of Accountants and the Financial Executives Institute.

4. The set of rules and guidelines for preparing financial statements are:
   a. GAAP.
   b. GAAS.
   c. GAAP and GAAS.
   d. FASB rules.

PROBLEMS

PROBLEM 1-1
L.O. 3

Forms of Business Organizations

James Jones is thinking of acquiring a franchise for the New World Basketball Conference. Since you have had some business courses, he asks you for your advice. Jones asks you about the different forms of business organizations, since he is not sure whether to have the team set up as a proprietorship, a partnership, or a corporation. The franchise will cost about $3 million to get started.

Required:
Identify the advantages and disadvantages of the different forms of business organizations and make a recommendation to James Jones.

PROBLEM 1-2
L.O. 3

Comparison of the Three Forms of Business Organizations

Mason Smith has a number of business investments. He is the sole proprietor of a grocery store, a partner in a hardware store, and a stockholder in a local chemical company. He also owns a summer home, a permanent residence, and several vehicles. The total value of assets owned by Smith is estimated at $4 million. Answer the following **independent** questions concerning Mason Smith:

1. Smith's banker has asked for financial statements for the grocery store and the hardware store businesses. Smith is unsure how to provide this information since he only owns part of the hardware store. How should these businesses be reported to Smith's banker?
2. A customer decides to sue for $2 million in damages due to faulty products purchased from the hardware store. Smith's ownership capital in the hardware store is only $500,000. How much might Smith lose if the customer wins the lawsuit?
3. The chemical company is sued by the Environmental Protection Agency for illegal dumping and is expected to have to pay $10 million. Smith paid $100,000 for his stock in the company. The chemical company has total stockholders' equity of $5 million, and total assets of only $8 million. How much does Smith stand to lose from this lawsuit?
4. Smith used a check from the grocery store's checking account to pay bills owed by the hardware store operations. What accounting assumptions, if any, are violated by such behavior?

PROBLEM 1-3
L.O. 3

Decision Making and Forms of Business Organizations

Jackson's General Store is 100% owned by Maureen Jackson. The general store has earned large profits in recent years, and Jackson is considering buying an interest in another business. Two attractive alternatives available to Jackson are described below.

Alternative 1:
The El Doughno Bakery is currently owned by two brothers. The bakery is going to expand to a second location in hopes of doubling the business and the profits. To do so, the

brothers are looking for a new partner to contribute $100,000 cash in exchange for a 50% partnership interest.

Alternative 2:
The Taco fast-food restaurant is owned by five stockholders. The restaurant is going to expand the size of its present location in an effort to provide more seating space for customers. The expansion is expected to cost $100,000 and will be financed by the sale of stock to a new stockholder. The new stockholder would then have one sixth of the total stock of Taco.

Jackson is not certain which alternative to choose. Both alternatives are expected to return about the same amount of profits to Jackson in the near future. Jackson is interested in your advice.

Required:
1. What kind of decision is Jackson making?
2. What kind of user of accounting information would we call Jackson in this specific decision?
3. What are the potential advantages of each alternative that you see?
4. What important difference should Jackson be aware of in the organizational structure of the two businesses?
5. What effect, if any, will the acquisition of either alternative have on the accounting system for Jackson's General Store? Explain your answer.

PROBLEM 1-4
L.O. 5, 6

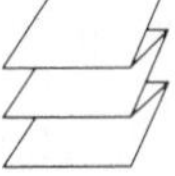

Event Analysis and Balance Sheet Preparation

The following balance sheet items pertaining to the Landis Corporation on December 31, 19x1, are listed in alphabetical order:

Accounts payable	$ 58,000
Building.	147,000
Cash	38,000
Equipment	240,000
Inventory	71,000
Land	62,000
Notes payable.	75,000
Other liabilities	88,000
Accounts receivable	43,000
Retained earnings	?
Capital stock	300,000

During January 19x2, the following events occurred:

a. Acquired inventory on account, $19,000.
b. Borrowed $50,000 cash from the bank signing a note.
c. Paid $28,000 cash on note payable.
d. Collected $23,000 on accounts receivable.
e. Issued Landis stock for $75,000 cash.
f. Paid $48,000 on accounts payable.

Required:
1. Prepare a spreadsheet analysis as illustrated in Exhibit 1-6, placing the beginning balances given in the balance sheet data of December 31, 19x1, on the first line of the spreadsheet. Fill in the missing amount for retained earnings as of December 31, 19x1.
2. Complete the spreadsheet analysis to account for the six events noted in the problem for January 19x2. Indicate the new balances for each balance sheet item after considering these six events.
3. Prepare the January 31, 19x2, balance sheet based on the spreadsheet analysis.

PROBLEM 1-5
L.O. 5, 6

Event Analysis and Balance Sheet Preparation

The Butler Corporation was formed in September 19xx. The following transactions occurred during the first three months:

19xx		
Sept.	1	Sold stock to stockholders for $1.5 million in cash.
	10	Acquired land and building for $1.2 million cash.
	30	Borrowed $800,000 cash from the bank.
Oct.	12	Purchased equipment costing $750,000, paying $250,000 cash. The balance due in 90 days was represented by a note signed by Butler.
	26	Purchased merchandise costing $85,000 on open account.
Nov.	10	An officer of Butler Corporation borrowed $5,000 from the corporation, signing a 90-day note.
	16	Returned merchandise purchased in October costing $7,000 for credit on account.
	17	Paid $45,000 cash on account for the merchandise purchased. The balance was to be paid in December.
	29	Paid cash of $150,000 on note signed October 12.

Required:

1. Prepare a spreadsheet analysis as illustrated in Exhibit 1-6 for Butler Corporation for the first three months of business.
2. Prepare the November 30, 19xx, balance sheet.

PROBLEM 1-6
L.O. 6

Balance Sheet Preparation

Bill and Sally Foster operate the Captain's Table Restaurant, and each has one half the owners' equity. At June 30, 19x1, the restaurant has equipment and furnishings for which they paid on June 20, $38,000; and eight months' rent has been paid in advance on the building at $2,400 per month. The food and supplies on hand cost $1,200 and the restaurant's checking account has $8,700 in it. An additional $200 is kept in the cash register at the restaurant. Suppliers are owed $1,100 and the restaurant still owes $15,000 on the note payable used to finance the equipment and furnishings.

Required:
Prepare a balance sheet for the Captain's Table Restaurant at June 30, 19x1.

PROBLEM 1-7
L.O. 5, 6

Balance Sheet Analysis

Valley Fashions, a sole proprietorship owned by J. Klein, started business on January 1, 19x1, with the following balance sheet:

Valley Fashions
Balance Sheet
January 1, 19x1

Cash	5,000	Accounts payable	11,000
Inventory	28,000	Long-term note payable	12,000
Store equipment	17,000	Mortgage payable	82,000
Building	92,000	Total liabilities	105,000
Land	15,000	J. Klein, capital	52,000
Total	157,000	Total	157,000

During 19x1, sales were very good. Two sales clerks were hired and advertisements were run in the newspaper and on T.V. Klein invested an additional $40,000 to refurbish the building, upgrade the store equipment, and expand storage space. At the end of 19x1 Klein drew up the balance sheet shown below:

Valley Fashions
Balance Sheet
December 31, 19x1

Cash	4,000	Accounts payable	62,000
Accounts received	12,000	Long-term note payable	12,000
Inventory	66,000	Mortgage payable	82,000
Store equipment	27,000	Total liabilities	156,000
Building	122,000	J. Klein, capital	90,000
Land	15,000		
Total	246,000	Total	246,000

Required:
Klein is very happy with the first year results since the assets of the business have increased by more than 50% and net assets have increased by $38,000. Comment on the performance of Valley Fashions for 19x1.

PROBLEM 1-8
L.O. 6

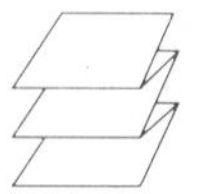

Income Statement and Statement of Cash Flows

The following items relate to National Corporation's fiscal year ended December 31, 19x1 (in thousands):

Sales revenue	$440.0
Interest expense	15.7
Salaries expense	163.3
Rent expense	47.0
Selling and administrative expense	25.1
Income tax expense	72.2
Cash from operations	138.2
Cash paid to acquire factory building	69.1
Cash from sale of stock	31.4
Cash paid for dividends	94.2

Required:
1. Prepare an income statement for the year ended December 31, 19x1.
2. Prepare a statement of cash flows for the year ended December 31, 19x1.

PROBLEM 1-9
L.O. 4

Assets, Liabilities, and Stockholders' Equity

Listed below are the descriptions of several items that pertain to the financial affairs of the Delta Company for January 19x1, its first month of operations:

a. Amount of loans on 1/15/x1 which must be paid back during January 19x2.
b. Cost of the Delta Company's warehouse paid on 1/20/x1.
c. Cost of unused supplies kept for use in the office.
d. Amount owed to suppliers of inventory at 1/31/x1.
e. Cash in the checking account at 1/31/x1.
f. Amount of money paid for stock by the owners as of 1/31/x1.
g. Amount owed at 1/31/x1 for items to be resold to customers.
h. Amount paid for office furniture on 1/29/x1.
i. Amount of sales planned for each line of product carried for February 19x1.

Required:
1. Indicate the balance sheet category to which each item belongs.
2. As what form of business entity is Delta organized? How do you know?

CASES

CASE 1-1
L.O. 4

Asset and Liability Valuation

James Jones and four other stockholders each contributed $500,000 to form a new WBC basketball team. The franchise was acquired on January 1, 19xx, at the cost of $2 million, of which $400,000 was paid immediately. A note was signed with the WBC league officials for the balance scheduled to be paid at the beginning of each of the next four years ($400,000 per year). The team signed up eight players resulting in a total annual salary commitment of $2 million. Also, the team paid a total of $1.5 million as signing bonuses to the top four players to get them to sign with the team. Prior to the start of the season, Jones' team, the Mildcats, reported the following balance sheet:

Mildcats, Inc.
Balance Sheet
September 30, 19xx

Assets		**Liabilities and Stockholders' Equity**	
Cash	$ 400,000	Liabilities:	
Equipment	200,000	Player contracts payable	$2,000,000
Player contracts	3,500,000	Total liabilities	$2,000,000
Franchise	400,000	Stockholders' equity:	
		Capital stock	$2,500,000
		Total stockholders' equity	$2,500,000
Total assets	$4,500,000	Total liabilities and stockholders' equity	$4,500,000

Required:
1. Critically evaluate the balance sheet as reported.
2. Indicate any items you feel should be eliminated, revised, or added.
3. What accounting concepts did you use to help you answer part 2 above?

CASE 1-2
L.O. 6

Financial Statement Disclosure

A standard set of financial statements includes change statements that provide details on two specific balance sheet amounts: the statement of cash flows and the statement of retained earnings. Comment on why you believe these amounts are the ones detailed. Why, for example, is there not also a statement of machinery and equipment? *(Hint: Consider the relative importance that different balance sheet amounts have for decision makers.)*

CASE 1-3
L.O. 2

Internal Users versus External Users

All major corporations record their operating assets for financial accounting purposes at their original (historical) costs. Several of these corporations, however, keep track of these same assets' current appraisal values (which may be higher than cost) for managerial decision-making purposes. Comment on this inconsistent practice from the view of the accounting profession.

EVALUATING FINANCIAL STATEMENTS

CASE 1-4
L.O. 4

Financial Statement Examination—Ralston Purina

Examine the annual report for Ralston Purina that is provided in Appendix E at the end of this textbook and give the amounts from the Consolidated Balance Sheet as of September 30, 1989:

1. Cash.
2. Notes payable.
3. Land.
4. Inventories.
5. Machinery and equipment.
6. Long-term debt.
7. Dividends payable.
8. Retained earnings.

CASE 1-5
L.O. 4, 6

Balance Sheet Preparation—IBM

International Business Machines Corporation (IBM) reported the following items in its 1986 annual report dated December 31, 1986 (in millions):

Accounts payable	$ 1,970
Cash	755
Capital stock	?
Loans payable	1,410
Notes and accounts receivable	9,971
Plant and other property	21,268
Other assets	25,820
Other liabilities	20,060
Retained earnings	28,053
Total assets	?
Total liabilities	?
Total stockholders' equity	34,374

Required:
1. Prepare a balance sheet using the above information for IBM for December 31, 1986.
2. Does the company have enough cash to pay the accounts payable? How will they pay these obligations?

CASE 1-6
L.O. 4–6

Balance Sheet Preparation and Analysis—McDonald's

The following summarized balance sheet is for McDonald's Corporation, the nation's leading fast-food chain, at the end of a recent year.

McDonald's Corporation
Balance Sheet
December 31
(in millions)

Assets		**Liabilities and Stockholders' Equity**	
Cash and receivables	$ 364	Liabilities:	
Inventories	38	Accounts payable	$ 461
Investments	182	Taxes and other liabilities	789
Property and equipment	4,878	Long-term debt	2,131
Intangible assets	232	Security deposits by franchisers	81
Other assets	275	Total liabilities	$3,462
		Stockholders' equity:	
		Capital stock	$ 130
		Retained earnings	2,377
		Total stockholders' equity	$2,507
Total assets	$5,969	Total liabilities and stockholders' equity	$5,969

The liability identified as *Security deposits by franchisers* represents advance payments for services to be received in the future by franchisers who are planning to open new McDonald's restaurants. In the month after this balance sheet was reported, assume that McDonald's received additional cash security deposits from future McDonald's restaurant owners of $25 million. At the same time McDonald's purchased new equipment costing $70 million by signing a long-term note for $50 million and paying the other $20 million in cash. Assume no other transactions have occurred since the reported balance sheet.

Required:

1. Prepare the revised balance sheet for McDonald's to reflect the impact of the investing and financing activity described in the problem.
2. Are the shareholders of McDonald's Corporation any better off now than they were at the time the original balance sheet was reported? Briefly explain your answer.

CASE 1-7
L.O. 5

Accounting Equation—Ralston Purina

Refer to the 1989 Ralston Purina Company annual report (Appendix E) and show that the following are true:

1. Change in assets from 1988–1989 = Change in liabilities from 1988–1989 + Change in stockholders' equity from 1988–1989

2. Change in Retained Earnings from 1988–1989 = Net income from income statement − Dividends from Statement of Shareholders' Equity

3. Change in cash + Marketable securities (Ralston's definition of cash) =
   Net cash flow from operations (+ or −)
   Net cash flow from investing activities (+ or −)
   Net cash flow from financing activities (+ or −)
   Effect of exchange rate on cash

APPENDIX CASE

CASE 1-8
L.O. 7

Accounting Environment—the Role of GAAP

General Motors Corporation has reporting responsibilities to many different groups and individuals including the SEC, the IRS, General Motors' current and future stockholders, and the financial institutions that may lend them money in the future.

Required:

1. Discuss the role financial statements based on generally accepted accounting principles play in meeting these reporting responsibilities.
2. What decision-making information does each of these groups likely need that is not provided in GAAP financial statements? How do these decision makers go about getting this other information?

CHAPTER 2

The Relationship between the Balance Sheet and the Income Statement

LEARNING OBJECTIVES

After studying Chapter 2, you should understand:

1. The concepts involved in analyzing balance sheet equation transactions, p. 52.
2. The purpose and use of the accounting equation, p. 53.
3. Revenue and expense measurement and recognition, pp. 53-55.
4. The complete balance sheet equation, pp. 55-57.
5. How to analyze the operating activities of a corporation, pp. 58-60.
6. The matching principle, p. 60.
7. Why adjustments are necessary, p. 65.
8. The distinction between the accrual basis and the cash basis of accounting, pp. 66-69.
9. The purpose of the income statement and its relationship to the balance sheet, p. 69.

The knowledge you acquired in Chapter 1 is background information to help you understand accounting and its function in our society. We also were introduced to some basic relationships found in financial statements, especially the balance sheet equation. While the Chapter 1 discussion on the balance sheet equation is only an introduction, this equation will be of importance to you throughout your study of accounting.

Objective 1
The concepts involved in analyzing balance sheet equation transactions.

As you followed the explanation in Chapter 1 of the effects of financing and investing activities on the balance sheet equation, you were told that a transaction must always keep the equation in balance. When an event changes the dollar amount of one side of the balance sheet equation, the event must also change the other side of the equation by the same dollar amount. This dual effect is the basis for the more complete version of the accounting equation, which you will begin to study in this chapter.

The balance sheet equation introduced in Chapter 1 was:

Assets (A) = Liabilities (L) + Owners' Equity (OE)

The term *owners' equity* in the equation is a broad term, as explained in Chapter 1, used to describe the owners' interests in the business. Except for appendixes, the remainder of this textbook will focus on corporations, whose owners are called *stockholders* or *shareholders.* Therefore, our balance sheet equation will contain the term **stockholders' equity** as follows:

Assets (A) = Liabilities (L) + Stockholders' Equity (SE)

Since the organization of corporations differs from the organization of proprietorships and partnerships, accounting for stockholders' equity is unique in some respects. However, most of the discussion in this and other chapters applies also to proprietorships and partnerships.

This chapter discusses the concepts involved in analyzing transactions, the complete balance sheet equation, and a more in-depth coverage of analyzing the financing, investing, and operating activities of a corporation. After following the effects of transactions for a corporation for an operating period, the chapter concludes with an analysis of the resulting financial statements and their meaning. It is crucial, for a thorough appreciation of accounting, that the goal of analysis and decision making always be kept in mind. Accounting, theory, methods, statements, and policymaking bodies would be meaningless if no relevant information were produced.

THE COMPLETE BALANCE SHEET EQUATION—ADDING REVENUES, EXPENSES, AND RETAINED EARNINGS

Analyzing and recording transactions requires the recognition of changes that business transactions cause in the balance sheet. In the accounting process, these changes involve the double effect of increasing and decreasing dollar amounts according to the equality that was explained earlier. Several possible combinations of increases and decreases are illustrated in Exhibit 2-1.

Earlier, we learned that all accounting transactions affect the dollar amount assigned to some combination of assets, liabilities, and stockholders' equity, even though the totals for any or all of these categories do not necessarily change. We

EXHIBIT 2-1

Possible Combinations of Effects of Transactions on the Balance Sheet Equation

Type of Dual Effect	Balance Sheet Equation Effects				
	A	=	L	+	SE
1. Only assets change:					
Increase one asset	+$100				
Decrease another asset	− 100				
2. Only liabilities change:					
Increase one liability.			+$250		
Decrease another liability			− 250		
3. Increase in assets:					
Increase an asset	+$380				
Increase a liability or stockholders' equity			+$380	or	+$380
4. Decrease in assets:					
Decrease an asset	−$420				
Decrease a liability or stockholders' equity			−$420	or	−$420
5. Other "complex changes," such as:					
Decrease one asset and	−$ 50				
Increase another asset.	+ 100				
Increase a liability or stockholders' equity			+$ 50	or	+$ 50

Objective 2
The purpose and use of the accounting equation.

also saw examples of financing and investing transactions and how they affected the balance sheet. In this chapter, we expand our analysis of transactions to include operating activities. First we expand our definitions of each of these terms:

1. **Financing activities** are those transactions involved with owners and creditors such as issuance of stock, sale of bonds, borrowing from banks and other institutions, payment of dividends to owners, repayment of loans, and other similar transactions.
2. **Investing activities** are those transactions that involve the acquisition or sale of productive assets such as plant, equipment, land, and other assets which are not completely consumed in the current period or offered for sale in the ordinary course of operations.
3. **Operating activities** are those transactions related to providing goods and services to customers, including sales to customers, receipts from customers, payments to suppliers, payments for taxes, payments for wages, the consumption of supplies, the using up of productive assets, and similar transactions.

Objective 3
Revenue and expense measurement and recognition.

Proper accounting for operating activities requires an understanding of revenues and expenses, and how the income statement illustrated in Chapter 1 is related to the changes in the balance sheet. The transactions illustrated in Chapter 1 for TSL were all the result of financing and investing activities; none pertained to operations. Operating transactions give rise to revenues and expenses and are intended to result in an increase in the net assets (assets minus liabilities) of the company although management's plans are not always successfully accomplished. Consider the following definitions of revenues and expenses:

Revenues are increases in net assets (defined as assets minus liabilities) that result from providing goods or services to customers. Revenues usually result in an increase in cash or promises to receive cash from customers.

Expenses are the decreases in net assets that occurred in order to earn revenues. Expenses usually result in decreases in assets or increases in liabilities to workers and suppliers.

These definitions enable us to think of revenues as the rewards of operations in the form of increases in assets, and expenses as the cost of achieving the rewards. If a business is **profitable**, it will have net income (often called *net profits* or *earnings*). All of these terms are used when revenues exceed expenses during a period of time resulting in an increase in net assets due to operating transactions. A **net loss** indicates the opposite; that is, expenses exceeded revenues. The increase in net assets from profitable operations is reflected in the balance sheet by increasing stockholders' equity. The stockholders' equity account that is increased along with the increase in the net assets is called **retained earnings.** To illustrate how the balance sheet reflects profitable operations, consider the examples which follow and their related effect on the balance sheet equation of the Z Company. The initial balance sheet amounts of: Assets = $12,000; Liabilities = $4,000; and Stockholders' Equity = $8,000 are assumed for illustration purposes.

Revenues

A revenue transaction is an operating transaction with an outside entity that increases net assets. For instance, if Z Company sells some goods to a customer and receives $1,000 in cash, that one transaction increases net assets by $1,000 as shown in the following analysis.

Z Company

	Assets	=	*Liabilities*	+	*Stockholders' Equity*
Initial balance	$12,000	=	$4,000	+	$8,000
Operating transaction:					
Revenue—Sale for cash . .	+ **1,000**				+ **1,000**
New balance	$13,000	=	$4,000	+	$9,000

Expenses

The expense from this transaction requires Z Company to provide goods which cost Z Company $800, thereby decreasing net assets:

Z Company

	Assets	=	*Liabilities*	+	*Stockholders' Equity*
Initial balance	$12,000	=	$4,000	+	$8,000
Operating transaction:					
Revenue	+ 1,000				+ 1,000
Expense—Cost of goods sold	− **800**				− **800**
New balance	$12,200	=	$4,000	+	$8,200

Note that the two operating transactions are shown separately with two separate effects, one increases net assets ($1,000) and the other decreases net assets ($800). Their combined effect resulted in an increase of net assets by $200, and $200 of income, which increases stockholders' equity.

Retained Earnings

Retained earnings is a category of stockholders' equity that captures revenue and expense effects and, as we will see below, also dividend effects. Let us expand the balance sheet equation to include the retained earnings category.

Z Company

						Stockholders' Equity		
	Assets	=	*Liabilities*	+	*Paid-in Capital*	+	*Retained Earnings*
Initial balance	$12,000	=	$4,000	+	$5,000		$3,000
Operating transaction:							
Revenue	+ 1,000						+ 1,000
Expense	− 800						− 800
New balance	$12,200	=	$4,000	+	$5,000	+	$3,200

The retained earnings classification of stockholders' equity also captures the effects of paying owners a return on their investment; that is, dividends. In our example, assume that Z Company pays dividends of $100 to owners.

Z Company

	Assets	=	*Liabilities*	+	*Paid-in Capital*	+	*Retained Earnings*
Initial balance	$12,000	=	$4,000	+	$5,000		$3,000
Operating transaction:							
Revenue	+ 1,000						+ 1,000
Expense	− 800						− 800
Financing transaction:							
Dividends	**− 100**						**− 100**
New balance	$12,100	=	$4,000	+	$5,000	+	$3,100

Objective 4
The complete balance sheet equation.

In studying the expanded balance sheet equation given above, note the following:

1. **Stockholders' equity** consists of.
   a. **Paid-in capital** (the amount paid for by owners for stock or capital stock).
   b. Retained earnings.
2. **Retained earnings** consists of the cumulative net effect on stockholders' equity of revenues, expenses, and dividends:
   a. Revenues (R) add to retained earnings.
   b. Expenses (E) reduce retained earnings.
   c. Dividends (D) reduce retained earnings, but dividends are not expenses or operating activities.

Now we can further expand the balance sheet equation as:

$$\text{Assets} = \text{Liabilities} + \overbrace{\text{Stockholders' Equity}}$$

$$\text{Assets} = \text{Liabilities} + \text{Paid-in Capital} + \overbrace{\text{Retained Earnings}}$$

$$\text{Assets} = \text{Liabilities} + \text{Paid-in Capital} + \text{Revenues} - \text{Expenses} - \text{Dividends}$$

or

$$A = L + SE$$

$$A = L + \overbrace{PIC + RE}$$

$$A = L + PIC + \overbrace{(R - E - D)}$$

The following diagram shows the relationship between the balance sheet equation, the operating activities that generate income (revenues and expenses), and dividend payments to stockholders. (Remember that dividend payments are not expenses or operating activities.) Look first at the right-hand column under RE. The excess of revenues over expenses increased retained earnings by $200. This same $200 is shown as an increase in net assets in the left-hand column under A = L. Now go to the right-hand column again and see that the owners were paid a cash dividend of $100. Go back to the left-hand column and note that net assets decreased $100 as a result of the payment of dividends. Note again that the same net money amounts are added and subtracted on both sides of the balance sheet equation.

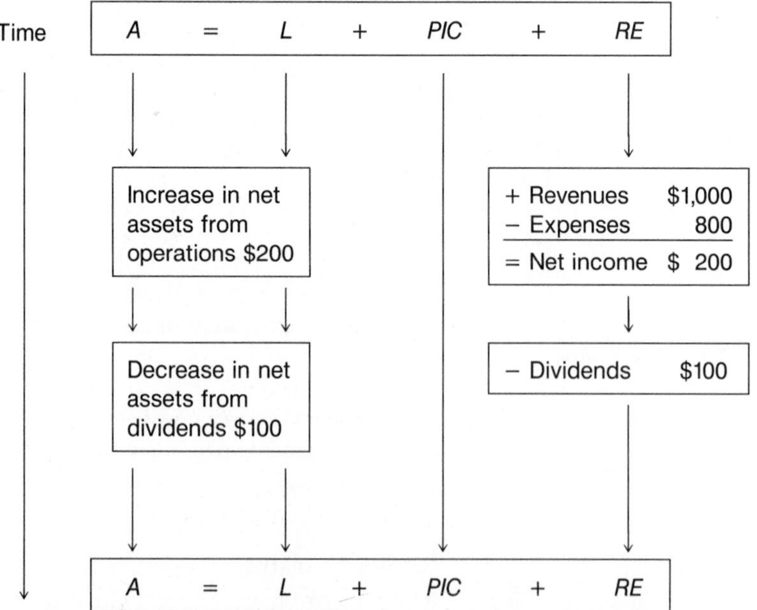

You now can relate the above diagram to Exhibit 2-1, which gave five possible combinations of transactions. The cumulative effect of the $200 increase in net income under RE and the increase in net assets of $200 belong to group 3—increase in assets and increase in stockholders' equity. The dividend decrease under RE of $100 and the decrease in net assets of $100 belong to group 4—decrease in assets and decrease in stockholders' equity. Cash dividends are payments to stockholders that reduce assets and also reduce retained earnings, thus, keeping the balance sheet equation in balance.

Noncash Operating Transactions

Revenue and expense transactions do not necessarily involve cash. To illustrate how cash flows and revenues and expenses may differ, consider the following examples:

	Effects of Transactions on the Balance Sheet Equation				
	A	=	*L*	+	*SE*
Example 1					
In year 1:					
Perform service for promise to receive cash and bill customer for $12 "receivable".	+$12 receivable				+$12 revenue
Collect receivable in cash. . .	−$12 receivable + 12 cash				
Example 2					
In year 1:					
Collect $15 cash from customer for services to be performed later. . . .	+$15 cash		+$15 customer advances		
In year 2:					
Perform service for customer			−$15 customer advances		+$15 revenue

In the first example, the revenue transaction increases retained earnings and an asset. When the customer later pays for the service, one asset (receivable) is decreased while another (cash) is increased by the same amount, $12. No revenue is reported simply from the collection of the receivable.

In the second revenue example, in year 1 a customer gave the company $15 for services to be performed in year 2. At the time the company received the cash advance, the asset cash increased; and because the company had not yet performed the service, an unearned revenue (called *customer advances*) in the liability section of the balance sheet is increased (you will learn more about this later). In year 2, when the service is performed, revenue is recorded as shown in example 2 by decreasing the liability and increasing retained earnings. In both examples, revenue is reported at a different point in time than when cash is received. Revenue need not be accompanied by cash and does not necessarily represent increases in cash when reported.

Since expenses result from an outflow of net assets, we can also reflect expenses with many different types of balance sheet effects, including asset decreases or liability increases. Note the following two examples:

	Effects of Transactions on the Balance Sheet Equation				
	A	=	*L*	+	*SE*
1. An expense that decreases an asset	−$8 stamps				−$8 expense
2. An expense that increases a liability			+$9 advertising payable		−$9 expense

The first expense might be the result of using $8 worth of postage stamps from those stamps on hand. The asset stamps would be decreased by $8, and postage expense would decrease stockholders' equity by $8. The second example might occur when a newspaper advertisement is purchased on account. A liability, advertising payable, would be increased by $9, and advertising expense would decrease stockholders' equity by $9. In both of these examples, the items go directly to expense because we assume their benefits are used up immediately and no future benefits remain. Both examples also involve outflows of net assets which do not affect cash, illustrating that expenses and cash consumption are not synonymous.

More on Operating Activities

Objective 5
How to analyze the operating activities of a corporation.

As we previously stated, operating transactions are those related to customers and suppliers of goods and services used in the pursuit of profits. Revenues and expenses result from operating transactions that increase or decrease net assets. For instance, consider the following four operating transactions:

1. Cash sales	$70
2. Cash expenses	60
3. Purchase of merchandise on credit	30
4. Payment of accounts payable.	20

All are operating transactions but not all represent revenues or expenses; that is, not all have an effect on net assets. Consider the following assumed balance sheet amounts for Robotics Company.

	Assets	=	*Liabilities*	+	*Paid-in Capital*	+	*Retained Earnings*
Initial balances	$100	=	$20	+	$30	+	$ 50

If we reformulate the equation to emphasize net assets, we get:

	Assets	–	*Liabilities*	=	*Paid-in Capital*	+	*Retained Earnings*
Initial balances	$100	–	$20	=	$30	+	$ 50
		Net assets ($ 80)		=Stockholders' equity ($ 80)			

Now, let us analyze the effects of each transaction.

	Assets	–	*Liabilities*	=	*Paid-in Capital*	+	*Retained Earnings*
Initial balances	$100	–	$20	=	$30	+	$ 50
Transaction 1:							
Cash sales	+ 70						+ 70
Balance after sales. . .	$170	–	$20	=	$30	+	$120
	Net assets ($150)			=Stockholders' equity ($150)			

The increase in retained earnings is a revenue because the operating transaction increased net assets.

Transaction 2, the payment of expenses, is also an operating transaction that changes net assets, in this case reducing net assets by $60 as follows:

	Assets	–	*Liabilities*	=	*Paid-in Capital*	+	*Retained Earnings*
Balance after sales. . .	$170	–	$20	=	$30	+	$120
Transaction 2:							
Cash expenses . . .	– 60						– 60
Balance.	$110	–	$20	=	$30	+	$ 60
	Net assets ($ 90)			=Stockholders' equity ($ 90)			

Therefore, the $60 is an expense because it is an operating transaction that reduces net assets, and it is reflected with a negative retained earnings effect.

But, not all operating transactions affect net assets; and, therefore, not all operating transactions are classified as revenues or expenses. For instance, transactions 3 and 4 are operating in that they reflect dealings with suppliers, but as you see below, these transactions have no effect on net assets or on retained earnings.

	Assets	–	*Liabilities*	=	*Paid-in Capital*	+	*Retained Earnings*
Balance after transactions 1 and 2. .	$110	–	$20	=	$30	+	$ 60
Transaction 3:							
Purchase on credit	+ 30		+ 30				
Transaction 4:							
Payment of accounts payable . . .	– 20		– 20				
Balance.	$120	–	$30	=	$30	+	$ 60
	Net assets ($ 90)			=Stockholders' equity ($ 90)			

Recognition of Revenues and Expenses. When the impact of revenue or expense transactions are reported (as in the examples illustrated above for transactions 1 and 2), they are said to be **recognized.** In accounting, to *recognize* simply means to record the effect of an event. Revenue and expense recognition is governed by certain accounting concepts. Before revenues and expenses can be recognized in the accounting records, they must be objectively measurable and meet the following criteria:

1. Revenues must be **realized** or **realizable**.
2. Revenues must be **earned**.

3. Expenses representing the outflow of net assets required to earn the revenue must be objectively **measurable**.

The **realization** of revenues occurs when the resulting inflow of net assets is in the form of cash or some other item that may be converted to a known amount of cash, usually as a promise from a customer to pay cash within some period of time, called **accounts receivable**. When the selling company receives cash, the revenue is realized. When accounts receivable are created, the revenue is considered to be realizable until cash is collected.

Before revenues are recorded, they must be **earned**. Revenues are generally considered to be earned when the business has provided the necessary goods or services that give rise to the revenues. For example, when a business delivers merchandise or provides services to customers, the business is generally considered to have *earned* revenue. As a result, the seller recognizes revenues normally at the time (1) the seller has performed the service and/or delivered the product and (2) the seller has received something of value that has been realized or is realizable.

Expenses are the outflows of net assets given up or **consumed** by the business to produce revenue. Expenses are often determined along with revenues, since revenues seldom occur without accompanying sacrifices or efforts that were necessary to earn revenues.

Objective 6
The matching principle.

The **matching principle** involves the process of relating the benefits from operations (revenues) with the efforts or costs of achieving those benefits (expenses) during an accounting period. The matching process addresses the question: What net assets were given up (consumed) by the business to obtain the recorded revenues (benefits)? Net income is the difference between the revenues and expenses from profit-seeking activities for a period. You will learn more about the matching principle later.

In the next section we see how financing, investing, and operating transactions affect the various balance sheet categories for a company that starts operations and experiences all three types of transactions during the accounting period.

COMPREHENSIVE EXAMPLE: TWIN PINES LABORATORIES

We will examine a series of economic activities that would commonly occur during the initial stages of a corporation's life. Our corporation—Twin Pines Laboratories—was organized as a testing laboratory specializing in technical aerospace instrumentation problems. We will emphasize: (1) the nature of the transaction—financing, investing, or operating; (2) the effect on the balance sheet equation; and (3) the specific increases and decreases in the balance sheet categories that result. As you study each of the following six business transactions of Twin Pines Laboratories, refer to Exhibit 2-2, the spreadsheet analysis for transactions 1 through 6. Later we will analyze transactions 7 through 22 plus adjustments at December 31 to complete the accounting period.

Transaction 1: Financing Activity—Issuance of Stock. On June 10, 19x1, Twin Pines Laboratories issued 2,500 shares of stock to each of four stockholders—a total of 10,000 shares. Each stockholder contributed $50,000—a total initial capital investment of $200,000. Both assets (cash) and stockholders' equity (capital stock) increased $200,000.

EXHIBIT 2-2

Spreadsheet Analysis of Transactions 1 through 6, Twin Pines Laboratories

Twin Pines Laboratories

		Assets				= Liabilities		+ Stockholders' Equity
Date of Event	Transaction No.	Cash	Supplies	Display	Prepaid Rent	Accounts Payable	Notes Payable	Capital Stock
6/10/x1	1	200,000						200,000
6/15/x1	2	−170,000			170,000			
6/21/x1	3			2,500		2,500		
6/25/x1	4		25,000			25,000		
6/29/x1	5	− 2,500				− 2,500		
6/30/x1	6	80,000					80,000	
6/30/x1		107,500	25,000	2,500	170,000	25,000	80,000	200,000
		$305,000				$305,000		

Assets, $305,000 = Liabilities, $105,000 + Stockholders' equity, $200,000

Transaction 2: Operating Activity—Renting Facilities and Equipment. On June 15, 19x1, Twin Pines rented for a year (July 1, 19x1 to June 30, 19x2) office and laboratory facilities for $120,000 and equipment for $50,000—a total of $170,000. This transaction involves the exchange of one asset—cash—for a new asset—prepaid rent. The asset cash is decreased by $170,000, and the $170,000 is used to create the new asset prepaid rent, leaving the balance sheet equation in balance. Prepaid rent represents objectively measurable future benefits controlled by the business for a one-year period, thus enabling Twin Pines to begin operations.

Transaction 3: Investing Activity—Purchasing Advertising Display. Businesses often increase their assets by increasing their liabilities. For example, on June 21, 19x1, Twin Pines purchased an outdoor advertisement from Ingenious Ads Company (IAC) for $2,500 on account. Twin Pines has 30 days to pay IAC for the display. This transaction created a $2,500 liability called *accounts payable* and a $2,500 asset called *display.* Note that net assets (assets minus liabilities) stayed the same; therefore, stockholders' equity remained unchanged at $200,000.

Transaction 4: Operating Activity—Purchasing Supplies on Account. On June 25, 19x1, Twin Pines purchased laboratory supplies for $25,000 from Hooker Supplies on a 30-day account. A new asset, supplies, was created for $25,000; and the liability, accounts payable, increased $25,000 (to $27,500).

Transaction 5: Operating Activity—Paying on Accounts Payable. On June 29, 19x1, Twin Pines paid IAC $2,500. The payment decreased the asset cash $2,500 and decreased the liability accounts payable $2,500.

Transaction 6: Financing Activity—Borrowing from a Bank. On June 30, 19x1, the day before beginning its lab operations, Twin Pines borrowed $80,000 from State Bank, signing a two-year note to repay the loan on June 30, 19x3. The asset cash increased $80,000 (to $107,500), and a new $80,000 liability, notes payable, was created.

Exhibit 2-3 shows the balance sheets of Twin Pines on June 10, 19x1, and June 30, 19x1. As you review the spreadsheet in Exhibit 2-2 and the balance sheets in Exhibit 2-3, note that transactions 2 through 6 did **not** change the initial net asset position of Twin Pines and did **not** result in profits for its owners. No changes in net assets were made despite the fact that the amount of total assets and total liabilities changed several times. To date, no profit was made by Twin Pines because no revenues or expenses have yet to be recorded.

We now resume our example of Twin Pines Laboratories, which works on a number of projects for three different customers between July 1, 19x1, and December 31, 19x1. The transactions that follow pertain to these three projects during that period. The numbering of these transactions begins with transaction 7, following on from transactions 1 through 6.

Date	*Transaction No.*	*Transaction*
19x1		
July 15	7	Purchased $30,000 of supplies on open account.
20	8	Billed client A for project Z-2, $45,000 due in 30 days.
21	9	Billed client B for project Z-X, $80,000 due in 30 days.
26	10	Paid $35,000 on accounts payable.
27	11	Received $50,000 from client B on accounts receivable.
30	12	Paid salaries, $65,000.

EXHIBIT 2-3

Comparison of Twin Pines Laboratories Balance Sheets, June 10, 19x1, and June 30, 19x1

Twin Pines Laboratories
Balance Sheet
June 10, 19x1

Assets		**Stockholders' Equity**	
Cash	$200,000	Capital stock	$200,000
Total assets	$200,000	Total stockholders' equity	$200,000

Twin Pines Laboratories
Balance Sheet
June 30, 19x1

Assets		**Liabilities and Stockholders' Equity**	
Cash	$107,500	Liabilities:	
Supplies	25,000	Accounts payable	$ 25,000
Display	2,500	Notes payable	80,000
Prepaid rent	170,000	Total liabilities	$105,000
		Stockholders' equity:	
		Capital stock	200,000
Total assets	$305,000	Total liabilities and stockholders' equity	$305,000

The effect of these transactions on the balance sheet equation is illustrated in the spreadsheet analysis in Exhibit 2-4. Notice that for transaction 8 (July 20, 19x1), revenue was recognized at the time the client was billed \$45,000, the agreed-upon price for hiring Twin Pines to do the project identified as Z-2. Twin Pines does not have to wait until cash is received to recognize revenue, since the inflow of assets is assumed to be measurable (equal to \$45,000), realizable (collectible from client A), and earned (Twin Pines had completed the work required on project Z-2). As a result, the billing of \$45,000 on July 20, 19x1, and \$80,000 on July 21, 19x1, give rise to revenue, while the collection of cash on July 27, 19x1, simply reduces the asset accounts receivable and increases the asset cash.

Notice also that the balance sheet equation totals given in Exhibit 2-4 maintain the equality, Assets = Liabilities + Paid-in Capital (Capital Stock) + Retained Earnings, after each transaction. The balance sheet totals for July 31, 19x1, are:

Twin Pines Laboratories
Balance Sheet
July 31, 19x1

Assets		**Liabilities and Stockholders' Equity**	
Cash	\$ 57,500	Liabilities:	
Accounts receivable	75,000	Accounts payable	\$ 20,000
Supplies	55,000	Notes payable	80,000
Display	2,500	Total liabilities	\$100,000
Prepaid rent	170,000		
		Stockholders' equity:	
		Capital stock	\$200,000
		Retained earnings	60,000
		Total stockholders' equity	\$260,000
		Total liabilities and	
Total assets	\$360,000	stockholders' equity	\$360,000

EXHIBIT 2-4

Spreadsheet Analysis of Transactions 7 through 12, Twin Pines Laboratories

Twin Pines Laboratories

		Assets					= Liabilities		+ Stockholders' Equity		
										Retained Earnings	
Date of Event	Transaction No.	Cash	Accounts Receivable	Supplies	Display	Prepaid Rent	Accounts Payable	Notes Payable	Capital Stock	Revenues	Expenses
7/1/x1	Bal.	107,500		25,000	2,500	170,000	25,000	80,000	200,000		
7/15/x1	7			30,000			30,000				
7/20/x1	8		45,000							45,000	
7/21/x1	9		80,000							80,000	
7/26/x1	10	− 35,000					−35,000				
7/27/x1	11	50,000	−50,000								
7/30/x1	12	− 65,000									−65,000
										125,000	−65,000
7/31/x1	Bal.	57,500	75,000	55,000	2,500	170,000	20,000	80,000	200,000	60,000	
		\$360,000					\$360,000				

Assets, \$360,000 = Liabilities, \$100,000 + Stockholders' equity, \$260,000

Continuing with the activities of Twin Pines for 19x1, the following transactions occurred:

Date	Transaction No.	Transaction
19x1		
Aug. 1	13	Received $40,000 on accounts receivable.
29	14	Billed clients A and C $120,000 for projects completed to date.
Sept. 15	15	Received $100,000 on accounts receivable.
20	16	Paid salaries, $105,000.
Oct. 20	17	Purchased supplies of $75,000 on account.
31	18	Billed clients A, B, and C $195,000 for projects completed to date.
Nov. 15	19	Received $230,000 on accounts receivable.
28	20	Paid $80,000 on accounts payable.
Dec. 15	21	Paid salaries, $150,000.
30	22	Billed clients A, B, and C $185,000 for projects completed to date.

The results of transactions 13 through 22 are summarized in Exhibit 2-5. Since the balance in retained earnings was zero on July 1, 19x1, and is reported at $305,000 on December 31, 19x1 (Exhibit 2-5), the change in retained earnings resulting from operating activities for the last six months of 19x1 appears to be $305,000. This amount represents net income after the results of transactions with outside parties.

EXHIBIT 2-5

Spreadsheet Analysis of Transactions 13–22, Twin Pines Laboratories

Twin Pines Laboratories

		Assets					=	Liabilities	+	Stockholders' Equity		
											Retained Earnings	
Date of Event	Transaction No.	Cash	Accounts Receivable	Supplies	Display	Prepaid Rent		Accounts Payable	Notes Payable	Capital Stock	Revenues	Expenses
7/31/x1	Bal.	57,500	75,000	55,000	2,500	170,000		20,000	80,000	200,000	125,000	– 65,000
8/1/x1	13	40,000	– 40,000									
8/29/x1	14		120,000								120,000	
9/15/x1	15	100,000	–100,000									
9/20/x1	16	–105,000										–105,000
10/20/x1	17			75,000				75,000				
10/31/x1	18		195,000								195,000	
11/15/x1	19	230,000	–230,000									
11/28/x1	20	– 80,000						–80,000				
12/15/x1	21	–150,000										–150,000
12/30/x1	22		185,000								185,000	
Preliminary balance,											625,000	–320,000
12/31/x1	Bal.	92,500	205,000	130,000	2,500	170,000		15,000	80,000	200,000	305,000	
		$600,000						$600,000				

Assets, $600,000 = Liabilities, $95,000 + Stockholders' equity, $505,000

Adjustments to the Balance Sheet

Objective 7
Why adjustments are necessary.

When the bank loaned Twin Pines $80,000 on June 30, 19x1 (transaction 6), Twin Pines agreed to present to the bank a formal balance sheet as of December 31, 19x1. The preliminary balances in Exhibit 2-5 are summarized in the following balance sheet of December 31, 19x1:

Twin Pines Laboratories
Preliminary Balance Sheet
December 31, 19x1

Assets		**Liabilities and Stockholders' Equity**	
Cash	$ 92,500	Liabilities:	
Accounts receivable	205,000	Accounts payable	$ 15,000
Supplies	130,000	Notes payable	80,000
Display	2,500	Total liabilities	$ 95,000
Prepaid rent	170,000		
		Stockholders' equity:	
		Capital stock	$200,000
		Retained earnings	305,000
		Total stockholders' equity	$505,000
		Total liabilities and	
Total assets	$600,000	stockholders' equity	$600,000

If you compare this balance sheet with the second balance sheet in Exhibit 2-3, you will note that both balance sheets show the item "Prepaid rent, $170,000." Now look at the dates of both balance sheets. The second balance sheet in Exhibit 2-3 is dated June 30, 19x1; the balance sheet above is dated December 31, 19x1. Six months have passed since Twin Pines prepaid one year's rent for its office and laboratory facilities and equipment. Obviously, the asset, prepaid rent, can no longer be valued at $170,000. You must decrease the asset by $85,000 (six months' rent) and increase the expense under retained earnings by $85,000. This leaves a remaining asset value of $85,000 for the next six months' rent (January 1, 19x2, to June 30, 19x2). This is called an **adjustment** because it adjusts the records to reflect certain operating effects. These adjustments which account for activities and transactions that do not directly involve outside parties are explained in the paragraphs that follow.

All the transactions we have considered before the prepaid rent discussion above have been external transactions. **External transactions** are triggered by economic events with outside parties. Usually external transactions are accompanied by the source documents such as sales invoices, purchase orders, checks, and shipping receipts. These transactions involve an exchange between two parties, each of which is looking out for its own best interest. This is called an **arm's length transaction** and it is generally considered that the exchange will be at the fair market value of the item. If this were not so, one of the parties would not agree to the exchange and there would not be a transaction.

The **adjustment** we must make for prepaid rent is called an *internal transaction*. **Internal transactions** are not directly triggered by economic events with outside parties or evidenced by source documents from outside parties. Accountants identify internal transactions by examining the preliminary balances at the end of an accounting period and record the effect needed to correctly state the assets, liabilities, and stockholders' equity of the business.

Some adjustments may be identified by looking at the preliminary balances of the balance sheet and thinking about the definitions of the balance sheet elements—as we did with the prepaid rent of Twin Pines. Other adjustments call for additional information and special procedures. You will learn more about adjustments in Chapter 4.

When we determined that the prepaid rent of Twin Pines was half used up on December 31, 19x1, we reduced the asset, prepaid rent, by one half and we increased expenses shown in retained earnings—to keep the balance sheet equation in balance. We used the matching principle because we were **matching the rent expense with the related period of benefit** (July 1, 19x1, to December 31, 19x1). If we waited until 19x2 to adjust the prepaid rent, the entire $170,000 would become an expense in 19x2 and nothing would have been expensed in 19x1.

We will also make adjustments for three other items that created expenses that must be matched to the revenues reported in 19x1:

- Interest payable for use of $80,000 borrowed on June 30, 19x1, for a six-month period—$4,000.
- Salaries for work performed by lab technicians since the last payday—$47,000.
- The consumption of supplies during the period—$102,000, explained below.

To properly state the balance sheet of Twin Pines on December 31, 19x1, the following four adjustments (labeled *a*, *b*, *c*, and *d*) must be made on December 31, 19x1:

Adjustment Reference	*Adjustments (internal transactions)*
a.	Decrease the asset prepaid rent by $85,000 for one-half year's use of facilities and equipment; decrease retained earnings $85,000 for rent expense.
b.	Increase the liability interest payable by $4,000 for interest owed to date; decrease retained earnings $4,000 for interest expense.
c.	Increase the liability salaries payable by $47,000 for unpaid salaries earned to date; decrease retained earnings $47,000 for salary expense.
d.	Decrease the asset supplies for the amount of supplies used during the period. A count of supplies on hand at the end of 19x1 revealed that $28,000 in supplies remained to be used in future periods. This means that $102,000 of supplies were consumed and should be shown as a reduction of the asset supplies and as an expense.

The spreadsheet analysis shown in Exhibit 2-6 summarizes all of the activities and adjustments for Twin Pines from June 10, 19x1, to December 31, 19x1, the first six months of the company's operations. The resulting balance sheet is shown in Exhibit 2-7.

Objective 8

The distinction between the accrual basis and the cash basis of accounting.

The adjustments that were made above for Twin Pines' first six-month period of operations were necessary according to generally accepted accounting principles (GAAP) and are the result of the accrual basis of accounting. The **accrual basis of accounting** states that revenues must be recorded when they are

EXHIBIT 2-6

Spreadsheet Analysis of All Transactions for 6/10 through 12/31/x1, Twin Pines Laboratories

Twin Pines Laboratories

	Assets					= Liabilities				+ Stockholders' Equity		
Date of Event	*Cash*	*Accounts Receivable*	*Supplies*	*Display*	*Prepaid Rent*	*Accounts Payable*	*Notes Payable*	*Interest Payable*	*Salaries Payable*	*Capital Stock*	*Retained Earnings*	*Explanation*
6/10/x1	200,000									200,000		Initial balance
6/15/x1	−170,000				170,000							Prepay rent
6/21/x1				2,500		2,500						Purchase display
6/25/x1			25,000			25,000						Purchase supplies
6/29/x1	− 2,500					− 2,500						Pay for display
6/30/x1	80,000						80,000					Borrow cash
7/15/x1			30,000			30,000						Purchase supplies
7/20/x1		45,000									45,000 (R)	Project revenue
7/21/x1		80,000									80,000 (R)	Project revenue
7/26/x1	− 35,000					−35,000						Pay for supplies
7/27/x1	50,000	− 50,000										Collect cash
7/30/x1	− 65,000										− 65,000 (E)	Salaries expense
8/1/x1	40,000	− 40,000										Collect cash
8/29/x1		120,000									120,000 (R)	Project revenue
9/15/x1	100,000	−100,000										Collect cash
9/20/x1	−105,000										−105,000 (E)	Salaries expense
10/20/x1			75,000			75,000						Purchase supplies
10/31/x1		195,000									195,000 (R)	Project revenue
11/15/x1	230,000	−230,000										Collect cash
11/28/x1	− 80,000					−80,000						Pay for supplies
12/15/x1	−150,000										−150,000 (E)	Salaries expense
12/30/x1		185,000									185,000 (R)	Project revenue
a.					− 85,000						− 85,000 (E)	Rent expense—facilities and equipment
b.								4,000			− 4,000 (E)	Interest expense
c.									47,000		− 47,000 (E)	Salaries expense
d.			−102,000								−102,000 (E)	Supplies expense
Balances, 12/31/x1	92,500	205,000	28,000	2,500	85,000	15,000	80,000	4,000	47,000	200,000	67,000	

Assets total: $413,000 — Liabilities and Stockholders' Equity total: $413,000

Assets, $413,000 = Liabilities, $146,000 + Stockholders' equity, $267,000

EXHIBIT 2-7

Balance Sheet of Twin Pines Laboratories at December 31, 19x1

Twin Pines Laboratories
Balance Sheet
December 31, 19x1

Assets		**Liabilities and Stockholders' Equity**	
Cash	$ 92,500	Liabilities:	
Accounts receivable	205,000	Accounts payable	$ 15,000
Supplies	28,000	Notes payable	80,000
Display	2,500	Interest payable	4,000
Prepaid rent	85,000	Salaries payable	47,000
		Total liabilities	$146,000
		Stockholders' equity:	
		Capital stock	$200,000
		Retained earnings	67,000
		Total stockholders' equity	$267,000
Total assets	$413,000	Total liabilities and stockholders' equity	$413,000

earned and expenses must be recorded in the periods that the efforts to achieve income occurred. Thus, if a sale of merchandise is made in December 19x1 but cash is not collected until early 19x2, accrual accounting would recognize the revenue in 19x1, along with the expenses associated with the sale. The asset, accounts receivable, is increased indicating that the money is owed to the business, and a revenue item under retained earnings is increased for an equal dollar figure.

If the sale is not recorded until the business collects the cash, the business would be using the cash basis of accounting. The **cash basis of accounting** is not generally accepted for financial reporting purposes; however, the cash basis is sometimes used for income tax accounting purposes.

Notice how the accrual basis of accounting is used in the Twin Pines example. The revenues and expenses are recognized or recorded as shown in the spreadsheet analysis, and revenue and expense recognition does **not** require the inflow or outflow of cash. When Twin Pines completes the projects, the cash to be received for the projects is recorded as accounts receivable for the amounts billed to their clients, and revenue is recorded in stockholders' equity. Likewise, Twin Pines recognizes expenses for supplies used and year-end unpaid salaries that are not accompanied by cash payments; these are recorded as decreases in the asset supplies and increases in the liability salaries payable, and in keeping with the double-entry accounting system, equal amounts of expense are recorded in the stockholders' equity section. None of these changes would be recorded on a strict cash basis of accounting.

As a final note, we should realize that many end-of-period adjustments are made automatically in computerized information systems. The timing and amount of many adjustments, including adjustments to record interest, unpaid wages, and reductions in prepaid expenses and supplies, can be anticipated at the time of the original transaction. As a result, these adjustments can be programmed into the computer at the date of the original transaction and made automatically at the end of the accounting period.

Income Statement

Objective 9
The purpose of the income statement and its relationship to the balance sheet.

The revenues and expenses identified in the "Retained Earnings" column of the spreadsheet analysis in Exhibit 2-6 represent the benefits (revenues) and costs (expenses) of the first six months of laboratory operations for Twin Pines. Since financial statement users are very concerned with the operating performance of a business, operating results are reported in a separate financial statement called the **income statement.**

The formal income statement provides a more convenient summary of the operating activities than the spreadsheet analysis. The income statement of Twin Pines for the six months ended December 31, 19x1, would be:

Twin Pines Laboratories
Income Statement
For the Six Months Ended December 31, 19x1

Project revenues		$625,000
Less expenses		
Salary expense	$367,000	
Supplies expense	102,000	
Rent expense	85,000	
Interest expense	4,000	
Total expenses		558,000
Net income		$ 67,000

Note that the income statement does not report the effects of financing or investing activities (e.g., borrowing money or buying land) that occurred during the six-month period.

The income statement and the balance sheet are both widely used formal financial statements. While the balance sheet provides a **snapshot of the financial position of a business at a point in time,** the income statement describes the operating transactions called **revenues and expenses that were experienced over a period of time.**

Exhibit 2-8 shows the relationship of the income statement and the balance sheet for Twin Pines for the period July 1, 19x1, to December 31, 19x1, in which only operating transactions took place. You can see that the $67,000 increase in net assets from the profitable operations is matched in the balance sheet equation by an increase of $67,000 in the stockholders' equity heading "Retained Earnings." Hence, the increase in retained earnings represents the increase in net assets from profit-seeking transactions that have been retained in the business for future use. In this example, we have no dividends which decrease both net assets and retained earnings. The amount of the increase in retained earnings is also reflected in increases in net assets in the balance sheet. Remember that net assets equal assets minus liabilities; and, therefore, net income which increases retained earnings also increases the net assets. In the Twin Pines example, the increase in net assets from $200,000 on July 1 to $267,000 on December 31 is the basis for the $67,000 amount in retained earnings.

Cash Flow Analysis of Twin Pines Laboratories' Results

Consider the following conversation between the president of Twin Pines Labs (a biochemist) and his chief accountant, which took place after the president received the financial statements, the balance sheet in Exhibit 2-7, and the income statement shown above.

EXHIBIT 2-8

Relationship of Net Income to Change in Net Assets and Retained Earnings

Twin Pines Laboratories
($000)

	Net Assets				*Stockholders' Equity*			
	Assets	–	*Liabilities*		*Capital Stock*	+	*Retained Earnings*	
	305	–	105	=	200	+	0	
Net assets (A – L), 7/1/x1		200				200		Total owners' equity, 7/1/x1
Operating activities— Effect on net assets: Net income, 7/1–12/31		+ 67				+ 67		Operating activities— Effect on owners' equity: Net income, 7/1–12/31
Net assets (A – L), 12/31/x1		267		=		267		Total owners' equity, 12/31/x1
	413	–	146	=	200	+	67	
	Assets	–	Liabilities	=	Capital stock	+	Retained earnings	

President: I want to fully understand the meaning of these financial statements; the real economic results for the period. How did each kind of activity affect our cash and net income?

Accountant: O.K., first let's talk about the three major categories of activities: financing, investing, and operating. Under financing, we issued stock and got a bank loan. Those transactions increased our total assets by $280,000.

President: Yes, but your balance sheet here shows assets of $413,000.

Accountant: Well, we also generated assets by earning net income of $67,000, and by, in essence, borrowing from our workers and suppliers another $66,000. Notice that we show three liabilities other than the note—accounts payable of $15,000, interest payable of $4,000, and salaries payable of $47,000. Each of these amounts is still owed.

President: Didn't we have any investing transactions?

Accountant: Not much, only the purchase of the display, which didn't affect net income but we paid $2,500 in cash. All of the rest is rented. Our operating activities resulted in net income of $67,000 but we had a negative cash flow from operations of $185,000—mostly because we still have $205,000 of accounts receivable owed us by customers and we prepaid rent of $85,000 that will not be expensed until next period.

President: With all those liabilities, how capable are we of paying them off. I only see cash of $92,500.

Accountant: Keep in mind we have a healthy $205,000 in receivables from customers, which should come in soon. So, our ability to pay is very good.

This conversation, though a bit rambling, is an example of the task accountants have in translating their statements into a language that is understood by nonaccountants.

Now consider a more rigorous analysis of the transactions that affected Twin Pines' cash. There were two financing transactions which had the following effects on cash:

Financing Activity	*Cash Effect*
Issued stock for cash.	+$200,000
Borrowed from bank	+ 80,000
Cash from financing activities	+$280,000

Note that income was not affected by these transactions, but cash increased by $280,000. The only investing activity during the period was the purchase of the display for $2,500 on credit and the subsequent payment of that amount:

Investing Activity	*Cash Effect*
Purchased display on credit.	$ 0
Paid the liability	− 2,500
Cash used by investing activities	−$ 2,500

Operating activity involved transactions with several external parties—customers, owners of rented building and equipment, suppliers, and workers, and several adjustments related to supplies consumed, unpaid salaries, recognition of prepaid rent used, and unpaid interest.

Operating Activity	*Cash Effect*
Sales on credit	$ 0
Received cash from customers	+ 420,000
Payment for rental of building and equipment . .	− 170,000
Adjustment to record rent expense.	0
Purchased supplies on credit	0
Payment to suppliers	− 115,000
Adjustment to record supplies used	0
Payment of salaries	− 320,000
Adjustment for unpaid salaries	0
Adjustment for unpaid interest.	0
Cash used by operating activities	−$185,000

Note that although net income is $67,000, the cash from operating activities was a negative $185,000.

Putting all three activities together gives a summary cash flow analysis:

	Cash Effect
Beginning cash amount	$ 0
Financing activities	+ 280,000
Investing activities	− 2,500
Operating activities	− 185,000
Ending cash amount, 12/31/x1.	$ 92,500

This type of analysis will be covered in detail in Chapter 14.

SUMMARY

This chapter illustrates that many aspects of accounting work together to provide external and internal users with financial statements—particularly the balance sheet and income statement. Again, as in Chapter 1, the balance sheet equation is highlighted as a major foundation of accounting. Just looking at the following complete balance sheet equation used by corporations should remind you of the contents of this chapter.

$$\text{Assets} = \text{Liabilities} + \text{Stockholders' Equity} \qquad (1)$$

$$\text{Assets} = \text{Liabilities} + \text{Paid-in Capital} + \text{Retained Earnings} \qquad (2)$$

$$\text{Assets} = \text{Liabilities} + \text{Paid-in Capital} + \text{Revenues} - \text{Expenses} - \text{Dividends} \qquad (3)$$

Before you analyze balance sheet equation transactions, you should understand some of the basic concepts and principles underlying the accounting model. In this chapter, we discussed how revenue recognition, the matching principle, and the accrual basis of accounting help us measure the assets, liabilities, and stockholders' equity (including revenues and expenses) of the business entity. These concepts will be further illustrated in the next two chapters.

From formula 2 you know that the stockholders' equity of a corporation contains paid-in capital (capital stock), which was invested by the stockholders, and retained earnings, which is further divided in formula 3 into revenues, expenses, and dividends.

If you change the first formula, you can see how the residual interest of the stockholders is equal to the net assets (assets minus liabilities) of the business:

$$\text{Assets} - \text{Liabilities} = \text{Stockholders' Equity}$$

$$\text{Net Assets} = \text{Stockholders' Equity}$$

From this last formula, you should try to understand that when operating transactions provide revenues, the result is an increase in net assets (i.e., selling goods and services to customers). Alternatively, when operating transactions cause net assets to decrease (i.e., assets being used up or liabilities being increased), the result is *expenses.* Because revenues and expenses are a part of retained earnings, you can see how revenues (increases in net assets) add to retained earnings and expenses (decreases in net assets) reduce retained earnings. In this way, you can describe the operating activities of a business in terms of their effect on the balance sheet equation. Dividends also reduce retained earnings, but dividends are unique in that they are not expenses or operating activities. Dividends return some of the profits of the business to the stockholders. The possible combinations of balance sheet equation increases and decreases given in the chapter will guide you in future chapters where you are called on to analyze business transactions.

The chapter concluded with the income statement—a summary of the operating activities of a business. The income statement shows how operating activities affect retained earnings on the balance sheet. Throughout the chapter, the financing and investing activities of a business were contrasted with the operating activities of a business. The overall picture of accounting relationships presented in this chapter will provide an important background for the chapters that follow.

DEMONSTRATION EXERCISE

WFT Tax Services, Inc., has the following balance sheet at December 31, 19x1:

WFT Tax Services, Inc.
Balance Sheet
December 31, 19x1

Assets		**Liabilities and Stockholders' Equity**	
Cash	$ 4,100	Liabilities:	
Accounts receivable	1,650	Accounts payable	$ 1,200
Note receivable	2,000	Total liabilities	$ 1,200
Prepaid rent	3,600		
Prepaid insurance	1,800	Stockholders' equity:	
		Capital stock	$10,000
		Retained earnings	1,950
		Total stockholders' equity	$11,950
Total assets	$13,150	Total liabilities and stockholders' equity	$13,150

During January 19x2, the following transactions and adjustments occurred:

1. Recorded cash sales of $3,515 and credit sales of $5,210. Also collected $4,950 from customers' accounts during the month.
2. Purchased supplies of $560 for cash to be completely consumed during January.
3. Paid tax preparers' salaries of $4,960.
4. Paid the January utility bill of $650 and the telephone bill of $324.
5. Prepaid rent represents three months' rent.
6. Prepaid insurance represents three months' insurance.
7. Interest revenue on the note receivable for the month of January is $30.
8. Unpaid salaries earned through the end of January amount to $575.

Using the spreadsheet analysis format, record the above transactions and prepare an income statement and a balance sheet.

Solution:

WFT Tax Services, Inc.

	Assets						= *Liabilities*		+ *Stockholders' Equity*	
Event	*Cash*	*Accounts Receivable*	*Note Receivable*	*Interest Receivable*	*Prepaid Rent*	*Prepaid Insurance*	*Accounts Payable*	*Salaries Payable*	*Capital Stock*	*Retained Earnings*
1/1/x1	4,100	1,650	2,000		3,600	1,800	1,200		10,000	1,950
1	3,515	5,210								8,725
	4,950	−4,950								
2	− 560									− 560
3	−4,960									−4,960
4	− 974									− 650
										− 324
5					−1,200					−1,200
6						− 600				− 600
7				30						30
8								575		− 575
1/31/x1	6,071	1,910	2,000	30	2,400	1,200	1,200	575	10,000	1,836

WFT Tax Services, Inc.
Income Statement
For the Month Ended January 31, 19x2

Revenues:		
Preparation revenue	$8,725	
Interest revenue	30	
Total revenues		$8,755
Expenses:		
Salaries expense	$5,535	
Supplies expense	560	
Rent expense	1,200	
Insurance expense	600	
Utilities expense	650	
Communications expense	324	
Total expenses		8,869
Net loss		$ (114)

WFT Tax Services, Inc.
Balance Sheet
January 31, 19x2

Assets:		Liabilities:	
Cash	$ 6,071	Accounts payable	$ 1,200
Accounts receivable	1,910	Salaries payable	575
Note receivable	2,000	Total liabilities	$ 1,775
Interest receivable	30		
Prepaid rent	2,400	Stockholders' Equity:	
Prepaid insurance	1,200	Capital stock	$10,000
		Retained earnings	1,836
		Total stockholders' equity	$11,836
Total assets	$13,611	Total liabilities and stockholders' equity	$13,611

KEY TERMS

Accounts receivable. Promise from a customer to pay cash sometime in the near future.

Accrual basis of accounting. Used for financial statements prepared in accordance with GAAP; records revenues when earned and expenses in periods that the efforts to achieve income occurred and not necessarily when cash flows.

Adjustments. Internal transactions of the business recorded at period end when receivables and payables and previously unrecognized revenues and expenses are recognized.

Arm's length transaction. An exchange between independent parties at fair value of the item(s) exchanged.

Cash basis of accounting. Method of accounting where revenues and expenses are not recognized until cash is received or paid; this method is not generally accepted for financial reporting purposes.

Expenses. Measures of decreases in owners' equity resulting from operating activities. Decreases in net assets that occur in order to earn revenues.

External transactions. Triggered by economic events with outside parties; these events affect the assets, liabilities, and stockholders' equity of the business.

Income statement. Financial statement used to evaluate the operating performance, revenues, and expenses of a business for a period of time.

Internal transactions. Adjustments needed to correctly state the assets, liabilities, and stockholders' equity of the business.

Matching principle. Concept employed by accountants to relate the benefits from operations (revenues) with the efforts or costs (expenses) of achieving these benefits during the accounting period.

Net loss. The excess of expenses over revenues for a period.

Paid-in capital. The amount paid by owners for stock.

Realization. The process by which revenue generates an inflow of cash or other item that can be converted into cash, at which time the revenue is said to be realized.

Recognition. Process of formally incorporating an item into the financial statements as an asset, liability, revenue, expense, or the like; to recognize means to record.

Retained earnings. Describes the cumulative net effect on stockholders' equity of revenues, expenses, and dividends from all prior periods.

Revenues. Measures of increases in owners' equity resulting from operating activities. Operating transactions resulting in net asset increases or inflows; measured at fair market value. Revenues increase stockholders' equity.

Stockholders' equity. Consists of paid-in capital (capital stock) and retained earnings.

SYNONYMS

Adjustments; internal transactions.

Capital stock; paid-in capital; stock.

Historical cost; original cost; fair value at acquisition date.

Income statement; earnings statement.

Net income; net profit; earnings.

Recognize; record.

Revenues; sales.

Stockholders' equity; owners' equity.

QUESTIONS

1. What are the components of stockholders' equity in the most detailed balance sheet equation?
2. How do increases in revenues affect stockholders' equity? Net assets?
3. How do increases in expenses affect stockholders' equity? Net assets?

4. What does the dual effect of transactions on the balance sheet require when a transaction has the effect of decreasing assets by $100?
5. What are financing activities?
6. What are investing activities?
7. What are operating activities?
8. Give two examples of financing activities that increase assets.
9. Give two examples of investing activities and tell what their effect is on total assets.
10. Give two operating activities and explain their effect on total assets and net assets.
11. What are revenues? Give an example and discuss its cash flow effects.
12. What are expenses? Give an example and discuss its cash flow effects.
13. When are revenues recorded?
14. Describe how revenues and expenses affect the balance sheet equation.
15. Who receives dividends? Out of what category are dividends paid?
16. Differentiate between operating and nonoperating transactions.
17. How do internal transactions, or adjustments, differ from external transactions?
18. How is the matching process related to the accrual basis of accounting?
19. How does the cash basis of accounting differ from the accrual basis of accounting?
20. Discuss why the information found on an income statement cannot be gotten off a balance sheet and a statement of cash flows.

EXERCISES

EXERCISE 2-1

L.O. 1

Concepts

1. Revenue recognition requires that:
   a. The revenues must be earned.
   b. The revenues are received in cash or some other asset, such as an account receivable, that can be converted to cash.
   c. The revenues must be realized or realizable.
   d. All of the above.
   e. None of the above.
2. The matching principle—
   a. Involves analysis of which costs were used up (consumed) in the process of earning the revenues reported for the period.
   b. Compares the cash received with the cash paid for goods and services.
   c. Calls for the measurement of net assets given up to obtain the net assets received or receivable from operating transactions.
   d. All of the above.
   e. Only (*a*) and (*c*) are correct.
3. Which of the following is accounted for differently under the cash and accrual bases of accounting?
   a. Receive cash from sale of merchandise to customer.
   b. Pay for services received.
   c. Prepay rent for two years.
   d. Pay salaries in cash.
   e. None of the above.
4. What tasks are required at the end of an accounting period in order to achieve the accrual basis of accounting?
   a. Investing activities.
   b. Dividend decisions.
   c. Adjustments (internal transactions).
   d. Financing activities.
   e. All of the above.

5. In the balance sheet equation, an increase in an asset—
   a. May be accompanied by an increase in a liability.
   b. May be accompanied by a decrease in an asset.
   c. May be accompanied by an increase in revenues.
   d. May be accompanied by an increase in paid-in capital.
   e. All of the above.

EXERCISE 2-2
L.O. 3, 6

Types of Business Transactions

The following business transactions occurred during the current accounting period:

a. Sold additional stock to shareholders for cash.
b. Purchased merchandise for sale to customers on account from a supplier.
c. Purchased new showcases for displaying merchandise to customers.
d. Borrowed cash from bank by signing a note due in monthly installments over the next three years.
e. Purchased a delivery van for cash.
f. Sold merchandise to customers on account.
g. Collected cash from customers owing money on their accounts.

Required:
Indicate whether each of the transactions described above is an operating, financing, or investing activity.

EXERCISE 2-3
L.O. 2

Asset and Liability Recognition

In each of the items below, determine if an asset, liability, or stockholders' equity should be recognized. If so, describe the elements of the balance sheet that are affected and the amount.

a. A famous actor contracts to be the company spokesperson for future compensation payments.
b. A landlord is paid $2,000 for the next quarter's rent.
c. First National Bank lends the company $50,000.
d. A malpractice suit is brought against a doctor. The outcome amount is unknown.
e. Shares of capital stock are sold to investors for $44,000.

EXERCISE 2-4
L.O. 2, 3

Stockholders' Equity

On April 1, 19xx, Bumbling, Inc., declares bankruptcy and reports the following balance sheet:

Bumbling, Inc.
Balance Sheet
April 1, 19xx

Assets		**Liabilities and Stockholders' Equity**	
Cash	$ 412	Liabilities:	
Accounts receivable	15,770	Accounts payable	$ 4,822
Supplies	914	Notes payable	10,000
		Total liabilities	$14,822
		Stockholders' equity:	
		Capital stock	$ 5,000
		Retained earnings	(2,726)
		Total stockholders' equity	$ 2,274
Total assets	$17,096	Total liabilities and stockholders' equity	$17,096

Required:
Determine the stockholders' interest in this company and explain what this amount relates to.

EXERCISE 2-5
L.O. 3

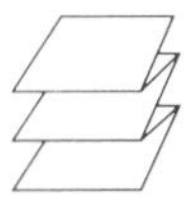

Balance Sheet Elements

Classify the following items as to whether they are assets (A), liabilities (L), or stockholders' equity (SE). If they are part of SE, tell whether they are stock (S), revenues (R), expenses (E), or dividends (D).

_______ *a.* Notes receivable.
_______ *b.* Cash.
_______ *c.* Inventory.
_______ *d.* Supplies.
_______ *e.* Capital stock.
_______ *f.* Dividends payable.
_______ *g.* Unearned revenue.
_______ *h.* Consulting fees.
_______ *i.* Salaries expense.
_______ *j.* Interest payable.
_______ *k.* Accounts receivable.
_______ *l.* Accounts payable.
_______ *m.* Dividends.

EXERCISE 2-6
L.O. 3

Determining Retained Earnings

On January 1, 19xx, FBON, Inc., had a $400,000 balance in Retained Earnings. During 19xx, FBON earned income of $50,000 and declared and paid dividends of $20,000. Also, FBON received cash of $15,000 as an additional investment in stock by its owners. Determine the balance of Retained Earnings on December 31, 19xx.

EXERCISE 2-7
L.O. 3

Balance Sheet Equation

The following information was taken from the financial statements of Aeroquip Corporation:

Total assets at 12/31/x2	$1,700,000
Net income of 19x2	70,000
Total liabilities at 12/31/x1	720,000
Total liabilities at 12/31/x2	650,000
Total assets at 12/31/x1	1,600,000

Required:
What was the apparent amount received by Aeroquip during 19x2 from the sale of Aeroquip stock? No dividends were declared or paid during the year.

EXERCISE 2-8
L.O. 3

Balance Sheet Equation

The following information is available for the Trying Corporation:

Total assets at 12/31/x2.	$250,000
Total liabilities at 12/31/x2.	80,000
Dividends paid during 19x2.	11,000
Total assets at 12/31/x1.	200,000
Net income for 19x2	31,000

No Trying Corporation stock was bought or sold during 19x2.

Required:
Compute the amount of total liabilities on December 31, 19x1.

EXERCISE 2-9
L.O. 3

Balance Sheet Equation

Fill in the missing number.

Cash	$ 5,625
Supplies	915
Accounts receivable	18,746
Equipment	20,000
Land	25,000
Accounts payable	4,669
Notes payable	10,000
Capital stock	50,000
Retained earnings	?

EXERCISE 2-10
L.O. 3

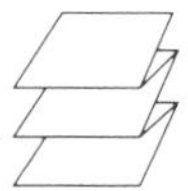

Balance Sheet

Prepare a balance sheet for the DRB Engineering Corporation as of November 30, 19xx, from the following information:

Cash	$ 16,200
Prepaid Rent	25,000
Supplies	5,800
Equipment	140,000
Accounts Receivable	91,500
Accounts Payable	?
Notes Payable	80,000
Capital Stock	120,000
Retained Earnings	41,750

EXERCISE 2-11
L.O. 3, 6

Operating, Investing, and Financing Activities

Baker, Inc., entered into a number of transactions described below. You are to indicate whether each of these transactions is an operating (O), a financing (F), or an investing (I) activity. Note that some transactions may have more than one purpose.

_______ *a.* Sold Baker capital stock to stockholders for cash.
_______ *b.* Sold inventory to customers on open account.
_______ *c.* Purchased equipment for cash.
_______ *d.* Borrowed cash from bank by signing a note payable.
_______ *e.* Provided services to customers for cash.
_______ *f.* Purchased merchandise inventory for cash from suppliers.
_______ *g.* Acquired land in exchange for stock.
_______ *h.* Recorded accrued salaries payable at the end of the accounting period.
_______ *i.* Recorded interest payable on bank loans.

EXERCISE 2-12
L.O. 6, 7

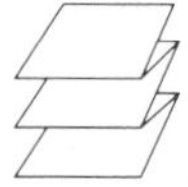

Events or Adjustments

Able Corporation entered into a number of transactions described below. Indicate whether these are transactions with outsiders (T) or adjustments (A) and whether they are investing (I), financing (F), or operating (O) activities.

_______ *a.* Recorded salaries payable at the end of the accounting period.
_______ *b.* Paid accounts payable with cash.
_______ *c.* Borrowed cash from the bank.
_______ *d.* Sold merchandise on open account.
_______ *e.* Recorded interest payable.

________ *f.* Recorded rent expense by reducing the asset prepaid rent.
________ *g.* Received cash for services to be provided by Able next accounting period.
________ *h.* Issued Able capital stock to stockholders.
________ *i.* Paid cash dividends to stockholders.

EXERCISE 2-13
L.O. 7

Matching Principle

At month-end, Katie's Answering Service has the following items:

a. Supplies inventory at the beginning of the month was $500. During the month, Katie's purchased $925 supplies; $315 is now in ending inventory.
b. At the beginning of the month, Katie's paid $52,000 cash to Shosing Realtors for four months' rent.
c. Switchboard operators have earned $5,300 since the last payday as of the end of the month.

Required:
Determine the amount to be recognized as revenue or expense for the month for each item.

EXERCISE 2-14
L.O. 8

Income Statement

Prepare an income statement for Schafer Electronics Corporation for the quarter ending March 31, 19xx, from the following information:

Interest Revenue	$ 5,000
Rent Expense	18,000
Salaries Expense.	32,000
Supplies Expense	2,100
Advertising Expense	12,000
Utilities Expense	10,000
Insurance Expense	6,000
Service Revenue	81,000

PROBLEMS

PROBLEM 2-1
L.O. 1

Concepts

For each statement below, identify the name of the principle or term described.

1. The process accountants go through to relate the benefits from operations with the efforts or costs of achieving these benefits.
2. Holds that revenue should be recognized in the period earned rather than when cash is received.
3. Triggered by economic events with outside parties.
4. Operating transactions resulting in net asset increases or inflows.
5. Formally incorporating an item into the financial statements as a component of assets, liabilities, and stockholders' equity.
6. Excess of revenues over expenses.
7. Recording events at their original transaction value.

PROBLEM 2-2
L.O. 2

Asset Valuation

In some transactions it appears as though the value of assets given equals the value of assets received, while in other transactions they do not seem to be equal. Consider the following transactions:

a. Company X purchases slippers for $8 a pair from a supplier and then sells them to customers for $18 a pair.
b. Company B sells land valued at $10,000 to Company J in exchange for stock with a market value of $10,000.

Required:
1. Are both transactions based on the fair value of the assets given and/or received? Explain.
2. Are both transactions considered arm's length?
3. In transaction (*a*) above, what is the fair market value of a pair of slippers at the date of purchase from the viewpoint of Company X?

PROBLEM 2-3
L.O. 3

Balance Sheet Equation; Net Assets from Operations

Assume the following balance sheet data are taken from three different companies after considering all transactions and adjustments (including stock and dividend transactions):

	Company A	*Company B*	*Company C*
Balance sheet data:			
Total assets, 1/1/xx	$100,000	$720,000	$380,000
Total assets, 12/31/xx	250,000	680,000	390,000
Total liabilities, 1/1/xx.	60,000	530,000	100,000
Total liabilities, 12/31/xx	130,000	450,000	140,000
Additional facts:			
Capital stock sold for cash in 19xx	50,000	50,000	40,000
Dividends declared and paid in cash in 19xx	10,000	20,000	0

Required:
Compute the increase or decrease in net assets for 19xx attributable to the operations (net income) of each company. How do your answers differ from the net income for each company.

PROBLEM 2-4
L.O. 3

Balance Sheet Equation; Net Income and Net Loss

Assume the following balance sheet data are the same for four different companies after considering all transactions and adjustments (including stock and dividend transactions):

	Total Assets	*Total Liabilities*
Beginning of the year	$ 85,000	$20,000
End of the year	100,000	10,000

Additional information that is already included in the amounts reported above for each company is as follows:

Company A: The company did not issue any additional stock and did not declare any dividends.

Company B: The company did not issue any additional stock but declared and paid dividends of $11,000.

Company C: The company issued $28,000 of additional stock but did not declare any dividends.

Company D: The company issued $10,000 of additional stock and declared dividends of $18,000.

Required:
On the basis of the above data, calculate the net income or net loss of each company for the year.

PROBLEM 2-5
L.O. 2, 6

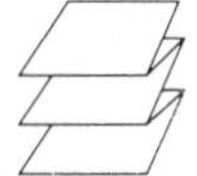

Transaction Analysis

During the month of September 19x1, the Winwood Realty Corporation completed the following transactions:

a. Purchased office supplies for inventory on account.
b. Paid rent for October.
c. Issued additional capital stock, receiving cash.
d. Recorded salaries paid to employees during the month.
e. Paid various office expenses incurred during September.
f. Earned service revenue, receiving cash.
g. Paid the amount owed to the vendor for the office supplies purchased in (*a*) above.
h. Used half of the supplies purchased in (*a*) above.
i. Declared and paid cash dividends to stockholders.
j. Paid interest due for September for a note payable to the bank.

Required:
Indicate the effect of each transaction on the balance sheet equation by the appropriate number from the following list:

1. Increase in one asset, decrease in another asset.
2. Increase in an asset, increase in a liability.
3. Increase in an asset, increase in stockholders' equity.
4. Decrease in an asset, decrease in a liability.
5. Decrease in an asset, decrease in stockholders' equity.

PROBLEM 2-6
L.O. 3, 6, 8

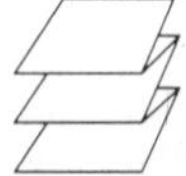

Preparing Financial Statements

On January 2, 19x5, your first day on the job as accountant for Young Corporation, you are given the following list of balance sheet and income statement items. You are told that all appropriate adjustments have been made as of December 31, 19x4, and that no transactions occurred on January 1.

Accounts payable	$ 22
Prepaid expenses	9
Service revenue received in advance	13
Inventory	46
Capital stock	90
Advertising expense	18
Sales revenue	254
Cash	15
Rent expense—facilities	49
Prepaid rent—facilities	72
Service revenue	42
Utilities expense	7

Salaries expense	54
Cost of goods sold	163
Notes payable	74
Accounts receivable	36
Retained earnings, 12/31/x1	13
Land	39

Assume that all of the balances given in the data above are normal and correct.

Required:

1. Prepare an income statement for 19x4.
2. Compute the amount to be reported in retained earnings as of December 31, 19x4.
3. Prepare a balance sheet as of December 31, 19x4.

PROBLEM 2-7
L.O. 4–8

Event Analysis

The Duotech Corporation reported the following balance sheet data at the end of 19x1:

Duotech Corporation
Balance Sheet
December 31, 19x1
(in millions)

Assets		**Liabilities and Stockholders' Equity**	
Cash	$ 19	Liabilities:	
Accounts receivable	22	Accounts payable	$ 20
Prepaid expenses	15	Income taxes payable	9
Inventory	31	Notes payable	75
Building	177	Total liabilities	$104
Land	20		
		Stockholders' equity:	
		Capital stock	$160
		Retained earnings	20
		Total stockholders' equity	$180
Total assets	$284	Total liabilities and stockholders' equity	$284

The following transactions (in millions) occurred during January 19x2:

a. Collected accounts receivable of $17.
b. Sold inventory costing $22 for $60 on account.
c. Purchased inventory costing $20 on account.
d. Paid income taxes payable of $9 in cash.
e. Paid accounts payable of $18 in cash.
f. Paid selling and administrative expenses of $5 in cash.
g. Collected accounts receivable of $35.

During January, Duotech used $8 of the prepaid expenses.

Required:

1. Using a spreadsheet analysis like that illustrated in Exhibit 2-6 (page 67), prepare a summary of the January transactions for Duotech.
2. Prepare an income statement for January 19x2 and the January 31, 19x2, balance sheet.

PROBLEM 2-8
L.O. 4–8

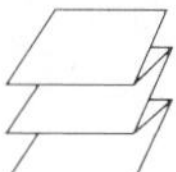

Event Analysis

Technavest, Inc., began operations in 19x1. During 19x1, the following transactions occurred (all amounts are in thousands):

19x1
Oct. 12 Sold Technavest stock for $200 cash.
15 Purchased computers for $80 on open account.
23 Rented facilities and equipment for one year starting November 1, 19x1, for $24 cash.
28 Purchased office supplies for $8 cash.
Nov. 1 Open for business.
15 Sold computers costing $25 for $38 on open account.
20 Borrowed $50 from bank for a two-year note.
22 Paid cash of $16 on accounts payable.
28 Collected cash of $32 on accounts receivable.
30 Paid salaries of $40 in cash.
Dec. 5 Sold computers costing $55 for $89 on open account.
6 Purchased computers for $95 on open account.
16 Paid advertising bill of $2 in cash.
18 Sold computers costing $63 for $115 on open account.
19 Paid salaries of $32 in cash.
22 Collected $150 on accounts receivable.
23 Paid accounts payable of $80 in cash.
25 Closed for holidays until next year.

Additional Data:
As of the end of the year, the following adjustments were needed:

a. Recognize rent expense.
b. Recognize unpaid salaries of $9.
c. Recognize unpaid interest on note of $1.
d. Recognize unused office supplies on hand at year-end of $5.

Required:
1. Using a spreadsheet analysis like the one illustrated in Exhibit 2-6 (page 67), prepare a summary of the transactions described in the problem.
2. Prepare an income statement for 19x1 and a balance sheet for Technavest at December 31, 19x1.

PROBLEM 2-9
L.O. 4–8

Event Analysis

The Dual Peaks Corporation started business in 19x1. The following transactions occurred:

19x1
Mar. 1 Sold Dual Peaks stock for $600,000 in cash.
15 Purchased land for $75,000 cash.
15 Rented a building by signing a one-year lease. Paid $84,000 for the first year's rent to begin May 1, 19x1.
23 Paid $35,000 for the rental of equipment for seven months starting May 1, 19x1.
31 Hired two managers to run business at an annual salary of $90,000 each.
31 Borrowed $30,000 from the local bank.
Apr. 10 Paid $16,000 cash for radio advertisements in April and May announcing grand opening.
15 Acquired $42,000 in inventory on open account.
18 Returned $3,000 in inventory for credit.
24 Purchased investments for $100,000 cash.

May 1 Sold goods costing $20,000 for $38,500 cash.
5 Purchased $60,000 of inventory on open account.
16 Sold goods costing $43,000 for $89,600 on account.
20 Paid $85,000 cash on accounts payable.
21 Purchased $68,000 of inventory on open account.
28 Sold goods costing $52,000 for $112,900 in cash ($47,000) and on open account ($65,900).
30 Collected cash of $63,000 on accounts receivable.
30 Paid wages and salaries of $62,000.

Additional Data:

a. Interest payable on the bank borrowing amounted to $690 as of the end of May.
b. One month's rent on the building and the equipment had expired by the end of May.

Required:

1. Using a spreadsheet analysis like the one illustrated in Exhibit 2-6 (page 67), prepare a summary of the transactions described in the problem. Identify those transactions that are adjusting transactions with an "A."
2. Prepare an income statement for the three months of business and a balance sheet at May 31, 19x1, for Dual Peaks.

PROBLEM 2-10
L.O. 4–8

Event Analysis—General Dynamics

General Dynamics manufactures many different products, including F-16 fighter jets, Tomahawk antiship cruise missiles, M1A1 Abrams Army Tanks, and Trident and Seawolf class submarines. The following balance sheet data are summarized from a recent December 31 annual report.

General Dynamics
Balance Sheet
December 31
(in millions)

Assets		**Liabilities and Stockholders' Equity**	
Cash	$ 195	Liabilities:	
Receivables	1,948	Current liabilities	$ 820
Inventory	380	Long-term liabilities	2,468
Property, plant, and equipment	1,364	Total liabilities	$3,288
Other assets	665	Stockholders' equity:	
		Paid-in capital	$ 80
		Retained earnings	1,184
		Total stockholders' equity	$1,264
Total assets	$4,552	Total liabilities and stockholders' equity	$4,552

Assume that the following items summarize the operations during January following the balance sheet data above (amounts in millions):

a. Military equipment carried in inventory at $300 was sold on account for $2,000.
b. Collected $2,548 cash from the U.S. government on accounts receivable.
c. Used up equipment costing $44 during the month of January (record as an expense).
d. Paid salaries of $757 in January.
e. Paid accounts payable of $163 in January.

f. Paid other current liabilities of $650 in January.
g. Prepaid expenses for rent of $42, included in "Other Assets," expired during the month of January.
h. Accrued salaries at the end of January were $187.
i. Accrued other liabilities (primarily for interest expense and income tax expense) at the end of January were $456.
j. Dividends of $200 were declared and paid in cash during January.

Required:

1. Using a spreadsheet analysis like the one illustrated in Exhibit 2-6 (page 67), fill in the beginning balances from the December 31 balance sheet and then prepare a summary of the effect of the data items above from January on the balance sheet equation. Compute ending balances in all balance sheet columns in the spreadsheet.
2. Prepare the January income statement and retained earnings statement, and the balance sheet as of January 31.

PROBLEM 2-11 Financial Statement Adjustments

L.O. 7, 8

The following financial statements were prepared by the Farber Company's accounting clerk:

Farber Company
Balance Sheet
December 31, 19x1

Assets:		Liabilities:	
Cash	$ 8,500	Accounts payable	$12,160
Accounts receivable	14,080	Revenue received in advance	1,200
Supplies	5,710	Note payable	22,540
Prepaid insurance	3,620	Total liabilities	$35,900
Building	45,900		
Land	20,000	Stockholders' equity:	
		Capital stock	$22,000
		Retained earnings	39,910
		Total stockholders' equity	$61,910
Total assets	$97,810	Total liabilities and stockholders' equity	$97,810

Farber Company
Income Statement
For Year Ended December 31, 19x1

Revenues		$184,350
Expenses:		
Cost of goods sold	$98,480	
Selling and administrative	30,700	
Salaries	42,160	
Total expenses		171,340
Net income		$ 13,010

In discussing these statements with the president of the company you learn that the following items have not been recorded:

a. Interest payable on the note for the year is $2,200.
b. The prepaid insurance was for a two-year policy and one year of it has expired.

c. Supplies of $3,000 remain in the supplies storeroom.
d. Three new trucks were ordered on January 1, 19x2, to be delivered in April at a cost of $22,000 each.
e. Salaries payable for work performed since the December 21, 19x1, payday is $1,800.
f. One half the revenue received in advance has been earned.

Required:

1. Discuss the adjustments indicated by the additional information supplied by the president.
2. Prepare a revised balance sheet and a revised income statement for Farber Company.

PROBLEM 2-12
L.O. 3, 4, 8

Balance Sheet Equation: Revenues and Expenses

Assume the following amounts are taken from the financial statements of three different companies:

	Co. A	*Co. B*	*Co. C*
Total assets, 1/1/xx	$440,000	$560,000	$668,000
Total assets, 12/31/xx	490,000	654,000	568,000
Total liabilities, 1/1/xx	250,000	203,000	316,000
Total liabilities, 12/31/xx	280,000	230,000	?
Total stockholders' equity, 1/1/xx	190,000	?	352,000
Total stockholders' equity, 12/31/xx	?	424,000	326,000

Required:

1. Company A had revenues for 19xx of $412,000, expenses of $397,000 and did not pay any dividends. What amount of capital stock was sold in 19xx?
2. Company B had revenues for 19xx of $748,000, sold $25,000 worth of stock, and paid $12,000 in dividends. What were expenses in 19xx?
3. Company C sold $20,000 worth of stock, paid no dividends, and had $593,000 in expenses in 19xx. What were revenues in 19xx?

PROBLEM 2-13
L.O. 3, 4, 8

Preparation of Financial Statements

PC Sales and Service, Inc., started business in early 19x1. The corporation initially raised capital by selling $100,000 in stock to a group of 10 investors. The managers then signed a one-year lease on a retail building to begin on March 1, 19x1, for $4,000 per month. They paid a year's rent in advance. Inventory was purchased and operations were started on March 1, 19x1. Sales were made on account to 17 customers during March. At the end of March, the firm had $34,700 in cash and owed the bank $10,000 on a note taken out on March 15. Full payment had been received from all customers except for the most recent sale of $12,000. In addition, $1,000 in down payments had been received from customers waiting for a new unit that will be available in June. An inventory of $58,500 is on hand on which a $25,000 payment is still owed to the supplier. Sales totaled $102,000 for the month and Cost of Goods Sold totaled $76,500. Salaries, advertising, and utilities totaled $8,300, all of which were paid in cash. Interest of $50 is owed to the bank for the note.

Required:

1. Prepare a balance sheet at March 31, 19x1, for PC Sales and Service, Inc.
2. Prepare an income statement for the month ended March 31, 19x1.
3. What would sales revenue be under the cash basis of accounting?

PROBLEM 2-14
L.O. 4

Revenue/Expense Recognition

Arnwood Machine Company produces special metalworking machines on order for its customers. The following transactions occurred during the month of December 19x1:

a. Received $20,000 as a down payment on a machine to be delivered next summer.
b. Purchased on account $5,000 of special supplies for January work.
c. Paid $17,000 to the factory workers for December employment.
d. Advanced $6,000 to salespersons for sales commissions expected to be earned on January 19x2 sales.
e. Received $12,000 from Buck Company in payment for three machines to be delivered during 19x2.
f. Paid $27,000 to Arnwood's steel supplier for steel received and used in November 19x1.
g. Received $44,000 payment on account for machines shipped during the prior year.

Required:
For each item listed, indicate whether the amount of any inflow should be recognized as a revenue in the financial statements and whether the amount of any outflow should be recognized as an expense. If the amount should not be recognized, state what else must occur for the revenue or expense to be recognized.

CASES

CASE 2-1
L.O. 1, 2

Measuring Balance Sheet Elements

You have been hired by a bank to examine the balance sheet of a potential borrower. The balance sheet contains the following items (in millions):

Assets:	
Prepaid advertising	$ 1
Land (at estimated fair market value)	15
Famous paintings (at original cost)	35
Estimated value of managerial talent	5
Inventory (at selling price)	46
Investment in stocks (at cost, market value equals $10)	8
Liabilities:	
Cash in bank	2
Notes payable	10
Wages payable	11
Taxes payable	6

Required:
Identify any items that appear to be incorrectly stated from an accounting point of view and indicate the correct treatment in each instance. As a potential lender what information would you like to know about each item.

CASE 2-2
L.O. 8

Comparison of Financial Statements

Discussions occasionally occur in accounting circles about which financial statement is the most useful. Of the four standard statements, select the financial statement you feel is the most useful, and outline the arguments supporting your choice.

CASE 2-3
L.O. 2, 3

Balance Sheet Equation

A newly formed company found itself without much cash in the early days of the business. Therefore, it decided to pay its workers partly with cash and partly with stock in the company. The workers could then sell some of the stock to others if they needed the cash.

Required:

1. What was the effect on the balance sheet of the August 19x1 payroll, which paid \$8,000 to employees in cash and issued \$8,000 in stock to employees for employee wages?
2. What was the effect on the balance sheet of the sale by the employees of \$4,000 of this stock to other investors?

EVALUATING FINANCIAL STATEMENTS

CASE 2-4
L.O. 3

Retained Earnings—Warner-Lambert

Warner-Lambert is a major worldwide company specializing in the development, production, and marketing of health care and consumer products. These products range from prescription and nonprescription pharmaceuticals to chewing gums, razors and blades, and home aquarium products. Warner-Lambert reported the following information in its 1985 statement of consolidated retained earnings (in thousands):

	Year Ended December 31	
	1985	*1984*
Retained earnings at beginning of year	\$1,456,062	\$?
Net income (loss)	?	223,887
Dividends declared	117,248	118,003
Retained earnings at end of year	\$1,023,218	?

Required:
Fill in the missing information and discuss the relationship of the retained earnings balance and the net income amount.

CASE 2-5
L.O. 8

Income Statement Preparation—General Mills

The following information is taken from the 1986 annual report of General Mills, a major competitor in consumer foods, restaurants, and specialty retailing with such familiar products as Cheerios and Hamburger Helper and the Red Lobster restaurant chain (in millions):

Cash	\$ 56.4
Cost of sales	2,563.9
Land	100.9
Interest expense	38.8
Miscellaneous expenses	113.1
Notes payable	4.7
Retained earnings	812.9
Sales	4,586.6
Selling, general, and administrative expenses	1,545.7

Required:
Prepare General Mills' income statement for the year. The statement should be for the year ended May 25, 1986. What effect does net income have on the balance sheet?

CASE 2-6
L.O. 4, 8

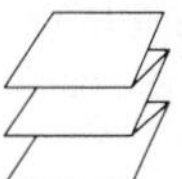

Income Statement—Ralston Purina

Examine the 1989 annual report for Ralston Purina Company provided in Appendix E at the end of this book.

Required:

1. Fill in the following amounts from the financial statements for the year ended September 30, 1989. What effect does net income have on retained earnings and net assets?
   a. Interest expense.
   b. Cost of products sold.
   c. Income tax expense.
   d. Net sales.
   e. Net income.
   f. Selling; general and administrative expense.
   g. Dividends.
   h. Advertising and promotion expense.
2. List Ralston Purina's exact titles for the four major financial statements.

CASE 2-7
L.O. 4

Recognition of Revenue—Dow Jones & Company

Shown below is a condensed version of a recent income statement from Dow Jones & Company, a financial news service firm that publishes, among other things, *The Wall Street Journal.*

Dow Jones & Company
Statement of Income
For the Year Ended Dec. 31
(in thousands)

Revenues:	
Advertising	$429,052
Circulation	193,930
Other	107,691
Total revenues	$730,673
Expenses:	
News, production, and royalty	214,495
Selling, administrative, and general	192,060
Newsprint	95,750
Postage	51,121
Depreciation	27,805
Total expenses	$581,231
Operating income	$149,442
Other income	7,113
Net income before taxes	$156,555
Income tax expense	68,452
Net income	$ 88,103

Required:

1. How do you think Dow Jones determines when advertising revenues are recognized?
2. How do you think Dow Jones determines when subscription (circulation) revenues are recognized?
3. When would you recognize revenues on a trial subscription in which customers get two weeks of papers and pay for them only if they continue?

C H A P T E R 3

Introduction to Recording, Reporting, and Analysis

LEARNING OBJECTIVES

After studying Chapter 3, you should understand:

1. How to analyze transactions (cycle step 1) and record them (cycle step 2) in the debit/credit format of the formal accounting system, pp. 102-4.
2. The relation between the journal and the ledger (cycle step 3), pp. 108-10.
3. The role of the trial balance as a check on the debit-credit convention and as a tool to help prepare adjustments (cycle step 4) and financial statements (cycle step 5), pp. 115-21.
4. How adjustments, based on past and/or expected future transactions, are recorded at the end of an accounting period (cycle step 4 developed further in Chapter 4), pp. 116-17.
5. The role of matching and revenue recognition in helping to guide the end-of-period adjusting entries, pp. 116-17.
6. The difference between the cash basis and the accrual basis of accounting, pp. 123-25.

In Chapter 2, you learned how the financing, investing, and operating activities of a business affect the complete balance sheet equation. After this initial sequence of financing and investing activities, there is a continuous mix of all three types of activities. As the operations of the business occur, the need for financing (e.g., borrowing) and investing (e.g., purchasing equipment) activities also occur. Thus, all three business activities occur on an ongoing basis. Accounting must provide an organized method of processing the results of operating, financing, and investing activities so that financial reporting can occur on a timely basis for managers and owners to evaluate the results of past transactions. In this chapter, the system used by accountants to quickly and efficiently report on the results of the many business transactions is illustrated.

Before you can process accounting information, you must understand the accounting system of debits and credits explained in the first section of this chapter. Then you are ready for an overview of the accounting cycle—six steps that end with the preparation of financial statements. This chapter explains the first three accounting cycle steps in detail and introduces the other steps, which are explained more fully in Chapter 4. These accounting cycle steps are integrated in an example of the financing, investing, and operating activities of a service corporation. It is important to keep in mind that the accounting system explained in Chapters 3 and 4 is simply a more efficient and systematic way of summarizing the effects of large numbers of transactions than that illustrated in Chapters 1 and 2. While these formal steps of the accounting cycle will replace the less formal spreadsheet analysis illustrated in Chapters 1 and 2, they will accomplish the same purpose: to capture and report the effects of business transactions in the financial statements.

Chapter 3 illustrates how most accounting systems actually translate financing, investing, and operating transactions into accounting information. After studying the basic flow of transactions to financial statements, you will be introduced to some of the methods used to analyze the financial results reported in the statements. A discussion of accrual accounting concludes the chapter.

THE ROLE OF DEBITS, CREDITS, AND T ACCOUNTS

In Chapters 1 and 2, we used the spreadsheet analysis to show how transactions affected the complete balance sheet equation. The columns of the spreadsheet referred to the assets, liabilities, and owner's equity of the business, with increases in any of these columns reported as positive numbers and decreases as negative numbers. In this chapter, and hereafter, we refer to each column as an **account**, such as the Cash account or the Land account. These accounts will report all of the activities which increase or decrease the account balance in a **T account** or ledger account. A T account is so named because it looks like a capital T, and it serves as a convenient and less formal way to illustrate a ledger account (for which it substitutes). The use of plus and minus notations in the columns of the spreadsheet is now replaced by left-side or right-side entries to these T accounts. All left-side entries to any T account are referred to as **debits** (abbreviated **Dr.**) and all right-side entries to any T account are referred to as **credits** (abbreviated **Cr.**). Therefore:

Debit = Dr. = Left-side entry

Credit = Cr. = Right-side entry

and the T account would appear as follows:

Title of Account (e.g., Cash)	
Debit (left) entries	Credit (right) entries

In keeping with the basic accounting equation (Assets = Liabilities + Stockholders' Equity), accountants developed a system of **account balances** (the difference between the sum of all the debits and the sum of all the credits) which results in assets having debit (left-side) balances and liabilities and stockholders' (owners') equity having credit (right-side) balances. Therefore, we can say the sum of the debit balances equals the sum of the credit balances instead of Assets = Liabilities + Stockholders' Equity!

Now consider the diagram in Exhibit 3-1 which relates the spreadsheet format used in Chapters 1 and 2 with the T account format using debits and credits to depict increases and decreases in the accounts. We can see how having asset accounts with debit balances and liabilities and stockholders' equity accounts with credit balances enables us to have Assets = Liabilities + Stockholders' Equity and, at the same time, have the sum of the debit balances equal the sum of the credit balances. This is accomplished by requiring debits and credits to have the opposite effects on assets than they have on liabilities and stockholders' equity. This opposite effect may be illustrated as follows:

1. First, review how the balance in any account is determined:

Any Account	*Beginning Balance*	+	*Increases*	−	*Decreases*	=	*Ending Balance*
(e.g., Cash).	$8,000	+	$7,000	−	$6,000	=	$9,000

2. Now summarize this effect using debits (Dr.) and credits (Cr.) as follows:

	Beginning Balance	+	*Increases*	−	*Decreases*	=	*Ending Balance*
Any asset	Dr.	+	Dr.	−	Cr.	=	Dr.
(e.g., Cash).	$8,000	+	$7,000	−	$6,000	=	$9,000
Any liability or stockholders' equity (e.g., Accounts	Cr.	+	Cr.	−	Dr.	=	Cr.
Payable)	$7,000	+	$9,000	−	$6,000	=	$10,000

The use of T accounts and debits and credits also pertains to the revenues and expenses which are now viewed as a separate set of T accounts which, when combined, represent the Retained Earnings T account as depicted in Exhibit 3-2. The normal account balance for Retained Earnings is a credit like any other liability or stockholders' equity account. Since revenues increase retained earnings, revenue accounts normally have credit (right-side) balances, as noted with the $XX in Exhibit 3-2. The balances in the expense accounts or the Dividend account are normally debits ($XX) because they reduce retained earnings. The system of using debits and credits in T accounts, as summarized in Exhibit 3-2, enables us to add to the rule: Assets = Liabilities + Stockholders' Equity +

EXHIBIT 3-1

Relation between Spreadsheet and T Accounts

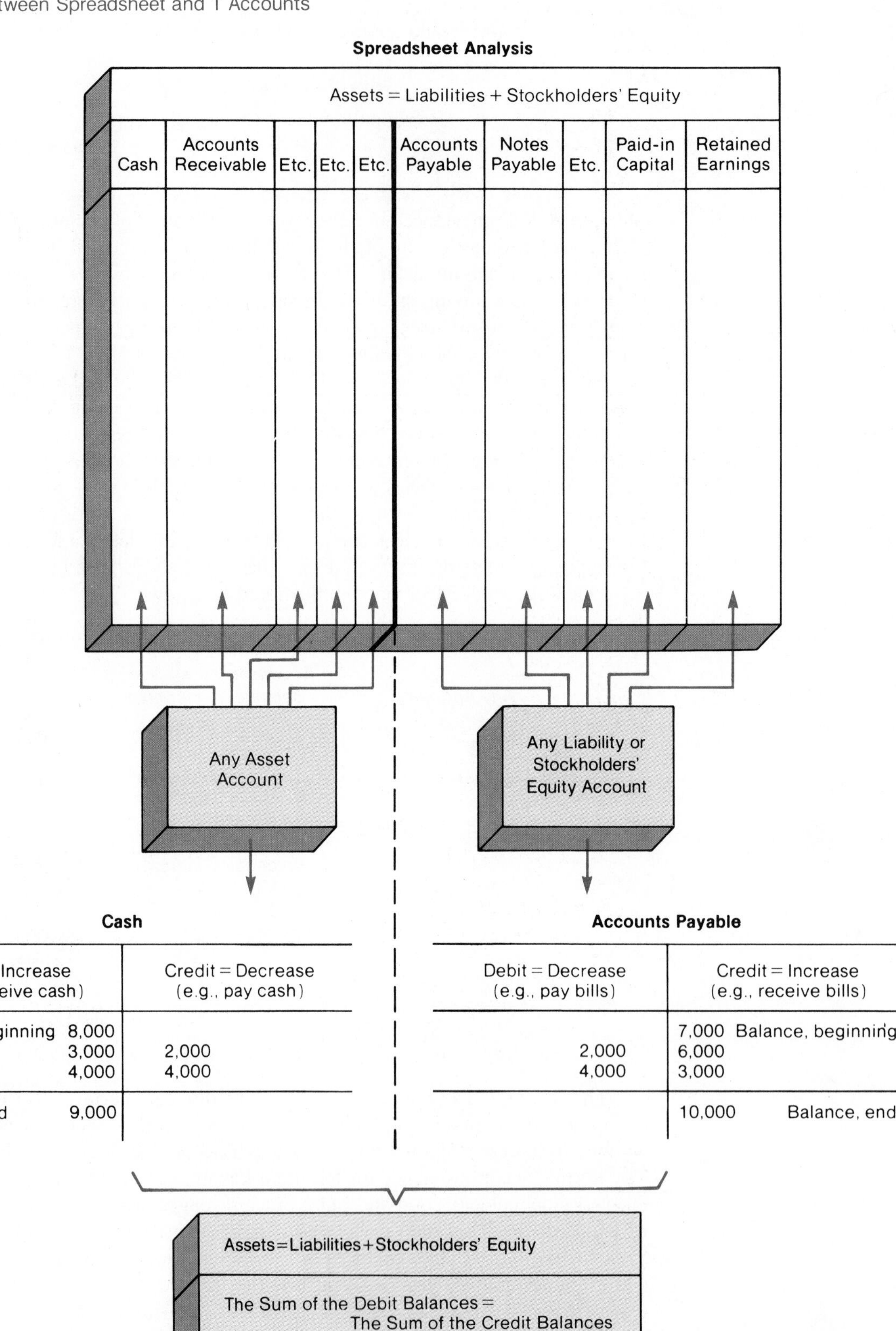

EXHIBIT 3-2

Relation between Spreadsheet and T Accounts

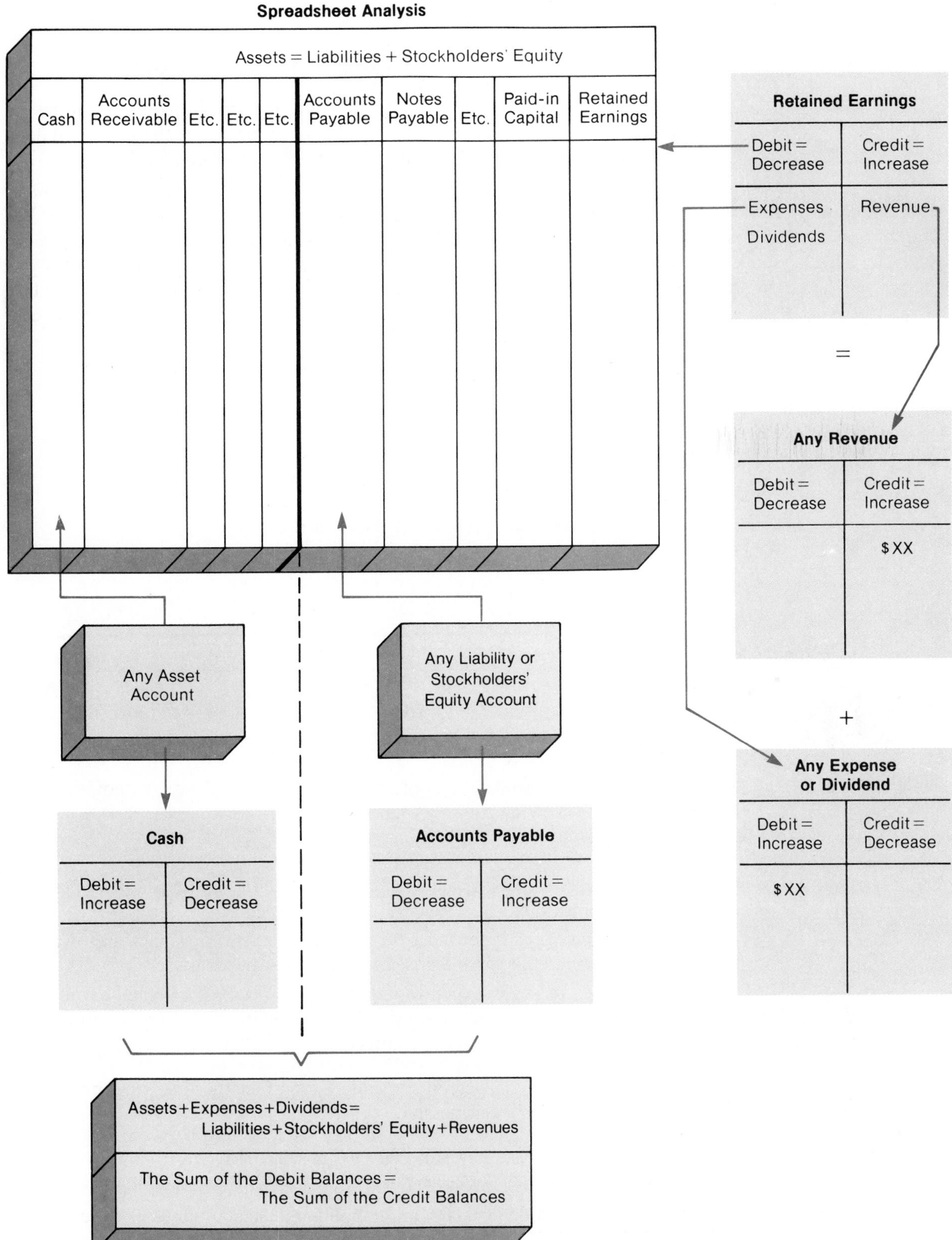

Revenues − Expenses − Dividends (or Assets + Expenses + Dividends = Liabilities + Stockholders' Equity + Revenues) a second important rule, which is:

For All Transactions, the Debits Must Equal the Credits.

This rule will be used throughout the text and provides us with a useful test to determine whether the accounting system is in balance since the sum of all debit balances must equal the sum of all credit balances at all times.

How Debits and Credits Are Used in Recording Transactions

The development of the complete balance sheet equation given in Chapter 2 is repeated below. Since we are discussing corporations, the term *stockholders' equity* is used instead of the broader term *owners' equity.* The equation elements are used as T account titles to indicate how the increases and decreases in all of the individual accounts (e.g., Cash) for each component of the equation (e.g., Assets) are recorded.

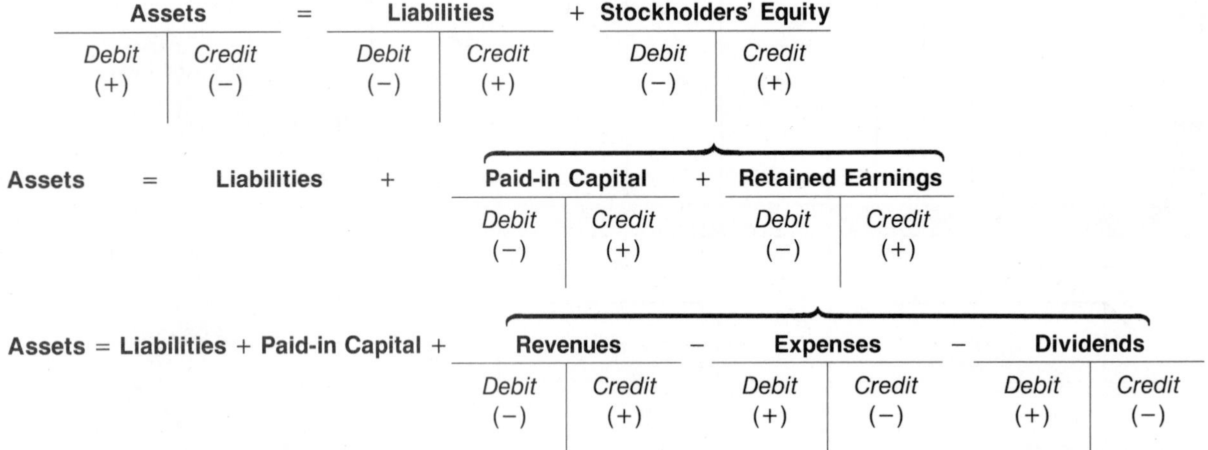

The increases and decreases of accounts illustrated above can now be translated into the following rules:

1. Increases in assets are debits, and decreases in assets are credits.
2. Decreases in liabilities and stockholders' equity are debits, and increases in liabilities and stockholders' equity are credits.
3. Since increases in revenues increase retained earnings, increases in revenues are credits, and decreases in revenues are debits.
4. Since increases in expenses and dividends decrease retained earnings, increases in expenses and dividends are debits, and decreases in expenses and dividends are credits.

To illustrate the debit-credit convention, consider the following three transactions at the start of a business:

1. The shareholders pay $100,000 for stock in the Delta Company.
2. Delta company borrows $60,000 from the bank on a long-term note.
3. Delta buys land ($50,000) and a building ($80,000) for $130,000 cash.

The T accounts for transaction 1 will be affected as follows:

Assets		=	Liabilities		+	Stockholders' Equity	
Debit (+)	*Credit* (−)		*Debit* (−)	*Credit* (+)		*Debit* (−)	*Credit* (+)

Cash		=		Capital Stock	
Debit	*Credit*			*Debit*	*Credit*
100,000					100,000

After transaction 2, we have:

Cash		=	Note Payable		Capital Stock	
Debit	*Credit*		*Debit*	*Credit*	*Debit*	*Credit*
100,000				60,000		100,000
60,000						
160,000						

After transaction 3, we have:

Cash		=	Note Payable		Capital Stock	
Debit	*Credit*		*Debit*	*Credit*	*Debit*	*Credit*
100,000				60,000		100,000
60,000						
160,000						
	130,000					
30,000						

Land	
Debit	*Credit*
50,000	

Building	
Debit	*Credit*
80,000	

The balance sheet equality is maintained after each transaction so that Assets = Liabilities + Stockholders' Equity. This system of recording transactions in accounts in such a way that **the sum of the debits for each transaction equals the sum of the credits** is known as the **double-entry system.** Notice that this double-entry effect holds for each of the three transactions illustrated above in the T accounts. Virtually all accounting is based on the double-entry system where at least two accounts are affected by each entry, and where the sum of the debits equals the sum of the credits for each entry. The third transaction illustrated above is called a **complex entry** because more than two T accounts are affected. However, the debits still equal the credits in the third transaction.

Since assets have debit balances, their balances are simply **summed** in the balance sheet. The same is true for liabilities and stockholders' equity which typically have credit balances. However, if, for instance, an asset account had a credit balance, it would be a negative number on the asset side of the balance sheet. This might occur if, for example, the Cash account represented an overdrawn checking account, resulting in a credit balance in cash.

Notice that rules such as "debits increase assets and expenses" are quite arbitrary. An opposite set of rules where all assets and expenses were increased with credits and all liability, stockholders' equity, and revenue accounts were increased with debits could also be employed. The point of the arbitrary rules is simply to maintain the fundamental equality of the balance sheet equation—Assets = Liabilities + Stockholders' Equity—by creating a system of accounts where the total debit balances always equal the total credit balances.

OVERVIEW OF THE ACCOUNTING CYCLE

The ultimate goal of all accounting activity is to communicate relevant financial information to decision makers on a timely basis. How often should accountants report? There is no obvious answer to this question. The corporate entity is viewed by accountants (as well as for legal purposes) as having an infinite life, with business activities continuing on an ongoing basis. The assumption that the corporation will have no end point is known as the **going concern concept** (or **going concern assumption**). Because of the going concern concept, there is assumed to be no end point, or settling up point, where a final accounting is made.

Because of the need to compare financial results across firms and over time on a systematic basis, accountants require that financial statements be prepared over standard intervals. Based on the **periodicity assumption,** accountants require financial statements to be prepared at least once per year. This accounting period is referred to as the company's **fiscal year.** This can be a calendar year—from January 1 to December 31—or another 12-month period, which may begin any time in one year and end 12 months later. Shorter reporting periods such as months or quarters are also used when desired or otherwise required.

The **accounting cycle** is the systematic sequence of steps or operations that are required to be performed in order to prepare periodic financial statements. In Chapters 1 and 2, we illustrated an informal cycle used to produce these financial statements. In Chapters 3 and 4, we introduce the formal accounting cycle, which consists of the following six steps:

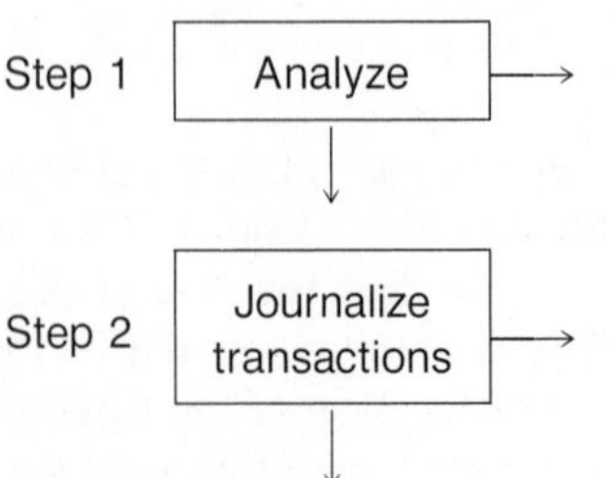

This step calls for source documents, such as invoices (bills) and other evidence to be examined to determine whether a transaction affecting the financial position of the business has occurred.

This step calls for those transactions which affect the financial position to be entered (or recorded) into the accounting system.

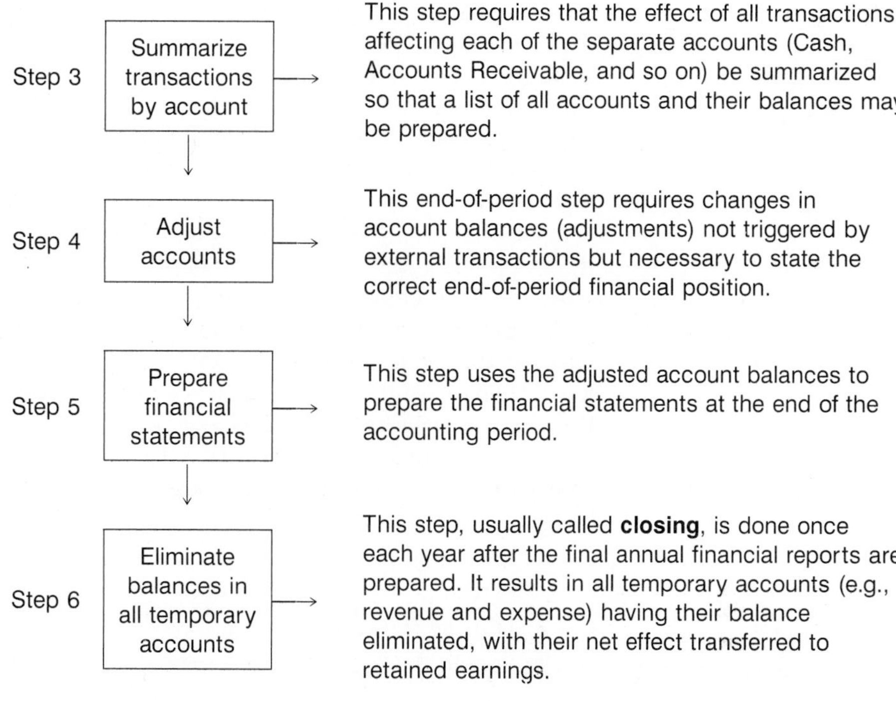

Step 3
Summarize transactions by account
This step requires that the effect of all transactions affecting each of the separate accounts (Cash, Accounts Receivable, and so on) be summarized so that a list of all accounts and their balances may be prepared.
Step 4
Adjust accounts
This end-of-period step requires changes in account balances (adjustments) not triggered by external transactions but necessary to state the correct end-of-period financial position.
Step 5
Prepare financial statements
This step uses the adjusted account balances to prepare the financial statements at the end of the accounting period.
Step 6
Eliminate balances in all temporary accounts
This step, usually called closing, is done once each year after the final annual financial reports are prepared. It results in all temporary accounts (e.g., revenue and expense) having their balance eliminated, with their net effect transferred to retained earnings.

These six steps require a good deal of additional explanation and illustration to be understood and are the focus of the remainder of Chapters 3 and 4.

Steps 1, 2, and 3 of the accounting cycle are used to summarize all the transactions of a business—financing, investing, and operating—and are explained in this chapter. You were introduced to step 4—adjusting the accounts—in Chapter 2. More is said about the adjustment process later in this chapter and again in Chapter 4. Step 5 is illustrated in this chapter and reviewed in Chapter 4 where step 6 is introduced.

As we illustrate these six steps of the formal accounting information system, keep in mind that their purpose is to provide the same set of financial statements that were illustrated in the first two chapters of the text. The major difference is that the formal accounting cycle explained in Chapters 3 and 4 provides a more systematic and efficient way for actual businesses to account for the large volume of operating, financing, and investing activities involved in running the business on a daily basis. The benefits of the more formal accounting cycle over the spreadsheet analysis approach illustrated in Chapters 1 and 2 is not always clear since the examples illustrated in this and other texts are not based on the same high volume of transactions that would normally occur in a real business.

ANALYZING TRANSACTIONS (ACCOUNTING CYCLE STEP 1)

Analyzing source documents and other evidence of external transactions—step 1 in the accounting cycle—is the key to accurately recording accounting information. **Source documents** are records usually retained in business files that provide evidence about the transactions which have actually occurred. Examples of source documents are sales receipts, invoices for merchandise purchased, utility bills, and so on. Other evidence such as contracts with suppliers and employees is also used to interpret transactions.

To correctly analyze transactions you must be able to recognize the effects that each transaction has on the accounts of the business. A thorough understanding of accounting concepts is necessary to master this first step in the accounting cycle, and errors in analyzing transactions may affect the entire accounting cycle and the resulting financial statements. As a result, our examples in the early chapters focus on relatively simple transactions so that their effects on the accounts of the business may be easily understood.

Since analyzing begins with recognizing the effects each transaction has on the assets, liabilities, and stockholders' equity of a business, it helps to understand the debit-credit relationships explained earlier in the chapter. In addition, you must become familiar with business terminology used to describe normal business transactions. To help familiarize you with these fundamentals, we follow a simple business through a series of transactions and observe the effect of these transactions on T accounts and formal ledger accounts. In this section, we begin with financing and investing activities. In studying each transaction, ask yourself the following three questions:

1. To what specific type of asset, liability, or stockholders' equity account (including the categories paid-in capital, retained earnings, revenues, expenses, and dividends) does the transaction belong?
2. Did the transaction increase or decrease the affected accounts?
3. Should the individual accounts affected be debited or credited?

Examples of Analyzing

To illustrate cycle step 1, we will begin to describe a business situation and follow it through to illustrate the complete six-step accounting cycle. Fitness Clinic, Inc., was organized as a service business providing individual and class instruction in physical fitness. Since the Fitness Clinic is a corporation, stockholders are the owners of the business.

Transaction 1: Financing Obtained. On December 28, 19x1, Fitness Clinic began operations with $100,000 cash received from the sale of stock to the stockholders.

Objective 1
How to analyze transactions (cycle step 1).

Analysis of transaction 1. Two accounts are affected—Cash (asset) and Capital Stock (stockholders' equity). Cash is increased (debited), and Capital Stock is increased (credited). The Cash and Capital Stock T accounts are affected as follows:

Cash

Debit = Increase	*Credit = Decrease*
19x1 Dec. 28 (1) 100,000	

Capital Stock

Debit = Decrease	*Credit = Increase*
	19x1 Dec. 28 (1) 100,000

Note that the date and transaction number are given to the left of the dollar amount to aid in our discussion. Dollar signs are not used in T accounts.

Transaction 2: Rental of Building and Office Equipment. On December 31, 19x1, Fitness Clinic paid $20,000 for two months' advance rental of a building and office equipment.

Analysis of transaction 2. Two accounts are affected—Cash (asset) and Prepaid Rent (asset). The asset cash is decreased (credited) and the asset prepaid rent is increased (debited). After transactions 1 and 2, the T accounts appear as follows:

Cash

Debit = Increase		*Credit = Decrease*	
19x1 Dec. 28 (1)	100,000	19x1 Dec. 31 (2)	20,000
Bal. Dec. 31	80,000		

Prepaid Rent

Debit = Increase		*Credit = Decrease*
19x1 Dec. 31 (2)	20,000	

Capital Stock

Debit = Decrease	*Credit = Increase*	
	19x1 Dec. 28 (1)	100,000

Note that the Cash account now has both a debit of $100,000, representing an increase, and a credit of $20,000, representing a decrease. The difference between debits and credits in any individual account at any point in time is called the **account balance.** For the Cash account, the balance is a debit balance of $80,000 after the second entry.

Every account has a balance at all times (even though the balance might not always be computed in manual systems). The accounting system of recording increases and decreases is arranged so that each type of account (e.g., asset accounts) has either a debit or a credit as its **normal balance.** Account groups with normal debit balances are assets, expenses, and dividends; account groups with normal credit balances are liabilities, paid-in capital (capital stock), retained earnings, and revenues. Knowing the normal balance of an account may help locate a recording error.

Trial Balance

When the rule of debit and credit is applied to all transactions, the summary results of all account balances will have equal debits and credits. This can be tested by a **trial balance.** A trial balance is a list of all **account balances with separate columns for debit and credit balances.** Since debits must equal credits, the totals of both columns must always be identical. Assuming that the Fitness Clinic has no other transactions for 19x1, we would have the following trial balance:

Fitness Clinic, Inc.
Trial Balance
December 31, 19x1

	Debits	*Credits*
Cash	$ 80,000	
Prepaid Rent.	20,000	
Capital Stock		$100,000
Totals.	$100,000	$100,000

A trial balance that does not balance indicates a recording error has occurred. In many computerized systems, a trial balance is effectively prepared after each entry to ensure that the total debit balances equal the total credit balances from all accounts. However, other kinds of recording errors can still occur (e.g., omitted entry) even if the trial balance is in balance. Notice that trial balances are different from balance sheets in that trial balances list the accounts and dollar balances without categorizing the accounts as assets, liabilities, or stockholders' equity. Also, as we will see in later trial balances, they include the balances in any revenue, expense, or dividend account when present.

JOURNALIZING TRANSACTIONS (ACCOUNTING CYCLE STEP 2)

In the examples above, we illustrated how T accounts give a status report on how the results of transactions affected the balance in each asset, liability, or stockholders' equity account. A complete set of accounts form the basic structure of the formal accounting system. Another important record used in an accounting system, however, is the journal. A **journal** is a chronological record where each accounting transaction is recorded in the order of the date that it occurred so that all of the accounts affected by a specific transaction, along with their respective debit or credit **impact**, are listed in one place. This record is called the **journal**, which is also known as the **book of original entry.**

The **general journal** is the most common and basic journal used by companies. The term *general journal* will be used in this textbook; however, the word *journal* used alone will also be used to refer to the general journal. Many companies have additional journals which are used in their accounting systems. These are referred to as *special journals*. Special journals are explained in the appendix to Chapter 7.

A **journal entry** (or **general journal entry**) is a record of an accounting transaction which lists all affected accounts and their respective debit or credit amounts. For each journal entry, the debits must equal the credits. For example, transaction 1 of the Fitness Clinic increased the asset account Cash by $100,000 (debit) and increased the stockholders' equity Capital Stock account by $100,000 (credit). Both the debit and credit effects of this transaction are shown in the following informal journal entry:

Objective 1
How to analyze transactions (cycle step 1) and record them (cycle step 2) in the debit/credit format of the formal accounting system.

Date	*Accounts*	*Debit*	*Credit*
19x1			
Dec. 28	Cash (A)*	100,000	
	Capital Stock (SE)		100,000
	To record the issuance of capital stock.		

*We are using the abbreviations "A" for assets, "L" for liabilities, "SE" for stockholders' equity other than revenues and expenses, "R" for revenues, and "E" for expenses to help familiarize you with the account categories that are affected by journal entries.

A more formal format for journal entries is as follows:

GENERAL JOURNAL					J1
Date		Account Titles and Explanation	Ref.	Debit	Credit
19x1 Dec.	28	Cash (A)	111	100,000	
		Capital Stock (SE)	311		100,000
		To record the issuance of capital stock.			

Note that in the above journal entry, the debit entry is written first. Then the credit entry is indented below the debit entry. This entry format is conventional and we use it throughout the text. Journal styles may vary as to the position of each entry's explanation line, with the style illustrated here used throughout this book. "J1" is the page number of the journal, and "Ref." refers to account numbers assigned to ledger accounts in each journal entry. Journal entries are recorded for each transaction in the order that they occur (chronological order). Then, periodically the debit-credit effects of each journal entry are also recorded in the separate ledger accounts through a procedure called **posting.** This **posting from the journal to the ledger** is usually done each day or after each journal page is complete in manual systems, and is done automatically as journal entries are made in computerized systems. The "Ref." column is completed as each entry is posted.

In this textbook, we use the informal or formal journal formats depending on the purpose of the example. In actual accounting systems, formal journal records are maintained either by hand or in computerized systems. Note that even in computerized systems, the journal entry for each transaction must be entered with the accounts, amounts, and debits or credits included.

POSTING FROM JOURNAL TO LEDGER ACCOUNTS (ACCOUNTING CYCLE STEP 3)

Before we illustrate how to post transactions from the journal to the ledger accounts, you should understand (1) the format of formal ledger accounts and how they are organized in a ledger and (2) the information that account balances communicate to decision makers.

As explained earlier, the informal T account is used for instructional purposes to represent the formal ledger account. While both account representations have a title, debit and credit columns, and a balance, the formal ledger account allows for more detail and the orderly handling of more transactions.

Exhibit 3-3 shows how the information in the Fitness Clinic's Cash, Prepaid Rent, and Capital Stock T accounts would be shown as formal ledger accounts. Note that in the formal ledger accounts (1) running balances are maintained after every entry; (2) in the Cash and Prepaid Rent asset accounts, the normal account balance is a debit, and any credit balances would be put in parentheses; and (3) in the Capital Stock stockholders' equity account, the normal account balance is a credit, and any debit balances would be put in parentheses.

A file that contains all the accounts used in an accounting system is called a **ledger.** Small companies may use only one file called a **general ledger.** Larger companies often use several subfiles called **subsidiary ledgers,** but they must also have a general ledger that contains the summary effects of the subsidiary ledgers. For example, most companies have subsidiary ledgers for cash, with a separate subsidiary ledger maintained for each separate cash account (i.e., checking, savings, payroll, and so on). However, the general ledger's Cash account includes the total balance of all the subsidiary cash accounts. Subsidiary ledgers are further explained in Chapter 5. When the term *ledger* is used alone in this textbook, the reference is to the general ledger.

Accounts within a ledger are organized as they appear in the financial statements—asset accounts, liability accounts, stockholders' equity accounts, including revenue, expense, and dividend accounts. Depending on the detail required, each group of accounts is assigned a multidigit number (e.g., assets to 100s,

EXHIBIT 3-3

Formal Ledger Accounts

GENERAL LEDGER

Cash Account No. 111

Date		Explanation	Ref.	Debit	Credit	Balance Debit (Credit)
19x1 Dec.	28	Issuance of capital stock	J1	100,000		100,000
	31	Prepayment of rent	J1		20,000	80,000

Prepaid Rent Account No. 131

Date		Explanation	Ref.	Debit	Credit	Balance Debit (Credit)
19x1 Dec.	31	Prepayment of rent	J1	20,000		20,000

Capital Stock Account No. 311

Date		Explanation	Ref.	Debit	Credit	Balance (Debit) Credit
19x1 Dec.	28	Issuance of capital stock	J1		100,000	100,000

liabilities to 200s), with individual accounts numbered within the range of the multidigit series for its group. For example, each asset can be assigned a three-digit number ranging from 100 to 199 or a four-digit number from 1000 to 1999. To locate a particular account and its number, companies prepare a list of account titles for each major balance sheet category. This list is called a **chart of accounts** (see Exhibit 3-4). We will be using the account titles shown in Exhibit 3-4 and many others throughout this textbook. The account numbers following the account titles are used in the reference ("Ref.") column of the journal (illustrated earlier) to facilitate cross-referencing between the journal and ledger. Likewise, the reference column in the ledger (see Exhibit 3-3) cross-references the page of the general journal that contains the complete transaction from which the ledger entry came.

Current and Noncurrent Accounts

Balance sheet accounts for assets and liabilities are frequently grouped into current and noncurrent categories. A **current asset** is one that is expected to be used up or converted to cash within one year or the operating cycle, whichever is longer. A **current liability** is one that is expected to require cash or other assets to be used within one year or the operating cycle, whichever is longer. Another

EXHIBIT 3-4

Chart of Accounts Example

Chart of Accounts

Account Titles	*Account Nos.*
Assets	100–199
Cash*	111
Accounts Receivable*	121
Prepaid Rent*	131
Supplies Inventory*	141
Land	151
Buildings	161
Equipment	162
Security Deposit	171
Liabilities	200–299
Accounts Payable*	211
Salaries Payable*	212
Income Taxes Payable*	215
Notes Payable*	217
Stockholders' equity	300–399
Capital Stock	311
Retained Earnings	331
Revenues	400–499
Consulting Fees	411
Service Revenue	421
Interest Revenue	441
Miscellaneous Revenue	491
Expenses	500–599
Salaries Expense	511
Commissions Expense	512
Travel and Entertainment Expense	513
Advertising Expense	521
Rent Expense	531
Office Supplies Expense	541
Utilities Expense	551
Communications Expense	552
Laundry Service Expense	553
Income Tax Expense	591
Dividends (or Dividends Declared)†	615

*Normally identified as current in classified balance sheet.

†Remember that Dividends Declared is a separate type of account that does not enter into the measurement of net income but does reduce retained earnings.

way to say this is that the items represented by the money amounts in current assets (e.g., accounts receivable) and current liabilities (e.g., account payable) will "turn over" in less than one year; therefore, their amounts are considered current. Balance sheets which separate current assets and liabilities from noncurrent assets and liabilities are called **classified balance sheets.** The assets and liabilities listed in Exhibit 3-4 that are marked with an asterisk (*) are normally identified as current accounts in classified balance sheets.

Temporary and Permanent Accounts

Because revenue and expense accounts are used to accumulate the effects of operating transactions for a period of time only, they are called **nominal** or **temporary accounts.** They are temporary because after a specified period of time, their balances are transferred to the retained earnings account (called *closing*). Retained earnings, like all balance sheet accounts, is a **permanent account,** which records the cumulative effect of revenues and expenses from all prior accounting periods. Dividends is also a temporary account which is closed to retained earnings. In Chapter 4, we will explain this closing process and show how it is that revenue, expense, and dividend accounts begin each new accounting period with no balances.

Posting to the Ledger (Required to Complete Cycle Step 3)

Objective 2
The relation between the journal and the ledger (cycle step 3).

Transactions 1 and 2 of Fitness Clinic affected three accounts—Cash, Prepaid Rent, and Capital Stock. The debits and credits shown in the journal must be posted to the accounts indicated. The journal entry for transaction 1 is posted to the Cash and Capital Stock accounts as follows:

Journal Entry

19x1			
Dec. 28	Cash (A)	100,000	
	Capital Stock (SE) . .		100,000
	To record the issuance of capital stock.		

Ledger Accounts

Cash

Debit	Credit
19x1 Dec. 28 (1) 100,000	

Capital Stock

Debit	Credit
	19x1 Dec. 28 (1) 100,000

Note that the $100,000 Cash debit in the journal entry is posted as a debit to the Cash account, and the $100,000 Capital Stock credit in the journal entry is posted as a credit to the Capital Stock account. Thus, posting is used to transfer the debit and credit effects of the activities of a business (financing, investing, and operating) from a chronological record (journal) to individual records (ledger accounts).

The journal entry for transaction 2 is posted as follows:

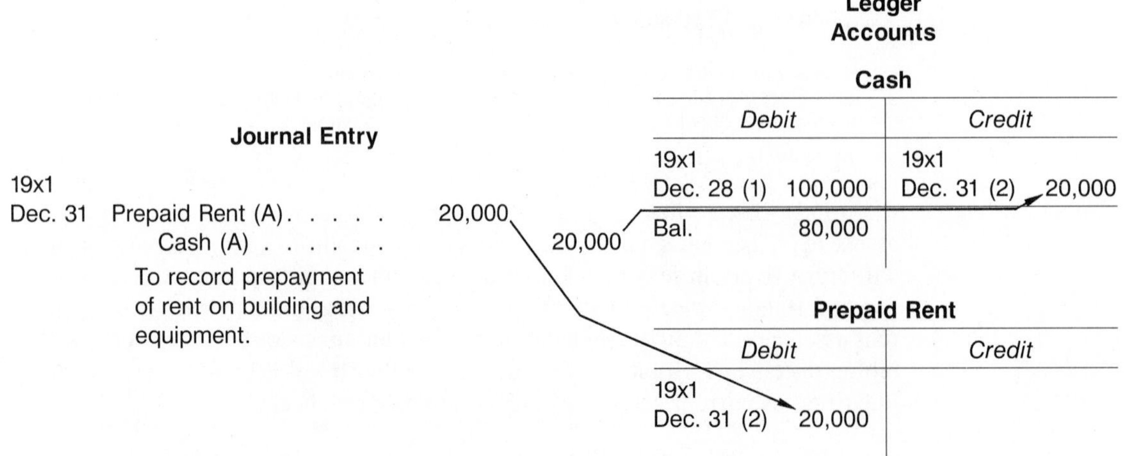

Ledger
Accounts
Cash
Debit
Credit
Journal Entry
19x1
Dec. 28 (1) 100,000
19x1
Dec. 31 (2) 20,000
19x1
Dec. 31 Prepaid Rent (A). 20,000
Cash (A) 20,000
Bal. 80,000
To record prepayment of rent on building and equipment.
Prepaid Rent
Debit
Credit
19x1
Dec. 31 (2) 20,000

The $20,000 debit for Prepaid Rent in the journal entry is debited to the Prepaid Rent account, and the $20,000 credit for Cash in the journal entry is credited to the Cash account. The balance in the Cash account is now $80,000.

Exhibit 3-5 illustrates the more detailed version of posting from the *formal* journal to the *formal* ledger accounts, and shows the cross-referencing that exists between the journal and the ledger accounts. Each ledger account is given the number indicated in the company's chart of accounts. When the accountant posts a journal entry to an account, the number of the account is inserted in the **Reference (Ref.) column** of the journal, and the number of the journal page is posted to the "Ref." column in the ledger account. This provides a system of cross-referencing that enables an accountant to check or trace the effect a transaction has on the accounting records.

Decision Implications

The first three steps of the cycle called for: (1) analyzing the effects of transactions on accounts; (2) recording the effects of transactions in chronological order in the journal; and (3) periodically posting the journal entries to the ledger accounts and obtaining ledger account balances. This formal accounting cycle has numerous advantages over the simpler spreadsheet analysis illustrated in the first two chapters. To illustrate, let us return to our case from Chapter 1.

Ann, Bill, and Connie, the three owners of Technotic Space Labs, started out their recordkeeping process with a large 20-column spreadsheet analysis worksheet with the names of the various accounts heading each of the columns and the date of each transaction listed down the far left-hand column. (Refer to Exhibit 2-6 on page 67 for an example.) Connie was placed in charge of maintaining the accounting records. After six months of operating activity, Ann, Bill, and Connie have a meeting to discuss some of their concerns. Let's sit in on their discussion.

Ann: You know Connie, I was looking over the spreadsheet analysis worksheet the other day trying to determine whether our new shipment of office supplies had arrived yet and I couldn't find any account called office supplies. The supplier was calling me about why we hadn't paid for them yet and I couldn't even tell if they had been received!

Connie: Well, if they had been received, they'd be in the column marked "Lab projects in progress," which is how I classify them.

Bill: But lab projects are what we sell, and office supplies are what we use to run the business. These aren't the same thing, are they?

Connie: Right, but you see I'm out of space on the worksheet. All 20 columns are being used. I've already included all of the prepaid rents for our cars, office space, and equipment in a single account to make more room. I'm looking into a 40-column worksheet but it's so big I'll have to post it up on the wall to use it. Each time I combine two accounts together to make room for a new category of item, it creates a big mess in the worksheet.

Bill: You know, another problem I'm having with that worksheet is that I can't seem to get information I need from it quickly and conveniently. Danko Co., one of our suppliers, called me July 2 and wanted to know when we would be able to pay them. He said we could have received a 5% discount if we would have paid invoice #1876 by June 25 and asked why we didn't take advantage of it. I know we have discounts available on many of our purchases but I can't tell whether the cash balance is positive without adding up a whole column of numbers. How can we possibly know which purchases to pay and when to pay them without more information about the discount period? I don't know if we can be competitive if we're loosing 5% discounts on our purchases.

EXHIBIT 3-5

Posting from the Journal to the Ledger

GENERAL JOURNAL J1

Date		Acct. Titles/Explanation	Ref.	Debit	Credit
19x1 Dec.	28	Cash (A)	111	100,000	
		Capital Stock (SE)	311		100,000
		To record the issuance of capital stock.			
	31	Prepaid Rent (A)	131	20,000	
		Cash (A)	111		20,000
		To record prepayment of rent on building and equipment.			

GENERAL LEDGER

Cash Account No. 111

Date		Explanation	Ref.	Debit	Credit	Balance Debit (Credit)
19x1 Dec.	28	Issuance of capital stock	J1	100,000		100,000
	31	Prepayment of rent	J1		20,000	80,000

Prepaid Rent Account No. 131

Date		Explanation	Ref.	Debit	Credit	Balance Debit (Credit)
19x1 Dec.	31	Prepayment of rent	J1	20,000		20,000

Capital Stock Account No. 311

Date		Explanation	Ref.	Debit	Credit	Balance (Debit) Credit
19x1 Dec.	28	Issuance of capital stock	J1		100,000	100,000

Connie: I know what you mean. I've also found myself making mistakes when I add or record, which can be costly to us. Once I made a cash entry positive instead of negative and several times I've added negatives to positives instead of subtracting them. There must be some other way to process all of our business transactions more efficiently than this spreadsheet analysis worksheet. Maybe a 40-column worksheet isn't the answer to our problems. Besides, how will we find account balances when the worksheet is posted on the wall? We'll have to stand there with a hand calculator adding up columns of numbers! There must be a better system to account for our transactions!

The discussion between Ann, Bill, and Connie points out several key limitations of the spreadsheet used in the first two chapters. We can already see how some of these limitations are addressed by the more formal accounting system discussed in this chapter. For example, the T accounts and the debit/credit convention help us keep more accurate records of the increases and decreases in accounts. We can also easily add to our chart of accounts anytime a new account is desired. The system of journalizing entries and then posting them to the ledger provides records which enable us to easily determine account balances and to find out what other accounts were affected by a particular transaction. For example, in examining our ledger, we might see the following detail:

GENERAL LEDGER (excerpt)

Accounts Payable Account No. 211

Date		Explanation	Ref.	Debit	Credit	Balance (Debit) Credit
						78,650
June	15	Danko invoice #1876	J100		14,365	93,015
	16	Payment to Bruce, invoice #B5632	J100	21,340		71,675
June	30	Balance				81,936
July	1	Check to Danko, invoice #1876	J112	14,365		67,571

This answers the question that Danko raised with Bill (who could now tell Danko the check was sent July 1 for invoice #1876). Also, if Danko always allowed 10 days to pay for a 5% discount, scanning the Cash and the Accounts Payable accounts would help determine if discounts were available and could be taken. In later chapters, we will learn about other detailed aspects of the formal accounting system which permit timely decisions concerning purchases and payments. However, even after considering the first three steps of the accounting cycle in a formal accounting system, we can begin to see its advantages for making business decisions.

ACCOUNTING DURING AN OPERATING PERIOD (ACCOUNTING CYCLE STEPS 1, 2, 3, AND 4)

Businesses are organized for many different reasons. However, companies can stay in business only if the business is profitable. A company's profitability is of interest to many people such as owners, suppliers, employees, government, and others who must make decisions based on evaluations of profitability. In response to this need for profitability information, accountants have developed a standardized system for measuring profitability to improve its usefulness for the many different types of decisions which are based on profits.

Recall that the accountant's basic measure of profitability is **net income,** which is:

Revenues − Expenses = Net Income

Another way of stating net income is:

$$\frac{\text{Resources Generated}}{\text{by Operations}} - \frac{\text{Resources Consumed}}{\text{by Operations}} = \text{Net Income}$$

Also, recall that net income is added to the retained earnings balance at the end of each period and, after deducting the dividends declared (announced dividends) for the period, provides the ending retained earnings needed to balance the balance sheet equation (Assets = Liabilities + Stockholders' Equity) as follows:

Retained earnings, beginning of the period	$ xxx
+ Net income (or subtract net loss).	xxx
− Dividends declared	(xxx)
Retained earnings, end of the period	$ xxx

To illustrate how accountants measure net income, we return to the Fitness Clinic example. As you recall, on December 28, 19x1, the stockholders of Fitness Clinic invested $100,000 cash in the corporation—a financing transaction. With their investment, the stockholders put resources into the corporation for which they expect to earn a return. Then on December 31, 19x1, rent ($20,000) was prepaid two months to provide Fitness Clinic with a place to conduct its operations.

In this section you will trace the transactions of Fitness Clinic for the month of January 19x2. You will see how an accounting cycle develops and how, after making the adjusting entries (accounting cycle step 4), the financial statements (accounting cycle step 5) are prepared from an adjusted trial balance.

Recording Transactions during an Operating Period (accounting cycle steps 1, 2, and 3)

In January 19x2, Fitness Clinic began its instruction in physical fitness. The following entries occurred during January:

Date	*Entry No.*	*Description of Entry*	*Amount*
19x2			
Jan. 14	3	Salaries paid in cash	$ 10,000
22	4	Salaries paid in cash	15,000
27	5	Utilities paid in cash	3,000
29	6	Laundry services paid in cash.	7,000
30	7	Service revenue collected in cash	100,000
30	8	Borrowed cash from bank.	35,000

Date	*Entry No.*	*Description of Entry*	*Amount*
Jan. 30	9	Purchased equipment for cash	110,000
31	10	Unpaid salaries	5,000
31	11	Consumed one half of prepaid rent during January.	10,000
31	12	Declared and paid dividends	5,000
31	13	Determined income taxes for the month . .	10,000

Each transaction (entries 3–9 and 12 above) and each adjustment (entries 10, 11, and 13 above) triggers a journal entry, the debits and credits of which are posted to ledger accounts. To help you understand the types of transactions, we have grouped them into operating activities, financing activities, and an investing activity.

Operating Activities. Most transactions of a business involve operating activities. A company's major sources and uses of cash usually involve its customers and the suppliers of goods and services used by the company; that is, from the operating activities of the company. You will see that Fitness Clinic has both cash and noncash operating transactions that must be fully understood if the results of its operations are to be properly interpreted.

Cash expenses. During the month of January 19x2, the journal of Fitness Clinic showed that the following cash expenses (transactions 3–6) were incurred:

GENERAL JOURNAL					J2
Date		Account Titles and Explanation	Ref.	Debit	Credit
19x2					
Jan.	14	Salaries Expense (E)	511	10,000	
		Cash (A)	111		10,000
		To record salaries paid.			
	22	Salaries Expense (E)	511	15,000	
		Cash (A)	111		15,000
		To record salaries paid.			
	27	Utilities Expense (E)	551	3,000	
		Cash (A)	111		3,000
		To record utilities paid.			
	29	Laundry Service Expense (E)	553	7,000	
		Cash (A)	111		7,000
		To record laundry service paid.			

Each transaction is supported by a source document—employees' timecards, utility bills, and laundry bills. All entries that record cash expenses depict the same basic kind of transaction. The company uses cash, and the credits to the Cash account record this fact. The debits to expense accounts represent the offsetting reductions in stockholders' equity (Retained Earnings).

Service revenue. Transaction 7—receipt of service revenue—occurred when the clients of Fitness Clinic paid for fitness instruction. The source documents for these revenues are copies of the receipts given to customers. As indicated in the journal below, Cash is increased by the debit entry, and Service Revenue is increased by the credit entry.

GENERAL JOURNAL						J2
Date		Account Titles and Explanation	Ref.	Debit	Credit
19x2 Jan.	30	Cash (A)	111	100,000	
		Service Revenue (R)	421		100,000
		To record service revenue.			

Financing Activities. As is often the case with a new business, additional sources of funds are needed if the business is expanding. On January 30, 19x2, Fitness Clinic borrows $35,000 from a bank. Fitness Clinic declared and paid a cash dividend of $5,000 to its stockholders. The journal entries for these two financing activities are:

GENERAL JOURNAL					J3
Date		Account Titles and Explanation	Ref.	Debit	Credit
19x2 Jan.	30	Cash (A)	111	35,000	
		Notes Payable (L)	217		35,000
		To record cash borrowed from the bank.			
	31	Dividends (SE)	615	5,000	
		Cash (A)	111		5,000
		To record dividends declared and paid to stockholders.			

This first entry records the increase in cash by the debit to the Cash account, and the credit to Notes Payable records the increase in the obligation to the creditor. The second entry records a decrease in retained earnings (stockholders' equity) with the debit to Dividends and the decrease in cash by the credit to the Cash account. If the dividends had been declared but not paid, a liability account, Dividends Payable, would have been credited instead of cash.

Investing Activity. Most businesses invest some of their funds in productive assets that will be used over several periods. Fitness Clinic purchased equipment on January 30, 19x2, as indicated by the following journal entry:

GENERAL JOURNAL					J3
Date		Account Titles and Explanation	Ref.	Debit	Credit
19x2 Jan.	30	Equipment (A)	162	110,000	
		Cash (A)	111		110,000
		To record purchase of equipment for cash.			

This entry shows that an asset acquisition is recorded with a debit entry, and the corresponding reduction of the asset cash is recorded with a credit.

Unadjusted Trial Balance

Objective 3
The role of the trial balance as a check on the debit-credit convention and as a tool to help prepare adjustments (cycle step 4) and financial statements (cycle step 5).

After the first three steps of the accounting cycle have been completed for a period of time, an unadjusted trial balance is often prepared prior to performing step 4: the adjusting process. While the unadjusted trial balance is not necessary, it often helps evaluate what adjusting entries need to be made. Note that a trial balance may be taken at any time. Trial balances are simply a list of all accounts and their balances. Different names for trial balances are used to help describe at what stage in the cycle the trial balance is taken. An **unadjusted trial balance,** such as the one shown in Exhibit 3-6 for Fitness Clinic, Inc., indicates that adjustments (cycle step 4) have not been made. An **adjusted trial balance** indicates cycle step 4 has been completed.

Introduction to Adjusting Entries (accounting cycle step 4)

Often resources are consumed and obligations incurred without a transaction with an outside party occurring at the **same** time, necessitating a periodic adjusting entry. **Adjusting entries** are journal entries used to record internal transactions at the **end of an accounting period.** Most internal transactions (or adjusting entries) stem from transactions with outside parties that have occurred before

EXHIBIT 3-6

Unadjusted Trial Balance

Fitness Clinic, Inc.
Unadjusted Trial Balance
January 31, 19x2

	Debits	*Credits*
Cash	$ 65,000	
Prepaid rent	20,000	
Equipment	110,000	
Notes payable		$ 35,000
Capital stock		100,000
Service revenue		100,000
Salaries expense	25,000	
Utilities expense	3,000	
Laundry service expense	7,000	
Dividends	5,000	
Totals	$235,000	$235,000

Objective 4
How adjustments, based on past and/or expected future transactions, are recorded at the end of an accounting cycle period (cycle step 4, developed further in Chapter 4).

the end of an accounting period or will occur after the end of an accounting period. Fitness Clinic has three such adjusting entries—unpaid salaries, consumption of a prepayment (rent), and unpaid taxes.

Unpaid Salaries. When employees have worked but have not yet been paid at the end of an operating period, the following type of adjusting entry is necessary to record the economic effect on the business:

GENERAL JOURNAL					J3
Date		Account Titles and Explanation	Ref.	Debit	Credit
19x2					
Jan.	31	Salaries Expense (E)	511	5,000	
		Salaries Payable (L)	212		5,000
		To record unpaid salaries.			

Objective 5
The role of matching and revenue recognition in helping to guide the end-of-period adjusting entries.

This adjusting entry (like many others) reflects the matching concept discussed in Chapter 2. The debit to Salary Expense is a reduction in stockholders' equity, and the credit to Salaries Payable is an increase in a liability. While the transaction to actually pay these salaries will occur in the future (February), this demonstrates how adjusting entries can match expenses (salaries) with revenues before assets (cash) are used to pay for these expenses. This adjustment also reports a new liability account, Salaries Payable, which will appear in the adjusted trial balance and in the January 31 balance sheet.

Consumption of a Prepayment. Another type of adjusting entry motivated by matching is required to account for prepaid rent, which was paid in an earlier transaction (in December) to cover expenses for January and February of 19x2 and is partially consumed in January.

GENERAL JOURNAL					J3
Date		Account Titles and Explanation	Ref.	Debit	Credit
19x2					
Jan.	31	Rent Expense (E)	531	10,000	
		Prepaid Rent (A)	131		10,000
		To record January rent.			

An expense represents the consumption of an asset or the incurrence of an obligation that will consume an asset at a later date. In this case, the asset, Prepaid Rent, is being consumed (reduced); thus the credit entry reducing the asset account.

Unpaid Taxes. On January 31, 19x2, after examining its revenues and expenses, Fitness Clinic determines it will owe the federal government $10,000 for income taxes. The adjusting entry to match this expense with January's revenues is:

GENERAL JOURNAL					J3
Date		Account Titles and Explanation	Ref.	Debit	Credit
19x2 Jan.	31	Income Tax Expense (E) Income Taxes Payable (L) To record income taxes owed for January.	591 215	10,000	 10,000

The ledger in Exhibit 3-7 indicates the accounts affected by all of Fitness Clinic's journal entries after posting. Note the "Ref." column in each account where the journal page has been inserted, as a way of identifying the source of the posted amount. Note that the source of the posted amount is indicated by inserting the journal page in the "Ref." column of each account.

After posting the January transactions and adjusting entries to the ledger and determining the balances of the accounts, the adjusted trial balance illustrated in Exhibit 3-8 can be constructed by listing all the account titles and their debit and credit balances in a two-column schedule. You will learn more about adjusting entries and trial balances in Chapter 4.

Financial Statements Preparation (accounting cycle step 5)

Once the adjusted trial balance is prepared, step 4 of the cycle is complete and financial statements (step 5 of the cycle) may be prepared just as we did in Chapter 2. The order for preparing the financial statements is important. The balance sheet cannot be prepared before the income statement and retained earnings statement since (1) net income must be computed in order to know how much to add to retained earnings; and (2) the new retained earnings balance—after adding net income (or deducting net loss) and deducting dividends (if any)—is needed to make the balance sheet balance. Exhibit 3-9 shows these three statements for Fitness Clinic, Inc., which are prepared in order by taking the appropriate account balances from the adjusted trial balance in Exhibit 3-8. The income statement accounts listed in the trial balance are included in the income statement; the net income from the income statement along with the dividends account are included in the retained earnings statement; the ending balance from the retained earnings statement along with all of the asset, liability, and stockholders' equity account balances from the adjusted trial balance are reported in the balance sheet. Note that while the revenue, expense, and dividends accounts all affect the balance sheet in some way, they are never listed in the balance sheet as separate accounts.

Analyzing the Effects of an Operating Period

In the Fitness Clinic example, the transactions recorded during its operating period changed the company's assets, liabilities, and stockholders' equity. Cash decreased, prepaid rent decreased, equipment increased, liabilities increased, capital stock remained unchanged, and retained earnings increased. The changing state of assets, liabilities, and stockholders' equity is illustrated in Exhibit 3-10. Note that cash has a net decrease of $15,000; prepaid rent decreased by $10,000; equipment has an increase of $110,000; obligations increased to employees by $5,000 and to creditors by $45,000; and the stockholders' residual interest increased by a net of $35,000, the amount of net income less dividends.

EXHIBIT 3-7

Fitness Clinic, Inc.'s Ledger Accounts on January 31, 19x2

GENERAL LEDGER

Cash Account No. 111

Date		Explanation	Ref.	Debit	Credit	Balance Debit (Credit)
19x1						
Dec.	28	Issuance of capital stock	J1	100,000		100,000
	31	Prepayment of rent	J1		20,000	80,000
19x2						
Jan.	14	Salaries paid	J2		10,000	70,000
	22	Salaries paid	J2		15,000	55,000
	27	Utilities paid	J2		3,000	52,000
	29	Laundry services paid	J2		7,000	45,000
	30	Service revenue	J2	100,000		145,000
	30	Proceeds from note	J3	35,000		180,000
	30	Equipment purchase	J3		110,000	70,000
	31	Dividends paid	J3		5,000	65,000

Prepaid Rent Account No. 131

Date		Explanation	Ref.	Debit	Credit	Balance Debit (Credit)
19x1						
Dec.	31	Prepayment of rent	J1	20,000		20,000
19x2						
Jan.	31	January rent expense	J3		10,000	10,000

Equipment Account No. 162

Date		Explanation	Ref.	Debit	Credit	Balance Debit (Credit)
19x2						
Jan.	30	Equipment purchase	J3	110,000		110,000

Salaries Payable Account No. 212

Date		Explanation	Ref.	Debit	Credit	Balance (Debit) Credit
19x2						
Jan.	31	Unpaid salaries	J3		5,000	5,000

Income Taxes Payable Account No. 215

Date		Explanation	Ref.	Debit	Credit	Balance (Debit) Credit
19x2						
Jan.	31	Jan. income taxes owed	J3		10,000	10,000

Notes Payable						Account No. 217
Date		Explanation	Ref.	Debit	Credit	Balance (Debit) Credit
19x2 Jan.	30	Bank note	J3		35,000	35,000

Capital Stock						Account No. 311
Date		Explanation	Ref.	Debit	Credit	Balance (Debit) Credit
19x1 Dec.	28	Issuance of capital stock	J1		100,000	100,000

Service Revenue						Account No. 421
Date		Explanation	Ref.	Debit	Credit	Balance (Debit) Credit
19x2 Jan.	30	Service revenue	J2		100,000	100,000

Salaries Expense						Account No. 511
Date		Explanation	Ref.	Debit	Credit	Balance Debit (Credit)
19x2 Jan.	14	Salaries paid	J2	10,000		10,000
	22	Salaries paid	J2	15,000		25,000
	31	Unpaid salaries	J3	5,000		30,000

Rent Expense						Account No. 531
Date		Explanation	Ref.	Debit	Credit	Balance Debit (Credit)
19x2 Jan.	31	January rent expense	J3	10,000		10,000

Utilities Expense						Account No. 551
Date		Explanation	Ref.	Debit	Credit	Balance Debit (Credit)
19x2 Jan.	27	Payment of utilities	J2	3,000		3,000

EXHIBIT 3-7 *(concluded)*

Laundry Service Expense						Account No. 553
Date		Explanation	Ref.	Debit	Credit	Balance Debit (Credit)
19x2 Jan.	29	Payment of laundry bill	J2	7,000		7,000

Income Tax Expense						Account No. 591
Date		Explanation	Ref.	Debit	Credit	Balance Debit (Credit)
19x2 Jan.	31	January income taxes	J3	10,000		10,000

Dividends						Account No. 615
Date		Explanation	Ref.	Debit	Credit	Balance Debit (Credit)
19x2 Jan.	31	Dividends paid	J3	5,000		5,000

EXHIBIT 3-8

Adjusted Trial Balance

Fitness Clinic, Inc.
Adjusted Trial Balance
January 31, 19x2

	Debits	*Credits*
Cash	$ 65,000	
Prepaid Rent	10,000	
Equipment	110,000	
Salaries Payable		$ 5,000
Income Taxes Payable		10,000
Notes Payable		35,000
Capital Stock		100,000
Service Revenue		100,000
Salaries Expense	30,000	
Rent Expense	10,000	
Utilities Expense	3,000	
Laundry Service Expense	7,000	
Income Tax Expense	10,000	
Dividends	5,000	
Totals	$250,000	$250,000

EXHIBIT 3-9

Income Statement, Retained Earnings Statement, and Balance Sheet

Fitness Clinic, Inc.
Income Statement
For the Month Ended January 31, 19x2

Service revenue		$100,000
Expenses:		
Salaries expense	$30,000	
Rent expense	10,000	
Utilities expense	3,000	
Laundry service expense	7,000	
Total expenses (excluding income tax)		50,000
Net income before taxes		$ 50,000
Income tax expense		10,000
Net income		$ 40,000

Fitness Clinic, Inc.
Retained Earnings Statement
For the Month Ended January 31, 19x2

Retained earnings, January 1, 19x2	$ 0
Net income for January	40,000
Dividends	(5,000)
Retained earnings, January 31, 19x2	$35,000

Fitness Clinic, Inc.
Balance Sheet
January 31, 19x2

Assets		**Liabilities and Stockholders' Equity**	
Current assets:		Current liabilities:	
Cash	$ 65,000	Salaries payable	$ 5,000
Prepaid rent	10,000	Notes payable	35,000
Total current assets	$ 75,000	Income taxes payable	10,000
Noncurrent assets:		Total current liabilities	$ 50,000
Equipment	$110,000	Stockholders' equity:	
Total noncurrent assets	$110,000	Capital stock	$100,000
		Retained earnings	35,000
		Total stockholders' equity	$135,000
Total assets	$185,000	Total liabilities and stockholders' equity	$185,000

Operating and Nonoperating Cash Flows. Decision makers are always interested in the status of a business's cash flow—the amount of cash flowing into the business and the amount of cash flowing out. Exhibit 3-11 analyzes Fitness Clinic's cash flow from all sources. Because all sales (service revenues) were for cash in January, sales provided $100,000 in positive cash flows. Remember that income statements represent more than just the cash flow of a business; they reflect the flow of net assets. Not all the expenses for the month of January 19x2

EXHIBIT 3-10

Fitness Clinic's Changes in Assets, Liabilities, and Stockholders' Equity

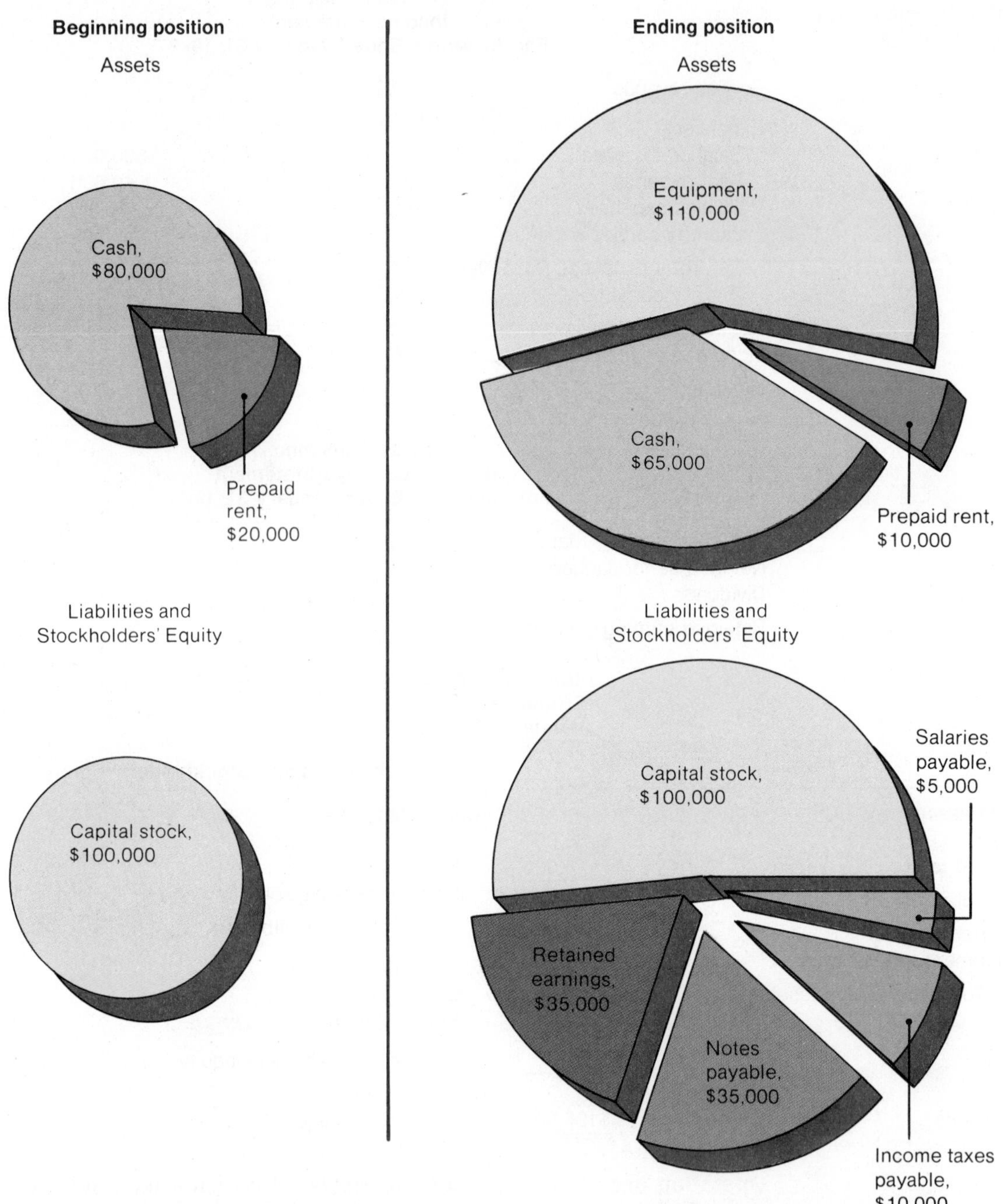

required cash payment. The rent was actually paid in December 19x1 (the previous period), but $10,000 of the original payment was consumed in January. The salaries still owed to employees at January 31 will be paid in February, but the $5,000 of salaries are shown in the January income statement because the value of the employees' services was consumed in January. The $10,000 of income tax

EXHIBIT 3-11

Comparison of Operating and Nonoperating Cash Flows, Fitness Clinic, Inc.

Income Statement		Cash Flow Analysis: January 19x2 Cash Flow	Cash Flow Analysis: Explanation for Cash Flow Effects
Revenue:			**Operating transactions:**
Service revenue	$100,000	$ 100,000	All sales were received in cash.
Expenses:			
Salary expense.	30,000	25,000	$5,000 is to be paid in February.
Utilities expense	3,000	3,000	All utilities are paid in cash.
Rent expense	10,000	0	$10,000 was prepaid in December.
Laundry expense.	7,000	7,000	All laundry services were paid for in cash.
Income tax expense	10,000	0	$10,000 is to be paid in February.
Net income	$ 40,000	$ 65,000	Cash flow from **operations.** (The difference of $25,000 between net income and cash flow from operations is because certain expenses did not require cash flow in January.)
			Financing transactions:
		$ 35,000	Note is to be paid off in the future.
		(5,000)	Cash dividends were paid to owners.
		$ 30,000	Increase in cash from **financing** activities.
			Investing transactions:
		$(110,000)	Cash was paid for equipment.
		$(110,000)	Decrease in cash from **investing** activities.
		$ (15,000)	Overall cash decrease.

expense is recognized in January because the $10,000 is an obligation to the government, but the tax obligation required no cash flow in January. Since Fitness Clinic only paid $35,000 in cash for expenses, the difference between the $100,000 cash from sales and the $35,000 cash paid for expenses resulted in $65,000 positive cash flow provided by operations.

In January 19x2, Fitness Clinic borrowed $35,000, paid dividends of $5,000 (financing activities), and purchased equipment for $110,000 (investing activity). Thus, the total inflow of cash totaled $100,000 (from operations $65,000 plus borrowing of $35,000), but the outflow of cash totaled $115,000 (for equipment purchase of $110,000 plus dividends of $5,000) and exceeded the inflow of cash by $15,000. Thus, cash decreased from $80,000 to $65,000.

ACCRUAL VERSUS CASH BASIS OF ACCOUNTING

In Chapter 2, you learned that financial statements for businesses are based on the *accrual basis of accounting.* **Accrual accounting** is the approach to accounting that allows recording of the effects of transactions in the period in which economic events take place even if cash flow from the transactions is at another point in time. In accrual accounting, revenues are recorded when revenue is earned and expenses are recorded when the effort to produce revenue is expended. Because of accrual accounting, the income statement for a period of time will usually not equal the cash flow from operations (as illustrated in Exhibit 3-11).

Objective 6
The difference between the cash basis and the accrual basis of accounting.

Accrual accounting permits revenues to be recorded before cash is collected and expenses to be recorded before bills are paid. Note that in an accrual system when cash is used to acquire an asset or reduce an obligation, it is called an **expenditure,** while an **expense** refers to the use of an asset or incurrence of an obligation in order to obtain revenue. Consider the following comparison between the cash basis and accrual basis of accounting:

	Journal Entries					
	Cash Basis			*Accrual Basis*		
Event	*Accounts*	*Dr.*	*Cr.*	*Accounts*	*Dr.*	*Cr.*
1. Buy merchandise for $50	Merchandise expense (E) Cash (A)	50	 50	Merchandise (A) Cash (A)	50	 50
2. Sell merchandise costing $50 for $100 on account	No entry			Accounts Receivable (A) Sales (R)	100	 100
	No entry			Merchandise Expense (E) Merchandise (A)	50	 50
3. Receive $100 cash on account	Cash (A) Revenue (R)	100	 100	Cash (A) Accounts Receivable (A)	100	 100
4. Receive a bill for newspaper advertising $30	No entry			Advertising Expense (E) Accounts Payable (L)	30	 30
5. Pay for advertising $30 cash	Advertising Expense (E) Cash (A)	30	 30	Accounts Payable (L) Cash (A)	30	 30

The pure cash basis of accounting only records inflows and outflows of cash, with revenues not recorded until cash is received and expenses not recorded until cash is paid. The difference between the cash basis and accrual basis is largely one of timing in that they recognize revenues and expenses at different points in time, often in different accounting periods (e.g., different years).[1]

Accrual accounting calls for the recognition of expenses in the period in which their economic benefits are received regardless of when cash is paid. Also, accrual accounting normally calls for the recognition of revenues in the period in which a sale is made, or a service rendered, even though cash might not be received until the following period. Often this results in a receivable being recorded for a sales transaction and a liability being recorded for an expense transaction, as we saw in our examples.

[1]Note that over the life of the firm the measurement of net income on a cash basis will be the same as on an accrual basis once the balance in all noncash assets and all liabilities become zero. This may be seen in the simple example provided here. There are no balances left in any of the assets or liabilities in this illustration (other than cash), and the ending cash balance of $20 equals the net income on both the cash basis and the accrual basis. Of course, in real cases it is doubtful that all noncash asset and liability balances will ever be zero at the same time.

Throughout this textbook, the principles of accrual accounting govern recognition decisions for balance sheet and income statement purposes. Of course, many business decisions are also concerned with cash flow and cash position. Because of this need for cash based data, GAAP also requires a statement of cash flows to accompany the accrual based statements.

Other Accounting Characteristics and Assumptions

In this chapter we have learned about several basic accounting concepts: revenue recognition; matching; going concern; periodicity. These concepts, along with certain qualitative characteristics, and assumptions provide direction to accountants and are often generally referred to as **accounting principles.** They all play a role in determining whether financial statements are prepared in accordance with generally accepted accounting principles (GAAP).

In recording the transactions in cycle steps 1 through 3 for the Fitness Clinic example, we were employing both the *historical cost assumption* and the qualitative characteristics of *objectivity* or *verifiability*. These features help to enhance the consistent qualities of the data found in financial statements. The **historical cost assumption** calls for all transactions to be recorded at their original (historical) transacted amounts. This use of historical cost is based on the assumption that the values of the recorded items will not change over time.[2] This prohibits companies from arbitrarily changing the values of their assets, liabilities, or stockholders' equity accounts. For example, if Fitness Clinic's capital stock, which originally sold for $100,000, later had a market value of $200,000, the historical cost assumption would prohibit Fitness Clinic from changing the historical value to the market value.

One of the reasons accountants have adopted the historical cost assumption is because the historical amounts of transactions are objectively measurable and independently verifiable. The **objectivity** (or verifiability) **quality** suggests that the data recorded in cycle steps 1 through 4 and reported in the financial statements be based on objective or verifiable evidence. If, for example, 20 people were asked to determine the market value of a plot of land in the heart of a city, their answers would probably vary considerably, making the market value of the land an unverifiable (or subjective) measure. However, if asked to determine the historical cost of the same land, their answers would likely be the same (providing they could locate the original purchase or sales documents). Because accountants place such a high value on the quality of objective or verifiable measurements, financial statements are based on historical costs, which are considered to be more objective or verifiable than other measures.

Another underlying principle in accounting is the *materiality* principle. The **materiality principle** requires the accounting information system to report all material events and transactions affecting the business entity. What is a **material amount?** While this question is not specifically answered in a measurable way, the accounting literature defines a **material amount** as **an amount that would probably affect the decision of a knowledgeable user** of accounting information. Note that applying this principle will generally prohibit a dollar amount to be identified for all situations. For example, a material dollar amount for Ford Motor

[2]The historical cost assumption is also sometimes thought of as the stable dollar assumption since it assumes that the value of the measurement unit (the dollar) does not change over time.

Company would be much larger than a material amount for your corner drugstore. While materiality is a somewhat abstract principle, it is an important feature of GAAP financial statements. Financial statement users may assume that there are no material omissions or misstatements if the statements are prepared in conformance with GAAP.

SUMMARY

The accounting process begins with analyzing transactions and determining how they affect the assets, liabilities, and/or stockholders' equity of a business. Then the economic effect of these transactions on the business is captured by journal entries, and the financial story of the business begins.

Because each transaction has equal debit and credit effects on the balance sheet equation, an orderly recording of transactions occurs as the accounting cycle moves from journal entries and posting to ledger accounts to preparing adjusting entries, and financial statements. The introduction to the first five steps in the accounting cycle in this chapter provides an aid to learning the fundamental nature of accounting relationships. Without this knowledge of the basis of accounting, the all-important analysis and communication of financial results for decision making would not be fully understood.

The financing, investing, and operating activities of a business generate transactions. The business records reflecting these three business activities culminate in financial statements—the income statement summarizing the operating activity of the accounting period and the balance sheet reflecting the results of all business activities as of the end of the accounting period. All this occurs because of the steps in the accounting cycle, of which the debit and credit procedures are one brief part. The main conceptual link among all the accounting cycle steps is the nature of the relationship between economic transactions and the balance sheet equation and its components. Chapter 4 elaborates more on the accounting cycle, with focus on the last three cycle steps.

DEMONSTRATION EXERCISE

Financial Planners, Inc., (FPI) began operations on February 1, 19x1, with the following transactions:

a. Sold capital stock for $50,000.

b. Paid $9,000 for three months' office rent plus another $2,400 for the security deposit. Also paid $500 for one month's rent of office equipment.

During the month of February, FPI also had the following activity:

c. Recorded consulting fees earned of $12,000. Received $4,500 in cash, and the remaining was recorded on account. (Hint: Accounts Receivable is recorded.)

d. Purchased office supplies to be used during the month for $190 cash.

e. Paid salaries of $6,000 and commissions of $3,000 in cash.

f. Received and paid the utility bill of $130 and the telephone bill of $312.

g. Paid entertainment expense of $950 in cash.

h. Recorded the invoice for an introductory ad in *The Wall Street Journal.* The ad, which appeared last month, cost $750, and payment is not due until next month.

i. At the end of the month, FPI purchased office furniture and equipment for $5,670 on account.

Required:

1. Record the above transactions and the adjusting entry required for rent in general journal form including explanations. Post the entries to the appropriate T accounts using the chart of accounts given in Exhibit 3-4, page 107.

2. Prepare a month-end income statement, and post net income or net loss to the Retained Earnings account.
3. Prepare a February 28, 19x1, balance sheet.

Solution:

GENERAL JOURNAL					J1
Date		**Account Titles and Explanation**	**Ref.**	**Debit**	**Credit**
19x1					
Feb.	1	Cash (A)	111	50,000	
		Capital Stock (SE)	311		50,000
		To record issuance of stock.			
	1	Prepaid Rent (A)	131	9,500	
		Security Deposit (A)	171	2,400	
		Cash (A)	111		11,900
		To record prepayment of rent.			
During Feb.		Cash (A)	111	4,500	
		Accounts Receivable (A)	121	7,500	
		Consulting Fees (R)	411		12,000
		To record revenue for the month.			
		Office Supplies Expense (E)	541	190	
		Cash (A)	111		190
		To record purchase of supplies.			
		Salaries Expense (E)	511	6,000	
		Commissions Expense (E)	512	3,000	
		Cash (A)	111		9,000
		To record salaries and commissions for the month.			
		Utilities Expense (E)	551	130	
		Communications Expense (E)	552	312	
		Cash (A)	111		442
		To record expense for the month.			
		Travel and Entertainment Expense (E)	513	950	
		Cash (A)	111		950
		To record expense for the month.			
		Advertising Expense (E)	521	750	
		Accounts Payable (L)	211		750
		To record invoice for *The Wall Street Journal* ad.			
19x1					
Feb.	28	Equipment (A)	162	5,670	
		Accounts Payable (L)	211		5,670
		To record purchase of equipment and furniture.			
	28	Rent Expense (E)	531	3,500	
		Prepaid Rent (A)	131		3,500
		To adjust for February rent.			

Cash 111

(*a*)	50,000	(*b*)	11,900
(*c*)	4,500	(*d*)	190
		(*e*)	9,000
		(*f*)	442
		(*g*)	950
Bal.	32,018		

Accounts Receivable 121

(*c*)	7,500		
Bal.	7,500		

Prepaid Rent 131

(*b*)	9,500	(*j*)	3,500
Bal.	6,000		

Equipment 162

(*i*)	5,670		
Bal.	5,670		

Security Deposit 171

(*b*)	2,400		
Bal.	2,400		

Accounts Payable 211

		(*h*)	750
		(*i*)	5,670
		Bal.	6,420

Capital Stock 311

		(*a*)	50,000
		Bal.	50,000

Consulting Fees 411

		(*c*)	12,000

Salaries Expense 511

(*e*)	6,000		

Commissions Expense 512

(*e*)	3,000		

Travel and Entertainment Expense 513

(*g*)	950		

Advertising Expense 521

(*h*)	750		

Rent Expense 531

(*j*)	3,500		

Office Supplies Expense 541

(*d*)	190		

Utilities Expense 551

(*f*)	130		

Communications Expense 552

(*f*)	312		

Financial Planners, Inc.
Income Statement
For the Month Ended February 28, 19x1

Revenue:		
Consulting fees		$12,000
Expenses:		
Salaries expense	$6,000	
Commissions expense	3,000	
Travel and entertainment expense	950	
Advertising expense	750	
Rent expense	3,500	
Office supplies expense	190	
Utilities expense	130	
Communications expense	312	
Total expenses		14,832
Net income (loss)		$(2,832)

Retained Earnings 331

	Debit	Credit
	2,832	
Bal.	2,832	

Financial Planners, Inc.
Balance Sheet
February 28, 19x1

Assets

Current assets:	
Cash	$32,018
Accounts receivable	7,500
Prepaid rent	6,000
Total current assets	$45,518
Noncurrent assets:	
Office equipment and furniture	$ 5,670
Security deposit	2,400
Total noncurrent assets	$ 8,070
Total assets	$53,588

Liabilities and Stockholders' Equity

Liabilities:	
Accounts payable	$ 6,420
Total liabilities	$ 6,420
Stockholders' equity:	
Capital stock	$50,000
Retained earnings	(2,832)
Total stockholders' equity	$47,168
Total liabilities and stockholders' equity	$53,588

KEY TERMS

Account. Provides a separate record for each asset, liability, and stockholders' equity item on the balance sheet and each temporary account such as revenue, expense, and dividends. Indicates increases and decreases based on debit and credit rules. Informal T account is used for instructional purposes, while the formal ledger account is used for both instructional purposes and actual accounting systems.

Account balance. Difference between debits and credits in any individual account at any point in time.

Accounting cycle. Six accounting steps that begin with analyzing transactions and end with closing journal entries.

Accrual accounting. The approach to accounting that allows recording of the effects of transactions in the period in which economic events take place even if cash flow from the transactions is at another point in time. In accrual accounting, revenues are recorded when revenue is earned and expenses are recorded when the effort to produce revenue is expended; contrasts with cash basis of accounting. (Accrual accounting is the same as accrual basis of accounting in Chapter 2 term list.)

Adjusted trial balance. The end-of-period trial balance taken after cycle step 4.

Adjusting entries. Journal entries used to record internal transactions at the end of an accounting period.

Chart of accounts. List of account titles and account identification numbers used by a business in its accounting system.

Classified balance sheet. A balance sheet that shows current and noncurrent classifications for assets and liabilities.

Complex entry. A journal entry that affects three or more accounts.

Credit. Right side of account or journal entry.

Current asset. An asset that is expected to be consumed or converted to cash in its entirety within one year or operating cycle, whichever is longer.

Current liability. A liability that is expected to utilize cash or other current assets within the next year or operating cycle, whichever is longer.

Debit. Left side of an account or journal entry.

Double-entry system. System whereby each transaction affects two or more accounts and where the total debits equal the total credits for each transaction.

Expenditure. An outflow of cash for the acquisition of a product, service, or the reduction of an obligation.

Fiscal year. Twelve consecutive months that may begin at any time in the calendar year. Most companies use January 1 through December 31 as their fiscal year thus making fiscal and calendar years identical.

General journal. Chronological record that records accounting transactions in the order of the date they occur so that all debits and credits for all transactions are listed in one medium of original entry; also called journal.

Going concern concept. The business entity is assumed to have an indefinite life; therefore, financial statements are based on the principle of continuous life.

Historical cost assumption. Requires that all transactions be recorded at their original (historical) transacted amounts.

Journal entry. Record of the effects of an accounting transaction with equal debit and credit effects; also called general journal entry.

Ledger. A file that contains all of the accounts used in an accounting system; also called general ledger.

Material amount. A material amount is one that would probably affect the decision of a knowledgeable user of accounting data.

Materiality principle. Requires the accounting system and resulting financial statements to reveal all material events or transactions affecting the business.

Normal balance. The side of the account (debit or credit) on which the increases are recorded. Assets, expenses, and dividends have normal debit balances, while liabilities and paid-in capital, retained earnings, and revenues have normal credit balances.

Objectivity. A preferred quality of accounting information. Accountants require that data recorded in the accounting records be based on objective or verifiable information.

Periodicity assumption. States that although business activity is continuous, financial statements divide this continuous flow into uniform time periods.

Permanent accounts. Accounts that appear on the balance sheet—assets and liabilities, and those stockholders' equity accounts that are not closed to Retained Earnings; also called real accounts.

Posting. Recording, transferring, or copying of the debit and credit dollar amounts from the journal into the appropriate ledger accounts.

Reference (Ref.) column. Column in the journal or a ledger account used as a cross reference to the location of the ledger account or journal page.

Simple entry. A journal entry that affects only two accounts.

Source documents. Records usually retained in business files that provide evidence about the transactions which have actually occurred.

Subsidiary ledgers. Subfiles providing detail for specific general ledger accounts.

Temporary accounts. The accounts that are closed to Retained Earnings including revenue, expense, and dividend accounts; also called nominal accounts.

Trial balance. A list of account balances with columns for debit and credit balances used to show the balance sheet equation remains in balance through equal debits and credits.

Unadjusted trial balance. Trial balance prepared before the adjustments (cycle step 4) have been made.

SYNONYMS

Complex entry; compound entry.

Expenditure; cash payment.

Fiscal year; 12-month accounting period.

Journal; general journal.

Ledger; general ledger.

Net income; profit.

Objectivity; verifiability.

Permanent accounts; real accounts; balance sheet accounts.

Temporary accounts; nominal accounts; income statement and dividend accounts.

QUESTIONS

1. What is the main purpose of the double-entry system in accounting and what role do debits and credits play in it?
2. How do debits affect assets? Liabilities? Stockholders' equity?
3. How do credits affect assets? Liabilities? Stockholders' equity?
4. What is the effect of debits and credits on revenues? Expenses? Retained earnings?
5. If revenues increase retained earnings and retained earnings normally has a credit balance, then what kind of balance will revenues normally have? How are revenues increased?
6. If expenses decrease retained earnings and retained earnings normally has a credit balance, then what is the normal balance for expense accounts? How are expenses decreased?
7. What is an account? A ledger account? A T account?
8. Describe the information contained in a formal ledger account.
9. How is a trial balance used, and how is it different than a balance sheet?
10. What is a journal? Describe the data that is entered into a journal entry. What role does the chart of accounts play in journalizing?
11. What triggers the need to record a journal entry?
12. Describe the process of posting. How often does posting take place?
13. What is a trial balance taken after the first three cycle steps called? What types of accounts does it consist of at this stage?
14. What does cycle step 4 accomplish?
15. How does matching affect cycle step 4?
16. Explain why the adjusting entries, all recorded at the end of an accounting period, are sometimes referred to as internal transactions. To what two types of external transactions are these adjustments related?
17. What is the trial balance called when prepared after cycle step 4?
18. Give an example of a journal entry describing an operating transaction.
19. Give an example of a journal entry describing a financing transaction.
20. Give an example of a complex journal entry for an investing transaction.
21. Give an example of an adjusting journal entry for an operating account. What original transaction does this adjusting entry refer to?
22. Which statement contains permanent accounts?
23. Which statement contains only temporary account balances? Where is the net effect of the temporary account balances of prior accounting periods reported?
24. Give journal entry examples of the following effects:
    a. Increase an asset and increase a liability.
    b. Increase an asset and increase stockholders' equity.
    c. Decrease an asset and decrease a liability.
    d. Increase one asset and decrease another asset.
    e. Increase a liability and decrease stockholders' equity.
25. When looking at the results of operations, what does the income statement show?
26. Why is net cash flow different from net asset flow?
27. What is accrual accounting? How does it differ from cash accounting?
28. What is the periodicity concept?
29. Differentiate between expenditures and expenses.
30. State the balance sheet classification of each of the following accounts (asset, liability, or stockholders' equity):
    a. Rent Expense.
    b. Prepaid Rent.
    c. Equipment.
    d. Accounts Payable.
    e. Retained Earnings.
    f. Salaries Payable.

31. Explain how the historical cost is related to the quality of objectivity.
32. Explain the materiality principle and define a material amount.

EXERCISES

EXERCISE 3-1
L.O. 1, 2

Describing Accounts

Listed below are some of the ledger accounts of the Johnson Corporation. Describe each account as either an asset, liability, or stockholders' equity account and tell if the account normally carries a debit or credit balance. If the account is a stockholders' equity account, describe the type of account. (paid-in capital, revenue, expense, etc.).

a. Cash.
b. Accounts Receivable.
c. Salaries Payable.
d. Capital Stock.
e. Prepaid Insurance.
f. Insurance Expense.
g. Interest Revenue.
h. Dividends.
i. Bonds Payable.
j. Machinery and Equipment.
k. Communications Expense.
l. Consulting Fees.
m. Unearned Consulting Fees.
n. Accounts Payable.
o. Land.
p. Notes Payable.
q. Prepaid Rent.
r. Retained Earnings.
s. Building.
t. Supplies.

EXERCISE 3-2
L.O. 1

Journal Entries and Accounts—Multiple Choice

1. Which group of accounts contains only those that normally have a debit balance?
   a. Accounts Receivable, Retained Earnings, and Equipment.
   b. Bond Investment, Cash, and Capital Stock.
   c. Prepaid Insurance, Equipment, and Interest Expense.
   d. Note Receivable, Salaries Payable, and Communications Expense.
   e. None of the above.
2. Which group of accounts contains only those that normally have a credit balance?
   a. Consulting Fees, Land, and Supplies.
   b. Capital Stock, Accounts Payable, and Taxes Payable.
   c. Interest Revenue, Land, and Furniture and Fixtures.
   d. Notes Payable, Retained Earnings, and Communications Expense.
   e. None of the above.
3. Hien Condiments, Inc., purchases manufacturing equipment by issuing a short-term note for $45,000. What is the journal entry to record this transaction?
   a. Debit Notes Payable and credit Equipment for $45,000.
   b. Debit Equipment and credit Cash for $45,000.
   c. Debit Equipment and credit Notes Payable for $45,000.
   d. Debit Inventory and credit Notes Payable for $45,000.
4. Which of the following entries increases total assets?
   a. Debit Cash; credit Accounts Payable.
   b. Debit Equipment; credit Notes Payable.
   c. Debit Cash; credit Capital Stock.
   d. All of the above.
   e. None of the above.
5. Which of the following transactions increases net assets (stockholders' equity)?
   a. Buy land for cash (one half) and notes payable (one half).
   b. Borrow cash from bank for note.
   c. Buy new equipment for cash.

d. Sell merchandise to a customer for a profit.
e. None of the above.

6. Which of the transactions in question 5 above are financing or investing activities?
a. (*a*) and (*c*) only.
b. (*b*) and (*d*) only.
c. (*a*), (*b*), and (*c*) only.
d. (*a*) and (*b*) only.
e. None of the above.

EXERCISE 3-3
L.O. 1

Effects of Transactions

Listed below are various transactions for the Byrne Company that occurred during 19xx. At the time the journal entries for these transactions were made, did the respective transactions **increase**, **decrease**, or cause **no change** in (1) the current cash balance and (2) the current period net income under the accrual basis of accounting? Remember, a transaction's effect on cash may differ from its effect on net income.

a. Declaration and payment of a cash dividend.
b. Sale of services on credit.
c. Issuance of a $10,000 note in return for cash.
d. Payment of an accounts payable on a purchase made in the current period.
e. Payment of 19xx rent on a building.
f. Payment of salaries.

EXERCISE 3-4
L.O. 1

Preparing Journal Entries

Prepare the journal entries in general journal form that the Sullivan Company would record for the following events during 19xx:

a. Purchased $400 of supplies on account on January 27.
b. Prepaid two months' rent of $5,000 in cash on February 1.
c. Provided $3,900 of services on account on May 31.
d. Issued additional capital stock for $10,000 on July 31.

EXERCISE 3-5
L.O. 1, 4, 6

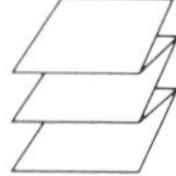

Preparing Journal Entries

Listed below is a series of transactions for the King Company that occurred in 19x2.

19x2		
Jan.	1	Paid $12,000 for 19x2 rent of office space.
Feb.	3	Purchased sewing machines at a total cost of $8,000; paid cash of $4,000 with the balance due on March 10, 19x2.
Mar.	5	Paid the outstanding balance on the sewing machines purchased on February 3.
Mar.	20	Collected $9,500 cash for credit sales recorded during 19x1.
Nov.	1	Paid $7,000 cash for a fire and theft insurance policy covering 19x3 and 19x4.
Dec.	31	Declared and paid a cash dividend of $10,000.
	31	Recorded rent expense for the year.

Required:
Prepare the journal entries in journal form for the above transactions.

EXERCISE 3-6
L.O. 1, 4, 6

Preparing Journal Entries

For transactions (*a*)–(*f*) below, give the appropriate journal entries in general journal form for the Miser Company.

a. Issued shares of capital stock to investors in exchange for $40,000 cash.
b. Purchased a piece of equipment for $50,000, for which Miser paid $30,000 cash and the remainder in the form of a long-term note.

c. Purchased supplies on credit for $5,000.
d. Paid the $5,000 owed in transaction (*c*).
e. Purchased an insurance policy for $1,000 cash. Coverage is for the next year.
f. Used up $600 of the supplies purchased in transaction (*c*).

EXERCISE 3-7
L.O. 1, 4, 6

Preparing Journal Entries

Consider the following selected business transactions of the Rocky Mountain Real Estate Company in September 19xx.

19xx

Sept. 1 Performed rental management services for apartment building for $4,000, of which $1,500 was collected in cash at the time the services were performed and the remainder was billed with payment expected in October.

9 Cash amounting to $75 was stolen from the company's cash drawer. The company's insurance does not cover this type of loss.

10 Declared and paid a cash dividend of $10,000 on the company's capital stock.

15 Paid $2,300 for 19xx taxes on business property. This amount was previously recorded on August 31, 19xx, with the following entry:

Property Tax Expense	2,300	
Property Taxes Payable.		2,300

19 Purchased three company cars at a total cost of $35,000. Paid $10,000 in cash and signed a $25,000, one-year, 10 percent note for the balance.

30 Utilities expense for the main office amounts to $5,000 for the month of September; $2,900 was paid on September 30, and $2,100 remains unpaid.

30 Real estate brokers working for the company earned commissions of $25,000 during September, of which $10,000 has been previously paid to the broker employees.

30 Estimated income tax for September is $9,500. No income tax was paid during the month.

Required:
Prepare journal entries in journal form to record the above transactions using appropriate revenue, expense, asset, liability, and stockholders' equity accounts. Prepare entries only for the transactions indicated on the dates indicated.

EXERCISE 3-8
L.O. 1, 2, 3, 5, 6, 7, 9

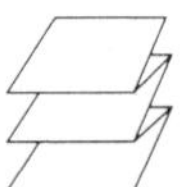

Journal Entries and Effect on Financial Statements

ABC Corporation was formed on January 1, 19xx. Assume that the following three transactions are the **only** transactions in which ABC was involved during 19xx:

a. Three investors contributed $10,000 each in return for the issuance of 100 shares of capital stock to each investor.
b. ABC Corporation incurred operating expenses of $8,500, $7,000 of which were paid in cash.
c. ABC Corporation earned revenues of $22,000, $15,000 of which were received in cash.

Required:
1. Prepare journal entries for the above transactions to record their proper effects.
2. Prepare the December 31, 19xx, balance sheet. What is the total dollar value of assets?
3. Compute the correct net income figure for ABC for 19xx using the accrual basis of accounting.

EXERCISE 3-9
L.O. 3

Trial Balance Preparation

Richmond Electronics general ledger consists of the following accounts on March 31, 19xx:

Accounts Receivable.	$ 18,000
Accounts Payable	12,000
Building	50,000
Capital Stock	30,000
Cash	7,000
Communications Expense	10,000
Interest Payable	1,500
Land	15,000
Notes Payable	20,000
Retained Earnings	5,500
Salaries Expense	60,000
Salaries Payable.	6,000
Service Revenue	100,000
Supplies Expense	15,000

Required:
Prepare the March 31, 19xx, trial balance. Assume all accounts carry their normal balances.

EXERCISE 3-10
L.O. 3

Trial Balance Preparation

The general ledger for Kasar, Inc., consists of the following accounts on December 31, 19xx:

	Normal (not normal)
Accounts Receivable	$ 9,500
Accounts Payable	12,700
Building	80,000
Capital Stock	150,000
Cash	?
Communications Expense.	5,000
Income Tax Expense	760
Income Taxes Payable	760
Interest Receivable	800
Interest Revenue	800
Land	60,000
Note Receivable	10,000
Rent Expense	6,000
Retained Earnings	(5,000)
Salaries Expense.	30,000
Salaries Payable	5,000
Service Revenue	55,000
Supplies Expense	10,000
Supplies Inventory	2,000
Utilities Expense	1,000

Required:
Prepare the December 31, 19xx, trial balance, filling in the missing amount. Unless otherwise indicated, assume all accounts carry their normal balances.

EXERCISE 3-11
L.O. 3

Determining Retained Earnings Account Balance

On January 1, 19xx, the Sky-High Company had a $20,000 credit balance in its Retained Earnings account. During 19xx, the Sky-High Company incurred a net loss of $5,000, declared and paid cash dividends of $4,000, and issued 1,000 new shares of stock for $3,500 cash. Compute the balance in the Retained Earnings account for the Sky-High Company on December 31, 19xx.

EXERCISE 3-12
L.O. 1

Cycle Steps 1 and 2

Record the following transactions in the journal on January 1, 19xx.

a. Paid $20,000 cash for five months' rent of equipment.
b. Agreed to pay a new manager $6,000 per month on the first day of each month starting February 1.
c. Purchased supplies for $750 cash.
d. Borrowed $10,000 cash by signing a note at the bank.

EXERCISE 3-13
L.O. 2

Cycle Steps 3 and 4

1. Consider the transactions in Exercise 3-12 above, and post their effects to the appropriate ledger accounts.
2. Prepare any necessary adjusting entries at January 31, 19xx, suggested by the operating transactions in Exercise 3-12.

EXERCISE 3-14
L.O. 3

Trial Balance

The income statement accounts prepared as of December 31, 19xx, the end of Howley Company's fiscal year, contain the following balances:

	Debits	*Credits*
Service Fees		$9,000
Rent Expense	$ 500	
Salaries Expense	2,600	
Supplies Expense	200	
Advertising Expense	300	
Income Tax Expense	540	

Included in other accounts are Dividends Declared and Paid of $1,000 and Retained Earnings of $12,500.

Required:
1. Prepare an income statement for the period ending December 31, 19xx.
2. Prepare a retained earnings statement for the period ending December 31, 19xx.

EXERCISE 3-15
L.O. 1, 2, 4, 5, 6

Multiple Choice

1. The accounting cycle—
   a. Includes analyzing source documents, entering transactions, and posting.
   b. Includes preparing trial balances.
   c. Includes adjusting entries, closing temporary accounts, and preparing financial statements.
   d. All of the above.
2. Posting, one of the mechanical steps in the accounting cycle, is done to—
   a. Tie the transactions entered in the journal to the individual accounts in the general ledger.

b. Create more clerical work.
c. Prepare the accounts for the closing process.
d. Analyze the source documents received from external users.

3. During its first year of operations, Sperry paid its employees $10,000 but owed its employees an additional $2,000. Assuming the accrual basis of accounting is used, the amount Sperry will recognize as salary expense at year-end on its income statement is:
   a. $10,000.
   b. $8,000.
   c. $20,000.
   d. $12,000.
4. Accountants recognizing transactions and amounts in one period even though the cash consequences may occur in different periods describes—
   a. Financial accounting.
   b. Cash basis of accounting.
   c. Accrual basis of accounting.
   d. Managerial accounting.

EXERCISE 3-16
L.O. 6

Accounting Principles

1. The going-concern assumption:
   a. Means a business has a life as long as its owners.
   b. Suggests that there is no end point in the life of a business.
   c. Requires that financial statements be prepared periodically.
   d. All of the above.
   e. None of the above.
2. The use of historical costs:
   a. Requires adjustments for periodic changes in the value of assets and liabilities.
   b. Is the basis for financial statements prepared in conformance with GAAP.
   c. Differs from the original transacted amounts used to record the events of the business.
   d. All of the above.
   e. None of the above.
3. A material amount is:
   a. $1,000,000 or more.
   b. $500,000 or more.
   c. $250,000 or more.
   d. Not defined in money amounts.
   e. None of the above.
4. Objectivity:
   a. Requires transactions to be recorded at amounts that are verifiable.
   b. Requires the use of historical costs or market value, whichever is more objective.
   c. Requires that no subjective judgments be used to record events or transactions.
   d. All of the above.
   e. None of the above.
5. Periodic financial statements must be prepared:
   a. At least once each year.
   b. At the end of the business operations.
   c. Whenever someone asks for them.
   d. Weekly, monthly, quarterly, and annually.
   e. None of the above.

EXERCISE 3-17
L.O. 1, 2, 3, 6

True or False Questions

Use T or F to indicate whether the following statements are true or false:

_____ 1. Periodicity is required because of the going-concern assumption.
_____ 2. The historical-cost principle is more consistent with the objectivity principle than a fair market value principle.
_____ 3. Matching requires first knowing the costs of the period and then finding their benefits.
_____ 4. The double-entry system requires exactly two accounts to be affected by each transaction.
_____ 5. The double-entry system requires that the total debits equal the total credits for each transaction.
_____ 6. A material omission could be so small that you would not have changed your decision had you known about it.
_____ 7. Asset accounts are all permanent accounts.
_____ 8. Revenue accounts are all permanent accounts.
_____ 9. Total debits must always equal total credits.
_____ 10. Debit means increase and credit means decrease.

EXERCISE 3-18
L.O. 3

Annual Report—Ralston Purina

Consider the 1989 Ralston Purina annual report reproduced in Appendix E at the end of this text. From the Consolidated Statement of Earnings, identify the following amounts for fiscal 1989.

1. Net sales.
2. Total costs and expenses.
3. Income taxes.
4. Net earnings.

PROBLEMS

PROBLEM 3-1
L.O. 1

Balance Sheet Equation

National Stock Investments (NSI) begins business on January 1, 19xx, by receiving $1 million from owners for capital stock and borrowing $500,000 from the local bank. During January, additional transactions were:

Transaction	*Date*	*Explanation*	*Amount*
a.	Jan. 1	Paid for January and February rent	$ 10,000
b.	4	Purchased office supplies on account	2,500
c.	10	Earned and collected sales commissions . . .	100,000
d.	15	Paid salaries	35,000
e.	30	Paid telephone and other utility bills	3,100
f.	31	Earned and collected sales commissions . . .	94,000
g.	31	Issued a note to purchase land for use as the site of an office building	100,000
h.	31	Paid salaries	40,000
i.	31	Made necessary adjusting entries for rent and office supplies.	

At month-end, $500 of office supplies were on hand. All sales commissions and purchases are on a cash basis.

Required:

1. Analyze each transaction in terms of debits and credits by filling out the following schedule. (Show revenues and expenses as changes in stockholders' equity.)

Transaction	*Assets*	=	*Liabilities*	+	*Stockholders' Equity*
Issued stock	Dr. $1,000,000				
Borrowed funds	Dr. 500,000		Cr. $500,000		Cr. $1,000,000
a.					
b.					
c.					
d.					
e.					
f.					
g.					
h.					
i.					

2. Prove the balance sheet equation remains in balance.

PROBLEM 3-2
L.O. 1

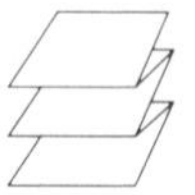

Transaction Analysis

For each of the following transactions indicate the accounts that would be debited and credited and the effect on the total assets reported on the balance sheet [increase (+), decrease (−), or no effect (NE)]:

a. The recording of a bill for a new machine for a factory; payment to be made later.
b. The entry to record the payment of the monthly utility bill.
c. The entry to record the advance payment for four months' rent.
d. The recording of an uninsured tornado loss on a building.
e. The entry made to record the interest accrued on a note payable.
f. Declaration and payment of a dividend.

PROBLEM 3-3
L.O. 1, 2

Journalizing and Posting

Audit, Inc., started business on April 1, 19x1, and had the following transactions during its first month of operations:

a. Sold stock for $40,000, 50% each to A. Andersen and C. Lybrand.
b. Acquired equipment from P. Mitchell Company with an invoice price of $12,500; $3,000 was paid in cash, and $9,500 is to be paid in one month.
c. Purchased office supplies for cash from T. Ross Company for $400.
d. Paid $1,800 salaries to A. Young for the month in cash.
e. Received $22,000 in cash from customers for services rendered.

Required:

1. Prepare the journal entries in journal form for the above transactions.
2. Set up the necessary ledger accounts and post the effects of the above entries into the appropriate ledger accounts.

PROBLEM 3-4
L.O. 2, 3

Recording and Reporting

Refer to the NSI transactions in Problem 3-1. In journal form, prepare the journal entries for each transaction using the appropriate revenue and expense accounts. Post the entries to the appropriate T accounts and construct the month-end income statement. Prepare the January 31, 19xx, balance sheet.

PROBLEM 3-5
L.O. 1–6

Comprehensive

Meyers Cleaning Service, Inc., has the following transactions during its first quarter of operations, which ended on June 30, 19xx:

a. Sold capital stock of $30,000 to investors.

b. Paid cash of $3,000 for three months' office space rent. Rent is expensed when paid.
c. Paid $15,000 for rental of cleaning equipment for the first quarter.
d. Purchased $5,000 cleaning supplies for cash; used $3,000 during the quarter.
e. Paid $1,000 for bonding of employees for six months, covering April through September.
f. Recorded cleaning service revenue of $42,000 for the period; $16,000 was received in cash, and the remainder on account.
g. Paid $12,000 in wages for cleaning employees and $4,000 in supervisor's salary.
h. Paid $716 for advertising in the local paper.
i. Received utility bill for $1,189 for the period (but did not pay it until July).
j. Received $17,000 from customers on account.
k. Recorded income tax expense for the period of $560, to be paid in July.

Required:

1. Record the above transactions and any necessary adjusting entries in journal form and post to the appropriate ledger accounts.
2. Prepare an adjusted trial balance.
3. Prepare an income statement and a retained earnings statement for the first quarter.
4. Prepare the June 30, 19xx, balance sheet.

PROBLEM 3-6
L.O. 1, 3

T Account Balances

Consider the following T accounts of the newly formed company, Alice's Decorating Service:

Cash	
55,000	28,000
10,000	4,000
14,000	950
	450
	200

Accounts Receivable	
32,000	14,000

Supplies Inventory	
900	650

Prepaid Rent	
4,000	2,000

Accounts Payable	
450	900

Notes Payable	
	10,000

Capital Stock	
	55,000

Service Revenue	
	32,000

Salaries Expense	
4,000	
7,000	
9,800	
7,200	

Rent Expense	
2,000	

Utilities Expense	
950	
200	

Supplies Expense	
650	

Required:

1. Compute the balance in each account and prepare a trial balance at September 30, 19xx.
2. Prepare the income statement and retained earnings statement.
3. Prepare the September 30, 19xx, balance sheet.

PROBLEM 3-7
L.O. 3

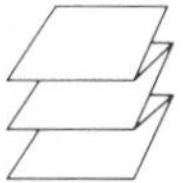

Preparing Financial Statements

Amalgamated Financial has the following adjusted trial balance at December 31, 19xx:

Amalgamated Financial
Adjusted Trial Balance
December 31, 19xx

	Debits	*Credits*
Cash	$ 6,300	
Accounts Receivable	45,900	
Note Receivable	8,000	
Supplies	400	
Prepaid Insurance	1,200	
Accounts Payable		$ 2,600
Income Taxes Payable		5,132
Capital Stock		20,000
Retained Earnings		13,540
Consulting Fees		105,700
Interest Revenue		960
Salaries Expense	72,000	
Supplies Expense	4,100	
Insurance Expense	1,200	
Utilities Expense	3,700	
Income Tax Expense	5,132	
Totals	$147,932	$147,932

Required:
Construct an income statement and retained earnings statement for the year and a year-end balance sheet.

PROBLEM 3-8

L.O. 3

Preparing Financial Statements

Consider the following adjusted trial balance for Genovesee's, Inc.:

Genovesee's, Inc.
Adjusted Trial Balance
December 31, 19xx

	Debits	*Credits*
Cash	$ 1,400	
Accounts Receivable	22,500	
Supplies	225	
Prepaid Rent	20,000	
Prepaid Insurance	6,250	
Accounts Payable		$ 3,000
Capital Stock		20,000
Retained Earnings		?
Advertising Fees		58,000
Salaries Expense	25,000	
Travel and Entertainment Expense	4,200	
Telephone Expense	800	
Rent Expense	10,000	
Insurance Expense	1,250	
Supplies Expense	500	
Utilities Expense	650	
Totals	$ 92,775	?

Required:

1. Prepare the income statement and the ending retained earnings balance for the year ended December 31, 19xx.
2. Prepare the December 31, 19xx, balance sheet.

PROBLEM 3-9
L.O. 3

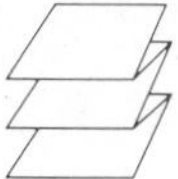

Preparing Financial Statements

The adjusted trial balance with the accounts in alphabetical order, of the Midland Goods Company at June 30, 19x2, is shown below.

Midland Goods Company
Adjusted Trial Balance
June 30, 19x2

	Debits	*Credits*
Accounts Payable		$ 2,350
Accounts Receivable	$ 18,300	
Advertising Expense	5,000	
Capital Stock		40,000
Cash	1,200	
Selling Expenses	142,600	
Dividends (declared and paid)	11,000	
Equipment	49,600	
Income Tax Expense	15,000	
Income Taxes Payable		11,600
Interest Receivable	1,100	
Interest Revenue		5,800
Inventory	21,000	
Note Receivable	50,000	
Miscellaneous Expenses	8,100	
Rent Revenue		18,510
Retained Earnings, 7/1/x1		55,390
Sales Revenue—Cash		93,000
Sales Revenue—Credit		98,500
Unearned Rent Collected in Advance		9,750
Utilities Expense	12,000	
Totals	$334,900	$334,900

Required:
1. Prepare Midland's income statement for the year.
2. Prepare the June 30, 19x2, balance sheet.

PROBLEM 3-10
L.O. 1, 3

Trial Balance

T accounts with their balances for the Super Company at the end of its fiscal year on December 31, 19xx, immediately following the posting of transactions and adjustments were as follows:

Cash	
4,594	

Property Taxes Payable	
	11,400

Maintenance Expense	
6,800	

Accounts Receivable	
1,200	

Income Taxes Payable	
	12,240

Salary Expense	
96,600	

Prepaid Insurance	
2,400	

Interest Payable	
	1,200

Interest Expense	
40,326	

Supplies Inventory	
400	

Mortgage Payable	
	476,074

Dividends Payable	
	50,000

Apartment Building	
770,000	

Capital Stock	
	100,000

Miscellaneous Expense	
8,400	

Retained Earnings	
	52,920

Insurance Expense	
2,400	

Utilities Expense	
9,000	

Dividends	
50,000	

Rent Revenue	
	310,126

Income Tax Expense	
12,240	

Property Tax Expense	
11,400	

Salaries Payable	
	1,800

Required:
Prepare a trial balance.

PROBLEM 3-11
L.O. 3

Preparing Financial Statements

Refer to Problem 3-10 and the Super Company.

Required:
1. Prepare an income statement and retained earnings statement for the year ended December 31, 19xx.
2. Prepare the December 31, 19xx, balance sheet.

PROBLEM 3-12
L.O. 1, 2

Preparing Journal Entries and Analyzing Their Effects

The following lettered transactions present summary information for the Typo Services Company for the fiscal year ending December 31, 19x2:

a. Typo collected cash of $27,000 for typing services performed: $4,000 of the fees collected were for services performed in 19x1, and $2,000 of the fees earned in 19x2 remained uncollected on December 31, 19x2.
b. The company paid office salaries of $9,000. However, the last payroll payment for fiscal year 19x2 was made on December 21, 19x2; salaries amounting to $450 were earned during the period December 22 through December 31, 19x2. No salaries for 19x1 remained unpaid at December 31, 19x1.
c. At the end of the year, Typo purchased typewriters, for which it paid $1,200 in cash and also issued a $1,200 note.
d. Typo paid a total of $4,100 for office rent in 19x2. This amount includes $300 for December 19x1 rent which was unpaid on January 1, 19x2.
e. The company paid $910 for utility and telephone bills; in addition the electricity bill for December 19x2, amounting to $55 remained unpaid at December 31, 19x2.

Required:
1. Prepare the journal entry (or entries) that is appropriate for each lettered item. Show calculations.
2. Indicate the effect of each item listed above on the company's assets, liabilities, and net income at December 31, 19x2. Also indicate the dollar amount of each effect.

PROBLEM 3-13
L.O. 1, 2

Transaction Analysis

A-1 Travel, Inc., starts the current year with the following balance sheet:

A-1 Travel, Inc.
Balance Sheet
December 31, 19x1

Assets		Liabilities and Stockholders' Equity	
Current assets:		Liabilities:	
Cash	$ 100,000	Accounts payable	$ 75,000
Accounts receivable	200,000	Salaries payable	15,000
Prepaid rent (for 10 months)	175,000	Total liabilities	$ 90,000
Total current assets	$ 475,000	Stockholders' equity:	
Noncurrent assets:		Capital stock	$1,200,000
Land	1,500,000	Retained earnings	685,000
		Total stockholders' equity	$1,885,000
Total assets	$1,975,000	Total liabilities and stockholders' equity	$1,975,000

During January 19x2, A-1 had operating, financing, and investing transactions with the following summary results:

a. Sales totaled $1,800,000, and accounts receivable had an ending balance of $400,000.
b. Expenses, including rent expense, totaled $1,300,000, and accounts payable and salaries payable had ending balances of $90,000 and $5,000, respectively. No rent was paid in January.
c. Office equipment was purchased and received on January 31, 19x2, for $29,000. A $29,000 note due on February 15, 19x2, is given in exchange for the equipment.
d. A-1 borrowed $250,000 on January 31, 19x2, to be paid back to the bank on June 30, 19x2.

Required:
1. In journal form, prepare the journal entries for the above transactions. Post the transactions to the proper ledger accounts.
2. Analyze the effects of transactions described in (*a*), (*b*), (*c*), and (*d*) by completing the following schedule:

Transaction	*Asset Effect*	*Income Statement Effect*	*Cash Flow Effect*
Example	−$1,000	−$1,000	No effect

PROBLEM 3-14
L.O. 3

Trial Balance, Financial Statements, and Operating Analysis

Refer to the A-1 Travel, Inc., facts in the preceding problem.

Required:
1. Prepare the income statement for the month and the January 31, 19x1, balance sheet. Ignore income taxes.
2. Analyze the cash flow during the month by listing sources and uses of cash from operating, financing, and investing activities in the following format:

A-1 Travel, Inc.
Statement of Cash Flows
For the Month Ended January 31, 19x2

Operating activities:

Investing activities:

Financing activities:

Change in cash flow

PROBLEM 3-15
L.O. 6

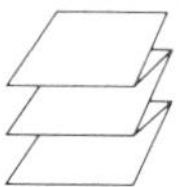

Cash and Accrual Accounting

Complete the table below for the effects of the following selected transactions from Clay's Ceramics Company. For both the cash basis of accounting and the accrual basis of accounting, indicate whether the Cash account and net income are increased (I), decreased (D), or not affected (NA).

a. Paid for the next three months' rent, $24,000.
b. Purchased office equipment for cash, $15,000.
c. Recorded end-of-period salaries to be paid next period, $10,000.
d. Purchased advertising in the local paper, $1,065 cash.
e. Received payment on a previously recorded credit sale, $5,600.
f. Paid salaries earned last period, $8,000.
g. Recorded cash sales, $3,000.
h. One month of prepaid rent has expired, $8,000.
i. Purchased office supplies, $875 cash.
j. Paid the monthly utility bill, $660 cash.

Example: Sold services on credit, $50,000.

	Cash Basis of Accounting		*Accrual Basis of Accounting*	
	Cash Account	*Net Income*	*Cash Account*	*Net Income*
Example:	NA	NA	NA	I
a.				
b.				
c.				
d.				
e.				
f.				
g.				
h.				
i.				
j.				

PROBLEM 3-16
L.O. 4, 5

Adjusting Entries

Several internal transactions of the Robar Company require adjusting entries at the end of the current accounting period, December 31, 19x1. The details of these transactions are:

a. $13,000 is owed to employees for work performed during the last week of 19x1.
b. $4,000 of the Supplies Inventory was used during the current period.
c. $2,200 of Prepaid Insurance expired during the current period.
d. $8,000 is owed for income taxes on 19x1 income.
e. $200 interest is owed on a note held by the bank.
f. $800 of Prepaid Rent expired during the current period.

Required:

1. Prepare adjusting journal entries to record the above internal transactions.
2. Set up the necessary ledger accounts and post the entries to the accounts.

PROBLEM 3-17
L.O. 1, 4, 5

Analysis of T Accounts

The accountant for New Process, Inc., has lost some of the details of the firm's accounting information for the month of February 19x1.

Missing Amount	*What is Known*
a. Collections of Accounts Receivable	Beg. Balance of Accounts Receivable $13,200. Credit Sales $65,000. End. Balance of Accounts Receivable $10,500.
b. Purchases of Supplies Inventory	Beg. Balance of Supplies $1,800. Supplies Expense $10,000. End. Balance of Supplies $2,500.
c. Beginning Balance in Prepaid Rent	End. Balance in Prepaid Rent $1,200. Rent Expense $6,200. Cash paid for rent $7,000.
d. Ending Balance in Salaries Payable	Beg. Balance in Salaries Payable $5,500. Salaries Expense $32,000. Cash paid for salaries $29,300.
e. Amount borrowed from the bank during the month	Beg. Balance in Note Payable $10,000. Payments made on principal $6,000. End. Balance in Note Payable $8,000.

Required:

Use your understanding of how transactions affect ledger accounts to help the accountant determine the missing amounts.

PROBLEM 3-18
L.O. 3

Finding Trial Balance Errors

Xebec Company prepared the following adjusted trial balance at December 31 of their first year of operations. All accounts have normal balances and all amounts are correct.

	Debit	*Credit*
Accounts Payable		$ 26,000
Accounts Receivable	$ 28,000	
Advertising Expense	12,000	
Capital Stock		250,000
Cash	45,000	
Equipment	180,000	
Income Tax Expense	4,500	
Income Tax Payable	4,500	
Insurance Expense	3,800	
Interest Revenue		1,600
Land	70,000	
Note Payable		20,000
Prepaid Insurance		1,800
Rent Expense	22,000	
Retained Earnings		0
Salaries Expense	85,000	
Salaries Payable		5,000
Service Revenue		180,000
Supplies Expense	28,000	
Supplies Inventory		4,000
Utilities Expense	3,000	
	$485,800	$488,400

Required:
1. Locate the errors that have caused the trial balance to be out of balance.
2. Prepare a corrected adjusted trial balance in proper format.

PROBLEM 3-19
L.O. 1

Recording from Source Documents

The following source documents support the day's transactions for Better Computer Services, Inc.:

a. Services Invoice for J. Brown:

Programming services	$12,000
Computer installation	3,000
Cleaning printer	45
Total	$15, 045
Less: Cash received	0
Total on account	$15,045

b. Services Invoice for T. Jones:

Programming services	$11,000
Software	900
Total	$11,900
Less: Cash received	1,000
Total on account	$10,900

c. Electric Bill for the current month (unpaid):

Total due	$ 723

d. Telephone Bill for the current month (paid by check):

Total paid	$ 437

e. Packing Slip in office furniture that arrived today:

3 Desks ($400 each)	$ 1,200
2 Tables ($150 each)	300
Total due on account	$ 1,500

f. Purchase Invoice for delivery truck picked up at the dealer today:

Delivery truck	$36,000
Dealer preparation	500
Total	$36,500
Less: Cash down payment	5,000
Total financed	$31,500

g. Checks received from customers on their accounts:

F. Smith	$ 600
M. Green	400

Required:
Analyze the source documents and prepare the journal entries necessary to record the effect of each transaction.

PROBLEM 3-20

L.O. 3

Trial Balance Errors

Federation, Inc., prepared the following adjusted trial balance at December 31, 19x1, and is concerned that it does not balance:

	Debit	*Credit*
Cash	$ 124,000	
Accounts Receivable	65,900	
Prepaid Rent	41,000	
Supplies Inventory	19,500	
Building	420,000	
Land	365,000	
Accounts Payable		$ 65,500
Notes Payable		145,000
Income Taxes Payable		10,500
Salaries Payable		11,400
Capital Stock		580,000
Retained Earnings		203,000
Service Revenues		318,000
Advertising Expense	35,000	
Salaries Expense	137,400	
Rent Expense	52,000	
Supplies Expense	65,000	
Income Tax Expense	10,500	
	$1,335,300	$1,333,400

The auditors have discovered the following errors that were made in posting the firm's journal entries:

a. A $1,000 debit to Cash was posted correctly but the credit to Accounts Receivable was posted for $100.
b. A $3,200 credit to Cash was posted correctly but the debit to Prepaid Rent was posted for $2,200.
c. A $2,000 debit to Accounts Receivable was posted correctly but the credit to Service Revenue was not posted.
d. A $5,000 debit to Accounts Payable and $5,000 credit to Cash were not posted.
e. A $600 credit to Cash was posted correctly but the $600 debit was incorrectly posted to Salaries Payable rather than Salaries Expense.

Required:

1. List each posting error and describe the account or accounts in error and how they were affected (e.g., account understated by $xxx).
2. Prepare a corrected trial balance.

CASES

CASE 3-1

L.O. 6

Accrual Accounting

Robin Matthews started an office machine repair business on January 1, 19x1, with cash of $1,000, and use of a building for six months without rental payments (however, rent of $400 per month will be charged from July 1, 19x1, to December 31, 19x1). The ordinary rental cost of this building is $200 per month. Robin has decided not to pay herself a salary for the first six months of operations and to live on $1,000 a month that she will withdraw from her personal savings.

Ms. Matthews makes the following estimates of operating activity for the four quarters of 19x1:

Estimates	*Quarter* 1	2	3	4
Revenues:				
Repair revenues (customers have 30 days to pay)* . . .	$8,000	$10,000	$11,000	$12,000
Expenses (all cash):				
Supplies	$1,000	$ 1,000	$ 1,000	$ 1,000
Utilities.	2,500	2,500	2,500	2,500
Rent—equipment	2,000	2,000	2,000	2,000
Rent—building	0	0	1,200	1,200
Salary	0	0	3,000	3,000
Total payments	$5,500	$ 5,500	$ 9,700	$ 9,700

*Assume that Accounts Receivable balance at quarter-end is 20 of sales for the quarter.

Required:
Robin comes to you for financial advice. She asks:

1. Am I going to make a profit this year?
2. Will I have to borrow money to stay in business?

Using your knowledge of accrual accounting, write a report that answers the above questions. List any assumptions you need to make to complete your analysis.

EVALUATING FINANCIAL STATEMENTS

CASE 3-2
L.O. 3

Preparing a Balance Sheet—R. J. Reynolds Industries, Inc.

R. J. Reynolds Industries, Inc., one of the world's leading consumer products businesses with interests in Nabisco Brands, Kentucky Fried Chicken, and others, has the following balance sheet accounts and account balances (amounts are in millions) on December 31, 1985:

Accounts and notes receivable.	$1,944
Accounts payable.	3,060
Capital stock	2,026
Cash	589
Current portion of long-term debt	172
Income taxes accrued	232
Inventories	3,209
Long-term debt	4,857
Notes payable	666
Other long-term assets	5,593
Other long-term liabilities	1,560
Prepaid expenses.	136
Property, plant, and equipment.	5,459
Retained earnings	4,357

Required:
Prepare the classified December 31, 1985, balance sheet. Be sure to categorize the assets and liabilities into current and noncurrent.

CASE 3-3
L.O. 1, 2

Transaction Analysis—Reebok International Ltd.

Selected accounts and account balances (amounts in thousands) from the December 31, 19x6, balance sheet of Reebok International Ltd., a leading producer of apparel and shoes are as follows:

	($000)
Accounts Receivable	$120,075
Accounts Payable	67,865
Capital Stock	119,961
Cash	66,077
Notes Payable	22,111
Prepaid Selling Expenses (Short-Term)	2,324

During January 1987, the following transactions occurred:

a. Issued 100,000 additional shares of capital stock for $3 per share.
b. Recorded sales of $87,546,000. Total selling expenses amounted to $43,773,000. Two thirds of the sales were on credit; the remainder for cash. Three fourths of the selling expenses were paid in cash.
c. Paid $500,000 to the local bank on a note payable plus an additional $60,000 for interest.
d. Received $97,053,000 from customers on accounts.

Required:
Record the above transactions in journal form and post to the appropriate ledger accounts. (Round all amounts to the nearest thousand.)

CASE 3-4
L.O. 3

Balance Sheet Preparation—AMR Corporation

On December 31 of a recent year, AMR Corporation, consisting primarily of American Airlines, reported the following balance sheet data (in millions):

Retained earnings	$1,368
Current liabilities	1,985
Flight equipment	?
Cash and securities	?
Long-term obligations under capital leases	1,183
Other long-term obligations	622
Accounts receivable	690
Deposits for purchase of flight equipment	145*
Inventories and other current assets	336
Total current assets	2,109
Property and facilities	907
Long-term investments and other assets	677
Capital stock	1,141
Long-term debt	1,229

*This is not considered a current asset by AMR Corporation.

Required:
Place the information provided into a classified balance sheet and solve for the amounts of the missing information.

CHAPTER 4

Completion of the Accounting Cycle

LEARNING OBJECTIVES

After studying Chapter 4, you should understand:

1. How the accounting concepts of revenue recognition, matching, and periodicity relate to adjusting entries, pp. 158-62.
2. The way the adjusting entries (in cycle step 4) place the account balances on an accrual basis so that financial statements may be prepared, pp. 164-70.
3. The relation between adjusting journal entries, ledger balances, and unadjusted and adjusted trial balances, pp. 170-72.
4. How the worksheet is used to summarize cycle steps 1 through 5, pp. 175-77.
5. How the formal closing process wipes the slate clean in the temporary accounts (revenues, expenses, and dividends) for the start of a new period and includes the last period's results in retained earnings, pp. 175-78.
6. How to correct the current period's errors, pp. 179-80.
7. How reversing entries are used (Appendix 4A), pp. 194-95.
8. How the income statement and balance sheet can be converted to common-size statements by using percentages of total revenues or total assets (Appendix 4B), pp. 196-98.

In Chapter 3 you learned about the first three steps in the formal accounting cycle [(1) analysis of transactions; (2) journalizing; and (3) posting to the ledger]. In addition, steps 4 (adjusting) and 5 (financial statement preparation) were introduced, with the help of the unadjusted and adjusted trial balances. Chapter 4 continues our examination of the formal accounting cycle, taking a closer look at steps 4 and 5, introducing step 6 (the closing process) and the post-closing trial balance. In addition, you will be introduced to a new version of an accounting worksheet, much different than the spreadsheet analysis used in the first two chapters, which is an important tool used in formal accounting information systems. You will learn the linkages between the worksheet and the formal journal and ledger with emphasis on how adjusting entries and their effects on the financial statements are shown in the worksheet. Other topics in the chapter include the correction of current period errors, reversing entries (Appendix 4A), and a simple analysis of financial statements (Appendix 4B).

REVIEW OF THE ACCOUNTING CYCLE

The six steps of the accounting cycle were introduced in Chapter 3. The key tasks of these six accounting cycle steps are as follows:

The Accounting Cycle

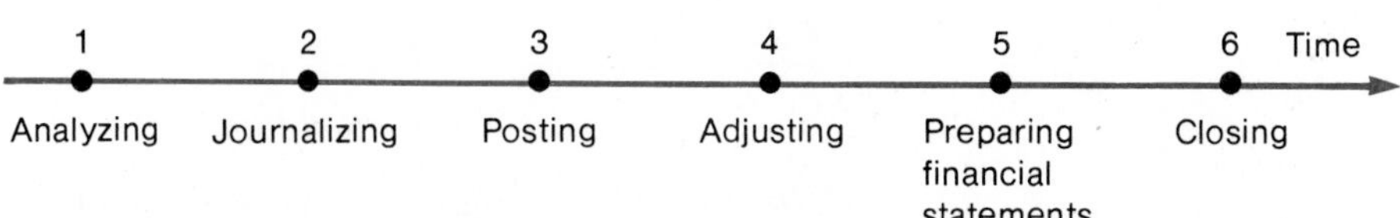

The first three accounting steps (analyzing transactions, journalizing or entering transactions into the journal, and posting from the journal to the ledger accounts) are triggered by evidence (invoices, checks, and so on) of transactions with external parties. Accounting cycle step 4—making the necessary adjusting entries—results from internal transactions usually documented by internally generated schedules of depreciation, schedules of interest, payroll records, and the like. From the adjusted trial balance following step 4, the financial statements of step 5 are prepared. Closing—accounting cycle step 6—is the most mechanical step in that all temporary account balances are merely transferred to Retained Earnings, as we shall see later in this chapter. Steps 4 and 6 both involve making journal entries and, therefore, include journalizing and posting. A more detailed depiction of the accounting cycle would be as follows:

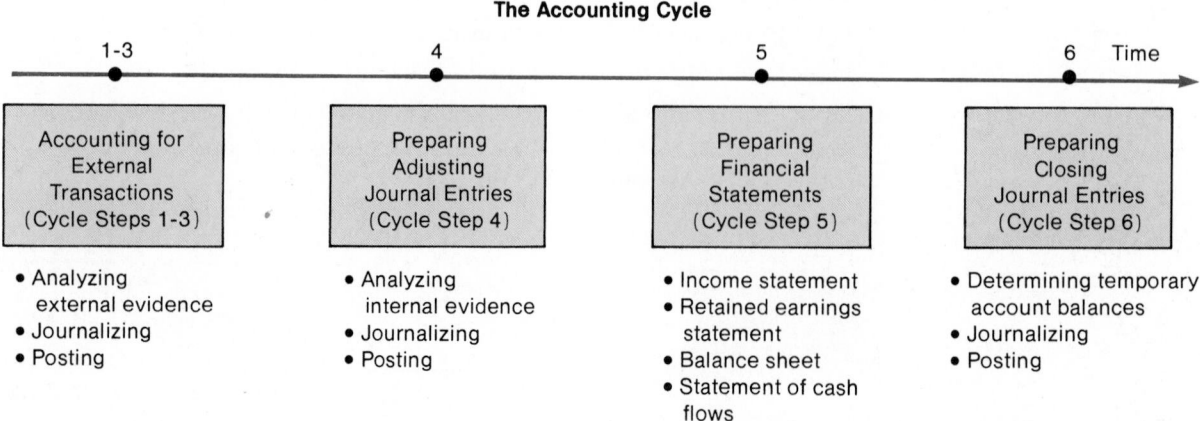

The Accounting Cycle

1-3 — 4 — 5 — 6 Time

Accounting for External Transactions (Cycle Steps 1-3)	Preparing Adjusting Journal Entries (Cycle Step 4)	Preparing Financial Statements (Cycle Step 5)	Preparing Closing Journal Entries (Cycle Step 6)
• Analyzing external evidence • Journalizing • Posting	• Analyzing internal evidence • Journalizing • Posting	• Income statement • Retained earnings statement • Balance sheet • Statement of cash flows	• Determining temporary account balances • Journalizing • Posting

The time period covered by the accounting cycle varies depending on the length of time between which financial statements are prepared. When preparing annual financial statements, the accounting cycle lasts one year. Companies also use monthly and quarterly accounting cycles. Business transactions—the raw inputs to the accounting system—occur intermittently throughout the accounting period.

Transactions occur in response to economic decisions and processes that are not necessarily related to standard time periods such as three months (a quarter) or a calendar year. For example, a payroll may be paid on December 28, but the accounting period ends on December 31; or a yearly insurance premium may be paid on November 18 and provide coverage that straddles two accounting periods. Since the periodicity concept (introduced in earlier chapters) calls for periodic financial statements which might not be the exact same period affected by all of the business transactions, accountants must convert the impact of the economic transactions into the uniform intervals of time covered by the financial statements. Periodicity is accomplished with the guidance of revenue recognition and matching discussed in earlier chapters.

Individual transactions trigger the analyzing, journalizing, and posting steps (steps 1, 2, and 3) of the accounting cycle. Posting to ledger accounts may take place at the same time as the transactions, or transactions may be accumulated and totals posted after a period of time (e.g., as each journal page is filled, or at the end of each day). In any event, steps 1, 2, and 3 of the accounting cycle are recorded as the underlying business transactions actually occur. At the same time, the needs of decision makers for timely information require that the accounting cycle summarizes the economic effects as of a specific date and for a distinct time period. As shown in the following diagram, the last three accounting cycle steps—adjusting, preparing financial statements, and closing—are end-of-period steps designed to facilitate these information requirements.

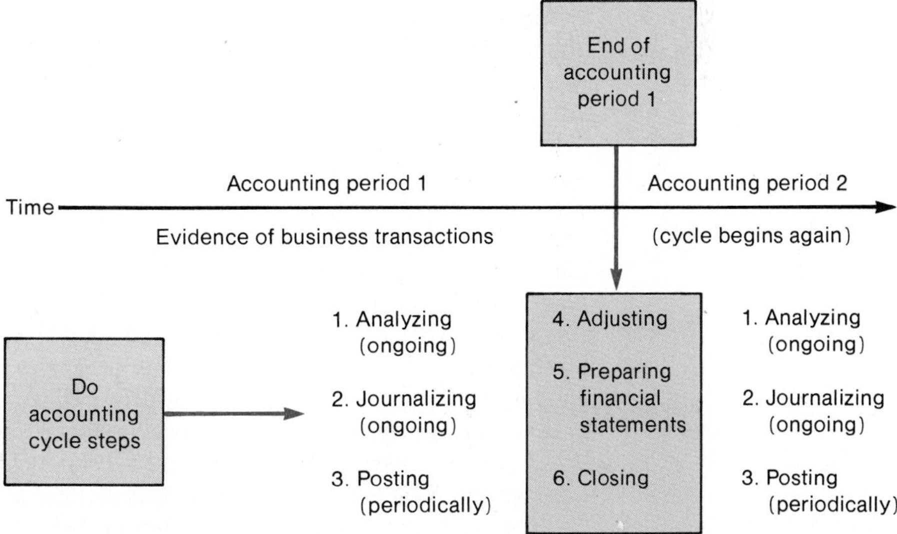

Depending on the size of the corporation, the six accounting cycle steps are based on hundreds, thousands, or possibly millions of specific accounting transactions. Summarization is necessary if all of the data are to be converted into meaningful financial statements. Balance sheets, income statements, and other financial statements should be viewed as informative summaries that communicate a company's economic conditions and flows.

ADJUSTING ENTRIES (ACCOUNTING CYCLE STEP 4)

As you know from Chapters 2 and 3, accountants use accrual accounting because (1) both cash and noncash transactions affect the economic status of a company and (2) periodic information is needed on the economic effects of a company's transactions. To comply with the accrual accounting concept, accountants prepare adjusting entries at the end of each accounting period. These adjusting entries reflect any changes in the economic status of the business which have not already been accounted for by the entries that were recorded during the accounting period. Thus, **adjusting entries** are period-end journal entries used to update accounts so that the financial statements reflect the current economic position of the company in conformance with the accrual concept.

The adjusting entries that must be recorded at the end of the accounting period can be grouped into two major categories: (1) *period-end allocations* (also called *deferrals*) involving the updating of existing account balances which originated from *past transactions*, and (2) *period-end accruals* involving business activities that will require known *future transactions* which have not yet been recorded. We will see that in the former case (allocations) the adjustments do not usually require new account titles to be developed, whereas with accruals we often need to develop new accounts to record the necessary adjusting entries. This section discusses period-end allocations and accruals, and gives an example of recording the period-end allocations and accruals of a service organization.

Period-End Allocations

Period-end allocations involve adjustments to account balances from original transactions whose current and/or future periods' effect on expenses and/or revenues have not yet been recorded. The allocation-type adjusting entries spread these amounts out over their current and future periods of benefit because of the concepts of **matching** expenses with related revenues and **periodicity** where financial statements are demanded at regular intervals. The revenue-related account balances from past transactions that must be adjusted are unearned revenues such as the subscription example given below; the expense-related account balances from past transactions are prepaid expenses such as the prepaid rent transaction explained in Chapter 3. Long-term assets, such as buildings and equipment, and short-term assets, such as prepaid insurance and supplies, also belong to the prepayments group, and their costs incurred in past transactions are allocated to current and future periods of benefit. When economic value still exists in an asset on hand at the end of a period, some portion of the original cost must remain as an asset. You should note here that the term *deferrals* is often used for delaying the effect of revenues and expenses on the income statement. Therefore, **deferred assets** are often delayed expenses, while **deferred liabilities** are often delayed revenues, and adjusting entries are often made when these deferred amounts are ready to be released (no longer need to be delayed) for purposes of measuring the current period's income. However, it is also common terminology to refer to this process of releasing delayed revenues and delayed expenses by way of end-of-period adjusting entries, as **allocations**. In this text, we will most frequently refer to this process as allocation.

Objective 1
How the accounting concepts of revenue recognition, matching, and periodicity relate to adjusting entries.

The following example of an end-of-period adjusting entry for a magazine advance subscription demonstrates the allocation procedure for a past transaction which was originally recorded as a liability—delayed revenue—when cash in advance was received. On January 1, 19x1, a publisher receives $600 cash for a three-year subscription to one of its publications. This original transaction will affect more than one accounting period. What are the income statement and balance sheet effects of this $600 revenue in years 1, 2, and 3?

Although cash of $600 is received in year 1, all three years are involved in the revenue-generating process. Since the revenue is not earned until the magazines are delivered to the customers and the deliveries will occur over three years, revenue must be recognized over three years. If the full $600 cannot be recognized as revenue in year 1, how is it accounted for? Exhibit 4-1 illustrates the alternative methods of handling the $600 so that each accounting period—year 1, year 2, and year 3—shows the revenue earned.

Note that in accounting alternative 1, the cash collected in advance (January 1, 19x1) was debited to Cash and credited to Subscriptions Revenue, an income statement account. Since the cash collection was initially recorded by increasing Cash and increasing Subscriptions Revenue, an adjusting entry is needed at year-end to reduce revenue and recognize a $400 liability—Unearned Subscriptions Revenue—for the $200 to be earned in year 2 and $200 to be earned in year 3. Thus, the adjusting entry is needed to allocate the original $600 to the three accounting periods of benefit and recognize the $400 obligation to the subscriber at the end of the first accounting period. In alternative 2, however, the initial entry records a liability—Unearned Subscriptions Revenue—which now requires an end-of-period adjustment to reduce the liability and record $200 revenue which has been earned by the end of the first year (December 31, 19x1). Which alternative is correct? Alternative 2 may be more correct on January 1, 19x1, because no revenue has been earned as of that date. In practice, we may find both approaches being used. However, looking at the income statement and balance sheet effects shown in Exhibit 4-1, you can see that the results on the income statement and balance sheet at the end of 19x1 are the same. A business should adopt one method and use it consistently. As long as the end-of-period adjustments are made correctly, the results will always be the same.

Many current-period transactions will create the need for end-of-period adjusting entries to allocate the recorded amounts to the current period and future periods. Notice that this first type of adjusting entry which allocates existing amounts reported in balance sheet accounts to current and future periods usually will not require new accounts to be established.

Period-End Accruals

Period-end accruals include (*a*) accrued revenues and (*b*) accrued expenses that are related to past and/or future transactions with outside parties. The word *accrue* means to record amounts of revenue or expense that have accumulated over the current period, but have not yet been accounted for in a transaction. Thus, accrued revenues and expenses have accumulated or accrued during the current accounting period and, therefore, must be recorded at the end of the period by way of adjusting entries. When the accrued revenues or expenses are recorded, a corresponding balance sheet account such as a receivable or payable is also recorded. An example of an accrued revenue is interest revenue that has been earned but is unrecorded at period end. For example, on October 1, 19x1, a company deposits $10,000 in an investment account that earns 12% annual interest with payments at the end of each three-month period. At December 31, 19x1, three months' interest ($10,000 × .12 × 3/12 = $300) has been earned on this account but no cash has been received. The following adjusting entry would be made:

19x1			
Dec. 31	Interest Receivable (A)	300	
	Interest Revenue (R).		300
	To record interest accrued at year-end ($10,000 × .12 × 3/12).		

EXHIBIT 4-1

Alternative Methods of Recording Revenue Earned

Date		*Purpose of Entry*	*Accounting Alternative No. 1*			*Accounting Alternative No. 2*		
1/1/x1	Cash transaction	To record receipt of cash.	Cash (A)	600		Cash (A)	600	
			Subscriptions Revenue (R)		600	Unearned Subscriptions Revenue (L)		600
12/31/x1	Adjusting entry	To allocate revenue between years 1, 2, and 3.	Subscriptions Revenue (R)	400		Unearned Subscriptions Revenue (L)	200	
			Unearned Subscriptions Revenue (L)		400	Subscriptions Revenue (R)		200
	Income statement effect		Revenue = $200			Revenue = $200		
	Balance sheet effect		Liability = $400			Liability = $400		
12/31/x2	Adjusting entry	To recognize revenue in year 2.	Unearned Subscriptions Revenue (L)	200		Unearned Subscriptions Revenue (L)	200	
			Subscriptions Revenue (R)		200	Subscriptions Revenue (R)		200
	Income statement effect		Revenue = $200			Revenue = $200		
	Balance sheet effect		Liability = $200			Liability = $200		
12/31/x3	Adjusting entry	To recognize revenue in year 3.	Unearned Subscriptions Revenue (L)	200		Unearned Subscriptions Revenue (L)	200	
			Subscriptions Revenue (R)		200	Subscriptions Revenue (R)		200
	Income statement effect		Revenue = $200			Revenue = $200		
	Balance sheet effect		Liability = $ 0			Liability = $ 0		

The balance sheet account, Interest Receivable, would not be required were it not for this adjusting entry. If interest revenue were only recognized (recorded) when cash was received (as in the cash basis of accounting), then only the cash and interest revenue accounts would be needed.

If we assume that a check for the interest is received on January 5, 19x2, the following entry would be made to record the receipt of cash:

19x2			
Jan. 5	Cash (A)	300	
	Interest Receivable (A)		300
	To record the receipt of three months' interest earned on the investment account.		

Why do we want to show $300 interest revenue in 19x1 instead of 19x2? The **revenue recognition concept** applies here, stating that the period in which revenue is both earned and either realized or realizable (soon expected to be received) should reflect the revenue. The revenue recognition concept provides accountants with guidance in answering the important question: When should revenue be reported? We will face many examples where this concept is employed as we move through the text.

A common example of accrued expenses is services performed by employees that are unpaid at the time the accounting period ends. For example, assume that a company pays its employees $1,500 per week each Friday and that the end of the company's accounting period—December 31, 19x1—falls on a Wednesday. As a result, on December 31, 19x1, three days of employees' salaries ($900) are due that have not been shown as an expense for the accounting period ending December 31, 19x1. This type of adjusting entry which is based on a yet to be recorded transaction is necessary to record the expense and obligation that exists on December 31, 19x1. The year-end adjusting entry for this accrued expense would be recorded as follows:

19x1			
Dec. 31	Salaries Expense (E)	900	
	Salaries Payable (L)		900
	To accrue three days' unpaid salaries at year-end.		

Notice that this accrual establishes an account balance for Salaries Payable. Without this year-end adjustment the balance in Salaries Payable would have been zero, and it may have been excluded from the unadjusted trial balance. This is why many accrual-type adjusting entries appear to require new balance sheet accounts to be reported.

Next assume that on January 2, 19x2, when the actual payroll of $1,500 is paid, the following entry is made:

19x2			
Jan. 2	Salaries Expense (E)	600	
	Salaries Payable (L)	900	
	Cash (A)		1,500
	To record the payroll for the week ending January 2, 19x2.		

This entry debits Salaries Expense for two days' payroll ($600) not yet recorded and debits Salaries Payable for the three days' payroll ($900) recorded as an adjustment at the end of the previous accounting period. The entire payroll for the week ($1,500) is then credited to Cash. This entry eliminates the balance in the Salaries Payable account and records $600 of expense in 19x2.

The guiding accounting concept for this and many other accrued expenses recorded by period-end adjusting entries is the **matching principle.** The matching principle (or **matching concept**) tells accountants to record expenses in that period where the related benefits (revenues) are recorded, thus fully matching costs (expenses) with benefits (revenues) so that the periodic accrual accounting measurements of net income will accurately portray the performance of the company for the stated time period. In the above case, we assume that $900 of salaries were paid for work performed in 19x1 which benefited 19x1 revenues. Without the employees working the last three days in 19x1, we might have expected 19x1 revenues to be less. Therefore, matching requires that these unpaid salaries for the end of 19x1 be charged against 19x1 revenues and not charged to 19x2 revenues when the three days of salaries are actually paid.

Remember that in an accrual accounting system, cash flow does not necessarily coincide with the amounts shown on the income statement. Thus, at the end of an accounting period, to achieve account balances in conformance with accrual accounting, previously unrecorded assets, revenues, liabilities, and expenses must be recorded, and often revenue-related and expense-related items must be allocated between two or more accounting periods.

Example of a Company's Adjusting Entries

On December 1, 19x1, Legislative Minds, Incorporated (LMI), was organized by three former members of Congress (Larry, Maureen, and Ian) for the purpose of providing lobbying services for special-interest groups. The initial financing and investing activities necessary to begin operations occurred in December. On January 2, 19x2, the operating activities of LMI began. The owners wanted financial statements prepared at the end of the company's first month of operation—January 31, 19x2.

Ian, who had taken a bit of accounting, prepared the unadjusted trial balance (after cycle steps 1 through 3) illustrated in Exhibit 4-2 at the end of January and distributed copies to Larry and Maureen at their regular weekly meeting on February 2, 19x2. The following discussion took place.

Larry: Well, it looks like we're off to a great start. If I can have my share of the $25,850 in net income for January soon, I may buy that new car I've been thinking about. Let's pay ourselves a dividend to celebrate.

Maureen: How can we do that, Larry? We only have about $1,200 in cash. How can net income be so good with so little cash left?

Ian: Wait a minute you guys. I'm not so sure we should be talking about paying any big dividends just yet. I prepared this statement based on what I could remember from my accounting class and with the help of my old textbook, but I know it's not exactly complete. First of all, I know that one of the reasons we have any cash at all in this trial balance is because a new client came in this morning and gave me some cash for consulting services that we haven't yet provided. Although I included it in the revenue account, Consulting Fees, I know we haven't earned it yet.

Maureen: Great! Then it's worse than I thought since net income is overstated and we wouldn't have as much as $1,260 cash were it not for this last new client. How can this be?

EXHIBIT 4-2

Unadjusted Trial Balance

Legislative Minds, Incorporated
Unadjusted Trial Balance
January 31, 19x2

	Unadjusted Trial Balance		*Income Statement**	
	Debits	*Credits*	*Debits*	*Credits*
Cash	$ 1,260			
Accounts Receivable	12,150			
Note Receivable	4,800			
Office Supplies	1,200			
Prepaid Rent	24,000			
Prepaid Insurance	12,000			
Office Equipment	3,000			
Trademark	12,000			
Accounts Payable		$ 4,560		
Capital Stock		40,000		
Consulting Fees		61,000		$61,000
Salaries Expense	27,000		$27,000	
Travel and Entertainment Expense	6,000		6,000	
Communications Expense	1,300		1,300	
Utilities Expense	450		450	
Postage Expense	400		400	
Totals	$105,560	$105,560	$35,150	$61,000
Net income (?)			25,850	
Totals			$61,000	$61,000

*Note: This is **not** the appropriate place to prepare an income statement, as the discussion in the LMI example points out.

Ian: Well, remember that measuring net income isn't the same as measuring cash, Maureen. Some of the revenues that we've received in cash have been put back into the business to pay for rent, insurance, and so on. Prepayments for future expenses have already been made for February and beyond in some cases, so we have something of real value here. Also, we spent a lot on developing our trademark so that everyone around Washington will recognize our logo, and that will hopefully have long-term benefits.

Larry: It's not as bad as it looks, Maureen. I know one client who owes us $5,000. He said he'll deliver the check to me tonight at our church meeting. That will bring in some cash.

Maureen: So, how much of a dividend can we pay ourselves anyway? What is our real net income for January and how much can we declare as a dividend without hampering our operations?

Ian: You know, those are really important and yet difficult to answer questions, Maureen. I may be in over my head with this accounting stuff. I'm thinking we should probably get some professional help.

Larry: I agree. That's a good idea. We've got to be able to answer Maureen's questions sooner or later, and the sooner the better. How can we make good business decisions if we don't know how much net income we've earned? We'll never be able to make a sound dividend decision unless we have confidence in how well we've done.

Ian: Okay. Let's postpone deciding about any dividen until I get some help with some of the adjustments that need to be made to this trial balance. I'll hire a real sharp accountant to help us out. I don't know what the final net income number will be, Maureen, but I expect it to be less than $25,000 for sure. What's the next topic on our agenda?...

The conversation between Larry, Maureen, and Ian points out the importance of accurate accrual accounting records to provide the basis for business decisions. The end-of-period adjustment process, guided by the important concepts of revenue recognition and matching (as well as other guiding concepts introduced later in the text) provide an important step in preparing financial statements that can be used as a basis for business decisions. For example, every business needs to know the answers to fundamental questions such as: "How is the business doing this period?" When the accrual accounting process is not complete, measures of periodic net income, and other basic business information cannot be determined.

Let's turn now to the period-end adjustment process that is being directed by the accountant Ian hired. In the following paragraphs you will learn how LMI's accountant performed the necessary adjustments so that the financial statements as of January 31, 19x2, would give an accurate economic picture of LMI.

Objective 2
The way the adjusting entries (in cycle step 4) place the account balances on an accrual basis so that financial statements may be prepared.

Exhibit 4-2 provides LMI's unadjusted trial balance as of January 31, 19x2. (You should ignore the shaded income statement columns in Exhibit 4-2 since they are not appropriate to use with an unadjusted trial balance.) We will examine several of the elements of LMI's unadjusted trial balance and describe the types of adjusting entries necessary to comply with the objectives of accrual accounting. The adjustments have been divided into the two main categories discussed above—period-end allocations and period-end accruals.

Period-End Allocations. As stated earlier, period-end allocations involve (*a*) unearned revenues that affect the current and/or future accounting periods and (*b*) prepayments that affect the current and/or future accounting periods. LMI's unearned revenue—Unearned Consulting Fees—is discussed first, followed by LMI's prepayments, including transactions related to Prepaid Rent, Prepaid Insurance, Depreciation and Amortization, and Office Supplies. These allocations requiring end-of-period adjusting entries are often identified by looking at the asset and liability amounts in the unadjusted trial balance and asking the question: Are there any amounts included in the account balances that should not be there as of the end of the period? (In other words, they no longer represent assets or liabilities equal to the stated amounts.)

Unearned consulting fees (unearned revenue). In LMI's unadjusted trial balance given in Exhibit 4-2, a balance of $61,000 is shown in the Consulting Fees revenue account. This balance resulted from transactions recorded by debits to Cash for cash fees, debits to Accounts Receivable for fees earned but not yet paid, and credits to Consulting Fees. Assuming that $2,000 of the amount now recorded as Consulting Fees represents a client's prepayment for services that have not yet been performed, this amount should be transferred from the Consulting Fees revenue account to the Unearned Consulting Fees liability account.

The $2,000 is an obligation of the company because the client is entitled to future services or the client may demand a return of the prepayment. To report the $2,000 unearned revenue, the Consulting Fees revenue account is debited to reduce the recognized revenue for the period, and the Unearned Consulting Fees liability account is credited to reflect the company's obligation to provide the service in the future. Thus, the adjusting entry on January 31, 19x2, is:

a. 19x2			
Jan. 31	Consulting Fees (R)	2,000	
	Unearned Consulting Fees (L)		2,000
	To allocate $2,000 of the fees collected in January to future periods.		

If LMI had known that the consulting services in the above entry would not be performed until the next period, LMI could have originally recorded this $2,000 as Unearned Consulting Fees; then no adjusting entry would have been required.

Prepaid rent (short-term prepayment). On January 2, 19x2, LMI paid $24,000 for the rent on office space from January 2 through March 31. Thus, on January 2, $24,000 is recorded in the Prepaid Rent account to represent advance payment of three months' rent. The following adjusting journal entry is necessary on January 31 because one month's portion of the economic value of the prepayment has been consumed:

b. 19x2			
Jan. 31	Rent Expense (E)	8,000	
	Prepaid Rent (A).		8,000
	To record one month's rent expense.		

The entry reduces the current asset, Prepaid Rent, with a credit and reduces stockholders' equity with a debit to the Rent Expense account. This is an example of an adjusting entry that allocates a prepayment by transferring an amount from an asset account to an expense account.

Exhibit 4-3 shows the flow of costs from Prepaid Rent, a current asset category on January 2, 19x2, to the income statement expense category over the three-month period. Allocations such as these are common adjustments. As you will see, the same basic process applies to other prepayments as well as to long-term assets.

Prepaid insurance (short-term prepayment). When insurance premiums are paid in advance, adjusting entries are needed to record that some of the insurance protection has been consumed. LMI's yearly insurance premium of $12,000 was paid on January 2, 19x2. At that time, the Prepaid Insurance asset account was debited $12,000 and Cash was credited $12,000. By January 31, LMI had consumed one twelfth (1/12) of the insurance protection, or $1,000, and the following adjusting entry is necessary:

c. 19x2			
Jan. 31	Insurance Expense (E).	1,000	
	Prepaid Insurance (A)		1,000
	To record one month's premium as insurance expense.		

This leaves $11,000 in the current asset Prepaid Insurance to be expensed in future months.

EXHIBIT 4-3

Allocations of Prepaid Rent

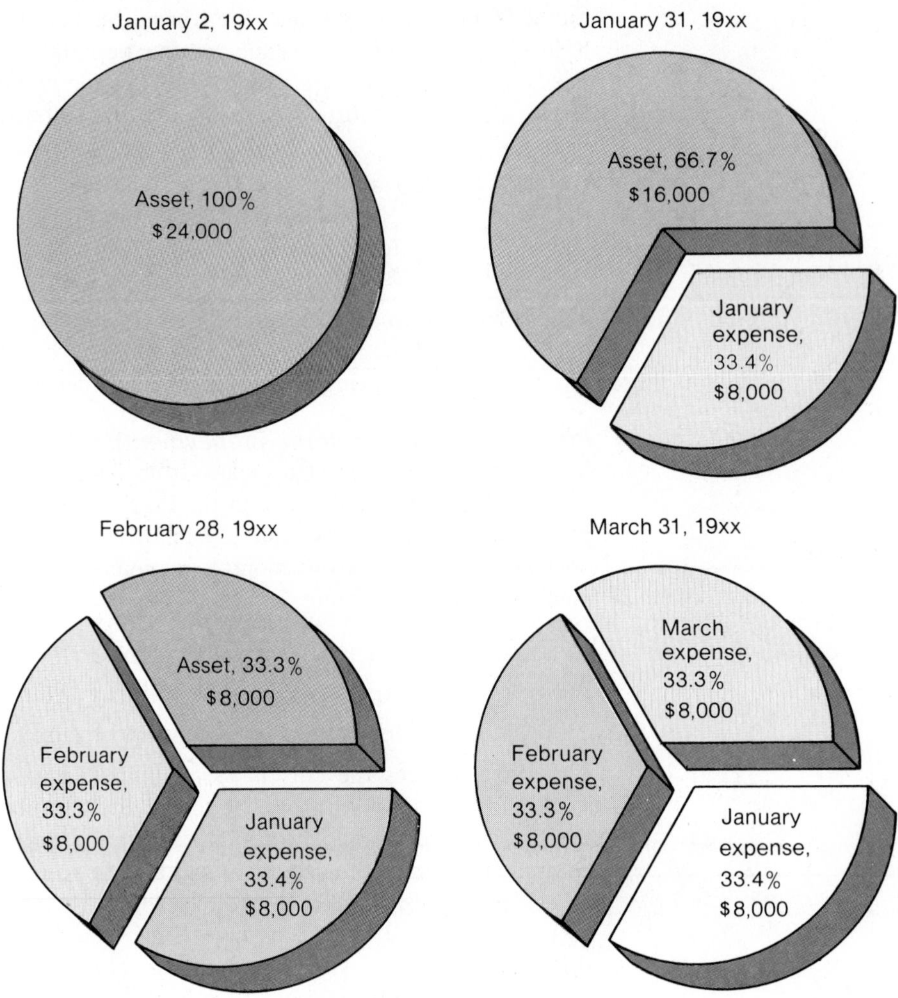

Office supplies (short-term prepayment). Office supplies are usually purchased in quantity and used as the need arises. The amount used in a given period is charged to Office Supplies Expense. The exact amount charged is usually determined by taking an inventory of the supplies and subtracting the ending amount of supplies on hand from the total of the beginning balance and the amount purchased during the current period. This method is easier than keeping track of the exact usage of supplies on a day-to-day basis. For example, LMI has supplies costing $300 on hand at January 31, 19x2. The $1,200 shown in the unadjusted trial balance of Exhibit 4-2 represents the amount of supplies available—the cost of the beginning supplies inventory plus supplies purchases for the month.

Cost of supplies available for use . . .	$1,200
Less ending inventory on 1/31/x2 . . .	300
Cost of supplies used in January . . .	$ 900

The $300 represents the amount left on January 31, 19x2, and available for consumption in subsequent periods. Thus, $900 must be charged to January's Office Supplies Expense as follows:

d.	19x2			
	Jan. 31	Office Supplies Expense (E)	900	
		Office Supplies (A)		900
		To record cost of supplies consumed in January.		

The above allocation process is depicted in Exhibit 4-4.

Depreciation and amortization (long-term prepayments). Closely related to the adjusting entries for the current assets is the allocation of the cost of a noncurrent asset. When an asset with a useful economic life exceeding one year is purchased, its cost is put into a noncurrent asset account. Such an asset is written off or expensed over its useful life because its economic potential is, in fact, being consumed by the operations of the business. LMI has two long-term assets that were partially consumed during January—office equipment and trademark. The trademark account represents costs incurred to develop the "mark" or business logo. These costs are normally amortized over the period of expected benefit, but never in excess of 40 years.

When **tangible assets** with physical form such as office equipment are expensed or written off over time, the term *depreciation* is used. When **intangible assets** with no physical form (which often exist only as legal documents) such as patents, copyrights, and trademarks or tradenames are expensed or written off over time, the term *amortization* is used.

Depreciation and **amortization** are processes that allocate original costs of noncurrent assets consumed by operating activities over the periods benefited by their consumption. These processes have the same purpose as other allocations of prepaid expenses—the costs of the assets consumed by operating activities must be allocated (matched) to the periods that benefit from their use. For example, LMI purchased $3,000 of office equipment on January 2, 19x2, and assigned the office equipment an estimated useful life of 60 months. Assuming that all of the equipment's value will be consumed during the next 60 months

EXHIBIT 4-4

The Effect of an Adjusting Entry on Office Supplies

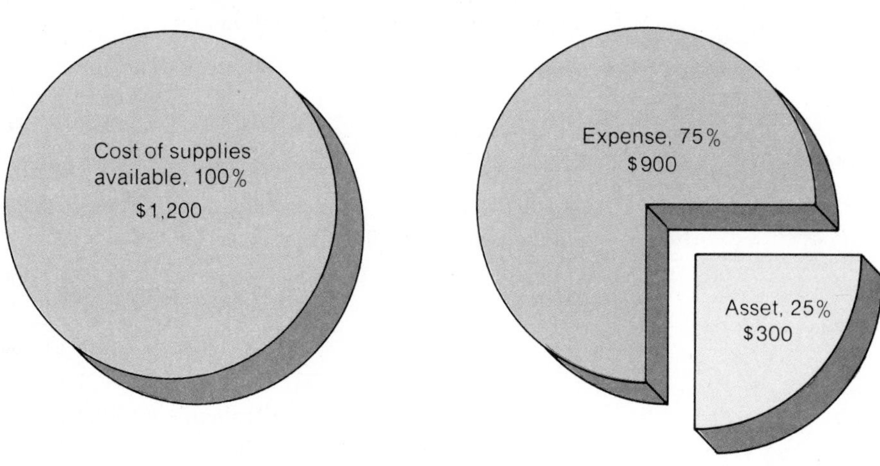

(i.e., the office equipment will have no value at the end of the 60 months), 1/60 of the cost of the asset is allocated to each month as depreciation expense. The entry to record this depreciation expense adjustment is:

e.	19x2			
	Jan. 31	Depreciation Expense—Office Equipment (E)	50	
		Accumulated Depreciation—Office Equipment (XA)*.		50
		To record depreciation of office equipment for January.		

*(XA) is the symbol for a contra asset to be discussed below.

What is the Accumulated Depreciation account, and why is it used instead of crediting the Office Equipment account directly? The Accumulated Depreciation account is called a **contra account** because its balance (a credit in the case of depreciation) is subtracted from the debit balance of the asset being depreciated, Office Equipment, to determine the **net book value of an asset** (the original cost minus the total amount expensed to date, or the original cost minus "Accumulated Depreciation" for buildings, plant, and equipment). The procedure of using a contra account for depreciation expense recorded in all periods to date makes the communication of the components of book value of depreciable assets clearer. Thus, for long-term tangible assets whose costs are allocated over several accounting periods, it is common practice in accounting to use the contra asset account Accumulated Depreciation because then both the original cost of the long-term asset and the amount depreciated to date can be shown. This is explained by the following table:

Date	*Original Cost*	*Office Equipment Account Balance*	*Depreciation Expense for the Month*	*Accumulated Depreciation Account Balance*
1/31/x2.	$3,000	$3,000	$50	$50

Balance sheet disclosure at January 31, 19x2:

Office equipment.	$3,000
Less: Accumulated depreciation	50
	$2,950

If we project forward to June 30, 19x4, when half of the asset's useful life has expired, we would see the following:

Date	*Original Cost*	*Office Equipment Account Balance*	*Depreciation Expense for the Month*	*Accumulated Depreciation Account Balance*
6/30/x4	$3,000	$3,000	$50	$1,500

Balance sheet disclosure at June 30, 19x4:

Office equipment.	$3,000
Less: Accumulated depreciation	1,500
	$1,500

The amortization of the **trademark** follows the same basic pattern as depreciation. The original cost is allocated to the periods benefiting from the use of the asset. However, contra accounts are not normally used when recording amortization of intangible assets such as trademarks.

Assume LMI has estimated the useful life of the trademark to be five years (60 months) from January 1, 19x2. The entry to record the appropriate adjustment is:

f.	19x2			
	Jan. 31	Amortization Expense (E)	200	
		Trademark (A).		200
		To record amortization of trademark for January.		

The Trademark account balance and balance sheet disclosures for January 31, 19x2, and June 30, 19x4, are as follows:

Date	*Original Cost*	*Amortization Taken to Date*	*Trademark Account Balance*	*Amortization Expense for the Month*
1/31/x2	$12,000	$ 200	$11,800	$200
6/30/x4	12,000	6,000	6,000	200

Balance sheet disclosure:

Date	*Noncurrent Assets*	
1/31/x2	Trademark	$11,800
6/30/x4	Trademark	6,000

Note that, in contrast to depreciation, because no contra account is used, only the net book value is shown on the balance sheet.

Period-End Accruals. Period-end accruals, as explained earlier, involve (*a*) accrued revenues and (*b*) accrued expenses. These revenues and expenses have accumulated but have not been recorded. LMI has two period-end accruals or balance sheet items that have not been recorded as of January 31, 19x2—interest receivable and salaries payable. Note that an accrued revenue usually results in a debit to an asset account and a credit to a revenue account; an accrued expense usually results in a debit to an expense account and a credit to a liability account. Accruals that require end-of-period adjustments are often identified by asking the question: Are there any assets or liabilities that are not in the unadjusted trial balance but should be there?

Interest receivable (accrued asset). On January 2, 19x2, LMI loaned $4,800 to one of its owners and received a one-year note with an annual interest rate of 16%. LMI, therefore, has earned $64 interest income on January 31, 19x2 ($4,800 at 16% for one month). This accrued receivable is recorded as follows:

g.	19x2			
	Jan. 31	Interest Receivable (A)	64	
		Interest Revenue (R)		64
		To accrue interest receivable on note: $4,800 × .16 × 1/12.		

Note that this entry records a new asset that did not previously exist. Since interest is earned as time passes, no interest had been earned on January 2; and, therefore, the recording of the interest receivable waited until the end of the period. This Interest Receivable item will remain on LMI's books and will be increased by other month-end accruals until the entire $4,800 plus all interest is received from the maker of the note. When payment is received, Cash would be debited for the amount received, Note Receivable would be credited for the $4,800 principal amount, and Interest Receivable would be credited for the interest. Because the asset has been earned as of January 31, stockholders' equity must be increased by means of the credit to Interest Revenue. The $64 revenue will be shown on LMI's income statement.

Salaries payable (accrued expense). Since LMI does not pay its employees until February 11, LMI has an unpaid payroll amount on January 31. The accrued salaries expense must be shown in the income statement; and if we assume that amount is $2,115, the following debit to Salaries Expense and credit to Salaries Payable is made:

h.	19x2			
	Jan. 31	Salaries Expense (E)	2,115	
		Salaries Payable (L)		2,115
		To accrue salaries unpaid at January 31, 19x2.		

Salaries Payable represents an obligation to employees that will be paid at the next payday, at which time the liability will be debited and Cash credited.

Income taxes payable (accrued expense). LMI must also record its income tax expense for the period. This is an accrual because it represents an unpaid obligation and expense that has not yet been recorded by period-end, thus requiring an adjusting entry. The entry, assuming a $2,330 income tax, is:

i.	19x2			
	Jan. 31	Income Tax Expense (E)	2,330	
		Income Taxes Payable (L).		2,330
		To accrue income taxes for January.		

LMI's adjusting entries are now completed. In the sections that follow you will learn how LMI's accountant uses the unadjusted trial balance amounts plus these adjusting entry amounts to prepare its financial statements.

RELATIONSHIP OF JOURNAL AND LEDGER TO UNADJUSTED AND ADJUSTED TRIAL BALANCES

LMI's accountant, you will recall, started with Ian's unadjusted trial balance (Exhibit 4-2) from LMI's ledger accounts before making the necessary adjustments. After the accountant completed the journal entries (*a*) through (*i*), these entries were posted to the ledger accounts. New ledger accounts were established for the new accounts required by the adjustments. Remember that adjusting entries **must** be journalized in the journal and posted to the ledger accounts, just as were all the transactions made during the month.

When the LMI accountant had finished journalizing and posting the adjusting entries to the ledger accounts, the accountant prepared a new trial balance from the ledger. Since all the necessary adjustments have now been made, this new trial balance is called the **adjusted trial balance.**

Objective 3
The relation between adjusting journal entries, ledger balances, and unadjusted and adjusted trial balances.

Exhibit 4-5 summarizes the effects that the adjusting entries (*a*) through (*i*) have on the existing accounts and newly generated accounts. Note that several new accounts have been added to the adjusted trial balance. Three permanent (balance sheet) accounts, Interest Receivable, Accumulated Depreciation—Office Equipment, and Retained Earnings, have been added to the list of accounts previously shown on the unadjusted trial balance because they were affected by adjusting entries but had no balances until that time. This schedule is

EXHIBIT 4-5

Flow of Information from Unadjusted Trial Balance to Adjusted Trial Balance

Legislative Minds, Incorporated
Trial Balances
For the Month Ended January 31, 19x2

	Unadjusted Trial Balance		*Adjustments*		*Adjusted Trial Balance*	
Account Titles	*Debit*	*Credit*	*Debit*	*Credit*	*Debit*	*Credit*
Cash	1,260				1,260	
Accounts Receivable	12,150				12,150	
Note Receivable	4,800				4,800	
Interest Receivable	*None*		(*g*) 64		64	
Office Supplies	1,200			(*d*) 900	300	
Prepaid Rent	24,000			(*b*) 8,000	16,000	
Prepaid Insurance	12,000			(*c*) 1,000	11,000	
Office Equipment	3,000				3,000	
Accumulated Depreciation—Office Equipment		*None*		(*e*) 50		50
Trademark	12,000			(*f*) 200	11,800	
Accounts Payable		4,560				4,560
Unearned Consulting Fees				(*a*) 2,000		2,000
Salaries Payable				(*h*) 2,115		2,115
Income Taxes Payable				(*i*) 2,330		2,330
Capital Stock		40,000				40,000
Retained Earnings, 1/1/x2		*None*				0
Consulting Fees		61,000	(*a*) 2,000			59,000
Salaries Expense	27,000		(*h*) 2,115		29,115	
Travel and Entertainment Expense	6,000				6,000	
Communications Expense	1,300				1,300	
Utilities Expense	450				450	
Postage Expense	400				400	
Totals	105,560	105,560				
Rent Expense			(*b*) 8,000		8,000	
Insurance Expense			(*c*) 1,000		1,000	
Office Supplies Expense			(*d*) 900		900	
Depreciation Expense—Office Equipment			(*e*) 50		50	
Amortization Expense			(*f*) 200		200	
Interest Revenue				(*g*) 64		64
Income Tax Expense			(*i*) 2,330		2,330	
Totals			16,659	16,659	110,119	110,119

not a substitute for the formal journalizing and posting of the adjusting entries that the LMI accountant has already performed. In fact, the schedule can be made before the adjusting entries are journalized and posted to the ledger accounts, but the adjusting entries will become part of the company's records by journalizing and posting these entries to the ledger. You will see later in this chapter how this schedule becomes part of a worksheet, which is an organizing tool accountants use at the end of the accounting period.

RELATIONSHIP OF ADJUSTED TRIAL BALANCE, INCOME STATEMENT, RETAINED EARNINGS STATEMENT, AND BALANCE SHEET

The adjusted trial balance has all the components needed to construct the period-end income statement, retained earnings statement, and balance sheet as illustrated in Chapter 3. To illustrate this process once again, the adjusted trial balance given in Exhibit 4-5 is repeated at the left of Exhibits 4-6 and 4-7. Exhibit 4-6 shows how the adjusted trial balance is used to prepare an income statement and a retained earnings statement, and Exhibit 4-7 shows how the adjusted trial balance is used to prepare a balance sheet. Refer to these two exhibits as you study the paragraphs that follow.

The format of LMI's income statement in Exhibit 4-6 shows two major sections—"Revenue" and "Expenses"—plus a section titled "Other revenue." The "Other" section can contain miscellaneous revenues and expenses that do not result from the main business activity of the company. When other revenues and expenses are insignificant in amount, companies include them under a miscellaneous or catchall category in the major section of their income statement.

In Chapter 3, you learned how both the permanent (balance sheet) accounts and temporary (income statement) accounts are listed in the unadjusted and the adjusted trial balances. In Exhibit 4-6, you can follow the arrows from the temporary accounts of LMI's adjusted trial balance to the components of LMI's income statement.

As you can see from studying the arrows from LMI's adjusted trial balance to LMI's balance sheet in Exhibit 4-7, both permanent account balances and the effects of temporary account balances (by means of the Retained Earnings account) are represented in the balance sheet. Note that all account balances, other than those shown in the income statement, are listed in the balance sheet as assets, liabilities, or stockholders' equity. For LMI, net income, which is the net of the income statement accounts, is then added to the beginning Retained Earnings account balance to arrive at the ending balance sheet total for retained earnings. As we discussed in Chapter 3, dividend declarations also create a temporary account that is closed to Retained Earnings. In the current example, LMI declared no dividends.

LMI's balance sheet classifies assets and liabilities as current and noncurrent. A **current asset** is one that is expected to be consumed or converted to cash in its entirety within one year or the company's operating cycle, whichever is longer. A **current liability** is expected to utilize cash or other current assets within the next year or the company's operating cycle, whichever is longer.

LMI's office equipment is classified as a noncurrent asset because, although part of the equipment is consumed through depreciation, the equipment will not be entirely consumed during the following year. The unearned consulting fees are classified as a current liability because the company expects that cash and other current assets will be consumed in providing services to customers in the next year and that the revenue will be recognized within a one-year period.

EXHIBIT 4-6

Adjusted Trial Balance and the Income Statement and Retained Earnings Statement

Legislative Minds, Incorporated
Adjusted Trial Balance
January 31, 19x2

	Debits	*Credits*
Cash	$ 1,260	
Accounts Receivable	12,150	
Note Receivable	4,800	
Interest Receivable	64	
Office Supplies	300	
Prepaid Rent	16,000	
Prepaid Insurance	11,000	
Office Equipment	3,000	
Accumulated Depreciation—Office Equipment		$ 50
Trademark	11,800	
Accounts Payable		4,560
Unearned Consulting Fees		2,000
Salaries Payable		2,115
Income Taxes Payable		2,330
Capital Stock		40,000
Retained Earnings, 1/1/x2		0
Consulting Fees		59,000
Salaries Expense	29,115	
Travel and Entertainment Expense	6,000	
Communications Expense	1,300	
Utilities Expense	450	
Postage Expense	400	
Rent Expense	8,000	
Insurance Expense	1,000	
Office Supplies Expense	900	
Depreciation Expense—Office Equipment	50	
Amortization Expense	200	
Interest Revenue		64
Income Tax Expense	2,330	
Totals	$110,119	$110,119

Legislative Minds, Inc.
Income Statement
For the Month Ended January 31, 19x2

Revenue:		
Consulting fees		$59,000
Expenses:		
Salaries expense		$29,115
Travel and entertainment expense		6,000
Communications expense		1,300
Utilities expense		450
Postage expense		400
Rent expense		8,000
Insurance expense		1,000
Office supplies expense		900
Depreciation expense—office equipment		50
Amortization expense		200
Total expenses		$47,415
Income before other revenue		$11,585
Other revenue:		
Interest revenue		64
Net income before taxes		$11,649
Income tax expense		2,330
Net income		$ 9,319

Legislative Minds, Inc.
Retained Earnings Statement
For the Month Ended January 31, 19x2

Retained earnings, January 1, 19x2	$ 0
Add: Net income	9,319
Less: Dividends	0
Retained earnings, January 31, 19x2	$ 9,319

EXHIBIT 4-7

Adjusted Trial Balance and Balance Sheet

Legislative Minds, Incorporated
Adjusted Trial Balance
January 31, 19x2

	Debits	*Credits*
Cash	$ 1,260	
Accounts Receivable	12,150	
Note Receivable	4,800	
Interest Receivable	64	
Office Supplies	300	
Prepaid Rent	16,000	
Prepaid Insurance	11,000	
Office Equipment	3,000	
Accumulated Depreciation—Office Equipment		$ 50
Trademark	11,800	
Accounts Payable		4,560
Unearned Consulting Fees		2,000
Salaries Payable		2,115
Income Taxes Payable		2,330
Capital Stock		40,000
Retained Earnings, 1/1/x2	0	
Consulting Fees		59,000
Salaries Expense	29,115	
Travel and Entertainment Expense	6,000	
Communications Expense	1,300	
Utility Expense	450	
Postage Expense	400	
Rent Expense	8,000	
Insurance Expense	1,000	
Office Supplies Expense	900	
Depreciation Expense—Office Equipment	50	
Amortization Expense	200	
Interest Revenue		64
Income Tax Expense	2,330	
Totals	$110,119	$110,119

Legislative Minds, Inc.
Balance Sheet
January 31, 19x2

Assets

Current assets:		
Cash	$ 1,260	
Accounts receivable	12,150	
Note receivable	4,800	
Interest receivable	64	
Office supplies	300	
Prepaid rent	16,000	
Prepaid insurance	11,000	
Total current assets		$45,574
Noncurrent assets:		
Office equipment	$ 3,000	
Less: Accumulated depreciation	50	$ 2,950
Trademark		11,800
Total noncurrent assets		$14,750
Total assets		$60,324

Liabilities and Stockholders' Equity

Liabilities:		
Accounts payable	$ 4,560	
Unearned consulting fees	2,000	
Salaries payable	2,115	
Income taxes payable	2,330	
Total liabilities		$11,005
Stockholders' equity:		
Capital stock	$40,000	
Retained earnings	9,319	
Total stockholders' equity		$49,319
Total liabilities and stockholders' equity		$60,324

THE WORKSHEET: AN ACCOUNTING TOOL

Objective 4
How the worksheet is used to summarize cycle steps 1 through 5.

Most businesses have the need to examine their financial statement performance many times throughout the year. This requires preparing steps 4 and 5 of the cycle—adjusting entries and financial statements. However, businesses may not wish to *formally* record the adjustments in their journal and ledger each time they want to examine a balance sheet or an income statement. To facilitate preparation of financial statements (cycle step 5) (whether or not adjusting entries are formally journalized and posted to the ledger), accountants often use a **worksheet.** The worksheet is a convenient tool for preparing steps 4 and 5 of the cycle from an unadjusted trial balance prepared after steps 1, 2, and 3. In Exhibits 4-6 and 4-7 we illustrated how the January 31, 19x2, financial statements were prepared from the information in the adjusted trial balance. Exhibit 4-8 illustrates this same statement preparation process in a 12-column worksheet format. This worksheet summarizes the results of steps 1 through 5 of the accounting cycle and contains the following accounting data:

Columns	*Data*	*Relation to Cycle Steps*
1–2	Unadjusted trial balance	After steps 1–3
3–4	Adjusting entries	Step 4
5–6	Adjusted trial balance	After step 4
7–8	Income statement	Part 1 of step 5
9–10	Retained earnings statement	Part 2 of step 5
11–12	Balance sheet	Part 3 of step 5

The adjusting entries in columns 3 and 4 explain the differences between the unadjusted trial balance (columns 1 and 2) and the adjusted trial balance (columns 5 and 6) since the balances in each account are simply summed across. The income statement is prepared in columns 7 and 8 with the debit of $9,319 at the bottom of column 7 (entry *j*) needed to balance columns 7 and 8 representing net income. The credit side of entry *j* for $9,319 is carried to column 10 and added to retained earnings. (If there were dividends for LMI, the balance would be carried across from column 1 to column 9, resulting in a deduction from retained earnings.) The debit of $9,319 for entry *k* at the bottom of column 9 needed to balance columns 9 and 10 is the sum of beginning retained earnings ($0 credit) plus net income ($9,319 credit) less dividends ($0 debit). This credit side of entry *k* is equal to the ending retained earnings balance and is carried to column 12 in the balance sheet as retained earnings. The mechanics of the worksheet in Exhibit 4-8 are only a slightly different way of preparing financial statements than that method illustrated in Exhibits 4-6 and 4-7. The resulting statements are, of course, the same. The worksheet is a commonly used tool in accounting, especially for preparing statements over periods of less than one year.

CLOSING ENTRIES (ACCOUNTING CYCLE STEP 6)

The final step in the accounting cycle is closing the books for the period. Closing the books requires recording and posting closing entries which eliminate the balance in all temporary (income statement) accounts. This step is not performed unless it is the last time that net income will be computed for the period—normally only once a year. In other words, if the first five cycle steps, which include the measurement of net income, are being made for purposes of evaluating the monthly or quarterly performance of the business, closing entries would not be required. To close the books for LMI at the end of January would result in formally eliminating the balances in all income statement accounts and starting

EXHIBIT 4-8

Preparing a Worksheet

Legislative Minds, Incorporated
Worksheet
For the Month Ended January 31, 19x2

	Unadjusted Trial Balance		*Adjustments*	
Account Titles	*(1) Debit*	*(2) Credit*	*(3) Debit*	*(4) Credit*
Cash	1,260			
Accounts Receivable	12,150			
Note Receivable	4,800			
Interest Receivable			(*g*) 64	
Office Supplies	1,200			(*d*) 900
Prepaid Rent	24,000			(*b*) 8,000
Prepaid Insurance	12,000			(*c*) 1,000
Office Equipment	3,000			
Accumulated Depreciation—Office Equipment				(*e*) 50
Trademark	12,000			(*f*) 200
Accounts Payable		4,560		
Unearned Consulting Fees				(*a*) 2,000
Salaries Payable				(*h*) 2,115
Income Taxes Payable				(*i*) 2,330
Capital Stock		40,000		
Retained Earnings, 1/1/x2		0		
Consulting Fees		61,000	(*a*) 2,000	
Salaries Expense	27,000		(*h*) 2,115	
Travel and Entertainment Expense	6,000			
Communications Expense	1,300			
Utilities Expense	450			
Postage Expense	400			
Rent Expense			(*b*) 8,000	
Insurance Expense			(*c*) 1,000	
Office Supplies Expense			(*d*) 900	
Depreciation Expense—Office Equipment			(*e*) 50	
Amortization Expense			(*f*) 200	
Interest Revenue				(*g*) 64
Income Tax Expense			(*i*) 2,330	
	105,560	105,560	16,659	16,659
Net income				
Retained Earnings, 1/31/x2				
Totals				

February with a set of income statement accounts with no balances. This would not permit a measure of two-month (January/February) or annual (19x2) net income by using the income statement accounts. As a result, closing entries to "wipe the slate clean" in the (temporary) income statement accounts are normally journalized and posted only once each year. This closing process is often aided by the use of a new temporary account, Income Summary, which is only used at the time of closing to facilitate both closing and income measurement. Although LMI would not ordinarily close its books at the end of one month, we

Adjusted Trial Balance		*Income Statement*		*Retained Earnings Statement*		*Balance Sheet*	
(5) Debit	*(6) Credit*	*(7) Debit*	*(8) Credit*	*(9) Debit*	*(10) Credit*	*(11) Debit*	*(12) Credit*
1,260						1,260	
12,150						12,150	
4,800						4,800	
64						64	
300						300	
16,000						16,000	
11,000						11,000	
3,000						3,000	
	50						50
11,800						11,800	
	4,560						4,560
	2,000						2,000
	2,115						2,115
	2,330						2,330
	40,000						40,000
	0				0		
	59,000		59,000				
29,115		29,115					
6,000		6,000					
1,300		1,300					
450		450					
400		400					
8,000		8,000					
1,000		1,000					
900		900					
50		50					
200		200					
	64		64				
		47,415	59,064				
2,330		2,330					
110,119	110,119						
		(*j*) 9,319			(*j*) 9,319		
				(*k*) 9,319			(*k*) 9,319
		59,064	59,064	9,319	9,319	60,374	60,374

Objective 5
How the formal closing process wipes the slate clean in the temporary accounts for the start of a new period and includes the last period's results in retained earnings.

will use the adjusted trial balance in Exhibit 4-8 (also found in Exhibits 4-6 and 4-7) to illustrate the closing process. Since only the temporary (nonbalance sheet) accounts are closed, let's consider the adjusted balances in these accounts. Their pre-closing T account balances, along with the closing entries, and post-closing T account balances for LMI's temporary accounts are illustrated in Exhibit 4-9. Notice how the closing entries simply force the post-closing balances in all temporary accounts to be zero (a clean slate) for next period and record their effect in the Income Summary account (a very temporary account), which is

EXHIBIT 4-9

Closing Entries (Step 6)

Pre-Closing Ledger Balances
Temporary Accounts

Consulting Fees

	59,000

Interest Revenue

	64

Salaries Expense

29,115	

Travel and Entertainment Expense

6,000	

Communications Expense

1,300	

Utilities Expense

450	

Postage Expense

400	

Rent Expense

8,000	

Insurance Expense

1,000	

Office Supplies Expense

900	

Depreciation Expense

50	

Amortization Expense

200	

Income Tax Expense

2,330	

Closing Journal Entries

	Account	Debit	Credit
(*l*)	Consulting Fees	59,000	
	Interest Revenue	64	
	Income Summary		59,064
	To close revenue accounts.		
(*m*)	Income Summary	49,745	
	Salaries Expense		29,115
	Travel and Entertainment Expense		6,000
	Communications Expense		1,300
	Utilities Expense		450
	Postage Expense		400
	Rent Expense		8,000
	Insurance Expense		1,000
	Office Supplies Expense		900
	Depreciation Expense		50
	Amortization Expense		200
	Income Tax Expense		2,330
	To close expense accounts.		
(*n*)	Income Summary	9,319	
	Retained Earnings		9,319
	To close income summary account.		

Post-Closing Ledger Balances
Temporary Accounts

Consulting Fees

(*l*)	59,000		59,000
		Bal.	-0-

Interest Revenue

(*l*)	64		64
		Bal.	-0-

Salaries Expense

	29,115	(*m*)	29,115
Bal.	-0-		

Travel and Entertainment Expense

	6,000	(*m*)	6,000
Bal.	-0-		

Communications Expense

	1,300	(*m*)	1,300
Bal.	-0-		

Utilities Expense

	450	(*m*)	450
Bal.	-0-		

Postage Expense

	400	(*m*)	400
Bal.	-0-		

Rent Expense

	8,000	(*m*)	8,000
Bal.	-0-		

Insurance Expense

	1,000	(*m*)	1,000
Bal.	-0-		

Office Supplies Expense

	900	(*m*)	900
Bal.	-0-		

Depreciation Expense

	50	(*m*)	50
Bal.	-0-		

Amortization Expense

	200	(*m*)	200
Bal.	-0-		

Income Tax Expense

	2,330	(*m*)	2,330
Bal.	-0-		

Income Summary

(*m*)	49,745	(*l*)	59,064
(*n*)	9,319	Bal.	9,319
			-0-

Retained Earnings

			-0-
	-0-		
		(*n*)	9,319
		Bal.	9,319

Dividends

-0-	-0-

then itself closed to the Retained Earnings account. The closing of the books on January 31, 19x2, will prohibit us from going back and changing the revenue and expense accounts from January, since their net income effect is in retained earnings once February begins.

POST-CLOSING TRIAL BALANCE AND NEW ACCOUNTING CYCLE

Exhibits 4-7 and 4-8 both illustrated how the balances of the permanent accounts become the balance sheet items. Assume that LMI's accountant has completed the LMI income statement and balance sheet, closed the temporary accounts, and is now ready for the new accounting period. To be sure that the account balances are correct, on January 31, 19x2, LMI's accountant takes a **post-closing trial balance.** The post-closing trial balance, illustrated in Exhibit 4-10, is a listing of all account balances just as the other trial balances were. However, after closing only the permanent balance sheet accounts are left with a balance.

Remember that all trial balances are internal documents used to help check completeness and accuracy. The unadjusted trial balance is prepared before the company has made its adjustments; the adjusted trial balance is prepared after the adjustments have been made; and the post-closing trial balance is prepared after the closing entries are made and before a new accounting period begins.

CORRECTION OF CURRENT PERIOD ERRORS

During an accounting period, errors may be made in recording and posting accounting entries. The most common errors involve improper amounts and improper classifications. Of course, when such errors are detected, they must be

EXHIBIT 4-10

Post-Closing Trial Balance

Legislative Minds, Incorporated
Post-Closing Trial Balance
January 31, 19x2

	Debits	*Credits*
Cash	$ 1,260	
Accounts Receivable	12,150	
Note Receivable	4,800	
Interest Receivable	64	
Office Supplies	300	
Prepaid Rent	16,000	
Prepaid Insurance	11,000	
Office Equipment	3,000	
Accumulated Depreciation—Office Equipment		$ 50
Trademark	11,800	
Accounts Payable		4,560
Unearned Consulting Fees		2,000
Salaries Payable		2,115
Income Taxes Payable		2,330
Capital Stock		40,000
Retained Earnings		9,319
Totals	$60,374	$60,374

Objective 6
How to correct the current period's errors.

corrected. When this **correction process** is performed in the same period in which the error occurs, the process is considered routine. For instance, assume that on October 15, 19x1, a company purchases land for $10,000 and erroneously debits Administrative Expense and credits Cash. If that error is detected at the end of the period (December 31, 19x1, in this case), the accountant would correct the error by debiting Land and crediting Administrative Expense, giving both accounts their appropriate balances.

Incorrect entry:

19x1			
Oct. 15	Administrative Expense (E)	10,000	
	Cash (A).		10,000
	To record purchase of land.		

Correcting entry:

19x1			
Dec. 31	Land (A).	10,000	
	Administrative Expense (E)		10,000
	To correct October 15, 19x1, entry.		

If such an error were left uncorrected, it would cause erroneous balances in several accounts that flow to the financial statements. In our example, net income, land (noncurrent assets), and retained earnings would all be understated in the year of the error. Also, unless corrected, both land and retained earnings would be understated in subsequent years.

Although this type of correction changes account balances, you must not consider a correction to be the same as an adjusting entry. For example, compare the correcting entry above to an adjusting entry to record depreciation expense. The depreciation adjustment is necessary because a portion of the economic life of an asset is consumed during the period. Although this adjusting entry is made at the end of the period and is similar in appearance to the correcting entry shown above, the adjusting entry does not correct an error but updates the accounts.

REVIEW OF THE COMPLETE ACCOUNTING CYCLE

To review the complete six-step process examined in Chapters 3 and 4, let's consider a new example. (For those who wish to skip this review, turn to the chapter summary on page 187.)

Trans Company was organized on January 1, 19x1, for the purpose of providing transportation. Data in summary form from the first year's operations are given below (all amounts are in thousands of dollars):

a. Transportation revenue earned from services performed on account, $2,500.

b. Cash receipts for the year:

Jan. 10	From stockholders for shares of stock . .	$5,000
June 30	From bank loan	2,000
Jan. 1–Dec. 31	From customers representing collections on account	1,850
		$8,850

c. Cash disbursements for the year:

Jan. 1	For purchase of land	$1,000
July 1	For advertising (3 years paid in advance)	3,540
Dec. 30	For dividends	100
	For interest on notes payable	5
Jan. 1–Dec. 31	For gasoline	250
Jan. 30–Dec. 15	For wages	1,200
Jan. 30–Dec. 31	For repairs.	125
Mar. 1–Dec. 1	For auto payments	400
		$6,620

d. Purchased autos costing $2,000 total on February 1 for no down payment. These autos were expected to have a 10-year life and no value at the end of 10 years. The autos were acquired with a loan from the dealer, and were to be paid for in 50 equal monthly interest-free payments of $40 each.

e. Unpaid wages as of December 31 are $100.

f. Unpaid gasoline invoices as of December 31 are $60.

g. Accrued interest payable as of December 31 is $5.

The analysis of transactions, journal entries, and ledger account balances for the first three cycle steps pertain to the transactions summarized in items *a* through *d* of our example. Items *e*, *f*, and *g* are accrual-type adjusting entries that would pertain to cycle step 4.

The following summary journal entries, ledger accounts, and unadjusted trial balance would result from the first three cycle steps:

Journal Entries (summarizing all transactions for the year):

Reference	*Accounts*	*Debit*	*Credit*
a.	Accounts Receivable (A)	2,500	
	Service Revenue (R)		2,500
	To record sale on account.		
b.	Cash (A)	8,850	
	Capital Stock (SE)		5,000
	Notes Payable (L)		2,000
	Accounts Receivable (A)		1,850
	To record cash receipts for year.		
c.	Land (A)	1,000	
	Prepaid Advertising (A)	3,540	
	Dividends (D)	100	
	Interest Expense (E)	5	
	Gasoline Expense (E)	250	
	Wages Expense (E)	1,200	
	Repairs Expense (E)	125	
	Auto Loan Payable (L)	400	
	Cash (A)		6,620
	To record cash disbursements for year.		
d.	Automobiles (A)	2,000	
	Auto Loan Payable (L)		2,000
	To record autos purchased with loan.		

Ledger Account Balances:

Assets:

Cash

(*b*)	8,850	(*c*)	6,620
Bal.	2,230		

Accounts Receivable

(*a*)	2,500	(*b*)	1,850
Bal.	650		

Prepaid Advertising

(*c*)	3,540		
Bal.	3,540		

Autos

(*d*)	2,000		
Bal.	2,000		

Land

(*c*)	1,000		
Bal.	1,000		

Liabilities:

Accounts Payable-Autos

(*c*)	400	(*d*)	2,000
		Bal.	1,600

Notes Payable

		(*b*)	2,000
		Bal.	2,000

Stockholders' Equity:

Capital Stock

		(*b*)	5,000
		Bal.	5,000

Service Revenue

		(*a*)	2,500
		Bal.	2,500

Interest Expense

(*c*)	5		
Bal.	5		

Gasoline Expense

(*b*)	250		
Bal.	250		

Wages Expense

(*a*)	1,200		
Bal.	1,200		

Repairs Expense

(*c*)	125		
Bal.	125		

Dividends

(*c*)	100		
Bal.	100		

Trans Company
Unadjusted Trial Balance
December 31, 19x1
(in thousands)

	Debits	*Credits*
Cash	$ 2,230	
Accounts Receivable	650	
Prepaid Advertising	3,540	
Autos	2,000	
Land	1,000	
Auto Loan Payable		$ 1,600
Notes Payable		2,000
Capital Stock		5,000
Service Revenue		2,500
Interest Expense	5	
Gasoline Expense	250	
Wages Expense	1,200	
Repairs Expense	125	
Dividends	100	
Totals	$11,100	$11,100

After the first three cycle steps are complete, the unadjusted trial balance (above) can be used to help identify any adjustments needed to complete cycle step 4.

Accrual-type adjustments are required for data items *e, f,* and *g* in this example. The year-end adjusting entries would be:

	Date	Account	Debit	Credit
e.	19x1 Dec. 31	Wages Expense (E)	100	
		Wages Payable (L)		100
		To accrue earned but unpaid wages at year-end.		
f.	Dec. 31	Gasoline Expense (E)	60	
		Accounts Payable (L)		60
		To accrue gasoline invoices unpaid as of year-end.		
g.	Dec. 31	Interest Expense (E)	5	
		Interest Payable (L)		5
		To accrue interest on bank note unpaid as of year-end.		

Notice that each of these accrual-type adjusting entries require a new liability account (not in the unadjusted trial balance) to be established.

We can examine the unadjusted trial balance and ask the following question: Are there any amounts listed as assets or liabilities which no longer represent assets or liabilities? Cash and accounts receivable are properly stated assets; however, prepaid advertising and autos are both overstated since some of their value has been consumed. The advertising was paid on July 1 for three years; therefore, 6 out of 36 months, or one sixth of this amount has expired. The following allocation-type adjusting entry would be recorded at year-end:

			Debit	Credit
h.	19x1			
	Dec. 31	Advertising Expense (E)	590	
		Prepaid Advertising (A)		590
		To allocate one sixth of prepaid advertising to expense.		

The autos were acquired on February 1 and have been in use for 11 months. They are expected to last 10 years, or 120 months, so 11/120 of their cost should be allocated to expense in 19x1. This allocation-type adjusting entry (rounded to the nearest $1,000) would be recorded as follows:

			Debit	Credit
i.	19x1			
	Dec. 31	Depreciation Expense (E)	183	
		Accumulated Depreciation (XA)		183
		To record 11 months of depreciation expense on autos.		

Other allocations are not apparent in this example based on the examination of the trial balance and the details provided.

After posting cycle step 4, we will be ready to prepare the adjusted trial balance and the three financial statements which are prepared from the listed account balances. To illustrate the recording and posting of adjustments (*e*) through (*i*) and the resulting financial statements, we provide the worksheet in Exhibit 4-11. From this worksheet, we can examine the results of cycle steps 1 through 3 in the first two columns and the effect of the adjustments made in cycle step 4 (columns 3 and 4) on the adjusted ledger balances (columns 5 and 6), from which the income statement (columns 7 and 8), retained earnings statement (columns 9 and 10) and balance sheet (columns 11 and 12) are prepared.

After the adjusting entries are actually posted to the ledger accounts, the balances illustrated on the next page will be reported in the **nominal** accounts (only) of Trans Company before and after closing entries at December 31, 19x1. The formal closing entries to eliminate all balances in these nominal accounts for 19x1 and close their net effect to retained earnings would be recorded in journal form as follows:

			Debit	Credit
j.	19x1			
	Dec. 31	Service Revenue	2,500	
		Income Summary		2,500
		To close revenue account.		
k.	Dec. 31	Income Summary	2,518	
		Interest Expense		10
		Gasoline Expense		310
		Wages Expense		1,300
		Repair Expense		125
		Advertising Expense		590
		Depreciation Expense		183
		To close expense accounts.		
l.	Dec. 31	Retained Earnings (Deficit)	18	
		Income Summary		18
		To close Income Summary account.		
m.	Dec. 31	Retained Earnings (Deficit)	100	
		Dividends		100
		To close Dividends account.		

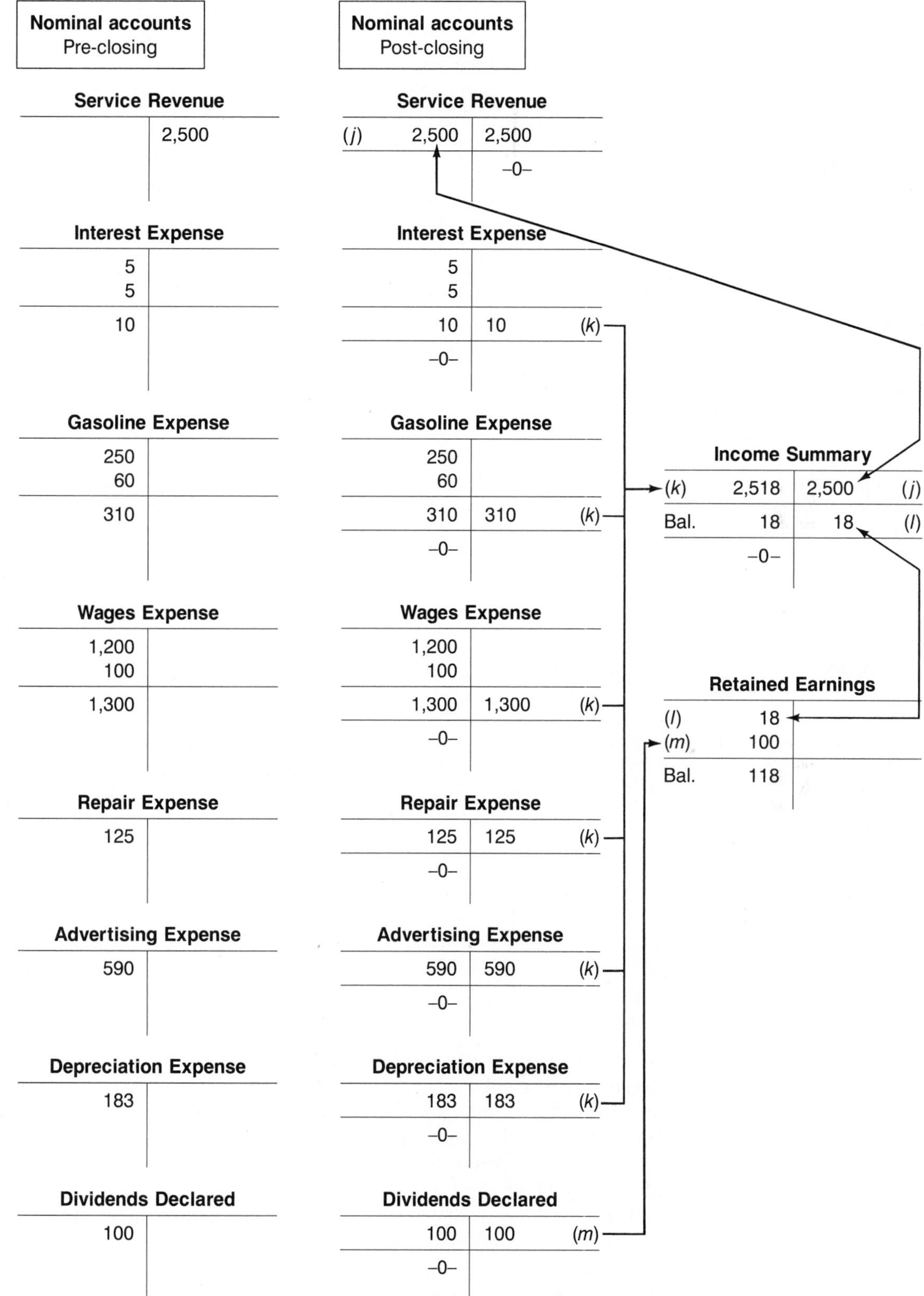
Nominal accounts
Pre-closing
Nominal accounts
Post-closing
Service Revenue
2,500
Service Revenue
(j) 2,500 | 2,500
-0-
Interest Expense
5
5
10
Interest Expense
5
5
10 | 10 (k)
-0-
Gasoline Expense
250
60
310
Gasoline Expense
250
60
310 | 310 (k)
-0-
Wages Expense
1,200
100
1,300
Wages Expense
1,200
100
1,300 | 1,300 (k)
-0-
Repair Expense
125
Repair Expense
125 | 125 (k)
-0-
Advertising Expense
590
Advertising Expense
590 | 590 (k)
-0-
Depreciation Expense
183
Depreciation Expense
183 | 183 (k)
-0-
Dividends Declared
100
Dividends Declared
100 | 100 (m)
-0-
Income Summary
(k) 2,518 | 2,500 (j)
Bal. 18 | 18 (l)
-0-
Retained Earnings
(l) 18
(m) 100
Bal. 118

EXHIBIT 4-11

Trans Company Worksheet

Trans Company
Worksheet
For the Year Ended December 31, 19x1

	Unadjusted Trial Balance		*Adjustments*	
Account Titles	*(1) Debit*	*(2) Credit*	*(3) Debit*	*(4) Credit*
Cash	2,230			
Accounts Receivable	650			
Prepaid Advertising	3,540			(*h*) 590
Autos	2,000			
Land	1,000			
Auto Loan Payable		1,600		
Note Payable		2,000		
Capital Stock		5,000		
Service Revenue		2,500		
Interest Expense	5		(*g*) 5	
Gasoline Expense	250		(*f*) 60	
Wages Expense	1,200		(*e*) 100	
Repair Expense	125			
Dividends	100			
	11,100	11,100		
Advertising Expense			(*h*) 590	
Depreciation Expense			(*i*) 183	
Accumulated Depreciation—Autos				(*i*) 183
Wages Payable				(*e*) 100
Accounts Payable				(*f*) 60
Interest Payable				(*g*) 5
			938	938
Net income or Loss				
Retained Earnings or Deficit				
Totals				

Since expenses exceeded revenues in 19x1 by $18, the retained earnings would have a debit balance and would be labeled retained deficit. It would not be unusual for companies to experience losses in the early years of operations. While Trans Company did declare and pay $100 of dividends in 19x1, further increasing the retained deficit to a $118 debit balance, such dividend payments are not typical. Some state laws would prohibit payment of a dividend if a retained deficit results. This will be discussed in more detail in Chapter 11.

The post-closing trial balance and formal balance sheet that would be reported for Trans Company at the end of 19x1 are provided in Exhibit 4-12. You should study this complete example carefully to review the six steps of the accounting cycle and the role of the accounting worksheet.

Adjusted Trial Balance		*Income Statement*		*Retained Earnings Statement*		*Balance Sheet*	
(5) Debit	*(6) Credit*	*(7) Debit*	*(8) Credit*	*(9) Debit*	*(10) Credit*	*(11) Debit*	*(12) Credit*
2,230						2,230	
650						650	
2,950						2,950	
2,000						2,000	
1,000						1,000	
	1,600						1,600
	2,000						2,000
	5,000						5,000
	2,500		2,500				
10		10					
310		310					
1,300		1,300					
125		125					
100				100			
590		590					
183		183					
	183						183
	100						100
	60						60
	5						5
11,448	11,448	2,518	2,500				
			(l) 18	*(l)* 18			
		2,518	2,518	118	0		
					118	118	
				118	118	8,948	8,948

SUMMARY

This chapter concentrated on the final steps in the accounting cycle which occur at the end of the accounting period—adjusting, preparing financial statements, and closing. The adjusting step was emphasized because adjusting entries are so pivotal in preparing accurate accrual based financial statements.

Adjustments are necessary because frequently balances in existing accounts must be modified and new accounts often must be created. Entries that involve revenue-related and expense-related account balances affecting more than one period must be spread among accounting periods. Unrecorded accrued revenues and expenses that have accumulated during the accounting period must be recorded as adjusting entries.

After the adjusting journal entries are journalized and posted to the ledger accounts, the adjusted trial balance is prepared. The adjusted trial balance has all the components needed to construct the period-end income statement, retained

EXHIBIT 4-12

Trial Balance and Balance Sheet at December 31, 19x1, Trans Company

Trans Company
Post-Closing Trial Balance
December 31, 19x1
(in thousands)

	Debits	*Credits*
Cash	$2,230	
Accounts Receivable	650	
Prepaid Advertising	2,950	
Autos	2,000	
Accumulated Depreciation—Autos		$ 183
Land	1,000	
Accounts Payable		60
Wages Payable		100
Auto Loan Payable		1,600
Interest Payable		5
Note Payable		2,000
Capital Stock		5,000
Retained Earnings	118	
Totals	$8,948	$8,948

Trans Company
Balance Sheet
December 31, 19x1
(in thousands)

Assets

Current assets:		
Cash	$2,230	
Accounts receivable	650	
Prepaid advertising	2,950	
Total current assets		$5,830
Noncurrent assets:		
Autos	$2,000	
Less: Accumulated depreciation	183	$1,817
Land		1,000
Total noncurrent assets		$2,817
Total assets		$8,647

Liabilities and Stockholders' Equity

Current liabilities:		
Accounts payable	$ 60	
Wages payable	100	
Interest payable	5	$ 165
Noncurrent liabilities:		
Auto loan payable	1,600	
Notes payable	2,000	3,600
Total liabilities		$3,765
Stockholders' equity:		
Capital stock	$5,000	
Retained deficit	(118)	
Total stockholders' equity		4,882
Total liabilities and stockholders' equity		$8,647

earnings statement, and balance sheet. All accounts on an adjusted trial balance affect some balance sheet category. The net effect of the income statement accounts becomes part of retained earnings, a permanent account; and all of the permanent accounts go directly into the body of the balance sheet.

In this chapter you learned how accountants prepare a worksheet to aid them in evaluating the financial position of the business. The first five steps in the accounting cycle are summarized in the elements of the worksheet, which is an informal representation of the accounting cycle. The worksheet shows the flow of data from the unadjusted trial balance to the financial statements.

The accounting cycle is completed with closing entries that return all temporary (income statement and dividend) accounts to zero in preparation for the next accounting period. The closing process is done with the aid of the Income Summary account, the balance of which is transferred to the Retained Earnings account.

Since errors are sometimes made during the recording and posting of transactions, the correction process is explained. You must not confuse the correction process with the adjustment process where no actual errors are made.

DEMONSTRATION EXERCISE

At the end of March 19x1, its second month of operations, Financial Planners, Inc. (FPI) had the following trial balance:

Financial Planners, Inc.
Trial Balance
March 31, 19x1

	Debits	*Credits*
Cash	$32,778	
Accounts Receivable	12,940	
Office Supplies	350	
Prepaid Rent	4,800	
Prepaid Insurance	3,600	
Security Deposit	2,400	
Office Equipment	5,670	
Accounts Payable		$ 4,500
Capital Stock		50,000
Retained Earnings	2,832	
Consulting Fees		32,000
Salaries Expense	12,000	
Commissions Expense	5,000	
Travel and Entertainment Expense	2,650	
Advertising Expense	715	
Communications Expense	580	
Utilities Expense	185	
Totals	$86,500	$86,500

The following end-of-month data is also available:

a. Prepaid rent of $1,600 is applicable to the month of March.

b. Depreciation for the month on the furniture and equipment is $95.

c. The insurance policy purchased at the beginning of the month is for 12 months.

d. Salaries and commissions earned at the end of the month but not yet paid amount to $1,325 and $900, respectively.

e. Consulting fees of $3,500 that were received but not yet earned have been recorded in Consulting Fees.

f. Office supplies on hand at the end of the month amount to $140.
g. FPI uses a 10% tax rate.

Required:

Prepare FPI's—

1. Complete worksheet for the month.
2. Adjusting journal entries in journal form.
3. Income statement for the month and March 31 balance sheet.
4. Closing entries for the end of the period.

Solution:

Financial Planners, Inc.
Worksheet
For the Month Ended March 31, 19x1

	Unadjusted Trial Balance		Adjustments		Adjusted Trial Balance		Income Statement		Balance Sheet	
Account Titles	(1) Debit	(2) Credit	(3) Debit	(4) Credit	(5) Debit	(6) Credit	(7) Debit	(8) Credit	(9) Debit	(10) Credit
Cash	32,778				32,778				32,778	
Accounts Receivable	12,940				12,940				12,940	
Office Supplies	350			(*f*) 210	140				140	
Prepaid Rent	4,800			(*a*) 1,600	3,200				3,200	
Prepaid Insurance	3,600			(*c*) 300	3,300				3,300	
Security Deposit	2,400				2,400				2,400	
Office Equipment	5,670				5,670				5,670	
Accumulated Depreciation—Office Equipment				(*b*) 95		95				95
Accounts Payable		4,500				4,500				4,500
Salaries Payable				(*d*) 1,325		1,325				1,325
Commissions Payable				(*d*) 900		900				900
Unearned Consulting Fees				(*e*) 3,500		3,500				3,500
Income Taxes Payable				(*g*) 294		294				294
Capital Stock		50,000				50,000				50,000
Retained Deficit, 3/1/x1	2,832				2,832				**2,832**	
Consulting Fees		32,000	(*e*) 3,500			28,500		28,500		
Salaries Expense	12,000		(*d*) 1,325		13,325		13,325			
Commissions Expense	5,000		(*d*) 900		5,900		5,900			
Travel and Entertainment Expense	2,650				2,650		2,650			
Advertising Expense	715				715		715			
Communications Expense	580				580		580			
Utilities Expense	185				185		185			
Rent Expense			(*a*) 1,600		1,600		1,600			
Depreciation Expense—Office Equipment			(*b*) 95		95		95			
Insurance Expense			(*c*) 300		300		300			
Office Supplies Expense			(*f*) 210		210		210			
							25,560	28,500		
Income Tax Expense			(*g*) 294		294		294			
	86,500	86,500	8,224	8,224	89,114	89,114				
Net income **(add to Retained Deficit)**							2,646			**2,646**
Totals							28,500	28,500	63,260	63,260

GENERAL JOURNAL					J9
Date		Account Titles and Explanation	Ref.	Debit	Credit
Adjusting entries:					
19x1					
Mar.	31	Rent Expense (E)		1,600	
		Prepaid Rent (A)			1,600
		To adjust for March rent expense.			
	31	Depreciation Expense—Equipment (E)		95	
		Accumulated Depreciation—Equipment (XA)			95
		To record depreciation expense.			
	31	Insurance Expense (E)		300	
		Prepaid Insurance (A)			300
		To adjust for insurance expense.			
	31	Salaries Expense (E)		1,325	
		Commissions Expense (E)		900	
		Salaries Payable (L)			1,325
		Commissions Payable (L)			900
		To accrue unpaid salaries and commissions.			
	31	Consulting Fees (R)		3,500	
		Unearned Consulting Fees (L)			3,500
		To adjust for fees received for services not yet performed.			
	31	Office Supplies Expense (E)		210	
		Office Supplies (A)			210
		To adjust for expense of office supplies used during the month.			
	31	Income Tax Expense (E)		294	
		Income Taxes Payable (L)			294
		To accrue income taxes for March.			

Financial Planners, Inc.
Income Statement
For the Month Ended March 31, 19x1

Revenue:		
Consulting fees		$28,500
Expenses:		
Salaries expense	$13,325	
Commissions expense	5,900	
Travel and entertainment expense	2,650	
Rent expense	1,600	
Insurance expense	300	
Depreciation expense—office equipment	95	
Office supplies expense	210	
Utilities expense	185	
Communications expense	580	
Advertising expense	715	
Total expenses		25,560
Net income before taxes		$ 2,940
Income tax expense		294
Net income		$ 2,646

Financial Planners, Inc.
Balance Sheet
March 31, 19x1

Assets		**Liabilities and Stockholders' Equity**	
Current assets:		Liabilities:	
Cash	$32,778	Accounts payable	$ 4,500
Accounts receivable	12,940	Salaries payable	1,325
Office supplies	140	Commissions payable	900
Prepaid rent	3,200	Unearned consulting fees	3,500
Prepaid insurance	3,300	Income taxes payable	294
Total current assets	$52,358	Total liabilities	$10,519
Noncurrent assets:		Stockholders' equity:	
Security deposit	$ 2,400	Capital stock	$50,000
Office equipment	5,670	Retained deficit	(186)
Less: Accumulated depreciation—office equipment	95		
Total noncurrent assets	$ 7,975	Total stockholders' equity	$49,814
Total assets	$60,333	Total liabilities and stockholders' equity	$60,333

GENERAL JOURNAL					J10
Date		Account Titles and Explanation	Ref.	Debit	Credit
Closing entries:					
19x1					
Mar.	31	Consulting Fees (R)		28,500	
		Income Summary (SE)			28,500
		To close revenue account.			
	31	Income Summary (SE)		25,854	
		Salaries Expense (E)			13,325
		Commissions Expense (E)			5,900
		Travel and Entertainment Expense (E)			2,650
		Advertising Expense (E)			715
		Communications Expense (E)			580
		Utilities Expense (E)			185
		Rent Expense (E)			1,600
		Depreciation Expense—Office Equipment (E)			95
		Insurance Expense (E)			300
		Office Supplies Expense (E)			210
		Income Tax Expense (E)			294
		To close expense accounts.			
	31	Income Summary (SE)		2,646	
		Retained Earnings (SE)			2,646
		To close the Income Summary account.			

A P P E N D I X 4 A

Reversing Entries

From the discussion on adjusting entries earlier in the chapter, you learned that certain amounts must be accrued at the end of the accounting period to correctly reflect receivables, liabilities, revenues, and expenses. For example, LMI made the following end-of-period adjusting entry for accrued salaries.

19x2			
Jan. 31	Salaries Expense (E)	2,115	
	Salaries Payable (L)		2,115
	To accrue month-end unpaid salaries.		

This entry affects the two ledger accounts as follows:

Salaries Expense						Account No. 511
Date		Explanation	Ref.	Debit	Credit	Balance Debit (Credit)
19x2						
Jan.	14	Payroll	J2	14,000		14,000
	28	Payroll	J4	13,000		27,000
	31	Adjusting	J5	2,115		29,115
	31	Close account	J6		29,115	0

Salaries Payable						Account No. 212
Date		Explanation	Ref.	Debit	Credit	Balance (Debit) Credit
19x2						
Jan.	31	Adjusting	J5		2,115	2,115

The $2,115 in the liability account, Salaries Payable, would normally be eliminated at the next payroll date. For example, if LMI has a $15,000 total payroll on February 11, 19x2, the following journal entry would be made:

19x2			
Feb. 11	Salaries Expense (E)	12,885	
	Salaries Payable (L)	2,115	
	Cash (A)		15,000
	To record February 11, 19x2, payroll.		

The person in charge of recording the payroll must be aware that $2,115 has already been accrued or else the February payroll expense will be overstated.

The potential confusion and the need to remember to reflect the accrual when the next payroll is processed can be removed by using a reversing entry. A

Objective 7
How reversing entries are used.

reversing entry is made at the beginning of a new accounting period to eliminate the effects of any previous accrual entries. This process allows the payroll journal entry to be simplified to its familiar form—a debit to Salaries Expense and a credit to Cash. In the LMI case, a reversing entry may be made relating to the payroll. The reversing entry along with the subsequent payroll entry would be as follows:

19x2			
Feb. 1	Salaries Payable (L)	2,115	
	Salaries Expense (E)		2,115
	To reverse January 31, 19x2, accrual.		
11	Salaries Expense (E)	15,000	
	Cash (A)		15,000
	To record February 11, 19x2, payroll.		

Let's see how the accrual-reversal payment process affects the ledger accounts in question.

Salaries Expense — Account No. 511

Date		Explanation	Ref.	Debit	Credit	Balance Debit (Credit)
19x2						
Jan.	14	Payroll	J2	14,000		14,000
	28	Payroll	J4	13,000		27,000
	31	Adjusting	J5	2,115		29,115
	31	Close account	J6		29,115	0
Feb.	1	Reversal	J7		2,115	(2,115)
	11	Payroll	J8	15,000		12,885

Salaries Payable — Account No. 212

Date		Explanation	Ref.	Debit	Credit	Balance (Debit) Credit
19x2						
Jan.	31	Adjusting	J5		2,115	2,115
Feb.	1	Reversal	J7	2,115		0

Note that as of February 11, Salaries Expense is $12,885, which is the amount earned by employees up to that point in February. This is the same amount that would be recorded in Salaries Expense if the reversing entry had not been made.

Keep this critical point in mind when thinking about reversing entries: **Reversing entries do not affect the income statement amounts or the period-end balance sheet amounts.** Because reversing entries are merely a clerical convenience, they have no impact on the financial statements. Also, not all adjusting entries can be reversed. Only those entries that require a related entry in the next period can be reversed. Finally, since reversing entries are not necessary, they are often not used.

APPENDIX 4B

Introducing a Simple Analysis of Financial Statements

After studying the beginning history of the Fitness Clinic in Chapter 3, you learned that income statements are tools for analyzing the operating results of a company and this shows how net assets flow from operating activities. In this appendix we continue to explore how financial statements are analyzed and used in business decisions.

The financial statements generated by the accounting cycle are themselves an analysis of the financial condition of a business. For example, the balance sheet in Exhibit 4-7 has a fairly standardized format, with assets divided into current and noncurrent portions and with certain accounts shown separately and other accounts combined. Income statements, too, organize the information in such a way that certain activities are highlighted and the net result, or net income, is given prominence.

If the basic financial statements are an analysis in themselves, is any further analysis necessary? The answer is yes, because different types of comparison across time or across businesses often require some simplifying transformation of the accounts that appear in financial statements.

When a bank reviews applications for loans, it may concentrate on **liquidity**, which can be defined as a business's ability to meet current obligations by means of available cash and other assets that can be converted to cash or used as cash. One means of making standardized comparisons across companies is to show percentages as opposed to dollar amounts. As illustrated below, LMI has only 2.1% of its assets in cash at the end of January, but its current assets, cash and those assets to be converted into cash or to be used up in the next year or operating cycle whichever is longer, represent 75.5% of its assets.

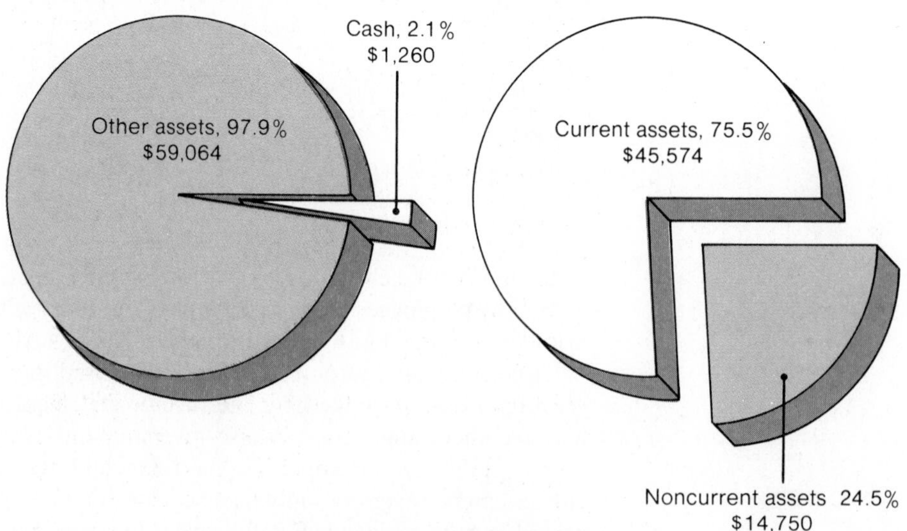

This relationship of cash to other assets is important in analyzing whether too little or too much cash is maintained. Idle cash earns no return, and good cash management involves keeping idle cash to a minimum.

The ratio of current to noncurrent assets varies with the economic characteristics of an industry. LMI has no inventory and has a modest accounts receivable, which would point to current assets being a smaller percentage of total assets than they would be in an industry with different characteristics. But LMI rents its facilities, and, therefore, its noncurrent assets are very low.

The amount of a company's liability balance relative to its stockholders' equity is also considered of critical importance in evaluating financial health. LMI has the following percentages of debt and stockholders' equity:

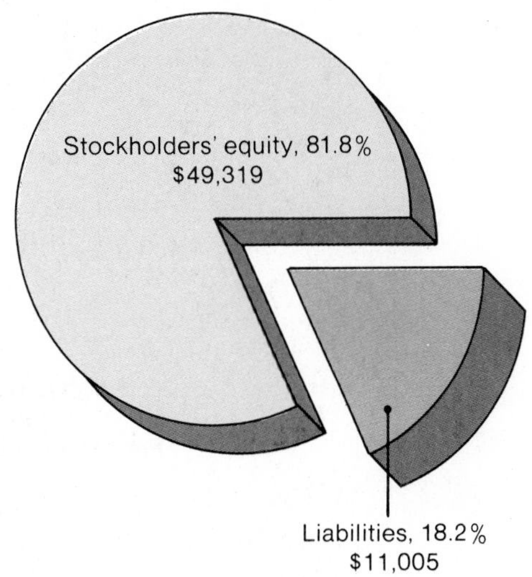

Total liabilities and stockholders' equity = $60,324

If a company has a relatively large percentage of debt outstanding relative to stockholders' equity, the company's ability to borrow additional funds may be questioned.

The liabilities of LMI are rather small in relation to the total stockholders' equity. This does not necessarily mean that LMI would be considered a good credit risk by bankers.

The relationship of items in LMI's income statement are of interest to management and to outside parties. One way of viewing the income statement that makes it more comparable to other companies and other periods is to show all major categories as percentages of total revenues. LMI had total revenues of $59,064 and net income of $9,319 or 15.8% of total revenues ($9,319/$59,064), as illustrated at the top of the next page.

Objective 8
How the income statement and balance sheet can be converted to common-size statements by using percentages of total revenues or total assets.

Exhibit 4B-1 shows all income statement categories in terms of their percentage of total revenues. The major expense categories are salaries, 49.3%; rent, 13.5%; travel and entertainment, 10.2%; income taxes, 3.9%; insurance, 1.7%; office supplies, 1.5%; and all other, 4.1%. Often these percentages are presented as **common-size** income statements, which show the percentage of total revenue represented by **each** item. These common-size statements help make comparisons within a given business over several accounting periods, or across businesses

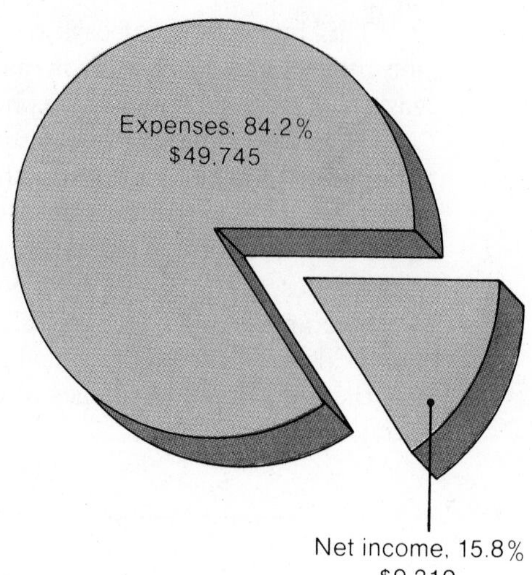

EXHIBIT 4B-1

Income Statement Showing Percentage of Total Revenues

Legislative Minds, Incorporated
Income Statement
For the Month Ended January 31, 19x2

	Dollar Amount	*Percentage of Total Revenues*
Revenue:		
Consulting fees	$59,000	99.9
Expenses:		
Salaries expense	$29,115	49.3
Travel and entertainment expense	6,000	10.2
Communications expense	1,300	2.2
Utilities expense	450	0.8
Postage expense	400	0.7
Rent expense	8,000	13.5
Insurance expense	1,000	1.7
Office supplies expense	900	1.5
Depreciation expense—office equipment	50	0.1
Amortization expense	200	0.3
Total expenses	$47,415	80.3
Income before other revenue	$11,585	19.6
Other revenue:		
Interest revenue	64	0.1
Net income before taxes	$11,649	19.7
Income tax expense	2,330	3.9
Net income	$ 9,319	15.8

at a point in time. Common-size balance sheets may also be prepared using total assets (= 100%) as the basis for comparison.

All individuals interested in a company may use accounting information to analyze the company's financial results and compare the company with similar companies. Potential and present stockholders, bankers, suppliers, and others must make decisions that require an analysis of financial statements. This subject is explored in greater detail in later chapters.

KEY TERMS

Adjusted trial balance. Trial balance after all the necessary adjustments have been made.

Adjusting entries. Period-end journal entries used to update accounts and construct financial statements that reflect all of a company's significant economic transactions in conformance with the accrual concept.

Amortization. Process that allocates original costs of intangible noncurrent assets consumed by operating activities over the periods benefited by their consumption.

Contra account. An account whose balance is subtracted from another account to get the net effect or book value. Accumulated Depreciation is an example of a contra account.

Correction process. Process used to correct errors; not to be confused with the adjusting process.

Depreciation. Process that allocates original costs of tangible noncurrent assets consumed by operating activities over the periods benefited by their consumption.

Intangible assets. Assets with no physical form such as patents, copyrights, or assets that can be used but are not owned, such as trademarks.

Net book value of an asset. Asset's original cost less the total amount written off to date, often the original cost minus accumulated depreciation for buildings, plant, and equipment.

Period-end accruals. Adjusting entries to record revenues, expenses, receivables, and payables that have accumulated during the accounting period but have not as yet been recorded.

Period-end allocations. Adjusting entries that involve (*a*) revenue-related and (*b*) expense-related account balances that affect more than one period and therefore must be spread among accounting periods.

Post-closing trial balance. Gives the period-end account balances after all temporary accounts have been closed to retained earnings.

Tangible assets. Assets with physical form such as land, buildings, and equipment.

Worksheet. Tool used by accountants to show the flow of account balances from an unadjusted trial balance to the financial statements; provides an overview of the end-of-period accounting cycle steps of adjusting, and preparing financial statements.

APPENDIX KEY TERMS

Liquidity. A business's ability to meet current obligations by means of available cash and other assets that can be converted to cash or used as cash.

Reversing entry. Entry made at the beginning of a new accounting period to eliminate the effects of a previous accrual entry; these entries do not affect the income statement amounts or the period-end balance sheet amounts.

SYNONYMS

Accounting cycle; accounting period.
Adjusting entries; period-end accruals and allocations.
Allocation; depreciation; amortization.
Post-closing trial balance; after-closing trial balance.
Tangible asset; physical asset.

QUESTIONS

1. Describe the six steps in the accounting cycle. Discuss the timing of each step in the accounting period.
2. Which of the steps of the accounting cycle occur only at the end of a company's accounting period? Why?
3. Describe the two major categories of adjusting entries.
4. Give two examples of period-end allocations.
5. Give two examples of period-end accruals.
6. How does the unadjusted trial balance differ from the adjusted trial balance?
7. What question is answered by allocation-type adjusting entries? What question is answered by accrual-type adjusting entries?
8. Consider the adjusting entry to record unpaid salaries. Is this entry based on the concept of revenue recognition or matching? Why?
9. What is a worksheet? What is its purpose?
10. Explain the relation between the 12 worksheet columns and the first five steps of the accounting cycle.
11. What cycle steps included in the worksheet must be formally performed elsewhere in records of the company to generate the same financial statement results reported in the worksheet?
12. What financial statements can be provided from a worksheet prepared at the end of the accounting period?
13. When does the closing process occur?
14. What accounts are affected by the closing process?
15. What is the purpose of the Income Summary account and in which step of the accounting cycle is it employed?
16. In what permanent account is the effect of net income or loss from all periods reported?
17. Define the correction process. Are correcting entries the same as adjusting entries?
18. Give two examples of when correcting entries are necessary.
19. What is the effect on the balance sheet when the JMK Company erroneously records the same payment of an account payable twice? Only one check was written.

APPENDIX QUESTIONS

20. What is a reversing entry? What is its purpose?
21. Describe a situation where a reversing entry is used.
22. Describe two percentage relationships that can be used to analyze financial statements.

EXERCISES

EXERCISE 4-1
L.O. 1

Recording Earned Revenue

Cash of $15,000 was collected in advance on magazine subscriptions and credited to the Unearned Subscriptions account. Of this $15,000, $9,000 was earned by delivery of magazines in June. Prepare the June 30 journal entry needed to record the deliveries. What was the cash flow related to this entry?

EXERCISE 4-2
L.O. 1

Determining Rent Payment

Company Z debits all rent payments for the facilities it uses to the Prepaid Rent account. On January 1, 19xx, the Prepaid Rent account had a $2,000 debit balance. The income statement for the first six months of 19xx showed $1,500 of rent expense, and the June 30, 19xx, balance sheet showed prepaid rent of $800. Compute the amount paid by Company Z for rent in the first six months of 19xx. What is the difference between rent expense and cash paid to the landlord and why?

EXERCISE 4-3
L.O. 1

Determining Insurance Expense

On September 30, 19xx, the Joy Company paid an $8,000 premium on a two-year insurance policy. The company's fiscal year ends on December 31. Journalize the amount the Joy Company would record as insurance expense for 19xx.

EXERCISE 4-4
L.O. 1

Depreciation

On April 1, 19xx, Birdwatchers, Inc., has a balance of $45,000 in its Equipment account and a balance of $7,600 in its Accumulated Depreciation—Equipment account. Depreciation expense for the quarter ending June 30, 19xx, is $3,800. Record the adjusting journal entry made at the end of the quarter and show the balance sheet presentation related to equipment for Birdwatchers, assuming no equipment was purchased or sold during the quarter.

EXERCISE 4-5
L.O. 1

Determining Supplies Purchased and Consumed

During 19x1, the Whitney Corporation purchased $12,150 of office supplies and recorded the purchases in the Office Supplies account. On January 1, 19x1, the corporation had a balance of $600 in the Office Supplies account. On December 31, 19x1, the corporation had $400 of office supplies on hand.

During the next year, Whitney consumed $6,100 of supplies and had $850 of office supplies on hand at the end of the year.

Required:

1. Determine the amount of supplies used during 19x1 and the amount of supplies purchased during 19x2.
2. Prepare the adjusting journal entries in general journal form that the Whitney Corporation made to record the supplies used during 19x1 and 19x2.

EXERCISE 4-6
L.O. 1

Alternative Recording Methods

Patrick's Toy Shop prepaid $2,400 for three months' rent on January 1, 19xx. Prepare the journal entries Patrick would make on January 1 and January 31 regarding rent, using two different methods:

a. Rent Expense is initially debited for $2,400.
b. Prepaid Rent is initially debited for $2,400.

EXERCISE 4-7
L.O. 1

Determining Accrued Salaries

A salesperson started working at Super Sam's Discount Store on August 1, 19x1, at a salary of $700 per month. The salesperson quit working at the store on January 15, 19x2. Super Sam's pays its salespeople on the 15th of each month for work done through that date. Determine the amount of salaries expense and prepare the summary journal entry that Super Sam's should record for this salesperson for the year ended December 31, 19x1. Assume each month has 30 days.

EXERCISE 4-8
L.O. 1

Journal Entries and Analyzing Their Effects

For the following transactions (1) record the journal entry or adjusting entry and (2) indicate the impact of the entry on net income and cash:

a. Recorded sales of $6,000 on open account.
b. Purchased supplies of $3,000 for cash.
c. Accrued income taxes of $800 as a year-end adjustment.
d. Recorded depreciation for the year of $1,200.
e. Received $1,500 for services to be performed next year.
f. Paid salaries of $14,000 in cash.
g. Recorded cash sales of $3,000.
h. Paid $8,000 cash for January and February rent on January 1, 19xx. Recorded January rent expense at this time.
i. Purchased a piece of office equipment for $2,000 cash.
j. Accrued $1,600 salaries at month-end.
k. Paid the monthly telephone bill of $400 in cash.
l. Received proceeds from a note receivable of $20,000 plus $1,000 of interest.
m. Paid a two-year insurance premium of $36,000 in advance.
n. Paid utilities for the month of $900 in cash.
o. Recorded monthly insurance expense paid for in (*m*) above.

EXERCISE 4-9
L.O. 1

Adjusting Entries

For the following transactions, record (1) the journal entry made; and (2) the effect and amount of the entry on net income, total assets, and cash.

a. Cash of $200 had been received last year for services performed during the current year. (Record entry for the current year only.)
b. During the last month of the year, $900 cash is received for services to be performed next year.
c. Interest for the year of $4,800 on a note payable is recorded but not yet paid.
d. Of the amount charged to Rent Expense during the year, $1,500 applies to the following year.

EXERCISE 4-10
L.O. 1, 8

Effect of Adjusting Entry Errors

At the end of 19x1, the Lawrence Company had balances as shown in column (*a*) below. If correct adjusting entries had been made, the adjusted balances would be as shown in column (*b*).

	(*a*) *Amount per Books*	(*b*) *Correct Amount*
a. Office Supplies	$500	$350
b. Prepaid Insurance	300	450
c. Unearned Revenue	700	580
d. Salaries Payable	500	300
e. Income Taxes Payable (the taxes were paid in January) . . .	500	775

Assume that the adjusting entries for 19x1 were not made. State the effect of each omission on 19x1 net income, using the following symbols:

Symbols	*Effect*
O	Overstatement
U	Understatement
N	No effect

EXERCISE 4-11
L.O. 6

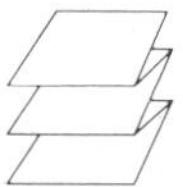

Error Correction

While preparing to close its year-end books, Insiders, Inc., discovers the following errors:

a. Depreciation expense of $5,200 for the year was charged to Travel and Entertainment Expense.
b. Salaries at the end of the year for $13,300 were accrued to the Notes Payable account.
c. An invoice received for $10,000 of supplies purchased on account during the year was recorded under Salaries Payable. When the invoice was paid, Accounts Payable was debited.

Required:
Show the incorrect journal entries that were initially made and the correct journal entries that should have been made. Prepare the journal entries to correct the errors.

EXERCISE 4-12
L.O. 6

Error Correction

In posting transactions for the month, the bookkeeper for Star Jewelry Company made the errors described below. For each error, indicate the amount by which the month-end trial balance totals would be out of balance because of that transaction. Also indicate whether the total for the debit or the credit column would be excessive. Consider each transaction independently.

Example: A debit to Cash of $88 was posted as $888. (The credit was properly posted.)
Answer: $800 excess debit to Cash.

a. A debit of $250 to Supplies Inventory was posted as $520. (The credit was properly posted.)
b. An entry debiting Salary Expense and crediting Cash for $300 was not posted.

c. A credit of $80 to Accounts Payable was not posted. (The debit was properly posted.)
d. A credit of $100 to Accounts Receivable was posted to Sales. (The debit was properly posted.)
e. A debit of $410 to Equipment was posted twice. (The credit was properly posted.)

EXERCISE 4-13
L.O. 3, 5

Multiple Choice

1. For the year ended December 31, 19x1, Murphy Corporation has net income of $74,500. The entry to close this amount to the balance sheet is—
   a. Debit net income and credit income summary.
   b. Debit retained earnings and credit net income.
   c. Debit income summary and credit retained earnings.
   d. Debit income summary and credit various revenue and expense accounts.
   e. None of the above.
2. At the end of 19x2, Jeffries Company had total expenses of $82,875, total revenues of $95,325, total dividends of $4,000, and a pre-closing retained earnings balance of $158,000. The ending retained earnings balance should be—
   a. $166,450.
   b. $141,550.
   c. $174,450.
   d. $149,550.
   e. None of the above.
3. Bests Foods contracted for $240,000 of newspaper advertising equal to 240 full-page ads to be used as desired over a two-year period beginning July 1, 19x1. At the end of 19x1, a total of 40 full-page ads had been run and another 10 had been slated to run the first week of 19x2. The balance in prepaid advertising at the end of 19x1 should be—
   a. $0.
   b. $180,000.
   c. $190,000.
   d. $200,000.
   e. None of the above.
4. Closing entries—
   a. Must be formally posted to the ledger accounts.
   b. Are recorded every time a worksheet is prepared.
   c. Eliminate the balance in all nominal accounts.
   d. Only (*a*) and (*c*) are correct.
   e. All of the above.
5. Z Company's year-end unadjusted trial balance reported retained earnings of $492,000. Dividends of $10,000 were declared and paid during the year. The year-end balance sheet reported retained earnings of $526,000. Net income for the year must have been—
   a. $24,000.
   b. $34,000.
   c. $54,000.
   d. $10,000.
   e. None of the above.

EXERCISE 4-14
L.O. 1

Ralston Purina Annual Report

Consider the Ralston Purina annual report reproduced in Appendix E at the back of this text.

Required:

1. From the Consolidated Statement of Earnings and the Consolidated Balance Sheet, identify the following amounts:
   a. Net earnings, fiscal 1989
   b. Retained earnings, September 30, 1988
   c. Retained earnings, September 30, 1989
2. Compute the amount of dividends declared during fiscal 1989 using the following relationship:

Retained earnings, beginning of period
Plus: Net earnings for period
Less: Dividends declared for period
Equals: Retained earnings, end of period

EXERCISE 4-15
L.O. 2

Recording and Analysis of Entries

The following independent transactions pertain to the operations of a management consulting company with a December 31 year-end.

a. Purchased $18,000 of office furniture for cash of $3,000 and a note of $15,000.
b. Borrowed $2,000 to be repaid next year.
c. Received $17,000 cash from the maturity value of an interest-bearing investment which had cost $15,500 earlier this year. The $1,500 in interest had not been accrued.
d. Recorded credit sales of $8,000.
e. Paid invoice of $15,000 on accounts due.

Required:

1. Record the necessary entries for *a* through *e* above.
2. Indicate the impact on *net income* and cash for item *a* through *e* above.
3. For each item *a* through *e* above indicate whether it represents an operating (O), financing (F), or investing (I) activity—or some combination of these.

EXERCISE 4-16
L.O. 1, 3

Multiple Choice

1. If X Company debits an expense account instead of the Land account when purchasing land, this error will:
   a. Overstate expenses.
   b. Understate retained earnings.
   c. Understate assets.
   d. All of the above.
   e. None of the above.
2. If, at the end of an accounting period, Z Company computes its depreciation for the period to be $15,000, they should:
   a. Debit the asset and credit Retained Earnings $15,000.
   b. Debit Depreciation Expense and credit Accumulated Depreciation $15,000.
   c. Debit Accumulated Depreciation and credit Depreciation Expense $15,000.
   d. Debit Retained Earnings and credit the asset $15,000.
   e. None of the above.

3. Z Company records $2,000 of wages payable on the last day of the accounting period.
   a. This is an allocation-type adjusting entry.
   b. This is an external transaction.
   c. This is an accrual-type adjusting entry.
   d. This is a simple payment of wages in cash.
   e. None of the above.
4. Which of the following adjusting entries addresses the question: Are all of the asset and liability amounts in the unadjusted trial balance appropriate?
   a. Adjusting for interest payable.
   b. Adjusting for wages payable.
   c. Adjusting for accumulated depreciation.
   d. Adjusting for interest receivable.
   e. None of the above.
5. Which of the following adjusting entries addresses the question: What amounts are not included as assets and/or liabilities in the unadjusted trial balance but are assets and/or liabilities?
   a. Adjusting for interest payable.
   b. Adjusting for accumulated depreciation.
   c. Adjusting for amortization of a trademark.
   d. Adjusting for part of a long-term prepaid asset.
   e. None of the above.

APPENDIX EXERCISES

EXERCISE 4-17
L.O. 7

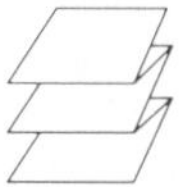

Reversing Entries

On December 31, 19x1, Miller, Inc.'s year-end, unpaid salaries amounted to $15,964. On January 7, 19x2, Miller pays $32,500 to its employees. Record the 19x1 year-end adjusting entry, and the reversing entry and entry to record the payment to employees made in 19x2.

EXERCISE 4-18
L.O. 8

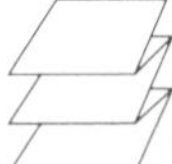

Common-Size Income Statement

BES, Inc., has the following excerpt from its adjusted trial balance on December 31, 19xx:

	Debits	*Credits*
Sales Revenue		$92,400
Salaries Expense	$53,000	
Communications Expense	4,830	
Utilities Expense	3,600	
Rent Expense	12,000	
Insurance Expense	1,800	
Depreciation Expense	2,100	
Advertising Expense	900	
Interest Expense	500	
Totals	$78,730	$92,400

Required:
Prepare a year-end income statement including each item's percentage of total revenue, thus converting it to a common-size income statement.

PROBLEMS

PROBLEM 4-1
L.O. 2, 3

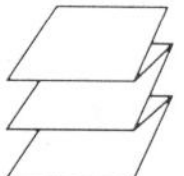

Preparing Financial Statements from the Adjusted Trial Balance

The Erie Company's adjusted trial balance for the year ended December 31, 19x1, appears below. The accounts are listed in alphabetical order.

Erie Company
Adjusted Trial Balance
December 31, 19x1

	Debits	*Credits*
Accounts Payable		$ 37,210
Accounts Receivable	$ 53,000	
Accumulated Depreciation—Buildings		30,000
Accumulated Depreciation—Equipment		36,000
Buildings	170,000	
Capital Stock		130,000
Cash	58,710	
Communications Expense	1,450	
Delivery Expense	1,800	
Depreciation Expense—Buildings and Equipment	13,000	
Equipment	90,000	
Income Tax Expense	12,960	
Income Taxes Payable		10,960
Insurance Expense	1,500	
Interest Expense	29,700	
Interest Revenue		6,500
Investments, Short Term	45,000	
Land	55,000	
Notes Payable, Long Term		235,000
Notes Receivable, Short Term	10,000	
Patents and Trademarks	50,000	
Prepaid Insurance	8,000	
Property Taxes Expense	9,000	
Property Tax Payable		15,000
Retained Earnings, 1/1/x1		33,000
Salaries Expense	60,100	
Salaries Payable		10,000
Service Revenue		154,750
Supplies	28,100	
Utilities Expense	1,100	
Totals	$698,420	$698,420

Required:

1. Using the accounts listed in the trial balance, prepare an income statement and a retained earnings statement for the year ended December 31, 19x1.
2. Prepare the December 31, 19x1, classified balance sheet for Erie. Remember to include current and noncurrent assets and liabilities.

PROBLEM 4-2

L.O. 2

Adjusting Entries

Preview Properties is a real estate company with the following transactions for 19xx:

19xx	
July 1	Prepayment of rent of $2,400 for two years is recorded in the Prepaid Rent account.
Sept. 30	Prepayment of insurance of $1,800 for one year is recorded in the Insurance Expense account.
Dec. 31	The company pays its employees on Fridays. The year 19xx ends on Wednesday when $2,500 is owed to employees for work performed. No entry has been made.
31	Depreciation of $3,000 on office equipment for 19xx is unrecorded.
31	A major sale was completed on December 29, 19xx, for $60,000. The salesperson's commission is $6,000. The sale was made on account and has not been recorded. The commission also has not been recorded or paid.

Required:
Record all necessary journal entries including adjusting entries at period-end based on the above facts.

PROBLEM 4-3

L.O. 2

Adjusting Entries

The fiscal year of the Blaze Corporation ends on December 31. Examination of the accounting records and related documents of the company on December 31, 19x1, provides the following information that should be considered for adjusting entries:

a. The company paid a $2,100 fire insurance premium covering the period from July 1, 19x1, through January 31, 19x2. The payment was recorded as follows:

Insurance Expense	2,100	
Cash		2,100

b. On October 1, 19x1, the company paid $2,400 to rent a machine for the six-month period ending March 31, 19x2. At the time of payment, Prepaid Rent was debited.

c. The bookkeeper recorded a $3,000 payment to rent a building for November 19x1 as a debit to Prepaid Insurance and a credit to Cash.

d. The company used a Supplies Inventory account to record purchases of supplies during the year. The balance in this account on January 1, 19x1, was $1,200. During the year, supplies were purchased in the amount of $6,000. On December 31, 19x1, an inventory count showed that supplies on hand amounted to $1,500.

e. On December 31, 19x1, the bookkeeper determined that employees had earned $12,090 in salaries which had not yet been paid.

Required:
Based on the above information, prepare in general journal form the adjusting or correcting journal entries required on December 31, 19x1. Assume that Blaze Corporation has not made any adjusting entries.

PROBLEM 4-4
L.O. 1–4

Adjusting Entries

Smintog Company has the following unadjusted trial balance at December 31, 19xx:

Smintog Company
Unadjusted Trial Balance
December 31, 19xx

	Debits	*Credits*
Cash	$ 1,000	
Accounts Receivable	500	
Prepaid Rent	3,000	
Supplies	600	
Equipment	4,000	
Accumulated Depreciation—Equipment		$ 800
Accounts Payable		400
Notes Payable		2,000
Capital Stock		4,000
Retained Earnings		500
Service Revenue		1,000
Sales Revenue		3,500
Salaries Expense	1,300	
Supplies Expense	1,800	
Totals	$12,200	$12,200

The following information is available at year-end:

a. Prepaid rent at December 31, 19xx, is $1,000.
b. The equipment has a useful life of 20 years, with no residual value. Unrecorded depreciation for the year is $200.
c. Supplies inventory remaining at December 31, 19xx, is actually $900.
d. Employees' salaries of $400 incurred at the end of 19xx were neither paid nor recorded.
e. Of the $1,000 of service revenue recorded, $500 was for deposits paid to Smintog from customers for services not performed as of December 31, 19xx.

Required:
Give the adjusting journal entries in general journal form for the Smintog Company using the unadjusted trial balance and the additional information.

PROBLEM 4-5
L.O. 1, 2, 4

Preparing a Worksheet

Edston's Plastics Company, Inc., has the following unadjusted trial balance at December 31, 19x1:

Edston's Plastics Company, Inc.
Unadjusted Trial Balance
December 31, 19x1

	Debits	*Credits*
Cash	$ 5,300	
Supplies Inventory	600	
Accounts Receivable	18,000	
Note Receivable	6,000	
Prepaid Rent	2,400	
Equipment	22,800	
Accumulated Depreciation—Equipment		$ 3,200
Accounts Payable		5,200
Notes Payable		15,000
Capital Stock		20,000
Retained Earnings		7,450
Sales Revenue		27,800
Rent Expense	2,400	
Salaries Expense	19,000	
Maintenance Expense	1,400	
Utilities Expense	750	
Totals	$78,650	$78,650

The following information is available at month-end:

a. Depreciation on the equipment for the month is $150.
b. Interest on the note receivable is $70 for the month.
c. Interest on the note payable is $225 for the month.
d. An inventory of supplies on hand shows $450 on December 31, 19x1.
e. Unpaid salaries at month-end are $1,850.
f. An unpaid invoice of $230 for maintenance expense has not been recorded.

Required:
Construct a partial worksheet with the following columns and record the above information into the worksheet:

Unadjusted Trial Balance		*Adjustments*		*Adjusted Trial Balance*	
Debit	*Credit*	*Debit*	*Credit*	*Debit*	*Credit*

PROBLEM 4-6
L.O. 2–4

Preparing a Worksheet, Adjusting Entries, and Financial Statements

The unadjusted trial balance and the adjusted trial balance of the Super Shape Health Club are shown below as of the end of the fiscal year December 31, 19xx:

	Unadjusted Trial Balance		*Adjusted Trial Balance*	
	Debits	*Credits*	*Debits*	*Credits*
Cash	$ 3,020		$ 3,020	
Accounts Receivable	2,200		2,200	
Prepaid Rent	1,250			
Office Supplies	160		50	
Exercise Equipment	23,170		23,170	
Accumulated Depreciation—Exercise Equipment		$ 4,230		$ 6,680
Salaries Payable		100		345
Interest Payable				500
Income Taxes Payable				2,275
Unearned Membership Fees		900		470
Notes Payable		4,000		4,000
Capital Stock		1,000		1,000
Retained Earnings, 1/1/xx		1,955		1,955
Membership Fees Earned		41,420		41,850
Interest Expense			500	
Office Supplies Expense	95		205	
Rent Expense	2,750		4,000	
Salaries Expense	20,960		21,205	
Depreciation Expense—Exercise Equipment			2,450	
Income Tax Expense			2,275	
Totals	$53,605	$53,605	$59,075	$59,075

Required:

1. Prepare the complete worksheet for Super Shape Health Club.
2. Using only the accounts listed above, show the adjusting entries that the club recorded at December 31, 19xx.
3. Prepare a balance sheet and an income statement.

PROBLEM 4-7
L.O. 3–5

Preparing a Worksheet and Adjusting Entries

Bart Computer Repairs, Inc., has the following unadjusted trial balance on December 31, 19x1:

Bart Computer Repairs, Inc.
Unadjusted Trial Balance
December 31, 19x1

	Debits	*Credits*
Cash	$ 8,000	
Accounts Receivable	6,000	
Office Supplies	1,000	
Building	50,000	
Land	12,000	
Accounts Payable		$ 8,500
Notes Payable		35,500
Capital Stock		7,000
Retained Earnings		6,900
Service Revenue		50,000
Salaries Expense	18,000	
Rent Expense	8,400	
Office Supplies Expense	1,500	
Utilities Expense	3,000	
Totals	$107,900	$107,900

The following information is available at year-end:

a. Sales on credit of $700 in the last week of December were not recorded because although the work has been completed, no invoices would be mailed until January 3.
b. All office supply purchases are recorded in Office Supply Expense. An inventory taken on December 31 revealed that $1,200 of office supplies are on hand.
c. The building is being depreciated over 20 years at $2,500 per year. No entry has been made for 19x1.
d. The $8,400 of rent expense includes all of 19x1 rent plus a prepayment of the rent for January and February 19x2. The monthly rental fee has remained unchanged during the year.
e. Employees have earned $2,000 for the last week of December but have not yet been paid.
f. Interest owed but not yet recorded on the note payable is $500.
g. The company uses a 20% tax rate.

Required:
1. Prepare a worksheet for Bart Computer Repairs, Inc.
2. Prepare the necessary adjusting journal entries in journal form.
3. Prepare the closing entries in general journal form for the year-end.

PROBLEM 4-8

L.O. 1, 2, 4, 5

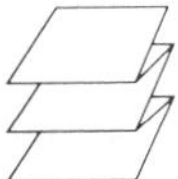

Transactions, Partial Worksheet, and Closing Entries

The balance sheet for Saturn Dry Cleaning at the end of its latest fiscal year appears as follows:

Saturn Dry Cleaning, Inc.
Balance Sheet
August 31, 19xx

Assets		**Liabilities and Stockholders' Equity**	
Current assets:		Liabilities:	
Cash	$ 3,200	Accounts payable	$ 1,940
Accounts receivable	900	Total liabilities	$ 1,940
Supplies	1,600	Stockholders' equity:	
Total current assets	$ 5,700	Capital stock	$ 4,000
Noncurrent assets:		Retained earnings	8,360
Equipment	$10,200	Total stockholders' equity	$12,360
Less: Accumulated depreciation	1,600		
Total noncurrent assets	$ 8,600	Total liabilities and	
Total assets	$14,300	stockholders' equity	$14,300

Business transactions during the accounting period for the month of September 19xx are summarized as follows:

a. Paid rent for the month of $360 in cash.
b. Purchased $100 supplies on account.
c. Received $3,600 from cash customers for dry cleaning sales.
d. Paid $1,620 on outstanding accounts payable for expenses incurred during August 19xx.
e. Charged $1,180 to customers for dry cleaning sales on account.
f. Paid the following expenses incurred in September in cash:

Salaries expense	$1,280
Utilities expense	450
Miscellaneous expense	540

g. Received $775 from customers for services performed before September.
h. Determined by taking an inventory that supplies amounting to $30 were used during the month.
i. Estimated $170 of depreciation on the equipment for the month.
j. Declared and paid cash dividends to stockholders of $500.

Required:

1. Prepare the journal entries in general journal form for the above transactions. All adjustments are included in the above items. Post the journal entries to the appropriate T accounts.
2. Prepare the adjusted trial balance columns, the income statement columns, and the balance sheet columns of a worksheet for Saturn.
3. Prepare and post the closing entries in journal form.

PROBLEM 4-9
L.O. 6

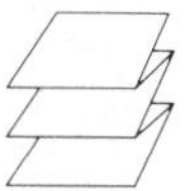

Effects of Errors

At the end of January 19xx, before adjusting entries for the month, the following accounts had balances as shown in column 1 below. If correct adjusting entries had been made, the adjusted balance in the accounts would be as shown in column 2. Assume that adjusting entries were not made. Indicate the effect (understated, overstated, or no effect) and the amount in dollars of the effect of each omission on January net income.

	(1) Amount per Books	*(2) Correct Amount*
a. Interest Payable	$ 130	$ 400
b. Accounts Receivable	2,100	3,300
c. Dividends Declared and Paid	0	1,000
d. Prepaid Rent	750	600
e. Accumulated Depreciation	1,700	2,100
f. Prepaid Insurance	600	375
g. Income Tax Expense	900	1,150
h. Supplies	600	700

PROBLEM 4-10
L.O. 6

Effects of Errors

During August 19xx, the accountant for Wacko Party Stores, Inc., made the accounting errors listed below. Assume Wacko's monthly financial statements are prepared on August 31, 19xx. Indicate the impact of each error on net income, total assets, total liabilities, and stockholders' equity using the following symbols:

Symbols	*Effect*
O	Overstatement
U	Understatement
NE	No effect

Note: Four responses are necessary for each error. Also, assume that net income for the year has been closed to Retained Earnings.

a. Failure to record the sale of land for cash. The selling price of the land was $5,000 more than it originally cost.
b. Dividends declared and paid in August were not recorded.
c. Store supplies purchased on credit and used up during August were not recorded. The supplies have not yet been paid for.
d. Cash receipt of $10,000 for the issuance of 100 shares of stock was not recorded.
e. One-year insurance premium for $2,000 was paid on August 1, 19xx. The full amount was debited to Prepaid Insurance, and no adjustment has been made.
f. September rent was paid in August and recorded as a debit to Rent Expense and a credit to Cash when paid.

PROBLEM 4-11
L.O. 2, 3

Adjusting Entries and Review

Fasco Motors, Inc., started business on December 1, 19x1, with the following balance sheet before operations commenced:

Fasco Motors, Inc.
Balance Sheet
December 1, 19x1

Assets		**Liabilities and Stockholders' Equity**	
Current assets:		Liabilities:	
Cash	$ 2,700	Accounts payable	$ 4,200
Supplies	1,600	Notes payable	5,000
Total current assets	$ 4,300	Total liabilit es	$ 9,200
Noncurrent assets:		Stockholders' equity:	
Equipment	$ 9,900	Capital stock	$20,000
Land	15,000	Total stockholders' equity	$20,000
Total noncurrent assets	$24,900	Total liabilities and	
Total assets	$29,200	stockholders' equity	$29,200

During the period from December 1, 19x1, to December 31, 19x1, the following transactions occurred:

a. Paid rent of $2,100 in cash for December 19x1 and January 19x2.
b. Sales of $24,000 were made, all in cash.
c. Salaries amounted to $3,800 paid in cash and $200 payable at year-end.
d. Borrowed $10,000 on a 90-day note to be paid back plus interest of $900 on March 15, 19x2.
e. The December telephone bill of $320 was received but not yet paid on December 31, 19x1.
f. Equipment is being depreciated over three years. One thirty-sixth of the cost is to be depreciated in December.

Required:
1. Prepare the journal entries and any adjustments required for the above transactions.
2. Prepare the income statement for the month and the December 31, 19x1, balance sheet in good form.
3. Compare the net cash flow and the net income for the month and explain the difference.

PROBLEM 4-12
L.O. 1–3

Analysis of T Accounts

The accountant for Wood Products, Inc., lost the details of some of the firm's accounting entries that were made during 19x1. All cash payments are debited to asset accounts (e.g., Prepaid Rent, Prepaid Insurance, Supplies Inventory) and adjusted to expense at year-end.

Missing Amount	*What is Known*
a. Ending balance in Supplies Inventory	Beginning balance in Supplies Inventory, $1,300 Supplies purchased in 19x1, $14,000 Adjusting entry debit to Supplies Inventory Expense, $14,400
b. Salaries Expense for 19x1	Beginning balance in Salaries Payable, $5,000 Cash paid for salaries, $57,000 Ending balance in Salaries Payable, $8,000
c. Rent Expense for 19x1	Beginning balance in Prepaid Rent, $800 Cash paid for prepaid rent, $6,000 Ending balance in Prepaid Rent, $1,400
d. Insurance Expense for 19x1	Beginning balance in Prepaid Insurance, $600 Cash paid for insurance policy, $3,600 Ending balance in Prepaid Insurance, $900
e. Credit sales for 19x1	Beginning balance in Accounts Receivable, $10,000 Ending balance in Accounts Receivable, $9,000 Beginning balance in Revenue Received in Advance, $0 Ending balance in Revenue Received in Advance, $2,000 Total cash received from customers, $216,000

Required:
Use your understanding of how normal journal entries and adjusting journal entries affect ledger accounts to provide the missing information.

PROBLEM 4-13
L.O. 3

Effects of Errors

The following accounting errors were made by the Maple Leaf Corporation during 19x1. Assume the financial statements have been prepared for 19x1 and that net income has been closed to retained earnings. Indicate the impact of each error on net income, total assets, total liabilities, and stockholders' equity using the following symbols:

Symbol	*Effect*
O	Overstatement
U	Understatement
NE	No effect

Note: Four responses are necessary for each error.

a. The adjusting entry for the expiration of Prepaid Rent was not made.
b. The adjusting entry for Accrued Salaries Payable was not made.
c. A cash purchase of office machinery was incorrectly recorded as a debit to Supplies Expense.
d. A $932 payment on Accounts Payable was incorrectly recorded as a credit to Cash and a debit to Accounts Payable of $923.
e. November credit sales of $13,000 were incorrectly recorded at $1,300.

PROBLEM 4-14
L.O. 1–3, review of Chapter 3

Comprehensive

Amanda and Melissa Darling both have had experience with large public relations companies and are now in the first month of operations with their own company, AMD, Inc. The following transactions have taken place during January 19x1:

a. Each owner purchased 5,000 shares of capital stock for $5 per share.
b. Borrowed $20,000 from the First Dallas National Bank to be paid back on July 5, 19x1. Interest of $180 per month is paid on the fifth of the next month.
c. Prepaid rent for January, February, and March totaled $3,000. Office equipment was rented for $750 per month, and the payment for January was made on January 2.
d. Sold services of $30,000, of which $20,000 was received in cash and the remainder is to be received from customers by February 10.
e. Paid the January telephone bill of $500 and utility bill of $190 in cash.
f. Salaries of $500 per week were paid on Friday of each week. January 31 was a Tuesday, and no entry has been made for the two unpaid workdays. So far, $2,000 cash for salaries has been paid.
g. Office supplies of $1,000 were acquired for cash on January 1, and $200 remained in stock on January 31.
h. Office furniture and equipment, purchased for $18,000, was delivered on January 1. The office equipment is expected to be used over a 10-year period and to have no residual value. Monthly depreciation expense is $150. No cash was paid in January. The invoice has a February 15, 19x1, due date.

Required:
1. Prepare in journal form the journal entries for the above transactions and the January 31 adjustments. Post the entries to the appropriate ledger accounts.
2. Prepare an adjusted trial balance for January 31, 19x1.
3. Prepare the income statement for the month and the balance sheet at January 31, 19x1.
4. (Optional) Discuss AMD's sources and uses of cash; compare them to net income.

PROBLEM 4-15
L.O. 2

Review of Cash to Accrual Basis

Saunders Engineering, Inc., has been in business several years and has prepared its most current comparative balance sheet for 19x2 with comparison to 19x1 as follows:

Saunders Engineering, Inc.
Comparative Balance Sheet

	12/31/x2	*12/31/x1*
Assets		
Current assets:		
Cash	$35,300	$ 5,100
Accounts receivable	28,300	31,200
Note receivable	0	8,000
Interest receivable	0	800
Total current assets	$63,600	$45,100
Noncurrent assets:		
Equipment	$45,000	$40,000
Less: Accumulated depreciation	36,000	24,000
Total noncurrent assets	$ 9,000	$16,000
Total assets	$72,600	$61,100
Liabilities and Stockholders' Equity		
Liabilities:		
Accounts payable	$ 1,000	$ 800
Notes payable	0	20,000
Interest payable	0	1,800
Salaries payable	1,890	2,250
Total liabilities	$ 2,890	$24,850
Stockholders' equity:		
Capital stock	$50,000	$30,000
Retained earnings	19,710	6,250
Total stockholders' equity	$69,710	$36,250
Total liabilities and stockholders' equity	$72,600	$61,100

The following transactions took place during the year 19x2:

Payments:	
a. Purchased equipment	$ 5,000
b. Paid salaries	76,000
c. Paid property taxes	9,200
d. Paid dividends	5,000
e. Paid utility bill	1,100
f. Paid note and interest	21,800
g. Paid on accounts payable	10,500
Receipts:	
h. Collected cash from customers	130,000
i. Sold stock	20,000
j. Collected interest on note receivable	800
k. Collected on note receivable	8,000

Required:
Construct an accrual-based income statement for 19x2 based on the above information. (Hint: Make up a set of T accounts as needed, starting with balance sheet accounts and their beginning and ending balances. Post entries for items *a–k* first.)

APPENDIX PROBLEMS

PROBLEM 4-16
L.O. 8

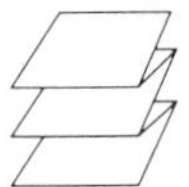

Common-Size Income Statement, Balance Sheet

Refer to the August 31, 19xx, balance sheet information given in Problem 4-8 for Saturn Dry Cleaning, Inc.

Required:
Prepare a common-size balance sheet.

PROBLEM 4-17
L.O. 8

Common-Size Income Statement and Balance Sheet

Refer to the unadjusted trial balance given in Problem 4-7 for Bart Computer Repairs, Inc. Assume there are no adjustments required for Bart.

Required:
1. Prepare a common-size income statement for 19x1 showing each item as a percent of revenues.
2. Compute the new retained earnings balance at December 31, 19x1, and prepare a common-size balance sheet at this date.

PROBLEM 4-18
L.O. 5, 6, 8

Common-Size Income Statement, Balance Sheet, Reversing Entry

Refer to the adjusted trial balance information given for Super Shape Health Club in Problem 4-6.

Required:
1. Prepare a common-size income statement showing each item's percentage to total revenues.
2. Prepare the December 31, 19xx, balance sheet.
3. Prepare the post-closing trial balance.
4. Prepare in general journal form the reversing entry for accrued salaries.

PROBLEM 4-19
L.O. 2, 7

Adjusting (and Optional Reversing) Entries

The following internal transactions of the International Corporation require adjusting entries at December 31, 19x1:

a. A balance of $19,000 is in the firm's Prepaid Insurance account. One half of this amount expired during the current period and the other half will expire at December 31, 19x2.
b. $1,100 of unrecorded interest on a $10,000 Note Payable is owed at December 31, 19x1. The interest will be paid in full on February 1, 19x2.
c. $15,000 of the $46,000 Supplies Inventory remains unused.
d. $34,000 of salaries are owed to employees for work done during the current period. The next scheduled payday is January 10, 19x2.
e. $600 of a total $900 in unrecorded service revenue has been earned on Contract #5263. The contract will be completed and the total revenues collected on January 3, 19x2.
f. $38,000 in income tax expense will be due on 19x1 income. The tax will be paid on March 1, 19x2, when the firm files its tax return.

Required:
1. Prepare adjusting entries for the above listed internal transactions.
2. (optional) Identify the adjusting entries above that could be reversed to save bookkeeping effort later in 19x2. Prepare those reversing entries.

PROBLEM 4-20
L.O. 2, 7

Adjusting (and optional reversing) Entries

The following internal transactions of American Services, Inc., require adjusting entries at December 31, 19x1:

a. $1,200 of supplies, used during the current period, remain in Supplies Inventory.
b. Depreciation for the period on the building is $27,000.
c. Interest of $480 has been earned on a Note Receivable the firm holds. The interest will be received in full on June 1, 19x2.
d. $18,000 remains in the Prepaid Rent account. All of it has expired except for two months of rent at $1,500 per month which will expire in 19x2.
e. Commissions earned during 19x1 but not yet paid to employees amount to $11,000. These will be paid on January 30, 19x2, along with those commissions earned in January 19x2.
f. Of the $640,000 paid by customers and recorded as service revenue during 19x1 only $635,000 has been earned. The remaining $5,000 will be earned in 19x2.

Required:
1. Prepare adjusting entries for the above-listed internal transactions.
2. (optional) Identify the adjusting entries above that could be reversed to save bookkeeping effort later in 19x2. Prepare those reversing entries.

CASES

CASE 4-1
L.O. 1, 3

Accrual versus Cash Accounting

Company A and Company B are identical in every way except for their accounting methods. One uses the cash basis and the other uses the accrual basis. Both started business on January 1, 19x1, and both had identical transactions. Consider the before-closing trial balances of each as of the end of 19x1.

	Company A		*Company B*	
	Debits	*Credits*	*Debits*	*Credits*
Cash	$ 80,000		$ 80,000	
Accounts Receivable	20,000			
Prepaid Rent	5,000			
Prepaid Insurance	3,000			
Land	40,000		40,000	
Buildings and Equipment	50,000		50,000	
Accumulated Depreciation—Buildings and Equipment		$ 5,000		
Accounts Payable		12,000		
Salaries Payable		8,000		
Capital Stock		158,000		$158,000
Sales		130,000		110,000
Rent Expense	10,000		15,000	
Insurance Expense	5,000		8,000	
Salaries Expense	45,000		37,000	
Depreciation Expense—Buildings and Equipment	5,000			
Other Expenses	50,000		38,000	
Totals	$313,000	$313,000	$268,000	$268,000

Required:
Discuss the differences and similarities in accounting treatment on an item-by-item basis. How would you describe Company A's accounting system and Company B's accounting system? What are the strengths and weaknesses of each system in terms of communicating economic status and operating results?

EVALUATING FINANCIAL STATEMENTS

CASE 4-2
L.O. 2

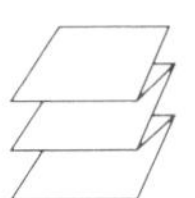

Adjusting Journal Entries—Detroit Edison Company

The Detroit Edison Company services a 7,600-square-mile area providing over half of Michigan's population with electric and steam energy. Assume Detroit Edison has the following transactions (in thousands) during 1985:

a. Depreciation for the year of $218,500.
b. Records rent expense of $900 that was prepaid in 1984.
c. Accrued $100 interest owed on a note payable.
d. Salaries earned but not yet paid are $142.
e. Accrues income tax for the year of $50,989.

Required:
Record the above transactions in general journal form.

CASE 4-3
L.O. 2

Preparation of Balance Sheet—Molson Companies Limited

The following information is taken from the 1985 annual report of Molson Companies, a Canadian corporation comprised of three principal businesses—Molson Breweries of Canada Limited, Diversey Corporation, and Beaver Lumber Company Limited. All amounts are in thousands.

	May 31	
	1985	*1984*
Accounts payable	$236,176	$216,476
Accounts receivable	191,537	174,104
Capital stock	64,565	63,168
Cash	?	112,064
Dividends payable	5,730	5,713
Equipment	406,912	377,842
Inventories	214,892	200,910
Notes payable, long term	238,777	237,999
Notes payable, short term	75,460	69,389
Other long-term assets	121,836	104,028
Other long-term liabilities	72,574	48,974
Prepaid assets, short term	28,747	17,741
Retained earnings	337,606	?
Taxes payable	3,014	25,289

Required:
Prepare the classified comparative balance sheets for the Molson Companies Limited. Assume dividends are paid once each year. What was the fiscal 1985 net income?

CASE 4-4
L.O. 1, 2

Adjustments—Hershey Foods Corporation

Consider the following data taken from Hershey Foods Corporation's 1987 financial statements:

Income statement data:	
Sales	$2,433,793
Costs and expenses	2,139,680
Interest expense	24,711
Income tax expense	121,231
Net income	148,171
Data on liabilities:	
Current liabilities:	
Accounts payable	$ 130,415
Accrued liabilities:	
Payroll	47,459
Advertising	31,144
Other	42,888
Accrued income taxes	16,414
Short-term notes	31,449
Total current liabilities	$ 299,769
Long-term liabilities	349,230
Memo:	
Dividends declared in 1987	$ 51,467

Required:

Give the best answer to the following multiple-choice questions.

1. Hershey's income tax expense—
   a. Is less than the amount currently owed to the government for income taxes.
   b. Is equal to the amount currently owed to the government for income taxes.
   c. Results in an accrued liability because a portion of 1987 tax obligation is unpaid at year-end.
   d. Has no effect on the balance sheet items listed above.
2. The accrued liabilities shown in Hershey's balance sheet—
   a. Were closed to the Income Summary account.
   b. Must be reversed in January 1988.
   c. Represent expenses that will affect the 1988 income statement.
   d. Were recorded in adjusting entries at year-end.
3. Hershey's net income amount—
   a. Represents cash inflow from customers minus any accounts receivable balance at year-end.
   b. Increased retained earnings more than dividends decreased retained earnings.
   c. Decreased retained earnings more than dividends increased retained earnings.
   d. Has no effect on the balance sheet accounts.

CASE 4-5
L.O. 3

Analysis of Results

Tax Advice Corporation (TAC) reported the following partial comparative balance sheet data at the end of 19x5:

Partial Balance Sheet Data
($000)

	December 31	
	19x5	*19x4*
Accounts receivable (asset)	$2,940	$2,620
Prepaid rents (asset)	615	750
Prepaid service revenue (liability)	730	850

During 19x5, TAC reported service revenue (its only revenue account) of $18,000,000. Accounts receivable, which only pertain to service customers, were decreased by $16,000,000 during 19x5 for payments on customer accounts. All of the prepaid service revenue from 19x4 was earned during 19x5. Also, all of the prepaid rent from 19x4 was expensed during 19x5, with total rent expense for 19x5 reported at $2,820,000. All rent must be paid in advance.

Required:

(*Hint: Use T accounts to help answer these questions.*)

1. How much of the 19x5 service revenue was paid for in cash during 19x5? How much of the 19x5 service revenue was on open customer accounts?
2. How much cash was paid for rent during 19x5?
3. What is the difference between total cash flows from these two items (service revenue, rent expense) and their income statement amounts?

PART 2

Accounting for Major Business Transactions

FINANCIAL STATEMENTS

FINANCIAL STATEMENT COMPONENTS EMPHASIZED IN CHAPTER 5

Hi-Tech Corporation
Income Statement
For 1991

Revenues

Cash sales
Credit sales
Less: Discounts
Returns
Net sales

Expenses

Beginning inventory
Net purchases
Ending inventory
Cost of goods sold

	1991	1990
Cash sales	$ XXX	$ XXX
Credit sales	XXX	XXX
Less: Discounts	(XX)	(XX)
Returns	(XX)	(XX)
Net sales	XXX	XXX

	1991	1990
Beginning inventory . . .	$XXXX	$XXXX
Net purchases	XXXX	XXX
Ending inventory	(XXXX)	(XXX)
Cost of goods sold	$XXXX	$XXXX

Hi-Tech Corporation
Balance Sheet
12/31/91

Current assets

Accounts receivable
Less: Allowance for bad debts
Net accounts receivable

Noncurrent assets

xxxx
xxxx

Current liabilities

xxxx
xxxx

Noncurrent liabilities

xxxx
xxxx

Stockholders' equity

xxxx
xxxx

	1991	1990
Accounts receivable . . .	$ XXX	$ XXX
Less: Allowance for bad debts	(XXX)	(XXX)
Net accounts receivable	XXX	XXX

Hi-Tech Corporation
Cash Flow Statement
For 1991

Operating activities

Cash received from customers
Cash paid to suppliers

Investing activities

xxxx
xxxx

Financing activities

xxxx
xxxx

	1991	1990
Cash received from customers	$XXXX	$ XXX
Cash paid to suppliers .	(XXX)	(XXX)

CHAPTER 5

Accounting for Merchandising Operations—Planning, Purchases, and Sales

LEARNING OBJECTIVES

After studying Chapter 5, you should understand:

1. The importance of preparing a business plan during the preoperating phase of a merchandising business, pp. 229-34.
2. How to account for merchandise inventory—net purchases, cost of goods available for sale, and cost of goods sold, pp. 234-41.
3. How to account for sales revenue, pp. 241-43.
4. The relationship between accounts receivable and bad debts, pp. 243-45.
5. How to account for sales returns and allowances, p. 245.
6. How to account for sales discounts, pp. 245-46.
7. Accounting for transactions not related to inventory and sales, pp. 247-48.
8. How to prepare a worksheet for a merchandising company, pp. 248-51.
9. How to analyze the effects of a merchandising company's operations, pp. 253-55.
10. Accounting for bad debts, credit card sales, and installment sales (Appendix), pp. 258-64.

Accounting information is the output of the accounting system and the input for the decision-making process. It helps to explain past performance and enables management to plan for the future. Accountants, as you learned in the first four chapters, use financial accounting to prepare financial reports that provide accounting information for decision making of external users and for those who manage the firm.

Decision makers outside the business need accounting information for purposes such as investing, lending, regulating, merging, and taxing. Decision makers inside the business need accounting information for purposes such as investing, financing, and planning and controlling the operations of the business. This chapter illustrates how an accounting system evolves in response to the needs of internal decision makers. By following a new business from its inception through an accounting cycle, you will learn how those responsible for planning, financing, and controlling operations create and use accounting systems.

The emphasis in this chapter is on a merchandising business—a business that buys items from suppliers (wholesalers and manufacturers) for sale to customers. The key characteristic being that a physical product acquired from a supplier is involved. Although the chapter discussion is in a merchandising context, the major issues we focus on pertain to all types of businesses.

The merchandising company we use as an example in this chapter is a retail computer supply store. You will learn the importance of accurate accounting for merchandise inventory and sales revenue in planning and controlling operations. The chapter concludes with an analysis of the first-quarter operations of a computer supply store. The appendix discusses accounting for bad debts in detail, as well as credit card sales and installment sales.

USE OF ACCOUNTING INFORMATION BY ENTREPRENEURS

Usually when people first conceive of a business venture, they have some idea of their goals, where they will obtain their resources, and how they plan to operate their business. Goals may vary from maximizing profits to fulfilling a lifetime desire to own a business, or a combination of goals may exist. Resources may include personal and creative skills, cash in a savings account, other personal assets, and various sources of credit. Plans may be sketchy, such as "purchase merchandise from manufacturers and sell this merchandise to a retail market," or plans may be elaborate, including detailed statistical analysis with specific operating, marketing, and financing strategies. The goals, resources, and plans are as varied as the people who become **entrepreneurs** (i.e., people who organize, manage, and assume the risks of a business).

In addition to goals, resources, and plans, a successful business must have a system that will help entrepreneurs organize their thoughts and visualize the probable effect of alternative courses of action. Accounting systems work well in this capacity for a wide variety of business settings. They are designed to measure the progress of a business venture and thus provide a useful structure for business management. Forward-looking data can be obtained from a well-structured accounting system, allowing decision makers to forecast the financial consequences of alternative business actions before the actions take place.

Before a business venture can begin, entrepreneurs must look to the future. A crucial step is to visualize the possible outcomes of the business effort. What will the company's status be after operating for a week, a month, or a year? To answer this question, decision makers must imagine future income statements and balance sheets when they plan operations, and they must also foresee the company's possible assets and obligations at future dates.

An accounting system can provide estimates of the possible outcomes that management can expect in the future. These estimates are in the form of **projected (forecasted) balance sheets** that provide possible financial states in the future and **projected (forecasted) income statements** that visualize the possible results of future operations. Projected balance sheets and income statements need not be different in format from the statements you have studied in the previous chapters. However, the data used to prepare the statements are derived from a combination of past events and estimates of future events.

Estimating future events for the operations of a business is beneficial in executing the plans of a business organization. Also, the information that accounting systems provide is valuable in controlling the actions of members of the business organization. Some of the questions the accounting system can help answer are: When should inventory be ordered? Are costs within reasonable bounds? Are customers paying invoices in a timely fashion? Are new sources of financing needed?

In summary, accounting is used to plan and control business operations as well as to provide historical summaries of operating results. Accounting also is an excellent tool of analysis. In all of its uses, accounting builds on several fundamental concepts, some of which were introduced in the first four chapters of this textbook.

In this chapter you will follow the exploits of two young entrepreneurs from the initiation of their merchandising business through their first operating period. The section that follows shows how accounting aids in the start-up of a business and when the business operations begin. Subsequent sections illustrate how accounting is used in other phases of business activity.

Preoperating Phase of a Business

Mary and Brad are recent college graduates with strong computer skills. They were both "bitten by the computer bug" early in life and developed compulsive study habits that involved solitary work with their computers as companions. Although Mary and Brad were successful students, their education was rather narrow and did not include any business courses.

A mutual friend introduced Mary to Brad at a computer software fair. They became good friends and had long conversations about computers and their future careers. Soon Mary and Brad realized their skills and personal compatibility could be the ingredients of a computer-related business venture. They believed that small businesses needed not only the software available from many sources but also the personal instruction and attention their expertise in computers could provide. The two friends decided that a computer supply store with a knowledgeable staff catering to small businesses would be successful because the sales personnel they had dealt with in the large chain stores were either not knowledgeable in computers or were unfriendly to customers.

Objective 1
The importance of preparing a business plan during the preoperating phase of a merchandising business.

In early December 19x1, Mary and Brad incorporated their venture as Byte-Size, Inc. Operations were scheduled to begin on January 2, 19x2. Mary and Brad prepared a planning document they called *First Quarter 19x2.* They each planned to purchase \$11,000 of Byte-Size stock, and they estimated their merchandise sales at \$125,000 for the first quarter. Mary and Brad's lack of business and accounting knowledge is clearly evident in their planning document shown in Exhibit 5-1.

EXHIBIT 5-1

The First-Quarter Planning Document

Byte-Size, Inc.
First Quarter 19x2

Starting cash		$ 22,000
Expected sales		+ 125,000
Expected payments:		
Merchandise	$100,000	
Other	10,000	− 110,000
Ending cash		$ 37,000

Mary and Brad soon realized that their planning of Byte-Size left much to be desired and that their document was not very helpful in actually planning their business operations. They knew that often cash would have to be paid in advance. For example, the landlord of the building they were to rent demanded up-front payments for a security deposit and rent; and their primary supplier, Computech, Inc., required payment for purchases within 20 days of delivery. Since Byte-Size would obviously not sell all of its merchandise in 20 days, some of the company's money would be tied up in merchandise.

Mary and Brad also knew they would have to provide credit for some of their customers, and they were vaguely aware of the advantages and disadvantages of customer credit. Although customer credit would generate more sales, there was the chance of not collecting the full amount that was owed to them.

Now Mary and Brad began to understand that their future success as entrepreneurs depended on many decisions and economic events, some of which were not within their control. Also, they realized that all of the hundreds of events—which they later learned were called *transactions*—involved in running a business affect the ongoing financial status of the business. Thus, for their business to remain financially solvent throughout a period, Mary and Brad knew they must be able to meet ongoing obligations. Our two aspiring entrepreneurs realized they needed a system that would help them see the probable outcomes of their expected actions.

What should these future business leaders do now? After pondering this for a while, Mary and Brad decided they needed advice from someone knowledgeable in business who could forecast the outcomes of their business venture. Brad's father was an accountant, but Brad had never been interested in his father's profession. In fact, Brad was not really sure what accountants did. However, since his father's advice would be free, Mary and Brad made a trip to Brad's hometown to talk to his father.

Brad's father was surprised that his son, who in the past had no interest in the world of business, was now planning to be an entrepreneur. "As future entrepreneurs," Brad's father explained, "you need the services of an accountant who will develop a comprehensive business plan and set up a system of record-keeping." Brad's father continued: "Go to the business school at your university and hire a graduate student. Graduate students are often looking for part-time work, and they are not expensive. I'll review the work to be sure everything is in order."

Constructing a Business Plan for a Merchandising Business

Mary and Brad took the advice of Brad's father and hired Frank McDonald-Mellon, or FM, a graduate accounting student. FM began by giving Mary and Brad the rudiments of an accounting vocabulary in the form of a review of the first four chapters of a financial accounting textbook. He explained terms such as assets, liabilities, owners' (stockholders') equity, revenues, expenses, transactions, journal entries, ledger accounts, and financial statements. Soon Mary and Brad realized their original planning document was of little help because it did not reflect the many transactions and relationships found in an actual business. After providing an introduction to accounting and business terminology, FM studied the needs of Byte-Size and constructed a projected balance sheet and income statement based on assumptions of Byte-Size's first quarter of operations.

To project a quarter-ending balance sheet and income statement, FM listed Byte-Size's starting cash, the timing of its initial cash payments, its expected cash inflow from sales and cash outflows for merchandise, and various other expenditures. Then he traced the expected journal entries to the period-end financial statements. FM discovered that based on the assumed timing of the transactions, the projected cash balance would be inadequate, and a cash shortage would occur during the quarter if planned operations actually took place.

To ensure continued operations, Byte-Size needed additional capital of at least $20,000. Under the assumption that Byte-Size could borrow $20,000 and repayment of the loan could be delayed for at least three months, FM traced the

EXHIBIT 5-2

First Quarter 19x2 Business Plan for Byte-Size, Inc.

Byte-Size, Inc.
Projected Balance Sheet
March 31, 19x2

Assets		Liabilities and Stockholders' Equity	
Current assets:		Liabilities:	
Cash	$ 9,200	Accounts payable	$ 2,000
Accounts receivable	20,000	Notes payable	20,000
Security deposit	4,500	Interest payable	750
Merchandise inventory	22,500	Total liabilities	$22,750
Total current assets	$56,200	Stockholders' equity:	
Noncurrent assets:		Capital stock	$22,000
Computer	5,000	Retained earnings	16,450
		Total stockholders' equity	$38,450
Total assets	$61,200	Total liabilities and stockholders' equity	$61,200

Byte-Size, Inc.
Projected Income Statement
First Quarter 19x2

Sales		$125,000
Cost of goods sold		93,750
Gross margin		$ 31,250
Salaries	$6,400	
Other expenses	8,400	14,800
Net income		$ 16,450

EXHIBIT 5-2 *(concluded)*

Byte-Size, Inc.
Projected Cash Flow Statement
From Inception to March 31, 19x2

Operating activities:	
Receipts from customers	$ 105,000
Payments to suppliers	(114,250)
Payments for rent	(9,000)
Payments for utilities	(900)
Payments for salaries	(6,400)
Payments for office supplies	(850)
Payments for insurance	(1,400)
Cash to be used in operating activities	$ (27,800)
Investing activities:	
Payment for computer	$ (5,000)
Cash to be used in investing activities	$ (5,000)
Financing activities:	
Receipt from sale of stock	$ 22,000
Receipt from bank loan	20,000
Cash to be provided by financing activities	$ 42,000
Projected 3/31/x2 cash balance	$ 9,200

Assumptions upon which projections are based:

Purchases on credit	$ 116,250
Cash payments to suppliers for first quarter: January, $52,000; February, $40,250; and March, $22,000, with $2,000 still outstanding at end of quarter (March 31, 19x2).	
Sales	125,000
Cash collections from customers for first quarter sales: January, $25,000; February, $35,000; March, $45,000, with $20,000 still outstanding at end of quarter (March 31, 19x2).	
Cost of merchandise sold	93,750
Security deposit payment for rented building	4,500
Rent payments	4,500
Utility payments	900
Salary payments	6,400
Proceeds from bank loan	20,000
Interest accrued on loan	750
Office supplies purchase	850
Insurance premiums payment	1,400
Computer purchase	5,000

effects of this additional cash on the projected financial statements. These forward-looking financial statements became the business plan for Byte-Size shown in Exhibit 5-2.

Note that three items occur in Byte-Size's projected statements that were not in the statements of service companies—merchandise inventory (an asset in the balance sheet), cost of goods sold, and gross margin (both found in the income statement). **Merchandise inventory** (or **inventory**) is an asset equal to the cost of merchandise on hand ready for sale. **Cost of goods sold** is an expense equal to the cost of merchandise sold to customers during the period. **Gross margin** (sometimes called **gross profit**) is a subtotal computed as sales less cost of goods sold. Merchandise inventory and cost of goods sold are discussed in detail in a following section titled "Accounting for Merchandise Inventory."

Projected financial statements such as Byte-Size's projected balance sheet, income statement, and cash flow statement given in Exhibit 5-2 are good planning tools. These projected statements are also useful at the end of a period when actual performance is evaluated. In the paragraphs that follow we review the accounting concepts and techniques used to convert actual transactions into financial statements. Later, you will learn how to compare actual results to projected statements.

Use of the Plan to Acquire Financing. Shortly after Byte-Size constructed its comprehensive business plan, a tangible benefit resulted. On December 30, 19x1, Mary and Brad took their business plan to a local bank and were able to negotiate a 15%, $20,000 loan due on June 30, 19x2. In explaining why she approved the loan, the banker said she was particularly interested in Byte-Size's projected liquidity (ability to have enough cash to meet obligations) as shown by the company's projected current ratio and quick ratio. From the expression on Mary and Brad's faces, the banker realized that they did not understand the terms *current ratio* and *quick ratio,* so she gave the following explanation:

Current ratio is the ratio of current assets to current liabilities, or

$$\frac{\text{Current assets}}{\text{Current liabilities}} = \text{Current ratio}$$

Higher ratios are viewed as signs of higher liquidity. Byte-Size projected current assets of $56,200 and current liabilities of $22,750:

$$\frac{\$56{,}200}{\$22{,}750} = \text{Current ratio of 2.47 to 1}$$

The banker told Mary and Brad that she always reviewed current ratio carefully for short-term loans, and she thought Byte-Size had a reasonable current ratio.

Quick ratio is the ratio of quick assets which are cash, receivables, and marketable securities to current liabilities, or:

$$\frac{\text{Quick assets}}{\text{Current liabilities}} = \text{Quick ratio}$$

Usually high quick ratios are considered indicators of quick convertibility to cash. Byte-Size projected quick assets of $29,200 and current liabilities of $22,750:

$$\frac{\$29{,}200}{\$22{,}750} = \text{Quick ratio of 1.28 to 1}$$

The banker told Mary and Brad that the quick ratio was a more stringent indicator of liquidity. She added that she also considered the projected quick ratio of Byte-Size to be reasonable.

The banker also emphasized that she approved the loan primarily because the business idea seemed to make good economic sense, the assumptions seemed valid, and the business plan reflected good planning and control skills. The $20,000 loan now gave Byte-Size the financial cushion that FM said was needed for continued business operations.

Accounting for Preoperating Transactions

On December 28, Mary and Brad purchased the Byte Size, Inc., capital stock for a total of $22,000. On December 30, they signed the bank note for $20,000 and received the cash. They also made three cash expenditures related to rent of their building and to acquire merchandise inventory. The five initial transactions in December 19x1 are as follows:

Date	*Description of Transaction*
19x1	
Dec. 28	Issued stock for $22,000.
28	Paid security deposit on their rented building, $4,500.
28	Paid three months' rent (January, February, and March) for the building, $4,500.
30	Signed bank note for $20,000.
30	Purchased a local bookstore's discontinued computer software line, $8,500.

Exhibit 5-3 shows Byte-Size's initial journal entries and the resulting December 31, 19x1, balance sheet.

The next section discusses the typical accounting decisions that must be made for a merchandising business. As you follow the history of Byte-Size, you will learn the first law of business—not everything goes according to plan. Many unexpected events confront businesses, and Byte-Size is no exception. At the end of the first quarter, we will compare Byte-Size's actual operations with their business plan and indicate how Mary and Brad can intelligently plan the operations of their next period.

ACCOUNTING FOR MERCHANDISE INVENTORY

Objective 2
How to account for merchandise inventory—net purchases, cost of goods available for sale, and cost of goods sold.

A merchandising business usually has its merchandise on hand ready to be sold. As mentioned earlier, items held for sale are called *merchandise inventory.* The method of handling merchandise ready for sale varies with the type of merchandising company. For example, the merchandise inventory of a supermarket is on open shelves, and customers have direct access to the specific items they want to purchase. However, in a carpet store, customers usually select carpets from small samples of merchandise, while the actual merchandise is either in a warehouse ready for delivery or must be ordered from a carpet manufacturer. On the other hand, mail-order merchandising operations use catalogs to promote their products, so the customer does not see the actual item purchased until it arrives by mail or delivery service. Some mail-order companies do not own a stock of merchandise but order from their suppliers only what is needed for specific customer orders, and the supplier ships the merchandise directly to the customer. Regardless of how the merchandise company provides its merchandise for sale, the basic accounting procedures illustrated in this chapter apply to all merchandising companies.

EXHIBIT 5-3

Initial Journal Entries and Balance Sheet of Byte-Size

General Journal J1

Date		Account Titles and Explanation	Ref.	Debit	Credit
19x1					
Dec.	28	Cash (A)	111	22,000	
		Capital Stock (SE)	311		22,000
		To record initial investment.			
	28	Security Deposit (A)	171	4,500	
		Cash (A)	111		4,500
		To record deposit on rented building			
	28	Prepaid Rent (A)	131	4,500	
		Cash (A)	111		4,500
		To record prepayment of three months' rent.			
	30	Cash (A)	111	20,000	
		Note Payable (L)	217		20,000
		To record 15 % loan, with principal and interest due June 30, 19x2.			
	30	Merchandise Inventory (A)	142	8,500	
		Cash (A)	111		8,500
		To record acquisition of merchandise from ABC Discount Stores			

Byte-Size, Inc.
Balance Sheet
December 31, 19x1

Assets		**Liabilities and Stockholders' Equity**	
Cash	$24,500	Liabilities:	
Merchandise inventory	8,500	Note payable	$20,000
Security deposit	4,500	Total liabilities	$20,000
Prepaid rent	4,500	Stockholders' equity:	
		Capital stock	$22,000
Total assets	$42,000	Total liabilities and stockholders' equity	$42,000

Byte-Size purchases its inventory from suppliers. Some of the inventory is on display in the front of the store. The excess inventory is stored in a storage area at the back of the store. At any financial statement date, the cost of the merchandise still on hand appears on the balance sheet as an asset, Merchandise Inventory, and the cost of the merchandise sold to customers during a period appears on the income statement as an expense, Cost of Goods Sold.

The simplest flow of merchandise inventory for an accounting period is:

Starting amount:	Beginning inventory.	$xxx
Additions:	Net purchases	xxx
Subtotal:	Cost of goods available for sale . .	$xxx
Deduction:	Ending inventory (asset on the balance sheet)	(xxx)
Amount sold:	Cost of goods sold (expense on the income statement)	$xxx

In the above table, purchases are shown as an addition to beginning inventory. However, purchases are actually **net purchases** computed as follows:

Gross purchases—invoice prices of merchandise acquired. . .		$xxx
Less: Purchase returns and allowances for damaged or unwanted items.	$(xx)	
Purchase discounts for prompt payment.	(xx)	(xx)
Plus: Freight-in.		xx
Net purchases.		$xxx

Usually the merchandising company (the purchaser) pays the freight for merchandise shipped from suppliers. The freight cost is called **freight-in** and is added to arrive at net purchases as shown above. Freight is sometimes paid by the shipper, as you will learn later.

This section concentrates on an inventory process called the **periodic inventory method** of determining cost of goods sold. This method requires a physical count of the units of inventory on hand *periodically* (hence, the term *periodic*) to measure the value of the ending inventory and cost of goods sold. The units on hand are multiplied by the cost per unit to determine the ending inventory. Then, cost of goods sold is computed using the calculation illustrated above. (Chapter 6 discusses the perpetual inventory method—a method that keeps a continuous record of cost of inventory items on hand and cost of goods sold.)

To understand the periodic inventory system, study the relationship of the three formulas below. Formula 1 states that to determine the cost of goods sold, you subtract the ending inventory from the cost of goods available for sale. Formula 2 states that to determine the cost of goods available for sale, you add net purchases to the beginning inventory. Formula 3 states that to determine net purchases, you subtract (*a*) purchase returns and allowances and (*b*) purchase discounts from gross purchases, then add freight-in.

Formula 1: **Cost of goods sold** = Cost of goods available for sale − Ending inventory

Formula 2: **Cost of goods available for sale** = Beginning inventory + Net purchases

Formula 3: **Net purchases** = Gross purchases (invoice prices of purchases acquired) − Purchase returns and allowances − Purchase discounts + Freight-in

In the periodic inventory method, the balance sheet account, Merchandise Inventory, is not affected until the end of the accounting period. Separate accounts are used for Purchases, Purchase Returns and Allowances, Purchase Discounts, and Freight-In, none of which appear on the financial statements. We will see shortly that all of the balances in these accounts flow into either inventory or cost of goods sold.

To understand formula 1, you must understand the terms in formulas 2 and 3. For this reason, we subdivide this section into determining net purchases, determining cost of goods available for sale, and determining cost of goods sold. Refer frequently to these three formulas as you study the paragraphs below.

Determining Cost of Goods Available for Sale

Net purchases (formula 3) is the total of gross purchases (invoice prices of merchandise acquired) minus purchase returns and allowances, minus purchase discounts, and plus freight-in. To determine the net purchases for an accounting period, you must understand gross purchases, purchase returns and allowances, and purchase discounts.

Gross Purchases. **Gross purchases** is the total invoice price of all merchandise purchases without regard to discounts, returns, or allowances. To record gross purchases, a Purchases account is used. Only merchandise bought for resale is recorded in the Purchases account.

During the first quarter in 19x2, Byte-Size received invoices totaling $145,500 for merchandise received from suppliers. These payments were recorded at various times throughout the quarter and are recorded in the following summary entry:

		Debit	Credit
(1)	Purchases (A)	145,500	
	Accounts Payable (L)		145,500

Some of the entries shown in this chapter are summary entries. They represent the effects of many separate entries made at different times throughout the quarter. Thus, no dates are given, and the explanation line is omitted. For convenience in referencing, from this point on, we have numbered all of Byte-Size's journal entries.

Purchase Returns and Allowances. Because of defects or errors, not all merchandise received from suppliers is acceptable. Therefore, allowances are often made for merchandise defects. If a defect is serious, the merchandise may be returned for full credit. If a defect is minor, the purchaser may decide to keep the merchandise providing the supplier agrees to reduce the price or amount owed. The term **purchase returns and allowances** includes merchandise returned for credit and merchandise on which allowances have been made for defects.

Byte-Size returned one shipment of diskettes for $2,600 credit and received a $600 credit for defective paper that would have to be sold at a reduced price. These credits are recorded in the Purchase Returns and Allowances account, a contra asset account (XA), as follows:

		Debit	Credit
(2)	Accounts Payable (L)	2,600	
	Purchase Returns and Allowances (XA)		2,600
	To record return of defective diskettes.		
(3)	Accounts Payable (L)	600	
	Purchase Returns and Allowances (XA)		600
	To record allowance for inferior paper.		

A contra account, you recall from Chapter 4, is an account whose balance is subtracted from another account to get the net amount. In this case the contra account will be subtracted from gross purchases to determine net purchases.

Purchase Discounts. Some suppliers give discounts to customers when bills are paid promptly. These discounts are called **purchase discounts** and reduce the buyer's cost of merchandise. Since discounts are a reduction of the purchase price, the Purchase Discounts account is a contra asset (XA) account.

During the first quarter of 19x2, Byte-Size paid invoices for purchases totaling $110,000. No discounts were offered on invoices totaling $70,000, and payment was recorded as follows:

(4)	Accounts Payable (L)	70,000	
	Cash (A)		70,000

Discounts were offered and taken on $40,000, and such payments are summarized as follows:

(5)	Accounts Payable (L)	40,000	
	Cash (A)		39,200
	Purchase Discounts (XA)		800

When a supplier offers discounts, they are usually stated on the invoice with a special designation such as 2/10, n/30, which means that a 2% discount may be taken if the invoice is paid within 10 days; and if the invoice is not paid in 10 days, the total amount would be due within 30 days. Thus, if a company chooses not to take the discount, payment will usually be made at the latest possible date, allowing the company to retain its cash as long as possible.

Is it a good business decision to take a discount when it is offered? The answer to this question depends, of course, on the terms of the discount. During the period shown in transaction 5, Byte-Size saved $800 by paying the invoice 20 days before the 30-day deadline. Since the use of money is often measured by its annual interest rate, let us determine the annual interest rate represented by 2% for 20 days. Two percent is to 20 days the same as the annual interest rate is to 360 days, or $.02/20 = x/360$, $x = .001(360)$, $x = 0.36$, or 36%. You can also compute the annual interest rate by multiplying 2% times 18 periods of 20 days each ($360 \div 20 = 18$). A 36% yearly interest rate is an extremely high rate of interest. Remember Byte-Size is only paying 15% on its borrowed funds. This high annual interest percentage for cash discounts is not only a recognition for quick payment of the invoice but also a marketing device used by suppliers to attract customers.

In entry 5 above, we illustrated the **gross method** of recording purchase discounts. This method initially records purchases at their total invoice amount and only records the discount when and if it is taken. However, the actual cost of the merchandise was the total price less the discount. It is up to Byte-Size to decide if the discount will be taken.

An alternative to the gross method that enables businesses to keep track of lost discounts is called the **net method**, which records purchases net of their discounts or records the purchases at their net cost. Then if the purchases are paid within the discount period, no adjustments are needed. The following table of journal entries compares how a $500 invoice with terms of 2/10, n/30 is recorded using the net method and the gross method when it is paid within the discount period and when it is paid after the discount period:

	Net Method Paid				*Gross Method Paid*			
Journal Entry	*Within Discount Period*		*After Discount Period*		*Within Discount Period*		*After Discount Period*	
Recording purchase:								
Purchases (A)	490		490		500		500	
Accounts Payable (L)		490		490		500		500
Recording payment:								
Accounts Payable (L)	490		490		500		500	
Discounts Lost (E)			10					
Purchase Discounts (XA) . .						10		
Cash (A)		490		500		490		500

When discounts are not taken, the net method records the discount amount as an expense. Only the net cost of the merchandise flows to the Merchandise Inventory and Cost of Goods Sold accounts. In all circumstances, therefore, under the net method, the costs after discount are inventoried in the asset Merchandise Inventory; and any lost discounts are highlighted as a separate expense in the income statement. This method makes management aware of lost discounts that become material. On the other hand, under the gross method, the cost of inventory depends on the decision whether or not to take a discount. If a discount is taken, the inventory costs go down; if the discount is not taken, inventory costs are higher.

The **cost of goods available for sale** during an accounting period (formula 2, page 236) is the beginning inventory plus net purchases. We have discussed how accountants record purchase returns and allowances and discounts. Now we will see how beginning inventory and freight-in become components of cost of goods available.

Beginning Inventory. During December, before Byte-Size opened its doors, Mary and Brad purchased the discontinued software line of a local bookstore. Included with the $8,500 invoice from the bookstore was a list of the items purchased and their cost. For Byte-Size—a new business—this was their **beginning inventory** for the first quarter of 19x2. During the first quarter, Byte-Size purchased more merchandise and sold some merchandise. At the end of the first quarter, then, the **ending inventory** contained the merchandise that remained after selling items from the beginning inventory and from the purchases made during the quarter.

Let's look again at formulas 1 and 2 (page 236) to see the relationship between the beginning and ending inventory.

Period 1: Cost of goods sold = Cost of goods available for sale − Ending inventory

Period 2: Cost of goods available for sale = Beginning inventory + Net purchases

In an ongoing business, the ending inventory of an accounting period becomes the beginning inventory of the next accounting period. Now the question is: How do we determine the ending inventory? This question is answered below under the heading "Determining Cost of Goods Sold."

Freight-In. In addition to beginning inventory, purchases, returns and allowances, and discounts, another common component of net purchases is freight-in paid by the buyer. These freight charges are accounted for in an account titled **Freight-In.**

During the first quarter, Byte-Size paid $1,264 for incoming freight as shown in the following summary entry:

(6) Freight-In (A)	1,264	
Cash (A)		1,264

Freight-In is a common account used by merchandising companies since companies usually pay the freight on the merchandise they buy for resale.

Byte-Size's Cost of Goods Available for Sale. Now that you understand the nature of gross purchases, purchase returns and allowances, purchase discounts, beginning inventory, net purchases, and freight-in, you are ready to determine Byte-Size's cost of goods available for sale.

Using the cost figures given for Byte-Size earlier in the chapter, cost of goods available for sale for the first quarter of operations can be summarized as follows:

Beginning inventory			$ 8,500
Purchases (gross)		$145,500	
Less: Purchase returns and allowances . .	$(3,200)		
Purchase discounts	(800)	(4,000)	
Add: Freight-in		1,264	
Net purchases.			142,764
Cost of goods available for sale			$151,264

Determining Cost of Goods Sold

The cost of goods sold (formula 1, page 236) is the cost of goods available for sale minus the ending inventory. Since you know how to determine the cost of goods available for sale, you have only to learn how accountants determine ending inventory.

Ending Inventory. In a periodic inventory system such as that used by Byte-Size, a physical count of the inventory on hand is taken at the end of an accounting period, and the cost of the actual units on hand is the amount recognized as the inventory balance on the period-end balance sheet. This **ending inventory** is the merchandise that *remains* available for sale at the end of an accounting period, the beginning inventory for the next period.

Byte-Size determined the dollar amount of its ending inventory on March 31, 19x2, by counting the merchandise displayed in the store and in storage. Then the number of units of the different inventory items was multiplied by the net cost per item after subtracting allowances and discounts from purchase cost.

We will assume that Byte-Size's ending inventory balance determined by the above procedure is $54,000. To determine cost of goods sold for the period,

Byte-Size uses the cost of goods available for sale, $151,264, minus the ending inventory balance, $54,000. To record cost of goods sold, two adjusting entries are needed.

The first adjusting entry establishes the Cost of Goods Sold balance with a journal entry that eliminates the balances in all the other inventory-related accounts. Thus, the net of all the related account balances are put into the Cost of Goods Sold account. This is accomplished by the following journal entry:

		Debit	Credit
(7)	Cost of Goods Sold (E)	151,264	
	Purchase Returns and Allowances (XA)	3,200	
	Purchase Discounts (XA)	800	
	Merchandise Inventory (beginning) (A)		8,500
	Purchases (A).		145,500
	Freight-In (A)		1,264
	To transfer the beginning inventory and the other accounts that relate to net purchases to Cost of Goods Sold.		

A second adjusting entry is required to debit Merchandise Inventory for the cost of merchandise on hand at the end of the period and to reduce Cost of Goods Sold by the same amount, thus establishing the correct inventory balance in Merchandise Inventory which will be carried to the next period.

		Debit	Credit
(8)	Merchandise Inventory (ending) (A)	54,000	
	Cost of Goods Sold (E)		54,000
	To establish the ending inventory.		

The following shows how the two entries result in the correct Cost of Goods Sold amount:

Beginning inventory	$ 8,500
Net purchases	142,764
Cost of goods available for sale	$151,264
Ending inventory	54,000
Cost of goods sold	$ 97,264

Exhibit 5-4 shows how entries 7 and 8 relating to ending inventory affect Byte-Size's accounts. Five items make up the $151,264 debit to Cost of Goods Sold: the beginning amount in Merchandise Inventory, Purchases, Purchase Returns and Allowances, Freight-In, and Purchase Discounts. This $151,264 is the cost of goods available for sale discussed earlier. The credit to Cost of Goods Sold of $54,000 comes from entry 8—the amount of the Merchandise Inventory's ending balance.

ACCOUNTING FOR SALES

Objective 3
How to account for sales revenue.

To account for the first-quarter sales of Byte-Size, Mary and Brad began by learning how to recognize and record a sale. Since Byte-Size offered credit to customers, Mary and Brad had to learn from their accountant, FM, how to account for accounts receivable and for customers who did not pay what was owed. Knowing Byte-Size would have some sales returns and allowances, FM also taught Mary and Brad the method accountants use to record (1) sales returns and allowances and (2) sales discounts given to customers for prompt payment.

EXHIBIT 5-4

Byte-Size's Accounts Related to Inventory

Merchandise Inventory

Beg. bal.	8,500	(7)	8,500
(8)	54,000		
Bal.	54,000		

To the balance sheet ← Bal. 54,000

Purchases

(1)	145,500	(7)	145,500
	–0–		

Purchase Returns and Allowances

(7)	3,200	(2)	2,600
		(3)	600
			–0–

Cost of Goods Sold

(7)	151,264	(8)	54,000
Bal.	97,264		

Closed to Income Summary ← Bal. 97,264

Purchase Discounts

(7)	800	(5)	800
			–0–

Freight-In

(6)	1,264	(7)	1,264
	–0–		

These accounts have zero balances after adjustment of inventory and recording of cost of goods sold.

Revenue Recognition

Although Mary and Brad knew that they must record their sales revenue for the first quarter of 19x2, they were not sure: (1) when a sales transaction was considered completed, (2) what was the appropriate time to record a sale, and (3) how to determine the amount of each sale. So FM gave them the following criteria to use for the evaluation of sales saying that when all four criteria were met, a sale could be recorded.

1. Delivery of merchandise—the point at which the buyer takes responsibility for the item.
2. Measurement of the selling price—the point at which the selling price is known by both parties.
3. Receipt of cash or a valid receivable or other asset—the point at which something of known value is being transferred to the seller.
4. Reasonable determination of all relevant costs—the point at which no material uncertainties exist about the cost of the item to the seller.

For a merchandising company such as Byte-Size, these four criteria are usually all met on the date the customer takes possession of the merchandise. FM instructed Mary and Brad to record credit and cash sales as follows (we are using summary entries):

		Debit	Credit
(9)	Accounts Receivable (A)	124,450	
	Sales (R)		124,450
(10)	Cash (A)	9,300	
	Sales (R)		9,300

As you will see in the following sections, special considerations are sometimes made for uncollectible receivables, sales returns and allowances, and sales discounts. These considerations can affect the amounts actually collected from customers.

Accounts Receivable and Bad Debts

Objective 4
The relationship between accounts receivable and bad debts.

Companies usually have many credit customers who owe the company for outstanding invoices. Companies expect that most of their customers will pay their bills within a normal period, but some customers will be delinquent, while others will default and never pay. Defaulted invoices are called **bad debts** (or **uncollectible accounts**).

To minimize bad debts, companies begin by carefully checking the creditworthiness of potential credit customers. Once credit is extended, a systematic approach should be taken to follow up on late accounts. Then, if necessary, appropriate collection procedures must be initiated for delinquent payers. However, even the best conceived and operated system of credit granting and follow-up will not eliminate all problems.

As with all business situations, companies must watch out for the "point of overkill." That is, the cost of the credit system could exceed its expected benefits. An extremely tight credit policy could actually screen out a significant number of reasonably safe customers, and a too aggressive collection process could drive away customers who would have paid anyway and perhaps become repeat customers. Regardless of the credit policy employed by a company, inevitably some potentially good customers will be lost or not accepted, and some bad customers will be granted credit.

Accountants have developed procedures to estimate and account for the many combinations of results that occur in dealing with credit customers. The following example from Byte-Size and the appendix at the end of this chapter illustrate the most important of these procedures.

On March 31, 19x2, Byte-Size had been in operation for three months, and no specific invoices had been determined uncollectible. However, Mary read in a trade journal (*Software Retailing*) that about 2% of all small retailer credit sales were ultimately "written off as bad debts." In talking with FM, Mary learned that this phrase meant that when customers could not be made to pay their obligations, the accounts receivable amounts were removed from the company's books by journal entries and usually never collected.

Mary was concerned about the possibility of bad debts. She wondered if the bad debts should be anticipated or should all accounts receivable amounts be recognized as assets until they are proven to be uncollectible? Mary knew that an asset such as accounts receivable represented economic value in the form of expected cash inflow. To Mary, it was apparent that if the book value of the receivable exceeds the expected cash inflow, the receivable should be reduced. Then the receivable would be properly valued and the negative impact of expected bad debts matched to the period of sale.

FM explained to Mary that if Byte-Size uses 2% of the first quarter's credit sales ($124,450 × .02) as its best estimate of future bad debts related to first-quarter sales, the following adjusting entry would be made:

(11)	19x1			
	Mar. 31	Bad Debts Expense (E)	2,489	
		Allowance for Bad Debts (XA)		2,489
		To record estimated uncollectible accounts.		

The **Allowance for Bad Debts** account is a contra asset account to the Accounts Receivable account representing an estimate of uncollectible accounts receivable. The balance in this contra account is subtracted from the balance in accounts receivable in the balance sheet to arrive at the net realizable value of accounts receivable, or net receivable.

To understand how the Allowance for Bad Debts contra account is used, you must realize that a business keeps a record of each individual customer's receivable balance. This is called a *subsidiary record,* and all individual customers' outstanding amounts are kept in a **subsidiary ledger.** The total of all balances in the subsidiary ledger is represented in the general ledger with one account called the control account (or primary account). We are concerned here with the Accounts Receivable control account in the general ledger. The appendix to this chapter and the appendix to Chapter 7 discuss the use of the control account and subsidiary ledger.

Adjusting entry 11 above reduces net income and the asset book value, although no subsidiary account for individual customers is affected by this entry. Remember that at this time it is not known which customers will not pay their bills. The 2% used above is an overall estimate of bad debts that may or may not turn out to be accurate. Neither the subsidiary customer balances nor the Accounts Receivable control account is affected by the adjustment and both remain equal to each other at all times.

When specific invoices are proven to be uncollectible, the following entry, referred to as a **write-off entry,** is made:

Allowance for Bad Debts (XA)	xxx	
Accounts Receivable (A)		xxx
To write off uncollectible accounts.		

It is at this time that the specific customer invoice is removed from the Accounts Receivable control account and the related subsidiary ledger account.

Throughout the accounting period, the amount of the Allowance for Bad Debts account fluctuates as specific bad debts are recognized. However, the Bad Debts expense account is recorded only in the period-end adjusting entry. The appendix at the end of the chapter gives more detail about accounting for bad debts.

Sales Returns and Allowances

Objective 5
How to account for sales returns and allowances.

After customers take possession of purchased goods, the merchandise may be returned if it is damaged, inferior, or unwanted. Customers do not have an absolute right to return purchased items, but most merchandisers allow some returns. Sometimes the merchandiser gives the customer a reduction in price if the merchandise is damaged and the customer decides to keep it. The term **sales returns and allowances** refers to the merchandise returned by customers or the reduction in sales price given to customers due to unsatisfactory merchandise.

To keep track of returned or damaged merchandise, a company records the amounts in a contra revenue account called *Sales Returns and Allowances.* Byte-Size allowed a credit customer to return some damaged diskettes for full credit. The entry to show this return is:

(12)	19x1			
	Mar. 3	Sales Returns and Allowances (XR)	4,125	
		Accounts Receivable (A)		4,125
		To record receipt of merchandise returned by a customer.		

Note that the original sale for the diskettes was a credit sale. If the customer had paid cash for the diskettes, then the customer would receive cash or credit toward the reduction in cost of a future purchase.

The Sales Returns and Allowances account is a contra revenue account because it is treated as a reduction in the Sales account. On income statements, sales returns and allowances are subtracted from sales to arrive at **net sales.**

Sales Discounts

Objective 6
How to account for sales discounts.

Just as purchase discounts discussed earlier in the chapter reduce net purchases, **sales discounts,** which are shown as reductions in sales for the period, are reductions given to customers for prompt payment. Byte-Size offers its customers credit terms of 1/10, n/30 (1% of invoiced amount can be deducted if customer pays within 10 days of invoice date or the total invoice price is due within 30 days of invoice date).[1]

[1]Note again that this gives customers a strong incentive to make early payments. The annual rate could be computed in the same means as shown on page 238 for purchase discounts: $0.01/20 = x/360$, $x = 0.0005(360)$, $x = .18$. An annual return of 18% may be considered a good return on funds by customers.

During the first quarter of 19x2, Byte-Size collected cash from its credit customers on invoices totaling $96,300. Of the $96,300, receipts on $54,200 were reduced by the 1% sales discount. The summary journal entries for these two transactions are:

		Debit	Credit
(13)	Cash (A)	53,658	
	Sales Discounts (XR)	542	
	Accounts Receivable (A)		54,200
	To record receipts on which 1% discounts were taken.		
(14)	Cash (A)	42,100	
	Accounts Receivable (A)		42,100
	To record receipts on which discounts were not taken.		

The Sales Discounts account is a contra revenue account to the Sales account and is shown as such on the income statement. Thus, to determine net sales, both sales returns and allowances and sales discounts are subtracted from sales.

The above example uses the **gross method** of recording sales and sales discounts. Just as purchase discounts can be recorded using the net method, sales can also be recognized using the **net method.** The net method initially records the sales at their cash equivalent value assuming the discounts will be taken. When the customer pays within the discount period, no reference to a Sales Discounts account is required. If, however, payment is made after the discount period, the account Sales Discounts Not Taken is credited. The following journal entries would be made by Byte-Size if the net method were used. These entries are alternatives to entries 9, 13, and 14, respectively.

	Debit	Credit
Accounts Receivable (A)	123,206	
Sales (R)		123,206
To record credit sales net of discount: ($124,450 – (.01)($124,450)		
Cash (A)	53,658	
Accounts Receivable (A)		53,658
To record collections of credit sales net of discount taken.		
Cash (A)	42,100	
Sales Discounts Not Taken (R)		421
Accounts Receivable (A)		41,679
To record collections of credit sales for which discounts were not taken.		

On the income statement, the sales discounts not taken would appear under the "Other revenue" section. Most companies do not use the net method because it highlights something that is usually immaterial.

ACCOUNTING FOR TRANSACTIONS NOT RELATED TO INVENTORY AND SALES

Objective 7
Accounting for transactions not related to inventory and sales.

Byte-Size had the following transactions during its first quarter that were not related to inventory and sales:

Date	*Transaction No.*	*Description*	*Amount*
19x2			
Jan. 2	15	Purchased six-month insurance policy.	$1,500
4	16	Purchased office supplies	300
5	17	Purchased computer for office use (five-year life, no estimated salvage value) . . .	9,000
Various dates	18	Paid salaries for January–March	6,400
Mar. 25	19	Paid utilities for January–March.	300

The journal entries for these transactions are given in Exhibit 5-5. Since we have used transactions similar to these in previous chapters, you should have no difficulty in understanding them.

At the end of the first quarter, Byte-Size must make adjusting entries for the accruals and allocations listed at the top of the next page.

EXHIBIT 5-5

Journalizing Byte-Size's Transactions Not Related to Inventory and Sales

GENERAL JOURNAL					J3
	Date	Account Titles and Explanation	Ref.	Debit	Credit
	19x2				
(15)	Jan. 2	Prepaid Insurance (A)	143	1,500	
		Cash (A)	111		1,500
		To record prepayment of insurance for six months.			
(16)	4	Supplies (A)	132	300	
		Cash (A)	111		300
		To record purchase of office supplies			
(17)	5	Equipment (A)	151	9,000	
		Cash (A)	111		9,000
		To record purchase of computer for office use.			
(18)	Various	Salaries Expense (E)	521	6,400	
		Cash (A)	111		6,400
		To record January–March salaries paid.			
(19)	Mar. 25	Utilities Expense (E)	522	300	
		Cash (A)	111		300
		To record January–March utilities expense.			

Transaction No.	*Transactions Requiring Adjusting Entries*
20	Three months of rent expense, \$4,500. (Recall this amount was prepaid in December 19x1.)
21	One half of insurance premium paid January 2 (transaction 15), \$750, expired.
22	Of \$300 supplies purchased January 4 (transaction 6), only \$75 remain. The supplies used (\$225) are expensed.
23	Three months' depreciation for computer purchased on January 5 (transaction 17) is \$450 (\$9,000/60 months × 3 months).
24	Three months' interest on note due June 30, 19x2, is \$750 (\$20,000 × 0.15 × 3/12).

Objective 8
How to prepare a worksheet for a merchandising company.

Exhibit 5-6 gives the journal entries for these adjustments. Remember that adjusting entries 7, 8, and 11 were covered previously. The resulting adjusted account balances before closing are shown in T accounts in Exhibit 5-7. Exhibit 5-8 (pages 252-53) shows a worksheet for Byte-Size that includes all of the transactions you have studied.

EXHIBIT 5-6

Journal Entries for Byte-Size's Adjusting Entries

GENERAL JOURNAL J4

	Date	Account Titles and Explanation	Ref.	Debit	Credit
	19x2				
(20)	Mar. 31	Rent Expense (E)	523	4,500	
		Prepaid Rent (A)	142		4,500
		To adjust January–March rent expense.			
(21)	31	Insurance Expense (E)	524	750	
		Prepaid Insurance (A)	143		750
		To adjust January–March insurance expense.			
(22)	31	Office Supplies Expense (E)	525	225	
		Supplies (A)	132		225
		To adjust office supplies used during the January–March period.			
(23)	31	Depreciation Expense—Equipment (E)	526	450	
		Accumulated Depreciation—Equipment (XA)	156		450
		To record depreciation expense on office equipment for January–March period.			
(24)	31	Interest Expense (E)	527	750	
		Interest Payable (L)	222		750
		To record January–March interest expense on the outstanding note.			

EXHIBIT 5-7

Byte-Size's Account Activity in T Accounts

Cash

Bal.	24,500	(4)	70,000
(10)	9,300	(5)	39,200
(13)	53,658	(6)	1,264
(14)	42,100	(15)	1,500
		(16)	300
		(17)	9,000
		(18)	6,400
		(19)	300
Bal.	1,594		

Accounts Receivable

(9)	124,450	(12)	4,125
		(13)	54,200
		(14)	42,100
Bal.	24,025		

Allowance for Bad Debts

		(11)	2,489
		Bal.	2,489

Merchandise Inventory

Bal.	8,500	(7)	8,500
(8)	54,000		
Bal.	54,000		

Purchases

(1)	145,500	(7)	145,500
Bal.	-0-		

Purchase Returns and Allowances

(7)	3,200	(2)	2,600
		(3)	600
		Bal.	-0-

Purchase Discounts

(7)	800	(5)	800
		Bal.	-0-

Freight-In

(6)	1,264	(7)	1,264
Bal.	-0-		

Supplies

(16)	300	(22)	225
Bal.	75		

Security Deposit

Bal.	4,500		

Prepaid Rent

Bal.	4,500	(20)	4,500
Bal.	-0-		

Prepaid Insurance

(15)	1,500	(21)	750
Bal.	750		

Equipment

(17)	9,000		
Bal.	9,000		

Accumulated Depreciation—Equipment

		(23)	450
		Bal.	450

EXHIBIT 5-7 *(concluded)*

Accounts Payable

	Debit		Credit
(2)	2,600	(1)	145,500
(3)	600		
(4)	70,000		
(5)	40,000		
		Bal.	32,300

Note Payable

	Debit		Credit
		Bal.	20,000

Interest Payable

	Debit		Credit
		(24)	750
		Bal.	750

Capital Stock

	Debit		Credit
		Bal.	22,000

Sales

	Debit		Credit
		(9)	124,450
		(10)	9,300
		Bal.	133,750

Sales Returns and Allowances

	Debit		Credit
(12)	4,125		

Sales Discounts

	Debit		Credit
(13)	542		

Cost of Goods Sold

	Debit		Credit
(7)	151,264	(8)	54,000
Bal.	97,264		

Salaries Expense

	Debit		Credit
(18)	6,400		

Utilities Expense

	Debit		Credit
(19)	300		

Rent Expense

	Debit		Credit
(20)	4,500		

Insurance Expense

	Debit		Credit
(21)	750		

Supplies Expense

	Debit		Credit
(22)	225		

Depreciation Expense—Equipment

	Debit		Credit
(23)	450		

Interest Expense

	Debit		Credit
(24)	750		

Bad Debts Expense

	Debit		Credit
(11)	2,489		

ANALYSIS OF THE EFFECTS OF BYTE-SIZE'S OPERATIONS

Objective 9
How to analyze the effects of a merchandising company's operations.

Now that Byte-Size has been in operation for three months, the time has come to compare the actual financial statements of Byte-Size on March 31, 19x2 (see Exhibit 5-9 on page 254), with the projected statements in the business plan prepared by FM at the beginning of the period (Exhibit 5-2, pages 231-32). When you compare these two sets of statements, you will note that **some** variations exist. Are the variations from the projected statements in the business plan good or bad? This question requires careful analysis.

The first thing you should know is that variations from plans normally occur, and these variations in and of themselves do not indicate a poor planning process. As a tool of analysis, accounting helps interpret the results of operations and aids in revising plans for the future. When you view the results of the first three months of Bite-Size's operations along with their original projections, you note that Byte-Size was close in projecting sales and cost of goods sold; therefore, the projected gross margin was fairly accurate. Also, other expenses were considerably less than projected resulting in greater net income than expected.

Bite-Size's projected and actual balance sheets show two significant differences. Merchandise Inventory and Accounts Payable are both much larger than expected. Now think about the relationship of these two accounts. Inventory was purchased on credit, thereby increasing Accounts Payable. What does this mean for short-run liquidity? If the Accounts Payable must be paid before cash can be collected from customers, Byte-Size may need to find a new source of financing. Also, the cash balance is less than first projected, primarily because of the greater than expected cost of the computer and inventory.

Byte-Size must carefully plan for the next period. A new loan or more capital from the two owners may be necessary. The first quarter's experience and the analysis of results show that the plan for the next quarter must consider the high level of investment in inventory that was underestimated in the original plan. Thus, Mary and Brad must seriously question the need for so much inventory on hand. If they decide that such a high level of inventory is necessary, they should consider investing more of their money or borrowing more money. Also Mary and Brad must make a cash flow forecast including due dates on loans.

To summarize this analysis of Byte-Size's first quarter of operations, we can conclude that the business is profitable, but it has a problem with short-term liquidity.

SUMMARY

This chapter begins by discussing the need for an accounting system when planning and operating a merchandising business. Compared to a service business, a merchandising business possesses unique accounting and operating problems relating to inventory. By following Byte-Size, Inc., from the planning stage to the operating stage and then analyzing its operations, the important accounting questions related to inventories were introduced.

In planning operations, merchandising managers must make crucial decisions about the nature and amounts of inventory to be purchased and maintained. This leads to questions of financing inventory purchases and the appropriate accounting for inventory. Inventory costs flow to cost of goods sold, an expense on the income statement, and merchandise inventory, a current asset account on the balance sheet. Understanding the formulas for cost of goods sold, cost of goods available for sale, and net purchases is necessary to see the relationship between

E X H I B I T 5-8

Worksheet for Byte-Size, Inc.

Byte-Size, Inc.
Worksheet
For the Quarter Ended March 31, 19x2

	Unadjusted Trial Balance		*Adjustments*		*Adjusted Trial Balance*		*Income Statement*		*Balance Sheet*	
Account Titles	*(1) Debit*	*(2) Credit*	*(3) Debit*	*(4) Credit*	*(5) Debit*	*(6) Credit*	*(7) Debit*	*(8) Credit*	*(9) Debit*	*(10) Credit*
Cash	1,594				1,594				1,594	
Accounts Receivable . .	24,025				24,025				24,025	
Allowance for Bad Debts				*(11)* 2,489		2,489				2,489
Merchandise Inventory .	8,500		*(8)* 54,000	*(7)* 8,500	54,000				54,000	
Purchases	145,500			*(7)* 145,500						
Purchase Returns and Allowances		3,200	*(7)* 3,200							
Purchase Discounts . .		800	*(7)* 800							
Freight-In	1,264			*(7)* 1,264						
Supplies	300			*(22)* 225	75				75	
Security Deposit	4,500				4,500				4,500	
Prepaid Rent	4,500			*(20)* 4,500						
Prepaid Insurance . . .	1,500			*(21)* 750	750				750	
Equipment	9,000				9,000				9,000	

Accum. Depreciation—Equipment				(23) 450		450				450
Accounts Payable		32,300				32,300				32,300
Note Payable		20,000				20,000				20,000
Interest Payable				(24) 750		750				750
Capital Stock		22,000				22,000				22,000
Sales		133,750				133,750		133,750		
Sales Returns and Allowances	4,125				4,125		4,125			
Sales Discounts	542				542		542			
Salaries Expense	6,400				6,400		6,400			
Utilities Expense	300				300		300			
Cost of Goods Sold			(7) 151,264	(8) 54,000	97,264		97,264			
Rent Expense			(20) 4,500		4,500		4,500			
Insurance Expense			(21) 750		750		750			
Supplies Expense			(22) 225		225		225			
Depreciation Expense—Equipment			(23) 450		450		450			
Interest Expense			(24) 750		750		750			
Bad Debts Expense			(11) 2,489		2,489		2,489			
Totals	212,050	212,050	218,428	218,428	211,739	211,739	117,795	133,750	93,944	77,989
Net income/Retained earnings							15,955			15,955
Totals							133,750	133,750	93,944	93,944

ending inventory, beginning inventory, freight-in, gross purchases, purchase returns and allowances, and purchase discounts.

Since merchandising businesses buy merchandise for resale to customers, accounting for sales must be understood before a business can accurately determine its net income. You must know when to recognize a sale, the appropriate time to record a sale, and the correct amount of a sale. Many sales are on credit, and credit sales involve accounts receivables and bad debts. Recording an expense and a reduction in the book value of accounts receivable for estimated bad debts is an application of the matching concept where all related expenses are matched

EXHIBIT 5-9

Simple Financial Statement Analysis

Byte-Size, Inc.
Balance Sheet Analysis
March 31, 19x2

	Actual	Business Plan	Variance (Actual − Plan)
Assets			
Current assets:			
Cash	$ 1,594	$ 9,200	−$ 7,606
Accounts receivable	24,025	20,000	+ 1,536
Allowance for bad debts	(2,489)		
Merchandise inventory	54,000	22,500	+ 31,500
Office supplies	75		+ 75
Security deposit	4,500	4,500	0
Prepaid insurance	750		+ 750
Total current assets	$82,455	$56,200	+$26,255
Noncurrent assets:			
Office equipment	$ 9,000		
Less: Accumulated depreciation	(450)		
Total noncurrent assets	$ 8,550	$ 5,000	+$ 3,550
Total assets	$91,005	$61,200	+$29,805
Liabilities and Stockholders' Equity			
Liabilities:			
Accounts payable	$32,300	$ 2,000	+$30,300
Note payable	20,000	20,000	0
Interest payable	750	750	0
Total liabilities	$53,050	$22,750	+$30,300
Stockholders' equity:			
Capital stock	$22,000	$22,000	$ 0
Retained earnings	15,955	16,450	− 495
Total stockholders' equity	$37,955	$38,450	−$ 495
Total liabilities and stockholders' equity	$91,005	$61,200	+$29,805

EXHIBIT 5-9 *(concluded)*

Byte-Size, Inc.
Income Statement Analysis
For the Quarter Ended March 31, 19x2

	Actual	Business Plan	Variance (Actual – Plan)
Sales	$ 133,750		
Less: Sales returns and allowances	4,125		
Sales discounts	542		
Net sales	$ 129,083	$ 125,000	+$4,083
Cost of goods sold	97,264	93,750	+ 3,514
Gross margin	$ 31,819	$ 31,250	+$ 569
Expenses:			
Salaries expense	$ 6,400	$ 6,400	$ 0
Bad debt expense	2,489		+ 2,489
Rent expense	4,500	4,500	0
Utilities expense	300	900	– 600
Other expense	2,175	3,000	– 825
Total expenses	$ 15,864	$ 14,800	+$1,064
Net income	$ 15,955	$ 16,450	–$ 495

Byte-Size, Inc.
Comparison of Actual and Projected Cash Flows
From Inception to March 31, 19x2

	Actual	Business Plan	Variance (Actual – Plan)
Operating Activities:			
Receipts from customers	$ 105,058	$ 105,000	$ 58
Payments to suppliers	(118,964)	(114,250)	– 4,714
Payments for rent	(9,000)	(9,000)	0
Payments for utilities	(300)	(900)	+ 600
Payments for salaries	(6,400)	(6,400)	0
Payments for office supplies	(300)	(850)	+ 550
Payments for insurance	(1,500)	(1,400)	– 100
Cash used in operating activities	$ (31,406)	$ (27,800)	–$3,606
Investing activities:			
Payment for computer	$ (9,000)	$ (5,000)	–$4,000
Cash used in investing activities	$ (9,000)	$ (5,000)	–$4,000
Financing activities:			
Receipt from sale of stock	22,000	22,000	0
Receipt from bank loan	20,000	20,000	0
Cash provided by financing activities	$ 42,000	$ 42,000	$ 0
3/31/x2 cash balance	$ 1,594	$ 9,200	–$7,606

to the period in which revenue is recognized. Some sales are returned, which involve sales returns and allowances. When discounts are allowed, accounting must provide for them. All of these items were discussed in this chapter.

This chapter concludes by using the output of the accounting system to analyze the operations of a merchandising company. As a tool of analysis, accounting not only records the history of a company but also helps in guiding its future. As you continue to study each chapter in this textbook, your appreciation for the effectiveness of the accounting system in planning and controlling businesses will increase.

DEMONSTRATION EXERCISE

The following information is taken from the accounting records of the Sell-It-Now Company for the end of the second quarter of 19xx:

Beginning inventory	$ 24,000
Purchases	145,000
Discounts taken on merchandise purchased	980
Merchandise returned to supplier because of damage or inferior quality	3,700
Freight costs incurred in bringing merchandise to the store	6,400
Ending inventory	18,300
Sales (gross)	268,000
Discounts taken by customers	3,900
Merchandise returned by customers	6,225
Freight costs incurred in delivering merchandise to customers	2,850
Invoice No. 217 determined to be uncollectible	425

Required:

1. Determine net sales for the quarter.
2. Determine cost of goods sold associated with those sales.
3. Determine bad debt expense for the period if Sell-It-Now estimates bad debts to be 2% of net sales. All sales are made on credit. Prepare the journal entry to record bad debt expense.
4. Prepare the journal entry that Sell-It-Now would make to write off invoice No. 217 on June 30, 19xx.
5. (*Appendix*) Prepare the journal entry(ies) that the company would make if on October 15, 19xx, payment for invoice No. 217 was unexpectedly received.

Solution:

1. Net sales for the period:

Sales		$268,000
Less: Sales returns and allowances	$ 6,225	
Sales discounts	3,900	10,125
Net sales		$257,875

2. Cost of goods sold for the period:

Beginning inventory		$ 24,000
Purchases	$145,000	
Less: Purchases discounts	980	
Purchase returns and allowances	3,700	$140,320
Plus: Freight-in		6,400
Net purchases		146,720
Cost of goods available for sale		$170,720
Ending inventory		18,300
Cost of goods sold		$152,420

3. Estimate of bad debts for the period:

Net sales	$257,875
Estimate percentage	× .02
	$ 5,158

Date	Account	Debit	Credit
19xx			
June 30	Bad Debt Expense (E)	5,158	
	Allowance for Bad Debts (XA)		5,158
	To record estimate for uncollectible accounts.		

4.

Date	Account	Debit	Credit
19xx			
June 30	Allowance for Bad Debts (XA)	425	
	Accounts Receivable (A)		425
	To write off invoice No. 217.		

5.

Date	Account	Debit	Credit
19xx			
Oct. 15	Accounts Receivable (A)	425	
	Allowance for Bad Debts (XA)		425
	To record previously written off account.		
	Cash (A)	425	
	Accounts Receivable (A)		425
	To record receipt of payment on invoice No. 217.		

APPENDIX

Bad Debts, Credit Card Sales, and Installment Sales

Objective 10
Accounting for bad debts, credit card sales, and installment sales.

This appendix continues the discussion of accounting for bad debts that began in the chapter. You will learn how a business estimates the amount of bad debts to be recognized, how to write off a bad debt, and how to record a collection of an account previously written off. The appendix ends with a section on accounting for credit card sales and installment sales.

ACCOUNTING FOR BAD DEBTS

In most businesses, the timing of cash inflows depends to a large extent on the contractual arrangements made with customers and others who ultimately pay cash into the business. In a standard credit sales transaction, the customer takes possession of the goods or receives the benefits of services and promises to pay the invoice price in the future. This contractual arrangement is not the same as receiving cash at the time of the sale; however, usually the time between the sale and receiving the cash is short.

When a credit sale is made, the business uses a current asset account called *Accounts Receivable* to carry the amount owed by customers between the point of sale and the receipt of cash. The Accounts Receivable account represents the total money amount of all outstanding invoices; however, the future economic benefit to be received by the company depends on the willingness and ability of customers to meet their obligations. The probability of collecting all receivables is usually less than 100%. Some risks always exist with outstanding receivables. Notes receivable and other receivables not necessarily related to sales also involve the risk of noncollection. How should we account for the risks inherent in such situations? This question is answered in the section that follows.

Estimating Bad Debts

Accountants make provision for the risks of not collecting accounts receivables by estimating the amount of bad debts a company may incur and showing these estimates as a contra account to the Accounts Receivable account. Then, accounts receivable is shown on the balance sheet as net of the estimated uncollectible bad debts.

Several methods are used by accountants to estimate bad debts. In this section we discuss the two methods used most often—the accounts receivable aging method and the percentage-of-sales method.

For our example, we are using Overnight Express, Incorporated (OEI). OEI began business operations on October 1, 19x1. It has many cash customers for whom OEI sends small individual shipments and a smaller number of commercial customers for whom it sends large shipments. OEI mails invoices to its commercial customers. For the fourth quarter of 19x1, OEI has the following sales experience:

Cash sales	$1,100,000
Credit sales	2,800,000
Cash collections from credit customers . . .	2,426,000

Aging of Accounts Receivable. As you can see in Exhibit 5A-1, OEI keeps two complementary records of its accounts receivable—the general ledger Accounts Receivable account and a subsidiary ledger. The balance of the Accounts Receivable account in the general ledger equals the total outstanding invoices of the separate customer accounts in the subsidiary ledger. As mentioned in the chapter, the general ledger account is often called the *control* or *primary account.* The subsidiary ledger allows management to keep track of each customer and each invoice issued to each customer.

EXHIBIT 5A-1

Control Accounts from the General Ledger

Accounts Receivable

Credit sales	2,800,000	Collections	2,426,000
Balance	374,000		

Subsidiary Customer Accounts

Air Products, Inc.

14,000	4,000
10,000	

Allcomp, Inc.

8,000	2,000
6,000	

•
•
•

Other subsidiary accounts for individual customers (not shown in this example).

•
•
•

Young Supply

21,000	16,500
4,500	

$374,000 = Total of all customer subsidiary ledger balances

Accountants make an analysis of the outstanding invoices, and they determine the probability of noncollection. This analysis (1) gives the company an opportunity to follow up on slow-paying customers and (2) provides the needed allowance for bad debts to be included in the balance sheet. The net book value of the receivable shown in the balance sheet should be the total amount that the company expects to collect. The current period should absorb the expense associated with any losses expected from noncollection.

One way that accountants estimate the uncollectibles is by making an **aging schedule** that lists each outstanding invoice and gives its probability of collection based on the number of days the invoice has been outstanding. Exhibit 5A-2 shows the aging schedule for OEI.

All of the invoices listed in OEI's aging schedule in Exhibit 5A-2 have some probability of not being collected, but OEI does not know which of these invoices will not be collected. Note that on December 31, invoice #1002 issued on September 15 has an estimated 50% chance of not being collected, which means that the expected future value is one half of the invoice amount.

Such probabilities as shown in Exhibit 5A-2 are based on the company's experience and/or on industry statistics. If in OEI's case these probabilities are accurate, $62,000 of the outstanding invoices on December 31, 19x1, will not be collected. This amount is the loss in economic benefits that can be expected if the probabilities of noncollection are accurate.

To provide for bad debts, OEI's accountant would make the following adjusting entry to record the expense and a reduction in the book value of the Accounts Receivable account:

19x1			
Dec. 31	Bad Debts Expense (E)	62,000	
	Allowance for Bad Debts (XA)		62,000
	To record estimated uncollectible accounts.		

Remember, this is OEI's first year of operations. Accounting for bad debts on an ongoing basis is shown below.

EXHIBIT 5A-2

Accounts Receivable Aging Schedule for OEI

Overnight Express, Incorporated
Accounts Receivable Aging Schedule
Outstanding Invoices at December 31, 19x1

Invoice No.	*Date Issued*	*Amount*	*Age in Days*	*Percent Probability of Noncollection*	*Expected Bad Debt Amount*
1002.	9/15/x1	$ 18,000	107	50%	$ 9,000
2076.	9/30/x1	47,500	87	40	19,000
3026.	10/15/x1	30,000	77	40	12,000
4053.	10/31/x1	22,500	62	40	9,000
5037.	11/15/x1	24,000	46	25	6,000
6021.	11/30/x1	12,000	31	25	3,000
7011	12/15/x1	20,000	16	10	2,000
8001–8086	After 12/15/x1	200,000	1–15	1	2,000
		$374,000			$62,000

Percentage-of-Sales Method. As an alternative to the aging method, uncollectibles can be estimated by the **percentage-of-sales method.** This method charges a percentage of credit sales for the period to Bad Debts Expense. For example, the industry average of uncollectible accounts for OEI is 2% of credit sales. The adjusting entry for OEI would be:

19x1			
Dec. 31	Bad Debts Expense (E)	56,000	
	Allowance for Bad Debts (XA)		56,000
	To record estimated uncollectible accounts ($2,800,000 × .02).		

The percentage could also be applied to net credit sales; that is, sales minus sales returns and allowances and sales discounts.

To summarize, the aging method calls for an analysis of outstanding invoices and results in an estimate of the uncollectible amount. The balance in the Allowance for Bad Debts account is made to equal this estimate by means of the adjusting entry which debits Bad Debts Expense and credits Allowance for Bad Debts. The method gives a balance in the allowance account which is the company's best estimate of uncollectible accounts. Alternatively, under the percentage-of-sales method, Bad Debt Expense is estimated and debited for the estimated amount (a percentage of net credit sales) and the allowance account is credited for the same amount. The aging method is more balance sheet oriented resulting in the best estimate of uncollectibles as the allowance account balance and the bad debts expense amount for the period is "forced." The percentage-of-sales method is more income statement oriented because the bad debt expense is estimated without regard to the resulting balance in the allowance account.

Writing Off Bad Debts and Accounting for Bad Debts Expense in a Subsequent Year

An invoice is determined to be uncollectible when a customer declares bankruptcy, dies, disappears without a trace, or is in some other way unable to pay. Assume that on January 2, 19x2, before any new credit sales are recorded, OEI determined invoice #1002 to be uncollectible. To write off this bad debt, OEI reduces the Accounts Receivable balance by $18,000 as follows:

19x2			
Jan. 2	Allowance for Bad Debts (XA)	18,000	
	Accounts Receivable (A).		18,000
	To record write-off of invoice #1002.		

The net book value of the accounts receivable is not affected by this entry, and net income is not directly reduced. Under the allowance method, the book value of the receivable and net income are directly affected only at period-end when the adjusting entry is made to record the bad debts expense.

You should note that the write-off of a specific customer's account must also be recorded in the customer's record in the subsidiary ledger so that the balance in the general ledger Accounts Receivable account and the total of the customer balances in the subsidiary ledger are equal. The effects of entries to record bad debts expense and to write off an account are as follows (assuming the aging method was used to estimate bad debts):

Date	*Outstanding Invoices*	–	*Allowance for Bad Debts*	=	*Net Book Value of Accounts Receivable*
12/31/x1 (before write-off) . . .	$374,000	–	$62,000	=	$312,000
1/2/x2 (after write-off)	356,000	–	44,000	=	312,000

Note also that the balance in the Allowance for Bad Debts is reduced from $62,000 to $44,000, and this reduction may affect the period-end adjustment for 19x2. For example, if the aging analysis of outstanding invoices on March 31, 19x2, shows expected bad debts of $120,000 and the Allowance for Bad Debts remains at $44,000 at the end of the quarter, an adjustment of $76,000 would be necessary to establish the proper balance in the allowance account. The journal entry for this would be:

19x2			
Mar. 31	Bad Debts Expense (E)	76,000	
	Allowance for Bad Debts (XA)		76,000
	To record estimated uncollectible accounts.		

Collection of a Previously Written Off Invoice

An invoice is written off when it is deemed uncollectible, but sometimes cash is collected on that invoice at a later date. When this occurs, the proper procedure is to reestablish the written off amount and then record the collection of cash in the usual manner. Assume that during 19x2, OEI wrote off an invoice as follows:

19x2			
May 15	Allowance for Bad Debts (XA).	980	
	Accounts Receivable (A)		980
	To record write-off of invoice.		

On July 2, a check is received for $980 from the errant customer, and the following entries are made:

19x2			
July 2	Accounts Receivable (A)	980	
	Allowance for Bad Debts (XA)		980
	To record reinstatement of invoice previously written off.		
	Cash (A)	980	
	Accounts Receivable (A)		980
	To record receipt of payment on account.		

Notice that these entries have no direct effect on net income. The period-end adjusting entries establish the bad debt expense which depends on the estimates of uncollectibility and the existing balance in the allowance for bad debts under the aging method.

CREDIT CARD SALES

Many retail businesses use bank cards such as VISA or Mastercard as their primary means of selling on credit. This relieves the company from the risk of noncollection because the credit card company assumes the risk. The credit card company charges the retail business a percentage of the original sales price as compensation for assuming this risk and providing the collection service.

EXHIBIT 5A-3

Retail/Credit Customer Relationship with and without Credit Cards

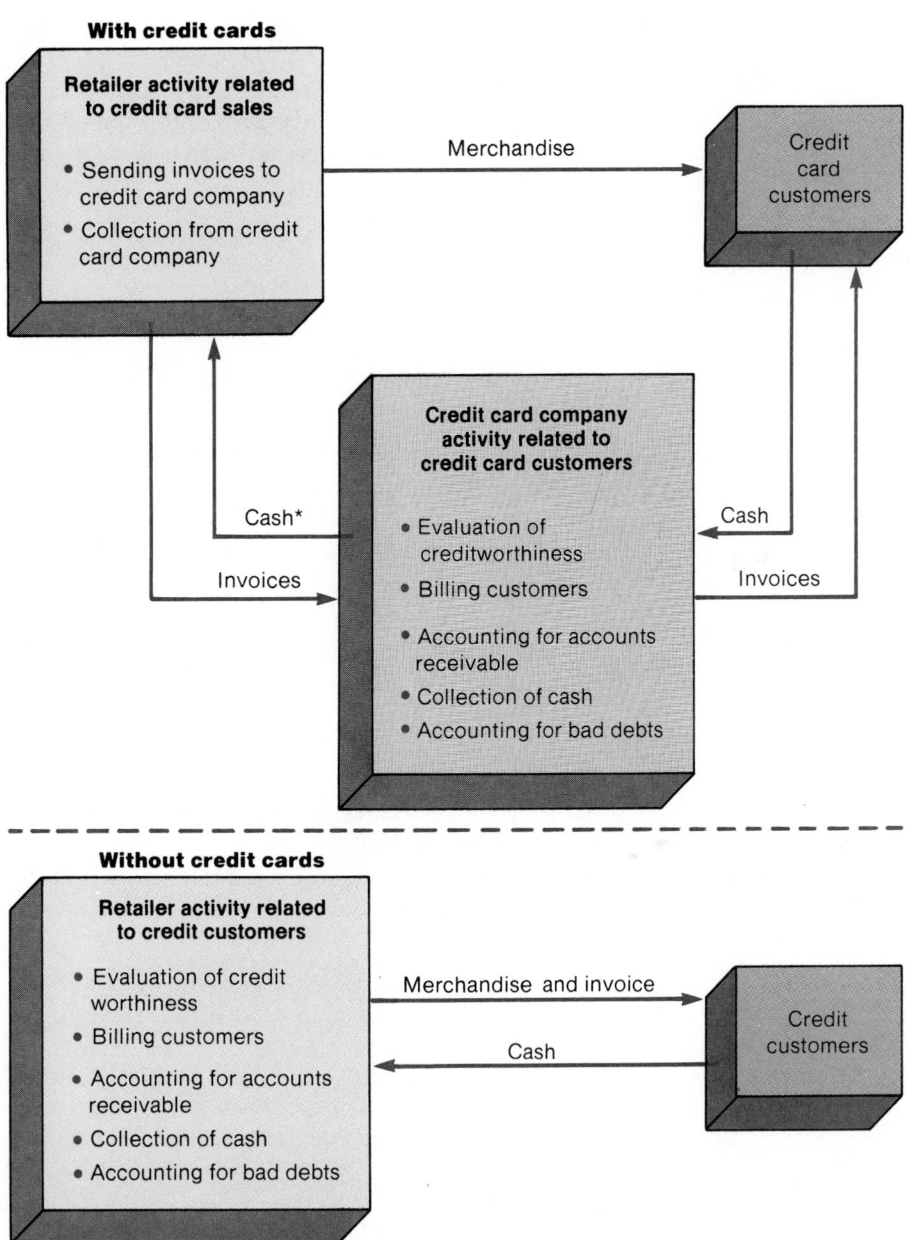

*Invoice amount less fee.

Since the credit card company assumes the risk and bills the customer, the retailer's accounting effort and clerical activity are much reduced. Exhibit 5A-3 shows the relationship of retailer and customer with and without credit cards.

The enormous popularity of retailer arrangements with credit card companies is testimony that these credit cards involve economic efficiencies. Generally, credit card companies are efficient at evaluating creditworthiness, collection, and recordkeeping.

Customers also find using national credit cards convenient. Carrying one or two of the major credit cards reduces the need for holding cash, and paying bills can be done with one or two checks rather than many checks to individual retailers.

The following example illustrates the retailer's accounting for a credit card sale: On March 1, 19x1, Otis, Inc., sells a spreadsheet program to Ms. Stockman for $450 by means of Americard which charges Otis, Inc., a 4% fee on the sales price. The entries to record the sale and collection are as follows:

19x1			
Mar. 1	Accounts Receivable, Americard (A)	432	
	Credit Card Fee Expense (E)	18	
	Sales (R)		450
	To record sale on credit card basis.		
Apr. 1	Cash (A)	432	
	Accounts Receivable, Americard (A)		432
	To record collection of account.		

Otis could have recorded the gross amount of receivables, but this would make the accrual of the credit card fee expense at the end of the accounting period necessary. For example, assume that Otis, Inc., has credit card sales of $100,000 through Americard in 19x1 and collected $90,000 of the sales by the end of the period. The following entries summarize the accounting if the gross receivables amount is recorded:

During 19x1	Accounts Receivable, Americard (A)	100,000	
	Sales (R).		100,000
	To record gross sales made on a credit card basis.		
	Cash (A)	86,400	
	Credit Card Fee Expense (E).	3,600	
	Accounts Receivable, Americard (A)		90,000
	To record collection of account from Americard.		
Dec. 31	Credit Card Fee Expense (E).	400	
	Allowance for Credit Card Fee (XA).		400
	To record accrual of credit card fee attributed to sales for which payment has not yet been received from Americard.		
19x2			
Jan. 15	Cash (A)	9,600	
	Allowance for Credit Card Fee (XA).	400	
	Accounts Receivable, Americard (A)		10,000
	To record collection of cash from Americard.		

The balance sheet at December 31, 19x1, would show the net receivable from Americard as a current asset.

INSTALLMENT SALES

Not all receivables are paid in one payment. Retailers, such as Sears, Roebuck and Co., have billions of dollars in **installment sales** that involve payment over several months or years with interest charges being added on the unpaid balance. Because these payment periods are usually considered to be within the operating cycle of the retailer, installment sales receivables are usually classified as current assets, even if they extend beyond one year. The tax considerations and specific accounting procedures applicable to installment sales are covered in intermediate or advanced courses in accounting.

KEY TERMS

Allowance for Bad Debts. Contra asset account to the Accounts Receivable account that represents the estimation of uncollectible accounts receivable.

Bad debts. Invoices that have been determined to be uncollectible; also called uncollectible accounts.

Beginning inventory. Cost of goods available for sale at the beginning of the operating period; ending inventory of previous accounting period.

Cost of goods available for sale. Total cost of all merchandise held for sale during the period; beginning inventory plus net purchases plus freight-in.

Cost of goods sold. Cost of merchandise sold to customers during the period; cost of goods available for sale minus ending inventory.

Current ratio. Ratio of current assets to current liabilities.

Ending inventory. Merchandise that remains available for sale at the end of an accounting period, becomes the beginning inventory for the next period.

Entrepreneur. One who organizes, manages, and assumes the risks of a business venture.

Freight-in. Cost of delivering the merchandise from supplier to the purchaser; part of cost of net purchases.

Gross margin. Sales less cost of goods sold; also called gross profit.

Gross method. Initial recording of sales or purchases at their total invoice amount without regard to potential discounts, returns, or allowances.

Gross purchases. Total invoice price of all merchandise purchases without regard to potential discounts, returns, and allowances.

Gross sales. Total invoice price of sales.

Merchandise inventory. Cost of merchandise on hand ready for sale; also called inventory.

Net method. Initial recording of sales or purchases net of their expected discounts, returns, and allowances.

Net purchases. Gross purchases minus purchase returns, allowances, and purchase discounts, and plus freight-in.

Net sales. Gross sales minus discounts, returns, and allowances.

Periodic inventory method. Method involving a physical count of units of inventory on hand at the end of a period and multiplying the units by the cost per unit based on the cost of goods available and the total units available for the period.

Projected (forecasted) balance sheets. Forecasted balance sheets based on hypothetical transactions.

Projected (forecasted) income statements. Forecasted income statements based on hypothetical transactions.

Purchase discounts. Discounts given by some suppliers to customers when bills are paid promptly.

Purchase returns and allowances. Credit given for returned merchandise; allowances made for defective merchandise.

Quick ratio. Ratio of quick assets such as cash and receivables to current liabilities.

Sales. The amount of revenue recorded for a period based on delivery of merchandise, measurement of selling price, receipt of cash or a valid receivable or other asset, and reasonable determination of all relevant costs.

Sales discounts. Reduction in sales price given to customers for prompt payment.

Sales returns and allowances. Merchandise returned by customers for which credit is given, or the reduction in sales price given to customers due to defects in merchandise.

Subsidiary ledger. Individual accounts that have a control account in the general ledger, such as individual customer accounts receivable.

Write-off entry. Entry to eliminate a specific customer receivable from the accounting records.

APPENDIX KEY TERMS

Aging schedule. List of outstanding invoices and their probability of collection based on the length of time the invoice has been outstanding.

Installment sales. Sales of merchandise that involve payment over several months or years with interest charges added on the unpaid balance.

Percentage-of-sales method. Method of estimating bad debts based on a percentage of credit sales.

SYNONYMS

Allowance for Bad Debts; Allowance for Uncollectibles; Allowance for Doubtful Accounts.

Bad debts; uncollectibles.

Control account; primary account.

Gross profit; gross margin.

Merchandise inventory; inventory.

Pro forma; projected.

QUESTIONS

1. Explain how a merchandising business differs from a service business.
2. Describe the process entrepreneurs go through to set up their businesses. Why go through this process?

3. What are projected financial statements? How do they differ from those statements generated by an accounting cycle?
4. In drawing up a plan, what items must be considered for a merchandising concern?
5. How does the preoperating phase differ from the operating phase of a business?
6. Describe the periodic inventory method.
7. Explain the costs included in the goods available for sale amount for a period. Explain the subcomponents of each cost.
8. Describe the gross and net methods for recording purchase discounts and sales discounts.
9. How is cost of goods sold determined? Differentiate between cost of goods sold and cost of goods available for sale.
10. Define sales and the four criteria evaluated to determine if a sale is made.
11. How are the projected financial statements made at the beginning of an accounting period used at the end of the accounting period?
12. Explain how accounts receivable are created. Will all accounts receivable be collected?
13. Define sales discounts and sales returns and allowances.

APPENDIX QUESTIONS

14. Give two reasons why accountants analyze their outstanding accounts receivable for uncollectible accounts.
15. There are several ways to estimate bad debt expense. Describe two of the methods.
16. The Brody Company writes off a $5,400 invoice to J. Jones as uncollectible in 19x1. In 19x2, after winning the lottery, Jones decides to pay the invoice. What is the balance sheet effect of the entries the Brody Company records on its books when the payment is received?
17. Differentiate between the accounting treatment for a credit sale and treatment for a credit card sale.
18. What are installment sales?

EXERCISES

EXERCISE 5-1
L.O. 2

Determining Beginning Inventory

Renner Company has net sales of $240,000 and a gross margin of $60,000. Determine the beginning inventory of merchandise if net purchases are $170,000 and year-end inventory is $40,000.

EXERCISE 5-2
L.O. 2

Determining Cash Payments to Suppliers

From the beginning to the end of January, the Merchandise Inventory account balance increased by $8,000 and the Accounts Payable account balance decreased by $4,000. Cost of goods sold during January was $44,000. All inventory purchases were made on open account, and no merchandise was returned to suppliers. Determine the amount of cash paid to suppliers of inventory during January.

EXERCISE 5-3
L.O. 2

Determining Purchases

On April 1, 19x1, Geriatrics Supply, Inc., had $412,000 of merchandise in beginning inventory. On March 31, 19x2, ending inventory was $394,000. Cost of goods sold was

$1,529,000 for the year. During the year, GSI took discounts of $15,200 and returned $8,315 of merchandise. Determine gross purchases for the fiscal year ending March 31, 19x2.

EXERCISE 5-4
L.O. 2

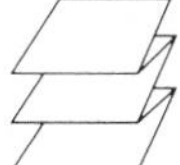

Recording Purchases

The following transactions are taken from the accounting records of Charles Plumbing Supplies, which records its merchandise inventory using the periodic inventory method:

Apr. 6 Purchase $25,000 of merchandise; terms 1/10, n/30, invoice No. 113.
8 Purchase $12,800 of additional merchandise; terms 2/10, n/20, invoice No. 21693.
10 Returned $900 of merchandise on invoice No. 21693 because of defects.
15 Paid invoice No. 113.
27 Paid invoice No. 21693.

Required:
Record the above transactions in general journal form using:

1. The net method.
2. The gross method.

EXERCISE 5-5
L.O. 2

Determining Cost of Goods Sold

Andrew's Country Store has the following information regarding its merchandise on December 31, 19xx, its year-end:

Beginning inventory	$ 31,000
Ending inventory	39,600
Freight-in	4,350
Purchases	465,900
Purchases discounts	2,525
Purchase returns and allowances	6,750

Required:
Prepare the adjusting entries at year-end to record cost of goods sold for the year.

EXERCISE 5-6
L.O. 2

Determining Cost of Goods Sold

Cannon, Inc., used the periodic inventory method. Prior to year-end adjusting entries, the following account balances were reported in the trial balance:

Purchases	$176,545	dr.
Freight-In	17,100	dr.
Sales Returns and Allowances	10,800	dr.
Purchase Returns and Allowances	21,400	cr.
Discounts Lost	9,500	dr.
Inventory, 1/1/xx	45,000	dr.
Inventory, 12/31/xx	40,000	dr.

Required:
Compute the cost of goods sold for the year.

EXERCISE 5-7
L.O. 3, 5, 6

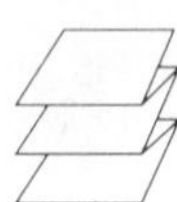

Sales, Sales Discounts, and Sales Returns and Allowances

Computer Parts, Inc. (CPI), has the following transactions relating to sales:

a. Sales of $36,000 on credit; terms 1/10, n/30.
b. Cash sales of $8,000.

c. Return of defective merchandise with a gross amount sold in (*a*) of $1,800.
d. Received payment within the discount period for $12,000 of the merchandise sold in (*a*).
e. Received payment for $10,000 of the merchandise sold in (*a*) after the discount period expired.

Required:
1. Record the above tr nsactions in journal form assuming CPI uses the net method to record its sales discounts.
2. Record the above transactions in journal form assuming CPI uses the gross method to record its sales discounts.

EXERCISE 5-8
L.O. 3

Determining Sales Revenue

The Jewel Corporation sells all merchandise on a credit basis. On January 1, 19x1, the Accounts Receivable account balance was $200,000. Cash received from customers in 19x1 was $470,000, of which $35,000 was advance payments on merchandise to be delivered in February 19x2. The Accounts Receivable account balance on December 31, 19x1, was $300,000. Compute the amount the Jewel Corporation should record as Sales Revenue for 19x1.

EXERCISE 5-9
L.O. 3–6

Determining Credit Sales and Bad Debts

Forward Auto Supply has the following information at their April 30 month-end:

Cash sales	$ 92,100
Cash collections on account	239,700
Sales discounts	1,250
Sales returns and allowances	3,100
Accounts receivable, 4/1	61,000
Accounts receivable 4/30	53,700

Returns and allowances were from credit customers. All sales are recorded using the gross method. No accounts receivable were written off during the year. Bad debts computed on the percentage-of-sales method is estimated at 1% of net credit sales.

Required:
1. Determine net credit sales for the month.
2. Prepare the adjusting journal entry to record estimated bad debts expense.

EXERCISE 5-10
L.O. 4

Accounts Receivable and Bad Debts

Nelson's trial balance before adjustments on December 31, 19xx, included the following accounts and balances:

	Debits	*Credits*
Accounts Receivable	$60,000	
Allowance for Bad Debts		3,000
Sales Revenue		$600,000

The company makes all sales on account. Using the aging method, the company estimates that $4,000 would be uncollectible. Accounts Receivable had a balance of $70,000 on January 1, 19xx, and the company wrote off specific bad accounts during 19xx in the amount of $5,500 which is reflected in the above account balances.

Required:
1. Prepare the summary journal entries for the 19xx transactions that resulted in the above trial balance amounts.

2. Prepare the necessary adjusting journal entry(ies) at December 31, 19xx, for the Nelson Company related to the above information.
3. Show how accounts receivable should be presented on Nelson's balance sheet at December 31, 19xx.

APPENDIX EXERCISES

EXERCISE 5-11
L.O. 3, 4, 6, 10

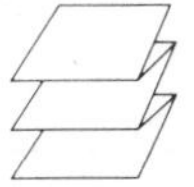

Accounts Receivable Related Transactions

Record the following transactions for World-Wide Toys, Inc.:

Oct. 16 Sold on account $64,500 of merchandise to Toys-R-Them; terms 2/10, n/30, invoice No. 31562. Sales discounts are recorded using the net method.
21 Wrote off as uncollectible invoice No. 16786 for $8,134 (net).
25 Received payment in full of invoice No. 31562.
30 Received $6,249 in payment of invoice No. 09553 which had previously been written off.
31 An aging of accounts receivable reveals $43,126 worth of accounts as uncollectible. The allowance account before adjustments has a $200 debit balance. Record the adjusting journal entry.

EXERCISE 5-12
L.O. 4, 10

Bad Debts

1. DRB Engineering had credit sales of $1,067,000 during 19xx. Prior experience has revealed 1% of these sales will be uncollectible. Bad debt expense for 19xx is:
   a. $21,340.
   b. $106,700.
   c. $10,670.
   d. None of the above.
2. Giles, Inc., has the following sales: cash sales, $68,000; credit sales, $740,500; credit card sales, $410,800. Giles estimates bad debts to be 1.5% of credit sales. Bad debts expense for the period is:
   a. $77,269.50.
   b. $11,107.50.
   c. $22,215.00.
   d. $18,289.50.
3. Baker Company had a beginning Allowance for Uncollectibles balance of $7,500 credit at January 1, 19xx, and an ending credit balance of $8,900 at December 31, 19xx. Bad debts expense for 19xx was $19,700. The write-offs of bad debts during 19xx were:
   a. $21,100.
   b. $19,700.
   c. $18,300.
   d. $8,900.
4. The Konrad News Agency has the following account balances before adjusting entries:

Accounts Receivable	$430,000 dr.
Allowance for Uncollectibles . .	3,260 cr.

   From an analysis of the customers' accounts using the aging method, it is determined $14,200 will be uncollectible. Bad debt expense for the period is:
   a. $4,300.
   b. $17,460.
   c. $43,000.
   d. $10,940.

EXERCISE 5-13
L.O. 4, 5, 10

Bad Debts

Village Depot, Inc., showed the following normal balances in its accounts prior to recording bad debt expense:

Gross Sales.	$185,000
Operating Expenses	93,500
Sales Returns and Allowances	14,000
Income Tax Expense.	12,500
Cost of Goods Sold	52,800
Allowance for Bad Debts	1,200

Forty percent of Village Depot's gross sales were on credit, and 55% of sales returns and allowances related to credit sales. The company uses the percentage of net credit sales method to estimate bad debt losses. Prepare the journal entry Village Depot would make to record its bad debt expense if the company estimates an expected loss rate on net credit sales of 7%.

EXERCISE 5-14
L.O. 10

Aging Accounts Receivable

Gorton's Jewelers, Inc., uses the aging of accounts receivable method to estimate its uncollectible accounts. Gorton's bookkeeper has compiled the following information from the company's accounts receivable subsidiary ledger:

Days Outstanding	*Total of Invoices*	*Estimated Uncollectible Percentage*
0–30 . . .	$115,000	10
31–60 . . .	90,000	15
61–90 . . .	48,000	25
91–120 . . .	15,500	50
121 + ...	1,000	80

On December 31, 19xx, the Allowance for Bad Debts account has a debit balance of $1,050.

Required:
Prepare the journal entry Gorton's would make to record its bad debts expense for 19xx.

EXERCISE 5-15
L.O. 10

Credit Card Sales

During 19xx, Carson's Fitness Center had total sales of $1,450,000. Customers used a major credit card on 30% of those sales. The credit card company charges a 1.5% fee. Record the journal entries Carson's would make to record the credit card sales and receipt of cash from the credit card company on those sales.

P R O B L E M S

PROBLEM 5-1
L.O. 2, 3, 7

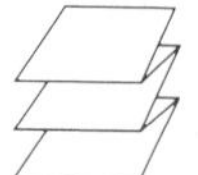

Purchases, Sales, and the Income Statement

The Maize-N-Blue Shop, Inc., had the following transactions during August 19xx:

a. Bought $25,000 worth of "M" shirts. Paid $10,000 in cash, the remainder on account.
b. Total cash sales for the month were $40,000.
c. Paid monthly salaries to employees of $5,000.

d. Paid $12,000 on account to supplier of shirts.
e. Incurred $4,000 of miscellaneous operating expenses. Paid $2,500 in cash with remainder on account.

Additional information:

a. Assume that all the shirts purchased were sold and that the shirts are the only product sold by the shop. All sales are for cash. There was no beginning inventory.
b. Interest expense on a note payable was $1,000 for the month of August.

Required:

1. Record the journal entries in journal form for the above transactions.
2. Prepare the income statement for the Maize-N-Blue Shop, Inc., for the month of August.

PROBLEM 5-2
L.O. 8

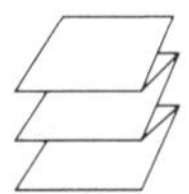

Preparation of Financial Statements

The adjusted trial balance for the Tinker Corporation at April 30, 19x2 (the end of its fiscal year) is shown below. The accounts are given in alphabetical order. Closing entries have not been made.

Tinker Corporation
Adjusted Trial Balance
April 30, 19x2

	Debits	*Credits*
Accounts Payable		$ 45,000
Accounts Receivable.	$ 103,400	
Accumulated Depreciation—Store Equipment		15,000
Accumulated Depreciation—General Office Equipment		1,000
Administrative Salaries Expense . .	42,500	
Advertising Expense	50,000	
Cash	47,000	
Cost of Goods Sold	604,000	
Capital Stock		312,000
Depreciation Expense—Store Equipment	3,750	
Depreciation Expense—General Office Equipment	250	
Income Tax Expense.	34,500	
Income Taxes Payable		7,500
Insurance Expense—Selling	4,500	
Interest Expense	14,000	
Interest Revenue.		3,250
Merchandise Inventory	377,500	
Miscellaneous Selling Expenses. . .	2,500	
Miscellaneous General and Administrative Expenses	750	
Notes Payable, Long Term		25,000
Note Receivable, Long Term	16,000	
Office Equipment	4,000	
Retained Earnings, 5/1/x1		115,900
Sales Returns and Allowances . . .	2,000	
Sales Revenues		905,000
Salaries Expense	89,000	
Store Equipment	37,500	
Salaries Payable		3,500
Totals	$1,433,150	$1,433,150

Required:
Using the above adjusted trial balance prepare an income statement and a balance sheet as would be required at April 30, 19x2.

PROBLEM 5-3
L.O. 2, 8

Determining Cost of Goods Sold and Preparing Financial Statements

The following trial balance was taken from the accounts of the Holmes Company at the end of its fiscal year. All adjusting entries have been made except for those to determine cost of goods sold. No closing entries have been made.

Holmes Company
Trial Balance
December 31, 19xx

	Debits	*Credits*
Cash	$ 3,350	
Accounts Receivable	5,720	
Allowance for Doubtful Accounts		$ 260
Merchandise Inventory 1/3/xx	20,760	
Purchases	112,650	
Purchase Returns and Allowances		680
Purchase Discounts		1,830
Freight-In	670	
Store Supplies	575	
Office Supplies	180	
Prepaid Insurance	935	
Store Equipment	19,410	
Accumulated Depreciation—Store Equipment		3,120
Office Equipment	4,210	
Accumulated Depreciation—Office Equipment		1,130
Accounts Payable		895
Salaries Payable		4,600
Capital Stock		20,000
Retained Earnings, 1/1/xx		4,585
Sales		200,195
Sales Returns and Allowances	510	
Sales Discounts	1,430	
Salaries Expense	31,950	
Rent Expense	9,000	
Bad Debt Expense	260	
Store Supplies Expense	3,550	
Depreciation Expense—Store Equipment	2,240	
Office Supplies Expense	840	
Depreciation Expense—Office Equipment	520	
Insurance Expense	935	
Communications Expense	2,500	
Utilities Expense	6,700	
Advertising Expense	8,400	
Totals	$237,295	$237,295

A year-end physical inventory disclosed that the ending merchandise inventory is $18,650.

Required:

1. Prepare in journal form the adjusting journal entries to determine cost of goods sold for the year and establish the December 31, 19xx, ending inventory balance.
2. Prepare an income statement for the year and a December 31, 19xx, balance sheet.

PROBLEM 5-4
L.O. 4, 7

Preparing Adjusting Entries

On December 31, 19x5 (Perlick Corporation's year-end), the following balances appeared in the accounts of the Perlick Corporation's unadjusted trial balance:

Perlick Corporation
Unadjusted Trial Balance
December 31, 19x5

	Debits	*Credits*
Cash	$ 15,970	
Accounts Receivable	23,100	
Allowance for Doubtful Accounts		$ 200
Merchandise Inventory	6,300	
Prepaid Insurance	3,360	
Note Receivable	10,000	
Equipment	86,600	
Accumulated Depreciation—Equipment		28,000
Accounts Payable		5,650
Notes Payable		8,000
Capital Stock		80,000
Retained Earnings, 1/1/x5		15,735
Sales Revenue—Credit		45,900
Sales Revenue—Cash		11,300
Cost of Goods Sold	37,180	
Rent Expense	5,500	
Salaries Expense	6,775	
Totals	$194,785	$194,785

Examination of the records and related documents provides the following additional information that should be considered for adjusting entries:

a. The Prepaid Insurance account is comprised of a $3,360 payment made on April 30, 19x5, for a two-year building insurance policy.

b. Perlick's credit manager estimates that the average expected loss rate for bad debt losses due to uncollectible accounts is 1% of 19x5 credit sales. It has also been determined that two individual customers' accounts totaling $375 will never be collected and should be written off. The company uses the percentage of sales method to record bad debt expense and estimates 19x5 bad debt expense to be $459.

c. The Note Receivable arose when the corporation loaned one of its employees $10,000 on August 1, 19x5. Both the $10,000 principal amount and interest are due on July 31, 19x7. Interest for 19x5 is $500.

d. The equipment was purchased on January 1, 19x1, at a total cost of $86,600 and is estimated to have a 12-year useful life to the company and a $2,600 residual value. Depreciation for 19x5 is $7,000.

e. Interest owed but not paid on the note payable is $800. Principal plus interest will be paid in 19x6.

Required:
Based on the above data, prepare the adjusting entries in journal form required on December 31, 19x5. New accounts may be needed.

PROBLEM 5-5
L.O. 8

Worksheet and Financial Statements

Taking the information from Problem 5-4, prepare a worksheet, income statement, and balance sheet.

PROBLEM 5-6
L.O. 4

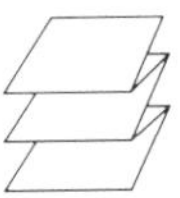

Bad Debts

The Wolverine Corporation's unadjusted trial balance at December 31, 19xx, shows a debit balance of $200,000 for Accounts Receivable. The Allowance for Bad Debts has a debit balance of $5,000. Net credit sales for the year were $2 million. The corporation uses the percentage of net credit sales method to record bad debts, and estimates 1% of net credit sales or $20,000 of those sales to be uncollectible.

Required:
1. Determine the bad debts expense for the Wolverine Corporation for 19xx.
2. Determine the balance in the Allowance for Bad Debts account for the Wolverine Corporation at December 31, 19xx, after adjusting entries.

PROBLEM 5-7
L.O. 2–6

Recording Purchases and Sales

The following transactions took place during the month of June 19xx for the Zach Company:

a. Purchased merchandise on account, $6,000; terms 2/10, n/30. All purchases are recorded using the gross method.
b. Purchased merchandise on account, $4,000; terms 1/15, n/45.
c. Purchased merchandise on account, $1,000; terms 2/10, n/30.
d. Purchased merchandise for cash, $1,500.
e. Purchased merchandise on account, $3,000; terms 1/10, n/30.
f. Made a sale on account, $1,000. All sales are made on terms of 1/10, n/30 and are recorded using the gross method.
g. Made a sale for cash, $200.
h. Because the customer had filed for bankruptcy, determined that an account receivable in the amount of $600 was uncollectible and wrote the account off.
i. Returned $300 of the merchandise purchased in item (*e*).
j. Made a sale on account, $3,000.
k. Made a sale on account, $4,000.
l. Paid for the merchandise in item (*a*) within the discount period.
m. Paid for the merchandise in item (*b*) but **not** within the discount period.
n. Collected on the sale referred to in item (*f*) within the discount period.
o. Recorded additional cash sales for the month, $3,200.
p. Recorded additional credit sales for the month, $29,000.
q. Recorded additional credit purchases for the month of $15,000. No discount terms were offered.
r. Paid for the merchandise referred to in items (*e*) and (*i*) within the discount period.
s. The customer who purchased merchandise in item (*k*) returned half of the order due to a mistake on the part of Zack Company.
t. Received payment for merchandise referred to in items (*k*) and (*s*) within the discount period.
u. Bad debt expense for the month is estimated to be $150.

Required:
Prepare in general journal form the journal entries for the above transactions.

PROBLEM 5-8
L.O. 7, 8

Posting Journal Entries and Preparing Financial Statements

On June 1, 19xx, Robins Merchandising, Inc., has the following trial balance:

Robins Merchandising, Inc.
Trial Balance
June 1, 19xx

	Debits	*Credits*
Cash	$ 9,000	
Accounts Receivable	20,000	
Allowance for Bad Debts		$ 1,000
Merchandise Inventory	18,000	
Accounts Payable		12,000
Capital Stock		20,000
Retained Earnings		14,000
Totals	$47,000	$47,000

Transactions and other information for June:

a. Credit sales	$400,000
b. Cash collections	395,000
c. Credit purchases	270,000
d. Payments to suppliers	275,000
e. Payments for salaries	65,000
f. Unpaid salaries at June 30	8,000
g. Payments for other expenses	48,000
h. Cost of goods sold	256,000
Merchandise inventory at June 30 . . .	32,000
i. Bad debts expense	4,000

Required:

1. Open T accounts for the above accounts with the balances provided. Post the transactions to the appropriate accounts opening any new ones as needed.
2. Foot the T accounts to the final month-end balances. Prepare the adjusting journal entry to determine cost of goods sold and post to the appropriate accounts.
3. Prepare a month-end income statement and the June 30, 19xx, balance sheet.

PROBLEM 5-9
L.O. 2, 3, 7

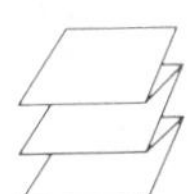

Filling in the Missing Data

Given below are various balance sheet accounts, income statement accounts, and other data for the Dolesky Corporation. Some amounts for accounts listed have been deliberately omitted. Not all accounts of the corporation are listed.

Selected Balance Sheet Accounts

	December 31, 19x2		*December 31, 19x1*	
	Debits	*Credits*	*Debits*	*Credits*
Cash	$82,000		$78,000	
Accounts Receivable	?		26,000	
Supplies Inventory	3,000		2,500	
Merchandise Inventory	45,000		50,000	
Equipment	40,000		40,000	
Accumulated Depreciation—Equipment		$16,000		$12,000
Income Taxes Payable		4,200		10,000
Retained Earnings		?		39,000

Selected Income Statement Accounts
For the Year Ended

	12/31/x2	*12/31/x1*
Sales	$108,000	$99,000
Cost of Goods Sold . .	?	44,000
Supplies Expense . . .	1,200	1,000
Net Income	20,000	16,000

Additional information for 19x2:

a. Credit sales $29,000
b. Purchases of inventory 27,000
c. Collections on accounts receivable 18,000
d. Dividends declared and paid by Dolesky. 4,000
e. Supplies are recorded as an asset when purchased

Required:
Using the information provided above, compute the following amounts for the Dolesky Corporation for 19x2:

1. Cost of goods sold for 19x2.
2. Depreciation expense for 19x2. No assets were purchased or sold during the year.
3. Accounts receivable at December 31, 19x2.
4. Cash sales for 19x2.
5. Purchases of supplies for 19x2.
6. Retained earnings at December 31, 19x2.

PROBLEM 5-10
L.O. 2–4

Accounts Receivable

Selected information at the conclusion of three consecutive years of operations of Floate Company follows:

	12/31/x3	*12/31/x2*	*12/31/x1*
Accounts receivable.	$ 500	$ 500	$400
Allowance for bad debts.	?	30	40
Inventory, beginning balance	?	70	60
Inventory, ending balance	?	?	70
Purchases (net).	?	810	?
Cost of goods available for sale . .	870	?	710
Sales	3,000	2,500	?
Cost of goods sold	810	790	?
Bad debts expense	24	17	20

The following additional information is available:

a. The balance in the Allowance for Bad Debts account was $38 at the beginning of 19x1.

b. Actual accounts receivable written off during these years were as follows:

19x1	?
19x2	?
19x3	$14

c. All sales are made on credit.

d. Bad debt expense is estimated at 1% of sales in 19x1.

Required:

Analyze the various accounts and determine the following:

1. Cost of goods sold for 19x1.
2. Cost of goods available for sale for 19x2.
3. Ending inventory balance for 19x2 and 19x3.
4. Purchases for 19x1 and 19x3.
5. Sales for 19x1.
6. Accounts receivable written off in 19x1 and 19x2.
7. Allowance for bad debts at 12/31/x3.
8. Cash collected on accounts receivable for 19x2 and 19x3.

PROBLEM 5-11
L.O. 2, 3, 5, 6

Sales and Cost of Goods Sold

The Joel Company uses the periodic method of recording its purchases of merchandise. The company's adjusted trial balance as of December 31, 19x2 (its fiscal year-end), appears below.

Joel Company
Adjusted Trial Balance
December 31, 19x2

	Debits	*Credits*
Cash	$ 63,200	
Accounts Receivable	10,000	
Allowance for Uncollectible Accounts		$ 2,200
Merchandise Inventory, 1/1/x2	40,000	
Purchases	110,000	
Purchase Returns and Allowances		2,000
Freight-In	1,000	
Store Equipment	60,000	
Accumulated Depreciation—Store Equipment		24,000
Accounts Payable		16,000
Income Taxes Payable		6,000
Capital Stock		80,000
Retained Earnings, 1/1/x2		18,000
Sales		204,000
Sales Returns and Allowances	4,000	
Administrative Expense	43,000	
Depreciation Expense	6,000	
Discounts Lost	4,000	
Income Tax Expense	6,000	
Dividends Declared and Paid	5,000	
Totals	$352,200	$352,200

A physical inventory count at December 31, 19x2, showed that the company's inventory on hand was $32,000.

Required

1. Prepare in journal form the adjusting entries to record the cost of goods sold for the period.
2. Analyze the above information and compute the following:
   a. Net sales.
   b. Net purchases.

c. Cost of goods sold.
d. Gross margin.

3. Prepare in journal form the closing entries and compute the retained earnings balance for the Joel Company on December 31, 19x2.

PROBLEM 5-12
L.O. 2–6

Sales

The Washington Company was formed on July 1, 19x1. It decided to use the periodic inventory system, offer terms of 2/10, n/30 on credit sales, record sales revenue under the net method, and to close its books annually on June 30. During its first year of operations, the following selected transactions occurred:

a. Sales for cash, $10,000.
b. Sales on credit, $120,000 gross price.
c. Allowances of $6,000 (gross price) were granted to credit customers who complained within the discount period about receiving damaged goods.
d. Returns of goods within the discount period by credit customers, $8,500 gross price.
e. Invoice price of collections from credit customers were on gross invoice amounts of $73,800 all of whom took discounts.
f. The credit manager estimated bad debts losses to be 2% of net credit sales for the year or $2,068.
g. Purchased $85,000 of merchandise, with no discount terms being offered.
h. A physical inventory indicated that $12,000 of inventory was on hand at June 30, 19x2.

Required:
Based on the above information, compute the following amounts for the company's first year of operation:

1. Sales discounts taken on cash collections from credit customers.
2. Net sales revenue.
3. Gross margin on sales.
4. Net accounts receivable in the balance sheet at June 30, 19x2.

PROBLEM 5-13
L.O. 1, 9

Operating Analysis

1. Projected or forecasted financial statements are used—
   a. Before operations begin.
   b. To provide insights to the future and visualize the possible results of future operations.
   c. At the end of an accounting period.
   d. All of the above.

Use the following data for 2 and 3.

Selected account balances from the Wolverine Company's general ledger are as follows:

Accounts Payable	$ 8,000
Accounts Receivable	45,000
Cash	15,600
Income Taxes Payable	5,000
Inventory	34,000
Notes Payable (due in 9 months)	30,000
Prepaid Rent	14,000
Salaries Payable	22,500
Supplies	3,000

2. Wolverine's current ratio is (round to two digits):
   a. 1.44.
   b. 1.95.
   c. 1.71.
   d. .93.
3. Wolverine's quick ratio is (round to two digits):
   a. 1.44.
   b. .93.
   c. .75.
   d. 1.70.
4. Accountants compare projected financial statements with actual financial statements to—
   a. Interpret the results of operations.
   b. Determine if potential problems exist.
   c. Revise plans for the future.
   d. All of the above.
   e. None of the above.

PROBLEM 5-14
L.O. 4

Receivables and Bad Debt Analysis

The Balance Corporation reported $35,850,000 in credit sales during 19x7. Credit receivables which were written off as uncollectible during 19x7 amount to $360,000. Bad debt expense for 19x7 is 1% (0.01) of credit sales for 19x7. The following balance sheet data are reported by Balance at the end of 19x7 (after adjusting entries):

Partial Balance Sheet Data

	December 31	
	19x7	*19x6*
Accounts Receivable	$2,700,000	$2,500,000
Less: Allowance for Bad Debts	160,000	150,000
Net Accounts Receivable	$2,540,000	$2,350,000

Required:
1. Reconstruct the journal entry(ies) to record the estimate for bad debt expense for 19x7.
2. Reconstruct the journal entry(ies) to record write-offs for 19x7.

PROBLEM 5-15
L.O. 9

Analysis of Balance Sheet Results

The following comparative balance sheet data were available for the Westend Corporation as of the end of 19x5:

Westend Corporation
Balance Sheet
December 31, 19x5
(in millions)

Assets	19x5	19x4	Liabilities	19x5	19x4
Cash	$ 3	$ 2	Accounts payable (Inventory only)	$10	$ 19
Accounts receivable	18	15	Notes payable	55	50
Inventory	47	50	Sales revenue received in advance	15	11
Equipment (net)	89	95	General expenses payable	18	12
Land	40	40	Total liabilities	$ 98	$ 92
Buildings	136	120	**Stockholders' Equity**		
Accumulated depreciation—building	(72)	(74)	Capital stock	125	125
			Retained earnings	38	31
Total assets	$261	$248	Total liabilities and stockholders' equity	$261	$248

Additional information ($000,000):

Dividends declared and paid to Westend's stockholders	$ 12
Cash payments on accounts payable during 19x5	103
Cash collected on accounts receivable during 19x5	148
Cost of building sold during 19x5	18
Accumulated depreciation on buildings sold during 19x5	5
Gain on sale of building sold in 19x5	7
Cost of equipment purchased during 19x5	6

Required:
Answer the following questions concerning Westend Corporation. (Hint: Set up T accounts to help solve for the missing information.)

1. How much depreciation expense was taken in 19x5 on equipment? No equipment was sold during 19x5.
2. What was Westend's net income for 19x5?
3. If total sales revenue reported for 19x5 was $170 million, what was the amount of 19x5 sales revenue from cash (versus credit) sales during 19x5? (Note that all $11 million of Sales Revenue Received in Advance from 19x4 was earned during 19x5. Also, there were no sales returns or refunds of any kind.)
4. How much inventory was acquired during 19x5?
5. What was the cost of inventory sold during 19x5?
6. Cash payments for general expenses during 19x5 were $60 million. What was the amount of general expense reported in the 19x5 income statement?

PROBLEM 5-16
L.O. 9

Analysis of Balance Sheet Results

Consider the following comparative balance sheet data (in millions) for American Brands, Inc., maker of tobacco products (Lucky Strike, Pall Mall), distilled spirits (Jim Beam, Gilbey's Gin), Titleist golf balls, Master locks, and many other consumer products:

Selected Balance Sheet Data	*As of December 31* 19x7	19x6
Assets:		
Accounts Receivable	$1,128	$ 692
Less allowance for uncollectibles	39	26
Accounts Receivable—Net	1,089	666
Inventories	1,693	1,264
Property plant and equipment	1,840	1,385
Less accumulated depreciation	775	640
Net property plant and equipment	1,065	745
Other assets	209	105
Liabilities:		
Accounts payable (all pertaining to inventory)	$ 316	$ 256
Accrued taxes payable	923	607
Long-term debt	1,631	671

The following additional data are assumed to be from either the income statement or the cash flow statement ($ in millions):

Cash received for plant and equipment sold during 19x7	$ 17
Loss on sale of plant and equipment sold in 19x7	20
Depreciation expense for 19x7	141
Taxes paid in cash during 19x7	349
Additional cash borrowed long term during 19x7	1,482
Other expenses for 19x7	950
Cash payments for inventory during 19x7	10,870
Bad debt expense for 19x7	118
Recoveries of prior year's write-offs during 19x7	3
Credit sales from 19x7	13,110

Additional assumptions:

a. All inventory is purchased on account.
b. Other assets are all for prepaid expenses.
c. Other expenses are all from expired prepaid expenses.

Required:

1. What was cost of goods sold for 19x7?
2. What were write-offs of bad debts for 19x7?
3. How much cash was collected on accounts receivable during 19x7?
4. How much cash was paid for prepaid expenses in 19x7?
5. What was 19x7 income tax expense?
6. How much long-term debt was retired in 19x7?

APPENDIX PROBLEMS

PROBLEM 5-17
L.O. 4, 10

Accounts Receivable

Zeron Nursery Company had the following before adjusting trial balance items at year-end on December 31, 19x1 (all accounts carry their normal balances):

Cash	$ 180,000
Accounts Receivable	2,200,000
Allowance for Uncollectibles . . .	228,000
Sales	10,500,000
Sales Returns and Allowances . .	300,000

Required:

1. Prepare adjusting journal entries for Zeron related to bad debts if—
   a. Two percent of net sales is used to estimate uncollectibles.
   b. The aging of Accounts Receivables method is used, and it is estimated that $380,000 of accounts receivable will not be collected.
2. Prepare the entries needed on January 25, 19x2, for the collection of a $12,800 account written off on December 1, 19x1.

PROBLEM 5-18
L.O. 10

Aging of Accounts Receivable

The Winston Company's accounting department has compiled the following information as of December 30 from its accounts receivable subsidiary ledger:

Month Issued	*Total of Outstanding Invoices*	*Estimated Uncollectible Percentage*
Dec.	$410,000	10%
Nov.	106,000	15
Oct.	62,000	25
Sept.	15,000	40
Aug.	16,000	60 (Aug.–Jan.)
July	5,400	
June	2,300	
May	1,100	
Apr.	0	
Mar.	4,200	
Feb.	0	
Jan.	10,000	

Winston writes all invoices off that are over a year old. The company uses percentages shown to estimate its bad debt expense.

At December 31, 19xx, the Accounts Receivable account has a debit balance of $632,000; the Allowance for Bad Debts account also has a debit balance of $1,350, before adjustments.

Required:

1. Prepare a schedule showing the aging of Winston's Accounts Receivable account.
2. Prepare the journal entry to record bad debt expense for the year.
3. Show the balance sheet presentation of accounts receivable on December 31, 19xx.

PROBLEM 5-19
L.O. 10

Receivables and Bad Debts Analysis

Bradley Corporation is a wholesaler doing business with a group of retail stores in the Los Angeles area on a credit basis. Bradley reported the following balance sheet data (after adjustment) as of the end of 19x4.

	December 31	
	19x4	*19x3*
Accounts Receivable—Retailers	$5,275,100	$2,967,800
Less: Allowance for bad debts	126,100	228,950
Net Accounts Receivable	$5,149,000	$2,738,850

Bradley estimates bad debt expenses at one half of 1% of credit sales. All sales are on credit. Bradley has experienced significant increases in sales during the past few years as noted in the following summary:

	For the Year		
	19x4	*19x3*	*19x2*
Credit sales (in millions)	$40.85	$32.70	$26.35

Required:
1. Reconstruct the adjusting journal entry that was recorded at the end of 19x4 to reflect the year-end estimate for bad debt expense.
2. Assume there are no collections on accounts once they are written off. What was the amount of write-offs recorded by Bradley during 19x4?
3. What was the amount of cash collected on accounts receivable during 19x4?
4. As a banker who has made large loans to Bradley, you are responsible for evaluating Bradley's credit position. Do you feel Bradley's creditworthiness is improving or worsening? Answer "improving" or "worsening" and give support for answer based **only** on the data provided—**do not** assume any additional facts.

CASES

CASE 5-1
L.O. 2, 7

Inventory and Cost of Goods Sold

Plastic Made, Inc., started business this year to purchase high-quality kitchen containers from several manufacturers for sale by mail order directly to customers. Now that the first year of operations is over, the accountant is trying to decide the best way to construct an income statement. The following facts are applicable to the first year:

Beginning inventory.	$ 0
Invoices received for merchandise during the year from the manufacturer	800,000
Damaged merchandise returned to the manufacturer	12,000
Invoices paid during the year on credit purchases	750,000
Freight-in paid by Plastic Made, Inc.	2,500
Freight paid by manufacturer	1,200
Inventory of merchandise on hand at year-end	30,000
Cost of supplies used in warehouse maintenance	500
Cost of wages for warehouseperson	22,000
Property taxes on merchandise	3,000
Cost of shipping to customers	4,000

Required:

1. Calculate and discuss how cost of goods sold is determined.
2. Discuss why certain items are not included in cost of goods sold and explain what effect they have on net income.

CASE 5-2
L.O. 8

Preparing an Income Statement—Monsanto Company

The following selected information appears in the 1985 annual report of the Monsanto Company, which provides a diverse product line ranging from chemical and agricultural products to low-calorie sweeteners and synthetic fibers (all amounts in millions):

Accounts payable	$ 522
Amortization expense	88
Cash	195
Cost of goods sold	4,841
Income tax expense	170
Interest expense	178
Interest revenue	63
Inventories	1,097
Land	101
Marketing and administrative expenses	919
Net sales	6,747
Other revenue	23
Technological expenses	548

There are several formats for income statements; two are shown below.

Format A:

Net sales	$xxx
Cost of goods sold	xxx
Gross margin	$ xx
Expenses	xx
Income from operations	$ xx
Other:	
Interest revenue or (expense)	xx
Miscellaneous revenue or (expense)	(xx)
Net income before taxes	$ xx
Income tax expense	xx
Net income	$ xx

Format B:

Revenues:	
Net sales	$xxx
Other revenue	xx
Total revenues	$xxx
Expenses:	
Cost of goods sold	$xxx
Detailed expenses	xx
Miscellaneous expenses	xx
Total expenses	$xxx
Net income before taxes	$ xx
Income tax expense	xx
Net income	$ xx

Required:
Prepare Monsanto's income statement for 1986 for each of the above formats. Discuss the differences in information transmitted by each.

CASE 5-3
L.O. 9

Cash Flow and Net Income

On November 10, 19x1, you, as a business consultant for MD Pizza, are present at the following conversation between two partners of a chain of pizza stores who are trying to decide if they should expand, starting January 1, 19x2, into a college town 50 miles west of their current region which currently includes 20 locations and a fleet of 40 delivery trucks.

"We need a loan to get started. Trucks are going to cost $200,000 and equipment $50,000. Leases on 10 locations, another $10,000 down. We have to lease the warehouse with a $5,000 deposit, and I project negative cash flow from operations of $10,000 for each of the first six months and breaking even for the second six months. That's another $60,000 we need plus interest on the amount borrowed at 10% minimum," says one partner.

"Without this new operation, we will probably have net income next year of about $600,000. If we go into it you mean we're going to have close to zero?" asked the other partner.

Required:
Explain to the partners the difference between cash flow and net income and discuss the effect of each item mentioned in the conversation above on both cash flow and net income. Assume that after starting operations all transactions are on a cash basis and that inventory levels for the new operations stay about the same at $200,000. Assume also that the company borrows the amount needed for the initial cash outflow and that any other cash deficiencies will be contributed by the partners.

CASE 5-4
L.O. 2

Analysis of Inventory Transactions—Gannett Company

Gannett Company is a diversified news and information company operating newspapers (including *USA Today*), television and radio stations, and other services. Their inventories consist largely of newsprint, printing ink, plate material, and production film for their publishing operations. A recent annual report included the following balance sheet data:

Excerpt from the Comparative Balance Sheets

	December 31	
	19x6	*19x5*
Inventories (asset) . .	$ 57,401,000	$53,999,000
Accounts payable . .	118,633,000	96,214,000

Assume that all inventory is purchased on account. Gannett reported expenses of $1,564,545,000 for 19x6. Assume cost of sales in 19x6 is $1,284,000,000 of this $1,564,545,000 amount.

Required:
1. How much cash was paid for inventory during 19x6? (Hint: Use T accounts to solve this case.)
2. How much of the inventory buildup (increase) required cash outflow?
3. Did the company's liquidity improve or worsen because of its inventory acquisition and payment activities?

APPENDIX CASE

CASE 5-5
L.O. 4

Accounts Receivable and Bad Debts—General Mills, Inc.

General Mills, a major competitor in consumer foods, restaurants, and specialty retailing with such popular items as Cheerios, Wheaties, and the Red Lobster restaurant chain, has the following information from its 1986 annual report:

General Mills, Inc., and Subsidiaries
Excerpt from Balance Sheet
(in millions)

	5/25/86	*5/26/85*
Accounts receivable	$220.0	$284.5
Allowance for doubtful accounts . . .	6.3	4.0

Assume General Mills writes off $4.2 million of accounts during the fiscal year 1986 and that they use the percentage-of-sales method to estimate bad debts. What effect does writing off bad debts have on cash flows, net income, and net assets? Explain.

FINANCIAL STATEMENTS

FINANCIAL STATEMENT COMPONENTS EMPHASIZED IN CHAPTER 6

Diamond Corporation
Income Statement
For 1991

Revenues
xxxx
xxxx
Expenses
Cost of goods sold

	1991	1990
Cost of goods sold . .	$XX,XXX	$XX,XXX

Diamond Corporation
Balance Sheet
12/31/91

Current assets
Inventory at FIFO cost
Less allowance to reduce inventory to market
Inventory at LCM
Noncurrent assets
xxxx
xxxx
Noncurrent liabilities
xxxx
xxxx
Stockholders' equity
xxxx
xxxx

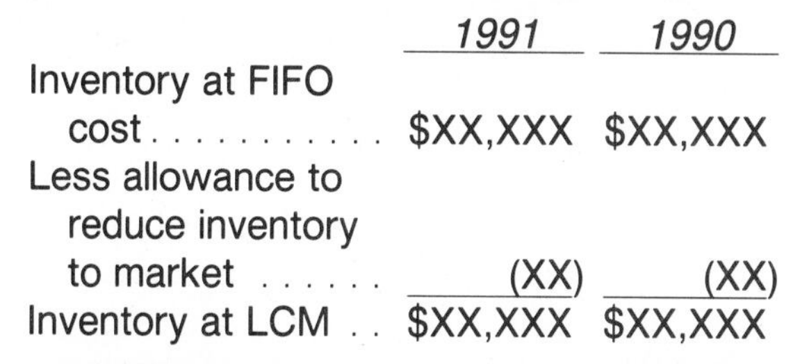

	1991	1990
Inventory at FIFO cost	$XX,XXX	$XX,XXX
Less allowance to reduce inventory to market	(XX)	(XX)
Inventory at LCM . .	$XX,XXX	$XX,XXX

Diamond Corporation
Cash Flow Statement
For 1991

Operating activities
Cash paid to suppliers
Investing activities
xxxx
xxxx
Financing activities
xxxx
xxxx

	1991	1990
Cash paid to suppliers	$XX,XXX	$XX,XXX

C H A P T E R 6

Inventory

LEARNING OBJECTIVES

After studying Chapter 6, you should understand:

1. The decision that managers must make in choosing between the periodic inventory system and the perpetual inventory system, pp. 291-93.
2. The four cost flow methods—specific identification (SI); first-in, first-out (FIFO); last-in, first-out (LIFO); and weighted average (WA)—and how they are used in periodic inventory systems, pp. 294-301.
3. The lower-of-cost-or-market measurement test, pp. 301-3.
4. The impact of inventory errors, pp. 303-4.
5. How to analyze inventory changes, pp. 304-8.
6. How to measure the cost of ending inventory using LIFO, FIFO, and moving average (MA) methods in a perpetual system (Appendix 6A), pp. 311-13.
7. The fundamentals of the retail method of estimating inventory value (Appendix 6B), pp. 315-17.
8. LIFO reserves and LIFO liquidation (Appendix 6C), pp. 317-19.

Along with investments in plant, property, and equipment, many businesses invest a large portion of their resources in inventories. The term *inventory* is used (1) to refer to a specific physical item of merchandise, (2) to identify a general category of merchandise, and (3) to refer to all merchandise that is included as an asset. Inventories are considered current assets since they will usually be converted to cash in less than one year (or, by definition, within the operating cycle).

Inventory consists of merchandise that is produced or obtained to be sold in the regular course of business for the purpose of making a profit. Companies can earn a profit from selling inventory because they add form, place, or time utility to the merchandise making it worth more to the buyer than the merchandise cost the seller. For example, a retail furniture store buys furniture from various parts of the world and provides place utility (through its retail location) and time utility (having the goods available when the customer wants them).

This chapter begins with a discussion of how managerial decisions affect the inventory costs reported in the financial statements. The major portion of the chapter examines the alternative decisions concerning (1) the selection of an inventory system, (2) the identification of inventory cost, (3) the selection of an inventory costing method, and (4) testing inventory cost relative to market value (lower of cost or market). The chapter also shows you how to analyze the inventory and cost-of-goods-sold figures on comparative financial statements, and concludes with three appendixes that provide additional inventory information.

IMPORTANCE OF INVENTORY

The efficient use of inventory has a significant effect on the performance of a business. For most merchandising and manufacturing businesses, inventory is the lifeblood of profitable business operations. (Although we do not discuss manufacturing companies in this textbook, manufacturing companies produce products that are sold to merchandising companies and other customers.)

Controlling the amount of inventory a business has on hand involves detailed planning. Merchandise that remains in inventory for long periods of time is not earning a return. In fact, merchandise that remains in inventory is costly to the business and results in (1) increased financing costs when merchandise is purchased with borrowed funds, (2) storage costs for space that could be available for other business operations, and (3) increased administrative costs to safeguard and keep track of the merchandise.

To finance inventory purchases, companies use the capital contributed by the owners, earnings from prior operations, or borrowed money. The more inventory the company has for sale, the larger the company's investment and the greater the need for funds to finance inventory purchases.

In the remainder of this chapter, you will learn some of the decisions that merchandising managers must make pertaining to inventory measurement. These decisions include:

1. Selection of an inventory system.
2. Identification of inventory cost.
3. Selection of an inventory costing method.
4. Testing inventory cost relative to market value (lower of cost or market).

The alternative choices examined in these sections are all within the framework of generally accepted accounting principles (GAAP), even though selection of alternative choices may lead to significant differences in inventory measurements and operating income, as you will learn.

SELECTION OF AN INVENTORY SYSTEM

Two types of inventory systems available to merchandising and manufacturing companies are the periodic inventory system and the perpetual inventory system. An **inventory system** enables the business to measure the cost of inventory on hand (the asset account) and the cost of inventory sold (the expense account). Recall that the **periodic inventory system** illustrated in Chapter 5 provided measures of ending inventory and cost of goods sold only (periodically) when a physical inventory count was taken and the ending inventory cost was computed. The set of accounts in a periodic system enabled the following computations to be made periodically:

Beginning inventory	$xxx	(from last period's physical count)
+Net purchases (computation below)	+ xxx	(from the purchases accounts)
Cost of goods available for sale	$xxx	
−Ending inventory.	− xxx	(from this period's physical count)
Cost of goods sold	$xxx	

The net purchases amount is computed from the following ledger accounts:

		Normal Balance
Purchases	$xxx	Debit
−Purchase returns and allowances (if any)	− xx	Credit
−Purchase discounts (if any)	− xx	Credit
+Freight-in (if any)	+ xx	Debit
Net purchases	$xxx	Debit

The periodic system was used by Byte-Size, Inc., in Chapter 5.[1]

The perpetual inventory system also permits the business to obtain a measure of ending inventory and cost of goods sold. However, the perpetual system does not use the purchases accounts to measure the asset and the expense related to inventory (ending inventory and cost of goods sold). Instead, in the **perpetual inventory system** records are kept so that the balance in Inventory and Cost of Goods Sold are continuously (perpetually) updated each time merchandise is purchased or sold. Rather than waiting until the end of an accounting period to measure Inventory and Cost of Goods Sold, these two accounts are

[1]You may wish to examine the periodic inventory system illustrated on pages 234-42 if you need to review this material.

updated on an ongoing basis. For example, consider the following comparisons for the purchase of $700 of merchandise inventory:

Entry to Purchase Merchandise

In a Periodic System			*In a Perpetual System*		
Purchases (A)	700		Inventory (A)	700	
Accounts Payable (L) . . .		700	Accounts Payable (L) . . .		700

The asset, inventory, is directly increased at the time merchandise is purchased in the perpetual system. Similarly, inventory is decreased and cost of goods sold is increased directly when merchandise is sold. Assume merchandise costing $500 is sold for $800. The following comparison may be made:

Entries to Sell Merchandise

In a Periodic System			*In a Perpetual System*		
Accounts Receivable (A) . . .	800		Accounts Receivable (A) . . .	800	
Sales (R)		800	Sales (R)		800
(no entry)			Cost of Goods Sold (E)	500	
			Inventory (A)		500

Objective 1
The decision that managers must make in choosing between the periodic inventory system and the perpetual inventory system.

Notice that the perpetual system records the use of merchandise at the time goods are sold, thus providing an up-to-date balance in inventory and cost of goods sold at all times. In a manual accounting system the continuous recording of additions (for purchases) and deletions (for sales) from each inventory item would make the perpetual system costly to use. However, with the increased usage of fast, high-powered computerized systems, more and more companies are using the perpetual system for inventories. Perpetual systems help reduce the chances of lost sales because of stockouts, and also help to reduce the quantity of inventory on hand by knowing when to reorder. Even department stores and grocery stores which carry hundreds of different low-cost items now use perpetual systems, many involving wands or electronic reading devices that scan sales tickets or coded labels to instantly reduce the inventory quantity of each specific item of merchandise as it is sold.

There are advantages and disadvantages to both perpetual and periodic systems. In general, periodic systems are simpler and less costly, while perpetual systems are somewhat more complex and more costly. However, even these generalizations may not always be true, and each specific situation should be evaluated to decide which system is most appropriate.

The journal entries and information provided by the periodic and perpetual systems are summarized in Exhibit 6-1. Note that both systems will not always provide the same results for the ending asset value and for cost of goods sold, as we will see in the next sections. You should carefully examine the similarities and differences in the two systems illustrated in Exhibit 6-1.

IDENTIFICATION OF INVENTORY COST

Costing inventory requires two pieces of information: (1) the number of units or other measure of inventory quantities (i.e., pounds, feet, and so on); and (2) the cost per unit. Below we consider these two components in order.

EXHIBIT 6-1

Accounting Entries for Periodic and Perpetual Accounting Systems

A. Comparison of Journal Entries to Record Events Concerning Inventory

Events	*Periodic*			*Perpetual*		
1. Buy goods on open account, terms 2/10, net 30.	**Purchases (A)**	600		**Inventory (A)**	600	
	Accounts Payable (L)		600	Accounts Payable (L)		600
2. Pay for freight on purchase of goods.	**Freight-In (A)**	60		**Inventory (A)**	60	
	Cash (A)		60	Cash (A)		60
3. Return 10% of goods purchased in (1) above.	Accounts Payable (L)	60		Accounts Payable (L)	60	
	Purchase Returns (XA)		60	**Inventory (A)**		60
4. Pay for 50% of goods purchased in (1) above within discount period.	Accounts Payable (L)	300		Accounts Payable (L)	300	
	Cash (A)		294	Cash (A)		294
	Purchase Discounts (XA)		6	**Inventory (A)**		6
5. Pay for 40% of goods purchased in (1) above after discount period.	Accounts Payable (L)	240		Accounts Payable (L)	240	
	Cash (A)		240	Cash (A)		240
6. Sell goods costing $410 for $700 cash.	Cash (A)	700		Cash (A)	700	
	Sales (R)		700	Sales (R)		700
				Cost of Goods Sold (E)	410	
				Inventory (A)		410

B. Ledger Balances before Adjusting and Closing Entries

Periodic		*Perpetual*	
Inventory (beginning)	$ 0	**Inventory (ending)**	**$184 Debit**
Purchases	600 Debit	**Cost of Goods Sold**	**410 Debit**
Freight-In	60 Debit		
Purchase Returns	60 Credit		
Purchase Discounts	6 Credit		

C. Adjusting and Closing Entries

	Periodic			*Perpetual*		
1. To adjust.	**Inventory (ending) (A)**	**184**		No entry.		
	Cost of Goods Sold (E)	**410**				
	Purchase Returns (XA)	60				
	Purchase Discounts (XA)	6				
	Inventory (beginning) (A)		0			
	Purchases (A)		600			
	Freight-In (A)		60			
2. To close.	Income Summary	410		Income Summary	410	
	Cost of Goods Sold (E)		410	Cost of Goods Sold (E)		410

D. Ledger Balances after Adjusting and Closing

Periodic		*Perpetual*	
Inventory	$184 Debit	Inventory	$184 Debit

Taking an Inventory Count

An inventory count must be taken at least once each year. This counting, called a **physical inventory count,** is required for both perpetual and periodic systems. In a periodic system it is needed to measure the ending inventory cost. In a perpetual system it is used to check on the accuracy of the perpetual records.

Taking a physical count requires special care for three types of inventory:

1. Inventory in transit.
2. Goods out on consignment.
3. Special-order goods.

When taking the physical inventory count, the inventory should normally include all merchandise owned by the business but not yet sold. This includes **inventory in transit** when the legal title to inventory has not passed to the buyer. The title to merchandise inventory **usually** passes to the buyer either at the time the merchandise is shipped by the seller or when the merchandise arrives at the buyer's location.

The seller's invoice usually indicates when the title of the goods passes to the buyer. For example, **FOB shipping point** indicates that the goods are free on board (FOB) to the seller's point of shipment only—the title passes to the buyer as goods leave the seller's location, and the buyer pays the freight from the point of shipment. **FOB destination** indicates that the goods are free on board (FOB) to the buyer's location. Title passes to the buyer as the goods are received at the buyer's location, and the seller pays the freight charges up to the point where the buyer takes delivery and title.

FOB shipping point and FOB destination are not the only possible inventory-in-transit situations. Title to inventory can pass to the buyer at any point agreed to by both buyer and seller.

Goods out on consignment are owned by the company but held by some agent of the company at another location for possible sale to customers. For example, farm equipment is usually owned by the manufacturer but held on consignment by farm implement sales agents in farming communities. The equipment is part of the manufacturer's inventory until sold by the agent.

When a customer places a special order for merchandise, the company usually assumes that it has made a sale as soon as the merchandise is ready to be delivered. In these cases, companies often ask for a down payment from the customer because the item is unique for that customer. If the **special-order goods** are on hand at the end of an accounting period waiting to be delivered to the customer, the company usually records the goods as a sale, and the item is not included in the company's inventory even though the company still has possession of the goods.

SELECTION OF AN INVENTORY COST FLOW METHOD

The identification of inventory cost is guided by a concept that applies to all assets. Inventory costs should include **all costs necessary to place the inventory into its intended useful state.** Application of the concept often requires professional judgment.

Costs that are assigned to units of inventory are called **product costs.** For a manufacturing company, accountants must use judgment to determine the product costs per unit for materials, direct labor, and other production costs. For a merchandising company, product costs usually consist of the invoice cost of merchandise, plus freight-in, and less any discounts for timely payment and for purchase returns and allowances.

While other costs may be included in merchandise inventory, in practice accountants rarely include them. Packaging costs, such as shopping bags, and assembly costs, such as costs for assembling bikes, could be assigned to merchandise inventory. However, most merchandisers expense these costs as *period costs* rather than include them in inventory as product costs. **Period costs** are costs incurred to generate revenue and are expensed in the period in which they occur (not assigned to inventory).

Because companies often purchase identical inventory items at different prices during the accounting period, accountants must use one of four alternative cost flow methods to measure the dollar value of inventory. These four methods, illustrated next, are: specific identification (SI); first-in, first-out (FIFO); last-in, first-out (LIFO); and weighted average (WA). Note that these four cost flow methods *describe* cost of goods sold and are used to measure ending inventory.

Inventory Cost Flow Methods: Periodic Inventory Systems

Accounting systems assign costs to inventories using the four common cost flow methods. However, before examining these methods, it is important to realize that the actual **physical flow** of inventory does not need to be the same as the **cost flow** used to measure inventory. In other words, physical flows of goods may be different than the cost flows **assumed** for inventory costing purposes.

If the cost of merchandise does not change over time, all four cost flow methods will result in the same measures of cost of goods sold and ending inventory. However, because the cost of most inventory items changes over time, the question that must be answered is: What unit costs should be assigned to the inventory units sold and what unit costs should be assigned to the inventory units remaining on hand at year-end?

When inventory is purchased at several different prices, some systematic cost flow method must be used to assign the actual unit costs paid to both the units sold and the units remaining at the end of the period. The method used to assign costs to units sold and units on hand does **not** need to be the same as the actual physical flow of goods and rarely is in practice. **However,** as illustrated below, **the total cost paid for all of the inventory available must equal the costs assigned (allocated) to the units sold (cost of goods sold) plus the costs assigned to the units remaining on hand (ending inventory) no matter which cost flow method is used.**

The four cost flow methods *describing* cost of goods sold are defined as follows:

1. **Specific identification (SI).** In the SI method, the actual cost of each specifically identified unit sold is charged to cost of goods sold. This method would be useful for inventories that are valuable and somewhat unique, such as precious jewels or automobiles. Specific identification is the only inventory costing method that values each unit of inventory at its actual cost. All other costing methods are based on *assumed* cost flows.
2. **First-in, first-out (FIFO).** The FIFO method assumes that the "first goods in" (beginning inventory, then the first purchases) are the first goods sold and assigns the actual cost of the "first goods in" to cost of goods sold.
3. **Last-in, first-out (LIFO).** The LIFO method assumes that "the last goods in" (most recent purchases) are the first goods sold and assigns the actual cost of the "last goods in" to cost of goods sold.

4. **Weighted average (WA).** The WA method measures the cost of the units sold (as well as the ending inventory) using the weighted average cost of all purchases. The weighted average cost is computed by taking the cost of goods available for sale and dividing by the number of units available for sale (beginning inventory plus purchases). This computation weights each purchase price in proportion to the quantity purchased. For example, 100 units at a cost of $5 each (total $500) plus 200 units at $4.25 each (total $850) results in a weighted average cost of $4.50 [($500 + $850)/(100 + 200)].

Jack and Maryann were both future accounting students at the University. They were hired by the Student Lounge to sell school supplies in the Lounge, which was owned by a local bookstore. Since this was a new venture for both the Lounge and the two students, they were not sure how to begin. Let's listen in on their conversation in April 19x1, their first year at the University.

Jack: Well, we at least have some kind of job to help us finance the cost of our introductory accounting course that we'll be taking in the spring term.

Maryann: Yea, but I'm not sure I know enough to develop an accounting system for these supplies we're supposed to sell.

Jack: Don't worry. The accounting professor we're going to have said to just keep track of our purchases and sales and by the end of spring term we'll know all we need to know about how to account for them.

Maryann: I hope she's right. I heard this course is a real killer.

Jack and Maryann are about to learn how to account for inventory for the Student Lounge. To illustrate the information needed and how it is used to cost out the ending inventory and measure cost of sales, we will focus on one of the items sold by the Lounge—a new erasable ink pen.

To illustrate these four methods, assume that during 19x1 the Student Lounge began selling a new erasable ink pen. The purchases and sales of the pens during 19x1 follow. Note that parentheses are used around the sales figures to remind you that these figures represent decreases in inventory.

	Units	*Unit Cost*	*Total Cost*	*Total Sales Revenue*
Beginning inventory	0	$ 0	$ 0	
Purchase, 5/1	40	6	240	
Sales, 5/1 to 8/30 at $8	(20)			$ 160
Purchase, 8/30	290	7	2,030	
Sales, 9/1 to 9/30 at $10	(245)			2,450
Purchase, 9/30	20	9	180	
Sales, 10/1 to 12/31 at $11	(35)			385
Units on hand at end of period	50			
Cost of goods available for sale			$2,450	
Sales revenue				$2,995

The specific identification method would not be appropriate for erasable ink pens which are low-value items with no specifically identifiable features. The other three methods would all be appropriate for costing something like erasable ink pens. The FIFO measure for cost of goods sold and ending inventory would be computed as follows:

FIFO cost of goods sold—Compute cost.
FIFO means earliest purchases are in cost of goods sold.

Units	×	*Unit cost*	=	*Total cost*
40	×	$6	=	$ 240
260*	×	$7	=	1,820
300				$2,060

*From the purchase of 290 units on 8/30.

FIFO ending inventory—50 units remaining.
FIFO means most recent purchases are in inventory.

Units	×	*Unit cost*	=	*Total cost*
20	×	$9	=	$180
30*	×	$7	=	210
50				$390

*From the purchase of 290 units on 8/30.

Since cost of goods sold plus ending inventory cost must always equal cost of goods available for sale ($2,450 in this example), **both** computations are not required. For example, given ending FIFO inventory of $390, we know that cost of goods sold must be $2,060 from the following:

Beginning inventory	$ 0
+Net purchases	+ 2,450
Cost of goods available for sale	$2,450
−Ending inventory (FIFO)	− 390
Cost of goods sold	$2,060

The LIFO cost of ending inventory and cost of goods sold for the Student Lounge data given above would be computed as follows:

LIFO cost of goods sold—Compute cost.
LIFO means most recent purchases are in cost of goods sold.

Cost of goods available for sale	$2,450
−Ending inventory (LIFO)	− 310
Cost of goods sold	$2,140

LIFO ending inventory—50 units remaining.

LIFO means oldest purchases are in inventory.

Units	×	*Unit cost*	=	*Total cost*
40	×	$6	=	$240
10*	×	$7	=	70
50				$310

*From the purchase of 290 units.

Be careful to note that, in this first illustration (summarized later in Exhibit 6-2), cost of goods available for sale is the **same** for FIFO, LIFO, and WA **because there is no beginning inventory.** Later on, when we illustrate the next period's results for the Student Lounge, you will see how each method results in a different (1) **beginning inventory;** (2) **cost of goods available for sale;** and (3) **ending inventory,** which is normally the case.

The **weighted average cost** for the Student Lounge example is computed to be $7 per unit, as follows:

$$\frac{\text{Cost of goods available}}{\text{Total units available (beginning inventory + purchases)}} = \frac{\$2{,}450}{350} = \$7.00$$

Therefore, ending inventory is $350 (50 units × $7) and cost of goods sold is $2,100 (300 × $7) using the weighted average method.

Objective 2
The four cost flow methods — specific identification (SI); first-in, first-out (FIFO); last-in, first-out (LIFO); and weighted average — and how they are used in periodic inventory systems.

The measurements of Student Lounge's ending inventory and cost of goods sold for 19x1 under the **assumed** cost flows—FIFO, LIFO, and WA—are compared in Exhibit 6-2. Remember that you do not have to actually sell the pens on a FIFO basis to use the FIFO cost flow method. Thus, the actual flow of the products need not be the same as the cost flows except when using the SI method. As a result, FIFO, LIFO, and WA are called **cost flow assumptions.**

Nature of Cost Flow Differences. Notice that the value of the Ending Inventory as reported in the balance sheet at the end of 19x1 and the amount of Cost of Goods Sold reported in the income statement of 19x1 will differ depending on which cost flow assumption is used. In the Student Lounge example, LIFO results in the lowest ending inventory value ($310) and the lowest gross margin ($855) but the highest cost of goods sold ($2,140), while FIFO results in the highest ending inventory value ($390) and the highest gross margin ($935) but the lowest cost of goods sold ($2,060).

In periods of increasing inventory costs, LIFO will generally result in the lowest net income and ending inventory value. Keep in mind, however, that the Student Lounge is really no better off using one cost flow assumption instead of another! The economic facts—the purchases and the sales—are constant, and the **cost flow assumption only affects the timing of when specific inventory costs are assigned to cost of goods sold.**

Jack and Maryann looked at the alternative results summarized in Exhibit 6-2 at the end of 19x1. The following conversation took place:

Jack: Well, we've got to decide which one of these cost flow assumptions to use.

Maryann: It looks like we are stuck with a periodic inventory system, which is

EXHIBIT 6-2

Student Lounge
Comparison of FIFO, LIFO, and WA for 19x1

	19x1		
	FIFO	*LIFO*	*WA*
Sales revenue	$2,995	$2,995	$2,995
Cost of goods sold:			
Beginning inventory	$ 0	$ 0	$ 0
Purchases:			
40 @ $6	$ 240	$ 240	$ 240
290 @ $7	2,030	2,030	2,030
20 @ $9	180	180	180
Cost of goods available for sale	$2,450	$2,450	$2,450
Less ending inventory (50 units):			
20 @ $9 and 30 @ $7	390		
40 @ $6 and 10 @ $7		310	
50 @ $7*			350
Cost of goods sold	$2,060	$2,140	$2,100
Gross margin	$ 935	$ 855	$ 895

*$2,450/350 units = $7 per unit weighted average cost.

good actually since it's so easy to use. Can you imagine keeping perpetual records for all these items?

Jack: Right! We could make a career out of this part-time job that way. Say, it looks to me like LIFO will give us the worst results since ending inventory is only $310 and cost of goods sold is the highest ($2,140). Maybe we should use it so students don't feel like we're ripping them off.

Maryann: Yes, but why not show the best results so we can ask for a raise? You know we're not exactly getting rich running this supply center. FIFO seems to make more profit since inventory is the highest while cost of goods sold is the lowest.

Jack: Yea, but don't forget, the Student Lounge has to file a tax return and pay taxes on its profits, so FIFO means paying more income tax too. That will actually result in less cash on hand to give us a raise or a year-end bonus.

The discussion between Jack and Maryann is one that has occurred many times in new businesses trying to decide which cost flow assumption to use. Does it really matter? Let's see what happens the following year. Assume that in 19x2, the Student Lounge had the following purchases and sales of erasable ink pens:

	Units	*Unit Cost*	*Total Cost*	*Total Sales Revenue*
Beginning inventory	50	?	?	
Sales, 1/1 to 3/31 @ $12	(40)			$ 480
Purchase, 4/1	100	$10	$1,000	
Sales, 4/1, to 9/30 @ $12	(110)			1,320
Units on hand at end of period	0			
				$1,800

By September 30, 19x2, all pens were sold, and the Student Lounge decided to discontinue the pens. The results shown in Exhibit 6-3 reflect the three alternative cost flow assumptions for 19x2, and for the years 19x1 and 19x2 combined.

Note that the **total cost of goods sold for the pens for the two years is the same for all three cost flow methods.** As a result, the total gross margin from the pens for the two years is the same—$1,345 for each cost flow method. However, the time when costs flow into income and when profit is recognized is different for each of the three cost flow assumptions. Thus, the Student Lounge example illustrates that total gross margin over the life of a business will be the same no matter which cost flow method is used, while timing is different.

Importance of Alternative Inventory Methods. Given the examples above, how should a company select a cost flow method? LIFO states the asset, inventory, at older costs but matches current costs against income. FIFO reports the asset at current costs but matches older costs against income. Under present accounting rules, no choice is available that would report both the asset and the cost of goods sold at the current cost of inventory when price changes occur.

From an economic standpoint, perhaps the method of inventory measurement that companies should use for financial reporting is the same method they use for income tax reporting. The tax laws are written in such a way that LIFO may be used for tax reporting purposes only if it is also being used for financial reporting purposes. This prevents companies experiencing increasing costs from showing high profits for financial reporting purposes (from using FIFO, for example) and lower profits for tax purposes by using LIFO. As a result, most com-

EXHIBIT 6-3

Cost Flow Assumptions of Student Lounge for 19x2 and Cost of Goods Sold for 19x1 and 19x2

		19x2		
	Units	*FIFO*	*LIFO*	*WA*
Sales revenue for 19x2		$1,800	$1,800	$1,800
Cost of goods sold:				
Beginning inventory	50	$ 390	$ 310	$ 350
Purchases (net)	100	1,000	1,000	1,000
Cost of goods available for sale	150	$1,390	$1,310	$1,350
Ending inventory	0	0	0	0
Cost of goods sold	150	$1,390	$1,310	$1,350
Gross margin for 19x2		$ 410	$ 490	$ 450
Total cost of goods sold:				
From 19x1		$2,060	$2,140	$2,100
From 19x2		1,390	1,310	1,350
		$3,450	$3,450	$3,450
Total gross margin:				
From 19x1 (see Exhibit 6-2)		$ 935	$ 855	$ 895
From 19x2 (see above)		410	490	450
		$1,345	$1,345	$1,345

panies experiencing rising costs (such as Student Lounge) should use the LIFO inventory method for financial reporting purposes so that they may currently minimize taxable income and income tax expense.

In the Student Lounge example, taxes would be lower in 19x1 under LIFO, which reports the lowest gross margin ($855). This temporary tax savings in 19x1 will eventually be offset, but at least temporarily the lower taxes will save the business cash, leaving more cash to invest or otherwise use to earn additional profits. In summary, while LIFO will generally provide the lowest net income for companies with increasing inventory costs, it will also result in lower income taxes and, therefore, cash savings available for use by the business. Since most companies have experienced increasing inventory costs over the past 20 years or so, it is not surprising that LIFO is the most popular inventory method among large publicly owned companies.[2] LIFO's real cash savings from reduced income taxes provides a greater benefit than the higher accrual net income that could be reported under FIFO or other alternatives.

Inventory Cost Flow Methods: Perpetual Inventory Systems

The four inventory cost flow methods that are used in periodic systems are also used in perpetual systems. However, LIFO and WA usually result in different inventory measures for perpetual and periodic systems. On the other hand, **SI and FIFO yield the same results in both perpetual and periodic systems.** In a perpetual system, the WA method is called **moving average (MA)** method because a new weighted average is computed each time goods are purchased.

Detailed examples of the LIFO, FIFO, and WA cost flow methods applied to the perpetual system using the Student Lounge data are provided in Appendix 6A.

Consistency and Inventory Measurement

One of the primary principles of accounting is the **consistency principle,** which means that accounting methods should be applied on a consistent basis from year to year whenever possible. When a company makes a change in the basis used to prepare its financial statements, the effect of the change must be adequately disclosed to financial statement users.

The consistency principle also suggests that a company should use the same inventory cost flow method each year. When reasonable justification results in changes in inventory cost flow methods, the effect of the change on the ending inventory and the net income must be fully disclosed in financial statements.

TESTING INVENTORY COST RELATIVE TO MARKET VALUE (LOWER OF COST OR MARKET)

In accounting, many instances occur where **conservative measurement procedures are used to recognize (record) all possible losses and costs as soon as they become apparent but to recognize (record) gains or profits only after they are clearly realized or realizable.** One of the areas in which these conservative rules apply is inventory measurement. Once a company has determined its inventory cost using one of the cost flow methods, the company must determine if the market value of the inventory is below cost. When market value is less than cost, the inventory must be written down to the market value according to the **lower-of-cost-or-market (LCM) valuation method.**

[2]See *Accounting Trends and Techniques: 1989* (New York: AICPA, 1989).

To compare the cost of inventory to market values, companies use the current cost to replace the existing inventory at the end of the period—called the inventory's **current replacement cost.** If the current replacement cost of the inventory on hand at the end of the year is less than its original cost, then an adjusting entry (LCM adjustment) such as the following is required:

19xx			
Dec. 31	Cost of Goods Sold (E)	xxx	
	Merchandise Inventory (A)		xxx
	To record write-down of inventory to its current replacement cost.		

To illustrate, in anticipation of the coming holiday season, Kay Dee Toys, Inc., acquired 1,000 cabbage batch rabbits for $15 per unit in September 19xx. The company expected the rabbits to be a big seller at $25 each, but a new product, cabbage batch dogs, turned out to be the most popular item in 19xx. By the end of 19xx, Kay Dee still had 500 unsold rabbits with a cost of $7,500 (500 × $15) in inventory. The replacement cost of the rabbits at the end of 19xx was $10 per unit and was not expected to increase in the near future. Kay Dee Toys was in the following position at the end of 19xx:

Item	*Quantity*	*FIFO Cost*	*Replacement Cost*	*Lower of Cost or Market*
Cabbage batch rabbits . .	500	$7,500	$5,000	$5,000

The entry at the end of 19xx would be:

19xx			
Dec. 31	Cost of Goods Sold (E)	2,500	
	Merchandise Inventory (A)		2,500
	To record write-down of inventory.		

Objective 3
The lower-of-cost-or-market measurement test.

The LCM method should be applied to inventory at the end of each accounting period. LCM may be applied to each type of inventory item separately (rabbits, dogs, and so on); to each category of inventory item (e.g., stuffed animals and dolls); or to inventory in total (e.g., all toys at their total cost versus their total replacement cost).

For example, assume that Kay Dee Toys has only two categories of inventory (cabbage batch group and train sets) on hand at the end of 19xx (see Exhibit 6-4). Note that the item-by-item basis of LCM shown in the exhibit results in the lowest possible LCM inventory measurement. This will always be true when the item-by-item basis is used.

Normally, the group-of-items basis and the total-inventory basis of applying LCM will generate different results as illustrated in Exhibit 6-4. In Exhibit 6-4, LCM on the total-all-items basis ($33,805) is equal to FIFO cost. LCM on the group basis ($33,435) and item-by-item basis ($30,755) are both less than FIFO cost and would require an adjusting entry similar to that illustrated for the rabbits above.

Inventory Errors

It is not uncommon to have some errors in inventory quantities and/or costs in companies which handle large quantities of many different types of merchandise. The physical count taken at the end of the accounting period and the costing of the quantities on hand will often locate these errors.

EXHIBIT 6-4

LCM Method As Used by Kay Dee Toys

	Quantity	FIFO Cost	Replacement Cost	LCM Basis: Item-by-Item LCM	Group-of-Items LCM	Total-All-Items LCM
		For individual LCM ↓	↓	↓		
Cabbage batch group:						
Rabbits	500	$ 7,500	$ 5,000	$ 5,000		
Dogs	300	6,000	7,500	6,000		
Infants	190	4,180	4,370	4,180		
Babies	350	6,300	7,525	6,300		
Total cabbage batch group		$23,980	$24,395	$21,480	$23,980	
		↑	↑	For group LCM	↑	
Train sets:						
L1450	90	$ 4,500	$ 4,680	$ 4,500		
J1620	75	3,375	3,150	3,150		
TYC050	65	1,950	1,625	1,625		
Total train sets		$ 9,825	$ 9,455	$ 9,275	$ 9,455	
		↑	↑	For group LCM	↑	
Grand total		$33,805	$33,850	$30,755	$33,435	$33,805
		↑	↑	For total inventory LCM		↑

Objective 4
The impact of inventory errors.

When errors are made and identified in the same accounting period, correcting entries are used to correct the books. For example, assume Marker, Inc., took a physical count at the end of 19x3 and found 100 units of chalk marking rods on hand. The perpetual records revealed that 120 units at $10 each should have been on hand. The 20 missing units could have been lost, damaged and thrown out, or stolen by employees or customers. In any case, the inventory must be written down to reflect the actual number of units on hand. The following error correction would be made:

19x3			
Dec. 31	Cost of Goods Sold (E)	200	
	Inventory (A)		200
	To write down the loss of 20 chalk marking rods.		

Most inventory errors are discovered in the same period that they occur as long as accurate physical counts are taken and costing the quantities is done correctly.

Inventory errors that effect more than one year are normally **self-correcting errors,** also called **counterbalancing errors.** These errors will correct themselves the next year in most cases. To illustrate a counterbalancing error, assume that at the end of 19x4 Marker, Inc., made an error in the physical count of the year-end inventory, reporting 120 units of an item on hand at $1,500 each instead of 102 units on hand at $1,500 each. Assume Marker uses a periodic inventory system and the cost of goods available for sale in 19x4 was $975,000. Further assume that net purchases for 19x5 were 500 units at $1,500 each ($750,000), and that the ending inventory count at the end of 19x5 correctly reported 115 units on hand at $1,500 each. The following analysis shows that the incorrect results for 19x4 are offset in 19x5, so that the sum of the two years' incorrect results equal the sum of the two years' correct results:

	Incorrect Results		*Correct Results*	
	19x4	*19x5*	*19x4*	*19x5*
Beginning Inventory	$ 0	$180,000	$ 0	$153,000
+Purchases (net)	975,000	750,000	975,000	750,000
Cost of Goods available	**$975,000**	$930,000	**$975,000**	$903,000
−Ending Inventory	180,000	**172,500**	153,000	**172,500**
Cost of Goods Sold	$795,000	$757,500	$822,000	$730,500
Total Cost of Sales: 19x4 + 19x5	**$1,552,500**		**$1,552,500**	

The inventory at the end of 19x5 is the same ($172,500) in both cases, and the total amount of expense (cost of goods sold) over the two-year period is also the same ($1,552,500)! While not all inventory errors are counterbalancing, most errors not found in the period they originate (i.e., 19x4 in the example above) will automatically correct themselves in the following period.

ANALYSIS OF INVENTORY CHANGES

So far this chapter has illustrated the alternative ways a company may elect to measure, record, and report its inventory. Like many other chapters, the illustrations of inventory systems and costing methods use more information than we normally find in a set of published financial statements. This section of the chapter makes an attempt to explain what inventory data are normally provided in financial statements, and illustrates how we can analyze these inventory data to obtain information not specifically reported in the statements.

Assume you are looking over a company's annual report. What information related to inventory is available in the financial statements? The following data should be available from the company's comparative balance sheets and income statement in virtually every case:

Balance sheet data:

- Beginning inventory balance (= last year's ending inventory balance).
- Ending inventory balance.
- Beginning accounts payable balance (= last year's ending balance).
- Ending accounts payable balance.

Income statement data:

- Cost of goods sold for the current period.

Note that in analyzing financial statements, the above data should be available regardless of whether a perpetual or periodic system is employed, since both systems must report ending inventory and cost of goods sold each period. *In fact, it is not possible to determine whether a perpetual or a periodic system is in use by looking at the published financial statements.*

While the financial statements do not normally tell us (1) the amount of inventory purchased (or made) during the year, or (2) the payments made to inventory suppliers, these data may be of interest to us. By understanding the interrelationship between the accounts used to measure and record inventory, as illustrated in the chapter, we will be able to estimate these two pieces of information, as well as others. First, let's summarize what we learned in the chapter concerning the general types of business transactions that result in increases or decreases in Inventory, Accounts Payable, and Cost of Goods Sold:

Objective 5
How to analyze inventory changes.

1. Inventory is decreased and Accounts Payable is increased when merchandise is acquired on account.
2. Inventory is decreased and Cost of Goods Sold is increased when merchandise is sold.
3. Accounts Payable is decreased and Cash is decreased when payment is made for merchandise acquisitions on account.

Note that these generalizations may not always be correct while accounting for ongoing transactions. For instance, the Inventory account is not increased when purchases are made in a periodic system, the Purchases account is increased instead. However, in looking back in time and analyzing the past financial statements of a company, we will see that these generalizations are always appropriate. Based on the effects of the three transactions summarized above and the financial statement balances in Inventory, Accounts Payable, and Cost of Goods Sold, the interrelationship between these three accounts is summarized in Exhibit 6-5.

The following example illustrates how to determine (1) the amount of inventory purchased during the year and (2) the payments made to the suppliers. To begin, assume the following facts are obtained from the two-year comparative balance sheets and income statement of the Arens Corporation, as shown below in T account form.

Accounts Payable

	Beg. bal., 1/1/xx	3,400
?		?
	End. bal., 12/31/xx	4,200

Cost of Goods Sold

47,800	

Merchandise Inventory

Beg. bal., 1/1/xx	7,200	
	?	?
End. bal., 12/31/xx	8,100	

EXHIBIT 6-5

Relationship to Accounts Payable, Cost of Goods Sold, and Cash to Merchandise Inventory

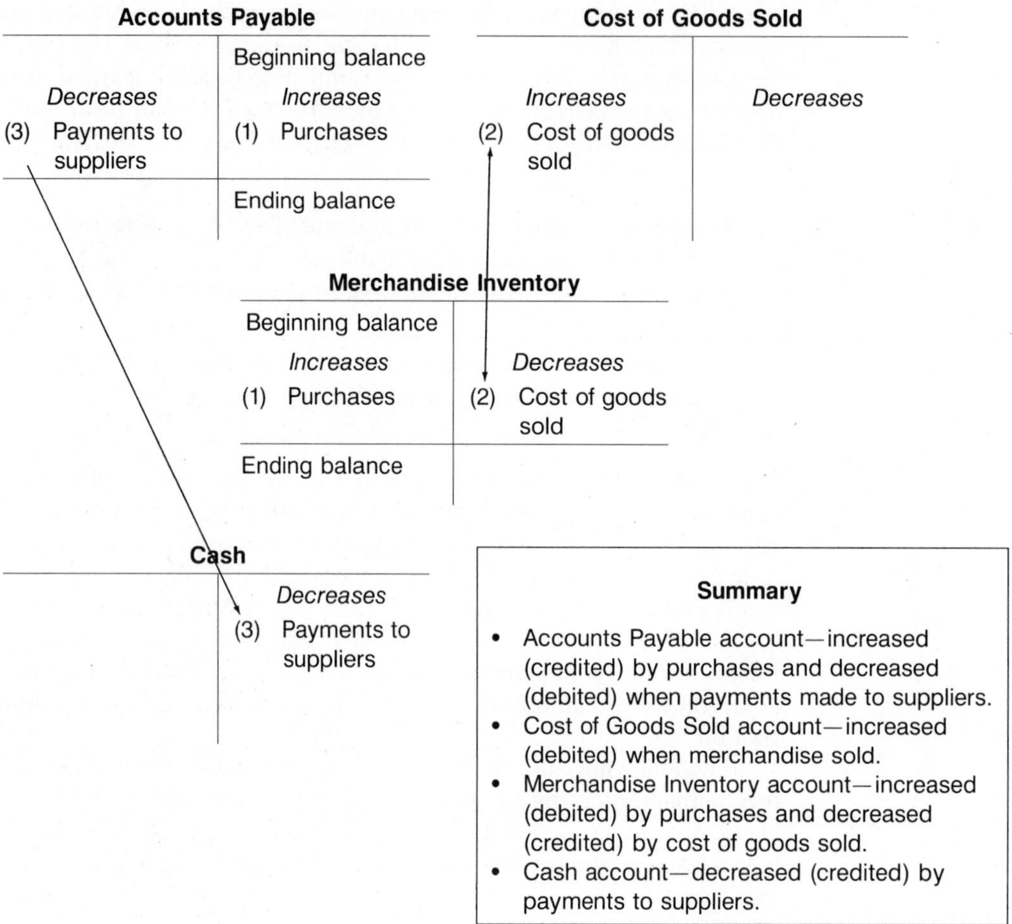

By using the following steps we will insert the missing information into the above accounts to arrive at the information given in Exhibit 6-6.

Step 1. The $47,800 debit (increase) shown in the Cost of Goods Sold above must also be shown as a decrease (credit) in the Merchandise Inventory account (see Exhibit 6-6). (This is the same as entry [2] in Exhibit 6-5.)

Step 2. By decreasing Merchandise Inventory $47,800, we must increase inventory by $48,700 to explain the $900 increase in the Merchandise Inventory balance. The following formula can be used to determine the amount of merchandise inventory purchases that should be placed on the debit side of Merchandise Inventory:

Ending inventory balance		Beginning inventory balance		Cost of goods sold		Merchandise inventory purchases
$8,100	−	$7,200	+	$47,800	=	$48,700

EXHIBIT 6-6

Determining Purchases and Accounts Payable for Year

Accounts Payable

			3,400
Step 3	47,900	Step 2	48,700
			4,200

Cost of Goods Sold

Step 1	47,800	

Merchandise Inventory

	7,200		
Step 2	48,700	Step 1	47,800
	8,100		

Cash

	Step 3	47,900

Summary

Merchandise purchased during year:
$8,100 – $7,200 + $47,800 = $48,700
Payments made on account:
$3,400 + $48,700 – $4,200 = $47,900

Now, we have answered the first question: How much inventory did Arens purchase during the year? Next, the amount of inventory purchases—$48,700—is inserted as a credit in the Accounts Payable account as shown in Exhibit 6-6 because we assume all purchases are made on credit. (This is entry [1] in Exhibit 6-5.)

Step 3. Since we know that $48,700 merchandise was purchased during the year and have inserted this amount in Accounts Payable, we are ready to answer the second question: How much did Arens pay suppliers during the year? This amount can be determined from the following formula:

Beginning Accounts Payable balance	+	Merchandise inventory purchases	–	Ending Accounts Payable balance	=	Amount paid on Accounts Payable
$3,400	+	$48,700	–	$4,200	=	$47,900

Accounts Payable can be forced to balance by decreasing (debiting) the Accounts Payable account $47,900 and decreasing (crediting) Cash as shown in Exhibit 6-6. (This is entry [3] in Exhibit 6-5.)

Note that it is possible that inventory is acquired for cash rather than on account. To the extent that there are cash purchases, both the increases and decreases to Accounts Payable are equally overstated. Notice, however, that this offsetting error created by the assumption of only credit purchases does **not** affect the accuracy of your answer to the second question: the amount of the payments to suppliers.

When you understand the interrelationships between inventory changes and cost of goods sold, accounts payable, and other accounts, you are better equipped to evaluate the financial position of a company. And you will be able to "read between the lines" of financial statements and obtain information about a company that is not specifically reported.

SUMMARY

This chapter began with a discussion of the four measurement decisions that managers must make pertaining to inventory. The four inventory measurement decisions examined in the chapter are:

1. Selection of an inventory system:
   a. Periodic system.
   b. Perpetual system.
2. Identification of inventory costs:
   a. Taking a physical inventory.
3. Selection of a cost flow method:
   a. Specific identification (SI) method.
   b. First-in, first-out (FIFO) method.
   c. Last-in, first-out (LIFO) method.
   d. Weighted average (WA) method (or moving average method).
4. Testing inventory cost relative to market value (lower of cost or market):
   a. Item-by-item basis.
   b. Group-of-items basis.
   c. Total-all-items basis.

The inventory measurement decisions made by a company will generally not have any serious economic consequences. While the different measurement methods (e.g., SI, FIFO, LIFO, and WA) will result in different asset and net income figures in any given period, over the life of the firm they will all generate the same total income. These different inventory measurement methods are essentially allocating a given pool of inventory dollars (equal to the total actual cost of inventory) to income at different points in time. As a result, the alternative inventory measurements may be viewed as being different in the timing of their release of inventory costs to periodic earnings.

The major exception to this general evaluation of "what's going on" with alternative inventory measurements stems from the income tax consequences resulting from the use of the LIFO method. Using LIFO rather than some other method in periods of increasing inventory costs will generally result in the real economic benefit of lower income taxes, all else being equal.

The lower-of-the-cost-or-market (LCM) test was illustrated after the coverage of cost flow methods. It should be noted, however, that the LCM test is a required aspect of inventory measurement, not an option. The impact of inventory errors was also illustrated in the chapter, with examples explaining the effect of errors on financial statements. The chapter concluded with an analysis of inventory changes. This aspect of the chapter showed you how to use information from comparative statements to determine new information—the amount of inventory purchased during the year and the amount paid to suppliers. If you have a chance to see an annual report of an actual company, practice your skill in applying this knowledge.

DEMONSTRATION EXERCISE

The A. J. Company had the following activity during the year:

Date	Transaction	Units	Unit Cost	Unit Selling Price
1/1	Beginning inventory. .	1,000	$2.00	
3/31	Purchase No. 1. . . .	2,000	2.75	
6/30	Sale No. 1	2,500		5.50
8/25	Purchase No. 2. . . .	2,000	3.50	
11/15	Sales No. 2	2,250		7.00

Selling price is always 200% of the most recent purchase cost per unit.

Required:
Calculate the total sales, cost of goods sold, and gross margin based on:

1. LIFO periodic.
2. Weighted average periodic.
3. FIFO periodic.

Solution:
Total sales:

Sale	Units		
No. 1	2,500	× $5.50 =	$13,750
No. 2	2,250	× 7.00 =	15,750
	4,750		$29,500

Cost of goods sold (4,750 total units sold):

LIFO periodic:

Units			
2,000	× $3.50 =	$ 7,000	
2,000	× 2.75 =	5,500	
750	× 2.00 =	1,500	
4,750		$14,000	Cost of Goods Sold

Weighted average periodic:

$$\frac{[(1{,}000 \times \$2.00) + (2{,}000 \times \$2.75) + (2{,}000 \times \$3.50)]}{5{,}000} = \$2.90$$

4,750 × \$2.90 = \$13,775 Cost of Goods Sold

FIFO periodic:

Units			
1,000 × $2.00 =	$ 2,000		
2,000 × 2.75 =	5,500		
1,750 × 3.50 =	6,125		
4,750	$13,625	Cost of Goods Sold	

Gross margin summary:

	LIFO	*WA*	*FIFO*
Sales	$29,500	$29,500	$29,500
Cost of goods sold . .	14,000	13,775	13,625
Gross margin.	$15,500	$15,725	$15,875

A P P E N D I X 6 A

Cost Flow Methods — Perpetual Inventory System

The Student Lounge example that we analyzed in the chapter used the periodic inventory system. In this appendix, the Student Lounge example is presented as using the perpetual system. This will illustrate how the cost flow computations of the perpetual inventory system are affected by the **pattern of purchases and sales.**

Consider once again the purchases and sales data in the Student Lounge example on page 296. Notice that the sales data were only used to compute total sales in the earlier examples. Since the periodic system only computes cost of goods sold at the end of the accounting period, there is no need to record the cost for each sale. However, the perpetual system records the cost of each sale and the reduction in inventory that results from each sale as follows:

Accounts Receivable (A)	xxx	
Sales (R)		xxx
To record sales on credit.		

Cost of Goods Sold (E)	yyy	
Merchandise Inventory (A)		yyy
To record the cost of sales.		

The cost to be recorded at the time of sales depends on the cost flow method used by the company.

LIFO PERPETUAL COST FLOW METHOD

Using the LIFO perpetual cost flow method for the Student Lounge data on page 296, the following computation schedule illustrates how to determine the costs for reducing inventory and increasing Cost of Goods Sold at the time of each (summary) sales entry.

LIFO Perpetual Record
Merchandise Inventory—Erasable Pens

Description and Computation	*Units*	*Unit Cost*	*Total Cost*
Beginning balance	0	$0	$ 0
Purchase 5/1	40	6	240
Sold 20 units @ $6 = $120	(20)	6	(120)
Balance: From 5/1, 20 @ $6 = $120	20	6	$ 120
Purchase, 8/30	290	7	2,030
Sold 245 units @ $7 = $1,715	(245)	7	(1,715)
Balance: From 5/1, 20 @ $6 = $120			
From 8/30, 45 @ $7 = $315			
65 $435	65		$ 435
Purchase, 9/30	20	9	180
Sold 35 units, 20 @ $9 = $180			
15 @ $7 = 105			
35 $285	(35)		(285)
Balance: From 5/1, 20 @ $6 = $120			
From 8/30, 30 @ $7 = 210			
50 $330	50		$330

The entries to record the purchases and sales are:

Date	*Accounts*	*Dr.*	*Cr.*
May 1	Inventory (A)	240	
	Accounts Payable (L)		240
May 2–Aug. 30	Cost of Goods Sold (E)	120	
	Inventory (A)		120
Aug. 30	Inventory (A)	2,030	
	Accounts Payable (L)		2,030
Aug. 31–Sept. 30	Cost of Goods Sold (E)	1,715	
	Inventory (A)		1,715
Sept. 30	Inventory (A)	180	
	Accounts Payable (L)		180
Oct. 1–Dec. 31	Cost of Goods Sold (E)	285	
	Inventory (A)		285

The inventory T account would show the following:

Inventory—Erasable Pens

Bal.	0		
5/1	240	5/1 to 8/30	120
8/30	2,030	9/1 to 9/30	1,715
9/30	180	10/1 to 12/31	285
12/31 Bal.	330		

MOVING AVERAGE COST FLOW METHOD

In the perpetual system, the moving average method requires that a new average inventory cost be computed *after each purchase*. The following computation schedule illustrates the moving average calculation procedures for the Student Lounge example. The ending balance of 50 units at $7.41 each (rounded) would result in a $371 ending inventory value.

Merchandise Inventory—Pens

	Units	*Computation of Average Unit Cost*	*Unit Cost*	*Total Cost*
Beginning balance	0	—	$0.00	$ 0
Purchase, 5/1	40	Not needed	6.00	$ 240
Sales, 20 units	(20)	—	6.00	(120)
Balance	20		6.00	$ 120
Purchase, 8/30.	290		7.00	2,030
Balance	310	$2,150/310 =	6.94	$2,150
Sold, 245 units.	(245)		6.94	(1,700)
Balance	65		6.94	$ 450
Purchase, 9/30	20		9.00	180
Balance	85	$630/85 =	7.41	$ 630
Sold, 35 units	(35)		7.41	(259)
Balance	50		7.41	$ 371

Objective 6
How to measure the cost of ending inventory using LIFO, FIFO, and moving average (MA) methods in a perpetual system.

Recall that **FIFO perpetual is the same as FIFO periodic in all cases.** As a result, using the FIFO computations from the chapter (page 297), the following summarizes the results of the alternative methods for 19x1:

From chapter:

	Periodic System	
Method	*Ending Inventory*	*Cost of Goods Sold*
FIFO. . . .	$390	$2,060
LIFO. . . .	310	2,140
WA	350	2,100

From Appendix 6A and chapter:

	Perpetual System	
Method	*Ending Inventory*	*Cost of Goods Sold*
FIFO. . . .	$390	$2,060
LIFO. . . .	330	2,120
WA	371	2,079

Other than the tax consequences of using LIFO noted earlier, these differences have no economic significance in and of themselves.

DEMONSTRATION EXERCISE

The A.J. Company had the following activity during the year:

Date	Transaction	Units	Unit Cost	Unit Selling Price
1/1	Beginning inventory. . .	1,000	$2.00	
3/31	Purchase No. 1.	2,000	2.75	
6/30	Sale No. 1	2,500		5.50
8/25	Purchase No. 2.	2,000	3.50	
11/15	Sale No. 2	2,250		7.00

Selling price is always 200% of the most recent purchase cost per unit.

Required:
Calculate the total sales, cost of goods sold, and gross margin based on:

1. LIFO perpetual.
2. Moving average perpetual.
3. FIFO perpetual.

Solution:
Total sales:

Sale	Units		
No. 1	2,500	× $5.50 =	$13,750
No. 2	2,250	× 7.00 =	15,750
	4,750		$29,500

Cost of goods sold (4,750 total units sold):

LIFO perpetual:
Sale No. 1:

2,000	× $2.75 =	$5,500	
500	× 2.00 =	1,000	$ 6,500

Sale No. 2:

2,000	× $3.50 =	$7,000		
250	× 2.00 =	500	7,500	
4,750			$14,000	C/G/S

Moving average:
Sale No. 1:

$$\frac{[(1{,}000 \times \$2.00) + (2{,}000 \times \$2.75)]}{3{,}000} = \$2.50$$

Sale No. 2:

$$\frac{[(500 \times \$2.50) + (2{,}000 \times \$3.50)]}{2{,}500} = \$3.30$$

Total cost of goods sold under MA method:

2,500 × $2.50 =	$ 6,250	
2,250 × 3.30 =	7,425	
4,750	$13,675	C/G/S

FIFO perpetual:

Sale No. 1:

1,000 × $2.00 =	$2,000	
1,500 × 2.75 =	4,125	$ 6,125

Sale No. 2:

500 × $2.75 =	$1,375		
1,750 × 3.50 =	6,125	7,500	
4,750		$13,625	C/G/S

Gross margin summary	*LIFO*	*MA*	*FIFO*
Sales	$29,500	$29,500	$29,500
Cost of goods sold . . .	14,000	13,675	13,625
Gross margin	$15,500	$15,825	$15,875

APPENDIX 6B

Inventory Estimation Methods

The major **drawback of the periodic inventory** method is that the cost of goods sold (and gross margin) cannot be computed without knowing the ending inventory. **Interim financial statements,** that is, statements prepared for periods of less than a year, cannot be prepared without a measure of ending inventory and cost of goods sold. Thus, managers are unable to evaluate how well the business is doing until the end of the accounting period when a physical inventory is taken. To illustrate, consider the following data normally known in a periodic system:

Sales (known from sales register) . .	$180,000
Cost of goods sold:	
Beginning inventory (known from last year's ending inventory). . .	$ 22,000
Add: Purchases (net)	196,000
Cost of goods available for sale . .	$218,000
Less: Ending inventory	?
Cost of goods sold.	$?
Gross margin	$?

Once the ending inventory is known, cost of goods sold and gross margin may easily be computed. However, since it is costly and time consuming to take a physical inventory during the accounting period, accountants have developed various methods to estimate the inventory balance at any point in time. This makes it possible for managers to evaluate performance without waiting for a physical inventory. In this appendix you will learn about the retail inventory estimation method.

RETAIL INVENTORY METHOD

If the relationship between retail prices and costs is not fixed, retailers may still estimate their inventory balance (and resulting cost of goods sold) by keeping track of the relationship between cost (amount retailer pays for merchandise) and retail prices (amount retailer sells the merchandise for). The retail (selling) price is normally stamped on each item. The **retail inventory method** requires records to keep track of:

1. Beginning inventory at cost and retail value.
2. Purchases at cost and at retail.

Combined with information about total sales (at retail prices), the above information enables retailers to estimate inventory value at any point in time. The ending inventory estimated using the retail inventory method can also be compared with the actual physical count of inventory to estimate inventory losses due to theft, disasters, and so on, for a period of time.

To illustrate the retail method, assume Prostyle Shoes reported sales in January of $740. In addition, the following information was available at the end of January 19xx:

	Cost Price	*Retail Selling Price*
Beginning inventory, 1/1/xx	$286	$ 305
Purchases (net)	544	695
Goods available for sale	$830	$1,000

Cost as a percent of retail: $830/$1,000 = 83% = 0.83

Objective 7
The fundamentals of the retail method of estimating inventory value.

The relationship in this example—called a **cost ratio**—indicates that costs are equal to 83% of selling prices. The ending inventory at **retail** selling prices is found by taking the retail value of goods available for sale ($1,000) less net sales ($740), or $260. The ending inventory **at cost** is then estimated by multiplying the ending inventory at retail by the cost ratio ($260 × 0.83 = $215.80). This computation and the resulting estimate of profit for the month of January may be illustrated as follows:

	Cost Price	*Retail Selling Price*	
Beginning inventory, 1/1/xx	$286	$ 305	Cost
Purchases (net)	544	– 695	ratio:
Goods available for sale	$830	$1,000	$830 / $1,000 = 0.83
Less net sales		– 740	
Ending inventory at retail prices		$ 260	
Cost ratio		× .83 ←	
Estimated ending inventory at cost prices		$215.80	= $216 rounded

Estimated Profit—January

Sales (net)		$740
Cost of goods sold:		
Beginning inventory	$286	
Purchases (net)	544	
Cost of goods available for sale	$830	
Estimated ending inventory (from above)	216	
Cost of goods sold		614
Gross margin		$126

This example illustrates the basic approach of the retail inventory method. Additional details can be included in retail estimation systems that add to both the complexity of the calculations and the accuracy of the resulting estimates of ending inventory. These estimation methods are accurate to the point where they are acceptable as a basis for financial statements as well as income tax returns. The additional complexities and other variations of the retail method are covered in detail in most intermediate accounting texts.

APPENDIX 6C

LIFO Reserves and LIFO Liquidation

Many companies using the LIFO inventory method for reporting purposes also keep records on a FIFO basis. These companies frequently use FIFO for internal reports throughout the year (due to simplicity and lower cost) and convert to LIFO at year-end using LIFO inventory estimation procedures.[3] This conversion to LIFO (from FIFO) at year-end is normally accomplished with the following type of adjusting entry:

19xx			
Dec. 31	Cost of Goods Sold (E)	xxx	
	LIFO Reserve (XA)		xxx
	To convert FIFO inventory to LIFO value.		

This adjusting entry increases expenses (cost of goods sold), and decreases assets (inventory) and net income. The LIFO Reserve account is a contra asset to merchandise inventory, and is shown as follows:

Partial Balance Sheet

Accounts receivable (net)		$187,550
Merchandise inventory (at FIFO)	$386,200	
Less: LIFO reserve	41,000	
Merchandise inventory (at LIFO)		345,200

[3] These procedures go beyond the scope of this text but are covered in detail in most intermediate accounting texts.

Since the LIFO value of inventory is less than FIFO the contra asset balance should be a credit. The credit balance reports the **cumulative difference** between LIFO and FIFO inventory value from all prior periods. The balance in the reserve is a measure of the cumulative impact of price increases on inventory value over time. However, it is possible for this reserve to experience a decrease (debit) in any given year. The two factors that could cause the year-end adjusting entry to decrease the reserve balance (make it a smaller credit balance) are:

Objective 8
LIFO reserves and LIFO liquidation.

1. A **decrease** in inventory costs (cheaper costs for inventory item).
2. A reduction in inventory quantities during the year below the beginning inventory level (forcing the sales to be costed out at costs of prior years) called **LIFO liquidations.** (LIFO liquidations are normally disclosed in the financial statement footnotes.)

The following T accounts explain how these factors could cause the reserve account to either increase or decrease from year to year:

Merchandise Inventory (FIFO)

Beginning balance at FIFO	
Increases	*Decreases*
Purchases at FIFO	Cost of goods sold at FIFO
Ending balance at FIFO	

LIFO Reserve

	Beginning balance
Decreases	*Increases*
1. Inventory costs decrease during the year. 2. Liquidation of beginning inventory at LIFO costs.	1. Inventory costs increase during the year.
	Ending balance

To illustrate, assume Technavest Corporation had the following balances at the end of 19xx prior to adjustment:

Merchandise Inventory (FIFO)

19xx		
Jan. 1	380,000	
	993,200	987,000
Dec. 31	386,200	

LIFO Reserve

	19xx	
	Jan. 1	46,200

The beginning balance in the LIFO reserve account ($46,200) represents the accumulated differences between FIFO and LIFO from all prior periods. If Technavest had always used FIFO instead of LIFO to measure inventory, the net asset Merchandise Inventory would be $46,200 larger and the total amount of inventory costs charged to cost of goods sold in all prior years would have been $46,200 less. If Technavest experienced no price changes and no reductions in beginning inventory levels during 19xx, then no adjusting entry to the LIFO reserve account would be necessary at the end of 19xx. Technavest would report inventory of $340,000 ($386,200 less LIFO reserve of $46,200) in the 19xx balance sheet and cost of goods sold of $987,000 (the decrease to inventory) in the 19xx income statement. Instead, assume that Technavest experienced a $5,200 decrease in its LIFO reserve during 19xx due to decreasing inventory costs during 19xx.[4] The following year-end adjusting entry would be made:

19xx			
Dec. 31	LIFO Reserve (XA)	5,200	
	Cost of goods Sold (E)		5,200
	To convert FIFO inventory to LIFO value.		

After this entry, the following account balances would be reported:

Balance Sheet Accounts

Merchandise inventory (FIFO)	$386,200
LIFO reserve	(41,000)
Inventory (LIFO)	$345,200

Income Statement

Cost of goods sold (LIFO) ($987,000 − $5,200)	$981,800

The adjusting entry to the LIFO reserve for 19xx cost decreases resulted in a $5,200 increase to assets and a $5,200 decrease in cost of goods sold. Adjustments to the LIFO reserve are normally made at the end of each accounting period when reports are prepared. This liquidation of a portion of the LIFO reserve is permanent. Future period price increases will increase the LIFO reserve, while future period price decreases and/or LIFO liquidations will decrease the LIFO reserve.

DEMONSTRATION EXERCISE

Jipper Corporation reported the following data in its 19x9 balance sheet (in $000):

	19x9	*19x8*
Inventory (at FIFO cost)	$258,730	$285,317
Less: LIFO reserve	95,817	84,317
Inventory (at LIFO cost)	$162,913	$201,000

Required:

1. Did inventory costs increase or decrease in 19x9?
2. What was the 19x9 year-end adjustment to the LIFO reserve assuming there were no LIFO liquidations?
3. What was the 19x9 year-end adjustment to the LIFO reserve assuming there was a $6,000,000 LIFO liquidation in 19x9?

[4]An explanation of the accounting procedures used to arrive at this estimated price decrease of $5,200 is beyond the scope of this textbook. These procedures are discussed in intermediate accounting texts.

Solution:

1. Inventory costs **increased** because the LIFO reserve increased. Note that while total inventory value declined, this was due to lower inventory **quantities**, not lower costs. The only way the LIFO reserve can increase is as a result of cost increases.
2. The year-end adjusting entry would have been:

Cost of Goods Sold (E)	11,500,000	
LIFO Reserve (XA)		11,500,000
To increase LIFO reserve.		

The T account analysis is:

LIFO Reserve

	84,317,000	Given 12/31/x8 balance
	11,500,000	Adjusting entry
	95,817,000	Given 12/31/x9 balance

3. If a $6,000,000 LIFO liquidation occurred in 19x9, the year-end adjustments would have been:

LIFO Reserve (XA)	6,000,000	
Cost of Goods Sold (E)		6,000,000
To record liquidation of LIFO inventory layers.		
Cost of Goods Sold (E)	17,500,000	
LIFO Reserve (XA)		17,500,000
To increase LIFO reserve.		

The T account analysis is:

LIFO Reserve

		84,317,000	Given 12/31/x8 balance
Given 19x9 liquidation	6,000,000	17,500,000	Adjusting entry (plug)
		95,817,000	Given 12/31/x9 balance

KEY TERMS

Consistency principle. Principle stating that accounting methods should be applied on a consistent basis from year-to-year whenever possible.

Cost flow assumptions. Another term to describe cost flow methods—LIFO, FIFO, and weighted average; term *assumption* used because the actual physical flow of goods need not be the same as the cost flow method used; only affects the timing of when specific inventory costs are transferred to cost of goods sold.

Counterbalancing or self-correcting error. Inventory error that corrects itself the next year.

Current replacement cost. The current cost to replace existing inventory.

First-in, first-out (FIFO). Cost flow method that *assumes* the "first goods in" were the first goods sold and assigns the actual cost of the "first goods in" to cost of goods sold.

FOB destination. Goods are free on board (FOB) to the buyer's location; the seller pays the freight charges up to the point where the buyer takes delivery and title passes to the buyer.

FOB shipping point. Goods are free on board (FOB) to the seller's point of shipment only—title passes to the buyer as goods leave the seller's location, and the buyer pays the freight from the point of shipment.

Goods out on consignment. Goods owned by company but held by some agent of the company at another location for possible sale to customers.

Inventory. Merchandise that is produced or obtained to be sold in the regular course of business for the purpose of making a profit.

Inventory in transit. Inventory that is between the seller and buyer but legally owned by one or the other, depending on shipping terms.

Last-in, first-out (LIFO). Cost flow assumption that *assumes* "the last goods in" (most recent purchases) were the first goods sold and assigns the actual cost of the "last goods in" to cost of goods sold.

Lower-of-cost-or-market (LCM) valuation method. Method used to write inventory down to its market value when the current replacement cost of the inventory is less than its original cost.

Moving average (MA). A cost flow assumption used in a perpetual inventory system; new weighted average is computed each time goods are purchased.

Period costs. Costs incurred to generate revenue; expensed in the period they occur (not assigned to inventory).

Perpetual inventory system. System that continuously updates the records for the quantity and cost of each type of item in inventory; the Merchandise Inventory account is increased when companies purchase merchandise and decreased when companies sell merchandise.

Physical inventory count. Count of actual inventory on hand; necessary in a periodic inventory system to determine cost of goods sold and ending inventory; necessary in a perpetual inventory system to ensure against errors.

Product costs. Costs assigned to units of inventory.

Special-order goods. Goods special ordered for a customer; if special-order goods are on hand at the end of an accounting period waiting to be delivered to customer, company usually records the goods as a sale, and the goods are not included in the company's inventory even though company still has possession of goods.

Specific identification (SI). Cost flow method where actual cost of each specifically identified unit sold is charged to cost of goods sold when units are actually sold. This is the only cost flow method that matches actual costs with the actual physical flow of goods.

Weighted average (WA). Cost flow assumption that measures the cost of the units sold using the weighted average cost of all purchases.

APPENDIX KEY TERMS

Cost ratio. Relationship of an inventory item's cost to its selling price.

Interim financial statements. Statements prepared during the accounting period on a monthly or quarterly basis.

Retail inventory method. Inventory estimation method based on the relationship between retail prices and costs.

SYNONYMS

Current cost; replacement cost; current replacement cost.
Counterbalancing error; self-correcting error.
Interim financial statements; monthly statements; quarterly statements.
Perpetual system; real-time system.
Physical inventory; actual inventory count.
Shrinkage; loss from theft and/or damaged goods.

QUESTIONS

1. What are three costs incurred by keeping inventory too long?
2. What are the two types of inventory systems?
3. What are the attributes of a periodic system?
4. What are the attributes of a perpetual system?
5. What are the advantages and disadvantages of a perpetual system?
6. Which inventory system requires a physical count of inventory at least once a year?
7. When does title to goods pass to the buyer?
8. What does the term *FOB destination* mean?
9. What is the effect on the income statement if a seller records the transfer of title to goods too soon? (Assume goods are sold at a profit.)
10. What are goods out on consignment and how do they affect inventory measurement?
11. What are special-order goods and how do they affect inventory measurement?
12. What are self-correcting errors?
13. What is the effect on earnings when ending inventory is overstated?
14. What costs are to be included in the asset inventory?
15. What are four common cost flow methods?
16. Which cost flow method is the only one that is always consistent with the actual physical flow of goods?
17. Which cost flow method results in the lowest earnings in periods of increasing inventory costs?
18. Which cost flow method results in the highest earnings in periods of decreasing inventory costs?
19. Over the life of a business, which cost flow method will result in the highest gross profits assuming increasing costs? Assuming decreasing costs?
20. For tax purposes, which inventory cost flow should be used in periods of increasing inventory costs? Why?

21. When and how does the lower-of-cost-or-market (LCM) method require a change in the inventory measurement?
22. How is market value measured in the LCM method?
23. Identify three ways that the LCM test may be applied to an inventory made up of many different types of merchandise.

APPENDIX QUESTIONS

24. Which cost flow methods will provide the same inventory measurements in both perpetual and periodic systems? Why?
25. Which cost flow methods will provide different inventory measurements in a perpetual system than in a periodic system? Why?
26. What information is needed to estimate inventory using the retail method?
27. What is a LIFO Reserve account? How is it used?

EXERCISES

EXERCISE 6-1
L.O. 1

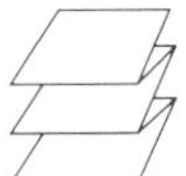

Perpetual/Periodic Recording

The following events of TOK Corporation, which records its purchases at their gross invoice amount, occurred during June of 19xx:

19xx
June 3 Purchased $45,000 of merchandise on open account from Vendor, Inc.; terms 2/15, n/30.
10 Paid $17,920 to Max Corporation for goods billed for $18,350, taking a $430 purchase discount.
12 Sold merchandise costing $40,000 to a client for $50,000 cash.
15 Paid $1,795 in freight bills for merchandise acquired.
17 Returned $7,000 of merchandise to Vendor, Inc., and paid balance of June 3 purchase in cash.
25 Acquired $39,500 in merchandise from XYZ, Inc.; terms 2/15, n/30.
28 Some of the merchandise sold on June 12 was returned for a full refund of the $5,000 selling price. The goods were expected to be resold.

Required:
1. Record these events assuming a periodic inventory system is used.
2. Record these events assuming a perpetual inventory system is used.

EXERCISE 6-2
L.O. 1

Perpetual/Periodic Recording

The following events occurred during July 19x5 for the Beat Corporation:

19xx
July 1 Purchased merchandise inventory on open account for $63,000, terms 2/10, n/30.
6 Purchased merchandise inventory on open account for $87,000, terms 2/15, n/30.
8 Returned $6,000 of July 1 purchase and paid the balance in cash.
10 Sold merchandise costing $50,000 for $95,000 on open account.
12 Purchased merchandise inventory on open account for $57,500, terms 2/10, n/30.

July 15 Received and paid freight bills of $1,640 in cash for merchandise purchased earlier on open account.
20 Paid for July 6 purchase in cash.
23 Returned $15,000 of July 12 purchase.
27 Paid balance due on July 12 purchase.
30 Half of merchandise sold on July 10 was returned for credit, and payment was received for the balance due.

Required:
1. Record these events assuming a periodic inventory system is used.
2. Record these events assuming a perpetual inventory system is used.

EXERCISE 6-3
L.O. 2

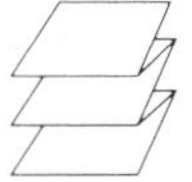

FIFO Periodic

Printer Supplies, Inc., which sells bottles of ink, had the following transactions in January related to the ink:

Jan. 1 Beginning inventory of 100 bottles and total cost of $600.
8 Purchased 400 bottles at a cost of $8 each.
22 Sold 450 bottles at $15 each.
30 Counted ending inventory of 50 bottles.

Printer Supplies uses a periodic inventory system and FIFO inventory costing method.

Required:
Compute the cost of the ending inventory and cost of goods sold.

EXERCISE 6-4
L.O. 2

LIFO Periodic

The following data are from the ledger of the Rose Company for 19xx:

Date	*Transaction*	*Units*	*Unit Cost*	*Total Cost*
1/1	Beginning inventory	200	$6.00	$1,200
2/10	Purchase.	600	7.00	4,200
4/15	Sale	400	—	—
6/30	Purchase.	100	8.00	800
8/16	Sale	400	—	—
10/31	Purchase.	300	8.50	2,550

Required:
Using a periodic inventory system and LIFO, determine the cost of the ending inventory and the cost of goods sold for 19xx.

EXERCISE 6-5
L.O. 2

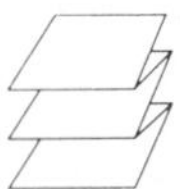

LIFO Periodic

The following table reflects inventory activity for Theisman Surgical Supplies, Inc., during 19xx:

Date	*Transaction*	*Units*	*Unit Cost*
1/1	Beginning inventory . . .	400	$1.00
2/15	Purchase.	200	1.25
6/30	Sale	300	—
9/20	Purchase.	300	1.50
11/30	Sale	500	—
12/15	Purchase.	100	1.75

Total sales for the year were $1,500.

Required:
Determine the cost of the ending inventory, cost of goods sold, and gross margin during 19xx if the company uses LIFO and a periodic inventory system.

EXERCISE 6-6
L.O. 2

Inventory Costing Methods/Periodic

The following information applies to the Ross Appliance Shop during 19xx:

Date	*Transaction*	*Units*	*Unit Selling Price*	*Units*	*Unit Cost*
1/1	Beginning inventory . .			200	$20
1/27	Sold	120	$32		
4/15	Purchase			190	22
7/16	Sold	140	35		
9/12	Purchase			160	24
11/20	Sold	180	36		
12/29	Purchase			110	25

Required:
Determine the ending inventory (units and dollar amounts), cost of goods sold, and gross margin at December 31, 19xx, under each of the following inventory costing methods using a periodic inventory system:

1. FIFO.
2. LIFO.
3. WA.

EXERCISE 6-7
L.O. 2

Inventory Costing Methods/Periodic

The inventory records for the Hope Corporation for January 19xx are as follows:

Date	*Transaction*	*Units*	*Unit Cost*	*Unit Selling Price*
1/1	Beginning inventory	100	$25	
1/6	Purchase	25	26	
1/10	Purchase	30	27	
1/17	Sold	45		$50
1/23	Purchase	20	27	
1/28	Sold	10		52

Required:
1. Assuming the Hope Company uses the periodic inventory method applied on a LIFO basis, determine the costs assigned to the ending inventory on January 31, 19xx.
2. Assume the Hope Company uses the periodic inventory system and the specific identification inventory costing method. All of the items sold on January 17 came from beginning inventory, and all of the items sold on January 28 came from the January 10 purchase. Based on these assumptions, determine the gross margin for January 19xx.
3. Assuming the Hope Company uses the periodic inventory system applied on a WA basis, determine the cost of goods sold (rounded to the nearest whole dollar) for January 19xx.

EXERCISE 6-8
L.O. 2

Inventory Costing Methods/Periodic

The following data are available for the Stockout Company at the end of 19xx:

Date		Units	Unit Cost	Total Cost
1/1	Beginning inventory . .	80	$10	$ 800
3/10	Purchase	100	9	900
6/26	Purchase	50	11	550
9/5	Purchase	60	10	600
11/15	Purchase	40	13	520
12/31	Purchase	70	14	980
		400		$4,350

The physical inventory count at year-end revealed 120 units on hand. Stockout uses a periodic inventory system.

Required:
1. Compute cost of goods sold for 19xx:
   a. Using the FIFO cost method.
   b. Using the LIFO cost method.
   c. Using the WA cost method.
2. Which method will result in the highest net income for 19xx?

EXERCISE 6-9
L.O. 3

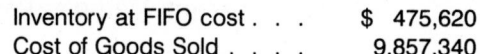

Lower-of-Cost-or-Market Method

Whembly Corporation reported the following balances as of the end of 19xx:

Inventory at FIFO cost . . .	$ 475,620
Cost of Goods Sold	9,857,340

The market value (replacement cost) of Whembly's inventory at the end of 19xx is $457,500. Whembly uses the lower-of-cost-or-market method.

Required:
1. What should Whembly report as the balance sheet value of inventory at the end of 19xx?
2. What should Whembly report as cost of goods sold for 19xx? Prepare the journal entry to record the LCM value.

EXERCISE 6-10
L.O. 3

LCM Test

The records of Nancy's Exterior Decorating, Inc., provide the following data relating to inventories for the years 19x6 and 19x7:

	Inventory (in thousands)		
	12/31/x7	12/31/x6	1/1/x6
At average cost.	$145	$123	$112
At lower-of-average-cost-or-market . . .	135	110	112

Required:
1. What should be reported as ending inventory at the end of 19x6?
2. What should be reported as ending inventory at the end of 19x7?

EXERCISE 6-11
L.O. 4

Inventory Errors

Answer the following independent questions, selecting the appropriate choice in each case.

1. The ending inventory mistakenly included goods that had been sold to a customer, therefore:
   a. Net income is overstated and assets are understated.
   b. Net income is understated and assets are overstated.
   c. Both net income and assets are overstated.
   d. Both net income and assets are understated.
2. A purchase of 1,000 units of merchandise on open account was somehow recorded twice in the company's periodic inventory system. As a result:
   a. The ending inventory is overstated.
   b. Cost of goods sold is understated.
   c. Cost of goods sold is overstated.
   d. The ending inventory is understated.
3. A quantity of inventory out on consignment was omitted from ending inventory. As a result:
   a. There is no error.
   b. The ending inventory is understated.
   c. Profits are understated.
   d. Both (*b*) and (*c*) are correct.
   e. None of the above.
4. A company using a periodic system was billed twice for the same inventory purchase, and paid both bills by mistake. As a result:
   a. Inventory is overstated and cash is understated.
   b. Cost of goods sold is overstated and cash is understated.
   c. Net income is overstated and cash is understated.
   d. Accounts payable is overstated and cash is understated.
5. A company using a perpetual system was billed twice for the same purchase, and paid both bills by mistake. As a result:
   a. Inventory is overstated and cash is understated.
   b. Cost of goods sold is overstated and cash is understated.
   c. Net income is overstated and cash is understated.
   d. Accounts payable is overstated and cash is understated.

EXERCISE 6-12
L.O. 4

Correcting Inventory

Consider the following transactions for Whiz Company:

a. Whiz Company recorded the following entry on July 1, 19xx:

Merchandise Inventory	42,500	
Accounts Payable		42,500

The invoice for this purchase was actually for $24,500. Record the correcting journal entry.

b. Whiz Company recorded the following entries on September 10, 19xx:

Accounts Receivable	25,000	
Sales		25,000
Cost of Goods Sold	15,000	
Merchandise Inventory		15,000

The merchandise recorded as sold was actually only sent to a distributor of Whiz Company for possible sale to customers. These goods are out on consignment and still belong to Whiz. Record the correcting entries.

EXERCISE 6-13
L.O. 2

Cost Flows

1. Acquisition cost for a heavily used raw material changes frequently. The book value of the inventory of this material at year-end will be the same if perpetual records are kept as it will be under a periodic inventory method only if the book value is computed under the
   a. Average cost method.
   b. First-in, first-out method.
   c. Last-in, first-out method.
   d. None of the above.
2. DEK Corporation's inventory cost on its statement of financial position would have been lower using FIFO than if LIFO had been used. Assuming no beginning inventory, in what direction did the cost of purchases move during the period?
   a. Up (increasing).
   b. Down (decreasing).
   c. Very constant.
   d. Cannot be determined.
3. In the periodic inventory method, which of the following generally would not be separately accounted for in the computation of cost of goods sold?
   a. Delivery charges on the sale of inventory.
   b. Cash (purchase) discounts on merchandise purchased during the period.
   c. Purchase returns and allowances on merchandise acquired during the period.
   d. Cost of freight-in for merchandise purchased during the period.
4. Which method of inventory pricing best approximates specific identification of the actual flow of costs and units in most perishable goods merchandising situations?
   a. Weighted-average cost.
   b. FIFO.
   c. LIFO.
   d. All of the above.

EXERCISE 6-14
L.O. 4, 5

Analysis of Inventory

1. If ending inventory of 19x5 is overstated, then the net income for 19x5 will:
   a. Be overstated.
   b. Be understated.
   c. Not be affected.
   d. Offset the error.
   e. None of the above.
2. B Company had cost of goods sold of $43,000 during the period. The balance in the accounts payable for merchandise *increased* $5,000 during the period. Inventory, all of which is acquired on account, had an ending balance of $60,000. Cash payments for inventory acquired on account totaled $50,000 during the period. What was the beginning balance in inventory?
   a. $72,000.
   b. $53,000.
   c. $48,000.
   d. $43,000.
   e. $67,000.
3. Suppose that D Corporation purchased 400 units of inventory on January 1, 19x5, for $700 per unit. The ending inventory consisted of 150 units, and sales for the period amounted to 410 units. If D Corp. uses FIFO perpetual and the total ending inventory cost is equal to the total beginning inventory cost what is cost of goods sold for the period?
   a. $280,000.
   b. $385,000.

c. $175,000.
d. Cannot be determined based on above data.
e. None of the above.

4. An understatement of $3,500 in inventory at the end of 19x3 would:
   a. Have no effect on net income of 19x3.
   b. Overstate the beginning inventory of 19x4.
   c. Overstate net income in 19x3.
   d. Overstate cost of goods sold for 19x4.
   e. None of the above.

EXERCISE 6-15
L.O. 5

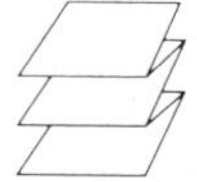

Evaluating Inventory Changes

Gulford Corporation reported the following data in its 19x2 annual report:

	19x2	*19x1*
Balance sheet data:		
Inventory	$187,600	$173,500
Accounts payable . .	67,450	73,900
Income statement data:		
Cost of goods sold . .	763,500	691,890

Assume Gulford purchases all inventory on account, and the Accounts Payable account is used only for purchases of inventory.

Required:
1. Compute net purchases for Gulford Corporation for 19x2.
2. Compute the amount of cash payments made during 19x2 on Accounts Payable.

APPENDIX EXERCISES

EXERCISE 6-16
L.O. 6

LIFO Perpetual (Appendix 6A)

The following table reflects inventory activity for Theisman Surgical Supplies, Inc., during 19xx:

Date	*Transaction*	*Units*	*Unit Cost*
1/1	Beginning inventory . . .	400	$1.00
2/15	Purchase.	200	1.25
6/30	Sale	300	—
9/20	Purchase.	300	1.50
11/30	Sale	500	—
12/15	Purchase.	100	1.75

Total sales for the year were $1,500.

Required:
Determine the cost of the ending inventory, cost of goods sold, and gross margin during 19xx if the company uses LIFO and a perpetual inventory system.

EXERCISE 6-17
L.O. 6

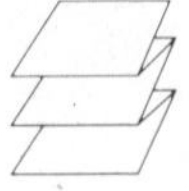

Inventory Costing Methods/Perpetual (Appendix 6A)

The following information applies to the Ross Appliance Shop during 19xx:

Date	*Transaction*	*Units*	*Unit Selling Price*	*Units*	*Unit Cost*
1/1	Beginning inventory . . .			200	$20
1/27	Sale	120	$32		
4/15	Purchase			190	22
7/16	Sale	140	35		
9/12	Purchase			160	24
11/20	Sale	180	36		
12/29	Purchase			110	25

Required:
Determine the ending inventory (units and dollar amounts), cost of goods sold, and gross margin at December 31, 19xx, under each of the following inventory costing methods using a perpetual inventory system.

1. FIFO.
2. LIFO.
3. MA.

EXERCISE 6-18
L.O. 6

Inventory Costing Methods/Perpetual (Appendix 6A)

The inventory records for the Hope Corporation for January 19xx are as follows:

Date	*Transaction*	*Units*	*Unit Cost*	*Unit Selling Price*
1/1	Beginning inventory	100	$25	
1/6	Purchase	25	26	
1/10	Purchase	30	27	
1/17	Sold	45		$50
1/23	Purchase	20	27	
1/28	Sold	10		52

Required:
1. Assuming the Hope Company uses the perpetual inventory method applied on a LIFO basis, determine the costs assigned to the ending inventory on January 31, 19xx.
2. Assume the Hope Company uses the perpetual inventory system and the specific identification inventory costing method. All of the items sold on January 17 came from beginning inventory, and all of the items sold on January 28 came from the January 10 purchase. Based on these assumptions, determine the gross profit for January 19xx.

EXERCISE 6-19
L.O. 6

Moving Average Method/Perpetual (Appendix 6A)

XYZ Company buys and sells grommets, using a perpetual system with the moving average inventory costing method. It had the following transactions in September:

Sept. 1 Beginning inventory 200 grommets; total cost $500.
5 Purchased 200 grommets at $3 each.
14 Sold 350 grommets at $5 each.
28 Purchased 50 grommets at $3.25 each.

Required:
1. Prepare a perpetual inventory record on a MA basis for the month of September assuming no other transactions are made.
2. Compute cost of goods sold for September and cost of the ending inventory as of September 30.

EXERCISE 6-20
L.O. 7

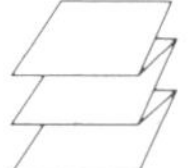

Retail Inventory Method (Appendix 6B)

Gerry's Department Store uses the retail method to value its inventory. The following data are available:

	Cost	*Retail*
Beginning inventory . .	$ 40,000	$ 70,000
Purchases	292,000	397,000
Sales.		390,000

Required:
Estimate the ending inventory cost, cost of goods sold, and gross profit. (Round the cost ratio to two decimal places.)

EXERCISE 6-21
L.O. 8

LIFO Reserve (Appendix 6C)

Majors, Inc., reported the following preliminary account balances at the end of 19xx before adjustments:

	Preliminary Balance
Inventory (FIFO)	$196,250 dr.
LIFO Reserve	34,100 cr.
Cost of Goods Sold . . .	515,840 dr.

Inventory costs increased rapidly during 19xx, with the resulting difference between FIFO and LIFO inventory value increasing by $14,300 for 19xx.

Required:
1. Record the 19xx year-end adjusting entry to the LIFO Reserve account.
2. Compute the amount to be reported for inventory and for cost of goods sold in Majors' 19xx financial statement (assuming no other adjustments to either account).

P R O B L E M S

PROBLEM 6-1
L.O. 2

Inventory Costing

Jacobs Corporation experienced the following inventory activity during the first four months of 19xx.

Date	*Transaction*	*Units*	*Unit Cost*	*Unit Selling Price*
1/1	Beginning inventory	60	$100	
1/19	Purchase	100	120	
2/20	Sold	75		$240
3/23	Purchase	180	130	
4/24	Sold	120		260

At the end of April, Jacobs decided to cut selling prices in order to try and improve profits. The results for the next four months were:

Date	Transaction	Units	Unit Cost	Unit Selling Price
5/3	Purchase	200	$140	
6/1	Sold	220		$210
6/5	Purchase	380	150	
7/18	Sold	360		225
8/4	Purchase	500	150	
8/29	Sold	460		225

Required:

1. Assume Jacobs uses the FIFO periodic inventory method. Compute ending inventory, cost of goods sold, and gross margin for each of the two separate four-month periods. (In other words, treat each four-month period like a separate year.)
2. Repeat requirement 1 using the LIFO periodic inventory method.
3. Compare your answers to parts (1) and (2) above. Did the cut in selling prices work as hoped? Is the effect of the price cut greater than the difference between LIFO and FIFO?

PROBLEM 6-2
L.O. 1

Comparison of Periodic/Perpetual Journal Entries

The following transactions involving the Fashion Friend Department Store were selected from the records of July 19xx:

a. Purchased merchandise on credit at an invoice cost of $2,300 with terms 2/10, n/30.
b. Returned damaged goods purchased in (*a*) with an invoice cost of $200 to the vendor. Fashion Friend received a credit against its outstanding account balance.
c. Sold merchandise for cash, $800, and on credit, $1,900. The inventory for this sale had a cost of $1,700. Fashion Friend's terms on credit sales are 2/10, n/30.
d. Paid invoice for the inventory purchases in (*a*) after the discount period.
e. Received payment from customer for sale made in (*c*) within the discount period.

Required:
Record all necessary entries that would be made for each transaction under a periodic inventory system and a perpetual inventory system. Use the gross method for sales and purchase discounts.

PROBLEM 6-3
L.O. 1

Recording in a Periodic System

During May 19xx, the following transactions occurred regarding Day Company's inventory:

19xx
May 2 Acquired on account $18,700 of merchandise inventory delivered by Rush Trucking whose freight bill for $600 was paid in cash by Day. The terms of the purchase were 2/10, n/30.
6 Sold merchandise costing $15,000 to a customer for $23,500 on open account; terms 2/10, n/30.
8 Acquired $26,000 in merchandise; terms 2/10, n/30, FOB destination. The freight bill was $500.
9 Returned $2,000 of merchandise acquired on May 2 for credit and paid for the balance due.

May 12 Sold merchandise costing $8,000 to a customer for $13,200 on open account; terms 2/10, n/30.
14 Collected cash from customer for May 6 sale.
23 Purchased merchandise on open account costing $17,000; terms 2/10, n/30. The freight bill of $480, FOB shipping point, was paid in cash.
25 Returned $4,000 worth of merchandise acquired May 8 for credit and received an allowance of $1,200 for damaged goods that were not returned by Day. Paid the balance of the May 8 purchase in cash.

Required:

1. Record all necessary entries assuming Day Company uses a periodic inventory system and records sales and purchase discounts taken in separate accounts.
2. Identify one advantage and one disadvantage of periodic systems.

PROBLEM 6-4
L.O. 1

Recording in a Perpetual System

Consider the facts in Problem 6-3 for Day Company:

Required:

1. Record the events, assuming Day Company uses a perpetual inventory system.
2. Identify one advantage and one disadvantage of perpetual systems.

PROBLEM 6-5
L.O. 2

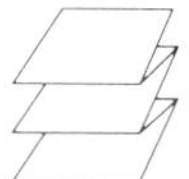

Inventory Cost Flows

The following information is taken from the records of Merkel Retail Store for the month of January 19x2.

Jan. 1 Beginning inventory is 150 units at $20 each.
5 Purchase 2,000 units at $18 each.
19 Sell 1,800 units.
25 Purchase 500 units at $22.70 each.
30 Sell 450 units.
31 Ending inventory is 400 units.

Merkel uses the periodic inventory system.

Required:
Compute the cost of the ending inventory and cost of goods sold for the following cost flow alternative:

1. FIFO.
2. LIFO.
3. Weighted average.

PROBLEM 6-6
L.O. 2

Inventory Costing Methods/Periodic/Perpetual

The following information applies to Widgets, Inc., for 19xx:

Inventory of Item X	*Units*	*Unit Price*
Beginning inventory, 1/1 . .	200	$3.00
Purchase, 2/10.	600	3.50
Sale, 4/15	400	—
Purchase, 6/30.	100	4.00
Sale, 8/16	400	—
Purchase, 10/31	300	4.25

Required:

1. Using a periodic inventory system and LIFO, determine:
   a. The cost of goods available for sale in 19xx.
   b. The cost of goods sold in 19xx.
2. Using a periodic inventory system and FIFO, determine the cost of goods sold during 19xx.
3. In 19xx, does using FIFO instead of LIFO result in a higher or lower balance in ending inventory? By what amount?
4. Using a perpetual inventory system and LIFO, determine the ending inventory cost and cost of goods sold for item X. *(Relates to Appendix 6A.)*

PROBLEM 6-7
L.O. 2

Inventory Costing Methods/Periodic

The following information relates to inventory purchases and sales of the Caribbean Company for May 19xx.

Date	*Transaction*	*Units*	*Unit Cost*	*Selling Price per Unit*
5/1	Beginning inventory	150	$6	
5/9	Purchase	130	7	
5/12	Sale	140		$20
5/17	Purchase	200	8	
5/21	Sale	130		20

Required:
Calculate the following amounts:

1. Number of units in ending inventory on May 31.
2. Cost of goods available for sale during May.
3. FIFO (periodic) cost of goods sold for May.
4. FIFO (periodic) ending inventory at May 31.
5. FIFO (periodic) gross margin for May.
6. WA (periodic) cost of goods sold for May.
7. WA (periodic) ending inventory at May 31.
8. Specific identification ending inventory at May 31. (Assume that the May 12 sale was made from units in beginning inventory and that the May 21 sale was made from units purchased on May 17.)

PROBLEM 6-8
L.O. 2

Inventory Costing Methods

The Martin Corporation reported the following inventory data for 19x1:

Beginning inventory	20 units costing $9 each
Purchases during the year:	
February 28	40 units @ $13 each
June 13	60 units @ $11 each
September 24	40 units @ $ 9 each
November 5	25 units @ $ 7 each

Required:

1. Compute the total cost of the remaining 55 units in the ending inventory using: (Hint: Will you use the periodic or perpetual inventory system?)
   a. The LIFO method.
   b. The FIFO method.
   c. The WA method.

2. Answer the following questions:
   a. Which method would result in the lowest net income? Why?
   b. Which method would result in the most current inventory value at the end of the year?
   c. Which method would result in the best "matching" of revenues and expenses for the current year?

PROBLEM 6-9
L.O. 3

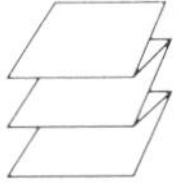

Lower-of-Cost-or-Market Method

The following inventory data are taken from the records of the Palmrose Floors Corporation at December 31, 19xx:

	Quantity in Square Yards	*Total FIFO Cost*	*Total Replacement Cost*
Indoor/outdoor carpets:			
Sil No. 87	9,817	$98,170	$100,250
Dray No. 76	6,215	79,420	80,690
Gard No. 97	1,940	31,500	27,150
Plush carpets:			
CC No. 452	1,830	15,790	14,650
Milih No. 841	3,205	29,750	31,490
Welb No. 543	2,906	18,725	18,100

Required:
1. Compute the ending inventory value for 19xx using the LCM method applied on an item-by-item basis.
2. Repeat part 1 above using the group-of-items basis.
3. Repeat part 1 above using the total-all-items basis.

PROBLEM 6-10
L.O. 3

LCM Tests

The following data relate to the ending inventory of the Somer Store:

Inventory Classification	*Quantity*	*Cost per Unit* FIFO	*Cost per Unit* Market
Rubber boats:			
5 person	200	$150.00	$175.00
4 person	100	125.00	110.00
Golf clubs:			
Irons	150	40.00	37.50
Woods	100	25.00	30.00
Fishing gear:			
Reels	60	12.50	14.00
Rods	40	5.00	4.00

Required:
Determine ending inventory based on FIFO cost or market, whichever is lower:

a. On an item-by-item basis.
b. On a group-of-items basis.
c. On a total-all-items basis.

PROBLEM 6-11
L.O. 4

Inventory Errors

St. Francis, Inc., recently discovered the following errors concerning inventory measurement in its periodic inventory system for the year ending December 31, 19x8:

a. The 19x6 ending inventory was understated $92,000.
b. Inventory costing $40,000 was assumed to be out on consignment as of the end of 19x7 when it had actually been sold in 19x7. The sale was recorded as revenue in 19x7. The $40,000 was not included in the 19x8 ending inventory.
c. Merchandise costing $51,000 was correctly included in the 19x7 ending inventory based on the physical count but was not recorded as a purchase until January 19x8.
d. Merchandise was recorded as a purchase in December 19x8 for $60,000 but the goods were not received until January 19x9. The goods were shipped on January 1, 19x9, by the vendor. The ending physical inventory count did not include this merchandise.

Required:
Explain the effect, if any, of each of the four items on the 19x8 net income, 19x8 net purchases, and the 19x8 ending inventory value, indicating the overstatement or understatement effect and the amount for each.

PROBLEM 6-12
L.O. 4

Inventory Errors/Periodic

The Gamma Corporation is a December 31, year-end company. At the end of the year before the books were finally closed, their internal auditor discovered the following errors which had occurred during the year, and noted the entry that should have been made in each case.

Erroneous Entry			*Entry That Should Have Been Made*		
1. Purchases	5,250		Purchases	2,550	
Accounts Payable		5,250	Accounts Payable		2,550
2. Accounts Payable	3,100		Accounts Payable	5,100	
Purchase Returns		3,100	Purchase Returns		5,100
3. Accounts Payable	16,500		Accounts Payable	18,000	
Cash		16,500	Purchase Discounts		1,500
			Cash		16,500
4. Purchases	18,700		Purchases	18,700	
Freight-In	1,200		Accounts Payable		18,700
Accounts Payable		19,900			
5. Advertising Expense	1,340		Purchases	1,340	
Accounts Payable		1,340	Accounts Payable		1,340

Required:
Record the entries to correct each of these five errors separately.

PROBLEM 6-13
L.O. 4

Impact of Inventory Errors

The Major Value Pak Corporation reported the following data in its 19x2 annual report (in millions):

Excerpt from Balance Sheet

	At December 31	
	19x2	*19x1*
Inventory	$167	$159

Excerpt from Income Statement

	For the Year Ended December 31	
	19x2	*19x1*
Net income.	$31	$28

Assume that in 19x3, it was discovered that a clerical error was made in valuing the 19x1 ending inventory, and the correct value should have been $164 million instead of $159 million. Assume the tax rate for 19x1 and 19x2 is 40%.

Required:
1. By how much are assets overstated or understated at the end of 19x1?
2. By how much is net income overstated or understated for 19x1?
3. By how much are assets overstated or understated at the end of 19x2?
4. By how much is net income overstated or understated for 19x2?

PROBLEM 6-14
L.O. 5

Evaluating Inventory Changes

During 19xx, the Railsback Company sold merchandise costing $876,300 for $2,387,500. The Merchandise Inventory increased by $37,200 during 19xx to a year-end balance of $239,800. Accounts Payable decreased by $8,950 during 19xx to a year-end balance of $114,000. All purchases and sales are made on account. Accounts Receivable increased by $14,900 during 19xx to a year-end balance of $154,000.

Required:
1. Compute Railsback's net purchases for 19xx.
2. Compute cash payments made on Accounts Payable during 19xx assuming only merchandise inventory affects the Accounts Payable balance.
3. Compute the cash receipts from customers during 19xx assuming Accounts Receivable are only for customer credit sales.

PROBLEM 6-15
L.O. 5

Evaluating Inventory Changes

During the past year, Siller Corporation sold merchandise on open account which had cost $1,857,000 to customers for $3,225,000. From its beginning balance of $650,000, the Merchandise Inventory increased by $53,650 during the year. The balance in Accounts Payable decreased by $45,820 during the year to a year-end balance of $387,200. Assume all purchases and sales are made on account. Accounts Receivable decreased by $21,500 during the year to a year-end balance of $487,630.

Required:
1. Compute Siller's inventory additions (purchases) for the year.
2. Compute cash payments on accounts payable during the year (assume accounts payable are all for inventory purchases only).
3. Compute the cash collected from customers during the year (assume accounts receivable are only for customers' sales).

APPENDIX PROBLEMS

PROBLEM 6-16
L.O. 6

Inventory Costing Methods/Perpetual (Appendix 6A)

Consider the data in Problem 6-7. Assume the Caribbean Company uses the perpetual inventory system.

Required:
Calculate the following:

1. LIFO cost of goods sold for May.
2. LIFO cost of ending inventory at May 31.
3. FIFO cost of goods sold for May.
4. FIFO cost of ending inventory at May 31.

PROBLEM 6-17
L.O. 6

Inventory Costing/Perpetual (Appendix 6A)

Refer to the data given for the Jacobs Corporation in Problem 6-1.

Required:
1. Assume Jacobs uses the FIFO perpetual inventory method. Compute ending inventory, cost of goods sold, and gross margin for each of the two separate four-month periods.
2. Repeat requirement 1 above using the LIFO perpetual inventory method.

PROBLEM 6-18
L.O. 7

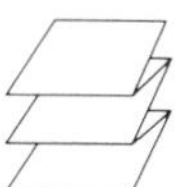

Retail Inventory Method (Appendix 6B)

The Retail Sales Company uses the retail inventory method to value its merchandise inventory. The following information is available:

	Cost	*Retail*
Beginning inventory	$139,780	$ 247,120
Purchases	996,320	1,720,880
Freight-in	42,750	
Purchase returns	(7,650)	(16,000)
Sales		1,703,000

Required:
1. What is the ending inventory at retail?
2. What is the cost to retail ratio?
3. What is the estimate of ending inventory and cost of goods sold?

PROBLEM 6-19
L.O. 7

Retail Inventory Method (Appendix 6B)

Flasks Department Store values its inventory using the retail method. The following data are available at January 31, 19x2:

	Cost/Price	*Retail Selling Price*
Inventory, 2/1/x1	$ 54,800	$ 65,200
Purchases	479,700	608,625
Purchase returns	(14,500)	(23,825)
Sales		587,930
Sales returns		(16,250)

Required:
Based on the data provided, compute the estimated cost of Flasks' ending inventory, cost of goods sold, and gross margin using the retail inventory estimation method.

PROBLEM 6-20
L.O. 8

LIFO Reserves (Appendix 6C)

The Balance Corporation reported the following data at December 31, 19x2:

	19x2	*19x1*
Inventory (FIFO)	$17,600	$16,900
Less LIFO reserve	2,850	3,150
Inventory (LIFO)	$14,750	$13,750

During 19x2, Balance discontinued several of its major lines of inventory, replacing them with newer, more efficient product lines. This change created LIFO liquidations that reduced the December 31, 19x1, LIFO reserve balance by $1,850. Balance has a tax rate of 40% on all income and reported net income of $3,440 in 19x2. Cost of goods sold for 19x2 was $83,200.

Required:
1. Did the cost of Balance's inventory acquired during 19x2 increase, decrease, or remain the same?
2. What was the 19x2 tax effect of the LIFO liquidations? (Indicate increase or decrease and amount.) In other words, how much more or less tax was paid in 19x2 because of the LIFO liquidations?
3. If the FIFO inventory method had been used during 19x2, what would cost of goods sold have been for 19x2? (Do not consider prior years, only 19x2.)

PROBLEM 6-21
L.O. 8

LIFO Reserves (Appendix 6C)

The following data pertain to Airy, Inc., as of December 31, 19x2:

	19x2	*19x1*
Balance sheet data:		
Inventory (FIFO value)	$10,000	$8,965
Less LIFO reserve	3,000	1,390
Inventory (LIFO value)	$ 7,000	$7,575
Other data:		
19x2 cost of goods sold (under LIFO)	$18,000	
19x2 tax rate	40%	
19x2 net income	2,250	

The LIFO reserve ($3,000 in 19x2) is the cumulative difference between the LIFO and FIFO inventory value over all prior years. The change in the LIFO reserve ($3,000 − $1,390) is the difference between LIFO and FIFO inventory values during 19x2. Since the reserve increased in 19x2, the difference between LIFO and FIFO became greater in 19x2.

Required:
1. What would the 19x2 cost of goods sold have been if the FIFO inventory method had been used in 19x2? (Do not consider prior years, only 19x2.)
2. What was the apparent 19x2 income tax savings attributable to the LIFO inventory method in comparison to the FIFO method?

PROBLEM 6-22

L.O. 8

LIFO Reserves/LIFO Liquidation (Appendix 6C)

The Taxing Corporation reported the following data in its 19x2 annual report?

	19x2	*19x1*
Balance sheet data:		
Inventory (FIFO)	$ 765,806	$ 820,000
Less LIFO reserve	188,506	159,400
Inventory (LIFO)	$ 577,300	$ 660,600
Other data:		
Cost of goods sold (LIFO). .	$10,954,000	$9,857,000

During 19x2, Taxing had LIFO liquidations of $40,000 from the elimination of one of its product lines.

Required:

1. Did Taxing's inventory costs increase or decrease during 19x2? By how much?
2. What would have been reported for cost of goods sold in 19x2 if Taxing had not liquidated LIFO inventory and if no cost increases or decreases had occurred?

CASES

CASE 6-1

L.O. 1

Inventory Systems

The Barnes Hardware Store has three stores in the area. The stores all carry the same items. About 50% of all merchandise carried has a cost of less than $5 per unit, with most of these low-priced items being carried in large quantities to avoid stockouts. The low-priced items represent about 60% of sales dollars. About 40% of all merchandise carried costs between $5 and $100 per unit, with the other 10% of the merchandise costing over $100 per unit. The mid-priced items account for 20% of sales dollars, while the high-priced merchandise accounts for the other 20% of sales dollars.

Barnes is currently using a periodic inventory system, but a computer salesperson has suggested that with some new sales register equipment and some computer support a perpetual system could be installed at a cost of about $250,000—a one-time cost. Barnes has annual sales of about $12 million and is presently carrying about $3 million in inventory.

Required:

1. What do you recommend Barnes do regarding its inventory system? Why?
2. What are the advantages and disadvantages of the present system?
3. What are the potential advantages and disadvantages of the proposed system?
4. What additional information would help you make a recommendation?

CASE 6-2

L.O. 2

Inventory Systems/Cost Flow Methods

Mason Jewelers has been in business for less than a year and is about to prepare its financial statements for the first time. Mason carries many standard items such as watches, gold chains, and so on that are not unique. They also carry some unique items such as valuable stones and gems that are priced and stored separately. The prices of most items have increased by over 10% during the past year, and Mason has replaced much of its original inventory several times at higher prices each time.

Mr. Mason, the owner, knows very little about accounting but has heard that different inventory methods can affect the amount of profit reported. Mason Jewelers has a $200,000 bank loan that is reviewed by the bank each year based on Mason's financial statements. Mr. Mason wants to put his best foot forward and report a healthy financial result to his bankers from the first year of operations. Also, he is considering an additional loan of $100,000 to expand his inventory. Mason Jewelers is expected to be in a 30% tax bracket this year.

Required:

1. Which inventory system or systems would you advise Mr. Mason to use? Explain your selections.
2. Assuming Mr. Mason decides he wants to maximize net income in the first year, which method should be used?
3. Assuming Mr. Mason wants to maximize cash flow in the first year, which method should be used?
4. Which method should Mason's bank prefer? Why?

CASE 6-3
L.O. 2

Inventory Cash Flow Choice

The Byte-Size Company has just finished its first year of operations. Its managers, Brad and Mary, were trying to decide which inventory method to use. Brad had made the following calculations:

Assume inventory was computed based on:

	LIFO	*FIFO*	*Weighted Average*
Ending Inventory	$1,755	$1,880	$1,800
Cost of Goods Sold	9,650	9,525	9,605

Brad favors using the LIFO method because it results in the highest cost of goods sold and, therefore, the lowest taxable income. He argues this will save on cash needed to pay taxes without making Byte-Size worse off. Mary favors using FIFO because it reports the highest net income. Besides, Mary argues that LIFO will just require more taxes to be paid in future periods to offset the lower taxes now, so how much better off is the company? Brad and Mary both seem committed to their positions.

Required:

1. Assume the inventory costs of Byte-Size are expected to increase each year in the future, which method do you favor? Explain your answer.
2. Assume the inventory costs are expected to decrease each year in the future, which method do you favor? Explain.
3. Identify any flaws in Brad's or Mary's arguments.
4. What reason can you give to help explain why all companies do not use LIFO?

CASE 6-4
L.O. 2

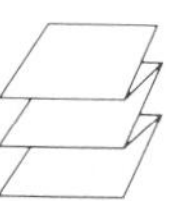

Cash Flow Choice and Purchase Decision

Raven Corporation started a new division of the business in 19x2 to acquire from wholesalers and sell to retail customers unfinished wooden kitchen sets. During the first year of operations, Raven made the following purchases:

Date (19x2)	*Units*	*Unit Cost*	*Total Cost*
January 19	1200	$180	$216,000
May 23	400	230	92,000
June 15	1200	240	288,000
Sept. 1	600	260	156,000
Nov. 15	800	270	216,000
	4200		$968,000

During 19x2 Raven sold 2,800 units for $900,000, with sales units increasing steadily throughout the year as people across the country heard of the economical high quality product from satisfied customers. Sales are expected to be brisk in 19x3, and management is considering purchasing an additional 2,000 units in December of 19x2 from the supplier at a unit price of $270. The supplier's costs have been increasing rapidly, and further cost increases are expected in 19x3. The offer for 2,000 units at $270 each will expire December 24, 19x2. No payments are required until April of 19x3 if the special offer is accepted by Raven.

Raven is a calendar year-end company. The wooden furniture division must decide which cost flow method will be used to cost out the sales in 19x2 and future years. Expenses other than for merchandise amounted to $128,000 in 19x2. Raven's year-end cash position is very low, but the bank has offered to extend additional credit to Raven. The income tax rate for 19x2 is 35%.

Required:

1. Ignore the offer to purchase an additional 2,000 units for a moment. Assuming Raven uses the periodic inventory system in the wooden furniture division, which cost flow method would you recommend for Raven? Explain.
2. Now consider the special purchase offer of 2,000 units for $270 each. Should Raven accept this offer? What affect would this decision have on your recommendation of a cost flow method?
3. Assume Raven is going to acquire the additional 2,000 units. Further assume the option to accept the special purchase offer has been extended until January 10, 19x3 (instead of December 24, 19x2). When would you make the purchase? Explain your choice.
4. Assume Raven decides to accept the special purchase offer in 19x2 and elects the LIFO method. Describe the effect on 19x2 net income and the effect on cash at year-end. (Assume taxes must be paid in cash at year-end.)
5. Assume Raven declines the special purchase offer and elects the FIFO cost flow method. Describe the effect on 19x2 net income and the effect on cash at year-end. (Assume taxes must be paid in cash at year-end.)

CASE 6-5
L.O. 2

LIFO Cost Flow and Taxes

Northern Power Company operates as an electric utility in northern Michigan. Its chief source of energy is coal, which provides fuel to power plants at six locations. The plants normally carry a minimum inventory of 6,000 tons of coal each during the winter months.

A coal miners strike during 19x5 is having a serious effect on Northern's operating results. Because Northern uses the LIFO periodic method and has a December 31 year-end, its year-end inventory is usually large and costed at very low (old) prices. For example, at the end of 19x4 Northern reported inventory of 42,000 tons: 40,000 tons at an average of $50 per ton from purchases which occurred 5 to 10 years earlier; and 2,000 tons from 19x4 purchases at $100 per ton. During 19x5, because of the strike, coal supplies are limited and Northern's cost per ton has reached $120.

The coal shortage has caused Northern's 19x5 year-end coal inventory to drop 32,000 tons to 10,000 tons. This, in turn, has caused Northern's profits to soar since low-cost coal inventory (including 26,000 tons at $50 per ton) from prior years (i.e., "LIFO layers") are being expensed against current revenues. The current revenue rates, set by the State Regulatory Commission (SRC), are based on coal costs of about $120 per ton. Because of the higher profits, the SRC is thinking about forcing Northern to give its customers a temporary rate reduction on electric bills in early 19x6. Also, because of the higher profits, 19x5 income taxes were about $400,000 higher than normal.

Required:

1. Northern is putting together a response to the SRC's proposal for a rate reduction. Identify any points you feel support Northern's case for no rate cuts.

2. Northern is developing a petition to the federal and state income tax authorities asking them to allow Northern to charge operations with coal at a cost of $120 per ton in computing taxable income. Northern would like your help in identifying factors supporting their argument. Northern plans to return its coal inventory to normal levels (about 40,000 tons) as soon as the strike is over.
3. Assume Northern wins its appeals for no rate reduction and for the use of the current $120 per ton cost in computing taxable income. **Before** Northern replaces the shortfall in the coal inventory (about 30,000 tons below normal levels at the end of 19x5), what will be the effect of the coal shortage on Northern's cash position? (Assume utility bills are paid in cash by customers each month.) What will be the effect on Northern's cash position after it replaces the shortfall in the coal inventory?

CASE 6-6
L.O. 2

Economic Effects of LIFO

The Star Share Corporation has been experiencing increasing inventory costs for years. Because of a conservative management team, however, Star Share has always used the FIFO inventory method. You have recently been promoted to chief financial officer (CFO) of the corporation, resulting in a large raise, a bonus based on net income, and a stock option plan. As one of your first projects, you investigate what would happen to Star Share if they changed to the LIFO inventory method. Your analysis provides the following results (amounts are in millions):

	Assumption	
	Continue to Use FIFO Method	*Switch to LIFO Method*
Ending inventory (asset) . . .	$ 435	$ 390
Cost of goods sold	3,850	3,895
Tax payments on income . . .	76.5	61.2
Net income	148.5	118.8
Dividends to stockholders. . .	80	80

Required:
Do you decide to switch to LIFO? Explain your decision, but confine your explanation to an evaluation of the cash flow effects of these alternatives.

EVALUATING FINANCIAL STATEMENTS

CASE 6-7
L.O. 5

Evaluating Inventory Changes—Dow Chemical Company

The following data are taken from a recent annual report of the Dow Chemical Company (in millions):

Balance Sheet

	19x2	19x1		19x2	19x1
Assets:			Liabilities:		
Cash.	$ 19	$ 12	Accounts payable . .	$947	$1,056
.					
.					
.					
Inventories	1,927	1,961			

Other data:

	19x2	*19x1*
Cost of goods sold	$9,516	$9,446

Assume that Dow's cost of goods sold consists only of inventory costs, and that all inventory is purchased on account.

Required:
1. How much inventory was acquired by Dow during 19x2?
2. How much cash was paid on accounts payable during 19x2?

APPENDIX CASES

CASE 6-8
L.O. 6

LIFO: Perpetual or Periodic? (Appendix 6A)

The Spear Company has been using the LIFO periodic inventory system for many years. The management is pleased with LIFO because of its tax savings feature. Spear has experienced cost increases in all inventory items each year, and had a balance in its LIFO Reserve account of $447,350 as of 19x3.

During 19x4, management asks you to explain whether LIFO perpetual offers any advantages over LIFO periodic. A business acquaintance of Spear's president claims that with LIFO perpetual he is able to achieve tax savings **and** increased profits when needed. Apparently, the increased profits stem from the timing of purchases in such a way that older (lower) LIFO prices are sometimes charged to cost of goods sold, resulting in larger profits.

To help explain how this might work, consider using the following example of one of Spear's main inventory items for the month of January 19x4:

	Units	*Unit Cost*	*Total*
Beginning LIFO inventory:			
From 19x8	50	$ 80	$4,000
From 19x0	40	100	4,000
	90		$8,000
Purchases 19x4:			
1/15/x4	45	160	$7,200
1/22/x4	60	162	$9,720
Sales 19x4:			
1/5/x4	10 units		
1/12/x4	35		
1/19/x4	20		
1/25/x4	35		
	100 units		

Required:
1. Explain to Spear's president how LIFO perpetual can result in higher profits than LIFO periodic.
2. Is it possible for LIFO perpetual to provide higher profits *and* greater tax savings than LIFO periodic?

3. Some people argue that LIFO perpetual results in *more taxes* than almost any other method (including FIFO) in those years where older, lower cost units are charged to cost of goods sold (e.g., when units costing $80 from 19x8 or $100 from 19x0 are sold in the example above). They say that this offsets the tax benefits of earlier years, making LIFO (or LIFO perpetual) a more costly inventory method with no real cash savings. The president asks for your comments on this potential criticism.

CASE 6-9
L.O. 7

Inventory Estimation Methods (Appendix 6B)

The Arbor Luggage Company had a fire in its warehouse on December 15, 19x2, that destroyed all of its inventory. The company needs to determine how much inventory was in the warehouse at the time of the fire in order to file a claim with its insurance company. Fortunately, the accounting records are thought to be accurate and up-to-date, with purchases of merchandise inventory recorded up to the time of the fire. Unfortunately, the company does not have a perpetual inventory system and does not know the amount of inventory that was in the warehouse at the time of the fire. The last physical count of the warehouse inventory took place on December 31, 19x1.

Required:
1. What accounting method might be available to help Arbor Luggage estimate the warehouse inventory lost in the fire?
2. Identify the accounting information required in order to make the estimate, and how it would be used to estimate the lost inventory.

CASE 6-10
L.O. 8

LIFO Reserve—General Motors (Appendix 6C)

General Motors Corporation uses the lower-of-cost-or-market (LCM) inventory method, where "cost" is based primarily on the LIFO method for domestic (U.S.) inventories. The following data were reconstructed from GM's 19x8 footnote disclosures.

	($ in millions)	
	19x8	*19x7*
Inventory at FIFO	$10,509.6	$10,299.6
LIFO reserve	2,525.3	2,359.9
Inventory at LIFO	$ 7,984.3	$ 7,939.7

GM reported no LIFO liquidations in 19x8.

Required:
1. What was the effect on GM's 19x8 pre-tax income from using LIFO rather than FIFO for 19x8? (Do **not** include the effect from before 19x8.)
2. What happened to GM's inventory costs during 19x8? Did costs increase, decrease, remain about the same, or can you determine this from the data given?
3. What is your estimate of the current cost of GM's 19x8 ending inventory?
4. GM's 19x8 return on asset ratio is computed as ($ in millions):

$$\frac{\text{19x8 Net income}}{\text{Ending total assets}} = \frac{\$4{,}856.3}{\$164{,}063.1} = 2.96\%$$

What would happen to GM's 19x8 return on assets ratio if GM had used FIFO in 19x8 and all prior years? Assume the tax rate for all years is 30%.

FINANCIAL STATEMENTS

FINANCIAL STATEMENT COMPONENTS EMPHASIZED IN CHAPTER 7

White Corporation
Income Statement
For 1991

Revenues
Interest income
Expenses
xxxx
xxxx

	1991	1990
Interest income	$XXX	$XXX

White Corporation
Balance Sheet
12/31/91

Current assets
Cash
Notes receivable
Less notes receivable discounted
Noncurrent assets
xxxx
xxxx
Current liabilities
xxxx
xxxx
Noncurrent liabilities
xxxx
xxxx
Stockholders' equity
xxxx
xxxx

	1991	1990
Cash	$XXX	$XXX
Notes receivable	XXX	XXX
Less notes receivable discounted	(XX)	(XX)

White Corporation
Cash Flow Statement
For 1991

Operating activities
Cash paid for interest
Investing activities
xxxx
xxxx
Financing activities
Cash from loan
Cash paid at maturity of note

	1991	1990
Cash paid for interest . .	$ (XX)	$(XXX)

	1991	1990
Cash from loan	$XXX	$ XX
Cash paid at maturity of note	(XX)	(XXX)

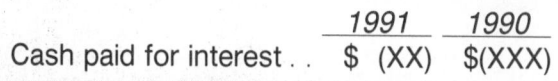

C H A P T E R 7

Internal Controls, Cash, and Notes Receivable

LEARNING OBJECTIVES

After studying Chapter 7, you should understand:

1. The five general principles of internal control, pp. 350-51.
2. The internal control procedures used to safeguard assets and assure the accuracy and reliability of accounting data, pp. 351-53.
3. The cost-benefit evaluation of internal controls, pp. 353-55.
4. The advantages of electronic data processing, pp. 355-58.
5. Cash flow management and cash control, pp. 358-64.
6. Cash reconciliation, pp. 364-69.
7. A petty cash imprest system, pp. 369-72.
8. Accounting for notes receivable, pp. 372-79.
9. Special journals and control accounts (Appendix), pp. 382-86.

Management has the obligation to safeguard assets and to assure that accounting information is accurate. The chapter begins with a discussion of the procedures businesses adopt to safeguard assets and follows with a discussion of accounting for cash and notes receivable.

Cash is the most flexible and most widely accepted asset. It is used in all kinds of transactions as a medium of exchange. The flow of cash in and out of the business provides the momentum that enables the business to continue its operations. Owners, customers, and creditors bring cash into the business; and cash flows out of the business to owners in the form of dividends, to suppliers for products and services, and to creditors in payment of obligations. Employees, governments, and many others have cash transactions with businesses. Another current asset that is often associated with cash is short-term investment in marketable securities. This topic is covered in Chapter 12 along with other investments.

Even when a transaction with an outside party does not immediately involve cash, it usually affects the company's cash flow sooner or later. For example, purchases and sales on credit eventually involve cash flow. Successful business operations depend on successful management of the company's cash.

In Chapter 5, you were introduced to the importance of credit sales and accounts receivable in businesses. This chapter continues the discussion on accounting for receivables by explaining how companies account for notes receivable. A note is a formal contract issued by the debtor as evidence of an obligation to pay a specific amount to the creditor at a specific time. Sometimes customers convert their accounts receivable into a note. The discussion on notes receivable includes discounting a note receivable at a bank. The appendix to the chapter gives additional information on special accounting journals and control accounts.

INTERNAL CONTROL

Businesses are risky; there are general business risks related to competition, regulation, failed customers, innovations, and many other normal business uncertainties. Also, there are risks associated with errors and irregularities, which can be intentional or unintentional. Management must attempt to control errors and irregularities by installing an adequate system of internal controls.

What Are Internal Controls?

Consider the following conversation between the controller (Bonnie) of Fashions Inc., and the manager (Jack) of one of its local department stores, who has just been promoted directly from a position in fashion design and buying.

Controller: Jack, we are instituting a new plan of internal control for all of our stores and I'm here to answer any of your general questions.

Store Manager: Remember Bonnie, I know nothing about accounting. Give me a simple definition of internal control. Is it kind of like intestinal fortitude? Ha, Ha.

Controller: Control is a term we use for a system to help assure us that the assets of the company are safeguarded, that all transactions are authorized, and that policies are followed and stuff like that. What I have brought with me is a checklist of things to be concerned about and a short write-up on implementing each item on that list. First we want you and your top people to read the write-ups and next month one of my people will come in to help with specifics.

Store Manager: Wait a minute. My people are honest and I keep a pretty close eye on everything. Isn't that enough?

Controller: I agree that most of our people are honest, the vast majority are, but remember that a person's situation may change, and sometimes we, as managers, don't understand the pressure some of the staff may be under, so temptation can overcome even those we trust.

Store Manager: Ok, give me a concrete example of what we're talking about.

Controller: Think of a basic transaction type like purchasing and think of all the opportunities there are for losses. The ordering process, for instance. Here we want separation of duties so that one person can't both perpetrate and hide an irregularity. So we want to make sure we have policies about authorizations of a purchase, ordering, taking custody of the merchandise, paying the bills, recording of the transactions, and so on. In general we don't want the same people doing all of those duties.

Store Manager: I see, but that might be a problem because we don't have that many different people to spread the duties out to.

Controller: Well, we have ways of judging just how fine the separation has to be. In some cases duties can be combined but never all of them. Going on with this type of transaction, in addition to separation of duties we would want to safeguard the inventory once we take possession, which means restricting access to the inventory itself and to the records of inventories. Also, authority and responsibility for inventory must be assigned to certain people so that there is no question as to who makes access decisions. Another general procedure we think is valuable is a system of reconciliations where we would count the inventory and make sure that the ending amount ties to the amount acquired less sales, tying accounts payable to the statement of our supplier and that kind of thing.

Store Manager: OK. I get the picture. What's in that ominous looking folder there?

Controller: This contains checklists for internal controls issues for all major types of transactions like sales, purchasing, cash receipts and payments, and production.

After reading the above narrative, you might conclude that internal controls seem like just good common sense and that is true, but as with our store manager, a trusting manager will not focus on all the potential problem areas and therefore careful study and continuous oversight is needed. We will now give more formal definitions of internal control. **Internal control** can broadly be defined as the firm's overall plan to (1) safeguard assets; (2) check the accuracy and reliability of accounting data; (3) promote efficiency; and (4) encourage adherence to managerial policies. The focus in this chapter will be on the first two elements since they are directly related to the firm's accounting system. Of course companies would like to prevent all errors and irregularities from ever occurring but, practically, the goal in most settings is to reduce the amounts of losses to a minimum and to increase the probability of detection for those that do occur.

The extent of the internal controls necessary to protect the operations of a business depends on the size and function of the business. In Chapter 5, you followed two entrepreneurs as they established their business goals, obtained resources, and developed plans for the operation of Byte-Size, Inc. With the help of a graduate accounting student, Byte-Size established an accounting system that enabled it to monitor operations and determine possible corrective action for their cash flow problem. As the enterprise grows, it must add internal controls to protect its assets and accounting data and to make sure its employees operate efficiently and comply with prescribed managerial policies.

The first topic in this section discusses the general principles of internal control. Then you will learn some of the procedures companies use to establish internal controls over assets and accounting data. An explanation of the cost-benefit evaluation of internal controls follows; and a discussion on electronic data processing concludes this section.

Before studying the topics that follow, you should realize that competent, honest employees are the foundation of all successful internal controls. No matter how well designed a system is, it will fail if the people charged with its operations do not perform adequately. Great care should be taken in screening new personnel, providing thorough employee training, placing employees in positions commensurate with their capabilities and interests, and providing feedback on employee performance. There is no substitute for motivated, honest employees.

General Principles of Internal Control

Objective 1
The five general principles of internal control.

Prior to establishing internal controls, a business must have an effective organizational plan or structure designed by management according to the goals and functions of the business. The type of organizational plan used by a business depends on many factors, such as size of the business, philosophy of management, and so on. For example, Byte-Size, Inc. (our Chapter 5 example), is a small business with only the owners, Mary and Brad, working in the business. Byte-Size, therefore, would have a simple organizational plan. Mary and Brad agreed before they organized Byte-Size how they would share the work and responsibilities. However, as the company grows and adds new employees, it must develop a more elaborate organizational plan. The internal controls the company builds into its organizational plan should be based on the following general principles:

1. **Authorization and responsibility.** Top management must authorize the lines of authority in the organization and determine the responsibilities of each employee. In addition, each employee in authority is responsible for his or her decisions and actions, and the performance of subordinates must be authorized by a supervisor.
2. **Separation of duties (division of work).** Separation of duties discourages employee theft and fraud. In addition, the work of one employee can provide an internal check on the work by another employee thus helping to avoid honest mistakes.
3. **Protection of assets.** Physical assets should be covered by insurance to ensure they will be replaced if a casualty occurs. To ensure against theft, employees in important asset-responsible positions should be rotated periodically; and employees handling cash should be bonded. **Bonding** is a type of insurance policy taken out on certain employees that will pay the company damages if an employee misappropriates assets. The actual control of the cash asset is discussed later in this chapter.
4. **Mechanical and electronic devices.** Various devices such as computers, cash registers, check protectors, and time clocks are valuable aids for internal control.

5. **Accounting system procedures.** Many different procedures can be used to ensure that the accounting system provides internal controls over the recording of transactions pertaining to assets, liabilities, revenues, and expenses. Some of the procedures used to protect the accounting system are discussed in the following subsection on internal control procedures.

These five general principles should make you aware of the importance of internal control. In fact, to protect stockholders of publicly owned corporations, the federal government established the Foreign Corrupt Practices Act in 1977. Although the act was originally established to prevent bribes of foreign officials by employees of publicly traded U.S. corporations, the act calls for a system of controls, and the management of the corporation must assume the responsibility to maintain accurate accounting records and a system of internal control over these records.

Internal Control Procedures

Objective 2
The internal control procedures used to safeguard assets and assure the accuracy and reliability of accounting data.

Put in accounting terminology, internal controls are the technical procedures of an accounting information system that are designed to ensure that (1) relevant transactions are recorded, (2) the financial statements are sound, and (3) the company's assets are protected. Since the primary duty of such internal controls is the safeguarding of assets and the accuracy and reliability of accounting data, the paragraphs that follow discuss these two topics in turn.

Safeguarding Assets. The following specific internal controls show specific approaches to the general goals discussed earlier.

1. **Separation of physical asset control from asset recordkeeping.** In Chapter 6, you learned the importance of inventory. Unfortunately, the theft of inventory by employees is a serious problem in many companies. Thus, internal controls should be established so that the same employee does not control the company's physical assets and keep the records for these assets. Cash, the most liquid of assets, is covered in detail in a separate section of this chapter. Much of that discussion deals with controls over cash.

2. **Periodic comparison of actual assets on hand with amount reported in the records.** The use of the physical inventory count studied in Chapter 6 is an important element of internal control. At least once a year a physical inventory count should be taken. The need for an asset count also applies to plant, property, and equipment items. Theft of small items, such as hand tools, is difficult to detect, but procedures that limit access and assign responsibility can discourage theft. For example, if a foreman knows that a detailed accounting of all hand tools in a department is necessary, he or she will devise methods to control access to the hand tools. Later in this chapter, under bank reconciliation procedures, we emphasize the importance of comparing actual cash on hand and in banks with cash records.

3. **Proof that a liability exists before payment is made.** The general principle of separation of duties is also effective in controlling theft associated with payments to suppliers. The employee who receives the merchandise should not authorize payment for the merchandise. Also, an invoice to a supplier should not be authorized for payment unless the purchase order (the document authorizing the purchase of the merchandise) and the receiving report (document prepared when merchandise is received) are attached to the invoice.

Ensuring the Accuracy and Reliability of Accounting Data. The accuracy and reliability of accounting data begins with authorized transactions. Again, some of the general internal control measures mentioned earlier are useful to ensure that the accounting data is accurate and reliable. In addition, companies can use various other procedures. Some of these procedures are discussed in the paragraphs that follow.

1. **Accuracy of source documents.** Since external transactions originate with source documents (checks, invoices, purchase orders, shipping and receiving reports), these documents should be prenumbered to discourage tampering. Companies also use other methods to promote and/or detect authenticity and accuracy of the documents, such as requiring employee signatures on various documents to indicate that the figures have been checked.

2. **Ensuring accurate recordkeeping.** Several procedures can be used to check the recordkeeping of employees. A valuable procedure is to separate recording duties so that related transactions are not recorded by one employee. Special journals—discussed in item 3 that follows—also help to ensure accurate recordkeeping.

3. **Special journals.** In Chapter 5, you were introduced to subsidiary ledgers and the relationship of subsidiary ledgers to the general ledger. In addition to providing the company with necessary and detailed information, subsidiary ledgers can promote separation of duties and double checks for the account balances.

Chapter 5 also stated that many companies use special journals in addition to the general journal. These **special journals** are books of original entry designed to efficiently process a class of repetitive transactions. They add efficiency in some applications and provide an opportunity to implement internal controls. Companies commonly keep special journals for sales, purchases, cash receipts, and cash disbursements. Thus, the sales transactions are entered only in the sales journal, the purchases transactions in the purchases journal, and so on. If scale of operations permits, separation of duties is possible by assigning different people to each journal. The appendix to this chapter illustrates the use of special journals and ledger control accounts.

Accounting systems that use special journals still need a general journal. Companies always have some transactions that occur infrequently or do not fall into the common categories represented by the special journals. For example, an unusual transaction such as the purchase of land for common stock would be recorded in the general journal.

The separation of groups of transactions into special journals creates a more efficient method of recording transactions and provides more control over accounting procedures. In manual accounting systems, special journals also lead to more efficient posting of transaction information to the ledger accounts.

4. **Regular evaluations of recordkeeping.** Every internal control system must include regular recordkeeping evaluations to make sure that all the appropriate control techniques are installed and followed. Owners of small businesses usually are personally involved in maintaining controls and evaluating the company's internal control system. Larger businesses often have **internal auditing departments** ensuring that internal controls are performing as designed. These departments make periodic internal audits.

In many large corporations the internal audit department is required to perform two types of audits—operational audits and financial audits. An **opera-**

tional audit focuses on management controls and how well various levels of management are performing under these controls, and it helps to determine if efficiency is achieved. The **financial audit** tests for conformance to accounting procedures and assures management that the controls in the accounting system are functioning as designed and the system is providing reliable information.[1]

Cost-Benefit Evaluation of Internal Controls

Objective 3
The cost-benefit evaluation of internal control.

An accounting system is subject to the same cost-benefit evaluation as any other business function. Companies must judge the costs of enlarging their accounting systems and implementing internal controls against the benefits they will receive. Costs are usually increased when companies (1) increase the amount of accounting information recorded and reported, (2) increase the speed with which this information is available, and (3) add internal controls to protect the accounting system. Generally, the larger the company, the greater is the need for enlarged accounting systems and increased internal controls. But managers must always question whether the increased costs are worth the benefits received.

For example, assume that a restaurant has one waiter who prepares the guest checks and also collects the money from the customers. Principles of good internal control would suggest that one employee records a customer's invoice (guest check) and another employee accepts the customer's payment. Thus, to avoid potential problems, the restaurant owner could hire a cashier. Then the waiter would prepare prenumbered guest checks, and the cashier would collect the money and retain the check. At the end of the day, the amount of money collected should equal the total amount of the guest checks. Any unaccounted guest check numbers could be investigated.

The separation of duties suggested above usually improves the accuracy of the accounting information and reduces the chance that any money or other asset will be misappropriated. Note, however, that if the restaurant owner hires a cashier, the cost of running the business may increase. The restaurant owner must weigh the cost of adding this internal control against the benefit that would be received. Often a manager finds that it is difficult to place a specific dollar value on such a potential change.

Electronic Data Processing

In this section, we will concentrate on illustrating the advantages of computers in the accounting system rather than how computers work, since most of you are familiar with computer systems. Consider the following features of a system:

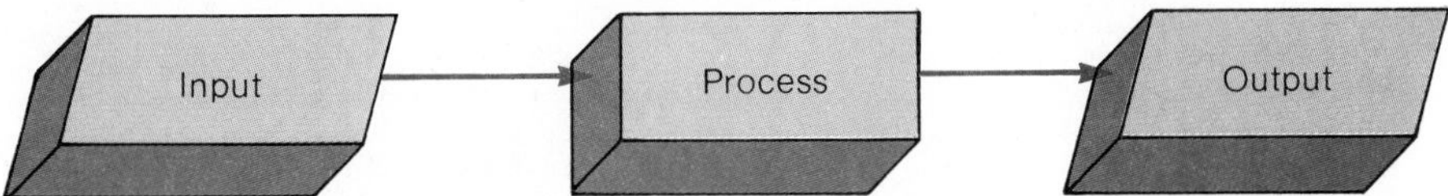

This general pattern applies to all kinds of systems; for example, in manufacturing where the inputs are raw materials, the process is the work of applying labor and equipment to materials, and the output is the finished product.

The electronic data processing system has the same basic structure with the final output being information and each step involving electronic devices to capture, process, and communicate the information.

[1]In addition to the internal audit, the books and records of many companies are subject to external audits, as introduced in Chapter 1. An **external audit** is a review by an outside independent auditor who is not an employee of the company. These audits are conducted by firms of certified public accountants and are part of the controls exercised by parties external to the company's management, such as stockholders and bankers.

Data input is accomplished in all sorts of ways but in all cases some change in the business occurs; for instance, inventory is increased or decreased, and that is entered by a person, or even automatically in some cases. The process would then update files related to inventory; and the output could be a check written to suppliers, an updated inventory report, or any other report of which inventory is a component. For instance, the income statement and balance sheet are affected by all the inventory transactions for a period, therefore the system has to keep track of all changes over many periods of time. Electronic output in the case of inventories could involve access to current balances by a production manager who needs to know how many specific items are available in order to schedule production.

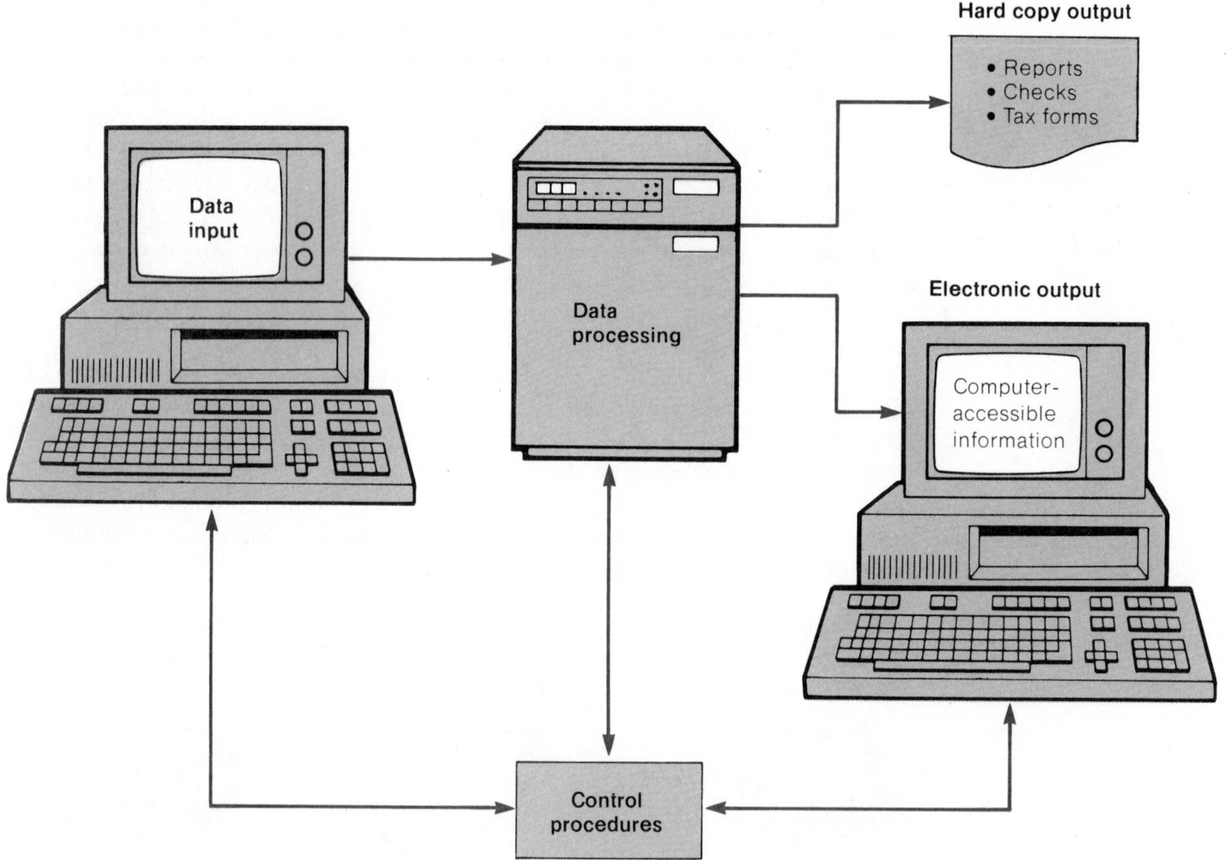

Because information is so crucial to organizational success, the concept of control of information is as important as control of any other resource. The above diagram shows that control functions are integrated into electronic data processing systems, where a key objective is to make sure that access to the system is proper and authorized.

Computer systems can range from the most sophisticated systems used by large corporations to the less complicated systems used by small businesses. With the decreasing prices of computers and the increasing computer training given to virtually all employees, some type of computer system is within the reach of all businesses regardless of size.

The widespread use of computers has resulted in significant changes in the gathering and processing of accounting data in accounting systems. Computers have increased the amount and kind of data that can be recorded, summarized, and analyzed for management's use. Also, the computer's capacity for massive storage and rapid calculation has resulted in quicker processing of transactions. As a result, managers are asking for more timely information than ever before. Although the per unit cost of processing the information has gone down, some contend the increase in total volume has driven overall costs up. In any event, new opportunities for increased efficiency have certainly been created, but new challenges for controlling business operations have also been created.

Since not all the decision-making information that managers need is financial, the accounting system is only part of the overall information system used to run a company. Managers must consider the financial and nonfinancial results of management action, and the accounting data must be carefully coordinated with the company's overall data information system.

Computerized processing is a blend of people, machine, programs, and procedures designed to add efficiency and effectiveness to the accounting system. The computer revolution provides several important advantages for the accounting process:

Objective 4
The advantages of electronic data processing.

1. **Quick processing**—especially for large-volume jobs such as invoices and payrolls.
2. **Timeliness of reports**—accounts can be updated instantaneously.
3. **Analysis**—results and forecasts of business operations can be prepared and compared immediately, allowing continuous reordering of inventory.
4. **Reducing certain risks**—credit cards can be authorized via telecommunications, for example.
5. **Increased accuracy**—computers seldom make computational or clerical errors.

Data can be entered into the computerized accounting system in batches or on a real-time basis. In a **batch system,** entries are collected for some period of time and entered into the computer periodically—daily or weekly. When a transaction is entered into the computer in a **real-time system,** it is immediately posted to the general and subsidiary ledger accounts and incorporated into reports. One entry in the system transfers data to several places and into various reports.

While a real-time system can work with one entry, manual systems often involve multiple entries requiring one entry in the general ledger accounts and another entry in the subsidiary accounts; and if the same information is needed for another report (such as for inventory records) a third entry is likely to be made. These multiple entries make the collecting of information costly and increase the chance for errors. In the computerized system, both the cost and number of error possibilities should decrease.

Although fewer clerical errors may occur in the computerized system, the errors that do occur may be difficult to track. The paper flow that characterizes manual systems makes tracing errors to sources relatively easy. The electronic trail in computer systems is elusive, and special control procedures are needed before such systems are auditable.

The speed of computerized data gathering and accounting entry processing is evident when you compare the computerized systems commonly used today in large grocery and retail stores with the method used in small retail businesses. In a small business, a sale is usually rung up on a cash register. The register clerk enters the price of each item purchased. Often a code is also entered that identifies the department that sold the item. The register can accumulate not only the customer's total purchase but also the total daily sales for each department and the entire store. At the end of the day, the results of the day's activities are printed out on a tape produced by the cash register. This tape contains the information that accountants enter into the accounting journals. For example, assume the tape for July 21, 19xx, showed the following information:

Department sales:	
Hardware	$1,026
Paint	3,079
Clothing	2,973
Sundries	375
Total department sales	$7,453
Sales tax	373
Total cash collected	$7,826

Accountants enter the above information into the journals, either at the end of that day or at some later time. The entry in the general journal is:

19xx			
July 21	Cash (A)	7,826	
	Hardware Sales (R)		1,026
	Paint Sales (R)		3,079
	Clothing Sales (R)		2,973
	Sundries Sales (R)		375
	Sales Taxes Payable (L)		373
	To record cash register sales.		

In addition to the sales transaction, the store must also account for the cost of the inventory sold, and it must have procedures to reorder necessary inventory.

Companies using modern electronic data processing systems design their computerized accounting system so that sales data immediately enters the entire accounting system. In addition, significantly more information is obtained at the time of the sale. This added information improves management's ability to manage the company.

For example, in a retail business with a modern electronic data processing system, the register clerk records most of the purchased products by entering the product's UPC (Uniform Product Code) directly into the computer (see Exhibit 7-1). The computer to which the cash register is attached enters the appropriate prices, identifies the department that made the sale, totals the sale, calculates the sales tax, and totals the amount owed by the customer. When the product has no UPC, the register clerk must use the cash register keys to enter the product's inventory number, and the computer completes the operation. Now the computer has the same information about the sale that was in the cash register totals of the previous example. In addition, as soon as the register clerk enters the product's UPC or inventory number, the computer records the data into the

EXHIBIT 7-1

Computerized Cash Register System

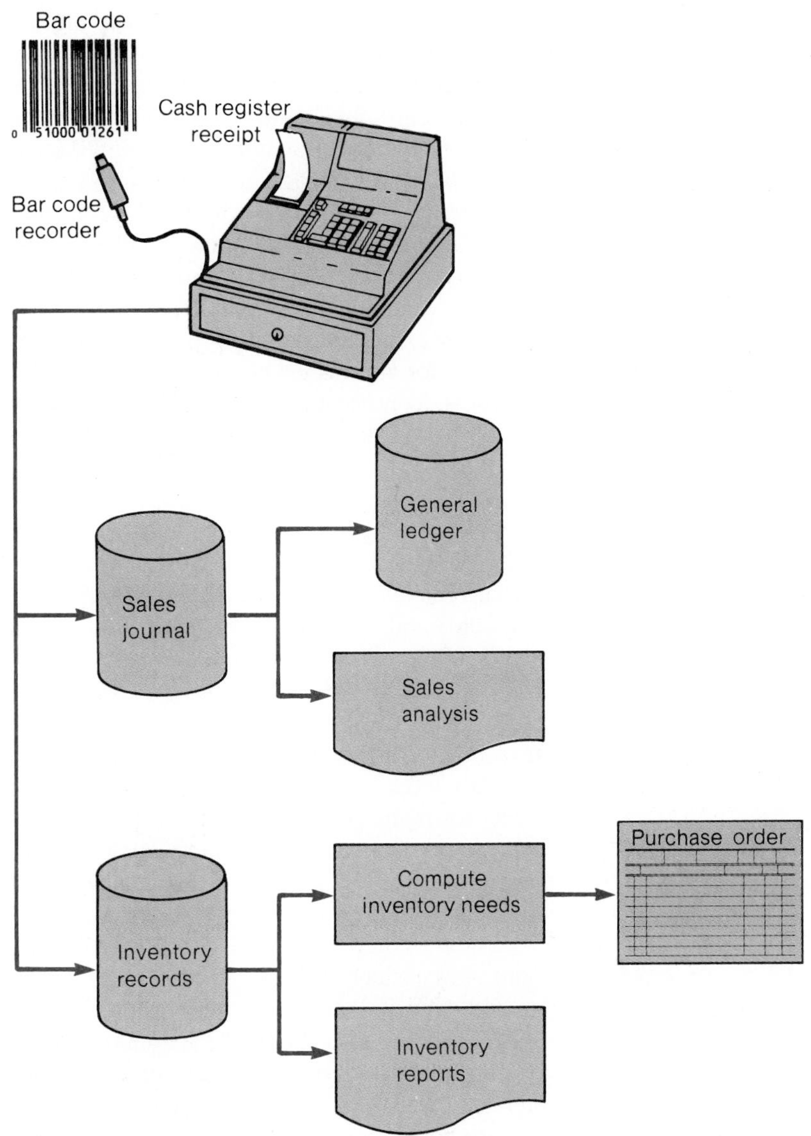

accounting system. Thus, entries into the accounting system are made almost instantaneously instead of waiting until the end of the day or some future time.

Computerized accounting systems also supply information valuable for inventory management. When a product's UPC or inventory number is entered into the computer, it automatically keeps track of the products that are sold. As a result, managers can prepare reports indicating what products must be ordered from the warehouse or purchased from suppliers.

Exhibit 7-1 shows how the computerized cash register system begins with a UPC and puts out recorded information into a sales journal and inventory records. The sales journal in the exhibit is a subsidiary journal mentioned earlier in the chapter and is discussed in detail in the appendix to this chapter.

As is true with all business decisions, a careful analysis of the **cost and benefits** of adopting new technology is imperative. Given the current level of competition, businesses simply must explore all avenues of reducing costs and increasing efficiency. In practice, because of the economies of scale, large and complex entities are utilizing more and more sophisticated electronic data processing systems, but smaller entities are also benefiting greatly from the improvements in power and flexibility of the small-scale systems currently available.

Although the introduction of electronic data processing has made possible the gathering of more decision-making information at relatively low cost, electronic data processing has some problems. The ease with which data can be recorded, transferred, and analyzed increases the need for special internal controls. For example, in a computer environment, separation of duties involves such steps as authorization of program changes and the use of different programmers for various elements of the accounting system. Security steps include passwords, identification numbers, machine readable codes, and automatic limits on certain transactions.

CASH

Cash is a word that we normally use in our everyday life when referring to coins and currency. Generally, we call it money. In accounting, **cash** includes more than coins and currency; it also includes amounts on deposit such as checking accounts, and checks and money orders made out to the business. Accountants define cash as money that a business actually has on hand and the money a business has a right to and easy access to, such as money orders, checks, and balances in checking accounts.

Cash is the most current and the most liquid of assets. It can be used immediately for many purposes in and out of business. While other business assets, such as raw materials, computers, delivery trucks, and buildings, have only specific uses, cash is acceptable as the general medium of exchange. Cash is flexible; it can be used to rent or purchase any number of products and services.

When a company uses a checking account, the checks written on the account are considered the same as cash payments. Checking accounts are called **demand deposits** because the depositor has free access to the cash without advance notification to the bank. If a bank requires notification before a business can use the money, these accounts are called **time deposits** and usually they earn interest. Because the business may not have immediate access to time deposits, they are not as liquid as cash and are classified as investments.

In addition to time deposits, short-term and long-term investments with withdrawal restrictions should not be classified as cash. Also, if a loan contract with a bank requires that the borrower deposit specific sums (called **compensating balances**) in a noninterest-earning account or an account that earns less than the market rate of interest, this money is classified as an investment or restricted cash, since the money is not freely available to the depositor. Usually, these compensating balances must be maintained as long as the loan is outstanding.

In contrast to investments, cash is completely liquid; and unless otherwise specifically stated in a contract, all business debts can be paid in cash. Businesses use cash to pay their employees, taxes, and dividends to stockholders. Customers use cash to pay for a company's services and products. Although cash can be used immediately for legitimate business purposes, it can be used just as easily for unauthorized purposes.

The flexibility of cash disappears when it is used to purchase another asset such as a piece of equipment or a building because the asset purchased may not be easily sold and turned back into cash. For example, if a company purchases a factory building to manufacture its products rather than subcontract the products from another company, the company has committed funds hoping to increase its efficiency in the long term. At the same time, however, future cash decisions have been restricted. The company also assumes that spending the cash for the building will increase the future flow of cash into the business, but it takes time for such returns to be earned.

One of management's greatest responsibilities is controlling cash flows. This section begins with the importance of cash flow management. Then a discussion on cash flow control continues the coverage of protection of assets begun earlier in the chapter.

WHY MINIMIZE CASH ON HAND?

Before we delve into the specifics of managing cash and accounting for cash transactions, consider the following conversation between Bonnie (recall she is the controller of Fashions, Inc., from our introduction to internal controls on page 348) and Jack (the store manager).

Controller: Another major area we need to work on is cash management. We want all of our people to adopt the philosophy that too much cash is bad.

Store Manager: Oh yea, empty your pockets. I'll take all you have.

Controller: Ha, Ha. Very funny. But in a way that proves my point. Cash is so liquid that it creates a control problem, especially if it's in currency. In addition, it doesn't earn us a return if it's idle.

Store Manager: Sure, so we deposit it in the bank on a daily basis.

Controller: Right, but ordinary checking, while safeguarding the asset, doesn't usually earn any interest. We want to establish procedures that safeguard the asset, maintain minimum necessary balances in noninterest-earning accounts, and have the maximum return on all of our cash.

Store Manager: We need to be a bit flexible. We can't work with zero in our checking accounts.

Controller: You're correct, but we want to always work toward minimizing the amount and also be able to pay obligations as they come due, and that means paying a lot more attention to the timing of payments. For example, your store's weekly payroll runs about $18,000, right? You issue those checks on Friday and they clear the banks on Monday. We want to put the money in the checking accounting at the latest time the bank will allow to cover the checks. Now some of our stores are keeping the payroll amount for a whole week before the checks are issued. Our investment people could be earning interest for all that time. Multiply that lost interest by our 30 stores for several weeks a year, and we're talking about a lot of lost revenues.

Cash Flow Management

Objective 5
Cash flow management and cash control.

You should be familiar with the importance of timing cash flows. As you recall, the Byte-Size Company of Chapter 5 had a cash flow problem. Even though the entrepreneurs followed their accountant's advice and borrowed money before they began their business, an analysis of the company's operations after three months showed that Byte-Size's liquidity problem had not been completely solved. A severe cash shortage was likely without more financing.

Small companies are not the only ones where cash is of major concern. In any one period, a large company may have millions of dollars of cash inflows and outflows while the company's cash balance may be a relatively small amount. Timing these cash inflows and outflows is one of the most important and difficult functions of managers.

Managers must time the inflow of cash so that enough cash is available to pay the company's obligations as they occur. If management fails to keep enough cash flowing in to meet the company's obligations, a serious situation can develop. Many companies have gone bankrupt because their cash flow was poorly timed and inadequate. Management also must not have too much cash on hand, since idle cash is not productive. Thus, the goal is to have just enough cash on hand to meet company obligations and also have a small cash cushion for emergencies.

Cash Control

You learned from the discussion on internal control that safeguarding assets is an important function of management. Because of the relative ease with which cash can be used for unintended purposes, special precautions must be taken to safeguard cash. Some of these precautions have been discussed earlier in the chapter. Additional procedures to ensure the safety of cash are discussed in the paragraphs that follow.

Prudent **cash control** usually involves the following steps:

1. Employees who handle cash should not record cash transactions.
2. Employees who handle cash receipts should not handle cash payments.
3. Significant amounts of cash should not be held as currency but should be deposited in the bank intact each day.
4. All cash disbursements should be made by check and approved by someone who is separate from the check writing and signing function.
5. Prenumbered checks should be used for disbursements except for small amounts for which a petty cash imprest system (to be defined later in the chapter) should be used.
6. Periodic bank reconciliations are prepared by employees who do not handle cash or record cash transactions.

You will notice that most of these safeguards, and many other safeguards used by companies, are designed to isolate functions so that no employee can misuse cash without the collusion of one or more other employees. The following example illustrates the importance of separation of duties pertaining to the handling of cash.

Employee A handles the receipt of money (currency, not checks) from customers and also records and deposits the money in the bank. Upon receipt of a $300 currency payment from customer X, employee A pockets the money and does not record the receipt until customer Y makes a payment of at least $300 in currency, at which time customer X's payment is recorded. Customer Y's payment is not recorded until customer Z pays, and so on. In this way, employee A has effectively taken $300 from the company by delaying the date when cash receipts are recorded and deposited. This activity is called **lapping** because the cash receipts of one customer are applied to the receivables of another customer. The separation of duties would force employee A to find other dishonest coworkers to help perpetrate and conceal the crime.

The above example is simplified to illustrate the importance of separation of duties. It would be more difficult for employee A to appropriate the money if checks made out to the company were involved. The endorsing of the checks may not be too difficult, but employee A would have to convert the checks into cash by, for example, establishing a bogus checking account.

The use of checks provides a method of internal control both to the business and the customer. The paragraphs that follow discuss checking accounts, bank statements, reconciliation of checking accounts, and the control of petty cash—a fund many companies use for small incidental expenses.

Checking Accounts. In most companies, the inflow of cash is in the form of checks. Checks made out to the company, money orders, and currency are usually deposited in a bank **checking account.** Often a company will keep several checking accounts at one or more banks. One checking account might be used exclusively for payroll while another might be used to pay suppliers. Such specialized checking accounts provide safeguards against misappropriation of funds.

The procedure of opening a company checking account is similar to opening a personal checking account. The employees authorized to sign checks must sign a bank signature card so that the bank can validate the check signatures if necessary. Banks generally provide printed deposit tickets and serially numbered checks printed with the company's name, address, and identification number. The company's identification number and the bank's identification number are printed in magnetic ink so that the checks can be processed by computer.

The company keeps a record of the checks written, deposits made, and the balance left in the checking account. Small businesses often use their check stubs as a record; large businesses enter this information directly into their computerized accounting system. No matter how cash is recorded, the company must reconcile the balance shown in its records with the balance in the bank's records.

The company's records and the bank's records register the same transactions and could, if it weren't for timing differences be viewed as mirror images of one another. You recall from Chapter 3 that increases in the Cash account are recorded as debits and decreases as credits, and at any point in time the company can determine the balance in the Cash account. When the company deposits cash in its checking account, the company becomes a creditor of the bank because the balance in the company's checking account is an obligation of the bank. The deposit increases (credits) the bank's demand deposit liability. Cleared checks,[2] withdrawals, and service charges are decreases (debits) in the bank's demand deposit liability. Thus, to the bank, the company is a depositor and a creditor because the balance in the company's checking account is an obligation of the bank. (Note the "Deposits/Credits" and "Checks/Debits" shown in the bank statement illustrated in Exhibit 7-2.)

Bank Statements. Periodically, usually monthly, the bank sends the company a **bank statement.** The bank statement is a document that shows the beginning and ending balances in the checking account and gives details of the deposits, withdrawals, bank service charges, and other activity. Exhibit 7-2 illustrates one

---

[2]A cleared check is one that has been processed by the bank and deducted from the checking account balance.

EXHIBIT 7-2

Bank Statement

Ameritex Bank
100 Main Street
Gainesville, TN 99999-0870

Statement Date: 10/31/xx
Account Number: 110-7777-6

Arrow, Inc.
579 Broadway Drive
Gainesville, TN 99999-0880

Summary for the Month:

Previous balance	$ 1,080
2 deposits totaling	20,500
33 checks or withdrawals	(21,080)
SC	(25)
Current balance	$ 475

Detail of Transactions:

Deposits/Credits

Date	*Amount*
10/22/xx	$ 8,500
10/30/xx	12,000
Total	$20,500

Checks (Withdrawals)/Debits

Date	*Check No.*	*Amount*
10/1/xx	1124	$ 82
10/16/xx	1155	197
.	.	.
.	.	.
.	.	.
10/28/xx	1197	600
Total		$21,080

Explanation of Symbols

EC	Error Correction	OD	Overdraft	MC	Miscellaneous Charges
SC	Service Charge	NSF	Not Sufficient Funds	IN	Interest Earned

form of bank statement. You will note that letter codes are listed at the bottom of the statement. The explanation of these common letter codes follows.

1. EC—error correction. When the bank makes an arithmetic error and corrects the error, the symbol EC follows the correction.

2. SC—service charge. A **service charge** is the fee charged by the bank for services to maintain a checking account. The service charge can be based on the number of transactions (checks cleared, deposits made, and so on), and often the average balance in the account has an effect on the amount of the charge. Sometimes a bank will waive service charges for customers with large average balances since the banks can earn revenue on these funds.

3. OD—overdrafts. An **overdraft** occurs when a combination of checks written and service charges incurred exceeds the amount on deposit. When the company has an overdraft, does it have a negative asset or a positive liability? Such credit balances are reported as current liabilities on the company's balance sheet because the deficiency must be made up by a payment or cash deposit to the bank.

4. NSF—nonsufficient funds (not sufficient funds). A **nonsufficient funds (NSF) check** is a check deposited in the company's checking account but not honored by the check writer's bank because the balance in the check writer's checking account is insufficient to cover the check. Some banks charge the depositor of the NSF check a small "charge-back" fee. The maker of the NSF check is always charged a fee for checks returned because of insufficient funds. Exhibit 7-3 illustrates a chain of events resulting from NSF checks. In this example, the depositor of the NSF check was not charged a fee.

Company A in Exhibit 7-3 pays an invoice with check No. 802 for $1,500 to Company B; however, Company A's checking account balance is only $950. Both Company A and Company B have checking accounts at First Bank. Company B deposits Company A's check. When First Bank processes the deposit and Company A's checking account does not have $1,500 to cover the check, Company A is charged a $50 penalty for the NSF check. Company A then cancels check No. 802 and records the penalty as a miscellaneous expense or part of the monthly service charge. Company B is notified that Company A's NSF check was returned. After these transactions, if no other cash has been paid or received, Company A has $900 in its checking account. Company A must still pay Company B for the invoice.

EXHIBIT 7-3

Example of NSF Check Transaction

Company A

Writes check No. 802 for $1,500:

Accounts Payable (L)	1,500	
Cash (A)		1,500

Company B

Receives check No. 802 for $1,500:

Cash (A)	1,500	
Accounts Receivable (A) . . .		1,500

First Bank

Deposited check returned to Company A's account as a NSF check; amount of check subtracted from Company B's account.

Company A

Cancels check No. 802 and records penalty:

Cash (A)	1,500	
Accounts Payable (L)		1,500
Service Charge (E)	50	
Cash (A)		50

Company B

Gets notice of NSF check:

Accounts Receivable (A)	1,500	
Cash (A)		1,500

5. MC—miscellaneous charges. Banks make **miscellaneous charges** against the checking accounts for items such as stopping payment on checks, printing checks, and transactions on promissory notes. All these charges are handled the same as service charges on the depositor's books.

6. IN—interest. Banks sometimes pay interest on the cash balances in checking accounts. This interest is reported on the bank statement and becomes a reconciling item that calls for a journal entry to increase Cash and record Interest Revenue.

Objective 6
Cash reconciliation.

Reconciliation of Checking Accounts. If you have a checking account, you know that time lags occur between the time: (1) you write the check and the check clears the bank, (2) you make a deposit and the bank records the deposit, and (3) the bank subtracts service charges from your checking account and you are notified of the deduction on your monthly bank statement. These time lags are the primary reason that your personal checking account balance does not agree with the balance on your bank statement. In addition to timing differences, discrepancies also occur due to errors.

When the company receives its bank statement, the company must compare and reconcile the bank's records with the company's records. Since the bank and the company maintain separate records, the **bank reconciliation** acts as an internal control for the company, as an independent check on the company's records. The following steps are commonly used in reconciling a bank statement:

1. Check the beginning balance on the bank statement to make sure it is the ending balance of the previous month's statement.
2. Compare the deposits made to the bank this month and any deposits in transit at the end of last month against the deposits shown on the bank statement. If the company shows more deposits than the bank, check to see if any deposits are in transit. **Deposits in transit** are deposits recorded in the company's records as of the bank statement date but not reflected in the current bank statement. These money amounts are legitimately recognized as cash by the depositor.
3. Compare the checks returned (cleared) by the bank with the record of checks written and with any outstanding checks at the end of last month to determine which checks have cleared the bank. **Outstanding checks** are checks that have been written and recorded by the company but have not cleared the bank at the time the bank statement was prepared. Also compare the amount on the check with the amount reported on the bank statement.
4. Check the bank statement for any increases (such as interest or the collection of a note receivable by the bank) and decreases (such as service charges or NSF checks) that are reported on the bank statement but have not been accounted for in the company's checking account record.

After performing steps 1–4, all the necessary amounts are known to explain the differences between the cash balance and the bank statement balance. Such an explanation or listing of differences is called a reconciliation.

Checking account reconciliation—a simple example. The following example begins with the transactions recorded in a company's Cash account and follows the procedure a company uses to check the account against the bank statement.

Arrow, Inc., has a Cash account with the following transactions close to the end of the month:

Cash						Account No. 111
Date		Description	Ref.	Debit	Credit	Balance Debit (Credit)
19x1 Oct.	1	Beginning balance				1,400
	28	Check No. 1197	J5		600	500
	29	Check No. 1198	J5		150	350
	30	Deposit	J6	100		450

On October 31, First Bank sends Arrow a bank statement that shows a $475 balance after deducting a service charge of $25. Also, the bank statement does not show either that check No. 1198 has cleared the bank or that the October 30 deposit was received. Since the bank shows a $475 balance and Arrow shows $450, obviously both the $475 and $450 cannot be the correct balance.

We must (1) determine the correct balance and (2) record any necessary adjustments to Arrow's records. Study Exhibit 7-4 as you follow Arrow's reconciliation procedure.

Arrow's ledger account balance of $450 and First Bank's statement balance of $475 are shown in the two bars at the left of the exhibit. Since First Bank has already taken the $25 service charge from its balance, Arrow must make the following entry to record the service charge shown in Exhibit 7-4:

19xx			
Oct. 31	Service Charge Expense (E)	25	
	Cash (A)		25
	To record service charge for October.		

As you can see in Exhibit 7-4, after recording the $25 service charge, the company ledger balance is $425. No other entries are necessary on Arrow's books.

First Bank shows a balance of $475, but the bank has not yet recorded the October 30 deposit of $100 and the October 29 check No. 1198 for $150. The bank will increase its obligation to Arrow $100 when it records the October 30 deposit and decrease the obligation by $150 when check No. 1198 clears. Both transactions will be reflected on the next bank statement. After Arrow allows for these two differences, the bank balance is also $425.

Comprehensive example. Now let's look at a more comprehensive example. The business of Depositor, Inc., began on January 1, 19xx, with a deposit of $100,000 at First Bank. Depositor's cash transactions for January are shown in Exhibit 7-5. First Bank records the January deposits, cleared checks, and service charges, which results in the bank statement shown in Exhibit 7-6 (the deposits are now credits and the checks cleared are debits).

EXHIBIT 7-4

Reconciliation Process

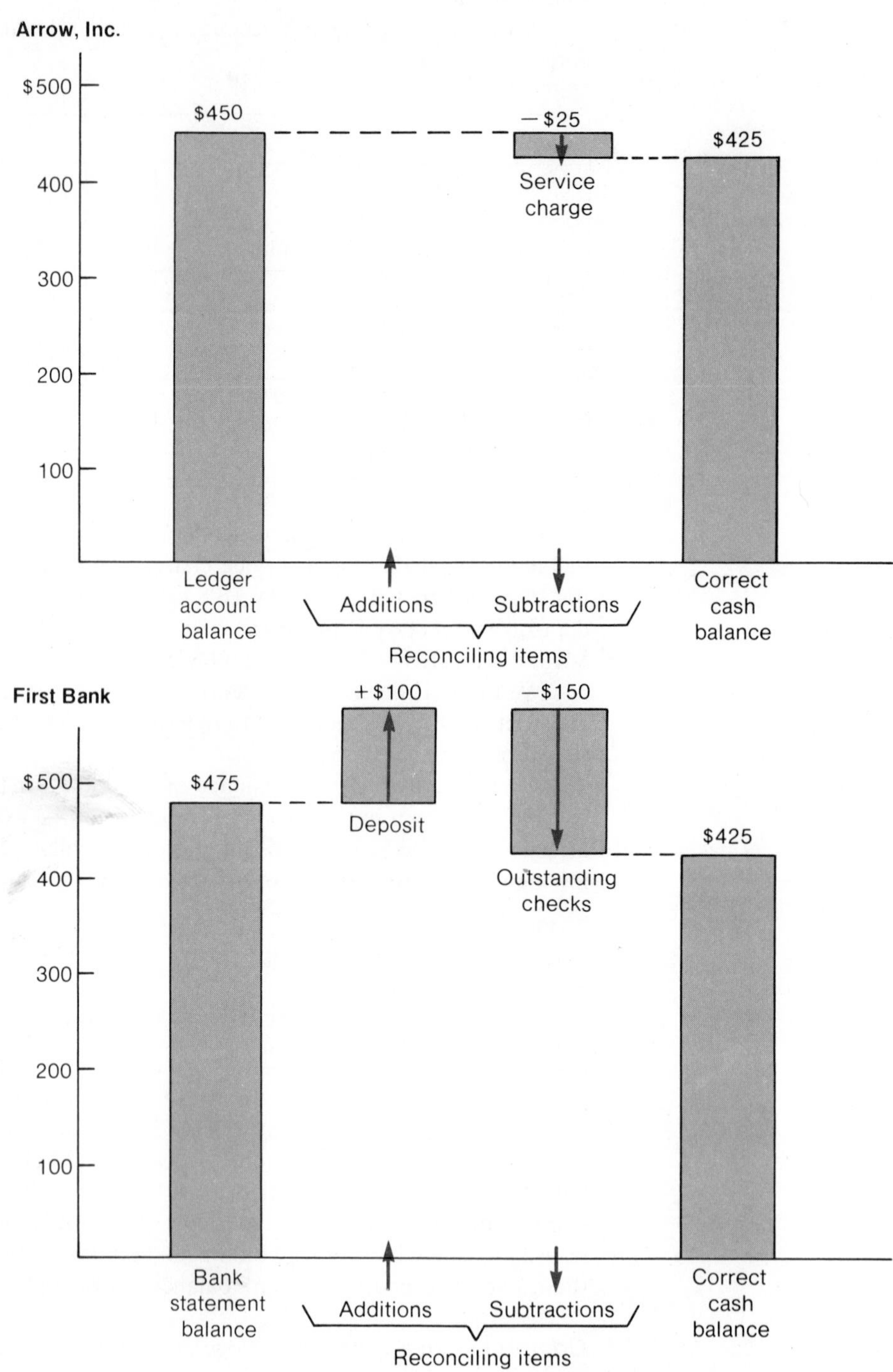

EXHIBIT 7-5

January Cash Transactions of Depositor, Inc.

Cash						Account No. 111
Date		Description	Ref.	Debit	Credit	Balance Debit (Credit)
19xx						
Jan.	1	Deposit		100,000		100,000
	2	Checks written			8,960	91,040
	4	Deposit		4,956		95,996
	6	Checks written			17,451	78,545
	7	Deposit		9,267		87,812
	8	Deposit		15,116		102,928
	10	Checks written			33,470	69,458
	13	Deposit		9,513		78,971
	17	Deposit		16,397		95,368
	19	Deposit		17,725		113,093
	20	Checks written			15,692	97,401
	25	Deposit		25,137		122,538
	26	Checks written			12,168	110,370
	30	Deposit		23,240		133,610
	31	Deposit		25,360		158,970
	31	Checks written			16,584	142,386
Totals				246,711	104,325	

Note that the balance in Depositor's Cash account (Exhibit 7-5) is $14,751 more than First Bank's balance ($142,386 − $127,635 = $14,751). This difference is made up of (1) deposits in transit of $48,600, which is the difference between total deposits of $246,711 and deposits recorded by the bank of $198,111; (2) outstanding checks of $34,334, which is the difference between total checks written of $104,325 and checks cleared of $69,991; (3) an unrecorded service charge of $135; (4) a check printing charge of $125; and (5) a NSF check of $225.

The bank reconciliation of Depositor's records and First Bank's records is shown below:

Depositor, Inc.
Bank Reconciliation
January 31, 19xx

Balance per statement from First Bank	$127,635	Balance per Depositor's Cash account	$142,386
Add:		Deduct:	
Deposits in transit	48,600	Service charge	(135)
Deduct:		Check printing charge	(125)
Outstanding checks	(34,334)	NSF check, customer No. 213	(225)
Adjusted bank balance	$141,901	Adjusted Cash account balance	$141,901

EXHIBIT 7-6

First Bank's January Transactions of Depositor, Inc.

First Bank
200 Main Street
White Cloud, MN 00000-1111

Statement Date: 1/31/xx
Account Number: 1350-999-999

Depositor, Inc.
17 Industrial Drive
White Cloud, MN 00000-1111

Summary for the Month:

Previous balance	$ 0
8 deposits totaling	198,111
33 checks or withdrawals	(69,991)
NSF	(225)
MC	(125)
SC	(135)
Current balance	$127,635

Detail of Transactions:

Deposits/Credits		Checks (Withdrawals)/Debits		
Date	*Amount*	*Date*	*Check No.*	*Amount*
1/2/xx	$100,000	1/6/xx	10001	$ 4,000
1/6/xx	4,956	1/6/xx	10002	10,000
1/8/xx	9,267	1/7/xx	10003	2,140
1/10/xx	15,116	.	.	.
1/14/xx	9,513	.	.	.
1/18/xx	16,397	.	.	.
1/21/xx	17,725	1/31/xx	10046	1,340
1/26/xx	25,137	1/31/xx	10049	692
	$198,111	Total		$69,991

Explanation of Symbols

EC	Error Correction	OD	Overdraft	MC	Miscellaneous Charges
SC	Service Charge	NSF	Not Sufficient Funds	IN	Interest Earned

The journal entries Depositor, Inc., makes to record the service charge, check printing charge, and reestablishment of the account receivable (the NSF check) are as follows:

19xx			
Jan. 31	Service Charge Expense (E)	135	
	Miscellaneous Expenses (E)	125	
	Cash (A)		260
	To record bank service charge and check printing charge.		
	Accounts Receivable (A)	225	
	Cash (A)		225
	To record NSF check returned by the bank.		

The Cash account has a debit balance representing an asset that is available for use in the business. After recording the above entries, the ending cash balance of $141,901 will appear on the balance sheet as a current asset. To summarize the effects of all January transactions, consider a summary of Depositor's cash transactions in the following T account.

Cash

Beg. bal.	0	Checks written	104,325
Deposits	246,711	Service charge	135
		Check printing charge	125
		NSF check	225
End. bal.	141,901		

Objective 7
A petty cash imprest system.

Petty Cash. A business has many miscellaneous uses for small amounts of cash, such as paying cab fares, postage, coffee supplies, delivery charges, and tips. It would be cumbersome and expensive to write checks to pay for these small items, but control and orderly recordkeeping are still necessary.

A **petty cash imprest system** allows for a fund of ready cash, usually a small amount of cash, while at the same time assuring systematic accountability. The fund begins with a stated amount (which can be increased or decreased as the need demands). As the fund is used, from time to time it is replenished to its original amount.

The petty cash imprest system calls for recordkeeping by the custodian of the fund. Usually, the petty cash fund is kept in a cash box. As money is used from the fund, the money is replaced by a signed receipt stating who received the money and how the money was spent. A unique feature of petty cash accounting is that even though the actual amount of cash on hand fluctuates, the Petty Cash asset account has an unchanging balance (unless the fund is increased or decreased).

When cash is initially given to the custodian, the Petty Cash account is debited and the Cash account is credited for the amount of the check, and the Petty Cash account balance remains at that amount. As the cash in the fund is used up, no entries are made in the Petty Cash account; but when the fund is replenished with a check, expense accounts representing the cash spent from the fund are debited and the Cash account is credited. Note that the Petty Cash account balance does not change.

Exhibit 7-7 illustrates the following example of establishing and using a petty cash fund. Study this exhibit as you read the example.

Joseph Karnes is the office manager of a business that initiates a petty cash system on July 1 by cashing a company check for $500 (circle 1, Exhibit 7-7). The following entry is made:

19xx			
July 1	Petty Cash (A)	500	
	Cash (A)		500
	To record establishment of petty cash system.		

EXHIBIT 7-7

Example of a $500 Petty Cash Fund (Currency plus Receipts)

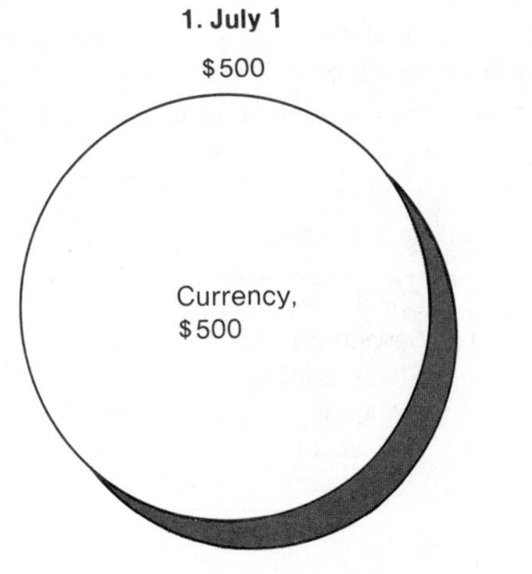

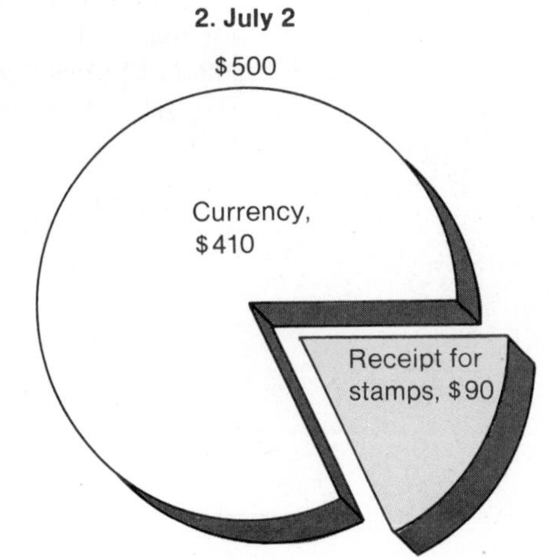

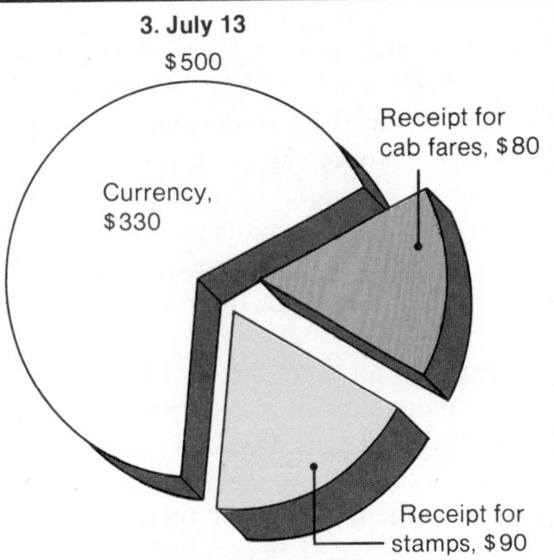

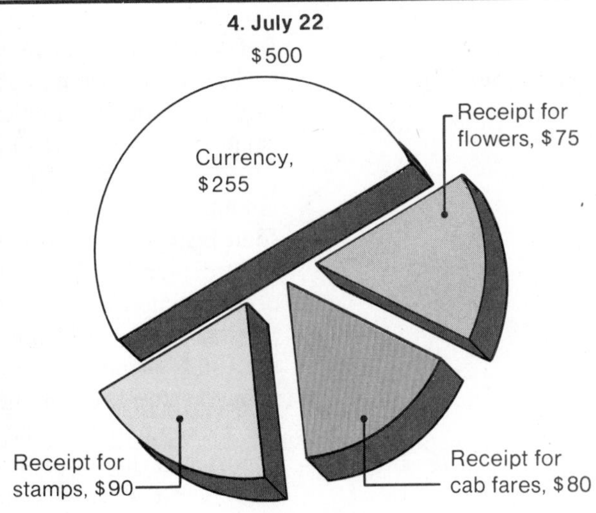

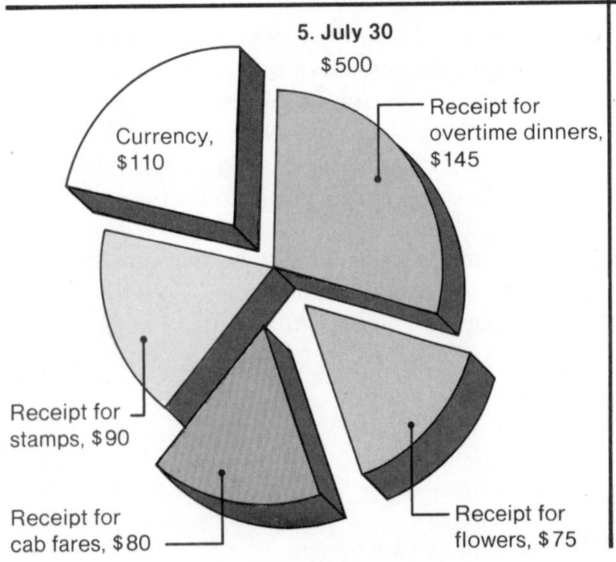

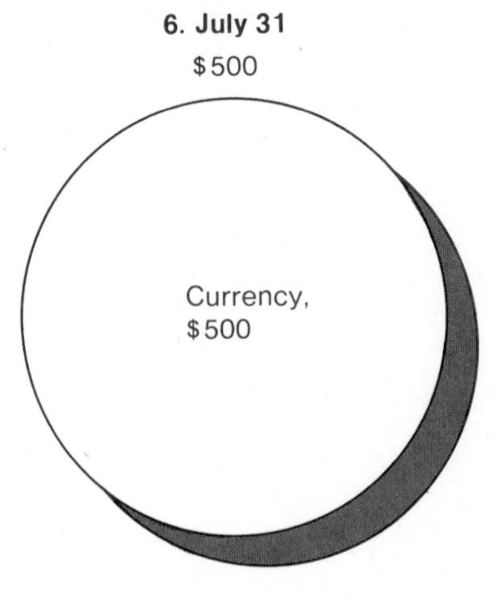

During July, Mr. Karnes disburses the following funds:

Date	*Transaction*
19xx	
July 2	Paid $90 for stamps (circle 2, Exhibit 7-7).
13	Paid $80 for cab fares for overtime workers (circle 3, Exhibit 7-7).
22	Paid $75 for flowers sent to an ill employee (circle 4, Exhibit 7-7).
30	Paid $145 for dinners for overtime workers (circle 5, Exhibit 7-7).

The receipt for each payment was kept in the cash box. On July 31, Mr. Karnes counted the remaining cash in the fund at $110. The following journal entry was made to replenish the fund:

19xx			
July 31	Postage Expense (E)	90	
	Miscellaneous Expense (E)	300	
	Cash (A)		390
	To record replenishment of petty cash fund.		

The Petty Cash account balance remains at $500 and is not affected by disbursements or replenishments. Circle 6 of Exhibit 7-7 shows the petty cash fund replenished to $500—which is the same beginning amount of the fund shown in circle 1.

Shortages and overages can occur in the petty cash fund due to oversight and error such as the failure to get a receipt for a cash payment for cab fare. For instance, if the currency in Mr. Karnes's petty cash fund equaled only $105 on July 31 and receipts added up to $390, a $5 shortage would be charged to Miscellaneous Expense as follows:

19xx			
July 31	Postage Expense (E)	90	
	Miscellaneous Expense (E)	305	
	Cash (A)		395
	To record replenishment of petty cash fund.		

Of course, material discrepancies should be investigated. If the discrepancies are immaterial, the Miscellaneous Expense account can be used to expense the difference. However, if a company wants to keep track of the discrepancies that occur, a Cash Over and Short account can be used. Some companies such as grocery stores, department stores, and banks, use the Cash Over and Short account because they have a greater chance of day-to-day discrepancies.

The petty cash fund can also be increased or decreased. To increase the fund, the person responsible for the fund will request additional cash when it is time to replenish the fund. The fund can also be decreased when it is replenished. If Mr. Karnes decided to reduce the $500 petty cash fund to $250, he would turn in all his receipts and request a check to bring the petty cash fund up to $250 rather than $500. The journal entry to do this is:

19xx			
July 31	Postage Expense (E)	90	
	Miscellaneous Expense (E)	300	
	Petty Cash (A)		250
	Cash (A)		140
	To record replenishment of petty cash fund and to reduce the fund from $500 to $250.		

You should note that the petty cash fund has its own system of internal control. One person is responsible for the fund. When the fund needs replenishing, the total amount of receipts (each of which is signed by the party who was issued the cash) in the cash box and the cash left in the cash box should equal the original amount of the fund. This is checked by another person who writes the check to replenish the fund and voids the receipts so they cannot be used again.

Because of the small balance kept in the petty cash fund, you rarely see petty cash as a separate item on the balance sheet. Usually, individual cash accounts such as Cash in Bank No. 1, Cash in Bank No. 2, Petty Cash, and similar unrestricted amounts of cash are combined and shown as one line item, Cash, on the balance sheet.

NOTES RECEIVABLE

In Chapter 5, we defined accounts receivable as the asset created between the point of sale and the receipt of cash. Thus, when a customer owes an outstanding invoice that the company expects to collect within a short period of time, the amount of the invoice is included in the accounts receivable asset on the balance sheet. The invoice is a document that indicates general contractual terms between a vendor and a customer. Generally, the printed form states what is expected of customers who purchase goods or services from the vendor. Because the customers accept the product or service, it is expected that they will comply with the terms of the invoice.

In contrast to accounts receivable, notes receivable represents a more formal contractual relationship evidenced by a document that is "custom-made" for a specific party. When a debtor of the business signs a document promising payment to the business of a specific amount at a specific time, the document signed is a formal contract called a **promissory note,** or note. It stipulates the terms governing cash payments including dates, amounts to be paid, and perhaps interest rates.

You may wonder why a company uses a formal note. Formal notes give a clear legal status and interpretation to the understanding between the creditor (the **payee**), the person or entity to whom the note is issued, and the debtor (the **maker**). All important terms are stipulated in the note and understood by all parties involved. Also, if cash is needed a note can often be turned into cash easily by means of bank discounting which will be described later in this chapter. Upon examining the note, the following facts should always be determinable even though some of the facts are not explicitly stated:

Term	*Meaning*
Principal amount	Amount lent or borrowed.
Maturity date	Date that the debtor is required to make the final payment on the note.
Maturity amount	Amount to be paid at the maturity date.
Interest	Amount the debtor pays for use of the money, which is the excess of the total payments to the creditor over the principal amount; Principal × Interest rate × Time period money is used = Interest.
Interest rate	Annual percentage that when applied to the principal for the time period(s) yields the interest amount.

What is the difference between notes receivable and accounts receivable? In some respects, all of the above facts given for a note can also be determined for accounts receivable. Although interest is often not charged on ordinary accounts receivable, some companies do charge interest when payment is delayed beyond 30 days. Both notes receivable and accounts receivable are contracts, but notes have more formality, with the basic facts written on a legal document that is signed by both the debtor and creditor. However, an ordinary sales agreement evidenced by an invoice is generally as enforceable as a note. Thus, when a seller has evidence that a debtor took possession of a product or was rendered a service, the law views the debtor as legally bound to pay the sale price to the seller. A note, however, is direct evidence of the debtor's obligations, and no other evidence is usually needed to establish the debtor's legal obligation.

In this section you will learn how to compute interest followed by a discussion of the accounting for a note receivable and the accounting for a dishonored note. The last topic in this section explains how a company discounts a note receivable at a bank when the company decides to convert the note to cash before the note's maturity date.

Computation of Interest

As stated earlier, interest is computed by applying an interest rate to an outstanding amount for the period involved. In this text, we use annual interest rates, but, as we will see, interest is frequently earned for only a portion of a year.

When a note is issued for less than a year, the company must determine the proportion of the year that the principal is used to compute the interest on the note. No fixed rules exist on how to determine this proportion, and companies differ in the methods they use. To see the effects of different methods, consider the following example.

A company has a $1,000 principal amount note with a 10% annual interest rate that is outstanding from July 1 through December 31. How much interest is applicable to July? For a full year the interest for the note would be $100 because the annual interest rate is 10%. Since July 1 to December 31 is one-half year, the interest for the six months is $50; and since July is one sixth of the half year, the interest for July would be $8.33 ($\frac{1}{6} \times \frac{1}{2} \times .10 \times \$1,000$, or $50 divided by 6).

You can also figure interest on a proportion of a year by using a daily basis. If the year has 365 days, based on a yearly 10% interest and 365 days in a year, each day would have $0.274 of interest ($\frac{1}{365} \times .10 \times \$1,000$). Therefore, interest for the month of July (31 days) would be $8.49 ($\frac{31}{365} \times .10 \times \$1,000$).

As you can see, the method chosen to determine the interest amount—monthly basis versus daily basis—results in minor differences in the interest amount. In this text, we assume that each month has 30 days and receives one twelfth of the annual interest. Therefore, a six-month note receives one half of the annual interest, a 90-day note receives one fourth, and a 60-day note receives one sixth, and so on. Thus, we assume that each year has 360 days; therefore, the computation of interest for July on the $1,000, 10% note above could be done as follows: $\$1,000 \times .10 \times \frac{1}{12} = \$8.33$.

Accounting for a Note Receivable

To illustrate how to account for a note receivable, the following example is given. This particular example is used because it contains a situation frequently encountered in the actual business world.

Objective 8
Accounting for notes receivable.

Electrostat, Inc., owes Express Overnight, Inc. (EOI), $50,000 for an outstanding invoice (No. 1278). When the invoice becomes due, Electrostat cannot make the $50,000 payment. On January 1, 19xx, EOI decides to accept Electrostat's one-year promissory note which calls for a December 31, 19xx, payment of $57,500. No interest rate is given on the note, but you can compute the rate by means of the following known relationships:

Analysis of Note Receivable from Electrostat

Principal amount:	$50,000 (the invoice amount).
Maturity amount:	$57,500 (the amount to be paid at maturity).
Maturity date:	December 31, 19xx.
Interest:	$7,500 ($57,500 − $50,000).
Interest rate:	15% ($7,500 ÷ $50,000).

EOI records the following entries for the note:

19xx			
Jan. 1	Notes Receivable (A)	50,000	
	Accounts Receivable (A)		50,000
	To record acceptance of note in place of accounts receivable.		
Dec. 31	Cash (A)	57,500	
	Interest Income (R)		7,500
	Notes Receivable (A)		50,000
	To record receipt of note payment.		

The time line shown in Exhibit 7-8 is helpful in studying the relationships created by the note. Since the note begins with a principal of $50,000 and at the end of the year is worth $57,500, the interest for the year is $7,500.

The interest of $7,500 earned during the one-year period represents the increase in the net assets of EOI that results from this transaction. You can verify the $7,500 interest amount by multiplying $50,000 by the 15% interest rate determined earlier which gives $7,500.

Now let's change the EOI example so that the interest earned straddles two accounting periods. Assume that EOI ends its accounting period on June 30 and that the facts relating to the note are the same as above. EOI would make the following entries:

19xx			
Jan. 1	Notes Receivable (A)	50,000	
	Accounts Receivable (A)		50,000
	To record acceptance of note in place of accounts receivable.		
June 30	Interest Receivable (A)	3,750	
	Interest Income (R)		3,750
	To record interest earned to date.		
Dec. 31	Cash (A)	57,500	
	Notes Receivable (A)		50,000
	Interest Receivable (A)		3,750
	Interest Income (R)		3,750
	To record receipt of note payment.		

EXHIBIT 7-8

Notes Receivable: Principal and Maturity Amounts

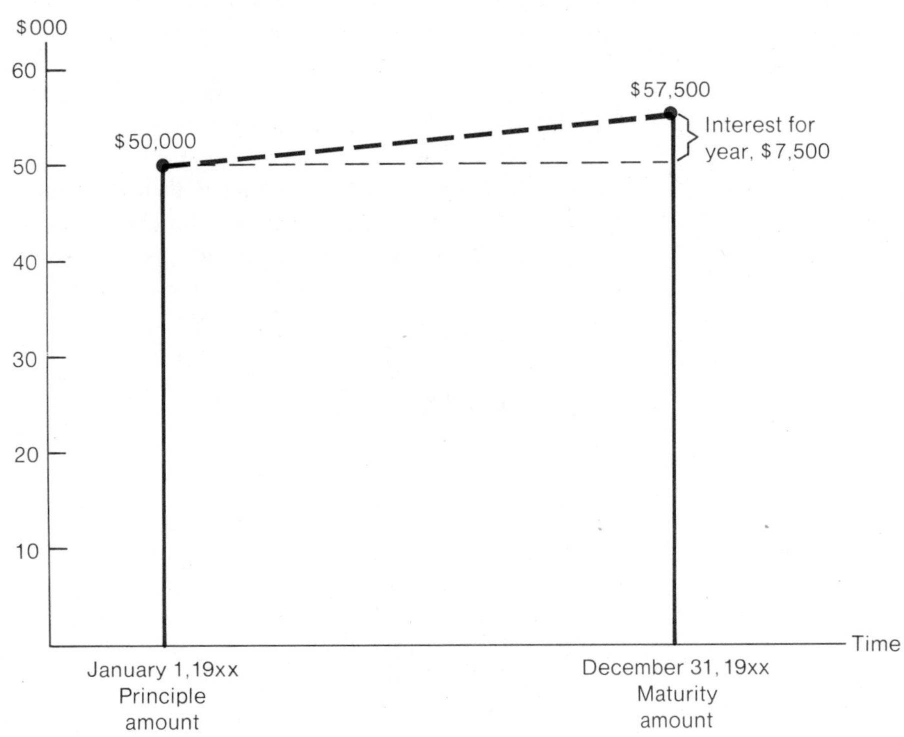

The balance sheet presentation at June 30, 19xx, shows the $50,000 principal in the Notes Receivable account and the $3,750 accrued interest in the Interest Receivable account. When only one account, Notes Receivable, is used, it includes both principal and interest.

Express Overnight, Inc.
Partial Balance Sheet
June 30, 19xx

Current assets:		
Cash		$xx,xxx
Accounts receivable	$xx,xxx	
Less: Allowance for bad debts	x,xxx	xx,xxx
Notes receivable		$50,000
Interest receivable		3,750
Total current assets		$xx,xxx

The reason we record the $3,750 is based on the revenue recognition concept. By June 30, EOI has earned interest because the debtor has held EOI's money for six months and there is a legitimate claim.

In the above discussion, we assume that Electrostat will honor its note. However, notes are not always honored at maturity. The following subsection explains how accountants record dishonored notes.

Accounting for a Dishonored Note

When a customer does not honor a note at maturity, the company has several options: (1) legal action to collect the amount, (2) renegotiation of the note, or (3) forgiveness of the debt and/or write-off of the receivable.

Before expensive legal action is taken, the company will usually discuss the matter with the debtor and attempt to develop an arrangement for payment. If that appears fruitless, then the company could initiate legal proceedings to force payment, if in fact the debtor has the assets to pay all or a part of the amount due. In either case, the note remains on the books of the creditor until it is collected or until it is determined that it will not be collected. Often, a past due debtor will eventually pay even though there has been a default at the maturity date. Creditors, who believe that with more time the payment will be made, could issue a new note to replace the old note in an amount equal to the old principal plus the earned but unpaid interest. Study the following example.

Good Guy, Inc., accepted a 12%, 60-day note on August 1, 19xx, from a customer, G. Holliday, for a $9,000 outstanding invoice that was not paid on its due date. The following entries were made by Good Guy to (1) record the note and (2) issue a new note with the same terms at the maturity date of the old note when the note was dishonored:

19xx			
Aug. 1	Notes Receivable (A)	9,000	
	Accounts Receivable (A)		9,000
	To record the receipt of a 12%, 60-day note for invoice No. 11078.		
Sept. 30	Notes Receivable (A)	9,180	
	Notes Receivable (A)		9,000
	Interest Income (R)		180
	To record the receipt of a 12%, 60-day note to replace former note (G. Holliday).		

As you can see, the new note has been increased by $180, which is the interest earned to date on the note ($\$9,000 \times .12 \times {}^{60}/_{360}$). Good Guy, Inc., will attempt to collect the receivable in the normal manner; and in the event of noncollection and no chance of collection, the $9,180 receivable will be written off.

If the new note is dishonored and no further attempt is made to collect, Good Guy would write off the note as follows.

12/1	Loss on Dishonored Note (E)	9,180	
	Notes Receivable (A)		9,180
	To record the write off of a dishonored note.		

Another approach to the write-off of the note would be to return the amount to Accounts Receivable and then to write it off as a normal bad debt. (See Chapter 5 for a discussion of the accounting methods used.)

12/1	Accounts Receivable (A)	9,180	
	Notes Receivable (A)		9,180
	To record the dishonored note of G. Holliday and to recognize the balance as an accounts receivable.		
12/1	Allowance for Bad Debts (XA)	9,180	
	Accounts Receivable (A)		9,180
	To write off the uncollectible account of G. Holliday.		

Decreasing the allowance account creates the need for a larger bad debts expense accrual at year-end, resulting in the same income statement effect as the write-off of the note shown above. One reason for using the accounts receivable and allowance for bad debts would be to have those involved with receivables know that the customer defaulted, in case future questions are asked about the customer's creditworthiness.

Discounting a Note Receivable at a Bank

If a company needs cash and it holds a note, the company (the payee) can endorse the note and sell it to a bank before the note matures. This transaction is called **discounting** because the bank deducts the interest it charges in advance and thus discounts the note. The amount of the discount depends on the maturity value of the note, the bank's discount rate, and the time period to maturity. The company receives the **proceeds** of the note from the bank—the maturity value of the note less the bank's fee for discounting.

If the maker of a discounted note defaults, the payee usually remains liable to pay the bank when the note matures. The note is then **discounted with recourse.** Recourse means that the ultimate risk of default is not passed on to the bank. The bank merely advances funds to the payee and earns a financing fee on the advanced amount. The following diagrams illustrate the events that occur when a note is discounted.

Inception of a note:	Maker	—— (Note) ——→ ←—— (Cash) ——	Payee
Date of discounting:	Payee	—— (Note) ——→ ←—— (Cash) ——	Bank
Maturity date:	Maker	—— (Cash) ——→	Bank

The bank earns money on this transaction by means of the discount rate applied to the maturity value of the note. The discount rate is usually higher than the original interest rate that the seller of the note was going to receive from the maker of the note. An example of a discounted note follows.

On January 1, 19x1, Maker, Inc., issues a 10%, $10,000 principal amount note with a maturity date of December 31. The payee of the note is Payee, Inc. On July 1, 19x1, Payee discounts the note at a local bank, and the discount rate is 20%. The key to understanding this transaction is knowing the meaning of the 20% discount rate.

The bank wants to earn a fee equal to 20% per year on the maturity value of a discounted note for the amount of time it will hold the note. The maturity value of a note is the principal plus interest. In this example, the maturity value is $11,000 [computed: $10,000 + ($10,000 × .10)], and the proceeds to be paid to Payee on July 1 are computed as follows:

Maturity amount	$11,000
20% for one-half year left until maturity.	× .10
Discounting fee	$ 1,100
Proceeds ($11,000 − $1,100)	$ 9,900

Payee, therefore, receives $9,900 from the bank on July 1. The bank now has the right to collect the payment from Maker on December 31. Payee makes the following entries to record the transactions related to the note:

19xx			
Jan. 1	Notes Receivable (A)	10,000	
	Cash (A) or Accounts Receivable		10,000
	To record receipt of note.		
July 1	Cash (A)	9,900	
	Financing Expense (E)	100	
	Notes Receivable Discounted (XA)		10,000
	To record discounting of note.		
Dec. 31	Notes Receivable Discounted (XA)	10,000	
	Notes Receivable (A)		10,000
	To record elimination of note when it is paid to the bank.		

The financing expense recorded above could be recorded as interest expense. However, by using financing expense, accountants indicate the results from netting the discounting fee charged by the bank, which in this example is $1,100, and the interest that would have been earned if the note had been held by Payee for the entire year, $1,000.

As a contra account to Notes Receivable, Notes Receivable Discounted is used when the bank has recourse to the payee in the event that the maker of the note defaults. By using the contra account, the book value of the note is reduced to zero, but the original notes receivable is maintained as a reminder that a real liability will result if the payee defaults. Such a situation results in a contingent liability, which means that an accounting liability may result if another specific event(s) occurs. Contingent liabilities are discussed in Chapter 9.

If the $10,000 note were **discounted without recourse,** then Payee would have credited Notes Receivable on July 1 because no contingency would exist. In this example, we assume that Maker is notified of the bank discounting the note and knows that the bank must be paid at maturity. Sometimes the maker is not notified and pays the payee at maturity. Then, the payee must forward the maturity amount to the bank.

Discounted Notes that Are Dishonored. It is possible that the dishonored note with recourse will not be paid by Maker at maturity. If such a default occurs, Payee would become liable to pay the bank the full $11,000 on December 31. Payee then records this payment as follows:

19x1			
Dec. 31	Notes Receivable Discounted (XA)	10,000	
	Notes Receivable (A)	1,000	
	Cash (A)		11,000
	To record payment to the bank for a discounted note that the maker dishonored.		

This illustrates how a contingent liability becomes a real liability. Maker is now obligated to pay Payee for the full maturity value of the note, which is the amount paid to the bank by Payee upon default. What remains on Payee's books is a receivable of $11,000 which will be eliminated as follows if cash is received from Maker.

19x2			
Jan. 5	Cash (A)	11,000	
	Notes Receivable (A)		11,000
	To record receipt of note payment.		

The effects of the above note transactions as related to the balance sheet and income statement follow.

Payee, Inc.

		Balance Sheet Effects		Income Statement
Date	*Transaction*	*Cash*	*Notes Receivable*	*Effects*
19x1				
Jan. 1	Receipt of note	$(10,000)	$ 10,000	$ 0
July 1	Discounting of note	9,900	(10,000)	(100)
Dec. 31	Dishonoring of note	(11,000)	11,000	0
19x2				
Jan. 5	Receipt of cash for note . .	11,000	(11,000)	0
	Net effect	$ (100)	$ 0	$(100)

The net effect on cash is equal to the net effect on the income statement: cash was reduced by $100, and income was reduced by $100. If this note had not been discounted and had been paid at maturity, the following effects would have resulted:

Payee, Inc.

		Balance Sheet Effects		Income Statement
Date	*Transaction*	*Cash*	*Notes Receivable*	*Effects*
19x1				
Jan. 1	Receipt of note	$(10,000)	$ 10,000	$ 0
Dec. 31	Receipt of cash for note . .	11,000	(10,000)	1,000
	Net effect	$ 1,000	$ 0	$1,000

When Payee discounted the note, it had an expense of $100. This is the net of the interest to be paid by Maker ($1,000) and the discounting fee earned by the bank ($1,100). Remember that it is possible for the discounting fee to be less than the interest earned at the time of discounting on the note, in which case Interest Income is credited and net income is increased.

SUMMARY

This chapter began with a definition of internal control. You then learned the five general principles involved in effective internal control (authorization and responsibility, separation of duties, protection of assets, electronic and mechanical devices, and accounting system procedures). Because of the importance of internal control procedures, these procedures were discussed in detail. You were cautioned to remember that the management principle of measuring costs of any operation against its benefits also pertained to internal control. An example illustrating the advantages of electronic data processing concluded the section on internal control.

Since cash is a cornerstone of successful business operations, an entire section in the chapter was devoted to cash. Because of its liquidity, considerable space was devoted to cash control, which involves checking accounts, bank statements, reconciliation of checking accounts, and the control of petty cash. The overlap between general internal controls and specific accounting internal controls—including cash control—was clearly evident by the frequent repetition in accounting internal control procedures of the importance of separation of duties.

The chapter concluded with an introduction to notes receivable, including interest computation and accounting for notes receivable and dishonored notes. You learned about discounting a note at a bank and how to record transactions pertaining to this procedure. The underlying importance of cash flow to successful business operations again becomes evident when companies find it necessary to turn a note receivable into a cash receipt before maturity.

DEMONSTRATION EXERCISE

The following selected transactions are from the records of Acro Services, Inc., for 19xx:

19xx

Feb. 19 Monthly bank statement is received. A check from C. Jones, a customer, for $1,700 was returned NSF, and a bank service charge for $84 appears on the statement.

Apr. 7 Request for $243 to reimburse the $300 petty cash fund is received. The following receipts are attached: $75 postage, $68 office supplies, and $95 delivery charges which are charged to miscellaneous expense.

June 1 Accepted a $35,000, 8%, 60-day note from customer, L. Zekan.

July 31 Received payment on note from L. Zekan.

Oct. 31 Discounted with recourse a $20,000, 12%, six-month note due on November 30, 19xx, at 24% at the local bank.

Dec. 1 Received notice from the local bank that the discounted note was not paid.

Required:

Prepare the journal entries in general journal form that Acro would have made for the above transactions. This is Acro's first year of operations, and December 31 is its year-end.

Solution:

GENERAL JOURNAL					J10
Date		Account Titles and Explanation	Ref.	Debit	Credit
19xx					
Feb.	19	Accounts Receivable (A)		1,700	
		Cash (A)			1,700
		To record customer's NSF check returned by the bank.			
		Service Charge Expense (E)		84	
		Cash (A)			84
		To record bank service charge for the month.			
Apr.	7	Postage Expense (E)		75	
		Office Supplies Expense (E)		68	
		Miscellaneous Expense (E)		100	
		Cash (A)			243
		To record replenishment of petty cash fund including a $5 shortage in Miscellaneous Expense.			
June	1	Notes Receivable (A)		35,000	
		Accounts Receivable (A)			35,000
		To record a 60-day, 8% note from customer.			
July	31	Cash (A)		35,467	
		Notes Receivable (A)			35,000
		Interest Income (R)			467
		To record payment received on note.			
Oct.	31	Cash (A)		20,776	
		Interest Income (R)			776
		Notes Receivable Discounted (XA)			20,000
		To record discounted note: Maturity = Principal ($20,000) + Interest ($20,000 × .12 × 6/12 = 1,200) = $21,200. Proceeds = Maturity ($21,200) − Discount fee ($21,200 × .24 × 1/12) = $20,776.			
Dec.	1	Notes Receivable Discounted (XA)		20,000	
		Notes Receivable (A)		1,200	
		Cash (A)			21,200
		To record payment to bank on defaulted note.			

APPENDIX

Special Accounting Journals and Control Accounts

Objective 9
Special journals and control accounts.

Prior to the availability of computers and electronic data processing, most companies used some form of a manual or mechanical system to record business transactions. Although computers are used in most small businesses today, some small companies still use the manual system of accounting. By using the special journals and control accounts discussed in this appendix, manual systems can handle large volumes of transactions efficiently and provide useful information to management. Many computer systems also use versions of the journals discussed in this appendix.

The typical small retail business uses the following special journals: sales, cash receipts, purchases, and cash disbursements. All accounting systems also have a general journal because, as was stated in the chapter, not all transactions will fit into the structure of the special journals.

The names of the special journals are self-explanatory. The **sales journal** records credit sales. The **cash receipts journal** records all cash receipts from cash sales, credit customers, and other sources (such as a bank loan). The **purchases journal** records purchases of merchandise inventory, supplies, and any other items purchased on credit. The **cash disbursements journal** records all checks written to pay suppliers, employees, and others.

Each special journal contains a series of columns into which transactions are entered. A "key" column records the common account feature of all the transactions entered into that journal. In the cash receipts journal, the key column is the Cash Dr. column. A transaction should not be entered into a special journal unless part of the transaction is recorded in the key column. Also, a separate column is established for each other account that requires frequent entries. For example, in the cash receipts journal, an Accounts Receivable Cr. column is required because much of the cash collected is from customers paying on account.

Along with the frequently used columns, most special journals have a general-purpose column where an account that is not included among the special columns can be identified and the amount entered. This column usually is called the Other Debits column or Other Credits column.

In this discussion on special journals, our example is the Wilco Company, a retailer of luggage and gifts. In addition to its cash sales, Wilco provides its own credit sales program to approved customers—the company does not accept other credit cards. Wilco uses four special journals—sales, cash receipts, purchases, and cash disbursements. The relationship of the subsidiary ledgers with the four journals is also explained. For illustration purposes, we examine only a limited number of transactions for Wilco during the month.

SALES JOURNAL

All credit sales are entered into the sales journal. Exhibit 7A-1 contains the sales journal for the Wilco Company. The columns of the sales journal include the following: Date; Customer; Ref.; Invoice No.; and Sales Cr., Accounts Receivable

EXHIBIT 7A-1

Wilco Company's Sales Journal

SALES JOURNAL					S1
Date		Customer	Ref.	Invoice No.	Sales Cr., Accounts Receivable Dr.
19xx					
Aug.	1	Rachel Allen	√	1343	450
	6	Jean Coll	√	1344	1,260
	13	Allo Corporation	√	1345	8,625
	29	Richard Smith	√	1346	550
					10,885
					(411) (121)

Dr. Since the amount of the sale and the amount of the accounts receivable are the same, only one amount column is necessary. All credit sales are entered into the journal in the numerical order of the invoices. Study the entry for invoice No. 1343. In addition to the date, the invoice number, and the amount, the customer's name (Rachel Allen, in this case) is inserted.

Periodically the sales journal is posted by first totaling the amount column. The sales journal is posted in two stages. First the $10,885 total of the Sales Cr., Accounts Receivable Dr. column is posted to the Sales account and the Accounts Receivable account. To indicate that posting is done, the account numbers are inserted in parentheses below the total of $10,885. The individual invoices are then posted to the customers' accounts in the subsidiary ledger and check marks inserted in the Ref. column to indicate posting is complete.

CASH RECEIPTS JOURNAL

Any cash received by Wilco is recorded in the cash receipts journal. The columns of the cash receipts journal include the following: Date, Name (cash source), Invoice No., Ref., Cash Dr., Accounts Receivable Cr., Sales Cr., and Other Credits. Payments from customers and cash sales comprise an important part of any company's receipts, which is the reason for the associated special columns in the cash receipts journal. The Other Credits column is used for occasional cash receipts that are not collections on account or sales, such as a refund from a utility company for overpayment of a previous bill. The Wilco Company cash receipts journal is shown in Exhibit 7A-2.

The posting of the cash receipts journal is very similar to the sales journal. Rather than posting one column to two separate accounts, however, you must verify that debits equal credits in the cash receipts journal. After the columns are totaled, the Cash Dr. column should equal the sum of the Accounts Receivable Cr., Sales Cr., and Other Credit columns. By its nature, the Other Credits column cannot be posted in total. Each entry must be posted and the appropriate account number inserted in the column to indicate posting is complete. If the debits do not equal credits, the mistake(s) must be discovered and corrected. Then the column totals are posted to the general ledger and account numbers

EXHIBIT 7A-2

Wilco Company's Cash Receipts Journal, Accounts Receivable Control, and Subsidiary Ledger Accounts

CASH RECEIPTS JOURNAL CR8

Date		Name	Invoice No.	Ref.	Cash Dr.	Accounts Receivable Cr.	Sales Cr.	Other Credits (Debits) Amount	Other Credits (Debits) Account
19xx									
Aug.	3	Cash sales			6,217		6,217		
	5	R. Smith	1285	√	1,250	1,250			
	13	Cash sales			4,217		4,217		
	17	R. Allen	1343	√	450	450			
	17	Electric Co.			45			45	561
	29	Cash sales			8,915		8,915		
					21,094	1,700	19,349	45	
					(101)	(121)	(411)		

GENERAL LEDGER

Accounts Receivable 121

Debit		Credit	
Beg. bal.	3,210	Cr.8	1,700
S1	10,885		
End. bal.	12,395		

ACCOUNTS RECEIVABLE SUBSIDIARY LEDGER

Allen, Rachel

Debit		Credit	
S1	450	Cr.8	450
End. bal.	-0-		

Allo Corporation

Debit		Credit
Beg. bal.	1,320	
S1	8,625	
End. bal.	9,945	

Coll, Jean

Debit		Credit
S1	1,260	

Exton Corporation

Debit		Credit
Beg. bal.	640	

Smith, Richard

Debit		Credit	
Beg. bal.	1,250	Cr.8	1,250
S1	550		
End. bal.	550		

inserted in the columns to indicate posting is complete. If a customer makes a payment on his accounts, that payment must be posted to the subsidiary ledger to update the customer's account. When that posting is completed, a check mark is inserted in the column. If no subsidiary ledger is involved in the transaction, the Ref. column will remain blank.

EXHIBIT 7A-3

Wilco Company's Purchases Journal

PURCHASES JOURNAL										P6
Date		Supplier	Invoice No.	Ref.	Accounts Payable Cr.	Merchandise Inventory Dr.	Supplies Dr.	Other Debits (Credits) Amount	Other Debits (Credits) Account	
19xx Aug.	3	Acme Leather	32756	√	11,450	11,000	450			
	16	Botts Gifts	A625	√	2,310	2,310				
	19	DS Displays	963	√	4,210			4,210	171	
	30	Tay Paper	2336	√	1,327		1,327			
					19,297	13,310	1,777	4,210		
					(211)	(131)	(141)			

As we discussed in Chapter 5, managers know the total amount of accounts receivables by referring to the Accounts Receivable **control account** (general ledger account that provides a summary total of underlying subsidiary accounts). They know the amount owed by each individual customer by referring to the subsidiary ledger. Exhibit 7A-2 illustrates Wilco's Accounts Receivable control account and the supporting subsidiary accounts, and their relationship with the sales journal and cash receipts journal. Note that the total of the subsidiary accounts receivable [Allen ($0) + Allo ($9,945) + Coll ($1,260) + Exton ($640) + Smith ($550)] equals the Accounts Receivable ledger (control) account of $12,395.

In addition to the Accounts Receivable control account, many other general ledger accounts may be supported by subsidiary accounts. Among them are Accounts Payable, Notes Receivable, Merchandise, Equipment, and Loans Payable. The techniques for operating such accounts are essentially the same as those illustrated for the accounts receivable subsidiary ledger.

PURCHASES JOURNAL

Exhibit 7A-3 illustrates the purchases journal the Wilco Company uses where all its credit purchases are entered. Since this journal includes all purchases made on credit, the key column of this journal is the Accounts Payable Cr. column. The Merchandise Inventory Dr. and Supplies Dr. columns are the other columns included since they are frequently used. The remaining columns include the following: Date, Supplier, Invoice No., Ref., and Other Debits. This latter column will handle those occasional purchases that are not for merchandise or supplies.

Again, the posting of this journal is very similar to the procedure used for the cash receipts journal. The columns must be footed and debits must equal credits. Wilco then posts the column totals to the appropriate accounts and inserts the account numbers to indicate posting is complete. The other debits are posted individually. For example, Wilco's bookkeeper will credit the $19,297 to Accounts Payable for the total purchases made on credit for the period. Wilco also uses a subsidiary ledger to detail its Accounts Payable control account. The suppliers' individual accounts are credited to update the balances owed to those suppliers. Check marks in the Ref. column indicate posting to the subsidiary ledger is complete.

CASH DISBURSEMENTS JOURNAL

Exhibit 7A-4 illustrates the Wilco Company's cash disbursements journal. As the name implies, the key column for this journal is the Cash Cr. column. For Wilco, debits to Accounts Payable and Salaries Payable are frequently made and these become the special columns in this journal. Additional columns of the cash disbursements journal include the following: Date, Payee, Check No., Ref., and Other Debits. Again, the Other Debits column is for transactions that do not fit in the specific account columns. Notice that the disbursements are entered into the journal in numerical order by check number. This sequential ordering is for control purposes to ensure against unrecorded disbursements.

The procedure for posting follows that used for the cash receipts and purchases journals. Columns are totaled; debits must equal credits. Posting to the general ledger is indicated by account numbers and to any subsidiary ledgers by using check marks.

EXHIBIT 7A-4

Wilco Company's Cash Disbursements Journal

CASH DISBURSEMENTS JOURNAL CD9

Date		Payee	Check No.	Ref.	Cash Cr.	Accounts Payable Dr.	Salaries Payable Dr.	Other Debits (Credits)	
								Amount	Account
19xx									
Aug.	4	Tay Paper	2735	√	650	650			
	14	Acme Leather	2736	√	14,803	14,803			
	18	K. Ball	2737		785		785		
	18	N. Alto	2738		639		639		
	23	Electric Co.	2739		410			410	561
	29	Daily News	2740		450			450	543
	31	K. Ball	2741		830		830		
	31	N. Alto	2742		684		684		
	31	C. Lerch	2743		214		214		
					19,465	15,453	3,152	860	
					(101)	(211)	(221)		

KEY TERMS

Bank reconciliation. Process by which a company's Cash account is compared to the bank statement to ensure against errors in the company's records and the bank's records.

Bank statement. A document prepared periodically by the bank that shows the beginning and ending balances in the checking account and gives details of the deposits, withdrawals, service charges, and other activities.

Batch system. Process by which entries are collected for some period of time and entered into the computer periodically—daily or weekly; compare to real-time system.

Bonding. Type of insurance policy taken out on certain employees that will pay the company damages if an employee misappropriates assets.

Cash. Money the bank will accept for deposit in checking accounts (coins, currency, checks written to depositor, traveler's checks, money orders) and demand deposits that are available to the business without restrictions; banks do not accept postage stamps, postdated checks, or notes receivable for deposit.

Cash control. Steps taken to safeguard the cash asset from dishonest employees and other persons who may have access to the company's cash.

Checking account. A demand deposit at a bank in which checks made out to the company and any money orders or currency are deposited and from which checks are written; also called a demand deposit account.

Compensating balances. Sums required by a bank loan contract to be deposited in a noninterest-earning account or an account that earns less than the market rate of interest.

Demand deposits. Checking accounts in which the depositor has free access to the cash without advance notification to the bank.

Deposits in transit. Deposits recorded in the company's records as of the bank statement date but not reflected in the current bank statement.

Discounted without recourse. Payee is not liable to pay the bank if the maker of a discounted note defaults.

Discounted with recourse. If the maker of a discounted note defaults, payee remains liable to pay the bank when the note matures.

Discounting. Transaction by which a business endorses a note and sells it to a bank before the note matures.

Financial audit. Tests for conformance to accounting procedures and to assure management that the controls in the accounting system are functioning as designed and the system is providing reliable information.

Interest. The amount paid for the use of money; the excess of the total paid back to the creditor over the principal.

Interest rate. Annual percentage that when applied to the principal of the note for the time period yields the interest amount.

Internal auditing department. Department in corporations that ensures internal controls are performing as designed.

Internal control. The plan of organization and all the methods and measures used to safeguard the company's assets, check the accuracy and reliability of its accounting data, promote operational efficiency, and encourage adherence to prescribed managerial policies.

Lapping. A form of theft where an employee takes the cash paid by one customer and then applies the payment of another customer to the accounts receivable of the first customer.

Maker. Person or entity that issues a note; the debtor.

Maturity amount. Amount to be paid at maturity date.

Maturity date. Date that the debtor is required to make the final payment on a note.

Miscellaneous charges. Charges made by the bank to the depositor for items such as stopping payment on checks, printing checks, and so on.

Nonsufficient funds (NSF) check. Check deposited in the company's checking account but not honored by the check writer's bank because the balance in the writer's checking account is insufficient to cover the check; also known as **not sufficient funds.**

Operational audit. Focuses on management controls and how well various levels of management are performing under these controls.

Outstanding checks. Checks that have been written and recorded by the company but have not cleared the bank at the time the bank statement was prepared.

Overdraft. Occurs when the company has written checks for more money than is in the company's checking account.

Payee. Person or entity to whom a note is issued; known as the creditor.

Petty cash imprest system. Method that allows for a fund of ready cash while at the same time assuring systematic accountability.

Principal amount. Initial value of the note.

Proceeds. Amount received by the company who discounts a note—maturity value of the note less the bank's fee for discounting.

Promissory note. Formal contract between a debtor and a creditor that stipulates the terms governing cash payments including dates, amounts to be paid, and perhaps interest rates; commonly called a note.

Real-time system. Used when computer posts transactions immediately to the general and subsidiary ledger accounts and into various other reports and records.

Service charge. The fee charged by the bank for services to maintain a checking account.

Special journals. Books of original entry designed to efficiently process a class of repetitive transactions.

Time deposits. Accounts on deposit at a financial institution that require notification before the business can use the money.

APPENDIX KEY TERMS

Cash disbursements journal. Special journal used to record all checks written to pay suppliers, employees, and others.

Cash receipts journal. Special journal used to record all cash receipts from cash sales, credit customers, and other sources.

Control account. General ledger account that provides a summary total of underlying subsidiary accounts.

Purchases journal. Special journal used to record purchases of merchandise inventory, supplies, and other items purchased on credit.

Sales journal. Special journal used to record credit sales.

SYNONYMS

Checking accounts; demand deposits.

Defaulted; dishonored.

Draft; check.

Maker; issuer of note; debtor on a note.

Not sufficient funds; insufficient funds; NSF.

Overdraft; overdrawn.

Payee; recipient; creditor.

Principal; face value.

Promissory note; note.

QUESTIONS

1. Briefly describe why a company should provide an internal control system. Differentiate between internal controls that are related to the firm's accounting system and other internal administrative controls.
2. Describe three reasons internal controls are used.
3. Internal controls are based on five principles. Describe in detail three of those principles.
4. Before a company installs or adds to its internal control system, the costs of the system are weighed against its benefits. Explain some of the costs and benefits of an internal control system.
5. Describe an electronic cash register system in terms of its hardware and software components.
6. Explain the concept of separation of duties and describe how this concept applies to the various functions associated with the recording and handling of cash in a business.
7. An employee who opens mail from customers is also assigned to maintain petty cash, prepare bank deposits, and prepare journal entries in the cash receipts journal. What are the dangers inherent in this situation from a cash control point of view?
8. If you were responsible for the operations of a school cafeteria, what controls would you establish for the handling of the cash paid by customers?
9. Define cash. How is it different from any other asset?
10. What types of cash may not be included in a company's balance sheet category cash?

11. Virtually all companies use checking accounts or demand deposits. Define a checking account and explain why it is used.
12. Because of the nature of cash, steps should be taken to control it. Describe these steps.
13. Companies prepare bank reconciliations for what reason(s)?
14. The Sedley Company is preparing its bank reconciliation statement for the month of November 19xx. What type of items would the company add to the "Balance per Bank Statement" as part of the process of determining the "Adjusted Bank Balance"? What types of items would be subtracted?
15. Describe and explain six different items that may appear on a bank statement.
16. Define a petty cash imprest system. Why is it used?
17. Define four terms used in describing a note.
18. Why would a company discount a note? Describe the discounting process.
19. On June 30, customer S. Merrill issues you a $2,000, 12%, 60-day note in payment on her account. On August 31, Merrill defaults on the note. On September 30, you receive a check for $2,040 from Merrill. Explain the nature of the asset you hold from Merrill on June 30 and August 31.
20. Assume you discount a note with recourse and the maker defaults. What responsibilities do you have to the bank where you discounted the note? Does your answer differ if the note were discounted without recourse?

APPENDIX QUESTIONS

21. Describe the advantages in using special journals.
22. What types of transactions are entered in the sales journal, the cash receipts journal, the purchases journal, and the cash disbursements journal?
23. How do special journals aid in establishing controls?

EXERCISES

EXERCISE 7-1
L.O. 1, 2, 4

Accounting Controls

1. Internal controls are—
   a. Methods used to safeguard assets.
   b. Procedures a company uses to keep its employees in check.
   c. Operational efficiency and adherence to managerial policies.
   d. Plans, methods, and measures a company uses to safeguard its assets, check the accuracy and reliability of its accounting data, promote operational efficiency, and encourage adherence to prescribed policies.
2. Internal controls are designed to ensure—
   a. Transactions are executed in accordance with management's authorization.
   b. Transactions are recorded as necessary.
   c. Access to assets are permitted only according to management's authorization.
   d. Comparison of the accounting records with the existing assets is performed and differences are corrected.
   e. All of the above.
3. As a company grows, a larger, more elaborate organizational plan is usually developed. This plan includes an internal control system based on some general principles including—
   a. Equality of assets and liabilities plus owners' equity; debits equal credits.
   b. Authorization and responsibility, protection of assets, separation of duties, and accounting system procedures.

c. Execution of transactions in accordance with management's authorization, access to assets in accordance with management's authorization, and recording of transactions as necessary.
d. Separation of physical asset control and recordkeeping, periodic comparison of actual assets with reported assets, and proof of liability existence.

4. Using a computerized accounting system provides several advantages over using a manual system. The advantages include:
   a. Increased efficiency through a reduction in the work force.
   b. Opportunity for risk reduction, increased accuracy, and quick processing for large-volume jobs thus providing reports and analysis on a timely basis.
   c. Elimination of number of journals that must be kept.
   d. All of the above.
   e. None of the above.

EXERCISE 7-2
L.O. 6

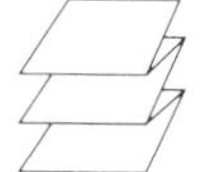

Bank Reconciliation

Given the following facts, prepare a bank reconciliation and determine the actual cash balance of the Simson Company. (Assume this is the only relevant information.)

Balance per bank statement	$10,000
Checks written by Simson	27,000
Checks clearing the bank	26,500
Deposits by Simson	12,000
Deposits recorded by the bank . . .	11,750
Bank service charges	300
Check written and accidentally recorded twice by Simson	575

EXERCISE 7-3
L.O. 6

Bank Reconciliation

Consider the following items in connection with a bank reconciliation:

a. The bank made an error on one of the company's checks by entering $100 on the records instead of $1,000.
b. A service charge of $322 appears on the bank statement.
c. An $8,539 deposit in transit does not appear on the bank statement.
d. Eight of the company's checks totaling $22,765 are still outstanding and do not appear on the statement.
e. A check from a customer, R. Dunne, for $579 was returned to the depositor's bank NSF.

Required:
If you start your reconciliation with the amount per the bank statement, what would you do with each of the above items to reconcile the company's (depositor's) Cash account balance and the bank statement balance?

EXERCISE 7-4
L.O. 6

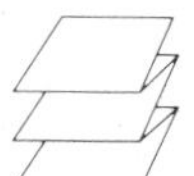

Bank Reconciliation

Each item in a bank reconciliation has one of the following effects:

1. Increase bank balance.
2. Increase book balance.
3. Decrease bank balance.
4. Decrease book balance.

Required:
Identify which type of effect each of the following items would have:

1. Error in the total on our deposit ticket noted by the bank in favor of the bank (for example, total was overstated).
2. Interest on checking account balance.
3. Checks that have been written but have yet to clear the bank.
4. Deposit in transit.
5. Bank service charge.
6. NSF checks.

EXERCISE 7-5
L.O. 7

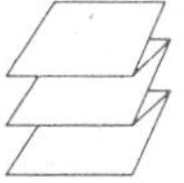

Petty Cash

Sue Coy of Great Ideas Advertising Agency was looking for an easier system to handle transactions of small amounts of cash where use of a check was inconvenient. A $100 petty cash system was established on September 1, 19xx, and shows the following on October 4, 19xx:

Receipt for postage	$24.16
Receipt for office supplies	38.21
Receipt for miscellaneous items. . . .	17.92
Cash on hand.	20.86

Required:
Prepare the journal entries to record the establishment and the replenishment of the fund.

EXERCISE 7-6
L.O. 7

Petty Cash

Prepare the journal entries to record the following:

Feb. 1 Establish a $250 petty cash fund.

15 Replenish fund. Cash on hand totaled $75.36. Receipts for the following included:

Stamps	$65.00
Flowers	49.50
Office supplies . . .	39.56
Lunch for client. . .	20.58

28 Replenish fund and increase it to $500. Cash on hand totaled $86.21. Receipts for the following included:

Stamps	$66.00
Office supplies . . .	79.21
Door lock	15.45

EXERCISE 7-7
L.O. 7

Petty Cash

In examining the $2,000 petty cash fund of Future Sound, Inc., you discover the following data:

Receipts	*Amount*
13—Cab fares	$ 506
18—Postage charges	230
1—Umbrella	26
21—UPS bills	770
1—Pocket calculator	84
14—Batteries for warehouse lights	20
2—Adding machine tapes	36
	$1,672
Over and short	(72)
Cash and bills	400
	$2,000

All items costing less than $200 are expensed. (Hint: Use miscellaneous expense for items which do not seem to fit in a major category.)

Required:
Record the entry or entries necessary to replenish the petty cash fund.

EXERCISE 7-8
L.O. 5, 7

Balance Sheet Classifications

Explain how each of the following should be reported on a balance sheet:

a. An IOU signed by an employee that promises to repay petty cash for $15 she took to pay for lunch when she had forgotten her money.
b. The amount in a checking account (demand deposit).
c. A money order made out to the company in payment of an invoice.
d. A $50,000 money market certificate in a local savings and loan. The money is available at any time with the payment of a penalty of one quarter's interest.
e. U.S. postal stamps in the amount of $3,000.

EXERCISE 7-9
L.O. 8

Interest Computation

Compute interest for the following notes. Consider each note separately.

a. Interest for 45 days on a $5,000, 8%, 60-day note.
b. One month of interest on a $25,000, 12%, one-year note.
c. Total interest on a $16,000, 11%, 45-day note.
d. One year's interest on a $50,000, 10%, three-year note.

EXERCISE 7-10
L.O. 8

Notes Receivable Related Transactions

Record the following transactions for the Easy-Money Corporation:

Feb. 1 Accepted a $15,000, 16%, 90-day note from Cye Lablanski for an outstanding invoice.
Mar. 15 Recorded receipt of quarterly interest payment of $900 from Joe Burroughs.
May 2 Recorded receipt of note payment from Lablanski at maturity.

EXERCISE 7-11
L.O. 8

Notes Receivable

Scholten Enterprises, Inc.'s notes receivable subsidiary ledger contains the following:

$ 10,000, 10%, 30-day note
150,000, 14%, 60-day note
45,000, 8%, 90-day note
300,000, 7%, 120-day note
250,000, 18.5%, 180-day note

Required:
Prepare the journal entries to:

1. Record the above notes. Assume that each involved a cash payment by Scholten.
2. Record the receipt of principal and interest on each note. Assume all transactions occur in the same fiscal year.

EXERCISE 7-12
L.O. 8

Recording of Interest

Jay Smithers, accounting clerk for Top Secret, Inc., has been asked to record receipt of principal and interest on the following notes:

a. $26,000, 12%, 60-day note; half of total interest has previously been accrued.
b. $64,000, 18% note dated April 15 and received payment September 1 of the same year.
c. $39,000, 6%, 30-day note.
d. $100,000, 13%, 45-day note; 15 days have previously been accrued.

Required:
Record the receipt of the principal and interest on the above notes.

EXERCISE 7-13
L.O. 8

Discounting a Note

Columbo Dairy holds the following note:

Face amount	$10,000
Annual interest rate	12%
Term.	90 days
Date of note	3/10/X1

The note is discounted at a bank on 4/1/x1 at a discount rate of 10%. The discounting contract is "with recourse."

Required:
What were the proceeds from the bank? Assume each month has 30 days.

EXERCISE 7-14
L.O. 8

Discounting a Note

On January 1, 19xx, Playthings, Inc., accepted an 11%, six-month note from a customer for $5,000, with principal and interest due on July 1, 19xx. Due to a cash shortage, Playthings decided to sell the note to Huckster Bank. Huckster discounted the note with recourse at a 20% annual discount rate on May 1, 19xx.

Required:
Determine how much Huckster must pay for the note.

EXERCISE 7-15
L.O. 8

Discounting a Note

On March 1, 19xx, Bob sold Sue a new stereo system for $3,000 and received a 12%, six-month note receivable. On June 1, 19xx, he discounted it at the bank at 15%.

Required:
Prepare the journal entry to reflect the June 1, 19xx, transaction assuming the note is discounted with recourse.

EXERCISE 7-16
L.O. 8

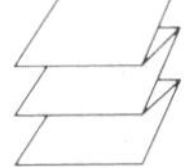

Dishonored Note

Stark Company discounted, with recourse, Burke's $44,000 note at the local bank. The note had a maturity value of $46,000. Burke defaulted on the note.

Required:
1. Record the journal entries Stark makes on the date of default and six months later when a $48,500 check is received from Burke in repayment of the note. (Note that more interest is paid for the period between maturity and payment date.)
2. What journal entries would Stark have to make on those dates if the note were discounted without recourse?

APPENDIX EXERCISES

EXERCISE 7-17
L.O. 9

Special Journals

Describe the special journals each of the following items would be recorded in:

a. Monthly payroll.
b. Payment received from a credit customer.
c. Cash sale.
d. Credit sale.
e. Invoice for merchandise purchased on account.
f. Deductions from employee paychecks.
g. Cash receipt from customer for prepaid subscriptions.
h. Payment to replenish petty cash fund.

EXERCISE 7-18
L.O. 9

Control Accounts

Warehouse Foods Company has a balance of $36,900 in its Accounts Receivable control account. This account is supported by the following subsidiary ledger:

Customer	*May 1 Amount*
T. Berry	$ 9,000
F. Channing . . .	6,400
R. Nixon.	3,550
B. Scott	4,000
G. Smith	3,700
F. Stone	5,600
L. Wilson	4,650
Total	$36,900

During the month of May 19xx, Warehouse had the following activity related to its Accounts Receivable account:

Customer	*Sales*	*Receipts*
T. Berry	$5,550	$13,000
F. Channing . .	0	4,000
R. Nixon	2,700	3,200
B. Scott	0	4,000
F. Stone	1,550	5,000
L. Wilson	1,200	0

Required:
Compute the ending balance in the Accounts Receivable account. Post the above transactions to the subsidiary ledger and prepare a schedule showing the ending balances in each customer's account.

PROBLEMS

PROBLEM 7-1
L.O. 7

Petty Cash

The P&G Company created a $350 petty cash fund for its accounting department on July 1, 19xx. During the next two months, the fund made the following payments:

Last-minute purchase of mailing labels . . .	$68
Dinner for overtime workers	56
Postage stamps	44
Cab fare for out-of-town visitor to the department manager	72

Cash on hand at August 29, 19xx, is $108.

Required:
1. Prepare the journal entry to create the fund on July 1, 19xx.
2. Prepare the journal entry for the replenishment of the fund on August 29, 19xx.

PROBLEM 7-2
L.O. 6

Bank Reconciliation

The Chung Company reported the following data related to its cash transactions for the month of March 19xx:

Balance per bank statement at the close of business, 3/31/xx	$40,000
Bank statement service charge for March 19xx . .	20
Collection of note by bank—reported on March bank statement	2,000
Deposit in transit, 3/31/xx	6,000
Outstanding checks, 3/31/xx	8,000
NSF check from J. Smith, a customer, returned by the bank with the March statement.	250

Required:
1. Determine the amount of cash that should appear on the company's balance sheet as of March 31, 19xx.

2. Record the journal entries in general journal form for the NSF check, the note collection, and the service charge.
3. What journal entry is required to record the $6,000 deposit in transit?

PROBLEM 7-3
L.O. 6

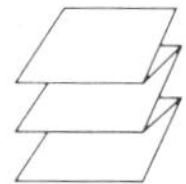

Bank Reconciliation

Katydid Enterprises' bank statement for the month ended July 31, 19xx, gave the following information:

Beginning balance, July 1	$3,500
Deposits during July	2,645
Checks cleared during July	3,217
NSF check (R. Maki)	63
Bank service charge	25
Ending balance, July 31	2,840

Katydid's general ledger Cash account for July showed the following:

Beginning balance, July 1	$3,500
Deposits made	2,800
Checks written	3,300
Ending balance, July 31	3,000

There were no deposits in transit or checks outstanding as of June 30, 19xx. However, there are outstanding checks and deposits in transit as of July 31, 19xx.

Required:
Reconcile the bank statement and prepare any journal entries Katydid Enterprises would need to make.

PROBLEM 7-4
L.O. 6

Bank Statement Reconciliation

The trial balance of the North Sales Company shows a balance of $8,000 in the Cash account at December 31, 19xx. The bank statement received after the trial balance was prepared indicates the following:

a. A check written for $89 in payment of an advertising bill for that amount had been erroneously recorded on the company's books as $98.
b. The bank deducted $30 for collection and service charges that have not been entered on the company's books.
c. A deposit for $243 which the company made in late December did not appear on the bank statement.
d. The bank collected a note receivable for the company in the total amount of $1,750 including $50 of interest; the company did not know that the bank made this collection until the bank statement was received.
e. The bank statement included a check written by North Star Salt Corporation which was charged against North Sales Company's account.

Required:
1. Prepare the appropriate journal entries North Sales Company would make to record the above.
2. What action, if any, would North Sales Company take for any of the items that did not require a journal entry to be made?

PROBLEM 7-5
L.O. 6

Bank Statement Reconciliation

You are the independent auditor for Systat Software, Inc., and you are currently comparing the cash balance as of December 31, 19xx, with the most recent bank statement dated December 31, 19xx. You are given the following summary information for the year from Systat's accountant:

Beginning cash balance, 1/1/xx . . .	$ 85,500
Deposits during 19xx	1,400,000
Checks written during 19xx.	(1,350,000)
Service charges for first 11 months of 19xx	(2,750)
Ending cash balance, 12/31/xx . . .	$ 132,750

You reconcile the bank statement and discover the following:

a. The service charge for December is $280, which was not recorded on Systat's books.
b. Eight checks totaling $9,000 and two checks totaling $3,500 written by Systat in November are still outstanding.
c. One check written in November to an advertising company for $10,800 was recorded as $1,080 in November, and it was included in the current bank statement at the correct amount. The original entry was:

19xx			
Nov. 30	Advertising Expense	1,080	
	Cash		1,080

d. Checks and cash totaling $8,750 were deposited after the bank closed on December 31, 19xx, and this did not show up on the current bank statement.

Required:
1. What is the correct cash balance at December 31, 19xx?
2. What cash-related journal entries, if any, are necessary on Systat's books at December 31, 19xx?

PROBLEM 7-6
L.O. 6

Bank Reconciliation

Greedy Corporation deposits all receipts intact each day and pays all debts by check. On July 31 of the current year, the balance of its Cash account was $2,105. However, the bank statement of that date showed a balance of $5,586. The following information is available from the records:

a. The June 30 bank reconciliation showed seven checks outstanding:

Check No.	*Amount*
764 . . .	$ 882
801 . . .	1,156
802 . . .	90
804 . . .	150
805 . . .	705
806 . . .	65
808 . . .	1,010

Of these checks, No. 764 and No. 808 were not returned with the July 31 bank statement.

b. July checks written but not returned with the bank statement totaled $2,859.

c. While comparing returned checks to the cash payments records, it was found that check No. 894 issued to the electric company and debited to Utilities Expense had been written for $908 and had cleared the bank at that amount but had been recorded on the books at $980.

d. The following items were returned with the bank statement:

1. Notification that a check for $260 written by a customer, Darwin Company, on their account, had been returned NSF.
2. Bank service charge for the month totaled $22.

e. The bank statement also contained a notification that the bank had deposited $641 to Greedy's account. This amount was net of the bank's collection fee of $15 and resulted from a transfer of 931 Canadian dollars from a Canadian bank. This transfer was in settlement of a $662 receivable balance in the account of Windsor Bros. Ltd., a Canadian firm. This arrangement is the normal method of doing business between Windsor Bros. and Greedy. Greedy applies any gains or losses on currency conversion to Miscellaneous Income or Expense. The $15 bank service fee is **not** included in the $22 of bank service charges for the month.

f. The bank erroneously cleared check No. 814 at $762. It had been written for $765 and was properly recorded in Greedy's records.

g. The July 31 deposit amounted to $1,704. This deposit had not been made in time to be included in the bank's records for July.

Required:

1. Prepare the July 31 bank reconciliation.
2. Prepare all journal entries required as a result of the reconciliation.

PROBLEM 7-7
L.O. 8

Interest

Star Equipment Company, which is in the business of designing, manufacturing, and selling equipment to move materials, accepts the following notes at the beginning of September:

a. $ 25,000, 8%, 180-day note
b. 50,000, 10%, 90-day note
c. 60,000, 12%, 120-day note
d. 100,000, 15%, 1-year note

Required:
Determine Star Equipment's interest income for the month of September.

PROBLEM 7-8
L.O. 8

Notes Receivable

Boxton, Inc., builds yachts on a custom-made basis and allows customers to delay payment for various periods. During the current year Boxton sold the following yachts where the customer signed notes as follows:

Yacht	*Delivery Date*	*Maturity Date of Note*	*Maturity Amount of Note*	*Selling Price of Yacht*	*Cost of Yacht*
13-A	1/31/x1	1/31/x2	$ 77,000	$ 70,000	$ 50,000
17-C	6/30/x1	6/30/x2	154,000	140,000	104,000
101-B	9/30/x1	9/30/x2	220,000	200,000	180,000

Required:

1. What was the annual interest rate on the notes?
2. What effect did these sales and notes have on the revenue of Boxton for the year ended December 31, 19x1? (Assume 30-day months for interest computation purposes.)
3. How would your answer to (2) above change if the yachts had been sold for cash?

PROBLEM 7-9
L.O. 8

Discounting a Note

On December 1, 19x1, Utopia sold $3,000 worth of merchandise to Moore in exchange for a $3,000, 12%, four-month note. The principal and interest on the note are payable on March 31, 19x2. Utopia's fiscal year ends on December 31.

Required:
1. On March 1, 19x2, Utopia discounts the note with recourse at a 20% discount rate at the First State Bank. Determine how much in proceeds Utopia will get from the discounting.
2. Record all of Utopia's entries for 19x1 and 19x2 related to the note.
3. Assume that Moore pays off the note to the bank on March 31, 19x2. Prepare any necessary journal entry or entries for Utopia on the date of payment.

PROBLEM 7-10
L.O. 8

Notes Receivable

A summary of the activity in the Accounts Receivable and Notes Receivable accounts of HiTech Consultants for 19xx appears below:

Accounts Receivable

Balance, 1/1/xx	$ 762,000
Credit sales for 19xx	12,050,000
Cash collections for 19xx	(10,660,000)
Acceptance of notes for two separate invoices	(430,000)
Default by maker of discounted note	199,500
Balance, 12/31/xx	$ 1,921,500

Notes Receivable

Balance, 1/1/xx	$ 0
Acceptance of notes for accounts receivable	430,000
Collection of one note	(240,000)
Default of discounted note	(190,000)
Balance, 12/31/xx	$ 0

Notes Receivable Discounted

Balance, 1/1/xx	$ 0
Discounting of note	190,000
Default of discounted note	(190,000)
Balance, 12/31/xx	$ 0

The two notes have the following features:

	Principal	*Interest*	*Maturity Amount*	*Proceeds from Discounting*
Note No. 1	$240,000	$12,000	$252,000	$ 0
Note No. 2	190,000	9,500	199,500	185,000

Required:
Show all journal entries in general journal form related to the above notes.

PROBLEM 7-11
L.O. 8

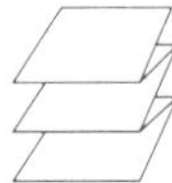

Notes Receivable Transactions and Discounting

Kaline Company has the following transactions affecting Notes Receivable during its first two years of operations:

19x1

Oct.	15	Made a sale to Caldwell Corporation and accepted a $2,000, 12%, 120-day note.
Nov.	1	Accepted a $3,600, 10%, 90-day note from S. Shelata in place of an accounts receivable.
	1	Accepted a $4,000, 12%, 60-day note from Brooks Company in place of an accounts receivable.
Dec.	1	The Brooks Company note was discounted with recourse at the bank at 14%.
	31	Accrued interest receivable is recorded for all notes receivable.

19x2

Jan.	1	Received notification from the bank that the Brooks Company note had been dishonored. Kaline paid the bank.
Feb.	1	Collected the Shelata, Inc., note.
	15	Collected the Caldwell Corporation note.
	15	Collected the Brooks Company note along with interest for the entire period it had been outstanding.

Required:
Prepare all journal entries in general journal form for the above events. Round all computations to the nearest dollar.

PROBLEM 7-12
L.O. 8

Notes Receivable Transactions

Benefit-for-Life, Inc., has the following transactions for the period:

a. Made a sale on account, $3,000; terms 1/10, n/30. All sales are recorded using the gross method.
b. Made a sale on account, $2,000; terms 1/10, n/30.
c. Made a sale accepting a 12%, 90-day note for $8,000 in payment.
d. Made a sale accepting a 10%, 120-day note for $6,000 in payment.
e. Accepted a note for a customer's account receivable in the amount of $4,000 to a 15%, 60-day note.
f. Collected the account receivable in (*a*) within the discount period.
g. Discounted at the bank the note referred to in (*c*) 60 days before maturity, at 15%, without recourse.
h. Discounted at the bank the note referred to in (*d*) 90 days before maturity at 16%, with recourse.
i. Collected the receivable referred to in (*b*) after the discount period expired.
j. Received notice from the bank that the note in (*h*) was dishonored. Paid the bank in full and reestablished the note on the books.
k. Collected the note referred to in (*e*).
l. Collected the note referred to in (*j*) with no additional interest.

Required:
Prepare the journal entries in general journal form required for the above transactions.

PROBLEM 7-13
L.O. 8

Notes Receivable

Plymouth Manufacturing has a large number of notes receivable and, accordingly, maintains a subsidiary ledger for them. You have recently been hired as an accounting clerk and have been assigned the maintenance of this ledger. You are told that there are "problems" with the ledger and that it does not balance with the general ledger control account Notes Receivable. Most of the problems result from the fact that the previous clerk made all general ledger journal entries, as you will, to maintain the account. This person, however, was not properly trained.

During your first month on the job, the following transactions and additional information come to your attention:

a. The subsidiary ledger that had previously been maintained by the previous clerk is shown below. The subsidiary ledger was accurate at the beginning of the month.

Maker	*Amount*	*Face Terms*
Bird Company	$ 4,000	11%, 90 days
Birr, Inc.	6,000	10%, 6 months
Floate, Inc.	1,000	14%, 90 days
Gregory Supply Company	7,500	12%, 60 days
Holmes Industries	12,000	12%, 90 days
Krissie Manufacturing	3,000	11%, 120 days
Paula's Kitchen Supply	9,000	10%, 30 days
Ray Farmer Building Company	11,000	14%, 120 days
Topsy Turvy Amusements.	2,000	14%, 6 months
Zach Company	5,000	15%, 1 year
Total	$60,500	

The balance in the general ledger control account of $63,710 is inaccurate at the beginning of the month because of *b*, *c*, and *d* below.

b. The general ledger account balance includes a credit for $150 arising from the collection of a note in the previous month. This amount arose when a $3,000, 10%, six-month note from Spencer Company was collected and the previous accounting clerk credited the entire proceeds to Notes Receivable.

c. One of the items in the general ledger account balance is a $12,000, 12%, 90-day note from Holmes Industries recorded at its maturity value of $12,360 with the $360 being properly credited to Interest Income. The previous accounting clerk frequently used this procedure for familiar customers who were known to be excellent about paying.

d. In the previous month the Bird Company's $4,000, 11% note was mistakenly recorded by a debit to Notes Receivable and a credit to Cash for $7,000.

e. The following notes were created during the month from sales:

Maker	*Face Amount*	*Terms*
Fox Company	$2,500	14%, 90 days
Zach Company	8,000	12%, 6 months
Gregory Supply	4,000	13%, 90 days
Bird Company	6,000	13%, 90 days

f. A 10%, 60-day note with face value of $3,000 was accepted in payment for an account receivable from Car-Mac Industries.

g. The following notes were collected during the month along with interest:

Paula's Kitchen Supply note of $9,000
Birr, Inc., note of $6,000

h. To generate cash for a payroll, the $7,500 Gregory Supply Company note was discounted, without recourse, at the bank at 16% 30 days before maturity.

Required:

1. Make the entries to record Notes Receivable transactions during the month and to correct the general ledger account balance.
2. Prepare a schedule of the notes outstanding that agrees with the appropriate balance in the general ledger.

APPENDIX PROBLEMS

PROBLEM 7-14
L.O. 9

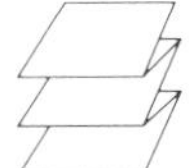

Special Journals

The following transactions were taken from Mott, Inc.'s accounting records for July 1, 19xx:

a. Received $1,600 from customer M. Logan, invoice No. 2333.
b. Paid Office Realty, Inc., $24,000 for six months of rent on office space.
c. Created a $200 petty cash fund.
d. Recorded weekly payroll to the following: A. Bird, $600; C. Sullivan, $900; D. Devol, $500; and P. Ross, $1,100.
e. Received payment from Comtype on invoice No. 2230, $1,000 less 2% discount. Comtype uses the gross method.
f. Paid Jenkins Glassworks $500 on invoice No. 216899.
g. Received payments on $10,000 note from G. Hanks plus $1,000 interest.
h. Received a $50 refund from the local utility company, Electric Works.
i. Paid monthly communications bill for $1,445 to On-Site Phone Company.
j. Paid $140 to American Company for renewal of annual magazine subscriptions.
k. Paid Schaffer Music Company $320 on invoice No. 11111.
l. Recorded cash sales of $3,600 for the day.

You have been called on to demonstrate the timesaving features of special journals.

Required:

1. Construct a cash receipts journal and a cash payments journal and record the entries above. Use account names for other debits and credits. Mott begins the month with check No. 107 and issues all checks consecutively.
2. Explain what the timesaving features are of the special journals.
3. Are there any other characteristics of special journals that make them desirable?

PROBLEM 7-15
L.O. 9

Control Accounts

Polo Fabrics, Inc., sells high-quality fabrics to customers throughout the United States. Invoices are sent for each shipment. One major customer was sent its shipments in May 19xx, and the following special journal transactions were recorded for the customer:

Excerpt from Sales Journal

Date	*Customer*	*Invoice No.*	*Sales Cr. Accounts Receivable Dr.*
5/2	Utah Shirts, Inc.	5-08	$18,000
5/8	Utah Shirts, Inc.	5-11	67,000
5/16	Utah Shirts, Inc.	5-24	13,800
5/30	Utah Shirts, Inc.	5-30	44,150

Excerpt from Cash Receipts Journal

	Invoice					*Other Credit (Debit)*	
Date	*Name*	*No.*	*Cash*	*Accounts Receivable*	*Sales*	*Amount*	*Account*
5/7 . .	Utah Shirt	4-11	$55,000	$55,000			
	Utah Shirt	4-15	43,500	43,500			
5/29 . .	Utah Shirt	5-08	18,000	18,000			
	Utah Shirt	5-11	67,000	67,000			

Required:

1. If invoice No. 4-11 and invoice No. 4-15 were the only outstanding invoices for Utah Shirts at the beginning of May, construct a subsidiary ledger account for Utah Shirts, Inc., for the May transactions.
2. What is the relationship of the Sales account and the Accounts Receivable Control account to the subsidiary ledger accounts? How do each affect the financial statements?

PROBLEM 7-16
L.O. 9

Special Journals and Control Accounts

Consider the following sales and purchases transactions for the first day of operations of TCI Company:

a. Sold $10,000 of merchandise to C. Steinacker on account. No terms were given.
b. Purchased $6,000 of merchandise from R. Ford on account.
c. Sold $7,000 of merchandise to T. Jones on account.
d. Purchased $900 of office supplies on account from Marsh's Office Supply Store.
e. Sold $200 of merchandise to M. Hambo for cash.
f. Purchased $4,000 of office furniture on account from Marsh's Office Supply Store.
g. Purchased merchandise worth $800 for cash.
h. Purchased $690 of merchandise on account of F. Stahl.

TCI posts from the special journal daily.

Required:

1. Record the above transactions, if appropriate, in either the sales or purchases journal.
2. Open and post the transactions to the appropriate general and subsidiary ledger T accounts as necessary at the end of the first day.

CASES

CASE 7-1

L.O. 2, 5

Control Systems

Burns Computer Supplies sells products for cash and on credit. Betty Burns has instituted a flow of duties chart that she believes provides good control over cash transactions (see Exhibit 7C-1).

EXHIBIT 7C-1

Flow of Duties Chart

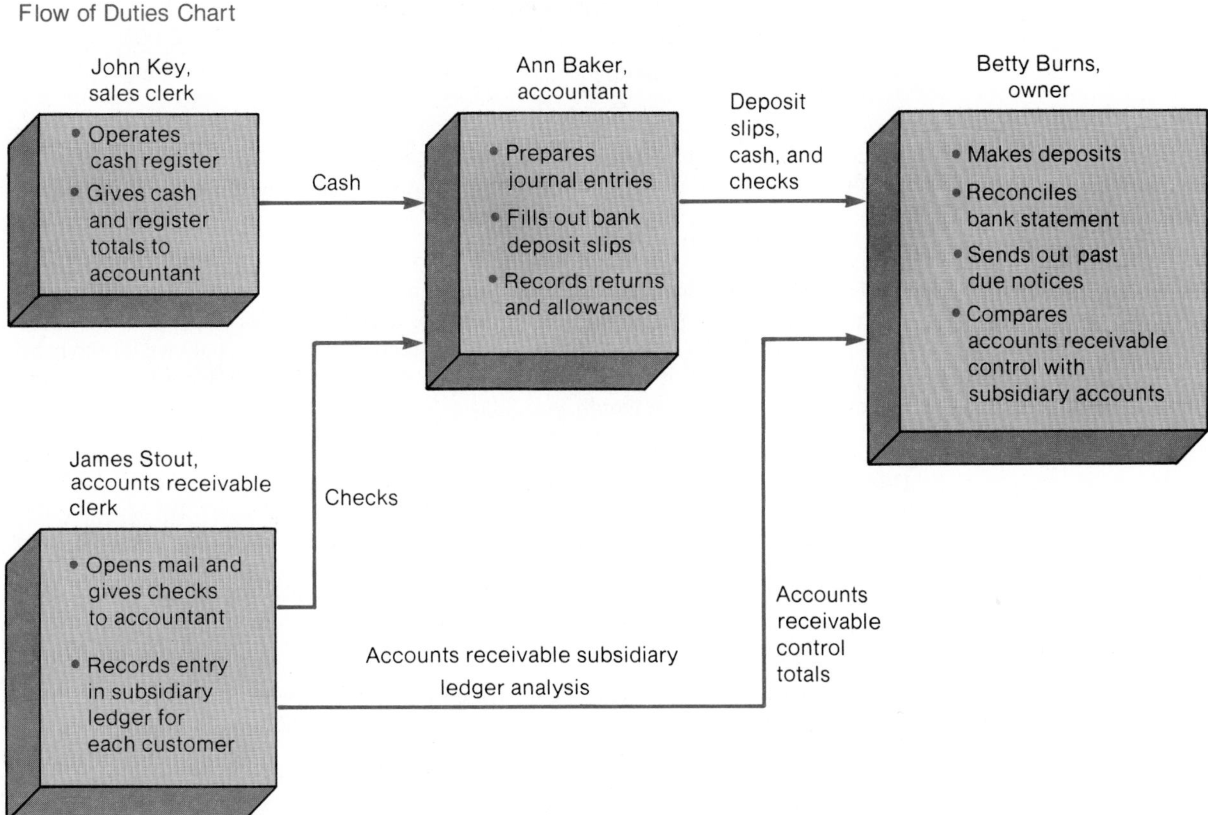

Ann Baker is in grave financial straights and has concocted the following fraudulent scheme. She plans to:

a. Record a fictitious return of damaged merchandise from a customer who has actually paid an invoice amount (say, $500).
b. Pocket cash equal to the fictitious return of damaged merchandise.

Her logic is that Betty Burns will rely on the subsidiary ledger to check on unpaid invoices, but her scheme will circumvent this check because the subsidiary ledger will show the invoice paid.

Required:

1. Will the scheme work? Why or why not?
2. How would you improve the control system and why?

CASE 7-2
L.O. 5

Definition of Cash

Environmental Impact Company has a Cash balance on its balance sheet of $38,500 at year-end. An examination of the transactions in the classification reveals the following:

Balance in Cash-in-Bank account	$10,500
Petty cash balance	500
Marketable securities market value	15,000
Savings account—36-month certificate, penalty for early withdrawal	7,500
Noninterest-earning bank account that must be maintained under a loan agreement with the bank	5,000
Total cash balance	$38,500

Required:
As Environmental's auditor, you are to explain the nature of cash and comment on the appropriate treatment of each item shown above as a component of cash.

CASE 7-3
L.O. 5, 6

Bank Reconciliation and Cash Control

While reviewing the bank statement of your company you find a $10,000 difference between the deposits on the bank statement and the deposits on the company's record. You note a specific $10,000 deposit on the company's records that was not shown on the bank statement. At the end of the next month you find that the $10,000 deposit was actually made at the middle of the month.

Required:
Does this set of facts indicate a cash control problem? What steps would you take?

CASE 7-4
L.O. 1, 2, 5, 7

Petty Cash and Control

You are about to organize your own consulting firm. You need to establish a petty cash fund of $500.

Required:
Discuss what types of needs you might have for petty cash, how you would keep record of the petty cash transactions, and discuss any concerns you might have for controlling petty cash.

CASE 7-5
L.O. 8

Discounting of Note and Liquidity Analysis

The following is an excerpt from the December 31, 1987, annual report of Clark Equipment Company and consolidated subsidiaries. Clark Equipment Company is an international manufacturer of heavy equipment including forklifts, endloaders, and other construction and manufacturing equipment.

	December 31	
	1987	*1986*
Current assets (in thousands):		
Cash	$115,599	$58,484
Accounts and notes receivable (less allowance for doubtful accounts of $4.3 million for each year)	63,044	34,819

Assume that the above balances were prepared before adjusting for the following hypothetical transaction:

On December 31, 1987, Clark discounted with recourse a 10%, 12-month, $15 million note due June 30, 1988. The bank requires a 15% annual discount rate. No interest has been accrued or received to date.

Required:

1. How much will the bank pay for the note?
2. How would Clark's balance sheet be affected by the discounting? Has Clark improved its liquidity by means of the discounting?

CASE 7-6
L.O. 8

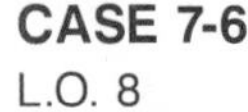

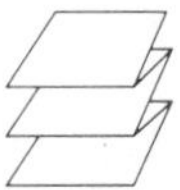

Notes Receivable and Business Decisions

West Coast Instruments, Inc. (WCI), is a producer of electronic equipment. One of its very important suppliers, Bently Plastics, Inc. (BP), has requested that WCI lend it $2,000,000 on a six-month note at 18% interest in order that BP expand its manufacturing facilities. The expansion would be devoted to supplying WCI exclusively. BP proposes the following schedule:

5/15	BP issues a note to WCI	$2,000,000
11/15	BP pays off the note plus interest.	2,180,000

WCI's president makes the following statement about the matter to his vice-president of finance: "Given we definitely want BP to expand to ensure our supply, why don't we go ahead and lend the money and that way we will earn the interest?" His vice-president replies: "We need all of our available cash for our own expansion. We would have to borrow ourselves if we give them the loan." The president then says: "Couldn't we lend the money and then discount the note and have use of the cash right on? Work up the numbers for me as soon as possible." The vice-president responds: "OK, but keep in mind that when you discount a note at a bank they charge a substantial discount rate, and we would be contingently liable if the maker defaults."

Required:

1. Show the journal entries necessary on WCI's books if they lend the money to BP and BP pays on time.
2. Show the journal entries necessary on WCI's books if it lends the money to BP and then immediately discounts the note at a bank at a 20% discount rate, with recourse. Assume the note is paid on time.
3. Under what conditions do you think lending money to a supplier makes good business sense?
4. Does it make good business sense to discount a note at a bank if, as is the case here, the discount fee is more than the interest that would have been earned on the note?

FINANCIAL STATEMENTS

FINANCIAL STATEMENT COMPONENTS EMPHASIZED IN CHAPTER 8

Rabic Inc.
Income Statement
For 1991

Revenues
XXXX
XXXX
Expenses
Depreciation expense
Amortization expense
Depletion expense

	1991	1990
Depreciation expense . .	$ XXX	$ XXX
Amortization expense .	XX	XX
Depletion expense	XX	XX

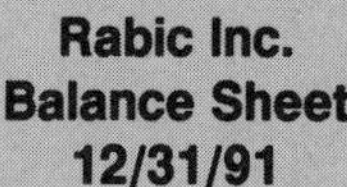

Rabic Inc.
Balance Sheet
12/31/91

Current assets
XXXX
XXXX
Noncurrent assets
Plant, property, and equipment
Less accumulated depreciation
Net plant assets
Natural resources (net)
Franchise rights (net)
Goodwill (net)
Current liabilities
XXXX
XXXX
Noncurrent liabilities
XXXX
XXXX
Stockholders' equity
XXXX
XXXX

	1991	1990
Plant, property, and equipment	$ XXX	$ XXX
Less accumulated depreciation	(XXX)	(XXX)
Net plant assets	XXXX	XXXX
Natural resources (net) .	XXX	XXX
Franchise rights (net) . .	XXX	XXX
Goodwill (net)	XX	XX

Rabic Inc.
Cash Flow Statement
For 1991

Operating activities
XXXX
XXXX
Investing activities
Investment in equipment
Sale of old equipment
Financing Activities
XXXX
XXXX

	1991	1990
Investment in equipment	$(XXXX)	$(XXX)
Sale of old equipment	XX	XXX

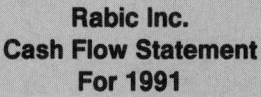

C H A P T E R 8

Long-Term Assets

LEARNING OBJECTIVES

After studying Chapter 8, you should understand:

1. How to measure the acquisition costs of tangible assets, including group asset purchases, pp. 411-13.
2. Four depreciation methods—straight-line, units of output, sum-of-the-years'-digits, and declining-balance, pp. 415-22.
3. How to determine depreciation for partial years, and how to make revisions in depreciation estimates, pp. 422-25.
4. When costs subsequent to acquisition are capitalized or expensed, pp. 425-28.
5. How to record disposals of tangible assets at net book value, disposals involving gains or losses, and disposals of fully depreciated assets, pp. 428-30.
6. The importance of evaluating changes in plant assets, pp. 430-32.
7. Accounting for long-term intangible assets, pp. 432-36.
8. Accounting for asset exchanges (Appendix 8A), pp. 438-40.
9. Accounting for natural resources (Appendix 8B), pp. 442-44.

In earlier chapters you learned that a company's assets: (1) arise from past transactions, (2) are controlled by the company, and (3) have measurable future benefits beyond the current accounting period. Both tangible and intangible assets have these characteristics. The difference between these two types of assets is the nature of their future benefits.

Tangible assets are financial resources having a physical form, such as buildings and equipment. Tangible assets normally represent a much larger dollar investment than intangible assets. Tangible assets are sometimes divided into two categories: (1) those that will be used up in the normal course of business; and (2) those that will not be consumed by business operations. The first category is often called **wasting assets** (or **productive assets** or **consumable assets**), and consists of the following types of tangible assets:

1a. Buildings (also called *Plant*).

1b. Equipment and machinery.

1c. Furniture and fixtures.

1d. Natural resources (minerals, oil, and so on).

Tangible assets that will not be consumed in the business are generally limited to land (or "property"), which will benefit future operations of the business for an indefinite time period. It is not uncommon to see land reported along with buildings, machinery, and equipment as a single amount in published balance sheets, and referred to by such captions as "plant, property and equipment," "plant assets," or some other similar terminology.

Intangible assets are financial resources with no physical substance, such as patents or copyrights. Intangible assets along with the first category of tangible assets noted above (wasting assets) do not last indefinitely, but are consumed through the normal course of business operations. The accrual accounting model requires that the cost of these long-term tangible and intangible assets be charged (expensed) against revenues over the periods of benefit. This process of assigning the cost of a long-term asset such as a piece of equipment to the years in which it will benefit the operations is most generally referred to **cost allocation,** which is any system of systematically assigning costs to accounting periods. More specifically, for tangible assets the cost allocation process is called **depreciation,** while for intangible assets it is called **amortization.** Both depreciation and amortization are simply systematic cost allocation methods of expensing the cost of long-term tangible and intangible assets to the income statements of the periods benefiting from their use.

Tangible assets have value to a business because of what they are and what they are capable of doing or providing—a value based on the asset's physical capability to provide benefits. The value of **intangible assets** to a business stems from what they **represent** rather than their physical existence. Most intangible assets consist of legal contracts or documents that entitle a business to certain rights representing future benefits. For example, a patent is a legal document that entitles a specified business to the exclusive rights to an invention or process. The patent itself is merely paper and has no physical substance; however, the patent represents rights that are important to the business.

For most businesses, plant and equipment represent the largest investment in long-term assets. Remember that these long-term assets are used for operating activities and are not held for sale. In this chapter we examine the following life cycle of long-term tangible assets:

1. Acquisition of long-term tangible assets.
2. Depreciation of long-term tangible assets—allocation of costs to periods of benefit.
3. Costs subsequent to acquisition—additions to long-term tangible assets.
4. Disposal of long-term tangible assets.

The discussion on the life cycle of long-term tangible assets is followed by an evaluation of changes in these assets. We conclude the chapter with a discussion of accounting for intangible assets. Two appendixes at the end of the chapter cover asset exchanges and natural resources.

Long-term tangible assets used in a company's production process represent one of the major investments of resources for most product-oriented businesses. Along with inventory, long-term tangible assets represent the primary operating assets of most business entities.

ACQUISITION OF LONG-TERM TANGIBLE ASSETS

The acquisition cost of all assets is the **current fair market value of the assets given or received, whichever is more objectively measurable.** This acquisition cost should include **all costs necessary to acquire the asset and to place the asset into its intended useful state.** In conceptual terms, these two sentences describe how acquisition costs are measured and what they include. Applications of these concepts may call for judgment on the part of the accountant and will not always lead to a clear or obvious solution to asset measurement problems.

Costs Included in the Original Cost of an Asset

Objective 1
How to measure the acquisition costs of tangible assets, including group asset purchases.

What is the total cost to be included in recording an asset? **The asset's recorded value should include all costs necessary to acquire the asset and to place the asset into its intended useful state.** For example, the cost to insure a new casting machine while it is in-transit to the buyer's plant would be included in the cost of the machine. However, insurance on the machine once it is placed into use would be charged to the period covered as insurance expense. When costs are added to an asset account, the costs are said to be capitalized, since they add to the assets of the business. When costs are not capitalized, they are expensed (or "charged") to the current period. The two examples of capitalized costs that follow are: (1) capitalization of costs necessary to place an asset into its intended useful state and (2) capitalization of interest costs.

Capitalization of Costs Necessary to Place an Asset into Its Intended Useful State. Assume Delta Corporation purchased land on which Delta intended to build a factory. However, before Delta could begin construction of the factory, it had to remove an old barn and prepare the building site. The events that follow occurred shortly after the $75,000 land purchase.

Delta paid a salvage company $2,000 to tear down the old barn and sold the wood for $2,200. To prepare the land for a building site, Delta paid $3,400 to have the land cleared and graded. The net cost of these three activities is $3,200 ($2,000 − $2,200 + $3,400). This cost should be added to the value of the Land account (capitalized) rather than expensed because these activities are necessary to prepare the land for its intended purpose.

EXHIBIT 8-1

Disclosure of Capitalization of Interest

The Dow Chemical Company

Excerpt from footnotes:

Interest cost reported in income statement

(in $ millions)	*19x3*	*19x2*
Total interest incurred on debt	$478	$579
Less—Interest capitalized	– 47	– 65
Net interest expense	$431	$514

Analysis of impact of interest capitalization

(in $ millions)	*19x3*	*19x2*
Reported net income	$334	$399
Capitalized interest as a percentage of reported net income	14.1%	16.3%

Interest Capitalization. Another component of an asset's cost may be interest incurred on borrowings. GAAP requires interest to be included as a cost of major long-term assets which require an extended length of time to prepare them for their intended purpose. Assets such as these (e.g., a new plant or warehouse) require a construction period during which interest costs are to be included as a cost of the asset. Interest costs are included as a cost of constructed assets regardless of whether self-constructed or constructed by an outside contractor/builder. The amount of interest to be included in the asset's cost depends on the accumulated cost of the asset throughout the construction period and the length of the construction period.[1]

Exhibit 8-1 shows the disclosure for interest capitalization reported by Dow Chemical Company in a recent annual report. The top of Exhibit 8-1 provides for footnote explanation of: the total amount of interest for each year (i.e., $478 million for 19x3); the amount of interest capitalized, or added to Dow's assets (i.e., $47 million in 19x3); and, the net amount of interest expensed each year (i.e., $478 – $47 = $431 million expensed in 19x3). In the lower part of Exhibit 8-1 we compute capitalized interest as a percent of reported net income to determine whether interest capitalization has a material effect on income. In 19x3, the interest capitalized by Dow ($47 million) was equal to about 14.1% of reported net income ($47/$334). In 19x2, the amount was 16.3% of net income. While the amount of interest capitalized by a company is usually only a fraction of its total interest costs for the period, its effect on net income is sometimes significant.

[1]This procedure is explained in some detail in *FASB Statement No. 34,* "Capitalization of Interest Cost" (Norwalk, Conn.: FASB, 1979). Note that if interest to be capitalized is not material in amount, capitalization may be ignored.

Group Purchases

The purchasing of assets as a group instead of in separate transactions creates special measurement problems. To illustrate, assume Campus Rentals, Inc., acquired three houses from another rental agency for a package price of $380,000. The three houses were to be renovated and rented as student housing. The following information is available:

House Address	*Square Feet*	*Property Tax Assessment Value*
1181 Summit Street	2,816	$121,600
2247 Hill Street	1,408	76,000
1818 Olivia Street	2,176	106,400
	6,400	$304,000

Note that the assessed value does not depend entirely on floor space. However, both the square feet and assessed value measures could be used to assign the total cost to the three separate properties. If we assume that the square footage of floor space determined the fair value of the three houses, the $380,000 total cost could be assigned (allocated) to the three houses as follows:

House	*Square Feet*	*Percent of Total Square Feet*	×	*Amount to be Allocated*	=	*Allocated Cost per House*
Summit. . . .	2,816	.44 (2,816/6,400)		$380,000		$167,200
Hill	1,408	.22 (1,408/6,400)		380,000		83,600
Olivia.	2,176	.34 (2,176/6,400)		380,000		129,200
	6,400	1.00 (6,400/6,400)		380,000		$380,000

The selection of the "most appropriate" basis for allocating the total cost of a **group purchase** (also called a **basket purchase**) can have a significant affect on the recorded cost of the individual assets. Since by definition the term *allocation* is used to identify an arbitrary process, obviously there is no single correct way to allocate any cost.

DEPRECIATION OF LONG-TERM TANGIBLE ASSETS

Productive assets such as plant, equipment, machinery, vehicles, and warehouses are tangible long-term assets representing future benefits to the business. However, in time, the operations of the business will "use up" or consume the future benefits of these tangible assets. As a result, the original cost of tangible assets minus their expected resale value when fully used (called **residual value** or **salvage value**) must be systematically expensed over their useful lives. For tangible assets, this systematic expensing or allocation process is called **depreciation. Depreciation expense** is the amount that is charged to current income to reflect the portion of the asset's benefit used during that period. The difference between an asset's original cost and its estimated salvage value is called its **depreciable base.** A portion of the depreciable base is allocated to income each period over the asset's **useful life,** which is the length of time the asset is expected to be used by the business.

To illustrate, assume a machine costing $900,000 was acquired on January 1, 19x1, for cash. The estimated salvage value was $100,000 and the estimated useful life was eight years. Further assume that the $800,000 depreciable base will be allocated equally to each of the eight years of use at the rate of $100,000 per year. The following entries would be recorded for 19x1 and 19x2:

19x1			
Jan. 1	Machine (A)	900,000	
	Cash (A)		900,000
Dec. 31	Depreciation Expense—Machine (E)	100,000	
	Accumulated Depreciation—Machine (XA) . .		100,000
19x2			
Dec. 31	Depreciation Expense—Machine (E)	100,000	
	Accumulated Depreciation—Machine (XA) . .		100,000

The same $100,000 depreciation expense entry would be recorded each year-end for the eight years of use. The account used to offset Depreciation Expense is a contra asset account, **accumulated depreciation**, which accumulates depreciation expense from all periods and is reported in the balance sheet as follows:

Partial Balance Sheet

	December 31	
	19x2	*19x1*
Machinery	$900,000	$900,000
Less Accumulated Depreciation	200,000	100,000
Net Book Value—Machinery	$700,000	$800,000

The difference between the original cost of depreciable assets and their accumulated depreciation is the assets' **net book value** (or just **book value**). Sometimes only the net book value of "plant assets" is reported in the balance sheet, with details about the nature of the assets and their accumulated depreciation reported in the footnotes following the financial statements.

The examples of depreciation illustrated above and in the earlier chapters were all based on a simple depreciation method which assigned the depreciable base of the asset equally to all time periods over the useful life of the asset. The alternative depreciation methods commonly used in practice are considered in the following sections, along with illustrations of how to determine a partial year's depreciation and how to account for depreciation expense when either the original estimated life or original estimated salvage value are revised.

Alternative Depreciation

Generally accepted accounting principles (GAAP) allow several methods of systematically depreciating (allocating) the depreciable base of an asset over its periods of benefit. These different methods permit businesses some flexibility in deciding how fast the depreciable base of an asset is assigned to the periods of benefit. To illustrate how this selection might be made, let's listen in on a conversation between Brad and Mary that occurred during their first year of operations for Byte-Size.

Brad: You know, we really need to decide what depreciation method we are going to use for our equipment, Mary. I don't know if we should use straight-line or some other method.

Mary: Well, what difference will it make, Brad?

Brad: Straight line will spread out or "allocate" the cost evenly over the life of the equipment, while the more rapid depreciation methods allocate more of the cost in the early years of use and less in later years. It is kind of like this. [*Brad sketches the following graph to show depreciation expense.*]

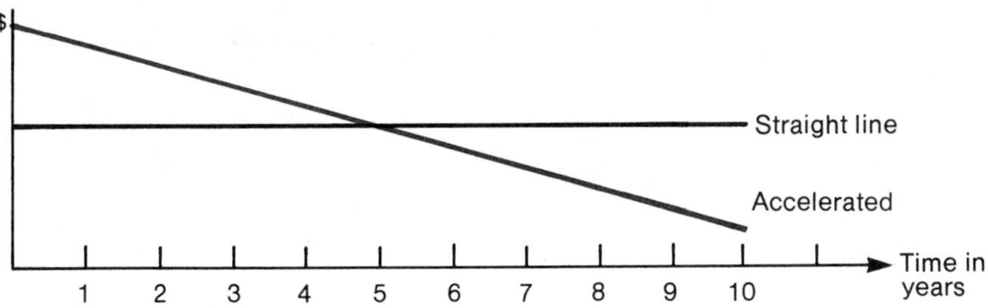

Mary: Is the total depreciation taken over the life of the equipment any different for one method or the other?

Brad: No, they are the same in total.

Mary: So an accelerated method will result in more expense in the first few years of use than straight line. Why should we consider doing that?

Brad: Well, what if a change in technology occurs? Our equipment may be less useful in the latter part of its useful life, therefore it might make sense to have less depreciation expense later on.

Mary: Yes, but the bank would feel better about lending us money if our expenses were lower in the first few years of our business. Lower expenses will make it easier for us to show a profit.

Brad: You know, since we don't need to use the same method for income tax purposes that we decide to use for financial reporting purposes, it really doesn't matter too much what method we decide on. The depreciation method that we choose for financial reporting purposes will not affect our cash flow.

Mary: Yes, but I wonder if the bank knows that? They aren't going to ask us for our tax return—only for the financial statements. I say we use straight line. Besides being simple to use, it will improve our first few income statements.

The discussion between Brad and Mary points to some common questions and concerns in the choice of a depreciation method. Before we consider these issues in more detail, let us consider an example of each of the following types of depreciation methods allowed within GAAP:

Objective 2
Four depreciation methods — straight-line, units of output, sum-of-the-years'-digits, and declining-balance.

1. Straight-line depreciation.
2. Units-of-output depreciation.
3. Accelerated depreciation:
   a. Sum-of-the-years'-digits depreciation.
   b. Declining-balance depreciation.

Straight-Line Depreciation. The example given in Exhibit 8-2, and examples illustrated earlier in the book, have all been based on straight-line depreciation.

EXHIBIT 8-2

Straight-Line Depreciation

Depreciation Schedule
Calculation: Straight Line

$$\frac{\$50{,}000 - \$10{,}000}{2 \text{ years}} = \$20{,}000 \text{ per year}$$

Date and Period	*Cost*	− *Accumulated Depreciation*	= *Book Value*	*Depreciation Expense*
1/1/x1.	$50,000	$ 0	$50,000	
19x1				$20,000
12/31/x1	50,000	20,000	30,000	
19x2				20,000
12/31/x2.	50,000	40,000	10,000	

The **straight-line depreciation method** assumes assets are equally useful over all time periods of use. Thus, a $50,000 asset with a two-year useful life and a $10,000 residual value would be depreciated (expensed) equally over the two years of use, or $20,000 depreciation expense per year.

Straight-line depreciation is the most common method used for preparing financial statements. You can use the following formula to measure straight-line annual depreciation:

$$\text{Straight-line annual depreciation expense} = \frac{\text{Cost} - \text{Residual (salvage) value}}{\text{Number of years of useful life}}$$

Exhibit 8-2 shows the straight-line depreciation for the $50,000 asset described above.

Units-of-Output Depreciation. The **units-of-output depreciation method** records depreciation expense based on the amount of use an asset receives during the period. For example, assume a machine costs $50,000, has a $10,000 residual value, and an estimated useful life of 10,000 hours of running time. If the machine is used for 6,000 hours in year 1 and 4,000 hours in year 2, depreciation amounts for each unit would be computed using the following equation:

$$\text{Units-of-output depreciation expense (per unit)} = \frac{\text{Cost} - \text{Residual (salvage) value}}{\text{Number of “units” in useful life}}$$

Exhibit 8-3 shows the units-of-output depreciation schedule for the $50,000 machine.

Accelerated Depreciation. Although depreciation is the allocation of an asset's original cost to the periods that benefit from the asset's use, each period will not always receive equal benefit from the use of an asset. Often the asset's early years will provide more benefits and trouble-free use than the later years.

EXHIBIT 8-3

Units-of-Output Depreciation

Depreciation Schedule
Calculation: Units of Output

$$\text{Hourly depreciation expense} = \frac{\$50{,}000 - \$10{,}000}{10{,}000 \text{ hours}} = \$4 \text{ per hour}$$

Year 1:	6,000 hours × $4 =	$24,000
Year 2:	4,000 hours × 4 =	16,000
	10,000 hours	$40,000

Date and Period	*Cost*	− *Accumulated Depreciation*	= *Book Value*	*Depreciation Expense*
1/1/x1	$50,000	$ 0	$50,000	
19x1				$24,000
12/31/x1	50,000	24,000	26,000	
19x2				16,000
12/31/x2	50,000	40,000	10,000	

When assets provide more benefits in earlier periods than in later periods, an accelerated depreciation schedule may be justified. **Accelerated depreciation** is a general term to describe depreciation methods that give higher depreciation expense amounts to the early years of the asset's useful life than are given to the asset's later years. Two accelerated depreciation methods are discussed in the paragraphs that follow: declining-balance depreciation and sum-of-the-years'-digits depreciation.

Declining-balance depreciation. To help you understand the declining-balance method of depreciation, we begin with an example of the straight-line depreciation method. Assume Arrow, Inc., purchases a delivery truck on January 1, 19x1, for $50,000. The truck has an estimated useful life of five years and an estimated residual value of $10,000. Straight-line depreciation would, therefore, be $8,000 per year, computed as follows:

Straight-Line Depreciation Computation

Cost	$50,000
Less residual value	− 10,000
Depreciable base	$40,000

$$\frac{\$40{,}000}{5 \text{ years}} = \$8{,}000 \text{ per year straight-line depreciation expense}$$

When the **declining-balance depreciation method** is used, the amount of depreciation expense is accelerated. To accomplish this acceleration, more than 100% of the straight-line depreciation rate is applied to the declining book value of the depreciable asset. The formula for declining-balance depreciation is:

$$\text{Asset book value at beginning of year} \times \text{Multiple of the straight-line rate} = \text{Declining-balance depreciation expense}$$

EXHIBIT 8-4

Declining-Balance Depreciation

Depreciation Schedule
Calculation: 150% Declining Balance

Straight-line rate = 100%/5 years = 20% per year = .20
150% declining balance = .20 × 1.50 = .30, or 30%

Year	*Book Value at Beginning of the Year* ×	*150% of the Straight-Line Rate* =	*Depreciation Expense Current Year*	*Accumulated Depreciation Balance*
1.	$50,000	30% (.30)	$15,000	$15,000
2.	35,000	30% (.30)	10,500	25,500
3.	24,500	30% (.30)	7,350	32,850
4.	17,150	30% (.30)	5,145	37,995
5*	12,005	30% (.30)	3,602	41,597
Total			$41,597	

**Alternatively:*

5	$12,005	Forced	$ 2,005	$40,000
			$40,000	

Using Arrow's delivery truck as an example, we will illustrate a depreciation schedule for 150% of the straight-line rate. The straight-line depreciation rate, stated as a percentage of the cost of the truck, is 20% (100%/5-year life = 20% per year = .20 or 20%). Therefore, the **150% declining-balance method** uses a 30% rate (150% × 20% = 1.50 × .20 = .30) and a **200% declining-balance method** (or **double-declining balance method**) would use a 40% rate (200% × 20% = .40).

The depreciation schedule for the truck using 150% declining-balance depreciation is given in Exhibit 8-4. Note that in declining-balance depreciation, the residual value is ignored in computing annual depreciation expense and **not** considered until the end of the asset's useful life. Also, depreciation expense is always a **constant** percent (30% in this example) of the declining balance. The book value in this example happens to be $8,403 ($50,000 cost less $41,597 accumulated depreciation) after five years. The final year's depreciation expense is sometimes "forced" to achieve the desired residual value. For example, if Arrow recorded $2,005 depreciation expense in year 5 instead of $3,602 as scheduled, the book value at the end of year 5 would equal $10,000, the estimated residual value. This approach is illustrated in the Exhibit 8-4 footnote.

Sum-of-the-years'-digits depreciation. The **sum-of-the-years'-digits (SYD) depreciation method** provides an accelerated schedule of depreciation. However, unlike the declining-balance method, this method considers the estimated residual value of the asset as did the straight-line and units-of-output methods. To use the SYD method, you must compute the sum of the number of years of useful life and use this sum as a denominator for each year. For Arrow's delivery

EXHIBIT 8-5

Sum-of-the-Years'-Digits Depreciation

Year	Depreciable Base	×	Sum-of-the-Years'-Digits Rate	=	Depreciation Expense Current Year	Accumulated Depreciation Balance
1. . . .	$40,000	×	5/15		$13,333	$13,333
2. . . .	40,000	×	4/15		10,667	24,000
3. . . .	40,000	×	3/15		8,000	32,000
4. . . .	40,000	×	2/15		5,333	37,333
5. . . .	40,000	×	1/15		2,667	40,000
Total . .			15/15		$40,000	

truck, which has a five-year life, the sum would be 5 + 4 + 3 + 2 + 1 = 15. The more general formula for an asset with an n-year life is:

$$\text{Formula for determining the sum of a series of numbers} = \frac{n(n+1)}{2}$$

$$\text{The sum of the series 1–5} = \frac{5(5+1)}{2} = 15$$

The formula for computing the depreciation expense for the period using the SYD method is:

$$\text{Asset's depreciable base} \times \frac{\text{Number of years of asset's remaining life}}{\text{Sum-of-the-years'-digits}} = \text{SYD depreciation expense for the period}$$

The depreciable base, which in our example is $40,000, is then multiplied by the fraction of the first year's digit, in this case five years over the total sum of the years, or 15. The first year's depreciation for an asset with a depreciable base of $40,000 × 5/15 = $13,333. Exhibit 8-5 shows the sum-of-the-years'-digits depreciation schedule for Arrow's truck.

Exhibit 8-6 uses the $50,000 truck example and compares the effects of straight-line depreciation, 150% declining-balance depreciation, and sum-of-the-years'-digits depreciation. Both of the accelerated methods provide more depreciation expense than straight line in the first two years of use and less in the last two years of use, as graphically illustrated at the bottom of Exhibit 8-6.

DEPRECIATION, TAXES, AND CASH FLOW

The depreciation methods illustrated in the previous section of this chapter are all acceptable for financial reporting purposes. The straight-line method is the most common, and is used by more than 90% of publicly traded corporations for financial reporting purposes.[2] However, most companies use an accelerated method of depreciation for income tax reporting purposes. Tax laws, which

[2] See *Accounting Trends and Techniques* (New York: AICPA, 1988).

EXHIBIT 8-6

Comparison of Straight-Line, 150% Declining-Balance, and Sum-of-the-Years'-Digits Depreciation

Asset's original cost: $50,000
Useful life: 5 years
Salvage value: $10,000

		Accelerated Methods	
Year	*Straight Line*	*150% Declining Balance*	*Sum-of-the-Years'-Digits*
1. . . .	$ 8,000	$15,000	$13,333
2. . . .	8,000	10,500	10,667
3. . . .	8,000	7,350	8,000
4. . . .	8,000	5,145	5,333
5. . . .	8,000	2,005 (forced)	2,667
Total . .	$40,000	$40,000	$40,000

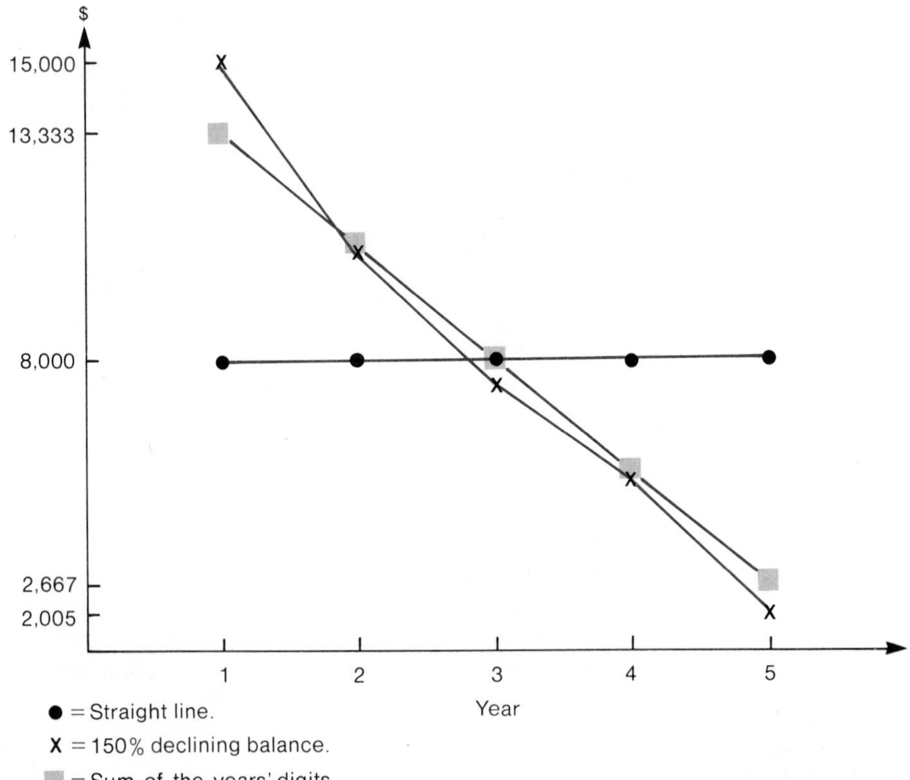

change frequently, normally allow companies to depreciate long-term tangible assets over a shorter period than their estimated economic life and at an accelerated rate. Since companies may wish to reduce taxable income for income tax reporting purposes, they often take a different depreciation expense deduction for tax purposes than that reported in the financial statements.

To illustrate the difference between book and tax depreciation, assume Liquid, Inc., acquired equipment on January 1, 19x1, for $800,000 cash. The equipment has an estimated useful life of eight years and no salvage value. Liquid uses straight-line depreciation for book purposes, but the tax laws allow the following depreciation schedule:

Year of Use	*Percentage of Cost to Be Depreciated*
1	20.00%
2	32.00
3	19.20
4	11.52
5	11.52
6	5.76
	100.00%

The difference between book depreciation expense and tax depreciation expense over the life of the asset is zero, as illustrated in the following schedule:

Year	*Computation of Income Tax Depreciation Expense*			*Straight-Line Book Depreciation Expense*		*Tax Expense over (under) Book Expense*
1	$800,000 × .2000 =	$160,000	−	$100,000	=	$ 60,000
2	800,000 × .3200 =	256,000	−	100,000	=	156,000
3	800,000 × .1920 =	153,600	−	100,000	=	53,600
4	800,000 × .1152 =	92,160	−	100,000	=	(7,840)
5	800,000 × .1152 =	92,160	−	100,000	=	(7,840)
6	800,000 × .0576 =	46,080	−	100,000	=	(53,920)
7	None	0	−	100,000		(100,000)
8	None	0	−	100,000		(100,000)
		$800,000	−	$800,000		$ 0

Notice that the depreciation expense allowed for both income tax purposes and book purposes is limited to the price paid for the equipment—$800,000. The cash outflow of $800,000 on January 1, 19x1, is offset by different patterns of depreciation expense, but total depreciation expense is $800,000 for both book and tax purposes.

Why should Liquid, Inc., use the accelerated method for tax purposes if it results in the same total depreciation expense? The answer to this question lies in the fact that money has "time value." In other words, $1 of cash today is worth more than $1 in five years, since it can be used to earn more cash in the five-year period. Liquid, Inc., will ultimately pay the same amount of total tax whether it uses straight-line or the allowable accelerated method of depreciation. However, by using the accelerated method, Liquid has more cash in the near term, which it can use to earn additional cash to help pay future taxes! The tax savings in the first three years can be computed by multiplying the tax rate times the difference between book and tax depreciation, as follows:

Year	*Tax Depreciation*		*Book Depreciation*		*Excess Tax over (under) Book*		*Tax Rate*		*Tax Savings (Additional Tax)*
1	$160,000	–	$100,000	=	$ 60,000	×	.34	=	$20,400
2	256,000	–	100,000	=	156,000	×	.34	=	53,040
3	153,600	–	100,000	=	53,600	×	.34	=	18,224
4	92,160	–	100,000	=	(7,840)	×	.34	=	(2,666)
5	92,160	–	100,000	=	(7,840)	×	.34	=	(2,666)
6	46,080	–	100,000	=	(53,920)	×	.34	=	(18,332)
7	0	–	100,000	=	(100,000)	×	.34	=	(34,000)
8	0	–	100,000	=	(100,000)	×	.34	=	(34,000)
	$800,000	–	$800,000		$ 0				$ 0

While the tax savings in the first three years ($20,400 + $53,040 + $18,224 = $91,664) is offset by the same amount of additional taxes in years 4–8, Liquid, Inc., still has the benefit of the tax savings in the early years when less cash must be paid out in taxes. If Liquid invested these cash savings over the first three years, it would help offset the additional taxes in years 4–8, resulting in a **real** benefit to Liquid, Inc.

From the analysis above, we should see why companies use accelerated depreciation for income tax purposes, while often using straight line for financial reporting purposes. The relation between depreciation, income taxes, and cash flows may be summarized by the following statements:

1. A cash outflow normally occurs when a depreciable asset is acquired.
2. Recording depreciation expense does **not** involve a cash outflow, since depreciation is a noncash expense which reduces income and reduces long-term tangible assets (by increasing accumulated depreciation—a contra asset) but does **not** reduce cash.
3. Over the depreciable assets' life, **total** depreciation expense will be the same for all depreciation methods.
4. For income tax purposes, accelerated depreciation methods are preferred because they result in tax savings in the early years of an asset's life. These early tax savings mean less cash is required to pay taxes, making more cash available for investing or operating activities.

Keeping these key facts in mind will keep you from becoming confused about decisions concerning depreciable assets.

Partial Year's Depreciation

Objective 3

How to determine depreciation for partial years...

How is depreciation expense computed for assets acquired during an accounting period rather than at the start of a year? Although many options are available, the two methods often used to determine depreciation for assets acquired during a period are:

1. Round purchase date to **nearest month** and prorate depreciation for number of months used.
2. Use one half of a year's depreciation on all assets acquired or sold during the year (known as the **half-year convention**).

EXHIBIT 8-7

Comparison of Nearest Month Approach and Half-Year Convention

Nearest Month Approach

Year	*Straight Line*	*150% Declining Balance*	*Sum-of-the-Years' Digits*
		Alternative Methods	
19x1 . . .	$8,000 × 8/12 = $5,333	$50,000 × .30 × 8/12 = $10,000	$40,000 × 5/15 × 8/12 = $ 8,889
19x2 . . .	$8,000	$40,000 × .30 = $12,000*	$40,000 × 5/15 × 4/12 = $ 4,444
			$40,000 × 4/15 × 8/12 = 7,111
			$11,555

*Note the second (and subsequent) year's depreciation expense may also be computed the long way as follows:

$50,000 × .30 × 4/12 = $ 5,000
+ 35,000 × .30 × 8/12 = 7,000
$12,000

Half-Year Convention

Year	*Straight Line*	*150% Declining Balance*	*Sum-of-the-Years'-Digits*
		Alternative Methods	
19x1 . . .	$8,000 × 1/2 = $4,000	$50,000 × .30 × 1/2 = $ 7,500	$40,000 × 5/15 × 1/2 = $ 6,667
19x2 . . .	$8,000	$42,500 × .30 = $12,750	$40,000 × 5/15 × 1/2 = $ 6,667
			$40,000 × 4/15 × 1/2 = 5,333
			$12,000

To illustrate these two methods, assume a company purchases a truck for $50,000 on May 7, 19x1, with an estimated life of five years and an estimated residual value of $10,000. Using the nearest month approach, eight months' depreciation (May to December) would be taken in 19x1. Referring to the annual amounts reported in Exhibit 8-6, the depreciation amounts for the first two years (19x1 and 19x2) for each of the three alternatives using the nearest month approach and the half-year convention would be as shown in Exhibit 8-7. A careful study of Exhibit 8-7 will indicate the differences in the results of the nearest month approach and the half-year convention.

In future examples and problems, you should assume that unless otherwise stated, monthly depreciation is taken for asset acquisitions and asset disposal or retirements that do not occur at the beginning or end of a year. If assets are purchased at the beginning of the year or sold at the end of the year, use a full year's depreciation.

Group Depreciation of Tangible Assets

Some low-cost assets providing benefits for long time periods are expensed as purchased. Most companies have policies indicating the minimum dollar amount an asset must cost before it is capitalized and depreciated. It is not unusual to see large corporations expense all asset purchases below $200 to $500.

In some cases even minor assets should be capitalized and expensed over their useful lives. When necessary to depreciate large numbers of minor assets such as power hand tools, accountants often use the **group depreciation method.** Under this method, large quantities of similar assets are capitalized as purchased and then depreciated on a group basis rather than individually. A fixed percentage of the total value of the group of assets is then taken as depreciation expense each year. Group depreciation methods are also used to account for most of the depreciable assets in some companies, not just minor assets. Group depreciation procedures are illustrated in most intermediate accounting texts.

Revisions in Depreciation Estimates

Objective 3

...and how to make revisions in depreciation estimates.

Since depreciation is based on **estimates** of the asset's useful life and residual value at the date of acquisition, what happens when these **estimates** are no longer appropriate? To illustrate, assume Provisions, Inc., acquires a machine for $46,000 cash on January 1, 19x1. At first the machine is expected to have a useful life of four years and a residual value of $2,000. The annual straight-line depreciation expense for the machine is computed as follows:

Cost	− Residual value	= Depreciable base
$46,000 −	$2,000	= $44,000

$$\frac{\$44,000}{4 \text{ years}} = \$11,000 \text{ per year depreciation expense}$$

Depreciation expense of $11,000 is recorded at the end of 19x1 and the end of 19x2. However, during 19x3, Provisions decides that the machine will last five years instead of four years and will have a residual value of $3,000 and not $2,000. The book value at the **beginning** of 19x3 (year 3) is as follows:

Machine cost	$46,000
Less: Accumulated depreciation	22,000
Book value	$24,000

When changes are made in depreciation estimates, the new estimates must be applied to the book value **as of the beginning of the year of the change.** For the machine of Provisions, then, the book value at the beginning of 19x3 is $24,000. Therefore, the new depreciation rate for the last three years of the asset's useful life is calculated as follows:

Book value, 1/1/x3		$24,000
Less new estimated residual value . .	−	3,000
Remaining depreciable base		$21,000
Dividend by remaining life	÷	3 years
New depreciation rate		$ 7,000 depreciation expense per year

Provisions will use the annual depreciation expense of $7,000 per year for 19x3, 19x4, and 19x5, the remainder of the machine's useful life. A complete depreciation schedule for the five-year life of the machine is:

As of	*Depreciation Expense*	*Accumulated Depreciation*	*Net Book Value*
1/1/x1 . . .	$ 0	$ 0	$46,000
12/31/x1 . . .	11,000	11,000	35,000
12/31/x2 . . .	11,000	22,000	24,000
12/31/x3 . . .	7,000	29,000	17,000
12/31/x4 . . .	7,000	36,000	10,000
12/31/x5 . . .	7,000	43,000	3,000
Total	$43,000		

Remember that this procedure for changes in either useful life, residual value, or both will **affect current and future years only.** No adjustments are made to prior years' depreciation amounts for changes in estimates.

COSTS SUBSEQUENT TO ACQUISITION

After tangible assets are acquired and placed into use, additional expenditures often occur. The accountant must determine whether these costs are *capital expenditures* or *periodic expenses.* **Capital expenditures** are those costs that provide future benefits to the asset either by extending its useful life or increasing its productive capacity or efficiency. If an additional outlay does not meet the conditions of a capital expenditure, it is charged to income in the period incurred. Capital expenditures are recorded as new assets or recorded as additions to the cost of existing assets.

Typical types of capital expenditures include:

Objective 4
When costs subsequent to acquisition are capitalized or expensed.

1. **Betterments** and **improvements** (e.g., partitions added to a building to improve customer traffic flow).
2. **Additions** (e.g., add 10 feet to rear of building for more inventory storage).
3. **Unexpected replacements** and **renewals** (e.g., a new roof on a two-year-old building).

Typical types of periodic expenses include:

1. **Repairs** (e.g., replace broken tiles in floor).
2. **Maintenance** (e.g., clean windows twice each year).
3. **Expected replacements** and **renewals** (e.g., carpeting for a customer entryway).

The most troublesome costs subsequent to acquisition are probably replacements and renewals. When these costs are **expected** to occur accountants normally expense them as routine costs. For example, tuning an engine, replacing spark plugs, replacing factory light bulbs, painting, and carpeting are examples of replacements and renewals that are expected to occur and are normally treated as periodic expenses.

Costs that significantly extend the life, productive capacity, or efficiency of an existing asset should be capitalized and depreciated over the remaining life of the asset. Also, unexpected replacements and renewals are usually capitalized.

Because of the conservative nature of accounting, when a question exists whether an item should be capitalized or expensed, the item is often expensed.

Capitalization of Subsequent Costs

When costly renewals or replacements are not expected to occur, their costs are normally capitalized as an additional cost of the asset. The capitalization of these subsequent asset costs involves increasing the recorded amount of the tangible asset, which in turn increases the amount of periodic depreciation expense. The following example illustrates this procedure.

Assume Technical Data Processing Corporation (TDP) owns a communications satellite for its long-distance data transmissions. On February 10, 19x5, the satellite, which originally cost $3 million, develops an unexpected malfunction. The net book value at the end of 19x4 was $2 million, with the remaining life estimated at 10 years and no residual value. A NASA space shuttle replaces the defective elements of the satellite on March 23, 19x5, at a cost of $800,000. This unexpected replacement cost is a capitalizable cost to TDP. Assuming the replacement did not extend the original useful life of the satellite and TDP uses straight-line depreciation to the nearest month, the following entries are recorded for 19x5:

19x5			
Mar. 23	Communication Satellite (A)	800,000	
	Cash (or Accounts Payable—NASA)		800,000
	To record cost of unexpected replacement.		
Dec. 31	Depreciation Expense (E)	261,538	
	Accumulated Depreciation—Satellite (XA) . .		261,538
	$2,000,000 ÷ 120 months × 3 months = $50,000 plus ($2,000,000 − $50,000 + $800,000) ÷ 117 months × 9 months = $211,538.		

Since the $800,000 repair cost was unexpected, it is added to the $1,950,000 remaining asset book value that is to be depreciated over the next 117 months.[3] Alternatively, if the replacement had been expected, the entire $800,000 cost would be expensed on March 23, 19x5, and annual depreciation would remain at $200,000 per year.

When costs incurred after the acquisition of an asset have short lives and/or are relatively immaterial, they are often considered periodic expenses. Alternatively, subsequent costs that have long lives or are relatively material in amount are usually capitalized. Exhibit 8-8 provides a decision table to aid in the evaluation of subsequent costs. Note that the table only examines four extreme situations. In practice, the cost and period of future benefit are not always easily classified as small and large or short and long. Some situations are more common and easier to decide than others, especially when the cost and useful life are both large and long or small and short as in cells A and D. The difficult decisions are those depicted in cells B and C, and as you approach the center intersection.

[3]Note that several other possible solutions could also be acceptable to account for these facts. For example, the $800,000 repair cost could be depreciated for one-half year in 19x5 instead of nine months. Also, the depreciation expense for the period the satellite was not working could be recorded as a loss instead of depreciation expense. As long as these alternatives do not result in material differences in operating results, they are all reasonable and acceptable.

EXHIBIT 8-8

Subsequent Costs

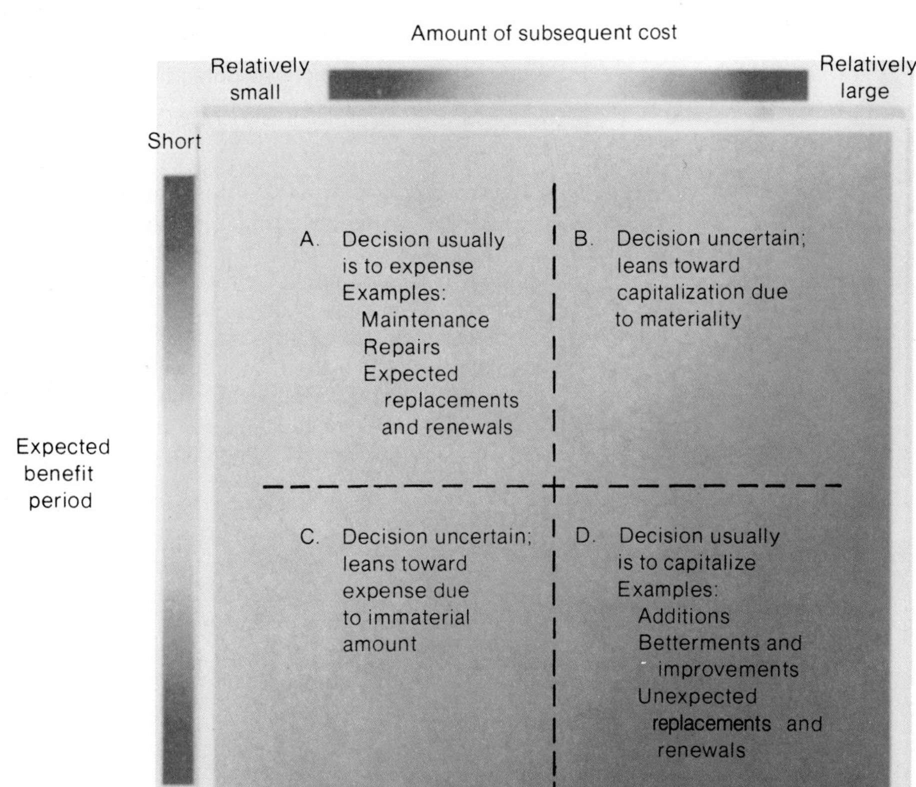

The annual report reproduced in Exhibit 8-9 for Atwood Oceanics, Inc. and Subsidiaries, gives an example of a cost like that shown in cell B of Exhibit 8-8. Under the heading "Deferred costs and expenses," the Atwood report explains that its vessels are brought into port about every two years for routine maintenance during drydocking. While two years is a fairly short benefit period, the costs must be relatively large (material) because Atwood expenses these costs "over the period to the next scheduled drydocking (normally two years)" rather than expensing the entire cost in the year of drydocking.

Errors in Accounting for Asset Costs after Acquisition

From discussions in earlier chapters, you should understand the importance of **accurately** recording costs incurred after the acquisition of assets. The incorrect expensing of a capital expenditure as a revenue expenditure results in: (1) understating the net income of the current period because the expense is too high; (2) a fully expensed asset with no depreciation expense left for future periods, resulting in an overstated future net income; and (3) understating the current and future years' assets because no assets are recorded. Thus, this type of error can seriously affect the measurement of periodic net income and results in mismatching of costs with their periods of benefit. To accurately report on a company's financial condition, you must apply the guidelines for capital and revenue expenditures in an appropriate and consistent way.

EXHIBIT 8-9

Annual Report Example

Atwood Oceanics, Inc. and Subsidiaries

Excerpt from footnotes to consolidated financial statements

(1) SUMMARY OF SIGNIFICANT ACCOUNTING POLICIES

Depreciation, maintenance and retirement policies—

Depreciation is provided on the straight-line method over the estimated useful lives of the various classifications of assets. Estimated useful lives are ten to twelve years for drilling vessels and equipment, three years for drill pipe and three to ten years for other equipment. Maintenance, repairs and minor replacements are charged against income as incurred; major replacements and betterments are capitalized and depreciated over the remaining useful life of the asset as determined upon completion of the work. The cost of assets sold, retired or otherwise disposed of and related accumulated depreciation are removed from the accounts at the time of disposition, and any resulting gain or loss is reflected in the statement of operations for the period.

Deferred costs and expenses—

It is the Company's policy when moving a drilling vessel to a new drilling area to defer and amortize, on a straight-line basis over the life of the applicable drilling contract, the net mobilization income or expense resulting from the move. There were no unamortized mobilization expense or unamortized mobilization income at September 30, 19xx.

The Company defers the cost of scheduled drydocking and the cost is charged to expense over the period to the next scheduled drydocking (normally two years).

Capitalization of interest during construction—

The Company capitalizes, as cost of drilling vessels and equipment, the interest costs incurred during the construction period on funds borrowed to finance the construction of drilling vessels.

DISPOSAL OF LONG-TERM TANGIBLE ASSETS

When a company disposes of tangible assets, all related account balances are updated and eliminated as of the date of the asset disposal. In addition, any proceeds from the sale of the asset increase the company's assets (cash). The difference between the sale proceeds and the eliminated account balances is either a gain or loss.

The updating of account balances that occurs at the time of asset disposal begins with the asset's depreciation expense. For tangible assets that are sold during the year, the depreciation expense is recorded for that portion of the year since the last depreciation entry was recorded, up to the date of asset disposal.

The half-year convention method explained earlier in the chapter is used by many companies for all assets eliminated during the year by taking a half-year's depreciation for the year of disposal (regardless of when the disposal occurs). In the paragraphs that follow, examples are given for asset disposals at net book value, disposals involving gains or losses, and disposals of fully depreciated assets. In these examples, we assume **book value of the assets has been adjusted to the date of disposal.**

Disposals at Net Book Value

Objective 5
How to record disposals of tangible assets at net book value, disposals involving gains or losses, and disposals of fully depreciated assets.

Assume Telex, Inc., sold 15 microcomputers on January 1, 19x5, for $9,000. Originally, the computers cost $3,500 each. They had an estimated residual value of $600 each and were fully depreciated as of December 31, 19x4. The balances in the computer-related accounts before recording the sale at January 1, 19x5, were:

Microcomputers (15)		Accumulated Depreciation—Microcomputers (15)	
52,500			43,500

The entry to record the disposal of the 15 microcomputers is:

19x5			
Jan. 1	Cash (A)	9,000	
	Accumulated Depreciation—Microcomputers (XA) . .	43,500	
	Microcomputers (A)		52,500
	To record sale of 15 microcomputers at net book value.		

Note that this entry records the inflows and outflows of net assets at the time of exchange. The outflows (assets given up) are recorded by eliminating the balances in all accounts pertaining to the microcomputers (the asset and the accumulated depreciation accounts). The inflows are recorded by an increase in cash, the asset received in the transaction. In this example, the net book value of the assets given up ($52,500 asset less $43,500 contra asset equals $9,000 net book value) and the asset received (cash, $9,000) are equal; therefore, the disposal of the computers did not result in a gain or loss.

Disposals Involving Gains or Losses

When the net book value of assets given up differs from the fair market value of the assets received in the exchange, a gain or loss occurs. In the computer example given above, we can assume that because an outside party was willing to pay $9,000 for the 15 used computers, the fair market value of the computers happened to equal their book value at January 1, 19x5. The following examples illustrate the more typical cases where book value differs from fair value at the time of disposal.

Proceeds in Excess of Net Book Value. To illustrate a gain on the disposal of assets, assume now that Telex, Inc., sold the 15 micros on January 1, 19x5, for $12,000 instead of $9,000. The following entry would be recorded:

19x5			
Jan. 1	Cash (A)	$12,000	
	Accumulated Depreciation—Microcomputers (XA) . .	43,500	
	Microcomputers (A)		52,500
	Gain on Sale of Computers (R)		3,000
	To record sale of microcomputers.		

Whenever the value of the assets received (cash of $12,000 in this case) is greater than the net book value of the assets disposed of, a gain will result. This situation occurs because the depreciation (cost allocation) process is *not* a valuation process. In other words, depreciation is not intended to reflect the change in an asset's market value. Depreciation is simply a way of assigning the asset's depreciable base (*original* cost less salvage value) to the years of benefit. Therefore, it is very unusual for the net book value to equal market value for depreciable assets during their useful life. And, at the end of the asset's useful life it is also common to have the *estimated* salvage value (usually estimated at the time of purchase) not equal the market value, since there is normally much uncertainty about the value of fully used assets.

Proceeds less than Book Value. To illustrate a loss on the disposal of an asset, refer again to the Telex example. Assume now that the computers are sold for $5,000 on January 1, 19x5.

The following entry would be recorded:

19x5			
Jan. 1	Cash (A)	5,000	
	Accumulated Depreciation—Microcomputers (XA)	43,500	
	Loss on Sale of Computers (E)	4,000	
	Microcomputers (A)		52,500
	To record sale of microcomputers.		

Whenever the value of assets received is less than the net book value of the assets disposed of, a loss will result.

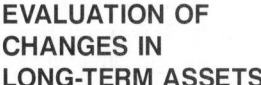

EVALUATION OF CHANGES IN LONG-TERM ASSETS

In previous chapters you were introduced to the importance of knowing how to evaluate a company's financial reports. Understanding the relationship between the long-term asset accounts (e.g., asset and accumulated depreciation) and other account balances is also useful in financial report analysis. Often this knowledge can be used to obtain information about the acquisitions and disposals of long-term assets that is not explicitly reported in the financial statements.

The relationship between long-term accounts and other accounts can best be understood by examining the reasons for changes in the account balances. For example, consider the following accounts associated with a tangible asset:

Balance Sheet Accounts:

Plant and Equipment	
Beg. bal.	
Increases	*Decreases*
(1) Buy new assets	(2) Sell or retire old assets
End. bal.	

Accumulated Depreciation—Plant and Equipment	
	Beg. bal.
Decreases	*Increases*
(2) Sell or retire old assets	(3) Depreciation expense on assets
	End. bal.

Income Statement Account:

Depreciation Expense	
Increases	
(3) Annual depreciation expense	

For example, assume that the following three entries summarize the three types of changes in these T accounts:

(1)	Plant and Equipment (A)	40,000	
	Cash (A)		40,000
	To record acquisition of new assets.		

		Debit	Credit
(2)	Cash (A)	400	
	Accumulated Depreciation—Plant Equipment (XA)	9,000	
	Plant and Equipment (A)		9,200
	Gain on Sale of Plant Equipment (R)		200
	To record sale of assets.		
(3)	Depreciation Expense (E)	8,000	
	Accumulated Depreciation—Plant and Equipment (XA)		8,000
	To record annual depreciation expense on plant assets.		

The published financial statements do not always provide information on the purchase and sale of plant assets (items 1 and 2 above); however, major purchases are often reported in the statement of cash flows as an investing activity of the company.

Objective 6
The importance of evaluating changes in plant assets.

To illustrate how you might use your understanding of these relationships, assume Ford, Inc., reported the following data:

	19x7	*19x6*
Balance sheet data:		
Equipment (at cost)	$12,000	$14,000
Accumulated depreciation—equipment	7,500	8,000
Income statement data:		
Depreciation expense—equipment	600	550
Statement of cash flows data:		
Investment in equipment	850	320

Using T accounts to evaluate the changes in equipment for 19x7, the following data are known:

Equipment

	Debit	Credit
(3)	14,000	
(1)	850	?
(3)	12,000	

Accumulated Depreciation—Equipment

Debit	Credit	
	8,000	(3)
?	600	(2)
	7,500	(3)

The numbers in the T accounts above refer to:

1. Purchases of equipment given in statement of cash flows.
2. Depreciation expense given in income statement.
3. Beginning and ending balances given in the balance sheet.

The credit to Equipment that is needed to balance the account is $2,850 ($14,000 + $850 − $12,000). Also, the debit to Accumulated Depreciation—Equipment must be $1,100 ($8,000 + $600 − $7,500). Apparently, Ford, Inc., sold equipment that had cost $2,850 with accumulated depreciation of $1,100 taken prior to the sale. The known elements of the entry to record this sale are:

	Debit	Credit
Cash (A)	?	
Accumulated Depreciation—Equipment (XA)	1,100	
Gain or Loss on Sale of Equipment (R or E)	?	?
Equipment (A)		2,850
To record sale of equipment.		

Investors may be interested in the additional insight that Ford, Inc., sold equipment that was less than 50% depreciated. This could indicate new technology in their manufacturing process, or perhaps equipment purchases that were not well planned in some prior year. In any case, understanding the relationship between long-term assets and other accounts is useful in acquiring data on asset disposals that might not be detailed in the financial statements.

INTANGIBLE ASSETS

As discussed earlier, intangible assets are those long-term assets that lack physical substance. The value of intangibles stems from the rights which they provide their owner rather than their physical form. Most intangibles are legal documents whose physical form is merely paper. However, the rights which intangibles document may be extremely important assets of a business. Intangible assets are often classified as identifiable and unidentifiable intangibles. **Identifiable intangibles** are separate and specifically identifiable items, while **unidentifiable intangibles** are **not** separate or observable assets. Examples of identifiable and unidentifiable intangibles follow.

Objective 7
Accounting for long-term intangible assets.

Identifiable intangibles:
- Patents
- Copyrights
- Trademarks and trade names
- Franchises and licenses
- Research and development (R&D)
- Computer software development
- Organization costs

Unidentifiable intangibles:
- Goodwill

These identifiable and unidentifiable intangibles are discussed in this section.

The costs of all intangibles are allocated (expensed) to the income statement of the benefit period by a process called **amortization.** Amortization expense for intangible assets is essentially the same as depreciation expense for tangible assets. **Intangibles must be amortized over a period of 40 years, their economic useful life, or legal life, whichever is less.**[4]

Accounting for Identifiable Intangibles

Accounting for the life cycle of intangibles is very similar to the accounting for tangible assets discussed in the first part of this chapter. Intangibles are recorded at the cost necessary to obtain them. The cost of intangibles is often small, consisting primarily of legal fees and perhaps the cost of a prototype or sample of the item to which the intangible pertains (e.g., patented invention).

Amortization of intangible assets is on a straight-line basis in virtually all cases, and contra asset accounts are usually not used. If an intangible asset cost $36,000 and has an estimated economic useful life of 18 years, the following entry is made each year for 18 years:

Amortization expense (E)	2,000	
Intangible asset (A)		2,000

$36,000/18 years = $2,000 per year amortization expense.

[4] See *APB Opinion No. 17*, "Intangible Assets" (New York: AICPA, 1970).

The paragraphs that follow discuss most common identifiable intangibles, including patents, copyrights, trademarks and trade names, franchises and licenses, research and development (R&D) costs, computer software development costs, and organization costs.

Patents. The federal government grants **patents** to the inventor of a new product or process. Patents entitle the inventor to the exclusive right to use the product or process, or to sell it to others for their use, for a 17-year period. Because patents often deal with products or processes that are subject to rapid technological change, their useful lives may often be less than their 17-year legal life.

The recorded cost of a patent is limited to its legal costs plus the actual cost of developing the prototype. If patents are purchased from their inventor, they are recorded at the price paid for the patent. The legal costs of successfully defending patent rights in court are capitalized as part of the patents asset. However, if the defense of a patent fails, the patent is apparently worthless and written off as a loss.

Copyrights. The federal government grants **copyrights** for literary or artistic works. When copyrights are granted to a business, the rights are for a 75-year period; when granted to an individual, the rights are for the life of the creator plus 50 years. The cost of developing copyrighted material is usually small; however, copyrights purchased from their creator may be costly. The useful lives of most copyrights are much less than their legal lives.

Trademarks and Trade Names. Words, symbols, or designs used to identify and distinguish a product or group of products are called **trademarks and trade names.** They are registered with the federal government and do not expire. The cost of developing trademarks or trade names at the time they are registered is usually insignificant. However, for successful products such as Coca-Cola or Chevrolet, these symbols or names can be valuable. No legal limit exists for the life of trademarks and trade names; therefore, their costs should be amortized over the lesser of 40 years or their expected economic life (as with all other intangibles).

Franchises and Licenses. **Franchises and licenses** are rights granted by a government or a private enterprise to distribute, sell, service, or otherwise handle a specified line of goods and/or services. Governmental units grant licenses to drive automobiles, sell liquor, fish, hunt, and so on. Private businesses grant franchises for Taco Bell restaurants, Days Inn motels, National Football League teams, and so on. The length of the rights granted by the license or franchise depends on the terms stipulated in each agreement. The cost of the license or franchise agreement should be recorded as an asset and amortized over its economic life, but not in excess of 40 years.

Research and Development (R&D) Costs. **Research and development (R&D) costs** are incurred in searching for new knowledge (research) that may be used to create new products or to improve old products or services (development). Some industries, such as aerospace, computers, and ethical drugs, undergo rapid change and spend considerable amounts on R&D activities to maintain their competitive advantage.

For the past two decades, accounting for R&D costs has been a controversial topic. The key issue is the uncertain and unmeasurable nature of the future benefits, if any, expected from the current period's R&D activity. Often judgment plays a crucial role in deciding whether any given expenditure or R&D project has future benefits (revenue), thus making the difference between capitalization or expensing huge expenditures. To avoid these measurement problems, the FASB has decided that all routine R&D costs should be expensed as incurred.[5] As a result, even though some R&D activity seems to represent an intangible asset with future economic benefits, R&D costs are not normally capitalized as intangible assets.

Computer Software Development. Many companies are in the business of developing computer software. Because the costs of developing the computer programs (the intangible assets) represent a major part of the "assets" for many software developers, the FASB established separate guidelines for these businesses.[6] Software developers are required to expense all R&D costs until the "technological feasibility" of the software product has been established. The detailed guidelines for determining exactly when technological feasibility of a product occurs (covered in more detail in *FASB Statement No. 86*) is ultimately dependent on professional judgment. After technological feasibility of a software product has been established, development costs are capitalized as assets. These capitalized costs are amortized over 40 years or the estimated product life, whichever is shorter.

Organization Costs. The costs incurred in establishing a business are called **organization costs.** They are normally capitalized as an intangible asset. These costs include expenditures for legal fees and the filing fees necessary to file for incorporation (or partnership papers, and so on) and to do business in a state or states; license fees; accounting fees for developing a recordkeeping system; computer software fees for developing an information processing system; cost of issuing initial stock offering (if a corporation); and other similar costs involved in preparation for business operations.

In theory, organization costs are either expenses or permanent assets. Thus, at the time the costs are incurred, they could have future benefit or have no future benefit. However, since organization costs are the costs of starting the business and a business is expected to continue indefinitely, it is unlikely that you would expect these costs to benefit only a portion of the life of the business. As a result, you might argue for either permanent (life of the business) capitalization or immediate expensing of such costs.

In practice, organization costs are normally capitalized and expensed (amortized) over a five-year period. This is the usual income tax treatment of these costs, and companies usually follow this same procedure for financial reporting purposes. In any case, GAAP requires all intangibles to be amortized over no longer than 40 years.

---

[5]See *FASB Statement No. 2,* "Accounting for Research and Development Costs (Norwalk, Conn.: FASB, 1974).

[6]*FASB Statement No. 86,* "Accounting for the Cost of Computer Software to Be Sold, Leased or Otherwise Marketed" (Norwalk, Conn.: FASB, 1985).

Accounting for Unidentifiable Intangibles

The primary unidentifiable intangible asset is goodwill. Since goodwill can have many possible characteristics, it is considered a complex and unusual asset to record. Goodwill can include a superior management talent, business location, product reputation, customer loyalty, and future earnings potential. All of these attributes can be unrecorded assets that lead to future benefits for the business. It is considered an unidentifiable intangible because its makeup is too complex to be attributed to any one of the many attributes which represent goodwill. As a result, **goodwill** is defined as representing the otherwise unrecorded assets of the business.

In many companies, goodwill exists but is not reported on their balance sheets. While every company probably believes it has goodwill, the accurate internal measurement of goodwill is likely to be biased and not reliable due to its subjective nature. The accounting system could not very well rely on management's own estimate of how much goodwill should be reported for their own company, since it would not represent an unbiased measure. As a result, companies cannot report their own assessment of goodwill. Generally accepted accounting principles require that goodwill **must be purchased from an outside party to be recorded as an asset.** Thus, goodwill is recorded only when one company purchases another company. This purchase by an outside party provides objective evidence of the value of the goodwill. Recorded goodwill is amortized over 40 years or the expected period of economic benefit, whichever is less.

The following information about Graphic Corporation on December 31, 19x1, illustrates how goodwill is measured and recorded:

Graphic Corporation
Balance Sheet Data
December 31, 19x1

Recorded Items on Books	*Estimated Market Value*	*Recorded Book Value*
Assets.	\$560,000	\$490,000
Liabilities	200,000	200,000
Net assets	\$360,000	\$290,000

Note that the recorded net assets have a book value of \$290,000 as of December 31, 19x1, and an estimated \$360,000 fair market value. Assume Baird Corporation pays \$400,000 to acquire the net assets of Graphic on January 1, 19x2. For accounting purposes, **goodwill is measured as the excess of the price paid over the fair market value of the *identifiable* net assets acquired.** In this case, goodwill is \$40,000 (\$400,000 − \$360,000) and would be recorded on Baird's books as follows:

19x2			
Jan. 1	Various assets (A)	560,000	
	Goodwill (A).	40,000	
	Various liabilities (L)		200,000
	Cash (A)		400,000
	To record the purchase of Graphic Corporation.		

Note that Graphic's book values are not used by Baird Corporation in recording the purchase. Assuming a 40-year amortization period, Baird would record the following entry each year-end:

19x2			
Dec. 31	Amortization Expense—Goodwill (E)	1,000	
	Goodwill (A)		1,000
	To record annual amortization of goodwill.		

From the above transaction, we can see why it is appropriate to define goodwill as the unrecorded assets of a business. Apparently, Baird was willing to pay $40,000 more than the fair market value of Graphic's **identifiable** net assets because of Graphic's **unrecorded** assets.

Companies such as Baird Corporation can use many ways to estimate the amount of unrecorded assets of an investment like Graphic Corporation. However, for accounting purposes, goodwill is always measured as the difference between the purchase price and the fair market value of the net assets acquired.

SUMMARY

This chapter introduced you to the life cycle of long-term assets, which involves their acquisition, depreciation, costs subsequent to acquisition, and disposal. Long-term asset acquisition cost includes all costs necessary to place the asset into its intended state.

The depreciation of tangible assets includes determining the asset's depreciable base and choosing a depreciation method. In this chapter we discussed straight-line depreciation, units-of-output depreciation, and two accelerated depreciation methods—declining-balance and sum-of-the-years'-digits. Tangible asset depreciation also involves knowing how to account for partial year depreciation as well as making revisions in depreciation estimates.

When additional expenditures occur after long-term tangible assets are acquired and placed into use, accountants must determine when these costs should be capitalized and when they should be expensed. Costs that provide future benefits to the asset are capitalized; other costs are expensed.

When a company disposes of a long-term asset, the company updates the asset's depreciation or amortization expense and eliminates all amounts related to the asset from its books. Examples were given in the chapter of disposals at net book value, disposals involving gains or losses, and disposals of fully depreciated assets.

You know from previous chapters that one of the goals of studying this textbook is to teach you how to evaluate a company's financial statements. This chapter included a section on financial statement evaluation as it pertains to changes in long-term assets. This evaluation can often result in knowledge not explicitly reported in the financial statements.

The last section of the chapter examined the identifiable intangibles (patents, copyrights, trademarks and trade names, franchises and licenses, R&D, computer software development, and organization costs) and goodwill. While a few unique features apply to intangibles, the majority of entries accounting for the life cycle of intangibles—from acquisition to disposal—are similar to those for long-term tangible assets.

Two appendixes follow this summary. They provide information on accounting for asset exchanges and natural resources. You will find this additional information helpful in establishing a complete picture of what accountants include in accounting for long-term assets.

DEMONSTRATION EXERCISE

Linear Graphics, Inc., purchased a new graphics printer on January 1, 19x1, for $75,000 with an estimated life of four years and a $15,000 residual value. It is also estimated the printer will be used by the company for a total of 30,000 hours. During 19x1, the printer was used for 12,570 hours, and 19x2 for 8,620 hours.

Required:

Compute depreciation expense for 19x1 and 19x2 using the following depreciation methods.

a. Straight-line.
b. Units of output.
c. Sum-of-the-years'-digits.
d. 150% declining-balance.

Solution:

Year	*Straight Line*	*Units of Output*	*Sum-of-the-Years'-Digits*	*150% Declining-Balance*
19x1 . . .	$15,000	$25,140	$24,000	$28,125
19x2 . . .	15,000	17,240	18,000	17,578

Computations:

Straight-line depreciation method:

$$\frac{\$75{,}000 - \$15{,}000}{4 \text{ years}} = \$15{,}000 \text{ depreciation expense per year}$$

Units-of-output depreciation method:

$$\frac{\$75{,}000 - \$15{,}000}{30{,}000 \text{ hours}} = \$2 \text{ depreciation expense per hour}$$

$$\text{19x1: } 12{,}570 \times \$2 = \$25{,}140$$

$$\text{19x2: } 8{,}620 \times \$2 = \$17{,}240$$

Sum-of-the-years'-digits depreciation method:

$$\text{Denominator} = 1 + 2 + 3 + 4 = 10$$

$$\text{19x1: } (\$75{,}000 - \$15{,}000) \times 4/10 = \$24{,}000$$

$$\text{19x2: } (\$75{,}000 - \$15{,}000) \times 3/10 = \$18{,}000$$

150% declining-balance depreciation method:

$$\text{Rate: Straight-line rate} \times 150\% = 150\% \text{ declining-balance rate}$$

$$.25 \times 1.5 = 37.5\% \text{ or } .375$$

$$\text{19x1: } \$75{,}000 \times .375 = \$28{,}125$$

$$\text{19x2: } (\$75{,}000 - \$28{,}125) \times .375 = \$17{,}578$$

APPENDIX 8A

Asset Exchanges

Sometimes companies exchange long-term assets for other assets before the original assets have been fully depreciated. When this occurs, accountants record the exchange in a manner similar to the disposal of assets that are **not** fully depreciated. The assets given up are recorded as outflows, the assets acquired are recorded as inflows, and any differences are recorded as gains or losses on the exchange. This general method of accounting for exchanges, called the **fair value method** (or the **fair market value method**), is the first topic discussed in this appendix.

Although the fair value method of recording asset exchanges is appropriate for most asset exchanges, this appendix also discusses two exceptions: (1) the exchange treatment due to income tax laws and (2) the special accounting rule for certain exchanges involving similar assets.

FAIR VALUE METHOD OF RECORDING ASSET EXCHANGES

The fair value method of recording exchanges treats the assets given up as outflows and the assets acquired as inflows. To illustrate, assume Baker Construction Company owned a grader originally costing $45,000 which had $26,000 recorded accumulated depreciation (net book value is $19,000) as of December 31, 19x1. On December 31, 19x1, Baker traded the grader for a new semitractor that would move machinery from one job to another. The semitractor had a fair market value (or cash price) of $88,000 and an expected useful life of five years (no scrap value). Baker acquired the semi by paying $70,000 cash plus the old grader. The fair value of the assets given and received is computed as follows:

	Fair Value of Assets Received		*Fair Value of Assets Given*
Semi. . . .	$88,000 (cash price)	Cash	$70,000
		Grader	18,000*
			$88,000

*Cash value of semi	$88,000
Less cash paid by Baker . . .	− 70,000
Fair value of used grader . . .	$18,000

The gain or loss on the transaction is computed by taking the difference between the fair market value and the book value of the assets given in the exchange (the same as in the asset disposals illustrated earlier) as follows:

Objective 8
Accounting for asset exchanges.

	Fair Value of Assets Given	−	*Less Book Value of Assets Given*	=	*Gain or (Loss) on Exchange*
Cash . . .	$70,000		$70,000		$ 0
Grader . . .	18,000		19,000		(1,000)
Total. . . .	$88,000		$89,000		$(1,000)

The book value of the grader ($19,000) was $1,000 more than the fair market value of the grader, resulting in a loss on the exchange. The entry to record this asset exchange is:

19x1			
Dec. 31	Equipment—Semitractor (A)	88,000	
	Accumulated Depreciation—Grader (XA)	26,000	
	Loss on Exchange (E).	1,000	
	Equipment—Grader (A)		45,000
	Cash (A)		70,000
	To record the exchange of a grader for a new semi.		

Notice that the fair market values of the assets received are known in the example above, since the semitractor's cash price was given as $88,000. This made it fairly easy to compute the apparent fair market value of the used grader because **the fair value of assets given and received must be equal in any arm's-length transaction.**[7] Sometimes, the fair market value of the asset received (the new asset) and the fair market value of the asset given (the used equipment) are both unknown, making it difficult to record the exchange transaction. Often the income tax method described below is used to record such exchange transactions.

INCOME TAX METHOD

Because of the difficulty in measuring the fair value of the assets given or received in many exchange transactions, the income tax laws normally require special treatment for asset exchanges. In general, **tax laws do not recognize gains or losses on the exchange of assets.** For tax purposes, any gain or loss is deducted or added to the book value of the newly acquired asset. To illustrate, for the semitractor example, Baker Construction would record the following:

19x1			
Dec. 31	Equipment—Semitractor (A)	89,000	
	Accumulated Depreciation—Grader (XA)	26,000*	
	Equipment—Grader (A)		45,000*
	Cash (A)		70,000*
	To record the exchange for tax purposes.		

Note that the figures marked with an asterisk (*) are the same as in the previous entry, which recorded the exchange using the fair market value method. These components of the entry that record the outflow of the old asset and the cash flow effect must always be the same no matter which method is used. To change these figures would be to change the economic facts of the situation. Since the grader no longer is Baker's asset, Baker must eliminate the original cost of the grader ($45,000) and its accumulated depreciation to date ($26,000). Also, the cash outflow must be recorded since it is the amount paid by Baker.

Note, however, that for the new asset, the income tax method results in a different asset value than the fair market value method. For tax purposes, Baker shows no loss, but the company will record depreciation expense of $89,000 over

[7]In other words, there is no reason to believe that the semi dealer would accept less than $88,000 in value for the semi from Baker Construction.

the life of the semi (assuming no scrap value), resulting in total changes to income of $89,000. For financial reporting purposes, Baker should use the fair market value method, which results in a $1,000 loss plus $88,000 depreciation expense over the life of the asset. Both methods result in total charges to earnings of $89,000.

SPECIAL EXCHANGE CASE

The accounting policymakers have ruled that a special gain recognition formula must be used that defers recognition of the resulting gain for asset exchanges when:

1. Similar productive assets are exchanged.
2. A gain would result using the fair market value.
3. Both assets given and received have the ability to generate future earnings.[8]

Only when these three conditions are present can companies use the special measurement method. Thus, many asset exchanges would not be affected by the special case procedures, and the fair market value method would be used for financial reporting purposes. Since gains and losses are normally not recorded for tax purposes, the special procedures do not apply to income tax reporting.

DEMONSTRATION EXERCISE

Andrew's Body Shop purchased a paint machine on March 31, 19x1, for $14,780. The machine had a salvage value of $500 and an expected life of seven years. Straight-line depreciation on a monthly basis was used in allocating the machine's cost over its useful life. On July 20, 19x5, J. Andrew sold the machine.

Required:

1. Assuming depreciation expense has been correctly recorded as of December 31, 19x4, record depreciation expense to date of disposal using the nearest month approach.
2. Record the journal entry if the machine is:
   a. Sold for cash equal to its net book value.
   b. Sold for $4,800 cash.
   c. Sold for $7,200 cash.
   d. Exchanged for a different type of equipment valued at $18,900; $12,500 in cash is also given for the new equipment. Use the fair value method to record this exchange.

[8] For an explanation of this procedure, see *APB Opinion No. 29,* "Accounting for Nonmonetary Transactions" (New York: AICPA, 1973).

Solution:

1. $\frac{\$14{,}780 - \$500}{7 \times 12 \text{ months}} = \$170$ depreciation per month

$\$170 \times 7$ months $= \$1{,}190$ depreciation expense for December 31, 19x4, to July 20, 19x5

19x5			
July 20	Depreciation Expense	1,190	
	Accumulated Depreciation—Equipment		1,190
	To record depreciation to date of disposal.		

2. Accumulated depreciation:

19x1:	9 × $170 =	$1,530
19x2:	12 × 170 =	2,040
19x3:	12 × 170 =	2,040
19x4:	12 × 170 =	2,040
19x5:	7 × 170 =	1,190
		$8,840

a. Cash (A)	5,940	
Accumulated Depreciation—Equipment (XA)	8,840	
Equipment (A)		14,780
To record disposal of equipment at NBV.		

b. Cash (A)	4,800	
Accumulated Depreciation—Equipment (XA)	8,840	
Loss on Sale of Equipment (E)	1,140	
Equipment (A)		14,780
To record disposal of equipment at less than NBV.		

c. Cash (A)	7,200	
Accumulated Depreciation—Equipment (XA)	8,840	
Equipment (A)		14,780
Gain on Sale of Equipment (R)		1,260
To record disposal of equipment for more than NBV.		

d. Equipment (A)	18,900	
Accumulated Depreciation—Equipment (XA)	8,840	
Equipment (A)		14,780
Cash (A)		12,500
Gain on Exchange (R)		460
To record exchange of equipment.		

APPENDIX 8B

Accounting for Natural Resources

Natural resources include iron ore, crude oil, natural gas, and timberlands; they are wasting assets like plant, equipment, furniture, and so on. Although natural resources are wasting assets, they are different in several respects. Instead of being purchased, natural resources are usually discovered. As a result, their cost does not represent their fair market value at time of acquisition but is usually far less than their fair value. For example, a company spent $25,000 to search for natural gas that was worth $1 million at the date of discovery. However, the cost of the resources is recorded as $25,000. Only when the resource is sold for $1 million can the profit of $975,000 be recognized.

Accounting for natural resources involves recording their depletion, recording changes in estimated amounts of natural resources, treating asset costs associated with extracting natural resources, and understanding statutory depletion rates. These topics are discussed in this appendix.

DEPLETION OF NATURAL RESOURCES

Objective 9
Accounting for natural resources.

The recorded cost of natural resources consists of the costs necessary and reasonable to purchase (or discover) the natural resources. Once extracted, natural resources are either sold to another company for further processing or they are processed further by the company that extracted them. In either case, the natural resources normally are reclassified from the asset Natural Resources to the asset Inventory once they are extracted. They remain in Inventory until they are expensed as cost of goods sold once a sale has occurred. The entries which follow record the discovery of oil in early 19x1, and the **depletion** (extraction) of the oil during 19x1 and 19x2, which transfers the recorded value of the natural resources from the long-term asset Oil Reserves to Oil Inventory. Note that depletion is an allocation process similar to depreciation and amortization in that it assigns the cost of a long-term asset to inventory, which in turn is expensed as goods are sold. To illustrate, assume that North Sea, Inc., spent $1 million in 19x1 on an oil discovery that was estimated to contain 500,000 barrels of oil. North Sea extracted 100,000 barrels of oil in 19x1 and 140,000 barrels in 19x2. The following entries are made to record the discovery and extraction of the oil:

19x1			
Jan. 1	Oil Reserves (A)	1,000,000	
to	Cash (A)		1,000,000
May 1	To summarize all discovery costs during 19x1.		

Depletion computation:

$$\frac{\text{Cost}}{\text{Barrels}} = \frac{\$1 \text{ million}}{500{,}000} = \$2 \text{ cost per barrel}$$

Dec. 31	Oil Inventory (A)	200,000	
	Oil Reserves (A)		200,000
	To record depletion for oil extracted during 19x1: 100,000 barrels × \$2 per barrel depletion.		
19x2			
Dec. 31	Oil Inventory (A)	280,000	
	Oil Reserves (A)		280,000
	To record depletion for oil extracted during 19x2: 140,000 barrels × \$2 per barrel depletion.		

The recording of depletion may be offset by either a credit to the Oil Reserves asset account or by a credit to the contra asset account Accumulated Depletion—Oil Reserves, which is similar to accumulated depreciation. Most companies directly reduce depletable assets, as in the entries above.

CHANGES IN ESTIMATED AMOUNTS OF RESOURCES

The estimated quantity of natural resources is similar to the estimated life of a building or machine in that the estimate may change over time. The accounting procedure to record these **changes in estimates** is the same as used for long-term assets.

To illustrate a common occurrence of changes in the estimated amount of natural resources, assume that at the start of 19x3 a new geological survey of North Sea, Inc., is conducted. Before the survey, the estimated undepleted oil reserve is 260,000 barrels [500,000 − (100,000 + 140,000)]. After the survey, it is estimated that 320,000 barrels remain to be extracted. To determine the new depletion rate, the remaining net book value of the asset **at the beginning of the period of change** is depleted over the new estimated number of barrels remaining to be depleted as follows:

Revised depletion rate:

$$\frac{\text{Remaining cost}}{\text{New estimate of remaining quantity}} = \frac{(\$1{,}000{,}000 - \$200{,}000 - \$280{,}000)}{320{,}000 \text{ barrels}} = \begin{matrix}\$1.625 \text{ cost} \\ \text{per barrel}\end{matrix}$$

If we assume 150,000 barrels were extracted during 19x3, the appropriate entry is:

19x3			
Dec. 31	Oil Inventory (A)	243,750	
	Oil Reserves (A)		243,750
	To record depletion of oil extracted during 19x3: 150,000 barrels at \$1.625 each.		

ASSET COSTS ASSOCIATED WITH RESOURCES

Often assets acquired for purposes of extracting resources have little or no value once the resources are completely extracted. Examples of such assets might include a shed or house constructed as a base camp for harvesting lumber in a remote forest, or an oil drilling platform constructed in the North Sea. These assets should be depreciated over their expected economic life, or the expected time required to extract the resources, whichever is the shorter period. Once the resources are extracted, these assets (such as a drilling platform in the North Sea) generally provide no future benefits, and therefore they should be fully depreciated. The amount to be depreciated includes the cost of these assets less any expected residual value once the natural resources are fully extracted.

STATUTORY DEPLETION RATES

For income tax purposes, the amount of depletion expense allowed in any period is normally based on the sales of the resources during the period multiplied by a legally set percentage called the **statutory depletion rate.** The statutory depletion rate varies depending on the type of natural resources being extracted. As a result, depletion for tax purposes is not based on the actual cost of the resources.

As designed by Congress, this tax law provides an incentive for business to explore for additional natural resources. In general, the more scarce the natural resource, the higher the statutory depletion rate. Since the tax depletion amounts are more than the depletion taken for financial reporting purposes, the statutory depletion percentages result in a greater allowable deduction for tax purposes than the actual depletion recorded in the financial statements.

KEY TERMS

Accelerated depreciation. Any depreciation method that results in higher depreciation expense in the early years of the asset's useful life than in the asset's later years.

Accumulated depreciation. The cumulative amount of depreciation expense taken in the current and prior periods; reported on the balance sheet as a contra asset.

Acquisition cost. Current fair market value of the assets given or received, whichever is more objectively measurable; should include all costs necessary to acquire the asset and place it into its intended useful state.

Amortization. Allocation process similar to depreciation used for intangible assets.

Basket purchase. Group purchase of assets.

Capital expenditures. Costs that provide future benefits and are, therefore, recorded as assets (or additions to existing assets).

Capitalized. When costs are recorded as an asset (as opposed to an expense).

Copyright. Intangible asset granted by the federal government for literary or artistic works.

Declining-balance depreciation method. An accelerated depreciation method.

Depreciable base. That portion of an asset's cost that is expected to be depreciated (consumed) over the asset's useful life.

Depreciation. Allocation process that systematically assigns the cost of a tangible asset to the income statements during the asset's useful life.

Depreciation expense. Amount of an asset's cost expensed to current income.

Franchises and licenses. Rights granted by a government or a private enterprise to distribute, sell, service, or otherwise handle a specified line of goods and/or services.

Goodwill. Represents the otherwise unrecorded assets of a business. The difference between the price paid and the fair market value of the identifiable assets acquired.

Group depreciation method. Where large quantities of similar assets are depreciated as a group rather than individually.

Half-year convention. Taking one half of a year's depreciation expense on all assets purchased and sold during the year.

Identifiable intangibles. Assets that are separate and specifically identifiable items such as patents, copyrights, trademarks, and so on.

Intangible assets. Financial resources with no physical substance, such as patents. Their value to the business stems from the rights they represent rather than their physical form.

Net book value. For a depreciable asset, this is the asset's cost less its accumulated depreciation; also called book value.

Organization costs. Costs incurred in getting a business started.

Patent. An intangible asset that entitles a specified entity to the exclusive rights to some invention or process.

Research and development (R&D) costs. Costs incurred in searching for new knowledge that may be used to create or improve new products or services.

Residual value. Asset's estimated market value at the end of its period of use; also called salvage value or scrap value.

Straight-line depreciation method. Method of depreciation that assumes assets are equally useful over all time periods of use.

Sum-of-the-years'-digits (SYD) depreciation method. An accelerated depreciation method.

Tangible assets. Assets that have physical substance (such as equipment) representing future benefits.

Trademarks and trade names. Words, symbols, or designs used to identify and distinguish a product or group of products.

Unidentifiable intangibles. Intangible assets that are not separate or observable (principally goodwill).

Units-of-output depreciation method. Method that records depreciation expense based on the amount of use an asset receives during the period.

Useful life. Length of time an asset is expected to be used by a business in the capacity for which it is purchased.

Wasting assets. Tangible assets whose benefits are essentially consumed or used up over time.

APPENDIX KEY TERMS

Depletion. Allocation process similar to depreciation used for natural resources.

Statutory depletion rate. The legally set percentage of sales allowed as depletion expense for natural resources for income tax purposes.

SYNONYMS

Assets; capitalized costs.
Basket purchase; group purchase.
Book value; net book value.
Building; plant; physical plant; facilities.
Current cost; replacement cost.
Expensed; charged.
Fair value; fair market value.
Long-term assets; noncurrent assets.
Natural resources; wasting assets.
Productive assets; wasting assets; consumable assets.
Residual value; salvage value; scrap value.
Revenue expenditure; period expense; expense.

QUESTIONS

1. Identify two categories of long-term assets that differ based on their physical substance.
2. Identify two types of tangible assets. How do they differ?
3. What is the major category of tangible assets?
4. How is the acquisition cost of an asset measured?
5. What types of costs may be capitalized as the cost of an asset?
6. Is interest cost a capitalizable cost? Explain.
7. How are costs measured when assets are purchased as a group?
8. What is depreciation? Depreciation expense? Accumulated depreciation?
9. What is the "depreciable base" of an asset?
10. Describe four alternative depreciation methods.
11. What is the basis of allocation in the straight-line method?
12. How does the declining-balance method differ from the other methods?
13. What is the formula for the sum-of-the-years'-digits?
14. What is the half-year convention, and how is it applied in computing depreciation expense?
15. Which depreciation method is the best to use for financial reporting purposes?
16. What happens if the actual life of an asset turns out to be longer or shorter than originally estimated?
17. Should companies have fully depreciated assets in use in their businesses?
18. Explain the difference between a capital expenditure and a revenue expenditure.
19. What costs are capitalized subsequent to the acquisition of an asset? Why?
20. What subsequent costs are expensed as incurred? Why?
21. What is the impact of expensing a subsequent cost that should have been capitalized?
22. What happens when assets are sold for more or less than their book value?
23. When assets are no longer in use, how are they treated?
24. What are intangible assets?
25. What are the two main categories of intangible assets?
26. Define four identifiable intangible assets and explain how each is amortized.
27. What are organizational costs and how are they amortized?
28. Define goodwill. When and how is goodwill measured in accounting?
29. Can any company report goodwill? Explain.

APPENDIX QUESTIONS

30. When one asset is exchanged for another asset and cash is also paid, how is the gain or loss determined in the fair value method?
31. For income tax purposes, what is the value of a new asset acquired in exchange for an old asset plus cash?
32. When are special rules required for recording asset exchanges?
33. What are natural resources, and how is their cost measurement different from most other assets?
34. How is depletion measured for financial reporting purposes?
35. What are statutory depletion rates?

EXERCISES

EXERCISE 8-1
L.O. 1

Group Purchase

Rent-a-Clunk purchased five used cars from U-Rent for $20,000 total. The following data were available from U-Rent at the time of the purchase:

Vehicle	*Original Cost*	*Book Value*
Tempo	$10,900	$ 2,500
Topaz.	11,650	3,000
Cougar	16,980	3,500
T-Bird.	15,550	3,500
Econoline	14,200	4,000
Total	$69,280	$16,500

Required:
1. Which value is more appropriate for allocation purposes, original cost or book value?
2. Record the value of each vehicle, assigning the $20,000 cost on the basis of their original cost. (Round all answers to the nearest dollar.)

EXERCISE 8-2
L.O. 2

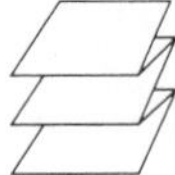

Depreciation Methods

On January 1, 19x1, the Tavares Company bought a record-making machine for $72,000. This machine had an expected useful life of 10 years with an estimated residual value of $8,000. The machine was expected to be able to produce 40,000 records during its life.

Required:
1. Compute the 19x1 depreciation expense on the machine using the sum-of-the-years'-digits depreciation method. (Round to nearest dollar.)
2. The machine actually produced 12,000 records in 19x1. Compute the 19x1 depreciation expense on the machine using the units-of-output depreciation method.

EXERCISE 8-3
L.O. 2

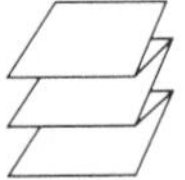

Depreciation Methods

Go Blue, Inc., purchased a machine on January 1, 19x1, for $55,000. The machine has an estimated residual value of $5,000 and a useful life of five years. The company uses the 200% declining-balance depreciation method.

Required:
1. Compute the amount Go Blue will record for depreciation on the machine in 19x2.
2. Compute the depreciation expense for 19x2 if Go Blue uses the straight-line method or the sum-of-the-years'-digits method rather than the declining-balance method.

EXERCISE 8-4
L.O. 2, 3

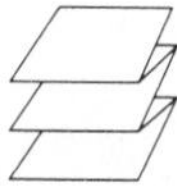

Depreciation Methods and Change in Estimate

Spud's Lounge purchased a dishwashing machine with an estimated 10-year useful life for $26,000. The estimated residual value is $2,000, and the accumulated depreciation at the end of year 5 for the machine is $12,000. It is now the beginning of year 6, and Spud reevaluated the estimated total useful life to be 13 years. Compute the depreciation expense for year 6.

EXERCISE 8-5
L.O. 3

Change in Estimate

On January 1, 19x1, Boose, Inc., purchased furniture for $218,000. The furniture was expected to last five years and to have a residual value of $18,000. Late in 19x4, Boose revised its estimate of the salvage value from $18,000 to $40,000. Boose uses straight-line depreciation.

Required:
Compute the depreciation expense for 19x1 and for 19x4.

EXERCISE 8-6
L.O. 3

Half-Year Convention

The Using Corporation acquired a machine on May 1, 19x1, at a cost of $78,000. The machine had an estimated useful life of 10 years and an estimated salvage value of $3,000. The half-year convention is used by the corporation.

Required:
Compute (round all answers to the nearest dollar) the depreciation expense for the second year of use (19x2) assuming:

1. The straight-line method is used.
2. The 175% declining-balance method is used.
3. The sum-of-the-years'-digits method is used.

EXERCISE 8-7
L.O. 3

Half-Year Convention

Lily Lumber reported the following activities during 19x5 concerning its depreciable assets.

Feb. 1 A power saw which had a net book value on January 1, 19x5, of $4,800 and annual depreciation of $1,200 per year (straight-line) was sold for $4,500 cash. The saw had originally cost $12,000.

Mar. 1 A new power saw was acquired for $15,800 cash. It has an expected useful life of eight years and no salvage value. The 200% declining-balance method will be used.

July 15 A new forklift truck costing $23,000, with an expected life of 60,000 hours of use and no scrap value was acquired for cash. The truck was used 500 hours in 19x5.

Oct. 31 A new warehouse was placed in service today. The new storage facility cost $125,000 cash and is expected to last 30 years and have no scrap value. Sum-of-the-years'-digits depreciation will be used.

Required:
Using the half-year convention, record all of the journal entries for 19x5 to account for the four events described in the exercise, including any adjusting entries to record depreciation. (Round all computations to nearest dollar.)

EXERCISE 8-8
L.O. 3

Nearest Month Depreciation

Janet's Jet Travel Service reported the following activities during 19x9 concerning depreciable assets.

Feb. 15 Purchased a new high-speed printer for $4,980 cash. The useful life is five years and the estimated scrap value is $480. The 150% declining-balance method is used.

May 20 Sold for $3,000 cash a used computer whose January 1, 19x9, net book value was $3,200. The computer, which had originally cost $10,000, was being depreciated on a straight-line basis at the rate of $900 per year.

Nov. 18 Purchased a new delivery car for $15,000 cash. The car is expected to be used 60,000 miles and to have a scrap value of $3,000. The car had been driven 2,150 miles by year-end.

Dec. 1 Purchased a new communications system for $23,600 cash. The system, which will be depreciated using the sum-of-the-years'-digits method, should last 8 years and have a salvage value of $1,600.

Required:
Using the nearest month approach, record all of the journal entries for 19x9 to account for the four events described in the exercise, including any adjusting journal entries to record depreciation. (Round all computations to nearest dollar.)

EXERCISE 8-9
L.O. 2

Depreciation and Taxes

Argo Corporation purchased equipment costing $85,000 on January 1, 19x1, for cash. The estimated useful life was four years and the estimated salvage value was $5,000. The tax rate is fixed at 30%.

Required:
1. What is the total depreciation expense over the life of the asset that may be taken for tax purposes?
2. What is the total depreciation expense over the life of the asset that may be taken for book purposes?
3. How much less income tax expense will Argo pay over the asset's life in comparison to the income taxes it would have paid if it had not purchased the equipment?

EXERCISE 8-10
L.O. 1, 4

Subsequent Costs/Basket Purchase

The Colette Corporation purchased a factory building and the land it was on for $210,000. At that time, the land had an appraised value of $100,000, and the building had an appraised value of $150,000. Colette then put a new roof on the factory building at a cost of $10,000. Compute the total amount debited to the Factory Building account.

EXERCISE 8-11
L.O. 4

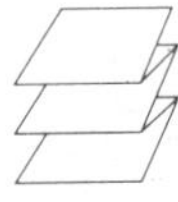

Subsequent Costs

For each of the situations described below, indicate whether the cost should be capitalized or expensed. Assume the company involved has total assets of $1,500,000 and average net income of $50,000.

a. Built an addition to the warehouse adding 2,000 square feet at a cost of $23,000.
b. Paid $280 to have windows in rented office building cleaned.
c. Added partitions to sales showroom for privacy in client meetings at a cost of $2,300.
d. Painted interior of showroom at a cost of $295 for the third time in two years due to heavy traffic.
e. Replaced chipped tiles in showroom floor at a cost of $675.
f. Replaced dead tree outside of showroom at a cost of $600. This was the only loss from the 10 trees planted five years earlier during landscaping renovations.

EXERCISE 8-12
L.O. 4

Subsequent Costs

The Gabel Cable TV Company invested $2,500,000 in a cable broadcasting system in January of 19x1. The new system was expected to handle all cable transmissions for eight years and was being depreciated on a straight-line basis (assuming no salvage value). In May 19x3, a severe thunderstorm destroyed a key component of the transmission system. The replacement, which cost Gabel $635,000, was not insured. While the replacement did not add to the useful life of the system, it was necessary for the system to be used, and it was installed on May 31, 19x3.

Required:
Record the journal entry to account for the replacement component, and record the journal entries to account for depreciation expense in 19x3 and 19x4. You should compute depreciation to the nearest month. (Round all computations to nearest dollar.)

EXERCISE 8-13
L.O. 5

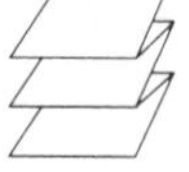

Disposal of Assets

Zeron Company owns a drill press. The press originally cost $35,000 and had a 10-year useful life with a $5,000 residual value. At December 31, 19x5, the drill press had accumulated depreciation of $12,000 (after all adjusting entries). Zeron uses straight-line depreciation to the nearest month.

Required:
1. How old was the machine at December 31, 19x5?
2. If the drill press were sold on March 31, 19x6, for $17,000 cash, what would be the journal entry (entries) on that date?

EXERCISE 8-14
L.O. 5

Disposal of Assets

On January 1, 19x1, Berry Corporation sold equipment that had originally cost $50,000 and had accumulated depreciation of $22,000 for $12,000 and a one-year note receivable. The note had a face value of $16,000 and paid interest of $3,000 at the end of one year.

Required:
Record the sale of the old equipment:

1. Using the above facts.
2. Same as above except $10,000 cash was received rather than $12,000.
3. Same as above except $14,500 cash was received rather than $12,000.
4. Assuming the equipment was scrapped rather than sold.

EXERCISE 8-15
L.O. 7

Patents

On January 14, 19xx, Johnson, Inc., filed a lawsuit against Jayco for a patent violation arguing that Jayco was using a patented process owned by Johnson to produce its products. Johnson spent $578,000 in legal fees to defend its exclusive right to the patented process.

Required:
1. Assume the lawsuit was successful for Johnson. How should Johnson treat the legal fees?
2. Assume the lawsuit was **not** successful. What should Johnson record regarding the legal fees? The patent?

EXERCISE 8-16
L.O. 7

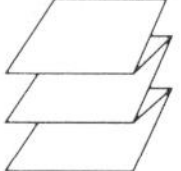

Goodwill

Baker Corporation acquired a small tool and die company for $480,000 on December 31, 19x1. The tool and die company reported the following data:

	Book Values	*Estimated Market Values*
Recorded assets . . .	$450,000	$550,000
Recorded liabilities . .	150,000	150,000
Net assets recorded. .	$300,000	$400,000

Baker amortizes goodwill over 40 years.

Required:
1. Compute goodwill, if any, included in this purchase.
2. Record the amortization of goodwill for 19x2 for Baker.

EXERCISE 8-17
L.O. 7

Intangibles

Select the best alternative for each of the following multiple-choice questions or statements.

1. The XYZ Company reported an asset, Patents, $38,000.
   a. Which were licensed by the federal government.
   b. Which represented the unamortized legal fees plus the cost to develop prototypes.
   c. Which would be amortized over no more than 17 years.
   d. All of the above are correct.
   e. None of the above is correct.
2. Research and development costs—
   a. Are costs of searching for new knowledge.
   b. Are costs of creating new products.
   c. Are very important activities in some industries leading to new products but are still not allowed to be recorded as assets in most cases.
   d. All of the above are correct.
   e. None of the above is correct.
3. In practice, organization costs—
   a. Are expensed as incurred.
   b. Are capitalized as a permanent asset.
   c. Are capitalized and amortized over 40 years.
   d. Are capitalized and amortized over five years.
   e. None of the above.
4. Copyrights granted to a business are:
   a. Granted by the federal government for a 75-year period of time.
   b. Amortized over not more than 40 years.
   c. Granted for original works of art and music.
   d. All of the above are correct.
   e. None of the above is correct.
5. On January 12, 19x5, XYZ Corporation paid legal fees of $35,000 to successfully defend its patent, which had a net book value of $5,000 and a remaining legal life of eight years at that time.
   a. The $35,000 should be capitalized as an asset in 19x5.
   b. The $35,000 should be expensed in 19x5.
   c. The amortization should be $625 per year for 19x5 and thereafter.
   d. Amortization expense for 19x5 should be $2,500.
   e. None of the above.

EXERCISE 8-18
L.O. 2, 5, 7, 9

Depreciation, Amortization, and Depletion Expense

For each of the following unrelated situations, calculate the annual depreciation, depletion, or amortization expense for the Andrews Company for its fiscal year ended December 31, 19x5.

1. A five-year-old patent was purchased for $480,000 on January 1, 19x5. The patent will probably be useful commercially for 12 more years.
   a. $12,000.
   b. $28,235.
   c. $40,000.
   d. $24,000.
2. Various building fixtures costing $56,000 were constructed and permanently installed on January 1, 19x5, in a building being rented from another company. The useful life of the fixtures was estimated to be 15 years, and the residual value was estimated to be $6,000. The rental agreement ends in eight years. The rent agreement contained no provision for the removal of fixtures.
   a. $3,333.
   b. $7,000.
   c. $3,733.
   d. $6,250.
3. On January 1, 19x3, the company purchased a machine at a cost of $25,000. The machine was estimated to have a useful life of four years, after which it could be sold for $1,000. The company is using the sum-of-the-years'-digits method to record depreciation on the machine.
   a. $5,000.
   b. $4,800.
   c. $2,400.
   d. $7,500.
4. On January 1, 19x4, the company purchased a building for $100,000. The company is using the 200% declining-balance method to record depreciation and estimates that the building has a $20,000 residual value. Depreciation expense on the building for 19x4 was $10,000.
   a. $18,000.
   b. $10,000.
   c. $9,000.
   d. $7,000.
5. (*Appendix 8B*) The company purchased a mining site for $290,000 on June 15, 19x5, containing an estimated one million tons of coal. Before starting mining operations, the company paid $5,000 in legal fees to acquire proper title. The company estimates that it can sell the mining site for $15,000 after all the coal has been extracted. During 19x5, 85,000 tons of coal were extracted and sold.
   a. $25,075.
   b. $24,650.
   c. $23,375.
   d. $23,800.

EXERCISE 8-19
L.O. 2, 4, 5, 7

Accounting Policies—Ralston Purina

Consider the Ralston Purina Company's (RPC's) annual report in Appendix E at the back of the text. Refer to the first page of footnotes, "Summary of Accounting Policies," in answering the following questions.

Required:
1. What is RPC's policy on costs subsequent to acquisition?
2. Where are gains or losses on the disposal of properties reported?

3. What is the method and useful life used for depreciable assets?
4. What is the method and useful life used for intangible assets?

EXERCISE 8-20
L.O. 5, 6

Asset Disposals—Ralston Purina

Consider the Ralston Purina Company's (RPC's) annual report in Appendix E. Refer to the footnote, "Analysis of Balance Sheet Changes" (page 30 of the annual report). RPC disposed of some property during fiscal 1989. From RPC's Cash Flow Statement, we know the cash proceeds of the property disposals were $16.3 million.

Required:
1. Compute the gain or loss (pretax) on the disposals for fiscal 1989.
2. What was the percentage of depreciation taken on these disposed-of assets prior to their sale?

APPENDIX EXERCISES

EXERCISE 8-21
L.O. 8

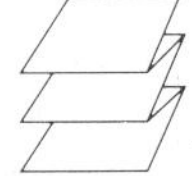

Asset Exchanges (Appendix 8A)

On January 1, 19xx, Danko, Inc., traded in a used truck in exchange for a new truck. The old truck cost $28,000 and had a net book value of $9,000 on the date of exchange. The new truck had a "list" price of $40,000 but could be purchased for $35,000 cash. Danko gave the old truck plus $27,000 cash in exchange for the new truck.

Required:
1. Record the exchange using the fair value method.
2. Record the exchange using the tax method.
3. Does this exchange qualify as a "special case" exchange? Explain.

EXERCISE 8-22
L.O. 8

Asset Exchanges (Appendix 8A)

Waite, Inc., acquired land from Bolding Corporation in exchange for 1,000 units of Waite's inventory. The inventory had cost Waite $76,800 to manufacture during the current year and had a regular selling price of $140 per unit. The land had been on Bolding's books at an original cost of $60,000 and was recently appraised at a value of $135,000 by an independent real estate agent.

Required:
Using the fair value method, answer the following questions:

1. What is the cost of the land to be recorded by Waite?
2. What is the cost of the inventory to be recorded on Bolding's books?
3. Is there a gain to be recorded by Bolding on this transaction? If so, how much?
4. Record the entry to acquire the land on Waite's books.

EXERCISE 8-23
L.O. 9

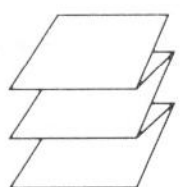

Natural Resources (Appendix 8B)

The North Shore Corporation spent $1,680,000 cash in 19x8 to discover 480,000 barrels of crude oil. During the remainder of 19x8, they extracted 80,000 barrels and sold them to a processing company for $5.50 per barrel. During 19x9 North Shore extracted 200,000 barrels of crude oil and sold them to a processing company for $6 per barrel. Extraction costs were $0.02 per barrel in both 19x8 and 19x9.

Required:
1. Record the discovery costs and the depletion for 19x8 and 19x9.
2. What was the gross profit on sales in 19x8? 19x9?

PROBLEMS

PROBLEM 8-1
L.O. 1

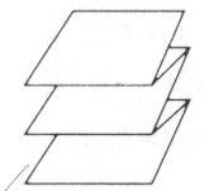

Acquisition Costs

Elton Corporation incurred the following costs in the process of buying new cutting equipment for its furniture manufacturing plants:

Invoice cost of cutting machines	$137,500
Installation labor	250
Installation materials	475
Freight charges for delivery	4,380
Insurance costs	2,000
Special cutting bands for machine	17,000
Supervisor's salary for day machines installed	200
Sales tax on machine (5%)	6,875
Sales tax on special cutting bands (5%)	850
Cost of materials used while adjusting machines. . . .	770

The installation labor was based on the actual cost of Elton's workers who installed the machinery. The freight charges were for both railroad fees ($2,300) and trucking fees ($2,080) using Elton's own trucks. Insurance costs were for a one-year insurance policy sold by the manufacturer to take effect on the first day of operation. The cutting bands were only useful in conjunction with the cutting machines, which could not be operated without the bands. The manufacturer offered a 4% discount on the invoice price of the cutting machines if paid within 30 days of delivery. Elton did not pay within the 30-day period.

Required:
1. Determine the cost of the cutting machines.
2. Record the appropriate entries to account for all of the costs noted in the problem.

PROBLEM 8-2
L.O. 1

Acquisition Cost Allocation

On May 1, 19x1, Danco, Inc., purchased a 10-acre parcel of land for $150,000 to be used as a future building site. On June 10, 19x4, Danco sold five acres of the land for $200,000 cash and constructed a warehouse on the remaining five acres at a cost of $180,000 cash.

Required:
1. What are some of the additional facts that you might like to know in order to record the sale on June 10, 19x4? Why?
2. Record the above facts assuming no additional information.
3. Explain how you decided to allocate the $150,000 original land cost to the two five-acre parcels on June 10, 19x4. Why did you choose this method?

PROBLEM 8-3
L.O. 1

Asset Acquisition/Basket Purchase

The Lime Tree Complex purchased three houses from Campus Realtors for a total price of $450,000. The three houses were to be made into apartments for student rentals. The following data were available concerning the three houses:

Unit	*Square Feet of Floor Space*	*Assessed Value*	*Campus Realtors Book Value*
A	3,496	$ 90,000	$120,000
B	2,944	70,000	90,000
C	2,760	60,000	100,000
Total	9,200	$220,000	$310,000

All three houses were between three and five years old. Unit A was assessed last year at $90,000, while units B and C were assessed this year. The assessed value is estimated to be 50% of the market value of each house. The current replacement cost of similar quality houses in the area is about $52 per square foot. All three houses are in excellent locations and should be easy to rent. The rental fee will be based on the size of the apartment units, since all will be similarly equipped.

Required:

1. Assume no goodwill exists in the purchase by Lime Tree. Allocate the $450,000 purchase price to the three units on a basis you believe is most equitable.
2. Explain why you did not choose the alternative methods for allocating the $450,000 cost.
3. (*Optional*) Assume Lime Tree sells unit A for $195,000 the day after its purchase from Campus Realtors. Does this affect your allocation method? Explain.
4. (*Optional*) Record the sale of unit A for $195,000 cash by Lime Tree the day after it is purchased from Campus Realtors.

PROBLEM 8-4
L.O. 2

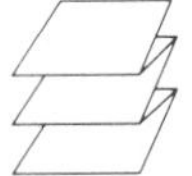

Depreciation Methods

On January 1, 19x1, Daydreamer Corporation purchased a "sleep" machine for $112,000. The estimated useful life is five years, and the residual value is $20,000. The estimated productive output is 50,000 hours of use. Daydreamer's fiscal year ends December 31.

Required:

1. Using the sum-of-the-years'-digits method, compute depreciation expense for 19x1 and 19x2 and the machine's book value at December 31, 19x2.
2. During 19x1, the machine was used for 12,000 hours. Compute 19x1's depreciation expense using the units-of-output method.
3. Using the 150% declining-balance method, compute 19x1's and 19x2's depreciation expense and the machine's book value at the end of both fiscal years.

PROBLEM 8-5
L.O. 2

Depreciation Methods

On January 1, 19x1, the Salinsky Company purchased a machine for $10,000. The machine has a 20-year life and no residual value. It is estimated the machine will be used 40,000 hours. During 19x1 and 19x2, the machine was used 3,000 and 2,500 hours, respectively. The company has a December 31 year-end and uses a monthly depreciation measurement.

Required:

Determine the depreciation expense amounts for 19x1 and 19x2 using the following depreciation methods (round answers to nearest dollar):

1. Straight-line.
2. Sum-of-the-years'-digits.
3. 200% declining-balance.
4. Units of output.

PROBLEM 8-6
L.O. 2, 3

Depreciation Methods/Nearest Month Approach

An asset that cost $50,000 with a $5,000 residual value and a five-year life was purchased on April 1, 19x1, by JKA Corporation. The company uses the nearest month approach to record depreciation expense.

Required:

Compute depreciation expense for the fiscal years ended December 31, 19x1, and 19x2, using the following depreciation methods:

1. Straight-line.
2. Sum-of-the-years'-digits.
3. 200% declining-balance.

PROBLEM 8-7
L.O. 2, 3

Depreciation Methods/Half-Year Convention

The Tooz Company installed a machine in its factory at a total cost of $15,800. Its useful life was estimated at five years or 50,000 units of product. The residual value is estimated to be $600. Production was 11,000 units for the first year of operation; 13,000 units for the second year; and 9,000 units for the third year. Tooz Company uses the half-year convention for measuring depreciation expense.

Required:
Compute the depreciation expense for the first three years of the machine's use under the following depreciation methods:

1. Straight-line.
2. Units of output. (Round to nearest cent per unit.)
3. Sum-of-the-years'-digits. (Round to nearest dollar.)
4. 200% declining-balance. (Round to nearest dollar.)

PROBLEM 8-8
L.O. 2, 3

Depreciation Methods/Partial Years

On May 15, 19x4, Mastco, Inc., acquired a new furnace for its glazing operations. The furnace cost $35,650. Freight costs amounted to $760 and the installation of the furnace cost $590. The estimated salvage value of the furnace in seven years is $2,000. The furnace is expected to be useful for 14,000 hours of glazing. It was used for 1,200 hours during 19x4 and 2,000 hours during 19x5.

Required:
Record the depreciation expense for 19x4 and 19x5 using the following alternative methods:

1. Straight-line, computed to closest month.
2. Sum-of-the-years'-digits, computed using the half-year convention.
3. 150% declining-balance, computed to the closest month (round rate to four decimals).
4. Units of output.

PROBLEM 8-9
L.O. 2

Depreciation and Taxes

Ladro Corporation reports income *before* considering depreciation expense and taxes of $200,000 every year. Ladro acquired depreciable assets at a cost of $250,000 on January 1, 19x1. The assets have a useful life of six years and no salvage value. The income tax rate is 34% every year.

Required:
1. Assume Ladro uses straight-line for books, but, for income tax purposes, Ladro depreciates the assets over five years as follows: 30% (year 1); 25% (year 2); 20% (year 3); 15% (year 4); 10% (year 5). Compute the tax savings or the additional taxes each year from 19x1 to 19x6 compared with the straight-line method.
2. Explain why Ladro should not use straight-line for income tax purposes too.

PROBLEM 8-10
L.O. 2

Depreciation and Taxes

Wayco, Inc., is considering the following depreciation schedules to apply to a $100,000 asset acquired on January 1, 19x1, and expected to have a five-year useful life and no salvage value.

Year	*Schedule 1*	*Schedule 2*
1 . . .	30%	20%
2 . . .	25	20
3 . . .	20	20
4 . . .	15	20
5 . . .	10	20
	100%	100%

Required:
1. Compute depreciation expense for each schedule.
2. Assume net income before taxes and depreciation expense is $65,000 each year, and the tax rate is 40%. Compute net income for 19x1 and 19x2 under each alternative.
3. Assume cash flow from operations before considering taxes and depreciation expense is $55,000 in 19x1 and $60,000 in 19x2. Taxes must be paid in cash each year. Compute cash flow from operations after taxes and depreciation expense for 19x1 and 19x2.

PROBLEM 8-11
L.O. 3

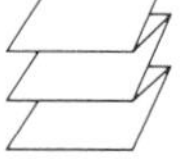

Change in Estimate

Paymor Corporation purchased equipment on January 1, 19x1, for $86,600. The equipment was expected to have a 15-year life and $3,600 residual value. Paymor uses straight-line depreciation. On December 31, 19x5 (the fifth year of use), the technology for this equipment changed significantly, and the estimated useful life was decreased from 15 years to 8 years with no change in residual value.

Required:
(Round to nearest dollar.)

1. Record depreciation expense for 19x1.
2. Record depreciation expense for 19x5 and 19x6.

PROBLEM 8-12
L.O. 3

Change in Estimate

Welden, Inc., discovered in 19x8 that it had been using fully depreciated equipment throughout the year and that the equipment was expected to be useful for at least three more years (after 19x8) with no residual value. The original cost of $480,000 had been fully depreciated over 12 years on a straight-line basis by the end of 19x7.

Required:
1. What should have been done prior to 19x8?
2. Assume that this situation was discovered before the books were closed for 19x7. What should Welden have depreciated for 19x7? For 19x8?
3. How could Welden prevent this situation from occurring in the future?

PROBLEM 8-13
L.O. 1

Errors in Recording Plant and Equipment

On May 20, 19xx, Bradley Corporation purchased land for $450,000 cash for a future building site. The following additional costs were incurred during 19xx and added to the "Land and Buildings" account on Bradley's books:

Date		*Item*	*Amount*
19xx			
June	10	Paid for cutting trees	$ 7,850
	15	Sold cut trees to local sawmill	(3,500)
	22	Destroyed old barn on land.	8,300
	23	Sold old barn wood to furniture company	(6,750)
	30	Paid for grading of land and excavation of building site . .	15,000
July	10	Paid for paved road to building site	110,000
	18	Paid first payment to construction company	1,300,000
	23	Paid for insurance to cover building during construction period	13,000
Aug.	31	Paid for final payment on building	700,000
	31	Paid interest on money borrowed to pay construction company initial payment	48,000
Sept.	30	Paid agency for grand opening fees including prizes given to public, promotions, etc.	19,500
		Balance: Land and buildings	$2,211,400

Bradley plans to depreciate this amount over 50 years on a straight-line basis.

Required:

1. Identify any errors made by Bradley in recording the transactions described above.
2. Determine the appropriate balances to be recorded in the following accounts: Land, Roadway, Buildings.
3. Prepare the necessary entries to correct the records of Bradley. Do not record any depreciation for 19xx.

PROBLEM 8-14
L.O. 5

Disposal of Assets

On September 14, 19x7, the Pullman Corporation disposed of two pieces of machinery from its office equipment division. The first machine had cost $28,750 on January 1, 19x1. It was originally expected to have a 10-year useful life and no scrap value. The machine was being depreciated using the 200% declining-balance method computed by the half-year convention. The machine was sold to a competitor for $8,300 cash.

The second machine was acquired on May 3, 19x1, at a cost of $33,700. It had an estimated useful life of eight years and an estimated residual value of $2,500. The second machine was being depreciated on a straight-line basis computed to the nearest month. It was sold for $7,500 cash.

Required:
(Round to nearest dollar.)

1. Compute the gain or loss from the sale of each machine separately.
2. Record the entries to dispose of the two machines.

PROBLEM 8-15
L.O. 2–5, 9

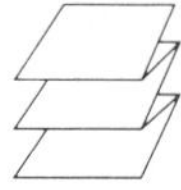

Depreciation, Depletion, and Disposal of Assets

Below is a schedule of selected account balances taken from the Apollo Corporation's adjusted trial balance at December 31, 19x8. The corporation's fiscal year ends on December 31.

	Debits	*Credits*
Delivery Truck	$ 10,000	
Accumulated Depreciation—Delivery Truck		$ 6,000
Machine A	50,000	
Accumulated Depreciation—Machine A		40,000
Machine B	60,000	
Accumulated Depreciation—Machine B		24,000
Machine C	78,000	
Accumulated Depreciation—Machine C		59,200
Building	200,000	
Accumulated Depreciation—Building		62,182
Land	100,000	
Mining Properties	150,000	
Accumulated Depletion—Mining Properties		50,000

During 19x9, the following transactions occurred related to the above accounts:

19x9

Jan. 1 Made substantial improvements costing $45,000 to Machine C. Machine C was purchased on January 1, 19x1, for $78,000 and has been depreciated on a straight-line basis. On January 1, 19x1, the corporation estimated that the machine had a useful life of 10 years and a residual value of $4,000. The corporation estimates that the improvements increased the machine's total useful life to 12 years and residual value to $13,000.

Feb. 1 Sold the delivery truck for $4,100 cash. The depreciation expense of $300 for the month of January on the truck has not yet been recorded.

Mar. 1 Machine A was destroyed by fire. The insurance proceeds amounted to $4,000. Depreciation expense on this item for January 1, 19x9, through March 1, 19x9, has not been recorded yet and amounts to $400.

May 1 Paid $400 cash for routine repairs to the machines.

Dec. 31 Made the adjusting entry for depletion of mining properties, which were originally acquired for $150,000. The corporation estimates that the properties will produce a total of 150,000 tons of ore during their useful life. During 19x9, 10,000 tons of ore were produced.

31 Made the adjusting entry for Machine B. Machine B was purchased on January 1, 19x8, at a cost of $60,000. The corporation is using the 200% declining-balance depreciation method to record depreciation on the machine and estimates that the machine has a $5,000 residual value.

31 Made the adjusting entry to record depreciation on the building. The building was purchased on January 1, 19x7, and has a 10-year useful life with a $20,000 residual value. The corporation is using the sum-of-the-years'-digits depreciation method to record depreciation.

31 Made the adjusting entry to record depreciation for Machine C.

Required:
Prepare the journal entries in general journal form for the above transactions.

PROBLEM 8-16
L.O. 4

Subsequent Costs

The Marecoor Corporation had a number of events recorded during 19xx that were being disputed by the company's auditors. The central question in each case is whether or not a capital expenditure took place.

Event A: Marecoor paid $156,000 in legal fees to *successfully* defend its right to the exclusive use of a patented product for data transmission.

Event B: Land held as a future building site was originally zoned for commercial use until a citizens group successfully had it rezoned in 19xx for residential use only. Marecoor sued the local zoning board to reverse their decision or pay damages but was not successful. Legal fees were $100,000.

Event C: Marecoor replaced the carpet and repainted two floors of its 10-story office building at a cost of $425,000. This process occurs about once every five years.

Required:
Indicate whether or not these items are capital expenditures. Record the entries to account for the costs in each event.

PROBLEM 8-17
L.O. 4

Subsequent Costs

For each of the situations described below, determine whether the expenditure involved should be capitalized or expensed and give the reason for your decision. Assume the assets of each company are about $1,500,000.

1. Apex Company had a car drive into their storefront on Main Street. The uninsured damage to the front of the building (doors, glass, brick, and so on) cost Apex $2,965 to fix.
2. In 19x3, Meal Furniture Store painted the exterior of its showroom facilities for only the third time in the company's 100-year history, at a cost of $3,215. The building was originally a red brick structure.
3. Arthur Marwick has two floors at the top of the World Center Building. The carpet has just been replaced at a cost of $60,000 to help celebrate 50 years of practice as a local CPA firm.
4. The Main Front Bookstore recently put a new roof on its building at a cost of $15,000. The old roof had been repaired several times in each of the last five years and was no longer worth repairing.
5. The Barnes Ace Hardware Store recently spent $6,950 to landscape its store and parking lot area as their part of a major local beautification project in Hill City.
6. Ace Moving and Storage had to pay $3,000 to replace engines on two moving vans. Both vans were purchased just 15 months earlier, and the replacements were not covered by warranty. This was the earliest such replacement in the company's history.

PROBLEM 8-18
L.O. 7

Goodwill

Sunoma Wines acquired the net assets of Hill Round Ltd. for $1,580,000 cash on January 1, 19xx. The following information was available for Hill Round on the date of purchase:

	Fair Market Value	*Book Value*
Cash	$ 115,000	$ 115,000
Inventory	285,000	120,000
Land	1,295,000	485,000
Buildings	460,000	340,000
Total assets	$2,155,000	$1,060,000
Liabilities	750,000	750,000
Net assets	$1,405,000	$ 310,000

Sunoma estimates that all intangible assets will have a 25-year economic life and uses straight-line amortization for all intangibles.

Required:
1. Compute the amount of goodwill purchased by Sunoma.
2. Record the purchase of Hill Round on Sunoma's books on January 1, 19xx.
3. Record amortization of goodwill by Sunoma on December 31, 19xx.

PROBLEM 8-19
L.O. 7

Goodwill

Gulf-Eastern Industries exchanged one of its communication satellites for a 100% interest in WAVO Radio Station. The following data are available about the exchange:

Satellite

	Book Value	*Estimated Fair Market Value*
Cost	$3,900,000	
Accumulated depreciation	820,000	
Net	$3,080,000	$4,300,000

WAVO Radio Station

	Book Value	*Estimated Fair Market Value*
Assets	$1,850,000	$3,980,000
Liabilities	790,000	790,000
Net assets	$1,060,000	$3,190,000

Assume that both WAVO Radio owners and Gulf-Eastern management agree that the fair market value (cash-equivalent price) of the satellite—Sitcom I—is $4.3 million. Also, both parties agree that WAVO Radio has future earnings potential that is not reflected in the recorded assets of WAVO.

Required:
1. What is the apparent amount of goodwill, if any, that Gulf-Eastern seems willing to pay for when buying WAVO Radio?

2. What is the fair market value of the net assets given (or received) to be used by Gulf-Eastern in recording the exchange transaction?
3. Assume that the net assets acquired by Gulf-Eastern have a fair value of $4.3 million. Record the exchange on Gulf-Eastern's books. Use a single asset account, "Investment in WAVO," to record the inflow of assets in this exchange.

PROBLEM 8-20
L.O. 6

Evaluating Changes in Plant Assets

Jay-Kay Products acquired equipment costing $48,000 in 19x2 and recorded depreciation expense on equipment of $26,000 for the year. The following balance sheet data were reported at the end of 19x2:

	December 31	
	19x2	*19x1*
Equipment (at cost)	$498,650	$487,500
Accumulated depreciation—equipment	130,000	115,950
Net book value—equipment	$368,650	$371,550

The sale of used equipment during the year produced a gain of $2,850.

Required:
1. Compute the original cost of the used equipment sold in 19x2.
2. Compute the accumulated depreciation on the used equipment sold in 19x2.
3. Record the sale of used equipment.

PROBLEM 8-21
L.O. 6

Evaluating Changes in Plant Assets

Assume that your examination of the Armco Steel's 19x2 annual report revealed the following facts (in millions):

	December 31	
	19x2	*19x1*
Machinery (at cost)	$28	$29
Accumulated depreciation—machinery	10	9

During 19x2, Armco purchased $3 million in new machinery and sold used machinery at a loss of $2 million. Depreciation expense on machinery for 19x2 was $2 million.

Required:
1. Compute the original cost of the used machinery sold at a loss.
2. Compute the amount of accumulated depreciation on the used machinery sold at a loss.
3. Record the sale of used machinery.
4. What percent of the used machinery had been depreciated before the sale?

PROBLEM 8-22
L.O. 6

Annual Report Analysis

The following information for the machinery and equipment of the Bardsley Corporation was taken from its 19x5 annual report:

	December 31		
	19x3	*19x4*	*19x5*
Machinery at cost net of accumulated depreciation	$2,875	$2,327	$2,756

	For the Year Ended December 31		
	19x3	*19x4*	*19x5*
Depreciation expense	$300	$315	$330

During 19x4, no acquisition of machinery occurred, but some machinery was sold by Bardsley for cash at a gain of $37. No machinery was sold in 19x5, but some new machinery was acquired for cash.

Required:
1. How much cash was provided by the sale of machinery in 19x4?
2. How much cash was used to acquire machinery in 19x5?

APPENDIX PROBLEMS

PROBLEM 8-23
L.O. 8

Asset Exchanges (Appendix 8A)

Barnett Company acquired a four-color printing press from Mr. Graves who was going out of business. The press had cost Mr. Graves $170,000 five years earlier. The current replacement cost of the press was $360,000. A printing industry publication listed the estimated market value of the press (and others like it) at $200,000. Barnett Company gave Mr. Graves a two-year $100,000 note that paid 10% interest each year, plus 2,000 shares of Barnett stock that were selling for $55 per share on the date of the exchange. Barnett stock was selling for $58 per share by the end of the accounting period. Use the fair value method to answer the requirements below.

Required:
1. What is the cost to be reported by Barnett at the date of the transaction?
2. Record the entry to account for the purchase of the press using the fair value method.
3. Assume now that no market price was available for Barnett's stock during the year of the purchase. What value would be assigned to the press at the date of purchase?

PROBLEM 8-24
L.O. 8

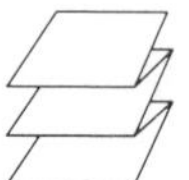

Assets Exchange (Appendix 8A)

Partners Pizza acquired a new delivery truck on July 1, 19x7, at a cost of $7,350 cash plus its old truck. The old truck had been acquired for $7,000 cash on July 1, 19x3, and was being depreciated on a straight-line basis using the half-year convention and assuming no scrap value. The estimated useful life of a delivery truck is five years. One of the delivery persons who worked for Partners offered to buy the truck for $900 cash. However, the new truck dealer wanted $8,500 cash for the new truck without the old truck as a trade-in, so Partners took the trade-in value of the old truck.

Required:

1. What is the fair value of the new truck?
2. Record the depreciation on the old truck to June 30, 19x7, for the year 19x7.
3. Record the asset exchange on July 1, 19x7, using the fair value method.
4. Record depreciation expense on the new truck for 19x7 using straight-line depreciation assuming no salvage value.
5. Repeat requirement (3) above using the income tax accounting method.

PROBLEM 8-25
L.O. 9

Natural Resources (Appendix 8B)

The Big Dig Mining Company negotiated a rental agreement with the government of Ziembaro to extract copper ore from government coastal property for an eight-year period. The copper ore mining rights cost Big Dig $2,260,000 cash. The following additional facts were provided to you by Big Dig at the end of 19x1, the year the rental agreement was negotiated:

Cost of mining roads.	$ 5,100,000
Cost of mining equipment and buildings	$ 9,440,000
Estimated physical life of equipment and buildings . .	15 years
Estimated tons of copper ore to be extracted	20,000,000 tons
Estimated maximum copper ore extraction possible per year starting in 19x2	2,000,000 tons

Because of the political climate in Ziembaro, the rent agreement, which expires at the end of 19x8, is not expected to be renewable. Also, because of the remote location of the mines, all of the equipment must be abandoned upon termination of the mining operations.

In 19x2, Big Dig extracted and sold 2,000,000 tons of copper ore at a selling price of $50 per ton.

Required:

1. Compute the depletion rate per ton of copper ore.
2. Record depletion for 19x2.
3. Assume mining and processing costs are $3.25 per ton during 19x2. Compute the total inventory cost of the copper ore sold in 19x2 and the gross profit on sales.

PROBLEM 8-26
L.O. 9

Depletion/Change in Estimate (Appendix 8B)

The Voldez Oil Corporation discovered 25 million barrels of oil in 19x1 in the Gulf of Alaska. The total cost of the discovery, including drilling costs, platforms, and so on, amounted to $18 million. During 19x1, Voldez extracted 8 million barrels of oil, which were sold to Standard of California for $120 million.

Required:

1. Compute the depletion for 19x1 for Voldez Oil.
2. Assume the statutory depletion rate for tax purposes is 29% of sales dollars. Compute the tax depletion for 19x1. How much more depletion can Voldez Oil report in 19x1 for tax purposes compared to the financial reports?
3. Assume that in 19x2 Voldez extracted another 10 million barrels of oil. Then, in early 19x3, a new survey reported that the estimated remaining amount of unextracted oil was 15 million barrels. Two million barrels had been extracted in 19x3 **prior** to this survey, and another 8 million barrels were extracted in 19x3 after the survey. What is the new depletion rate as a result of this change in estimate? What is the amount of depletion to be reported in 19x3 by Voldez Oil?

CASES

CASE 8-1
L.O. 2, 3

Depreciation

Rawlings, Inc., acquired equipment on June 15, 19x1, at a cost of $140,000. The equipment was expected to last 10 years and have a $20,000 residual value. Rawlings used straight-line depreciation, resulting in $12,000 depreciation per year. Rawlings took one-half year's depreciation ($6,000) in 19x1. On September 30, 19x7, Rawlings sold the equipment for $70,000 cash to Wilson Corporation. Rawlings took $6,000 depreciation expense on the equipment for 19x7 in accordance with the half-year convention and recorded the following entry at the time of sale:

19x7			
Sept. 30	Cash	70,000	
	Accumulated Depreciation.	72,000	
	Equipment.		140,000
	Gain on Sale of Equipment		2,000

Rawlings' auditor is contending that Rawlings never specified it was using the half-year convention, and that nine months of depreciation (or $9,000) should have been taken in 19x7. This would have turned the $2,000 gain into a $1,000 loss.

Required:

1. Are the numbers in the case correct?
2. Assume the numerical data provided are all correct. Is the auditor's position correct or not?
3. If Rawlings refused to go along with the auditor, how much more income before tax would be reported in 19x7?
4. Is your answer to part 3 peculiar to this case or does it apply in general?
5. What additional information could be viewed to help solve this dispute, assuming Rawlings had been in business for many years?

CASE 8-2
L.O. 7

Goodwill

Consider the facts in Problem 8-3 concerning the basket purchase of three houses by Lime Tree Complex. Is there any goodwill in this transaction? Explain your position referring to the definition of goodwill.

CASE 8-3
L.O. 1

Acquisition Costs

West Corporation acquired the following assets from Baiman, Inc., on January 1, 19xx, at a total cost of $2,875,000:

- Land (corner lot at Stadium and Main, Atherton, Ohio).
- Building (brick construction, built 25 years ago, 4 stories).
- Equipment (average remaining life, six years).

The book values of these assets on Baiman's books at the date of purchase were:

	Book Values
Land	$ 75,000
Building (net)	1,080,000
Equipment (net)	620,000
Total	$1,775,000

On January 10, 19xx, before West did anything with the idle Baiman facilities, the equipment was sold to Jarrell Corporation for $750,000.

Required:

1. How might West assign the $2,875,000 purchase price to the three different assets?
2. What method of asset valuation would be most appropriate for West if any value desired were available?
3. What is the gain or loss, if any, that you think should be recorded on January 10, 19xx, by West from the sale of the equipment?
4. If Baiman had sold the equipment directly to Jarrell, what would be your estimate of the selling price of the equipment?

CASE 8-4
L.O. 4

Subsequent Costs

L & M Real Estate owns four furnished rental houses in Chelsea near Community University. The following expenditures took place in 19x5 concerning these rental properties:

Property 1:
- Interior painting, $780.
- Replace rear door, $650.
- Replace screens and storms, $800.
- Replace some furniture, $1,360.

Property 2:
- Replace carpeting in living room and stairs, $1,650.
- Replace some furniture, $760.

Property 3:
- Resurface gravel driveway, $435.
- Paint exterior, $1,290.
- Replace furniture in kitchen, $1,500.

Property 4:
- Paint interior, $695.
- Paint exterior, $1,150.
- Replace sliding glass door, $520.

Required:
Determine which expenditures should be expensed in 19x5 and which should be capitalized. Give the reason for each of your decisions.

CASE 8-5
L.O. 4

Subsequent Costs

The Briarwood Mall is a major shopping center located on a 30-acre site near Centerville. The complex has just undergone a major renovation to celebrate its 25th anniversary of being in business. The following expenditures were incurred during the renovation.

Item	*Cost*	*Estimated Useful Life*
1. Landscaping	$120,000	15 years
2. Parking lot light fixtures	180,000	20 years
3. New high-intensity bulbs in all fixtures	15,000	18 months
4. Repair parking lot surface holes	95,000	5 years
5. Sealant to parking lot surface	32,000	2 years
6. Repaint exterior of buildings	63,000	4 years
7. Repaint interior of mall	79,000	3 years
8. New interior benches for seating	125,000	8 years

The net book value of the mall before renovations was $5,600,000.

Required:

1. Explain which items you believe should be capitalized as assets and which items you believe should be expensed. In each case, explain the reason(s) supporting your decisions.
2. Which decision in your answer above are you least confident in? What are the factors which might support an alternative treatment of these costs?

CASE 8-6
L.O. 2

Depreciation and Taxes

Wellman Corporation acquired new lab equipment on January 1, 19x3, at a cost of $520,000. The equipment is expected to have a 10-year life and a $20,000 salvage value. Wellman reports income before taxes and before depreciation expense of $250,000 in 19x3 and $300,000 in 19x4. The income tax rate is 34% and taxes must be paid in cash.

Required:

1. Which of the following depreciation methods will result in the lowest income tax payments for 19x3 and 19x4 combined?
   a. Straight-line.
   b. 150% declining-balance.
   c. Sum-of-the-years'-digits.
2. Which depreciation method results in the highest net income for 19x3 and 19x4 combined?
3. Assuming you are Wellman's chief accountant, which method would you advise them to use? Explain your choice.

CASE 8-7
L.O. 2

Depreciation and Taxes

The Lakeland Corporation has been in business for less than one year. The owner, Mr. Griffin, has been asked by his accountant to select a depreciation method to use for financial reporting purposes. The accountant told Mr. Griffin that he was going to use the most accelerated method possible for income tax purposes, with most major assets to be depreciated over 18 years even though they are expected to be useful for 60 plus years. The accountant has told Griffin that this selection for financial reporting purposes will have an impact on earnings with straight-line resulting in the highest profits.

Lakeland's profits before income taxes and depreciation for the initial year of operations was about $170,000. The depreciation expense taken for tax purposes was $410,000. The range of possible depreciation expense measures for financial reporting purposes is $70,000 to $240,000.

Mr. Griffin is totally confused by this information and uncertain of the accountant's ethics given all the conflicting information. He knows you are an accounting major and asked you a number of questions at a recent dinner party with your family (friends of Griffin's).

Required:

1. What should be Lakeland's profit objective for income tax purposes?
2. What should be Lakeland's profit objective for financial reporting purposes?
3. How much better off will Lakeland be if it elects to use the $70,000 depreciation expense method rather than the method that results in $240,000 depreciation purposes? How much more cash will Lakeland have using one versus the other?
4. Is Mr. Griffin's accountant violating any accounting principles or procedures?

EVALUATING FINANCIAL STATEMENTS

CASE 8-8
L.O. 3

Change in Estimates—GM

General Motors Corporation leases automobiles to customers through its many GM dealerships. These automobiles are reported as assets on GM's books and are depreciated over their estimated useful lives. In 19x7, GM reported net income of $3,550.9 million compared to 19x6 income of $2,994.7 million, or a 20.5% increase in 19x7. However, in its financial statement footnotes, GM revealed the following information:

> In the first quarter of 19x7, (GM) revised the rates of depreciation on automobiles . . . [leased] to retail customers. . . . These revisions had the effect of increasing [GM's] 19x7 net income by $254.7 million.
>
> GM also noted the following change in the estimated life of its plant and equipment:
>
> "In the third quarter of 19x7, [GM] revised the estimated service lives of its plants and equipment and special tools [effective] January 1, 19x7. These revisions . . . had the effect of reducing 19x7 depreciation and amortization (expense) by $1,236.6 million . . ."

Assume the effect of the second change on GM's 19x7 net income was $816.1 million ($1,236.6 × (1 − tax rate) = $1,236.6 × .66).

Required:

1. What direction was the change in the life of leased automobiles?
2. What direction was the change in the life of plants, equipment, and special tools?
3. What would GM have reported as net income in 19x7 if these changes in estimates had not been made? What would have been the percentage change in 19x7 net income over 19x6 net income?
4. Was GM correct in making a change in estimate in the third quarter but carrying the effect of the change back to the beginning of the year of change?

CASE 8-9
L.O. 6

Annual Report Analysis—IBM

The following balance sheet data were reported by International Business Machines Corporation (IBM) in a recent annual report (in millions of dollars):

	19x6	*19x5*
Plant, machines, and property	$38,121	$34,483
Less: Accumulated depreciation . . .	16,853	14,803
Net book value	$21,268	$19,680

Assume that from the other financial statement data you learn that IBM recorded depreciation expense of $3,316 million and that they sold machines with a net book value of $647 million during 19x6?

Required:
What is the apparent amount of additional investment in plant, machines, and property during 19x6?

CASE 8-10
L.O. 6

Annual Report Analysis—General Electric

A recent annual report for General Electric Corporation (GE) reported the following balance sheet data:

Property, Plant, and Equipment
December 31
(in millions)

	19x6	*19x5*
Land	$ 271	$ 178
Buildings	4,087	3,449
Machinery and equipment	12,061	10,218
Other plant assets	1,955	1,861
Total original cost	$18,374	$15,706
Less:		
Accumulated depreciation balance at January 1	$ 7,806	$ 7,089
Current year expense	1,460	1,249
Asset disposals	(733)	(532)
Balance at December 31	$ 8,533	$ 7,806
Net book value	$ 9,841	$ 7,900

During 19x6, GE acquired $3,680 million in property, plant, and equipment. This included $1,638 million in assets acquired through their purchase of RCA in 19x6.

Required:
1. What was the apparent original cost of assets disposed of during 19x6 by GE?
2. What was the approximate percentage of depreciation taken on assets disposed of during 19x6 prior to their disposal?

CASE 8-11
L.O. 2, 6, 7

Analysis of Intangibles—Ralston Purina

Consider the Ralston Purina Company's (RPC's) annual report in Appendix E at the back of the text. Refer to the two footnotes, "Supplemental Balance Sheet Information" and "Analysis of Balance Sheet Changes" along with the combined amount of "depreciation and amortization" reported in the fiscal 1989 Statement of Cash Flows.

Required:
1. How much was amortization expense for fiscal 1989? (Hint: use T accounts.)
2. How much was depreciation expense for fiscal 1989?
3. What was the cost of intangibles acquired during fiscal 1989? (Hint: use T accounts.)

FINANCIAL STATEMENTS

FINANCIAL STATEMENT COMPONENTS EMPHASIZED IN CHAPTER 9

Massy Corporation
Income Statement
For 1991

Revenues
xxxx
xxxx
Expenses
Interest expense

	1991	1990
Interest expense	$ XX	$ XX

Massy Corporation
Balance Sheet
12/31/91

Current assets
xxxx
xxxx
Noncurrent assets
xxxx
xxxx
Current liabilities
Accounts payable
Notes payable
Salaries payable
Taxes payable
Current portion of long-term debt
Noncurrent liabilities
xxxx
xxxx
Stockholders' equity
xxxx
xxxx

	1991	1990
Accounts payable	$ XX	$ XX
Notes payable	XX	XX
Salaries payable	XX	XX
Taxes payable	XX	XX
Current portion of long-term debt	XX	XX

Massy Corporation
Cash Flow Statement
For 1991

Operating activities
Cash paid for interest
Investing activities
xxxx
xxxx
Financing activities
Cash from loan
Cash paid at maturity of note

	1991	1990
Cash paid for interest . .	$ (XX)	$ (XX)

	1991	1990
Cash from loan	$XXX	$ XX
Cash paid at maturity of note	(XX)	(XXX)

CHAPTER 9

Current Liabilities and Payroll

LEARNING OBJECTIVES

After studying Chapter 9, you should understand:

1. Accounting for definitely determinable liabilities, which include accounts payable, short-term notes payable, dividends payable, and the current portion of long-term debt, pp. 472-82.
2. Accounting for estimated liabilities, which include income taxes, property taxes, vacation pay, and warranties, pp. 482-90.
3. Accounting for contingent liabilities, pp. 490-91.
4. The importance of a payroll system to a company, pp. 491-92.
5. The effect of payroll deductions and employer taxes, pp. 494-97.
6. The nature of deferred income taxes (Appendix), pp. 500-502.
7. The financial statement effects of deferred income taxes (Appendix), pp. 502-5.

Liabilities were defined in Chapter 1 as claims by outsiders to receive cash, other assets, or services from the business at some future date. These claims require future sacrifice and arise from past transactions. In Chapter 2, you learned that liabilities are debts of the business that are recorded in the accounting records. Another way of saying the same thing is that liabilities are the obligations of the business to deliver assets or perform services for which money amounts can be assigned.

If at the balance sheet date, a liability is such that the cash, goods, or services owed are to be paid, provided, or performed within one year or one operating cycle, whichever is longer, the liability is current or short term; otherwise, the liability is noncurrent or long term. This chapter focuses on **current liabilities.** Noncurrent or long-term liabilities are discussed in Chapter 10.

The key to determining whether a liability is short term or long term is the expected timing of the flow of assets or services that are required to eliminate the obligation. Current liabilities can arise from transactions with suppliers, banks, employees, governments, and many other entities. Most current liabilities are paid off in a routine, ongoing manner. Suppliers' invoices usually call for payment within a month of receipt; payrolls are paid weekly, semimonthly, or monthly; taxes have defined payment dates; notes usually have fixed interest and principal payment dates. And long-term liabilities become short term when payment is scheduled within a year or operating cycle, whichever is longer, of the balance sheet date.

Appendix E of this book shows the current liabilities in an annual report of Ralston Purina Company. Although this represents typical current liability disclosure, it demonstrates that a great deal of variation exists in the terminology used to describe current liabilities. The word *payable* is often used as in "Accounts payable"; the word *accrued* is also used as in "Accrued liabilities." While no formal rules exist governing such terminology, accrual usually represents the result of adjusting entries that record payables at year-end. For some current liabilities, neither term is used, as in "Income taxes" in the "Current liabilities" section of Ralston's balance sheet.

In this chapter we categorize current liabilities as (1) definitely determinable current liabilities, (2) estimated liabilities, and (3) contingent liabilities. Although payroll is a definitely determinable current liability, we discuss it in a separate section titled "Payroll Accounting" because in most businesses payroll is a major expense that generates several liabilities. An Appendix to the chapter discusses deferred income taxes.

DEFINITELY DETERMINABLE CURRENT LIABILITIES

Objective 1
Accounting for definitely determinable liabilities.

A **definitely determinable current liability** is an existing current liability of a precisely measurable amount. The definitely determinable current liabilities discussed in this section are accounts payable, short-term notes payable, dividends payable, and the current portion of long-term debt. Later in the chapter, we discuss other liabilities that exist but whose amounts must be estimated. We also discuss several situations where a liability may result if certain future events take place.

Before looking at specifics, consider the following dialog as an introduction to the concept of definitely determinable liabilities.

Do All Liabilities Appear on the Balance Sheet?

Two friends, a bank president and a CPA partner, are having lunch and engaging in their usual kidding about each other's professions; but in this case there is a serious theme, which is a good introduction to accounting for liabilities:

Banker: Look, I lend money to companies and I rely on their financial statements, particularly the reported liabilities, because if I give them the loan, that loan will show up there on the right side of the balance sheet (It *is* the right side, correct?) along with all the rest of the debts. The more creditors the higher my risks of not being paid back.

Accountant: O.K., so what's the problem? If there is one thing we beancounters are good at it's coming up with a pretty reliable number for liabilities.

Banker: I agree with that, for the liabilities you actually put on the balance sheet, like accounts payable, salaries payable, notes payable, and all that. What I worry about are the quote liabilities unquote that you don't necessarily show. For instance, I gave a $4 million, one-year loan to a seemingly healthy company last year. It turns out that they were being sued by the government for a toxic waste spill and it could possibly take $30 million to clean it up. Now, that amount was *not* on the balance sheet even though the spill took place before the year-end.

Accountant: Listen, I don't know about that case specifically, but this is in general how I would approach such a situation. At the balance sheet date, if an event has taken place that has created a definite liability, like unpaid salary or borrowing, I would record it. If an event like a toxic spill had taken place that might create a liability in the future, whether I record it or not depends on the probability of the future actions, like the outcome of lawsuits. Now we have rules about how we determine the probabilities.

Banker: So you are admitting that it could be okay for this potential liability not to be on the balance sheet?

Accountant: It depends on the probabilities involved. When we are 100% sure that an obligation exists (that is, if it is definitely determinable), we record it even if we have to estimate the amount, like is often the case for taxes. If we are not sure, but something has happened already that makes it probable that there will be an obligation we will estimate it and record and/or disclose something according to our rules.

Banker: All I know is that it is what I don't know that can hurt me and if it's not shown on the balance sheet, how do you expect me to know about it?

Accountant: I'll bet you the price of lunch that if your people looked closely at the notes to that balance sheet they would find that something was mentioned about the problems of that toxic spill.

Banker: Maybe, but that's not the same as being shown on the balance sheet.

This conversation touches on many issues we will formally cover in the sections that follow, and it focuses on the fact that accountants must use professional judgment in all aspects of their job, even in determining whether or not a liability exists.

Accounts Payable

Accounts payable is a current liability used to record the purchase of goods and services on credit. For example, when a purchaser receives goods shipped on open account from suppliers, the transaction causes an entry of the following kind to be recorded on the customer's books:

19xx			
Apr. 1	Purchases (A).	1,000	
	Accounts Payable (L)		1,000
	To record purchase of merchandise on account.		

When the Accounts Payable account is used to record a liability, it usually means that the obligation will be paid off soon with no interest charged on the outstanding amount, although cash discounts are often given for early payment. (See Chapter 5 for a discussion of cash discounts.) If payment were made on the liability recorded above and no discount was taken, the following entry would be recorded:

19xx			
Apr. 15	Accounts Payable (L)	1,000	
	Cash (A)		1,000
	To record payment of invoice dated April 1.		

The balance sheet of a company shows the total liabilities to be paid. The accounts payable amount is based on the assumption that the company normally expects to pay all invoice amounts less the discounts offered and expected to be taken. Companies do not make an estimation of nonpayment for accounts payable such as the estimation of noncollection for accounts receivable that you learned about in Chapter 5. If the entity is a going concern (i.e., expected to stay in business for the foreseeable future), the accountant assumes that all debts will be paid according to the contractual terms that govern them. Creditors have the legal right to payment, and it is reasonable to assume that they will pursue that right to receive payment even to the point of forcing the sale of the debtor's assets.

Interest—Simple and Compound

Consider the following simple borrowing transaction by Borrower Corporation.

Borrows	*Pays*
$10,000	$11,000
1/1/x1	12/31/x1

What do you believe determined the amount paid back of $11,000? The difference between the amount received upon borrowing and the amount paid back is the interest on the loan. Interest is determined by multiplying the amount borrowed (principal) by the interest rate (a percentage applied to principal). The formula for computing interest is:

$$(\text{Interest per period}) = (\text{Principal})\begin{pmatrix}\text{Interest rate}\\ \text{per period}\end{pmatrix}(\text{Number of periods})$$

Applying the specific amounts from the case of Borrower Corporation to the above formula we get:

$$\$1{,}000 = (\$10{,}000)\,(.10)\,(1)$$

How was the interest rate determined? In this case we know that if we start with a liability of $10,000 (the principal) and we pay back $11,000 (the maturity amount) in one year, interest equals $1,000. The interest amount for a period divided by the principal at the beginning of the period is the interest rate for the period; that is, $1,000 divided by $10,000 = 10%.

If we change our example to a two-period example we can make a distinction between two methods of computing interest: simple and compound. Consider the following transaction, again at a 10% interest rate:

Method 1			*Method 2*		
Borrows		*Pays*	*Borrows*		*Pays*
$10,000		$12,000	$10,000		$12,100
1/1/x1	12/31/x1	12/31/x2	1/1/x1	12/31/x1	12/31/x2

Why is the total interest under method 1 less than under method 2? In this case the total interest for the two-year period is $2,000 for method 1 and $2,100 for method 2, computed as follows:

		Interest Computation Method 1	*Interest Computation Method 2*
1/1/x1	Principal at 1/1/x1	$10,000	$10,000
	Interest for year x1 at 10%. . . .	1,000	1,000
	Balance owed at 12/31/x1	11,000	11,000
	Interest for year x2 at 10%. . . .	1,000	1,100
	Total maturity amount	$12,000	$12,100

Method 1 demonstrates what is called **simple interest** where the interest earned in the first period is ignored in the computation of the interest for the second period; that is, we simply multiply the initial principal by the stated interest to get the interest for any period. Method 2 is an example of a **compound interest** calculation where the interest in the first period is added to the principal for the next period's computation of interest. Note that under simple interest all periods have the same interest amount; that is, (initial principal) (interest rate). Under compound interest each period has a different interest amount. Year 1 is $1,000 the same as under simple interest, but year 2 is $1,100 computed as follows: (initial principal plus unpaid interest to date) (interest rate). Throughout this text we assume compound interest. Unless otherwise stated, interest is compounded annually. Compound interest will be covered more thoroughly in Chapter 10.

Short-Term Notes Payable

A **short-term note payable** is a liability with many of the same attributes as accounts payable except that a note is a formal contract of indebtedness between a debtor (the **maker** of the note) and a creditor (the **payee** of the note). Short-term notes are usually interest bearing, but they can also be noninterest bearing. The paragraphs that follow discuss both interest-bearing short-term notes and noninterest-bearing short-term notes.

Interest-Bearing Short-Term Notes. An **interest-bearing short-term note** issued to a creditor by a debtor specifies the principal amount of the note (i.e., the

EXHIBIT 9-1

Interest-Bearing Short-Term Note

(Location)		(Date)
(Maker of note) promises to pay (Payee)		
on (Due date)	$ (Principal)	plus
interest at (Interest rate) percent per annum.		
		(Signature)

EXHIBIT 9-2

Jetstar Labs, Inc., Note

Jackson, Wyoming November 1, 19x1

Jetstar Labs, Inc., promises to pay National Bank on May 1, 19x2, one hundred thousand dollars ($100,000) plus interest at twelve (12) percent per annum.

J. R. Jet

J. R. Jet, President

initial amount borrowed), the interest rate, and the maturity date. Exhibit 9-1 gives the general format of an interest-bearing short-term note. To illustrate a short-term interest-bearing (and later noninterest-bearing) note, we will follow the transactions of Jetstar Labs, Inc.

On November 1, 19x1, Jetstar Labs, Inc. (which has a December 31 year-end), borrowed $100,000 from National Bank and signed a six-month note (see Exhibit 9-2) at an annual interest rate of 12%. Often, in this text and in the real world, the phrase *annual interest rate* and *interest rate* are used interchangeably. Unless stated otherwise, assume that *interest rate* means annual interest rate. The principal and interest are to be paid on May 1, 19x2. The initial liability of Jetstar is the face amount or principal of the note, $100,000. The additional liability for interest is recorded at year-end in a separate account called Interest Payable. The total amount paid at maturity is $106,000, which is the principal plus interest for the six-month period. The interest accrued at year-end is recorded by means of an adjusting entry and represents two months' interest on the $100,000 principal. The journal entries to record the note on Jetstar's books, the accrued interest, and the payment of the note at maturity are:

19x1			
Nov. 1	Cash (A)	100,000	
	Short-Term Notes Payable (L)		100,000
	To record 12%, six-month note.		

Dec. 31	Interest Expense (E).	2,000	
	Interest Payable (L)		2,000
	To record interest for two-month period: $100,000 × .12 × 2⁄12 = $2,000.		
19x2			
May 1	Interest Expense (E)	4,000	
	Interest Payable (L)	2,000	
	Short-Term Notes Payable (L)	100,000	
	Cash (A)		106,000
	To record payment of principal plus interest and record interest expense for four-month period in 19x2.		

The entries above indicate that at December 31, 19x1, Jetstar was liable for the $100,000 principal plus $2,000 interest, or $102,000.

At December 31, 19x1, does Jetstar owe $102,000 or is this merely an accounting representation of an economic theory? This question is difficult to answer because the note contract indicates that principal plus interest is due on the maturity date; it does not say how much Jetstar legally owes on December 31, 19x1. Accountants, however, are in the business of communicating economic substance rather than legal form; and standard accounting principles state that interest accrues under the assumption that each month covered by the note gets the same benefit from a short-term loan. If the note were to be paid off early, say, on December 31, the $102,000 is a reasonable approximation of what National Bank would accept. Unless specified in the contract, the bank is not obligated to accept the early payment, and certainly it cannot force the debtor to make an early payment.

We will now review the fundamental concept of the effects of interest accumulated on the total liability related to the obligation by means of the analysis of Exhibit 9-3.

At the date the note is issued, the principal of $100,000 (the amount of cash received) is the liability balance. Interest accumulates evenly throughout the term of the note. At 12/31/x1, $2,000 of interest has accumulated so the total obligation related to the note is $102,000. At 5/1/x2, the maturity date, another $4,000 of interest has accumulated which gives a total liability related to the note of $106,000 and this is the cash payment to the maker of the note. Therefore total interest is the total *cash out* of $106,000 *minus* the total *cash in* of $100,000 or $6,000. The $6,000 is recognized as interest expense over two periods; 19x1 gets $2,000 and 19x2 gets $4,000 of interest expense.

Noninterest-Bearing Short-Term Notes. A **noninterest-bearing short-term note** does not specify an interest rate, and its maturity value is the face value of the note. For example, on November 1, 19x1, Jetstar could have promised to pay National Bank $106,000 on May 1, 19x2. Although the face value of the note is $106,000, Jetstar does not receive $106,000 from the bank. Instead, interest is taken into consideration, and Jetstar receives something less than $106,000, depending on the "implied" interest rate. Assume Jetstar receives $100,000; the $6,000 difference between what is received and paid in a noninterest-bearing note is the bank's interest charge for the use of the $100,000. Although the interest rate is not specified, the interest of $6,000 on the $100,000 borrowed is for one

EXHIBIT 9-3

Cash Flow and Interest Accumulation on a Note

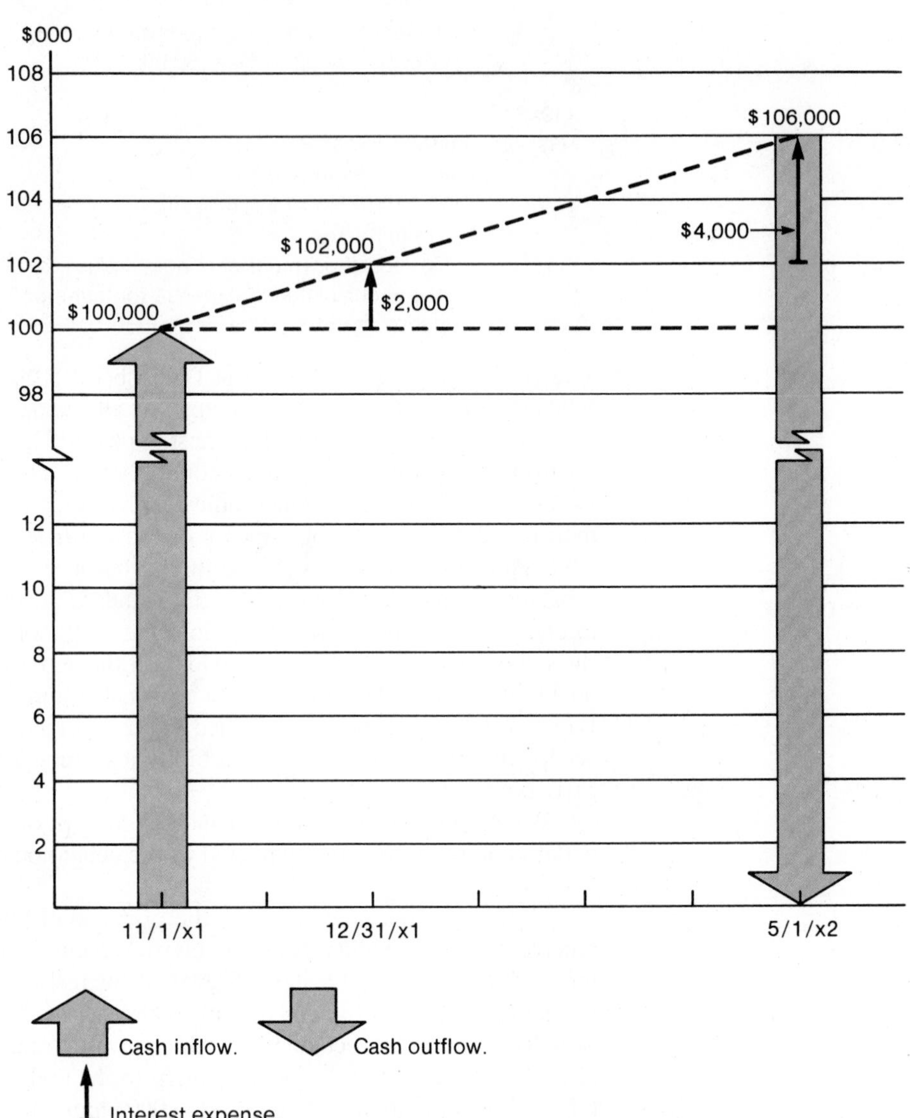

half of a year and the interest rate is seen to be 12%. This interest rate is then used to make the interest calculations.

The journal entries to record the noninterest-bearing note are:

19x1			
Nov. 1	Cash (A)	100,000	
	Discount on Notes Payable (XL)	6,000	
	Short-Term Notes Payable (L)		106,000
	To record noninterest-bearing note.		
Dec. 31	Interest Expense (E)	2,000	
	Discount on Notes Payable (XL)		2,000
	To record interest for two-month period: $100,000 \times .12 \times {}^2/_{12} = \$2,000$.		

19x2			
May 1	Interest Expense (E)	4,000	
	Short-Term Notes Payable (L)	106,000	
	Discount on Notes Payable (XL)		4,000
	Cash (A)		106,000
	To record payment of principal plus interest and record interest expense for four-month period.		

Note that the economic substance of the noninterest-bearing note is no different than an interest-bearing note. Compare the balance sheet and income statement disclosure under each type of note:

Interest Bearing:

Jetstar Labs, Inc.
Partial Balance Sheet
December 31, 19x1

Current liabilities:	
Notes payable.	$100,000
Interest payable	2,000
	$102,000

Jetstar Labs, Inc.
Partial Income Statement
For the Year Ended December 31, 19x1

Expenses:	
Interest expense	$ 2,000

Noninterest Bearing:

Jetstar Labs, Inc.
Partial Balance Sheet
December 31, 19x1

Current liabilities:	
Notes payable.	$106,000
Discount on notes payable.	(4,000)
	$102,000

Jetstar Labs, Inc.
Partial Income Statement
For the Year Ended December 31, 19x1

Expenses:	
Interest expense	$ 2,000

The account, Discount on Notes Payable, is a contra account (one that is subtracted from another account—Notes Payable, in this case). Since the noninterest-bearing note has the maturity value stated on the note, that amount is often recorded as notes payable, but the contra account is used to reduce the liability to its appropriate balance.

Dividends Payable

A corporation's board of directors has the right to decide whether or not to distribute earnings to its stockholders in the form of **cash dividends** and must decide on the amount to be paid on outstanding stock. Once cash dividends are declared, they become definite obligations of the company. As an obligation, declared cash dividends are recorded as a current liability. If no dividends are declared, no obligation exists, and no liability is recorded.

Time usually elapses between the **declaration date** and the **payment date** of cash dividends, and the establishment of the liability on the declaration date recognizes that the company owes money to the stockholders at that point. For example, if on December 15, 19x1, Los Alamos, Inc., has one million common shares outstanding and declares a $0.25 per share dividend to be paid on January 15, 19x2, the journal entries for the declaration and payment are:

19x1			
Dec. 15	Dividends (SE)	250,000	
	Dividends Payable (L)		250,000
	To record declaration of dividend: 1,000,000 × $0.25 = $250,000.		

19x2			
Jan. 15	Dividends Payable (L)	250,000	
	Cash (A)		250,000
	To record payment of dividend.		

When dividends are discussed in detail in Chapter 11, you will learn that not all forms of dividends and other disbursements to stockholders have such clear-cut accounting treatment.

Current Portion of Long-Term Debt

As stated at the beginning of this chapter, **long-term liabilities** are those liabilities that are not expected to be paid to creditors within one year or one operating cycle, whichever is longer. However, the current portion of a long-term debt is classified on the balance sheet as a current liability. For example, assume that a company borrows \$300,000 and signs a three-year note on December 31, 19x1, to be paid in three payments on December 31, 19x2, 19x3, and 19x4, plus 10% annual interest on the unpaid balance. Exhibit 9-4 shows the relationship of cash in, cash out, interest, and the liability balances on each date after each payment. Again, the total interest is the total cash out of \$360,000 minus the total cash in of \$300,000 or \$60,000 allocated to 19x2, 19x3, and 19x4 (\$30,000, \$20,000, and \$10,000, respectively). The following series of journal entries are recorded:

19x1			
Dec. 31	Cash (A)	300,000	
	Notes Payable (L)		300,000
	To record 10%, three-year note.		
19x2			
Dec. 31	Interest Expense (E)	30,000	
	Notes Payable (L)	100,000	
	Cash (A)		130,000
	To record payment of \$100,000 on the principal and \$30,000 in interest (\$300,000 × .10 = \$30,000).		
19x3			
Dec. 31	Interest Expense (E)	20,000	
	Notes Payable (L)	100,000	
	Cash (A)		120,000
	To record payment of \$100,000 on the principal and \$20,000 in interest (\$200,000 × .10 = \$20,000).		
19x4			
Dec. 31	Interest Expense (E)	10,000	
	Notes Payable (L)	100,000	
	Cash (A)		110,000
	To record payment of \$100,000 on the principal and \$10,000 in interest (\$100,000 × .10 = \$10,000).		

The following table shows how the current liability and long-term liability of this \$300,000 note is related to its total liability during the three-year period from December 31, 19x1, to December 31, 19x4:

		Balance Sheet Classification	
Date	*Total Liability* =	*Current Liability** +	*Long-Term Liability*†
12/31/x1	$300,000	$100,000	$200,000
12/31/x2	200,000	100,000	100,000
12/31/x3	100,000	100,000	0
12/31/x4	0	0	0

*To be paid within one year or one operating cycle if longer.
†To be paid after one year or one operating cycle if longer.

EXHIBIT 9-4

Cash Flows and Interest Amounts on a Long-Term Note

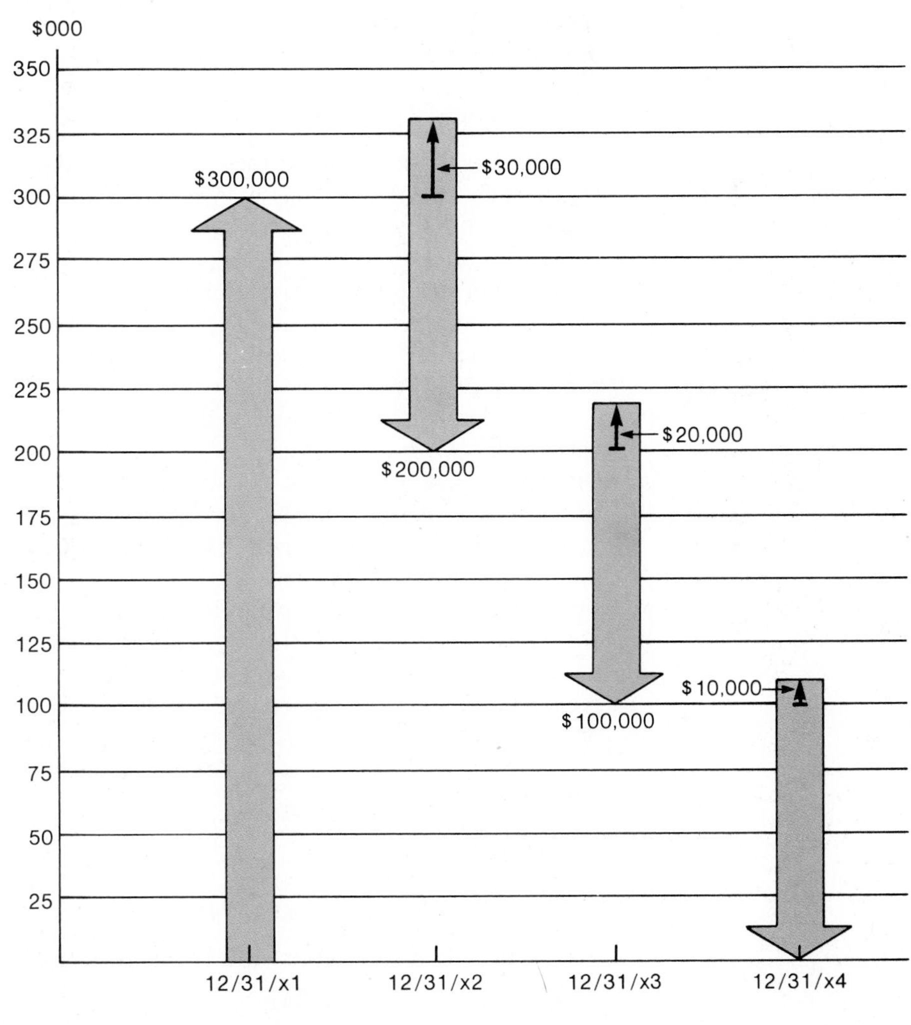

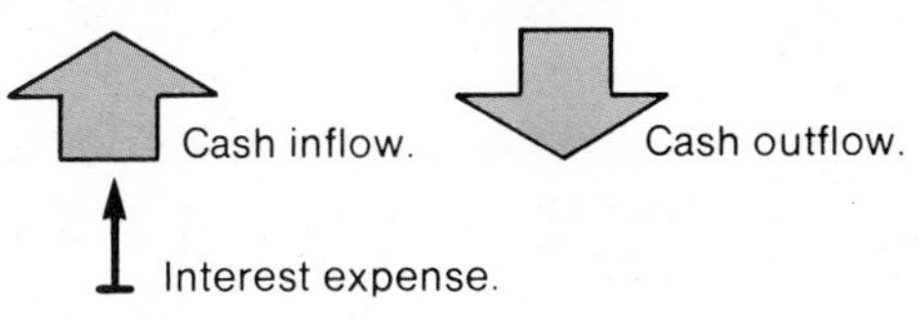

It is important to see that in this case, no interest is accrued at year-end either because no time has elapsed (as on December 31, 19x1) or because the interest has been paid up-to-date (as is the case on December 31, 19x2, 19x3, and 19x4). Also, because interest is paid each year, there is no compounding of interest even though this note extends beyond one year. Although it is expected that the interest amounts will be paid as scheduled, no liability exists for interest until time has elapsed.

ESTIMATED LIABILITIES

Not all liability amounts are known with certainty at financial statement dates. When a company has a liability with a reasonable basis for estimating or measuring the amount that must be paid, the company makes the estimate and records the liability; these are **estimated liabilities.** Liabilities are commonly estimated for income taxes, property taxes, vacation pay, warranties, and many other obligations where precise amounts are not known.

Income Taxes

Federal, state, and local governments levy **income taxes** on a business's taxable income. Businesses compute their income tax obligations on income tax forms that include the tax versions of revenues and expenses called *taxable revenue* and *deductions*, respectively. The rules for determining taxable revenues and tax deductions often differ from the rules for inclusion of revenues and expenses on income statements. In this subsection, we examine the current liability created by the income tax obligation. The appendix to this chapter discusses the accounting treatment for differences between accounting and tax measurements of pre-tax income.

Objective 2
Accounting for estimated liabilities, which include income taxes, property taxes, vacation pay, and warranties.

Why doesn't a company know its exact income tax obligation at the balance sheet date of each accounting period? Because of the complexity of the tax law, the time needed to complete the tax return for one year usually extends far into the next year. For this reason, the tax obligation shown on income statements may be different from the final tax obligation. By the filing deadline, the company often pays an estimated amount and files for an extension, which allows the company to delay submitting its final tax return for several months after the normal tax deadline. Thus, the Income Tax Payable account shown on many balance sheets is an estimate based on knowledge as of the date the balance sheet is prepared. Such an estimate creates a current liability that will be paid later and one which will probably be adjusted further when the final tax filing is made.

Consider the following example of cash payments and accruals for Universal Alliance, Inc.:

19x1			
Dec. 31	Income Tax Expense (E).	720,000	
	Income Taxes Payable (L)		720,000
	To record estimated tax expense for 19x1.		
19x2			
Apr. 15	Income Taxes Payable (L)	720,000	
	Cash (A)		720,000
	To record cash payment of estimate when filing for an extension.		

July 1	Income Tax Expense (E).	40,000	
	Cash (A)		40,000
	To record the payment of $40,000 on the final filing of 19x1 income tax return, representing additional tax of $39,000 plus a $1,000 interest charge.		

Note that the tax expense for 19x1 was underestimated by $39,000, and the government charges interest of $1,000 on the underestimated amount. Changes in estimates such as this are usually recorded as expense in the period the company makes the final determination of the correct amount. For Universal Alliance, the $720,000 estimated tax expense was recorded in 19x1, and the additional $40,000 expense from 19x1 was recorded in 19x2. This agrees with the general principle that changes in estimates are reported in the current period, or current and future periods only.

Most companies pay income taxes during the year; therefore, the liability balance at year-end does not equal the total obligation for taxes for the entire year. To illustrate the procedure companies generally use to record taxes, assume Print, Inc., has a 30% tax rate. The schedule that follows summarizes Print's activity for each quarter in the 19x1 operating year by listing its net income before taxes (NIBT), tax expense, taxable income, tax payments, and current liability at quarter-end.

	NIBT	*Tax Expense*	*Taxable Income*	*Payment to Government*	*Current Liability at Quarter-End*
3/31/x1 . . .	$ 300,000	$ 90,000	$ 300,000	$ 0	$90,000
4/15/x1 . . .				90,000	
6/30/x1 . . .	300,000	90,000	300,000	0	90,000
7/15/x1 . . .				90,000	
9/30/x1 . . .	300,000	90,000	300,000	0	90,000
10/15/x1. . . .				90,000	
12/31/x1. . . .	300,000	90,000	300,000	0	90,000
1/15/x2 . . .				90,000	
Total	$1,200,000	$360,000	$1,200,000	$360,000	

Note that in this example even if tax expense exactly equals tax liability at each quarter-end balance sheet date, we still have a current liability at the balance sheet date because the actual payment to the government comes after the end of the accounting period.

The summary journal entries made in 19x1 for Print's 19x1 taxes are:

Income Tax Expense (E)	360,000	
Income Taxes Payable (L)		360,000
To record four quarters of tax expense.		
Income Taxes Payable (L)	270,000	
Cash (A)		270,000
To record payment of taxes to the government at the end of quarters 1, 2, and 3.		

The Income Taxes Payable account balance of $90,000 is a current liability for the unpaid taxes at the balance sheet date, December 31, 19x1.

Estimated Property Tax

For many local governments such as cities and counties, the property tax is a major source of tax revenue. **Property taxes** are usually based on a stated percentage of assessed values of real property (land and building) and personal property (property, other than real property, such as furniture, automobiles, jewelry, inventory, and sometimes stocks and bonds). Businesses must pay property taxes the same as individuals, and the differences in the time periods covered by the property tax bill and the business's fiscal periods often lead to the necessity of estimates.

The following example illustrates how companies use estimates for property taxes. Motion Electric, Inc., a corporation located in Arbor City with a December 31 year-end, began business operations on January 1, 19x1. On September 1 of each year, Arbor City sends out property tax bills (due September 30) for the period January 1 through December 31 of that year. Motion Electric estimates that property taxes for 19x1 will total $60,000. Since Motion Electric prepares quarterly financial statements, it estimated its property tax for quarters 1 and 2 and made the following journal entries on March 31 and June 30:

19x1			
Mar. 31	Property Tax Expense (E)	15,000	
	Property Taxes Payable (L)		15,000
	To record estimated property tax for the first quarter.		
June 30	Property Tax Expense (E)	15,000	
	Property Taxes Payable (L)		15,000
	To record estimated property tax for the second quarter.		

The diagram and bar chart in Exhibit 9-5 illustrate Motion Electric's accounting for property tax. To study Exhibit 9-5, begin with the horizontal axis on the diagram and bar chart that show the four quarters of 19x1. In the diagram, the heavy dot represents the cumulative property tax expense, and the square represents the cumulative cash paid. The $15,000 located at the heavy dot above quarter 1 in the diagram indicates that Motion Electric recognized this $15,000 as an expense and as a current liability. The square on the horizontal axis above quarter 1 indicates that the cash paid to March 31 is zero. The $15,000 is also shown in the bar chart above quarter 1. The June 30 entry is indicated in the diagram and bar chart in the same manner as the March 31 entry. Since Motion Electric has not paid any cash on June 30, the square in the diagram is at zero; however, the cumulative expense is increased to $30,000 as indicated by the heavy dot, and the current liability has grown to $30,000.

On September 30, 19x1, Motion Electric paid the $72,000 property tax bill and made the following entry:

19x1			
Sept. 30	Property Tax Expense (E)	24,000	
	Property Taxes Payable (L)	30,000	
	Prepaid Property Taxes (A)	18,000	
	Cash (A)		72,000
	To record payment of 19x1 property tax bill.		

Above quarter 3 in the diagram of Exhibit 9-5, the square indicating cumulative cash paid has moved to $72,000. The heavy dot indicating cumulative expense has moved to $54,000. The increase from $30,000 cumulated expense to $54,000 is explained in the bar chart above quarter 3. When Motion Electric esti-

EXHIBIT 9-5

Relationship among Property Tax Cash Flow, Expense, Liability, and Prepayments

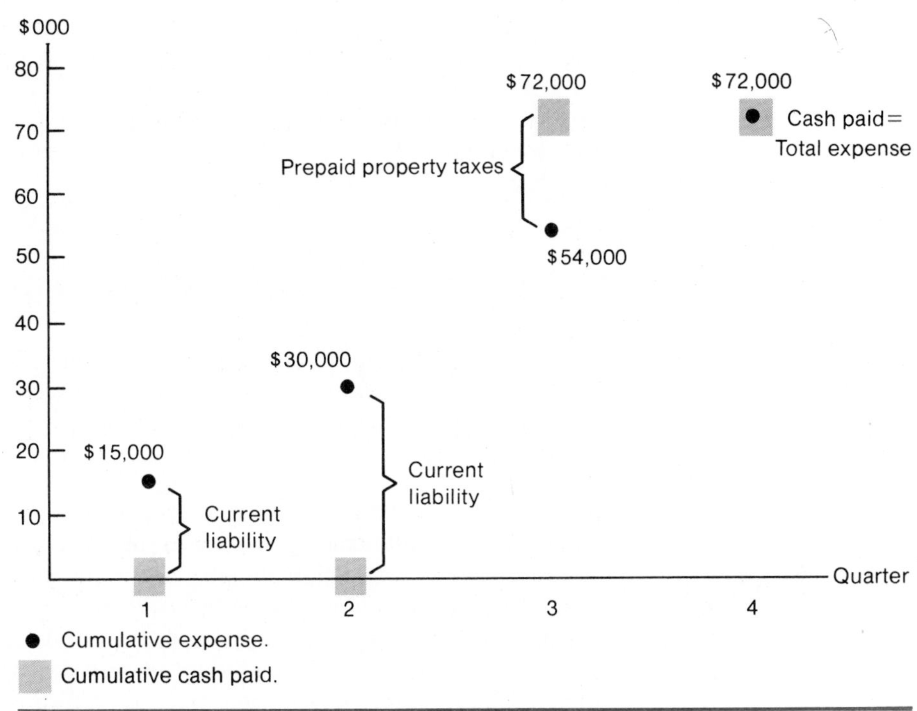

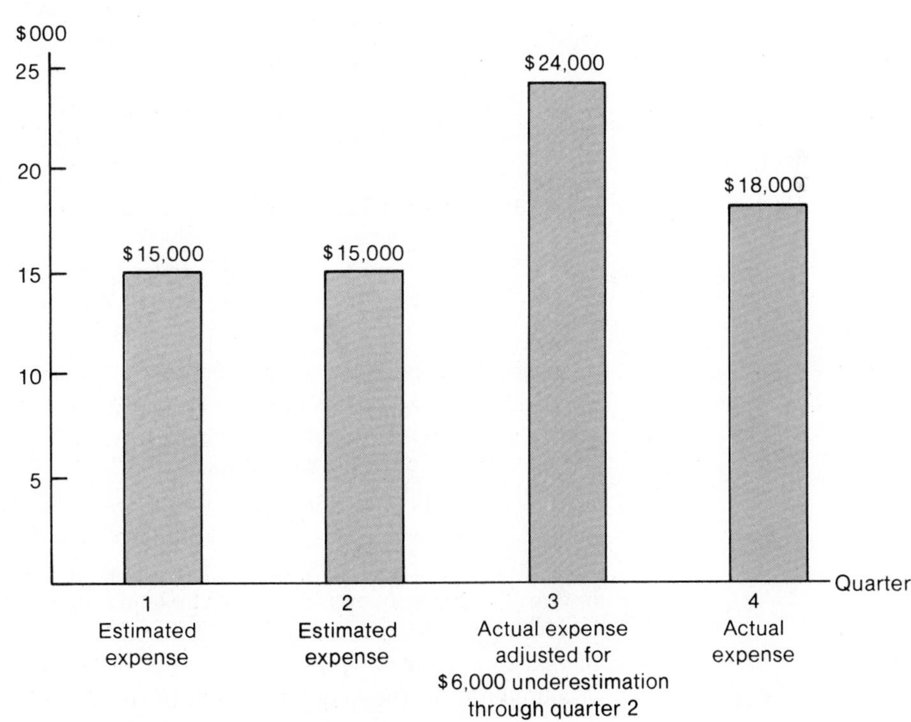

mated its yearly property tax at $60,000, $15,000 was allotted to each quarter. Since receiving the $72,000 tax bill, Motion Electric knows that each quarter should have been allotted $18,000 ($72,000 ÷ 4 quarters = $18,000 per quarter);

thus, expense through quarter 2 was underestimated by $6,000. When this $6,000 underestimate is added to the $30,000 already expensed plus the $18,000 for quarter 3, the cumulative expense through quarter 3 is $54,000. Since Motion Electric paid the entire $72,000 on September 30, the $18,000 allotted to quarter 4 is a prepaid asset.

At year-end Motion Electric records the following journal entry for the fourth quarter:

19x1			
Dec. 31	Property Tax Expense (E)	18,000	
	Prepaid Property Taxes (A).		18,000
	To allocate prepaid property tax to the fourth quarter.		

The final $18,000 expense entry on December 31, 19x1, eliminates the prepayment. Above quarter 4 in the diagram, the cumulative expense equals the cash paid for the year (the heavy dot is inside the square), and no liability or expense remains on the books at the end of quarter 4.

Vacation Pay

Some businesses allow employees to accumulate, rather than use, vacation time. The amount of time employees have earned and not taken at the end of an accounting period is **vacation liability** and represents an obligation of the business.[1] Usually, the fiscal period in which the vacation is earned absorbs the expense associated with paying employees for time off. Any unclaimed vacation pay at period end is accounted for by an accrual entry based on an estimate of the cost of providing the vacation time in the future.

Assume that a company has an employee who earns one day of vacation for each full month worked and that the employee's salary is $100 per day in 19x1 and 19x2. The employee took no vacation in 19x1 and worked all 12 months. During January 19x2, the employee took all 12 days of vacation accumulated through December 31, 19x1. The journal entries to account for the 19x1 vacation pay are:

19x1			
Dec. 31	Vacation Expense (E)	1,200	
	Estimated Vacation Liability (L)		1,200
	To record unused vacation for 19x1: 12 months × 1 day of vacation × $100 = $1,200		
19x2			
January	Estimated Vacation Liability (L)	1,200	
	Salaries Payable (L)		1,200
	To record vacation taken: 12 days × $100 = $1,200.		

Note that 19x2 is not charged with vacation expense for vacation earned in 19x1. Year 1 was charged with 12 months' salary expense (months worked in year 1) and 12 days' vacation expense (vacation earned in year 1 but taken in year 2). This is an application of the matching principle, where the period that received the benefit is charged with the resulting expense. Of course, at the end of year 2, any outstanding vacation time earned in 19x2 by that date would be accounted for in the manner shown above.

[1]See *FASB Statement No. 43,* "Accounting for Compensated Absences" (Norwalk, Conn.: FASB, 1980), for more details.

Warranties

Many businesses guarantee their products against defects for a certain period of time after the sale. The expected costs of honoring **warranty commitments** should be assigned to the period in which the revenue for the sale of the warranted item is earned. Again, the objective is to match the expense with the period of benefit, and it is assumed that offering warranties enhances sales. Thus, the period of sale should absorb the associated warranty expense.

To record estimates of outstanding warranty commitments at the end of each accounting period, adjusting entries are used. Because the actual expenditures are usually different from the estimates, subsequent periods' income statements will be affected by the difference.

Assume that Orange Computer, Inc., begins to manufacture and sell printers for microcomputers during May 19x1 and stops manufacturing the printers in 19x2 with no sales after December 31, 19x2. No warranty expenditures are expected after December 31, 19x3. At December 31, 19x3, the following facts and estimates are known:

	19x1	*19x2*	*19x3*
Sales	$18,000,000	$20,000,000	0
Total estimated warranty cost for annual sales	2% of sales (= $360,000)	2% of sales (= $400,000)	0
Actual warranty costs incurred during the year	$ 0	$ 410,000	$390,000

On December 31, 19x1, Orange Computer made the following entry:

19x1 Dec. 31	Warranty Expense (E)	360,000	
	Warranty Payable (L)		360,000
	To record estimated warranty costs at 2% of sales.		

During 19x2, Orange Computer made the following summary entry for amounts expended on warranty activities:

During 19x2	Warranty Payable (L)	410,000	
	Cash, Supplies, Wages, etc.		410,000
	To record settlements of warranty claims.		

Since Orange Computer spent $410,000 for warranty activities during 19x2, Warranty Payable has a $50,000 debit balance before adjustment on December 31, 19x2; that is, the net of the beginning credit balance of $360,000 and the debit of $410,000 is a debit of $50,000. The entry to record the adjustment for the warranty expense at December 31, 19x2, is:

19x2 Dec. 31	Warranty Expense (E)	400,000	
	Warranty Payable (L)		400,000
	To record estimated warranty costs associated with 19x2 sales: $20,000,000 × .02.		

The following T account depicts the 19x1 and 19x2 activity:

Warranty Payable

		19x1 Dec. 31	360,000
19x2	410,000	19x2 Dec. 31	400,000
		Bal.	350,000

During 19x3, the company paid out $390,000 in warranties and made the following entry:

During 19x3	Warranty Payable (L)	350,000	
	Warranty Expense (E)	40,000	
	Cash, Supplies, Wages, etc.		390,000
	To record settlements of warranty claims.		

The Warranty Payable account as of December 31, 19x3, is as follows:

Warranty Payable

		19x1 Dec. 31	360,000
19x2	410,000	19x2 Dec. 31	400,000
		Bal.	350,000
19x3	350,000		
		Bal.	0

Let's review the economic flows, expenses, and liabilities related to Orange's warranty commitments. In 19x1, Orange Computer had no outflows related to warranties, but it recognized $360,000 in warranties expense and, therefore, $360,000 in the current liability Warranty Payable. In 19x2, Orange Computer had outflows of $410,000 related to actual warranty claims. These claims could have stemmed from sales made in either 19x1, 19x2, or both. At December 31, 19x2, Orange Computer must recognize a liability equal to the best estimate of the future outflows for warranties. If we assume that 2% of sales is still the best estimate of warranty costs at the end of 19x2, then $400,000 should be recorded as warranty expense for 19x2, leaving a liability of $350,000 for estimated future claims. The cumulative estimated warranty commitment to date of $760,000 (2% of cumulative sales of $38 million) minus the cumulative warranty payments to date of $410,000 equals the current Warranty Payable at December 31, 19x2, of $350,000.

Exhibit 9-6 shows the three-year history of Orange Computer's warranty obligation. The heavy dot in the exhibit represents the cumulative warranty expense (the total recognized expense for the current and previous periods), and the square represents the cumulative outflows (the total cash payments and other outputs related to warranties of the product for the current and previous

EXHIBIT 9-6

Relationship between Orange Computer's Warranty Expense, Cash Payments, and Warranty Payable

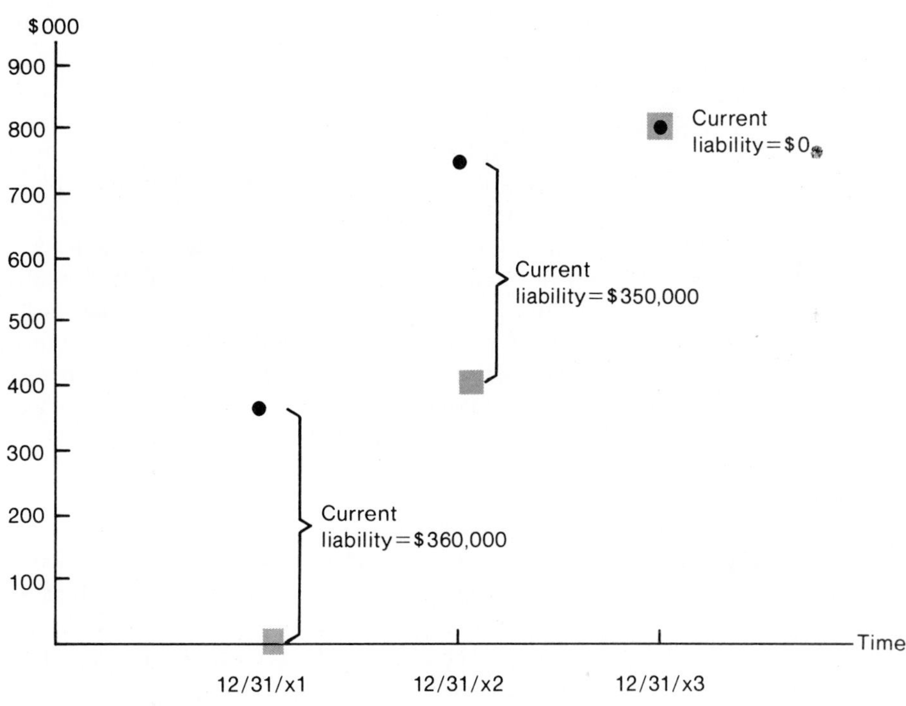

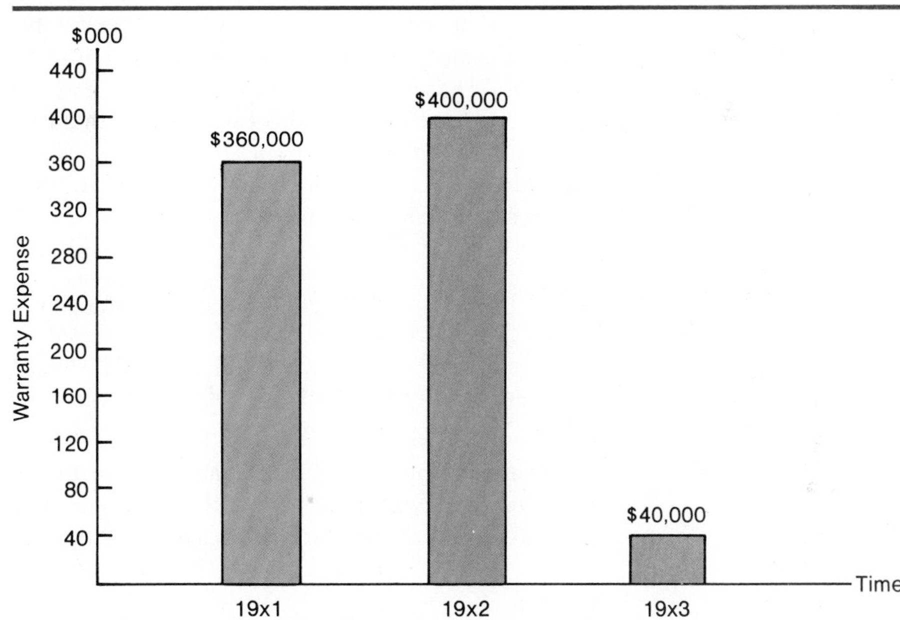

periods). As indicated on December 31, 19x1, the current liability is $360,000 because the expense charged to date exceeds the payments to date (indicated by the square above 12/31/x1 on the time line) by that amount. On December 31, 19x2, the current liability is $350,000 because new sales have increased the cumulative expense to date to $760,000 (indicated by the heavy dot above 12/31/x2 on the time line) and the cumulative payments to date (indicated by the square above 12/31/x2) amount to only $410,000. On December 31, 19x3, because the printer line has been discontinued and under the assumption that no further warranties are in effect, the total payments to date equal the total obligation estimated for the printers sold (indicated by the heavy dot inside the square above 12/31/x3 on the time line), and no liability remains. The bar chart shows the warranty expense charged each year. Note that year 3, in which no sales of printers were made, is charged with $40,000 of warranty expense. Again, this is an application of the general principle that the current year absorbs the effects of previous inaccuracies in estimates. Total cumulative expense over the three years for warranties exactly equals $800,000, which is the total amount of payments made to settle warranty claims.

CONTINGENT LIABILITIES

Contingent liabilities occur when a company does not actually have a current obligation but a real possibility exists that an obligation will develop based on the resolution of a past event. Review the discussion on page 473, "Do all liabilities appear on the balance sheet?" as an introduction to the following material on contingent liabilities.

Objective 3
Accounting for contingent liabilities.

A chemical company has a toxic spill, and some of the surrounding farmland may have been affected. However, the company disputes all claims made by the owners of the farmland, and a $30 million lawsuit ensues. At year-end, the lawsuit is yet to be resolved. Should the accountant for the chemical company record a liability because of this **contingency** (the possibility of a future payment or sacrifice because of a past event)? The answer depends on the probability of an ensuing legal claim. In this case, assume that the chemical company loses the suit in 19x2, and a judgment of $12 million is made on June 30, 19x2. Of course, the outcome was unknown on December 31, 19x1. Let's review the facts by means of the following time line:

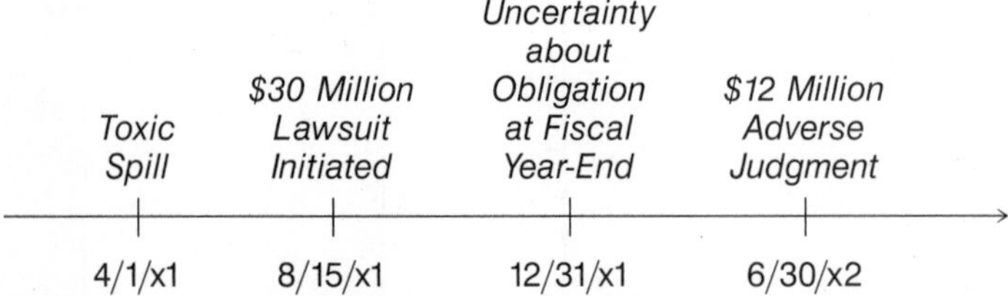

If at December 31, 19x1, the attorney for the company believed that an adverse judgment was probable and that the best estimate of the amount the company would be required to pay was $10 million, the following entries would be made:

19x1			
Dec. 31	Loss—Toxic Spill (E)	10,000,000	
	Estimated Lawsuit Liability (L)		10,000,000
	To record the estimated loss resulting from a toxic spill.		

19x2			
June 30	Loss—Toxic Spill (E)	2,000,000	
	Estimated Lawsuit Liability (L)	10,000,000	
	Cash (A).		12,000,000
	To record settlement of lawsuit.		

Note that the chemical company did not record an amount at the time of the spill because at that time the company did not believe it was liable. Since the company believed that by year-end $10 million would probably have to be paid, the estimated liability was recorded even though it was possible that the verdict would be favorable, and no payment would be made. Although the contingency is created at the time of the spill, an estimated liability was recorded only when the payment was deemed probable and a reasonable estimate could be made of the amount.

When a company believes it will be liable for some damages but is unsure of the estimated amount, a footnote disclosure is required in the balance sheet.[2] Companies may also use footnotes to explain details about contingent liabilities reported in the balance sheet.

Another type of contingency exists when a company may have to pay a third party if another party does not perform according to a contract. In this contingency, the money amounts may be known, but the unanswered question is whether a payment is necessary. For example, assume Company A guarantees the debt of one of its suppliers, Company B. Company A may have made this guarantee so that Company B could secure a bank loan to finance the facilities needed to manufacture a product for Company A. Because it is important to Company A that Company B get the loan, Company A is willing to guarantee that default by Company B will be reimbursed by Company A. In such a case, Company A is said to be contingently liable in the event of Company B's default. A similar situation is created when a company discounts a note with recourse. If the maker defaults, the payee who discounted the note must pay (see Chapter 7). When the amounts involved are significant, these contingencies are usually reported in a footnote to the balance sheet.

The excerpts from several financial statements appear in Exhibit 9-7. The Allis Chalmers and Warner-Lambert excerpts illustrate a common type of contingent liability. The companies state that certain contingencies exist but that management and legal counsel do not believe that the resolutions of these contingencies will materially affect the financial statements. The Owens-Illinois example is more precise in that a specific reason and amount are stated. Remember that these disclosures are in notes to the financial statements and not recorded as liabilities. They represent unresolved matters that may require the recording of measurable liabilities in the future.

PAYROLL ACCOUNTING

Objective 4
The importance of a payroll system to a company.

In most companies, the payroll (salaries and wages) is a recurring and important function. The company's unpaid salaries and wages at the end of an accounting period are shown as current liabilities on the balance sheet. Since most companies withhold taxes, insurance, and other amounts from an employee's paycheck,

[2]For more details regarding when footnote disclosure is required, see *FASB Statement No. 5,* "Accounting for Contingencies" (Norwalk, Conn.: FASB, 1975).

EXHIBIT 9-7

Examples of Annual Report Disclosures of Contingent Liabilities

Allis Chalmers

Excerpt from footnotes:

Commitments and Contingent Liabilities
There are various lawsuits pending against the Company and its subsidiaries arising in the normal course of business. Management believes, based on the opinion of counsel, that final disposition of these actions will not have a materially adverse effect on financial position or results of operations.

Warner-Lambert Company

Excerpt from footnotes:

NOTE 11
Contingencies
Various claims, suits and complaints, such as those involving government regulations, patents and trademarks and product liability claims, arise in the ordinary course of Warner-Lambert's business. In the opinion of Warner-Lambert, all such pending matters are without merit or are of such kind or involve such amounts, as would not have a material adverse effect on the consolidated operating results or financial position of Warner-Lambert if disposed of unfavorably.

Owens-Illinois

Excerpt from footnotes:

Contingencies. Owens-Illinois was contingently liable at December 31, 1985, under guarantees of loans and other obligations in the principal amount of $29.5 million. . . . The Company is one of a number of defendants (typically ten to twenty) in a substantial number of lawsuits by persons alleging personal injury as a result of exposure to dust from asbestos fibers.

these withholdings, or **payroll deductions,** create current liabilities owed to many different entities and are also shown on the balance sheet if they are unpaid at the end of an accounting period.

A company usually follows a routine process or system to prepare its payroll. The size of the company and its individual needs dictate the type of system used. Payroll systems range from the simplest manual system used for four or five employees to the sophisticated data processing system used by large companies with thousands of employees. This section begins with a brief introduction to the payroll system. Discussions on social security taxes, federal and state income tax withholding, other payroll deductions, and unemployment taxes follow.

Payroll System

The payroll process has received much attention because of its importance and the relatively large money amounts involved. Companies must maintain accurate employee records on the employee's date of employment, name, address, pay rate, age, dependents for personal income tax withholding purposes, hours worked, vacation time allowed and taken, and much more.

Payroll systems must also be controlled so that companies can prevent payroll fraud. Internal control methods are designed to prevent the issuing of payroll checks to nonexistent workers and the payment of incorrect amounts. Controlling payroll fraud requires an integration of efforts and records across several departments of a business.

EXHIBIT 9-8

Payroll System for Factory Assembly Workers

Departments			
Personnel	**Worker's factory department (assembly)**	**Accounting**	**Treasurer**
Hiring Promotion Termination	Authorization of hours worked	Preparation of payroll checks Maintenance of records	Signing of checks Distribution of checks

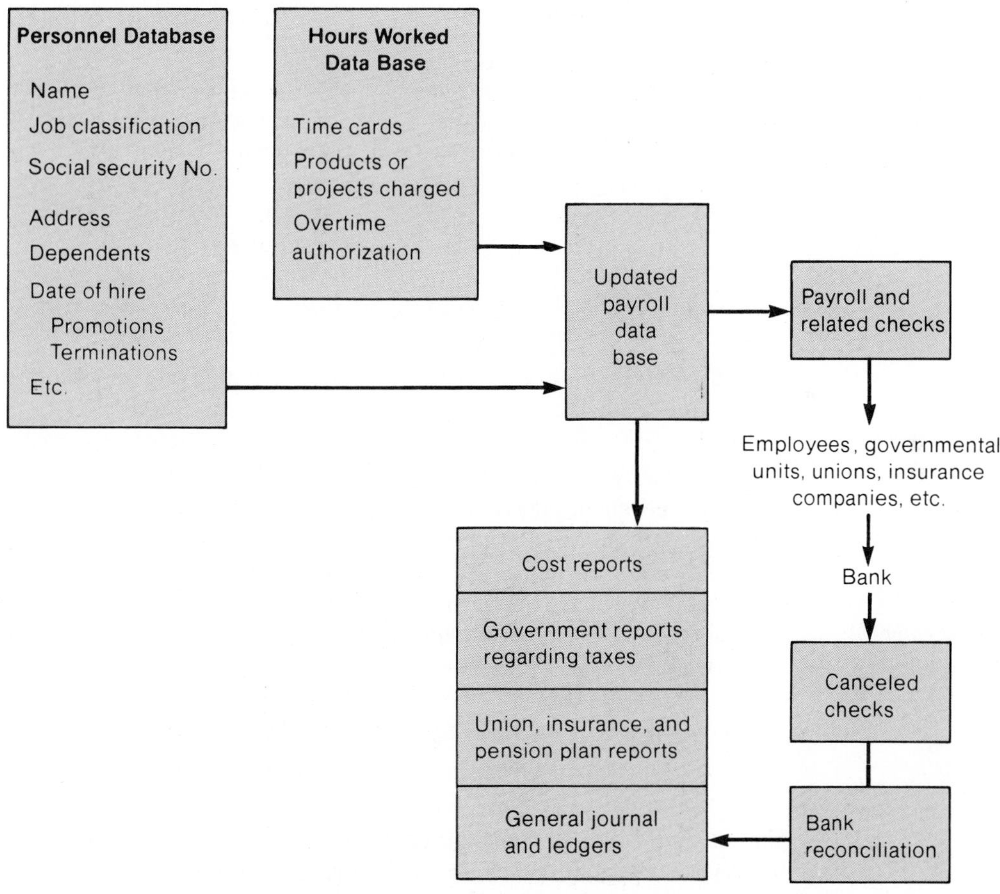

Exhibit 9-8 illustrates some of the main features of a factory assembly payroll system in which information is accessible electronically by various departments. Notice the separation of duties across the departments. In the example shown in Exhibit 9-8, the stored Personnel Database may be accessed by more than one department for various purposes. For instance, the accounting department needs some of the information to process the payroll. This accessibility creates both new control problems and opportunities to solve old control problems.

The preparation of payroll checks and maintenance of the payroll records shown in Exhibit 9-8 includes keeping track of deductions made from employees' pay such as those made for social security taxes, federal and state income taxes, insurance premiums, pension contributions, and so on. Employers must also pay certain payroll taxes such as social security, federal unemployment taxes, state unemployment taxes, and workmen's accident compensation taxes. Thus, you should remember that in addition to acting as collection agents for social security taxes and income taxes, employers must pay certain payroll taxes based on the gross earnings of employees.

The following summarizes the payroll responsibilities of employees and employers often found in practice:

Employee Responsibilities (Withholdings from Employees' Pay)	*Employer Responsibilities (Paid by Employer)*
FICA (social security)	Wages
Federal income taxes	FICA (social security)
State income taxes	Federal unemployment taxes
Local income taxes	State unemployment taxes
Other:	Other:
Pension	Pension
Insurance	Insurance
Credit union	Vacation
Union dues	

Not all payrolls contain all of these items. We will give examples of each major item in the following sections.

FICA (Social Security) Taxes

Objective 5
The effect of payroll deductions and employer taxes.

One of the largest social programs administered by the federal government is the system of retirement, disability, hospitalization, and survivors' benefits called the *social security system.* Both employer and employee contribute to social security in the form of taxes applied to wages up to a certain maximum amount each year for each employee. In 1990, the maximum applicable wage was $50,400. At this writing, the tax rates levied under the **Federal Insurance Contributions Act (FICA)** are:

	1988	*1989*	*1990*
Rate . . .	7.51%	7.51%	7.65%

The monies withheld from the employee's paycheck and an equal amount paid by the employer are called **social security taxes** or **FICA taxes,** with the employer acting as the collection agent.

To illustrate the payment of FICA taxes, consider an employee, Jennifer Smith, whose gross wages are $3,000 in January 19x1. Assuming the FICA rate for year 19x1 is 7% the employee's net pay would be reduced by $210 ($3,000 × .07). At the same time, the employer would be responsible for an additional $210—the employer's FICA tax. The employer now owes the Social Security Administration $420, of which half is a payroll deduction and half is an expense to the employer.

Federal and State Income Tax Withholding

Each employee must file a W-4 form (an Employee's Withholding Exemption Certificate) establishing the employee's exemptions and thereby the income tax withholding amount. The employer is responsible for withholding the appropriate amount of federal income tax. Most of the states and some cities require similar procedures to determine the appropriate amount of state and city income taxes to be withheld.

To illustrate, consider again the employee with a gross wage of $3,000 and total FICA tax of $420. Assume that the amount to be withheld for federal and state income taxes are $600 and $120, respectively. The employer withholds from the employee's wages $210 FICA tax plus $600 federal income tax plus $120 state income tax, a total of $930. The employer matches the employee's $210 FICA tax and sends the government $420, which is applied to the employee's FICA account. In addition, the employer must send $600 to the Internal Revenue Service and $120 to the state income tax authority. The employer does not contribute to the employee's state and federal income taxes.

Other Payroll Deductions

Companies often withhold amounts other than taxes from employee's pay and remit these amounts to third parties such as unions, insurance companies, savings plans, and pension plans. Assuming the employee discussed above participates in an insurance plan that costs the employee $85 per month and a retirement plan that costs $105 per month, the table below summarizes the computation of this employee's net pay:

Jennifer Smith
Payroll Computation for January 19x1

Gross pay		$3,000
Withholdings:		
FICA	$210	
Federal income tax	600	
State income tax	120	
Insurance	85	
Pension	105	
Total withholding		1,120
Net pay		$1,880

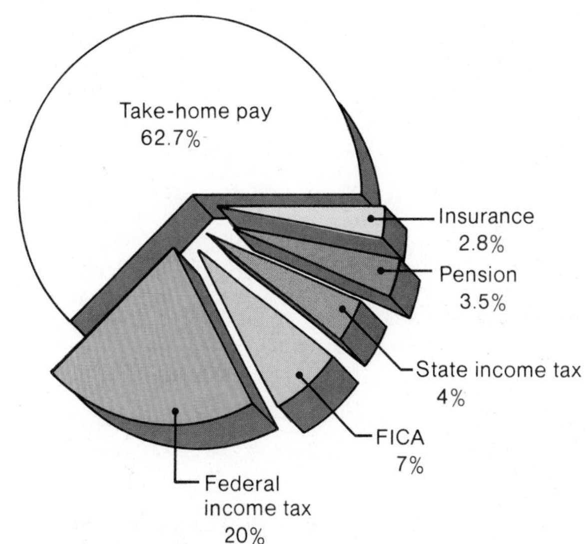

As you can see, a considerable difference exists between Jennifer's gross pay and net pay. Jennifer's "take-home" pay is only 62.7% of her gross pay. The 37.3% difference is owed by the employer to various agencies. This relationship of Jennifer's deductions to her gross pay is illustrated above in pie chart format beside the table. Remember that each employee's situation is different, and this is but one example.

Unemployment Taxes

The federal and state governments have a joint program to fund employment benefits paid to unemployed workers. The **Federal Unemployment Tax Act (FUTA)** imposes a tax on wages paid by employers. The amount levied is 6.2% of the first $7,000 wages of each employee. States are allowed to levee up to 5.4% to be paid to the state, leaving only .8% payable to the federal government. The state varies the amount of tax each employer must pay depending on the employer's claim experience. Employers with more employee unemployment claims pay a higher rate than those with fewer claims.

To illustrate, assume Jennifer Smith's wages are subject to a .8% FUTA tax, a 3% state unemployment tax, and the employer matches Jennifer Smith's pension and insurance payments. The complete payroll computation for Jennifer Smith is as follows:

Schedule of Current Liabilities Related to Jennifer Smith's January 19x1 Wage

	Employee's Portion	*Employer's Portion*	*Total Liability to Third Parties*
Payee:			
Federal government:			
FICA	$ 210	$210	$ 420
Income tax	600		600
FUTA		24	24
State government:			
Income tax	120		120
Unemployment		90	90
Other agencies:			
Pension	105	105	210
Insurance	85	85	170
Total	$1,120	$514	$1,634

The journal entry to record Jennifer Smith's wages and deductions is:

19x1			
Jan. 31	Salaries Expense (E)	3,000	
	FICA Payable (L)		210
	Federal Income Tax Withholding Payable (L)		600
	State Income Tax Withholding Payable (L)		120
	Pension Contribution Payable (L)		105
	Insurance Premium Payable (L)		85
	Cash (A)		1,880
	To record Jennifer Smith's wages.		

The journal entry to record the employer's portion of the payroll liabilities is:

19x1			
Jan. 31	Payroll Expense (E)	514	
	FICA Payable (L)		210
	FUTA Payable (L)		24
	State Unemployment Tax Payable (L)		90
	Pension Contribution Payable (L)		105
	Insurance Premium Payable (L)		85
	To record employer's payroll-related expenses.		

Salaries Expense includes Jennifer Smith's $3,000 gross pay, and Payroll Expense includes the $514 of various payments to be made to the government and other agencies which are the employer's responsibility. Note that the employee's portion ($1,120) is called withholdings, and the employer merely acts as an agent of the employee in making these payments. In the normal course of business, an employer would usually issue checks for the amounts withheld for all employees and the employer's portion during the month following the payroll payment.

SUMMARY

This chapter deals primarily with the business transactions that create short-term obligations. Some of the transactions involve liabilities with known money amounts and payment dates (definitely determinable current liabilities), such as invoices from suppliers, notes, dividends, and the current portion of long-term debt. Other transactions require estimations (estimated liabilities), such as income taxes, property taxes, vacation pay, and warranties. Sometimes a past event creates the need to disclose a potential obligation even though no payment may actually become necessary (contingent liabilities). Such contingencies are recorded if a loss is probable and a reasonable estimate can be made of the amounts involved.

The payroll process involves maintaining accurate employee records and a control system that will prevent payroll fraud. Payrolls create current liabilities for unpaid salaries and for payments that the employer makes to third parties such as government agencies, insurance companies, unions, and so on. Withholdings from employees' wages for income taxes, FICA taxes, insurance, unions, and several others are deductions from gross pay that are subsequently transmitted to the third parties. Some of the payroll-related liabilities are for costs borne solely by the employer, such as certain insurance payments and unemployment taxes.

In this chapter the focus was on current or short-term liabilities. Chapter 10 discusses noncurrent or long-term liabilities. Remember that the key to determining whether a liability is short term or long term is the expected timing of the flow of assets or services that are required to eliminate the obligation.

DEMONSTRATION EXERCISE

Selected transactions from the fiscal year 19x1 for Kangaroo Electronics (KE) follow:

19x1

Jan. 14 Received $4,300 of merchandise inventory on account. KE uses the perpetual inventory system. No discount is given.

Mar. 30 Borrowed $5,000 from the local bank for one year at 8% interest.

May 15 Declared a $0.10 dividend on the 100,000 outstanding shares of common stock to be paid on June 1.

June 1 Paid cash dividend.

June 15 Filed the previous year's income tax return that reported taxes of $54,000 owed to the government. On April 15, KE paid $56,000, which had been fully accrued on December 31 of the previous year, and filed for an extension.

Aug. 15 Recorded August 15 payroll. Gross pay for all employees is $15,900. Deductions from employees included: $1,113 for FICA, $950 for federal income tax, $576 for state income tax, and $200 for insurance premiums. KE's expenses to the payroll include: matching amounts for FICA and insurance, $600 for retirement benefits, and $636 for FUTA.

Dec. 15 The property tax bill is received for $88,000 for 19x1. For the first three quarters, KE estimated the annual property tax to be $80,000. The bill is paid on December 24.

31 Employees' unused vacation time amounts to $2,380.

31 KE estimates that warranty payments on the current year's sales will equal 2.5% of total sales of $5,670,000.

31 Recorded interest expense on the March 30 note.

Required:

Record in general journal form the journal entry for each of these transactions.

Solution:

GENERAL JOURNAL

Date		Account Titles and Explanation	Ref.	Debit	Credit
19x1					
Jan.	14	Inventory (A)		4,300	
		Accounts Payable (L)			4,300
		To record merchandise purchased.			
Mar.	30	Cash (A)		5,000	
		Notes Payable (L)			5,000
		To record bank loan.			
April	15	Tax Payable		56,000	
		Cash			56,000
		To record payment of tax.			
May	15	Dividends (SE)		10,000	
		Dividends Payable (L)			10,000
		To record dividends declared.			
June	1	Dividends Payable		10,000	
		Cash			10,000
		To record dividend payment.			
June	15	Income Tax Receivable (A)		2,000	
		Income Tax Expense (E)			2,000
		To record overpayment to government of income taxes.			

Aug.	15	Salaries Expense (E)		15,900	
		Payroll Expense (E)		2,549	
		FICA Payable (L)			2,226
		Federal Income Tax Withholding Payable (L)			950
		State Income Tax Withholding Payable (L)			576
		FUTA Payable (L)			636
		Pension Contribution Payable (L)			600
		Insurance Premium Payable (L)			400
		Cash (A)			13,061
		To record payroll.			
Dec.	24	Property Tax Expense (E)		28,000	
		Property Taxes Payable (L)		60,000	
		Cash (A)			88,000
		To record payment of property tax bill.			
	31	Vacation Expense (E)		2,380	
		Estimated Vacation Liability (L)			2,380
		To record unused vacation for the year.			
	31	Warranty Expense (E)		141,750	
		Estimated Warranty Liability (L)			141,750
		To record estimated warranty costs.			
	31	Interest Expense (E)		300	
		Interest Payable (L)			300
		To record interest expense on the bank loan: ($5,000 × .08 × 9/12).			

APPENDIX

More on Income Taxes

Objective 6
The nature of deferred income taxes.

Because tax laws often are aimed at affecting business policies, the net income before taxes (NIBT), which is based on accounting principles and methods, and the taxable income, which is based on IRS regulations, may differ. Some differences are permanent in that an amount that appears as a revenue or expense on the income statement never affects the tax return, and other differences are temporary with the difference reversing over time.

In this appendix, we look closely at differences between accounting (book) items and tax return items. A major topic is the concept of deferred taxes where a new class of liability is recorded. The liability is titled **deferred taxes,** and it represents the differences between the amount charged to income tax expense and the sum of the amounts already paid and currently payable to the government through the current period.

Temporary differences are differences between the tax basis and the book basis of certain items that reverse over time. For example, accountants often depreciate assets over estimated useful lives on a straight-line basis, while using accelerated schedules for tax purposes. The government allows faster depreciation for tax purposes to encourage investment in plant and equipment. If different schedules for depreciation are adopted for book and tax purposes, different tax amounts for book and tax purposes will result when the same tax rate is applied to both NIBT to arrive at tax expense and taxable income to arrive at tax liability.

ACCOUNTING FOR TEMPORARY DIFFERENCES

To become familiar with the basics of the current principles governing income tax accounting,[3] we will follow the simple example of Depo, Inc., for its 19x1, 19x2, and 19x3 taxable years. This is merely an introduction to a very complex area of accounting, but a careful analysis of the Depo case will give you a foundation for an understanding of the income tax reporting practices of corporations. First, you must appreciate the contrasts between the "books" of the corporation (i.e., the formal accounting records and statements) and the income tax return. Exhibit 9A-1 shows excerpts from Depo's income statements and tax returns for 19x1, 19x2, and 19x3. Although, as mentioned later in the appendix, several types of business events can create book/tax differences, we will concentrate on the depreciation differences in our coverage.

[3]*FASB Statement No. 96,* "Accounting for Income Taxes" (Norwalk, Conn.: FASB, 1987).

EXHIBIT 9A-1

Comparison of Depo, Inc.'s Books and Tax Return

Depo, Inc.
For the Years Ended December 31
(in thousands)

	19x1	*19x2*	*19x3*	*Total 19x1-x3*
Excerpt from income statement:				
Income before depreciation expense	$200	$200	$200	$600
Depreciation expense	40	40	40	120
Net income before taxes (NIBT)	$160	$160	$160	$480
Income tax expense (at 30%)	48	48	48	144
Excerpt from tax return:				
Taxable income before depreciation	$200	$200	$200	$600
Depreciation deduction	80	40	0	120
Taxable income	$120	$160	$200	$480
Current tax obligation (at 30%)	36	48	60	144

Deferred Tax Liability

In Exhibit 9A-1, consider the **net income before taxes** versus the **taxable income** amounts and the **income tax expense** versus the **current tax obligation** amount. What causes the differences? To answer this question we must know more about the asset being depreciated by Depo which is given in the following schedule:

Data on Depo's Depreciable Equipment

Purchased on January 1, 19x1	$120,000
Estimated useful life	3 years
Estimated salvage value	$0
Applicable tax rate for all years	30%
Method of depreciation used for books	straight-line

	19x1	*19x2*	*19x3*	*Total*
Depreciation expense per books (in thousands)	$40	$40	$40	$120
Depreciation deduction per tax return (in thousands)	80	40	–0–	120

Depo's differing depreciation schedules for books and tax return creates **temporary differences,** which are defined as the difference between the book carrying amounts and the tax bases of assets and liabilities that will affect the tax return in the future. The **book carrying amount** (book basis) is the purchase price of $120,000 minus the depreciation expense charge through the current balance sheet date (accumulated depreciation) or the asset's net book value as discussed in Chapter 8. The **tax basis** is the purchase price minus the depreciation deduction taken to date on tax returns. Depo's equipment has the following history:

	(in thousands) 19x1	19x2	19x3
Books:			
Original purchase price	$120	$120	$120
Cumulative depreciation expense to date	40	80	120
Year-end book carrying amount (book basis)	$ 80	$ 40	$ 0
Tax:			
Original purchase price	$120	$120	$120
Cumulative depreciation deduction to date	80	120	120
Tax basis	$ 40	$ 0	$ 0

Consider the $40,000 difference between the book carrying amount and the tax basis on December 31, 19x1. This is a temporary difference because the cumulative difference in depreciation for book and tax purposes reverses and is eliminated by the end of the equipment's useful life. For tax purposes, 19x1, received a deduction of $80,000 leaving only $40,000 to be deducted in future years. For book purposes, the opposite is true; $80,000 remains to be charged in future years after year 19x1.

Objective 7
The financial statement effects of deferred income taxes.

How do the temporary differences affect the financial statements? Refer to Exhibit 9A-1. Depreciation for books and tax, while both adding to $120,000 over three years, are different each year. The current tax obligation is 30% of taxable income each year, while tax expense is 30% of NIBT each year. In 19x1 $36,000 is due the government for taxes but $48,000 is charged to tax expense. The $12,000 difference is 30% of the temporary book/tax difference in bases of the asset being depreciated; that is ($80,000 − $40,000) × 30% = $12,000. The following schedule gives the computation of deferred tax liability for each year:

	(in thousands) 19x1	19x2	19x3
Book basis	$80	$40	$0
Tax basis	40	0	0
Cumulative temporary difference	$40	$40	$0
Deferred tax liability at 30%	12	12	0

The **deferred tax liability** then is the cumulative temporary difference at the balance sheet date multiplied by the current tax rate.

In 19x1 the tax expense is $48,000, $36,000 of which is currently payable and $12,000 is deferred; that is, payable in the future. The liability account Deferred Tax Liability is, therefore, increased by $12,000 in 19x1. Because the cumulative temporary difference remains at $40,000 at December 31, 19x2, no change is made to the Deferred Tax Liability account. At December 31, 19x3, the cumulative temporary difference is zero; and, therefore, the deferred tax liability is zero also. The journal entries to accomplish proper reporting are as follows (in thousands):

	December 31, 19x1		*December 31, 19x2*		*December 31, 19x3*	
Account Title	*Debit*	*Credit*	*Debit*	*Credit*	*Debit*	*Credit*
Income Tax Expense . .	48		48		48	
Deferred Tax Liability . .		12		0	12	
Income Taxes Payable. .		36		48		60

The sum of the tax currently payable ($36,000 at December 31, 19x1) and the increase in deferred tax liability ($12,000 at December 31, 19x1) equals the total tax expense for 19x1. For 19x2, there is no change in the deferred tax liability; therefore, the tax currently payable is equal to the expense for the year. The tax payable at December 31, 19x3, is $60,000, but the expense is $48,000. The $12,000 difference is the reversal of the amount deferred in 19x1.

The balance sheet classification of deferred tax liability is a noncurrent liability at December 31, 19x1, and a current liability on December 31, 19x2. The current/noncurrent designation depends on when the temporary differences reverse. Exhibit 9A-2 depicts the reversal of a temporary difference.

Deferred Tax Assets

Our example concentrated on a temporary difference created by using accelerated depreciation for income tax purposes versus straight-line depreciation for book purposes. Such a difference creates a deferred tax liability in the early years which reverses in the later years. Temporary differences can create *deferred tax assets* as well as liabilities.

A **deferred tax asset** is created when the cumulative temporary difference is associated with an initial excess of tax currently payable to the government over the tax expense reported on the income statement. An example of an event that creates this situation is warranty costs. While GAAP allows for warranty costs to be estimated and accrued thus matching revenues and expenses, the tax laws permit warranty costs to be deducted from revenues only when actual warranty expenditures are made. The procedures for determining and recording deferred tax assets are similar to those described for deferred tax liabilities, but there are limitations and complexities involved which are beyond the scope of this text.

ACCOUNTING FOR OTHER BOOK/TAX DIFFERENCES

Without considering temporary differences, accounting net income before taxes (NIBT) may not equal taxable income because certain items that appear on the income statement may not appear on the tax return. An example of such a difference is interest on municipal bonds, which is revenue for accounting purposes but is not taxable. Jefferson Investment, Inc., has two sources of revenue, real

EXHIBIT 9A-2

Reversal of Temporary Differences

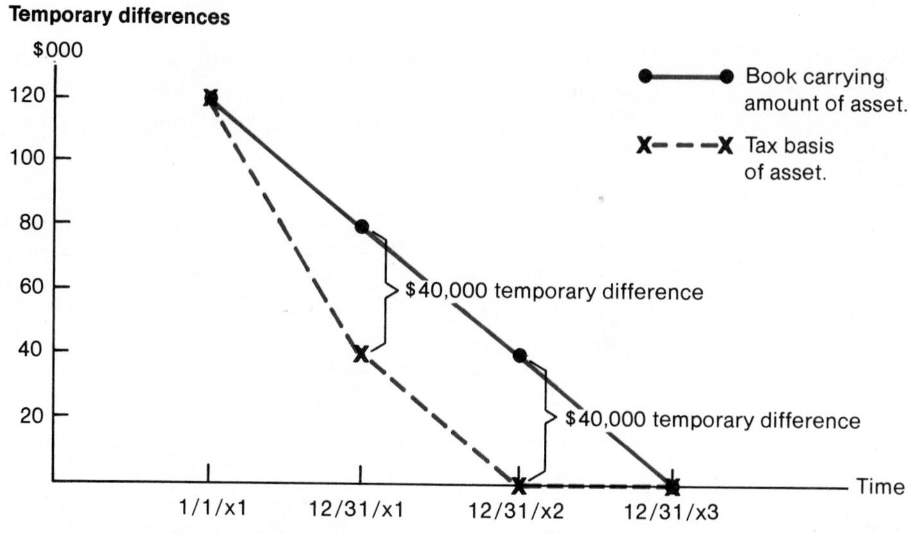

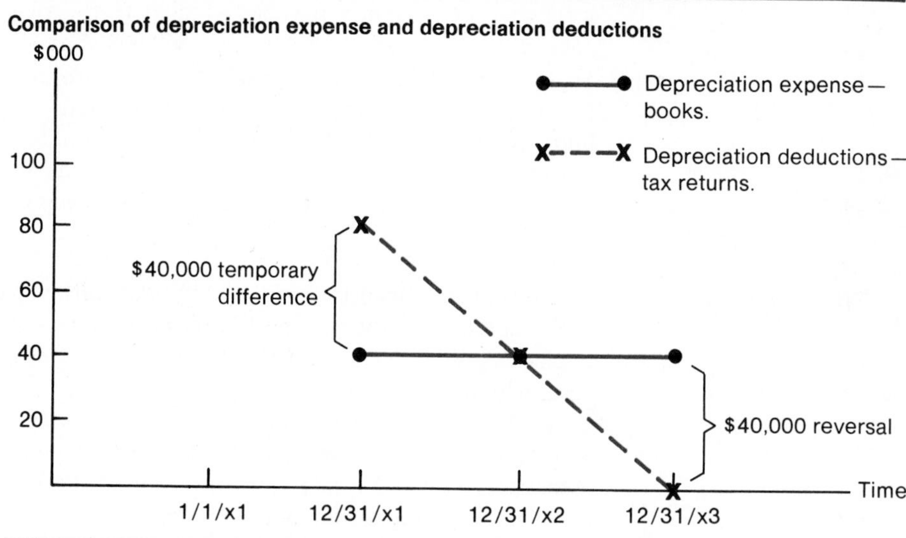

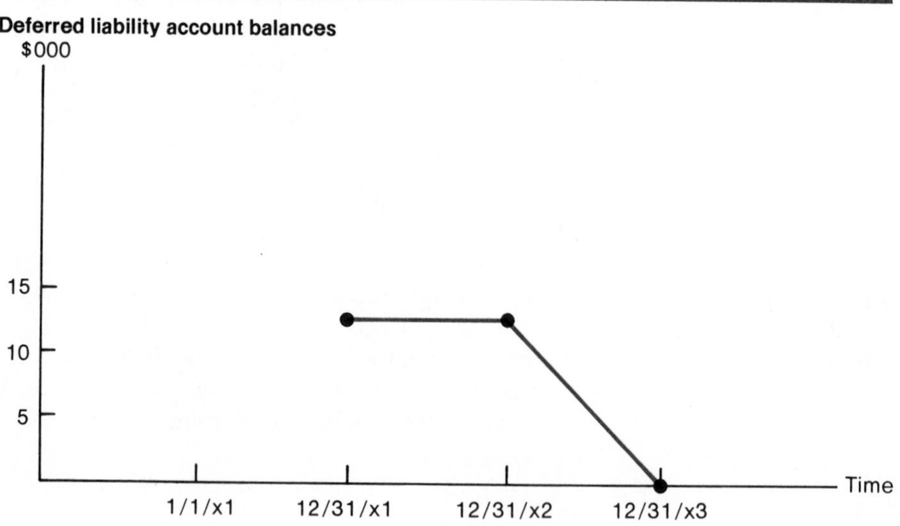

estate commissions, and municipal bond interest, resulting in the following summarized partial income statement:

Jefferson Investment, Inc.
Summarized Partial Income Statement
For the Year Ended December 31, 19xx

Revenues:		
Real estate commissions . . .	$100,000	
Municipal bond interest . . .	50,000	$150,000
Expenses.		80,000
Net income before taxes		$ 70,000

If the applicable tax rate is 30%, how much should be recognized as tax expense for the period? To answer this you must examine Jefferson Investment, Inc.'s tax return.

Jefferson Investment, Inc.
Summary of Tax Return

Taxable revenue . . .	$100,000
Deductions.	80,000
Taxable income . .	$ 20,000
Tax rate	.30
Tax obligation	$ 6,000

Jefferson will record only $6,000 tax expense on net income before taxes (NIBT) of $70,000 because the $50,000 of municipal interest will never be taxed. Such a difference between taxable income and NIBT changes the percentage relationship of tax expense to NIBT. Normally, you would expect tax expense to be 30% (or whatever the tax rate is for the period) of NIBT; but in this case it turns out to be less than 10% ($6,000/$70,000). The journal entry to record tax expense is:

19xx			
Dec. 31	Income Tax Expense (E).	6,000	
	Income Taxes Payable (L)		6,000
	To record tax obligation for the period.		

The resulting summarized income statement would be

Jefferson Investment, Inc.
Summarized Income Statement
For the Year Ended December 31, 19xx

Revenues:		
Real estate	$100,000	
Municipal bond interest . . .	50,000	$150,000
Expenses.		80,000
Net income before taxes		$ 70,000
Tax expense		6,000
Net income		$ 64,000

Accounting for income taxes can be a complicated topic. A more complete treatment of this subject can be found in a more advanced accounting text.

KEY TERMS

Accounts payable. A current liability used to record the purchase of goods and services on credit.

Cash dividends. Earnings distributed to stockholders; corporation's board of directors declares cash dividends and the amount to be paid on outstanding stock becomes a legal obligation.

Compound interest. Interest earned on both the principal and on accrued interest.

Contingency. A situation that creates a possibility for a liability to be created because of a past event.

Contingent liabilities. Occur when a company does not actually have a current obligation but a real possibility exists that an obligation will develop based on the resolution of a past event.

Current liabilities. Liabilities that are due within one year or one operating cycle, whichever is longer.

Declaration date. Point in time that board of directors declares a dividend to stockholders and a current liability is established.

Definitely determinable current liability. An existing current liability of a precisely measurable amount.

Estimated liability. An existing liability for which the amount is not precisely known, but for which a reasonable estimate can be made.

Federal Insurance Contributions Act (FICA). Law setting up the social security program which is a system of retirement, disability, hospitalization, and survivors' benefits.

Federal Unemployment Tax Act (FUTA). Law that set up the joint program between federal and state governments to fund benefits for unemployed workers through taxation of employers.

Income taxes. Taxes levied by federal, state, and local governments against a business's taxable income and against employees' earnings.

Interest-bearing short-term note. Specifies the principal amount of the note, the interest rate, and the maturity date.

Long-term liabilities. Liabilities that are not expected to be paid to creditors within one year or one operating cycle, whichever is longer.

Noninterest-bearing short-term note. Does not specify an interest rate, and its maturity value is the face value of the note.

Payment date. Date on which dividends are paid in cash.

Payroll deductions. Amounts withheld from employees' earnings by the employer for income taxes, FICA taxes, and other purposes.

Property taxes. Major source of tax revenue for local governments; usually based on a stated percentage of assessed values of real property (land and buildings) and personal property (property other than real property, such as furniture, automobiles, jewelry, inventory, and sometimes stocks and bonds).

Short-term note payable. A liability with many of the same attributes as accounts payable except that a note is a formal contract of indebtedness between a debtor (the **maker** of the note) and a creditor (the **payee** of the note). It can be either interest-bearing or noninterest-bearing.

Simple interest. Interest charged on only the unpaid principal.

Social security taxes. Monies levied under the Federal Insurance Contributions Act—a portion paid by employees and the other portion paid by the employer. Also called FICA taxes.

Vacation liability. Cost of vacation earned by employees but not taken at the end of an accounting period; represents an obligation of the business that must be matched with the period in which it is earned, thus creating a current liability on the books.

Warranty commitments. Obligations created when businesses guarantee their products against defects for a certain period of time after the sale.

APPENDIX KEY TERMS

Book carrying amount. Amount of an asset or liability on the accounting records.

Deferred tax asset. Created when the cumulative temporary difference is associated with an initial excess of tax currently payable to the government over the tax expense reported on the income statement.

Deferred tax liability. The cumulative temporary difference at the balance sheet date multiplied by the current tax rate.

Tax basis. Amount of an asset or liability on the tax records.

Temporary differences. The difference between the book carrying amounts and the tax bases of assets and liabilities that will affect the tax return in the future.

SYNONYMS

Beancounters; accountants, used affectionally.

Principal; amount borrowed or loaned.

Net pay; take-home pay.

Payable; accrued.

Social security tax; FICA tax.

Taxes currently payable; current tax obligation.

Tax expense; tax provision.

Timing difference; temporary difference.

Warranty; guarantee.

Withholding; payroll deductions.

QUESTIONS

1. Define current liabilities.
2. Why does a company not record an estimate for the possibility of nonpayment of accounts payable?
3. Define five parts of a promissory note.

4. Dividends are paid to a company's stockholders. What do the dividends represent to those stockholders? What comparable payments are made to creditors?
5. Describe the two significant dates involved in the issuance of dividends and what each date means.
6. Why are accountants concerned with determining when long-term notes become short term?
7. Distinguish between definitely determinable current liabilities and estimated liabilities. Describe four different types of estimated liabilities.
8. Why is it necessary to estimate income taxes? Property taxes?
9. What is the purpose of accruing vacation pay?
10. In estimating warranty liability for the year, what is the accountant concerned with in making the estimate?
11. In what ways do contingent liabilities differ from definitely determinable and estimated liabilities?
12. Describe how contingent liabilities are treated in the financial statements.
13. If a contingent liability is recorded on the books, how is it disclosed?
14. Why are organizations so concerned with their payroll systems?
15. Describe the different departments' responsibilities in the payroll system.
16. Describe three employer expenses associated with payroll.
17. Describe four items deducted from an employee's pay and explain how they are treated by the employer.

APPENDIX QUESTIONS

18. Define temporary differences.
19. Contrast book carrying amount and tax basis of a depreciable asset.
20. Over the life of the business, what are the effects of temporary differences? Why?
21. Contrast deferred tax liability and taxes payable.
22. How would you decide on the balance sheet classification of a deferred tax liability account?

EXERCISES

EXERCISE 9-1
L.O. 1

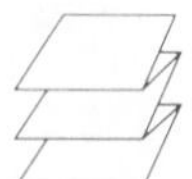

Accounts Payable

Prepare the journal entries related to the following events for Sapak Forestry. Sapak uses the periodic inventory system and the net method for recording purchases.

a. Received goods from Supplier A on February 10 for $10,000. Terms are 2/10, n/30. Paid for goods on February 20.
b. Purchased supplies on account for $550 on February 20. Terms are 2/10, n/30, but Sapak did not pay the supplies until after the discount period expired.

EXERCISE 9-2
L.O. 1

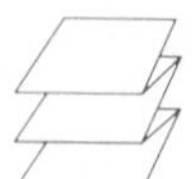

Note Payable

The Graham Company issued a 10%, two-year note payable to the Friendly Bank for a $60,000 loan of cash on October 1, 19xx.

Required:
1. Prepare in general journal form the entry Graham Company recorded on October 1, 19xx.
2. Prepare in general journal form the adjusting journal entry recorded by the Graham Company on December 31, 19xx (its fiscal year-end).

EXERCISE 9-3
L.O. 1

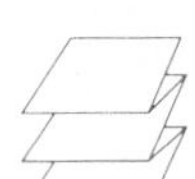

Noninterest-Bearing Note Payable

Needs-the-Money, Inc., issued a one-year noninterest-bearing note for $35,000 cash on September 1, 19x1. The implied interest rate on the note is equal to 10%. Prepare the journal entries on September 1, 19x1, December 31, 19x1, and September 1, 19x2, related to interest expense.

EXERCISE 9-4
L.O. 1

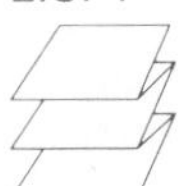

Dividends

On March 15, 19xx, National Motors Company declared a $0.15 dividend on each of its 500,000 shares of common stock to be paid on May 15, 19xx. In general journal form, record the journal entries made on the declaration and payment dates.

EXERCISE 9-5
L.O. 1

Long-Term Interest-Bearing Note and Reclassification to Current

On October 1, 19x1, Datanow Company took out a $500,000, 12%, four-year note with $125,000 due on September 30 of each year of the note. Interest is paid on September 30 of each year. Datanow's fiscal year ends on December 31 of each year.

Required:
Prepare in journal form all journal entries related to the note over the four years.

EXERCISE 9-6
L.O. 2

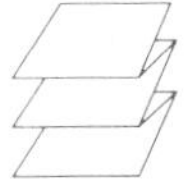

Income Taxes

Rent-It-All Company estimates its 19x1 income taxes to be $125,000 when it closes its books for the fiscal year ending December 31, 19x1. When Rent-It-All prepares its income tax return and files it on March 31, 19x2, the actual income tax due and paid to the government is $132,000.

Required:
Prepare the journal entries related to the income taxes.

EXERCISE 9-7
L.O. 2

Property Taxes

On January 1, 19xx, Flights on the Wing, Inc., estimates its property tax for 19xx to be $60,000 and uses that estimate in preparing its quarterly financial statements. On September 15, Flights receives its tax bill, which it pays immediately for $52,000.

Required:
Record all journal entries during the year related to property taxes.

EXERCISE 9-8
L.O. 2

Vacation Pay

Mabel's Furniture Company accrued vacation pay at December 31, 19x1, and 19x2, of $760 and $940, respectively. Mabel's paid $570 of the 19x1 accrued vacation pay in 19x2.

Required:
1. In general journal form, prepare the journal entries Mabel's Furniture Company makes related to accrued vacation pay during 19x1 and 19x2.
2. Determine the liability related to vacation pay on December 31, 19x2.

EXERCISE 9-9
L.O. 2

Warranties

Breitmeyer's Micro, Inc., a producer of the latest in high-tech microwave ovens, has sales of $2,796,400 during 19x1, its first year of operations. Breitmeyer's estimates the warranty work required to be 3% of sales. During 19x2, warranty expenditures were $56,000, and sales were $3,209,000. There were no warranty expenditures during 19x1.

Required:
1. In general journal form, record the journal entry Breitmeyer's made at December 31, 19x1, its fiscal year-end.
2. Record any journal entries related to warranties during 19x2.

EXERCISE 9-10
L.O. 3

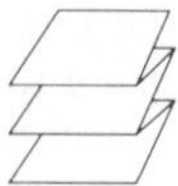

Contingent Liabilities

On September 30, 19x1, Chemicals, Inc.'s year-end, corporate executives know of a pending lawsuit filed on June 20, 19x1, by one of its former employees on the grounds of known dangerous working conditions. The lawsuit has been filed for $750,000, but the corporate legal department believes it will be settled for $100,000.

Required:
1. Prepare any journal entries required by the above lawsuit.
2. Prepare the footnote disclosures Chemicals would show in its 19x1 annual report.
3. If on August 14, 19x2, the lawsuit is settled for $150,000, what journal entry would Chemicals make on that date?

EXERCISE 9-11
L.O. 5

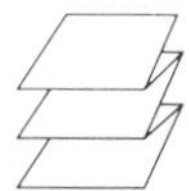

Payroll

Carol's Country Crafts (CCC) pays its employees twice a month. The August 15 payroll includes $1,527 paid to employees and withholdings of $145 for FICA, $132 for federal income tax, $97 for state income tax, and $200 for direct deposit in the local credit union. CCC is also responsible for FICA of $145, FUTA of $50, and health insurance premiums of $130.

Required:
Prepare the journal entries in general journal form CCC makes for the August 15 payroll.

EXERCISE 9-12
L.O. 5

Payroll

Anita's Fine Confections has gross pay for the payroll period ending April 30, 19xx, of $146,200. The FICA rate is 7.51% for both Anita and her employees. Federal income tax and state income tax withholdings amounted to $7,850 and $5,699, respectively. Retirement benefits of $2,000 and health insurance benefits of $3,600 were paid completely by the employer. Anita must also pay FUTA at a rate of .4% and state unemployment tax at a rate of .35%. All employees are below the applicable maximum wages for FICA, FUTA, and SUTA.

Required:
Prepare the journal entries to record the above payroll.

EXERCISE 9-13
L.O. 1, 2

Accounts Payable, Dividends, and Warranties

1. During June 19x7, Tri-State Furniture Company pays $16,892 to suppliers, purchases $19,236 of goods on account, and has an ending balance in its Accounts Payable account of $4,816. The account's beginning balance is:
   a. $7,160.
   b. $2,344.
   c. $2,472.
   d. $7,288.
2. On December 31, the end of Conte, Inc.'s first year of operations, the board of directors declared a $0.35 dividend on each of its 250,000 shares of outstanding common stock. No other dividends were declared during the year. Total dividends paid during the year were:
   a. $87,500.
   b. $0.
   c. $125,000.
   d. $85,700.

3. Terres Company, a leading seller of computer software, guarantees its products for one year from date of purchase. During 19x6, Terres has sales of $15,875,500 and expects to pay 2% on the warranties. During 19x6 Terres pays $530,000 on warranty repairs. The beginning balance in the Warranty Payable account is $641,000. The ending balance in the account is:
   a. $317,510.
   b. $269,755.
   c. $853,490.
   d. $428,510.

APPENDIX EXERCISES

EXERCISE 9-14
L.O. 6, 7

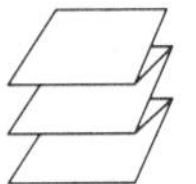

Deferred Taxes

Esther's Eatery, which has a calendar fiscal year, purchased kitchen equipment for $70,000. The equipment has a seven-year life and no salvage value. Esther uses straight-line depreciation for book purposes and sum-of-the-years' digits for tax purposes. This is the only temporary difference. For years 19x1, 19x2, and 19x3, net income before depreciation and taxes is $150,000, $135,000, and $100,000, respectively. The income tax rate is 40%.

Required:
1. Compute the cumulative temporary difference for each of the three years.
2. Prepare the journal entries relating to income tax expense and deferred taxes.

EXERCISE 9-15
L.O. 6, 7

Deferred Taxes

Howell Auto Parts, Inc., has the following information from its books and tax return for the last three years:

	NIBT	*Taxable Income*
19x1	$1,400,000	$1,000,000
19x2	1,900,000	1,500,000
19x3	1,800,000	1,900,000

Net income before taxes in each year includes $150,000 of interest revenue earned from municipal bonds which is not considered taxable income. All other differences are created by different depreciation methods used for book and tax purposes. The tax rate is 30%.

Required:
Prepare the journal entries related to income tax expense and deferred taxes.

PROBLEMS

PROBLEM 9-1
L.O. 1

Accounts Payable

Airtex, Inc., a manufacturer of pollution control monitoring equipment with a December 31 fiscal year-end, purchases gauges from one primary supplier, White Supply Company. During 19x1, Airtex had cash flow problems and requested that White allow delay of payment of three invoices. White agreed to delayed payment of the invoices if Airtex signed three three-month notes with 10% annual interest paid as follows:

Date	*Invoice No.*	*Invoice Amount*	*Date of Note*	*Due Date*
6/30	1001	$100,000	7/31	10/31
9/1	2107	50,000	10/1	12/31
11/2	3612	36,000	12/1	2/28
		$186,000		

Required:
1. Record Airtex's journal entries for the transactions with White during 19x1. (Assume 30-day months for interest calculations and that Airtex uses the perpetual inventory system.)
2. Describe how current liabilities on the December 31, 19x1, balance sheet are affected by these transactions.

PROBLEM 9-2
L.O. 1

Interest and Recording Notes Payable

Smith Company has to finance the $10,000 purchase of a new generator. First Bank offers the following terms:

Principal	$10,000
Annual interest rate	12%, compounded annually
Payment schedule	Interest and principal at maturity
Maturity date	December 31, 19x2
Inception of note	January 1, 19x1

Second Bank offers the following terms with the same effective interest rate as above:

Maturity amount	$12,544
Payment schedule	$12,544 at maturity
Inception of note	January 1, 19x1
Maturity date	December 31, 19x2

Required:
1. For each note described above, record all journal entries related to the notes for 19x1 and 19x2, assuming Smith Company has a December 31 year-end.
2. Which note is "interest bearing"? What is the annual interest rate for each note?

PROBLEM 9-3
L.O. 1

Short-Term Notes

Clearly Corporation typically arranges short-term financing with its bank to provide operating cash as needed. Interest expense is recorded upon payment of the note and at the end of each quarter for financial reporting purposes if this occurs sooner.

During 19xx, Clearly Corporation had the following activity in short-term financing:

19xx	
Jan. 15	Borrowed $50,000 at 12% on a 60-day note.
Feb. 28	Borrowed $100,000 at 10% on a six-month note.
Mar. 15	Paid the note of January 15 plus interest.
30	Accrued interest as required for quarterly statements.
May 1	Borrowed $100,000 on a 9%, 90-day note.
June 30	Accrued interest as required for quarterly statements.
July 15	Borrowed $50,000 on a 10%, six-month note.
Aug. 1	Paid the note of May 1 plus interest.
30	Paid the note of February 28.
Sept. 30	Accrued interest as required for quarterly statements.
Nov. 1	Borrowed $50,000 on an 8%, 90-day note.
Dec. 31	Accrued interest as required.
31	Closed the Interest Expense account for the year.

Required:
In general journal form, prepare all journal entries the Clearly Corporation made during 19xx for the above notes. Round all computations to the nearest dollar.

PROBLEM 9-4
L.O. 1, 2

Balance Sheet Classification

Lonestar, Inc., shows "Accounts Payable . . . . $34,300" on its balance sheet at December 31, 19x1, under the "Current liabilities" section. Upon investigation of the subsidiary records, the following details were revealed about the $34,300 amount:

a. Unpaid invoices for office equipment, supplies, and inventory total $24,800. This includes one invoice of $1,500 for a typewriter that was returned to the vendor because it was not the model ordered. The $24,800 credit is part of the Accounts Payable balance.
b. Estimated income taxes to be received from the federal government are $10,500. This represents the estimated overpayment of the current year's taxes. The $10,500 is part of the Accounts Payable balance.
c. Notes payable to bank total $20,000. This is the principal amount of a promissory note issued to a bank which is due on December 31, 19x3. The interest on those notes is paid semiannually. The $20,000 is part of the Accounts Payable balance.

Required:
1. Comment on the appropriate balance sheet classification of each item.
2. Make any necessary journal entries to correct the classifications, if any.

PROBLEM 9-5
L.O. 1, 2

Dividends, Property Taxes, and Contingent Liabilities

Prepare the journal entry, or state why no entry is required for each of the following items. Consider each case separately.

Case 1:

a. December 31, 19x1. The board of directors declares a dividend of $0.50 per share; 250,000 shares of common stock are outstanding.
b. January 30, 19x2. The dividend declared on December 31, 19x1, is paid.

Case 2:

a. March 31, 19x1. One quarter of the year's estimated property taxes of $800,000 is recorded.
b. June 30, 19x1. The second quarter of estimated property taxes is recorded.
c. September 30, 19x1. The tax bill for the calendar year 19x1 is received and paid. The bill is for $780,000.

Case 3:

a. A company is a defendant in a lawsuit alleging patent infringement. The lawsuit is for $300,000, an amount that is material to the company. Management and the company's attorney believe the lawsuit is entirely without merit, and the company will prevail.
b. A company is a defendant in a product liability lawsuit of $1 million. This amount is material to the company, and management and the company's attorneys feel they will lose the case. However, management is reluctant to record the liability as they intend to fight the case and eventually settle for $500,000 "a few years" away.
c. Same as situation *(b)* except the amount is not material, and the court's decision is due within the next 60 days.

PROBLEM 9-6
L.O. 2

Property Taxes

The city of Johnsonville levies a yearly property tax equal to 1% of the fair value of real estate. The payment is due on July 1 of each year for the year then ending, and the tax bill is mailed on June 15. Levity, Inc., is a calendar-year company that has paid the following property tax in the last two years:

Period Covered by Tax	*Assessed Fair Value*	*Tax Paid*
7/1/x1–6/30/x2	$10,000,000	$100,000
7/1/x2–6/30/x3	16,000,000	160,000

On December 31, 19x3, Levity estimates that the tax for the July 1, 19x3, to June 30, 19x4, period will be $180,000. The estimate made on December 31, 19x2, was exactly correct.

Required:

1. Record the journal entries made for property tax on December 31, 19x2, and on July 1, 19x3.
2. Record the journal entry made on December 31, 19x3, for property tax.

PROBLEM 9-7
L.O. 2

Vacation Pay

Tysen Produce, Inc., has three employees all of whom earn one day of vacation for each month of employment. The following schedule shows each employee's vacation status for 19x1:

Employee No.	*Vacation Days Earned*	*Vacation Days Taken*	*Vacation Days Carried Over to 19x2*
1.	12	0	12
2.	6	0	6
3.	12	5	7

Tysen has recorded all payroll-related expenses in one account labeled "Salary Expense." The expense amount per day of work recorded for each employer during 19x1 was: employee No. 1, $330; employee No. 2, $230; and employee No. 3, $100. Nothing has been separately recorded for vacations during the current year.

Required:

1. Record the necessary adjustment for vacation time.
2. Discuss the implication of the unused vacation time at December 31 for Tysen financial statements and explain why the adjustment is necessary.

PROBLEM 9-8
L.O. 2

Vacation Pay

Techtronics, Inc., has five employees who worked for the entire year from January 1, 19x2, to December 31, 19x2. Each employee is entitled to 1 day vacation for each 25 days of work to a maximum of 10 vacation days per year, so that in one year, when an employee works for 250 days (50, 5-day weeks), he or she would be entitled to 10 days of vacation (two 5-day weeks) at full pay. There were no carryovers from 19x1, but in 19x2, the work schedule was so tight that most employees did not take all of their earned vacation. The following schedule shows vacation time earned and taken by each employee:

Employee No.	*Weeks Worked*	*Vacation Weeks Taken*	*Weekly Pay*
1	52	0	$850
2	51	1	700
3	50	2	750
4	52	0	900
5	52	0	800

Required:

1. Ignoring all taxes and withholdings, show any entry necessary at December 31, 19x2, to account for vacation pay. Explain your answer.
2. If all current and carryover vacation time is taken in 19x3 and the weekly pay stays the same, show a summary entry to record wage expense for 19x3. (Again, ignore taxes and withholdings.)

PROBLEM 9-9
L.O. 2

Warranties

In 19x1, Foley, Inc., started manufacturing high-quality video cassette recorders and selling them via mail order. One feature of this product that the company feels will be attractive to the prime market target group is the unlimited returns policy for three years. Under this warranty program, Foley will replace any defective set with a new one. Because of the high quality, Foley expects only a 1% return. During 19x1, no returns were made on the following sales:

Units Sold	*Sales Price per Unit*	*Manufacturing Cost per Unit*	*Units Replaced*	*Estimated Handling Cost per Unit Replaced*
1,200	$1,350	$650	0	$102

Required:

Prepare the December 31, 19x1, journal entry and the accounting disclosures in the financial statements (if any) required because of the warranty policy.

PROBLEM 9-10
L.O. 3

Contingent Liabilities

Sunbelt Charters, Inc., operates a small airline that specializes in interisland flights in Hawaii. Sunbelt carries liability insurance of $10 million for injury to passengers, but the insurance contract terms call for Sunbelt to pay the first $100,000 of claims for each incident. During 19x1, two incidents occurred which have not yet been settled.

a. On October 12, 19x1, an overhead compartment door opened on landing and a carry-on bag fell on a passenger causing a head injury. The passenger filed a lawsuit on April 15, 19x1, and Sunbelt's attorney has been instructed to settle out of court. At December 31, 19x1, the attorney has a strong belief that the out-of-court settlement will take place on January 20, 19x1, for $85,000.

b. On November 30, 19x1, four passengers were badly injured upon debarking when the portable ramp collapsed. Lawsuits totaling $1.8 million have been filed against Sunbelt and the airport that owned the ramp. On December 31, Sunbelt's attorneys believe strongly that if the lawsuits were taken to trial, they would result in payment of $1.8 million to the injured passengers, but that Sunbelt should be found innocent while the airport will be found negligent and made to pay the damages.

Required:

1. Discuss the nature of the obligations created by these two incidents. Do they create estimated or contingent liabilities?
2. Describe the accounting treatment of each incident, showing any necessary journal entries at December 31 and describing any financial statement effects.

PROBLEM 9-11
L.O. 5

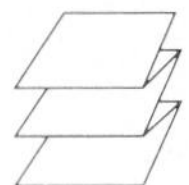

Payroll

Farmland Products, Inc., has three employees who were paid the following amounts for December 19xx:

Employee No.	*Gross Pay*	*Federal Income Tax Withheld*	*FICA Tax Withheld (Employee's Portion)*	*Insurance Withheld*	*State Income Tax Withheld*
1	$7,000	$2,500	$ 0	$50	$190
2	5,000	1,200	350	50	120
3	2,000	600	140	50	100

In addition to the above items, Farmland initiated a hospitalization plan on December 1, 19xx, which will cost $200 per employee per month for the insurance. The employee pays nothing for this benefit. The payments are made in advance for six-month periods. On December 2, 19xx, Farmland made the following entry for the insurance:

Salaries Expense	3,600	
Cash.		3,600

Required:

1. Record the journal entries for the payroll at December 31, 19xx, and for any necessary adjustments.
2. Discuss how balance sheet classifications are affected by the above transactions.

PROBLEM 9-12
L.O. 5

Payroll

The following payroll data is available for the three employees in the sales department of Malmac Corporation:

Employee	*Earnings to Date**	*Rate*
Cobb, T. R.	$43,360	$2,710 per pay period
Gehrig, H. L.	16,000	$10.00 per hour
Williams, T. S.	22,800	$12.00 per hour

*As of beginning of the current period.

During the current period, Gehrig worked 80 hours and Williams worked 77. In addition to FICA, amounts withheld during the period are as follows:

	Cobb	*Gehrig*	*Williams*
Federal income taxes	$894.30	$210.00	$250.00
State income taxes	130.00	38.40	44.35
City income taxes	59.60	17.60	20.30
Health insurance premium	38.00	38.00	13.00
Savings plan	100.00	0	25.00

Assume that FICA taxes are 7% for both the employee and the employer on the first $43,800 of wages earned during the year.

Required:

1. Prepare a schedule computing for each employee gross pay, individual deductions, and net pay.
2. Prepare the journal entry(ies) to record the payroll including the employer's portion of FICA taxes.

APPENDIX PROBLEMS

PROBLEM 9-13
L.O. 6

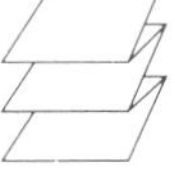

Deferred Taxes

Zach, Inc., purchased a machine for $80,000. It has an estimated life of five years and a salvage value of $5,000. It will be depreciated by the straight-line method for book purposes and by the sum-of-the-years'-digits method for tax purposes which will result in depreciation expense as follows:

Year	*Straight Line*	*Sum-of-the-Years' Digits*
1	$15,000	$25,000
2	15,000	20,000
3	15,000	15,000
4	15,000	10,000
5	15,000	5,000

Income before taxes and depreciation each year is $150,000. A tax rate of 40% should be used for all purposes.

Required:

1. Prepare a schedule that shows:
   a. Net income before taxes.
   b. Taxable income for each of the first five years involved.
2. Prepare the journal entries to record the tax liability for years 1, 3, and 5.

PROBLEM 9-14
L.O. 6

Deferred Taxes

Stanley Company has two depreciable assets that create timing differences. Depreciation is recorded on the straight-line basis for book purposes and on an accelerated basis for tax purposes.

Asset No.	*Depreciation Expense on Income Statement* 19x1	19x2	19x3	*Depreciation Expense on Tax Form* 19x1	19x2	19x3
1. . . .	$100,000	$100,000	$100,000	$300,000	$200,000	$100,000
2. . . .	0	42,000	42,000	0	90,000	40,000

Stanley's income before depreciation and taxes for 19x1, 19x2, and 19x3 was $420,000, $602,000, and $480,000, respectively. The tax rate for all three years was 30%, and this rate is expected to continue into the future.

Required:

1. Show all journal entries for income taxes for the years 19x1, 19x2, and 19x3.
2. Discuss the balance sheet classification for 19x1 affected by the temporary differences.

PROBLEM 9-15
L.O. 1, 2, 5

Short-Term Liabilities and Business Decisions

You are a bank loan officer and a potential client, Professional Financial Services, Inc. (PFS), has applied for a loan of $300,000. The proposed note would be issued on 1/1/x2 to be paid back on 2/1/x2 with interest at 20%. On 12/31/x1, PFS supplies the following information:

1. Schedule of expected liability balances at the 12/31/x1 year-end:

Current liabilities:		
Accounts payable.	$120,000	(due Jan. 10, 19x2)
Salaries payable	62,000	(due Jan. 6, 19x2)
Notes payable	660,000	(see schedule*)
Interest payable.	18,717	(see schedule†)
Total current liabilities	$860,717	

***Schedule of Notes Payable:**

Note	*Note Made to*	*Term of Note*	*Interest Principal*	*Rate*	*Interest Payment*
1	Scott Products	10/1/x1 to 4/1/x2	$300,000	15%	4/1/x2
2	First Bank	11/30/x1 to 2/28/x2	200,000	16%	End of each month
3	National Mortgage	9/1/x1 to 2/28/x2	160,000	14%	2/28/x2

†Schedule of Interest Payable (rounded):

Note 1 ($300,000) (.15) (3/12) = $11,250
Note 3 ($160,000) (.14) (4/12) = 7,467
$18,717

2. Schedule of expected cash payments for January 19x2:

Payroll	Jan. 6	$125,000
	Jan. 20	125,000
Accounts payable	Jan. 10	120,000
	Jan. 28	60,000
Notes (interest)	Jan. 31	2,667
Other expenses	Jan. 15	15,000
	Jan. 31	30,000

3. Schedule of cash receipts for January 19x2:

From customers	Jan. 10	$150,000
	Jan. 20	50,000
	Jan. 30	50,000
From bank—new note	Jan. 1	300,000

4. Expected cash balance on 12/31/x1, $130,000.

Required:
1. Show all of PFS's journal entries for the expected January 19x2 transactions assuming all payments are made on time and all receipts are collected as scheduled. (Round all amounts to nearest dollar.)
2. Give your opinion about the banker's decision on granting the loan, backed up by an analysis of cash available to pay off the new note when it is due.

CASES

CASE 9-1
L.O. 3

Contingent Liabilities

Precision Company, Inc., was notified on December 31, 19x1, the end of its fiscal period, that a lawsuit had been initiated against them for $10 million. The lawsuit claims that one of Precision's delivery people drove a truck into a pedestrian walkway and injured two people. The police report noted that the driver claims that the pedestrians were walking against the light. Precision's insurance coverage for such accidents has a limit of $1 million. Precision's attorney expects that an out-of-court settlement will be reached for no more than $1 million, but she cannot rule out the possibility of a larger adverse payment.

Required:
Discuss the accounting issues involved in this case. How should Precision disclose this situation in its financial statements?

EVALUATING FINANCIAL STATEMENTS

CASE 9-2
L.O. 1

Dividends Payable

During 1986, General Electric Company declares dividends of $1,081 million. GE reported the following current liabilities in its December 31, 1986, statement of financial position.

	(in millions) December 31	
	1986	*1985*
Current liabilities:		
Short-term borrowings	$ 1,813	$1,297
Accounts payable	2,594	2,204
Progress collections and price adjustments accrued	2,273	2,257
Dividends payable	287	264
Taxes accrued.	1,153	751
Other costs and expenses accrued	3,341	2,146
Current liabilities.	$11,461	$8,919

Required:
Compute dividends General Electric paid during 1986 and discuss the effects that dividends have on cash flows and current liabilities.

CASE 9-3
L.O. 3

Contingent Liabilities

E. I. Du Pont de Nemours and Company reports the following in its 1986 consolidated balance sheet (in millions):

	December 31	
	1986	*1985*
Other liabilities	$1,669	$1,475

The footnotes to the financial statements include this excerpt:

Other Liabilities

	December 31	
	1986	*1985*
Reserves for employee-related costs including coal workers' pneumoconiosis.	$ 814	$ 753
Miscellaneous	855	722
	$1,669	$1,475

Required:

1. Describe the nature of this liability. What does this liability represent?
2. Do you think this liability is current or noncurrent? Why?

CASE 9-4
L.O. 1

Accounts Payable and Reclassification of Long-Term Debt

The following is an excerpt from the December 31, 1986, balance sheet of Ford Motor Company and consolidated subsidiaries:

	(in millions) 1986	1985
Current liabilities:		
Accounts payable:		
Trade	$5,752.3	$4,751.9
Other	2,546.1	1,825.6
	$8,298.4	$6,577.5

Required:

1. If 1986 purchases on trade accounts were $8,000 million, what was the amount of cash paid to trade creditors for the year?
2. Is it possible that any of the $5,752.3 million will not be paid in 1987? Explain.
3. Assume that $1,500 million of the $2,546.1 million is reclassified long-term debt. What is the justification for classifying the $1,500 million as current?

CASE 9-5
L.O. 3

Contingent Liabilities—Warranties

Dunn Equipment Co. manufactures lightweight, compact electric motors for industrial customers. For the past several years about 1% of the engines have been returned for full credit because of defects. Dunn allows full credit on returns within a year of sale because the transportation and repair costs on average for repairing the used engines would exceed the manufacturing cost of the new engines. Whenever a customer reports a defect within the warranty period, Dunn's standard accounting is to Debit Sales and Credit Inventory for the cost of the new engine.

Required:

Write a memo to management explaining the proper accounting treatment for such a situation. Give the financial statement effects of your suggested accounting.

CASE 9-6
L.O. 1

Noninterest-Bearing Note

As auditor of Kansas Glass Works, Inc. (KGW), you come upon the following history of a transaction involving the purchase of equipment by means of a six-month noninterest-bearing note.

KGW's accountant recorded the following journal entries:

5/1/x1	Equipment	80,000	
	Notes Payable		80,000
	To record the signing of a noninterest-bearing note with a maturity value of $84,000 for the purchase of equipment costing $80,000.		
11/1/x1	Interest Expense	4,800	
	Notes Payable	80,000	
	Cash		84,000
	Gain on Interest		800
	To record interest expense at 12% per annum and the payment of the maturity value of the note.		

Upon questioning the accountant, you find the 12% was the interest rate charged by a bank for a loan made during October.

Required:
Criticize the handling of the transactions and tell how you would have recorded them.

CASE 9-7
L.O. 3

Contingency

In June 19x1, All-Right Rental, Inc., rented a chain saw to a minor who was using his older brother's driver's license as identification. The young man was severely injured while using the saw and initiated a $10 million lawsuit against All-Right on November 15, 19x1. At the end of All-Right's fiscal year, December 31, 19x1, the company's attorney is working on an out-of-court settlement that calls for All-Right to pay $1 million in medical expenses and $2 million in damages. The attorney believes that the plaintiff will not accept the offer and will push ahead with the suit. If a trial ensues, the attorney states, "We will probably lose, and if we do, the minimum we will pay is $4 million; but that payment will not come until 19x3 at the earliest."

Required:
Discuss how the concepts of periodicity, matching, measurement, and objectivity affect the accounting for the above facts and describe what the accounting should be for the All-Right contingency.

CASE 9-8
L.O. 3

Contingency

Read the "Legal matters" section of the "Commitments and contingencies" note to Ralston Purina Company's annual report in Appendix E. Also review Ralston's balance sheet in Appendix E.

Required:
1. Does Ralston have a contingent liability as of the balance sheet date? Explain.
2. Did Ralston record a liability related to "legal matters" on its balance sheet? Explain.

FINANCIAL STATEMENTS

FINANCIAL STATEMENT COMPONENTS EMPHASIZED IN CHAPTER 10

Somers Corporation
Income Statement
For 1991

Revenues
xxxx
xxxx
Expenses
Interest expense

	1991	*1990*
Interest expense......	$ XX	$ XX

Somers Corporation
Balance Sheet
12/31/91

Current assets
xxxx
xxxx
Noncurrent assets
xxxx
xxxx
Current liabilities
xxxx
xxxx
Noncurrent liabilities
Notes payable
Bonds payable
Leases payable
Stockholders' equity
xxxx
xxxx

	1991	*1990*
Notes payable	$XXX	$XXX
Bonds payable	XXX	XXX
Leases payable	XXX	XXX

Somers Corporation
Cash Flow Statement
For 1991

Operating activities
Payment of interest
Investing activities
xxxx
xxxx
Financing activities
Cash from loans
Cash from sale of bonds
Payments to retire debt

	1991	*1990*
Payment of interest ...	$ (XX)	$ (XX)

	1991	*1990*
Cash from loans......	$XXX	$XXX
Cash from sale of bonds	XXX	XXX
Payments to retire debt	(XXX)	(XXX)

CHAPTER 10

Long-Term Liabilities — Notes and Bonds

LEARNING OBJECTIVES

After studying Chapter 10, you should understand:

1. Debt financing and the importance of risk assessment, pp. 524-26.
2. The common traits among noncurrent liabilities, pp. 526-31.
3. Accounting for interest-bearing and noninterest-bearing long-term notes, pp. 532-34.
4. The characteristics of bonds, pp. 535-36.
5. Bonds sold at face value, at discount, and at premium, pp. 536-48.
6. Retirement of bonds, pp. 548-49.
7. Bond conversions, p. 549.
8. Bond sinking funds, pp. 549-51.
9. Bonds sold between interest dates, pp. 551-52.
10. Future values and present values (Appendix 10A), pp. 554-60.
11. Present value problems relating to bonds, leases, and pensions (Appendix 10B), pp. 563-69.

In this chapter the focus is on accounting for long-term debt financing—how accounting is affected by the contractual terms of certain noncurrent liabilities such as notes, bonds, leases, and pensions. As you study the chapter, you will note that a key factor in all decisions on noncurrent liabilities is the effect of interest on cash flow and on the financial statements. Once you understand the effects of interest, the accounting procedures follow a standard pattern.

Why is interest so important in noncurrent liabilities? Interest is the cost of using borrowed funds. The amount of interest over the entire term of a loan is the total cash outflow minus the total cash inflow related to the loan. The longer the time frame of a liability, the greater is the interest amount relative to the initial amount of the liability. The chapter begins with a discussion of four examples of loan repayment, illustrating the effect of alternative repayment patterns on the total amount of cash a company pays to the creditor of a long-term liability.

Within the chapter, accounting for long-term interest-bearing and noninterest-bearing notes is discussed. Then accounting for bonds is explained. Appendix 10A is concerned with techniques used to compute the time value of money—the future and present values; and Appendix 10B discusses special present value problems for bonds, leases, and pensions. The chapter is organized so that each topic builds on the previous topic. Should you have any difficulty with one topic, restudy it and the previous topics before moving on.

TYPES OF LONG-TERM FINANCING

Objective 1
Debt financing and the importance of risk assessment.

The two common types of long-term financing used by corporations are *debt financing* and *equity financing.* Long-term **debt financing** is a long-term borrowing from creditors; **equity financing** is the issuance of capital stock to the stockholders of a business. The providers of debt financing (creditors) and equity financing (stockholders) demand a monetary return. For debt financing, the return is interest; for equity financing, the return is dividends and/or share price appreciation of stock. As you might expect, debt financing and equity financing have advantages and disadvantages, and the terms of the contracts governing them are quite different.

A major difference between debt financing and equity financing is that interest expense is tax deductible to the business while dividend payments to stockholders are not. For income statement purposes, interest expense reduces net income, while dividend payments are not part of income measurement.

Debt financing creates constraints on a corporation that equity financing does not. Debt interest and principal must be paid when the contractual terms dictate or creditors can take legal action against the corporation. Often the loans made by creditors are **secured** by assets that are pledged as collateral on the loan (property pledged by the borrower to protect the lender in case of default). Thus, if bankruptcy occurs, the secured creditors have the right to the value of specific assets before other nonsecured creditors and equity holders are paid.

Long-term creditors often require specific provisions, called **covenants**, that limit management actions relating to paying dividends or acquiring more loans while their debt is outstanding. For example, a corporation could borrow money from a bank under a long-term note with a covenant requiring the corporation to maintain a specified ratio of total liabilities to total equity (called the *debt-to-equity ratio*). If the debtor violated the covenant provision, the bank would be entitled to take certain actions such as demanding immediate repayment.

Equity owners (stockholders) cannot demand dividend payments, and if the business terminates, they have a lower priority claim on the assets of the business than do creditors. Also, stockholders may prefer that a company use debt financing rather than equity financing because (1) debt financing does not dilute the stockholders' ownership interests; and (2) if a rate of return in excess of the cost of debt financing is earned, the excess return increases the stockholders' interest. You will learn more about equity financing in Chapter 11.

Remember that debt and equity do not have the same contractual rights. When a business terminates, providers of debt financing and equity financing are categorized as to their order of payment because the law gives different rights to different parties. In general, creditors have priority over equity holders, but a "pecking order" exists among creditors. **Senior debt** includes debt secured by mortgages that are pledged to specific assets. **Junior debt,** often called **unsecured** or **subordinated debt,** relies on the general creditworthiness of the debtor. In liquidation, after the pledged assets are used to pay off secured creditors, if the secured creditors are not fully paid, they have equal claims with the unsecured creditors to the remaining assets. Upon liquidation of a business, stockholders typically are not paid anything until all other claimants are paid in full.

Junk Bonds and High Risk

Consider the following conversation between a young stockbroker who has just started his first job on Wall Street and his father who is about to retire.

Father: Junior, my pension plan report says that 20% of the assets in the pension fund are in "unsecured, high yield, subordinated bonds." Someone at work says that's what they call **junk bonds.** Should I be worried? I don't like the idea of my pension payments depending on junk or whatever they call it.

Son: In the past few years, a lot of bonds were issued to finance **leveraged buyouts (LBOs).** That usually involves management or someone else arranging for all the stock of a company to be bought and, as part of the financing the company often issues these kinds of bonds. So, in essence, the management becomes the owners and the institutions like banks and pension funds get these high-yield debt instruments.

Father: I see, but why are they called junk and why would a pension fund buy them?

Son: Well, they are viewed as more risky than other debt of the issuing company. They usually are subordinated, which means they would have a lower priority of payment in case of bankruptcy. But, they pay high rates of interest, so, they are attractive to some investors.

Father: Should I be worried about my pension?

Son: That depends. First, only 20% of the assets of your fund are invested in them. I assume the rest of the assets are less risky. Most people believe that if the economy has a major recession, some of the companies that issued a lot of junk bonds would not be able to meet the heavy interest payments and some could go bankrupt. But, on the other hand, most issues of that type have paid on time and are yielding high returns. What I would suggest, Pop, is that you make sure that at least some of your other personal investments are in less risky assets.

Father: That's good advice, but I think I'll write the trustees of the fund a little note expressing my concern.

Son: You have that right and maybe if enough others do the same, they'll reconsider their investment strategy.

The preceding conversation highlights the trade-off between risk and return that all investors must make. Issuance of risky, high return securities such as junk bonds, has significant cash flow implications which must be thoughtfully considered by both the issuers and investors.

In this text we focus on going concerns rather than with terminating businesses, but the priority of rights of the various suppliers of funds affects how many ordinary business transactions are recorded and disclosed. In this chapter and the next one, we will discuss accounting for various types of financing activities.

The next section discusses the common traits, or characteristics, of debt financing of noncurrent liabilities. You will find this section important in providing a background for the remainder of the chapter.

COMMON TRAITS AMONG LONG-TERM LIABILITIES

Objective 2
The common traits among noncurrent liabilities.

When a company borrows money by means of long-term liabilities, the bank or lending institution first considers the amount of risk involved in the transaction. Risk is the probability of nonpayment or delay in payment of scheduled amounts. Banks evaluate risk by checking the creditworthiness of a company and studying its financial statements before lending money.

A lender wants to be compensated for (1) the risk of loss in case the borrower does not repay the loan and (2) the time value of money during the time the borrower uses the money. These two factors—risk and time—affect the total cash (principal plus interest) that a debtor returns to its creditor. In effect, given a certain amount borrowed (principal), the debtor's risk level and the timing of its cash payments determine the total cash returned to its creditor.

To help you understand the effect of timing on the total amount of cash a debtor pays to a creditor, this section discusses four general cases illustrating loan repayment: (1) principal and interest paid back in one lump sum, (2) principal paid back in equal amounts along with interest, (3) equal periodic total payments, and (4) interest paid each year and principal paid at maturity. The same basic interest rate, principal amount, and time period are used in all four cases—a $100,000, 10%, three-year loan. The total interest is always measured as the **total cash outflow minus total cash inflow.** Note, however, that the actual amount of interest (and total cash outflow) varies depending on the repayment schedule called for in each separate case.

Case 1—Debtor Pays Loan and Interest Back in One Lump Sum

A company borrowed $100,000 on January 1, 19x1. In this case assume the company paid the lender the total amount of interest and principal in one payment on December 31, 19x3, as shown in the following time line:

Case 1:

	1/1/x1	12/31/x1	12/31/x2	12/31/x3
	Borrow $100,000	*Pay $0*	*Pay $0*	*Pay $133,100*

Cash outflow. . . .	$133,100
Cash inflow	100,000
Interest	$ 33,100

On December 31, 19x3, the $33,100 interest the debtor pays back has been **compounded over the three-year period. Compound interest** is interest charged on both the unpaid principal and on any unpaid interest accrued after the inception of the liability. Since the interest rate is 10%, the unpaid amount of interest in the first year is $10,000 ($100,000 × .10 = $10,000), resulting in a $110,000 (principal plus interest) unpaid balance at the beginning of year 2. This $110,000 results in interest of $11,000 for year 2 ($110,000 × .10), and so on. The amortization schedule for this first case over the life of the liability follows:

Amortization Schedule for Case 1
($100,000, 10%, Three-Year Loan with Lump-Sum Payment)

(1) Date	(2) Cash Inflow (Outflow)	(3) Interest, 10% of Prior Column 5 Balance	(4) Change in Net Liability	(5) Net Liability (Book Value of the Obligation)
1/1/x1	$ 100,000	$ 0	$100,000	$100,000
12/31/x1	0	10,000	(10,000)	110,000
12/31/x2	0	11,000	(11,000)	121,000
12/31/x3	0	12,100	(12,100)	133,100
12/31/x3	(133,100)	0	(133,100)	0
	$ (33,100)	$33,100		

Each column of this amortization schedule communicates important facts about the life of the liability. Column 1 lists the critical dates, beginning with the inception of the $100,000 liability and ending with December 31, 19x3, when the principal plus interest is paid to the creditor. Column 2 shows the cash flows. The net cash flow is negative; $33,100 more cash flowed out than in. Remember, this difference in cash outflows over inflows represents the total interest on the loan. Column 3 shows how the $33,100 of total interest accrued each year. The change in the book value of the liability is shown in Column 4, and the balance at each date is shown in Column 5.

Now study the graphic explanation of Case 1 in Exhibit 10-1. Note how the cash inflow of $100,000 is indicated by the large arrow pointing upward above the 1/1/x1 date on the time line. On 12/31/x1, the point of the small arrow, which represents the net liability balance, is at $110,000. On 12/31/x2, the point of the small arrow is at $121,000. On 12/31/x3, the total obligation grows to $133,100 before the final payment—indicated by the large arrow pointing downward—in which the company paid the loan plus interest, leaving the liability $0. The figures in Case 1 of Exhibit 10-1 are the same as the figures in the amortization schedule of Case 1 given above.

Case 2—Principal Paid Back in Equal Amounts along with Interest

In Case 2, the principal is paid back in equal amounts of $33,333 each period, along with interest of 10% on the reducing unpaid principal as shown in the following time line:

Case 2:

1/1/x1	12/31/x1	12/31/x2	12/31/x3
Borrow $100,000	*Pay $43,333*	*Pay $40,000*	*Pay $36,667*

Cash outflow. . . .	$120,000
Cash inflow	100,000
Interest	$ 20,000

At the end of year 1, interest is $10,000 (10% of $100,000). The unpaid balance at the beginning of year 2 is $66,667, and interest for year 2 is, therefore,

EXHIBIT 10-1

Comparison of Different Cash Flow, Interest, and Net Liability Patterns

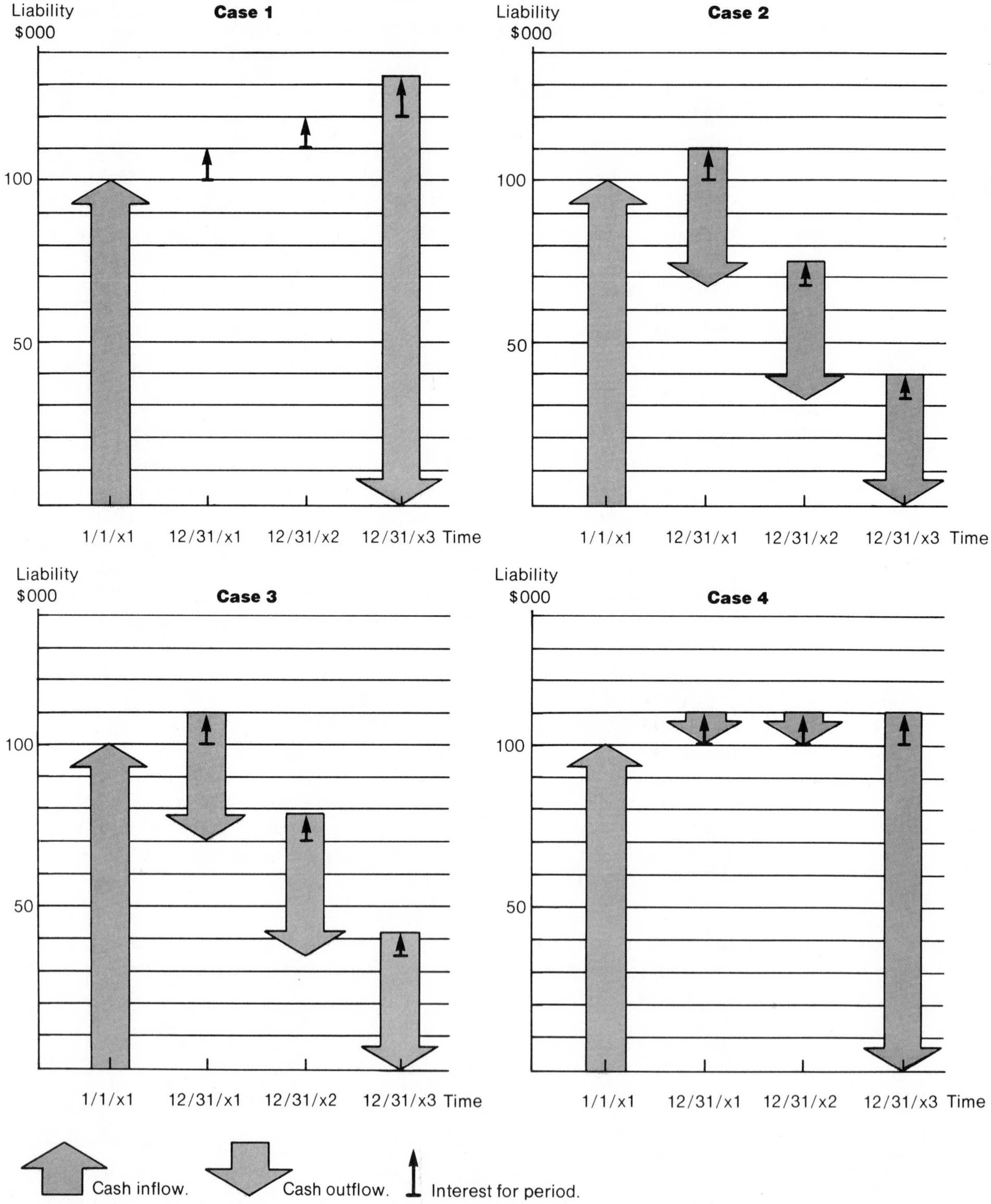

$6,667, and so on. Again, the events and balances related to the liability can be summarized as follows:

Amortization Schedule for Case 2 ($100,000, 10%, Three-Year Loan with Equal Amount Principal Reductions)

(1) Date	(2) Cash Inflow (Outflow)	(3) Interest, 10% of Prior Column 5 Balance	(4) Change in Net Liability	(5) Net Liability (Book Value of the Obligation)
1/1/x1	$100,000	$ 0	$100,000	$100,000
12/31/x1	(43,333)	10,000	(33,333)	66,667
12/31/x2	(40,000)	6,667	(33,333)	33,334
12/31/x3	(36,667)	3,333*	(33,334)	0
	$ (20,000)	$20,000		

*Rounded.

The graphic explanation of Case 2 in Exhibit 10-1 begins with the cash inflow arrow at $100,000 above 1/1/x1 on the time line. The first payment of $33,333 principal plus $10,000 interest is shown as a total cash outflow of $43,333 above 12/31/x1. The second payment results in an outflow of $33,333 principal plus $6,667 interest above 12/31/x2. The last outflow of cash shown above 12/31/x3 is $33,334 principal plus $3,333 interest. By comparing Case 2 in Exhibit 10-1 with the above amortization schedule, you can see how the numbers in the amortization schedule are depicted graphically.

Case 3—Equal Principal and Interest Payments

In Case 3, we illustrate a repayment schedule calling for a series of equal payments, which is often referred to as an *annuity* payment schedule. As shown in the following time line, the company pays the $100,000 borrowed on January 1, 19x1, with three equal payments of $40,211 at the end of each year, which includes the payment of principal and interest.

Case 3:

Borrow $100,000	*Pay $40,211*	*Pay $40,211*	*Pay $40,211*
1/1/x1	12/31/x1	12/31/x2	12/31/x3

Cash outflow. . . .	$120,633
Cash inflow	100,000
Interest	$ 20,633

While an annuity repayment schedule holds the payment constant each period, the amounts of interest in the payment decrease each year and the amount of principal reduction increases each period, as summarized in the following amortization schedule:

**Amortization Schedule for Case 3
($100,000, 10%, Three-Year Loan
with Equal Total Annual Payments)**

(1) Date	(2) Cash Inflow (Outflow)	(3) Interest, 10% of Prior Column 5 Balance	(4) Change in Net Liability	(5) Net Liability (Book Value of the Obligation)
1/1/x1	$100,000	$ 0	$100,000	$100,000
12/31/x1	(40,211)	10,000	(30,211)	69,789
12/31/x2	(40,211)	6,979	(33,232)	36,557
12/31/x3	(40,211)	3,654*	(36,557)	0
	$ (20,633)	$20,633		

*Rounded.

The even payment (annuity) method illustrated in Case 3 is frequently used for term loans of three to five years to finance purchases of automobiles, computers, or equipment. Annuity contracts are also often used over longer time periods (e.g., 30 years) to finance the purchase of houses (home mortgages) or facilities. Appendix 10B shows that the above pattern of payments is also used in leasing contracts with equal payments over several periods.

Now look at the graphic representation for Case 3 in Exhibit 10-1. The cash inflow arrow above 1/1/x1 is again at $100,000. Since the three payments are equal, the three cash outflow arrows are the same size. The figures for Case 3 in the exhibit again match the figures in the amortization schedule above.

Case 4—Interest Paid Each Year and Principal Paid at Maturity Date

In Case 4, the company pays its loan obligation with three equal year-end interest payments of $10,000 and at the end of the three-year period it also pays the $100,000 principal, as shown in the following time line:

Case 4:

Borrow $100,000	Pay $10,000	Pay $10,000	Pay $110,000
1/1/x1	12/31/x1	12/31/x2	12/31/x3

Cash outflow	$130,000
Cash inflow	100,000
Interest	$ 30,000

The payment of equal yearly interest makes the following amortization schedule relatively simple:

**Amortization Schedule for Case 4
($100,000, 10%, Three-Year Loan with Interest Paid
Annually and a Lump-Sum Principal Payment)**

(1) Date	(2) Cash Inflow (Outflow)	(3) Interest, 10% of Prior Column 5 Balance	(4) Change in Net Liability	(5) Net Liability (Book Value of the Obligation)
1/1/x1	$ 100,000	$ 0	$ 100,000	$100,000
12/31/x1	(10,000)	10,000	—	100,000
12/31/x2	(10,000)	10,000	—	100,000
12/31/x3	(110,000)	10,000	(100,000)	0
	$ (30,000)	$30,000		

This pattern of loan repayment, where interest is paid each period and the principal is paid at maturity, is often used in bond contracts.

Refer to Case 4 Exhibit 10-1. The cash inflow arrow is again at $100,000 above 1/1/x1 on the time line. The two cash outflow arrows above 12/31/x1 and 12/31/x2 indicate two payments of $10,000 interest. The cash outflow arrow above 12/31/x3 includes both the yearly interest payment and the principal.

The Common Elements in Long-Term Liabilities

Even though the contractual terms that determine the repayment schedules of the above cases differ and each may be called by a different name, the following three generalizations can be made:

1. In all cases, the net liability starts out at the amount borrowed, $100,000. This is called the *principal.*
2. When interest is compounded annually, the interest expense for each period is based on the balance of the liability at the beginning of the period (or the end of the prior period). Note that in all four cases the interest for year 1 is $10,000 (.10 × $100,000). The different cash payments in each case create different beginning-of-the-year net liabilities for years 2 and 3. As a result, each case shows different interest amounts for years 2 and 3.
3. The **net** cash outflow over the life of the liability exactly equals the total cumulative interest for all periods. In all four cases, the principal is $100,000, but interest varies from a low of $20,000 in Case 2 to a high of $33,100 in Case 1. The interest differences result from the differing net liability amounts that are outstanding or unpaid at the beginning of each year. In Case 1, both the principal and accumulated interest are outstanding for the entire life of the liability; while in Case 2, one third of the principal is paid off each year, quickly reducing the outstanding balance on which interest is computed.

The graphic representations of the four cases in Exhibit 10-1 verify these three generalizations on cash flow, interest, and net liability. Patterns of cash flow and the interest rate determine all other amounts used in accounting for noncurrent liabilities. To the extent that repayment of either principal or interest is delayed, the total cash outflow increases. Given that all cases have the same cash inflow ($100,000 on January 1, 19x1) and the same interest rate (10%), the varying interest for each case is a function of the different patterns of cash outflow.

ACCOUNTING FOR LONG-TERM NOTES

As explained in Chapter 7, a promissory note is a formal contract that stipulates the terms governing cash payments including dates, amounts to be paid, and perhaps interest rates. In Chapter 9, you learned that a short-term note can be interest bearing—the face of the note specifies the principal, interest rate, and maturity date—or noninterest bearing—the face of the note does not specify an interest rate, and its maturity value is the face value. The same is true for long-term notes.

Before discussing interest-bearing and noninterest-bearing long-term notes, you should remember from Chapter 9 that both interest-bearing and noninterest-bearing notes charge the debtor interest. The interest rate is not given on the noninterest-bearing note, but the debtor is charged interest and the rate can be determined from the cash flows and dates given on the note. The term *noninterest bearing* is an example of the imprecise use of accounting language that has become commonplace. Interest is almost always a factor in accounting for borrowing transactions, and the accountant's challenge is to determine the amount of interest and when and how it should be recognized. Accountants always strive to report the economic substance of transactions. In the case of liabilities, often the legal form of the contract obscures the substance, as illustrated in the wording of a note that seems to imply that there was no interest or that an unrealistically low interest rate was charged for the use of borrowed money.

Interest-Bearing Notes

Accounting for interest-bearing, long-term notes follows the pattern shown in the four cases discussed in the previous section. Interest expense is recorded each period based on the net liability at the beginning of the period and the period of time the liability amount is outstanding. In the four cases, the money was borrowed at the beginning of the first year. In the following example, the money is borrowed during the calendar year.

Company A, a calendar-year company, borrowed $10,000 on October 1, 19x1, to be paid back in 24 months with interest at 12% per year payable at maturity. Since the interest is stated on the face of the note, the rate of interest is called the **face interest rate** or **nominal interest rate.** The amortization schedule for this note is as follows:

Objective 3
Accounting for interest-bearing and noninterest-bearing long-term notes.

(1) Date	(2) Cash Inflow (Outflow)	(3) Interest, 12% of Prior Column 5 Balance	(4) Change in Net Liability	(5) Net Liability (Book Value of the Obligation)
10/1/x1	$ 10,000	$ 0	$ 10,000	$10,000
9/30/x2	—	1,200	1,200	11,200
9/30/x3	(12,544)	1,344	(11,200)	0
	$ (2,544)	$2,544		

Because such a note affects a company's financial position at the date of borrowing and throughout the life of the note, accountants make a series of journal entries. In this example, the fiscal year-end of December 31 does not coincide with the cash flows of October 1, 19x1, and September 30, 19x3. This necessitates accrual entries at December 31, 19x1, and December 31, 19x2, to record the interest for the months that have elapsed to that time.

The following journal entries capture the economic effects of the various phases in the life of the note. Compare the amortization schedule above and the series of journal entries.

19x1			
Oct. 1	Cash (A)	10,000	
	Notes Payable (L)		10,000
	To record proceeds from note.		
Dec. 31	Interest Expense (E)	300	
	Interest Payable (L)		300
	To accrue interest on note: 3/12 × $10,000 × .12 = 3/12 × **$1,200** = $300.		

19x2			
Dec. 31	Interest Expense (E)	1,236	
	Interest Payable (L)		1,236
	To accrue interest on note: 9/12 × \$10,000 × .12 = 9/12 × **\$1,200** = \$ 900 3/12 × \$11,200 × .12 = 3/12 × **\$1,344** = 336 \$1,236		

19x3			
Sept. 30	Interest Expense (E)	1,008	
	Interest Payable (L)	1,536	
	Notes Payable (L)	10,000	
	Cash (A)		12,544
	To record the payment of the note at maturity and interest from January 1, 19x3, to September 30, 19x3: 9/12 × \$11,200 × .12 = 9/12 × **\$1,344** = \$1,008.		

Interest expense is recorded each period: \$300 in 19x1, \$1,236 in 19x2, and \$1,008 in 19x3, totaling \$2,544, and the computations are given after each journal entry. Notice that even though the total interest of \$2,544 is recorded over the life of the note, the precise interest expense for an accounting period was computed according to the months the note was outstanding during that period.

Noninterest-Bearing Notes

The note described in the example above would be a noninterest-bearing note if the maturity amount of \$12,544 were described on the note and no mention were made of the interest rate. Remember that if the amount of the original transaction is the same for both interest-bearing and noninterest-bearing notes, the actual economic substance is the same. Thus, a company pays the same amount of interest for a \$10,000, 12%, two-year interest-bearing note as it pays for a \$12,544 face value, two-year noninterest-bearing note. In both cases the borrower receives \$10,000 and repays \$12,544 including \$2,544 interest.

As discussed in Chapter 9, when an obligation takes the form of a noninterest-bearing note, accountants show the maturity amount of the note reduced by a discount equal to the unrecorded interest to date. The note, therefore, is carried at maturity value, in this case \$12,544, with a contra account labeled Discount on Notes Payable used to bring the net book value of the note down to outstanding principal plus accrued and unpaid interest to date. The following entries to record the noninterest-bearing note are different than for the interest-bearing note above, but they convey the same economic message.

19x1			
Oct. 1	Cash (A)	10,000	
	Discount on Notes Payable (XL)	2,544	
	Notes Payable (L)		12,544
	To record proceeds from note.		
Dec. 31	Interest Expense (E)	300	
	Discount on Notes Payable (XL)		300
	To record interest on note: 3/12 × \$10,000 × .12 = 3/12 × **\$1,200** = \$300.		

19x2			
Dec. 31	Interest Expense (E)	1,236	
	Discount on Notes Payable (XL)		1,236
	To record interest on note: 9/12 × $10,000 × .12 = 9/12 × **$1,200** = $ 900 3/12 × $11,200 × .12 = 3/12 × **$1,344** = 336 $1,236		
19x3			
Sept. 30	Interest Expense (E)	1,008	
	Notes Payable (L)	12,544	
	Discount on Notes Payable (XL)		1,008
	Cash (A)		12,544
	To record the payment of the note at maturity and interest from January 1, 19x3, to September 30, 19x3: 9/12 × $11,200 × .12 = 9/12 × **$1,344** = $1,008.		

When a company uses a noninterest-bearing note, the balance sheet disclosure is different than when a company uses an interest-bearing note. However, the **net liability is the same.** As emphasized by the following table, the net liability shown on a balance sheet is not affected by use or nonuse of the contra account Discount on Notes Payable.

Interest-Bearing Note: *No Discount on Notes Payable Account*		*Noninterest-Bearing Note:* *Discount on Notes Payable Account*	
Excerpt from December 31, 19x1, Balance Sheet		**Excerpt from December 31, 19x1, Balance Sheet**	
Noncurrent liability:		Noncurrent liability:	
Notes payable.	$10,000	Notes payable	$12,544
Interest payable	300	Less discount	2,244
	$10,300		$10,300
Excerpt from December 31, 19x2, Balance Sheet		**Excerpt from December 31, 19x2, Balance Sheet**	
Current liability:		Current liability:	
Notes payable.	$10,000	Notes payable	$12,544
Interest payable	1,536	Less discount	1,008
	$11,536		$11,536

Review the noncurrent and current classifications in the above illustration. The note is first classified at December 31, 19x1, as noncurrent, which means maturity is more than a year off, and is then reclassified as current on December 31, 19x2, when the maturity is less than a year off. Recall that the current/noncurrent balance sheet classification is based on the "one year or operating cycle if longer" rule first introduced in Chapter 3.

ACCOUNTING FOR BONDS

The word **bonds** describes a whole series of debt contracts with varying terms. In this section, we concentrate on the basic principles for measurement and disclosure of bond liabilities and therefore discuss only a subset of the variations of bonds found in financial markets. This section begins with the characteristics of bonds, followed by discussions on bonds sold at face value, bonds sold at a discount, bonds sold at a premium, bond conversions, bond sinking funds, and bonds sold between interest dates.

Characteristics of Bonds

Corporations, governmental units, charitable organizations, and other entities issue bonds to raise money from the public. Since many potential creditors can be offered bonds, the advantage of bonds over bank loans is that the corporation has a broadly based potential source of capital. Often privately placed debt or notes with individual banks may not provide the magnitude of financing needed by large corporations. However, many large corporations find it advantageous to have both private and public debt.

Exhibit 10-2 lists the common types of bonds classified according to their security, interest payment, maturity date, and termination characteristics. We discuss these characteristics and their special accounting effects throughout the chapter. Keep in mind that one bond issue may have several of the characteristics listed. For instance, unsecured, coupon, term, convertible bonds are common as well as many other combinations of the characteristics given in Exhibit 10-2.

Objective 4
The characteristics of bonds.

Before issuing bonds, a corporation usually must get approval from its board of directors and stockholders—and the Securities and Exchange Commission if the bonds are to be sold publicly. Then the corporation usually selects a trustee—a bank or trust company—to represent the bondholders. For the protection of bondholders, a **bond indenture** is prepared that describes all rights and obligations of all parties to the bond.

Corporations usually issue bonds in a group, called a *bond issue.* The face value or maturity amount of each bond is often $1,000. The term of a bond can vary from 3 years to 30 years. When the bond indenture is prepared for a bond issue, the stated interest rate on the bonds is usually close to the market interest rate. However, since interest rates go up and down as the economy changes, the stated interest rate and the market interest rate are often not the same by the time the bond is sold to the public.

Usually, corporations hire an investment company, or underwriter, to market their bonds. The investment company makes a profit by selling the bonds to the public at a slightly higher price than the company paid the corporation and/or by charging the corporation a fee. The purchaser of a bond receives a bond certificate which states the terms of the bond. A bondholder may not want to keep a bond until it matures, which could be as much as 20 or 30 years after issuance. To facilitate change of bond ownership, some bonds are traded daily on bond markets similar to stock markets. Bond prices are quoted as a percentage of the bond's maturity value. Thus, a $1,000 bond may be sold on any given day at 95, which is 95% of $1,000 or $950, or at 105, which is 105% of $1,000 or $1,050.

EXHIBIT 10-2

Common Types of Bonds Categorized by Major Characteristics

Major Characteristics of Bonds	Type of Bond	Explanation of Varying Characteristics
Security	Secured (mortgage) bonds	Bonds backed by a physical asset as collateral, such as a building.
	Unsecured (debenture) bonds	Bonds backed only by the credit standing of the company.
Interest and principal payments	Registered bonds	Names and addresses of bond owners kept on file with the company or trustee so interest and principal are paid directly to the registered owner.
	Coupon (bearer) bonds	Coupons attached to bonds for each interest payment that state interest amount due and payment date; bondholder endorses coupon when payment is due and presents it to a bank for payment.
Maturity date	Term bonds	Principal paid in full on a specified maturity date.
	Serial bonds	Principal paid on a series of specified future dates.
Termination	Callable bonds	Bonds can be called in or repurchased by issuer prior to maturity; call price is usually higher than maturity value.
	Convertible bonds	Under specified conditions, bonds can be exchanged for capital stock.
	Redeemable bonds	Under specified conditions, bonds can be presented to the issuer for a specified cash payment.

Objective 5
Bonds sold at face value, at discount, and at premium.

Assume that on January 1, 19x1, a bondholder acquires a $1,000 face value, 10%, three-year bond for $1,000 cash. The bondholder would receive the following cash payments:

Beginning of year 1	End of year 1	End of year 2	End of year 3
	Interest Payment $100	*Interest Payment $100*	*Interest Payment Plus Maturity Amount Payment $1,100*

This bond contract calls for equal annual interest payments of $100, and the final payment includes the bond principal. Recall that this is the same pattern we introduced in Case 4 on page 530. Should the bondholder decide to sell the bond, the bond market (potential buyers and sellers of bonds) decides how much to pay for the remaining payments at the date of sale. If the market considers 10% to be the appropriate return for the bond, then buyers should be willing to pay $1,000. If the market determines that something **less than** 10% is an acceptable return for the remaining payments, then more than $1,000 per bond would be paid. When a bond sells for more than face value, it sells at a **premium,** and this indicates that the stated rate of interest on the bond is above the rate required by the market. When a bond sells for less than face value, it sells at a **discount** suggesting the market considers the stated interest rate to be lower than the required rate of interest. The rate of interest required by the market for a particular bond issue at the date of sale is called the **yield rate** or the **effective-interest rate.**

Bond contracts usually call for semiannual interest payments. The contract of the bond example used above stipulated annual payments. If semiannual payments were stipulated in the contract, the payments would be $50 every six months rather than $100 every year, but the bond would still be a 10% bond. When a $1,000 face value, 10%, three-year bond pays interest semiannually, the interest payments of $50 are computed as follows: (½)(10%)($1,000) = $50.

Bonds Sold at Face Value

When a bond is sold at face value, the bond is sold for the principal amount, and it yields the interest rate stated on the bond. To illustrate the accounting for these bonds, assume that 100 of Company A's $1,000, 10%, three-year bonds are sold for $1,000 each on January 1, 19x1. As shown in Exhibit 10-3, the cash inflow arrow (broken because of space limitations) is at $100,000, which indicates the company's initial liability is $100,000. Because interest is paid each year, as indicated by the three cash outflow arrows indicating interest paid, the liability at the end of each year remains at $100,000 for the entire life of the bond. The last cash outflow arrow indicates the payment, consisting of the $100,000 principal plus the final $10,000 interest payment. The amortization schedule at the bottom of the exhibit also shows these transactions. The journal entries are as follows:

Date	Account	Debit	Credit
19x1			
Jan. 1	Cash (A)	100,000	
	Bonds Payable (L)		100,000
	To record issuance of bonds.		
Dec. 31	Interest Expense (E)	10,000	
	Cash (A)		10,000
	To record annual interest payment on bonds.		
19x2			
Dec. 31	Interest Expense (E)	10,000	
	Cash (A)		10,000
	To record annual interest payment on bonds.		
19x3			
Dec. 31	Interest Expense (E)	10,000	
	Cash (A)		10,000
	To record last annual interest payment on bonds.		
	Bonds Payable (L)	100,000	
	Cash (A)		100,000
	To record retirement of bonds.		

EXHIBIT 10-3

Patterns of Cash Flows and Amortization Schedule—Bonds Issued at Face Value

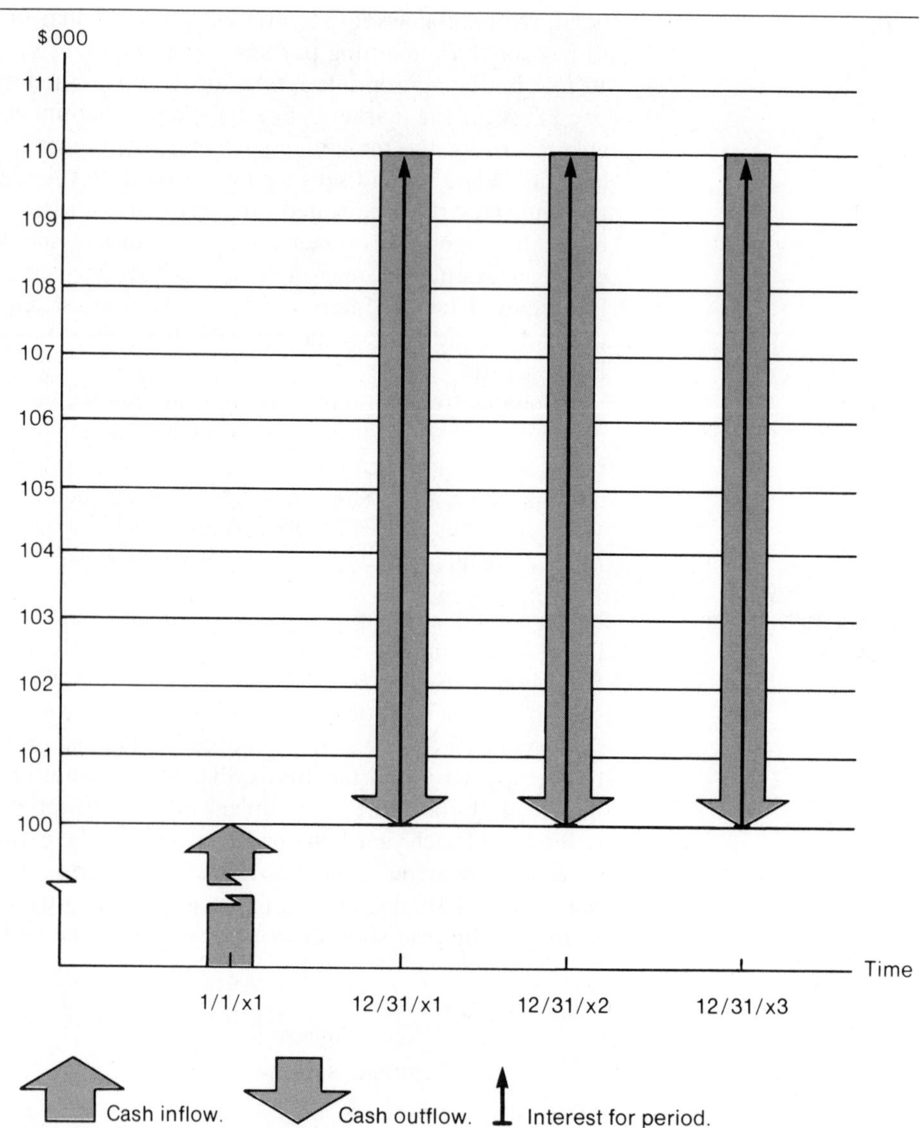

Amortization Schedule

Date	Cash Inflow (Outflow)	Interest Expense	Change in Net Liability	Net Liability (Book Value of the Obligation)
1/1/x1	$ 100,000	$ 0	$ 100,000	$100,000
12/31/x1	(10,000)	10,000	0	100,000
12/31/x2	(10,000)	10,000	0	100,000
12/31/x3	(10,000)	10,000	0	100,000
12/31/x3	(100,000)	0	(100,000)	0
	$ (30,000)	$30,000		

Total interest expense for any borrowing, including bonds, is always **total cash outflow minus total cash inflow.** For the above bonds, the total interest expense is $130,000 − $100,000 = $30,000, or $10,000 per year, for three years.

Bonds Sold at a Discount

Because bond terms, such as the maturity value, the number of periods, and the timing and amount of interest payments, are fixed, the bond issue price depends upon the effective interest the market establishes for the particular bond issuance. If $100,000 is paid for the bonds with a face value of $100,000 and a stated interest rate of 10%, then exactly 10% is earned each year; that is, 10% × $100,000 = $10,000. Remember that the bond contract is fixed in terms of cash flows to the holder. If bondholders demand less or more than a 10% return, the only way to affect the rate actually earned is to vary the purchase price. Thus, if the market for the bond described above will accept less than a 10% return, it will bid the purchase price of the bonds up above $100,000, effectively reducing the effective interest on the bonds. Alternatively, if the market for the bonds requires more than a 10% return, it will bid the purchase price of the bonds down below $100,000, thus increasing the effective interest on the bonds.[1] Furthermore, for bonds that have already been issued, the market value of the bonds will change as economy-wide changes in interest rates fluctuate. As market interest rates go up, bond selling prices go down and vice versa.

If Company A's $100,000 face value, 10%, three-year bonds discussed above were sold for $95,198, the discount would be $4,802, and the net liability or carrying value on the date of sale would be $95,198. The following journal entry records the sale of the bonds.

19x1			
Jan. 1	Cash (A)	95,198	
	Discount on Bonds (XL)	4,802	
	Bonds Payable (L)		100,000
	To record issuance of bonds.		

The discount account is a contra account to the long-term liability account, Bonds Payable. The net book value of the liability is the Bonds Payable amount (the maturity value of the bonds outstanding) minus the Discount on Bonds Payable account balance.

How much total interest expense is associated with this bond issue over the life of the issue? Again total interest expense equals cash outflow minus cash inflow. In this case, $130,000 is the total cash payment to bondholders called for in the bond contracts, and $95,198 is total cash paid in. Total interest expense then is $130,000 minus $95,198 or $34,802 over the life of the issue. This total is composed of (1) $30,000 in nominal interest payments and (2) the $4,802 discount upon issuance. Accountants have developed procedures to record the full $34,802 as an interest expense over the bond issue life. As we will see below, this involves "amortizing" or writing off the discount amount according to a certain

[1]Note that the total interest on any bond contract is simply the difference between the cash paid and the cash received. As a result, paying less than $100,000 (say, $97,000) for a bond with fixed payments of $10,000 per year "stated" interest plus $100,000 face value at maturity will increase total actual interest by the amount of the discount ($100,000 − $97,000 = $3,000 more interest). For premiums, the effective interest is less than the nominal interest by the amount of the premium paid over the face value.

schedule. We will see in the following sections that each year's interest expense for a bond issued at a discount is the sum of the cash paid and the amortization of the discount for that year. We will discuss two methods accountants use to amortize the bond discount—straight-line method and effective-interest method.

Amortization of Discount—Straight-Line Method. The Discount on Bonds account is a contra account to Bonds Payable that accountants amortize over the life of the bond. The simplest way to amortize the discount is the **straight-line method** where equal amounts are amortized each period [$4,802/3 = $1,601 (rounded) each period]. Exhibit 10-4 summarizes the cash flow, interest expense, and net liability amounts for the three-year period. Again, total interest expense of $34,802 for the life of the bonds is equal to the total cash outflow ($130,000) minus total cash inflow ($95,198). Using straight-line amortization, each period is charged with the same amount of interest expense. Interest expense for any period equals the sum of the cash payment for nominal interest and the amortization of discount for the period.

The journal entries at December 31 of each year are:

19x1			
Dec. 31	Interest Expense (E)	11,601	
	Discount on Bonds Payable (XL)		1,601
	Cash (A)		10,000
	To record annual interest payment.		
19x2			
Dec. 31	Interest Expense (E)	11,601	
	Discount on Bonds Payable (XL)		1,601
	Cash (A)		10,000
	To record annual interest payment.		
19x3			
Dec. 31	Interest Expense (E)	11,600	
	Discount on Bonds Payable (XL)		1,600
	Cash (A)		10,000
	To record last annual interest payment.		
	Bonds Payable (L)	100,000	
	Cash (A)		100,000
	To record retirement of bonds.		

Amortization of Discount—Effective-Interest Method. A more precise method of amortizing the discount is called the **effective-interest method.** Under this method, the interest expense is computed by applying the market interest rate to the net liability balance (carrying value) at the beginning of the period.

Assume that for Company A, 12% is the **effective-interest rate** at the date of bond issuance. (See Appendix 10B for the method of computing selling prices of bonds given the effective-interest rate.) The interest rate stated on the bond, you recall, is 10%. The bond sold for a discount because the effective-interest rate demanded by the market was higher—12%. Exhibit 10-5 summarizes the patterns of cash flow, interest, and net liability balance that apply to the three years the bonds are outstanding.

EXHIBIT 10-4

Patterns of Cash Flows and Amortization Schedule—Bonds Sold at a Discount

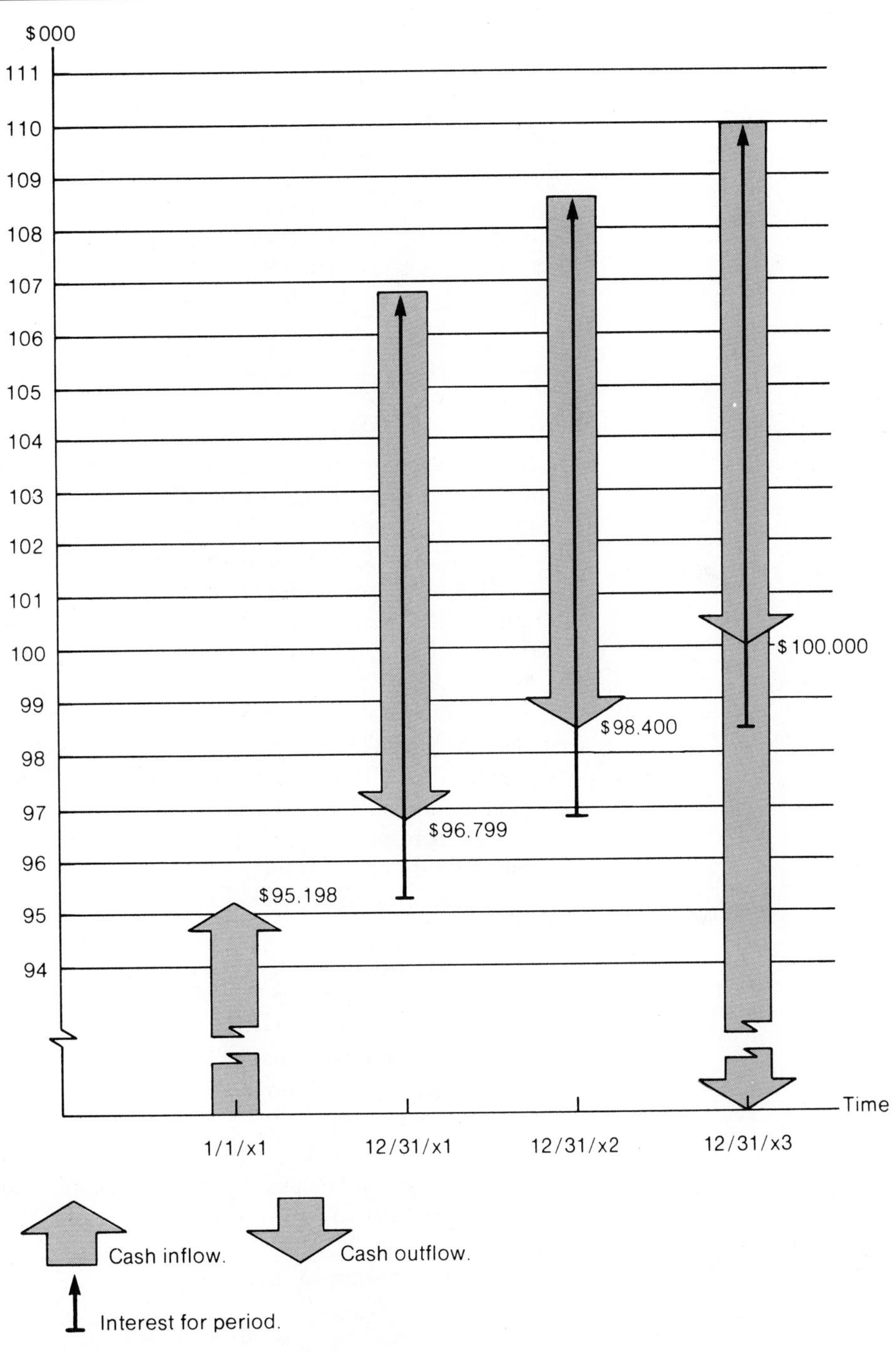

Note: The amortization schedule is at the top of the next page.

EXHIBIT 10-4 *(concluded)*

Amortization Schedule—Straight-Line Method

Date	*Cash Inflow (Outflow)*	*Interest Expense*	*Amortization of Discount*	*Change in Net Liability*	*Net Liability*
1/1/x1	$ 95,198	$ 0	$ 0	$ 95,198	$ 95,198
12/31/x1	(10,000)	11,601	1,601	1,601	96,799
12/31/x2	(10,000)	11,601	1,601	1,601	98,400
12/31/x3	(10,000)	11,600*	1,600	1,600	100,000
12/31/x3	(100,000)	0	0	(100,000)	0
	$ (34,802)	$34,802	$4,802		

*Rounded.

Interest expense for any period is the effective-interest rate applied to the beginning-of-the-period net liability balance: 19x1 interest is $95,198 × .12 = $11,424; 19x2 interest is $96,622 × .12 = $11,595; and 19x3 interest is $98,217 × .12 = $11,783 (rounded).[2] The amortization of the discount each year is the difference between the interest expense and the cash payment for nominal interest for the year: 19x1 amortization is $11,424 − $10,000 = $1,424; 19x2 amortization is $11,595 − $10,000 = $1,595; and 19x3 amortization is $11,783 − $10,000 = $1,783.

Again, interest expense of $34,802 for the entire life of the bond issue is total cash outflow ($130,000) minus total cash inflow ($95,198). The net liability or carrying value is the $100,000 face value minus the discount balance which is gradually amortized over the life of the bond. Interest expense increases because the net liability increases as the discount is amortized.

The journal entries to record the issuance of the bonds, the payment of interest, and the maturity payment are:

19x1			
Jan. 1	Cash (A)	95,198	
	Discount on Bonds Payable (XL)	4,802	
	Bonds Payable (L)		100,000
	To record issuance of bonds.		
Dec. 31	Interest Expense (E)	11,424	
	Cash (A)		10,000
	Discount on Bonds Payable (XL)		1,424
	To record annual interest payment and interest expense ($95,198 × .12).		
19x2			
Dec. 31	Interest Expense (E)	11,595	
	Cash (A)		10,000
	Discount on Bonds Payable (XL)		1,595
	To record annual interest payment and interest expense [($95,198 + $1,424) × .12].		

[2] $98,217 × .12 = $11,786; but we use $11,783 as interest expense to force the net liability to equal $100,000.

EXHIBIT 10-5

Patterns of Cash Flows and Amortization Schedule—Bonds Issued at a Discount

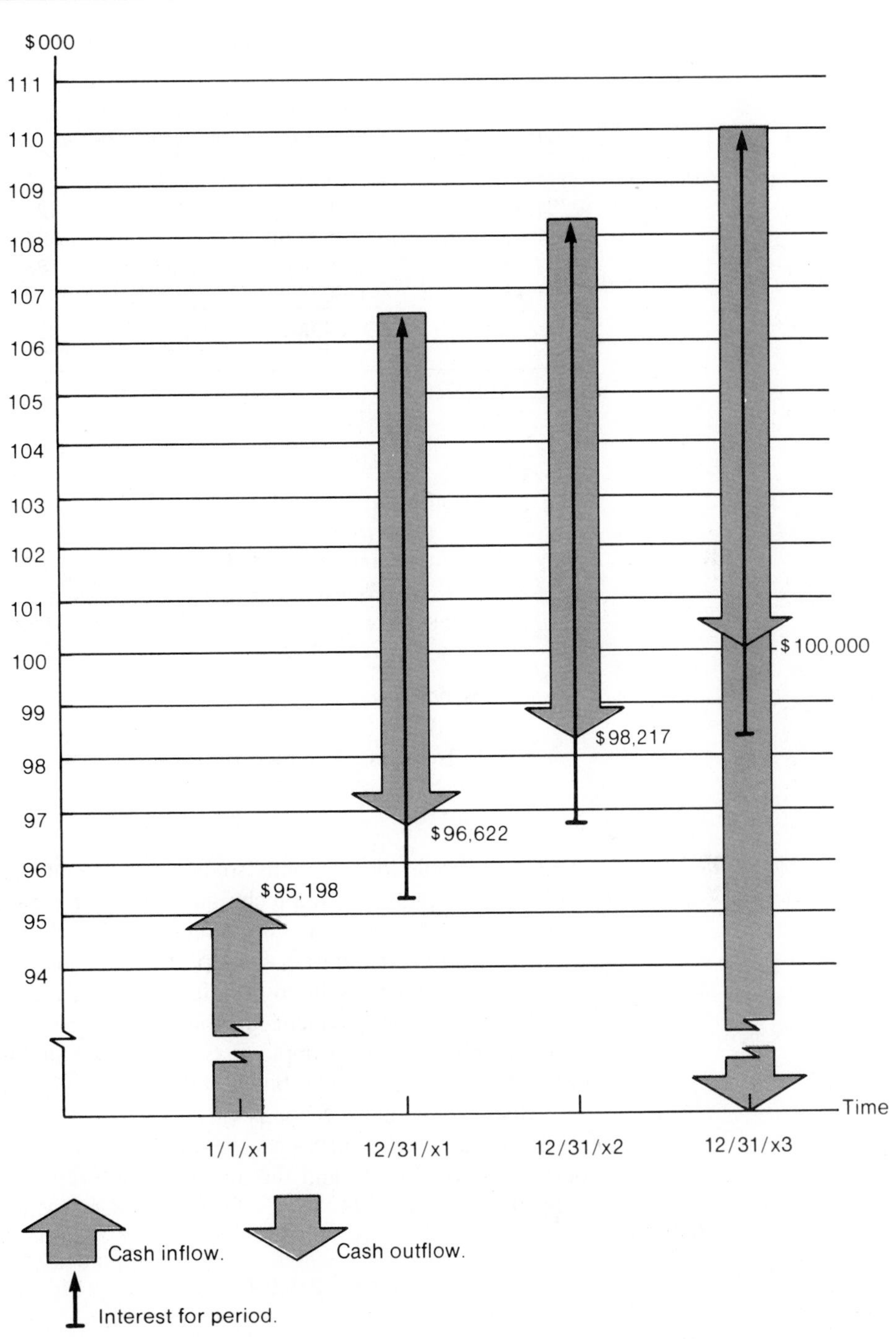

Note: The amortization schedule is at the top of the next page.

EXHIBIT 10-5 *(concluded)*

Amortization Schedule

Date	*Cash Inflow (Outflow)*	*Interest Expense*	*Amortization of Discount*	*Change in Net Liability*	*Net Liability*
1/1/x1	$ 95,198	$ 0	$ 0	$ 95,198	$ 95,198
12/31/x1	(10,000)	11,424	1,424	1,424	96,622
12/31/x2	(10,000)	11,595	1,595	1,595	98,217
12/31/x3	(10,000)	11,783*	1,783	1,783	100,000
12/31/x3	(100,000)	0	0	(100,000)	0
	$ (34,802)	$34,802	$ 4,802		

*Rounded.

19x3			
Dec. 31	Interest Expense (E)	11,783	
	Cash (A)		10,000
	Discount on Bonds Payable (XL)		1,783
	To record last annual interest payment and interest expense [$95,198 + $1,424 + $1,595) × .12 = $11,783]:*		
	Bonds Payable (L)	100,000	
	Cash (A)		100,000
	To record retirement of bonds.		

*Rounded.

Bonds Sold at a Premium

Recall our discussion of bonds sold at a discount. The same logic applies to bonds sold at a premium and techniques for amortizing bond premiums are similar to those used to amortize discounts. Bonds sell at a premium if the interest rate demanded by the market for a particular bond issue is less than the stated interest rate. Amortizing bond premiums has the effect of reducing periodic interest below the cash payment for nominal interest.

Going back to our example of Company A's $100,000 maturity, 10%, three-year bonds, assume that the bonds sell for $105,151. Why would the market pay more than face value for bonds (in this case, $5,151 more)? The premium of $5,151 represents the difference between the stated interest payments in the bond contract ($30,000) and the amount of interest required by bondholders for Company A's bonds ($24,849). Note the following cash outflows for this contract:

Issuance	*$10,000*	*$10,000*	*$100,000* *$10,000*	
1/1/x1	12/31/x1	12/31/x2	12/31/x3	Time

The $105,151 selling price of the bonds above is $5,151 more than the maturity value of the bond. This $5,151 is called the premium on bond payable and is recorded in an adjunct account (AL) which is the opposite of a contra account. A contra account such as Discount on Bonds Payable is subtracted from its related primary account. The adjunct account Premium on Bonds Payable is added to the primary account, Bonds Payable. The journal entry to record the sale of the bonds at a premium is:

19x1			
Jan. 1	Cash (A)	105,151	
	Bonds Payable (L)		100,000
	Premium on Bond Payable (AL)		5,151
	To record issuance of bonds.		

Both the straight-line method and the effective-interest method are also used in the amortization of bonds sold at a premium.

Amortization of Premium—Straight-Line Method. For bonds sold at a premium, interest expense each period is equal to the cash payment for nominal interest minus the amount of premium amortization. The initial premium on the bonds is amortized in equal amounts over the three-year period so that the net liability at the date of maturity is $100,000 as shown in Exhibit 10-6.

The journal entries for each payment date are:

19x1			
Dec. 31	Interest Expense (E)	8,283	
	Premium on Bonds Payable (AL)	1,717	
	Cash (A)		10,000
	To record annual interest payment.		
19x2			
Dec. 31	Interest Expense (E)	8,283	
	Premium on Bonds Payable (AL)	1,717	
	Cash (A)		10,000
	To record annual interest payment.		
19x3			
Dec. 31	Interest Expense (E)	8,283	
	Premium on Bonds Payable (AL)	1,717	
	Cash (A)		10,000
	To record last annual interest payment.		
	Bonds Payable (L)	100,000	
	Cash (A)		100,000
	To record retirement of bonds.		

Amortization of Premium—Effective-Interest Method. Just as with bond discount, a more precise method of calculating the interest expense is to apply the effective market interest rate to the beginning-of-the-period net liability amount. In this case, the **effective-interest rate** is 8%. (See Appendix 10B for the method of computing bond selling price given the effective-interest rate.) Exhibit 10-7 summarizes the pattern of cash flow, interest, and net liability balance applicable to the three years the bond is outstanding. Just as with bond discounts, the interest expense for a year is the effective-interest rate applied to the beginning-of-the-period net liability balance: 19x1 interest is $105,151 × .08 = $8,412; 19x2 interest is $103,563 × .08 = $8,285; and 19x3 interest is $101,848 × .08 = $8,152 (rounded). The amortization of premium is the cash flow for nominal interest minus the interest expense for each year: 19x1 amortization is

EXHIBIT 10-6

Patterns of Cash Flows and Amortization Schedule—Bonds Sold at a Premium, Straight-Line Method

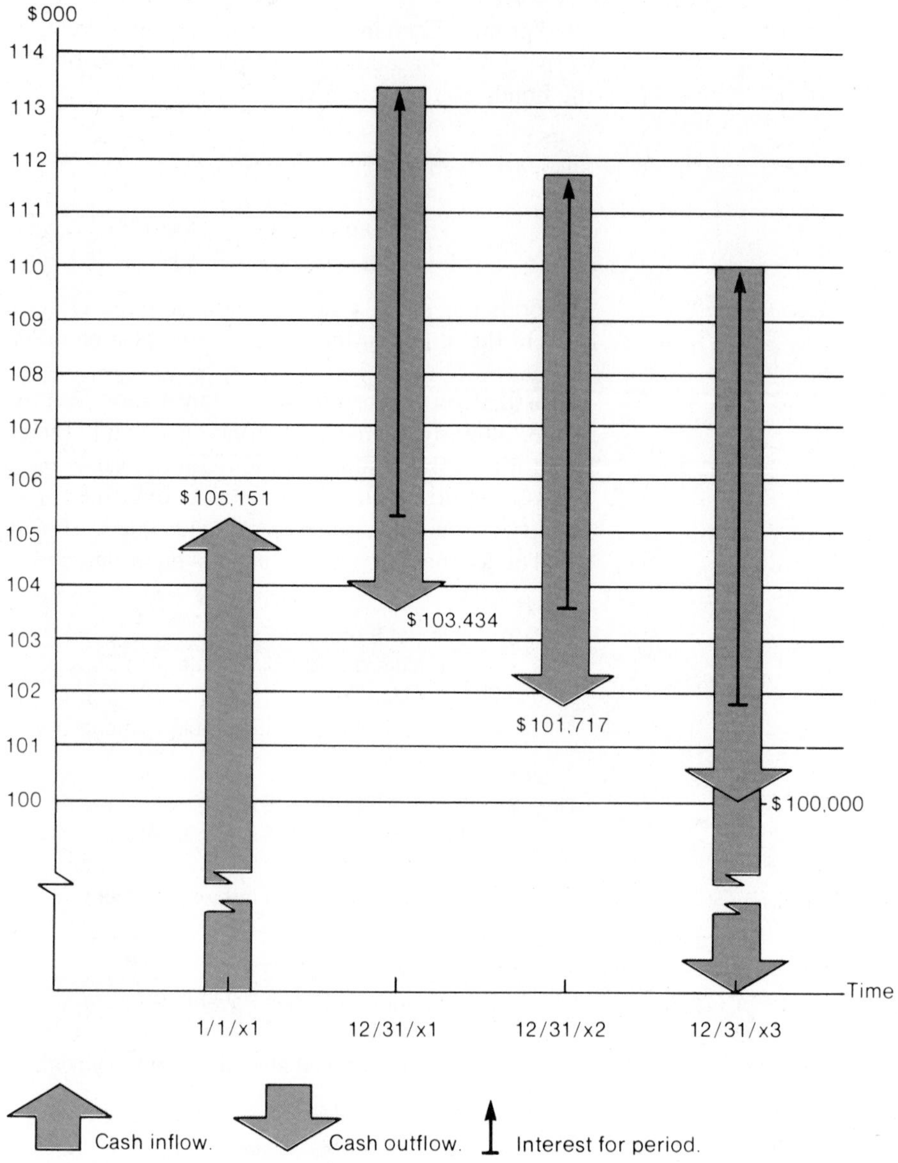

$000

114
113
112
111
110
109
108
107
106
105
104
103
102
101
100

$105,151
$103,434
$101,717
$100,000

Time

1/1/x1
12/31/x1
12/31/x2
12/31/x3

Premium Amortization Schedule—Straight-Line Method

Date	*Cash Inflow (Outflow)*	*Interest Expense*	*Amortization of Premium*	*Change in Net Liability*	*Net Liability*
1/1/x1	$ 105,151	$ 0	$ 0	$ 105,151	$105,151
12/31/x1	(10,000)	8,283	1,717	(1,717)	103,434
12/31/x2	(10,000)	8,283	1,717	(1,717)	101,717
12/31/x3	(10,000)	8,283	1,717	(1,717)	100,000
12/31/x3	(100,000)	0	0	(100,000)	0
	$ (24,849)	$24,849	$5,151		

E X H I B I T 10 - 7

Patterns of Cash Flows and Amortization Schedule—Bonds Sold at a Premium, Effective-Interest Method

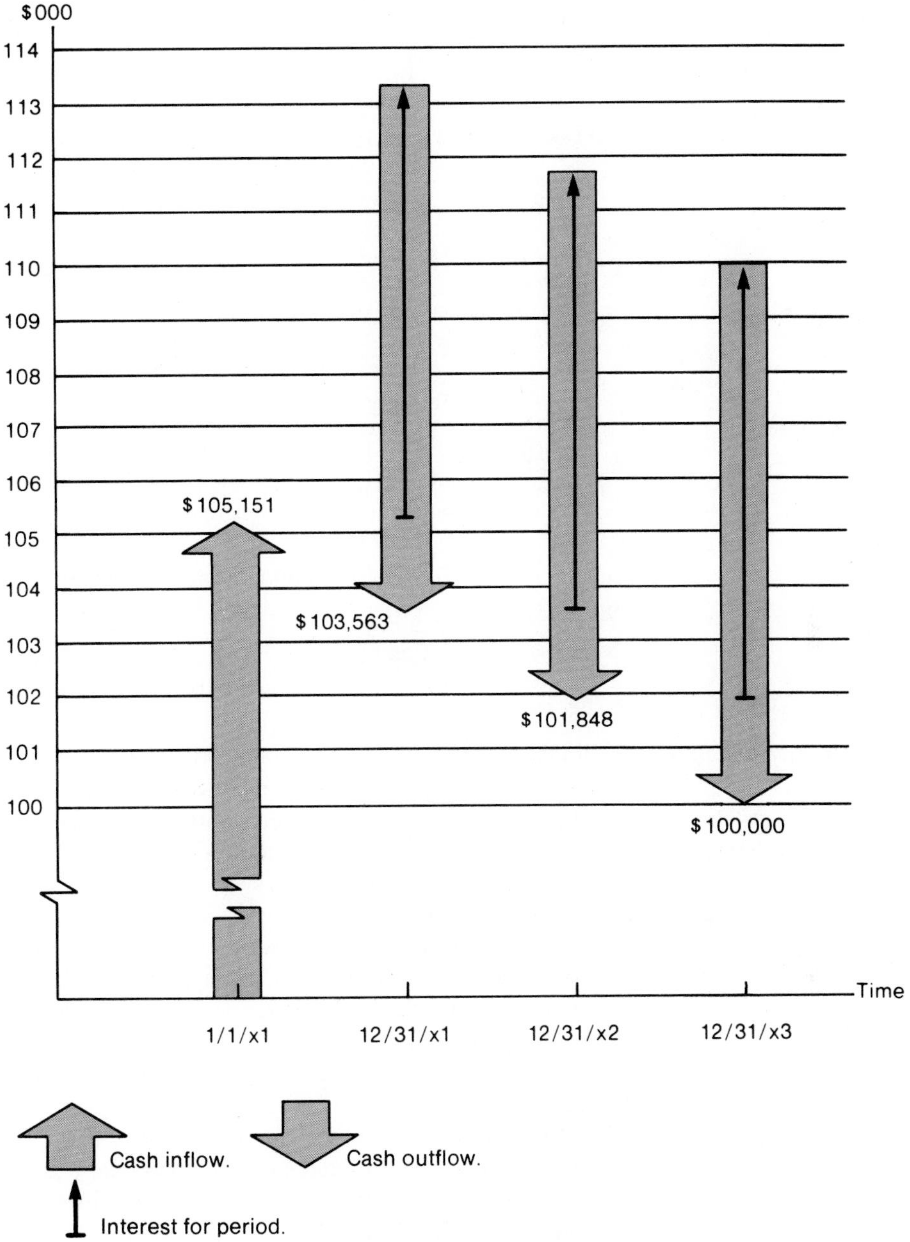

$000

114
113
112
111
110
109
108
107
106
105
104
103
102
101
100

$105,151
$103,563
$101,848
$100,000

Time

1/1/x1
12/31/x1
12/31/x2
12/31/x3

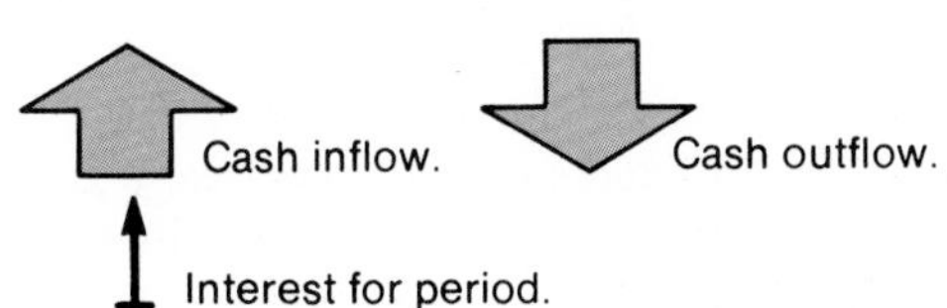

Amortization Schedule

Date	Cash Inflow (Outflow)	Interest Expense	Amortization of Premium	Change in Net Liability	Net Liability
1/1/x1	$ 105,151	$ 0	$ 0	$ 105,151	$105,151
12/31/x1	(10,000)	8,412	1,588	(1,588)	103,563
12/31/x2	(10,000)	8,285	1,715	(1,715)	101,848
12/31/x3	(10,000)	8,152	1,848	(1,848)	100,000
12/31/x3	(100,000)	0	0	(100,000)	0
	$ (24,849)	$24,849	$5,151		

\$10,000 − \$8,412 = \$1,588; 19x2 amortization is \$10,000 − \$8,285 = \$1,715; and 19x3 amortization is \$10,000 − \$8,152 = \$1,848.

Date	Account	Debit	Credit
19x1			
Dec. 31	Interest Expense (E)	8,412	
	Premium on Bonds Payable (AL)	1,588	
	Cash (A)		10,000
	To record annual interest payment.		
19x2			
Dec. 31	Interest Expense (E)	8,285	
	Premium on Bonds Payable (AL)	1,715	
	Cash (A)		10,000
	To record annual interest payment.		
19x3			
Dec. 31	Interest Expense (E)	8,152	
	Premium on Bonds Payable (AL)	1,848	
	Cash (A)		10,000
	To record last annual interest payment.		
	Bonds Payable (L)	100,000	
	Cash (A)		100,000
	To record retirement of bonds.		

Retirement of Bonds

Objective 6
Retirement of bonds.

Bond contracts expire on the maturity date, at which time the face value of the bonds must be paid to the bondholder. If bonds are outstanding until maturity, all premiums and discounts are amortized by the maturity date, the book value of the bonds is equal to the required maturity cash payment, and no gain or loss is realized on the retirement.

Bonds often contain a provision giving the issuer the right to retire or **call** the bonds before maturity at a price specified in the bond contract. If a call provision does not exist, issuers can retire bonds by simply making an open-market purchase. Issuers can also offer new debt contracts to the holders of old bonds. Since several methods exist for bond issuers to retire existing debt and corporations frequently make use of these methods, you may question what would motivate a bond issuer to retire bonds.

The decision to retire bonds is based on the following logic. Outstanding bonds require certain fixed cash outflows over a known period of time in the future, but the early retirement of bonds requires a certain immediate cash outflow. Although the decision to retire bonds early involves many factors that are beyond the scope of this text, the comparisons of the returns expected from alternative uses of cash are important in the decision of whether or not to retire bonds early. If the only alternative use of idle cash is the retirement of bonds, then, of course, retirement would always be advantageous. In most cases, positive return opportunities are available for new investments such as expansion of productive capacity, purchase of equity securities of other corporations, and so on. Often the extinguishment of existing debt or the substitution of new debt for existing debt perhaps in combination with other financing and investing transactions is expected to yield the most desirable results.

When bonds are retired, for whatever reason, the Bonds Payable account balance and any balance in the premium or discount account are eliminated, and a gain or loss is recognized for the difference between the amount paid for the bonds and the carrying value. For example, if the bonds described in the amortization schedule in Exhibit 10-6 were purchased from bondholders on January 1, 19x3, for $106,000, the following journal entry would be made:

19x3			
Jan. 1	Loss on Retirement of Bonds (IS)	4,283	
	Bonds Payable (L)	100,000	
	Premium on Bonds Payable (AL)	1,717	
	Cash (A)		106,000
	To record retirement of bonds.		

Note that no interest would be paid for year 3 because the bond liability would have been eliminated on retirement as of the beginning of year 3.

Gains or losses on early retirement of debt of any kind are included on the income statement (IS); and if the aggregate of all such items is material, then the total gains or losses must be shown as a separate extraordinary item. (See Chapter 13 for a discussion of extraordinary items.)

Bond Conversions

Objective 7
Bond conversions.

Some bonds are issued with a provision that the bondholder may convert the bond into capital stock. This **convertibility** gives the bondholder flexibility in managing investments. Initially, the fixed interest and maturity payments may be desirable for the bondholder, but if bonds have a conversion feature and the value of capital stock goes up relative to the bonds, the bondholder may want to convert bonds into stocks.

At the time the **convertible bonds** are issued, they are accounted for in the same manner as all other bonds with no recognition of the convertibility feature. When the bonds are converted, the Bonds Payable account along with the premium or discount account are eliminated, and the appropriate stock accounts are recorded.

As an example of accounting for convertible bonds, assume a company issues $1,000 face value bonds that currently have a book value of $1,040 and have all interest recorded to date. Each bond is convertible into 50 shares of capital stock valued at $20.80 per share. The journal entry to record the conversion of one bond is as follows:

Bonds Payable (L)	1,000	
Premium on Bonds Payable (L)	40	
Capital Stock (SE)		1,040
To record conversion of one bond into 50 shares of capital stock.		

Notice that no gain or loss is recorded upon conversion, regardless of the fair values of the stocks or bonds.

Bond Sinking Funds

Objective 8
Bond sinking funds.

When companies issue bonds, there comes a time when plans must be made for the payment of the maturity amounts. Since large cash amounts are usually involved, it is often the case that a company will not have enough idle cash to pay the maturity amount. Companies sometimes issue new debt to pay off the old debt, or a **bond sinking fund** is established that accumulates cash over the life of the bond issue. A bond sinking fund is money put aside for the purpose of retiring bonds. Usually a bond sinking fund is accumulated because the bond contract calls for annual contributions of certain amounts to be invested annually and allowed to grow for the exclusive purpose of paying bond obligations to the bondholders at maturity. The example that follows illustrates accounting for a bond sinking fund.

Sunshine Flowers has a $100,000, five-year bond issue outstanding. At the end of years 1 through 5, Sunshine Flowers put $16,000 into a bond sinking fund. Management intends to use the proceeds from the fund to pay the maturity amount of the bonds. If the fund earns $2,000 in year 2 and $3,000, $3,500, and $3,800 in the subsequent years, the fund would grow as follows:

	Payments into Fund	*Investment Revenue*	*Sinking Fund Balance*
12/31/x1.	$16,000	$ 0	$16,000
12/31/x2.	16,000	2,000	34,000
12/31/x3.	16,000	3,000	53,000
12/31/x4.	16,000	3,500	72,500
12/31/x5.	16,000	3,800	92,300

Journal entries for the accumulation of the bond sinking fund would be as follows:

19x1			
Dec. 31	Bond Sinking Fund (A)	16,000	
	Cash (A)		16,000
	To record annual payment to fund.		
19x2			
Dec. 31	Bond Sinking Fund (A)	2,000	
	Investment Revenue (R)		2,000
	To record interest earned on fund.		
31	Bond Sinking Fund (A)	16,000	
	Cash (A)		16,000
	To record annual payment to fund.		
19x3			
Dec. 31	Bond Sinking Fund (A)	3,000	
	Investment Revenue (R)		3,000
	To record interest earned on fund.		
31	Bond Sinking Fund (A)	16,000	
	Cash (A)		16,000
	To record annual payment to fund.		
19x4			
Dec. 31	Bond Sinking Fund (A)	3,500	
	Investment Revenue (R)		3,500
	To record interest earned on fund.		
31	Bond Sinking Fund (A)	16,000	
	Cash (A)		16,000
	To record annual payment to fund.		

19x5			
Dec. 31	Bond Sinking Fund (A)	3,800	
	Investment Revenue (R)		3,800
	To record interest earned on fund.		
31	Bond Sinking Fund (A)	16,000	
	Cash (A)		16,000
	To record annual payment to fund.		

When the bonds are retired, the following entry would be made:

19x5			
Dec. 31	Cash (A)	92,300	
	Bond Sinking Fund (A)		92,300
	To reclassify sinking fund to cash.		
31	Bonds Payable (L)	100,000	
	Cash (A)		100,000
	To record retirement of bonds.		

In the case of Sunshine Flowers, the sinking fund balance was less than the amount needed to retire the bonds at maturity. In other cases, companies could have surpluses. Obviously, the bond issuer must pay any deficiency in the sinking fund out of cash and can retain any surplus in the sinking fund as long as all contractual provisions of the bond issue have been met.

Bonds Sold between Interest Dates

Objective 9
Bonds sold between interest dates.

Even though the bond indenture agreement states the interest periods such as January through June and July through December, bonds may not always be sold at the beginning of the first interest period. Consider the following case:

> One thousand $1,000 face value bonds with 12% annual interest paid semiannually (i.e., $60 per bond on June 30 and December 31) starting in year 1.

If instead of being issued on January 1, the bonds are issued on March 1, what happens to the January and February interest? Although the bonds are outstanding for only four months of the first interest period, on June 30, 19x1, the corporation pays the bondholders the nominal interest for the entire six months. Assuming the bonds have an effective-interest rate of 12% (no premium or discount), the purchaser must pay the accrued January and February interest in addition to the face value of the bond. In this case, if the bonds have a total face value of $1 million, interest would be added to the selling price and computed as follows: \$1 million $\times$ .12 $\times$ $\frac{2}{12}$ = \$20,000. The journal entries for the first interest period are:

19x1			
Mar. 1	Cash (A)	1,020,000	
	Bonds Payable (L)		1,000,000
	Interest Payable (L)		20,000
	To record issuance of bonds and cash received for interest.		
June 6	Interest Expense (E)	40,000	
	Interest Payable (L)	20,000	
	Cash (A)		60,000
	To record first interest payment.		

The March 1, 19x1, $20,000 payment by the bondholders for interest is returned to the bondholders on June 30, 19x1, with the remainder of the semiannual interest; and the income statement of the issuer is not affected by the first two months' interest. Note that all bondholders would receive the same interest payment (face value times stated interest rate) regardless of when the bonds were issued during the interest period. Since it is commonplace to issue bonds in large numbers over a period of time, this method avoids the high clerical cost that would be incurred if interest payments to bondholders depended on the date of issuance to each bondholder.

SUMMARY

Corporations use two types of long-term financing—debt financing and equity financing. Debt financing is long-term borrowing. Equity financing is the issuance of stock. This chapter focuses on debt financing that generates long-term (noncurrent) liabilities.

Several types of noncurrent liabilities have common traits. They are governed by contractual terms that determine the pattern of cash (or other asset) flows between the creditor and the debtor. Two important generalizations underlie much of the accounting for long-term liabilities:

1. The total interest on a debt contract is the total cash paid to creditors minus the total cash received from creditors.
2. The interest charge for a period is the effective interest rate times the beginning of the period liability balance.

Notes and bonds are common noncurrent liabilities, and the same basic principles govern each. A note is an obligation to one creditor where the amount borrowed, the amount to be paid back, and the payment dates are all stated in the form of a contract between the debtor and a lending institution or other individual creditor. Bonds are contracts printed in anticipation of offering them for sale to many different creditors, or bondholders. Because bond contracts are made to be sold to many people, the terms such as *interest paid* and *dates of payment* are determined in advance, and the market determines at the date of sale the amount to be paid for the bond. Differences in effective and face interest rates cause bonds to be sold at premiums or discounts, and the sale of bonds between interest dates creates additional accounting problems.

DEMONSTRATION EXERCISE

The following transactions relate to a $1 million bond issue by Memory Datalink. The 1,000 bonds are $1,000 face value, 8%, five-year bonds with a maturity date of December 31, 19x5.

a. Sell 500 bonds on January 1, 19x1, for a total of $520,792 yielding a 7% effective-interest rate.

b. Sell remaining 500 bonds on March 31, 19x1, for a total of $510,000, yielding an 8% effective-interest rate.

c. Pay interest on the bonds on June 30, 19x1, and December 31, 19x1.

d. Retire 250 of the bonds sold in (*a*) on January 1, 19x2, for a total of $252,000.

Required:
Prepare the journal entries to record the above transactions using the effective-interest method to amortize bond discounts and premiums.

Solution:

Date	Account	Debit	Credit
19x1			
Jan. 1	Cash (A)	520,792	
	Bonds Payable (L)		500,000
	Premium on Bonds Payable (AL)		20,792
	To record issuance of 8% bonds at 7% effective-interest rate.		
Mar. 31	Cash (A)	510,000	
	Bonds Payable (L)		500,000
	Interest Payable (L)		10,000
	To record issuance of 8% bonds at an 8% effective-interest rate.		
June 30	Interest Expense (E)	18,228	
	Premium on Bonds Payable (AL)	1,772	
	Cash (A)		20,000
	To record semiannual interest payment and amortization of bond premium for bonds issued 1/1/x1. $20,000 − ($520,792 × .07 × 6/12).		
30	Interest Expense (E)	10,000	
	Interest Payable (L)	10,000	
	Cash (A)		20,000
	To record semiannual interest payment for bonds issued 3/31/x1.		
Dec. 31	Interest Expense (E)	18,166	
	Premium on Bonds Payable (AL)	1,834	
	Cash (A)		20,000
	To record semiannual interest payment and amortization of bond premium for bonds issued 1/1/x1.		
31	Interest Expense (E)	20,000	
	Cash (A)		20,000
	To record semiannual interest payment for bonds issued 3/31/x1.		
19x4			
Jan. 1	Bonds Payable (L)	250,000	
	(Debit) Premium on Bonds Payable (AL)	8,593*	
	Gain on Retirement of Bonds (R)		6,593
	Cash (A)		252,000
	To record retirement of 250 bonds issued 1/1/x1.		

*($20,792 − $1,772 − $1,834) × 1/2.

APPENDIX 10A

Future Values and Present Values

A dollar in your hand today is worth more than the promise of receiving a dollar one year in the future. Why? First, the promise of receiving a dollar in a year involves risk—something could happen so that you may not receive the promised dollar. Second, money has time value, and you could invest the dollar so that in a year its value would grow.

Because money has time value, if someone wants to borrow $100 from you today with a promise to pay it back in one year, you would probably charge interest for the use of the money. In the following time line, the present value of your $100 is $100. However, the future value of your $100 has grown to $110; the $10 difference is the interest.

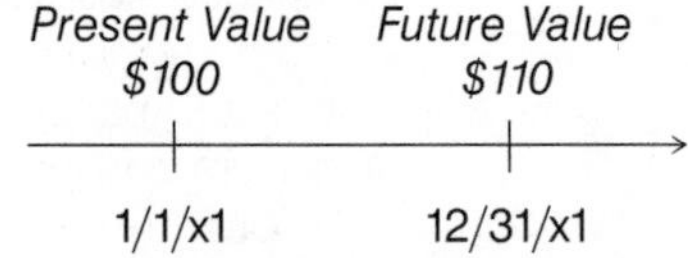

Everything of value commands a price, and owners of valuable items will charge that price for its use. Interest is the price paid for use of money just as rent is the price paid for use of an apartment.

This appendix explains in greater detail what you were introduced to about interest in the chapter. Then future values and present values are discussed.

COMPOUND VERSUS SIMPLE INTEREST

Simple interest is computed by the following formula:

$$\text{Principal} \times \text{Rate} \times \text{Time}$$

If $10,000 is borrowed on January 1, 19x1, at 10% simple interest and paid back on December 31, 19x2, the simple interest is $10,000 × .10 × 2 = $2,000.

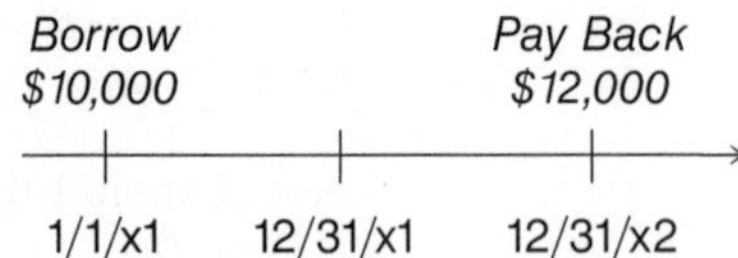

Compound interest uses the time value of money on the entire outstanding amount **including** interest. Thus, **compound interest** is interest charged on both the unpaid principal and any unpaid interest accrued after the inception of the liability. For example, if we change the terms of the $10,000, 10%, two-year loan so that interest compounded annually is paid at maturity, we have the following time line:

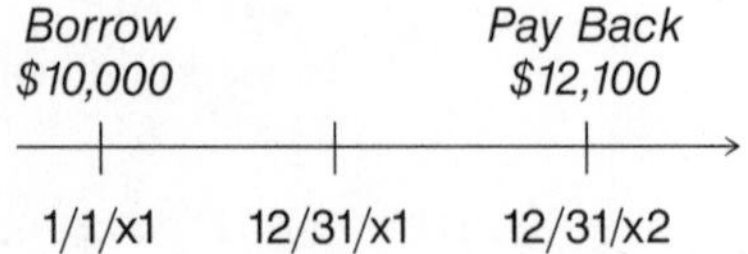

The compound interest amount is computed as follows:

	Amount Outstanding				Interest
Interest—year 1	$10,000	×	.10	=	$1,000
Interest—year 2	11,000	×	.10	=	1,100
Total interest					$2,100

The $100 differential between the $2,000 simple interest illustrated earlier and the $2,100 compound interest is the interest charged on the previous unpaid interest for year 1. The diagram in Exhibit 10A-1 illustrates how the $10,000 borrowed on January 1, 19x1, grows to $12,100 on December 31, 19x2.

FUTURE VALUES

Future value is the value that an investment today will grow to, by a stated time in the future at a specified interest rate. In this section, you will learn how to compute the future value of a single amount and the future value of an ordinary annuity.

Future Value of a Single Amount

Objective 10
Future values. . . .

If $20,000 is invested on January 1, 19x1, at 10% compound interest, how much will the $20,000 grow to in three years? In other words, what is the maximum that could be withdrawn at the end of three years? The answer is that the $20,000 will grow to its **future value,** which is the sum of the principal and compound interest for the time the investment is held. You can compute the exact amount of future value in several ways. In the discussion on compound interest, you saw that each year more interest is accumulated, which increases the amount outstanding by more each period.

The following table illustrates one method of computing future value:

	Amount Outstanding		Interest Rate		Interest Amount
Interest—year 1.	$20,000	×	.10	=	$ 2,000
Interest—year 2.	22,000	×	.10	=	2,200
Interest—year 3.	24,200	×	.10	=	2,420
Total interest					$ 6,620
Principal					20,000
Future value					$26,620

This type of computation can be time consuming. Therefore, precomputed table factors are available to aid in the computation of compound interest. Table 10A-1 (at the end of this appendix) shows the amount $1 will grow to for different numbers of periods outstanding and different interest rates. In our example, we have three periods at 10% per period. The intersection of the column for interest rate and the row for number of periods gives the appropriate table factor. The future value factor is 1.331, which is applied to the principal of $20,000 as follows:

(Principal) (Future value factor) = Future value
($20,000) (1.331) = $26,620

EXHIBIT 10A-1

Growth of the Total Amount Outstanding under Compound Interest

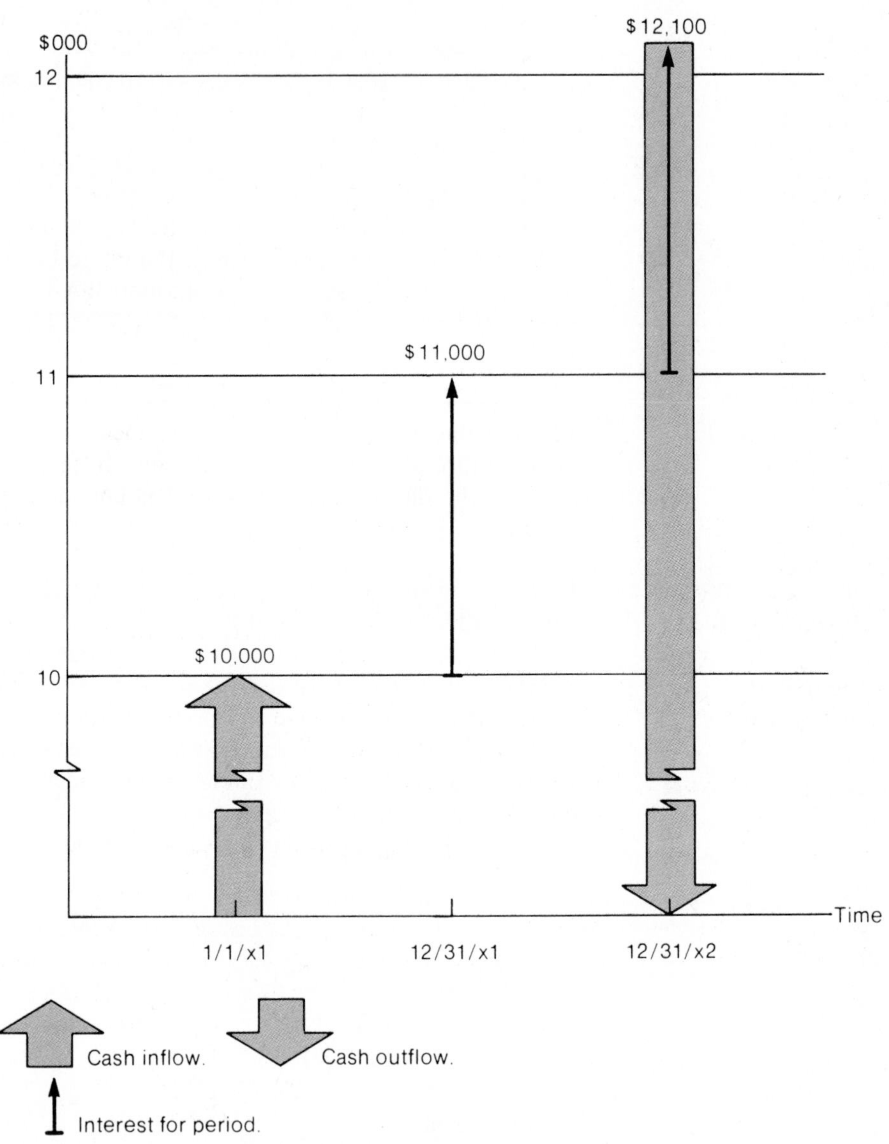

Future Values of an Ordinary Annuity

Sometimes payments are made in several periodic amounts rather than as a single payment. The same basic pattern is followed for determining the future value of a series of amounts as used to determine the future value of a single amount. For example, assume that payments are made into a fund for $10,000 a year at each year-end for three years and that the fund earns 10% per year. Such patterns of equal amounts separated by equal periods are called **annuities.**

The following time line shows the equal payments into the fund:

1/1/x1	12/31/x1	12/31/x2	12/31/x3
	Ordinary Annuity $10,000	*Ordinary Annuity $10,000*	*Ordinary Annuity $10,000*

Because money is coming into the fund in the form of an **ordinary annuity,** that is, payments at the end of each period, year 1 has no interest, year 2 earns interest only on the December 31, 19x1, payment, and year 3 earns interest on both the December 31, 19x1, and 19x2, payments, but none on the December 31, 19x3, payment. This is shown in the following table:

	Interest Earned during			
	Year 1	*Year 2*	*Year 3*	*Total*
Annuity payment 1	$0	$1,000	$1,100	$2,100
Annuity payment 2	0	0	1,000	1,000
Annuity payment 3	0	0	0	0
Total	$0	$1,000	$2,100	$3,100

The diagram in Exhibit 10A-2 shows how the payments and compound interest grow to a future amount of $33,100 on December 31, 19x3.

To arrive at the future value of an ordinary annuity, we could make the individual computations or use a table of factors. Table 10A-2 is similar to Table 10A-1 except that Table 10A-2 is for an ordinary annuity of $1. The future value factor for three years and 10%—3.310—is found at the intersection of the 10% interest column and the three-year row. The computation therefore is:

(Annuity) (Future value factor) = Future value
($10,000) (3.310) = $33,100

PRESENT VALUES

Objective 10
. . . and present values.

Sometimes managers know future amounts such as maturity values of bonds and want to compute the present value. This is the "other side of the coin" of the future value concepts and computations discussed above.

If someone promises to pay you $100,000 including principal and interest in three years, what is the **present value** of the future cash receipt? Or, put differently, what would you pay now for the promise of $100,000 in three years? Study the following time line:

Present Value = ?			*Future Value = $100,000*
1/1/x1	12/31/x1	12/31/x2	12/31/x3

As you probably have decided for yourself, the answer depends a great deal on interest rate considerations. If you can now earn large returns on invested money, $100,000 three years hence would be worth less than if you can earn only small returns. And, of course, your confidence in the ultimate receipt of the future payment is a crucial consideration also. From the use of future value

EXHIBIT 10A-2

Growth of Investment by Payments and Compound Interest

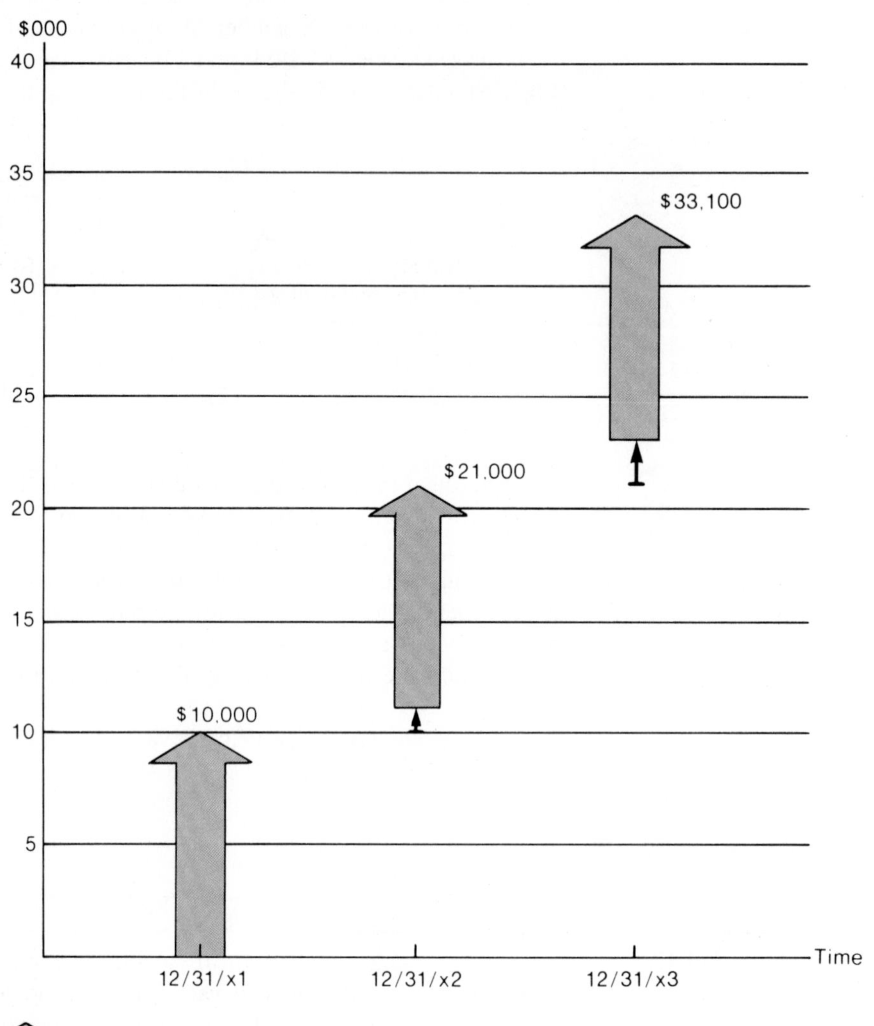

tables, we know that for any given interest rate the following algebraic relationship exists between present values and future values.

$$\text{Present value of \$1} \times \text{Table factor for future value of \$1} = \text{Future value of \$1}$$

Therefore,

$$\text{Present value of \$1} = \frac{\text{Future value of \$1}}{\text{Table factor for future value of \$1}}$$

Hence, the present value factors are the reciprocals of the future value factors. Table 10A-3 shows the present value factors that are the reciprocals of the factors in Table 10A-1. For example, the future value factor for three years at 10% is 1.331. The present value factor for three years at 10% is .7513, and 1/1.331 equals .7513 (rounded).

Going back to our example, the time line is as follows:

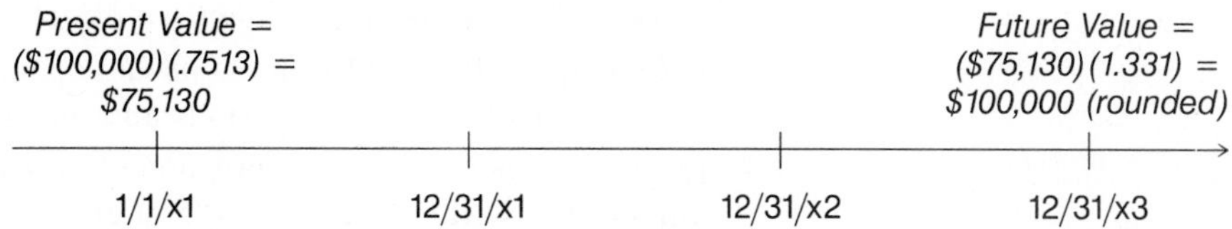

Present Value of an Ordinary Annuity

Just as the present values of future amounts must sometimes be computed, often the present value of future annuities must be computed. For example, how much would you have to invest now to withdraw $20,000 at the end of three subsequent years? The time line for this example is as follows:

Present Value = ?	Annuity $20,000	Annuity $20,000	Annuity $20,000
1/1/x1	12/31/x1	12/31/x2	12/31/x3

To answer this question, you must compute the present value of these amounts. Assuming an 8% interest rate, the present value of each annuity payment is computed separately and added together to sum the total present value as follows:

Present Value of $20,000

	Future Amount		Table 10A-3 Factor (8%)		Present Value
1 year	$20,000	×	.9259	=	$18,518
2 years	20,000	×	.8573	=	17,146
3 years	20,000	×	.7938	=	15,876
Total present value. . . .					$51,540

Table 10A-4 saves computational time by giving the necessary factors to compute the present value of annuities for different interest rates and time periods. Thus, using the following formula, we can arrive at the same answer as above:

(Annuity amount) (Table 10A-4 factor) = Present value
($20,000) (2.5771) = $51,540 (rounded)

Notation Commonly Used in Future and Present Value Computations

We have discussed four tables used for four different but closely related computations. A shorthand notation is used to designate each computation. Note the following relationship with the four tables of factors in Appendix 10A: In Table 10A-1, Future Value of a Single Amount, factors are designated $(F/P, n, i)$, where n is the number of periods and i is the effective-interest rate; in Table 10A-2,

Future Value of an Ordinary Annuity, factors are designated $(F/A, n, i)$; in Table 10A-3, Present Value of a Single Amount, factors are designated $(P/F, n, i)$; and in Table 10A-4, Present Value of an Ordinary Annuity, factors are designated $(P/A, n, i)$.

The reading of each notation is as follows:

1. $(F/P, n, i)$ reads "The future value (F) computed from a known present amount (P) with (n) periods and an effective-interest rate of (i)."
2. $(F/A, n, i)$ reads "The future value (F) computed from a known ordinary annuity (A) with (n) periods and an effective interest rate of (i)."
3. $(P/F, n, i)$ reads "The present value (P) computed from a known future amount (F) with (n) periods and an effective-interest rate of (i)."
4. $(P/A, n, i)$ reads "The present value (P) computed from a known ordinary annuity (A) with (n) periods and an effective-interest of (i)."

TABLE 10A - 1 Future Value of a Single Amount

n	1%	2%	3%	4%	5%	6%	7%	8%	9%	10%	11%	12%	13%	14%	15%	16%	17%	18%	19%	20%
1	1.0100	1.0200	1.0300	1.0400	1.0500	1.0600	1.0700	1.0800	1.0900	1.1000	1.1100	1.1200	1.1300	1.1400	1.1500	1.1600	1.1700	1.1800	1.1900	1.2000
2	1.0201	1.0404	1.0609	1.0816	1.1025	1.1236	1.1449	1.1664	1.1881	1.2100	1.2321	1.2544	1.2769	1.2996	1.3225	1.3456	1.3689	1.3924	1.4161	1.4400
3	1.0303	1.0612	1.0927	1.1249	1.1576	1.1910	1.2250	1.2597	1.2950	1.3310	1.3676	1.4049	1.4429	1.4815	1.5209	1.5609	1.6016	1.6430	1.6852	1.7280
4	1.0406	1.0824	1.1255	1.1699	1.2155	1.2625	1.3108	1.3605	1.4116	1.4641	1.5181	1.5735	1.6305	1.6890	1.7490	1.8106	1.8739	1.9388	2.0053	2.0736
5	1.0510	1.1041	1.1593	1.2167	1.2763	1.3382	1.4026	1.4693	1.5386	1.6105	1.6851	1.7623	1.8424	1.9254	2.0114	2.1003	2.1924	2.2878	2.3864	2.4883
6	1.0615	1.1262	1.1941	1.2653	1.3401	1.4185	1.5007	1.5869	1.6771	1.7716	1.8704	1.9738	2.0820	2.1950	2.3131	2.4364	2.5652	2.6996	2.8398	2.9860
7	1.0721	1.1487	1.2299	1.3159	1.4071	1.5036	1.6058	1.7138	1.8280	1.9487	2.0762	2.2107	2.3526	2.5023	2.6600	2.8262	3.0012	3.1855	3.3793	3.5832
8	1.0829	1.1717	1.2668	1.3686	1.4775	1.5938	1.7182	1.8509	1.9926	2.1436	2.3045	2.4760	2.6584	2.8526	3.0590	3.2784	3.5115	3.7589	4.0214	4.2998
9	1.0937	1.1951	1.3048	1.4233	1.5513	1.6895	1.8385	1.9990	2.1719	2.3579	2.5580	2.7731	3.0040	3.2520	3.5179	3.8030	4.1084	4.4355	4.7854	5.1598
10	1.1046	1.2190	1.3439	1.4802	1.6289	1.7908	1.9671	2.1589	2.3674	2.5937	2.8394	3.1059	3.3946	3.7072	4.0456	4.4114	4.8068	5.2338	5.6947	6.1917
11	1.1157	1.2434	1.3842	1.5395	1.7103	1.8983	2.1049	2.3316	2.5804	2.8531	3.1518	3.4786	3.8359	4.2262	4.6524	5.1173	5.6240	6.1759	6.7767	7.4301
12	1.1268	1.2682	1.4258	1.6010	1.7959	2.0122	2.2522	2.5182	2.8127	3.1384	3.4984	3.8960	4.3345	4.8179	5.3503	5.9360	6.5801	7.2876	8.0642	8.9161
13	1.1381	1.2936	1.4685	1.6651	1.8856	2.1329	2.4098	2.7196	3.0658	3.4523	3.8833	4.3635	4.8980	5.4924	6.1528	6.8858	7.6987	8.5994	9.5964	10.6993
14	1.1495	1.3195	1.5126	1.7317	1.9799	2.2609	2.5785	2.9372	3.3417	3.7975	4.3104	4.8871	5.5348	6.2614	7.0757	7.9875	9.0075	10.1473	11.4198	12.8392
15	1.1610	1.3459	1.5580	1.8009	2.0789	2.3966	2.7590	3.1722	3.6425	4.1772	4.7846	5.4736	6.2543	7.1379	8.1371	9.2655	10.5387	11.9738	13.5895	15.4070
16	1.1726	1.3728	1.6047	1.8730	2.1829	2.5403	2.9522	3.4259	3.9703	4.5950	5.3109	6.1304	7.0673	8.1373	9.3576	10.7480	12.3303	14.1290	16.1715	18.4884
17	1.1843	1.4002	1.6528	1.9479	2.2920	2.6928	3.1588	3.7000	4.3276	5.0545	5.8951	6.8661	7.9861	9.2765	10.7613	12.4677	14.4265	16.6723	19.2441	22.1861
18	1.1961	1.4282	1.7024	2.0258	2.4066	2.8543	3.3799	3.9960	4.7171	5.5599	6.5435	7.6900	9.0243	10.5752	12.3755	14.4625	16.8790	19.6733	22.9005	26.6233
19	1.2081	1.4568	1.7535	2.1068	2.5269	3.0256	3.6165	4.3157	5.1417	6.1159	7.2633	8.6128	10.1974	12.0557	14.2318	16.7765	19.7484	23.2145	27.2516	31.9480
20	1.2202	1.4859	1.8061	2.1911	2.6533	3.2071	3.8697	4.6609	5.6044	6.7275	8.0623	9.6463	11.5231	13.7435	16.3666	19.4608	23.1056	27.3931	32.4294	38.3376
25	1.2824	1.6406	2.0938	2.6658	3.3864	4.2919	5.4274	6.8485	8.6231	10,8347	13.5854	17.0001	21.2306	26.4260	32.9190	40.8743	50.6579	62.6688	77.3881	95.3963
30	1.3478	1.8114	2.4273	3.2434	4.3219	5.7435	7.6122	10.0626	13.2677	17.4494	22.8922	29.9600	39.1160	50.9503	66.2119	85.8500	111.0650	143.3710	184.6750	237.3760
40	1.4889	2.2080	3.2620	4.8010	7.0400	10.2857	14.9744	21.7244	31.4094	45.2591	65.0006	93.0513	132.7820	188.8840	267.8650	378.7220	533.8690	750.3810	1051.6700	1469.7700

Notation: $(F/P, n, i)$ where F = Future value; P = Present amount; n = Number of periods; and i = Interest rate.

TABLE 10A - 2 Future Value of an Ordinary Annuity

n	1%	2%	3%	4%	5%	6%	7%	8%	9%	10%	11%	12%	13%	14%	15%	16%	17%	18%	19%	20%
1	1.0000	1.0000	1.0000	1.0000	1.0000	1.0000	1.0000	1.0000	1.0000	1.0000	1.0000	1.0000	1.0000	1.0000	1.0000	1.0000	1.0000	1.0000	1.0000	1.0000
2	2.0100	2.0200	2.0300	2.0400	2.0500	2.0600	2.0700	2.0800	2.0900	2.1000	2.1100	2.1200	2.1300	2.1400	2.1500	2.1600	2.1700	2.1800	2.1900	2.2000
3	2.0301	3.0604	3.0909	3.1216	3.1525	3.1836	3.2149	3.2464	3.2781	3.3100	3.3421	3.3744	3.4069	3.4396	3.4725	3.5056	3.5389	3.5724	3.6061	3.6400
4	4.0604	4.1216	4.1836	4.2465	4.3101	4.3746	4.4399	4.5061	4.5731	4.6410	4.7097	4.7793	4.8498	4.9211	4.9934	5.0665	5.1405	5.2154	5.2913	5.3680
5	5.1010	5.2040	5.3091	5.4163	5.5256	5.6371	5.7507	5.8666	5.9847	6.1051	6.2278	6.3528	6.4803	6.6101	6.7424	6.8771	7.0144	7.1542	7.2966	7.4416
6	6.1520	6.3081	6.4684	6.6330	6.8019	6.9753	7.1533	7.3359	7.5233	7.7156	7.9129	8.1152	8.3227	8.5355	8.7537	8.9775	9.2068	9.4420	9.6830	9.9299
7	7.2135	7.4343	7.6625	7.8983	8.1420	8.3938	8.6540	8.9228	9.2004	9.4872	9.7833	10.0890	10.4047	10.7305	11.0668	11.4139	11.7720	12.1415	12.5227	12.9159
8	8.2857	8.5830	8.8923	9.2142	9.5491	9.8975	10.2598	10.6366	11.0285	11.4359	11.8594	12.2997	12.7573	13.2328	13.7268	14.2401	14.7733	15.3270	15.9020	16.4991
9	9.3685	9.7546	10.1591	10.5828	11.0266	11.4913	11.9780	12.4876	13.0210	13.5795	14.1640	14.7757	15.4157	16.0853	16.7858	17.5185	18.2847	19.0859	19.9234	20.7989
10	10.4622	10.9497	11.4639	12.0061	12.5779	13.1808	13.8164	14.4866	15.1929	15.9374	16.7220	17.5487	18.4197	19.3373	20.3037	21.3215	22.3931	23.5213	24.7089	25.9587
11	11.5668	12.1687	12.8078	13.4864	14.2068	14.9716	15.7836	16.6455	17.5603	18.5312	19.5614	20.6546	21.8143	23.0445	24.3493	25.7329	27.1999	28.7551	30.4035	32.1504
12	12.6825	13.4121	14.1920	15.0258	15.9171	16.8699	17.8885	18.9771	20.1407	21.3843	22.7132	24.1331	25.6502	27.2707	29.0017	30.8502	32.8239	34.9311	37.1802	39.5805
13	13.8093	14.6803	15.6178	16.6268	17.7130	18.8821	20.1406	21.4953	22.9534	24.5227	26.2116	28.0291	29.9847	32.0887	34.3519	36.7862	39.4040	42.2187	45.2445	48.4966
14	14.9474	15.9739	17.0863	18.2919	19.5986	21.0151	22.5505	24.2149	26.0192	27.9750	30.0949	32.3926	34.8827	37.5811	40.5047	43.6720	47.1027	50.8180	54.8409	59.1959
15	16.0969	17.2934	18.5989	20.0236	21.5786	23.2760	25.1290	27.1521	29.3609	31.7725	34.4054	37.2797	40.4175	43.8424	47.5804	51.6595	56.1101	60.9653	66.2607	72.0351
16	17.2579	18.6393	20.1569	21.8245	23.6575	25.6725	27.8881	30.3243	33.0034	35.9497	39.1899	42.7533	46.6717	50.9804	55.7175	60.9250	66.6488	72.9390	79.8502	87.4421
17	18.4304	20.0121	21.7616	23.6975	25.8404	28.2129	30.8402	33.7502	36.9737	40.5447	44.5008	48.8837	53.7391	59.1176	65.0751	71.6730	78.9792	87.0680	96.0218	105.9306
18	19.6147	21.4123	23.4144	25.6454	28.1324	30.9057	33.9990	37.4502	41.3013	45.5992	50.3959	55.7497	61.7251	68.3941	75.8364	84.1407	93.4056	103.7403	115.2659	128.1167
19	20.8109	22.8406	25.1169	27.6712	30.5390	33.7600	37.3790	41.4463	46.0185	51.1591	56.9395	63.4397	70.7494	78.9692	88.2118	98.6032	110.2846	123.4135	138.1664	154.7400
20	22.0190	24.2974	26.8704	29.7781	33.0660	36.7856	40.9955	45.7620	51.1601	57.2750	64.2028	72.0524	80.9468	91.0249	102.4436	115.3797	130.0329	146.6280	165.4180	186.6880
25	28.2432	32.0303	36.4593	41.6459	47.7271	54.8645	63.2490	73.1059	84.7009	98.3471	114.4133	133.3339	155.6196	181.8708	212.7930	249.2140	292.1049	342.6035	402.0425	471.9811
30	34.7849	40.5681	47.5754	56.0849	66.4388	79.0582	94.4608	113.2832	136.3075	164.4940	199.0209	241.3327	293.1992	356.7868	434.7451	530.3117	647.4391	790.9480	966.7122	1181.8815
40	48.8864	60.4020	75.4013	95.0255	120.7998	154.7620	199.6351	259.0565	337.8824	442.5926	581.8261	767.0914	1013.7043	1342.0251	1779.0903	2360.7573	3134.5218	4163.2130	5529.8289	7343.8577

Notation: $(F/A, n, i)$ where F = Future value; A = Ordinary annuity; n = Number of periods; and i = Interest rate.

TABLE 10A - 3 Present Value of a Single Amount

n	1%	2%	3%	4%	5%	6%	7%	8%	9%	10%	11%	12%	13%	14%	15%	16%	17%	18%	19%	20%
1	.9901	.9804	.9709	.9615	.9524	.9434	.9346	.9249	.9174	.9091	.9009	.8929	.8850	.8772	.8696	.8621	.8547	.8475	.8403	.8333
2	.9803	.9612	.9426	.9246	.9070	.8900	.8734	.8573	.8417	.8264	.8116	.7972	.7831	.7695	.7561	.7432	.7305	.7182	.7062	.6944
3	.9706	.9423	.9151	.8890	.8638	.8396	.8163	.7938	.7722	.7513	.7312	.7118	.6931	.6750	.6575	.6407	.6244	.6086	.5934	.5787
4	.9610	.9239	.8885	.8548	.8227	.7921	.7629	.7350	.7084	.6830	.6587	.6355	.6133	.5921	.5718	.5523	.5337	.5158	.4987	.4822
5	.9515	.9057	.8626	.8219	.7835	.7473	.7130	.6806	.6499	.6209	.5934	.5674	.5428	.5194	.4972	.4761	.4561	.4371	.4190	.4019
6	.9420	.8880	.8375	.7903	.7462	.7050	.6663	.6302	.5963	.5645	.5346	.5066	.4803	.4556	.4323	.4104	.3898	.3704	.3521	.3349
7	.9327	.8706	.8131	.7599	.7107	.6651	.6228	.5835	.5470	.5132	.4817	.4524	.4251	.3996	.3759	.3538	.3332	.3139	.2959	.2791
8	.9235	.8535	.7894	.7307	.6768	.6274	.5820	.5403	.5019	.4665	.4339	.4039	.3762	.3506	.3269	.3050	.2848	.2660	.2487	.2326
9	.9143	.8368	.7664	.7026	.6446	.5919	.5439	.5002	.4604	.4241	.3909	.3606	.3329	.3075	.2843	.2630	.2434	.2255	.2090	.1938
10	.9053	.8204	.7441	.6756	.6139	.5584	.5084	.4632	.4224	.3855	.3522	.3220	.2946	.2697	.2472	.2267	.2080	.1911	.1756	.1615
11	.8963	.8043	.7224	.6496	.5847	.5368	.4751	.4289	.3875	.3505	.3173	.2875	.2607	.2366	.2149	.1954	.1778	.1619	.1476	.1346
12	.8874	.7885	.7014	.6246	.5568	.4970	.4440	.3971	.3555	.3186	.2858	.2567	.2307	.2076	.1869	.1685	.1520	.1372	.1240	.1122
13	.8787	.7730	.6810	.6006	.5303	.4688	.4150	.3677	.3262	.2897	.2575	.2292	.2042	.1821	.1625	.1452	.1299	.1163	.1042	.0935
14	.8700	.7579	.6611	.5775	.5051	.4423	.3878	.3405	.2993	.2633	.2320	.2046	.1807	.1597	.1413	.1252	.1110	.0986	.0876	.0779
15	.8614	.7430	.6419	.5553	.4810	.4173	.3625	.3152	.2745	.2394	.2090	.1827	.1599	.1401	.1229	.1079	.0949	.0835	.0736	.0649
16	.8528	.7284	.6232	.5339	.4581	.3936	.3387	.2919	.2519	.2176	.1883	.1631	.1415	.1229	.1069	.0930	.0811	.0708	.0618	.0541
17	.8444	.7142	.6050	.5134	.4363	.3714	.3166	.2703	.2311	.1978	.1696	.1456	.1252	.1078	.0929	.0802	.0693	.0600	.0520	.0451
18	.8360	.7002	.5874	.4936	.4155	.3503	.2959	.2502	.2120	.1799	.1528	.1300	.1108	.0946	.0808	.0691	.0592	.0508	.0437	.0376
19	.8277	.6864	.5703	.4746	.3957	.3305	.2765	.2317	.1945	.1635	.1377	.1161	.0981	.0829	.0703	.0596	.0506	.0431	.0367	.0313
20	.8195	.6730	.5537	.4564	.3769	.3118	.2584	.2145	.1784	.1486	.1240	.1037	.0868	.0728	.0611	.0514	.0433	.0365	.0308	.0261
25	.7798	.6095	.4776	.3751	.2953	.2330	.1842	.1460	.1160	.0923	.0736	.0588	.0471	.0378	.0304	.0245	.0197	.0160	.0129	.0105
30	.7419	.5521	.4120	.3083	.2314	.1741	.1314	.0994	.0754	.0573	.0437	.0334	.0256	.0196	.0151	.0116	.0090	.0070	.0054	.0042
40	.6717	.4529	.3066	.2083	.1420	.0972	.0668	.0460	.0318	.0221	.0154	.0107	.0075	.0053	.0037	.0026	.0019	.0013	.0010	.0007

Notation: $(P/F, n, i)$ where P = Present value; F = Future amount; n = Number of periods; and i = Interest rate.

TABLE 10A - 4 Present Value of an Ordinary Annuity

n	1%	2%	3%	4%	5%	6%	7%	8%	9%	10%	11%	12%	13%	14%	15%	16%	17%	18%	19%	20%
1	.9901	.9804	.9709	.9615	.9524	.9434	.9346	.9259	.9174	.9091	.9009	.8929	.8850	.8772	.8696	.8621	.8547	.8475	.8403	.8333
2	1.9704	1.9416	1.9135	1.8861	1.8594	1.8334	1.8080	1.7833	1.7591	1.7355	1.7125	1.6901	1.6681	1.6467	1.6257	1.6052	1.5852	1.5656	1.5465	1.5278
3	2.9410	2.8839	2.8286	2.7751	2.7232	2.6730	2.6243	2.5771	2.5313	2.4869	2.4437	2.4018	2.3612	2.3216	2.2832	2.2459	2.2096	2.1743	2.1399	2.1065
4	3.9020	3.8077	3.7171	3.6299	3.5459	3.4651	3.3872	3.3121	3.2397	3.1699	3.1024	3.0374	2.9745	2.9137	2.8550	2.7982	2.7432	2.6901	2.6386	2.5887
5	4.8534	4.7135	4.5797	4.4518	4.3295	4.2124	4.1002	3.9927	3.8897	3.7908	3.6959	3.6048	3.5172	3.4331	3.3522	3.2743	3.1993	3.1272	3.0576	2.9906
6	5.7955	5.6014	5.4172	5.2421	5.0757	4.9173	4.7666	4.6229	4.4859	4.3553	4.2305	4.1114	3.9976	3.8887	3.7845	3.6847	3.5892	3.4976	3.4098	3.3255
7	6.7282	6.4720	6.2302	6.0021	5.7864	5.5824	5.3893	5.2064	5.0330	4.8684	4.7122	4.5638	4.4226	4.2883	4.1604	4.0386	3.9224	3.8115	3.7057	3.6046
8	7.6517	7.3255	7.0197	6.7328	6.4632	6.2098	5.9713	5.7466	5.5348	5.3349	5.1461	4.9676	4.7988	4.6389	4.4873	4.3436	4.2072	4.0776	3.9544	3.8372
9	8.5660	8.1622	7.7861	7.4353	7.1078	6.8017	6.5152	6.2469	5.9953	5.7590	5.5371	5.3282	5.1317	4.9464	4.7716	4.6065	4.4506	4.3030	4.1633	4.0310
10	9.4713	8.9826	8.5302	8.1109	7.7217	7.3601	7.0236	6.7101	6.4177	6.1446	5.8892	5.6502	5.4262	5.2161	5.0188	4.8332	4.6586	4.4941	4.3389	4.1925
11	10.3676	9.7868	9.2526	8.7605	8.3064	7.8869	7.4987	7.1390	6.8052	6.4951	6.2065	5.9377	5.6869	5.4527	5.2337	5.0286	4.8362	4.6560	4.4865	4.3271
12	11.2551	10.5753	9.9540	9.3851	8.8633	8.3839	7.9427	7.5361	7.1607	6.8137	6.4924	6.1944	5.9177	5.6603	5.4206	5.1971	4.9884	4.7932	4.6105	4.4392
13	12.1338	11.3484	10.6349	9.9857	9.3936	8.8527	8.3577	7.9038	7.4869	7.1034	6.7499	6.4235	6.1218	5.8424	5.5832	5.3423	5.1183	4.9095	4.7147	4.5327
14	13.0037	12.1062	11.2961	10.5631	9.8986	9.2950	8.7455	8.2442	7.7862	7.3667	6.9819	6.6282	6.3025	6.0021	5.7245	5.4675	5.2293	5.0081	4.8023	4.6106
15	13.8651	12.8492	11.9379	11.1184	10.3797	9.7123	9.1079	8.5595	8.0607	7.6061	7.1909	6.8109	6.4624	6.1422	5.8474	5.5755	5.3242	5.0916	4.8759	4.6755
16	14.7179	13.5777	12.5611	11.6523	10.8378	10.1059	9.4467	8.8514	8.3126	7.8237	7.3792	6.9740	6.6039	6.2651	5.9542	5.6685	5.4053	5.1624	4.9377	4.7296
17	15.5623	14.2919	13.1661	12.1657	11.2741	10.4773	9.7632	9.1216	8.5436	8.0216	7.5488	7.1196	6.7291	6.3729	6.0472	5.7487	5.4746	5.2223	4.9897	4.7746
18	16.3983	14.9920	13.7535	12.6593	11.6896	10.8276	10.0591	9.3719	8.7556	8.2014	7.7016	7.2497	6.8399	6.4674	6.1280	5.8179	5.5338	5.2732	5.0333	4.8122
19	17.2260	15.6785	14.3238	13.1339	12.0853	11.1581	10.3356	9.6036	8.9501	8.3649	7.8393	7.3658	6.9380	6.5504	6.1982	5.8775	5.5845	5.3163	5.0701	4.8435
20	18.0456	16.3514	14.8775	13.5903	12.4622	11.4699	10.5940	9.8181	9.1285	8.5136	7.9633	7.4694	7.0248	6.6231	6.2593	5.9289	5.6278	5.3528	5.1009	4.8696
25	22.0232	19.5234	17.4132	15.6221	14.0940	12.7834	11.6536	10.6748	9.8226	9.0770	8.4217	7.8431	7.3300	6.8729	6.4641	6.0971	5.7662	5.4669	5.1952	4.9476
30	25.8077	22.3964	19.6005	17.2920	15.3725	13.7649	12.4091	11.2578	10.2737	9.4269	8.6938	8.0552	7.4957	7.0027	6.5660	6.1772	5.8294	5.5168	5.2347	4.9789
40	32.8347	27.3555	23.1148	19.7928	17.1591	15.0464	13.3317	11.9246	10.7574	9.7791	8.9510	8.2438	7.6344	7.1051	6.6418	6.2335	5.8713	5.5482	5.2582	4.9966

Notation: $(F/A, n, i)$ where F = Future value; A = Ordinary annuity; n = Number of periods; and i = Interest rate.

APPENDIX 10B

Special Present Value Problems: Bonds, Leases, and Pensions

VALUATION OF BONDS

Objective 11
Present value problems relating to bonds, leases, and pensions.

As discussed in the chapter, a bond is a contract between a debtor (the bond issuer) and a creditor (the bondholder) that promises distinct future cash flows at specific points in time. When a bond is offered to the market, the riskiness of the investment is evaluated by the potential buyers. Riskiness is a function of the probability of default or failure to pay the promised cash payments. For any given bond contract, the higher the perceived risk, the lower the selling price of the bond, all other factors equal.

The selling price of a bond is the present value of future cash flows. Bonds usually have two types of cash payments: (1) a maturity amount and (2) an annual or semiannual annuity payment called nominal interest.

To illustrate how to determine bond selling prices, the following data for a bond is used:

Issue date:	January 1, 19x1
Maturity date:	December 31, 19x3
Maturity value:	$10,000
Nominal interest rate:	10% per year
Semiannual interest payment dates:	June 30 and December 31

Remember that no matter what the bond sells for, this bond will pay the following fixed stream of payments:

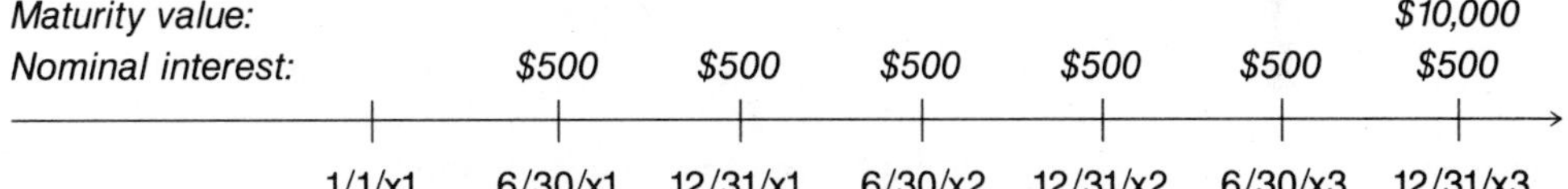

Total cash outflow per bond for the bond issuer is $13,000; that is, six $500 payments plus $10,000 at maturity. What are potential bondholders willing to pay?

Assume that the market demands a 12% per year return on bonds in this risk class. The 12% is this bond's **effective-interest rate.** The selling price, or **proceeds**, would be the sum of the present values of the annuity amounts and the maturity amount computed at 6% for six payments (half the annual rate and twice the number of years) because the bonds pay interest semiannually. Note that the effective-interest rate is used to value the bonds. The nominal rate merely establishes the cash flows.

$(P/A, 6, .06)\$500$	$= (4.9173)\$500$	$= \$2,459$
$(P/F, 6, .06)\$10,000$	$= (.705)\$10,000$	$= 7,050$
Selling price		$9,509

Recall from Appendix 10A that the notation $(P/A, n, i)$ reads "The present value (P) computed from a known ordinary annuity (A) with (n) periods and an effective interest rate of (i)."

If the bonds paid interest annually and all other terms remained the same, the present values would be based on a 12% effective-interest rate for three periods, which is computed as follows:

Annual Payments

$(P/A, 3, .12)\$1{,}000$	$= (2.4018)\$1{,}000$	= $2,402
$(P/F, 3, .12)\$10{,}000$	$= (.7118)\$10{,}000$	= 7,118
Selling price		$9,520

This bond sells for a discount, which would be recorded as described earlier in this chapter.

Semiannual and annual payment schedules give slightly different total interest expense amounts because of more frequent compounding in the semiannual payments. Compare the amounts of total interest expense for the three years for each situation below:

Effective Annual Interest Rate	*Timing of Payments*			
	Semiannual		*Annual*	
12%	Cash outflow	$13,000	Cash outflow	$13,000
	Cash inflow	9,509	Cash inflow	9,520
	Total interest expense . .	$ 3,491	Total interest expense .	$ 3,480
8%	Cash outflow	$13,000	Cash outflow	$13,000
	Cash inflow	10,524	Cash inflow	10,515
	Total interest expense . .	$ 2,476	Total interest expense .	$ 2,485

Note that interest expense is total cash outflow to bondholders minus the cash inflow from the bondholders at issuance. Total nominal interest in all cases is $3,000. Selling the bonds at an effective-interest rate above the nominal interest rate increases the interest expense above $3,000, and selling the bonds at an effective-interest rate below the nominal interest rate decreases the interest expense below $3,000.

LEASES

Leases are contracts that give the **lessee** (the renter) the right to the use of property, plant, or equipment for a fixed amount of time with a fixed schedule of payments to the **lessor** (the owner). Consider the following lease contract:

> A **lessor** owns an automobile that costs $18,000 on January 1, 19x1, and leases it to the **lessee** for five years after which the title to the automobile is transferred to the lessee.

Since this lease contract transfers most of the rights and obligations of ownership to the lessee, it is called a **capital lease** and is recorded as a purchase of equipment by means of long-term borrowing. However, leases where the lessor, the legal owner, keeps the risks and obligations of ownership are called **operating leases,** and payments for operating leases are recorded as rent expense. The paragraphs that follow discuss the capital lease of the automobile given in the lease contract example above.

If, in the automobile lease contract, the payments from the lessee to the lessor are equal year-end payments, can we compute the amount of each payment? This is an annuity valuation problem because the payments are equal payments separated by equal periods. If we assume that the lessor wants cash flows sufficient to recapture the $18,000 investment in the automobile plus an annual rate of return of 14%, the Table 10A-4 factors can be used in the following formula to determine the annuity payments:

$$(P/A, 5, .14)\,(\text{Annual lease payment}) = \$18{,}000$$

$$(\text{Annual lease payment}) = \$18{,}000/(P/A, 5, .14)$$

$$= \$18{,}000/3.4331$$

$$= \$5{,}243$$

The five $5,243 annual lease payments, therefore, have a present value of $18,000:

$$(P/A, 5, .14)\,(\$5{,}243) = \$18{,}000$$

$$(3.4331)\,(\$5{,}243) = \$18{,}000$$

Should the automobile be recorded on the lessee's books? A leased asset under the terms described above is recorded as an asset on the lessee's books, and a long-term liability is also recorded. The contract gives the lessee the right to use the automobile for five years and then the title is transferred to the lessee. In substance, that is the same as an outright purchase. The lessor effectively sold the automobile for the present value of the lease payments.

The following schedule summarizes the accounting for such a lease:

Date	*Cash Flow*	*Interest*	*Change in Lease Receivable or Payable*	*Lease Receivable or Payable*
1/1/x1	$ 0	$ 0	$18,000	$18,000
12/31/x1 . . .	5,243	2,520	2,723	15,277
12/31/x2 . . .	5,243	2,139	3,104	12,173
12/31/x3 . . .	5,243	1,704	3,539	8,634
12/31/x4 . . .	5,243	1,209	4,034	4,600
12/31/x5 . . .	5,243	643*	4,600	0
	$26,215	$8,215		

*Rounded.

The journal entries to record the lease on the lessor's and lessee's books would be as follows:

Date	*Lessor's Books*			*Lessee's Books*		
19x1						
Jan. 1	Lease Receivable (A) . . .	18,000		Leased Auto (A)	18,000	
	Automobile (A)		18,000	Lease Payable (L) . . .		18,000
	To record lease.			To record lease.		
Dec. 31	Cash (A)	5,243		Interest Expense (E)	2,520	
	Lease Receivable (A) .		2,723	Lease Payable (L)	2,723	
	Interest Revenue (R) . .		2,520	Cash (A)		5,243
	To record receipt of lease payment.			To record payment on lease.		
19x2						
Dec. 31	Cash (A)	5,243		Interest Expense (E)	2,139	
	Lease Receivable (A) .		3,104	Lease Payable (L)	3,104	
	Interest Revenue (R) . .		2,139	Cash (A)		5,243
	To record receipt of lease payment.			To record payment on lease.		
19x3						
Dec. 31	Cash (A)	5,243		Interest Expense (E)	1,704	
	Lease Receivable (A) .		3,539	Lease Payable (L)	3,539	
	Interest Revenue (R) . .		1,704	Cash (A)		5,243
	To record receipt of lease payment.			To record payment on lease.		
19x4						
Dec. 31	Cash (A)	5,243		Interest Expense (E)	1,209	
	Lease Receivable (A) .		4,034	Lease Payable (L)	4,034	
	Interest Revenue (R) . .		1,209	Cash (A)		5,243
	To record receipt of lease payment.			To record payment on lease.		
19x5						
Dec. 31	Cash (A)	5,243		Interest Expense (E)	643	
	Lease Receivable (A) .		4,600	Lease Payable (L)	4,600	
	Interest Revenue (R) . .		643	Cash (A)		5,243
	To record receipt of lease payment.			To record payment on lease.		

Note that in this case the lessor does not make a profit or gain on the "sale" of the automobile. When the lessor is a manufacturer, there is usually gross profit recognized in the normal way by recording sales revenue and cost of goods sold. Sales equal the present value of the future lease payments, and cost of goods sold equals the cost of inventory sold. The lessee would also depreciate the automobile over its useful life in the normal fashion.

The critical issue in accounting for leases is to determine whether the lease is to be accounted for as a capital-type lease (a purchase), as illustrated above, or simply a rental agreement (operating-type lease). To help determine whether or not a lease is a capital lease, the FASB identified the following four conditions, any one of which causes the lease to be treated as a capital lease by the lessee:[3]

[3]Refer to *FASB Statement No. 13,* "Accounting for Leases" (Norwalk, Conn.: FASB, 1976).

1. Transfer of title to the lessee.
2. An option allowing the lessee to purchase the asset in the future at a bargain price (a price below its fair market value).
3. Lease term of 75% or more of the leased property's economic life.
4. Present value of the minimum scheduled lease payments equal to at least 90% of leased property's fair market value.

These conditions also apply to the lessor; and, therefore, when a lessee treats a lease as a long-term purchase agreement (a capital lease), the lessor normally treats it as a sale where financing is provided to facilitate the lessee's purchase. Many variations in lease payments exist, all of which may affect the accounting of lessors and lessees. These topics are covered in detail in intermediate accounting texts.

A Conversation about Substance over Form—The Effect of Lease on the Financial Statements

Jill Petro, the president of Petro Advertisers, is discussing the purchase of a company aircraft with her chief accountant, Bernie Best. Bernie has just concluded his presentation of an analysis of the relative costs of the staff flying on commercial carriers versus a company-owned jet.

Accountant: J. P., from a pure dollars and cents perspective, it is cheaper to use the airlines, but that doesn't factor in the delay time and customer satisfaction. I look at this as having a customer relations aspect, anyway, so it's hard to quantify the benefits. The bottom line, J. P., is that I recommend the purchase.

President: O.K! Review the major costs for me once more.

Accountant: I'll put up slide 1 again.

SLIDE 1
Estimated Yearly Costs of Purchasing and Operating a Surecraft 505.M

Aircraft purchase price		$5,000,000
Aircraft yearly cost:	Salaries	150,000
	Hanger fees, fuel, insurance, and maintenance	200,000
	Depreciation (book)	500,000
	Tax savings	(100,000)
	Total yearly cost	$ 750,000
Yearly airline travel to be eliminated		600,000
Excess yearly cost		$ 150,000

President: I think it would be worth $150,000 in customer relations alone. I know of several cases where we could have landed big accounts if we had that kind of flexibility to bring people together. Now how do we pay for it? Can we lease it and not have to borrow more money?

Accountant: Well, Surecraft has a leasing option, but even if we lease it, we still probably would have to show the liability on the balance sheet, for the amount of the purchase price initially, and of course reduced by the principal payments after that.

President: You mean for one year's rent, don't you?

Accountant: No, for the present value of the required payments under the lease, which in this case equals the total purchase price.

President: You're telling me, that if I rent this plane and have a legal lease contract, your accounting rules would still force me to show a liability, just as if I had borrowed money to purchase it?

Accountant: Listen, J. P., think about it from our bankers' perspective. We sign this noncancellable contract that obliges us to make periodic payments whose present value equals the purchase price, and we use the equipment for its useful life, pay the insurance, and do the maintenance and everything else an owner would do. Does a banker who reads our balance sheet care if it's a loan or a lease?

President: What about for taxes? Do they allow us to deduct depreciation as if we had purchased it?

Accountant: For the most part, that's our option and in this case, given the contract Surecraft has offered, I believe we will be able to capitalize and depreciate the aircraft for tax purposes.

President: So, for accounting and tax purposes, you guys just look at it as if it were a purchase. Our bankers won't like that liability, but I guess they'll get used to it.

The above conversation makes two major points. First, the business decision to purchase the aircraft did not depend on a purely quantifiable analysis. As you can see, the purchase option is expected to cost the company $150,000 more than the status quo, but there are other benefits that overcome this. Second, it provides an example of why the economic substance of a contract or transaction is more important than its form. Keep in mind, however, that it is often crucial that the form be completely understood in order that the substance not be overlooked.

PENSIONS

Pension plans are of two major types: (1) **defined contribution plans** where certain amounts are contributed with no guarantees about future retirement benefits, and (2) **defined benefit plans** where the employer guarantees specific amounts of benefits during retirement. Accounting for defined contribution plans is simple, the contribution to the plan is merely debited to Pension Expense and credited to Cash.

Accounting for defined benefit plans is quite complex, however, and we will only touch on the fundamentals here. The major challenge is determining the expense amounts applicable to any one period. For instance, a plan gives an employee $3,000 at the end of each year of retirement for each year of service. The employee works for five years and is expected to collect five years of pension payments. How much is charged to each of the five years of service?

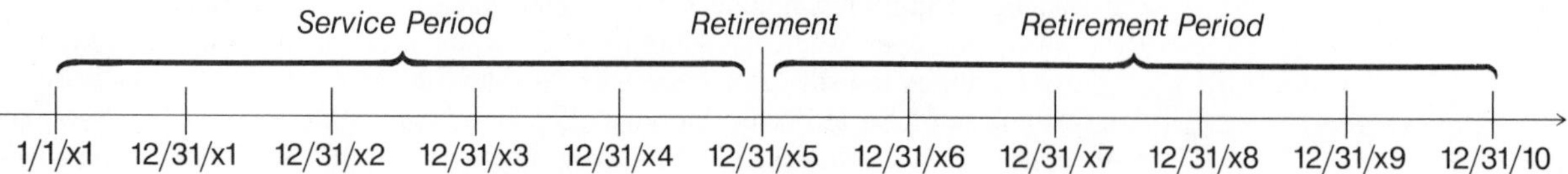

For year 1, what is the employer's obligation at December 31, 19x1? What amount must the employer put aside to provide the employee with retirement benefits in the future? The benefit the employee has earned after working one year is $3,000 for each year of retirement. If we assume a 10% interest rate for all computations, the obligation at December 31, 19x1, is the present value of an annuity of $3,000 per year for five years starting on December 31, 19x6.

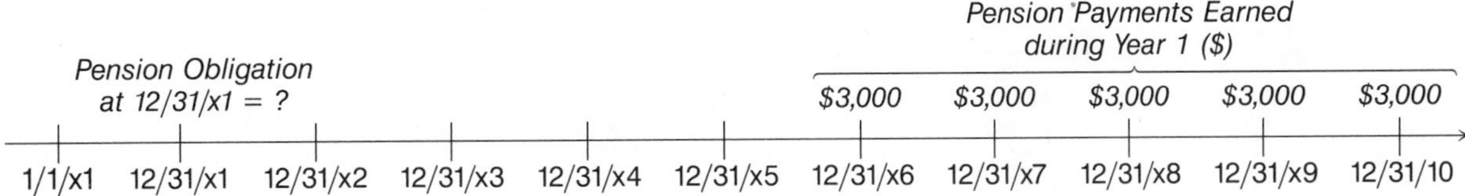

The computation is as follows:

1. $(P/A, 5, .10)\$3,000$ = Present value at 12/31/x5
$(3.7908)\$3,000$ = $11,372

2. $(P/F, 4, .10)\$11,372$ = Present value at 12/31/x1
$(.683)\$11,372$ = $7,767.

The first part of this two-part computation requires the computation of the present value of the retirement annuity as of the retirement date. This gives the sufficient amount needed on December 31, 19x5, to provide withdrawals of $3,000 per year for five years: $(P/A, 5, .10)\$3,000 = \$11,372$. The second part is the computation of the amount at December 31, 19x1, that if invested at compound annual interest of 10% would provide a fund of $11,372 at December 31, 19x5: $(P/F, 4, .10)\$11,372 = \$7,767$. As depicted in Exhibit 10B-1, the pension obligation is $7,767 at December 31, 19x1; and if cash is paid, the accounting entry would be:

19x1			
Dec. 31	Pension Expense (E)	7,767	
	Cash (A)		7,767
	To record 19x1 pension expense.		

The year 19x1, therefore, has pension expense of $7,767. That amount is put into a fund that will grow to $11,372 by the date of retirement if 10% is earned and compounded. The fund will continue to grow, and $3,000 per year could be paid to the retiree for five years before the fund would be depleted. Of course, years 2, 3, 4, and 5 would have to be funded in a like manner if the employee is to receive the full pension of $15,000 per year during retirement, 19x6–10.[4]

The actual computations and accounting rules used in pensions are beyond the scope of this text and are covered in intermediate accounting texts.

[4] *FASB Statement No. 87*, "Employer's Accounting for Pensions" (Norwalk, Conn.: FASB, 1985).

EXHIBIT 10B-1

History of Pension Fund Needed for 19x1 Service

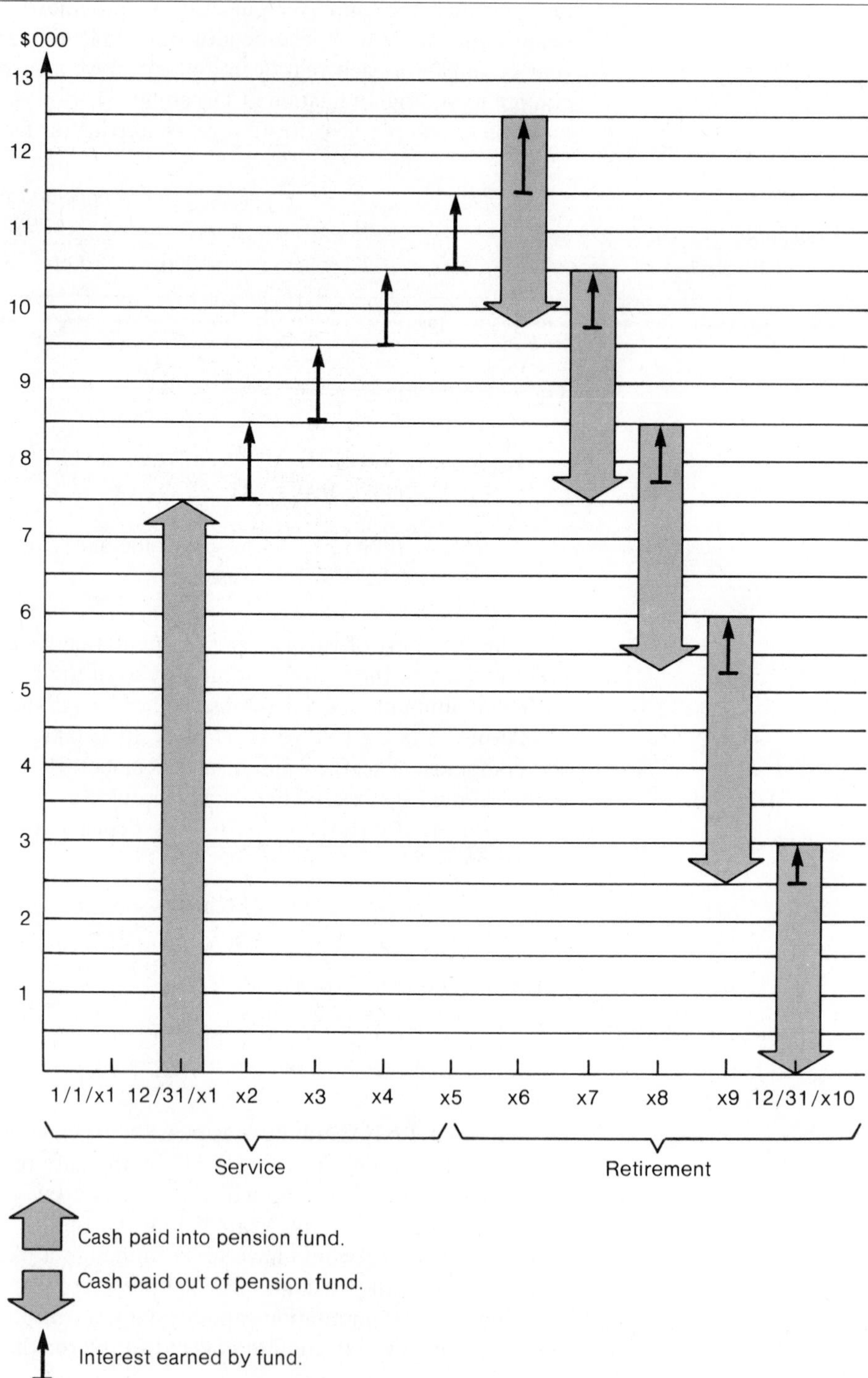

KEY TERMS

Bond indenture. Contract that describes all rights and obligations of all parties to the bonds.

Bonds. General term used for a whole series of debt contracts with varying terms, usually involving fixed interest payments, semiannual or annual, and a fixed maturity amount.

Bond sinking fund. Cash set aside and accumulated over the life of the bond issue to be used to pay off the bonds at maturity.

Compound interest. Interest charged on both the unpaid principal and any unpaid interest accrued after the inception of the liability.

Convertibility. Feature in bonds that allows for the bond to be converted into capital stock.

Covenants. Provisions in loan agreements that govern certain debtor actions and specify conditions under which loans must be repaid before maturity.

Debt financing. Long-term borrowing from creditors.

Discount. Created when a bond sells for less than the face value, suggesting the market considers the stated interest rate to be lower than the market's required rate of interest.

Effective-interest method. Interest expense for the period is computed by applying the market interest rate to the net liability balance (carrying value) at the beginning of the period.

Effective-interest rate. The rate of return on an investment determined by market forces; also called yield rate.

Equity financing. Issuance of capital stock to the stockholders of a business.

Junior debt. Unsecured or subordinated debt that relies on the general creditworthiness of the debtor; also called unsecured or subordinated debt.

Junk bonds. High-yield, subordinated debentures.

Leveraged buy outs. Financing arrangements where management and/or others gain control of a corporation by means of stock purchases financed by combinations of new investment and the issuance of debt, often in the form of junk bonds.

Nominal interest rate. Interest rate stated on the face of a debt instrument, such as a note or a bond.

Premium. Created when a bond sells for more than its face value, indicating that the stated rate of interest on the bond is above the rate required by the market.

Secured. A loan backed by assets that are pledged as collateral.

Senior debt. Liabilities that are secured by mortgages pledged to specific assets.

Simple interest. Interest charged on only the unpaid principal.

Straight-line method. Method used to amortize a bond premium or discount where equal amounts are amortized each period.

APPENDIX KEY TERMS

Annuities. Payments of equal amounts separated by equal periods of time. Ordinary annuities are paid at the end of each period.

Capital lease. Lease contract that transfers most of the rights and obligations of ownership to the lessee; recorded as purchase of equipment by means of long-term borrowing.

Defined benefit plans. Pension plans where the employer guarantees specific amounts of benefits.

Defined contribution plans. Pension plans where certain amounts are contributed with no guarantees about benefits.

Future value. Value that an investment today will grow to in a stated time in the future at a specified interest rate.

Leases. Contracts that give the lessee the right to the use of property, plant, or equipment for a fixed amount of time with a fixed schedule of payments to the lessor (the owner).

Lessee. The renter named in a lease.

Lessor. The owner named in a lease.

Operating leases. Leases where the lessor, the legal owner, keeps the risks and obligations of ownership.

Present value. The current value of a future payment given an effective-interest rate and a known number of periods.

Proceeds. The net amount received in a bond transaction; the selling price.

SYNONYMS

Collateral; pledged asset; mortgaged asset; security.
Coupon bonds; bearer bonds.
Covenants; loan provisions.
Creditors; providers of debt financing.
Debt financing; borrowing.
Default; nonrepayment.
Equity financing; stock issuance.
Equityholders; stockholders; equity owners.
Face interest rate; nominal interest rate; coupon rate.
Face value; maturity value.
Junior debt; unsecured debt; subordinated debt.
Market interest rate; yield rate; effective-interest rate.
Nominal interest rate; face interest rate.
Principal; amount borrowed.
Unsecured; debentured; subordinated.
Unsecured bonds; debentures.

QUESTIONS

1. Differentiate between debt financing and equity financing. How does each group receive a return on its investment?
2. Describe four common cash flow patterns regarding long-term liabilities.
3. What is the difference between an interest-bearing note and a noninterest-bearing note? How are they similar?
4. Describe two different methods of recording a note payable.
5. Define bonds. Describe the differences when bonds are sold at face value, at a discount, or at a premium.
6. Why do bonds sell in the market for more or less than their face value?
7. What is the market saying when a $1,000, 8%, 10-year bond is sold at 104?
8. Describe the two methods for amortizing a bond discount or a bond premium.
9. What is the difference between an adjunct account and a contra account?
10. Explain the convertibility feature of a bond.
11. Describe the use of a bond sinking fund.
12. Compute the total amount of cash received from the sale of a $1,000, 6%, five-year bond that pays interest semiannually on June 30 and December 31 and is sold on March 1 at 95. Why does this bond sell at a discount?
13. What is an amortization schedule? How does it relate to the account balances?
14. Given that you know the amount borrowed and the date of maturity, does it make a difference in the total cash paid back if the periodic payments of interest are annual or semiannual?
15. What is the general rule for determining the effective interest expense for an outstanding liability?

APPENDIX QUESTIONS

16. Differentiate between compound and simple interest.
17. Define the term *annuity*.
18. List the four conditions used to test whether a lease is a capital or an operating lease.
19. What two major types of pensions exist? How are they different?
20. What makes defined benefits plans so complex?
21. Why is the determination of substance over form crucial in accounting for leases?
22. If the future value of an obligation is fixed, how will varying the interest rate affect the present value?

EXERCISES

EXERCISE 10-1
L.O. 2

Common Traits of Long-Term Liabilities

Jack's Carwash borrows $600,000 at 8% on January 1, 19x1, to be repaid on December 31, 19x4. Consider the following payment terms independently:

a. December 31 year-end payments of $150,000 plus interest on the unpaid balance.
b. Payment of interest only on December 31 of each year and principal on December 31, 19x4.
c. Payment of principal and total interest on December 31, 19x4.
d. Four equal payments of $181,152 on each year-end.

Required:
Prepare an amortization schedule for each of the above payment schemes showing cash inflow and outflow, interest expense for each period, and the net liability at the end of each of the four years. (Round to nearest dollar.)

EXERCISE 10-2
L.O. 3

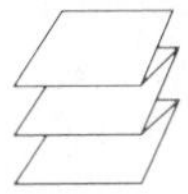

Long-Term Note Payable

On January 1, 19x1, the Alpha Company negotiated a $200,000 mortgage loan from the Beta Bank. The loan principal and interest is to be repaid in five equal annual installments of $52,760 beginning January 1, 19x2. The loan bears interest at an annual interest rate of 10%. Prepare the journal entries to record the issuance of the note, interest expense, and the five annual installments. Alpha Company's year-end is December 31. (Round to nearest dollar.)

EXERCISE 10-3
L.O. 3

Interest-Bearing and Noninterest-Bearing Notes

The following two notes are issued on January 1, 19x1:

a. $200,000, 10%, two-year note with principal and interest due on December 31, 19x2.
b. $242,000 note due on December 31, 19x2.

The company received $200,000 for each note on January 1, 19x1.

Required:
1. Prepare the journal entries in general journal form to record the issuance of each note, any adjusting entries required, and payment of each note on December 31, 19x2.
2. Show the balance sheet disclosure for each note on December 31, 19x1.

EXERCISE 10-4
L.O. 5, 6

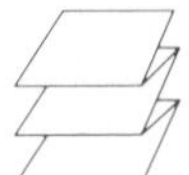

Bond Issuance, Interest, and Retirement

On January 1, 19x1, the King Corporation issued 7%, 20-year bonds at their face value of $1 million. Interest is payable semiannually on June 30 and December 31.

Required:
Prepare the journal entries in general journal form to record:

1. The bond issuance.
2. The first two years of interest payments.
3. Retirement of the bonds at face value at the end of year 20.

EXERCISE 10-5
L.O. 5

Bonds, Discount, and Straight-Line Amortization

On January 1, 19x4, the Holst Company issued and sold 600, $1,000 par value, 10%, 10-year bonds when the market interest rate was 8%. The bonds sold for $668,709. Interest is payable each January 1. Holst uses the straight-line amortization method for amortizing bond discount or premium. Show the balance sheet presentation of these bonds on December 31, 19x4. (Round to the nearest dollar.)

EXERCISE 10-6
L.O. 5

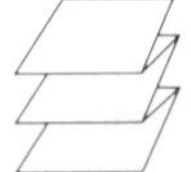

Bonds Sold at a Discount

Holland Corporation issued $100,000 of five-year bonds with a face value of $1,000 each and 8% interest payable semiannually. The bonds were sold on January 1, 19x1, for $92,278 yielding a 10% effective-interest rate. Compute the total amount of interest expense on these bonds over their five-year life.

EXERCISE 10-7
L.O. 5

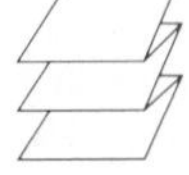

Bonds Sold at a Premium

Maker Corporation issued $100,000 in 12% bonds on January 1, 19x1. The bonds pay semiannual interest on June 30 and December 31 each year and were sold for $112,463 for an effective-interest rate of 10%. The bonds mature in 10 years. Compute the interest expense for the first six months of 19x1 using the effective-interest method. (Round to nearest dollar.)

EXERCISE 10-8
L.O. 7

Bond Conversion

On March 31, 19x4, Turner Electronics converts 100, $1,000 face value bonds with a net book value of $98,800 to 1,000 shares of its capital stock valued at $98.80 per share. The bonds pay 10% semiannually on June 30 and December 31. Bond interest for the period has not yet been paid but has been accrued to compute the net book value of the bonds.

Required:
Prepare the journal entries to record the interest payment and conversion of the bonds.

EXERCISE 10-9
L.O. 8

Bond Sinking Fund

The Sommers Company established a bond sinking fund to provide funds for the repayment of a $300,000 outstanding bond issue. The bonds mature on December 31, 19x6. The company will make six equal deposits of $43,000 each to the fund each December 31 with the first deposit being made on December 31, 19x1. Deposits to the fund earn interest at a 6% annual interest rate.

Required:
1. Prepare the journal entries in general journal form for the establishment of the fund and the annual payments and interest earned on the fund.
2. Prepare the journal entries in general journal form for the payment of the bonds on December 31, 19x6.
3. Compute total interest earned by the bond sinking fund over the six-year period.

EXERCISE 10-10
L.O. 5, 9

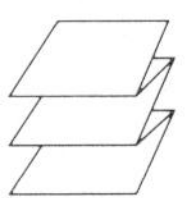

Bond Issuance between Interest Dates

Bozo Corporation issued $100,000 of 12% stated interest, five-year bonds on April 1, 19x5. The bonds pay interest semiannually on June 30 and December 31 and straight-line amortization is used. The total cash received at the date of sale was $103,000.

Required:
1. Show the necessary journal entry(ies) on April 1, 19x5.
2. Show the necessary journal entry(ies) on June 30, 19x5.
3. Show the necessary journal entry(ies) on December 31, 19x5.

EXERCISE 10-11
L.O. 5, 9

Bond Issuance between Interest Dates

On September 1, 19x1, the Yates Company, which has a December 31 year-end, sold 1,000, $10,000, 8%, five-year bonds at face value plus accrued interest. The bonds were dated June 30, 19x1, and interest is payable annually each June 30.

Required:
Prepare the journal entries in general journal form to record (round to nearest dollar):

1. The sale of the bonds on September 1, 19x1.
2. Adjustment on December 31, 19x1.
3. The first interest payment.

EXERCISE 10-12
L.O. 5

Bonds Sold at a Discount

Dorek, Inc., issued $400,000 of ten-year bonds, each with a face value of $10,000 and a coupon interest rate of 10%, payable annually. The bonds all sold on January 1, 19x4, for $316,524, resulting in an effective interest rate of 14%.

Required (round all answers to dollars):
1. Compute the interest expense to be recorded in 19x4.
2. Compute the total cash interest payments over the life of the bonds.
3. Compute the total interest expense recorded over the life of the bonds.

EXERCISE 10-13
L.O. 5

Coupon versus Effective Interest

Some years ago Brant Corporation issued bonds having a maturity value of $100,000 on November 1, 19x6. A portion of the bond amortization table relating to the issue appears below:

Date	Annual Interest Payment	Annual Interest Expense	Premium Amortization	Net Liability
—	—	—	—	—
11/1/x1	—	—	—	$102,195
11/1/x2	$5,000	$4,599	$401	101,794
11/1/x3	5,000	4,581	419	101,375
11/1/x4	5,000	4,562	438	100,937
11/1/x5	5,000	4,531	458	100,479
11/1/x6	5,000	4,521	479	100,000

Required:

1. What was the effective interest rate on these bonds at issuance?
2. What is the coupon rate of interest on these bonds?
3. Assume the bonds had been issued on November 1, 19x1, for $102,195. What would be the total interest expense over the life of the bond issue? What would be the total cash outflow minus the total cash inflow over the life of the bond issue?

APPENDIX EXERCISES

EXERCISE 10-14
L.O. 10

Present Values

1. Compute the future value of:
   a. $16,000 in eight years at 6% compounded annually.
   b. $25,000 in 10 years at 8% compounded semiannually.
   c. $82,000 in two years at 16% compounded quarterly.
2. Compute the present value (compounded annually) of:
   a. $100,000, 6%, five years.
   b. $19,000, 10%, 10 years.
   c. $35,000, 12%, three years.
3. Compute the future value (compounded annually) of the following ordinary annuities:
   a. $6,000, five years, 10%.
   b. $3,000, 10 years, 15%.
   c. $150,000, three years, 12%.
4. Compute the present value (compounded annually) of the following ordinary annuities:
   a. $25,000, 4%, eight years.
   b. $160,000, 10%, five years.
   c. $100,000, 5%, 10 years.

EXERCISE 10-15
L.O. 10, 11

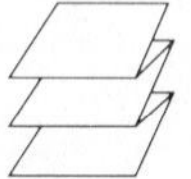

Bond Issuance—Computing Proceeds

On January 1, 19x6, the King Corporation issued $1 million face value, 7% 10-year bonds. Interest is payable semiannually on June 30 and December 31.

Required:
1. Calculate the proceeds of the bond issue if the market interest rate is 8%.
2. Calculate the proceeds of the bond issue if the market interest rate is 6%.

EXERCISE 10-16
L.O. 10

Computing Bond Proceeds (Appendix 10B)

On January 1, 19x1, Jaybar Corporation sold 5% bonds with a face value of $100,000. These bonds mature in 20 years, and interest is paid annually on December 31. The bonds were sold to yield 6%.

Required:
1. Compute the proceeds from the sale of Jaybar bonds.
2. Using the effective-interest method of computing interest, how much should be charged (debited) to interest expense in 19x1?

EXERCISE 10-17
L.O. 10, 11

Financing Alternatives

Jacobs Corporation has the option of purchasing a computer system in one of two ways:

1. $118,250 cash now.
2. $17,425 at the end of each of the next 10 years ($0 down), starting one year from now.

Required:
1. Determine which option is the best one to take.
2. Would your answer differ if option 2 required 10 year-end payments of $25,000? Of $11,825?

EXERCISE 10-18
L.O. 10, 11

Leases

Baker entered into a lease purchase agreement for a fleet of ships. The ships had a fair market value of $196,360,000 at the date of the lease, were expected to last 20 more years (no scrap value, straight-line depreciation), and the lease called for annual year-end payments of $20 million for the next 20 years. This results in an implicit interest rate of 8%.

Required:
1. Determine the total interest expense over the life of the lease.
2. What would be the balance in the net lease liability at the end of 15 years (after the payment for year 15)? Hint: Calculate the present value of the remaining payments.

EXERCISE 10-19
L.O. 10, 11

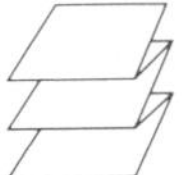

Leases

Bartlett Corporation leased equipment from Henderson, Inc., on January 1, 19x1, by signing a five-year lease contract calling for $80,000 payment on January 1, 19x1, and five additional annual payments of $100,000 each subsequent December 31. The effective-interest rate in the lease agreement is 10%.

Required:
Compute the total amount of interest expense for Bartlett Corporation over the life of the lease. Hint: Compute the present value of all cash payments and compare that amount to the total cash payments.

PROBLEMS

PROBLEM 10-1
L.O. 5

Straight-Line and Effective-Interest Amortization Methods

Assume a company sells the following bonds:

Face value:	$100,000
Interest rate:	8%
Interest payment dates:	April 1 and October 1
Date sold:	April 1, 19x1
Term:	Four years

Required:
1. Complete an amortization table using the straight-line method assuming the bond selling price $93,552 provides an effective-interest rate of 10%. (Round all calculations to the nearest dollar.)
2. Complete an amortization table using the effective-interest method assuming the bond selling price $93,552 provides an effective-interest rate of 10%. (Round all calculations to the nearest dollar.)

PROBLEM 10-2
L.O. 5, 9

Bonds Issued between Interest Dates

The Ogihara Company is authorized to issue 1,000, $1,000, 9%, 10-year bonds. The bonds are dated March 1, 19x1, and interest is payable semiannually on March 1 and September 1. The following transactions occurred regarding the bonds:

19x1
Apr. 1 Sold 500 bonds at $500,000 plus accrued interest.
Sept. 1 Paid the semiannual interest.
Dec. 1 Sold the remaining 500 bonds at $500,000 plus accrued interest.
31 Accrued interest for the year-end financial statements.
19x2
Mar. 1 Paid the semiannual interest.

Required:
Record the above transactions assuming premiums and discounts are amortized at each interest payment date and at year-end using the straight-line method. Record all computations to nearest dollar.

PROBLEM 10-3
L.O. 5

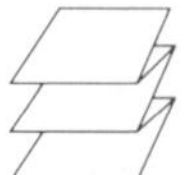

Bonds and Discounts

The Brandy Company issued 2,000, $1,000, 8%, 10-year bonds on July 1, 19x1, when the market interest rate was 10%. The proceeds from the issue were $1,750,776. Interest is paid semiannually on June 30 and December 31 of each year, with the first payment being made on December 31, 19x1. The company closes its books on December 31 and recognizes amortization at the time of each interest payment.

Required (round to nearest dollar):
1. Prepare the journal entry to record the issuance of the bonds on July 1, 19x1.
2. Prepare the journal entries related to the bond issue on December 31, 19x1, and June 30, 19x2, assuming the company uses the straight-line method for amortization of bond discount or premium.
3. Repeat part 2 using the effective-interest method for amortization of bond discount or premium.

PROBLEM 10-4
L.O. 5

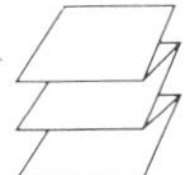

Bonds and Premiums

The Enchilada Corporation issued $100,000 of 10% interest, 20-year bonds on January 1, 19x6. The bonds pay interest semiannually on July 1 and January 1. The bonds were issued for $119,765 to yield an effective-interest rate of 8%. The fiscal year-end is December 31.

Required (round to nearest dollar):
1. Prepare the entry(ies) to record the issuance and account for the interest on these bonds for the remainder of 19x6. Use the effective-interest method for amortization of any discount or premium.
2. Compute the total interest expense recorded over the 20-year life of the bond issue.
3. Repeat parts 1 and 2 using the straight-line method for amortization of any discount or premium.

PROBLEM 10-5
L.O. 5

Bond Discount and Premium

The Winston Company sold 50, $1,000, 14% bonds on January 1, 19x1. Interest is payable on June 30 and December 31 of each year. The bonds mature on December 31, 19x4. The company uses the effective-interest amortization method of amortizing bond discount or premium.

Required:
1. Prepare a bond amortization schedule for the four-year period assuming the proceeds from the bond issue are $53,105. The market interest rate on January 1, 19x1, is 12%. (Round numbers to the nearest dollar.)
2. Prepare a bond amortization schedule for the four-year period assuming the proceeds from the bond issue are $47,125. The market interest rate on January 1, 19x1, is 16%. (Round number to the nearest dollar.)

PROBLEM 10-6
L.O. 5

Bonds Sold at a Discount

Superior Corporation sold a $200,000, 12% bond issue on November 1, 19x1, at 96.5% of maturity value. The bonds were dated November 1, 19x1, and pay interest semiannually on April 30 and October 31. The bonds mature on October 31, 19x5. Superior Corporation uses the straight-line method of amortizing bond discount or premium. Superior's fiscal year ends on December 31.

Required (round to nearest dollar):
1. Prepare the journal entry to record the sale of the bonds on November 1, 19x1.
2. Prepare the adjusting journal entry required at December 31, 19x1.
3. Show how bonds payable should be reported on the December 31, 19x1, annual financial statement.
4. Prepare the journal entry to record the interest payment on April 30, 19x2.

PROBLEM 10-7
L.O. 5, 6

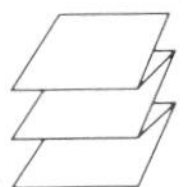

Bond Issuance at a Premium, Interest, and Retirement

On January 1, 19x1, the Illini Company issues 10-year bonds of $100,000 at $114,877 for an effective-interest rate of 6%. Interest is payable on December 31 and June 30 at an annual rate of 8%. On July 1, 19x4, the Illini Company reacquires and retires 20% of its own $1,000 bonds at 98. The fiscal period for the Illini Company is the calendar year. The company uses the effective-interest rate method of bond discount or premium amortization.

Required:
1. Prepare the journal entries to record the issuance of the bonds and an amortization schedule through June 30, 19x4.
2. Prepare the journal entries relating to the payment of interest and amortization of discount or premium on December 31, 19x3.
3. Prepare the journal entries to record the reacquisition and retirement of 20% of the bonds on July 1, 19x4.

PROBLEM 10-8
L.O. 5, 6, 9

Bond Issuance at a Discount, Interest, and Retirement

Floate Company sold 100 of their $1,000, 8%, 10-year bonds at $87,539; a price that creates an effective interest of 10%. The bonds were sold on January 1, 19x1, with interest payable on June 30 and December 31. The following transactions occurred regarding these bonds:

a. Sale of the bonds on January 1, 19x1.
b. Payment of the semiannual interest and amortization of the discount on June 30, 19x1.
c. Payment of the semiannual interest and amortization of the discount on December 31, 19x1.
d. Assuming that the unamortized discount amounted to $1,862 on December 31, 19x9, after recording the 12/31/x9 payment, make the entry to record the final two interest payments and to retire the bond at maturity.

Required:
Prepare the journal entries in general journal form using the effective-interest method of amortizing the discount for the above transactions. Round all computations to the nearest dollar.

PROBLEM 10-9
L.O. 7, 9

Bond Sale and Conversion

Arb Products authorized the issuance of $400,000 of 10-year bonds with a 9% coupon on January 1, 19x1. The bonds pay interest semiannually on June 30 and December 31, and mature on December 31, 19x10. All of the bonds are convertible into common stock of Arb Products after December 31, 19x5, at the rate of 20 shares of Arb no par common for every $1,000 face value bond. Arb common was selling for $35 per share on March 1, 19x1, but by January 31, 19x6, Arb common was trading at $62 per share. On January 31, 19x6, one-half of the bonds were exchanged for 4000 shares of Arb common stock. Arb uses straight-line amortization for bond discounts or premiums. Accrued interest is paid to the bondholders who convert to common stock up to the date of the exchange.

Required:
1. Record the issuance at face value of these bonds on March 1, 19x1.
2. Record the interest payments for 19x1.
3. Record the conversion of one-half of the bonds on January 31, 19x6.
4. Record the interest payment for June 30, 19x6, for the remaining one-half of the bonds.

PROBLEM 10-10
L.O. 5, 6

Premium Bonds and Partial Retirement

Protak Corporation issued $400,000 of five-year bonds on January 1, 19x4. The bonds had a stated interest rate of 10%, paid semiannually, and were sold for $432,458 at a yield of 8%.

Required:
1. Compute the interest expense to be recorded in 19x4.
2. Compute the total cash interest payments over the life of the bonds.

3. Compute the total interest expense recorded over the life of the bonds.
4. Assume Protak repurchases and retires $100,000 face value of bonds on January 1, 19x5, for $105,000. Record the retirement of these bonds.

PROBLEM 10-11
L.O. 2, 3

Alternative Repayment Schemes

On January 1, 19x3, the General Trucking Company borrows $20 million from Union Bank. The loan is at 10% annual interest for four years.

Required:
1. Assume the loan requires one lump sum payment at 12/31/x4. Prepare an amortization schedule for General Trucking that shows interest expense for each year and in total.
2. Assume General Trucking agrees to repay the loan with equal principal payments of $5 million each December 31, plus accrued interest for the year. Prepare an amortization schedule that shows interest expense for each year and in total.
3. Assume General Trucking agrees to repay the $20 million on December 31, 19x4, and accrued interest once each year on December 31. Prepare an amortization schedule that shows interest expense for each year and in total.
4. Assume General Trucking agrees to repay the loan with four equal payments of $6,309,347. Prepare an amortization schedule that shows interest expense each year and in total.
5. Which repayment scheme calls for the most interest? Why?
6. Which repayment scheme is like a zero coupon (noninterest-bearing) bond or note (also called a deep discount bond/note)?
7. Which repayment scheme is like a bond sold at face value?

APPENDIX PROBLEMS

PROBLEM 10-12
L.O. 5, 10, 11

Bonds—Determining Proceeds

Determine the proceeds that will be received if bonds are sold under the following circumstances. Prepare the journal entries in general journal form to record these sales:

a. $3 million of 8%, 10-year bonds sold on January 2 with interest payable June 30 and December 31 priced to yield an effective rate of 8%.
b. $3 million of 8%, 10-year bonds sold on January 2 with interest payable June 30 and December 31 priced to yield 12%.
c. $3 million of 12%, 10-year bonds sold on January 2 with interest payable June 30 and December 31 priced to yield 16%.
d. The bonds described in item (*c*) priced to yield 10%.
e. $1 million of 12%, 10-year bonds with interest payable June 30 and December 31 issued at face value on March 1.

PROBLEM 10-13
L.O. 10

Present Value

Assume in each of the following cases that the number of years is five and the interest rate is 13%. The following information is also given:

Future value of $1	1.8424
Present value of $1	.5428
Future value of a $1 annuity . . .	6.4803
Present value of a $1 annuity . . .	3.5172

Required:
Compute:

1. The amount of each year-end payment required to repay a $5,000 interest-bearing loan.
2. How much a $3,000 deposit will accumulate in five years.
3. How much should you put in the bank on the last day of the next five years to accumulate $4,000 for a trip to Europe when you finish law school.
4. How much cash will the bank give you for a noninterest-bearing note with a face value of $7,000.

PROBLEM 10-14
L.O. 10

Present Value

The state helps a rural county maintain an old bridge and has agreed to pay $6,000 on December 31 of each year for five years toward the expenses. The first payment is to be made on December 31, 19x6. The state wishes to discharge its obligation by paying a single sum to a trust on January 1, 19x6, in lieu of the first payment due on December 31, 19x6, and all future payments. Calculate the amount the state should pay the trust on January 1, 19x6, assuming the trust earns interest at a rate of 8% compounded annually.

PROBLEM 10-15
L.O. 10, 11

Bonds

Aerotech reported Bonds Payable on their December 31, 1986, balance sheet that had a maturity value of $10 million. The bonds mature in three years. The bonds were issued on January 1, 1968, at a yield at 10%. The bonds pay semiannual interest of $400,000 on June 30 and December 31. Aerotech has a December 31 year-end and uses the effective-interest method for amortization.

Required:
1. What is the net book value of the Bonds Payable in Aerotech's 1986 annual report?
2. What is the amount of interest expense reported in Aerotech's 1986 annual report?

PROBLEM 10-16
L.O. 10, 11

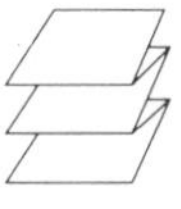

Leases

Chattanooga Locomotive, Inc., manufactures locomotives which it sells to customers using one of two alternative plans:

Plan 1: Payment of $3 million cash at date of purchase.

Plan 2: A lease of 10 years with equal annual payments of $488,233 due at the end of each year for 10 years. The title to the locomotive passes to the buyer at the end of the 10-year lease. The implicit interest rate in the lease is 10%.

The expected life of a locomotive is 10 years, and its expected salvage value is zero.

Choo Choo Company leases a locomotive from Chattanooga on January 2, 19x5, using Plan 2. Choo Choo uses straight-line depreciation on all assets.

Required:
1. Record the lease transaction on January 1, 19x5, on Choo Choo's books.
2. Calculate the total expense recorded by Choo Choo for 19x5 in connection with this leased asset and lease obligation.
3. Calculate the total expense recorded by Choo Choo in 19x6 in connection with this leased asset and lease obligation.

PROBLEM 10-17
L.O. 10, 11

Leases

Hauler, Inc., leased 10 tractor trailers from Fuqua Corporation on January 1, 19x1. The fair market value of the trailers was $8.1 million total, and their expected useful life was 12 years with no scrap value. Hauler paid Fuqua $1,605,000 on January 1, 19x1, and agreed to pay an additional $1 million each subsequent January 1 for the next 11 years. The appropriate rate of interest for this lease is 10% for both the lessor and the lessee.

Required:
1. Compute the total amount of interest expense to be paid by Hauler over the life of the lease.
2. Using straight-line depreciation, determine how much total expense Hauler will charge to income in 19x1 for the lease obligation and the leased assets.
3. Compute the net lease liability balance on January 2, 19x6 (the day after the fifth $1 million payment), on Hauler's books.

PROBLEM 10-18
L.O. 10, 11

Leases

Lessee, Inc., agrees to lease a machine from January 1, 19x1. The machine could have been purchased for $2 million cash. The lease is for five years with annual payments of $544,816 due at the end of each of the next five years and the ownership of the machine is transferred to Lessee, Inc., after the final payment. The expected life of the machine for amortization purposes is 10 years. Lessee uses straight-line depreciation on all assets and assumes a zero salvage value. The agreement is a capital lease. Assume a 12% interest factor.

Required:
1. Show all journal entries relating to the leased asset and obligation for the years 19x1, 19x2 on the books of Lessee, Inc.
2. Show how the asset would be reported on Lessee's balance sheet at the end of 19x2.

PROBLEM 10-19
L.O. 11

Leases

BREZ Air Corporation agreed to pay $35,000,000 at the end of each year for the next 20 years in order to acquire two DC10-30 aircraft from Wells Fargo Bank (the lessor). These aircraft have a fair market value of $171,816,750 each at the time the lease is signed. Assume the aircraft will be depreciated over 20 years on a straight-line basis by BREZ, with the aircraft reverting to the lessor after 20 years. This lease is a capital lease for BREZ.

Required:
1. What is the interest rate implied by this lease agreement?
   (Hint: (P/A)A = $171,816,750 × 2.)
2. Record the lease at its inception.
3. Compute the balance in the leased assets and lease liability at the end of 10 years.

CASES

CASE 10-1
L.O. 10, 11

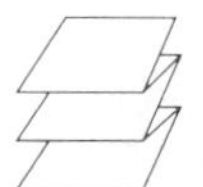

Financing Alternatives

Hatfield Company has to purchase two large generators for its plant on January 1, 19x1. Each generator will cost $500,000. Two alternative payment schemes have been proposed. The first is to borrow $1 million at 12% from a bank with two year-end payments at December 31, 19x1, and December 31, 19x2, equal to one-half of the unpaid principal plus interest for the period. The second is to purchase the generators on time from the manufacturer. The manufacturer's financing plan calls for a down payment of $100,000 per unit plus payments of $200,000 plus interest at 12% for each unit—one payment 12 months and the other 24 months after delivery of the generator. Hatfield Company has a December 31 year-end.

Required:

1. Construct a schedule that shows the cash outflow patterns for each alternative financing method.
2. Discuss the reasons for choosing each method over the other.

CASE 10-2
L.O. 1, 4, 5

Bonds

Campbell Company issued $1,000,000 of 10-year, 8% bonds on January 1, 19x1, for $875,480. On the same date, Martin Company issued $1,000,000 of 10-year, 12% bonds for $1,124,720. Both sets of bonds pay interest on June 30 and December 31 of each year, both have similar risk characteristics, and both were issued to yield 10%.

Required:

1. Discuss the factors that must be considered when issuing bonds at a premium and at a discount.
2. Why did Martin receive much higher cash proceeds from their issue when both firms issued the same dollar amount of bonds at the same market rate of interest?
3. Compute the interest expense related to these bonds for each company for 19x1 and 19x2 using the effective-interest method. Why did interest expense in 19x2 increase for Campbell but decrease for Martin?
4. Show the presentation of each bond issue on the two companies' 19x2 balance sheets. Does this presentation accurately reflect the economic substances of these two similar bond issues?

CASE 10-3
L.O. 1, 2

Comparison of Financing Methods and Business Decisions

Assume that World Concessions, Inc. (WCI), has the opportunity to operate the main food concession at a world exhibition which is to run for a two-year period, 1/1/x1 through 12/31/x2. The following are the important amounts involved:

Expected cash sales per year	$6,000,000
Expected cash expenses per year . . .	$2,500,000
Interest rate for all transactions.	10%
Dividend payments	Net income for period

Other information: The Tucson Convention Center owns all of the structures and equipment at the exhibit and it will take possession of all assets on 12/31/x2. WCI has four options: (1) Use its own cash for the initial payment of $5,000,000. (2) Rent the concession assets for a $3,000,000 payment on 12/31/x1 with an option for a second-year rental. (3) Borrow $5,000,000 by signing a two-year note to be paid back in two year-end payments. Each payment reduces the principal by equal amounts and pays interest on the unpaid balance at the beginning of the period. (4) Sign a two-year noncancelable lease agreement with required payments of $2,881,014 on 12/31/x1 and 12/31/x2.

On 1/1/x1 WCI has only one asset: $10,000,000 in a bank account that earns 10% and it has common stock with a book value of $10,000,000.

Required:

1. Consider the four alternative ways that WCI can get the right to operate the concession. Use the format below to analyze the balance sheet and income statement effects of the WCI's transactions for 19x1. (Hint: The transactions shown here are for Financing Method 1. You may have to modify the format for other methods.)

2. Answer this question: Does the method of financing a particular asset acquisition affect the financial statements?

World Concessions, Inc.
Balance Sheet Analysis
(Financing Method 1)

Bank Account	*Concession Assets*	*Liabilities*	*Common Stock*	*Retained Earnings*
Beginning balances $	$	$	$	$
Purchase assets				
Sales				
Cash expenses				
Depreciation expense				
Interest revenue				
Dividend ______	______	______	______	______
End balance ______	______	______	______	______

Net assets = $______

Net income = $______

CASE 10-4
L.O. 1, 3, 4

Riskiness of Collateralized Notes and Debentures

Kingston Ferry Service, Inc., is negotiating for the purchase of two new vessels. Two alternative financing plans are proposed by the corporate treasurer: (1) issuance of debentures bonds at an effective-interest rate of 18%, and (2) a note with the vessels used as collateral to be repaid one third each year-end plus interest at an interest rate of 12%.

Required:
Explain why the interest rates vary across the two alternatives and the effect each alternative has on the income statement and balance sheet.

CASE 10-5
L.O. 5

Straight-Line versus Effective-Interest Methods of Discount Amortization

In January Parr Foods, Inc., issued 10-year debenture bonds having total face value of $10,000,000 at a significant discount. The company has a December 31 year-end and pays interest on June 30 and December 31 of each year. The president of the company wants an explanation of the effects on the income statement of the following alternatives: (*a*) amortization of the discount by the effective interest method, and (*b*) amortization of the discount by the straight-line method.

Required:
Write a memo explaining the impact of each alternative on the income statement. Give arguments in favor of each.

CASE 10-6
L.O. 3

Zero Coupon Note

Consider the following excerpt from a footnote in a recent published annual report:

Note Six: Long-Term Debt

In Millions	*May 28, 1989*	*May 29, 1988*
Zero coupon notes, yield 11.14% $555.5 due August 15, 2013.	$41.1	$37.6
Zero coupon notes, yield 14⅝% $49.2 due June 30, 1991	36.7	31.9

Zero coupon notes (and bonds) require the debtor to pay back the borrowed amount plus accumulated interest in one lump sum at the maturity date. The reported amounts on the right represent the total obligation (principal plus all interest to date, since no payments have been made) at the end of fiscal 1989 and 1988. The amounts due at maturity ($555.5 million and $49.2 million, respectively) are given after the effective interest dates.

Required:
1. For the first notes (11.14%), what is the total remaining interest expense to be recorded between May 28, 1989, and maturity (August 15, 2013)?
2. For the second notes (14⅝%), what is the apparent compounding period (e.g., quarterly, annually, and semiannually)?
3. For the 14⅝% notes, what was the apparent amount of interest expense for fiscal 1989?

APPENDIX CASES

CASE 10-7
L.O. 10, 11

Bonds and Leases

At January 1, 19x3, the long-term liability section of ABC Company balance sheet contained the following items:

Long-Term Liabilities

Bonds payable, 9%, due 19x6 . . .	$1,000,000	
Add: Unamortized premium	100,000	$1,100,000
Capitalized lease obligations		600,000
Deferred income taxes.		150,000
Total long-term liabilities		$1,850,000

Required:
1. Discuss the nature of the cash flows that will be required to satisfy each category of long-term liability on this balance sheet.
2. Explain why the cash received in excess of the face amount to be paid back on the bonds was not recorded as a gain on the sale of the bonds when they were issued in 19x1.
3. On January 15, 19x3, these bonds were selling in the bond market at 97. What economic event would cause the switch from premium to discount? What accounting entry would be required by ABC to account for this economic event?
4. What factors were considered in determining which of ABC's leases would be shown as liabilities?

CASE 10-8
L.O. 10

Present Values and Interest Rates

Consider a case where two customers, Allen Co. and Baker, Inc., have notes made out to your company with the same required cash flows; that is, five year-end note payments of $5,000 each with an effective-interest rate of 14%. The notes were made on January 1 of the current year. Your company charges 18% to some customers that are considered more risky. Assume that Allen Co. is in strong financial shape and has a reputation of paying on time. It has been discovered that Baker, Inc., on the other hand, is in weak financial shape and has missed payments to other creditors in the past. This was not known when the contract was signed. It is now at the first year-end and the first payments have been received.

Required:
As accountant for your company, you are to write a memo explaining how these receivables are to be valued on the year-end balance sheet and what effect they will have on the income statement.

CASE 10-9
L.O. 10, 11

Noninterest-Bearing Notes and Present Values

Quake Winery purchased a new harvester on September 1, 19x1, and signed a three-year note that calls for one payment three years hence of $266,200, including principal and interest.

Required:
Answer the following questions:

1. If the note does not explicitly state an interest rate, what evidence can be used to determine the purchase price of the equipment and the liability as of the date of purchase?
2. Would changes in the interest rate change the book value of the note and the equipment? Why?
3. Would the income statement be affected by the choice of interest rate? How?

FINANCIAL STATEMENTS

FINANCIAL STATEMENT COMPONENTS EMPHASIZED IN CHAPTER 11

Siller Corporation
Income Statement
For 1991

Revenues
xxxx
xxxx
Expenses
xxxx
xxxx

Siller Corporation
Balance Sheet
12/31/91

Current assets
xxxx
xxxx
Noncurrent assets
xxxx
xxxx
Current liabilities
Dividends payable
Noncurrent liabilities
xxxx
xxxx
Stockholders' equity
Common stock—par
Preferred stock—par
Additional paid-in capital
Common
Preferred
Retained earnings

	1991	1990
Dividends payable	$XXX	$XXX

	1991	1990
Common stock—par . .	$XXX	$XXX
Preferred stock—par . .	XXX	XXX
Additional paid-in capital		
Common	XXX	XXX
Preferred	XXX	XXX
Retained earnings	XX	XX

Siller Corporation
Cash Flow Statement
For 1991

Operating activities
xxxx
xxxx
Investing activities
xxxx
xxxx
Financing activities
Cash from sale of stock
Cash payments for dividends

	1991	1990
Cash from sale of stock	$XXX	$XXX
Cash payments for dividends	(XXX)	(XXX)

CHAPTER 11

Noncorporate and Corporate Business Organizations

LEARNING OBJECTIVES

After studying Chapter 11, you should understand:

1. The legal and accounting aspects of noncorporate and corporate business organizations, pp. 590-94.
2. Accounting for owner's equity in a proprietorship, pp. 594-96.
3. Partnerships—ease of formation, classes of partners, limited life, and mutual agency, pp. 596-98.
4. The advantages and disadvantages of the corporate form of business organization, pp. 598-600.
5. Accounting for corporate organization costs and issuance of stock, pp. 600-604.
6. The corporate balance sheet presentation of contributed capital, p. 606.
7. Accounting for the reacquisition and retirement of stock, pp. 607-9.
8. Accounting for donated capital, cash dividends, and stock dividends and splits, pp. 610-13.
9. The special features of preferred stock, pp. 613-15.
10. Some of the accounting challenges created by partnerships (Appendix), pp. 619-31.

This chapter discusses the noncorporate (proprietorships and partnerships) and the corporate (corporations) business organizations. To understand how accounting is affected by the form of business organization, you must first have some knowledge of fundamental legal and economic factors that shaped the evolution of those forms. In this chapter you are introduced to many of these issues. The general nature of proprietorships and partnerships and their major underlying accounting concepts are also explained. The appendix to the chapter is an introduction to the accounting for partnerships.

The accounting for the rights and responsibilities of corporate stockholders is discussed in detail in this chapter because accounting reflects these relationships and the transactions that occur between corporations and stockholders. The corporate organization gives business advantages such as the **potential to raise large amounts of capital and to continue in operation when ownership changes.** Stockholders of corporations also have an advantage because they are **not personally responsible for the obligations of the business.** Corporations and stockholders have a legal relationship that is governed by state and federal law. Payments to stockholders, in the form of dividends or upon liquidation, are constrained by the laws of the state in which the corporation is registered. The formal rules that govern the stockholder and the corporation contrast with the ease and informality of asset flow from business to owner found in noncorporate business organizations.

You will note in this chapter that accounting reflects the underlying economics of the noncorporate and corporate business organizations and not merely the legal relationship of businesses to owners. However, in corporations, legalities can affect economic aspects, especially in the realm of stockholder rights and obligations.

LEGAL AND ACCOUNTING ASPECTS OF NONCORPORATE AND CORPORATE BUSINESSES

Objective 1
The legal and accounting aspects of noncorporate and corporate business organizations.

The business entity concept is one of the fundamental principles of accounting. Throughout this textbook we have illustrated that in accounting, the business entity is a separate economic unit. Accountants always consider the rights and obligations of a business as being separate from its individual owners or other entities. Employees, suppliers, governments, and even owners are not the entity being accounted for in the business's financial records.

As you recall from Chapter 1, although accountants view the business as a separate entity, the extent of the legal liability of business owners depends on how the business is organized. For **proprietorships** (single-owner, noncorporate businesses) and **partnerships** (multiowner, noncorporate businesses), the owners' legal liability from business activities is unlimited; for corporations, this legal liability is limited to the owners' (stockholders') investment in the business entity. In this section you will learn more about the differences in the legal and accounting (business entity) aspects of noncorporate and corporate businesses.

In the typical corporate balance sheet (1) assets are listed without reference to their sources, (2) creditors' names do not appear next to liability accounts, and (3) stockholders' equity accounts do not indicate the identities of individual stockholders. Also, in the corporate income statement, no reference is made to how specific stockholders participate in earnings. In a noncorporate business, the basic elements of assets, liabilities, revenues, and expenses in the financial statements are essentially the same as for corporations, but owners have a different legal relationship to the noncorporate business than stockholders have to the corporation. This special legal relationship affects the accounting and reporting for noncorporate businesses, especially owners' equity, and is explained in the paragraphs that follow.

You must distinguish between the legal and accounting aspects of corporate and noncorporate businesses to understand the differences between these two forms of business organizations. The assets, liabilities, revenues, and expenses of a corporation are legally separated from stockholders. Thus, creditors of the corporation usually cannot sue stockholders when the company defaults on payment of debts. Also, stockholders usually cannot withdraw assets from the corporation at will. By contrast, the legal view of proprietorships and partnerships does not separate them from their owners. In general, owners are responsible for the debts of their partnership or proprietorship and can withdraw assets at will according to prescribed formulas.

As an example, consider two businesses: Corporation A, owned exclusively by Ms. Andrews, and Company B, a proprietorship owned exclusively by Mr. Brown. Both owners contributed $20,000 to start the business. The two businesses are identical in every way except that A is a corporation and B is a proprietorship.[1] The individual balance sheets include the following items:

Corporation A	
Cash.	$100,000
Liabilities	80,000
Stockholders' equity. . .	20,000

Company B	
Cash	$100,000
Liabilities.	80,000
Brown, capital . . .	20,000

Assume that both businesses lose lawsuits for damages of $300,000 because of defective products. How would the **entity** be viewed from the legal and accounting perspectives for each business? In the corporate organization, Andrews is not at risk of losing any of her personal assets beyond what she has already invested in the corporation ($20,000). Her personal assets are viewed as separate from the obligations of the corporation. From the corporate entity or accounting entity point of view, the lawsuit creates a liability and a reduction of owners' equity resulting in the following balance sheet for Corporation A, but the liability in no way affects the stockholders' personal obligations.

Corporation A Balance Sheet (after lawsuit)	
Cash	$ 100,000
Liabilities	$ 380,000
Stockholders' equity	(280,000)
Total liabilities and stockholders' equity . . .	$ 100,000

[1]While in most states it is necessary to have more than one stockholder to form a corporation (usually three or more stockholders are required), this case assumes a single stockholder for simplicity.

Obviously the corporation cannot pay off the total liability without obtaining more assets by borrowing more money, selling more stock, or operating profitably. If no additional funds are obtained and bankruptcy is declared, the creditors will not be paid their full amounts, and the stockholder (Andrews) is not liable for the deficiency.

The legal concept of business entity applies differently in the proprietorship, although the balance sheet appears much the same. Because Mr. Brown, as a proprietor, is personally liable for the debts of the business, the law considers the debt of the entity a responsibility of the owner, so the owner must use personal funds to settle the debt. Of course, if Mr. Brown does not have sufficient personal assets, he can declare personal bankruptcy.

From an accounting perspective, the business entity and the owner are kept separate. An accountant does not mingle personal and business assets but awaits a transfer of personal assets into the business before recording it, as follows:

1. After the lawsuit liability amount is determined, the business entity is reported as follows:

Company B (after recording loss)	
Cash	$ 100,000
Liabilities	$ 380,000
Brown, capital	(280,000)
Total liabilities and owner's equity	$ 100,000

   Note that the $300,000 loss has reduced "Brown, capital" from a positive $20,000 to a deficit of $280,000.

2. The deficit or negative capital amount of $280,000, which is the $380,000 liability minus the cash in the business, is a legal obligation of the owner. However, from an accounting perspective, the balance sheet shows only business assets and obligations. If Brown were to contribute $300,000 to the business, the following balance sheet would result:

Company B (after contribution from owner)	
Cash	$400,000
Liabilities	$380,000
Brown, capital	20,000
Total liabilities and owner's equity	$400,000

Now Company B can pay off the new debt of $300,000 and still be in the same financial position as before the loss. Although the law makes no distinction between the proprietor and the business, accountants do not automatically combine personal and business assets and liabilities. Accounting reports reflect only business assets and liabilities. When personal assets or liabilities are transferred into the business (e.g., Brown's $300,000 capital contribution), they are shown in the accounting records and financial statements. Of course, the transfer of assets into the business may be motivated by the law as was the case in this example. In the above example, if Brown had not transferred cash into the business, he would still have been responsible for the debt.

To summarize, in corporate accounting, the legal and business entity concepts are similar. The stockholders' personal assets and obligations are viewed as completely separate from the corporation. For unincorporated businesses, although the business and personal entities are not merged, the special rights and obligations of owners have some effect on what is reported and how it is reported, and these rights and obligations can lead to real asset flows such as was the case when Mr. Brown transferred cash into the business to pay off the business's obligation.

TAX AND THE FORM OF THE ORGANIZATION

One very important legal consideration concerning the organizational form of a business is its tax status. Consider the case of Jack Lundlum who just resigned as a jeweler for a large retailer and is now going to open his own exclusive shop to design and manufacture custom-made, fine jewelry. The following is a conversation between Jack and a CPA who is advising him on his options about the various forms of business.

Jack: There are two main things I'm really concerned about. One is legal liability and the other is taxation of earnings. Can you sketch out my options?

CPA: I agree, those are the critical factors for you. You've got the capital you need, so that's not a problem at this stage, anyway; and you are not concerned about continuation of the business if you depart. That leaves taxes and legal liability as major factors. There are three basic categories for tax purposes: (1) unincorporated, which means a proprietorship or a partnership, (2) a C corporation, and (3) an S corporation. In terms of your obligation for business liabilities, there are really two options—to incorporate or not to incorporate.

Jack: Before I get completely confused, let's talk about the liability issue first. If I incorporate, the debts of the corporation are not my personal debts, right, and in a proprietorship or a partnership, the opposite holds, am I correct?

CPA: That's correct. If you have a partner, he or she shares in the responsibility of the business's debt and agreements among the partners determine how it is shared. If you don't have a partner, you are fully responsible. With a corporation, all you can lose, is your investment.

Jack: OK, I think I understand that. What about this business of a C corporation and an S corporation for tax purposes? What's the difference?

CPA: An S corporation gives most of the benefits of the corporate form but income is taxed like a proprietorship or a partnership, that is, the income, if any, flows to the owners in proportion to stockholdings, just like an unincorporated business, even if no dividends are paid to the owners. But when dividends are paid they are not taxed again. In a C corporation, the corporation is considered a taxpayer and pays taxes on income each year, and dividends are taxed to the individual when dividends are paid.

Jack: That doesn't seem fair. That's what they mean by double taxation, right?

CPA: Yes, but a large corporation with many stockholders can't elect to be an S corporation. In your case, because you are the primary owner and you don't expect to have many other owners, you will have that option.

Jack: So, in the eyes of the law, a proprietorship or partnership is not a separate entity for liability or tax purposes, an S corporation is viewed as a separate entity for liability purposes but not for taxes and a C corporation is a separate entity for both liability and tax purposes.

CPA: That's about it.

In the sections that follow, we will discuss the accounting concepts and procedures that are used in accounting for ownership interest in noncorporate and corporate forms of business. Specifics about differences in the taxation of entities can be found in texts on taxation.

NONCORPORATE FORM OF BUSINESS ORGANIZATION

Objective 2
Accounting for owner's equity in a proprietorship.

While assets and liabilities are accounted for and reported similarly in noncorporate and corporate balance sheets, major differences occur in the owners' equity accounts. In a noncorporate business, owners can withdraw assets and reduce owners' equity at will, and one account is used to represent the overall ownership capital balance. In a corporate business, payments to stockholders are generally limited to retained earnings, and accountants use different accounts to keep track of the several categories of stockholders' equity.

This section discusses the two noncorporate business forms—proprietorships and partnerships. Under proprietorships, you will learn how to record owner's capital and withdrawals. The discussion on partnerships explains some of the accounting complexities created when a business is owned by more than one owner. An appendix introduces some details of partnership accounting.

Proprietorships

To reflect the owner's interest in a proprietorship, accountants use the **owner's capital account.** All owner contributions (investments) into the business are credited to this capital account; and income, losses, and owner's withdrawals flow in and out of the owner's capital account. For example, M. Maples, M.D., had the following transactions in 19xx:

1. Invested $25,000 in the business January 1, 19xx.
2. Earned $100,000 in fees (all cash).
3. Paid $20,000 for expenses (all cash).
4. Withdrew $95,000 in cash.

The journal entries to record these transactions are:

Date	Account	Debit	Credit
19xx			
Jan. 1	Cash (A)	25,000	
	M. Maples, Capital (OE)		25,000
	To record initial investment.		
During 19xx	Cash (A)	100,000	
	Fees Revenue (R)		100,000
	To record cash revenue from services rendered.		

Date	Account	Debit	Credit
	Expenses (E)	20,000	
	Cash (A)		20,000
	To record the payment for expenses during the year.		
	M. Maples, Drawing (OE)	95,000	
	Cash (A)		95,000
	To record the withdrawal of cash by M. Maples during the year.		
Dec. 31	Fees Revenue (R)	100,000	
	Expenses (E)		20,000
	Income Summary (OE)		80,000
	To close revenue and expenses to Income Summary account.		
	Income Summary (OE)	80,000	
	M. Maples, Capital (OE)		80,000
	To close Income Summary account to permanent capital account.		
	M. Maples, Capital (OE)	95,000	
	M. Maples, Drawing (OE)		95,000
	To close drawing account to permanent capital account.		

Note that the **owner's drawing account** is not the same as a company's Salaries Expense account. Owners are different from salaried employees because owners have direct access to the assets of the business irrespective of the effort they put into the job. For this reason, the owner's withdrawal of cash is not recorded as an expense of the business. Instead, the payments made to an owner are recorded as withdrawals of capital.

The following **statement of owner's equity** for M. Maples, M.D., at December 31, 19xx, shows how the various transactions during the year affected the owner's capital account.

M. Maples, M.D.
Statement of Owner's Equity
For the Year Ended December 31, 19xx

M. Maples, capital, January 1, 19xx	$ 0
Plus: Investments	25,000
Net income for year 19xx	80,000
	$105,000
Less: Withdrawals	95,000
M. Maples, capital, December 31, 19xx	$ 10,000

The ending balance sheet of M. Maples, M.D., would appear as follows:

M. Maples, M.D.
Balance Sheet
December 31, 19xx

Assets		Owner's Equity	
Cash	$10,000	M. Maples, capital	$10,000

Note that only one capital account appears on the balance sheet showing the final owner's equity result of the transactions of the period. This is shown in the following T accounts:

Cash

(1)	25,000	(3)	20,000
(2)	100,000	(4)	95,000
	10,000		

M. Maples, Capital

(7)	95,000	(1)	25,000
		(6)	80,000
			10,000

M. Maples, Drawing

(4)	95,000	(7)	95,000
	0		

Income Summary

(6)	80,000	(5)	80,000
			0

Fees Revenue

(5)	100,000	(2)	100,000
			0

Expenses

(3)	20,000	(5)	20,000
	0		

Description of numbered entries:

1. The investment transaction is recorded.
2. The revenue transactions are recorded.
3. The expense transactions are recorded.
4. M. Maples withdrawal of $95,000 is recorded.
5. The revenue and expense accounts are closed to the Income Summary account.
6. The Income Summary account is closed to the M. Maples, Capital account.
7. The M. Maples, Drawing account is closed to the M. Maples, Capital account.

Partnerships

Objective 3
Partnerships — ease of formation, classes of partners, limited life, and mutual agency.

As explained in Chapter 1, a noncorporate business with more than one owner is called a *partnership.* The association of individuals as partners creates unique legal rights and obligations resulting in accounting complexities for partnership capital that do not occur in proprietorships. The concept that a proprietorship is legally indistinguishable from the business is relatively simple because the rights and responsibilities of business ownership are under one person's control. In a partnership, however, two or more people have joint ownership, which creates a need for rules to govern the sharing of the joint rights and responsibilities.

A partnership can be created either without a formal agreement among the partners or with a formal agreement. If no formal agreement exists, state laws applicable to partnerships control the legal relationship. The **Uniform Partnership Act (UPA)** governs the formation, operation, and liquidation of partnerships in most states when no formal agreement exists. When a formal agreement is created, it is called a **partnership agreement,** or articles of co-partnership. The partnership agreement gives the details of the understanding among the partners on the ownership percentages, procedures for asset withdrawals, sharing of profits and losses, and other issues. Specific partnership agreement stipulations may differ from those in the UPA, but the UPA governs in the absence of a partnership agreement.

The paragraphs that follow discuss the ease of partnership formation, classes of partners, limited life of partnerships, and mutual agency.

Ease of Partnership Formation. Partnerships are easy to initiate. Unlike corporations, usually no legal forms or government approvals are necessary. The legal status of a partnership is established when two or more parties commit resources to a venture and agree to act as partners.

This ease of partnership formation does not mean that complexities cannot occur. Partners must give serious thought to the outcome of many possible events and their implications for the business and the various partners. Even though the formation of a partnership is simple, the smooth operation of a partnership can be extremely difficult unless a partnership clearly stipulates partners' rights and obligations. The appendix to this chapter discusses some of the accounting challenges partnerships create.

Classes of Partners. In all partnerships, there must be at least one partner with unlimited liability. Just as in the case of a sole proprietor, at least one person in an unincorporated business takes full responsibility for the debts of the entity. The general provisions of the UPA are that all partners have joint and equal responsibilities and rights. When the partnership agreement does not specify otherwise, each partner is called a **general partner**, with unlimited responsibility for the liabilities of the partnership.

All partners are considered to be general partners unless the partnership agreement specifically limits their liability. In states that allow **limited partners,** the limited partners' responsibilities are no more than the assets contributed to the partnership or some other specific amount.

General partners may be called upon to contribute additional capital if the assets of the partnership are insufficient to pay for legitimate creditor claims. Such contributions create a claim by the contributing partner against other general partners of the partnership. A limited partner, however, would not be required to contribute additional capital. The most a limited partner could lose is the amount previously invested in the partnership or the amount specified.

Limited Life of Partnerships. Unless the partnership agreement states otherwise, a partnership dissolves upon the admission of a new partner or the withdrawal of an old one. The partnership agreement can modify these general conditions. For instance, consider the partnership of David Smith and Carla Jones. If Smith dies, the partnership is dissolved, and the remaining assets of the partnership are divided among Smith's heirs and Jones. If the partnership agreement stipulated that upon a partner's death, a specific person (e.g., Smith's child) would take over the capital amount without interruption, Smith's death would not lead to an ending of the business but merely a name change in the capital accounts.

Often the operation of a business is not disturbed by the legal dissolution of the partnership. It is certainly possible for the business to continue without interruption if the old and new partners cooperate in an orderly transition of ownership. If, on the other hand, the departing partner or the survivors demand specific assets from the business, then operations of the business most likely will be interrupted.

Mutual Agency. All general partners can act as agents for the partnership; that is, they have the legal right to commit partnership assets in transactions with outsiders. The partnership agreement can stipulate restrictions on the agency status of one or more partners. However, in the absence of specific restrictions, all partners are said to have **mutual agency**, allowing each partner to borrow money, purchase assets, commit to sales contracts, and engage in other transactions in the name of the partnership. Of course, this gives the partnership great flexibility, but at the same time, it creates a control problem. Because authorization of other partners is not required for a general partner to commit partnership resources, general partners should know and trust one another. Each general partner's business and personal assets can be affected by another partner's decisions. The appendix discusses accounting for partnerships.

CORPORATE FORM OF BUSINESS ORGANIZATION

Accounting for corporate businesses differs in several ways from accounting for noncorporate businesses. The important differences center on the relationship of the entity with its stockholders, and the remainder of this chapter focuses on this relationship, beginning with the advantages and disadvantages of a corporation. Then we discuss corporate organization costs, the issuance of stock, balance sheet presentation of contributed capital, reacquisition and retirement of stock, donated capital, cash dividends, stock dividends, and special features of preferred stock.

Advantages and Disadvantages of Corporations

Objective 4
The advantages and disadvantages of the corporate form of business organization.

To begin, study the following two definitions of a corporation:

- A group of people who get a charter granting them as a body certain of the legal powers, rights, privileges, and liabilities of an individual, distinct from those of the individuals making up the group.[2]
- An association of individuals created by law and existing as an entity with powers and liabilities independent of those of its members.[3]

These definitions give two major concepts. First, a **corporation** is an **association of individuals** that is recognized by the law. Second, a corporation has rights and responsibilities **separate** from those of its members. When applied in a business context, these characteristics help explain why corporations are the dominant business form of organization in the United States and control the vast majority of business assets. Because corporations can be associations of large numbers of owners (stockholders), **large amounts of capital can be generated** allowing corporations to accumulate the necessary assets to operate on a large and often more efficient scale.

The separation of the corporation entity from its owners encourages stockholder investment because the **liability of stockholders is limited.** This is a major advantage of the corporation from the stockholders' viewpoint. Remember, however, that although corporation stockholders are not personally responsible for corporate debts, in case of bankruptcy or poor performance, stockholders could lose all of their investment in the corporation. In general, the losses of stockholders are limited to the amount of their investment.

Other advantages of the corporate form of business include:

- Ease of transferability of ownership.
- Continuity of existence.

---

[2]*Webster's New World Dictionary,* 2nd college edition, 1978.

[3]*The Random House College Dictionary,* 1975.

- Separation of management and owners.
- Advantageous tax status.

In contrast to a noncorporate business, a change of stock ownership does not affect the corporation's legal status. The corporation exists independent of the specific owners, and there is **continuity of existence** when one owner sells to another. In publicly traded corporations, there is **ease of transferability of ownership** because a market exists where shares can be bought and sold. This ease of ownership transfer is conducive to large-scale investments and operations.

When the shares of a corporation are owned by a small number of stockholders the company is said to be a "closely held" corporation with no public trading of shares. These corporations enjoy the benefit of the corporate form but usually operate on a much smaller scale than large corporations. Privately held corporations far outnumber those corporations that trade on the stock exchanges, as there are three million corporations in the United States, and less than 1% are publicly traded.

Because stockholders are not necessarily part of management, the **separation of management and owners** makes it possible for corporations to assemble specialized management talent. The stockholders who are willing to take the risks of ownership can indirectly employ managers who have the needed managerial and technical skills but who may not want to assume the business risks of business ownership. This flexibility of assembling management talent often results in individuals with different preferences and skills contracting with the business entity in a mutually beneficial manner.

The separation of owners and management prevalent in most large corporations can also be a **disadvantage.** Stockholders must make sure that managers operate in the stockholders' best interests. Corporations use many mechanisms to control management actions, starting with the board of directors who are individuals elected by the stockholders to represent their interests. The board appoints top management and makes major decisions about corporate policy, strategy, compensation, and dividend policy. In addition, the board is responsible for the overall **monitoring** and **control** of management, which involves a relationship with internal and external auditors. The following general hierarchical relationships are common in large corporations:

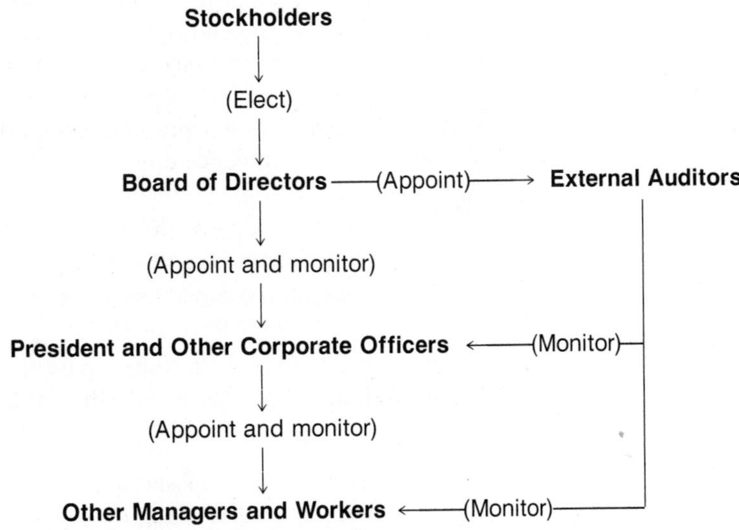

Another disadvantage of publicly traded corporations from management's perspective is the increasing threat of hostile takeovers by outside groups who, if successful, will often replace top management. Seen from another perspective, the threat of hostile takeovers encourage managers to be as efficient as possible.

The corporate system of election, appointment, and monitoring, along with reward structures, is designed to create a consistency of purpose where the goals of the stockholders are fostered by the actions of each member in the corporate hierarchy. Accounting systems designed to successfully accomplish this play a major role in the corporate management process. In addition to the financial accounting systems introduced in this text, corporations also employ managerial accounting systems that provide the information management needs to plan, monitor, and control operations.

Another advantage of the corporate form is that the government considers it a separate taxable entity, which can give stockholders an advantageous tax status.[4] The profits of the corporation are generally not taxable to the stockholders until funds are distributed in the form of dividends, unlike the noncorporate businesses, in which the income is taxable whether or not it is distributed. For small corporate businesses, this separate tax liability could be viewed as a disadvantage because of the added complexity in recordkeeping. Since corporate profits are taxed and dividend distributions to stockholders are taxed again, the possibility of double taxation exists. This creates a complexity that may be quite costly, and great care must be taken to minimize the tax burdens of the stockholders.

When individuals in a proprietorship or partnership or individuals thinking about beginning a new business find that the advantages of the corporate business form outweigh the disadvantages, they may decide to apply to a state for a corporate charter. Often **incorporators** or **promoters** are employed to help organize corporations. These promoters often become owners as well. The efforts of promoters involve developing ideas and plans, attracting potential investors, and drafting a corporate charter or articles of incorporation, which is part of the application necessary to gain a state's permission to form a corporation.

Organization Costs

Objective 5
Accounting for corporate organization costs and issuance of stock.

Lawyers, promoters, and accountants involved in the creation of a business eventually are paid either in shares of corporate stock, or in cash after stock has been sold to others. Expenditures incurred in organizing a corporation, such as legal fees, taxes, stock issuance costs, and promotional fees are recorded generally as an intangible asset account called Organization Costs. For example, assume a corporate charter has been issued to Filex Corporation on January 1, 19xx, and the first recorded transaction is:

19xx			
Jan. 1	Organization Costs (A)	84,000	
	Accounts Payable (L)		84,000
	To record the incurrence of cost during the formation of the corporation.		

Filex may liquidate the accounts payable liability by cash payments or by issuing capital stock. In any event, the intangible asset organization costs are

[4] Refer to the discussion of S and C corporations on p. 593.

amortized over some period of time, usually no less than 5 years but never more than 40 years. If Filex decides to amortize the organizational costs over 10 years, the year-end adjusting entry would be:

19xx			
Dec. 31	Amortization of Organization Costs (E)	8,400	
	Organization Costs (A)		8,400
	To record the amortization of organization costs.		

Issuance of Stock

Since the issuance of stock is the main source of capital for corporations, we begin with a discussion of the two major types of stock—common stock and preferred stock. Then, to understand how stock is recorded and disclosed, you should be familiar with the par or stated value of stock. This subsection also shows you how to record the direct sale of stock and the sale of stock by stock subscriptions.

Common Stock. As you know, a major advantage of the corporate business form is that corporations can raise capital from a large number of investors. The primary corporation investors are called **common stockholders,** and they purchase corporate securities called **common stock.**

Stockholders who own common stock have the following legal rights:

1. Each share of common stock carries an equal vote for the election of members to the board of directors. This **voting right** is important because the board has the authority to control all major corporate decisions.
2. Common stockholders may have a **preemptive right** that allows them to maintain a proportionate share of ownership. For example, if a stockholder owns 10% of a corporation's common stock, the stockholder must be offered 10% of any new stock issuance before the new shares are offered to others.
3. Common stockholders have **dividend rights,** that is, the right to share in any distribution of earnings in the form of dividends if the board of directors decides to distribute such dividends.
4. Common stockholders have the **right to the residual assets (residual asset right)** of the corporation upon its liquidation, after all other claims are met.

These four basic rights are features of common stock, and common stock is the one class of stock issued by all corporations.

Preferred Stock. Another class of stock, **preferred stock,** may be issued but with modifications in the rights discussed for common stock. Preferred stock usually does not carry voting and preemptive rights, and the rights to receive dividends and residual value are usually restricted to specifically stated amounts per share. However, preferred stock carries certain preferences over common stock that makes it attractive to some investors. For example, a preferred stockholder is usually paid a fixed dividend amount per share per period before common stockholders are paid anything. Also, should the business liquidate or terminate, preferred stockholders are paid a fixed amount per share before common stockholders are given any residual. These features make preferred stock less risky than common stock.

A disadvantage of preferred stock is that it has limited "upside" potential. This means that in contrast to common stock which can increase in value if the corporate fortunes improve, preferred stock is rather limited in its appreciation potential because of the fixed nature of its dividend and liquidation preferences. Remember that all stocks, including preferred stock, are riskier than debt, which has preference over both common and preferred stock.

Par or Stated Value. Stock shares often have an amount of money assigned to them called **par value** (also called **stated value**). Common stock par values range from $0.01 to $50 or more per share. Preferred stock usually has $10, $50, or $100 per share par value. If no par value is assigned to the stock, the stock is called **no-par stock.**

Stock par values have a long history. They were initially required as a minimum investment per share to protect creditors of corporations. Although most state laws continue to allow par values, their effectiveness as protection for creditors has always been in doubt. Stock with a par value of $1 may sell for $100 or more. Having a par value may assure creditors that at a minimum $1 was contributed by stockholders, but par value usually has little economic significance.

State laws often require that a **stated value** per share be assigned to no-par stock. However, the stated value also has little significance. When a stated value is assigned to no-par stock, the stated value can be no less than the lowest price received from the sale of the no-par stock.

Another term you should become familiar with is **legal capital,** which usually refers to the amount of par or stated value of the stock outstanding for a corporation. For example, a corporation may have 100,000 shares of $1 par common stock and 10,000 shares of $50 preferred stock outstanding (shares in the hands of owners) which sold for $8 and $55 per share, respectively. The distinction between **contributed capital** (the total money contributed by owners, which is legal capital plus any money contributed in excess of legal capital) and legal capital is as follows:

			Contributed Capital			
			Legal Capital			
Class of Stock	*Number of Shares Outstanding*	*Selling Price per Share*	*Par Value per Share*	*Total Par Value*	*Contributed Capital in Excess of Par*	*Total Contributed Capital*
Common	100,000	$ 8	$ 1.00	$100,000	$700,000	$ 800,000
Preferred	10,000	55	50.00	500,000	50,000	550,000
				$600,000	$750,000	$1,350,000

Recording Sale of Stock. Corporations usually issue stock for cash, but occasionally they accept other things of value in exchange for shares of stock. Often an attorney, accountant, or promoter will accept shares of stock in lieu of a cash payment for services performed in organizing a corporation. Similarly, partners in a business will often accept shares of stock for the assets they transfer into a newly formed corporation. In the following example, Dynamics Corporation is formed on January 1, 19xx, and issues a total of 17,000 shares of $1 par value stock in exchange for $100,000 cash, an attorney's services valued at $10,000, and a building worth $60,000. This initial issuance is recorded as follows:

19xx			
Jan. 1	Cash (A)	100,000	
	Organization Costs (A)	10,000	
	Building (A)	60,000	
	Common Stock—Par (SE)		17,000
	Contributed Capital in Excess of Par—Common (SE)		153,000
	To record the issuance of 17,000 shares of common stock with $1 par value.		

The Common Stock—Par account represents the legal capital of the business at the time of the initial issuance. This means that the $17,000 recorded in the Common Stock—Par account has special legal status and must be shown separately in financial statements. If the corporate charter for the corporation in our example did not mention par value for common stock, the no-par stock would be recorded as follows:

19xx			
Jan. 1	Cash (A)	100,000	
	Organization Costs (A)	10,000	
	Building (A)	60,000	
	Common Stock (SE)		170,000
	To record the issuance of 17,000 shares of no-par common stock.		

The total amount contributed by stockholders is the same for both par value stock and no-par stock, but corporations make no distinction between par and contributed capital in excess of par when it issues no-par stock. In some states, true no-par stock can be issued. In other states, a stated value must be assigned to each share, and this stated value per share has the same legal status as par value per share.

The Contributed Capital in Excess of Par account (sometimes called *Paid-In Capital in Excess of Par*) represents the excess paid by stockholders over the par value. The word **premium** is sometimes applied to this amount, although the existence or magnitude of such an excess does not necessarily signify relative economic strength. Because the amount of the par value per share is set arbitrarily, neither the par nor the excess of par means much by itself. What is of real economic importance is the total amount paid in per share.

The function of par value is more significant in preferred stock where dividend amounts and liquidation values are often stated in terms of par value. For example, on January 1, 19xx, the Essex Corporation issued 10,000 shares of $100 par value preferred stock for $105 per share. Essex recorded this as follows:

19xx			
Jan. 1	Cash (A)	1,050,000	
	Preferred Stock—Par (SE)		1,000,000
	Contributed Capital in Excess of Par—Preferred Stock (SE)		50,000
	To record the issuance of 10,000 shares of preferred stock.		

Preferred stock certificates usually give the par value and the dividend rate, which is often stated as a percentage of par value. If the dividend rate is

10%, then each stockholder receives $10 for each share of $100 par value preferred stock owned each year before any distributions are made to common stockholders.

Stock can also be sold for amounts equal to and less than par value. For example, on January 1, 19xx, Zeron Corporation issued 5,000 shares of $5 par value common stock for $4 per share and recorded the following:

19xx			
Jan. 1	Cash (A)	20,000	
	Discount on Common Stock (XSE)	5,000	
	Common Stock—Par (SE)		25,000
	To record issuance of 5,000 shares of common stock at $4 per share.		

Zeron's total contributed capital is only $20,000, but par value is recorded at the legal amount of $25,000. Just as premiums are added to par value to determine total contributed capital, discounts are subtracted from par value to arrive at total contributed capital. The Zeron example is a rare event because issuing stock below par (or stated value) is illegal in some states; and when issuing stock below par is allowed, this often means that original stockholders are liable for the discount amount in the event of corporate liquidation. Such an issuance of stock at a discount can negate some of the limited liability advantages of the corporate form of business. In any event, in the rare event it is recorded, the discount account is shown as a contra to par value on corporate balance sheets.

Recording Stock Subscriptions. Corporations sometimes accept a promise to pay for stock shares in the form of **subscription contracts.** In a subscription contract, prospective stockholders enter into an agreement by which they pay for the stock in installments over some future period of time. Stock is issued only upon final payment of the contract. The end result is the same as an initial cash sale, but because of the time lapse, special accounting treatment is needed.

For example, on January 1, 19xx, Hickman Corporation accepted an $80,000 subscription agreement for 4,000 shares of $2 par value stock to be paid in two installments of $40,000 each on July 1, 19xx, and December 31, 19xx. Hickman recorded the following:

19xx			
Jan. 1	Subscriptions Receivable—Common (A) . .	80,000	
	Common Stock Subscribed (SE)		8,000
	Contributed Capital in Excess of Par—Common Stock (SE)		72,000
	To record subscription agreement for 4,000 shares.		
July 1	Cash (A)	40,000	
	Subscriptions Receivable—Common (A)		40,000
	To record receipt of first installment payment.		
Dec. 31	Cash (A)	40,000	
	Subscriptions Receivable—Common (A)		40,000
	To record receipt of second and final installment payment.		

Dec. 31	Common Stock Subscribed (SE)	8,000	
	Common Stock—Par (SE)		8,000
	To record the issuance of 4,000 shares of $2 par value common stock.		

In our example, the Common Stock Subscribed account has no balance at year-end and would not appear on the 12/31 balance sheet. When a balance sheet is made before subscribed stock is issued, the Common Stock Subscribed account is shown as stockholders' equity on the balance sheet in the same section as par value. The Subscriptions Receivable—Common is a current asset and treated much the same as Accounts Receivable. The Contributed Capital in Excess of Par account is used regardless of whether stock is sold outright or through subscriptions.

Balance Sheet Presentation of Contributed Capital

The balance sheet or a footnote to the balance sheet should indicate the par value of the company's stock and the number of shares authorized, issued, and outstanding. The number of **authorized shares** is the maximum number of shares allowed to be issued by the corporate charter; the number **issued** represents the shares sold to owners; and the number **outstanding** are the shares currently in the hands of owners. These three numbers may be different. All shares authorized may not be issued. Some shares that have been issued may be bought back and held as treasury stock; and although treasury shares are considered issued, they would not be considered outstanding.

Exhibit 11-1 shows a corporate annual report disclosure of contributed capital. Note that the par value of Reebok's common stock is listed as $0.01 per share. Compare Reebok's 1985 total contributed capital of $43,622,000 with its legal capital (par) of $160,000. This means the average share of common stock

EXHIBIT 11-1

Example of Annual Report Disclosure of Contributed Capital

Reebok International Ltd.
Partial Balance Sheet
December 31

	(000,000) 1985	*(000,000)* 1984
Stockholders' equity (Notes 7 and 11):		
Common stock, par value $0.01 per share; authorized 20,000,000 shares; issued and outstanding 15,983,259 shares in 1985, 13,053,601 in 1984	$ 160	$131
Additional paid-in capital	43,462	37

Analysis of Shares Issued in 1985

	Number of Shares Outstanding	*Rounded* *$.01 Par Value*	*Rounded* *Additional Paid-In Capital*
January 1, 1985	13,053,601	$131,000	$ 37,000
Issued during 1985	2,929,658	29,000	43,425,000
December 31, 1985	15,983,259	$160,000	$43,462,000

Objective 6
The corporate balance sheet presentation of contributed capital.

was sold by the company for about $2.73 per share, but each share has a par value of only $0.01 per share. Exhibit 11-1 also shows an analysis of the change in Reebok stock from January 1, 1985, to December 31, 1985. The 13,053,601 shares previously issued had an average selling price of just over $0.01 per share, while the 2,929,658 shares issued in 1985 had an average selling price of over $14 per share. The great differences in the amount per share are not uncommon when a long period of time separates the two issuances of stock. The initial issuance sold for close to par, while the later issuance reflects increased market value.

An important point to remember about shares of stock is that after a corporation issues the shares, they may change hands among investors, but this has no effect on the issuing corporation's accounting for contributed capital. The market value of a share after issuance by a corporation may be greater or less than the initial selling price.

REACQUISITION AND RETIREMENT OF STOCK

A Case of Murky Motivations

In what follows you will eavesdrop on the quarterly board of directors meeting of Kenco, Inc., a major manufacturer of shoes, as they discuss their president's plan to reacquire half of the company's stock.

President: Ladies and gentlemen, we have paid our shareholders $0.25 per share for the last 40 quarters. I believe that we have tremendous potential growth in our earnings per share and I believe that the stockholders want more cash flow. So, I propose that we do two things. Buy back and retire half of the outstanding stock and then increase our dividend each quarter for the next eight quarters until we reach $0.50 per share per quarter. We will pay $2 in excess of the current market price of $24 so those interested in immediate cash will be satisfied and then those remaining will be very happy with the increased future dividends and stock value appreciation. Look at Chart 1 to see our projections of the balance sheet effects of the reacquisition assuming everything else remains constant. Note that we will have to use $500 million of cash and securities and a loan of $2.1 billion to make the deal.

Chart 1

	($000)	
	Now	After Repurchase*
Cash and marketable securities	$1,000,000	$ 500,000
Other assets	4,000,000	4,000,000
	$5,000,000	$4,500,000
Liabilities	$ 500,000	$2,600,000
Common stock (no par)	3,000,000	1,500,000
Retained earnings	1,500,000	400,000
	$5,000,000	$4,500,000

*The journal entry to record the reacquisition and retirement of half of the stock:

	(000)	
Common Stock	1,500,000	
Retained Earnings	1,100,000	
Cash		500,000
Liabilities		2,100,000

Note that retained earnings can be reduced when stock is retired at amounts in excess of the original selling price.

Board member: That really seems to hurt our liquidity with our debt going from $500,000 to $2,600,000. I don't see what we gain by this.

President: Well, we believe that our stock at $24 a share is very much undervalued. If our income increases over the next two years as expected, we believe that the price per share will triple. So buying our own stock is our best investment.

Board member: If that's true, are we hurting ourselves by reducing our future borrowing capacity? We won't be able to build the plant we need to expand our production.

President: No, I don't think so. We could always sell more shares of stock later at the higher price.

Board member: We are reducing our retained earnings by $1.1 billion. Won't that limit future dividends?

President: No, because our projected earnings over the next few years will add considerably to the retained earnings balance.

The preceding conversation hints at the complexity behind many of the buybacks of stock that have been so prevalent in the stock market of late. What are the president's motivations? Is he or she and management considering a **leveraged buyout,** where a small group borrows money against the assets of the business and buys out all or most of the other shareholders? Or, maybe the president and a group of managers own enough shares to have significant influence in board selection if the total number of shareholders is reduced. Another motivation could be that a **hostile takeover,** where an outside party tries to acquire enough shares to get control, is anticipated and, by borrowing money and perhaps eliminating shareholders who might vote against management, the corporation will be less attractive as a takeover target. Of course, it is also possible that the president is sincerely interested in the welfare of the current shareholders and the competitive position of the company. We leave further discussion of these issues to more advanced accounting and finance texts.

We will now cover the accounting for reacquisitions followed by accounting for dividends and related issues.

Treasury Stock

Objective 7
Accounting for the reacquisition and retirement of stock.

Although issued stock remains **outstanding** in the hands of owners for long periods of time, sometimes corporations reacquire their shares and reissue them for various purposes. When a company holds reacquired shares, they are called **treasury stock** (or treasury shares).

If stock is reacquired and retired, the corporation reduces its asset and capital balances permanently. Retirement of stock cancels the shares, and they cannot be reissued. Treasury stock, however, is normally intended for purposes such as employee compensation plans and does not indicate a permanent reduction in the number of shares outstanding.

Treasury shares held by the issuing corporation have a special status that falls somewhere between issued and unissued shares. Because a corporation cannot own itself, corporate management cannot vote the treasury shares, and the corporation cannot pay itself dividends on the treasury shares it holds. In this sense, treasury shares are similar to unissued shares. Also, treasury shares can be resold without triggering the preemptive right provision that is present in authorized and unissued shares.

Treasury shares are disclosed on the balance sheet as a contra account to all of stockholders' equity. For example, Fuelmakers, Inc., issued all of its 20,000 authorized shares of $1 par value common stock for $5 per share on July 1, 19x1.

On December 1, 19x1, Fuelmakers purchased 800 shares of its issued stock on the open market for $6 per share. The journal entries to record these transactions are:

19x1			
July 1	Cash (A)	100,000	
	Common Stock—Par (SE)		20,000
	Contributed Capital in Excess of Par—Common (SE)		80,000
	To record issuance of 20,000 shares of common stock at $5 per share.		
Dec. 1	Treasury Stock—Common (XSE)	4,800	
	Cash (A)		4,800
	To record the acquisition of 800 shares of common stock for $6 per share.		

The December 31, 19x1, balance sheet would include the following stockholders' equity section, assuming net income was $40,000 and no dividends were paid.

Fuelmakers, Inc.
Partial Balance Sheet
December 31, 19x1

Stockholders' equity:		
Contributed capital:		
Common stock ($1 par) 20,000 shares authorized and issued and 19,200 shares outstanding	$20,000	
Contributed capital in excess of par—common	80,000	$100,000
Retained earnings		40,000
		$140,000
Less treasury stock at cost—800 shares		(4,800)
Total stockholders' equity.		$135,200

Note the location of the debit balance of $4,800 for treasury stock as contra to all of stockholders' equity. The number of shares authorized and issued are not affected by treasury stock acquisition, but treasury shares do reduce the number of shares outstanding.

Treasury stock can be resold later. No matter what the selling price may be, no gain or loss is recognized on the income statement. Likewise, retained earnings cannot be increased by transactions in a company's own stock; therefore, selling treasury stock for an amount exceeding purchase price does not affect retained earnings. Accountants consider a "gain" on treasury stock sales to be additional contributed capital, much the same as contributed capital in excess of par. For instance, if Fuelmakers sells 400 treasury shares for $8 each ($2 per share more than what they paid for the treasury shares) on January 15, 19x2, the following entry would be recorded:

19x2			
Jan. 15	Cash (A).	3,200	
	Treasury Stock—Common (XSE).		2,400
	Contributed Capital from Treasury Stock Transactions (SE).		800
	To record the sale of 400 shares of treasury stock for $8 per share.		

Treasury stock could be sold for less than the original purchase price. In such cases, the "loss" on the transaction is applied first to any existing credit balance in Contributed Capital from Treasury Stock Transactions. If the "loss" exceeds previous "gains", Retained Earnings or Contributed Capital in Excess of Par may be debited for the excess. For instance, if Fuelmakers sells 200 shares at $3 each on June 12, 19x2, and 200 shares at $2 per share on October 31, 19x2, the $800 balance in Contributed Capital from Treasury Stock Transactions account would first be eliminated and then Retained Earnings would be reduced.

19x2			
June 12	Cash (A)	600	
	Contributed Capital from Treasury Stock Transactions (SE)	600	
	Treasury Stock—Common (XSE)		1,200
	To record the sale of 200 shares of treasury stock for $3 per share.		
Oct. 31	Cash (A)	400	
	Contributed Capital from Treasury Stock Transactions (SE)	200	
	Retained Earnings (SE)	600	
	Treasury Stock—Common (XSE)		1,200
	To record the sale of 200 shares of treasury stock for $2 per share.		

If stock is reacquired for purposes of cancelling the shares, then such a retirement is recorded by debits to the Common Stock—Par and the Contributed Capital in Excess of Par—Common for the amounts initially paid in. If more is paid upon retirement than was initially paid in, Retained Earnings is debited for the excess. For example, if Fuelmakers, Inc., purchased 1,000 shares at $6.00 per share on December 15, 19x2, the following entry would be made:

19x2			
Dec. 15	Common Stock—Par	1,000	
	Contributed Capital in Excess of Par—Common	4,000	
	Retained Earnings	1,000	
	Cash		6,000
	To record the retirement of 1,000 shares of common stock.		

If the reacquisition was at an amount less than the initial paid-in amount, say $4 per share, then the following entry would be made:

19x2			
Dec. 15	Common Stock—Par	1,000	
	Contributed Capital in Excess of Par—Common	3,000	
	Cash		4,000
	To record the retirement of 1,000 shares of common stock.		

DONATED CAPITAL, DIVIDENDS, AND SPLITS

Donated Capital

Objective 8

Accounting for donated capital, cash dividends, and stock dividends and splits.

Sometimes corporations receive assets from outsiders, such as land donated by a municipality as an inducement to open a facility. In cases like these where no payment of cash or stock is involved, the corporation credits a contributed capital account, **Donated Capital,** for the fair value of the asset. The balance in the Donated Capital account is an addition to contributed capital along with par value and contributed capital in excess of par. Such contributions have no initial income statement effect. For example, if the Montreux Corporation accepts a building site worth $100,000 from the city of Mount Blanc, the asset Land would be recorded as follows:

19xx			
Jan. 1	Land (A)	100,000	
	Donated Capital (SE)		100,000
	To record receipt of land from the city of Mount Blanc with a fair value of $100,000.		

Because Montreux issued no stock, the city of Mount Blanc has no ownership interest in the company. Of course, Montreux would have an obligation to locate on the Mount Blanc site. If the land is actually worth $100,000 on the date of donation and Montreux can use the land in the same manner as land purchased outright, the financial statements would not distinguish the donated land from other owned land. The Donated Capital balance would stay on the books permanently, even if the land is eventually sold or written off.

You should understand that contributors of capital (whether donated or by purchase of stock) transfer something of value to the company, usually cash but sometimes other assets. Once the company receives the asset, it is accounted for according to its subsequent use in the business. If a building were donated to a business, the fair value of the building would be recorded and depreciated in the normal fashion.

Cash Dividends

Stockholders invest in corporations to earn a return on their investments. One element of the return on investment is dividend payments. A **dividend** is a distribution of earnings to stockholders in cash or something else of value. Corporations distribute dividends on a **pro rata** basis; that is, in strict proportion to the number of shares held by the stockholder. For example, if Tymekeep, Inc., has 100,000 shares of common stock issued and outstanding and Ms. Kelp owns 10,000 shares, she will receive 1/10 of total dividend payments. Also, if Tymekeep Inc., has 100,000 shares issued and 10,000 shares are held in treasury, Ms. Kelp's 10,000 shares would give her the right to 1/9 of any dividends distributed because dividends are paid only on outstanding shares.

The board of directors controls the payment of dividends, and no liability exists for payment of dividends until the board makes a formal **declaration** of dividends. However, the board is constrained in dividend policy in several ways. First, state laws usually limit dividend distributions to the amount of a positive Retained Earnings balance. This usually means that profitable operations must precede dividend payments. Second, even if a corporation has a positive Retained Earnings balance, it still must have assets to distribute, usually cash. As discussed in earlier chapters, profitable operations do not assure available cash. Third, when different classes of stock exist, the corporation must consider dividend preferences. Preferred stock must be paid the proper amount per share before common stock stockholders are paid anything.

Dividend distributions involve a standard series of events:

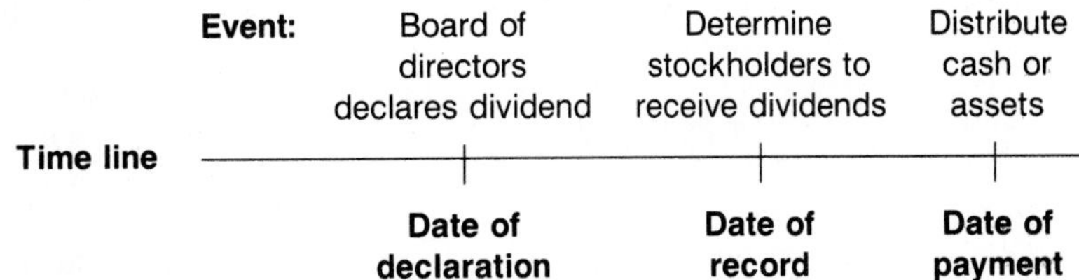

As an example, assume the Wiretron Corporation has the following stockholders' equity:

Wiretron Corporation
Partial Balance Sheet
December 31, 19x1

Stockholders' equity:		
Contributed capital:		
Common stock—$2 par, 100,000 shares authorized, issued, and outstanding	$ 200,000	
Contributed capital in excess of par—common . . .	1,500,000	
Preferred stock—10%, $50 par, 10,000 shares authorized, issued, and outstanding	500,000	$2,200,000
Retained earnings		1,200,000
Total stockholders' equity.		$3,400,000

On January 1, 19x2, the board of directors of Wiretron declares a total cash dividend of $250,000 to be paid on January 31, 19x2, to stockholders of record on January 15, 19x2. The board has a policy of paying dividends once a year in this manner. The following series of entries would record the transactions:

19x2			
Jan. 1	Retained Earnings (SE)	250,000	
	Cash Dividends Payable—Common (L) . . .		200,000
	Cash Dividends Payable—Preferred (L) . . .		50,000
	To record the declaration of $250,000 in cash dividends to be distributed to preferred stockholders on the basis of 10% of $500,000 or $5 per share and $2 per share to common stockholders.		
15	No entry is made on the date of record.		
31	Cash Dividends Payable—Common (L)	200,000	
	Cash Dividends Payable—Preferred (L)	50,000	
	Cash (A)		250,000
	To record payment of cash dividends declared on January 1, 19x2.		

On the **date of declaration,** a current liability is recorded because the corporation has an obligation to pay its stockholders once a declaration has been made. For large corporations with thousands of stockholders and active trading of shares, the task of determining the stockholders who are to receive dividends can be a difficult one. For corporations with a small number of shares, it is easier to determine the list of outstanding stockholders. Determining the stockholders who are to be paid dividends does not affect any accounts, and no entry is made on the **date of record.** The elimination of the liability is recorded on the **payment date.**

In the above example, the account Retained Earnings was debited on the declaration date. Often an account titled "Dividends" is debited. This is a temporary account that is closed to retained earnings in the closing entries.

Stock Dividends

As a substitution for or in conjunction with cash dividends, corporations sometimes issue additional shares of stock to existing stockholders. These distributions, called **stock dividends,** are governed by the preemptive rights of existing stockholders. Therefore, each stockholder would get a pro rata increase in the number of shares owned. Distributing shares rather than cash could be motivated by a desire to issue a dividend at a time of cash shortage. Corporations also issue stock dividends to reduce the market value per share of the outstanding stock.

Small Stock Dividend. If the number of shares distributed is small in proportion to the shares outstanding, this distribution is called a **small stock dividend,** and Retained Earnings is reduced by the market value of the new shares at the time of the declaration. For instance, assume that on June 30, 19xx, a corporation has 500,000 shares of $1 par value common stock issued and outstanding with a market value of $6 per share and declares a stock dividend to be paid on July 31, 19xx. The number of shares to be distributed pro rata to stockholders of record on July 15, 19xx, is 25,000 shares, or 5% of the outstanding shares. The following journal entries would record the transactions:

Date	Account	Debit	Credit
19xx			
June 30	Retained Earnings (SE)	150,000	
	Stock Dividend Distributable—Common (SE)		25,000
	Contributed Capital in Excess of Par—Stock Dividend (SE)		125,000
	To record the declaration of a 5% stock dividend (25,000 shares at $6) to stockholders of record on July 15, 19xx.		
July 15	No entry on date of record.		
31	Stock Dividend Distributable—Common (SE)	25,000	
	Common Stock—Par (SE)		25,000
	To record the issuance of 25,000 shares of common stock.		

Accountants do not classify the Stock Dividend Distributable—Common account as a liability but consider it a contributed capital account and list it in the stockholders' equity section of the balance sheet. Although rarely done, the board can rescind stock dividends before the issuance date. This potential recall supports the practice of classifying Stock Dividend Distributable as stockholders' equity rather than as a liability, as is the case with cash dividend declarations.

Large Stock Dividends and Splits. Large percentage distributions of stock to existing stockholders are called **large stock dividends** and **stock splits.** Accountants view any dividend distribution above 20 to 25% of the shares outstanding as a large stock dividend. These large stock dividends are accounted for by a debit to Retained Earnings for only the par or stated value per share; fair market values are ignored. The credit is to the Common Stock—Par account for large stock dividends. For stock splits, no journal entries are necessary because only the number of shares outstanding and the par value per share, if any, are affected.

Stock splits involve the issuance of new shares at a lower par value to replace the old shares, thus increasing the number of shares outstanding without changing the total dollars of contributed capital. The motivation for a stock split usually relates to a policy of keeping the market price per share within a certain range so that the stock will be more marketable.

The economic effect of a stock split is the same as a large or small stock dividend. In all three cases, the individual stockholders each own the same percentage interest in the entity before and after the split or dividend. Neither the total value of the entity nor their individual percentage ownership in the entity has changed as a result of the split or dividend, and net assets (or total stockholders' equity) remains the same.

The following example shows how large stock dividends and splits can affect the corporation's balance sheet and stock prices. Valuedate Corporation has 20,000 shares of $2 par value common stock issued and outstanding on April 1, 19x1, with a market price of $70 per share. A 100% stock dividend would double the number of $2 par value shares outstanding. A 2-for-1 stock split would double the number of shares outstanding, and at the same time reduce the par value per share to $1. In both cases, the market would revalue the stock adjusting the price to approximately $35 per share.

Exhibit 11-2 shows the effects of the 100% stock dividend and the 2-for-1 split on Valuedate Corporation's balance sheet and per share market values. Note that no economic impact occurs in terms of total market value of all shares outstanding. Within the stockholders' equity section of the balance sheet, however, the description of shares outstanding and the par value per share amounts have changed. In the case of a large stock dividend with par value stock, Retained Earnings is reduced by the amount of the credit to the par value account, which is simply the number of shares times the par value.

Special Features of Preferred Stock

Objective 9
The special features of preferred stock.

Preferred stock may have several contractual stipulations that are not found in common stock. Most preferred stock is **cumulative.** Thus, dividends not paid in one period accumulate and must be paid in subsequent periods before common stockholders are paid any further dividends.

If cumulative preferred stock dividends are not paid in one year, they are **dividends in arrears.** For example, if a corporation issues 100,000 shares of $100 par value cumulative 8% preferred stock on January 1, 19x1, and pays no dividends in 19x1 and 19x2, the dividends in arrears as of December 31, 19x2, would be $1.6 million [$10 million × .08 (percent dividend) × 2 (years)]. Before common stockholders could receive any dividends in 19x3, the preferred stockholders would have to receive $1.6 million dividends in arrears plus $800,000 of current preferred dividends applicable to 19x3. Dividends in arrears are not liabilities since no liability exists until dividends are declared. However, once dividends are declared, dividends in arrears have preference and must be paid first.

Sometimes preferred stocks are allowed to participate in cash dividends in excess of the dividend amount stated per share. This is called **participating preferred stock.** Preferred stock may carry with it a conversion privilege that allows

EXHIBIT 11-2

Comparison of the Effect of Large Stock Dividends on Stock Splits on the Stockholders' Equity Section of the Balance Sheet

Valuedate Corporation

Before Dividend/Split		*After 100% Dividend*		*After 2 for 1 Split*	
Stockholders' equity:		Stockholders' equity:		Stockholders' equity:	
Common stock—$2 par, 20,000 shares issued and outstanding	$ 40	Common stock—$2 par, 40,000 shares issued and outstanding	$ 80	Common stock—$1 par, 40,000 shares issued and outstanding	$ 40
Contributed capital in excess of par	85	Contributed capital in excess of par	85	Contributed capital in excess of par	85
	$125		$165		$125
Retained earnings	150	Retained earnings	110	Retained earnings	150
Total stockholders' equity	$275	Total stockholders' equity	$275	Total stockholders' equity	$275

Market value analysis:

Shares Outstanding	*Market Value per Share*	*Total Market Value*	*Shares Outstanding*	*Market Value per Share*	*Total Market Value*	*Shares Outstanding*	*Market Value per Share*	*Total Market Value*
20,000	$70	$1,400	40,000	$35	$1,400	40,000	$35	$1,400

	After 100% Dividend — **Journal entry:**			After 2 for 1 Split — **Journal entry:**
	Retained Earnings	40		No entry necessary for a stock split.
	Common Stock—Par		40	
	To record stock dividend.			

Note: Dollars are in thousands.

the holder under certain conditions to trade a share of preferred stock for a fixed number of common shares. This is called **convertible preferred stock.** These and many other possible features of preferred stock are discussed in intermediate accounting texts.

Preferred stock contracts often allow the issuing corporation to purchase the preferred stock back from the stockholders by paying a stated amount per share, usually the par value plus a redemption premium. These are known as **callable preferred stock.** Preferred stock can also be reacquired by making a **tender offer,** which involves offering holders of preferred stock an amount in excess of market value.

Upon issuance, callable preferred stock is accounted for the same as noncallable preferred stock, with Preferred Stock and Contributed Capital in Excess of Par—Preferred being credited for the contributed capital. The entry to record a redemption includes an elimination of the applicable par balance and contributed capital in excess of par balance for the shares redeemed and a credit to Cash. If less is paid to redeem the shares than was received at issuance, a new account, Contributed Capital from Redemption of Preferred Stock, is credited.

For example, on January 1, 19xx, the Mirror Corporation has 10,000 shares of $100 par value preferred stock outstanding with contributed capital in excess of par of $100,000, or $10 per share. Assume that all shares of preferred originally sold for $110 per share. On January 10, 19xx, 4,000 shares are purchased on the open market at $105 per share. The journal entry recorded on that date would be:

19xx			
Jan. 10	Preferred Stock (SE).	400,000	
	Contributed Capital in Excess of Par— Preferred (SE).	40,000	
	Contributed Capital from Redemption of Preferred Stock (SE).		20,000
	Cash (A)		420,000
	To record redemption of preferred stock.		

Mirror was able to redeem the stock for $105 per share, or $20,000 less than the original selling price. This excess is credited to a contributed capital account identifying the $20,000 capital as being created by a redemption of preferred stock. If more is paid to redeem the preferred stock than was originally received upon issuance, Retained Earnings is debited for the amount of the excess. In our example, if Mirror had paid $112 per share (instead of $105 per share) to redeem 4,000 shares, the redemption entry would have been:

19xx			
Jan. 10	Preferred Stock (SE).	400,000	
	Contributed Capital in Excess of Par— Preferred (SE).	40,000	
	Retained Earnings (SE)	8,000	
	Cash (A)		448,000
	To record redemption of preferred stock.		

In this case the capital in excess of par of $10 per share contributed initially was eliminated, and retained earnings equal to the difference between the original issue price ($110) and the redemption price ($112) of $2 per share was also eliminated.

SUMMARY

This chapter began with a discussion on how the form of business organization—noncorporate or corporate—affects some aspects of accounting, especially those related to owners' equity. Many other important aspects of accounting are not affected by the form of business organization, such as accounting for most assets, liabilities, revenues, and expenses. Noncorporate businesses are viewed by the law as, in essence, combining the owner and the business for certain purposes. In corporate businesses, the stockholders and the business entity are viewed as separate, both by the law and by accountants.

Corporations provide several advantages over other forms of business—the major advantage for the corporation is the ability to raise large amounts of capital. Limited liability of stockholders, continuity of business, and ease of ownership transfer aid in pooling the financial resources needed for a large business. The economies provided by specialized management also make corporations desirable in today's highly specialized business world.

These and other features of corporations have implications for accounting and business decisions. Balance sheets communicate certain features of stockholder rights, such as the breakdown between par value and contributed capital in excess of par, and the distinction between common and preferred stock and contributed capital and retained earnings. Corporations' stockholders' equity disclosures make these and other distinctions, some of which are purely legalistic while others are reflective of economic transactions.

Although dividend policy is a very complex issue, accountants must record the effects of dividend declarations and payments. Preferred and common stocks' dividends are controlled by different contractual terms. Several of the common transactions were introduced in this chapter.

DEMONSTRATION EXERCISE

Flatbush Products, Inc., is formed on September 20, 19x1. The following selected transactions occur during 19x1 and 19x2:

19x1

Sept. 20 Incur $10,000 in legal fees for the organization of the corporation. These fees are paid with 1,000 shares of $10 par value common stock.

30 Issue 10,000 shares of $10 par value common stock for $15 per share and 500 shares of 5%, $100 par value preferred stock for $115 per share.

19x2

Feb. 1 Accept a $36,000 stock subscriptions agreement for 2,000 shares of common stock. One half of the subscriptions are paid for on March 1, and the remainder paid on April 1, when all of the 2,000 shares are issued.

June 30 Purchase 100 shares of previously issued stock at $12 per share. Resell 50 shares on July 15 for $10 per share and another 25 shares on August 31 for $15 per share.

Sept. 30 Declare the preferred stock dividend and a $0.40 per share cash dividend on outstanding common stock of record on October 31. The dividends are to be paid on November 15, 19x2.

Oct. 1 Declare a 10% common stock dividend on outstanding shares with a market value of $18 per share. The dividend is to be issued on November 15 to stockholders of record on October 31.

Dec. 15 Declare a 2-for-1 stock split effective December 31.

31 The organization costs are amortized over a 20-year period starting January 1, 19x2.

Required:

Prepare the journal entries in general journal form for the above transactions.

Solution:

19x1			
Sept. 20	Organization Costs (A)	10,000	
	Common Stock—Par (SE)		10,000
	To record legal fees for organization.		
30	Cash (A)	150,000	
	Common Stock—Par (SE)		100,000
	Contributed Capital in Excess of Par—Common (SE)		50,000
	To record issuance of 10,000 shares of common stock.		

Date	Account	Debit	Credit
Sept. 30	Cash (A)	57,500	
	Preferred Stock (SE)		50,000
	Contributed Capital in Excess of Par—Preferred (SE)		7,500
	To record issuance of 500 shares of preferred stock.		
19x2			
Feb. 1	Subscriptions Receivable—Common (A)	36,000	
	Common Stock Subscribed (SE)		20,000
	Contributed Capital in Excess of Par—Common Stock (SE)		16,000
	To record subscription agreement for 2,000 shares.		
Mar. 1	Cash (A)	18,000	
	Subscriptions Receivable—Common (A)		18,000
	To record receipt of payment on subscription agreement.		
Apr. 1	Cash (A)	18,000	
	Subscriptions Receivable—Common (A)		18,000
	To record receipt of final payment on subscription agreement.		
	Common Stock Subscribed (SE)	20,000	
	Common Stock—Par (SE)		20,000
	To record issuance of 2,000 shares of common stock.		
June 30	Treasury Stock (XSE)	1,200	
	Cash (A)		1,200
	To record purchase of 100 shares at $12 per share of issued stock.		
July 15	Cash (A)	500	
	Retained Earnings (SE)	100	
	Treasury Stock (XSE)		600
	To record sale of 50 shares of treasury stock at $10 per share.		
Aug. 31	Cash (A)	375	
	Treasury Stock (XSE)		300
	Contributed Capital in Excess of Par—Treasury Stock (SE)		75
	To record sale of 25 shares of treasury stock at $15 per share.		
Sept. 30	Retained Earnings (SE)	7,690	
	Dividends Payable (L)		7,690
	To record preferred and common stock dividends declared: Preferred: 500 shares × $5 = $2,500. Common: (1,000 + 10,000 + 2,000 − 25) × $0.40 = $5,190.		

Date		Account	Debit	Credit
Oct.	31	No journal entry on date of record.		
Nov.	15	Dividends Payable (L)	7,690	
		Cash (A)		7,690
		To record payment of dividends.		
Oct.	1	Retained Earnings (SE)	23,355	
		Stock Dividend Distributable—Common (SE)		12,975
		Contributed Capital in Excess of Par—Stock Dividend (SE)		10,380
		To record declaration of small stock dividend: 12,975 shares × .10 × $18 = $23,355.		
	31	No journal entry on date of record.		
Nov.	15	Stock Dividend Distributable—Common (SE) . .	12,975	
		Common Stock—Par (SE)		12,975
Dec.	15	No journal entry for split.		
Dec.	31	Amortization of Organization Costs (E)	500	
		Organization Costs (A)		500
		To record amortization or organization costs.		

APPENDIX

Accounting for Partnerships

Objective 10
Some of the accounting challenges created by partnerships.

Proprietorship and partnership accounting differ because of the complexity that multiple owners create in terms of rights and duties. Accounting records must reflect legal partnership relationships, especially in the critical area of capital accounts. For example, each partner has a capital account and a drawing account, and the amounts that go into these accounts are strictly governed by the partnership agreement or the Uniform Partnership Act if the partnership agreement is silent or nonexistent. This appendix discusses the accounting for the following critical partnership topics: original investment by partners, partnership profits and losses, return on capital allowance, salaries of partners, financial statements of a partnership, and dissolution of a partnership.

ORIGINAL INVESTMENT BY PARTNERS

The partnership agreement governs the initial dollar amount assigned to each partner's capital contribution as well as the percentages used to distribute subsequent profits and losses of the partnership. For example, the partnership agreement of the ABC Travel Agency, organized on January 1, 19x1, established that partners A, B, and C should make the following contributions:

Partner	*Asset Contributed*	*Agreed-Upon Fair Value*
A	Cash	$10,000
B	Furniture and equipment	8,000
C	Prepaid one year of rent on office space	12,000
	Total contribution	$30,000

The journal entry to record the formation of the partnership is:

19x1			
Jan. 1	Cash (A)	10,000	
	Furniture and Equipment (A)	8,000	
	Prepaid Rent (A)	12,000	
	A, Capital (OE)		10,000
	B, Capital (OE)		8,000
	C, Capital (OE)		12,000
	To record initial investment in partnership.		

Note that the furniture contributed by B is recorded at a fair value of $8,000 at January 1, 19x1. This furniture may have been purchased previously and used in another business. You may wonder how the $8,000 fair value is established. The $8,000 is not necessarily the original cost or the current book value on B's individual records. The partners simply agreed on the value among themselves.

It is possible that partners could agree to assign capital to owners in some proportion not equal to the actual value of asset contribution. Assume X, Y, and Z form a partnership. Z has great experience in the industry, and X and Y, who are less knowledgeable, are willing to contribute assets and give Z credit for his experience. The partnership agreement could give each one third of the capital, although the asset contribution comes entirely from X and Y as follows:

Partner	*Asset Contributed*	*Fair Value of Tangible Assets Contributed*	*Capital Allocation*
X	Cash	$30,000	$20,000
Y	Equipment	30,000	20,000
Z	None	0	20,000
		$60,000	$60,000

The journal entry to record the formation of XYZ partnership would be:

Cash (A)	30,000	
Equipment (A)	30,000	
X, Capital (OE)		20,000
Y, Capital (OE).		20,000
Z, Capital (OE)		20,000
To record the formation of XYZ partnership.		

After the formation of XYZ partnership, each partner has co-ownership of the contributed assets. X's cash and Y's equipment are commingled, and Z has as much right to them as do the others.

PARTNERSHIP PROFITS AND LOSSES

How do the profits and losses affect the capital accounts? The answer depends completely on the partnership agreement, which usually includes a formula for the division of profits and losses. If nothing is stated in the partnership agreement about profits and losses, an equal amount is assigned to each partner. Obviously, such an equal division may not be acceptable when partners make unequal contributions of capital or make unequal efforts in running the business. Several variations of profit and loss division formulas found in practice will be analyzed. Keep in mind that the partnership agreement can include any formula agreed upon by the partners.

The wording of the partnership agreement is crucial to a partnership, especially on the all-important distribution of profits to partners. Any number of distribution schemes can be devised. This section discusses accounting for partnership earnings under a series of simple assumptions and four earnings distribution cases based on the following stated ratios:

1. Equal earnings distribution to each partner.
2. Earnings distribution based on beginning capital balances with no withdrawals.
3. Earnings distribution based on beginning capital balances with withdrawals.
4. Earnings distribution based on average capital balances.

Case 1: Equal Earnings Distribution to Each Partner

The simplest formula for the distribution of earnings is to give each partner equal amounts of earnings. If C contributes $20,000 and D contributes $30,000 on January 1, 19x1, and earnings for years 1 and 2 are $60,000 and $100,000, respectively, the following journal entries summarize the effects of equal distribution of partnership earnings:

19x1			
Jan. 1	Cash (A)	50,000	
	C, Capital (OE)		20,000
	D, Capital (OE)		30,000
	To record the formation of partnership.		
Dec. 31	Income Summary (OE)	60,000	
	C, Capital (OE)		30,000
	D, Capital (OE)		30,000
	To close the Income Summary account to the partners' capital accounts.		
19x2			
Dec. 31	Income Summary (OE)	100,000	
	C, Capital (OE)		50,000
	D, Capital (OE)		50,000
	To close the Income Summary account to the partners' capital accounts.		

Case 2: Earnings Distribution Based on Beginning Capital Balances with No Withdrawals

If the partnership agreement states that the beginning capital balance ratio governs earnings distribution of each period, the following computations would be made for C and D in years 1 and 2:

	19x1 Beginning Balance	*Ratio*		*19x1 Earnings*		*Distribution of Earnings*	*19x1 Ending Capital Balance*
C, capital . . .	$20,000	40%	×	$60,000	=	$24,000	$ 44,000
D, capital . . .	30,000	60	×	60,000	=	36,000	66,000
	$50,000	100%				$60,000	$110,000

	19x2 Beginning Balance	*Ratio*		*19x2 Earnings*		*Distribution of Earnings*	*19x2 Ending Capital Balance*
C, capital . . .	$ 44,000	40%	×	$100,000	=	$ 40,000	$ 84,000
D, capital . . .	66,000	60	×	100,000	=	60,000	126,000
	$110,000	100%				$100,000	$210,000

Journal entries closing the Income Summary to the partners' capital accounts would be made for each year as in Case 1.

Case 3: Earnings Distribution Based on Beginning Capital Balances with Withdrawals

Often partners withdraw cash or other assets from the partnership, thereby reducing their capital balances. This, of course, changes capital ratios. In our example, if C and D withdraw $30,000 and $20,000, respectively, during both 19x1 and 19x2, the following journal entry would be made for the withdrawals:

C, Withdrawals (OE)	30,000	
D, Withdrawals (OE)	20,000	
Cash (A)		50,000
To record withdrawals of money during year by the partners.		

Year 1's earnings distribution would not be changed because the beginning balance for 19x1 is not affected by the withdrawal, but year 2's earnings distribution is changed because of the withdrawal's effect on the capital balances of each partner. Study the following tables:

Partner	*1/1/x1 Beginning Balance*	*Ratio*		*19x1 Earnings*	*Distribution of Earnings*	*Capital Balance before Withdrawal*	*19x1 Withdrawal*	*19x1 Ending Capital Balance*
C, capital	$20,000	40%	×	$60,000	$24,000	$ 44,000	$30,000	$14,000
D, capital.	30,000	60	×	60,000	36,000	66,000	20,000	46,000
	$50,000	100%			$60,000	$110,000	$50,000	$60,000

Partner	*1/1/x2 Beginning Balance*	*Ratio*		*19x2 Earnings*	*Distribution of Earnings*	*Capital Balance before Withdrawal*	*19x2 Withdrawal*	*19x2 Ending Capital Balance*
C, capital. . . .	$14,000	23%	×	$100,000	$ 23,000	$ 37,000	$30,000	$ 7,000
D, capital. . . .	46,000	77	×	100,000	77,000	123,000	20,000	103,000
	$60,000	100%			$100,000	$160,000	$50,000	$110,000

Again, journal entries closing Income Summary to C's and D's capital accounts would be made at year-end, and the withdrawals would be closed to the capital accounts.

Case 4: Earnings Distribution Based on Average Capital Balances

C and D could decide to distribute earnings on any formula they choose. For example, if the weighted average capital balances are used and 19x1 earnings are not considered until year-end, the computations for 19x1 assuming a withdrawal of $30,000 for C on October 31 would be as follows:

C, Capital Balance		*Fraction*		*Weighted Average Balance*
$ 20,000	×	10/12	=	$16,668
(10,000)	×	2/12	=	(1,667)
				$15,001

The beginning capital balance for C is $20,000, the amount contributed at the creation of the partnership, and this balance remains for 10 months. C's withdrawal of $30,000 on October 31, 19x1, reduces the capital balance to a negative $10,000, and the balance remains for two months until December 31, 19x1.

If D withdrew $20,000 on October 31, the following computation of weighted average capital balance would be:

D, Capital Balance		*Fraction*		*Weighted Average Balance*
$30,000	×	10/12	=	$25,002
10,000	×	2/12	=	1,667
				$26,669

The earnings distribution would be:

Partner	*Weighted Average Capital Balance*	*Ratio*		*Earnings*	*Distribution*
C	$15,001	36%	×	$60,000	$21,600
D	26,669	64	×	60,000	38,400
	$41,670	100%			$60,000

The ratios are the weighted average capital balance for each partner divided by the weighted average capital of the partnership: for C $15,001/$41,670 = 36% and for D, $26,669/$41,670 = 64%.

RETURN ON CAPITAL ALLOWANCE

Often partners desire a return on their invested amounts before earnings are distributed. When partners are given an allowance for a return or interest on the capital amounts, this reduces the amount to be distributed based on the earnings distribution formula. For example, in the C and D partnership of the previous section, $60,000 was earned in 19x1. If a return on partners' capital balances is allowed, the earnings distribution involves two steps: first, a return is computed for each partner; and second, the residual amount of earnings after subtracting the return on capital is distributed according to the agreed-upon formula.

Assume that (1) C and D agree to a 12% return on average capital balances and (2) the residual amount of earnings after the return on capital is distributed equally. The following schedule shows the computation of income distribution for 19x1:

Partner	*12% Return on Weighted Average Capital Balance*		*Equally Distributed Residual Earnings*		*Total 19x1 Distribution*
C	$1,800	+	$27,500	=	$29,300
D	3,200	+	27,500	=	30,700
	$5,000	+	$55,000	=	$60,000

C's 12% return allowance is based on a $15,001 weighted average capital balance, and D's is based on $26,669 as computed in the previous example. The $27,500 residual earnings distribution to each partner is 50% of the earnings remaining after the allowance of the 12% return.

SALARIES OF PARTNERS

Often partners contribute different levels of service to the business, and this is reflected in differential salary amounts credited to capital accounts before the residual earnings (after the salaries and capital return allowance, if any) are distributed. For example, X and Y agree to share residual earnings equally, but first X is to be credited for $20,000 in salary and Y, $10,000. Assume the following two earnings distribution cases:

Case 1. Earnings before salaries, $100,000.
Case 2. Earnings before salaries, $25,000.

Case 1: Earnings before Salaries, $100,000

In Case 1, X and Y are first credited for their respective salaries, $20,000 and $10,000, which totals $30,000. Since the earnings before salaries are $100,000, the residual earnings is $70,000, which is divided equally between X and Y as shown in the following table:

	X	*Y*	*Total*
Salary allowance	$20,000	$10,000	$ 30,000
Residual earnings distribution	35,000	35,000	70,000
Distribution	$55,000	$45,000	$100,000

Case 2: Earnings before Salaries, $25,000

In Case 2, the earnings before salary is only $25,000. The salary allowances create a negative residual earnings of $5,000, which must be distributed equally to X and Y. Thus, the total increase in capital accounts is $25,000, but it is distributed as follows:

	X	*Y*	*Total*
Salary allowance.	$20,000	$10,000	$30,000
Residual earnings distribution	(2,500)	(2,500)	(5,000)
Distribution	$17,500	$ 7,500	$25,000

Although the residual earnings amount is negative, this does not affect the basic form of the entry to close the Income Summary account but does make a considerable difference in the amount credited to each partner's capital.

FINANCIAL STATEMENTS OF A PARTNERSHIP

Partnership financial statements are similar in many ways to those of corporations and proprietorships; however, there are differences in the owners' equity section. A special statement titled **Statement of Partners' Capital** may be shown in addition to the capital accounts given on the balance sheet. The earnings statement often has a section that shows the allocation of net income (loss) to partners. Exhibit 11A-1 highlights the special features of partnership financial statements. Note that there is no income tax expense in PQ's income statement because the partners declare their share of the partnership's income on their own personal income tax returns.

DISSOLUTION OF A PARTNERSHIP

Unless the partnership agreement contains a special provision, the legal status of a partnership changes whenever the identity of the partners changes as the result of events such as admitting a new partner, withdrawal of a partner, death of a partner, and reduction or increase of interest of an old partner. Often when such a change is made and the business continues, the business routine is uninterrupted. From the legal perspective, however, the old partnership is dissolved, and a new one is created.

EXHIBIT 11A-1

Special Features of Partnership Financial Statements

PQ Partnership
Income Statement
For the Year Ended December 31, 19x1

Fees revenue	$165,000
Expenses:	
Salaries expense	$ 45,400
Rent expense	24,000
Insurance expense	3,600
Supplies expense	15,600
Utilities expense	18,400
Interest expense	8,000
Total expenses	$115,000
Net income	$ 50,000
Distribution of income:	
50% to P	$ 25,000
50% to Q	25,000
Net income	$ 50,000

PQ Partnership
Statement of Partnership Capital
For the Year Ended December 31, 19x1

	P	*Q*	*Total*
Beginning capital, 1/1/x1	$40,000	$40,000	$ 80,000
Add: Net income for the year	25,000	25,000	50,000
Total available capital	$65,000	$65,000	$130,000
Less: Withdrawals	5,000	15,000	20,000
Ending capital, 12/31/x1	$60,000	$50,000	$110,000

PQ Partnership
Balance Sheet
December 31, 19x1

Assets		**Liabilities and Owners' Equity**	
Current assets:		Liabilities:	
Cash	$ 45,200	Accounts payable	$ 13,200
Accounts receivable	82,100	Notes payable	80,000
Office supplies	1,200	Salaries payable	12,800
Prepaid rent	8,500	Taxes payable	24,600
Prepaid insurance	3,600	Total liabilities	$130,600
Total current assets	$140,600	Owners' equity:	
Land	100,000	P, capital	$ 60,000
		Q, capital	50,000
		Total owners' equity	$110,000
Total assets	$240,600	Total liabilities and owners' equity	$240,600

Usually, when a partner is added or withdrawn, assets are added to or taken away from the partnership. In this section we discuss the five major categories of partner changes shown in the following matrix:

Typical Patterns of Asset Flows		
Adding a partner	**Case 1** New assets added to partnership	**Case 2** New assets go to continuing partners
Withdrawal of a partner	**Case 3** Payment from partnership assets	**Case 4** Payment from partners' personal assets
Adding a partner and withdrawal of a partner	**Case 5** New assets given to old withdrawing partner	

Within each major category, several specific cases are discussed.

Adding a New Partner

Case 1: Assets from New Partner Added to the Partnership. In the first example, Partnership CD, with capital accounts of $100,000 each for C and D, admits a new partner, E, who contributes $100,000 in cash to the partnership.

Old Partnership CD	**New Partnership CDE**
Total Capital = $200,000	**Total Capital = $300,000**

The journal entry to record the admission of E is:

19x1			
Jan. 1	Cash (A)	100,000	
	E, Capital (OE)		100,000
	To record the admission of E to CDE partnership.		

Note that the entity has grown in size because new assets were added. The partners should prepare a new partnership agreement.

Bonus. Assume that the CD Partnership is such a good business opportunity that E is willing to contribute $100,000 for a 20% interest. The cash goes to the partnership, increasing the net assets and capital by $100,000; and the ending capital of CDE is allocated 40% to C, 40% to D, and 20% to E.

Old Partnership CD	**New Partnership CDE**
Total Capital = $200,000	**Total Capital = $300,000**

The journal entry to record the capital contribution is:

19x1			
Jan. 1	Cash (A)	100,000	
	C, Capital (OE)		20,000
	D, Capital (OE)		20,000
	E, Capital (OE)		60,000
	To record the admission of E to CDE partnership.		

This situation is called the bonus method because E is willing to pay an amount in excess of the capital credited to him or her, which can be said to be a bonus for the old partners.

In some situations, a partnership may need the talents of a prospective partner enough to offer to pay a bonus to entice him or her into joining the firm. For instance, C and D invite E to become an equal partner for a contribution of only $70,000 in cash. The partnership is $70,000 larger after the admission of E, but C and D have smaller capital balances as follows:

Old Partnership CD	New Partnership CDE
Total Capital = $200,000	**Total Capital = $270,000**

In this situation, the bonus of $20,000 goes to E and the transaction recorded as follows:

19x1			
Jan. 1	Cash (A)	70,000	
	C, Capital (OE)	10,000	
	D, Capital (OE)	10,000	
	E, Capital (OE)		90,000
	To record the admission of E to CDE partnership.		

Of course, C and D could agree to share the bonus given to E in some other way. It is not necessary that they share it equally. Note that all three partners now have capital of $90,000 or one third of the $270,000 total.

Case 2: New Assets Go to Continuing Partners. What if E pays $60,000 personally to both C and D for a one-third share of the partnership?

Old Partnership CD	New Partnership CDE
Total Capital = $200,000	**Total Capital = $200,000**

The business entity, in this case, has not increased in size because the asset flow was from the new partner to the old partners, bypassing the business completely. The journal entry shows that C and D's capital accounts are reduced by equal amounts and then E is credited with $66,667 even though the payment to C and D totaled $120,000. The cash received by C and D did not affect the total capital of the partnership.

19x1			
Jan. 1	C, Capital (OE)	33,333	
	D, Capital (OE)	33,334	
	E, Capital (OE)		66,667
	To record the admission of E to CDE partnership.		

Withdrawal of a Partner

When a partner withdraws from a partnership, the remaining partnership legally becomes a new partnership just as when a new partner is admitted. The partnership agreement usually gives details as to the disposition of assets in the case of a withdrawal. A partner has a right to his or her share of the net assets of the partnership, but the book value may be more or less than the fair value of the assets. Consider the MNO partnership with the following balance sheet on January 1, 19x2:

MNO Partnership
Balance Sheet
January 1, 19x2

Assets		**Liabilities and Owners' Equity**	
Current assets:		Liabilities:	
Cash	$ 20,000	Accounts payable	$ 10,000
Accounts receivable	60,000	Notes payable	50,000
Inventories	100,000	Total liabilities	$ 60,000
Total current assets	$180,000	Owners' equity:	
Noncurrent assets:		M, capital	$120,000
Equipment (net)	$ 40,000	N, capital	120,000
Building (net)	200,000	O, capital	120,000
Total noncurrent assets	$240,000	Total owners' equity	$360,000
		Total liabilities and	
Total assets	$420,000	owners' equity	$420,000

If the partnership agreement allows any partner to withdraw his or her share of assets at any time, some procedure is necessary to appraise the assets for their fair value and then to distribute the fair value according to the formulas prescribed in the partnership agreement. Several variations will be examined.

Case 3: Payment from Partnership. On January 1, 19x2, O withdraws from the partnership. The partnership agreement states that a withdrawing partner is entitled to one third of the fair value of the net assets in cash. If M and N want to continue the business, they first must have the net assets appraised and then generate enough cash to pay O. Consider the following appraised values as compared to book values:

	Book Value	*Appraised Value*	*Difference*
Cash	$ 20,000	$ 20,000	$ 0
Accounts receivable	60,000	55,000	(5,000)
Inventory	100,000	150,000	50,000
Equipment	40,000	60,000	20,000
Building	200,000	225,000	25,000
Accounts payable	(10,000)	(10,000)	0
Notes payable	(50,000)	(50,000)	0
Net assets	$360,000	$450,000	$90,000

The assets of the partnership are first revalued to fair value with the following journal entry:

19x2			
Jan. 1	Inventory (A)	50,000	
	Equipment (A)	20,000	
	Building (A)	25,000	
	Accounts Receivable (A)		5,000
	M, Capital (OE).		30,000
	N, Capital (OE).		30,000
	O, Capital (OE).		30,000
	To record revaluation of MNO partnership.		

Rather than liquidate the business or sell off some of the assets, M and N decide to have the partnership borrow the $150,000 necessary to pay off O:

19x2			
Jan. 1	Cash (A).	150,000	
	Notes Payable		150,000
	To record note taken to pay O.		
Jan. 1	O, Capital (OE).	150,000	
	Cash (A).		150,000
	To record withdrawal of O from partnership.		

The following illustrate the changing capital structure of the partnership:

MNO Capital Balance before Restructure, $360,000	MNO Capital Balance after Restructure, $450,000	MN Capital Balance after Withdrawal of O, $300,000

Note that the total capital always equals the net assets of the business. Borrowing the $150,000 does not increase the net assets because the increase in cash is offset by the increase in a liability, notes payable.

Bonuses can be paid to the withdrawing partner which means the agreement gives a withdrawing partner more assets than his or her capital balance would warrant. This may result from the partnership agreement, or it may be determined that the business would benefit from the departure and a bonus is offered.

Case 4: Payment from Remaining Partners' Personal Assets. Consider the KLM partnership where partnership capital is equally divided at $100,000 for each partner. Assume that L sells her share directly to K and M for $120,000. K and M agree the capital of the new partnership would be divided equally between K and M.

Old Partnership KLM Total Capital = $300,000	New Partnership KM Total Capital = $300,000

The fact that L receives $20,000 more than book value is not recorded on the journal of the partnership.

19x1			
June 30	L, Capital (OE)	100,000	
	K, Capital (OE).		50,000
	M, Capital (OE).		50,000
	To record transfer of L's share of the partnership to K and M.		

The key to understanding the effect of such transactions on partnerships is the entity concept. In this case, the asset flow circumvented the business entity; and, therefore, the overall size of the entity stayed the same. The capital account changes reflect the changing ownership of the business entity.

Case 5: New Assets Go to Withdrawing Partner. Another possibility is for the departing partner to sell his or her share to a new partner; that is, a simultaneous adding and withdrawing of partners. In this case, the partnership does not change size or the relative capital balances of the remaining partners. For instance, assume in our KLM example, L sells, with permission of K and M, her one-third share to O for $120,000. Because the partnership does not receive any cash, the following relationship of capital balances applies:

Old Partnership KLM	New Partnership KMO
Total Capital = $300,000	**Total Capital = $300,000**

The entry would merely record the fact that L's share is being taken over by O.

19x1			
June 30	L, Capital (OE)	100,000	
	O, Capital (OE)		100,000
	To record transfer of L's share of the partnership to O.		

Various factors could motivate O to pay more or less than book value for the share of the business. As stressed many times, asset book values do not necessarily represent fair values; and when a business is sold in total or in part, the selling parties usually demand fair value.

Liquidation of a Partnership

When partners agree to liquidate or dissolve the partnership, they usually convert all assets to cash, pay off all creditors and then distribute the remaining cash on the basis of balances in the capital accounts. Complexities can arise when partners have negative balances in their capital accounts. The following shows how liquidation normally is recorded, and, as always, the partnership agreement can stipulate otherwise.

The PQ partnership has the following balance sheet items before conversion of all assets to cash and after conversion and payment of liabilities, assuming that P and Q share profits and losses equally:

	Book Value	*Cash Value*	*Gain or (Loss)*	*Book Values after Conversion of Assets to Cash and Payment of Liabilities*
Cash	$110,000	$110,000	$ 0	$100,000
Accounts receivable.	50,000	20,000	(30,000)	
Building (net)	400,000	200,000	(200,000)	
Liabilities	230,000	230,000	0	
P, capital	65,000		(115,000)	(50,000)
Q, capital	265,000		(115,000)	150,000

The journal entries to record the sale of assets and payment of the liabilities are:

19x1			
Sept. 30	Cash (A)	220,000	
	P, Capital (OE)	115,000	
	Q, Capital (OE)	115,000	
	Accounts Receivable (A)		50,000
	Building (A)		400,000
	To record liquidation of partnership's assets and allocation of associated losses of $230,000, equally.		
	Liabilities	230,000	
	Cash (A)		230,000
	To record payment of partnership's liabilities.		

Because the conversion of the assets to cash results in losses totaling $230,000, each partner absorbs $115,000, reducing their capital balances. After posting the journal entries to record the losses, P's and Q's capital accounts would have the following balances:

P, Capital	
	65,000
115,000	
50,000	

Q, Capital	
	265,000
115,000	
	150,000

Before the partnership is liquidated by means of a payment of the remaining cash to the partners, P must pay $50,000 to the partnership to eliminate the deficit in his account.

19x1			
Sept. 30	Cash (A)	50,000	
	P, Capital (OE)		50,000
	To record the payment by P of the deficit capital balance.		

This entry gives P a zero capital balance and the $150,000 of cash is paid to Q.

19x1			
Sept. 30	Q, Capital (OE)	150,000	
	Cash (A)		150,000
	To record the liquidation of the PQ partnership.		

This example shows a partner's capital account having a debit (negative) balance which represents an obligation to the remaining partner upon liquidation. During ongoing operations, such negative balances may appear from time to time, and they can be eliminated through profitable operations or additional contributions. This example demonstrates the unlimited liability of general partners to creditors and the possible obligation that results when a partner's capital account is negative.

KEY TERMS

Authorized shares. Maximum number of shares that the corporate charter allows to be issued.

Callable preferred stock. Preferred stock that allows the issuing corporation to purchase the preferred stock back from stockholders by paying a stated amount per share, usually the par value plus a redemption premium.

Common stock. Corporate securities that have voting rights, preemptive rights, rights to share in dividends, and rights to the residual assets.

Common stockholders. Investors of corporations who own common stock.

Contributed capital. Total money contributed to the business by the owners.

Convertible preferred stock. Preferred stock that allows the holder under certain conditions to trade a share of preferred stock for a fixed number of common shares.

Corporation. An association of individuals recognized by law that has rights and responsibilities separate from its members.

Cumulative. Characteristic of preferred stock where unpaid dividends accumulate and must be paid in subsequent periods before common stockholders are paid any dividends.

Date of declaration. Date on which dividends are declared.

Date of payment. Date on which payment to stockholders for dividends is made.

Date of record. Date on which stockholders who will receive dividends is established.

Dividend. Distribution of earnings to stockholders in cash or something else of value.

Dividend rights. Stockholders' rights to share in the distributions of earnings in the form of dividends.

Dividends in arrears. Cumulative preferred stock dividends that have not been paid over the years.

Donated Capital. An owners' equity account that is credited when a corporation receives assets that are donated to the corporation; usually this donation is from a government unit that is attempting to encourage a business to locate in its area.

General partners. Owners of a partnership that have unlimited responsibility for the partnership's liabilities.

Hostile takeover. An outside party tries to acquire enough shares of a corporation to gain control, without the cooperation of management.

Incorporators. Individuals who organize a corporation who may or may not become owners; also called promoters.

Issued. The number of shares that have been sold to owners of a corporation.

Large stock dividends; stock splits. Issuance of stock (usually 20 to 25% of the outstanding stock) to stockholders as a dividend.

Legal capital. Amount of par or stated value of stock outstanding.

Leveraged buyout (LBO). A small group arranges a borrowing against the assets of the business and buys out all or most of the other shareholders.

Limited partners. Owners of a partnership whose liability responsibility is limited to the assets contributed to the partnership or some other specific amount.

Mutual agency. Allows each partner to borrow money, purchase assets, commit to sales contracts, and so on, in the name of the partnership without the other partners' consent.

No-par stock. Stock that has no-par-value assigned to it.

Outstanding. Shares previously issued that are currently held by owners.

Owner's capital account. Account used in a proprietorship or partnership to reflect the owner's interest.

Owner's drawing account. Account used in a proprietorship or partnership to keep track of the owner's withdrawals from the business during the period.

Participating preferred stock. Preferred stock that is allowed to participate with common stock in cash dividends in excess of the dividend amount stated per share.

Partnership. Multiowner, noncorporate business.

Partnership agreement. Formal agreement that lists the rights and responsibilities of partners.

Par value. Arbitrary value per share assigned to a share of stock; also called stated value; usually is the minimum amount a share can be issued for.

Preemptive right. Common stockholders' right to maintain their percentage of ownership.

Preferred stock. Class of stock that has different rights from common stock including various preferences.

Premium. Excess paid by stockholders over the stock's par value; also called contributed capital in excess of par.

Proprietorship. Single-owner, noncorporate business.

Residual asset right. Common stockholders' right to the resident assets of a corporation upon liquidation.

Small stock dividends. Small number of shares (usually less than 20% of outstanding shares of stock) relative to total outstanding shares issued to stockholders in the form of a dividend.

Statement of owner's equity. Financial statement in a proprietorship and partnership which shows the owner's interest in a business over a period of time.

Stock dividend. Issuance of additional shares of stock to existing stockholders as a substitution for or in conjunction with cash dividends.

Subscription contracts. Promises to pay the corporation for shares of stock at a future date.

Treasury stock. Shares of previously issued stock reacquired by the company but not retired.

Uniform Partnership Act (UPA). Law that governs the formation, operation, and liquidation of partnerships in most states.

Voting right. Common stockholders' right to elect a board of directors.

SYNONYMS

Corporate charter; articles of incorporation.
Incorporators; promoters.
Large stock dividend; stock split.
Paid-in capital; contributed capital.
Par value; stated value.
Premium; contributed capital in excess of par.
Treasury stock; treasury shares.

QUESTIONS

1. Define three different forms of business organization and describe the major differences among them.
2. Describe four characteristics of partnerships.
3. Describe the advantages and disadvantages of forming a corporation.
4. Describe the process of forming a corporation.
5. What is common stock? Give four characteristics of common stock.
6. Define preferred stock and list several characteristics. Name two special types of preferred stock.
7. Define par value. Why is it important?
8. How is the accounting treatment different for stock subscriptions versus the issuance of shares of stock for cash?
9. Describe the difference between authorized, issued, and outstanding shares of stock.
10. Define treasury stock. Why would a company repurchase its own stock?
11. If treasury stock is sold for more than it was purchased, what ledger accounts are affected? If it is sold for less than its purchase cost, what accounts are affected?
12. Where does donated capital appear on the balance sheet? Why?
13. What are cash dividends? Why are they issued?
14. In the chapter, three different dates associated with dividends were described. Give those dates and explain why they are important.
15. Define a stock dividend. Differentiate between small and large stock dividends. How does the difference affect the accounting treatment they receive?
16. Illustrate the difference between a large stock dividend and a stock split.

APPENDIX QUESTIONS

17. Jane, John, and Joe form a partnership by each contributing $50,000. Discuss different ways the first year's profits of $21,000 can be distributed if Jane, John, and Joe withdraw $20,000, $5,000, and $10,000, respectively, on June 30 of the first year.
18. How are the financial statements for a partnership similar to the financial statements for a corporation? How are they different?
19. Describe five different ways the composition of a partnership's ownership can change.

EXERCISES

EXERCISE 11-1
L.O. 1

Entity Concept

Two businesses identical in every way except one is a corporation and the other is a partnership find themselves facing the same outcome in a lawsuit—pay the plaintiff $1 million in damages. After completing the appeal process, the damages are reduced to $500,000. Both the corporation and partnership have $300,000 in net assets, and the owners of each business each have $500,000 in personal assets.

Required:
Determine the amount the plaintiff will receive in each case.

EXERCISE 11-2
L.O. 2

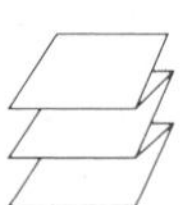

Establishment of a Proprietorship

Harvey James decides to go into business for himself by starting a gourmet catering business. On March 1, 19xx, he contributes the following to the business:

	James' Original Cost	*Fair Market Value*
Cash	$ 3,000	$ 3,000
Kitchen equipment.	10,000	18,000
Serving equipment.	1,000	1,900
Paper supplies	750	800
His expert culinary skills . .		5,000

Required:
Record the journal entry in general journal form that Harvey made on March 1, 19xx.

EXERCISE 11-3
L.O. 2, 5

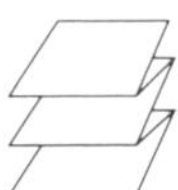

Preparing Journal Entries (Proprietorship versus Corporation)

Selected transactions for the Caro Company are as follows:

a. Original investment in the business is $150,000.
b. A salary of $5,000 for the month is paid to the owner (manager of the business).
c. Revenues of $80,000 are earned during the month (all in cash).
d. Expenses (excluding salaries) of $62,000 are incurred on account during the month.
e. Accounts payable paid during the month totaled $56,000.
f. The income for the month is closed to the appropriate owners' equity account. Assume all appropriate closing entries are made to the Income Summary account.

Required:
1. Prepare the journal entries in general journal form for the above items assuming Caro's is organized as a proprietorship.
2. Prepare the journal entries in general journal form for the above items assuming Caro's is organized as a corporation. The original investment is evidenced by 10,000 shares of $10 par value common stock.

EXERCISE 11-4
L.O. 5

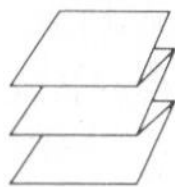

Issuance of Stock

Henry's Fitness Center has the following transactions involving stock issuance:

19xx

Apr. 5	Issues 10,000 shares of $1 par value common stock for $5 per share.
16	Issues 1,000 shares of $100 par value preferred stock at par.
May 1	Issues an additional 5,000 shares of the common stock for $6 per share to a friend of Henry's.
June 30	Accepts a $20,000 stock subscription for 5,000 shares of common stock.
July 31	Receives payment for one half of the stock subscriptions.
Aug. 31	Receives final payment for the stock subscriptions and issues the stock.

Required:
Record journal entries for the above transactions in general journal form.

EXERCISE 11-5
L.O. 7

Reacquisition of Stock

The Movers Corporation bought 1,000 shares of its previously issued common stock outstanding at $12 per share on October 15, 19x1. On February 21, 19x2, the corporation sold 500 of these shares at $14 per share for cash. On April 14, 19x2, the corporation sold 250 shares at $10 per share for cash. The remaining 250 shares were sold on June 28 at $5 per share for cash.

Required:
Prepare the journal entries in general journal form for the above treasury stock transactions.

EXERCISE 11-6
L.O. 7

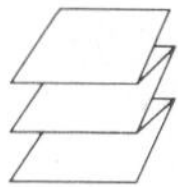

Reacquisition of Stock

Guiffre International Corporation had the following transactions during 19xx regarding repurchase of its stock:

19xx

Apr. 20	Repurchases 5,000 shares of $1 par common stock at $7 per share. Guiffre plans to hold the stock for future reissuance.
July 21	Repurchases and retires 3,000 shares of common stock at $4 per share.
Sept. 5	Sells 2,000 shares of treasury stock for $10 per share.
Nov. 30	Sells 1,000 shares of treasury stock for $5.50 per share.

Assume that the stock was originally issued on Jan. 1, 19xx, for $5 per share.

Required:
Prepare the journal entries in general journal form for these transactions.

EXERCISE 11-7
L.O. 8

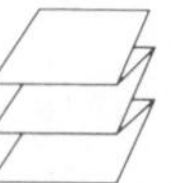

Cash Dividends

On October 30, 19x5, MasterCraft, Inc., declares a $0.35 cash dividend on its 60,000 shares of common stock to stockholders of record on November 15, 19x5, to be paid on November 30, 19x5. Prepare the journal entries required, if any, on each of the dates.

EXERCISE 11-8
L.O. 8

Stock Dividends

The Banner Corporation had 50,000 shares of $20 par value common stock outstanding at January 1, 19xx. On June 15, 19xx, the board of directors declared a 15% stock dividend on the outstanding common stock. The market value of the stock was $31 per share on June 15, 19xx. The stock was issued on July 30. Prepare Banner's journal entries related to dividends.

EXERCISE 11-9
L.O. 8

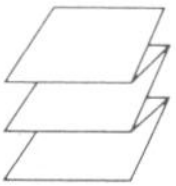

Stock Dividends

Swann's Discounters, Inc., has 100,000 shares of $4 par value common stock with a current market value of $10 per share. Consider the following three items independently and prepare the appropriate journal entries for each case:

a. Declares and issues a 5% stock dividend.
b. Declares and issues a 50% stock dividend.
c. Declares and issues a 2-for-1 stock split.

EXERCISE 11-10
L.O. 5, 7, 8

Changes in Stockholders' Equity

Assume the following transactions occur during 1986 for the General Electric Company, which is involved in technology, services, manufacturing, and other areas. Indicate the effect of each item (increase, decrease, no effect) on total stockholders' equity.

a. Issue 100,000 of additional shares of common stock.
b. Repurchase 1,000 shares of common stock for $43,000.
c. Sale of 25 shares of common stock from J. Blumberg to T. Jones.
d. Sale of 150 shares of treasury stock purchased in (*b*) for $6,000.
e. Sale of 200 shares of treasury stock purchased in (*b*) for $9,000.
f. Declare a cash dividend.
g. Declare a 2-for-1 stock split.

EXERCISE 11-11
L.O. 5

Stock Subscriptions

Wiretex, Inc., was organized on April 1, 19x1. One million shares of $3.00 par value common stock were authorized. Two hundred thousand shares were issued for cash at $4.00 per share on 4/1/x1 to A. Hall, and 800,000 shares were subscribed to by two stockholders under the following payment schedule:

		Payments		
Stockholder	*Shares*	*4/1/x1*	*10/1/x1*	*3/31/x2*
J. Leno	200,000	$300,000	$300,000	$200,000
J. Carson	600,000	900,000	900,000	600,000

All payments are made on schedule.

Required:
1. Show journal entries at each date.
2. Show how effects of these transactions would be reported on the 12/31/x1 balance sheet.

APPENDIX EXERCISES

EXERCISE 11-12
L.O. 10

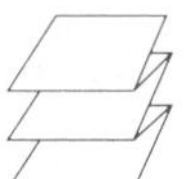

Establishment of a Partnership and Distribution of Net Income

On August 15, 19x1, Sarah, Sue, and Sally entered into a partnership called SuperFitness Salon. Sarah contributes $10,000. Sue contributes equipment with a fair market value of $5,000, and Sally brings to the partnership her experience as an aerobics instructor. It is decided the partnership will be a 50:25:25 split, respectively, and all profits after salaries will be allocated accordingly. During the first year, which ends on July 31, 19x2, a profit of $12,000 is made. During that same year, Sarah withdraws $5,000, Sue withdraws $2,000, and Sally withdraws nothing but earns a salary of $15,000.

Required:

1. Record the journal entry in general journal form made on August 15, 19x1, to set up the partnership.
2. Record the journal entry in general journal form to allocate the profits and close out the drawing accounts to the capital accounts on July 31, 19x2.

EXERCISE 11-13
L.O. 10

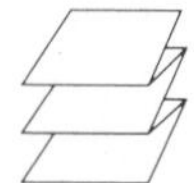

Addition of a New Partner

New Town Relocation Services is a partnership owned by John and Joe with total capital of $150,000 which is shared equally. A new partner, Jim, wants to enter the partnership.

Required:

1. Record the journal entry in general journal form if Jim contributes $75,000 to enter the partnership as an equal partner.
2. Record the journal entry in general journal form if Jim contributes $105,000 to enter the partnership as an equal partner.
3. Record the journal entry in general journal form if Jim contributes $55,000, but he is to be an equal partner in the business.

EXERCISE 11-14
L.O. 10

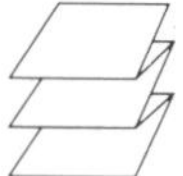

Withdrawal of a Partner

On April 30, 19x6, Willis decides to withdraw from the Baker, Jones, Willis Surveying Company. On that date the fair market value of the net assets is $540,000. Total book value of the partnership capital is $480,000, which the partners share equally.

Required:

1. Record the journal entry(ies) made if Baker and Jones buy Willis' share of the partnership for fair market value with personal assets. Assume that assets are not revalued on partnership books.
2. If assets of the company are sold and the company liquidated, record the journal entry(ies) for the final payment to owners.
3. Record the journal entry(ies) made if Baker and Jones pay Willis $200,000 to withdraw Willis' personal assets from the partnership. Assume that assets are not revalued on partnership books.
4. Record the journal entry(ies) made if a new partner purchases Willis' share from him for $250,000. Assume that assets are not revalued on partnership books.

EXERCISE 11-15
L.O. 10

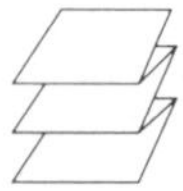

Liquidation of a Partnership

The Many Legal Services partnership decides to liquidate on September 30, 19x7. The firm, which shares all profits and losses equally, has the following assets, liabilities, and capital accounts prior to liquidation:

	Book Value	*Fair Market Value*
Cash	$ 20,000	$20,000
Accounts receivable	16,000	12,500
Equipment (net)	8,000	2,500
Liabilities	8,700	8,700
Ross, capital	(22,000)	
Streeter, capital	57,300	

Required:

1. Determine the book values after conversion of assets to cash and payment of liabilities and record any journal entry(ies) in general journal form made in conversion.
2. Record the journal entries made in liquidating the partnership.

EXERCISE 11-16
L.O. 10

Addition of a Partner

The partnership of Jones and Kane had the following summary balance sheet at June 30, 19xx.

Assets	$200,000
Liabilities	$ 50,000
Jones, capital	100,000
Kane, capital	50,000
Total liabilities and owners' equity . .	$200,000

The partners share profits and losses equally.

On June 30, the partners decide to admit Lance to the partnership. Prepare the journal entries in general journal form to record the admission of Lance under the following independent assumptions:

a. Lance will contribute cash of $50,000 for a 25% interest.
b. Lance will contribute cash of $50,000 for a 40% interest.
c. Lance will contribute cash of $50,000 for a 20% interest.
d. Lance will contribute cash of $150,000 for a 50% interest.
e. Lance will give Kane $40,000 for Kane's one-third interest in the existing partnership.
f. Lance will give Jones $80,000 for Jones' two-thirds interest in the existing partnership.
g. Lance will pay Jones and Kane personally $50,000 and $25,000, respectively, for a 30% interest in the newly created partnership.

For *b, c,* and *d,* assume that old partners share the bonus equally.

EXERCISE 11-17
L.O. 10

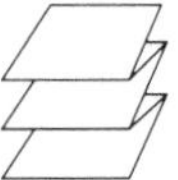

Distribution of Partnership Profits and Losses

Partners A, B, and C distribute profits and losses as follows: Salaries of $12,000 to A and B and $18,000 to C; a return of 8% on the original investment; and the residual is divided equally. The original cash investments made in 19x1 are: A, $60,000; B, $50,000; and C, $40,000.

Net income (loss) for the first four years of operations is as follows:

19x1	$ 66,000
19x2	99,900
19x3	45,000
19x4	(63,000)

Required:
Prepare a schedule computing the amounts allocated to each partner for the first four years of operation.

PROBLEMS

PROBLEM 11-1
L.O. 5

Organization Costs

Derry Corporation was organized on August 10, 19x1. The corporate charter stated that 80,000 shares of $1 par value common stock was authorized. Consider each of the following items independently:

a. 80,000 shares are sold for $4 per share on August 15, 19x1, and $20,000 is paid to organizers of the corporation as compensation for legal and accounting services during the organization period.

b. 75,000 shares are sold for $4 per share, and 5,000 shares are distributed to organizers for promotion, legal, and accounting services during the organization period.

Required:
Prepare the journal entries in general journal form for each case above.

PROBLEM 11-2
L.O. 5

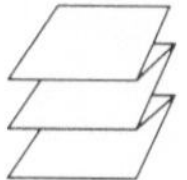

Stock Transactions

Storey Corporation was organized on December 1, 19x1. One hundred twenty thousand shares of $0.25 par value common stock and 10,000 shares of $100 par value preferred stock were authorized. During the month, the following transactions related to stock took place:

19x1
Dec. 2 Issued 100,000 shares of common stock for $8 per share.
14 Received subscriptions for 10,000 shares of common stock for $3 per share down payment plus $5.50 per share to be paid on June 30, 19x2.
16 Issued 10,000 shares of preferred stock for cash of $105 per share.
20 Issued 5,000 shares of common stock in exchange for the following assets:

	Fair Value
Trucks	$17,000
Computer	10,500
	$27,500

Required:
Prepare the journal entries for the above transactions.

PROBLEM 11-3
L.O. 5, 6

Issuance of Common Stock

Maher Corporation received authorization for 100,000 shares of common stock on September 1, 19x1, and some of the stock is sold on September 10, 19x1. Consider the following items independently.

a. Common stock has a par value of $2 per share, and 50,000 shares sell for $3.50 per share.
b. Common stock has no-par value, and 50,000 shares sell for $3.50 per share.
c. Common stock has par value of $2 per share, 50,000 shares sell for $3.50 per share, and 10,000 shares are given to the owner of an office building for purchase of the building. The building had been advertised at a selling price of $40,000.

Required:
1. Show the journal entries for each case.
2. Show the balance sheet disclosure of contributed capital for each case.

PROBLEM 11-4
L.O. 6

Stockholders' Equity Section of Balance Sheet

Strickling Corporation has a fiscal year ending December 31, and on December 31, 19x1, the following information is available.

	Debits	Credits
Retained earnings	$1,150,000	
Contributed capital in excess of par—common stock		$1,200,000
Treasury stock.	215,000	
Common stock—par		2,100,000
Common stock subscribed		125,000
Subscriptions receivable	140,000	
Preferred stock—par		900,000
Discount on preferred stock. . . .	100,000	

Required:
Show the stockholders' equity section of Strickling Corporation's balance sheet on December 31, 19x1. Explain how any account not shown in owners' equity would be disclosed.

PROBLEM 11-5
L.O. 5, 6

Stock Subscriptions

Jones, Inc., was authorized to issue 200,000 shares of $0.50 per share par value common stock on January 1, 19x1. One hundred twenty thousand shares were immediately sold for cash for $2 per share, and 40,000 shares were subscribed to at a subscription price of $2.50 per share to be paid in equal payments on June 30, 19x1, and December 31, 19x1. During 19x1, Jones, Inc., had net income of $30,000 and no dividends were paid.

Required:
1. Record all journal entries related to stock for 19x1.
2. Prepare the stockholder's equity section of Jones, Inc., balance sheet on December 31, 19x1.

PROBLEM 11-6
L.O. 6, 7

Treasury Stock

The stockholders' equity section of the Johnson Corporation appears as follows on the December 31, 19x1, balance sheet:

Stockholders' equity:	
Contributed capital:	
Common stock, par $1 per share, 2 million shares authorized, 1.5 million shares issued and outstanding.	$1,500,000
Contributed capital in excess of par . .	3,000,000
Retained earnings	450,000
Total stockholders' equity	$4,950,000

On January 10, 19x2, Johnson Corporation purchased 20,000 shares of common stock on the open market for $4 per share. On October 1, 19x1, 10,000 shares were sold for $5 per share, and on December 15, 19x2, 5,000 shares were sold for $4 per share. At December 31, 19x2, 5,000 shares were still held as treasury stock. Net income for the year was $200,000 and no dividends were declared.

Required:
1. Record all journal entries during 19x2 related to treasury stock.
2. Prepare the stockholders' equity section of Johnson Corporation's balance sheet on December 31, 19x2.

PROBLEM 11-7
L.O. 5, 6, 8

Organization Costs and Donated Capital

On June 1, 19x1, HiTech, Inc., was issued a corporate charter with authorization of 500,000 shares of no-par common stock. The following transactions took place in the first week following the issuance of the charter:

a. 400,000 shares were issued for cash of $4 per share.
b. $15,000 was paid to the accounting firm that acted as consultant during the organization period.
c. The city of Jacksonville gave the company the title to a parcel of land on which the headquarters of HiTech is to be constructed. The land has an appraised value of $200,000.

At December 31, 19x1, the end of its first fiscal period, HiTech, Inc., reported net income of $120,000 and declared no dividends.

Required:
1. Record journal entries for transactions (*a*), (*b*), and (*c*) above.
2. Prepare the stockholders' equity section of HiTech, Inc., on December 31, 19x1.

PROBLEM 11-8
L.O. 6, 7

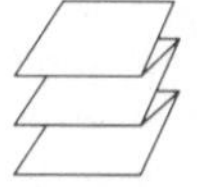

Cash Dividends and Treasury Stock

On December 31, 19x1, Starke, Inc., reported a retained earnings balance of $1,850,000 and a Contributed Capital in Excess of Par of $750,000. During 19x2, Starke had the following transactions related to its $1 par value stock (50,000 shares of common stock are authorized, issued, and outstanding as of December 31, 19x1):

19x2	
June 10	Declared a $.50 per share cash dividend to be paid on July 10, 19x2, to stockholders of record on June 30, 19x2.
July 10	Paid the cash dividend.
20	Purchased 4,000 treasury shares for $10 per share.
Sept. 20	Sold 2,000 treasury shares for $15 per share.
Dec. 10	Declared a $.50 per share cash dividend to be paid on January 10, 19x3, to stockholders of record on December 31, 19x2.
31	Closed the Income Summary account and recognized net income of $800,000.

Required:
1. Prepare journal entries in general journal form for the above transactions.
2. Prepare the stockholders' equity section of the balance sheet on December 31, 19x2.

PROBLEM 11-9
L.O. 6, 8

Stock Dividends and Balance Sheet Presentation of Stockholders' Equity

The stockholders' equity section of Russell, Inc., on December 31, 19x1, showed one million shares of $1 par value common stock issued and outstanding, contributed capital in excess of par of $5 million, and retained earnings of $2.3 million. During 19x2, net income amounted to $650,000.

Although Russell, Inc., generated a considerable amount of cash during 19x2, most of it was used to purchase long-term assets. Management declared a 15% stock dividend on December 10, 19x2, in lieu of a cash dividend to be distributed on January 10, 19x3, to stockholders of record on December 30, 19x2. The stock was selling for $5 per share on the date of declaration.

Required:
1. Prepare all journal entries related to common shares from December 10, 19x2, through January 10, 19x3.
2. Prepare the stockholders' equity section of Russell, Inc.'s balance sheet on December 31, 19x2.

PROBLEM 11-10
L.O. 1, 5, 7, 8

True/False

1. _____ Par value is the same as the current fair market value.
2. _____ Par value is the same as the original selling price.
3. _____ Par value of common is always equal to liquidation value.
4. _____ Par value of preferred can be equal to liquidation value.
5. _____ Par value of preferred always exceeds par value of common.
6. _____ Preferred stock dividends have preference over bond interest.
7. _____ Total common stock dividends may exceed total preferred stock dividends.
8. _____ Treasury stock is valued at the fair market value on the balance sheet date.
9. _____ Treasury stock transactions can never result in gains or losses on the income statement.
10. _____ Treasury stock transactions can constrain a company's dividends declarations.
11. _____ Preferred stock always has a maturity date.
12. _____ Preferred stockholders can sue the company for undeclared dividends just as bondholders can sue the company for unpaid interest.
13. _____ Contributed capital is synonymous with par or stated value.
14. _____ Subscriptions receivable is a current asset account.
15. _____ Large stock dividends and stock splits have no effect on contributed capital.

APPENDIX PROBLEMS

PROBLEM 11-11
L.O. 10

Establishment of a Partnership

Annabel and Beatrice form a partnership where Annabel contributes cash of $100,000 and Beatrice contributes a proprietorship which has the following trial balance.

	Debits	*Credits*
Cash	$ 8,000	
Accounts Receivable (net)	26,000	
Inventory	29,000	
Building and Equipment	58,000	
Accumulated Depreciation		$ 9,000
Accounts Payable		12,000
Beatrice, Capital		100,000
Totals	$121,000	$121,000

Annabel and Beatrice agree that Beatrice's assets' book values are equal to their fair values. Annabel and Beatrice agree to share the responsibility for the proprietorship's liabilities.

Required:
Make the entries necessary to set up the Annabel and Beatrice partnership.

PROBLEM 11-12
L.O. 10

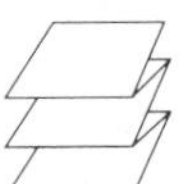

Distribution of Partnership Profits

The Smith & Brown Group had the following stipulations in its partnership agreement:

- Each partner is allowed 10% return on the beginning capital balances.
- Smith is allowed a salary of $40,000 per year, and Brown is allowed a salary of $30,000 per year.
- The remaining net income or loss after the effect of the return on capital and salary allowance is distributed equally to Smith and Brown.

Smith's beginning capital balance on January 1, 19x2, was $60,000, and Brown's was $50,000. During 19x2, Smith withdrew $35,000, and Brown withdrew $25,000. Net income for 19x2 before allowances for return on capital and salaries was $120,000.

Required:
Prepare a schedule showing how each partner's capital is affected by the above transactions.

PROBLEM 11-13

L.O. 10

Distribution of Partnership Profits

Schrafts and Lotto invest $140,000 and $100,000, respectively, in a partnership on January 1, 19x1. During 19x1 and 19x2, the partnership has earnings of $80,000 and $120,000, respectively.

Required:
Prepare a schedule showing how each partner's capital is affected under each of the following independent assumptions:

1. The partnership agreement does not mention the distribution of earnings.
2. The partnership agreement calls for a 12% return on beginning capital balance with the remainder of earnings being distributed equally.
3. Earnings and losses are to be shared equally after salary allowances of $60,000 for Schrafts and $20,000 for Lotto.

PROBLEM 11-14

L.O. 10

Establishment of a Partnership

Inkling and Macburg each run separate fast-food businesses. On January 1, 19x1, they agree to form the Burger partnership. The balance sheets of Inkling and Macburg on January 1, 19x1, are as follows:

Inkling's Operations

	Book	Fair Market Value
Cash	$ 8,000	$ 8,000
Accounts receivable (net)	26,000	23,000
Inventory	114,000	130,000
Building and equipment (net)	65,000	100,000
Land	10,000	60,000
Total	$223,000	$321,000
Accounts payable	$ 40,000	$ 40,000
Notes payable	10,000	10,000
Owners' equity	173,000	271,000
Total	$223,000	$321,000

Macburg's Operations

	Book	Fair Market Value
Cash	$ 1,000	$ 1,000
Accounts receivable (net)	8,000	8,000
Inventory	42,000	50,000
Total	$51,000	$59,000
Accounts payable	$ 1,500	$ 1,500
Owners' equity	49,500	57,500
Total	$51,000	$59,000

Because Macburg's business seems more dynamic and has more potential, it is decided that Macburg would be given credit for $100,000 in capital over the fair value of Macburg's assets minus liabilities. It is decided that notes payable are not to be transferred to the partnership.

Required:
Record the formation of the Burger partnership.

PROBLEM 11-15
L.O. 10

Withdrawal of a Partner

Hogan and Jones have been partners in Delta Records for several years, and the accounting records show the following account balances at December 31, 19xx. It is believed that the book values and fair values of assets and liabilities are approximately the same.

	Debits	*Credits*
Cash	$ 18,500	
Accounts Receivable (net) . . .	32,000	
Inventory	105,000	
Building and Equipment	95,000	
Accounts Payable		$ 10,000
Notes Payable		7,000
Hogan, Capital		166,500
Jones, Capital		95,000
Hogan, Drawing	18,000	
Jones, Drawing	10,000	

Jones wants to retire effective December 31, 19xx, and the partners decide on the following terms: Jones will get $10,000 of the cash plus a promissory note from Delta Records for $100,000 to be paid in five annual year-end installments—$20,000 each plus interest at 10%.

Required:

1. Prepare the journal entry in general journal form made by the partnership to record the retirement of Jones.
2. Prepare Delta Records' December 31, 19xx, balance sheet.

PROBLEM 11-16
L.O. 10

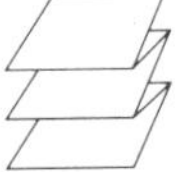

Distribution of Partnership Profits

The partnership of A, B, and C was formed in 19x1. Initial investments were: A, $10,000; B, $20,000; and C, $30,000. Net income over a two-year period is as follows:

19x1	$72,000
19x2	18,000

The partners had withdrawals during this period as follows:

	A	*B*	*C*
19x1	$16,000	$20,000	$60,000
19x2	3,000	24,000	7,000

Required:
Prepare a schedule showing the allocations of profits for each year to each partner's capital account under the following independent assumptions:

a. Profits are divided equally.
b. Profits are divided: 37.5% to A; 37.5% to B; and 25% to C.
c. Profits are divided based on the original investments.
d. During 19x1 and 19x2, salaries are assigned to A, B, and C at $10,000, $10,000, and $4,000, respectively. The balance is divided based on original investments.
e. Profits are divided based on the beginning of the year capital balances.

CASES

CASE 11-1
L.O. 1

Entity Concept

Haney owns two businesses that are run as proprietorships—an appliance repair shop and a car wash. After hearing the explanation of his rights and responsibilities as a proprietor, Handy asks, "Why should I keep separate accounting records for these two businesses when the law makes no distinction between any of my assets and obligations including those in the business?"

Required:
Draft a response to Haney's question.

CASE 11-2
L.O. 1, 2, 4

Forms of Business

Joe Blunt is a leather craftsman who is going to open a retail store and must decide on the form of business to adopt. He wants to know the legal and accounting differences between the proprietorship and the corporate form of business organizations.

Required:
Write a short response to Mr. Blunt which explains how proprietorships and corporations differ from accounting and legal perspectives.

CASE 11-3
L.O. 5

Issuance of Stocks and Organization Costs

Lucas, Inc., was organized on January 1, 19x1, with 200,000 shares of 1 par common stock being authorized. The following transactions affecting stock took place during 19x1:

1. On January 1, 19x1, five investors each paid $50,000 for 10,000 shares of stock.
2. On January 1, 19x1, Ms. Spike, the organizer of the corporation, was issued 40,000 shares of common stock for $180,000 in cash. Ms. Spike had incurred $20,000 in legal and other costs during the organization phase. She had paid all costs out of her own pocket, and it was agreed that the "bargain" price she paid for these shares would compensate her for the $20,000.
3. On January 2, 19x1, 50,000 shares were issued to Ms. Spike for a parcel of land she owned. The original cost to her was $200,000.

The following journal entries were made for the above transactions:

a. Cash	$250,000	
Common Stock-Par		50,000
Contributed Capital in Excess of Par		200,000
b. Cash	180,000	
Common Stock-Par		40,000
Contributed Capital in Excess of Par		140,000
c. Land	50,000	
Common Stock-Par		50,000

Required:
1. Discuss each accounting transaction and show how you would have recorded it.
2. Show how the contributed capital accounts should appear on the 12/31/x1 balance sheet.

CASE 11-4
L.O. 5, 7

Balance Sheet Disclosure

Two stockholders' equity accounts, Treasury Stock and Subscriptions Receivable, have generated considerable controversy in the past because of debate over their proper balance sheet classification. Both accounts have debit balances but are normally located in different sections of the balance sheet. Treasury Stock is normally shown as a contra to total stockholders' equity and Subscriptions Receivable is normally shown as a current asset.

Required:

1. Discuss the justification of the normal disclosures of these two items.
2. Discuss the possible justification for showing Treasury Stock as an asset and Subscriptions Receivable as a contra stockholders' equity account.

APPENDIX CASES

CASE 11-5
L.O. 10

Allocation of Profits

You overhear the following conversation between your friend, Samantha, and her business partner, Al.

Al: If we form a partnership, we have to share all profits equally which means that we should contribute the same amounts initially.

Samantha: No, I believe that we must share profits according to our relative capital balances.

Required:

Clarify their misconceptions with a short summary statement of the allowable relationship between capital contributions, capital balances, and profit sharing among partners.

EVALUATING FINANCIAL STATEMENTS

CASE 11-6
L.O. 1–4, 6

Elements of Stockholders' Equity and Rights of Shareholders

A corporation may have several categories of stockholders' equity. Each category represents the results of transactions and each in one way or another says something about the rights of stockholders. List the stockholders' equity categories and describe the transactions which affect those categories. Also, discuss the rights of stockholders and tell how some aspect of those rights is related to each category.

CASE 11-7 Treasury Shares

L.O. 7

In a recent annual report, General Motors showed their treasury stock as an asset labeled "Common Stock Held for the Incentive Program" as follows:

General Motors
Consolidated Balance Sheet (excerpt)
(in $ millions)

Assets:	
Current assets:	
Cash	$ 369.5
U.S. government and other marketable securities and time deposits—at cost, which approximates market of $5,834.6	5,847.4
Total cash and marketable securities	6,216.9
Accounts and notes receivable—less allowances	6,964.2
Inventories	6,621.5
Prepaid expenses and deferred income taxes	997.2
Total current assets	20,799.8
Equity in net assets of nonconsolidated subsidiaries and associates	4,450.8
Other investments and miscellaneous assets	1,222.5
Common stock held for the Incentive Program (Note 3)	**56.3**
Property:	
Real estate, plants and equipment	37,777.8
Less accumulated depreciation	20,116.8
Net real estate, plants and equipment	17,661.0
Special tools	1,504.1
Total property	19,165.1
Total assets	$45,694.5

The following is from Note 3 of GM's balance sheet:

Note 3 (excerpt)

Common stock held for the Incentive Program is stated substantially at cost and used exclusively for payment of Program liabilities (in millions).

	Shares	*Amount*
Balance at Jan. 1	592,207	$ 35.2
Acquired during the year	592,680	42.6
Delivered to participants	(358,614)	(21.5)
Balance at Dec. 31	826,273	$ 56.3

Required:

1. Explain the normal balance sheet location of treasury stock.
2. Give the pros and cons of reporting treasury stock as an asset.

CASE 11-8
L.O. 5–7

Changes in Stockholders' Equity

The following partial owners' equity section of a balance sheet (in thousands) was reported on a recent published annual report.

Preferred stock:	
$1 par value, 2,077,189 shares authorized, 421,694 shares outstanding	$ 422
Common stock:	
$1 par value, 30,000,000 shares authorized, 13,269,650 shares issued	13,270
Capital in excess of par value	149,472
Retained earnings	522,532
	$685,696
Less cost of 209,525 shares of common stock in treasury	8,060
	$677,636

The following is an excerpt from a note to the balance sheet:

	Preferred Stock $1 Par Value	*Common Stock $1 Par Value*	*Treasury Stock*	
			Shares	*Cost*
Beginning balance	$ 590,528	$13,209,875	(420,021)	$(16,887,000)
Purchase of treasury stock	—	—	(97,000)	(3,727,000)
Conversion and retirements of preferred stock and exercise of options	(168,834)	59,775	307,496	12,554,000
Ending balance	$ 421,694	$13,269,650	(209,525)	$ (8,060,000)

Required:
Study the balance sheet and note excerpt, and write a paragraph explaining how each category (except for retained earnings) was affected by transactions during the year. Be as explicit as possible and state any assumptions you make.

FINANCIAL STATEMENTS

FINANCIAL STATEMENT COMPONENTS EMPHASIZED IN CHAPTER 12

Barker Corporation
Income Statement
For 1991

Revenues
XXXX
Dividend income
Investment income—
Equity investees
Minority interest in income
Expenses
XXXX
XXXX

	1991	1990
Dividend income	$XXX	$XXX
Investment income—		
Equity investees	XXX	XXX
Minority interest in income	(XXX)	(XXX)

Barker Corporation
Balance Sheet
12/31/91

Current assets
XXXX
XXXX
Noncurrent assets
Investments at LCM
Equity investments in unconsolidated subsidiaries
Current liabilities
XXXX
XXXX
Noncurrent liabilities
XXXX
XXXX
Stockholders' equity
XXXX
XXXX

	1991	1990
Investments at LCM . . .	$XXX	$XXX
Equity investments in unconsolidated subsidiaries	XXX	XXX

Barker Corporation
Cash Flow Statement
For 1991

Operating activities
XXXX
XXXX
Investing activities
Purchase of investments
Sale of investments in bonds
Financing activities
XXXX
XXXX

	1991	1990
Purchase of investments	$ XXX	$ XXX
Sale of investments in bonds	XXXX	0

C H A P T E R 12

Investments

LEARNING OBJECTIVES

After studying Chapter 12, you should understand:

1. The three primary business purposes behind investment activities, pp. 652-53.
2. The cost method (used for temporary investments in nonequity securities) and the amortized cost method (used for long-term investments in certificates of deposit [CDs], bonds, and notes), pp. 653-58.
3. The lower-of-cost-or-market (LCM) method (used for all temporary investments in marketable equity securities plus long-term investments in marketable equity securities of less than a 20% interest), pp. 659-64.
4. The equity method (used when the investor company has enough voting stock to influence the operations of the investee company), pp. 664-66.
5. The consolidation method (used when the investor company owns over 50% of the investee company and controls its operations), pp. 666-75.
6. Additional aspects of consolidation (Appendix 12A), pp. 680-84.
7. Pooling of interests (Appendix 12B), pp. 685-86.

Chapters 10 and 11 discussed the accounting for capital that companies acquired by debt and equity financing. In this chapter you will learn why some companies invest in such assets as bonds or stocks, of other businesses. Then the chapter introduces the four methods used to account for investments—cost, lower of cost or market (LCM), equity, and consolidation. The method companies use depends on the length of the investment—temporary or long term—and the type of asset acquired and the percentage of the company acquired.

This chapter will help you understand the nature of different types of investments and to read and evaluate published financial statements of businesses with significant investment activities.

NATURE AND PURPOSE OF INVESTMENTS

Objective 1
The three primary business purposes behind investment activities.

When a company acquires assets with the expectation of receiving interest, dividends, or price appreciation, these assets are called **investments.** Most business investments are made up of bonds, notes, or stocks of another entity. However, land, rare works of art, or other valuable assets are sometimes acquired as investments too. Usually, the company's purpose for investing determines the nature of the assets that a company acquires as an investment.

The primary business purposes behind investment activities are:

1. As a temporary use of idle cash that the company will need for operating purposes in the not-too-distant future.
2. As a part of a "savings" program designed to build up a pool of liquid assets for a major purchase (such as a new plant), to refund long-term debt when it matures (a sinking fund), or to accomplish some other long-term objective.
3. As a part of a program designed to gain a significant investment interest or ownership control in another business entity.

While the last two purposes noted above are long term in nature, the first one has a short-term time horizon. Because the time frame of an investment is considered to be important information, investments are categorized as temporary and long term. The following table lists the accounting methods discussed in this chapter for various types of temporary and long-term investments:

Length of Investment	*Type of Invested Asset*	*Accounting Method*
A. Temporary	1. Bonds, notes, certificates of deposit (CDs).	Cost method
	2. Equity securities.	Lower of cost or market (LCM)
B. Long term	1. Bonds, notes, CDs.	Cost method
	2. Equity securities:	
	a. Ownership interest of less than 20%.	Lower of cost or market (LCM)
	b. Ownership interest of 20% to 50%.	Equity method
	c. Ownership interest of over 50%.	Consolidation

Note that, in general, for **nonequity investments** (bonds, notes, CDs—investments other than voting stocks of publicly traded companies), accountants use the cost method. However, for **equity investments** (voting stocks of corporations), the method accountants use varies depending on the extent of the investor's ownership in the investee company's stock. The following diagram identifies the accounting method to be used for investments of 0–20%, 20–50%, and 50–100% of the investee's common stock:

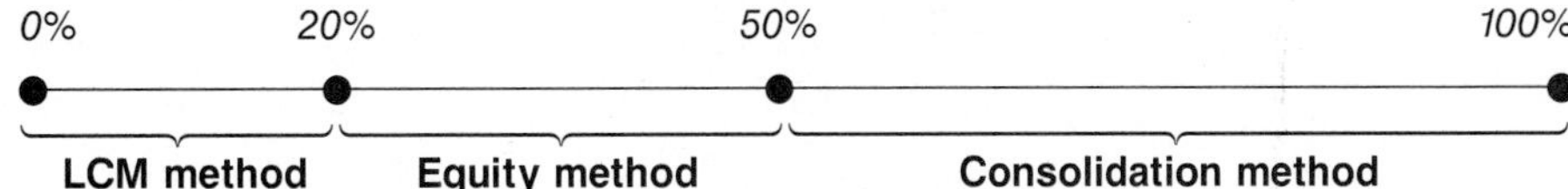

The four basic methods of accounting for investments—cost, LCM, equity, and consolidation—are discussed in the four sections of this chapter.

COST METHOD

Accountants generally apply the **cost method** to all temporary and long-term nonequity investments such as bonds, notes, and CDs. The cost method is relatively straightforward when applied to most nonequity investments. However, accountants use one of two variations of the cost method depending on the intended holding period of the investments.

To account for temporary nonequity investments, accountants use the *cost method;* and to account for long-term nonequity investments, accountants use the *amortized cost method.* Amortization of bonds was introduced in Chapter 10 when bonds were discussed from the issuer's point of view. In this chapter, we discuss the cost method and the amortized cost method from the investor's point of view.

Cost Method—Temporary Investments

Objective 2

The cost method (used for temporary investments in nonequity securities)....

The **cost method** applies to all temporary investments in nonequity securities. These investments include a savings account; a short-term certificate of deposit, such as a 90-day *CD;* a *U.S. Treasury bill;* a *note* of another entity (also called *commercial paper*) promising to pay the amount borrowed plus a stated interest at a specific future date (such as a 10%, 100-day note due January 19, 19xx); and a corporate bond (normally publicly traded on bond exchanges) with a stated interest rate, maturity date, and principal amount. As applied to temporary investments, the cost method records the investment at original cost and does not adjust the recorded cost until the investment is sold. Any interest on these securities is recognized as interest income in the period that the interest is earned.

Although the market value of nonequity investments often changes between the time of purchase and time of sale, these changes are not recorded. Accountants only record the gain or loss from short-term investments at the time of sale under the cost method. The theory behind this method is that wide fluctuations in the market value of these securities, which are of relatively low risk to the investor because of fixed interest rates and maturity dates, will not occur during the short period the investments are held by the company. As a result, these changes are "settled up" when the temporary investments are sold, and the accounting system does not record the changes as they occur.

Because the purpose for owning temporary investments is the utilization of temporarily idle cash, companies look for the following characteristics in such investments:

1. Good return on investment.
2. Low risk of loss of invested amount.
3. Ease of convertibility back to cash (liquidity).

Short-term CDs and high-quality, publicly traded corporate bonds are common examples of **temporary investments** that meet these three requirements. Remember that temporary investments are investments that management intends to keep less than one year or operating cycle, whichever is longer.

Purchase at Other than Face Value. As you learned in Chapter 10, bonds sold above or below their face value (maturity value) are purchased at a **premium** or a **discount**. When the bond investment is classified as temporary, the cost method does **not** require amortization of any discount or premium. The investment would remain at cost until sold. Any difference between the original cost and the proceeds at the time of sale, not including interest, would be recorded as a gain or loss.

If, on January 1, 19x3, Investor Corporation paid $975 for a 10%, $1,000 face value bond maturing on December 31, 19x3, how would you record the purchase using the cost method? Entries for the bond purchased at a $25 discount ($975) would be:

Bond Investment

19x3			
Jan. 1	Temporary Investments—Bonds (A)	975	
	Cash (A).		975
	To record purchase of bond.		
June 30	Cash (A).	50	
	Interest Income (R)		50
	To record interest received: $1,000 × .10 × 6/12 = $50.		
Dec. 31	Cash (A).	50	
	Interest Income (R)		50
	To record interest received: $1,000 × .10 × 6/12 = $50.		
31	Cash (A).	1,000	
	Temporary Investments—Bonds (A)		975
	Gain on Bond (R).		25
	To record bond maturity.		

The gain recorded at December 31 reflects the fact that more cash was received at maturity than was paid out at date of purchase. If Investor Corporation purchased the bond for $1,050 on January 1, 19x3, a $50 loss would have been recorded on December 31, 19x3, when the bond matured.

Sale before Maturity. Now assume that the 10%, $1,000 bond acquired on January 1, 19x3, for $975 is sold on August 31, 19x3, for $985, which includes two months' accrued interest. This accrued interest is \$17 rounded (\$1,000 × .10 × 2/12 = \$16.67 = \$17 rounded); therefore, the proceeds on the bond alone are \$968 (\$985 − \$17 accrued interest), resulting in a \$7 loss (\$975 paid − \$968 received = \$7 loss in principal) on August 31, 19x3. Investor Corporation would record this purchase and sale as follows:

19x3			
Jan. 1	Temporary Investments—Bonds (A)	975	
	Cash (A)		975
	To record purchase of bond.		
June 30	Cash (A)	50	
	Interest Income (R)		50
	To record interest received: \$1,000 × .10 × 6/12 = \$50.		
Aug. 31	Cash (A)	985	
	Loss on Sale of Bonds (E)	7	
	Temporary Investments—Bonds (A)		975
	Interest Income (R)		17
	To record sale of bond and interest income.		

Note that the selling price of a bond includes accrued and unpaid interest as of the date of sale unless otherwise stated. The loss represents the difference between the original price paid for the bond (\$975) and the proceeds from the bond alone (\$968 without interest) at the time of the sale.

Normally, investors do not trade CDs or notes like they trade bonds. CDs are usually issued on the date purchased by the individual investor, with the maturity date a specified number of days from the issue date (e.g., a 180-day CD). The amount invested is normally equal to the maturity value for notes or CDs. However, for temporary investments in bonds, the amount invested and the proceeds at the time of sale will frequently differ due to changes in market value. Exhibit 12-1 summarizes the basic approach for measuring and recording temporary investments in notes and bonds.

Amortized Cost Method—Long-Term Investments

Accountants also use the cost method for **long-term investments** (investments longer than one year) in CDs, bonds, and notes. However, when companies acquire these "fixed income" investments with stated interest rates and maturity amounts at a premium or a discount, accountants use the **amortized cost method** and amortize the premium or discount over the remaining life of the security. These **long-term investments are assumed to be held to maturity;** therefore, differences between the price paid and maturity value (discount or premium) should be eliminated (amortized) over the remaining life of the securities.

As illustrated in Chapter 10, the amortization process systematically allocates the discount or premium to the income statement. In the case of the bondholder the discount or premium is eliminated by adding (for a discount) or deducting (for a premium) the periodic amortization to or from the stated (nominal) amount of interest payment. This method is consistent with the fact that bonds purchased at discount provide effective interest **greater** than the stated (nominal) interest rate on the bond. Alternatively, bonds purchased at a premium provide effective interest **less** than the stated rate.

EXHIBIT 12-1

Cost Method: Temporary Investments in Notes and Bonds

Event	*Entry to Be Recorded*
Purchase	Record at the price paid for the note or bond.
Receipt of interest	Record cash received for interest as interest income. Interest income should be based on the maturity value of the bond or note and the stated rate of interest.
End of accounting period	Record an adjusting entry for accrued interest earned but not received as of financial statement date, increasing an asset (interest receivable) and a revenue (interest income).
Sale of investment	1. Record any interest income earned since the last interest payment date. 2. Increase assets for the cash or other assets received. 3. Decrease temporary investments for the original cost of the investment. 4. Calculate (or plug) the difference as a gain or a loss. A gain (credit) is recorded when the total proceeds exceed the original cost of the investment plus any accrued interest. A loss (debit) is recorded when the total proceeds are less than the original cost of the investment plus any accrued interest.

You should use the effective-interest method (illustrated in Chapter 10) for the amortization of bond premiums and discounts unless no material difference exists between the effective-interest method and the straight-line method. Also, note that for long-term investments in bonds, separate discount or premium accounts are rarely (if ever) used. Investors use the remaining life of the bond from date of purchase as the amortization period for discounts and premiums on long-term bond investments.

Objective 2
The . . . amortized cost method (used for long-term investments in certificates of deposit [CDs], bonds, and notes).

To illustrate the amortized cost method, assume that on January 1, 19x1, Alcan Pipe, Inc., purchased 10 bonds with a maturity value of $10,000 each for "94" (94% of their maturity value) or $94,000 total. The bonds mature in five years (December 31, 19x5) and have an annual interest rate of 8% paid semiannually on June 30 and December 31. Assume the $6,000 total discount on these bonds (.06 × 10 bonds × $10,000 each = $6,000) is amortized on a straight-line basis over the next five years (60 months) at the rate of $100 per month ($6,000/60 months = $100 per month). The entries to record the purchase and the first year's interest payments and discount amortization would be:

19x1			
Jan. 1	Bond Investments (A)	94,000	
	Cash (A)		94,000
	To record purchase of $100,000 bonds at 94.		
June 30	Cash (A)	4,000	
	Bond Interest Income (R)		4,000
	To record six months of bond interest.		
30	Bond Investments (A)	600	
	Bond Interest Income (R)		600
	To amortize six months of bond discount.		

EXHIBIT 12-2

Amortization Table for a Long-Term Investment in Bonds

Purchase price: $94,000
Purchase date: January 1, 19x1
Maturity value: $100,000
Maturity date: December 31, 19x5
Nominal annual interest: $8,000 (8%)
Interest payment dates: June 30, December 31
Amortization method: Straight-line

	Semiannual			
Date	*Cash Interest (Nominal) Received*	*Amortization of Bond Discount or Premium*	*Interest Income*	*Balance in Investment Account*
1/1/x1. . . .	$ 0	$ 0	$ 0	$ 94,000
6/30/x1. . . .	4,000	600	4,600	94,600
12/31/x1. . . .	4,000	600	4,600	95,200
6/30/x2. . . .	4,000	600	4,600	95,800
12/31/x2. . . .	4,000	600	4,600	96,400
6/30/x3. . . .	4,000	600	4,600	97,000
12/31/x3. . . .	4,000	600	4,600	97,600
6/30/x4. . . .	4,000	600	4,600	98,200
12/31/x4. . . .	4,000	600	4,600	98,800
6/30/x5. . . .	4,000	600	4,600	99,400
12/31/x5. . . .	4,000	600	4,600	100,000
	$40,000	$6,000	$46,000	

Dec. 31	Cash (A).	4,000	
	Bond Interest Income (R)		4,000
	To record six months of bond interest.		
31	Bond Investments (A)	600	
	Bond Interest Income (R)		600
	To amortize six months of bond discount.		

Exhibit 12-2 gives the complete bond amortization table for the Alcan Pipe bond. The exhibit illustrates how the book value of the bond systematically increases to the face value by the date of maturity. Note also that the total interest income reported by the investor over the life of the bond ($46,000) is equal to the total cash interest payments ($40,000) plus the $6,000 excess of the maturity value received on December 31, 19x5 ($100,000) over the price paid on January 1, 19x1 ($94,000). Hence, the income statement reflects the total difference between the cash received ($140,000) and the cash paid $(94,000) as interest income during the life of the bond investment.

Sale before Maturity. Assume that Alcan Pipe decided to sell the bonds on August 31, 19x4 (16 months before maturity) for $100,333, which includes $1,333 accrued interest ($100,000 × .08 × 2/12 = $1,333 rounded). The entries to record the sale would first record accrued interest receivable plus two months' discount amortization. Then, the sale would be recorded to eliminate all accounts pertaining to the bonds, as follows:

19x4			
Aug. 31	Interest Receivable (A)	1,333	
	Bond Investments (A)	200	
	Bond Interest Income (R)		1,533
	To record two months' interest and discount amortization.		
31	Cash (A)	100,333	
	Bond Investments (A)		98,400
	Interest Receivable (A)		1,333
	Gain on Sale of Bonds (R)		600
	To record sale of bonds.		

Note that the $98,400 reduction in the Bond Investments account is the sum of the balance at June 30, 19x4 ($98,200 in Exhibit 12-2) plus the $200 discount amortization recorded in the first August 31, 19x4, entry above.

Purchase between Interest Dates. Now assume that a company purchases bonds between interest dates at a premium. In this example, the company purchases a 9%, $10,000 bond on May 1, 19x6, for $10,800 plus accrued interest. The bond pays semiannual interest of 4.5% ($450) on June 30 and December 31 and matures at the end of 19x7 (20 months). The following entries would be required for 19x6:

19x6			
May 1	Bond Investments (A)	10,800	
	Interest Receivable (A)	300	
	Cash (A)		11,100
	To record purchase of bond plus accrued interest: $10,000 × .09 × 4/12 = $300.		
June 30	Cash (A)	450	
	Interest Receivable (A)		300
	Interest Income (R)		150
	To record receipt of six months of bond interest and two months of interest income.		
30	Interest Income (R)	80	
	Bond Investments (A)		80
	To amortize two months of bond premium on a straight-line basis: $800/20 months = $40.		
Dec. 31	Cash (A)	450	
	Interest Income (R)		450
	To record receipt of six months' interest.		
31	Interest Income (R)	240	
	Bond Investment (A)		240
	To amortize six months' bond premium on a straight-line basis. $40 × 6 = $240.		

As noted earlier, the assumption underlying accounting for long-term bond investments is that they will be held until they mature. Therefore, discounts and premiums are always amortized over the remaining life of the bonds. Cash interest, of course, is recorded as received, with the amount of interest income affected by the amortization of discounts or premiums as illustrated above.

LOWER-OF-COST-OR-MARKET (LCM) METHOD

Accountants use the **lower-of-cost-or-market (LCM) method** for all temporary investments in marketable equity securities plus those long-term investments in marketable equity securities of less than a 20% interest.[1] The LCM method is slightly different for temporary investments than for long-term investments. The basic concept, however, is the same: On the balance sheet, the total value of all marketable equity securities (**temporary** or **long term**) is reported at the lower of their **total** original cost or their **total** market value. The detailed procedures for temporary and long-term stock investments, which are reported separately, are discussed in this section.

LCM Method: Temporary Stock Investments

The lower-of-cost-or-market (LCM) method is used for **marketable equity securities** consisting of common stocks that are publicly traded on stock exchanges, thus the adjective "marketable" which indicates that they are easy to sell.[2] The cost of equity investments includes all costs necessary to acquire the asset (stocks), which normally includes the market price plus brokerage fees. Equity investments are classified as **temporary** if management **intends** to convert them to cash within one year (or the normal operating cycle, whichever is longer).

Using the LCM method, marketable equity securities are reported on the balance sheet at the lower of the portfolio's total cost or the total current market value. The LCM method results in a loss if the total market value drops below total cost as of a balance sheet date, but the LCM method does not permit a gain for market values in excess of actual cost. When total market value is less than total cost, a contra asset account (Allowance to Reduce Temporary Investments to Market Value) is used to reduce the balance sheet value of the portfolio below total cost. At the end of each accounting period, the total market value is compared to the total cost. If the allowance balance needs to be increased (credited), a loss (debit) is recorded; if the allowance balance needs to be decreased (debited), an unrealized revenue (i.e., Recovery of Unrealized Loss on Temporary Investments) is recorded. However, total Recovery of Unrealized Loss on Temporary Investments cannot exceed the beginning balance in the Allowance to Reduce Temporary Investments to Market account.

---

[1]For details of this requirement, see *FASB Statement No. 12,* "Accounting for Certain Marketable Securities" (Norwalk, Conn.: FASB, 1975).

[2]If the temporary investments in stocks are not readily marketable (e.g., stocks of closely held private corporations), the cost method should be used. However, it is unlikely that a temporary investment would be made in nonmarketable stocks since their conversion to cash could be difficult to achieve on a timely basis.

Objective 3
The lower-of-cost-or-market (LCM) method (used for all temporary investments in marketable equity securities plus long-term investments in marketable equity securities of less than a 20% interest).

To illustrate the LCM method for temporary investments in stock, assume Ritter Corporation, a calendar-year company, made the following purchases during 19x1:

Date	Acquired	Total Cost (Including Fees)
7/19	10 shares of MAX common stock at $25	$ 250
8/20	20 shares of ILCO common stock at $40. . . .	800
10/23	15 shares of ARCO common stock at $65 . . .	975
	Total cost of portfolio	$2,025

The entries to record these purchases would be:

19x1			
July 19	Temporary Investments—Stock (A).	250	
	Cash (A).		250
	To record purchase of stock.		
Aug. 20	Temporary Investments—Stock (A).	800	
	Cash (A).		800
	To record purchase of stock.		
Oct. 23	Temporary Investments—Stock (A).	975	
	Cash (A).		975
	To record purchase of stock.		

At the end of 19x1, the total portfolio cost is compared to the total market value of the stocks at December 31, 19x1:

Stocks	Original Cost	12/31/x1 Market Value	Difference if Total Cost Is More than Total Market
MAX.	$ 250	$ 350	
ILCO.	800	700	
ARCO	975	875	
Total portfolio.	$2,025	$1,925	$100

The LCM method requires the $2,025 balance in Temporary Investments—Stocks account be reduced by $100 ($2,025 − $1,925)—**the excess of cost over market value** as of December 31, 19x1. The adjusting entry would be:

19x1			
Dec. 31	Unrealized Loss on Temporary Investments (E)	100	
	Allowance to Reduce Temporary Investments to Market (XA)		100
	To reduce temporary investments to their LCM value.		

This year-end adjusting entry reduces income for the unrealized loss and increases the Allowance to Reduce Temporary Investments to Market contra asset account, thereby decreasing total assets. The $100 credit balance in the contra asset account will remain until the next accounting period when it must be reconsidered in relation to the **new** required balance in the allowance account, if any.

The LCM method has no effect on how dividends are recorded. If $300 in dividends were received during December of 19x1, they would be recorded as follows:

19x1			
Dec. 15	Cash (A)	300	
	Dividend Income (R)		300
	To record cash dividends received from temporary investments in stocks.		

The dividend income is reported on the income statement as an additional revenue item—interest and dividend income—while the unrealized loss of $100 is reported as a reduction in income (probably as a part of "Other gains and losses"). The partial balance sheet and income statement for Ritter would show:

Ritter Corporation
Partial Balance Sheet
December 31, 19x1

Assets:		
.		$ xxx
.		xxx
.		xxx
Temporary investments—stocks . . .	$2,025	
Less: Allowance to reduce temporary investments to market	100	1,925
.		xxx

Ritter Corporation
Partial Income Statement
For the Year Ended December 31, 19x1

Revenues and other income:	
Sales revenue.	$ xxx
Interest income	xxx
Dividend income	300
Expenses and other costs:	
.	xxx
.	xxx
Unrealized loss on temporary investments	100
.	xxx
.	xxx
Net income.	$ xxx

The adjusting entry made in applying the LCM method is only **required at the end of an accounting period.** The LCM method does not require any adjustments to the allowance account for sales or purchases of stocks but only requires evaluations and possible adjustment at the end of each accounting period (when other adjusting entries are also recorded). The LCM method may not be applied to temporary investments on an **individual** security basis.

Under the LCM method. adjusting entries made to the allowance account at the end of an accounting period are used to properly value the asset, temporary investments, in the balance sheet. The sale of the stocks is recorded as if no contra asset account existed. To illustrate using the data provided in the above example, assume that on May 10, 19x2, Ritter sold all 15 shares of ARCO that had originally cost $975, for $900 cash. The following entry would be recorded.

19x2			
May 10	Cash (A)	900	
	Loss on Temporary Investments (E).	75	
	Temporary Investments—Stocks (A)		975
	To record sale of ARCO stock.		

The decrease to the Temporary Investments—Stocks asset account is for the original cost of the ARCO stock, $975. The $100 balance in the Allowance to Reduce Temporary Investments to Market account is not affected by the sale of stock and is not reconsidered for possible adjustment until the end of the current accounting period. Assume that at the end of 19x2, Ritter has the following information about its portfolio of temporary stock investments:

Stock	*Original Cost*	*12/31/x2 Market Value*	*Difference if Total Cost Is More than Total Market*
MAX.	$ 250	$ 400	
ILCO.	800	725	
Total portfolio. . .	$1,050	$1,125	$0

The 19x2 year-end adjusting entry will eliminate the $100 balance in the allowance account since the total market value of the remaining temporary investments now exceeds the total cost at the end of the accounting period. The following adjusting entry is recorded to bring the net book value of investment back to the original cost:

19x2			
Dec. 31	Allowance to Reduce Temporary Investments to Market (XA)	100	
	Recovery of Unrealized Loss on Temporary Investments (R).		100
	To increase temporary investments to their LCM value.		

At the end of each accounting period, the allowance account is evaluated; it does not have any effect on the purchase or sale of stock or on the receipt of dividends. If total market exceeds total cost, the allowance account is eliminated, as done for Ritter at the end of 19x2.

Exhibit 12-3 summarizes the measurement and recording process for temporary marketable equity investments that use the LCM method. Note that **only** for the last two situations is the allowance account adjusted.

LCM Method: Long-Term Stock Investments

The LCM method is also required for long-term investments in marketable equity securities when the corporation ownership is less than 20%. However, unlike temporary investments where the LCM method reports unrealized losses on the income statement, the **unrealized losses on long-term LCM investments are disclosed as a contra stockholders' equity account** and **not** on the income statement. The reasoning here is that gains and losses will even out in the long run; therefore, they need not be reported in the income statement for long-term investments.

EXHIBIT 12-3

LCM Method: Temporary Investment in Marketable Equity Securities

Situation	*Entry to Be Required*
Purchase	Record at cost.
Receive dividend	Record cash and dividend income
Sell stock at a realized gain or realized loss	1. Record cash proceeds; 2. Reduce Temporary Investment account for the original cost of the stocks sold; and 3. If a **credit** is needed to balance the entry, record this difference as a **Realized Gain;** if a **debit** is needed to balance the entry, record it as a **Realized Loss.**
At the end of accounting period when total cost is greater than total market value	1. Make the balance in the allowance account equal to total cost less total market value of the stocks on hand; 2*a*. If a debit entry to the allowance account is needed to achieve this balance, record a **Recovery of Unrealized Loss** as the offsetting credit; or 2*b*. If a credit entry to the allowance account is needed to achieve this balance, record an **Unrealized Loss** as the offsetting debit.
At the end of accounting period when total cost is less than total market value	1. Make the balance in the allowance account equal to zero. 2. Offsetting credit (if any) is to a **Recovery of Unrealized Loss** account.

To illustrate the LCM method for long-term investments, assume that Sportex, Inc., holds the following long-term investments at the end of 19x2:

Stocks	*Original Cost*	*12/31/x2 Market Value*	*Difference if Total Cost Is More than Total Market*
Wilco common.	$ 7,320	$ 6,985	
Spear preferred	5,475	6,100	
DeVeaux common . . .	3,920	2,250	
Total portfolio	$16,715	$15,335	$1,380

At the end of 19x2, the market value of these stocks is $1,380 below cost. Let's also assume that before the 19x2 year-end adjustment, the credit balance in the Allowance to Reduce Long-Term Investments to Market account was $1,000. The following adjusting entry must be made at the end of 19x2:

19x2			
Dec. 31	Unrealized Loss on Long-Term Investments (XSE)	380	
	Allowance to Reduce Long-Term Investments to Market (XA)		380
	To increase allowance balance to $1,380.		

This entry is similar to the entry required for temporary investments using the LCM method except that the Unrealized Loss on Long-Term Investments account is a separate contra stockholders' equity account whose yearly change ($380 in 19x2 for Sportex) is reported as a component of stockholders' equity rather than on the income statement. Thus, except for the nature of and disclosure of the Unrealized Loss on Long-Term Investments account, the accounting methods are the same for long-term and temporary investments using the LCM method.

Sportex would report the following financial statement effects:

Sportex, Inc.
Partial Balance Sheets
As of December 31

	19x2	*19x1*
Long-term assets:		
Investments (at cost)	$ 16,715	$ 16,715
Allowance to reduce investments to current market value	(1,380)	(1,000)
	$ 15,335	$ 15,715
Land.	195,000	195,000
.	.	.
.	.	.
.	.	.
Stockholders' equity:		
Common stock (at par $5)	$4,800,000	$4,800,000
Unrealized loss on long-term investments . . .	(1,380)	(1,000)

Sportex would not report any effects on its income statement due to the LCM adjustments. However, any dividends received on these stocks would be included in the income statement as dividend income and any gains or loss on sales of individual stocks would be reported as realized on the income statement.

EQUITY METHOD

Accountants use the **equity method** whenever the investor has enough voting stock to **influence the operations of the investee.** Normally, this "influence" includes placing people on the investee's board of directors, hiring top managers, and other actions made possible by exercising ownership voting rights. In practice, such influence is usually assumed to exist if the investor owns between 20 and 50% of the investee's voting stock.[3] When an investor owns over 50% of an investee, the investor has a **controlling interest** in the investee.

The equity method records the purchase of an investment at the total cost incurred to acquire the securities. Beyond the date of purchase, the **Investments** asset account (also called Equity Investments or Long-Term Investments) is increased for the investor's proportional share of the investee's net income and decreased for dividends received from the investee. These equity procedures result in the investor increasing (decreasing) its recorded assets and reported net income for its proportional share of the investee's net income (loss) regardless of whether the investee paid any dividends to the investor.

[3]For more complete details concerning the equity method, see *APB Opinion No. 18,* "The Equity Method of Accounting for Investments in Common Stock" (New York: AICPA, 1971), or most intermediate accounting texts.

Objective 4
The equity method (used when the investor company has enough voting stock to influence the operations of the investee company).

To illustrate the equity method, assume that on January 1, 19x1, Logo Gifts, Inc., acquires a 40% interest in Stadium Foto by purchasing 40% of Stadium's common stock for $60,000 cash. On the date of acquisition, Stadium had the following balance sheet data:

Stadium Foto
Summarized Balance Sheet
January 1, 19x1

Assets		**Liabilities and Stockholders' Equity**	
Current assets:		Liabilities:	
Cash.	$ 14,000	Accounts payable	$ 35,000
Accounts receivable. . . .	86,000	Notes payable.	165,000
Lab supplies	65,000	Total liabilities	$200,000
Total current assets . .	$165,000		
Noncurrent assets:		Stockholders' equity:	
Equipment	185,000	Total stockholders' equity. .	150,000
Total assets	$350,000	Total liabilities and stockholders' equity	$350,000

Logo's purchase of 40% of Stadium's common stock outstanding for $60,000 makes Logo a 40% owner of Stadium Foto, and Logo records the investment as follows using the equity method:

19x1			
Jan. 1	Equity Investments (A)	60,000	
	Cash (A)		60,000
	To record purchase of Stadium stock.		

Stadium does not record an entry to reflect the change in its stockholders.

Now assume that Stadium reports a 19x1 net income of $40,000 and pays its stockholders $25,000 in dividends on December 31, 19x1. Logo, a 40% owner, makes the following entries:

19x1			
Dec. 31	Equity Investments (A)	16,000	
	Investment Income (R)		16,000
	To record 40% of investee's net income for 19x1.		
31	Cash (A).	10,000	
	Equity Investments (A)		10,000
	To record 40% of investee's dividends.		

In the first entry, Logo increases its assets and income by $16,000 to reflect Stadium's $40,000 net income in 19x1, 40% of which is Logo's. In the second entry, Logo records the receipt of some of Stadium's income in the form of cash dividends. Because these dividends are a distribution of Stadium's income, Logo reduces the Investment in Subsidiary asset account and increases the Cash asset account by $10,000, which is Logo's 40% share of Stadium's cash dividends. Note that Logo's $16,000 investment income is **not** affected by the dividend payment and remains at $16,000 with or without cash dividends. The receipt of a cash dividend merely requires a reclassification from the Equity Investments asset account to the Cash asset account. Once the $16,000 Investment Income account is closed out to Retained Earnings, the ending balance sheet effect can be reconciled as follows:

Net Effects in Balance Sheet Accounts Caused by Equity Method Following Purchase

Assets:		Liabilities:	
Cash	+$10,000		
Equity investments	+ 6,000		
		Stockholders' equity:	
		Retained earnings	+$16,000

Exhibit 12-4 gives the Logo and Stadium example illustrating the equity method and shows how the change in the investment is reported in the investor's balance sheet. Note that the balance in the investor's asset equals the investee's net assets (stockholders' equity) times the percent of ownership.

The Logo and Stadium example of the equity method is based on two assumptions:

1. The purchase price paid for a 40% interest in Stadium Foto is equal to 40% of Stadium Foto's book value. In other words, book value equals market value in this case.
2. No business transactions occurred between Logo and Stadium during 19x2.

Although these two assumptions are usually unrealistic in practice, they make it possible to consider the fundamental aspects of equity method investments at a basic level. Intermediate and advanced accounting textbooks discuss the details of equity method investments.

CONSOLIDATION METHOD—CONSOLIDATED FINANCIAL STATEMENTS

Objective 5
The consolidation method (used when the investor company owns over 50% of the investee company and controls its operations).

Investor companies owning over 50% of an investee can exercise their voting rights to **control the operations of the investee.** These voting rights can determine the members of the board of directors, the top officers and managers of the investee company, declaration of dividends, and other top-level business decisions. Between financial reporting dates, the investor entity will normally account for all equity investments in excess of 20% by using the equity method; however, the investor must report all investments in excess of a 50% interest on a consolidated basis.[4] The following sections illustrate the basic principles of consolidation.

An investor company with a controlling interest is usually called a **parent** company, while the investee company is often called a **subsidiary** or "sub." Although the parent and subsidiary remain as two separate legal entities, they are accounted for, using the consolidation techniques described below, as one economic entity. The owners of the parent company are in control of the resources of both companies, even though they might not own all of the subsidiary's stock.

[4]This requirement for consolidation is imposed and described in more detail in *Financial Accounting Standards Board Statement No. 94,* "Consolidation of All Majority-Owned Subsidiaries" (Norwalk, Conn.: FASB, 1987), which modifies the basic principles of consolidation as required by *APB Opinion No. 16,* "Business Combinations" (New York: AICPA, 1970).

EXHIBIT 12-4

Equity Method Investments

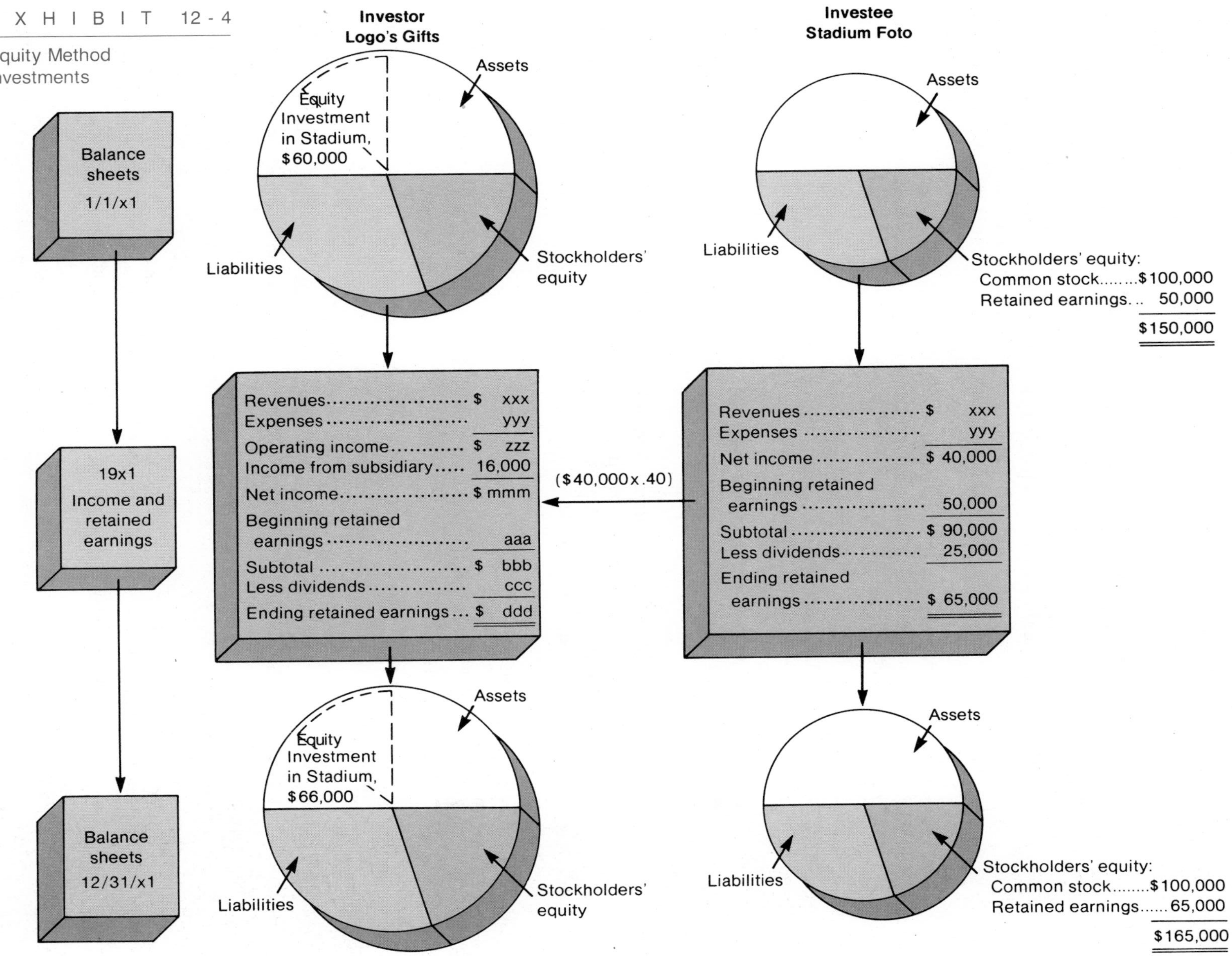

Balance sheets 1/1/x1
19x1 Income and retained earnings
Balance sheets 12/31/x1
Investor Logo's Gifts
Equity Investment in Stadium, $60,000
Assets
Liabilities
Stockholders' equity
Revenues .... $ xxx
Expenses .... yyy
Operating income .... $ zzz
Income from subsidiary 16,000
Net income .... $ mmm
Beginning retained earnings .... aaa
Subtotal .... $ bbb
Less dividends ccc
Ending retained earnings ... $ ddd
Equity Investment in Stadium, $66,000
Assets
Liabilities
Stockholders' equity
Investee Stadium Foto
Assets
Liabilities
Stockholders' equity:
Common stock........$100,000
Retained earnings... 50,000
$150,000
($40,000 x .40)
Revenues .... $ xxx
Expenses .... yyy
Net income .... $ 40,000
Beginning retained earnings 50,000
Subtotal .... $ 90,000
Less dividends 25,000
Ending retained earnings .... $ 65,000
Assets
Liabilities
Stockholders' equity:
Common stock........$100,000
Retained earnings...... 65,000
$165,000

To indicate the unique relationship of parent and subsidiary, accountants prepare **consolidated financial statements** with the aid of a **consolidation worksheet** in order to combine the independent financial statements of the parent (investor) and the subsidiary (investee), both of whom remain as separate entities with separate journals, ledgers, and so on. These consolidation worksheets are not a formal part of the separate accounting systems of either the investor or investee companies but are schedules that draw data from the separate entities and calculate the adjustments necessary to prepare consolidated financial statements. This separate nature of investor and investee companies enables them to report separately and on a consolidated basis. The investment in the subsidiary appears like an equity investment on the separate books of the parent company prior to consolidation. Upon consolidation, the single Investment in Subsidiary account is eliminated and replaced with the specific assets and liabilities of the subsidiary.

Simple Situation: Purchase 100% of Subsidiary

To illustrate the consolidation process, we will examine the following example: Book value of acquired net assets equals market value; purchase 100% of subsidiary. This example will enable us to look at the fundamentals of consolidated financial statements needed to understand the financial reports of the thousands of large publicly held companies with consolidated subsidiaries.

Consolidation at Date of Acquisition. Assume that on December 31, 19x1, Big, Inc., acquires a 100% interest in Kidco by purchasing all of Kidco's stock from its owners for $70,000. Just prior to the purchase, the following balance sheet data are available:

Big, Inc.*
Balance Sheet
December 31, 19x1

Assets	
Cash	$100,000
Other assets	500,000
Total assets	$600,000
Liabilities and Stockholders' Equity	
Liabilities:	
All liabilities	$300,000
Stockholders' equity:	
Common stock	$200,000
Retained earnings	100,000
Total stockholders' equity	$300,000
Total liabilities and stockholders' equity	$600,000

Kidco*
Balance Sheet
December 31, 19x1

Assets	
Other assets	$100,000
Total assets	$100,000
Liabilities and Stockholders' Equity	
Liabilities:	
All liabilities	$ 30,000
Stockholders' equity:	
Common stock	$ 50,000
Retained earnings	20,000
Total stockholders' equity	$ 70,000
Total liabilities and stockholders' equity	$100,000

*The detailed description of the assets and liabilities of the balance sheets are omitted here for simplicity of illustration.

The purchase by Big should be recorded on its books as:

19x1			
Dec. 31	Investment in Kidco (A)	70,000	
	Cash (A)		70,000
	To record purchase of 100% of Kidco stock.		

After Big purchased Kidco, the **unconsolidated** balance sheet of Big and the balance sheet of Kidco would appear as follows:

Big, Inc.
Unconsolidated Balance Sheet
December 31, 19x1

Assets

Cash	$ 30,000
Investment in Kidco	70,000
Other assets	500,000
Total assets	$600,000

Liabilities and Stockholders' Equity

Liabilities:	
All liabilities	$300,000
Stockholders' equity:	
Common stock	$200,000
Retained earnings	100,000
Total stockholders' equity . .	$300,000
Total liabilities and stockholders' equity	$600,000

Kidco
Balance Sheet
December 31, 19x1

Assets

Other assets	$100,000
Total assets	$100,000

Liabilities and Stockholders' Equity

Liabilities:	
All liabilities	$ 30,000
Stockholders' equity:	
Common stock	$ 50,000
Retained earnings	20,000
Total stockholders' equity . .	$ 70,000
Total liabilities and stockholders' equity	$100,000

Note that Kidco's balance sheet is **not** affected by the purchase since only the names of Kidco's stockholders have changed. Also, at this point the financial statements of Big **look no different than they would if the equity method were used.**

Next, assume that Big wants to prepare a consolidated balance sheet as of December 31, 19x1. This requires the following entry on the **consolidation worksheet:**

Consolidation Worksheet Entry

19x1			
Dec. 31	Common Stock (Kidco)	50,000	
	Retained Earnings (Kidco)	20,000	
	Investment in Kidco (Big)		70,000
	To eliminate intercompany accounts.		

The **worksheet entry** is NOT made in the journal or ledger of Big or Kidco but is only made on a worksheet to facilitate the consolidation of the financial statements. The debits to the Common Stock and Retained Earnings accounts on Kidco's balance sheet should leave these accounts with a zero balance (for consolidation worksheet purposes only). The credit to the Investment in Kidco asset account on Big's balance sheet also leaves it with a zero balance. This consolidation worksheet entry enables the balance sheets of the two separate

EXHIBIT 12-5

Consolidated Balance Sheet

Big, Inc.
Consolidated Balance Sheet
December 31, 19x1

Assets

Cash	$ 30,000
Other assets	600,000
Total assets	$630,000

Liabilities and Stockholders' Equity

Liabilities:	
All liabilities	$330,000
Stockholders' equity:	
Common stock	$200,000
Retained earnings	100,000
Total stockholders' equity	$300,000
Total liabilities and stockholders' equity	$630,000

companies to be added together (combined) to form a consolidated balance sheet at the end of 19x1.

Understand that the purpose of consolidation worksheet entries is to eliminate any duplication that might otherwise result when the financial statements of the parent are added together (combined) with those of the subsidiary. Such consolidation worksheet entries are sometimes referred to as **elimination entries.**

Next, you add the remaining assets, liabilities, and stockholders' equity accounts of Big and Kidco together as shown in Exhibit 12-5.

This entire consolidation process can also be illustrated using a consolidation worksheet as shown in Exhibit 12-6. Whether the worksheet entry or the formal worksheet is used, the consolidated balance sheet of Big at the end of 19x1 includes all the assets, liabilities, and stockholders' equity of the combined consolidated entity. The consolidation process replaces the single equity method asset account, Investment in Kidco, of $70,000 found on Big's **unconsolidated** balance sheet with all of Kidco's assets ($100,000) and liabilities ($30,000).

Accounting for 100% Owned Subsidiary after Acquisition. To continue the Big and Kidco example, let's examine how Kidco's operations after the date of acquisition affect the consolidation process. Assume the 19x2 operating results and balance sheet effects for Big and Kidco are as shown in Exhibit 12-7. Note that in 19x2, Big had a $50,000 operating income from its operations plus $30,000 income from its 100% interest in Kidco's operations — a total of $80,000 net income. The $30,000 net income from Big's investment in Kidco:

1. Increased Big's Investment in Kidco balance at December 31, 19x2, by $10,000 (from $70,000 to $80,000) for Kidco's 19x2 net income that remained in Kidco ($30,000 earnings less $20,000 cash dividends).
2. Increased Big's cash at December 31, 19x2, by $20,000 for the dividends from Kidco.

EXHIBIT 12-6

Worksheet for Consolidated Balance Sheet as of Date of Acquisition

	Separate Balance Sheets		Worksheet Elimination Entries		Big, Inc. Consolidated Balance Sheet 12/31/x1
	Big, Inc.*	Kidco	Debit	Credit	
Assets:					
Cash.	30,000				30,000
Investment in Kidco . .	70,000			70,000	
Other assets	500,000	100,000			600,000
Total assets	600,000	100,000			630,000
Liabilities:					
All liabilities.	300,000	30,000			330,000
Stockholders' equity:					
Common stock	200,000	50,000	50,000		200,000
Retained earnings. . .	100,000	20,000	20,000		100,000
Total liabilities and stockholders' equity. .	600,000	100,000	70,000	70,000	630,000

*Unconsolidated.

The $50,000 net income from Big's own operations is assumed to have increased Big's other assets by $50,000.[5] The unconsolidated balance sheet of Big at the end of 19x2 (lower left part of Exhibit 12-7) reports the effects of Big's and Kidco's 19x2 operations. However, Big's income from Kidco's operations are reported as a $30,000 single-line item in Big's unconsolidated 19x2 income statement, and Big's unconsolidated balance sheet shows Kidco's net assets, which are owned by Big, as a single asset of $80,000. Because the equity method reports all of the investee's net assets owned by the investor as a single asset account, and all of the investee's net income owned by the investor as a single line item in the income statement, **the equity method is sometimes referred to as "one-line consolidation."** Big's 19x2 entries to account for Kidco are the same as those used for equity investments.

Journal Entries—Big's Books

19x2			
Dec. 31	Investment in Kidco (A)	30,000	
	Income from Kidco (R)		30,000
	To record share of Kidco's 19x2 earnings.		
31	Cash (A)	20,000	
	Investment in Kidco (A)		20,000
	To record share of Kidco's dividends.		

[5]For illustration purposes, we assume liabilities remain unchanged for both parent and sub during 19x2. Also we **assume** that the cash dividends are the only source of cash for the parent, Big. These assumptions are not important, but simply help to follow the nature of changes in the balance sheets.

EXHIBIT 12-7

Effect of Operating Results for 19x2 on Unconsolidated Statements

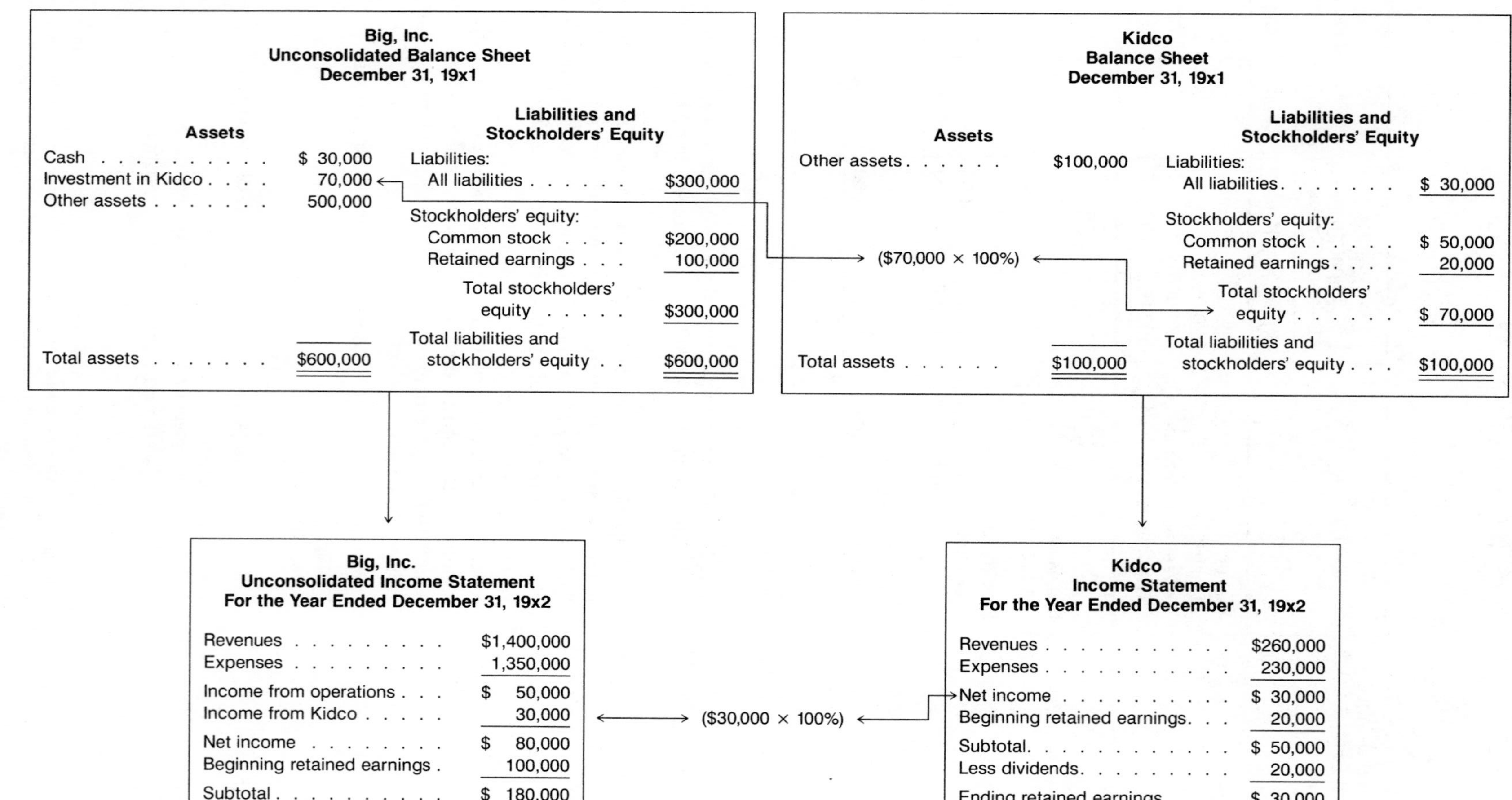

Big, Inc.
Unconsolidated Balance Sheet
December 31, 19x1

Assets		Liabilities and Stockholders' Equity	
Cash	$ 30,000	Liabilities:	
Investment in Kidco	70,000	All liabilities	$300,000
Other assets	500,000	Stockholders' equity:	
		Common stock	$200,000
		Retained earnings	100,000
		Total stockholders' equity	$300,000
Total assets	$600,000	Total liabilities and stockholders' equity	$600,000

Kidco
Balance Sheet
December 31, 19x1

Assets		Liabilities and Stockholders' Equity	
Other assets	$100,000	Liabilities:	
		All liabilities	$ 30,000
		Stockholders' equity:	
		Common stock	$ 50,000
		Retained earnings	20,000
		Total stockholders' equity	$ 70,000
Total assets	$100,000	Total liabilities and stockholders' equity	$100,000

($70,000 × 100%)

Big, Inc.
Unconsolidated Income Statement
For the Year Ended December 31, 19x2

Revenues	$1,400,000
Expenses	1,350,000
Income from operations	$ 50,000
Income from Kidco	30,000
Net income	$ 80,000
Beginning retained earnings	100,000
Subtotal	$ 180,000
Less dividends	0
Ending retained earnings	$ 180,000

($30,000 × 100%)

Kidco
Income Statement
For the Year Ended December 31, 19x2

Revenues	$260,000
Expenses	230,000
Net income	$ 30,000
Beginning retained earnings	20,000
Subtotal	$ 50,000
Less dividends	20,000
Ending retained earnings	$ 30,000

Big, Inc.
Unconsolidated Balance Sheet
December 31, 19x2

Assets		Liabilities and Stockholders' Equity	
Cash	$ 50,000*	Liabilities:	
Investment in Kidco	80,000[†]	All liabilities	$300,000
Other assets	550,000[‡]	Stockholders' equity:	
		Common stock	$200,000
		Retained earnings	180,000
		Total stockholders' equity	$380,000
Total assets	$680,000	Total liabilities and stockholders' equity	$680,000

*$30,000 beginning balance + $20,000 cash dividend from Kidco.
[†] $70,000 beginning balance + $30,000 Kidco net income − $20,000 cash dividend.
[‡] $500,000 beginning balance + $50,000 parent's separate net income.

Kidco
Balance Sheet
December 31, 19x2

Assets		Liabilities and Stockholders' Equity	
Other assets	$110,000	Liabilities:	
		All liabilities	$ 30,000
		Stockholders' equity:	
		Common stock	$ 50,000
($80,000 × 100%)		Retained earnings	30,000
		Total stockholders' equity	$ 80,000
Total assets	$110,000	Total liabilities and stockholders' equity	$110,000

Preparing the consolidated balance sheet for 19x2 requires the following consolidation worksheet entry:

Consolidation Worksheet Entry

19x2			
Dec. 31	Common Stock (Kidco)	50,000	
	Retained Earnings (Kidco)	30,000	
	Investment in Kidco (Big)		80,000
	To eliminate intercompany accounts for consolidation.		

Exhibit 12-8 shows the complete consolidation worksheet. Note that the total assets for the consolidated company ($710,000) are **not** the same as the sum of the two separate companies' total assets ($680,000 + $110,000 = $790,000). The **net** assets of Kidco ($80,000) at the end of 19x2 are already in Big's unconsolidated balance sheet. The consolidation process merely replaces the single equity method asset of $80,000 (representing Big's share of Kidco's net assets) with all of Kidco's assets ($110,000) and liabilities ($30,000). Also, note that the stockholders' equity in Big's *unconsolidated* balance sheet is the same as the *consolidated* stockholders' equity (stock, $200,000, and retained earnings, $180,000).

To prepare a consolidated income statement, you apply the same concepts used to create the consolidated balance sheet—**replace the single account with**

EXHIBIT 12-8

Case A: Worksheet for Consolidated Balance Sheet as of December 31, 19x2

	Separate Balance Sheets		Worksheet Elimination Entries		Big, Inc. Consolidated Balance Sheet 12/31/x1
	Big, Inc.*	Kidco	Debit	Credit	
Assets:					
Cash.	50,000				50,000
Investment in Kidco . .	80,000			80,000	
Other assets	550,000	110,000			660,000
Total assets	680,000	110,000			710,000
Liabilities:					
All liabilities.	300,000	30,000			330,000
Stockholders' equity:					
Common stock	200,000	50,000	50,000		200,000
Retained earnings. . .	180,000	30,000	30,000		180,000
Total liabilities and stockholders' equity. .	680,000	110,000	80,000	80,000	710,000

*Unconsolidated.

the detailed accounts. For Big's consolidated income statement, replace the income from Kidco with all of Kidco's income statement accounts, as follows:

	Unconsolidated Big	+	*Kidco*	=	*Consolidated Big*
Revenues	$1,400,000		$260,000		$1,660,000
Expenses	– 1,350,000		– 230,000		– 1,580,000
Net income	$ 50,000		$ 30,000		$ 80,000
Income from Kidco	30,000		– 30,000		0
Net income	$ 80,000		$ 0		$ 80,000

The preceding example illustrates the basic principles of consolidation. Its purpose is to provide a fundamental understanding of what it means to report on a consolidated versus an unconsolidated basis. Unconsolidated financial statements report subsidiary investments as a single asset account on the parent company's unconsolidated balance sheet, and a single net revenue or income item on the parent's unconsolidated income statement. This type of presentation in **unconsolidated** financial statements **looks** the same for both equity investments (20 to 50% interest) and subsidiaries where there is a controlling interest (over 50% interest). However, equity investments (those between 20 and 50% ownership) are not subject to the consolidation process.

Disclosure Implications. In examining financial statements it is helpful to know whether the reporting entity is made up of equity investments and/or consolidated subsidiaries. If a reporting entity includes consolidated subsidiaries, the following should hold:

1. The titles to the financial statements should include the word *consolidated.*
2. The footnotes should include the names and/or descriptions of the consolidated subsidiaries. This information would include the percentage of ownership in consolidated subsidiaries.

If a reporting entity includes equity investments, the following should hold:

1. The income statement should include income from the equity investee(s) as a separate line item to reflect the parent's share in net income from equity (or "unconsolidated") subsidiaries.
2. The balance sheet should include a single asset amount reflecting the parent's share in net assets of the equity investee(s).
3. The footnotes to the financial statements should identify all equity investees and the net asset investment in each.

These features should help you to identify the important components of the reporting entity. A reporting entity with no equity investees or consolidated subsidiaries is generally going to be easier to evaluate than one which is made up of many equity investees and consolidated subsidiaries, particularly when these investments are in unrelated lines of business. To evaluate reporting entities with stock investments in excess of 20% in other unrelated companies first requires breaking the reporting entity down into components that are similar (i.e., electric appliances, aerospace, and so on). Understanding the characteristics of equity investments and consolidated subsidiaries described above is an important first step in evaluating reporting entities with significant investment interests in other companies with unrelated operations.

There are many other aspects of equity investments and consolidation not illustrated in this chapter. In Appendix 12A, we expand on the example above by illustrating two additional common features of consolidations: (1) when the subsidiary is less than 100% (but over 50%) owned and there exists a minority interest; and (2) when the purchase price does not equal the book value of the subsidiary. In Appendix 12B, we explain the difference between the purchase method and the pooling of interests method of accounting for investments in consolidated subsidiaries. These two appendixes may be omitted for those who are not interested in more details concerning consolidations. Accounting for consolidated investees is much more complex than what we illustrate in this text. Advanced accounting texts review the material included in this introduction to consolidations and cover the subject in much greater detail.

SUMMARY

In this chapter we examined the fundamental nature of investments in bonds, stocks, and other securities. For accounting purposes, the primary factors are the term of the investment, either temporary or long term, and the type of investment. Exhibit 12-9 outlines the various types of investments discussed in the chapter and their appropriate accounting method.

Temporary investments normally consist of bonds, notes, and stocks. Since management intends to convert temporary investments to cash in the short term, these investments must be readily marketable. Also, they should be low-risk investments since it would be poor management to invest idle cash at a loss. Usually, temporary investments are a minor current asset and are often reported in the balance sheet with cash under the heading "Cash and temporary investments" or some similar title.

Long-term investments are generally more important than temporary investments in terms of both their purpose and relative size. The purpose of long-term investments may be to gain influence in another entity or to build up a liquid asset for future cash needs. If the corporations's goal is to gain influence over another entity, common stock must be purchased; but if the corporation's goal is long-term planning for future cash requirements, any type of marketable security could be purchased.

Financial statement users must understand the fundamentals of alternative accounting methods for investments to evaluate the performance of an entity and its subsidiaries. For example, an equity investment will report investment income equal to the parent's share of the equity investee's earnings whether or not these earnings are distributed by the investee in the form of dividends. On the other hand, an LCM investment will report investment income equal to the dividends declared but will not recognize the investor's share of the investee's net income. If an investor owned an interest in a growth company with rapidly increasing sales and net income but with no dividends, the difference in that investor's net income between a 19% interest and a 21% interest in the growth company's stock could be substantial.

EXHIBIT 12-9

Summary of Investments

	Type of investment	Correct accounting method	Income statement effects
Temporary investments	a. Notes, CDs.	Cost method	Interest income
	b. Bonds.	Cost method	Interest income
	c. Stocks—nonmarketable.	Cost method	Dividend income
	d. Stocks—marketable.	LCM method	Dividend income Unrealized gains or losses
Long-term investments	a. Notes, CDs.	Cost method	Interest income
	b. Bonds.	Cost method	Interest income
	c. Stocks—nonmarketable.	Cost method	Dividend income
	d. Stocks—marketable with ownership below 20%.	LCM method	Dividend income
	e. Voting stocks, 20-50% ownership.	Equity method	Pro rata share of investor's net income (with adjustments and eliminations)
	f. Voting stocks, over 50% ownership.	Consolidation	Pro rata share of investor's net income (with adjustments and eliminations)

Investors, creditors, managers, and other users must have a basic understanding of the effects of the alternative methods used to account for investments if they are to properly compare and evaluate financial statements of business entities. The four methods of accounting for investments—cost, lower of cost or market, equity, and consolidation—introduced in this chapter provide a basis for comparing and evaluating the performance of complex business entities reported in published financial statements.

DEMONSTRATION EXERCISE

Critchett Company has the following information regarding its investments during 19x2: 19x2:

a. Purchases as a temporary investment 50 shares of common stock of the Alexander Corporation at \$80 per share. Alexander pays a \$1.50 per share dividend. The market price per share at the end of the year is \$62.

b. Purchases 30% of the common stock of Christine's Fashions for \$50,000 cash. Christine's has net income of \$90,000 and declares total dividends of \$50,000 during 19x2.

c. Purchases as a temporary investment 100 shares of common stock of the Zacher Company at $42 per share. No dividends are paid during the year. The market price per share at the end of the year is $45.

d. Sells 75 shares of Cleary common stock for $36 per share. These shares were purchased as a temporary investment in 19x1 at $30 per share. They were the only temporary investment Crichett held during 19x1.

e. Purchases a 100% interest in HiTech, Inc., for $810,000. HiTech's fair market value equals its book value. During the year HiTech has net income of $150,000 and declares dividends of $40,000.

f. The balance in Crichett's Allowance to Reduce Temporary Investments to Market at December 31, 19x1, is a $900 credit.

Required:

1. Prepare the journal entries, including year-end adjusting entries, the Crichett Company makes during the year regarding its investments.
2. Prepare the worksheet entries Crichett makes to consolidate its investment in HiTech at acquisition and at December 31, 19x1, year-end. Use a Stockholders' Equity account instead of Common Stock and Retained Earnings for HiTech.

Solution:

Requirement 1:

a.	Temporary Investments (A)	4,000	
	Cash (A)		4,000
	To record investment in Alexander.		
	Cash (A)	75	
	Dividend Income (R)		75
	To record dividends received.		
b.	Investment in Christine's (A)	50,000	
	Cash (A)		50,000
	To record investment in Christine's Fashions.		
	Investment in Christine's (A)	27,000	
	Investment Income (R)		27,000
	To record net income of Christine's.		
	Cash (A)	15,000	
	Investment in Christine's (A)		15,000
	To record dividends received.		
c.	Temporary Investments (A)	4,200	
	Cash (A)		4,200
	To record investment in Zacher.		
d.	Cash (A)	2,700	
	Temporary Investments (A)		2,250
	Gain on Sale of Temporary Investment (R)		450
	To record sale of Cleary stock.		
e.	Investment in HiTech (A)	810,000	
	Cash (A)		810,000
	To record investment in HiTech, Inc.		

Investment in HiTech (A)	150,000	
Investment Income (R)		150,000
To record net income of HiTech.		
Cash (A)	40,000	
Investment in HiTech (A)		40,000
To record dividends received.		
f. Allowance to Reduce Temporary Investments to Market (XA)	300	
Recovery of Unrealized Loss on Temporary Investments (E)		300
To record temporary investments at their LCM value: \$900 − \$600 = \$300.*		

*Total portfolio market value at December 31, 19x1, was \$900 less than cost. At December 31, 19x2, the carrying value of the temporary investments must be adjusted upward by \$300 since total portfolio value is only \$600 less than cost as can be seen from the following table:

	Original Cost	*12/31/x2 Market Value*
Alexander . . .	\$4,000	\$3,100
Zacher.	4,200	4,500
	\$8,200	\$7,600

Requirement 2:

Worksheet entry at date of acquisition:

Stockholders' Equity (HiTech)	810,000	
Investment in HiTech		810,000

Worksheet entry at December 31, 19x2:

Stockholders' Equity (HiTech)	920,000	
Investment in HiTech		920,000

APPENDIX 12A

Additional Aspects of Consolidation

This appendix builds on the example illustrated in the chapter, explaining two additional common aspects encountered in consolidations:

a. What happens if less than 100% of the subsidiary is acquired by the parent as an investment?

b. What happens if the purchase price is greater than the book value of the assets acquired?

If a parent acquires less than 100% of a subsidiary, the stock not owned by the parent is called the **minority interest** in the subsidiary. The minority interest could be between 1% and 49% for a consolidated subsidiary. In the example below we illustrate how the minority interest case is like the example in the chapter in that 100% of the subsidiary's net assets and net income are added into the parent's financial statements. The difference is that the minority interest's share of the net assets is reported like an additional liability in the consolidated balance sheet, and the minority interest's share of net income is reported like an additional expense in the consolidated income statement.

The example which follows will also illustrate how to account for a consolidation when the price paid exceeds the book value of the net assets purchased by the parent. This difference between the value of the net assets on the parent's books and the value of the net assets on the separate books of the subsidiary is not unusual and will require the parent to make adjusting journal entries for this difference in accounting for the net income and net assets of the subsidiary before consolidation takes place.

Objective 6
Additional aspects of consolidation.

To illustrate these two additional features of consolidated investments, consider again the acquisition of Kidco by Big, Inc., December 31, 19x1. Now assume Big pays $72,000 cash for a 90% interest in Kidco by acquiring 90% of Kidco's stock in the open market. Just prior to the acquisition, their book values are:

Big, Inc.*
Balance Sheet
December 31, 19x1

Assets	
Cash	$100,000
Other assets	500,000
Total assets	$600,000
Liabilities and Stockholders' Equity	
Liabilities:	
All liabilities	$300,000
Stockholders' equity:	
Common stock	$200,000
Retained earnings	100,000
Total stockholders' equity	$300,000
Total liabilities and stockholders' equity	$600,000

Kidco
Balance Sheet
December 31, 19x1

Assets	
Other assets	$100,000
Total assets	$100,000
Liabilities and Stockholders' Equity	
Liabilities:	
All liabilities	$ 30,000
Stockholders' equity:	
Common stock	$ 50,000
Retained earnings	20,000
Total stockholders' equity	$ 70,000
Total liabilities and stockholders' equity	$100,000

*The detailed description of the assets and liabilities of the balance sheets are omitted here for simplicity of illustration.

Why would Big pay $72,000 for a 90% interest when 100% of the net book value of Kidco is only $70,000? Two reasons could be that Kidco's net assets are undervalued (book value is less than fair market value) and/or Kidco has unrecorded assets (goodwill) for which Big is willing to pay.[6]

When a parent acquires a controlling interest in a subsidiary, the parent must determine the fair value of all purchased assets and liabilities. Some of the assets may be carried on the books of the subsidiary at less than current value and some at more. The books of the subsidiary, however, remain at their original book values. Once the parent has determined the fair value of the recorded assets (and liabilities) of the subsidiary, any excess of the price paid over the fair value of the assets acquired is attributable to goodwill.

In this example assume that Big's purchase price is above Kidco's book value because Big believes (1) Kidco has goodwill and (2) all of Kidco's recorded assets are already recorded at their fair market value. Big views Kidco's fair market value balance sheet as follows:

Kidco
Fair Market Value Balance Sheet
December 31, 19x1

Assets		**Liabilities and Stockholders' Equity**	
Other assets	$100,000	Liabilities:	
Goodwill	10,000	All liabilities	$ 30,000
		Stockholders' equity:	
		Common stock	$ 50,000
		Retained earnings	30,000*
		Total stockholders' equity	$ 80,000
Total assets	$110,000	Total liabilities and stockholders' equity	$110,000

*Includes $10,000 for value of goodwill.

Although Kidco's actual (historical cost) balance sheet does **not** show goodwill (and only has $20,000 retained earnings), Big is willing to pay $72,000 for a 90% interest in Kidco (Kidco's $80,000 assumed net assets × 90% = $72,000) based on **Big's own separate assessment of the value of Kidco.** The entry to record the 90% purchase of Kidco would be:

Entry on Big's Journal

19x1			
Dec. 31	Investment in Kidco (A)	72,000	
	Cash (A)		72,000
	To record purchase of 90% of Kidco's stock.		

No entry is made on Kidco's books to reflect goodwill or the purchase by Big. The necessary consolidation worksheet entry to achieve the consolidated balance sheet at the date of purchase would be:

[6]Note that most companies' stocks sell in the market in excess of their book value per share because of these two reasons. As a result, it is uncommon to see a company acquired for a price that is at or below book value.

Consolidation Worksheet Entry

19x1			
Dec. 31	Common Stock (Kidco)	50,000	
	Retained Earnings (Kidco)	20,000	
	Goodwill (New)	9,000	
	Investment in Kidco (Big)		72,000
	Minority Interest (New).		7,000
	To eliminate intercompany accounts and record goodwill and minority interest in the consolidated balance sheet.		

The consolidation worksheet entry eliminates the intercompany accounts:

Common Stock (Kidco)	$50,000
Retained Earnings (Kidco) . . .	20,000
Investment in Kidco (Big) . . .	72,000

The entry establishes two new accounts that did **not** appear in the separate (unconsolidated) financial statements:

An asset—Goodwill	$9,000
A liability—Minority Interest . .	7,000

The asset account, Goodwill, represents 90% of the goodwill that Big believes exists in Kidco, which is the portion actually paid for by Big.[7] (By paying more than book value for Kidco, Big provided real evidence of the existence of this asset that was not recorded on Kidco's books.) Goodwill will be reported as an asset on Big's consolidated balance sheet. The minority interest account represents the 10% of the net assets of Kidco (at their book value) which are not owned by Big. Since Big will report 100% of the assets of Kidco (including $9,000 of goodwill) in Big's consolidated balance sheet, the credit balance of the Minority Interest account serves like a contra net asset account in reducing the consolidated net assets of Big. The **Minority Interest account** looks like a liability and is typically reported as a separate item between liabilities and stockholders' equity in consolidated balance sheets. Minority interest should equal the net book value of the subsidiary times the percentage of minority ownership, even when the fair value of the subsidiary exceeds its book value.

Exhibit 12A-1 illustrates the worksheet of the separate and consolidated balance sheet of Big and Kidco at December 31, 19x1.

Next, assume the 19x2 operations of Big and Kidco were the same as in the chapter, with Big reporting separate net income of $50,000 and Kidco reporting net income of $30,000 and dividends of $20,000. Recall from Chapter 8 that goodwill must be amortized over not longer than 40 years. Assume that Big amortizes goodwill over 20 years in this example. Annual goodwill amortization would be $450 per year ($9,000/20 years = $450 per year). In 19x2, Big records the following journal entries to account for its investment in Kidco:

Entries on Big's Journal

19x2			
Dec. 31	Investment in Kidco (A)	27,000	
	Income from Kidco (R)		27,000
	To record 90% of Kidco's 19x2 net income.		

[7]For a review of goodwill, refer to Chapter 8, pp. 435-36.

EXHIBIT 12A-1

Worksheet for Consolidated Balance Sheet

	Separate Balance Sheets		Worksheet Elimination Entries		Big, Inc. Consolidated Balance Sheet 12/31/x2
	Big, Inc.*	Kidco	Debit	Credit	
Assets:					
Cash	28,000				28,000
Investment in Kidco . .	72,000			72,000	—
Other assets	500,000	100,000			600,000
Goodwill	—	—	9,000		9,000
Total assets.	600,000	100,000			637,000
Liabilities:					
All liabilities	300,000	30,000			330,000
Minority interest	—	—		7,000	7,000
Stockholders' equity:					
Common stock	200,000	50,000	50,000		200,000
Retained earnings . . .	100,000	20,000	20,000		100,000
Total liabilities and stockholders' equity . .	600,000	100,000	79,000	79,000	637,000

*Unconsolidated.

Dec. 31	Cash (A)	18,000	
	Investment in Kidco (A)		18,000
	To record 90% of Kidco's 19x2 dividends.		
31	Income from Kidco (R)	450	
	Investment in Kidco (A)		450
	To amortize 1/20 of 90% of Kidco's goodwill: \$9,000/20 years = \$450.		

The third entry is an equity method adjustment made by Big because Kidco's net income for 19x2 (\$30,000) does not include amortization of Kidco's goodwill. Since goodwill is not recognized on the separate books of Kidco but was recognized by Big in its investment account (as evidenced from Big's payment of \$72,000 for a 90% interest), Big must adjust Kidco's net income for the purchased goodwill. Recall that Big's investment in Kidco (\$72,000) includes \$9,000 for purchased goodwill. To be consistent in its investment account, Big must adjust the 19x2 net income of Kidco for the amortization of the purchased goodwill. The consolidation worksheet entries for the end of 19x2 would be:

Consolidation Worksheet Entry

19x2			
Dec. 31	Common Stock (Kidco)	50,000	
	Retained Earnings (Kidco)	30,000	
	Goodwill (new)	8,550	
	Investment in Kidco (Big)		80,550
	Minority Interest (New).		8,000
	To eliminate intercompany accounts and record goodwill and minority interest in the consolidated balance sheet.		

Exhibit 12A-2 provides a complete consolidation worksheet and consolidated income statement for the end of 19x2. Note that although this example illustrates several complexities, the basic principles illustrated earlier in the chapter still apply. The single asset on Big's unconsolidated statements ($80,550 as of the end of 19x2) is being eliminated and replaced with all of Kidco's assets and liabilities, including the unrecorded assets represented by goodwill. Also, Big's stockholders' equity is the same before and after consolidation. Consolidation does not change the substance of the financial reports—only the form of the reports is altered.

EXHIBIT 12A-2

Worksheet for Consolidated Balance Sheet as of December 31, 19x2

Sheet	Separate Balance Sheets		Worksheet Elimination Entries		Big, Inc. Consolidated Balance Sheet 12/31/x2
	Big, Inc.*	Kidco	Debit	Credit	
Assets:					
Cash	46,000				46,000
Investment in Kidco	80,550			80,550	
Other assets	550,000	110,000			660,000
Goodwill			8,550		8,550
Total assets	676,550	110,000			714,550
Liabilities:					
All liabilities	300,000	30,000			330,000
Minority interest	—	—		8,000	8,000
Stockholders' equity:					
Common stock	200,000	50,000	50,000		200,000
Retained earnings	176,550	30,000	30,000		176,550
Total liabilities and stockholders' equity	676,550	110,000	88,550	88,550	714,550

*Unconsolidated.

Big, Inc.
Consolidated Income Statement
For the Year Ended December 31, 19x2

Revenues	$1,660,000
Expenses	1,580,000
Amortization of goodwill	450
	$ 79,550
Less minority interest	3,000*
Net income	$ 76,550

*Kidco's net income	$30,000
Minority share	× .10
Minority net income	$3,000

APPENDIX 12B

Pooling of Interests

The examples illustrated in the chapter and Appendix 12A have all assumed that the parent company was **purchasing** an interest in the subsidiary by paying cash for the stock of the subsidiary. This is the most common form of acquisition known as the **purchase method.**

In the purchase method, the parent records the investment at cost. If the cost of the subsidiary is greater than its book value, the recorded value of the subsidiary may be "written up" above its book value in the parent's unconsolidated statements and in the consolidated statements as illustrated in Appendix 12A. This write-up could result in the addition of "new" asset accounts (such as goodwill) that were not on the subsidiary's books or the revaluation of existing book values reported by the subsidiary. As a result, the parent revalues the assets of the subsidiary at the date of acquisition even though the assets remain at their book values on the subsidiary's books.

Objective 7
Pooling of interests.

In addition to the purchase method of acquisition, an alternative form of acquisition occurs that is called **pooling of interests.** The basic concept supporting the pooling method is that the two entities are "pooling" assets and liabilities; and, therefore, revaluation is not necessary. What evidence can support the contention that the two entities are pooling resources rather than one buying the other? The most common indicator is the nature of the exchange transaction. Purchase transactions are primarily for cash and pooling transactions are primarily exchanges of stock. In general then, the pooling of interests method is used in cases where 90% or more of the subsidiary is acquired by exchanging stock or other securities of the parent for the subsidiary's stock.[8] The main effect of pooling is the ignoring of the fair value of the stock (given or received). Accounting for the parent's investment in the subsidiary is based only on the subsidiary's book value. Therefore, the two balance sheets are combined with no adjustments for goodwill or fair values.

If we assumed the same facts as in the example illustrated in the chapter except that (1) the market value of Kidco was something greater than book value and (2) Big had acquired Kidco with Big common stock rather than for cash, then the chapter illustration would be an example of the pooling of interests method. Thus, in *the pooling of interests method, the book values of the subsidiary are added to the book values of the parent in the consolidation process, regardless of whether the fair value of the subsidiary is greater (or less) than book value*.

In practice, the use of pooling of interests method is rare because it is difficult to convince 90% of the stockholders of a public company to exchange their stock for the stock (or other securities) of another company. Such acquisitions usually require the agreement of the boards of directors of both companies, which makes the acquisition a "friendly takeover." In recent years, the number

[8]The specific rules governing the use of the pooling method are beyond the scope of this text. These rules and the accounting techniques used to create pooled statements can be found in advanced accounting texts.

of companies using the pooling of interests method of accounting for acquisitions has been about 10% of all companies reporting acquisitions.[9] Cash purchases of securities are much more common than pooling of interests.

In evaluating investments, it is important to know whether the purchase or pooling method is used to account for a company's consolidated subsidiaries. In general, the pooling method results in lower consolidated total assets, which results in a higher return on assets ratio, all else being equal. The pooling method will also normally result in higher consolidated profits (e.g., no recognition of asset value in excess of their book values) than the purchase method, all else being equal. This also results in a better ratio of net income to net assets (or return on equity) for the pooling method, all else being equal. However, these differences are based strictly on the method of consolidation, not real economic differences. As a result, it is necessary for investors to attempt to estimate the differences between purchase and pooling methods when comparing investment alternatives that use different methods for consolidation purposes.

KEY TERMS

Amortized cost method. Used when companies acquire long-term investments with stated interest rates and maturity amounts at a premium or a discount and the premium or discount must be amortized over the remaining life of the security.

Consolidated financial statements. Financial statements that present the parent and subsidiary as one entity.

Consolidation worksheets. Aids that are not a formal part of the separate accounting systems of either the investor or investee companies but are schedules that draw data from the separate entities and calculate the adjustments necessary to prepare consolidated financial statements.

Controlling interest. Occurs when the investor owns over 50% of an investee. Disclosures of investees that are controlled are reported using principles of consolidation.

Cost method. Accounting method applied to all temporary and long-term nonequity investments such as bonds, notes, and CDs; depending on holding period of investments, accountants use variations of the cost method.

Elimination entries. Consolidation worksheet entries used to eliminate duplication in the parent's and subsidiary's formal accounting records.

Equity investments. Investments of between 20 and 50% of another company's voting stocks.

Equity method. Accounting method used for equity securities when the investor has enough voting stock to influence the operations of the investee, usually between 20 and 50%.

Investments. Assets acquired by a company with the expectation of receiving interest or dividends and/or price appreciation.

[9] See *Accounting Trends & Techniques 1988* (New York: AICPA, 1988).

Long-term investments. Investments longer than one year.

Lower-of-cost-or-market method. Accounting method used for all temporary investments in marketable equity securities plus those long-term investments in marketable equity securities of less than a 20% interest.

Marketable equity securities. Stocks publicly traded on stock exchanges.

Nonequity investments. Bonds, notes, and CDs—investments other than voting stocks of publicly traded companies.

Parent. Investor in a subsidiary.

Subsidiary. Investee company.

Temporary investment. Investment that management intends to keep less than one year or operating cycle, whichever is longer.

APPENDIX KEY TERMS

Minority Interest account. Similar to an "allowance" account. The minority shareholders' interest in the net assets of the investee firm.

Pooling of interests. Alternative form of recording an acquisition that records the acquired company at book value if 90% or more of the subsidiary is acquired by exchanging stock or other securities of the parent for the subsidiary's stock.

Purchase method. Form of recording an acquisition where the parent pays cash for the subsidiary and records the fair market value of the sub on its books.

SYNONYMS

Certificates of deposit; CDs.

Corporate notes; commercial paper.

Ease of conversion back to cash; liquidity.

Elimination entries; consolidation worksheet entries.

Equity investee; unconsolidated subsidiary.

Investment income; equity investment income; income in unconsolidated subsidiaries.

Investments; equity investments; long-term investments.

Parent; investor company.

Subsidiary; sub; investee company.

U.S. Treasury notes; T bills.

QUESTIONS

1. What are the primary business purposes for investments?
2. What are three features desired for temporary investments of idle cash?
3. What types of investments are best suited as temporary investments?
4. What types of investments are best suited as long-term investments?
5. What accounting method is used for temporary investments in bonds and notes?

6. What accounting method is used for temporary investments in marketable securities?
7. When is the only time that an entry is made to the Allowance to Reduce Temporary Investments to Market account? Explain.
8. When is the LCM method used for long-term investments?
9. How does the LCM method for long-term investments differ from its use for temporary investments?
10. What method is used to account for long-term investments in bonds? What is the assumed holding period for these investments?
11. When is the equity method used to account for investments?
12. How do earnings of an equity method investee affect the earnings of the investor?
13. How do cash dividends received from an equity method investee affect the earnings of the investor?
14. When is the consolidation method used for investments?
15. What is the impact of subsidiary earnings on the parent's unconsolidated balance sheet and earnings statement?
16. How does the consolidation process eliminate the parent's asset account, Investment in Subsidiary, in order to prepare consolidated financial statements?
17. What is the effect of the consolidation process on the parent's unconsolidated owners' equity section of the balance sheet?
18. What effect does the consolidation process have on the formal journals and ledgers of the parent? The subsidiary?
19. What effect do consolidation worksheet entries have on the formal journals and ledgers of the parent and the subsidiary?

APPENDIX QUESTIONS

20. When a parent acquires less than a 100% investment in a subsidiary, what new accounts (not found in the separate unconsolidated financial statements of the parent or the subsidiary) are found in the consolidated financial statements? What is the purpose of these accounts?
21. When a parent pays more than book value for a subsidiary, what effect does it have on the subsidiary's separate (unconsolidated) financial statements?
22. What is a pooling of interests?
23. How does the pooling of interests method differ from the purchase method?

EXERCISES

EXERCISE 12-1

L.O. 2

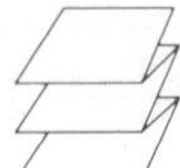

Cost Method—Temporary Investments

Butler Corporation purchased a U.S. Treasury bill for $97,000 plus accrued interest on June 1, 19x1. The T bill pays semiannual interest at the rate of 8% per year (4% semiannually) on June 30 and December 31. The face (maturity) value of the T bill is $100,000, and the maturity date is December 31, 19x6. Butler holds the T bill until January 31, 19x2, and then sells it for $97,300 plus accrued interest.

Required: (Round to nearest dollar.)
Record the entries necessary to account for this investment on Butler's books from the date of purchase to the date of sale.

EXERCISE 12-2
L.O. 2

Cost Method—Temporary Investments

Chartex Corporation purchased General Boaters Corporation bonds on May 1, 19x4, for $53,800 including accrued interest. The bonds have a face value of $50,000, pay interest at the rate of 9% per year, with semiannual interest payments made on July 1 and January 1 each year. The bonds mature on January 1, 19x7. Chartex Corporation held the bonds as a temporary investment until March 15, 19x5, when they were sold for $53,900 including accrued interest. Chartex has a December 31 year-end.

Required: (Round answers to nearest dollar.)
Record all of the journal entries necessary to account for Chartex's bond investment from the date of purchase to the date of sale.

EXERCISE 12-3
L.O. 2

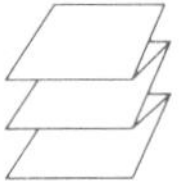

Cost Method—Long Term

Whalen, Inc., purchased $150,000 face value of 8% corporate bonds on May 1, 19x1, for $138,800 cash plus accrued interest. The bonds pay interest semiannually on June 30 and December 31 and mature on December 31, 19x5. Whalen accounts for this investment using the amortized cost method with straight-line amortization of the discount.

Required: (Round to nearest dollar.)

1. Record any necessary journal entries for 19x1 to account for this investment.
2. Prepare the bond amortization table for the remaining life of the bond.

EXERCISE 12-4
L.O. 2

Cost Method—Long Term

Hurd Corporation purchased $200,000 face value 10% bonds on July 1, 19x1, for $212,000. The bonds pay semiannual interest on June 30 and December 31 and mature on December 31, 19x4.

Required: (Round answers to the nearest dollar.)

1. Assuming Hurd uses straight-line amortization on this long-term investment, record the necessary entries for 19x1.
2. Prepare the amortization table for the bonds assuming they are held to maturity.
3. Assume Hurd uses the effective-interest (present value) amortization method as illustrated in Appendix 10B and that the effective annual interest rate is 8%. Record the necessary entries for 19x1 and prepare the amortization table assuming the bonds are held to maturity.

EXERCISE 12-5
L.O. 2

Long-Term Bond Investments

Madden Corporation began investing in high-grade corporate bonds in 19x2 as long-term investments for financing future expansion. On July 1, 19x4, Madden paid $139,798 cash for Star Corporation 10% bonds which had a face value of $150,000 and paid semiannual interest on June 30 and December 31. The bonds mature on December 31, 19x8.

Required:

1. Prepare a bond amortization table based on straight-line amortization of the bond discount or premium.
2. Record the entries required from the date of purchase to July 1, 19x5.
3. *(Optional)* Assume the effective interest on the bonds is 12%. Repeat requirements 1 and 2 above using the effective-interest method of amortizing the discount or premium.

EXERCISE 12-6
L.O. 2, 3

Temporary Investments

CENBO, Inc., purchased equity securities of ABC and XYZ during 19x1. All securities were properly classified as short term. The number of shares, purchase prices, and market prices at December 31, 19x1, are shown below:

Company	*Number of Shares*	*Purchase Price per Share*	*12/31/x1 Market Price per Share*
ABC.	1,500	$105	$110
XYZ.	400	80	50

During 19x2, CENBO, Inc., sold the 1,500 shares of ABC for $115 and purchased 1,000 shares of HIJ for $45 per share cash. The information on the portfolio held at December 31, 19x2, is as follows:

Company	*Number of Shares*	*Purchase Price per Share*	*12/31/x2 Market Price per Share*
XYZ.	400	$80	$82
HIJ	1,000	45	30

Required:
Record all journal entries for 19x1 and 19x2 related to marketable equity securities, including any year-end entries that may be necessary.

EXERCISE 12-7
L.O. 2

Temporary Investments

Marsten, Inc., uses idle cash to invest in stocks as temporary investments. At the start of 19x2, Marsten's investments were as follows:

Stock	*Number of shares*	*Price per Share*	
		Original	*12/31/x1*
General Mills.	100	$ 45.50	$ 39.75
IBM.	100	132.00	109.75
Reebok	250	14.75	15.25

During 19x2, the following events took place:

a. Sold 100 shares of Reebok for $16 per share.
b. Sold 100 shares of IBM for $125 per share.
c. Sold 100 shares of General Mills for $43 per share.
d. Purchased 100 shares of Ford for $52 per share.
e. Purchased 400 shares of Detroit Edison for $17.50 per share.
f. Purchased 200 shares of Apple Computer for $47.50 per share.
g. Received $150 in Ford dividends.
h. Received $185 in IBM dividends.

The market values of stocks held at December 31, 19x2, were:

Reebok	$14.00 per share
Ford.	54.00 per share
Detroit Edison	16.00 per share
Apple Computer	49.50 per share

Required:
Record all journal entries for 19x2 related to Marsten's temporary investments in common stock. Include any year-end adjusting entries that may be necessary.

EXERCISE 12-8
L.O. 3

Long-Term Investments

At the end of its fiscal year, the Sunshine Corporation's unadjusted trial balance showed a credit balance of $24,000 in the Allowance to Reduce Long-Term Investments to Market account. Sunshine's long-term investment portfolio at the end of the year had an original cost of $170,000 and a year-end market value of $160,000. Based on this information, prepare Sunshine's adjusting entry related to its long-term investments valuation.

EXERCISE 12-9
L.O. 3

Long-Term Stock Investments

Masten, Inc., holds several stocks of other companies as long-term investments. At the end of 19x4, the total cost of these stocks exceeded their market value by $4,850. Masten did not have any sales or purchases of long-term stock investments during 19x5. At the end of 19x5, the following data are reported by Masten's accountant.

	December 31, 19x5		
Stock	*Original Cost*	*Market Value*	*19x5 Cash Dividend*
Zerox	$13,850	$16,225	$850
Campbell	15,735	13,975	150
Rockwell	12,950	11,115	225

Required:
Prepare any entries required by Masten, Inc., for 19x5.

EXERCISE 12-10
L.O. 4

Equity Method (CPA Adapted)

1. Hysen, Inc., owns 40% of the outstanding stock of Legander Company. During 19x9, Hysen received a $4,000 cash dividend from Legander. What effect did this dividend have on Hysen's 19x9 financial statements?
   a. Increased total assets.
   b. Decreased total assets.
   c. Increased income.
   d. Decreased the investment account.
2. Slayton, Inc., owns a 40% interest in Johnson Corporation. During the calendar year 19x4, Johnson had net income of $100,000 and paid dividends of $10,000. Slayton mistakenly recorded these transactions using the cost method rather than the equity method of accounting. What effect would this have on (1) the Long-Term Investment in Johnson account, (2) net income, and (3) retained earnings, respectively?
   a. Understate 1, overstate 2, overstate 3.
   b. Overstate 1, understate 2, understate 3.
   c. Overstate 1, overstate 2, overstate 3.
   d. Understate 1, understate 2, understate 3.
3. A parent corporation that uses the equity method of accounting for its investment in a 40% owned subsidiary, which earned $20,000 and paid $5,000 in dividends, made the following entries:

Investment in Subsidiary (A)	8,000	
Earnings in Unconsolidated Subsidiary (R)		8,000
Cash (A)	2,000	
Dividend Revenue (R)		2,000

   What effect will these entries have on the parent's balance sheet?
   a. Financial position will be fairly stated.
   b. Investment in subsidiary will be overstated; retained earnings, understated.
   c. Investment in subsidiary will be understated; retained earnings, understated.
   d. Investment in subsidiary will be overstated; retained earnings, overstated.

4. On January 1, 19x6, Schonfeld Corporation acquired, as a long-term investment, a 40% common stock interest in Action Company for $130,000. On that date, Action had net assets of $325,000. During 19x6, Action reported net income of $60,000 and declared and paid cash dividends of $15,000. What is the amount of income that Schonfeld can report from this investment for the calendar year 19x6?
   a. $6,000.
   b. $18,000.
   c. $23,750.
   d. $24,000.

EXERCISE 12-11
L.O. 4

Equity Method

P Company purchased 30% of the outstanding stock of S Company on December 31, 19x1, for $1 million cash. In 19x2, S Company reported net income of $80,000. In 19x2, S Company declared and paid dividends of $10,000.

Required:

1. Record the journal entries P Company makes in recording its interest in S Company.
2. Determine the balance on P's books of its Investment in S Company at the end of 19x2.

EXERCISE 12-12
L.O. 3, 4

LCM and Equity Methods

The following information pertains to the long-term investments of the Lullo Company purchased on January 1, 19x4:

Investment	*Number of Shares Purchased*	*Percentage of Total Outstanding Shares of Company*	*Cost*	*Market Price per Share at 12/31/x4*	*Earnings of Company for 19x4*
Maize common stock . . .	10,000	15	$25,000	$2	$75,000
Blue common stock	6,000	30	60,000	9	50,000

Neither Maize nor Blue declared dividends on its common stock in 19x4. Determine the carrying value the Lullo Company will report to its total long-term investment account on its December 31, 19x4, balance sheet.

EXERCISE 12-13
L.O. 4

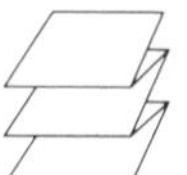

Equity Method

On January 1, 19x1, the Reece Corporation purchased, as a long-term investment, 10,000 shares of the outstanding common stock of the Luke Corporation at $60 per share. Both the Reece Corporation and Luke Corporation fiscal years end on December 31, 19x1. During 19x1, the following events occurred with respect to the Luke Corporation:

Net income reported for 19x1	$40,000
Dividends declared and paid (per share)	.75
Market price per share of common stock on December 31, 19x1	56.00
Number of outstanding shares during all of 19x1 for Luke Corporation	40,000

Required:

1. Prepare the journal entry to record the stock purchase.
2. Prepare the journal entry to recognize the Luke Corporation's net income for 19x1.
3. Prepare the journal entry to record the cash dividend declared and paid by the Luke Corporation.
4. Prepare any required adjusting entries at December 31, 19x1.

EXERCISE 12-14
L.O. 3, 4

Long-Term Investments

On January 1, 19xx, the Denver Corporation purchased, as long-term investments, 8% of the voting stock of the Green Corporation for $200,000 and 35% of the voting stock of the Blue Corporation for $400,000. During 19xx, Green Corporation had net income of $80,000 and paid dividends of $50,000. During 19xx, the Blue Corporation had net income of $40,000 and paid dividends of $20,000. The market value of neither investment declined during the year.

Required:
Prepare Denver's journal entry(ies) pertaining to its investments in the Green Corporation and the Blue Corporation.

EXERCISE 12-15
L.O. 2–5

Methods of Recording Investments

Fill in the blanks.

1. Under this method, the purchase of the investments are recorded at cost: ________.
2. Under this method, it is not appropriate for the investment to be consolidated in preparing the financial statements: ________________________.
3. Under this method, year-end adjustments to an asset account are made if the market value of the investment account is below cost: ________________________.
4. Under this method, the investor records as investment revenue the net income of the investee company multiplied by the investor's ownership percentage in the investee: ________________________________.

EXERCISE 12-16
L.O. 5

Consolidation

BOT, Inc., acquired 100% of Top Corporation's common stock for $1,500,000 on January 1, 19x1. Top Corporation had the following activity and facts for 19x1.

	1/1/x1
Assets	$2,800,000
Liabilities	1,300,000
Stockholders' equity	1,500,000
19x1 net income	500,000
19x1 dividends declared and paid	200,000

Required:
1. Prepare the journal entries in general journal form that BOT will make during 19x1 regarding its interest in Top Corporation.
2. Prepare the consolidation worksheet entry BOT will make to consolidate Top Corporation at the end of 19x1.

EXERCISE 12-17

L.O. 5

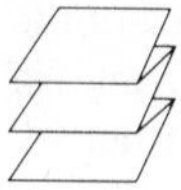

Consolidation at Acquisition

Bates Corporation acquired 100% of Terry, Inc., common stock for $148 million cash on January 1, 19x3. The separate balance sheets of the two companies just prior to the purchase by Bates were as follows:

Bates Corporation
Balance Sheet
December 31, 19x2
(in millions)

Assets		Liabilities and Stockholders' Equity	
Cash	$153	Liabilities:	
Accounts receivable	98	Accounts payable	$108
Inventory	86	Notes payable	250
Plant assets (net)	218	Other liabilities	37
Investments	12	Total liabilities	$395
		Stockholders' equity:	
		Common stock	$100
		Retained earnings	72
		Total stockholders' equity	$172
Total assets	$567	Total liabilities and stockholders' equity	$567

Terry, Inc.
Balance Sheet
December 31, 19x2
(in millions)

Assets		Liabilities and Stockholders' Equity	
Cash	$ 11	Liabilities:	
Accounts receivable	101	Accounts payable	$162
Inventory	112	Taxes payable	30
Plant assets (net)	249	Advances from customers	11
Investments	108	Notes payable	230
		Total liabilities	$433
		Stockholders' equity:	
		Common stock	$ 42
		Retained earnings	106
		Total stockholders' equity	$148
Total assets	$581	Total liabilities and stockholders' equity	$581

Required:

1. Record the journal entry to account for the purchase by Bates and the consolidation worksheet entry on January 1, 19x3.
2. Prepare a consolidated balance sheet on January 1, 19x3.

APPENDIX EXERCISES

EXERCISE 12-18
L.O. 5

Consolidation—Minority Interest

Wright, Inc., owns 80% of April Corporation. The following data are available:

Wright, Inc.
Balance Sheets (Unconsolidated)
December 31

	19x7	*19x6*
Assets		
Cash	$ 196,000	$ 166,000
Investment in April	504,000	384,000
Other assets	9,800,000	9,450,000
Total assets	$10,500,000	$10,000,000
Liabilities and Stockholders' Equity		
Liabilities	$ 2,700,000	$ 2,700,000
Common stock	2,300,000	2,300,000
Retained earnings	5,500,000	5,000,000
Total liabilities and stockholders' equity	$10,500,000	$10,000,000

April Corporation
Balance Sheets
December 31

	19x7	*19x6*
Assets	$850,000	$700,000
Liabilities and Stockholders' Equity		
Liabilities	$220,000	$220,000
Common stock	280,000	280,000
Retained earnings	350,000	200,000
Total liabilities and stockholders' equity	$850,000	$700,000

No dividends were declared by either company in 19x7.

Required:

1. Prepare the consolidation worksheet entry at December 31, 19x7, needed to prepare the consolidated balance sheets.
2. Prepare the consolidated balance sheet for Wright, Inc., as of December 31, 19x7.
3. What was Wright's consolidated net income for 19x7?

EXERCISE 12-19
L.O. 5

Annual Report Disclosures

Anderson Company discloses the following items on its consolidated income statement:

Total net income	$12,889,000
Less minority interest	480,000
Consolidated net income . . .	$12,409,000

Required:

1. If the percentage of ownership by Anderson is 60%, what was the subsidiary's separate net income? Show computations.
2. What reference to minority interest would you expect to see on Anderson's consolidated balance sheet?

PROBLEMS

PROBLEM 12-1
L.O. 2, 3

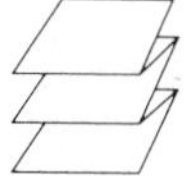

LCM Method—Temporary Investments

The December 31, 19x7, balance sheet for Farm Products, Inc., reported the following data for their temporary investments in stocks:

Temporary investments (at original cost) . . .	$87,500	
Less: Allowance to reduce temporary investment to market value	4,900	$82,600

During 19x8, Farm Products received $2,400 in dividends on these stocks. Also, on June 30, 19x8, Farm Products sold stock originally costing $58,000 for $63,000 cash. On December 15, 19x8, Farm Products acquired stock for $49,000 cash to be held as a temporary investment.

Required:

1. Record dividends for 19x8.
2. Record the sale of stock on June 30, 19x8.
3. Record the purchase of stock on December 15, 19x8.
4. Assume the total market value of the temporary investments at December 31, 19x8, is $77,500. Record any necessary adjusting entry to account for this fact.
5. Ignore (4) above. Assume instead that the total year-end market value is $72,000. Record any necessary adjusting entry at year-end.
6. Ignore (4) and (5) above. Assume instead that the total year-end market value is $80,000. Record any necessary entry at year-end.

PROBLEM 12-2
L.O. 2, 3

LCM Method—Temporary Investments

The Ski Shop started in business on July 1, 19x3, and has a June 30 year-end. The company invests idle cash in the off season in marketable equity securities. Each year the stocks are sold as cash is needed, or acquired when there is idle cash. The investment performance over each of the first three years of operations are summarized as follows:

Fiscal Year	*Gain (Loss) on Sale of Stock*	*Dividends Declared and Received*	*Total Original Cost*	*Total Market Value at Year-End*
19x3–x4	$ 7,350	$ 650	$ 91,500	$ 89,350
19x4–x5	(2,100)	1,975	105,600	102,100
19x5–x6	4,950	860	87,950	91,400

Required:

1. Record the necessary adjusting entries at the end of each of the first three years in accordance with the lower-of-cost-or-market method.
2. Illustrate how the asset account would appear in each of the three year-end balance sheets.
3. Compute the total effect on net income for each year (separately) as a result of the investing activities summarized above.

PROBLEM 12-3
L.O. 2, 3

Temporary Investments—Stocks and Bonds

The Wagman Corporation reported the following balance sheet account balances pertaining to their temporary investments on December 31, 19x4. Wagman has no long-term investments in stocks or bonds.

FMC Bonds—face value $100,000, 12% semiannual interest, mature on 9/30/x9	$101,425
JRT Common Stock—4,000 shares, original cost $33	132,000
Cort, Inc., Common Stock—5,000 shares original cost $15	75,000
Allowance to Reduce Temporary Investments to Market Value	1,050
Accrued Interest Receivable—FMC Bonds	3,000

Wagman uses straight-line amortization on bond discounts and premiums. The following activities took place during 19x5 concerning Wagman's temporary investments:

19x5	
Jan. 28	Received cash dividends of $1.25 per share on JRT common.
Feb. 20	Received cash dividends of $0.50 per share on Cort common.
Mar. 31	Received semiannual bond interest on FMC bonds.
Apr. 18	Purchased 5,000 shares of ICC common stock for $25 per share including brokerage fee.
May 5	Sold 2,000 shares of JRT common for $35 per share cash.
June 30	Sold half of the FMC bonds ($50,000 face value) for $54,000 cash.
July 18	Received cash dividends of $0.50 per share on Cort common and $1.25 per share on JRT common.
Aug. 10	Sold 5,000 shares of Cort, Inc., for $13.50 per share cash.
Sept. 30	Received semiannual bond interest on FMC bonds.
Oct. 31	Purchased $75,000 face value TRW bonds for $73,635 plus accrued interest. The bonds mature at the end of 19x8 and pay 10% interest semiannually on June 30 and December 31.
Nov. 8	Received an additional 200 shares of JRT common as a result of a 10% stock dividend.
Dec. 31	Dividends declared, but unpaid, at year-end were:

JRT common:	$1.25 per share
ICC common:	$1.50 per share

The market values of the stocks at year-end were:

JRT common:	$32.00 per share
ICC common:	$24.50 per share

Required:

1. Record the journal entries necessary to account for the transactions and related adjusting entries for the year 19x5 on Wagman's books.

2. Determine the balance in all balance sheet accounts pertaining to Wagman's investments at December 31, 19x5.
3. Determine the total income or loss from Wagman's investment activities to be reported in the 19x5 income statement by source (e.g., interest, dividends, gains and losses on sale of stocks and bonds, unrealized gain or loss on temporary investments).

PROBLEM 12-4
L.O. 2

Bond Investment—Long Term

On December 31, 19x2, Investor Corporation acquired as a long-term investment $500,000 maturity value bonds of Debt, Inc., for 104.32% of face value. The bonds mature at the end of 19x8 and pay interest on June 30 and December 31 each year at an annual rate of 12%. Investor Corporation's year ends on September 30 each year. Investor uses straight-line amortization on all bond investments.

Required:
1. Record the bond purchase by Investor Corporation.
2. Record the entries for Investor Corporation for 19x3 and 19x4.
3. Assume Investor Corporation sold one half of these bonds on January 1, 19x5, for 104% of maturity value. Record the sale.
4. Assume instead that Investor acquired the bonds as a temporary investment rather than as a long-term investment. Record the entries for 19x3 and 19x4 to account for the bonds.
5. Again assuming the investment in bonds is temporary, record the sale of one half of the bonds on January 1, 19x5, for 104% of maturity value.

PROBLEM 12-5
L.O. 2

Bond Investment—Long Term

On January 1, 19x3, KMI, Inc., acquired GM bonds with a maturity value of $500,000 as a long-term investment. The bonds mature at the end of 19x9 and pay 10% interest on a semiannual basis, with payments made each June 30 and December 31. KMI paid $453,525 for the bonds, providing them with an effective interest rate of 12%.

Required: (Round amounts to nearest dollar.)
1. Record the purchase of the bond by KMI.
2. Record the entries for KMI's bond investment for 19x3 and 19x4. Use straight-line amortization for the bond discount.
3. *(Optional)* Record the entries for KMI's bond investment for 19x3 and 19x4. Use the effective-interest method to amortize the bond discount.

PROBLEM 12-6
L.O. 3, 4

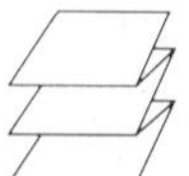

Long-Term Investments

On January 2, 19x4, Big Company acquired some of the total 10,000 outstanding voting common shares of Small Corporation as a long-term investment. The annual accounting period of each company is December 31.

The following events occurred:

Alternative 1:

19x4

Jan.	2	Big purchased 1,000 shares of Small stock at $14 per share.
Dec.	15	Small declared a dividend of $1.50 per share, payable January 15, 19x5.
	30	Big learned that Small would report earnings for 19x4 in the amount of $10,000.
	31	The market price of Small's stock was $12 per share.

Alternative 2:
All of the facts are the same as in Alternative 1 except that on January 2, Big purchased 3,000 shares of Small (instead of 1,000 shares).

Required:
Prepare the journal entries for the above transactions in general journal form for the Big Company under each alternative. Consider each alternative separately.

PROBLEM 12-7
L.O. 3

LCM Method—Temporary/Long-Term Investments

The following data are reported for the Harried Corporation:

	December 31		
	19x8	19x7	19x6
Temporary investments in stocks (at cost)	$68,300	$73,500	$54,200
Less: Allowance to reduce temporary investment to market	1,100	6,800	3,350
Temporary investments in stocks (at market)	$67,200	$66,700	$50,850

Before 19x6, Harried had no temporary investments in stocks. Over the period 19x6 to 19x8 many purchases and sales of stocks held as temporary investments have occurred, and dividends have been received each year.

Required:
1. Prepare the year-end adjusting entry for each of the three years based on the data provided.
2. If the Harried investments in stock had been long term instead of temporary, and the LCM method were still appropriate, how would your answer to part 1 above differ?

PROBLEM 12-8
L.O. 2–4

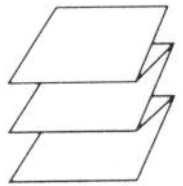

Comparison of Cost and Equity Methods

Serious Corporation acquired a 40% interest in Supplier Company for $10 million in cash at the end of 19x1. During 19x2 Supplier Company reported net income of $6 million and paid cash dividends of $2 million.

Required:
1. Report the effect on Serious' assets, liabilities, stockholders' equity, and net income for 19x2 assuming Serious used the cost method. Ignore income taxes.
2. Repeat requirement 1 above assuming Serious uses the equity method.
3. Repeat requirements 1 and 2 above assuming the facts as given *except* that no cash dividends were paid by Supplier in 19x2.

PROBLEM 12-9
L.O. 2–4

Long-Term Investments: LCM/Equity

Rokport, Inc., acquired 200,000 shares of Raybok stock for $50 per share on January 1, 19x8, as its only long-term investment in stock. The following data concern the Raybok investment for 19x8 and 19x9:

	December 31 Market Price per Share	Reported Net Income (Net Loss)	Dividends Declared and Paid
19x8	$48	$ (5,500,000)	None
19x9	53	15,140,000	$5,000,000

Required:

1. Assume that Raybok had 2 million shares of stock outstanding throughout 19x8 and 19x9. Record any entries needed to account for Rokport's investment in Raybok during 19x8 and 19x9 using the appropriate accounting method.
2. Assume instead that Raybock had 800,000 shares of stock outstanding through 19x8 and 19x9. Record any entries needed to account for Rokport's investment in Raybok during 19x8 and 19x9 using the appropriate accounting method.

PROBLEM 12-10
L.O. 4

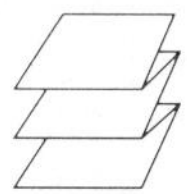

Equity Method

On January 2, 19x1, Major Corporation purchased 20,000 shares of Minor Corporation at $30 per share. During 19x1, Minor had net income of $500,000 and declared and paid dividends of $50,000. During 19x2, Minor had net income of $400,000 and declared and paid dividends of $60,000. On January 2, 19x3, Major sold its investment in Minor at $32 per share.

Required:
Prepare all journal entries Major will make regarding its investment in Minor Corporation assuming Minor has 50,000 shares of common stock issued and outstanding.

PROBLEM 12-11
L.O. 4, 5

Comparison of Equity and Consolidation Methods

Massive, Inc., acquired a 100% interest in Banker Corporation at the end of 19x1 for $20 million cash. The condensed financial statements of these two companies *just before* the purchase were as follows (in millions):

	Massive	*Banker*
Total assets (12/31/x1)	$380	$450
Total liabilities (12/31/x1)	190	430
Total stockholders' equity (12/31/x1)	190	20
Reported 19x1 net income	19	2

Required:

1. Assume the purchase is accounted for as an equity investment. Compute Massive's 19x1 return on assets (net income/total assets) and return on equity (net income/total stockholders' equity) before the purchase.
2. Indicate what changes, if any, would occur in the condensed financial statement data *after* the purchase assuming the equity method is used. Recompute Massive's return on assets and return on equity. (Hint: Banker's 19x1 net income is not added to Massive's since the purchase took place at the end of 19x1 after the income was reported by Banker and purchased by Massive.)
3. Repeat requirement 2 above assuming Massive prepares consolidated financial statements at the end of 19x1 after purchasing Banker.

PROBLEM 12-12
L.O. 5

Consolidation at Acquisition—100%

On January 1, 19x2, Giant Corporation acquired a 100% interest in Knat, Inc., by paying $500,000 cash for all of Knat's common stock. The following balance sheet data are available immediately before this acquisition.

Balance Sheet
December 31, 19x1
(in thousands)

	Giant	*Knat*
Cash	$4,000	$400
Other assets (total)	6,000	200
Liabilities (total)	5,000	100
Stockholders' equity (total)	5,000	500

Required:

1. Prepare the entry to record the purchase of Knat by Giant.
2. Prepare the consolidation worksheet entry on January 1, 19x2, needed to prepare a consolidation balance sheet on that date.
3. Prepare the consolidated balance sheet at January 1, 19x2.

PROBLEM 12-13
L.O. 5

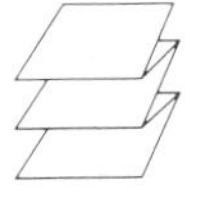

Consolidation at Acquisition—100% Interest

On June 30, 19x1, Bellows, Inc., acquired a 100% interest in Olson Corporation by paying $900,000 in cash to Olson's shareholders for their stock. The following balance sheet data were prepared by Olson at June 30, 19x1:

Olson Corporation
Balance Sheet

Cash	$ 25,000
Land	200,000
Other assets	975,000
Total assets	$1,200,000
Liabilities	$ 300,000
Shareholders' equity	900,000
Total liabilities and shareholders' equity	$1,200,000

Bellows reported the following balance on June 30, 19x1, just before the cash purchase of Olson:

Bellows Corporation
Balance Sheet

Cash	$ 2,000,000
Land	5,000,000
Other assets	3,000,000
Total assets	$10,000,000
Liabilities	$ 6,000,000
Shareholders' equity	4,000,000
Total liabilities and shareholders' equity	$10,000,000

Required:
1. Prepare the journal entry to record the purchase on June 30, 19x1, on Bellows' books.
2. Prepare the consolidated worksheet entry on June 30, 19x1, needed to prepare the consolidated balance sheet.
3. Prepare the consolidated balance sheet at June 30, 19x1.

PROBLEM 12-14
L.O. 5

Consolidation—100% Interest

The Major Corporation acquired a 100% interest in Minor, Inc., on January 1, 19x8, by purchasing all of Minor's common stock for $700,000 in cash. The following balance sheet data were available immediately after the purchase.

Balance Sheet
January 1, 19x8
(in thousands)

	Major	*Minor*
Cash	$5,000	$200
Investment in Minor	700	0
Other assets (total)	8,300	700
Liabilities (total)	6,000	200
Stockholders' equity (total)	8,000	700

During 19x8, Major reported net income of $1 million which included $100,000 of income from its investment in Minor. Minor declared and paid dividends of $50,000 in 19x8. Major declared no dividends in 19x8.

Required:
1. Record any entries necessary to account for Major's investment in Minor for 19x8, including the entry to purchase Minor.
2. Assume the liabilities of both Major and Minor were unchanged during 19x8. Prepare a consolidation worksheet for 19x8 including the consolidated balance sheet at December 31, 19x8.

APPENDIX PROBLEMS

PROBLEM 12-15
L.O. 10

Consolidation at Acquisition—90% Interest

Consider the data in Problem 12-13 above for Bellows, Inc. Assume that on June 30, 19x1, Bellows acquired a 90% interest in Olson by paying $810,000 cash for Olson's stock. All other information remains the same as in the earlier problem.

Required:
1. Prepare the journal entry to record the purchase on June 30, 19x1, on Bellows' books.
2. Prepare the consolidation worksheet entry on June 30, 19x1.
3. Prepare a consolidated balance sheet at June 30, 19x1.

PROBLEM 12-16
L.O. 6

Consolidation—90% Interest

The King Corporation acquired a 90% interest in Jackson, Inc., on May 1, 19x1, purchasing Jackson stock in the open market for $1,800,000 in cash. The following balance sheet data were prepared on May 1, 19x1, immediately after the purchase.

	Jackson	*King*
Cash	$ 500,000	$1,000,000
Investment in Jackson	0	1,800,000
Other assets	5,000,000	6,000,000
Liabilities	3,500,000	3,000,000
Stockholders' equity	2,000,000	5,800,000

During the remainder of 19x1, Jackson reported net income of $200,000 and declared and paid cash dividends of $100,000. King reported net income for the remainder of 19x1 of $500,000, **not** including any income from Jackson. King paid no dividends in 19x1.

Required:

1. Record any journal entries on King's books to account for the purchase and subsequent earnings and dividends of Jackson.
2. Assume the liabilities of both King and Jackson were unchanged during the remainder of 19x1. Prepare a consolidation worksheet at December 31, 19x1.
3. Prepare a consolidated balance sheet of King and Jackson at December 31, 19x1. Assume no cash inflow from operations for either company.

PROBLEM 12-17
L.O. 6

Consolidation—80% Interest

On January 1, 19x1, Parent Company acquired an 80% voting stock interest in Kidco. The following data are available immediately after the acquisition:

Balance Sheet Data
January 1, 19x1
(in thousands)

	Parent	*Kidco*
Cash and other assets. . . .	$250	$550
Investment in Kidco	200	0
Liabilities	50	300
Stockholders' equity.	400	250

During 19x1, Parent Company earned income of $125 **before** considering income from Kidco, and paid cash dividends of $50. Kidco earned income of $60 during 19x1, and paid cash dividends of $30.

Required:

1. Prepare the consolidation worksheet entry necessary to prepare a consolidated balance sheet on January 1, 19x1.
2. Compute the total owners' equity in the consolidated balance sheet at January 1, 19x1.
3. Assume the total liabilities for both Parent ($50) and Kidco ($300) are the same on December 31, 19x1, as they were on January 1, 19x1. What would the total assets in the consolidated balance sheet be on December 31, 19x1?
4. Compute consolidated net income for 19x1.
5. What is the balance in Parent Company's asset "Investment in Kidco" on December 31, 19x1, after adjusting for Kidco's 19x1 earnings but before consolidation?

PROBLEM 12-18
L.O. 6

Consolidation Balance Sheet—85% Interest

The Bien Hoa Corporation acquired an 85% interest in Soo Lin, Ltd., on January 1, 19x6, for $255 million. At the date of acquisition, after recording the purchase, the following data were available:

Bien Hoa Corporation
Balance Sheet
January 1, 19x6
(in millions)

Assets:		Liabilities	$370
Investment in Soo Lin	$255	Stockholders' equity	415
Other assets	530	Total liabilities and	
Total assets	$785	stockholders' equity	$785

Soo Lin, Ltd.
Balance Sheet
January 1, 19x6
(in millions)

Assets	$700	Liabilities	$400
		Stockholders' equity	300
		Total liabilities and	
Total assets	$700	stockholders' equity	$700

Required:

1. What is consolidated stockholders' equity on January 1, 19x6?
2. What is minority interest on January 1, 19x6?
3. Assume liabilities for both companies remain the same during 19x6. During 19x6, the **separate** net income of Bien Hoa was $120 million and the separate net income of Soo Lin was $90 million. There were no dividends or stock transactions during 19x6. Prepare the consolidated balance sheet at the end of 19x6.
4. What was consolidated net income for 19x6?

PROBLEM 12-19
L.O. 6

Consolidation and Goodwill—90% Interest

Big, Inc., purchased a 90% interest in Kidco for $630 million cash on January 1, 19x4. The book value and fair market value of Kidco's net assets at the date of acquisition were both equal to $600 million. Immediately after the acquisition the following balance sheet data were available.

Balance Sheet
January 1, 19x4
(in millions)

	Big, Inc.	*Kidco*
Investment in Kidco	$ 630	$ 0
Other assets	2,000	1,800
Liabilities	1,200	1,200
Stockholders' equity	1,430	600

Required:

1. How much "goodwill" is included in the $630 million purchase price paid for Kidco?
2. Record the consolidation worksheet entry at the date of purchase to prepare consolidated statements as of January 1, 19x4.

3. Assume Big, Inc., amortizes goodwill over 30 years. During 19x4, Kidco reported net income of $100 million. Big's **separate** net income (before considering Kidco's net income) was $150 million for 19x4. Compute the consolidated net income (net of the minority interest's share) for 19x4.

CASES

CASE 12-1
L.O. 1, 3, 4

Investment Methods

Brasco, Inc., acquired an 18% interest in the common stock of Vista Crafts in 19x5 for $1.5 million. Brasco has since managed to place two of its top managers on Vista Crafts' board of directors.

As of December 15, 19x9, Brasco had experienced below-average sales and profits on its primary operations for the 19x9 calendar year. Brasco had managed to report an increase in earnings in each of the eight years prior to 19x9, but it looked like their record of increases would not be achieved in 19x9. Vista Craft had a great year in 19x9 and was expecting to report record profits.

Required:

1. Assume you are manager for Brasco and that your annual bonus (which normally makes up about 25% of your total income) is based on the increase in this year's Brasco's bottom-line earnings over the prior year's. What might you do to improve Brasco's 19x9 earnings outlook, despite the late date?
2. Assume you are a major stockholder in Brasco, and that you are aware of all the facts presented in the case. How would you structure the bonus plan for your top managers to avoid the potential problems of the bonus plan described in (1) above? Be specific and remember the bonus should give managers an incentive to increase earnings.

CASE 12-2
L.O. 4

Equity Investments

Flestex Corporation reported the following financial statement data for its equity investments in its 19x9 annual report (in millions):

	19x9	*19x8*
Balance sheet (noncurrent assets):		
Equity investments in affiliates	$437	$492
Income statement:		
Equity income and gains (losses) from sale of affiliates (pre-tax)	$171	$ 93

In 19x9, Flestex sold all of its stock in one of its affiliated companies for $167 million cash, resulting in a gain of $49 million before taxes.

Required:
Assume Flestex originally paid a price for its equity investments equal to book value of the investee companies at the date of purchase. (In other words, Flestex did not pay any premium above the book value of the investees.) What were the cash dividends received by Flestex in 19x9? (Hint: Use a T account to explain the change in the asset account.)

CASE 12-3
L.O. 4, 5

Investments—Ralston Purina Company

Ralston Purina Company includes a number of subsidiaries, as noted in their report in Appendix E at the end of this text. Most of these investments are 100% owned, but some are equity investments in "affiliated companies" and others are less than 100% owned consolidated investments where a minority interest is present. Consider the footnote titled "Supplemental Balance Sheet Information" in answering these questions.

Required:

1. What is the balance in "investments in affiliated companies" at the end of fiscal 1988? 1989?
2. What types of transactions or events could explain the change in "investments in affiliated companies"?
3. What is the balance in "minority interests" at the end of fiscal 1988? 1989?
4. What types of transactions or events could explain the change in minority interests?

EVALUATING FINANCIAL STATEMENTS

CASE 12-4
L.O. 3

Long-Term Investments—General Motors

Consider the following footnote disclosure from General Motors' 19x6 annual report. This footnote is describing details of GM's balance sheet account—appearing in the stockholders' equity section of the balance sheet. As noted, the account reflects holding gains or losses from (1) translation of foreign currency (to be discussed in Appendix B) and (2) long-term investments in marketable equity securities (discussed in this chapter).

Excerpt from Footnote 15

(Dollars in Millions)	*19x6*	*19x5*	*19x4*
Accumulated foreign currency translation and other adjustments:			
Balance at beginning of the year:			
Accumulated foreign currency translation adjustments	$ (675.0)	$ (789.5)	$ (661.8)
Net unrealized gains on marketable equity securities	130.0	71.7	91.3
Changes during the year:			
Accumulated foreign currency translation adjustments	192.2	114.5	(127.7)
Net unrealized gains (losses) on marketable equity securities	30.8	58.3	(19.6)
Balance at end of the year	$ (322.0)	$ (545.0)	$ (717.8)
Total stockholders' equity.	$30,678.0	$29,524.7	$24,214.3

Required:

1. What accounting method is GAAP for long-term marketable equity securities representing less than a 20% interest in an investee for those investors **who are not** primarily concerned with buying and selling securities? (Name the method.)
2. GM is using a stockholders' equity account to report unrecognized gains or losses on marketable equity securities. By the end of 19x6, what is the net unrecognized gain or loss? (State amount and whether it is a gain or a loss.)
3. What method is apparently being used by GM for valuing its investments in marketable equity securities reported in this footnote? (Name the method.)

CASE 12-5
L.O. 2, 3

Investments—General Electric

General Electric (GE) reported the following footnote data in their 19x6 annual report.

Note 9 Cash and marketable securities

Deposits restricted as to usage and withdrawal or used as partial compensation for short-term borrowing arrangements were not material.

Carrying value of marketable securities was substantially the same as market value at year-end 19x6 and 19x5. Equity securities in the portfolio were carried at a cost of $48 million and $206 million at December 31, 19x6 and 19x5, respectively.

Note 14 Other investments

December 31 (in millions)	*19x6*	*19x5*
1. Equity investments	$3,468	$2,604
2. Miscellaneous investments (at cost)[a]		
Government and government-guaranteed securities	177	158
Other	258	344
3. Marketable equity securities[b]	74	81
Less allowance for losses	(63)	(37)
	$3,914	$3,150

[a]Estimated realizable value about the same as cost at year-end.
[b]Carried at cost. Aggregate market value was $65 million and $209 million at year-end 19x6 and 19x5, respectively. Gross unrealized gains were $16 million and gross unrealized losses were $25 million at December 31, 19x6.

Note 9 pertains to a current asset account in GE's balance sheet, while note 14 explains part of their long-term account called "Other Investments" in the balance sheet. The balances reported in these two accounts in GE's balance sheets were:

December 31 (in millions)

	19x6	*19x5*
Marketable securities (note 9)	$ 221	$ 951
Other investments (note 14)	3,914	3,150

After reading over the footnote disclosures, answer the following questions:

1. What is the apparent balance, if any, in GE's Allowance to Reduce Temporary Investments in Marketable Equity Securities to Market account?
2. Are all of GE's temporary investments in marketable securities invested in stocks? If not, what amount is invested in other marketable securities as of the end of 19x6?
3. What is the apparent balance, if any, in GE's Allowance to Reduce Long-Term Investments in Marketable Equity Securities to Market account?
4. What was the amount of the change in the Allowance to Reduce Long-Term Investments in Marketable Equity Securities to Market account in 19x6?

CASE 12-6
L.O. 4

Equity Investments—Ford Motor Company

Ford Motor Company reported the following amounts in a recent annual report:

	19x6	*19x5*
Balance Sheet–Assets		
Equity in net assets of unconsolidated subsidiaries	$5,088.4	$4,176.4
Income Statement		
Equity in new income of unconsolidated subsidiaries	816.9	598.1
Statement of Cash Flows		
Purchase of an unconsolidated subsidiary (First Nationwide Financial Corporation)	381.7	

Assume there were no other items affecting Ford's balance sheet account other than the dividends Ford received from unconsolidated subsidiaries.

Required:
Compute the dividends received by Ford in 19x6 from its unconsolidated subsidiaries.

CASE 12-7
L.O. 4

Equity Investments—Ford Motor Company

Ford Motor Company reported the following financial statement data for its equity investments in its 19x8 annual report (in millions):

	19x8	*19x7*
Balance sheet (noncurrent assets):		
Equity in net assets of affiliated companies.	$2,102.7	$2,001.2
Income statement:		
Equity in net income/(loss) of affiliated companies	$ 147.8	$ (136.6)

Required:
Assume that Ford paid a price equal to book value for these equity investees (affiliates). What were the cash dividends received by Ford Motor from its affiliates in 19x8? (Hint: Use a T account to explain changes in the asset.)

CASE 12-8
L.O. 4

Equity Investments—USX Corporation

USX Corporation (formerly U.S. Steel) reported the following in their 19x8 annual report (in millions):

	19x8	*19x7*
Balance sheet (equity investments):		
Investments in partially owned companies and partnerships	$657	$679
Income statement:		
Income (loss) from equity method affiliates.	$ 39	$ 13

Required:
Assume USX paid a price equal to book value for its equity investments. What were the apparent dividends received by USX in 19x8 from its equity investments?

CASE 12-9
L.O. 4, 5

Equity versus Consolidation—General Electric

A recent FASB ruling eliminated the use of the equity method of accounting for companies that were over 50% owned by a parent company, requiring consolidation to be used. An example of the impact of this standard is illustrated below.

In 19x6, General Electric reported the following data, which is condensed from their annual report.

General Electric
Balance Sheet Data
December 31, 19x6
(in millions)

Assets		Liabilities and Stockholders' Equity	
Equity investments in GE Financial Service Corp. . .	$ 2,994	Liabilities	$19,482
Other assets	31,597	Stockholders' equity	15,109
Total assets	$34,591	Total liabilities and stockholders' equity	$34,591

General Electric
Income Statement Data
For the Year Ended December 31, 19x6
(in millions)

Revenues	$36,221
Expenses	33,033
	$3,188
Equity income from GE Financial Service Corporation.	504
Income tax expense	(1,200)
Net income	$ 2,492

Required:

1. Compute GE's return on assets ratio (net income/assets).
2. Compute GE's debt-to-equity ratio (liabilities/stockholders' equity).
3. Now, consider the following data regarding GE Financial Services Corporation (GEFS), a 100% owned subsidiary of GE, which is accounted for in the condensed data above like an equity investment.

GEFS Balance Sheet Data
(in millions)

Assets	$53,823
Liabilities	$50,829
Stockholders' equity	2,994
Total	$53,823

Recompute the two ratios required in parts 1 and 2 above by using the GEFS data to prepare fully consolidated financial statement amounts for total assets, total liabilities, and stockholders' equity. Note, consolidated net income will still be $2,492 million.

4. Evaluate the impact of full consolidation versus equity method accounting on GE's performance ratios.

APPENDIX CASE

CASE 12-10
L.O. 7

Purchase versus Pooling Method (Appendix 12B)

The directors of Korbet, Inc., are considering a bid for its common stock made by Prentice Corporation. Prentice's 2 million shares of common stock are currently selling for $100 per share, while Korbet's 100,000 shares of common stock are currently selling for $80 per share. Korbet has a net **book value** (net assets) of $6 million as of the end of 19x8. Prentice has made the following offers to Korbet's board for 100% interest in Korbet:

a. 100,000 shares of Prentice in exchange for all 100,000 shares of Korbet; or
b. $9 million cash in exchange for all 100,000 shares of Korbet.

Required:

1. What accounting method would be used if Korbet accepted the first offer?
2. What accounting method would be used if Korbet accepted the second offer?
3. What asset(s) would Prentice report on its unconsolidated financial statements if the first offer were accepted by Korbet?
4. What asset(s) would Prentice report on its unconsolidated financial statements if the second offer were accepted by Korbet?
5. As a director for Korbet, which alternative offer would you prefer? Explain your answer.

P A R T 3

Reporting and Evaluating Financial Results

FINANCIAL STATEMENTS

Reynolds, Inc.
Income Statement
For 1991

Revenues
XXXX
XXXX
Expenses

Income from continuing operations
Discontinued operations (net of taxes)
Extraordinary gain (net of taxes)
Change in accounting method (net of taxes)
Net income

Earnings per share:
Earnings per share from continuing operations
Discontinued operations per share
Extraordinary gain per share
Change in accounting method per share
Earnings per share

Reynolds, Inc.
Balance Sheet
12/31/91

Current assets
XXXX
XXXX
Noncurrent assets
XXXX
XXXX
Noncurrent liabilities
XXXX
XXXX
Stockholders' equity
XXXX
XXXX

Reynolds, Inc.
Cash Flow Statement
For 1991

Operating activities
XXXX
XXXX
Investing activities
XXXX
XXXX
Financing activities
XXXX
XXXX

FINANCIAL STATEMENT COMPONENTS EMPHASIZED IN CHAPTER 13

	1991	*1990*
Income from continuing operations	$X,XXX	$X,XXX
Discontinued operations (net of taxes)	(XXX)	(XXX)
Extraordinary gain (net of taxes)		XXX
Change in accounting method (net of taxes)	XXX	
Net income	$ XXX	$ XXX
Earnings per share:		
Earnings per share from continuing operations	$ XXX	$ XXX
Discontinued operations per share	(XX)	(XX)
Extraordinary gain per share		XX
Change in accounting method per share	XX	
Earnings per share	$ XXX	$ XXX

CHAPTER 13

Understanding the Income and Retained Earnings Statements

LEARNING OBJECTIVES

After studying Chapter 13, you should understand:

1. The criteria for recognizing revenues and expenses, pp. 718-19.
2. Accounting for changes in estimates, pp. 719-20.
3. How to differentiate gains and losses from revenues and expenses, p. 721.
4. The nature and purpose of items receiving separate income statement disclosures, including discontinued operations, extraordinary items, and accounting changes, pp. 723-28.
5. The preparation of a retained earnings statement or a statement of changes in stockholders' equity, pp. 729-30.
6. Computation of EPS for a simple capital structure, pp. 731-34.

So far in this textbook, the discussion of specific accounting topics has centered on the balance sheet. Whenever it was appropriate, as we discussed the balance sheet items, we also looked at their impact on the income statement. By now we should understand the important relationship between changes in the balance sheet and their effect on the income statement. For all operating transactions, increases in net assets (total assets less total liabilities) result in increases in income, while decreases in net assets result from expenses or losses and therefore decreases in net income. Thus, when a company earns net income, its net assets must increase to maintain the balance sheet equation as illustrated below:

	Assets	=	*Liabilities*	+	*Stockholders' Equity*
Beginning	$50,000	=	$20,000	+	$30,000
	↓		↓		↓
Ending.	$70,000	=	$25,000	+	$45,000

Note that **net assets** (assets − liabilities) increased by $15,000 from operations: from $30,000 ($50,000 − $20,000) at the beginning of the period to $45,000 ($70,000 − $25,000) at the end of the period. This illustrates the fact that net income results in an increase in net assets. The example illustrated above is not the only way that net income of $15,000 from operations could have increased net assets but is merely one possibility. Other examples of balance sheet changes resulting in net assets increasing by $15,000 to reflect net income of $15,000 would include:

	Assets	=	*Liabilities*	+	*Stockholders' Equity*
Beginning	$50,000	=	$20,000	+	$30,000
	↓		↓		↓
Ending.	$50,000	=	$ 5,000	+	$45,000

or:

	Assets	=	*Liabilities*	+	*Stockholders' Equity*
Beginning	$50,000	=	$20,000	+	$30,000
	↓		↓		↓
Ending.	$65,000	=	$20,000	+	$45,000

The first section of this chapter reviews the various types of transactions giving rise to revenues, expenses, gains, and losses. These transactions are reported in summary form in the income statement, but they also affect the balance sheet accounts.

The second section of this chapter discusses the statement of changes in stockholders' equity, which examines all balance sheet changes from the viewpoint of the owners. Periodic net income, which is added to the retained earnings balance, explains changes in stockholders' equity from nonowner transactions. To stress this point, some companies use the title **statement of operations** instead

EXHIBIT 13-1

Changes in the Balance Sheet

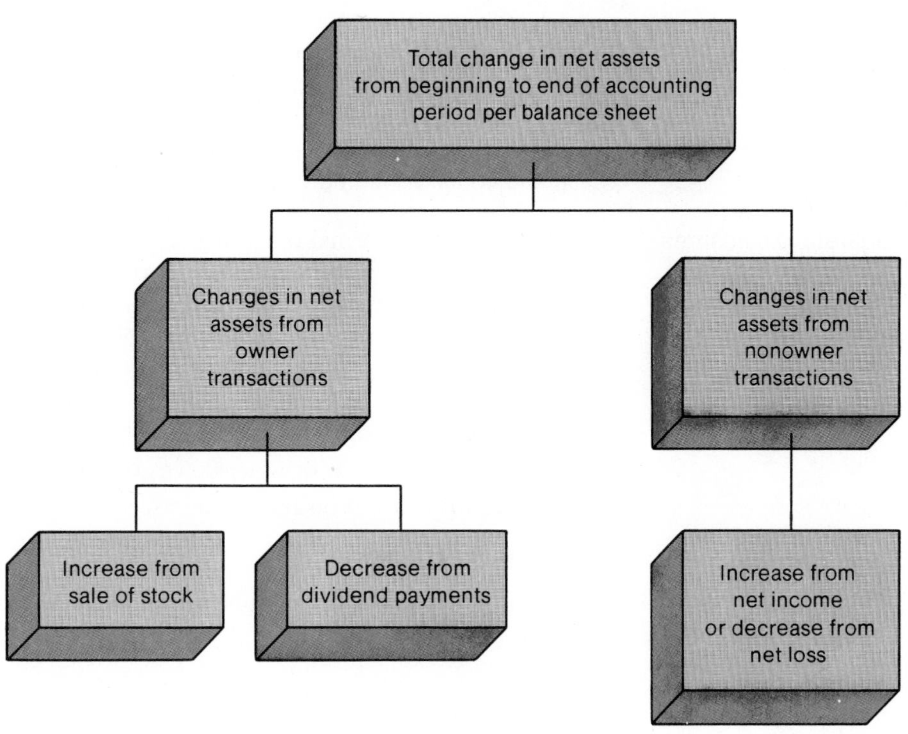

of **income statement** or **earnings statement.** The statement of changes in stockholders' equity summarizes balance sheet changes from owner transactions (such as new stock issues and the payment of dividends) and nonowner transactions. We can look at changes in the balance sheet from the owners' point of view in Exhibit 13-1.

In the third section of this chapter you will become familiar with earnings per share (EPS) measurement. Since a company's EPS is often quoted as an indication of the company's financial performance, the information in this section is important.

The focus of this chapter is to discuss and illustrate both routine and unusual operating-related transactions that are reported in the income statement. The objective is to introduce and explain the nature of the various income statement disclosures that could be encountered in reading published, detailed income statements.

INCOME STATEMENT

Chapter 1 introduced the basic format of the income statement, which is revenues less expenses equals net income. As we added details to the accounting information system in Chapters 3 through 5, the income statement illustrations gradually became larger and more complete. Exhibit 5-9, page 000, gives a reasonably complete representation of the operating revenues and expenses of a merchandising company.

The income statement in Exhibit 13-2 is representative of the common operating disclosures made by larger corporations. Note that it presents income statements for the current year and the previous year. Normally, publicly traded companies present income statements for the current year and two prior years to facilitate comparison and evaluation of a company's operating results.

Separate Disclosures

In addition to normal operating revenues and expenses, income statements may report on the results of transactions or activities that are not directly related to ongoing operations. These items should receive separate disclosure. Such separately disclosed items would include the following examples:

Unusual items:

- Gains and losses from the sale of equipment, land, or facilities.
- Losses from write-offs or write-downs of assets (e.g., obsolete inventory).
- Gains or losses from insurance claims.

Discontinued operations:

- Operating income/loss from operations that have been discontinued.
- Gain or loss from the sale of the assets of a discontinued operation (line of business).

Extraordinary items:

- Gain or loss on the retirement of bonds payable before maturity.
- Gain or loss from an earthquake.

EXHIBIT 13-2

Common Disclosures Given in an Income Statement

Orange Company
Income Statement
For the Years Ending December 31

	19x5	*19x4*
Revenues:		
Sales revenue	$ 700,000	$ 650,000
Service revenue	250,000	200,000
Interest and dividend income	50,000	50,000
Total revenues	$1,000,000	$ 900,000
Expenses:		
Cost of goods sold	$ 275,000	$ 270,000
Cost of services	70,000	65,000
Selling and advertising expenses	65,000	60,000
Administrative expenses	75,000	70,000
Interest expense	15,000	15,000
Total expenses	$ 500,000	$ 480,000
Income from operations before taxes	$ 500,000	$ 420,000
Provision for income taxes (or income tax expense)	(190,000)	(184,000)
Net income	$ 310,000	$ 236,000

Accounting method change:

Cumulative effect on prior years' income of a change in an accounting method used to measure income.

Exhibit 13-3 illustrates an income statement in its most complete (complex) form to show how each of these items would be separately disclosed. Unusual items (categories 3 and 4 in Exhibit 13-3) are normally disclosed separately and explained in the financial statement footnotes. These unusual gains and losses are, however, included in income from continuing operations. Category 5 in Exhibit 13-3 represents the income tax expense associated with the items reported in categories 1 through 4. Specific accounting rules require that the last three items (categories 6, 7, and 8) of Exhibit 13-3 are reported as separate items and that the income tax effect be reported with each separate item (i.e., the amount reported for each separate item is net of any taxes).[1] These three items,

EXHIBIT 13-3

Components of the Income Statement—Most Complete Form

Ozello Company
Income Statement
For the Year Ending December 31

Category of Items		*19x8*	*19x7*
1	Revenues:		
	Sales revenue	$ 700,000	$ 650,000
	Service revenue	250,000	200,000
	Interest and dividend income	50,000	50,000
	Total revenues	$1,000,000	$ 900,000
2	Expenses:		
	Cost of goods sold	$ 275,000	$ 270,000
	Cost of services	70,000	65,000
	Selling and advertising expenses	65,000	60,000
	Administrative expenses	75,000	70,000
	Interest expense	15,000	15,000
	Total expenses	$ 500,000	$ 480,000
3	Gains	75,000	—
4	Losses	(25,000)	(10,000)
	Income from continuing operations before taxes	$ 550,000	$ 470,000
5	Income tax expense on continuing operations	(200,000)	(180,000)
	Income from continuing operations	$ 350,000	$ 290,000
6	Discontinued operations (net of taxes)	(35,000)	2,000
7	Extraordinary items (net of taxes)	10,000	—
8	Cumulative accounting adjustment (net of taxes)	15,000	—
	Net income	$ 340,000	$ 292,000

[1]See *APB Opinion No. 20,* "Accounting Changes" (New York: AICPA, 1971), and *APB Opinion No. 30,* "Reporting the Results of Operations" (New York: AICPA, 1973), for details on these disclosure requirements beyond what is discussed later in this chapter.

which are reported separately net of their respective income tax effects, are discussed in some detail later in this chapter.

Before studying these separately disclosed items, let's first review the guiding accounting principles for the measurement and disclosure of normal operating revenues and expenses and changes in accounting estimates.

Revenues and Expenses (Categories 1 and 2)

Objective 1
The criteria for recognizing revenues and expenses.

The measurement of revenues and expenses is based on the recognition criteria discussed in Chapters 2 and 3. Because expense recognition is partially dependent on when revenues are recognized, we can think of revenue recognition decisions as coming before expense recognition.

Revenues must be (1) measurable, (2) realized or realizable, and (3) earned before accountants recognize (or record) them on the income statement.[2] This means that the amount of net assets to be received (e.g., cash or accounts receivable) from the transactions must be **measurable** with a reasonable degree of precision before income can be reported. Cash sales can, of course, be measured with precision. Because of the possibility of bad debts, the increases in net assets from credit sales are more difficult to measure. However, accountants usually consider the increases in net assets from credit sales to be measurable with reasonable precision. In contrast, a sale of unique inventory in exchange for another company's common stock that is not traded on a public stock exchange may not meet the measurability criterion (until the stock is sold for cash).

The second criterion—realized or realizable—means that before accountants record revenue, the inflow of net assets must be **realized** (as in a cash sale) or **realizable** (as in a credit sale expected to be collected). Finally, the revenue must be **earned** to be recorded. The revenue from a sale has been earned if the goods have been accepted by the buyer. However, when a customer pays cash for future services, revenue is not earned until the service is performed. To indicate this, accountants record unearned revenue as a liability until it is earned; and once earned, the revenue is recorded (recognized) as revenue in the income statement.

It is important to note that revenue recognition, based on the three criteria described above, may take place before or after the point of sale. While most companies do recognize revenue at or near the point of sale, there are common examples of recognition before the point of sale (such as with long-term construction projects or mining precious metals) and after the point of sale (such as retail land sales or installment sales). The three criteria above serve as the primary accounting rule (test) to determine when to recognize revenue. In general, whenever these three criteria are satisfied, revenue may be recognized.

Expenses represent **outflows of net assets** (e.g., a decrease in an asset like inventory or an increase in a liability like salaries payable). Accountants record expenses based on (1) matching, (2) direct expensing, or (3) systematic allocation.

Matching occurs when the costs of achieving the recorded revenues are recognized (recorded) as expenses in the same period as their related revenues. Thus, to correctly measure income for the month of May, revenues from the sale of goods in May should be matched with the cost of goods sold, wages necessary to complete the sale, transportation costs to deliver the goods, and so on. Matching is generally associated with the direct costs which give rise to revenue, such as inventory use, the wages or salaries directly linked to the sale (i.e., salespersons' commissions), and packaging and delivery costs.

---

[2]Recall that **to recognize** revenue or expense is the same as **to record.** Recognition of a revenue or an expense in the income statement requires that an entry be recorded.

Direct expensing records expenses as they occur based on the assumption that the revenues associated with these expenses have also been recorded. Examples of direct expense recognition include those costs that are difficult to associate with specific periods of future benefit such as advertising costs, most research and development costs, and costs of top administrators' salaries.

To accurately measure net income, some costs require **systematic allocation** to be recognized as expenses. Allocated costs include depreciation of plant and equipment, amortization of intangible assets, and so on. These allocation processes were introduced in Chapter 4 and discussed in detail in Chapter 8. Note that allocated costs normally are recorded at the end of an accounting period by making **adjusting entries to balance sheet accounts** (assets or liabilities). For example, the expiration of prepaid rent expense, prepaid insurance, and other prepaid expenses are charged to expense through systematic allocations based on the passage of time, use, or some other predetermined basis.

Recording expenses is based on one of the three processes noted above: (1) matching, (2) direct expensing, or (3) systematic allocation. The process used for a given type of expense may vary from company to company depending on the specific expensing policies employed. However, once a policy is established it should consistently assign costs to expense by one of these three processes.

Changes in Cost Estimates

Recall from earlier discussions of depreciation expense, bad debt expense, and other allocated and matched costs that the recorded amounts of these expenses are normally based on estimates. For example, depreciation expense **seems to be** the result of an exact process that systematically assigns the cost of depreciable assets to their periods of use. However, to determine an asset's depreciation schedule, the useful life and the salvage value **must be estimated.** Likewise, to properly match revenues with bad debt expense, you must estimate the amount of the current period's credit sales that will not be collected.

Whenever you estimate expenses (or revenues), the passage of time often reveals new information suggesting that your earlier estimates should be revised. For example, you may originally estimate a truck to have a three-year useful life, but after two and one-half years of use, you believe the truck will last four or five years. Chapter 8 illustrated the accounting procedure used for a change in an estimate of an asset's useful life.

The basic method of changing estimates illustrated in Chapter 8 applies to other estimate changes as well. Changes in estimates are accounted for by applying the new estimate to the book value of the item as of the beginning of the period of the estimated change. This charges current and future periods with amounts that are based on current estimates of the benefit period.

Objective 2
Accounting for changes in estimates.

For example, consider a change in an estimate for warranty costs that are normally measured as a percentage of sales. Assume Appliance Mart Corporation estimated its warranty expense to be 2% of sales. The balance in the Estimated Warranty Liability account at the beginning of 19x7 was $85,000. During 19x7, sales were $4,850,000. The actual cost of warranty claims made in 19x7 from 19x7 sales and sales of prior years still covered by warranty amounted to $65,000. At the end of 19x7, the following entry was made:

19x7			
Dec. 31	Warranty Expense (E)	97,000	
	Estimated Warranty Liability (L)		97,000
	To record estimated warranty expense on 19x7 sales: $4,850,000 × .02.		

The balance in the Estimated Warranty Liability account at the end of 19x7 is:

Estimated Warranty Liability

		Bal. Jan. 1	85,000
(19x7 actual claims)		(19x7 estimate)	
Jan.-Dec.	65,000	Dec. 31	97,000
		Bal. Dec. 31	117,000

During 19x8, sales were $5 million, and the actual cost of warranty claims made in 19x8 for sales made in 19x8 and prior years was $80,000. Assume that toward the end of 19x8, Appliance Mart managers decided that due to the steady increase in the warranty liability balance over the past several years, a more accurate estimate of the warranty cost would be 1.5% of sales. To change the estimate from 2% to 1.5% of sales, you simply apply the new estimate to 19x8 (the entire current year) and future periods. The sales for all of 19x8 times the new estimate results in a year-end adjusting entry of $75,000 (.015 × $5 million), which is recorded as follows:

19x8			
Dec. 31	Warranty Expense (E).	75,000	
	Estimated Warranty Liability (L)		75,000
	To record estimated warranty expense on 19x8 sales.		

The balance in the warranty liability at the end of 19x8 would be:

Estimated Warranty Liability

		Bal. Jan. 1	117,000
(19x8 actual claims)		(19x8 estimate)	
Jan.-Dec.	80,000	Dec. 31	75,000
		Bal. Dec. 31	112,000

Note that **changes in estimates do not affect the prior years' results.** On the other hand, a change in estimate made anytime during the current accounting period is applied as if it were made on the **first day of the period.** Accountants apply changes in estimates as of the beginning of the period of the change to allow the new (hopefully improved) estimate to be reflected in the statements for the **entire** period. For Appliance Mart, even though management decided toward the end of 19x8 that the estimated warranty cost should be changed, the change was applied to all of 19x8 as if the managers decided to make change on the first day of 19x8.

Normally, no disclosure is required in the financial statements when the revenues and expenses of a business are changed due to changes in accounting estimates. However, if a change in estimate has a material impact on the financial

EXHIBIT 13-4

Annual Report Example of Disclosure of Change in Accounting Estimate

Union Carbide

Excerpt from footnotes:

3. Change in Accounting Estimate

As explained in Note 1, during 1985 Union Carbide revised, retroactive to January 1, 1985, the estimated useful lives used to depreciate the cost of machinery and equipment. The effects of this change in accounting estimate were to increase 1985 depreciation expense by approximately $57 million, and to decrease 1985 net income by approximately $34 million, or $0.16 per share.

statements, the notes to the financial statements should disclose the effect. Exhibit 13-4 gives an example of such a disclosure.

Unusual Items—Gains and Losses (Categories 3 and 4)

Objective 3

How to differentiate gains and losses from revenues and expenses.

Gains and **losses** (categories 3 and 4 in Exhibit 13-3), sometimes referred to as "unusual items," differ from revenues and expenses in that they are not the result of the planned **operating activities** of the entity. However, most gains and losses result from activities that are peripheral to normal operations, often involving investing activities related to future operations. Typically, gains occur when a company sells old machinery, buildings, temporary investments, or other assets for more than their book value, thereby resulting in an increase in net assets. Losses occur when a business sells these types of assets for less than their book value, which results in a decrease in net assets.

While gains and losses do not reflect the operating activities of the entity, they may be an indirect result of operations or the result of planned (nonoperating) actions by management (e.g., replacement of equipment). As a result, most gains and losses are reported as separate items in income from continuing operations, as shown in Exhibit 13-3. Sometimes companies combine and report gains and losses from separate transactions as a single item on the income statement, such as "Other income" or "Unusual items."

Income Tax Expense—Intraperiod Tax Allocation (Category 5)

When separately disclosed items (categories 6, 7, and 8 in Exhibit 13-3) are included on the income statement, the total income tax expense of the entity (often called *Provision for taxes*) is not reported as a single expense. Instead, **intraperiod tax allocation** requires that the tax effects associated with each special item are reported with the special item. Only the income tax effects associated with income from continuing operations are reported as income tax expense (category 5 in Exhibit 13-3). To charge the operations of the business with the tax effects of all the special items would distort "Income from continuing operations."

To illustrate the effect of intraperiod tax allocation, assume Jason Software Design, Inc., had a total operating income before income tax expense for 19x5 of $50,000 plus a before-tax extraordinary gain of $10,000. Assume a flat tax rate of 25% is in effect. The tax expense on operations is $12,500, and the tax expense on the extraordinary gain is $2,500, making a total income tax expense of $15,000. The following summary compares the income statement with and without intraperiod tax allocation:

Software Design, Inc.
Income Statement
For the Year Ended December 31, 19x5

	Correct Method: with Intraperiod Tax Allocation	*Incorrect Method: without Intraperiod Tax Allocation*	
Revenues	$ 490,000	$ 490,000	
Expenses	(440,000)	(440,000)	
Pre-tax income	$ 50,000	$ 50,000	
Income tax expense	(12,500)	(15,000)	(overstated)
Income from continuing operations	$ 37,500	$ 35,000	(understated)
Extraordinary gain	7,500	10,000	(overstated)
Net income	$ 45,000	$ 45,000	

Note that the earnings total is **not affected** by intraperiod tax allocation, but the subtotals in the income statement are different. With tax allocation, continuing operations are only charged with the $12,500 tax expense related to the $50,000 in pre-tax income (based on the assumed uniform tax rate of 25% on all elements of income). The extraordinary gain of $10,000 is reduced by $2,500 for taxes (again, a 25% tax rate), resulting in a net extraordinary gain of $7,500. Without intraperiod tax allocation, the income from continuing operations in this example would be understated by $2,500, and extraordinary gain would be overstated by $2,500.

We should mention two additional aspects of intraperiod tax allocation. First, the tax effects of a special item that results in a loss could be negative, resulting in a tax savings (a credit to tax expense). Second, depending on the specific tax laws, the tax rate applicable to various items may be different from the tax rate on operating income. To illustrate these two points, assume an extraordinary loss of $20,000 before taxes is subject to a tax credit (or "tax refund") of 20% and that ordinary pre-tax income from operations of $80,000 is taxed at a 30% rate. The total tax bill and the appropriate reporting of intraperiod tax allocation would be:

Tax Bill Computation

	Income (Loss)	×	*Rate*	=	*Tax*
From operations	$ 80,000	×	.30	=	$24,000
From extraordinary loss	(20,000)	×	.20	=	(4,000)
Total taxes					$20,000

Partial Income Statement

Revenues	$ xxx
Expenses	xxx
Income from operations before taxes	$ 80,000
Income tax expense	24,000
Income from continuing operations	$ 56,000
Extraordinary loss (net of taxes)	(16,000)
Net income	$ 40,000

Reconciliation:

Income from operations before taxes . .	$ 80,000
Extraordinary loss before taxes	(20,000)
Pre-tax earnings—all sources	$ 60,000
Total taxes—all items	(20,000)
Net income	$ 40,000

Intraperiod tax allocation provides more meaningful information in the income statement by reporting special items net of their separate taxes.

Discontinued Operations (Category 6)

Most large, publicly held companies have multiple business lines. A line of business, or **business segment,** consists of a "separate major line of business or class of customers."[3] When an entity eliminates one of its business segments, **discontinued operations** (category 6 in Exhibit 13-3) result. Discontinued operations do **not** include the elimination or phase out of a product line, class of service, or part of a business line.

Companies often discontinue business segments because they are not profitable. A company with three profitable business lines and one unprofitable line might have higher total future profits if the unprofitable operation is discontinued. However, sometimes plant closings and layoffs associated with discontinued operations may be costly to the company for reasons such as the effect on the company's business reputation.

Objective 4
The nature and purpose of items receiving separate income statement disclosures, including discontinued operations, extraordinary items, and accounting changes.

When a company decides to discontinue a business segment, a separate disclosure is made on the income statement. Usually discontinued operations result in two disclosures:

1. The profit or loss for the period from the **operating activities** that have been discontinued, net of taxes.
2. The gain or loss from the **sale of the assets** of the discontinued operations, net of taxes.

Some companies combine these disclosures as a single item on the income statement and describe the separate effects (if any) in the footnotes to the statements, while other companies report two separate items in the income statement.

To illustrate income statement disclosures for discontinued operations, assume KLM, Inc., discontinued its tool and die operations in 19x5, with an operating loss after taxes for 19x5 of $450,000. KLM sold the assets of the tool and die operations in 19x5 at a gain of $250,000 net of taxes. The other 19x5 operations of KLM resulted in after-tax income of $1 million. The partial income statement in Exhibit 13-5 shows how this would be disclosed. Separate disclosure

EXHIBIT 13-5

Discontinued Operations

Partial Income Statement

	19x5	*19x4*
Income from continuing operations	$1,000,000	$ 900,000
Discontinued operations:		
Operating loss (net of taxes)	(450,000)	(300,000)
Gain on sale of assets (net of taxes) . . .	250,000	—
Net income	$ 800,000	$ 600,000

[3] *APB Opinion No. 30.*

of discontinued operations enhances the comparability and consistency of the accounting data and provides relevant data for predicting the future business operating results. When comparative income statements are shown, the data from prior years are restated to separate out the income or loss from the discontinued operations. This is shown in Exhibit 13-5.

Extraordinary Items (Category 7)

Objective 4
The nature and purpose of items receiving separate income statement disclosures, including discontinued operations, extraordinary items, and accounting changes.

The second possible category of separately disclosed items included in the measurement of earnings is **extraordinary items,** net of taxes (category 7 in Exhibit 13-3). Based on the environment in which the entity operates, an extraordinary item is generally defined as an event that is:

1. **Highly** unusual in nature, **and**
2. Not expected to occur again in the foreseeable future.[4]

Most large complex companies will typically have a number of transactions each year that are included in the income statement because they give rise to gains or losses, but that are **not** normal operating activities. These transactions are often referred to as **unusual events,** a broad category of events that are not directly a part of the business operations. Within this broad category, those unusual events that also meet the two criteria for extraordinary items noted above receive separate disclosure (see category 7 in Exhibit 13-3). However, most unusual events include items like the following:

- Write-down or write-off of inventory due to obsolescence or reduced marketability.
- Gains or losses on sale of plant assets.
- Gains or losses on sale of securities.
- Write-offs of large amounts of accounts receivable.
- Losses caused by a strike.[5]

While these events are somewhat unusual, they are **not extraordinary items** because they do not qualify as being so unusual that a person could not "expect them to occur again in the foreseeable future."[6] The events listed above would typically be reported as gains and losses in the income statement, while losses from major earthquakes, floods, and certain other natural disasters will normally qualify as extraordinary items. However, if a company operates in an environment where floods or severe weather is not extremely uncommon, the general definition above would suggest losses from these events may not be extraordinary!

In addition to transactions that qualify as extraordinary based on the general definition, one other event has been singled out for special disclosure by accounting rule makers: gains or losses from the retirement (extinguishment) of long-term debt (bonds payable, notes payable, etc.) before their maturity date.[7] Other than this one situation, accountants report few items as extraordinary.[8]

---

[4]Ibid.

[5]Ibid. par. 23.

[6]Ibid.

[7]*FASB Statement No. 4,* "Reporting Gains and Losses for Extinguishment of Debt" (Norwalk, Conn.: FASB, 1975).

[8]Prior to *FASB Statement No. 96,* issued in 1987, the tax benefits of tax loss carryforwards were also reported as extraordinary items.

Thus, income from continuing operations may include the effects of many events that do not appear to be "operating" events but still do not qualify for separate disclosure as an extraordinary item. For this reason, total revenues less total expenses before considering gains and losses (items 3 and 4 in Exhibit 13-3), may be a more useful subtotal for evaluating the operating performance of the business when separately disclosed items are present.

Keep in mind that one of the most important functions of the income statement is to help users predict the **future** performance of a business. What good is knowing where you have been if you do not know something about where you might be going next? By providing clear and separate disclosure for all unusual items, past income statements should be more relevant for helping users predict future income from operations. Items that are not expected to continue in the future are of less relevance to investors and creditors for predicting future performance of the business.

The income statement and explanatory footnotes of the Ralston Purina Company shown in Exhibit 13-6 provide a good example of the three separately disclosed items that we have discussed so far: (1) unusual gains and losses, (2) discontinued operations, and (3) extraordinary items. Note how the disclosures permit the reader to estimate that portion of the operating results expected to

EXHIBIT 13-6

Annual Report Disclosure of Unusual Gains and Losses, Discontinued Operations, and Extraordinary Items

Ralston Purina Company and Subsidiaries
Consolidated Statement of Earnings
Year Ended September 30
(in millions)

	19x6	*19x5*	*19x4*
Net sales	$5,514.6	$5,299.4	$4,351.8
Costs and expenses			
Cost of products sold	$3,177.9	$3,229.2	$3,130.5
Selling, general, and administrative	1,094.2	1,033.8	379.5
Advertising	584.6	497.5	395.8
Unusual or nonrecurring items	32.2		38.0
Interest	134.6	111.5	34.8
Investment income	(35.6)	(8.1)	(5.3)
	$4,987.9	$4,863.9	$3,973.3
Earnings from continuing operations before income taxes and extraordinary item	$ 526.7	$ 435.5	$ 378.5
Income taxes	263.1	205.6	167.3
Earnings from continuing operations before extraordinary item	$ 263.6	$ 229.9	$ 211.2
Earnings from discontinued operations		26.5	31.5
Gain on disposal of discontinued operations	148.8		
Earnings before extraordinary item	$ 412.4	$ 256.4	$ 242.7
Extraordinary item—Loss on early retirement of debt	(23.7)		
Net earnings	$ 388.7	$ 256.4	$ 242.7

EXHIBIT 13-6 *(concluded)*

Partial excerpts from footnotes:

Extraordinary Item

During 19x6, the Company retired, through repurchase and the exercise of redemption provisions under related indentures, approximately $300.8 of its outstanding long-term debt prior to its scheduled maturity. . . . The debt extinguishment results in an extraordinary loss of $23.7 after an income tax benefit of $22.7.

Discontinued Operations

In fiscal 19x6, the Company discontinued its restaurant operations through two separate transactions. In October 19x5, the Company sold its Foodmaker, Inc., restaurant subsidiary. . . . The sales price was $450.0 which consisted primarily of cash. . . . A gain on sale of $148.8 after applicable taxes of $59.2 was recognized. . . .

Sales of the discontinued operations of $564.5 in 19x5 and $628.3 in 19x4 have been excluded from net sales in the consolidated statement of earnings. Earnings of discontinued operations in 19x5 and 19x4 of $26.5 and $31.5, net of income taxes of $19.4 and $27.8, respectively, have been segregated and reported separately from results of continuing operations.

Unusual or Nonrecurring Items

These items represent provisions established (i) in fiscal 19x6 of $32.2 before applicable tax benefits of $7.7 representing the loss on sale of the Company's tuna cannery and related operations in Ecuador and a provision for write-down of tuna boats and related operations and (ii) in fiscal 19x4 for estimated losses of $38.0, before applicable tax benefits of $18.1, related to the closing of the San Diego tuna cannery. These provisions reduced earnings after taxes of $24.5 or $.32 per share in 19x6 and $19.9 or $.22 per share in 19x4.

continue in future periods by eliminating the effects of these separate items from net income.

Illustrating Reporting of Accounting Method Changes (Category 8)

Objective 4
The nature and purpose of items receiving separate income statement disclosures, including discontinued operations, extraordinary items, and accounting changes.

Accountants prepare financial statements on the basis of many specific accounting methods (sometimes called *accounting principles*). Management selects some of these accounting methods from a number of acceptable alternatives. For example, the method of measuring inventory is selected from a group of acceptable methods such as LIFO, FIFO, and average cost. When a company switches from one generally accepted accounting method to another, the effect of this change must be disclosed.[9]

The reporting of changes in accounting principles involves two steps:

Step 1: Compute the differential effect (if any) on net income of all prior years from using the newly elected method instead of the old (formerly used) method. This difference is called the *cumulative prior years' effect*

[9]Note that companies use separate procedures when switching from an unacceptable (non-GAAP) method to an acceptable one. The procedures are discussed in *APB Opinion No. 20.*

on net income and measures the difference that would have been reported in net income of all prior years if the new method had been in use since the beginning of the business.

Step 2: Apply the newly elected method to the current and future period's financial statements as if it had been used throughout the current period.

Accountants follow the second step for all changes in accounting methods. Also, step one is **measured** (if measurable) the same way for each method, but accountants disclose this measurement in one of two different ways, depending on the type of accounting change involved. These two different types of disclosure are explained below.

In most accounting changes, the cumulative prior years' effect is disclosed as a separate item (net of taxes) in the bottom portion of the income statement, as illustrated in category 8 of Exhibit 13-3. This first method is known as **current treatment** since the total of all prior years' effects is reported as a single item in the current year's income statement, and the results of prior years are not adjusted from their original reported amounts. For some accounting changes, accountants use a second method of disclosure referred to as **retroactive treatment,** which applies the cumulative prior years' effect by restating the results of prior years. This is done by adjusting the beginning retained earnings of the year of the change. The retroactive treatment is generally used when the accounting change seriously limits the comparability of the current year's results with prior years' results. For retroactive treatment the prior years' results are restated.

To illustrate the current and retroactive treatments, assume that during the current year a change in inventory method resulted in an increase in both the beginning asset balance and prior periods' income by $50,000 (assume no tax effect). This is the "cumulative prior years' effect" from step 1 above. To record this change using the **current treatment** (category 8 in the income statement), the following entry would be recorded for the prior years' effect of the change:

Inventory (A)	50,000	
Cumulative Effect of Change in Accounting Method (R)		50,000
To record change in method of accounting for inventory.		

Note from the above entry that the current treatment reports the prior years' effect of an accounting method change as a separate component in the current year's income statement.

As shown in the following entry, the **retroactive treatment** directly increases retained earnings for the prior years' effect of the accounting change.

Inventory (A)	50,000	
Retained Earnings (SE)		50,000
To record change in method of accounting for inventory.		

The retroactive treatment is not shown directly on the income statement but appears as an adjustment to the beginning retained earnings balance in the retained earnings statement. Exhibit 13-7 illustrates the current and retroactive treatments.

EXHIBIT 13-7

Reporting Accounting Changes: The Effect on Prior Years' Income

Method A: Current Treatment

Kelly Company
Partial Income Statement
For the Years Ending December 31

	19x7	*19x6*
Income from continuing operations	$4,897,000	$4,300,000
Discontinued operations (net of taxes)		(350,000)
Extraordinary loss (net of taxes)	(200,000)	
Change in accounting method—prior years' effect (net of taxes)	50,000	
Net income	$4,747,000	$3,950,000

Method B: Retroactive Treatment

Kelly Company
Retained Earnings Statement
For the Year Ending December 31, 19x7

Retained earnings, 1/1/x7	$17,847,000
Change in accounting method (net of taxes)	50,000
Revised 1/1/x7, balance	$17,897,000
Net income for 19x7	4,697,000*
Dividends for 19x7	(2,000,000)
Retained earnings, 12/31/x7	$20,594,000

*Net income of $4,747,000 per method A less the $50,000 effect of the accounting change would result in net income per method B of $4,697,000. The $50,000 effect of the accounting change is reported as an adjustment to Retained Earnings in method B.

Whichever treatment is required to record the accounting change, the new accounting method is applied to the current year's financial statements (step 2) to measure net income. The only difference between the current and retroactive treatments is where and how the cumulative prior years' effect (step 1) is disclosed. Most types of accounting changes are covered by special rules that specify whether current treatment or retroactive treatment must be used. These rules are not covered in this text.

Sometimes, it is impossible or impractical to measure the cumulative prior years' effect. Then, the new accounting method is applied to the current and future periods only, and no prior years' effect is recorded or reported. Generally, accounting changes are infrequent, and many accounting changes result from changes in accounting rules that eliminate one or more previously acceptable methods. Intermediate accounting textbooks discuss this subject in detail.

RETAINED EARNINGS STATEMENT

The retained earnings statement is sometimes reported as a separate statement, but it may be included as a part of the statement of changes in stockholders' equity. Exhibit 13-8 illustrates a comprehensive example of a retained earnings statement.

EXHIBIT 13-8

Comprehensive Example of Retained Earnings Statement

Teltex Corporation
Retained Earnings Statement
For the Year Ending December 31, 19x9

Category of Items		
	Retained earnings, 1/1/x9	$4,720,000
1	Prior period adjustment due to errors affecting prior years (net of taxes)	(140,000)
2	Change in accounting method (net of taxes)	(30,000)
	Adjusted retained earnings balance, 1/1/x9	$4,550,000
3	Net income for the period (from the income statement)	325,000
4	Dividends declared for 19x7 (cash and stock dividends)	(120,000)
	Retained earnings, 12/31/x9	$4,755,000

Prior Period Adjustments

Objective 5
The preparation of a retained earnings statement....

The beginning **retained earnings** balance captures the effects of net income and dividends for all prior years. This balance is the cumulative earnings amount from all prior years that has not been paid out to stockholders but has been **retained** in the business. If material errors were made in measuring net assets and operating profits in prior years, retained earnings must be corrected by making an adjustment to the beginning balance—a **prior period adjustment.** For example, assume a $10,000 credit sale from 19x1 was not recorded. The error was discovered on March 23, 19x3, when a customer paid $10,000 for an unrecorded account receivable. The error could be corrected as follows:

19x3			
Mar. 23	Accounts Receivable (A)	10,000	
	Retained Earnings (SE)		10,000
	To record the credit sale from 19x1.		
23	Cash (A)	10,000	
	Accounts Receivable (A)		10,000
	To record the collection of the receivable from 19x1.		

Consider the Teltex example in Exhibit 13-8. A $140,000 error, such as the example discussed above, is reported (net of taxes, if any) as a prior period adjustment, adding to the beginning retained earnings balance in the retained earnings statement (category 1 in Exhibit 13-8). Prior period adjustments are rare, and corrections due to errors of prior periods are seldom observed in actual published financial reports.

In addition to prior period adjustments for errors, the beginning retained earnings balance might be adjusted for accounting changes receiving retroactive treatment (category 2 in Exhibit 13-8). Retained earnings is then increased for net income of the period, or decreased for a net loss (category 3 in Exhibit 13-8). Finally, dividends are deducted from retained earnings (category 4 in Exhibit 13-8) to arrive at the ending retained earnings balance.

STATEMENT OF CHANGES IN STOCKHOLDERS' EQUITY

Objective 5
The preparation of... a statement of changes in stockholders' equity.

The statement of changes in stockholders' equity (SCSE) is designed to explain the cause of all changes in stockholders' equity accounts from the beginning to the end of the period. The example in Exhibit 13-9 assumes that (1) \$500,000 of no-par common stock was issued by Teltex Corporation during 19x9 and (2) **unrealized gains** of \$20,000 occurred during the period.

Unrealized items are typically from gains or losses on foreign currency translations for foreign operations (see Appendix B at the end of this text for a more complete discussion) or from long-term investments in stocks (as discussed in Chapter 12). Such gains or losses are not reported in net income or retained earnings but are reported as a separate account balance within stockholders' equity.

The SCSE reconciles all changes in stockholders' equity during the period; these changes equal the changes in net assets. As illustrated in Exhibit 13-9, the SCSE divides the change in stockholders' equity, which is always equal to the change in net assets, into three components:

1. Changes due to corrections or restatements (a \$170,000 decrease) resulting in an adjusted balance in stockholders' equity of \$14,830,000.
2. Changes in net assets from nonowner-related transactions (a \$345,000 increase).

EXHIBIT 13-9

Example of a Statement of Changes in Stockholders' Equity (SCSE)

Teltex Corporation
Statement of Changes in Stockholders' Equity
For the Year Ended December 31, 19x9

	Stockholders' Equity Accounts			
Cause of Change in Net Assets	*Retained Earnings*	*Common Stock (No-Par)*	*Accumulated Unrealized Gains*	*Total Stockholders' Equity*
Beginning balances	\$4,720,000	\$10,000,000	\$280,000	\$15,000,000
Error correction	(140,000)			(140,000)
Retroactive accounting change.	(30,000)			(30,000)
Adjusted balances.	\$4,550,000	\$10,000,000	\$280,000	\$14,830,000
Net income	325,000			\$ 325,000
Unrealized gains			20,000	20,000
Net nonowner transactions				\$ 345,000
Balances after nonowner transactions	\$4,875,000	\$10,000,000	\$300,000	\$15,175,000
Cash dividends	(120,000)			\$ (120,000)
Sale of stock		500,000		500,000
Net owner transactions . .				\$ 380,000
Ending balances	\$4,755,000	\$10,500,000	\$300,000	\$15,555,000

3. Changes in net assets from owner-related activities (a $380,000 increase).

The format for the SCSE may vary in practice from that shown in Exhibit 13-9. However, the purpose of the statement is always the same—explain all of the changes in stockholders' equity. Because of the balance sheet equality (A = L + SE), the changes in stockholders' equity must be equal to the changes in net assets.

The complete SCSE should be reported whenever any significant changes occur in stockholders' equity accounts other than retained earnings. Accountants may use only the retained earnings statement, which is reported in the first column of the SCSE, when retained earnings is the only stockholders' equity account that changed during the period.

EARNINGS PER SHARE

The remainder of this chapter discusses the measurement of earnings per share, the most widely cited piece of accounting data. **Earnings per share (EPS)** is a basic financial ratio **measuring the periodic earnings of the entity on a "per share of common stock" basis.**

EPS measurements must be reported on the face of the income statement for all publicly traded companies, but EPS need not be reported for private entities. Together with the market price and the dividends per share of common stock, EPS provides stockholders with summarized financial results that are easy to understand and helps them compare the corporation's performance from period to period on a per share basis.

The computation of EPS is essentially the net income of the entity divided by the number of outstanding shares of common stock. The objective is to measure the corporation's earnings that are available for the common stockholders. In some cases, this is a fairly simple computation, but the computation may be complicated by a number of factors. The following examples of computing EPS progress from the simplest situation to more complex situations.

Definitions of Simple and Complex Capital Structures

The capital structure of an entity may be described as either simple or complex. A **simple capital structure** has only one class of voting common stock and no other securities that have the potential to be converted to common stock. A **complex capital structure** has securities that may be converted to additional shares of common stock in certain situations. Examples of securities that may be converted to common stock include convertible preferred stock and convertible bonds. In this text we only illustrate EPS computations for simple capital structures. Intermediate and/or advanced accounting texts cover this topic in greater detail.

Examples of Simple Capital Structure EPS Computations

The three examples of EPS computations that we discuss are: example No. 1, constant shares outstanding; example No. 2, weighted average shares outstanding; and example No. 3, preferred stock outstanding. A discussion on the effect of separate disclosures on EPS measurements follows these examples.

Objective 6
Computation of EPS for a simple capital structure.

Constant Shares Outstanding. Let's begin illustrating EPS computations by assuming a simple capital structure consisting of 400,000 shares of common stock that are issued and outstanding throughout the year. Assume there are no preferred stocks and no convertible securities. Net income for the year is $2 million. The EPS computation for example No. 1 follows.

Example No. 1:

$$\text{EPS} = \frac{\text{Net income}}{\text{Number of shares of common stock}}$$

$$\text{EPS} = \frac{\$2{,}000{,}000}{400{,}000} = \underline{\underline{\$5}} \text{ per share}$$

This $5 EPS measure simply means that net income for the year amounted to $5 for every share of stock outstanding. Hence, each share earned $5 of net income.

Weighted Average Shares Outstanding. What if the number of shares outstanding changes during the year? In such cases, the net income is divided by the weighted average number of shares outstanding during the year. To illustrate, assume the following facts:

Date	*Number of Shares Issued*	*Total Shares Outstanding*
1/1/x3	0	400,000
5/1/x3	120,000	520,000
11/1/x3	120,000	640,000
12/31/x3	0	640,000

Assume there are no preferred stocks and no convertible securities. The 400,000 shares outstanding at the start of the year increase to 640,000 shares at year-end as a result of the two additional issuances of 120,000 each. Earnings for the year are $2 million. Since earnings are assumed to be generated throughout 19x3, the $2 million is divided by the weighted average number of shares of stock outstanding throughout 19x3 to compute EPS. The weighted average number of shares can be computed several ways, but each approach should always yield the same answer. For the data given above, two alternative computations would be as follows:

Computation Method A: Cumulative Approach

Balance in Total Number of Shares Outstanding	×	*Fractions of Year (in Months) Balance Was Maintained without Change*	=	*Weighted Average Number of Shares of Common Stock Outstanding*
400,000	×	4/12	=	133,333
520,000	×	6/12	=	260,000
640,000	×	2/12	=	106,667
Weighted average shares.				500,000

Computation Method B: Incremental Approach

Source of Layer	Number of Shares in Each Layer	×	Fraction of Year Each Layer Was Outstanding	=	Weighted Average Number of Shares of Common Stock Outstanding
Beginning balance	400,000	×	12/12	=	400,000
May 1 issuance	120,000	×	8/12	=	80,000
November 1 issuance	120,000	×	2/12	=	20,000
Weighted average shares . .					500,000

Method A will be used in the remainder of the chapter illustrations, but either method is acceptable. The EPS computation for this second example can now be made given the weighted average number of shares as computed above:

Example No. 2:

$$\text{EPS} = \frac{\text{Net income}}{\text{Weighted average number of shares of common stock}}$$

$$\text{EPS} = \frac{\$2{,}000{,}000}{500{,}000} = \underline{\underline{\$4}} \text{ per share}$$

Preferred Stock Outstanding. Next, assume the same facts as in example No. 2 above except that preferred stock is also outstanding and the total preferred stock dividend for 19x3 is $375,000. Since preferred stock dividends must be paid before dividends to common stockholders, they are deducted from net income to compute EPS to common stockholders. The revised EPS computation would be:

Example No. 3:

$$\text{EPS} = \frac{\text{Net income} - \text{Preferred stock dividends}}{\text{Weighted average number of shares of common stock}}$$

$$\text{EPS} = \frac{\$2{,}000{,}000 - \$375{,}000}{500{,}000 \text{ shares}} = \underline{\underline{\$3.25}} \text{ per share}$$

All three EPS computations examined so far have been examples of **simple capital structures,** which require only one EPS measurement per year. The practice of subtracting preferred dividends from net income in example no. 3 highlights the goal of EPS disclosure: to communicate the effects of earnings of the period on common stockholders' interests. Conceptually, common stockholders' ability to receive dividends is limited by both earnings and preferred dividend obligations.

Effects of Separate Disclosures. What should be disclosed for EPS when earnings include separate items such as discontinued operations and/or extraordinary items? These separate items normally are provided separate EPS

EXHIBIT 13-10

EPS Presentation of Discontinued Operations and Extraordinary Items

Maria's Company
Condensed Income Statement
For the Year Ended December 31, 19x3

Sales	$10,000,000
Cost of sales, taxes, and other expenses (details omitted)	6,375,000
Income from continuing operations	$ 3,625,000
Loss from discontinued operations (net of taxes)	(750,000)
Extraordinary loss (net of taxes)	(875,000)
Net income	$ 2,000,000
Earnings per share of common:	
From continuing operations	$ 6.50*
Discontinued operations	(1.50)†
Extraordinary loss	(1.75)‡
Net income	$ 3.25§

*($3,625,000 − $375,000 P.S. dividends)/500,000 shares.
†$750,000/500,000 shares.
‡$875,000/500,000 shares.
§($2,000,000 − $375,000 P.S. dividends)/500,000 shares.

presentation, since stockholders are most interested in the EPS from continuing operations. To illustrate, assume that the $2 million net income in the previous example included an extraordinary loss of $875,000 and a loss from discontinued operations of $750,000. Exhibit 13-10 shows an appropriate EPS presentation of discontinued operations and extraordinary items.

In most instances, the EPS number referred to in the financial news media is EPS from continuing operations. This is the amount of income from ongoing operations that might be expected to continue in future periods. Given investors' interest in future economic flows of an entity, it is widely assumed that the continuing components of net income are the most relevant for predicting future economic performance.

SUMMARY

This chapter has examined the income statement, retained earnings statement, statement of changes in stockholders' equity, and earnings per share.

In its most complex form, the income statement may include the results of many different types of nonowner transactions giving rise to revenues, expenses, gains, and losses. The format of the income statement is designed to permit readers to separate the strict operating activities of the entity giving rise to revenues and expenses from the other activities resulting in nonoperating gains and losses. Several special classes of transactions require separate disclosure net of taxes, including: (1) discontinued operations, (2) extraordinary items, and (3) those changes in accounting methods receiving "current treatment."

The components of the retained earnings statement could include adjustments to the beginning balance for prior period adjustments such as retroactive-effect-type accounting changes, as well as increases for net income and decreases for dividends. The SCSE is somewhat more comprehensive than a retained earnings statement in that it reconciles all changes in stockholders' equity from both nonowner-related (net income) and owner-related (e.g., dividends, new stock issues, and so on) transactions.

The final segment of the chapter discusses how to measure earnings per share. The chapter illustrates fundamental measurement procedures for simple capital structures. You may wish to examine the consolidated statements of earnings and retained earnings and the related footnotes for the Ralston Purina Company which are included at the end of the text (Appendix E) for a real world example of applications of the subjects considered in this chapter.

DEMONSTRATION EXERCISE

Czerkas Industries, Inc., has the following information available at March 31, 19x2, its year-end:

a. Revenues for the period were $4,360,000. Total expenses for the period were $2,875,000.
b. Used equipment was sold for a gain of $40,000.
c. Czerkas recorded a loss of $400,000 from an employee strike that occurred at the beginning of the year.
d. A major line of business was discontinued during the year and its assets sold. During last year, a $200,500 net loss from operations was incurred. The net assets of the discontinued operations were sold for a gain of $100,000.
e. Bonds due to mature in 19x5 were retired early for a $350,000 gain.
f. An accounting method was changed in 19x2. The cumulative effect of this change on income of all prior years (before 19x2) was to increase prior years' income by $240,000 before taxes. The effect of this accounting change in 19x2 has already been included in item (*a*) above. This change is to receive retroactive treatment disclosure in the 19x2 financial statements.
g. An error in a prior period's financial statements was discovered. If the error had not been made, reported income before taxes for that period would have been $500,000 less.
h. The income tax rate for income from continuing operations and the prior period error is 30%. For all other items, the income tax rate is 20%.
i. Retained earnings at April 1, 19x1, was $10,280,000. Czerkas Industries declared and paid preferred stock dividends of $100,000 and common stock dividends of $75,000 during the period.
j. On April 1, 19x1, 600,000 shares of common stock were issued and outstanding. An additional 90,000 shares of common stock were sold on November 30, 19x1. The company purchased 60,000 shares of its own common stock on January 31, 19x2.

Required:

1. Prepare the Czerkas Industries, Inc., combined income and retained earnings statement for the year.
2. Prepare Czerkas Industries, Inc.'s detailed EPS information for the period.

Solution:

Requirement 1:

Czerkas Industries, Inc.
Combined Income and Retained Earnings Statement
For the Year Ended March 31, 19x2

Revenues	$ 4,360,000
Expenses	(2,875,000)
Gain on sale of equipment	40,000
Loss from employee strike	(400,000)
Income from continuing operations before taxes	$ 1,125,000
Income tax expense on continuing operations	337,500
Income from continuing operations	$ 787,500
Discontinued operations:	
Net operating loss (net of taxes)	(160,400)
Gain on sale of assets (net of taxes)	80,000
Extraordinary gain on early debt retirement (net of taxes)	280,000
Net income	$ 987,100
Retained earnings, 4/1/x1	$10,280,000
Prior period adjustment due to error affecting prior year (net of taxes)	(350,000)
Cumulative effect of accounting method change (net of taxes)	192,000
Adjusted retained earnings balance	$10,122,000
Net income	987,100
Dividends declared and paid	(175,000)
Retained earnings, 3/31/x2	$10,934,100

Requirement 2:
Weighted average number of common stock shares:

Shares Outstanding	×	*Period of the Year*	=	*Weighted Average No. Shares Outstanding*
600,000	×	8/12	=	400,000
690,000	×	2/12	=	115,000
630,000	×	2/12	=	105,000
Total weighted average number of shares				620,000

EPS computations:

$$\text{Continuing operations} = \frac{\$787{,}500 - \$100{,}000}{620{,}000} = \$1.11$$

$$\text{Discontinued operations} = \frac{\$(80{,}400)}{620{,}000} = \$(0.13)$$

$$\text{Extraordinary gain} = \frac{\$280{,}000}{620{,}000} = \$0.45$$

$$\text{Net income} = \frac{\$987{,}100 - \$100{,}000}{620{,}000} = \$1.43$$

Czerkas Industries, Inc.
EPS Information
For the Year Ended March 31, 19x2

From continuing operations	$ 1.11
From discontinued operations . . .	(0.13)
From extraordinary gain	0.45
Net income	$ 1.43

KEY TERMS

Business segment. A major line of business or class of customers.

Complex capital structure. One that includes securities that may be converted to additional shares of common stock in certain situations.

Current treatment. Treatment accorded accounting method changes where the effect of the change is recorded in the current period's income statement.

Direct expensing. Records expenses as they occur based on the assumption that the revenues associated with these expenses have also been recorded.

Discontinued operations. An entity's business segment that has been eliminated requiring special disclosures in financial statements.

Earnings per share (EPS). Basic financial ratio measuring the periodic earnings of the entity on a "per share of common stock" basis.

Extraordinary items. Based on the environment in which the entity operates, an extraordinary item is both highly unusual in nature and not expected to occur again in the foreseeable future.

Gains. Increases in income attributable to a nonoperating activity.

Intraperiod tax allocation. When reporting special items, this calls for the separate associated tax effects to be reported with the special item rather than on the line with tax expense on continuing operations.

Losses. Decreases in income attributable to a nonoperating activity.

Matching. Occurs when the costs of achieving the recorded revenues are recognized (recorded) as expenses in the same period as their related revenues.

Prior period adjustments. Treatment accorded certain accounting method changes and error corrections that require a restatement of prior years' retained earnings balance.

Retroactive treatment. Treatment accorded certain accounting method changes whereby the cumulative prior years' effect is reported as an adjustment to the beginning retained earnings of the year of the change.

Simple capital structure. Has only one class of voting common stock and no other securities that have the potential to be converted to common stock.

Systematic allocation. Method of expensing costs. Examples include depreciation and amortization.

Unusual events. Infrequent events not directly related to operations. Extraordinary items are a special category of unusual events.

SYNONYMS

Accounting methods; accounting principles; accounting procedures.
Direct expensing; period costs.
Discontinued operations; sale of a business segment.
Errors of prior years; prior period adjustments.
Income statement; earnings statement; statement of operations.
Income tax credits; income tax reductions.
Income tax expense; provision for income taxes.
Net income; earnings; net profits.
Statement of changes in stockholders' equity; statement of stockholders' equity; changes in shareholders' equity.
Unusual items; nonoperating gains and losses.

QUESTIONS

1. What is the relation between net income and the change in the balance sheets from the start of the period to the end of the period?
2. What are the two main categories of transactions that result in changes in net assets? Give an example of each.
3. What criteria are required to recognize revenue?
4. What criteria are required to recognize expenses?
5. Some assets call for estimates in order to be measured. Give two examples.
6. How are changes in estimates accounted for?
7. How do gains and losses differ from revenues and expenses?
8. Where are most gains and losses reported?
9. What is intraperiod tax allocation?
10. What portion of income taxes is reported as income tax expense in the income statement?
11. What are discontinued operations?
12. What is the definition of an extraordinary item?
13. What is the most common example of extraordinary items?
14. How many ways are there to report changes in accounting methods? Explain each.
15. What are prior period adjustments?
16. What is included in the statement of changes in owners' equity (SCOE)?
17. What is EPS?
18. What is the difference between a simple and a complex capital structure?

EXERCISES

EXERCISE 13-1 — Expense Recognition
L.O. 1

For the following list of expenses, indicate which of the following three processes will normally cause the expense to be recognized in income measurement:

Process:
a. Matching.
b. Direct expensing.
c. Systematic allocation.

Expenses:

1. Depreciation—building.
2. Cost of goods sold.
3. Freight-in for merchandise purchases.
4. Freight-out for merchandise sold.
5. Packaging costs for bagging sold merchandise.
6. Advertising for past months' newspaper ads.
7. Office supplies.
8. Amortization of special tools used to service merchandise sold.
9. Research and development.
10. Administrators' salaries.
11. Income taxes.
12. Salespersons' commissions.

EXERCISE 13-2
L.O. 1

Expense Recognition

For each of the following balance sheet accounts, indicate the process by which they would ordinarily become recognized as expenses in the income statement:

Process:

a. Matching against revenue.
b. Direct expensing.
c. Systematic allocation to expense.

Balance Sheet Account:

1. Prepaid insurance.
2. Inventory-finished products ready for sale.
3. Machinery and equipment for service department.
4. Prepaid advertising.
5. Goodwill.
6. Wages payable—service repair.
7. Consultant's fees payable.
8. Interest payable on long-term note.
9. Natural resources—crude oil.
10. Patents.
11. Prepaid property taxes.
12. Prepaid officers' salaries.

EXERCISE 13-3
L.O. 1

Revenue Recognition

For each situation below, indicate when is the earliest possible acceptable point for revenue to be recognized. Provide the reasons for your answers. Assume all companies have December 31 year-ends.

Case A: A major league baseball franchise sells season tickets each year, with the average number of seats sold by December 31 each year for the forthcoming season equal to 18,000 over the past five years. By December 31, 19x4, the franchise has sold 22,000 season tickets for a total of $17,600,000 cash for the 19x5 season.

Case B: Big Ed's Discount Store has been in business for two years. Ed sells major household appliances to customers in a northeastern city on the following terms: $0 down, 10 equal monthly payments beginning in the fourth month after the month of sale. Ed does a credit check on each customer when they first buy an item, but after the first purchase a repeat customer simply needs to present the invoice from any earlier sale and Ed grants them "instant credit." Ed's sales and accounts receivable balances have grown steadily over the past two years. It is estimated that repossessed appliances account for about 30% to 35% of the first year's sales.

EXERCISE 13-4
L.O. 1

Revenue Recognition

For each situation below, indicate when is the earliest possible acceptable point for revenue to be recognized. Provide the reasons for your answers. Assume companies have December 31 year-ends.

Case A: A forthcoming concert at your school is sold out several weeks beforehand. The promoters collected all $3 million from ticket sales by November 14. All fees, salesagent wages, and commissions had been paid by December 10. The rock star's fee is known in advance (a flat $1 million). The concert dates are January 17 and 18. When can the promoter recognize revenue (and expenses) for this event?

Case B: An exploration firm discovered a large deposit of precious stones on December 13, 19x2. The stones are all of a high grade, and are traded on commodity exchanges throughout the world at prices which have ranged between $1,000 and $1,200 per carat over the past five years. The firm keeps the stones in its inventory until December 28, 19x7, when it sells all of them for $1,020 per carat.

EXERCISE 13-5
L.O. 2

Change in Estimate

The Martin Corporation provided a two-year warranty on all of its products. The actual sales and warranty cost history since the company first offered the warranty in 19x2 has been (in thousands):

	19x6	*19x5*	*19x4*	*19x3*	*19x2*
Sales	$7,050	$7,135	$6,820	$6,353	$6,101
Actual cost of warranty repairs . . .	136	122	141	127	143

Martin has been estimating warranty expense at 2.5% of sales each year since 19x2. During 19x7, Martin reported sales of $7,412,000 and incurred actual warranty repair costs of $170,000. Due to the favorable experience, Martin decided to change its estimate of warranty expense to 2% of sales on December 31, 19x7.

Required:
1. What was the balance in the Estimated Warranty Liability account at the start of 19x7?
2. What would be reported as warranty expense for 19x7?
3. What would be the balance in the Estimated Warranty Liability account at the end of 19x7?
4. When and how would the change in estimate affect Martin's financial statements?
5. Would you recommend a warranty expense allowance different than the 2% of sales?

EXERCISE 13-6
L.O. 2

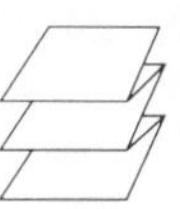

Change in Estimate

The Jackson Corporation purchased equipment at the start of 19x1 at a cost of $157,000. The equipment was expected to last 10 years and to have a salvage value of $12,000. Straight-line depreciation has been used on the equipment.

During 19x6, Jackson's management decided that the equipment would need to be replaced by the end of 19x7 due to obsolescence. The scrap value is still estimated to be $12,000.

Required:
1. What is the book value of the equipment on December 31, 19x5?
2. What should Jackson record for depreciation expense for 19x6?
3. How will this change in estimate be identified by financial statement users?

EXERCISE 13-7
L.O. 1, 3, 4

Multiple Choice (CPA Adapted)

1. Expense recognition is based in part on—
   a. Systematic allocations.
   b. Random events.
   c. The reliability of the system.
   d. None of the above.
2. Revenue recognition—
   a. Takes place at the point of sale.
   b. Takes place when goods are received.
   c. May take place only after a purchase order is signed.
   d. Is an objectively determinable point in time requiring little or no judgment.
   e. None of the above.
3. The determination of expenses of an accounting period is based partly on—
   a. Application of the cost principle.
   b. Application of the consistency principle.
   c. Application of the matching principle.
   d. Application of the objectivity principle.
   e. None of the above.
4. A transaction that is material in amount, unusual in nature, but not infrequent in occurrence should be presented separately as—
   a. A component of income from continuing operations, but not net of applicable income taxes.
   b. A component of income from continuing operations, net of applicable income taxes.
   c. An extraordinary item, net of applicable income taxes.
   d. A prior period adjustment, but not net of applicable income taxes.
5. An extraordinary item should be reported separately as a component of income.
   a. Before cumulative effect of accounting changes and after discontinued operations of a segment of a business.
   b. Before cumulative effect of accounting changes and before discontinued operations of a segment of a business.
   c. After cumulative effect of accounting changes and after discontinued operations of a segment of a business.
   d. After cumulative effect of accounting changes and before discontinued operations of a segment of a business.

EXERCISE 13-8
L.O. 3, 4

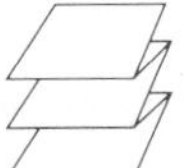

Income Statement Preparation

Bartlett Corporation reported the following account balances in the 19x7 pre-closing trial balance (in millions):

Account	*Debit (Credit)*
Cost of Goods Sold	$ 953
Loss on Sale of Factory Equipment	14
Loss on Retirement of Debt	35
Sales	(3,106)
Gain on Sale of Assets from Bakery Subsidiary	(79)
Loss on Operations from Bakery before Discontinuance	15
Gain on Sale of Temporary Investments	(22)
Selling Expenses	786
Administrative Expenses	857
Interest on Long-Term Debt	32
Dividends Declared by Bartlett	115

Bartlett has an income tax rate of 30% on all items affecting income.

Required:
Prepare Bartlett's 19x7 income statement using proper intraperiod tax allocation.

EXERCISE 13-9
L.O. 3, 4

Income Statement Preparation

Strake, Inc., reported the following account balances (in thousands) at the end of 19x4:

Gain on Sale of Discontinued Inventory	$ 33
Operating Loss from Fabric Division	497
Cost of Goods Sold	14,896
Explosion Loss in Chemical Plant	2,300
Interest Expense	248
Interest Income	169
Sales	35,871
Gain on Sale of Assets from Fabric Division	630
Loss on Retirement of Debt	220
Selling and Administrative Expenses	8,463

Assume that the appropriate tax rate on all items is 30%. No taxes have been included in the amounts reported above.

Required:
1. Prepare an income statement for 19x4 using proper intraperiod tax allocation.
2. What is your best guess at net income for 19x5?

EXERCISE 13-10
L.O. 3, 4

Income Statement Preparation

Drake, Inc., reported the following account balances (in thousands) at the end of 19xx:

Sales	$7,837
Cost of Goods Sold	5,736
Gain on Early Retirement of Debt	347
Fire Loss in Paint Division	186
Selling and Administrative Expenses	943
Operating Loss from Plastics Division	147
Gain on Sale of Assets from Plastics Division	321
Interest Expense	129
Loss on Sale of Discontinued Inventory Items	37

Assume that Drake has not considered the tax effect of the data reported above, and that a 30% tax rate is appropriate for all items.

Required:
Prepare an income statement for 19xx using proper intraperiod tax allocation.

EXERCISE 13-11
L.O. 5

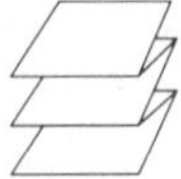

Retained Earnings Statement

Marglett Corporation reported the following balance sheet (in thousands) at December 31, 19x5:

	19x5	*19x4*
Stockholders' Equity		
Common stock—($1 par)	$ 80	$ 75
Capital in excess of par	356	290
Retained earnings	228	193
Total stockholders' equity	$664	$558

On April 1, 19x5, Marglett issued 5,000 additional shares of common stock. Marglett paid out $28,000 in cash dividends during 19x5.

Required:
Prepare a retained earnings statement for 19x5.

EXERCISE 13-12
L.O. 5

Statement of Changes in Stockholders' Equity

The Weltex Corporation began 19x1 with the following stockholders' equity account balances (in thousands):

Common Stock (1,000,000 shares)	$ 8,500
Unrealized Gains and Losses	(267)
Retained Earnings	4,387
Total Stockholders' Equity	$12,620

During 19x1, the following occurred:

a. Declared and paid $400,000 cash dividends to Weltex shareholders.
b. Issued another 200,000 shares of common stock on June 30, 19x1, for $15 per share.
c. Reported net income of $1,430,000 for 19x1.
d. Reported unrealized gains of $48,000.

Required:
Prepare a statement of changes in stockholders' equity for 19x1.

EXERCISE 13-13
L.O. 5

Statement of Changes in Stockholders' Equity

The Marslong Corporation reported the following account balances as of December 31, 19x4 (in thousands):

Common Stock (no par)	$2,675
Unrealized Gains and Losses	143
Retained Earnings	1,431
Total Stockholders' Equity	$4,249

The following occurred during 19x5:

a. Reported net income of $386,000.
b. Declared cash dividends of $128,000.
c. Paid cash dividends of $120,000.
d. Issued 4,500 shares of stock to corporate managers for $72,000 cash.
e. Reported unrealized holding losses of $15,000.

Required:
Prepare a statement of changes in stockholders' equity for 19x5.

EXERCISE 13-14
L.O. 6

EPS Computation

Refer to the data in Exercise 13-11 for the Marglett Corporation.

Required:
Compute EPS for 19x5 for Marglett's stockholders.

EXERCISE 13-15
L.O. 6

EPS Computation

Refer to the data in Exercise 13-12 for Weltex Corporation.

Required:
Compute EPS for Weltex for 19x1.

EXERCISE 13-16
L.O. 6

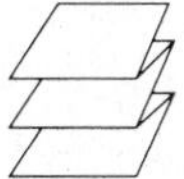

Weighted Average Number of Shares—EPS

Owens Engineering, Inc. (OEI), reported earnings of $2,014,000 for the year ending December 31, 19xx. During 19xx, OEI had several changes in the number of outstanding shares of stock. At the start of 19xx, OEI had 710,000 shares outstanding. On April 30, 19xx, OEI issued 40,000 shares of stock to company officials as a part of their stock incentive plan. On July 1, 19xx, OEI repurchased 50,000 shares of stock in the open market at $24.50 per share. On September 30, 19xx, OEI issued an additional 140,000 shares as partial compensation for the acquisition of Pell Engines Company.

Required:
1. Compute the weighted average number of shares of OEI stock for 19xx.
2. Compute EPS for 19xx (rounded to the nearest cent).

EXERCISE 13-17
L.O. 6

Weighted Average Number of Shares

The Travis Corporation had several changes in its capital structure for the year 19xx as follows:

Date	*Description*
1/1 . . .	400,000 shares of common stock outstanding
2/28 . . .	Issued 25,000 shares of common stock
6/30 . . .	Issued 50,000 shares of common stock
9/30 . . .	Issued 40,000 shares of preferred stock

Required:
Compute the weighted average number of shares of common stock for 19xx.

EXERCISE 13-18
L.O. 6

EPS Computation

The Eagle Corporation reported net income of $1,987,000 for 19x1. Eagle declared and paid preferred stock dividends of $367,000 and common stock dividends of $285,000 during 19x1. Eagle started 19x1 with 220,000 shares of common stock and sold an additional 60,000 shares on June 30, 19x1.

Required:
Compute Eagle's EPS for 19x1.

P R O B L E M S

PROBLEM 13-1
L.O. 1

Revenue Recognition

The following events occurred during December of 19x1 for the Robinson Corporation, a calendar-year company:

a. Collected cash of $1,800 from a customer on an account receivable. The sale occurred in 19x1.
b. Collected cash of $2,400 from a customer as a deposit for equipment to be delivered and installed by Robinson at the customer's plant in January 19x2.
c. Sold equipment on account to a customer for $8,000. The equipment was installed in December 19x1.
d. Collected cash of $650 from a customer for an account receivable originally recorded in 19x6 and written off as uncollectible early in 19x1.
e. Received a purchase order from a customer for equipment of $18,000 that Robinson has in inventory. The customer plans to install the equipment in January 19x2.

Required:
1. Record the journal entries in general journal form for the above events.
2. For each entry, identify the year in which revenue from the transaction should be recognized in the income statement.
3. What year is revenue recorded for each of these events?
4. Are there any differences between your answers to parts 2 and 3 above? Explain why.

PROBLEM 13-2
L.O. 1

Expense Recognition

The Orbiter Corporation reported the following activities in the last month of 19xx:

a. Paid salaries to top corporate executives of $180,000.
b. Recorded depreciation for the year of $425,000.
c. Recorded reduction in inventory of $487,500 in conjunction with a credit sale to a customer.
d. Recorded purchase of $2,100 in office supplies on open account on December 31.
e. Paid advertising invoices of $37,800 for newspaper ads from the current month.
f. Recorded accrued interest payable of $8,750 on long-term debt at year-end.
g. Recorded accrued salaries payable of $17,500 at year-end.
h. Purchased $64,000 of machinery with a 10-year economic life for cash.

Required:
1. Record the journal entries in general journal form for the above activities on Orbiter's books.
2. Indicate which year or years each item will be recognized as an expense.
3. Indicate which of the following processes is (or will be) used to recognize the expense for each item recorded in part 1:
   a. Matching.
   b. Direct expensing.
   c. Systematic allocation.

PROBLEM 13-3
L.O. 2

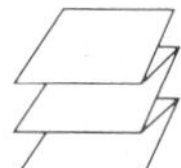

Change in Estimate

Jason Appliances has previously estimated its warranty expense at 2% of annual net sales. The following data are reported at the end of 19x4:

Net sales	$4,000,000
Estimated Warranty Liability account (1/1/x4 balance)	60,000 credit
Payments made during 19x4 for warranty parts and service by Jason	75,000

At the end of 19x4, Jason decides to decrease warranty expense estimates to 1.5% of annual net sales.

Required:
Record the 19x4 warranty expense. What is the Estimated Warranty Liability account balance as of the end of 19x4?

PROBLEM 13-4
L.O. 2

Change in Estimate

The Towers, Inc., owns a hotel that is being depreciated on a straight-line basis. The original estimated useful life of the hotel was 50 years, with a $1 million salvage value. The hotel, which originally cost $301 million, had a net book value of $187 million as of December 31, 19x6. During 19x7, certain improvements to the hotel, costing $12 million, were added to the Building account. During 19x7, Towers also revised the expected total useful life from 50 to 60 years, and the salvage value from $1 million to $3 million.

Required:
Record the depreciation expense on the hotel for 19x7.

PROBLEM 13-5
L.O. 2

Change in Estimate

The Whade Corporation had purchased equipment at the start of 19x1 at a cost of $400,000. The equipment was expected to last five years and had no expected salvage value at the time of the purchase.

The following is the **preliminary** income measurement for Whade for 19x3:

Whade Corporation
Income Statement
For the Year Ending December 31, 19x3

Sales	$4,382,000
Cost of goods sold	3,845,000
Gross margin	$ 537,000
Selling and administrative expenses	423,000
Depreciation expense—equipment	80,000
Interest expense	57,000
Net loss	$ (23,000)

Before the books are closed for 19x3, Whade's management reviewed the equipment and decided that the original estimated life of five years was not appropriate, but that an eight-year life was more realistic. Also, Whade's management believes the equipment will have a scrap value of $12,000 instead of zero after it is fully depreciated. Whade uses straight-line depreciation.

Required:

1. Prepare the entry needed to record the change in estimate for 19x3 assuming the books have not yet been closed.
2. Prepare the revised 19x3 income statement. (Ignore income taxes since Whade makes this change in estimate for financial reporting purposes only.)
3. If Whade's management had made this change in estimate early in 19x4 but before the 19x3 financial statements had been issued to stockholders, how would your answer to part 2 above have changed?

PROBLEM 13-6
L.O. 1, 3, 4

Income Statement Preparation

Consider these account balances of the Edge Corporation as of December 31, 19x1:

Salespersons Commissions	$ 39,000
Sales Returns	61,000
Depreciation Expense	185,000
Gain on Early Retirement of Debt	120,000
Cost of Goods Sold	5,295,000
Selling and Administrative Expenses	315,000
Gain on Sale of Assets from Discontinued Operations	395,000
Operating Loss on Operations Discontinued in 19x1	175,000
Sales	7,532,000
Interest Expense	140,000
Loss on Sale of Discontinued Inventory	77,000
Gain on Sale of Temporary Investments	36,000
Research and Development Expense	93,000

Assume that all items are taxed at the 40% rate and that no income taxes are included in the items listed above.

Required:

Prepare the 19x1 income statement for Edge Corporation using appropriate intraperiod tax allocation.

PROBLEM 13-7
L.O. 1, 3–5

Income Statement/Retained Earnings Statement

The following information was summarized from the adjusted trial balance of the Right Company at the end of 19xx:

	Debits	Credits
Sales		$3,507,000
Cost of Goods Sold	$1,500,000	
Selling Expenses	185,000	
Administrative Expenses	218,000	
Other Gains and Losses		35,000
Discontinued Operations	132,000	
Extraordinary Gain		47,000
Prior Period Adjustment	13,000	
Retained Earnings (1/1/xx balance)		3,840,000
Common Stock (1/1/xx balance)		2,900,000
Dividends Declared—19xx	125,000	
Accounting Change (retroactive treatment)		22,000
Accounting Change (current treatment)	41,000	

Ignore income taxes.

Required:

1. Prepare the 19xx income statement.
2. Prepare the 19xx retained earnings statement.

PROBLEM 13-8
L.O. 1, 3–5

Income Statement/Retained Earnings Statement

The following data are from the financial statements of Curry Corporation at December 31, 19xx (its year-end):

	Debits	Credits
Gain from sale of land	$	$ 38,000
Prior period adjustment due to error	42,000	
Operating loss on discontinued operations	209,000	
Gain on sale of net assets in discontinued operations		480,000
Income from continuing operations		1,050,000
Change in accounting method	75,000	
Gain from early retirement of debt		79,000
Loss from earthquake	410,000	
Beginning retained earnings		3,565,000
Dividends declared (but unpaid)	50,000	

The change in accounting method is to receive retroactive treatment. None of these data has reported the impact of taxes, which are at a 40% rate.

Required:

Using proper intraperiod tax allocation, prepare a partial income statement beginning with "Income before taxes," and a retained earnings statement.

PROBLEM 13-9
L.O. 4, 5

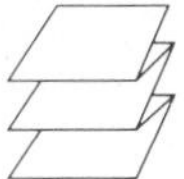

Income and Retained Earnings Statements

The following year-end balances were taken from the pre-closing trial balance of Trebble, Inc., on December 31, 19x9 (in thousands):

Sales	$ 577 Cr.
Gain on retirement of debt	32 Cr.
Dividends declared	18 Dr.
Dividend and interest income	26 Cr.
Correction of prior period's error	34 Dr.
Cumulative effect of change in accounting method	12 Dr.
Selling and administrative expenses	108 Dr.
Interest expense	16 Dr.
Loss from uninsured earthquake damages	60 Dr.
Loss on restructuring of steel operations and closing of one steel plant	14 Dr.
Cost of goods sold	321 Dr.
Loss on sale of obsolete equipment	7 Dr.
Retained earnings (December 31, 19x8)	1,399 Cr.

The appropriate income tax rate is 30% on all items.

Required:
Prepare income and retained earnings statements for 19x9.

PROBLEM 13-10
L.O. 1, 3–5

Income Statement and Stockholders' Equity

Shanklin, Inc., a multisegment San Francisco-based company, experienced the following changes during 19x1:

a. Debt due to mature in 19x2 was retired at a gain of $140,000.
b. Made a change in accounting method calling for retroactive treatment that resulted in a gain of $280,000.
c. Sold obsolete inventory at a loss of $95,500.
d. Incurred $75,000 in damages to several structures due to a minor earthquake registering 5.2 on the Richter scale.
e. Discontinued all retail operations during 19x1. These operations were sold at their market value, which exceeded book value by $650,000. The retail stores had lost $194,000 during 19x1 prior to their closing.
f. Sold securities held for the past 28 years at a gain of $1,850,000. These were the only long-term investments owned by Shanklin.

In addition to these changes, Shanklin reported the following data:

Common stock (no par) (1/1/x1)	6,800,000
Retained earnings (1/1/x1)	4,875,000
Sales	6,730,000
Cost of sales	5,295,000
Selling and administrative expenses	986,000
Interest expense	135,000
Dividends declared and paid	247,000

None of the information provided above has considered income taxes, which are 40% on all items.

Required:
1. Prepare an income statement for 19x1 in good form. Include all items in their appropriate place using proper intraperiod tax allocation.

2. Prepare a retained earnings statement for 19x1.
3. Assume there were 300,000 shares of common stock outstanding during 19x1. Prepare the EPS data to accompany the income statement.
4. What were the changes (increases/decreases) in net assets during 19x1 from:
   a. Operations?
   b. Earnings?
   c. All nonowner transactions?

PROBLEM 13-11
L.O. 5

Statement of Changes in Stockholders' Equity

Langstrom Corporation reported the following data (in thousands) at the end of 19x5:

	19x5	*19x4*
Stockholders' Equity		
Common stock ($2 par)	$ 8,400	$ 8,000
Capital in excess of par	21,000	19,960
Unrealized losses on long-term investments	(189)	(214)
Retained earnings	13,105	12,732
Total stockholders' equity	$42,316	$40,478

During 19x5 the following activities took place:

a. Issued 200,000 shares of common stock on May 1, 19x5.
b. Declared and paid cash dividends of $745,000 during 19x5.

Required:
Prepare a statement of changes in stockholders' equity for 19x5.

PROBLEM 13-12
L.O. 5

Reconciling Changes in Stockholders' Equity

During 19x2, the following changes occurred in the balance sheet of Kwicker, Inc.:

Kwicker, Inc.
Balance Sheet
December 31
(in millions)

	19x2	*19x1*
Assets		
Current assets:		
Cash	$ 2	$ 3
Other current assets	19	17
Total current assets	$21	$20
Noncurrent assets:		
Long-term depreciable assets (net)	$15	$12
Long-term investments	4	5
Total noncurrent assets	$19	$17
Total assets	$40	$37

Liabilities and Stockholders' Equity

Liabilities:		
Current liabilities	$ 7	$ 6
Long-term liabilities	11	12
Total liabilities	$18	$18
Stockholders' equity:		
Common stock (no par)	$15	$13
Retained earnings	7	6
Total stockholders' equity	$22	$19
Total liabilities and stockholders' equity	$40	$37

During 19x2, Kwicker declared and paid cash dividends of $2 million.

Required:

1. What is the apparent change (increase/decrease) in net assets during 19x2 from nonowner-related transactions?
2. What is the apparent change during 19x2 from owner-related transactions?
3. Determine net income for 19x2.

PROBLEM 13-13
L.O. 4

Discontinued Operations

In its 19x2 annual report, Multi Corporation disclosed the following results (in thousands):

	19x2	*19x1*
Sales	$1,826	$1,714
Cost of sales	(730)	(702)
Depreciation	(112)	(105)
Administrative and other expenses	(701)	(655)
Pretax income	$ 283	$ 252
Income tax expense (30%)	(85)	(76)
Net income	$ 198	$ 176

During 19x3, Multi Corporation discontinued one of its lines of business. The discontinued operation had performed poorly over the past few years with the following **separate** results (in thousands):

	19x3	*19x2*	*19x1*
Sales	$145	$ 292	$ 286
Cost of sales	(77)	(163)	(151)
Depreciation	(13)	(21)	(22)
Administrative and other expenses	(75)	(140)	(135)
Pre-tax loss	$ (20)	$ (32)	$ (22)
Income tax credit (30%)	6	10	7
Net loss	$ (14)	$ (22)	$ (15)

The sale of the net assets of the discontinued operations in September of 19x3 resulted in a pre-tax gain of $100,000. During 19x3, Multi reported the following results (in thousands) **without** considering the discontinued operations:

	19x3
Sales	$1,986
Cost of sales	(835)
Depreciation	(107)
Administrative and other expenses	(697)
Pretax income	$ 347

Assume that the appropriate tax rate for all years is 30% and that all amounts are rounded to the nearest thousand.

Required:
1. Prepare the comparative income statements for Multi Corporation for 19x3, 19x2, and 19x1 as they would appear in the 19x3 year-end financial statements.
2. What was the total tax expense for Multi Corporation for the year 19x3?

PROBLEM 13-14
L.O. 4

Accounting Method Changes

Westwick, Inc., reported the following **preliminary** results for 19x1:

Westwick, Inc.
Combined Statement of Income and Retained Earnings
For the Year Ended December 31, 19x1
(in thousands)

Sales revenues		$12,875
Less:		
Cost of sales	$6,923	
Depreciation expense	743	
Administrative and other expenses	820	8,486
Income before taxes		$ 4,389
Income tax expense		1,317
Net income		$ 3,072
Beginning retained earnings		14,023
		$17,095
Less dividends		2,000
Ending retained earnings		$15,095

Assume that after examining these preliminary figures, Westwick decides to change its inventory accounting method. In computing the effects of this change, Westwick's accountant determined the following:

a. The cumulative effect on all years **prior** to 19x1 is to reduce income by $2,686,000 after considering tax credits of $1,100,000. (The before-tax reduction is $3,786,000.)
b. The effect on 19x1 results would be to increase cost of sales from $6,923,000 to $7,400,000.
c. The appropriate tax rate for 19x1 is 30%.

Required (round all amounts to the nearest thousand):
1. Assume this accounting method change should receive current treatment (as illustrated in Exhibit 13-7). Prepare the revised 19x1 income and retained earnings statement for Westwick.
2. Assume this accounting method change should receive retroactive treatment (as illustrated in Exhibit 13-7). Prepare the revised 19x1 income and retained earnings statement for Westwick.
3. What is the total 19x1 tax expense for Westwick from all items including the accounting method change?
4. What was the apparent 19x1 tax savings resulting from this change?

PROBLEM 13-15
L.O. 4

Accounting Method Change and Discontinued Operations

During 19x1, Theta Corporation changed its method of accounting for inventory and also discontinued one of its major lines of business. The effects from these two items were:

a. 19x1 cost of goods sold increased by $34 million due to the accounting method change.
b. Net income before taxes for years prior to 19x1 decreased by $127 million due to the accounting method change.
c. Operating losses before taxes in 19x1 from the discontinued operations were $50 million.
d. The net assets of the discontinued operations were sold at a pretax gain of $50 million.
e. In 19x1, Theta declared and paid dividends of $45 million.

The preliminary income statement results (in millions) **before** considering the accounting change and **after** eliminating the effects of the discontinued operations were:

	19x1
Sales revenue	$1,029
Cost of goods sold	$ 387
Depreciation expense	93
Selling and administrative expense	176
Other expenses	38
Total expenses	$ 694
Pre-tax income from operations	$ 335

The retained earnings balance of Theta at the start of 19x1 was $795 million. The appropriate tax rate for all of Theta's transactions is assumed to be 30%.

Required (round all answers to the nearest million):

1. Assume the accounting method change is disclosed as a current treatment type of change. Prepare Theta's income statement and retained earnings statement for 19x1.
2. Assume the accounting method change is disclosed as a retroactive treatment type of change. Prepare Theta's income statement and retained earnings statement for 19x1.
3. What is the total tax expense of Theta for all transactions described in this problem for 19x1.

PROBLEM 13-16
L.O. 3, 4

Special Disclosures

Fractor Corporation reported several special items in 19x2 in addition to its normal ongoing operations. The ongoing operations generated the following results (in millions):

	19x2	*19x1*
Sales	$661	$602
Less:		
Cost of sales	$279	$263
Selling and administrative expenses	201	189
Depreciation expense	64	57
Other losses (gains)	13	(5)
Total	$557	$504
Pre-tax income from operations	$104	$ 98

In addition to these operating results, you have learned about the following items:

a. Included in other losses (gains) for 19x2 and 19x1 were the following items (in millions):

	19x2	*19x1*
Write-off of obsolete inventory . . .	$15	
Uninsured fire loss		$ 5
Gain on early debt retirement . . .		(10)
Gain on sale of used assets	(2)	
Total loss (gain).	$13	$ (5)

b. The tax rate on all items is assumed to be fixed at 30%.

c. The discontinued operations of Fractor Corporation generated the following results before taxes (in millions):

	19x2	*19x1*
Loss from operations	$(10)	$(20)
Gain from sale of assets	30	—
Net	$ 20	$(20)

Note that these results are **not** included in the results from ongoing operations provided above.

d. The company changed an accounting method in 19x2. The cumulative effect of this change on income of all prior years (**before** 19x2) is to increase prior years' income by $40 million **before taxes.** The effect of this accounting change on 19x2 is already included in "Pre-tax income from operations." This change is to receive current treatment disclosure in the 19x2 financial statements.

Required:

1. Prepare the comparative income statements for 19x2 and 19x1 for Fractor Corporation as they should be reported at the end of 19x2 after considering additional items (*a*) through (*d*) above. Be sure to employ proper intraperiod tax allocation.
2. Compute the total tax expense for 19x2 from all items included in the income statement in 19x2.

PROBLEM 13-17
L.O. 6

Computing EPS with Preferred Stock

Hay Corporation issued 600,000 shares of common stock when originally organized in 19x1. On July 15, 19x5, Hay issued 400,000 shares of preferred stock, which had no voting rights and was **not** convertible in any way. Hay reported net income during 19x6 of $7,720,000. Hay also declared and paid $1,800,000 cash dividends to common stockholders, and $880,000 cash dividends to preferred stockholders.

Required:
Compute Hay's EPS for 19x6.

PROBLEM 13-18
L.O. 6

EPS with New Shares and Preferred Stock

Danoff, Inc., reported net income of $1,832,000 for 19x7. The following new common stock issues occurred during 19x7:

Jan. 1 1,000,000 common shares outstanding (from prior issuances).
July 31 Issue 120,000 shares of common stock.
Sept. 30 Issue 200,000 shares of common stock.

During 19x7 Danoff declared and paid $380,000 cash dividends to preferred stockholders, and $612,000 cash dividends to common stockholders.

Required:
1. Compute the weighted average number of common shares outstanding during 19x7.
2. Compute EPS on common stock for 19x7.

PROBLEM 13-19
L.O. 6

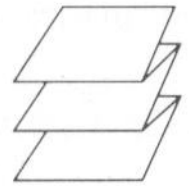

EPS with New Shares and Preferred Stock

Darren Corporation reported net income for 19x8 of $1,410,000. The following new common stock issues occurred during 19x8:

January	1	450,000 common shares outstanding (from prior issuances).
May	31	Issued 60,000 shares of common stock.
July	31	Issued 90,000 shares of common stock.

During 19x8 Darren declared and paid $365,000 cash dividends to preferred stockholders, and $490,000 cash dividends to common stockholders.

Required:
1. Compute the weighted average number of common shares outstanding during 19x8.
2. Compute EPS on common stock for 19x8.
3. Assume no new stock was issued in 19x9. Darren paid the same preferred dividends in 19x9, and reported net income of $1,500,000. Compute EPS for 19x9.

PROBLEM 13-20
L.O. 6

EPS: New Common and Preferred Issuances

Edge Corporation began 19x5 with 500,000 shares of common stock and 300,000 shares of preferred stock. On May 31, 19x5, Edge issued 240,000 additional shares of common stock. On June 30, 19x5, Edge issued 300,000 additional shares of preferred stock. The preferred stock pays a $0.75 per share dividend twice each year, on April 1 and October 1. Edge reported net income of $2,819,000 for 19x5. There were no new stock issues in 19x6, when Edge reported net income of $3,083,000.

Required:
Compute EPS on common stock for 19x5 and 19x6.

CASES

CASE 13-1
L.O. 3, 4

Disclosure

Each of the following items has occurred during the current year. Indicate the specific financial statement, if any, in which each would appear, and briefly discuss where and how each item would appear in that statement. State any assumptions made in arriving at your decisions.

a. Loss from tornado damage.
b. Losses from sale of assets of a discontinued segment.
c. Loss on discontinuance of certain operations that are a segment of the entity.
d. Gain on sale of marketable securities properly classified as a current asset.
e. Resignation of the company's president.
f. Write-off of a material amount of intangible assets.

CASE 13-2
L.O. 3, 4

Disclosure

Each of the following items has occurred during the current year. Indicate the specific financial statement, if any, in which each would appear, and briefly discuss where and how each item would appear in that statement. State any assumptions made in arriving at your decisions.

a. Gain on sale of fixed assets.
b. Error in recording depreciation for the past three years.
c. Loss on early extinguishment of long-term debt.
d. Write-down of accounts receivable.
e. Change from the FIFO inventory measurement method to LIFO (a current treatment accounting change).
f. Gain on sale of intangible assets.
g. Loss due to the effects of a strike.
h. Loss on disposal of a major segment of an entity—the only segment producing furniture.

CASE 13-3
L.O. 4

Disclosure Decisions

During your first year as staff auditor for a large local CPA firm, you encounter the following difficult situations requiring your judgment as to how they should be disclosed.

a. A company involved in the manufacture of flour had several different operations: growing wheat on company-owned land; storing wheat from its own crops and other companies' crops; milling the wheat into finished products. During the current year, all company land used for growing wheat was sold to another company, along with the equipment used for these operations.
b. During the current period, a company that had previously used the LIFO inventory method changed to FIFO to be consistent with current industry methods.
c. A local farm moved its farming operations to another location up the coast. The costs of this move were high, equal to 50% of revenues for the period. However, the move is expected to improve production for many years.
d. An earthquake damaged the structure of the Bank of Kansas City's main office in downtown Kansas City. The cost to repair the structure will be about 30% of last year's profits. This damage was unusual in that few people actually observed the quake and only a few other companies reported any damage. No one could recall a similar disaster ever having occurred before in Kansas.
e. During the past period, a client with many foreign operations experienced an unusually large gain from the translation of foreign currency into U.S. currency for financial reporting purposes, five times larger than the largest gain previously reported, and three times larger than all other sources of income for the period.

Required:
Explain how each of these situations should be reported in the financial statements.

EVALUATING FINANCIAL STATEMENTS

CASE 13-4
L.O. 3, 4

Annual Report Disclosures—Ralston Purina

Consider the annual report disclosures for Ralston Purina reported in Exhibit 13-6 of the chapter. Answer the following questions:

a. What is the before-tax amount of the "Unusual or nonrecurring items" for 19x6?
b. What is the before-tax amount of the "Gain on disposal of discontinued operations" for 19x6?

c. What is the before-tax amount of the extraordinary loss for 19x6?
d. What was the estimated total "Income taxes" (income tax expense) for Ralston Purina for 19x6 from all components of the earnings statement?
e. What did Ralston Purina probably report for 19x5 "earnings from continuing operations" in 19x5? If this differs from what is reported for 19x5 in 19x6 ($229.9), explain why.

CASE 13-5 Annual Report Disclosures—Union Carbide

L.O. 3, 4

The following data are excerpted from the 19x5 annual report of Union Carbide Corporation (UCC) (amounts are in millions):

Partial Income Statement
For the Year Ended December 31

	19x5	*19x4*
Net sales	$ 9,003	$9,508
Cost of sales	6,252	6,702
Research and development	275	265
Selling, administrative, and other expenses	1,289	1,221
Depreciation	596	507
Interest on debt	292	300
Other expenses (income)	173	(77)
Unusual charges	1,168	—
Income (loss) before income taxes	$(1,042)	$ 590
Income tax credit	441	(227)
Income (loss) of consolidated companies	$ (601)	$ 363

In the financial statement footnotes, Union Carbide disclosed the following details concerning its 19x5 "unusual charges" of $1,168,000.

Excerpt from footnotes:

The following is a summary of the items comprising the 19x5 unusual charges:

Millions of dollars	*19x5*
Inventory write-downs	$ 78
Fixed asset write-downs, write-offs and related items:	
Net fixed assets	615
Mine development expenses	24
Foreign currency equity adjustment	45
Write-downs of other assets and facility closing costs	202
Staff reduction costs	204
	$1,168

Required:
Consider these data and answer the following questions:

1. Are the "unusual charges" the same thing as extraordinary items?
2. Do any of the unusual charges seem to be items that require separate disclosure as extraordinary items, discontinued operations, or accounting changes?

3. Are the unusual charges stated before tax?
4. What kind of a year did Union Carbide have in 19x5 excluding the unusual items?
5. What would probably happen to earnings in 19x6 and future years if the $1,168,000 in write-downs, write-offs, etc., taken in 19x5 were more than an unusual charge than was actually warranted? In other words, what effect would it have in future periods if inventory (for example) was written down by $78 million when it should have only been written down by say $30 million?

CASE 13-6 Annual Report Disclosures—General Electric

L.O. 3, 4

The following summarized data are abstracted from a recent General Electric (GE) annual report:

General Electric Company and Consolidated Affiliates
Statement of Earnings
For the Years Ended December 31
(in millions)

	19x6	*19x5*
Revenues	$36,725	$29,252
Cost and expenses:		
Cost of goods sold and services sold	$26,187	$20,843
Selling, general, and administrative expense	5,963	4,594
Interest and other financial charges	625	361
Unusual items:		
(Gains) from sales of assets	(50)	(518)
Provisions for business restructuring activities	311	447
Special payment to non-exempt and hourly employees		93
Total costs and expenses	$33,036	$25,820
Earnings before income taxes and minority interest	$ 3,689	$ 3,432
Provision for income taxes	(1,200)	(1,143)
Minority interest in earnings of consolidated affiliates	3	(12)
Net earnings	$ 2,492	$ 2,277
Net earnings per share (in dollars)	$ 5.46	$ 5.00

In addition, GE reported the following data in its financial statement footnotes:

Excerpt from footnotes:

Regarding Accounting Change

Restatement of prior years' financial statements for the change in method of accounting for oil and gas properties. In 19x6, the Company changed its method of accounting for oil and gas properties from the "full cost" method to the "successful efforts" method.... This change in method must be applied retroactively. Accordingly, previously reported net earnings have been restated downward by $233 million.

Unusual items

Unusual items include pretax gains from certain asset sales and pretax expense provisions for costs of several different types of transactions. Gains from sales of assets which management has determined are not complementary to the Company's future business focus were $50 million in 19x6, and $518 million in

19x5. Total unusual expenses aggregated $311 million in 19x6, and $540 million in 19x5. Details of these unusual gains and expenses follow.

Unusual gains in 19x6 arose from the sale of a small foreign affiliate ($12 million) and adjustments to previous unusual disposition provisions ($38 million).

Unusual costs in 19x6 include the following:

Expense provisions to cover corporate restructuring were $311 million in 19x6. These represent the provisions for expenses of refocusing a wide variety of business and marketing activities and reducing foreign and domestic risk exposures. These provisions include costs of rationalizing and improving a large number of production facilities, rearranging production activities among a number of existing plants, and reorganizing, phasing out or otherwise concluding other activities no longer considered essential to the conduct of the Company's business.

Required:

1. What type of treatment did GE give its accounting method change—current or retroactive?
2. Where else will the $233 prior years' impact of the change from the full cost method to the successful efforts method be disclosed in GE's financial statements (besides the footnote)?
3. Was the sale of GE's foreign affiliate, reported in the "Unusual items" footnote, a discontinued operation? Explain why you believe it was or was not.
4. Are any of the $311 million costs of restructurings discontinued operation costs? Explain why you believe they are or are not.

CASE 13-7 L.O. 2 Changes in Estimates—General Motors

General Motors (GM) has reported a positive trend in earnings on its ($1-2/3 per share par value) common stock. In the past three years, EPS on this stock has been:

	1988	*1987*	*1986*
EPS on $1-2/3 par value common	$7.17	$5.03	$4.11

Included in GM's 1988 annual report was the following footnote regarding depreciation and amortization of assets.

Depreciation and Amortization

Depreciation is provided based on estimated useful lives of groups of property generally using accelerated methods, which accumulate depreciation of approximately two-thirds of the depreciable cost during the first half of the estimated useful lives.

Expenditures for special tools are amortized over their estimated useful lives. Amortization is applied directly to the asset account. Replacement of special tools for reasons other than changes in products is charged directly to cost of sales.

GMAC provides for depreciation of automobiles and other equipment on operating leases or in company use generally on a straight-line basis.

In the first quarter of 1987, GMAC revised the rates of depreciation for automobiles on operating leases to retail customers to give effect to current experience with respect to the residual values of leased vehicles. These revisions had the effect of increasing GMAC's 1987 net income by $254.7 million, or $0.41 per share of $1-2/3 par value common stock (post-split).

In the third quarter of 1987, the Corporation revised the estimated service lives of its plants and equipment and special tools retroactive to January 1, 1987. These revisions, which were based on 1987 studies of actual useful lives and periods of use, recognized current estimates of service lives of the assets and had the effect of reducing 1987 depreciation and amortization charges by $1,236.6 million or $1.28 per share of $1-2/3 par value common stock (post-split).

Required:

1. Assume GM made the changes in estimates for assets under "operating leases to retail customers" and "plants and equipment and special tools" for both book and tax (IRS) reporting purposes. Further assume the effective tax rate for GM was 30% in each year. Provide the impact on both *depreciation expense* and *net income* for each change in estimate separately in the schedule below. (Give dollars in millions.)

	1987	
	From change in estimate for operating leases	*From change in estimate for plants and equipment and special tools*
Effect on depreciation expense (+ or −) . .	$	$
Effect on net income (+ or −)	$	$

2. Compute the amount of EPS on ($1-2/3 par) common stock that would have been reported in 1987 if these two changes in estimates had not occurred.
3. GM says it "revised the estimated service lives of its plants and equipment and special tools retroactive to January 1, 1987." This retroactive change was made even though it was not decided to change the estimated lives of these assets until the third quarter! Did GM follow GAAP here?
4. Was the change in estimates pertaining to operating leases made *during* the first quarter of 1987 also applied retroactive to January 1, 1987?

FINANCIAL STATEMENTS

FINANCIAL STATEMENT COMPONENTS EMPHASIZED IN CHAPTER 14

Reilly Corporation
Income Statement
For 1991

Revenues
xxxx
xxxx
Expenses
xxxx
xxxx

Reilly Corporation
Balance Sheet
12/31/91

Current assets
xxxx
xxxx
Noncurrent assets
xxxx
xxxx
Current liabilities
xxxx
xxxx
Noncurrent liabilities
xxxx
xxxx
Stockholders' equity
xxxx
xxxx

Reilly Corporation
Cash Flow Statement
For 1991

Operating activities
xxxx
xxxx
Investing activities
xxxx
xxxx
Financing activities
xxxx
xxxx

Reilly Corporation
Statement of Cash Flows
For the Year Ended December 31, 1991
(in $000)

Cash flows from operating activities:		
Cash received from customers	$X,XXX	
Cash paid to suppliers of inventory	(X,XXX)	
Cash paid to workers	(X,XXX)	
Cash paid to income taxes	(X,XXX)	
Cash paid for interest	(XXX)	
Net cash provided by operating activities		$ XXX
Cash flows from investing activities:		
Cash paid for purchase of building	$(X,XXX)	
Cash paid for purchase of securities	(XXX)	
Cash received from disposal of land	XXX	
Cash received from disposal of securities	XXX	
Net cash used by investing activities		$(X,XXX)
Cash flows from financing activities:		
Cash received from issuing stock	$X,XXX	
Cash paid for dividends	(XXX)	
Net cash provided by financing activities		X,XXX
Net increase (decrease) in cash		$ (XXX)

C H A P T E R 14

Statement of Cash Flows

LEARNING OBJECTIVES

After studying Chapter 14, you should understand:

1. Why information on operating, financing, and investing cash flows is important to decision makers, p. 762.
2. The format of the statement of cash flows, pp. 763-64.
3. How to analyze the operating, investing, and financing transactions of a company and prepare its statement of cash flows, pp. 769-76.
4. The relationship of balance sheets, income statements, and cash flow statements, pp. 769-76.
5. The effect of noncash transactions on the statement of cash flows, p. 776.
6. The difference between preparing a statement of cash flows with the direct and indirect methods, pp. 777-80.
7. The use of cash flow information in evaluating the performance and prospects of a business, pp. 780-82.
8. The use of a worksheet in preparing a statement of cash flows (Appendix), pp. 786-88.

Objective 1
Why information on operating, financing, and investing cash flows is important to decision makers.

Although the balance sheet, income statement, and statement of retained earnings provide decision makers with useful information, some decisions require information not found in these statements or their accompanying notes. For instance: How much cash did the company's operating activities provide? How much cash did the company use to purchase plant and equipment? How much cash did the company generate from the sale of securities? The answers to such questions are important in appraising a business's viability. While the income statement is based on accrual concepts that do not necessarily hinge on whether or not revenues have generated cash or whether or not expenses have consumed cash during a period, the **statement of cash flows (SCF)** analyzes the effects of cash flow transactions and communicates this information to decision makers.

While the SCF gives details as to the inflows and outflows of cash in the period just ended and is not a projection of future cash flows, decision makers do use the SCF as a basis for future projections. In order to plan the financing of operations, the paying of obligations, and the providing of adequate returns to investors, managers must project and budget cash flows. Present and potential owners of stock need information on the probable future dividends and the ability of the company to grow through cash reinvestment in operations. In general, a need exists for all types of decision makers to have information about a business's inflows and outflows of cash related to operations, issuance of debt, issuance of stock, investments in assets, dividends, and other types of business transactions.

Chapter 7 introduced you to the accounting definition of cash, defined as money that a business actually has on hand and money that a business has a right and easy access to such as money orders, checks, and balances in checking accounts. Businesses often invest their idle cash in short-term, highly liquid investments called **cash equivalents,** such as money market funds, U.S. Treasury bills, and commercial paper. Generally accepted accounting principles (GAAP) exclude equity securities (i.e., investments in the stock of other companies) from the definition of a cash equivalent.[1] The SCF explains the change in cash and cash equivalents in terms of major categories of business activity. Although this chapter concentrates on cash, you should understand that in analyzing cash flows, most balance sheets include under the caption "Cash" both cash and liquid, short-term investments, or cash equivalents. The SCF, therefore, analyzes the change in the appropriate balance sheet category for that company. This implies that items not meeting the definition of cash and cash equivalents, such as investments in equity securities, should not be combined with cash in the balance sheet.

This chapter begins with a study of the format of the SCF. The elements in the SCF will be familiar to you since they were introduced in Chapters 1 and 2, and throughout the text we have stressed the three major classes of transactions: operating, investing, and financing. The remainder of the chapter illustrates the actual preparation of the SCF and emphasizes the relationship of cash flow and accrual-based income statement items.

[1]*Financial Accounting Standards Board Statement No. 95,* "Statement of Cash Flows" (Norwalk, Conn.: FASB, November 1987).

FORMAT OF THE STATEMENT OF CASH FLOWS

Objective 2
The format of the statement of cash flows.

The SCF summarizes the following three major groups of activities affecting cash:

1. Operating activities.
2. Investing activities.
3. Financing activities.

Each group of activities can result in inflows and outflows of cash, and the SCF is, in essence, a listing of all such flows of cash classified under the three groups of activities.

Exhibit 14-1 illustrates a general format of SCFs and gives some examples of the categories often found in published statements. Note that cash flows can be positive or negative. Each type of transaction listed in the SCF reflects an increase or a decrease of cash. Visualize the typical journal entry related to each type of transaction. Cash received from customers results in debits to Cash. The outflow of cash paid to suppliers results in a credit to Cash, and the parentheses around a figure indicate a negative flow of cash. The format in Exhibit 14-1 is called the *direct method* format because, in the operations section, it lists the amounts received from customers and others and the amounts paid to suppliers and others. Another format, introduced later in this chapter, is called the *indirect method* format because it starts with net income and adds and subtracts reconciling items to derive "Net Cash Flow Provided by Operating Activities." Note that the specific items shown in Exhibit 14-1 are examples and not comprehensive. We will see many other items in the following analyses.

EXHIBIT 14-1

General Format of Statement of Cash Flows—Direct Method

Corporate Name
Statement of Cash Flows
For the Year Ended (Fiscal Year-End)

		Increase (Decrease)
Cash flows from operating activities:		
Cash received from customers		$ xxx
Cash paid to suppliers of inventory		(xxx)
Cash paid to workers		(xxx)
Cash paid for income taxes		(xxx)
Cash paid for interest		(xxx)
Net cash flow provided by operating activities .		$ xxx
Cash flows from investing activities:		
Cash paid for purchases of land	$(xx)	
Cash received from sales of investments . . .	xx	
Net cash used by investing activities		(xx)
Cash flows from financing activities:		
Cash received from sale of stock	$ xx	
Cash paid for dividends	(xx)	
Net cash provided by financing activities . . .		xx
Net increase (decrease) in cash		$ xx

Operating Activities

A common long-term and ongoing goal of businesses is to make a profit by providing goods and services to customers. As you recall, the activities necessary to provide goods and services are called **operating activities.**

Cash provided by operations are the **cash effects** of many of the transactions included in determining income, but not all. Receipts from customers, payments to suppliers, payments for taxes, and payments for wages are all examples of cash flows related to operations that would be reported in the SCF as operating activities. Payments of interest on loans and receipt of interest and dividends are also considered operating activities.

Investing Activities

Businesses must put resources to use in order to earn a return for investors. Investing in productive assets, such as plant, equipment, land, and other long-term items, is an important management task. Utilizing idle cash by making loans to others and acquiring securities can be very important in a company's overall profitability, and these also are classified as investing activities.

The statement of cash flows shows the cash results of all **investing activities** including cash paid for long-term assets, cash received on the disposition of such assets, and cash paid and received for the principal amount of loans made to others. Therefore, the word *investing* is used in a broad way, including the acquisition of long-term assets, as well as the acquisition of securities and the making of loans.

Financing Activities

Before a business can operate or invest, it must obtain financing by means of receipts of cash from owners for shares of stock or from borrowing from bondholders and other creditors such as banks. These activities are called **financing activities;** they are presented in the financing section of the SCF, which shows certain cash flows related to owners and creditors. Many types of these cash flow transactions can occur, including cash inflows from sales of the company's own stocks and bonds and from borrowings and cash outflows such as the repayment of loans, redemption of stock, payment of dividends, and retirement of stock.

Some ambiguities can exist in classifying certain transactions. For example, borrowing activities are considered financing transactions, but the purchase of supplies on credit is an operating transaction. The operating classification also applies to other short-term liability transactions such as those involving salaries payable, taxes payable, and many other payables of that kind.

Another example of a transaction that might cause confusion is when a building or piece of equipment is constructed to be sold but is rented for a period before the sale. Production and sale indicates an operating transaction, but holding an asset to generate rent revenue indicates that the asset is an investment because most assets are held for that purpose for more than one accounting period. In a case where the most important element is the sale, all cash flows related to the item would be classified as an operating activity. If, in this example, it is determined that the building was going to be held for rental rather than sale, the cash flows related to its acquisition or construction would be classified as an investing transaction.

Exhibit 14-2 gives several examples of how specific transactions are classified on SCFs.

Understanding the Basics of Cash Flows

In this section we show the basic relationships between the beginning and ending balance sheets, the income statement, and the statement of cash flows by means of a very simple example. Later in this chapter we cover a more realistic

EXHIBIT 14-2

Example of Cash Flow Transactions

Operating Inflows	Operating Outflows
Receipts from customers.	Payments to employees, suppliers, and governments.
Receipts of interest and dividends.	Payments of interest.
Other receipts, such as insurance proceeds, refunds from suppliers, tax refunds, and many others.	Other payments, such as payments for lawsuits, refunds to customers, and many others.
Investing Inflows	**Investing Outflows**
Receipts from sales of long-term assets, such as property, plant, and equipment, and from investments in equity and debt securities other than cash equivalents.	Payments for long-term assets, such as property, plant, and equipment, and equity and debt securities other than cash equivalents.
Receipts from debtors for the principal amount of loans.	Payments to debtors for principal amounts of loans.
Receipts from selling notes receivables.	
Financing Inflows	**Financing Outflows**
Receipts from issuance of stock, bonds, and notes.	Payments to stockholders for dividends, retirement of stock, purchase of treasury stock.
Receipts from creditors for the principal amount of loans.	Payments to creditors for the principal amount of loans.

example. Consider the following items for Bare Bones, Inc., for the current operating period:

Bare Bones, Inc.
Comparative Balance Sheets
(in thousands)

	Beginning Balance	*Ending Balance*	*Change*
Cash	$10	$17	+$ 7
Land	0	12	+ 12
Total assets	$10	$29	+$19
Liabilities	$ 3	$10	+$ 7
Common stock	5	11	+ 6
Retained earnings	2	8	+ 6
Total liabilities and stockholders' equity	$10	$29	+$19

Transactions (in thousands):

Sales (all cash)	$100
Expenses (all cash)	90
Sale of stock for cash	6
Borrowing of cash from bank	7
Payment of dividends	4
Purchase of land for cash	12

Before we construct a statement of cash flows for Bare Bones, Inc., it is valuable to understand the relationship of change in cash to the change in all other balance sheet accounts.

Recall the basic balance sheet relationship:

$$\text{Assets} = \text{Liabilities} + \text{Stockholders' Equity}$$

Bare Bones, Inc., has the following specific accounts:

$$\text{Cash} + \text{Land} = \text{Liabilities} + \text{Common Stock} + \text{Retained Earnings}$$

An algebraically equivalent equation shows that the cash balance on the previous page is a function of all other balance sheet accounts:

$$\text{Cash} = \text{Liabilities} + \text{Common Stock} + \text{Retained Earnings} - \text{Land}$$

Further algebraic manipulation tells us that the change (designated Δ) in cash for a period equals the change in all other accounts:

$$\Delta\text{Cash} = -\Delta\text{Land} + \Delta\text{Liabilities} + \Delta\text{Common Stock} + \Delta\text{Retained Earnings}$$

$$\$7 = -\$12 + \$7 + \$6 + \$6$$

$$\$7 = \$7$$

Exhibit 14-3 shows how Bare Bones, Inc.'s transactions this period resulted in the positive change in cash of $7,000.

The statement of cash flows describes how operating, investing, and financing transactions changed cash during an accounting period. In the case of Bare Bones, Inc., categorization of transactions is simple. Note that the numbers in parentheses are negative cash flows.

Change in Cash		=	*Change in Cash from Operating Transactions*		+	*Change in Cash from Investing Transactions*		+	*Change in Cash from Financing Transactions*	
			Cash from customers	$100		Cash paid for purchase of land	$(12)		Cash from common stock	$6
			Cash paid for expenses	(90)					Cash from loan	7
									Cash paid for dividends	(4)
Net cash change	$7	=		$ 10	+		$(12)	+		$9

Exhibit 14-4 shows how the various categories of transactions are arranged into a formal statement of cash flows.

In the next section we cover a more complex and complete set of transactions. When necessary, the student should refer back to the Bare Bones example as a general guide.

EXHIBIT 14-3

Effects of Bare Bones' Transactions on Cash and Other Accounts (in thousands)

Transactions	*Cash*	=	*−Land*	+	*Liabilities*	+	*Common Stock*	+	*Retained Earnings*
Sales	$100								$100
Expenses	(90)								(90)
Sale of common stock .	6						$6		
Borrowing of cash . . .	7				$7				
Payment of dividends .	(4)								(4)
Purchase of land. . . .	(12)		$12		—		—		—
Net change	$ 7	=	−$12	+	$7	+	$6	+	$ 6

EXHIBIT 14-4

Statement of Cash Flows

Bare Bones, Inc.
Statement of Cash Flows
For the Year Ended (Fiscal Year-End)
(in thousands)

	Increase (Decrease)
Cash flows from operating activities:	
Cash received from customers	$100
Cash paid for expenses	(90)
Net cash flow provided by operating activities . .	$ 10
Cash flows from investing activities:	
Cash paid for purchase of land	$ (12)
Net cash used by investing activities	$ (12)
Cash flows from financing activities:	
Cash received from sale of stock	$ 6
Cash received from borrowing	7
Cash paid for dividends	(4)
Net cash provided by financing activities	$ 9
Net increase (decrease) in cash	$ 7

PREPARING A STATEMENT OF CASH FLOWS

"What Happened to Your Cash?"

Ms. Julie Perez, president of DataCo, Inc., a distributor of computer software, has a problem. It is January 4, 19x3, and although her company has just completed its best year in terms of sales and net income, she is gravely concerned about liquidity, especially since she has an opportunity to expand into a new region if she moves fast. Her company needs a $2 million, six-month loan, but her banker (who has just reviewed the 19x2 income statement and the comparative 19x1 and 19x2 balance sheets shown in Exhibits 14-5 and 14-6) is not impressed with the company's cash generating ability.

Banker: Julie, what happened to your cash? You started the year with $248,000 and now there's only $34,000. Your income was good and you even issued stock during the year. Where's your cash flow statement? That should answer most of my questions.

EXHIBIT 14-5

DataCo's Comparative Balance Sheet

DataCo, Inc.
Comparative Balance Sheets
(in thousands)

	December 31	
	19x2	*19x1*
Assets		
Current assets:		
Cash	$ 34	$ 248
Accounts receivable	2,685	965
Inventory	1,750	1,015
Prepaid insurance	6	12
Marketable securities	250	—
Total current assets	$4,725	$2,240
Noncurrent assets:		
Land	$ 800	$1,100
Building	4,800	2,700
Accumulated depreciation—building	(1,120)	(850)
Total noncurrent assets	$4,480	$2,950
Total assets	$9,205	$5,190
Liabilities and Stockholders' Equity		
Current liabilities:		
Accounts payable	$ 75	$ 200
Notes payable	460	360
Salaries payable	130	150
Income taxes payable	168	40
Total current liabilities	$ 833	$ 750
Noncurrent liabilities:		
Bonds payable	2,200	2,200
Total liabilities	$3,033	$2,950
Stockholders' equity:		
Common stock	$3,664	$1,500
Retained earnings	2,508	740
Total stockholders' equity	$6,172	$2,240
Total liabilities and stockholders' equity	$9,205	$5,190

Ms. Perez: My controller is working on that now. I was in a hurry to talk to you and get the ball rolling on this loan. I'll get it to you as soon as possible. He worked up these preliminary statements for our meeting. I have got to move fast. Is there anything in particular you want more detail on now?

Banker: Let's wait until I have a chance to review the cash flow statement. It will break out the cash flows from operations, financing, and investing activities. As soon as possible of course, we'll need formal statements audited by your CPAs. First things first. The cash flow statement should answer most of my questions.

EXHIBIT 14-6

DataCo's Income Statement

DataCo, Inc.
Income Statement
For the Year Ended December 31, 19x2
(in thousands)

Sales		$10,870
Cost of goods sold		5,300
Gross margin		$ 5,570
Expenses:		
Administrative expense	$640	
Marketing expense	660	
Interest expense	220	
Depreciation expense	270	
Total		1,790
Net income before taxes		$ 3,780
Income tax expense		1,512
Net income		$ 2,268

The banker then gave Ms. Perez a list of other statements that would have to be worked up in addition to complete financial statements, such as projections of cash flows for one year ahead and a detailed statement of what the money would be used for and how it would be repaid. At the end of the chapter we will return to Ms. Perez and her banker, but first we must explore the concepts and methods that underlie DataCo's statement of cash flow. In the sections that follow we will see how a thorough understanding of the cash and accrual effects of each transaction is the key to understanding a cash flow statement.

You can determine the net change in DataCo's cash by computing the difference between the 19x1 cash balance and the 19x2 cash balance shown in DataCo's comparative balance sheets of Exhibit 14-5. DataCo had a net outflow or decrease of $214,000, which is the difference between the $248,000 beginning balance and the $34,000 ending balance. The comparative balance sheets also show the net change in all noncash accounts, but they do not provide an analysis of the operating, investing, and financing cash flow transactions.

Cash flow cannot be determined directly from the income statement because its revenues and expenses are based on accrual accounting, which allows recognition of revenues and expenses regardless of the actual cash effects in the current period. Many transactions other than revenues and expenses affect cash, and the SCF focuses directly on the cash effects of all transactions.

The following section focuses on how to analyze the operating, investing, and financing transactions of a company. Three additional topics are discussed based on the DataCo example—interest paid and received, noncash transactions, and the indirect method of SCF preparation.

Analysis of Operating Transactions

A most important operating transaction is cash received from customers; and, in the case of a merchandising concern such as DataCo, operating transactions include cash paid to suppliers. We will see that DataCo also paid cash for salaries, taxes, and interest, all of which are operating activities.

Objective 3
How to analyze the operating, investing, and financing transactions of a company and prepare its statement of cash flows.

Cash Received from Customers. How much cash did DataCo generate from customers during the period? As you have learned, sales to customers in a period are usually not the same as the cash received from customers in the same period because of changes in the balance of the Accounts Receivable account. During 19x2, DataCo had sales on account of $10,870,000 and collected $9,150,000 cash from customers. Consider the following journal entries relating to customers during 19x2, and the effect the transactions had on DataCo's cash flow:

Summary Entries			*Cash Flow Effect*
Accounts Receivable (A)	10,870,000		None
Sales (R)		10,870,000	
Cash (A)	**9,150,000**		**+$9,150,000**
Accounts Receivable (A)		9,150,000	

Recall that **summary entries** like those above indicate that the one entry shown represents the sum of the many entries of its kind actually recorded during the period. Obviously, DataCo had more than one sales transaction during 19x2, but for convenience, we show one summary entry. To follow the relationship of sales and receivables to cash, consider the following T accounts.

Sales

	Credit sales	10,870,000

Accounts Receivable

Bal.	965,000	Cash collections	9,150,000
Credit sales	10,870,000		
Bal.	2,685,000		

Cash

Bal.	248,000	XXX
	XXX	XXX
Receipt of cash from credit sales	9,150,000	XXX
		XXX
Bal.	34,000	

Objective 4
The relationship of balance sheets, income statements, and cash flow statements.

DataCo's SCF will show the $9,150,000 inflow of cash from customers in the "operating activities" section along with the other operating effects to be discussed below. Exhibit 14-7 shows where the cash flow of $9,150,000 appears on the SCF. As we follow through and develop DataCo's SCF, each new cash flow item will be highlighted until the complete SCF has been prepared. Also note in Exhibit 14-7 that DataCo's net decrease in cash is shown in the last line of its SCF.

Cash Paid to Suppliers. The "cost of goods sold" item in DataCo's income statement is not the amount of cash flow to suppliers because DataCo purchases its merchandise on credit, and during 19x2, DataCo increased its inventory level by purchasing more than it consumed. Merchandise of $6,035,000 was purchased,

EXHIBIT 14-7

Statement of Cash Flows: Cash Received from Customers Highlighted

DataCo, Inc.
Partial Statement of Cash Flows
For the Year Ended December 31, 19x2
(in thousands)

Cash flows from operating activities:		
Cash received from customers	**$9,150**	
Cash paid to suppliers of inventory	(xx)	
Cash paid to workers	(xx)	
Cash paid for income taxes	(xx)	
Cash paid for interest	(xx)	
Net cash provided by operating activities		$ xx
Cash flows from investing activities:		
Cash paid for purchases of land	$ (xx)	
Cash received from sales of investments	xx	
Net cash used by investing activities		xx
Cash flows from financing activities:		
Cash received from sale of stock	$ xx	
Cash paid for dividends	(xx)	
Net cash provided by financing activities		xx
Net increase (decrease) in cash		$(214)

but only $5,300,000 was consumed. Cash payments to suppliers amounted to $6,160,000. The transactions related to inventory and their cash flow effects can be summarized as follows:

Summary Entries			*Cash Flow Effect*
Inventory (A)	6,035,000		None
Accounts Payable (L)		6,035,000	
Accounts Payable (L)	6,160,000		
Cash (A)		**6,160,000**	**−$6,160,000**
Cost of Goods Sold (E)	5,300,000		None
Inventory (A)		5,300,000	

The entry to record the purchase of inventory does not affect cash, and likewise the entry to record the cost of goods sold has no cash effect. Only the payments to suppliers change the cash balance. As you can see, DataCo's cash is decreased by $6,160,000 through payments to suppliers, but its income statement shows an expense of only $5,300,000 for cost of goods sold.

Cash Paid for Salaries, Income Taxes, and Interest. DataCo incurred several expenses during 19x2, but not all had cash flow effects. The following administrative and marketing expenses totaling $1,300,000 are composed of amounts for salaries and insurance:

Summary Entries			Cash Flow Effect
Administrative Expense (E)	640,000		
Marketing Expense (E)	660,000		None
Salaries Payable (L)		1,294,000	
Prepaid Insurance (A).		6,000	
Salaries Payable (L)	1,314,000		
Cash (A)		**1,314,000**	**−$1,314,000**

Cash of $1,314,000 was paid to workers, but only $1,294,000 was charged to expense for the current year. Salaries Payable was reduced by $20,000 during the year because more cash was paid out than was expensed. Refer to the balance sheet in Exhibit 14-5 to confirm that Salaries Payable was reduced by $20,000. Although $6,000 of insurance premiums was expensed in 19x2, no cash was paid for insurance during that year. Insurance premiums were actually paid in the previous year (19x1), and the asset prepaid insurance is being amortized.

Income taxes of $1,384,000 were paid during 19x2, but $1,512,000 was expensed. The difference of $128,000 is the increase in the amount of Income Taxes Payable on the balance sheet during the year.

Summary Entries			Cash Flow Effect
Income Tax Expense (E)	1,512,000		None
Income Taxes Payable (L)		1,512,000	
Income Taxes Payable (L)	1,384,000		
Cash (A)		**1,384,000**	**−$1,384,000**

Interest expense was paid in full to creditors with no amount still outstanding at December 31, 19x2.

Summary Entry			Cash Flow Effect
Interest Expense (E)	220,000		
Cash (A)		**220,000**	**−$220,000**

We can now complete the "operating activities" section of the SCF by putting together all of the cash flow effects from the preceding analysis. As can be seen in Exhibit 14-8, a net of $72,000 cash was provided by operating activities.

It is important to compare the net income figure of $2,268,000 with the $72,000 net cash provided by operating activities. Later in the chapter, we will analyze all the differences between net cash provided by operations and the accrual-based income statement amounts. For now, it is sufficient to say that net income is designed to communicate the economic effect of operations which includes both cash and noncash transactions such as depreciation and the changes in receivables and payables. By contrast, cash from operations focuses exclusively on cash flows.

Analysis of Investing Transactions

Although returns from operations may be the ultimate goal of a business, returns come only after assets are invested in productive projects. **Investing transactions** involve the dedication of assets to a particular return-generating task. For instance, the purchase of a factory building for cash is an investing transaction

EXHIBIT 14-8

Partial Statement of Cash Flows: Operating Cash Payments Highlighted

DataCo, Inc.
Partial Statement of Cash Flows
For the Year Ended December 31, 19x2
(in thousands)

Cash flows from operating activities:		
Cash received from customers	$ 9,150	
Cash paid to suppliers of inventory	**(6,160)**	
Cash paid to workers	**(1,314)**	
Cash paid for income taxes	**(1,384)**	
Cash paid for interest	**(220)**	
Net cash provided by operating activities		**$ 72**
Cash flows from investing activities:		
Cash paid for purchases of land	$ (xx)	
Cash received from sales of investments	xx	
Net cash used by investing activities		xx
Cash flows from financing activities:		
Cash received from sale of stock	$ xx	
Cash paid for dividends	(xx)	
Net cash provided by financing activities		xx
Net increase (decrease) in cash		$(214)

because the building is used to generate profits. Thus, the acquisition of any long-term productive asset is classified as an investing transaction. Also, the sale of such assets often generates cash flows, which are classified as investing transactions.

In addition to the acquisition and sale of long-term productive assets, businesses are involved in other investing transactions. Often businesses purchase securities of other businesses and governments. Businesses also make loans to other entities. Cash flows out when investments are purchased and loans are made, and cash flows in when investments are sold and debtors pay back their loans. All these effects of investing transactions are summarized in the SCF.

Cash Paid for Purchase of Building and Securities. DataCo purchased a building by means of a $1,640,000 cash payment and the issuance of a $460,000 note. The journal entry and cash flow effect of this transaction follows:

Summary Entry			*Cash Flow Effect*
Buildings (A)	2,100,000		
Cash (A)		**1,640,000**	**−$1,640,000**
Notes Payable (L)		460,000	

The entire $2,100,000 is the cost of the buildings, but the cash outflow is only $1,640,000.

DataCo also used cash to acquire securities that will be held as investments:

Summary Entry			*Cash Flow Effect*
Marketable Securities (A)	600,000		
Cash (A)		**600,000**	**−$600,000**

Both the building and securities acquisitions are classified in the SCF as investing activities. Note that if the securities in question were considered cash equivalents (see page 762), then the effect of the transaction would not be shown on the SCF as an investing activity that used cash. Here we are explicitly assuming that the asset Marketable Securities is not a cash equivalent.

Cash Received from the Disposal of Land and Securities. Companies can sell assets such as land, buildings, equipment, and securities to generate positive cash flows. In 19x1, DataCo had two such classes of transactions—the sale of land for $300,000 cash and the sale of some of its investment in marketable securities for $350,000. In both transactions, the amount received equaled the book value of the asset, so no gains or losses were recorded. The journal entries and cash flow effect of these transactions are as follows:

Summary Entries			*Cash Flow Effect*
Cash (A)	**300,000**		**+$300,000**
Land (A)		300,000	
Cash (A)	**350,000**		**+$350,000**
Marketable Securities (A)		350,000	

We can now construct the "Cash flows from investing activities" section of DataCo's SCF shown in Exhibit 14-9.

EXHIBIT 14-9

Partial Statement of Cash Flows: Investing Activities Highlighted

DataCo, Inc.
Partial Statement of Cash Flows
For the Year Ended December 31, 19x2
(in thousands)

Cash flows from operating activities:		
Cash received from customers	$ 9,150	
Cash paid to suppliers of inventory	(6,160)	
Cash paid to workers	(1,314)	
Cash paid for income taxes	(1,384)	
Cash paid for interest	(220)	
Net cash provided by operating activities		$ 72
Cash flows from investing activities:		
Cash paid for purchase of building	**$(1,640)**	
Cash paid for purchase of securities	**(600)**	
Cash received from disposal of land	**300**	
Cash received from disposal of securities	**350**	
Net cash used by investing activities		**(1,590)**
Cash flows from financing activities:		
Cash received from sale of stock	$ xx	
Cash paid for dividends	(xx)	
Net cash provided by financing activities		xx
Net increase (decrease) in cash		$ (214)

Analysis of Financing Transactions

Businesses must accumulate the necessary funds to carry out operating and investing activities. As you learned in previous chapters, the corporate form of business has many advantages in attracting financing from a wide variety of sources such as common stockholders, preferred stockholders, bondholders, and financial institutions. To obtain funds, businesses must demonstrate that the suppliers of capital have a high probability of earning an adequate return on their money—a return in the form of interest payments and principal payments for creditors and dividend payments and/or appreciation of stock prices for equity holders. The financing section of the SCF helps in making such judgments.

Cash Received from the Issuance of Stock. During 19x1 and 19x2, DataCo sold stock that generated $1,804,000 in positive cash flow, as shown in the following summary entry and cash flow effect:

Summary Entry			*Cash Flow Effect*
Cash (A)	**1,804,000**		**+$1,804,000**
Common Stock (SE)		1,804,000	

A company could have transactions where the issuance of stock did not result in positive cash flow, such as when stock is issued to pay off a liability or in exchange for assets such as land and buildings. These may be significant events even though no cash changes hands. Later in the chapter you will see how accountants report such noncash transactions along with the SCF.

Dividends Paid. Financing activities such as issuing stocks are usually expected to be followed after a period of profitable operations by dividend payments to stockholders. DataCo declared and paid $500,000 in dividends, which had the following cash flow effect:

Summary Entries			*Cash Flow Effect*
Retained Earnings (SE)	500,000		None
Dividends Payable (L).		500,000	
Dividends Payable (L).	500,000		
Cash (A)		**500,000**	**−$500,000**

Often dividends are declared and unpaid at period-end. Remember that the declaration of dividends does not affect cash flow; instead, a credit is made to Dividends Payable. When the company actually pays the dividends to stockholders, cash is of course reduced by the payment amount.

Now that we have analyzed the cash flow effects of all of DataCo's operating, investing, and financing activities, the DataCo SCF is complete, as shown in Exhibit 14-10. The year resulted in a negative cash flow of $214,000—the amount of the change in cash that was determined from DataCo's balance sheet shown in Exhibit 14-5.

Interest Paid and Received

Note that DataCo shows interest payments as an operating item, and this is consistent with current accounting practice. Interest payments could be viewed as the result of financing activities, and interest received could certainly be viewed as the results of investing activities. The reason accountants include interest in

EXHIBIT 14-10

Completed Statement of Cash Flows: Financing Activities Highlighted

DataCo, Inc.
Statement of Cash Flows
For the Year Ended December 31, 19x2
(in thousands)

Cash flows from operating activities:		
Cash received from customers	$ 9,150	
Cash paid to suppliers of inventory	(6,160)	
Cash paid to workers.	(1,314)	
Cash paid for income taxes	(1,384)	
Cash paid for interest	(220)	
Net cash provided by operating activities. . .		$ 72
Cash flows from investing activities:		
Cash paid for purchase of building.	$(1,640)	
Cash paid for purchase of securities	(600)	
Cash received from disposal of land	300	
Cash received from disposal of securities . .	350	
Net cash used by investing activities.		(1,590)
Cash flows from financing activities:		
Cash received from issuing stock	**$ 1,804**	
Cash paid for dividends	**(500)**	
Net cash provided by financing activities . .		**1,304**
Net increase (decrease) in cash		$ (214)

the operating section of the SCF is because accounting policy makers wanted, to the extent possible, to have the operating section of the SCF include the cash effects of transactions affecting income.

Noncash Transactions

Objective 5
The effect of noncash transactions on the statement of cash flows.

As mentioned earlier, some very significant investing and financing transactions do not affect cash at all or only partly affect cash. For instance, in 19x2, DataCo, Inc., paid off a long-term note with a carrying value of $360,000 by issuing stock. This financing transaction involved no cash. It is not necessary to discuss why the creditor accepted stock instead of demanding cash in payment for the note. Such noncash trades do, in fact, take place from time to time, and the major concern of the accountant is determining the fair value of the items traded. If market values are known (such as through quotations from a stock exchange), valuation is straightforward. This is not always the case, and appraisals may be necessary to determine value. In any event, it is usually possible to estimate the cash equivalent amount of the trade.

Summary Entry			*Cash Flow Effect*
Notes Payable—Long Term (L)	360,000		None
Common Stock (SE)		360,000	

Such significant noncash transactions must be disclosed in a separate schedule that is shown along with the SCF. DataCo had two noncash trade transactions.

In addition to the issuance of stock to pay off the note, a long-term note of $460,000 was used in partial payment of a building, as shown on page 773. Both are shown on the following schedule:

DataCo, Inc.
Statement of Cash Flows
Schedule of Noncash Investing and Financing Activities

Acquisition of building by means of long-term note	$460,000
Stock issued to settle debt	$360,000

Indirect Method

Objective 6
The difference between preparing a statement of cash flows with the direct and indirect methods.

The SCF in Exhibit 14-10 has an operating section that shows the cash received from customers and paid to suppliers of goods and services. This is called the **direct method.** Another form of analysis, called the **indirect method,** begins with net income and adds and subtracts noncash income statement items to arrive at net cash provided by operations. The direct method illustrated earlier follows an income statement-type format by listing the cash from customers followed by the cash paid to suppliers and employees. The indirect method starts with the bottom line of the income statement (net income) or some near bottom line subtotal such as "income from continuing operations" and deletes revenues and expenses and gains and losses, which do not have a cash flow effect.

The format of the operating section of the SCF using the indirect method is as follows:

Cash flows from operating activities:	
Net income	$ xxx
Adjustments to reconcile net income to net cash provided by operating activity:	
Additions	xxx
Subtractions	(xxx)
Net cash provided by operating activities	$ xxx

In the indirect format we reconcile net income and net cash provided by operating activities. As we will see below, items such as depreciation expense reduce net income but have no effect on cash; and transactions such as paying off accounts payable decrease cash but have no effect on net income. All such reconciling items are analyzed below.

Several operating transactions, such as depreciation expense, have no direct cash flow effect. DataCo's $270,000 depreciation expense was recorded as follows:

Summary Entry			*Cash Flow Effect*	*Net Income Effect*	*Reconciling Amount*
Depreciation Expense (E)	270,000		None	−270,000	+270,000
Accumulated Depreciaton (XA)		270,000			

The depreciation entry, therefore, reduced net income by $270,000, but cash was not affected. Therefore, in order to reconcile net income to net cash provided by operating activities, the $270,000 must be added to net income.

Net income includes all sales and not just cash sales. Because credit sales generate accounts receivable, an increase or decrease in accounts receivable during the year would indicate a difference between sales recognized on the accrual basis and cash flow from customers. DataCo's Accounts Receivable account increased $1,720,000 during the year.

Summary Entries			*Cash Flow Effect*	*Net Income Effect*	*Reconciling Amount*
Accounts Receivable (A)	10,870,000		None	+10,870,000	−1,720,000
Sales (R)		10,870,000			
Cash (A)	9,150,000		+9,150,000	None	
Accounts Receivable (A)		9,150,000			

In reconciling net income to net cash provided by operating activities, $1,720,000 must be subtracted from net income.

During 19x2, DataCo's inventory increased by $735,000, which was the result of DataCo purchasing more inventory than it sold to customers. In addition the Accounts Payable account decreased by $125,000. Assuming a perpetual inventory system, the following entries summarize this activity:

Summary Entries			*Cash Flow Effect*	*Net Income Effect*	*Reconciling Amount*
Inventory (A)	6,035,000		None	None	−860,000
Accounts Payable (L)		6,035,000			
Accounts Payable (L)	6,160,000			None	
Cash (A)		6,160,000	−6,160,000		
Cost of Goods Sold (E)	5,300,000		None	−5,300,000	
Inventory (A)		5,300,000			

This same type of analysis will show how changes in salaries payable, taxes payable, and prepayments create a reconciling item between net income and net cash provided by operations.

Summary Entries			*Cash Flow Effect*	*Net Income Effect*	*Reconciling Amount*
Administrative Expenses (E)	640,000			−1,300,000	−14,000
Marketing Expenses (E)	660,000		None		
Salaries Payable (L)		1,294,000			
Prepaid Insurance (A)		6,000			
Salaries Payable (L)	1,314,000			None	
Cash (A)		1,314,000	−1,314,000		
Income Tax Expense (E)	1,512,000		None	−1,512,000	+128,000
Income Taxes Payable (L)		1,512,000			
Income Taxes Payable (L)	1,384,000			None	
Cash (A)		1,384,000	−1,384,000		

Exhibit 14-11 summarizes some of the situations where reconciliation of the net income to net cash is needed if the operating activities in a statement of cash flows is to be shown using the indirect method. Exhibit 14-12 shows how the operating section of DataCo's SCF is prepared using the indirect method.

EXHIBIT 14-11

Common Adjustments to Net Income—Indirect Method

Items that Appear as Adjustments to Net Income	*Explanation of Cash versus Income Statement Effect*	*Adjustment*
Depreciation, depletion, and amortization	These expense items reduce net income but have no cash effect.	Add back depreciation expense to net income.
Increase in accounts receivable and accrued receivables	As accounts receivable and accrued receivables increase, net income increases but cash is not affected.	Deduct increase in receivables from net income.
Decrease in accounts receivable and accrued receivables	A reduction in receivable balances indicates cash receipts but not income recognition.	Add decrease in receivables to net income.
Increase in inventory	Purchases for the period are not reflected in expenses (cost of goods sold).	Deduct increase in inventory from net income.
Decrease in inventory	Expenses (cost of goods sold) for the period include items purchased in prior periods.	Add decrease in inventory to net income.
Increase in prepayments	Payments for certain services exceed related expenses on income statement.	Deduct increase in prepayments from net income.
Decrease in prepayments	Expenses on income statement exceed related cash payments for services.	Add decrease in prepayments to net income.
Increase in current liabilities	Expenses exceed related payments to suppliers and others.	Add increase in current liabilities to net income.
Decrease in current liabilities	Cash payments to suppliers and others exceed related expenses.	Deduct decrease in current liabilities from net income.
Increase in unearned revenue	Cash receipts from customers exceed amounts recognized as revenue.	Add increase in unearned revenue to net income.
Decrease in unearned revenue	Revenue recognized exceeds amount of cash receipts from customers.	Deduct decrease in unearned revenue from net income.

EXHIBIT 14-11 *(concluded)*

Items that Appear as Adjustments to Net Income	*Explanation of Cash versus Income Statement Effect*	*Adjustment*
Increase in Deferred Income Tax Liability account	Income tax expense on the income statement exceeds amount currently payable to the government.	Add increase in the Deferred Income Tax Liability account to net income.
Decrease in Deferred Income Tax Liability account	Amount currently payable to the government exceeds income tax expense for the period.	Deduct decrease in the Deferred Income Tax Liability account from net income.
Gain on sale of assets	The gain increases net income but the cash effect of the transaction is shown in the investing section.	Deduct the gain from net income.
Loss on sale of assets	The loss decreases net income but the cash effect of the transaction is shown in the investing section.	Add the loss back to net income.

"This Is What Happened to Our Cash"

Objective 7
The use of cash flow information in evaluating the performance and prospects of a business.

We now return to the negotiations between the banker and Ms. Perez, DataCo's president. As you recall from page 767, the banker asked Ms. Perez, "What happened to your cash?" after he reviewed the preliminary comparative balance sheets and an income statement at their first meeting to discuss a loan. Now it is three days later, and Ms. Perez is armed with two statements of cash flow, one with cash from operations shown using the direct method (our Exhibit 14-10), and the other using the indirect method (Exhibit 14-12). Having reviewed the causes of all cash flows with her controller, she is more confident than ever that her business is sound and worthy of quick action on the loan request. Refer to the exhibits as you read the next section.

Ms. Perez: Let's start with operations. [She was pointing to specific items on the SCF, our Exhibit 14-12.] Our net income was $2,268,000 but most of it came late in the year, 60% in the last quarter, so we built up accounts receivable by $1,720,000 over the previous year. That may look odd, but we have an aggressive marketing effort and credit sales are important to that effort. My people tell me that our current receivables are very sound. We expect to collect all of them within 30 days. The same can be said for our inventory buildup. We added $735,000 to inventories to support our increasing sales. Again, our inventory is all first rate, with increasing fair values. So even though operations show only $72,000 in positive cash flow, our receivables and inventories are high quality and of real value and their increases account for most of the difference between net income and cash flow from operations.

Banker: I want to talk to your CPA about those two items. If they are as you say, then your actions to increase credit sales and expand inventories probably

EXHIBIT 14-12

Statement of Cash Flows: Indirect Method

DataCo, Inc.
Statement of Cash Flows
For the Year Ended December 31, 19x2
(in thousands)

Cash flows from operating activities:			
Net income			**$ 2,268**
Adjustments to reconcile net income to cash provided by operating activities:			
Depreciation		**$ 270**	
Increase in accounts receivable		**(1,720)**	
Increase in inventory	**$(735)**		
Decrease in accounts payable	**(125)**	**(860)**	
Decrease in salaries payable	**$ (20)**		
Decrease in prepayments	**6**	**(14)**	
Increase in income taxes payable		**128**	**(2,196)**
Net cash provided by operating activities			$ 72
Cash flows from investing activities:			
Cash paid for purchase of building		$(1,640)	
Cash paid for purchase of securities		(600)	
Cash received from disposal of land		300	
Cash received from disposal of securities		350	
Net cash used by investing activities			(1,590)
Cash flows from financing activities:			
Cash received from issuing stock		$ 1,804	
Cash paid for dividends		(500)	
Net cash provided by financing activities			1,304
Net increase (decrease) in cash			$ (214)

make good business sense. Are there any other significant items that affected cash?

Ms. Perez: Our financing and investing activities were important and we believe successful. We issued stock for $1,804,000 and we used most of the cash to purchase our new building for $1,640,000. We increased our investment in securities by $250,000 and the value of that portfolio has grown about 30% since that time.

Banker: Let's review your cash performance. [He was referring to the SCF in Exhibit 14-10 and to DataCo's income statement.] You received just over $9 million from customers with sales of just under $11 million. That's where the buildup in receivables came from, and though your cost of goods sold is only $5.3 million, you paid suppliers $6.2 million. Yep, there's no doubt, my people will want to make sure about those receivables and inventory. The rest of it looks good. That building is in a good location with strong real estate values. Now I think I know what happened to your cash.

The above discussion points to the importance of a thorough understanding of the relationship between accrual-based statements such as the income statement and the balance sheet and the nonaccrual-based cash flow statement. Sound business decisions can be made only if both perspectives are fully understood.

SUMMARY

In evaluating the future of a business, the prospects for future cash flow is almost always crucial. How can decision makers rationally evaluate cash flow prospects? Decision makers can begin by understanding a company's past cash flows. This information is acquired from the statement of cash flow, which reports the cash flow from the operating, investing, and financing activities of a business. The SCF gives information that cannot be found in balance sheets and income statements.

The question is: How well can the historical SCF predict future trends? We believe that, although all financial statements are based on historical records, this look into the past, along with sound projections, can give insights into the future.

In this chapter you learned about the general formats of the SCF. Then by analyzing DataCo, Inc., you were instructed how to construct an SCF. For example, you can prepare the operating section of the SCF either directly by reviewing the cash received from customers and the cash paid to suppliers and others, or indirectly, beginning with net income and adding or subtracting noncash items to arrive at cash provided by operations. In addition to operations, the SCF emphasizes the major managerial functions of investing and financing. You were given the concepts and procedures necessary to identify and report the cash flow effects of investing and financing transactions.

An important theme in this chapter is that accrual accounting focuses on income determination and historic cost-based balance sheets, which is crucial to understanding the economic flows and states of an entity. The cash flow statement gives another critical perspective—the cash effects of transactions for a period. Neither is the one and only correct approach. They are complementary, providing different insights about a business's activities, current state, and future prospects.

DEMONSTRATION EXERCISE

Saleco, Inc., has the following December 31, 19x1, and 19x2 balance sheets, 19x2 income statement, and additional information regarding transactions for 19x2.

Saleco, Inc.
Balance Sheet
At December 31

	19x2	*19x1*
Assets		
Cash	$ 201,400	$ 43,000
Accounts receivable	102,000	42,000
Prepaid rent	1,800	1,200
Plant assets	1,575,000	1,050,000
Less: Accumulated depreciation	(565,000)	(690,000)
Long-term investment, Kalmor stock	400,000	—
Land	500,000	500,000
	$2,215,200	$ 946,200

Liabilities and Stockholders' Equity

Liabilities:		
Accounts payable	$ 5,500	$ 34,000
Notes payable	600,000	—
Salaries payable	24,000	12,000
Interest payable	10,000	—
Income taxes payable	100,470	—
Total liabilities	$ 739,970	$ 46,000
Stockholders' equity:		
Common stock	$ 300,000	$ 250,000
Contributed capital in excess of par	770,200	320,200
Retained earnings	405,030	330,000
Total stockholders' equity	$1,475,230	$ 900,200
Total liabilities and stockholders' equity	$2,215,200	$ 946,200

Saleco, Inc.
Income Statement
For the Year Ended December 31, 19x2

Revenues:		
Sales revenue		$600,000
Expenses:		
Depreciation expense	$ 75,000	
Salaries expense	210,000	
Rent expense	12,500	
Interest expense	10,000	
Miscellaneous expense	27,000	
Total expenses		334,500
Operating income		$265,500
Gain on sale of plant assets		30,000
Income before taxes		$295,500
Income tax expense		100,470
Net income		$195,030

Additional data:

a. Plant assets with original cost of $250,000 and accumulated depreciation of $200,000 were sold for $80,000 cash.
b. Dividends declared and paid of $120,000.
c. Issued common stock with a total par value of $50,000 for $500,000 cash.
d. Borrowed $600,000 cash on November 1, 19x2, to be paid back with annual interest of 10% on June 1, 19x3.
e. Sales of $600,000 on credit.
f. Collected $540,000 from credit customers.
g. Incurred salaries expense of $210,000 for the year.
h. Paid $198,000 for salaries.
i. Depreciation expense of $75,000.
j. Purchased plant assets for $775,000 in cash.
k. Incurred miscellaneous expenses of $27,000 on credit.
l. Purchased 5,000 shares of Kalmor Corporation for $400,000 cash.
m. Paid $55,500 of accounts payable.
n. Paid $13,100 for prepaid rent.
o. Incurred rent expense of $12,500.
p. Incurred interest expense of $10,000 on a short-term note of $600,000 acquired on November 1, 19x2.
q. Incurred income tax expense of 34% of income before taxes.

Required:

1. Prepare a statement of cash flows for Saleco for 19x2 using the direct method.
2. Prepare a statement of cash flows for Saleco for 19x2 using the indirect method.

Solution:

Direct Method:

Saleco, Inc.
Statement of Cash Flows
For the Year Ended December 31, 19x2

Cash flows from operating activities:		
Cash received from customers	$ 540,000	
Cash paid to suppliers and employees	(266,600)	
Net cash flow from operating activities		$ 273,400
Cash flows from investing activities:		
Proceeds from sale of plant assets	$ 80,000	
Payment for purchase of plant assets	(775,000)	
Payment for purchase of Kalmor stock	(400,000)	
Net cash flow from investing activities		(1,095,000)
Cash flows from financing activities:		
Net borrowings	$ 600,000	
Proceeds from issuance of stock	500,000	
Dividends paid	(120,000)	
Net cash flow from financing activities		980,000
Net increase in cash		$ 158,400
Cash at beginning of year		43,000
Cash at end of year		$ 201,400

Indirect Method:

Saleco, Inc.
Statement of Cash Flows
For the Year Ended December 31, 19x2

Cash flows from operating activities:		
Net income		$ 195,030
Adjustments to reconcile net income to cash flow from operations:		
Depreciation	$ 75,000	
Gain on sale of plant assets	(30,000)	
Change in current assets and liabilities:		
Increase in accounts receivable	(60,000)	
Increase in prepaid rent	(600)	
Decrease in accounts payable	(28,500)	
Increase in salaries payable	12,000	
Increase in interest and income taxes payable	110,470	
Total adjustments		78,370
Net cash provided by operating activities		$ 273,400
Cash flows from investing activities:		
Proceeds from sale of plant assets	$ 80,000	
Payment for purchase of plant assets	(775,000)	
Payment for purchase of Kalmor stock	(400,000)	
Net cash used by investing activities		(1,095,000)
Cash flows from financing activities:		
Net borrowings	$ 600,000	
Proceeds from issuance of stock	500,000	
Dividends paid	(120,000)	
Net cash provided by financing activities		980,000
Net increase in cash		$ 158,400
Cash at beginning of year		43,000
Cash at end of year		$ 201,400

APPENDIX

Worksheet for Statement of Cash Flows

Objective 8
The use of a worksheet in preparing a statement of cash flows.

A working paper technique, called the **worksheet method,** can be used to help construct an SCF. The same concepts underlie this technique as those discussed in the chapter, and the unique organization on the working paper provides some computational efficiencies.

The working paper in Exhibit 14A-1 uses reconciliations of beginning and ending balance sheet amounts as its major technique. The top half has all the beginning (December 31, 19x1) and ending (December 31, 19x2) balance sheet amounts listed in the first and fourth columns, respectively. The second and third columns reconcile the two balances; that is, the money amounts in those columns show the amounts by which each account increased or decreased during the period. For example, Cash, the object of this analysis, decreased a total of $214,000; therefore, a credit entry is shown in the third column. Accounts Receivable, on the other hand, increased $1,720,000, and this shows in the second column as a debit. Keep in mind that these debit and credit entries are not journal entries but are merely used as a clerical device to make the worksheet balance. Of course, they do reflect the net debit and credit changes from all journal entries that affected each account during the period.

The bottom half of the working paper also utilizes the second and third columns to classify the cash flow effects of the changes in account balances from the top half. This classification scheme is the same as the formal SCF illustrated in the chapter: cash from operating activities, cash from investing activities, and cash from financing activities. The object is to describe the net change in cash. For example, find entry number 11 in the upper half. It shows that the Land account decreased by $300,000 during the period. This number shows up in the lower half as an investing activity ("Disposal of land"), that provided cash of $300,000. Because every entry on the upper half has a counterpart on the lower half, the worksheet is self-balancing.

Although the worksheet format is concise and lends itself to mechanical manipulation, remember that it is only a tool for organization and computation. The real challenge is the mastering of the concepts that allow a cash flow analysis to be prepared from accrual-based records.

We shall reconstruct each working paper entry in terms of its effect on operating, investing, and financing activities. You should first concentrate on the lower half of the working paper and then trace the effect to the upper half.

OPERATING ACTIVITIES

The placement of entry 1 indicates that net income is usually a major source of cash; thus, it is shown as the starting point in the lower part of the worksheet. Find entry 1 in Exhibit 14A-1. Because net income is a major reconciling item between beginning and ending retained earnings, it is shown alone as an increase in retained earnings. Of course, net income does not represent cash flow;

EXHIBIT 14A-1

DataCo, Inc.
Working Paper for Statement of Cash Flows
For the Year Ending December 31, 19x2

	12/31/x1	Transactions for Year 2 Debit	Transactions for Year 2 Credit	12/31/x2	
Cash	248		(X) 214	34	
Accounts Receivable	965	(3) 1,720		2,685	
Inventory	1,015	(4) 735		1,750	
Prepaid Insurance	12		(7) 6	6	
Marketable Securities		(10) 600	(12) 350	250	
Building	2,700	(9) 2,100		4,800	
Accumulated Depreciation	(850)		(2) 270	(1,120)	
Land	1,100		(11) 300	800	
Totals	5,190			9,205	
Accounts Payable	200	(5) 125		75	
Notes Payable	360	(13) 360	(9) 460	460	
Salaries Payable	150	(6) 20		130	
Taxes Payable	40		(8) 128	168	
Bonds Payable	2,200			2,200	
Common Stock	1,500		(13) 2,164	3,664	
Retained Earnings	740	(14) 500	(1) 2,268	2,508	
Totals	5,190	6,160	6,160	9,205	
Operating Activities:					
Net Income		(1) 2,268			Net Cash Flow from Operating Activities +$72
Add: Depreciation Expense		(2) 270			
Decrease in Prepayments		(7) 6			
Increase in Taxes Payable		(8) 128			
Subtract:					
Increase in Accounts Receivable			(3) 1,720		
Increase in Inventories			(4) 735		
Decrease in Accounts Payable			(5) 125		
Decrease in Salaries Payable			(6) 20		
Investing Activities:					
Acquisition of Building			(9) 1,640		Net Cash Used by Investing Activities −$1,590
Acquisition of Securities			(10) 600		
Disposal of Land		(11) 300			
Disposal of Securities		(12) 350			
Financing Activities:					
Issuance of Common Stock		(13) 1,804			Net Cash Provided by Financing Activities +$1,304
Payment of Dividends			(14) 500		
Decrease in Cash		(X) 214			
Totals		5,340	5,340		

therefore, several other balance sheet changes must be analyzed before cash provided by operations is determined.

Entries 2, 7, and 8 are all reconciling items between net income and cash from operating activities, which are added to the net income amount. Depreciation of $270,000 is an expense that did not consume cash in this period. Prepayments of $6,000 were expensed this period but cash flowed in the previous period and the increase in Taxes Payable of $128,000, although expensed this period, will not be paid until 19x3.

Entries 3, 4, 5, and 6 are reconciling items shown as subtractions from net income. Accounts Receivable increased by $1,720,000 which, of course, increased net income but cash has not yet been received. Inventories increased by $735,000 representing purchases during the year in excess of deliveries to customers. Such purchases are eventually paid for with cash although net income will not be reduced until the merchandise is sold to customers. Accounts Payable decreased by $125,000 by means of cash payments to suppliers, thereby creating a negative cash flow of $125,000 more than is reflected in the expenses shown in the income statement. Likewise, salaries payable decreased by $20,000 reflecting more cash flow to workers than is shown as salary expense. In summary, although net income is shown on the income statement at $2,268,000, operations generated only $72,000 of net cash.

INVESTING ACTIVITIES

Entries 9, 10, 11, and 12 all relate to the cash flow from investing activities. A building costing $2,100,000 was acquired by means of a cash payment of $1,640,000 and a note issuance of $460,000. Securities of $600,000 were acquired using cash. Land and securities were sold for cash of $300,000 and $350,000, respectively. The net effect was $1,590,000 negative cash flow from investing activities.

FINANCING ACTIVITIES

Entries 13 and 14 show cash inflows and outflows from financing activities. Common stock issuance generated $1,804,000 in cash as the result of issuing stock of $2,164,000 for a combination of cash $1,804,000 and the payment of a liability of $360,000. The dividend payment decreased cash and is part of the reconciliation of retained earnings balance. Financing activities, therefore, generated a net positive cash flow of $1,304,000.

The entry marked (X) is shown in the upper half as the cash reconciliation credit and as the balance "Decrease in cash" amount below.

Refer to Exhibit 14-12 earlier in the chapter to see that the formal SCF reflects all the changes analyzed in the working paper in Exhibit 14A-1.

KEY TERMS

Cash equivalents. Short-term, highly liquid investments that can be converted to cash so quickly as to be considered equivalents of cash. Investments in equity securities are not considered cash equivalents.

Direct method. Method of determining cash from operations by analyzing the cash received from customers and the cash paid to suppliers and others.

Financing activities. Activities that involve receipt and payments of cash or other assets from and to owners or from borrowing from bondholders and other creditors such as banks.

Indirect method. Method of determining cash from operations that begins with net income and adds or subtracts any noncash income statement items to arrive at cash from operations.

Investing activities. Activities involving acquisition and disposal of long-term assets as well as cash paid and received for securities and for the principal amount of loans made to others.

Operating activities. Activities necessary to provide goods and services to customers.

Statement of cash flows (SCF). Financial statement that analyzes the effects of cash flow transactions and gives details as to the inflows and outflows of cash during a period.

Summary entries. Entries used for convenience that represent the sum of several like entries that have been recorded in a journal during the period.

APPENDIX KEY TERM

Worksheet method. A working paper method used to help construct an SCF.

QUESTIONS

1. What information does the statement of cash flows provide that is not provided in the income statement and comparative balance sheets?
2. Define cash equivalents and explain why these are included in analyzing changes in cash from one period to the next.
3. Describe the difference among operating, investing, and financing activities.
4. Why is interest received and paid considered operating activities?
5. List three types each of operating, investing, and financing inflows and outflows.
6. Which of the three cash flow activities would ordinarily be considered of the greatest long-term importance to the firm?
7. Describe the change in cash in relation to the change in other balance sheet accounts.
8. How are significant investing and financing transactions that do not affect cash, such as the issuance of stock to acquire a building, disclosed in the statement of cash flows?
9. Give three examples of noncash transactions that would be disclosed in the manner described in the answer to the previous question.
10. How does the statement of cash flows differ from the other financial statements?
11. Would it be possible for a firm to report a net loss in its income statement and an increase in cash in its statement of cash flows for the same year? If so, how could this happen?
12. If a deduction for depreciation of assets is not made on the statement of cash flows, as it is on the income statement, when is the deduction for the assets made?
13. Explain the difference between the direct and indirect methods of preparing the statement of cash flows.
14. What advantage does the worksheet method provide in preparing a statement of cash flows?

EXERCISES

EXERCISE 14-1
L.O. 1

Classifying Transactions

The following selected transactions have been taken from the Western Company. Classify each transaction as to whether it is an operating (O), investing (I), or financing (F) activity:

a. Salaries were paid to employees.
b. Shares of Western's common stock were repurchased and held in treasury.
c. A short-term note receivable was received from a customer.
d. Office supplies were purchased.
e. Land was sold for $100,000 cash.
f. Interest on a long-term note was paid.
g. The principal portion of the long-term note in (*f*) was paid.
h. Dividends were declared and paid.

EXERCISE 14-2
L.O. 1

Classifying Transactions

The following transactions from the month of January 19x2, have been taken from the accounting records of Garth Computers, Inc. Classify each transaction as to what amount and where that amount would appear on the statement of cash flows. The direct method was used.

a. A $500,000 long-term note was paid off with $100,000 cash and the issuance of $400,000 in common stock.
b. During the month, merchandise was sold for $60,000 to customers on account. Collections on account amounted to $58,000.
c. Dividends of $20,000 were declared in December 19x1 and paid during January 19x2.
d. Equipment with a net book value of $2,500 was sold for cash at a $300 loss.
e. Temporary marketable equity securities were purchased for $75,000.
f. During the month $40,000 of inventory was purchased on account. Payments to suppliers for the month were $48,000.
g. Interest of $8,000 on short- and long-term notes was paid.
h. A $40,000 settlement from the insurance company was received for building destroyed by fire last year.

EXERCISE 14-3
L.O. 3–5

Multiple Choice

1. On its statement of cash flows for the period, Donahue, Inc., reports net cash provided by operating activities of $85,000. For the period, Donahue reports depreciation expense of $20,000 and a $6,000 loss on sale of plant equipment. Net income for the period is—
   a. $65,000.
   b. $105,000.
   c. $59,000.
   d. $111,000.
2. On its statement of cash flows for the period, Winfrey, Inc., reports net cash flow from operating activities of $(14,000). The following information is also available: depreciation expense of $10,000; gain on sale of land, $4,000; an increase in accounts receivable, $5,000; and an increase in accounts payable, $2,000. Net income (loss) for the period is—
   a. $(17,000).
   b. $(23,000).
   c. $3,000.
   d. $(3,000).

3. A company purchases a building valued at $150,000 by paying cash of $50,000 and issuing the remainder in common stock. On the statement of cash flows this would appear as—
   a. $150,000 outflow for financing activities.
   b. $50,000 outflow for investing activities.
   c. $50,000 outflow for financing activities.
   d. $150,000 outflow for investing activities.
4. During the year, Bubbles Company writes off an old invoice for $4,000 as a bad debt. On the statement of cash flows using the direct method for the period this would appear as a—
   a. $4,000 outflow for operating activities.
   b. $4,000 outflow for investing activities.
   c. $4,000 outflow for financing activities.
   d. This item would not appear on the SCF.

EXERCISE 14-4
L.O. 2

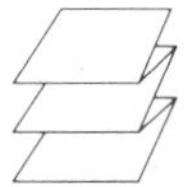

Format of Statement of Cash Flows

During its 19x1 fiscal year which ended on December 31, Fledgling Industries, Inc., has the following summarized data from its general ledger Cash account:

Receipts from customers	$250,000
Payment for income taxes	8,500
Interest payment on note	20,000
Proceeds from sale of common stock	100,000
Dividends declared and paid	50,000
Payment to employees	75,000
Payments to suppliers of inventory	90,000
Proceeds from sale of equipment	28,400
Payment for miscellaneous expenses	22,500
Payment of the long-term note principal	88,000

Required:
Prepare a statement of cash flows in proper format for Fledgling Industries for 19x1.

EXERCISE 14-5
L.O. 5

Effect of Noncash Transactions

Selected investing and financing activities for Fiber Optics, Inc., follow:

a. Declares and pays a $40,000 cash dividend.
b. Purchases a parcel of land for $50,000 and a $400,000 note.
c. Sells a piece of equipment with a net book value of $30,000 for a $4,000 gain. Payment is accepted in the form of $9,000 cash and the remainder in a note.

Required:
Describe how each of the above transactions would be disclosed on Fiber Optics' statement of cash flows or on any supporting schedules.

EXERCISE 14-6
L.O. 5

Effect of Noncash Transactions

Selected information of Niehaus Financing Company for the fiscal year 19x1 is as follows:

a. Purchases a building valued at $750,000 by issuing 15,000 shares of common stock with a per share par value of $10. The current market price of the stock is $50 per share.
b. Pays off a $100,000 short-term note by issuing a $100,000 long-term note.
c. Purchases a $250,000 piece of equipment by paying $50,000 and the remainder in a note.

Required:
Describe how each of the above transactions would be disclosed on Niehaus Financing's statement of cash flows or on any supporting schedules.

EXERCISE 14-7
L.O. 3, 4

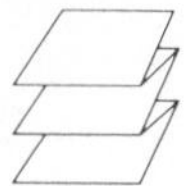

Cash Provided by Operating Activities—Direct Method

The following selected information is available for the Salesky Company for the year ended December 31, 19x2 (all amounts in thousands):

	December 31	
	19x2	*19x1*
Balance sheet data:		
Accounts receivable	$ 50	$52
Inventory	27	31
Prepaid expenses	12	11
Accounts payable	9	11
Salaries payable	14	11
Income taxes payable . . .	17	19
Income statement data:		
Sales revenue	$400	
Cost of goods sold	136	
Salaries expense	92	
Depreciation expense	25	
Other expenses	15	
Income tax expense	30	
Loss on sale of building . . .	29	

Additional data:

a. Purchases of inventory during the period totaled $132,000. All purchases are made on credit and the Accounts Payable account is only used for purchases of inventory.
b. All sales were made on credit.

Required:
Prepare the cash provided by operations section of Salesky's statement of cash flows for 19x2 using the direct method.

EXERCISE 14-8
L.O. 6

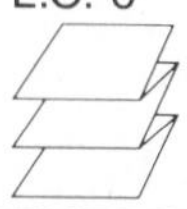

Cash Provided by Operating Activities—Indirect Method

Refer to the information in Exercise 14-7. Prepare the cash provided from operations section of Salesky's statement of cash flows using the indirect method.

EXERCISE 14-9
L.O. 3, 4

Statement of Cash Flows—Direct Method

Saunders Engineering, Inc., has been in business several years and has prepared its December 31, 19x2, comparative balance sheet and 19x2 income statement as follows:

Saunders Engineering, Inc.
Comparative Balance Sheet

	12/31/x2	*12/31/x1*
Assets		
Current assets:		
Cash	$35,300	$ 5,100
Accounts receivable	28,300	31,200
Note receivable	0	8,000
Interest receivable	0	800
Total current assets	$63,600	$45,100
Noncurrent assets:		
Equipment.	$45,000	$40,000
Less: Accumulated depreciation . . .	36,000	24,000
Total noncurrent assets	$ 9,000	$16,000
Total assets	$72,600	$61,100

Liabilities and Stockholders' Equity

Liabilities:		
Accounts payable	$ 1,000	$ 800
Note payable	0	20,000
Interest payable	0	1,800
Salaries payable	1,890	2,250
Total liabilities	$ 2,890	$24,850
Stockholders' equity:		
Capital stock	$50,000	$30,000
Retained earnings	19,710	6,250
Total liabilities and stockholders' equity	$72,600	$61,100

Saunders Engineering
Income Statement
For the Year Ended December 31, 19x2

Sales revenue		$127,100
Expenses:		
Salaries expense.	$75,640	
Depreciation expense.	12,000	
Property tax expense.	9,200	
Utilities expense	1,100	
Other expenses	10,700	
Total expenses		108,640
Net income		$ 18,460

The following cash transactions took place during the year:

Payments:	
a. Purchased equipment	$ 5,000
b. Paid salaries	76,000
c. Paid property taxes	9,200
d. Paid dividends	5,000
e. Paid utility bill	1,100
f. Paid note and interest.	21,800
g. Paid on accounts payable	10,500
Receipts:	
a. Collected cash from customers.	130,000
b. Sold stock	20,000
c. Collected interest on note receivable . . .	800
d. Collected on note receivable.	8,000

Required:
Prepare Saunders' statement of cash flows for 19x2 using the direct method.

EXERCISE 14-10
L.O. 6

Statement of Cash Flows—Indirect Method

Refer to the information in Exercise 14-9.

Required:
Prepare Saunders' statement of cash flows for 19x2 using the indirect method.

EXERCISE 14-11
L.O. 7

Evaluating Performance via Statement of Cash Flows

Refer to this chapter's Demonstration Exercise and solution on pages 784-85. Evaluate Saleco's performance by comparing the balance sheets and income statement with its statement of cash flows.

APPENDIX EXERCISE

EXERCISE 14-12
L.O. 8

Use of a Worksheet in Preparing a Statement of Cash Flows

Refer to the Demonstration Exercise for this chapter on pages 784-85. Using the data for Saleco, Inc., prepare the worksheet to aid in completing the 19x2 statement of cash flows for the company.

PROBLEMS

PROBLEM 14-1
L.O. 6

Indirect Method

The following information is available regarding the current asset and current liability accounts of Searching, Inc. (all carry normal balances and are in thousands):

	December 31	
	19x2	*19x1*
Cash	$ 120	$ 140
Receivables	975	950
Inventory	1,960	2,120
Prepaid Insurance	17	21
Accounts Payable	840	805
Revenue Received in Advance	26	32
Salaries and Wages Payable	140	115

The following additional data are available (all amounts in thousands):

a. Plant assets, sold at a $300 loss had originally cost $2,700 and had accumulated depreciation of $1,800 at the time of sale. The sale was for cash.
b. Cash dividends declared in 19x2 were $500.
c. Net income for 19x2 was $495. Depreciation expense was $310 for 19x2, and amortization of intangible assets for 19x2 was $36. Also, cash paid for depreciable equipment in 19x2 amounted to $750.

Required:
1. Compute cash provided by operations for 19x2.
2. Compute the total change (increase or decrease) in cash for 19x2.
3. Compute the cash inflow resulting from the sale of plant assets.

PROBLEM 14-2
L.O. 6

Indirect Method

The following information is available for Taxing Company:

	December 31	
	19x2	19x1
Assets		
Cash	$ 41	$ 31
Accounts receivable	25	18
Inventories	35	24
Land	70	95
Building, net of depreciation	460	380
Patents, net of amortization	22	17
Total assets	$653	$565
Liabilities and Stockholders' Equity		
Liabilities:		
Accounts payable	$ 41	$ 60
Salaries payable	10	9
Dividends payable	8	7
Notes payable (long-term)	170	120
Total liabilities	$229	$196
Stockholders' equity:		
Common stock, no-par	$280	$260
Retained earnings	144	109
Total stockholders' equity	$424	$369
Total liabilities and stockholders' equity	$653	$565

	For the Year Ended December 31, 19x2
Net income	$ 53
Depreciation of buildings in 19x2	25
Purchase of new building	170
Cash dividends declared in 19x2	18
Gain on sale of buildings (a nonoperating gain included in net income)	10
Purchase of new patent	9

Required:
Using the information presented above, compute cash provided by operations for the year ended December 31, 19x2.

PROBLEM 14-3
L.O. 6

Indirect Method

The following data are taken from the financial statements of Speed Sprocket, Inc. (all accounts carry their normal balances):

Comparative Balance Sheet Data ($000):

	December 31	
	19x2	*19x1*
Accounts Receivable—Services	$150	$ 85
Accrued Interest Receivable	25	30
Plant and Equipment (cost)	695	645
Accumulated Depreciation	130	145
Accounts Payable	71	64
Prepaid Service Revenue	45	25
Notes Payable	120	110

Income Statement Date ($000):

	For the Year Ended December 31, 19x2
Service Revenue	$560
Interest Revenue	54
Depreciation Expense—Plant and Equipment	28

During 19x2 Speed Sprocket, Inc., acquired new equipment for cash at a cost of $110, and also sold some old equipment.

Required:

1. Speed Sprocket, Inc., has no uncollectible accounts. Compute the amount of cash received during 19x2 from customers.
2. Compute the **original cost** and the **accumulated depreciation** on equipment that was disposed of during 19x2.
3. Compute the amount of cash received for interest during 19x2.

PROBLEM 14-4
L.O. 6

Indirect Method

The Bardsley Corporation, a large retail clothing store, reported the following balances in its accounts at December 31, 19x2 (all accounts carry their normal balances and are in thousands):

Sales Revenue	$15,700
Interest Revenue—Customers	900
Cost of Goods Sold	7,800
Depreciation Expense	400
Amortization Expense	300
Gain on Sale of Land Held as a Long-Term Investment	120
All other expenses—primarily salaries and wages	5,500
Net income	$ 2,720

The following balance sheet changes occurred in the current assets and current liabilities during 19x2 (all in thousands):

	December 31		Change Increase (Decrease)
	19x2	19x1	
Cash	$ 470	$ 410	$ 60
Receivables	4,974	4,900	74
Inventory	4,551	4,500	51
Other current assets	930	908	22
Accounts payable	5,102	5,140	(38)
Dividends payable	110	100	10
Other current liabilities . . .	2,940	2,890	50

The following additional data are available (in thousands):

a. Land, sold at a $120 gain had originally cost $4,000. The sale was for cash.

b. Cash dividends declared in 19x2 were $760.

Required:

1. Compute the cash provided by operations for 19x2.
2. Compute the amount of cash paid for dividends in 19x2.
3. Compute the cash inflow resulting from the sale of land.

PROBLEM 14-5
L.O. 6

Indirect Method

Clark Company is in the process of preparing the annual financial statements on December 31, 19x2, including a statement of cash flows. The balance sheet and income statement have been completed and are summarized below:

Clark Company
Balance Sheet
At December 31

	19x2	19x1
Assets		
Cash	$ 25,500	$ 42,000
Accounts receivable.	93,500	75,500
Inventory.	63,000	75,000
Prepaid insurance.	6,000	15,500
Investments (long-term)	0	25,000
Property, plant, and equipment (net)	180,000	120,000
	$368,000	$353,000
Liabilities and Stockholders' Equity		
Liabilities:		
Accounts payable.	$ 38,500	$ 37,400
Accrued salaries payable	6,000	3,500
Notes payable, short-term	38,000	19,100
Mortgage payable (long-term)	80,000	105,000
Total liabilities	$162,500	$165,000
Stockholders' equity:		
Common stock	$120,000	$100,000
Contributed capital in excess of par. . . .	26,000	20,000
Retained earnings.	59,500	68,000
Total stockholders' equity	$205,500	$188,000
Total liabilities and stockholders' equity . . .	$368,000	$353,000

Clark Company
Income Statement
For the Year Ended December 31, 19x2

Sales		$275,000
Cost of goods sold		218,000
Gross margin		$ 57,000
Expenses:		
Depreciation expense	$20,000	
Other operating expenses . . .	17,000	37,000
Income before taxes		$ 20,000
Income tax expense		6,000
Net income		$ 14,000

Additional data:

a. 200 shares of common stock par value $100 were sold for $130 per share.
b. Dividends of $22,500 were paid on August 30, 19x2.
c. A storage building was purchased for $55,000.
d. The company acquired a machine worth $25,000 in exchange for the General Motors stock being held as an investment. In addition, obsolete equipment that had cost $35,000 and was fully depreciated was scrapped.

Required:

Prepare a statement of cash flows for the Clark Company for the year ended December 31, 19x2, using the indirect method. Use appropriate headings and subheadings.

PROBLEM 14-6
L.O. 6

Statement of Cash Flows—Indirect Method

You are the independent auditor for Rex Tours, Inc., whose fiscal year ended on December 31, 19x3. Your assistant has developed the following analysis to be used for the preparation of Rex Tours' statement of cash flows:

	Increase (Decrease)	*Details*	
Assets:			
Cash and cash equivalents . .	$ 4,000		
Accounts receivable (net) . . .	7,000	Bad debt expense	$ 3,000
		Accounts receivable increase . .	10,000
Notes receivable (long-term) . . .	(8,000)	Cash received	8,000
Property, plant, and		Purchased equipment for cash . .	16,000
equipment (net)	12,000	Depreciation expense	4,000
	$15,000		
Liabilities:			
Accounts payable and		Accrued expenses	$ 3,000
accrued liabilities	$ 9,000	Accounts payable increase . . .	6,000
Notes payable	(3,000)	Paid off note, 2/25/x3	12,000
		Borrowed cash, 11/15/x3	9,000
Common stock	3,000	Issued stock for cash	3,000
Retained earnings	6,000	Income statement items:	
	$15,000	Sales	$32,000
		Selling and administrative expense	14,000
		Depreciation expense	4,000
		Income tax expense	6,000
		Net income	$ 8,000
		Dividends paid	$ 2,000

Required:
Prepare a statement of cash flows using the indirect method for the operating section.

PROBLEM 14-7
L.O. 3, 6

Statement of Cash Flows—Direct Method

Consider the following income statement, balance sheet, and summary journal entries made for MACC Corporation for the year 19x2 (all in thousands).

MACC Corporation
Income Statement
For the Year Ended December 31, 19x2

Sales	$20,400	
Cost of goods sold	12,240	
Gross margin		$8,160
Operating expenses:		
Salaries and wages	$ 3,500	
Repairs and maintenance	90	
Rent expense	110	
Miscellaneous expense	70	
Depreciation expense	540	
Interest expense	300	
Unrealized loss on temporary investments	20	4,630
Income from operations		$3,530
Gain on sale of long-term assets	$ 200	
Earnings of subsidiary	130	
Interest revenue	40	
Total other revenue		370
Income before taxes		$3,900
Income tax expense		1,326
Net income		$2,574

NOTE: Land with a book value of $410,000 was sold for $610,000.

MACC Corporation
Balance Sheet
At December 31

	19x2	19x1
Assets		
Current assets:		
Cash	$ 2,552	$ 2,332
Accounts receivable	1,420	2,020
Marketable (equity) securities)	738	738
Less: Allowance to reduce to LCM	(82)	(62)
Inventory	1,980	1,120
Accrued interest receivable	10	10
Prepaid miscellaneous expenses	122	72
Total current assets	$ 6,740	$ 6,230

Noncurrent assets:		
Bonds of A Corporation (8%, semiannual payment on 3/31 and 9/30)	$ 500	$ 500
Equity investment in subsidiary—S Corp. (40% owned)	872	742
Machinery and equipment	4,482	3,842
Less: Accumulated depreciation	(1,429)	(1,129)
Buildings and land improvements	7,280	7,280
Less: Accumulated depreciation	(2,650)	(2,410)
Land	2,690	3,100
Total noncurrent assets	$11,745	$11,925
Total assets	$18,485	$18,155

Liabilities and Shareholders' Equity

Current liabilities:		
Accounts payable	$ 1,410	$ 510
Salaries and wages payable	120	70
Short-term note payable—suppliers	600	750
Income taxes payable	550	220
Total current liabilities	$ 2,680	$ 1,550
Noncurrent liabilities:		
Bonds payable (10%; interest due 6/30 and 12/31)	$ 3,000	$ 3,000
Deferred taxes	1,884	1,208
Total noncurrent liabilities	$ 4,884	$ 4,208
Shareholders' equity:		
Common stock	$ 5,050	$ 4,550
Retained earnings	5,871	7,847
Total shareholders' equity	$10,921	$12,397
Total liabilities and shareholders' equity	$18,485	$18,155

Summary entries during the year:

		Debit	Credit
a.	Accounts Receivable	20,400	
	Sales		20,400
b.	Cost of Goods Sold	12,240	
	Inventory		12,240
c.	Inventory	13,100	
	Accounts Payable		13,100
d.	Cash	21,000	
	Accounts Receivable		21,000
e.	Accounts Payable	12,200	
	Cash		12,200
f.	Prepaid Expenses	120	
	Cash		120
g.	Cash	40	
	Interest Revenue		30
	Accrued Interest Receivable		10
h.	Machinery	640	
	Cash		640

	Account	Debit	Credit
i.	Cash	610	
	Land		410
	Gain on Sale		200
j.	Salaries Expense	3,500	
	Salaries and Wages Payable		3,500
k.	Salaries and Wages Payable	3,450	
	Cash		3,450
l.	Cash	400	
	Short-Term Notes Payable		400
m.	Short-Term Notes Payable—Supplies	550	
	Cash		550
n.	Taxes Payable	220	
	Cash		220
o.	Interest Expense	300	
	Cash		300
p.	Cash	500	
	Common Stock		500
q.	Dividends	4,550	
	Cash		4,550
r.	Repairs and Maintenance Expense	90	
	Cash		90
s.	Rent Expense	110	
	Cash		110

Entries at the end of the year:

	Account	Debit	Credit
t.	Unrealized Loss on Short-Term Investments	20	
	Allowance to Reduce Short-Term Investments to Market		20
u.	Miscellaneous Expense	70	
	Prepaid Expenses		70
v.	Accrued Interest Receivable	10	
	Interest Revenue		10
w.	Equity Investment in Subsidiary—S Corporation	130	
	Investment Income		130
x.	Depreciation Expense	300	
	Accumulated Depreciation—Machinery and Equipment		300
y.	Depreciation Expense	240	
	Accumulated Depreciation—Buildings		240
z.	Income Tax Expense	1,326	
	Deferred Taxes		676
	Income Taxes Payable		550
	Cash		100

aa.	Sales	20,400	
	Interest Revenue	40	
	Gain on Sale of Long-Term Assets	200	
	Investment Income	130	
	Income Summary		20,770
bb.	Income Summary	16,260	
	Cost of Goods Sold		12,240
	Salaries Expense		3,500
	Interest Expense		300
	Repairs and Maintenance Expense		90
	Rent Expense		110
	Unrealized Loss on Short-Term Investments		20
cc.	Income Summary	610	
	Depreciation Expense		540
	Miscellaneous Expense		70
dd.	Income Summary	1,326	
	Tax Expense		1,326
ee.	Retained Earnings	1,976	
	Income Summary	2,574	
	Dividends		4,550

Required:
Prepare a statement of cash flows for 19x2 using the direct method.

PROBLEM 14-8
L.O. 6

Statement of Cash Flows—Indirect Method

Refer to the information for Problem 14-7.

Required:
Prepare a statement of cash flows for 19x2 using the indirect method.

PROBLEM 14-9
L.O. 3, 5

Statement of Cash Flows—Direct Method

SKM, Inc., has the following income statement for 19x2, comparative balance sheets at December 31, 19x1, and 19x2, and 19x2 summary journal entries:

SKM, Inc.
Income Statement
For the Year Ended December 31, 19x2
(in thousands)

Sales		$1,200
Cost of goods sold		560
Gross margin		$ 640
Expenses:		
Salaries and wages expense	$215	
Rent expense	80	
Interest expense	25	
Depreciation expense	60	
Total expenses		380
Income before taxes		$ 260
Income tax expense		108
Net income		$ 152

SKM, Inc.
Comparative Balance Sheets
December 31
(in thousands)

	19x2	*19x1*
Assets		
Current assets:		
Cash	$ 125	$131
Accounts receivable (net)	125	40
Inventory	80	50
Total current assets	$ 330	$221
Noncurrent assets:		
Machinery and equipment	$ 500	$400
Accumulated depreciation	(100)	(40)
Land	80	—
Total noncurrent assets	$ 480	$360
Total assets	$ 810	$581
Liabilities and Stockholders' Equity		
Current liabilities:		
Accounts payable	$ 50	$ 65
Salaries payable	10	10
Income taxes payable	22	5
Accrued interest	5	—
Total current liabilities	$ 87	$ 80
Noncurrent liabilities:		
Bonds payable (10%; paid 6/30 and 12/31)	$ 150	$150
Long-term note payable	100	—
Total noncurrent liabilities	$ 250	$150
Stockholders' equity:		
Common stock	$ 200	$200
Retained earnings	273	151
Total stockholders' equity	$ 473	$351
Total liabilities and stockholders' equity	$ 810	$581

NOTE: Machinery and equipment were acquired during 19x2 by the issuance of a $100,000 long-term note (interest payable on January 1 and July 1 at 10%). Land was purchased for $80,000 cash.

Summary journal entries for the year 19x2 are as follows (all amounts in thousands):

a.	Accounts receivable	1,200	
	Sales		1,200
b.	Cost of Goods Sold	560	
	Inventory		560
c.	Salaries and Wages Expense	215	
	Salaries Payable		215

d.	Salaries Payable	215	
	Cash		215
e.	Rent Expense	80	
	Cash		80
f.	Interest Expense	25	
	Cash		20
	Accrued Interest		5
g.	Depreciation Expense	60	
	Accumulated Depreciation		60
h.	Cash	1,115	
	Accounts Receivable		1,115
i.	Inventory	590	
	Accounts Payable		590
j.	Accounts Payable	605	
	Cash		605
k.	Machinery and Equipment	100	
	Note Payable		100
l.	Land	80	
	Cash		80
m.	Income Tax Expense	108	
	Income Taxes Payable		108
n.	Income Taxes Payable	91	
	Cash		91
o.	Dividends	30	
	Cash		30
p.	Sales	1,200	
	Income Summary		1,200
q.	Income Summary	1,048	
	Cost of Goods Sold		560
	Salaries and Wages Expense		215
	Rent Expense		80
	Interest Expense		25
	Depreciation Expense		60
	Income Tax Expense		108
r.	Income Summary	152	
	Retained Earnings		152
s.	Retained Earnings	30	
	Dividends		30

Required:
Prepare a statement of cash flows for 19x2 using the direct method.

PROBLEM 14-10
L.O. 6

Statement of Cash Flows—Indirect Method

Refer to the information for Problem 14-9.

Required:
Prepare a statement of cash flows for 19x2 using the indirect method.

PROBLEM 14-11
L.O. 3, 5

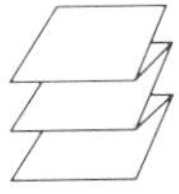

Statement of Cash Flows—Direct Method

Gamen Company, Inc., has the following income statement for 19x2, comparative balance sheets at December 31, 19x1, and 19x2, and additional data:

Gamen Company, Inc.
Income Statement
For the Year Ended December 31, 19x2

Sales		$105,740
Cost of goods sold		68,731
Gross margin		$ 37,009
Expenses:		
Bad debt expense	$ 114	
Depreciation and amortization expense	870	
Interest expense	3,200	
Total expenses		4,184
Operating income before taxes		$ 32,825
Loss from sale of equipment		1,500
Income before taxes		$ 31,325
Income tax expense (34%)		10,651
Net income		$ 20,674

Gamen Company, Inc.
Comparative Balance Sheets
At December 31

	19x2	*19x1*
Assets		
Cash	$ 6,685	$ 4,300
Accounts receivable	18,505	12,800
Less: Allowance for doubtful accounts	(370)	(256)
Notes receivable	2,200	2,200
Inventory	60,569	17,300
Investments (long-term)	3,210	3,210
Property, plant, and equipment	114,771	92,771
Less: Accumulated depreciation	(8,310)	(9,770)
Intangible assets	520	550
Total assets	$197,780	$123,105
Liabilities and Stockholders' Equity		
Liabilities:		
Accounts payable	$ 60,800	$ 13,800
Interest payable	1,700	300
Income taxes payable	10,731	2,080
Short-term debt	13,600	13,600
Long-term debt	0	15,000
Total liabilities	$ 86,831	$ 44,780
Stockholders' equity:		
Common stock ($5 par)	$ 12,500	$ 10,000
Contributed capital in excess of par	52,500	40,000
Retained earnings	45,949	28,325
Total stockholders' equity	$110,949	$ 78,325
Total liabilities and stockholders' equity	$197,780	$123,105

Additional data for 19x2:

a. Cost of goods sold for the year was $68,731. Total sales were $105,470 of which $90,000 was paid in cash with the remainder on account.
b. Cash of $10,035 collected on outstanding accounts receivable.
c. Gamen maintains a 2% allowance for doubtful accounts on the year-end balance in accounts receivable.
d. Equipment was sold for $9,700 cash. Equipment had a book value of $13,500 and accumulated depreciation of $2,300 at date of sale.
e. Inventory of $112,000 was purchased on credit.
f. Payment of $65,000 to suppliers for merchandise purchased earlier on credit.
g. Purchased a plant for $20,500 cash and the issuance of 500 shares of common stock at $30 per share.
h. Retired $15,000 of long-term debt at year-end. Interest was also paid on the debt at the rate of 12%.
i. Declared and paid dividends of $3,050.
j. Interest expense for the period was $3,200.
k. Depreciation on property, plant, and equipment was $840 for the period.
l. Amortization expense on intangibles for the period was $30.
m. Gamen is subject to a 34% tax rate on income before taxes.

Required:
Prepare a statement of cash flows for 19x2 using the direct method.

PROBLEM 14-12
L.O. 6

Statement of Cash Flows—Indirect Method

Refer to the information for Problem 14-11.

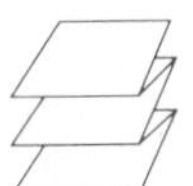

Required:
Prepare a statement of cash flows for 19x2 using the indirect method.

PROBLEM 14-13
L.O. 3, 5

Statement of Cash Flows—Direct Method

Perlon, Inc., has the following income statement for 19x2, comparative balance sheets at 12/31/x1 and 12/31/x2, and additional data (in thousands).

Perlon, Inc.
Income Statement
For the Year Ending December 31, 19x2

Revenues:		
Sales revenue	$37,000	
Investment revenue	600	
Total revenues		$37,600
Salary expense	$ 5,000	
Depreciation expense	4,640	
Interest expense	2,500	
		12,140
Income before taxes		$25,460
Income tax expense		3,996
Net income		$21,464

Perlon, Inc.
Comparative Balance Sheets
at December 31

	19x2	19x1
Assets		
Cash	$ 47,110	$12,800
Accounts receivable	10,190	21,440
Interest receivable	600	0
Long-term investment	7,500	0
Equipment (net)	63,220	61,560
Total assets	$128,620	$95,800
Liabilities and Stockholders' Equity		
Interest payable	$ 2,500	$ 0
Income tax payable	2,646	2,350
Long-term note payable	42,400	38,400
Total liabilities	$ 47,546	$40,750
Common stock ($1 par)	1,200	1,000
Contributed capital in excess of par	26,600	22,000
Retained earnings	53,274	32,050
Total stockholders' equity	$ 81,074	$55,050
Total liabilities and stockholders' equity	$128,620	$95,800

Additional information for 19x2 (amounts in thousands):

a. Sales on credit amounted to $37,000.
b. Equipment was purchased by issuing a note for $4,000.
c. Common stock with total par of $200 was issued for cash of $2,500 and new equipment of $2,300.
d. A long-term investment costing $7,500 was purchased for cash.
e. Income tax expense for 19x2 was $3,996.
f. Depreciation expense for 19x2 was $4,640.
g. Cash dividends paid were $200.

Required:
Prepare a statement of cash flows for 19x2 using the direct method.

PROBLEM 14-14
L.O. 6

Statement of Cash Flows—Indirect Method

Refer to the information for Problem 14-13.

Required:
Prepare a statement of cash flows for 19x2 using the indirect method.

PROBLEM 14-15
L.O. 6

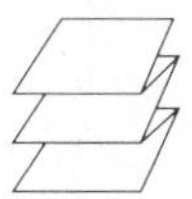

Statement of Cash Flows—Indirect Method

Trident Corporation's assistant controller roughed out the preliminary draft of a 12/31/x1 statement of cash flows:

Operations:	
Net Income.	$ 4,500,000
Add: Depreciation Expense	1,200,000
Cash from Operations.	$ 5,700,000
Other Cash Effects:	
Issuance of Stock.	$ 1,200,000
Issuance of Bonds	3,300,000
Payment of Dividends	(900,000)
Payment for a Building	(1,215,000)
Net Other Cash Effects	$ 2,385,000
Cash Increase for Period.	$ 8,085,000

The assistant controller is confused because the cash account shows a decrease of $3,165,000 for the period. As Trident's auditor you discover that the assistant controller failed to consider the following accounts:

Accounts Receivable

1/1/x1 Balance	$ 2,400,000	Collections from customers	$13,500,000
Sales	16,500,000		
12/31/x1 Balance	$ 5,400,000		

Accounts Payable

		1/1/x1 Balance	$ 1,257,000
Payments	$17,250,000	Purchases	18,500,000
		12/31/x1	$ 2,507,000

Inventory

1/1/x1 Balance	$ 4,500,000	Cost of goods sold	$9,000,000
Purchases	18,500,000		
Balance 12/31/x1	$14,000,000		

Required:
Use the above information to construct a statement of cash flows in good form.

APPENDIX PROBLEM

PROBLEM 14-16
L.O. 8

Worksheet for Preparing Statement of Cash Flows

Pioneer Bakery, Inc., has the following comparative balance sheets for 19x1 and 19x2:

	19x2	*19x1*
Assets		
Current assets:		
Cash	$ 600	$ 400
Marketable securities	160	0
Accounts receivable (net)	1,680	1,160
Inventory	1,320	840
Prepaid insurance	200	100
Total current assets	$3,960	$2,500
Plant, property, and equipment	$2,260	$1,200
Less: Accumulated depreciation	220	100
	$2,040	$1,100
Total assets	$6,000	$3,600
Liabilities and Stockholders' Equity		
Current liabilities:		
Accounts payable	$1,060	$ 880
Accrued expenses	280	260
Dividends payable	140	0
Total current liabilities	$1,480	$1,140
Bonds payable—long-term	1,000	0
Total liabilities	$2,480	$1,140
Stockholders' equity:		
Common stock, no par	$2,400	$1,800
Retained earnings	1,120	660
Total stockholders' equity	$3,520	$2,460
Total liabilities and stockholders' equity	$6,000	$3,600

Pioneer Bakery's comparative income statement is as follows:

	Years Ended December 31	
	19x2	*19x1*
Net revenues	$12,800	$8,000
Cost of goods sold	10,000	6,400
Gross profit	2,800	1,600
Expenses	2,000	1,040
Net income	$ 800	$ 560

Required:
Using the above information, prepare a working paper for Pioneer's statement of cash flows.

CASES

CASE 14-1
L.O. 1

Basic Purpose of Cash Flow Statement

As assistant controller for Arrow Software, Inc., you are assigned to run an introduction to financial accounting workshop for programmers who have little or no financial accounting knowledge. After introducing the basic techniques and financial statements, you are asked the two following questions:

a. What is the key difference between the information found in an income statement and a statement of cash flows?
b. I notice that depreciation is added back to net income on the statement of cash flows. How does depreciation generate cash?

Required:
Write one-paragraph answers to each question. Remember these programmers are accounting wimps.

CASE 14-2
L.O. 1, 5, 7

Using Cash Flow Information to Evaluate Performance

The following statement was made by the president of a publicly held corporation in a published annual report.

> Because of the depression in the international price of crude oil, the company saw further deterioration of sales and net income, both of which were 15% lower than the prior year. Net cash flow from operations was strong primarily because of tightening of credit which reduced our outstanding receivables and the adoption of accelerated depreciation for tax and book purposes as of January 1 which reduces cash flow for taxes by $8,400,000 and which resulted in the add back to net income of $20,000,000 as shown on the statement of cash flows.

Required:
Critique the logic behind the reasons given for the cash flow experience.

CASE 14-3
L.O. 3

Interest and Dividends as Investing Activities

While the majority of the FASB (four members) voted affirmatively for *SFAS No. 95,* three members dissented giving the following explanation: "... interest and dividends received are returns on investments in debt and equity securities that should be classified as cash inflows from investing activity.... Interest paid is a cost of obtaining financial resources that should be classified as a cash outflow for financing activities."

The current rule (*SFAS No. 95*) requires that interest and dividends received and interest paid be reported as cash flows from operating activities. What are some arguments for this treatment?

CASE 14-4
L.O. 6

Direct versus Indirect Method

Two formats are allowed for reporting cash flow from operations on the statement of cash flows: (1) the direct method, which shows major classes of cash receipts and payments such as cash received from customers and cash paid to employees summing to net cash flow from operating activities, and (2) the indirect method, which begins with net income and adds and subtracts amounts that were not the result of operating cash flows during the period. The sum of the net income number and the adjustments equals net cash flow from operating activity.

Required:
What are the advantages of the direct method and the indirect method?

CASE 14-5
L.O. 2–4

Analysis of Cash Flows—Hershey Foods Corporation

Hershey Foods Corporation showed the following charts in their 1987 annual report.

Three-Year Sources of Cash and Short-Term Investments (in millions)

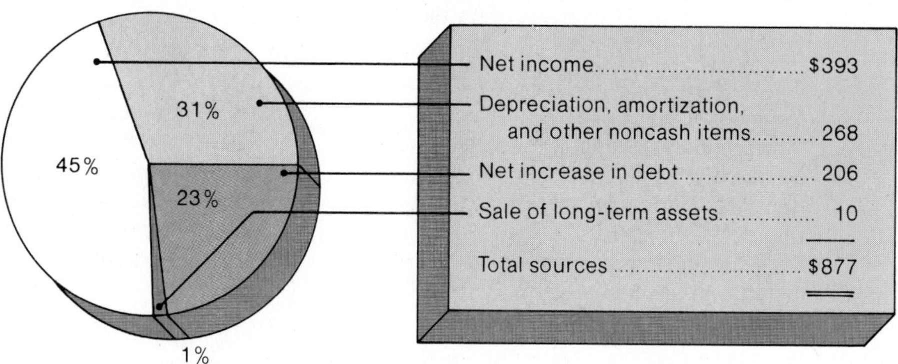

Three-Year Uses of Cash and Short-Term Investments (in millions)

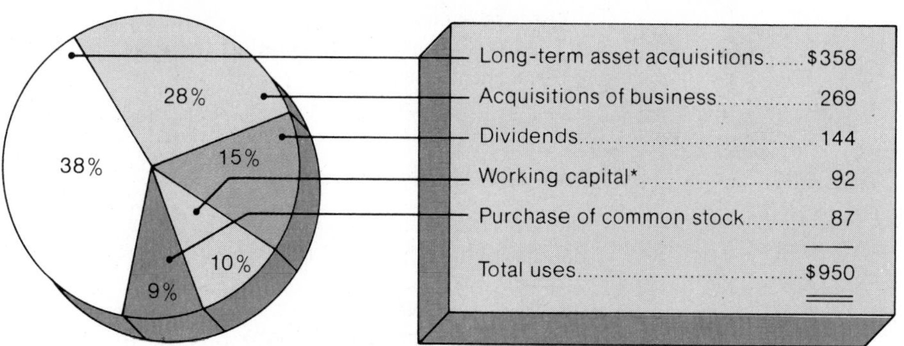

*Net change in inventories, accounts receivable, prepayments, and accounts payable; that is, the increase in current assets not including cash and short-term investments over the increase in current liabilities for the three-year period.

Required:

1. Why are items such as depreciation shown as sources of funds?
2. If Hershey's book value of cash and short-term investments at January 1, 1985, was $88,000,000, what was the book value of their cash and short-term investment on December 31, 1987?
3. Construct a three-year summary statement of cash flows from the information given. Assume that cash is defined as cash plus short-term investments.

CASE 14-6
L.O. 3, 4, 6, 7

Recasting Financial Analysis into a Statement of Cash Flows

Morgan Investments and you are currently working on a corporate acquisition deal between your client American Rental, Inc., and a privately owned regional rental company (New England Rental). NER provides the following analysis of cash flows for the year just ended (in thousands):

Sources of Cash		*Uses of Cash*	
Net income	$5,327	Purchase of land	$2,550
Sale of marketable equity securities	29	Payment of dividends	2,285
Issuance of long-term notes	300	Purchase of building	1,500
Issuance of common stock	750	Purchase of equipment	750
Depreciation expense	780	Increase in inventory	225
Decrease in accounts receivable	120	Decrease in taxes payable	75
Increase in account payable	75		
Total sources	$7,381	Total uses	$7,385

Required:
1. Critique the categorization of "sources" and "uses" of cash in the analysis of cash flows presented.
2. Discuss the meaning of operating, investing, and financing transactions as shown on a statement of cash flows.
3. Recast the given analysis as a formal statement of cash flows.

CASE 14-7
L.O. 3, 4, 6, 7

Analysis of Cash Flows

You are a bank lending officer and a potential customer has provided an income statement, a balance sheet, and the following cash flow analysis:

Net income	$ 3,750,000
Issuance of stock	1,000,000
Issuance of bonds	2,750,000
Payment of dividends	(750,000)
Purchase of building	(1,012,500)
Net cash effects	$ 5,737,500

Upon scrutinizing the accounting records you determine that the following T account activities were ignored in the cash flow analysis:

Accounts Receivable

Beginning balance	$ 2,005,000	Collections	$11,250,000
Sales	13,750,000		
Ending balance	$ 4,505,000		

Accumulated Depreciation

		Beginning balance	$8,450,000
		Depreciation for year	1,000,000
		Ending balance	$9,450,000

Accounts Payable

		Beginning balance	$ 1,047,500
Payments	$14,375,000	Purchases	15,125,000
		Ending balance	$ 1,797,500

Inventory

Beginning balance	$ 3,750,000		
Purchases	15,125,000	Cost of goods sold	$7,500,000
Ending balance	$11,375,000		

Required:
1. Critique the cash flow analysis given.
2. Recast the analysis into a formal cash flow statement.

CASE 14-8
L.O. 2

Analysis of Cash Flow Disclosure—Ralston Purina Company

Refer to the Ralston Purina Company (RPC) financial statements in Appendix E at the end of this book.

Required:
1. Identify the balance sheet items used in the definition of "cash and cash equivalents" in the statement of cash flows. What can you infer about the noncash items included?
2. Does RPC use the direct or indirect method to report the "operations" portion of the SCF?

FINANCIAL STATEMENTS

FINANCIAL STATEMENT COMPONENTS EMPHASIZED IN CHAPTER 15

Whitaker Corporation
Income Statement
For 1991

Revenues
xxxx
xxxx
Expenses
Research and development
Advertising
Bad debts

	1991	*1990*	*Percent change*
Research and development	XX.X%	XX.X%	+ XX.X%
Advertising . . .	XX.X	XX.X	− XX.X
Bad debts	XX.X	XX.X	− XX.X

Whitaker Corporation
Balance Sheet
12/31/91

Current assets
xxxx
xxxx
Noncurrent assets
Plant assets (net)
Intangible assets
Goodwill
Current liabilities
xxxx
xxxx
Noncurrent liabilities
xxxx
xxxx
Stockholders' equity
xxxx
xxxx

	1991	*1990*	*Percent change*
Plant assets (net)	XX.X%	XX.X%	− XX.X%
Intangible assets	XX.X	XX.X	+ XX.X
Goodwill	XX.X	XX.X	+ XX.X

Whitaker Corporation
Cash Flow Statement
For 1991

Operating activities
xxxx
xxxx
Investing activities
From operations
For investments
From financing
Total cash flow
Financing activities
xxxx
xxxx

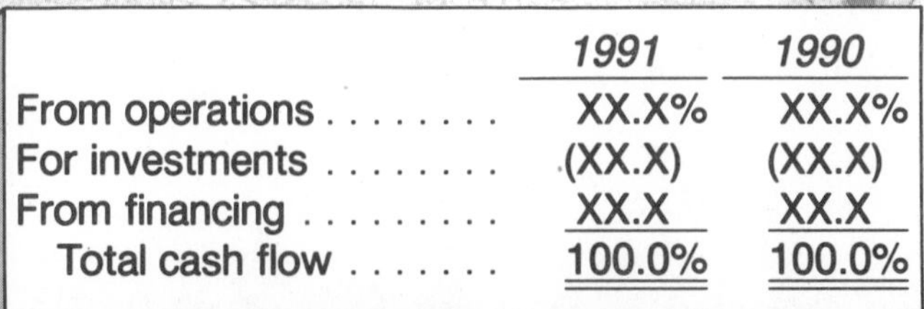

	1991	*1990*
From operations	XX.X%	XX.X%
For investments	(XX.X)	(XX.X)
From financing	XX.X	XX.X
Total cash flow	100.0%	100.0%

CHAPTER 15

Accounting Theory and Financial Statement Analysis

LEARNING OBJECTIVES

After studying Chapter 15, you should understand:

1. The objectives of financial accounting and the qualitative characteristics of accounting information, pp. 816-20.
2. The importance of the elements of financial statements and measurement and recognition in financial statement analysis, pp. 821-22.
3. The common types of analysis used to evaluate financial statements—horizontal, vertical, vertical/horizontal, trend, and ratio analysis, pp. 829-34.
4. How to prepare accounting performance, market performance, liquidity, leverage, and activity ratios, pp. 835-45.

This chapter reviews the conceptual framework of accounting and introduces the fundamental concepts of financial statement analysis. To evaluate financial statements, you must understand their purpose and the underlying principles and concepts used to prepare them. Part A of this chapter ties together the concepts used throughout the text as the basis for accounting choices. This review will help you understand the structure underlying financial statements prepared in accordance with generally accepted accounting principles (GAAP). Part B of this chapter identifies sources of accounting data used to evaluate business entities and provides an introduction to analytical methods of evaluating financial statements.

PART A: ACCOUNTING THEORY—THE CONCEPTUAL FRAMEWORK OF ACCOUNTING

Throughout this textbook we have integrated the underlying theory that ties accounting practices together to form a cohesive body of knowledge. Without these underlying theoretical concepts, accounting would be a set of disjointed rules with no relation to one another. Some of the more obvious underlying concepts include the matching principle employed in the income measurement process and the principle of original (historical) costs that is used as a basis for the recognition and measurement of many balance sheet elements.

In Part A of this chapter, we discuss the theoretical framework that guides the development of accounting practice. This theoretical framework is perhaps best represented by the results of the FASB's Conceptual Framework Project, which was intended to aid the development of accounting practices. This project, initiated soon after the FASB was formed in 1973, has resulted in six *Statements of Financial Accounting Concepts (SFACs)* published between 1978 and 1985. The hierarchy shown in Exhibit 15-1 represents this framework and its four related *Concept Statements* as they apply to business enterprises.[1] In this part of the chapter, you will study the first four components in the hierarchy—objectives of financial accounting, qualitative characteristics of accounting information, elements of financial statements, and measurement and recognition (nature and content of financial statements). The foundation of the hierarchy—generally accepted accounting principles (GAAP)—has been referred to throughout the text.

OBJECTIVES OF FINANCIAL ACCOUNTING

Objective 1
The objectives of financial accounting and the qualitative characteristics of accounting information.

The objectives of financial accounting are **to collect, measure, and communicate economic information for business decisions.** To accomplish these objectives, goals of accounting include helping decision makers:

1. **Assess the future cash-generating ability** of the entity, or some subset of the entity's operations.
2. **Evaluate the past performance** of the entity and its managers through the evaluation of the financial statements.[2]

[1] *SFAC No. 4* and *SFAC No. 6* pertain to nonbusiness organizations, which are discussed in Appendix D at the end of this text.

[2] *Statements of Financial Accounting Concepts No. 1,* "Objectives of Financial Reporting by Business Enterprises" (Norwalk, Conn.: FASB, 1978).

EXHIBIT 15-1

Framework of Accounting Theory

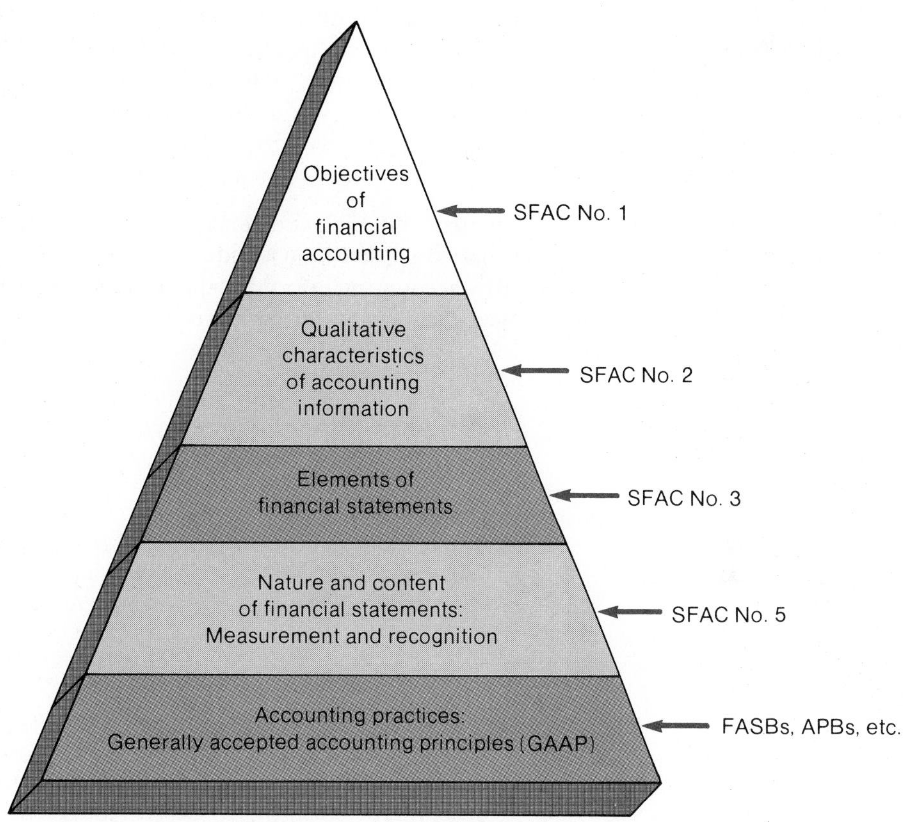

The quality and value of the financial data provided by the accounting information system is based on the extent to which these goals and objectives are achieved.

The future cash-generating ability of an entity's overall operations and its individual components of operations are important for determining the value of the entity. In theory, the value of the entity is equal to the present value of the entity's expected future cash flows. The same could be said for specific assets or groups of assets. As a result, information that helps predict future cash flows is important to decision makers for investing, credit granting, and other business decisions.

You can evaluate the past performance of an entity and its managers by analyzing the past financial statements of the entity. This evaluation process helps determine why the entity achieved its results, which in turn helps to provide expectations about future cash flows from operations. Since evaluating past performance helps predict future performance, past and current financial statements are important elements in achieving the overall objective of accounting. The combination of historical and forward-looking financial statement data helps management plan future operating decisions and also helps investors and creditors make investment and credit-granting decisions.

QUALITATIVE CHARACTERISTICS OF ACCOUNTING INFORMATION

To achieve its overall objective of providing decision makers with information to make decisions, accounting information must possess certain qualities. It is generally agreed that these qualities should consist of *relevance, reliability, comparability,* and *consistency.*[3] Although these four qualities have been discussed in earlier chapters, they are now reviewed in outline form as presented in Exhibit 15-2.

Primary Qualities of Accounting Information

By studying Exhibit 15-2, you can see that the two primary qualities of accounting information are **relevance** and **reliability.** Although you already know some reasons why accounting information must be relevant and reliable, the discussion that follows focuses your attention on these two important qualities.

EXHIBIT 15-2

Qualities of Useful Accounting Data

Quality	*Examples*
Primary qualities:	
1. Relevance. *a.* Timeliness. *b.* Usefulness.	1. Using information regarding inventory on hand provides useful information for timely reordering of inventory, avoiding both lost sales from stockouts and excessive costs from carrying too much inventory.
2. Reliability. *a.* Measurability. *b.* Verifiability (or objectivity). *c.* Unbiased.	2. The periodic physical counts of cash on hand, marketable securities, inventory, machines, and so on, enhance the reliability of the accounting data.
Secondary qualities:	
3. Comparability.	3. Disclosure requirements for discontinued operations (see Chapter 13) help improve the consistency of this year's operating income with prior years.
4. Consistency	4. Using the same accounting methods each year enhances consistency.
Constraining qualities:	
5. Materiality considerations.	5. A company may have a policy of directly expensing hand tools which have about a five-year life rather than setting them up as an asset and depreciating them over five years because the differential effect on income is **not** material.
6. Cost-benefit considerations.	6. The cost of obtaining better estimates of the amount of oil and/or gas discovered may exceed the economic benefits of such data.

[3] *Statement of Financial Accounting Concepts No. 2,* "Qualitative Characteristics of Accounting Information" (Norwalk, Conn.: FASB, 1980).

Relevance. Accounting data used in business decisions must be relevant, which means that the data should be both **timely** and **useful**. Information is **timely** if it helps evaluate a future event or outcome of interest. For example, a report that estimates manufacturing costs of a special-order product before it is produced would be timely if the information were received in time for the salesperson to quote a price to the potential customer. A net income figure is timely if it can be used in negotiations with a potential lender who wants to see past results *before* making a loan. Information is **useful** if it helps reduce uncertainty about *future* events or outcomes of interest to the decision maker. For example, potential investors in a company may be more certain of the company's prospects for future profits, cash flows, and dividends after studying the company's most recent financial statements. Thus, relevant accounting information should be both timely and useful to decision makers.

Reliability. If decision makers are going to use accounting information to make decisions, this information must obviously be reliable. **Reliable information** is characterized by data that are **measurable with a reasonable degree of precision,** free from bias, and verifiable.

The **measurability attribute** of accounting data explains why certain procedures based on historical cost are used while other procedures based on current cost or market values are not normally used. Sometimes decision makers may want to know the market values or current costs of a company's land, office building, or other assets. However, these data are usually **not measurable with a reasonable degree of precision and are not considered to be reliable.** Except in certain instances where market value falls below cost (e.g., when the LCM method is used for investments in stocks and for inventories), most components of the financial statements remain at their original historical cost.

The accounting system provides **unbiased** data as long as the measurements produced are not systematically too large or too small in relation to some underlying standard. For instance, in lower-of-cost-or-market (LCM) comparisons, an **unbiased** measure of market value would neither systematically overstate nor understate the market value. Most accounting measures are the result of arm's-length transactions between two or more independent entities, with each entity seeking to promote its own self-interest. Accounting measurements arrived at through arm's-length transactions (i.e., purchase price of an asset) are considered to be unbiased.

Verifiable (or **objective**) accounting data are those which can be reproduced by another system (or measurer) and result in the same or similar measures. For example, if management's accounting system measures the cost of its inventory at $10,000 and a physical inventory taken by an independent accountant results in about a $10,000 measurement, management's inventory measurement system is verifiable, or objective.

Reliable accounting data, then, are data that are verifiable, unbiased, and measurable with reasonable precision. Taken together, relevance and reliability are the primary qualities of accounting information—qualities that accounting data should have to be useful for decision-making purposes.

Secondary Qualities of Accounting Information

As indicated in Exhibit 15-2, the secondary qualities that accounting data should possess are comparability and consistency.

Accounting data are **comparable** when different companies experience the same or similar events and report the same results. For example, **comparability** would be high if all companies in the steel industry recognized sales revenue at the time goods were shipped (or some other common standard). Comparability is a "between entities" concept unless more than one accounting period is being considered.

Consistency in accounting data means that a given entity uses the same measurement procedures from year to year so that the same or similar events occurring in consecutive years are reported in the same manner through time. Consistency is a "within entity" concept. For example, the timing of revenue recognition must be **consistent** from year to year for each specific entity. If all entities in an industry recognized revenues at the same point (e.g., at the time of sale) over a number of consecutive accounting periods, revenue recognition would be **comparable** across entities and **consistent** within entities over time.

Constraining Qualities of Accounting Information

The **constraining qualities** of accounting information are considerations that might override the primary and secondary qualities discussed above. Two constraining qualities are **materiality** and **cost-benefit** considerations.

Accountants strive for relevance, reliability, comparability, and consistency unless the amounts involved are immaterial. What is an immaterial amount? In some cases, accounting policymakers have specified materiality limits. For example, special disclosures are required if a single customer represents a material portion of a company's business, with material defined in this situation as 10% of sales. In most cases, however, a material amount is a subjective value based on the judgment of the preparer of the accounting data. As a general guideline, a **material amount** is an amount that could affect the decision of a reasonably knowledgeable user of accounting data. Professional judgment usually is the basis for materiality considerations.

Cost-benefit considerations suggest that the cost of providing the accounting data should not exceed the potential benefits that users will receive from the data. This means that some accounting information may be more costly to produce than their beneficial effects for users.

A good example of a cost-benefit determination affecting accounting policy is the controversy over whether or not companies should be required to use footnotes to their annual stockholders' reports that disclose the effects of price changes on net income. (Accounting for changing prices is discussed in Appendix C to this textbook.) The SEC and the FASB have wavered on this issue due to cost-benefit considerations. While policymakers believe the impact of price changes on net income is relevant information, managers have argued that this information is too costly to produce. In many questions concerning cost-benefit considerations, exact measures of costs and benefits are usually difficult or impossible to obtain. As a result, cost-benefit issues, like materiality issues, are often resolved by the professional judgment of accountants.

In conclusion, for accounting data to be useful for business decisions, the data should possess the qualities of relevance, reliability, comparability, and consistency to the greatest feasible extent. The more closely accounting data reflect these qualities, the more useful the data will be for business decision making. These four qualities provide accountants with guidance that gives valuable direction in helping to enhance the usefulness of accounting information.

You realize, of course, that relevance, reliability, comparability, and consistency are subjective qualities and do not lend themselves to precise identification or measurement. In other words, you cannot readily measure the amount of relevance, reliability, and so on, in a given accounting report or specific accounting data. Yet these quality judgments provide the accounting profession and its data users with confidence in the overall quality of a company's accounting information. Professional judgments regarding the presence of these four qualities in financial accounting data have a significant effect on how informed users employ accounting in making business decisions.

ELEMENTS OF FINANCIAL STATEMENTS

Objective 2

The importance of the elements of financial statements and measurement and recognition in financial statement analysis.

The definitions of the elements of financial statements provide additional guidance for the preparation of useful accounting data. These elements (assets, liabilities, equity, investments by owners, distributions to owners, revenues, expenses, gains, and losses) and their definitions were presented throughout Part 1 of this textbook, and we referred to them several times to resolve measurement and reporting issues. Exhibit 15-3 reviews the elements of financial statements and their definitions.[4]

Recall from Chapters 1 and 2 that the definitions of assets and liabilities are important for understanding many other elements of financial statements. Once you understand the definitions of assets and liabilities, all other financial state-

EXHIBIT 15-3

Elements of Financial Statements Defined

Element	*Definition*
Assets	Assets are probable future economic benefits obtained or controlled by a particular entity as a result of past transactions or events.
Liabilities	Liabilities are probable future sacrifices of economic benefits arising from present obligations of a particular entity to transfer assets or provide services to other entities in the future as a result of past transactions or events.
Equity	Equity is the residual interest in the assets of the entity that remains after deducting its liabilities. In a business enterprise, the equity is the ownership interest and equals the net assets of the business.
Investments by owners	Owner transactions resulting in an increase in net assets (e.g., owners purchase more stock).
Distributions to owners	Transactions between owners and the entity that result in a decrease in net assets (e.g., dividends).
Revenues	Increases in net assets resulting from operating activities.
Expenses	Decreases in net assets resulting from operating activities.
Gains and losses	Increases and decreases in net assets that are the result of nonowner events unrelated or indirectly related to normal operating activities.

[4]*Statement of Financial Accounting Concepts No. 3,* "Elements of Financial Statements of Business Enterprises" (Norwalk, Conn.: FASB, December 1980).

ment elements can be defined in the context of assets and liabilities. To do this, remember that net assets are assets minus liabilities. After defining assets and liabilities, the other financial statement elements can be defined in terms of the related effect on net assets, as in Exhibit 15-3.

We can also relate the definitions of the elements of financial statements to the four qualities—relevance, reliability, comparability, and consistency—that accounting data should possess. For example, assets are probable future benefits that are controlled by an entity as a result of past transactions. To be recorded, asset measurements must be reliable; that is, asset measurements must be measurable with a reasonable degree of precision and be unbiased and verifiable. If you cannot reliably record assets, they are not assets in an accounting sense. Potential assets such as those represented by managerial talent, business location, or customer relations have no recorded asset value even though these assets may represent "real" future benefits. When future benefits cannot be reliably estimated, they may not be recorded as assets.

MEASUREMENT AND RECOGNITION

Guidance as to when and how information about business transactions should be incorporated into the financial statements is provided by the *FASB Statement of Financial Accounting Concepts No. 5 (SFAC No. 5)*, "Recognition and Measurement in Financial Statements of Business Enterprises." This statement—the most specific of the concepts statements—has been integrated into various sections of earlier chapters.

Recall from Chapter 2 that in accounting, "to recognize" means "to record." In concept, *SFAC No. 5* provides guidance as to when to record and how to measure accounting data. For example, two key measurement and recognition issues involve revenues and expenses. We introduced these topics in Chapter 2, developed them in Chapters 3 through 5, and reviewed the more detailed aspects of revenue and expense recognition and measurement in Chapter 13. In essence, the underlying recognition and measurement concepts examined in *SFAC No. 5* have been fully integrated into earlier chapters. Since all financial statement data must meet the recognition (recording) and measurement criteria to be reported, the scope of these concepts includes the entire set of accounting data reported in the financial statements.

While accounting theory does aid the continuing development of accounting practice, accounting theory does not eliminate the need for professional judgments by policymakers or practicing accountants. Furthermore, the dynamic and complex nature of the business environment makes it unrealistic to expect accounting theory to provide a rigid framework for practice.

PART B: FINANCIAL STATEMENT ANALYSIS

Part B of this chapter examines the various sources of financial accounting information and some of the basic methods of analyzing accounting data within and among business entities.

SOURCES OF FINANCIAL DATA

Many sources and forms of financial data exist. In general, the data provided to and used by external users (investors, bankers, and so on) come from the same accounting information system as the data used by the entity's internal managers. The major difference is that external users generally use highly summarized and aggregated data about the entity, while most internal managers use detailed accounting reports about their specific area of authority and responsibility because they are concerned with subcomponents of the entity's overall operations.

The nature and source of financial accounting data may vary widely depending on the type of ownership structure of the entity and the interests of creditors. Exhibit 15-4 attempts to summarize the relationship between ownership structure and financial accounting information requirements. In general, the quantity and quality of information provided to external users is related to the significance of external users' interests in the company: the greater the external interest, the greater the quantity and quality of the financial accounting data demanded by these outside (stockholder and creditor) interests.

EXHIBIT 15-4

Relationship between Financial Accounting Information and Ownership Structure

Type	*Ownership Structure/Size*	*Information Required or Needed*
1	Publicly owned companies with stock traded on a public stock exchange.	Full disclosure of financial statements prepared in conformance with GAAP and independently audited as required by the SEC and all major stock exchanges.
2	Closely held companies *not* publicly traded; organized as a corporation, partnership, or proprietorship.	Disclosure requirements are not governed by SEC or other regulators but may be equivalent to SEC requirements, depending on the extent of nonowner (creditor) interests in the company and their demands. *a.* If no debt (no creditors other than suppliers, labor, and so on), no information need be provided to outsiders unless owners desire it. *b.* If material amount of debt (banks or public debt holders), creditors normally require that information be audited in conformance with GAAP resulting in disclosures like Type 1 companies.
3	Companies where managers are also owners and there are no significant outside interests.	Disclosures may be no more than the tax returns for these companies, which are not publicly available. However, financial services, such as Dun & Bradstreet, attempt to provide some financial data on all business entities.

For large publicly traded companies governed by SEC requirements, the primary financial accounting data sources are:

1. Annual reports to stockholders (and proxy statements).
2. Quarterly reports to stockholders.
3. Securities and Exchange Commission (SEC) reports.

ANNUAL REPORTS TO STOCKHOLDERS (AND PROXY STATEMENTS)

A company's stockholders receive annual reports to help evaluate what the managers have accomplished with the resources entrusted to them. All publicly traded companies are required to prepare annual reports in accordance with GAAP, and most medium to large, closely held companies also prepare GAAP financial statements for creditors and/or internal users. The annual reports of publicly owned companies normally contain the elements outlined in Exhibit 15-5. The three main sections of the annual report are the management's discussion, the formal financial statements, and other financial and demographic data.

Section 1. As shown in Exhibit 15-5, the first section of the annual report usually includes financial highlights of the company's operations, such as sales and earnings per share (EPS) for the current and prior year(s). Also, this first section normally contains a letter from the chief executive officer (CEO) or president and/or the chief financial officer (CFO) or financial vice president evaluating the past results and discussing the future plans and goals of the business. In addition, a number of pages are usually devoted to pictures and descriptions of the various new or existing products and/or services and new or existing production facilities.

EXHIBIT 15-5

Content of Annual Reports

Section 1: Management discussion	Normally contains: • Financial highlights • Letter to stockholders • Data on various operations
Section 2: Financial statements	Normally contains: • Income statement • Balance sheet (or statement of financial position) • Statement of cash flows • Statement of changes in stockholders' equity • Footnotes to the statements • Management's report and independent auditor's report
Section 3: Other data	Normally contains: • Historical summary of key financial data for the past 5 to 10 years • List of members of the Board of Directors • List of top executives, office locations, plants, etc.

Section 2. The second section of the annual report usually contains the formal financial statements of the overall (consolidated) entity along with a report of management and the report of the independent auditor. The income statement is most often the first statement presented. The balance sheet, or statement of financial position, is usually the second statement, followed by statement of cash flows and the statement of changes in stockholders' equity.

The footnotes to the formal financial statements contain detailed explanations of the data reported in the formal statements. The first footnote identifies the major accounting methods and policies that the entity followed in preparing its financial statements. This footnote helps users understand the nature of inventory measurements, depreciation methods, and other accounting methods to facilitate firm-specific evaluations over many years (consistency) as well as for comparisons across firms at a specific point in time (comparability).

The footnotes to the annual report may also include a summary of (1) **revenues**, (2) **net income,** and (3) **net assets employed** for each of the different major **industry groups** represented by the formal financial reports. If a company operates in multiple industries, it must disclose these three items of financial data for each **major industrial segment.**[5] In addition, the same three items (revenues, net income, and net assets) must be disclosed for each **major geographical segment,** such as North America, Europe, and Asia. Sometimes companies provide these segment data as part of management's discussion of the operations of the business which occurs before the formal financial statements. Exhibit 15-6 illustrates a typical example of segmental disclosures.

In recent years, a few companies have moved to a shortened version of the financial data normally found in annual reports. In these instances, the details of the formal financial statements needed to comply with GAAP and SEC requirements have typically been moved to the *proxy statement.* All stockholders usually receive the proxy statement before the annual stockholders' meeting and after they receive the annual report. The purpose of a **proxy statement** is to announce the time and place of the annual meeting and describe any agenda items to be voted on by the stockholders (i.e., who will be on the board of directors, selection of a CPA firm to conduct the audit, and so on). The proxy statement will usually include a stockholder ballot and other relevant data to help the stockholder decide how to vote.

Included as key components of Section 2 of the annual report are reports from management and from the independent (outside) auditor. The management report is not always present, but when included it usually contains a statement identifying management's responsibility for the financial statements and the system of internal controls for safeguarding the firm's assets. This report often identifies the audit committee of the board of directors and its role in hiring the independent auditor and maintaining the integrity of the company's financial reporting system. The report of the independent auditor, while normally addressed to the board of directors, provides useful information about the financial statements to all outside users and should be read whenever the financial statements are to be used as a basis for business decisions. For companies with publicly traded securities, the independent audit report is a required part of the financial

[5]*FASB Statement No. 14,* "Financial Reporting for Segments of a Business Enterprise" (Norwalk, Conn.: FASB, 1976).

EXHIBIT 15-6

Annual Report Example of Segmental Disclosures

General Mills, Inc.
Excerpt from footnotes:
Note Seventeen: Segment information [in millions]

	Consumer Foods	*Restaurants*	*Specialty Retailing*	*Unallocated Corporate Items*	*Consolidated Total*
Sales:					
19x7	$3,449.9	$1,249.1	$490.3		$5,189.3
19x6	3,061.3	1,051.0	383.6		4,495.9
19x5	2,771.3	1,140.1	294.8		4,206.2
Operating profits (losses):					
19x7	369.5	92.5	30.7	$ (59.5)	433.2
19x6	284.2	84.8	11.6	(63.9)	316.7
19x5	245.3	45.9	(40.7)	(58.0)	192.5
Identifiable assets:					
19x7	1,211.7	594.0	177.8	296.9	2,280.4
19x6	1,091.8	467.8	128.2	398.4	2,086.2
19x5	1,000.1	424.6	136.8	1,092.5	2,654.0
Capital expenditures:					
19x7	151.5	145.3	30.1	2.2	329.1
19x6	153.6	74.0	13.7	3.6	244.9
19x5	103.2	40.5	27.0	39.0	209.7
Depreciation expense:					
19x7	78.9	39.4	9.0	1.4	128.7
19x6	69.2	32.7	7.2	0.7	109.8
19x5	60.9	37.5	6.3	1.7	106.4

statements. These two reports are usually found at the start or end of the Section 2 formal financial statement data.

The Audit Report. After the auditors conduct their audit, they issue an **auditor's report or opinion** as to whether the company's financial statements and accompanying footnotes fairly present the results of its operations and financial position. A "clean" or "unqualified" opinion, like that provided in Exhibit 15-7, informs owners that the auditors believe management's financial statements fairly present the results of the company's actual operations. The auditor's opinion provides the owners with a statement as to whether or not the financial statements of management included in the annual report were prepared in accordance with generally accepted accounting principles (GAAP). To provide some structure as to how the audit is conducted, the CPA profession, through the American Institute of Certified Public Accountants (AICPA), has established generally accepted auditing standards (GAAS). In a "clean" opinion, the CPA states that the statements are "fairly present(ed)" in accordance with GAAP, and that the audit was conducted in accordance with GAAS. Note that a clean audit opinion, such as the one reported in Exhibit 15-7, includes a statement in the second paragraph describing the basic requirements of GAAS and the underly-

EXHIBIT 15-7

Annual Report Disclosure of Auditor's Opinion—Example

To the Board of Directors and Stockholders
Prime Motor Inns, Inc.

We have audited the accompanying consolidated balance sheets of Prime Motor Inns, Inc. and Subsidiaries as of June 30, 1989 and 1988, and the related consolidated statements of income, stockholders' equity and cash flows for each of the three years in the period ended June 30, 1989. These financial statements are the responsibility of the Company's management. Our responsibility is to express an opinion on these financial statements based on our audits.

We conducted our audits in accordance with generally accepted auditing standards. Those standards require that we plan and perform the audit to obtain reasonable assurance about whether the financial statements are free of material misstatement. An audit includes examining, on a test basis, evidence supporting the amounts and disclosures in the financial statements. An audit also includes assessing the accounting principles used and significant estimates made by management, as well as evaluating the overall financial statement presentation. We believe that our audits provide a reasonable basis for our opinion.

In our opinion, the consolidated financial statements referred to above present fairly, in all material respects, the financial position of Prime Motor Inns, Inc. and Subsidiaries as of June 30, 1989 and 1988, and their results of operations and cash flows for each of the three years in the period ended June 30, 1989, in conformity with generally accepted accounting principles.

J.H. Cohn & Company

J.H. Cohn & Company

Roseland, New Jersey
August 23, 1989

ing limitations of the audit process. It states that the audit is designed to obtain "reasonable assurance" that the financial statements are "free of material misstatement." This does not represent a guarantee and cannot be viewed as such. We should also note that the audit report does not say whether management is doing a good job, but only indicates whether management has fairly disclosed the results of its activities. Audit reports should be read carefully. In the event that a "qualified" report is issued, the audit report will normally explain the basis for the qualification preventing the CPA firm from rendering a "clean" opinion.

Section 3. The third and final section of the annual report often contains summary financial information which has not been audited by the independent auditor. Unaudited financial statement data is usually marked "unaudited." The financial data in Section 3 is often in the form of a 5- or 10-year history of key financial highlights (i.e., sales, net income, EPS, dividends, total assets, total liabilities, and so on) and certain financial ratios (i.e., return on assets, return on equity, debt to equity, and so on). In addition to these financial highlights, the last section of the annual report also identifies the names of the board of directors and their affiliation with the reporting company or some other company. Board members not affiliated with the company are called "outside" directors. Outside directors usually make up all or most of the **audit committee** which is that segment of board members responsible for hiring and contracting with the independent auditors. Finally, the last section normally lists the top managers of the company, the location of its headquarters and its other principal offices or places of business. Other information such as the company's outside law firm, the name and phone number of the company's media and/or investor relations contact, and the date, time, and location of the annual stockholders' meeting are also sometimes reported in the final section of the annual report.

Quarterly Reports to Stockholders

In addition to the annual reports, most publicly held companies also provide stockholders with quarterly financial statements. These interim reports contain less data than annual reports. The data required on a quarterly basis for publicly traded companies include:[6]

1. Income statement data:
   a. Sales.
   b. Income tax expense (estimated).
   c. Extraordinary items.
   d. Effect of changes in accounting principles.
   e. Net income.
   f. Earnings per share.
2. A discussion of the following, when appropriate:
   a. Seasonal nature of revenues and/or expenses.
   b. Change in method of computing estimated taxes.
   c. Discussion of any unusual items, disposals of segments, and so on.
   d. Discussion of any contingent obligations.
   e. Significant changes in the balance sheet.
   f. Discussion of any changes in accounting policies.

Some companies provide more than the required disclosures, including both a balance sheet and an income statement, while still other companies may also provide a statement of cash flows. However, unlike the annual reports which include discussions by management, future plans, independent audit reports, and so on, the formal income statement is often the only financial statement provided in quarterly reports.

Securities and Exchange Commission (SEC) Reports

Over the past decade, the SEC adopted the policy of making its reports conform more to the annual and quarterly reports provided to owners of publicly held companies. The SEC, which has the authority to determine financial reporting

[6] *APB Opinion No. 28,* "Interim Financial Reporting" (New York, AICPA, 1973).

requirements of publicly owned companies that are traded on U.S. stock exchanges, requires that these companies file financial statements with the SEC on an annual and quarterly basis. The annual report filed with the SEC is called Form 10-K, while the quarterly report is called Form 10-Q.

The SEC Forms 10-K and 10-Q are not really "forms" like those required for tax returns, but they are simply a set of guidelines describing the required disclosures. For most companies, the 10-K and 10-Q are somewhat more detailed than annual and quarterly reports to stockholders. The 10-K and 10-Q include data in stockholder reports and also require data on inside ownership (stock owned by corporate management) and trades by insiders in the company's own stock, greater detail about management compensation, and several other items typically not found in annual reports to stockholders. However, stockholders may request a company's 10-K and 10-Q.

In addition to the 10-K and 10-Q, the SEC requires public companies to file a Form 8-K within 15 days of any major event that may have a significant effect on the entity. These 8-K reports are filed for major changes in ownership of an entity, when an entity files for bankruptcy, when a change is made in outside auditors, and for other similarly significant developments.

EVALUATING FINANCIAL STATEMENTS

So far in this chapter you considered the nature, sources, and quality of formal accounting information. This section discusses the different methods used to evaluate financial statements. Remember that the evaluation of financial statements is worthwhile only if the quality of the underlying accounting data (discussed in Part A of this chapter) is at an acceptable level. For example, if the underlying data are **unreliable** (e.g., biased) or lacking **consistency** or **comparability**, then evaluating the resulting financial statements may produce useless information. Most financial analysts agree that evaluating financial reports for companies with poor accounting quality provides little or no information for investment or credit-granting decisions.

Financial reports may be evaluated using a number of different techniques. The following types of analysis are examined in this section:

Objective 3
The common types of analysis used to evaluate financial statements — horizontal, vertical, vertical/horizontal, trend, and ratio analysis.

1. Horizontal analysis—analysis of changes between two years of data.
2. Vertical analysis—analysis of a single year's data.
3. Trend analysis—analysis of data over three or more years.
4. Ratio analysis—analysis of one financial statement component relative to another component.

You may use these techniques separately or in conjunction with one another. While all these techniques are different in approach, they have one common feature in that they attempt to eliminate the size effects of dollar measures found in the financial statements. The size effects are eliminated by stating the financial statement data in terms of percentages or ratios. Eliminating the effects of dollar measures helps analysts make two fundamental types of comparisons:

1. Comparisons of a specific entity's performance from one period of time to another.
2. Comparisons of a number of different entities for a specific period of time.

EXHIBIT 15-8

Financial Statement Data

Cybron G.T. Corporation
Balance Sheet
At December 31
(in millions)

Assets	*19x7*	*19x6*
Current assets:		
Cash	$ 7	$ 5
Accounts receivable (net)	36	33
Inventory	42	48
Prepaid insurance	3	2
Prepaid rent	6	9
Total current assets	$ 94	$ 97
Noncurrent assets:		
Land	$ 20	$ 20
Buildings and equipment (net)	154	146
Equity investments	38	34
Intangible assets	9	8
Total noncurrent assets	$221	$208
Total assets	$315	$305

Liabilities and Stockholders' Equity	*19x7*	*19x6*
Current liabilities:		
Accounts payable	$ 30	$ 35
Notes payable	10	10
Other payables	7	6
Total current liabilities	$ 47	$ 51
Noncurrent liabilities:		
Bonds payable	$ 70	$ 70
Leases payable	23	25
Total noncurrent liabilities	$ 93	$ 95
Total liabilities	$140	$146
Stockholders' equity:		
Common stock (par)	$ 98	$ 98
Contributed capital in excess of par	21	21
Retained earnings	56	40
Total stockholders' equity	$175	$159
Total liabilities and stockholders' equity	$315	$305

Horizontal Analysis

The term **horizontal analysis** is used to describe any evaluation of financial statement data that looks at the change in a specific financial statement item from one period to another. Normally, accountants apply horizontal analysis to the financial reports of a specific entity. However, horizontal analysis could also be used with data summarized for an entire industry or for data on segments of a particular company. Horizontal analysis requires **two periods of data and evaluates the change in data items on a percentage basis.**

To illustrate horizontal analysis, study the summarized balance sheet and income statement data of Cybron G.T. Corporation given in Exhibit 15-8. The financial statement data of Cybron will serve as our example for several types of

EXHIBIT 15-8 *(concluded)*

Cybron G.T. Corporation
Income Statement
For the Years Ended December 31
(in millions)

	19x7	*19x6*
Sales (net)	$ 321	$ 303
Cost of goods sold	(230)	(215)
Gross margin on sales	$ 91	$ 88
Selling, general, and administrative expenses	(62)	(56)
Interest expense	(8)	(8)
Income from equity investments	7	6
Income before income taxes	$ 28	$ 30
Income tax expense	(8)	(12)
Net income	$ 20	$ 18
Other data (in millions, except per share data):		
Average number of shares of common stock	4	4
Cash dividends paid	$ 4	$ 4
Stock price per share, end of year	37.50	31.50
Net credit sales	276	241.80
Beginning net receivables	33	29
Beginning inventory	48	52
Beginning total assets	305	295

analysis. The Cybron income statement below represents an example of horizontal analysis. (All percentages are rounded to a single decimal point.)

Cybron G.T. Corporation
Horizontal Analysis
Income Statement
For the Years Ending December 31
(in millions)

	19x7	*19x6*	*19x7 Less 19x6 as a Percent of 19x6 Increase (Decrease)*
Net sales	$ 321	$ 303	5.9 %
Cost of goods sold	(230)	(215)	7.0
Gross margin	$ 91	$ 88	3.4
Selling, general, and administrative expenses	(62)	(56)	10.7
Interest expense	(8)	(8)	—
Income from equity investments	7	6	16.7
Income before income taxes	$ 28	$ 30	(6.7)
Income tax expense	(8)	(12)	(33.3)
Net income	$ 20	$ 18	11.1

Note that horizontal analysis may also be applied to other statements as well as the income statement.

Like all methods of analysis, horizontal analysis has both strong points and limitations. In its favor, horizontal analysis identifies how key variables changed from one period to the next. Looking at the 19x7 and 19x6 dollar data, the only clear fact is that net sales, cost of goods sold, and gross margin all increased. Looking at the percentage change data, you can quickly see that cost of goods sold increased more (7.0%) than net sales (5.9%) in 19x7, resulting in only a 3.4% increase in gross margin.

Note the following limitations of horizontal analysis:

1. The percentages in the analysis are not intended to "add up" vertically.
2. Small base year numbers (near zero) may result in large change percentages.
3. Base year numbers of zero or a negative amount cannot be used to compute change percentages.

When you examine the results of horizontal analysis, remember these limitations. Horizontal analysis is designed to evaluate year-to-year changes in specific items of accounting data, thus providing financial analysis over time.

Vertical Analysis

The term **vertical analysis** describes any evaluation of financial statement data for a particular time period without comparison to other time periods. Some might think of vertical analysis as static analysis since only a single period's financial data is required.

Like horizontal analysis, vertical analysis restates dollar amounts to percentages. For balance sheet data, all items are usually expressed as a percent of total assets, with total assets equal to 100%. For income statements, all items are usually expressed as a percent of net sales, with net sales equal to 100%. For a statement of cash flows, all items may be expressed as a percent of net sources of cash in the event of a net increase in cash, or as a percent of net uses of cash in the event of a net decrease in cash.

To illustrate vertical analysis, the following restatement could be made of the Cybron earnings data for 19x7 and 19x6:

Cybron G.T. Corporation
Vertical Analysis
Income Statement
For the Years Ending December 31
(in millions)

	19x7		*19x6*	
	Dollars	*Percent*	*Dollars*	*Percent*
Net sales	$ 321	100.0 %	$ 303	100.0 %
Cost of goods sold	(230)	(71.7)	(215)	(71.0)
Gross margin	$ 91	28.3 %	$ 88	29.0 %
Selling, general, and administrative expenses	(62)	(19.3)	(56)	(18.5)
Interest expense	(8)	(2.5)	(8)	(2.6)
Income from equity investments	7	2.2	6	2.0
Income before income taxes	$ 28	8.7 %	$ 30	9.9 %
Income taxes	(8)	(2.5)	(12)	(4.0)
Net income	$ 20	6.2 %	$ 18	5.9 %

Note that in vertical analysis, percentages "add up," thus providing a view of the financial data stated in percentages rather than dollars. Vertical analysis reveals information such as the gross margin percentage (28.3% for 19x7) and effective tax expense rate on sales (2.5% for 19x7) at a glance. For the income statement, vertical analysis breaks down each cost or other revenue item in terms of each dollar of sales. For example, in 19x7, cost of goods sold averaged $0.717 per $1 of sales, while interest expense averaged $0.025 per $1 of sales.

Vertical/Horizontal Analysis

Accountants often follow vertical analysis with a horizontal analysis of the vertical percentage data. For example, once vertical analysis states everything as a percent of sales (or total assets, and so on) horizontal analysis may be used on these percentages. For the Cybron income statement data above, the following extension could be made:

Cybron G.T. Corporation
Vertical/Horizontal Analysis
Income Statement
For the Years Ending December 31

	Vertical Analysis		*Horizontal Analysis*	
	19x7	*19x6*	*Percentage Change*	*Relative Percentage Change Increase (Decrease)*
Net sales	100.0 %	100.0 %	0.0 %	— %
Cost of goods sold	(71.7)	(71.0)	(0.7)	1.0
Gross margin	28.3 %	29.0 %	(0.7)%	(2.4)
Selling, general, and administrative expenses	(19.3)	(18.5)	(0.8)	4.3
Interest expense	(2.5)	(2.6)	0.1	(3.8)
Income from equity investments	2.2	2.0	0.2	10.0
Income before income taxes	8.7 %	9.9 %	(1.2)%	(12.1)
Income taxes	(2.5)	(4.0)	1.5	(37.5)
Net income	6.2 %	5.9 %	0.3 %	5.1

The first two columns simply report the results of vertical analysis, with no dollar data provided. Two forms of horizontal analysis for the percentages in the first two columns are reported in the last two columns of the example. Both the "percentage change" and the "relative change" columns provide horizontal analysis beyond that of the vertical analysis in the first two columns. The "percentage change" column is simply the 19x7 percent less the 19x6 percent. This tells us **how each income statement item changed from one year to the next as a percentage of net sales.** For example, gross margin on sales decreased by .7% of net sales (seven tenths of 1%, or .007) in 19x7 due to a .7% increase in cost of goods sold (from 71.0 to 71.7%). Selling, general, and administrative expenses went up .8% of sales, while interest expense went down .1% of sales.[7] Note that the "percentage change" column adds up, with positive changes (as they affect earnings) listed as positive percentages, and negative changes listed as negative percentages.

[7]While the **dollar amount** of interest expense was the same for 19x7 and 19x6, it is not the same when stated as a percent of each year's net sales.

The last column in the above vertical/horizontal analysis of Cybron reports the relative **percentage** change in each income statement item. Note that this is not the same as the first column in the horizontal analysis, which measures the percent change in the dollar amounts. The limitations of horizontal analysis cited earlier apply to this column of data. The 4.3 relative percentage change in selling, general, and administrative expense (SGA expense) is computed as:

$$\frac{\text{Percentage change}}{\text{19x6 (base year) percent}} = \frac{.8}{18.5} = 4.3\%$$

The selling, general, and administrative expense percentage increased from 18.5% of sales to 19.3% of sales, which is a 4.3% increase in SGA expense as a percent of 19x6 sales.

A partial vertical/horizontal analysis of Cybron's balance sheet data could be prepared as follows:

Vertical/Horizontal Analysis
Partial Balance Sheet Data
(Total assets = 100%)

	Vertical Analysis		*Horizontal Analysis*	
	19x7	*19x6*	*Percentage Change Increase (Decrease)*	*Relative Percentage Change Increase (Decrease)*
Liabilities:				
Accounts payable	9.5%	11.4%	(1.9)%*	(16.7)%†
Notes payable	3.2	3.3	(0.1)	(3.0)
Other payables	2.2	2.0	.2	10.0
Total current liabilities	14.9%	16.7%	(1.8)%	(10.8)%

*9.5% − 11.4% = −1.9%
†−1.9%/11.4% = −16.7%

Note that total assets (which equals total liabilities plus stockholders' equity) equals 100% for balance sheet analysis. Accounts payable decreased from 11.4% of the balance sheet total ($35/$305) at the end of 19x6 to 9.5% ($30/$315) at the end of 19x7, resulting in a 1.9% (9.5% − 11.4% = −1.9%) decrease in the percentage of the balance sheet total represented by accounts payable. This change in accounts payable also represented a relative decrease of 16.7% (−1.9%/11.4%) in the proportion of the balance sheet total represented by accounts payable at the end of 19x6.

Horizontal analysis, vertical analysis, and vertical/horizontal analysis can be performed on any financial statement. Most forms of spreadsheet analysis performed by computer software will prepare these analyses automatically once the financial statement data are provided in the database.

Trend Analysis

The term **trend analysis** describes horizontal analysis over three or more time periods. Usually between 5 and 10 years of data are required for trend analysis. The objective of trend analysis, as the name implies, is to look for trends or patterns in the accounting data that might help predict future outcomes. Accounting income data are the most common object of trend analysis.

Accountants use many forms of trend analysis. Some techniques examine horizontal percentage over many years; some graphically plot the results obtained over the past 5 or 10 years on a weekly, monthly, quarterly, or annual basis; and still others use statistics to evaluate a series of historical data. Statistical methods of trend analysis include time-series analysis, regression analysis, and many other methods of evaluating the historical trends in elements of financial data. All of these techniques are based on the assumption that the historical trend in data is valuable for predicting the future. To the extent that this assumption is correct, trend analysis provides a useful tool for financial planning and forecasting.

In practice, accountants often combine trend analysis with other sources of information about future events when preparing financial plans. These methods are discussed in greater detail in most cost accounting and business statistics textbooks.

Ratio Analysis

Objective 4
How to prepare accounting performance, market performance, liquidity, leverage, and activity ratios.

A widely used method of evaluating financial data is ratio analysis, which **expresses the relationship between two numbers as a ratio of one to the other.** Analysts use many different types of ratios to evaluate financial data. Once these ratios are prepared, they may be used as the basis for further analysis, such as trend analysis, horizontal analysis, and so on.

The following five major categories of ratios will be discussed:

Overall performance measures:

1. Accounting performance ratios.
2. Market performance ratios.

Detailed performance measures:

3. Liquidity ratios.
4. Leverage ratios.
5. Activity ratios.

In each of these five categories, we examine several of the more commonly used ratios. Like the other types of analysis discussed above, these ratios eliminate the size effects of actual dollar measures and permit the analyst to make clearer comparisons within an entity over time and across entities at a given point in time.

Accounting Performance Ratios. The evaluation process used by external and internal users of financial data normally includes one or more measures of overall performance. The most common examples of these overall accounting-based performance ratios and their definitions are:

1. Accounting performance ratios:

a. $$\text{Earnings per share (EPS)} = \frac{\text{Net income} - \text{Preferred stock dividends}}{\text{Average shares of common stock outstanding}}$$

b. $$\text{Return on assets (ROA)} = \frac{\text{Net income}}{\text{Average total assets}}$$

c. $$\text{Profit margin} = \frac{\text{Net income}}{\text{Net sales}}$$

You will frequently find these ratios used to express the performance of the entire entity or of its separate components.

Earnings per share (EPS). External statement users and stockholders often refer to EPS as the single most important performance measure. As you recall from Chapter 13, EPS is the amount of earnings left after paying the preferred stock dividends divided by the average number of shares of common stock outstanding during the period.[8] As such, EPS states the net income of a company on a per share of common stock basis.

Using the Cybron data from Exhibit 15-8, Cybron's EPS computations are:

$$\text{EPS} = \frac{\text{Net income} - \text{Preferred stock dividends}}{\text{Average shares of common stock outstanding}}$$

$$\text{19x7 EPS} = \frac{\$20{,}000{,}000}{4{,}000{,}000 \text{ shares}} = \$5.00 \text{ per share}$$

$$\text{19x6 EPS} = \frac{\$18{,}000{,}000}{4{,}000{,}000 \text{ shares}} = \$4.50 \text{ per share}$$

Since Cybron has no preferred stock, preferred stock dividends are not deducted from net income. When a company has outstanding preferred stock, the declared dividends for the year are deducted from net income; and for cumulative preferred stock, the declared or undeclared dividends for the year are deducted from net income to compute EPS. As a result, EPS measures net income pertaining only to the common stockholders on a per share basis.

Return on assets (ROA). The most widely used ratio by external users is probably the return on assets (ROA) ratio. This ratio measures performance for the period relative to the amount of resources employed (average total assets) and informs users what they earned relative to what they invested in or loaned to the business entity. For Cybron, the ROA ratios are:

$$\text{ROA} = \frac{\text{Net income}}{\text{Average total assets}}$$

$$\text{19x7 ROA} = \frac{\$20{,}000{,}000}{(\$315{,}000{,}000 + \$305{,}000{,}000)/2} = \frac{\$20{,}000{,}000}{\$310{,}000{,}000}$$

$$= \underline{\underline{.0645}} \text{ or } \underline{\underline{6.45\%}}$$

$$\text{19x6 ROA} = \frac{\$18{,}000{,}000}{(\$305{,}000{,}000 + \$295{,}000{,}000)/2} = \frac{\$18{,}000{,}000}{\$300{,}000{,}000}$$

$$= \underline{\underline{.06}} \text{ or } \underline{\underline{6.0\%}}$$

For 19x7, the average total assets employed was computed as the ending 19x7 assets plus the ending 19x6 assets (also the **beginning** 19x7 assets) divided by 2, or: $315,000,000 + $305,000,000 = $620,000,000/2 = $310,000,000. Cybron's ROA

[8] You may want to refresh your memory on EPS by reviewing pages 731-34 of Chapter 13.

for 19x7 was 6.45% (or .0645). The average assets for 19x6 was $300,000,000 ($305,000,000 + $295,000,000 = $600,000,000/2 = $300,000,000; see "Other data" in Exhibit 15-8), resulting in a 6% ROA for 19x6. An increase in ROA is generally considered to mean improved performance. However, you should always try and understand the cause of such changes in ROA (or any other ratio).

If ROA went up because of growth in net income, this is usually good news. But if Cybron entered into some **operating** leases for $100,000,000 of operating equipment early in 19x7 and none of this equipment appeared on Cybron's balance sheet, it might not be fair to compare the ROA of 19x7 with 19x6. In such a case, the **book value** of recorded assets would remain the same in 19x7 as in 19x6, but revenues and earnings from the use of the $100,000,000 in (unrecorded) leased equipment could cause 19x7 net income to increase, making it appear as though the increase in the 19x7 ROA ratio was achieved by earning more net income from the **same** resources as employed in 19x6 (instead of the 19x7 resources **plus** the new leased equipment).

In a similar situation, it would not be relevant to compare ROA for a steel company using new (higher cost) equipment with the ROA for a steel company with old (lower cost and partly depreciated) equipment. Assuming that each company's equipment is used to produce identical revenues for each company, the company with the older equipment will have higher net income due to lower depreciation expenses. The company with the older equipment will also have lower asset values. Therefore, ROA for the company with the older equipment would normally appear to be much higher than ROA for the company with the newer equipment all else being equal. Appendix C at the end of this text examines the effects of price changes on historical cost financial statements in more detail.

Profit margin. The annual profit margin informs statement users what percentage of net sales remained as earnings after deducting all expenses. For Cybron, this margin is computed as:

$$\text{Profit margin} = \frac{\text{Net income}}{\text{Net sales}}$$

$$\text{19x7 profit margin} = \frac{\$20{,}000{,}000}{\$321{,}000{,}000} = \underline{\underline{6.23\%}}$$

$$\text{19x6 profit margin} = \frac{\$18{,}000{,}000}{\$303{,}000{,}000} = \underline{\underline{5.94\%}}$$

Sometimes profit margins are computed using profit subtotals before the net income number. For example, the profit margin from operations would be computed by dividing operating income (net sales less operating expenses) by net sales, to eliminate the effects of nonoperating items on the profit margin measurement. In general, analysts feel that the higher the profit margin, the better the performance. However, it is not unusual for profit margins to be fairly small, below 5%, for large publicly owned companies.

Market Performance Ratios. The following three commonly referenced performance ratios are based in part on market prices of an entity's stock.

2. Market performance ratios:

a. $$\text{Price to earnings or P-E ratio} = \frac{\text{Ending market price per share of common stock}}{\text{EPS}}$$

b. $$\text{Dividend yield} = \frac{\text{Annual cash dividends per share}}{\text{Ending market price per share of common stock}}$$

c. $$\text{Systematic market risk (beta)} = \frac{\text{Covariance of returns}}{\text{Variance of returns of the market}}$$

These three ratios describe the performance of the company relative to the market price of the company; they are aimed primarily at stockholders and other external users.

Price to earnings (P-E) ratio. The price to earnings ratio, or P-E ratio is perhaps the most popular measure of overall performance used by stock analysts. The P-E ratio describes the relation between a stock's year-end market price to the EPS for the period.[9] This ratio, also called the **earnings multiple,** expresses the company's year-end stock price per share as a multiple of the past year's earnings per share. For Cybron, these ratios would be:

$$\text{P-E ratio} = \frac{\text{Ending market price per share of common stock}}{\text{EPS}}$$

$$\text{19x7 P-E ratio} = \frac{\$37.50 \text{ per share}}{\$5.00 \text{ per share}} = \underline{\underline{7.5:1}}$$

$$\text{19x6 P-E ratio} = \frac{\$31.50 \text{ per share}}{\$4.50 \text{ per share}} = \underline{\underline{7.0:1}}$$

In the United States, most P-E ratios are between 5 and 20 to 1 (i.e., most stocks sell for between 5 and 20 times annual earnings), with low P-E stocks generally considered to be less speculative and high P-E stocks considered more speculative, all else being equal. P-E ratios vary among industries and are sometimes reported on a daily basis in the financial press along with the current market price of the stock.

Dividend yield. The dividend yield measures the payment stockholders receive on their stock. The annual cash dividends per share divided by the ending stock

[9]Note that for both the P-E ratio and the dividend yield we suggest using the year-end market price per share. However, other sources do not all agree on this share price, and some suggest the average price for the past year or past month is more representative. When stock prices vary widely from day to day, some average may be preferred.

price forms the basis for computing the dividend yield. For Cybron, the dividend yield percent calculations are:

$$\text{Dividend yield percent} = \frac{\text{Annual cash dividends per share}}{\text{Ending market price per share of common stock}}$$

$$\text{19x7 dividend yield percent} = \frac{\$1.00}{\$37.50} = \underline{\underline{2.67\%}}$$

$$\text{19x6 dividend yield percent} = \frac{\$1.00}{\$31.50} = \underline{\underline{3.17\%}}$$

Making generalized statements about dividend yields is difficult. For Cybron, the dividend payment to common shares was $1 per share in both 19x7 and 19x6. Often annual dividends remain the same from year to year. However, if dividends stay constant and stock prices increase, then the dividend yield will drop as in the Cybron example. While higher dividend yields are often desirable, a decrease in the dividend yield is not necessarily bad news for stockholders.

Systematic market risk (beta). A commonly cited measure of the riskiness of a stock is its systematic market price risk, or its "beta." Beta is a ratio of how a specific stock's market price varies in relation to all other stocks in the market (known as the covariance of the stock with the market) divided by the variance in overall market prices. Normally, beta varies between .5 and 2.5, with the following interpretations:

Beta	*Interpretation*
Less than 1.0	The price of a stock with a beta less than 1.0 will tend to vary less than market prices as a whole. When market prices as a whole are up, the price of low beta stocks will tend to be up by less than the market. When market prices fall, the price of these stocks will tend to fall less than the market as a whole.
Equal to 1.0	This means that the stock's price tends to vary in the same direction and magnitude as the prices of the market taken as a whole.
Greater than 1.0	The price of stocks with betas greater than 1.0 will tend to vary more than the market as a whole. When market prices are up, these stocks will tend to be above average in their percentage price increase, and when market prices fall, they will tend to fall further than average price decreases.

Beta measures relative stock price volatility, with high beta stocks indicating risky investments and low beta stocks indicating more conservative investments. While the computation of beta is based on the relationship of a company's stock prices to the stock prices of all other companies in the market, a relationship also exists between beta and accounting measures of financial leverage (i.e., the ratio of debt to equity based on book values). Companies with higher measures of accounting leverage usually have higher beta values; and companies with relatively lower measures of accounting leverage usually have lower beta values and are considered less risky, all else being equal. Therefore, accounting-based leverage is also an important measure of risk. Many investment services, such as *Value Line,* report the beta for each company's common stock. This ratio is discussed more completely in most finance texts.

Liquidity Ratios. In addition to the overall performance ratios discussed above, analysts can use many detailed financial ratios. Creditors often suggest that the most important of these detailed ratios are the liquidity ratios that describe the resources of the company in terms of their convertibility to cash in a reasonably short time period. The two most common liquidity ratios are:

3. Liquidity ratios:

a. $$\text{Current ratio} = \frac{\text{Current assets (end of period)}}{\text{Current liabilities (end of period)}}$$

b. $$\text{Quick ratio} = \frac{\text{Cash + Temporary investments + Receivables}}{\text{Current liabilities}}$$

Current ratio. The current ratio measures the relationship between current assets and current liabilities. This ratio indicates whether the assets expected to be converted back to cash in the next year (or operating cycle) are greater than the liabilities expected to use cash in the next year (or operating cycle). A current ratio of less than 1.0 may signal financial problems. Many analysts consider a 2.0 (or 2:1) current ratio to be a safe and desirable target. The current ratios for Cybron are computed as follows:

$$\text{Current ratio} = \frac{\text{Current assets}}{\text{Current liabilities}}$$

$$\text{19x7 current ratio} = \frac{\$94{,}000{,}000}{\$47{,}000{,}000} = \underline{\underline{2.0:1}}$$

$$\text{19x6 current ratio} = \frac{\$97{,}000{,}000}{\$51{,}000{,}000} = \underline{\underline{1.9:1}}$$

Note that many of these ratios can be expressed several different ways. For example, the 19x7 current ratio could be stated as 2:1, or 2.0, or 200%.

The current ratio is a convenient way to describe the working capital position of a company for comparison with other companies in the same or similar industries.

Quick ratio. The quick ratio measures how quickly and easily a company's assets can be converted to cash in relation to its current liabilities. This ratio indicates whether a company's current liabilities can be paid with the company's current assets that can be quickly converted to cash. Normally, quick assets include cash, temporary investments, and net accounts receivable. Cybron's quick ratios are computed as:

$$\text{Quick ratio percent} = \frac{\text{Cash + Temporary investments + Receivables}}{\text{Current liabilities}}$$

$$\text{19x7 quick ratio percent} = \frac{\$43{,}000{,}000}{\$47{,}000{,}000} = \underline{\underline{91.5\%}} \text{ (or .915:1)}$$

$$\text{19x6 quick ratio percent} = \frac{\$38{,}000{,}000}{\$51{,}000{,}000} = \underline{\underline{74.5\%}} \text{ (or .745:1)}$$

$$\text{19x6 quick ratio percent} = \frac{\text{Cash + Temporary investments + Receivables}}{\text{Current liabilities}}$$

The quick ratios show the improvement in Cybron's liquid position from the end of 19x6 to the end of 19x7.

Leverage Ratios. Leverage ratios are generally considered to be accounting measures of risk. The more financial leverage a company has, the higher the risk. The two primary leverage ratios are:

4. Leverage ratios:

a. $$\text{Debt to equity} = \frac{\text{Total liabilities}}{\text{Total equity}}$$

b. $$\text{Times interest earned} = \frac{\text{Operating income before interest expense and taxes}}{\text{Interest expense}}$$

Debt-to-equity ratio. The debt-to-equity ratio—the primary accounting measure of leverage—is related to systematic market risk (beta). As a general rule, high debt-to-equity ratios are associated with higher beta values and low debt-to-equity ratios are associated with lower beta values. The debt-to-equity ratio can be measured in different ways. For example, some analysts only look at long-term debt to equity rather than total debt to equity. Usually the debt-to-equity ratio ranges between 1.0 and 4.0. For Cybron, the debt-to-equity ratios are:

$$\text{Debt to equity} = \frac{\text{Total liabilities}}{\text{Total stockholders' equity}}$$

$$\text{19x7 D/E ratio} = \frac{\$140{,}000{,}000}{\$175{,}000{,}000} = \underline{\underline{.80:1}}$$

$$\text{19x6 D/E ratio} = \frac{\$146{,}000{,}000}{\$159{,}000{,}000} = \underline{\underline{.92:1}}$$

Cybron's debt-to-equity ratio was less than 1.0 for both years, indicating a fairly conservative debt position. A ratio below 1.0 indicates that creditors have invested less than owners in the company's resources. All else being equal, a company with a debt-to-equity ratio below 1.0 would likely be able to borrow more funds at a lower rate of interest than a company with a ratio above, say, 2.5.

Times interest earned (TIE) ratio. The times interest earned (TIE) ratio—ratio of operating income before interest expense and taxes to interest expense—is a rough approximation of how difficult it will be for a company to make its interest payments. The lower the ratio, the more difficult to make interest payments; and higher ratios suggest a company may be able to take on more borrowing. For Cybron, the times interest earned ratios are computed as follows:

$$\text{Times interest earned (TIE)} = \frac{\text{Operating income before interest expense and taxes}}{\text{Interest expense}}$$

$$\text{19x7 TIE} = \frac{\$36{,}000{,}000}{\$8{,}000{,}000} = \underline{\underline{4.50}}$$

$$\text{19x6 TIE} = \frac{\$38{,}000{,}000}{\$8{,}000{,}000} = \underline{\underline{4.75}}$$

Cybron's interest expense was the same for both years, but their interest coverage ratio was higher in 19x6 due to higher pre-tax profits.

Activity Ratios. Many different types of activity ratios can be used to help evaluate the productivity of various asset investments. Three common activity ratios are:

5. Activity ratios:

a. $$\text{Receivable turnover ratio} = \frac{\text{Net credit sales}}{\text{Average net accounts receivable}}$$

b. $$\text{Inventory turnover ratio} = \frac{\text{Cost of goods sold}}{\text{Average inventory}}$$

c. $$\text{Asset turnover ratio} = \frac{\text{Net sales}}{\text{Average total assets}}$$

These three activity ratios may vary considerably from industry to industry. For example, you would expect inventory turnover to be more important to manufacturers who normally have sizable inventory than to service companies which normally have little inventory. Also, the investment in plant assets and total assets would probably be higher for manufacturing industries, making asset turnover lower in manufacturing industries than in service industries, which normally require relatively small investments in plant and equipment. Retailers that grant credit to customers may be expected to have lower receivables turnover than a wholesaler that provides supplies to only a few retail establishments. Since activity ratios may vary considerably, they are difficult to evaluate without considering industry averages.

Receivables turnover ratio. The accounts receivable turnover ratio measures the multiple of net credit sales to net receivables, indicating how many times receivables "turn over" in a year. The higher the turnover ratio, the smaller the ratio of receivables to credit sales. If a company collected all of its accounts receivable every day, this ratio would be about 365, which is virtually the highest possible ratio. If receivables take an average of 100 days to collect, the ratio would be 3.65. A high receivables turnover ratio normally indicates good collection procedures. For Cybron, the receivables turnover ratios are:

$$\text{Receivable turnover} = \frac{\text{Net credit sales}}{\text{Average net accounts receivable}}$$

$$\text{19x7 receivable turnover} = \frac{\$276{,}000{,}000}{\$34{,}500{,}000} = \underline{\underline{8.0}}$$

$$\text{19x6 receivable turnover} = \frac{\$241{,}800{,}000}{\$31{,}000{,}000} = \underline{\underline{7.8}}$$

While Cybron's receivables increased in 19x7, credit sales increased at a rate **greater than** 7.8 times the increase in receivables, resulting in an increase in the turnover rate from 7.8 to 8.0 for 19x7.[10]

Inventory turnover ratio. Like most activity ratios, the inventory turnover ratio is generally considered better when it is higher than prior years, or on an increasing trend. For Cybron, the ratios are computed as follows:

$$\text{Inventory turnover} = \frac{\text{Cost of goods sold}}{\text{Average inventory}}$$

$$\text{19x7 inventory turnover} = \frac{\$230{,}000{,}000}{\$45{,}000{,}000} = \underline{\underline{5.11}}$$

$$\text{19x6 inventory turnover} = \frac{\$215{,}000{,}000}{\$50{,}000{,}000} = \underline{\underline{4.30}}$$

Cybron's increasing turnover ratio is due to both lower average inventory levels and higher cost of sales. This could be caused in part by higher sales and in part by more efficient inventory stocking and ordering procedures, both of which would be positive factors in an evaluation of activity ratios. However, this increase could have also been caused by a change in inventory method during 19x7. It is helpful if you try to rule out artificial causes for changes in ratios. One way you can do this is to study the footnotes to the financial statements that describe the accounting policies the company uses.

[10]This analysis of the change can also be directly computed by dividing the increase in net credit sales ($276,000,000 − $241,800,000 = $34,200,000) by the increase in average receivables ($34,500,000 − $31,000,000 = $3,500,000) or $34,200,000/$3,500,000 = 9.77. Since a 9.77 ratio for the change is greater than the first year's ratio of 7.8, we know the overall ratio must increase in the second year. See "Other data" in Exhibit 15-8 for 1/1/x6 balances.

Asset turnover ratio. The asset turnover ratio is a rough approximation of how efficiently a company used its assets in its revenue generating process. For Cybron, the asset turnover ratios are computed as follows:

$$\text{Asset turnover ratio} = \frac{\text{Net sales}}{\text{Average total assets}}$$

$$\text{19x7 asset turnover ratio} = \frac{\$321{,}000{,}000}{\$310{,}000{,}000} = \underline{\underline{1.04}}$$

$$\text{19x6 asset turnover ratio} = \frac{\$303{,}000{,}000}{\$300{,}000{,}000} = \underline{\underline{1.01}}$$

Like the receivables turnover ratio and the inventory turnover ratio, an increase in total asset turnover is generally a good news signal. However, the average age and composition of the assets should be considered in making evaluations, as noted earlier for the return on assets ratio.

The ratios we have studied in this section are summarized in Exhibit 15-9. Remember that the ratios are only as good as the underlying accounting data on which they are based. The better the accounting quality, the more useful the various forms of analysis will be to evaluate financial statements and aid in business decisions. When the accounting data are of a poor quality, no amount of analysis will help make their evaluation useful.

SUMMARY

In this chapter you were given an overview of financial statement analysis. The chapter was divided into two parts. Part A discussed how accounting data should be evaluated to determine if their quality justifies further analysis. Part B discussed (1) the various sources where accounting data useful for analysis purposes may be found, and (2) the various methods used to perform financial statement analysis on accounting data.

Part A essentially draws on our ability to apply accounting theory. The qualitative attributes identified by theorists are to be used to judge the quality of the accounting data. When accounting data are judged to be relevant, reliable, comparable, and consistent, the quality is judged to be high. However, these qualitative attributes are not readily observable, and assessing accounting quality requires professional judgment.

The various sources of accounting data discussed in Part B provide some insights into the types of analysis that are possible. The general-purpose financial statement data normally available to external users in annual reports provide the basis for most of the analysis performed by external users. However, SEC reports are also commonly used as a basis for financial statement analysis by sophisticated creditors and/or investors. Also, the many possible additional special reports not specifically illustrated in this chapter are subject to the same methods of analysis as those reports that provide the most common basis for analysis.

Part B concluded with an introduction to the various methods of financial statement analysis. The central advantage of these methods is in their ability to evaluate the relative performance of one company over many periods, as well as the relative performance of one company in comparison to others at the same point in time. These techniques, despite certain limitations noted in the chapter, add to the comparability of the accounting information and are extremely useful and widely used for performance evaluation purposes.

EXHIBIT 15-9

Summary of Key Financial Ratios

Overall Performance Measures

1. Accounting performance ratios:

a. $$\text{Earnings per share (EPS)} = \frac{\text{Net income} - \text{Preferred stock dividends}}{\text{Average shares of common stock}}$$

b. $$\text{Return on assets (ROA)} = \frac{\text{Net income}}{\text{Average total assets}}$$

c. $$\text{Profit margin} = \frac{\text{Net income}}{\text{Net sales}}$$

2. Market performance ratios:

a. $$\text{Price to earnings or P-E ratio} = \frac{\text{Ending market price per share of common stock}}{\text{EPS}}$$

b. $$\text{Dividend yield percent} = \frac{\text{Annual cash dividends per share}}{\text{Ending market price per share of common stock}}$$

c. $$\text{Systematic market risk (beta)} = \frac{\text{Covariance of returns}}{\text{Variance of returns of the market}}$$

Detailed Analysis Measures

3. Liquidity ratios:

a. $$\text{Current ratio} = \frac{\text{Current assets}}{\text{Current liabilities}}$$

b. $$\text{Quick ratio} = \frac{\text{Cash} + \text{temporary investments} + \text{receivables}}{\text{Current liabilities}}$$

4. Leverage ratios:

a. $$\text{Debt to equity} = \frac{\text{Total liabilities}}{\text{Total stockholders' equity}}$$

b. $$\text{Times interest earned} = \frac{\text{Operating income before interest expense and taxes}}{\text{Interest expense}}$$

5. Activity ratios:

a. $$\text{Receivable turnover ratio} = \frac{\text{Net credit sales}}{\text{Average net accounts receivable}}$$

b. $$\text{Inventory turnover ratio} = \frac{\text{Cost of goods sold}}{\text{Average inventory}}$$

c. $$\text{Asset turnover ratio} = \frac{\text{Net sales}}{\text{Average total assets}}$$

DEMONSTRATION EXERCISE

The Rulkowski Company's comparative balance sheet at December 31, 19x2, and the income statement for the year 19x2 are as follows:

Rulkowski Company
Balance Sheet
At December 31

	19x2	19x1
Assets		
Cash	$ 25,500	$ 42,000
Accounts receivable	93,500	75,500
Inventory	63,000	75,000
Prepaid insurance	6,000	15,500
Investments (long-term)	0	25,000
Property, plant, and equipment (net)	180,000	120,000
Total assets	$368,000	$353,000
Liabilities and Stockholders' Equity		
Liabilities:		
Accounts payable	$ 38,500	$ 37,400
Accrued salaries payable	6,000	3,500
Notes payable, short-term	38,000	19,100
Mortgage payable (long-term)	80,000	105,000
Total liabilities	$162,500	$165,000
Stockholders' equity:		
Common stock	$120,000	$100,000
Contributed capital in excess of par	26,000	20,000
Retained earnings	59,500	68,000
Total stockholders' equity	$205,500	$188,000
Total liabilities and stockholders' equity	$368,000	$353,000

Rulkowski Company
Income Statement
For the Year Ended December 31

	19x2	19x1
Sales	$275,000	$255,000
Cost of goods sold	208,000	183,000
Gross margin	$ 67,000	$ 72,000
Expenses:		
Salaries expense	$ 10,000	$ 12,000
Rent expense	5,000	4,000
Depreciation expense	20,000	18,000
Other operating expenses	5,000	6,000
Interest expense	7,000	5,500
Total expenses	$ 47,000	$ 45,500
Income before taxes	$ 20,000	$ 26,500
Income tax expense	6,000	7,950
Net income	$ 14,000	$ 18,550

Required:

1. Prepare a vertical/horizontal analysis of the above financial statements for the Rulkowski Company. Assume all sales are on account.
2. Using the summary of ratios in Exhibit 15-9 on page 845, prepare as many ratios as possible using the above information. During 19x1 and 19x2 Rulkowski Company averaged 50,000 and 55,000 shares of stock outstanding, respectively.

Required:

Requirement 1:

Rulkowski Company
Vertical/Horizontal Analysis
Balance Sheet
At December 31

	Vertical Analysis		*Horizontal Analysis*	
	19x2	*19x1*	*Percentage Change Increase (Decrease)*	*Relative Percentage Change Increase (Decrease)*
Assets				
Cash	6.9%	11.9%	(5.0)%	(42.0)%
Accounts receivable	25.4	21.4	4.0	18.7
Inventory	17.1	21.2	(4.1)	(19.3)
Prepaid insurance	1.7	4.4	(2.7)	(61.4)
Investments (long-term)		7.1	(7.1)	(100.0)
Property, plant, and equipment (net)	48.9	34.0	14.9	43.8
Total assets	100.0%	100.0%	0.0 %	
Liabilities and Stockholders' Equity				
Liabilities:				
Accounts payable	10.5%	10.6%	(0.1)%	(0.9)
Accrued salaries payable	1.7	1.0	0.7	70.0
Notes payable, short-term	10.3	5.4	4.9	90.7
Mortgage payable (long-term)	21.7	29.7	(8.0)	(26.9)
Total liabilities	44.2%	46.7%	(2.5)%	(5.4)
Stockholders' equity:				
Common stock	32.6%	28.3%	4.3 %	15.2
Contributed capital in excess of par	7.0	5.7	1.3	22.8
Retained earnings	16.2	19.3	(3.1)	(16.1)
Total stockholders' equity	55.8%	53.3%	2.5 %	4.7
Total liabilities and stockholders' equity	100.0%	100.0%	0.0 %	

Rulkowski Company
Vertical/Horizontal Analysis
Income Statement
For the Year Ended December 31, 19x2

	Vertical Analysis		*Horizontal Analysis*	
	19x2	*19x1*	*Percentage Change Increase (Decrease)*	*Relative Percentage Change Increase (Decrease)*
Sales	100.0 %	100.0 %	0.0 %	— %
Cost of goods sold	(75.6)	(71.8)	(3.8)	5.3
Gross margin	24.4 %	28.2 %	(3.8)%	(13.5)
Expenses:				
Salaries expense	(3.6)%	(4.7)%	1.1 %	(23.4)
Rent expense	(1.8)	(1.5)	(0.3)	20.0
Depreciation expense	(7.3)	(7.1)	(0.2)	2.8
Other operating expenses	(1.8)	(2.4)	0.6	(25.0)
Interest expense	(2.6)	(2.1)	(0.5)	23.8
Total expenses	(17.1)%	(17.8)%	0.7 %	(3.9)
Income before taxes	7.3 %	10.4 %	(3.1)%	(29.8)
Income tax expense	(2.2)	(3.1)	0.9	29.0
Net income	5.1 %	7.3 %	(2.2)%	(30.1)

Requirement 2:

EPS: $19x2 = \frac{\$14{,}000}{55{,}000} = \$0.25$ $19x1 = \frac{\$18{,}550}{50{,}000} = \$0.37$

ROA: $19x2 = \frac{\$14{,}000}{(\$353{,}000 + \$368{,}000)/2} = 3.9\%$

Profit margin: $19x2 = \frac{\$14{,}000}{\$275{,}000} = 5.1\%$ $19x1 = \frac{\$18{,}550}{\$255{,}000} = 7.3\%$

Current ratio: $19x2 = \frac{\$25{,}500 + \$93{,}500 + \$63{,}000 + \$6{,}000}{\$38{,}500 + \$6{,}000 + \$38{,}000} = 2.28:1$

$19x1 = \frac{\$42{,}000 + \$75{,}500 + \$75{,}000 + \$15{,}500}{\$37{,}400 + \$3{,}500 + \$19{,}100} = 3.47:1$

Quick ratio: $19x2 = \frac{\$25{,}500 + \$93{,}500}{\$38{,}500 + \$6{,}000 + \$38{,}000} = 1.44:1$

$19x1 = \frac{\$42{,}000 + \$75{,}500}{\$37{,}400 + \$3{,}500 + \$19{,}100} = 1.96:1$

Debt-to-equity: $19x2 = \frac{\$162{,}500}{\$205{,}500} = .79:1$ $19x1 = \frac{\$165{,}000}{\$188{,}000} = .88:1$

Times interest earned: $19x2 = \frac{\$27{,}000}{\$7{,}000} = 3.86$ $19x1 = \frac{\$32{,}000}{\$5{,}500} = 5.82$

Receivable turnover: $19x2 = \frac{\$275{,}000}{(\$75{,}500 + \$93{,}500)/2} = 3.25 \text{ times}$

Inventory turnover: $19x2 = \frac{\$208{,}000}{(\$75{,}000 + \$63{,}000)/2} = 3.01 \text{ times}$

Asset turnover: $19x2 = \frac{\$275{,}000}{(\$353{,}000 + \$368{,}000)/2} = .76 \text{ times}$

KEY TERMS

Auditor's report or opinion. The report made by auditors after they conduct an audit; states whether the company's financial statements and notes fairly present the results of its operations and financial position.

Comparability. Accounting data is comparable when different companies experience the same or similar events and report the same results.

Consistency. When a given entity uses the same measurement procedures from year to year so that the same or similar events occurring in consecutive years are reported in the same manner from year to year.

Constraining qualities. Considerations that might override the primary and secondary qualities of accounting information, namely materiality and cost-benefit considerations.

Horizontal analysis. Used to describe any evaluation of financial statement data that looks at the change in a financial statement item between two years.

Material amount. Amount that could affect the decision of a reasonably knowledgeable user of accounting data.

Proxy statement. Usually announces the time and place of the annual meeting and describes any agenda items to be voted on by the stockholders.

Ratio analysis. Expresses relationship between two numbers as a ratio of one to the other (see Exhibit 15-9 for summary of ratios).

Relevance. Information must be timely and helpful to users in making judgments about the future performance of an entity; **relevant** information is **timely** when it helps evaluate a future event or outcome of interest and **useful** when it helps reduce uncertainty about future events or outcomes of interest to the decision maker.

Reliability. Information must consist of unbiased and verifiable measurements; data that are measurable with a reasonable degree of precision, free from bias, and verifiable.

Trend analysis. Horizontal analysis over three or more time periods.

Verifiable. Accounting data produced by one accounting system can be reproduced by another system (or measurer) and results in the same measures.

Vertical analysis. Any evaluation of financial statement data for a particular time period without comparison to other time periods.

SYNONYMS

Accounting principles; accounting practices; GAAP.

Auditor's opinion; auditor's report.

Objective information; verifiable information.

P-E ratio; P/E ratio; earnings multiple.

Ratio analysis; fundamental analysis.

Recognize; record.

Systematic risk; market beta; beta.

Trend analysis; time-series analysis.

Unbiased; neutral.

Unqualified audit report; clean opinion.

QUESTIONS

Part A

1. What is the objective of financial accounting?
2. How do financial statements help decision makers?
3. What four accounting qualities help financial statements achieve their objective?
4. What are two constraining qualities of accounting information?
5. How is relevant information identified?
6. How is reliable information identified?
7. What makes accounting information comparable?
8. What makes accounting information consistent?
9. What are the elements of financial statements?
10. Define five elements in terms of their effect on net assets.

Part B

11. Identify three separate sources of financial statement data.
12. Identify the three sections of an annual report.
13. Besides the formal financial statements, identify two other items of **financial** information found in most annual reports.
14. Identify three financial reports typically found in most publicly owned companies besides the formal financial statements.
15. Identify four types of analysis.
16. Define horizontal analysis.
17. Define vertical analysis.
18. Define trend analysis.
19. Define ratio analysis.
20. Identify and define two accounting performance ratios.
21. Identify and define two market performance ratios.
22. Identify and define two liquidity ratios.
23. Identify and define two leverage ratios.
24. Identify and define two activity ratios.
25. What ratio results when you multiply the profit margin ratio times the asset turnover ratio?

EXERCISES

EXERCISE 15-1
L.O. 1, 2

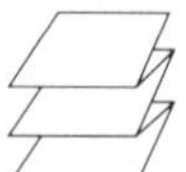

Reliability—Balance Sheet

Recall from the chapter that reliable information is measurable, verifiable, objective, and unbiased. The following balance sheet accounts are typically found in most companies. Each account is measured based on varying degrees of reliability. Using the following classifications, indicate the degree of reliability you believe to be present in each of the balance sheet accounts listed:

A = A *very reliable* account.
B = A *reliable* account.
C = A *relatively unreliable* account.

Balance sheet accounts:

a. Estimated warranty liability.
b. Cash.
c. Land.
d. Net accounts receivable.
e. Goodwill (net of amortization).
f. Marketable equity securities at lower of cost or market.
g. Accounts payable.
h. Buildings at original cost.
i. Buildings net of accumulated depreciation.
j. Inventory at lower of average cost or market.
k. Patents.
l. Bonds payable.

(Hint: In making your classifications, ask yourself whether the same account balances would have been arrived at if a dozen separate accountants had measured these account balances.)

EXERCISE 15-2
L.O. 1, 2

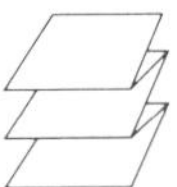

Relevance—Balance Sheet

Recall from the chapter that relevant information is both timely and useful for decision making. Assume you are evaluating financial statements **for purposes of making an equity investment** (between 20 and 50% ownership) in another company. Using the following classifications, indicate the degree of relevance present in each of the listed balance sheet accounts for assisting you in your investment decision:

A = A *very relevant* account.
B = A *relevant* account.
C = A *relatively irrelevant* account.

Balance sheet accounts:

a. Estimated warranty liability.
b. Cash.
c. Land.
d. Net accounts receivable.
e. Goodwill (net of amortization).
f. Marketable equity securities at lower of cost or market.
g. Accounts payable.
h. Buildings at original cost.
i. Buildings net of accumulated depreciation.
j. Inventory at lower of average cost or market.
k. Patents.
l. Bonds payable.

(Hint: In making your classifications, ask yourself how useful the information about each particular account balance would be in helping you make a buy/**not** buy decision.)

EXERCISE 15-3
L.O. 2

Elements of Financial Statements

Based on your understanding of accounting theory, which of the following would qualify as an asset? Explain the amount, if any, and the justification for your answer.

1. A contract between the Denver Broncos and John Elway for exclusive service rights for the next three years. The present value of the contracted salary payments is $3 million.
2. A contract between Ford Motors and Donald Peterson, who will agree to be president for the next two years at a salary of $2 million per year.
3. The discovery of a vaccine to eliminate chicken pox, valued at $1 billion by competitors who wish to acquire the patent rights.

EXERCISE 15-4
L.O. 1, 2

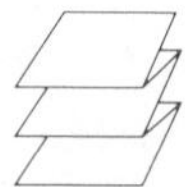

Comparability—Balance Sheet

Recall that comparable data are those which are meaningful when compared across firms. Assume you are doing a comparative analysis of a group of companies. Using the following classifications, indicate the degree of comparability present in each of the listed balance sheet accounts:

A = A *very comparable* account.
B = A *comparable* account.
C = A *relatively uncomparable* account.

Balance sheet accounts:

a. Estimated warranty liability.
b. Cash.
c. Land.
d. Net accounts receivable.
e. Goodwill (net of amortization).
f. Marketable equity securities at lower of cost or market.
g. Accounts payable.
h. Buildings at original cost.
i. Buildings net of accumulated depreciation.
j. Inventory at lower of average cost or market.
k. Patents.
l. Bonds payable.

EXERCISE 15-5
L.O. 1, 2

Reliability

Recall from the chapter that reliable information is measurable, verifiable, objective, and unbiased. Using the following classification, indicate the degree of reliability in each of the income statement accounts listed.

A = A *very reliable* account.
B = A *reliable* account.
C = A *relatively unreliable* account.

Income statement accounts:

a. Net sales.
b. Bad debt expense.
c. Goodwill amortization expense.
d. Depreciation expense—buildings.
e. Salaries expense.
f. Advertising expense.
g. Cost of goods sold (based on LIFO cost flow).
h. Cost of goods sold (based on FIFO cost flow).
i. Interest income.
j. Interest expense.
k. Realized loss on sale of marketable securities.
l. Unrealized loss on marketable securities.

EXERCISE 15-6
L.O. 1, 2

Relevance and Comparability

The financial statements should include the following summary data:

a. Income from continuing operations.
b. Net income.
c. Cash flow from continuing operations.
d. Net cash flow.
e. Total assets.
f. Net assets.

Required:

1. Rank these six data items from 1 (*most* relevant) to 6 (*least* relevant) for purposes of making an investment decision.
2. Rank these six data items from 1 (*most* comparable) to 6 (*least* comparable) for purposes of making an investment decision.

EXERCISE 15-7
L.O. 2

Elements of Financial Statements

Based on your understanding of accounting theory, which of the following would qualify as an asset or a liability? Explain your answers.

a. A customer advances your firm $20,000 cash for engineering services, which you plan to perform during the next fiscal year.
b. A customer falls while in your store and ruins five pieces of artwork costing $15,000 which were being sold for $30,000. You sue for $30,000. The customer, who broke his leg in the fall, sues you for $100,000. Both cases are waiting to come to trial. Your insurance does not cover either possible loss.
c. Z Company, with office equipment recorded at $2.3 million, buys its 125 department-level managers each a $2.50 paperweight with the company's logo for their desk at work. Z Company reports $18 million in sales last year. The paperweights are expected to have a 10-year useful life.

EXERCISE 15-8
L.O. 3

Vertical Analysis—Income Statements

The following condensed income statement data are taken from the year-end statements of Basic Elements Labs (in thousands):

	19x2	*19x1*
Sales	$1,850	$1,650
Cost of goods sold	1,320	1,240
Selling and administrative expense	216	187
Interest expense	120	105
Other gains (losses)	50	(28)
Income tax expense	62	25

Required:
1. Prepare comparative income statements for 19x2 and 19x1.
2. Evaluate the income statement data using vertical analysis.
3. What is the profit margin for 19x2 and 19x1?

EXERCISE 15-9
L.O. 3

Vertical/Horizontal Analysis—Income Statements

Consider the data in Exercise 15-8 for Basic Elements Labs.

Required:
1. Prepare comparative income statements for 19x2 and 19x1.
2. Evaluate the income statement data using vertical/horizontal analysis as illustrated in the chapter. (Round answers to the nearest tenth of a percent.)

EXERCISE 15-10
L.O. 3

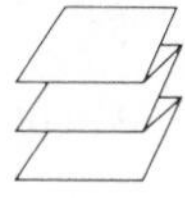

Horizontal Analysis—Balance Sheets

Consider the following balance sheet data for Westwick, Inc. (in thousands):

	December 31	
	19x2	*19x1*
Cash	$ 356	$ 287
Receivables	420	530
Inventory	680	720
Other current assets	403	380
Land	600	600
Plant and equipment (net)	1,806	1,675
Total assets	$4,265	$4,192
Accounts payable	$ 510	$ 488
Other current payables	420	540
Long-term debt	2,000	2,000
Common stock (par $10)	110	110
Other contributed capital	630	630
Retained earnings	595	424
Total liabilities and stockholders' equity	$4,265	$4,192

Required:
1. Prepare a horizontal analysis of the Westwick balance sheets for 19x2 and 19x1. Round all percents to a single decimal place (xx.x% or .xxx).
2. Assume Westwick declared and paid dividends of $55,000 in 19x2. Compute EPS and dividends per share for 19x2.

EXERCISE 15-11
L.O. 3

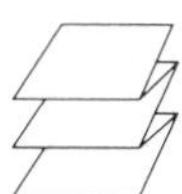

Vertical Analysis—Balance Sheets

Consider the balance sheet data of Westwick provided in Exercise 15-10 above.

Required:
Prepare a vertical analysis of these balance sheets as illustrated in the chapter. Let total assets equal 100%. (Round to xx.x% or .xxx.)

EXERCISE 15-12
L.O. 3

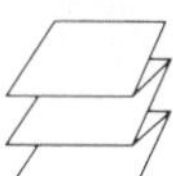

Vertical/Horizontal Analysis—Balance Sheets

Consider the balance sheet data of Westwick, Inc., provided in Exercise 15-10 above.

Required:
1. Prepare a vertical/horizontal analysis of these balance sheets as illustrated in the chapter. Let total assets equal 100%. (Round all answers to tenths of a percent.)
2. Evaluate the changes in the current accounts of Westwick (the current ratio). Did Westwick's current liquid position improve during 19x2? Explain your answer.

EXERCISE 15-13
L.O. 4

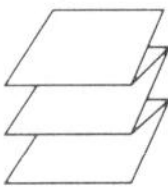

Ratio Analysis

The following data are taken from the records of the Taylor Wine Company as of the end of 19x2 (in thousands):

	19x2	*19x1*
Cash	$ 185	$ 198
Accounts receivable	548	502
Allowance for bad debts	(16)	(14)
Wine inventory	832	786
Current prepaid expenses	54	46
Total current assets	$1,603	$1,518
Total current liabilities	1,122	1,139
Total long-term liabilities	2,000	2,000
Total stockholders' equity	1,800	1,700

Other data for 19x2:

Accounts Receivable Turnover Ratio	4.5
Inventory Turnover Ratio	3.2

Required:
Compute the following data:

a. Net sales for 19x2.
b. Cost of sales for 19x2.
c. Gross margin for 19x2.
d. Quick ratio for 19x2.
e. Current ratio for 19x2.
f. Asset turnover ratio for 19x2.

EXERCISE 15-14
L.O. 4

Ratio Analysis

Braxton Corporation reported the following data analysis for the most recent year:

Total asset turnover ratio	2.25 times
Average total assets	$8,000,000
Income tax expense	2,100,000
Times interest earned	2.80 times
Gross margin as percentage of sales	65%
Operating income before interest expense and tax as a percentage of sales	35%

Note that interest expense has not been deducted in computing operating income. Also, gross margin is sales less cost of goods sold only.

Required:
1. Prepare an income statement for Braxton to include the following components:
   a. Sales.
   b. Cost of sales.
   c. Other operating expenses.
   d. Interest expense.
2. Compute the profit margin for the year.

EXERCISE 15-15
L.O. 4

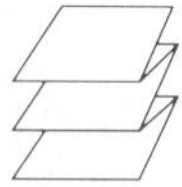

Ratio Analysis

Jansen, Inc., reported the following financial data for the most recent year of operations.

Income tax expense.	$462,000
Income tax rate.	30%
Return on assets	8%
Leverage (debt-to-equity) ratio	3.0 times
Asset turnover	1.8 times

Assume that Jansen's total assets were constant throughout the year.

Required:
Based on these facts, answer the following questions (not necessarily in order):

1. What is net income?
2. What are total assets?
3. What is total debt?
4. What are total sales?
5. What is pre-tax income?
6. What is stockholders' equity?

EXERCISE 15-16
L.O. 4

Ratio Analysis—General Electric

The following data are summarized from General Electric financial statements and stock exchange data as of October 14, 1987 (the Wednesday before "Black Monday").

Market price per share of common stock	$61.375
Earnings per share, most recent four quarters combined	$ 3.85
Cash dividend per share most recent four quarters combined . . .	$ 1.32

Required:
1. Compute the price-earnings ratio for GE (round to two decimal places).
2. Compute the dividend yield ratio for GE (round to two decimal places).

EXERCISE 15-17
L.O. 4

Ratio Analysis—Ford Motor Company

The following data are taken from the 1986 annual report of the Ford Motor Company.

Average total asset during 1986.	$34.75 billion
Pre-tax operating income as a percentage of sales	8.08%
Pre-tax operating rate of return on average total assets	14.59%

Required:
Compute the following information based on the data provided above:

1. Sales dollars (to nearest $100 million).
2. Pre-tax operating income (to nearest million).
3. Total asset turnover (to nearest single decimal place).

PROBLEMS

PROBLEM 15-1
L.O. 1

Relevance/Reliability/Comparability

Consider the following facts. Each of 20 different companies owns a portfolio of stocks purchased at various dates over the past 12 years that consist of the exact same securities:

100 shares of X Company common.
200 shares of Y Company common.
300 shares of Z Company common.
150 shares of B Company common.

On December 31, 19x5, each of these 20 companies reports the value of this portfolio as a long-term asset at the lower-of-cost-or-market (LCM) value. The prices paid and current market value at the end of 19x5 were:

Security	*Range of Original Cost per Share*	*Market Value per Share*
X common	$10–$15	$18
Y common	12– 18	14
Z common	20– 27	29
B common	45– 59	52

Required:
1. Discuss the relevance, reliability, and comparability of the LCM method.
2. Discuss the relevance, reliability, and comparability of the market value method.
3. Which method seems most relevant for comparison and performance evaluation?

PROBLEM 15-2
L.O. 1

Relevance/Reliability/Comparability

Assume two utility plants can each produce 100 million kilowatt-hours of power per month, at capacity. Both plants run at 80% of capacity and charge an equal fee for each kilowatt of power. Plant A was built in 1946 at a cost of $10 million and is expected to last 80 years. Plant B was built in 1986 at a cost of $120 million and is expected to last 80 years. Straight-line depreciation is used by both. Assume that each plant is a separate entity, with separate shareholders, and so on. In 1990 each entity reports $4 million income from operations before depreciation and taxes. Each entity is subject to a 35% tax rate and has 1 million shares of stock.

Required:
1. Compute 1990 earnings per share and return on assets for each entity. (Assume no other assets.)
2. How relevant, reliable, and comparable are the net income and return on asset measures for these two plants.
3. Assume utility regulators allow utilities to set prices so that all utilities receive an equal return on assets. What problems do you foresee in such a regulatory system?

PROBLEM 15-3
L.O. 1

Relevance versus Reliability

Banner Corporation is a closely held family business whose common stock is not publicly traded. Banner common stock has a par value of $10 per share. On November 1, 19x1, there are 100,000 shares outstanding, held by the Banner family. On November 2, 19x1, Banner Corporation issued 10,000 shares of stock in exchange for 50 acres of land which is to be used for a future operating location near Boyne Falls. Just prior to this transaction, Banner reported net assets of $2,850,000. The business was also appraised during the summer of 19x1, and the net assets were estimated to be worth between $4 and $5 million. The realtor who sold the land to Banner indicated that the owner had recently turned down an offer of $425,000 for the land before selling it to Banner for the stock.

Required:

1. Indicate the *most reliable* basis for recording the land on Banner's books. Explain why you believe this measure is the *most reliable.*
2. Indicate the *most relevant* basis for recording the land on Banner's books. Explain your choice.
3. What would you use as the recorded value of the land if you were Banner's accountant? Explain your choice.

PROBLEM 15-4
L.O. 2

Elements of Financial Statements

Based on your understanding of accounting theory, how would the following situations be reflected in the financial statements, if at all?

a. B Company owns a fleet of oil tankers. In November 19x3 a tanker, with a book value of $2 million, sinks in a North Atlantic storm. In December 19x3 the insurance company agrees to pay B Company $3 million for the loss.
b. A forest fire destroys an apartment complex owned by Delta Corporation. The book value of the complex was $10 million and was about 30% of the assets owned by Delta Corporation. There was no insurance coverage for losses due to forest fire.
c. The city of Detroit agreed to not charge GM property taxes for a 30-year period for a site where a new plant was to be built. The property taxes would have been $530,000 in 19x3, the first year of the agreed tax waiver period.

PROBLEM 15-5
L.O. 2

Elements of Financial Statements

Based on your understanding of accounting theory, how would you report the following items in the financial statements, if at all?

a. B Company buys a patent from its competitor for $50,000 cash. The patent has a remaining legal life of eight years. B Company does not intend to use the patent for production purposes.
b. C Company gives $250,000 (market value) of its own stock to a contractor who has agreed to build a new office building for C Company which will cost $8,000,000. The stock has a par value of $10,000.
c. The local government of Mayville is planning to build a new civic center on the site of your present downtown warehouse facility. The warehouse has a book value of $25,000 and the land originally cost $10,000. Mayville has agreed to pay you $350,000 for the land and warehouse at the beginning of the next fiscal year.

PROBLEM 15-6
L.O. 4

Ratio Analysis

Consider the condensed financial statement data for Garfield Fish, Inc., provided below (all amounts are in thousands):

Garfield Fish, Inc.
Balance Sheets
At December 31

	19x2	19x1	19x0
Cash	$ 21	$ 24	$ 20
Marketable securities	149	100	61
Receivables (net)	232	190	204
Inventory	229	244	260
Total current assets	$ 631	$ 558	$ 545
Plant and equipment (net)	1,400	1,360	1,390
Land	310	310	310
Total assets	$2,341	$2,228	$2,245

	19x2	19x1	19x0
Liabilities:			
Accounts payable	$ 187	$ 193	$ 204
Taxes payable	49	77	82
Other current	63	39	68
Total current liabilities	$ 299	$ 309	$ 354
Long-term debt	1,020	985	985
Common stock	680	680	680
Retained earnings	342	254	226
Total liabilities and stockholders' equity	$2,341	$2,228	$2,245

Garfield Fish, Inc.
Earnings Statements
For the Years Ending December 31

	19x2	19x1
Revenues	$4,508	$3,752
Cost of goods sold	3,606	3,077
Gross margin	$ 902	$ 675
Other gains and (losses)	(14)	15
Interest expense	(105)	(102)
Earnings before taxes	$ 783	$ 588
Income tax expense	(303)	(274)
Earnings	$ 480	$ 314

Par value for Garfield common stock is $1.00 per share. Market value of the stock was $2.75, $2.50, and $2.25 per share at the end of 19x2, 19x1, and 19x0, respectively.

Required:
Compute all of the ratios summarized in Exhibit 15-9 that are possible for 19x2 and 19x1 based on the data provided. (Round all ratios to two decimal places.)

PROBLEM 15-7
L.O. 3

Horizontal/Vertical Analysis

Consider the data in Problem 15-6 for Garfield Fish, Inc.

Required:
1. Prepare a horizontal analysis of the balance sheet data for Garfield Fish, Inc., for 19x2 and 19x1.
2. Prepare a horizontal analysis of the income statement data for 19x2 and 19x1.
3. Prepare a vertical analysis of the income statement data for 19x2 and 19x1.
4. Prepare a vertical/horizontal analysis of the income statement data for 19x2 and 19x1.

PROBLEM 15-8
L.O. 3

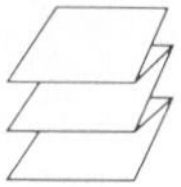

Horizontal Analysis—McDonald's

The following data are summarized from a recent income statement of McDonald's Corporation, the world's largest fast-food restaurant chain (in millions):

	Years Ended December 31	
	19x2	*19x1*
Revenues:		
Sales by company-operated restaurants	$3,106	$2,770
Revenues from franchised restaurants	1,037	924
Other revenues	97	66
Total revenues	$4,240	$3,760
Costs and expenses:		
For company-operated restaurants	$2,579	$2,278
For franchised restaurants	169	140
Total costs and expenses	$2,748	$2,418
Gross profit	$1,492	$1,342
General, administrative, and selling expenses	471	419
Interest expense	173	141
Income before taxes	$ 848	$ 782
Income tax expense	368	349
Net income	$ 480	$ 433
Net income per common share	$3.73	$3.32
Dividends per common share	0.65	0.59

Required:
Prepare a horizontal analysis for McDonald's similar to that illustrated in the chapter.

PROBLEM 15-9
L.O. 3

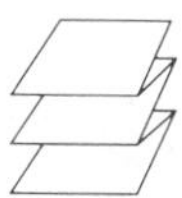

Vertical Analysis—McDonald's

Consider the McDonald's income statement data provided in Problem 15-8.

Required:
Prepare a vertical analysis of each year's income statement data for McDonald's as illustrated in the chapter.

PROBLEM 15-10
L.O. 3

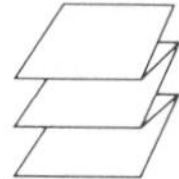

Vertical/Horizontal Analysis—McDonald's

Consider the McDonald's income statement data provided in Problem 15-8.

Required:
Prepare a vertical/horizontal analysis of the McDonald's income statement as illustrated in the chapter.

PROBLEM 15-11
L.O. 3

Horizontal Analysis—Ralston Purina

Consider the balance sheets of the Ralston Purina Company provided in Appendix E at the end of this text.

Required:
Prepare a horizontal analysis of the balance sheets. To reduce computations, treat all of shareholders' equity as a single account (amount), including the redeemable preferred stock and the unearned ESOP compensation.

PROBLEM 15-12
L.O. 3

Vertical Analysis—Ralston Purina

Consider the balance sheets of the Ralston Purina Company provided in Appendix E.

Required:
Prepare a vertical analysis of the balance sheets, stating all amounts as a percentage of total assets. To reduce computations, treat all of shareholders' equity as a single account, including the redeemable preferred stock and the unearned ESOP compensation.

PROBLEM 15-13
L.O. 3

Vertical/Horizontal Analysis—Ralston Purina

Consider the balance sheets of the Ralston Purina Company (Appendix E).

Required:
Prepare a vertical/horizontal analysis of the balance sheets as illustrated in the chapter letting total assets equal 100%. To reduce computations, treat all of shareholders' equity as a single account, including the redeemable preferred stock and the unearned ESOP compensation.

PROBLEM 15-14
L.O. 4

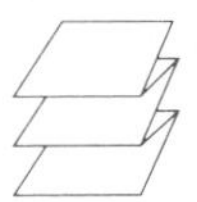

Ratio Analysis—Westinghouse

The following data are summarized from a recent annual report of Westinghouse Electric Corporation, a diversified technology-based corporation providing products and services for industrial, construction, and electric utility applications, and equipment for power generation.

Westinghouse Electric Corporation
Condensed Balance Sheet Data
At December 31
(in millions)

	19x2	*19x1*
Assets		
Cash and marketable securities	$ 598	$ 702
Receivables	1,905	2,032
Inventories	1,391	1,262
Prepaid and other current assets	741	625
Total current assets	$4,635	$4,621
Investments	894	762
Plant and equipment	2,189	3,300
Intangibles and other noncurrent assets	764	1,028
Total assets	$8,482	$9,711
Liabilities and Stockholders' Equity		
Accounts payable	$ 646	$ 625
Unearned revenues	1,129	1,097
Short-term debt	597	2,039
Other current liabilities	1,824	1,492
Total current liabilities	$4,196	$5,253
Long-term liabilities	1,252	1,190
Minority interest	24	33
Total stockholders' equity	3,010	3,235
Total liabilities and stockholders' equity	$8,482	$9,711

Westinghouse Electric Corporation
Condensed Income Statement Data
For the Year Ended December 31
(in millions)

	19x2	*19x1*
Sales	$10,731	$10,700
Cost of sales	7,771	7,738
Depreciation and amortization	371	449
Interest expense	146	185
Other expenses (net)	1,643	1,534
Pre-tax income	$ 800	$ 794
Income tax expense	129	189
Net income	$ 671	$ 605

In addition to the condensed data above, Westinghouse reported its weighted average number of shares of common stock outstanding for 19x2 and 19x1 were 157 million shares and 179 million shares, repectively. The market price of Westinghouse common was $55.75 and $44.50 per share at the end of 19x2 and 19x1, respectively.

Required:

1. Compute earnings per share for 19x2 and 19x1.
2. Compute the price-earnings ratio for 19x2 and 19x1.
3. Compute the quick ratio for 19x2 and 19x1.
4. Compute the debt-to-equity ratio for 19x2 and 19x1.
5. Compute the inventory turnover ratio for 19x2 only.

PROBLEM 15-15
L.O. 4

Ratio Analysis—Westinghouse

Consider the Westinghouse data provided in the previous problem.

Required:

1. Compute the return on assets ratio for 19x2.
2. Compute the profit margin for 19x2 and 19x1.
3. Compute the current ratio for 19x2 and 19x1.
4. Compute the times-interest-earned ratio for 19x2 and 19x1.
5. Compute the receivables turnover ratio for 19x2.
6. Compute the asset turnover ratio for 19x2.

PROBLEM 15-16
L.O. 3

Analysis of Performance—Westinghouse

Consider the Westinghouse data provided in Problem 15-14. Your objective in this problem is to better understand the improved net income of Westinghouse in 19x2 versus that of 19x1.

Required:

1. First, perform a vertical analysis of the two separate income statements for 19x2 and 19x1.
2. Which expenses decreased as a percentage of sales during 19x2 relative to 19x1?
3. Which expenses increased in 19x2?
4. What was the percentage increase in sales in 19x2 over 19x1?
5. What was the percentage increase in net income in 19x2 and 19x1?
6. Do you think cash flows from operations improved in 19x2? Explain.

PROBLEM 15-17
L.O. 4

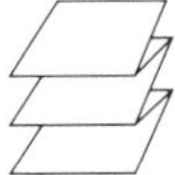

Ratio Analysis—Ralston Purina

Consider the financial statements of the Ralston Purina Company (Appendix E). Include redeemable preferred stock and unearned ESOP compensation as shareholders' equity.

Required:
Compute:

1. Return on assets for 19x7.
2. The profit margin for 19x7.
3. The current ratio for 19x7 and 19x6.
4. The quick ratio for 19x7 and 19x6.
5. The debt-to-equity ratio for 19x7.
6. The times-interest-earned ratio for 19x7.
7. The receivables turnover ratio for 19x7.
8. The inventory turnover ratio for 19x7.
9. The asset turnover ratio for 19x7.

PROBLEM 15-18
L.O. 3

Trend Analysis

Consider the following data from the reports of Whetherwax, Inc. (in millions):

	19x5	*19x4*	*19x3*	*19x2*	*19x1*
Sales	$950	$838	$748	$687	$ 0
Cost of sales	710	630	560	515	0
Net accounts receivable	130	108	89	75	67
Net income	41	38	37	35	0

Assume Whetherwax faced a constant tax rate throughout this four-year period.

Required:

1. Prepare a combination of horizontal and vertical/horizontal analysis, plus receivable turnover analysis to evaluate the performance of Whetherwax over the past four years.
2. What, if any, are your major concerns over the growth being experienced by Whetherwax?
3. What is the apparent trend in operating expenses?

PROBLEM 15-19
L.O. 3

Trend Analysis

The Bellstrom Furniture Company reported the following historical financial statement data (in millions):

	For the Year Ended			
	19x4	*19x3*	*19x2*	*19x1*
Sales	$203	$182	$96	$57
Cost of goods sold	138	119	58	38
Net income (loss)	45	35	15	(3)

	As of December 31				
	19x4	*19x3*	*19x2*	*19x1*	*19x0*
Inventory	$ 37	$ 33	$28	$14	$10
Net accounts receivable	71	59	26	12	10

Assume Bellstrom has a 30% tax rate from 19x2 to 19x4 and that no taxes were paid in 19x1.

Required:

1. Prepare a combination of horizontal and vertical/horizontal analysis for income statement data over the past four years.
2. Prepare turnover ratios for the past four years.
3. Analyze the trends from your answers to parts 1 and 2 above. Should Bellstrom be concerned about any of its trends?

PROBLEM 15-20
L.O. 4

Ratio Analysis—Leverage

The Modular Corporation reported the following data at the end of 19x1:

Assets	$400,000
Liabilities	100,000
Stockholders' equity	300,000
Interest expense	5,000
Net income	30,000
EPS (on 30,000 shares)	$1.00

During 19x2, the Modular Corporation expanded and financed the expansion with debt. The growth took place on the first day of 19x2, and the following results were reported at the end of 19x2:

Assets	$800,000
Liabilities	500,000
Stockholders' equity	300,000
Interest expense	45,000
Net income	70,000
EPS (on 30,000 shares)	$2.33

Income tax rate for both years is 30%.

Required:

1. Compute the following ratios before (19x1 data) and after (19x2 data) the expansion.
   a. Return on year-end assets (net income/ending assets).
   b. Return on year-end stockholders' equity (net income/ending stockholders' equity).
   c. Times interest earned (net income before interest expense and taxes/interest expense).
   d. Debt-to-equity ratio (liabilities/stockholders' equity).
2. What Modular has done with its debt financing of the expansion has had both positive and negative effects on the stockholders. What are some of the negative effects that could affect stockholders in future periods?

PROBLEM 15-21
L.O. 4

Ratio Analysis

The following condensed data are taken from the 19x3 annual report of Gotham, Inc. (in millions):

	Year Ended December 31	
	19x3	*19x2*
Sales	$387	$356
Cost of goods sold	212	193
Interest expense	8	8
Net income	20	17
Income tax rate	30%	30%

	December 31		
	19x3	*19x2*	*19x1*
Assets			
Current assets:			
Cash	$ 15	$ 13	$ 12
Accounts receivable	61	57	52
Inventories	53	48	43
Other current assets	9	8	7
Total current assets	$138	$126	$114
Plant and equipment	$127	$115	$120
Less accumulated depreciation	(39)	(36)	(40)
Net plant and equipment	$ 88	$ 79	$ 80
Total assets	$226	$205	$194
Liabilities and Stockholders' Equity			
Current liabilities:			
Accounts payable	$ 47	$ 39	$ 36
Accrued liabilities	18	19	20
Other current liabilities	12	15	13
Total current liabilities	$ 77	$ 73	$ 69
Long-term liabilities	93	88	86
Total liabilities	$170	$161	$155
Stockholders' equity:			
Contributed capital	$ 20	$ 20	$ 20
Retained earnings	36	24	19
Total stockholders' equity	$ 56	$ 44	$ 39
Total liabilities and stockholders' equity	$226	$205	$194

Required:

1. Compute the following ratios for 19x3 and 19x2:
   a. Current ratio.
   b. Quick ratio.
   c. Debt-to-equity ratio.
   d. Times-interest-earned ratio.
   e. Accounts receivable turnover ratio.
   f. Inventory turnover ratio.
   g. Asset turnover ratio.
   h. Profit margin.
   i. Return on assets.
2. Compute the apparent amount of dividends for 19x3 and 19x2 declared and paid by Gotham, Inc.
3. Assume that Gotham's contributed capital consists of common stock with a par value of $100 per share which was sold for $200 per share at the time the company was formed. No sales have occurred since the original issuance. Compute EPS for 19x3 and 19x2.
4. Gotham common stock performed as follows:

	December 31	
	19x3	*19x2*
Market price per share	$450	$425

   Compute the dividend yield for 19x3 and 19x2.

PROBLEM 15-22
L.O. 2

Analysis of Changes in Accounts

Refer to the financial statement data provided in Problem 15-21 for Gotham, Inc. The following additional data are obtained from the footnotes to Gotham's 19x3 annual report (in thousands):

	19x3	*19x2*	*19x1*
Bad debt expense	$ 937	$ 889	—
Depreciation expense	3,685	2,900	—
Gain (loss) on sale of depreciable assets	(1,300)	1,500	—
Other data:			
Allowance for doubtful accounts, December 31	$ 1,935	$1,780	$ 1,520
New purchases of plant and equipment	15,000	5,000	12,000
New issuance of long-term debt	10,000	8,000	—
Amortization of premium/discount on long-term debt	0	0	0
Cash paid to retire long-term debt before maturity	4,580	5,000	—

Required:

1. Compute the amount of accounts receivable written off in 19x3 and 19x2. (Hint: Set up T accounts to solve.)
2. Compute the cash received from the sale of depreciable assets in 19x3 and 19x2. (Hint: Use T accounts.)
3. Compute the pre-tax extraordinary gain or loss from the early retirement of long-term debt in 19x3 and 19x2. (Hint: Use T accounts.)

CASES

CASE 15-1
L.O. 1

Accounting Qualities

Accounting data are expected to represent the qualities of relevance and reliability. Evaluate the reliability of the following assets:

a. Cash.
b. Accounts Receivable.
c. Inventory.
d. Equipment (net of depreciation).
e. Equity Investment in Subsidiary.

CASE 15-2
L.O. 4

Bad Debt Analysis

The Builtmore Products Company reported total accounts receivable of $468,000 at the end of 19x5 and $535,000 at the end of 19x6. The allowance for bad debts was $37,000 at the end of 19x5 and $49,000 at the end of 19x6. All sales were made on account during 19x6 except for $389,000 of cash sales. The accounts receivable turnover ratio for 19x6 was 3.8.

Required:
Compute Builtmore's net sales for 19x6.

CASE 15-3
L.O. 4

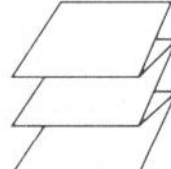

Ratio Analysis

A newspaper report on Express Star, Inc., contained the following statements about the company's annual earnings:

> The earnings for the current year resulted in a 12% return on total assets of $850 million, or 5 cents for each dollar of sales revenue. These earnings also resulted in a 25.5% return on average net assets for the past year.

Required:
Based on this information, compute the following data:

a. Average shareholders' equity.
b. Earnings.
c. Total revenues.
d. Asset turnover ratio.

CASE 15-4
L.O. 4

Debt-to-Equity

In a recent report to shareholders, top management of Executech Software, Inc., identified a need for new sources of funds to support rapidly increasing sales. The president of Executech warned that additional long-term borrowing from banks would significantly increase the financial leverage of the company. The president expressed hope that additional stock could also be issued to reduce or offset the shareholder risk from additional borrowing. Explain the effects on leverage and "shareholder risk" from:

a. Increases in borrowing.
b. Increases in stock issued.
c. Increases of equal size to both.

CASE 15-5
L.O. 4

Market and Accounting Risk

Consider two power generation companies in an unregulated market setting. Each company has a physical plant which cost $800 million to acquire in 19x1 and represents 80% of their total assets. Company A has total debt and equity equal to $500 million each. Company B is 100% equity (no debt) and is the exact same size as Company A. Company A is paying 8% per year on its debt. The tax rate for both companies is 40%. Over the past year, both companies reported income before interest and taxes of $80 million. In the coming year, the forecast of income before interest and taxes is uncertain with estimates ranging between $30 million and $130 million.

Required:
Discuss the difference between Company A and Company B in terms of accounting leverage and return measures, and market risk and return measures. Try to explain the relationship, if any, between the accounting measures and market measures of risk and return. (Which company has the highest expected return? Why? Which has the highest risk [beta]? Why?)

EVALUATING FINANCIAL STATEMENTS

CASE 15-6
L.O. 2

Inventory Valuation—LIFO versus FIFO—General Mills

The following footnote is taken from a recent annual report for General Mills Corporation:

Note Six: Inventories

The components of year-end inventories are as follows (in millions):

	May 31, 19x7	*May 25, 19x6*
Raw materials, work in process, and supplies	$156.4	$141.8
Finished goods	259.0	230.2
Grain	24.7	24.7
Reserve for LIFO valuation method	(51.5)	(45.8)
Total inventories	$388.6	$350.9

General Mills uses the LIFO method of valuing inventory. General Mills reported net income before taxes of $433 million and $317 million for fiscal 19x7 and 19x6, respectively. Cost of goods sold for fiscal 19x7 was $2,834 million. Assume General Mills' income tax rate is 35% for all periods.

Required:

1. What would cost of goods sold have been for 19x7 if General Mills' LIFO Reserve account had not changed in fiscal 19x7?
2. What was the fiscal 19x7 tax savings attributable to the use of LIFO?
3. What is the total tax savings for all years before fiscal 19x7 attributable to LIFO?

CASE 15-7
L.O. 2

Analysis of LIFO Inventory—Vader Corporation

The Vader Corporation reported the following partial income statement data (in millions):

	For the Year Ended December 31	
	19x2	*19x1*
Cost of sales	$1,689.0	$1,557.0
Net income before tax	187.5	140.0
Income tax expense (40%)	75.0	56.0
Net income	112.5	84.0

The following balance sheet data (in millions) pertain to inventories, which are valued at FIFO during the year but converted to LIFO each year-end by way of adjustments to the LIFO Reserve account:

	December 31	
	19x2	*19x1*
Inventories at FIFO	$597	$520
Less LIFO Reserve	(86)	(75)
Inventories at LIFO	$511	$445

During 19x2 Vader liquidated some of its LIFO inventories, resulting in a decrease (debit) in the LIFO reserve of $10 million.

Required:
1. Compute the tax savings from using LIFO for 19x2 only, based on the data provided.
2. Compute the additional taxes paid in 19x2 because of the LIFO liquidations.
3. What was the dollar effect of 19x2 price changes on Vader's inventory value (amount and increase or decrease)?
4. What would cost of goods sold have been in 19x2 if there had been no 19x2 price changes in inventory and no LIFO liquidations?

CASE 15-8
L.O. 2

Analysis of Sale of Plant Assets—Westinghouse

Consider the condensed financial statement data for Westinghouse presented in Problem 15-14. Assume that in 19x2 Westinghouse spent $440 million on new plant and equipment. Depreciation on plant and equipment in 19x2 was $320 million. Westinghouse disposed of plant and equipment during 19x2, resulting in a pre-tax gain on sale of $650 million. Westinghouse also wrote off plant and equipment with a net book value of $250 million during 19x2.

Required:
1. What was the net book value of the plant and equipment sold at a gain of $650 million?
2. What was the apparent cash flow from the disposal of these assets?

CASE 15-9
L.O. 2

Receivables Valuation

Bradley Corporation is a wholesaler doing business with a group of retail stores in the Los Angeles area on a credit basis. Bradley reported the following balance sheet data as of the end of 19x4.

	December 31	
	19x4	19x3
Accounts receivable—Retailers . .	$5,275,100	$2,967,800
Less: Allowance for bad debts . . .	126,100	228,950
Net accounts receivable.	$5,149,000	$2,738,850

Bradley estimates bad debt expenses at 0.5% (one-half of 1%) of credit sales. All sales are on credit. Bradley has experienced significant increases in sales during the past few years, as noted in the following summary (in millions):

	For the Year		
	19x4	19x3	19x2
Credit sales . . .	$40.85	$32.70	$26.35

Required:
1. Reconstruct the adjusting journal entry that was recorded at the end of 19x4 to reflect the year-end estimate for bad debt expense.
2. Assume there are no collections on accounts once they are written off. What was the amount of write-offs recorded by Bradley during 19x4?
3. What was the amount of cash collected on accounts receivable during 19x4?
4. As a banker who has made large loans to Bradley, you are responsible for evaluating Bradley's credit position. Do you feel Bradley's creditworthiness is improving or worsening? Answer "improving" or "worsening" and give support for your answer based **only** on the data provided—**do not** assume any additional facts.

CASE 15-10 Analysis of Equipment

L.O. 2

Barth Corporation reported the following data:

	From the Balance Sheet As of December 31	
	19x9	*19x8*
Equipment at original cost	$239,500	$223,800
Less accumulated depreciation	64,600	62,000
Net equipment	$174,900	$161,800

On January 1, 19x9, Barth sold some of its equipment, which had originally cost $26,000, for $5,000 cash. This sale resulted in a pre-tax loss of $8,000. No other equipment sales took place in 19x9. You may wish to use T accounts to help you solve this problem.

Required:

1. What was the amount of accumulated depreciation on the equipment sold in 19x9?
2. What was depreciation expense for 19x9?
3. What was the original cost of new equipment acquired during 19x9?
4. Assume all equipment has **no** salvage value and is being depreciated on a "straight-line" basis (an equal amount of depreciation expense for each year of use). What is the estimated remaining useful life of Barth's equipment at the end of 19x9? (Round your answer to the nearest year. Label computations and show your work for credit.)

P A R T 4

Appendixes

APPENDIX A

Ethics and Accounting Judgments

LEARNING OBJECTIVES

After studying Appendix A, you should understand:

1. The meaning and importance of ethical behavior, pp. 874-76.
2. Some common situations that threaten ethical behavior by accountants, pp. 876-77.
3. Ethical considerations for each of the three groups of individuals in the environment of financial accounting: (*a*) managers; (*b*) owners, creditors, and other financial statement users; and (*c*) auditors, pp. 877-87.

Note: This appendix can be covered as a reading assignment any time after the completion of Chapter 2. However, some of the end-of-appendix materials require knowledge of text material through Chapter 11.

THE CONCEPTS OF ETHICS AND MORALS AND THEIR BUSINESS DIMENSIONS

Objective 1
The meaning and importance of ethical behavior.

The objective of this appendix is to introduce important aspects of ethics in business and accounting and to demonstrate their application through a series of business cases. To discuss all relevant dimensions of ethics as related to accounting and financial reporting is beyond the scope of this text. However, ethics is so fundamental to accounting judgment and to a proper understanding of business decisions that an introduction to some of the key elements is warranted.

The dictionary definitions of the word *ethics* are a bit vague, starting usually with academic and impersonal sounding phrases such as, "The study of standards of conduct and moral judgment."[1] Alternative definitions stress legalisms such as, "The rules or standards governing the conduct of the members of a profession."[2] While these definitions hint at the personal responsibilities for decisions, we must look to the definition of morals to get closer to the role of the individual: "Of or concerned with the judgment *principles of right and wrong* in relationship to *human actions or characters.*"[3] In accounting and business we are concerned with both the standards of conduct and the personal responsibility for the effects of decisions on other people and organizations.

In this appendix, we concentrate on the difficult decisions business people have to make when there are perceived rights and wrongs on both sides of an issue and when guidelines or standards do not resolve the moral dilemma. Our purpose is to initiate thought about such conflicts and to demonstrate that certain approaches, while seldom providing absolute certainty, can help a person understand the nature of the trade-offs that must be made in many business and accounting settings.

Ethics relate to how people should behave in their dealings with other people and entities, when the choice to be made has the potential to hurt or benefit others. To act in an ethical way is to choose an action that the decision maker believes is morally correct; that is, to choose what is believed to be right over what is believed to be wrong. There are many cases where most would agree on the morally correct choice, where we can easily determine who is benefiting and who is hurt and where the degree of justice of the result is clear.

In cases of murder or robbery, the immorality of the act is apparent because an unjustifiable hurt has been inflicted on the victim. Personal morals, public opinion, and laws all more or less agree that such actions are immoral. In many business situations, however, we are confronted with ethical dilemmas that cannot be so readily categorized. For instance, a scientist involved in basic research on pesticides may sincerely believe that his or her discoveries will help feed the world's people, but the same product may also endanger wildlife and humans. Typically, such a scientist in a big organization does not have the ability to determine the way a product is marketed, labeled, or packaged. If that person comes to believe that some harm is possible, should he or she cross lines of responsibility in the business organization and trace the ultimate effect of the discoveries on the ultimate user? Is it ethical to rely on government regulators to make sure all such products are safe—regulators who may not know all the effects of the product? Who is hurt by action or inaction? Who benefits?

[1]*Webster's New World Dictionary of the American Language,* 2nd college edition (World Publishing Company, 1978).

[2]*The American Heritage Dictionary* (New York: Houghton Mifflin, 1982).

[3]*Ibid.*

Business decisions affect individuals, entities, and even whole societies. Should all parties affected by a decision be viewed as capable of enjoying benefits and suffering harm? Who is hurt when a taxpayer is "over aggressive" in claiming deductions? Who benefits? Who is hurt when an insurance claim is exaggerated? Who benefits? In purely personal situations, the answers are reasonably straightforward, but what if you are the tax expert for a client who expects you to stretch the rules as far as possible, or what if you are the person responsible for making damage claims to insurance companies for your employer? Is it ethical to rely on the belief that it is up to the government or the insurance company to audit your returns or claims?

In addition to the problems created when an individual must consider the welfare of the organization as well as personal ethics, in some business settings we are confronted with even more ambiguous ethical decisions, where cultural norms may be in conflict. Consider the following case involving a U.S. company that is trying to start operations in an economically underdeveloped Eastern Bloc country. You are heading up the management team assigned to deal with officials. You find that it is common practice for certain officials who approve business permits to take bribes. Such payments are clearly illegal, but it seems that all businesses pay them and that the government is fully aware of the practice. Your management back in the states wants the new venture to get off the ground and your reputation for being an up-and-coming executive is tied to your success in this assignment. Who, besides you will benefit from going along with the local custom? The society of the underdeveloped country will benefit from the expanded consumer choices your operations will provide and there will be good jobs for local workers. Of course, the bribe-taking officials will benefit from the cash they receive. Who is harmed? General disregard for the laws of the host country certainly does not bode well for the legal system. In addition, you find out that there are U.S. laws prohibiting the giving of bribes by U.S. firms in foreign countries, even when it is an accepted local custom. This case involves trading off legal and business considerations; and, of course, lawbreaking in any jurisdiction is a serious matter and should be avoided, no matter what the seeming justification.

Consider the following case involving cross-cultural frictions, which does not hinge on an illegality. A very profitable U.S. company has the opportunity to change its raw materials supplier from a relatively high-priced local firm to a low-priced foreign firm which is located in a country run by a notorious dictator. Who would be hurt by such a decision? Employees of the domestic supplier in the local community may lose their jobs, but workers in the foreign country will be employed. Can it be said that the foreign society will be hurt by, in effect, supporting a repressive regime? On the other hand, the company might, by being an important part of the foreign economy, be able to use its influence to improve conditions there. The owners of the company will benefit from higher profits, and the consumers of the company's products will benefit from lower costs.

The cases we have discussed up to now raise many questions and point to the ethical challenges in today's business environment. While our introduction does not give a formula or rule for making such decisions, two observations might be of help in approaching such issues. First, before a person can even hope to be ethical in a complex business situation, he or she must have the competence to understand the problem. Perhaps the most common form of unethical behavior in business occurs when individuals are unwilling to admit that they might not have an appropriate grasp of the facts, or the skills to act in a certain capacity. Second, a clear and honest listing of who benefits and who is harmed by a business decision would seem to be a prerequisite to deciding what the ethical choice should be.

Ethics and Morals in an Accounting Setting

Objective 2
Some common situations that threaten ethical behavior by accountants.

While the above discussion of ethics helps us understand ethical behavior in a general sense, how does ethics relate to accounting specifically? At first you might think that accounting in conformance with generally accepted accounting principles (GAAP) defines what is ethical, while non-GAAP accounting is unethical. However, as we will see ethical choices in accounting involve more than merely determining whether the treatment of a particular transaction is in conformance with GAAP, or even if the overall financial statements are in conformance with GAAP. First, often GAAP treatment is not clear cut and also it is not unusual that the issues involved go beyond the determination of GAAP. We will see that accounting decisions have the same potential for ethical conflict as do other business decisions.

In a study conducted by Touche Ross (now Deloitte & Touche), a major international CPA firm, key business leaders, deans of business schools, and members of Congress were asked to identify which conditions threaten to undermine ethical business behavior. Of the more than 1,000 respondents to the survey, 94% said that the business community is troubled by ethical problems. The four major areas of concern, identified in Exhibit A-1, include the emphasis on short-term accounting income, which ranked as the second most important area of concern, after concern with the perceived general deterioration of our

EXHIBIT A-1

Most Threatening Conditions for American Business Ethics

Which conditions most threaten to undermine American business ethics today? Rank them from first to fourth. (Ranking points: Possible, 4,000.)

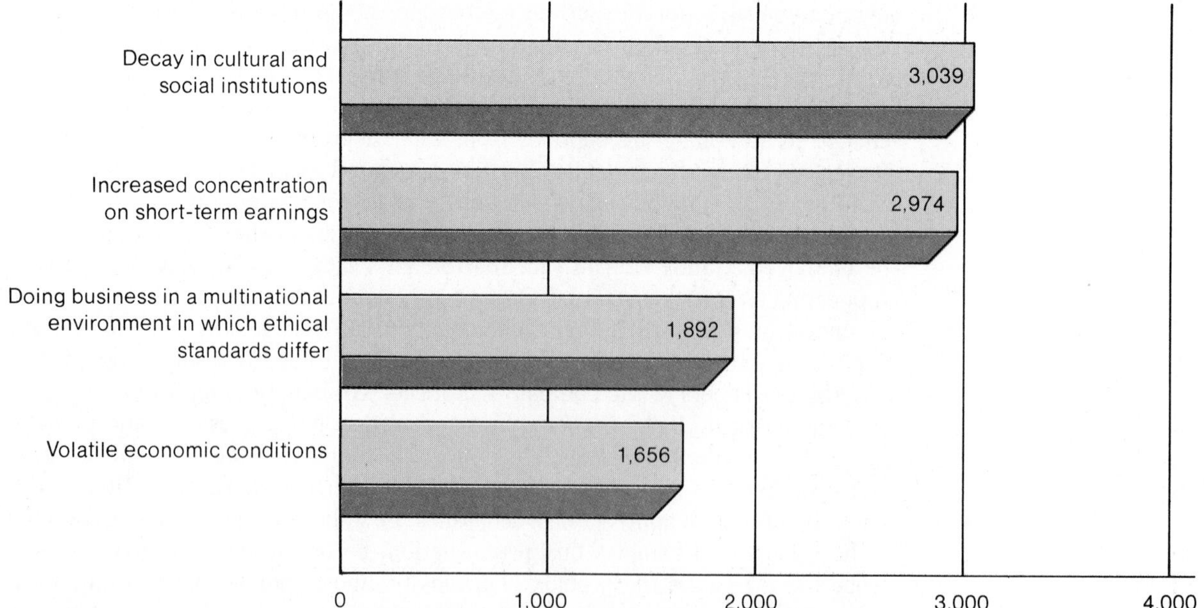

SOURCE: *Ethics in American Business* (New York: Touche Ross and Company, 1988), p. 5.

institutions. Doing business in a multinational environment and pressures related to economic volatility also were seen as putting strain on business ethics.

In what follows, we focus first on the roles of accountants and some of the formal structures designed to guide ethical behavior. Later we discuss cases where choices about accounting reports create ethical dilemmas.

Our purpose is not to identify what is morally correct in accounting reporting. Instead, we attempt to identify some basic attributes of the financial reporting environment that frequently create the need for ethical choices. While ethical standards and codes of conduct exist for both management accountants and independent public accountants,[4] these sources fail to define what is morally correct behavior. The accountant must consider his or her specific charge, the environment, and the potentially conflicting benefits and harm to all parties related to or influenced by the decision at hand.

ENVIRONMENT OF FINANCIAL ACCOUNTING

Objective 3

Ethical considerations for each of the three groups of individuals in the environment of financial accounting: (a) *managers;* (b) *owners, creditors, and other financial statement users; and* (c) *auditors.*

We will discuss how ethical considerations affect these three key groups with special interests in accounting information:

1. Managers, including managerial accountants.
2. Owners, creditors, governments, and other "external" users.
3. Independent auditors.

In most privately held corporations, partnerships, and proprietorships, some overlap exists between managers and owners. As a result, the interests of these first two groups overlap significantly; and in some small businesses, there may be no real need for the third group—independent auditors—unless the owners decide to employ an auditor to independently verify the results of the company's information system or for consulting or income tax purposes. On the other hand, even small companies may have a need for an independent audit of their accounting statements, particularly if outsiders, such as bankers or other creditors, have a significant interest in the company. Therefore, although independent audits are only legally required of publicly traded companies, many closely held corporations, partnerships, and proprietorships also employ independent auditors for various reasons.

Auditor's Responsibility

In most large companies, there is a potential conflict of interests between managers and owners. While owners are generally assumed to be interested in maximizing their wealth, the managers may key on their own compensation and their consumption of resources. As a basis for performance evaluation, managers must then report back to the owners periodically on the results of operations. Published financial statements prepared in accordance with GAAP are an important reporting mechanism in this process.

To reduce the likelihood of inaccurate reporting in management's financial statements, independent public accountants are employed to verify that the periodic financial statements of management were, in fact, prepared in conformance

[4]Specifically, the National Association of Accountant's Management Accounting Practices Committee has issued in "Standards of Ethical Conduct for Management Accountants," *Statements on Management Accounting 1C,* which provides guidance for what is appropriate ethical behavior. Also, the AICPA has a *Code of Professional Conduct* (AICPA, 1988) providing similar guidance to public accountants.

EXHIBIT A-2

Standard Audit Report

Independent Auditor's Report

Coopers & Lybrand

certified public accountants

To the Board of Directors and Stockholders
Ford Motor Company

We have audited the consolidated balance sheets of Ford Motor Company and Subsidiaries at December 31, 1988 and 1987, and the related consolidated statements of income, stockholders' equity and cash flows for each of the three years in the period ended December 31, 1988. These financial statements are the responsibility of the Company's management. Our responsibility is to express an opinion on these financial statements based on our audits.

We conducted our audits in accordance with generally accepted auditing standards. Those standards require that we plan and perform the audit to obtain reasonable assurance about whether the financial statements are free of material misstatement. An audit includes examining, on a test basis, evidence supporting the amounts and disclosures in the financial statements. An audit also includes assessing the accounting principles used and significant estimates made by management, as well as evaluating the overall financial statement presentation. We believe that our audits provide a reasonable basis for our opinion.

In our opinion, the financial statements referred to above present fairly, in all material respects, the consolidated financial position of Ford Motor Company and Subsidiaries at December 31, 1988 and 1987, and the consolidated results of their operations and their cash flows for each of the three years in the period ended December 31, 1988, in conformity with generally accepted accounting principles.

As required by a new statement of the Financial Accounting Standards Board, in 1988 the Company consolidated certain subsidiaries previously accounted for by the equity method. Financial statements for prior years have been restated to conform with the 1988 presentation, as discussed in Note 1 to the financial statements.

Coopers & Lybrand

400 Renaissance Center
Detroit, Michigan 48243
313-446-7100
February 9, 1989

SOURCE: Ford Motor Company, *1988 Annual Report*.

with GAAP and "fairly state the position and results of operations" for the periods covered by the financial statements. The standard report provided by the independent auditor, illustrated in Exhibit A-2, gives owners some confidence that management's reports are properly stated.[5]

In essence, when owners are not involved in the management of a business, they hire: (1) managers who administer the company's resources and prepare standard financial reports (e.g., balance sheets, income statements, and so on) to inform owners of their performance, and (2) independent accountants, who report to owners on the fairness of presentation of management's financial reports in conformance with GAAP. Note that independent accountants do not work for

[5]Note the similarity between this example of an audit report and that disclosed in Exhibit 15-7 (page 827) of Chapter 15, Part A. The wording is similar in both examples, as well as in other "clean" (or unqualified) audit reports.

managers, and in fact must be unrelated to management.[6] Independent auditors, therefore, first must be competent to evaluate financial reports, and also they must be independent of management so that auditors are free to express their judgments about financial statements.

Manager's Responsibility

Managers are generally hired to manage the net assets of the business because of their special management skills (i.e., marketing, financing, operating, and so on). These managers have a legal and an ethical obligation to manage the business for the benefit of the owners. They also have an obligation to follow explicit and implicit contractual terms of employment. They are stewards for the owners and their stewardship over resources has an ethical dimension. Frequently contracts between the entity and its managers provide incentive clauses to encourage managers to earn profits for the owners. For example, bonuses to managers are often not paid unless management achieves some minimum level of profits. Also, in an effort to encourage key managers to act in the best interests of the owners, businesses often reward key managers with shares of stock if they perform well. By making managers part owners in the entity, some of their wealth becomes tied to the performance of the company.

In addition to the incentives in compensation agreements and the verification of management's financial statements by the independent auditors, managers' behavior is governed by various legal responsibilities. One source of managers' legal responsibilities is defined by the Foreign Corrupt Practices Act (FCPA) passed by Congress in 1977. This act of Congress is broader than the name implies and covers the legal responsibilities of managers to safely control the entity's resources and report on the transactions and events that affect the entity's resources.[7] Businesses need not be involved with foreign entities to be covered by the FCPA.

Management accountants have a special role in safeguarding the assets of the business (the stewardship function) in that they are charged with providing information that is timely and useful for business decision making. The information provided by management accountants helps other managers make internal business decisions regarding the operating, financing, and investment activities of the entity. Management accountants also prepare the publicly disclosed financial statements for use by outside creditors, stockholders, and other potential investors to use in their investment and credit-granting decisions. It is important to understand that management prepares and has the primary responsibility for the published financial statements. Exhibit A-3 shows an example of the formal management statement regarding its responsibility for the financial statements found in published annual reports. Hence, the management accountant is charged with developing an accounting information system that has the integrity, breadth, and detail needed to provide useful information for the business decisions of both internal and external users of accounting information.

---

[6]Unrelated is used here to mean the auditor and manager have no mutually beneficial reasons for deceiving the owners. There are detailed professional standards that spell out what relationships between auditors and managers are violations of auditor independence. These are covered in detail in auditing texts.

[7]For a discussion of the Foreign Corrupt Practices Act and its implications, see *Internal Control in U.S. Corporations* (New York: Financial Executives Research Foundation, 1980).

EXHIBIT A-3

Formal Management Statement

RESPONSIBILITY FOR FINANCIAL STATEMENTS

Hershey Foods Corporation is responsible for the financial statements and other financial information contained in this report. The Corporation believes that the financial statements have been prepared in conformity with generally accepted accounting principles appropriate under the circumstances to reflect in all material respects the substance of applicable events and transactions. In preparing the financial statements, it is necessary that management make informed estimates and judgments. The other financial information in this annual report is consistent with the financial statements.

The Corporation maintains a system of internal accounting controls designed to provide reasonable assurance that financial records are reliable for purposes of preparing financial statements and that assets are properly accounted for and safeguarded. The concept of reasonable assurance is based on the recognition that the cost of the system must be related to the benefits to be derived. The Corporation believes its system provides an appropriate balance in this regard. The Corporation maintains an Internal Auditing Department which reviews the adequacy and tests the application of internal accounting controls.

The financial statements have been examined by Arthur Andersen & Co., independent public accountants, whose appointment was ratified by stockholder vote at the stockholders' meeting held on April 27, 1987. Their report expresses an opinion that the Corporation's financial statements are fairly stated in conformity with generally accepted accounting principles, and they have indicated to us that their examination was performed in accordance with generally accepted auditing standards and, accordingly, included reviewing the internal accounting controls and conducting other auditing procedures they deemed necessary.

The Audit Committee of the Board of Directors of the Corporation, consisting solely of outside directors, meets regularly with the independent public accountants, internal auditors and management to discuss, among other things, the audit scopes and results. Arthur Andersen & Co. and the internal auditors both have full and free access to the Audit Committee, with and without the presence of management.

SOURCE: Hershey Foods Corporation, *1988 Annual Report.*

ETHICAL JUDGMENT AND THE MEANING OF GAAP

One of the most important parts of the standard audit report is that which tells the owners (and other users) that the accounting reports of management were prepared in accordance with GAAP. The meaning of GAAP, however, is a matter of judgment. Sometimes a specific rule may apply to a transaction, but it is possible that no rule fits the facts exactly. In such cases accountants have a hierarchy of authoritative sources to consult. If a question concerning whether something is a generally accepted accounting principle is not addressed by the first level of authority, the second level should then be considered, and so on, until some basis for choice can be established. Exhibit A-4 summarizes the three levels of authority that comprise GAAP.[8] In essence, to say that a practice or procedure is in conformance with GAAP requires either a specific reference to an authoritative source (e.g., *FASB Statements*), or a reference to the general use and acceptance of the practice or procedure.

While the sources of authoritative support for GAAP are voluminous, many specific transactions or adjustments encountered in practice are not explicitly addressed. These situations require in-depth knowledge of business practices, ac-

[8]For a discussion of GAAP, see "The House of GAAP," *Journal of Accountancy* (June 1984), pp. 122–29. For authoritative reference to sources of GAAP, see *Statement on Auditing Standards No. 43* (New York: AICPA, 1982).

EXHIBIT A-4

Authoritative Sources for Determining What Procedures Constitute Generally Accepted Accounting Principles (GAAP)

Level One:

1. *FASB Statements* (1974 to the present)
2. *APB Opinions* (1960–73).
3. *AICPA Accounting Research Bulletins* (1953–59)
4. *FASB Interpretations* (1974 to the present)

Level Two:

1. *AICPA Accounting Interpretations* (1960–73)
2. *FASB Technical Bulletins*
3. *AICPA Statements of Position*

Level Three:

1. Documented prevalent industry practices and procedures
2. *FASB Concepts Statements*
3. *APB Statements*
4. Documented textbook procedures
5. Documented acceptance from other professional or academic literature

counting theory, and professional judgment on the part of both management's internal accountants and the independent auditors. Ethical considerations are perhaps most important and most difficult to apply in these judgment situations. Where there is no direct authoritative guidance, managers may be inclined to account in a way that maximizes their own welfare. On the other hand, the auditor may disagree with management's judgment. In such uncertain situations where there is no clear authoritative basis, it may be difficult to convince management that a different accounting treatment is necessary to avoid a qualification of the audit opinion.

Two Cases Concerning GAAP and Ethical Judgments

To illustrate such reporting dilemmas, consider the following two cases, Fly-by-Night Travel and "20/20 hindsight." Fly-by-Night is a new travel agency that specializes in booking flights to Florida over winter and spring breaks at deep discount fares. Its first four flights for spring break of 19x2 are sold out by December 31, 19x1. There is also a waiting list of 250 students who want tickets. Refund of ticket prices to students requires a cancellation notice by January 31, 19x2, for a full refund, and by February 28, 19x2, for a partial refund. The manager of Fly-by-Night is paid a salary based on reported net income and wants to include all bookings for the 19x2 spring break as sales revenue for the 19x1 income statement instead of recording them as 19x2 sales. The owners of Fly-by-Night Travel have no other travel agencies (yet) but have employed you to audit this new venture as well as their other 35 unrelated business operations. You are not sure whether to permit Fly-by-Night to record sales revenues for these four sold-out flights in the 19x1 income statement. How do you decide?

Note that while GAAP does provide rather specific directives as to when to recognize revenue, the ultimate decision is still based on professional judgment. The auditor must decide whether to disagree with the manager of Fly-by-Night, and if so, on what grounds. To disagree will cost the manager salary, providing economic incentives for the manager to argue in support of recording the revenue in 19x1. Who can be hurt by recording revenue in 19x1? If the financial statements are relied upon by creditors or stockholders and it turns out that the revenues are not legitimate, then those parties could be hurt. If the auditor forces the issue, the client may choose to change auditors; and, therefore, both the auditor and the audit firm may be harmed. How does one decide when ordinary sources do not answer the question? Auditors could use industry practice as one basis for making a determination. Another pervasive approach to such gray areas is to reason by analogy. If GAAP covers a closely related type of transaction, the arguments may be compelling for the case at hand.

The Fly-by-Night case is but one example of the potential conflict of interests between owners, managers, and auditors. Each year there are literally thousands of conflicts whose resolutions have a material impact on the financial reports of publicly owned companies.

The second case, aptly named "20/20 hindsight," focuses on a Senate hearing. Consider the following exchange between a U.S. senator and a senior partner of a CPA firm during a hearing before a congressional committee concerning the savings and loan crisis. The senator is referring to the chart shown here.

Senator: You are familiar with the MII, FSI, DLI affiliation as is shown on Chart A.

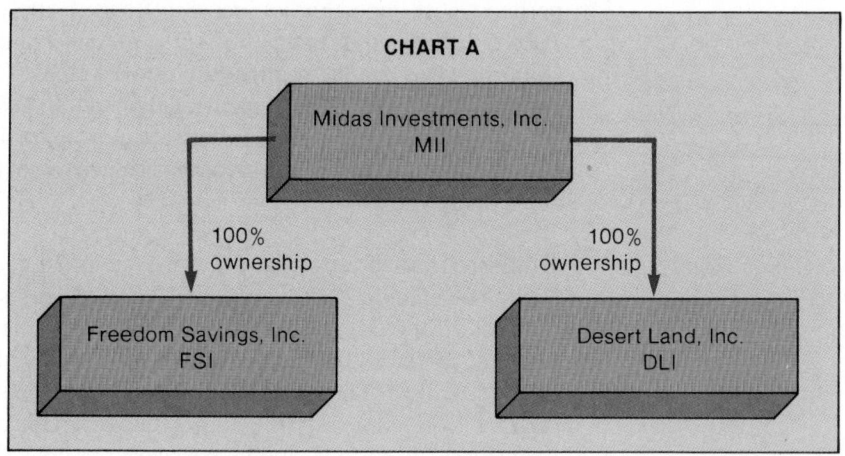

CPA: Yes, my firm was the external auditor of MII and subsidiaries from 1980 until we resigned from the engagement in 1988.

Senator: Now, I want you to verify that the series of transactions depicted in Chart B approximately describes the major cash flows within the group made up by MII and its subsidiaries during the period 1985–87.

As you know, our problem is that $300,000,000 of federally insured FSI depositor accounts will now have to be paid by the government because the notes FSI accepted and the land which is the collateral on those notes are now worth, on average, 10 cents on the dollar. Do you agree that this is in general what happened?

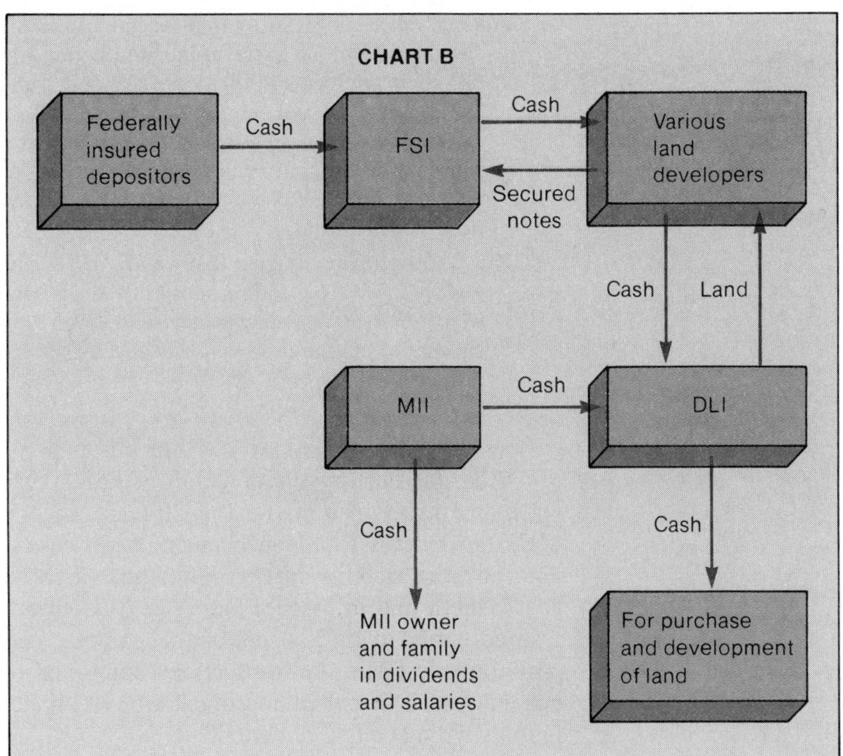

CPA: Yes, Senator, I believe that you have summarized the major features, but please keep in mind that we, as independent CPAs, didn't know back when FSI recorded those notes and DLI recognized the revenue on the sale of the land that the various land developers were not financially viable and that the land would reduce in value. At the time, we believed that the sale met all GAAP requirements and in the two years following, we have forced write-downs of the notes on FSI's balance sheet as we saw problems of collectibility emerge.

Senator: Yes, but didn't you sketch out this pattern yourself before you gave clean opinions in 1986 and 1987? Couldn't you tell that this whole scheme of cash flows from insured depositors to the MII owners didn't seem quite right?

CPA: In hindsight, it looks obvious, but remember, Senator, that the regulations governing S&L investments were liberalized in the 80s to allow a great variety of investments and certainly many S&Ls were engaged in similar transactions, most of which were approved by the regulators at the time.

Senator: I always felt that when you issued a clean opinion on the overall financial statements that you investigated the underlying economics of the transactions and made sure that they were real and made economic sense.

CPA: I can assure you, Senator, that at the time we analyzed every major transaction, our working papers prove that, and we applied generally accepted auditing standards in all cases. In hindsight, we, like everyone else, see that the land values were overstated and that the cash actually flowed out of FSI to the parent company and because of a general collapse in the real estate market, the parent is now bankrupt. But we contend that your own regulators, in essence, approved of such transactions at the time; therefore, it was normal industry practice.

Senator: All I know, Sir, is that federally insured deposits were used to finance speculation and an extravagant lifestyle for a handful of corporate executives and their families and that your issuing a series of clean opinions was a contributing factor. You can say that you were in conformance with GAAP but I say that you had a professional responsibility to make sure that the economics were sound and that Federal Savings did not engage in such risky loans or at least that the cash could not flow from insured deposits to the owners' business the way it did.

CPA: I respectfully disagree that we are responsible for the actions of the parties involved. We have the responsibility to determine if the financial statements were reported in conformance with GAAP, and we did that. If a business chooses to engage in risky loans and if the regulations allow that, we are not responsible for such losses.

Who was hurt by the downfall of FSI? Who benefited? Does this case involve an ethical dilemma for the CPA, the accounting profession, the owners of MII, the Congress? Obviously much of this case depends on the valuation of the land and the viability of the purchasers of the land. If these "sales" were not arm's length and in essence were just a scheme to divert cash from a federally insured entity to the owners of the parent company, and if the CPAs did not properly investigate the transactions, then a professional lapse certainly did occur, but can it be called an ethical lapse without a conscious decision to take a morally wrong course of action?

In both of these cases, there was obvious pressure on the auditor to agree with management's interpretation of the appropriate accounting for the transactions at issue. Auditors must be both competent and independent so that they can judge for themselves what the appropriate treatment should be, and so that they will be free to report their positions regardless of management's desires.

To maintain an independent position as a representative of owners and other parties places an important responsibility on the auditor. A contributing environmental factor is that the auditor interacts relatively less with the true client (the owners, creditors, and general public) than with management and representatives of outside groups when performing the audit. Nonetheless, auditors must maintain both an ethical and an independent attitude, particularly in gray areas where professional judgment is called upon to decide whether management's chosen accounting procedures are acceptable. Yet, without an ethical and independent posture, the services of the independent auditor are of no value to creditors, stockholders, or the public at large. As such, ethical and independent behavior and competence must be the hallmarks of the public accounting profession.

PROFESSIONAL ETHICS

Independent public accountants have met the challenges of a changing, increasingly more complex business environment. In the Touche Ross study noted earlier, participants were asked to identify the professions which they thought had the highest ethical standards. The results, reported here in Exhibit A-5, reveal that accountants are ranked second only to clergy in terms of their ethical standards and were perceived somewhat more ethical than both teachers and engi-

EXHIBIT A-5

Most Ethical Professions

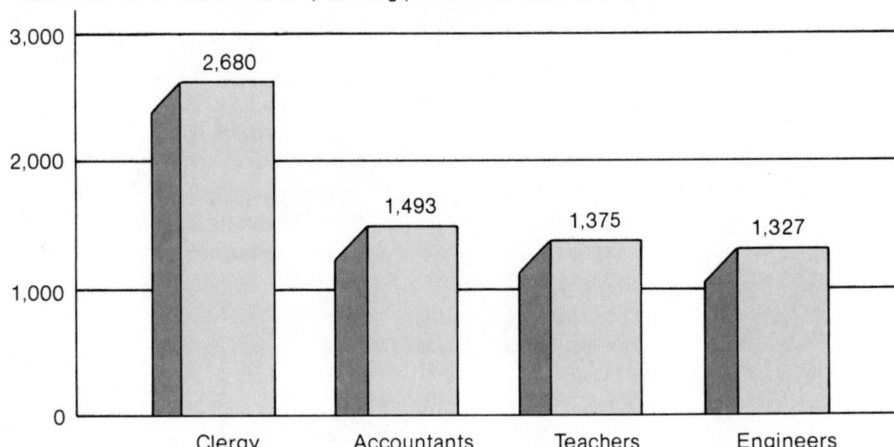

SOURCE: *Ethics in American Business* (New York: Touche Ross and Company, 1988), p. 7.

neers. Still, the challenge to improve the quality of audit services continues, and the auditing profession has responded with changes in their ethical structure in an effort to meet these challenges.

Supporting Ethical Structure

What can be done to enhance ethical behavior in business and accounting? The participants of the Touche Ross study were asked to identify measures which were most and least likely to encourage ethical business behavior. The results, reported in Exhibit A-6, reveal a considerable amount of disagreement. The strongest response found that 55% of the participants thought **new legislation** would be the **least effective** way to encourage ethical behavior, while 20% thought it would be most effective. Codes of business ethics were considered to be the most effective way to encourage ethical behavior by 39% of the respondents, followed by 30% who felt business education could enhance ethical behavior.

To enhance the ethical behavior and independent image of the auditor, the public accounting profession and individual CPA firms have both established several supporting structures. Most notable are:

1. The profession's Public Oversight Board (POB) and the Peer Review Process.
2. The profession's Code of Professional Conduct and the AICPA's Professional Ethics Executive Committee.
3. Audit firms' quality control procedures.

The first two structures provide an audit quality assurance program (monitored by the POB) and a vehicle for resolving questions concerning ethical practices and positions. The third structure is used within each firm to assure that individual auditors perform in a professional manner.

EXHIBIT A-6

Most and Least Effective Measures for Encouraging Ethical Business Behavior

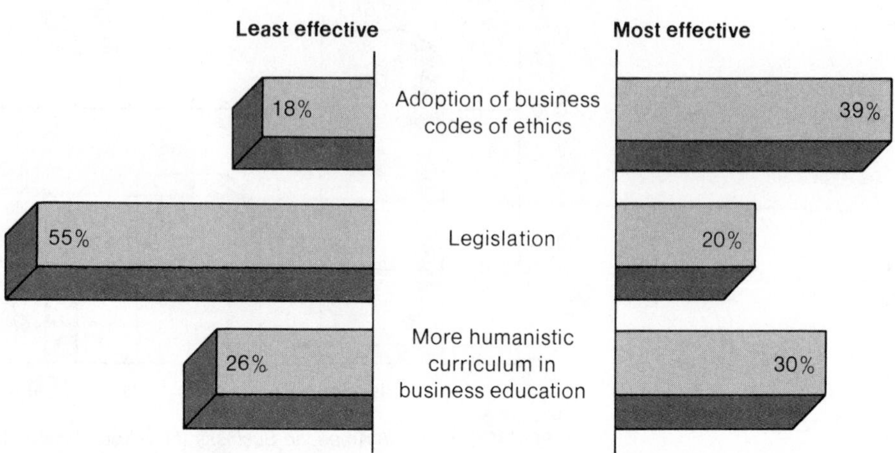

SOURCE: *Ethics in American Business* (New York: Touche Ross and Company, 1988), p. 14.

The POB and the Peer Review Process

The **Public Oversight Board (POB)** and **peer review process** were established as an outgrowth of public concern over the ethical and independent behavior of the public accounting profession. In the mid-1970s, Congress conducted an investigation of the "Accounting Establishment," which was critical of the public accounting profession. Citing those rare cases of audit failure, Congress recommended more professional oversight of public accounting practices. As a result of the congressional inquiry and the 1976 staff report on its findings, the POB and peer review process were established. (Peer review calls for the auditing and reporting practices of each CPA firm conducting audits of publicly owned corporations—those firms with clients that are registered with the SEC—to be examined once every three years by another CPA firm.) Since the process began in 1979, some 3,000 peer reviews have been conducted. In most reviews, suggestions for improvements are made, followed by responses to suggestions made by the firm being reviewed. A more complete diagram of the structure and procedures of the POB and the peer review process is provided in Exhibit A-7.

The **Code of Professional Conduct** and the **AICPA's Professional Ethics Executive Committee** provide a second major source of structure for accounting ethics. The Code of Ethics consists of 11 rules of conduct to guide auditors in determining appropriate behavior and to enhance the quality of audit services. The role of the Professional Ethics Executive Committee is to provide interpretations and rulings regarding the Code of Conduct. The committee is also in charge of the joint ethics enforcement program between the AICPA and the (50) individual state societies.

The audit practitioner, either as a firm or as an individual, has a great incentive to be perceived as both competent and independent. These attributes create the value of audit services; and, therefore, there is a self-governing mecha-

EXHIBIT A-7

The POB and the Peer Review Process

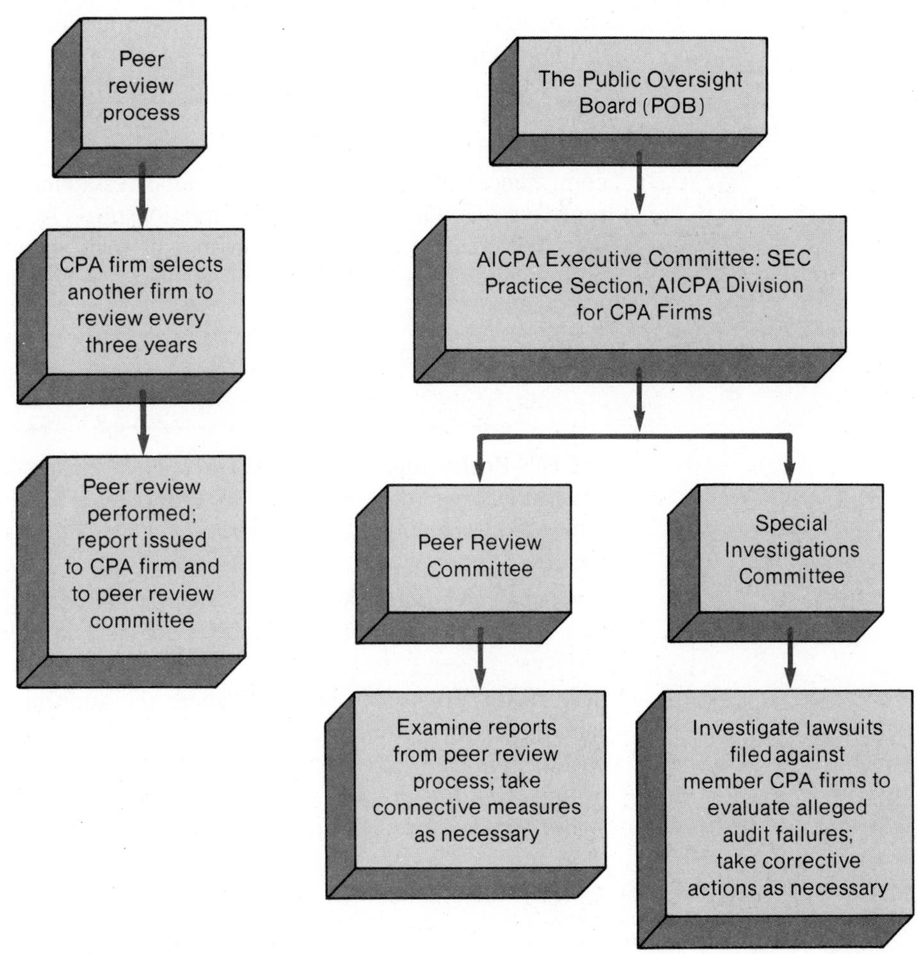

nism at work in the auditing profession. Because auditors are keenly aware of the value of professional reputation, they establish many procedures to maintain ethical standards. One such procedure would be to rotate auditors on specific client engagements. Another would be to have staff who are not assigned to the specific client review the audit procedures and the resulting audit report. Auditing textbooks cover many similar procedures which are instituted in the private sector to promote professionalism.

SUMMARY

While ethical considerations are important to the integrity of all activities of a business enterprise—from marketing to production to warranty service after the sale—they are the lifeblood of accounting. In particular, the practices of public accounting would not exist were it not for the independent ethical behavior of CPAs, and the value of managerial accountants would be diminished if they absolved themselves from the resolution of ethical dilemmas. Ethics, therefore, is a cornerstone of the accounting process.

This appendix discussed the structure and environmental factors affecting ethics in business and accounting. Judgments about justification of the harm and the benefit resulting from chosen courses of action lie at the heart of ethical decision making.

Accountants are charged with providing information about all types of relationships among people, business entities, not-for-profit entities, and governmental units. If their services are to enhance society, accountants must have competence and integrity. That is, financial statements must be viewed as representative of underlying economic relationships. Accountants, who are charged with the creation and communication of such statements, must be considered both competent and ethical by all parties.

KEY TERMS

AICPA's Professional Ethics Executive Committee. Provides interpretations and rulings regarding the Code of Professional Ethics and is in charge of the ethics enforcement program between the AICPA and the (50) individual state societies.

Code of Professional Conduct. Consists of 13 rules of conduct to guide auditors in determining appropriate behavior and to enhance the quality of audit services.

Peer review process. Process where the auditing and reporting practices of each CPA firm conducting audits of publicly owned corporations are examined once every three years by another CPA firm.

Public Oversight Board (POB). Structure to provide an audit quality assurance program and to resolve questions concerning practices and positions.

CASES

CASE A-1 GAAP Disclosures

L.O. 2, 3

United Mines, Inc., has copper and gold mining operations throughout the world. You as the new controller must decide on the amount of detailed geographical breakdown to show in the current year's financial statements. GAAP states that if at least 10% of sales or 10% of identifiable assets are related to a specific nondomestic geographical area then net revenue, operating profit, and identifiable assets for that foreign operation must be identified and disclosed in a footnote to the financial statement.

You have the following summary of operations (in thousands):

	U.S.	*Argentine*	*Brazil*	*The Union of South Africa*	*Zimbabwe*	*Total*
Sales	57,570	14,780	28,600	40,500	21,400	162,850
Operating profit	5,400	1,800	3,500	6,900	2,100	19,700
Identifiable assets	80,000	20,500	58,200	72,900	12,500	244,100

The president of the company tells you that because investment in South Africa is controversial and that it might offend some stockholders, she wants you to disclose the following breakdown of foreign operations (in thousands) which she says is in conformance with GAAP.

	U.S.	*South America*	*Africa*	*Total*
Sales	57,570	43,380	61,900	162,850
Operating profit. . . .	5,400	5,300	9,000	19,700
Identifiable assets. . .	80,000	78,700	85,400	244,100

Required:
Assuming that the suggested disclosure is in conformance with GAAP, is there an ethical dilemma? Who can be hurt by the alternative chosen? Who can benefit?

CASE A-2
L.O. 2, 3

Banking

You are a loan officer for First City Bank and you have the following dilemma. A minority owned construction contractor has applied for a loan of $2,000,000 and has provided you with financial statements that show reasonably profitable operations and a reasonable balance sheet. The major item of value is a warehouse building that currently has a book value of $3,500,000 and it would be the major collateral for the loan. You visit the sight and determine that it is a sound business and suitable for the purpose, but it is located in a part of town where property values have plummeted in recent years because of urban flight and arson. You consult a real estate expert and he says that the building has little resale value, perhaps only $800,000. Your problem is that if the loan is granted the building will be used profitably, and that a substitute in a more desirable part of town would cost in excess of $8,000,000. If the asset is revalued, the balance sheet ratios used in determining creditworthiness will call for a rejection of the loan, but if the historic book value is maintained the loan will meet the technical hurdles. You consult a CPA who says that businesses do not revalue assets such as buildings to market value as long as it is expected that the assets will be utilized in the expected fashion and that the business is a going concern. Of course, ordinary depreciation is taken.

You believe that if the loan is not forthcoming there is grave doubt about the future of the business.

Required:
1. What is the ethical consideration in this case and how does accounting interact with it?
2. Who can be hurt and who can be helped by your decision and what is the justification for those possible effects?

CASE A-3
L.O. 2, 3

Accounting Judgment

Zero Queen, Inc., owns 10 factories which manufacture sports equipment. You are auditing one of these plants where they make ski equipment. The inventory records revealed the following data:

	Units of Inventory		
Item	*Beginning Inventory*	*Made during Year*	*Ending Inventory*
Pro K-3	1,000	13,500	600
Status RX7	2,800	36,500	2,000
ZQ 442	4,200	0	3,800
North Slop 88	3,600	45,000	2,900
Air Tuk 4ZK	1,800	53,000	2,000

The ZQ 442s represent about 40% of the reported cost of ending inventory. The material used to make these skis is no longer used in production. Newer makes use material that maintains its flexibility three times longer than the material used in the ZQ model. You recommend that the company write down the inventory or write it off. When presented with this suggestion, the controller tells you she is confident that all remaining units will eventually be sold at cost or above.

Required:
1. What is the ethical decision choice situation depicted in this exercise?
2. Identify factors that could convince you the controller's judgment is morally correct.
3. Identify factors that could convince you the controller's judgment is wrong.
4. Would you require a write-down of the inventory based on the facts provided?

CASE A-4
L.O. 2, 3

Ethical Behavior

In January 1988, XYZ Publishing Company published a new introductory marketing textbook designed for the basic undergraduate marketing course taught in most colleges and universities. As is common practice in the textbook publishing industry, the company and its sales staff identified the people at each school who had recently taught the introductory marketing course and sent them a "desk copy" of the text (at no charge to the recipient) to encourage teachers to look their product over for possible selection as the book to be used in the introductory classes.

These desk copies were clearly stamped "complimentary copy—for professional use only—NOT for resale." This label is designed to keep the faculty from taking their desk copies and selling them to the "used" book salespersons who come to faculty offices offering to buy these desk copies for cash. Working in coordination with college textbook stores, these book salespersons then sell these desk copies to students as new books, or perhaps at a slight discount from the price of a new book.

The book introduced in January 1988 was for a fairly large market. A total of 5,000 complimentary copies were sent to marketing faculty as desk copies. For the first year of sales, the book sold 10,000 units, of which 4,000 were desk copies and 6,000 were units on which the publisher (and the authors) earned profits. Because the break-even point for this book is 8,000 units per year, XYZ is probably not going to revise the text and publish a second edition.

Required:
Identify at least one ethical decision choice situation in this case. Indicate what the appropriate (morally correct) choice should be from your viewpoint. Who are the "winners" and "losers" in this situation?

CASE A-5
L.O. 2, 3

Ethical Behavior

In early January 19x8, the controller of the Wardel Corporation began to worry about the level of the corporation's profits for the most recently completed year. While the final results for 19x7 were not yet known, it appeared as though profits would not enable top management to maximize their bonus plan for 19x7. The 19x7 bonus plan is structured as follows:

*Profit Range**	*Bonus Pool*
Below $20 million	0% of profits
$20–$29 million	2% of profits
$30–$39 million	3% of profits
$40–$49 million	4% of profits
$50 million or more	5% of profits

*Profit is net income before taxes and bonuses per GAAP (rounded to the nearest million).

The preliminary estimate by the corporate controller is that profits will be about \$27 million. The controller has also made the following estimates of the effect on profits of certain possible year-end adjusting entries that are being considered:

Possible Adjustment	*Affect on Profits*
a. Change estimated life of factory building . . .	+\$10 million
b. Change estimate of warranty costs	+ 3 million
c. Change amount of estimated bad debts	+ 1 million
	+\$14 million

The controller is in his last year of employment before retirement. His retirement plan provides an amount during each year of retirement that is based on the average of his last five years' income (salary plus bonus).

Required:

1. Identify the decision choice situation in this case.
2. From the stockholders' point of view, what is the morally correct decision choice?
3. From the controller's point of view, what is the morally correct decision choice?
4. If you were the controller, what arguments could you make in support of the three possible adjustments?
5. Assume the controller makes all three adjustments and that profit turns out to be \$39.6 million. As the independent auditor of Wardel Corporation, what would you do?

CASE A-6
L.O. 2, 3

Ethical Decisions

Acquire Chemicals, Inc. (ACI), has been manufacturing sealants and adhesives at its plant just outside a major metropolitan area for 30 years. The state's Department of Natural Resources has started an investigation into accusations of illegal dumping of dangerous chemicals by ACI at its plant site and by the independent waste disposal company, Caper Sanitation, Inc. (CSI), that has been disposing of all of ACI's waste for the past eight years.

It is now February 10, 19x2, and you, as controller of ACI, are trying to decide if some mention of the investigation is warranted in the annual report for the year ended 12/31/x1. Your independent auditor gives the following advice:

> The department's report will not be made public until at least June. We now have no way of knowing what the outcome will be, what their recommendation will be, what the cleanup costs, if any, will amount to, and we don't even know how much the insurance company or CSI would pick up if some cleanup is necessary. So, I say we are completely justified in ignoring this one for the time being. Companies are investigated all the time. If we mentioned every one before something reasonably concrete is known or at least some indication is given, our annual reports would be as thick as telephone books.

What your auditor doesn't know is that your sister-in-law, who works for the Department of Natural Resources, told you "off the record" that preliminary findings were that a massive cleanup would probably be necessary, both at the plant site and by CSI, which it turns out was not properly licensed for such work. There is no way for you to get official confirmation of her statement without violating her confidence. On your own, you have studied other cleanup cases in the state and you estimate that if what your sister-in-law says is true, the range of costs to the company would be from \$25,000,000 to \$75,000,000. ACI's net income for 19x1, a very profitable year, before consideration of the cleanup was just over \$20,000,000.

You report directly to the president of the company and she has made it quite clear that she expects to see a healthy bottom line in the 19x1 income statement and in general an upbeat annual report, because she plans several major financing initiatives including bank borrowings and the issuance of preferred stock.

Required:

1. Who could be helped or hurt by mention of the investigation in the annual report?
2. What steps would you go through to determine the best course of action?
3. Assume that you decide to recommend a full discussion of all possible outcomes in the annual report, and the president of the company consults with and agrees with the auditor that no mention should be made. What steps would you take?

APPENDIX B

International Accounting

LEARNING OBJECTIVES

After studying Appendix B, you should understand:

1. How to measure and disclose foreign currency transaction gains and losses, pp. 898-900.
2. How to "hedge" to avoid transaction gains and losses, p. 901.
3. How to measure and disclose translation gains and losses, pp. 901-3.
4. The general nature of differences between U.S. GAAP and foreign financial reporting rules, pp. 903-7.

Note: This appendix may be covered anytime after Chapter 6. It works well when combined with Appendix C on price changes, since both appendixes involve conversion of unlike measures to like measures on two somewhat different dimensions. This appendix is probably most effective if covered after Chapter 12 or toward the end of the course.

Due largely to faster and more efficient transportation and communication systems, the magnitude and importance of international business have increased dramatically in the past few decades. Today, most large businesses in developed nations view the world as their marketplace, and virtually all countries have businesses with significant international operations. We hear news about "the dollar" and its gains against the British pound or losses against the French franc as often as news about changes in stock price indexes like "the Dow" (the Dow Jones Index of 30 Industrial Stocks) or "the NYSE Index" (the New York Stock Exchange Index of 500 stocks).

The objective of this appendix is to introduce the language and basic accounting concepts of international business operations. While international accounting is not covered completely in this appendix, the basic accounting concepts of international businesses explained here should facilitate reading financial statements of companies with foreign operations.

STRENGTH OF THE DOLLAR

What does it mean to have a strong or weak dollar? The strength of the U.S. dollar is measured by how many units of a foreign currency the dollar will purchase, known as its **exchange rate.** Exchange rates may fluctuate daily and are published each day in the financial press. Exhibit B-1 provides a sample of exchange rates for the U.S. dollar. On the Thursday reported in Exhibit B-1, a U.S. dollar would purchase 144.15 Japanese yen, or 1.1875 Canadian dollars, or 1.4875 Swiss francs.

The exchange rate changes are based on the supply and demand of various currencies, which in turn are based on the relative demand for a country's goods and services. If the change in exchange rates enables the dollar to purchase more Japanese yen, the dollar is said to be "stronger" against the yen, and the cost of Japanese goods in U.S. dollars should become cheaper, all else being equal. At the same time, the cost of U.S. goods in Japanese yen would become more expensive. Therefore, if you were spending U.S. dollars in Japan you would want the dollar to strengthen against the yen so your dollars would buy more. However, if you were exporting U.S. products to Japan, a stronger dollar would probably cause you to increase your selling prices in yen and therefore would reduce sales of your products. As a result, it is not obvious whether a stronger dollar is good news or bad news!

To U.S. exporters, the weakening of the U.S. dollar is usually good news and would tend to improve the U.S. "balance of payments," which is based on whether a nation imports more than it exports. To U.S. travelers in foreign countries, a weaker U.S. dollar is bad news since it will take more U.S. dollars to acquire food, lodging, and so on. As the U.S. dollar weakens against foreign currencies, we expect U.S. goods and services to be more attractive to foreign consumers, and foreign goods and services to be less attractive to U.S. consumers.

How are changes in exchange rates reflected in financial reports of U.S. companies doing business in foreign countries? Publicly owned businesses that operate in more than one country are called **multinational corporations.** The U.S. financial statements of multinational corporations report the position and operating results of both foreign and U.S. activities together, stated in U.S. dol-

EXHIBIT B-1

Exchange Rates

CURRENCY MARKETS

EXCHANGE RATES

Thursday, January 25, 1990

The New York foreign exchange selling rates below apply to trading among banks in amounts of $1 million and more, as quoted at 3 p.m. Eastern time by Bankers Trust Co. Retail transactions provide fewer units of foreign currency per dollar.

	U.S. $ equiv.		Currency per U.S. $	
Country	**Thurs.**	**Wed.**	**Thurs.**	**Wed.**
Argentina (Austral) ...	.0005587	.0005587	1790.03	1790.03
Australia (Dollar)	.7587	.7625	1.3180	1.3115
Austria (Schilling)	.08420	.08391	11.88	11.92
Bahrain (Dinar)	2.5971	2.5971	.3851	.3851
Belgium (Franc)				
Commercial rate	.02834	.02823	35.29	35.42
Financial rate	.02833	.02823	35.30	35.43
Brazil (Cruzado)	.06361	.06517	15.72	15.35
Britain (Pound)	1.6575	1.6517	.6033	.6054
30-Day Forward	1.6485	1.6424	.6066	.6089
90-Day Forward	1.6306	1.6250	.6133	.6154
180-Day Forward	1.6058	1.6002	.6227	.6249
Canada (Dollar)	.8421	.8428	1.1875	1.1865
30-Day Forward	.8391	.8398	1.1917	1.1907
90-Day Forward	.8342	.8351	1.1987	1.1975
180-Day Forward	.8288	.8297	1.2065	1.2052
Chile (Official rate) ...	.003875	.003875	258.09	258.09
China (Yuan)	.211775	.211775	4.7220	4.7220
Colombia (Peso)	.002314	.002314	432.18	432.18
Denmark (Krone)	.1531	.1535	6.5300	6.5150
Ecuador (Sucre)				
Floating rate	.001443	.001443	693.00	693.00
Finland (Markka)	.25157	.25157	3.9750	3.9750
France (Franc)	.17445	.17382	5.7324	5.7530
30-Day Forward	.17411	.17345	5.7435	5.7652
90-Day Forward	.17328	.17261	5.7709	5.7935
180-Day Forward	.17205	.17138	5.8124	5.8350
Greece (Drachma)	.006345	.006321	157.60	158.20
Hong Kong (Dollar) ...	.12801	.12801	7.8120	7.8120
India (Rupee)	.05900	.05900	16.95	16.95
Indonesia (Rupiah)	.0005571	.0005571	1795.01	1795.01
Ireland (Punt)	1.5712	1.5719	.6365	.6362
Israel (Shekel)	.5319	.5319	1.8799	1.8799
Italy (Lira)	.0007967	.0007938	1255.26	1259.76
Japan (Yen)	.006937	.006867	144.15	145.62
30-Day Forward	.006946	.006877	143.96	145.41
90-Day Forward	.006958	.006889	143.71	145.16
180-Day Forward	.006977	.006907	143.32	144.78
Jordan (Dinar)	1.5399	1.5399	.6494	.6494
Kuwait (Dinar)	3.4403	3.4403	.2907	.2907
Lebanon (Pound)	.001808	.001808	553.00	553.00
Malaysia (Ringgit)	.3699	.3698	2.7035	2.7045
Malta (Lira)	2.9851	2.9851	.3350	.3350
Mexico (Peso)				
Floating rate	.0003698	.0003698	2704.02	2704.02
Netherland (Guilder) .	.5260	.5242	1.9010	1.9075
New Zealand (Dollar)	.5950	.5925	1.6807	1.6878
Norway (Krone)	.1534	.1534	6.5200	6.5175
Pakistan (Rupee)	.0471	.0471	21.25	21.25
Peru (Inti)	.00008057	.00008057	12411.57	12411.57
Philippines (Peso)	.04598	.04598	21.75	21.75
Portugal (Escudo)	.006628	.006628	150.88	150.88
Saudi Arabia (Riyal) ..	.26681	.26681	3.7480	3.7480
Singapore (Dollar)	.5329	.5333	1.8765	1.8750
South Africa (Rand)				
Commercial rate	.3906	.3912	2.5602	2.5562
Financial rate	.3034	.3007	3.2960	3.3256
South Korea (Won)	.0014624	.0014624	683.80	683.80
Spain (Peseta)	.009141	.009113	109.40	109.73
Sweden (Krona)	.1622	.1626	6.1670	6.1500
Switzerland (Franc) ..	.6723	.6689	1.4875	1.4950
30-Day Forward	.6713	.6658	1.4897	1.5020
90-Day Forward	.6696	.6641	1.4935	1.5058
180-Day Forward	.6676	.6617	1.4978	1.5112
Taiwan (Dollar)	.038387	.038535	26.05	25.95
Thailand (Baht)	.03883	.03883	25.75	25.75
Turkey (Lira)	.0004310	.0004310	2320.02	2320.02
United Arab (Dirham)	.2723	.2723	3.6725	3.6725
Uruguay (New Peso)				
Financial	.001248	.001248	801.50	801.50
Venezuela (Bolivar)				
Floating rate	.02299	.02299	43.50	43.50
W. Germany (Mark) ..	.5928	.5907	1.6870	1.6930
30-Day Forward	.5929	.5908	1.6867	1.6926
90-Day Forward	.5928	.5907	1.6868	1.6928
180-Day Forward	.5922	.5902	1.6887	1.6944

SDR	1.31967	1.32042	.75777	.75733
ECU	1.20616	1.20910	....	....

Special Drawing Rights (SDR) are based on exchange rates for the U.S., West German, British, French and Japanese curren-cies. Source. International **Monetary Fund**.

European Currency Unit (ECU) is **based on a basket** of community currencies. Source: **European Community** Commission.

Source: *The Wall Street Journal,* January 26, 1990.

lars. The process of converting financial statements of those U.S. corporations with foreign businesses and subsidiaries into U.S. dollars for financial reporting purposes can result in two different types of gains and losses:[1]

1. Foreign currency **transaction** gains and losses.
2. Foreign currency **translation** gains and losses.

These two types of gains and losses are accorded different treatment by U.S. corporations, and each is explained in some detail in the sections that follow.

[1] *Statement of Financial Accounting Standards No. 52,* "Foreign Currency Translation" (Norwalk, Conn.: FASB, 1981).

FOREIGN CURRENCY TRANSACTIONS

Objective 1
How to measure and disclose foreign currency transaction gains and losses.

When U.S. companies purchase or sell goods or services with foreign companies, these transactions may result in a **transaction gain or loss.** If the transactions with foreign companies are expressed (i.e., paid off or settled) in terms of U.S. dollars, no transaction gains or losses will result for the U.S. company. However, when the transactions are expressed in terms of foreign currency (i.e., their contract calls for future payment in foreign currency), the U.S. company is "exposed" to gains or losses from currency exchange rate fluctuations between the date the transaction is originally recorded and the date a cash settlement is made. If the dollar becomes **stronger** during the "exposed" period, a transaction **gain** will result for the U.S. company making **purchases,** while a transaction **loss** will occur for U.S. companies making **sales**.

Purchase: Transaction Gain

To illustrate a transaction gain on a foreign purchase, assume U.S.A., Inc. (a U.S. company), purchases West German steel on June 2, 19x7, when the German mark is selling for U.S. \$0.50 (1 mark = U.S. \$0.50; or U.S. \$1 = 2.00 marks). The purchase price of the steel is 200,000 marks. This purchase would be recorded on the U.S. company's books in U.S. dollars as follows:

19x7			
June 2	Inventory—Steel (A)	100,000	
	Accounts Payable—W. German (L)		100,000
	To record steel purchase: 200,000 marks at U.S. \$0.50 each.		

Assume the account payable is settled in cash on June 30 when the exchange rate is U.S. \$0.40 = 1 mark (the mark has become \$0.10 cheaper, so the U.S. dollar is "stronger" against the mark). To pay off the payable still requires 200,000 marks, but the dollar cost of 200,000 marks is now only U.S. \$80,000 (200,000 marks × \$0.40 each = \$80,000), resulting in a transaction gain of \$20,000. The payment of the account payable on June 30, 19x7, would be recorded as follows:

19x7			
June 30	Accounts Payable—W. German (L)	100,000	
	Foreign Exchange Gain (R)		20,000
	Cash (A).		80,000
	To pay account for W. German steel.		

Note that if the terms of the purchase had been stated as U.S. \$100,000 instead of 200,000 marks, the U.S. company would have been required to pay \$100,000, and no foreign exchange gain or loss would have resulted for the U.S. company. (However, the West German company would then have been "exposed" to an exchange gain or loss!)

Sale: Transaction Loss

To illustrate how sales have the opposite effect of purchases, assume a U.S. company sold computer equipment to a West German shipbuilder on June 2, 19x7 (mark selling for U.S. \$0.50). The sale price is expressed as 300,000 marks, which is recorded by the U.S. company as follows:

19x7			
June 2	Accounts Receivable—W. German (A)	150,000	
	Sales Revenue (R)		150,000
	To record sale of computers for 300,000 marks.		

On June 30, 19x7, the West German company settles its obligation by paying 300,000 marks to the U.S. company, which have a dollar value of only U.S. $120,000 on that date (Exchange rate = U.S. $0.40 per mark on June 30, 19x7). The U.S. company would receive only U.S. $120,000 (300,000 marks × $0.40 each = $120,000) and would record a $30,000 foreign exchange loss as follows:

19x7			
June 30	Cash (A)	120,000	
	Foreign Exchange Loss (E)	30,000	
	Accounts Receivable—W. German (A) . . .		150,000
	To record receipt of 300,000 marks.		

Once again, if the sale contract on June 2 called for payment of U.S. dollars, no gain or loss would have resulted for the U.S. company, and U.S. $150,000 would have been received regardless of exchange rate fluctuations.

Purchase Losses and Sales Gains

Note that in the examples above, the U.S. dollar is becoming stronger against the West German mark, going from $0.50 per mark to $0.40 per mark. If the dollar had weakened, it would have resulted in a foreign exchange loss on the purchase and a foreign exchange gain on the sale. The effects of changing exchange rates on transaction gains and losses is summarized in Exhibit B-2. Whether a gain or loss occurs on a sale or purchase depends on whether the dollar is becoming weaker or stronger between the date the sale/purchase is first recorded and the date it is settled. For cash sales or purchases in any currency, there would be no foreign exchange gains or losses (since the date of first record is also the settlement date).

Unsettled Purchases and Sales

What if receivables or payables with foreign countries are not settled at year-end? Accounting rules require that "unrealized gains and losses" be measured and recorded for all unsettled foreign accounts as of the balance sheet date.[2] As a result, any unsettled receivables or payables would be adjusted at year-end to reflect year-end exchange rates, with gains or losses recorded as needed.

EXHIBIT B-2

Determining Transaction Gains and Losses

A. When the change in exchange rates between the original date of a transaction is recorded and the settlement date (date paid) enables a U.S. dollar to buy:	B. Transactions expressed in the foreign currency that are:	
	B1. Credit sales will result in a transaction	B2. Credit purchases will result in a transaction
A1. More foreign currency (e.g., dollar becomes stronger).	Loss	Gain
A2. Less foreign currency (e.g., dollar becomes weaker).	Gain	Loss

[2]Ibid.

To illustrate unrealized gains and losses, assume U.S.A., Inc., had the following information regarding its year-end receivables and payables:

	Exchange Rate at Date Purchase/ Sales Recorded	*Year-End Exchange Rate*	*Original Transaction Amount*	*Balance at Year-End before Adjustment*
Receivables:				
W. Germany . . .	$0.50 per mark	$0.40 per mark	30,000 marks	$15,000
Japan	0.01 per yen	0.02 per yen	2,000,000 yen	20,000
Payables:				
Swiss	1.50 per S. franc	1.20 per S. franc	12,000 S. francs	18,000

The unrealized gains and losses would be computed as follows:

	Original Transaction Amount	×	*Year-End Exchange Rate*	=	*Year-End Amount in U.S.*	–	*Unadjusted Year-End Balance*	=	*Resulting Gain or (Loss)*
Receivables:									
W. Germany . . .	30,000 marks	×	$0.40	=	$12,000	–	$15,000	=	$ (3,000)
Japan	2,000,000 yen	×	0.02	=	40,000	–	20,000	=	20,000
									$17,000
Payables:									
Swiss	12,000 S. franc	×	1.20	=	14,400	–	18,000	=	3,600
Net gain or (loss) . .									$20,600

U.S.A., Inc., would record the following year-end adjusting entry:

19x7			
Dec. 31	Accounts Payable—S. Franc (L)	3,600	
	Accounts Receivable—Japan (A)	20,000	
	Accounts Receivable—W. Germany (A)		3,000
	Foreign Exchange Gain—Unrealized (R)		20,600
	To record net unrealized gain on exchange rate changes.		

Disclosure

The total year-end balance in the foreign exchange gain or loss account from both realized and unrealized **transaction** gains or losses would be reported in the income statement below other gains and losses but before taxes on continuing operations, as follows:

U.S.A., Inc.
Partial Income Statement
For the Years Ending December 31
(in millions)

	19x7	*19x6*
Operating income	$287	$263
Other gains (losses)	11	(2)
Foreign exchange gains (losses) . . .	**(3)**	**6**
Income before income taxes	$295	$267
Income tax expense	(67)	(48)
Net income	$228	$219

Often the net transaction gain or loss is not material enough to appear as a separate item in the income statement. In such cases, the amount of the transaction gain or loss for the period is often reported in the "Notes to Financial Statements." The third page of the footnotes in the Ralston Purina annual report provided in Appendix E illustrates such footnote disclosure.

HEDGING AGAINST GAINS AND LOSSES

Objective 2
How to "hedge" to avoid transaction gains and losses.

Multinational corporations can **hedge** (or protect) **against gains and losses** from foreign exchange fluctuations in a number of ways. Hedging is like betting on each of two teams that are playing one another. One way to hedge against a foreign exchange loss from a **credit purchase** costing 200,000 Swiss francs (S. Fr.) would call for a **credit sale** for 200,000 Swiss francs to be made at the same time. The exchange gains or losses from the account payable and account receivable, both for S. Fr. 200,000, would offset one another as long as they were initiated on the same date and were outstanding for the same length of time. While such exact offsetting is not usually possible, hedging against large gains or losses can be accomplished by keeping approximately the same balance in receivables and payables that must be settled in any given foreign currency.

When companies cannot keep their foreign denominated receivables approximately equal to their payables, they can still hedge against losses by purchasing or selling futures contracts. **Futures contracts** (also called **forward exchange contracts**) are rights to receive a specific amount of foreign currency in exchange for a fixed number of dollars at a specified future date. To illustrate, assume a U.S. company purchased goods from Japan for 6 million yen on June 1, 19x1, on open account, to be paid on June 30, 19x1. The U.S. company could protect against exchange gains or losses by purchasing a futures contract on June 1, 19x1, to receive 6 million yen on June 30, 19x1. The purchase of this account receivable for 6 million yen would hedge the account payable for 6 million yen, preventing any gain or loss from the credit purchase. If foreign receivables are to be hedged, the U.S. company would **sell** futures contracts to other investors (e.g., foreign banks) to avoid exchange gains or losses. Of course, the easiest way to avoid transaction losses (and gains) is to negotiate all credit purchases and credit sales in terms of U.S. dollars rather than foreign currencies. This approach passes the concern over exchange rate fluctuations on to the foreign seller or buyer, who may then incur a gain or loss.

Hedging may be accomplished by (1) balancing foreign receivables with foreign payables and (2) buying or selling futures contracts to offset unhedged foreign receivables or payables. Some companies use these hedging strategies to avoid risk of foreign exchange losses. Others that are not hedged are said to be "exposed" to the risks of exchange losses. Still other companies are hedged in some foreign currencies and exposed in others.

FOREIGN CURRENCY TRANSLATION

The transaction gains or losses discussed above result from business transactions between U.S. companies and **independent** foreign companies. If the U.S. company owns a controlling interest in the foreign company, principles of consolidation require that the foreign company's financial results be reported as a part of the U.S. parent company's consolidated financial statements. The consolidation process first requires that the foreign subsidiary's financial statements be translated into U.S. dollars. This translation normally results in a **translation gain or loss,** which is accounted for in a different way than **transaction** gains or losses.

Objective 3
How to measure and disclose translation gains and losses.

Translating foreign financial reports into U.S. dollars is guided by specific accounting rules. The following exchange rates are to be applied to this translation process:

Accounts		*Exchange Rate*
• All assets and liabilities	⟶	• **Current rate** at date of the balance sheet
• Stockholders' equity accounts **other than** retained earnings	⟶	• **Historical rate** from date item was originally recorded
• Retained earnings	⟶	• Not adjusted
• Income statement accounts	⟶	• **Average rate** for the period covered by the income statement

Application of these exchange rates will normally result in a balance sheet that is out of balance, necessitating a "plug" to a special account in the stockholders' equity section of the balance sheet. To illustrate the translation process, assume that Mardot Company is a wholly owned French subsidiary of the U.S. company—Bardens, Inc. On January 1, 19x9, Mardot began its operations and was acquired by Bardens. The financial data of Mardot are stated in French francs (F. Fr.). The following exchange rate data are available on December 31, 19x9:

Time Period	*Exchange Rates (U.S.$ per F. Fr.)*
December 31, 19x9 (current)	$0.40
Historical rate for Mardot's stockholders' equity accounts . .	0.44
Average for the year 19x9	0.42

The exchange rates are applied to the French company's income statement and balance sheet to convert them to U.S. dollars, as illustrated in Exhibit B-3. Several simplifying assumptions have been made in the example illustrated. Since Mardot is 100% owned and in its first year of operations, net income for 19x9 in U.S. dollars is the same as retained earnings in U.S. dollars at the end of 19x9. The ending retained earning balance would normally be the beginning balance (in U.S. dollars), plus net income (in U.S. dollars), less dividends if any (in U.S. dollars). The plug needed to make the balance sheet (in U.S. dollars) balance—a $900,000 translation loss in this example—is the **cumulative** foreign currency translation gain or loss from all prior periods as of the end of 19x9. This is shown in a special account in stockholders' equity section of the balance sheet.[3]

The role of this special account is similar to the role of the contra stockholders' equity account used to record **unrealized losses** on marketable equity securities held as a noncurrent asset (as discussed in Chapter 12). Cumulative unrealized foreign currency translation **gains as well as losses** can be recorded in this special account. Since 19x9 is the only year of operation, the cumulative loss of $900,000 is also the loss for the year 19x9. The **change** in this cumulative

[3]See the stockholders' equity section of the Ralston Purina report in Appendix E for an example of this balance sheet disclosure.

EXHIBIT B-3

Translation of Foreign Currency

Mardot Company
Income Statement
For the Year Ended December 31, 19x9

	French Francs	*Exchange Rate*	*U.S. Dollars*
Sales	85,950,000	0.42	$ 36,099,000
Cost of goods sold	(47,280,000)	0.42	(19,857,600)
Gross margin	38,670,000	0.42	$ 16,241,400
Other expenses	(21,440,000)	0.42	(9,004,800)
Other gains (losses)	(2,950,000)	0.42	(1,239,000)
Pre-tax income	14,280,000	0.42	$ 5,997,600
Tax expense	(6,830,000)	0.42	(2,868,600)
Net income	7,450,000	0.42	$ 3,129,000

Mardot Company
Balance Sheets
December 31, 19x9

	French Francs	*Exchange Rate*	*U.S. Dollars*
Cash	1,900,000	0.40	$ 760,000
Receivables	3,875,000	0.40	1,550,000
Inventory	6,620,000	0.40	2,648,000
Plant and equipment	16,940,000	0.40	6,776,000
	29,335,000		$11,734,000
Payables	3,110,000	0.40	$ 1,244,000
Common stock	18,775,000	0.44	8,261,000
Retained earnings	7,450,000	See net income	3,129,000
Cumulative translation gains (losses)	0	Plug	(900,000)
	29,335,000		$11,734,000

translation gain or loss account from the beginning of a year to the end of that year is the annual translation gain or loss. In the example given, the dollar strengthened against the French franc during 19x9, causing an unrealized translation loss of $900,000. Bardens, Inc.'s ownership of net assets in France during a period when the French franc fell in price against the dollar caused this translation loss.

INTERNATIONAL ACCOUNTING STANDARDS

Evaluating financial reports of multinational companies is facilitated by the measurement and reporting of transaction and translation gains and losses illustrated above. However, there are many accounting differences other than currency to be considered in comparing and evaluating foreign operations. For example, while LIFO is a popular inventory method for U.S. companies, Australian accounting rules prohibit the use of LIFO inventory methods.

To help resolve these differences and to promote uniformity, the International Accounting Standards Committee (IASC) was formed in 1973 by accounting organizations in the United States, Canada, Mexico, Australia, Japan, the United Kingdom, France, West Germany, and the Netherlands. Today, more than 100 accounting organizations from 74 countries are effectively represented by the IASC, which has issued over 30 pronouncements identifying International Accounting Standards for financial reporting. At present these Standards have no real authoritative support, and have been developed to facilitate the international effort to unify accounting methods, an effort referred to as **harmonization.**[4] Multinational firms often reference these standards in their financial reports.

Differences in Financial Accounting Methods

Objective 4

The general nature of differences between U.S. GAAP and foreign financial reporting rules.

Accounting methods often differ across countries because of the varying information needs of people in different countries and because of different accounting conventions (or "habits") which have developed over time.[5] Variations in accounting methods sometimes result in substantive differences while in other cases they are simply differences in the format of presentation. For example, while U.S. firms show accumulated depreciation as a contra asset in their balance sheets, Italian firms show the accumulated depreciation on the liability side of their balance sheets! This format difference could affect the comparability of many financial statement ratios, such as return on assets, between U.S. and Italian firms, yet it is not an important difference in accounting methods. Examples of some of the more important accounting method differences are discussed next.

Asset Costs

Differences in accounting methods across countries often lead to differences in how asset costs are measured, and in some cases whether they are measured at all. For example, firms in the United States include the full cost of manufactured inventories which consists of direct material used, direct labor, and manufacturing overhead (consisting of such costs as factory supervisors' salaries and depreciation on factory buildings and equipment). This procedure, known as *full absorption costing,* is followed by many other countries too, including Japan and Great Britain. However, in countries such as India, Denmark, and Chile only the direct material and direct labor costs are included as an asset in inventory, with all manufacturing overhead costs charged against revenue in the period incurred.

In Chapter 8 of the text we noted that U.S. firms include some of the interest incurred on debt during the period when major long-term assets are being constructed as a cost of such assets. This procedure is similar to the normal treatment for interest during the construction period in over 30 countries, but it

---

[4]It is interesting to note that another international group, the International Federation of Accountants (IFAC), was established in 1977 in an effort to harmonize, or unify, international auditing standards. To date, about 30 International Auditing Guidelines (IAGs) have been developed by the IFAC's International Auditing Practices Committee.

[5]For example, in socialist and communist countries the accounting systems are usually very uniform across entities, with the government dictating a uniform set of accounts and accounting procedures in many cases. This is done to facilitate planning at the national level since the government is the primary user of accounting data in these countries.

is not permitted for French or Belgian firms where all interest is expensed in the period incurred.

As one last example of asset differences, U.S. and German firms must expense most research and development (R&D) costs as incurred. However, most other countries treat these costs as assets when they can be associated with projects that are expected to lead to future revenues in excess of their costs. These R&D assets are then expensed over their expected useful lives.

These examples are but a few of the many differences in asset measurement across countries. At first glance it would seem the use of financial ratios such as return on assets or return on stockholders' equity might enable us to evaluate a firm's relative performance and abstract away from the problems of different currencies in comparing firms from different countries. However, since the measurement of assets (or liabilities and equity) may also vary significantly from country to country, such comparisons must be made with caution. A thorough understanding of how differences in accounting methods affect the financial statements is needed before precise and meaningful comparisons can be made across countries.

Using "Reserves"

One of the major differences between U.S. accounting procedures and those of other countries is in the use of "reserves" or "appropriations." Firms in the United States, under GAAP, use allowances, which are similar to reserves, to estimate bad debts and estimated warranty costs among other things. These allowances essentially reduce the net assets in the balance sheet and reduce income (via Bad Debt Expense, Warranty Expense, and so on) as well. Such reserves (or allowances) are used in an effort to better match revenues of a period with (actual and estimated future) expenses of the period. However, U.S. firms are not allowed to use reserves or appropriations to reduce current income for expected future problems or needs such as for self-insurance or for possible shortfalls in future profits as do many foreign firms.

In many foreign countries, these "set asides" (reserves) are used to reduce income and to make offsetting reserves which usually appear either in stockholders' equity (like separate "appropriated" retained earnings accounts) or above stockholders' equity (like a liability). In some foreign firms up to 80% of stockholders' equity is made up of such reserves or appropriations. The purpose of these reserves varies, but their use often has the affect of smoothing the net income results over time. For example, Swedish companies may appropriate up to 40% of pre-tax profits, thereby avoiding taxes on these "reserves" and enabling the firm to call these pre-tax profits back into income in later years when the firm is experiencing less profitable operations. In many countries the reporting rules make it difficult to determine the nature of changes in these reserves.

Exhibit B-4 illustrates the consolidated statement of income for Saab-Scania Group, the Swedish car and truck manufacturer. Notice that the "appropriations" of 1,344 million SEK (Swedish krona) are deducted from income before "income before taxes." Saab is setting aside 1,344 million SEK of 1987 income to reserve for the items noted in their footnote 9 which is partially reproduced at the bottom of Exhibit B-4. The consolidated balance sheet of Saab-Scania is provided in Exhibit B-5. Note the large (10,328 million SEK) balance in Untaxed Reserves as well as the Statutory Reserves (1,499 million SEK) which represent about 32% of Saab's total liabilities and stockholders' equity. These reserves and appropriations represent a common feature of financial statements in many foreign countries, but they are not allowed by U.S. GAAP.

EXHIBIT B-4

Saab-Scania Group Consolidated Statement of Income (in SEK millions)

			1987		1986
Operating revenue	Sales		**41,403**		35,222
Operating expenses	Manufacturing, selling and administrative expenses		**−37,163**		−31,224
Operating income before depreciation			**4,240**		3,998
Depreciation according to plan			**−1,377**		−1,202
Operating income after depreciation			**2,863**		2,796
Financial income and expenses	Dividends	**5**		2	
	Interest income	**1,222**		909	
	Interest expenses	**−791**		−732	
	Currency differences	**6**	**442**	151	330
Income after financial income and expenses			**3,305**		3,126
Share of income of associated companies			**240**		163
Income before extraordinary income and expenses			**3,545**		3,289
Extraordinary income and expenses			**85**		38
Allocation to the Jubilee Fund for Group Employees			**−50**		—
Income before appropriations and taxes			**3,580**		3,327
Minority interest in subsidiaries' income			**−44**		−37
*Appropriations (Note 9)**			***−1,344***		*−1,204*
Income before taxes			**2,192**		2,086
Taxes, of which SEK 73 m. (22) is a tax to the wage-earner fund (profit-sharing tax)			**−746**		−780
Net income			**1,446**		1,306

***Note 9—Appropriations**

	Group	
SEK millions	*1987*	*1986*
Reversed excess depreciation	**182**	139
Transfer to:		
General investment reserve	**−1,399**	−1,296
Inventory reserve	**−112**	−22
Contingency reserve	**−15**	−25
Internal profit reserve		
Group contribution received and given, respectively		
Total	**−1,344**	−1,204

EXHIBIT B-5

Saab-Scania Group Consolidated Balance Sheet (in SEK millions)

			1987		1986
Assets					
Current assets	Cash and marketable securities	**5,927**		5,113	
	Accounts receivable	**5,807**		4,944	
	Prepaid expenses and accrued income	**687**		521	
	Inventories	**9,446**	**21,867**	8,767	19,345
Blocked accounts with the Bank of Sweden			**60**		239
Obligations of the Kingdom of Denmark			**76**		101
Fixed assets	Long-term receivables	**880**		462	
	Shares, bonds and other securities	**2,683**		1,650	
	Property, plant and equipment, etc.	**11,373**	**14,936**	9,666	11,778
Total assets			**36,939**		31,463
Liabilities and stockholders' equity					
Current liabilities	Bank loans, etc.	**1,478**		1,289	
	Accounts payable, etc.	**3,756**		3,006	
	Accrued expenses and prepaid income	**3,925**		2,966	
	Other current liabilities	**1,490**		1,466	
		10,649		8,727	
	Advance payments from customers	**2,800**	**13,449**	2,679	11,406
Bond loans secured by the Kingdom of Denmark			**75**		100
Long-term liabilities	Long-term loans	**3,803**		2,947	
	Provision for pensions	**2,146**		1,962	
	Provision for vehicle damage guarantee	**121**	**6,070**	101	5,010
Minority interest in subsidiaries			**323**		287
Untaxed reserve			***10,328***		*8,992*
Stockholders' equity	Restricted stockholders' equity				
	Capital stock				
	67,894,192 common shares, par value SEK 25	**1,697**		1,212	
	240,000 preferred shares, par value SEK 25	**6**		6	
	Statutory reserves	***1,499***		*1,641*	
		3,202		2,859	
	Unrestricted stockholders' equity				
	Unappropriated earnings	**2,046**		1,503	
	Net income	**1,446**		1,306	
		3,492	**6,694**	2,809	5,668
Total liabilities and stockholders' equity			**36,939**		31,463

SUMMARY

The world is rapidly becoming one large marketplace rather than a group of separate markets. Multinational firms and multinational stock investors are becoming more commonplace, and are creating a greater need for understanding international accounting. With trade barriers (i.e., tariffs on imports or exports) being eliminated or reduced by more and more nations, business entities are freer to deal with anyone anywhere without having to consider economic barriers. By 1992 the European Common Market countries are expected to have no remaining trade barriers, and may someday have a single central bank system and a common currency.

The American Assembly of Collegiate Schools of Business (AACSB) recognized the need to integrate international dimensions into the business curricula in 1974 when it began to require such coverage by AACSB-accredited schools. This introduction to international accounting has highlighted the primary aspects of international accounting, and it should help you understand the impact of international operations on U.S.-based firms as well as the general nature of differences between U.S. and foreign business entities.

KEY TERMS

Exchange rate. Number of units of foreign currency a U.S. dollar will purchase.

Futures contracts (forward exchange contracts). Agreements to exchange currencies with another country at a specified rate at a specified future date.

Harmonization. Effort on the part of international firms and standard setters to unify accounting methods.

Hedge against gains or losses. To offset potential transaction gains or losses by purchasing or selling future contracts in the exposed currency.

Multinational corporations. Publicly owned businesses that operate in more than one country.

Transaction gain or loss. Results from a change in the exchange rate between the functional currency and the foreign currency used to express the transaction amount between the date the transaction is recorded and the date it is settled (paid).

Translation gain or loss. Results from restating financial statements of a foreign subsidiary (investee) from a foreign (functional) currency to the reporting currency of the parent at the time financial statements are prepared.

QUESTIONS

1. If the U.S. dollar is strengthening against the British pound, is this good news for those who buy from or sell to Great Britain?
2. If the German mark is costing less to buy in U.S. currency, will this result in gains or losses between U.S. firms selling goods to German firms?
3. Where are transaction gains and losses reported by U.S. firms doing business with foreign companies?

4. How can U.S. firms avoid transaction gains or losses when doing business with foreign firms without hedging?
5. What does a hedge do for U.S. firms with foreign transactions?
6. Where are translation gains and losses reported?
7. At what exchange rate are income statement accounts translated?
8. At what exchange rate are assets and liabilities translated?
9. At what exchange rate are stockholders' equity accounts other than retained earnings translated?
10. What authority do international accounting standards (IASs) have?

EXERCISES

EXERCISE B-1
L.O. 1

Transaction Gains/Losses

The Stripes Corporation exports some of its merchandise to France and also does business with a French exporter. The following transactions occurred during 19xx for Stripes:

19xx
June 21 Purchased goods on account for 85,000 francs.
30 Sold goods on account to a French client for 12,000 francs.
July 30 Paid for June 21 purchase in cash.
Aug. 15 Received payment in cash for sale of goods from June 30.

The exchange rates on these dates were:

Date	*U.S. Dollar per Franc*
June 21	0.18
30	0.19
July 30	0.17
Aug. 15	0.20
Dec. 31	0.21

Required:
Record these transactions on Stripes' books in U.S. dollars.

EXERCISE B-2
L.O. 1

Transaction Gains/Losses

ITECK, Inc., a U.S. company, sold computers to Boyds, Ltd., an English company, for 400,000 pounds on December 1, 19xx. The sale was on open account, and Boyd was to make four installments of 100,000 pounds at the end of each month (no interest). Boyd paid the first 100,000 pounds on December 31, 19xx. The pound sold for $1.35 on December 1, 19xx, but had fallen to $1.25 by year-end.

Required:
1. Record the sale on December 1, 19xx, on ITECK's books.
2. Record the receipt of the first payment on December 31, 19xx.
3. Record any unrealized exchange gains or losses as of December 31, 19xx.
4. What would be reported on ITECK's 19xx pre-tax income as a result of the above entries?

EXERCISE B-3
L.O. 3

Translation—Income Statement

Consider the consolidated income statement of Saab-Scania in Exhibit B-4. Assume the average exchange rate during 1987 was 6.3 krona per U.S. dollar.

Required:
Prepare Saab's 1987 income statement in U.S. dollars, rounding each amount to the nearest $ million.

EXERCISE B-4
L.O. 3, 4

Translation—Balance Sheet

Assume an Indian Corporation reported the following balance sheet at the end of 19x4 in pounds.

Bombay Hose, Inc.
Balance Sheet
December 31, 19x4
(in millions of pounds)

Assets		**Liabilities and Stockholders' Equity**	
Current assets	475,650	Liabilities:	
Plant and equipment	812,040	Current liabilities	495,100
Investments	196,190	Long-term debt	316,750
Intangibles	87,660	Total liabilities	811,850
		Stockholders' equity:	
		Paid-in capital	300,000
		Retained earnings	459,690
		Total stockholders' equity	759,690
Total assets	1,571,540	Total liabilities and stockholders' equity	1,571,540

Assume the appropriate current rate for translation to U.S. dollars is $3.75 per pound, and the appropriate historical rate *for all of stockholders' equity* is $3.20 per pound.

Required:
1. Prepare a balance sheet for Bombay Hose, Inc., in U.S. dollars.
2. What is the ratio of current assets to current liabilities in pounds? In dollars?
3. What is the ratio of long-term debt to total assets in pounds? In dollars?

PROBLEMS

PROBLEM B-1
L.O. 3

Translation Gains/Losses

The Ruhle Company was formed in West Germany on January 1, 19x1, by a U.S. Corporation—Starstake, Inc. Ruhle is owned 100% by Starstake. During 19x1, the following exchange rates were noted:

Date/Period	*Exchange Rate (U.S. $ per West German mark)*
January 1, 19x1	$0.56
December 31, 19x1	0.60
Average for 19x1	0.58

Ruhle reported the following financial data at the end of 19x1:

Ruhle Company
Income Statement
For the Year Ended December 31, 19x1
(in West German marks)

Revenues	24,789,640
Expenses	22,801,440
Operating income	1,988,200
Other gains	483,800
Net income	2,472,000

Ruhle Company
Balance Sheet
December 31, 19x1
(in West German marks)

Assets		**Liabilities and Stockholders' Equity**	
Cash	2,805,000	Liabilities:	
Receivables	6,907,000	Payables	3,108,000
Inventory	10,518,000	Long-term notes	10,000,000
Plant assets	40,350,000	Total liabilities	13,108,000
		Stockholders' equity:	
		Common stock	45,000,000
		Retained earnings	2,472,000
		Total stockholders' equity	47,472,000
Total assets	60,580,000	Total liabilities and stockholders' equity	60,580,000

Required:
Translate Ruhle's 19x1 income statement and year-end balance sheet into U.S. dollars.

PROBLEM B-2
L.O. 3

Translation Gains/Losses

Macadona Corporation was formed in Japan on January 1, 19x4, by a U.S. corporation—Micky Dees, Inc. Macadona is 100% owned by Micky Dees. During 19x4, the following exchange rates were noted:

Date/Period	*Exchange Rate (U.S. $ per yen)*
January 1, 19x4	$0.0070
December 31, 19x4	0.0080
Average for 19x4	0.0075

Macadona reported the following financial statements at the end of 19x4:

Macadona Corporation
Income Statement
For the Year Ended December 31, 19x4
(in millions of yen)

Net sales	2,673
Cost of goods sold	(1,021)
Other costs and expenses	(896)
Net income	756

Macadona Corporation
Balance Sheet
December 31, 19x4
(in millions of yen)

Assets		Liabilities and Stockholders' Equity	
Cash	971	Liabilities:	
Receivables	1,125	Payables	2,167
Inventory	3,081	Long-term notes	19,000
Plant assets	19,746	Total liabilities	21,167
		Stockholders' equity:	
		Capital stock	3,000
		Retained earnings	756
		Total stockholders' equity	3,756
Total assets	24,923	Total liabilities and stockholders' equity	24,923

Required:
Translate Macadona's income statement and balance sheet from yen to U.S. dollars.

PROBLEM B-3
L.O. 1

Transaction Gains/Losses

Sport Corporation purchases supplies from Britain and manufactures goods in the United States for sale to France. The following transactions occurred recently:

May 1 Purchased supplies on account for 28,000 pounds.
May 15 Sold goods on account for 180,000 French francs.
May 25 Sold goods on account for 420,000 French francs.
May 25 Purchased supplies on account for 50,000 pounds.
May 30 Collected on sale made May 15.
May 30 Paid for purchase made May 1.
May 31 Collected on the May 25 sale and paid for the May 25 purchase.

The exchange rates in May were:

	U.S. Dollars per	
Date	*French Franc*	*British Pound*
May 1	$0.20	$1.50
May 15	0.21	1.55
May 25	0.22	1.60
May 30	0.24	1.65
May 31	0.24	1.65

Required:
Compute the exchange gains or losses on these transactions.

PROBLEM B-4
L.O. 3, 4

Translation of Balance Sheet

The following comparative balance sheet is for CAP Gemini Sogeti S.A., a large French-based international company specializing in computer information systems, data processing and systems consulting. The balance sheets are expressed in French francs. CAP's net income for 1987 was 103,230,224 francs.

Assume the following exchange rates:

	Dollars per Franc
At December 31, 1987	.18
Weighted average historical rate at the date stockholders' equity accounts other than retained earnings were created	.20

Further assume that the amount of retained earnings in U.S. dollars (from the restated income statements of all prior years, which are not provided here) is U.S. $110,000,000.

Required:

1. Prepare a balance sheet in U.S. dollars for CAP Gemini Sogeti as of December 31, 1987. (Round all amounts to the nearest thousand.)
2. What is the cumulative translation gain or loss?

PROBLEM B-5
L.O. 3, 4

Translation of Balance Sheet

Consider the consolidated balance sheet in Exhibit B-5 of Saab-Scania, the Swedish manufacturer of cars, trucks, and jet aircraft. Assume that one Swedish krona (SEK) is equal to $0.155 at the end of 1987. Further assume that appropriate historical rate for all stockholders' equity accounts (including retained earnings) is .172.

Required:

1. Prepare a December 31, 1987, balance sheet for Saab in U.S. dollars.
2. What is the cumulative translation gain or loss?
3. Over Saab's life has the U.S. dollar strengthened or weakened against the Krona?

CAP GEMINI SOGETI S.A.
Balance Sheet
At December 31, 1987
(expressed in French francs)

ASSETS	1986	1987
Cash	605,380,288	175,797,733
Accounts and notes receivable	1,638,604	1,992,975
Other receivables	3,928,532	21,128,225
Affiliated Companies	93,873,405	59,936,715
Other current assets	9,152,718	7,431,953
TOTAL CURRENT ASSETS	**713,973,547**	**266,287,601**
Consolidated investments in affiliates	304,772,518	1,051,336,405
Other investments	1,698,233	2,839,597
Other noncurrent assets	352,718,085	309,779,486
Property, plant and equipment, net of accumulated depreciation	18,730,402	19,220,862
Intangible assets	13,072,500	13,317,215
TOTAL NONCURRENT ASSETS	**690,991,738**	**1,396,493,565**
TOTAL ASSETS	**1,404,965,285**	**1,662,781,166**

LIABILITIES AND SHAREHOLDERS' EQUITY	1986	1987
Financial debt	643,822,248	850,386,245
Operating debt	11,263,967	13,022,034
Other current debt	23,698,961	29,659,734
Unrealized exchange gain	746,432	247,500
TOTAL CURRENT LIABILITIES	**679,531,608**	**893,315,513**
NONCURRENT LIABILITIES		
Provisions for risks and charges	30,408,077	20,709,595
SHAREHOLDERS' EQUITY		
Common stock, authorized and issued	70,687,500	77,837,800
Retained earnings	519,466,898	540,740,727
Foreign investment tax provision	33,747,307	26,947,307
Shareholders' equity	623,901,705	645,525,834
Net income for the year	71,123,895	103,230,224
Total shareholders' equity before appropriation of income	**695,025,600**	**748,756,058**
TOTAL LIABILITIES AND SHAREHOLDERS' EQUITY	**1,404,965,285**	**1,662,781,166**

CASES

CASE B-1
L.O. 3

Foreign Currency—General Motors

Consider the following footnote disclosure from the 19x6 annual report of General Motors (GM). This footnote is describing details of GM's balance sheet account Accumulated Foreign Currency Translation and Other Adjustments appearing in the stockholders' equity section of the balance sheet. As noted, the account reflects holding gains or losses from translation of foreign currency discussed in Appendix B.

Excerpt from Footnote 15:

(dollars in millions)	*19x6*	*19x5*	*19x4*
Accumulated Foreign Currency Translation and other Adjustments:			
Balance at beginning of year:			
Accumulated foreign currency translation adjustments	$(675.0)	$(789.5)	$(661.8)
Net unrealized gains on marketable securities	130.0	71.7	91.3
Changes during the year:			
Accumulated foreign currency translation adjustments	192.2	114.5	(127.7)
Net unrealized gains (losses) on marketable securities	30.8	58.3	(19.6)
Balance at end of the year	$(322.0)	$(545.0)	$(717.8)

Required:

1. The cumulative **prior years'** effect of foreign currency translation adjustments have resulted in how much of a holding gain or loss as of January 1, 19x6? (Be sure to indicate amount as well as gain or loss.)
2. What was the effect of translation for 19x6? (Give amount and whether it was a gain or loss.)

CASE B-2
L.O. 1, 3

Foreign Currency—Union Carbide

Consider the following footnotes taken from a recent annual report of Union Carbide Corporation (UCC):

Excerpt from footnotes:

Foreign Currency Translation

The following is an analysis of Equity Adjustment from Foreign Currency Translation which reduces stockholders' equity:

Millions of dollars	
Balance at beginning of year . .	$(374)
Translation adjustments	34
Balance at December 31	$(340)

Other Expense (Income)

The following is an analysis of Other Expense (Income):

Millions of dollars	
Investment income (principally from short-term investments)	$ (42)
Foreign currency adjustments	(3)
Net discount expense on sales of customer obligations to Ucar Capital Corporation . . .	18
Special litigation costs	185
Costs relating to self-tender offer	58
Sales and disposals of business and other assets	(63)
Other	20
Total	$173

Required:

1. What was UCC's translation gain or loss for the year?
2. What is the apparent gain or loss from **transaction** adjustments included in UCC's income statement account Other Expenses (Income)?
3. Did the U.S. dollar become stronger or weaker in the year reported in this case? Explain.

CASE B-3
L.O. 4

French Balance Sheet

Consider the consolidated balance sheet and income statement of Pernod Ricard, the French manufacturer of liquors, wines, and soft drinks, reproduced on the following pages. (When Pernod uses the term *group,* it is the same as saying the consolidated parent company.)

Required:

1. Identify four differences between Pernod's balance sheet and those of U.S. firms.
2. What is the apparent exchange rate used for converting Pernod's assets from francs to dollars?

Pernod Ricard
Consolidated Income Statement
For the Years Ended December 31
(in millions)

	U.S. $ 1987	*F. Fr. 1987*	*F. Fr. 1986*
SALES NET OF VAT	**2,344**	**12,516**	**11,773**
Excise taxes and duties	(339)	(1,812)	(1,757)
SALES NET OF TAX	**2,005**	**10,704**	**10,016**
Cost of sales	(838)	(4,476)	(4,246)
GROSS MARGIN	**1,167**	**6,228**	**5,770**
Outside services	(417)	(2,228)	(1,973)
INCOME FROM OPERATIONS	**750**	**4,000**	**3,797**
Taxes	(41)	(219)	(213)
Payroll	(386)	(2,059)	(2,019)
GROSS OPERATING PROFIT	**323**	**1,722**	**1,565**
Other income	25	131	106
Other expense	(33)	(173)	(140)
Depreciation	(68)	(362)	(336)
OPERATING PROFIT BEFORE INTEREST EXPENSE	**247**	**1,318**	**1,195**
Net interest expense	(15)	(82)	(91)
OPERATING PROFIT	**232**	**1,236**	**1,104**
Provision for employee profit-sharing	(15)	(78)	(69)
Gains (losses) on disposal of assets	5	26	40
Other income (expense)	(13)	(67)	(12)
INCOME BEFORE INCOME TAXES	**209**	**1,117**	**1,063**
Income taxes	(92)	(492)	(521)
Interest in earnings (losses) of equity companies	2	10	5
NET INCOME	**119**	**635**	**547**
Minority interests	(5)	(28)	(31)
GROUP INTEREST IN NET INCOME	**114**	**607**	**516**

Pernod Ricard
Consolidated Balance Sheet
At December 31
(in millions)

Assets	*U.S. $ 1987*	*F. Fr. 1987*	*F. Fr. 1986*
CAPITAL ASSETS	**587**	**3,136**	**2,664**
Intangibles	46	245	539
Plant, property, and equipment	346	1,847	1,794
Goodwill	36	195	27
Financial investments	159	849	304

Assets	U.S. $ 1987	F. Fr. 1987	F. Fr. 1986
CURRENT ASSETS	**1,105**	**5,900**	**6,259**
Inventories	446	2,381	2,453
Customer and other receivables	575	3,069	2,865
Marketable securities	15	82	418
Cash	69	368	523
ACCRUED INCOME AND PREPAID EXPENSE	**18**	**97**	**83**
CURRENCY TRANSLATION ADJUSTMENT	**1**	**5**	**5**
TOTAL ASSETS	**1,711**	**9,138**	**9,011**
Liabilities and Shareholders' Equity			
SHAREHOLDERS' EQUITY	**718**	**3,835**	**3,907**
Of which Group interest in net income	114	607	516
MINORITY INTERESTS IN SHAREHOLDERS' EQUITY	**45**	**239**	**299**
Of which minority interest in net income	5	27	31
PROVISIONS FOR RISK AND EXPENSE	**46**	**245**	**199**
DEFERRED INCOME TAXES	**6**	**30**	**88**
DEBT	**895**	**4,780**	**4,514**
Financial debt	291	1,557	1,335
Containers on deposit	55	293	303
Accounts payable and other	452	2,414	2,279
Other debt	97	516	597
PREPAID INCOME AND ACCRUED EXPENSE	**1**	**6**	**1**
CURRENCY TRANSLATION ADJUSTMENT	**—**	**3**	**3**
TOTAL LIABILITIES AND SHAREHOLDERS' EQUITY	**1,711**	**9,138**	**9,011**

CASE B-4 French Income Statement

L.O. 4

Consider the income statement for Pernod Ricard provided in Case B-3. In its income statement, Pernod refers to "VAT," which is a tax (value added tax) paid in certain European firms based on the total value added to a product (both costs and profits). A VAT provides incentives for firms to cut costs and increase profits since they will be taxed on the total.

Required:

1. Does Pernod Ricard have equity method investments in other firms (i.e., unconsolidated subsidiaries)?
2. Does Pernod Ricard have any consolidated subsidiaries?
3. How does "net income" reported ($119) differ from "net income" for a U.S. firm that has consolidated (but not 100% owned) subsidiaries?

APPENDIX C

Accounting for Changing Prices

LEARNING OBJECTIVES

After studying Appendix C, you should understand:

1. The limitations of the stable dollar assumption underlying the historical cost model, p. 920.
2. How to measure the effects of general price changes on accounting disclosures, pp. 920-24.
3. How to measure the effects of specific price changes and when they may be more relevant than general price changes, pp. 923-28.
4. How to measure monetary gains or losses and their effect on the business entity, pp. 929-32.

Note: This appendix introduces students to the measurement issues which reduce the relevance of the historical cost model, and also illustrates how to adjust for general and specific price changes. The appendix does **not** illustrate the alternatives to historical cost on a comprehensive model basis. However, based on the material provided, students should get an understanding of the nature of the problems created by changing prices and the methods that are available to adjust for the effects of general and specific price change.

This appendix could be introduced anytime after Chapter 6. Two chapters where the effects of price change would be of more than average relevance would be after Chapter 6 (inventories) or after Chapter 8 (long-term assets). Also, some instructors teach inventory cost flows (Chapter 6), foreign currency adjustments (Appendix B), and price changes (Appendix C) as a unit, focusing on the measurement issues which are the core of all three topics.

Objective 1
The limitations of the stable dollar assumption underlying the historical cost model.

This textbook introduces generally accepted accounting principles (GAAP) to students. For the most part, GAAP is based on the historical cost principle, which reports elements of financial statements at their original (historical) cost, less any depreciation, amortization, or depletion where appropriate. The major exception to historical cost within GAAP is the lower-of-cost-or-market (LCM) procedures which apply to marketable securities (Chapter 13) and to inventory (Chapter 6). The LCM procedures permit the use of current "market" values only if they are below historical cost. As a result, based on **conservatism,** accountants use LCM, which allows write-downs of assets below their historical cost.

While historical cost-based financial statements are used to aid many business decisions, they are not without serious limitations in some decision-making situations. GAAP financial statements are based on the assumption that the dollar measurement unit is an equal unit of measure over all time periods, which is referred to as the **stable dollar assumption.** When prices do change, GAAP financial statements become more difficult to compare and evaluate. In this appendix, several concepts and procedures are introduced that should help you evaluate financial statements in periods of changing prices and compensate for these changing prices in the preparation and/or evaluation of a company's financial results. This appendix discusses the following:

1. Types of price changes.
2. Using general and specific price changes:
   a. Constant dollar analysis using general price changes.
   b. Current cost analysis using specific price changes.
3. Monetary gains and losses.

Understanding the effects of price changes on financial statements is very important since it can significantly affect evaluations of a single company from year to year and evaluations comparing several companies at a single point in time. We will see from the examples presented here that consideration of the impact of price changes on GAAP financial statements may change our evaluations of how well a company is doing in comparison to prior years or in comparison to other companies.

We begin by explaining the two basic types of price changes and how we can measure their effect on elements of financial statements.

TYPES OF PRICE CHANGES

While price changes may be defined and reported in various ways, all price changes can be expressed in the form of a price index. A **price index** is the ratio of current prices to some previous year's prices, with the previous year selected usually referred to as the *base year*. The two basic types of price indexes are the general price index and the specific price index.

A **general price index** measures the changes in prices of a group of items. The most common example of a general price index is the consumer price index (CPI), which measures the change in prices of all goods and services normally acquired by individual consumers. The CPI attempts to track the change in prices of a "market basket" of goods and services typically consumed by individual households. The price and price change for each good or service included in a general index such as the CPI is weighted in proportion to its relative importance to the "average" consumer. For example, housing prices may be weighted

20% of the total of all goods and services a consumer purchases; food, 25%; transportation, 15%; and so on. Another index that is broadly based is the gross national product (GNP) index, which measures the change in price of all items *produced* in the United States.

A **specific price index** measures the price and change in price of a specific good or service. The specificity of an index may vary, depending on what type of items are priced in the index. For example, one specific price index may measure hourly labor costs in general, while other specific indexes may measure hourly skilled labor and hourly unskilled labor separately. The specific price index for a product or service is constructed by measuring its current cost over time. To illustrate, assume the cost of steel is reported on the dates given as follows:

Date	*Average Price per Ton of Cold Rolled Steel, 1/8"*
12/31/x1	$1,900
12/31/x2	1,875
12/31/x3	2,150
12/31/x4	2,370

The price of steel can be stated in index form using the actual price reported in 19x1 of $1,900 per ton as the basis for comparison as follows:

Year	*Actual Historical Cost Price per Ton* ÷	*Actual Price in 19x1 per Ton*	= *Specific Price Index Stated as a Percent**
19x1. . . .	$1,900	$1,900	100.0%
19x2. . . .	1,875	1,900	98.7
19x3. . . .	2,150	1,900	113.2
19x4. . . .	2,370	1,900	124.7

*19x1 = Base year.

The specific price index can use any year desired as the base year, since a base year is simply a point in time used as the basis for price comparison. If you wish to know what current prices are compared to 1967, then 1967 would be the base year. It is most common for specific price indexes to use either the current year's prices or some arbitrary prior year's prices (often 1967) as the base year for preparing a specific price index. In the example above, 19x1 is the base year, and the specific price index measures changes in prices from 19x1 to 19x4 **relative to** 19x1's prices.

Using General or Specific Price Changes

General and specific price indexes may be used to evaluate the impact of price changes on historical cost data. The financial statement data prepared in accordance with GAAP on a historical cost basis are often referred to as **nominal dollar** financial statements because they do not differentiate the various dollar units that originated from transactions over many different accounting periods. The balance sheet, for instance, may sum dollar units from 35 years ago when 100 acres of land were purchased for $10,000 with dollar units from the current year when one acre of land was purchased for $10,000 without differentiating between these two $10,000 amounts. Since the nominal dollar amounts of these two transactions both have the same historical cost, GAAP would report their sum at

$20,000. However, if we wish to account for the fact that prices have changed over the last 35 years, we can restate the value of the land using general or specific price changes, thereby developing new information which could be more relevant for certain types of business decisions. The examples that follow illustrate how we can use information about changing prices to restate financial report data, separating the effects of price change from the real performance and position of the reporting entity. When price changes are large, these procedures are important for meaningful financial statement analysis.

Objective 2
How to measure the effects of general price changes on accounting disclosures.

Constant Dollar Analysis Using General Price Changes. Data that have been adjusted for the effects of changes in the general price index are called **constant dollar** data or **general price level adjusted (GPLA)** data. To illustrate constant dollar data, assume that SPA-Tech, Inc., reported the following historical summary of earnings per share (EPS) for the past five years:

SPA-Tech, Inc.
Historical Cost Results

	19x5	*19x4*	*19x3*	*19x2*	*19x1*
Earnings per share (EPS) . . .	$3.30	$3.23	$3.15	$3.05	$3.00

These results reveal an increasing trend in earnings on a historical cost basis. However, assume that the general consumer price index from 19x1 to 19x5, measured using 1967 prices as the base (or reference) year, changed as follows:

End of Year	*Consumer Price Index (CPI) (1967 = 100)*
19x1 . . .	280.0
19x2 . . .	299.6
19x3 . . .	326.6
19x4 . . .	359.3
19x5 . . .	388.0

The historical results can now be examined on a constant dollar basis, which means that we can control the effects of changes in the purchasing power of the dollar over time. We can restate the historical results in terms of 1967-sized dollars, or 19x5-sized dollars, or any other point of reference desired. To restate all amounts to 1967-sized dollars, we would simply divide each year's historical data by the year-end CPI as follows (all amounts rounded to nearest cent):

SPA-Tech, Inc.
EPS Restatement—1967 Dollars

Year	*Historical EPS Reported*	×	*1967 CPI Divided by Respective Year's CPI*	=	*Equivalent 1967 Constant Dollar Amount*
19x5 . . .	$3.30	×	(100/388.0)	=	$0.85
19x4 . . .	3.23	×	(100/359.3)	=	0.90
19x3 . . .	3.15	×	(100/326.6)	=	0.96
19x2 . . .	3.05	×	(100/299.6)	=	1.02
19x1 . . .	3.00	×	(100/280.0)	=	1.07

In terms of 1967-sized dollars, we now see that EPS has actually been decreasing from 19x1 to 19x5! Restated in 1967 dollars (constant 1967 dollars), EPS has decreased from $1.07 per share in 19x1 to $0.85 per share in 19x5. This reversal of the trend first reported on a historical (nominal) basis, from $3.00 to $3.30 per share, results from the fact that general price changes increased more rapidly than EPS each year. For example, the change in the CPI during 19x2 was about 7% [(2.996 − 2.800)/2.800 = +.07], while the change in EPS during 19x2 was only about 2% [($3.05 − $3.00)/$3.00 = +.017]. The changes observed in the constant dollar or GPLA data are often referred to as "real changes," since they examine the reported earnings measures (e.g., $3.00 to $3.05) **after** removing the effects of general price changes.

Constant dollar data may be stated in other than base year dollars, which are 1967 dollars in the example above. Many analysts feel that restating all nominal dollars in terms of current year constant dollars is more appropriate than restating all amounts to some previous base year (e.g., 1967) dollars. To restate the EPS data in 19x5-sized constant dollars requires adjusting all amounts except 19x5 as follows (rounded to nearest cent):

SPA-Tech, Inc.
EPS Restatement—19x5 Dollars

Year	*Historical (Nominal) Dollar Amount*	×	*19x5 CPI over Original Year's CPI*	=	*19x5 Constant Dollar Amount*
19x5 . . .	$3.30	×	(3.88/3.88)	=	$3.30
19x4 . . .	3.23	×	(3.88/3.593)	=	3.49
19x3 . . .	3.15	×	(3.88/3.266)	=	3.74
19x2 . . .	3.05	×	(3.88/2.996)	=	3.95
19x1 . . .	3.00	×	(3.88/2.800)	=	4.16

Notice that all prior years' EPS amounts are larger when restated at 19x5-sized constant dollars. Restatement of the historical cost data in this example to constant dollars shows the same decreasing trend in EPS regardless of whether 1967, 19x5, or some other base year is used as a reference point. The restated constant dollar EPS amounts tell the reader that the real trend in EPS has been decreasing in this example from 19x1 to 19x5 because increases in the CPI have outpaced increases in nominal dollar EPS amounts.

When these constant dollar results are compared among firms, it could give a different perspective to the evaluation of a firm's relative performance, as noted in the comparison of Company A and Company B in Exhibit C-1.

While Company A reveals steady real growth in constant dollar EPS measures, Company B actually appears to be on a declining constant dollar EPS trend since 19x3! Constant dollar analysis can add new insights to conventional accounting data, particularly in periods of rapidly changing prices.

Current Cost Analysis Using Specific Price Changes. While constant dollar analysis adjusts nominal historical cost data for changes in general price levels, not all accounting data are affected by general price changes. For example, what if your business is experiencing decreasing inventory costs in a period where prices in general are *increasing* (general inflation)? Would it make

EXHIBIT C-1

Comparison of EPS Performance of Company A and Company B

Year-End	Historical Cost EPS: Company A	Historical Cost EPS: Company B	× 19x5 CPI over the Original Year's CPI	= 19x5 Constant Dollar EPS: Company A	19x5 Constant Dollar EPS: Company B
19x5	$8.35	$8.35	(3.88/3.88)	$8.35	$8.35
19x4	7.51	7.85	(3.88/3.593)	8.11	8.48
19x3	6.67	7.27	(3.88/3.266)	7.92	8.64
19x2	6.05	6.48	(3.88/2.996)	7.84	8.39
19x1	5.55	5.55	(3.88/2.800)	7.69	7.69

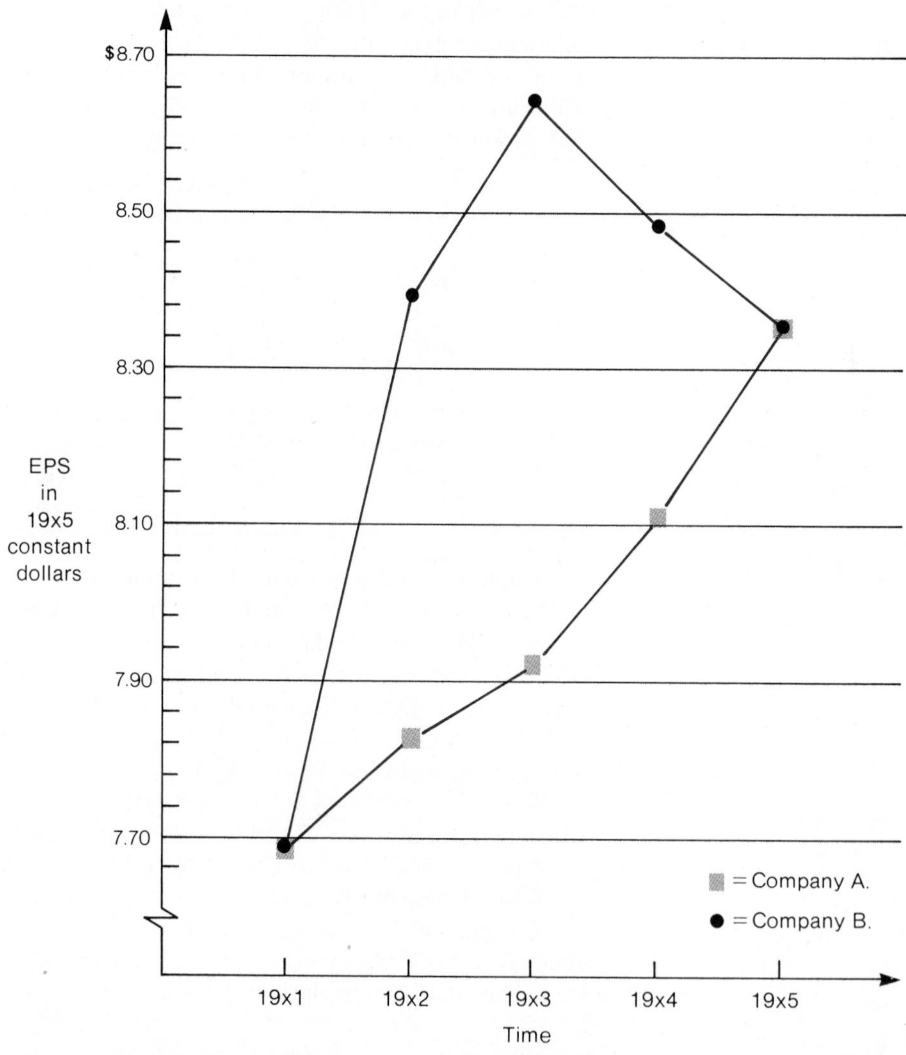

sense to increase the value of inventory to reflect general price increases? Many accountants feel that while constant dollar adjustments may be insightful for the evaluation of EPS, dividends per share, or other overall financial statement results, the effect of specific price changes may be more useful for assessing other financial statement components whose prices are not changing the same as changes in the general price index. Specifically, inventory and plant, property, and equipment might be better evaluated by considering how they are affected by specific price changes.

Historical cost (nominal dollar) accounting data that have been adjusted for the effects of specific price changes are called **current cost** data (also known as **replacement cost,** or **specific price level adjusted (SPLA)** data). These current cost data are prepared by using specific price indexes to convert the historical cost (nominal dollar) amounts to current costs. The only difference between the current cost adjustment process and the constant dollar process illustrated earlier is the index. The current cost adjustments would use a **separate specific price index** to convert each class of items (i.e., machinery, raw materials inventory, and so on) to its current costs, while the constant dollar model uses a single general price index for all conversions to constant dollars.

Objective 3
How to measure the effects of specific price changes and when they may be more relevant than general price changes.

To illustrate current cost adjustments, assume a retail carpet store reported the following ending inventory values for its carpet inventory, which is valued on a FIFO basis.

Year-End	*FIFO Value of Ending Inventory*
19x4	$435,000
19x3	408,030
19x2	389,550
19x1	382,500

Further assume that the specific price index of carpeting has been increasing during this four-year period as follows:

Year-End	*Specific Price Index for Carpeting (1967 ≡ 100)*
19x4	300
19x3	290
19x2	265
19x1	250

By looking at the historical FIFO value only, it appears as though the quantity of inventory on hand at year-end has increased in each of the last three years since 19x1. However, using the information about specific price changes, we can see that the quantity of inventory (the "real" investment in inventory) actually decreased in 19x2 and 19x3 before increasing in a real sense in 19x4. Converting all of the year-end FIFO values to 19x4 current costs provides the following results:

	Ending Inventory				
Year-End	*FIFO Value*	×	*19x4 Specific Index/Respective Year-End Index*	=	*19x4 Current Costs*
19x4	$435,000		(300/300)		$435,000
19x3	408,030		(300/290)		422,100
19x2	389,550		(300/265)		441,000
19x1	382,500		(300/250)		459,000

The current cost measures computed above for the carpet inventory reveal a different pattern of "real" inventory change than the nominal FIFO values. The current cost measures show that there were decreases in the real quantity of inventory in both 19x2 and 19x3. The decrease is obscured by the FIFO measures because of the specific price change in the carpet inventory during 19x2 and 19x3. The increase in the specific index for carpet during 19x2 and 19x3 was greater than the increase in the FIFO inventory value. As a result, even though the total FIFO ending inventory value increased in both 19x2 and 19x3 (due to specific price increases), the real quantity of carpet on hand actually decreased in both 19x2 and 19x3. In 19x4, both specific prices and real quantities increased. Using the 19x4 current costs, the graph in Exhibit C-2 illustrates the changes in inventory on both a nominal cost and current cost basis.

Overall Effect of Specific Price Changes on Performance Measures

The effect of specific price changes on inventory in the example above may also be applied to other balance sheet items using other appropriate specific price indexes. These adjustments for specific price changes can be *very* important in measuring the performance of companies or parts of companies. The more long-term assets a company has, the greater the potential effect of specific price changes on a company's relative performance. To further illustrate how these specific price changes might affect performance measures, consider the following example:

> Company A and Company B are both lumber companies. Their primary assets are land and trees. Company A acquired most of its land in the 1920s at an average price of $200 per acre. Company B acquired most of its land in the 1970s at an average price of $2,000 per acre. Both companies started by borrowing half of the cost of the land initially, and have continued to maintain this same level of debt. The other half of the land cost was paid for from the sale of common stock. Assume both companies have 100,000 acres of timberland, and each year they cut and sell 5,000 acres of timber and replant new seedlings on the harvested area. In 19x5, both companies reported net income of $5,000,000. By 19x5, the current cost of land for both companies was $2,300 per acre. Assuming there were no other specific price changes affecting these companies, Exhibit C-3 shows how historical cost performance measures can lead to incorrect comparisons. Exhibit C-3 also shows how current costs can result in more comparable performance ratios when results are very similar, as they were for companies A and B.

Based on the historical cost data, it looks as though Company A is much more efficient with its assets, since its ROA is more than four times that of Company B. Also, Company A has a much higher ROE than Company B. Yet the assumptions in this case revealed that both companies were very similar in their assets and operations. The current cost comparison in Exhibit C-3 reveals the real similarity between companies A and B. Both companies have identical ROAs of 1.9%. Also, since Company B is newer and has more debt, its ROE on a current cost basis is higher than that of Company A.

In Exhibit C-3, the increase in Company A's Land account from its historical cost of $200 per acre to its current cost of $2,300 per acre results in a *holding gain* of $2,100 per acre. A **holding gain** is the increase in the value of any asset over its original cost that results over time as the asset is held. **Holding losses** measure decreases in value over original cost. Inventory, buildings, and land often increase in value as they are held. In historical cost-based accounting, these holding gains are not recognized until the asset is sold. In current cost-based sys-

EXHIBIT C-2

Change in Inventory on Nominal Cost and Current Cost Basis

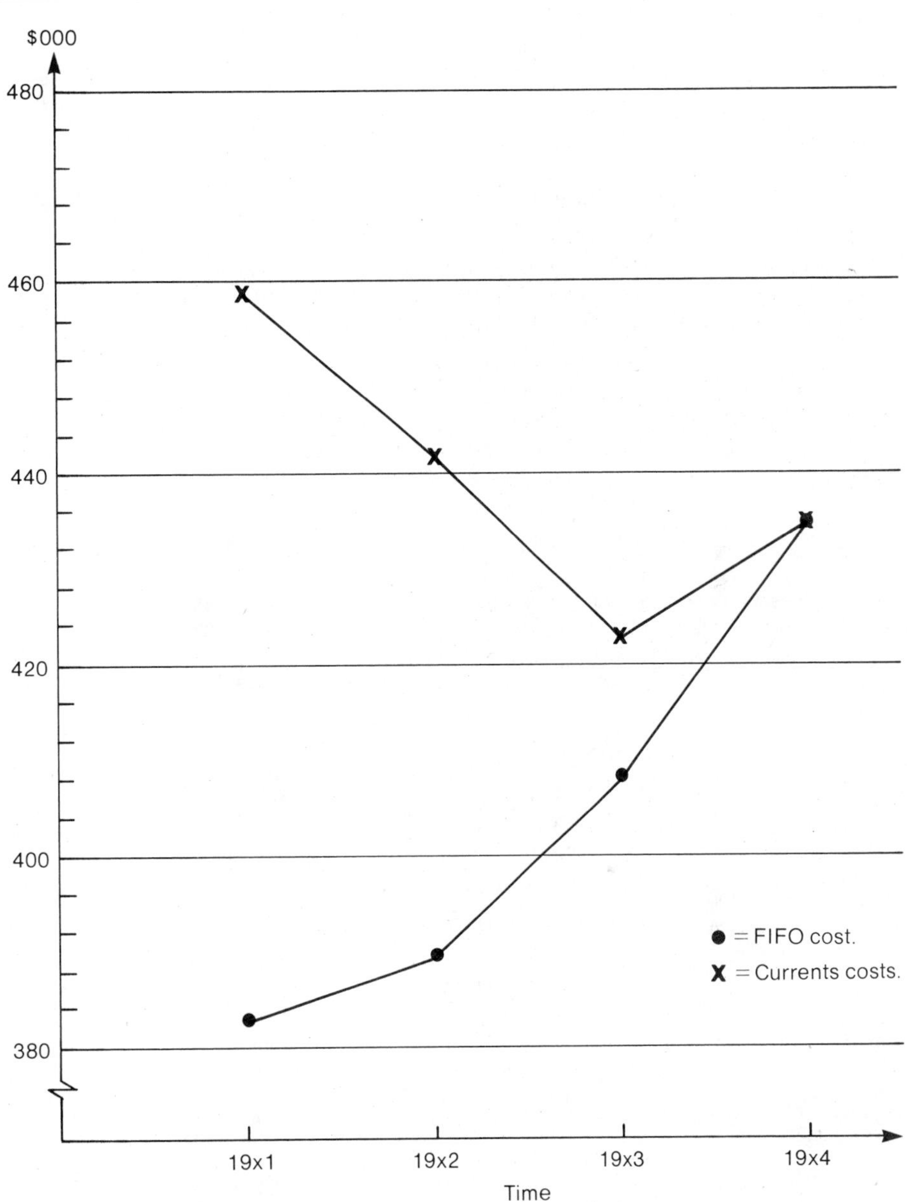

tems, holding gains or losses are recognized in income each period that the specific prices of assets change.

The example in Exhibit C-3 is simplified to illustrate the potential importance of current cost information in comparing one company to another (or one operating plant to another within the same company). However, the potential effect of specific price changes and their importance is very real. In capital-intense industries failure to consider the effects of specific price changes can lead to inappropriate operating, financing, and investing decisions which can eventually lead to bankruptcy. The U.S. steel industry is an excellent example of how

EXHIBIT C-3

Comparison of Historical Cost and Current Cost Performance Measures

Historical Cost Balance Sheets
(in millions)

Company A

Assets:		Liabilities:	
Other assets	$ 5	Other liabilities	$ 5
Inventory	25	**Debt**	10
Land	20	Total liab.	$15
		Stockholders' equity:	
		Capital stock	10
		Retained earnings	25
Total assets	$50	Total liabilities and stockholders' equity	$50

Return on assets (ROA) = $5/$50 = 10%
Return on equity (ROE) = $5/$35 = 14.3%

Company B

Assets:		Liabilities:	
Other assets	$ 5	Other liabilities	$ 5
Inventory	25	**Debt**	100
Land	200	Total liab.	$105
		Stockholders' equity:	
		Capital stock	100
		Retained earnings	25
Total assets	$230	Total liabilities and stockholders' equity	$230

ROA = $5/$230 = 2.2%
ROE = $5/$125 = 4.0%

Current Cost Balance Sheets
(in millions)

Company A

Assets:		Liabilities:	
Other assets	$ 5	Other liabilities	$ 5
Inventory	25	**Debt**	10
Land	230	Total liab.	$ 15
		Stockholders' equity:	
		Plug total	245
Total assets	$260	Total liabilities and stockholders' equity	$260

$$ROA = \frac{\$5}{\$260} = 1.9\%$$

$$ROE = \frac{\$5}{\$245} = 2.0\%$$

Company B

Assets:		Liabilities:	
Other assets	$ 5	Other liabilities	$ 5
Inventory	25	**Debt**	100
Land	230	Total liab.	$105
		Stockholders' equity:	
		Plug total	155
Total assets	$260	Total liabilities and stockholders' equity	$260

$$ROA = \frac{\$5}{\$260} = 1.9\%$$

$$ROE = \frac{\$5}{\$155} = 3.2\%$$

failure to consider the effects of specific price changes contributed to the demise of this country as a world leader in steel production.

While constant dollar and current cost measurements may be useful and interesting when applied to certain elements of financial statement data, they are not appropriate for restating current balances of those assets and liabilities that represent specific claims to receive (assets) or pay (liabilities) fixed money amounts. These balance sheet items represent **fixed claims to receive or pay money,** and are called **monetary assets** and **monetary liabilities.** Monetary assets such as cash and accounts receivable entitle the entity to receive a fixed money amount regardless of whether prices are increasing or decreasing. Yet these fixed claims to receive (in the case of monetary assets) or pay (in the case of monetary liabilities) specified money amounts are somehow affected by changing prices. The final section of this appendix explains how to measure the impact of changing prices on monetary assets and liabilities.

Monetary Gains and Losses

As prices change, the values of some assets and liabilities change while the values of other assets and liabilities remain fixed. For example, the amount of cash you can receive from a customer with a $100 outstanding accounts receivable balance does not change over time. However, the amount of cash you can receive for unsold inventory will normally increase as prices increase and decrease as prices decrease.

Cash and accounts receivable are examples of **monetary assets** because they represent **fixed claims to a specified number of dollars.** Inventory and land are examples of **nonmonetary assets** that do not represent fixed claims but instead represent assets whose values may change as prices change. Since most liabilities represent fixed claims to a specified number of dollars, most liabilities are monetary liabilities.

Typical examples of monetary and nonmonetary assets and liabilities are listed in the following table.

Assets	*Liabilities and Stockholders' Equity*
Monetary items:	**Monetary items:**
Cash	Accounts payable
Accounts receivable	Notes payable
Notes receivable	Salaries payable
Leases receivable	Taxes payable
Long-term investment in bonds	Bonds payable
	Dividends payable
Nonmonetary items:	**Nonmonetary items:**
Inventories	Estimated liabilities
Most investments in stocks	Advances from customers
Land	Preferred stock
Building	Convertible bonds and stocks expected to be converted to common stock
Equipment	Common stock
Intangible assets	

These assets, liabilities, and stockholders' equity items are classified as monetary or nonmonetary depending strictly on whether they represent fixed claims to receive (or pay) a specified number of dollars that will not vary as prices change.

Whenever a balance sheet item represents a fixed claim to receive or provide a specified number of dollars, it is a monetary item. While the recorded measures of monetary items do not change, their economic value to the company holding the asset or liability does change as prices change. For example, if you hold cash for one year and general price levels increase by 10% during that time, the cash will buy 10% less at the end of the year, resulting in a "monetary loss." Thus, if you hold monetary assets in a period of increasing prices, a **monetary loss** results. However, holding monetary liabilities in a period of increasing prices will result in **monetary gains** because you can pay off these liabilities with "cheaper dollars," dollars that can buy less than the dollars originally borrowed.

Monetary gains and losses (also called **purchasing power gains or losses**) resulting from holding monetary items in periods of changing prices are not reported in conventional GAAP financial statements, but their effects are measurable and may be of interest to decision makers.

Objective 4
How to measure monetary gains or losses and their effect on the business entity.

To illustrate, assume Company X borrows $100,000 cash from Company Y at 0% interest on January 1, 19x9. (The effect of interest rates is examined in more advanced accounting texts.)[1] The general price index increases from 160 to 192 during 19x9, an increase of 20% [(192 − 160)/160 = 32/160 = .20 = 20%)]. On December 31, 19x9, Company X repays the $100,000 cash to Company Y. Because of the note payable to Company Y, Company X experienced a monetary gain of $20,000, the difference between the nominal dollar value and the constant dollar value of the note, computed as follows:

19x9	*Note Payable*	*Nominal Dollars*	×	*Conversion Ratio*	=	*Year-End Constant Dollars (192)*
Jan. 1	Beginning balance	$ 100,000	×	192/160	=	$ 120,000
Dec. 31	Change (repayment) . . .	(100,000)	×	192/192	=	(100,000)
31	Ending balance	$ 0		→		$ 20,000
					−	0
	Monetary gain					$ 20,000

The recorded value of the note payable remains at $100,000 on the books of Company X until paid at year-end. However, the value (or size) of the dollars used to repay the loan are not the **same** as those received on January 1! The dollars borrowed on January 1, 19x9, are size 160 index dollars, whereas the dollars used to repay the note on December 31, 19x9, are size 192 index dollars. In other words, it would take $192 at the end of 19x9 to buy the same things that $160 could have purchased at the start of 19x9, resulting in a 20% decline in purchase power [($160 − $192)/$160 = −.20 = −20%]. The purchasing power of the dollar has declined during 19x9, and the $100,000 cash at year-end will buy 20% less than the $100,000 cash at the start of the year. If Company X had taken the $100,000 cash on January 1 and invested it in the items making up the general price index (e.g., the "market basket" of goods and services), these items would be worth $120,000 at year-end. Company Y, holding a note receivable throughout 19x9, would have experienced a monetary loss of $20,000 from this loan.

[1]Interest rates on debt are generally established based on expected future inflation. As such, an interest rate may be viewed as consisting of two parts: one part to compensate the lender for expected future inflation plus a second part to provide the lender with a **real** return on his or her capital. A 10% interest rate might be based on 4% for expected inflation plus 6% for the real return. A borrower would only obtain a *real* benefit from a monetary gain if the actual rate of inflation exceeded the lender's expected rate of inflation. However, a monetary gain will still result in any case where there is a net monetary liability position in a period of inflation, as in the example later in this section. Without knowing the expected rate of *inflation* included in the lender's interest rate, it is not possible to determine whether monetary gains represent real gains to the borrower or real losses to the lender. This same uncertainty exists for monetary losses if the lender was expecting some unknown rate of deflation.

Note that in the example above, if Company X had simply held onto the $100,000 cash until the year-end repayment, it would have had a $20,000 monetary loss from holding cash to offset against the $20,000 monetary gain from the note payable. To illustrate how to compute the **net monetary** gain or loss for a company, assume the following data for the Tran Corporation:

Tran Corporation
Balance Sheet
December 31

Assets	19x7	19x6	Liabilities and Stockholders' Equity	19x7	19x6
Cash	$ 5,000	$ 8,000	Liabilities:		
Accounts receivable	28,000	22,000	Accounts payable	$ 5,000	$ 7,000
Inventory	42,000	45,000	Notes payable	40,000	40,000
Land	65,000	65,000	Total liabilities	$ 45,000	$ 47,000
			Stockholders' equity:		
			Common stock	$ 80,000	$ 80,000
			Retained earnings	15,000	13,000
			Total stockholders' equity	$ 95,000	$ 93,000
Total assets	$140,000	$140,000	Total liabilities and stockholders' equity	$140,000	$140,000

Assume that during 19x7, the general price index went from 150 at the start of the year to 200 by year-end, with the average price index equal to 180 during 19x7. Note that the average price level would be the sum of the daily price levels divided by 365 days and need not be exactly between the high and low price level for the year. Tran has two monetary assets (cash and accounts receivable) and two monetary liabilities (accounts payable and notes payable). In the previous example of Company X, note that the only change in the monetary account took place at the end of the year. Here we have several monetary accounts that could change daily. To simplify our analysis, *we assume that all account balance changes occurred evenly throughout the year,* unless otherwise stated. The total net monetary gain or loss for all four monetary accounts can be computed together, as follows:

	Monetary Liabilities (*Accounts Payable* + *Notes Payable*)	−	*Monetary Assets* (*Cash* + *Accounts Receivable*)	=	*Net Monetary Liability (Asset)*
Beginning balance	($7,000 + $40,000)	−	($8,000 + $22,000)		
	$47,000	−	$30,000	=	$17,000
Ending balance	($5,000 + $40,000)	−	($5,000 + $28,000)		
	$45,000	−	$33,000	=	12,000
Net increase (decrease) in net monetary liability					$ (5,000)

	Nominal Dollars	Conversion Ratio	Year-End Constant Dollars (200)
Beginning net monetary liability	$17,000	200/150*	$22,667
19x7 decrease in net monetary liability	(5,000)	200/180†	(5,556)
Ending net monetary liability	$12,000	→	$17,111
			− 12,000
Net monetary gain. . .			$ 5,111

*End of period index/Beginning of period index.
† End of period index/Average of period index.

Since the Tran Company was in a net monetary liability position (monetary liabilities exceed monetary assets) throughout 19x7 (a period of general inflation), the difference between their nominal dollar and constant dollar net liability position results in a monetary gain.

While monetary gains and losses are not recorded or reported in GAAP financial statements, they may be computed from the comparative balance sheet data for any company, and might be useful for evaluating the management of a company. Since a monetary gain will result from being in debt during a period of inflation, and since most people believe we will continue to experience some inflation in the future, it would appear that being in debt would be a good strategy! However, the monetary gains from being in debt during a period of inflation must be weighed against the actual interest cost paid on the debt.

This example helps to illustrate the fundamental effects of price changes on monetary assets and liabilities, which may be summarized as follows:

1. In periods of inflation (prices increasing):
   a. Holding monetary assets results in a monetary (purchasing power) loss.
   b. Holding monetary liabilities results in a monetary (purchasing power) gain.
2. In periods of deflation (decreasing prices):
   a. Holding monetary assets results in a monetary (purchasing power) gain.
   b. Holding monetary liabilities results in a monetary (purchasing power) loss.

In general, increasing prices benefit companies that have a net monetary liability position. Alternatively companies holding net monetary assets will incur monetary losses in periods of increasing prices.

DEPRECIATION AND PRICE CHANGES

In evaluating long-term assets in financial reports, an important aspect to consider is the effect of price changes throughout the useful lives of the assets. The longer the useful life of an asset, the greater the potential impact of price changes on its recorded book value. Over the last 40 to 50 years, most assets have experienced significant price increases. How do these price changes affect financial reports? To answer this question, consider the following example of two steel plants (dollar figures in thousands):

	Plant A	*Plant B*
Year assets purchased	1986	1979
Cost of assets	$40,000	$10,000
Maximum production per year	50 million tons	50 million tons
Annual cost of maximum production in 1988 excluding depreciation expense	$35,000	$35,000
Depreciation per year (straight line, 10 years)	$ 4,000	$ 1,000
Annual revenues per year at maximum production	$40,000	$40,000

Assuming maximum production, the 1988 income statements for each plant would be (in thousands):

	Plant A	*Plant B*
Revenues	$40,000	$40,000
Expenses:		
Material, labor, etc.	$35,000	$35,000
Depreciation	4,000	1,000
Total expenses	$39,000	$36,000
Pre-tax income	$ 1,000	$ 4,000
Income tax expense (40%)	400	1,600
Net income	$ 600	$ 2,400

Notice that both plants are identical in their operations except for the amount of depreciation charged and the related income tax effects. The depreciation difference occurs because Plant A was purchased in 1986 and is more expensive than Plant B purchased in 1979.

Several questions may be interesting to consider. Which plant is more profitable? Which plant provides more cash flow? If one of the two plants had to be closed, which one would you close? It seems that Plant B is more profitable than Plant A. However, since depreciation expense does **not** use cash, the cash flow from operations after taxes is higher for Plant A! If we assume all revenues are for cash and all expenses other than depreciation use cash, the following results:

	Plant A	*Plant B*
Cash inflows (revenues)	$ 40,000	$ 40,000
Less cash outflows:		
Materials, labor, etc.	(35,000)	(35,000)
Taxes	(400)	(1,600)
Net cash inflow	$ 4,600	$ 3,400

EXHIBIT C-4

Current Cost Annual Report Disclosure—Excerpt from Footnotes

The Quaker Oats Company and Subsidiaries
Comparison of Selected Supplementary Financial Data
Adjusted for the Effects of Changing Prices

(in millions)

For the Years Ended June 30	*1986*	*1985*	*1984*	*1983*
Net assets at year-end:				
—Current cost	$1,196.9	$1,194.5	$1,548.7	$1,184.6
—Historical	831.1	824.8	758.6	680.7
Increase in the general price level over/(under) increase in specific prices of inventories and property, plant, and equipment	$ (68.4)	$ (48.7)	$ (12.8)	$ (32.2)*

*Increase in general prices faster (slower) than specific price changes.

EXHIBIT C-5

Former Disclosures for Changing Prices

Standard Oil Company (Indiana)
Statement of Net Income
Adjusted for Changing Prices
For Year Ended December 31, 1984
(average 1984 dollars, in millions)

	As Reported (historical cost)		*As Adjusted for Changing Prices (current costs)*
Total revenues	$29,008		$29,008
Purchases and operating expenses	**16,126**		**16,133**
Exploration expenses		1,286	1,286
Selling and administrative expenses		1,302	1,302
Taxes other than income taxes		3,825	3,825
Depreciation, depletion, and amortization		**2,090**	**2,651**
Interest expense		446	446
Total costs and expenses	25,075		25,643
Income before income taxes	3,933		3,365
Income taxes	1,750		1,750
Net income	$ 2,183		$ 1,615
Unrealized gain from decline in purchasing power of net amounts owed			$ 267
Increase in specific prices (current cost) of inventories and property, plant, and equipment held during the year*			$ 5
Increase due to general inflation			1,043
Difference between increase in specific prices and the increase due to general inflation			$ (1,038)

*At December 31, 1984, current cost of inventory was $3,550 and current cost of property, plant, and equipment (net) was $23,643.

EXHIBIT C-5 *(concluded)*

Five-Year Comparison of Selected Financial Information Adjusted for Effects of Changing Prices (average 1984 dollars, in millions except as noted)

	1984	*1983*	*1982*	*1981*	*1980*
Total revenues:					
As reported	**$29,008**	$29,494	$29,783	$31,729	$27,832
Adjusted for general inflation	**$29,008**	$30,749	$32,049	$36,237	$35,083
Net income from operations:					
As reported	**$ 2,183**	$ 1,868	$ 1,826	$ 1,922	$ 1,915
Current costs	**$ 1,615**	$ 1,217	$ 1,058	$ 1,090	$ 1,180
Net income from operations per share:					
As reported	**$ 7.70**	$ 6.39	$ 6.25	$ 6.56	$ 6.54
Current costs	**$ 5.69**	$ 4.16	$ 3.62	$ 3.72	$ 4.03
Cash dividends per share:					
As reported	**$ 3.00**	$ 2.80	$ 2.80	$ 2.60	$ 2.00
Adjusted for general inflation	**$ 3.00**	$ 2.92	$ 3.01	$ 2.97	$ 2.52
Net assets at year-end:					
As reported	**$12,524**	$12,440	$11,426	$10,665	$ 9,385
Current costs	**$20,324**	$21,993	$22,721	$24,353	$24,543
Difference between increase in specific prices and the increase due to general inflation	**$ (1,038)**	$ (818)	$ (880)	$ 86	$ 776
Unrealized gain from decline in purchasing power of net amounts owed	**$ 267**	$ 264	$ 279	$ 567	$ 666
Percentage of net income to average shareholders' equity:					
As reported	**17.5%**	15.7%	16.5%	19.2%	21.6%
Current costs	**7.6%**	5.4%	4.5%	4.5%	5.0%
Market price per share at year-end:					
As reported	**$52⅞**	$50⅝	$39¾	$52	$ 79⅞
Adjusted for general inflation	**$52⅞**	$52¾	$42¾	$59⅜	$100⅝
Average consumer price index (1967 = 100)	**311.1**	298.4	289.1	272.4	246.8

Plant A paid less taxes due to its higher depreciation expense and therefore had $1.2 million more net cash inflow from operations. This makes the question of which plant to close more difficult to answer. Plant A has higher cash flow, but Plant B has higher profits. Most businesses would prefer the cash flows provided by Plant A and would close down Plant B.

The effect of price changes on depreciable assets makes comparisons within a company and between companies more difficult. Between 1976 and 1984, companies were required to provide supplementary schedules reporting the effects of changing prices on plant assets and inventory. Today, these disclosures are voluntary and need not be reported. Exhibit C-4 provides an example of a voluntary disclosure. Exhibit C-5 provides an example of the disclosures previously required by *FASB Statement No. 33* and several other related pronouncements.

In some industries where assets are, on average, rather old, the difference between historical cost depreciation expense and current cost depreciation expense can be large. It is possible that the additional depreciation expense on a current cost basis could change profits to losses if used to measure income. As a result, the current cost of depreciation should be considered in evaluating financial statements whenever possible.

SUMMARY

While current cost or constant dollar financial data are not currently required under GAAP, they were required as supplemental disclosures for many companies between 1976 and 1984. The contribution for decision making of current cost and/or constant dollar financial statements is greatest in economies experiencing significant price changes. However, when prices are relatively stable over time, the alternative to the historical cost (nominal dollar) financial statements are of less interest to financial statement users. Still, we should recognize the potential important effect of price changes on accounting data in making business decisions. Trying to compare the financial performance of a new steel company to one that was started 50 years earlier would be difficult without some consideration of the effect of price changes on measures of net income and return on assets. Over time, a series of relatively small price changes can have a significant effect, particularly on the values reported in the balance sheet for long-term assets. We should not lose sight of the effects of changing prices on financial statements in making decisions about the performance of companies at a point in time, or over time.

KEY TERMS

Constant dollar. Data that have been adjusted for the effects of changes in the general price index; also called general price level adjusted (GPLA) data.

Current cost. Accounting data that have been adjusted for the effects of specific price changes; also called replacement cost or specific price level adjusted (SPLA) data.

General price index. Measures the changes in prices of a group of items.

Monetary assets. Represent fixed claims to receive a specified number of dollars.

Monetary liabilities. Fixed claims to pay a specified number of dollars.

Nominal dollar. Units of dollars that do not differentiate by accounting periods. GAAP financial statements are reported in nominal dollars.

Nonmonetary assets. Assets whose value may change as prices change.

Price index. The ratio of current prices to some previous year's prices, with the previous year selected usually referred to as the "base year."

Specific price index. Measures the price and change in price of a specific good or service.

Stable dollar assumption. Assumption that the dollar measurement unit is an equal unit of measure over all time periods.

SYNONYMS

Constant dollar; general price level adjusted (GPLA).
Current cost; replacement cost; specific price level adjusted (SPLA).
Monetary gain (loss); purchasing power gain (loss).

QUESTIONS

1. Identify two cases where GAAP permits market values of assets to be reported.
2. Give an example of a general price index and tell what it measures.
3. Give an example of a specific price index and tell what it measures.
4. If the general price index increased by 10%, what do we know happened to the price of automobile tires?
5. If the specific price index for automobile tires increased by 15%, what do we know happened to the general price index?
6. Assume there is no change in the general price index. If the specific price index for food increased by 10%, what else must have happened?
7. How many different sized (indexed) dollars would typically appear in the balance sheet of a large publicly traded company? What is the effect of this on the comparability of one company's balance sheet with another?
8. Would it make more sense to restate the historical cost of ending inventory for specific price changes or general price changes? Explain.
9. Identify common examples of monetary assets and liabilities. Why are they monetary items?
10. What information is normally not available but is needed to measure the actual net monetary gain or loss that would result from borrowing $1 million at 10% annual interest per year during a period of inflation?

EXERCISES

EXERCISE C-1
L.O. 2

Constant Dollar Measurements—Earnings

The Brazil Corporation reported the following earnings results for the past four years:

Year	*Reported Earnings (in thousands)*
19x4	$3,547
19x3	2,956
19x2	2,274
19x1	1,895

During this same time period, Brazil's economy experienced rapid inflation, with the value of the dollar decreasing by 25% per year as follows:

Average for Year	*General Price Index*
19x4	244.1
19x3	195.3
19x2	156.3
19x1	125.0

Required:

1. Restate Brazil's earnings results for each year using average 19x4 constant dollars. (Round answers to the nearest thousand.)
2. Did Brazil have real growth in earnings during any of the last three years?

EXERCISE C-2
L.O. 4

Monetary Gain or Loss

Jensen Corporation started 19x1 with cash of $175,000. At the end of 19x1 the cash balance had increased to $275,000. During 19x1 the consumer price index (CPI) went from 300 to 330. Assume Jensen's changes in the cash balance and changes in the CPI both occurred evenly throughout 19x1.

Required:

1. Compute the monetary gain or loss that resulted from Jensen's holding cash during 19x1.
2. How would your answer to requirement 1 have changed if the CPI had decreased during 19x1?

EXERCISE C-3
L.O. 3

Current Cost Measures—Inventory

Drasko Corporation reported the following data concerning its inventory:

December 31	*Reported Book Value of Inventory at FIFO Cost*	*Specific Price Index at Year-End for Inventory*
19x4 . . .	$850,000	229.9
19x3 . . .	825,000	209.0
19x2 . . .	770,000	200.0

The FIFO inventory value states the ending inventory at year-end prices each year.

Required:

1. Restate the reported value of the ending inventory for 19x3 and 19x2 in terms of 19x4 year-end current costs.
2. Did Drasko have a real increase in inventory during 19x4 or 19x3?

EXERCISE C-4
L.O. 2

Constant Dollar Measurements—EPS

The Traster Corporation reported the following earnings over the past four years:

Year	*Reported Earnings (in thousands)*
19x4	$7,000
19x3	6,600
19x2	6,000
19x1	5,200

The general price index over this same period of time increased steadily, as follows:

Year-End	*General Price Index*
19x4	405
19x3	385
19x2	350
19x1	330

Required:

1. Restate Traster's earnings for 19x1 to 19x4 using 19x4 year-end constant dollars. (Round answers to the nearest thousand.)
2. In which years did Traster report real growth in earnings?

EXERCISE C-5
L.O. 4

Monetary Gain or Loss

Baily Corporation began 19x5 with accounts payable of $82,875. Baily made purchases on account of $473,800 evenly throughout 19x5, and payments on account of $465,300 evenly throughout 19x5. The consumer price index increased steadily from 320 at the start of 19x5 to 352 by the end of 19x5.

Required:
Compute the net monetary gain or loss attributable to accounts payable for 19x5.

EXERCISE C-6
L.O. 4

Monetary Gain or Loss

Arrow Corporation began 19x5 with accounts receivable of $95,000. Arrow recorded credit sales of $3,600,000 evenly throughout 19x5 and received $3,200,000 cash on accounts receivable evenly throughout 19x5. The consumer price index increased steadily from 320 at the start of 19x5 to 352 by the end of 19x5.

Required:
Compute the net monetary gain or loss from accounts receivable for 19x5.

PROBLEMS

PROBLEM C-1
L.O. 2

Constant Dollar Measures—Earnings

The Red and White Companies have been in competition with one another for some time. Their operating results for the past several years are summarized as follows:

	Earnings (in thousands)	
Year	*Red Company*	*White Company*
19x4 . . .	$650,000	$325,000
19x3 . . .	558,382	298,465
19x2 . . .	542,118	289,481
19x1 . . .	526,329	263,164

Throughout this time period, Red Company has had twice as many assets and liabilities as White Company. The general price index has increased steadily over the past four years as follows:

Year	*General Price Index*
19x4.	274.5
19x3.	261.4
19x2.	253.7
19x1.	235.0

Required:

1. Recompute the reported earnings of both Red and White in 19x4 constant dollars for all four years.
2. In which years, if any, did Red Company experience a real increase in earnings?
3. In which years, if any, did White Company experience a real increase in earnings?
4. Which company appears to have the most consistent real growth in earnings?

PROBLEM C-2
L.O. 3

Current Cost Measurements—Inventory

The Waymire Corporation reported the following balances in their retail furniture inventory over the past several years:

Year	*Ending FIFO Inventory Value*
19x4	$737,124
19x3	702,023
19x2	644,058
19x1	596,350

During the same interval the specific price index of furniture costs from manufacturers to retail outlets (like Waymire), as reported by the Bureau of Labor, changed as follows:

Year	*Specific Price Index—Retail Furniture*
19x4	287.9
19x3	279.5
19x2	254.1
19x1	231.0

Required:

1. Compute the restated ending inventory balance for 19x1 to 19x4 in terms of 19x4 current costs.
2. In which of the last three years did Waymire have a real increase in inventory?

PROBLEM C-3
L.O. 2

Constant Dollar Adjustments

The following data summarize the financial statements of Parrot, Inc., as of December 31, 19x6. The index data stated in parentheses to the right of each historical (nominal) dollar value indicate the general price index in effect when the original transaction giving rise to each item took place. (When more than one transaction affects an account balance, the index represents the weighted average index value.) The current general price index (at the end of 19x6) is 300.

Balance Sheet Data (in $000)

Cash	$ 130 (28b)	Accounts Payable	$ 293 (275)
Accounts Receivable	286 (264)	Wages and Taxes Payable	346 (300)
Inventory	620 (180)	Long-Term Debt	2,500 (160)
Plant Assets	4,180 (160)	Common Stock	2,000 (140)
Land	1,200 (140)	Retained Earnings	1,277 (?)
	$6,416		$6,416

Required:
Prepare a general price level adjusted balance sheet for December 31, 19x6. Round all answers to the nearest thousand. (Hint: Treat retained earnings as a plug; do not try to price level adjust this balance.)

PROBLEM C-4
L.O. 2, 3

Price Changes and Inventory

During 19x1 Darren, Inc., purchased 10,000 units of product X for $10 each at a time when the general price index was 200. At the end of 19x4 these 10,000 units of product X were sold for $15 per unit, when the general price index was 280. An additional purchase of 10,000 units of product X was made at the end of 19x4 at a then-current cost of $13 per unit.

Required:

1. Compute cost of goods sold and gross profit for 19x4 for product X on a historical cost basis.
2. Repeat requirement 1 using current costs.
3. Repeat requirement 1 using constant dollars (general price level adjusted amounts).
4. Compare your answers in 1 and 2 above. What is the apparent "holding gain" included in gross profit in the historical cost income statement?
5. Which measure of gross profit do you believe to be the most relevant for measuring Darren's operating performance concerning product X during 19x4? Explain your answer.

PROBLEM C-5
L.O. 4

Monetary Gain or Loss

The Print Corporation reported the following comparative balance sheets:

Print Corporation
Balance Sheet
At December 31

Assets	*19x2*	*19x1*	**Liabilities and Stockholders' Equity**	*19x2*	*19x1*
Cash	$ 12,500	$ 10,000	Liabilities:		
Accounts receivable	21,350	30,000	Accounts payable	$ 18,300	$ 15,400
Inventory	41,400	39,800	Notes payable	60,000	60,000
Land	60,000	60,000	Total liabilities	$ 78,300	$ 75,400
			Stockholders' equity:		
			Common stock	$ 25,000	$ 25,000
			Retained earnings	31,950	39,400
			Total stockholders' equity	$ 56,950	$ 64,400
Total assets	$135,250	$139,800	Total liabilities and stockholders' equity	$135,250	$139,800

During 19x2, the consumer price index increased by 14% (.14), with the average increase for the year equal to 7% (.07).

Required (round all amounts to the nearest dollar):
1. Compute the net monetary gain or loss from monetary assets (combined) for 19x2.
2. Compute the net monetary gain or loss from monetary liabilities (combined) for 19x2.
3. Compute the total net monetary gain or loss for 19x2.

CASES

CASE C-1
L.O. 3

Current Costs—LIFO Inventory

The Weber Company uses the LIFO inventory method to account for its various product lines. During 19x7, Weber eliminated one of these product lines, causing it to liquidate its LIFO layers from beginning inventory. The beginning inventory for product Z on January 1, 19x7, was made up of the following layers:

Year Added	*Units Added*	×	*Unit Price in Year Added*	=	*LIFO Cost*
19x1	2,000		$10		$20,000
19x3	1,200		12		14,400
19x5	1,800		14		25,200
19x6	1,000		15		15,000
	6,000				$74,600

During 19x7 Weber acquired 2,500 units of product Z at $16 per unit for a total cost of $40,000. By the end of 19x7, all 8,500 units of product Z had been sold for $32 per unit.

Required:
1. Compute the gross margin (sales less cost of sales) from sales of product Z for 19x7.
2. Assume next that Weber did not have any beginning inventory of product Z at the start of 19x7, but that they purchased (for $16 each) and sold (for $32 each) 8,500 units during 19x7. Compute the gross margin from sales of product Z for 19x7.
3. Your answer to part 2 above is equivalent to the current cost measure of gross margin. What is the amount of holding gains included in the gross margin measured in part 1 above? In part 2?
4. If you were top management of Weber and were attempting to compensate the sales force for their efforts to sell product Z during 19x7, which gross margin measure do you think would be most equitable? Explain your choice briefly.

CASE C-2
L.O. 4

Monetary Gains and Losses

During 19x3 Weber Corporation borrowed $1 million from State Bank, signing a five-year, 10% note on January 1 of the year. The note calls for annual interest payments, with the principal to be paid at maturity. The corporation, which was owned by the Weber family, had never borrowed on a long-term basis before, and the president, John Weber, was nervous about doing so in 19x3 because of the changing economic climate. The inflation rate over the past three years (19x0 to 19x2) had been quite low, averaging about 2% per year. However, during 19x3 inflation began to climb, and by 19x4 it was up to about a 6% annual rate. Weber's chief accountant seemed happy with the increase in inflation and reported to John Weber at the end of 19x4 that the corporation was experiencing a large monetary gain from the $1 million bank loan. John Weber is having a difficult time understanding how being in debt can result in a gain. The financial statements do not report any such gain, but do report $100,000 interest expense in the 19x4 income statement.

Required:

1. Write a short note explaining to Mr. Weber how the recent inflationary trend might be viewed as a gain.
2. What information would you need to determine whether or not a real gain existed in this case?

CASE C-3
L.O. 2, 3

General versus Specific Price Changes

Assume you are an investor who owns stock in about 25 large publicly traded corporations which you have held for the past five years. You invested $500,000 in these stocks five years ago because of their dividends, which is your major source of income. Over the past five years, your total dividends from these same investments have been as follows:

Year	*Dividends Received*
19x9	$67,350
19x8	63,200
19x7	61,940
19x6	60,015
19x5	57,330

Your accountant has frequently discussed the effects of changing prices on your investments with you. You understand that there are both specific price changes, which affect each of your companies somewhat differently, and general price changes which affect the economy as a whole. You realize that over the past five years there have been some rather significant general and specific price changes which have affected your investments. You begin to wonder whether *you* are really better off in 19x9 than you were in 19x5.

Required:

What general or specific price adjusted information might help you decide whether or not *you* are better off in 19x9 than you were in 19x5? Would general or specific price adjusted data be more useful to you? Explain your answer.

CASE C-4
L.O. 2, 3

General versus Specific Price Changes

Assume you are the chief operating officer for the Norfold plant of the Beldon Corporation. As the plant's top manager, you are held responsible for its performance by corporate management. The main asset controlled by your plant is inventory. Inventory costs have fluctuated widely over the past six years, with costs continuously experiencing rather large increases or decreases. The economy has experienced a steady increase in inflation over this same time period, causing selling prices to climb steadily. Your plant uses the LIFO method for costing inventories. You realize that the reported asset value for inventory is not realistic since it consists primarily of costs from many years ago. This is having a serious effect on your analysis of your investment in inventory, inventory turnover ratios, etc. You would like to evaluate inventory using measures which better represent the current economic conditions. Most of your competitors are using the FIFO method of costing their inventory and are less affected by price changes.

Required:

What general or specific price adjusted information might best help you evaluate your investment in inventory over the past six years compared to both yourself (year-to-year) and your competitors? Explain your answer.

APPENDIX D

Accounting for Not-for-Profit Entities

LEARNING OBJECTIVES

After studying Appendix D, you should understand:

1. The difference between not-for-profit and business entities, pp. 946-47.
2. The nature of fund accounting, including fund accounting statements and types of funds, pp. 947-52.
3. The three key features of fund accounting—modified accrual accounting, accounting for encumbrances, and accounting for budgets, pp. 952-60.
4. Reporting for multiple funds and evaluating not-for-profit entities, pp. 960-65.

Note: This appendix could be covered anytime after Chapter 8. It is probably best to cover this appendix near the end of the course if inclusion is elected. It is somewhat longer and more mechanically involved than Appendixes A, B, or C.

ACCOUNTING FOR NOT-FOR-PROFIT ENTITIES—FUND ACCOUNTING

Although this textbook has concentrated on profit-seeking business entities, a great many resources in the United States are controlled by approximately 1,000,000 not-for-profit entities which include federal, state, and local governments; universities; hospitals; religious organizations; and various public service organizations (e.g., the United Way). These organizations are also frequently referred to as nonbusiness entities. In this appendix you will learn some of the basic concepts of accounting for not-for-profit entities.

Objective 1
The difference between not-for-profit and business entities.

Not-for-profit entities are organizations established to provide goods and/or services on a nonprofit basis. As you know, **business entities** are established to provide goods and/or services at a profit. The lack of a profit motive may seem like a minor difference separating business entities from nonbusiness entities; however, this profit motive difference is associated with major differences in the accounting systems of business and nonbusiness entities. For example, the lack of a profit motive creates problems in evaluating the performance of not-for-profit entities.

The three major categories of entities using not-for-profit systems are:

1. Federal, state, and local governmental units.
2. Hospital and health care entities.
3. Colleges and universities.

Specialized accounting standards and special-interest groups affect the accounting information systems of these three groups of not-for-profit entities. For example, the Municipal Finance Officers Association has established a National Council on Governmental Accounting (NCGA) which has published several statements on financial reporting principles.[1] Special-interest groups like the NCGA have in some cases helped formulate generally accepted accounting principles (GAAP) for not-for-profit entities.

In 1984, the Financial Accounting Foundation (which is also the "parent" of the FASB) organized the **Government Accounting Standards Board (GASB)** to establish GAAP for governmental units. In its first GASB statement, *GASB No. 1*, "Authoritative Status of NCGA Pronouncements and AICPA Industry Audit Guide," the GASB recognized the authority of the pronouncements of these two unrelated organizations (NCGA and AICPA) in establishing GAAP. The AICPA (American Institute of Certified Public Accountants) has also been influential in defining GAAP for hospitals, colleges, and universities. In general, the GASB is now responsible for formulating GAAP for governmental units, while the FASB remains involved in establishing GAAP for hospitals, colleges, universities, and most other not-for-profit organizations. Still many other organizations play an important part in the establishment of GAAP for not-for-profit entities.

Although we cannot adequately cover GAAP for all not-for-profit entities in this appendix, we do introduce the basic underlying concepts. Also, the basic differences between not-for-profit accounting and for-profit accounting are discussed. Some advanced accounting textbooks discuss not-for-profit accounting systems in much greater detail.

[1]For example, see NCGA, "Government Accounting and Financial Reporting Principles, Statement 1" (Chicago: Municipal Finance Officers Association of the United States and Canada, 1979).

You should be aware that GAAP for not-for-profit entities is changing rapidly, with standard setting becoming most active during the past two decades. This increased activity reflects a greater public awareness and concern with how efficiently the vast amounts of resources controlled by the not-for-profit organizations are being utilized. With the federal government alone spending over $1 trillion a year, this increased interest is surely warranted. The expected trend for the future is to make not-for-profit accounting systems more like those of business entities, moving toward a more complete accrual accounting approach to permit costs and benefits to be assessed by taxpayers, insurers, patients, and other providers of funds to not-for-profit entities.

Accounting systems for nonbusiness entities are typically referred to as **fund accounting systems.** The term *fund* used in nonbusiness accounting has a special meaning, as defined in the sections to follow. Three key features of most fund accounting systems that differ from accounting for profit-oriented businesses include:

1. A modified accrual system.
2. A different type of a liability, called *Reserve for Encumbrance*, which is formally recorded when funds are committed (e.g., a purchase agreement).
3. Budgets that are formally recorded in the accounting system.

We begin with a general discussion of the nature of fund accounting. Then, we examine the above three key features that make fund accounting systems different from profit-oriented business accounting. We conclude with a brief discussion of reporting for multiple funds and evaluating not-for-profit entities.

NATURE OF FUND ACCOUNTING

A fund is an accounting entity within the larger nonbusiness entity with a self-balancing set of accounts that is usually defined by its purpose. Like any entity, a fund consists of resources, which equal the claims against these resources. In fund accounting, **fund assets** are those resources controlled by the fund that are available to carry out the specified purpose(s) of the fund.[2] **Fund liabilities** represent those claims or other uses or proposed uses of fund assets that have yet to be paid.[3]

In business entities, the difference between assets and liabilities is called *owners' equity;* however, in nonbusiness entities, fund assets less fund liabilities is known as the **fund balance.** Thus, the fund balance represents the difference between the resources available to carry out the activities of the fund and the claims against these resources. The statement reporting the resources, claims, and balance of the fund is the balance sheet, which looks much like the balance sheet of any business entity.

Objective 2
The nature of fund accounting, including fund accounting statements and types of funds.

While the financial statements of profit-oriented business entities include an income (or earnings) statement, no income statement is prepared for not-for-profit entities. Instead, the not-for-profit accounting system uses a **statement of revenues, expenditures, and changes in fund balance (SRECFB)**, which focuses on the flow of resources into and from the fund and reconciles changes in the

[2]See *Statement of Financial Accounting Concepts No. 6,* "Elements of Financial Statements" (Norwalk, Conn.: FASB, 1985).

[3]Ibid.

fund balance sheet during the period. Also referred to by other names, such as an activity statement, statement of inflows and outflows, and so on, the SRECFB identifies the sources of resources coming into the fund and their uses for a specified period of time. If sources exceed uses during the period, the "fund balance" in the balance sheet increases much like retained earnings increases with net income. If uses exceed sources during the period, the "fund balance" decreases.

Many nonprofit entities (e.g., city or state governments) are required by law to maintain a positive fund balance. However, the federal government has for some time had a large negative fund balance that we know as the national debt or deficit. Deficit spending by the federal government means that the uses of funds exceed the sources of funds for a specified period of time. Often, federal deficit spending is financed by issuing U.S. government debt (e.g., the federal government issues U.S. Treasury Bonds), thus the accumulated outstanding deficit is often call the national debt.

Fund Accounting Statements

To illustrate the fund balance sheet and SRECFB, consider the balance sheet and SRECFB of Pioneer City High School (Exhibit D-1). For fund assets, Pioneer reports cash and receivables from various funding agencies available for running the operation of the high school. The fund liabilities are unpaid expenditures necessary to operate the school.

The SRECFB reports the sources of the revenues received by Pioneer City High School Fund and how the school used these resources. Note that the 19x2 increase in fund balance ($14,460) represents the excess of revenues less expenditures and the change in the fund balance between 19x2 and 19x1 ($103,040 – $88,580 = $14,460).

The purpose of the Pioneer City High School Fund is to account for the day-to-day operations of the high school. As a result, the statements of this fund only report on these responsibilities. Other funds (entities) may also exist for activities such as Pioneer City Elementary School, Pioneer City Fire Department, Pioneer City Police, Pioneer City Public Library, and so on.

Also, within a given entity, special-purpose funds might exist that require separate fund accounting. For example, within the Pioneer City High School Fund, there may be special funds for band, athletics, or the drama club. These funds may report separately, and they may also be included in the overall statements illustrated in Exhibit D-1. Similarly, Pioneer City might report separate statements for the high school fund, fire department fund, and so on, or Pioneer City might report a single set of statements for all activities under the jurisdiction of Pioneer City. This is similar to the separate/combined reporting that business entities use when a parent company has a number of 100% owned subsidiaries (see Chapter 12 on investments).

No rule exists that states when an activity should be reported as a separate fund or as part of a fund. A separate set of fund accounts and statements may be prepared for any specific activity. The domain of a fund and what it accounts for depends on the specified purpose or *charge* of the fund's activity.

Types of Funds

Objective 2
The nature of fund accounting, including fund accounting statements and types of funds.

Although any not-for-profit entity may include many separate funds, accountants have identified and defined categories of funds to help determine the type of fund involved and its related accounting system attributes. Different types of funds have somewhat different accounting attributes. In governmental accounting, the GASB has identified seven types of funds, while colleges and universities usually use six different types of funds. The titles and brief descriptions of these types of funds are summarized in Exhibit D-2.

EXHIBIT D-1

Fund Accounting Statements

Pioneer City High School
Balance Sheet
At December 31

	19x2	*19x1*
Assets:		
Cash	$ 23,200	$ 19,800
Taxes receivable	187,950	162,800
Federal funding receivable	71,240	68,440
State funding receivable	13,010	9,960
Total assets	$ 295,400	$ 261,000
Liabilities:		
Accounts payable	$ 105,420	$ 108,990
Salaries and benefits payable	86,940	63,430
Fund equity:		
Fund balance	103,040	88,580
Total liabilities and fund equity	$ 295,400	$ 261,000

Pioneer City High School
Statement of Revenues, Expenditures, and Changes in Fund Balance for the Years Ending December 31

	19x2	*19x1*
Revenues:		
From property taxes	$2,897,205	$2,599,603
From federal agencies	383,291	382,000
From state agencies	200,000	200,000
From school fund-raising activities	185,200	173,550
Total revenues	$3,665,696	$3,355,153
Expenditures:		
For faculty salaries	$1,488,960	$1,376,220
For administration salaries	370,469	330,105
For student aid	187,500	182,500
For the library	310,000	300,000
For texts, supplies, and other	1,294,307	1,162,738
Total expenditures	$3,651,236	$3,351,563
Net increase in fund balance	$ 14,460	$ 3,590

Since this textbook only introduces the basic concepts of not-for-profit accounting, we will not give detailed explanations and examples of all the various types of funds that can be found in not-for-profit entities. Instead, we will summarize all the different fund categories into three types of funds and discuss their basic aspects as follows:

1. General funds (or unrestricted funds).
2. Special-purpose funds.
3. Revenue-producing funds.

EXHIBIT D-2

Types of Funds

Government accounting systems:

1. General fund—for all activities not accounted for elsewhere.
2. Special revenue funds—funds accounting for specific sources of revenues.
3. Capital project funds—funds accounting for acquisition of major capital assets.
4. Debt service funds—funds accounting for payments of interest and principal on long-term debt.
5. Enterprise funds—funds operating similar to a business enterprise, to provide some public goods or services usually with fees for users.
6. Internal service funds—funds operating to provide some service to another fund (e.g., government printing office).
7. Trust and agency funds—funds responsible for holding resources to be used by some outside (private) agency or other governmental unit.

College and university funds:

1. Current funds—funds established to carry out the operations of the college or university (e.g., food service, housing, instruction).
2. Loan funds—funds established to account for loans to students, faculty, and other school organizations.
3. Plant funds—funds established to account for the acquisition, renewal, and replacement of facilities, and the repayment of debt incurred to acquire the facilities.
4. Endowment funds—funds established to account for resources received from donors, and the disbursement of the income from these resources for general or specific purposes as stipulated by the donor.
5. Annuity and income funds—funds accounting for donated resources, making payments to individuals in a stipulated way.
6. Agency funds—funds for which the college or university is a custodian on behalf of an individual student or faculty, or some group (usually affiliated with the school).

General Funds (or Unrestricted Funds). Most not-for-profit entities have a fund that is viewed as a **general fund** and is commonly known as an **unrestricted fund.** As the name implies, a general fund accounts for all activities that the entity (e.g., city) is responsible for that have not otherwise been assigned to another fund (e.g., a special-purpose fund). A general fund usually has the broadest set of responsibilities and the most diverse set of activities. If an entity has no revenue-producing funds or special-purpose funds, then the general fund accounts for all of the entity's activities.

Special-Purpose Funds. As implied by the name, **special-purpose funds** have specific responsibilities. These funds are specifically limited in their authority and responsibility. Some are designed to only account for expenditures, others are accountable only for inflows of resources, and still others do both. Common examples of special-purpose funds include:

Plant asset funds—These funds account for the long-term assets of a nonbusiness entity once they are acquired. One of the primary objectives of these funds is to facilitate the timing of when assets must be replaced, repaired, or renewed. This group of funds includes capital projects funds and plant funds as described in Exhibit D-2.

Investment funds—These funds take some of the resources of the nonbusiness entity and invest them in stock, bonds, and so on, to generate income for use by the entity. In those cases where the originally invested amount cannot be spent, the fund is called an **endowment fund.** Other funds that could be included in this category are trust and agency funds, annuity funds, and income funds.

Debt service funds—These funds are established for the purpose of paying the interest and principal on the debt (bonds or notes) of the nonbusiness entity. Usually resources are transferred from a general fund or an investment fund to the debt service fund so that interest and principal payments can be made.

Special-purpose funds in not-for-profit organizations can be grouped in many possible ways. One special-purpose fund is distinguished from another by the specific **charge** or task assigned to the fund describing the purpose of the fund and the authority and responsibility of the fund's managers.

The performance of special-purpose funds is evaluated on the basis of how well the funds achieve their purpose. Usually, when a specified purpose for a fund is not being achieved, the fund managers will request more resources or modify its operations in another way. However, the relationship between a fund's resources and its ability to accomplish its purpose is not always clear, making management performance evaluation more difficult in a not-for-profit entity than in its profit-seeking counterpart.

Revenue-Producing Funds. While general and special-purpose funds employ special-fund accounting procedures (illustrated in this chapter), revenue-producing funds do not. A **revenue-producing fund** may employ a regular for-profit-type full accrual accounting system. The major difference between the financial statements of revenue-producing funds and those of business entities is the use of a fund balance in place of owners' equity. Examples of revenue-producing funds include enterprise funds, possibly internal service funds, and certain current funds or loan funds (see Exhibit D-2), depending on the structure and purpose of the fund.

Whenever a nonbusiness entity conducts activities that involve receiving revenues based on the provision of some service or product, the entity may elect to establish a separate **revenue-producing fund** to account for these activities. Revenue-producing funds are similar to the enterprise funds described in Exhibit D-2. For example, a state may set up its state parks as a revenue-producing fund since the parks charge a user fee for their services (e.g., campsites).

Revenue-producing funds may be designed to lose money in that revenues are not expected to cover expenses. It is becoming more popular to identify those funds with distinguishable revenue-producing activities as revenue-producing funds and to account for them on a full accrual system just as for-profit entities. This approach allows users of financial statements to evaluate the fund's costs and benefits. The increased use of revenue-producing funds is expected to enhance the efficient use of public funds (e.g., taxes).

To illustrate, assume the state capital has a central copy center for copying all types of state government documents (i.e., an internal service fund). Assume the copy center is accounted for as a revenue-producing fund, with fees for copy services charged to each state government unit using these services. If the copy center is established as a revenue-producing fund with user fees charged to those who use the copy services, the efficiency of the government's copy center may be compared to that of other local private (for-profit) copy services. If a local private copy service could do the same job at a lower cost to the state government (and the taxpayers), state officials might consider switching to a private copy service (eliminating the government-run service) as a source of cost savings to the public.

Without information provided by a revenue-producing fund using conventional business (accrual) accounting systems, an evaluation of a fund's effectiveness or efficiency in its use of public resources is difficult, if not impossible. Therefore, revenue-producing funds are viewed as a means of improving the efficiency of certain nonprofit operations.

Not-for-profit entities use many types of funds. These funds may be categorized in other ways than the system described above which places all funds into one of three broad categories. Since revenue-producing funds are capable of operating on a full accrual accounting system like that discussed elsewhere in this textbook, the remainder of this appendix focuses on the fundamental accounting procedures applicable to general funds and special-purpose funds.

MODIFIED ACCRUAL ACCOUNTING

Objective 3
The three key features of fund accounting—modified accrual accounting, accounting for encumbrances, and accounting for budgets.

The modified accrual method of accounting is the first key feature of fund accounting systems mentioned at the beginning of this appendix. Most general- and special-purpose funds use a modified accrual system rather than the full accrual system employed by most businesses or the cash system used by many individuals for tax purposes.

As illustrated throughout this textbook, **accrual accounting recognizes revenues as they are earned and matches expenses with revenues.** On the other hand, the **cash basis of accounting recognizes revenues as cash is received and expenses as cash is paid.** Since most fund accounting activities are not involved in the process of generating revenues by providing goods or services as we normally understand that process, the full accrual method is not applicable. Also, the cash basis of accounting has limitations caused by differences in the timing of when cash is actually needed and when cash inflows occur. This inconsistency between inflows and outflows could result in overspending or underspending if funds were run on a cash basis. The most common solution to these problems is to use a modified accrual system for fund accounting.

The **modified accrual system** recognizes revenues as soon as their amount is known and their collectibility is reasonably assured. This revenue recognition point often coincides with when revenues are billed, since at the billing date the goods or services have been provided or another event (e.g., the passage of time) has already occurred giving rise to the right to collect revenues. For example, property tax revenue, city water revenue, and other city services (e.g., trash collection) are normally recognized at the time they are billed. Also, tuition revenue may be recognized at the time it is billed. Alternatively, some revenues such as sales taxes, late fees or fines (e.g., libraries), user permits (e.g., parks), and licenses (e.g., fishing, drivers'), are recognized when cash is received.

In a modified accrual system, **expenditures recognition** takes the place of expense recognition under the matching concept employed in an accrual system. Expenditures occur when the fund recognizes outflows of resources either from payments or from recording obligations of the fund. Note that in a full accrual system, **expense** recognition does not occur until resources are consumed. Hence, **expenditure recognition in an accrual system often precedes expense recognition** in the modified accrual system. For example, if supplies were purchased on account for $1,000, the accrual (for-profit) example would record an asset (supplies) and a liability (accounts payable) while the modified accrual system used by not-for-profit entities would record an expenditure and a liability. We will illustrate this difference between for-profit and not-for-profit entities more completely in the examples that follow.

Revenues—Modified Accrual

To illustrate the modified accrual system, assume Pioneer City assesses property taxes on all homes and businesses once a year. The assessed value of all property and the tax rate per $1,000 of assessed value are known on the first day of each fiscal year when tax bills are sent out. Note that when revenues for the year are known or reasonably estimable at the start of the year, they may be recorded on the first day of the year even if the revenue bills are not sent out until later in the year.

On July 1, 19xx, the start of the current fiscal year for Pioneer City, collectible taxes of $44,890,000 are billed to property owners. Assume that estimated uncollectible taxes are 2% of this total. The following entry would be recorded on July 1, 19xx:

19xx			
July 1	Property Taxes Receivable (A)	44,890,000	
	Allowance for Uncollectible Taxes (XA)		897,800
	Property Tax Revenue (R)		43,992,200
	To record property tax revenue for fiscal year.		

The asset, Property Taxes Receivable, and the contra asset, Allowance for Uncollectible Taxes, would be reported in the balance sheet. The Property Tax Revenue account would be reported in the SRECFB as a revenue.

Expenditures—Modified Accrual

Unlike the matching procedures used for expense recognition, the modified accrual basis reports expenditures for outflows of resources as soon as the fund becomes obligated to pay for goods or services. In other words, an expenditure is recorded, regardless of when the benefits resulting from the expenditure are to be used.

Exhibit D-3 compares the modified accrual system with the accrual accounting system. Note that fund assets are seldom created by the acquisition of goods or services by a fund. **Assets of a fund are those resources available to carry out the stated purpose of the fund.** The acquisition of supplies is viewed as an expenditure that has accomplished an objective of the fund (e.g., to buy supplies enabling the fund to repair school desks, projectors, driveways, and so on). The supplies are not considered assets because modified accrual accounting considers the supplies as no longer available to acquire the goods and services. Instead, the supplies are expenditures reported in the SRECFB as reductions in revenues. In general, expenditures in the modified accrual system precede expensing in an accrual system. Also, the modified accrual system has few year-end adjustments.

EXHIBIT D-3

Comparison of Modified Accrual and Accrual Methods

Event	*Fund Accounting—Modified Accrual*			*Business Accounting—Accrual*		
Buy supplies on October 1, 19x0.	Expenditures . .	7,500		Supplies Inventory	7,500	
	Cash		7,500	Cash		7,500
On June 30, 19x1, record use of $5,000 of supplies during year.	No entry.			Supplies Expense.	5,000	
				Supplies Inventory . .		5,000
Purchase insurance on facilities for the next 18 months on January 1, 19x1, for cash of $2,400.	Expenditures . .	2,400		Prepaid Insurance.	7,500	
	Cash		2,400	Cash		7,500
Six months' worth of insurance used—adjusting entry on June 30, 19x1.	No entry.			Insurance Expense	5,000	
				Prepaid Insurance. . .		5,000

New standards continue to reduce the differences between full accrual and modified accrual accounting allowed for not-for-profit entities. For many years, not-for-profit entities recorded expenditures for depreciable capital assets, such as furniture, fixtures, equipment, and so on, in the year of acquisition and did not record depreciation expense like accrual accounting (e.g., as in Chapter 8). Recently, the FASB issued a statement requiring that not-for-profit entities governed by FASB standards (e.g., schools and hospitals) also issue general-purpose financial statements to record depreciation on long-term depreciable assets.[4] Although GASB has not ruled on this issue for government entities, the trend is toward a more complete accrual system for all not-for-profit entities.

If a not-for-profit entity with a December 31 year-end used the modified accrual basis for a depreciable-type asset purchased on June 30, 19x1, for $60,000 cash, the entry would be:

19x1			
June 30	Expenditures.	60,000	
	Cash		60,000
	To record the purchase of an asset.		

At the end of 19x1, no asset would be reported on the balance sheet. If this asset had a five-year life and no salvage value (using straight-line depreciation), *an accrual accounting system* would have recorded the following entries in 19x1:

19x1			
June 30	Asset	60,000	
	Cash		60,000
	To record the purchase of an asset.		

[4]*Statement of Financial Accounting Standards No. 93,* "Recognition of Depreciation by Not-for-Profit Organizations" (Norwalk, Conn.: FASB, 1987).

Dec. 31	Depreciation Expenditure (E)	6,000	
	Accumulated Depreciation (XA)		6,000
	To record depreciation: $60,000/5 years = $12,000/year = $1,000/month.		

The year-end balance sheet would report a net asset of $54,000 ($60,000 – $6,000), and expenditures would be $54,000 less than in the modified accrual system. While most government entities (e.g., cities, states) still employ the modified accrual system, schools and hospitals now are required to use accrual techniques for depreciable assets.

ACCOUNTING FOR ENCUMBRANCES

Objective 3
The three key features of fund accounting—modified accrual accounting, accounting for encumbrances, and accounting for budgets.

The second key feature of a fund accounting system is that the fund recognizes commitments to spend fund resources before an accrual system would recognize them. This early recognition of commitments is called **encumbrance accounting.** Encumbrances are like expenditures in that they indicate fund resources have been spoken for. Encumbrances are recorded at the time funds are committed, before the recording of expenditures. The objective of encumbrance accounting is to prevent the fund from making commitments of fund resources in excess of the fund balance. An encumbrance is recorded like an estimated expenditure and is later converted from an encumbrance to an expenditure when the amount becomes known and an obligation exists. When these estimated future expenditures are recorded as encumbrances, fund managers can tell how much of the fund's resources have been spoken for at any point in time.

To illustrate encumbrance accounting, assume Pioneer City High School orders 50 new lockers on June 15, 19xx. An encumbrance is recorded on the date the order is placed, with the lockers expected to cost about $35 each at this time. The lockers arrive on September 1, 19xx, and the total actual invoice price is then determined to be $1,825, or $36.50 each. The encumbrance is converted to an expenditure on September 1, 19xx, the time the actual cost of the obligation is known. Assume the high school pays the invoice on September 30, 19xx. The four entries to record (1) the encumbrance, (2) the actual obligation, and (3) the payment are:

19xx			
June 15	Encumbrances (E)	1,750	
	Reserve for Encumbrances (L)		1,750
	To record estimated expenditure: 50 units at $35 each.		
Sept. 1	Reserve for Encumbrances (L)	1,750	
	Encumbrances (E)		1,750
	To reverse estimated expenditure.		
1	Expenditures (E)	1,825	
	Accounts Payable (L)		1,825
	To record actual invoice for expenditure.		
30	Accounts Payable (L)	1,825	
	Cash (A)		1,825
	To record payment for lockers.		

The June 15 entry records an encumbrance, which appears like an expenditure in the SRECFB (e.g., at June 30, 19xx) as an outflow or use of fund resources. The encumbrance represents the **estimated** cost of the 50 new lockers. Encumbrance accounts are closed to the fund balance at the end of each accounting period and are listed in the SRECFB with expenditures of the same category (e.g., equipment). Note that the debit to encumbrances of $1,750 on June 15, 19xx, would be closed to the fund balance on June 30, 19xx (the fiscal year-end for Pioneer City High School). The credit to encumbrances for $1,750 on September 1, 19xx, would leave a credit balance in the encumbrances account until other new encumbrance debits (like that on June 15) were added to its balance. At the end of any fiscal year, the balance in most encumbrance accounts will usually be net debit; but, if credit balances exist, they would offset the debit balances in the appropriate expenditures accounts.

The credit to Reserve for Encumbrances establishes a balance sheet account that represents an **estimated fund liability** which is reported in the balance sheet as a component of the fund balance until it is reversed on September 1, 19xx. As a result, the fund balance reported in the balance sheet has two components: (1) reserve for encumbrances and (2) fund balance (unencumbered).

Exhibit D-4 illustrates how the reserve for encumbrances and the fund balance appear in the balance sheet. In Pioneer's June 30 financial statements, the Reserve for Encumbrances account would alert the financial statement reader that funds of approximately $42,103 had been committed but not yet spent. In general, fund managers should have fund assets greater than or equal to fund liabilities plus Reserve for Encumbrances to prevent deficit spending.

EXHIBIT D-4

Balance Sheet Disclosure of Fund Balance

Pioneer City High School
Balance Sheet
June 30, 19xx

Assets	
Cash	$ 18,120
Taxes receivable	99,650
Federal funding receivable	13,105
State funding receivable	8,650
Total assets	$139,525
Liabilities and Fund Equity	
Liabilities:	
Accounts payable	$ 47,350
Salaries and benefits payable	19,730
Total liabilities	$ 67,080
Fund equity:	
Reserve for encumbrances	**$ 42,103**
Fund balance	**30,342**
Total fund equity	$ 72,445
Total liabilities and fund equity	$139,525

ACCOUNTING FOR BUDGETS

Objective 3
The three key features of fund accounting—modified accrual accounting, accounting for encumbrances, and accounting for budgets.

The third key feature of a fund accounting system is that the annual budget is formally recorded in the accounting records. While budgets are important accounting tools for both profit and not-for-profit entities, budgets have an added significance for not-for-profit entities. For example, in state and local governments, budgets often define the legal limit on expenditures (plus encumbrances) for specific fund activities. In most government entities, budgets establish spending limits that may not be exceeded without formal legislative approval for modification of the budget. As a result, the accounting records are designed to permit continuous comparison between **budgeted** revenues and expenditures and **actual** revenues and expenditures.

To illustrate how budgets are recorded in the accounting records, assume the Pioneer City High School has budgeted revenues of $3,800,000 for 19x2 and budgeted expenditures (normally called **appropriations**) of $3,600,000 for 19x2, resulting in a budgeted increase in the fund balance of $200,000 for 19x2 ($3,800,000 − $3,600,000 = $200,000). On the first day of the new budget year, the following entry would be recorded:

		Debit	Credit
(*a*)	Estimated Revenues	3,800,000	
	Appropriations		3,600,000
	Fund Balance		200,000
	To record the budget for the year.		

These three new budget accounts are like revenue and expenditure accounts in that they are nominal (or temporary) in nature and must be closed out at the end of each accounting period. Entry (*a*) in Exhibit D-5 shows a more detailed example of the summary entry provided above for the Pioneer City High School's annual budget. Note that debit/credit balances in the entry to record the budget are the opposite of **actual** revenues and expenses. For example, budgeted revenues have debit balances while actual revenues have credit balances.

Next, assume that actual revenues for 19x2 are $3,700,000 and actual expenditures are $3,580,000. The following entries which summarize these actual results for the year are provided in somewhat greater detail in (*b*) and (*c*) of Exhibit D-5:

		Debit	Credit
(*b*)	Cash (and/or Receivables)	3,700,000	
	Revenues		3,700,000
(*c*)	Expenditures (and/or Encumbrances)	3,580,000	
	Cash (and/or Payables; and/or Reserve for Encumbrances)		3,580,000

The following two T accounts would be reported prior to closing:

Nominal Accounts

Estimated Revenues

Debit	Credit
(*a*) 3,800,000	

Revenues

Debit	Credit
	(*b*) 3,700,000

Appropriations

Debit	Credit
	(*a*) 3,600,000

Expenditures/Encumbrances

Debit	Credit
(*c*) 3,580,000	

EXHIBIT D-5

Detailed Journal Entries for 19x2

Budget entry:

		Debit	Credit
(*a*)	Estimated Property Tax Revenues	2,900,000	
	Estimated Federal Program Revenues	400,000	
	Estimated State Program Revenues	300,000	
	Estimated Fundraising Revenues	200,000	
	Appropriations—Faculty Salaries		1,900,000
	Appropriations—Administrative Salaries		350,000
	Appropriations—Student Aid		150,000
	Appropriations—Library		350,000
	Appropriations—Texts, Supplies, etc.		850,000
	Fund Balance		200,000
	To record the annual budget.		

Summary entries of actual events:

		Debit	Credit
(*b*)	Cash	3,200,000	
	Receivable from Property Taxes	250,000	
	Receivable from Federal Programs	125,000	
	Receivable from State Programs	125,000	
	Revenues from Property Taxes		2,880,000
	Revenues from Federal Programs		400,000
	Revenues from State Programs		291,000
	Revenues from Fundraisers		129,000
	To record summary entry for revenues for the year.		
(*c*)	Expenditures—Faculty Salaries	1,895,000	
	Expenditures—Administrative Salaries	345,000	
	Expenditures—Student Aid	85,000	
	Encumbrances—Student Aid	45,000	
	Expenditures—Library	260,000	
	Encumbrances—Library	140,000	
	Expenditures—Texts, Supplies, etc.	695,000	
	Encumbrances—Supplies and Other	115,000	
	Cash		3,237,000
	Accounts Payable		105,000
	Salaries and Benefits Payable		38,000
	Reserve for Encumbrances		200,000
	To record summary entry for expenses for the year.		

To close budget accounts against actual accounts:

		Debit	Credit
(*d*)	Revenues from Property Taxes	2,880,000	
	Revenues from Federal Programs	400,000	
	Revenues from State Programs	291,000	
	Revenues from Fundraisers	129,000	
	Fund Balance	100,000	
	Estimated Property Tax Revenues		2,900,000
	Estimated Federal Program Revenues		400,000
	Estimated State Program Revenues		300,000
	Estimated Fundraising Revenues		200,000
	To close budget accounts.		

EXHIBIT D-5 *(concluded)*

		Debit	Credit
(e)	Appropriations—Faculty Salaries	1,900,000	
	Appropriations—Administrative Salaries	350,000	
	Appropriations—Student Aid	150,000	
	Appropriations—Library	350,000	
	Appropriations—Texts, Supplies, etc.	850,000	
	Expenditures—Faculty Salaries		1,895,000
	Expenditures—Administrative Salaries		345,000
	Expenditures—Student Aid		85,000
	Encumbrances—Student Aid		45,000
	Expenditures—Library		260,000
	Encumbrances—Library		140,000
	Expenditures—Texts, Supplies, etc.		695,000
	Encumbrances—Supplies and Other		115,000
	Fund Balance		20,000
	To close expenditures, encumbrances, and budgeted appropriations.		

Balance Sheet Accounts

Cash

	Debit		Credit
(b)	3,700,000	*(c)*	3,580,000

Fund Balance

	Debit		Credit
		(a)	200,000

At the end of 19x8, the following closing entries would be made to eliminate both the budget accounts and the actual accounts with the difference between actual revenues and actual expenditures ($3,700,000 − $3,580,000 = $120,000) left in the balance sheet account, Fund Surplus:

		Debit	Credit
(d)	Revenues	3,700,000	
	Fund Balance	100,000	
	Estimated Revenues		3,800,000
	To close revenues and budgeted revenues.		
(e)	Appropriations	3,600,000	
	Expenditures/Encumbrances		3,580,000
	Fund Balance		20,000
	To close expenditures, encumbrances, and budgeted appropriations.		

The detailed entries for the summary entries in (*b*), (*c*), (*d*), and (*e*) are also provided in Exhibit D-5. After posting these entries, the following balances would result:

Nominal Accounts

Estimated Revenues

	Debit		Credit
(a)	3,800,000	*(d)*	3,800,000
	0		

Revenues

	Debit		Credit
(d)	3,700,000	*(b)*	3,700,000
			0

Appropriations

(e)	3,600,000	(a)	3,600,000
			0

Expenditures/Encumbrances

(c)	3,580,000	(e)	3,580,000
	0		

Balance Sheet Accounts

Cash

(b)	3,700,000	(c)	3,580,000
	120,000		

Fund Balance

		(a)	200,000
(d)	100,000	(e)	20,000
			120,000

The budget accounts have been eliminated and would not appear in any of the year-end statements. Budget accounts are only used for interim reporting purposes to reveal how actual revenue and expenditures are doing compared to the budgeted amounts. This helps keep not-for-profit entities within their budgeted (or authorized) spending limits, reducing the chance of unexpected deficit spending.

REPORTING FOR MULTIPLE FUNDS

Objective 4
Reporting for multiple funds and evaluating not-for-profit entities.

Not-for-profit organizations often have several different funds, each with a separate set of self-balancing accounts. When financial reports are prepared for the entire organization, some form of consolidation of funds is necessary, just as in entities with subsidiary investments in excess of 50% ownership. Not-for-profit entities will typically report these results as illustrated in Exhibit D-6, a recent annual report of the American Accounting Association (AAA).

EVALUATING NOT-FOR-PROFIT ENTITIES

Some concern exists over the limitations of the accounting systems for not-for-profit entities. Without a "bottom-line" profit measure, it is difficult to compare and evaluate the effectiveness and efficiency of a not-for-profit entity. While the measurement of net income for businesses is not without its limitations, it does afford users some basis for comparing and evaluating the relative performance of business entities. Without the benefit of such a bottom-line measure, how can the effectiveness and efficiency of various not-for-profit entities be compared and evaluated? How can the demand for additional public resources by the fire department be compared to the need for more resources requested by the police department or the public schools? How can the resources used by the emergency room of a hospital be compared to those used by the cardiac care unit, or the intensive care unit, or the home health care unit of the hospital? How can the cost of the English department at a state university be compared to the Medical School or the Law School or the Business School?

Many important decisions concerning the allocation and use of public and private resources must be made by not-for-profit entities without the aid of uniform or comparable measures of effectiveness and efficiency. Each nonprofit entity, such as a fire department, is established for a specific purpose, such as fire prevention and control. It is often difficult to determine how successful the entity is at accomplishing its purpose. (For example, if you put out more fires this

AMERICAN ACCOUNTING ASSOCIATION

REPORT OF INDEPENDENT ACCOUNTANTS

To the Executive Committee of the American Accounting Association

In our opinion, the accompanying balance sheets and the related statements of support and revenue, expenses and changes in fund balances and of changes in financial position present fairly, in all material respects, the financial position of the American Accounting Association at August 31, 1989 and 1988, and the results of their operations and their changes in financial position for the years then ended in conformity with generally accepted accounting principles. These financial statements are the responsibility of the Association's management; our responsibility is to express an opinion on these financial statements based on our audits. We conducted our audits of these statements in accordance with generally accepted auditing standards which require that we plan and perform the audit to obtain reasonable assurance about whether the financial statements are free of material misstatement. An audit includes examining, on a test basis, evidence supporting the amounts and disclosures in the financial statements, assessing the accounting principles used and significant estimates made by management, and evaluating the overall financial statement presentation. We believe that our audits provide a reasonable basis for the opinion expressed above.

Our examination was made for the purpose of forming an opinion on the basic financial statements taken as a whole. The Statement of Contributions Earned is presented for purposes of additional analysis and is not a required part of the basic financial statements. Such information has been subjected to the auditing procedures applied in the examination of the basic financial statements and, in our opinion, is fairly stated in all material respects in relation to the basic financial statements taken as a whole.

Tampa, Florida
October 20, 1989

PRICE WATERHOUSE
Certified Public Accountants

AMERICAN ACCOUNTING ASSOCIATION

BALANCE SHEET

	August 31, 1989						August 31, 1988	
	Unrestricted	Restricted						
ASSETS	General Fund	Sections Fund	Fellowship Fund	Educational Research Fund	Regions	Total all Funds	General Fund	Total all Funds
Current assets:								
Cash and temporary investments	$ 762,735					$ 762,735	$ 990,774	$ 990,774
Current portion of pledges receivable	232,539	$ 264	$ 2,895			235,698	131,911	143,688
Accounts and interest receivable	59,033					59,033	50,402	50,402
Publications inventory	38,318					38,318	46,158	46,158
Prepaids and other assets	15,228					15,228	7,317	7,317
Due from (to) other funds	(372,023)	203,221	50,377		$118,425		(388,210)	
Total current assets	735,830	203,485	53,272		118,425	1,111,012	838,352	1,238,339
Pledges receivable, less current portion	477,250					477,250	246,666	246,666
Restricted assets, marketable securities	59,400					59,400	35,800	35,800
Property and equipment, net	165,055					165,055	160,746	160,746
	$1,437,535	$203,485	$53,272	$ 0	$118,425	$1,812,717	$1,281,564	$1,681,551
LIABILITIES AND FUND BALANCES								
Current liabilities:								
Accounts payable and accrued liabilities	$ 81,074	$ 6,501	$35,000			$ 122,575	$ 157,233	$ 204,194
Current portion of deferred revenue	160,553	18,031				178,584	192,447	214,202
Current portion of deferred support	175,676					175,676	72,905	77,905
Total current liabilities	417,303	24,532	35,000			476,835	422,585	496,301
Deferred compensation	59,400					59,400	35,800	35,800
Deferred revenue, less current portion	37,531					37,531	25,186	25,186
Deferred support, less current portion	477,250					477,250	246,666	246,666
	991,484	24,532	35,000			1,061,016	730,237	803,953
Fund balances:								
Unrestricted	446,061					446,061	551,327	551,327
Restricted		178,953	18,272		$118,425	315,650		326,271
Total fund balance	446,051	178,953	18,272		118,425	761,701	551,327	877,598
	$1,437,535	$203,485	$53,272	$ 0	$118,425	$1,812,717	$1,281,564	$1,681,551

The accompanying Notes to Financial Statements are an integral part of these financial statements.

— ANNUAL REPORT

AMERICAN ACCOUNTING ASSOCIATION

STATEMENT OF SUPPORT AND REVENUE, EXPENSES AND CHANGES IN FUND BALANCES

	For the year ended August 31, 1989						For the year ended August 31, 1988	
	Unrestricted	Restricted						
	General Fund	Sections Fund	Fellowship Fund	Educational Research Fund	Regions	Total all Funds	General Fund	Total all Funds
Support and revenue:								
Membership dues	$ 392,088	$114,153				$ 506,241	$ 379,277	$ 479,779
Subscriptions	154,705					154,705	143,150	143,150
Advertising	107,800	2,020			$ 69,767	179,587	98,031	98,031
Publications	73,928	22,850				96,778	46,595	67,141
Contributions	434,437	36,865	$36,843			508,145	294,191	354,280
Interest and dividend income	63,416				740	64,156	54,206	54,206
Annual convention	319,512					319,512	399,084	399,084
Other revenue (primarily programs and seminars)	168,923	68,585			149,349	386,857	134,936	389,489
	1,714,809	244,473	36,843		219,856	2,215,981	1,547,470	1,985,160
Expenses:								
Cost of publications	542,450	62,481				604,931	488,405	564,376
Programs and seminars	438,073	68,572				506,645	286,500	532,550
Research and education	7,021	1,053				8,074	2,529	2,529
Committees	57,802					57,802	46,614	46,614
Officers' meetings	52,411					52,411	48,431	48,431
Administration	435,388	101,958			199,850	737,196	421,200	475,811
Financial Accounting Foundation contribution	11,002					11,002	10,987	10,987
Fellowship grants			35,000			35,000		30,000
Annual convention	278,470	5,390				283,860	326,741	336,801
Other expenses	38,481		(3,524)			34,957	33,751	33,751
	1,861,098	239,454	31,476		199,850	2,331,878	1,665,158	2,081,850
Excess (deficiency) of support and revenue over (under) expenses	(146,289)	5,019	5,367		20,006	(115,897)	(117,688)	(96,690)
Fund balances, beginning of year	551,327	173,934	37,905	$16,013	98,419	877,598	674,015	974,288
Transfers in (out)	41,013		(25,000)	(16,013)		-	(5,000)	
Fund balances, end of year	$ 446,051	$178,953	$18,272	$ 0	$118,425	$ 761,701	$ 551,327	$ 877,598

The accompanying Notes to Financial Statements are an integral part of these financial statements.

AMERICAN ACCOUNTING ASSOCIATION

STATEMENT OF CHANGES IN FINANCIAL POSITION

	For the year ended August 31, 1989						For the year ended August 31, 1988	
	Unrestricted	Restricted						
	General Fund	Sections Fund	Fellowship Fund	Educational Research Fund	Regions	Total all Funds	General Fund	Total all Funds
Sources of cash:								
From operations:								
Excess (deficiency) of support and revenue over (under) expenses	($146,289)	$ 5,019	$ 5,367		$20,006	($115,897)	($ 117,688)	($ 96,690)
Charges (credits) not affecting cash in the current period:								
Depreciation	15,243					15,243	13,871	13,871
Deferred revenue - current and long-term	(19,549)	(3,724)				(23,273)	3,569	3,163
Deferred support - current and long-term	333,355		(5,000)			328,355	225,033	225,033
Deferred compensation	23,600					23,600	18,200	18,200
Cash provided from operations	206,360	1,295	367		20,006	228,028	142,985	163,577
Transfer between funds	41,013		(25,000)	($16,013)			(5,000)	
(Increase) decrease in:								
Pledges receivable - current and long-term	(331,212)	3,913	4,705			(322,594)	(239,778)	(205,367)
Accounts and interest receivable	(8,631)					(8,631)	2,068	2,068
Publications inventory	7,840					7,840	(1,351)	(1,351)
Interfund borrowings	(16,187)	15,252	4,928	16,013	(20,006)		36,131	
Total sources of cash	(100,817)	20,460	(15,000)			(95,357)	(64,945)	(41,073)
Uses of cash:								
(Increase) decrease in:								
Prepaids and other assets	(7,911)					(7,911)	5,488	5,488
Decrease in:								
Accounts payable and accrued liabilities	(76,159)	(20,460)	15,000			(81,619)	(34,796)	(92,581)
Purchase of property, plant and equipment	(19,552)					(19,552)	(5,191)	(5,191)
Increase in restricted assets	(23,600)					(23,600)	(18,200)	(18,200)
Total uses of cash	(127,222)	(20,460)	15,000			(132,682)	(52,699)	(110,484)
	(228,039)	-	-	-	-	(228,039)	(117,644)	(151,557)
Cash and temporary investments, beginning of year	990,774	-	-	-	-	990,774	1,108,418	1,142,331
Cash and temporary investments, end of year	$762,735	$ -	$ -	$ -	$ -	$762,735	$ 990,774	$ 990,774

The accompanying Notes to Financial Statements are an integral part of these financial statements.

(Continued)

NOTES TO FINANCIAL STATEMENTS

NOTE 1 - SUMMARY OF SIGNIFICANT ACCOUNTING POLICIES:

Basis of Accounting

The financial statements of the American Accounting Association (the "Association") are prepared in accordance with the Statement of Position (SOP) 78-10 entitled "Accounting Principles and Reporting Practices for Certain Nonprofit Organizations" issued by the American Institute of Certified Public Accountants.

The financial statements include the general, sections, fellowship, educational research and regions funds of the Association.

Pledges

Pledges are recorded as receivables in the year the pledge is made. Pledges for support of future periods are recorded as deferred amounts in the respective funds to which they apply. Support restricted by the donor for use in specified programs is recognized when the related program expenses are incurred. Non-restricted pledges, including pledges for publications, are included in the general fund.

Publications Inventory

Publications inventory is stated at the lower of cost or market. Cost is determined using the first-in, first-out (FIFO) method.

Property and Equipment

Property and equipment are stated at cost less accumulated depreciation.. Depreciation is computed using the straight-line method over the estimated useful lives of the assets which range from 5 to 20 years.

Membership Dues and Subscriptions

Membership dues and subscriptions are recognized in the applicable membership and subscription period.

Publication Revenue

Publication revenue is recognized when the related publications are issued.

Fellowship Grants

Fellowship grants are expensed at the time the grant is approved by the Association.

Research Projects

Research project expenses relate to projects authorized by the Director of Research and Director of Education and are accrued in the year the projects are authorized.

Income Taxes

Pursuant to a determination letter received from the Internal Revenue Service, the Association is generally exempt from Federal income tax under Section 501(c)(3) of the Internal Revenue Code and, accordingly, income taxes have not been provided in the accompanying financial statements.

NOTE 2 - DESCRIPTION OF FUNDS:

The assets, liabilities and fund balances of the Association are reported in five self-balancing funds, as follows:

General Fund

The General Fund is used to account for the operations of the Association, as well as those operations and activities not accounted for in other established funds.

Sections Fund

This fund was established to account for the activities of the Association's special-interest membership groups, such as the auditing section and public sector section.

Fellowship Fund

This fund was established to record the operations of the Fellowship program. Fellowships are awarded using funds generated by contributions to this fund.

Educational Research Fund

This fund was established to record research projects which are directly funded by the related pledges received. The educational fund was terminated during the current year.

Regions

This fund was established to record the operations of regional groups. These groups represent geographic areas, the purpose of which is holding annual meetings for the presentation and discussion of subjects in accounting and allied fields of interest to members of the Association. Funds are generated by collections for these meetings at the regional level.

NOTE 3 - CASH AND TEMPORARY INVESTMENTS:

	August 31	
	1989	1988
Cash and money market funds	$ 62,735	$290,774
Certificates of deposit	700,000	700,000
	$762,735	$990,774

NOTE 4 - PROPERTY AND EQUIPMENT:

	August 31,	
	1989	1988
Land	$ 29,748	$ 29,748
Land improvements	15,252	15,252
Building	173,271	173,271
Furniture and equipment	104,456	84,904
	322,727	303,175
Less accumulated depreciation	(157,672)	(142,429)
	$165,055	$160,746

NOTE 5 - EMPLOYEE BENEFIT PLAN:

The Association has a contributory money purchase pension plan which covers substantially all employees. During fiscal years 1989 and 1988, contributions to the plan were based upon 15% of qualifying employee compensation, and approximated $27,690 and $28,900, respectively.

NOTE 6 - EMPLOYEE AGREEMENT:

The Association entered into an employee agreement, effective September 1, 1985, requiring the payment of a minimum annual salary of $54,400 to its Executive Director. In addition, the agreement requires that the Association set aside a minimum of $5,600 per year for purposes of deferred compensation payments upon the retirement or termination of the Executive Director. At August 31, 1989 and 1988, $59,400 and $35,800 were accrued for deferred compensation and were invested in securities designated for such purposes. The agreement expires on August 31, 1990.

(Continued)

Notes to Financial Statements *(Continued)*

STATEMENT OF CONTRIBUTIONS EARNED

	For the year ended August 31, 1989	1988
General Fund:		
Arthur Andersen & Co. Foundation	$ 78,000	$ 58,000
Arthur Young Foundation	10,000	5,000
Coopers & Lybrand Foundation	18,500	21,709
Deloitte, Haskins & Sells Foundation	67,937	65,593
Exxon Corporation	4,000	4,000
Ford Motors	3,500	3,000
Price Waterhouse Foundation	17,500	7,500
The Touche Ross Foundation	175,000	129,389
Peat Marwick Foundation	10,000	—
Ernst & Whinney Foundation	10,000	—
Boise Cascade Corporation	10,000	—
Hewlett-Packard Company	10,000	—
Monsanto Company	10,000	—
Wells Fargo Bank	10,000	—
	434,437	294,191
Sections Fund:		
Other	36,865	14,299
Fellowship Fund:		
American Accounting Association Members and Others	11,843	14,170
Arthur Young Foundation	5,000	5,000
Coopers & Lybrand Foundation	5,000	5,000
Ernst & Whinney Foundation	5,000	5,000
Price Waterhouse Foundation	5,000	5,000
The Touche Ross Foundation	5,000	5,000
	36,843	39,170
Educational Research Fund:		
Coopers & Lybrand	—	6,620
Total Contributions Earned	$508,145	$354,280

year than last, is that good or bad?) It is even more difficult to compare the success of one type of fund (e.g., fire department) with another (e.g., police department) since each is established for a different purpose and with different objectives. While for-profit businesses have the virtue of a common objective—to earn profits for owners, not-for-profit entities seldom have common objectives or objectives that are readily measurable using accounting data. As a result, not-for-profit entities are frequently considered to be inefficient and ineffective at utilizing resources. This complaint seems to be particularly problematic in government entities where those providing funds (the public by way of income, property, and/or some other taxes) are only remotely influential in important decisions such as how much funding is required, for what purposes, and whether the existing level of funding is being efficiently and effectively utilized.

Because of the frustration with these limitations of not-for-profit accounting systems, more emphasis is being placed on using revenue-producing funds to account for activities whenever possible. Application of business accounting methods (especially full accrual accounting) to those activities of not-for-profit entities that generate some revenue from products or services is viewed by many as the primary tool to enhance the usefulness of accounting information. As for now, the arena of political debate and social choice makes the ultimate decisions about most nonbusiness entities. It is hoped that improvements in accounting for such entities may make for more rational social decisions.

SUMMARY

This appendix introduced the basic concepts of accounting for not-for-profit entities. We examined the nature of fund accounting and noted the differences and similarities of fund accounting statements and the statements of profit-oriented businesses. The fund accounting balance sheet is similar to that of a business, except that owners' equity is replaced by a fund balance. The statement of revenues, expenditures, and changes in fund balance (SRECFB) reports on the nature of balance sheet changes for a period of time.

The three key features that help to differentiate fund accounting are: (1) the modified accrual method, (2) the use of encumbrances, and (3) the formal recording of budgeted amounts. Each of these key features was illustrated in the chapter.

We concluded with a discussion on reporting for multiple funds and on evaluating fund accounting statements. This introduction to fund accounting, while brief, should be helpful for reading financial reports of not-for-profit entities and understanding some of the fundamental differences between business and not-for-profit accounting systems. Advanced accounting texts usually provide more detailed coverage of accounting for not-for-profit entities.

DEMONSTRATION EXERCISE

Paradise City realizes revenues from two sources—property taxes from city property owners and income taxes from employees within the city. During fiscal year 19x1, the following information is available for Paradise City government:

a. On January 1, 19x1, budgeted property tax revenue for the year is $15,481,685. Budgeted income tax revenue is $10,900,000. Paradise budgets expenditures for the year to be $26,100,000.

b. Paradise City bills property owners $15,960,500 for property taxes. Historically 3% of those taxes are not collected.

c. During the year, property tax collections total $15,725,000 and income tax collections total $10,461,300. All payments are received in cash.

d. Encumbrances for 19x1 total $9,860,500 of which $8,900,000 has been received and included in actual expenditures for the year. Expenditures for the year total $25,000,950 of which $22,105,000 has been paid in cash and the remainder is in accounts payable.

Required:

1. Prepare the journal entries to record Paradise City's 19x1 budget.
2. Prepare the journal entries to record actual revenues, encumbrances, and expenditures for 19x1.
3. Prepare the journal entries to close the appropriate accounts at the end of 19x1.

Solution:

Requirement 1:

Date	Account	Debit	Credit
19x1			
Jan. 1	Estimated Property Tax Revenue	15,481,685	
	Estimated Income Tax Revenue	10,900,000	
	Appropriations		26,100,000
	Fund Balance		281,685
	To record the budget for the year.		

Requirement 2:

Account	Debit	Credit
Property Taxes Receivable	15,960,500	
Allowance for Uncollectible Taxes		478,815
Property Tax Revenue		15,481,685
To record property tax revenue for the year.		
Cash	26,186,300	
Property Taxes Receivable		15,725,000
Income Tax Revenue		10,461,300
To record collections of property taxes and income tax revenue for the year.		
Encumbrances	9,860,500	
Reserve for Encumbrances		9,860,500
To record encumbrances for the year.		
Reserve for Encumbrances	8,900,000	
Encumbrances		8,900,000
To reverse estimated expenditures for the year.		
Expenditures	25,000,950	
Cash		22,105,000
Accounts Payable		2,895,950
To record expenditures for the year.		

Requirement 3:

19x1			
Dec. 31	Property Tax Revenues	15,481,685	
	Income Tax Revenues	10,461,000	
	Fund Balance	439,000	
	Estimated Property Tax Revenues		15,481,685
	Estimated Income Tax Revenues		10,900,000
	To close revenues and budgeted revenue accounts.		
Dec. 31	Appropriations	26,100,000	
	Encumbrances		960,500
	Expenditures		25,000,950
	Fund Balance		148,550
	To close expenditures, encumbrances, and budgeted appropriations accounts.		

KEY TERMS

Appropriations. Budgeted expenditures for nonbusiness entities.

Business entities. Established to provide goods and/or services at a profit.

Charge. Purpose given to a specific fund.

Encumbrance accounting. Early recognition of commitments.

Endowment fund. An investment fund where the original amount invested is not allowed to be spent.

Fund accounting systems. Term used to describe the accounting systems used by nonbusiness entities.

Fund assets. Those resources controlled by the fund that are available to carry out the specified purpose(s) of the fund.

Fund balance. Difference between fund assets and fund liabilities in a non-business entity.

Fund liabilities. Those claims or other uses or proposed uses of fund assets that have yet to be paid.

General fund. Accounts for all activities the entity is responsible for that have not otherwise been assigned to another fund; also called unrestricted fund.

Government Accounting Standards Board (GASB). Organization whose task is to establish uniform accounting standards (GAAP) for governmental units.

Modified accrual system. Accounting system used in nonbusiness entities which recognizes inflows of resources as soon as their amount and collectibility are reasonably assured and also recognizes outflows when a commitment of resources is made by the fund.

Not-for-profit entities. Organizations established to provide goods and/or services on a nonprofit basis; also called nonbusiness entities.

Revenue-producing fund. Fund a nonbusiness entity elects to establish when it conducts activities that involve taking in revenues based on the provision of some service or product.

Special-purpose fund. Fund with limited authority and responsibility designed for specific responsibilities.

Statement of revenues, expenditures, and change in fund balance (SRECFB). Statement that identifies the sources of funds coming into the fund and the uses of the resources of the fund for a specified period of time.

SYNONYMS

Encumbered; restricted (fund balance).

Fund purpose; fund charge.

General fund; unrestricted fund.

Not for profit; nonbusiness; nonprofit.

Unencumbered; unrestricted (fund balance).

QUESTIONS

1. What is a fund and how is it usually defined? Give an example.
2. What are fund assets and liabilities?
3. What is the fund balance?
4. What is deficit spending?
5. What are the three broad categories of funds?
6. Which broad category of funds employs the same accounting procedures as business entities? Why?
7. What is the fundamental difference between general funds and special-purpose funds?
8. Identify three types of special-purpose funds.
9. What are three key features of a fund accounting system?
10. In the modified accrual system used for fund accounting, when are inflows of resources recognized? When are outflows recognized?
11. What is an encumbrance and when is it recorded?
12. What is the role of budgets in a fund accounting system?
13. What are the two primary budget accounts?
14. What is the major limitation in evaluating the performance of most funds?

EXERCISES

EXERCISE D-1

L.O. 3

Recording Revenues

The city of Westbranch estimated its gross revenues from property taxes for the coming year ending June 30, 19x6, to be $3,875,000. In the past few years uncollected property taxes were about 2% of those levied. On August 31, 19x5, tax bills of $3,875,000 were sent to property owners in Westbranch. Cash collections between July 1, 19x5 (the start of the fiscal year), and August 31, 19x5, for property taxes were $1,000,000. (These were actually collected in advance of the billing.) Property taxes for the 19x5–x6 year, still uncollected at June 30, 19x6, were $56,300.

Required:

1. Record the July 1, 19x5, entry for property taxes, if any.
2. Record collections of the first $1,000,000 of taxes.
3. Record the entry for the August 31, 19x5, billing, if any.

EXERCISE D-2
L.O. 3

Recording Revenues

Millvale City estimated total property tax revenue to be $985,000 for the year starting July 1, 19x8. The expected uncollectible taxes are 1% of the total taxes. Millvale also has had revenue from parking tickets in the past. This revenue has varied between $4,000 and $1,800 over the past five years.

Required:
Record any entries required or implied by the above data. Be sure to date any entries.

EXERCISE D-3
L.O. 3

Recording Expenditures

The city of Westbranch has the following selected transactions for the year:

a. Westbranch officials obtained $5,000 of furniture for city offices on open account on July 1, 19x6. Payment for the furniture took place on July 20, 19x6. The fiscal year ends June 30. The furniture has a five-year expected life and no salvage value.
b. Westbranch officials purchased a new city car with a four-year life and no salvage value for $18,000 cash on June 29, 19x7.
c. Westbranch officials purchased $1,500 of office supplies on open account on June 30, 19x7. The supplies are expected to last for six months.

Required:

1. Record the journal entries for the year ending June 30, 19x7, for these three events using the modified accrual procedures of a fund accounting system (i.e., do not record depreciation).
2. Record the journal entries for the year ending June 30, 19x7, for these three events assuming conventional accrual accounting had been used. Use straight-line depreciation where necessary.

EXERCISE D-4
L.O. 3

Recording Expenditures

Selected events from the records of the Howell Public School District, which has a fiscal year-end of September 30, are:

a. Pays first annual interest payment of $20,500 on school bonds on June 30, 19x7.
b. On August 20, 19x7, purchases, on account $2,400 of art supplies for all elementary schools. Payment is made on the due date, October 10, 19x7. Half of the supplies are used by September 30, 19x7.
c. On September 1, 19x7, $15,000 of monies received from a federal grant is spent to purchase 10 computers with expected useful lives of five years each for the high school computer lab.

Required:

1. Record the journal entries required by these events assuming a modified accrual system is used by Howell.
2. What is the total expenditure to be reported for the year ending September 30, 19x7, for these three events using the modified accrual procedures of a fund accounting system?
3. What would be reported as an expenditure (expense) for the year ending September 30, 19x7, if conventional accrual accounting had been used? Assume all depreciable assets have no scrap value and employ straight-line depreciation.

EXERCISE D-5
L.O. 3

Recording Encumbrances

On June 15, 19x3, Knollville officials ordered a new fire truck. The estimated cost of the truck, fully equipped, was $38,000. Several companies were involved in building the truck and the final cost of $42,875 was not known until September 30, 19x3, when the truck was delivered. Knollville's fiscal year ends on June 30.

Required:
1. Record the entries necessary to account for the acquisition of the fire truck.
2. In which fiscal year will the fire truck appear as an expenditure? Explain.

EXERCISE D-6
L.O. 3

Recording Encumbrances

Rural School District orders five new buses on August 28, 19x3. The assistant superintendent of finance estimates the total cost of the buses to be $280,000. When the buses are delivered on December 1, 19x3, the actual invoice amount is $259,632. The district's fiscal year ends on September 30.

Required:
1. Record the journal entries necessary to account for the acquisition of the buses.
2. In which fiscal year will the buses appear as an expenditure? Explain.

EXERCISE D-7
L.O. 3

Accounting for Budgets

Cedarville has a June 30 fiscal year-end. The budget for the coming year calls for revenues of $4,500,000 and appropriations of $4,350,000. During the year, actual revenues were $4,800,000 and expenditures were $4,300,000. Encumbrances at year-end (June 30, 19x4) were $250,000.

Required:
1. Record the entries for the budgeted revenues and appropriations.
2. Record the actual revenues and expenditures. Assume revenues and expenditures were all for cash.
3. Record encumbrances.
4. Record the closing entries to eliminate the budget accounts and the other nominal accounts.
5. What is the change in the fund balance for the year ending June 30, 19x4?

EXERCISE D-8
L.O. 3

Accounting for Budgets

The city of Ishpeming has a September 30 fiscal year-end. The budget for the coming year calls for revenues of $16.8 million and appropriations of $16.1 million. During the year, actual revenues were $16.5 million and expenditures were $16.2 million. Encumbrances at September 30, 19x2, were $350,000.

Required:
1. Record the entries for the budgeted revenues and appropriations.
2. Record the actual revenues and expenditures. Assume revenues and expenditures were all for cash.
3. Record encumbrances.
4. Record the closing entries to eliminate the budget accounts and the other nominal accounts.
5. What is the change in the fund balance for the year ending September 30, 19x2?

EXERCISE D-9
L.O. 2–4

Multiple Choice

1. What type of account signals financial statement readers that funds are being earmarked to pay for goods or services that are ordered but not yet received?
   a. Appropriations.
   b. Reserve for Encumbrances.
   c. Encumbrances.
   d. Expenditures.
   e. Contingent Liabilities.
2. In fund accounting systems—
   a. The budget accounts appear in the balance sheet at year-end.
   b. The budget accounts appear in the SRECFB for the period.
   c. Some budget accounts appear in the balance sheet and some appear in the SRECFB.
   d. Budget accounts do not appear in either the balance sheet or the SRECFB.
3. In governmental accounting, when a legislative body designates that a certain amount of funds may be spent for a specific purpose (e.g., fire protection)—
   a. It is referred to as an appropriation.
   b. It becomes part of that government's budget accounts.
   c. It is the legal limit that may be spent for that purpose without further legislative approval.
   d. All of the above.
   e. None of the above.
4. When estimated revenues are less than actual revenues for the year—
   a. The fund balance must be negative.
   b. The fund balance must report a decrease for the year.
   c. The fund balance cannot increase for the year.
   d. All of the above.
   e. None of the above.
5. If the budget called for estimated revenues to exceed appropriations by $48,000 and actual revenues exceeded expenditures and encumbrances by $60,000, the fund balance for the period will—
   a. Increase by $12,000.
   b. Decrease by $12,000.
   c. Increase by $48,000.
   d. Increase by $60,000.
   e. None of the above.

EXERCISE D-10
L.O. 2, 4

Multiple Choice

1. In governmental entities, a fund that behaves like a regular business entity is referred to as—
   a. A profit center.
   b. A general fund.
   c. An enterprise fund.
   d. An internal service fund.
2. Virtually every government has—
   a. A debt service fund.
   b. A general fund.
   c. An enterprise fund.
   d. A capital projects fund.

3. The two broad categories of funds employed by not-for-profits that are usually on a modified accrual basis are—
   a. General funds and special-purpose funds.
   b. Special-purpose funds and revenue-producing funds.
   c. General funds and revenue-producing funds.
   d. All of the above.
   e. None of the above.
4. Examples of funds that could be considered revenue producing are—
   a. Enterprise funds and internal service funds.
   b. Debt service funds and capital project funds.
   c. Agency funds and plant asset funds.
   d. Endowment funds and enterprise funds.
   e. All of the above.
5. The purpose of a general fund is—
   a. To raise funds for other funds.
   b. To pay government salaries.
   c. For miscellaneous purposes.
   d. To account for all activities not accounted for by other funds.
   e. None of the above.

PROBLEMS

PROBLEM D-1
L.O. 3

Encumbrance Accounting

The Mason County Road Commission reported the following balances at June 30, 19x1:

Account	*Balance Debit (Credit)*
Reserve for Encumbrances . . .	$ (38,600)
Expenditures	263,100
Encumbrances	18,600

Required:
Use T accounts to help you answer the following questions:

1. What was the apparent beginning balance in the Reserve for Encumbrances account?
2. What is the total amount to be charged against revenues in 19x1?
3. If revenues during 19x1 are $300,000, what is the change in the total fund equity during 19x1?

PROBLEM D-2
L.O. 3

Balance Sheet

The general fund of Ski Town USA reported the following account balances at June 30, 19x1, just before closing journal entries were prepared:

	Pre-Closing Trial Balance	
	Debit	*Credit*
Revenues		$330,500
Taxes Receivable	$ 47,600	
Allowance for Uncollectible Taxes . . .		3,100
Accounts Payable		6,300
Notes Payable		58,800
Notes Receivable	39,500	
Appropriations		315,000

	Pre-Closing Trial Balance	
	Debit	*Credit*
Encumbrances	3,500	
Estimated Revenues	320,000	
Reserve for Encumbrances		13,000
Fund Balance		35,300
Expenditures	314,300	
Cash	37,100	
Totals	$762,000	$762,000

Required:

1. Prepare the necessary closing journal entries for all temporary accounts.
2. Prepare Ski Town USA's balance sheet at June 30, 19x1.

PROBLEM D-3
L.O. 3

Budgets/Closing Entries

The following account balances (all with normal balances) were available from the Jonville City ledger at the end of fiscal 19x3:

Appropriations	$356,000
Encumbrances	39,500
Expenditures	279,800
Estimated Revenues	340,000
Revenues	318,600
Reserve for Encumbrances	36,900
Fund Balance	8,200

Required:

1. Prepare the necessary closing entries.
2. What is the new fund balance at the end of 19x3?

PROBLEM D-4
L.O. 3

Encumbrance Accounting

The Town of Dent reported the following comparative balance sheet data (in millions):

	December 31	
	19x2	*19x1*
Fund equity:		
Reserve for encumbrances	$ 59.6	$ 84.3
Fund balance	163.2	118.9
Total fund equity	$222.8	$203.2

During 19x2, encumbrances of $189.9 million were charged against revenues. Also during 19x2 bills for goods and services totaling $237.8 million were received for items originally recorded as encumbrances of $214.6 million. Cash payments of $200 million were made during 19x2 on these billed amounts.

Required: (Hint: You may find a T account helpful.)

1. What is the change in fund equity during 19x2?
2. Record the encumbrances incurred in 19x2.
3. Record the reversal of encumbrances that occurred in 19x2.
4. Record the expenditures for the actual cost of encumbered goods and services in 19x2.
5. Record the payments made in 19x2.

APPENDIX E

1989 Annual Report — Ralston-Purina Company

Ralston Purina Company and Subsidiaries

THE COMPANY

Company's Businesses – The Company is presently comprised of three Business Segments – Human and Pet Foods, Other Consumer Products, and Agricultural Products.

The Human and Pet Foods segment consists of the Grocery Products Group, Continental Baking Company and the consumer products operations of the Ralston Purina International Division. The Company's Grocery Products Group produces and sells dog and cat foods under the *Purina* name, including *Dog Chow, Cat Chow* and numerous other dog and cat food brands. Also, the Group manufactures and sells *Chex* and other cereals, and a variety of snacks. The Company's Continental Baking Company subsidiary manufactures and sells bakery products principally under the trademarks *Wonder* for bread and *Hostess* for sweet baked goods. The consumer products operations of the Ralston Purina International Division produce and sell dog and cat food in 11 countries. The Company operates 65 manufacturing facilities in the United States and worldwide for the production of human and pet foods.

The Other Consumer Products segment consists primarily of the battery products business and the protein technologies business. The battery products business manufactures and sells primary batteries, rechargeable batteries and battery-powered lighting products in the United States and worldwide, principally under the trademarks *Eveready* and *Energizer.* The Company's domestic and foreign battery operations have been organized as Eveready Battery Company, Inc., and Ralston Purina Overseas Battery Company, respectively, both wholly-owned subsidiaries of the Company. Forty manufacturing facilities are operated in the United States and worldwide for the production of battery products. The protein technologies business has been organized as Protein Technologies International, Inc., a wholly-owned subsidiary of the Company. This subsidiary manufactures primarily food protein and industrial polymer products in six plants, four of which are located in the United States. Also included in Other Consumer Products is Keystone Resort. A wholly-owned subsidiary of the Company is the general partner of, and owns 50 percent equity in, the partnership owning the Resort, and another wholly-owned subsidiary manages the Resort.

The Agricultural Products segment consists primarily of the business of manufacturing *Chow* brand formula feeds and animal health products in 63 Ralston Purina International Division facilities outside the United States.

The Company acquired, in November 1989, the Beech-Nut baby food business which is engaged in the manufacturing and selling of prepared baby food, baby cereal and baby fruit juices.

Financial information relating to the Company's businesses is summarized beginning on page 9.

Distribution – Human and pet foods are marketed primarily in the United States through direct sales forces and food brokers to grocery and retail chains and other customers. Battery products and food protein and industrial polymer products are marketed in the United States and internationally primarily through direct sales forces. Agricultural products are distributed primarily through a network of approximately 3,500 independent dealers outside the United States.

Employment – More than 20 years have passed since Ralston Purina Company developed its first equal employment opportunity policy statement and affirmative action program. It is the continuing policy of the Company to provide equal opportunity for all its employees and job applicants on the basis of merit without discrimination because of race, sex, color, age, religion, national origin, veteran status, or physical or mental disability. In addition to providing equal employment opportunity, affirmative action is taken at each step in the employment process which includes but is not limited to the following: employment, promotion, demotion or transfer; compensation and employee benefits; selection for training including apprenticeship; and social and recreation programs sponsored by the Company. The Company realizes that only through the cooperation of all employees can the Company's nondiscrimination policy be meaningful.

Ralston Purina Company and Subsidiaries

FINANCIAL REVIEW

The following discussion is a summary of the key factors management considers necessary for an assessment of the Company's results of operations, liquidity and capital resources, and operating segment results. Additional information concerning the Company's results of operations and financial position are contained in the Chairman's Letter to Shareholders and the Review of Operations sections of this report.

Highlights

The Company sold its Van Camp seafood operations in November 1988 recognizing a gain on the sale of $70.2 million, net of taxes of $42.5 million. The gain on sale in 1989 and results of operations for all periods presented have been reclassified as discontinued operations.

In January 1989, the Company acquired a French-based battery products manufacturer for $124.0 million. The acquisition was accounted for using the purchase method of accounting and, accordingly, the results of operations are included in the consolidated results of the Company from that date.

The Company's Agricultural Products division acquired substantially all the remaining interest in its Mexican operations in May 1988. The results of operations, which were previously accounted for using the equity method, have been accounted for using the purchase method of accounting since the date of acquisition of a controlling interest.

In October 1986, the Company sold its domestic agricultural products business (Purina Mills) recognizing an after-tax gain of $209.3 million or $2.89 per primary share. In August 1987, the Company sold its Drake Bakeries, Inc. subsidiary (Drake), and recognized an after-tax gain on the sale of $43.0 million or $.60 per primary share.

OPERATING RESULTS

Net Sales

Net sales increased 13% in 1989 primarily on higher selling prices in most businesses and on the strength of international acquisitions in the battery products and agricultural products businesses. In 1988, higher sales prices and volumes in most businesses, particularly in international operations, offset the effect of the Drake disposition and accounted for the 5% increase. Comments on sales changes by business segment may be found on page 13 of this report.

Gross Profit

Consolidated gross profit increased 9% in 1989 following a 4% increase in 1988. Cost of products sold as a percent of sales increased from 53% in 1988 to 55% in 1989 after a slight increase in 1988. Increases in both years reflect higher ingredient costs in the Human and Pet Foods segment and, in 1989, increased raw material costs in the domestic battery products business.

Operating Expenses

Selling, general and administrative expenses increased $153.5 million in 1989, following a slight decline in 1988, primarily as a result of variable selling and distribution expenses. Selling, general and administrative expenses as a percentage of sales have declined slightly to 21% in 1989 compared to 22% and 23% in 1988 and 1987, respectively. Advertising and promotion expenses have remained at 12% of sales over the past three years, due in large part to costs associated with advertising programs designed to support product introductions in the Human and Pet Foods segment.

In 1989, the Company announced the planned closure or restructuring of certain battery manufacturing and bakery operations, and administrative restructuring. In connection with these decisions, the Company provided $31.4 million, before tax benefit of $11.9 million, or $.31 per primary share, in the fourth quarter of fiscal 1989 for costs associated with these actions.

Interest Expense and Investment Income

Interest expense declined slightly in 1989 to $217.7 million compared to $218.5 million in 1988 and $200.9 million in 1987. The increase in 1988 resulted primarily from higher foreign interest expense. Investment income was $33.5 million in 1989 compared to $18.2 million and $11.8 million in 1988 and 1987, respectively. Proceeds from the sale of businesses and net cash flow generated from operations provided the Company with additional temporary investments during 1989 and 1988.

Ralston Purina Company and Subsidiaries

FINANCIAL REVIEW

(continued)

OPERATING RESULTS

(continued)

Income Taxes

Income taxes, which include federal, state and foreign taxes, were 39.0% of pre-tax earnings from continuing operations in 1989, 40.0% in 1988 and 46.6% in 1987. These rates generally reflect statutory tax rates. The lower effective tax rate in 1988 reflects a reduction of the Company's statutory federal rate to 34%. The 1987 rate includes a statutory federal tax rate of 43% adjusted for capital gains treatment, net of depreciation recapture, of the sales of Purina Mills and Drake and a provision of $5.8 million representing the reversal of investment tax credit recognized in fiscal 1986.

In December 1988, the Financial Accounting Standards Board (FASB) deferred the implementation of Statement No. 96 – "Accounting for Income Taxes" – until the fiscal year beginning October 1, 1990 (fiscal 1991). The standard will significantly change current accounting methods for income taxes. The Company is currently evaluating the Statement's effects and determining the method and timing of its adoption. The FASB is currently considering postponing the Statement's mandatory effective date until fiscal 1992.

Discontinued Operations

Net earnings of seafood operations for the three years ended September 30, 1989 have been reclassified as discontinued operations. In 1989, the gain on the sale of discontinued seafood operations added $1.10 per share to primary earnings per share.

Extraordinary Item

The extraordinary item represents the after-tax loss on early retirement of debt of $3.3 million, or $.04 per share. Retired debt consisted primarily of the Company's outstanding 12% notes.

Net Earnings

Earnings from continuing operations declined $12.2 million or 3% in 1989 due primarily to the restructuring provision. Excluding the provision, earnings from continuing operations in 1989 increased slightly over prior year results. Earnings from continuing operations decreased 29% in 1988 due to gains on sales of businesses recognized in 1987. Excluding those gains, earnings from continuing operations increased substantially over the prior year on improved operating performance and lower tax rates.

Including the impact of discontinued operations, net earnings increased 9% over 1988. Net earnings decreased 26% in 1988 as the impact of the gains on sale of businesses in 1987 was partially offset by increased earnings from discontinued operations in 1988 and the extraordinary loss on early retirement of debt in 1987.

Excluding the gains on the sale of businesses, restructuring provision, discontinued operations and extraordinary items, earnings and primary earnings per share would have been $370.7 million and $5.63, $363.4 million and $5.28, and $258.3 million and $3.56 in 1989, 1988 and 1987, respectively.

Earnings Available to Common Shareholders

On February 1, 1989, the Company issued $500.0 million of preferred stock to the Company's leveraged employee stock ownership plans and their related trust (ESOP). Earnings available to common shareholders are reduced by preferred stock dividends of $13.7 million, net of tax benefit of $8.8 million.

Primary earnings per common share increased 14% in 1989. The percentage change in primary earnings per share is more favorable than for net earnings due to a reduced number of common shares outstanding partially offset by the impact of the preferred stock dividends.

Fully diluted earnings per share were $6.09 and $5.57 for 1989 and 1988, respectively, an increase of 9%. Fully diluted earnings per share give effect to the preferred stock and other dilutive convertible securities.

On June 29, 1989, the Emerging Issues Task Force (EITF) of the Financial Accounting Standards Board reached a consensus opinion on the calculation of fully diluted earnings per share as it relates to leveraged ESOPs with preferred stock that is convertible into common stock. Subsequent deliberations by the EITF have raised a number of issues relating to the proper accounting treatment for leveraged ESOPs including issues surrounding the calculation of earnings per share. A determination of the impact of changes that may be required, if any, based on the eventual outcome of these deliberations cannot be made at this time. The Company has adopted the consensus, although management believes that its provisions, relating to the calculation of fully diluted earnings per share, are not necessarily indicative of the actual impact of the ESOP on the Company's financial statements, nor does it necessarily reflect the economic substance of the ESOP transaction.

Ralston Purina Company and Subsidiaries

FINANCIAL REVIEW

(continued)

QUARTERLY FINANCIAL INFORMATION

(unaudited)

(Dollars in millions except per share data)	Quarter			
Fiscal 1989	First	Second	Third	Fourth[a]
Net sales	$1,681.1	$1,589.3	$1,624.1	$1,763.8
Gross profit	788.4	717.8	723.1	775.8
Earnings from continuing operations	131.4	90.8	83.8	45.2
Earnings from discontinued operations	71.3			
Net earnings	202.7	90.8	83.8	45.2
Earnings per common share –				
Primary				
Continuing operations	1.94	1.39	1.27	.65
Discontinued operations	1.05			
Net earnings	2.99	1.39	1.27	.65
Fully diluted				
Continuing operations	1.92	1.32	1.18	.61
Discontinued operations	1.04			
Net earnings	2.96	1.32	1.18	.61
Dividends paid	.375	.4125	.4125	.4125
Market price range of	88⅜-	85¾-	96½-	101½-
common stock	74¾	78¾	81½	85
Fiscal 1988				
Net sales	$1,511.4	$1,407.1	$1,405.6	$1,551.8
Gross profit	725.6	664.8	654.7	716.1
Earnings from continuing operations	122.2	88.7	73.1	79.4
Earnings from discontinued operations	10.2	4.6	4.1	5.5
Net earnings	132.4	93.3	77.2	84.9
Earnings per share –				
Primary				
Continuing operations	1.76	1.28	1.07	1.16
Discontinued operations	.15	.07	.06	.08
Net earnings	1.91	1.35	1.13	1.24
Fully diluted				
Continuing operations	1.74	1.26	1.06	1.15
Discontinued operations	.14	.07	.06	.08
Net earnings	1.88	1.33	1.12	1.23
Dividends paid	.31	.375	.375	.375
Market price range of	83½-	78¾-	78⅜-	80⅞-
common stock	57⅝	63¾	68	74

[a] Earnings for the fourth quarter were decreased by $19.5 million or $.31 per primary share due to a provision for restructuring expenses.

LIQUIDITY AND CAPITAL RESOURCES

Operations and Sources of Liquidity

Cash flow from continuing operations, which is the Company's primary source of liquidity, was $446.0 million in 1989 compared to $553.6 million in 1988. This measure was determined in accordance with FASB Statement No. 95 "Statement of Cash Flows" which was adopted by the Company in fiscal 1988. As permitted by the Statement, prior year cash flow information presented in the Consolidated Statement of Changes in Financial Position on page 19, including cash flow from continuing operations of $397.5 million in 1987, was not restated.

The Company's working capital (current assets less current liabilities) was $505.2 million at September 30, 1989 compared to $612.7 million and $295.6 million at September 30, 1988 and 1987. The working capital ratio was 1.4 to 1 at the end of 1989 compared to 1.6 to 1 and 1.3 to 1 at the end of 1988 and 1987, respectively. At September 30, 1989, current liabilities included $76.4 million of current maturities of long-term debt relating to 12% notes due 1994, on which the Company had exercised early redemption provisions. At September 30, 1988, current assets included $152.1 million net assets of discontinued seafood operations. Financial flexibility and liquidity are also provided by $380.6 million of cash and cash equivalents at September 30, 1989.

Ralston Purina Company and Subsidiaries

FINANCIAL REVIEW

(continued)

LIQUIDITY AND CAPITAL RESOURCES

(continued)

The Company's working capital requirements for inventories and receivables are influenced by changes in raw material costs, the availability of raw materials and seasonality, and as a result, may fluctuate widely. The Company has traditionally used short-term debt to finance these seasonal and other working capital requirements and from time to time to finance capital expenditures on a temporary basis. Bank lines of credit are maintained which provide future credit availability and support the sale of commercial paper. Payment for lines of credit is effected primarily through fees. On September 30, 1989, the total unused lines of credit were $275.0 million. In October 1989, the Company issued $200.0 million principal amount of 9.25% bonds due 2009 from its current shelf registration. Following this issue, the Company has available for issuance approximately an additional $100 million in principal amount of debt securities under the shelf registration.

Investing Activities

During the three year period ended September 30, 1989, the Company generated a significant source of cash through the disposition of businesses, including Van Camp ($260.0 million) in 1989, and Purina Mills ($364.5 million) and Drake Bakeries ($151.6 million) in 1987. In 1989, the acquisition of a French-based battery products business represented a significant investment.

Capital expenditures for new facilities and improvements were $221.6 million, $224.4 million and $196.9 million in fiscal years 1989, 1988 and 1987, respectively. Depreciation aggregating $548.3 million in the three years ended September 30, 1989 represented 85% of the reinvested capital in property during the period. Capital expenditures are expected to be approximately $330 million in 1990. The Company anticipates that the necessary funds for capital expenditures will be derived from operations.

On November 3, 1989, the Company acquired the assets and assumed certain liabilities of the Beech-Nut baby food business from affiliates of Nestle Enterprises, Inc. The acquisition is not expected to have a significant impact on the financial position of the Company.

Financing Activities

Long-term financings are arranged as determined necessary to meet the Company's capital or other requirements, with the timing of issue, principal amount and form depending on the prevailing securities markets and general economic conditions. The Company received $39.6 million and $149.4 million in proceeds from new debt issuances in 1989 and 1988, respectively. In addition, the Company received $500.0 million in proceeds from the issuance of preferred stock to the Company-sponsored leveraged ESOP. The ESOP funded the purchase of the preferred stock through the issuance of $500.0 million principal of fixed rate funds. The debt is guaranteed by the Company and is included in the consolidated balance sheet.

Long-term debt as a percentage of total capitalization was 67.5% at September 30, 1989 compared to 57.7% at the end of 1988 and 59.3% at the end of 1987 on a historical cost basis. On a current equity market basis, long-term debt as a percentage of total capitalization is approximately 24% at September 30, 1989 compared to 21% at September 30, 1988. For purposes of these ratios, the guarantee of the ESOP debt is treated as long-term debt and redeemable preferred stock and related unearned compensation are treated as capital. These ratios also reflect early retirements of higher rate long-term debt in 1989 and 1987, and common stock repurchases in all three years. An additional source of funds in 1987 resulted from the execution of an interest rate swap transaction intended to protect the Company's short-term cash and marketable securities position.

The Company returned a significant amount of cash to its common shareholders during the three years ended September 30, 1989 through common stock dividends and common stock repurchases. These outflows totalled $578.1 million and $101.1 million for common stock repurchases and dividends, respectively, in 1989 compared to $178.7 million and $99.2 million in 1988 and $492.5 million and $87.5 million in 1987. As of November 16, 1989, 1,430,863 shares of the current Board of Directors' authorization for the purchase of up to two million shares remain outstanding.

Inflation

Management recognizes that inflationary pressures may have an adverse effect on the Company through higher asset replacement costs and related depreciation and higher material costs. The Company attempts to minimize these effects through cost reductions and productivity improvements as well as price increases to maintain reasonable profit margins. However, it is management's view that inflation has not had a significant impact on operations in the three years ended September 30, 1989.

BUSINESS SEGMENT INFORMATION

BUSINESS SEGMENTS

Summarized financial information on a worldwide basis by business segments for the three years ended September 30, 1989 is set forth below. During these years the segments comprised the following:

Human and Pet Foods
Bakery products
Pet foods
Cereals
Other specialty grocery products, including crackers, cookies and snacks

Other Consumer Products
Battery products
Isolated soy protein and industrial polymer products
All-seasons resort

Agricultural Products (International)
Animal and poultry feeds
Poultry products

REVIEW OF SEGMENT FINANCIAL INFORMATION

Human and Pet Foods' sales increased 10% in 1989 following a 3% increase in 1988. Sales of domestic pet foods increased in both years on higher prices and in 1988 on higher volume. Bakery products sales increased 9% in 1989 on higher prices and bread volume. Excluding Drake, bakery products sales increased in 1988 on higher prices. Sweet baked goods volume declined in both years. Cereal sales increased on higher prices and volume, despite declines in the *Chex* brand in 1989, and on higher overall volumes in 1988. Operating profit of the segment was off 4% in 1989 compared to an increase of 13% in 1988 (excluding the gain on sale of Drake in 1987). Increased advertising and promotion spending to support product introductions, higher ingredient costs and an unfavorable shift in sales mix resulted in an 8% decline in pet foods operating profit. Operating profit was up in cereals on higher volumes partially offset by increased advertising and promotion expense. Bakery products operating profit increased slightly, primarily as a result of labor strikes in the prior year, as pricing and volume gains were nearly offset by increased ingredient costs and marketing and distribution costs. In 1988, strong pet food performance on higher margins and volumes, especially in the last quarter of the year, relating to the timing of price increases, and higher gross profit margins and lower advertising and promotion expenditures in bakery products were the primary factors accounting for the increase.

Other Consumer Products' sales increased 19% in 1989 primarily on the strength of international acquisitions in the battery products business and volume increases in most areas of the world for both battery products and soy protein products. Sales increased 3% in 1988 due to higher worldwide volume for soy protein products and higher battery products volume primarily in Asia and Europe. Operating profit declined 9% in 1989 as a result of the restructuring provision recognized in the battery products business. Excluding the restructuring provision, operating profit increased 4% on higher margins and volume in the soy protein products business and improved battery products performance. Domestically, battery products volume growth was partially offset by lower margins as a result of raw material price increases. Internationally, operating profit was off as a significant decline in South American operations, which was adversely affected by deteriorating economic conditions, more than offset improvements in all other world areas. Operating profit improved in 1988 due to the higher protein volumes and the strong performance of international battery operations. Domestically, battery products volume increased in 1988, although operating profit margins declined, on lower average selling prices and higher advertising and promotional spending due to competitive trade discounting. International performance was enhanced in 1988, primarily in the fourth quarter, by the inclusion of eighteen months of operating results from Australia and New Zealand operations after issues surrounding the purchase of that business from Union Carbide Corporation were resolved.

Agricultural Products' segment sales increased 22% in 1989 reflecting the inclusion of the Mexican operations for the entire year (seven months in 1988) and improved volumes in most areas. Sales for the segment increased 23% in 1988 due to a continuing shift in sales mix to higher priced products, stronger foreign currencies and higher tonnage in most areas. Operating profit of the international operations increased in 1989 and 1988 primarily as a result of margin and volume improvements.

Ralston Purina Company and Subsidiaries

BUSINESS SEGMENT INFORMATION

(continued)

(Dollars in millions)	1989	1988	1987
Sales by Product Lines and Segments			
Human and Pet Foods			
Bakery Products	**$1,940.6**	$1,782.5	$1,842.0
Pet Foods	**1,684.5**	1,549.5	1,442.1
Cereals	**414.1**	338.9	301.6
Other	**92.7**	100.0	69.1
Subtotal	**4,131.9**	3,770.9	3,654.8
Other Consumer Products			
Battery Products	**1,351.1**	1,139.1	1,126.6
Soy Protein Products	**221.6**	182.0	157.1
Subtotal	**1,572.7**	1,321.1	1,283.7
Agricultural Products	**953.7**	783.9	639.4
Total	**$6,658.3**	$5,875.9	$5,577.9
Operating Profit			
Human and Pet Foods	**$ 579.3**	$ 604.1	$ 602.2[b]
Other Consumer Products	**176.7[a]**	194.2	173.3
Agricultural Products	**53.2**	45.2	412.6[c]
Total	**809.2**	843.5	1,188.1
Unallocated Corporate Expenses, Net	**(49.3)**	(37.4)	(42.9)
Interest Expense	**(217.7)**	(218.5)	(200.9)
Investment Income	**33.5**	18.2	11.8
Earnings from Continuing Operations before Income Taxes and Extraordinary Item	**$ 575.7**	$ 605.8	$ 956.1
Assets at Year End			
Human and Pet Foods	**$1,406.9**	$1,330.4	$1,294.3
Other Consumer Products	**2,042.7**	1,736.4	1,787.3
Agricultural Products	**248.1**	258.0	161.2
Subtotal	**3,697.7**	3,324.8	3,242.8
Corporate Assets	**684.0**	567.5	441.8
Net Assets of Discontinued Operations		152.1	
Total Assets of Discontinued Operations			179.1
Total	**$4,381.7**	$4,044.4	$3,863.7
Depreciation Expense			
Human and Pet Foods	**$ 93.3**	$ 89.1	$ 88.8
Other Consumer Products	**65.4**	61.4	55.7
Agricultural Products	**14.4**	12.6	7.8
Property Additions			
Human and Pet Foods	**107.1**	128.0	128.9
Other Consumer Products	**78.1**	61.5	43.7
Agricultural Products	**21.7**	14.8	6.9

[a] Includes restructuring provision of $24.9.
[b] Includes gain of $69.7 from sale of Drake Bakeries, Inc.
[c] Includes gain of $376.8 from sale of Purina Mills.

BUSINESS SEGMENTS
(continued)

Export sales and sales between business segments were immaterial. No single customer accounted for 10% or more of sales. Minority interests in earnings of certain subsidiaries and the Company's equity in earnings of unconsolidated 20% through 50%-owned companies were not significant and have been included in operating profit.

Summarized financial information for foreign continuing operations for the past three years, excluding Puerto Rico, is set forth below. No foreign geographic area accounted for 10% or more of consolidated sales or assets.

(Dollars in millions)	**1989**	1988	1987
Sales	**$1,832.1**	$1,434.6	$1,258.0
Operating Profit	**146.3**	143.2	109.9
Assets at Year End	**1,022.9**	747.3	710.2

RESPONSIBILITY FOR FINANCIAL STATEMENTS

The preparation and integrity of the financial statements of Ralston Purina Company are the responsibility of its management. These statements have been prepared in conformance with generally accepted accounting principles and in the opinion of management fairly present the Company's financial position, results of operations and cash flows or changes in financial position.

The Company maintains accounting and internal control systems which it believes are adequate to provide reasonable assurance that assets are safeguarded against loss from unauthorized use or disposition and that the financial records are reliable for preparing financial statements. The selection and training of qualified personnel, the establishment and communication of accounting and administrative policies and procedures, and an extensive program of internal audits are important elements of these control systems.

The report of Price Waterhouse, independent accountants, on their examinations of the accompanying financial statements is shown below. This report states that the examinations were made in accordance with generally accepted auditing standards. These standards include a study and evaluation of internal control for the purpose of establishing a basis for reliance thereon relative to the scope of their examinations of the financial statements.

The Board of Directors, through its Audit Committee consisting solely of nonmanagement directors, meets periodically with both management and the independent accountants to discuss audit and financial reporting matters. To assure independence, Price Waterhouse has direct access to the Audit Committee.

REPORT OF INDEPENDENT ACCOUNTANTS

To the Shareholders and Board of Directors of Ralston Purina Company

In our opinion, the accompanying consolidated balance sheet and the related consolidated statements of earnings, of shareholders equity, of cash flows and of changes in financial position present fairly, in all material respects, the financial position of Ralston Purina Company and its subsidiaries at September 30, 1989 and 1988, and the results of their operations and their cash flows or changes in their financial position for each of the three years in the period ended September 30, 1989, in conformity with generally accepted accounting principles. These financial statements are the responsibility of the Company's management; our responsibility is to express an opinion on these financial statements based on our audits. We conducted our audits of these statements in accordance with generally accepted auditing standards which require that we plan and perform the audit to obtain reasonable assurance about whether the financial statements are free of material misstatement. An audit includes examining, on a test basis, evidence supporting the amounts and disclosures in the financial statements, assessing the accounting principles used and significant estimates made by management, and evaluating the overall financial statement presentation. We believe that our audits provide a reasonable basis for the opinion expressed above.

As described on page 21, in 1988 the Company adopted prospectively the provisions of Statement of Financial Accounting Standards No. 95, "Statement of Cash Flows."

Price Waterhouse

St. Louis, Missouri
November 1, 1989

Ralston Purina Company and Subsidiaries

CONSOLIDATED STATEMENT OF EARNINGS

Year ended September 30

(Dollars in millions except per share data)	1989	1988	1987
Net Sales	**$6,658.3**	$5,875.9	$5,577.9
Costs and Expenses			
Cost of products sold	**3,653.2**	3,114.7	2,931.0
Selling, general and administrative	**1,422.2**	1,268.7	1,274.8
Advertising and promotion	**791.6**	686.4	673.4
Provision for restructuring	**31.4**		
Interest	**217.7**	218.5	200.9
Investment income	**(33.5)**	(18.2)	(11.8)
Gain on sale of businesses			(446.5)
	6,082.6	5,270.1	4,621.8
Earnings from Continuing Operations before Income Taxes and Extraordinary Item	**575.7**	605.8	956.1
Income Taxes	**224.5**	242.4	445.5
Earnings from Continuing Operations before Extraordinary Item	**351.2**	363.4	510.6
Earnings from Discontinued Operations	**1.1**	24.4	15.8
Gain on Disposal of Discontinued Operations	**70.2**		
Earnings before Extraordinary Item	**422.5**	387.8	526.4
Extraordinary Item – Loss on Early Retirement of Debt			(3.3)
Net Earnings	**422.5**	387.8	523.1
Preferred Stock Dividend, Net of Taxes	**13.7**		
Earnings Available to Common Shareholders	**$ 408.8**	$ 387.8	$ 523.1
Earnings per Share			
Primary			
Continuing operations	**$ 5.32**	$ 5.28	$ 7.05
Discontinued operations	**1.12**	.35	.22
Extraordinary item			(.04)
Net earnings	**$ 6.44**	$ 5.63	$ 7.23
Fully Diluted			
Continuing operations	**$ 5.04**	$ 5.22	$ 6.94
Discontinued operations	**1.05**	.35	.21
Extraordinary item			(.04)
Net earnings	**$ 6.09**	$ 5.57	$ 7.11

The above financial statement should be read in conjunction with the Notes to Financial Statements on pages 21 to 30.

Ralston Purina Company and Subsidiaries

CONSOLIDATED BALANCE SHEET

September 30

(Dollars in millions)	1989	1988
Assets		
Current Assets		
Cash	**$ 28.6**	$ 23.8
Marketable securities	**352.0**	337.1
Receivables, less allowance for doubtful accounts	**636.3**	526.9
Inventories	**677.8**	559.9
Other current assets	**126.3**	94.7
Net assets of discontinued operations		152.1
Total Current Assets	**1,821.0**	1,694.5
Investments and Other Assets	**795.1**	638.0
Property at Cost		
Land	**98.6**	88.6
Buildings	**612.9**	598.5
Machinery and equipment	**1,926.6**	1,763.5
Construction in progress	**80.2**	81.1
	2,718.3	2,531.7
Accumulated depreciation	**952.7**	819.8
	1,765.6	1,711.9
Total	**$4,381.7**	$4,044.4
Liabilities and Shareholders Equity		
Current Liabilities		
Current maturities of long-term debt	**$ 225.6**	$ 60.3
Notes payable	**142.0**	150.2
Accounts payable and accrued liabilities	**824.9**	753.1
Dividends payable	**33.8**	25.6
Income taxes	**89.5**	92.6
Total Current Liabilities	**1,315.8**	1,081.8
Long-Term Debt	**1,790.7**	1,486.5
Deferred Income Taxes	**172.9**	142.6
Other Liabilities	**242.0**	243.6
Commitments and Contingencies		
Redeemable Preferred Stock – Series A 6.75%, $1 par value, authorized 4,600,000 shares – Issued 4,511,414 shares in 1989	**500.0**	
Unearned ESOP Compensation	**(471.4)**	
Shareholders Equity		
Preferred stock, $1 par value, authorized 1,400,000 shares – None outstanding		
Common stock, $.41⅔ par value, authorized 380,000,000 shares – Issued 114,604,912 in 1989 and 114,556,330 in 1988	**47.8**	47.7
Capital in excess of par value	**261.8**	252.0
Retained earnings	**2,919.7**	2,612.9
Cumulative translation adjustment	**(33.3)**	(33.3)
Common stock in treasury, at cost, 53,004,774 shares in 1989 and 46,358,013 in 1988	**(2,350.1)**	(1,766.5)
Unearned portion of restricted stock	**(14.2)**	(22.9)
Total Shareholders Equity	**831.7**	1,089.9
Total	**$4,381.7**	$4,044.4

The above financial statement should be read in conjunction with the Notes to Financial Statements on pages 21 to 30.

Ralston Purina Company and Subsidiaries

CONSOLIDATED STATEMENT OF CASH FLOWS

Year ended September 30

(Dollars in millions)	1989	1988
Cash Flow from Operations		
Earnings from continuing operations	**$351.2**	$363.4
Adjustments to reconcile earnings to net cash flow provided by continuing operations		
Depreciation and amortization	**223.1**	214.6
Deferred income taxes	**18.4**	32.7
Provision for restructuring	**31.4**	
Changes in operating assets and liabilities used in continuing operations		
Increase in accounts receivable	**(60.5)**	(57.3)
Increase in inventories	**(86.2)**	(64.1)
Increase in other current assets	**(36.7)**	(11.0)
Increase in accounts payable and accrued liabilities	**16.9**	17.3
(Decrease) increase in other current liabilities	**(34.4)**	35.5
Other, net	**22.8**	22.5
Net cash flow from continuing operations	**446.0**	553.6
Earnings from discontinued operations	**71.3**	24.4
Adjustments to reconcile earnings to net cash flow provided by discontinued operations		
Gain on sale of discontinued operations	**(70.2)**	
Depreciation	**.5**	7.7
Deferred income taxes		(4.7)
Changes in operating assets and liabilities used in discontinued operations	**12.9**	(24.5)
Net cash flow from discontinued operations	**14.5**	2.9
Net cash flow from operations	**460.5**	556.5
Cash Flow from Investing Activities		
Proceeds from sale of discontinued operations	**260.0**	
Acquisition of battery products business	**(124.0)**	
Property additions	**(221.6)**	(224.4)
Property disposals	**16.3**	36.6
Other, net	**(99.6)**	(17.6)
Net cash used by investing activities	**(168.9)**	(205.4)
Cash Flow from Financing Activities		
Proceeds from sale of long-term debt	**39.6**	149.4
Principal payments on long-term debt, including current maturities	**(78.5)**	(216.7)
Net increase in notes payable	**4.4**	86.1
Proceeds from sale of preferred stock	**500.0**	
Proceeds from sale of common stock		8.6
Treasury stock purchases	**(578.1)**	(178.7)
Dividends paid	**(114.8)**	(99.2)
Net cash used by financing activities	**(227.4)**	(250.5)
Effect of Exchange Rate Changes on Cash	**(44.5)**	(11.1)
Net Increase in Cash and Cash Equivalents	**19.7**	89.5
Cash and Cash Equivalents, Beginning of Year	**360.9**	271.4
Cash and Cash Equivalents, End of Year	**$380.6**	$360.9

The above financial statement should be read in conjunction with the Notes to Financial Statements on pages 21 to 30.

Ralston Purina Company and Subsidiaries

CONSOLIDATED STATEMENT OF CHANGES IN FINANCIAL POSITION

Year Ended September 30

(Dollars in millions)	1987
Cash Flow from Operations	
Earnings from continuing operations before extraordinary item	$510.6
Non-cash items included in income	
Depreciation and amortization	205.4
Deferred income taxes	36.9
Gain on sale of businesses	(252.3)
Net increase in working capital (see below)	(103.1)
Net cash flow from continuing operations	397.5
Net cash flow from discontinued operations	41.0
Net cash flow from operations	438.5
Cash Flow from Investing Activities	
Proceeds from sale of businesses, net of taxes	516.1
Property additions	(196.9)
Disposals of property	30.4
Other, net	5.0
Net cash provided by investing activities	354.6
Cash Flow from Financing Activities	
Decrease in long-term debt	(146.2)
Extraordinary loss on retirement of debt	(3.3)
Add conversion of debentures	.8
Net cash flow from long-term debt	(148.7)
Issuance of common stock	6.7
Less issuance from conversion of debentures	(.8)
Cash proceeds of stock issuance	5.9
Dividends paid	(87.5)
Treasury stock purchases	(492.5)
Proceeds from interest rate swap transaction	103.7
Net decrease in current maturities of long-term debt and notes payable	(275.3)
Net cash used by financing activities	(894.4)
Net Decrease in Cash and Marketable Securities	($101.3)
(Increase) Decrease in Working Capital Used in Continuing Operations	
Receivables	($ 74.1)
Inventories	2.9
Other current assets	(28.3)
Accounts payable and accrued liabilities	(4.4)
Other current liabilities	.8
Net increase in working capital used in continuing operations	($103.1)

The above financial statement should be read in conjunction with the Notes to Financial Statements on pages 21 to 30.

Ralston Purina Company and Subsidiaries

CONSOLIDATED STATEMENT OF SHAREHOLDERS EQUITY

Three years ended September 30, 1989

	Number of Shares (In thousands)		Amount (Dollars in millions)					
	Common Stock	Common Stock in Treasury	Common Stock	Capital in Excess of Par Value	Retained Earnings	Cumulative Translation Adjustment	Common Stock in Treasury	Unearned Portion of Restricted Stock
Balance October 1, 1986	114,493	(38,249)	$47.7	$228.0	$1,893.3	($37.5)	($1,099.4)	($33.2)
Treasury stock purchased		(6,512)					(492.5)	
Common stock issued on conversion of debentures	54			.8				
Activity under stock plans		383		6.0			.2	(2.2)
Market value adjustment on restricted stock				9.4				(9.4)
Amortization of restricted stock								11.6
Translation adjustments						3.8		
Net earnings					523.1			
Dividends declared on common stock					(88.2)			
Balance September 30, 1987	114,547	(44,378)	47.7	244.2	2,328.2	(33.7)	(1,591.7)	(33.2)
Treasury stock purchased		(2,630)					(178.7)	
Common stock issued on conversion of debentures	9			.1				
Activity under stock plans		650		8.0			3.9	(3.0)
Market value adjustment on restricted stock				(.3)				.3
Amortization of restricted stock								13.0
Translation adjustments						.4		
Net earnings					387.8			
Dividends declared on common stock					(103.1)			
Balance September 30, 1988	114,556	(46,358)	47.7	252.0	2,612.9	(33.3)	(1,766.5)	(22.9)
Treasury stock purchased		(6,892)					(578.1)	
Common stock issued on conversion of debentures	49		.1	.7				
Activity under stock plans		245		4.1			(5.5)	(.7)
Market value adjustment on restricted stock				5.0				(5.0)
Amortization of restricted stock								14.4
Translation adjustments								
Net earnings					422.5			
Dividends declared on common stock					(102.0)			
Dividends declared on preferred stock, net of taxes					(13.7)			
Balance September 30, 1989	114,605	(53,005)	$47.8	$261.8	$2,919.7	($33.3)	($2,350.1)	($14.2)

The above financial statement should be read in conjunction with the Notes to Financial Statements on pages 21 to 30.

NOTES TO FINANCIAL STATEMENTS

(Dollars in millions except per share data)

SUMMARY OF ACCOUNTING POLICIES

The Company's significant accounting policies, which conform to generally accepted accounting principles and are applied on a consistent basis among years, are described below:

Principles of Consolidation – The consolidated financial statements include the accounts of the Company and its majority-owned subsidiaries. All significant intercompany transactions are eliminated. Investments in affiliated companies, 20% through 50%-owned, are carried at equity.

Minority interests in earnings of consolidated subsidiaries and the Company's share of the net earnings (losses) of unconsolidated companies carried at equity are included in selling, general and administrative expenses.

Foreign Currency Translation – Foreign currency financial statements of foreign operations where the local currency is the functional currency are translated using exchange rates in effect at period end for assets and liabilities and average exchange rates during the period for results of operations. Related translation adjustments are reported as a separate component of shareholders equity. For foreign operations where the U.S. dollar is the functional currency and for countries which are considered highly inflationary, translation practices differ in that inventories, properties, accumulated depreciation and depreciation accounts are translated at historical rates of exchange and related translation adjustments are included in earnings. Gains and losses from foreign currency transactions are generally included in earnings.

Statement of Cash Flows – In November 1987, the Financial Accounting Standards Board (FASB) issued Statement No. 95, "Statement of Cash Flows." As permitted under the Statement, the Company has adopted the statement prospectively and accordingly has presented statements of cash flows for 1989 and 1988 and a statement of changes in financial position, which was prepared under previous accounting principles, for 1987. For purposes of the statement of cash flows, cash equivalents are considered to be all highly liquid investments with a maturity of three months or less when purchased.

Marketable Securities are valued at cost which approximates market.

Inventories are valued generally at the lower of average cost or market. The Company hedges certain of its grain and commodity purchases as considered necessary to reduce the risk associated with market price fluctuations. Gains and losses on hedges of future grain and commodity purchases are recognized in the same period as the related purchase transaction.

Property at Cost – Expenditures for new facilities and those which substantially increase the useful lives of the property, including interest during construction, are capitalized. Maintenance, repairs and minor renewals are expensed as incurred. When properties are retired or otherwise disposed of, the related cost and accumulated depreciation are removed from the accounts and gains or losses on the dispositions are reflected in earnings.

Depreciation is generally provided on the straight-line basis by charges to costs or expenses at rates based on the estimated useful lives of the properties. Estimated useful lives range from 5 to 25 years for machinery and equipment and 10 to 40 years for buildings.

Intangible Assets, which are included in Investments and Other Assets, represent the excess of cost over the net tangible assets of acquired businesses and are amortized over estimated periods of related benefit ranging from 2 to 40 years.

Income Taxes – Deferred income taxes are recognized for the effect of timing differences between financial and tax reporting. No additional U.S. taxes have been provided on earnings of foreign subsidiaries expected to be reinvested indefinitely. Additional income taxes are provided, however, on planned repatriations of foreign earnings after taking into account tax-exempt earnings and applicable foreign tax credits.

Earnings per Share – Primary earnings per share are based on the average number of shares outstanding during the year (63,518,000 in 1989, 68,873,000 in 1988 and 72,379,000 in 1987). Fully diluted earnings per share assume the conversion of the Series A 6.75% preferred stock (Redeemable Preferred Stock) into Company common stock from their issuance on February 1, 1989 and other dilutive securities. For purposes of calculating fully diluted earnings per share, net income has been adjusted for the additional contribution to the Company's employee stock ownership plans and their related trust (ESOP) that would have been required had the Redeemable Preferred Stock been converted as of February 1, 1989 (effective date of the ESOP adoption).

Ralston Purina Company and Subsidiaries

NOTES TO FINANCIAL STATEMENTS

(Dollars in millions except per share data)

BUSINESS SEGMENT INFORMATION

The financial information on the Company's business segments appearing on pages 13 through 15 herein, except for the narrative appearing under the heading "Review of Segment Financial Information," is an integral part of these financial statements.

DISPOSITIONS

On October 3, 1986, the Company sold its domestic agricultural products business to a subsidiary of The British Petroleum Company for $545.0 in cash. The Company recognized a gain on the sale during the first quarter of fiscal 1987 of $376.8, before taxes of $167.5 (net of $209.3 or $2.89 per primary share).

On August 21, 1987, the Company sold its Drake Bakeries, Inc. subsidiary to a private group led by Drake management and supported by Rock Capital Partners, L.P. for $176.0 in cash. The Company realized a gain on the sale in the fourth quarter of fiscal 1987 of $69.7, before taxes of $26.7 (net of $43.0 or $.60 per share).

ACQUISITIONS

In January 1989, the Company acquired the net assets of a French-based battery products manufacturer for $159.6, including cash acquired of $35.6. The acquisition was accounted for using the purchase method of accounting, and accordingly, the results of operations are included in the consolidated statement of earnings from the date of acquisition. Assuming the acquisition had occurred as of October 1, 1988, it would not have had a material effect on net sales, earnings from continuing operations or earnings per share.

During 1988, the Company acquired substantially all of the remaining outstanding shares of its Mexican agricultural and consumer products affiliate. This operation was formerly accounted for as an investment under the equity method. During 1987, the Company acquired Benco Pet Foods, Inc., a manufacturer of soft-moist and canned pet food. Neither acquisition was significant to the Company's consolidated financial position.

PROVISION FOR RESTRUCTURING

In the fourth quarter of fiscal 1989, the Company provided $31.4, before applicable tax benefit of $11.9, for costs associated with the planned closure or restructuring of certain battery manufacturing and bakery operations, and administrative restructuring.

DISCONTINUED OPERATIONS

On November 15, 1988, the Company completed the sale of its Van Camp Seafood division to a group of investors led by PT Management Trust, a privately-held Indonesian concern, for $260.0 in cash. The Company recognized a gain on the sale in the first quarter of fiscal 1989 of $70.2, net of taxes of $42.5 or $1.10 per primary share. The results of operations of Van Camp have been reported as discontinued operations for the three-year period ended September 30, 1989. Sales of Van Camp of $19.8, $299.9 and $290.1 for 1989, 1988 and 1987, respectively, have been excluded from net sales in the consolidated statement of earnings. Earnings of the discontinued operations of $1.1 or $.02 per share (excluding the gain on sale), $24.4 or $.35 per share and $15.8 or $.22 per share for 1989, 1988 and 1987, net of income tax expense of $.3, $8.8 and $1.7, respectively, have been segregated and reported separately from the results of continuing operations. The net assets of the discontinued operations, which were transferred to the purchaser, were included in the consolidated balance sheet at September 30, 1988 as a single amount which consisted primarily of receivables, inventories, fixed assets and certain liabilities assumed by the purchaser.

EXTRAORDINARY ITEM

During 1987, the Company extinguished, through repurchase, $29.2 of its outstanding long-term debt prior to its scheduled maturity. The debt extinguished consisted primarily of 12% notes due November 1996 and resulted in an extraordinary loss of $3.3, after income tax benefit of $2.9. Funds for the extinguishment were provided from the proceeds of dispositions and working capital.

NOTES TO FINANCIAL STATEMENTS

(Dollars in millions except per share data)

INCOME TAXES

The provisions for income taxes consisted of the following:

	1989	1988	1987
Currently payable			
United States	**$196.8**	$163.2	$346.4
State	**20.4**	27.6	52.5
Foreign	**31.7**	32.9	29.4
Total current	**248.9**	223.7	428.3
Deferred			
United States	**16.3**	24.3	11.9
State		.5	(.2)
Foreign	**2.1**	2.7	4.3
Total deferred	**18.4**	27.5	16.0
	267.3	251.2	444.3
Income taxes – discontinued operations	**(42.8)**	(8.8)	(1.7)
Income tax benefit – extraordinary item			2.9
Income taxes – continuing operations	**$224.5**	$242.4	$445.5

Deferred income taxes, reflecting timing differences between financial and tax reporting, relate primarily to depreciation, deferred incentive compensation, pensions and self-insurance reserves.

The source of pre-tax earnings follows:

	1989	1988	1987
United States	**$588.2**	$506.4	$862.3
Foreign	**101.6**	132.6	105.1
	689.8	639.0	967.4
Pre-tax earnings – discontinued operations	**(114.1)**	(33.2)	(17.5)
Extraordinary loss			6.2
Pre-tax earnings – continuing operations	**$575.7**	$605.8	$956.1

Income taxes were 38.8% of pre-tax earnings in 1989, 39.3% in 1988 and 45.9% in 1987. A reconciliation of income taxes with the amounts computed at the statutory federal rate follows:

	1989	1988	1987
Statutory tax rate	**34%**	34%	43%
Computed tax at statutory rate	**$234.5**	$217.3	$416.0
State income taxes, net of federal tax benefit	**13.5**	18.5	29.8
Investment tax credit reversal			5.8
Capital gains at lower rate, net of recapture			(10.8)
Other, net	**19.3**	15.4	3.5
	$267.3	$251.2	$444.3

The fiscal 1987 investment tax credit reversal presented above represents the credit recognized in fiscal 1986 for additions during the period from January 1, 1986 to September 30, 1986. Investment tax credit for this period was subsequently repealed by the Tax Reform Act of 1986. In accordance with the guidelines of the FASB, the tax effect of this retroactive provision was recognized as a component of income tax expense in the first quarter of fiscal 1987.

Ralston Purina Company and Subsidiaries

NOTES TO FINANCIAL STATEMENTS

(Dollars in millions except per share data)

INCENTIVE COMPENSATION

The Company's 1988 Incentive Stock Plan (1988 Plan) was adopted in January 1988 to replace the 1982 Incentive Stock Plan (1982 Plan). Remaining reserved shares of stock under the 1982 Plan, which will continue in effect until awards granted thereunder are exercised or otherwise terminated, will be used for the 1988 Plan. No additional awards may be granted under the 1982 Plan.

The 1988 Plan provides that eligible employees may receive stock option awards at an option price of not less than 100% of the fair market value of the shares optioned at the date of grant and other stock awards payable in whole or part by the issuance of stock. Changes in incentive and nonqualified stock options outstanding are summarized as follows:

	Shares Under Option
Outstanding October 1, 1988 ($11⅞ to $81¾ per share)	1,483,616
Granted	
Exercised ($11⅞ to $26⅛ per share)	(329,125)
Cancelled	(16,500)
Outstanding September 30, 1989 ($11⅞ to $81¾ per share)	1,137,991
Exercisable at September 30, 1989	186,491

At September 30, 1989 and 1988, there were 3,618,318 and 3,611,225 shares available for future awards, respectively.

Since all option prices are 100% of market value at date of grant, no charge is made against earnings for stock option awards and the proceeds from sales thereof are credited to the appropriate capital accounts. Restrictions on shares of restricted stock issued to eligible employees lapse over periods ranging from three to nine years provided continued employment and, in certain cases, that minimum stock price requirements are met. Compensation cost is recognized ratably over this vesting period. Charges to earnings were $16.2 in 1989, $16.4 in 1988 and $14.6 in 1987.

PENSION PLANS AND OTHER POSTEMPLOYMENT BENEFITS

The Company has several noncontributory defined benefit pension plans covering substantially all full-time employees in the United States who are not participating in a multiemployer pension plan, and certain employees in other countries. The plans, which are subject to modification at any time, provide retirement benefits based on years of service and earnings. It is the Company's practice to fund pension liabilities in accordance with the minimum and maximum limits imposed by the Employee Retirement Income Security Act of 1974 (ERISA) and federal income tax laws. The Company also contributes to jointly administered multiemployer defined benefit pension plans covering certain of its union employees.

In fiscal 1988, the Company adopted FASB Statement No. 87, "Employers' Accounting for Pensions," for its principal foreign defined benefit plans. The provisions of the Statement were adopted prospectively without restatement of the related prior year expense. Other foreign pension arrangements, which include various retirement and termination benefit plans, some of which are required by local law or coordinated with government-sponsored plans, are not material in the aggregate and are not included in these disclosures.

Pension cost included the following components:

	1989	1988	1987
Defined benefit plans			
Service cost for benefits earned during the year	**$23.8**	$23.4	$24.1
Interest cost on projected benefit obligation	**49.7**	45.0	41.4
Return on plan assets	**(154.1)**	1.1	(174.2)
Net amortization and deferral	**80.6**	(71.9)	115.8
Subtotal	**–**	(2.4)	7.1
Multiemployer plans	**51.6**	48.1	49.2
Defined contribution plans	**21.7**	7.9	6.7
Principal foreign plans not under SFAS No. 87			2.0
Total pension cost	**$73.3**	$53.6	$65.0

NOTES TO FINANCIAL STATEMENTS

(Dollars in millions except per share data)

PENSION PLANS

(continued)

The following table presents the funded status of the Company's principal defined benefit plans and amounts recognized in the balance sheet at September 30:

	1989	1988	1987
Actuarial present value of			
Vested benefits	**($473.5)**	($427.6)	($374.4)
Nonvested benefits	**(31.5)**	(28.4)	(25.1)
Accumulated benefit obligation	**(505.0)**	(456.0)	(399.5)
Effect of future salary increases	**(162.2)**	(150.1)	(141.7)
Projected benefit obligation	**(667.2)**	(606.1)	(541.2)
Plan assets at fair value	**919.6**	812.1	787.6
Plan assets in excess of projected benefit obligation	**252.4**	206.0	246.4
Unrecognized net gain	**(161.7)**	(114.8)	(169.1)
Unrecognized prior service cost	**1.1**	(4.4)	(7.2)
Unrecognized net asset at transition, net of amortization	**(43.2)**	(46.4)	(38.5)
Prepaid pension cost included in Investment and Other Assets	**$ 48.6**	$ 40.4	$ 31.6

The assumptions used in determining the information above, which reflect weighted averages for the component plans, were as follows:

	1989	1988	1987
Discount rate	**8.17%**	8.13%	8.13%
Rate of increase of future salary levels	**6.40%**	6.39%	6.50%
Long-term rate of return on assets	**8.94%**	8.94%	9.00%

Assets of the plans consist primarily of listed common stocks and bonds, including 745,732 shares of the Company's common stock having an aggregate market value of $66.3 at September 30, 1989.

In November 1988, the Company amended certain of its defined contribution benefit plans to include a Company-sponsored leveraged ESOP. Substantially all full-time administrative and non-union production employees in the United States are eligible to participate in the ESOP. The Company makes a matching contribution of up to 100% of the participant's contribution based on specified limits of the participant's salary.

The cost of the ESOP is recognized as incurred and was $18.4 for the period February 1, 1989 (effective date of adoption) through September 30, 1989. Company contributions include $4.7 of additional employer contributions necessary to meet the debt service requirements of the leveraged ESOP's long-term debt as discussed in the Long-Term Debt footnote which follows.

Prior to February 1, 1989, the Company sponsored several defined contribution benefit plans covering a majority of its domestic administrative and certain of its non-union hourly employees. Company contributions were based on a percentage of employee contributions up to specified limits.

The Company also provides health care and life insurance benefits for its retired employees who meet specified age and years of service requirements. The cost of health care benefits is recognized as incurred. The cost of life insurance benefits is recognized as insurance premiums are paid. The total of these costs to the Company approximated $5.0 in 1989, $4.4 in 1988 and $4.4 in 1987. Coincident with the adoption of the ESOP, the Company is phasing out its subsidy of medical benefits for future retirees. The Company will continue to provide all, or some portion of, the subsidy for retirement medical benefits for current retirees and a limited group of active employees.

In February 1989, the FASB issued an exposure draft – "Employers' Accounting for Postretirement Benefits Other Than Pensions" (OPEBs). The proposed standard would require the recognition of OPEB's expense on an accrual basis and the recognition of a minimum liability for the amount of unfunded accumulated postretirement benefit obligation. Management is currently evaluating the impact of the proposed standard and the method and timing of its adoption.

Ralston Purina Company and Subsidiaries

NOTES TO FINANCIAL STATEMENTS

(Dollars in millions except per share data)

NOTES PAYABLE

Information relative to short-term debt borrowings for the three years ended September 30, 1989 follows:

	1989	1988	1987
Notes payable			
Ending balance	**$142.0**	$150.2	$ 82.7
Weighted average interest rate	**18%**	36%	27%
Outstanding during period[a]			
Maximum	**$367.2**	$216.9	$161.6
Average	**178.0**	121.4	107.7
Weighted average interest rate	**23%**	32%	26%
Commercial paper			
Outstanding during period[a]			
Maximum	**$225.5**	$139.5	$106.4
Average	**32.2**	21.1	24.9
Weighted average interest rate	**9%**	8%	7%

[a] Based on month-end balances.

Notes payable are primarily foreign. Higher weighted average interest rates reflect local currency borrowings in highly inflationary economies. The effective net cost of borrowing in these economies is expected to be substantially less due to devaluation of the applicable local currencies against the U.S. dollar.

On September 30, 1989, the total unused lines of credit were $275.0.

LONG-TERM DEBT

The detail of long-term debt as of September 30 follows:

	1989	1988
Sinking fund debentures		
7.70% due 1996	**$ 15.0**	$ 16.4
9½% due 2016	**300.0**	300.0
9⅜% due 2016	**200.0**	200.0
10.45% due 2018	**150.0**	150.0
Other debt		
ESOP debt guarantee	**471.4**	
Medium-term Notes, 7.15% to 8.25%	**49.1**	96.3
12¾% Notes due 1989	**100.0**	100.0
Swiss Franc Notes due 1992, variable	**13.1**	18.6
12¾% Swiss Franc Bonds due 1994[a]	**50.1**	50.1
12% Notes due 1994[b]	**76.4**	76.4
11¾% Notes due 1995	**132.3**	132.3
9% Notes due 1996	**200.0**	200.0
12% Notes due 1996	**37.8**	35.7
7¾% Notes due 1998	**43.5**	47.8
Variable Rate Notes due 1996[c]	**37.8**	
Capitalized lease obligations, 3.1% to 11⅛%	**21.4**	22.2
Industrial revenue bonds, 4⅜% to 12¾%	**58.0**	60.2
Other	**60.4**	40.8
	2,016.3	1,546.8
Less current portion	**(225.6)**	(60.3)
	$1,790.7	$1,486.5

[a] Represents the equivalent principal amount and approximate effective interest rate of the 5⅜% Bonds under related currency exchange arrangements.

[b] As of September 30, 1989, notice of mandatory redemption had been given to holders of these notes. The entire amount outstanding as of that date was reclassified to current.

[c] The Company has entered into interest rate swap agreements on these notes, converting the variable rates into a fixed rate of 9.32%.

Aggregate maturities on all long-term debt, exclusive of debentures held in treasury, are $12.8, $13.6, $9.6 and $46.2 for the years ending September 30, 1991 through 1994, respectively. These aggregate maturities do not include the future maturities of the ESOP debt guarantee.

Ralston Purina Company and Subsidiaries

NOTES TO FINANCIAL STATEMENTS

(Dollars in millions except per share data)

LONG-TERM DEBT
(continued)

In August 1989, the Company filed a shelf registration statement for $200.0 principal amount of debt securities which may be issued from time to time under Rule 415 of the Securities Act of 1933. In October 1989, the Company issued $200.0 principal amount of 9.25% bonds due 2009 from this registration statement and amounts remaining under a previous registration statement filed in December 1987. Following this issue, the Company may issue approximately an additional $100.0 of debt securities under the current shelf registration statement.

To fund its purchase of the Company's preferred stock, the Trust for the Company-sponsored ESOP borrowed $500.0 principal amount in ten-year 8.25% notes (ESOP loan). The ESOP loan is unconditionally guaranteed by the Company and is included in the Company's consolidated balance sheet as long-term debt, along with the corresponding Unearned ESOP Compensation. Both the long-term debt and the unearned ESOP compensation will be reduced as employee and employer contributions to the ESOP are used to reduce the outstanding ESOP loan. During 1989, the ESOP incurred $26.9 of interest expense on the ESOP loan.

REDEEMABLE PREFERRED STOCK

At September 30, 1989, the Company had 6,000,000 shares of $1 par value preferred stock authorized, of which 4,600,000 shares were authorized as Series A 6.75% preferred stock. On February 1, 1989, 4,511,414 shares were issued to the Company's ESOP. Series A 6.75% preferred stock is convertible into the Company's common stock at a ratio of one-to-one and currently has a guaranteed minimum value of $110.83 per share. The shares have preference in liquidation and each share has one voting right. Dividends are cumulative, compounded and payable semi-annually. In accordance with financial reporting requirements of the Securities and Exchange Commission, the preferred stock has been classified outside of permanent equity as Redeemable Preferred Stock.

Preferred stock shares are held, on behalf of the ESOP, by the ESOP's trustee and are allocated to individual participants' accounts based on the amount of employee and employer matching contributions to the ESOP. Dividends on unallocated Redeemable Preferred Stock are used to fund the debt service requirements of the ESOP.

The trustee, as holder of the preferred stock, may convert its shares into Company common stock at any time, or may require the Company to redeem the preferred stock shares, under certain limited circumstances, at the guaranteed minimum price, in cash or common stock. The Company may elect to redeem the preferred stock, under limited circumstances, in cash or common stock.

SHAREHOLDERS EQUITY

On March 31, 1989, the Board of Directors approved a plan to purchase an additional 2,000,000 shares of the Company's common stock. As of November 16, 1989, 1,430,863 shares of this authorization remain outstanding.

On January 17, 1986 and as amended on May 26, 1989, the Board of Directors declared a dividend distribution of one share purchase right (Right) for each outstanding share of the Company's common stock. Each Right entitles shareholders to purchase from the Company one common share at an exercise price of $150 per share subject to antidilution adjustments. The Rights become exercisable and transferable apart from the common stock ten days after an acquiring person or a group acquires 20% or more, or announces or commences a tender offer for 20% or more, of the Company's common stock. If, after the Rights become exercisable, an acquiring person or group acquires 20% or more of the Company's common stock without proposing to acquire the remainder in a tender or exchange offer approved by the Board of Directors, merges into or recapitalizes the Company or engages in certain other specified transactions, holders of Rights (other than the acquiring person or group) may purchase common stock of the Company at one-third of its then market price. In the event that the Company merges with, or transfers 50% or more of its assets or earning power to any person or group after the Rights become exercisable, holders of Rights may purchase, at the exercise price, common stock of the acquiring entity having a value equal to twice the exercise price. The Rights can be redeemed by the Board of Directors at $.05 per Right only up to the date a person or group acquires 20% or more of the Company's common stock. Also, following the acquisition by a person or group of beneficial ownership of at least 20% but less than 50% of the Company's common stock, the Board may exchange the Rights for common stock at a ratio of one share of common stock per Right. The Rights expire on January 27, 1996.

At September 30, 1989, there were 4,511,414 shares of common stock reserved for conversion of Redeemable Preferred Stock, 55,544 shares of common stock reserved for conversion of the 5¾% subordinated debentures, convertible at 65.217 shares for each $1,000 principal amount, and 5,890,719 shares reserved under various employee incentive compensation and benefit plans.

Ralston Purina Company and Subsidiaries

NOTES TO FINANCIAL STATEMENTS

(Dollars in millions except per share data)

COMMITMENTS AND CONTINGENCIES

Legal Matters

On September 11, 1989, a class action lawsuit styled *Bauder v. Ralston Purina Company* was filed in the U.S. District Court for the Eastern District of Pennsylvania, on behalf of all purchasers (other than for resale) of the Company's product *Purina Puppy Chow* brand puppy food, during the period October 1, 1985 to July 30, 1989. A similar lawsuit styled *Castle v. Ralston Purina Company* was filed in the same court on September 14, 1989. Both petitions allege that the Company violated the federal Racketeer Influenced and Corrupt Organizations Act ("RICO"), as well as committed violations of common law and state statutes, in the advertising and sale of *Puppy Chow*, and seek treble damages and other appropriate relief. The petitions make reference to another lawsuit, *Alpo Petfoods Inc. v. Ralston Purina Company*, in which the U.S. District Court for the District of Columbia determined certain *Puppy Chow* advertising claims made between August, 1985 and November, 1986 to be violations of the federal Lanham Act. The *Alpo* case is being appealed, and the Company believes its position is meritorious. The *Bauder* and *Castle* cases are in a very preliminary stage, and no determination has been made that they may proceed as class actions.

In the opinion of management, the ultimate liability of the Company, if any, arising from the foregoing, all other pending legal proceedings, as well as from asserted legal claims and known potential legal claims which are probable of assertion, should not have a material adverse effect on the consolidated financial position of the Company at September 30, 1989.

Other Contingencies

In June 1987, the Company entered into a five-year $300.0 notional amount interest rate swap transaction to fix the rate of interest earned on the Company's current and short-term cash and marketable securities position. In lieu of periodic fixed rate payments, the Company elected to receive a single cash payment of $103.7 representing the present value of the total fixed rate payments to be received over the term. The unamortized balance of this payment is included in Other Liabilities as a deferred credit. The Company in turn makes quarterly payments based upon a London Interbank Offering Rate (LIBOR)-related floating rate. In a separate transaction, the Company purchased an 8% interest rate cap on $200.0 of the notional amount to reduce its exposure to significant increases in the floating rate.

The Company sells certain of its trade accounts receivable to others subject to defined limited recourse provisions. The Company is responsible for collection of the accounts and remits the proceeds to the purchaser on a monthly basis. During 1989, the Company sold, on average, accounts totaling $50.0 each month. At September 30, 1989, $.4 of transferred receivables were outstanding and subject to recourse provisions.

During 1986, the Company sold $47.7 of long-term notes receivable subject to defined recourse provisions which include the repurchase by the Company of delinquent notes. The Company is responsible for collection of the accounts and remits the principal amount collected plus a floating rate of interest to the purchaser on a monthly basis. At September 30, 1989, $10.9 of the notes remain uncollected and subject to recourse provisions.

Lease Commitments

Future minimum rental commitments under noncancellable operating leases in effect as of September 30, 1989 were: 1990 – $29.6, 1991 – $26.6, 1992 – $19.4, 1993 – $10.9, 1994 – $8.7, thereafter – $37.8.

Total rental expense for all operating leases was $56.0 in 1989, $58.2 in 1988 and $50.7 in 1987.

Ralston Purina Company and Subsidiaries

NOTES TO FINANCIAL STATEMENTS

(Dollars in millions except per share data)

SUPPLEMENTAL INCOME STATEMENT INFORMATION

	1989	1988	1987
Maintenance and repairs	**$164.5**	$172.8	$158.3
Research and development	**67.5**	65.5	61.9
Translation and exchange gains (losses)	**(3.6)**	8.9	7.2

SUPPLEMENTAL BALANCE SHEET INFORMATION

	1989	1988
Receivables (current) –		
Trade	**$534.7**	$434.8
Notes and other	**113.0**	100.4
Allowance for doubtful accounts	**(11.4)**	(8.3)
	$636.3	$526.9
Inventories –		
Raw materials and supplies	**$245.3**	$224.5
Work in process	**53.6**	56.4
Finished products	**378.9**	279.0
	$677.8	$559.9
Other Current Assets –		
Prepaid expenses	**$ 95.9**	$ 76.3
Deferred income tax benefits	**30.4**	18.4
	$126.3	$ 94.7
Investments and Other Assets –		
Intangible assets (net of accumulated amortization – 1989 – $122.2 and 1988 – $87.4)[a]	**$550.0**	$454.1
Investments in affiliated companies	**51.3**	42.8
Deferred charges and other assets	**193.8**	141.1
	$795.1	$638.0
Accounts Payable and Accrued Liabilities –		
Trade accounts payable	**$382.7**	$366.0
Incentive compensation, salaries and vacations	**98.2**	91.8
Accrued interest	**71.8**	69.4
Other items	**272.2**	225.9
	$824.9	$753.1
Other Liabilities –		
Self-insurance reserves	**$ 71.1**	$ 56.3
Deferred credit – interest rate swap transaction	**62.5**	80.8
Minority interests	**9.2**	22.9
Deferred compensation and other	**99.2**	83.6
	$242.0	$243.6

[a] Intangible assets for 1989 reflect the acquisition of a French-based battery products manufacturer.

Ralston Purina Company and Subsidiaries

NOTES TO FINANCIAL STATEMENTS

(Dollars in millions except per share data)

ANALYSIS OF BALANCE SHEET CHANGES

	1989	1988	1987
Allowance for Doubtful Accounts –			
Balance, beginning of year	**$ 8.3**	$ 8.0	$ 13.1
Provision charged to expense	**7.0**	5.2	7.4
Writeoffs, less recoveries	**(3.9)**	(4.4)	(12.5)
Transfers		(.5)[c]	
Balance, end of year	**$ 11.4**	$ 8.3	$ 8.0
Property at Cost –			
Balance, beginning of year	**$2,531.7**	$2,415.6	$2,647.7
Additions	**219.5**	222.9	196.9
Acquisitions	**44.4**[a]	80.3[d]	
Disposals	**(74.7)**	(99.0)	(405.9)
Adjustment	**1.0**[b]		(29.9)
Foreign translation	**(3.6)**	2.6	6.8
Transfers		(90.7)[c]	
Balance, end of year	**$2,718.3**	$2,531.7	$2,415.6
Accumulated Depreciation –			
Balance, beginning of year	**$ 819.8**	$ 684.3	$ 674.7
Depreciation provision	**188.3**	185.2	174.8
Acquisitions		48.2[d]	
Disposals	**(54.6)**	(58.5)	(169.3)
Foreign translation	**(.8)**	(1.8)	4.1
Transfers		(37.6)[c]	
Balance, end of year	**$ 952.7**	$ 819.8	$ 684.3

[a] Represents net property of French-based battery products manufacturer at acquisition.

[b] Represents adjustment to the preliminary purchase price allocation for Eveready and, in 1989, certain foreign affiliates of Eveready.

[c] Represents the transfer of the net assets of discontinued seafood operations to "Net Assets of Discontinued Operations" in the consolidated balance sheet. See the Discontinued Operations note on page 22.

[d] Represents property at cost and accumulated depreciation at acquisition of substantially all of the remaining outstanding shares of the Company's Mexican agricultural and consumer products affiliate. This operation was formerly accounted for as an investment under the equity method.

[e] Includes $282.1 and $53.0 property at cost and $123.6 and $5.3 accumulated depreciation of domestic agricultural products business and Drake, respectively, at disposition.

SUPPLEMENTAL CASH FLOW STATEMENT INFORMATION

	1989	1988
Interest paid	**$187.9**	$210.7
Income taxes paid	**229.4**	172.6

SUBSEQUENT EVENT

On November 3, 1989, the Company acquired the assets and assumed certain liabilities of the Beech-Nut baby food business from affiliates of Nestle Enterprises, Inc.

Ralston Purina Company and Subsidiaries

FIVE YEAR FINANCIAL SUMMARY

(In millions except per share and percentage data)

OPERATING RESULTS

(for the year ended September 30)

	1989[a]	1988	1987[cd]	1986[d]	1985
Net Sales	**$6,658.3**	$5,875.9	$5,577.9	$5,243.8	$5,046.4
Earnings from Continuing Operations before Income Taxes	**575.7**	605.8	956.1	537.8	410.9
Income Taxes	**224.5**	242.4	445.5	264.5	200.0
Earnings from Continuing Operations[b]	**351.2**	363.4	510.6	273.3	210.9
As a Percent of Sales	**5.3%**	6.2%	9.2%	5.2%	4.2%
Per Share – Primary	**$ 5.32**	$ 5.28	$ 7.05	$ 3.56	$ 2.59
Net Earnings	**422.5**	387.8	523.1	388.7	256.4
Per Share – Primary	**6.44**	5.63	7.23	5.06	3.15
Earnings Available to Common Shareholders	**408.8**	387.8	523.1	388.7	256.4
Common Shares Outstanding (average)	**63.5**	68.9	72.4	76.8	81.3
Dividends Declared on Common Stock	**$ 102.0**	$ 103.1	$ 88.2	$ 83.8	$ 80.4
Per Share	**1.65**	1.50	1.24	1.10	1.00

FINANCIAL POSITION

(as of September 30)

	1989	1988	1987	1986	1985
Working Capital	**$ 505.2**	$ 612.7	$ 295.6	$ 96.7	$ 241.1
Property at Cost, Net	**1,765.6**	1,711.9	1,731.3	1,973.0	1,501.4
Additions (during year)	**219.5**	222.9	196.9	193.6	239.4
Depreciation (during year)	**188.3**	185.2	174.8	141.1	154.4
Total Assets	**4,381.7**	4,044.4	3,863.7	4,209.9	2,630.5
Long-Term Debt	**1,790.7**	1,486.5	1,403.0	1,549.2	889.6
As a Percent of Total Capitalization	**67.5%**	57.7%	59.3%	60.8%	49.0%
Redeemable Preferred Stock	**$ 500.0**				
Shareholders Equity	**831.7**	$1,089.9	$ 961.5	$ 998.9	$ 924.5
Per Common Share	**13.50**	15.98	13.70	13.11	11.53
Common Shares Outstanding	**61.6**	68.2	70.2	76.2	80.2
Market Price Range of Common Stock	**101½-74¾**	83½-57⅝	94-63	77-44¼	46⅞-30½

[a] Provision for restructuring reduced earnings by $19.5 in 1989.
[b] Exclusive of discontinued seafood operations for fiscal years 1985-1989 and discontinued restaurant operations for fiscal years 1985-1986.
[c] Includes gains on sale of businesses which increased earnings from continuing operations by $252.3.
[d] Before extraordinary charges of $3.3 ($.04 per share) and $23.7 ($.31 per share) in 1987 and 1986, respectively.

Index